AN APT BIOGRAPHICAL PARTNERSHIP

The initial compilations for WHO'S WHO IN AMERICA were under way in 1897. Continuously since their first issuance, these compilations have been thoroughly revised and brought down to currency. Issuance is biennial; the latest (Vol. 34) being the current "WHO'S WHO."

WHO'S WHO IN AMERICA endeavors to supply a brief, crisp personal sketch of every *living* American whose position or achievements make his personality of general interest; to provide just the facts every intelligent person wants to know about those who are outstanding in every reputable walk of life. Since the selected biographees themselves supply the necessary information and have the opportunity of revising it before publication, these sketches may be considered condensed autobiographies.

Being a compilation of living men and women in whom there is general interest, necessarily each revision of WHO'S WHO IN AMERICA adds biographies of those coming into the public eye and drops the biographies of those who have died. Therefore, before the advent of WHO WAS WHO considerable searching—unless the date of death and all the earlier volumes of "WHO'S WHO" were at hand—had been required to locate the last published sketch of a deceased biographee.

WHO WAS WHO IN AMERICA saves time by frequently obviating the necessity for such a search, for it contains the last-published sketches of biographees known by its Editors to have died previous to the publication of the latest volume of it, with dates of death, interment locations and requested revisions appearing in their files, appended. It also saves valuable space, as non-current editions of WHO'S WHO IN AMERICA need not be consulted as frequently as would otherwise be necessary. Hence its place is as an appropriate companion volume to WHO'S WHO IN AMERICA, totally aside from its general usefulness as an unusual biographical—perhaps more accurately, an autobiographical —dictionary of those who have been most outstandingly significant in the making of post-Civil-War America. WHO WAS WHO IN AMERICA is issued on a decadal schedule, each ten-year (following the first issue, which drew on all Editions of "WHO'S WHO" from the First to, and including, the Twenty-first) volume of it picking up the work's continuous and unique necrological service from the preceding one.

In no other biographical reference work will there be found the biographies of non-living noteworthy men and women which were published in WHO'S WHO IN AMERICA.

THE THIRD VOLUME (1951-1960)

Now again Available in the Third Printing (1966)
959 pages; 12,828 biographies
(Drawing from Vols. 26-31, inclusive, of "Who's Who")

THE SECOND VOLUME (1943-1950)

Now again available in the Fifth Printing (1966)
614 pages; 8,500 biographies
(Drawing from Vols. 22-26, inclusive, of "Who's Who")

THE FIRST VOLUME (1897-1942)

Now again available in the Sixth Printing (1966)
1,408 pages; 27,458 biographies
(Drawing from Vols. 1-21, inclusive, of "Who's Who")

THE HISTORICAL VOLUME (1607-1896)

Now again available in the Revised Edition (1966)
690 pages; 13,500 biographies
(Consisting of originally researched data)

MARQUIS—WHO'S WHO

INCORPORATED

(The A. N. Marquis Company—Founded 1897)

Marquis Publications Building

210 East Ohio Street   Chicago, Illinois 60611

WHO WAS WHO

®

IN AMERICA

—

A COMPONENT VOLUME OF
WHO'S WHO IN AMERICAN HISTORY

VOL. 3

(1951-1960)

A Third Printing (1966)

Sketches of Who's Who in America biographees, as last published in Volumes 27 to 31
inclusive (1951-1960)—or in any preceding volume if not in hand for inclusion in
Volumes I or II of Who Was Who in America, which compile, respectively,
"Who's Who" biographies from Volumes 1 to 21 inclusive (1897-1942)
and Volumes 22 to 26 inclusive (1943-1950)—with dates of
death, interment locations and requested revisions appearing in the Editors' files, appended.

MARQUIS—WHO'S WHO

INCORPORATED

(The A. N. Marquis Company—Founded 1897)

CHICAGO, ILLINOIS 60611

Library of Congress Catalogue Card Number 43-3789

THIRD VOLUME

(1951-1960)

Manufactured in The United States of America
by The Von Hoffmann Press, Inc., St. Louis, Missouri

CONTENTS

PREFACE

WHY THE "WAS" BIOGRAPHICAL DICTIONARIES ARE UNIQUE

The 12,828 biographies removed, because of deaths of biographees, from the five volumes of WHO'S WHO IN AMERICA published since the 1950-51 biennial volume, are contained—with, if brought to the Editors' attention, dates of deaths and places of interment appended—in this third volume of its companion book, WHO WAS WHO IN AMERICA. The first "Was" volume—now in a fourth printing—contained over 27,000 similar biographies removed from "Who's Who" since its founding in 1897 to—and including—the twenty-first volume. The second volume, now in a third printing, contained over 8,500 biographies drawn from "Who's Who" volumes Twenty-two to Twenty-six.

A primary advantage which results is the increased facility with which sketches of deceased biographees can now be located. Unless the year of death happened to be at hand, this has usually required volume-by-volume inspection of back issues of "Who's Who" until the biography last published was located. Now, the biography is ready to hand in WHO WAS WHO IN AMERICA.

Of equal practical value is the saving in space which results, particularly when preferred library shelving, for which there is insistent demand, is involved. The three volumes of "Who Was Who" now available and the current volume of "Who's Who" (1960-61) are in normal usage equivalent to thirty-one volumes, and require but 8½ inches of shelving, while the 31 issued "Who's Who" volumes would require 7½ feet. And hereafter only the volumes of WHO'S WHO IN AMERICA issued biennially until the fourth issuance of WHO WAS WHO IN AMERICA (about a decade hence, in 1970) will be required to maintain this complete Civil-War-to-date coverage of American biography.

Perhaps as important as these purely utilitarian advantages are the unique characteristics which the "Was" books legitimately inherit from "Who's Who" itself, and which therefore will be found in no other biographical dictionary.

The sketches, for example, have not only been prepared from information originally supplied by the biographees themselves, but have been approved personally—and frequently revised—before publication in a "Who's Who" during the subject's lifetime. Many have been finally scrutinized and revised by relatives or legal representatives of the deceased biographees before being published in "Who Was Who," but, except for resulting changes, and occasional variations interjected by the compilers, the "Was" biographies are purposely printed exactly as they last appeared in "Who's Who," even in respect to tense and the like. As a result, many contain personal data not readily available elsewhere. The preface to the first volume of WHO'S WHO IN AMERICA selected this fact as one of that volume's outstanding characteristics, and stated: "The book is autobiographical, the data having been obtained from first hands." It follows that WHO WAS WHO IN AMERICA is autobiographical to a distinctive degree, which makes it, in that respect, unique among American biographical dictionaries. And although condensed to the concise style which "Who's Who" has made famous, the sketches contain all essential facts.

There results far more than a biographical dictionary of 48,786 non-living American notables within the covers of three volumes. It is as well a vital portion of American history from the Civil War through the Second World War and the booming Fifties, written in the lives of those who made this history, as the subjects themselves recorded the details.

It is this distinguishing characteristic which qualifies WHO WAS WHO IN AMERICA as an exceptional reference work, essential to many—students, journalists, business executives, lecturers, public officials, editors, writers, educators—and of daily usefulness in the home, particularly now that the state of world affairs makes a comprehensive but convenient American biographical compilation a "must" in order to keep abreast.

An interesting instance of the timely usefulness of WHO WAS WHO IN AMERICA is to be found in Clare Boothe Luce's vivid introduction to "The Valor of Ignorance" (Harper & Brothers) by Homer Lea, who 50 years ago warned the United States of the course foreign aggression would take. Mrs. Luce writes: "I returned to the library. No, there was no biography. No, he was not in the 1941 Encyclopædia Britannica. I sought 'Who's Who' for 1912, the year his last book was published. He was there: 'Lea, Homer, author, soldier; b. Denver, Nov. 17, 1876 . . .' And with this as a clue to other clues . . . I finally came upon one of the strangest, most adventurous and significant stories that America ever knew—and had ever forgotten . . ."

Had WHO WAS WHO IN AMERICA been published when Mrs. Luce sought information about Lea, her key "clue to other clues" would have been at her finger tips, along with thousands of easy-to-use references to significant non-living Americans whose lives, like his, reflect in today's events. For instance, only three of the twelve presidents of the United States whose biographies have been published in "Who's Who" are currently sketched in it. The sketches of the other nine of course appear in the "Was" books.

That "Who Was Who" serves an urgent reference need is decisively demonstrated by the fact that the first volume is currently going into a fourth printing, and the second volume into a third, and the widespread commendation the work has received and continues to receive. The following comments are typical: A journalist—"Your idea of a 'Who Was Who in America' is an excellent one"; an historian—"The idea is fine, the 'Was' volume will be a great convenience"; an educator—". . . will be of extraordinary value to our libraries and to the public"; an administrator—" . . . think publication of the new volume . . . an excellent idea . . ."; a sociologist—" . . . a must for most libraries . . ."; a businessman—". . . not only saves valuable library space, but endless hours of time"; a secretarial executive—". . . is a reference book that has long been needed"; an editor—". . . fills a great need . . ."; an author—"the bibliographical possibilities are tremendous"; a newspaperman—"I shall use it almost daily"; an association executive—". . . will prove immensely popular and widely used"; a White House staff official—". . . will be a very helpful reference book for 1600 Pennsylvania Avenue (The White House)."

WHO WAS WHO IN AMERICA is not only a companion reference work to WHO'S WHO IN AMERICA, but in reality a supplement. For *supplemented* by the "Was" volumes now published, the current edition of WHO'S WHO IN AMERICA provides over 100,000 significant biographies and four-fifths-of-a century coverage of both living and deceased biographees of current and recurring general interest. These two publications provide a biographical reference service that is obviously unique— reaching back 95 years and up to "last night"— and surprisingly compact.

This rounding out, through the publication of WHO WAS WHO IN AMERICA, of the undertaking which the first Marquis biographical compilations initiated over sixty years ago, recalls two sentences from the preface of the first WHO'S WHO IN AMERICA which, by direct inheritance, become descriptive also of the "Was" books:

"Without claiming infallibility or inerrancy, it is believed that this publication will be a welcome addition to the list of handy helps that make up the library of indispensable books. Certainly nothing has been omitted that painstaking care, persistent effort, or expenditure of money could supply toward making the volume fully fill the purposes of its compilation."

THE EDITORS.

Chicago, April 1, 1960.

PREFACE TO THE THIRD PRINTING

The First and Second Printings of Volume III of WHO WAS WHO IN AMERICA having already been exhausted, a third was decided upon as immediately necessary to supply the continuous demand for this volume by reference users, to be printed as were prior editions on paper providing the unusual compactness desirable for a reference work, and to be bound in buckram with careful consideration given to obtaining exceptional sturdiness suitable for constant reference usage. This volume is the result.

As would naturally be inferred from the urgency of the demand for Volume I of WHO WAS WHO IN AMERICA and the cordial reception accorded Volumes II (1943-1950) and III (1951-1960), all of which are now available in reprintings, WHO WAS WHO has established itself as an indispensable reference work and as the companion to WHO'S WHO IN AMERICA.

As was also to be expected—in view of the prepublication commendation mentioned above in the original preface—the publishers have since its publication received a steady flow of favorable, even enthusiastic comment regarding WHO WAS WHO IN AMERICA, which is serving important reference needs in innumerable instances.

A new volume of WHO WAS WHO IN AMERICA has been published, which is originally researched, subtitled the "Historical Volume," and includes in the famous Marquis format biographies-in-brief of 13,500 figures prominent in American history from the founding of Jamestown Colony in 1607 to 1896, thus spanning the period between the origins of American history and Volume I of WHO WAS WHO IN AMERICA. The Historical Volume (now in a revised edition) together with Volumes I, II, and III of WHO WAS WHO IN AMERICA and the current volume of WHO'S WHO IN AMERICA, collectively constitute WHO'S WHO IN AMERICAN HISTORY, the only such complete compilation extant of sketches of famous Americans, past and present.

THE EDITORS

Chicago, August 4, 1966.

ABBREVIATIONS

The following abbreviations are frequently used in this book:

*Following a sketch signifies that the published biography could not be verified.

A.A., Associate in Arts.
A.A.A., Agricultural Adjustment Administration; Anti-Aircraft Artillery.
A.A.A.S., American Association for the Advancement of Science.
AAC, Army Air Corps.
a.a.g., asst. adjutant general.
AAF, Army Air Forces.
A. and M., Agricultural and Mechanical.
A.A.O.N.M.S., Ancient Arabic Order of the Nobles of the Mystic Shrine.
A.A.S.R., Ancient Accepted Scottish Rite (Masonic).
A.B.C.F.M., American Board of Commissioners for Foreign Missions (Congregational).
A.B. (also **B.A.**), Bachelor of Arts.
A.,B.& C. R.R., Atlanta, Birmingham & Coast R.R.
ABC, American Broadcasting Company.
abt., about.
AC, Air Corps.
acad., academy; academic.
A.C.L. R.R., Atlantic Coast Line R.R.
A.C.P., American College of Physicians.
A.C.S., American College of Surgeons.
actg., acting.
a.d.c., aide-de-camp.
add., additional.
adj., adjutant; adjunct.
adj. gen., adjutant general.
adm., admiral.
administr., administrator.
administrn., administration.
administrv., administrative.
adv., advocate; advisory.
advt., advertising.
A.E., Agricultural Engineer.
AEC, Atomic Energy Commission.
A.E. and P., Ambassador Extraordinary and Plenipotentiary.
AEF, American Expeditionary Forces.
aero., aeronautics, aeronautical.
A.F.D., Doctor of Fine Arts.
A.F. and A.M., Ancient Free and Accepted Masons.
AFL (or **A.F. of L.**), American Federation of Labor.
agr., agriculture.
agri., agricultural.
agt., agent.
Agy., Agency.
a.i., ad interim.
A.I.A., American Institute of Architects.
A.I.M., American Institute of Management.
A.L.A., American Library Association.
Am., American, America.
A.M. (also **M.A.**), Master of Arts.
A.M.A., American Medical Association.
A.M.E., African Methodist Episcopal.
Am. Inst. E.E., American Institute of Electrical Engineers.
Am. Soc. C.E., American Society of Civil Engineers.
Am. Soc. M.E., American Society of Mechanical Engineers.
A.N.A., Associate National Academician.
anat., anatomical.
ann., annual.
ANTA, American National Theatre and Academy.
anthrop., anthropological.

antiq., antiquarian.
A.O.H., Ancient Order of Hibernians.
appmnt., appointment.
apptd., appointed.
apt., apartment.
a.q.m., assistant quartermaster.
A.R.C., American Red Cross.
archeol., archeological.
archtl., architectural.
Arts D., Doctor of Arts.
arty., artillery.
AS, Air Service.
A.S.C.A.P., American Society of Composers, Authors and Publishers.
ASF, Air Service Force.
assn., association.
asso., associate; associated.
asst., assistant.
astron., astronomical.
astrophys., astrophysical.
A.T.S.C., Air Technical Service Command.
A.,T.& S.F. Ry., Atchison, Topeka & Santa Fe Ry.
atty., attorney.
AUS, Army of the United States.
Av., Avenue.

b., born.
B., Bachelor.
B.A. (also **A.B.**), Bachelor of Arts.
B.A.A.S., British Association for the Advancement of Science.
B.Agr., Bachelor of Agriculture.
Balt., Baltimore.
Bapt., Baptist.
B.Arch., Bachelor of Architecture.
B.& A. R.R., Boston & Albany R. R.
B.A.S. (or **B.S.A.**), Bachelor of Agricultural Science.
batn., batln., batt., battalion.
B.B.A., Bachelor of Business Administration.
B.B.C., British Broadcasting Company.
B.C., British Columbia.
B.C.E., Bachelor of Civil Engineering.
B.Chir., Bachelor of Surgery.
B.C.L., Bachelor of Civil Law.
B.C.S., Bachelor of Commercial Science.
bd., board.
B.D., Bachelor of Divinity.
B.Di., Bachelor of Didactics.
B.E. (or **Ed.B.**), Bachelor of Education.
BEF, British Expeditionary Force.
bet., between.
B.F.A., Bachelor of Fine Arts.
bibl., biblical.
bibliog., bibliographical.
biog., biographical.
biol., biological.
B.J., Bachelor of Journalism.
Bklyn., Brooklyn.
B.L. (or **Litt.B.**), Bachelor of Letters.
Bldg., building.
blk., block.
B.L.S., Bachelor of Library Science.
Blvd., (also **boul.**), Boulevard.
B.& M. R.R., Boston & Marine R.R.
Bn. (or **Batn.**), Battalion.
B.O. (or **O.B.**), Bachelor of Oratory.
B.& O. R.R., Baltimore & Ohio R.R.
bot., botanical.
B.P., Bachelor of Painting.
B.P.E., Bachelor of Physical Education.
B.P.O.E., Benevolent and Protective Order of Elks.
B.Pd. (or **Pd.B.**, or **Py.B.**), Bachelor of Pedagogy.
br., branch.

brig., brigadier, brigade.
brig. gen., brigadier general.
Brit., British; Britannica.
Bro., Brother.
B., R. & P. Ry., Buffalo, Rochester & Pittsburg Ry.
B.S. (also **S.B.** or **Sc.B.**), Bachelor of Science.
B.S. in Ry. M.E., Bachelor in Railway Mechanical Engineering.
B.S.D., Bachelor of Didactic Science.
B.Th., Bachelor of Theology.
bull., bulletin.
bur., bureau.
bus., business.
B.W.I., British West Indies.

C.A., Central America.
CAC, Coast Artillery Corps.
Cal. (or **Calif.**), California.
Can., Canada.
Cantab., of or pertaining to Cambridge University, Eng.
capt., captain.
C. & A. R.R., Chicago & Alton R.R., now Alton Ry. Co.
Cath., Catholic.
cav., cavalry.
CBI, China - Burma - India theater of operations.
C.,B.& Q. R.R., Chicago, Burlington & Quincy R.R.Co.
CBS, Columbia Broadcasting System.
CCC, Commodity Credit Corporation.
C.,C.,C.& St.L. Ry., Cleveland, Cincinnati. Chicago & St. Louis Ry.
C.E., Civil Engineer (degree); Corps of Engineers.
CEF, Canadian Expeditionary Forces.
C.& E.I. R.R., Chicago & Eastern Illinois R.R.
C.G.W. R.R., Chicago Great Western Railway.
ch., church.
Ch.D., Doctor of Chemistry.
chem., chemical.
Chem.E., Chemical Engineer.
Chgo., Chicago.
Chirurg., Chirugical.
chmn., chairman.
chpt., chapter.
Cia, (Spanish), Company.
CIA, Central Intelligence Agency.
CIC, Counter Intelligence Corps.
C.,I.&L. Ry., Chicago, Indianapolis & Louisville Railway.
Cin., Cincinnati.
CIO, Congress of Industrial Organizations.
civ., civil.
Cleve., Cleveland.
climatol., climatological.
clin., clinical.
clk., clerk.
C.L.S.C., Chautauqua Literary and Scientific Circle.
C.L.U., Certified Life Underwriter.
C.M., Master in Surgery.
C. M., St.P.&P.R.R., Chicago, Milwaukee, St. Paul & Pacific R.R. Co.
C. N. Ry., Canadian Northern Ry.
C.& N.-W. Ry., Chicago & Northwestern Railway.
Co., Company; County.
C. of C., Chamber of Commerce.
C.O.F., Catholic Order of Foresters.
C. of Ga. Ry., Central of Georgia Ry.
col., colonel.
coll., college.

com., committee.
comd., commanded.
comdg., commanding.
comdr., commander.
comdt., commandant.
commd., commissioned.
comml., commercial.
commn., commission.
commr., commissioner.
Com. Sub., Commissary of Subsistence.
condr., conductor.
conf., conference.
confed., confederate.
Congl., Congregational; Congressional.
Conglist., Congregationalist.
cons., consulting, consultant.
consol. (or **con.**), consolidated.
constl., constitutional.
constn., constitution.
constrn., construction.
contbd., contributed.
contbg., contributing.
contbn., contribution.
contbr., contributor.
conv., convention.
coöp. (or **co-op.**), cooperative.
corpl., corporal.
corp., corporation.
corr., correspondent; corresponding; correspondence.
C & O. Ry., Chesapeake & Ohio Ry. Co.
C.P.A., Certified Public Accountant.
C.P.H., Certificate of Public Health.
cpl. (or **corpl.**), corporal.
C.P. Ry., Canadian Pacific Ry. Co.
C. R.I.& P. Ry., Chicago, Rock Island & Pacific Ry. Co.
C.R.R. of N.J., Central Railroad Co. of New Jersey.
C.S., Christian Science.
C.S. Army, Confederate States Army.
C.S.B., Bachelor of Christian Science
C.S.D., Doctor of Christian Science.
C.S.N., Confederate States Navy.
C.& S. Ry. Co., Colorado & Southern Ry. Co.
C.,St.P.,M.&O. Ry., Chicago, St. Paul, Minneapolis & Omaha Ry. Co.
Ct., Court.
C.T., Candidate in Theology.
C.Vt. Ry., Central Vermont Ry.
C.& W I. R.R., Chicago & Western Indiana R.R. Co.
CWS, Chemical Warfare Service.
cyclo., cyclopedia.

d. (also **dau.**), daughter.
D.Agr., Doctor of Agriculture.
D.A.R., Daughters of the American Revolution.
D.C., District of Columbia.
D.C.L., Doctor of Civil Law.
D.C.S., Doctor of Commercial Science.
D.D., Doctor of Divinity.
D.D.S., Doctor of Dental Surgery.
dec., deceased.
Def., Defense.
deg., degree.
Del., Delaware.
del., delegate.
Dem., Democratic.
D.Eng. (also **Dr. Engring.**, or **E.D.**), Doctor of Engineering.
denom., denominational.
dep., deputy.
dept., department.
dermatol., dermatological.
desc., descendant.
D.H.L., Doctor of Hebrew Literature.

D.& H. R.R., Delaware & Hudson R.R. Co.
dir., director.
disch., discharged.
dist., district.
distbg., distributing.
distbn., distribution.
distbr., distributor.
div., division; divinity; divorce proceedings.
D.Litt., Doctor of Literature.
D.L.& W.R.R., Delaware, Lackawanna & Western R.R. Co.
D.M.D., Doctor of Medical Dentistry.
D.M.S., Doctor of Medical Science.
D.O., Doctor of Osteopathy.
DPA, Defense Production Administration.
D.P.H. (also **Dr.P.H.**), Diploma in Public Health or Doctor of Public Health or Doctor of Public Hygiene.
Dr., Doctor, Drive.
D.R., Daughters of the Revolution.
D.R.E., Doctor of Religious Education.
D.& R.G.W. R.R. Co., Denver & Rio Grande Western R.R. Co.
D.Sc. (or **Sc. D.**), Doctor of Science.
D.S.C., Distinguished Service Cross.
D.S.M., Distinguished Service Medal.
D.S.T., Doctor of Sacred Theology.
D.T.M., Doctor of Tropical Medicine.
D.V.M., Doctor of Veterinary Medicine.
D.V.S., Doctor of Veterinary Surgery.

E., East.
E. and P., Extraordinary and Plenipotentiary.
ECA, Economic Cooperation Administration.
eccles., ecclesiastical.
ecol., ecological.
econ., economic.
ECOSOC, Economic and Social Council of UN.
ed., educated.
E.D. (also **D.Eng.,** or **Dr.Engring.**), Doctor of Engineering.
Ed.B., Bachelor of Education.
Ed.D., Doctor of Education.
edit., edition.
Ed.M. (or **M.Ed.**), Master of Education.
edn., education.
ednl., educational.
E.E., Electrical Engineer.
E.E. and M. P., Envoy Extraordinary and Minister Plenipotentiary.
Egyptol., Egyptological.
elec., electrical.
electrochem., electrochemical.
electrophys., electrophysical.
E. M., Engineer of Mines.
ency., encyclopaedia.
Eng., England.
engr., engineer.
engring., engineering.
entomol., entomological.
e.s., eldest son.
E.S.M.W.T.P., Engring. Science and Management War Training Program.
ethnol., ethnological.
ETO, European Theater of Operations.
Evang., Evangelical.
exam., examination; examining.
exec., executive.
exhbn., exhibition.
expdn., expedition.
expn., exposition.
expt., experiment.
exptl., experimental.

F., Fellow.
F.A., Field Artillery.
F.A.C.P., Fellow American College of Physicians.
F.A.C.S., Fellow American College of Surgeons.
FAO, Food and Agriculture Organization.
FBI, Federal Bureau of Investigation.
FCA, Farm Credit Administration.
FCC, Federal Communications Commission.
FCDA, Federal Civil Defense Administration.
FDA, Food and Drug Administration.
FDIA, Federal Deposit Insurance Administration.

F.E., Forest Engineer.
Fed., Federal.
Fedn., Federation.
Fgn., Foreign.
FHA, Federal Housing Administration.
FOA, Foreign Operations Administration.
Found., Foundation.
frat., fraternity.
F.R.C.P., Fellow Royal College of Physicians (England).
F.R.C.S., Fellow Royal College of Surgeons (England)
frt., freight.
FSA, Federal Security Agent.
Ft., Fort.
FTC, Federal Trade Commission.

G.-1 (or other number), Division of General Staff.
G.A.R., Grand Army of the Republic.
G.,C.& S.F. Ry., Gulf, Colorado & Santa Fe Ry. Co.
G.D., Graduate in Divinity.
g.d., granddaughter.
gen., general.
geneal., genealogical.
geod., geodetic.
geog., geographical; geographic.
geol., geological.
geophys., geophysical.
g.g.d., great granddaughter.
g.g.s., great grandson.
G.H.Q., General Headquarters.
G.,M.& N. R.R., Gulf, Mobile & Northern R.R. Co.
G., M.& O. R.R., Gulf, Mobile & Ohio R.R. Co.
G.N. Ry., Great Northern Ry. Co.
gov., governor.
govt., government.
grad., graduated; graduate.
g.s., grandson.
Gt., Great.
G.T. Ry., Grand Trunk Ry. System.
G.W. Ry. of Can., Great Western Ry. of Canada.
gynecol., gynecological.

Hdqrs., Headquarters.
H.G., Home Guard.
H.I., Hiwaiian Islands.
hist., historical.
H.M., Master of Humanics.
HOLC, Home Owners Loan Corporation.
homeo., homeopathic.
hon., honorary; honorable.
Ho. of Reps., House of Representatives.
hort., horticultural.
hosp., hospital.
Hts., Heights.
H.Ty. (or **H.T.**), Hawaiian Territory.
Hwy., Highway.
hydrog., hydrographic.

IBM, International Business Machines Corporation.
ICC, Interstate Commerce Commission.
I.C.R.R., Illinois Central R.R. System.
I.G.N. R.R., International - Great Northern R.R.
ILO, International Labor Organization.
illus., illustrated.
Inc., Incorporated.
Ind., Indiana, Independent.
Indpls., Indianapolis.
indsl., industrial.
inf., infantry.
ins., insurance.
insp., inspector.
inst., institute.
instn., institution.
instr., instructor.
instrn., instruction.
internat., international.
intro., introduction.
I.O.B.B., Independent Order of B'nai B'rith.
I.O.G.T., Independent Order of Good Templars.
I.O.O.F., Independent Order of Odd Fellows.

J.B., Jurum Baccalaureus.
J.C.B., Juris Canonici Bachelor.
J.C.L., Juris Canonici Lector.

J.D., Doctor of Jurisprudence.
j.g., junior grade.
jour., journal.
jr., junior.
J.S.D., Doctor of Juristic Science.
Jud., Judicial.
J.U.D., Juris Utriusque Doctor: Doctor of Both (Canon and Civil) Laws.

K.C., Knight of Columbus.
K.C.C.H., Knight Commander of Court of Honor.
K.P., Knight of Pythias.
K.C.S. Ry., Kansas City Southern Ry.
K.T., Knight Templar.

lab., laboratory.
lang., language.
laryngol., laryngological.
lectr., lecturer.
L.H.D., Doctor of Letters of Humanity.
L.I., Long Island.
L.I. R.R., Long Island R.R. Co.
lit., literary; literature.
Lit. Hum., Literae Humanores (classies Oxford U., Eng.).
Litt.B. (or **B.L.**), Bachelor of Letters.
Litt.D., Doctor of Letters.
LL.B., Bachelor of Laws.
LL.D., Doctor of Laws.
LL.M. (or **M.L.**), Master of Laws.
L.& N. R.R., Louisville & Nashville R.R.
L.O.M., Loyal Order of Moose.
L.R.C.P., Licentiate Royal Coll. Physicians.
L.R.C.S., Licentiate Royal Coll. Surgeons.
L.S.A., Licentiate Society of Apothecaries.
L.S.& M. S. Ry., Lake Shore & Michigan Southern Ry.
lt, or (**lieut.**), lieutenant.
Ltd., Limited.
Luth., Lutheran.
L.V. R.R., Lehigh Valley R.R. Co.

m., marriage ceremony.
M.A. (or **A.M.**), Master of Arts.
mag., magazine.
M.Agr., Master of Agriculture.
maj., major.
M.Arch., Master in Architecture.
math., mathematical.
M.B., Bachelor of Medicine.
M.B.A., Master of Business Administration.
MBS, Mutual Broadcasting System.
M.C., Medical Corps.
M.C.S., Master of Commercial Science.
mcht., merchant.
M.C. R.R., Michigan Central R.R.
M.D., Doctor of Medicine.
M.Di., Master of Didactics.
M.Dip., Master in Diplomacy.
mdse., merchandise.
M.D.V., Doctor of Veterinary Medicine.
M.E., Mechanical Engineer.
mech., mechanical.
M.E. Ch., Methodist Episcopal Church.
med., medical.
Med. O.R.C., Medical Officers' Reserve Corps.
Med. R.C., Medical Reserve Corps.
M.E.E., Master of Electrical Engineering.
mem., member.
Meml. (or **Mem.**), Memorial.
merc., mercantile.
met., metropolitan.
metall., metallurgical.
Met.E., Metallurgical Engineer.
meteorol., meteorological.
Meth., Methodist.
metrol., metrological.
M.F., Master of Forestry.
M.F.A., Master of Fine Arts.
mfg., manufacturing.
mfr., manufacturer.
mgmt., management.
mgr., manager.
M.I., Military Intelligence.
micros., microscopical.
mil., military.
Milw., Milwaukee.
mineral., mineralogical.
M.-K.-T. R.R., Missouri - Kansas-Texas R.R. Co.

M.L. (or **LL.M.**), Master of Laws.
M.Litt., Master of Literature.
Mlle., Mademoiselle (Miss).
Mme., Madame.
M.M.E., Master of Mechanical Engineering.
mng., managing.
Moblzn., Mobilization.
M.P., Member of Parliament.
Mpls., Minneapolis.
M.P. R.R., Missouri Pacific R.R.
M.Pd., Master of Pedagogy.
M.P.E., Master of Physical Education.
M.P.L., Master of Patent Law.
M.R.C.P., Member Royal College of Physicians.
M.R.C.S., Member Royal College of Surgeons.
M.R.E., Master of Religious Education.
M.S. (or **M.Sc.**), Master of Science.
M.S.F., Master of Science of Forestry.
M.S.T., Master of Sacred Theology.
M.& St. L. R.R., Minneapolis & St. Louis R.R. Co.
M.,St.P.& S.S.M. Ry., Minneapolis, St. Paul & Sault Ste. Marie Ry.
Mt., Mount.
mtn., mountain.
M.T.O.U.S.A., Mediterranean Theater of Operations, U.S. Army.
mus., museum; musical.
Mus.B., Bachelor of Music.
Mus.D. (or **Mus. Doc.**), Doctor of Music.
Mus. M., Master of Music.
Mut., Mutual.
M.V.M., Massachusetts Volunteer Militia.
M.W.A., Modern Woodmen of America.
mycol., mycological.

N., North.
N.A., National Academician; North America; National Army.
N.A.A.C.P., National Association for the Advancement of Colored People.
NACA, National Advisory Committee for Aeronautics.
N.A.D., National Academy of Design.
N.A.M., National Association of Manufacturers.
NASA, National Aeronautics and Space Administration.
nat., national.
NATO, North Atlantic Treaty Organization.
N.A.T.O.U.S.A., Northern African Theater of Operations, U.S. Army.
nav., navigation.
N.B., New Brunswick.
NBC, National Broadcasting Co.
N.,C.& St.L. Ry., Nashville, Chattanooga & St. Louis Ry.
NDRC, National Defense Research Committee.
N.E., Northeast; New England.
N.E.A., National Education Association.
N.G., National Guard.
N.G.S.N.Y., National Guard State of New York.
NLRB, National Labor Relations Board.
N.Ph.D., Doctor Natural Philosophy.
N.P. Ry., Northern Pacific Ry.
No., Northern.
NPA, National Production Authority.
nr., near.
NRA, National Recovery Administration.
NRC, National Research Council.
N.S., Nova Scotia.
NSC, National Security Council.
NSRB, National Security Resources Board.
N.T., New Testament.
numis., numismatic.
N.W., Northwest.
N.& W. Ry., Norfolk & Western Ry.
N.Y.C., New York City.
N.Y. Central R.R. (or **N.Y.C. R.R.**), New York Central Railroad Company.
N.Y.,C.& St.L. R.R., New York, Chicago & St. Louis R.R. Co.
N.Y.,N.H.& H. R.R., New York, New Haven & Hartford R.R. Co.

N.Y.,O.& W. Ry., New York, Ontario & Western Ry.

O.B., Bachelor of Oratory.
obs., observatory.
obstet., obstetrical.
OCDM, Office of Civil and Defense Mobilization.
ODM, Office of Defense Mobilization.
O.E.S., Order of the Eastern Star.
ofcl., official.
Ont., Ontario.
OPA, Office of Price Administration.
ophthal., ophthalmological.
OPM, Office of Production Management.
OPS, Office of Price Stabilization.
O.Q.M.G., Office of Quartermaster General.
O.R.C., Officers' Reserve Corps.
orgn., organization.
ornithol., ornithological.
O.S.B., Order of Saint Benedict.
O.S.L. R.R., Oregon Short Line R.R.
OSRD, Office of Scientific Research and Development.
OSS, Office of Strategic Services.
O.T., Old Testament.
O.T.C., Officers' Training Camp.
otol., otological.
O.T.S., Officers' Training School.
O.U.A.M., Order United American Mechanics.
OWI, Office of War Information.
O.-W.R.R.& N. Co., Oregon-Washington R.R. & Navigation Co.

Pa. R.R., Pennsylvania R.R.
pass., passenger.
path., pathological.
Pd.B. (or B.Pd., or Py.B.), Bachelor of Pedagogy.
Pd.D., Doctor of Pedagogy.
Pd.M., Master of Pedagogy.
P.E., Protestant Episcopal.
Pe.B., Bachelor of Pediatrics.
P.E.N., Poets, Playwrights, Editors, Essayists and Novelists (Internat. Assn.).
penol., penological.
pfc., private first class.
PHA, Public Housing Administration.
pharm., pharmaceutical.
Pharm.D., Doctor of Pharmacy.
Pharm.M., Master of Pharmacy.
Ph.B., Bachelor of Philosophy.
Ph.C., Pharmaceutical Chemist.
Ph.D., Doctor of Philosophy.
Ph.G., Graduate in Pharmacy.
Phila., Philadelphia.
philol., philological.
philos., philosophical.
photog., photographic.
phys., physical.
Phys. and Surg., Physicians and Surgeons (college at Columbia University).
physiol., physiological.
P.I., Philippine Islands.
Pitts., Pittsburg.
Pkwy., Parkway.
Pl., Place.
P.& L.E. R.R., Pittsburgh & Lake Erie R.R.
P.M., Paymaster.
P.M. R.R., Pere Marquette R.R. Co.
polit., political.
poly., polytechnic.
pomol., pomological.

P.Q., Province of Quebec.
P.R., Puerto Rico.
prep., preparatory.
pres., president.
Presbyn., Presbyterian.
presdl., presidential.
prin., principal.
Proc., Proceedings.
prod., produced (play production).
prodn., production.
prof., professor.
profl., professional.
Prog., Progressive.
propr., proprietor.
pros. atty., prosecuting attorney.
pro tem, pro tempore (for the time being).
psychiat., psychiatrical; psychiatric.
psychol., psychological.
P.T.A., Parent-Teacher Association.
PTO, Pacific Theatre of Operations.
pub., public; publisher; publishing; published.
publ., publication.
pvt., private.
Py. B., Bachelor of Pedagogy.

q.m., quartermaster.
Q.M.C., Quartermaster Corps.
q.m. gen., quartermaster general.
Q.M.O.R.C., Quartermaster Officers' Reserve Corps.
quar., quarterly.
Que., Quebec (province).
q.v., quod vide (which see).

radiol., radiological.
R.A.F., Royal Air Force.
R.A.M., Royal Arch Mason.
R.C., Roman Catholic; Reserve Corps.
RCA, Radio Corporation of America.
R.C.S., Revenue Cutter Service.
Rd., Road.
R.D., Rural Delivery.
R.E., Reformed Episcopal.
rec., recording.
Ref., Reformed.
Regt., Regiment.
regtl., regimental.
Rep., Republican.
rep., representative.
Res., Reserve.
ret., retired.
Rev., Reverend, Review.
rev., revised.
RFC, Reconstruction Finance Corporation.
R.F.D., Rural Free Delivery.
rhinol., rhinological.
R.N., Registered Nurse.
röntgenol., röntgenological.
R.O.S.C., Reserve Officers' Sanitary Corps.
R.O.T.C., Reserve Officers' Training Corps.
R.P., Reformed Presbyterian.
R.P.D., Rerum Politicarum Doctor (Doctor Political Science).
R.R., Railroad.
R.T.C., Reserve Training Corps.
Ry., Railway.

s., son.
S., South.
S.A., South America.
S.A. (Spanish) Sociedad Anónima, (French) Société Anonyme.
S.A.L. Ry., Seaboard Air Line Ry.
san., sanitary.

S.A.R., Sons of the Am. Revolution.
S.A.T.C., Students' Army Training Corps.
Sat.Eve.Post, Saturday Evening Post.
Savs., Savings.
S.B. (also **B.S. or Sc.B.**), Bachelor of Science.
S.C., South Carolina; San. Corps.
Sc.D. (or D.Sc.), Doctor of Science.
S.C.D., Doctor of Commercial Science.
sch., school.
sci., science; scientific.
S.C.V., Sons of Confederate Veterans.
S.E., Southeast.
SEC, Securities and Exchange Commission.
sec., secretary.
sect., section.
seismol., seismological.
Sem., Seminary.
sgt. (or sergt.), sergeant.
SHAEF, Supreme Headquarters, Allied Expeditionary Forces.
SHAPE, Supreme Headquarters Allied Powers in Europe.
S.I., Staten Island.
S.J., Society of Jesus (Jesuit).
S.J.D., Doctor Juristic Science.
S.M., Master of Science.
So., Southern.
soc., society.
sociol., sociological.
SOS, Services of Supply.
S. of V., Sons of Veterans.
S.P. Co., Southern Pacific Co.
spl., special.
splty., specialty.
Sq., Square.
S.R.C., Signal Reserve Corps.
sr., senior.
S.R., Sons of the Revolution.
S.S., Steamship.
SSS, Selective Service System.
St., Saint; Street.
sta., station.
statis., statistical.
Stblzn., Stabilization
S.T.B., Bachelor of Sacred Theology.
S.T.D., Doctor of Sacred Theology.
S.T.L., Licentiate in Sacred Theology; Lector of Sacred Theology.
St.L.-S.F. R.R., St. Louis - San Francisco Ry. Co.
supr., supervisor.
supt., superintendent.
surg., surgical.
S.W., Southwest.

T. and S., Trust and Savings.
Tb (or TB), tuberculosis.
Tchrs., Teachers.
tech., technical; technology.
technol., technological.
Tel.&Tel., Telephone and Telegraph.
temp., temporary.
T.H. (or H.T.), Territory of Hawaii.
Th.D., Doctor of Theology.
Th.M., Master of Theology.
theol., theological.
Tng., Training.
topog., topographical.
T.P.A., Travelers Protective Assn.
T.&P. Ry., Texas & Pacific Ry. Co.
trans., transactions; transferred.
Transl., translation; translations.
treas., treasurer.
TV, television.
TVA, Tennessee Valley Authority.
Twp., Township.

Ty. (or Ter.), Territory.
typog., typographical.

U. (or Univ.), University.
UAW, United Automobile Workers.
U.B., United Brethren in Christ.
U.C.V., United Confederate Veterans.
U.D.C., United Daughters of the Confederacy.
UN, United Nations.
UNESCO, United Nations Educational, Scientific and Cultural Organization.
UNRRA, United Nations Relief and Rehabilitation Administration.
U.P., United Presbyterian.
U.P. R.R., Union Pacific R.R.
urol., urological.
U.S., United States.
U.S.A., United States of America.
USAC, United States Air Corps.
USAF, United States Air Force.
USCG, United States Coast Guard.
U.S.C.T., U.S. Colored Troops.
USES, United States Employment Service.
USMC, United States Marine Corps.
USMHS, United States Marine Hospital Service.
USN, United States Navy.
USNA, United States National Army.
U.S.O., United Service Organizations.
USNG, United States National Guard.
USNRF, United States Naval Reserve Force.
USPHS, United States Public Health Service.
U.S.R., U.S. Reserves.
U.S.R.C.S., U.S. Revenue Cutter Service
U.S.S., United States Ship.
USSR, Union of Soviet Socialist Republics.
U.S.V., United States Volunteers.

v., vice.
VA, Veterans Administration.
vet., veteran; veterinary.
vice pres. (or v.p.,), vice president.
vis., visiting.
vol., volunteer; volume.
vs., versus (against).

W., West.
WAC, Women's Army Corps.
Wash., Washington (state).
W.C.T.U., Women's Christian Temperance Union.
WHO, World Health Organization.
W.I., West Indies.
W.& L.E. Ry., Wheeling & Lake Erie Ry. Co.
WPB, War Production Board.
W.P. R.R. Co., Western Pacific R.R. Co.
WSB, Wage Stabilization Board.

YMCA, Young Men's Christian Association.
YMHA, Young Men's Hebrew Association.
YM and YWHA, Young Men's and Young Women's Hebrew Association.
Y.& M.V. R.R., Yazoo & Mississippi Valley R.R.
yrs., years.
YWCA, Young Women's Christian Association.

zoöl., zoölogical.

AARON, Marcus, mfr.; b. Pitts., Dec. 14, 1869; s. Louis I. and Mina (Lippman) A.; ed. prep. dept. Western U. Pa.; matriculated in the Univ. and left soon afterwards on account of illness; LL.D., U. Pitts., 1924; m. Stella Hamburger, Nov. 23, 1898 (died Feb. 23, 1950); children—Marcus Lester, Fannie Hamburger (Mrs. Louis K. Friedman, dec.). Chmn. bd. Homer Laughlin China Co., mfrs. semi-vitreous tableware; pres. Newell Co., Newell Bridge & Ry. Co. (Newell, W.Va.). Mem. Bd. Public Edn., Pitts., 1911-46, pres. 1922-42; mem. State Bd. of Edn. of Pa., 1916-21; mem. State Council of Edn., 1921-23 and since 1940; mem. board Union of Am. Hebrew Congregations; trustee Jewish Publ. Soc.; pres. Rodef Shalom Congregation, 1930-41, hon. pres. 1941——. Republican. Home: 5564 Aylesboro Av. 17. Office: Union Trust Bldg., Pitts. Died June 21, 1954; buried West View Cemetery, Ross Twp., Allegheny County, Pa.

ABBELL, Maxwell, accountant, lawyer; b. Poland, Feb. 22, 1902; s. Maurice and Frieda (Alpert) A.; brought to U.S., 1905; A.B. magna cum laude, Harvard, 1922; M.B.A., Northwestern, 1925; grad. student U. of Chicago, 1926-28; J.D. cum laude, Loyola U., 1938; LL.D., (hon.), Jewish Theol. Sem. Am., 1954; m. Fannie Edelman, Aug. 21, 1923; children—Samuel, Nahami, Miriam, Ruth, Michael. Social worker Jewish Social Service Bur. of Chicago, 1922-23; factory personnel worker Hart, Schaffner & Marx, 1923; staff accountant John K. Laird & Co., 1923-25; sec., asst. dir. Jewish Charities of Chicago, 1925-37; sr. partner Maxwell Abbell & Co., 1937—; admitted to Ill. bar, 1938; sr. mem. Abbell & Abbell, 1944—; director, v.p. Am. Palestine Trading Corporation, 1949-53; member board of directors American Financial & Development Corp. for Israel; officer and dir. numerous bus. corps. Dir. bd. Jewish Edn., Chgo., 1937-54; dir. So. Side Hebrew Congregation, 1936-55, financial sec., 1937-38, pres. 1950-51; sec. Congregation B'nai Israel of Austin, 1926-28; dir. Young Men's Jewish Council of Chicago, 1935-39, sec. 1938, v.p. 1939; chmn. President's com. on Govt. Employment Policy, 1955-56. Mem. exec. com. Jewish Nat. Fund of Chicago, 1944—; mem. bd. govs. Coll. of Jewish Studies, Chicago, 1946-54, chmn. bd., 1950-54; gov. Hebrew U. of Jerusalem, 1955——; mem. nat. bd. dirs. Am. Friends of Hebrew U.; director Jewish Theol. Sem. of Am. 1948—— (mem. vice chmn. bd. overseers, chmn. nat. planning com., 1947-51). Hon. fellow Hebrew U. of Jerusalem. Mem. Am., Ill. and Chicago bar assns. Am. Acad. Polit. and Social Sci., Ill. Soc. C.P.As., Am. Inst. Accountants, Zionist Orgn. of Chicago (exec. com., 1944——), Phi Beta Kappa. Jewish religion (pres. United Synagogue of Am. 1950-53). Clubs: Harvard, Northwestern, Standard, Covenant (Chicago). Home: 6918 S. Euclid Av., Chgo. 49. Office: 59 E. Van Buren St., Chgo. 5. Died July 9, 1957.

ABBETT, Merle J., supt. schools; b. Franklin, Ind., Sept. 7, 1885; s. Lawson Oliver and Harriett (Mitchell) A.; A.B., Franklin Coll., 1907; A.M., Columbia, 1918, supt's. diploma Tchrs. Coll., 1918; LL.D., Franklin Coll., 1948; m. Janet Van Nuys, Nov. 29, 1916; children—Elizabeth Ann, Rebecca Jane. Supt. Hopewell (Ind.) Sch., 1908-15; tchr. pub. schs. Indpls., 1915-16; prin. Sr. High Sch., Bedford, Ind., 1916-24; supt. schs., Bedford, 1924-32, Ft. Wayne, 1932—. Mem. bd. dirs. Fed. Relief Agencies, C. of C. (v.p.), YMCA, Boy Scouts Am. (all Ft. Wayne); nat. adviser Girl Scouts Am.; mem. bd. dirs. Franklin Coll.; mem. Gov.'s Com. of Licensing Tchrs. (Ind.), 1936; mem. Nat. Com. on Phys. Edn. Program for Pub. Schs. of U.S.; del. Internat. Rotary Conv., Belgium, 1927, and inspected English and Continental schs.; exec. chmn. for war bonds Ft. Wayne and Allen County; chmn. adv. com. Youth in Selective Service, congl. del. Life mem. Ind. Congress Parents and Tchrs.; mem. N.E.A. (life; sec. discussion group, forum supt. div.), Ind. State Tchrs.

Assn. (pres. 1919), Ind. State Supts. Schs. (pres. 1931), N.E. Ind. Tchrs. Assn. (pres. 1933; chmn. exec. com. 1936), Ind. Prins. of Schs. (ex-pres.), Ind. Sch. Men's Club (pres. 1940), Horace Mann League, Phi Delta Theta, Phi Delta Kappa. Presbyn. Mason (K.T., Shriner). Clubs: Ft. Wayne Quest, Rotary (pres.). Author of Character Education for Public Schools; also of courses of study for public schools of Bedford and Ft. Wayne. Speaker and writer on ednl. subjects. Home: 4024 Harrison Blvd. Office: 1230 S. Clinton St., Ft. Wayne, Ind. Died May 5, 1956; buried Hopewell Cemetery, Franklin, Ind.

ABBIATI, F. Alexander (ab-ē-a'tē), chem. exec.; b. Barre, Vt., Dec. 30, 1904; s. Charles and Regina (Comolli) A.; B.S., U. N.H., 1927; m. Virginia M. McCrillis, Sept. 21, 1929; children—Melvin A., M. Virginia. Asst. sales mgr. Merrimac div. Monsanto Chem. Co., Everett, Mass., 1927-38, plastics div., Springfield, Mass., 1938-39, asst. gen. mgr. sales, 1939-44, gen. mgr. sales, 1944-47, asst. gen. mgr., 1947-50, gen. mgr. since 1950, v.p. Monsanto Chem. Co. since 1951; dir. Shawinigan Resins Corp.; dir. Union Trust Co.; corporator Hampden Savs. Bank. Dir. Future Springfield; mem. adv. com. Salvation Army, Springfield. Trustee Proctor Acad., Andover, N.H. Mem. Mfg. Chemists Assn., Employers Assn. Western Mass. (dir.), Am. Chem. Soc., Soc. Plastics Industry, Springfield C. of C. (dir.). Clubs: Colony (Springfield, Mass.); Metropolitan (N.Y. City); Longmeadow (Mass.) Country. Home: 130 Ellington St., Longmeadow. Office: Monsanto Chemical Co., Plastics Div., Springfield 2, Mass. Died Aug. 13, 1952; buried Longmeadow (Mass.) Cemetery.

ABBINK, John (ăb-bĭnk), publisher; b. Gibbsville, Wis., Mar. 24, 1890; s. Henry Garret and Deliah (Flipse) A.; student Wis. Meml. Acad., Cedar Grove, Wis., 1904-08, Hope Coll., Holland, Mich., 1908-11; m. Emily Catherine Seeboth, June 16, 1920; children—John Basil, Lois Marian. Engaged in newspaper writing and editing, 1911-14; public relations work, 1914-17; world travel in electrical industry, 1917-22; publishing, technical and world trade field, 1922-49; now partner Abbink and Drumm, consultants in fgn. trade and overseas bus. investments. Chmn. Nat. Fgn. Trade Council, 1945-49; co-chmn. Brazil-U.S. Tech. Commn. with rank of minister, 1949-50; cons. U.S. State Dept., 1950—; chief Delegation for study Italian mech. industries, 1951——. Clubs: Metropolitan, India House (N.Y.C.); Larchmont Shore (Larchmont, N.Y.). Home: 81 Colonial Av., Larchmont, N.Y. Office: 17 E. 42d St., N.Y.C. Died Aug. 3, 1958.

ABBOTT, Allan, educator; b. Bklyn., Feb. 15, 1876; s. Albert Allen and Susan Wildes (Hayes) A.; A.B., Harvard, 1896, A.M., 1911; Litt.D., Dickinson Coll., 1933; m. Mary Allen Rand, Dec. 27, 1900 (dec. May 1945); children—Elizabeth (dec.), Mary; m. 2d, Mrs. Amy Shaw Hock, Oct. 10, 1947. Tchr. St. James Sch., Md., 1896-1900; tchr. English, Washington Sch. for Boys, 1900-02, Horace Mann Sch., N.Y.C., 1902-13; asst. prof. English, Tchrs. Coll., Columbia, 1913-21, asso. prof., 1921-28, prof., 1928-42, ret. 1942; vis. prof. Wabash Coll., 1942-43; editor coll. English texts Am. Book Co., 1944-54. Mem. Nat. Council Tchrs. English (pres. 1917), Modern Lang. Assn. Am., N.E.A., Harvard Tchrs. Assn., Kappa Delta Pi, Delta Upsilon. Episcopalian. Contbr. English Jour., Tchrs. Coll. Record. Home: 90 Morningside Dr., N.Y.C. Died Mar. 21, 1956.

ABBOTT, Christopher J(oseph), cattleman, banker; b. Bird City, Kan., Oct. 11, 1889; s. Arthur J. and Hannah E. (Minor) A.; student Univ. Neb., 1911, 12, Univ. Mich., 1909-11; m. Helen Sears, July 10, 1914; children—Arthur Glaideth, Phyllis Drummond; married second Ethel Schmitz Page, August 26, 1933. President Guardian State Bank of

Alliance, Neb., 1928—; Bank of Chadron, 1946—, Bank of Hyannis, 1940——; pres. The Abbott Co., Hyannis, 1928——, Stansbie and Engel Co., 1940—; dir. Northwestern Bell Telephone Co. Mut. Benefit Health and Accident Assn., Omaha, Union Stock Yards Co. of Omaha, Omaha Nat. Bank. Mem. U.S. C. of C. (dir., 1942-48, v.p. 1948-49), Sigma Alpha Epsilon. Republican. Mason; Elk. Address: Hyannis Neb. Died Jan. 10, 1954.

ABBOTT, Edith, social worker, educator; b. Grand Island, Neb., Sept. 26, 1876; d. Othman A. and Elizabeth (Griffin) Abbott; prep. edn. Brownell Hall, Omaha; A.B., U. of Neb., 1901, Litt.D., 1917; fellow polit. economy, U. Chgo., 1903-05, Ph.D., 1905; studied U. London, 1906-07; LL.D., Beloit Coll., 1924, Oberlin, 1937, Tulane, 1942, U. Denver, 1952. Instr. polit. economy, Wellesley Coll., 1907-08; asso. dir. Chgo. Sch. Civics, 1908-20; resident Hull-House, 1908-20, 49-53; mem. faculty U. Chgo., 1913-53, prof., dean Sch. of Soc. Service Adminstrn., 1924-42, dean emeritus, 1942-53. Recipient survey award, Nat. Conf. Social Workers, 1952. Fellow Am. Statis. Assn.; mem. Am. Econ. Assn., Am. Assn. U. Women, Nat. Child Labor Com. Mem. Am. Econ. Assn., Am. Assn. Social Workers, Women's Trade Union League, Phi Beta·Kappa, Delta Gamma. Pres. Nat. Conf. of Social Work, 1937, Ill. Conf. of Social Work, 1939. Clubs: College (Chgo.), Cosmopolitan (N.Y.C.). Author: Women in Industry, 1910; Immigration—Select Documents and Case Records, 1923; Historical Aspects of the Immigration Problem, 1926; Social Welfare and Professional Education, 1931; Crime and the Foreign Born (Vol. VII. Repts. of Wickersham Com.), 1931; The Tenements of Chicago, 1936; Some American Pioneers in Social Welfare, 1937; Public Assistance, 1939; also (with Sophonisba P. Breckinridge) The Delinquent Child and the Home, 1912; Truancy and Non-attendance in Chicago, 1917. Editor Social Service Review. Home: Grand Island, Neb. Died July 28, 1957; buried Grand Island (Neb.) Cemetery.

ABBOTT, Edward Farrington, shoe mfr.; b. Lake City, Colo., Apr. 3, 1882; s. Jacob Jackson and Jenny Lind (Farrington) A.; A.B., Bowdoin Coll., 1903; m. Mary Hale Dana, June 7, 1906; children—Helen Dana, Margaret Farrington, Edward Farrington, Ruth Livingston, Luther Dana, John Cushman. Pres. Cushman-Hollis Co. since 1919; pres. Webster Rubber Co., Charles Cushman Company. Member School Board, Auburn, 1916-19, City Council, 1918-24; president Auburn C. of C., 1918-20; pres. Auburn Y.M.C.A., Auburn Harpswell Assn.; trustee Bowdoin Coll. Mem. Theta Delta Chi. Republican. Conglist. Mason (32°, Shriner). Clubs: Rotary (Auburn); Riverton (Lewiston, Me.). Home: Auburn, Me. Died Dec. 1, 1952.

ABBOTT, Leonard Dalton, editor, author, publicist; b. Liverpool, Eng., May 20, 1878; s. Lewis L. and Grace (Van Dusen) A.; m. Rose Yuster, Apr. 9, 1915 (dec. Dec. 21, 1930); children—Voltairine (dec.), William Morris, Ellen. Came to U.S., 1897; joined staff of Literary Digest, 1899; asso. editor Current Literature (later Current Opinion), 1905-25; editor Physical Culture, 1926-27; mem. staff Ency. of Social Sciences, 1929-34; research editor Fed. Writers Project, Works Progress Adminstrn., Washington, 1935-39. Identified with the Socialist movement, 1895-1905; pres. Thomas Paine Nat. Hist. Assn. 1910; pres. Free Speech League, 1910-14; pres. bd. trustees Bronx Free Fellowship, 1925-35. A Founder Rand Sch. Social Sci., Intercollegiate Socialist Soc. (now League for Indsl. Democracy), Poetry Soc. Am., Ferrer Colony, and of Ferrer Sch., Stelton, N.J. Active in behalf of Sacco and Vanzetti, 1927. Author: Ernest Howard Crosby, a Valuation and a Tribute, 1907. Editor: Sociological sect. of Science-History of the Universe, 1909; Francisco Ferrer, His Life, Work and Martyrdom, 1910; Masterpieces of Economics, 1946; Masterworks of Government, 1947. Home: 49 Grove St., N.Y.C. Died Mar. 19, 1953.

ABBOTT, Theodore Jacob, physician; b. Cornwall-on-Hudson, N.Y., July 20, 1872; s. Lyman and Abby Frances (Hamlin) A.; ed., The Hill Sch., Pottstown, Pa.; A.B., Harvard, 1896; M.D., Coll. Physicians and Surgeons (Columbia), 1900; m. Marie Matthiessen, June 8, 1907; children—Frances Sophie, Beatrice Vail. Practiced at N.Y. City since 1900; clin. prof. medicine New York U., 1915, now retired; formerly visiting physician Bellevue Hosp.; consultant U.S. Vet. Bur., Hosp. for Ruptured and Crippled (New York). Served as maj. M.C., U.S.A., with A.E.F. in France, World War. Mem. A.M.A. Republican. Conglist. Club: Harvard (New York). Home: Cornwall-on-Hudson, N.Y. Died Mar. 3, 1951.

ABDUL-HUDA, Tawfiq Pasha, premier of Hashemite Kingdom of Jordan, July 1951—; served several times previously as prime minster and minister of fgn. affairs. Address: Amman, Jordan. Deceased.

ABDUL-ILAH HASHIMI, Crown Prince, heir presumptive to throne of Iraq; b. Nov. 14, 1913; uncle of King Feisal II; ed. pvtly. and at Victoria Coll., Alexandria, Egypt. Governed as regent of Iraq during minority of King Feisal II, 1939-57. Address: The Royal Palace, Baghdad, Iraq. Died July 14, 1958.

ABDULLAH, Ibn al Hussein, King of Hashemite Kingdom of Jordan. Assassinated July 20, 1951.

ABEL, John A(very), nat. pres. Fraternal Order of Eagles; b. Prospect, O., Jan. 14, 1886; s. John Christian and Catherine (Isler) A.; ed. Harding High Sch., Marion, O., 1900-04, Marion Bus. Coll., 1904-05; m. Florida A. Churchill, Feb. 4, 1907; children—Dorothy Catherine (Mrs. James W. Rein), Marion Lucile (dec.), John Churchill (dec.). Sec., mgr. Marion Brewing Co., 1906-19; owner Marion Exide Battery Co., 1919-25; mgr. Marion Eagles Bldg., 1925-33; dir. Fed. Relief and Employment, 1933-36; supr. Ohio State Treasurer's Office, 1937-38; sec.-treas. Betty Zane Corn Products Co., Marion, 1937—; v.p., sec. Lautenslager Oldsmobile Co.; sec.-treas. Marion Land Co. Grand worthy pres. Fraternal Order of Eagles, 1939. Democrat. Methodist. Mem. Elks, Druids, K.P. Clubs: Kiwanis, Eagles (Marion). Home: Pleasant Acres, Marion, O. Office: Bellefontaine Av., Marion, O. Died Nov. 17, 1955.

ABELLS, Harry Delmont, educator; b. Hatfield, Mass., Oct. 18, 1872; s. Nathaniel T. and Ruth Elizabeth (Livermore) A.; grad. Mt. Hermon Sch., Mass., 1891; S.B., U Chgo. 1897, postgrad. work, 1897-98; m. Helena M. Sadd, Dec. 27, 1897; children—Sumner Delmont (dec.), Ruth Helene. Gen. sec. Englewood dept. YMCA, Chgo., 1898; acad. asst. introductory yr., Morgan Park Acad., U. Chgo., 1898-1901, continuing as asso. and instr. in physics and chemistry; prin. Morgan Park Mil. Acad., 1907-19, supt. 1919—; supt. Morgan Park Jr. Coll., 1933—. Pres. Sch. Bd., Morgan Park, 1910-12; mem. Chgo. Adv. Sch. Plan Commn., 1921-23. Col. Ill. N.G. Mem. Central Assn. Science and Mathematics Tchrs. (pres. 1918), Pvt. Schs. Assn. Central States (treas. 1931-32), N.E.A., Am. Chem. Soc., Alpha Delta Phi. Conglist. Club: Executives (Chgo.). Home: Morgan Park Sta., Chgo. Died Mar. 2, 1958.

ABEND, Hallett Edward (ā'bĕnd), foreign corr.; b. Portland, Ore., Sept. 15, 1884; s. Alexander and Kittie (Hallett) A.; student Stanford U., 1904-06; unmarried. Reporter Spokesman-Rev., Spokane, Wash., 1906-08; telegraph editor, gen. asst. editor Spokane Chronicle, 1908-13; city editor Honolulu Star-Bull., 1915-16; mng. editor Idaho Statesman, Boise, 1916-20; city editor Los Angeles Times, 1920-24; script and title writer for Talmadge Sisters, Hollywood, Calif., 1924-25; free lance writing in China, 1926-27; with N.Y. Times, 1927-42, as China correspondent, 1937-41; joined Washington, D.C. Bureau, New York Times, May, 1941; now free lance writer and lecturer; asso. editor Marshalltown (Ia.) Times-Republican, 1951-55. Mem. Kappa Sigma. Republican. Author: Tortured China, 1930; Can China Survive (with Anthony Billingham), 1936; Chaos in Asia, 1939; Japan Unmasked, 1941; Ramparts of The Pacific, 1942; Pacific Charter, 1943; My Life in China, 1943; Treaty Ports, 1944; Reconquest, Its Results and Responsibilities, 1946; The God from the West, 1947; Half Slave, Half Free, 1950; also author articles in Saturday Evening Post, Am. Mercury, McLean's, Reader's Digest, Look, Cosmopolitan, etc. Home: Moccasin, Cal. Died Nov. 27, 1955; buried Hyde Park, Vt.

ABERN, Oscar G. (a'bern), lawyer, govt. ofcl.; b. Mpls. June 10, 1903; s. William and Amelia (Solomon) A.; A.B., U. Minn., 1924, LL.B., 1926; m. Sally Rubin, Feb. 6, 1929; children—Jerome Myron, Wendell Samuel. Admitted to Minn. bar, 1926, N.D. bar, 1927; practiced in Wishek, N.D., 1927-34; atty. Home Owners Loan Corp., Omaha, 1934-38, N.D. state counsel, 1938-40, sr. atty., Omaha, 1940-42; atty., regional rent atty. OPA, Chgo., 1942-46, regional rent atty., N.Y.C., 1946-47; regional dir. Office of Rent Stblzn., and predecessor orgns., (nine Midwest states), Chgo., since 1947. Compiled, revised ordinances City of Wishek, N.D. Address: 125 W. Arikara St., Bismarck, N.D. Died Oct. 27, 1954; buried Mpls.

ABERNATHY, Milton Aubrey, gas exec.; b. Whitney, Tex., Dec. 11, 1892; s. William Harvel and Minnie Annetta (Overton) A.; B.S., Texas A. and M. Coll., 1916; m. Ernestine Olivia Faulk, Oct. 16, 1923. Various positions r.r. maintenance, location, constrn., 1916-20; engr. Magnolia Petroleum Co., Dallas, 1920-24; supt. Magnolia Gas Co., Dallas, 1924-30; gen. supt. transmission United Gas Pub. Service Co., Houston, 1930-37; v.p., dir. United Gas Pipe Line Co. since 1937, United Gas Corp. since 1947; dir. Union Producing Co., Shreveport, La., since 1947, v.p. since 1952. Mem. gas. industry adv. council, oil and gas div. U S. Dept. of Interior. Mem. bd. nat., so. YMCA's. Trustee Tex. A. and M. Coll. Research Found., Centenary Coll. Served as lt., 315th C.E., World War I. Mem. Am. (director), So. gas assns., Am. Petroleum Inst., Mid-Continent Oil and Gas Assn. Methodist. Clubs: Engineers (N.Y. City); Country, Petroleum, Rotary (Shreveport); Petroleum (New Orleans). Home: 555 Southfield Rd. Office: United Gas Bldg., Shreveport, La. Died Nov. 2, 1955; buried Forest Park Cemetery, Shreveport.

ABERNETHY, Charles Laban, ex-congressman; b. Rutherford College, N.C., Mar. 18, 1872; s. John Turner and Martha Anna (Scott) A.; student Rutherford Coll., 1891; studied law U. N.C., 1895; m. Minnie M. May, Dec. 19, 1895; 1 son, Charles Laban. Admitted to N.C. bar, 1895, practicing at Beaufort; solicitor 3d Jud. Dist., later 5th Dist., 12 yrs.; elected to 67th Congress to fill unexpired term of S. M. Brinson, reelected 68th to 73d Congresses, 3d N.C. Dist. Formerly mem. Dem. Exec. Com. of N.C., Dem. presdl. elector, 1900, 04. Methodist. Mason (K.T., 32°, Shriner), Odd Fellow, P.P., Red Man, Elk, Woodman; mem. Jr. Order of United Am. Mechanics. Home: New Bern, N.C. Died Feb. 23, 1955; buried Cedar Grove Cemetery, New Bern.

ABERNETHY, Robert Swepston, ret. army officer; b. Gonzales County, Tex., Aug. 5, 1874; s. Benjamin Roberts and Anna Elizabeth (Swepston) A.; grad. U.S. Mil. Acad., 1897; grad. Sch. Submarine Defense, 1905-06, Army War Coll., 1911-12. Commd. 2d lt. arty. U.S. Army, 1897, promoted through grades to brig. gen., 1932; temporary major U.S. Vols., 1899-1901; temp. col. Nat. Army, 1917-20. Served in Spanish-Am. War, in Philippines, 1898-1901; comdr. 165th F.A. Brigade, AEF, served in France and Germany, 1917-18; last command, San Francisco Port of Embarkation, Fort Mason, Cal.; retired, 1938. Decorated Silver Star with two clusters, Order of Purple Heart, with one cluster. Nat. pres. Nat. Sojourners, Inc., 1937-40. Mason (33°, hon.). Home: Summerton, S.C. Died June 10, 1952.

ABERNETHY, William Ellis, lecturer; b. Rutherford Coll., N.C., May 28, 1860; s. Rev. R. L. A. (D.D.); grad. Rutherford Coll., 1878; read law with Col. Geo. N. Folk, Lenoir, N.C., 1880; m. Bertha Thomas Winn, June 11, 1899. Prof. Latin and Greek, Rutherford Coll., 1881-99, pres. 1894-99; has published volume of lectures. Twice nominated for State senate by dominant party in his county, but declined. Address: Rutherford College, N.C. Died Mar. 15, 1936; buried Rutherford College.

ABRAMS, Stanley L., lawyer; b. North East, Md., Nov. 4, 1899; s. Rudolph T. and Viola M. (Lupold) A.; LL.B., Temple U., 1931; m. Mary J. Holland, June 29, 1926; children—Donald H., Richard J., William S. Admitted to Del. bar, 1931; with E. I. du Pont de Nemours & Co., Wilmington, Del., since 1916, asst. dir. legal dept., 1940-50, dir. since 1950, gen. counsel since 1951. Home: 2200 Park Dr. Office: 1007 Market St., Wilmington, Del. Died May 8, 1954.

ABT, Isaac Arthur, pediatrist; b. Wilmington, Ill., Dec. 18, 1867; s. Levi and Henrietta (Hart) A.; completed preliminary med. course Johns Hopkins, 1889; M.D., Chicago Med. Coll., 1891; interne Michael Reese Hosp., Chicago, 1891-93; post-grad. work in Vienna and Berlin, 1893-94; Sc.D., Northwestern U., 1931; m. Lena Rosenberg, Aug. 20, 1897; children—Arthur F., Lawrence E. Prof. diseases of children Northwestern U. Woman's Med. Sch., 1897-1901; asso. prof. diseases of children Rush Med. Coll., 1902-08; professor diseases of children Northwestern University Medical School, 1909-42, prorfessor emeritus, 1942—; cons. physician diseases of children at Children's Memorial Hosp., Sarah Morris Children's Hosp., St. Luke's Hosp.; was attending physician diseases of children Passavant Hosp. Honorary mem. Deutsche Gesellschaft für Kinderheilkunde; mem. Am. Pediatric Soc. (pres. 1926-27), Am. Acad. Pediatrics (pres. 1930-31), A.M.A., Chicago Med. Soc. (pres. 1927), Chicago Pediatric Soc., Central States Pediatric Soc., Am. Assn. Teachers of Diseases of Children (pres. 1922), Children's Hosp. Assn. of American, Washington Med. and Surg. Soc. (hon.), Alpha Omega Alpha (hon. Minnesota Chapter). Distinguished Service Award, A.M.A., 1948, Chevalier of Legion of Honor (France). Clubs: City, Ill. Athletic (Chicago). Author: The Baby's Food, 1917, The Baby Doctor, 1944. Editor vol. on Pediatrics in the Practical Medicine Series; also editor, A System of Pediatrics. Has written many monographs on subjects relating to diseases of children. Home: 4747 S. Kenwood Av., Chgo. 15. Office: 104 S. Michigan Av., Chgo. Died Nov. 22, 1955; buried Rosehill Cemetery, Chgo.

ACHER Howard Mossman (a'ker), hotel exec.; b. at Cleveland, Dec. 10, 1889; son of Albert Milton and Frances Annetta (Hilands) A.; Ph.B., Grove City Coll., 1913; m. Ruth Byerly Spearman, June 2, 1922. Dir. of athletics, Du Bois (Pa.) High Sch., 1913-14, Grove City Coll., 1915-17 and 1919-20; with Gen. Electric Co., 1921; dir. of athletics, U. of Tulsa, 1922-25; pres. Morris Plan Co. of Okla., 1926-32, Southwest Homes Corp., 1927-32, Industrial Bancstock Corp., 1928-32, Mid-Continent Bancshares, Inc., 1932; in investment banking business, 1932-35 and 1937-38; engaged in ranching and farming, 1935-38; real estate, Tucson, Ariz., 1939-41; hotel exec., Denver, 1950—. Supt., hotels and restaurants, Atomic Energy Commn., Los Alamos, 1943-48. Served as lt. United States Army, World War I; war construction work, 1942-43; awarded Army Service Forces Commendation for Meritorious Civilian Service. President Tulsa County Council Boy Scouts, 1931; chairman of Advanced Gifts Committee of Tulsa Community Fund, 1931. Mem. American Legion. Republican. Presbyterian. Clubs: Tulsa, Tulsa Country, Spavinaw (Okla.); Los Alamos Officers, Los Alamos Civic. Address: 516 Dartmouth Pl., S.E., Albuquerque, N.M. Died May 10, 1957.

ACHESON, Barclay (ăch'ĕ-sŭn), b. Virden, Manitoba, Can., June 3, 1887; s. T. Davis and Mary E. (Huston) A.; A.B., Macalester Coll., LL.D., 1933; student San Francisco and McCormick theol. sems.; D.D., Dubuque U., 1928; m. Louise M. Patteson, Aug. 26, 1914; 1 dau., Judy. Teacher at Am. Univ., Beirut; later pastor of a Presbyn. ch., Raymond, Wash.; sec. Portland (Ore.) Y.M.C.A. during World War; became asso. gen. sec. and field dir. New Era Movement of the Presbyn. Ch., Nov. 1918; later had charge field orgn. of China Famine Fund; asso. gen. sec. Near East Relief, 1921-29, exec. sec. 1929-44, trustee 1932-44, also dir. overseas operations, 1924-29; exec. sec. Near East Foundation, 1930-37, v.p. bd. dirs., 1937—; asso. editor Reader's Digest, 1936-40, roving editor, 1949-42, now dir. internat. editions. Pres. Community Ch. Workers Am., 1936-38; mem. U.S. Nat. Commn. for UNESCO, 1946-51; former mem. Am. Arbitration Assn.; mem. Finance Com. Fed. Council Chs., 1944-50; mem. Laymen's com. 1950-55; mem. gen. budget and bus. and finance coms., Nat. Council Chs.; mem. bd. dirs. Export Advertising Assn. Inc., 1946-48; mem. of bd. dirs., Camp Sloane, Inc.; dir. of Y.M.C.A. Uptown Branch, N.Y. City, 1937-40; mem. bd. trustees Macalester Coll., St. Paul; mem. advisory bd. Com. on Citizenship Training, N.E.A.; mem. Health Sect. and American Advisory Com., World Fedn. Edn. Assns.; mem. Advisory Council, Department of Oriental Languages and Literatures, Princeton, 1944-53; mem. bd. trustees U.S. Council, Internat. C. of C.; director Reader's Digest Found. Decorated Greek Red Cross medal, 1927; Comdr. Order of Phoenix (Greece), 1930; Commander Order of Redeemer (Greece), 1935; Chevalier, Legion of Honor (France), 1952; Royal Order North Star Knighthood First Class (Sweden), 1953. Mem. Nat. Pubs. Assn., Internat. Advt. Assn., Ecuadorean Am. Assn., Pan Am. Soc. U.S. Republican. Clubs: Cloud, New York Athletic, Overseas Press of America, Triton Fish and Game, Old English Sheep Dog of America. Home: Todd Lane, Briarcliff Manor, N.Y. Address: care The Reader's Digest, Pleasantville, N.Y. Died Dec. 4, 1957; buried Ferncliff Mausaleum, Hartsdale, N.Y.

ACKERMAN, Ralph Henry, ex-ambassador; b. W. Hoboken, N.J., July 23, 1892; s. Alva Scott and Grace (Knox) A.; student Emerson Inst., Washington, 1913, U. Chattanooga, 1914-15; m. Jessica M. Simmons, Jan. 14, 1916; children—Ralph Simmons, William Knox. Chief clk. S.A. agy. So. Ry., Chattanooga, 1913-17; partner Harry F. Flachs & Co., Buenos Aires, Argentina, 1917-18; mgr. Boomer & Co., N.Y.C., 1919; mgr. S.A. dept. Quaker City Corp., 1919-21; chief of Latin Am. div., U.S. Dept. Commerce, 1922-23; comml. attaché, Santiago, 1923-33, Rio de Janeiro, 1933-37, Madrid, 1939-46; chief dir. reporting services State Dept., 1946-47; counselor Am. Embassy, Lima, Peru, 1947-48; became A.E. and P. to Dominican Republic, 1948. Econ. expert 5th Pan-Am. Conf., Santiago, 1923, First Pan-Am. Comml. Conf. Buenos Aires, 1935. Decorated Officer Order of Merit (Chile). Address: Walterboro, S.C. Died Jan. 12, 1957.

ACKERMAN, R(obert) B(urke), business exec.; b. New York, N.Y., Oct. 19, 1886; s. William and Mary Jane (Fallon) A.; ed. in pub. schs.; m. Margaret Crane, Feb. 17, 1931; 1 dau., Margaret Crane. Vice pres., treas., dir. Am. Ship Bldg. Co., 1947-53, pres., 1953-57. Clubs: Union, Mayfield Country (Cleve.). Home: 2859 Sedgewick Rd., Cleve. 20. Office: The American Ship Building Co., foot of W. 54th St., Cleve. 2. Died Apr. 29, 1958; buried Cleve.

ACOSTA GARCIA, Julio (ä-kōs'tä gär-thē'ä), sec. of state, minister fgn. affairs, Costa Rica; b. Province of Alajuela, Costa Rica, May 23, 1872; s. Juan Vicente and Jésus (Garcia) A.; student of distinction, Colls. of San José and Cartago; m. Elena Gallegos, April 16, 1910; 1 child, Zulay, Governor Province of Alajuela; dep. to Congress from Alajuela and San José; consul of Costa Rica in San Salvador; head diplomatic missions on various occasions for the govt. and other states of Central Am.; sec. of state and minister fgn. affairs, 1915; pres. Rep. of Costa Rica, 1920-24; sec. of state and minister fgn. affairs, 1944-48. Decorated Benemerito de la Patria, 1954. Home: Calles 7-9, Avenida, 9, San Jose, Costa Rica, C.A. Died July 6, 1954; buried San José.

ACREE, Solomon Farley (ā'krē), chemist; b. McGregor, Tex., Dec. 18, 1875; s. George Wren and Elizabeth Virginia (Grimes) A.; B.S., U. Tex., 1896, M.S., 1897; Ph.D., C. Chgo., 1902; grad. study U. Berlin, 1903-04; Johnston scholar Johns Hopkins, 1904-06; m. Ruby Jarvis Tiller, May 1, 1917; children—Ruby Jane de Haven, George Wren. Asst. in chemistry U. Tex., 1896-97; fellow and asst. in chemistry U. Chgo., 1898-1901; asst. prof. chemistry U. Utah, 1901-04; asst. and asso. prof. Johns Hopkins, 1906-14; prof. forest chemistry U. Wis., 1914-17, prof. and chief of chem. sect., Forest Products Lab., 1914-17; prof. forest chemistry Syracuse U., 1917-19; v.p. Internat. Chem. Products Co. and pres. Grahame Chem. Co., 1920-24; prof. physical organic chemistry, George Washington U., 1924-26; prin. chemist U.S. Bur. Standards, Washington, 1927—, chief of sect. Fiber Structures and Hydrogen Ion Measurements, 1931—. Fellow A.A.A.S., Texas Acad. Science, Chemical Soc. (London); mem. Am. Chem. Soc., German Chem. Soc., Phi Beta Kappa, Sigma Xi. Baptist. Writer of Graphs and Theory of Errors, Physical Organic Chemistry, Reactions of Ions and Molecules (in mimeographed form). Contbr. to Jour. Am. Chem. Soc., Am. Chem. Jour., Jour. Physical Chemistry, Science, Jour. Chem. Soc., Berichte Chemische Gesellschaft, etc. Research on utilization of agrl. and lumber waste; pH standards; etc. Home: 3259 R St. N.W., Washington 7. Office: Bureau of Standards, Washington. Died Oct. 23, 1957.

ACRET, George Edward (ā'krĕt), lawyer; b. Brooklyn, N.Y., Dec. 23, 1886; s. George W. and Katherine (Franklin) A.; student Brooklyn Manual Training High Sch., 1902-05, Worcester Poly. Inst., 1905-06, U. of Wis., 1906-09; legal edn. in law office; m. 3d, Marian McMillan, July 1, 1943; children by previous marriage—Mary, John, James. Admitted to Wash. bar, 1919, to Calif. bar, 1923, and since practiced at Los Angeles; admitted to bar of Wash., D.C., 1938; formerly asso. with firm of Hanna & Morton; formerly asso. with late Sen. William G. McAdoo; dist. atty. Grays Harbor Co., Wash., 1921-22; city atty. Venice, Calif., 1923-25; apptd. mem. Nat. Bituminous Coal Commn., 1935-37; acting dir. div. of trials and hearings, 1937-38. In air service, A.E.F., World War, 1917-19, and with Wash. Nat. Guard, 1920-22, retiring as capt. Mem. State Bar of Calif., Los Angeles Bar Assn., Lawyers Club, Am. Legion. Democrat. Episcopalian. Home: El Rancho Paraiso, 10428 Penrose St., Sun Valley, Calif. Office: 650 S. Grand Av., Los Angeles. Deceased.

ACUFF, Herbert (ā'kŭf), surgeon; b. Washburn, Tenn., Aug. 22, 1886; s. Joel and Sarah A.; Pharm.G., Ky. Sch. of Pharmacy, 1911; M.D., U. of Louisville Med. Sch., 1911; Honoris Causa, U. of Argentina; m. Lola Pruden, Oct. 20, 1915; 1 dau., Betty Rose (Mrs. Lawrence Barker). In practice at Knoxville, Tenn.; chief of staff, St. Mary's Memorial Hospital; vis. surg. East Tenn. Bapt. Hosp., Knoxville General Hospital, Fort Sanders Hospital, cons. surgeon and chmn. operating com., Beverly Hills Sanatorium; chief cons. surgeon of Pruden Coal & Coke Co., surgeon, Southern Ry. System; pres. and surg. dir. surgery, Acuff Clinic.Served as maj., Med. Corps, U.S. Army, World War I. Mem. Tenn. Hosp. Licensing Bd.; sec. Internat Bd. Cancerology. Life fellow Am. Coll. Surgeons, Southeastern Surg. Congress (pres., 1947-48), Internat. Coll. Surgeons (treas., 1946-48; pres. U.S. Chapt., 1946-48; founder fellow Qualification Bd. since 1947; pres. since 1950); hon. fellow Med. and Surg. Society of Sao Paulo, Brazil, Surg. Soc. of Rome, Italy, Piemontese Soc. of Torino, Italy; mem. Am. Goiter Assn., American Coll. Chest Physicians (asso.), Am. Cancer Soc. (bd. dirs., 1945-46; bd. dirs. and service dir., Tenn. div. since 1945), World Med. Assn. (mem. bd. dirs., U.S. Com., Inc.), Knoxville Acad. Medicine (pres. 1945-46), Am. Assn. Ry. Surgeons. Clubs: Civitan (internat. pres. 1926-27), Cherokee Country. Contbr. papers to med. lit. on surg. subjects. Home: 632 Cherokee Blvd. Office: 514 Church Av., Knoxville, Tenn. Died Nov. 2, 1951.

ADAIR, Henry Porterfield, lawyer; b. Red Sulphur Springs, W.Va., Aug. 26, 1883; s. Lewis Cass and Sidney (Taylor) A.; m. Marie Manning, June 1, 1910; children—Polly Manning, Louise Manning, Sidney Taylor. Admitted to Fla. bar, 1911; mem. Knight & Adair, Jacksonville, 1911-25, Cooper, Knight, Adair, Cooper & Osborne, 1925-29, Knight, Adair, Cooper & Osborne, 1929-38, Adair, Cooper, Osborne & Copp, 1938, Adair, Kent, Ashby & McNatt, 1939-52, now Adair, Ulmer, Murchison, Kent & Ashby; dir. Fla. Nat. Bank of Jacksonville, St. Joe Paper Co. Chmn. State Bd. Control, Fla. Instns. of Higher Learning 1939-45; chmn. Duval Co. Budget Commn., 1931-34. Chmn. bd. mgrs. The Nemours Found. Mem. Am., Fla. State, Jacksonville bar assns., Am. Law Inst., Assn. Bar City N.Y., Newcomen Soc. N.A., Lawyers Club, C. of C. (ex-pres.). Democrat. Episcopalian. Clubs: Seminole; Timquana Country, Florida Yacht; Farmington Country (Charlottesville, Va.). Address: 1867 Edgewood Av., Jacksonville, Fla. Died May 9, 1955; buried Evergreen Cemetery, Jacksonville.

ADAIR, Jackson Leroy, ex-congressman, judge; b. Clayton, Ill., Feb. 23, 1887; s. Henry L. and Sarah Emily (Pevehouse) A.; student Illinois Coll., 1907-08; B.L., U. of Mich., 1911; married Apr. 15, 1911. Admitted to bars of Mich., Okla. and Ill.; practiced at Muskogee, Okla., 1911-13; returned to Quincy, Ill.; city atty.. Quincy, Ill., 1914-16, state's atty. Adams Co., 1916-20 and 1924-28; state senator, 1928-32; mem. 73rd and 74th Congresses (1933-37), 15th Ill. Dist. U.S. Dist. judge Southern Dist. Ill., since 1937. Mem. Ill. State and Am. bar assns., Rho Sigma Rho. Democrat. Conglist. Mason, Elk, Moose, Eagle. Clubs: Peoria, Quincy Country. Home: 2101 Grove Av. Office: Fed. Bldg., Quincy, Ill. Died Jan. 19, 1956; buried South Side Cemetery, Clayton, Ill.

ADAMIC, Louis (ăd'ăm-ĭk), writer; b. village of Blato, Slovenia, Yugoslavia, Mar. 23, 1899; son of Anton and Ana (Adamic) A.; student Gymnasium, Lyublyana, Yugoslavia, 1910-13; hon. D.Litt., Temple U., 1941; m. Stella Sanders, June 15, 1931. Came to U.S., 1913, naturalized, 1918. Served in U.S. Army during World War I. Member American Legion. Awarded Guggenheim fellowship, 1932-33; awarded a grant-in-aid, Rockefeller Foundation, 1937, Carnegie Foundation, 1939, 40, 41; received $1000 John Anisfield award for book, From Many Lands, 1940. Awarded Order of National Unity by Marshal Tito, of Yugoslavia, 1944. Mem. Authors League of America Writers War Board, American Historical Association, Society of American Historians, Emergency Com. to Save Jewish People of Europe (1944); president United Com. of South-Slavic Americans, 1943; hon. pres. United Com. of South-Slavic Americans, 1944; hon. pres. Slovenian Am. Nat. Council, 1942-45; dir. American Institute Ethnic Affairs, 1946. Author: Dynamite, 1931 (revised 1934), Laughing in the Jungle, 1932; The Native's Return, 1934; Grandsons, 1935; Cradle of Life, 1936; The House in Antigua, 1937; My America, 1938; From Many Lands, 1940; Two-Way Passage, 1941; What's Your Name, 1942; My Native Land, 1943; A Nation of Nations, 1945; Dinner at the White House, 1946; The Eagle and the Roots, 1952. Publisher-editor of the Trends and Tides since 1945; gen. editor The Peoples of America series, since 1943. Editor Common Ground, 1940-41. Contbr. articles and fiction to mags. Address: R.F.D. 1, Milford, N.J. Died Sept. 4, 1951.

ADAMS, Arthur Frank, banking, mfg., pub. utilities; b. Aurorahville, Wis., Jan. 3, 1881; s. Harrison Emil and Susan (Coville) A.; high sch., Berlin, Wis.; studied elec. engring, through corr. course and in the field; m. Louetta M. Spalding, Sept. 10, 1902; children—Mrs. Ruth Kline (dec.), Mrs. Marjorie Nelle Swanson; m. 2d, Alice E. Clark, August 9, 1942. Began business in employ telephone company at Berlin, Wis., 1898; worked as telephone engr. in Wis., Minn., Ill., Mo. and Kan.; chmn. Theodore Gary & Co. (Kansas City); chmn. Anglo Canadian Telephone Co. (Montreal), Automatic Electric Co. (Chicago), Asso. Telephone and Telegraph Co., Telephone Bond and Share Co., Gary Services and Investment Co. (Wilmington, Del.); chairman Theodore Gary & Co. (London); president Almera Electrical Co. (Wilmington, Del.), and other corporations. Member General Operating Board in charge federal operation of telegraph and telephone systems, by appointment of Postmaster General Burleson, December 13, 1918-July 31, 1919. Trustee Liberty Memorial Association of Kansas City. Republican. Presbyterian. Clubs: Kansas City Country; Surf (Miami Beach); Union League (New York); Chicago (Chicago); Army-Navy Country, Congressional Country (Washington); Junior Carlton, Royal Thames Yacht (London). Home: 4450 Alton Road, Miami Beach, Fla. and 70 Cheyne Walk, Chelsea, London, Eng. Office: 1100 King St., Wilmington, Del. Died Mar. 28, 1958; buried Woodlawn Mausoleum, Miami Beach, Fla.

ADAMS, Benjamin Cullen, utilities exec.; b. Madison, Wis., Apr. 1, 1880; s. Henry Cullen and Anna Berkeley (Norton) A.; B.S. in elec. engring. U. Wis., 1903; m. Rachel Lloyd Nicholson, June 3, 1908; children—Florence (Mrs. Robt. H. McDonnell), Benjamin Cullen. Tester electric meters, later supt. distbn. Madison (Wis.) Gas & Electric Light Co., 1903-06; supt., later gen. mgr. Lincoln (Neb.) Gas & Electric Light Co., 1906-13; v.p., gen. mgr. Spokane (Wash.) Gas & Fuel Co., Eng. in Brazil, 1914-15; v.p., gen. mgr. Montgomery (Ala.) Light & Water Power Co., 1915-16, Empire Dist. Electric Co., Joplin, Mo., 1916-20, St. Joseph (Mo.) Ry., Light, Heat and Power Co., 1920-22. Toledo Edison Company; pres. Community Traction Co. 1922-25; v.p., gen. mgr. Gas Service Co., Kansas City, Mo., 1925-40, pres., gen. mgr., dir. 1940; exec. v.p., dir. Kansas City (Mo.) Gas Co., 1925-40, pres., 1940-47; exec. v.p., dir. Wyandotte County Gas Co., 1925-40, pres., 1940-47; Kansas City Gas Co. and Wyandotte Gas Co. merged with Gas Service Co. 1947-56; chmn. bd., 1956—; dir. Commerce Trust Co., Mo. Mem. bd. govs. Am. Royal Live Stock and Horse Show; mem. bd. dirs. A.R.C.; trustee Midwest Research Inst. Mem. Am. Gas Assn. (dir.). Clubs: Kansas City, Kansas City County, Mission Hills Country, University, Saddle & Sirloin, River (Kansas City, Mo.); Tennis, Racquet, Committee of Twenty-Five (Palm Springs, Cal.). Home: 420 E. Armour. Office: Scarritt Bldg., Kansas City, Mo. Died Oct. 14, 1959; buried Mt. Moriah Cemetery, Kansas City, Mo.

ADAMS, Bristow, educator; b. Washington, Nov. 11, 1875; s. of C. C. and Ada G. (Harrison) A.; art edn. Spring Garden Inst., Phila., Corcoran Sch. Art, Washington, Barron Studios, Stanford U.; A.B., Stanford, 1900; m. Luella Farmer, Apr. 23, 1902; children—Eleanor, Gertrude, Everett W., Bristow. Co-founder, 1892, asso. editor, 1892-96, The Pathfinder; artist Bering Sea Fur Seal Commn., 1897-98, illustrating govt. reports of fur seal investigations from life sketches made on Pribilof Islands. At Stanford founded the Chaparral; asso. editor Forestry and Irrigation, 1902-04; co-founder, 1903, mng. editor, 1903-05, Washington Life; editor Am. Spectator, 1905-06; forest examiner in charge Office of information U.S. Forest Service, 1906-14; developed information service N.Y. State Coll. of Agr., at Cornell U., and edited Cornell agrl. and home econs. publs.; taught journalism, 1914-45, now prof. emeritus, painting and exhibiting oils. With office of information U.S. Dept. Agr., 1917-18; mil. intelligence div. of Gen. Staff U.S. Army, 1918. Dir. publicity, World's Dairy Congress, 1923; studied farming methods in France, 1924, Eng., 1926; trips around world studying farm methods, 1930, 37. Tchr. drawing, painting Cornell Summer Sch., 1923-26, 45-49, Colo. State Coll., summer 1937, 38, 40, 50. Alderman, City of Ithaca, 1946—, acting mayor, 1949-53. Mem. Soc. Am. Foresters, Am. Assn. Tchrs. Journalism, Am. Assn. Agrl. Coll. Editors (pres. 1918), Am. Assn. Coll. News Bureaus (pres. 1920), N.Y. Press Assn., Nat. Editorial Assn., A.A.A.S., Sigma Xi, Sigma Delta Chi (nat. hon. pres. 1920). Clubs: National Press (Washington), University (pres. 1920), Salvage (Ithaca). Illustrator and contbr. to mags.; compiler Farmers' Bull. 1902, an Agricultural Almanac for U.S. Dept. Agr., 1921; editor Home Maker dept. True Story Mag., 1929-42. Editor The Cornell Plantations; co-editor Farm Research 1943-45; reg. broadcasts WGY and WHCU. Home: 202 Fall Creek Dr. Address: Cornell University, Ithaca, N.Y. Died Nov. 19, 1957.

ADAMS, Charles Christopher, ecologist; b. Clinton, Ill., July 23, 1873; s. William Henry Harrison and Hannah Westfall (Concklin) A.; B.S., Ill. Wesleyan U, 1895; M.S., Harvard, 1899. Ph.D., U. Chgo., 1908; Sc.D., Ill. Wesleyan U., 1920; m. Alice Luthera Norton, Oct. 3, 1908 (dec. Sept. 1, 1931); 1 dau., Harriet Dyer. Asst. in biology Ill. Wesleyan U., 1895-96; asst. entomologist Ill. State Lab. of Natural History, 1896-98; curator U. Museum, U. Mich., 1903-06; dir. Cin. Soc. Natural History, 1906-07; asso., animal ecology U. Ill., 1908-14; asst. prof. forest zoölogy N.Y. State Coll. Forestry, Syracuse U., 1914-16, prof. 1916; dir. Roosevelt Wild Life Forest Expt. Sta., 1919-26; N.Y. State Mus., 1926-43, retired. Mem. Am. Soc. Naturalists, Assn. Am. Geographers, Ecol. Soc. Am., A.A.A.S., History Sci. Soc., Sigma Xi. Author: Guide to the Study of Animal Ecology, 1913. Contbr. sci. mags. and reviews. Address: 149 Manning Blvd., Albany 3, N.Y. Died May 22, 1955; buried Burlington, Wis.

ADAMS, Charles Edward; b. Toledo, O., Oct. 29, 1881; s. Charles Frederick and Anne Hewitt (Baldwin) A.; grad. St. Paul's Sch., Concord, N.H., 1900; A.B., Yale, 1904; m. Phyllis Shearson, Feb. 3, 1917; children—Phyllis Anne, Janet Shearson. Sec. to Robert C. Pruyn, Albany, N.Y., 1904-07; with F. S. Butterworth & Co., stock brokers, New Haven, Conn., 1907-10, Callaway Fish & Co., N.Y. City, 1910-16; mem. Foster & Adams, 1917-18; treas. Air Reduction Co., New York, 1918-20, v.p., 1920-21, pres., 1921-37, chmn. 1937-47, chmn. bd., 1947—; chmn. bd. U.S. Industrial Alcohol Co. (now U.S. Industrial Chemicals), 1927—, Pur Carbonic, Inc.; dir. Nat. Carbide Corp., Dry Ice, Inc. Comml. Acetylene Supply Company Incorporated, Cuban Air Products Corporation, Sterno Corporation, Vanadium Corp. of Am. National Distillers Prod. Corp.; trustee Mutual Life Ins. Co. of N.Y.; dir. Fed. Reserve Bank, N.Y. Div. adminstr. N.R.A., summer of 1934; vice president Chamber of Commerce, State of N.Y. Served with Industrial Materials Dept., Advisory Commn. to Council of National Defense as exec. officer and consultant June-Dec. 1940, and as sr. consultant with Priorities Div. Office of Prodn. Management from Jan.-Mar. 1941; Nat. Defense Mediation Bd., Apr.-Dec. 1941; chief iron and steel branch, War Prodn. Bd., Dec. 1941-May 1942. Trustee and member exec. com. Presbyn. Hosp. Mem. Alpha Delta Phi, Skull and Bones (Yale). Republican. Episcopalian. Clubs: Chemists, Links, Yale, Downtown, Uptown, Cloud, Union (New York); Southside Sportsmen's. Home: 455 E. 57th St., N.Y.C. 22. Office: 60 E. 42d St., N.Y.C. 17. Died Jan. 27, 1957; buried Woodlawn Cemetery.

ADAMS, Charles Francis, lawyer, ex-secretary of navy; b. Quincy, Massachusetts, August 2, 1866; s.

John Quincy and Fanny (Crowninshield) A.; great-great-grandson of John Adams; A.B., cum laude, Harvard, 1888; LL.B., 1892; read law in office of Sigourney Butler, of Boston; admitted to Suffolk bar, 1893; m. Frances Lovering, April 3, 1899. Began practice with his law preceptor, but later with Judge Everett C. Bumpus until death of father, 1894; became interested in many business enterprises in Boston, Mass., and elsewhere; secretary of navy, by appointment President Hoover, Mar. 4, 1929-Mar. 4, 1933; now chmn. bd. State Street Trust Co., Boston; dir. many corps. Mem. Quincy City Council, 1893-95, mayor, 1896, 97. Treasurer of Harvard Coll., 1898-1929; elected pres. Harvard Alumni Assn., 1933. Amateur skipper on yacht "Resolute" which won Internat. Yacht Races, 1920. Clubs: Eastern Yacht, Quincy Yacht, etc. Home: 177 Commonwealth Av., Boston; summer address: The Glades, Minot, Mass. Office: 15 State St., Boston. Died June 11, 1954; buried Quincy, Mass.

ADAMS, Claude Mitchell, govt. ofcl.; b. Humboldt, Tenn., Oct. 2, 1895; s. Jeremiah John Robert and Annie (Senter) A.; ed. Fitzgerald-Clarke Sch., U. of Tenn., grad. Inf. Sch., Command and Gen. Staff Sch.; m. Ruth Cornelia Graves, Sept. 14, 1921. Enlisted N.G. of Tenn., June, 1916; served as 1st lt. in 119th Inf., 30th Div., World War I, and advanced through the grades to brig. gen., 1943; served as adjutant, executive officer and aide-de-camp to Gen. G. C. Marshall, Chief of Staff, U.S. Army; served as military attache to Brazil, 1942-44; state dir. Civil Def., 1951-52; exec. asst. Gov. Browning, 1952. Awarded Order of Military Merit (Brazil); Legion of Merit (U.S.); Legion of Honor (France); Medalha de Guerre (Brazil). Mem. Sigma Alpha Epsilon. Clubs: Cumberland (Nashville); Arlington (Portland, Ore.); Army and Navy (Washington); Humboldt Country. Home: Humboldt, Tenn. Died Mar. 26, 1958; buried Rose Hill Cemetery, Humboldt.

ADAMS, Comfort Avery, electrical engr.; b. Cleveland, Nov. 1, 1868; s. Comfort Avery and Katherine Emily (Peticolas) A.; S.B., Case Sch. of Applied Science, Cleveland, 1890, E.E., 1905, Dr. Engring., 1925; hon. Dr. Engring., Lehigh U., 1938; student mathematics and physics, Harvard, 1891-93; m. Elizabeth Challis Parsons, June 21, 1894; children—John, Clayton Comfort. Asst. in physics, Case School of Applied Science, 1886-90; designing engr., 1890-91; instr., 1891-95, asst. prof., 1896-1905, prof. elec. engring., 1906-16, Lawrence prof. of engring., Harvard U., 1914-36, Gordon McKay prof. of elec. engring., 1935-36, emeritus since 1936; dean Harvard Engring. Sch., 1919; chmn. div. engring. Nat. Research Council, 1919-21; consulting engr. for Am. Tool & Machine Co., Boston, 1905-30, The Okonite Co. since 1915, Okonite Callender Cable Co. since 1925, Babcock and Wilcox Co. since 1926, General Electric Co., 1927-32, The Budd Company, 1934-47. Member International Jury of Awards (department electricity), St. Louis Expn., 1904. Unitarian. Fellow Am. Acad. Arts and Sciences, Am. Inst. Elec. Engrs. (pres. 1918-19), Am. Soc. Mech. Engrs., A.A.A.S.; mem. Nat. Acad. of Sciences, Instn. Elec. Engrs., Société Francaise 'des Electricienes, Am. Soc. C.E., Soc. Promotion Engring. Edn., Am. Physical Soc., Am. Welding Soc. (pres. 1919-20), American Bureau Welding (dir. 1919-36), Engineering Foundation (hon. chmn. welding research council since 1949), American Engineering Standards Committee (chairman 1918-20). Mem. John Fritz Medal Bd. of Award (pres. 1922), Edison Medal Bd. of Award (chmn. 1920). Chmn. Gen. Engring. Com. of Council Nat. Defense, during war period, also as chmn. Welding Com. of Emergency Fleet Corp. Clubs: Engineers (Philadelphia) (New York); Cedarbrook Country. Author: Dynamo Design Schedules; also articles on kindred subjects. Received 1st award of Miller medal, "for conspicuous contributions to the art of welding," 1929; Lamme medal from Am. Inst. E.E. for contributions to theory and design of alternating current elec. machinery and to electric welding, 1940. Edison Medal 1956 by Am. Inst. E.E. Home: 417 W. Price St., Phila. 44. Died Feb. 21, 1958.

ADAMS, Earl Frederick, clergyman; b. Palmyra, N.Y., May 28, 1900; s. Floyd Holden and Evelyn Sarah (Parkes) A.; A.B., Denison U., 1921; B.D., Colgate-Rochester Divinity Sch., 1925; student U. of Chicago, 1929-30; D.D., Hillsdale Coll., 1939, Denison U., 1941; m. Dorris Victoria Booth, June 24, 1925; children—Robert Winn, James Hubert, Mary Louise. Ordained to ministry Bapt. Ch., 1925; pastor Coll. Bapt. Ch., Hillsdale, Mich., 1925-29, Irving Park Bapt. Ch., Chicago, 1929-30, Delaware Av. Bapt. Ch., Buffalo, N.Y., 1931-39; gen. dir. Promotion, Northern Bapt. Conv., 1939-45; exec. dir. Protestant Council, City of N.Y., 1945-48; visiting prof. Yale Div. Sch., 1947-49; exec. sec. planning com., National Council of Churches of Christ in U.S.A., 1948-50, asst. gen. sec., 1950—, general director Washington office. Trustee Denison U. Served as pvt. U.S. Army, 1918. Mem. exec. com. Baptist World Alliance; cofounder of United Church Canvass; bd. mgrs. Ch. World Service; mem. nat. com. on Closer Relationship Between Interdenominational Agencies; mem. Assn. of Council Secs. Author nat. broadcasts on theme, Thinking Beyond Today. Mem. Phi Beta Kappa (p. Western N.Y.), Beta Theta Pi, Phi Mu Alpha, Delta Theta Chi. Mason (32°). Clubs: Westchester Country, Nat. Arts, Quill (N.Y.); Corinthian, Cosmos (Washington). Co-author: Christian Leadership in a World Society. Contbr. religious journals. Home: 2122 Massachusetts Av., Washington. Office: 122 Maryland Av. N.E., Washington; also 297 Fourth Av., N.Y.C. 10. Died Nov. 1, 1956; buried Fort Lincoln Cemetery, Washington.

ADAMS, Edwin Plimpton, educator; b. Prague, Jan. 23, 1878; s. Edwin Augustus and Caroline Amelia (Plimpton) A.; B.S., Beloit (Wis.) Coll., 1899, Sc.D., 1931; M.S., Harvard, 1901, Ph.D., 1904; studied univs. of Berlin, Gottingen, Trinity Coll., Cambridge U. Prof. physics Princeton, 1906-41. Served as capt. Brit. Army, World War I. Mem. Am. Phys. Soc., Am. Math. Soc., Am. Philos. Soc., Beta Theta Pi. Clubs: University, Harvard, Princeton (N.Y.C.); Royal Societies (London). Home: 105 Plimpton St., Walpole, Mass. Died Dec. 31, 1956; buried Maple Grove Cemetery, Walpole.

ADAMS, Elizabeth Kemper, educator; b. Nashotah, Wis., Oct. 24, 1872; d. Francis Kemper and Mary Lee (Whiting) A.; grad. Kemper Hall, Kenosha, Wis., 1889; B.A., Vassar, 1893; Ph.D., U. Chgo., 1904. Tchr. Kemper Hall, 1893-99; instr. English, Vassar, 1899-1901; instr. philosophy and edn. Coll. for Women, Western Res. U., 1904-05; instr., asso. prof. and prof. psychology and edn. Smith Coll., 1905-14; asst. chief profl. sect. U.S. War Emergency Employment Service, 1918-19; ednl. sec. Girl Scouts, Inc., 1922—. Alumnae trustee Vassar, 1918-24. Mem. Am. Assn. U. Women, Am. Assn. Social Workers, N.E.A., Nat. Conf. Social Work, Phi Beta Kappa. Clubs: Vassar, Town Hall (N.Y.C.). Author: The Aesthetic Experience, 1907; Women Professional Workers, 1921; also articles and verse in mags. Home: Half-a-Loaf, Conway, Mass. Address: 670 Lexington Av., N.Y.C. Died Dec. 14, 1948; buried Conway.

ADAMS, Elmer E., editor, banker; b. Waterbury, Vt., Dec. 31, 1861; s. Daniel K. and Olive Ann (Hale) A.; student Morrisville (Vt.) Acad.; A.B., U. Minn., 1884; m. Fanny K. Cowles, Aug. 28, 1890; children—Marjorie, Samuel P., Dorothy Quincy (Mrs. A. C. Eschwerler, Jr.). Editor Fergus Falls Daily Jour., 1885-1933; pres. First Nat. Bank, Fergus Falls, 1912—; pres. First State Bank of Underwood, Fergus Journal Co.; treas. Beall-McGowan Co.; sec. Red River Milling Co. Mem. Minn. Ho. of Reps., 1905-19; mem. State Senate, 1930-34; candidate for Rep. nomination for congressman, 1932. Regent U. Minn., 1898-1905. Club: Chippewa (Fergus Falls). Home: Fergus Falls, Minn. Died June 24, 1950; buried Oak Grove Cemetery, Fergus Falls.

ADAMS, Frank Hicks, engring. exec.; b. Lamar, Mo., Mar. 28 1886; s. Edmund Hamilton and Caroline (Hicks) A.; B.S., U. Mo., 1908; m. Mary Jones, June 21, 1911; children—Edmund, Carroll Josephine. Draftsman Denver Reservoir Irrigation Co., 1908-12; chief engr. irrigation projects, spl. assignments Henry L. Doherty & Co., Denver, 1913-24; pres., dir. Surface Combustion Corp., Toledo, 1925—, Webster Engring. Co., Tulsa, 1934—; dir. Toledo Trust Co. Republican. Conglist. Clubs: Toledo, Rotary, Inverness (Toledo). Home: 60 Birckhead Pl., Toledo. Office: 2375 Dorr St., Toledo 1. Died Apr. 6, 1958; buried Woodlawn Cemetery Toledo.

ADAMS, George Wendell, director Christian Science Mother Church, Boston; b. Kingston, Massachusetts, son Horatio and Charlotte Goodrich (Russell) A.; student Phillips Exeter Acad., 1889-90; grad. Chauncy Hall, 1894; student Mass. Inst. of Tech., 1894-95; C.S.B., Mass. Metaphysical Coll., under personal instruction of Mary Baker Eddy, 1898; unmarried. Practitioner of Christian Science since 1895; teacher of Christian Science since 1898; clerk Christian Science Ch., Boston, 1922-25; dir. Christian Science Mother Ch. since 1925; trustee Estate of Mary Baker Eddy under her will since 1925; trustee Christian Science Benevolent Assn., Christian Science Pacific Coast Sanatorium, Christian Science Pleasant View Home; trustee F. C. Adams Pub. Library, Kingston, Mass., 1921-36. Republican. Clubs: University, Boston Yacht (Boston). Home: 310 Bellevue Rd., North Quincy 71, Mass. Office: 107 Falmouth St., Boston 15. Died Oct. 22, 1953.

ADAMS, James Barton, poet; b. Jefferson County, O., Apr. 17, 1843; s. John B. and Sarah A.; ed. Richmond, O., and Mt. Pleasant, Ia.; m. Lydia Louise Troub, June 28, 1898. Served in 6th Ia. Inf., 1861-5; served in Indian wars, 1873-77, western Neb., Kan., Wyo., as scout and officer of Indians enlisted as scouts. Republican. Author: Breezy Western Verse, Denver, 1898. His poems printed in Denver Post, especially those treating of frontier life and customs, in western dialect and cowboy vernacular, are widely reproduced by the press. He has also contributed short western stories and poems to various publs. Editor Rocky Mountain Elk. Home: 1250 University Av., Myrtle Hill. Office: 1646 Arapahoe St., Denver. Deceased.

ADAMS, James McKee, theological seminary prof.; b. Raleigh, N.C., Oct. 17, 1886; s. David Thomas and Anne Marie (Nowell) A.; A.B., Wake Forest (N.C.) Coll., 1909, M.A., 1910; student Crozer Theol. Sem., Chester, Pa., 1910-11; Th.M., Southern Baptist Theol. Sem., Louisville, Ky., 1920, Ph.D., 1929; m. Claudia Aycock, 1911; 1 dau., Elizabeth (Mrs. Stanley Unruh); m. 2d, Lucy Oliver, Aug. 3, 1922; children—James McKee, Anne Moseley. Pastor, Ebenezer Bapt. Ch. (South Carolina), 1912-16; asst. prof. theology Southern Bapt. Theol. Sem.; 1921-24, prof. biblical introduction since 1924; sabbatical year in Near East, specializing in orientation studies, 1927-28; made 11 trips to Europe and Near East in connection with archeology and research work. Mem. Oriental Soc. Research. Author: Syllabus for Biblical Introduction Studies, 1926; Biblical Backgrounds (translated into several languages for use in schools and seminaries), 1934; The Heart of the Levant: Palestine and Syria, 1937; Our Bible, 1937; Ancient Records and the Bible, 1946. Contbr. numerous articles to mags. Home: 2407 Longest Av., Louisville 4. Died Sept. 17, 1945.

ADAMS, James Randolph, advt. exec.; b. Monroe City, Ind., June 19, 1898; s. George Washington and Ellen Mariah (Loveless) A.; student Vincennes U., 1916-17, Ind. U., 1918, Notre Dame U., 1921-22, m. Bertha DeChant, May 15, 1923; children—Marilyn Jean (Mrs. Robert Heckenkamp), Charles Francis, Ellen Ann. Sch. tchr., Vincennes, Ind., 1917-18; editorial staff mem. South Bend (Ind.) Tribune, 1919-20; editor employee mag. Studebaker Corp., 1920-21; dir. advt. and sale promotion Straube Piano Co., 1922-24; mem. creative staff Critchfield & Co., Chgo., 1925-26; v.p., dir. Campbell-Ewald Co., Det., 1927-34; founding partner MacManus, John & Adams, Inc., advt. agy., Detroit, 1934, v.p., 1934-37, exec. v.p. 1937-45, became pres., 1945, later chmn. bd. Served in O.T.C., U.S. Army, World War I. Mem. Detroit Port Authority, 1942-44. Mem. Detroit Bd. Commerce, Ind. Soc. Chgo., Am. Assn. Advt. Agencies (dir. 1945-48). Clubs: Athletic, Recess, Country, Adcraft (Detroit); Bloomfield Hills (Mich.) Country; Lotus (N.Y.C.). Author: More Power to Advertising, 1937; Sparks Off My Anvil, 1956. Home: Rathmoor Rd. Office: Woodward at Long Lake, Bloomfield Hills, Mich. Died Nov. 5, 1956; buried Holy Sepulchre Cemetery, Detroit.

ADAMS, Jedidiah Howe, physician, author; b. Union Springs, N.Y., Aug. 19, 1866; grad. Haverford Coll., Pa., 1877; med. dept. U. Pa., 1889; m. Margaret Agnew Stuart, May 6, 1889; 1 son, D. Hayes Agnew. Editor Univ. Med. Mag. Mem. Sons Revolution; Phila., County Med. Soc. Club: University. Contbr. to leading mags. on lit. subjects. Author: Life of D. Hayes Agnew, 1892. Address: Paoli, Pa. Died May 2, 1919.

ADAMS, John Stokes, lawyer; b. Phila., Mar. 22, 1864; s. Greenfield and Josephine Lippincott (Stokes) A.; prep. edn. Christ's Ch. Sem., Lexington, Ky.; grad. Emerson Inst., Washington, 1880; A.B., U. Pa., 1884, LL.B., 1886; m. Heloise Zelina Root, Apr. 23, 1890; children—Henry Clay, Randolph Greenfield, John Stokes. Admitted to Pa. bar, 1886, since practiced in Phila.; mem. Adams, Childs, McKaig and Lukens; lectr. on law of mines U. Pa. Law Sch., 1907-29. Mem. Am., Pa., Phila. bar assns., Am. Hist. Assn., Phi Kappa Psi, Phi Beta Kappa. Democrat. Club: University. Author: The Law of Mines and Mining in the U.S. (with D. M. Barringer), 1897. Editor: An Autobiographical Sketch by John Marshall, 1937. Home: Deepdale Rd., Strafford. Office: 1528 Walnut St., Phila. 2. Died Apr. 3, 1954; buried West Laurel Hill Cemetery, Bala-Cynwyd, Pa.

ADAMS, L. Sherman, ret. trustee; b. Lowell, Mass., July 17, 1887; s. Lewis Sherman and Sophia (Barrows) A.; student pub. schs.; m. Helen Hewitt, May 25, 1914; children—Sarah (Mrs. James H. Stannard), Jeannette (Mrs. Charles W. Ireland III), Helen (Mrs. Helen A. Gates), Lewis S. Began in stock brokerage bus. under name L. Sherman Adams, 1912; mem. Boston Stock Exchange; formed the Mass. Investors Trust, 1924, becoming trustee, and now retired as trustee; dir. Bklyn. Union Gas Co., Eastern Mass. St. Ry. Co., Twentieth Century Fox-Film Corp. Clubs: Algonquin, Indian Creek Country, Beacon Soc., Downtown, Bostonian Soc., Wellesley Country. Home: 105 Benvenue Street, Wellesley 81, Mass. Office: John Hancock Building, 200 Berkeley St., Boston 16. Died Mar. 12, 1959.

ADAMS, Maude, actress; b. Salt Lake City, Utah, Nov. 11, 1872; d. of James and Annie (Adams) Kiskadden. (Her mother, stage name Adams, was leading woman of stock co. at Salt Lake City.) Appeared on stage in child's parts; went to school; joined E. H. Sothern Co., New York, at 16; ingénue rôle in the "Midnight Bell"; afterward in Charles Frohman's stock company; later supported John Drew, 5 yrs.; starred as Lady Babbie, in "Little Minister," 1897-98; as Juliet in "Romeo and Juliet," 1899; in "L'Aiglon," 1900-01; in "Quality Street," 1902; in "The Pretty Sister of José," 1903; in "The Little Minister," and Hop o' My Thumb," 1905; "Peter Pan," 1905-07; "What Every Woman Knows," 1908-09; "Joan of Arc," 1909; "As You Like It," 1910; "Chantecler," 1910-11; Peter Pan, 1913; The Legend of Leonora, 1914; The Ladies Shakespeare, 1914;

Quality Street; The Little Minister, 1915-16; A Kiss for Cinderella, 1916-18; The Merchant of Venice, 1931; Twelfth Night, 1934. Hon. LL.D., U. of Wis., 1927; M.A. (hon.), Union Coll., Schenectady, 1921. Mem. faculty, Stephens Coll., Columbia, Mo. Address: Stephens Coll., Columbia, Mo.; (summer) Renkonkoma, L.I., N.Y. Died July 17, 1953.

ADAMS, Morgan, finance; b. Dayton, O., Apr. 14, 1886; s. James H. and Lillian (Turner) A.; student Am. Coll., Strassburg, Germany, 1902-04; B.A., Stanford, 1908; m. Aileen McCarthy, Feb. 14, 1915; children—Morgan, James H.; m. 2d, Virginia Phillips, Mar. 14, 1931. Salesman, James H. Adams & Co., bonds, Los Angeles, Calif., 1909-12; v.p. Mortgage Guarantee Co., Los Angeles, 1912-22, president since 1922; president Bond Investment Company to 1946; chairman board Western Mortgage Corporation; pres. Mortgage Oil Co. Lt. comdr. U.S.N.R.F., World War I; spl. asst., Sec. of Navy, World War II. Mem. Phi Beta Kappa, Delta Kappa Epsilon. Republican. Clubs: California, Los Angeles Yacht. Home: 2780 San Pasqual St., Pasadena 10, Calif. Office: 1500 Wilshire Blvd., Los Angeles 14. Died Aug. 6, 1951; buried Inglewood, Cal.

ADAMS, R. R., transportation exec. Exec. v.p., dir. Grace Line, Inc.; exec. v.p. Maritime Assn., Port of N.Y. Office: 10 Hanover Sq., N.Y.C. Died Jan. 1953.

ADAMS, Randolph Greenfield, librarian; b. Phila., Pa., Nov. 7, 1892; s. John Stokes and Heloise Zelina (Root) A.; A.B., Univ. of Pa., 1914, Ph.D., 1920; studied law, same univ., 1 year; LL.D., Albion Coll., 1938; m. Helen Newbold Spiller, June 16, 1917; children—Thomas Randolph, Richard Newbold. Asst. in history, U. of Pa., 1915-16; fellow in history, U. of Chicago, 1916-17, Carnegie fellow in internat. law, U. of Pa., 1919-20; asst. prof. history, Trinity Coll. (now Duke U.), 1920-23; dir. William L. Clements Library Am. History, U. of Mich., since 1923; rank of prof., visiting Carnegie prof. Am. hist., St. Andrews Univ., Scotland, 1929, Rosenbach fellow in bibliog., U. of Pa., 1938. Served as pvt., U.S. Army, 1917, attached to Base Hosp. 20, in France with U. of Pa. Unit, May 1918, 2d lt. Q.M.C., Sept. 5, 1918; hon. disch., May 5, 1919. Trustee, The Franklin D. Roosevelt Library, Inc. Mem. American Hist. Assn., Am. Bibliog. Soc. (pres. 1940-41), Am. Antiquarian Society, New York Historical Society, Mass. Historical Society, American Library Institute, Grolier Club, Phi Kappa Psi, Phi Beta Kappa. Episcopalian. Author: Political Ideas of the American Revolution, 1922; A History of American Foreign Policy, 1924; Passports printed by Benj. Franklin, 1925; A Gateway to American History, 1927; The British Headquarters Maps, 1776-1782, 1928; Pilgrims, Indians, and Patriots, 1928; Three Americanists, 1939. Home: 2030 Norway Rd., Ann Arbor, Mich. Died Jan. 4, 1951; buried West Laurel Hill Cemetery, Philadelphia.

ADAMS, Raymond Fletcher, lawyer; b. Phila., Aug. 27, 1900; s. Raymond Edmond and Eleanore Hoffman (Fletcher) A.; B.S., Pa. State Coll., 1921; student George Washington U. Law Sch., 1921-22; m. Blanche Lucas Milliken, June 3, 1922; children—Raymond M., Mary Eleanore, Phoebe Jane, Richard F. Joined firm of Pennie, Davis, Marvin & Edmonds, N.Y. City, as clk., 1922, partner, 1930; admitted to N.Y. State bar, 1925; established own firm Adams, Forward & McLean, 1949. Served with U.S. Army, World War I. Mem. Lambda Chi Alpha, Phi Kappa Phi, Phi Lambda Upsilon. Clubs: The University (Chicago and New York); Chemists (N.Y. City). Home: 370 Lenox Av., South Orange, N.J. Office: 115 Broadway, N.Y.C. 6. Died May 17, 1955.

ADAMS, Robert Brooks, agrl. real estate and investments; b. Hopkinton, Mass., Apr. 14, 1887; s. William Phipps and Nettie Elizabeth (Moore) A.; student The Hill Sch., 1903-07; m. Jessie M. Helsell, Oct. 6, 1909; children—William Phipps, Robert Brooks, Barbara (Mrs. Searles), John Malcom. Operator and owner Fairview Farm, Odebolt, Ia., 1935—; real estate, Chgo., 1907—, investments, 1907—; trustee Equitable Life Ins. Co. of Ia. Trustee Grinnell Coll. Mem. regional exec. com. No. div. Boy Scouts Am.; regional com. Zone 4, Am. Horse Shows Assn. Clubs: The Bath, Indian Creek Country (Miami Beach, Fla.); Chicago Athletic Association; The Des Moines; The Omaha. Home: Odebolt, Ia., and 1204 West Av., Miami Beach, Fla. Office: Odebolt, Ia. Died June 27, 1956; buried Odebolt.

ADAMS, Robert Simeon, educator; b. Richwood, O., Aug. 9, 1897; s. Frank Leslie and Ellen Maude (Perry) A.; A.B., Ohio State U., 1925; A.M., Western Res. U., 1932; m. Mary Leone Thurness, May 3, 1925; 1 son, Hazard. Prin. schs., Sparta, O., 1921-22; prin. high sch., Milford Center, O., 1922-23; asst. English dept. Ohio State U., 1924-25; head English dept. Hawken Sch., Cleve., 1925-34; headmaster Lakeside Sch., Seattle, 1934—. Mem. Seattle Community Fund. First pres. Pacific N.W. Assn. Ind. Schs.; mem. Interstate Com. on High Sch. Coll. Relations, 1948. Served in USN, World War I. Mem. Progressive Edn. Assn., Wash. Mental Hygiene Assn., Delta Tau Delta. Clubs: Rotary, China (bd. trustees), Monday (sec.) (Seattle). Author: Poems, 1952; also contbr. verse to mags. Address: The Lakeside Sch., Seattle. Died Oct. 5, 1950.

ADAMS, Samuel Hopkins, author; b. Dunkirk, N. Y., Jan. 26, 1871; s. Myron and Hester Rose (Hopkins) A.; A.B., Hamilton Coll., Clinton, N.Y., 1891, L.H.D., 1926; m. Elizabeth R. Noyes, 1898; children—Hester Hopkins, Mrs. Cecil C. Adell; married 2d, Jane Peyton Van Norman, 1915. Reporter and special writer N.Y. Sun, 1891-1900; managing editor McClure's Syndicate, 1900-01; advertising manager McClure, Phillips & Co., publishers, 1901-02; mem. staff McClure's Magazine, 1903-05. Ex-trustee Hamilton Coll. Hon. fellow Am. Antiquarian Soc., N.Y. State Hist. Assn. Democrat. Clubs: Century, Players, Dutch Treat (N.Y.), Owasco Country (Cayuga Co., New York). Author: The Great American Fraud, 1906; The Mystery (with Stewart Edward White), 1905; The Flying Death, 1906; Average Jones, 1911; The Secret of Lonesome Cove, 1913; The Clarion, 1914; Little Miss Grouch, 1915; The Unspeakable Perk, 1916; Our Square and the People in It, 1917; Common Cause, 1918; Wanted, a Husband, 1919; Success, 1921; From a Bench in Our Square, 1922; Siege, 1924; The Piper's Fee, 1925; Revelry, 1926; The Flagrant Years, 1929; The Godlike Daniel, 1930; The Gorgeous Hussy, 1934; It Happened One Night (motion picture), 1934; Perfect Specimen, 1936; Maiden Effort, 1937; The World Goes Smash, published 1938; Incredible Era, 1939; Whispers, published 1940; Both Over Twenty-one, 1941; The Harvey Girls, 1942; Tambay Gold, 1942; Canal Town, 1944; A. Woolcott: His Life and His Works, 1946; Banner by the Wayside, 1947; Plunder, 1948; Sunrise to Sunset, 1950; The Pony Express, 1950; The Santa Fé Trail, 1952; The Erie Canal, 1953; Grandfather Stories, 1955. Home: R.D. 2, Auburn, N.Y. Died Nov. 15, 1958.

ADAMS, Walter Sydney, astronomer; b. Antioch, North Syria, Dec. 20, 1876; s. Lucien Harper and Dora (Francis) A.; A.B., Dartmouth, 1898; D.Sc., 1913; A.M., U. Chgo., 1900, U. Munich, 1901; LL.D., Pomona, 1926; D.Sc., Columbia, 1926. U. So. Cal., 1930, U. Chgo., 1945, Princeton, 1947; m. Lillian M. Wickham, June 2, 1910 (died 1920); m. 2d, Adeline L. Miller, June 15, 1922; children—Edmund Miller, John Francis. Asst. 1901-03, instr. 1903-04, Yerkes Obs., asst. astronomer, 1904-09, astronomer 1909—, acting dir., 1910-11, asst. dir., 1913-23, dir., 1923-46, Mt. Wilson Obs. of Carnegie Instn., Pasadena, Cal., research asso., 1946-47. Mem. Am. Astron. Soc. (pres. 1931-34), Astron. Soc. Pacific (pres. 1923), Royal Acad. Sciences of Upsala, Astron. Union (v.p. 1935-38), Am. Philos. Soc.; fgn. mem. Royal Society of London, Royal Astronomical Society (London), Institute of France (Acad. of Sciences), Royal Swedish Acad. of Scis. Gold medal Royal Astron. Soc., 1917, Draper medal Nat. Acad. Sciences, 1918; Janssen medal, Societé Astronomique de France, 1926; Bruce medal, Astron. Soc. Pacific, 1928; Janssen medal, Paris Acad. of Sciences, 1935. Clubs: Athenaeum, Twilight. Writer numerous papers on solar and stellar spectroscopy, radial velocities and distances of stars. Home: 873 N. Hill Av., Pasadena 7, Cal. Died May 11, 1956; buried Derry, N.H.

ADAMS, Wayman, portrait painter; b. Muncie, Ind., Sept. 23, 1883; s. Nelson Perry and Mary Elizabeth (Justice) A.; studied John Herron Art Inst., Indianapolis, 1905-09, also studied in Italy, 1910, Spain, 1912; honorary Dr. Fine Arts, Syracuse U., 1945; m. Margaret Graham Boroughs, Oct. 1, 1918; 1 son, Wayman. Awarded 1st prize Muncie, (Ind.) Art Assn., 1910; Thomas R. Proctor prize, Nat. Acad. Design N.Y.C., 1914; Mary T. R. Foulke prize, Art Assn., Richmond, Ind., 1915; J. I. Holcomb prize, Indiana Artists' Exhbn., 1916; Mr. and Mrs. Frank G. Logan medal (with $1,500), Art Inst. Chgo., 1918; 1st prize, Newport (R.I.) Art Assn., 1918; Indpls. Star portrait prize, Hoosier Salon, Chgo., 1925, 1929; Richard S. Geenough meml. prize, Newport, 1925; State of Tenn. Medal, Portraits Distinguished Americans, 1925; John C. Shafer prize, Hoosier Salon, Chgo., 1926; silver medal, Sesquicentennial, Phila. 1926; first Altman prize ($1,000), Nat. Acad. Design, 1926; portrait prize, Art Assn., Springfield, Mass., 1926; Dana water color gold medal, Pa. Acad., 1929; medal of honor, Allied Artists of America, 1930; William Church Osborne prize, Am. Water Color Soc., 1930; hon. mention, 2d Internat. Exhbn. Lithography and Wood Engraving, Art Inst., Chgo., 1930; hon. mention for lithography, Print Club of Phila., 1931; John T. McCutcheon prize for lithographs, Hoosier Salon, Chgo., 1931; Joseph S. Isador prize for lithograph, Salmagundi Club, 1931; Nat. Arts Club Maida Gregg Meml. Prize, 1932; Artists Poplar Vote Prize Hoosier Salon, Chgo., 1932; 2d Altman prize ($500), Nat. Acad. of Design, 1932; Walter Lippincott prize, Pa. Acad. of Fine Arts, 1933; gold medal for achievement in portraiture, Holland Soc. of N.Y., 1933; portrait prize, Hoosier Salon, Chgo., 1935; Shaw purchase prize, Salamagundi Club, 1940; medal, Sanity in Art Exhbn., Chgo., 1941; first prize ($1,000) "Painting, in U.S." exhibition. Carnegie Inst., Pitts., 1943; Medal of Honor, Allied Artists of America, 1948; Ind. Pubs. prize, Hoosier Salon 1950, 51, 52; National Academician; mem. Nat. Inst. Arts and Letters, N.Y. Soc. of Painters, Nat. Assn. Portrait Painters, Am. Water Color Soc., Allied Artists of America, N.Y. Water Color Club, Art Club of Phila., Phila. Water Color Club, Audubon Artists, Houston Art League; hon. mem. New Orleans Art League, Saranac Lake Art League, Kappa Pi; elected laureate mem. Delta Phi Delta, 1948. Clubs: Indiana Artists (hon.), Phila. Art, Phila. Sketch; Salmagundi, Nat. Arts (life), Lotos (life), New York Athletic, Century (New York). Home: 2815 San Gabriel St., Austin, Tex. Studio: Elizabethtown, N.Y. Died Apr. 7, 1959.

ADAMS, William H., ex-gov.; b. Blue Mounds, Wis., Feb. 15, 1861; s. John and Eliza (Blanchard) A.; ed. pub. schs., Black Earth, Wis., and Pueblo, Colo.; m. Hattie Mullins, 1916 (died 1918). County commr. Conejos County, Colo., 1882-84; cattle raiser, Alamosa, 1883—; mayor, Alamosa, 1884-85; mem. Colo. Ho. of Rep., 1887-89, Senate, 1889-1927; gov. Colo., 3 terms, 1927-33. Democrat. Conglist. Home: Alamosa, Colo. Died Feb. 4, 1954.

ADAMS, William Milton, plastic surgeon; b. Ripley, Miss., Apr. 26, 1905; s. Dr. R. M. and Patty Etter (Murray) A.; B.S., U. Miss., 1928; M.D., Tulane, 1930; m. Catherine Taylor, May 22, 1934; children—William Milton, Robert Franklin, Ann Taylor, Catherine Sue. Intern N.Y. Post Grad. Hosp., N.Y. City, 1931-32; resident Brooklyn Eye and Ear Hosp., 1931-32; asso. prof. surgery U. Tenn., 1951—, chief plastic surgery dept. U. Tenn., John Gaston Hosp., 1935—; chief surgery Meth. Hosp., 1947, chief staff, 1948; senior attending plastic surgery Bapt. Meml., John Gaston, Meth., St. Joseph's hosps.; chief cons. plastic surgery Kennedy V.A., U.S. Marine hosps. Mem. Examining Bd. Plastic Surgery, 1947—. Diplomate Am. Bd. Plastic Surgery. Fellow Internat. Coll. Surgeons, A.C.S.; mem. Am. Soc. Plastic and Reconstructive Surgery (pres. 1954; asso. editor Jour.), Am., Brit. assns. plastic surgeons, American Association Surgery Trauma, Am. Med. Assn., Southern, Tenn., Shelby Co., Memphis med. assns., Southeastern Surg. Congress, Southwestern Surg. Assn., Memphis Surg. Soc., La.-Miss. Ophthal. and Otolaryngol. Soc. (hon. mem.). Clubs: Rotary, Memphis Country (Memphis). Contributor articles medical journals. Home: 689 East Drive., Memphis 2. Office: 1073 Madison St., Memphis 3. Died Apr. 4, 1957; buried Memorial Park, Memphis.

ADCOCK, Edmund David, lawyer; b. Galesburg, Ill., Apr. 29, 1877; s. William and Mary Jane (Henderson) A.; A.B., Knox Coll., Galesburg, 1898; LL.B., Northwestern U., 1902; m. May Rex, Aug. 31, 1905 (died June 15, 1918); 1 son, Edmund Rex; m. 2d, Evelyn E. Ringland, Dec. 12, 1924. Admitted to Ill. bar, 1902; asso. in practice with Otis H. Waldo, 1902-04; mem. Wood, Fyffe & Adcock, 1905-07, Fyffe & Adcock, 1907-12; atty. for Sanitary Dist. of Chicago, 1912-19; mem. firm Haight, Adcock, Haight & Harris, 1919-24, Haight, Adcock & Banning, 1924-33, Spitz & Adcock, 1933-43, Adcock, Fink & Day, 1943-49, Adcock and Fink since 1949; apptd. referee in bankruptcy, July 18, 1933, resigned Mar. 18, 1935. Mem. Chicago Bar Assn., Law Club, Phi Delta Theta Democrat. Clubs: Midday, Chicago, Chicago Athletic. Assn. (Chicago); Midlothian (Ill.) Country. Home: Midlothian Country Club, Midlothian, Ill. Office: 134 S. LaSalle St., Chicago. Died Oct. 4, 1951.

ADDICKS, Frank F(loris), business exec.; b. Roanoke, Va., Mar. 25, 1892; s. John H. and Marie M. (Ris) A.; M.E., Cornell U., 1913; m. May G. VanSlingerlandt, Dec. 11, 1915; children—John H., Margaret F. (Mrs. David Henderson). Engring. asst. N.Y. Telephone Co., N.Y. City, 1913-17, engr., 1921-25, gen. plant supervisor, New Jersey area, hdqrs. Newark, 1925-27, div. plant supt., Newark, 1927-28, and with succeeding N.J. Bell Telephone Co., 1928-33, gen. plant mgr., 1933-46, vice pres. and gen. mgr. and dir., 1946-49, vice pres. in charge of revenue and finance and dir., 1945-53, ret. Served as lt. USN, 1917-20; mem. USN, Manpower Survey Bd., 1943-44. Dir. Newark C. of C. since 1947. Republican. Baptist. Clubs: Essex, Athletic (Newark); Manufacturers (West Hudson); Cornell (New York); Echo Lake Country (Westfield, N.J.); Hyannisport (Mass.). Home: 12-A English Village, Cranford, N.J. Office: 540 Broad St., Newark 1. Died Dec. 7, 1954.

ADDISON, James Thayer, clergyman; b. Fitchburg, Mass., Mar. 21, 1887; s. Charles Morris and Ada (Thayer) A.; student Groton Sch., 1900-05; A.B., Harvard, 1909; B.D., Episcopal Theol. Sch., Cambridge, Mass., 1913; S.T.M., Harvard Div. Sch., 1917; D.D., Theol. Sem. of Va., 1931; m. Margaret B. Crocker, Dec. 18, 1917; children—Helen Crocker, Martha Lothrop. Ordained to ministry P.E. Ch., 1913; minister in charge St. Mark's Ch., Nowata, and St. Paul's Ch., Claremore, Okla., 1913-15; lecturer Episcopal Theol. Sch., 1915-17, asst. prof. history of religion and missions, 1919-26, prof., 1926-40; acting master Kirkland House, Harvard, 1932-33; vice president National Council of the Protestant Episcopal Church, 1940-46. Chaplain 1st Gas Regt., A.E.F., France, 1918-19. Trustee Am. Univ., Cairo, Egypt. Author: Story of the First Gas Regiment, 1919; Chinese Ancestor Worship, 1925; Our Father's Business,

1927; Our Expanding Church, 1930; Life Beyond Death, 1932; The Way of Christ, 1934; The Medieval Missionary, 1936; The Lord's Prayer, 1937; Parables of Our Lord, 1940; The Christian Approach to The Moslem, 1942; The Episcopal Church In The United States, 1789-1931, 1951. Mem. Phi Beta Kappa. Address: 401 Beacon St., Boston. Died Feb. 13, 1953; buried Fitchburg, Mass.

ADKINS, Curtis D., bank executive; born at Odenville, Ala., Jan. 24, 1897; s. Joseph William and Carrie (Cole) A.; student pub. schs.; m. Erin Westbrook, Jan. 24, 1922; children—Joe W., Carolyn (Mrs. James Max Spann). Tax collector, St. Clair Co., Ala., 1920-27, probate judge, 1927-33; pres. Asheville Sav. Bank, also dir. Sec.-treas. Rep. State Exec. Com., mem. Nat. Com., 1950-54; Ala. state dir. U.S. Savs. Bond Sales, 1954. Del. Rep. Nat. Conv., 1936-42. Served as sgt. U.S. Army, World War I. Baptist. Mason. Club: Lions. Home: Ashville, Ala. Died Feb. 22, 1956.

ADKINS, Homer (Burton), univ. prof.; b. Newport, Washington County, O., Jan. 16, 1892; s. Alvin and Emily (Middleswart) A.; B.Sc., Denison Univ., 1915, D.Sc., 1938; M.A., Ohio State U., 1916, Ph.D., 1918; m. Louise Spivey, Feb. 21, 1917; children—Dorothea, Nancy, Roger. Began as instr. chemistry, Ohio State U., 1918; asst. prof. organic chemistry, U. of Wis., 1919-24, asso. prof., 1924-28, prof. since 1928. Mem. division 9, National Defense Research Com. Awarded Medal for Merit. Mem. Nat. Acad. of Scis., Am. Chem. Soc. (past chmn. organic div.), A.A.A.S., Chemical Society (London), Phi Beta Kappa, Phi Delta Theta, Phi Lambda Upsilon, Alpha Chi Sigma, Sigma Xi. Author: Practice of Organic Chemistry, 1925; Elementary Organic Chemistry, 1928; Reactions of Hydrogen, 1937; also about 160 scientific papers. Mem. bd. editors, Organic Chemistry, 1938; Organic Syntheses (annual vols.) and Organic Reactions. Home: 2103 Rowley Av., Madison, Wis. Died Aug. 10, 1949; buried Forest Hills, Madison.

ADKINS, Jesse Corcoran, judge; born Knoxville, Tenn., Apr. 13, 1879; s. Milton T. and Sarah Elizabeth (Walker) A.; ed. grade schs. and Business High Sch., Washington, D.C.; LL.B., Georgetown U. Law Sch., 1899; LL.M., 1900, LL D., 1932; m. Bertha McNaught, July 14, 1903; children—Mrs. Sidney L. Eaton, Archibald W. Asst. U.S. atty., Washington, D.C., 1905-08; spl. asst. to atty. gen., 1908-11; mem. Beach & Adkins, 1908-11; asst. atty. gen. of U.S., 1912-14; special asst. atty. gen. U.S., 1914-16; mem. Adkins & Nesbit, Washington, D.C., until 1930; apptd. asso. justice Supreme Court of D.C. (now judge of U.S. Dist. Court for District of Columbia), June 1930; instr. and prof., Georgetown U. Law Sch., 1936-44. For many yrs. chmn. grievance com. Bar Assn. D.C.; chmn. jud. sect. Am. Bar Assn. 1935. Mem. Am. Bar Assn., Bar Assn. D.C. (pres 1928), Assn. Bar City of N.Y.; hon. mem. Taft Chapter, Phi Alpha Delta (Georgetown). Republican. Mason (32°). Clubs: Chevy Chase, Cosmos, Lawyers' (Washington). Retired Oct. 1946. Home: 2219 California St., Washington 8. Died Mar. 29, 1955.

ADLER, David, architect; b. Milw., Jan. 3, 1883; s. Isaac and Therese (Hyman) A.; student Lawrenceville (N.J.) Sch., 1898-1900; A.B., Princeton, 1904; student Ecole des Beaux Arts, Paris, 1906-11; m. Katherine Keith, June 1, 1916. Began practice of architecture with Henry Corwith Dangier, Chgo., 1912; partner firm David Adler & Robert Work, Inc., 1917-28, alone, 1928—. Trustee Art Inst., Chgo. Fellow A.I.A.; mem. Nat. Inst. Arts and Letters. Home: Libertyville, Ill. Office: 220 S. Michigan Av., Chgo. Died Sept. 27, 1949.

ADLER, F. Charles, conductor; b. London, Eng., July 2, 1889; s. Julius and Frieda (Ulmer) A.; grad. Royal Acad. Music, Munich; studied conducting with Felix Mottl and Gustav Mahler; m. Hannah Moriarta, June 6, 1936; 1 dau., Annemarie. Asst. to Felix Mottl, Royal Opera, Munich, 1908-11; tours North and South America, 1908-11; asst. at Bayreuth (Germany) Music Festival, 1910; condr. for Max Reinhardt, 1911, 1913; 1st condr. of opera at Duesseldorf, 1913-14; Symphonic Concert series at Munich, Hamburg, Berlin, Russia, Austria, and Italy, also appeared in radio concerts, 1919-33, also 1952-58; made La Argentina tour, 1927; condr. Berlin State Radio, 1924-33; condr. Gadski tour, U.S., 1930-31; founder and owner Edition Adler, Berlin, 1931-33; with UFA and Emelka film prodns., 1924-33; dir. Saratoga Music Festival, 1927, 46, 47; condr. radio concerts, and N.Y. Chamber Orchestra, 1944-47; weekly column Listen in New Enterprise, Corinth, N.Y., 1948-50; lectr. R.P.I., Union and Skidmore colls. Artistic dir., condr. S.P.A. Records, Inc., 1951—. Recipient Bruchner Mahler Soc. medal, Schoenberg medal. Contbr. various mags. Home: Long Look, R.D. 2, Gansevoort, N.Y. Died Feb. 16, 1959.

ADLER, Julius Ochs, journalist; b. Chattanooga, Tenn., Dec. 3, 1892; s. Harry Clay and Ada (Ochs) A.; student Baylor Univ. Sch., Chattanooga; grad. Lawrenceville (N.J.) Sch., 1910 (valedictorian); A.B., Princeton, 1914; m. Barbara Stettheimer, Aug. 27, 1922; children—Julius Ochs, Jr., Barbara Squier, Nancy Jean. With New York Times, 1914—, first vice president, general manager; also president and pub., Chattanooga Times, 1935; dir. The New York Times Co., Times Printing Co. (Chattanooga Times), Spruce Falls Power and Paper Co., Ltd., Toronto, Can.; vice chmn. dir. Interstate Broadcasting Co., Inc. N.Y.; chmn, bd. dirs. Chattanooga (Tenn.) Pub. Co.; v.p. and dir., Times Facsimile Corp. Civilian aide to Sec. of War, 2d Corps Area, 1932-40; mem. Army com. on Civilian Components, Reserve Forces Policy Board (rep. O.R.C.) since 1949. Commd. 2d lt., Cavalry, ORC, 1917; served continuously as reserve officer advancing through grades to maj. gen.; 306th Inf, 77th div., World War I.; 44th, 4th and 6th inf. div., World War II; comdr. 77th inf. division, U.S. Army Reserve, 1946-54. Decorated D.S.C., Silver Star (2 Oak-Leaf Clusters), Order of Purple Heart, New York State Conspicious Service Cross (World War I and World War II), Officer of the Legion d'Honneur, Croix de Guerre with Palm, France; Croce de Guerra, Italy, World War I; Legion of Merit, Bronze Star Medal, World War II. Pres. Senior Res. Comdrs. Assn., Army of U.S. Chmn. exec. bd., Greater N.Y. Councils Boy Scouts of Am. Pres. Tenn. Soc. in N.Y., 1929-30; pres. Class of 1914 (Princeton), 1934-39. Received Daily Princetonian Alumni award, 1939. Alumni trustee-at-large Princeton U., 1940-44, rep.-at-large, graduate council; pres. Daily Princetonian, Inc.; mem. bd. trustees, Internat. House, Nat. Jewish Hosp. (Denver); trustee Grover Cleveland Birthplace Assn.; mem. gov. bd. Bur. Advt., Am. Newspaper Publishers Assn.; adv. council, Better Bus. Bur. of Greater N.Y.C., Inc; bd. dirs., N.Y. Conv. and Visitors Bur.; chmn., nat. exec. com., Mil. Tng. Camps Assn. of U.S.; mem. bd. dirs., Citizens Com. for Mil. Training, Civilian Mil. Edn. Fund; mem. Am. Soc. of French Legion of Honor, Inc.; pres. 77th Div. Assn., 1945-46; chmn., First Army Adv. Com. for Greater N.Y. Clubs: Pilgrims of U.S., Princeton, Advertising, Mountain City (Chattanooga); Army-Navy (Washington). Editor in chief History of the 77th Division, A.E.F., 1919; editor History of 306th Infantry, 1935. Home: 2 E. 67th St., N.Y.C. 21. Office: 229 W. 43d St., N.Y.C. 36. Died Oct. 3, 1955; buried Arlington Nat. Cemetery.

ADLER, Max, philanthropist, ret. corp. exec.; b. Elgin, Ill., 1866; m. Sophie Rosenwald, 1897; children—Cyrus, Robert, Mrs. Leonard Sperry, Mrs. Bernard Mayers. Joined Sears, Roebuck & Co., Chgo., 1897, was v.p., gen. mgr. on retirement 1928. Donated Planetarium and Astronomical Mus. to Chgo. Home: Beverly Hills, Cal. Died Nov. 4, 1952.

ADNEY, Edwin Tappan, artist; b. Athens, O., July 13, 1868; s. Col. and Prof. W. H. G. and Ruth (Shaw) A.; ed. U. N.C.; student Art Students League, N.Y. City, 3 yrs.; m. Minnie Bell Sharp, Sept. 12, 1899; 1 son, Glenn. Artist, spl. corr. Harper's Weekly and London Chronicle, the Klondike, 1897-98, Colliers' Weekly at Cape Nome, 1900; painter, writer on outdoor subjects. Commd. lt. Canadian Engrs., C.E.F., Sept. 23, 1916; charge constrn. mil. models for instrn., by spl. order of chief of staff, Mar. 16-Dec. 19, 1919; also same work on staff Royal Mil. Coll., Kingston, Ont. Expert, cons. in heraldic design, Montreal, 1923-32; conducted research in langs., canoes, gen. ethnology of Am. Indian, 1932-50. Author: The Klondike Stampede, 1899; also unpublished mss relating to canoes (Mariners Mus., Newport News, Va.) and Am. Indian langs. and ethnolcgy (Peabody Mus., Salem, Mass.). Home: Woodstock, N.B. Died Oct. 10, 1950; buried Upper Woodstock, N.B.

ADOUE, Jean Baptiste, Jr. (ăd'dōō), banker, city ofcl.; b. Dallas, Nov. 4, 1884; s. Jean Baptiste and Mittie N. (Simpson) A.; LL.B., U. of Tex., 1906; m. Hester A. Allen, Oct. 12, 1909 (dec.); children—Jean Baptiste III, Bertrand Allen (dec.); m. 2d, Mary J. Wilson, May 12, 1937. Began with Nat. Bk. of Commerce, Dallas, 1906, pres. since 1924; chmn. bd. Met. Bldg. & Loan Assn., Gulf Ins. Company; Universal Life & Accident Ins. Co.; dir. Graham-Brown Shoe Co., First Tex. Chem. Co., Cosmopolitan Hotel Company; president Dallas Clearing House Assn., 1954. Mayor City of Dallas, 1951-53; former v.p., dir. Nat. War Fund; mem. exec. com. Dallas Community Chest; bd. trustees Southwestern Med. Found.; dir. Dallas Citizens Council, Better Bus. Bur., Dallas Clearing House, Dallas S.P.C.A. Recipient Linz award, 1943. Mem. Am., Tex. State, Dallas Co. bar assns., Am. Arbitration Assn., C. of C. (past pres., treas. 1950), Am. Soc. Internat. Law, Internat., U.S. (past dir.) lawn tennis assns., Newcomen Soc. Eng., Phi Delta Theta. Episcopalian. Clubs: Dallas Athletic, Dallas Lawn Tennis (secretary, treasurer), Cedar Springs Lawn Tennis, Dallas Country, Brookhollow Country, Rotary, Petroleum, City; Bankers Club (N.Y.). Home: 3428 Cedar Springs Rd. Address: National Bank of Commerce, Dallas, Tex. Died Nov. 17, 1956; buried Crown Hill Memorial Mausoleum, Dallas, Tex.

ADRIAN, G(ilbert), dress designer; b. Naugatuck, Conn., Mar. 3, 1903; student Sch. Fine and Applied Arts, N.Y.C., and in Paris; m. Janet Gaynor, Aug. 14, 1939; 1 son, Robin Gaynor. Spl. art work Music Box Revue, N.Y.C., 1921; formerly asso. with Metro-Goldwyn-Mayer, Hollywood; designer for ballet, later originator of custom-made costumes. Office: 233 N. Beverly Dr., Beverly Hills, Cal. Died Sept. 13, 1958.

ADSON, Alfred Washington, surgeon; b. Terril, Ia., Mar. 13, 1887; s. Martin and Anna (Bergeson) A.; B.Sc., U. of Neb., 1912, A.M., 1918; M.D., U. of Pa., 1914; M.S. in surgery, U. of Minn., 1918; hon. D.Sc., U. of Neb., 1948, St. Olaf Coll.; m. Lora G. Smith, Aug. 3, 1911; children—William Walter, Mary Louise, Martin Alfred. Successively fellow in surgery, Mayo Clinic, 1st asst., jr. surgeon, neurol. surgeon, chief neurol. surgeon; now senior neuro-surgeon professor neuro-surgery Mayo Foundation Grad. Sch. of U. of Minn. Colonel Med. R.C., United States Army. Mem. Minn. State Board of Med. Examiners since 1929, pres., 2 years. Mem. Medical Council of the Veterans Administration, Council on Medical Service and Public Relations of A.M.A., adv. com. Med. Unit of Div. of Social Welfare of Minn. Dept. of Social Security; mem. Commn. on Associated Med. Care Plans; chmn. Minn. State Med. Service Com.; pres. Northwest National Conference. Fellow American College of Surgeons; member A.M.A., American Surg. Assn., American Neurol. Assn., American Neurosurgical Assn. (pres. 1932), Internat. Neurol. Assn., Internat. Congress of Surgeons, Western Surg. Assn. (v.p. 1936), Minn. State Med. Assn. (pres. 1937; del. to A.M.A.), Am. Bd. Neurol. Surgery (chmn.), Minn. Soc. of Neurology and Psychiatry (pres. 1943), also numerous local, state and district medical societies, Phi Rho Sigma, Sigma Xi, Alpha Omega Alpha. Republican (chmn. co. com.). Mason (32°, K.T., Shriner). Clubs: University, Golf. Contbr. more than 242 articles to med. jours. in development and improvement of surg. technique in removal of brain and spinal cord tumors; development of operations for treatment of glossopharyngeal neuralgia, cervical ribs, Reynaud's disease, Hirschsprung's disease and essential hypertension. Home: 831 9th Av. S.W., Rochester, Minn. Died Nov. 12, 1951.

AGA KHAN, Aga Sultan Mohamad Shah; b. 1877; m. Teresa Magliano, 1908; 1 son; m. 2d, Andreé Carron, 1929; 1 son; m. 3d, Yvette Labrousse, 1944. Mem. Viceroy's Council, 1902-04; leader Moslem deputation to Lord Minto, 1906; founder Moslem U., Aligarh, 1910; chmn. Brit.-Indian delegation Round Table Conf., London, 1930-31; Indian rep. World Disarmament Conf., Geneva, 1932; leader Indian delegation League Nations Assembly, 1932, 34-37, pres. League Nations Assembly, 1937. Decorated Order Brilliant Star of Zanzibar, Prussian Order of Royal Crown, Order Star of India, Order of Indian Empire, Knight Grand Cross Royal Victorian Order. Address: Villa Barakat, Versoix, Suisse. Died July 11, 1957.

AGASSIZ, George Russell (ă'gá-sē), trustee; b. Nahant, Mass., July 21, 1862; s. Alexander and Anna (Russell) A.; LL.D., Harvard U., 1938; m. Mabel Simpkins, June 27, 1902. Dir. Calumet and Hech Mining Co. since 1933; former pres. Harvard Bd. of Overseers. Fellow Am. Acad.; mem. Mass. Historical Soc. (past pres.), Harvard Alumni Assn. Faculty Museum Comparative Zoölogy (Harvard). Author: Letters and Recollections of Alexander Agassiz, 1913; Meade's Headquarters, 1927. Contbr. articles to jours. Home: Dedham, Mass. Office: 14 Ashburton Place, Boston. Died Feb. 5, 1951.

AGNEW, Andrew Davison, lawyer; b. County Antrim, Ireland, Nov. 18, 1867; s. William and Sarah H. (Waters) A.; LL.B., Marquette U.; m. Harriett E. Kobs. Has resided in Milw., 1871—, practicing law there until retirement. Grand Comdr. K.T., State of Wis., 1920-21. Dep. for Wis., Supreme Council, A.A.S.R. 33°, N.M.F., 1927—; Grand Master Grand Encampment K.T., U.S.A., 1932-37. Mem. Wis., Milw. bar assns., Wis State Hist. Soc. Republican. Presbyn. Clubs: Milwaukee Athletic, Old Settlers. Home: 4845 N. Lake Dr. Office: 110 E. Wisconsin Av., Milw. Died Dec. 20, 1951.

AGNEW, Hugh Elmer, marketing consultant; b. Hillsdale Co., Mich., Jan. 31, 1875; s. Allen and Rhoda Ann (Mason) A.; student Hillsdale (Mich.) Coll., 1893-96; Mich. State Teachers Coll., Ypsilanti, 1896-98, M.Pd., 1920; A.B., U. of Mich., 1902; grad. student Univ. of Washington, 1913-15; Litt.D., Huntington (Ind.) College, 1935; LL.D., Hillsdale College, 1942; m. Marie Jeanne LeGault, August 26, 1902; children—Clifton Allen, Mary Grace. Supt. of schs., Portland, Mich., 1898-1901, Howell, Mich., 1902-03; publ. Dowagiac (Mich.) Republican, 1903-12; mgr. Canton (Ill.) Daily Ledger, 1912-13; instr. U. of Wash., 1913-16; sales mgr. A. Schilling & Co., San Francisco, Calif., 1916-18; editor Western Advertising, 1918-20; editorial staff Printers' Ink, 1920-22; prof. of marketing, New York U., 1920-43, chairman department, 1928-43, prof. emeritus since 1943; visiting professor, Ohio State University, 1945; dir. of research Periodical Pubs. Assn., 1922-25; chmn. advisory bd. Fact Finders Assos.; mem. Nat. Com. Economic Development since 1942. Mem. Am. Marketing Assn. (sec. 1929-36; pres. 1937), Research Council of New York, Am. Econ. Assn., Beta Gamma Sigma, Phi Delta Pi, Alpha Delta Sigma. Clubs: Faculty (N.Y.U.). Author Cooperative Advertising by Competitors, 1926; Advertising Principles (with G. B. Hotchkiss), 1926, rev. 1930 and '41.

Advertising Media—How to Weigh and Measure, 1932; Outlines of Marketing (with Jenkins and Drury), 1936, revised (with Conner and Doremus), 1950; Advertising Media (with W. B. Dygert), 1938; Outdoor Advertising, 1938; Marketing Policies (with Dale Houghton), 1941, revised 1950. Contbr. articles on advertising and marketing for Encyclopaedia Britannica, 1928, 1940, 1950. Died July 30, 1955; buried Locust Valley Cemetery, L.I., N.Y.

AGNEW, P(aul) G(ough), engineer; b. Hillsdale Co., Mich., July 3, 1881; s. Allen and Rhoda Ann (Mason) A.; B.L., Hillsdale Coll., 1901; A.M., U. of Mich., 1902; Ph.D., Johns Hopkins, 1911; m. Ethna Mercedes Heebner, Sept. 27, 1911. Instr. physics, high schs., Monroe and Pontiac, Mich., 1902-05; physicist Bur. Standards, 1906-19, v.p., sec. Am. Standards Assn., 1920-47, consultant to the association, 1948-51, awarded Standards medal, 1951. Mem. Am. Ins. E.E., A.A.A.S., Washington Acad. Scis. Clubs: Cosmos (Washington, D.C.); Town Hall (New York). Author of papers on physics, elec. engring. and standardization. Home: 325 E. 72d St., N.Y. City. Died Jan. 9, 1954.

AGNEW, William John Clarke, med. officer; b. High Falls, N.Y., Dec. 6, 1891; s. William J. C. and Mary Martha (Stephens) A.; student L.I. Coll. Hosp., Bklyn., 1910-11; M.D., U. Vt., 1914; m. Drika Fisher, Apr. 29, 1937. Interne, St. Johns Riverside Hosp., Yonkers, N.Y., 1914-16; resident N.Y., Nursery and Childs Hosp., N.Y.C., 1916, N.Y. Orthopedic Hosp., N.Y.C., 1916-17; entered M.C., U.S. Navy, 1917; promoted through grades to rear adm., Sept. 1942; now dist. med. officer, 11th Naval Dist. Fellow A.C.S.; mem. Alpha Kappa Kappa, Theta Nu Epsilon. Clubs: Army and Navy (Washington); Chevy Chase, Columbia Country (Chevy Chase, Md.). Editor: Handbook of the Hospital Corps, U.S. Navy, 1939. Home: 1041 Encino Row, Coronado, Cal. Address: District Medical Officer, 9th Naval District, Great Lakes, Ill. Died Jan. 26, 1955.

AGOOS, Solomon, business exec.; b. Krinik, Poland, Oct. 2, 1880; s. Lassor Agoos; student Newburyport Grammar School; Chelsea High School; Harvard Univ., 1899-1900; m. Florence Montwid, June 6, 1911. With L. Agoos & Co., 1901-15; pres., Standard Kid Co., 1915-29; pres., Allied Kid Co., Boston, Mass., 1929-45, chmn. bd. since 1945. Home: 62 Beech Rd., Brookline, Mass. Office: 209 South St., Boston, Mass. Died Jan. 30, 1953.

AGRY, Warren C(ram) (ā'grē), publisher; b. Newtonville, Mass., Nov. 17, 1889; s. George and Pamelia Warren (Cram) A.; B.S., Dartmouth, 1911; m. Marian A. Stutson, Dec. 29, 1914; children—Marian (wife of Dr. Robert C. Berson), Ann, Warren C. Advt. rep., Peoples Home Jour., 1911-18, western mgr., 1918-27; advt. rep. Cosmopolitan, 1927-29, advt. mgr. 1929; advt. mgr. Good Housekeeping, 1930-33, bus. mgr., 1933-41, pub., 1941-44; advt. dir. The American Home, 1944-52, v.p., asst. to pub., 1952—. Past pres. Nat. Better Bus. Bur., 1st vice chmn., 1952-55, chmn. bd., 1955—. Mem. Casque and Gauntlet, Psi Upsilon. Clubs: Apawamis, Manursing Island (Rye, N.Y.); Union League, Dartmouth College (N.Y.C.); University (Chgo.). Home: 29 Cayuga St., Rye, N.Y. Office: 444 Madison Av., N.Y.C. 22. Died Jan. 18, 1958.

AGUILAR, Roberto Trigueros, El Salvador diplomat; b. San Salvador, Rep. of El Salvador, C.A., Nov. 5, 1888; s. Eugenio and Angela (Trigueros) A.; student pvt. sch., London, Eng., 1897-1902 and pub. schs., Dresden, Germany; m. Maria Luisa Meardi, Feb. 11, 1916 (div.); children—Fermina, Roberto Ricardo, Mauricio, Federico, Maria Marina (Mrs. Gorge Lopez); m. 2d, Gwendolyn Frances Doty, May 9, 1939. Mayor, City of San Salvador, 1912-13; sec. to delegation First Pan Am. Financial Conf., Washington, 1915; treas. gen. of El Salvador, 1918-19, acting minister of finance, 1919-20; rep. Coffee Growers Assn. of El Salvador in N.Y., 1932-56; comml. attaché to embassy, Washington, 1946-56. Del. to Inter-Am. Coffee Bd.; pres. Pan-Am. Coffee Bur.; N.Y., 1937-49; del. to 2d session Gen. Assembly of UN, and 2d spl. session, also del. to interim com. of UN; del. to I.T.O. Conf., Havana, Cuba, 1947-48; del. to Inter-Am. Econ. and Social Council Orgn. of Am. States, Washington, 1948. Roman Catholic. Home: 127 W. 96th St., N.Y.C. 25. Offices: 120 Wall St., N.Y.C. Died Jan. 1959.

AHALT, Arthur M(ontraville) (ā'-hält), agrl. educator; b. Monesson, Pa., July 8, 1907; s. Alonza Joshua and Hattie Mozell (Flook) A.; B.S. (first honors), U. of Md., 1931; M.S., Pa. State Univ., 1937; student part time George Washington U., 1943-46; m. Mary Jane Zeigler, Mar. 29, 1935; children—Mary Jane, Arthur Montraville. Teacher vocational agr., Dorchester County, Md., 1931-34, Frederick County, Md., 1934-39; mem. faculty, U. of Md. since Sept. 1939, prof. and head agr. edn. since 1947, part time teaching in agrl. edn. as asst. prof. and asso. prof. agrl. edn. and part time research worker in agr. economics, Agr. Expt. Sta., as asst. prof. and asso. prof. agr. economics, 1939-47. Cons. specialist in agricultural education Inter-American Seminar in Vocational Education, U. of Maryland, 1952. Mem. Am. Assn. Univ. Profs., Future Farmers of Am. (hon.), N.E.A., Am. Vocational Assn., Nat. Vocational Agr. Teachers Assn., Am. Assn. Adult Edn., Md. Vocational Assn. (bd. dirs., 1947-55), Md. Vocational Agr. Teachers Assn. (sec.-treasurer 1935-36, pres., 1936-37), Md. State Teachers Assn., Phi Kappa Phi, Alpha Zeta, Phi Delta Kappa, Alpha Gamma Rho, Alpha Tau Alpha, Kappa Phi Kappa. Mem. Grange (local master, 1937-39). Lutheran. Author expt. sta. bulletins; contbr. numerous articles in Vocational Agricultural Education. Home: 7007 Rhode Island Av., College Park 1, Md. Died Sept. 12, 1958; buried Lutheran Cemetery, Middletown, Md.

AHERN, Michael Joseph, clergyman; b. N.Y.C., May 25, 1877; s. Maurice and Mary Ellen (Brophy) A.; A.B., St. Francis Xavier's Coll., N.Y.C., 1896; A.M., Woodstock Coll. Md., 1902; S.T.D., Innsbruck U. Austria 1911; Ph.D. Gregorian U., Rome, 1931; LL.D., Canisius, 1941; hon. D.Sc., Tufts, 1942. Joined Soc. of Jesus (Jesuits), 1896; instr. chemistry Boston Coll., 1902; instr. geology Woodstock Coll., 1906; head dept. chemistry Canisius Coll., Buffalo, 1911-15, Boston Coll., 1915-19; pres. Canisius Coll., 1919-23; head dept. chemistry Holy Cross Coll., 1923-25; head dept. geology Weston Coll., 1926—. Fellow A.A.A.S., Am. Geog. Soc., Am. Acad. Arts and Scis.; mem. councillor Am. Chem. Soc.; mem. Boston Soc Natural History, Buffalo Acad. Sci. Lectr., writer religious and sci. subjects. Address: Weston Coll., Weston, Mass. Died June 5, 1951.

AILSHIE, Margaret Cobb, pub.; b. Chgo., Mar. 27, 1886; d. Calvin and Fannie (Lyon) Cobb; ed. pvt. schs. in Boise, Ida., Chgo., Farmington, Conn.; m. James F. Ailshie, Jr., 1929 (dec.). Became pub. of Idaho Statesman upon death of father in 1929; now owner Daily Statesman, Ida. Evening Statesman, Ida. Sunday Statesman, Boise, Ida. Dir. Boise chpt. A.R. C.; dir. Booth Meml. Hosp. (Boise). Home: 212 W. Idaho St. Office: Statesman Bldg., 601 Main St., Boise, Ida. Died Aug. 26, 1959.

AIRD, Alexander N(eilson), industrialist; b. Jersey City, Sept. 7, 1903; s. Alexander and Grace (Smith) A.; M.E., Cornell U., 1927; m. Ola E. Odendhal, Sept. 15, 1946; children—Alexander N., Douglas B. With Revere Copper & Brass, Inc., 1927—, successively mech. engr., mech. supt., chief engr., works mgr., v.p., 1953—. Mem. Saint Andrews Soc., Alpha Chi Rho. Republican. Clubs: Baltimore Country, Merchants, Cornell. Home: 1208 Robin Hood Circle, Towson, Md. Office: 1301 Wicomico St., Balt. 30. Died Sept. 7, 1958.

AITKEN, Robert Grant, astronomer; b. Jackson, Calif., Dec. 31, 1864; s. Robert and Wilhelmina (Depinau) A.; A.B., Williams Coll., 1887, A.M., 1892; hon. Sc.D., U. of the Pacific, 1903, Williams Coll., 1917, U. of Ariz., 1923; LL.D., U. of Calif., 1935; m. Jessie L. Thomas, June 19, 1888; children—Wilhelmine, Robert Thomas, Malcolm Darroch, Douglas Carryl. Instr. mathematics, Livermore Coll., 1888-91; prof. mathematics and astronomy, U. of Pacific, 1891-95; astronomer at Lick Obs., 1895-1935, asso. dir., 1923-30, dir., 1930-35, emeritus dir. and astronomer since 1935. Discovered 3,100 double stars since 1899. Lalande prize, Acad. of Sciences of France, 1906, for double star discoveries; Bruce gold medal "for distinguished services to astronomy," 1926; gold medal of Royal Astron. Soc., 1932. George Darwin lecturer, Royal Astron. Soc., 1932. Lecturer astronomy, U. of Calif., summers, 1908-09, 1913, 1919; mem. Lick Obs. Eclipse Expdn. to Flint Island, 1908. Mem. Phi Beta Kappa, Sigma Xi, Nat. Acad. Sciences (chmn. sect. of astronomy, 1929-32), Am. Philos. Soc., Am. Astron. Soc. (v.p., 1929-31, pres. 1937-40), Internat. Astron. Union (chmn. double star commn., 1918-28), Astron. Soc. Pacific; fellow A.A. A.S. (pres. Pacific div., 1925-36; v.p. sect. D, 1926-27), Calif. Acad. Science; fgn. asso. Royal Astronomical Soc. Editor Publs. Astronomical Society Pacific, 1897-1908 and 1911-1942. Official delegate U.S.A. to Fifth Pacific Science Congress, Victoria, B.C., 1933. Author: Publs. Lick Obs., vol. XII, 1914; The Binary Stars, 1918, 2d edit., 1935; New General Catalogue of Double Stars within 120° of the North Pole, 1932. Editor and contbr. Adolfo Stahl Lectures in Astronomy, 1919. Contbr. astron. and other scientific jours. Address: 1109 Spruce St., Berkeley 7, Calif. Died Oct. 29, 1951; buried Oakland, Calif.

AKINS, Zoë, author; b. Humansville, Mo., Oct. 30, 1886; d. Thomas J. and Elizabeth (Green) A.; ed. at home, Monticello Sem., Godfrey, Ill., and Hosmer Hall, St. Louis; m. Hugh (Hugo) Cecil Levinge Rumbold of London, (capt. grenadier guards), March 12, 1932 (dec.). Contributor poems, criticisms, etc., Reedy's Mirror, St. Louis; later contributor to leading magazines. Member Poetry Soc. America, Artists' Guild of St. Louis, Am. Dramatists and Composers Soc., Authors League Am. Author: Interpretations (poems), 1911; (plays) Papa, prod. 1919, pub. 1914; The Magical City, prod. 1919; Déclassée, prod. 1919, pub. 1923; Foot-Loose, prod. 1920; Daddy's Gone a-Hunting, prod. 1921, & pub. 1923; The Varying Shore, prod. 1921; Greatness (The Texas Nightingale), prod. 1922, pub. 1923; A Royal Fandango, 1924; Thou Desperate Pilot, prod., 1927; The Furies, prod., 1928; The Greeks Had A Word For It, produced 1929-30; The Morning Glory produced as moving picture, 1932; The Old Maid, dramatized from story by Edith Wharton, produced at Empire Theatre, Jan. 7, 1936, also published, 1936; O Evening Star, prod. 1936; The Little Miracle (play in verse), pub. 1936; The Hills Grow Smaller (poems), 1937; The Human Element (adaptation; prod. in Budapest under title, "The Devil and the Woman"), 1939; Forever Young (novel), 1941; The Happy Days (play adapted from French), prod. 1941; Mrs. January and Mr. Ex., 1944, produced in Stockholm under title "Tomorrow's Plans," 1946; (play) Another Darling, prod. 1950; (dramatization) The Old Maid (Pulitzer Prize); (play) The Greeks Had a Word for It; (poems) The Hills Grow Smaller; (novel) Forever Young. Winner of Pulitzer drama prize for 1934-35. Home: 324 S. Ardmore Av., Los Angeles 5. Office: Care Samuel French Co., 25 W. 45th St., N.Y.C. Died Oct. 29, 1958.

ALABASTER, Francis Asbury, educator; b. Rochester, N.Y., June 10, 1866; s. Rev. John and Harriet Ann (Bemish) A.; A.B., Northwestern U., 1890; A.M., U. Neb., 1898; post-grad., 1898-99, U. Chgo., summers 1901, 02; Litt.D., Dickinson Coll., 1918; m. Blanche Robinson, 1895; children—Wendell Robinson, Francis Theodore, Ruth Clara (Mrs. Clair Weatherhogg). Prof. Latin, Neb. Wesleyan U., 1893-1912, prof. Greek, 1898-1928, prof. of classics, 1928—, dean College of Liberal Arts, 1911-36, 38-39, dean emeritus, 1936—. Mem. Neb. Tchrs. Assn. (life). Phi Kappa Psi, Phi Beta Kappa, Phi Kappa Phi, Pi Gamma Mu. Republican. Methodist. Club: Lions. Home: 5226 Madison Av., Lincoln, Neb. Died June 22, 1946; buried Lincoln Meml. Park.

ALANSON, Bertram Edward, investment broker; b. San Francisco, Calif., Jan. 8, 1877; s. Alexander and Fanny (Weinberg) A.; student Colegio Universitario de Esponda, Guatemala City, Guatemala, 1885-90, Berkeley (Calif.) Gymnasium Prep. Sch., 1890-93; m. Mabel Bartholomew, May 23, 1924. Investment broker, mem. Alanson Bros. & Co., San Francisco, since 1907; vice president Federal Telegraph Co., 1921-23; vice president E. C. Horst Co.; dir. Alaska Salmon Co. Vice-pres. San Francisco Stock & Bond Exchange, 1914-15, chmn. exec. com., 1914-18; pres. San Francisco Stock Exchange, 1930, later chmn. finance com.; Fellow American Geog. Soc. of N.Y. Vice president Pan-American Society. Clubs: Argonaut (pres. 1918), Lakeside, Stock Exch. (chmn. bd. since 1949) (San Francisco); First Edition (London, Eng.). Home: 828 Francisco St., San Francisco 9, Calif. Office: 400 Montgomery, San Francisco 4. Died May 25, 1958.

ALBANI, Madame, prima donna; b. (Marie Louise Emma Cecile Lajeunesse) Chamblay, nr. Montreal, Can., Nov. 1, 1851; ed. Convent of Sacred Heart, Montreal, and at Albany, N.Y., where she became locally famous as a singer. A concert was given there to raise funds to complete her musical ed'n at Paris and, under Lamperti, at Milan. Made début as opera singer at Messina, Italy, 1870, taking the stage name "Albani" as a compliment to the city which had aided her career. Has since been very prominent as an operatic prima donna in Europe and America; m. Ernest Gye, the impressario, 1878. Address: Park House, Earl's Court Rd., S.W., London, Eng. Died Apr. 3, 1930.

ALBEE, Percy F., artist; b. Bridgeport, Conn.; June 26, 1883; s. William A. and Amelia Ann (Holt) A.; ed. Pa. Acad. Fine Arts, 1900-04; R.I. Sch. of Design, 1905-07; m. Grace Arnold, May 10, 1913; children—Edward F., John F., Nathaniel E., William C., Percy F. Mural painter, 1910—; decorations in Museum R.I. Sch. Design, St. Stephens Ch., Providence, Brown and Sharpe Mfg. Co., Brown U., R.I. Country Club, Bridgham High Sch. Exhibits in most museums, art socs. and galleries here and in Europe, Asso. N.A.D.; mem. Artists for Victory, Inc., Pa. Acad. Fellowship, Conn. Acad. Fine Arts, Soc. Am. Etchers, New Hope Hist. Soc., Springtown Recreational Center. Recipient Gedney Bunce prize, 1942, Conn. Academy; Salmagundi Water Color Prize, 1946; hon. mention, Allied Artists of America, Soc. Am. Graphic Artists. Represented Met. Mus. Clubs: Providence Art; Salmagundi (mem. Jury of Award, 1937, 48, 49; pres. 1949-53, dir.) (N.Y.); Philadelphia Water Color. Home: Hidden Spring, Springtown, Pa.; (mailing address) R.D. 1, Hellertown, Pa. Died Nov. 1959.

ALBERS, William Henry, market chain exec.; b. Cin., May 23, 1880; s. Henry A. and Anna (Alf) A.; student pub. and parochial schs.; m. Dorothy Brown, 1913 (dec. Nov. 30, 1951); children—Irene (Mrs. J. Harry Dornheggen), Jeanette (Mrs. A. J. Long, dec.). Began career in father's grocery in Cin., later with D. McKim Cooke & Co., mdse. brokers, also Schneider Bros. Co. of which he was sec. upon consolidation with Kroger Grocery & Baking Co., became asst. sec. Kroger's, 1910, mgr. St. Louis br., 1912-15, v.p., gen. mgr., Cin., 1915, later pres.; purchased controlling interest A. Nash Co., 1930, organized Nash Crusaders of the Golden Rule; opened first Super-Market under name Albers Super Markets, Inc., 1933, now pres., operating 65 super markets in Ohio and Ky.; chmn. bd. Sperti, Inc., Sperti Products, Inc.; pres. Schock Gusmer, Inc., Sperti Faraday,

Inc., Sperti Foods, Inc.; dir. Cooper Hewitt Electric Co., First Nat. Bank of Cin. Chmn. Bd. Park Commrs. Hamilton Co.; former chmn. Cin. Community Chest; life mem. nat. exec. bd. Boy Scouts Am.; dir. Cath. Youth Orgn., Nat. Council Cath. Men; chmn. adv. bd. St. Mary's Hosp.; mem. Food Adv. Council OPA and War Food Council, Dept. Agr., Washington, and chmn. rationing sub-com. of Food Industry War Com. during World War II. Trustee, treas. Coll. Music Cin.; trustee Cath. U., Washington; lay adv. bd. Xavier U., Cin. Decorated Knight Comdr. Order St. Gregory; named Jet Jockey by Air Proving Ground Elgin Air Force Base, Fla. Mem. Cin. Art Mus., Ohio C. of C., Cin. C. of C., Ohio Soc. N.Y., Hist. and Philos. Soc. Ohio. K.C. (4°). Clubs: Queen City, Camargo (Cin.); Everglades (Palm Beach, Fla.); Biltmore Forest Country (Biltmore, N.C.). Home: "Alberly Manor" 9200 Shawnee Run Rd., Indian Hill, Cin. 43. Office: 266 W. Mitchell Av., Cin. 32. Died June 6, 1954; buried Gate Haven Cemetery, Cin.

ALBERT, Elma Gates, judge; b. Hampton, Pa., June 5, 1866; s. Daniel and Margaret (Getz) A.; LL.B., Drake U., 1891; m. Alice Kester, June 16, 1897; children—Helen Margaret, John W. Admitted to Ia. bar, 1892, and began practice at Grand Junction; county atty., Green County, Ia., 1900-06; asso. justice Supreme Ct. of Ia., 1925-30. Republican. Mason. Home: Jefferson, Ia. Deceased.

ALBERTSON, Charles Carroll, clergyman; b. Plainfield, Ind., Feb. 11, 1865; s. Benjamin and Martha (Bowman) A.; ed. for law; studied theology in Garrett Bibl. Inst.; D.D., Allegheny Coll., 1899; m. Florence Edith Romer, 1899 (died 1926); 1 dau., Katherine; m. 2d, Permelia Hogg Lindridge, 1928. Pastor, Goshen, Ind., 1888-92, Jamestown, N.Y., 1892-95, Buffalo, 1895-99, Philadelphia, 1899-1904, Central Presbyn. Ch. Rochester, N.Y., 1904-13, Lafayette Av. Ch., Bklyn., 1913-28; lectr. homiletics, Bibl. Sem., 1928—. Chaplain Pratt Inst., Bklyn., 1924-28. Founder and pres. Book Lovers' Guild (Phila.). Editor: Gems of Truth and Beauty; Pearls from Many Seas; Light on the Hills, 1904; Lyra Mystica, 1934. Author: Safe Counsel and Sweet Comfort, 1891; The Gospel According to Christ, 1898; Many Voices, 1904; Death and Afterwards, 1907; College Sermons, 1912; Distinctive Ideas of Jesus, 1915; Chapel Talks, 1916; Prophets and the War, 1918; The Reality of Religion, 1928; Ministers' Book of Prayer, 1942; Voices in the Night, 1943; numerous poems and essays. Contbr. Christian Herald, Association Men, etc. Clubs: Wyandauch (L.I.); Union Interalliée (Paris). Home: 952 Fifth Av., N.Y.C. Died May 14, 1959.

ALBERTSON, Ralph, business man; b. Jamesport, N.Y., Oct. 21, 1866; s. Richard and Sarepta Y. (Aldrich) A.; ed. Greenport (N.Y.) Acad., 1880-84, Oberlin Coll. and Theol. Sem., 1888-91, and by pvt. study; m. Irene Mulford, Aug. 6, 1886; m. 2d, Hazel Hammond, May 8, 1904; m. 3d, Dorothy G. Stewart, September 2, 1934. Ordained Congregational ministry, 1890; pastor Penfield, O., 1889-91, Springfield, O., 1891-5; took a leading part in organization and mgmt. of Christian Commonwealth, Andrews, N.C., and Commonwealth, Ga., 1895-1900; pres. Twentieth Century Co., pub. The Twentieth Century Mag., also pres. Cooperative Pub. Co., publishers of The Boston Common; gen. mgr. Wm. S. Butler & Co., dept. store, Boston, 1910-12; pres. Albertson, Beckhand & Allen, Inc., N.Y.C. Decorated Cross of St. George. Editor: Social Gospel, 1897-1900, the Am. Co-operator, Lewiston, Me., 1902-04. Author: Fighting Without a War, 1920. Clubs: Town Hall (N.Y.C.); Cosmos (Washington); Liberal. Home: 3387 Stuyvesant Pl. N.W., Washington. Died Jan. 22, 1951.

ALBRIGHT, Adam Emory (awl'brīt), artist; b. Monroe, Wis., Aug. 15, 1862; s. Zachariah and Catherine (Kepler) A.; art edn. Art Inst. Chgo., 1881-83, Pa. Acad. Fine Arts, Phila., 1883-86, Munich and Paris, 1887-88; m. Clara Amelia Wilson, Dec. 24, 1888 (dec.); children—Lisle Murillo, Ivan Lorraine and Malvin Marr (twins). Painter Am. country children; shown at many exhbns. in America; represented at Chgo. Expn. in 1893, also N.Y., Phila., Boston, Washington, Carnegie Inst. (Pitts.), Buffalo, St. Louis, Chgo., Paris Salon, Panama-Pac. Internat. Expn., San Francisco. Represented in permanent collection of City Art Mus., St. Louis, Toledo Mus. Art, Municipal Art League, Chgo., state mus., Springfield, Ill., libraries, clubs, schs., etc. Awarded Grower Prize, Art Inst. Chgo., 1907, 1914; Martin B. Cahn Prize, Chgo., 1908; Gold Medal, Chgo. Painters and Sculptors, 1947. Del. for Chgo. Soc. Artists and Soc. Western Artists, at 1st Nat. Art Conv., Washington, 1909, for Chgo. Soc. Artists to Am. Fedn. of Arts, Chgo., 1914. Mem. Soc. Western Artists, Fellowship of Pa. Acad. Fine Arts, Phila., Chgo. Soc. Artists (pres. 1915-16), Chgo. Water Color Club (dir., ex-pres.), Chgo. Acad. Design, Am. Water Color Soc., N.Y. (life), N.Y. Water Color Club, Chgo. Galleries Assn. Clubs: Chgo. Painters and Sculptors; Salmagundi (N.Y.C.). Author: For Arts Sake, 1953. Home: Warrenville, Ill. Died Sept. 14, 1957.

ALBRO, Mrs. Curtis Sanford, city official; b. Passaic, N.J., Jan. 14, 1893; d. George and Jeanie (Mac Vicar) Warwick; grad. Adelphia Coll., Seattle, Wash., 1913; student U. of Wash.; m. Curtis Sanford Albro, June 17, 1926. Loan and discount clerk Canadian Bank of Commerce, Seattle, 1917-19; loan clerk Security First National Bank, Los Angeles, 1920-26. Mem. bd. of police commissioners, Los Angeles, since 1946. Dir. Citizens Nat. Com., Washington; dir. women's div. Los Angeles Chamber of Commerce; founder, chmn. Woman's Tax Study Group of Los Angeles; dir. Calif. War Chest (state exec. com.); chmn. women's com. Los Angeles War Chest; mem. Community Chest of Los Angeles; vice pres. U.S.O. Area Bd. of Los Angeles, 1941-47. Chmn. Woman's Civic Conf., U. of Southern Calif., Los Angeles, 1945; vice pres. Volunteers of America (Los Angeles), nat. chmn. youth activities; mem. bd. of Church Welfare Bur., Los Angeles, 1943-47. Mem. membership commn. Nat. Y.W.C.A.; pres. Los Angeles Y.W.C.A., 1939-44, and since 1946. Board mem. and officer Woman's Club of Hollywood, 5 yrs., Friday Morning Club of Los Angeles, 2 yrs. Republican. Methodist. Home: 665 S. Orange Dr., Los Angeles 36. Office: Los Angeles Police Commission, City Hall, Los Angeles. Died July 31, 1950; buried Forest Lawn Meml. Park Mausoleum, Glendale, Calif.

ALCOCK, Nathaniel Graham (awl'kŏk), urologist; b. 1881; B.S., Northwestern U., 1907, M.S., 1908, M.D., 1912. With State U. of Ia., 1915—, prof. and head dept. of genito-urinary surgery, 1923—. Mem. A.M.A., Am. Assn. Genito-Urinary Surgeons, Am. Urol. Assn., others. Home: 430 E. Brown St. Office: 105 E. Iowa Av., Iowa City, Ia. Died 1953.

ALCORN, Hugh Mead, lawyer; b. at Suffield, Conn., October 24, 1872; s. of Hugh Glen and Susan (Ford) A.; grad. Conn. Literary Instn., Suffield, 1894; hon. M.A., Dartmouth, 1928; m. Cora Terry Wells, June 28, 1900; children—Howard Wells, Hugh Mead, Robert Hayden. Admitted to Conn. bar, 1897, and practiced since at Hartford; state's atty., Hartford Co., 1908-42; special assistant to United States Attorney General (trial case United States vs. Rumely et al, United States Dist. Ct., N.Y. City), 1920. Mem. Conn. Ho. of Rep., 1903, 05, State Civil Service Commn., 1915-18; del. to Rep. Nat. Convns., 1912, 20, 36. Recipient U.S. Flag Assn. award for Law Enforcement, 1933. Mem. Am. Bar Association, Connecticut State Bar Assn. (pres. 1934-36), Hartford Co. Bar Assn. (pres. 1932-34), Am. Judicature Soc., Am. Law Inst., Acad. Am. Trial Bar, Conn. Hist. Soc., Sons Union Vets. of Civil War. Republican. Conglist. Home: Suffield, Conn. Office: 750 Main St., Hartford, Conn. Died May 26, 1955.

ALDEN, Charles Henry, architect; b. Hingham, Mass., Sept. 27, 1867; s. Charles Henry and Katharine Russell (Lincoln) A.; student U. Minn., 1884-87; B.S. in Architecture, Mass. Inst. Tech., 1890. Began practice in Boston, 1897; with Howard and Galloway, supervising architects Alaska Yukon Pacific Expn. and U. Wash., 1906-09; in charge specifications and archtl. dept., div. of works Panama-Pacific Expn., 1913-15; practiced at Seattle, 1909—; lectr. on architecture U. Wash. Mem. Mass. N.G., 1891-1900; commd. capt., O.R.C., U.S. Army, 1917; apptd. supply officer, 311th Sanitary Train, 86th Div., later asst. depot q.m., Boston, 1917; asst. q.m. 6th A.C., 1918; adj. 122d Engrs. supply officer and asst. to engr. officer in charge constrn., Am. Embarkation Center, Le Mans, France, 1918-19; maj. to col. Q.M. Res. Corps, 1919-31. Mem. Seattle Zoning Commn., Building Code Revision Commn., Seattle City Planning Commn. (chmn. zoning commn.), King County Planning Commn., 1939; state chmn. Pub. Works of Art Project, 1933-34; mem. Com. on City and Local Planning of Wash. Planning Council, 1934; chmn. planning com. Assn. of Wash. Cities, 1940; trustee Seattle Traffic and Safety Council, 1937. Engr. Seattle Municipal Def. Commn. Fellow A.I.A. (pres. Wash. chpt.); mem. Fine Arts Soc. of Seattle (pres.), Pacific N.W. Acad. Arts, Mil. Order Loyal Legion, Municipal League of Seattle (dir.), Chi Psi. Episcopalian. Clubs: University, Cosmos. Home: University Club, 1004 Boren Av. Office: Arcade Bldg., Seattle. Died 1951.

ALDEN, Edward S., mfg. exec.; b. Boston, Jan. 28, 1888; s. Edward and (Madan) A.; student Bryant & Stratton Comml. Coll., Boston; m. Una Elliott, June 1, 1910; children—Barbara, Janet. With United Drug Co., Boston, 1907-13, treas. subsidiary Guth Chocolate Co., 1912-13; with Scovill Wellington & Co., Boston, 1916-18; trustee Whitinsville (Mass.) Savs. Bank since 1928; chmn. security investment com. Whiten Machine Works since 1918, dir. and treas. since 1928, vice president, 1951—; also vice president Whitensville Nat. Bank since 1935, now dir. and v.p. Conglist. Clubs: Algonquin (Boston); Whitinsville Golf. Home: 88 Ledgeways, Wellesley. Office: Whitin Machine Works, Whitinsville, Mass. Died Jan. 10, 1953.

ALDEN, Herbert Watson, engring. exec.; b. Lyndonville, Vt., Dec. 20, 1870; s. Horace Allen and Elizabeth (Eaton) A.; S.B., Mass. Inst. Tech., 1893; m. Madelaine Grier, Dec. 27, 1893 (div.); children—Horace Allen, Douglas Grier, Madelaine (Mrs. William H. Hynard). Asst. engr. Am. Projectile Co., Lynn, Mass., 1893-95, Pope Mfg. Co., 1895-1906, Timken Roller Bearing Co., 1906-09; chief engr. Timken-Detroit Axle Co., 1909-13, v.p., 1913-25, chmn. bd., 1926-41, now dir. engring. Recipient Scott Medal from Army Ordnance Assn. for work on indsl. preparedness, 1941; Distinguished Service citation Automobile Old Timers, 1946. Commd. maj., 1917, lt. col., 1918; now col. O.R.C. Decorated D.S.M. (U.S.). Founder mem. Soc. Automotive Engrs. (past pres). Fellow Am. Soc. M.E.; mem. Army Ordnance Assn., Automobile Old Timers Assn. (charter mem.), Delta Kappa Epsilon. Republican. Conglist. Club: Athletic (Detroit). Home: 2645 Riverside Dr., Trenton, Mich. Office: The Timken-Detroit Axle Co., Detroit. Died Nov. 10, 1950.

ALDEN, William Tracy, lawyer; b. Pleasanton, Ia., Sept. 20, 1866; s. William and Leath (Rock) A.; Ph.B., Northwestern U., 1891, LL.B., 1893; m. Marjorie Edwards, Oct. 24, 1923; children—William Tracy, John Edwards. Admitted to bar, 1893; law clk. Chgo., 1893-95; mem. Wilber, Eldredge & Alden, 1895-99, Alden, Latham & Young, 1899—. Mem. Am., Ill. State, Chgo. (pres. 1921-22) bar assns., Art Inst. Chgo. (life), Field Mus. Natural History, Chgo. Hist. Soc. Democrat. Clubs: Chicago, University, Union League, Glenview Golf (Chgo.); University (N.Y.C.). Home: 1320 N. State St. Office: 134 S. La Salle St., Chgo. Deceased.

ALDER, Byron, coll. prof.; b. Manti, Utah, Nov. 18, 1883; s. Alfred and Alvira Jane (Cox) A.; student Brigham Young U., 1903-06; B.S., Utah State Agr. Coll., 1912; m. Jennie May Westenskow, Aug. 28, 1907; children—Horace Byron, Dorothy May (Mrs. Ralph M. Porter). Teacher mathematics Manti High Sch., 1912; head dept. poultry husbandry Utah State Agr. Coll. since 1913, professor emeritus of poultry husbandry since 1949. Mem. Am. Poultry Sci. Assn., World's Poultry Sci. Assn., Phi Kappa Phi. Republican. Mem. Ch. of Jesus Christ of Latter-Day Saints. Author and co-author of Utah Agr. Expt. Sta. bulls., circulars, spl. reports on research on poultry husbandry problems. Home: 332 N. 4th E St., Logan, Utah. Died Apr. 7, 1951; buried Logan City Cemetery.

ALDER, Kurt, scientist; b. Germany, 1902; s. Joseph and Maria (Lammel) A.; student U. Berlin, 1922; Ph.D., Kiel U., 1922-26; M.D. (hon.), Cologne U., 1950; Dr. E. h., der Universitat Salamanca, 1954. Extraordinary professor Christian Albrechts U., Kiel, Germany, 1934-36; research lab. staff Bayer Dye Works, Leverkusen, 1936-40; prof. chemistry Cologne U. since 1940, dean faculty of philosophy, 1949-50, engaged in organic research since 1926. Awarded Nobel prize for chemistry (with Diels), 1950. Hon. mem. Real Sociedad Española de Fisica y Quimica (Madrid), Censejo Superior de Investigationes Cientificas (Madrid). Home: Köln, Zülpicherstr. 47. Office: Chemisches Instut der Universitat Cologne, Cologne, Germany. Died June 20, 1958.

ALDRICH, Bess Streeter (Mrs. Charles S. Aldrich) (aw'drĭch), writer; b. Cedar Falls, Ia., Feb. 17, 1881; d. James Wareham and Mary Wilson (Anderson) Streeter; grad. Ia. State Teachers Coll., Cedar Falls, Ia., 1901; hon. Litt.D., U. of Neb., 1934; m. Charles S. Aldrich, banker, Sept. 24, 1907 (died May 3, 1925); children—Mary Eleanor (Mrs. Milton P. Beechner), James Whitson, Charles S., Robert Steeter. Teacher pub. schs., Ia., and Salt Lake City, Utah, 5 yrs.; asst. supervisor primary training, Ia. State Teachers Coll., 1 yr. Methodist. Mem. O.E.S., Altrusa P.E.O., Chi Delta Phi, Theta Sigma Phi; hon. mem. Neb. State Press Assn. Clubs: Southern California Press Assn., The Midland Authors. Contbr. short stories to American Mag., Ladies' Home Jour., Woman's Home Companion, Delineator, Cosmopolitan, Good Housekeeping, Harper's Weekly, etc. Used pen name Margaret Dean Stevens, 1911-18; writing under own name 1918—. Author: Mother Mason, 1924; The Rim of the Prairie, 1925; The Cutters, 1926; A Lantern in Her Hand, 1928; A White Bird Flying, 1931; Miss Bishop, 1933; Spring Came On Forever, 1935; The Man Who Caught the Weather, 1936; Song of Years, 1939; The Drum Goes Dead, 1941; The Lieutenant's Lady, 1942; Journey Into Christmas, 1949; The Bess Streeter Aldrich Reader, 1950. Home: 1000 S. 52d St., Piedmont, Lincoln, Neb. Died Aug. 3, 1954; buried Elmwood, Neb.

ALDRICH, Edward Burgess, newspaper exec.; b. Providence, Sept. 28, 1871; s. Nelson Wilmarth and Abby (Pearce) A.; grad. Brown U., 1893; m. Lora Lawson, 1910; children—Suzanne Aldrich (Mrs. Philip Drinker), Robert B., Ruth Aldrich (Mrs. Samuel Lines). Pres., dir. Pawtucket (R.I.) Times since 1916; dir. Gorham Co., Trustee Lora Lawson Aldrich estate. Mem. C. of C. Republican. Conglist. Clubs: Hope, Turks Head, Brown, Republican (Providence); to Kolan (Pawtuckett); Bankers, Brown, D.K.E. (New York City); Squantum (East Providence); Warwick Country. Home: Warwick, R.I. Office: 1121A Industrial Trust Bldg., Providence. Died Oct. 24, 1957.

ALDRICH, John Gladding, mfr.; b. Providence, R.I., Nov. 24, 1864; s. Elisha Smith and Anna (Gladding) A.; B.S. in M.E., Worcester Poly. Inst., 1885; m. Margaret Calder, Oct. 12, 1891; children—John Gladding, Putnam Calder, David. Supt. Foundry Builders Iron Foundry, Providence, 1889-

1900; supt., 1900-04, v.p., gen. mgr. 1904-15, pres., 1915-45, N. E. Butt Co.; dir. Apponaug Co. Mem. Am. Soc. M. E., Providence C. of C. Unitarian. Club: Art. Home: 223 Bowen St. Office: 304 Pearl St., Providence. Died Jan. 20, 1952; buried Swan Point Cemetery, Providence.

ALDRICH, Morton Arnold, educator; b. Boston, Jan. 6, 1874; s. Charles A. and Helen F. (Mowry) A.; A.B., Harvard, 1895; student univs. of Berlin, Munich and Halle, Ph.D., 1897; grad. study in economics; m. Zoe Worthington Fiske, 1902. Formerly instr. in economics, Harvard, and asst. prof. economics, Stanford U.; asso. prof. economics and sociology, Tulane U., 1901-05, prof., 1905-39, dean Coll. of Commerce and Business Adminstrn., 1914-39, dean and prof. emeritus 1939—. Mem. Am. Econ. Assn.; ex-pres. Tulane Soc. Economics; ex-pres. Harvard Club of La. Home: 722 Cherokee St., New Orleans. Deceased.

ALDRIDGE, Walter Hull, mining engr.; b. Bklyn., Sept. 8, 1867; s. Volney and Harriet Elizabeth (Hull) A.; E.M., Sch. of Mines, Columbia U., 1887 (hon Sc.D., 1929); m. Maude Miller, Mar. 18, 1914. Assayer, chemist and metallurgist, Colo. Smelting Co., Pueblo, until 1892; mgr. United Smelting & Refining Co., Mont., 1892-97; in charge mining and metall. work Canadian Pacific Ry., 1897-1911; mng. dir. Consol. Mining and Smelting Co. of Can.; was at various times mng. dir. Inspiration Copper Co.; pres. Magma Copper Co.; v.p. Mines Co. of America; pres. Tex. Gulf Sulphur Co., 1918-51, chmn. bd., 1951-57, chmn. emeritus, dir., 1957—. Recipient John Fritz medal for 1949. Mem. Am. Inst. Mining and Metall. Engrs., Mining and Metall. Soc. America, Am. Electrochem. Soc., Canadian Inst. Mining Engrs., Instn. Mining and Metallurgy (London), Newcomen Soc. England. Republican. Episcopalian. Clubs: Union League, Down Town, Columbia University, Apawamis, Shenorock Shore. Home: 71 E. 71st. N.Y.C. Office: 75 E. 45th St., N.Y.C. 17. Died Aug. 1959.

ALEXANDER, Donald, bus. exec.; b. Canton, O., June 21, 1891; s. Wes Lawrence and Caroline (Renick) A.; M.W., Cornell U., 1914; m. Elsie Downing, Dec. 4, 1920 (dec.); children—Beatrice Downing, Donald Lawrence, Malcolm Graham; m. 2d, Kathleen Jones Hocker, Jan. 31, 1945. Sales engr., Edw. G. Budd Mfg. Co., and Budd Wheel Co., 1919-21, asst. to v.p. and gen. sales mgrs., 1921-29; v.p. charge sales, Budd Co., 1929-49, dir., 1929—. Served as capt., Ordnance Dept., U.S. Army, 1918-19, World War I. Corr. mem. Am. Entomol. Soc., Entomol Soc., Brasil. Mem. Cornell Soc. Engrs., Army Ordnance Assn., Alpha Delta Phi. Clubs: Detroit Athletic, Detroit Country, Detroit, Grosse Pointe (Detroit); University (N.Y.C.); Racquet, Phila. Country, Rittenhouse, Gulph Mills Country (Phila.); Merion Cricket (Merion, Pa.); Chevy Chase (Chevy Chase, Md.). Home: The Barclay, 18th and Rittenhouse Sq. Address: 2450 Hunting Park Av. 3, Phila. 32. Died July 20, 1959.

ALEXANDER, Henry Martyn, lawyer; b. N.Y.C., Jan. 25, 1869; s. James W. And Elizabeth Beasley (Williamson) A.; A.B., Princeton, 1890, A.M., 1893; m. Helen Manice, Dec. 4, 1896; children—Helen Gertrude (wife of Philip K. Rhinelander, now deceased), DeForest Manice. Admitted to N.Y. bar, 1892, and since engaged in practice, N.Y.C.; mem. firm Alexander & Keenan; dir. Equitable Life Assurance Soc. of U.S. Mem. N.Y. Bar Assn. Clubs: University (N.Y.C.); Nassau, Ivy (Princeton, N.J.). Home: 24 W. 55th St. Office: 42 Broadway, N.Y.C. Deceased.

ALEXANDER, Hubbard Foster, shipping; b. Colorado Springs, Colo., Aug. 14, 1879; s. Edward Sime and Emma (Foster) A.; ed. Powellson's Acad. and High Sch., Tacoma, Wash.; m. Ruth Caldwell, Apr. 30, 1902; 1 dau., Mrs. Winston Jeide. Began as wharf agent Dodwell, Carlill & Co., Ltd., Tacoma, Wash., 1894; gen. mgr. Commercial Dock Co., Tacoma, 1900-01, pres., 1901-27; pres. Alaska Pacific S.S. Co., 1907-08, Alaska Coast Co., 1908-11, Pacific Alaska Navigation Company, 1908-26, Pacific Steamship Co. (Admiral Line), 1916-30, Complete Combustion Co. Chmn. Trailerships, Inc., N.Y.-Albany Route; pres., chmn. bd. Pacific Coast Steamship Company. Mem. Loyal Legion. Republican. Episcopalian. Mason (32°). Clubs: Transportation of Seattle (hon. life); Transportation (hon. life), Pacific Union, Bohemian (San Francisco); India House, Racquet and Tennis (New York). Home: 1215 Fifth Av. Office: 274 Madison Av., N.Y.C. 16. Died Feb. 17, 1952, buried Tacoma.

ALEXANDER, Jerome, chemist; b. New York, N.Y., Dec. 21, 1876; s. Isaac and Annie Josephine Lewis (Jackson) A.; B.S., Coll. City of New York, 1896, M.Sc., 1899; m. Gertrude Eleanor Hammerslough, Apr. 9, 1903 (died Dec. 25, 1945); children—Dr. Eleanor Gertrude Jackson, Mrs. Dorothy Alexander Livingston (dec.). Consulting chemist and chem. engr. Past chmn. spl. com. on colloids of Nat. Research Council. Fellow A.A.A.S., Am. Inst. Chemists (hon. mem.); mem. Am. Inst. Chem. Engrs. (hon.), Am. Chem. Soc., Assn. Cons. Chemists and Chem. Engrs., Soc. de Chimie Industrielle (hon. sec. Am. sect.; hon. mem. parent société), American Genetics Association, N.Y. Micros. Soc., Sons of Confed. Vets. (historian), Phi Beta Kappa Associates (dir.) Phi Beta Kappa (past president N. Y. Alumni), Pi Gamma Mu, Pi Lambda Phi, Tau Beta Pi (hon.). Decorated Officer de l'Instruction Publique (France), 1931, also Chevalier de la Légion d'Honneur, 1936; Townsend Harris Medal, 1943. Mason. Clubs: Chemists (New York); Authors' (London). Author: Colloid Chemistry, 1919, and subsequent editions: Glue and Gelatin (American Chemical Soc. monograph), 1923; also chapters on "Glue and Gelatin" and "Colloid Chemistry" Rogers' Industrial Chemistry, 1942; chapter on "Albuminoids or Seleroproteins," in Allen's Commercial Organic Analysis, 1913 and 1931; chapter on "Colloid Chemistry" in Liddell's Handbook for Chemical Engineers, 1920; Colloid Chemistry, Theoretical and Applied (in collaboration with about 450 men of all nations). Volume I, 1926, II, 1928, III, 1931, IV, 1932, V, 1944, VI. 1946, VII, 1950, volume VIII in preparation; (verses) "Essences from Life's Alembic" and "Retorts from a Chemist's Laboratory," 1941; Tribute to Gertrude, 1946; "Life—Its Nature and Origin," 1948 Translator: Colloids and the Ultramicroscope, by Prof. Dr. Richard Zsigmondy, 1909. Pioneer worker with the ultramicroscope in America; specialist in colloid chem. and its scientific and indsl. applications. Address: 390 Riverside Dr., N.Y.C. 25. Died Jan. 18, 1959.

ALEXANDER, John, surgeon; b. Phila., Pa., Feb. 24, 1891; s. Lucien Hugh and Mazie (Just) A.; student Episcopal Acad., Phila., 1903-04, Chestnut Hill Acad., 1904-08; B.S., U. of Pa., 1912, M.A., 1913, M.D., 1916 (hon. Sc.D., 1940); m. Emma Ward Woolfolk, July 11, 1936. Formerly mem. surg. and teaching staff U. of Pa.; now prof. surgery, U. of Mich.; surg. in charge sect. thoracic surg., U. of Mich. Hosp.; chief surg., Mich. State Sanatorium; cons. thoracic surg., various sanatoria and hosps. Surg. with French Army; lt. U.S.M.C., World War I. Awarded Samuel D. Gross prize of Phila. Acad. Surgery, 1925; Henry Russel award, U. of Mich., 1930; Trudeau medal, Nat. Tuberculosis Assn., 1941. Henry Russel lectureship, U. of Mich., 1944. Fellow Am. Coll. Surgeons; mem. Am. Surg. Assn., Soc. of Thoracic Surgery of Great Britain and Ire. (hon.), Sociedad de Argentina de Cirujanos (hon.); Société Belge de Chirurgie (hon.); Sociedad Parguaya de Tisiologia (hon.); Sociedad de Tisiologia de Cordoba, Argentina (corr.); Tuberculosis Assn. of India (corr.); Detroit Heart Club; Am. Trudeau Soc. (pres. elect 1946), Am. Bd. Surg. (founders' group), Soc. of Clin. Surg., Internat. Soc. of Surgery, Am. Assn. for Thoracic Surg. (p. 1935), Detroit Acad. of Surgery (hon.), Central Surg. Assn. (founders' group), A.M.A., Mich. State Med. Soc. (chmn. sect. on surgery, 1932), Mich. Tuberculosis Assn. (trustee 1936-42, pres. 1938-39), Nat. Tuberculosis Assn. (dir. 1941-44, v.p. 1945), Mich. Trudeau Soc., Alpha Omega Alpha, Alpha Mu Pi Omega, Nu Sigma Nu (hon.), Sigma Xi, Phi Kappa Phi, Delta Tau Delta. Republican. Presbyterian. Author: The Surgery of Pulmonary Tuberculosis, 1925; The Collapse Therapy of Pulmonary Tuberculosis, 1937; also articles on thoracic surgery. Mem. adv. editorial bd. Journal of Thoracic Surgery. Home: 788 Arlington Blvd. Office: U. of Mich. Hospital, Ann Arbor. Died July 16, 1954; buried Forest Hills Cemetery.

ALEXANDER, John Macmillan, clergyman; b. Jackson, Miss., Oct. 31, 1891; s. Charlton Henry and Matilda (Macmillan) A.; student Southwestern Coll. (now in Memphis, Tenn.), 1906-09; A.B., Princeton, 1914; B.D., Union Theol. Seminary of Va., 1921, D.D., 1926; m. Victoria M. Holladay, June 19, 1923; children—Victoria Holladay (Mrs. Henry Sharp), Matilda Caroline (Mrs. George W. Bryan) John Macmillan. With A.E.F., France, World War, 1917-19; 1st lt. Med. Dept. Sanitary Corps, 1918-19; ordained ministry Presbyn. Ch. in U.S., 1921; pastor First Ch., Columbia, Mo., 1924-32, First Church, Birmingham, Ala., 1932-39, First Church, Fayetteville, N.C., 1939-46; dir. radio com., Presbyn. Church U.S., 1946—. Moderator of Synod of Mo., 1930; Synod of Ala., 1936; commr. Gen. Assembly Presbyn. Ch. in U.S., 1927, 30, 32, 34, 43, 46; mem. Assembly's Com. on Union of Presbyn. and Reformed Chs., 1930-33, and mem. Assembly's Ad-Interim Com. on Salaries and Retirement Allowances, 1933-34; chmn. Assembly's Ad-Interim Com. on Minimum Income for Ministers, 1934-35; chmn. Assembly's Ad-Interim Com. on Pastoral Changes, 1935-36; mem. Assembly's Com. on Stewardship and Finance, 1935-39; chmn. Assembly's special com. on radio, 1943—; pres. Birmingham Protestant Pastors' Union, 1934-35; del. from Presbyn. Ch. of U.S. to World's Conf. on Life and Work, Oxford, 1937, and World's Conf. on Faith and Order, Edinburgh, 1937; interchange preacher representing American Committee in France and Great Britain, 1937; chairman Defense Service Council, Synod of N.C., 1941-46; member Assembly's Defense Service Council, 1944-46; mem. executive com., Federal Council of Chs. of America, 1941-51, N.C. Council of Chs. 1941-46; fraternal del. Assembly of Presbyn. Ch., U.S.A., 1943; sec. div. Radio and TV, Presbyn. Ch., U.S.A.; mem. exec. com. broadcasting and film commn. Nat. Council Chs.; pres. Protestant Radio and TV Center, Inc.; Rep. Presbyn. Bd. World Missions in Radio Survey Brazil, 1952. Received citation Nat. Council Chs. for work in religious radio. Mem. Kappa Sigma. Democrat. Clubs: Kiwanis. Athletic (Atlanta). Asso. editor Presbyterian Outlook. Home: 16691 Dyson Dr., N.E., Atlanta 7. Office: 1717 Clifton Rd. N.E., Atlanta. Died Aug. 7, 1957; buried Jackson, Miss.

ALEXANDER, John Romich, missionary; b. Wooster, O., May 23, 1849; s. Samuel K. and Leah (Romich) A.; A.B., Ohio Central Coll., 1871; B.D., Xenia Theol. Sem., 1874; hon. M.A. U. Wooster, 1878; D.D., Monmouth Coll., 1895; LL.D., Westminster Coll., 1910; m. Carrie A. Elder, Nov. 25, 1875 (dec. Jan. 9, 1936;); children—May (wife of Prof. Thompson), Leigh, Mrs. Pauline R. Owens, Mrs. Bertha B. Bradstreet. Ordained to United Presbyn. ministry, 1875; began missionary work in Egypt, Mar. 1875; gen. supt., 1875-87, pres. 1887-1910, Assiût Col.; coll. pastor and librarian, 1910-13; prof. ch. history and ch. govt., Mission Theol. Sem., Cairo, 1913-25. Dir. Protestant ednl. work in Egypt, 1880-1903; moderator Synod of Nile, 1911-12; chmn. coms. in Presbytery of Egypt and Synod of Nile, especially of joint mission and Synodical Com. on Pslater (in Arabic) for Evangelical Ch., Egypt, 1912-17; retired. Author of The Alexanders of Martic Forge, Pa., 1922, Knowest Thou Yesterday, and many articles on mission and college work in Egypt. Address: American Mission, Assiût, Egypt. Died Apr. 16, 1940.

ALEXANDER, Julian Power, judge; b. Jackson, Miss., Dec. 7, 1887; s. Charlton Henry and Matilda (Macmillan) A.; student Millsaps Coll. (Jackson, Miss.), Southwestern Presbyn. U. (Clarksville, Tenn.); A.B., Princeton, 1908; LL.B., U. of Miss., 1910; m. Corabel Wharton Roberts, Dec. 16, 1913; children—Seta Wharton, Julian P., Clay Roberts. Mem. Brooke & Alexander, Meridian, Miss., 1911-13, Alexander & Alexander, later Alexander, Alexander & Satterfield, Jackson, 1913-19; served as asst. U.S. dist. atty., 1916-19, dist. atty., 1919-22, Southern Dist. of Miss.; apptd. judge Circuit Court, 7th Dist., Miss., Apr. 28, 1934, and elected for full term, 1935-39; asso. Justice Miss. Supreme Court since Jan. 1941. One of framers of commn. plan of govt. for cities of Miss. Mem. Am. and Miss. State bar assns., The Newcomen Soc., Kappa Sigma, Phi Delta Phi. Democrat. Presbyterian. Scottish Rite Mason, Shriner. Rotarian (hon.). Author: Code Chapter on Oil and Gas Conservation. Home: 1616 Poplar Blvd. Office: State Capitol, Jackson, Miss. Died Jan. 1, 1953.

ALEXANDER, Lester Fisher; b. Dallas County, Texas, Feb. 3, 1879; s. Charles Pinckney and Nancy C. (Fisher) A.; ed. pub. and night schs. commercial course; m. Gladys M. Billero, June 5, 1929; children—Lester Fisher, William Billero. With F. M. Hammond Co., Lancaster, Texas, 1896-98; clerk and chief clerk, U.S. Engrs., Havana, Cuba, 1899-1902; inspector, U.S. Enging. Dept. La., 1902-09; gen. supt. Christie & Love, contractors, La., 1909-10; pres. and gen. mgr. Lester F. Alexander Co., Inc., New Orleans, 1910-40, now partner Lester F. Alexander Co.; pres. Alexander Shipyards, Inc.; partner United Marine Co.; dir. New Orleans Pub. Service, Inc. Pres. New Orleans Tidewater Development Assn. Recipient, Silver Antelope and Silver Beaver awards Boy Scouts Am. Mem. La. Enging. Soc., Soc. Am. Mil. Engrs. Clubs: Army and Navy (Washington); Boston, New Orleans Country, Southern Yacht, Rotary, Army and Navy (New Orleans). Home: 28 Audubon Pl. Office: Audubon Bldg., New Orleans. Died Dec. 12, 1954.

ALEXANDER, M(alcolm) Moss, corp. exec.; pres. and dir. Mo. Portland Cement Co., also dir. Portland Cement Assn., First Nat. Bank, St. Louis. Home: 4931 Lindell Blvd. Office: 3615 Olive St., St. Louis 8. Died Feb. 26, 1959; buried Rose Hill Mausoleum, Oklahoma City.

ALEXANDER, Walter R(ichardson), clergyman; b. Phila., Pa., Sept. 23, 1889; s. William Booth and Martha Kay (Foreman) A.; A.B., Central High Sch., Phila., 1907; student, Temple Univ., 1908-09; grad., Crozer Theol. Sem., 1916; D.D., Furman Univ., 1931; m. Eva Elizabeth Edge, June 28, 1911; 1 dau., Ruth (wife of the late Rev. John C. Cowell, Jr.). Ordained minister, Baptist Ch., 1916; pastor, 1st Baptist Ch., Winchester, Va., 1916-18, Stamford, Tex., 1918-21, Mantua Baptist Ch., Phila., 1921-22, 1st Baptist Church, Rock Hill, S.C., 1922-28, Florence, S.C., 1928-42; asso. exec. sec., Relief and Annuity Bd. of So. Baptist Conv., 1942-47, exec. sec., since 1947. S.C. bd. mem., Relief and Annuity Bd. of So. Baptist Conv., 1940-42; pres., Federated Forces of S.C. for Temperance and Law Enforcement, 1940-42; member of the board of corporators, Presbyterian Ministers Fund, Philadelphia, since 1952. Trustee, Coker College, Hartsville, S.C., 1930-40, Baptist Bible Inst. (now Baptist Theol. Sem.), New Orleans, La., 1930-40, Baptist Hosp., Columbia, S.C., 1930-35. Mem. Ch. Pensions Conf. of U.S. and Can. (interdenominational) (pres., 1951). Clubs: Rotary (pres., Rock Hill, S.C., 1925); Kiwanis, Plain Dealers (Florence, S.C.). Author: All Out for God, 1946; Holy Hours in the Holy Land, 1946; Doing Likewise, 1947; Two O'clock in the Morning, 1956. Contbr. articles to denominational papers. Travel in Brit. Isles, Europe, Egypt and Palestine. Home: 7308 Turtle Creek Blvd., Dallas 25. (summer) Renascence, Ridgecrest, N.C. Office: Baptist Bldg., Dallas 1. Died Dec. 13, 1954; buried West Laurel Hill Cemetery, Bala-Cynwyd, Pa.

ALEXANDER, Wilford S., ex-govt. ofcl.; b. Eastport, Me., Sept. 25, 1878; s. Wilford F. and Nellie M. (Swett) A.; grad. Boynton High Sch., Eastport, 1896; m. Mary P. White, July 19, 1905 (died Apr. 1, 1948); children—Katherine Marcia (Mrs. Cyril Coleman), Sheila (Mrs. Richard Joyce Smith), Agnes, Alison (Mrs. Edward C. Tredennick), Wilford S., Jr. (1st lt. USMC, killed in action, Okinawa, May 5, 1945). Clerk Eastport Savings Bank, 1896; was asst. cashier Frontier Nat. Bank, Eastport; then cashier Oxford Paper Co., Rumford, Me.; securities salesman Paine, Webber & Co., Boston until 1920; treas. Puritan Bank & Trust Co., Meriden, Conn., 1920-27, pres., 1927-36; adminstr. Fed. Alcohol Adminstrn. 1936-40 (dept. merged with alcohol tax unit under President's reorgn. plan); dist. supr. and dist. co-ordinator Dist. No. 1 Alcohol Tax Unit, Bur. of Internal Revenue, Me., Vt., N.H., Mass., R.I. and Conn., 1940-49; city mgr. City of Eastport, Me., 1950-53. Served as capt. inf., U.S. Army, 5 mos. on Mexican Border and 20 mos. in France, World War. Expres. Meriden Pub. Health and Visiting Nurse Assn., Meriden C. of C.; past dept. comdr. Conn. Am. Legion. Home: 139 Main St., Southport, Conn. Died Apr. 24, 1959.

ALEXANDER, Will Winton, ret. authority on race relations; b. Marrisville, Mo., 1884; s. William Baxter and Arabella A. (Winton) A.; A.B., Scarritt-Morrisville (Mo.) Coll., 1908; B.D., Vanderbilt U., 1912; hon. degs. Berea Coll., So. Coll., Boston U., La. State U.; m. Mabelle A. Kinkead, Oct. 1914; children—Edgar Kinkead, John Winton, William McLees. Ordained to ministry Meth. Ch. South, 1901; pastorates at Nashville and Murfreesboro, Tenn., 1911-17; withdrew from ministry, 1917; exec. dir. Commn. on Interracial Coop., 1919-30; acting pres. Dillard U., New Orleans, 1931-35; asst. adminstr., U.S. Resettlement Adminstrn., 1935-36; adminstr. Farm Security Adminstrn., U.S. Dept. Agr., 1937. V.p. Julius Rosenwald Fund. Served as exec. sec. Army Y.M.C.A., Southeastern Mil. Dept., 1917-19. Chmn. adv. com. on race studies of problems and policies com. Social Sci. Research Council, 1927-28; Am. del. to Internat. Conf., Jerusalem, 1928; Weil lectr. U. N.C., 1929; mem. Com. on Minority Groups in Econ. Recovery, 1934-35; mem. on care and edn. of Am. youth, Am. Council Edn. Vice pres., treas. Am. Council Race Relations and Staff War Manpower Commn., World War II. Recipient Harmon Nat. Award for service in Am. peace relations, 1928. Trustee Antioch Coll., Bethune-Cookman Coll., Atlanta U., Morehouse Coll., Spelman Coll. Mem. Alpha Tau Omega. Democrat. Club: Cosmos (Washington). Co-author: Collapse of Cotton Tenancy, 1935. Home: R.R. 3, Chapel Hill, N.C. Deceased.

ALEXANDER, Sir William, business exec.; b. Glasgow, Scotland, May 4, 1874; s. Thomas and Isabella (Hill) A.; student Kelvinside Acad., Glasgow U., U. Göttingen; m. Beatrice Evelyn Ritchie, June 1911 (dec. 1928); m. 2d, Ruby May Spencer, Jan. 1930; children—William Bryce, John Ritchie, Charles Stuart, Kenneth Alston. Commd. lt. Territorial Force (6th Black Watch), 1899, advanced through grades to brig. gen., 1917; served European War, 1914-18. M.P., Central Glasgow, since 1923; dir. Celanese Corp. Am., Canadian Celanese, Ltd. Home: Grey Gables, St. Aubin, Jersey, C.I. Office: 14 Waterloo Pl., London, Eng. Died Dec. 29, 1954; buried St. Brelades Bay.

ALEXANDER, William McFaddin, clergyman; b. Union, W.Va., Nov. 7, 186; s. Michael Caperton and Sarah (McFaddin) A.; student, Washington and Lee U., class of '84; grad. Union Theol. Sem., Va., 1887; D.D., Washington and Lee, 1898, Southwestern Presbyn. U., 1898; LL.D., U. of Ga., 1911; m. Ceneilla Bower, June 24, 1891; 1 dau., Miriam Caperton (Mrs. Matthew T. McClure). Ordained Presbyn. ministry, 1887; pastor Bainbridge, Ga., 1887-90, Alabama St. Ch., Memphis, Tenn., 1890-99, Prytania St. Ch., New Orleans, from 1899, now pastor emeritus. Trustee Southwestern at Memphis, Tenn. Mem. Pan-Presbyn. Council, Washington, 1899; mem. Council of Reformed Churches, 1907-20. Elected moderator of Gen. Assembly of Presbyn. Church in U.S. (Southern) for 1915. Club: Round Table. Home: 2328 Coliseum St., New Orleans. Died Mar. 29, 1944; buried Metairie Cemetery, New Orleans.

ALFARO, Colon Eloy (äl-fä'rō), Ecuadorian diplomat; b. Guayaquil, Ecuador, Jan. 1, 1891; s. Eloy (ex-president Ecuador) and Ana Paredes (y Arosemena) A.; ed. Colegio Nacional Vicente Rocafuerte (Guayaquil), pvt schs. and spl. tutors, Ecuador, U.S. Mil. Acad. (West Point); Cavalry Sch., Germany; LL.D., George Washington U., U. Florida; Litt.D., Andhra Research U., 1942, academicum corr., 1951; academicum corr. U. Mexico, 1952; Ph. D., Coll. of Sequoias, 1952; m. Bianca Puig Arosemena; children—Eloy, Jaime Eduardo, Olmedo. Served as lieutenant, regiment 15th Hussars, 9th Army Corps, Germany, cav. regt., "Yaguachi" No. 1, Ecuador; capt., minister's adj., Ministry of War, Quito; capt., adj., and prof., Mil. Acad., Quito; mil. attache, Legation of Ecuador, London and Belgium; consul gen., charge d'affaires, minister resident, Panama; consul gen., Canal Zone; E.E. and M.P., Mex. (twice), Panama, Nicaragua, Guatamala, El Salvador, Honduras, Costa Rica, Colombia (twice), Dominican Republic; E.E. and M.P. to U.S., 1933-36, A.E. and P., 1936-44; ambassador, rep. Eduador on governing bd. Pan Am. Union, Washington, 1947-48; A.E. and P. to U.S., 1952; ambassador on various spl. missions to fgn. countries. Mem. Eloy Alfaro Internat. Found.; exec. dir. Simon Bolivar Meml. Found., San Martin Meml. Found. (both Washington). Founder Cia Alfaro, S.A.; mem... board directors Flanigan, Loveland Shipping Company, Del., Ecuadorean Army to coronation of King George V of Eng.; E.E. and M.P. in spl. mission to Congress of Bolivar, Panama, 1926, spl. mission to Cuba, 1929, spl. mission to Nicaragua, 1931; ambassador extraordinary in spl. mission to Panama, 1924, 1928; del. inauguration of monument to Vasco Nunez de Balboa, Panama, to 6th Pan. Am. Conf., Havana, 1928; del. Govt. of Ecuador, municipalities of Quito, Guayaquil and Montecristi to inauguration of monument and Square "Eloy Alfaro," Havana, 1929, Inter-Am. Econ. and Financial Adv. Com., Washington, rep. from Ecuador, com. on provisional adminstrn. of European colonies and possessions in the Americas, Washington, Inter-Am. Econ. and Social Council, 1948. Decorations: Cross and Medal of Eloy Alfaro Internat. Found., Star of Abdon Calderon (1st class), Grand Cross Order Al Merito, Grand Officer Order Merito Agricola (Ecuador); Grand Cross Order Juan Pablo Duarte (Dominican Republic); Grand Cross Vasco Núñez de Balboa, Medal of Solidarity (Panama); Grand Cross Order Petion et Bolivar, Order of Merit (Haiti); Grand Cross Mil. Merit, Grand Officer Order Carlos Manuel de Céspedes, Comdr. Cross of Honor and Merit, Distinguished Mil. Service Medal, 4th of Sept. Mil. Medal, Medal Cuban Geog. Soc. (Cuba); Grand Officer Order Aquila Azteca, Medal Ateneo de Ciencias y Artes (Mex.); Grand Officer Order Al Merito (Chile); Grand Officer Order Cruz de Boyaca, Medal of Bolivarin Soc., Medal Guard of the Liberator (Colombia); Grand Cross Order Condor de los Andes, Comdr. Order Mil. Merit (Bolivia); Grand Officer Al Merito (Praguay); Grand Cordon Order Busto del Liberatador (Venezuela); Presdl. Medal (Nicaragua); medal 6th Pan-American Conference (Havana); Medal of George V, English Military Medal (England), Gold Medal Pan-Am. Soc., Medal Liga International de Acción Bolivariana. Medal of Freedom with Silver Palm; Grand Cross Order of St. John Baptist of Am., Collar, Internat. Inst. Am. Ideals, Grupo America, Blue Cross, Nat. Legion Greek-Am. W.V., Cross, Nat. Legion Greek-Am. Meritorious War Service Order, Cross 33°, Supreme Council (So. Jurisdiction) (U.S.), Medal of Red Cross (Costa Rica); Grand Cross Order S.S. Salvador and St. Brigida (Sweden), Cross Order of St. John of Jerusalem (Denmark), Grand Cross Grand Prix Humanitaire (Belgium), Medal of Lit. and Artistic Inst., Medal of Historic and Heraldic Inst. (France); Grand Cross Order of Spada d'Oro; Gold medal of S.S. Maritime Alps; Grand Cross Medal of St. George, Knight; Medal of Grand Duke Cyril (Russia); Knight Order of Constructores Masones (Internat.). Fellow Am. Geog. Soc.; mem. Am. Inst. Internat. Law, Acad. Polit. Sci. Columbia U., Geog. Soc. Cuba, Am. Legion, Inter-Am. Military Assn. Washington (pres.), Inst. Sanmartiniana Bogota, Bolivarian Soc., Liga Internacional de Acción Bolivariana N.Y.C., Internat. Inst. Am. Ideals, Italian-Panama Soc., Am. Soc. Heraldry, Spanish Cultural Center Washington (pres.), other sci. instns., clubs, etc. Mason (33°, Shriner). Clubs: Army and Navy, University, Nat. Press, Fencers (pres.) (Washington, D.C.); Bankers (N.Y. City); Export Managers (Chicago); Union, Golf (Panama). Author: Principle of Strategy, Eloy Alfaro and American International Law. Address: P.O. Box 200, Panama City, Republic of Panama. Died Apr. 12, 1957.

ALFORD, Mrs. Nell, Dem. nat. committeewoman; vorn at Quincy, Florida; daughter Benjamin Harvey and Alice (Sheppard) Flournoy; grad. Orlando (Fla.) High School; married Neil Alford, January 31, 1927 (deceased January 1954). Engaged as owner and operator of millinery store and greeting card business, Jacksonville, Fla., 1932-42; elected to State Democratic Exec. Com. for Duval County, Fla., 1936, finance chmn. since 1939; nat. Dem. committeewoman since 1945. Chmn. Americanization and civil def. com. Am. Legion Auxiliary Post 9; past chmn. A.R.C. Motor Service; past pres. Proto Club, Duval Co. Fedn. Women's Clubs. Mem. Hotel Greeters, Polit. Sci. Group Columbia U., League Women Voters, Peace Officers Assn. (hon.), Am. Flag Guard Assn., Am. War Mothers (past pres. state chapter; third national vice pres.; ways and means chairman). Presbyn. (past pres. Women's auxiliary, past pres. Motion Picture council). Mem. Rebecca, Moose, Eastern Star (White Shrine). Club: Coin, Womens, Friday Musicale, Garden Circle. Home: 807 St. Johns Apts., Jacksonville 4, Fla. Died Nov. 1957.

ALI KHAN, Liaquat, prime minister of Pakistan; b. Karnal, East Punjab, Oct. 1, 1895; s. Ruknud-daullah Shamsher Jang Nawak Rustam Ali Khan; student Aligarh, 1910; M.A.O. Coll. (Aligarh) (affiliated with Allahabad Univ., 1910-19; LL.B., Exeter Coll., Oxford Univ., 1921; m. Raana Begum, 1933; children—Ashraf, Akbar. Called to Bar, England, 1922; returned to India, 1922, joined the Muslim League, 1923; advocate of the Punjab High Court, since 1922. Mem. United Provinces Legislative Council, 1926-40, Central Legislative Assembly, 1940-47; dep. pres., United Provinces Legislative Council, 1931-36; mem. Indo-British Trade Delegation, London, 1937; hon. general sec., All-Indian Muslim since 1936; dep. leader, Muslim League Party since 1940; mem. court and exec. council M.U. Aligarh, 1941-46; chmn. of Central Parliamentary Bd., All-India Muslim League; rep. of the Muslim League, Simla Conf., 1945, 1946; mem. Viceroy's Exec. Council, 1946; held the portfolio of Finance, 1946-47; mem. conf., London, Dec., 1946, apptd. mem. of the Partition Council to represent future govt. of Pakistan; prime minister of Pakistan since 1947. Address: Prime Minister, Karachi, Pakistan. Assassinated Oct. 16, 1951.

ALLDREDGE, Eugene Perry, clergyman, statistician; b. Brooksyille, Ala., May 30, 1875; s. P. G. Alldredge (M.D.) and Emma Vicie (South) A.; B.A., Baylor U., 1900, M.A., 1901, Th.B., 1903, Th.M., Southern Bapt. Theol. Sem., Louisville, Ky., 1904; D.D., Ouachita Coll., Arkadelphia, Ark., 1917, Baylor U., 1920; state oratory honors, Tex., 1899; m. Barbara M. Taliaferro, Oct. 4, 1904 (dec.); children—Eugene Perry, Mary (Mrs. E. A. Sanders, Jr.); m. 2d, Mrs. Elkin Lightfoot Lockett, Nov. 27, 1940. Ordained ministry Baptist Ch., 1899; pastor, Amarillo and Dallas, Tex., 1905-07; state sec. of missions in N.M., Southern Bapt. Conv. 1911-12; pastor Immanuel Bapt. Ch., Little Rock, Ark., 1913-19; state exec. sec. Ark. Bapt. Conv., 1919-20; sec. of survey statistics and information, Southern Baptist Conv., 1920-45. Member Constl. Conv. of Ark., 1916 (only minister in that body); mem. Charities and Corrections Commn. of Ark. 4 yrs. Mem. Am. Statis. Association, American Academy Political and Social Science, American Economic Assn. Democrat. Author: Southern Baptist Hand Book, yearly 1921-45; Southern Baptists Working Together, 1924; The New Challenge of Home Missions, 1926; One Hundred Successful Country Churches, 1922; Southern Baptists in World Service, 1936; 101 Expository Sermons, 1941; Forty Serman Studies, 1942; Soul-Winning Sermons, 1943; Sunshine and Shadows (poems), 1944; Cowboys and Coyotes, 1945; The New Racial Situation, 1946; Unionizing Southern Baptists, 1948; While Southern Baptists Sleep, 1949, Editor: Quarterly Review, 1941-46. Home: 1407 Elmwood Av., Nashville. Died Feb. 22, 1953; buried Woodlawn Cemetery, Nashville.

ALLEE, Warder Clyde (ăl-lē'), zoölogist; b. nr. Bloomingdale, Ind., June 5, 1885; s. John Wesley and Mary Emily (Newlin) A.; S.B., Earlham Coll., Ind., 1908, LL.D., 1940; S.M, U. of Chicago, 1910, Ph. D., 1912; m. Marjorie Hill, Sept. 4, 1912 (dec. 1945); children—Warder (dec.), Barbara Elliott, Mary Newlin; married 2d, Ann Silver, June 26, 1953. Assistant in zoölogy, University of Chicago, 1910-12; instr. in botany, U. of Ill., 1912-13, in zoölogy, Williams Coll., 1913-14; asst. prof. zoölogy Okla. U., 1914-15; prof. biology, Lake Forest Coll., 1915-21; asst. prof. zoölogy, 1921, asso. prof., 1923, prof., 1928-50, U. of Chicago, prof. of zoology emeritus since 1950. dean in the colleges. 1925-27; head professor biology University of Florida, 1950-55; instructor Marine Biol. Lab., Woods Hole, Mass., summers 1914-21, invertebrate course, 1918-21; lecturer in zoölogy, U. of Calif., winter 1923; prof. zoölogy, Nat. Summer Sch., Logan, Utah, 1924-26. Alumni trustee, Earlham Coll., 1925-39; trustee Marine Biol. Lab. since 1932. Fellow Am. Assn. Advancement Sci. (v.p. 1942), Am. Soc. Entomologists, Am. Acad. Arts and Scis.; mem. Am. Soc. Zoologists (pres. 1936), Nat. Acad. Sci., Ecol. Soc. Am. (pres. 1929), Am. Soc. Naturalists, Gamma Alpha, Phi Beta Kappa, Sigma Xi, Soc. Friends. Club: Quadrangle. Author: Animal Aggregations, 1931; Animal Life and Social Growth, 1932; The Social Life of Animals, 1938; Cooperation among Animals, with Human Implications, 1951. Co-author: Jungle Island (with Marjorie Hill Allee), 1925; Nature of the World and Man, 1926; The World and Man, 1937; Ecological Animal Geography, 1937; A Laboratory Introduction to Animal Ecology and Taxonomy, 1939; Principles of Animal Ecology, 1949. Managing editor Physiological Zoology, 1930-55. Chmn. com. on revision of Zoological articles, Encyclopedia Britannica, 1944-50. Contributor technical articles to professional journals. Home: 1080 S.W. 11th Terrace, Gainesville, Fla. Died Mar. 18, 1955.

ALLEMAN, Herbert Christian, theologian; b. Bloomsburg, Pa., May 13, 1868; s. Benjamin F. (D.D.) and Charlotte (Benson) A.; A.B., 1st honor, Pa. Coll., Gettysburg, 1887; grad. Luth. Theol. Sem., Gettysburg, 1891; U. Pa., 1908-11; D.D., Temple U., 1907, Gettysburg Coll., 1923; LL.D., Franklin & Marshall Coll., 1936; m. Julia Suesserott, July 8, 1897; 1 son, Benson Suesserott.

Ordained Lutheran ministry, 1891; pastor Trinity Church, Chambersburg, Pa., 1891-96, College Ch., Gettysburg, Pa., 1896-1900, Messiah Ch., Phila., 1900-11; prof. O.T. lit. and theology Luth. Theol. Sem., 1911—. Trustee Luth. Publ. Soc., Phila., 1900-11; mem. bd. of Publ. of United Luth. Ch., 1925-31; incorporator Presbyn. Ministers' Fund. Mem. Soc. Bibl. Lit. and Exegesis, Phi Gamma Delta, Phi Beta Kappa. Democrat. Author: The Gist of the Sermon, 1905; The Book—A Brief Introduction to the Bible, 1908; Prayers for Boys, 1925; The Old Testament—A Study, 1934; The New Testament—A Study, 1934; New Testament Commentary, 1936. Home: Gettysburg, Pa. Died Feb. 8, 1953.

ALLEN, Arthur Moulton, lawyer; b. Providence, R.I., Mar. 3, 1876; s. Marvin E. and Sarah A. (Moulton) A.; A.B., Brown U., 1897; LL.B., cum laude, Harvard, 1900; m. 2d, Martha Baird, May 20, 1930. Admitted to R.I. bar, 1900, began practice, Providence; mem. Hinckley, Allen, Tillinghast & Wheeler. Dir. Phenix Nat. Bank of Providence, J. & P. Coats (R.I.), Inc., Baltic Mills Co. (exec. com.), Baltic Water Co., Sprague Warehouses, Inc. Named by New England Power Assn. and asso. cos., June 18, 1945, as dir. successor co., N.E. Electric System, confirmed by Securities and Exchange Commn., Mar. 1946, and U.S.D. Ct. (Mass.) June, 1946, and CCA (1st), Apr. 1947, elected dir. June 3, 1947. Mem. vis. com. on econ., Brown U., 1930-36. Trustee Homeopathic Hosp. of R.I. (sec.), Knight Meml. Library Assn. Mem. N.E. Conf. Def. Mem. Mfrs. Assn. Conn. (dir. 1939-42). Dir. Cotton Textile Inst. (exec. com. 1942-49). Mem. Am. (mem. tax and corp. divs.), R.I., N.Y. State bar assns., Am. Judicature Soc., Am. Law Inst., Phi Beta Kappa (v.p. 1940-43, pres., 1943-45, Alpha chpt.). Rep. Conglist. Clubs: Hope, Providence Art, Turks Head, Agawam Hunt (Providence); North East Harbor Golf; University (N.Y.). Contbr. Harvard and Columbia law revs. Home: 184 Upton Av., Providence 6. Died May 6, 1950; buried Swan Point Cemetery, Providence.

ALLEN, Arthur Wilburn, surgeon; b. McKinney, Ky., Nov. 30, 1887; s. James Hayden and Emma (Arthur) A.; A.B., Georgetown Coll., 1909, D.Sc. (hon.), 1943; M.D., Johns Hopkins, 1913; D.Sc. (hon.), Harvard, 1952; m. Vida Weddle, July 9, 1913; 1 son, Arthur Wilburn, Jr. Chief east surg. service Mass. Gen. Hosp., 1936-48, cons. in surgery, 1948—; lectr. surgery Harvard Med. Sch., 1936-48. Served as capt. M.C., U.S. Army, 1917-19. Diplomate Am. Bd. Surgery. Fellow A.C.S. (pres. 1947-48, chmn. bd. regents 1948-51), Royal Coll. Surgeons Eng. and Edinburgh (hon.), Royal Soc. Medicine Eng. (hon.); mem. Am. Acad. Arts and Scis., Am., So., New Eng. surg. assns., Pan-Pacific (pres. 1954—), Eastern (hon., 1954—), N.E., Boston (pres. 1942-44) surg. socs., A.M.A., Boston Med. Library (pres. 1953—), Soc. Clin. Surgery, Mass. Med. Soc. (pres. 1949-50). Republican. Mason. Clubs: Harvard, Somerset, Tavern (Boston); The Country (Brookline). Home: 191 Commonwealth Av. Office: 266 Beacon St., Boston. Died Boston Mar. 18, 1958; buried West Boxford, Mass.

ALLEN, Benjamin, publisher; b. Phila., Pa., Nov. 27, 1896; s. Charles H. and Mary (King) A.; grad. William Penn Charter Sch., Phila., 1915; m. Eleanor Christine, Mar. 4, 1922; children—Christine, Charles A. H., David Bell. Salesman Hames, Jones & Cadbury, Inc., 1915-17; jr. exec. circulation dept., Curtis Pub. Co., 1921-23, mgr. sales adminstrn., 1923-32, asst. circulation mgr., 1932-35, circulation dir. 1935—, director 1937—, v.p., then sr. v.p.; pres. Curtis Circulation Co. since 1946; Dir. Audit Bur. of Circulations, Bantam Books, Inc., Moore-Cottrell Subscription Agencies, Wonder Books, Inc., Treasure Books, Inc., Nat. Mag. Service Co., Transworld Pub. Co. of London Eng. Enlisted in U.S.N.R., 1917, commd. ensign, 1918; ensign to lt. (j.g.), U.S.N., 1918-19. Republican. Mem. Soc. of Friends. Clubs: Union League, Down Town (Phila.); Aronimink Golf; Tavern (Chgo.). Home: 343 S. Smedley St., Phila. Office: Independence Sq., Phila. Died Oct. 1958.

ALLEN, Carlos Eben, coll. pres.; b. Fillmore, Ill., Feb. 7, 1873; s. Lyman Copeland and Alice Direxia (Bliss) A.; A.B., Carleton Coll., Northfield, Minn., 1894; A.M., U. Chgo., 1903, Ph.D., 1913; m. Maude Vrooman Willsey, Aug. 28, 1895; children—Marjorie Copeland (Mrs. King Cook), William Willsey, Ned Bliss, Carlos Eben, Elizabeth Winslow (Mrs. David Marvel). Head of dept. fgn. langs., So. Ill. Normal U., Carbondale, 1894-1918, v.p. and registrar, 1913-18; pres. State Tchrs. Coll., Valley City, N.D., 1918—. Pres. So. Ill. Tchrs. Assn., 1915-16. Mem. N.E.A. (life), N.D. Edn. Assn. (pres. 1925-26), Phi Beta Kappa, S.A.R. Conglist. Mason. Rotarian. Home: College Campus, Valley City, N.D. Died 1945.

ALLEN, Charles Curtis, landscape painter; b. Leominster, Mass., Dec. 13, 1886; s. Charles Curtis and Mary Jane (Bartlett) A.; ed. Worcester (Mass.) Art Mus. Sch.; m. Mrs. Frances Sandra Woodland, June 23, 1919; 1 step-dau., Sarah Woodland. Bronze medal Panama-Pacific Expn.; water color prize, Boston Water Color Soc.; gold medal, Boston Art Club; medal for distinction in landscape painting, Boston Tercentenary, 1930; 1st prize in Audubon group, 1944; Salmagundi Club lay members prize, 1944. Represented by water colors in Clark Univ. Collection, Worcester, Mass.; The New Rockland (Me.) Museum; rep. by 2 in oil "Road to Boothbay" and "November Cloud" in the Currier Art Museum, Manchester, N.H. Paintings in permanent exhibitions Worcester Art Museum, Leominster and Fitswilliam pub. libraries, Brown University, Andover College; water color "Westwood Hillside," purchased, 1935, by Boston Mus. of Fine Arts. Academician, 1945; mem. Boston Water Color Soc. (v.p.), Guild of Boston Artists, Vermont Artists' Guild, Inc., Grand Central Galleries (N.Y.), Ogunquit Arts Assn. (hon.), Am. Water Color Soc., Rockport Art Assn., North Shore Art Assn. Republican. Episcopalian (New York). Club: Phila. Water Color. Home: 21 Kewadin Rd., Waban, Mass. Died June 28, 1950; buried Forest Hills Cemetery, Mass.

ALLEN, Charles Elmer, botanist; b. Horicon, Wis., Oct. 4, 1872; s. Charles and Eliza (North) A.; B.S., U. Wis., 1899, Ph.D., 1904; Sc.D., U. Chgo., 1941; m. Genevieve Sylvester, June 20, 1902; children—Edith (Mrs. C. R. Slater) Harold Sylvester, Charles Rittenhouse. Ct. reporter, 1890-1901; instr. botany U. Wis., 1901-04, asst. prof., 1904-07, asso. prof., 1907-09, prof., 1909-43, emeritus prof., 1943—; research asst. Carnegie Inst. of Washington, at Univ. of Bonn, 1904-05; vis. prof. Columbia U., 1924. Mem. NRC, 1925-31, chmn. div. biology and agr., 1929-30. Fellow A.A.A.S. (v.p. and chmn. Sect. G 1928); mem. Nat. Acad. Sciences, Am. Society Naturalists (pres. 1936), Genetics Soc. Am., Am. Genetic Assn., Am. Microscopic Soc. (pres. 1944), Am. Philos. Soc., Bot. Soc. Am. (pres. 1921), Wis. Acad. Sci. Arts and Letters (pres. 1930-33), Hist. Soc. Wis., Am. Assn. U., Profs., Delta Upsilon, Phi Beta Kappa, Sigma Xi, Phi Sigma. Author: A Textbook of Botany (with Edward M. Gilbert), 1917; A Textbook of General Botany (with Gilbert M. Smith and others), 1924, 4th ed., 1942. Editor-in-chief Wis. Alumni Mag., 1899-04, Am. Jour. of Botany, 1918-26. Contbr. to scientific publs. Home: 2014 Chamberlin Av., Madison 4, Wis. Died June 24, 1954.

ALLEN, Charles Metcalf, hydraulic engr.; b. Walpole, Mass., Dec. 12, 1871; s. Melzar Waterman and Martha (Metcalf) A.; B.S., Worcester Poly. Inst., 1894, M.S., 1899, hon. D.Eng., 1929; m. Eva May Taylor, Mar. 27, 1907; children—Virginia, Lucian Taylor, Jeannette. Instr. exptl., mech. and hydraulic engring., Worcester Poly. Inst., 1894-1906; prof. hydraulic engring., 1906-45; prof. emitus, hydraulic engring., 1945—; dir. Alden Hydraulic Lab., also practicing engr. Mem. A.A.A.S., Am. Soc. M.E., Am. Soc. C.E., Soc. Promotion Engring. Edn., Boston Soc. C.E. Republican. Conglist. Clubs: Worcester, Rotary (Worcester). Home: 1 Lincoln Av., Holden, Mass. Died Aug. 15, 1950; buried Maple Grove Cemetery, Walpole, Mass.

ALLEN, Claxton Edmonds, electrical engr.; b. Seven Islands, Va., Feb. 4, 1881; s. George Hunt and Mollie (Edmonds) A.; grad. high sch., Covington, Va., 1897; B.S. in E.E., Va. Poly. Inst., 1901; m. Lydia Ann Kimbrough, Apr. 7, 1908 (deceased 1943); children—Claxton Edmonds, Lydia Ann (Mrs. I. A. Long). Electrical apprentice with General Electric Co., Lynn, Mass., 1901-03, designing engr. and research work, Lynn, 1903-07, commercial engr. and instr. of salesmen, at Schenectady, N.Y., 1907-09; with Westinghouse Electric & Mfg. Co., successively mgr. transformer dept., at East Pittsburgh, Aug.-Nov. 1909, asst. mgr. and mgr. supply dept., N.Y.C., until 1914, mgr. supply and Central Sta. depts., Chgo., 1914-22, dist. mgr., St. Louis, 1922-30, v.p. charge merchandising, 1930-47; vice president Comml. Electric Supply Co.; dir. Electric Appliance Co., Columbia Electric Co. Dept. fuel administrator of Ill., World War. Fellow Am. Inst. E.E.; mem. Electric Light Assn., St. Louis Elec. Bd. of Trade (pres.). Episcopalian. Clubs: Noonday, Bellerive Country, Racquet; University (Pitts.). Inventor: Original distributed core transformer; maximum demand electric meter; electric relay. Home: 4626 Maryland Av. Office: 411 N. 7th St., St. Louis. Deceased.

ALLEN, Devere, editor; b. Providence, June 24, 1891; s. Henry L. and Sarah Elizabeth (Champlin) A.; A.B. cum laude, Oberlin (O.) Coll., 1917; m. Marie Hollister, Aug. 22, 1917; children—Jean Fern (Mrs. Hugh N. Young), Shirley April (Mrs. Louis Katona). Editor The Rational Patriot, 1917-18, Young Democracy, 1918-21; mng. editor The World Tomorow, 1921-25, editor, 1925-31, 32-33; spl. corr. in Europe for Am. Newspapers and mags., 1930-31; asso. editor The Nation, 1931-32; founder, editor, dir. Worldover Press (formerly Nofrontier News Service), dir. European bur., Brussels, Belgium, 1939-40, Latin-Am. bur., Havana, Cuba, 1942, Mexico City, 1942-44; lectured Harvard Summer Sch., Williamstown Inst. Politics, Am. Acad. Polit. and Social Scis.; mem. faculty Inst. Internat. Relations. Candidate for U.S. Senate from Conn. on Socialist ticket, 1932, 34, for gov. of Conn. on Labor Party ticket, 1938. Former mem. World Council War Resisters' Internat., League for Indsl. Democracy (dir.). Mem. Commn. for Return of Confiscated German and Japanese Property; exec. v.p. Am. Inst. Internat. Information. Mem. Workers' Def. League (nat. council), Fellowship of Reconciliation (internat. policy com.), Am. Acad. Polit. and Social Sci., Am. Fedn. Tchrs., Am. Civil Liberties Union, Americans for Dem. Action, Authors League of Am., R.I., Westerly hist. socs., New Eng. Historic Geneal. Soc., Phi Beta Kappa. Mem. Soc. of Friends (peace com. yearly meeting). Clubs: Foreign Correspondents (Mexico); Overseas Press. Author: The Fight for Peace, 1930; Some Prudence Island Allens, 1946; (pamphlets) Will Socialism End the Evil of War?, 1932: The Caribbean-Laboratory of World Cooperation, 1943; What Europe Thinks About America, 1948. Editor: Pacifism in the Modern World, 1929; Adventurous Americans, 1932; Am. editor: Above All Nations, 1948. Home: Godfrey Pl., Wilton, Conn.; also North Stonington, Conn. Died Aug. 27, 1955; buried Wheeler Cemetery, North Stonington, Conn.

ALLEN, Duff S(hederic), surgeon; b. Lebanon, Mo., July 7, 1895; s. William Thomas and Mary Elizabeth (Casey) A.; grad. Druy Acad., Springfield, Mo., 1913; student Washington U., 1913-15, M.D., 1919; m. Mildred Lucille Burns, 1926. House physician St. Luke's Hosp., 1919; asst. in surgery Washington U., 1921-24, instr. in surgery, 1924-26, asst. prof., 1926—; resident surgeon Barnes Hosp., 1923-24, now asst. surgeon; asst. surgeon St. Louis Maternity Hosp.; vis. surgeon and chief of unit St. Louis City Hosp. Editor Washington U. Med. Alumnus, 1924; asso. editor Journal of Thoracic Surgery, Diplomate Am. Bd. Surgery. Mem. Phi Beta Pi (nat. pres.). Republican. Catholic. Worked out surg. procedure for reconstruction of the esophagus; devised needle which reduces time required for an operation 5 minutes; devised first method for doing operations inside a living heart under direct vision. Contbr. studies on goitre and on the etiology of empyema and abscess of the lung and the mechanism of secretion of the gastric juice and method of absorption of egg white from gastro-intestinal tract. Address: 10 Oakleigh Lane, St. Louis. Died Dec. 7, 1958; buried Calvary Cemetery, St. Louis.

ALLEN, Edward Ellis, educator; b. West Newton, Mass., Aug. 1, 1861; s. James Theodore and Caroline Augusta (Kittredge) A.; prep. edn., English and Classical Sch., West Newton, Mass., and pvt. sch., Zurich, Switzerland; A.B., Harvard, 1884; student med. dept., Harvard, 1884-85; D.Sc., U. of Pa., 1930; m. Katharine Francena Gibbs, 1891; children—Isabel Sturtevant (Mrs. Charles Huntingford Malan), Caroline Kittredge (Mrs. Percival William Davis), Edward Ellis. Tchr. Royal Normal Coll. for the Blind, London, 1885-88; head tchr. Perkins Instn., Watertown, Mass. 1888-90; prin. Pa. Instn. for the Blind, Phila., 1890-1907; dir. Perkins Instn., 1907-31, now emeritus; lectr. on edn. of blind, Grad. Sch. of Edn., Harvard. Rebuilt Pa. Instn. and Perkins Instn.; introduced field sports and athletics for the blind; pioneer in spl. tng. of tchrs. of blind. Mem. State Commn. for the Blind (now Div. of the Blind) 1909—; v.p. Mass. Assn. for Adult Blind; ex-pres. Am. Assn. Instrs. of Blind, etc. Republican. Unitarian. Clubs: Twentieth Century, Unitarian, Lions. Home: Cambridge, Mass. Died Apr. 14, 1950.

ALLEN, Edward Tyson, ret. forester; b. New Haven, Dec. 26, 1875; s. Oscar Dana and Fidella Roberts (Totman) A.; student pvt. schs.; m. Matilda Price Riley, Oct. 20, 1902 (died 1927); children—Olmsted Tyson (Mrs. Donald Plimpton Abott), Barbara (Mrs. Robert E. Burns); m. 2d, Mildred Grudolf-Smith, Feb. 18, 1928. Forest ranger, 1898; entered Bur. Forestry, U.S. Dept. Agr., 1899; Cal. state forester, 1905-06; in U.S. Forest Service, 1906-09, charge establishment and adminstrn. nat. forests in far west; organized, 1909, and managed Western Forestry and Conservation Assn., an alliance of all pvt., state and fed. forest agencies in Mont., Ida., and Pacific Coast states; counsel to Nat. Lumber Mfrs. Assn. for many yrs., also to U.S. Treasury Dept., FTC, Dept. Interior, Dept. Agr., ret. from active service, 1932. Was specialist on forest econs., taxation and preservawas specialist on forest econs., taxation and preservation. Charter mem. Soc. Am. Foresters. Author many articles for popular, sci. and trade mags.; manuals for field officers and briefs for lawyes and legislators. Home: Otis, Ore. Died 1942.

ALLEN, Ezra Griffen, naval officer; b. Scranton, Pa., Mar. 11, 1885; s. Thomas H. and Maria (Smith) A.; B.S., U.S. Naval Acad., 1907; m. Elizabeth F. Travers, June 11, 1931. Commd. ensign U.S. Navy, 1907, and advanced through the grades to rear adm. Decorated Navy Cross (U.S.); Chevalier Legion of Honor (France). Mason. Clubs: Army and Navy, Army and Navy Country, Chevy Chase (Washington); New York Yacht (N.Y.C.). Home: 2419 California St., Washington. Died Jan. 4, 1952.

ALLEN, Frank Bigelow, newspaper corr.; b. Earlville, Ia., July 12, 1900; s. Johnson and Ruth (Bigelow) A.; student Ia. State Teachers Coll., and Ia. State Coll., 1922-26; m. Iola Meeker, Oct. 25, 1930; children—Diana, Jacqueline. Reporter, Waterloo (Ia.) Trbiune, 1927-1930; publisher, Waterloo (Ia.) Herald (weekly), 1933-35; courts and political reporter, Waterloo (Ia.) Courier, 1935-42; joined Internat. News Service, 1942, served as Senate Reporter, Washington, 1943-49, covered Bikini atomic tests, 1946, head senate staff, 1949-53; mil. writer, 1953—. Former chairman United States Capitol standing committee of correspondents. Mem. White House Corr. Assn., S.A.R., Am. Legion. Club: National Press. Home: 808 N. Danville St., Arlington, Va. Office: Times-Herald Bldg., Washington 5. Died Sept. 26, 1957; buried Arlington Nat. Cemetery.

ALLEN, Frank G., ex-governor; b. Lynn, Mass., Oct. 6, 1874; s. Frank M. and Abbie L. (Gilman) A.; ed. high sch., Lynn; m. Clara Winslow, Dec. 2, 1897 (now dec.); 1 dau., Mrs. Mary Winslow Crane; m. 2d, Eleanor Hamilton Wallace, Nov. 26, 1927; children—Frank Gilman, Marjorie Wallace. Began leather business with Black & Newhall, Boston, and later with Lyman W. Smith Sons Co., and J. W. Kennan Co.; with firm of Winslow Bros., which bought out Lyman Smith Sons Co.; firm name changed to Winslow Bros. & Smith (sheepskins), of which was president, 1911-29, chairman board, 1929-49; director C. Moulton Stone Company, Providence; dir. State Street Trust Co., Norwood (Mass.) Co-operative Bank, John Hancock Life Ins. Co., Dewy & Almy Chem. Co., Union Freight R.R., Boston & Providence R.R.; trustee of Franklin Savings Bank (Boston), Consolidated Investment Trust (Boston). Pres. Massachusetts Senate, 1921-22, 23-24, lt. governor of Massachusetts, 2 terms, 1925-28; gov. of Mass. term, 1929-30. Trustee Wellesley Coll., Boston Univ., Norwood Hospital; chmn. trustees Wrentham School, Wrentham, Mass.; v.p. Boston Chamber Commerce. Republican. Conglist. Clubs: Algonquin, University, Union, Tennis and Racquet (Boston); Eastern Yacht, Corinthian Yacht (Marblehead Neck); Essex County Country, Tedesco Country, Dedham Country and Polo, Salem Country. Home: 88 Marlborough St. Office: 248 Summer St., Boston 10. Died Oct. 9, 1950; buried Highland Cemetery, Norwood, Mass.

ALLEN, Fred (John Florence Sullivan), radio comedian; b. Cambridge, Mass., May 31, 1894; ed. Boston U.; m. Portland Hoffa, 1927. Began as juggler in vaudeville and toured U.S. and Australia; appeared in musical comedy, Poly; began work on radio, 1932; appears on TV; starred in motion pictures Thanks a Million, Sally, Irene and Mary, Love Thy Neighbor. Author: Treadmill to Oblivion, 1954. Address: care William Morris Agency, 1270 Sixth Av., N.Y.C. Died Mar. 17, 1956.

ALLEN, Frederick Lewis, magazine editor; b. Boston, Mass., July 5, 1890; s. Rev. Frederick B. and Alberta Hildegarde (Lewis) A.; A.B., Harvard, 1912, A.M., 1913; Litt.D. (hon.), Northeastern U., 1946, Dartmouth, 1951; m. Dorothy Penrose Cobb, Nov. 29, 1918; children—Elizabeth Penrose (dec.), Oliver Ellsworth; m. 2d, Agnes Rogers (Hyde), Sept. 29, 1932. Asst. in English, Harvard U., 1912-14; asst. editor Atlantic Monthly, 1914-16; mng. editor Century Magazine, 1916-17; with Council of Nat. Defense, 1917-19; sec. Corp., Harvard University, 1919-23; assistant editor Harper's Mag., 1923-31, associate editor, 1931-41, editor, 1941-53. Vice president Harper & Bros., publishers; director of Ford Foundation, 1953—. Trustee, Bennington College, 1937-44. Overseer Harvard U., 1942-48, and since 1950. Dir., Fgn. Policy Assn., 1945-50, now hon. dir. Clubs: Harvard, Century, Coffee House (New York). Author: Only Yesterday, 1931; The Lords of Creation, 1935; Since Yesterday, 1940; The Great Pierpont Morgan, 1949. also text for The American Procession, 1933; Metropolis, 1934; I Remember Distinctly, 1947; The Big Change, 1952. Contbr. articles and essays to mags. Home: 121 E. 35th St. Office: 49 E. 33d St., N.Y.C. 16. Died Feb. 13, 1954.

ALLEN, George Henry, educator; b. Grand Rapids, Mich., July 28, 1876; s. George Roderick and Viola (Miller) A.; A.B., Univ. of Michigan, 1898, A.M., 1899, Ph.D., 1904; student Am. Sch. of Classical Studies in Rome, 1900-02, U. of Paris, 1902-03, U. of Berlin, 1911-14; m. Wilifred Morris, Jan. 1, 1907; 1 son, George Edmund Morris; m. 2d, Ilène Martin, Dec. 20, 1932. Asst. in Latin, U. of Michigan, 1899-1900; fellow in classical archaeology, Am. Sch. Classical Studies, Rome, Italy, 1900-02; instr. Latin, U. of Cincinnati, 1903-06, asst. prof., 1906-11; dir., Bureau of University Travel, Berlin, 1911-14, manager home office Newton, Mass., 1920-21, dir., Paris, 1921-29; prof. Latin and the fine arts, Lafayette Coll., Easton, Pa., 1929-47. Mem. bd. trustees Bureau of Univ. Travel, Newton, Mass. Served as translator, mil. intelligence div., Gen. Staff of U.S. Army, Washington, 1917-20. Mem. Classical Assn. of Atlantic States, Archaeological Inst. America, Phi Beta Kappa, Delta Upsilon. Editor: Forum Conche (Fuero de Cuenca) (Latin text of municipal charter and laws of City of Cuenca, Spain), 1910. Author: The Great War (with others), 1921; The French Revolution, 1925. Contbr. articles on archeol. and antiquarian subjects to scientific periodicals. Home: 382 Washington Av., Dumont, N.J. Died Nov. 20, 1950; buried Oak Hill Cemetery, Grand Rapids, Mich.

ALLEN, Grosvenor Noyes, chmn., v.p. Oneida Ltd.; b. Kenwood, Oneida, N.Y., Jan. 13, 1874; s. Henry G., and Portia (Underhill) A.; m. Christine Hamilton, Nov. 23, 1905; children—Harriet, Hamilton, Henry G. Grad. Yale (Sheffield), 1895. With Pope Mfg. Co., Hartford, Conn., 1895-98; with Oneida Ltd., Oneida, N.Y., 1898—, now hon. chmn., v.p., dir. Home: Kenwood, N.Y. Office: Oneida, Ltd., Oneida, N.Y. Died Sept. 5, 1954; buried Oneida Community Cemetery.

ALLEN, James Henry, paper mfg. exec.; b. Neodesha, Kan., Nov. 19, 1880; s. Patric C. and Lottie Viola (Jones) A.; grad. Pine Bluff (Ark.) High Sch.; m. Lutie Ella Laine, Dec. 2, 1902 (dec.); children—James Laine (dec.), William Frank (dec.), Robert Hays. Began with newspaper agency Hanf & Allen, Pine Bluff, Ark., 1899; gen. mgr. J. H. Allen & Co., 1901-03; v.p. Bastrop Lumber Co., timber investments, 1903-36; v.p., dir. Union Bag and Paper Corp., Bastrop, La., 1936-40; pres., dir. Fla. Pulp & Paper Co., Pensacola, Fla., 1940-49, Ala. Pulp & Paper Co., Pensacola, 1945-49; dir., vice chmn. bd. St. Regis Paper Co., N.Y.C., 1949—. Pres. citizens com. Pensacola Jr. Coll., 1948-49. Mem. Fla. Indsl. Commn., Inst. Religious Sci. and Philosophy at Los Angeles. Democrat. Elk. Club: Pensacola Country. Home: 1928 E. Blount St. Office: San Carlos Hotel, Pensacola, Fla. Died Dec. 18, 1950.

ALLEN, John Clayton, ex-congressman; b. Hinesburg, Vt., Feb. 14, 1860; s. John H. and Elizabeth (Burns) A.; student pub. schs. Hinesburg, and Beeman Acad., New Haven, Vt.; m. Abbie Stapleford, Aug. 2, 1881; 1 son, Ralph C.; m. 2d Eudora Durell, Jan. 30, 1902; children—John C., Theodore D. Mayor of McCook, Neb., 1890; sec. of state Neb., 1891-95; settled at Monmouth, Ill., 1896; pres. John C. Allen Co., dry goods, Peoples Nat. Bank; mem. 69th to 72d U.S. Congresses, 14th Ill. Dist.; dir. Western Stone Ware Co. Pres. Bd. of Edn., Monmouth, 20 yrs. Chmn. Rep. County Central Com., Warren County, Ill., 1906. Presbyn. Mason (32°, Shriner), K.P., Elk, Woodman. Was instrumental in securing apptmt. John J. Pershing as mil. instr. U. Neb., 1891. Home: Monmouth, Ill. Deceased.*

ALLEN, M(arcus) Marshall, clergyman, educator; b. Fayette County, Ky., Aug. 24, 1862; s. Heman H. (D.D.) and Mary Washington (Marshall) A.; A.B., Centre Coll., Danville, Ky., 1884, A.M., 1888, D.D., 1915; grad. Princeton Theol. Sem. 1888; m. Lettie Cowan Craig, Feb. 11, 1902; children—Heman Hawthorne Allen (by 1st marriage), John Craig Allen (by 2d marriage). Ordained Presbyn. ministry, 1888; pastor Bessemer, Mich., 1888-95, Ishpeming, 1895-1915; pres. Ky. Coll. for Women, 1915-22; pastor Caldwell group of Chs., 1915—. Stated clk. Lake Superior Presbytery, 1897-1915. Mem. Sigma Chi. Repubulican. Mason (32°). Home: Danville, Ky. Deceased.

ALLEN, Richard Frazer, former Red Cross exec.; b. Craig, Mo., Nov. 29, 1890; s. Frank K. and Ella Scott (McKee) A.; student Craig High Sch. and Mo. U. Teachers College High Sch., 1905-09, U. of Mo., 1909-11; unmarried. Postmaster, Craig, Mo., 1911-14; with Morris & Co., packers, 1915-17; lt. of inf., U.S. Army, May 1917-Mar. 1919; apptd. mem. European Commn. of Am. Red Cross, May 1919; dir. Personnel dept. Am. Red Cross in Europe (hdqrs. in Paris), July 1919, aide to deputy commr., Nov. 1920; commr. of Am. Red Cross to Poland, Oct. 1920-Aug. 1921, deputy commr. to Europe, 1921-22; traveled around world, 1922-23; asst. to pres., gen. mgr. and dir. Rogers Peet Co. of N.Y., 1923-31; traveled and studied econ. and social problems of South Am. countries and West Indies, 1931-32; gen. administrative asst. of cotton program of Am. Red Cross, 1932-33; mgr. Eastern Area, Am. Red Cross, 1933-40; del. to Europe, 1940-41; vice chmn. insular and fgn. operations, Jan. 1942-Nov. 1945; spl. missions to Iceland, Great Britain, N. Africa, Middle East, France, Italy, India and Switzerland; adminstr. Fgn. Relief Fund, 1947-48; Chief Mut. Security Adminstrn., for Yugoslavia, Dec. 1950-52. Decorations: Polish Government; Polish Red Cross; Russian Red Cross; Order of St. Ann, Montenegran Govt.; Belgian Red Cross; Officer of Legion of Honor, Comité Francais de Service Social, city of Marseille; Grand Priory of British Realm of St. John of Jerusalem; Comdr. Royal Order of the Netherlands. Address: Cosmos Club, 2121 Massachusetts Av., Washington. Died Aug. 25, 1957; buried Caveau des Cendras, Cemetery de St. Georges, Geneva, Switzerland.

ALLEN, Robert Emmet, banker; b. Greenville, S.C., Feb. 26, 1890; s. Henry Wilson and Mary Irene (Mendenhall) A.; student Chicora Coll., Greenville, S.C., 1897-1901, Furman Fitting Sch., 1901-04; B.A., Furman U., 1909, M.A., 1914, LL.D. (hon.), 1937; m. Ellen Douglas Boykin, Nov. 5, 1919; 1 dau., Ellen Douglas (Mrs. George W. Kinchwey, III). Bank clk. Norwood National Bank (Greenville), National Bank of Commerce (Baltimore), Newberry (S.C.) Savings Bank, 1910-14; prof. Sch. Fine Arts, dept. of music, Chicora Coll. for Women, Columbia, S.C., 1915-17; clerk, Central Union Trust Co. of N.Y., 1919-21; asst. treas. Central Union Trust Co. of N.Y. (now The Hanover Bank, 1921-25, v.p. 1925-47; practicing as financial consultant since 1948. Past v.p., mem. bd., treas., mem. fin. com. N.Y. Post-Grad. Med. Sch. (now part of N.Y. University Bellevue Medical Center); past treasurer, mem. board, member finance, chairman executive com. Josiah Macy Jr. Foundation. Enlisted as pvt., World War I; with A.E.F., Savenay, France, 1918-19; commd. 1st lt., 1918. Past vice pres. Furman Univ. Alumni Association (ex-pres. New York chapter), Tokenoke Assn. (past pres.), Uptown Bankers Assn. (p.p.), Mil. Order Fgn. Wars, N.Y. Southern Soc., S.R., Pi Kappa Phi. Episcopalian. Home: 611 McDaniel Av., Greenville, S.C. Office: S.C. Nat. Bank Bldg., Greenville, S.C. Died Aug. 7, 1955; buried Quaker Cemetery, Camden, S.C.

ALLEN, Samuel G., ret. mfg. exec.; b. Warren, Pa., 1870; m. Emily Myers. Chmn. bd. Combustion Engring.-Superheater, Inc., Franklin Ry. Supply Co. Address: Pinehurst, N.C. Died Oct. 16, 1956.

ALLEN, Sidney J., chmn. Allen Industries, Inc. Home: 1920 Lincolnshire Dr. Office: Leland & Grand Trunk R.R., Detroit. Died Apr. 8, 1958.

ALLEN, Sturges, clergyman; b. Hyde Park, N.Y., June 25, 1850; s. Theodore and Catharine (Reed) A.; B.S., Coll. City of N.Y., 1869; B.D., Gen. Theol. Sem., 1880. Deacon P.E. Ch., 1880, priest, 1882; curate St. Mary's Ch., Kansas Ciyt, Mo., 1880-1, St. George's Ch., Newburgh, N.Y., 1881-4; with Holy Cross Mission Ch., N.Y.C., 1884-89; professed in Order of Holy Cross, 1888; Superior Order of the Holy Cross, 1888-94, 1907-15. Lived in New York, 1889-92, Westminster, Md., 1892-04; missionary in Liberia, 1923-29. Democrat. Home: West Park, N.Y. Died Mar. 26, 1929; buried Holy Cross Mission, Bolahun, Liberia.

ALLEN, Walter Barth, banker; b. Woonsocket, S.D., Sept. 21, 1892; s. William Henry and Rosa Jane (Barth) A.; student U. of S.D.; m. Florence Samuels, Dec. 23, 1937; children—Hazen Martin, Janet Ann. Asst. cashier Woonsocket (S.D.) State Bank, 1919-23; treas. Thompson & Co., Inc., Vermillion, S.D., 1923-24; receiver closed banks, S.D. Banking Dept., 1924-26; with Continental & Commercial Nat. Bank & Trust Co., Chicago, 1926-29; v.p. Continental Ill. Nat. Bank & Trust Co. since 1933. Served as lt. Motor Transport Corps, A.E.F., 1917-19. Mem. Sigma Alpha Epsilon. Republican. Episcopalian. Club: Hinsdale (Ill.) Golf. Home: 229 W. Ogden Av., Hinsdale, Ill. Office: 231 LaSalle St., Chicago 90. Died Oct. 8, 1951.

ALLEN, William Fitch, educator; b. Oneonta, N.Y., Nov. 11, 1875; s. Horace Hews and Frances (Fitch) A.; student Cornell U., 1896-98; A.B., Stanford, 1900, A.M., 1902; Ph.D., U. Minn., 1915; Sc.D., U. Ore., 1945; m. Augusta Annette Nahl, Sept. 11, 1908; 1 son, Horace Hews. Research asst. to Mr. Edward P. Allis, Pacific Grove, Cal., 1901-06, to Jacques Loeb, Monterey, Cal., 1906-10; instr. zoology, U. Ill., 1910-11; instr. anatomy, U. Minn., 1911-16; prof. anatomy, head dept., U. Ore., 1916-46; prof. emeritus, 1946—. Mem. Wash., N.Y. acads. sci., Am. Assn. Anatomists, Am. Physiol. Soc., Anatomischen Gesellschaft; Soc. Exptl. Biology and Medicine, A.A.A.S., Sigma Xi. Author many publs. on anatomy and physiology of nervous, blood and lymphatic systems. Home: 3947 S.E. Salmon St., Portland 15, Ore. Died Mar. 11, 1951; buried Portland Crematorium and Mausoleum.

ALLEN, William Ray, educator; b. Ossian, Ind., Mar. 8, 1885; s. Elza and Ellen (Chupp) A.; A.B., Ind. U., 1913, A.M., 1914; student Cornell, 1916-17; Ph.D., Ind. U., 1920; m. Lura Belle Devin, June 14, 1922; children—Martha Jane (Mrs. W. B. Jackson), Barbara Janet, Ellen Claire. Newspaper, advt. work, 1903-07; tchr., prin. Hartford City, Ind., 1907-12; asst. Carnegie Sta. Exptl. Evol., Cold Spring Harbor, L.I., N.Y., 1914; instr. zoology, Kan. State Coll., 1914-16; asst. biology, Cornell U., 1916-17; instr. Ind. U., 1918-19; traveling fellow, U. Ill., Peru, Bolivia, Chile, 1918-19, Ind. U., 1920-21; asst. prof. zoology, Municipal U. Akron, 1921-22; asst. prof. zoology, U. Ky., 1922-25, asso. prof., 1925-30, prof., 1930—, head dept., 1948-50. Mem. Am. Soc. Zoologists, Am. Ecol. Soc., Am. Microscop. Soc., Am. Soc. Ichtyologists and Herpetologist, Am. Fishery Soc., Am. Soc. Limnologists, Oceanographers, Am. Assn. U. Profs., Ind., Ky. Acads. Sci., Phi Beta Kappa (sec., pres. Ky. chpt.), Sigma Xi (treas., v.p., pres. Ky. chpt.). Author: Fishes of Western South America, 1942 (with C. H. Eigenmann); Nature Sketch Book, 1935; Laboratory Guide to Zoology, 1916. Editor: Genera Insectorum, Family Membracidae, Genera Insectorum, 1951. Home: 417 Clifton Av., Lexington, Ky. Died Apr. 7, 1955; buried Oak Lawn Cemetery, Ossian, Ind.

ALLEN, William Sims, educator; b. Hico, Tex., Oct. 27, 1888; s. Abel Orville and Maggie (LeNoir) A.; grad. high sch., Hico, 1907; A.B., Baylor U., 1912; A.M., Columbia, 1915, Ph.D., 1923; studied U. of Chicago 8 mos., 1919; m. Gertrude Eudaly, June 22, 1914. Prin. high sch. Italy, Tex., 1912-14, Waco, 1915-16; with Baylor U., 1916-34, successively instr. Latin, 1916-17, asst. prof., 1917-18, prof. secondary edn., 1919-34, also dean Coll. Arts and Sciences, 1924-34, acting pres., June 1, 1931-June 1, 1932, v.p., dean, and chmn. of Sch. of Edn., 1932-34; president John B. Stetson University, 1934-47; now emeritus. Member S.A.T.C., Ft. Sheridan, Ill., summer 1918.

Pres. Fla. Bapt. Conv., 1940 and 41; pres. Fla. Assn. Colls. and Univs., 1945; mem. at-large Nat. Council Boy Scouts of America, past pres. Central Florida Council. Mem. N.E.A., De Land C. of C. (dir., hon. life mem.), Am. Polit. Sci. Assn., Am. Acad. Political and Social Science, Phi Delta Kappa (Zeta Chapter), Kappa Delta Pi. Democrat. Kiwanian. Author: A Study in Latin Prognosis, 1923. Contbr. to mags. Address: 131 Chevy Chase Dr., San Antonio. Died June 1, 1951.

ALLEN, Wilmar Mason, hosp. adminstr.; b. Chattanooga, Tenn., Oct. 20, 1894; s. William Mason and Mary Henry (Drake) A.; student William Penn Charter Sch. (Phila.), 1910-12; A.B., Haverford (Pa.) Coll., 1916; M.D., Johns Hopkins, 1920; m. Erma Helen Smale, Aug. 5, 1925; children—Erma Barbara, Nancy Elizabeth. Intern, Henry Ford Hosp., Detroit, 1920-21; dir. Central Lab., Saginaw, Mich., 1921-22; asst. resident, instr. Johns Hopkins Hosp. and Johns Hopkins U. Med. Sch., 1922-25; pathologist, bacteriologist Hartford Hosp., 1925-36, dir. of hosp. cons. pathologist, 1936—. Served in M.C., U.S. Army, 1917-18; S.A.T.C., Johns Hopkins, 1918. Fellow A.C.P., Am. Coll. Hosp. Adminstrs.; mem. A.M.A., Am., New Eng., Conn. hosp. assns., Conn. State, Hartford med. socs., Hartford Co. Med. Assn., Nu Sigma Nu, Phi Beta Kappa, Alpha Omega Alpha. Conglist. Address: Morgan Creek Rd., Chapel Hill, N.C. Died Jan. 14, 1956; buried New Hartford, Conn.

ALLENDOERFER, Carl W., banker; b. Carlinville, Ill., May 15, 1880; s. Charles and Margarette Maria (Fishback) A.; ed. high sch.; m. Winifred Barnett, Jan. 23, 1909; 1 son, Carl Barnett. Began as bookkeeper First Nat. Bank, Concordia, Kans.; successively auditor, asst. cashier, v.p., pres., now chmn. bd. First Nat. Bank, Kansas City, Mo.; dir. Sunshine Biscuits, Inc., Gleaner Harvester Corp., Pitts. Midway Coal Mining Co. Republican. Conglist. Club: Mission Hills Country. Home: 10 E. 56th St. Terrace. Office: First National Bank, Kansas City, Mo. Died July 3, 1955; buried Mt. Moriah Cemetery, Kansas City, Mo.

ALLER, Howard Lewis (ăl'lẽr), pub. utility exec.; b. Richmond Hill, L.I., N.Y., Nov. 26, 1883; s. Amos and Katharine (Lewis) A.; M.E., Cornell U., 1906; m. Catherine Goddard, Aug. 14, 1907; children —Elizabeth Alden (Mrs. Richard Bullwinkle III). Howard Lewis, Rodney Goddard. Engr. and salesman Gen. Electric Co., Schenectady, N.Y., and Denver, Colo., 1906-12; mgr. and pres. Central Ariz. Light & Power Co., Phoenix, 1912-25; operating sponsor Electric Bond and Share Co., 1925-35; pres. and chmn. bd. Am. Power & Light Co., 1935-53; pres. and dir. Texas Utilities Co.; dir. Texas Power & Light Co., Texas Electric Service Co., Dallas Power & Light Company. Member Theta Xi. Club: Cornell (New York City). Home: 1509 Anyan St., Dallas, also Lakeville, Conn. Office: 1506 Commerce St., Dallas. Died Apr. 20, 1954.

ALLEZ, George Clare (ăl-lā), librarian; b. Bath, N.Y., Sept. 25, 1897; s. George Thomas and Grace Irene (Allen) A.; student Wash. State Normal Sch., Bellingham, 1925-27; B.A. in Edn., U. Wash., 1928; B.S. in Library Sci., Columbia, 1929, M.S., 1932; m. Martha Viola Anderson, Aug. 26, 1927; 1 son, George Nicholas. Librarian Central State Tchrs. Coll., Stevens Point, Wis., 1929-38; acting asst. dir. Library Sch., U. Wis., 1938-39, asso. dir., 1939-41, dir., 1941—. Served as pvt., 1st class, 314th Field Signal Batt., 89th Div., World War; 18 mos. overseas. Recipient Carnegie Fellowship for study in library sci., 1932. Mem. Am., Wis. Library Assos., Assn. Am. Library Schs. (pres. 1947-48), Am. Legion. Democrat. Episcopalian. Home: 2302 Keyes Av. Office: Library School, U. Wis., 811 State St., Madison, Wis. Died Apr. 26, 1950; buried Bellingham, Wash.

ALLIN, Roger, ex-gov. N.D.; b. Bradworthy, Eng., Dec. 18, 1848; student Canadian schs.; m. Isabella McKenzie, Mar. 22, 1881. Lived in Can. until 1878, then in Mich. until 1879, when he settled in Dakota, filing on land he now farms, nr. Grafton. Mem. Territorial Council, 1886-89, Constnl. Conv., 1889, 1st legislative assembly N.C., 1889; lt. gov. N.D., 1890, gov., 1894-97. Republican. Address: Grafton, N.D. Died 1936.

ALLIS, Louis, mfr. motors; b. Milw., Dec. 30, 1866; s. Edward Phelps and Margaret Maria (Watson) A.; prep. edn. Markham Acad., Milw.; C.E., Pa. Mil. Coll., Chester, 1888, hon. Dr. Elec. Engring., 1937; m. Carol Yates, Sept. 17, 1890; 1 son, Edward Phelps; m. 2d, Louise Hegen, May 1, 1911; children—Louis, John Watson, William White, Robert Thomas. Began as asst. shipping clk. in father's firm E. P. Allis Co. of Milw., purchasing agent and gen. mfg. asst. until 1893, also supervised 80,000 acres of father's estate in No. Peninsula of Mich.; after sale of E. P. Allis Co. to Allis-Chalmers Co., asso. with Mechanical Appliance Co. Milw. (later renamed The Louis Allis Co.), 1902—, now chmn. bd. Hon. dir. Milw. Country Day Sch. Mem. Nat. Elec. Mfrs. Assn., Elec. Mfrs. Club. Clubs: Milwaukee, Milwaukee Country. Home: Route 9, River Hills, Wis. Office: 427 E. Stewart St., Milw. 7. Died May 8, 1950.

ALLPORT, Fayette Ward, European mgr., Motion Picture Association of America, Incorporated; born in St. Louis, Mo., Jan. 25, 1893; son John Edward and Nellie Edith (Wise) A.; A.B., Western Reserve U., 1917, student Law Sch.; m. Mildred Dorcas Burt, Feb. 9, 1918; children—Peter Ward, Alexander Wise; m. 2d Toni Worthington, May 7, 1946. With U.S. Foreign Commerce Service, 1920-23; clerk to trade commissioner, Vienna and Warsaw, 1920-22; asst. trade commr., Vienna, Mar. 1922-Apr. 1923; trade commr., Berlin, Apr. 1923-Aug. 1924; asst. commercial attaché, Berlin, Aug. 1924-Jan. 1925; commercial attaché, Brussels and The Hague, Jan. 1925-Mar. 1926, Berlin, Mar. 1926-Sept. 1929, Paris, Sept. 1929-July 1933. Lt. U.S. Army, 1917-19; 327th Machine Gun Batn., A.E.F., France, later G.H.Q., A.E.F. Decorated Chevalier of Legion of Honor (France). Mem. Soc. Colonial Wars, Phi Gamma Delta, Delta Theta Phi. Club: American Club (London). Author of many official and pvt. studies of Am. foreign trade policy and practice. Home: 7 Park Av., N.Y. City. Office: 28 W. 44th St., N.Y.C. 18. Died 1958.

ALLRED, James V., judge; b. Bowie, Tex., Mar. 29, 1899; s. Renne and Mary (Hinson) A.; LL.B., Cumberland U., 1921; m. Jo Betsy Miller, June 20, 1927; children—James V., David, Sam Houston. Admitted to Tex. bar, 1921, began practice at Wichita Falls, dist. atty., 1923-25; atty. gen. of Tex., 2 terms, 1931-35; gov. State of Tex., 1935-39; U.S. dist. judge, So. Dist. of Tex., 1939-42; engaged in practice of law; U.S. dist. judge, So. Dist. Tex., 1951—. Served U.S. Navy, World War. Mem. Am. Legion. Democrat. Mem. Disciples of Christ Ch. Mason (32°, Shriner, K.C.C.H.), Elk. Club: Optimist of Wichita Falls (ex-pres.). Home: 4720 Bellaire. Office: Electric Bldg., Houston 2. Died Sept. 24, 1959.

ALLYN, Harriett May, coll. dean emeritus; b. New London, Conn., May 4, 1883; d. Charles and Helen Louisa (Starr) Allyn; A.B., Mt. Holyoke College, 1905, LL.D. (hon.), 1948; M.S., U. Chgo., 1910, Ph.D., 1912, Gen. sec. YWCA, Mt. Holyoke Coll., 1905-07; instr. zoölogy, Lake Erie Coll., Painesville, O., 1908-09, Vassar Coll., 1912-13, Hackett Med. Coll., Canton, China, 1913-19, dean 1915-19; instr. zoölogy, Mt. Holyoke Coll., 1920-21; dean, instr. zoölogy, Hackett Med. Coll., Canton, China, also mem. bd. dirs. Chan Kwang Sch., Canton, 1921-23; prof. zoölogy, Montecello Sem., Godfrey, Ill., 1923-24; instr. zoölogy, Vassar Coll., 1924, asst. prof., 1925-28, asso. prof., 1928-29, on leave; academic dean, prof. anthropology, Mt. Holyoke Coll., 1929-48. Rep. U.S. Govt. 2d Congress Prehistoric and Protohistoric Sci., Oslo, Norway, 1936. Formerly chmn. Cina div. of administrative com., foreign div., nat. bd. YWCA. Mem. N.E. Conf. Grad. Edn. (v.p. 1944-45), Nat. Assn. Deans Women (1st v.p. 1933-36, pres. 1937-39, cons. 1939-40), N. E.A. (mem. adv. com. in individual guidance 1937), N.E. Assn. Colls. and Secondary Schs. (chmn. com. instns. higher edn. 1940-41), Council Guidance and Personnel Assns. (chmn. 1940-42), Am. Anthrop. Assn., A.A.A.S. (fellow), Am. Assn. U. Women, Am. Schs. Oriental Research, China Soc., Mass. Archeol. Soc. (charter mem.), Mass. Soc. Prevention Cruelty to Animals, Soc. Am. Archeology, Soc. Woman Geographers, Ednl. Policies Commn., Phi Beta Kappa, Sigma Xi. Club: College (Boston). Home: 26 Jewett Lane, South Hadley, Mass. Died July 7, 1957.

ALMACK, John C(onrad) (aw-măk), author, educator; b. nr. Houston, Mo., Oct. 15, 1883; s. John Cullison and Amanda (Purcell) A.; B.A., U. Ore., 1918, M.A., 1921; Ph.D., Stanford, 1922; m. Alice Ethel Jaeger, Nov. 25, 1905 (died 1936); children —Grace Mildred (Mrs. W. F. Dietrich), Malcolm Dean; m. 2d, Evelyn M. Foster, Oct. 14, 1937. Tchr. pub. schs., 1905-15; editor country paper, 1915-16; tchr. English, 1916-17; acting dir. extension U. Ore., 1918-20; prof. edn. Stanford, 1921—. Mem. Palo Alto (Cal.) Bd. Edn. Mem. Nat. Soc. Study Edn., N.E.A., Am. Assn. U. Profs., Phi Delta Kappa. Republican. Methodist. Odd Fellow, K.P., Modern Woodman, Woodman of the World. Club: Crossroads. Author: Educator for Citizenship, 1924; The School Board Member, 1926; Research and Thesis Writing, 1929; Modern School Administration, 1933; Track of the Sun (verse), 1937; First Facts About Narcotics, 1939; A Clear Case Against Narcotics, 1929; Straight Thinking on Narcotics, 1940; The Painted Pony, 1944; (with A. R. Lang) Problems of the Teaching Profession, 1925, The Beginning Teacher, 1928; (with J. F. Bursch) Administration of Village Schools, 1926; (with L. M. Terman) Hygiene of the School Child, 1929; (with E. D. Adams) Historyo of the United States, 1931; (with E. H. Staffelbach) The Stanford Speller, 7 vols. 1931; (with Lillian E. Billington) The Laurel Handwriting Series, 1937; (with Evelyn M. Almack) Golden Keys, 1941, Doors to Open, 1941, Social Living, 1941; (with C. W. Wilson) American Health Series. Home: 683 Alvarado Row, Stanford University, Cal. Died Oct. 5, 1953.

ALMAND, Claude Marion, univ. dean, composer; b. Winnsboro, La., May 31, 1915; s. Claude F. and Pearl (Harrison) A.; A.B., La. Coll., 1934, Mus.B., 1934; student Sherwood Sch. Music, Chgo., 1934-35; Mus.M., La. State U., 1938; Ph.D., U. Rochester, 1940; m. Lenoir Patton, July 27, 1950. Asso. prof. music George Peabody Coll. for Tchrs., 1940-43, prof., 1943-44; prof. music, sch. ch. music So. Bapt. Theol. Sem., 1944-48, lectr. theory, composition, musicology, 1948-53; prof. composition, condr. chorus U. Louisville, 1944-48, asst. to dean, prof. music, head theory dept., 1948-53, dir. grad. dept., 1952-53; dean. sch. music Stetson U., 1953—. Recipient state, nat. honors Nat. Fedn. Music Clubs Composition Contest, 1940; one of six contemporary composers awarded commns. Louisville Orchestra, 1948, 49. Mem. Chamber Music Soc. Louisville (dir.), Louisville Community Concerts Assn., Daytona Beach Symphony Soc. (dir.), Fla. Music Tchrs. Assn. (v.p.), Phi Kappa Phi, Phi Mu Alpha (province gov.), Delta Omicron (nat. patron), Lambda Chi Alpha, Kappa Phi Kappa, Phi Delta Kappa. Clubs: Arts, Torch (Louisville); Athenian (DeLand). Composer: Pondy Woods, 1938; The Legend of Last Isle, 1939; The Waste Land, 1940; String Quartet, 1941; Chorale, 1943; Toccata, 1944; John Gilbert—A Steamboat Overture, 1949; Concerto, 1949; Roustabout, 1952, also piano sonatas, chamber music, songs choral works, piano and organ pieces. Works performed by Eastman-Rochester Orchestra, New Orleans Orchestra, Peabody Chamber Orchester, Little Symphony Nat. Gallery Art, Louisville and Cin. orchestras. Home: 210 W. Washington Av., Deland, Fla. Died Sept. 12, 1957.

ALONSO, Amado, philologist; b. Lerin, Spain, Sept. 13, 1896; s. Wenceslao and Clementa (García) A.; Ph.D., U. of Madrid, 1928; Ph.D. (hon.), U. of Chicago, 1941; A.M. (hon.), Harvard, 1947; m. Joan Cann Evans, Jan. 10, 1928; children—Ramón, William, Juan Manuel, Fernando. Came to U.S., 1946. Instr. U. of Hamburg, 1922-23; prof. philology Centro de Estudios Históricos, Madrid, 1923-27; dir. Philol. Inst., prof. Romance Linguistic U. of Buenos Aires, 1927-46; prof. Romance langs., lit. Harvard since 1947, Smith prof. since 1950. Hon. mem. Facultad de Filosofía, U. Chile, 1943. Mem. Am. Philos. Soc., Am. Acad. Arts and Scis. (fgn. hon. mem.), Modern Lang. Assn. of Am. (hon. mem.) Roman Catholic. Author: Problems de dialectologia Hispanoamericana, 1930; El problema de la lengua en América, 1935; Castellano, español, idoma nacional, Historia espiritual de tres nombres, 1938; Poesía y estilo de Pablo Neruda, 1940; Estudios Linguísticos (Temas españoles), 1951. Promoter, dir. and co-author: Biblioteca de Dialectologia Hispanoamericana, I-VII vols., 1930-49; Colección de Estudios Estilísticos, I-III vols., 1932-42; Filosofía y Teoría del lenguaje, I-IV vols., 1941-45. Editor: Revista de Filología Hispánica, Buenos Aires, 1939-46, The Nueva Revista de Filología Hispánica since 1947. Contbr. articles on Spanish and Latin-Am. lang., lit. to profl. revs. Home: 8 Kensington Rd., Arlington 74, Mass. Office: Widener Library, Harvard, Cambridge 38, Mass. Died May 26, 1952; buried Mount Auburn Cemetery, Cambridge.

ALSOP, Joseph Wright, (awl'sŭp); insurance; b. Middletown, Connecticut, April 2, 1876; s. Joseph Wright and Elizabeth Winthrop (Beach) A.; attended Groton Sch., Groton, Mass., 1889-93; Ph.B., Sheffield Scientific Sch. (Yale), 1898; U. of Berlin, 1893-94; m. Corinne Roosevelt Robinson, Nov. 5, 1909; children—Joseph W., Corinne Roosevelt, Stewart J. O., John de K. Insurance and farmer. Director U. of Conn., Connecticut Agricultural Expt. Sta., 1911-41. Member Connecticut House of Representatives, 1907-09, Senate, 2 terms, 1909-13. Member Republican State Central Com. of Conn., 1909-12, chmn. Progressive State Central Com. of Connecticut 1912; mem. Prog. Nat. Com., 1912-16; mem. Conn. Com. on Food Supply, 1917, Conn. State Council Defense, 1917. Commr. Conn. Pub. Utilities Commn., 1917-43; mem. Conn. State Planning Board, 1934. Pres. The Purebred Dairy Cattle Assn., Hartford County Mutual Fire Ins. Co., Conn. Valley Mutual Hail Ins. Co. Mem. NRA Dist. Recovery Bd. of New England. Episcopalian. Mem. Delta Psi. Clubs: Yale (New York); Hartford (Hartford); Graduate (New Haven). Home: Avon, Conn. Office: 750 Main St., Hartford, Conn. Died Mar. 17, 1953; buried Middletown, Conn.

ALTE, Visconde de (José de Horta Machado da Franca), Portuguese diplomat; asst. sec. fgn. affairs in Portugal, 4 yrs.; diplomatic service at various capitals; chargé de affaires of Portuguese Legation at St. Petersburg until 1902; became E.E. and M.P. from Portugal to U.S., 1922, now hon. counsellor of Legation. Address: 1944 B St., Washington. Deceased.

ALTGLASS, Max Mayer (awlt'gläs), teacher, vocal artist; b. Warsaw, Poland, February 16, 1895; son of Simon and Rachel (Koltun) Altglass; educated high school and commercial school, Warsaw, and in music at Conservatory, Berlin; m. Tema Lui, August 19, 1919; children—Adam, Edward. Began as lyric tenor at Frankfort a/M, Germany, 1915, later appeared in Warsaw, Vienna, Berlin, Prague, etc.; came to U.S., 1923; connected with Metropolitan Opera Company, 1924-40; principal roles in Rigoletto, Trovatore, Traviata, Carmen, Lohengrin, Bartered Bride, La Juive, Turandot, Coque D'or, Donna Juanita, Aida, Tosca, Mignon, Magic Flute, Tales of

Hoffman, etc. Home: 415 Central Park West, New York, N.Y. Died Feb. 13, 1952.

ALTHOUSE, Paul Shearer (ält'hous), operatic tenor; b. Reading, Pa., Dec. 2, 1889; s. Harry and Laura (Shearer) A.; student Bucknell U., Lewisburg, Pa.; hon. Doctor of Music, Doctor of Literature; m. Elizabeth Breen, June 20, 1914; children—Ritamary, Pauline; m. second Cecilia Glynn, June 3, 1950. Made début at Metropolitan Opera Co., New York, as Dimitri, in Boris Godounov, Mar. 19, 1913 (first Am. tenor without European training to make début in leading rôle with Met. Opera Co.); repertoire includes leading tenor parts in "Aïda," "Cavalleria Rusticana," "Pagliacci," "Carmen," "Tosca," "La Bohême," "Butterfly," "Faust," "Tristan and Isolde," "Tannhauser," "Walküre," "Parsifal," "Samson et Delilah," etc. Has appeared at music festivals in U.S. and with the leading orchestras; toured in Australia and New Zealand, 1922-25; formerly mem. Chicago Civic Opera Co., and San Francisco Opera; in Grand Opera 30 years; now voice diagnostician and teacher. Mem. Am. Acad. Teachers of Singing. Tenor Berlin, Stuttgart and Stockholm operas. Studio: 260 W. 72d St., New York, N.Y. Died Feb. 6, 1954, buried Ferncliff, Hartsdale, N.Y.

ALTMAIER, Clinton John, surgeon; b. Columbus, O., Dec. 14, 1882; s. Martin and Sophia (Stark) A.; D.D.S., Ohio State U., 1901, M.D., 1905; m. Ada My Henry, Sept. 26, 1906; children—Cloavis J., Jean E. (dec.). Dentist in Columbus O., 1901-02; practiced medicine in Wood County, O., 1905-09, Columbus, O., 1909-13; med. examiner Ohio Indsl. Commn., 1913-15; surgeon Marion (O.) Steam Shovel Co., 1915-44; gen. practice and surgery, Marion, O., 1927—. Served with M.C., U.S. Army, World War I. Mem. Ohio State Democratic Com., 8th Dist., 1932-46. Trustee Ohio State U., 1937-44, chmn., 1944. Mem. A.M.A., Ohio State Med. Assn., Northwestern Med. Soc., Marion (O.) Med. Acad., Sigma Nu, Alpha Mu Pi Omega, Am. Legion (40 and 8). Mason, Elk, Odd Fellow, K.P., Eagle, Moose. Home: 424 S. Prospect St. Office: 336 W. Center St., Marion, O. Died Jan. 10, 1950.

ALTROCCHI, Rudolph, prof. of Italian; b. Florence, Italy, Oct. 31, 1882; s. Giovanni and Pauline (Zamvòs) A.; A.B., Harvard, 1908, A.M., 1909, Ph.D., 1914; m. Julia Cooley, Aug. 26, 1920; children—John Cooley, Paul Hemenway. Instr. Romance langs., Columbia, 1910-11, U. of Pa., 1911-12, Harvard, 1912-15; asst. prof., U. of Chicago, 1915-22; asso. prof. Italian, U. of Chicago, 1922-27; prof. Italian, Brown, 1927-28; prof. Italian and chmn. department U. of Calif., 1928-47, professor emeritus. Member of the American Bureau of Public Information, Rome, 1918; dir. oral propaganda in Italy, 1918; 2d lt. inf., Liaison Service, A.E.F., Lyons, France, 1918-19. Decorated Officer of Academy (France), 1919; Chevalier of the Crown of Italy, 1921. Mem. Modern Language Assn. America, American Association University Professors, Am. Assn. Teachers of Italian (pres. 1929), Philol. Assn. of Pacific Coast (v.p. 1936, pres. 1937). Republican. Clubs: Literary (Chicago); Harvard (pres. 1932-34, 36-38); Asso. Harvard (v.p. 1934-41, pres., 1941-46). Editor: (with others) Italian Short Stories, 1912; Giacosa's Tristi amori, 1920; Bracco's Il Piccolo Santo, 1929. Translator; Sommi-Picenardi's Snow and Steel, 1926. Author: Deceptive Cognates, Italian-English and English-Italian, 1935; Sleuthing in the Stacks, 1944. Contributor numerous articles on Italian lit. to learned and lit. journals, also essays and poems to mags. Founder and editor, Italica, 1924-28, issued by Am. Assn. Teachers of Italian. Home: 129 Tamalpais Rd., Berkeley 8, Cal. Died May 13, 1953; buried Sunset View Cemetery, Berkeley.

ALTVATER, H(enry) Hugh, educator; b. Fowler, Mich., May 28, 1897; s. Henry H. and Mary Eva (Neurenberg) A.; A.B. and artist diploma, U. of Mich., 1920; Mus. M., hon., Southwestern Coll., 1925, Univ. Sch. of Music, Ann Arbor, 1929; studied in Paris and Fontainbleau, France, 1925 and 1928; m. Amelia Carolyn Miller, Nov. 27, 1919; children—Hubert Mark, Arnold Hugh. Head of violin dept. and dean Sch. of Fine Arts, Southwestern Coll., Winfield, Kan., 1920-36; condr. string choir, 1921-33, Winfield Oratorio Soc., Southwestern a Cappella Choir, 1932-34; state supervisor Federal Music Project of Kansas, 1935-36; dean of School of Music, Woman's College of University of North Carolina since 1936. Founder Greensboro Symphony Orchestra, 1939, and since served as conductor; condr. Greensboro Community Chorus since 1945; chmn. N.C. State Music Contest Festival system since 1937; contest adjudicator and guest condr. Served as examiner and past chmn. commn. on publicity Nat. Assn. Schs. of Music. Mem. Music Teachers Nat. Assn., Music Educators Nat. Conf., Am. String Teachers Assn., N.C. State Music Teachers Assn. (past pres.), Woman's Coll. Creative Arts Forum Com., Greensboro Civic Music Assn. (pres.), Fedn. of Music Clubs (past chmn. N.C. composers div.), Phi Beta Kappa, Pi Kappa Lambda. Lutheran. Composer: Three Portraits for Four Violins, 1924; (song) Break, Break, Break, 1924; (song) She Walks in Beauty, 1942; (song) Out in the Fields with God, 1942. Contbr. articles to professional publs. Home: 1205 Madison Av., Greensboro, N.C. Died Mar. 9, 1952.

ALWOOD, Olin Good, editor; b. Delta, O., Aug. 13, 1870; s. Rev. Josiah Kelley (D.D.) and Sarah Susanna (Hodges) A.; grad. High Sch., Morenci, Mich., 1888; student Hartsville Coll., Ind., 2 yrs., 1889-91; D.D. Huntington (Ind.) Coll., 1906; m. Mollie Leora Scudder, June 20, 1893; children—Mrs. Marjorie Luella Johnson, Ruth Athena, William Linford, Grace Elizabeth. Ordained ministry United Brethren in Christ Ch. (old constitution), 1892; pastor, Camden, Mich., 1892-94, Stryker, O., 1894-96, Pioneer, O., 1896-99, Blissfield, Mich., 1899-1902, Montgomery, Mich., 1902-03; presiding elder 1903-05; bishop charge Eastern, Southwest, Pacific and North dist. each one term, 1905-21. Trustee Huntington Coll. (Ind.). Editor Christian Conservator, 1921-25. Home: Huntington, Ind. Deceased.

AMBERG, Julius H. (am'berg), lawyer; b. Grand Rapids, Mich., Feb. 27, 1890; s. David M. and Hattie (Houseman) A.; A.B., Colgate U., 1912; LL.B. (Fay diploma), Harvard, 1915; hon. J.D., Detroit Coll. Law, 1940; m. Callie Sutherland Smith, Oct. 10, 1916; children—David M., Hazel F. Admitted to Mich. bar, 1915; clerk Butterfield & Keeney, Grand Rapids, 1915-16, partner, 1916—, firm name now Butterfield, Amberg, Law & Buchen; spl. asst. sec. war, Washington, 1941-45. Former pres. Grand Rapids Community Chest; chmn. Kent County Relief Commn., 1933-36; chmn. com. 100 (to study relief), 1932. Served as seaman 2d class, U.S. Navy, 1918, awarded Presdl. Medal for Merit, 1945. Mem. Mich. Bar Assn. (pres. 1939-40), Delta Upsilon, Phi Beta Kappa, Delta Sigma Rho. Democrat. Clubs: Kent Country, Univ. (Grand Rapids). Author articles on law and relief (awarded 1st prize for soc. work pub., Nat. Conf. of Soc. Work, 1935); formerly note editor Harvard Law Review. Home: 530 Madison Av., S.E. Office: Michigan Trust Bldg., Grand Rapids 2, Mich. Died Jan. 23, 1951.

AMBLER, Charles Henry, prof. emeritus; b. New Matamoras, O., Aug. 12, 1876; s. Lutellus and Ella Rebecca (Wells) A.; grad. West Liberty (W. Va.) State Normal Sch., 1900; A.B., W.Va. U., 1901, A.M., 1905; Ph.D., U. Wis., 1908; m. Helen Mary Carle, Sept. 4, 1920; children—Mary Elizabeth (Mrs. C. W. Lewis), Helen Louise (Mrs. Harold G. Godfrey). Prof. history, polit. science, Randolph-Macon Coll., Ashland, Va., 1908-17; prof. history W.Va. U., 1917-47, head dept. history, 1929-46; prof. summer sessions. U. Tex., 1918-20, 24; visiting prof. Ohio State U., 1928-29. Pres. Ashland (Va.) Sch. Bd., 1908-17, Monongalia County (W.Va.) Sch. Bd., 1933-39; sheriff Pleasants County, W.Va., 1900-01, Del. W.Va. legislature, 1951, 53. Mem. Am., So., Miss. Valley (pres. 1942-43) hist. assns., Sigma Nu, Phi Beta Kappa, Tau Kappa Alpha. Author: Sectionalism in Virginia from 1777 to 1861, 1910; Thomas Ritchie—A Study in Virginia of Politics, 1912; Life of John Floyd, 1918; A History of Transportation in the Ohio Valley with Special Reference to Waterways, 1932; A History of West Virginia, 1933; George Washington and the West, 1936; Francis H. Pierpont, Union War Governor of Virginia and Father of West Virginia, 1937; West Virginia Stories and Biographies, 1937; West Virginia, the Mountain State, 1940; A History of Education in West Virginia from Early Colonial Times to 1949; A History in West Virginia, 1951; Waitman Thomas Willey, 1954; West Virginia, the Mountain State, 1958; also pamphlets and articles. Editor: John P. Branch Hist. Papers, 1908-17; Letters and Papers of R. M. T. Hunter; Diary of John Floyd; Recollections of Peace and War, 1861-1868, by Ann Pierpont Siviter, 1938. Joint editor: Debates of First Constl. Conv. of W.Va. (3 vols.), 1943. Home: Morgantown, W.Va. Died Aug 31, 1957; buried Lawnwood Cemetery, Morgantown, W.Va.

AMBROSE, Arthur Warren, oil exec.; b. Lockeford, Calif., April 20, 1889; s. W. B. and Alice (Stephens) A.; A.B. in Geology, Stanford, 1914, E.M., 1920; m. Alma Locke, Apr. 9, 1916. Began in maintenance of way dept., Southern Pacific Co., 1907-09, geologist Shell Co., 1914-17; geol. Engr., Pomeroy & Hamilton, 1917; petroleum technologist, U.S. Bur. of Mines, Washington, D.C., 1918-19; supt. Petroleum Expt. Sta., Bartlesville, Okla., 1920; chief petroleum technologist, U.S. Bur. of Mines, Washington, 1921-22; asst. dir., 1922-23; mgr. Land and Geol. Depts., Empire Gas & Fuel Co., Bartlesville, 1923-25; mgr. prodn. Empire Cos., 1925-30; v.p. and asst. gen. mgr., Empire Oil & Refining Co., 1930-37; v.p. Cities Service Gas Co., 1937-44; v.p. and asst. gen. mgr. Cities Service Oil Co., 1937-41, exec. v.p. and asst. gen. mgr., 1941-46, pres. since 1946; p. pres. and dir. Cities Service Oil Co., Ltd., Toronto, Ont., since 1947, Cities Prod. Corp., since 1946, Cities Service Pipe Line Co. since 1946; dir. Petroleum Advisers, Inc., Empire Gas & Fuel Co., Cities Service Co., Texas-Empire Pipeline Co. (all Del.), Cities Service Petroleum Co., Am. Gas Production Company, Cities Service Oil Co., Union Nat. Bank, Prunty Prodn. Co., Terminal Facilities, Inc., Great Lakes Pipeline Co., Richfield Oil Corp., Am. Petroleum Inst. Dir. Y.M.C.A. Home: 300 E. 11th St. Office: Bartlesville, Okla. Died Dec. 28, 1952.

AMEND, Bernhard Gottwald, chemist; mem. firm of Eimer & Amend; v.p. German Exchange Bank; mem. N.Y. Acad. Sciences; N.Y. chpt. Am. Chem. Soc., N.Y. Mineralogical Club, Am. Chem. Soc. Residence: 120 E. 19th St. Office: 211 3d Av., N.Y.C. Died 1917.

AMES, Adelbert, Jr., educator; b. Lowell, Mass., Aug. 19, 1880; s. Adelbert and Blanche (Butler) A.; student Phillips Andover Acad., 1896-98; A.B., Harvard, 1903, LL.B., 1906; hon. A.M., Dartmouth, 1921, LL.D., 1955; m. Fanny Vose Hazen, Jan. 3, 1920; children—Adelbert 3d, Priscilla Vose. Admitted to Mass. bar, 1906, practiced law, 1906-10; studied art and painted, 1910-14; research fellow Clark U., Worcester, Mass., 1914-17; research prof. dept. re search in physiological optics Dartmouth, 1919-46; research prof. Dartmouth Eye Inst., 1946—; research dir. Inst. Asso. Research, Princeton. Served as aerial observer, U.S. Army, 1917-19. Recipient Egdar D. Tillyer medal Optical Soc. Am., 1955. Mem. Acad. Arts and Scis., Optical Soc. Am. Address: Rope Ferry Rd., Hanover, N.H. Died July 3, 1955.

AMES, Butler, ex-congressman; b. Lowell, Mass., Aug. 22, 1871; s. Adelbert (q.v.) and Blanche (Butler) A.; g.s. Gen. B. F. Butler; grad. U.S. Mil. Acad., 1894; apptd. 2d lt. 11th Inf., but resigned; B.A., Mass. Inst. Tech., 1896; unmarried. Engaged in mfg., 1896—; mech. and elec. engr. Was adj. 6th Mass. Vols., promoted col. after skirmish of Guanica and Yauco road, P.R. Mem. Lowell Common Council, 1896; mem. Mass. Ho. of Rep., 1897, 1898, 1899; mem. 58th-62d Congresses (1903-13), 5th Mass. Dist.; Republican. Address: Lowell, Mass. Died Nov. 6, 1954.

AMES, Edward Elbridge, mfg. exec.; b. Lowell, Ind., June 25, 1881; s. Edward P. and Nannie (Wason) A.; A.B., and hon. A.M., Wabash Coll.; m. Elsie Louise Russell, Sept. 28, 1904. Vice pres. and dir. sales, Gen. Box Co., Chicago, 1922-46, dir. 1946—, chmn. bd. until ret.; alumni sec. Wabash Coll. Mem. Linseed Oil Mfrs. Code Authority (past v.p.). Home: 416 W. Wabash Av., Crawfordsville, Ind. Died Sept. 28, 1952; buried Oak Hill Cemetery.

AMES, Edward Scribner, educator, clergyman; b. Eau Claire, Wis., Apr. 21, 1870; s. Lucius Bowles and Adaline (Scribner) A.; A.B., Drake U., 1889, A.M., 1891, LL.D., 1924; B.D., Yale Div. Sch., 1892; grad. student in philosophy, Yale, 1892-94; fellow in philosophy U. Chgo., 1894-95, Ph.D., 1895; m. Mabel Van Meter, July 6, 1893; children—Van Meter, Damaris (Mrs. Bernadotte E. Schmitt), Adelaide (Mrs. Harald Schade), Polly. Instr. Disciples Div. House, U. Chgo., 1895-97, docent philosophy, 1896-97, asso. in philosophy, 1900-01, instr., 1901-09, asst. prof., 1909-18, asso. prof., 1918-26, prof. 1926-35, chmn. dept. philosophy, 1931-35, emeritus, 1935—, dean Disciples Divinity House, 1927-45, emeritus, 1945—; pastor U. Church of Disciples of Christ, Chgo. 1900-40, emeritus preacher Harvard, 1912-14; editor The Scroll, 1925-51, Mem. Am. Psychol. Assn., A.A.A.S., Western Philos. Assn. (pres. 1921), Chgo. Hist. Soc., Art Inst. Chgo. (life), Mus. Natural History (life). Clubs: Quadrangle (president 1927), University, Chicago Literary. Author: Psychology of Religious Experience, 1910; Divinity of Christ, 1911; The Higher Individualism, 1915; The New Orthodoxy, 1918; Religion, 1929; Letters to God and the Devil, 1933; also beyond Theology: Autobiography, 1959. Also co-author: Varieties of American Religion, 1936; American Philosophies of Religion, 1936. Contbr. to Contemporary American Theology, 1933; The Church at Work in the Modern World, 1935. Home: 5834 Stony Island Av., Chgo. 37. Died June 29, 1958.

AMES, Jesse Hazen, ret. normal sch. pres.; b. Shiocton Wis., May 25, 1875; s. George Gordon Ames and Nancy D. (Main) A.; grad. State Normal Sch., Stevens Point, Wis., 1902; Ph.B., U. Wis., 1907; m. Lou I. Hitchcock, Jan. 1903. Tchr. pub. schs., Wis., 1895-97; supervising prin. high schs. and supt. schs. until 1910; head history dept., River Falls (Wis.) State Normal Sch., 1910-13; rep. extension div. U. Wis., 1913-15; supr. tng. sch. dept. River Falls State Normal Sch., 1915-17, pres., 1917-47. Mem. State Hist. Soc., Am. Hist. Assn. Conglist. Home: River Falls, Wis. Died Apr. 12, 1957; buried Greenwood Cemetery, River Falls.

AMES, John Griffith, educator; b. N.Y.C., Sept. 28, 1872; s. John G. and Elizabeth (Delano) A.; A.B., Johns Hopkins, 1894; B.Litt., Oxford U., Eng., 1899; post grad. work, Harvard; m. Elinor Kirk, Oct. 11, 1898; children—John G. III, Isabel (Mrs. James B. Overton), Desault Kirk, Elinor (wife of Dr. A. K. Rule). Instr. and asst. prof. English, Kenyon Coll., Gambier, O., 1895-97; became asst. prof. English, Ill. Coll., 1900, later prof. and head of dept., acting pres., 1929-30, 32-33. Mem. Phi Beta Kappa, Alpha Delta Phi. Republican. Episcopalian. Club: Rotary. Home: 1061 Grove St., Jacksonville, Ill. Died Apr. 29, 1945.

AMES, Louis Annin, mfr.; b. Island St. Helena, S.C., Sept. 5, 1866; s. Jacob Meech and Phebe (Palmer) A.; ed. pub. and high schs., Jersey City, N.J.; m. Abby Whitney Crowell, Jan. 20, 1909 (deceased). Pres. Annin & Co. (flag. mfrs.), Old Glory Realty Co., Annin Real Estate Company, North 16th St. Realty Company, Park Lane Realty Company. Democrat. Past pres. Universalist Church of America; trustee Grover Cleveland Birthplace Assn. Past pres. gen. Nat. Soc. S.A.R.; former gov.-gen. of Founders and Patriots of Am.; president Am. Friends of Lafayette; mem. Soc. Colonial Wars, S.R., Soc. Am. Wars, St. Nicholas Soc., N.Y. Hist. Soc., (life mem.). Mem. Chamber of Commerce of State of N.Y., Commerce and Industry Assn., of N.Y., Bd. of Trade, Fifth Avenue Assn. (dir), Broadway Assn., Nat. Aero Association, Washington Continental Guard, councilor Boy Scouts; trustee Universalist Pub. House, David Pierson Memorial Assn.; dir. and mem. Institute de Washington; life mem. Soc. Mechanicians and Traders. Life member Kane Lodge No. 454. Clubs: Aero, Kiwanis, Metropolitan, Military and Naval, Salmagundi, Universalist, Advertising (New York); Essex Fells Country. Home: Essex Fells, N.Y. Office: 85 Fifth Av., New York 3, N.Y. Died Nov. 28, 1952; buried Kensico.

AMES, Oakes, botanist, trustee; b. North Easton, Mass., Sept. 26, 1874; s. Gov. Oliver and Anna Coffin Ray A.; A.B., Harvard, 1898. A.M., 1899; Sc.D., Washington U., 1938; m. Blanche Ames, May 15, 1900; children—Pauline, Oliver, Amyas, Evelyn. Asst. in botany, Harvard, 1898-1900, instr., 1900-10; asst. dir. Bot. Garden of Harvard, 1899-1909, dir. from 1909-22; apptd. asst. prof. botany, Harvard, 1915, prof. botany, 1926-32, Arnold prof. botany, 1932-35, research prof. botany, 1935-41, research prof. botany, emeritus, 1941-—, curator Bot. Mus., Harvard, 1923-27; supr. Bot. Mus., Arnold Arboretum, Atkins Inst. Arnold Arboretum, Cuba (Harvard), 1927-35; dir. Bot. Mus., 1936-45, asso. dir., 1945-—, also chmn. Council Bot. Collections, Harvard, 1926-35; dir. 1st Nat. Bank of Easton. Awarded gold medal for eminent service to orchidology, Am. Orchid Soc., 1924; Centennial medal for same, Mass. Hort. Soc., 1929; George Robert White medal of honor for eminent service in horticulture, 1935. Fellow A.A.A.S., Linnaean Soc. London, Am. Acad. Arts and Scis., Am. Orchid Soc. (v.p.); mem. Am. Soc. Naturalists, N.Y. Acad. Scis, Nat. Inst. Social Scis., N.E. Bot. Club, Mass. Horticultural Soc., Boston Soc. Natural History, Washington Acad. Scis., Biol. Soc. Washington, Assn. Internat. des Botanistes, Orchid Circle of Ceylon, Canal Zone Orchid Soc. (hon. pres.), Sigma Xi. Unitarian. Club: Harvard. Author numerous papers mainly dealing with orchids, in botany periodicals, and contbrs. on orchid flora of Fla., serial work entitled "Orchidaceae" (7 vols.); also Enumeration of the Orchids of the U.S., Can., Economic Annuals and Human Cultures, 1939. Home: "Borderland," North Easton, Mass.; and Ormond, Fla. Office: 81 Ames Bldg., Boston. Died Apr. 28, 1950; buried North Easton, Mass.

AMES, William Lafayette, farmer; b. Dane County, Wis., Apr. 4, 1857; s. John N. and Mary A. (Ball) A.; student North Western Acad., Madison, Wis.; m. Julia A. Travis, Feb. 27, 1894. Engaged in farming at Oregon Wis. Mem. exec. com. Farmers' Nat. Congress, 1901-06, treas., 1906-13, elected pres., 1913, reëlected, 1915 (chmn. exec. com. 3 yrs.); hon. mem. Wis. Exptl. Assn.; v.p. Dane County Agrl. Soc.; 3d v.p. Farmers' Nat. Life Ins. Co.; dir. First Nat. Bank; active in promotion advanced methods in agr. and in community work. Home: Oregon, Wis. Died May 29, 1951; buried Mound Cemetery, Oregon, Wis.

AMEY, Harry Burton, lawyer; b. Pittsburg, N.H., Dec. 21, 1868; s. John Tillotson and Emily (Haynes) A.; A.B., Dartmouth, 1894; m. Garcia A. Norton, Apr. 1897 (died 1930); children—Henry T., Alpha N.; m. 2d, Harriet Hardy Bailey, Oct. 3, 1932. Admitted to N.H. bar, 1898, began practice at Milton; moved to Island Pond, Vt., 1902; states atty. Essex County, Vt., 1904-08, 10-12; mem. Vt. Ho. of Reps., 1910-12, mem. Vt. Senate, 1919, 20; U.S. dist. atty., Burlington, Vt., 1922-32; now practicing law. Mem. Vt., N.H. hist. socs. Republican. Unitarian. Mason (K.T., Shriner), Elk. Home: Box 33, Island Pond, Vt. Died Dec. 6, 1949; buried Indian Stream Cemetery, Pittsburg, N.H.

AMEZAGA, Juan José (ä-mä'sa-ga), pres. of Uruguay; b. Montevideo, Uruguay, 1882; s. Juan Jose and Josefa (Landaraso) A.; grad. with degree in law and social sciences, U. Montevideo, 1905; student scholarship, Paris and Berlin, 1906-07. Prof. penal law and later prof. civil law, U. Montevideo (taught civil law 23 yrs.); began pub. career, 1907; dep. Dept. Durazno, 1907-11; mem. com. to study and formulate nat. pub. assistance law, 1908; dir. Nat. Labor Office; minister of industry, 1915-17; became pres. State Ins. Bank, 1917, also Nat. Postal Savs. Bur.; chmn. Export and Import Control Commn.; assisted in drafting new constitution, 1942; pres. of Uruguay since Mar. 1, 1943. Rep. of Uruguayan govt. to League of Nations, Geneva, 1923. Del. Internat. Conf. Am. States, Buenos Aires, 1918, Santiago, 1923, Havana, 1928, Montevideo, 1933; del. Meeting of Jurists, Montevideo, 1939. Pres. Athenaeum of Montevideo; mem. Secondary Edn. Council, Nat. Pub. Assistance Bd., Bd. for Protection of Minors. Hon. dir. Law Sch. Library; mem. governing bd. House of Studies. Author numerous works on penal and civil Law. Address: Montevideo, Uruguay. Died Aug., 1956.

AMIDON, Beulah, editor; b. Fargo, N.D., Aug. 19, 1895; d. Charles Fremont and Beulah (McHenry) Amidon; A.B., Barnard Coll., 1915; student U. of So. Calif. and New Sch. for Social Research; m. Capt. Paul Grady Ratliff, Feb. 27, 1919 (died 1926); children—Beulah Curtis (Mrs. Thorold J. Deyrup), Philip Grady. Press sec. Nat. Woman's Party, 1916-17; spl. writer Com. on Pub. Information, 1917-18; feature and editorial writer, newspapers Non-partisan League, 1918-19; asso. editor The Survey, 1926-52; editor publs. The Twentieth Century Fund, 1952-54; now editorial staff member St. George's Church. Mem. bd. Public Affairs Com.; mem. Phi Beta Kappa. Episcopalian. Clubs: Barnard College; Pen and Brush. Editor: Windows on Henry Street, by Lillian D. Wald, 1934; Organized Labor and Production, by Morris Llewellyn Cooke and Philip Murray, 1940; Democracy's Challenge to Education by various authors, 1940. Author numerous mag. articles and pamphlets. Home: 450 E. 20 St., N Y.C. 9. Office: 206 E. 16 St., N.Y.C. Died Sept. 1958.

AMORY, William (ĕm'ĕr-ĭ), mfr.; b. Boston, Mass., Sept. 19, 1869; s. Charles Walter and Elizabeth (Gardner) A.; A.B., Harvard, 1891; m. Mary R. Stockton, Oct. 14, 1903. With Amory Mfg. Co., Boston, 1892-97, Amoskeag Mfg. Co., 1897-1907; treas., Boston office, Pepperell Mfg. Co., mfrs. cotton sheetings, flannels, shirtings, of Biddeford, Me., 1907-19, pres., 1919-48, chairman bd. since 1948. Served as lt., Battery A., 1st Arty., M.V.M., 1895-1904. Clubs: Somerset, Tennis and Racquet, Country. Home: 179 Commonwealth Av. Office: 160 State St., Boston, Mass. Died Jan. 16, 1954.

AMOSS, Harold L(indsay) (ā'mŏs), physician; b. Cobb, Ky., Sept. 8, 1886; s. David Alfred and Carolyn Waters (Lindsay) A.; B.S., State U. Ky., 1905, M.S., 1907; M.D., Harvard, 1911, Dr. P. H., 1912; hon. Sc.D., George Washington U., 1922; m. Marguerite Dupree Moore, May 17, 1917; children—Harold Lindsay, Dudley Moore. Chemist Ky. Agrl. Expt. Sta., 1905; asst. chemist Hygienic Lab., USPHS, 1905-07, Bur. Chemistry U.S. Dept. Agr., 1907-09; physiol. chemist Western Pa. Hosp., 1909; instr. preventive medicine and hygiene, Harvard Med. Sch., 1909-12; asst. in pathology and bacteriology, 1912-14, asso., 1914-19, asso. mem., 1919-22, Rockefeller Inst. Med. Research; asso. prof. medicine Johns Hopkins U. and asso. physician Johns Hopkins Hosp., 1922-30; prof. medicine, Duke, 1930-33. Cons. in medicine Greenwich, Grasslands, White Plains, United and No. Westchester Hosps. editor "Medicine," 1922-25. Commd. 1st lt. Med. R.C., 1915, capt. M.C. N.A., 1917; maj., 1918; honorably discharged, July 15, 1919. Chmn. Med. Adv. Bd. No. 5, Conn. Med. Adv. Food Panel. Mem. A.M.A., A.C.P., A.A.A.S., Assn. Am. Physicians, Assn. Am. Chest Physicians, Am. Soc. Clin. Investigation, Am. Soc. Exptl. Pathology, Am. Climatol. Soc., Am. Assn. Immunologists Am. Heart Assn., Harvey Soc., Interurban Clin. Club, So. Interurban Clin. Club, Sigma Xi, Phi Beta Kappa, Omicron Delta Kappa, Pi Kappa Alpha, Phi Chi. Independent. Episcopalian. Mason. Contbr. various articles on physiol. chemistry, infectious diseases, immunology, epidemiology and clin. medicine. Home: 68 Deerfield Dr., Greenwich, Conn. Died Nov. 2, 1956; buried Maplewood Cemetery, Princeton, N.Y.

AMSBARY, Wallace Bruce, lectr.; b. Pekin, Ill., Feb. 13, 1867; s. William Wallace and Harriet (Harlow) A.; m. Bertha Louise Margan, May 18, 1903; 1 dau., Dorothy Morgan. On stage, 1886-97; supported Marie Wainright, Thomas Q. Seabrooke and Nat Goodwin. Author: The Ballades of Bourbonnais, 1904; M'sieu Robin (legends, lyrics, ballads of Jean Baptiste and his friends), 1925. Lectures upon Kipling, Riley, The Folk Lore of Tolstoi, The Hunor of Shakespeare, The French-Canadian in Song and Story, Robert Louis Stevenson, William Sidney Porter (O. Henry), Jean Bateese and His Bretrhen, etc., Lyceum work, 1897-—; v.p. Internat. Lyceum and Chautauqua Assn. Profl. lectr. in gen. lit. Armour Inst. Tech., Chgo.; also Laughter and Life. Master of Writers' Guild Chgo., 1922-24. Mason. Clubs: Kiwanis, Forty (hon. mem. of both). Home: 4724 Greenwood Av., Chgo. Deceased.

ANDERES, Robert L., veterinarian; b. Kansas City, Mo., July 14, 1902; son of Otto L. and Hazel (Zick) A.; B.S., Kan. State Coll., 1925, D.V.M., 1934; m. Flo Catherine Busey, Mar. 18, 1939; children—Kay Sandra, Robert Lawrence. Practice of vet. medicine, K.C., Mo., since 1934; with dept. clin. medicine Jensen-Salsbery Labs., 1936-40; pres., treas. Vet. Med. Publ. Co., 1949-—, pub., editor Vet. Medicine, 1949-—. Served with Vet. Corps, AUS, 1940-46; col., Res. since 1946. Mem. Am. Vet. Med. Assn., Soc. for Animal Prodn., Mo., Kan., K.C vet medicine assns. Contbr. profl. publs. Home: 6509 Belinder Av., K.C. 13. Office: Livestock Exchange Bldg., K.C. 2, Mo. Died July 21, 1958; buried Johnson County Meml. Gardens, Johnson County.

ANDERSEN, Albert M., corp. exec.; b. Nevada, Ia., Dec. 13, 1898; s. Hans F. and Matilda (Mathison) A.; LL.D., Carthage Coll., 1956; m. Mary Jo Smith, June 16, 1928; 1 dau., Karin. With Reuben H. Donnelley Corp., Chgo., 1922-—, beginning as salesman, successively sales mgr., br. mgr., mgr. direct mail div., v.p., 1922-50, exec. v.p., 1950-—, also dir. Mem. adv. council U.S. Senate Post Office Com.; dir. Chgo. Area Project. Mem. president's council Carthage Coll. Mem. Asso. Third Class Mail Users (dir.). Clubs: Mail Advertising (dir.), Union League (Chgo.); Flossmoor (Ill.) Country. Home: 2448 Braeburn Rd., Flossmoor, Ill. Office: Prudential Plaza, Chgo. 1. Died Oct. 1959.

ANDERSEN, Arthur Olaf, composer; born Newport, R.I., Jan. 30, 1880; s. Anders and Helen (Monsen) A.; ed. Newport High Schs.; studied with Guiraud, Guillmant and Vincent d'Indy, Paris, Giovanni Sgambati, Rome, and Herman Durra, Berlin; Dr. Music, Am. Conservatory of Music, 1934; m. 2d, Helen Somerville, July 12, 1937. Began as teacher musical theory, 1904; head theory dept., American Conservatory of Music, 1929-34; head theory dept., director School of Music, U. Ariz. since 1934, dean coll. fine arts, 1934-52, now dean emeritus. Member National Music Teachers Association (chmn. ethics com. 1939), Ariz. Music Teachers Assn. (pres.), Am. Soc. Composers, Authors and Publishers, Nat. Collegiate Players, Phi Kappa Phi, Alpha Rho Tau, Kappa Kappa Psi. Democrat. Episcopalian. Clubs: Cliff Dwellers (Chicago); Old Pueblo (Tucson). Author: Harmony, First Forty Lessons, 1923, Second Forty Lessons, 1923; Musical Theory, Books I and II, 1926; Manual to Books I and II, 1929; Strict and Free Counterpoint, 1931; Practical Orchestration, 1929; Harmony, Modern Resources, 1938. Composer of 150 choruses, songs, etc Contbr. to music mags. Home: Catalina Foothills, Tucson, Ariz. Died Jan. 11, 1958; buried Evergreen Cemetery, Tucson.

ANDERSON, Andrew Runni; b. Norway, July 8, 1876; s. Hakon and Clara Marie (Lystad) A.; brought to U.S., 1884; ed. pub. schs. LaCrosse, Wis.; A.B., U. Wis., 1900; Ph.D., Harvard, 1903; m. Phoebe Margaret Van Hook, July 12, 1911; children—Laurens Van Hook, Norman La Rue, Marcia Lee. Instr. in Greek, U. Wis., 1904-05; preceptor in classics, Princeton, 1905-09; asst. prof. Latin, Northwestern U., 1909-15; prof. ancient langs. and lit., U. of Utah, 1915-29, prof. of Latin, Duke U., Durham, N C., 1929-—. Mem. Am. Philological Assn., Classical Assn. Middle West and South, Am. Assn. Univ. Profs., Soc. for Advancement of Scandinavian Study, Archaeol. Inst. America, Kappa Sigma, Phi Beta Kappa, Phi Kappa Phi. Conglist. Contbr. to Trans. Am. Philol. Assn., Classical Jour., Scandinavian Studies and Notes, etc. Home: Durham, N.C. Died July 8, 1936.

ANDERSON, Carlotta Adele (Mrs. J. Scott Anderson; maiden name Charlotte Augusta Bloss), educator, writer; b. N.Y.C., Mar. 15, 1876; d. Newell Willard and Emma Cathrine (Jones) Bloss; academic course, Claverack (N.Y.) Coll., 1893, postgrad. work, 1894; trained as oral teacher of deaf, Wright-Humason Sch., N.Y.C.; student Columbia, Swarthmore Coll.; B.S. in Edn., U. Pa., 1918, M.A., 1922; student Montessori method under Signora Galli-Saccenti, Rome; m. J. Scott Anderson, June 2, 1897; children—David Roy, Dorothy Scott. Tchr. Wright-Humason Sch., 1894-97; owner oral schs. for the deaf and tchr.-tng. schs., N.Y.C., Swarthmore and Torresdale, Pa., 1901-16; organizer, directress Torresdale House (All Saints' Ch.). 1st bldg. erected in Am. especially for Montessori work (tchr.-tng. Montessori, primary, grammar and high schs.), 1912-17; prin. academic dept., N. J. State Sch. for the Deaf, charge tng. tchrs. of the deaf. State Normal Sch., Trenton, N.J., 1918-21; tchr. in sight saving class, later of deaf, Phila. pub. schs., 1921-42. Several years hon. mem. Internat. Com. of Congresses on Home Edn. and Parent-Teacher Unions; del. 3d congress (Brussels, 1910), from U.S. Govt., Commonwealth Pa., City Phila. Mem. Am. Acad. Polit. and Social Sci., Am. Assn. to Promote Teaching of Speech to the Deaf, Swarthmore Women's Club, Phila. New Century Club, Pub. Edn. Assn. Founder, 1911, 1st pres. Swarthmore Safe and Sane Fourth of July Assn.; originator and sometime editor Dept. Home Training of the Young Deaf Child, Volta Review, Washington, D.C. Organized 1st symposium of physicians and instrs. of the deaf, Washington, 1910. Unitarian. Home: 174 Wellington Rd., Stonehurst, Upper Derby, Pa. Died Mar. 6, 1956; buried Arlington Cemetery, Drexel Hill, Pa.

ANDERSON, Donald Brown, judge; b. Cardston, Alberta, Can., Oct. 28, 1904; s. James H. and Lillie (Brown) A.; LL.B., U. Ida., 1927. Admitted to Ida. bar, 1927; practiced in Caldwell; probate judge Canyon County, Ida., pros. atty., Canyon County; spl. agt. FBI; spl. asst. U.S. atty. gen.; dist. judge 7th Jud. Dist., 1951-55; justice Ida. Supreme Ct., 1955-—. Mem. Ida., 7th Jud. Dist. bar assns. Home: 1902 Cleveland Blvd., Caldwell, Ida. Died Dec. 16, 1956.

ANDERSON, Douglas Smith, ret. elec. engr.; b. Lexington, Va., Sept. 6, 1871; s. John Randolph and Martha Adkins (Heiskel) A.; A.B., Washington and Lee U., 1890, D.Sc., 1933; M.A., Tulane U., 1892, LL.D., 1937; student U. Berlin, Zurich Poly. Sch.; m. Harriet Stetson Mason, June 14, 1898; m. 2d, Marjorie Harrison, 1942. Asst. prof. physics Tulane U., 1892-95, asso. prof. physics and elec. engring., 1896-99, asso. prof. elec. engring., 1901-14, became prof., 1914, dean Coll. Engring., 1919-36, dean emeritus, 1936—; prof. elec. engring. U. Miss., 1900-01. Dir. War Tng. Sch. for Radio Operators, Tulane U., World War. Fellow A.A.A.S.; mem. Am. Inst. E.E., Soc. Promotion Engring. Edn., La. Engring. Soc. (ex-pres.), Phi Beta Kappa, Phi Phi, Tau Beta Pi. Presbyn. Clubs: Cliff Country; Ogunquit (Me.). Home: Ogunquit, Me. Died Mar. 2, 1954.

ANDERSON, Dwight, publicist; b. Cleveland, O., Apr. 13, 1882; s. Alfred Travers and Harriet Emily (McGibeny) A.; student Western Reserve Academy, 1900-02, Ohio State U., 1902-04; LL.B., Wester Reserve U., 1906; m. Marie Lee Warner, Jan. 1, 1924. Publicity consultant Nat. Tuberculosis Assn., 1925-35; publicity consultant Maternity Center Assn., 1930-35; dir. pub. relations, Med. Soc. State N.Y., 1935-45, exec. sec., 1945-51; ret. 1951; dir. pub. relations Am. Assn. of Orthodontists, 1939-42; lecturer Yale Sch. Alcoholic Studies, 1943-45; consultant to various other sci., profl. welfare orgns. on relations with the public. Mem. Mil. Order of the World War, Soc. Med. Jurisprudence, Nat. Assn. Pub. Relations Counsel (chmn. 1942-43), became director of the National Association for Education on Alcoholism 1944; now council; Swedenborg Foundation, New York Fed. Grand Jurors Assn., Kappa Sigma. Clubs: University, Chemists, The Fossils (N.Y. City). Author: Making Things Happen in the Christmas Seal Sale, 1934-44; What it Means to be a Doctor, 1939; When Doctors are Rationed, 1942; Alcohol and Public Opinion, 1942; The Other Side of the Bottle, 1950. Named in his honor The Dwight Anderson Meml. Library on Alcoholism, established 1957. Home: Center Moriches, L.I., N.Y. Died Dec. 13, 1953.

ANDERSON, Edward Delmar, business exec.; b. LaPorte, Ind., Jan. 1, 1902; s. Edward O. and Ida (Anderson) A.; B.S. in mech. engring., Purdue U., 1924, M.E., 1930; m. Imogen Voorhees, Jan. 30, 1926; children—Mary Katherine, David Voorhees, Jean Adel. Vice pres. LaPorte Heat Corp. since 1945, Shore Line Shops since 1939; v.p., dir. No. Ind. Pub. Service Co. since 1938. Pres. Hammond (Ind.) Plan Commn.; mem. bd. trustees Purdue U.; chmn. Purdue Adv. Com. (Calumet area). Mem. Ind. Gas Assn. (dir.), Ind. Electric Assn. (dir.), Purdue Alumni Assn. Club: Kiwanis. Home: 6419 Forest Av. Office: 5265 Hohman Av., Hammond, Ind. Died Feb. 18, 1956.

ANDERSON, Ernest, ret. educator; b. Kaufman, Tex., Feb. 1, 1881; s. William Robert and Emily (Muckleroy) A.; A.B., Trinity Univ., 1902; B.S., Univ. of Tex., 1903, M.S., 1905; Ph.D., Univ. of Chicago, 1909; m. Lillian Hilliard, Dec. 25, 1907; children—William Ernest, Frank Hilliard. Research asst., Univ. of Chicago, 1909-12; prof. chemistry, Mass. State Coll., 1912-17, Univ. of South Africa, Pretoria, 1917-20, Univ. of Neb., 1920-23; prof. chemistry and head dept., U. Ariz., 1923-52, ret. 1952; temp. asso., Carnegie Inst., Palo Alto, California, summers, 1932-36; research asso., institute of Paper Chemistry, summers, 1941-48. Mem. Phi Beta Kappa, Sigma Xi, Phi Kappa Phi. Protestant. Contributor research articles on sugars and related carbohydrates to chem. jours. Home: 1930 E. Hawthorne St., Tucson, Ariz. Office: Dept. of Chemistry, Univ. of Arizona, Tucson. Died Feb. 19, 1954; buried South Lawn Meml. Park.

ANDERSON, Frank, ch. ofcl.; b. Wilmington, Del., Mar. 4, 1876; s. Andrew Peter and Clara Matilda (Johnson) A.; A.B., Bucknell U., 1901, A.M., 1903; student Crozer Theol. Sem., 1901-03; D.D., No. Bapt. Sem. Chgo., 1934; m. Anna H. Bergen, Sept. 23, 1901 (died Jan. 29, 1903); 1 son, Frank Bergen (dec.); m. 2d, Clara E. Bergen, June 10, 1908; children—Jeanette Irwin (Mrs. Edwin Richard Gustafson), Leona Mae. Ordained to ministry Bapt. Ch., 1901; pastor, Dividing Creek, N.J., 1901-04, First Ch., Millville, N.J., 1904-09, First Ch., Johnstown, N.Y., 1909-12; field sec. Baraca Bible Class movement, 1912-14; pastor, Collingswood, N.J., 1914-17, Watertown, N.Y., 1917-20; spl. work with N.Y. Sunday Sch. Assn., 1920-23; pastor, Ilion, N.Y., 1923-26; exec. sec. Ia. Bapt. Com., 1926-43; pastor First Bapt. Ch., Merrill, Wis., 1943—. County supt., N.J. State Christian Endeavor, 1904-08; boys' work dir. N.J. Sunday Sch. Assn., 1915-17; bd. mgrs. N.J. Bapt. Conv., 1916-17, N.Y. Bapt. Conv., 1918-19; bd. dirs. Northwestern Hosp. Assn., St. Paul, 1927—, N.W. Bapt. Home, Winnebago, Minn., 1928—; bd. trustees Sioux Falls Coll., No. Bapt. Sem.; pres. Anti-Saloon League Ia., 1936-43; mem. council finance and promotion, No. Bapt. Conv. Served as religious work dir., Camp Lee, Petersburg, Va., during World War. Mem. Phi Gamma Delta. Found. mem. Nu Chapter Phi Beta Kappa est. at Bucknell U., 1940. Mason. Club: Kiwanis (Des Moines). Author devotional booklets; contbr. religious jours.; tchr. in religious summer schs. Home: 403 N. Prospect St., Merrill, Wis. Died Mar. 1956.

ANDERSON, George Minor, physician, state health officer; b. Santa Rosa, Cal., July 12, 1873; s. Rev. John (D.D.) and Virginia (Drace) A.; A.B. and A.M., Central Coll., Fayette, Mo., 1898; student U. Mo., 1900; M.D., U. Chgo., 1903; postgrad. Sch. Pub. Health, U. Cal., 1938; m. Nancy Esther Holden, Jan. 5, 1903; children—Stephen M., Virginia Lewis (Mrs. James H. Carlisle), Dorothy (Mrs. Morrie Dowd). Intern Chgo. Lying-In Hosp., 1903; practiced medicine, Casper, Wyo., 1917-23; state health officer and sec. Wyo. State Bd. of Health, 1923—. Mem. bd. regents U. Denver, 1912-14. Mem. exec. com. Assn. State and Territorial Health Officers, 1937-38. Served as capt. M.C., U.S. Army, World War I. Mem. A.M.A., Wyo. State Med. Soc., Cheyenne Forum, Am. Legion, Sigma Nu. Democrat. Presbyterian. Home: 220 East 3d Av. Office: State Board of Health, Capitol Bldg., Cheyenne, Wyo. Died May 20, 1958.

ANDERSON, Harold Durbin, bus. exec.; b. East Liverpool, O., May 5, 1887; s. John Edwin Stanton and Maria Elizabeth (Bannon) A.; grad. East Liverpool High Sch., 1904; m. Cecile Jane Stewart, Dec. 12, 1912; children—Harold Durbin, William Stewart. Vice pres., sec., dir. Am. Gas & Electric Co., N.Y.C.; v.p., dir. Am. Gas & Electric Service Corp., Central Appalachian Coal Co., Kanawaha Valley Power Co., Ky. and W.Va. Power Co., Inc., Kingsport (Tenn.) Utilities, Inc.; v.p. Appalachian Electric Power Co., Duncan Falls (O.) Co., Ind. and Mich. Electric Co., Holston River Power Co., O. Power Co., W.Va. Power Co., Wheeling (W.Va.) Electric Co.; dir. Franklin Real Estate Co., Mem. Controllers Inst. Am. Rep. Presbyn. Mason. Clubs: Railroad-Machinery (N.Y.); Egypt Mills (Bushkill, Pa.). Home: Parker Rd., Chester, N.J. Office: 30 Church St., N.Y.C. Died June 23, 1950; buried East Liverpool, O.

ANDERSON, Harry William, corp. exec.; b. Cadillac, Mich., Dec. 25, 1891; s. Peter G. and Augusta M. (Benson) A.; LL.B., Detroit Coll. Law, 1913. With Union Title & Guaranty Co., Det., 1913-19; began with Gen. Motors Corp., Detroit, 1919, formerly v.p., now ret. Served in U.S. Army, World War I. Clubs: Detroit Golf; Recess; Detroit Athletic. Address: General Motors Bldg., Detroit. Died Nov. 18, 1959.

ANDERSON, Henry Watkins, lawyer; b. Dinwiddie County, Va., Dec. 20, 1870; s. Dr. William W. and Laura (Marks) A.; LL.B., Washington and Lee U., 1898, LL.D., 1916. Practiced at Richmond, 1898—, mem. Hunton, Williams, Anderson, Gay & Moore, 1901—. Rep. nominee for gov. of Va., 1921; apptd. trustee by U.S. Govt. for Armour and Swift interests in stock yards, 1921; special asst. to atty. gen. U.S., 1922-23; U.S. agent Mexican Claims Commn., 1924-26; counsel for receivers of Seaboard Air Line Ry., 1931-32, co-receiver, 1933-46; now chmn. bd. dirs. Seaboard Air Line R.R. Co. Mem. Nat. Commn. Law Observance and Enforcement, 1929. Pres. War Relief Assn. Va., 1915-17; chmn. Richmond chpt., dir. for Va., A.R.C., 1917; chmn. Roumanian Commn. Am. Nat. Red Cross, rank lt. col. in Roumania, fall of 1917-18; commr. of A.R.C. to Balkan States with rank lt. col., charge relief work there, Oct. 1918-Nov. 1919. Grand Comdr. Order of St. Sava, 1st Class, also 2d Class, and Red Cross (all of Serbia); Comdr. Order of Regina Maria, 1st Class, Cross Order of Regina Maria, 2d Class, Grand Officer Order of the Star, Comdr. of Crown, with swords (all of Roumania); Comdr. Royal Order of Saviour (Greece); Comdr. Order of St. Anne, with swords (Russia); Comdr. Order of Prince Danilo I (Montenegro); War Cross of Czechoslovakia; War Medal (Italy). Clubs: Commonwealth, Country of Va. (Richmond); Metropolitan (Washington). Home: 913 W. Franklin St., Richmond 20, Va., (country) Whippernock Manor, Sutherland P.O., Dinwiddie County, Va. Office: Electric Bldg., Richmond 19, Va. Died Jan. 7, 1954; buried Hollywood Cemetery, Richmond, Va.

ANDERSON, John, prof. civil engring.; b. Glasgow, Scotland, May 9, 1888; s. David and Marion (Millar) A.; came to U.S., 1898; naturalized 1918; student Franklin and Marshall Acad., 1902-04, Glasgow U., 1904-05; grad. Royal Tech. Coll., Glasgow, 1909; m. Elizabeth Franklin Thomas, June 24, 1924; 1 son, John Thomas. Rodman N.Y.C.&H.R. R.R., 1909-10; instrument man W. W. Young and Clyde Potts, 1910-13; junior mem. Kastenhuber & Anderson, civil engrs., 1913-19; asst. prof. of civil engring., The Citadel, Charleston, S.C., 1919-20, asso. prof., 1920-22, prof., 1922-57, acting head department of civil engring. 1952-53, head department civil engring., 1953-57, ret. Mem. Bd. of Adjustment, Charleston City Zoning Ordinance. Served as sergt., then 2d lt., C.A.C., 310th F.A., U.S. Army, 1917-19. Mem. Am. Soc. C.E., Am. Soc. Engring. Edn., S.C. Soc. of Engrs. (past pres.). Episcopalian. Address: 17 Moore Dr., Westwood, Charleston 42, S.C. Died Feb. 17, 1957; buried Old St. Andrews Churchyard.

ANDERSON, John (Ure), steel exec.; b. Youngstown, O., 1891; s. Hugh and Jane (Ure) A.; A.B., Williams Coll., 1914; m. Gertrude Woodcock, Jan. 4, 1919; children—Mary Jean, John Ure, Marjorie (Mrs. Robert Farr), Gertrude (Mrs. James Wimmer). Vice pres. finance Pitts. Steel Co. since 1942; dir. Nat. Fireproofing Corp., Pa. Bank Shares, Johnson Steel & Wire Co., Inc. Mem. Phi Beta Kappa, Delta Upsilon. Republican. Episcopalian. Clubs: Duquesne, Pitts. Athletic Assn., Oakmont Country (Pitts.); Williams (N.Y.C.). Home: Schenley Apts., Pitts. 13. Office: Grant Bldg., Pitts. Died Apr., 1953.

ANDERSON, John August, astronomer; b. Rollag, Minn., Aug. 7, 1876; s. Brede and Ellen Martha (Berg) A.; Concordia Coll., Moorhead, Minn., 1891-93; State Normal Sch., Moorhead, 1893-94; B.S., Valparaiso Coll., 1900; Ph.D., Johns Hopkins, 1907; m. Josephine Virginia Barron, June 9, 1909. Asso. prof. astronomy, Johns Hopkins, 1908-16; physicist at Mount Wilson (Cal.) Obs., 1916-43, retired 1949; exec. officer Obs. Council, Cal. Inst. Tech., 1928—. Asso. editor Am. Optical Journal. Mem. Am. Optical Soc., Am. Astron. Soc., A.A.A.S., Am. Seismol. Soc., Am. Phys. Soc., Am. Chem. Soc., Nat. Acad. of Sciences, Phi Beta Kappa. Club: University. Author: Absorption Spectra of Solutions (with H. C. Jones), 1908. Received Howard N. Pott's gold medal, Franklin Inst., 1924. Home: 978 E. Poppyfields Dr., Altadena, Cal. Died Dec. 1959.

ANDERSON, John Benjamin, clergyman, educator; b. Wisbech, Eng., Dec. 28, 1869; s. Joseph and Mary Jane (Thomson) A.; student Colgate Acad., 1886-89; A.B., Colgate U., 1896, B.D., 1899; postgrad. U. Berlin, 1906-07, U. Göttingen, 1907; D.D., U. Rochester, 1916; m. Rosena Downing Rowe, Apr. 5, 1899; m. 2d, Bertha May Shirley, June 20, 1925. Instr. ecclesiology and English Bible, Colgate Theol. Sem., 1900-06, asso. prof., 1906-08, prof., 1908-19, prof. N.T. interpretation, 1919-23, prof. Christian theology, 1923-28; prof. Christian theology and ethics Colgate-Rochester Div. Sch., 1928-36, emeritus, 1936—. Mem. Phi Beta Kappa, Delta Kappa Epsilon. Baptist. Author: Notes on Ecclesiology, 1901; New Thought—Its Lights and Shadows, 1911. Address: 417 E. Orange St., Lakeland, Fla. Died Oct. 17, 1952; buried Lakeland.

ANDERSON, John F., physician; born Fredericksburg, Va., Mar. 14, 1873; s. John Kerwin and Lucy Ella (Hundley) A.; ed. in pub. schs., Fredericksburg, Locustdale, Bowling Green, Va., and Washington; M.D., U. of Va., 1896; student Pathologische Institut, Vienna; Thompson Yates Labs., Liverpool, Eng., and Liverpool Sch. of Tropical Medicine, 1899-1901; m. Lucy Temple Hundley, Nov. 6, 1899; children—John Layton (dec.), Richard Hundley, Beverley Whiting (dec.). Asst. surgeon U.S.P.H. and Marine Hosp. Service, 1898; passed asst. surgeon, 1903; on epidemic duty in connection with yellow fever, 1898; quarantine officer Dry Tortugas, 1898-99; immigrant insp., Ellis Island, 1899; sanitary observer at Glasgow, Oporto and Liverpool, 1899-1900; sanitary attaché U.S. consulates-gen., Barcelona, Marseilles, Vienna, London and Liverpool 1899-1901; asst. dir. Hygienic Lab., Washington, 1902-09. dir. 1909-16; dir. research and biological labs., E. R. Squibb & Sons, 1916, also v.p.; vice-pres. chmn. bd. New Brunswick Savings Inst. Fellow A.A.A.S.; mem. Am. Assn. Pathologists and Bacteriologists (past pres.), Soc. Am. Bacteriology, Soc. Exptl. Medicine and Biology, A.M.A., Am. Pub. Health Assn. (past pres.), Assn. Am. Physicians, Phi Beta Kappa and Alpha Omega Alpha; Am. Drug Mfrs. Assn. (p.p.), S.A.R. Episcopalian. Author tech. articles. Home: 195 College Av., New Brunswick, N.J. Died Sept. 30, 1958; buried Rose Hill Center Cross, Va.

ANDERSON, John Murray, theatrical and motion picture dir.; b. St. John's, Newfoundland; s. John and Amelia (Murray) A.; student Edinburgh Acad., Scotland, and Lausanne U., Switzerland; m. Genevieve Lyon, 1914 (dec.). Came to U.S., 1910. Has written, devised, and staged more than 40 mus. comedies, revues, and spectacles, and numerous shows, masques and pageants for asso. producers; dir. in chief of presentations for Paramount-Publix Theatres, 1926-29; dir. Radio City Music Hall, N.Y., 1933; stage dir. Metro-Goldwyn-Mayer Pictures Corp., 1943. Served under George Creel in Bureau of War Information, World War I. Mem. Author's League of Am., Dramatists Guild, A.S.C.A.P. Presbyn. Author lyrics for about 50 songs for own productions, which productions include the six original Greenwich Village Follies, What's in a Name, Murray Anderson's Almanac in U.S., also in London, Eng., The League of Notions, Bow Bells, 1931, Fanfare, 1932, Home and Beauty (with Charles B. Cochran), 1937; created and directed first all-color mus. motion picture The King of Jazz, 1930; staged last edit. of Music Box Revue, Dearest Enemy (for asso. producers). Productions include Life Begins at 8:40, 1934; Jumbo, N.Y. Hippodrome, 1935; Ziegfeld Follies, 1934, 1936, 1943; Casa Manana revues Texas Centennial, Fort Worth, 1936-37; One for the Money, 1939, Two for the Show, 1940; The Aquacade, N.Y. World's Fair, 1939-40, and Golden Gate Exposition, San Francisco, 1940; Ringling Bros., Barnum and Bailey Circus, 1942-43, 47, 48, 49, 50, 51; Laffing Room Only, 1944; Three to Make Ready, 1946; New Faces, 1952; Two's Company, 1952; John

Murray Anderson's Almanac, 1953. Home: 15 Park Av., N.Y.C. 16. Died Jan. 30, 1954; buried Woodlawn Cemetery.

ANDERSON, Joseph Starr, investment banker; b. Rockford, Ill., May 25, 1884; s. Joseph Schuyler and Frances Deborah (Corson) A. Securities sales rep. W. C. Langley & Co., 1915-43, partner since 1943. Home: 140 E. 56th St., N.Y.C. 22. Office: 115 Broadway, N.Y.C. 6. Died Feb. 1, 1959.

ANDERSON, Karl, painter; b. Oxford, O., Jan. 13, 1874; s. I. M. and Emma (Smith) A.; ed. public schs., Art. Inst. of Chicago, and in Paris art schs.; m. Helen Edgerton Buell, Sept. 1, 1904; children—Alice Melissa, James Buell. Painted in Holland, Spain and Italy; exhibited in Paris Salon, St. Louis Expn., San Francisco Expn., N.A. and Society Am. Painters exhbns. Silver medal, Carnegie Internat. Exhbn., 1910, Lippincott prize, Pa. Acad. Phila., 1915; also first and second Altman prizes, Nat. Acad. of Design; French gold medal, Art Inst. Chicago; also gold medal Nat. Arts Club, New York, Isador prize, Salmagundi Club. Rep. in permanet collection of Art Inst. of Chicago, Nat. Arts Club, New York, Pa. Acad. Fine Arts, Phila., City Art Mus., St. Louis, Cleveland Art Museum, Art Museum, Detroit, Art Museum, Los Angeles, High Art Museum, Atlanta, Yale, Kenyon Coll., Boston Museum of Fine Arts; Art Mus., Houston, Tex., Nat. Assn. Portrait Painters. Illustrator for Scribner's Mag., Collierr's Weekly, Saturday Evening Post and other periodicals; has illustrated many books; has also painted numerous portraits; painted 2 murals for U.S. Govt. Nat. Academician. Mem. Nat. Soc. Mural Painters. Club: Nat. Arts. Home: Narrow Rock Rd., Westport, Conn. Died May 18, 1956; buried Westport, Conn.

ANDERSON, Louis Francis, prof. Greek; b. Morris, Ill., July 31, 1861; s. Alexander Jay and Maria Louisa (Phelps) A.; father 1st pres. Whitman Coll., 1882-91; A.B., U. of Wash., 1882, A.M., 1885; post-grad. work, Johns Hopkins, 1893-94, Columbia, 1913-14; Am. Sch. Archaeology at Athens, Greece, 1900, 1906-07; L.H.D., Whitman Coll., Walla Walla, 1922; m. Mabel Ida, Oct. 30, 1890 (died Aug. 16, 1915); m. 2d, Florence Mary Bennett, June 26, 1918. Instr. Latin and Greek, 1882-85, prof., 1885-93, prof. Greek, 1895-—, v.p., 1908-25, Whitman Coll., trustee, 1904-34; lay reader Missionary Dist. of Spokane, P.E. Ch.; corporate mem. A.B.C. F.M. Trustee St. Paul's Sch. for Girls, 1932-46. Mem. Am. Philol. Assn., Archaeol. Inst. Am. (v.p.; hon. sec. Walla Walla Soc.), Soc. Promotion Hellenic Studies (London), Nantucket, Ore. hist. socs., C. of C., Phi Beta Kappa, Beta Theta Pi; life fellow Am. Geog. Soc. Republican. Episcopalian. Clubs: Pacific, Winter (Nantucket, Mass.); Inquiry, (Walla Walla). Author: The Educational Value of Latin, 1939. Lectr., writer on classics and edn. Home: 364 Boyer Av., Walla Walla, Wash. Died Nov. 12, 1950.

ANDERSON, Maxwell, author, playwright; b. Atlantic, Pa., Dec. 15, 1888; s. William Lincoln and Premely (Stevenson) A.; B.A., U. of N.D., 1911; M.A., Stanford, 1914; m. Margaret Haskett, 1911 (died 1931); children—Quentin Alan Terence; m. 2d, Gertrude Maynard, 1933 (deceased 1953); 1 child Hesper; married 3d, Gilda Oakleaf, 1954. Taught school, N.D. and Calif.; instr. English department, Stanford, 1914; successively with Grand Forks (N.D.) Herald, San Francisco (Calif.) Chronicle and San Francisco Bulletin until 1918; editorial writer on New Republic, Evening Globe and Morning World, N.Y. City, until 1924. Mem. of the American Academy Arts and Letters. Author: (plays) White Desert, 1923; (with Laurence Stallings) What Price Glory, 1924; The Buccaneer, and First Flight (both with same), 1925; Outside Looking In, 1925; Saturday's Children, 1927; Gypsy, 1928; Gods of the Lightning (with Harold Hickerson), 1928; Elizabeth the Queen, 1930; Night over Taos, 1932; Both Your Houses (Pulitzer prize), 1933; Mary of Scotland, 1933; Valley Forge, 1934; Winterset (Critics' prize), 1935; The Masque of Kings, The Wingless Victory, High Tor (Critics' prize), 1936; Star-Wagon, 1937; Knickerbocker Holiday, 1938; Key Largo, 1939; Journey to Jerusalem, 1940; (1-act plays) The Feast of Ortolans; Second Overture; (poems) You Who Have Dreams; (essays) The Essence of Tragedy and others; Candle in the Wind, 1941; Eve of St. Mark, 1942; Storm Operation, 1944; Truckline Cafe, 1945; Joan of Lorraine, 1946; Anne of the Thousand Days, 1947; Lost in the Stars, 1949; Barefoot in Athens, 1951; Bad Seed, 1954; The Golden Six, 1958. Hon. cons. Am. Letters, Library of Congress, 1958. Home: 141 Downes Av., Stamford, Conn. Office: 1545 Broadway, N.Y.C. Died Feb. 28, 1959.

ANDERSON, Nelson Paul, physician; b. Galva, Ill., Oct. 2, 1899; s. Nels Frederick and Mary Winn (Williams) A.; B.S., U. of Chicago, 1923; M.D., Rush Med. Coll., Chicago, 1926; m. Dorothy Dederick, July 7, 1933; children—Paul Dederick, Maryanna. Interne, Cook County Hosp., Chicago, 1925-27; post grad. training New York Post-Grad. Med. Sch. and Hosp., 1927-30; pvt. practice of medicine, Los Angeles, Calif., 1930-—; instr. in dept. dermatology and syphilology Coll. of Med. Evangelists, Los Angeles, 1930-34, asst. prof., 1934-38, asso. prof., 1938-46; clinical prof. medicine, dermatology, U. of Southern California, 1946-54; chmn. staff, dept. dermatology and syphilology Los Angeles General Hospital, 1949-51. Diplomate Am. Bd. of Dermatology and Syphilology (pres. 1954, 55-57; dir.). Mem. A.M.A. (sec. sect. on dermatol. and syphilol., 1942-46, chmn. 1946-47), Am. Dermatol. Assn., Soc. Investigative Dermatol. Am. Acad. Dermatol. and Syphilology (pres. 1957), So. Calif. Med. Assn. (sec. 1942-47), Los Angeles Dermatol. Soc. (sec. 1933-34, pres. 1935), Cal. State Med. Assn. (sec. sect. on dermatology and syphilology, 1938, chmn. 1940), Pacific Dermatological Association (pres. 1952), Phi Beta Kappa, Alpha Omega Alpha. Home: 900 S. Longwood Av., Los Angeles 6. Office: 2007 Wilshire Blvd., Los Angeles 57. Died Dec. 1, 1957.

ANDERSON, Paul Lewis, photog. expert; b. Trenton, N.J., Oct. 8, 1880; s. Edward Johnson and Belle (Lewis) A.; E.E., Lehigh U., 1901; m. Mary Lyon Green, Aug. 22, 1910; children—Priscilla, Ruth. With Westinghouse Electric & Mfg. Co., Pitts., 1901; engring. and testing depts., Sprague Electric Co., Watsessing, N.J., 1902-04; engring. dept. N.Y. Telephone Co., 1904-07; a founder and mem. Struss-Anderson Labs., mfrs. "Kalogen" (photog. developer), of which was originator. Has exhibited photographs in leading cities of Am., also London, Hamburg and Budapest. Mem. Orange Camera Club (pres. 1938-40), Author's League Am. Author: Pictorial Landscape Photography, 1914; Pictorial Photography, Its Principles and Practice, 1917; The Fine Art of Photography, 1919; The Cub Arrives, 1927; Half-Pint Shannon, 1928; With the Eagles, 1929; A Slave of Catiline, 1930; For Freedom and for Gaul, 1931; The Knights of St. John, 1932; Swords in the North, 1935; Pugnax the Gladiator, 1939; The Technique of Pictorial Photography, 1939. Contbr. short stories to mags. Home: 27 Hillside Av., Short Hills, N.J. Died Sept. 15, 1956.

ANDERSON, Robert Campbell, clergyman; b. nr. Martinsville, Va., July 26, 1864; s. Robert Campbell and Justina Caroline (Armistead) A.; A.B., Hampden-Sydney Coll., 1887; grad. Union Theol. Sem., Va., Richmond, 1890; post. grad. Free Ch. Coll., U. Edinburgh, Scotland, 1895-96; D.D., Davidson (N.C.) Coll., 1923; m. Katie P. Walker, Dec. 24, 1890; m. 2d, Sadie K. Gaither, Nov. 11, 1896. Ordained to ministry Presbyn. Ch.; pastor San Angelo, Tex., 1890-92, 2d Ch., Roanoke, Va., 1892-97, Shelbyville Tenn., 1898-1905, 1st Ch., Gastonia, N.C., 1905-11; pres. Mountain Retreat Assn. (instn. Montreat (N.C.), home Gen. Assembly Presbyn. Ch. U.S. and Center of religious work), 1911-—; founder, 1916, since pres., mgr., treas. Montreat Coll. for Girls; designer, supr. Pub. Bldg. Montreat; del. Sesqui-Centennial Celebration, Presbyn. Ch. U. S.A., Phila., 1938. Trustee Davidson Coll. Recipient Algernon Sydney Sullivan medallion award Hampden-Sydney Coll. Va., 1939. Mem. Schoolmasters Club of Buncome County, Phi Gamma Delta, Pi Gamma Mu. Democrat. Mason (32°). Home: Montreat, N.C. Died Feb. 20, 1955; buried Elmwood Cemetery, Charlotte, N.C.

ANDERSON, Robert Gordon, author; b. Somerville, New Jersey; s. William Wallace and Mary (Davis) A.; student New York University in class of 1902; also studied for several years abroad; m. Marion Blake, 1911; children—Jean, Malcolm Gordon, Margot. Identified with various newspapers as reporter and columnist; with publishing houses as sales and promotion mgr. and as lit. adviser, 1911-23. Mem. Authors' League America, Delta Phi, The Players Club (N.Y.). Author: Not Taps But Reveille, 1918; The Little Chap, 1919; Leader of Men, 1920; Seven o'Clock Stories (juvenile), 1920; Half-Past Seven Stories, 1922; The Isle of Seven Moons, 1922; Eight o'Clock Stories, 1923; For Love of a Sinner, 1924; Over the Hill Stories (juvenile), 1925; Those Quarrelsome Bonapartes, 1927; An American Family Abroad, 1931; The Tavern Rogue, 1934; Villon (grand opera libretto and poem), 1937; The Biography of a Cathedral (The French edit. with forward by Archbishop Roger Beaussart deposited in Archives of Notre Dame Cathedral), 1944; The City and the Cathedral, 1948. Also contbr. to mags. and collaborator on several well-known books. Many titles pub. in fgn. editions. Home: 79 Summit Road, Port Wahhington, L.I., N.Y. Died Sept. 25, 1950; buried Somerville, N.J.

ANDERSON, Wells Foster, mfr.; b Tomah, Wis., July 14, 1902; s. Cassius Lionel and Laura Adele (Spaulding) A.; B.A., U. Wis., 1925; M.S., 1927, Ph.D., 1930; m. Eunice H. Avery, Sept. 28, 1929; children—Nancy Louise, Wells Avery, Susan Allis, Sally Eunice. Geologist Consol. Mining & Smelting Co., 1925-27; gen. tech. dir., mgr. gypsum operations U.S. Gypsum Co., 1929-44; gen. prodn. mgr. Reynolds Metals Co., 1944-50; v.p. Robertshaw Fulton Controls Co., 1950-51; v.p. mfg. Nat. Gypsum Co., Buffalo, 1951-54, v.p. operations, 1954-56, sr. v.p. operators, dir., 1956-—. Mem. Sigma Xi, Theta Delta Chi. Clubs: Buffalo Country, Buffalo. Home: 111 Brantwood Rd., Snyder, N.Y. Office: 325 Delaware Av., Buffalo 2. Died Sept. 21, 1958; buried Mount Albion Cemetery, Albion, N.Y.

ANDERSON, Wendell W., mfg. exec.; b. Detroit, May 27, 1901; s. John Wendell and Gustava (Doelitz) A.; B.A., Yale, 1922; m. Kathryn; children—John Wendell II, Wendell W., Mrs. Charles P. Sagar. Pres., treas. Bundy Tubing Co. 1929-—. Home: 211 Vendome Rd., Grosse Pointe Farms, Mich. Office: 8109 E. Jefferson Av., Detroit; also Penobscot Bldg., Detroit. Died Oct. 20, 1959.

ANDERSON, William A., judge; b. Adams Co., Wis., Oct. 19, 1873; s. Daniel and Cynthia E. (Harrison) A.; LL.B., Northwestern Coll. Law, 1914; m. Myra Blackmun, Nov. 25, 1897; children—Clara B. (Mrs. Walter W. Johnson), Wilbur A. Formerly pub. sch. tchr., employe paper co., grain buyer, auditor for orgn. of millers, v.p., sales mgr. for milling co., sec. Indsl. Commn., N.D.; asst. atty. gen., N.D., 1921; mem. Bd. Park Commrs., Mpls., 1917-19; mayor Mpls., 1931-33; was mem. firm Ellsworth, Clinite, Anderson, Dills & Dahl; v.p. Mpls. Artificial Limb County; mem. faculty Mpls. Coll. Law; spl. investigator for Minn. Tax Commn., atty. for Income Tax Dept. of Minn. Tax Commn., 1933-36; apptd. judge of Municipal Ct. of Mpls., 1936, elected for term of 6 years, 1937; elected judge Dist. Ct. of Hennepin County, Minn., Nov. 3, 1943, for term of 6 years. Mem. Am., Hennepin County bar assns., Hennepin County Bar Assn., Modern Woodmen Am., Sons of Norway, Ind. Order of Foresters. Methodist. Clubs: Commonwealth, Business and Professonal Men's, Saturday Lunch. Home: 1835 Morgan Av. N. Office: 234 Court House, Mpls. Died Dec. 12, 1954.

ANDERSON, William D(ickson), mfr. cotton goods; b. nr. Marietta, Ga., July 9, 1873; s. William Dickson and Louisa J. (Latimer) A., A.B., U. of Ga., 1891; studied law in office of R. N. Holland, Marietta; m. Linda M. McKinney, Dec. 12, 1897; children—Linda Katherine (Mrs. Van McKibben Lane), William Dickson (deceased); married second Jennie Loyall Anderson. Admitted to the bar, and practiced at Marietta; became salesman for Marietta Paper Mfg. Co., later supt. and gen. mgr.; began with Bibb Mfg. Co., as salesman, now chmn. bd. Chmn. 1st Bd. of Regents, University System of Georgia. Served as 2d lt. Marietta Rifles. Mem. Phi Beta Kappa. Methodist. Clubs: Idle Hour, Satilla River (Macon); Merchants (N.Y.). Home: 2545 Vineville Av., Macon, Ga. Died Jan. 20, 1957; buried Riverside Cemetery, Macon.

ANDERSON, William Hamilton, assn. exec.; b. Carlinville, Ill., Aug. 8, 1874; s. William E. P. and Nellie (Hamilton) A.; B.S., Blackburn Coll., Carlinville, 1892; LL.B., U. Mich., 1896; LL.D., Ill. Wesleyan U., 1919; m. Clarice Otwell, Oct. 23, 1901 (dec. 1947); children—Frederick Otwell, Elinor Hamilton. Taught sch., 1892-94; practiced law, Carlinville, 1896-1900; became atty. Anti-Saloon League of Ill., 1900, state supt. 1900-06; drafted the Ill. local option law and federated the chs. of the state into orgn. that secured its passage; asso. supt. N.Y. Anti-Saloon League, 1906-07; state supt. Anti-Saloon League of Md., 1907-14; gen. state supt. Anti-Saloon League of N.Y., 1914-24; secured from N.Y. new congressional votes necessary to submit 18th Amendment and built up state orgn. that ratified it and passed N.Y. State dry enforcement law. Acting legislative supt. of Anti-Saloon League Am., 1909. Mem. exec. and legislative com. Anti-Saloon League Am., 1912-24; mem. exec. com. World League Against Alcoholism, 1920-24. Lay mem. Gen. Conf. M.E. Ch., 1904, 08, 12, 20, and sec. temperance com. each time; chmn. legislative com., 1904-16, and nat. legislative supt., 1912-16, and chmn. com. on public policy, 1919-24, Bd. of Temperance, Prohibition and Pub. Morals, M.E. Ch. "Indicted July 1923 by the Tammany he had defeated on the liquor issue, in proceeding unamimously denounced by the Anti-Saloon League bd. of dirs. as 'a monstrous perversion of justice,' for an 'alteration' of the League books which the dirs. and their auditors had officially approved; convicted 1924, and sent to state prison for nine months, covering the Madison Sq. Garden Dem. Nat. Conv. and the 1924 presdl. election"; founded Am. Christian Alliance, gen. sec. 1926-—, now dir. gen; originated a proposed "Citizen Representation" amendment to the U.S. Constitution (pending 1951), to cut aliens from population count for membership U.S. House of Reps. Mason (32°). Author: The Church in Action Against the Saloon, 1906, 2d edit., 1910; The "Yonkers Plan" for Prohibition Enforcement, 1921; Am. Christian Alliance, 1955. Home: 65 Elliott Av., Yonkers 5, N.Y. Office: 41 E. 42d St., N.Y.C. 17. Died Sept. 4, 1959; buried Carlinville, Ill.

ANDERSSON, Alfred Oscar; b. Liverpool, Eng., dec. 10, 1874; s. Alfred Carolus and Elizabeth A. (Falk) A.; brought to U.S., 1888; prep. edn. in Eng., Germany and Central High Sch., Kansas City, Mo.; student Princeton, 1893-95; m. Dorothy W. Smart, 1900 (died 1911); 1 dau., Dorothy Elizabeth (Mrs. Harry G. Kraus); m. 2d, Ruth H. Harper, June 21, 1913; children—Alfred Chandler, Alice Ellen (wife of Col. J. H. N. Hudnall, Marine Corps), Ruth (Mrs. Lewis L. May). Reporter, subeditor, Kansas City, St. Louis, Chgo., 1895-1906; war corr., Cuba and Puerto Rico, 1898; established

Dallas Dispatch, 1906; Houston Press, 1911; former pres. Dallas Dispatch Co., Houston Press Co., Memphis Press Co., Denver Express Co., Newspaper Enterprise Assn., Dispatch-Journal Co., Dallas; ret. 1938. Episcopalian. Clubs: Town and Gown, Athletic, Dallas Country, La Jolla (Cal.) Country. Home: 5023 Lilac Lane, Dallas 9. Office: Liberty Bank Bldg., Dallas. Died May 11, 1950.

ANDRESEN, August Herman, congressman; b. Newark, Kendall County, Ill. Oct. 11, 1890; s. Rev. Ole and Anna (Lunke) A.; B.A., Red Wing (Minn.) Sem., 1912; B.A., St. Olaf Coll., Northfield, Minn., 1912; B.L., St. Paul Coll. of Law, 1915; m. Julia Lien, Aug. 12, 1914. Spl. investigator and prosecutor Minn. Railroad and Warehouse Commn., 1913-15; admitted to Minn. bar, 1914; practiced law in Red Wing since 1915; Rep. County chmn., Goodhue County, 1916-20; mem. 69th to 72d Congresses (1925-33), 3d Minn. Dist. and 74th to 85th Congresses First Minn. District Member Minn. Home Guard, 1917-20. Pres. Red Wing Chamber Commerce, Red Wing Fair Assn., Goodhue County Soldiers' Memorial Assn. and Red Cross. Lutheran. Home: Red Wing, Minn. Died Jan. 14, 1958; buried Red Wing, Minn.

ANDREW, Hardage L., business exec.; b. Boonville, Mo., Oct. 25, 1889; s. Charles E. and Jennie (Dobyns) A.; B.S., U. Mo.; m. Mitte Huff, Jan. 12, 1917; children—Hardage L., John Hampton. Test dept. Gen. Electric Co., Schenectady, N.Y., 1910-13, ry. motor design dept., 1913-17, ry. traction engine dept., 1917-27, asst. engr. ry. and traction, 1927-29, chief engr. ry. and traction, 1929-34, v.p. charge ry. electricity N.Y., 1934-39, charge appliance and mdse. dept., Bridgeport, 1939-50, exec. v.p. Gen. Electric Co., N.Y., 1950-51; pres., dir. Jones & Lamson Machine Co., Springfield. Vt., since 1953; dir., mem. exec. com. Manning-Maxwell & Moore, Bridgeport. Mem. Advisory Council, Dept. of Defense. Mem. Am. Inst. E.E., N.A.M. (mem. bd. of govs.), A.S.M.E., Nat. Investment Soc., Newcomb Society. Mason. Clubs: Brooklawn Country (Bridgeport); Mohawk (Schenectady, N.Y.). Home: Collingwood Rd., Bridgeport, Conn. Office: Jones & Lamson Machine Co., Springfield, Vt. Died Aug. 4, 1955.

ANDREWS, Avery DeLano, lawyer, ret. army officer; b. Massena, N.Y., Apr. 4, 1864; s. Hannibal and Harriet (DeLano) A.; Williston Sem., 1881-82; B.S., U.S. Mil. Acad., 1886; served as 2d and 1st lt. U.S. Army, resigned 1893; LL.B., Columbian (now George Washington) U., 1891; LL.B., N.Y. Law Sch., 1892 (apptd. prize tutor); m. Mary C. Schofield, Sept. 27, 1888; children—Schofield, DeLano. Began practice at N.Y.C., 1891; became gen. counsel Barber Asphalt Paving Co., 1897, v.p., 1902, and later also of Gen. Asphalt Co., Uintah Ry. Co., and other associated corps.; Am. rep. Royal Dutch Petroleum Co. of Holland and Shell Trading & Transport Co. of London, and chmn. bds. of various subsidiaries, 1919—; dir. Irving Trust Co. (N. Y.C.), Central Nat. Bank (Phila.), others. Police commr., N.Y.C., 1895-98. Maj. and staff engr. officer 1st Brig., 1893-98; maj. comdg. Squadron A N.Y. N.G. to Jan. 1899; adj. gen. N.Y. and chief of staff to Gov. Roosevelt, Rank of brig. gen., 1899; lt. col. U.S. Vols., Spanish-Am. War, Camp Thomas, Tenn.; dir. mil. service of Com. of Safety of Pa., 1917; col. Engrs. U.S. Army, with AEF in France, 1917-19, dep. dir. gen. transportation, 1917-18; dep. chief of utilities, Mar.-1918; dep. asst. chief of staff, Hdqrs. S.O.S., until 1918; duty with 1st sect., Gen. Staff, Gen. Hdqrs. AEF; apptd. chief of 1st sect. Gen. Staff, and asst. chief of staff to Gen. Pershing, Aug. 1918; promoted brig. gen., Gen. Staff, Oct. 1918; brig. gen. O.R.C., U.S. Army, Apr. 7, 1921. Decorated D.S.M. (U.S.); Comdr. Legion of Honor (France); Comdr. Order of Crown (Belgium and Italy). Dir. Am. Soc. of the French Legion of Honor. Mem. Soc. Fgn. Wars, Mil. Order World War, Assn. Grads. U.S. Mil. Acad. Trustee George Washington U., Grant Monument Assn. Clubs: Century, University, Church (N.Y.C.); Army and Navy (Washington). Author: My Friend and Classmate, John J. Pershing, 1939. Home: 500 Interlachen Av., Winter Park, Fla. Retired. Died Apr. 19, 1959.

ANDREWS, Bert, newspaperman; b. Colorado Springs, Colo., June 2, 1901; s. Bertrand A. and Laura (Whitaker) A.; student Stanford U., 1921-24; m. Martha Nadine Wright; children—John Wright, Peter Ferguson. Reporter Sacramento (Calif.) Star, 1924-25; successively reporter, city editor and columnist San Diego Sun, 1925-27; reporter Chicago Herald Examiner, Dec. 1927-Feb. 1928, Detroit Times, 1928-29, Paris (France) Herald, July-Dec. 1929, New York American, 1930-37; asso. with New York Herald Tribune since 1937, chief Washington corr. since 1941. Recipient Raymond Clapper Award, 1945; winner Pulitzer Prize, 1947, for Washington correspondence; winner, Heywood Broun Award, 1947; New York Newspaper Guild, 1947. Mem. Beta Theta Pi. Clubs: Gridiron, Nat. Press, Overseas Writers (Washington). Author: Washington Witch Hunt, 1948. Home: 2636 16 St. N.W. Office: National Press Bldg. Washington, D.C. Died Aug. 21, 1953; buried Cedar Hill, Washington.

ANDREWS, Charles Edgar, Jr., banker; b. New Bethlehem, Pa., June 22, 1881; s. Firman L. and A. Blanche (Craig) A.; A.B., cum laude, and hon. mention in economics, Harvard, 1904; m. Marjorie Edinger, Aug. 13, 1928. Financier and corp. exec., 1905—; chmn., dir. Charles E. Andrews, Jr. & Co. (personal holding Co., New Bethlehem), The Meadow River Lumber Co. (Rainelle, W.Va.); v.p. dir. C. E. Andrews Lumber Co., Andrews Real Estate Co. (New Bethlehem); dir., chmn. New Bethlehem office adv. bd. First Seneca Bank and Trust Co. (Oil City, Pa.); dir. The Meadow River Coal and Land Co., Citizens Water Co. Republican. Baptist. Clubs: Duquesne (Pitts.); Harvard (N.Y.C.); Surf (Miami Beach, Fla.). Home: 312 Penn St., New Bethlehem, Pa. Died Oct. 14, 1958; buried New Bethlehem.

ANDREWS, Eliphalet Frazer, portrait painter; b. Steubenville, O., June 11, 1835; s. Alexander Hull and Eliza Ann (Frazer) A.; grad. Marietta (O.) Coll., 1853; student art in Europe under Ludwig Knaus, and at Düsseldorf Acad.; m. Emma Stewart, 1857 (died 1889); m. 2d, Marietta Minnigerode, Sept. 25, 1895. Went to Washington, 1877; under patronage W. W. Corcoran, founded the Corcoran Sch. Art, 1877, was dir., 1877-1902; represented by portraits of Martha Washington, Jefferson, Buchanan, Jackson, Taylor, Johnson and Garfield, in the White House; also represented in various pub. and pvt. collections U.S. and abroad. Club: Metropolitan. Address: Theological Seminary, P.O., Va. Died May 30, 1932; buried Steubenville, O.

ANDREWS, Fannie Fern (Phillips), author, publicist; b. Margaretville, N.S.; d. William Wallace and Anna Maria (Brown) Phillips; grad. Salem (Mass.) Normal Sch., 1884; studied Harvard Summer Sch., 2 summers; A.B., Radcliffe, 1902, A.M., 1920, Ph. D., 1923; m. Edwin G. Andrews, July 16, 1890 (died 1935). Lectr. Am., Europe on European diplomacy; sec., organizer Am. Sch. Citizenship League, 1908; organizer, pres., 1914-18, Boston Home and Sch. Assn.; special collaborator U.S. Bur. Edn., 1912-21; rep. U.S., The Netherlands Govt. (1912-13) in interests of Internat. Conf. on Edn.; apptd. by Pres. Wilson to represent U.S. at Internat. Conf. Edn. (The Hague), Sept. 1914; rep. of U.S. at Com. of Jurists at The Hague, 1915, mem. exec. com. of same and internat. corr. sec., 1915-23; apptd. by Pres. Wilson to Peace Conf., Paris, 1919; del. Internat. Council Women, Conf. Women Suffragists Allied Countries, Paris, 1919; apptd. by late William Howard Taft, rep. League to Enforce Peace, Allied Conf., Peace Conf., Paris, 1919; addresses League of Nations Commn. on plan for Internat. Bur. Edn., Paris, 1919; mem. Internat. Bur. Edn., Geneva, 1929—; apptd. by Pres. Roosevelt, rep. U.S. at 3d Internat. Conf. Pub. Instrn., 1934, wrote ofcl. report for State Dept. lectured results of investigations, apptd. by Pres. Roosevelt 5th Conf., 1936. Made trip through Egypt and Near East to study mandatory system, 1925; made investigation of European diplomacy in ten countries, 1936, 37, 38. Trustee Radcliffe Coll., 1927-33; mem. exec. com. Yugoslav Relief Fund Boston. Fellow Am. Geog. Soc.; mem. Nat. Inst. Social Scis., Am. Acad. Polit. and Social Sci., Am. Soc. Internat. Law, A.A.A.S., Am. Polit. Sci. Assn., Boston League Women Voters, N.E. Woman's Press Assn., U.N. Assn., Am. Assn. U. (pres. Boston br. 1923-25; chmn. internat. relations com., 1925-32), English-Speaking Union, Nat. Com. on Prisons and Prison Labor, Boston Br. Fgn. Policy Assn. (program com. 1926-27, mem. council 1926—), Nat. Edn. Assn., Nat. Council Social Studies World Center for Women Archives, Nat. League Am. Pen Women (v.p. Boston br., 1941-42), Women's Internat. Week, Budapest, Phi Beta Kappa (pres. Iota of Mass. 1929-32; chairman committee on encouragement of scholarship, 1925-29; elected Phi Beta Kappa Assos., 1942), Bostonian Soc. Clubs: Twentieth Century, College, Authors (Boston); Women's Republican of Mass.; American Univ. Women's Paris Club; Ried Hall; Nat. Club of Am. Assn. Univ. Women (Washington). Author: The War—What Should Be Said About It in the Schools?, 1914; The Central Organization for a Durable Peace 1915; Freedom of the Seas, 1917; Course in Foreign Relations (prepared for Army Edn. Commn., Paris), 1919; The Mandatory System after the World War (thesis), 1923; The Holy Land Under Mandate (2 vols.), 1931; Memory Pages of My Life. Editor: American Citizenship Course in U.S. History, with Type Studies (5 vols.), 1921; Official Report of the Third Internat. Conf. on Public Instruction (for State Dept.), 1934; Education of the Jewish and Arab Population in Palestine, 1934. Writer Assos., many articles in mags. and profl. jours. Visted "danger spots" in Europe, 1938, assisted by Am. Foreign Service. Now studying the diplomacy of World War II. Presented her research and personal library to Harvard, 1942. Home: 100 Highland Av., Somerville, Mass. Died Jan. 23, 1950.

ANDREWS, John, clerk U.S. House Reps.; b. Salem, Mass., Sept. 18, 1894; s. John Joseph and Catherine F. (Stanton) A.; ed. Salem pub. schs. and Comml. Sch.; student Nat. U., 1922-25; m. Catherine R. Spaight, Sept .12, 1945. Clerk Ho. Reps., 80th Congress, 1947-49. Served with U.S. Army, 1918-19. Mem. Am. Legion. Republican. Roman Catholic. Elk. Home: 12 Hodges Court, Salem, Mass. Office: U.S. Capitol Bldg., Washington 25. Died May 22, 1950.

ANDREWS, Lincoln Clark, ret. army officer; b. Owatonna, Minn., Nov. 21, 1867; s. Charles T. and Mary (Clark) A.; student Cornell U., 1888-89; grad. U.S. Mil. Acad., 1893; m. Charlotte Graves, Oct. 5, 1899; 1 son, John Graves. Commd. 2d lt., 3d Cav., June 12, 1893; promoted through grades to lt. col., June 28, 1917; served as brig. gen., U.S. Army, Aide to Gen. Sumner, comdg. cav. div., Battle of Santiago, 1898; instr. physics, U.S. Mil. Acad., 1899; in Philippines, 1899-1903; 1st gov. Island of Leyte; participated in campaign against Lake Lanoa Moros; instr. cav. tactics, U.S. Mil. Acad., 1903-06; in Cuba, 1908-09; insp., instr. cav. N.Y. Nat. Guard, 1911-15; charge cav. instrs. 1st Plattsburg (N.Y.) Tng. Camp, 1915; duty, Philippines, 1916-17; insp. gen. and charge tng. and instrn. of officers P.I. Div. Nat. Guard; col. inf., Camp Dix, N.J., organized 3rd O.T.C., Dec. 1917, 304th Cav., U.S. Army, Leon Springs, Tex., Feb. 1918; brig. gen. 172d Inf. Brigade, 86th Div., Camp Grant, Ill.; took brigade to France, Aug. 1918; after armistice served as dep. provost marshal gen. at G.H.Q. till end of orgn.; ret. from active service at own request after 30 yrs. service, Sept. 30, 1919. In charge mil. tng. N.Y. State Universal Tng. Commn., Nov. 1920-May 1921; chief exec. N.Y. Transit Commn., May 1921-Jan. 1923; apptd. to receivership N.Y. and Queens County Ry. Co., 1923; asst. sec. of treasury, Apr. 1, 1925-Aug. 1, 1927; pres. Guradian Investment Trust, Hartford, Conn., Nov. 1, 1927-June 1928; pres. The Rubber Inst., Inc., June 1928-May 15, 1929; became chmn. bd. Internat. Development Corp., 1930. Author: Basic Course for Cavalry, 1914; Fundamentals of Military Service, 1916; Leadership and Military Training, 1918; Man Power, 1921; Military Man Power, 1921. Address: Grand Isle, Vt. Died Nov. 23, 1950.

ANDREWS, Roger Mercein, newspaper pub.; b. Stamford, Conn., Apr. 2, 1874; s. Joseph Ferry and Mary Mercein (Barry) A.; ed. Mohegan Lake Sch., Peekskill, N.Y., Centenary Collegiate Inst., Hackettstown, N.J., Yale Law Sch.; m. Mary Theresa Erdlitz; children—Charles H., Lucy H. (Mrs. R. B. Davy), Roger M., Marjorie M. (Mrs. Eugene C. Marble), Marion R. Began as free lance reporter, Washington, 1894; purchased Menominee (Mich.) Herald-Leader, 1901; served as pres. and pub. Detroit Times; pub. Cloverland Mag.; v.p. Citizens Nat. Bank, Los Angeles, 1923-25, Bank of America, San Diego, Cal., 1925-27; dir. Chgo. Herald & Examiner, Milw. Sentinel and News. Mem. Council Nat. Defense (labor com.), 1917-18; col. on staff of Gov. A. E. Sleeper of Mich., 1917-18. Commr. of mineral statistics, Mich., 1907-10. Pres. Mackinac Island (Mich.) State Park Commn. Ex-pres. Mich. Editorial Assn. Home. Mem. Soc. Colonial Wars, S.A.R. Mason (32°, K.T., Shriner), Elk, K.P. Clubs: Internat. Rotary (former dir.); Detroit, Detroit Athletic, Players, Detroit Golf; Union League (Chgo.). Home: Menominee, Mich. Died Aug. 9, 1943.

ANDREWS, Steffan, newspaperman; b. Mar. 25, 1914; s. Jan and Katharine (D'zurilla) A.; A.B., Western Reserve U., Cleveland, 1936, LL.B., 1939; M.S., Columbia U., 1940. Admitted to Ohio bar, 1939. Reporter Salt Lake Telegram, 1940-41, Pittsburgh Post-Gazette, 1941-42; Cleveland Plain Dealer, 1942-43, Wash. corr., 1943-44; war corr. China, Burma, India, Mongolia, Manchuria and Japan, N. Am. Newspaper Alliance and Cleveland Plain Dealer, 1944-46; Wash. corr. N. Am. Newspaper Alliance, 1946-53, chief Wash. Bur. since 1946; fgn. corr. in Venezuela, 1949, Formosa, Japan and intermittently the Philippines, 1950, Italy and France, 1951, England and Germany part of 1952. Assistant professor, Graduate School of Journalism. Columbia Univ., Chungking, China, 1944, 45; writer syndicated column The Washington Angle, since 1946. Awarded Warion Trophy, Western Reserve University, 1936; co-recipient Nathan Burkan law prize, 1939. Mem. Overseas Writers, White House Corr. Assn., Ohio Bar Assn. Roman Catholic. Clubs: Columbia University (Cleveland); Foreign Correspondents of China (Chungking, Shanghai); National Press (sec. since 1951). Author: Newspaper Copyright Law, 1939. Contbr. to various mags. Home: York Apts., 532 20th St., N.W. Office: National Press Bldg., Washington. Deceased.

ANDREWS, Wilfred Leslie, corp. exec.; b. Province of Ont., Can., Nov. 25, 1898; s. Matthew Henry and Jennie (Cardiff) A.; student Collegiate Inst., Moose Jaw, Can., 3 yrs.; m. Rowena C. Senick, June 11, 1927; children—Betty Jean, Gordon Robert. Came to U.S., 1923, naturalized, 1937. Asst. accountant Bank of Montreal, Can., 1916-23; statis. work Saskatchewan Creamery Co., Ltd., Moose Jaw, 1923; salesman and partner Andrews & Rutherford, Los Angeles, 1923-24; accountant and chief clk. Bank of Am. Nat. Trust & Savs. Assn., 1924-30; v.p., treas. and dir. Corp. of Am., 1940—; v.p. Transamerica Corporation, 1940-52, senior vice president, 1952—, treasurer, 1937—, director, 1949—; chmn. bd. Premier Ins. Co., 1950—, dir., 1941—; pres. and dir. Coast Service Co., 1942—, Inter-America Corp., 1947—; dir. Gen. Metals Corp., Mfrs. Casualty Ins. Co., Mfrs. Fire Ins. Co. Presbyn. Home: 2995 Lake St., San Francisco 21. Office: 4 Columbus Av., San Francisco 11. Died Nov. 14, 1954; buried Holy Cross Cemetery, San Francisco.

ANGELL, Montgomery B(oynton), lawyer; b. Rochester, N.Y., May 18, 1889; s. Edward B. and Florence (Montgomery) A.; Litt.B. cum laude, Princeton, 1911; LL.B. cum laude, Harvard U., 1915; m. Ellen Shipman, Sept. 8, 1917; children—Montgomery B., Ellen Whitney (Mrs. Frank Streeter), Nicholas Biddle. Admitted to N.Y. bar, 1916, D.C. bar, 1921; with ICC, Washington, 1915-17; gen. counsel's office Fed. Res. Bd., Washington, 1919-21; with Stetson, Jennings & Russell and successor firms, now Davis, Polk, Wardwell, Sunderland & Kiendl, 1921—, mem. firm, 1927—. Commr. Taconic State Park Commission of N.Y., 1948-58. Served as a major in the infantry of the U.S. Army, 1917-19. Decorated Croix de Guerre with gold star, French Army Corps citation. Mem. Am., N.Y. State bar assns., N.Y. Co. Lawyers' Assn., Bar Assn. City N.Y. Clubs: Century Assn., Princeton, Down Town Assn. (N.Y.C.). Author: Valuation Problems, 1945. Contbr. articles law revs. Home: 1 E. 87th St., N.Y.C. 28. Office: 15 Broad St., N.Y.C. 5. Died Nov. 1959.

ANGLE, Jay Warren, trust co. exec., ret.; b. Union County, Pa., Aug. 2, 1867; s. Jacob J. and Elisa Fulmer (Keyser) A.; student Lafayette Coll., Pa., 1885-86; Ph.G., Phila. Coll. Pharmacy, 1892; m. Ella May Boone, Aug. 1894; children—Jay Warren, Elizabeth (Mrs. Clarence B. Schaefer), Edith Albertson. Pharmacist, Hot Springs, Ark. for many years from 1892; an organizer and v.p. Ark. Trust Co. Mem. S.A.R., Delta Upsilon. Republican. Episcopalian. Mason (K.T., Shriner). Clubs: University, Hot Springs Country, Hot Springs Gun, Traveler and big game hunter. Home: 710 Quapaw Av. Office: Arkansas Trust Co., Hot Springs, Ark. Died Aug. 12, 1929.

ANGLY, Edward (ăng'lĭ), newspaper corr.; b. Palestine, Tex., Jan. 29, 1898; s. Joseph Edouard and Anna (Carson) A.; A.B., U. of Tex., 1919; m. Elizabeth Mary Wadsworth, Aug. 2, 1945; 1 dau., Patricia. Sports writer Galveston News, 1919-20; correspondent for Associated Press in N.Y. City, 1920-22, in London, Paris, Berlin, Moscow, 1922-30; with N.Y. Herald Tribune, 1930-34; free lance contbr. to Saturday Evening Post, The New Yorker, Vanity Fair, Forum, etc., 1934-36; again with N.Y. Herald Tribune, 1936-41 (became head London bureau Sept. 1939; with B.E.F. and Royal Air Force in retreat from Flanders, May 1940, from Bordeaux, June 1940; covered battle for Britain, June 1940-Feb. 1941; chief corr. in Middle East, Greece and Crete, Mar.-July 1941); apptd. Far Eastern corr. for Chicago Sun, Dec. 1941 (was one of 1st three Am. corrs. to reach Pearl Harbor from U.S. after Dec. 7, 1941; was first corr. to report arrival U.S. forces in Australia, Mar. 1942; covered New Guinea and Southwest Pacific throughout 1942); was one of two fgn. corrs. in Teheran during Roosevelt-Churchill-Stalin Conf., Nov.-Dec. 1943; (other being Lloyd Stratton of The Asso. Press); in Soviet Union and on eastern front in Roumania, Poland, Baltic states, Jan.-Nov. 1944; covered western front during Battle of Germany; head Paris Bureau, Chicago Sun, Dec. 1944-Nov. 1945; free lance writer since 1945. Served in U.S. Army, 1918. Mem. Delta Tau Delta, Sigma Delta Chi, Nat. Press (Washington), Anglo Am. Corrs. (Paris), Assn. Am. Corrs. (London). Author: Oh, Yeah!, 1932; (with Jesse Jones) Fifty Billion Dollars, 1950. Address: 333 Central Park West, N.Y.C. Died Dec. 7, 1950; buried Palestine, Tex.

ANKCORN, Charles M., brig. gen. U.S. Army, ret. Address: care Office of the Adjutant General, Dept. of the Army, Pentagon, Arlington, Va. Died Oct. 1, 1955.*

ANNAND, Percy Nicol (ăn'ănd), entomologist; b. Telluride, Colo., Nov. 16, 1898; s. James and Indiana (Nicol) Annand; student Colo. Coll., 1916-17; B.S., Colo. State Coll., 1920, D.Sc., 1945; A.M., Stanford, 1922, Ph.D., 1928; m. Ruth E. Lovett, Sept. 20, 1921; children—Richard Jay, Doris Marye. Asst. entomologist Great Western Sugar Co., Longmont, Colo., 1920-21; asst. in instrn., Stanford, 1921-22; head dept. biology, San Mateo Jr. Coll., 1922-29; asso. entomologist U.S. Bur. Entomology and Plant Quarantine, 1929-30, charge research on sugar beet insects, 1930-32, asst. chief Div. of Truck Crop Insect Investigation, 1932-34, chief Div. Cereal and Forage Insect Investigation, 1934-36, asst. chief Bur. Entomology an dPlant Quarantine, charge research, 1936-41, chief of bur., 1941—. Fellow A.A.A.S., Am. Entomol. Soc., Am. Assoc. Econ. Entomologist (pres. 1943), Entomol. Soc. Wash. (pres. 1944), Nat. Research Council, Sigma Xi, Alpha Zeta, Sigma Chi, Pi Kappa Delta. Conglist. Clubs: Cosmos (Washington); Washington Golf and Country (Arlington, Va.). Contbr. tech. jours. Home: 4247 Vacation Lane, Arlington, Va. Office: Dept. of Agriculture, Washington. Died Mar. 29, 1950.

ANSTED, Harry Bidwell, educator, clergyman; b. Temperance, Mich., Dec. 17, 1893; s. Lewis and Marrietta (Hayden) A.; grad. Spring Arbor Sem., 1911; student Hillsdale Coll., 1911-13; B.B.A., Greenville Coll., 1922, A.B., 1923; A.M., U. of Southern Calif., 1924, student, U. of Calif., 1925; student, U. of Mich., 1928-29; fellow Institute of Commerce, England, 1930; LL.D., Wessington Springs College, 1944, Seattle Pacific College, 1948; married Grace Marie Quimby, February 22, 1913; children—Eva Marie (Mrs. D. G. Wilder), Harry Burton. Served as pastor, churches in Mich., 1916-21; successively cost accountant, factory accountant, paymaster, office mgr. Studebaker, Sparks Withington Co., Gen. Motors Corp., 1913-21; dir. Sch. of Commerce, Greenville Coll., 1921-23; prof. social science, Los Angeles Pacific Coll., 1923-24; pres., bus. mgr. Wessington Springs Coll., 1925-36; dir. pub. relations, bursar, dean Coll. of Commerce Seattle Pacific Coll., 1936-44; pres. Seoul National University, Korea, 1946-47, chancellor since 1947; director and American manager, Heung Han Foundation since 1947; Am. rep. Whashin Indsl. Co., Inc., Korea, Japan, since 1949; exec. sec. Laymen's Missionary Movement, 1950-53; adminstrv. dir. United Temperance Movement, 1953—. Bd. mgrs. United Ch. Men; Dir. Evangelical Welfare Agy., Internat. Christian Leadership Inc. Served as chaplain, Leyte, P.I. and Korea, 1944-46; mem. O.R.C. Mem. Am. Economic Assn., Am. Hist. Soc., N.E.A., Washington Edn. Assn., Royal Econ. Soc., Washington Temperance Assn., Nat. Assn. Evangelicals. Republican. Free Methodist. Clubs: Commercial, Rotary, Breakfast (Seattle). Editor: Men and Missions Literature, The Spotlight. Home: 11986 Lakeside Pl., N.E., Seattle 55; also 4545 York Av. N., Mpls. 22. Office: Lumber Exchange Bldg., Mpls. 1. Died Dec. 16, 1955; buried Washelli, Seattle, Wash.

ANTHEIL, George (ăn'tīl), composer; born Trenton, New Jersey, July 8, 1900; son of Henry William and Wilhelmina (Huse) A.; student Trenton High Sch., 1914-18, Sternberg Cons., 1914-18; m. Elizabeth Markus, Oct. 4, 1925; 1 son, Peter Richard. Concert pianist, 1922-26; directing own compositions since 1928; became asst. music dir. Berlin State Theater, being 1st Am. born musician to hold this position; returned to U.S., 1933; music dir. Eastern Paramount Studios, 1934-35; composer for Hollywood Paramount Studios and Columbia Studios since 1936; lecturer on musical composition, Stanford University, 1940. Decorated: Societe Academique, France, 1933. Mem. League of Composers (N.Y. City), Screen Composers Assn. Democrat. Mem. Evangelical Ch. Author: Death in the Dark (glandular criminology), 1930; Everyman His Own Detective (glandular criminology), 1937; The Shape of the War to Come, 1940; Bad Boy of Music, (also pub. in Eng.) 1945; also articles in Esquire and Modern Music. Composer 3-act comic opera, Volpone (based on Ben Jonson's play), 1953; ballet based on Hemingway's Capital of the World; cantata, Cabeza de Vaca. Has made extensive study of glandular criminology. Address: 8161 Laurel View Dr., Hollywood 46, Cal. Died Feb. 12, 1959; buried Trenton, N.J.

ANTHONY, Arthur Cox, sec. Mass. Inst. Tech.; b. Boston, Jan., 1866; s. Nathan and Clara (Reed) A.; B.S., Mass. Inst. Tech., 1886. Mem. Townsend, Anthony & Tyson, stock brokers; sec. Mass. Inst. Tech. Mem. Boston Stock Exchange. Club: University (Boston). Office: 8 Congress St., Boston. Died 1931.

ANTHONY, Luther B., editor; b. Fort Scott, Kan., May 9, 1876; s. Capt. Jacob Merritt and Mary (Luther) A.; largely self-ed.; m. Charlotte Sutherland, May 14, 1910; children—Grace D., Daniel S., Susan B., Charlotte S. Formerly was an actor and entertainer; dir. Drexel Orchestra, Phila., 1898-99; dir. dramatics in schs. and colls., including Muhlenberg and Lafayette colls., Bucknell U., Lehigh U., until 1903. Collaborates in constrn. of plays with playwrights, mgrs., actors and novelists; founder, 1909, and editor The Dramatist (the only mag. of dramatic technology in the world); founder and pres. Inst. of the Drama. Republican. Free Thinker. Mem. Phi Gamma Delta. Contbr. to mags. Author: Dramatology, 1914; Eleven P.M. (with Paul M. Potter, play); Tootlums (with William H. Buckingham, play). Lectures on the drama; expert in copyright infringement litigations. Home: Easton, Pa.; (summer) Raubsville, Pa. Died Apr. 1955.

ANTRIM, Ernest Irving; b. Germantown, O., Feb. 21, 1869; s. Francis T. and Mary (Kemp) A.; A.B., De Pauw U., 1889; A.M., Boston U., 1890; Ph.D., Göttingen U., 1897; m. Saida Brumback, Oct. 17, 1899. Instr. Greek and English, Belmont Coll., College Hill, Cin., 1890-92; instr. English, Boston U., 1892-93; prof. English, Wyoming U., 1893-94; lectr. in English, W.Va. U., 1898; v.p. Van Wert (O.) Nat. Bank, 1904-28. Mem. Ohio Constl. Conv., 1912; trustee Ohio U., 1922-25; pres. Ohio Library Assn., 1921-22; organizer and 1st pres. Community Assn. of Van Wert; trustee M.E. Ch., 1916-28; del. Gen. Conf. M.E. Ch., 1916, 20. Mem. Beta Theta Pi. Republican. Author: The County Library (with wife), 1914; Fifty Million Strong (a study of rural life), 1916; active in social betterment work. Home: 220 N. Jefferson St., Van Wert, O. Died Jan. 6, 1953.

ANTRIM, Eugene Marion, clergyman, educator; b. Harveysburg, O., July 12, 1874; s. Charles Lewis and Emma (Macy) A.; A.B., U. Denver (winner Colo. state oratorical contest), 1896; S.T.B., Boston U. Sch. Theology, 1900, Jacob Sleeper fellow study and travel in Europe, 1901, Ph.D., 1904; D.D., U. Denver, 1914; L.L.D., Kansas Wesleyan U., 1927; m. Mary Winifred Vaughn (dec. Oct. 21, 1932); 1 son, Roderic Theodore (adopted); m. 2d Bertha Browning Hubbard, 1937. Ordained ministry M.E. Ch., 1900; pastor Trinity Ch., Springfield, Mass., 1902-10, N. Woodward Ch., Detroit, 1910-13, Decatur, Ill., 1913-16, Danville, 1916-17; dist. supt., Springfield Dist., Ill., 1917-23; pres. Oklahoma City U., 1923-34; pastor of the First Methodist Church of Woodward, Oklahoma, 1940-46, retired 1946. Member of the M.E. Ch. Gen. Conf., 1920, 28. Made mem. Okla. Hall of Fame, by Okla. Meml. Assn. for distinguished service to edn., 1934. Mem. Sigma Alpha Epsilon, Pi Gamma Mu. Republican. Mason (32°, K.T., Shriner). Address: Crescent, Okla. Died June 2, 1953.

APPENZELLAR, Paul (ăp-pĕn-zĕl'lẽr), retired banker; b. Chambersburg, Pa., Oct. 24, 1875; s. David K. and Elizabeth (Fohl) A.; prep. edn., Chambersburg Acad. and Dickinson Prep. Sch., Carlisle, Pa.; grad. Dickinson Coll., 1895; m. Edna Frances Howell, Mar. 2, 1909. Teacher, Dickinson Prep. Sch., 1895-97; engaged in banking and brokerage as mem. Swartwout and Appenzellar, members N.Y. Stock Exchange and N.Y. Cotton Exchange, 1899-1927; served as chmn. bd. Dictaphone Corp., Intertype Corp., (now chmn. exec. com.) also served as v.p. and dir. Am. Lafrance Fire Engine Co.; chmn. bd. Fundamental Investors (investment trust); dir. Bronxville (N.Y.) Trust Co., Internat. Grt. Northern R.R., N.Y. Railways Co., Pierce Oil Corp., Calco Chemical Corp., Ansco Photoproducts Corp., Service Fire Ins. Co., Morris & Essex Railroad. Formerly trustee and chmn. finance com. Dickinson Coll. Mem. Phi Beta Kappa, Beta Theta Pi. Clubs: Union League, University (New York); National Republican; Sleepy Hollow Country. Addresses: Bronxville, N.Y.; also Waldorf Astoria, N.Y.C. Deceased.

APPENZELLER, Alice Rebecca, coll. pres., missionary; b. Korea, Nov. 9, 1885 (1st Am. child born in Korea); d. Rev. Henry G. and Ella (Dodge) A. (pioneer M.E. missionaries to Korea); A.B., Wellesley Coll., 1909; A.M., Tchrs. Coll., Columbia, 1922; summer sch. student Harvard, 1910, Columbia, 1930, N.Y.U. in Seoul, Korea, 1927; Pd.D. (hon.), Boston U., 1937. Tchr. Shippen Sch., Lancaster, Pa., 1909-14; commd. missionary of Women's Fgn. Missionary Soc., M.E. Ch., 1914; with Ewha Womans U., Seoul, Korea (only coll. for women in Korea), 1914—, v.p. coll. and affiliated schs., 1917-22, pres. coll. and Kindergarten Tng. Sch., 1922-39, hon. pres. 1939; ordained ministry Korean M.E. Ch., 1932. Recipient Blue Ribbon medal, by Japan for service to edn., 1935; commemorative sun-dial placed on Ewha Coll. campus on 20th anniversary of service, 1935. Mem. Royal Asiatic Soc., Agora (Wellesley), Phi Delta Gamma. Clubs: Women's Music, Seoul Union (Seoul). Contbr. articles to missionary and ch. periodicals. Address: Ewha Womans University, Seoul, Korea. Died Feb. 20, 1950; buried Yang Wha Do (cemetery for fgn. people), Seoul, Korea.

APPLETON, Floyd, clergyman; b. Morrisania, N.Y., Aug. 20, 1871; s. William Gardner and Catherine (Ritter) A.; B.A., Columbia, 1893, Ph.D., 1906; grad. Gen. Theol. Sem., 1896 (Seymour prize); S.T.M., Phila. Div. Sch., 1922; m. Mildred Elsegood Miller, June 15, 1910; children—Lucy, David Elsegood, Robert Floyd. Deacon, 1896, priest, 1898, P.E. Ch.; chaplain Tombs, and Ludlow St. Jail, 1896; curate Grace Ch., Plainfield, N.J., 1896-1901; vicar St. Luke's Chapel, Bklyn., 1901-02; asst. Christ Ch., Bklyn., 1902-04; rector St. Clement's Ch., Bklyn., 1904-14, St. Paul's Ch., Harrisburg, Pa., 1914-21, Christ Church, Danville, Pa., 1921-25, Trinity Ch., Anderson, Ind., 1925-30, St. Paul's Ch., Woodbury, Conn., 1930-37, St. Stephen's Ch., South Ozone Park, L.I., 1937-40. In charge of St. James', Bury St. Edmunds, Eng., 1909, 11. Mem. Social Service Com., Diocese of L.I., 1906-14; mem. Standing Com., Diocese of Harrisburg, 1916-19, 21-25; Am. commissary archbishop of West Indies, 1918—. Vol. chaplain Ind. State Reformatory, 1926-30; mem. All Saints' Cathedral Chpt., Indpls., 1927-30. Pres. Ind. Soc. War of 1812, 1928-30. Republican. Author: Church Philanthropy in New York, 1906; The Seven Ages of the Church, 1931; also various brochures and pamphlets. Editor Harrisburg Churchman, 1914-21. Home: 143-13 Beech Av., Flushing, N.Y. Died Mar. 17, 1952.

APPLETON, William Hyde, educator; b. Portland, Me., June 10, 1842; s. Elisha Williams and Martha Wylly (Hyde) A.; A.B., Harvard, 1864, A.M., 1867, LL.B., 1869; Ph.D. (hon.), Swarthmore Coll.; 1888; student Greek and philology, univs. Berlin and Bonn, 1870-71, Athens, 1881-82; m. Esther Townsend Moore, July 12, 1900. Tutor in Greek, Harvard, 1868-70; prof. Greek and German, Swarthmore Coll., 1872-88, acting press., pres., 1889-91, prof. Greek and early English, 1891-95, prof. Greek lang. and lit., 1905-09, prof. emeritus, 1909. Mem. Am. Philos. Soc. Club: Union League (Phila.). Author: Greek Poets in English Verse, 1893. Address: Swarthmore, Pa. Died Apr. 3, 1926.

ARAKI, Eikichi, Japanese diplomat; b. Isikawa, Japan, Apr. 24, 1891; s. Tokutaro and Taka (Yasui) A.; Degree of Hogakushi, dept. law Tokyo Imperial U., 1916; m. Takiko Matumoto, 1920 (dec.); children—Yoshiyo, Fumio, Nobuo, Tomiko. Dir. Bank of Japan, 1942-45, vice gov., 1945, gov., 1946—; mem. bd. Tokyo Electric Power Co., 1950—; Japanese ambassador E. and P. to U.S., 1952-54. Clubs: Chevy Chase, Metropolitan. Home: Tokyo, Japan. Died Feb. 1, 1959.

ARANNA, Oswaldo (ä-rän'ya), Brazilian lawyer, statesman; b. Alegrete, Rio Grande do Sul, Brazil, Feb. 15, 1894; student Mil. Coll. of Rio de Janeiro, LL.D., George Washington, Columbia, Harvard and Washington & Jefferson Universities; married; has four children. Practiced law, Rio de Janeiro, for many yrs.; fought in local revolutionary battles and was seriously wounded, 1923-26; successively prefect of Alegrete, 1926, rep. in state legislature, 1927, fed. dep. from Rio Grande do Sul, 1928, sec. of state of Rio Grande do Sul (under Vargas), 1929; was one of leaders in Vargas Revolution, 1930, and has been closest friend of Vargas, 1930—; became minister of justice, 1930, minister of finance, 1931; served as ambassador to U.S., 1934-38; minister of foreign affairs, 1938-44; resumed law practice, 1944. Hon. Brig. Gen. Brazilian Army. Apptd. Chief Brazilian del. to U.N., 1947; pres. Security Council and U.N. Gen. Assembly, 1947. Home: Rua Campo Bello, 199. Office: Avenida Pres. Antonio Carlos 207, 6 Andar, Rio de Janeiro, Brazil. Died Jan. 1960.

ARBUCKLE, Charles Nathaniel, clergyman; b. Newark, N.J., May 22, 1879; s. Charles John and Mary Augusta (Lee) A.; ed. pub. schs. and by pvt. instruction; grad. Crozer Theol. Sem., Chester, Pa., 1902; D.D., Brown U., 1920, Colby Coll., 1928; m. Ruth Reeder, Oct. 17, 1905. Ordained to Bapt. Ministry, 1902; asso. pastor Warburton Av. Ch., Yonkers, N.Y., 1902-04; pastor Ch. of the Redeemer, Yonkers, 1904-19, First Ch., Newton Centre, 1919-48; lectr. Andover Newton Theol. Sch., 1920-29, prof. preaching, 1929-46; lectr. in homiletics Grad. Sch. Religion, U. So. Cal., 1948-49, 1950-51; interim preacher Claremont Community Ch., 1949-50. Mem. Corp., Pilgrim Place, Claremont, Cal., 1948-55. Mem. bd. fellows Brown U., 1929-46; trustee Crozer Theol. Sem., 1930-47, New Eng. Baptist Hosp., 1935-45. Mem. Mass. Council Religious Edn. (pres. 1924), Am. Bapt. Publ. Soc. (dir. 1922-41; chmn. bd. mgrs., 1941-43), Nat. Assn. Biblical Instrs. Preacher in schs., colleges. Home: 715 Plymouth Rd., Claremont, Cal. Dec. Jan. 17, 1955; buried Oak Park Cemetery, Claremont.

ARCHAMBAULT, A(nna) Margaretta (är-shăm-bō), artist; b. Phila.; d. Achille Lucien and Henrietta Bennett (Haupt) Archambault; student pvt. sch. of Miss Mary Anna Longstreth, Phila. Dir. Phila. Sch. Miniature Painting. Has exhibited widely at exhbns. of miniatures; awarded Medal of Honor, Pa. Soc. Miniature Painters, 1922. Painted miniatures from life of Presidents Warren G. Harding and Calvin Coolidge, for the Butler Art Inst., Youngstown, O.; oil portrait of Michael Hillegas, 1st treas. of U.S., for Independence Hall collection, Phila., and for Treasury Bldg., Washington; oil portrait of Prof. Lewis M. Haupt, for Engring. Dept., U. of Pa., of Admiral Stephen Bleecker Luce of U.S. Naval Acad., Annapolis, Md., of Robert W. Lesley, Esq., for Merion Golf Club, of Dr. Harrison Allen, for Coll. of Physicians, Phila., Mrs. J. Willis Martin, for Strawberry Mansion, Fairmount Park, Phila., Rev. William Ashmead Schaeffer, for Lutheran Theol. Sem., Mt. Airy; miniatures of Lord Edward Strachie of England, late Hon. Archie Gordon, owned by the late Lady Aberdeen of Scotland. Awarded the Emily Drayton Taylor gold medal for distinguished service in Art, 1939; the Howell Tracy Fisher Memorial award, 1940 (both in Pa. Soc. of Miniature Painters). Mem. Pa. Soc. Miniature Painters, Fellowship Pa. Acad. Fine Arts, Hist. Soc. Pa., Bot. Soc. Pa., Bartram's Garden Assn., Church Hist. Soc., Huguenot Soc. Republican. Episcopalian. Clubs: Plastic (charter mem.). Civic. Author: Art, Architecture and Historic interests in Pennsylvania, 1924. Home: 444 Overbrook Rd., Ridgewood, N.J. Died June 29, 1956; buried Woodlands Cemetery, Phila.

ARCHER, John Clark, clergyman, educator; b. Wilna, Md., Dec. 23, 1881; s. John and Virginia Augusta (Clark) A.; B.A., Hiram (O.) Coll., 1905; B.D., M.A., Yale, 1914, Ph.D., 1922, grad. study, Harvard, 1914-15; m. Cathaline Brewster Alford, Feb. 26, 1906; children—Alford, Virginia Clark (Mrs. T. R. Blakeslee II). Ordained Disciples of Christ Ch., 1905. Pastor Newton Falls, O., 1905-07; ednl. missionary, Jabalpur, India, 1907-11; pres. Y.M.C.A., 1910; mgr. Christian Mission Press, 1909-11; pastor Avon, Conn., 1912-14; asst. minister South Ch., Brockton, Mass., 1914-15; lectr. Yale. 1915-16, asst. prof. missions, 1916-24, asso. prof., 1924-27, prof. missions and comparative religion, 1927-32, Hoober prof. comparative religion, 1932-50, prof. emeritus, 1950—; lectr. Hartford (Conn.) Sem. Found., 1919-22, 1933, 1935-36, Chautauqua Summer Schs., 1920-22, Garrett Bibl. Inst., Evanston, 1926, Khalsa Coll., Amritsar, India, 1937, 46, Bklyn. Inst., 1944; librarian Day Missions Library, 1925-32; curator collector in comparative religion Yale, 1932-35; sec. Yale Div. Sch., 1920-50. Served as ednl. sec. YMCA with British-Indian Army, Iraq, 1917-18. Treas. and chmn. publ. com. Am. Oriental Soc., 1923-36. Ind. Democrat. Clubs: Graduates (mem. bd. govs. 1941-44), Oriental, Faculty, High Lane. Author: Mystical Elements in Mohammed, 1924, China in the Local Parish, 1924; A New Approach in Missionary Educator, 1926; Java, Garden of Insulinde, 1930; Youth in a Believing World, 1931; Faiths Men Live By, 1934; The Sikhs, a Study in Comparative Religion, 1946. Contbr. (chapter) "The Function of the Theological Seminary in the Enterprise of Missions," in Education for Christian Service, 1922; "Moslem Ethics," in Sneath's Evolution of Ethics, 1927, "Hinduism" in Jurji's Great Religions, 1946; also articles relating to history of religions in Collier's Nat. Cyclopedica, 1932, 48, and in Scribners Dictionary of American History, numerous sketches in Dictionary of Am. Biography. Contbr. to Review of Religion, Christendom, Moslem (now Muslim) World, Am. Scientist, The Aryan Path and other domestic and Indian periodicals. Home: 1712 Whitney Av., Hamden, Conn. Died July 7, 1957; buried Union Chapel Cemetery, Wilna, Md.

ARCHER, Ralph Curtis, machinery mfr.; b. Great Bend, Kan., July 28, 1892; s. Charles Lemuel and Margaret (Sample) A.; B.S., Ft. Hays (Kan.) State Coll., 1918; m. Meda Harriet McCarter, June 3, 1922; children—Margaret Ann (Mrs. William S. Fields), Ralph C. With Internat. Harvester Co., Chgo., 1919—, domestic sales mgr., 1941, dir. domestic and Canadian sales, 1942, v.p., 1945—; dir. LaSalle Nat. Bank, Chgo. Mem. Soc. Automotive Engrs. Mason (32°). Clubs: Knollwood Country, Chicago Athletic Assn. Home: R.D. 2, Box 245, Mundelein, Ill. Office: 180 N. Michigan Av., Chgo. 1. Died Aug. 11, 1957.

ARCHIBALD, Maynard Brown, judge; b. Nova Scotia, Jan. 26, 1891; ed. Dalhousie U.; called to N.S. bar, 1919; practiced in Picton, 1919-20, Halifax, 1920-37; justice Supreme Court of N.S., 1937-48; judge, Exchequer Court, 1949—; also chief commr. Bd. Transport Commrs. for Can., 1948-51. Address: Ottawa, Ont. Can. Died July 9, 1956.

ARCHIBALD, Raymond Clare, mathematician; b. Colchester County, N.S., Can., Oct. 7, 1875; s. Abram Newcomb and Mary (Mellish) A.; B.A., U. of Mt. Allison Coll., N.B., 1894, LL.D., 1923; Harvard, 1895-98; B.A., 1896, M.A., 1897; U. of Berlin, 1898-99; U. of Strassburg, 1899-1900, Ph.D., 1900; Sorbonne, Paris, France, 1909-10; U. of Rome, 1922; hon. doctor, U. of Padua, 1922; unmarried. Prof. mathematics, librarian, head violin dept. Mt. Allison Ladies' Coll.. Sackville, N.B., 1900-07; prof. mathematics Acadia U., Wolfville, N.S., 1907-08; instr. mathematics, 1908-11, asst. prof., 1911-17, asso. prof. 1917-23, prof. 1923-43; prof. emeritus since 1943, Brown University; lecturer University of California, 1924, Harvard, 1931, Columbia, 1939-40. Del. to congress univs. of Brit. Empire, London, 1912; del. to celebration 700th anniversary of founding U. of Padua, 1922; rep. for U.S. and Can. of Euler Commn. of Swiss Society of Naturalists, 1922-39; del. to opening of Gennadius Library (Athens), 1926; mem. Am. sect. Internat. Math. Union (mem. Internat. Com. on Bibliography 1924-28). Methodist. Fellow Am. Acad. Arts and Sciences, A.A.A.S. (sec. sect. A, 1925-27, v.p. and chmn. 1928; v.p. and chmn. sect. L 1937); mem. Div. of Phys. Sciences, National Research Council, 1928-31, 1940-43 and 1944-47, chmn. Internat. Com. on Math. Tables and Other Aids to Computation, 1939-50; fgn. fellow Masarykova Akademie Prace (Czecho-Slovakia), Societatea de Stiinte of Cluj (Rumania); hon. mem. Polish Math. Soc., Math. Assn. (Eng.), Phi Beta Kappa (Harvard Chapter); mem. Sigma Xi, London Math. Soc., Deutsche Mathematiker Vereinigung, Edinburgh Math. Soc., Unione Matematica Italiana, Am. Math. Soc. (council, 1918-41; librarian, 1921-41; trustee 1923), Math. Assn. America (pres. 1922. trustee, 1923-30), History of Science Soc. (council 1924-40, mem. com. on publs., 1923-30. Founder Mary Mellish and Archibald Mem. Library English and Am. Poetry and Drama, Mt. Allison U., Sackville, New Brunswick, Can., 1905-55. Author: The Cardioid and Some of Its Related Curves, 1900; Bibliography of Life and Works of Simon Newcomb, 1905, 24; Carlyle's First Love, Margaret Gordon, Lady Bannerman, 1910; Mathematical Instruction in France, 1910; Euclid's Book on Divisions of Figures with a Restoration, 1915; The Training of Teachers of Mathematics for the Secondary Schools of the Countries Represented in the International Commission on the Teaching of Mathematics, 1918; Benjamin Peirce (1809-1880), 1925; Bibliography of Babylonian and Egyptian Mathematics, 1927-29; Klein's Famous Problems of Elementary Geometry, rev. edit., 1930; Outline of the History of Mathematics, 1932, 6th edit., 1949, The Scientific Achievements of Nathaniel Bowditch, 1937; Semicentennial History American Mathematical Soc., 1888-1938, 1938; Fifty Mathematical Table-Makers, 1948; articles in Encyclopedia Britannica, 1929, Dictionary of Am. Biography, 1929-36, 1942; Historical Notes on the Education of Women at Mount Allison University, 1854-1954, 1954. Editor: with Introduction and notes of an English transl. of J. Steiner's, Geometrical Constructions With a Ruler—Given a Fixed Circle, 1949; asso. editor of the Bulletin of American Math. Society, 1914-20, of American Math. Monthly, 1917-18; editor in chief latter, 1919-21; Revue Semestrielle des Publications Mathématiques, 1921-34, of Isis since 1924, Scripta Mathematica since 1932; founder, editor Math. Tables and Aids to Computation (quar.), 1943-49. Extensive contbr. to math. jours. and revs. Address: 392 Benefit St., Providence. Died July 26, 1955; buried Halifax, N.S.

ARCTOWSKI, Henryk, scientist, explorer; b. Warsaw, Poland, July 15, 1871; studied chemistry and geology, univs. of Paris, Liege and Zurich, 1888-96; British Mus., London, 1896-7; Ph.D., U. Lemberg, 1912; m. Arian Jane Addy, Mar. 28, 1900. In charge phys. observations, Belgian Antarctic Expdn., 1897-9; discovered and studied geology of Antarctic Andes and established the first complete record of meteorol. observations made in south polar regions; afterwards assisted at Royal Ob. of Belgium until coming to America, 1909; visited Spitzbergen, 1910; chief of science div. N.Y. Pub. Library, May, 1911-19. Sec. for meteorology Belgian Astron. Soc.; mem. Belgica Commn.; Internat. Polar Conf.; fellow Royal Geog. Soc. (London), A.A.A.S., N.Y. Acad. Sciences, Assn. Am. Geographers; mem. Nat. Inst. Social Sciences; corr. mem. Belgian Geol. and Geog. socs. Knight of Order of Leopole; medals and hon. distinctions from Belgian Royal Acad., City of Antwerp, Geog. Soc., London, etc. Author: Die Antarktischen Eisverhaltnisse, 1903; L'Enchainement des Variations Climatiques, 1909; Study of the Changes in the Distribution of Temperature, 1916; also reports pub. by the Belgian Govt. and contbr. to Am. and European scientific jours. Prepared for Am. Delegation to Peace Conf. 14 reports on the geog., mineral resources, ethnography, demography, agr. and industy of Poland and many maps; in Poland with Inter-Allied Commn., Feb.-Mar. 1919. Address: 1 Livingston Av., Yonkers, N.Y. Died Feb. 21, 1958.

ARENSBERG, Walter Conrad (är'ĕns-bĕrg), author; b. Pittsburgh, Pa., Apr. 4, 1878; s. Conrad Christian Arensberg and Flora Belle (Covert) A.; A.B., Harvard U., 1900; m. Mary Louise Stevens, June 1907. Formed with Mrs. Arensberg the Louise and Walter Arensberg Collection of Pre-Columbian Art and Art of the Twentieth Century, donated to the Philadelphia Museum of Art. Trustee Southwest Museum. Clubs: Harvard (New York); University (Los Angeles, California). Author: Poems, 1914; Idols, 1916; The Cryptography of Dante, 1921; The Cryptography of Shakespeare, 1922; The Secret Grave of Francis Bacon at Lichfield, 1923; The Burial of Francis Bacon and His Mother in the Lichfield Chapter House, 1925; Baconian Keys, 1927; The Shakespearean Mystery, 1928; Francis Bacon, William Butts, and the Pagets of Beaudesert, 1929; The Magic Ring of Francis Bacon, 1930. The Skeleton Text of the Shakespeare Folio, 1952. Pres. Francis Bacon Foundation, Inc. Home: 7065 Hillside Av., Hollywood, Cal. Died Jan. 29, 1954.

ARGETSINGER, J(ames) C(ameron) (är'gĕt-sĭng-ĕr), lawyer; b. Burdett, N.Y., Dec. 12, 1883; s. Lafayette William and Eulalia (Reynolds) A.; A.B., Cornell U., 1905, LL.B., 1907; LL.D., Youngstown Coll., 1947; m. Louise Williams, Sept. 16, 1916; 1 s., Cameron Reynolds. In Philippine Insular Serv. 1907-09; editor Watkins (N.Y.) Express, 1910-11; practiced law, Elmira, N.Y., 1911-15; in legal dept. Erie R.R. Co., New York, 1916-17; mem. Manchester, Ford, Bennett & Powers, 1917-23, asst. gen. counsel Youngstown Sheet & Tube Co., 1923-30, gen. counsel, 1930-48, sec., 1932-49, vice president, 1935-51; mem. bd. dirs. and exec. com. Dollar Savings and Trust Co.; dir. Home Savings & Loan Co. (both of Youngstown, O.). Member Gov.'s Tax Commn. (Ohio), 1932; mem. and vice chmn. Mahoning County Charter Comm., 1934-35. Mem. Ohio Postwar Program Commn., 1943-44. Pres., trustee Youngstown Public Library Assn.; industrial councillor Ohio State L. Research Foundation (Columbus, O.); pres. and mem. bd. trustees Lucy R. Buechner Corp.; mem. and v. chmn. bd. govs. and exec. com. Youngstown Coll.; v.p. and trustee Y.M.C.A. (Youngstown); dir. Mahoning Valley Indsl. Council; trustee Henry H. Stambaugh Auditorium Assn.; dir. Youngstown C. of C. (past pres.), Ohio Mfrs. Assn. Mem. Am., Ohio State and Mahoning County bar assns., Cornell Law Assn. Republican. Presbyn. Mason. Clubs: Youngstown, Youngstown Country, Exchange (past pres.). Home: 251 Redonda Road. Office: Youngstown Sheet and Tube Co., Youngstown, O. Died June 16, 1955; buried Burdett, N.Y.

ARLEN, Michael (name changed from Dikran Kouyoumdjian), author; b. Roustchouk, Bulgaria, Nov. 16, 1895; s. Armenian parents; ed. Malvern Cll.; m. Atatanta Mercati, 1928; 2 children. Author: London Venture, 1920; Romantic Lady, 1921; Piracy, 1923; Green Hat, 1924; These Charming People, 1924; May Fair, 1925; Young Men in Love, 1927; Ace of Cads, 1927; Lily Christine, 1928; Babes in the Wood, 1929; Ghost Stories, 1930; Ancient Sin, and Other Stories, 1930; Men Dislike Women, 1931; Man's Mortality, 1933; Short Stories, 1933; Hell! Said the Duchess, 1934; Crooked Coronet, 1937; Flying Dutchman, 1939; (plays) Green Hat, 1925;

These Charming People, 1925. Club: Garrick (London, Eng.). Address: 812 Park Av., N.Y.C. Died June 25, 1956.

ARMAS, Carlos Castillo, Pres. of Guatemala; b. Santa Lucia Cotzumalguapa, Escuintla, Nov. 4, 1914; s. Raymundo and Josefina (Castillo) A.; Artillery diploma, Polytechnic Sch., 1936; student U.S. Army Sch., Ft. Leavenworth, Kan., 1945-46; m. Odilia Palomo. Commd. sub-lt. arty., lt. inf. Guatemalan Army, 1936; advanced through grades to lt. col. gen. staff, 1947; has served as supernumary officer Polytechnic sch., sub-director, and dir.; supernumary officer, mil. instr. Ft. Matamors; chief arty. Def. of Atlantic, Puerto Barrios; instr. arty. Fort of San Jose; chief 4th dept. Gen. Command of Army, chief 3d dept.; comdt. Cav. Div., chief 4th Mil. Zone, Mazatenango; mem. commn. for revision draft of new Constitutive Law of Army, 1945; mem. adv. bd. Nat. Def., 1945; mem. commn. Bilateral Conf., Mil. Staff U.S. and Guatemala, 1945; pres. Guatemala, 1954-—. Decorated Medal Mil. Merit (Mexico), 1948. Club: Military (v.p. exec. bd. 1944-45). Home: President of the Republic, Guatemala, Republic of Guatemala, C.A. Assassinated July 26, 1957.

ARMBRUSTER, Adolph Henry (arm'broo-ster), educator; b. Auburn, N.Y., Jan. 23, 1895; s. Carl Frederick and Gottlieben (Elsasser) A.; B.A., Western Res. U., 1918; M.B.A., Harvard, 1921; D.Ed. (honorary), Suffolk University, 1950; married Bertha Florentine Schewe, Aug. 5, 1929; 1 dau., Flora Lucille. Accountant Price, Waterhouse & Co., N.Y.C., 1921-22; asst. prof. accounting Yale, 1922-26; student counsellor, asst. dean, acting dean U. Pitts. Sch. Bus. Adminstrn., 1926-34; now prof. finance, dean Coll. Commerce, Ohio U. With U.S. Army, 1917-19. Mem. Am. Econ. Assn., Phi Gamma Delta, Omicron Delta Kappa, Phi Beta Kappa, Alpha Kappa Psi. Mem. Ch. of Christ. Mason, Rotarian. Home: Route 3, Athens, O. Died May 5, 1951.

ARMISTEAD, Henry Beauford, ex-sec. state Ark.; b. Upperville, Va., Oct. 19, 1833; grad. Va. Mil. Inst. Served as pvt. C.S. Army, 1861-65, since mcht. and farmer. Brig. gen. Ark. Militia during Brooks-Baxter gubernatorial war, 1874; state senator, 1877-99; dep. sec. of state Ark., 1889-93, sec. of state, 1893-97. Del. Dem. Nat. Conv., 1884. Address: Charleston, Ark. Deceased.

ARMISTEAD, Henry Marshall, lawyer; b. Fauquier County, Va., May 15, 1874; s. Bowles Edward and Elizabeth Lewis (Marshall) A.; LL.B., U. of Ark., 1895; m. Elizabeth Joan Murphy, Nov. 2, 1903; children—Marshall Murphy (dec.), George Murphy (dec.), Henry Marshall (dec.), Lewis Addison. Admitted to Ark. bar, 1895, and since practiced at Little Rock; partner Cockrill & Armistead, 1908-32, Cockrill, Armistead & Rector, 1932-40, Armistead, Rector and Armistead, 1940—; director E. L. Bruce Co. Mem. Am. and Ark. State bar assns. Democrat. Episcopalian. Home: 2901 Izard St. Office: Pyramid Bldg., Little Rock, Ark. Died Mar. 10, 1958; buried Roselawn Cemetery.

ARMISTEAD, Jesse Warren (ärm'stĕd), architect, engr.; b. Atlanta, June 29, 1899; s. Jesse Warren and Mary Elizabeth (King) A.; student Ga. Sch. Tech., 1921; m. Margaret Beachamp, June 22, 1921; children—John Beauchamp, Ann (Mrs. Daniel Bearse), Carol, Stanley. Practice of architecture since 1936. Mem. Met. Planning Commn., City of Atlanta, Fulton, DeKalb counties, Ga. Served as pvt. U.S. Army, 1918. Registered architect Ga., Fla., Ala., Miss., La., Tenn., Ky., S.C., N.C., Va., N.Y. Fellow A.I.A.; mem. Ga. Engring. Soc., Phi Gamma Delta. Rotarian. Home: 205 Peachtree Circle, N.E. Office: 739 W. Peachtree, Atlanta 5. Deceased.

ARMOUR, A(ndrew) Watson, meat packer; b. Kansas City, Mo., Apr. 4, 1882; s. Kirkland B. and Annie P. (Hearne) A.; ed. Andover, Mass.; m. Elsa, d. Augustus A. Parker, Nov. 20, 1907. Identified with packing bus., 1903—; dir., mem. exec. com. Armour & Co.; dir., chmn. bd. Nat. Aluminate Corp.; dir. No. Trust Co., Commonwealth Edison Co. Trustee St. Luke's Hosp. Clubs: Chicago, Racquet, Tavern, Casino, Onwentsia, Shoreacres, Old Elm. Home: 1500 Lake Shore Dr., Chicago 10, (summer) 900 Waukegan Rd. North, Lake Forest, Ill. Office: 316 S. La Salle St., Chgo. 4. Died Nov. 6, 1953.

ARMOUR, Laurance Hearne; b. Kansas City, Mo., Mar. 8, 1888; s. Kirkland B. and Annie P. (Hearne) A.; educated at Saint Paul's Sch., Concord, N.H.; m. Lacy Withers, Jan. 11, 1911; 1 son, Lauranee Hearne. Identified with packing business since beginning of active career, 1909; settled in Chicago, 1910; dir. Armour & Co.; chmn. bd. La Salle Nat. Bank, Chicago; dir. Automatic Canteen Co. of America. Episcopalian. Maj. AEF, 1917-19. Clubs: Chicago, Onwentsia, Shoreacres, Old Elm. Home: Lake Forest, Ill. Died Dec. 29, 1952; buried Lake Forest.

ARMOUR, Philip Danforth; b. 1893; s. Philip Danforth and May (Lester) A.; m. Gwendolin Condon, Jan. 8, 1915 (dec. 1950); m. 2d, Dorothy Braman, Aug. 23, 1951. Began with Armour & Co. (founded by grandfather), as a clerk to learn the business, 1914, resigned as 1st v.p., 1931; dir. 1st Nat. Bank, Lake Forest, Ill., Zonolite Co. Chmn. Chicago Community Fund Drive, 1935. Chmn. Army Air Force Price Adjustment Sect., Midcentral Dist., A.T.S.C. Home: Lake Forest, Ill. Office: 135 S. La Salle St., Chgo. Died Jan. 19, 1958.

ARMS, John Taylor, etcher; b. Washington, Apr. 19, 1887; s. John Taylor and Kate (Watkins) A.; prep. edn., Lawrenceville (N.J.) Sch., 1904-05; student Princeton, 1905-07, M.A. (hon.), 1947; B.S., Mass. Inst. Tech., 1911, M.S., 1912; M.A. (hon.), Wesleyan U., 1939; Litt.D. (hon.), Hobart Coll., 1940; pupil of Ross Turner, D. A. Gregg, Felton Brown and Despradelles; m. Dorothy Noyes, May 17, 1913; children—Margery, John Taylor, Henry Bowes. Represented in permanent collections of pub. instns. throughout U.S. and abroad, including: Bklyn., Los Angeles, Cleve., Toledo, San Diego, Worcester, Delgado (New Orleans), and Peabody (Salem, Mass.) museums, U.S. Nat. Mus., Art Inst. Chgo., N.Y. Pub., Congressional, Cal. State and Birmingham (Ala.) pub. libraries, Mattatuck Hist. Soc. (Waterbury, Conn.), Mus. Princeton U., Art Gallery Toronto, High Mus. (Atlanta), Mus. Fine Arts in Boston, Fogg Mus., Met. Mus. Art, Pa. Mus. Fine Arts, Corcoran Art Galleries, Detroit Inst. Arts, Hackley Art Gallery, Omaha Art Inst., Bibliothèque Nationale Paris, Musée de Rouen, Brit. Mus., Victoria and Albert Mus. (London), Internat. Gallery, Internat. Gallery Venice, M. H. de Young Mem. Mus. (San Francisco), Cin. Mus. Art, Albright Gallery, Montclair Art Mus., Yale U. Gallery Fine Arts, Seattle Art Mus., Mus. History, Sci. and Art (Los Angeles), Vanderpoel Mem. (Chgo.), Salina (Kan.) Art Assn., Carnegie Inst. (Pitts.), William P. Chapman, Jr., Collection (Cornell), Hispanic Soc. Am., Internat. Bus. Machines Corp., Bethany Coll., Skidmore Coll., Hobart Coll., Wesleyan U. Recipient numerous prizes since 1919, from: Bklyn. Soc. Etchers, Chgo. Soc. Etchers, Soc. Am. Etchers, Nat. Acad. Design, Salmagundi Club, Lotos Club, Nat. Arts Club, Bridgeport (Conn.) Art League, Arts and Crafts Assn. of Meriden (Conn.), Balt. Water Color Club, Conn. Acad. Fine Arts, Irvington (N.J.) Art and Museum Assn., Northwest Printmakers, Painters and Sculptors of N.J., Pa. Acad., Print Club of Phila., Print Makers Soc. Cal., Soc. Sanity in Art, So. Print Makers Soc., So. States Art League, Am. Vets. Soc. Artists, Boston Printmakers, 1951, Oakland Art Gallery, 1947, 51, Print Club of Albany, 1951, 1st nat. Exhbn. Fla. So. Coll., 1952, Soc. Am. Graphic Artists, 1952; gold medals: Dealers' Assn. of N.Y., 1934, Paris Internat. Expn., 1937, A.I.A., 1945, Audubon Artists, 1948. Elected trustee Louis Comfort Tiffany Found., 1938, pres. since 1940. Mem. Pennell Fund com. Library of Congress; mem. Smithsonian art commn. Smithsonian Instn.; mem. jury of selection Internat. Graphic Arts Soc., 1951-52. Vis. lectr. on graphic art Wesleyan U., 1938-39, annual demonstration and talk on The Making of an Etching since 1939. Served as ensign, convoy duty, U.S.N., World War I; as civilian artist executed series of etched plates of U.S.N. combat vessels for future records of Bur. of Ships, World War II. Made Chevalier Legion of Honor, 1933, Officier, 1951. Asso. Royal Etcher, 1934. Nat. Academician, 1933. Mem. Nat. Acad. Design, Soc. Am. Graphic Artists (formerly Soc. Am. Etchers, Gravers, Lithographers and Woodcutters) (pres.), Nat. Inst. Arts and Letters, Am. Acad. Arts and Letters, Am. Color Print Soc. (v.p.), Chgo. Soc. Etchers, Print Makers Soc. Cal., Am. Fedn. Arts, Am. Artists Profl. League, Cleve. Print Club, Balt., Phila., Washington water color clubs, North Shore Arts Assn., Art Assn. Newport, So. States Art League, Northwest Print Makers, Cleve. Print Makers, Miniature Painters, Sculptors, and Gravers of Washington, (asso.) Royal Soc. Painter-Etchers and Engravers, (asso.) Société des Beaux Arts (France), Soc. Canadian Painter-Etchers and Engravers, Academic Artists Assn., New Haven Paint and Clay Club, Soc. of Medalists, Soc. Print Connoisseurs, Artists Equity Assn. (v.p.), Prairie Print Makers, Phila. Art Alliance, Am. Soc. French Legion of Honor, Marblehead Art Assn., Mus. Modern Art, Met. Mus. Art (ex-officio fellow in perpetuity), Am. Vets. Soc. Artists, Conn. Acad. Fine Arts, Friends of Contemporary Prints, Nat. Commn. to Advance Art (mem. governing bd.), La. Soc. Etchers, Studio Guild, Inc. (founder mem.), Springfield Art Assn. (Ill.), Springfield Art League (Mass.), Archtl. League of N.Y., Am. Brit. Art Center (artist mem.), Arts and Crafts Assn. (Meriden, Conn.), Princeton Print Club, Boston Printmakers, Palm Beach Art League, Audubon Artists (mem. bd.), Carmel Art Assn. (Cal.), Mid-Vermont Artists. Republican. Episcopalian. Clubs: Salmagundi, Grolier, Century Assn., Nat. Arts (v.p.), Lotos, Princeton (N.Y.C.). Author: Handbook of Print Making and Print Makers, 1934; Design in Flower Arrangement (with Dorothy Noyes Arms), 1937. Illustrator (with drawings and etchings) Churches of France, also Hill Towns and Cities of Northern Italy (both by Dorothy N. Arms). Contbr. to Print mag. Home: Greenfield Hill, Fairfield, Conn. Died Oct. 13, 1954.

ARMSTEAD, George Brooks, editor; b. New Haven, May 30, 1883; s. James Benson and Louisa Matilda (Brooks) A.; Ph.B., Sheffield Sci. Sch. (Yale), 1906; m. Marion Gorham, Oct. 7, 1908 (died Sept. 27, 1912); 1 son, James Gorham; m. 2d, Frances J. Lakin, Jan. 5, 1927; children—George Brooks, Jessie Louise. Began as reporter New Haven Leader, 1904, city editor, 1908-09; editor Lynn (Mass.) News, 1909-11; Sunday editor New Haven Union, 1911-13, editor, 1913-16; city editor New Haven Jour.-Courier, 1917; asst. mng. editor Hartford Courant, 1921-23, mng. editor, 1924-40, lit. editor, 1941-1942. News commentator, Radio Station WDRC, Hartford Conn., 1943-46; compiler studies in adminstrn., State Conn., 1946-—. Served with A.E.F. in France, 1918-19; with British E.F. in Palestine and Egypt, 1919-20. Mem. Fgn. Policy Assn., Meteoritical Soc. Mineral. Soc. Hartford, S.A.R., Am. Revolution, Yale Alumni Assn., Alpha Chi Rho. Clubs: University, Twentieth Century. Address: 83 Stillwood Rd., Wethersfield, Conn. Died Mar. 7, 1950; buried Village Cemetery, Wethersfield, Conn.

ARMSTRONG, A. Joseph, library adminstr.; b. Louisville, Mar. 29, 1873; s. Andrew Jackson and Lotta (Froman) A.; A.B., Wabash Coll., 1902, A.M., 1904, Litt.D., 1932; Ph.D., U. Pa., 1908; student Brit. Mus., 1909, 10; Litt.D., Georgetown (Ky.) Coll., 1925; L.H.D., Shurtleff Coll., 1947; LL.D., Baylor U., 1951, So. Meth. U., 1952; m. Mary Maxwell, Jan. 24, 1911; 1 son, Richard Maxwell. Prof. English, Broadus Coll., 1903-04, Ill. Wesleyan U., Bloomington, Ill., 1904-07; prof. English (ad interim) Baylor U., 1908-09.: prof. English, Georgetown Coll., 1909-12; prof. English, head dept. Baylor U., 1912-52, dir. Armstrong-Browning Library since 1952. Lectr. on Browning and other lit. subjects. Presented to Baylor U. a collection of Browningiana, considered to be largest in world; raised funds to purchase portrait of Browning by his son, Robert Barrett Browning; secured from Lilian Whiting, Boston, gift of original Clasped Hands by Harriet Hosmer; also raised funds for building to house the collection (dedicated 1951). Del. World's Bapt. Alliance, Stockholm, 1923, Internat. Conf. Profs. English, N.Y., 1923; spl. rep. Tex. at dedication Library of U. Louvain, 1929. Mem. (life) Tex. State Tchrs. Assn., Dante Soc. Am. (nat. com.; rep. Dante Sei-Centennial, Ravenna, Italy 1921), Modern Lang. Assn. Am., Nat. Travel Soc., Shakspere Assn. Am., Am. Research Soc., Poetry Soc. London (v.p.), Linguistic Soc. Am., Ky. Pioneer Mem. Soc., Sigma Tau Delta (historian; mem. council), Sigma Upsilon; asso. mem. Poetry Soc. Am. hon. mem. N.Y., Boston, L.A. and K.C. Browning socs.; corr. academician Internationale di Lettere e Scienze (Naples). Democrat. Baptist. Kiwanian. Author: Operatic Performances in Eng. Before Handel, 1918; Baylor Men in Military Service, 1919; Browning Through French Eyes, 1932. Editor of several books, including, Letters of Vachel Lindsay, 1940. Contbr. to Agonia (Buenos Aires, Argentina). Home: 625 Dutton St., Waco, Tex. Died Mar. 31, 1954; buried Oakwood Cemetery, Waco.

ARMSTRONG, Anne Wetzell (Mrs. Robert F. Armstrong), writer; b. Grand Rapids, Mich., Sept. 20, 1872; d. Henry Bower and Lorinda (Snyder) Wetzell; student Mt. Holyoke (Mass.) Coll., 1889-91; spl. course, U. Chgo., 1898; m. Robert Franklin Armstrong, June 14, 1905; 1 son, Roger Franklin (dec.). Personnel dir. Nat. City Co., N.Y.C., 1918-19; asst. mgr. indsl. relations, Eastman Kodak Co., Rochester, N.Y., 1919-23. First woman to speak before Amos Tuck Sch. of Bus., Dartmouth coll., and Harvard Sch. Bus. Adminstrn. Democrat. Author: (novels) The Seas of God, 1915; This Day and Time, 1930. Contbr. to mags. Home: Emmett, Tenn. Died Mar. 17, 1958.

ARMSTRONG, C(harles) Dudley, ret. co. exec.; b. Wilkinsburg, Pa., Aug. 21, 1888; s. Charles D. and Gertrude V. (Ludden) A.; student Hill Sch.; A.B., Yale, 1910; m. Mary J. Hilliard, July 1, 1916; children—Barbara H. (Mrs. W. M. Dunlap, Jr.), John L., Virginia D. (Mrs. J. J. Kohlhas), Thomas M., Henry H. With Armstrong Cork Co., Lancaster, Pa., 1910-—, v.p., sec., 1937-53, retired Sept. 1, 1953; dir. Union Nat. Bank of Pitts. Republican. Episcopalian. Home: Abbeville, Lincoln Highway W., Lancaster, Pa. Died June 8, 1954.

ARMSTRONG, Edwin H(oward), elec. engr.; b. New York, N.Y., Dec. 18, 1890; s. John and Emily Gertrude (Smith) A.; E.E., Columbia, 1913, Sc.D., 1929; Sc.D., Muhlenberg College, 1941; married Marian MacInnis, December 1, 1923. Assistant in dept. elec. engring., Columbia, 1913-14; asso. with Prof. Michael I. Pupin in research, Marcellus Hartley Research Lab., at Columbia U., 1914-35; prof. of elec. engring., Columbia, since 1934. Served as capt. and major, Signal Corps, with A.E.F., 1917-19. Chevalier, Legion d'honneur, 1919. Awards: Medal of Honor, Inst. of Radio Engrs., 1917; Egleston medal, Columbia U., 1939; "Modern Pioneer" plaque, Nat. Assn. Mfrs., 1940; Holley medal, Am. Soc. Mech. Engrs., 1940; Franklin medal, Franklin Inst., 1941; John Scott medal, Bd. of City Trusts, City of Phila., 1941; Edison medal, Am. Inst. of Elec. Engrs., 1943; award to be known as Armstrong Medal, established by Radio Club of America, 1935; Medal for Merit, 1947; Washington award for 1951 Western Soc. Engrs. Mem. Inst. Radio Engrs. Rep. Presbyn. Contributor to tech. jours. Inventions: regenerative circuit, 1912; superheterodyne, 1918; super-regenerative circuit, 1920; method of eliminating static in radio by means of frequency modulation, 1939. Home: 435 E. 52d St., N.Y. City. Died Feb. 1, 1954; buried Locust Grove Cemetery, Merrimack, Mass.

ARMSTRONG, Gayle Geard, general contractor, rancher; b. Roswell, N.M., June 15, 1900; s. Geard R. and Clara H. (Gayle) A.; student Peddie Inst., 1917-18, Washington and Lee U., 1918, N.M. Mil. Inst., 1918-19; m. Murphy Shannon, June 18, 1919; children—Billie Bert, Gayle. Operator cattle ranch, 1919-21; partner highway constrn. bus. Armstrong & Armstrong, since 1922, added ranching activities, 1929, irrigated farms, 1937, mgr. firm since 1937; gen. mgr. Allison, Smith, Fellows & Armstrong for constrn. ordnance dept. Ft. Wingate, 1941, Allison, Armstrong & Thygesen for constrn. U.S. Army airfields, 1942-43. Spl. asst. U.S. Sec. of Agr., 1945-46; dep. adminstr. prodn. and marketing adminstrn., v.p Commodity Credit Corp., 1945; designated govt. rep. to operate strike-bound packing plants, Jan. 1946. Served as pvt. S.A.T.C., 1918. Pres. Spring Ranch Sheep Co.; treas. Foundation Investment Co.; partner San Pedro Land Co. Pres. Pecos Valley Farmers Assn., Roswell C. of C., 1945-46, Asso. Contractors of N.M., 1940-45, N.M. Mil. Inst. Alumni Assn., 1938-42, mem, exec. com. Asso. Gen. Contractors of Am., Sigma Chi. Mem. Christian Ch. Mason (Shriner). Club: Rotary. Home: 215 West Seventh St. Office: Box 873, Roswell, N.M. Died Oct. 15, 1950; buried South Park, Roswell.

ARMSTRONG, Moses Kimball, banker, author; b. Milan, O., Sept. 19, 1832; ed. Huron Inst. and Western Res. Coll.; m. Martha Bordeno, 1872. Went to Minn., 1856, and held local offices there; moved to Yankton, Dak.; published first Democratic newspaper in the territory; served 10 yrs. in territorial house and senate; with speaker house and pres. senate; delegate in Congress, 1871-75; Dem.; pres. Old Bank of St. James, Minn. Author: Early History of Dakota Territory, 1866; Empire Builders of the West, 1901 (for which two States have named counties to perpetuate his memory). Address: St. James, Minn. Deceased.

ARMSTRONG, Paul Galloway, state dir. Selective Service; b. Leadville, Colo., Oct. 26, 1890; s. Rev. Arthur Edson and Luvia Adelma (Russell) A.; student Fairmount Sch. (Denver) and West Denver High Sch.; m. Blanche Astrid Larson, Dec. 4, 1916; children—Don Wellington, Patricia Lorraine. With Parker, Schmidt and Tucker Paper Co., Chgo., 1919—, as clk., salesman and v.p.; dir. 1st Mutual Savings Assn.; state director S.S.S. for Illinois, 1940—. Served with 8th U.S. Regular Inf. in France, World War I. Awarded Legion of Merit; Médaille de la France Libér'e for World War II services. Mem. S.A.R., Am. Legion (past state commander). Republican. Presbyterian. Mason (Shriner, 33°). Clubs: Lake Shore, Illinois Athletic. Address: 1831 S. Holmes St., Springfield, Ill. Died Jan. 11, 1958; buried Rosehill Cemetery, Chgo.

ARMSTRONG, Richard H., lawyer; b. Biddeford, Me., Mar. 26, 1903; s. John and Abbie (Moore) A.; LL.B., Mercer U., 1924; B.S., Portland U., 1925; LL.M., Ph.D., McKinley-Roosevelt U., 1930; LL.D. Washington Nat. U.; m. Irma Dawson, Jan. 29, 1927 (div. 1933); 1 son, Richard H.; m. 2d, Beatrice Menard, May 28, 1934; children—Brent P., Maurice H. Began as lawyer and law writer, 1924; mem. Georgia and Maine bars; mem. Armstrong & Spill, Biddleford, Me., 1933-47; Armstrong, Wheeler & Pomeroy, Portland, 1947—, Armstrong, Marshall, Melnick & Caron, Biddeford, 1952—; dean emeritus, prof. pub. law, Portland U. Law Sch.; asst. atty. gen. Maine, 1936-37, chief atty. Office of Price Adminstrn., Maine, 1943-46; city solicitor, Saco, Me., 1944. Lt. col. staff of Gov. of Ga., 1945. Member Am., Maine and York bar assns., assn. of Trial Lawyers (dir.), Internat. (life mem., dir.), Am. (dir.) criminology assns. Author: Florida Chancery Jurisprudence, 1927; Index to Maine Statutes, 1944; Nursing Jurisprudence, 1945, Doctrines of Criminal Law; also articles for law revs. Home: 325 Pool Rd. Office: Journal Bldg., Biddeford, Me. Died Dec. 1959.

ARMSTRONG, Robert John, bishop; b. San Francisco; s. William and Margaret (Ryan) A.; grad. Gonzaga U., Spokane, Wash., 1904, A.M., 1912. Priest. R.C. Ch., 1910; curate Our Lady of Lourdes, Spokane, 1910-14; pastor St. Paul's Ch., Yakima, Wash., 1914-29; bishop Diocese of Sacramento, Cal., since Mar. 12, 1929. Mem. K.C. Home: 4300 Fair Oaks Blvd., Sacramento. Died Jan. 14, 1957; buried Bishops' Chapel, St. Mary's Mausoleum, Sacramento.

ARN, Elmer Raymond, surgeon; b. Arnhelm, O., July 8, 1886; s. Ad and Mary Elizabeth (Schatzman) A.; Miami U., 1904-06; M.D., U. of Cincinnati, 1911; post-grad work, U. of Berlin and U. of Vienna; m. Mina Marie Wannagat, Aug. 27, 1913; children—Elmer Raymond, Kenneth. Practiced at Dayton, since 1912. Surgeon Miami Valley Hospital and Nat. Mil. Home. Past pres. Dayton Bur. Community Service, 1937-39. Mem. Founders Group of Am. Bd. Surgery. Mem. bd. trustees, Miami Valley Hosp., Dayton Art Inst., pres. of Dayton Philharmonic Orchestra. Fellow A.C.S. (governor of Ohio); mem. A.M.A., Ohio State Med. Assn., Am. Assn. for Study of Goiter (ex-pres.), Alpha Kappa Kappa. Mason (33°) former Grand Master of Ohio, dep. for Ohio, Ancient and accepted Scottish Rite Bodies. pres. George Washington Nat. Masonic Meml. Assn.; mem. bd. of trustees Ohio Masonic Home. Mem. Dayton Rotary Club. Lutheran. Contbr. on goiter to med. jours. Home: 429 Ridgewood Av. Office: Fidelity Bldg., Dayton, O. Died Dec. 24, 1951.

ARNDT, Karl M(atthews), economist; b. Evanston, Ill., Aug. 27, 1901; s. Charles and Rose Agatha (Wahle) A.; Litt. B., U. of Notre Dame, 1922; student U. of Louvain, Belgium, 1922-24; m. Dorothy Welch, Aug. 8, 1929. Asst. prof. economics Creighton U., Omaha, Neb., 1924-25; prof. economics Canisius Coll., Buffalo, 1925-26; instr. in economics U. of Neb., 1926-29, asst. prof., 1929-33, asso. prof., 1933-45, professor of economics 1945-52 (on leave since Sept. 1, 1950); sr. staff economist Council Econ. Advisers, 1950-53; profl. lectr. Am. U. Washington, 1951-53; cons. economist N.Y.U. Workshop on economic edn., summer 1952, econ. adviser Mut. Security Mission to China, Taipei, Taiwan, 1953; financial economist Govt. Union of Burma, 1953-54; asst. dir. Fgn. Operations Adminstrn., Mut. Security Mission to China, Taipei, Taiwan, 1954—. Mem. Am. Econ. Assn., Am. Finance Assn., Beta Gamma Sigma, Delta Sigma Pi, Theta Chi. Specialist in money (monetary systems and monetary policy) and banking. Home: 4812 Drummond Av., Chevy Chase 15, Md. Died Feb. 22, 1956.

ARNDT, William Frederick (ärndt), educator; b. Mayville, Wis., Dec. 1, 1880; s. Christian and Mary (Oertwig) A.; student Concordia Coll., St. Paul, 1894-97, Concordia Coll., Milw., 1897-1900, Concordia Sem., St. Louis, 1900-03; A.M., U. Chgo., 1923; Ph.D., Washington U., St. Louis, 1935; D.D., Concordia Coll., Adelaide, Australia, 1930; m. Emma Vetter, July 23, 1907 (died June 18, 1933); children—Erna Hedwig, Ilse Lenore. Ordained to ministry Luth. Ch. (Mo. Synod), 1903, pastor, Bluff City, Tenn., 1903-05, St. Peters Ch., St. Joseph, Mo., 1905-10, Bethlehem Ch., Bklyn., 1910-12; teacher of Latin, Greek and Hebrew, St. Paul's Coll., Concordia, Mo., 1912-21; prof. N.T., Concordia Sem., St. Louis, 1921-51, prof. emeritus, 1951-57. Mem. Foreign Missions Bd., Luth. Mo. Synod, 1921-56; mem. com. on Luth. union, Luth. Mo. Synod, 1935-50. Mem. Church Craft Expedition, Palestine, 1947. Mem. Classical Club of St. Louis, Club Classical Philology (St. Louis), Mo. Acad. Science, Hist. Soc. Mo., Archaeol. Inst. Am., Soc. Bibl. Lit. and Exegesis. Author: Does the Bible Contradict Itself, 1926; Siehe, ich stehe vor der Tuer (German sermons), 1929; Bible Difficulties, 1932; Popular Symbolics (with others), 1934; Christian Prayer, 1937; Fundamental Christian Beliefs, 1938; New Testament History, 1939; Life of St. Paul, 1944; St. Luke (Bible commentary), 1956; Greek-English Lexicon of the New Testament (with F. W. Gingrich), 1957. Mng. editor Theol. Monthly, 1926-30, Concordia Theol. Monthly, 1938-50. Home: 7126 Northmore Dr., St. Louis. Died Feb. 25, 1957.

ARNEILL, James Rae (år-nēl), physician; b. De Pere, Wis., Mar. 6, 1869; s. John and Elizabeth (Rae) A.; A.B., Lawrence U. (Wis.), LL.D., 1923; M.D., U. Mich., 1894; m. Sarah Hyatt Taylor, Sept. 1900. Instr. clin. medicine U. Mich., 1897-1903; settled in Denver; was prof. medicine U. Colo. Mem. bd. regents A.C.P.; mem. A.M.A., Colo. Med. Soc. Served as capt., M.C., U.S. Army, World War. Author: Clinical Diagnosis and Urinalysis, 1905. Contbr. Reference Handbook of Med. Scis. Home: 741 Washington St. Office: 1765 Sherman St., Denver. Died Jan. 27, 1950; buried Fairmont Cemetery, Denver.

ARNESON, Ben, coll. prof.; b. Barneveld, Wis., May 22, 1883; s. Timan and Inger (Ruste) A.; grad. Whitewater Normal Sch., 1908; B.A., U. of Wisconsin, 1913, M.A., 1914, Ph.D., 1916; LL.D., Bowling Green State Univ., 1950; m. Elsie E. Baade, 1909; 1 dau., Esther Mildred. Teacher pub. schs., Barneveld and Sheboygan Falls, Wis., 1 yr. in German-English Acad., Milwaukee, 1909-10; taught polit. science at U. of Wis. and U. of Minn.; prof. polit. sci., Ohio Wesleyan U., 1917-53, also head dept.; dir. Ben. A. Arneston Inst. Practical Politics, 1947—; taught at Miami Univ., summers, 1929 and 1934, Ohio State U., summer, 1932, American U., summer, 1935; visiting prof. polit. science, American U., 1936-38. Administrative Consultant, United States Bureau of the Budget, summers, 1939 and 1940; review and negotiations officer, U.S. Civil Service Commn., summer 1942, consult., summer 1944. Mem. Am. Polit. Sci. Assn., Phi Beta Kappa, Alpha Tau Omega, Omicron Delta Kappa, Pi Sigma Alpha (nat. pres. 1948-50). Methodist. Kiwanian (governor Ohio district 1935). Co-author: A Gateway to the Social Sciences, 1926. Author: Elements of Constitutional Law, 1928; The Democratic Monarchies of Scandinavia, 1939 (rev. 1949). Home: 92 Montrose Av., Delaware, O. Died Feb. 13, 1958; buried Oak Grove Cemetery, Delaware.

ARNETT, Trevor, b. Little Hereford, Eng., Nov. 1870; s. John Bill and Sarah E. (Rowbotham) A.; student U. Minn., 1890-92; A.B., U. Chgo., 18[illegible]; post-grad., 1898-99; fellow, 1899-1900; Sc.D., Carleton Coll., 1926; LL.D., Colby Coll., 1939, Kalamazoo Coll., 1947; m. Bertha M. Stetson, Apr. 21, 1900. Accountant, chief clerk auditor's office C.G.W.Ry., 1893-96; chief accountant, 1899-1900, auditor, 190[illegible]-22, v.p., bus. mgr., 1924-26, U. Chgo. Trustee Rockefeller Inst. Med. Research (resigned 1937); mem. Rockefeller Found., Gen. Edn. Bd. (sec. 1920-24; pres. 1928-36), Internat. Edn. Bd. (pres. 1928-36); ret. 1936. Auditor Bapt. Theol. Union, 1901-22; trustee U. Chgo., Atlanta U., Rockford, Spelman, Morehouse colls. Recognized as an authority on coll. finance. Republican. Baptist. Clubs: Men's Faculty, Columbia University, Quadrangle. Wrote: Fraternity Accounting for Chapters, 1910; Teachers' Salaries in Certain Endowed Colleges and Universities in the United States, 1921 and 1928; College and University Finance, 1922; also various articles on coll. and univ. finance. Home: Grand Beach, Mich. Died Mar. 31, 1955; buried Kalamazoo, Mich.

ARNEY, C. E., Jr., assn. exec.; b. Idaho Falls, Ida., Jan. 9, 1891; s. C. E. and N. Gertrude (Jenks) A.; LL.B., U. Wash., 1915; m. Sherlie Rude, Oct. 16, 1943; children by previous marriage—Patricia Marie (Mrs. Clyde W. Stepheson) and Kathleen Jeanne (Mrs. N. N. Benson) (twins). Admitted to bar, 1915; clk. Wash. Atty. Gen.'s Office, 1915-18; asst. counsel U.S. Shipping Bd. Emergency Fleet Corp., 1918-20; asst. mgr. Seattle C. of C., 1920-22; exec. mgr. Wash. Fedn. Tax Payers Assns., 1922-30; radio commentator and pub. relations dir., radio sta. KOMO-KJR, Seattle, 1934-40; sec.-treas. Nat. Assn. Radio and TV Broadcasters, 1940—. Mem. Phi Delta Phi, Sigma Nu. Office: 1771 N St. N.W., Washington 6. Died Nov. 1, 1956; buried Mt. Pleasant Cemetery, Seattle.

ARNN, Charles Edward, adv. sales cons.; b. Jackson, Tenn., Apr. 1, 1897; s. James Walter and Lelia (Keiser) A.; student Northwestern, 1915-17; A.B. Stanford, 1921; LL.D., Coll. Osteopathic Phys. and Surgs., 1947; m. Paulyne McKinney, Dec. 31, 1920; children—Sally Nell, Sue Carolyn. Advt. mgr. Crescent Creamery Co., Los Angeles, 1921-22; sales engr. Young & McCalister, 1922-25; advt. mgr. Bullock's, Inc., 1928-31; sales mgr. Forest Lawn Meml. Park, 1925-28; sales promotion mgr. Desmond's, 1932-36; advt. dir. Los Angeles Daily News, 1936-40, v.p. 1940-51, exec. v.p., 1951-53, propr. Arnn & Associates, public relations and sales consultant 1953—; director of the Standard Paper Box Co. Pres. U.N. War Relief Council of So. Cal. 1944-45. Chmn. bd. trustees Coll. Osteopathic Physicians and Surgeons. Served as pharmacists mate, U.S.N., World War I. Mem. Am. Newspaper Pubs. Assn., Newspaper Advt. Execs. Assn. (dir.), So. Cal. Alumni Assn. (past pres.), Lambda Chi Alpha, Alpha Delta Sigma, Sigma Delta Chi. Clubs: Kiwanis (past pres.), Advertising (past pres.), Jonathan Country (Los Angeles). Home: 2738 Forrester Dr. Los Angeles 64. Office: 609 S. Grand Av., Los Angeles 17. Died Aug. 12, 1955; buried Forest Lawn Meml. Park.

ARNOLD, Almon Al, coll. prof.; b. Ft. Wayne, Ind., Apr. 13, 1887; s. Charles M. and Almira Elizabeth (Boger) A.; A.B., Wittenberg Acad. and Coll., 1912, M.A., 1920; student U. of Minn., summer 1915, Certificado de Suficiencia, Centro de estudios históricos, Universidad Central de España, 1920; m. Ada C. Bosserman, Aug. 19, 1914; children—Charles David, Dorothea Mae (Mrs. Stephen Ray), Arthur Lee, Marvin Eugene. Instr. in German, Wittenberg Coll., summer 1912; science teacher Richmond (Ind.) High Sch., 1912-13; instr. fgn. langs. Okla. A. and M. Coll., 1913-19, asso., 1917-19, acting head, 1919-20, prof. fgn. langs., 1919—, head dept. fgn. langs. 1919—, vice dean of Sch. of Arts and Scis., 1926—, French teacher Army Specialized Training Program mil. unit, 1916-17, head fgn. lang. mil. units, 1943-45. Mem. Modern Lang. Assn. (S. Central), Am. Assn. Teachers of Spanish and Portuguese, Phi Kappa Phi. Democrat. Presbyterian. Lecturer before civic, ch. and professional groups. Author: Minimum Spanish Essentials (N.Y.A. mimeograph service, A. & M. Coll.), 1936. Home: 1606 E. Third Av., Stillwater, Okla. Died May 15, 1955; buried Fairlawn Cemetery, Stillwater.

ARNOLD, Ben, judge; b. Newark, Ark., Oct. 24, 1892; s. Martin Luther and Elizabeth (Hughes) A.; student U. of Ark., 1911-13; A.B., U. of Okla., 1920, LL.B., 1925; m. Florence Melton, Mar. 19, 1920; 1 dau., Ella Beth. Prin. Afton (Okla.) High Sch., 1914-17, Oilton (Okla.) High Sch., 1920-23; teacher Univ. Model High Sch. and Norman High while studying law at U. of Okla.; admitted to Okla. bar, 1925, and began practice in Oklahoma City; elected dist. judge, 13th Judicial Dist., Okla., 1934, reëlected, 1938; elected justice, 3d Dist., Supreme Ct. of Okla., three terms, 1941-58, vice-chief justice Supreme Ct., 1949-51, chief justice,

1951-53. Served with 42d (Rainbow) Division, U.S. Army, with A.E.F., 1917-19. Mem. Dist. Judges Conf. (mem. legislative com. 1935-41). Mem. Okla. State and County bar assns., Am. Legion, Phi Delta Phi. Democrat. Mem. Christian Ch. Mason (32°, Shriner), K.P. Address: Edmond, Okla. Died Sept. 30, 1955; buried Meml. Park Cemetery, Oklahoma City.

ARNOLD, Constantine Peter, lawyer; b. Ashtabula County, O., Feb. 7, 1860; s. Franklin A.; A.B., Wabash Coll., 1881; m. Annie B. Arnold, June 4, 1887; children—Thurman W., Carl F. Practiced in Laramie; Dem. candidate for congress, 1896; mem. Wyo. State Bd. Law Examiners, 1908—. Mem. Am. (v.p.), Wyo. (1st pres. 1914) bar assns., Colo.-Wyo. Acad. Science, Wyo. Pioneer Assn. (pres. 1929), Phi Gamma Delta, Phi Beta Kappa (hon.). Presbyn. Author: Athletics of the Mind, 1917; Winter Picnics, 1924; Modern Prayer Book for Western Plants, 1925; The Coroner's Jury, 1926. Home: Laramie, Wyo. Deceased.

ARNOLD, Earl Caspar, lawyer; b. Iola, Kan., June 8, 1884; s. Charles Lawrence and Mary Elizabeth (Jacoby) A.; A.B., Baker U., 1906, LL.D., 1930; LL.B., Northwestern U., 1909; m. Mabel E. Weaver, Oct. 5, 1910 (died 1922); children—Marjorie (Mrs. E. M. Kirby), Charles W.; m. 2d, Susan F. Vaughan, June 24, 1940. Admitted to practice of law by bars, D.C., Idaho, Ill., Ohio, Tenn., and Supreme Court of U.S.; practiced at Boise, Ida., 1909-12; asst. to solicitor U.S. Dept. Agr., 1912-14; prof. law U. Ida., 1914-17, U. Fla., 1917-19, U. Cincinnati, 1919-23, George Washington U., 1923-30; dean Vanderbilt U. Sch. of Law, 1930-46; dean emeritus, 1946—; prof. law Northwestern U. Law Sch., summers 1921, 25, George Washington Law Sch., summer 1944, Western Reserve U. Sch. of Law, summer 1947; engaged in business and farming, 1947—. Member executive com. Assn. American Law Schools, 1943. Mem. Am. Bar Assn., Am. Law Inst., S.A.R. (pres. Andrew Jackson chapter, 1933; pres. Tenn. state soc., 1934), Order of Coif, Sigma Phi Epsilon, Delta Theta Phi, Delta Sigma Rho, Omicron Delta Kappa. Mason (K.T.). Club: Kiwanis of Nashville (pres. 1935; lt. gov. Div. 6, Ky.-Tenn. Dist. of Kiwanis Internat., 1940; gov. same, 1941). Author: Outlines of Suretyship and Guaranty, 1927. Extensive contbr. to legal mags. Home: 3705 Rosemont Av., Nashville 4, Tenn. Died Nov. 21, 1949.

ARNOLD, Edward (Guenther Schneider), actor; b. N.Y.C., Feb. 18, 1890; s. Charles and Elizabeth Schneider; student pub. schs. N.Y.C.; m. Harriet Marshall, Apr. 1916; children—Elizabeth Ohse (wife of Dr. William F. Orlando), William Edward, Dorothy Jane; m. 2d, Olive Emerson, Jan. 15, 1929 (div. 1949); m. 3d, Cleo P. Arnold, Oct. 7, 1951; 1 stepson, Michael Paris. Actor, 1907—, playing with Ben Greet Players, 2 yrs., Maxine Elliott, 2 yrs., Ethel Barrymore, 3 yrs., in stock cos., 11 yrs., played in Broadway prodns., The Storm, 1919, Nervous Wreck, 1922, Third Little Show, Music Box Revue, Miracle of Verdun, Whistling in the Dark; in motion pictures, 1932—, starring in Diamond Jim Brady, Come and Get It, You Can't Take It With You, Mr. Smith Goes to Washington, Meet John Doe, The Devil and Daniel Webster, The Ambassador's Daughter, and many others. Mem. Hollywood br. Nat. Def. Com. Vice pres. Permanent Charities Com. of Motion Picture Industry. Trustee So. Cal. Symphony Assn.; mem. bd. dir. Screen Actors' Guild; mem. Am. Fed. Radio Artists (nat. and local bd. mem.); hon. mem. Hollywood C. of C. Clubs: Breakfast (Los Angeles); Bohemian (San Francisco). Author: Lorenzo Goes to Hollywood (autobiography with F. F. Dubuc), 1940. Home: 10425 Bainbridge Av., Los Angeles 24. Address: 17349 Rancho St., Encino, Cal. Died Apr. 26, 1956; buried San Fernando (Cal.) Mission.

ARNOLD, Francis Joseph, physician; b. Burlington, Vt., Oct. 10, 1872; s. Joseph and Mary S. (Cummings) A.; M.D., U. of Vt., 1901; unmarried. Interne Mary Fletcher Hosp., Burlington, 1901-03; grad. work in diseases of eye, ear, nose and throat Phila. Hosps., 1903-04; practiced at Burlington since 1904; specializes in diseases of the eye, ear, nose and throat. Mem. staffs Mary Fletcher, Bishop DeGoesbriand Memorial and Fanny Allen hosps. and Providence Orphan Asylum and Hosp. Mem. A.M.A., Am. Acad. Ophthalmology and Otolaryngology, Vermont State Med. Soc., Chittenden Co. Med. Soc., New Eng. Otolaryngol. Soc. Catholic. Clubs: Knights of Columbus, Ethan Allen. Home: 94 North Av. Office: 182 Pearl St., Burlington, Vt. Died July 19, 1950.

ARNOLD, Frank Atkinson; b. Westboro, Mass., June 2, 1867; s. Daniel W. and France (Fay) A.; high sch. and coll. preparatory edn., also spl. study; m. Harriet Eudora Gurney, Nov. 27, 1890; children—Dorothy Faye (Mrs. W. O. Graham), Hilda Gurney (Mrs. F. S. Pease), Cyril Durrell, Donald Woodward, Frank Denman, Phyllis Eudora (Mrs. C. D. Rudolph). Engaged in mercantile business to 1893; editor, pub. The Trade Monthly, Boston, 1894-97; asst. advt. mgr. The Christian Endeavor World, Boston, and editor Literary Bulletin, 1898-99; on staff Boston Journal, 1900; editor, gen. mgr. Dry Goods Chronicle, and Modern Merchant, N.Y.C., 1900-02; v.p., sec. Colonial Press, Boston, pubs. The Suburban, 1904-07; v.p., sec. Suburban Press, N.Y.C., 1907-10, pres. and pub. Suburban Life Mag., afterwards Countryside Mag., 1911-16; spl. lit. work for Arnold Arboretum, Boston, 1917; sec., dir. Frank Seaman, Inc., adv. agency, N.Y.C., 1917-26; dir. of development NBC, 1926-32; v.p. Albert Frank-Guerther Law, Inc., 1932-33; cons. radio broadcasting, 1933—; lectr. Coll. of City N.Y.; nat. export chmn. Am. Assn. Adv. Agencies; trade adviser Nat. Fgn. Trade Council; v.p., asso. mng. dir. Inst. Pub. Relations; v.p. Edwin Bird Wilson, 1938. Mem. Mayor's Com. on Nat. Defense N.Y.C. Republican. Conglist. Mason. Club: Advertising, Twenty Year Radio Club (charter mem. 1942). Author: Broadcast Advertising—the Fourth Dimension, 1931, television edit., 1933; Do You Want to Get Into Radio?, 1940. Lectr. and writer on subject of radio. Home: Upper Montclair, N.J. Died July 16, 1958; buried Mt. Hebron Cemetery, Upper Montclair.

ARNOLD, Hazen S., investment banker; b. Toledo, Sept. 16, 1901; s. George D. and Elizabeth (Kirchgessner) A.; grad. Dundee (Mich.) High Sch., 1919; m. Louise Ann Warren, Feb. 14, 1925; children—Hazen, Helen (Mrs. Frederick Kent, Jr.). Municipal bond business, 1919—, with W. L. Slayton & Co., Toledo, 1919-26, Braun Bosworth & Co., 1926—, becoming exec. v.p., then pres., 1951—; dir. Indiana Glass Co. Former mayor Ottawa Hills, O.; chmn. bd. N.C. Municipal Adv. Council. Dir. Crippled Childrens Home, Toledo. Mem. Investment Bankers Assn. (past chmn. municipal securities com., past v.p.). Clubs: Inverness Country (past pres.), Toledo (v.p.). Home: 2841 Westchester Rd., Toledo, Died Sept. 13, 1953; buried Calvary Cemetery, Toledo.

ARNOLD, Henry J., coll. pres. emeritus; b. Sterling, Neb., Feb. 11, 1887; s. Henry and Rebecca (Menken) A.; A.B., U. Neb., 1917; A.M., U. Ia., 1924; Ph.D., Ohio State U., 1929; m. Hannah Julia Ehmen, Dec. 21, 1909; children—Harold Wilfred, Verna Gretchen. Prin. Bristow (Neb.) High Sch., 1908-09; asst. prin. Sterling (Neb.) Acad., 1910-13; prin. Wartburg Acad., Waverly, Ia., 1913-16; dean and instr. in psychology and edn. Wartburg Normal Coll., Waverly, Ia., 1917-23; instr. psychology U. Ia., 1923-25; asst. prof. psychology and dir. Extension Dept., Wittenberg Coll., 1925-27, asso. prof. and dir. Div. of Spl. Schs., 1928-35, prof. of psychology, 1935-39; instr. psychology Ohio State U., 1927-28; dean Wittenberg-Dayton Jr. Coll., 1929-39; pres. Hartwick Coll., Oneonta, N.Y., 1939-53, pres. emeritus, 1953—; exec. v.p. Iron Mountain Atomic Storage Corp., Hudson, N.Y. Sec., Commn. of Adjudication, United Luth. Ch. in Am., 1942—. Carl Schurz Meml. Found. fellow to make survey of adult edn. in Germany and Austria, 1932. Pres. Adult Edn. Council of Springfield, 1934-39; mem. Ohio Assn. for Adult Edn. (pres. 1932-39), Nat. Luth. Ednl. Conf. (treas., mem. exec. com. 1922-35, sec.-treas. 1936-47), Internat. Congress of Psychology, Am. Psychol. Assn., Mid-Western Psychol. Assn., N.E.A., Ohio Coll. Assn., Ohio Acad. Science, Phi Delta Kappa, Kappa Phi Kappa, Delta Sigma Phi, Psi Chi. Lutheran. Rotarian. Co-Author: Research Adventures in University Teaching, 1927. Contbr. to jours. Home: Saugerties, N.Y. Died Apr. 5, 1959; buried Hartwick Seminary Cemetery, N.Y.

ARNOLD, John Carlisle, justice Supreme Ct. Pa.; b. Curwensville, Pa., Mar. 10, 1887; s. William C. and Jane Patton (Irvin) A.; LL.B., University of Pennsylvania, 1909, LL.D. (hon.), Dickinson Coll.; m. Clare E. Platt, Sept. 17, 1913; children—Jane A. (Mrs. Mann), John Carlisle, Dan P., Mary A. (Mrs. Brandis). Admitted to Pa. bar, 1910; practice of law, Clearfield, Pa., 1910-45; dist. atty. Clearfield Co., 1918-25; judge Superior Ct. (Appellate) of Pa., 1945-53; justice Supreme Court, 1953—. Trustee of the Dickinson Law School and College. Mem. American, Pennsylvania (pres. 1942-43) bar assns., Delta Chi. Republican. Methodist (trustee). Mason (33°). Clubs: Duquesne (Pitts.); Union League (Phila.). Home: 113 Elizabeth St. Office: Box 711, Clearfield, Pa. Died 1958.

ARNOLD, Samuel Tomlinson, univ. provost; b. Fall River, Mass., Aug. 23, 1892; s. Henry and Annie (Tomlinson) A.; A.B., Brown U., 1913, Sc.M., 1914, Ph.D., 1916; Sc.D., R.I. Coll. Pharm., 1947, Franklin and Marshall Coll., 1949, U. R.I., 1953; LL.D., Tufts Coll., 1950; m. Vera Stockard, June 1920; children—David Stockard, Samuel Tomlinson, Henry Jerome. Instr. in chemistry Brown U., 1916-17, asst. prof., 1917-22, asso. prof., 1922-30, prof., 1930—, also acting dean, 1929-30, dean of undergrads., 1930-37, dean of coll., 1937-46, dean of univ., 1946-49, provost, 1949—; cons. War Dept., Corps Engrs., 1943-46; dir. Narragansett Electric Co.; trustee Citizens Savings Bank. Mem. R.I. State Council of Def.; chmn. Gov.'s Adv. Commn. on Ednl. TV; chmn. exec. com. Coll. Entrance Exam. Bd., 1952—. Mem. Am. Chem. Soc. (chmn. R.I. sect. 1922-25), Eastern Assn. Deans and Advisers of Men (pres. 1936-37), Nat. Collegiate Athletic Assn. (v.p. 1st dist. 1934-35), Arts Program Assn. Am. Coll. (dir. 1940-42), Am. Council on Edn. (2d v.p. 1946), New Eng. Assn. Colls. and Secondary Schs. (pres. 1947), Nat. Assn. Student Personnel Adminstrs., Nat. Assn. Acad. Deans (v.p. 1949-50), Eastern Coll. Personnel Officers, Assn. N.R.O.T.C. Colls. (pres. 1948-50), Phi Beta Kappa, Sigma Xi. Conglist. Clubs: Faculty, Art (Providence); Brown University (N.Y.C.). Home: 10 Euclid Av., Providence 6. Died Dec. 12, 1956; buried Swan Point Cemetery, Providence.

ARNOLD, William C., commissioner, territorial commander Southern Territory of the Salvation Army, 1939-48, ret. Address: 675 Seminole Av. N.E., Atlanta 7. Died Aug. 19, 1955.

ARNOLD, W(illiam) F(rederick), corp. exec.; b. Cin., 1898; s. Peter Edward and Mary (Widmer) A.; student U. Cin., 1920-22; m. Lola Werner, Aug. 1942; children—Robert William (by a former marriage), Thomas Frederick, George William. V.p. Underwood Corp., N.Y.C., 1944—. Republican. Clubs: Advertising, Sales Executives (dir.), N.Y. Sales Managers (past pres.) (N.Y.C.). Home: 1061 Park Av., N.Y.C. 28. Office: 1 Park Av., N.Y.C. Died Aug. 20, 1959; buried Ferncliff Cemetery, Hartsdale, Y.N.

ARNOLD William Wright, ex-congressman; ret. judge Tax Court of U.S.; b. Oblong, Crawford Co., Ill., Oct. 14, 1877; s. Berzelius M. and Mary Catherine (Baker) A.; student Austin Coll., Effingham, Ill., 1 yr.; LL.B., U. of Ill., 1901; m. Kate Wheeler Busey, Oct. 1909; children—William Busey, Mary Alice. Admitted to Ill. bar, 1901; began practice at Robinson; mem. firm McCarty & Arnold, 1901-22; mem. 68th to 74th Congresses (1923-37), 23d Ill. Dist.; resigned, Sept. 15, 1935, to become mem. U.S. Bd. of Tax Appeals (now The Tax Court of the U.S.). Mem. Ill. State and Crawford Co. bar assns., Sigma Alpha Epsilon. Democrat. Mason (32°, K.T., Shriner), Odd Fellow, K.P., Elk, Woodman. Club: Crawford County Country. Retired. Home: Robinson, Ill. Died Nov. 23, 1957; buried Robinson Cemetery.

ARONSON, Albert Y. (ăr'ŏn-sŭn), newspaperman; b. Cedar Rapids, Ia., Feb. 27, 1886; s. Louis and Yetta (Schnadig) A.; student U. Ind., 1904-06; m. Rose Schonwald, Mar. 28, 1916. Reporter Detroit News, June-Nov. 1906, Port Huron (Mich.) Herald, 1906-07, Louisville Courier-Journal, 1907-10; with Louisville Times, 1910—, mng. editor, 1923-52, columnist, 1952—. Sec. Louisville Vice Commn., 1916. Mem. exec. com. Asso. Press Mng. Editors Assn. 1941-48, chmn., 1946-47; mem. Phi Delta Theta. Jewish religion. Home: 1578 Cherokee Rd., Louisville 5. Died April, 1957; buried Adath Israel Cemetery.

ARONSON, Jacob, ry. official; b. Brooklyn, N. Y., Jan. 2, 1887; s. William and Hannah (Kalins) A.; LL.B., St. Lawrence U., Brooklyn, 1906, LL.D., 1934; m. Sadie Michaels, Aug. 30, 1914; children—Ruth (Mrs. Peter Meyer), Hubert. Admitted to N.Y. bar, 1908. Entered the employ of N.Y.C. R.R. Co., 1906; thereafter asst. atty., asst. gen. atty., 1922-26, asst. gen. counsel, 1926-29, gen. counsel, 1929-33, v.p. 1933, vice president and general counsel since 1947. Director M.C. R.R., C., C., C.&St.L. Ry. (Big Four), New York & Harlem R.R. and other affiliated and subsidiary companies of N.Y.C. R.R. Company; dir. Century Fed. Savings & Loan Assn., Searsdale Nat. Bank & Trust Co. Mem. Board of Appeals, Village of Scarsdale. Mem. Am., N.Y. State, and City of New York bar assns. Republican. Reform Jewish religion (hon. chmn. exec. bd. Union Am. Hebrew Congregations), Mason. Clubs: Quaker Ridge Golf, Traffic (N.Y.). Home: Scarsdale, N.Y. Office: 466 Lexington Av., N.Y. City 17. Died Jan. 13, 1951.

ARONSTAM, Noah Ephraim ăr' ŭn-stăm), physician; b. Libau, Latvia, Feb. 18, 1872; s. C. N. and Yetta (Nieburg) A.; grad. Gymnasium, 1888; M.D., Mich. Coll. Medicine and Surgery, 1898; post-grad. U. Berlin, 1907; m. Sarah Blumberg, 1899; children—Ralph Godfrey (dec.), Theodora Judith. Practiced at Detroit, 1898—; lectr. on dermatology and venereal disease, Mich. Coll. Medicine and Surgery, 1905, apptd. prof., 1906. Mem. Am., Mich., Wayne County med. assns., Am. Med. Editors' Assn., Maimonides Soc. of Detroit (pres. 1916), Zionist Dist. of Detroit (pres. 1918), Phi Lambda Kappa, Pi Gamma Mu. Del. to British Congress on Tb, 1902; hon. mention Internat. Exhibit of Hygiene, Dresden, 1912. Authorized delegate of A.M.A. to World Congress of Jewish Physicians at Jerusalem, Israel, 1952. Founder, Detroit Philos. Soc., 1899; chmn. Mich. Spinoza Tri-centennial Com., 1932. Mem. Mich. Authors' Assn. Author: Sociological Studies of a Medico-Legal Nature (with Louis J. Rosenberg), 1902; Manual on Venereal Diseases; Jewish Dietary Laws from a Scientific Standpoint, 1912; The Lost Nation, 1940; also poetry local newspapers. Address: N.Y.C. Died Sept. 30, 1957; buried Clover Hill Park Cemetery, Detroit.

ARROWOOD, Charles Flinn, univ. prof.; b. Cabarrus County, N.C., Nov. 9, 1887; s. Rev. Robert Sylvanus and Mary Louise (Dickson) A.; A.B., Davidson (N.C.) Coll., 1909, D.Litt., 1941; B.D., Union Theol. Sem., Richmond, Va., 1915; A.B., Rice Inst., Houston, Tex., 1918, M.A., 1921; Ph.D., U. of Chicago, 1924; m. Flora Kathleen Register, 1914. Teacher high sch., Hemp, N.C., 1909, and 1912; prin. schs., St. Pauls, N.C., 1910-11; ordained Presbyn. ministry, 1915; pastor various Tex. chs., 1915-20; resigned ministry, 1930; fellow in edn., Rice Inst., 1918-20; prof. philosophy, S.W. Presbyn. U. of Tenn., 1920-23; asst. in philosophy, U. of Chicago, 1923-24; instr. in edn., Rice Inst., 1924-26, asst. prof., 1926-28; prof. history and philosophy of edn., U. of Tex., since 1928; mem. grad. faculty since 1934; lecturer Teachers Coll., Columbia U., summer 1928; vis. prof. U. of Ill., summers, 1937, 47, Colo., 1940, 48, 50, Duke, 1941. Del. of U.S. to 4th Internat. Conf. on Edn., Geneva, 1935. Mem. Nat. Soc. Coll. Teachers of Edn. (exec. com., 1937-40), Texas State Teachers Association, Phi Beta Kappa, Phi Delta Kappa, Phi Kappa Sigma. Presbyterian. Mason. Clubs: University, Scholia. Author: Thomas Jefferson and Education in a Republic, 1930; Development of Modern Education (with F. Eby), 1934; The History and Philosophy of Education, Ancient and Medieval (with same), 1940; Theory of Education in Political Philosophy of Adam Smith, 1945. George Buchanan on the Powers of the Crown in Scotland, 1948; Consultant "Documentary History of Edn. in the South." Contbr. to Dictionary of Am. Biography, to Twenty-Fifth Yearbook, Nat. Soc. Coll. Teachers of Edn. and to mags. Home: 2919 West Av., Austin, Tex. Died Feb. 6, 1951; buried Clinton, N.C.

ARSCOTT, A. E., banker; b. Walkerton, Ont., Aug. 25, 1889; s. John and Jennia (Herbert) A.; ed. pub. and high schs., Walkerton, Ont. Began as junior in The Canadian Bank of Commerce, 1905, asst. inspector, 1919-20, asst. mgr., Ottawa, 1920-22, asst. mgr., Toronto, 1922-28, asst. gen. mgr. head office, 1929-37, apptd. gen. mgr., 1937; dir. 1938, vice pres. 1940, exec. vice pres. 1942, pres. 1944-48, chmn. bd. since 1948; dir. Canadian Gen. Electric Co. Ltd., Canada Life Assurance Co., Russell Industries Ltd., Canada Cycle & Motor Co., Ltd., Canadian Acme Screw & Gear, Ltd. Decorated Commander Order of the British Empire. Clubs: York (Toronto); Mount Royal (Montreal); Rosedale Golf (Toronto). Home: "Sunningdale," 20 Sandringham Dr. Office: 25 King St., W., Toronto, Ont., Can. Died Feb. 6, 1951.

ARTERS, John Manley, clergyman; b. Deals Island, Md., Aug. 13, 1877; s. Joseph Allen and Nancy (Smith) A.; grad. Wilmington Conf. Acad., Dover, Del., 1896; A.B., Dickinson Coll., 1899, D.D., 1929; m. Anna Louise Morris, Apr. 24, 1901. Ordained ministry M.E. Ch., 1899; pastor Fairlee, Md., 1899-1901, Odessa, Del., 1902-04, Wilmington, Del., 1904-08, Portland, Me., 1911-14, Rumford, Me., 1915-17. Del. state supt. Anti-Saloon League, 1908-11; supt. Portland dist. Me. Conf. M.E. Ch., 1919-25; gen. sec. Me. Council Religious Edn., 1925; pastor Clark Meml. M.E. Ch., Portland, Me., 1925-28; pastor Grace Ch., Bangor, Me., 1929-32; supt. Bangor dist., Me. Conf. M.E. Ch., 1933-39; leave of absence, 1939; sec. gen. conf. M.E. Ch., 1928-40. Served with YMCA, in army camps in U.S. during World War. Republican. Home: 587 Shore Road, Cape Elizabeth, Me. Died Feb. 18, 1943; buried Falmouth Foreside, Me.

ASCH, Sholem (Shalom) (ăsh), author; b. Kutno, Poland, Nov. 1, 1880; s. Moishe and Malka (Wydawski) A.; ed. Hebrew schs. and Rabbinical Coll., Poland; hon. D.H.L., Inst. Jewish Religion, N.Y. City; m. Mathilda Spira, Dec. 1901; children—Nathan, Moe, John, Ruth. Came to U.S., 1910, naturalized, 1920. Writer, 1901—. Mem. Joint Distribution Com., N.Y. City; mem. Jewish Agency of Jerusalem. Decorated Officer Polonia Restituta (Poland). Hon. mem. P.E.N., London; hon. pres. Jewish P.E.N., Buenois Aires, Argentina. Author: (all translated from Yiddish originally and from German translations) Three Cities, 1933; Salvation, 1934; Mottke the Thief, 1935; In the Beginning, 1935; Mother, 1937; The War Goes On, 1937; Three Novels, 1938; Song of the Valley, 1939; The Nazarene, 1939; What I Believe, 1941; Children of Abraham, 1942; The Apostle, 1943; One Destiny, 1945; East River, 1946; Tales of My People, 1948; Mary, 1949; Moses, 1951; A Passage in the Night, 1953; The Prophet, 1955. Office: care G. P. Putnam's Sons, 210 Madison Av., N.Y.C. 16. Died July 10, 1957.

ASCHAM, John Bayne (ăs'kăm), clergyman; born Vanlue, O., Feb. 12, 1873; s. Frederick Augustus and Minnie (Ault) A.; A.B., Ohio Wesleyan U., 1900 (Phi Beta Kappa), A.M., 1902; A.M., Harvard, 1906; Ph.D., Boston U., 1907; spent 6 mos. in travel and study, Italy and Germany, 1907; spl. student, Am. Sch. Oriental Research, Jerusalem, 1913, and made extensive tour of Palestine; m. Jessie Biggs, Aug. 15, 1895; 1 dau., Mrs. Margaret Greene. Entered ministry, M.E. Ch., 1897; served Marysville (Ohio) Circuit, 1897-98, 1900-01, Spencerville Circuit, 1901-02; ordained, 1899; pastor Trinity Ch., Delphos, O., 1902-05, 1907-10, Epworth Church, Toledo, 1910-16, Avondale Church, Cincinnati, Sept. 1916-Sept. 1925; retired since May 1, 1943. Trustee Ohio Wesleyan University, Ohio Methodist Children's Home, etc. First lt., assimilated rank, U.S. Army; chaplain Base Hosp. No. 25, Allerey, France, July 1918-Feb. 1919; sr. chaplain of hosp. center at Allerey; capt.-chaplain inactive, O.R.C., U.S. Army. Special visitor from Am. Waldensian Aid Soc. to The Waldensian Ch. of Italy, 1921; del. Fifth Ecumenical M.E. Conf., London, 1921. Traveled in Europe as corr. Christian Advocate, etc., summers 1922, 23, 24. Social service rep. of The A. Nash Co., and ednl. adviser of Turk Ojaq, of Turkey, 1925-28. Exec. v.p., The Children's Home, Cincinnati, 1928-43; chmn. children's div. Ohio Welfare Conf., 1933. Mem. Nat. Council for Social Work, Am. Sociol. Soc., Am. Acad. Polit. Science, Am. Assn. on Mental Deficiency, Am. Psychol. Assn., Nat. Com. for Mental Hygiene, Am. Eugenics Soc., Am. Assn. of Church History, Am. Assn. of Social Workers, Am. Legion. Republican. Mason (32°, Shriner). Clubs: Cincinnati, Torch, Clergy. Author: Help from the Hills, 1910; A Syrian Pilgrimage, 1914; The Religion of Israel, 1918; The Religion of Judah, 1919; Apostles, Fathers, and Reformers, 1921. Home: The Cincinnati Club, Cincinnati. Died Nov. 14, 1950; buried Spring Grove Cemetery, Findlay, O.

ASHBROOK, Ernest Shepardson, ins. exec.; b. Granville, O., Oct. 12, 1879; s. Milan P. and Lucy P. (Shepardson) A.; A.B., Denison U., 1902; m. Betty M. Hughes, Nov. 21, 1925. Cashier and later asst. credit man, Lyons Candy Co., Chicago, 1902-04; salesman Baker-Vawter Co., N.Y. City, 1905, St. Joseph, Mo., 1906-09; with North Am. Life Ins. Co., Chicago, 1909—, successively mgr. in Topeka, Kan., 1910, mgr. S.W. dept., Kansas City, 1911-19, v.p., Chicago, 1919-26, pres., 1927-50, treas., 1944-50, chmn. bd., 1951—. Pres. Chicago Cubs Baseball for Boys, Inc. Republican. Mason. Club: Chicago Athletic Assn. Address: 501 Cadagua Av., Coral Gables, Fla. Died Mar. 28, 1956; buried Granville, O.

ASHBY, George Franklin, railroad ofcl.; b. Mt. Airy, N.C., Sept. 3, 1885; s. George Whitfield and Rozella (Bunker) A.; grad. Mt. Airy (N.C.) High Sch.; m. Nelle Ross, May 1, 1913. Clerk purchasing dept. A.C.L. R.R., 1906; with accounting dept. S.A.L. Ry., 1906-11; with engring., operating and exec. depts. Ore.-Wash. R.R. and Nav. Co., 1911-21; with operating dept. U.P. R.R. Co., 1921-34, asst. to exec. v.p., 1934-37, asst. to pres., 1937-41, v.p. (U.P. R.R. and lessor cos.), 1941-44, exec. v.p., 1944-46, pres., dir., 1946-49, retired; pres., dir. Ore. Short Line R.R., Ore.-Wash. R.R. and Nav. Co., Los Angeles and Salt Lake R.R., St. Joseph and Grand Island Ry., Laramie, North Park and Western R.R., Saratoga and Encampment Valley R.R. Co., Des Chutes R.R., Kansas City Indsl. Land Co., Las Vegas Land and Water Co., Union Land Co., Utah Parks Co., Utah Parks Co. of Ariz.; v.p. Interstate Transit Lines, Interstate Transit Lines, Inc., Union Pacific Stages, Inc.; dir. No. Pacific Terminal Co. of Ore. Served as pvt., 382d Co., Tank Corps, U.S. Army, World War I. Mason (Shriner). Clubs: Country, Athletic (Omaha, Neb.); California; Denver. Address: Las Vegas, Nev. Died May 15, 1950.

ASHCRAFT, Lee, business exec.; b. Ashland, Ala., Jan. 14, 1871; s. Andrew Jackson and Eleanor (Wiley) A.; student Ala. State Tchrs. Coll; grad. Ala. Poly. Inst., 1893; m. Mary Bayless, Aug. 14, 1902; 1 dau., Rebecca Bayless (Mrs. R.D. Warren). Chmn., dir. Ashcraft-Wilkinson Co., fertilizer materials and feed stuff, Atlanta, since 1929; chmn., dir. Interstate Milling Co., Cairo, Ill., Cairo Fertilizer Co., Agrl. Sulphur & Chem. Co., Dothan, Ala., Flag Sulphur & Chem. Co., Tampa, Fla., Valley Chem. Co., Greenville, Miss.; dir., mem. exec. and trust coms. First Nat. Bank, Atlanta; dir. West Point (Ga.) Mfg. Co., Lanett Bleachery & Dye Works, Columbus (Ga.) Mfg. Co., Cabin Crafts, Inc., Wellington Sears Co., Continental Gin Co., Anderson (S.C.) Fertilizer Co., Dixie Cotton Mills. Decorated Chevalier Legion of Honor (France). Mem. Atlanta Art Assn. (dir.), Newcomen Soc. Eng. (chmn. Ga.), English Speaking Union (chmn. bd. dirs.). Democrat. Baptist. Mason (Shriner). Clubs: Presidents (pres.), Piedmont Driving, Capitol City, Homosassa Fishing (Atlanta). Home: 1341 Ponce De Leon Av. N.E., Atlanta. Office: 601 Trust Co. of Georgia Bldg., Atlanta 3. Died Jan. 26, 1953.

ASHE, Bowman Foster (ăsh), univ. pres.; b. Scottdale, Pa., Apr. 3, 1885; s. Andrew Jackson and Martha Ann (Plotner) A.; student Mount Union Coll. Alliance, O., 1901-05; B.S. in Economics, U. of Pittsburgh, 1912, grad. study, 1913-14, LL.D., 1927; LL.D., John B. Stetson University; Litt.D., Florida Southern College; married Marie Ida Rose, 1917; children—Dorothy (Mrs. Edward F. Dunn), Barbara. Teacher elementary and high school, 1903-10; teacher recreation centers, Pittsburgh, 1910-12; supt. schools, Parnassus, Pa., 1912-13; teacher Industrial Schs., Pittsburgh, 1913-14; employment mgr. Am. Zinc & Chem. Co., Pittsburgh, 1914-20; asso. prof. economics, U. of Pittsburgh, 1920; student counselor and univ. examiner same, 1921-26; exec. sec. U. of Miami, 1926, pres. since 1926. Regional dir. Social Security Bd. for Southeastern States, 1936-38. Regional dir., War Manpower Committee for Southeastern States, 1942. Mem. Sigma Alpha Epsilon, Omicron Delta Kappa, Beta Gamma Sigma. Methodist. Mason. Clubs: University (Pittsburgh); Century (Coral Gables); Committee of One Hundred. Home: 2475 S. Bayshore Drive, Coconut Grove, Miami. University of Miami, Coral Gables, Fla. Died Dec. 16, 1952; buried Woodlawn Mausoleum, Miami.

ASHFORD, Mahlon, surgeon; b. Washington, Mar. 24, 1881; s. Francis Asbury and Isabella Walker (Kelley) A.; M.D., Georgetown U. 1904; grad. U.S. Army Med. Sch., 1908, U.S. Army War Coll., 1925; m. Elizabeth Beale, Dec. 20, 1911; 1 son, Beale. Commd. 1st lt., M.C., U.S. Army, 1908, advanced through the grades to col., 1934; chief surgeon Panama Dept., 1935-36; retired from army, 1936; exec. sec. com. on med. edn., N.Y. Acad. Medicine, editor Bull. of N.Y. Acad. Medicine, 1936-51, ret. Fellow A.C.S., A.C.P.; mem. Theta Delta Chi. Presbyn. Club: Army and Navy (Washington). Home: Washington. Deceased.

ASHLEY, Frederick William, librarian; b. Mansfield, O., Jan. 12, 1863; s. George and Rachel (Adams) A.; grad. Western Res. Acad., 1880; B.A., Western Res U., 1885, M.A., 1888, Litt.D., 1935; studied Yale, Harvard, N.Y. State Library Sch.; m. Mary M. Cole, June 29, 1893; children—Ruth Mavérette (Mrs. Philip Cyrus Gunion), Mary Rachel (Mrs. Irving Sametz). Instr. in Latin, St. Charles (Mo.) Coll., 1886-87, Western Res. Acad., Hudson, O., 1887-91, prin. 1892-97; librarian Morley Meml. Library Painesville, O., 1897-98; with Library of Congress 1900—, supt. reading room, 1915-27, chief asst. librarian, 1927-36, retired. Fellow Am. Library Inst., A.A.A.S.; mem. A.L.A., Bibliog. Soc. Am., Wiegendruck Gesellschaft, D.C. Library Assn. (pres. 1927-29), Delta Upsilon. Presbyn. Author: Catalogue of the John Boyd Thacher Collection of Incunabula, 1915; Three Eras in the Library of Congress, 1929; Catalogue of Miscellaneous Books in the Thacher Collection, 1931; The Vollbehr Incunabula and the Book of Books, 1932; A Look Back, 1934; In Praise of Print, 1934; Story of the Vollbehr Collection of Incunabula, 1934; History of the Library of Congress, 1897-1939, 1939. Contbr. several sketches to Dictionary of Am. Biography. Home: (winter) 820 Castile Av., Coral Gables 34, Fla.; (summer) Hills Point Rd., Westport, Conn. Died June 14, 1943; buried Westport.

ASHLEY, George Hall, geologist; b. Rochester, N.Y., Aug. 9, 1866; s. Roscoe B. and Anna (Hall) A.; M.E., Cornell Univ., 1890, A.M., 1892; Ph.D., Stanford Univ., 1894; Sc.D., Lehigh U., 1937; m. Mary E. Martin, July 11, 1895; children—Carlyle, Jr., Dorothy (Mrs. R. H. Ross). Paleontologist, Rochester, N.Y., 1889-91; asst. geologist, Geol. Survey of Ark., 1891-93; teaching in Calif., 1894-96; asst. state geologist of Ind., 1896-1900; prof. biology and geology and curator of museum, Coll. of Charleston, S.C., 1900-03; prof. pharmacognosy, Med. Coll. State of S.C., 1901-03; asst. geologist, 1901-05, geologist, 1905-12, administrative geologist, 1912-19, U.S. Geol. Survey; state geologist of Pennsylvania, 1919-46; consulting mining geologist since 1946. Acting prof. geology, Vanderbilt U., 1917. Fellow A.A.A.S.; Fellow Geological Soc. of Am., Pa. Acad. Scis., Am. Inst. Mining and Metall. Engrs.; mem. Coal Mining Inst. America, Soc. Econ. Geol. (pres. 1948); hon. mem. Tenn. Acad., Ind. Acad. Science, S.C. Pharm. Assn.; ex-pres. Internat. Assn. of Torch Clubs. Author of numerous geol. reports and articles in lit. and tech. jours. Home: 3037 N. Front St., Harrisburg, Pa. Died May 28, 1951.

ASHWORTH, Robert Archibald, clergyman; b. Glasgow, Scotland, July 26, 1871; s. John W. and Emma (Gregson) A.; A.B., Columbia, 1892, A.M., 1894; grad. Union Theol. Sem., 1896; D.D., Brown U., 1912; m. Mabelle Edgerton, Oct. 28, 1902; children—Katharine Edgerton (Mrs. A. G. Baldwin), Dorothy Gregson (Mrs. R. H. Nathan). Ordained Bapt. ministry, 1896; pastor Minerva, N.Y., 1896-98, Bridgeton, N.J., 1898-1900, 1st Ch., Meriden, Conn., 1900-11, 1st Ch., Milwaukee, Wis., 1911-21, Ch. of the Redeemer, Yonkers, N.Y., 1921-30; editor of The Baptist, 1930-33; editorial sec. Nat. Conf. of Christians and Jews, 1933-52; also mem. exec. com. commn. on chs. abroad, commn. on a just and durable peace and chairman committee on publications, of Federal Council of Churches of Christ in America 1916-46, mem. dept. of research and edn. pres. Milwaukee Fed. of Chs., 1912-14; delegate World Conferences on Faith and Order (Lausanne 1927, Edinburgh 1937), Oxford World Conference on Church, Community and State, 1937, Utrecht Conf. on World Council of Churches, 1938; member American Com. for The World Council of Churches, 1938-45; mem. Am. Christian Com. for Refugees 1934-47, Ministers and Missionaries Benefit Bd. of Northern Bapt. Convention; mem. bd. of Yonkers Community Chest; mem. bd. Yonkers Tuberculosis and Health Assn.; chmn. Yonkers Social Planning Council. Mem. Alpha Delta Phi, Phi Beta Kappa. Clubs: Quill (pres. 1940-41); Q Club. Author: The Union of Christian Forces in America, 1915 (winner of $1,000 prize offered by Am. Sunday Sch. Union); Being a Christian, 1924. Mem. exec. bd. of editors, and contbr. to The Outline of Christianity; contbg. editor Christian Century, 1934-44. Lecturer Union Theol. Sem., Baptist Principles and Polity., 1931-41. Contbr. to religious periodicals. Home: 30 Gray Pl., Yonkers, N.Y. Died May 8, 1959.

ASKEW, Thyrza Simonton, educator; b. Dayton, Ala., July 16, 1879; d. Warren Simonton and Laura Earle (Boardman) A.; prep. edn., Girls' High Sch., Atlanta, and Agnes Scott Coll., Decatur, Ga.; B.A., Cornell U., 1914. Prin. North Av. Presbyn. Sch., Atlanta, 1917—. Mem. Phi Beta Kappa. Presbyn. Home: 331 Ponce de Leon, N.E., Atlanta. Deceased.

ASPINWALL, William Billings, coll. pres. emeritus; b. Loudonville, N.Y., Nov. 13, 1874; s. William F. and Sarah (Sterry) A.; A.B., Harvard, 1896; Pd.B., Pd.M., State Coll. for Tchrs., Albany, 1900-01; A.M., Ph.D., Ill. Wesleyan U., 1901-02; docteur de l'université, U. Paris, 1904; m. Aurelia Hyde, Apr. 8, 1908. Asst. prin. Union Female Coll., Eufaula, Ala., 1898-99; asst. prin. and prin. N.Y. State Normal High Sch., Albany, 1900-06; dean, prof. edn. State Coll. for Tchrs., Albany, 1906-12; pres. State Tchrs. Coll. (formerly State Normal Sch.), Worcester, Mass., 1912-40; mem. faculty summer sch. U. Vt., 1915-16. Vice pres. bd. trustees Leicester (Mass.) Jr. Coll., 15 yrs., mem. 1918-43; moderator Mass. Congl. Conf., 1918; del. from State Conf. to Nat. Council Congl. Ch., 1923-27. Mem. N.E.A., Mass. State Tchrs. Coll. Assn. (pres. 1926), Mass. Schoolmasters' Club (pres. 1924), Worcester County Supts. Club, Mass. State Supts. Assn., N.E. Supts. Assn., City Missionary Soc. (pres. 1918-26), Worcester Pub. Edn. Assn. (past pres., exec. com.), Delta Upsilon, Pi Gamma Mu, Kappa Delta Pi, etc. Clubs: Harvard, Economic (pres. 1928), Shakespeare (pres. 1929-30), Bohemian (pres. 1933), Rotary (pres. 1926-27). Author: Outlines of the History of Education, 1911. Address: 4 Dean St., Worcester 2, Mass. Died Jan. 5, 1955; buried Albany (N.Y.) Rural Cemetery.

ASPLUND, Rupert Franz (ăsp'lŭnd), tax investigator; b. Little Indian, Ill., June 26, 1875; s. John and Clara (Johnson) A.; B.A., Ill. Coll., Jacksonville, 1896, hon. M.A., 1921, LL.D., 1946; m. Julia Duncan Brown, Aug. 3, 1905; 1 dau., Carolyn E. (Mrs. Monroe K. Ruch). Teacher, public schs., Ill., 1896-98; instr. Whipple Acad. and Ill. Coll., 1898-1900; prin. Whipple Acad. and instr. Latin and Greek, Ill. Coll., 1900-02; prof. Latin and Greek, U. of N.M., 1902-09; chief clerk State Dept. of Edn., N.M., 1909-16; sec. State Tax Commn., 1917-18; dir. Taxpayers' Assn. of N.M. since 1918; editor and mgr. N.M. Jour. of Edn., 1907-19; dir. N.M. State Budget, 1919-41; comptroller state N.M., 1930; pres. Mutual Building & Loan Association. Member Nat. Tax Assn., Nat. Municipal League, Governmental Research Assn., Phi Beta Kappa. Republican. Episcopalian. Mason (33°); Grand Master of Grand Lodge of N.M., A.F. and A.M., 1947-48; dep. of Supreme council of Scottish Rite, Southern Jruisdiction since 1935. Author: New Mexico Tax Structure, 1946. Home: 217 Marcy St., Santa Fe, N.M. Died Dec. 7, 1952; buried Fairview Cemetery, Santa Fe.

ASSMUTH, Joseph, clergyman, educator; b. Germany, Feb. 21, 1871; s. John and Bernardina (Geilen) A.; ed. Gymnasium, Paderborn, Westphalia; B. A. and M.A., House of Studies, Valkenburg, Holland, 1905; Ph.D., U. of Leipzig, and U. of Berlin, 1910; studied Louvain U., and Oudenbosh, Holland. Joined Soc. of Jesus, 1893; ordained priest R.C. Ch., 1905; began teaching at St. Xavier's Coll., Bombay, India, 1898; ex-senator U. of Bombay; came to U.S., 1924; prof. biology, Fordham U., 1924—. Has specialized in study of ants and termites and their guests. Mem. Am. Micros. Soc., Am. Zoöl. Soc., Deutsche Zoöl. and Deutsche Entomol. Gesellschaft. Author: Termitoxenia assmuthi (anatomical and hist. study), 1910; Haeckel's Frauds and Forgeries, 1914; also many articles and original researches in scientific jours. Address: Fordham University, N.Y.C. Died June 11, 1954.

ASTOR, (William) Vincent; b. New York, Nov. 15, 1891; s. John Jacob and Ava Willing A.; now head of Astor family in U.S.; ed. St. George's Sch. and Harvard, 1911-12; m. Helen Dinsmore Huntington, Apr. 30, 1914 (div.); m. 2d, Mary Benedict Cushing, Sept. 27, 1940 (div. 1953); married 3d, Brooke Russell Marshall. Chmn. bd. Weekly Publs., Inc.; dir. U.S. Lines Co. Gov. New York Hospital; trustee N.Y. Pub. Library. Served as ensign, lt. (j.g.) and lt., U.S. Navy, World War I, active duty in European waters; capt., U.S. Naval Res.; on active duty with U.S. Navy, World War II. Mem. War Soc. of Cruiser and Transport Force, Humane Soc. of N.Y. (life), Am. Museum Natural History (life), Saint Nicholas Soc. (life); Navy League of U.S. (life), Society Naval Architects and Marine Engrs. (asso.), U.S. Naval Inst., Naval History Soc., Honor Legion of Police Dept., City of N.Y. (hon. mem.), Holland Lodge (life), U.S. Naval Reserve Officers Assn., Dutchess County Soc. of City of N.Y. (life), Nat. Assn. Audubon Socs. (life), Mil. Order World War (life); charter mem. Geog. and Hist. Soc. of the Americas. Clubs: City (life), Harvard (life), Nat. Golf Links America, The Brook (life), The Links Golf, Racquet and Tennis (life), N.Y. Yacht (life), Cedar Creek, Aero of America (life), India House; River of New York; Newport Reading Room (Newport, R.I.); Ft. Orange (Albany, N.Y.); Clove Valley Rod and Gun. Office: 405 Park Av., N.Y.C. 22. Died Feb. 3, 1959; buried Ferncliff, Rhinebeck, N.Y.

ASWELL, Edward C., editor, pub.; b. Nashville, Tenn., Oct. 9, 1900; s. McCoy Campbell and Carrie (Campbell) A.; A.B. magna cum laude; Harvard, 1926; m. Mary Louise White, Jan. 1, 1935 (div. 1946); children—Edward Duncan, Mary Elizabeth; m. 2d, Knyvett Lee, June 14, 1947 (deceased May 18, 1957). Member of the editorial staff Forum magazine, 1926, asst. editor, 1928-30; asst. editor Atlantic Monthly, 1930-35; asst. ed. of gen. books, Harper Brothers, 1935-43, editor-in-chief, director 1943-47; v.p. McGraw-Hill Book Co. 1947-56, editor-in-chief Trade Book Department, 1947-56; senior editor of Doubleday & Co., 1956—; trustee Eugene Saxton Memorial Trust, 1944-47; adminstr. Thomas Wolfe estate since 1947; member Yale editorial com. to pub. pvt. papers of James Boswell 1949—. Member of fraternity of Phi Beta Kappa. Clubs: Harvard (New York City and Westchester), Century. Editor: (posthumously from manuscript left by Thomas Wolfe) The Web and the Rock, 1939; You Can't Go Home Again, 1940; The Hills Beyond, 1941. Home: 1177 Hardscrabble Rd., Chappaqua, N.Y. Office: 575 Madison Av., N.Y.C. 22. Died Nov. 5, 1958.

ATEN, Fred N. (ā'tĕn), labor official; b. Crawford County, Ill., Feb. 21, 1885; s. William and Mary (Overly) A.; ed. in public schools; m. Margaret Johnson, Dec. 4, 1930. Mechanic in railroad shops, 1910-17; Grand Lodge Officer of Brotherhood Railway Carmen of America, 1917-46; asst. to pres. of Railway Employes Dept. of A. F. of L., 1938-46, pres. of the dept. since July 1946. Elk. Home: 425 Surf St., Chicago 14. Office: 608 S. Dearborn St., Chicago 5, Ill. Died Apr. 30, 1951.

ATHEARN, Fred Goodrich, lawyer; b. nr. Anaheim, Cal., Mar. 26, 1874; s. Frederick William and Susan (Goodrich) A.; student Pomona (Cal.) Coll., 1898; A.B., U. Cal., 1900; m. Evelyn Bottomes, Aug. 21, 1901 (dec.); children—Folger, Leigh. Prin. high sch., 1900-01; head dept. edn. San Francisco State Normal Sch. for Tchrs., 1901-03; head bur. econs. and efficiency expert S.P. Co., 1903-12; practice of law in San Francisco, 1912—; sr. mem. Athearn, Chandler & Hoffman, 1921—; formerly first dir. Investment for State Calif; formerly state commr. corps. Cal. Author: Outline of Course in Railroading. Home: 134 La Goma Av., Mill Valley, Cal. Office: Balboa Bldg., San Francisco 5. Died Oct. 27, 1956.

ATHERTON, John C., artist; b. Brainerd, Minn., June 7, 1900; s. James C. and Carrie (Martin) A.; ed. in pub. schs., Spokane, Wash., Coll. of the Pacific, San Jose, Calif., and Calif. Sch. of Fine Arts, San Francisco; m. Maxine Breese, Nov. 6, 1926; 1 dau., Mary. Joined navy, 1918; worked in mines, shipyards, as sign painter, clerk, musician, etc., 1919-25; advt. artist, on Pacific Coast and N.Y. City, since 1926; has painted in spare time since art study, 1923. Mem. faculty Famous Artists Schs., Westport, Conn. Has exhibited paintings at Julien Levy Gallery (N.Y. City), 1939-1942, museum in North America, Latin America and Europe; represented in collections of Museums Modern Art, Whitney Mus. Am. Art, Metropolitan Mus. Art (New York), Wadsworth Athenaeum (Hartford), Art Inst. of Chicago, Pa. Acad. Fine Art (Phila.), Albright Art Gallery (Buffalo). Served as seaman 2d class, U.S. Navy, 1918-19. Winner in competition, war posters, Mus. Modern Art, 1941, poster competition for World's Fair, New York, $2,000 4th prize artists for victory exhbn. Metropolitan Mus., N.Y., 1942. Club: Angler's of New York. Author: The Fly and the Fish. Home: Arlington, Vt. Died Sept. 17, 1952.

ATHERTON, Louis M(orse), stock broker; born Saugus, Mass., Dec. 15, 1878; s. Horace H. and Hannah P. (Oliver) A.; ed. public schools, Lynn, Mass.; m. Marion Childs Porter, June 2, 1904. Stenographer, Old Colony Trust Co., Boston, 1897-1907; reporter with Boston News Bureau, 1907-16; with Schirmer, Atherton & Co., stock brokers, Boston, since 1916. Clubs: Union, Downtown, Merchants (Boston); Tedesco Country (Swampscott); Yacht (Marblehead); Tin Whistles (Pinehurst, N.C.). Home: Tip Top Rd., Littles Point, Swampscott, Mass. Office: 50 Congress St., Boston. Died Feb. 24, 1950; buried Riverside Cemetery, East Saugus, Mass.

ATKESON, Floyd Warnick, educator; b. Butler, Mo., Nov. 28, 1893; s. William Oscar and Lizzie Wheat (Warnick) A.; B.S. in Agr., U. Mo., 1918; M.S., Kan. State Coll., 1929; m. Ferol Anna Richardson, July 23, 1931; 1 son, George William. Mgr. Belleview Farm, 1915-16; tchr. agr. Cape Girardeau (Mo.) State Normal, 1918; instr. dairy husbandry Kan. State Coll., 1918-20; fieldman Am. Jersey Cattle Club, 1920-21; head dept. dairy husbandry U. Ida., 1921-35, Kan. State Coll., 1935—. Mem. Am. Dairy Sci. Assn., Am. Soc. Animal Prodn., Am. Genetic Assn., Farm House, Alpha Zeta, Phi Kappa Phi, Gamma Sigma Delta. Episcopalian. Mason (Shriner), Rotarian. Author articles profl. jours. Home: 1820 Claflin Rd., Manhattan, Kan. Died Apr. 4, 1958; buried Sunset Cemetery, Manhattan, Kan.

ATKIN, Isaac Cubitt Raymond, banker; b. Springfield, Ont., Can., Jan. 2, 1892; s. William Isaac and Martha (Calk) A.; ed. Springfield, Ont., pub. and high schs.; m. Alice Winnifred Flanagan, Sept. 27, 1922; children—Donald Raymond, Frances Winnifred (dec.), James Blakesley. Came to U.S., 1925, naturalized, 1940. Asso. with Traders Bank of Can. and Royal Bank of Can., 1909-25; with J. P. Morgan & Co. since 1925, partner, 1939-40, vice-pres. and dir. since incorp., Apr. 1, 1940; dir. Johns-Manville Corp., Can. Life Assurance Co. Internat. Nickel Co. of Can., Ltd., Monsanto Can., Ltd. Served as capt. 102d Can. Inf. Batt., C.E.F., 1915-19. Decorated Mil. Cross and bar. Episcopalian. Clubs: Baltusrol Golf, Short Hills (Short Hills, N.J.). Home: 95 Knollwood Rd., Short Hills, N.J. Office: 23 Wall St., N.Y. City. Died Jan. 25, 1957.

ATKINS, Albert Henry, sculptor; b. Milw.; s. Henry L. and Ida Maria (Harrison) A.; studied at Cowles Art Sch., Boston, 1896-98; Académie Julien, and Académie Colorossi, Paris, 1898-1900; m. Louise Allen (Hobbs), 1927. Mem. faculty R.I. Sch. Design, Dept. Sculpture, 1909-26. Fellow Nat. Sculpture Soc.; mem. Archtl. League N.Y., Copley Soc. Boston, Am. Art Assn. (Paris), Providence Art Club, Salmagundi Club (N.Y.C.), N. Shore Arts Assn. (Gloucester, Mass.). Prin. works: Stations of the Cross, Trinity Chapel, Washington; Copenhagen Meml. Fountain, City of Boston; Lapham Meml., Milw.; archtl. sculptures, Christ Ch., Ansonia, Conn., All Saints Ch., Dorchester, Mass., Nazareth Hall, St. Paul; seven bronze chancel grilles and four marble chapel statues St. Paul Cathedral, St. Paul; baptismal font Cathedral of St. John the Divine, N.Y.C.; 13 statues and bronze gate for altar rail of St. Patrick's Cathedral, N.Y.C.; altar decorations St. Paul's Ch., Chestnut Hill, Phila.; many portraits, ideal sculptures, others; designer peace memls. Exhibited N.A.D. (N.Y.C.), Pa. Acad. Fine Arts (Phila.), Albright Galleries (Buffalo), Art Inst. (Milw.), Mus. R.I. Sch. Design (Providence), Carnegie Inst. (Pitts.), others. Permanently represented Museum R.I. Sch. Design and Toledo Museum Fine Arts. Decorated silver medal Art Inst., Milw.; North Shore Arts Assn. purchase prize; gold medal Garden Club Am.; gold medal Boston Tercentenary Fine Arts Exhibit. Studio: Gloucester, Mass. Died Mar. 10, 1951.

ATKINS, Mrs. Louise Allen, sculptor; b. Lowell, Mass.; d. Charles Herbert and Harriet C. (Dean) Allen; father 1st gov. of Porto Rico; studied art, R.I. Sch. of Design and Boston Mus. Fine Ar s; m. 2d, Albert Henry Atkins, 1927; (by 1st marria e) 1 son, Allen Hobbs (capt. U.S. Navy). Exhibited Pennsylvania Academy Fine Arts, National Academy, New York, Art Institute, Chicago, Albright Galleries, Buffalo, Museum Fine Arts, Providence, Rhode Island, Nat. Sculpture Soc. Represented in Cleveland Museum and the Hillyer Collection, Smith College. Prin. works: World War memorial, East Greenwich, R.I.; World War tablet, Gloucester, Mass.; memorial tablet, Bancroft Hall, Annapolis, Maryland; memorial, Rogers Hall, Lowell, Mass.; also many ideal bronzes, portraits, etc. Hon. mention, Boston Tercentenary Exhbn., 1930; Esther Groome memorial prize North Shore Arts Assn.; 1930. Fellow Nat. Sculpture Society; mem. Rockport Art Assn., Providence Art Club, North Shore Arts Assn. of Gloucester. Mem. faculty, R.I. Sch. of Design, 1925-32. Studio: 11 Lincoln St., West, Gloucester, Mass. Died Sept. 23, 1953.

ATKINSON, Benjamin Searcy, ry. official; b. Tuscaloosa, Ala., May 20, 1870; s. Joseph and Fannie Leonore (Hunter) A.; ed. pub. schs.; m. Berta Burch, Nov. 19, 1890; children—Annie Claire, Joseph Burch, Searcy Hunter. With Vicksburg, Shreveport & Pacific Ry. in various capacities, 1888-98; auditor and traffic mgr. Ark., La. and Southern Ry., 1898-1900; agent La. & Ark. Ry., at Minden, La., 1900-01, asst. gen. freight and passenger agent, 1901. gen. freight and passenger agent, 1901-16, traffic mgr., 1916-28, v.p., 1928-29, sr. v.p. 1929 until July 1, 1940; retired; also pres. and dir. Magnolia Ice & Coca-Cola Bottling Co.; dir. La. & Ark. Ry. Co., Columbia Ice Co., Gen. Am. Oil Co. of Tex. Mem. Louisiana Historical Soc., American Museum of Natural History, American Forestry Assn., Chamber of Commerce of the State of New York, Texarkana Chamber of Commerce. Methodist. Mason. Clubs: Asso. Traffic Clubs of America, Kansas City Traffic, New Orleans Traffic, Westchester Country, Missouri Athletic. Home: Twin Gardens, Sixth & Hickory St., Texarkana, Ark.; (winter) San Juan. Tex. Died Feb. 26, 1948; buried Hillcrest Meml. Park.

ATKINSON, Donald Taylor, physician; b. Shemogwe, New Brunswick, Can., May 31, 1874; s. Joseph Silliker and Elizabeth (Grant) A.; M.D., Hosp. Coll. of Medicine, Louisville, Ky., 1902; K.K. Allgemeines Krankenhaus, Vienna, Austria, 1906-07; student Royal London (Eng.) Ophthal. Hosp., 1907; Sc.D., Center College, Danville, Ky., 1944; LL.D., honoris causa, Huron (S.D.) College, 1945; m. Wanda Wiley, 1937. Became naturalized U.S. citizen, 1916. Engaged in practice of medicine at San Antonio, Tex., since 1902; mem. staff of Nix Hospital, Santa Rosa Infirmary, Medical and Surgical Hosp., San Antonio; specialist in diseases of eye; senior partner Atkinson & DeGasperi; asso. editor Eye, Ear, Nose and Throat Jour.; editor ophthalmic dept. Texas Med. News, 1905-09. Awarded Patronis Medal Award, U. Florence, 1951; selected outstanding author of yr., 10th annual Writers Roundup, Theta Sigma Phi, 1958. Fellow of the American College of Surgeons, Am. Acad. Ophthalmology and Otolaryngology, Royal Acad. Medicine (Ireland), Internat. Coll. Surgeons (Geneva, member of the adv. bd., school surgical history), National Surgical Soc. of Italy, 1951; mem. Am. Med. Editors and Authors Assn., A.A.A.S., Am. Med. Assn. of Vienna (life), Am., Southern, Bexar County and Tex. State Med. assns., Nat. Tuberculosis, Am. Genetic and Am. Social Hygiene assns., Nat. Soc. Arts and Letters, Nat. Assn. Authors and Journalists, The River Art Group. Republican. Club: Oak Hills Country. Author: Social Travesties, 1912; A Treatise on Cataract, 1913; Great Medical Innovations, 1915; External Diseases of the Eye, 1934, 2d edit., 1936; The Problem of the Secondary Cataract, 1934; Magic Myth and Medicine (World Publishers), 1936; The Ocular Fundus in Diagnosis and Treatment, 1937, many scientific essays including The Artifical Pupil in the Restoration of Vision. Art collaborator Southall's Introduction to Physiological Optics; Rea's System of Neuro Ophthalmology; Texas Surgeon (autobiography), 1958. Illustrates his technical books himself; reproductions of his illustrations in several med. books. Originator of Atkinson trocheo laryngoscope. Home: Rt. 11, Box 121. Office: 827 Medical Arts Bldg., San Antonio, Tex. Died Mar. 20, 1959; buried Grove Hill Meml. Park Cemetery, Dallas.

ATKINSON, Henry Avery, clergyman; b. Merced, Cal., Aug. 26, 1877; s. Thomas Albion and Sarah Jane (Yeargin) A.; A.B., Pacific Meth. Coll., Santa Rosa, Cal., 1897; student in Garrett Bibl. Inst. (Northwestern U.); D.D., Rollins Coll., Winter Park, Fla., 1913; m. Grace Olin, May 29, 1901. Ordained Congl. ministry, 1902; pastor 1st Ch., Albion, Ill., 1902-04, 1st Ch., Springfield, O., 1904-08, Central Ch., Atlanta, Ga., 1908-11; sec. Social Service Commn. of Congl. Chs. in the U.S., 1911-18; now gen. sec. Ch. Peace Union and World Alliance for Internat. Friendship. Prof. sociology, Atlanta Theol. Sem., 1904-08. Chevalier Legion of Honor (France), 1929. Trustee of Rollins Coll., Winter Park, Fla. Democrat. Clubs: Clergy, Quill (New York). Author: The Church and Industrial Warfare, 1914; The Church and the People's Play, 1915; Men and Things, 1918; Causes of War (in collaboration), 1932; Prelude to Peace, 1937. Contbr. to mags. Address: 70 5th Av., N.Y.C. Died Jan. 1960.

ATKINSON, Herbert Spencer, lawyer, ins. agt.; b. Fremont, O., Oct. 2, 1887; s. William A. and Mary Ann (Arnold) A.; LL.B., Ohio State U., 1913; m. Laura L. Harrison, Aug. 9, 1918; children—Griffin Arnold, Ann Pauline. Admitted to Ohio bar, 1913, practiced law, Columbus, O., 1913-30; gen. agt. for ins. cos., Columbus, O., 1930-—; dir. Ohlen-Bishop Mfg. Co. State rep., 83, 84th and 85th Ohio gen. assemblies, minority floor leader, 84th and 85th. Mem. Ohio Bd. of Agr., 1934-38. Mem. bd. trustees Ohio State U., 1925-—; mem. athletic bd. of univ. Dir. Columbus C. of C., Franklin County War Chest, Franklin City chpt. A.R.C., Am. Automobile Club. Mem. Alpha Sigma Phi, Bucket and Dipper, Sphinx (hon.). Mason (32°, Shriner), Elk, Odd Fellow, Eagle. Clubs: Columbus, State University Faculty (Columbus). Home: Grifana Farm, Blacklick, O. Office: 33 N. High St., Columbus 15, Ohio. Died Jan. 10, 1952.

ATKINSON, William Yates, asso. justice Supreme Court of Ga.; b. Newnan, Ga., Jan. 18, 1887; s. William Yates (gov. of Ga., 1894-98) and Susie Cobb (Milton) A.; student Ga. Mil. Acad., 1899-1901, Gordon Inst., Barnesville, Ga., 1902-04; LL.B., U. of Ga., 1915; m. Lourette Simms, Dec. 1, 1909; 1 son, William Yates. Admitted to Ga. bar, 1915, and since practiced in Newnan; referee in bankruptcy, 1918-20; solicitor gen. Coweta Judicial Circuit, 1921-43; asso. justice Supreme Court of Ga., 1943-48, presiding justice since 1948. Chairman Georgia Democratic Executive Committee, 1942. Director Newnan Building and Loan Association, Newnan Cotton Mills, Piedmont Hotel Co., Parrott Properties, Inc., Atlanta, Ga. Mem. Ga. Bar Assn. (pres. 1940-41), Kappa Alpha. Mason. Home: 73 Greenville St., Newnan, Ga. Address: Supreme Court, 326 State Capitol, Atlanta, Ga. Died Nov. 28, 1953.

ATLEE, John Light, surgeon; b. Lancaster, Pa., June 26, 1875; s. William Augustus and Elizabeth (Champneys) A.; A.B., Franklin and Marshall Coll., 1896, D.Sc., 1915; M.D., U. of Pa., 1900; m. Frances Rine Baer, 1903; children—John Light (M.D.), Frances (Mrs. William Kiner), Elizabeth (Mrs. George England), William Augustus (M.D.). Practiced at Lancaster since 1900; cons. surgeon Lancaster General Hosp., St. Joseph's Hosp. Trustee Y.M.C.A., Franklin and Marshall College. Fellow Am. Medical Assn., Am. Coll. Surgeons, Am. Assn. for Surgery of Trauma; mem. Medical Soc. State of Pa., Lancaster County Med. Soc., Phi Beta Kappa, Sigma Xi, Phi Alpha Sigma, Pi Gamma Mu. Republican. Episcopalian. Clubs: University (Phila.); Hamilton, Lancaster Country. Home: "Wild Acres," Bausman, Lancaster County. Office: 37 E. Orange St., Lancaster, Pa. Died Apr. 3, 1950; buried Woodward Hill Cemetery.

ATTEBERY, Olin Moody, banker; b. La Plata, Mo., Aug. 1, 1887; s. Benjamin F. and Lessie (Caldwell) A.; student pub. schs. La Plata and St. Louis; m. Katharine May Fairbrother, Jan. 27, 1915; 1 dau., Marjorie (wife of Dr. Edward K. Du Vivier). With Am. Nat. Bank, St. Louis, 1904-14, Ft. Dearborn Nat. Bank, 1910; cashier Badger State Bank, Cassville, Wis., 1911; mgr. transit dept. Fed. Res. Bank of St. Louis, 1914-17, asst. cashier, 1917-19, cashier, 1919, dep. gov., 1919-36, 1st v.p., 1936. Club: Missouri Athletic (St. Louis). Home: Park Plaza Hotel. Office: 411 Locust St., St. Louis. Died Sept. 23, 1954; buried Bellefontaine Cemetery, St. Louis.

ATTERBURY, Grosvenor (ăt'tēr-bēr-i), architect; b. Detroit, July 7, 1869; s. Charles Larned and Katharine Mitchill (Dow) A.; B.A., Yale, 1891; student Sch. Architecture (Columbia), 1892, École des Beaux Arts, Atelier Blondel, 1894; m. Dorothy A. Johnstone, Mar. 1923. Specialty, town planning, indsl. housing, model tenements and hospitals. Consultant Johns Hopkins U.; architect of Forest Hills Gardens, L.I. (model town built by Russell Sage Foundation), and indsl. communities, Indian Hill, Worcester, Mass., Erwin, and Kingsport, Tenn., etc.; architect for restoration of New York City Hall, Phipps Inst., Phila., Psychiatric Clinic of Johns Hopkins Hosp., Am. Wing of Met. Museum (New York), various buildings for N.Y. Hosp. at Bloomingdale, Hartford Orphan Asylum, Russell Sage Foundation Building and Sch. of Social Work, Inst. of Human Relations and Medical Library at Yale U., Stone Ashley, Tucson, Ariz., etc.; research asso. prof. Yale School of Architecture. Former member Squadron A, National Guard of N.Y. Awarded silver medal in architecture, St. Louis Expn.; recipient Gold Medal of Honor N.Y. A.I.A., 1953. Chmn. war industry housing com. Nat. Housing Assn. (dir.); mem. Army Ednl. Commission, A.E.F.; supervising archt. A.E.F. Univ., Beaune, France; mem. N.Y. Tenement House Commn., Community Service Soc. Com. on Housing. Academician Nat. Acad. Fellow A.I.A.; past pres. N.Y. Chapter A.I.A. and Archtl. League of New York; mem. Nat. Inst. Social Sciences, Soc. Beaux Arts Architects, Soc. Columbia Architects, Yale Elizabethan Club, Phi Beta Kappa (Yale), Psi Upsilon, Chi Delta Theta. Episcopalian. Clubs: Century, Dutch Treat, Digressionist. Inventor of method, apparatus & designs incorporated in the Atterbury rapid, mechanized, mass-prodn. manufacture of building units for low cost housing as further developed in private research lab. for Fireproof Bldgs., Inc., established 1953. Home: P.O. Box 1006, Southampton, N.Y. Died Oct. 18, 1956; buried Greenwood Cemetery, Bklyn.

ATWATER, Henry G., corp. exec.; b. Piscataway Twp., N.J., Mar. 26, 1879; s. Theron Skeel and Elmyra Maria (Donaldson) A.; student Rutgers, 1900-01; m. Elinor D'Arcy Armstrong, June 5, 1912; children—Henry G., D'Arcy Elmyra. Various positions with N.Y. Telephone Co., 1901-12, and Am. Tel. & Tel. Co., N.Y.C., 1912-21, asst. v.p., 1919-21; with G. M. P. Murphy & Co., bankers, 1921-25; v.p. Osborn Development Co., 1925-36; v.p., dir. Intercontinental Rubber Co., Continental Rubber Co., N.Y.; dir. Westfield Trust Co. Mem. Alpha Rho Alumni Assn. (trustee), Chi Psi. Republican. Presbyn. Home: 33 Washington Square, N.Y.C. 11; also Clearwater, Fla. Died July 20, 1950; buried Clearwater, Fla.

ATWATER, Mary Meigs, hand weaver; b. Rock Island, Ill., Feb. 28, 1878; d. Montgomery and Grace (Lynde) Meigs; prep. edn., pvt. tutor, Keokuk, Ia., and Miss Wheeler's Sch., Providence; studied Art Inst. Chgo., Chgo. Art Acad., pvt. classes of Raphael Collin, Fontenay-aux-Roses, France, and Julian and Colorossi Acads., Paris, France; m. Maxwell Wanton Atwater, 1903 (dec.); children—Montgomery Meigs, Elizabeth Joan Rodgers. Decorative designer Winslow Bros. Co., Chgo., 1902; tchr. decorative design, art sch., Seattle, 1921; organizer, 1922, since pres. Shuttle-Craft Guild, Weaving instrn., Seattle, until 1923, then Cambridge, Mass., later Basin, Mont.; pres. Black Beaver Fur Farms, Basin, Mont. Occupational therapist, Army Hosp. Service, 1919-20, at Base Hosp., Camp Lewis, Wash., Letterman Hosp., San Francisco, Ill. State Service, Watertown State Hosp., Moline, Ill., 1920-21. Mem. Am. Assn. Occupational Therapy, Art Alliance America, Arts and Craft Soc. of Boston, Needle and Bobbin Club of N.Y. Republican. Club: Helena Woman's. Author: Shuttle-Craft Course of Instruction, 1923; The John Landis Book of Designs for Weaving, 1925; Shuttle-Craft Book of American Hand-Weaving, 1928; ShuttleCraft Guild Recipe Book (pattern book for hand weavers), 1933; (mystery novel) Crime in Corn Weather, 1935; ShuttleCraft Guild Bulletin (monthly). Contbr. to leading mags. Died Sept. 1956.

ATWATER, Reginald Myers, physician, pub. health official; b. Canon City, Colo., Aug. 6, 1892; s. Samuel Henry and Selina (Myers) A.; A.B., Colo. Coll., 1914, LL.D., 1949; M.D., Harvard, 1918; M.P.H., Johns Hopkins, 1920, Dr. P. H., 1921; m. Charlotte Martin Penfield, July 10, 1919; children—Caroline Penfield (Mrs. Edwin Slater Leonard), Martha Martin (Mrs. John Bodine Duncan), Constance Avery (Mrs. Edward J. Bowser, Jr.), John Bancroft, David Sterling. Med. house officer Peter Bent Brigham Hosp., Boston, 1918-19; fellow in pub. health Rockefeller Foundation, 1919-21; cons. epidemiologist N.C. State Bd. of Health, 1920; asso. prof., hygiene, Hunan-Yale Coll. of Medicine, Changsha, Hunan, China, 1921-25; med. officer of health, Kuling Estate, Kiangsi, China, 1922-25; instr. preventive medicine and hygiene, Harvard Med. Sch., 1925-27; instr. epidemiology, Harvard Sch. Pub. Health, 1925-27; commr. of health, Cattaraugus County Dept. of Health, Olean, N.Y., 1927-35; exec. sec. Am. Pub. Health Assn., N.Y. City, since 1935; mng. editor Am. Jour. Pub. Health; spl. cons. U.S.P.H.S.; bd. dirs. Nat. Health Council; adv. com. Cleveland Health Museum. Served in Med. R.C., U.S. Army, 1918-19. Decorated Order of Carlos J. Finlay, Republic of Cuba, 1939; received Sedgwick Memorial Medal, 1947; received the Lasker award in public health, 1957. Fellow American Public Health Assn., American Med. Assn. (honorary) Royal Sanitary Inst. (Eng.); member New York State Med. Soc., Phi Beta Kappa, Alpha Omega Alpha, Delta Omega. Democrat. Mem. The Riverside Ch., N.Y. City. Contbr. to jours. Home: 2 Crows Nest Rd., Bronxville, N.Y. Office: 1790 Broadway, New York 19, N.Y. Died Oct. 18, 1957; buried Brookside Cemetery, Englewood, N.J.

ATWOOD, Arthur R., banker; b. Champlain, N.Y., Nov. 21, 1891; s. Levi E. and Ida M. (Waters) A.; m. Florence E. Doane, July 6, 1920; 1 son, John Deane (killed World War II). With U.S. Treasury Dept., 1931-35; dir. and v.p. Colonial Trust Co., Pitts., 1935-—, now exec. v.p., sec. dir. McClane Mining Co., P. McGraw Wool, U.S. Concrete Pipe Co., Pa. Industries, Inc., Ft. Pitt Coal & Coke Corp., Harmon Creek Coal Corp., Unity Rys. Co., The Waverly Oil Works Co.; partner A.R.M. Coal & Coke Sales Agy. Capt., 367th F.A. Res. Presbyn. Mason. Clubs: Duquesne, Pittsburgh Field. Home: 78 Woodhaven Dr., Mt. Lebanon, Pa. Office: Colonial Trust Co., 414 Wood St., Pitts. 22. Died June 13, 1954; buried Champlain, N.Y.

ATWOOD, Elmer Bugg, clergyman, educator; b. Clinton, Ky., Sept. 14, 1874; s. Thomas Letcher and Hettie Frances (Bugg) A.; grad. Clinton Coll., 1896; A.B., Georgetown (Ky.) Coll., 1900; Th.M., So. Bapt. Theol. Sem., Louisville, 1904, Th.D., 1911; m. Mabel Bagby, June 11, 1903; children—John Leland, Elmer Bagby. Ordained to ministry Bapt. Ch., 1896; pastor Yoakum, Tex., 1905-07, Alpine, Tex., 1907-11; gen. sec. Bapt. Conv. N.M., 1912-19; pres. Wayland Coll., Plainview, Tex., 1919-24; prof. religious edn. Hardin-Simmons U., 1925-50. Rotarian. Editor Bapt. New Mexican, 1912-19. Home: 2110 Grape St., Abilene, Tex. Died Nov. 30, 1957.

ATWOOD, Harrison, advertising; b. Auburn, Me., Sept. 30, 1886; s. Tascus and Helen (Jameson) A.; A.B., summa cum laude, Bowdoin Coll., 1909; m. Lena Paul, June 16, 1915; children—Catherine, Patricia, Harriet. Vice pres. The H. K. McCann Co., advt. agency, N.Y. City, 1915-30; vice pres. McCann-Erickson, Inc., N.Y. City, 1930-48; vice-chmn. board and chmn. finance com., 1948-55, vice chmn. bd., mem. finance com., 1955-—, chmn. exec. com. until 1956. Bd. Overseers, Bowdoin Coll. Mem. Phi Beta Kappa. Republican. Presbyterian. Clubs: University, Union League (N.Y. City); Scarsdale Golf; American Yacht. Home: 1170 Fifth Av., N.Y.C. 29. Office: 50 Rockefeller Plaza, N.Y.C. 20. Died Nov. 22, 1956; buried Mt. Auburn Cemetery, Auburn, Me.

ATWOOD, Henry (Elkins), banker; b. Keeseville, N.Y., Nov. 22, 1892; s. John N. and Harriet (Jocelyn) A.; A.B., Dartmouth, 1913; A.M., Harvard, 1914; m. Marion Woodward, June 19, 1917; children—John A., Roger W., Carol (Mrs. Harvey N. Daniels). Instr. in French, Syracuse (N.Y.) U., 1914, U. Minn., 1915-17; investment business, Mpls., 1919-24; bond officer Mpls. Trust Co., 1924-33; v.p. First Nat. Bank of Mpls., 1933-36, pres., 1945-—, also dir.; v.p. B. F. Nelson Mfg. Co., Mpls., 1936-45; v.p., dir. First Bank Stock Corp.; dir. First Service Corp., B. F. Nelson Mfg. Co., 1st Bancredit Corp., N.W. Fire & Marine Ins. Co., N.W. Nat. Life Ins. Co., Soo Line R.R. Co., Mpls. & Eastern Ry. (pres.). Trustee Mpls. Found.; dir., mem. exec. com. Minn. Community Research Council, Inc. Mem. Fed. Adv. Council. Served as capt. Cav., U.S. Army, World War I. Clubs: Minneapolis, Minikahda (Mpls.); Minnesota (St. Paul); Woodhill Country (Wayzata); Chicago. Home: Maplewoods, Wayzata, Minn. Died Aug. 27, 1950.

ATWOOD, John Murray, coll. dean; b. Brockton, Mass., Sept. 25, 1869; s. Isaac Morgan and Almira (Church) A.; ed. Canton (N.Y.) High Sch.; B.A., Coll. of Letters and Science (St. Lawrence U.), 1889, M.A., 1900; B.D., Canton Theol. Sem. (St. Lawrence University), 1893; D.D., Lombard Coll., 1906, LL.D., St. Lawrence U., 1939; m. Addie B. Ford, July 18 1894; children—Ruth Tuttle (Mrs. M. S. Black, Helen Ford (Mrs. R. C. Harwood), John Murray. Ordained Universalist ministry, 1893; Pastor Clifton Springs, New York, 1893-95, Minneapolis, Minnesota, 1895-98, Portland, Maine, 1899-1905; instructor, 1898-99, professor sociology and ethics, 1905-13, Canton Theological Sch.; Gaines prof. philosophy, Coll. Letters and Science, St. Lawrence University, 1913-14, dean theology dept. of univ. since 1914, mem. bd. of adminstration since 1919. President and chairman bd. trustees Universalist Gen. Conv., 1923-27; pres. N.Y. State Conv. of Universalists, 1927-29 and 1940-42. Mem. Beta Theta Pi, Phi Beta Kappa, Torch Club. Home:

25 College St., Canton, N.Y. Died Nov. 4, 1951; buried Evergreen Cemetery, Canton.

AUBREY, Edwin Ewart, educator, theologian; b. Glasgow, Scotland, Mar. 19, 1896; s. Edwin and Elizabeth Jane (Evans) A.; came to U.S., 1913, naturalized, 1918; prep. edn., pub. schs., Wales and Taunton Sch., England; Ph.B., Bucknell U., 1919, D.D., 1939; A.M., U. of Chicago 1921, D.B., 1922, Ph.D., 1926; m. Gladys Marsh Topping, Aug. 11, 1923; children—Nancy Jean, Donald Topping. Asso. prof. of Bible, Union Theol. Coll., Chicago, 1920-22; instructor, sociology and Bible, Carleton Coll., Northfield, Minn., 1922-23; asst. prof. sociology, Miami U., Oxford, Ohio, 1923-25; asso. professor sociology, 1925-26, asso. prof. Bibl. lit., Vassar Coll., 1926-27, professor, 1927-29; professor Christian theology and ethics, University of Chicago, 1929-44; chairman dept. 1933-35 chmn. theol. field, 1935-44; pres. Crozer Theological Sem., and prof. Christian social philosophy, 1944-49; professor religious thought, U. of Pa., 1949—; Cole lecturer, Vanderbilt University, 1940; pres. U. of Chicago Settlement, 1941-44; visiting lecturer in ethics, Calif. Inst. Tech., 1942; visiting professor of philosophy of religion, Union Theol. Sem., summers, 1942, 43, 45, 46, 49; Ingersoll lectr. Harvard, 1949. Served as corpl., U.S.A. Ambulance Service, 1917-19. Trustee Crozer Theological Sem., 1944-50, Bucknell Univ., 1944-48. Fellow Nat. Council Religion in Higher Edn.; chmn. com. on internat. justice and goodwill, Fedn. Council of Churches; consultant 1st assembly, World Council of Churches, Amsterdam, Holland, 1948; member American Society of Church History, American Theological Soc., Phi Beta Kappa, Delta Upsilon. Baptist. Author: Religion and the Next Generation, 1931; Present Theological Tendencies, 1936; Living the Christian Faith, 1939; Man's Search for Himself, 1940; Secularism a Myth, 1954; Humanistic Teaching and the Place of Ethical and Religious Values in Higher Education, 1959 (pub. posthumously). Book review editor, Journal of Religion, 1943-44. Contbr. Dictionary of Am. Biography, and various theol. jours. Home: 708 Argyle Rd., Wynnewood, Pa. Office: University of Pa., Phila. Died Sept. 10, 1956; buried Elgin, Ill.

AUCHTER, Eugene Curtis (ŏk'tēr), horticulturist; b. Elmgrove, N.Y., Sept. 14, 1889; s. William David and Florence Monroa (Curtis) A.; B.S., Cornell U., 1912, M.S., 1918, Ph.D., 1923; m. Catherine Elizabeth Beaumont, Aug. 25, 1914. Asst. in pomology, Cornell U., 1911-12; asst. and asso. prof. of horticulture, W.Va. U., 1912-17; head dept. of horticulture, U. of Md., 1918-28; prin. horticulturist in charge div. of fruit and vegetable crops and diseases, U.S. Dept. of Agr., 1928-38, asst. chief Bureau of Plant Industry, 1935-38, chief of Bureau of Plant Industry, 1938-42, administrator of Agricultural Research, 1942-45; pres. and dir. Pineapple Research Inst. of Hawaii, also v.p. Pineapple Growers Assn. since 1945. Mem. bd. of mgrs. New York Botanical Gardens. Hon. fellow Royal Hort. Soc. of London; fellow A.A.A.S.; mem. Am. Soc. Plant Physiologists, Wash. Acad. Sci., Am. Soc. Naturalists, Bot. Soc. of Washington, American Phytopathology Society, Am. Soc. Hort. Science, Am. Genetics Assn., Sigma Xi, Phi Kappa Phi, Alpha Zeta. Clubs: Cosmos (Washington, D.C.); Rotary, Pacific, Oahu Country, (Honolulu, Hawaii). Author: (with H. B. Knapp) Orchard and Small Fruit Culture, 1929; Growing Tree and Small Fruit, 1929. Home: 4471 Kahala Av., Honolulu, Hawaii. Office: Pineapple Research Institute, 2500 Dole St., Honolulu, T.H. Died July 8, 1952; buried Oahu Cemetery, Honolulu.

AUERBACH, Erich, lit. historian, educator; b. Berlin, Germany, Nov. 9, 1892; s. Herman and Rosa (Block) A.; student univs. Berlin, Freiburg, München; Dr. iur., U. Heidelberg, 1913; Dr. phil., U. Greifswald, 1921; m. Marie Mankiewitz, Feb. 27, 1923; 1 son, Clemens. Came to U.S., 1947, naturalized. 1953. Librarian, Prussian State Library, Berlin, 1923-29; prof. romance philology U. Marburg, 1929-35; prof. Turkish State U., Istanbul, 1936-47; vis. prof. Pa. State U., 1948-49; mem. Inst. Advanced Study, Princeton, N.J., 1949-50; prof. French and romance philology Yale, 1950—, Sterling prof., 1956. Mem. Modern Lang. Assn., Medieval Acad., Renaissance Soc., Dante Soc., Conn. Acad. Author several books in field romance philology, mediaeval Latin. Italian and French lit., including: Mimesis, 1953 (also pub. in German, Spanish, Italian, Hebrew); also articles hist. criticism. Home: 438 Whitney Av., New Haven 11. Died Oct. 13, 1957.

AULT, Otto Thurman, lawyer; b. Pikeville, Tenn., Oct. 9, 1892; s. George and Vesta (Darwin) A.; student Emory and Henry Coll., 1909; LL.B., Vanderbilt U., 1915; m. Eliza Swafford, Apr. 1, 1930. Admitted to Tenn. State bar, 1915, and practiced in Pikeville, 1915-48; mem. firm Ault & Clemmer; asst. state atty. gen., Pikeville, Tenn., 1937-39; asst. U.S. atty., Chattanooga, 1939-48, U.S. atty. 1948-53. Mem. Tenn. State Bar Assn., Am. Legion. Mason. Address: Pikeville, Tenn. Died July 6, 1954.

AUMAN, Orrin W. (aw'măn), clergyman; b. Dakota, Ill., Jan. 2, 1873; s. William R. and Susan (Lattig) A.; graduate College of Northern Illinois, 1893; D.D., University of Denver, 1912; m. Jessie S. Small, July 5, 1902; 1 dau., Jean (Mrs. Edward D. Dickerman). Entered ministry Methodist Church, 1900; pastor Farnhamville, Ia., 1900-01, Goldfield and Lamar, Colo., until 1907, First Ch., Pueblo, 1907-10, Grant Av. Ch., Denver, 1910-16; supt. Denver dist., M.E. Church, 1916-24; treas. World Service Commn., M.E. Church, 1924-40; treasurer General Commission on World Service and Finance of the Methodist Ch., 1940-44, treas. emeritus since 1944; retired Sept. 1, 1944. Mem. Gen. Conf. M.E. Church, 1920, 28, 36, 40 and Uniting Conf. at Kansas City, 1939. Ecumenical Methodist Conf., London, 1921. The Iliff School of Theology. Republican. Mason. Author: By the Help of the Infinite, 1928. Home: 2238 Sherman Av., Evanston, Ill. Died Mar. 29, 1951; buried Cedarville, Ill.

AUSTIN, Dwight Bertram, corp. exec.; b. Cedar Rapids, Ia., July 15, 1898; s. Alvia James and Jeanette (Togerson) A.; grad. Canton (Ill.) High Sch., 1916; m. Madeleine Drake, Oct. 23, 1920; children—Stephen, Patricia Jane (Mrs. J. D. Lewis), Betty Jane (Mrs. Arthur Bergman, Jr.). Formerly with Parlin & Orendorff, Canton, Ill., and Western Electric Co., Chgo.; warehouse supt. The Great Atlantic & Pacific Tea Co., Chgo., 1919—; dir. operations Middle Western div., 1925, divisional v.p., 1931, divisional pres., 1947—, also dir. Mem. Ill. Farm Bur., Ill. C. of C., Chgo. Assn. Commerce and Industry, Chgo. Better Bus. Bur. Presbyn. Elk. Clubs: Union League, Chicago Athletic, Executives (dir.), Rotary, Lions (Chgo.); Oak Park (Ill.) Country; River Forest (Ill.) Tennis. Home: 1046 Franklin Av., River Forest, Ill. Office: 2622 N. Pulaski Rd., Chgo. 39. Died Mar. 7, 1955; buried Greenwood Cemetery, Canton, Ill.

AUSTIN, Ennis Raymond, architect; b. Owasco, Cayuga County, N.Y., Aug. 30, 1863; s. John Rooks and Louise Ann (Prentice) A.; B.S. in Architecture, Cornell U., 1886; m. Elsie E. Woodworth, Oct. 5, 1887 (died Mar. 19, 1937); m. 2d, Melvina Brady, Jan. 11, 1940. Began with N. LeBrun & Sons, architects, N.Y. City, 1887; with John Du Fais, and Tiffany Glass & Decorating Co., 1888-92; mem. firm of Parker & Austin, architects, South Bend, Ind., 1892-1901; supt. of constrn., U.S. Treasury Dept., 1901-06; firm of Schneider & Austin, South Bend, 1906-09; mem. Austin & Shambleau, 1909-40; firm designed South Bend Federal Bldg., Building & Loan Tower, several city sch. bldgs., etc.; now retired. Fellow American Inst. of Architects; mem. Ind. Chapter A.I.A. (pres., 1911-12), Ind. Soc. Architects, South Bend Architectural Club (pres., 1910, 11, 12). Republican. Presbyterian. Clubs: Rotary, Indiana. Home: R.R. 1, Box 379, Osceola, Ind. Died Jan. 15, 1951; buried Owasco (N.Y.) Rural Cemetery.

AUSTIN, James Harold, prof. research medicine; b. Phila., Pa., Sept. 22, 1883; s. James Smith and Louisa McKee (Sloan) A.; B.S., University of Pennsylvania, 1905; M.D., 1908; married Thelma Frances Wood, June 21, 1924; children—Thelma Frances Wood (Mrs. W. Warrin Fry), James Harold, John Brander, 3d. Interne Univ. Hosp., Phila., 1908-10; asst. demonstrator in pathology, U. of Pa. 1910-11, asso. in research medicine and medicine, 1911-17; asst. Rockefeller Inst., New York, 1919-20, asso., 1920-21; prof. of research medicine, University of Pennsylvania, 1922-50, emeritus prof. since 1950. Dir. William Pepper Lab. of Clin. Medicine, 1942-50; exec. sec. Coll. Physicians of Philadelphia since 1949. Successively 1st lt., captain, major Medical Corps, U.S. Army, 1917-19. Mem. A.A.A.S., A.M.A., Assn. Am. Physicians, Assn. of Pathol. Bacteriology, Soc. Exptl. Biology, Soc. Clin. Investigation, Soc. Biol. Chemistry, Harvey Soc., Coll. of Physicians of Phila., Phi Beta Kappa, Sigma Xi, Alpha Omega Alpha, Delta Upsilon. Episcopalian. Club: University (Phila.). Editor Jour. Clin. Investigation, 1926-35; asso. editor Medicine since 1929. Home: 138 Chamounix Rd., St. Davids, Pa. Office: 19 S. 22d St., Phila. 3. Died Mar. 29, 1952; buried West Laurel Hill Cemetery, Bala Cynwyd, Pa.

AUSTIN, William Lacy, gen. ins. broker; b. Albanly, N.Y., Sept. 1, 1872; s. Thomas and Annie (Lansing) A.; m. Mary Catherine Sheldon, Oct. 14, 1908; 1 son, Thomas Sheldon. With Mechanics & Farmers Bank, Albany, N.Y., 1889-96; partner with father in gen. ins. bus., Austin and Co., Albany, N.Y., 1898-1942. retired, 1942; dir. Morris Plan Bank and Consolidated Car Heating Co., Albany; trustee, v.p. Nat. Savings Bank. Trustee First Church of Albany. Mason, Elk. Clubs: Fort Orange (life mem.), Albany Country, Schuyler Meadows Country (Albany); Lake Placid (N.Y.) (life mem.). Home: 399 Loudon Rd., Loudonville. N.Y. Office: 91 State St., Albany 7, N.Y. Died June 14, 1958; buried Albany Rural Cemetery.

AUSTRIAN, Charles Robert, physician; born Baltimore, Maryland, May 28, 1885; s. Robert and Belle (Bernei) A.; A.B., Johns Hopkins University, 1904, M.D., 1909; m. Florence Hochschild, Dec. 9, 1914; children—Robert, Janet (Mrs. Burton R. Fisher). Intern, asst. resident physician, Johns Hopkins Hospital, 1909-14; visiting physician since 1915; asst. instr. and asso. in medicine, Johns Hopkins U., 1910-23, asso. prof., 1923-50, asso. prof. emeritus since 1950; physician in chief Sinai Hosp., Baltimore, 1921-44, chief medical cons. since 1947; mem. staff Union Memorial Hosp., Hosp. for Women of Md. gen. chmn. of med. advisor to State Director, Selective Service System; formerly chairman medical advisory board, Johns Hopkins Hospital; former mem. State Bd. of Welfare. Served as mem. Med. Advisory Bd., No. 7, U.S. Army, 1917-18. Mem. bd. trustees Peabody Conservatory Music; formerly pres. and mem. bd. trustees, Park Sch., Baltimore. Awarded gold medal by Phi Lamda Kappa Soc., 1935; mem. Johns Hopkins Med. Soc. (former pres), Baltimore City Med. Soc. (former pres.), Council of Med. and Chirurg. Faculty of Md. (pres. 1943) A.M.A., Southern Med. Assn., Assn. Am. Physicians, American Climatol. and Clinical Association, Association Am. Pathologists and Bacteriologists, Cosmopolitan Clin. Club, Phi Beta Kappa, Sigma Xi, Alpha Omega Alpha. Clubs: Johns Hopkins, The 14 West Hamilton Street, University, Suburban (Baltimore); Laurel-on-the Severn (Annapolis). Mem. editorial bd. Bulletin of Johns Hopkins Hosp. Contbr. many papers to med. socs., etc. Home: 1417 Eutaw Pl., Balt. Died July 13, 1956.

AVENT, Joseph Emory (ā-vĕnt'), ednl. psychology; b. Wake County, N.C., Apr. 3, 1878; s. James Wesley and Martha Cornelia (Womble) A.; grad. Raleigh (N.C.) Male Acad., 1897; A.B., U. of N.C., 1901; M.A., Columbia Univ., 1913, Ph.D., 1925. Prin. high sch., Morven, N.C., 1901-02; successively supt. schs. Maxton, Bessemer City, Morganton, and Goldsboro (all in N.C.) until 1912; prof. edn., State Teachers Coll., Radford, Va., 1913-21; pres. Martha Washington Coll., Abingdon, Va., 1922-23; prof. ednl. psychol., U. of Tenn., 1923-47; dir. Tenn. State Testing Program (U. of Tenn.), 1947-49. Mem. Phi Delta Kappa, Kappa Delta Pi, Pi Gamma Mu, Phi Kappa Phi. Dem. Methodist. Clubs: Lions, Kiwanis. Author: Summer Sessions of State Teachers Colleges, 1925; Beginning Teaching, 1926; The Excellent Teacher, 1931; Excellences and Errors in Teaching Methods, 1931; Excellences and Errors in Class-room Management, 1934; Standard Testing Reduced to Lowest Terms, 1936; Educational Psychology, 1951. Home: 2007 Lake Av., Knoxville 16, Tenn. Ret. Died 1958.

AVERILL, George G., physician; b. Lincoln, Me., Dec. 5, 1869; s. David F. and Leah S. (Lowell) A.; M.D., Coll. Phys. and Surg., Boston, 1892; M.D., Tufts Coll. Med. Sch., 1896, L.H.D., 1941; LL.D., Colby Coll., 1942; m. Frances B. Mosher, Feb. 2, 1921. Practiced medicine, 1892-1911; retired because of ill health; later interested in mfg. bus. and various other businesses in Cal., now chiefly engaged in philanthropic activities, with particular interest in Good Will Home Assn. Mem. Mass. Med. Soc. Mason. Home: 109 Silver St., Waterville, Me. Died Sept. 19, 1954.

AVERY, Christopher Lester (ā'vēr-ĭ), judge; b. Groton, Conn., Sept. 4, 1872; s. Christopher Lester and Ellen Barber (Copp) A.; prep. edn. Norwich (Conn.) Free Acad.; A.B., Yale, 1893, LL.B., 1897; m. Betsy Ann Bouse, 1901 (died 1903); 1 son, Christopher Lester III; m. 2d, Elizabeth Anderson Brander, 1906 (died 1915); children—Betsy Ann, Catherine Barber, William Brander, Elizabeth Brander; m. 3d, Ethel Gray Bailey, 1917; 1 dau., Mary Gray. Admitted to N.Y. bar, 1897, and began practice at N.Y. City; moved to New London, Conn., 1903; mem. firm Waller, Waller, Avery & Gallup, 1903 to 1920; judge, Superior Court, Conn., 1920-29; apptd. justice Supreme Ct. of Conn., 1929, retired 1942; now state referee. Served as Q.M. USN, in U.S.S. Jason, Spanish-American War. Mem. Conn. Ho. of Reps., 1913; mem. Commn. on Uniform State Laws, Conn., 1914; mem. Commn. Rivers, Harbors and Bridges, Conn., 1915; chmn. Draft Bd., New London, 1917. Chmn. bd. Savings Bank of New London, 1939; chmn. Groton & New London Bridge Commn., 1939. Trustee Conn. Coll. for Women. Democrat. Conglist. Mason. Home: 306 Brandegee Av., Groton, Conn. Died May 6, 1956.

AVERY, Oswald Theodore, physician; b. Halifax, N.S., Oct. 21, 1877; A.B., Colgate; M.D., Coll. Phys. and Surg., Columbia, 1904; Sc.D., Colgate, 1921; LL.D., McGill U., 1935. Mem. Rockefeller Inst. for Med. Research, 1923-43, researcher emeritus, 1943-48, research in pneumococcus infections. Mem. Assn. Am. Physicians, Am. Soc. for Clin. Investigation, Am. Assn. Pathologists and Bacteriologists, Am. Soc. for Exptl. Pathology, Soc. Am. Bacteriologists, N.Y. Acad. Medicine, Am. Acad. Arts and Sciences, Nat. Acad. Sciences, Der Norski Videnskaps Akademi (Olso), Académi Royale de Medécine de Belgique, Société Philomathique de Paris. Address: Nashville. Died Feb. 20, 1955.*

AVITABILE, Salvatore (ä-vē-tä'bē-le), opera condr.; b. Cicciano, Naples, Italy, Jan. 1, 1873, came to U.S. 1893, naturalized 1908; s. Vincent and Maria (d'Avanzo) A.; Master Music, Royal Coll. of Music, Naples, Italy, 1893; m. Frances Mary Mauro, Aug. 19, 1899; children—Mrs. Altana Watson, Mrs. Alberta Tobie, Adrian R., Arnold C. Asst. prof. composition, harmony, piano and singing Royal Conservatory of Music, Naples, 1892-93; condr. grand opera with opera companies in Europe, 1892-93; vocal tchr., operatic coach, 1893; conducted grand opera for Henry Savage Opera Co., Aborn English Opera Co., Russian Opera Co. and many others. Apptd. by Duke of Abruzzi to direct orchestra at Carnegie Hall at memorial services for King Humbert I. Winner in musical composition contest sponsored by Artistic Soc. of Palermo (symphonic composition, La Fortis Joventus); 1892. Hon. mem. Artistic Soc. of Palermo. Republican. Roman Catholic. Tchr. Marion Talley and Marion Chamlee. Home: 384 9th St., Bklyn. 15. Office: Metropolitan Opera House Studios, 1425 Broadway, N.Y.C. Died May 17, 1957; buried Calvary Cemetery.

AVNSOE, Thorkild, corp. exec.; b. Copenhagen, Denmark, 1884. Exec. v.p. Lone Star Cement Corp., N.Y.C., v.p. Cuban Portland Cement Corp. Home: 59 Ontario Rd., Bellrose, L.I., N.Y. Office: 100 Park Av., N.Y.C. Died Sept. 11, 1958.

AXTELL, Harold Lucius, educator; b. West Medway, Mass., May 24, 1876; s. Seth Jones and Mary Caroline (Fletcher) A.; A.B., Kalamazoo Coll., 1897; A.B., U. Chgo., 1898, A.M., 1900, Ph.D., 1906; traveling fellow U. Chgo. and student Am. Sch. Classical Studies in Rome, 1901-02; m. Gertrude S. Bouton, June 30, 1908; children—Mildred Marion, Gertrude Mary, Richard William, Eleanor Grace, Muriel Beth. Prof. Latin, Des Moines Coll., 1898-1900; instr., prin. Prep. Sch., U. Ida., 1902-05, prof. classics, 1906-46, prof. emeritus, 1946—, prof. modern lang., 1920-23, also acting dean of College of Letters and Science, 1930-31. Served as YMCA sec. Ft. Stevens, Ore., 1918. Mem. Pacific Classical Assn., Am., Philol. Assn., Am. Classical League, Phi Beta Kappa. Republican. Author: The Deification of Abstract Ideas in Roman Literature and Inscriptions, 1907. Contbr. to professional jours. Home: 1106 E. 6th St., Moscow, Ida. Died May 8, 1955; buried Moscow, Ida.

AYDELOTTE, Frank (a'dĕ-lŏt), ret. coll. pres.; b. Sullivan, Ind., Oct. 16, 1880; s. William E. and Matilda (Brunger) A.; A.B., Ind. U., 1900, LL.D., 1937; A.M., Harvard, 1903; Rhodes Scholar from Ind. to Oxford U. 1905-07, B.Litt., 1908; LL.D., Allegheny Coll., 1923, Yale, 1928, N.Y.U., Dickinson 1940, Pomona Coll., U. Ia., 1941, U. Cal., 1942; L.H.D., U. Pa., 1924, Swarthmore, 1940; D. Litt., U. Pitts., 1925, Oberlin, 1926; D.C.L., Oxford U., 1937, U. South 1949; hon. fellow, Brasenose Coll., Oxford; m. Marie Jeannette Osgood, June 22, 1907 (dec. June 14, 1952); 1 son, William Osgood. Instr. English, Southwestern State Normal Sch., California, Pa., 1900-01; instr. English, Ind. U., 1901-02, Louisville Boys' High Sch., 1903-05; asso. prof. English, Ind. U., 1908-15; prof. English, Mass. Inst. Tech., 1915-21; pres. Swarthmore Coll., 1921-40; dir. Inst. Advanced Study, 1939-47, now dir. emeritus, Am. sec. Rhodes trustees 1918-53; pres. Assn. Am. Rhodes Scholars, 1930-56; trustee Carnegie Found. for Advancement of Teaching, 1922-53; nat. dir. War Issues Course, War Dept. Com. on Edn. and Spl. Tng. 1918; chmn. com. on sci. personnel Office Sci. Research and Development, 1942; chmn. N.J. Enemy Alien Hearing Bd., 1941-42; mem. Anglo-Am. Com. of Inquiry on Palestine, 1945-46; trustee Tchrs. Ins. and Annuity Assn. America, 1923-27, Inst. Internat. Edn., 1925-41; chmn. edn. advisory bd. John Simon Guggenheim Memorial Foundation, 1925-50, chmn. emeritus and consultant to Found., 1950-56; trustee World Peace Foundation 1927-56, Inst. for Advanced Study, 1930-56; mem. board managers Swarthmore College, 1945-56; Mem. Modern Lang. Assn. Am., Am. Hist. Assn., Am. Philos. Soc. (mem. council 1935-38 and 1943-46; v.p. 1941-43), Council on Fgn. Relations, Am. Acad. Polit. and Social Sci., Phi Beta Kappa (mem. senate 1931-49; dir., v.p. Assos. 1946-56), Sigma Nu; mem. Coll. Electors, Hall of Fame, N.Y. U., 1944-56; pres. Assn. Am. Colls., 1925; hon. mem. Am. Assn. U. Profs.; bd. dirs., Am. Friends Service Com., 1940-46, P.E.N. Democrat. Clubs: Cosmos (Washington); Thames, New London; Century, Harvard (N.Y.C.); Franklin Inn, University (Phila.); Harvard (Boston); Nassau (Princeton); Athenaeum (London). Author: Elizabethan Rogues and Vagabonds, 1913; College English, 1913; The Oxford Stamp, 1917. Editor: Materials for the Study of English Literature and Composition, 1914; English and Engineering, 1917; Oxford of Today (with L. A. Crosby and A. C. Valentine), 1922, 2d edit., 1927; Honors Courses in American Colleges and Universities (Nat. Research Council), 2d edit., 1925; Breaking the Academic Lock Step, 1944; The Am. Rhodes Scholarships, 1946 (pub. in Eng. as The Vision of Cecil Rhodes, 1946. Contbr. articles on English lit. edn. and pub. affairs. Home: 88 Battle Rd. Office: Inst. for Advanced Study, Princeton, N.J. Died Dec. 17, 1956.

AYER, Charles Fanning, financier; b. Lowell, Mass., 1865; A.B. Harvard, 1887. Pres. Boott Mills; dir. Am. Woolen Co., Columbian Nat. Life Ins. Co., Lamson Co., N.E. Tel. & Tel. Co., Old Colony Trust Co.; trustee Oliver Building Trust. Home: Hamilton, Mass. Office: 53 State St., Boston. Died Jan. 15, 1956.

AYERS, Lemuel (airs), theatrical producer and designer; b. N.Y.C., Jan. 22, 1915; s. Dr. Lemuel Delos and Hazel Carleton (Bisland) A.; A.B. in Architecture, Princeton, 1936; M.A. in Drama, Ia. U., 1938; m. Shirley Osborn, May 11, 1939; children—Jonathan Osborn, Sarah Lemuel Rockefeller Found. fellowship, 1937-38; designed scenery and costumes for Angel Street, St. Louis Woman, Cyrano, Kiss Me Kate, Out of this World, The Harvest According (ballet), See the Jaguar (producer), My Darlin' Aida, Camino Real, Kismet, The Pajama Game; designed scenery for The Pirate, Oklahoma, Harriet, Inside U.S.A., A Star Is Born (motion picture); designed (for M-G-M Studios) Meet Me in St. Louis; directed prodn. numbers in Ziegfeld Follies; co-producer Kiss Me Kate, 1948, Out of This World, 1950. Recipient Donaldson Award for best costume design, also best scenic design, Kiss Me Kate, 1948-49, Camino Real, 1952-53, best costume design, My Darlin' Aida, 1952-53, Kismet, 1953-54. Home: 233 East End Av., N.Y.C. Office: 17a W. 57th St., N. Y.C. 19. Died August 14, 1955.

AYERS, Roy E., ex-gov. Mont., ex-congressman; b. on ranch in Central Mont., Nov. 9, 1882; s. George W. and Mary E. (Sullenger) A.; LL.B., Valparaiso U., 1903; m. Ellen Simpson, June 7, 1905; children—Elnore, Arthur, Donald. Admitted to Mont. bar, 1903; county atty. Fergus County, Mont., 1905-09; judge 10th Dist. Mont., 1913-22; mem. law firm Ayers & Ayers; engaged in live stock bus., 1903—; mem. 73d-74th Congresses, 2d Mont. Dist.; gov. of Mont., 1936-41. Mem. Mont. Bd. Edn., 1908-12. Mem. Am., Mont. State bar assns. Democrat. Mason. Home: Lewiston, Mont. Died May 23, 1955.

AYLESWORTH, Merlin Hall (āls'wûrth), lawyer, corp. exec.; b. Cedar Rapids, Ia., July 19, 1886; s. Barton Orville and Georgia (Shores) A.; student Colo. Agricultural Coll., U. of Colo., U. of Wis., Denver U., Columbia U.; LL.B., U. of Denver, 1908; LL.D., Drake U., 1932; m. Blanche Parrett, Oct. 19, 1909; children—Barton Jerome, Dorothy; m. 2d, Caroline Andrews McEnteer, July 1, 1945. Practiced law at Ft. Collins, Colo., 1908-14; chmn. Colo. Pub. Utilities Commn., 1914-18; exec. v.p. Utah Power & Light Co., Salt Lake City, 1918-19; mng. dir. Nat. Electric Light Assn., 1919-26; pres. Nat. Broadcasting Co., 1926-36, vice-chmn. bd., 1936; pres., chmn. bd. Radio-Keith-Orpheum Corp., RKO Radio Pictures, Pathe News, Inc., dir. Keith Albee Orpheum Corp., B. F. Keith Corp., until Mar. 1, 1937; mem. Scripps-Howard Management, 1937-38; pub. N.Y. World-Telegram, 1938-40; chmn. bd. Radio City Music Hall 1934-45. Exec. Consultant, Office of Coordinator of Inter-Am. Affairs 1941-45, chmn. exec. com. Ellington & Co., Inc., N.Y.; mem. Appeal Bd., Selective Service. Trustee Drake U. Mem. Sigma Chi. Republican. Mem. Christian Ch. Clubs: National Golf Links of America; Deepdale Country (Great Neck, N.Y.). Home: Redding Ridge, Conn. Office: RCA Bldg., 30 Rockefeller Plaza, N.Y. City 20. Died Sept. 30, 1952.

AYRES, Frank C., C.S. lecturer; b. Indianapolis, June 11, 1886; s. Alexander C. and Anna (Fay) A.; A.B., U. Mich., 1908, LL.B., J.D., 1910; m. Myrtle Craft, Jan 15, 1926. Admitted to Ind. bar, 1910, practiced law, Indianapolis, 1910-27; C.S. com. publ. for Ind., 1927-29, 35, 40-48, began practice C.S., 1927, 1st reader Third Ch. Christ Scientist, Indianapolis, 1930-32; apptd. C.S. lectr. by The Mother Ch., Boston, 1950. Home: 1321 N. Meridian St., Indpls. Office: Merchants Bank Bldg., Indpls. 4. Deceased.

AYRES, William Augustus, federal trade commr.; b. Elizabethtown, Ill., Apr. 19, 1867; s. William Warren and Catherine (Drumm) A.; ed. Garfield (now Friends') University, Wichita, 1888-90, LL.D., Friends' Univ., 1942; m. Dula Pease, Dec. 30, 1896; children—Margaret Eleanor (Mrs. W. F. Weigester) and Kathryn Elizabeth (Mrs. H. J. Nichols, Jr.) (twins). Mrs. Pauline Williams. Admitted to Kansas bar, 1893, and practiced at Wichita. Served as clerk of Court of Appeals, Kansas, 1897-1901; pros. atty., Sedgwick County, Kan., 1907-11; mem. 64th to 66th Congresses (1915-21) and 68th to 72d Congresses (1923-33), 8th Kan. Dist., and 73d Congress (1933-35), 5th Kan. Dist., resigned upon appointment as fed. trade commr., Aug. 1934; reappointed fed. trade commr., May 14, 1940 and for term beginning Sept. 26, 1947. Democrat. Mem. Christian Ch. Mason (33°, Shriner). Home: Kennedy Warren, Washington. Office: 6th and Constitution Av. N.W., Washington. Died Feb. 17, 1952; buried Old Mission Cemetery, Wichita.

AZAD, Abul Kalam Maulana, Indian statesman. Founder Urdu weekly, Al-Hilal, later founded Al-Balagh; active Khilafat, Non-coop. and Civil Disobedience movements; mem. Congress Working Com., also All-India Congress Com.; pres. Indian Nat. Congress, 1923, 39-46; mem. Indian Interim Govt., 1947; minister edn. Govt. of India, 1947—, minister natural resources and sci. research, 1952—; pres. 9th session Gen. Conf. UNESCO, New Delhi, 1956. Author Commentary on Koran, and other books. Address: Ministry of Edn. and Scientific Research, New Delhi, India. Deceased.

AZEVEDO, Philadelpho, judge; b. Rio de Janeiro, Brazil, Mar. 13, 1894; s. José C. Barros e Azevedo and Julieta Derreira (Lima) A.; ed. Colegio Pedro II, Faculdade Livre de Ciencias Juridicas e Sociais do Rio de Janeiro, Ecole de Sciences Politiques, Paris, France; m. Vera Leite Guinarães, Apr. 29, 1919; children—Gustave Philadelpho, Gilda. Prof. of philosophy Coll. Pedro II, Rio de Janeiro, 1917-37; prof. civil law, Law Sch., Rio de Janeiro U., 1932-42, dean of law school, 1937-38; asso. justice Brazilian Supreme Court, 1942-46; mayor of Rio de Janeiro, 1945-46; judge at Internat. Court of Justice, The Hague, Holland, since 1946. Mem. Nat. Teaching Council (1925), Univ. Council (vice rector of Univ. of Brazil, 1938), Brazilian Bar Assoc. (pres. 1937), many commissions working in tech. subjects of law and Brazilian rep. in many nat. and internat. reunions and congresses of law. Author: Fraude contra credores, 1920; Registros publicos, 1924; Direito moral do escritor, 1930; Destinação do imovel, 1932; Execuções de sentenças, 1936; Discurso de paraninfo, 1939; Registro de imoveis, 1941; Projeto de Codigo de Processo, 1934; Projeto de Codigo de Obrigações, 1940; Valor da Transcrição, 1942. Home: Avenida Princeza Isabel, 11 (Leme), Rio de Janeiro, D.F., Brasil. Office: International Court of Justice, Peace Palace, The Hague, Holland. Died May 7, 1951.

AZUOLA, Eduardo (ä-zōō-ō-lä), Guatemalan consul; b. San José, Costa Rica, Nov. 15, 1892; s. Luis Eduardo and Elena (Aubert) A.; A.B., Valparaiso U., 1919, A.M., 1920, hon. Litt. D., 1925; D.D.S., Marquette U., 1925; Ph.D., Bogotá U., Colombia, 1938; grad. student, Boston Univ., 1936-38; m. Consuelo Trigo, Dec. 24, 1929; children—Luis Felipe, Consuelo Elena. Prof. of Spanish, Marquette Univ., 1920-26; traveling clinician, S.S. White Dental, Europe, Latin Am., 1926-36; prof. Spanish, Boston Coll., since 1936; prof. fgn. trade, Fisher sch., Boston, 1940-41; export mgr., Myerson Tooth Corp., Cambridge, Mass., since 1940; consul gen. of Costa Rica, Boston, since 1940; consul of Guatemala, Boston, since 1948; del. of Costa Rican Chamber of Commerce and Tourist Bd., Boston; lecturer on Latin Am. affairs. Mem. Pan Am. Soc. of Mass., Modern Lang. Assn., Acad. of History (Colombia). Roman Catholic. Clubs: Export of N.E. (dir.), Spanish. Author: Pequenos Cuentos, 1922, Understanding Latin Americans, 1938, Zorrilla, 1946, Espronceda, 1947, Campoamor, 1948. Home: 51 Mt. Alvernia Rd., Chestnut Hill 67, Mass. Office: 90 Hamilton St., Cambridge, Mass. and 230 Clarendon St., Boston. Died Mar. 1950.

B

BAAB, Otto J(ustice) (bŏb), educator; b. Chgo., July 6, 1896; s. William George and Mary (Haffner) B.; student Winona (Minn.) State Tchrs. Coll., 1917-18; B.A., Hamline U., 1921, D.D., 1956; M.A., Northwestern U., 1927; B.D., Garrett Bibl. Inst., 1927; Ph.D., U. Chgo., 1928; m. Eunice Beatrice Bothe, June 7, 1922; 1 dau., Mary Beatrice. Ordained to ministry Meth. Ch., 1927; minister Nashwauk, Minn., 1921-24, Mt. Greenwood, Ill., 1925-26, Hegewisch, Ill., 1926-27; instr. U. Chgo., 1929-30; prof. religion Ill. Wesleyan U., Bloomington, Ill., 1930-34; prof. Garrett Bibl. Inst., 1934—, acting pres., 1953-55. Mem. War Labor Bd., 1942-45; mem. WSB, 1951-52. Exec. sec. Citizens Com. Indsl. Relations, Chgo., 1948-48. Mem. Am. Arbitration Assn., Fed. Mediation and Conciliation Service, Nat. Acad. Arbitrators, Chgo. Soc. Bibl. Research, Soc. Bibl. Lit., Am. Oriental Soc., Phi Kappa Phi, Pi Gamma Mu. Author: Jesus Christ Our Lord, 1937; The Theology of the Old Testament, 1949; Prophetic Preaching, 1958. Contbr. articles The Bible Today and Tomorrow, 1946; Labor Arbitration Reports, 1946-58; Ency. Britannica, 1953; Schaff-Herzog Ency. Religious Knowledge, 1956. Home: 2417 Hartzell St. Office: 2121 Sheridan Rd., Evanston, Ill. Died Sept. 28, 1958; buried St. Paul, Minn.

BAAR, Arnold R(udolph Ruprecht) (bär), judge; b. Jersey City, June 12, 1891; s. Rudolph F. and Anna F. (Drake) Ruprecht; step-father Paul F. Baar; Ph.B., U. Chicago, 1912, J.D. cum laude, 1914; m. Mary L. Hoyt, Aug. 17, 1916; 1 dau., Doris Ruprecht (Mrs. R. W. Poole). Admitted to Ill. bar, 1914; with law firm Mayer, Meyer, Austrian & Platt, 1914-17; mem. firm KixMiller & Baar, 1918-26, KixMiller, Baar & Hoffman, 1926-35, KixMiller, Baar and Morris 1935—; judge of Tax Court of United States, 1954; director. Selected Am. Shares, Inc., Opelika Mfg. Corp., Record Controls, Inc. President Citizens Schs. Com., 1937-40, City Club, 1932-34, 1938-39, Civic Fedn., 1948-50 (trustee since 1933). Mem. Am., Ill. and Chicago bar assns., American Technical Society (pres. 1940-52, now director), National Tax Assn., Am. Law Inst., Order of Coif, Phi Beta Kappa, Delta Sigma Rho, Delta Chi. Club: Law. Joint author and editor: Hidden Taxes in Corporate Reorganizations, 1935; United States Income and War Tax Guide, 1917-28 (yearly revisions); other income tax publs. of Commerce Clearing House; also articles in mags. Home: 642 Cherry St., Winnetka, Ill. Office: Roanoke Tower, 11 S. La Salle St., Chgo. 3. Died Oct. 14, 1954; buried Weedsport, N.Y.

BABBITT, Juliette M., b. Hancock County, Ill.; d. Joseph and Susanne Younger; ed. in Iowa; m. Charles Henry Babbitt, Dec. 19, 1863. Writer of short stories, mag. articles, Washington gossip for Western papers, syndicate matter; Washington representative N.Y. Mirror, 1879-91; N.Y. Home Jour., spl. articles and letters, 1888-1900; Washington corr.

Boston Ideas; librarian, League of Am. Pen Women, 1898-1900, v.p. 1900-1901, pres. 1901-1901, historian, chmn. bd. dirs. 1902-1903. Address: Washington. Died Oct. 16, 1930.

BABCOCK, Ernest Brown, prof. genetics; b. Edgerton, Wis., July 10, 1877; s. Emilus Welcome and Mary Eliza (Brown) B.; student Lawrence Coll., Appleton, Wis., 1895-96; grad. State Normal Sch., Los Angeles, 1898; B.S., U. of Calif., 1906, M.S., 1911, LL.D., 1950; m. Georgia Bowen, June 24, 1908. First instr. in agrl. nature study State Normal Sch., Los Angeles, 1906-07; instr., asst. prof. plant pathology, 1907-10, asst. prof. agrl. edn., 1910-13, prof. genetics 1913-47, professor emeritus 1947—, University of California; faculty research lecturer for the University of Calif., 1944; exec. v.p. Forest Genetics Research Found., 1952-54, pres., 1954. Y.M.C.A. ednl. dir., with A.E.F., Jan.-Apr. 1919; mem. Army Ednl. Corps, A.E.F., Apr.-June 1919. Research Asso., Carnegie Inst., 1925-37. President section of experimental taxonomy, VII International Botany Congress, Stockholm, 1950. Mem. A.A.A.S., American Soc. Naturalists (vice pres. 1934), Genetics Soc. Am., Western Soc. Naturalists, Am. Genetics Assn., Bot. Soc. Am., California Academy Sciences (1st vice president, 1947-54, pres. 1954), California Botany Society (president 1940), Washington (D.C.) Academy Sciences, Nat. Acad. Sciences, Phi Beta Kappa, Sigma Xi, Alpha Zeta, Phi Sigma; hon. mem. Royal Bot. Soc. (Belgium), Japanese Bot. Soc. Congregationalist. Clubs: Faculty, City Commons (Berkeley, Calif.). Author: Genetics in Relation to Agriculture, (with Dr. Roy E. Clausen), 1918, 27; Genetics Laboratory Manual (with Dr. J. L. Collins), 1918; The Genus Crepis (in Bibliog. Genetica), (with Dr. M. Navashin), 1930; The Genus Youngia (with Dr. G. Ledyard Stebbins, Jr.), 1937; The Am. Species of Crepis, 1938; The Genus Crepis, Univ. Calif. Publ. Botany, vols. 21 and 22, 1947. Home: 1828 Hopkins St., Berkeley 7. Office: University of California, Berkeley 4, Cal. Died Dec. 8, 1954; buried Edgerton Fassett Cemetery, Edgerton, Wis.

BABCOCK, Harriet (Mrs. H. Hobart Babcock), psychologist; b. Westerly, R. I.; B.S., Columbia, 1922, A.M., 1923, Ph.D., 1930. Psychologist, Manhattan State Hosp., 1924-25; chief psychologist Bellevue Hosp., 1926-28; began research in measurement of mental deterioration, 1924; engaged in clinical work in efficiency phase of mental functioning since 1931. Fellow Am. Assn. Applied Psychology, N.Y. Acad. Science. Am. Psychol. Assn., A.A.A.S.; mem. eastern and local psychol assns.. Fgn. Policy Assn., Nat. Arts Club, N.Y. Pen and Brush. Author: An Experiment in the Measurement of Mental Deterioration, 1930; Dementia Praecox; A Psychological Study, 1933; Revised Examination for the Measurement of Efficiency of Mental Functioning, 1941; Time and the Mind, 1941. Contbr. to tech. and sci. jours. Originator method of measuring and evaluating efficiency of mental functioning in normal and abnormal mental conditions by controlling abstract-verbal development; determined place of psychogenic psychoses between the normal and definitely abnormal; stated the level-efficiency theory of intelligence; and showed the relation of personality to basic mental functioning. Home: 15 Gramercy Park, New York 3. Office: 119 E. 19th St., New York, N.Y. Died Dec. 12, 1952.

BABCOCK, Howard Edward, agricultural organizer, exec., teacher; b. Gilbertsville, N.Y., Feb. 23, 1889; s. Howard Worden and Mary Emma (Donahue) B.; B.A., Syracuse U., 1911 (hon. LL.D., 1941); m. Hilda Wall Butler, Oct. 23, 1913; children—Howard E., Barbara Elizabeth, John Butler. Teacher Elmira (N.Y.) Free Acad., 1912-13; county agt. Cattaraugus and Tompkins counties, 1913-14; asst. state dir. Farm Bureaus, N.Y., 1914-15; sec. Agrl. Conf. Bd., N.Y. State, 1917-21; sec. N.Y. State Farm Bur. Federation, 1919-21; state dir. Farm Bureaus, 1915-19; leave of absence, 1917-18, to serve on N.Y. State Food Conservation Commn.; prof. of marketing, Cornell U., 1920-22; gen. mgr. Coöp. Grange League Federation Exchange, 1922-32, 1935-36; pres. Coöp. G.L.F. Holding Corp., 1932-35; pres. Coöp. G.L.F. Products, Inc., 1937-40; dir. The G.L.F. School of Coöp. Adminstrn., 1940-43; dir. research (G.L.F.), 1943-45; mem. bus. advisory council for U.S. Dept. Commerce, 1944-45; mem. Nat. Research Adv. Com. since 1946; asst. chmn. Federal Farm Bd., 1933; dir. Central Bank for Coöp., 1933-39. Special consultant Farm Credit Adminstrn; president Nat. Council Farmer Cooperatives, 1943. Chmn. N.Y. State Emergency Food Commn., 1943. Trustee Cornell U. (chmn. bd. 1940-47). Mem. Gov. Roosevelt's Agrl. Advisory Com., N.Y. State Council Farms and Markets, Guernsey and Aberdeen-Angus Breeders Assn., Delta Chi. Owns and operates poultry and stock farms totalling 1000 acres. Contbr. to agrl. jours. Conglist. H. Edward Babcock Fund for promotion of studies in nutrition established in his honor at Cornell U. Home: Ithaca, N.Y. Died July 12, 1950.*

BABCOCK, Richard Earle, patent lawyer; b. Washington, Jan. 13, 1889; s. William Henry and Anne Johns (Earle) B.; LL.B., George Washington U., 1911, M.P.L., 1911; m. 1st, Georgie Hays Wright, Mar. 20, 1911; children—Georgie Wright (Mrs. James A. Ostrand), Richard Earle, Jr., William Henry; m. 2d Amelia Garden Clarkson, Jan. 3, 1924. Office boy, patent law office of father, 1907; admitted to D.C. bar, 1910, Va. bar, 1943, and since practiced in Washington specializing in patent law; sheep farmer near Herndon, Virginia, until 1956, retired. Member American Arbitration Association, the American Patent Law Assn., Am., D.C. bar assns. Republican. Episcopalian. Rotarian. Home: Stoney Hill Farm, Herndon, Va. Office: 1346 F St., Washington 4. Died June 1957.

BACH, Oscar Bruno (bäk), indsl. designer, craftsman for metals; b. Germany, Dec. 13, 1884; s. Adolpho and Ernestine (Marco) B.; student Cath. Higher Gymnasium, 1890-98, Royal Art Acad., Berlin, Germany, 1898-1902; m. Pauline Marie Di Rufolo, Apr. 12, 1916. Came to U.S., 1913, naturalized, 1926. Began as designer of metallic architecture and sculpture in Berlin, Germany, mostly for German, British and Italian govts., at age of 20; came to U.S. before the World War, retained as indsl. designer for such cos. as Remington-Rand, Manning-Bowman, Edw. Budd Mfg. Co., Oneida Ltd., Baldwin Locomotive Works, Am. Radiator Co., Tappan Stove Co., etc.; maintained research labs. for metall. and engring. work; pres. Oscar B. Bach Studios, Inc.; pres. Bachite Development Corp. Recipient gold medal for native indsl. design and craftsmanship Archt. League of N.Y. Works include metall. design and execution for S.S.'s Washington and Manhattan, Empire State Bldg., Bank of Manhattan, Bank of N.Y. and Trust Co., Riverside Ch., Arilines Terminal Bldg., Rockefeller Center, Dept. of Health Bldg. (all in N.Y.), Williamsburgh Savings Bank, Bklyn., Toledo Mus. Art, other museums, Yale U., Telephone Bldg., Cin., Christ Ch., Sch. Indsl. Art, Cranbrook, Mich. Developed Bachite process, a treatment giving color, corrosion and abrasion resistance to all ferrous metals; designs for automobile bodies, trains, airplanes, building material, etc. Lecturer. Contbr. to tech. jours. Office: La Maison Française, 610 Fifth Av., N.Y.C. Deceased.*

BACHARACH, Isaac, ex-congressman; b. Phila., Pa., Jan. 5, 1870; grad. Atlantic City (N.J.) High Sch., 1885; m. Florence Scull (dec. 1904). Pres. Bacharach Real Estate Co. Mem. N.J. Ho. of Rep., 1911; mem. 64th to 74th Congresses (1915-37). 2d N.J. Dist. Republican. Home: Brigantine, N.J. Office: Schwehm Bldg., Atlantic City, N.J. Died Sept. 5, 1956; buried Mt. Sinai Cemetery, Phila.

BACHEM, Albert, prof. biophysics; b. Bonn, Germany, Feb. 26, 1888; s. Dr. Joseph and Gertrude (Tonger) B.; Ph.D., U. of Bonn, 1910; m. Erica Pietsch; children—Erica, Wolfgang Albert. Came to U.S., 1921, naturalized 1931. Served as asst. prof. physics, Univ. of Bonn and Univ. of Frankfurt; prof. biophysics, U. of Ill. Coll. of Medicine, since 1924. Mem. Am. Physiol. Soc., Soc. Experimental Biology and Medicine, Am. Congress Physical Therapy, Sigma Xi. Author: Principles of X-Ray and Radium Dosage; also 6 physical therapy charts. Home: 1337 Winona St. Office: 1853 Polk St., Chicago, Ill. Died April 3, 1957.

BACHKE, Halvard Huitfeldt, Norwegian diplomat; b. Trondhjem, Norway, Dec. 13, 1873; s. Halvard and Marie Arilda (Huitfeldt) B.; student U. of Christiania; m. Ragna Thoresen. Entered fgn. service, 1899; chief of bur. Fgn. Office, Oslo, later chief sec. until 1909; counselor of legation, Paris and Berlin, 1910-19; envoyé to Argentine Republic, Uruguay and Paraguay, 1919-24, to Finland, Esthonia and Latvia, 1924-27; E.E. and M.P. to U.S., 1927-34, to France 1934-40. Died Jan. 20, 1948.

BACHMAN, Paul Stanton, coll. pres.; b. Adamsville, O., June 24, 1901; s. Herman H. and Clara Anita (Tussing) B.; B.S., Ohio State U., 1922; M.A., U. Wash., 1925, Ph.D., 1927; m. Vera Grieser Neese, Jan. 19, 1929; children—Stanton Leonard, Steven Bruce. Instr. polit. sci., U. Hawaii, 1927-28, asst. prof., 1928-34, asso. prof., 1934-37, prof. govt., 1937—, dir. grad. studies, 1934-42, dean faculties, 1942-55, dir. summer session, 1939-55, v.p., 1951-55, pres., 1955—; dir. Ewa Plantation Co., Ewa, Oahu, T.H. Mem. Am. Soc. Internat. Law, Am. Polit. Sci. Assn., Phi Kappa Phi. Clubs: Pacific; Honolulu. Author: Government of Hawaii, 1931; World Revolution, Marx to Stalin, 1951. Home: 2732 Manoa Rd., Honolulu, T.H. Died Jan. 9, 1957.

BACHMANN, Werner Emmanuel (bäk'män), prof. chemistry; b. Detroit, Mich., Nov. 13, 1901; s. Arnold William and Bertha (Wurster) W.; student Detroit Jr. Coll., 1919-21; B.S.E., U. of Mich., 1923, M.S., 1924, Ph.D., 1926; m. Marie Knaphurst, Sept. 14, 1927; children—Joan Marie, Roger Werner. Instr. chemistry, U. of Mich., 1925-29, asst. prof., 1929-35, asso. prof., 1935-39, prof. 1939-47, Moses Gomberg Univ. prof., 1947-51; asst. prof. U. of Illinois, summer, 1931, U. of Zurich, 1928-29, Royal Cancer Hosp., London, 1935, U. of Munich, 1935-36. Recipient of Henry Russel award, Naval Ordnance Award, Presdl. Certificate of Merit. King's Medal (Br.), 1948. Mem. Am. Chem. Soc., Nat. Acad. Scis., Sigma Xi, Phi Lambda Upsilon, Gamma Alpha, Tau Beta Pi, Alpha Chi Sigma. Author: Laboratory Manual of Organic Chem. (with L. C. Anderson), 1930. Member bd. editors Jour. of Organic Chemistry, and Organic Reactions. Home: 1608 Brooklyn Av., Ann Arbor, Mich. Died Mar. 22, 1951.

BACHMEYER, Arthur Charles (bäk'mī-ēr), med. adminstr.; b. Cincinnati, O., Dec. 6, 1886; s. Henry and Caroline (Weist) B.; M.D., U. of Cincinnati, 1911, hon. D.Sc., 1935; D.Sc. (honorary), University of Nebraska, 1949; m. Lulu K. Troeger, Nov. 23, 1911 (died May 3, 1933); children—Robert Wesley, William Leonard, Janet Ann; m. 2d Mary L. Hicks, July 5, 1934. Interne and resident surg. Cinn. Gen. Hosp., 1911-13, asst., later acting supt., 1913, supt., 1914-35, also supt. Cincinnati Tuberculosis Sanatorium, 1914-35; prof. hosp. admn., 1920-35; dean College of Medicine, U. of Cincinnati, 1925-34; prof., asso. dean biol. div., dir. of clinics, U. of Chicago, 1935-52; asso. dean biol. scis., prof. emeritus since 1952; vice chairman Commission on Survey of Medical Edn., since 1948. First lt., Med. Corps, O.N.G., 1916; capt. and maj. Med. R.C., U.S. Army, 1917-19; lt. col. Med. O.R.C. since 1919. Recipient Award of Merit, Am. Hosp. Assn., 1943. Dir. of study, Commn. on Hosp. Care, 1944-46, mem. exec. com. Commn. on Financing Hosp. Care since 1951. Mem. A.M.A., Ohio State Med. Assn., Chgo. Hosp. Council, Chgo. Hosp. Service Corp. (mem. bd.), Am. Coll. Hospital Administrators (pres. 1940-41; hon. mem. 1952), Assn. Am. Med. Colls. (treas. 1938-49, president 1950-51), National Security Resources Board, (med. adv. committee 1948-50), Cincinnati Acad. Medical, Inst. Med. of Chicago, American Hospital Assn. (past pres., treasurer since 1946), Am. Pub. Health Assn., A.A.A.S., Am. Acad. Polit. and Social Sciences, Alpha Kappa Kappa, Alpha Omega Alpha. Methodist. Mason. Chmn. editorial bd., Modern Hosp. Author: Hospital in Modern Society (with G. Hartman), 1943; Hospital Care in U.S. (report), 1947; Hospital Trends and Developments, 1948; Medical Schs. of Western Europe, 1952. Address: Box 180, R.D. 2, Loveland, O. Died May 22, 1953; buried Spring Grove Cemetery, Cin.

BACIGALUPI, James Augustus (bă-chē-găl'ōō-pē), lawyer; b. Santa Clara, Calif., Aug. 2, 1882; s. Angelo and Luigia (Nascio) B.; A.B., Santa Clara Coll., 1903; LL.B., Hastings Coll. of Law (U. of Calif.), 1907; LL.D., U. of Santa Clara, Calif., 1926; m. Mary Ellen Jones, July 20, 1909; children—Louise Catherine, Eugenia Marie, James Augustus, Mary Anne. Admitted to Calif. bar, 1907, and began practice at San Francisco; counselor Bank of Italy, predecessor of Bank of America, Nat. Trust & Savings Assn., representing the bank in purchase of banks acquired in creating the Branch Bank orgn.; v.p. Bank of Italy, 1917, and organized its trust dept., pres. and chmn. exec. com., Oct. 1924-Oct. 1929; gen. counsel Transamerica Corp., 1928-30, pres., 1931-32. Past dir. San Francisco Chamber of Commerce and San Francisco Community Chest. Mem. Native Sons of the Golden West, Young Men's Inst., K.C. Democrat. Catholic. Clubs: San Francisco Commercial, Olympic. Home: Oak Glen Park, Los Gatos, Calif. Died July 27, 1950.

BACKUS, August Charles (bă'kŭs), lawyer; b. Kewaskum, Wis., Apr. 24, 1877; s. August F. and Caroline (Spiegel) B.; student Oshkosh (Wis.) Normal Sch., 1891-95; LL.B., U. Wis., 1895-1900; LL.D., Marquette U., 1918; m. Elizabeth Hausmann, Aug. 21, 1902; children—Charlotte Caroline (wife of Dr. Claus Jordan), Lucille Teckla (wife of Dr. Alvah Newcomb), Walter A., August C. Admitted to Wis. bar, 1900, began practice in Milw.; became asst. dist. atty. Milwaukee County, 1905, dist. atty., 1909; judge Municipal Court, city and county of Milw., 1910-24; became pres., pub. Milw. Sentinel, 1924; mem. firm Backus & Parson; prof. criminal law, Marquette U. Declined appointment as Federal Judge. First pres. of Federal Loan Bank, 1932-33. Active in many civic drives Milw., also numerous community and nat. drives; founder adult probation system (first offenders). Chmn. bd. adviser Marquette U., trustee med. sch.; regent U. Wis., 12 years. Pres. Am. Crime Com. Mem. Wis. Bar Assn. Recipient gold medal Am. Legion for distinguished service. Chmn. Bd. Appeals on selective draft. Home: 722 E. Lakeview Av., Milw. Died Mar. 7, 1952.*

BACKUS, Edwin Burdette, clergyman; b. Blanchester, O., Dec. 27, 1888; s. Wilson Marvin and Stella (Campbell) B.; A.A., Lewis Inst., Chgo., 1907; A.B., U. Mich., 1909; B.D., Meadville (Pa.) Theol. Sch., 1912, D.D., 1940; work at Berlin and Jena Univs., 1912-13; m. Irene May Garrett, July 25, 1914; children—Virginia Louise (Mrs. Waldo Kampmeier Lyon), Mary Katherine (Mrs. Robert E. Goebel). Served as minister Unitarian Soc., Lawrence, Kan., 1913-17; 1st Unitarian Soc., Erie, Pa., 1917-20; 1st Unitarian Ch., Los Angeles, 1920-32, Humanist Soc. Chgo., 1933-34, 1st Unitarian Ch., Des Moines, 1935-38, All Souls Unitarian Ch., Indpls., 1938-53, 1st Unitarian Ch., Tacoma, Wash., 1954, Phoenix, 1954-

55. Vice pres. Western Unitarian Conf., 1946-50; pres. Am. Humanist Soc., 1944-46. Weekly broadcasts, sta. WFBM. Mem. Am. Unitarian Assn., Indpls. Council Soc. Agencies, Ind. Soc. for Mental Hygiene. Mason. Clubs: Indianapolis Athletic, Wranglers. Author: The Pattern on the Mountain, 1939, 1946; Lectures on the Bible (pub. in Danish translation) 1925; (book) If Thought Be Free, 1946; Sheep and Goats, 1948. Home: 5022 Narragansett, San Diego, Cal. Died July 7, 1955.

BACON, Francis Leonard, university professor; b. Kingman, Kan., July 30, 1889; s. Samuel and Alice (Dukes) B.; grad. Kingman County High Sch., 1908; A.B., Southwestern Coll., Winfield, Kan., 1912, LL.D., 1931; A.M., Columbia Univ., 1916; studied Yale and Harvard univs.; L.H.D., William, 1937; m. Ruth Siefkin, 1937. Teacher and prin. high schs., Blackwell, Okla.; later prin. high sch., Meriden, Conn.; then prin. Newton (Mass.) Classical High Sch., dir. sr. and jr. high schs., asst. supt. Newton schs.; later prin. J. Sterling Morton High Sch., Cicero, Illinois, supt. Evanston Twp. (Ill.) High Schs. Lecturer summer schs., Yale, 1920-24, Boston Univ., 1925, Harvard, 1925-28, Univ. of Wis., 1932, U. Wash., 1936, U. Mich., 1951; lecturer Northwestern U. Sch. of Edn., 1933-48; visiting prof. Teachers Coll., Columbia Univ., 1948, Univ. Cal., 1949. Member National Prins. Assn. (pres. 1926), Nat. Assn. Secondary Sch. Prins. (chmn. com. on planning), Headmasters Assn., Am. Council on Edn. (com. on research 1940-45; v. chmn. 1946-47), Nat. Safety Council (mem. com. on edn.), National Education Association (chmn. ednl. policies com. 1945-48); mem. Nat. Com. on Life Adjustment Edn.; mem. nat. planning com. Midcentury White House Conf., 1949-50; chmn. adv. com. Secondary Schs. Ednl. Testing Service. Mem. Kappa Delta Pi, Phi Gamma Mu, Phi Delta Kappa. Served as 1st lt., inf., United States Army, 1917-19. Conglist. Mason (32°). Editor of Mod. Promptbook of Shakespeare's Taming of the Shrew. Part author: The Administration of Am. Secondary Schl; Founds. of Health; Old Europe and Our Nation, Our Life Today; Youth Thinks It Through; Fact and Opinion Just for Sport; Our Democracy. Author: Outwitting the Hazards; The War and America. Contbr. to sch. mags. Home: 935 Las Alturas Rd., Santa Barbara, Cal. Died Jan. 20, 1958.

BACON, George Wood, mech. engr.; b. Greenwich, N.J., May 6, 1869; s. Josiah and Caroline (Wood) B.; grad. Westtown (Pa.) Boarding Sch., 1888; M.E., Cornell U., 1892; m. Caroline Tilden Mitchell, June 1, 1904; 1 dau., Elizabeth Mitchell (Mrs. Ferdinand K. Rodewald); m. 2d, Elizabeth Ann Mitchel, June 11, 1943. A founder, mem. Ford, Bacon & Davis, Inc., pub. utility and indsl. engrs., 1894-1946, offices also in Phila., Chgo., Los Angeles, Monroe, La., Mexico City; identified with electrification of New Orleans street rys.; v.p. United Rys. Investment Co. (owners pub. utilities, Pittsburgh and San Francisco) for 8 yrs.; former pres. Sierra & San Francisco Power Co. hydro-electric power and transmission system; served as head of export dept. of J. P. Morgan & Co., 1915, making extensive purchases in U.S. of munitions for British and French govts.; pres., dir. East Long Beach (L.I.) Corp.; former chmn. bd. Ford, Bacon & Davis, Inc., ret. 1946. Fellow Nat. Geog. Soc.; mem. Am. Soc. M.E., Army Ordnance Assn., C. of C. State N.Y., Met. Mus. Art, Am. Museum Natural History, Cornell Soc. Engrs., Acad. Polit. Sci., Nat. Aero. Assn., N.J. Hist. Soc. Republican. Mem. Soc. of Friends. Clubs: University, Cornell, Economic (N.Y.C.); Recess, Piping Rock, St. George's Golf and Country. Home: 435 E. 52d St., N.Y.C. 22. Deceased.

BACON, Leonard, author; b. Solvay, N.Y., May 26, 1887; s. Nathaniel Terry and Helen (Hazard) B.; grad. St. George's Sch., Newport, R.I., 1905; A.B., Yale, 1909, hon. M.A., 1941; m. Martha Sherman Stringham, May 16, 1912; children—Martha Sherman, Helen Hazard, Alice. Instr. in English and asst. prof. English, U. of Calif., 1910-23; devoting time to writing since 1923. Served as 2d lt., U.S. Air Service, 1917-18. Awarded Cervantes Medal of the Hispanic Inst. in Fla., 1950. Mem. Alpha Delta Phi. Elected mem. Nat. Inst. Arts and Letters, 1941, Am. Acad. Arts and Letters, 1951; elected fellow Am. Acad. Arts and Scis., 1943. Clubs: Century (N.Y.); Faculty (Univ. of Cal.); Tavern (Boston). Author: (verse): Ulug Beg, 1923; Ph.Ds., 1925; Animula Vagula, 1926; Guinea Fowl and Other Poultry, 1927; The Legend of Quincibald, 1928; Lost Buffalo, 1930; The Furioso, 1932. Translator: (with G. R. Noyes) Heroic Ballads of Servia, 1913; The Song of Roland, 1914; (with R. Selden Rose) The Lay of the Cid, 1919; Dream and Action, 1934; The Voyage of Autoleon, 1935; The Goose on the Capitol, 1936; Rhyme and Punishment, 1936; Bullinger Bound, 1938; Semi-Centennial, 1939; Sunderland Capture, 1940, Day of Fire, 1943; The Lusiads of Luis de Camoens (translation), 1950. Contbr. to mags. Awarded Pulitzer prize for verse, 1941. Home: The Acorns, Peace Dale, R.I. Died Jan. 1, 1954.

BACON, Raymond Foss, chem. engr.; b. Muncie, Ind., June 29, 1880; s. Rev. Charles and N. V. (Wiggs) B.; direct desc. of Bacons who settled in Mass., 1640; B.S., DePauw U., 1899, M.A., 1900. Ph.D., U. of Chicago, 1904; D.Sc., U. of Pittsburgh, 1918, DePauw, 1919; m. Edna Hine, Aug. 4, 1905. Chemist in U.S. Bur. of Science, Manila, P.I., 1905-10; asst. chemist Bur. of Chemistry, Washington, D.C., 1910-11; sr. fellow Petroleum Fellowship, Dept. Indsl. Research, U. of Pittsburgh, 1911-12; asso. dir., 1912-14, dir., 1914-21, Mellon Inst. Indsl. Research, U. of Pittsburgh; cons. chem. engr., New York, since Oct., 1921; scientific adviser to Philippine Govt., 1939. Col. Chem. Warfare Service, U.S. Army, Dec. 1, 1917-Dec. 16, 1918, spending 9 months in France as chief Tech. Div., C.W.S., A.E.F. Awarded D.S.M., 1922. Mem. Am. Inst. Chem. Engrs., A.A.A.S., Société de Chimie Industrielle, Chem. Soc. of London, D.K.E., Alpha Chi Sigma, Phi Lambda Upsilon. Clubs: Chemists', Siwanoy Country, Union League, Hudson River Country. Author: (with W. A. Hamor) American Petroleum Industry (2 vols.), 1916; (with same) American Fuels (2 vols.), 1922; also numerous papers on chemistry, technology of essential oils, reports, etc. Inventor of processes for mfr. of gasoline, recovery of cuprous sulphide from ores, for hydrogenating vegetable oils and for mfr. of sulphur from sulphide ores. Home: 98 Rockledge Rd., Bronxville, N.Y. Office: 500 Fifth Av., New York, N.Y. Died Oct. 14, 1954.

BACON, William Stevens, former chmn. Am. Paper Goods Co.; b. Bklyn., Sept. 11, 1877; s. William P. and Emma (Whittemore) B.; student pub. schs.; m. Margaret Bradley, June 15, 1904; children—Robert Bradley, William Plumb, Margaret (Mrs. Eric Warner). With Am. Paper Goods Co., 1895——, pres., 1929, chmn. bd., 1945——. Mem. Soc. of Cincinnati. Home: Moorland Hill Rd. Kensington, Conn. Died Mar. 18, 1955.

BADGER, Oscar Charles, corporation consultant, naval officer, retired; born in Washington, June 26, 1890; son of Charles Johnston (rear admiral, U.S. Navy), and Sophia Jane (Champlin) B.; student St. John's Coll., Md., 1905-07; B.S., U.S. Naval Academy, 1911; grad. Naval War College, 1932; married Isabelle Edna Austen, October 31, 1917; children—Isabelle Edna (Mrs. John Power Schroeder), Jane Austen (Mrs. Frederick John Leary). Commd. ensign, U.S. Navy, 1911 and advanced through the grades to vice admiral, 1945; served on USS Utah—landings at Vera Cruz, 1914; USS Porter—European waters, 1917; comd. USS Sultana and USS Worden, 1918; gunner officer Squadron 15, destroyers Atlantic Fleet, 1922; aide to CinCAsiaticFlt., 1923; at Bureau of Ordnance, 1923-25, 1928-31; USS Maryland, 1925-28; duty at Naval Acad., 1933-36; sec. of General Board Navy Dept., 1939-40; chief of staff to CinCUSLantFlt, 1940-41; comd. USS North Carolina, 1941-42; comd. destroyers Atlantic Fleet, 1942; asst. chief, Naval Operations for Logistics Plans, 1943-44; comdr. Service Squadrons South Pacific Force, 1944; tactical comdr. Heavy Striking Force of Third Fleet, 1944-45; comdr. Service Force U.S. Pacific Fleet, 1945-47; comdt. 11th Naval Dist., 1947-48; comdr. U.S. Naval Forces Far East, 1948-49; special adv. on Far Eastern matters at Navy Dept., 1949-50; comdr. Eastern Sea Frontier, comdr. Atlantic Reserve Fleet, 1950-52, retired with rank of adm., 1952; consultant Sperry Corp., 1952——; dir. Prudential Ins. Co. Sr. naval representative of Joint Chiefs of Staff on military staff committee of Security Council UN, 1951; commr. Civil Def., 1952-53; chmn. U.S.O. Defense Fund, 1952-53. Recipient of Congressional Medal of Honor; Navy Cross; Legion of Merit with three gold stars; Mexican Service Medal; Victory Medal with destroyer clasp; American Defense Service Medal with fleet clasp; American Campaign Medal; Asiatic-Pacific Campaign Medal; European-Africa-Middle Eastern Campaign Medal; World War II Victory Medal; China Service Medal; Philippine Liberation Ribbon with two bronze stars, Order of the British Empire (Honorary Commander). Clubs: N.Y. Yacht; Army-Navy, Army-Navy Country (Wash.); Garden City Golf; Seawanhaka-Corinthian Yacht; Piping Rock. Address: 57 Duck Pond Rd., Glen Cove, N.Y. Died Nov. 30, 1958; buried Arlington Nat. Cemetery.

BADGER, Walter Lucius, chem. engr.; b. Mpls., Feb. 18, 1886; s. Minor Campbell and Mary Helen (Albro) B.; B.A., U. Minn., 1907, B.S. in Chemistry, 1908, M.S., 1909; m. Helen Elizabeth Franklin, Apr. 8, 1913; 1 dau., Elizabeth Helen. Instr. chemistry U. Minn., 1908-09, spring 1910; chemist Gt. Western Sugar Co., fall 1909; asst. in chem. div. U.S. Bureau Standards, 1910-12; with U. Mich., 1912-37, prof. chem. engring., 1917-37; in charge research on water purification Detroit Edison Co., 1914-16; dir. research and cons. engr. Swenson Evaporator Co., 1917——; mgr. cons. engring. div. Dow Chem. Co., 1936-44; cons. chem. engr., 1944——; pres. W. L. Badger and Assos., Inc., 1957——. Recipient Wm. H. Walker award, 1940. Mem. Am. Chem. Soc., Am. Inst. Chem. Engrs., Sigma Xi, Tau Beta Pi, Alpha Chi Sigma, Phi Lambda Upsilon, Phi Delta Chi, Gamma Alpha. Conglist. Club: Chemists (N.Y.C.). Author: Heat Transfer and Evaporation, 1925; Inorganic Chemical Technology (with E. M. Baker), 1928; Elements of Chemical Engineering (with W. I. McCabe), 1931; Introduction to Chemical Engineering (with J. T. Bancherd), 1955. Home: 1055 Cedar Bend Dr. Office: 309 S. State St., Ann Arbor, Mich. Died Nov. 19, 1958.

BAEKELAND, Céline (bāk'lănd), artist; b. Ghent, Belgium; student Inst. de Kerchove, Ghent; studied music and painting with pvt. tchrs. in Belgium; student of Hobart Nichols in U.S.; m. Dr. Leo Hendrick Baekeland; children—George, Nina Baekeland Wyman. Came to U.S. as bride, naturalized by marriage, 1897. Painter in oils of flowers and of landscapes depicting scenes in both Europe and America. Solo exhibitions at N.J. State Museum, S.I. Mus., Brooks Museum, Memphis, Bruce Museum, Greenwich, Mattatuck Hist. Soc., Conn., Mint Museum, Charlotte, S.C., Art League of Upper Carolinas, Speed Museum, Louisville, Ky. Exhibited at 60th St. Art Gallery, N.Y.C., 1942; work featured by Am. Fedn. Arts for 2 yrs. and sent on tour of U.S.; many of her paintings have been acquired by museums for their permanent collections. Recipient Queen Elizabeth (Belgium) decoration for services during World War I. Life fellow N.A.D.; mem. Nat. Arts Club, Am. Fedn. Arts, Palm Beach (Fla.) Fedn. Art, Soc. Four Arts, Blue Dome Fellowship Miami, Southern States Art Assn., Art Assn. Yonkers, Hudson River Painters Assn., Studio Guild (N.Y.C.), Springfield Art League, Art Assn. Newport, Nat. Assn. Women Artists (hon. v.p.), Allied Artists Am. Republican. Clubs: Colony (N.Y.C.); National Arts, National Women's Republican. Home: Yonkers, N.Y. Died Feb. 27, 1957.

BAENSCH, Emil, lawyer; b. Manitowoc, Wis., June 12, 1857; student U. Wis.; m. Nov. 13, 1882, Ida Koehler. Justice of peace, 1882-84; city clk. 1885-88; county judge, 1888-94; lt. gov. Wis., 1894-98. Capt. Co. H, 2d Wis. N.G., 1882-88. Curator Wis. Hist. Assn. Publisher Manitowoc Post. Republican. Address: Manitowoc, Wis. Deceased.

BAEPLER, Walter A., educator, clergyman; b. Ft. Wayne, Ind., Sept. 21, 1893; s. Andrew and Sophia (Birkner) B.; ed. St. Paul's Coll., Concordia, Mo., 1904-10, Province Normal Sch. of Manitoba, 1921, U. Alberta, 1929-35; D.D., Concordia Seminary, 1914; m. Martha Fritz, July 5, 1921; children—Walter J., Marjorie Griffin, Richard, Donald. Pastor, Haultain, Sask., 1915-16; missionary, McEacherin, Sask., 1916-18; supt. missions, Manitoba and Sask., 1918-21; pastor, Winnipeg, 1921-23; prof. Concordia Coll., Edmonton, Alberta, 1923-35, Concordia Seminary, Springfield, Ill., since 1936, pres. since 1953. Vice pres. Manitoba and Sask. dist., Evangelical Luth. Synodical Conf. Am., 1922-23, pres., 1952——, chmn. com. doctoral unity, 1950——. Author: A Century of Blessings, 1946; A Century of Grace, 1947. Home: 1500 Concordia Ct. Office: 1301 Concordia Ct., Springfield, Ill. Died Oct. 9, 1958; buried Oak Ridge Cemetery, Springfield.

BAER, Joseph Louis, surgeon; b. Chicago, Apr. 29, 1880; B.S., U. of Chicago, 1902, M.S., 1903, M.D., Rush Med. Coll., 1904; post-grad. studies, Berlin and Vienna, 1908; married Gretchen Winslow Shattuck, July 28, 1913 (died Mar. 2, 1926); m. 2d, Janet Bachrach, Jan. 22, 1931. Interne Michael Reese Hosp., Chicago, 1904-07, anaestetist, 1907-13, attending obstetrician and gynecologist, 1913-36, sr. attending gynecologist and obstetrician, 1936——. Instr. dept. gynecology and obstetrics, Rush Med. Coll., 1917-21, asst. prof., 1921-27, asso. prof. 1927-35, prof., 1935-46, prof. emeritus, 1946——; bd. dirs. Blue Cross Plan for Hosp. Care, 1937——. Vice pres. and dir. Am. Bd. Obstetrics and Gynecology, 1927——. Captain Medical Corps, United States Army, Base Hospital, Camp Custer, Michigan, November 1918-Jan. 20, 1919. Fellow Am. Coll. Surgeons, Am. Gynecol. Soc.; mem. A.M.A., Chicago Gynecol. Soc., Chicago Inst. of Medicine. Mason. Contbr. articles to med. press. Home: 1642 E. 56th St. Office: 104 S. Michigan Av., Chgo. Died Dec. 8, 1954.

BAER, Sidney R., retail and realty exec.; b. Ft. Smith, Ark., Mar. 21, 1891; s. Sigmond P. and Marie (Pappenheimer) B.; grad. Yale, 1912; m. Marguerite S. Strecker, June 1, 1914; children—Sidney R., S. Charles. Vice chmn. bd., treas., dir. Stix, Baer & Fuller Co., St. Louis; pres. Grand Leader Realty Co., Premium Realty & Investment Co.; dir. Associated Merchandising Corp. dir. Govtl. Research Inst., Central Inst. for Deaf (both St. Louis). Pres. Leader Found. Home: Park Plaza Hotel, 220 N. Kingshighway, St. Louis 8. Office: 601 Washington Av., St. Louis 1. Died Aug. 25, 1956.

BAER, William Bush (bâr), dean; b. Peoria, Ill., July 15, 1902; s. John Valentine and Louise D. (Ely) B.; B.A., Hamilton Coll., Clinton, N.Y., 1924; M.A., Harvard U., 1926; unmarried. Instr. English, Univ. College of Arts and Science, New York U., 1926-30, counselor of studies, 1930-34, asst. dean University Coll., 1934-42, asst. prof., 1938-45, asso. prof. 1945——; dean, 1942——; writer, producer, narrator of Our Goodly Heritage, for CBS-TV, 1952——. Mem. Eastern Assn. of Coll. Deans and Advisers of Men, Alpha Delta Phi, Phi Beta Kappa. Clubs: Harvard, Fire Bell (New York). Home: 130 W. 183d St., N.Y.C. 53. Died Jan. 21, 1958.

BAGAR, Robert, writer; b. N.Y.C., Jan. 6, 1899; s. Anthony and Maria (Conti) Bagarozy; student Fordham Prep. Sch., 1914-18, Fordham U., 1919-22, Bellevue Med. Coll., 1923, Flower Med. Sch., 1923-25, Fordham Law Sch., 1926; pvt. music edn., 1907-18; m. Laura Boldt, June 28, 1927; 1 son, Robert Anthony. Mgr. Cosmopolitan Broadcast Bur., N.Y.C., 1927-33; asst. music critic N.Y. World-Telegram and Sun, 1933-41, music critic, 1941-55; asst. music editor and record reviewer The New Yorker, 1937-46; program annotator Philharmonic-Symphony Soc., 1941-49; mem. bd. experts Met. Opera Quiz, 1944—; painist and composer; works performed on radio and in concert. Co-author: The Concert Companion, 1947. Editor: Victor Book of the Opera, 1949; also numerous brochures on mus. history and biography. Contbr. to periodicals and mags.; writer of scripts; has appeared on various mus. radio programs. Roman Catholic. Home: 2440 Tiebout Av., N.Y.C. Died May 6, 1957.

BAGNELL, Robert, minister; b. Phila., Aug. 10, 1865; s. John and Eliza (Curran) B.; studied under pvt. tutors; A.M., Columbia, 1909, Ph.D., 1911; D.D., Cornell Coll., Ia., 1905; m. Mary E. Wallace, Mar. 17, 1886; 1 son, Robert Harold. Ordained M.E. ministry, 1888; various pastorates in Ia. until 1901; pastor Met. Temple, N.Y.C., 1901-07, Janes Ch., Bklyn., 1907-14, Park Av. Ch., Phila., 1914-17, Grace Church, Harrisburg, Pa., 1917-33, First Ch., Charleston, 1933-37; now retired. Mem. Continuation Com. on Faith and Order, 1925—; mem. World Conf. on Faith and Order, Laussanne, 1927, Edinburgh, 1937. Special rep. of Com. on Pub. Information, and spl. sec., YMCA in France and Eng., 1918. Mason (32°, K.T.). Author: Economic and Moral Aspects of the Liquor Business, 1912. Home: 243 Tulpehocken St., Germantown, Phila. Died Apr. 24, 1946.

BAHL, William Edgar, mfg. exec.; b. Zimmerman, Ohio, Feb. 8, 1889; s. John Edgar and Jennie May (Goodill) B.; ed. pub. schs. of Dayton, O.; m. Margaret May Brown, July 11, 1908; children—Edgar Noble, Thomas William. Apprentice, The Nat. Cash Register Co., 1906, traveling mech. insp., 1910-20, asst. head of repair sch., 1920-24, asst. in supt. office, 1924-37, supervisor of unit assembly, 1937-45, asst. factory mgr., 1945-46, factory mgr., 1946-47, v.p. in charge of mfg. since 1947. Mem. Nat. and Dayton chambers of commerce. Mason (past master). Club: Engineers' (Dayton). Home: 43 Monteray Rd., Dayton 9. Office: The National Cash Register Co., Dayton 9, O. Died March 1958.

BAILEY, Alfred Halsey, church ofcl.; b. Camden, Mich., Jan. 20, 1869; s. Orange James and Louisa (Burr) B.; Ph.B., Kalamazoo (Mich.) Coll., 1899; student Hamilton Theol. Sem. (Colgate U.), 1901-02; Summer Sch., theol. dept. U. Chgo.; D.D., Linfield Coll., 1920; m. Alvena Mauerhan, M.D., Oct. 24, 1895 (died July 4, 1922); m. 2d, Leila Margaret Skow, June 10, 1925; 1 son, Alfred Francis. Began preaching, 1889; ordained ministry Bapt. Ch., 1893; pastor in Mich. until 1906, Cal. until 1910; asst. sec. So. Cal. Bapt. Conv., at Los Angeles, 1910-16; gen. supt. East Wash. and North Ida. Bapt. Conv., 1916-27; editor E. Wash. and N. Ida. Bapt. Bull., 1916-27; pastor Central Bapt. Ch., Spokane, Wash., 1927-35, First Bapt. Ch., Raymond, Wash., 1935-40, First Bapt. Ch., Elma, Wash., 1940—. Trustee Wash. Bapt. Conv., 1931-41, mem. exec. com., 1939-41, mem. Dept. of Promotion, 1941—. Mem. S.A.R. Republican. Mason (Shriner); mem. Order Eastern Star. Home: 606 W. Main St., Elma, Wash. Died June 20, 1948; buried Masonic Cemetery, Elma.

BAILEY, Charles Franklin, mech. engr.; b. Greensboro, Vt., Aug. 29, 1863; s. Charles Minor and Mary (Blake) B.; B.S. in Mech. Engring., Worcester Poly. Inst., 1888, D.Eng., 1928; m. Almeria Isabel Adgate, Aug. 18, 1891 (died May 19, 1937); children—Almeria Pitkin, Albert Adgate, Mary Joyce. Machinist N.P. Ry., Tacoma, 1888-89; draftsman Tacoma Foundry & Machine Co., 1889-90, Neafie & Leavy Ship & Engine Bldg. Co., Phila., 1890-91; chief draftsman Newport News Shipbuilding and Drydock Co., 1891-1900, chief engr., 1900, dir., 1918-37, engring. dir. until 1934, ret. 1934; cons. engr. Westinghouse Elec. & Mfg. Co., 1915-21; dir. Newport News Constrn. Corp., Newport News Land Corp. Sch. trustee Elizabeth City County, Va., 1912-16; trustee Worcester Poly. Inst., 1925-38; trustee, v.p. The Mariners Mus., 1930-40; dir. The Mariners' Mus. Land Co. of Cal.; trustee, sec. Brookgreen Gardens, S.C., 1931-37, now hon. v.p. Mem. Soc. Naval Architects and Marine Engrs. (hon. v.p.); former mem. Tech. com. Am. Bur. Shipping; former mem. Am. Soc. Naval Engrs., Am. Soc. M.E.; Va. C. of C. (mem. com. for development Hampton Rds., 1927-29). Rep. Conglist. Home: 1224 Chesapeake Av., Hampton, Va. Died June 23, 1949.

BAILEY, Frank, banker; b. Chatham, N.Y., Jan. 5, 1865; s. William Cady and Julia M. (Utley) B.; A.B., Union Coll., Schenectady, 1885, LL.D., 1905; m. Marie Louise Lambert, July 6, 1905; 1 dau., Barbara. In banking bus. in Bklyn., 50 yrs., now ret.; pres. Bensonhurst Co.; dir. Am. Zinc. Lead & Smelting Co., L.I. Safe Deposit Co., Bklyn. Edison Co. Treas., trustee Union Coll.; trustee Mus. City N.Y. Mem. Columbia County Assn., S.R., Soc. of the Cincinnati, Phi Beta Kappa. Clubs: Uptown (N.Y.C.); Nassau Country, Wyandanch, Nassau. Home: Locust Valley, L.I., N.Y. Office: 17 E. 42d St., N.Y.C. 17. Died Aug. 26, 1953; buried Green-Wood, Bklyn.

BAILEY, John Ora, judge; b. Grinnell, Ia.; Sept. 26, 1880; s. John Sherbourne and Hariet C. (Kingsley) B.; studied in Europe, 1900-01; A.B., Harvard, 1905-06; student Harvard Law Sch., 1905-06; m. Verna Chase, Aug. 3, 1911; children—Frances Harriet (Mrs. O. V. White), Jason Samuel, Robert Chase (died Apr. 9, 1939), Barbara Jean (Mrs. Vernon R. Hedges). Admitted to Washington bar, 1907, and practiced in Spokane until 1910, in Portland with Platt & Platt, 1910-15; asst. atty. gen., Ore., 1915-20; partner Perkins & Bailey, Portland, 1920-33; judge Supreme Ct. of Ore., 1933-51. Mem. Ho. of Rep., Ore., 1925-29, State Senate 1929-33; mem. Sch. Bd., Portland, 1927-30. Republican. Conglist. Mason (K.T.), Elk, K.P. Club: Multnomah Athletic. Home: 7412 N. Chase Av., Portland, Ore. Died Feb. 16, 1959; buried Portland, Ore.

BAILEY, Liberty Hyde, author, botanist, horticulturist; b. South Haven, Mich., Mar. 15, 1858; s. Liberty Hyde and Sarah (Harrison) Bailey; reared on farm; B.S., Mich. Agrl. Coll., 1882, M.S., 1886; LL.D., U. of Wis., 1907, Alfred U., 1908; Litt.D., U. of Vt., 1919; D.Sc., U. of Puerto Rico, 1932; m. Annette Smith, June 6, 1883 (deceased); children—Sara May (deceased), Ethel Zoe. Has given particular attention to botany, horticulture and other biological subjects and to rural problems and education; asst. to Asa Gray, Harvard, 1882-83; prof. horticulture and landscape gardening, Mich. Agrl. Coll., 1885-88; prof. horticulture, Cornell U., 1888-1903, dir. and dean Coll. of Agr., 1903-13. Awarded Veitchian silver medal, 1898, gold medal, 1927; George Robert White medal, 1927; gold medal Nat. Inst. Social Sciences, 1928; grande médaille Société Nationale d'Acclimatation de France, 1928; gold medal of honor, Garden Club of America, 1931; Arthur Hoyt Scott medal and award, Swarthmore Coll. and Hort. Socs., 1931; Distinguished Service Award, Am. Assn. of Nurserymen, 1931; Centennial Medal, Am. Pomol. Soc.; Green Thumb Medal, Nat. Victory Garden Inst.; Johnny Appleseed Medal, Men's Garden Club of Am.; Medal Award, Nat. Garden Inst. 1948. Chmn. Roosevelt Commn. on Country Life, 1898. Fellow Am. Acad. Arts and Scis., A.A.A.S. (pres. 1926); mem. Nat. Acad. Scis., Am. Philos. Soc., Bot. Soc. Am. (pres. 1926), Am. Soc. Naturalists; hon. mem. Royal Hort. Soc. (London), Hort. Soc. Norway, Japan Agrl. Soc., Hort. Soc. Japan, Chinese Soc. Hort. Science, hort. societies Mass., R.I. and Ind., New Zealand Inst. Horticulture, Am. Soc. Hort. Science (1st pres.); corr. mem. Phila. Acad. Natural Science, Royal Acad. Agr. (Turin), Société Lyonnaise d'Horticulture; honorary member Botanical Society of Edinburgh. Author numerous publications relating to field. Editor: Cyclopedia of American Horticulture, 4 vols.; Cyclopedia of American Agriculture, 4 vols.; Standard Cyclopedia of Horticulture, 6 vols. (reprinted in 3 vols.); Rural Science series; Rural Textbook series; Rural Manual series; Rural State and Province series. Home: Ithaca, N.Y. Died Dec. 25, 1954; buried Lake View Cemetery, Ithaca.

BAILEY, Mervyn J(oy), educator; b. Gouldsborough, Me., Mar. 21, 1894; s. George Mervyn and Jessie H. (Sprague) B.; A.B., Boston U., 1915, A.M., 1917, Harvard, 1929; student Brown U., 1916-17, U. of Leipzig, 1924-25; m. Elsa M. Canell, July 1, 1916; children—Marshall Perrin, Judith; m. 2d Helen M. Farwell, Dec. 24, 1940. Mem. faculty Boston U. since 1919, prof. fine arts since 1934, chairman of department of fine arts since 1936. Mem. Sch. Com., Sherborn, Mass. Mem. Coll. Art Assn., New Eng. Gladiolus Soc., Am. Begonia Soc., Am. Assn. U. Profs., Phi Beta Kappa. Club: Boston Mineral. Home: White Oaks Farm, Sherborn, Mass.; (summer) Swans Island, Me. Office: Boston University, Boston 15. Died Apr. 6, 1955.

BAILEY, Morton, publishing exec.; b. Canon City, Colo., Nov. 5, 1895; s. Morton Shelley and Lutie (Wilkin) B.; student U. Colo., 1917; m. Jessica Burnette, Mar. 25, 1921; 1 son, Morton. With Capper Publs., N.Y.C., 1920-26; with Curtis Pub. Co., 1926—, Pacific Coast mgr., 1929-47, mgr. Sat. Eve. Post Phila., 1947-54, advt. dir.,1954—, v.p. Curtis Pub. Co., 1954—. Served as 1st lt. U.S. Army, 1917-19. Clubs: Merion Golf, Down Town, Mid Day (Phila.); Bohemian (San Francisco). Home: 1025 Fifth Av., N.Y.C. Office: Curtis Publishing Co., Independence Sq., Phila. Died Sept. 2, 1957.

BAILEY, Ray W(entworth), newspaperman; born Brooklyn, N.Y., Mar. 20, 1887; s. Frank Fields and Myra Eva (Wallace) B.; ed. pub. schs. and Heffley Sch., m. Margaret S. Hibbard, Mar. 27, 1912; children—Ray Wentworth, Robert Hibbard, Doris Catherine (Mrs. William F. Weber). Police reporter and gen. reporter, N.Y. Tribune, 1901-12; with N.Y. Herald assigned to police hdqrs. and rewriting, 1912-17; financial news depts., N.Y. Telegram and Sun-Herald, 1917-24, financial copyreader, 1924-27, Automobile Editor, 1927-31; religious editor, N.Y. Sun, 1927-42; and since 1946, news picture editor, 1931-46, asst. to financial editor, since 1946. Member The Silurians. Contbr. feature article series on New York City (Facts about New York, 1927, New York in Pictures, 1928, Around New York in an Airplane, 1931, Old New York in Pictures, 1939) to N.Y. Sun. Home: 18 Lincoln Av., N.Y. Died Feb. 22, 1951; buried Greenfields, Hempstead, L.I., N.Y.

BAILEY, (Irene) Temple, author; b. Petersburg, Va.; d. Milo Varnum and Emma (Sprague) Bailey; student pvt. schs., spl. coll. courses unmarried. Clubs: Chevy Chase, Washington Club, Arts (Washington); Author's (Boston); Pen and Brush (N.Y.C.). Republican. Presbyn. Author: Glory of Youth, 1913; Contrary Mary, 1915; Mistress Anne, 1917; Adventures in Girlhood, 1917; The Tin Soldier, 1919; The Trumpeter Swan, 1920; The Gay Cockade, 1921; The Dim Lantern, 1923; Peacock Feathers, 1924; The Holly Hedge, 1925; The Blue Window, 1926; Wallflowers, 1927; Silver Slippers, 1928; Burning Beauth, 1929; Wild Wind, 1930; So This Is Christmas, 1931; Little Girl Lost, 1932; Enchanted Ground, 1933; The Radiant Tree, 1934; Fair as the Moon, 1935; I've Been to London, 1937; Tomorrow's Promise, 1938; The Blue Cloak, 1941; The Pink Camellia, 1942; Red Fruit, 1945. Contbr. short stories, serials and essays to mags. Home: Wardman Park Hotel, Washington. Died July 6, 1953.

BAILEY, Theodore Mead, lawyer; b. Sioux Falls, Dak. Ty., Jan. 14, 1888; s. Charles Olin and Mary Emma (Swan) B.; prep. edn., Morgan Park Acad., Chicago, Ill.; student Dartmouth, 1906-09; B.A., U. of Mich., 1910; studied law, U. of S.Dak., 1910-11, LL.B., honoris causa, same, 1939; m. Marguerite Wadsworth, Sept. 3, 1912; 1 son, Theodore Mead; m. 2d, Anna Boudoin Munck, June 10, 1931; 1 dau., Julie Anne. Admitted to S.D. bar, 1911, U.S. Supreme Ct., 1925; began practice at Sioux Falls, 1911; mem. S.D. Ho. of Rep., 1921-23, Senate, 1925-27; chmn. Joint Com. of Senate and House for investigation of S.D. rural credit system involving $47,500,-000; v.p. and gen. counsel Queen City Fire Ins. Co.; mem. Bailey, Voorhees, Woods & Fuller. Dir. Assn. Against Prohibition Amendment, 1931-34; mem. advisory council Am. Liberty League, Board of Bar Commrs., S.D., 1937-40. Pres. S.D. Soc. S.A.R., 1927; dir. S.D. Hist. Soc., 1935—. Mem. Am. Bar Assn., S.Dak. Bar Assn., Alpha Delta Phi, Phi Delta Phi. Republican. Episcopalian. Mason (32 ' K.C.C.H.; Past Potentate El Riad Temple), Elk. Home: No. 1 Julie Pl. Office: Bailey-Glidden Bldg., Bldg., Sioux Falls, S.D. Died Jan. 28, 1949.

BAILEY, Vernon Howe, artist; b. Camden, N.J., Apr. 1, 1874; s. Amasa P. and Abby S. (Wise) B.; student Friends' Central School, Pa. Museum Sch. of Art, and Pa. Acad. Fine Arts, Phila.; Academie de l'Ecluse; Academie Bilouil, Paris; m. Lillian M. Cate, Nov. 4, 1896 (died 1900); m. 2d, Edith O'Brien Carr, Jan. 23, 1902. Staff artist, Phila. Times, 1892-94, Boston Herald, 1894-1901 (spl. artist at coronation of Edward VII); artist contbr. Graphic, Mail and Express, Lodon, The Studio, London, 1902, and since to Am. mags. and newspapers, Century, Scribner's, Harper's, also New York Herald, Sun, Times, World, others. Exhibited 1st at Pa. Acad. Fine Arts, Phila., 1891; later Archtl. League, N.Y., Albright Gallery, Buffalo, Cleve. Mus. Art, Detroit Inst. Art, Newport Art Assn., Salon des Beaux Arts, Paris; represented in permaent collections Detroit Inst. Art, Minn. State Art Soc., St. Paul, N.Y. Pub. Library, Hispanic Soc. Am. N.Y. (197 drawings of Spain), Musée de la Guerre of France (lithographs of Am. war subjects), Mus. City of N.Y.; Nat. Library, Madrid, Library for Am. Studies, Rome, Vatican Library. First artist on declaration of war, 1917, authorized by U.S. Govt. to make drawings of navy yards, munition factories, American fleet, etc., drawings exhibited in leading museums and pub. in mags.; received official thanks USN; complete collection of 80 drawings purchased and presented to Smithsonian Instn. Nat. Gallery of Art, Washington, 1923; made 2d tour of Spain, 1925; exhibited 41 lithographs of N.Y. skyscrapers in New York, 1927, later in London, Madrid and Rome; received royal decree of thanks from Alphonso XIII of Spain; received in pvt. audience by Mussolini; made first comprehensive collection, 1932-33, of 100 water colors and drawings of Vatican Palace including pvt. apts. of Pope, exhibited same in Am. Art Assn., Anderson Galleries, N.Y., 1933, Mass. Inst. Tech., U. Laval (Quebec), 1943, Museum Fine Arts, Montreal, 1944; made 830 drawings, 1934-37, pub. as daily feature, under title of Intimate Sketches of New York, and Sketches of New York Suburbs in N.Y. Sun, also exhibited in New York, and pub. as books, Magical City, 1935. Travel and work in countries of Western and Central Europe, 1937-38; make a pictorial record of defense activities in navy yards, naval air stations and other naval bases for Navy Dept., 1941; visited every leading navy yard and air station exhibited under Navy auspices, Corcoran Galery of Art, Washington, 1942, and art museum throughout country for 2 years. Mem. Soc. Colonial Wars, S.R.; corr. mem. Hispanic Soc. Am., Royal Acad. Fine Arts of San Fernando, Madrid. Author: Little Known Towns of Spain, 1927; 67 Water colors and drawings pub. in U.S., Gt. Britain and in France under title Visions d'Espagne, les cités trop peu connues; New Trails in Old Spain, 1927; Skyscrapers of New York (with intro. by Cass Gilbert), 1927; 25 drawings for book, The Empire State, by Col. W. A. Starrett, 1931. Address: The Gotham, 5th Av. at 55th St., N.Y.C. 19. Died Oct. 27, 1953.

BAILEY, William Bacon, economist; b. Springfield, Mass., May 7, 1873; s. William Leonard and Ellen Henrietta (Bacon) B.; A.B., Yale, 1894, Ph.D., 1896; m. Sheila Mackenzie Jewett, of Syracuse, N.Y., June 15, 1905; 1 dau., Dorothy. Asst. 1897-99, instr., 1900-04, asst. prof. polit. economy, 1905-14, asst. prof. social service, 1913-17, Gilbert L. Stark prof. practical philanthropy, 1917-21, Yale U.; also instr. Yale Sch. of Religion, 1901-13; economist Travelers Ins. Co., 1921—. Pres. Conn. Prison Assn.; fellow Casualty Actuarial Soc.; mem. Am. Econ. Assn., Nat. Municipal League, Beta Theta Pi; fellow Am. Statis. Assn.; dir. Conn. State Farm for Women. Clubs: Hartford, University. Author: Modern Social Conditions, 1906; Statistics, 1918; Children Before the Courts of Connecticut, 1919; Social Work as a Profession, 1922. Home: 68 Niles St. Office: Travelers Insurance Co., 700 Main St., Hartford, Conn. Died Jan. 10, 1952.

BAILLIE, Archie Fraser, business exec.; b. Montreal, P.Q., Can., Dec. 21, 1887; s. John and Maggie (Fraser) B.; B.S., McGill Univ., Montreal, 1909; married Norah Deane McKiel, 1912. President of the Dominion Oilcloth & Linoleum Co., Ltd., Montreal, since 1943; pres. Can. Linseed Oil Mills, Ltd., Montreal, Penmans, Ltd., Paris, Ont., Barry & Staines Linoleum (Can.), Ltd., Montreal; Mfrs. Holdings, Ltd., vice pres., dir. Congoleum Canada, Ltd., Montreal; dir. Montreal Cottons, Ltd., Standard Life Assurance Co. (Can.), Guardian Ins. Co. of Can., Dominion Textile Co., Ltd., Drummondville Cottons, Ltd. Mem. Montreal Bd. of Trade, Canadian Mfrs. Assn., C. of C. Presbyterian. Clubs: University, Royal Montreal Golf, Mount Bruno Country, Mount Royal, St. James's, Forest and Stream, Montreal Indoor Tennis, Montreal, Canadian, Montreal Light Aeroplane, Royal Automobile. Home: 1547 MacGregor St., Montreal; (country) Norwood, Knowlton, P.Q. Office: 2200 St. Catherine St., E. Montreal, P.Q., Can. Died June 19, 1954.

BAIRD, David, Jr., ex-senator; b. Camden, N.J., Oct. 10, 1881; s. David and Christiana B.; student, Raymond Acad., Camden, Penn Charter Sch., Phila., and Lawrenceville (N.J.) Sch.; C.E., Princeton, 1903; m. Mrs. Frances H. Smith, June 21, 1930. Pres., treas. David Baird Co., lumber, Camden; pres. Market Bldg. & Loan Assn.; pres. Smith Austermuhl Co.; dir. 1st Camden Nat. Bank & Trust Co., West Jersey & Seashore R.R. Co., N.Y. & Long Branch R.R., Roanoke R.R., & Lumber Co., Camden Fire Ins. Assn. Apptd. U.S. senator from N.J., Nov. 30, 1929, to fill unexpired term (1925-31) of Senator Walter E. Edge, resigned; nominee for gov. of N.J., 1931. Home: Faughan River Farm, Evesham Road, Marlton, N.J. Office: 431 Market St., Camden, N.J. Died Feb. 28, 1955.

BAIRD, James, business exec.; b. Vanceburg, Ky., May 18, 1873; s. Lyman Beecher and Frances Amelia (Halbert) B.; C.E., U. Mich., 1896, Eng.D., 1933; m. Cornelia Curtis, Mar. 28, 1900; children—John Curtis, Charles. Timekeeper Guaranty Constrn. Co., Chgo., 1895-96; engr. Moulton-Starrett Co., Columbus, O., and Pitts., 1896-98; supt. George A. Fuller Co., N.Y.C., 1899-1900, gen. supt. Boston, 1902-03, mgr. Washington, 1904-10, v.p. 1910-22, pres., 1922-24; supt. Thompson-Starrett Co., N.Y.C., 1900-01; pres. U.S. Realty & Improvement Co., N.Y.C., 1924-25; v.p. Plaza Hotel Operating Co., N.Y.C., 1924-25, Trinity Bldg. Corp., 1924-25, Copley-Plaza Hotel Co., Boston, 1924-25; pres. James Baird Co., Inc., N.Y. C., 1925—. Trustee Village of Scarsdale, N.Y., 1926-27. Clubs: Golf of Scarsdale (ex-pres.); University of Michigan (N.Y.C., Tucson); Cosmos (Washington); Am. Guernsey Cattle (Peterboro, N.H.); El Rio Country (Tucson). Directed the constrn. of the Lincoln Memorial and Arlington Memorial Amphitheater, Folger Shakespeare Library and Freer Collection Bldg. (Washington), Aeolian Bldg. and Ferncliff Mausoleum (N.Y.C.). Donor James Baird State Park, Dutchess Country, to State of N.Y., 1939. One of organizers, and v.p., dir. Tucson Cancer Clinic, Inc. (non-profit orgn.). Home: 4111 Calle El Centro, Tucson. Died May 16, 1953; buried Oakwood Cemetery, Chgo.

BAIRD, Richard F., insurance exec.; b. Buchanan County, Mo., Dec. 16, 1884; s. George and Belle (Hendrickson) B.; student pub. schs. of Fairfax, Mo.; m. Kate Robinson, May 1, 1908; 1 son, Richard F. Admitted to Supreme Court bar, Okla., 1913; counsel Lincoln Nat. Life Ins. Co., Ft. Wayne, Ind., 1925-27, general counsel, 1928-51, v.p. 1936-51, dir. since 1929, mem. finance com., 1939-51. Member Fort Wayne Chamber of Commerce (dir. 1949-51), Allen County Bar Assn., Ind. State Bar Assn., Association Life Insurance Counsel, Am. Life Convention (past pres. legal sect.), Internat. Assn. of Ins. Counsel. Republican. Presbyterian. Clubs: Quest (pres. 1944-45), Country (Ft. Wayne, Ind.). Retired. Home: 1502 Pemberton Drive, Ft. Wayne, Ind. Died Sept. 30, 1951.

BAIRD, William Jesse, coll. pres., lecturer; b. Artemus, Ky., April 12, 1890; s. Rev. Andrew Calvin and Rhoda (Broyles) Baird; B.S., Berea Coll., 1919, LL.D., 1944; M.S., Cornell Univ., 1927; graduate study, Columbia Univ., Univ. Wisconsin, Univ. of Kentucky; m. Agnes Ruth Tyler, June, 1915; one son, David Halsey. Teacher four years in Kentucky public schools; dir. department of agriculture, Berea Coll., 1925-30; dean, Foundation School, 1925-44; traveled in Europe, 1929; dir. Teacher Training, Berea Coll., 1939-44; appointed pres. Berry Schools, Mt. Berry, Ga., 1944; pres. Morehead (Ky.) State College, since 1946. Trustee Kentucky Female Orphans Sch., Midway, Ky. Mem. safety commn., State of Ky.; Conf. Southern Mountain Workers; Ky. Educational Planning Board; curriculum com. and philosophy of edn. sect., Kentucky Edn. Assn.; com. Annual Kentucky Mountain Laurel Festival; mem. Phi Delta Kappa, Pi Gamma Mu, Phi Kappa Phi. Home: Morehead, Ky. Died Feb. 19, 1951; buried Berea, Ky.

BAJPAI, Sir Girja Shankar (bäj'pä-ē), agent gen. for India; b. Lucknow, India, April 3, 1891; s. Rai Bahadur Sir Seetla Prasad Bajpai and Ruknine Shukla; B.S., Muir Central Coll., Allahabad, India; B.A., Merton Coll., Oxford, Eng.; m. Marharaj Dulari Misra; children—Lakshmi (wife of Sharad Chandra Misra), Tara (wife of Gauri Shankap Tiwari), Krishna, Bhagwati, Uma, Durga, Kayatyani. Mem. Indian Civil Service, 1915; under-sec. to Govt. of the United Provinces, India, 1920-21; sec. for India at the Imperial Conf., London, 1921, at the Conf. for Limitation of Armaments, Washington, 1921-22; sec. to Govt. of India, 1927-29; dep. to Geneva, 1929-30, to Indian Round Table Conf., London, 1930-31; temp. mem. of Viceroy's Exec. Council, 1935-36; advisor to Indian delegation to Imperial Conf., 1937; sec. to Govt. of India, Dept. of Edn., Health and Lands, 1932-40; mem. Viceroy's Exec. Council, 1940-41; chmn. Indian delegation, United Nations Food Conf., Hot Springs, Va., May 1943; mem. UNRRA Council; chmn., Indian Delegation to Internal Conference on Civil Aviation, Chgo., 1944; agt. gen. for India in U.S. 1941-47; Sec. Gen. Indian Ministry of External Affairs, 1947-52; Gov. of Bombay State, 1952—. Address: Bombay, India. Died Dec. 5, 1954.*

BAKER, Arthur Josiah Mountford; b. Birmingham, Eng., Apr. 22, 1881; s. Arthur and Ellen (Mountford) B.; prep. edn., St. John's Sch. and Tech. Sch., both Birmingham; student Mason College, Birmingham, 1897-99; married Miss Keren Culbertson; one son, Robert Mountford. Came to United States, 1905, naturalized citizen, 1920. Began as draftsman with Charles Taylor, Birmingham, 1899; later with Garrard Mfg. Co., Birmingham, and with Alfred Herbert, Coventry, Eng., with Cincinnati Milling Machine Co., 1905-20; chief engr. in charge of car design, Willys Overland Co., Toledo, O., 1920-32; with Hercules Motor Corp., Canton, O., 1932-38; Dep. Dir. Gen., Brit. Purchasing Commn., 1939-43; gen. mgr., Crocker-Wheeler Div., Joshua Hendy Co., 1943-45, v. p. E. W. Bliss Co., Brooklyn; exec. v. p. Melvin Pine & Co., Inc. Dir., industry div., E.C.A., Greece Apr.-Sept., 1948; chief, Methods and Equipment Div., Mut. Security Adminstrn., since 1950. Mem. Council Nat. Defense, and War Industries Bd., World War I. Comdr., Order of the British Empire. Home: Towers Hotel, Bklyn. Office: U.S. Embassy, London, Eng. Died Sept. 12, 1953.

BAKER, Crosby Fred, coll. prof.; b. Hampden, Me., Feb. 15, 1887; s. Fred Crosby and Cora Ida (Cole) B.; B.S., Tufts Coll., Mass., 1910, M.S., 1911; m. Ruth Ellingwood, June 15, 1914; children—Crosby F., Barbara (Mrs. Stuart McKenzie), Betsy R. Instr. in chemistry, Tufts Coll., 1911-19, asst. prof., 1919-24, prof., 1924-46, Henry Bromfield Pearson prof. natural science, 1946-49, Robinson professor since 1949, secretary department of chemistry and chem. engring., 1939-46, chmn. dept. chem. since 1946; cons. metallurgist, Eastern Smelting & Refining Co., 1915-20; metall. patent work, 1920-30, cons. and chem. engr. textile and finishing oils, since 1930; cons. Pepsodent Co. Sugar Foundation, since 1945; mgr. Three Mile Island Camp, Appalachian Mt. Club, since 1920. Instr. first aid, leadership training, Boy Scouts of Am., 1936-40, chmn. leadership training, 1936-40. Mem. Am. Chem. Soc., Am. Inst. Mining & Metall. Engrs., Soc. Chem. Industry (London), Am. Soc. for Metals, Boston Microchem. Soc., Phi Beta Kappa, Sigma Xi, Alpha Kappa Pi. Republican. Methodist (trustee). Mason (trustee). Club: Appalachian Mountain. Home: 53 Johnson Av., W. Medford 55, Mass. Office: Pearson Memorial Lab., Tufts College, Mass. Died Dec. 9, 1954.

BAKER, David Dudrow, clergyman; b. Green Springs, O., Nov. 11, 1897; s. George W. and Mary Jane (Dudrow) B.; A.B., Heidelberg, Tiffin, O., 1921, D.D., 1940; B.D., McCormick Theol. Sem., Chgo., 1928; student U. Edinburgh, 1928-29, Heidelberg, Germany, summer 1929; m. Helen Elizabeth Otte, Oct. 28, 1924; 1 dau., Elizabeth Louise. Staff mem. Robert Coll., Istanbul, Turkey, 1921-24, North Japan (Sendai) Coll., 1924-25; asst. minister Old Cannongate Ch., Edinburgh, Scotland, 1928-29; faculty mem. Am. Sch. for Boys, Baghdad, Iraq., 1929-34, acting prin., 1932-33; ordained to ministry of Evangelical and Reformed Ch., 1928; minister St. Paul's Ch., Balt., 1935-37; dir. Coop. Council of Missionary Edn., 1937-42, exec. sec. Emergency War Relief, 1940-42, editor The Messenger (official bi-weekly organ of ch), St. Louis, 1942-50. Pres. Associated Church Press, 1948-50. Dir. Friends' Work Camp, U.S. Refugee Shelter, Oswego, N.Y., 1945. Nettie F. McCormick fellow U. Edinburgh, 1928-29. Mem. Pi Kappa Delta. Author: (with Nevin C. Harner) Missionary Education in Your Church, 1942; New World Ahead, 1947. Contbr.: Windows of Worship, 1941; Gates of Beauty, 1945. Home: 7818 Grove Av., Webster Groves, Mo. Died June 27, 1950; buried Green Springs, O.

BAKER, Earle A., clergyman, coll. adminstr.; b. Edmund, Wis., Mar. 22, 1884; s. William Henry and Mary Ann (Richards) B.; A.B., Cornel Coll., 1908, D.D., 1924; B.D., Drew Sem., 1911; m. Grace Eloise Terrill, Sept. 20, 1910; children—Ruth Marie, Richard Terrill, Beth Eloise, Marjorie Grace. Ordained to ministry Meth. Ch., 1910, pastor, Coggon, Waterloo, Greene and Marion, Ia., 1911-27; dist. supt., Davenport. Ia., 1927-33; pastor Cedar Falls, Ia., 1933-42; dist. supt., Upper Ia. Conf. Waterloo, 1942-48; v.p. Cornell Coll., 1948—. Del. Gen. Conf. Meth. Ch., 1932-48. Mem. Phi Beta Kappa. Mason. Club: Lions. Home: 1221 College St., Cedar Falls, Ia. Office: Cornell College, Mount Vernon, Ia. Died Nov. 5, 1958; buried Elmwood Cemetery, Mason City, Ia.

BAKER, Edna Dean, coll. pres. emeritus; b. Normal, Ill.; d. Joshua Edmund and Olive Elmira (Clark) Baker; grad. high sch., Bellingham, Wash., 1902; grad. Nat. Coll. Edn., Evanston, Ill., 1913; B.Edn., Northwestern U., 1920, B.A., 1921, M.A.; studied summers, Columbia; D.Litt., Georgetown Coll., 1941; Ed.D. (hon.), Western Mich. Coll. Edn., Kalamazoo, 1949. Dir. Evanston Elementary Sch. (pvt.), 1909-16; asst. to pres. Nat. Coll. Edn., 1916-19, pres. 1920-49, pres. emeritus, 1949—. Mem. exec. bds. Nat. Council of Parent Edn. and Nat. Assn. for Nursery Edn.; mem. adv. bd. Edn. Digest 1938-46, bd. editors Jour. Childhood Edn., 1935-47; mem. com. of six acting as Nat. Adv. Com. for Emergency Nursery Schs. Fed. Govt., 19434-39; mem. Adv. Com. for Fed. Family Life Edn. under Works Progress Adminstrn., 1939-42; mem. White House Conf. on Child Health and Protection, 1930; mem. gen. adv. com. U.S. Office Edn. on its Inter-Am. edn. program, 1941-46; mem. nat. and state adv. coms. for WPA Child Protection Program, 1942-43; chmn. tng. com. Vol. Child Care Aides, Met. Chgo., 1942-45. Mem. N.E.A., Internat. Kindergarten Union (sec. 1921-22), Assn. for Childhood Edn. (pres. 1933-35), Phi Beta Kappa, Pi Lambda Theta, Pi Gamma Nu, Delta Kappa Gamma (hon.). Methodist. Clubs: Woman's City, Cordon. Author: The Beginner's Book in Religion, 1921; Parenthood and Child Nurture, 1922; Kindergarten Method in the Church School, 1925; The Worship of the Little Child, 1927; (with C. B. Baker) The Bible in Graded Story, 1922, The Bobbs-Merrill Readers, 1924, 39, The True Story Readers, 1928, 38; (with C. B. Baker and Mary Reed) The Curriculum Readers, 1934, 38. Home: Riverside, Cal. Died Mar. 1956.

BAKER, Everett Moore, educator; b. Newtonville, Mass., Aug. 28, 1901; s. George David and Mary Virginia (Hutton) B.; B.S., Dartmouth Coll., 1924; student theol. sch. Harvard, 1929; D.D., Tufts Coll., 1937; m. Helen Macdonald, Dec. 9, 1928; children—David Everett, Sidney Macdonald. Ordained to ministry Unitarian Ch., 1929; pastor Westminster Ch., Providence, 1929-37, First Ch., Cleve., 1942-46; lectr. sociology Cleve. Coll., 1944-45; dean of students Mass. Inst. Tech., 1947—. Exec. v.p. Am. Unitarian Assn., Boston, 1937-42, regional dir., 1943-46; nat. pres. Unitarian Ministerial Union, 1944-46. Pub. panel mem. Reg. 5, W.L.B. 1943-45; mem. nat. panel of arbitrators Am. Arbitration Assn., 1944—. Chmn. bd. dirs. Nat. Consumers League; mem. bd. Council World Affairs, Mental Hygiene Assn., Youth Bur., Travelers Aid Soc., Welfare Bd. (all Cleve.), Community Relations Board; mem. adv. bd. Nat. Student Assn. Trustee Proctor Acad., Andover, N.H., 1938-44, Hawken Sch., Cleve. Mem. bd. dirs. Unitarian Assn.; pres. Dartmouth Alumni Assn.; mem. Delta Kappa Epsilon. Compiler: Think on These Things (anthology of poetry and prose for men and women in service), 1940. Home: 43 Garden Road, Wellesley Hills, Mass. Office: Mass. Institute of Technology, Cambridge, Mass. Died Aug. 31, 1950.

BAKER, Harold Griffith, lawyer; b. East St. Louis, Ill., Feb. 16, 1899; s. Martin D. and Gertrude (McLean) B.; prep. edn. Manual Tng. Sch., Smith Acad., St. Louis; LL.B., U. Ill., 1921; m. Bernice Kraft, Dec. 10, 1927; children—Harold Griffith, William D., Martin D. Admitted to Ill. bar, 1921; Ill. state bank examiner, 1921-22; began practice at East St. Louis; U.S. atty. for Eastern Dist. Ill., 1926-31; in practice at East St. Louis, mem. Baker, Kagy & Wagner. Pres. mem. bd. Edn. Sch. Dist. 181, 1935-50; mem. Ill. Public Aid Commn., 1941—, sec., 1943—. Mem. bd. govs. St. Louis Unit, Shriners Crippled Children Hosp., 1938-41; pres. Law Alumni, U. Ill., 1937-39; bd. dirs. U. Ill. Alumni Assn., 1947-50. Served as 2d lt. inf. U.S. Army, 1918-19. Fellow Am. Coll. Trial Lawyers; mem. Internat. Assn. Ins. Counsel. Mem. Am., East St Louis, Illl State (bd. govs. 1937-38) bar assns., C. of C. (dir.

1937-38), Sigma Chi, Phi Delta Phi. Republican. Methodist. Mason (33° Shriner, Potentate Ainad Temple, 1938-39). Clubs: Union League (Chgo.); Missouri Athletic (St. Louis); City Club of East St. Louis; St. Clair Country. Home: 8 Country Club Drive, Belleville, Ill. Office: Murphy Bldg., East St. Louis, Ill. Died June 16, 1956; buried Mt. Hope Cemetery, Belleville, Ill.

BAKER, Harry (Harold) B(abcock), editor; b. Brooklyn, N.Y., Apr. 7, 1895; s. Maximillian and Catherine (Babcock) B.; ed. grade and high schs., Brooklyn; m. Caroline A. Rieger, May 16, 1920; children—Kathryn Virginia, Marilyn Joan (Mrs. Robert J. Cowhey). Entered newspaper work with New York (N.Y.) Globe, 1912, newspaper syndicate field with Asso. Newspapers, 1913-17; with Internat. Newsreel, 1918-21; news editor, Pacific and Atlantic Photos, 1921-23, gen. mgr., 1923-30; Eastern editor, Central Press Assn., 1930-36; gen. mgr. and editor, Internat. News Photos, 1936-40; photo editor, PM, N.Y. City, 1940-42; editor and gen. mgr., Chicago (Ill.) Sun Syndicate, 1940-47, Chicago Sun-Times Syndicate, 1947—. Roman Catholic. Home: 409 Washington Blvd., Oak Park, Ill. Office: 211 W. Wacker Dr., Chgo. Died Dec. 10, 1956; buried Queen of Heaven Cemetery, Hillside, Ill.

BAKER, Harvey Almy, lawyer; b. Warwick, R.I., Apr. 24, 1881; s. Benjamin and Lucy Anna (Sisson) B.; A.B., Brown U., 1903; LL.B., Harvard, 1906; m. Marion North Brown, Sept. 30, 1908. Practiced at Providence since 1906; U.S. atty., Dist. of R.I., 1914-20; pub. dir. (rep. City of Providence) United Electric Ry. Co. since 1921. Dir. Industrial Trust Co., Equitable Fire and Marine Insurance Company, The Gerry Estates Inc., New York. Member staff of Gov. Higgins, 1906-08. Mem. Bd. of Recreation, Providence, 1913-28. Mem. Am. and R.I. bar assns., American Judicature Society, Alpha Delta Phi. Phi Beta Kappa. Democrat. Clubs: Hope, Squantum, Dunes. Home: The Ledge, Hammond Hill, Saunderstown, R.I.; and 252 Bowen St., Providence, R.I. Office: Industrial Trust Bldg., Providence, R.I. Died Mar. 28, 1951.

BAKER, Holmes Davenport, banker; b. Frederick, Md., Apr. 11, 1880; s. Joseph Dill and Emma Newkirk (Cunningham) B.; student Frederick Acad., 1890-95; A.B., Western Md. Coll., Westminster, Md., 1899; m. Geraldine Frost, Sept. 16, 1922; children—Geraldine Frost, Holmes Davenport (dec.), Joseph Dill, II. Began as clk. Citizens Nat. Bank, 1900, pres., 1922—; v.p., dir. Frederick Hotel Co.; dir. Union Mfg. Co., Frederick, Md.; dir. Balt. br. Fed. Res. Bank of Richmond, Va. Mem. Dept. Geology, Mines and Water Resources of Md. Trustee, v.p. Buckingham Sch., Buckeystown, Md.; trustee Frederick Female Sem. Bd., Home for the Aged, Hood Coll., Frederick, Md. Mem. Md. Com. for Expenditure. Pub. Works, Fund, 1933, recovery bd. for Norfolk, Va. dist., NRA, 1933; chmn. Frederick County Welfare Bd., 1933; pres. Md. Bankers Assn., 1925-26; mem. exec. council Am. Bankers Assn., 1937; pres. Fed. Charities of Frederick, Md.; dir. local Community Chest; mem. Bowman Com. on Structure of Md. State Govt.; chmn. Region 2, Md. Victory Fund Com.; chmn. Frederick County War Price and Rationing Bd.; mem. State Com. for Economic Development; mem. exec. com. Md. War Chest, Inc. Served from 2d to 1st lt. U.S. Army, World War I. Mem. C. of C. (dir.). Democrat. Episcopalian. Clubs: Rotary past pres.); Merchants, Maryland (Balt.); Woodmont Rod and Gun (Hancock, Md.). Home: Frederick, Md. Died Apr. 15, 1950.

BAKER, Horace Forbes, lawyer; b. Mayville, N.Y., Apr. 15, 1878; s. George Albert and Julia Brewster (Hurlbert) B.; A.B. magna cum laude, Harvard, 1901, LL.B., 1903; m. Jane Torrance, Apr. 16, 1914; children—Francis J. Torrance, Mary Rachel. Admitted to Pa. bar, 1904, began practice at Pitts.; asso. A. O. Fording in gen. practice; asst. to gen. counsel Wabash R.R. Lines East of Toledo, 1905-08, atty. for receivers, 1908-12, receiver, 1912-16; gen. counsel and v.p. reorganized co. The Pittsburgh & W.Va. Ry. Co., 1917-22; gen. practice, 1917—; mem. Baker, Watts & Woods; dir. St. Paul Coal Co., Castle Shannon Coal Corp.; trustee, solicitor Dollar Savings Bank (Pitts.). Mem. bd. dirs. Public Charities Assn. Pa.; trustee Family and Children's Service; dir. Fedn. Social Agencies; dir. Woods Run Settlement. Trustee, chmn. exec. com. Sewickley Hosp. Mem. Am., Pa., Allegheny County bar assns., Am. Civic Assn., Sigma Alpha Epsilon. Republican. Episcopalian. Mason. Clubs: Harvard of Western Pa., Harvard-Yale-Princeton, Pittsburgh, Duquesne (Pitts.); Allegheny Country; Edgeworth. Home: 1008 Beaver Rd., Sewickley, Pa. Office: Union Trust Bldg., Pitts. Died Feb. 24, 1950.

BAKER, Hugh Potter, univ. pres. emeritus; b. St. Croix Falls, Wis., Jan. 20, 1878; s. Maj. J(oseph) Stannard and Alice (Potter) B.; B.S., Mich. State Coll., 1901; M.F., Yale, 1904; Dr. Econs., U. Munich, 1910; LL.D., Syracuse U., 1933, LL.D., R.I. State Coll., 1945, Amherst Coll., U. Mass., 1947; D.Sc. in Edn., Boston U., 1945; m. Fleta Paddock, Dec. 27, 1904 (now dec.); children—Carolyn, Steven Paddock (dec.), Clarence Potter; m. 2d, Richarda Sahla, Nov. 27, 1929. For 10 yrs. with the U.S. Forest Service, examining pub. lands for forest reserves in Central Ida., Wyo., Neb., N.M., Wash., and Ore. Prof. forestry, Ia. State Coll., 1904-07, Pa. State Coll., 1907-12; dean and prof. silviculture, N.Y. State Coll. Forestry, Syracuse, 1912-20, dean, 1930-33; exec. sec. Am. Paper and Pulp Assn., 1920-28; mgr. trade assn. dept. C. of C. of U.S., 1928-30; pres. Mass. State Coll., 1933-47. Mem. 2d R.O.T.C., Ft. Sheridan, Ill., Aug.-Nov. 1917; with 46th Inf., and mem. Gen. Staff; maj. O.R.C. Fellow A.A.A.S., Royal Geog. Soc. (London); mem. Soc. Am. Foresters, S.A.R., Loyal Legion. Mason. Clubs: Cosmos (Washington); University (Boston, N.Y.C.). Address: U. Mass., Amherst, Mass. Died May 24, 1950; buried St. Croix Falls, Wis.

BAKER, John Earl, retired exec.; b. Eagle, Wis., Aug. 23, 1880; s. Francis and Lydia Ann (Duffin) B.; grad. Whitewater (Wis.) Normal Sch., 1901; Ph.B., U. Wis., 1906, M.A., 1908, LL.D., 1936; law dept. George Washington U., 1907-08; m. Willie Kathryn Smith, Dec. 30, 1908; children—Frances Lydia (Mrs. Howard F. Ross), Barbara Smith (Mrs. George William Louden), John Earl. Tchr. pub. schs. until 1903; clk. ICC, 1907-09; clk. Census Bureau, 1909-10; statistician Brotherhood of Locomotive Firemen and Enginemen, 1910; service insp. S.P. Co, 1910-11, statistician, 1922-6; adviser on ry. mgmt. to Ministry of Communications, China, 1916-26; trustee China Found. for Promotion of Edn. and Culture, 1925-47. Dir. A.R.C. China Famine Relief, 1920-21, constructed 850 miles of highway in 4 provinces of China as means of giving employment to the destitute, gave considerable impetus to highway program and relief-through-work in China; gen. sec., China Famine Relief, U.S.A., 1928; exec. sec. Am. Adv. Com. on Famine Relief, 1929; adviser to Ministry of Rys., Nanking, China, 1930-31; dir. relief operations China Internat. Famine Relief Commn., 1930; in charge of custody and transportation Am. wheat and flour for Nat. Flood Relief Commn., 1931-32; mgr. Chinese-Am. Wheat Syndicate (Ministry of Finance), 1933-35; adviser Central Trust of China (Ministry of Finance), Nat. Relief Commn.; exec. sec. China Internat. Famine Relief Commn., 1937-40; also dir. Shanghai Internat. Red Cross, 1937-39; dir. A.R.C. in China, 1940-41; insp.-gen. Yunnan-Burma Highway Commn., 1941-42; cons. Fgn. Econ. Adminstrn., 1942-45; with UNRRA, 1945-46. Member of joint commission on rural reconstruction in Taiwan (Formosa), 1948-52. Member of Chinese Society and Political Science Association, Phi Beta Kappa, Alpha Tau Omega, Delta Sigma Rho. Decorated Order of Bountiful Harvest, 3d class, by Pres. of China, 1918, 2d class with sash, 1922; Order of Brilliant Jade, 1936. Methodist. Clubs: Commonwealth (San Francisco); American (Shanghai). Author: Explaining China, 1927; Chinese Railway Accounts. Home: 516 Throckmorton Av., Mill Valley, Cal. Died July 27, 1957; buried Eagle, Wis.

BAKER, Leonard Theodore, educator; b. Charleston, S.C., Jan. 22, 1868; s. Edward and Maxene (Blanchard) Baker; A.B., Coll. of Charleston, S.C., 1888, A.M., 1893, LL.D., 1926, Litt. D. (hon.) U.S.C., 1952; married Lucretia Douglas Lang, July 31, 1895; 1 dau., Lucretia Douglas; m. 2d, Ellen Deas Lang, Dec. 19, 1906; 1 dau., Harriet Kershaw. Teacher high schs., 1889-98; supt. schs., 1898-1906; prof. history and adminstrn. of edn., 1906—, dean, 1914—, acting pres., 1926-27, and 1931-32, president 1932-36, v.p. and dean of faculty, 1936-44, acting pres. 1944-45, v.p. and dean of faculty, 1945—, president emeritus, 1946—. U. of South Carolina. Mem. Nat. Educational Assn., S.C. State Teachers Assn. (pres. 1908-09), Soc. for Advancement of Education, Chi Phi, Phi Beta Kappa, Omicron Delta Kappa; pres. Assn. Colls. and Secondary Schs. of Southern States, 1924, sec. Assn. Colleges of S.C., 1914-40; pres. S.C. Conf. of Social Welfare, 1925. Democrat. Episcopalian. Mason. Lecturer on edn. before summer schs. for teachers. Clubs: Kosmos (ex-pres.), Rotary (Columbia). Home: 820 Henderson St., Columbia 1, S.C. Died Jan. 5, 1955; buried Quaker Cemetery, Camden, S.C.

BAKER, Marjorie Montgomery Ward (Mrs. Robert R. Baker); b. Chgo.; d. (A.) Montgomery and Elizabeth (Cobb) Ward; ed. by pvt. tutors and at finishing sch., Ogontz, Pa.; m. Robert R. Baker, 1932. Life trustee Northwestern U.; mem. Women's Bd., Passavant Hosp., Convalescent Home for Crippled Children, Wesley Hosp. (Chgo.). Clubs: Arts, Casino, Woman's Athletic, South Shore Country (Chgo.); Woman's Athletic (Los Angeles); Lake Placid (life mem.) (Essex County, N.Y.); Woman's Club of Wisconsin (Milw.). Home: 209 Lake Shore Dr., Chgo.; also "Knollward," Oconomowoc, Wis. Office: 30 N. Michigan Av., Chgo. Died July 7, 1959.

BAKER, William Jesse, urologist; b. Dallas City, Ill., May 1, 1894; s. Eugene Hamilton and Elizabeth Edith (Prescott) B.; B.S., Knox Coll., 1917; M.D., Rush Med. Coll., 1923; m. Eloise Parsons, Aug. 30, 1923; children—William, Robert. Intern, resident intern urology Cook County Hosp., Chgo., 1924-26, asso. urologist, 1932-46, chief urol. dept., 1946—; urologist St. Luke's Hosp., 1926—; prof. urology Northwestern U. Med. Sch., 1955—; cons. urologist Municipal Contagious Hosp. Served with med. dept. U.S. Army, 1917-19, as lt. col., M.C., AUS, World War II. Fellow A.C.S.; mem. A.M.A., Am. Urol. Assn., Am. Assn. Genito-Urinary Surgeons, Clin. Soc. Genito-Urinary Surgeons, Internat. Soc. Urologists, Chgo. Urol. Soc., Am. Neissereian Soc., Tau Kappa Epsilon, Delta Sigma Rho, Nu Sigma Nu, Alpha Omega Alpha, Pi Kappa Epsilon. Conglist. Mason. Clubs: University, South Shore Country (Chgo.). Home: 5830 Stony Island Av., Chgo. Office: 7 W. Madison Street, Chgo. 2. Died Dec. 3, 1958.

BAKETEL, H. Sheridan (bāk-tĕl), physician, med. editor; b. Hopedale, O., Nov. 15, 1872; s. Oliver Sherman (D.D.) and Rosie Lueretia (Mack) B.; student Phillips Exeter Acad., Boston U.; M.D., Dartmouth, 1895; postgrad. work Harvard, also abroad; A.M., Holston Coll., 1908; m. Zada Call; m. 2d, Corinne Phillippi Sellers; children—Mary (dec.), H. Sheridan. Editor Gaillard's Med. Jour., 1905-08, Med. Times, 1908-15; began practice urology, N.Y., 1910; became lectr. med. econs. L. I. Coll. Medicine, Bklyn., 1915, pres. preventive medicine, 1915-31, emeritur prof., 1931— (trans. to med. coll. State U. Med. Center of N.Y.C.); co-founder 1923, since editor-in-chief Med. Economics; pres. physiol. labs. Reed & Carnrick, Jersey City, 1925-51; chmn. Reed & Carnrick Inst. for Med. Research, 1946-51; some time urologist to N.Y. hosps. Chmn. bd. trustees Columbia U. Coll. Pharmacy, 1938-42. Del. to U.S. Pharm. Conv., 1930-40. Served with Med. R.C., U.S. Army, 1912-17; col. M.C. AUS, ret. 1949. Fellow A.C.P., Am. Pub. Health Assn., N.Y. Acad. Medicine; pres. Am. Pharm. Mfg. Assn. 1929-31; mem. A.M.A., Am. Urol. Assn. (life), A.M.A., Am. Med. Editors Assn. (pres. 1920), N.H. Med. Soc., S.A.R., Mil. Order World War, Am. Legion, Dartmouth Med. Alumni Assn. (pres. 1922-29), Newcomen Soc., Beta Theta Pi (past v.p.). Episcopalian. Mason (32°, Shriner). Clubs: Dartmouth, Nat. Republican, Pilgrims, Beta Theta Pi (N.Y.C.); Army and Navy (Washington); University (Jersey City); Connaught (London); Athenaeum (Portsmouth, N. H.). Author: The Treatment of Syphilis, 1920; also monographs. Asso. editor publ. Alpha Kappa Kappa. Home: 238 62d Av. S., Bahama Shores, St. Petersburg 5, Fla.; (summer) 309 Midland Av., St. Davids, Pa. Died July 7, 1955; buried Mt. Auburn Cemetery, Cambridge, Mass.

BAKEWELL, Charles Montague, ex-congressman, educator; b. Pitts., Apr. 24, 1867; s. Thomas and Josephine Alden (Maitland) B.; A.B., U. Cal., 1889, LL.D., 1943; A.M., Harvard, 1892, Ph.D., 1894; student univs. of Berlin, Strassburg and Paris, 1894-96; hon. A.M., Yale, 1905; m. Madeline Palmer, Dec. 21, 1899 (died May 15, 1947); children—Henry Palmer, Bradley Palmer (dec.), Mildred Palmer (Mrs. Richard Hooker, Jr.). Instr. philosophy Harvard, 1896-97; instr. philosophy U. Cal., 1897-98, asso. prof., 1900-03, prof., 1903-05; asso. prof. philosophy Bryn Mawr Coll., 1898-1900; prof. philosophy Yale, 1905-33, now emeritus; mem. 73d Congress, Conn. at large. Mem. Conn. Senate, 1920-24 (chmn. edn. com.); chmn. Commn. to Revise and Codify Edn. Laws of Conn. Mem. Am. Philos. Assn. (pres. 1910), A.A.A.S., Nat. Inst. Social Scis., Brit. Inst. Philosophy, N.H. Hist. Soc. Author: Source Book in Ancient Philosophy, rev. edit. 1939; Story of the American Red Cross in Italy; George Herbert Palmer (with W. E. Hocking). Also various essays in ethical and philos. criticism; editor and part author, Thomas Davidson's The Education of the Wage Earners; editor Everyman edit. of William James' Selected Papers on Philosophy, and Emerson's Poems, and Plato's Republic in Scribner's philosophy series. Insp. and historian with rank of maj., and dep. commr. Italian Commn. of A.R.C. in Italy, 1918-19. Decorated Order of The Crown (Italy); Silver Medal of Honor (Italian Red Cross). Mem. Beta Theta Pi, Phi Beta Kappa. Republican. Clubs: Century (N.Y.C.); Graduate, New Haven Country (New Haven); Metropolitan (Washington); Hammonassett Fishing Assn. Address: 437 Humphrey St., New Haven. Died Sept. 19, 1957.

BAKEWELL, Donald Campbell, steel mfr.; b. Salem, O., Dec. 5, 1887; s. Thomas Howard and Annie Esther (Mullins) B.; grad. Hotchkiss Sch., Lakeville, Conn., 1904; A.B., Yale, 1908; postgrad. Mass. Inst. Tech.; m. Margaret Jenifer Jennings, June 7, 1913; children—Donald Campbell (dec.), Richard Jennings, Margaret Jenifer, Dorothy Evan. Began in steel mfg. bus. with Pa. Co., Altoona, Pa., 1910; pres. Duquesne Steel Foundry Co., Pitts., 1917-37; pres. Pitts., Forge & Iron Co.; mem. exec. com. Ill. Zinc Co.; mem. exec. com., v.p. Blaw-Knox Co.; v.p., dir. E. H. Jennings Bros. Co.; dir. Coraopolis Trust Co. Mem. Nat. Founders Assn. (exec. com.), Alpha Delta Phi. Republican. Episcopalian. Clubs: Pittsburgh, Duquesne, Allegheny Country, Rolling Rock (Pitts.); University, Links (N.Y.C.). Home: Sewickley, Pa. Deceased.

BAKHMETEFF, Boris Alexander (bäk-mä'têf), civil engr.; b. Tiflis, Caucasus, Russia, May 14, 1880; s. Alexander Paul and Julia (Novitsky) B.; grad. Classical Gymnasium Tiflis, 1898; C.E., Inst. of Engrs. of Ways of Communication, St. Petersburg, 1903; studied at Poly. Inst., Zurich, 1903-04; D.Eng., Poly. Inst., St. Petersburg, 1911; m. Helen Speransky, July 15, 1905 (died 1921); m. 2d, Marie Helander Cole, June 7, 1938. Came to U.S., 1917, naturalized, 1935. Asst. dozent and prof. of gen. and advanced hydraulics, hydraulic structures, water power engring., theoretical mechanics and applied mechanics Polytech. Inst. Emperor Peter the Great, St. Petersburg, 1905-17; cons. engr. specializing on water power, St. Petersburg, 1907-15; enlisted with Red Cross, beginning of World War; chief plenipotentiary Central War Indsl. Com. to U.S., 1915-16; mem. Anglo-Russian Purchasing Commn., 1915-16; apptd. under-sec. of state (vice minister) Ministry for Commerce and Industry of Provisional govt. of Russia under premiership of Prince Lvov, 1917; apptd. head Extraordinary Russian Commn. to U.S. and Russian ambassador representing Provisional (Kerensky) Govt., 1917; continued as ambassador of the State of Russia until 1922; cons. engr. N.Y.C., 1923—; chmn. bd. Lion Match Co.; pres., dir. No. Mercury Felt Corp.; dir. Potash Co. Am., Research Corp.; prof. civil engring., Columbia, 1931, hon. prof., 1951; mem. bd. cons. engrs. Panama Canal, 1946-47. Dir. Humanities Fund, Russian Student Fund. Recipient Grand Medal, Soc. Drs. Engring., 1946, Order of Officer of Pub. Instrn., 1947 (France). Fellow Am. Geog. Soc., Fgn. Policy Council, N.Y. Acad. Scis., Inst. Aero. Scis. (asso.); mem. A.A.A.S., Am. Soc C.E. (hon. 1946; chmn. com. research; mem. bd. engring. found.), Am. Soc. M.E., Engring. Inst. (Can.), Conn. Acad. Arts and Scis., Sigma Xi, Tau Beta Pi. Mem. Russian Orthodox Ch. Clubs: Century, University (N.Y.C.); Metropolitan (Washington). Author: Lectures on Hydraulics (Russian), 1912; Varied Flow of Liquid in Open Channels (Russian), 1912; Variable Flow of Liquids (Russian), 1914; Hydraulics of Open Channels, 1932; Mechanics of Turbulence, 1936. Contbr. to Foreign Affairs, Slavonic Review and jours. of Am. Soc. C.E., Am. Soc. M.E., others. Home: 876 Park Av., N.Y.C. Died July 21, 1951.

BALABAN, John, motion pictures exec.; b. Chgo., Oct. 15, 1894. In motion picture industry, 1911—; successively with Gen. Feature Film Co.; theatre mgr. Balaban & Katz circuit; sec.-treas., sec. Publix-Gt. States circuit; pres. Balaban & Katz, 1949—. Mem. Motion Picture Pioneers. Home: 1000 Lake Shore Dr. Office: 175 N. State St., Chgo. Died Apr. 4, 1957; buried Waldheim No. 1 Cemetery, Forest Park, Ill.

BALCH, Franklin Greene, surgeon; b. Jamaica Plain, Mass., Apr. 26, 1864; s. Joseph W. and Agnes L. (Greene) B.; A.B., Harvard, 1888, A.M., 1892, M.D., 1892; m. Lucy R. Bowditch, Nov. 7, 1894; children—Franklin G., Charles B., Lucy B. (Mrs. Augustus L. Putnam), Henry G., Cornelia (Mrs. Leonard Wheeler, Jr.), Katharine (Mrs. Arthur D. Baldwin). Practiced in Boston, 1892—; hon. surgeon Mass. Gen. Hosp.; cons. surgeon Faulkner Hosp., Lawrence Meml. Hosp. Diplomate Am. Bd. Surgery. Fellow Am. Surg. Assn., A.A.A.S., A.C.S.; mem. A.M.A., Mass. Med. Soc., New Eng., Boston surg. socs. Republican. Unitarian. Clubs: Harvard (Boston); Tavern. Home: 109 Moss Hill Rd. Office: 330 Dartmouth St., Boston. Died Sept. 1958.

BALDERSTON, John Lloyd, writer; b. Phila., Pa., Oct. 22, 1889; s. Lloyd and Mary F. (Alsop) B.; student Columbia U., 1911-14; m. Marion Rubicam, Mar. 6, 1921; 1 son, John Lloyd, Jr. New York corr. Phila Record, 1912-14; went to Europe as free lance war corr., 1915; war corr. McClure Newspapers, 1916-18; dir. information, Gt. Britain and Ireland, for U.S. Govt. Com. on Pub. Information, 1918-19; editor The Outlook, London, 1920-23; chief London corr. New York World, 1923-31; took part through writings, broadcastings, etc., in defense movement, 1940-41; Washington observer for Com. to Defend America by Aiding the Allies, 1940; organized and conducted William Allen White Com. News Service from Washington, 1940; lectr. drama, U. of So. Cal., 1952—. Clubs: Century (New York); Athenaeum. Savile (London). Author: Genius of the Marne, 1919; A Morality Play for the Leisure Class, 1924; Berkeley Square, 1929; Chicago Blueprint, 1943; A Goddess to a God: also author Cleopatra and Caesar (play) (London), 1952. Co-author (plays): Dracula, 1927; Frankenstein, 1931; Red Planet, 1932; Farewell Performance, 1936; (motion pictures) Lives of a Bengal Lancer, Berkeley Square, Smilin' Through, Gaslight, Tennessee Johnson, Prisoner of Zenda, and others. Home: 615 N. Rodeo Dr., Beverly Hills, Cal. Died Mar. 8, 1954; buried Colora, Md.

BALDWIN, Alexander Richards, lawyer; b. San Francisco, Calif., Oct. 19, 1874; s. Alexander R. and Elizabeth G. (Stoutenborough) B.; Ph.B., U. of Calif., 1896; LL.B., Hastings Coll. of the Law, 1899; m. Jessie E. Glascock, June 7, 1899 (died Feb. 2, 1913); children—John G., Mary G., Frances S. Practiced law in Calif. since 1898; receiver D.&R.G. R.R. Co., 1918-21; pres. Western Pacific R.R. Corp., 1921-26; v.p. W.P. R.R. Co., 1916-26. Mem. Sigma Chi. Republican. Presbyterian. Clubs: University (San Francisco); Pacific-Union (San Francisco). Home: Woodside, R.F.D., Redwood City, Cal. Office: Mills Bldg., San Francisco. Died Feb. 27, 1956.

BALDWIN, Arthur Charles, clergyman; b. Rochester, N.Y., Aug. 9, 1875; s. Charles J. and Adelaide L. (Fosdick) B.; A.B., Denison U., Granville, O., 1896, D.D., 1916; Rochester Theol. Sem., 1900; m. Nellie T. Forbes, Apr. 17, 1901; 1 son, Schuyler Forbes. Ordained Bapt. ministry, 1900; pastor Ballston Spa, N.Y., 1900-06, 1st Ch., Aurora, Ill., 1906-08, First Ch. Fall River, Mass., 1908-14; fgn. sec. Am. Bapt. Foreign Missionary Soc., 1914-15, mem. of bd. of mgrs. 1915-40; pastor Park Av. Baptist Ch., Rochester, N.Y., 1915-16, First Ch., Montclair, N.J., 1916-18, Chestnut St. Ch., Phila., 1919—. Army Y.M.C.A. service, overseas, 1918-19. Del. bd. mgrs. Am. Bapt. Foreign Missionary Soc. to W. African and Congo Jubilee Conf., Sept. 1928; pres. Pennsylvania Bapt. Conv., 1939-40. Acting pres. Bapt. Inst. for Christian Workers, 1941-43. Mem. Sigma Chi. Rep. Clubs: Union League, Phi Alpha Clerical Club. Author: Inevitable Dawn, 1939. Home: 4510 Osage Av., Philadelphia, Pa. Died Feb. 24, 1960.

BALDWIN, Clarke Edward, lawyer; b. Canandaigua, Mich., Nov. 24, 1872; s. Edward C. and Marilda Elizabeth Baggerly B.; ed. pub. schs., 1877-88; grad. Adrian High Sch., 1892; Adrian Coll., 1893; grad. law dept., U. Mich., LL.B., 1896; m. Adelia Alice Wing Nov. 14, 1900. Admitted to bar, 1896, now mem. law firm Smith, Baldwin & Alexander; counsel for Wabash Ry. Co., Cincinnati Northern Ry. Co., Page Woven Wire Fence Co., etc.; v.p. Gilford Mfg. Co.; dir. Banner Fence Co., Adrian Pin & Tack Co.; treas. Citizens' Light & Power Co. Mem. Mich. Nat. Guard 6 yrs.; sec. to Congressman H. C. Smith, 1898-1900. Mem. Sigma Alpha Epsilon, Mich. State Bar Assn.; del. Universal Congress of Lawyers and Jurists, St. Louis, 1904. Episcopalian. Republican. Address: Adrian, Mich. Died Apr. 5, 1932.

BALDWIN, Francis Everett, mgr.; b. Otego, N.Y., Aug. 30, 1856; s. John Jackson and Sallie M. (Beardslee) B.; student Oneonta Acad.; m. Anna E. Grandin, May 7, 1882. Admitted to bar, 1881, practiced at Elmira, 20 yrs.; pres. Thatcher Mfg. Co. Prohibitionist (nat. com.). Methodist. Clubs: National Arts (N.Y.C.); Century (Elmira). Address: Elmira, N.Y. Deceased.

BALDWIN, Francis Marsh, prof. zoölogy; b. West Upton, Mass., Jan. 16, 1885; s. Ellory Albee and Rosa Arbella (Wood) B.; A.B., Clark U., 1906, A.M., 1907; Ph.D., U. of Ill., 1917; m. Bessie Mae Seay, July 15, 1912 (died Nov. 11, 1949); children—Gwendolyn, Francis Marsh; m. 2d Esther Pardee Harper, Aug. 5, 1950. Instr. nature and science, Ky. Normal Sch., 1908-11; independent investigator, U.S. Bureau Fisheries, Woods Hole, summers 1911-14; prof. biology, Western Maryland Coll., 1911-15; asst. zoölogy, U. of Ill., 1915-17; research, Marine Biol. Lab., Woods Hole, summer 1915; asst. prof. zoölogy, Ia. State Coll., 1917-19, asso. prof. 1919-20, prof. physiology, 1920-27; prof. zoölogy, Southern Calif., since 1927, chmn. dept., 1929-36; dir. Marine Biological Station, 1928-36; chmn. Biological Div., 1936; spl. investigator, Marine Biol. Lab., summer 1919; U.S. Biol. Survey, Barbary Erad, U.S.D.A., summer 1920; research, Freshwater Biol., Lakeside Lab. (Ia.) summers 1924-25. Fellow Ia. Acad. Science; mem. A.A.A.S., Am. Assn. Univ. Profs. (pres. local chapter 1931), Am. Physiological Soc., Soc. Exptl. Biol. and Medicine; mem. corp., Marine Biol. Lab., Woods Hole, Mass.; mem. So. Calif. Acad. Science, Sigma Xi (pres. local chapter 1943-44), Phi Kappa Phi (charter mem. local chapter). Author and contbg. editor: Elementary Manual for Physiology, 1927; Practical Exercises in Human Anatomy, 1932; Manual for Advanced Physiology (metabolism), 1933; Manual for Neurology, 1935. Contbr. articles on marine biology to Ency. Britannica, Book of the Year, 1937-46; "Ten Eventful Years," Ency. Brit.; collaborator for biol. abstracts. Frequent contbr. scientific articles to jours. Home: 5015 Angeles Vista Blvd., Los Angeles 43. Office: 3551 University Av., Los Angeles 7, Cal. Died Feb. 2, 1951; buried Forest Lawn Cemetery, Glendale, Cal.

BALDWIN, Frank A., editor; b. Des Moines, Ia., Dec. 27, 1891; s. Frank and Comfort L. (Baldwin) B. (both dec.); A.B., U. of Ia., 1913; m. Miriam Helen Pool, July 29, 1932. Admitted to Ia. bar, 1915; editor News-Tribune and Times-Herald, Waco, Tex., since 1917; mem. Tex. state legislature, 1929-30; newspaper reporter, European traveler and lecturer, 1937-41; mem. Tex. state bd. of edn., 1930. Democrat. Home: Route 1, Box 23. Office: News-Tribune and Times-Herald, Waco, Tex. Died Aug. 6, 1951; buried Waco.

BALDWIN, Geoffrey P., army officer; b. Madison Barracks, N.Y., May 10, 1892; s. John Arthur and Lucy Frances (Prescott) B.; B.S., U.S. Mil. Acad., 1916; grad. Inf. Sch., 1922; distinguished grad. Command and Gen. Staff Sch., 1926; grad. Army War Coll., 1928; unmarried. Commd. 2d lt., U.S. Army, 1916, and advanced through the grades to brig. gen., 1942; served as capt. and maj. (temp.) with 5th Div., A.E.F., France, 1918; formerly assigned to War Dept. Manpower Bd., Washington; retired from service, 1946; chief of CARE mission in Italy since May 1946. Decorated D.S.C., Silver Star, Victory Medal with three battle clasps (U.S.), Knight Comdr. (Mil. Class) Order St. Gregory the Great (Papal), Knight Comdr. Order of la Concordia (Italy). Hon. mem. Scabbard and Blade. Roman Catholic. Clubs: Army and Navy (Washington); University (Boston). Home: care The Adjutant General, Washington. Office: CARE, Inc., Via Lucullo 6, Rome, Italy. Died Aug. 30, 1951.

BALDWIN, Hadley, civil engr.; b. Marshallton, Pa., Feb. 24, 1867; s. Barkley Cloud and Emily Kelly (Dowell) B.; B.S. in Civil Engring., U. Mich., 1893; m. Emily Wilson, Nov. 7, 1903; children—Wilson Barkley, Betty. With C.,C.,C.&St.L. Ry. Co., 1893—, successively masonry insp. and asst. engr., until 1896, supr. track, 1896, resident engr., at E. St. Louis, 1896-97, supr. track, 1897-98, engr. maintenance of way, Indpls., 1898-1902, engr. constrn., Cin., 1902, supt. St. Louis div., 1902-15, asst. chief engr., 1915-24, chief engr., 1924-31; chief engr. N.Y.C. R.R. Co. (C.C.C.&St.L. Region), 1931-32; chief engr. Cin. No. R.R. Co. and Evansville, Indpls. & Terre Haute Ry. Co.; spl. engr. N.Y.C. R.R. Co., 1932—. Mem. Am. Ry. Engring. Assn. Republican. Unitarian. Clubs: Literary, Torch, Cincinnati Country. Home: 2565 Villa Lane. Address: Big Four Bldg., Cin. Died Nov. 22, 1949; buried Marshallton, Pa.

BALDWIN, Harry Streett, ex-congressman; b. Baldwin, Md., Aug. 21, 1894; s. Harry W. and Mary Elizabeth (Whiteford) B.; student U. Md., 1912-13; m. Mary Virginia Smith, July 14, 1917; children—John Streett, Harry Wallace, Maurice Whiteford, Mary Louise, William Smith. Operator large truck farm. Elected mem. Md. House of Dels., 1931; county commr. Baltimore County, 1934-38, pres. of bd. of county commrs., 1938-42; dir. Civil Def. for Baltimore County, 1941-42; mem. 78th and 79th Congresses, 2d Md. Dist. Democrat. Presbyn. Elk. Odd Fellow. Club: Country of Md. (Rogers Forge). Home: Hydes, Baltimore County, Md. Died Oct. 19, 1952; buried Chestnut Grove Presbyn. Ch., Sweetair, Md.

BALDWIN, Joseph Clark, ex-congressman; b. N.Y.C., Jan. 11, 1897; s. Joseph Clark and Fanny (Taylor) B.; B.A., Harvard, 1920; m. Marthe Guillon-Verne, Dec. 5, 1923; children—Fanny Taylor, Joseph Clark, Jeanne Neumayer, Stephen Verne. Was reporter N.Y. Tribune; asso. editor North Westchester Times; asso. editor The Independent; contbg. editor The Independent Outlook; salesman Russell Miller & Carey; asst. v.p. Murray Hill Trust Co.; now sr. partner Baldwin, Munson & Mann; v.p., dir. Nitralloy Corp.; v.p. Dunn & Fowler; pres., dir. United Dydwood Corp. Mem. Bd. of Aldermen, N.Y.C., 1928-34, minority leader, 1929-34; mem. N.Y. State Senate, 1934-36, Constnl. Conv., N.Y., 1937, N.Y.C. Council, 1937-41; mem. 77th-79th Congresses, 17th N.Y. Dist. Served in USN, 1917, U.S. Army with AEF, 1918; commd. 2d lt., 1918; now capt. Inf. Res. Decorated Officer French Legion of Honor. Republican. Episcopalian. Mason, Elk. Clubs: Racquet and Tennis, Brook, National Republican (N.Y.C.); Porcellian (Harvard). Home: 222 E. 71st St., N.Y.C. 21. Died Oct. 27, 1957; buried Woodlawn Cemetery, N.Y.C.

BALDWIN, Martin Mortimer, lawyer; b. Fitzpatrick, Ala., Aug. 26, 1873; s. Phillips Bernard and Sallie (Crews) B.; A.B., U. Ala., 1894, LL.B., 1895; m. Fannie Howry Dunn, June 14, 1917; 1 dau., Frances (Mrs. Meade Whitaker). Admitted to Ala. bar, 1895; practiced at Union Springs, 1895-1903, Birmingham, 1903—; partner White, Bradley, Arant, All & Rose, and predecessors, 1941—; specialized in corp. law. Mem. Ala. Ho. of Rep., 1900-01; apptd. sr. judge criminal court, Jefferson County, 1906; declined to run for election; dir. Protective Life Ins. Co. Trustee Children's Hosp., Birmingham; chancellor of P.E. Ch. in Diocese of Ala., 1933—. Mem. Ala., Birmingham bar assns. Democrat. Club: Mountain Brook. Home: 4141 Crescent Road. Office: Comer Bldg., Birmingham, Ala. Died Mar. 5, 1955; buried Elmwood Cemetery, Birmingham.

BALDWIN, Minor Coe, organist; b. Middletown, Conn., Feb. 21, 1856; s. Minor W. and Alvina E. (Coe) B.; studied N.E. Conservatory of Music, and with tchrs. in U.S. and Eng.; Mus.D., German Conservatory of Music, N.Y.C., 1888; unmarried. Gave organ recitals at World's Fair, Chgo., 1893, Omaha Expn., 1898, Charleston Expn., 1902, St. Louis Expn., 1904, etc.; gave series of concerts at Royal Albert Hall, London, Eng., 1906, at Chautauqua Assembly, N.Y., 1910; has appeared in leading cities of U.S., Can. and Europe. Republican. Episcopalian. Mason. Composer 18 pieces and transcripts for organ, also various selections for piano and voice. Author: Book of Poems of a Lyric Nature. Home: Orlando, Fla. Died June 21, 1950.

BALDWIN, Roland Dennis, banker, Masonic exec.; b. Yonkers, N.Y., May 29, 1896; s. William Delavan and Helen Runyan (Sullivan) B.; student The Lawrenceville (N.J.) Sch., 1911-13, Berkley-Irving Sch., N.Y. City, 1913-16; m. Pearl Sheldon Smith,

Apr. 4, 1925; children—William Delavan, Sheldon Smith. Pres. Baldwin Lumber Co., Jacksonville, Fla., 1919-22; asst. vice pres., Barnett Nat. Bank, Jacksonville, 1922-29; partner firm of Vanderholf & Robinson, mems. of N.Y. Curb Exchange, N.Y City, 1929-32; mgr. Jacksonville office of Merrill, Lynch, Pierce, Fenner & Bean, 1932-42, 1944-45; asst. vice pres., Atlantic Nat. Bank since 1945. Enlisted U.S. M.C., 1917; service in France; disch. as sergt., 1920; commd. 1st lt., 1942; returned to inactive service as capt., 1944. County chmn., 6th, 7th, and 8th War Loan Drives; treas. local U.S.O., 1942; treas. Greek Relief, 1942. Recipient Purple Heart, World War I. Mem. Am. Legion (mem. since inception; treas. 1926-27), Am. Cancer Soc. (local treas., 1946-49), Fla. C. of C., Children's Home Soc. of Fla. (state dir., 1935-50), Jacksonville Jr. C. of C. (charter mem., treas., 1925-29), Jacksonville C. of C. (gov., 1941-42, treas., 1942), Gen. Soc. Mayflower Descendants (life mem.), S.A.R. Episcopalian. Mason; mem. since 1921; R.A.M. (life mem., treas. 1928-29) K.T. (life mem., treas., 1928-29); 32° (life mem., Knight Comdr. of Court of Honour, 1947); Royal Order Jesters (dir., 1940, 41, 42); Royal Select and Super Excellent Master (1943); Hon. mem. of De Molay (1950); Shrine (treas., 1928-29, potentate, 1938, Imperial rep. to Imperial Council, 1938-42, mem. Imperial Divan of Imperial Council, 1942, deputy Imperial Potentate of Imperial Council, 1950-51; chmn. Shrine Room Com., The George Washington Nat. Masonic Memorial Bldg., 1946; mem. bd. trustees, Shriners' Hosps. for Crippled Children, 1949). Mem. Y.M.C.A. (dir., 1944-45, advisory com., 1945-46). Clubs: Rotary (past dir., Jacksonville), Timuquana Country, Florida Yacht (Jacksonville, Fla.). Home: 1846 Montgomery Pl., Jacksonville 5. Office: 121 Forsyth St., Jacksonville 2, Fla. Died May 29, 1951.

BALDWIN, William Alpheus, sch. adminstr.; b. Volney, N.Y., Aug. 16, 1859; s. Reuben C. and Josephine R. B.; grad. Oswebo (N.Y.) Normal Sch., 1884; student Cornell U., U. Chgo.; B.S., Harvard, 1897; m. Jennie M. Skinner, 1893. Prin. Hyannis (Mass.) Normal Sch., 1897—. Address: Hyannis, Mass. Deceased.

BALK, Robert, geologist; b. Reval, Estonia, May 31, 1899; s. Hugo and Mary (Koch) B.; ed. Gymnasium, Düsseldorf, Germany; Ph.D., U. Greifswald, Göttingen, Breslau, Ger., 1924. Came to U.S., 1924, naturalized citizen. Independent field work since 1923 in Italy, Germany, Norway, U.S.A.; geologist, N.Y. State Mus., 1925-26, Minn. Geol. Survey, 1930, U.S. Geol. Survey, 1938-45; instr. Hunter Coll., 1925-28, asso. prof., 1928-35; vis. prof., Stanford U., 1934; asso. prof., Mt. Holyoke Coll., 1935-37, head dept. geol. and geography since 1935, prof. 1937-47, prof. geology U. Chgo., 1947-52; Prin. geologist N.M. Bur. Mines and Mineral Resources, 1952—. Fellow Geological Society America, Society Rheology, Am. Geophys. Union, Norsk Geol. Forening; mem. Phi Beta Kappa, Sigma Xi. Author: Structural Behavior of Igneous Rocks, 1937. Editor, Geology of North America, 1936-39. Office: N.M. Bureau of Mines, Socorro, N.M. Died Feb. 19, 1955.

BALL, George Alexander, glass mfr.; b. Greene, O., Nov. 5, 1862; s. Lucius Stiles and Maria P. (Bingham) B.; ed. pub. schs. and Canandaigua (N. Y.) Acad.; hon. LL.D. Ind. U.; m. Frances Emily Woodworth, Oct. 24, 1893; 1 dau., Elisabeth W. Began mfr. of glass in partnership with four brothers at Buffalo, N.Y., 1888; moved to Muncie, Ind., same yr.; chmn. bd. Ball Bros. Co.; chmn. Mchts. Nat. Bank; dir. Mchts. Trust Co.; mem. Nat. Trust (London). Mem. Rep. Nat. Com., 1932-37. Trustee Riley Meml. Children's Hosp.; pres. Ball Meml. Hosp., Ball Brothers Found., George and Frances Ball Found. Mason (33°). Presbyn. Club: Columbia (Indianapolis). Home: Minnetrista Blvd., Muncie, Ind. Died Oct. 22, 1955.

BALL, Gordon Reginald, banker; b. Toronto, Ont., Can., Aug. 17, 1897; s. William John and Hannah (King) B.; student pub. schs. Toronto; D.C.L., Bishop's U., 1955; LL.D., U. Montreal, 1956; m. Helen Horlick St. John, Aug. 12, 1929; children—Sheila St. John, Gordon Reginald. Joined Mchts. Bank of Can. (merged with Bank of Montreal, 1922), 1914, trans. to N.Y.C. agy., 1924, mgr. securities dept., 1929-34, 3d agt., 1934-38, 2d agt., 1938-45, 1st agt., 1945, gen. mgr., Montreal, 1947, v.p., gen. mgr., dir., mem. exec. com., 1951, pres., chief exec. officer, Bank of London and Montreal Ltd., 1952; Chmn. Royal-Liverpool Ins. Group (Canadian sect.), v.p., dir. Royal Trust Co.; dir. Internat. Nickel Co. of Can., Ltd., Ogilvie Flour Mills Company, Ltd., Sun Life Assurance Co. of Canada, C.P. Ry., Bowater Power Co., Ltd., Steel Co. of Canada, Ltd. Mem. Canadian council of Nat. Indsl. Conf. Bd.; mem. Royal-Liverpool Insurance Group; mem. Dollar-Sterling Trade Council; gov. Welfare Fedn. Montreal; gov., mem. exec. com. Royal Victoria Hosp.; councillor Montreal Mus. Fine Arts; advisory council school commerce McGill U.; dir. Montreal Symphony Orchestra; Canadian Mental Health Assn. Hon. v.p. Boy Scouts Montreal. Served with C.E.F., 1915-19. Recipient Mil. Medal (Can.). Clubs: Toronto; Gatineau Fish and Game (Point Comfort, Que.); Mount Royal, St. James's, St. Denis, Royal Golf, Mount Bruno Country (Montreal, Que.); Seigniory (Montebello, Que.); Forest and Stream; Lavalsur-du-Lac Golf. Home: 1 Braeside Pl., Westmount. Office: 119 St. James St. W., Montreal, Que., Can. Died Feb. 28, 1959.

BALL, John Rice, geology and paleontology; b. Fremont, O., June 26, 1881; s. Oscar and Mary Ellen (Amsden) B.; prep. edn., Coll. of Puget Sound, Tacoma, Wash.; B.A., Northwestern U., 1913, M.A., 1917; B.D., Garrett Bibl. Inst., 1913; Ph.D., U. of Chicago, 1927; m. Cora Lena Goodman, Dec. 21, 1905; children—Clayton Garrett, Dorothy Margaret. With Northwestern University since 1916, asso. prof. geology and paleontology, 1928-45, prof. since 1945; with Univ. of Kansas City, 1946-51, U. of N.C. since 1951. Served on Illinois State Geological Survey, 1927, 1944; named several new fossils in the Silurian formations of Southeastern Missouri; served on North Dakota Geological Survey, summer, 1946; visiting and regular prof. geology and geography, U. of Kansas City, since June 1946. Fellow Geological Soc. America, A.A.A.S., Am. Paleontol. Soc.; mem. Am. Assn. Petroleum Geologists, Soc. of Economic Paleontologists and Mineralogists, Ill. Acad. Science, Chicago Acad. Science, Am. Assn. Museums, Sigma Xi. Methodist. Mason. Contbr. articles and brochures on researches. Address: University of Kansas City, Kansas City 4, Mo. Died Mar. 1, 1953.

BALL, Max W(aite), geologist; b. Henry Co., Ill., Sept. 9, 1885; s. Lewis Henry and Jennie Ann (Hoffstatter) B.; E.M., Colo. Sch. of Mines, 1906; LL.M., Nat. U., Washington, 1914; m. Amalia Maeder, Aug. 18, 1915; children—Douglas Schelling, Jean Katherine (Mrs. I. R. Kosloff). With U.S. Geol. Survey, 1906-16, chmn. oil bd., 1910-16; mining engr., law officer, U.S. Bur. of Mines, 1916-17; chief geologist, Royal Dutch Shell oil interests, Rocky Mountain region, 1917-18, gen. mgr., 1918-21; pres. Western Pipe Line Co., 1921-27, Marine Oil Co. and asso. cos., 1922-28, Argo Oil Co., 1925-28; consulting practice 1928-46; pres. Abasand Oils Ltd., 1930-43, Royal Royalties Ltd., Denver, 1931-44; spec. asst. to dep. petroleum adminstr., Petroleum Adminstrn. for War, 1944-46; dir. oil and gas div., Dept. Interior, 1946-48, oil and gas cons., 1948—, cons. to govt. Israel, drafting petroleum laws, 1950-53, govt. Turkey, 1953-54. Trustee Colo. Sch. of Mines, 1923-31. Recipient Medal of Merit for distinguished achievement Colo. Sch. of Mines, 1947; Gold Medal for distinguished service Dept. of Interior, 1948; Gold Medal for contbns. to Am. way of life, Freedom Founds. Inc., 1950. Fellow Am. Geog. Soc., Geol. Soc. of Am.; mem. Acad. of Polit. Sci., Am. Inst. Mining and Metall. Engrs. (vice chmn. Colo. chpt. 1923, 1926), Am. Assn. Petroleum Geologists (v.p. 1922-23; pres. 1923-24), Am. Petroleum Inst., Canadian Inst. Mining and Metallurgy (chmn. No. Alberta sect. 1942-43), Sigma Gamma Epsilon, Tau Beta Pi. Conglist. Club: Cosmos. Author: This Fascinating Oil Business; also bulls., articles on geology, econs., internat. relationships, etc. Home: 4705 Berkleley Terrace, Washington 7. Office: 1025 Vermont Av., Washington 5. Died Aug. 28, 1954.

BALL, Otho Fisher, publisher; b. Waterloo, Ia., June 20, 1875; s. Dr. James Moores and Martha G. (Glover) B.; ed. Waterloo, Ia., 1880-92, and spl. science course, U. of Wis., 1892-93; M.D., St. Louis Coll. Physicians and Surgeons, 1897, and Post-Grad. Med. Sch., New York, 1898; m. Leonora M., (d. Col. J. J. Clague, U.S. Army), Feb. 19, 1901, (now dec.); children—Elizabeth (Mrs. Gerald Wellesley), Peter. Publisher The Modern Hospital, The Nation's Schools, College and University Business, The Hospital Purchasing File, El Libro del Hospital Moderno. Home: 1325 Astor St. Office: 919 North Michigan Av., Chgo. Died July 19, 1953; buried Lakewood Cemetery, Mpls.

BALLANTINE, Henry Winthrop, prof. law.; b. Oberlin, O., Oct. 12, 1880; s. William Gay and Emma Frances (Atwood) B.; A.B., Harvard, 1900; LL.B., 1904; LL.D., Marietta, 1940; m. Grace Wetherell, July 22, 1906; 1 dau., Betty Winthrop. Admitted to Calif. bar, 1904; lecturer on law, U. of Calif., 1905-09; asst. prof. law, Hastings Coll. of Law, San Francisco, 1905-09; dean Law Sch. of U. of Mont., 1911-13; prof. of law, Law Sch. U. of Wis., 1913-16; dean, Coll. of Law Univ. of Ill., 1916-20; prof. law, U. of Minn., 1920-24; prof. law, U. of Calif. since 1924. Draftsman, com. on revision corp. laws, Calif. State Bar. Member of Delta Kappa Upsilon. Author: Corporations, 1946; Manual of Corporation Law and Practice, 1930; Problems in Law, with Solutions, 2d edit., 1937, 3d edit., 1948. Co-author: California Corporation Laws, 2d edit., 1938, 3d edit., 1949; Cases and Materials on Corporations, 1939. Contbr. on law topics. Club: Faculty. Home: 816 Oxford St., Berkeley 7, Cal. Died Dec. 4, 1951.

BALLARD, Ernest Schwefel, lawyer; b. Philadelphia, Pa., Aug. 29, 1885; s. Ellis Ames and Nina (Schwefel) B.; prep. edn. William Penn Charter Sch., 1894-1903; A.B., Yale, 1907; LL.B., U. of Pa., 1910; m. Elisabeth Sloan Duryee, Aug. 27, 1913; children—Elisabeth Sloan (Mrs. Frank F. Fowle, Jr.), Susan Rankin (Mrs. Stewart Boal), Ellis Ames, Joseph Duryee, Mary (Mrs. John H. Hobart), Ernest Schwefel, Jr., Samuel Sloan. Began practice as asst. to gen. solicitor N.Y. Central Lines, N.Y. City, 1910, commerce counsel at Chicago, 1915-17, asst. gen. solicitor at Chicago, 1917-19; partner Pope & Ballard and predecessor firms since 1919. Commissioned 1st lt. February 5, 1918; with A.E.F. in France, 1918-19; appointed officer General Staff A.E.F., Feb. 17, 1919; promoted captain, Feb. 19, 1919; honorably discharged, May 19, 1919. Knight Order of Black Star (France), 1919. Pres. Winnetka Bd. of Edn., 1923-30. Pres. Chicago Br. English-Speaking Union, 1930-32. Senior Warden Christ Church, Winnetka, Ill.; trustee Glenwood Manual Training Sch. Mem. Ill. and Chicago bar assns., Assn. I.C.C. Practitioners, Psi Upsilon, Order of Coif. Ind. Republican. Episcopalian. Clubs: Chicago, Indian Hill, Commercial, Commonwealth Church (Chicago); Century (N.Y.). Home: 6 Kent Road, Hubbard Woods, Ill. Office: 33 N. La Salle St., Chgo. Died Mar. 18, 1952.

BALLARD, Nathaniel Harrison, state supt. schs.; b. Pumpkin Town Plantation, Campbell County, Ga., Dec. 22, 1866; B.E., U. Ga., 1886; s. Levi and Sarah Smith (Harrison) B.; m. Frieda Geissler, Apr. 29, 1897. Pres. Lineville (Ala.) Coll., 1887; chemist, Woodstock Iron Co., Anniston, Ala., 1888-93; Prin., Meson Acad., Lexington, Ga., 1893-96; supt. schs., Greensboro, 1896-1900, Brunswick and Glynn counties, Ga., 1900-19; state supt. schs., Ga., 1922—. Democrat. Baptist. Mason (33°, Grand Master Ga. F. and A.M., 1914-16). Home: 856 Piedmont Av. Address: Capitol, Atlanta. Deceased.

BALLARD, W(illiam) C(yrus), Jr., educator, engr.; b. Balt., Sept. 1, 1888; s. William C. and Roberta (Franklin) B.; M.E., Cornell, 1910; m. Ruth Murphy, Dec. 22, 1910; children—Grace (Mrs. E. H. Lotspeich), Ruth (Mrs. Robert O. Klausmeyer), Evelyn (Mrs. H. O. Dunn). Mem. faculty Cornell, 1910—, prof. elec. engring., 1920—; cons. engr., 1926—. Fellow Am. Inst. E.E.; mem. Inst. Radio Engrs., Sigma Xi, Eta Kappa Nu, Phi Kappa Phi. Presbyn. (organist 1st Ch., Ithaca, 1918-38). Author: Elements of Radio Telephony, 1922. Contbr. articles engring. jours. Home: 204 Kline Woods Rd., Ithaca. Died June 11, 1953.

BALLENGER, William Sylvester, business exec.; b. Cambridge City, Ind. Dec. 5, 1866; s. William Sylvester and Frances Sina (Semans) B.; grad. Cambridge City High Sch., Chaffee's Bus. Inst., Oswego, N.Y.; m. Minnie Irene Wheeler, Dec. 16, 1891; children—Frances Louise (Mrs. Elmer J. Kinsinger), William Sylvester. Sec., treas. The Flint Wagon Works (Mich.), 1888-1910; treas. Chevrolet Motor Co., Flint, 1911-25; dir. Indsl. Raymon Corp., Cleve., 1930—; dir. chmn. bd. Citizens Comml. & Savings Bank, Flint. Republican. Presbyn. Mason (33°), Elk. Home: 914 Church St. Office: P.O. Box 358, Flint, Mich. Died Feb. 28, 1951; buried Glenwood Cemetery.

BALLIN, Hugo (băl'lin), artist; b. New York; s. Julius and Tillie (Rothschild) B.; student Art Students' League, New York, and in Rome and Florence; m. Mabel Croft, 1909. Awarded scholarship Art Students' League; Shaw Prize Fund, 1905; Thomas B. Clarke prize, 1906 and 1940; Architectural League medal, 1906 and 1907; medal, Buenos Aires International Exposition, Hallgarten prize, 1907; Isidor Gold medal, 1907; Anthony Dyer prize; First Prize, City of Los Angeles Art Week, 1947; Gardena Purchase Prize, 1948; Rhode Island Work reproduced in Critic, Century, Kunst and Künstlewerk (Vienna), International Studio, etc. Specialty, mural decorations. Works: executive chamber, Madison, Wis.; room in home of Oliver Gould Jennings, N.Y.C., E. D. Brandegee of Boston, and Milton E. Getz; decoration, History of the Jews, B'nai B'rith Temple, Los Angeles; decorative pictures in many pvt. collections; also represented in Nat. Museum, Washington, D.C.; Montclair Museum, N.J.; Ann Mary Mem., R.I.; murals in Edison Bldg., New County Hosp., Title Ins. & Trust Bldg., Guarantee Bldg., Robinson Restaurant, New Times Bldg. (Los Angeles), Carew Mem. Chapel (San Francisco), First Nat. Bank (La Jolla, Cal.); murals and ceiling, Griffith Obs., Hollywood; The Winds, 2 murals Golden Gate Internat. Expn., 1939; 2 murals Burbank City Hall, 1942; Mural in Administration Bldg., Burbank, Cal., 1949. N.A., 1940; mem. Nat. Inst. Arts and Letters. Produced and mounted over 100 feature motion pictures, including East Lynne, Pagan Love, Baby Mine, The Journey's End, Jane Eyre, Vanity Fair, Married People. Author: Stigma; The Woman at the Door; The Broken Toy; Dolce far Niente; Mr. Claus Goes Shopping; And They Hang Pictures. Awarded Certificate of Honor, San Diego Chapter Am. Inst. Architects. Home: 567 Almoloya Dr., Pacific Palisades, Cal. Died Dec. 7, 1956.

BALLOU, Frank Washington (băl-loo'), ret. supt. schs.; b. Fort Jackson, N.Y., Feb. 22, 1879; s. Hiram and Jennie E. (Foster) B.; grad. State Normal Tng. Sch., Potsdam, N.Y., 1902; B.S., Tchrs. Coll. (Columbia), 1904; M.A., U. Cin., 1908; Ph.D., Harvard, 1914; m. Catharine L. Knapp, Apr. 6, 1912 (died Nov. 1945); children—Mrs. Elizabeth Leedy, Robert; m. 2d, Mrs. Adeline J. Hamilton, Nov. 6, 1946. Prin. tech. sch. U. Cin., 1904-07, asst. prof.

edn. Coll. for Tchrs., 1907-10; dir. Dept. Edn., Investigation and Measurement, Boston, 1914-17 asst. supt. schs., Boston, 1917-20, supt. schools, Washington, 1920-43, retired, 1943—. Mem. N.E.A. (pres. Am. Assn. Sch. Adminstrs. 1925-26), Nat. Soc. Study Edn., Nat. Assn. Dirs. Ednl. Research, Commn. on Licensure by Law, Fed. Schoolmen's Club, Kappa Delta Pi, Phi Delta Kappa. Republican. Universalist (ch. moderator 1930-34, ch. trustee; nat. trustee 1929-37). Clubs: Torch, Rotary. Author: High School Organization, 1913; Harvard-Newton Scales for the Measurement of English Composition, 1915; The Appointment of Teachers in Cities, 1915. Co-author: Practical Exercieses in Mental Arithmetic, 1920. Home: 3130 Wisconsin Av. N.W., Washington 16. Died Feb. 2, 1955; buried Cedar Hill Cemetery, Washington.

BALLOU, Levi Herbert, textile exec.; b. Mar. 1, 1883; widower. With Kendall Co., Boston, 1917—, plant supt. charge Walpole, Mass., factory; now chmn. finance com. Home: Hotel Puritan, 390 Commonwealth Av., Boston. Office: United Shoe Machinery Bldg., 140 Federal St., Boston. Died Jan. 6, 1958.

BALMER, Edwin (bäl' mẽr), author, editor; b. Chgo., July 26, 1883; s. Thomas and Helen Clark (Pratt) B.; A.B., Northwestern U., 1902; A.M., Harvard, 1903; m. Katharine MacHarg, June 10, 1909 (dec. Nov. 1925); children—Caroline (Mrs. Joseph S. Thomas), Thomas, Katharine Ruth (Mrs. Wm. S. McChesney); m. 2d, Grace A. Kee, Feb. 5, 1927. Reporter Chgo. Tribune, 1903; asso. Graham Taylor in publ. The Commons, 1904-05 when it merged with Charities, N.Y.C.; editor Red Book mag., 1927-49, asso. pub., 1949-53, ret.; leader novel workshop Writer's Conf., U. Colo., 1955. Dir. Tarrytown (N. Y.) Hosp. Assn.; mem. adv. com. Christian Herald book club and Family Bookshelf. Mem. Soc. Midland Authors (pres. 1918-19, 24-25), Mag. Pub. Assn. (chmn. editorial com. 1949-53), Phi Beta Kappa, Phi Kappa Psi. Clubs: University (Chgo.); Union League, Dutch Treat, Harvard (N.Y.C.); P.E.N. Author: Waylaid by Wireless, 1909; The Science of Advertising, 1910; A Wild Goose Chase, 1915; Ruth of the U.S.A., 1919; Resurrection Rock, 1920; The Breath of Scandal, 1921; Fidelia, 1924; That Royle Girl, 1925; Flying Death, 1927; Dangerous Business, 1927; Dragons Drive You, 1934; The Torn Letter, 1941; In His Hands, 1954; The Candle of the Wicked, 1956; With All the World Away, 1958; (with William MacHarg); The Achievements of Luther Trant, 1910, The Surakarta, 1913, The Blind Man's Eyes, 1916, The Indian Drum, 1917; (with Philip Wylie); Five Fatal Words, 1932, When Worlds Collide, 1933, The Golden Hoard, 1935, After Worlds Collide, 1935; The Shield of Silence, 1936. Author many short stories, some produced as plays, motion pictures, on television, also pub. in Europe in fgn. langs. Formerly editorial adviser, contbr. Hampton's Mag., contbr. others. Home: Sunnyside Lane, Irvington-on-Hudson, N.Y. Died Mar. 21, 1959.

BALMER, Frank Everett, agrl. educator and investment counselor; b. Woodston, Kan., Oct. 29, 1883; s. Elmer Denizen and Mary (Jencks) B.; B.S. in agr., Kansas State College 1905, also post grad. work, 1909; post grad. work Kansas University, June-August, 1909, U. Minn., 1924-26; m. Bertha Mabel Eastman, August 25, 1910 (she died July 18, 1942). Rural school teacher Rooks County, Kansas, 1900-01 and 1907-08; farm mgr., 1906-08; dir. agrl. dept., Lewiston, Minn., 1909-11; prin. La Crosse County Sch. of Agr. and Domestic Sci., 1911-13; dist. supervisor county agrl. agts., West Central Minn., U. Minn., June 1913-Sept. 1914; asst. state leader county agt. work, U. Minn. Farm (St. Paul), Sept. 1914-July 1915; state county agt. leader, 1915-30; dir. agrl. extension, State Coll. of Wash. (Pullman), 1930-42; field representative Investors Syndicate and Investors Mutual Inc., Investors Stock Fund, Inc., Investors Selective Fund, Inc., Mpls., since 1942; conducted research in Minnesota relative cost of agricultural extension work also alfalfa prodn. possibilities. Awarded certificate of recognition for outstanding extension work, October, 1942. Member Agr. Hist. Soc. Am. Country Life Assn., Abraham Lincoln Assn., Acacia, Alpha Zeta, Epislon Sigma Phi, Mu Beta Beta. Presbyn. Mason. Clubs: Nat. Travel, Kiwanis, Pullman Toastmasters (Pullman). Collector of Lincolniana and Jeffersonia. Writer numerous articles on agr. and investment analysis. Home: Elmburst Apts. C. Pullman, Wash. Died July 23, 1954; buried Riverside Park Cemetery, Spokane, Wash.

BALMER, Thomas, ry. official, lawyer; b. Danville, Ill., July 29, 1888; s. Adam and Mary Ann (Williams) B.; student U. of Wash. Law Sch., 1908-09; hon. LL.M., Gonzaga U., Spokane, Wash., 1914; m. Lidie Virginia Herren, Sept. 6, 1911; children—Carolyn, Jeanne. Stenographer G.N. Ry., Seattle, 1907-09; admitted to Washington bar, 1909, Idaho bar, 1912, Minnesota bar, 1926; assistant attorney G.N. Ry., Spokane, 1912-18, atty. for Ida. and Eastern Wash., 1918-19, Ore. and Western Wash., 1919-26, asst. gen. counsel, St. Paul, Minn., 1926-29, Western counsel, Seattle, 1929-37, v.p. and Western counsel 1937-58; pres., Pacific Coast Railroad 1949-58; dir., mem. exec. com. National Bank of Commerce, Seattle, Pacific American Fisheries, Bellingham; trustee Washington Mutual Savings Bank, Seattle; dir. chmn. exec. com. Crow's Nest Pass Coal Co. Fernie, B.C.; dir. Crow's Nest Pass Oil & Gas Co., Ltd., Crow's Nest Pass Light & Power Co., Ltd., Morrissey, Fernie & Michel Ry. Co., Queen City Broadcasting Co. Pres. Bd. of Regents, U. Wash., 1938-40, 45-46, 57-58. Mem. Am., Wash., Seattle bar assns. Clubs: University, Rainier, Seattle Golf & Country. Home: 3001 W. Laurelhurst Dr., Seattle 5. Office: White-Henry-Stuart Bldg., Seattle 1, Wash. Died Aug. 1, 1959.

BALTZELL, Robert C. (bält' zẽl), judge; b. Lawrence County, Ill., Aug. 15, 1879; s. Henry H. and Margaret C. (Roderick) B.; student Northern Ill. Normal Coll., Dixon, Ill., 1899, Marion (Ind.) Normal Sch., 1903-04; LL.B., Marion Law Sch., 1904; m. Vienna N. Carlton, Mar. 28, 1904 (dec.); 1 son, Robert Carlton (dec.). Teacher public schools in Ill , 1898-1903; admitted to Ind. bar, 1904, and began practice with brother, Charles O., at Princeton; elected judge of Gibson Circuit Court, Princeton, Nov. 1920, served until Jan. 19, 1925; U.S. district judge, by apptmt. of President Coolidge, since Jan. 19, 1925. Served as maj. inf., Dec. 26, 1917-May 10, 1919, World War. Mem. Ind. State Bar Assn., Am. Bar Assn. Mem. Christian (Disciples) Ch. Mason. Club: Columbia (Indianapolis). Home: 5637 Central Av. Address: Federal Bldg., Indianapolis. Died Oct. 18, 1950.

BALZ, Albert George Adam (bawlts), prof. philosophy; b. Charlottesville, Va., Jan. 3, 1887; s. Henry Justus and Mary (Hartman) B.; A.B., U. of Va., 1908, A.M., 1909; fellow in philosophy, Columbia, 1912-13, Ph.D., 1916; m. Dorothy Dean, June 6, 1917; children—Patricia Goodwin, Albert Dean (dec.), Albert George Adam. Asst. prof. philosophy, U. of Va., 1913-16, asso. prof., 1916-20, prof., since 1920; Corcoran prof. philos. since 1938. Chmn. Charlottesville Sch. Bd., 1939-45. Chmn. So. Humanities Conf., 1952—. Served as 2d lt. inf., U.S. Army, 1918. Recipient Butler Medal in Silver, Colo. U., 1953. Mem. Am. Psychol. Assn., Am. Philosophical Association (president Eastern division 1955), Metaphys. Soc. Am., So. Society for Philosophy of Religion, So. Soc. Philos. and Psychology, Societas Spinozana, Phi Beta Kappa, Theta Delta Chi. Democrat. Clubs: Colonnade, Lotos, Farmington. Author: Cartesian Studies, 1951; Descartes and the Modern Mind, 1952. Contbr. to Jour. Philosophy, Philos. Review, Studies in the History of Ideas, etc. Home: 2011 Lewis Mountain Rd., Charlottesville, Va. Died Oct. 1, 1957.

BAMBERGER, Ernest (băm'bẽr-gẽr), mining; b. Salt Lake City, Utah, Aug. 11, 1877; A.B., Williams Coll., 1898; E.M., Columbia, 1900; LL.D., University of Utah. Assistant general manager of the Daly West Mining Co., 1902-04 gen. mgr., 1904-11; pres. and gen. mgr. Keystone Mining Co. 1920-45, Ontario Silver Mining Co., 1907-24, Utah mem. Rep. Nat. Com., 1920-38 and 1932-36; member board directors Asso. Oil Co. of Cal., 1923-33, Bank of Utah. Republican nominee for United States Senator, 1922, 28. Chmn. Draft Bd., Salt Lake City, 1917-18; head of chem. sect. materials dept. Fgn. and U.S. Air Craft Production, and chief materials dept., 1918. Regent U. of Utah, 1912-24. Mem. Agrl. Loan Com. for Utah, War Finance Corps., 1921. Mem. Chi Psi. Clubs: Flat Rock, Alta. Home: 524 E. South Temple St. Office: 163 S. Main St., Salt Lake City. Died Jan. 11, 1958.

BANCROFT, Charles Grey, lawyer, ofcl.; b. Lancaster, Mass., Dec. 3, 1867; s. Andrew J. and Mary A. (Clough) B.; Phillips Exeter Acad.; LL.B., Boston U., 1889; m. Blanche M. Hight, Dec. 10, 1890; children—Stowell H., Winthrop. Practiced at Clinton, Mass., 1889-1900, Boston, 1900—; for many yrs. counsel for Arkwright Club; receiver Jewelers Nat. Bank, 1908-12; pres. Lincoln Trust Co. until 1914, when it was merged into the Internat. Trust Co., pres. until merger with First Nat. Bank; former pres., dir. Central Aguirre Sugar Co., Machete Sugar Co., Santa Isabel Sugar Co., Ponce & Guayama R.R. Co., Central Aguirre Associates; pres. Porto Rico Sales Corp.; retired v.p., mem. exec. com. United Shoe Machinery Corp.; dir. Thomson Electric Welding Co., Am. Surety Co., Dorchester Mutual Fire Ins. Co., Liberty Mut. Ins. Co., Economic Machinery Co. Trustee permanent funds Am. Humane Edn. Soc.; dir. mem. exec. com. and trustee permanent funds Mass. Soc. Prevention of Cruelty to Animals. Republican. Unitarian. Mason, Odd Fellow. Club: Algonquin. Home: Framingham Center, Mass. Died Jan. 1, 1955; buried Framingham Center.

BANCROFT, Francis Sydney, business exec.; b. Knowlton, Que., Can., June 8, 1881; s. Charles and Eunice (Foster) B.; student Knowlton Acad., St. John's Sch., Montreal, Trinity Sch., N.Y.; m. Beatrice Fairfax Jordan, Nov. 16, 1904; children—Francis Sydney, Harding Foster, Costance Jordan (Mrs. William M. Doolittle). With Excelsior Savs. Bank, N.Y.C., 1945—, v.p., 1933-45, active v.p., 1945-49, pres., 1949-56, chmn. bd., 1956—, trustee, 1931—; v.p., dir. Pease & Elliman, Inc., 1952—; pres. 103 E. 75th St. Apts., Inc., N.Y.C., 1925—; sec. dir. Park Av. and 77th St. Corp., N.Y.C.; treas., dir. 535 Park Av. Corp.; dir. 928 Park Av. Apts., Inc., N.Y.C., 1021 Park Av. Corp; adv. bd. Mfrs. Trust Co., N.Y.C. Mem. Real Estate Bd., N.Y., Pilgrims Soc. Republican. Episcopalian. Clubs: Church, Murray Bay (Can.) Golf; Eternity Fish and Game; Gavelle Fishing. Home: 103 E. 75th St., N.Y.C. 21; also Murray Bay, Que., Can. Office: 221 W. 57th St., N.Y.C. 19. Died Oct. 21, 1957; buried Knowlton, P.Q., Can.

BANCROFT, Levi Horace, lawyer, judge, mayor; b. Bear Valley, Wis., Dec. 26, 1861; s. George I. and Helen M. (Randolph) B.; LL.B., U. Wis., 1884; m. Myrtle DeLap, June 11, 1890; children—Blaine D., Carolyn (Mrs. R. A. Heilman). Admitted to Wis. bar, 1885, began practice at Richland Center; dist. atty. Richland County, 1886-88; county judge Richland County, 1898-1902, 37—; 1st asst. atty. gen. Wis., 1902-04, atty. gen., 1910-12; judge Circuit Ct., 5th Wis. Circuit, 1920-22; U.S. dist. atty. Eastern Dist. Wis., 1924-32; resumed practice of law; mayor of Richland Center. Mem. Wis. Assembly, 1907-09, speaker, 1909. Judge adv. Wis. N.G., 1907-13. Republican. Mason. Clubs: Milwaukee, Madison. Home: Richland Center, Wis. Died Sept. 5, 1918; buried Richland Center.

BANCROFT, Wilder Dwight, chemist; b. Middletown, R.I., Oct. 1, 1867; s. John Chandler and Louisa Mills (Denny) B.; A.B., Harvard, 1888; Ph.D., U. Leipzig, 1892; post-grad. Harvard, 1888-89, Strassburg, 1889-90, Berlin and Amsterdam, 1892-93; D.Sc. (hon.), Lafayette, 1919, Cambridge, 1923; LL.D., U. So. Cal. 1930; m. Katharine Meech Bott, June 19, 1895; children—Mary Warner, Hester, John Chandler, George, Jean Gordon. Asst. prof. phys. chemistry Cornell U., 1895-1903, prof., 1903-37, emeritus. Editor Jour. Phys. Chemistry, 1896-1932; asso. editor Jour. Franklin Inst., 1913—; chmn. div. chemistry NRC, 1919-20; adv. com. C.W.S. Tallman prof. Bowdoin Coll., 1937. Lt. col. C.W.S., 1918-19. Bd. visitors, Bur. Standards, 1922-25; v.p. Internat. Union Chemistry, 1922-25. Fellow Am. Acad. Arts and Scis. hon. mem. Am. Electro-chem. Soc. (pres. 1905, 1919), Am. Electroplaters Soc., English French, Polish chem. socs.; mem. Am. Chem. Soc. (pres. 1910), Am. Phys. Soc., Nat. Acad. Sci., Am. Philos. Soc. Author: The Phase Rule, 1897 Appled Colloid Chemistry, 1932; also numerous articles sci. jours. Address: 7 East Av., Ithaca N.Y. Died Feb. 7, 1953.

BANDARANAIKE, Solomon West Ridgeway Dias, prime minister Ceylon; b. Colombo, Celyon, Jan. 8, 1899; s. Sir Solomon Dias Bandaranaike and Daisy Obesekera; student St. Thomas Coll., Mt. Lavinia, Ceylon, 1914-18; B.A. (hon.), Oxford; m. Sirimawo Ratwatte, Oct. 4, 1940. Mem. State Council, 1931-37; minister local adminstrn., 1937-47; minister health and local govt., leader Ho. of Reps., 1947-52; leader of opposition, 1952-56; prime minister of Ceylon, 1956—. Clubs: Orient (Colombo); Tennis (Bandarawela). Home: 65 Rosmead Pl., Colombo 7, Ceylon. Died Sept. 25, 1959.

BANDLER, Clarence G., surgeon, b. Owego, N.Y., Nov. 6, 1880; s. William and Eva (Fox) B.; A.B., Columbia, 1901, M.D., 1904; m. Miriam R. Zack, Aug. 17, 1951. Intern Bellevue Hosp., N.Y.C., 1904, adjunct attending urologist, chief of clinic, dept. urology, 1906-12; inst. asso. in urology, med. dept. Columbia, 1906-25; prof. urology N.Y. Post-Grad. Med. Sch. and Hosp. of Columbia U., 1909—; attending urologist Post-Grad. Hosp., 1934—, dir. dept. urology; cons. surgeon Home for Aged and Infirm, Yonkers, N.Y., 1908—; cons. urologist St. Francis Hosp., Port Jervis, N.Y., St. Vincent's Hosp., S.I., N.Y., U. Hosp., N.Y. U. Bellevue Med. Center, Bd. dirs. Asso. Hosp. Service. Served as capt., Med. Officers Res. Corps, World War I; sec. med. adv. bd. for draft registrants; with procurement and assignment com. Med. Adv. for Selective Service, World War II; with emergency med. service Office Civilian Def. Recipient Certificate, Medal of Merit, World War II. Diplomate Am. Bd. Urology (v.p.). Fellow A.C.S.; mem. Associete 'Internationale d'Urologie, N.Y. State, N.Y. County med. socs. Clubs: Columbia University (N.Y.C.); Fairview Country, (Elmsford, N.Y.). Author numerous med. articles, including Tumors of the Urogenital Tract in the Young, Nephroptosis and Nephropexy, Urinary Obstruction. Home: 440 Park Av., N.Y.C. 22. Office: 77 Park Av., N.Y.C. 16. Died Nov. 15, 1957.

BANE, Juliet Lita, educator; b. nr. Dana, Ill., Sept. 15, 1887; d. Milton M. and Florence (Clegg) Bane; B.S., U. Ill., 1912; A.M., U. Chgo., 1919; grad. study U. Chgo. and Columbia, 1925-26; D.Sc., Kan. State Coll., 1938. Asst. prof. home econs. Wash. State Coll., 1914-17; asst. state leader, home economics extension U. Ill., 1918-20, state leader, asst. prof., 1920-23; exec. sec. Am. Home Econs. Assn., Washington, 1923-25; asst. prof. home econs. U. Wis., 1926-28, asso. prof., in charge univ. extension in home econs. and health, 1928-29; asso. editor Ladies' Home Journal, 1929-34; collaborator in Parent Edn., Extension Service, U.S. Dept. Agr., 1935-36; prof. home econs., U. Ill., 1936—, head dept. and vice dir. Home Economics Extension, 1936-48. Mem. Am. Home Econs. Assn. (pres. 1926-28),

Phi Kappa Phi, Gamma Phi Beta, Omicron Nu, Phi Upsilon Omicron, Kappa Delta Pi. Presbyn. Home: 701 Pennsylvania Av., Urbana, Ill. Died Feb. 5, 1957; buried Meml. Park, Pontiac, Ill.

BANFIELD, Thomas Harry, mfg. exec.; b. Portland, Ore., Dec. 20, 1885; s. Jacob and Mary Ann (Mildren) B.; student pub. schs.; m. Margaret Elizabeth Weston, Oct. 18, 1921. Pres., dir. Iron Fireman Mfg. Co., Portland, Ore., Portland Wire & Iron Works, Parker & Banfield, also Parker-Banfield Holding Co.; dir. U.S. Nat. Bank, Oregon War Industries, Inc., Portland Gas & Coke Co. Chmn. Ore. State Hwy. Commn., 1943—. Clubs: Bohemian, Arlington (pres. 1940), Waverley Country, Multnomah Athletic (Portland). Home: 2370 S.W. Park Pl. Office: 4784 S.E. 17th Av., Portland, Ore. Died Aug. 31, 1950.

BANGS, George Archer, ins. exec.; b. LeSueur, Minn., Nov. 8, 1867; s. Alfred Walstein and Sarh D. (Plowman) B.; student Grand Forks (N.D.) High Sch., 1884-86; m. Cyrilla Agnes Behme, Jan. 21, 1922; 1 son, Donald Alfred Walstein (adopted). Admitted to N.D. bar, and practiced at Grand Forks, 1893-1933; city atty. Grand Forks, 1898-1914, states atty. Grand Forks County, 1902-04, spl. asst. atty. gen. of N.D., 1924-29; pres. United Mutual Life Ins. Co., 1933-37; mng. dir. of American United Life Ins. Co., 1937-39, pres. 1939-48, retired 1948. Pres. N D. State Capitol Commn., 1931-33. Served as maj. judge advocate, U.S. Army, 1919. Hon. mem. Butler U. Ins. Soc. Member American Bar Assn., Phi Delta Phi (hon.), Order of the Coif (U. of N.D.). Republican. Episcopalian. K. of P., Elk. Club: Columbia. Home: Marott Hotel. Office: 30 W. Fall Creek Parkway, Indpls. Died June 15, 1955; buried Meml. Park Cemetery, Grand Forks, N.D.

BANISTER, Marion Glass, asst. treas. of U.S.; b. Lynchburg, Va.; d. Maj. Robert Henry and Meta (Sandford) Glass; ed. in public and private schools in Va.; m. Blair Banister; 1 dau., Margaret Sandford. Began career as teacher, later being newspaper and magazine writer, pioneering in special editorial writing; became mem. editorial staff Public Information Service, Dept. of Labor, 1918; asst. to vice chmn. Democratic Nat. Com., and publicity dir. in charge of women's activities, 1921-24; dir. of publicity and advertising for a Washington hotel, 1924-28; publisher and editor The Washingtonian mag., 1929-33; asst. treas. of U.S. since 1933. Democrat. Episcopalian. Club: Woman's National Democratic. Author: (articles) The Tariff as a Tax on Women; Civil Service—Clean or Corrupt; The Lands Ye Possess; Progress of Democracy in America; also series of political articles now in Library of Congress. Home: Stonleigh Court, 1025 Connecticut Av., Washington 6. Office: Treasury Bldg., Washington 25. Died Sept. 30, 1951.

BANKS, A. A., clergyman; b. Webberville, Tex., June 25, 1890; s. David and Eliza B.; B.Th., Guadalupe Coll., 1912; m. Idell Dewey, Dec. 18, 1912; children—A. A., Jr., Patricia. Ordained to ministry Nat. Bapt. Evang. Life and Soul Saving Assembly U.S.A.; organizer People's Missionary Baptist Assn., 1915, People's Missionry Bapt. Ch., Dallas, 1925; founder, pres. Automatic Evang. Corr. Sch. Author: The Negro Woman, 1924; Banksology: Witty Sayings, 1944; Evangelogy and Missionaryology, 1945. Founder, editor, pub. The Peoples Soul Saving Radio Mag. Address: 1020 S. 4th St., Muskogee, Okla.; also 1319 River St., Boise, Ida. Died Feb. 17, 1954.

BANKS, Edgar James, archaeologist; b. Sunderland, Mass., May 23, 1866; s. John Randolph and Julia Maria (Dunklee) B.; student Amherst, 1886-87; A.B., Harvard, 1893, A.M., 1895; Ph.D., U. Breslau, 1897; m. Emma L. Lyford, July 16, 1893; m. 2d, Minja Miksich de Also Lukavecz; children—Edgar de Miksich, Daphne. Am. consul, Bagdad, Turkey, 1897-98; organized, 1899, expedition to excavate Babylonian city of Ur, but Sultan refused permission after 2 years waiting; acting prof. ancient history Robert College, Constantinople, 1902-03; pvt. sec. to Am. minister to Turkey, 1903; excavated Babylonian ruin, Bismya, 1903, for U. Chgo., discovering several thousand inscribed objects from 4500 B.C. to 2800 B.C. and the white statue of King David, a pre-Babylonian king of 4500 B.C. (oldest statue in the world); also much earlier ruins; field dir. of Babylonian expdn. and instr. Turkish and Semitic langs., U. Chgo., 1903-06; prof. Oriental langs. and archaeology Toledo U., 1909; lectr. on Babylonia, Arabia, Turkey, etc., 1906—. Dir. Sacred Films, Inc., 1921-22; pres. Seminole Films Co., Inc. Climbed to summit of Mt. Ararat, 17,212 ft., Aug. 20, 1912 (1st Am.); crossed the Arabian desert by camel, 1912, on an exploring expdn. Author: Babylonische Hymnen der Berliner Sammlung, 1897; Jonah in Fact and Fancy, 1899; Bismya, or The Lost City of Adab, 1912; Bible and the Spade, 1913; Armenian Princess, 1914; Seven Wonders of the Ancinet World, 1917. Also several hundred articles on archaeol. and other subjects. Address: P.O. Box 519, Eustis, Fla. Died May 5, 1945.

BANKS, E(manuel) S(imon) (Cy), financial editor; b. New York, N.Y., Sept. 5, 1900; s. John and Hannah (Cohan) B.; grad., Baltimore (Md.) City Coll., 1917; student, Johns Hopkins Univ., 1920; m. Helen Block, Aug. 23, 1927; children—John Richard, Jill Cele. Reporter, Baltimore American, 1915-22; reporter, Chicago (Ill.) Journal, 1923-25; news picture editor, Curtis-Martin Newspapers, 1925-35; financial writer, Phila. Inquirer, 1943-45, business editor, 1948-50, financial editor, 1950—. Received M. L. Annenberg Memorial Award for special merit in 1948. Mem. Am. Management Assn., Md. Society of Pa. Contbr. to financial jours. Home: 72-19 Drexelbrook Drive, Drexel Hill, Pa. Office: The Phila. Inquirer, Broad and Callowhill Sts., Phila. 1. Died Oct. 19, 1956.

BANKS, Frank Arthur, civil engr.; b. Saco, Me., Dec. 4, 1883; s. Otis Calvin and Emma (Chase) B.; B.S. in Civil Engring., U. Me., 1906, Eng.D., 1940; LL.D., Wash. State Coll. 1944; m. Theodora Livingston Drummond, Mar. 2, 1911; children—Laurina Margaret, John Vallery. Engring. aid U.S. Reclamation Service, Lower Yellowstone Project, Mont., 1906-09; designing engr., Boise, Ida., 1909-13; constrn. engr. Jackson Lake Dam, Wyo., 1913-16, Minidoka Project, 1916-20, Am. Falls Dam, 1920-26, Owyhee Dam & Project, 1926-33; supervising engr. Grand Coulee Dam, 1933-43, acting adminstr. Bonneville Power Project, 1939; regional dir., Region 1, U.S. Bureau of Reclamation, 1943-45; dist. mgr., Columbia River Dist., 1945—. Asso. mem. Am. Soc. C.E.; mem. Alpha Tau Omega, Phi Kappa Phi, Sigma Tau, Tau Beta Phi. Mason. Address: U.S. Bureau of Reclamation, Coulee Dam, Wash. Died Dec. 14, 1957.

BANKS, Harry Pickands, chem. exec.; b. Chgo., Feb. 19, 1884; William H. and Charlotte L. (Pickands) B.; Chem.E., U. Mich., 1907; m. Louise F. Chase, Apr. 12 1910; children—Vera L. (Mrs. Fred G. Galer), Betty C. (Mrs. H. R. Rayner). Chemist Boston & Mont. Copper Co., Gt. Falls, Mont., 1907-08, Falkenburg & Laucks, cons. chemists, Seattle, 1909-10; assayer, engr. Mt. Andrew Mine, Alaska, 1910-12; testing engr. Stone & Webster and So. Cal. Edison Co., Los Angeles, 1912-18; v.p., mgr. I.F. Laucks, Inc., Seattle, 1918-44, pres., 1944-47; v.p., gen. mgr. Western div. Monsanto Chem. Co., Seattle, 1947-49. Fellow Am. Inst. Chemists; mem. Civic Arts Com. Seattle, Am. Inst. Mining and Metall. Engrs., Am. Chem. Soc., Inst. Chem. Engrs. Clubs: Rainier, Washington Athletic (Seattle). Home: 2846 W. Viewmont Way, Seattle 99. Deceased.

BANKS, James Jones, lawyer; b. Enon, Ala., Apr. 27, 1861; s. Jabez Benoni and Jane Rebecca (Harvey) B.; A.B., Agrl. and Mech. Coll., Auburn, Ala., 1882; LL.B., U. Ala., 1885; m. Lee Frazer, Dec. 7, 1887; children—Lee Frazer, James Jones. Admitted Ala. bar, 1885, began practice at Birmingham; corp. counsel Birmingham, 1890-92; judge 10th Jud. Circuit Ala., 1892-99; asst. U.S. atty, Hawaii, 1917-19; judge First Circuit Court of T.H., 1919-26; became justice Supreme Court of T.H., 1926; later gen. practice of law. Mem. Alpha Tau Omega. Democrat. Methodist. Club: Pacific. Home: Pacific Club, Honolulu, Hawaii. Deceased.*

BANKS, John Wallace, ret. justice; b. Bethlehem, Conn., Sept. 22, 1867; s. George Wallace and Eliza Frances B.; grad. Guilford (Conn.) Inst., 1885; A.B., Yale, 1889, LL.B. (asso. editor law jour.), 1893; m. Mary Cowles Gay, May 7, 1895. Admitted to Conn. bar, 1893, began practice at Bridgeport; referee in bankruptcy, 1902-20; judge Superior Court, Conn., 1920-27; justice Supreme Court, Conn., 1927-37, ret. Mem. Phi Beta Kappa. Republican. Conglist. Clubs: University, Brooklawn Country (Bridgeport); Graduate (New Haven); Yale (N.Y.C.). Home: 70 Rusling Pl. Office: County Court House, Bridgeport, Conn. Died Mar. 8, 1958.*

BANKS, Nathan, entomologist; b. Roslyn, N.Y., Apr. 13, 1868; s. Daniel Gerow and Maria (Hawxhurst) B.; B.S., Cornell, 1889, M.S., 1890; m. Mary A. Lu Gar, June 2, 1897 (dec. Feb. 24, 1956); children—Ruth, Bessie, Harold Bryant, Nellie May, Gilbert Shelley, Waldo Hawthorne, Dorothy Alice, Elsie Lucile, Douglas Hartley (dec.). Asst. entomologist U.S. Dept. Agr., 1900-16; curator insects, Mus. Comp. Zoology, Harvard, 1916-36; also associate professor of zoology, Harvard University 1928-36, emeritus since 1936. Has largest collection of Arachnida and Neuroptera in United States. Member various entomological socs., Sigma Xi; fellow Am. Acad. Arts and Sciences. Prohibitionist. Wrote: Treatise on the Acarina, 1940; Catalogue of the Acarina, 1907; Catalogue Nearctic Neuroptera, 1909; How to Collect and Preserve Insects, 1909; Catalogue Nearctic Spiders, 1910; Catalogue Nearctic Heteroptera, 1911; Index Economic Entomology, 1917. Contbr. many scientific and tech. papers to leading scientific jours. Home: Holliston, Mass. Died Jan. 24, 1953; buried Lake Grove Cemetery, Holliston.

BANNISTER, Lucius Ward, lawyer; b. Des Moines, Ia., Mar. 30, 1871; s. Lucius George and Alice (Ward) B.; student Drake U., Des Moines, Ia., 1889, State U. of Iowa, 1899-90; A.B., Stanford U., 1893; LL.B., Harvard, 1896; m. Helen Allabach, 1902; 1 s., Wayne (dec.). Began practice at Des Moines, 1896; 1st asst. city atty., Des Moines, 1898-99; removed to Denver, Colo., 1899; general practice; member firm Bannister, Weller & Friedrich. Joint author of workmen's compensation and industrial commission laws of Colo., and counsel for first commn organized thereunder; regarded as an authority on water rights in the western states; spl. lecturer on the subject of water rights in Harvard, Denver, Columbia and Cornell law schools for many years. Special counsel of Colo., 1922-23, at various times since, in the state's interstate water controversies; spl. counsel, Denver, Colo. River matters, 1926-29. Member Colo. State Board of Pardons, 1907-08; pres. Denver C. of C., 1924-26, Colo. River League, 1925. Pres. Colorado-Hoover-for-President, and Colorado-Hoover-Curtis clubs, and dir. club activities in Colo. under Rep. Nat. Com., 1928; legal adviser to Oil Conservation Conf., by appointment of sec. of interior, 1929; mem. Com. on Interstate Streams of Denver C. of C. since 1929; chmn. Colo. World Court Com.; hon. life. mem. Denver C. of C. Mem. Com. on Organization of the Executive Branch of the Government (Hoover Com.), 1947-49. Mem. Am. Law Inst., Am. Bar Assn. (former mem. ho. of dels.), Colorado Bar Assn., Denver Art Assn., Denver C. of C. (past pres.; past nat. councilor and dir.; former dir. now mem. international relations and labor coms. U.S. C. of C.). Decorated Order of Crown of Rumania; officer Order of Crown of Italy, Delta Tau Delta, Phi Delta Phi. Republican. Clubs: Denver, Mile High, Denver Country, Rotary (former pres.), Denver City, St. Vrain Ranch; Harvard (N.Y.C.). Home: 849 Race St., Denver 6. Office: Equitable Bldg., Denver 2. Died Jan. 17, 1958; buried Fairmount Mausoleum, Denver.

BANNON, Henry Towne, ex-congressman; b. Scioto County, O., June 5, 1867; s. James W. and Mary E. (Smith) B.; B.Litt., U. of Mich., 1889; m. Jessie Damarin, May 25, 1893; children—Elizabeth Ferguson, Louis D. Admitted to Ohio bar, 1891, and began practice at Portsmouth; pros. atty. Scioto County, O., 1897-1903; mem. 59th and 60th Congresses (1905-09), 10th Ohio Dist.; atty. in Ohio for N.&W. and C.&O. rys. Del. to Republican Nat. Conventions, 1924, 28, 32, 36, 40. Club: Boone and Crockett (New York). Hunter of big game in the West, Alaska and Northern B.C. Author: Scioto Sketches, 1920; Stories Old and Often Told, 1927. Contbr. on wild life. Home: 1926 Franklin Av. Office: 325 Masonic Bldg., Portsmouth, O. Died Sept. 6, 1950.

BANZHAF, Henry Leo (bănz'häf), dental educator; b. Hartford, Wis., Oct. 15, 1865; s. Jacob and Marie (Rasch) B.; D.D.S., U. Mich., 1886; B.S., Marquette U., 1907; LL.D., U. Pitts., 1934; m. Ida Schuette, Oct. 5, 1898; children—George, Henry. Practiced dentistry, 1886-1902, part time thereafter, 1902-20; now bus. mgr. Marquette U., Milw.; dean Marquette U. Dental Sch., 1902-42, trustee Sch. Medicine; mem. Wis. State Bd. Dental Examiners, 1898-1902. Maj. Dental R.C., U.S. Army; apptd. col. on staff of gov. of Ky., 1932; dental examiner, Wis. for Army Dental Corps, World War; mem. Bd. of Edn., Milw., 1911-19, pres., 1914-15; trustee Pub. Library, 1914-15, mem. Art Commn.; treas. 7th Internat. Dental Congress, 1925-31. Hon. mem. La sociedad Odontologica de Chile, sociedad Dental de Caracas (Venezuela), La Asociacion Dental de Puerto Rico, Colegio de Cirujanos Odontologos (Paraguay); fellow Am. Coll. Dentists (v.p. 1925, pres. 1927-29), Am. Acad. Dental Surgery; mem. Assn. Am. Dental Schools (pres. 1923-24), Nat. Assn. Dental Faculties (ex-pres.), Dental Ednl. Council America (sec. 1909-19, pres. 1931-37), Am. Council on Edn., 1931-35, Am. Dental Assn. (pres. 1926-27), Milw. County Dental Soc., Wis. Dental Soc. (pres. 1910), Omicron Kappa Upsilon, R.I. (hon.), Ky. (hon.) dental socs. Republican. Episcopalian. Writer, lectr. dental, econ. subjects. Home: 3234 N. Hackett Av. Office: 615 N. 11th St., Milw. Died Mar. 5, 1951; buried Evergreen Cemetery, Manitowoc, Wis.

BAPST, Robert Thomas, educator; b. Buffalo, N.Y., Jan. 2, 1880; s. William John and Margaret Jane (Hardy) B. A.B., Canisius Coll., Buffalo, 1900, M.A., 1901, L.H.D., 1946; grad. study Canisius Coll. and St. Louis U., 1900-02; Ph.D. St. Louis U., 1908; LL.D., Niagara U., Niagara Falls, N.Y., 1937; unmarried. Instr. English and math. Canisius High Sch., 1902-06; instr. Canisius Coll., 1906-08; prin. elementary sch., Buffalo, 1908-14; prin. S. Park High Sch., 1914-32; lectr. ethics, philosophy of edn., Canisius Coll., 1928-32; asso. supt. of secondary edn. Buffalo Pub. Schs., 1932-36, supt., 1936-49; ordained priest Roman Catholic Ch., 1951; asst. pastor St. Louis Ch., Buffalo, lectr. Canisius Coll. Home: 388 Franklin St., Buffalo, N.Y. Died Oct. 18, 1959.

BARA, Theda, moving picture actress; b. Cincinnati, O., July 20, 1890; d. Bernard and Pauline Louise Françoise (de Coppet) B.; ed. in U.S. and abroad. m Charles Brabin 1921. Began as a "vampire" in moving pictures under direction of William Fox, 1915; appeared in Cleopatra, Salome, Camille, DuBarry, Carmen, A Fool There Was, etc. Home: Beverly Hills, Cal. Died Apr. 7, 1955.

BARACH, Frederica Pisek (Mrs. Alvan L. Barach), editor; b. Lake Hopatcong, N.J., Aug. 1, 1904; d. Godfrey Roger and Rosalie Scranton (Paul) Pisek; A.B., Vassar Coll., 1925; m. Franklin Field, May 29,

1926; m. 2d, Dr. Alvan L. Barach, Apr. 24, 1933; children—Jeffrey, John Paul. Began as editorial asst. Golden Book Mag., 1925, asso. editor, 1928-30, editor in chief, 1930-33; with Review of Reviews, 1926-28; taught creative writing, Sarah Lawrence Coll., 1928-30. Mem. Phi Beta Kappa. Democrat. Club: Cosmopolitan. Author: One Hundred Best Books, 1931. Home: 142 E. 71st St. N.Y.C. Deceased.

BARACH, Joseph H., physician, research medicine b. Calvary, Poland-Russia, 1883; s. Zorach and Deborah (Oppenheim) B.; came to U.S., 1888, citizenship derived from father; student Park Inst., 1895-99; M.D., Univ. of Pittsburgh, 1903; post grad. student, Columbia, 1903; m. Edna S. Levy, Sept. 21, 1915; children—Joseph L., Richard L. Resident pathologist and interne West Pa. Hosp., Pittsburgh, 1904; asso. prof. medicine U. Pitts., also med. dir. U. Clins. Sch. Medicine, 1930—; sr. staff med. center hosps. 1910—; cons. dept. health Carnegie Inst. Tech., Pitts., 1910; cons. in medicine, Sewickley (Pa.) Valley Hosp., 1925—. Chmn. metabolism and endocrinology sect., research grants div. U.S.P.H.S., 1946-51, nat. council arthritis and metabolism sect., research grants div. since 1952. Served as capt. med. corps., World War I; chief selective service Dist. 1, Western Pa., World War II. Name inscribed on the Wall of Fame of the American Common—World's Fair of 1940, New York, for "having made notable contribution to our living, ever-growing democracy devoted to peace and freedom." Fellow A.A.A.S., A.C.P., Am. Diabetes Assn. mem. council 1941, pres., 1944-46, chmn. sect. on metabolic and endocrine diseases, etc., member A.M.A., Sigma Xi. Republican-Liberal. Mem. Congregation Rodef Shalom, Pitts. Clubs: Cosmos (Washington); Concordia, Deep Creek Yacht. Author: Self Help for the Diabetic, 1934; Diabetes and Its Treatment, 1946; Diabetes, The Patients Book, 1948; Diabetes and Its Treatment, 1949; Diabetes, The Foods and Facts on Diabetes, 1949. Contributor many articles to med. lit. in U.S. and abroad. Home: 5745 Beacon St., Pittsburgh 17, (summer) Manteo, N.C., Roanoke Island. Office: 3601 Fifth Av., Univ. Clinic Med. Center, Pitts. 13. Died Mar. 7, 1954.

BARBEE, David Rankin (bär'bē), writer; b. Murfreesboro Tenn., Oct. 15, 1874; s. Rev. James Dodson (D.D.) and Margaret Roberson (Rankin) B.; student Emory and Henry Coll., LL.D., 1935; student Vanderbilt U.; m. Elina Guzman, Apr. 15, 1913; children—Mary (Mrs. Robert C. Maxwell), Susan Guzman (Mrs. Hugh F. Smith). Reporter for Nashville Banner, 1896-99, Nashville American, 1901; telegraph editor Memphis Commercial Appeal, 1901-08, news editor, 1908-10; editor Chattanooga Star, 1908; mng. editor Montgomery (Ala.) Advertiser, 1910-11, Mobile Ala.) Register, 1911-18; news editor New Orleans States, 1918-26; mng. editor Asheville (N.C.) Citizen, 1926-28; feature writer Washington Post, 1928-32; asst. to sec. of commerce, 1933; spl. asst. to adminstr. Fed. Alcohol Adminstrn., 1933-40; with public relations dept. U.S. Treasury, 1940-42. Mem. com. Am. History and So. Hist. Society, Kappa Sigma. Democrat. Presbyn. Club: Ntional Press. Author: (pamphlet) An Excursion in Southern History; Washington—City of Mighty Events. Contbr. to hist. mags. Home: 2019 30th St., Orange, Tex. Died Mar. 7, 1958; buried Cedar Hill Cemetery, Washington.

BARBER, Charles Newell, ret. univ. adminstrv. officer; b. Barre, Vt., Sept. 8, 1884; son Charles Newell and Ella Laura (Granger) B.; B.S. in civil engineering, Norwich University, Northfield, Vermont, 1908, D.Sc., 1952; married Ida Demis Stickney, May 12, 1917; children—Jane (Mrs. Marc Martin Lainwohl), Caroline. Instructor in physics, Norwich U., 1908-16, asst. mathematics and physics, 1916-24, asso. prof. physics, 1924-34, sec.-treas. of the univ. since 1934, now retired; director Selective Service, State of Vt., 1940-47; v.p., dir. Northfield Trust Co. Rep. to General Assembly of Vt., 1953. Chairman of advisory committee for rent control for Washington and Caledonia counties, 1948-49; mem. Governor's adv. council on education, 1956—. Member Vt. Nat. Guard, 1904-19 and 1920-41; retired with rank of major; col. comdg. Vt. State Guard, 1941-42; U.S. Property and Disbursing Officer, Vt., 1921-38; Mexican Border Service, 1916; U.S. Army, 1917-19. Awarded President's Certificate of Merit, 1946. Trustee Vt. Soldiers Home since 1924, president bd. since July, 1946. Dem. candidate (Vt.) lt. gov., 1924, 34. Del. Constl. Conv. State of Vt., 1933. State chmn. Infantile Paralysis Fund, 1940-45. Mem. Am. Legion (dept. comdr., 1923-24; mem. nat. com. edn. of orphans of veterans). Mil. Order Fgn. Wars (dept. comdr., 1924-25), Vt. Soc. Profl. Engrs., Vt. Hist. Soc., Newcomen Soc., Theta Chi. Mason, K.P., Granger, Elk. Home: Jefferson Av., Northfield, Vt. Died Apr. 22, 1958.

BARBER, Edward John, ocean commerce; b. Liverpool, Eng., Mar. 9, 1887; s. James and Catherine (Gandy) B.; brought to U.S., 1887; grad. St. John's Mil. Acad., Manlius, N.Y., 1906; m. Gladys Lemmel, July 4, 1912 (divorced); children—Gladys Katherine, Mary Helen, Edward John, James Laurance; m. 2d, Ethel Amweg Scott, Apr. 1925; adopted dau., Willetta Ann Barber (née Scott). Began with Internat. Merc. Marine Co., 1906; entered service 1907, of Barber & Co., established by father and uncle; pres. and dir. Barber Co., Inc., N.J., Barber Securities Corp., Battery Place Securities Corp., Pier Machine Works, Inc., Camelback Mountain Corp., Edjobar Co., Nassau Properties, Ltd.; chmn. bd. and dir. Am.-West African Line, Inc., Atlantic Piers Co., Inc., Atlantic Stevedoring Co., Inc., Barber West African Line, Inc., Barber Steamship Lines, Inc., Va. Coaling Corp.; dir. Barber Steamship Lines, Ltd. (London), Bankers & Shippers Ins. Co. of N.Y., Columbia Casualty Co., Commercial Union Fire Ins. Co., Jersey Ins. Co., N.Y., Pacific Fire Ins. Co., Pouch Terminal, Inc. Mem. U.S. C. of C., N.Y. Produce and Maritime exchanges, St. George's Soc. Republican. Episcopalian. Dir. Beekman Downtown Hosp., Seamen's Ch. Inst. Clubs: Union League, Metropolitan, Downtown, Everglades, Seminole Golf (Palm Beach, Fla.), Traffic, India House, Whitehall, Sleepy Hollow Country, Ridgewood Country (Danbury, Conn.), Knollwood Country, Apawamis Golf, Blind Brook Golf, Seaview Golf, Silver Spring Country, Metropolitan Advertising Golf, Tin Whistle, Bohemian, San Francisco Golf (San Francisco); Burlingame (Calif.) Country, Augusta (Ga.) Nat. Golf, Coombe Hill Golf (England), Oslo Golf (Oslo, Norway). Home: Ridgefield, Conn. Office: 17 Battery Pl., N.Y.C. Died June 13, 1953.

BARBER, Henry A., Jr., army officer; b. Ft. Reno, Okla., July 31, 1896; s. Henry Anson and Inez (Smith) B.; B.S., U.S. Mil. Acad., 1917; grad. Inf. Sch., Ft. Benning, Ga., 1922. Command and Gen. Staff Sch., Ft. Leavenworth, Kan., 1935, Army War Coll., 1937; m. Margaret Wahl, Aug. 16, 1920; children—Henry Anson, III, Natalie (dec.), Anne. Commd. 2d lt. Inf. U.S. Army, 1917, advanced through grades to brig. gen., 1943; served on War Dept. Gen. Staff, 1937-38, 41-43; participated in seizure of Adak, Aleutian Islands, 1942. Decorated D.S.C. (U.S.); Legion of Honor, Croix de Guerre with Palm (France), World War I. Died Apr. 29, 1956.

BARBER, Herbert Goodell, lawyer; b. Wardsboro, Vt., Aug. 14, 1870; s. Daniel Miller and Lydia E. (Barnard) B.; student pub. schs.; m. Florence H. Whittier, Oct. 20, 1909; children—Wendell Whittier, Elizabeth Lydia, Clarence Edward. Admitted to Vt. bar, 1893, began practice at Brattleboro; state's atty. Windham County, Vt., 1898-1900; mem. Gen. Assembly, Vt., 1908-10, 35-37, State Senate, 1912-14; atty. gen. of Vt., 1914-18. Mem. Vt. Rep. State Com., 1910-14. Mem. Am., Vt. bar assns. Universalist. Mason, Odd Fellow. Home: 18 Oak St. Office: 68 Main St., Brattleboro, Vt. Died Oct. 5, 1947.

BARBER, Raymond Jenness, cons. engr., mus. curator; b. Epping, N.H., Aug. 12, 1884; s. Albert Gilman and Annie Estelle (Skerrye) B.; S.B., Mass. Inst. Tech., 1906; m. June 1906; children—Raymond Jenness, Cedric Leonard; m. 2d, Edith Hudson MacLeod, Apr. 19, 1922. Mine rodman, Bingham Canyon, Utah, 1906; mining in Mexico, 1907; invention and mfg. small telephones for secret service Boston, 1907-10; mining exploration, appraisal, development, Los Angeles, 1910-13; asso. with Timothy W. Sprague, cons. engr., Boston, 1913-16; general mgr. Roxbury mines, Siskiyou Country, Cal., 1916-18; cons. engr. to shipyards, U.S. Shipping Bd., 1918-19; cons. engr. Gilboa Dam of Catskill Water Supply, N.Y., 1919; pres., mgr. Roxbury Gold Mines, Cal., 1920-21; cons. engr., San Francisco, 1921-37; research in nitrocellulose lacquers, Boston, 1924-25; chemist, dir. Hydro-Carbon Cos., San Francisco, 1926-42; cons. in geology, Div. of Hwys., State of Cal., 1934-35; lectr. in placer mining, Stanford, 1927-29, 1935-36; prof. geology, mining, dean Sch. of Mines, U. Alaska, 1937-40; mining engr. mem. Bd. Engrs. and Architects' Examiners, Territory of Alaska, 1939-45; engring. personnel counselor Lockheed (Vega) Aircraft Corp., Burbank, Cal., 1941-46; lectr. engring., geology U. So. Cal., 1946-48, vis. asso. prof. gen. engring., 1948-52; ret.; curator mineralogy, petrology Los Angeles County Mus., 1950—. Fellow Royal Soc. Arts London; Mem. Am. Inst. Mining and Metall. Engrs., Soc. for Promotion Engring. Edn., Nat. Highways Assn., Delta Tau Delta. Republican. Episcopalian. Mason. Clubs: Technology (N.Y.C.); Delta Tau Delta (Boston); Engineers (San Francisco). Contbr. to tech. jours. Home: 2637 Severance St., Los Angeles 7. Died Oct. 28, 1955; buried Utica, N.Y.

BARBEY, John Edward, textile mfr.; born Reading, Pa., 1890; s. John and Mary Ellen (Garst) B.; grad. Hill Sch., Pottstown, Pa., 1908; Ph.B., Yale, 1911; m. Catharine E. Quier, June 3, 1925; children—John E., Jr., Pierre G. (dec.), Mary Glyde, Edwin Quier, Helen Hawley. Asso. with Vanity Fair Mills, Inc., mfrs. underwear and hosiery, Reading, since 1912, gen. mgr., since 1916, now pres. Capt. A.S., U.S. Army, 1917-18. Mem. Book and Snake, Yale. Christian Scientist. Clubs: Denver (Colo.); Berkshire Country, Wyomissing; Metropolitan (N.Y.C.). Home: Greenfields, Reading. Office: Vanity Fair Mills, Inc., Reading, Pa.; also N.Y.C. Died. Oct. 21, 1956.

BARBOUR, Frank Alexander, civil engr.; b. St. John, N.B., Can., May 5, 1870; s. George L. and Elizabeth (Thompson) B.; A.B., U. N.B., 1888; m. Dorothy Boswell, 1916. Mem. Am. Soc. C.E., Am. Soc. for Testing Materials, Am., New Eng. water works assns., Am. Pub. Health Assn., Boston Soc. Mason. Clubs: Boston City, Engineers, Framingham Country. Home: Framingham Center, Mass. Office: Tremont Bldg., Boston. Died May 24, 1947.

BARBOUR, John S(trode), lawyer; b. nr. Brandy Station, Va., Aug. 10, 1866; s. James and Fanny Thomas (Beckham) B.; student Cables Acad., 1881-82; LL.B., U. Va., 1888; m. Mary Browning Grimsley, Apr. 4, 1894. Admitted to Va. bar, 1887; law clk. Commonwealth's Atty. for Culpeper Co., 1888-1911; established, pub. Piedmont Advance weekly newspaper, Culpeper, 1886-88; candidate for Commonwealth's atty., 1891; mayor, Culpepper, 1897; elected to represent Culpeper, Co. Va. Constl. Conv., 1901-02; mem. Barbour, Garnett, Pickett & Keith, and predecessors, Fairfax, Va. and Washington, 1907-13, since 34; gen. atty. Washington Ry. & Electric Co., Potomac Electric Power Co., Washington Utilities Co., and other affiliates, Washington, 1913-34. Served as pvt. to 1st sgt. Culpeper Minute Men, 3d Regt., inf., Va. N.G.; commd. capt., adj., 3d Regt.; maj., asst. adj. gen., 1st Brigade. Mem. Am., D.C., Va. State (nat. v.p.), Fairfax Co. bar assns., Clubs: Lawyers, University (Washington); Washington Golf and Country (Arlington, Va.); Fairfax Hunt (Sunset Hills, Va.); Court House Country (Fairfax, Va.). Home: The Oaks, Fairfax, Va. Died May 6, 1952.

BARBOUR, William Tefft, executive; b. Detroit, Mich., Apr. 4, 1877; s. Edwin Samuel and Ella Holbrook (Tefft) B.; ed. Phillips Acad., Andover, Mass.; m. Margaret Bispham Chittenden, June 10, 1902; children—Irene Tefft (Mrs. Jorden Mott), Ella Chittenden (Mrs. Harland G. Walter), William Tefft, Alpheus Williams (dec.), Thomas Edwin. Purchasing agt. Detroit Stove Works, 1895, pres. since 1897; pres. Art Stove Co. since 1923, Mich. Stove Co. since 1925; pres. Detroit-Mich. Stove Co., 1926-35, chmn. bd., 1935-54, ret.; v.p. Detroit Mfrs. R.R. Chmn. charter commn. City Bloomfield Hills. Chmn. Detroit com. Fatherless Children of France, 1917-24; mem. Liberty Loan Drive com., Oakland County, Mich., World War; mem. Bishop Williams Memorial Fund, 1924, nat. com. Japanese Reconstruction Fund, 1924. Pres. bd. trustees Grace Hospital Detroit, 1917-54, honorary president, 1954—. Delegate to General Convention P.E. Ch., New Orleans, 1925, Washington, 1928, Denver, 1931, Atlantic City, 1934, Cincinnati, 1937, Kansas City, Mo., 1940, Cleveland, 1943, Philadelphia, 1946; chmn. finance com. Centennial Fund P.E. Church, Diocese of Mich., standing com., 1932-54; commissioner Detroit Zoölogical Park, 1932-54; dir. Community Fund. Fellow Am. Geog. Soc.; mem. Am. Econ. Assn., Acad. Polit. Science, Nat. Econ. League, Nat. Assn. Gardeners, Nat. Assn. Audubon Societies, Am. Hort. Soc., Bloomfield Hills and Dist. Hort. Soc., English-Speaking Union, Izaak Walton League of America, Detroit Historical Society, American Hosp. Assn., Newcomen Soc. of Eng. Navy League of U.S., Order Americans of Armorial Ancestry, Soc. of Descendants of Knights of Most Noble Order of the Garter; asso. mem. Am. Museum Natural Hist. Harding Meml. Assn.; hon. mem. Grosse Pointe and Eastern Mich. Hort. Soc., Mich. Naval Force; patron Mil. Training Camps Assn. of U.S., Detroit Arctic Expdn. Republican. Episcopalian. Clubs: Detroit, Yondotega, Detroit Boat, Grosse Pointe (Detroit); Bloomfield Hills (Michigan) Country, Question, Country of Detroit. Home: 43 Old Brook Lane, Grosse Pointe Farms 36, Mich. Office: 20233 Mack Av., Grosse Pointe Woods 36, Mich. Died Sept. 29, 1955.

BARCLAY, Bertram Donald, botanist; b. Champaign, Ill., Nov. 9, 1898; Bachiller en Humanidades, Deutsche Schule, Santiago Chile, 1916; S.B., Coll. of Wooster 1923; S.M., W. Va. U., 1926; Ph.D., U. of Chicago, 1928; m. Harriet George, Sept. 4, 1928; children—Bertram Donald, Arthur Stewart. Instr. botany, W. Va. U., 1924-26, prof. botany, head dept., U. of Tulsa (Okla.), since 1929; staff, Rocky Mountain Biol. Lab., Crested Butte, Colo., since 1929, v.p., since 1940, acting dir., 1948. Fellow A.A.A.S., 1930; mem. Bot. Soc. of Am., Okla. Acad of Sciences (pres. 1937), Ecol. Soc. of Am, Phi Beta Kappa, Sigma Xi, Phi Sigma, Pi Gamma Mu, Gamma Alpha. Republican. Presbyterian. Author: Origin and Development of Adventitious Roots in Hedera Helix L. (unpub.), 1926; Organography of Elephantella Groenlandica at Varying Altitudes (unpub.), 1936; Origin and Development of Tissues in Stem of Selaginella Wildenovi, Botan. Gazette, 1931; contbd. articles. Home: R.D. 10, Box 56, Tulsa. Died June 6, 1953.

BARCLAY, William Kennedy, Jr., investment banker; b. Philadelphia, Pa., Mar. 30, 1896; s. William Kennedy and Florence Elizabeth (Brunner) B.; student William Penn Charter Sch., 1902-12; B. of Econ., Univ. of Pa., 1916; m. Grace Maxine Westervelt, Feb. 8, 1936; 1 son, William Kennedy. Partner Barclay Moore & Co., Phila., Jan. 1921-Dec. 1941; partner Stein Bros. & Boyce since Jan. 1942; dir. E. F. Houghton & Co., Bentley Harris Mfg. Co.,

Philadelphia-Baltimore Stock Exchange, Automatic Pinsetter Co., Inc.; pres. Phila. Stock Exchange since 1948. Served as lieutenant (junior grade) U.S.N.R.F., 1917-19; served as chairman investment bankers and brokers division United Campaign, 1944-45. Recipient Victory medal, overseas 1919; Treasury Citation, War Bond Activities, 1944, 45. Mem. Nat. Assn. Securities Dealers, Inc. (past gov. mem. exec. com., treas. and chmn.) Investment Bankers Assn. of Am. (past. gov. Pa.); The Penn Charter Alumni Society, Republican. Episcopalian. Clubs: Bond, Union League, Midday, Philadelphia; The Little Egg Harbor Yacht (past commodore). Home: 1405 Hillside Road, Wynnewood, Pennsylvania. Office: 123 S. Broad St., Phila. 9. Died Mar. 19, 1954.

BARD, A. T., mfg. exec.; b. New Carlisle, Ind., Mar. 18, 1889; s. John Edward and Emma Christine (Nicklas) B.; m. Anna Mickelsen, Nov. 25, 1911; children—Albert O., Robert E.; m. 2d, Mrs. Flavius Gentry Pernoud, Feb. 16, 1956. With Reliance Mfg. Co., 1901-54, successively cutting room foreman, factory supt., dist. supt., dir. mfg., v.p., exec. v.p., 1901-44, pres., 1944-54; pres. Rice-Stix, Inc., St. Louis, 1954—. Swedish Lutheran. Mason. Home: 3615 Utah Pl., St. Louis 16. Office: 1000 Washington Av., St. Louis 1. Died May 26, 1959.

BARD, Guy Kurtz, lawyer, b. Lincoln, Pa., Oct. 24, 1895; s. Silas E. and Miranda S. (Kurtz) B.; grad. Denver, Pa., High Sch.; grad. Millersville State Teachers College; A.B., Franklin and Marshall College, LL.D. (honorary), 1947; LL.B., University of Pennsylvania; unmarried. Lived on farm as a boy and later learned printing trade father's country newspaper; sch. teacher, Lancaster County, Pa., 1911-12; prin., Warwick Twp. High Sch., Lititz, Pa., 1913-15; teacher mathematics and sch. management, Millersville State Normal Sch., 1915; supervising prin., Ephrata (Pa.) Schs., 1916-18; admitted to Pa. bar, 1922, and practiced at Lancaster to 1939; admitted to practice Supreme Court of Pa. and U.S. and Federal courts; special asst. to U.S. atty. gen., 1934-37; U.S. atty. Eastern Pa. Dist., 1937; mem. Pa. Pub. Utility Commn., 1937-38; atty. gen. of Pa. 1938-39; U.S. Dist. judge, Eastern Dist. Pa., 1939-52, resigned 1952; member of law firm of Folz, Bard, Kamsler, Goodis & Greenfield since 1953; secretary Democratic Com. Lancaster County, 1920-24; chmn. 1925-34; Pa., del. at large Dem. Nat. Conv., Chicago, 1932 (mem. com. on resolutions, drafted prohibition repeal plank); Dem. nominee for lt. gov. of Pa., 1930. for U.S. Senator, 1952. Served with U.S. Army, with A.E.F., 1918-19. Member board of trustees Millersville State Teachers Coll., Muhlenberg Coll. Member Am., Pa. and Lancaster Co. bar assns., Am. Judicature Soc., Am. Acad. Polit. and Social Science, Acad. Polit. Science, Am. Legion (past comdr. Denver, Pa., post), Vets. Fgn. Wars, Phi Kappa Tau, Delta Theta Phi. Democrat. Lutheran. Mason. Elk (past exalted ruler), Moose. Clubs: Hamilton (Lancaster), University (Phila.). Home: Ephrata, R. 2, Pa. Office: 1315 Walnut St., Phila. 7. Died Nov. 23, 1953; buried Fairview Cemetery, Denver, Pa.

BARD, Harry Erwin, b. Crawfordsville, Ind., Aug. 22, 1867; s. Henry and Catherine (Yoder) B.; A.B., Wabash Coll., 1894, A.M., 1898; A.M., Columbia, 1907, Ph.D., 1909; Doctor's Diploma in Administration of Edn., Teachers Coll. (Columbia), 1909; m. Isabella Jane Wilkie, 1902. Instr. Wabash Coll., 1894-5; instr. Adams Collegiate Inst., New York, 1895-6, prin., 1896-8; div. supt. schs., Philippine Islands, 1901-6; research scholar, Teachers Coll. (Columbia), 1907-9; official advisor, Ministry of Instruction, Lima, Peru, 1909-12; research work in Paris, France, 1912-13; organizing dir. Pan Am. Div., Am. Assn. Internat. Conciliation, New York, 1913-15; sec. Pan Am. Soc. of U.S., 1915-19; official advisor Ministry of Instrn., Lima, Peru, 1919—. Assisted in preparing organic sch. law of Peru, 1910-12; was pres., commn. to visit capitals of S.A., under Carnegie Endowment for Internat. Peace, 1914; dir. gen. Pub. Instruction, Peru, 1920, in charge of the reorganization of pub. sch. system under new school law. Mem. Nat. Geog. Soc., Nat. Economic League, Nat. Inst. Social Sciences, etc. Am. Soc. Internat. Law, Am. Defense Soc. Clubs: Columbia Univ. (New York); Phoenix, Golf (Lima). Author: The City School District, 1909; Intellectual and Cultural Relations Between the United States and the Other Republics of America, 1914; South America, 1916. Contbr. to Cyclo. of Edn., etc. Home: Ridgefield, Conn. Address: Lima, Peru. Died July 11, 1955.

BARD, Roy Emerson, securities and grain broker b. Cleve., May 20, 1888; s. George Morris and Helen (Norwood) B.; student Lawrenceville Sch., 1906-07; Litt.B., Princeton, 1911; m. Dorothy Channon, Nov. 2, 1921. With bond dept. Harris Trust & Savings Bank, Chgo., 1911-20; partner firm of Bard, Esch & Co., 1920-25; v.p. Ralph A. Bard & Co., 1926-28; partner Bard & Co., 1928-30, Sutro Bros. & Co., 1930-41, Clement, Curtis & Co., 1941-45, Shearson, Hammill & Co., 1945—; dir. Chgo. Rivet & Machine Co. Served as capt., F.A., U.S. Army, World War I. Republican. Presbyn. Clubs: University, Attic (Chicago); Indian Hill (Winnetka). Home: 526 Greenwood, Kenilworth, Ill. Office: 208 S. LaSalle St., Chgo. 4. Died Aug. 1959.

BARDWELL, Rodney Jewett, lawyer; b. Tunkhannock, Wyo. County, Pa., Aug. 17, 1870; s. Hiram Webster and Gertrude Elizabeth (Jewett) B.; student Md. Mil. and Naval Acad., Oxford, Md., 1885-86; grad. Phillips Exeter Acad., Exeter, N.H., 1890; m. Iva Shepard, Feb. 20, 1900; children—Eva Gertrude (Mrs. Jackson Brown, Jr.), Rodney Jewett, James Shepard, Edith Burger (Mrs. Britton White). Admitted to Pa. bar, 1894, began practice in Wyo. County, Pa., 1894; moved to Denver, Colo., 1895; pres. Denver Gas & Electric Light Co.; gen. counsel and dir. Pub. Service Co. of Colo. Pres. bd. Colo. Sch. of Mines. State senator, Colo., 1907-11. Served 5 yrs. in Colo. N.G. Mem. Am. and Denver bar assns., S.A.R. Republican. Episcopalian. Mason (32°); K.C.C.H.; past Eminent Comdr. Coronal Commandery, K.T.; past Potentate El Jebel Temple, A.A. O.N.M.S., Phi Delta Theta. Clubs: Denver, Denver Country, Denver Athletic, Mile High Duck (Denver); Wigwam Fishing (Deckers, Colo.). Home: 2240 Ash St. Office: First Nat. Bank Bldg., Denver, Colo. Died Jan. 17, 1950.*

BARHAM, Charles (bar-ham), ry. ofcl.; b. Goldsboro, N.C., Apr. 16, 1867; s. Claudius and Alexine Goldborough (Ballard) B.; grad. Durham (N.C.) High Sch., 1884; m. Mary Hannah Wilkinson, Feb. 20, 1889 (dec.); children—Earle, Janie Alexine (Mrs. Robert H. Peoples), Helen Louise (dec.), Martha Elizabeth, Charles. With Richmond & Danville R.R., 1886-90, asso. Rys. of Va. and Carolinas, 1890-95, So. Ry., 1895-98; successively chief clerk to traffic mgr., asst. gen. freight agt., gen. freight agt. N.C. &St.L. Ry., 1898-1921; chmn. So. Freight Assn., 1922-28; v.p., traffic mgr. N.C.&St.L. Ry., 1928-39, v.p., 1939—. Served as traffic mgr. U.S. Food Adminstr., southern dist., 1917-18. Mem. C. of C. (past pres.). Episcopalian. Mason (33°, K.T., past grand master Tenn.). Clubs: Rotary (past pres.), Round Table; Traffic (Atlanta, Nashville, Chgo.). Home: 115 Louise Av. Office: Union Station, Nashville. Deceased.

BARHAM, Frank Forrest, publisher; b. Anaheim, Calif., May 24, 1879; s. Richard Marion and Martha Medora (Arnold) B.; Dr. medicine and surgery, Coll. of Physicians & Surgeons, U. of Southern Calif., 1906; m. Jessica Viola Gorham, Jan. 31, 1908 (divorced 1927); 1 dau., Patricia Ann; m. 2d, Arline Cadmus Belcher, Oct. 9, 1928 (div.). Propr., Guy B. Barham Co., gen. ins. and custom house brokerage; pres. and dir. Frank F. Barham Co., Barham & Mitchell, Incorporated. Mason. Clubs: California, Bohemian, Los Angeles Athletic, Jonathan, Los Angeles Country, Calif. Yacht, Newport Harbor Yacht. Home: 3480 Barham Blvd., Los Angeles 28. Office: 354 S. Spring St., Los Angeles 13. Died Aug. 6, 1953.

BARJA, Cesar (bär'hä), univ. prof.; b. Guitiriz, Lugo, Spain, Oct. 1, 1890; s. Manuel and Angela (Carral) B.; ed. Inst. of Lugo, 1900-06, U. of Santiago, 1906-09, U. of Madrid, 1909-12 (Doctor en Derecho), 1914-15, U. of Leipzig, Germany, 1913-14, Harvard, 1916-17; m. Jeannette Goldson, Feb. 11, 1927. Came to U.S., 1915, naturalized, 1931. Instr. in Spanish, Conn. Coll., New London, 1917-20, U. of Mich., 1920-21; asst. prof. Spanish, Smith Coll., 1921-24; lecturer in Spanish, U. of Calif. at Los Angeles, 1924-27, asso. prof., 1927-29, prof. Spanish lit. since 1929. Awarded fellowship by Spanish Govt. for study in Germany, 1913-14, U.S., 1915-17; Diploma of Honor by the Mexican Acad., 1939. Del. of U. S. Commn. to the Meeting of Intellectual Cooperation, Havana, 1941. Corr. mem. Real Academia Española, 1947, Real Academia Gallega, 1949. Mem. Modern Lang. Assn., Am. Assn. Teachers of Spanish, Sigma Delta Pi, Pi Delta Phi. Author: Libros y Autores Clasicos, 1922; Libros y Autores Modernos, 1925; En Torno al Lirismo Gallego, 1926; Libros y Autores Contemporaneos, 1935; The War and Cultural Relations, 1941; The Outlook for European Culture, 1945. Editor of Modern Language Forum, 1934-37. Contbr. to professional jours. Home: 10721 Wellworth Av., Los Angeles 24, Cal. Died June 17, 1951.

BARKAN, Otto, ophthalmologist; b. San Francisco, Apr. 5, 1887; s. Adolph and Louise (Desept) B.; B.A., Oxford, 1909, M.D., Munich, 1914; mem. Royal Coll. Surgeons, London, 1915; m. Margit Park, 1921; children—Park Otto, Thomas Adolph. House physician St. Mary's Hosp., London, 1915-16; with eye clinics, univs. of Munich and Vienna, 1916-17; asst. U. Munich, 1917-19, U. Zurich, 1919-20; practice of medicine, San Francisco, 1921—; mem. surg. staff San Francisco Hosp., 1921; asso. clin. prof. Stanford U. Med. Sch., 1921—; cons. opthalmologist Veterans' Hosp. Recipient Howe medal for development surgery to relieve glaucoma in infants A.M.A., 1954. Mem. Am. Acad. Ophthalmology, Western Ophthal. Soc., A.M.A., Cal. Med. Assn., Assn. for Research in Ophthalmology, Pacific Coast Oto-Ophthal. Soc., Brit. Ophthal. Soc., Alpha Kappa Kappa. Episcopalian. Clubs: Burlingame Country, Olympic. Contbr. articles on ocular surgery to med. jours. Home: 3435 Pacific Av. Office: 490 Post St., San Francisco. Died Apr. 26, 1958.

BARKDULL, Charles J., oil co. exec.; m. Florence Barkdull; 1 dau., Mrs. James Van Pelt. With Standard Oil Co. (Ind.), 1907—; auditor Midwest Refining Co., a subsidiary, 1921, returned to Chgo. as gen. 1924, as gen. auditor Standard Oil Co. (Ind.), 1924, treas., 1927-39, dir., 1928—, v.p., 1929, exec. v.p. 1933-45; retired. Home: Evanston, Ill. Office: 910 S. Michigan Av., Chgo. Died Apr. 20, 1953.

BARKER, Elsa, author; b. Leicester, Vt.; d. Albert G. and Louise Maria (Taylor) B.; ed. pvt. instrs. Formerly tchr., shorthand reporter, newspaper writer; asso. editor Consol. Encyclopaedic Library, 1901; lectr. N.Y. Bd. Edn., 1904-05; editorial staff Hampton's mag., 1909-10. Author: The Son of Mary Bethel, 1909; The Frozen Grail and Other Poems, 1910; Stories from the New Testament for Children, 1911; The Book of Love (poems), 1912; Letters from a Living Dead Man, 1914; War Letters from the Living Dead Man, 1915; Songs of a Vagrom Angel, 1916; Last Letters from the Living Dead Man, 1919; Fielding Sargent (novel), 1922; The Cobra Candlestick, 1928; The C.I.D. of Dexter Drake, 1929; The Redman Cave Murder, 1930. Wrote labor play, The Scab, produced N.Y.C., Boston, 1904-05. Contbr. poetry, short stories, articles to mags. Home: 52 Irving Pl., N.Y.C. Died Aug. 21, 1954.

BARKER, John Tull, lawyer; b. Carrollton, Missouri; son of Lucian and Mary (Withers) B.; student public schools; married Mayme Fisher; one dau., Mildred. Admitted to Mo. bar, and began practice at LaPlata; mem. Mo. Ho. of Rep. 3 terms, 1907-11 (speaker of House 1911); atty. gen. of Mo., 1913-17; corp. counsel Kansas City under city mgr. form of govt., 1926-29; spl. counsel state of Mo., fire ins. rate litigation, 1922-35; spl. counsel state of Ky. fire ins. rate litigation, 1928-29. Special asst. to Atty. Gen. of United States, 1946-51. Director Missouri Law School Foundation. President Nat. Assn. Atty. Gens., 1915; mem. Am. (ho. of dels. 1935-48), Mo. (pres. 1926), Kansas City (pres. 1942) bar assns., Am. Law Inst., Am. Judicature Soc. (dir.) Vets. Assn. Am., Legion of Honor De Molay (hon.), Alumnus Mo. Univ. (hon.), Phi Delta Phi (hon.). Democrat. Presbyn. Mason (32°), DeMolay (internat. supreme council), Elk. Clubs: Ambassadors, Kansas City. Author: Missouri Lawyer; Aaron Burr the Lawyer; Washington Personalities; Missouri Personalities; Trial of Frank James. Author numerous legal articles. Home: Kansas City Club. Office: 1228 Baltimore Av., Kansas City, Mo. Died 1958.

BARKER, Ralph Malcolm, tobacco co. exec.; b. Covington, Ky., Nov. 22, 1875; s. Myron Irving and Virginia Adalaide (Clark) B.; student pub. schs., Cin., Nelson's Bus. Coll.; m. Margaret Virginia Evans, Apr. 15, 1920 (dec.); 1 son, Myron Irving. In tobacco business in Ky., 1889—; pres. R. M. Barker Tobacco Co., gen. leaf tobacco; pres. Carrollton Tobacco Warehouse Co.; owner Richlawn Farm, breeder of Hereford cattle, Duroc Jersey swine (132 premiums for swine and 69 for cattle in 1924), Great Dane dogs and Percheron horses. An organizer Burley Tobacco Growers' Co.; built first telephone lines in Carroll County, Ky. Mayor of Carrollton 4 yrs. Pres. Ky. Holstein Club, Carrollton C. of C. Methodist. Home: Carrollton, Ky. Died Mar. 28, 1952; buried I.O.O.F. Cemetery, Carrollton, Ky.

BARKER, Walter R., business exec.; b. N.Y.C., July 15, 1890; s. England J. and Mathilda (Leard) B.; m. Margaret Gregson, Aug. 6, 1914; children —Gregson Leard, Margaret, Natalie, Consuelo. Chmn. bd. Uarco Inc., Chgo., 1956—. Republican. Clubs: Commonwealth, Chicago, Union League (Chgo.). Home: Santa Fe, N.M. Office: 141 W. Jackson Blvd., Chgo. 4. Died Aug. 19, 1959.

BARKLEY, Alben William, ex v.p. of U.S., senator; b. Graves County, Ky., Nov. 24, 1877; s. John Wilson and Electra (Smith) B.; A.B., Marvin Coll., Clinton, Ky., 1897; student Emory Coll., Oxford, Ga., 1897-98, U. Va. Law Sch., 1902; LL.D. (hon.), U. Louisville, U. Ky., Center Coll., Nat. U., Emory U., Ky. Wesleyan Coll., Mich. State Coll., De Paul U., Westminster College, Rider College; D.H.L. (honorary) U. Fla., Dropsie College for Hebrew and Cognate Learning; M.S. in Bus. Adminstrn., Bryant Coll.; m. Dorothy Brower, June 23, 1903 (deceased Mar. 10, 1947); children—David Murrell, Marian Frances (Mrs. Max O'Rell Truitt), Laura Louise (Mrs. Douglas MacArthur III); married second (Jane) Mrs. Carleton S. Hadley, November 18, 1949. Admitted to the Kentucky bar, 1901; pros. atty. McCracken Co., Ky., 1905-09; judge McCracken Co. Ct., 1909-13; mem. 63d to 69th Congresses (1913-27), 1st Ky. Dist.; U.S. senator, 4 terms, beginning Mar. 4, 1927; Mar. 4, 1933, Jan. 3, 1939, Jan. 3, 1945; majority leader, 1936-47, minority leader, 1947-49, majority leader, Jan. 3-20, 1949; vice pres. U.S., 1949-53, senator 1954—. Temporary chmn. Dem. Nat. Conv., 1932, 36; permanent chmn., Chicago, 1940, temporary chmn. and keynote speaker, Phila., 1948 (where nominated v.p.). Recipient Collier's Award for 1947 for distinguished Congl. service; Ky. Press Assn. award to Ky.'s outstanding citizen, 1948; Franklin D. Roosevelt Four Freedoms award, 1949; Algernon Sydney Sullivan award, U. Ky., 1949; awarded gold medal by Act of Congress, Aug. 12,

1949, in recognition of distinguished public service; Jr. C. of C. award for outstanding public service in government, 1953; citation, Transylvania Coll., 1954. Hon. mem. Gamma of Ga. chpt. Phi Beta Kappa. Pres. Am. Group, Interparliamentary Union. Mem. Delta Tau Delta, Phi Alpha Delta. Democrat. Methodist. Author: That Reminds Me, 1954. Address: Paducah, Ky.; Senate Office Bldg., Washington. Died Apr. 30, 1956; buried Paducah, Ky.

BARLOW, Fred, Jr., landscape architect; b. Colorado Springs, Colo., Dec. 20, 1902; s. Frederick Walter and Mabel (Crane) B.; student Stanford, 1922-23; B.S., U. Cal., 1925; m. Gwen Witherspoon, June 27, 1931; m. 2d Ruth T. Heartwell, Nov. 1, 1941; children—Marilyn, Patricia, Lee, Frederick alter, III. Staff Paul G. Thiene, 1926-29, Katherine Bashford, 1930-33, Nat. Park Service, Yosemite, 1934-36; partner Bashford & Barlow, 1936-42; ind. practice Fred Barlow Jr., since 1943. Recipient distinguished honor award for landscape architecture, A.I.A., 1946. Mem. Am. Soc. Landscape Architects (trustee 1947-50, v.p. since 1951, past pres., sec.), Am. Inst. Planners, Phi Kappa Psi, Theta Nu Epsilon. Republican. Episcopalian. Home: 230 N. Grand Av., Pasadena 3. Cal. Office: 3444 W. First St., Los Angeles 4. Died Mar. 12, 1954.

BARLOW, Harry Elmore, ry. ofcl.; b. Baraboo, Wis., Mar. 25, 1880; s. Henry P. and Alice R. B.; C.E., U. Minn., 1903; m. Jessie V. Lamb, June 8, 1904; children—Helen Lucile, Philip Elmore, Stephen Henry, Betty Alice. Began as office boy C.,St.P., M.&O. Ry., 1896, and has continued with same road (except when attending schs. and colleges) consecutively as chainman, 1899-1901, rodman and instrumentman, 1901, asst. engr., 1903-20, chief engr. 1920—. Mem. Am. Ry. Engrig. Assn., Engrs. Soc. St. Paul, Tau Beta Pi, Beta Theta Pi. Republican. Protestant. Club: St. Paul Athletic. Home: 2352 Bourne Av. Office: 275 E. 4th St., St. Paul. Died 1935.

BARNARD, Harrison Bernard, builder and contractor; b. Seville, O., May 11, 1872; s. William Edwin and Emily (Nye) B.; student prep. sch., Wooster (O.) U.; A.B., U. of Chicago, 1895; m. Elizabeth Tidholm, June 30, 1917; children—Harrison Blake, William Brewster, Marshall Nye, Burton Wayne, John Brewster. In business at Chicago as builder and contractor since 1892. Trustee (honorary) Univ. of Chicago, John G. Shedd Aquarium, Washington and Jane Smith Home, Chicago Home for Girls. Mem. Society Mayflower Descendants, Society Colonial Wars, Sons American Revolution, Order of Founders and Patriots of America, Delta Tau Delta. Republican. Baptist. Clubs: Union League (pres., 1927-28), South Shore Country, Beverly Country. Home: 7143 Princeton Av. Office: 38 S. Dearborn St., Chgo. Died Aug. 14, 1952; buried Mount Hope Cemetery, Chgo.

BARNARD, William O., ex-congressman; b. Union County, Ind., Oct. 25, 1852; acad. edn. Taught sch. 5 yrs.; admitted to bar; elected pros. atty., 1886, 1888, 1890; judge 53d Jud. Circuit of Ind., 1897-1903; mem. 61st Congress (1909-11) 6th Ind. Dist.; Republican. Address: Newcastle, Ind. Died Apr. 8, 1939.

BARNES, Charles Albert, lawyer; b. Alton, Ill., July 4, 1855; s. William and Eunice A. (Hubbard) B.; M.A., Ill. Coll., 1876; LL.B., U. Mich., 1878; m. Madge M. Martin, Feb. 19, 1899. Admitted to bar, 1878; city atty. Jacksonville, Ill., 1882; state's atty. Morgan County, Ill., 1884-92, county judge, 1897-1906. Del. Universal Congress Lawyers and Jurists, St. Louis, 1904. Trustee Ill. Coll., Jacksonville Female Acad. Mem. Ill. N G., 1870-78. Democrat. Presbyn. Grand chancellor K. P. Ill., 1892-93, supreme vice chancellor, 1904. supreme chancellor, 1906. Address: Jacksonville, Ill. Died Dec. 28, 1913.

BARNES, Charles P., ret. judge; b. Houlton, Me., Oct. 12, 1869; s. Francis and Isa A. (Putnam) B.; A.B., Colby Coll., 1892, A.M., 1893, LL.D., 1926; A.M., U. Me., 1923; m. Annie M. Richardson, Aug. 19, 1896; children—Phinehas Putnam, Charles Francis (dec.), John Albert, George Butler, Margaret Louise, Francis. Prin. pub. high schs., Lisbon and Norway, Me., Attleboro, Mass., 1892-99; supt. schs., Norway, Me., 1899-1910; admitted to bar, 1900; county atty., Oxford County, Me., 1904-09; asst. atty. gen. Me., 1909-11; mem. Hersey & Barnes, Houlton, Me., 1911-17; asso. justice Supreme Ct. Me., 1924-39, chief justice, 1939; retired. Mem. Me. legislature, 1917-23; speaker of house, 1921-23. Trustee Ricker Classical Inst. Republican. Baptist. Mason (K.T.). Home: Houlton, Me. Died Dec. 14, 1952; buried Evergreen Cemetery, Houlton, Me.

BARNES, Floyd Morgan, mfg. exec.; b. Cin., Mar. 16, 1877; s. Henry and Anna B. (Davis) B.; ed. pub. schs. Cin.; m. Lula May Lindsay, Sept. 26, 1901; children—Luella May (Mrs. Joseph B. Shirley). With Cincinnati, Hamilton & Dayton R.R. (now part of Baltimore & Ohio R.R.), Cin., 1896-99; asst. to traffic mgr., The Proctor & Gamble Co., Cin. office, 1899-1906, asst. mgr. cottonseed oil dept. and mgr. export oil sales dept., 1906-17, mgr. cottonseed oil dept., 1917-20, in charge of all buying of the co., 1920-31, vice pres. in charge of purchases 1931-46, dir., 1934—; ret. as v.p., 1946, again active as v.p., 1954—. Decorated Knight of St. Olaf by King Haakon VII of Norway, 1929. Mem. N.Y. Produce Exchange, Oil Trades Assn. of N.Y., Navy League of U.S., Cin. C. of C. Republican. Baptist. Mason (Scottish rite, Shriner). Clubs: The Cincinnati, Hyde Park Golf and Country, Queen City. Home: 3526 Raymar Blvd., Cin. 8. Office: Gwynne Bldg., Cin. 2. Died Mar. 14, 1957.

BARNES, Fred Asa, educator; b. Stockbridge, Mass., June 17, 1876; s. Albert Wheeler and Una Miriam (Thompson) B.; C.E., Cornell U., 1897, M.C.E., 1898; m. Bertha Lula Birdsall, Apr. 15, 1903; 1 dau., Mrs. Mary Louise Eddy. With dist. engrs.' office, Washington, D.C., 1898; draftsman, U.S. Navy, Santiago de Cuba, 1899; asst. and res. engr., Dept. of Santiago, 1899-1901; civ. engr., Ponupo and Cienfuegos, Cuba, 1901-02; instr. civ. engring., 1902-05, asst. prof. railroad engring., 1905-15, prof., 1915-44, prof. emeritus, 1944—; dir. School of Civil Engineering, 1921-30, Cornell U. Conglist. Fellow A.A.A.S.; life mem. Am. Soc. C.E., Am. Railway Engring. Assn., Soc. Promotion Engring. Edn.; mem. Soc. for Advancement of Education, Nat. Soc. Professional Engrs., Sigma Xi, Phi Kappa Phi, Tau Beta Pi, Chi Epsilon, Pi Gamma Mu fraternities. Co-author: (with late C. L. Crandall) Railroad Surveying and Railroad Construction. Author: Notes on Locomotive Rating, Engineering Construction. Contbr. articles on railroads and annual articles on transportation to Collier's Yearbook. Asso. editor: section on steam railways in Am. Civil Engineers Pocketbook and lectures on engineering in Popular Educator. Home: 409 Elmwood Av., Ithaca, N.Y. Died April 5, 1950.

BARNES, Fuller Forbes, business exec.; b. Bristol, Conn., Mar. 6, 1887; s. Carlyle Fuller and Lena H. (Forbes) B.; grad. Andover Prep. Sch., 1906; A.B., Yale, 1910; m. Myrtle Aurelia Ives, Oct. 1, 1913; children— Louise (Mrs. Paul W. Adams), Carlyle F., Aurelia (Mrs. William S. Bristow). Pres., dir. Asso. Spring Corp., Bristol, since 1923; chmn. bd. Wallace Barnes Co., Ltd.; dir. Veeder-Root, Inc., Conn. Light & Power Co., So. New Eng. Telephone Co., Bristol Brass Corp. Mem. Bd. Relief, Bristol, 1913-28, Bd. Finance, 1933-52; Conn. State senator 5th dist., 1929-31. Pres. Bristol Hosp., Inc., since 1921; mem. com. div. med. affairs Yale since 1949. Mem. Spring Mfrs. Assn. (dir.), A.S.M.E., Beta Theta Pi. Conglist. Mason (32°). Clubs: Farmington (Conn.) Country; Chippanee Golf (Bristol); Seigniory (Quebec). Author: Ten Generations of The Barnes Family, 1946. Home: Copper Ledges. Office: 18 Main St., Bristol, Conn. Died June 18, 1955; buried Bristol, Conn.

BARNES, Harold Arthur, army officer; b. Oneida, N.Y., Aug. 7, 1887; commd. 1st lt. Q.M. Corps, 1917, advanced through the grades to brig., 1943; became officer in charge, Civilian Conservation Corps br., Office Q.M. Gen., Washington, 1940; exec. to Q.M. Gen. for civilian personnel affairs, 1940; named chief, Organized Planning and Control Div., Office Q.M. Gen., Wasington, 1942; named dep. Q.M. Gen., 1943. Address: Quartermaster General's Office, War Dept., Washington. Died Aug. 7, 1953.

BARNES, Helen Florence, YWCA worker; b. Ottawa, O., Mar. 9, 1863; d. Revv. Adam Clark (D.D.) and Harriet P. (Gee) Barnes; student Ohio No. U., Ada, O., 1885; B.A., Ohio Wesleyan U., 1889, also M.A.; spl. course in sociology Columbia, 1907; LL. D., Lincoln Meml. U., 1920. Acting dean of women, Drury Coll., Springfield, Mo., 1894-95; state sec. YWCA, Neb. and Mo., 1892-94, 95-98, Wis., Minn. Ohio, Mich., 1880-1900, 1st nat. indsl. sec., 1900-07, 1st nat. country sec., 1909-11, 1st nat. sec. YW CA for Australia and New Zealand, 1911-17; war work for Nat. YWCA, 1918-19; nat. sec. for Secretarial Retirement and Annuity Fund, 1920-22; mem. Nat. YWCA, del. World's Conf., London, 1898, Paris, 1906, Stockholm, 1914; made study of indsl. work in Europe, 1906; pioneer YWCA indsl. and county work; retired from active work, 1923. Visited Greece in interests of Near East Relief, 1927; lectured for Near East Relief, 1927; visited Egypt, Palestine and Syria, 1930, in interests of YWCA and missions and lectured on history and life of same, 1931; del. World's W.C.T.U. Conf.; Stockholm, World's YWCA, Geneva, 1935; visited British Guiana, Windward Islands and Virgin Islands, 1937; lectured on life and customs of same. Made local preacher, 1926, by Ohio Conf. M.E. Ch.; apptd. local head of woman's dept., NRA, 1933. Mem. Ohio br. League of Nations, 1932-36; pres. Findlay Fedn. Women's Clubs, 1933-38; pres. W.C.T.U., 1928-39. Mem. Ohio Com., N.Y. World's Fair, 1939. Mem. Phi Beta Kappa, Altrusa. Toured S.A. and visited Meth. missions and Y.W. C.As., 1938. In 1940 visited Alaska, observing mission work of the churches. Home: 432 W. Sandusky St., Findlay, O. Died Dec. 29, 1953; buried Pomeroy Cemetery, Ottawa, O.

BARNES, Irving Franklin, clergyman; b. Worcester, Mass., May 12, 1872; s. Franklin D. and Mary J. (Higgins) B.; B.D., Oskaloosa (Ia.) Coll., M.A., 1924; spl. student Brown U.; special student Harvard U., two years, 1928-31; D.D., Aurora (Ill.) Coll., 1927; m. Idealla W. Bacon, Dec. 10, 1894 (now deceased); children—Ruth W. (Mrs. Guy Hayes, dec.), Rhobe A. (Mrs. Maurice A. Lohnes), Marion D. (Mrs. H. H. Reynolds); m. 2d, Cora C. Day, Sept. 1, 1928. Ordained ministry Advent Christian Ch., 1892; pastor successively at Webster and Fiskdale, Mass., Castleton, Vt. and Low Hampton, Hoosick and Hudson Falls, N.Y., Portsmouth, N.H., Bridgeport, Conn., Bangor, Me., Providence, R.I., and Somerville, Mass.; pres. Advent Christian Publ. Soc., Boston, 1923-34; pres. Advent Christian Gen. Conf. of America, 1920-38; traveling pastor at large, 1934-36; pastor Providence, R.I., 1937-40, Somerville, Mass., May 1940-44; pastor Dover, N.H., 1945-48, organized church and preached in Alton Bay, N.H., summers, Clearwater, Fla., winters until 1955; now lecturing on history and prophecy. Address: Alton Bay, N.H. Died Dec. 25, 1958; buried Bangor, Maine.

BARNES, James Martin, lawyer; b. Jacksonville, Ill., January 9, 1899; son of Charles A. and Madge (Martin) B.; B.A., Ill. Coll., 1921; LL.B., Harvard, 1924; m. Betty Grove, July 15, 1945. Admitted to Ill. bar, 1924, and began practice in Jacksonville; county judge, Morgan County, Ill., 1926-34; mem. 76th, also 77th, Congress (1939-43), 20th Ill. Dist. (mem. of judiciary com.); administrative assistant to President, U.S., 1943-45; dir. Nat. Savings and Trust Company. Trustee Illinois College. Served with U.S. Marines in France during World War I. President Illinois County and Probate-Judges Assn., 1929, 30. Mem. Am., Ill. State, D.C. bar assns., American Legion. Democrat. Presbyterian. Mason, Elk. Clubs: Chevy Chase, Metropolitan, National Press (Washington), Burning Tree. Home: 2548 Massachusetts Av., N.W. Office: 1025 Connecticut Av., Washington 6. Died June 8, 1958; buried Arlington Nat. Cemetery.

BARNES, John Bryson, soldier, author; b. Pennsboro, W.Va., Sept. 18, 1876; s. Henry and Adaline (Hupp) B.; ed. pub. schs.; distinguished grad. Army Sch. of Line, 1906; grad. Army Staff Coll., 1907, Army War Coll., 1920; m. Caroline Rayfield Bitting, Aug. 31, 1904; 1 son, John Bryson. Enlisted in U.S. Army, 1895; served through Spanish-Am. War, Philippine Insurrection and Cuban Pacification; commd. 2d lt. from ranks, Feb. 2, 1901; promoted through grades to col., June 21, 1930; maj., lt. col. and col. N.A., 1917-19; retired on account of physical disability Nov. 15, 1922. With Isthmian Canal Commn., 1908-09; insp.-instr. Vt. N.G., 1911-12; asst. chief of staff (operations), 5th Div., 80th Div. and 9th Corps, A.E.F.; mem. Gen. Staff, Washington, 1921-22; prof. Kemper Mil. Sch., Boonville, 1922-34. Awarded D.S.M. (U.S.); Officer Étoille Noir, and Croix de Guerre with Palm (French). Republican. Methodist. Mason (32°, Shriner). Clubs: Army and Navy (Washington and New York); Sojourners, Rotary. Author: Elements of Military Sketching, 1911; A Plattsburg Patriot, 1917. Home: Boonville, Mo. Died Oct. 23, 1956.

BARNES, John Hampton, laywer; b. Pitts., Dec. 24, 1860; s. William Henry and Eva (Hampton) B.; A.B., Yale, 1881; studied Columbia Law Sch., 1882-83; m. Emily Leland Harrison, Apr. 21, 1892; children—Dorothy Hampton (Mrs. Jewett Newton), Sylvia Leland (Mrs. Forde Todd), Cecily Weldon (Mrs. Emile Geyelin); m. 2d, Eleanor Kearny Riddle, Apr. 14, 1904; children—Eleanor Biddle (Mrs. H. Gates Lloyd, Jr.), John Hampton. Law practice, Phila., 1883; mem. firm Barnes, Dechert, Price & Smith; counsel Pa. R.R. Co., Girard Trust Co., Westmoreland Coal Co., Phila. Nat. Bank, Berwind White Coal Mining Co.; dir. Phila. Nat. Bank, Phila. Contributionship for Ins. of Houses from Loss by Fire; mgr. Phila. Savs. Fund Soc. Mem. Am. Inst. Law, Pa., Phila Assn. (former chancellor) bar assns., Delta Kappa Epsilon, Scroll and Key. Republican. Clubs: Philadelphia (Phila.); University, Yale (N.Y.); Graduate (New Haven). Home: West Acres, Devon, Chester County, Pa. Office: Packard Bldg., 15th and Chestnut Sts., Phila. Died May 14, 1952.

BARNES, John Peter, judge; b. Ohio Township, Beaver County, Pa., Mar. 15, 1881; s. Albert and Olive A. (Jack) B.; B.S., Geneva Coll. (Beaver Falls, Pa.), 1904, hon. LL.D., 1936; LL.B., U. Mich., 1907, hon. LL.M., 1933; LL.D., John Marshall Law S. 1954; m. Sara A. Darr, 1908; children—John Peter, Rufus Darr (dec.), Mrs. Sara Louise Suster, Mrs. Catherine Olive Hooper, Paul Harry (dec.), Hugh Douglas (dec.). Pvt. practice of law, Chgo., 1907-31, except for 1913-14, when first asst. county atty., Cook County; judge U.S. Dist. Court, No. Dist. of Ill., 1931-57. Northwestern U., Centennial Award, 1951; Jesuit Centennial citation, 1957; Pub. Service award, Chgo. Grad chpt., Tau Epsilon Rho, 1958. Mem. Am., Ill. State, Chgo. bar assns. Student editor Mich. Law Rev., 1906-07. Basset hound breeder, co-owner Barook Kennels, 1957-59. Home: Avalon, R.D. 3, Elgin, Ill. Office: U.S. Courthouse, Chgo. Died Apr. 10, 1959.

BARNES, Julius Howland, corp. ofcl.; b. Little Rock, Ark., Feb. 2, 1873; s. Lucien J. and Julia M. (Hill) B.; student pub. schs., Duluth, Minn., and Washington, D.C.; hon. A.M., Harvard, 1921, Dartmouth, 1921; LL.D., U. Pitts., 1923; Dr. Bus.

Adminstrn., Syracuse U., 1924; m. Harriet Carey, June 30, 1896. Pres. U.S. Food Adminstrn. Grain Corp., 1917-19; pres. U.S. Grain Corp., 1919-20. apptd. by Pres. Wilson U.S. wheat dir., 1919-20; pres. Intercontinental Development Co.; pres. Am. Industries, Inc.; chmn. bd. Klearflax Linen Looms, Inc., Barnes-Duluth Shipbuilding Co.; pres. Erie & St. Lawrence Corp., McDougall-Duluth Co. Pres. C. of C. of U.S., 1921-24, chmn. bd., 1929-31. Decorated Comdr. Order of the Crown (Belgium), 1919; Officer Légion d'Honneur (France), 1919; Comdr. Order of the Crown (Italy), 1920; Comdr. Polish Order Restituta, 1920; Comdr. Order of White Rose (Finland), 1920; Order Civil Mérite (Bulgaria), 1922. Hon. Phi Beta Kappa, William and Mary, 1921. Republican. Clubs: N.Y. Athletic, India House (N.Y.C.); Duluth Athletic, Kitchi Gammi (Duluth). Home: 25 S. 26th Av., Duluth, Minn.; also 10 Gracie Square, N.Y.C. Office: 19 Rector St., N.Y.C. Died Apr. 1959.

BARNES, Nathaniel Waring, educator, cons. bus. communications; b. Newburgh, N.Y., July 25, 1884; s. James Waring and Sarah Frances (Owen) B.; A.B., Columbia, 1903, A.M., 1905; m. Mabel Bonnell, Dec. 15, 1908; m. 2d, Kathleen Bassett, Mar. 31, 1929. Prof. English composition DePauw U., 1907-16; lectr. bus. writing U. Chgo., 1914-17, asst. prof. comml. orgn., 1917-23, asso. prof. marketing, sch. commerce and adminstrn., 1923-29; profl. lectr. bus. corr. sch. commerce Northwestern U., 1921-27; lectr. sch. bus. and U. extension Columbia. 1930—. Dir. Bur. Research and Edn., Internat. Advt. Assn., 1927-30. Specialist on bus. Eng. and asso. dir. field work in English for AEF, Army Ednl. Corps, 1919. Exec. sec. Assn. Cons. Mgmt. Engrs., 1932—; exec. sec., treas. 7th Internat. Mgmt. Congress, 1937-39. Mem.Am. Marketing Soc. (ex-nat. sec.), Nat. Assn. Tchrs. Marketing and Advt. (ex-pres.), Am. Mgmt. Assn., Am. Bus. Writing Assn., Soc. Advancement Mgmt., S.A.R., Phi Beta Kappa, Sigma Delta Chi, Delta Sigma Pi, Pi Gamma Mr. Mason (K.T., Shriner). Club: Columbia University (N.Y. C.). Author: The Art of Writing English (with E. W. Brown), 1913; How to Teach Business Correspondence, 1916; Manual of Business Communication, 1918; Marketing Management (with L. S. Lyon), 1923; Business Letters (with L. H. Grinstead), 1927; Business Writing Manual, 1935; Management Engineering—A Vocational Monograph, 1944; articles on bus. letters and mgmt. counsel. Home: 345 E. 57th St., N.Y.C. 22. Office: 347 Madison Av., N.Y.C. 17. Deceased.

BARNES, Parry, accountant; b. Kansas City, Kan.; Nov. 10, 1892; s. Edwin Burdette and Alfreda Sloane) B.; C.P.A. holding certificates granted by Mo., 1923, Kan., 1924, Okla., 1929, N.Y., 1931; m. Anne Cecil McShane, Sept. 15, 1928; children—Parry, Earl McShane. Began career as staff accountant with J. M. Mactaggart & Co., chartered accountants, Kansas City, Mo., 1918-22; mgr. Wichita, Kans. office, Smith Brodie and Lunsford; partner Smith, Lunsford and Wright, 1924, Lunsford, Barnes and Co., 1926; instr. in fed. taxation, U. of Kansas City, 1943-44. Mem. Am. Accounting Assn., Am. Inst. of Accountants (v.p., 1946), Nat. Assn. Cost Accountants (sec. Kansas City chapt. 1937-48, pres. 1948-49), N.Y. and Mo. socs. C.P.A. (pres. Mo. soc., 1936-38). Mem. bd. Kansas City Area Council Boy Scouts of Am. Independent. Protestant. Mason (32°, K.T., Shriner). Mem. Royal Order of Jesters. Club: Kansas City. Home: 800 W. 59th St., Kansas City 2. Office: 21 W. Tenth St., Kansas City 6, Mo. Died Jan. 11, 1950.

BARNETT, Bion Hall, banker; b. Ind., 1857; s. William Boyd B.; m. Caroline L. H. L'Engle, Apr. 8, 1880; children—Madeleine Hall (Mrs. Charles W. Camp), William L'Engle and Bion Hall (twins), Donald Murray (dec.). Hon. chmn. bd. Barnett Nat. Bank. Address: Jacksonville, Fla. Died Oct. 30, 1958.

BARNETT, Claribel Ruth, librarian; b. Kent, O., Mar. 26, 1872; d. George and Lucina (Deuel) Barnett; Western Res. Acad. 1887-89; Ph.B., U. of Mich., 1889-93; B.L.S., New York State Library Sch., 1920. With library of U.S. Dept. of Agr., 1895-1940, 1st as cataloguer, asst. librarian, 1901, librarian, July 1907-Nov. 15, 1940. Organized agrl. libraries sect. of A.L.A. (chmn. 1910-14, 27); mem. Library Advisory Wage Com. of Joint Congl. Commn. on Reclassification of Salaries, 1919-20. Mem. A.L.A. (2d v.p. 1921, 22), D.C. Library Assn. (pres. 1929-30), Agrl. Hist. Soc., Am. Assn. Univ. Women, Washington Acad. Sciences, Pi Gamma Mu, Phi Beta Kappa; fellow Am. Library Inst., A.A.A.S. Episcopalian. Club: A.A.A.W. Home: 1661 Crescent Pl. N.W., Washington 9. Died Mar. 6, 1951; buried Kent. O.

BARNETT, Harry, bishop; b. Jan. 25, 1888; ed. public schools of Indianapolis; married Victoria; one foster daughter Donna May. Bishop, Pentecost Assemblies of the World, serving in Minn. and Wis. area, 1934-51, hon. bishop since Aug. 1951. Home: 1324 N. 5th St., Niles, Mich. Died July 7, 1952; buried Garden of Memories, Silver Brook Cemetery, Niles.

BARNETTE, William Jay, naval officer; b. Morrisville, N.Y., Feb. 2, 1847; s. Dr. Milton and Caroline (Shepherd) B.; grad. U.S. Naval Acad., 1868; m. Evelyn G. Hutchins, Nov. 29, 1877. Served midshipman Asiatic Fleet, 1868; ensign, Apr. 19, 1869; master, July 12, 1870; lt., Dec. 28, 1872; lt.-comdr., Apr. 16, 1894; comdr., Mar. 3, 1899; capt., Oct. 11, 1903; rear-adm., Aug. 1, 1908. Comd. Dorothea, June, 1898, Saratoga, 1898-1901; mem. Gen. Bd. (Navy), 1902-04; mem. Joint Bd. (Army and Navy), July 21, 1903, to June 14, 1904; comdg. U.S. battleship Kentucky, June, 1904-Jan., 1906; mem. Gen. Bd. and Joint Bd., Jan., 1906; retired, Feb. 2, 1909. Republican. Clubs: University (N.Y.C.) Rittenhouse, University (Phila.), Metropolitan (Washington). Address: care Navy Dept., Washington. Deceased.

BARNEY, Charles Neal, corp. exec., counsel; b. Lynn, Mass., June 27, 1875; s. William Mitchell and Mary Louise (Neal) B.; A.B., Tufts Coll., Medford, Mass., 1895, A.M., hon., 1909; LL.B., Boston U., 1898; m. Maizie Blaikie, June 27, 1901; children—Virginia, Stuart Neal (dec.). Began as lawyer, Boston, 1898; partner Lummus & Barney, Lynn, Mass., 1900-15, Barney & Woodruff, 1915-18; officer Worthington Pump and Machinery Corp., Harrison, N.J., since 1918, vice pres. since 1942; lecturer Northeastern Law Sch., Boston, 1908-18, Boston U. Law Sch., 1911. Mayor, Lynn, Mass., 1906-07; presidential elector, Mass., 1908; chmn. legal adv. bd. for draft, Lynn, 1917. Trustee Tufts Coll., Boston, 1908-23. Pres. Maria Mitchell Assn. operating astron. obs., Nantucket. Recipient Ballou medal, Tufts College, 1949. Mem. Am., Mass. and N.Y. bar assns., Soc. of Mayflower Descendants (N.Y.), Newcomen Soc. of Eng., Phi Beta Kappa, Theta Delta Chi. Republican. Clubs: University (New York); Fox Meadow Tennis (Scarsdale, N.Y.); Pacific (Nantucket, Mass.). Author: Equity and Its Remedies, 1915. Home: 15 Barclay Rd., Scarsdale, N.Y. Office: Worthington Pump and Machinery Corp., 2 Park Av., N.Y. City. Died Apr. 24, 1949.

BARNEY, William Joshua, corp. exec.; b. Detroit, Mar. 11, 1884; s. Joshua Carroll and May Florence (Kelly) B.; C.E., U. of South, 1905; m. Lilian Warner, Oct. 17, 1910 (dec.); 1 son, William Joshua. Various engring. positions, 1905-11; dep. commr. docks, N.Y. City, 1911-14; cons. engr. Harbor and Port Installations, and mem. bd. cons. engrs. for laying out port of Portland, Ore., 1914-17; founder W. J. Barney Corp., specializing in designing and bldg. indsl. plants N.E. sect. country, N.Y. City, 1917, pres., 1917-50, chmn. bd. since 1950. Mem. Am. Soc. C.E. (past chmn. constrn. div.), N.Y. Bldg. Congress (past treas. and mem. bd. govs.), Bldg. Trades Employers Assn. of N.Y. (mem. bd. govs.), Asso. Gen. Contractors (past dir. and chmn. apprenticeship com.), Soc. of the Cincinnati, Soc. Colonial Wars, Alpha Tau Omega. Club: University (N.Y. City). Home: 103 E. 75th St., N.Y. City 21. Office: 101 Park Av., N.Y.C. 17. Died Dec. 12, 1954; buried Woodlawn Cemetery, N.Y.C.

BARNHART, Thomas Frederick (bärn'härt), univ. prof.; b. Snohomish, Wash., Oct. 26, 1902; s. Frederick and Ellen Agnes (Flynn) B.; B.A. U. Wash., 1930; M.A., U. Minn., 1937; m. Annice Rebecca Mars, Dec. 22, 1926; children—Thomas Frederick, Laurane, Robert Lee, Barbara Ellen. Mem. staff Snohomish Tribune, 1920-25; asst. Sch. Journalism U. Wash., also asst. to field mgr. Wash. Press Assn., 1927-28, 29-30; asso. editor and editor, U. Wash. Daily, 1928-29; mem. staff Snohomish Tribune, June-Oct. 1930; advertising and publicity mgr. Everett (Wash.) C. of C., 1930-31; asst. prof. journalism, U. Minn. 1931-35, asso. prof., 1935-37, prof., 1937—; consultant to Northwest Daily Press Assn., Minn. Editorial Assn. Mem. Am. Assn. Univ. Profs., Assn. for Edn. in Journalism, Am. Acad. Polit. and Social Sci., Sigma Delta Chi, Kappa Sigma, Kappa Tau Alpha. Clubs: Advertising of Minneapolis (president 1947-48), Campus. Author: Weekly Newspaper Management, 1936; Newspaper Sales Promotion, 1939; Weekly Newspaper Makeup and Typography, 1949; Weekly Newspaper Writing and Editing, 1949. Editor: The Weekly Newspaper: A Bibliography—1925-41, 1951. Advisory editor The Scholastic Editor, 1935—. Speaker at many state press groups. Home: 5228 Lake Nokomis Pky., Mpls. 7. Died Jan. 7, 1955; buried G.A.R. Cemetery, Snohomish, Wash.

BARNWELL, Middleton Stuart, bishop; b. Louisville, Sept. 9, 1882; s. Stephen Elliott and Elizabeth (Cleland) B.; A.B., Centre Coll., Danville, Ky., 1900; B.D., Va. Theol. Sem., 1909, D.D.; m. Margaret Thorne Lighthall, June 24, 1912. Deacon, 1908, priest, 1908, P.E. Ch.; asst. rector Christ Ch., Balt., 1909-11; rector St. Andrew's Ch., New Bedford, Mass., 1911-13, Ch. of the Advent, Birmingham, Ala., 1913-23; field sec. Nat. Council P.E. Ch., 1924-25; consecrated bishop of Ida., Dec. 3, 1925; pres. Boise Jr. Coll.; bd. trustees. St. Luke's Hosp., St. Margaret's Sch.; elected bishop of Georgia, 1935. Mem. Sigma Alpha Epsilon. Home: 732 E. 45th St., Savannah, Ga. Died May 6, 1957; buried Bonnaventure Cemetery, Savannah, Ga.

BARR, G(ranville) Walter, writer, physician; b. Medway, O., Oct. 25, 1860; s. Dr. Jacob Cullen and

Kate (Doll) B.; student Asbury (now DePauw) U., 1877-80; Rush Med. Coll., Chgo., 1882-83; M.D., Jefferson Med. Coll., Phila., 1884; m. Annabelle Applegate, Apr. 12. 1884. In newspaper work, Ind., 1877-80; surgeon Ill. div. Sons of Vets., 1890; prof. materia medica, therapeutics Coll. Phys. and Surg., Keokuk, Ia., 1890-8. Edited dept. materia medica and therapeutics, Iowa State Medical Journal, 1893-4; mng. editor Keokuk Gate City; 1899-1900, city editor, 1900-02; editor and propr. Keokuk Standard, 1902-10; in charge dept. of pub. relations Miss. River Power Co., 1911-15; efficiency engr. and prof. materia medica Highland Park Coll. of Pharmacy, Des Moines, Ia., 1915-16. Lecturer on popular science, economics; sec. bd. of edn., Keokuk, Ia., 1898-15; trustee pub. library, Keokuk, 1908-15. Exec. for Lee Co. in war aid work, Liberty bonds, food administration, thrift stamps, 1917-18; Med. R.C. 1918—. Chmn. pub. comfort commn., City of Keokuk, 1920—. Spl. writer, Burlington, Ia., Gazette. Republican. Clubs: High Tension, Iowa Authors. Author: Shacklett, 1901. Home: Keokuk, Ia. Deceased.

BARR, Richard Alexander, surgeon; b. Sumner County, Tenn., Sept. 8, 1871; s. B. B. M. L. and Mary Laura (Alexander) B.; B.A., Vanderbilt U., 1892, M.D., 1894; m. Sarah Elizabeth Kirkpatrick, Nov. 18, 1897; 1 son, Richard A. Practiced in Nashville, 1895—; prof. clinical surgery Vanderbilt U., 1902—. Maj. surgeon, 1st Tenn. Vol. Inf., Spanish-Am. War and Philippine insurrection, 1898-99; lt. col. M.C., U.S. Army, comdg. officer Hosp. Unit "S" (Vanderbilt), AEF, France, 1918, 19. Fellow A.C.S.; mem. A.M.A., So. Surg. Assn., Phi Delta Theta, Phi Beta Kappa. Presbyn. Address: R. 4, Gallatin, Tenn. Deceased.

BARR, Samuel Davis, educator; b. Gouverneur, N.Y., July 7, 1826; s. Elisha and Laura (Mix) B.; ed. Wesleyan Sem., Gouverneur; grad. Williams Coll., 1853; m. 1st, Olive Eddv, 1854; m. 2d, Maria O. Smith, 1869; m. 3d, Mrs. Mary Burhans Smith, 1890. Prof. mathematics and natural sciences Wesleyan Sem., Gouverneur, N.Y., 1853-6; prof. mathematics, Black River Literary and Religious Inst., 1856-58; practiced law at Watertown, N.Y., 1858-65; dep. supt. pub. instrn. N.Y., 1865-69; tchr. mathematics Mil. Collegiate Inst., Rochester, 1869-70; prin. Penn Yan Acad., 1870-73; prin. West High Sch., Cleve., 1874-80; prof. mathematics, Albion (Mich.) Coll., 1882-98; retired. Mem. Phi Beta Kappa; was pres. N.Y. State Tchrs. Assn. Address: Albion, Mich. Deceased.

BARR, Samuel Fleming, ex-congressman; b. Coleraine, Ireland, June 15, 1829; reared nr. Pitts.; pub. sch. edn. First terminal freight agt. Pitts., Ft. Wayne & Chgo. R.R. after consolidation with Pa. R.R., at Allegheny City, Pa.; assisted mgmt. r.r. service organized by govt. for supplying fed. army in Washington at outbreak of Civil War; re-entered Pa. R.R. service at close of war and continued until retirement; mem. 47th and 48th Congresses, 14th Pa. Dist. Del. Ren. Nat. convs. that nominated Hayes and Garfield. Home: Seal Harbor, Me. Deceased.

BARRETT, Channing Whitney, gynecologist; b. Blissfield, Mich., Dec. 14, 1866; s. David Fowler and Martha C. (Dewey) B.; student Fayette (O.) Normal U., Hillsdale (Mich.) Coll.; M.D., Detroit Coll. Medicine, 1895; m. Luella May Alvord, July 22, 1896; children—Russell Alvord, Florence Louise, Helen Elizabeth, Ruth Esther. Intern St. Luke's Hosp., Detroit, 1893-95; house phys. Harper Hosp., Detroit, 1895-96; asst. surgeon Marion Sims. Hosp., Chgo., 1893—; prof. gynecology Chgo. Clin. Sch., 1900-06; prof. gynecology Chgo. Policlinic Sch.; prof., chief dept. gynecology U. Ill. Med. Sch. to 1930; now prof. gynecology Loyola U. Med. Sch.; chief dept. of gynecology Cook County Hosp. Maj. M.C. World War. Fellow Assn. Obstetricians and Gynecologists, Am. Gynecol. Soc., Chgo. Gynecol. Soc. (ex-pres.); mem. A.M.A., and kindred orgns. Cited for Legion of Honor by French govt. Republican. Methodist. Clubs: City, Press. Contbd. med. jours. Home: 6224 Kenmore Av. Office: 6 N. Michigan Av., Chgo. Died Jan. 29, 1958; buried Montpelier, O.*

BARRETT, Edward F., utilities official; b. New York, N.Y., Apr. 5, 1888; s. Thomas F. and Jane (Cordial) B.; ed. pub. schs.; m. Elizabeth Schoder, Oct. 24, 1911; children—Virginia (Mrs. Richard N. Rand), Dorothy J. (Mrs. Ernest M. Fuller), Edward Mitchell. Dep. chamberlain, City of N.Y., 1914-18; with Nat. City Co., 1918-21, beginning as sec. to pres. and advanced to asst. sec. with Nat. City Bank, 1921-34, v.p., 1926-34; with Long Island Lighting Co. since Apr. 1934, v.p. in charge financial operations. 1934-37, pres., 1937-53, chairman board. 1953-57, dir., chmn. pension com. 1957-58; trustee, 1st vice pres., East River Savings Bank. Home: 67 Hilton Av., Garden City, L.I., N.Y. Office: 250 Old Country Rd., Mineola, L.I., N.Y. Died June 30, 1958.

BARRETT, Jesse W., lawyer; b. Canton, Mo., Mar. 17, 1884; s. Harry Hooven and Jeanette Amelia (Bushman) B.; A.B., cum laude, Christian U. (now Culver-Stockton Coll.), Canton, Mo., 1902, LL.D., 1923; LL.B., George Washington U., 1905; m. Ethelyn Louthan, June 19, 1912 (died Dec. 25, 1913); m. 2d, Mary Louise Church, Feb. 21, 1925. Began practice at St. Louis, Mo., 1906; spl. asst. U.S. atty., 1909-10; sec. Rep. State Com., 1919; atty. gen. of Mo., 1921-25; now in practice in St. Louis; counsel for State of Mo. in anti-trust proc. vs. Standard Oil Co. and spl. counsel St. Louis Police Bd., 1926; mem. of law firm Barrett, Cook and Fairfield. Successfully prosecuted bldg. material combine and cement "open price" assns.; expelled 3 per cent housing trusts from Mo.; won Mo. corp. franchise tax case; soldier bonus bonds case; Nat. branch banking case in U.S. Supreme Court; atty. for Mo. Press Assn. in freedom of press litigation, 1940. Vice pres., dir. Mo. Press Brick Co. Candidate for Republican nomination for U.S. Senate, 1922; Rep. nominee for governor, 1936; mem. advisory com. Bd. Draft Appeals, 1940. Chmn. St. Louis Bd. Election Commrs., 1941-45; chmn. Mo. Supreme Court's Com. on Bar Integration, 1944; mem. State Bd. Edn., 1921-25; pres. Assn. Young Republicans of Mo., 1914; pres. Alumni Assn. Culver-Stockton Coll., 1923; pres. bd. Kingdom House (social settlement); trustee St. John's Meth. Ch. Culver-Stockton Coll. (v. chmn.); pres. Meth. Club (St. Louis), 1940; mem. Meth. Commn. on Interdenom. Rel. Hon. life mem. Nat. Assn. Attys. Gen.; charter and life mem. Am. Inst. Law; mem. Internat. Assn. Attys. Gen., Am. Acad. Polit. Sci., Am., Mo. (pres. 1934), St. Louis bar assns., Mo. Inst. for Adminstrn. Justice (dir.). Mo. Hist. Soc., (dir. and mem., exec. com.), St. Louis Chamber of Commerce (mem. board of directors), St. Louis Authors Soc., Newcomen Soc. of England, Mo. Republican Editorial Assn., Vets. Welfare Assn. (trustee), Am. Legion (state comdr. 1933; mem. nat. legislative com. and chmn. nat. com. for entertainment of distinguished guests, 1935), Phi Sigma Kappa, Phi Delta Phi (pres. alumni assn. of St. Louis 1931), Pi Kappa Delta (hon.). Wrote "Limitations of the Anti-Trust Laws" and "Economics and Statutory Law"; joint author with Herbert S. Hadley, of report for Mo. Crime Survey on "Specific Recommendations." Methodist. Mason (33° Hon.); orator, Missouri Grand Lodge, 1923-24. Clubs: Noonday, Jefferson City Country, Scottish Rite Club (pres. 1926), Nat. Sojourners (hon. mem.), Contemporary (chmn. 1945). Home: 4950 Lindell Blvd. Office: 506 Olive St., St. Louis, Mo. Deceased.

BARRETT, Otis Warren, agriculturist; b. Clarendon, Vt., Apr. 18, 1872; s. James and Alice W. (Kelley) B.; B.Sc., U. of Vermont, 1896; also certificate of proficiency in modern langs. (hon. D.Sc., 1934); m. Bessie Lou Stearns, Ph.B., Apr. 27, 1898. In Jamaica, 1894, in employ of West India Improvement Co.; apptd., 1898, traveling agt. of the commn. for the Mexican exhibit of Paris Expn. of 1900; hon. curator entom. collections of Museo de la Comisión Geográfico-Exploradora at Tacubaya, Fed. Dist., Mexico, 1898-1900; entomologist and botanist to P. R. Agrl. Expt. Sta., 1901-05; plant introducer, Office Seed and Plant Introduction and Distribution, U.S. Dept. Agr., 1905-08. Specially commd. by Agrl. Soc. of Trinidad and Tobago, B.W.I., to report upon cacao diseases in Trinidad, 1907; dir. of agr. for Mozambique, Portuguese E. Africa, 1908-10; chief of divisions expt. stas. and horticulture, Bur. of Agr., Manila, P.I., 1910-14; horticulturist of Canal Zone, 1914-17; mgr. coconut plantations in Nicaragua, Mar.-Sept., 1917; with U.S. Dept. Agr., 1917; carbon expert, U.S. War Dept., 1918-19; agrl. adviser to Liberia, 1920-21; agrl. survey of Haiti, 1922; with Dept. of Agr., San Juan, P.R., 1923-29; horticulturist of U. of Hawaii, 1929-30. Mem. Vermont Bot. Club, Bot. Soc. Washington, Entomol. Soc. Washington, Soc. of Am. Mammalogists, Philippine Acad., Porto Rico Ateneo, S.A.R.; fellow A.A.A.S. Club: Philippine. Author: The Changa, or Mole Cricket, in Porto Rico, 1902; The Yautias, or Taniers, of Porto Rico, 1905; Promising Root Crops for the South, 1910; Coconut Culture, 1911; The Philippine Coconut Industry, 1913; The Food Plants of Porto Rico, 1925; The Tropical Crops, 1928; The Animals on Postage Stamps, 1936. Address: N. Clarendon, Vt. Died Oct. 6, 1950; buried Clarendon Flats Cemetery.

BARRETT, Robert South; b. Richmond, Va., Mar. 30, 1877; s. Rev. Robert S. Barrett (D.D.) and Kate (Waller) B. (M.D.); ed. U. of the South (Dr. Civil Laws) and George Washington U.; m. Viola Tupper, Nov. 17, 1898; children—Robert Tupper, Clifton Waller, John Paul Barker, Robert South (dec.), Viola Haywood. Editor and pub. Mexico City Daily Record, 1904-07, Alexandria (Va.) Gazette, 1911-16; trade commr., U.S. Dept. Commerce to S. America, 1916-17; comml. attaché to Am. Embassy, Buenos Aires, Argentina, 1918; rep. of War Trade Bd., 1918; v.p. Portalis & Co., bankers, Paris and Buenos Aires, 1919; pres. Nat. Florence Crittenden Mission since 1925. Pres. Va. Press Assn., 1915-16; treas. Commn. on Faith and Order of P.E. Ch. since 1931. Fellow Royal Geog. Soc. (London); mem. Delta Tau Delta. Democrat. Episcopalian. Mason (33°, K.T., Shriner), grand master, Grand Lodge of Va.; sovereign grand inspector gen. and grand almoner supreme council. Elk (grand exalted ruler for U.S.A., 1944-45, grand treas., 1938-41; grand trustee since 1941). Author: Standard Guide to Mexico, 1900; Blue Book of Mexico, 1905; The Care of the Unmarried Mother; Fifty Years Work with Girls; I Was an Unmarried Mother; also of many monographs on S. Am. trade. Clubs: National Press (Washington); Jockey, American (Buenos Aires). Donor of public buildings (hosp., library, boys' club, auditorium, dormitory) to various instns. in Va. Contributed with Mrs. Barrett $1,000,000 to establish Barrett Found. Inc., 1947. Home: 404 Duke St., Alexandria, Va. Died Feb. 24, 1959; buried Aquia Churchyard, Stafford Co., Va.

BARRETT, Wilbert Hamilton, retired mfr.; b. Cumberland County, N.J., Feb. 26, 1858; s. Reuben T. and Lucinda Maxson (Tomlinson) B.; student Union Acad., Shiloh, N.J., and South Jersey Inst., Bridgeton; m. Elizabeth Benner, May 18, 1881; 1 son, Roland Benner. Organizer, 1904, and pres. until retirement, 1925, Acme Preserve Co., mfrs. spl. food products, Adrian, Mich.; dir. Commercial Savings Bank of Adrian. Pres. Adrian (Mich.) Water Board. Past pres. Mich. Soc. S.A.R.; served as dir. gen. nat. orgn. S.A.R. and pres., 1926-27. Mem. S.R., Soc. Colonial Wars Republican. Bapitst. Mason (32°, K.T.); past comdr. Adrian Comdry. Home: 225 Toledo St., Adrian, Mich. Deceased.

BARRETT, William Felton, born Dayton, Ohio; Ph.B., Yale University, 1904; D.Sc., University of Pittsburgh, 1925; married Margery Barker, October 18, 1911; children—Julian Shumway, William Felton, David Barker. Began business career as civil engineer, Buffalo, Rochester & Pittsburgh Ry., 1904; with Ogden Gas Co., later Peoples Gas Light & Coke Co., Chicago, 1905-13; works mgr. The Linde Air Products Co., 1913-18, v.p., 1918-25, pres., 1925-29, chmn. bd., 1929-44; v.p. and dir. Union Carbide & Carbon Corp., 1926-44; chmn. bd. Carbide & Carbon Chems. Corp., Carbide & Carbon Chemicals, Ltd., Dominion Oxygen Co., Ltd., Prest-O-Lite Co., Inc., Prest-O-Lite Co. of Can., Ltd.; dir. Dominion Mines & Quarries, Ltd., Bakelite Corp., Electro Metall. Co., Elec. Furnace Products Co., Ltd., Nat. Carbon Co., The Oxweld R.R. Service Co., Union Carbide & Carbon Research Labs., Inc., Mich. Northern Power Co., United Chromium, Inc., Carbide & Carbon Realty Co., Inc., until 1944, now retired. Mem. bd. mgrs. N.Y. Bot. Garden. Mem. Am. Chem. Soc., Am. Soc. M.E., Chi Phi. Clubs: Links, University, Yale, The River, Cloud (N.Y.C.); Wyantenuck Country (Great Barrington, Mass.). Address: "Sky Farm," Great Barrington, Mass. Died May 24, 1955.

BARRON, Carter Tate, theatre exec.; b. Clarkesville, Ga., Jan. 30, 1905; s. David J. and Florence (Crow) B.; B.S., Ga. Inst. Tech., 1927; m. Velna Snelling, June 6, 1928; 1 son, Carter Tate, Mgr. Fairfax Theatre, East Point, Ga., 1927; asst. mgr. Capitol Theater, Atlanta, 1927; became mgr. Metropolitan Theater and converted it to talking pictures, 1928; mgr. The Capitol and Fox, 1932; city mgr. Loew's Washington Theaters, 1934; mgr. Loew's Eastern Div. of Theaters, including D.C., Md., Va., Del. and Pa., since 1934; Washington rep. Metro-Goldwyn-Mayer since 1942; v.p. Kes-Bar, Inc.; dir. Washington Bd. of Trade since 1949. Exec. vice chmn. Nat. Capitol Sesqui-Centennial Commn. since 1948; asst. chief barker Variety Clubs Internat., 1942-49; chmn, entertainment com. President's Birthday Balls, 1934-46; dir. D.C. chapter Nat. Cancer Soc.; mem. exec. com. Nat. Foundn. for Infantile Paralysis; dir. Metropolitan Boys Clubs, treas. Am. Foundn. for Physically Handicapped; co-chmn. Amusement Div. War Bond Campaigns, 1942-45; treas. Nat. Jefferson-Jackson Day Dinner Com. since 1945; head of music and entertainment Nat. Dem. Conv., 1940; chmn. entertainment com. President's Inaugural Gala, 1941; chmn. parade and special events com. Presdl. Inaugural, 1949. Mem. Sigma Alpha Epsilon. Democrat. Baptist. Mason. Clubs: National Press, Alfalfa, Rotary, Variety, Touchdown, Chatterbox. Home: 6661 Barnaby St., Washington 4. Office: Loew's Capitol Theatre, Washington 4. Died Nov. 16, 1950; buried West View Cemetery, Atlanta, Ga.

BARRON, E. S. Guzman, biochemist; b. Huari, Peru, Sept. 18, 1898; s. Sebastian and Agripina (Barron) G.; M.D., U. San Marcos, Lima, 1924; D.Sc., U. Trujillo, Peru, 1947, U. Brazil, 1956; m. Cora Durkee, Aug. 8, 1930; 1 son, Richard. Came to U.S., 1926, naturalized, 1939. Fellow The Rockefeller Found., 1927-28; professor biochemistry U. Chicago; honorary professor of medicine, Faculty of Medicine, Lima, 1949; hon. prof. medicine and chemistry University Uruguay, 1956; hon. prof. science U. Arequipa, 1956. Recipient prize for study abroad, Faculty of Medicine, Lima, 1925-26. Mem. Am. Soc. Biol. Chemists, Am. Assn. Physicians, Am. Chem. Soc., Soc. Exptl. Biology and Medicine. Home: 5642 Kimbark Av., Chgo. 37. Died June 25, 1957; buried Woods Hole, Mass.

BARROWS, Anna, educator, lectr., writer; b. Fryeburg, Me.; d. George Bradley and Georgiana (Souther) Barrows; grad. Fryeburg Acad., Boston Cooking Sch., 1886. Tchr. pub. schs. in Me. and N.H.; tchr. cookery North Bennet St. Indsl. Sch., Boston, 1886-91, Sch. of Domestic Science, Boston, 1891-95, Lasell Sem., Auburndale, Mass., 1891-1900, Robinson Female Sem., Exeter, N.H., 1895-1905, Chautauqua (N.Y.) Sch. of Domestic Sci., 1900-20; lectr. Sch. of Practical Arts, Tchrs. Coll. (Columbia), 1905-32; sec. Am. Home Econs. Assn., 1914-15; asst., extension work with women, U.S. Dept. Agr., 1917-18. Has lectured widely on cooking and other phases of domestic sci. Mem. Boston Sch. Com., 1900-03. Mem. N.E. Woman's Press Assn., Am. Home Econs. Assn., Gen. Fedn. Women's Clubs, D.A.R. Conglist. Has pub. books on Eggs, Principles of Cooking, others. Writes for agrl., religious and household papers. Home: Fryeburg, Me. Died Feb. 11, 1948; buried Pine Grove Cemetery, Fryeburg.

BARROWS, Harold Kilbrith, cons. engr.; b. Melrose, Mass., Nov. 9, 1873; s. Cyrus Moulton and Augusta (Kilbrith) B.; B.S. in Civil Engring., Mass. Inst. Tech., 1895; m. Mabel R. Jordan, Feb. 11, 1907 (died Dec. 24, 1953); 1 son, Kilbrith Jordan. With city engr., Newton, Mass., later with Met. Water Bd., Boston; asso. prof. civil engring. U. Vt., 1901-04; dist. engr. U.S. Geol. Survey, New Eng. and N.Y., 1904-08; cons. hydraulic engr., Boston, 1907-—; asso. prof. hydraulic engring. Mass. Inst. Tech., 1909-21, prof., 1921-41, in charge of hydro-electric option in civil engring., prof. emeritus, 1941-—. Cons. on water power, water supply and flood control for numerous state public utility and power commns., atty. gen.'s offices, etc., for many municipalities and pvt. corps.; mem. and cons. Adv. Com. Flood Control., State Vt., 1928-31; regional cons. Nat. Resources Com., 1934-41. Fellow Am. Acad. Arts and Scis.; mem. Am. Inst. Cons. Engrs., Am. Soc. C.E., Boston Soc. C E. (past pres.), Chi Epsilon. Author: Water Power Engineering, 1927, 3d edit. 1943; Floods—Their Hydrology and Control, 1948; also many state and national reports upon water power, storage, water supply, and flood control. Home: 332 Highland Av., Winchester, Mass. Office: 6 Beacon St., Boston. Died Mar. 15, 1954; buried Wildwood Cemetery, Winchester.

BARROWS, Nathaniel Haven, textile exec.; born South Berwick, Me., July 7, 1877; s. Albert C. and Elizabeth Cogswell (Clark) B.; grad. Dartmouth, 1900; m. Julia Rutter, Feb. 6, 1901; 1 son, Nathaniel Haven. Supt., Burlington mill, Am. Woollen Co., 1906-09; v.p., gen. mgr. Wyandotte Worsted Co., 1909-32, pres. since 1932. Mason, Elk, Rotarian. Clubs: Waterville Country; Algonquin (Boston); Bald Peak Colony. Home: Park St. Office: Head of Falls, Waterville, Me. Died Sept. 8, 1952; buried North Parish Cemetery, Plaistow, N.H.

BARROWS, Raymond H(ayes), welfare exec.; b. Northampton, Mass., July 8, 1899; s. Howard S. and Jennie M. (Hayes) B.; B.S., U. of Vt., 1925; student in social and group work, Fordham U., 1935-36, U. of Chicago, 1937-38, Northwestern, 1938-39; m. Martha Frances Church, July 10, 1926; children—Howard S., Virginia Sue, Nancy Jane. Civil engr., New England Power Co., Boston, 1919-21; building designer, James B. Black Co., Chicago, 1926-28; construction engr., Pachen Bros. Construction Co., 1928-30; wholesale beverage operation of Burlington, Vt., 1931-32; sales work for Oil Burner Equipment Co., 1932-33; supervisor CCC camps, Dept. of Interior, 1933-37; supt. Lawrence Hall Home for Boys, Chicago, 1937-41; dir. disaster service, Midwestern area Am. Nat. Red Cross, 1941-43, dep. mgr. Pacific area, San Francisco, 1943-48, v.p. and area mgr., 1948-51; exec. v.p. Nat. Foundation for Infantile Paralysis, 1951-—, now Nat. Found. Chairman adv. com. to Social Work Placement Service of Calif. Dept. of Employment since 1949; mem. council Govs. Calif. State Disaster Council since 1947; mem. bd. Nat. Publicity Council. Mem. Nat., Am. assns. social workers, A.I.M., Soc. Western Engrs. Clubs: Kiwanis (Chgo.); Rotary (N.Y.C.; San Francisco). Home: 10 North Pl., Pleasantville, N.Y. Office: 800 2d Av., N.Y.C. Died Oct. 22, 1958.

BARRY, John H., newspaper exec. Treas., gen. mgr., sec., dir. Chgo. Daily News, Inc., Miami Herald; gen. mgr., sec., treas. and dir. Beacon Journal Publishing Co., Detroit Free Press, Knight Newspapers, Inc. Home: 830 Mayfair Rd. Office: Knight Newspapers, Inc., Akron, O. Died Nov. 4, 1955.

BARRYMORE, Ethel (Mrs. Russell Griswold Colt) (băr'ĭ-mōr), actress; b. Phila., Aug. 15, 1879; d. late Maurice (Herbert Blythe) and Georgiana (Drew) B.; niece of John Drew; ed. Convent of Notre Dame, Phila.; m. Russell Griswold, s. Samuel Pomeroy Colt (divorced 1923); children—Samuel Pomeroy, John Drew, Ethel B. Made début in John Drew's Co., 1896; played Priscilla, in "Secret Service," London; later appeared in leading rôles with Henry Irving; first starred in "Captain Jinks," 1900; later starred in "Cousin Kate"; in "Sunday," 1906; "A Doll's House," 1905; "Alice Sit-by-the-Fire," 1906; "The Constant Wife," 1926; (with brothers) "Rasputin and the Empress," 1933; The Corn Is Green, 1942. Recipient Academy award for supporting role, 1944 in picture None But the Lonely Heart; recent pictures: Great Sinner, That Midnight Kiss, Pinky, Red Danube, Kind Lady, Secret of Convict Lake, Just For You, It's a Big Country, Deadline U.S.A., Story of Three Loves, Main Street to Broadway; also TV film series. Home: Mamaroneck, N.Y. Died June 18, 1959.

BARRYMORE, Lionel, actor; s. Maurice (Herbert Blythe) and Georgiana (Drew) B.; m. Doris Rankin; m. 2d, Irene Fenwick (Mrs. James F. O'Brien), July 14, 1923 (dec.). Debut in "The Rivals," 1893, in which his grandmother, Mrs. John Drew, was appearing as Mrs. Malaprop; also appeared with her in "The Road to Ruin"; played leading parts in "Squire Kate," "Cumberland '61," "Arizona"; with his uncle, John Drew, in "The Second in Command," and "The Mummy and the Humming Bird"; played in "Pantaloon," "The Fires of Hate," "The Still Small Voice," etc.; starred in numerous motion pictures; on radio in title role of Mayor of the Town, also as host-narrator-star in Hallmark Playhouse; annually appears on radio in role of Scrooge in A Christmas Carol; guest star on numerous radio programs; also on TV. Author: Mr. Cantonwine: A Moral Tale, 1953. Address: care C.B.S., 485 Madison Av., N.Y.C. 22. Died Nov. 15, 1954.

BARSTOW, Edith, choreographer; b. Ashtabula, Ohio; daughter of Thomas Arthur and Ada Mary (Hatton) B.; studied with private tutors. Began in show bus., 1916; danced, appeared stock cos. on tour Mont., Tex., Okla., 1918-21; appeared Midnight Frolics, Chgo., 1924-25, The Palace, N.Y.C., 1925; toured U.S., 1926-27; with brother appeared in featured musical comedies, Australia, 1927, London, on tour Europe, 1928-30, The Palace, N.Y.C., 1930-39; originated toe-tap dancing on a staircase; choreography, prodn. Merriel Abbott, 1943-48, took group Merriel Abbot dancers on tour, Italy, France, 1950; choreographer Wayne King TV, also Don McNeil shows; staged TV show Garraway-at-Large, Chgo., N.Y.C., 1953-54, also with TV shows Today, Colgate Comedy Hour, Milton Berle show, Buick Circus Hour, Kate Smith show; asso. prod. Eddie Albert TV show, 1953; choreographer Greatest Show on Earth, Ringling Bros. Barnum & Bailey Circus, 1952—; staged, directed, choreographed Champagne on Ice, London Hippodrome, 1953; prod., write, directed, staged with brother Motorama shows Gen. Motors, N.Y.C. and on tour, also Powerama, Chgo., 1955, prod., staged, directed (with brother) Am. Youth Expn., N.Y.C., 1959; other comml. films, indsl. shows, night club acts, TV shows. Recipient TV awards, including Look award, 1950. Home: 212 E. 54th St., N.Y.C. 22. Died Jan. 1960.

BARTEL, William Edwin, mfg. exec.; b. Waltham, Mass., Sept. 12, 1903; s. William Philip and Julia (O'Donnell) B.; B.S., Harvard, 1925; m. Mary E. Vahey, Feb. 25, 1938; children—Julia, Jonathan Peter, Anne, Christopher William. With Judson L. Thomson Mfg. Co., Waltham, 1925—, successively clk., asst. treas., treas., pres., 1954—, dir.; pres. Thomson (Can.) Rivet Co., Gananoque, Ont., 1953—, dir.; dir. Waltham Citizens Nat. Bank. Home: 12 Robin Rd., Weston 93. Office: Judson L. Thomson Mfg. Co., Waltham 54, Mass. Died Dec. 17, 1958.

BARTELS, Vernon C(arl), banker; b. Chicago, Oct. 5, 1905; s. Charles Fredrick and Anna Fredricka (Bowman) B.; student eve. sch. commerce Northwestern U., 1931-36; m. Anna C. Chvalovsky, Aug. 29, 1931; children—Vernon C., Roger Allan. Vice pres. operating div. First Nat. Bank of Chgo.; dir. Nat. Safe Deposit Co. Sec.-treas. North Side Animal Shelter, Chgo. Conglist. (trustee). Home: 1220 N. Grove Av., Oak Park, Ill. Office: 38 S. Dearborn St., Chgo. 90. Died May 23, 1957.

BARTELT, Edward F. (bär-tĕlt'), govt. ofcl.; b. Quincy, Ill., June 17, 1895; s. G. Henry and Emily (Goessling) B.; student pub. schs. of Quincy; m. Mildred Smith, June 5, 1917; children—Betty, Ruth, John. Chief div. of bookkeeping and warrants Treasury Dept., 1927—; commr. of accounts U.S. Treasury, 1934—; asst. sec. of the Treasury, 1945—; U.S. rep. on Fiscal Commn., UN. Interdeptl. chmn. U.S. Savings Bonds Com., 1942—; nat. chmn. for Fed. employees, Am. Cancer Soc., 1946— (v.p. D.C. div.); v.p. Nat. Soc. Crippled Children and Adults, Inc.; nat. chmn. for fed. employees Crusade for Freedom. Club: Columbia Country. Home: 3017 Stephenson Pl., N.W. Office: Treasury Dept., Washington. Died Sept. 16, 1958.

BARTHOLOMEW, Tracy, research engr.; b. Austin, Tex., Nov. 14, 1884; s. George Wells and Hettie Julia (Cole) B.; student Ohio State U., 1902-03; E.M., Colo. Sch. of Mines, 1906; m. Sarah Jane Anderson, Oct. 6, 1921; children—George Anderson, Jane Anderson. Construction engr. Federal Lead Co., Flat River, Mo., 1906-07; designing and test engr. Nev. Consol. Copper Co., McGill, Nev., 1907-09; gen. mgr. Alkali-Proof Cement Div. of Colo. Portland (now Ideal) Cement Co., Denver, Colo., 1909-11; mgr. Rico Tropical Fruit Co., Garrochales, P.R., 1911-21, pres. since 1921; sr. fellow Mellon Inst. of Industrial Research, Pittsburgh, 1921-39; mgr. of research Duquesne Slag Products Co., 1929-40; cons. engr. since 1940. Served as captain 374th Inf., United States Army, 1918-19. Mem. A.A.A.S, American Institute Mining and Metallurgical Engineers, American Society Civil Engineers, Am. Chem. Soc., Am. Ceramic Soc., Am. Soc. Municipal Engrs., Am. Soc. Testing Materials, Am. Concrete Inst., Engrs. Soc. of Western Pa., Beta Theta Pi, Phi Lambda Upsilon. Republican. Presbyterian. Mason (K.T., Shriner.). Clubs: Faculty (U. Pittsburgh); Longue Vue. Home: 1545 Beechwood Blvd., Pitts. 17. Died Dec. 7, 1951.

BARTKY, Walter, educator; b. Chicago, Sept. 21, 1901; s. Adolph and Louisa (Schaar) B.; B.S., U. of Chicago, 1923, Ph.D., 1926; m. Elizabeth Inrig Roberston, of Glasgow, Scotland, Jan. 9, 1932; children—Walter, Ian Robertson. Began as instr. U. of Chicago, 1926, asst. prof. of astronomy, 1927-32, associate professor, 1932-42; prof. applied mathematics; asso. dean, Div. of Physical Sciences, 1943-45, dean, 1945-55, vice pres. charge spl. scientific programs, 1955—; consulting mathematician to Western Electric Company, 1926-30. Mem. A.A.A.S., Am. Mathematical Society, American Astron. Soc., Chicago Astron. Soc., Chaos Club, Sigma Xi, Phi Beta Kappa. Club: Quadrangle. Home: 5451 S. Hyde Park Blvd., Chgo. Died Mar. 19, 1958.

BARTLETT, Sir Charles John, mfg. exec.; b. Bilbury, Glos., Dec. 12, 1889; student Bibury Glos., and Bath Tech. Coll.; m. Emily May Pincombe, 1925. With Vauxhall Motors, Ltd., 1921—, mng. dir., 1930-53, chmn., 1953—; mem. bd. Gen. Motors, Ltd., Vauxhall & Gen. Finance Corp. Fellow Royal Soc. Arts. Address: Whitewalls, Kinsbourne Green, Harpenden, Herts., Eng. Died Aug. 10, 1955; buried Golders Green Crematorium, London.

BARTLETT, Clarence, physician; b. Bklyn., May 22, 1858; s. William F. and Margaret (Ritter) B.; M.D., Hahnemann Med. Coll. and Hosp., 1879; m. Anna C. Miller, Sept. 29, 1885 (died Nov. 3, 1910); m. 2d, Mrs. Mary G. Wright, Apr. 4, 1912. Practiced in Phila., 1879—; was prof. and head dept. medicine Hahnemann Med. Coll. and Hosp., now emeritus. Mem. Alumni Assn. Hahnemann Med. Coll. (pres.), Am. Inst. Homoeopathy (hon. pres. 1923), Pa. Homoeopathic Soc., Phila. Acad. Medicine; hon. mem. N.Y., Va., Pa. (pres. 1922) homoeopathic med. socs., Brit. Homoeopathic Soc., others. Republican. Club: Union League. Author: Clinical Medicine—Diagnosis, 1903; Clinical Medicine—Treatment, 1904; Practice of Medicine, 3 vols. 1923. Many yrs. editor Hahnemannian Monthly. Home: Merion, Pa. Deceased.

BARTLETT, Edward Randolph, educator; born Ft. Madison, Iowa, November 10, 1889; s. Thompson Hall and Sarah Isadora (Maguire) B.; A.B., Ia. Wesleyan Coll., 1912, D.D., 1926; S.T.B., Boston U. Sch. of Theology, 1917; post grad. work Boston U., 1918, U. of Chicago, 1925; Ph.D., Northwestern U., 1933; m. Edna Ruth Pace, June 14, 1912; children—Elizabeth Ruth (dec.), James Randolph, Barbara Jean. Ordained ministry M.E. Ch., 1911; pastor Grandview, Ia., 1911-14, Newburyport, Mass., 1915-16; extension lecturer Boston U., 1916-18; dir. of religious edn., First Ch., Topeka, Kan., 1918-19; ednl. supt. Minneapolis Council of Religious Edn., 1919-20. Detroit Council of Chs., 1920-23; asso. prof. De Pauw U., 1924, prof. and head dept. of religious edn., 1925-47; professor Old Testament 1938-47, dean 1941-47; pres. The Iliff School of Theology since 1947. Pres. Indiana Council of Churches, 1946-47; pres. Wabash Valley Council, Boy Scouts of Am., 1946-47: chairman American Assn. of Academic Deans, 1946-47. Mem. chaplain's training sch., Camp Zachary Taylor, 1918. Mem. Internat. Council of Religious Education. Mem. Am. Assn. Univ. Profs., Mid-West Assn. Teachers Religion, Religious Edn. Assn., Mid-Western Psychol. Assn., Soc. of Bibl. Lit. and Exegesis, Phi Delta Kappa, Pi Gamma Mu, Delta Chi, Phi Mu Alpha Sinfonia. Mason. Club: Rotary. Writer on religious subjects, also lecturer. Address: Iliff School of Theology, Denver 10. Died Apr. 15, 1952; buried Denver.

BARTLETT, Edwin Rice, company exec.; b. Hanover, N.H., May 12, 1883; s. Edwin Julius and Caroline Elizabeth (Rice) B.; A.B., Dartmouth, 1904; m. Margaret Jeffrey Porter, June 2, 1915 (dec.); children—Edwin Porter, Elizabeth Langmuir, Margaret, Julia Jeffrey, John Alexander; m. 2d Katherine Nye Kirkpatrick, Nov. 23, 1939. Accountant Am. Light & Traction Co., N.Y.C., 1904-07; timekeeper Development & Funding Co., Niagara Falls, N.Y., 1907-08; purchasing agt. Hooker Electro-Chem. Co., Niagara Falls, 1908-09, office mgr., purchasing agt., 1909-12, asst. supt., 1912-15, supt., 1915-19, works mgr., 1919-24, v.p., works mgr., dir. since 1924, exec. v.p., 1941-45, president, 1945-51, chairman of board, 1951-55, chairman finance com., 1955—. Chairman adv. bd. Airport Commrs., Niagara Falls. Mem. Am. Chem. Soc., A.A.A.S., Engring. Soc. Buffalo, Army Ordnance Assn., S.A.R., Psi Upsilon. Clubs: Chemists, Dartmouth (N.Y.C.); Niagara, Univ., Country, Rotary (Niagara Falls, N.Y.); Univ. (Buffalo). Home: Fourth St., Lewiston. Office: Buffalo Av. and 47th St., Niagara Falls, N.Y. Died Dec. 10, 1957.

BARTLETT, Frederic Clay, artist; b. Chgo., June 1, 1873; s. Adolphus Clay and Mary H. (Pitkin) B.; student Harvard Sch., St. Paul's Sch., Concord, N.H., Royal Acad. Art, Munich, Germany, and studied art in Paris under Collin, Aman-Jean, Whistler; m. Dora Tripp, Oct. 4, 1898 (died 1917); m. 2d, Helen Louise Birch, Jan. 1919 (died 1925); m. 3d, Evelyn Fortune, June 1, 1931. Artist in mural decorations; has done work in U. Chgo., 2d Presbyn. Ch., University Club, Chgo.; mural decorations in Council Chamber of Chgo. City Hall, New 4th Presbyn. Ch., others. Recipient Silver medal St. Louis Expn., 1904, San Francisco Expn., 1915; hon. mention Carnegie Inst., Pitts. Represented in permanent collections Art Inst. Chgo., Carnegie Inst., Pitts., Corcoran Gallery, Washington. Mem. Nat. Inst. Arts and Letters. Clubs: Century, Nat. Arts, Coffee House (N.Y.C.); Chicago, University, Cliff Dwellers, Casino, Tennis and Racquet (Chgo.). Address: 2201 Howard St., Chgo. Died June 25, 1953.

BARTLETT, John Henry; b. Sunapee, N.H., March 15, 1869; s. John Z. and Sophronia A. (Sargent) B.; A.B., Dartmouth, 1894, A.M., 1920; LL.D., U. N.H., 1920; m. Agnes Page, June 1, 1900; 1 son, Calvin Page. Teacher in grammar schs. and high sch., Portsmouth, 4 yrs.; admitted to N.H. bar, 1898; practiced at Portsmouth since 1898; now mem. law firm Bartlett and Mitchell; postmaster, Portsmouth, 1899-1908; mem. staff of Gov. John McLane, 1905-06, rank of col.; elected gov. of N.H., 1918, term 1919-21; pres. Civil Service Commn., Washington, D.C., 1921-22; 1st asst. p.m. gen., Mar. 1922-May 1929; chmn. U.S. Sect. Internat. Joint Commission, U.S. and Can., 1929-39; pres. Portsmouth Trust & Guarantee Co., 1920-40. Pres. N.H. Soc. for Prevention of Cruelty to Children and Animals. Club: National Press. Author: Spice for Speeches, 1926; Folks is Folks, 1927; Legend of Ann Smith, 1931; The Bonus March and the New Deal, 1937; A Synoptic History of the Granite State. Home: Portsmouth, N.H. Died Mar. 19, 1952.

BARTLETT, Margaret Abbott, editor; b. Stoneham, Mass., Aug. 9, 1892; d. Albert Howard and Georgiana Grace (Perry) Abbott; grad. Pinkerton Acad., Derry, N.H., 1910; m. John Thomas Bartlett, Sept. 7, 1912 (died Jan. 23, 1947); children—Forrest Abbott, John Thomas, Richard Adams, Margaret Emily. Tchr. Newton, N.H., 1910-12; contbr. articles on domestic, nature, bus., and other subjects to nat. pubs., 1917—; free lance writer juvenile fiction and verse, 1919—; editor and pub. (with husband) The Author & Journalist 1940-47, sole editor and pub., 1947—; mng. editor Bartlett Service (nat. editorial service conducted with husband), 1921—; editor and pub. Boulder (Colo.) Daily Doings, 1930—; editor, pub. The Mountain Hardware and Implement Dealer, 1947-48. Sec. Mountain States Hardware and Implement Assn., 1947-48; mem. Nat. Fedn. Press Women (winner 1st award in feature and poetry contests, 1943; 3d award best mag. pub. by a woman, 1948), Colo. Authors' League, D.A.R. (state chmn. press relations, 1938-40). Republican. Conglist. Club: Soroptimist. Died Nov. 28, 1949.

BARTON, Charles William, editor, pub.; b. Oberlin, O., Nov. 24, 1887; s. Rev. William E. (D.D.) and Esther Treat (Bushnell) B.; matriculated Amherst Coll.; B.S., Berea (Ky.) Coll., 1909; Ph.B., U. Chgo., 1910; m. Violet Hullinger, of Huntington, Ind., Nov. 27, 1912; 1 dau., Barbara; m. 2d, Virginia Lee Nelson, Mar. 10, 1928. In mail-order business, Sears, Roebuck Co.; later bus. mgr. The Advance (religious weekly), Chgo., asst. pub. New York Telegraph, 1919-21; owner Casper (Wyo.) Tribune, 1922-23; purchased Sheridan Post and Sheridan Enterprise, 1923, and consolidated them into the Sheridan Post Enterprise of which was editor and pub. until sold; founded Northwestern Farmer and Rancher (mag.), 1929; purchased Casper (Wyo.) Independent, weekly, 1930; changed name to Casper Times, pub. daily; owner Charles W. Barton, pubs. rep. orgn., N.Y.C.; resigned as partner Worthman-Barton & Co., Inc., advt. agy., 1937; joined nat. advt. staff The Knoxville News-Sentinel, a Scripps-Howard newspaper, Knoxville, Tenn. Served as naval aviator, World War. Mem. Alpha Delta Phi. Republican. Conglist. Mason (32°), Rotarian, Elk, Moose. Home: Worcester, Mass. Died Oct. 21, 1956.

BARTON, Olive Roberts, (Mrs. James Lowrie Barton), writer; b. Allegheny, Pa., July 26, 1880; d. Thomas Beveridge and Cornelia (Gilleland) Roberts; sister of Mary Roberts Rinehart; grad. high sch., Allegheny, 1897, grad. study, 1898; m. Lt. Col. James Lowrie Barton, June 19, 1902; children—Eleanor Ains (dec.), Virginia-Anne, Mary Roberts (Mrs. R. L. Brummage, Jr.). Tchr. pub. schs., Allegheny, 1898-1902, Butler, Pa., 1905-06, 17-18; free lance writer, 1905-19; feature writer Newspaper Enterprise Assn. (Scripps Howard Syndicate), 1919-25; daily serial for children, Adventures of the Twins; daily editorials, features, 1925-28; daily column on child tng. and family mgmt., 1928—. Mem. Nat. League Am. Penwomen. Republican. Episcopalian. Clubs: Twentieth Century, Authors (Pitts.). Author: Cloud Boat Stories, 1916; Wonderful Land of Up, 1918; Helter Skelter Land, Land of Near By, Scrub Up Land and Topsy Turvy Land (series), 1920; Story Riddles in Rime and Prose, 1928; Bramble Bush Riddles, 1930. Editorial writer. Home: Whitemarsh, Pa. Died Aug. 14, 1957.

BARTOW, Charles K., ret. banker; b. Pontiac, Mich., 1889. Sr. v.p., dir. Mfrs. Nat. Bank of Detroit, ret. 1956. Address: 151 W. Fort St., Detroit. Died Nov. 17, 1957.*

BARTOW, Edward, chemist; b. Glenham, New York, January 12, 1870; s. Charles Edward and Sarah Jane (Scofield) B.; B.A., Williams Coll., 1892; Ph.D., U. Göttingen, 1895, Golden diploma, 1956; D.Sc., Williams Coll., 1923; m. Alice Abbott, Sept. 3, 1895 (dec. May 15, 1951); 1 dau., Virginia. Assistant in chemistry, 1892-94, instructor 1895-97, Williams Coll.; instr. in chemistry, 1897-99, asso. prof., 1899-1905, U. of Kan.; asso. prof., 1905-06, prof. sanitary chemistry, 1906-20, U. of Ill. Dir. State Water Survey, 1905-17; chief Water Survey Div., Dept. Registration and Education, Illinois, 1917-20; prof. and head dept. of chemistry and chem. engring., State Univ. of Ia., 1920-40, prof. emeritus, since 1940; research consultant, Johns-Manville Corp. 1940-1941. Del. 9th Internat. Congress Chemistry, Madrid, 1934, 10th, Rome, 1938; mem. council Internat. chem. Union, 1922-25, 27-30, 33-38, v.p. for U.S.A., 1934-38. Sec. Lake Mich. Water Commn., 1908; Commn. on Standards of Water for Interstate Carriers, 1913, 22; sec.-treas. Ill. Water Supply Association, 1909-17. Served from maj. to lt. col., san. corps, U.S. Army, A.E.F., 1917-19. Awarded Medaille d'Honneur, des Epidémies, d'Argent (France). Mem. of American Chemical Society (dir. 1933, pres. 1936), A.A.A.S., Societé Chim. Industrielle (France), Soc. Chem. Industry (Great Britain), Am. Water Works Assn. (trustee, 1913; v.p., 1921; pres., 1922), Am. Inst. Chem. Engrs. (dir. 1923-25, 1936-39), Am. Soc. Civil Engrs. (life mem. 1946), Am. Assn. U. Profs., Franklin Inst., Am. Pub. Health Assn., Kan. Acad. Sci. (pres. 1904), Am. Soc. Testing Materials, American Soc. for Engineering Education, Am. Public Works Assn., Nat. Security League, Mil. Order World War, Nat. Inst. Social Science, Acad. Polit. Science, Am. Veterans Assn., Am. Legion, Illinois Acad. Science, Iowa Engring. Society, Ia. Acad. Science (vice-president, 1933, president, 1934), Am. Inst. Chemists, American Philatelic Society, Society Philatelic Americans, Spanish Academy Science (corresponding mem.), Trans-Miss. Stamp Soc., Phi Beta Kappa Assos., Sigma Xi, Alpha Chi Sigma, Tau Beta Pi, Theta Delta Chi, Phi Lambda Upsilon. Conglist. Clubs: University, Chaos (Chgo.); Chemists (N.Y.C., Chgo.). Author 14 vol. report on Ill. waters; also papers relating to field. Asst. editor Chem. Abstracts, 1911—. Home: 304 Brown St. Office: Chemical Bldg., Iowa City, Ia. Died Apr. 12, 1958; buried Fishkill, N.Y.

BARUCH, Herman Benjamin (bá-rōōk'), diplomat; b. Camden, S.C., Apr. 28, 1872; s. Simon and Belle (Wolfe) B.; B.S., City Coll., N.Y., 1892; M.D., Columbia University, 1895; married Rosemary Emetaz, February 5, 1908; children—Robert P., Marina Symmers; married 2d, Anna Marie, Baroness Mackay of the Hague, Holland, October 22, 1949. Practiced medicine, N.Y., 1895-1903; mem. Baruch Bros. (N.Y Stock Exchange), 1903-18; H. Hentz and Co., bankers and commn. merchants (Chicago, Pittsburgh, Detroit), N.Y. City, 1918-42; owns and operates Bagetelle Nursery, Huntington, L.I. Served as special rep. of Bd. of Economic Warfare in Brazil and as special economic adviser to the U.S. Ambassador to Brazil, 1943; Ambassador Extraordinary and Plenipotentiary of U.S. to Portugal, 1945-47; Ambassador Extraordinary and Plenipotentiary to The Netherlands, 1947-49. Presidential elector, Dem., 1932; member Alien Enemy Review Bd. Pres. The Doctor Simon Baruch Found. (for med. research). Awarded Grand Cross of the Royal Order of Netherlands Lion, 1949; Grand Cross of the Order of Christus (Portuguese), 1950. Mem. N.Y. Acad. Medicine, Am. Arbitration Assn. (dir.), Phi Beta Kappa, Kappa Sigma; mem. alumni assns. of U. of Va., City Coll. (N.Y.), Sloane Maternity and Mt. Sinai Hosps. Democrat. Home: Bagatelle, Wyandanch, L.I., N.Y. Office: 60 Beaver St., N.Y.C. Died Mar. 15, 1953.

BARUCH, Sydney Norton, research engr.; b. Mamaroneck, N.Y., Mar. 14, 1895; s. Joseph and Sophia (Van Kitzinger) B.; E.E., Cooper Union, 1911; D.Sc., Royal (Eng.), 1921; student special courses in engring. Cooper Union; spl. study elec. phenomenon, U. Cal.; unmarried. Chief engr. Fed. Telephone Co., radio div. Postal Telegraph Co., 1919-20, Gen. Petroleum Co. of Am., 1921; pres. Pub. Service Corp. of Cal., 1916-20; condr. pvt. research labs., N.Y.C., 1930—; dir., controller United Broadcasting chain of radio stations; chief research engr. Gen. Arc Lighting Co. Builder high power radio broadcast chain, 1925; designer broadcasting stations, CHCR, WBNY, WKBK, WKBQ, LIY (Bordeaux, France); cons. engr. (U.S. Signal Corp, 1948. Awarded gold medal Internat. Jury of Scientists, 1915. Cons. engr., special weapons div. U.S. Air Force, 1943—. Fellow Royal Soc. of London; mem. Am. Inst. Radio Engrs., Soc. Motion Picture Engrs. Mason (Shriner). Inventor thermo relay and other devices, also thyraton and nortron type mercury rectifier tubes and sound recording on film, 1934; inventor depth bomb successfully used in destruction of submarines in World War I and World War II. Designer 300,000 volt direct current transmission system for Bonneville Project, U.S. Dept. Interior, 1941. Invented guided missile using jet propulsion. Home: 145 E. 54th St. Office: 1476 Broadway, N.Y. C. Died Sept. 22, 1959.

BASH, Louis Hermann, army officer; b. Chicago, Ill., Mar. 7, 1872; s. Daniel N. and Virginia (Ballance) B.; prep. edn., Lake Forest (Ill.) Acad.; grad. U.S. Mil. Acad., 1895, Army Sch. of Line, Ft. Leavenworth, Kan., 1920; m. Bertha Runkle, October 26, 1940 (deceased January 4, 1958). Commissioned 2d lieutenant inf., U.S. Army, June 12, 1895, and advanced through grades to col., July 1, 1920; brig. gen., Sept. 19, 1929. Served in Cuba, Spanish-Am. War, participating in assault on San Juan Hill and siege of Santiago; served in P.I., Filipino Insurrection; aide de camp to Gen Loyd Wheaton, 1900-02; service in field, Cavite Province, Jan.-July 1905; chief commissary, Dept. Mindanao, Apr. 1906-Sept. 1907; chief commissary, Dept. Tex., 1907-09; maj., inf., Mexican border and Mexican punitive expdn., 1916-17; served as adj. gen., Service of Supply, France, Feb. 1918-July 1919; transferred to Q.M.C., 1920; asst. to q.m., 4th Corps Area, 1920-21; gen. supt. army transport service, Port of New York, Apr.-Oct. 1921, asst. gen. supt., 1921-23; q.m. supply officer and gen. supt. army transport service, San Francisco, 1924-28; asst. to q.m. gen., chief of constrn. service, 1929-34; apptd. q.m. gen., with rank of maj. gen., 1934; retired from active service account of disability, Mar. 31, 1936. D.S.M.; silver star citation "for gallantry in action" at Battle of Santiago de Cuba; decorated Officer Legion of Honor (France). Home: Palo Alto, Cal. Died May 24, 1952; buried Presidio of San Francisco.

BASINGER, William S., ry. ofcl.; b. Savannah, Ga., Aug. 28, 1873; A.B., U. of Ga., 1890. Began as clk. in auditor's office, K.C., F.S.&M. Ry., at Kansas City, Mo., 1891, later clk. freight dept. U.P. R.R.; gen. freight and pass. agt. Leavenworth, Kan. & Western Ry., at Leavenworth, Kan., 1897-1905, also supt. same rd. and supt., sec. and treas. Leavenworth Depot & Ry. Co., 1903-05; trainsmaster U.P.R.R., at Kansas City, 1905-07; asst. gen. pass. agt. same rd., at Omaha, 1907-10, in office of dir. traffic U.P., and S.P. systems, Chgo., 1910-11; asst. to dir. of traffic, same systems, Chgo., 1911-12, N.Y.C., 1912-13; same position S.P. Co., Feb.-Mar. 1913; gen. pass. agt. U.P. R.R., at Omaha, 1913-18; asst., div. of traffic, U.S. R.R. adminstrn., Washington, 1918-20; asst. pass. traffic mgr. U.P. System, Mar.-Sept. 1920; pass. traffic mgr. same, 1920—. Office: 1416 Dodge St., Omaha, Neb. Died Nov. 28, 1948.

BASKERVILL, William Malone, editor; b. Nashville, Tenn., Feb. 1, 1888; s. William Malone and Janie (McTyeire) B.; ed. Vanderbilt U. and U. of the South; m. Evelyn Frances Lynch, Apr. 25, 1916; children—Dorothy Frances, Evelyn Katherine, Janie Cecelia. Began as reporter Nashville Tennessean, 1907, later with Commercial Appeal, Montgomery Advertiser and New York Journal; telegraph editor Atlanta Journal, 1910-11; news editor Asso. Press, southern div., 1911-14; asst. gen. news mgr. Internat. News Service, N.Y. City, 1919-20; asst. mngr. editor New York Journal, 1921-22; mng. editor Atlanta Georgian-American, 1922-26, Baltimore News (now News-Post and Sunday American, since 1926; mem. bd. dirs. Hearst Consolidated Publs., since 1938. Mem. Phi Delta Theta. Club: Baltimore Country. Home: 3917 Juniper Rd. Address: Baltimore News-Post, Balt. Died May 18, 1953.

BASS, Elizabeth (Mrs. George Bass); b. Buxton, Me.; d. Roscoe and Catherine (Douglas) Merrill; student pub. schs. and under pvt. tutors; m. George Bass, Aug. 8, 1894. Ex-pres. Chicago Woman's Club; active for many yrs. in promoting welfare of dependent and neglected girls; was mem. original Juvenile Ct. Com. of Ill., also of Marriage and Divorce Commn., etc. Mgr. Woman's Bur. of Dem. Nat. Campaign, 1916; chmn. Nat. Woman's Bur. of Dem. Nat. Com., 1916-45, ret. Apptd. by Sec. of Treasury mem. Woman's Liberty Loan Com., 1917. Mem. D.A.R. Episcopalian. Clubs: Woman's (Chgo.); Woman's City (Washington). Home: Manitowoc, Wis. Died Aug. 25, 1950.

BASS, Frederic Herbert, civil engr.; b. Hyde Park, Mass., June 19, 1875; s. George Walter and Elizabeth (Bellamy) B.; S.B., Mass. Inst. Tech., 1901; m. Lillian Leggett, June 27, 1903; children—Jason Parker, Elizabeth Bellamy. With engring. dept., Met. Water Works, of Mass., dam, aqueduct and filter constrn., 1896-99, 1901-02; with U.S. engr. corps, Boston Harbor Improvement, 1900; instr. in civ. engring., 1901-04, asst. prof., 1904-10, prof. municipal and sanitary engring., Dec. 1910-19, head of civil engring. dept., 1919-43, U. of Minn.; exec. dir. American Public Works Assn., 1943-45; vice pres., Minn. State Bd. of Health, 1932-44, pres., 1936-39; mem. bd. engrs. Minneapolis-St. Paul San. Dist. Designed numerous water works, sewerage systems and other pub. works; retired 1947. Unitarian. Mem. Am. Soc. C.E., 1911. Am. Soc. Promotion Engring. Edn., Sigma Xi, etc. Mason. Clubs: Engineers, St. Paul Athletic. Address: 515 6th St. S.E., Mpls. Died May 13, 1954; buried Forest Hills Cemetery, Boston.

BASS, Leo, editor; b. Hamburg, Germany, Nov. 30, 1878; s. Nathan and Laura (Ludwig) B.; student pvt. schs., Germany; m. Frida Haas, Nov. 10, 1920; 1 dau., Laurette Kassner. Came to U.S., 1900, naturalized, 1905. Began as reporter Gross-New Yorker Zeitung and German Herold, 1902; reporter New Yorker Staats-Zeitung, 1905-20, editor, 1920—. Author: Reimschmieds Betrachtungen, 1920. Home: 1483 Grand Concourse, N.Y.C. 52. Died Feb. 20, 1951.

BASS, Lyman Metcalfe, lawyer; student Yale, 1897; LL.B., Harvard, 1900; m. Grace Holland; children—Susan, Frances, Grace. Mem. law firm Kenefick, Cooke, Mitchell, Bass & Letchworth; U.S. atty. Western Dist. of N.Y., 1906-08. Home: 129 Oakland Pl. Office: Marine Trust Bldg., Buffalo, N.Y. Died July 9, 1955.*

BASS, Ray Spurgeon, business exec.; b. Oconee, Ill., Dec. 14, 1895; s. Henry Martin and Susan E. (McNichols) B.; B.S., James Millikin U., 1919; m. Ruth Lois Rogers, Dec. 25, 1917; children—Ray Spurgeon, William Wilberforce, Mrs. Suzanne Elizabeth Curry. With A. E. Staley Mfg. Co., Decatur, Ill., since 1919, treas. since 1935, dir. since 1942, mem. exec. com. since 1947; asst. sec. and asst. treas. Staley Sales Corp., Decatur, Ill.; treas., director, mem. exec. com. Staley Internat., Inc., Decatur, 1953—; dir. Am. Motorists Insurance Company; mem. Ill. Mfrs. Adv. Bd.; dir. Am. Farmers Mutual Ins. Co., 20 N. Wacker Corp., Lumbermen's Mutual Casualty Co. Dir. chmn. supervisor committee Staley Credit Union (dir. to 1948). Mem. James S. Kember Found., 1953—. Dir. Risk Research Inst., N.Y.C., 1941-51, Decatur Hosp. Service Corp. (Blue Cross), 1945-48; mem. Decatur Council on Edn., 1944-48 (chmn. 1946-47); nat. asso. Boys Clubs of Am.; mem. bd. dirs. Blue Cross Plan for Hosp. Care (Chicago), 1949—. Mem. bd. mgrs. James Millikin U., 1944—, v.p., 1945—, trustee, 1953—. Director, 1st v.p. Nat. Ins. Buyers Assn., Inc., 1950-53; national asso. Boys Clubs Am.; member National Association Credit Men, N.A.M., Illinois Credit Union League (dir. and mem. exec. com. 1940; chmn. exec. com. 1941-42; 1st vice pres. 1944), Ill. State C. of C. (mem. fed. tax and ins. com.), Ill. Mfr. Assn. (mem. workmens compensation, health and safety com. 1944-48, congl. legislative, fed. tax coms.), Asso. Employers of Ill. (dir.), Nat. Ins. Buyers Assn., Inc. (dir., 1st v.p.), Mid-West Ins. Buyers Assn. (dir. 1945-47), Decatur Assn. of Commerce (dir., 1937-39; treas. 1940-43); vice pres. heading ins. div. Am. Management Assn., 1947-49, dir., 1949-51; Illinois representative of federal expenditures com. Nat. Council of State C.'s of C., 1946-53; mem. govt. expenditure com. U.S. C. of C., 1953—. Mem. Controllers Inst. Methodist. Clubs: Decatur, Staley Fellowship (treas. 1931-48 (Decatur). Home: 151 N. Fairview Av., Decatur 24. Office: P.O. Box 151, Decatur, Ill. Died March 8, 1954.

BASSET, William Rupert, industrial engineer; b. Boston, Nov. 12, 1883; s. William and Mary (Simpson) B.; ed. under pvt. tutors; m. Frances Warner, Mar. 2, 1907 (dec.); 1 dau., Beatrix; m. 2d, Mary McClane, 1914 (divorced); m. 3d, Amy Strand, Feb. 19, 1929; children—Amy Jane, William Rupert (dec.). Pres. Miller, Franklin, Basset & Co., indsl. engrs., & Co., 1909-28; partner Spencer Trask & Co., bankers, New York, 1928-39; partner Jas. B. Colgate & Co., brokers; pres. Basset, Colgate & Co. (indsl. engrs.), 1939-41; now practicing as indsl. and financial advisor; dir. and mem. exec. committee Colgate-Palmolive-Peet Co., Container Corp. Am., Vick Chem. Co.; dir. and chmn. of exec. com. Reinsurance Corp. of New York, National Reins Company; director Budd Company, Interstate Bakeries Corp. Clubs: Union League, Greenwich Country, Round Hill, Field, Special Car (Greenwich). Author: Accounting as an Aid to Business, 1918; When the Workmen Help You Manage, 1919; The Organization of Modern Business, 1921; Production Engineering and Cost Keeping for Machine Shops (with Johnson Heywood), 1922; Taking the Guesswork Out of Business, 1924; How to Solve Typical Business Problems, 1928; Operating Aspects of Industrial Mergers, 1930. Contbr. to Nation's Business, Saturday Evening Post, Colliers. Home: Old Church Rd., Greenwich, Conn. Died Jan. 9, 1953.

BASSETT, Carroll Phillips, cons. engr.; b. Bklyn., Feb. 27, 1863; s. Allen Lee and Caroline (Phillips) B.; C.E., Lafayette Coll., 1883, E.M., 1884, Ph. D., 1888, Sc.D., 1942; m. Margaret Condit Kinney, Apr. 14, 1904; children—Carroll Kinney, Estelle Condit (Mrs. R. Watson Pomery), Wm. B. K. Designed and erected water works, electric light, drainage, sewerage disposal plants, in N.Y., N.J., Pa., Conn., W.Va. and S.C., 1886-1910; established and operated water and electric utility companies, 1900-22; cons. engr.; pres. Bassett Estates, Inc., Commonwealth Land Company, Commonwealth Water & Light Co., Lakewood Water & Coast Electric Company and subsidiaries; vice president Summit Home Land Company; chairman of the board of First Nat. Bank and Trust Co. (Summit); dir. State Title & Mortgage Guaranty Co., Firemen's Ins. Co., Commercial Casualty Co. (Newark). Trustee N.J. Hist. Soc. Lafayette Coll., YMCA (Summit); mem. exec. com. Sentinels of the Republic. Fellow Am. Geog. Soc.; mem. Am. Soc. C.E., Am., New Eng. water works assns., N.J. Public Utilities Assn., N.J. Soc. Colonial Wars., N.J. Hist. Soc., N.J. Washington Assn., Phi Beta Kappa, Tau Beta Pi, Phi Delta Theta (ex-pres.). Republican. Presbyn. Mason. Clubs: University (N.Y.C.); Baltusrol Golf, Canoe Brook Country. Home: Beacon Hill, Summit. Office: 382 Springfield Av., Summit, N.J. Died Jan. 9, 1952; buried Mt. Pleasant Cemetery, Newark.

BASSETT, George Jarvis, banking; b. New Haven, Conn., Nov. 23, 1869; s. John Edwards and Sarah Beach (Pratt) B.; student New Haven High Sch., 1882-86; m. Lillian C. Bond, June 25, 1921. Clerk in hardware store of John E. Bassett & Co., 1886-89, treas., 1889-1931, pres. since 1896; v.p. New Haven Bank, 1923-31; bank commr. State of Conn., 1931-33; pres. Conn. Savings Bank, 1933-48, chmn. since 1948; dir. New Haven Bank, New Haven Gas Light Co., New Haven Water Co., Evergreen Cemetery Assn. (past president). Lt. in Connecticut State Guard, 1918. Police Commr., New Haven, 1913-24, chmn. Traffic Commn., 1927-29; mem. City Plan Commn., 1935-48. President Young Men's Inst., 1917-43. Mem. Savings Bank Assn. of Conn. (pres. 1939-41), Nat. Association Mutual Savings Banks (pres. 1943), New Haven Colony Hist. Soc. (dir.), New Haven Chamber of Commerce (pres. 1923-24), Conn. Acad. of Arts and Sciences, Soc. of Colonial Wars, Founders and Patriots of America, S.A.R., Newcomen Society. Episcopalian. Clubs: Quinnipiack, Lawn, Rotary, Social Science (New Haven); New Haven Country. Home: 409 Humphrey St. Office: 47 Church St., New Haven, Conn. Died Feb. 24, 1954.

BASSETT, John, publisher; b. Omagh, County Tyrone, Northern Ireland, Feb. 7, 1886; s. Edward and Elizabeth (Tough) B.; student National Sch. and Christian Bros. Sch. of Omagh; Royal U. of Ireland; D.C.L. (hon.), Bishop's U., Lennoxville, Quebec, 1939; LL.D., U. New Brunswick, 1947, McGill University, Montreal, Canada, 1955; married Marion Wright Avery, Sept. 21, 1914; children—Elizabeth (Mrs. Baldwin Smith), John. Parliamentary corr. Montreal Gazette, Ottawa, 1911-26 (pres. Parliamentary Press Gallery, 1925-26), dir. Gazette Printing Co., Ltd., Montreal, 1913-20, v.p. and dir., 1920-37, president and managing director, 1937-56, chairman of the board, 1956—; president and publisher Sherbrooke Daily Record, 1936—; chancellor Bishop's U., Lennoxville, Que., 1950—. Staff ofcr. to Lt. Gen. Hon. Sir Sam Hughes in Can., England, Belgium and France, 1914-16. Decorated by Belgian Govt. with Ordre de Reconnaissance, 1918. Can. del. to Third Imperial Press Conf., Australia, 1926. Clubs: Mt. Royal, St. James's (Montreal); Rideau (Ottawa); St. George's (Sherbrooke, P.Q.). Home: 1227 Sherbrooke St. W., Montreal; also Bondville, P.Q., Can. Office: 1000 St. Antoine St., Montreal, P.Q. Died Feb. 12, 1958; buried Knowlton (Que.) Cemetery.

BASSETT, Neal, ret. ins. exec.; b. Huntsville, Ala., Sept. 3, 1871. Former chmn. bd. Girard Fire & Marine Ins. Co., Nat. Ben Franklin Fire Ins. Co., Concordia Fire Ins. Co., Milw. Mechanics Ins. Co., Met. Casualty Co., Comml. Casualty Ins. Co., pres. Firemen's Ins. Co., Mechanics Ins. Co., Superior Fire Ins. Co. (Newark), retired 1934. Office: 10 Park Place, Newark 1. Died May 4, 1947.

BASSFORD, Horace Richardson, actuary; b. Nutley, N.J., Dec. 17, 1889; s. Ethan Frost and Kate (Hobby) B.; B.A., Trinity Coll., 1910, hon. M.S., 1948; m. Madeleine Veyer, June 30, 1917. Instr. Trinity Chapel Sch., N.Y. City, 1910-14; research lab. Thomas A. Edison, West Orange, N.J., 1914-15; actuarial div. Met. Life Ins. Co., N.Y. City, 1915-22, asst. actuary, 1922-36, actuary 1936; v.p. and chief actuary since 1945. Served as lt. C.A.C., 1917-18. Mem. Soc. of Actuaries (pres. Actuarial Soc. of Am. 1947-49), Inst. of Actuaries (London), Spanish Inst. of Actuaries (hon. mem.), Internat. Congress of Actuaries (council), Am. Math. Society, French Inst. Actuaries, S.A.R., Alpha Chi Rho. Republican. Episcopalian. Club: Montclair Golf. Contbr. numerous articles to various publs. Home: 89 Clinton Av., Montclair, N.J. Office: 1 Madison Av., N.Y.C. Died Mar. 12, 1952.

BASSILL, John E., business exec.; b. Norristown, Pa., 1896; grad. Wharton Sch. Finance, U. Pa., 1924. Pres., dir. American Enka Corp., N.Y.C. Office: 530 Fifth Av., N.Y.C. 36. Died Apr. 17, 1959; buried Gate of Heaven, Valhalla, N.Y.

BASSLER, Anthony, physician, author; b. N.Y.C., May 24, 1874; s. Louis and Louisa (Black) B.; M.D., Bellevue Hosp. Med. Coll., 1898; m. Harriette Matilda Seeley, July 1917; (died Dec. 14, 1951); children—Joan Mary, Anthony Seeley professor gastroenterology, N.Y. Polyclinic Medical School and Hospital, 1911-25, Fordham U., 1915-20; consultant in gastroenterology and internal medicine to 14 New York hosps.; sub chief advisory med. bds. of State of N.Y. Fellow Am. Coll. of Physicians; mem. A.M.A., Acad. of Medicine, Nat. Gastroenterologic Assn., N.Y.C., Internat. gastroenterol. assns., Am. Roentgen Ray Soc., Assn. for Study of Internal Secretions, Am. Therapeutic Soc. Clubs: Pilgrims Soc., Canadian (N.Y.C.); Westchester Country. Author: Diseases of Stomach and Upper Alimentary Tract, 1907; Diseases of Intestines and Lower Alimentary Tract, 1920; Intestinal Toxemia, Biologically Considered, 1930; also author of over 200 monographs and papers on med. subjects. Home: 121 E. 71st St., N.Y.C.; (summer) Rye, N.Y. Died Aug. 20, 1959; buried Gate of Heaven Cemetery, Valhalla, N.Y.

BASTEDO, Paul Henry (băs-tē'dō), naval officer (ret.); b. Buffalo, Feb. 25, 1887; s. Walter Stanley and Catherine Ann (Henry) B.; B.S., U.S. Naval Acad., 1908; m. Helen Prindeville Griffin, May 4, 1920; stepchildren—Rosemary (wife of Capt. John F. Greenslade), Thomas Francis Griffin, Richard Bulen. Commd. ensign USN, 1910, advanced through grades to capt. 1936; staff officer to comdr. U.S. Naval Forces, European waters, World War I, acting chief of staff to comdr., Europe, World War II; naval aide to Pres. F. D. Roosevelt, 1936-37; naval attache, London, Eng., 1943; ret. with rank of rear adm., 1944 and continued on active duty until 1946. Trustee and treas. Naval Hist. Found. Decorated D.S.M., Cuban Pacification, Mexican, World War I, German occupation, Am. Defense, European Theatre medals; Valore medal silver and Fatiche di Guerra medal (Italy); Order of Leopold II (Belgium); Comdr. Order of the So. Cross (Brazil). Presbyn. Clubs: Alibi, Chevy Chase, Metropolitan (Washington); N.Y. Yacht (N.Y.C.). Home: 73 Catherine St., Newport, R.I. Deceased.

BASTIN, Edson Sunderland (băs'tĭn), mining geologist; b. Chicago, Ill., Dec. 10, 1878; s. Edson Sewell and Christina (Boyd) B.; A.B., U. of Mich., 1902; M.S., Univ. of Chicago, 1903; Ph.D., 1909; Sc.D., hon., U. of Mich., 1941; m. Elinor Norton, June 30, 1910 (dec. Aug. 12, 1949). With U.S. Geol. Survey, in Me. and in western mining dists., 1904-16; examination of copper properties in Chile, 1916-17; mineral statis. and informational work, U.S. Govt., 1917-19; apptd. chief Div. of Mineral Resources, U.S. Geol. Survey, Jan. 1, 1919 (resigned); prof. economic geology, Univ. of Chicago, 1920-44 (retired); also chmn. Dept. of Geology, 1922-44; chmn. Div. of Geology and Geography of Nat. Research Council, 1935-37; mem. Ill. Bd. of Natural Resources and Conservation, 1922-44; cons. geologist. Fellow Geol. Soc. America)v.p. 1935), American Assn. for Advancement of Science (v.p. 1930), Am. Inst. Mining and Metall. Engrs., Soc. Econ. Geologists (pres. 1933); mem. Sigma Nu, Phi Beta Kappa, Sigma Xi. Unitarian. Author of numerous repts. pub. by U.S. Geol. Survey, also articles in geol. and mining jours. Home: 205 Bryant Av., Ithaca, N.Y. Died Oct. 9, 1953.

BATCHELDER, Ann (băch'ĕl-dẽr), editor; b. Windsor, Vermont, Mar. 21, 1881; d. William and Julia Elizabeth (Kennedy) Batchelder; educated by tutors and at Bishop Hopkins Hall, Burlington, Vt.; L.H.D. (hon.), Bowling Green (O.) University, 1950. Began as bank sec., later reporter and newspaper feature writer and asst. in law office; food editor Delineator Mag., 1928-34; asso. editor Ladies Home Jour., 1934—. Served as sec. Vt. Equal Suffrage Assn. Adviser to faculty Dunbar-Danforth Sch. for Girls, Worcester, Mass. Mem. Soc. of Descendants of the Colonial Clergy, Mamaroneck Historical Society; hon. mem. Vermont Soc. of Bridgeport, Conn. Episcopalian. Author: Ann Batchelder's Own Cook Book, 1941; Journal's End—Ladies Home Journal (poems). East of Bridgewater, 1943; Start to Finish, 1954. Former column in Delineator—If I Know What I Mean. Home: Woodstock, Vt. Office: 1270 Sixth Av., N.Y.C. Died June 18, 1955; buried Riverside Cemetery, Woodstock.

BATCHELDER, Charles Foster, naturalist; b. Cambridge, Mass., July 20, 1856; s. Francis Lowell and Susan Cabot (Foster) B.; A.B., Harvard, 1878, C.E., 1882; m. Laura Poor Stone, Feb. 19, 1895. Asso. editor The Auk, 1887-93; editor Proc. N.E. Zoölogical Club, 1899-1947. Associate Museum of Comparative Zoölogy; fellow Am. Ornithologists' Union (pres. 1905-08), A.A.A.S., Am. Acad. Arts and Sciences; mem. Boston Soc. Natural History (v.p. 1917-19), Nuttall Ornithol. Club, N.E. Bot. Club, Biol. Soc. Washington. Home: Peterborough, N.H. Died Nov. 7, 1954; buried Cambridge, Mass.

BATCHELDER, Edward Trumbull, mfg. and assn. exec.; b. Salem, Mass., Apr. 13, 1906; s. Samuel Henry and Mabel Augusta (Trumbull) B.; A.B. cum laude, Harvard, 1930, M.B.A., 1932; m. Wilma Eliza Hemenway, Feb. 25, 1933; children—William Henry, Stephen Hemenway. Salesman R. H. Macy & Co., N.Y.C., summer 1931; sales Hampden Mfg. Co., 1932-33; dept. mgmt. B. Altman & Co., 1932-34; exec. asst. Hygrade-Sylvania Corp., 1934; treas. Ultrex Chemical Products, Inc., 1935-36; with Assn. Nat. Advertisers, Inc., N.Y.C., 1936—, sec. 1944-48, v.p., 1948—; dir. Hampden Mfg. Co., 1936—, v.p., 1948—. Mem. Salem Marine Soc., Harvard Bus. Sch. Alumni Assn., Am. Marketing Assn. Republican. Unitarian. Clubs: Harvard, Harvard Business School (past pres.) (N.Y.C.). Home: 215 Farrington Av., N. Tarrytown, N.Y. Office: 285 Madison Av., N.Y.C. 17. Died Apr. 17, 1950.

BATCHELDER, Nathaniel Horton, educator; b. Salem, Mass., June 13, 1880; s. Henry Morrill and Martha Osgood (Horton) B.; desc. Meshech Weare, gov. N.H. Colony; A.B., Harvard, 1901, A.M., 1902; hon. A.M., Trinity, 1918; m. Gwendolen Sedgwick Mead, Nov. 24, 1910 (died Feb. 23, 1917); 1 son, Nathaniel Horton; m. 2d, Mary Evelyn Beatrice Longman, June 28, 1920 (dec.). Master, Hackley Sch., Tarrytown, 1903-07; sr. English master, Hotchkiss Sch., Lakeville, Conn., 1907-12; headmaster, Loomis Institute, Windsor, Connecticut, 1912-49. President Headmasters' Club of Connecticut, 1918, Northeast Federated Harvard Clubs, 1921; vice president Harvard Alumni Assn., 1924-25; dir. Am. Unitarian Assn., 1931-33; pres. Conn. branch, League of Nations Assn., 1934-38; pres. Conn. Peace Conference, 1938-46. Member New England Assn. Colls. and Secondary Schs., Headmasters' Association (sec. 1922-26; president 1928), State Council Merit System Assn. Former trustee Proctor Academy and Hackley School; trustee West Parish Meml. Found. Independent. Unitarian. Author: The Headmasters Association, A Half Century of Retrospect. Address: Box 236, Osterville, Mass. Died. Jan. 22, 1956.

BATCHELLER, Tryphosa Bates, author, singer, poet; b. North Brookfield, Mass.; d. Theodore Cornelius and Emma Frances (Duncan) Bates; ed. pvt. schs. in America and Paris, France, and tutors; Radcliffe Coll.; studied with Mme. Marchesi, Paris, with Leopoldo Mugnone, Florence, Giraudet, Panzani, Henschel; m. Francis Batcheller. Given invitation by President and Mrs. Theodore Roosevelt to sing at White House; presented at the Court of England, the Court of Italy, and at the courts of Germany, Portugal, Spain, Holland, Austria, Belgium, Sweden, Denmark and Norway; also received in spl. pvt. audience by Pope Pius X, Pope Benedict XV, Pope Pius XI; received by Mussolini in 1927; has sung before nearly every court in Europe and in charity concerts. Decorated Order of Mercy, 1913, by King George V of England; awarded gold medal special merit by Italian Red Cross, 1919; received decoration of Order of Elizabeth (Belgium), 1922; Order of Alfonso XII (Spain), 1922; Officier d'Académie (France), 1923; Chevalier of Legion d'Honneur (France), 1929, also decorated Officer of Legion d'Honneur; Officier d'Instruction Publique (France); Officer of Order of Jade (Chinese Govt.), 1937, only foreign woman to be decorated by China; won second prize for sonnet "Old Glory." Mem. Incorporated Soc. of Authors of England, National League of American Penwomen, Pen and Brush Club of N.Y., English Speaking Union of U.S., Colonial Dames of America, Daughters of the Founders and Patriots of America, Am. Soc. Psychical Research, Alliance Française, Soc. Am. Women (London), Nat. Soc. Americans of Royal Descent, Nat. Soc. Daughters of Barons of Runnemede, Order of Crown, Soc. Mayflower Descendants, Daughters of Colonial Wars, Union Interalliée (Paris), Daughter of Society of Cincinnati, Magna Carta Dames, American Poetry Society, France-Amérique, Société des Poetes Français (only American member), Société des Gens de Lettres de France, Italy-America Society. Invited to sing at White House by President and Mrs. Harding, and given personal commendation of work for Belgium, Italy and France by President Harding. Clubs: Boston Authors; American Women's, St. Cloud Country, Paris-Polo (Paris); Lyceum (London); Sulgrave (Washington, D.C.). Author: Glimpses of Italian Court Life, 1906; Italian Castles and Country Seats, 1911; Royal Spain of Today, 1913; Une amitié Historique (publ. in French and dedicated to Maréchal Foch, 1924; The Soul of a Queen, 1942 (pub. in English, Spanish, French, Polish, Portuguese, Italian, now being translated into Chinese); France in Sunshine and Shadow (English and French), 1944; A Short History of the Units of the D.A.R. Outside of the U.S.A. (privately pub.), Tryphosa Bates-Batcheller collection established in Congressional Library, 1931. Founder and hon. regent of Rochambeau Chapter, D.A.R. (St. Cloud, France), and ex-state regent for France, N.S. D.A.R. Address: care Coudert Brothers, 2 Rector St., N.Y.C. Died Sept. 9, 1952.

BATDORF, Grant David, bishop; b. at Lickdale, Pa., Apr. 30, 1874; s. William and Amelia (Sattazahn) B.; B.S., Pa. State Normal Sch., Millersville, Pa., 1893; grad. Bonebrake Theol. Sem., Dayton, O., 1898; special student Lehigh U. and U. of Chicago; Ph.B., Ill. Wesleyan U., 1902, Ph.D., 1910; D.D., Otterbein Coll., 1921., LL.D., Lebanon Valley Coll., 1936; m. Lydia A. Zellers, Apr. 25, 1894; children—Agnes Luella, Hillis Gordon. Ordained ministry United Brethren in Christ Ch., 1898; pastor successively at Allentown, Harrisburg, Reading and Lancaster, Pa., until 1920, First Ch., Dayton O. (the outstanding ch. in the denomination), 1920-29; elected bishop, May 14, 1929, and assigned to the East Dist. Has received nearly 2,000 members into ch. fellowship and raised over $1,000,000 for ch., ednl. and benevolent enterprises. Special lecturer in dept. of preaching, Bonebrake Theol. Sem. Trustee Bonebrake Theol. Sem. (chmn. exec. com.; business mgr., Jan.-July 1929); pres. Ministerial Pension Fund, Pa. State Council of Chs., Pa. Anti-Saloon League, Quincy Orphanage and Home; chmn. bd. Christian Edn. of U.B. Ch.; member Commn. on Ch. Union; member executive, Federal Council of Churches, also of com. on worship; trustee Lebanon Valley Coll. Mem. Pa. German Soc., Am. Geog. Soc., Dayton Chamber Commerce. Republican. Club: Dayton City.

Author: The Pastor; The Pivotal Man (brochure), 1915; Jesus' Money Gospel (brochure), 1920; Progressive Teacher Training Course (with others), 1923. Made world tcur for study and lecture on foreign missions, 1936-37. Home: 1575 Campus Dr., Dayton 6, O. Died Sept. 21, 1954.

BATEMAN, Herbert D., banker; b. Washington Co., N.C., Oct. 21, 1877; s. Richard M. and Sarah E. (Everett) B.; student The Acad., Plymouth, N.C., 1894-97, U. N.C., 1897-1900; m. Ida Tucker, 1902 (dec. Nov. 3, 1921); children—Richard H. (dec.), Mrs. W. A. McQueen, Mrs. Junius S. Williams; m. 2d, Mrs. Lottis Skinner Cooper, 1927; children—Harry Skinner (lt. USAAF), Mrs. Lloyd K. Newman. Tchr. pub. schs., N.C., 1895-97, Plymouth, N.C., 1900-01, Bath Acad., 1901, Windsor Acad., 1902; bookkeeper Gilliam & Lyon, 1902; organizer Citizens Bank of Windsor, 1902, cashier, 1902-07; paying teller So. Nat. Bank, Wilmington, 1907; asst. cashier Bank of Greenville, 1908-11; state bank examiner, N.C., 1911-16; cashier Branch Banking & Trust Co., Wilson, N.C., 1916-24, v.p., 1918-24, pres., 1924, now sr. cons.; mem. exec. com. Gt. Am. Ins. Co. Group for N.C. Trustee Univ. N.C.; member trustees budget com. and director Home Economics Found., Woman's Coll., Greensboro, N.C. Home: Wilson, N. C. Office: Branch Banking & Trust Co., Wilson, N.C. Died Aug. 18, 1956.

BATEMAN, John, sculptor; b. Cedarville, N.J., Feb. 14, 1877; s. Joseph and Harriet (Hulings) B.; student Sch. of Industrial Art (Phila.); Pa. Acad. Fine Arts (summer scholarship abroad, 1905, 2-yr. scholarship abroad, 1906, 07); m. Caroline Ware, June 27, 1900; 1 son, John. Instructor in Arts in Ceramics. Exhibited in Salon, Paris, and principal art centers in United States. Works: Bronze Soldiers' Memorial Fountain, Doylestown, Pa.; Bronze Seal of Atlantic City; large group "Machinery" and three hist. panels, Pa. Bldg. and 13 bronze tablets for the 13 original states, Forum of the Founders, Sesquicentennial, Phila., 1926; seated figure Abraham Lincoln, Gillespie Schools, Phila., Pa., 1934; bust of Walt Whitman, Camden, N.J.; Peter Pan fountain, Haddonfield, N.J. Hon. mention, San Francisco Expn., 1915. Mem. Nat. Sculpture Soc., Fellowship Pa. Acad. Fine Arts. Mason. Address: 111 29th St., Ship Bottom, N.J. Died Jan. 5, 1955.

BATEMAN, John H(enry), univ. prof.; b. Huron County, Mich., Mar. 20, 1892; s. Eli and Grace (McMillan) B.; B.S. in Civil Engring., U. of Mich., 1915, C.E., 1922; m. Marie Theresa Hoheisel, Aug. 1, 1915; 1 dau., Ruth (Mrs. G. R. Ferguson). Inspector, U.S. Engr. Corps., 1912-13; engr. Mich. State Highway Dept., 1915-24; dir. State Highway Lab. and asso. prof. civil engring. U. of Mich., 1919-24; prof. highway engring. La. State U., 1925-29; engr. of materials La. Highway Commn., 1925-29; engr. in charge, engring. dept., Barrow-Agee Labs., Inc., Memphis, 1929-30; consultant Gov.'s Com. on Highway Financing and Taxation, Mich., 1931-32; engr.-mgr. Berrien County (Mich.) Road Commn., 1932-36; prof. civil engring. La. State U. since 1936; cons. engr. on operation and control of ready-mixed concrete plants. Mem. Nat. Soc. Profl. Engrs., Am. Soc. Civil Engineers, Am. Concrete Inst., Am. Road Builders Assn (vice-pres. edn. div., So. Dist.; com. on advancement of highway engring.), Am. Soc. for Metals, Highway Research Bd. (asso.), La. Engring. Soc., Baton Rouge Indsl. Forum, Sigma Xi, Tau Beta Pi. Author: Introduction to Highway Engineering, 5th edit., 1948; (textbook) Materials of Construction, 1950. Contbr. articles on highway engring. and materials of constrn. to tech. jours. Home: 434 Highland Park Dr., Baton Rouge 8, La. Died Aug. 23, 1953; buried Greenoaks Meml. Park, Baton Rouge.

BATES, Albert H(arlan), patent lawyer; b. Cin., Jan. 24, 1869; s. Cyrus S. and Laverna (Sutherland) B.; student Kenyon Mil. Acad., 1884, Brooks Mil. Acad., 1885-86; M.E., Lehigh U., 1889; LL.B., Ohio State U., 1892; m. Kathleen Jones, Oct. 11, 1904; children—Margaret Sutherland (Mrs. Walter V. Diener), Darwin Sutherland. Admitted to Ohio bar, 1892; asso. legal dept. Brush Electric Co., Cleve., 1892-93, Robert H. Parkinson, patent lawyer, Chgo., 1893-96; practice patent, trademark, copyright law, Cleve., 1896-1951, ret. Mem. A.S.M.E. (50 yr. mem.), Am. Bar Assn., Am., Cleve. (past pres.) patent law assns. New Eng. Soc. Cleve. and Western Res., Cleve. Engring. Soc., No. Ohio Lehigh Assn., Psi Upsilon. Home: 813 W. Loucks St., Sheridan, Wyo. Died Apr. 26, 1952.

BATES, Frederick (John), phys. chemistry; b. Marysville, Kan., Jan. 2, 1877; s. Charles A. and Harriett (Roberts) B.; B.S., U. Kan., 1900; A.M., U. Neb., 1902; m. Gertrude C. Coyle, Jan. 5, 1905. Chief magneto-optical and carbohydrate sect. Nat. Bureau of Standards, 1903-—; chief, optics div., 1941-47; cons. carbohydrate chemistry and optics, 1948; devised methods and prepared Treasury Dept. regulations for weighing, gauging, sampling, classifying and testing imported sugars; supr. govt. sugar labs. of the Customs Service, Treasruy Dept.; pres. Internat. Commn. for Uniform Methods of Sugar Analysis. Developed sensitive strip spectral polarizing system; Bates quartz compensating polariscope with adjustable sensibility; Bates cadmium-vapor arc lamp, Bates polariscope tubes, Bates sugar balance, etc.; has pursued investigation of inversion of quartz and of rotary polarization of magnetic elements at high temperatures. Mem. Am. Chem. Soc., Am. Phys. Soc., Washington Philos. Soc., Am. Optical Soc., Internat. Soc. Sugar Cane Technologists, Internat. Union of Pure and Applied Chemistry, Sigma Xi. Republican. Methodist. Clubs: Cosmos, Columbia Country. Contbr. extensive researches in natural and magnetic rotary polarizations of light, and in the transformations in silica, especially anomalous rotary dispersion; co-author of Bur. of Standards of Baumé scale. Co-author (circular) Polarimetry, Saccharimetry, and the Sugars. Home: 1649 Harvard St., Washington. Office: Nat. Bur. of Standards, Washington 25. Died Nov. 1, 1958; buried Rock Creek Cemetery, Washington.

BATSON, William Howard, dir. sch. edn.; born Martinsville, O., Sept. 18, 1881; s. James and Mary (Crawford) B.; A.B., Antioch Coll., Yellow Springs, O., 1907; Ph.D., U. of Mich., 1915; m. Mary Winifred Creamer, Aug. 26, 1914. Supt. schs., Osborn, O., 1907-11; prof. psychology and edn., Tex. Christian U., 1913-17; prof. edn. and dir. Training Sch., Southwestern State Normal Sch., Weatherford, Okla., 1917-18; prof. edn., U. of S.Dak., since 1919, formerly dir. Sch. of Edn. and dir. Summer Sch. Mem. Com. on Edn. and Spl. Training, Washington, D.C., 1918-19, serving as 2d and 1st lt., Gen. Staff Div. in connection with S.A.T.C. and R.O.T.C. Mem. Am. Psychol. Assn., A.A.A.S., Am. Assn. Univ. Profs., S.D. Edn. Assn. (pres. 1930-31), Sigma Xi. Republican. Episcopalian. Wrote: (monograph) Acquisition of Skill, 1916; South Dakota Group Intelligence Test for High Schools, 1922; (monograph) High School Scholastic Contests in South Dakota, 1946. Home: 421 S. University, Vermillion, S.D. Died Dec. 28, 1954; buried Bluff View Cemetery, Vermillion.

BATTEN, Joseph Minton, educator; b. Smithfield, Va., May 25, 1893; s. Ernest Lee and Sallie Jane (Minton) B.; A.B., Randolph-Macon Coll., 1912; B.D., Princeton Theol. Sem., 1917; A.M. (Gelston-Winthrop fellow ch. history, 1917-18), 1918; Ph.D., U. Chicago, 1930; m. Lina Cofer, June 20, 1918. Instr. English and Latin Randolph Macon Acad., 1912-14; instr. history and Bible Ferrum (Va.) Tng. Sch., 1920-23; prof. ch. history and Bible Scarritt Bible and Tng. Sch., Kansas City, Mo., 1923-24; prof. ch. history Scarritt Coll., Nashville, 1924-45, registrar, 1924-45, dean, 1943-45; prof. ch. history Garrett Bibl. Inst., Evanston, Ill., 1945-46, Vanderbilt U. Sch. Religion, Nashville, since 1946; vis. prof. history George Peabody Coll. Tchrs., summer sessions since 1931. Mem. Am. Soc. Ch. History, Am. Hist. Assn., Am. Acad. Polit. and Social Sci. Methodist (mem. Va. Ann. Conf.). Author: John Dury, Advocate of Christian Reunion, 1944; Protestant Backgrounds in History, 1951. Contbr. essays to Protestantism (edited by W.K. Anderson), 1944; Methodism (edited by W.K. Anderson), 1947. Home: 4021 Overbrook Dr., Nashville 7. Died June 10, 1954; buried Woodlawn Meml. Park, Nashville.

BATTEN, Loring Woart, clergyman; b. Gloucester County, N.J., Nov. 17, 1859; s. Thomas G. and Emeline (Zane) B.; A.B., Harvard, 1885; B.D., Phila. Div. Sch., 1887; Ph.D., U. Pa., 1893; S.T. D., Hobart, 1903; m. Clara B. Ware, Mar. 18, 1886. Deacon, 1886, priest, 1887, P.E. Ch.; instr. and prof. O.T., Phila. Div. Sch., 1888-99; rector St. Mark's Ch., N.Y.C., 1899-1911; lectr., prof. O.T., Gen. Theol. Sem., 1904-33, now emeritus. Mem. Am. Oriental Soc., Soc. Bibl. Lit. and Exegesis, Oriental clubs of New York and Phila. Clubs: Century, Harvard, The Club, The Clericus, Authors' (London). Author: Old Testament From the Modern Point of View, 1889; The Hebrew Prophet, 1905; Ezra-Nehemiah in the Internat. Critical Commentary, 1913; The Relief of Pain by Mental Suggestion, 1917; Good and Evil, 1918; The First Book of Samuel, 1919; also articles in Hastings' Dictionary of the Bible and articles in Semitic and Oriental jours. and periodicals. Home: 560 Riverview Rd., Swarthmore, Pa. Died Jan. 1946.

BATTIN, Charles Reginald, business exec.; b. Toronto, Ont., Can., Mar. 19, 1880; s. William Sanders and Isabella Fearon (Clark) B.; ed. in public schs., Can.; m. Charlotte Johnston Smith, Apr. 18, 1925. Connected with Goldsmiths Stock Co., Toronto, 1896-1907, Pogson-Peloubet & Co., Butte, Montana, 1910-11, Price, Waterhouse & Co., Toronto, Chicago, Mexico City and Havana, 1912-27; officer of Addressograph-Multigraph Corp., Cleveland, O., 1927-47, dir. and v.p. since 1929, treasurer, 1929-47; director and vice pres. Addressograph-Multigraph of Canada, Ltd., Toronto; dir. Addressograph-Multigraph, Ltd., London, Eng. Mem. Church of England (Anglican). Clubs: Union, Mid-Day (Cleveland). Home: Wade Park Manor, Parklane at E. 107th St. Office: care Addressograph-Multigraph Corp., 1200 Babbitt Road, Cleve. 17. Died 1950.

BATTLE, William James, univ. prof.; b. Raleigh, N.C., Nov. 30, 1870; s. Kemp Plummer and Martha Ann (Battle) B.; A.B., with honors, U. of North Carolina, 1888; A.M., Harvard, 1891, Ph.D., 1893 (Thayer scholarship 1 yr., Morgan fellowship 2 yrs.); D.C.L., from U. of the South, 1922; LL.D., Southwestern U., 1929, U. of North Carolina, 1940; unmarried. Instr. Latin, U. of North Carolina, 1889-90; tutor in Latin, U. of Chicago, 1893; asso. prof. Greek, 1893-98, prof., 1898-1917, dean Coll. of Arts, 1908-11, dean of faculty, 1911-17, acting pres., 1914-16, U. of Tex.; prof. Greek, U. of Cincinnati, 1917-20; professor classical Languages University of Texas, 1920-49, professor emeritus since 1949. Visiting lecturer, Harvard, 1923. Mem. American Philol. Assn., Archæol. Inst. America, Hellenic Soc. (London), Texas Hist. Assn., Tex. Fine Arts Assn. (pres. 1920-29), Tex. Philos. Soc. (pres. 1941), Classical Assn. Middle West and South (pres. 1929-30), Phi Beta Kappa, Zeta Psi. Clubs: University (ex-pres.), Town and Gown (pres.), Harvard Club of Austin (ex-pres.), Scholia. Author: The Story of All Saints Chapel, Austin, Texas, 1900-1950; co-author: Battle Book, 1931; editor Memories of an Old-Time Tar Hel, by Kemp Plummer Battle, 1945; contbr. articles and pamphlets. Address: University of Texas, Austin 12, Tex. Died Oct. 8, 1955.

BATTS, Arthur Alanson, chmn. bd. Corborundum Co., ret.; b. Syracuse, June 25, 1884; s. Joseph Henry and Jenny (Smith) B.; ed. Niagara Falls High Sch. and extension courses in accounting; m. Mabel B. Bradley, Sept. 9, 1909; 1 son, Arthur Alanson. With The Carborundum Company, 1901-05, bookkeeper, 1905-11, office mgr., 1911-20, asst. sec., 1920-27, sec., 1927-42, president 1942-46, chairman of the board since 1947, now retired; auditor Meltone Corporation; director Powder City Trust Co. Republican. Episcopalian. Mason. Clubs: Niagara Rotary, Niagara Falls Country. Home: Lewiston Heights, Lewiston, N.Y. Office: Buffalo Av., Niagara Falls, N.Y. Died Jan. 8, 1953.

BAUER, Harold, pianist; b. London, Eng., Apr. 28, 1873; studied violin with father and Adolph Pollitzer. Debut as violinist, in London, and toured 9 yrs.; upon recommendation of Paderewski, went to Paris to study piano; began as pianist, 1893; toured principal cities of Europe; appeared in U.S. with Boston Symphony Orchestra, 1900; has played with leading orchestras of America and given numerous recitals. Died Mar. 12, 1951.

BAUER, Marion Eugénie, composer, writer; b. Walla Walla, Wash., Aug. 15, 1887; d. Jacques and Julie (Heyman) Bauer; ed. St. Helen's Hall, Portland, Ore.; studied music with Eugene Heffley, Henry Holden Huss, Emilie Frances Bauer, Walter Henry Rothwell, André Gedalge, Raoul Pugno. M.A. (hon.), Whitman Coll., 1932; Mus.D. (hon.) N.Y. Coll. Music, 1951. Asso. prof. music dept. N.Y.U., 1930-51; mem. faculty Inst. of Mus. Art, Juilliard Sch., 1940, and since 1944; mem. faculty Mills Coll., summer 1935, Carnegie Inst. Tech., summers 1936, 39, Tchrs. Coll., Columbia, 1940, Juilliard Summer Sch., 1941-52; N.Y. editor Musical Leader, 1926-54, music critic, 1954-—. Mem. Nat. Music Council (dir.), Am. Composers Alliance, League of Composers (exec. com.), Soc. for Publ. Am. Music, Am. Musicol. Soc. (N.Y. sect.); allied colonist and corporate member MacDowell Assn.; hon. mem. Phi Beta. Composer of 30 songs, 20 piano pieces, 2 sonatas for violin and piano, string quartet, suite for chamber music orchestra, viola sonata, piano sonata, suite for oboe and clarinet, quintet for soprano and string quartet, orchestral tone poem, Sun-Splendor, concertino for oboe, clarinet, strings, symphonic suite for string orchestra, Symphony No. 1 (1948), concerto for piano and orchestra, Trio-Sonata for flute, cello, and piano, China, and other choral works. Author: How Music Grew, 1925, rev. 1940; Music Through the Ages, 1932, rev. 1946 (both with Ethel Peyser); Twentieth Century Music, 1933, rev. edit., 1947; Summary of Twentieth Century Music, 1935; Musical Questions and Quizzes, 1941; How Opera Grew (with Ethel Peyser), 1955. Contributor on various musical subjects, The Great Modern Composers (Oscar Thompson), 1941, Book of Modern Composers (David Ewen), 1942, Musical Quarterly 1936, 1942, 1943. Lectr. at Chautauqua, N.Y., 1928-29, 1932-52. Asso. editor Internat. Cyclopedia of Music and Musicians. Recipient award of Soc. for Publ. Am. Music, 1950. Home-Studio: 115 W. 73d St., N.Y.C. Died Aug. 9, 1955; buried Kensico Cemetery, Valhalla, N.Y.

BAUER, Ralph Stanley, law educator; b. Stonington, Ill., Sept. 25, 1883; s. Josiah Thomas and Katie (Smith) B.; A.B., U. Ill., 1904, student law, 1906-08; A.M., James Millikin U., 1906; J.D., U. Chgo., 1909; m. Edna Stetson, Aug. 12, 1914; children—Janet (dec.), Ann Stetson. Asst. prof. law John B. Stetson U., 1913-14, prof., 1914-17; prof. law Emory U., 1917-18; instr. business law U. Ill., 1919-20, asso., 1920-21, asst. prof., 1921-24; prof. law De Paul U., 1924-—. Mem. Am., Chgo. bar assns., Pi Gamma Mu (gov. Ill. province 1936-39), Sigma Pi (past grand v.p.), Sigma Delta Kappa. Republican. Conglist. Mason. Clubs: Interfraternity, Sigma Pi. Author: Essentials of the Law of Damages, 1919; Cases on Damages, 1923, 3d edit., 1940; Business Law, 1930; Illinois Supp. to Bohlen's Cases on Torts, 1939. Co-author: Cases on Business Law (with W. E. Britton), 1922, 3d edit., 1941; Cases on Business Law (with E. R. Dillavou), 1925; Cases on Carriers (with Edgar Watkins), 1928;

The Law of Business (with Laurence P. Simpson), 1936; 2d edit., 1946. Editor: John's Am. Notaries (4th edit.), 1931. Contbr. law journals. Home: 1116 Randolph St., Oak Park, Ill. Office: 64 E. Lake St., Chgo. Died Apr. 5, 1950; buried Chapel Hill Gardens, West, Elmhurst, Ill.

BAUER, William Hans, pathologist; b. Prague, Austria; s. Aloysius Bauer; M.D., St. Charles U. Prague, 1912; Research fellow histology, med. sch., U. Imsbruck, Austria, 1912-14; m. Mary Elizabeth Bauer, Nov. 4, 1913; children—John D. (M.D.), Inge Hynes, Annliese Lamb. Asst., Med. Sch., U. Imsbruck, 1912-14, 1918-24, privat dozent, 1925-38, associate prof., 1931-34, prof. and dir., 1934-38; prof. and dir. pathology, sch. dentistry, St. Louis U., 1938—, affiliated with dept. pathology, med. schs., St. Louis U., also Marquette U.; coordinator Cancer Control Program (sch. dentistry). Served in M.C., Austrian Army, 1914-18. Asso. A.M.A.; mem. Am. Assn. Pathologist and Bacteriologist, Internat. Dental Research Assn., A.A.A.S., St. Louis Soc. Pathology, Sigma Xi. Collaborator of Pathology by W. A. D. Anderson, 1948. Home: 3117 Russell St. Office: 3556 Caroline St., St. Louis 4. Died June 14, 1956; buried Calvary Cemetery, St. Louis.

BAUM, Harry, educator; b. Cracow, Austria, July 11, 1882; s. Jacob and Anna (Weitzenblum) B.; brought to U.S., 1883, naturalized Am. Citizen; B.S., Coll. City of N.Y., 1902; E.E., Columbia, 1908; m. Celia Bernstein, Apr. 5, 1914; children—Helen Gertrude (Mrs. Yale J. Laitin), Marian. With test, small motor, power and mining depts., Gen. Electric Co., 1909-14; Am. rep. and engr., Rich Marine Fire Indicating System, 1915-16; mgr. engring. dept., James Milaw, Inc., 1917-18; lectr. on fuels and fuel economy, Coll. City of N.Y., 1917-20, instr. U.S. Signal Corps sch. 1918, instr. in physics, 1918-19, supr. charge rehabilitation of disabled World War veterans, 1919-24, asst. prof. elec. engring., Sch. of Tech., 1924-28, asso. prof., 1928-34, prof., 1935-49, chmn. dept. elec. engring., 1938-49, prof. emeritus 1949—; engr., tech. adv. Bd. Higher Edn., N.Y.C., 1926-42; engring. consultant Polymet Mfg. Co., 1926-27, Godward Gas Generator, Inc., 1927-31, Phila. Rapid Transit Co., 1927-31. Mem. Am. Inst. E.E., Soc. Promotion Engring. Edn. Am. Assn. Univ. Profs., N.Y. State and Nat. socs. of profl. engrs., Eta Kappa Nu. Mason. Home: 150 Bennett Av., N.Y.C. 33. Office: 139th St. and Convent Av., N.Y.C. 31. Died June 6, 1959.

BAUM, Walter Emerson (bawm), artist; b. Sellersville, Pa., Dec. 14, 1884; s. Harvey W. and Mary Ellen B.; editor Pennsylvania Academy Fine Arts (student of William Trego); Doctor Humane Letters (hon.) Lehigh University, 1946; m. Flora Billger Barndt, November 16, 1904; children—Marian Eleanor (Mrs. J. Lawrence Grim), Robert Emerson, Ruth Lynnette (Mrs. Robert G. Young), Edgar S. (M.D.). Painter of landscapes since 1910; editor Sellersville Herald, 1920-42; art dir. Phila. Evening Bulletin; dir. Allentown (Pa.) Art Museum; dir. Kline-Baum Art Sch. Exhibited at Pa. Acad., Phila. Art Club, Corcoran Art Gallery (Washington), Nat. Acad. Design (New York), Chicago Art Inst., also in galleries, etc., St. Louis, Buffalo, Fort Worth, Baltimore, San Francisco, Cleveland, etc. Represented in permanent collections of Irene Rich Art Assn., Norfolk, Va.; State Coll., Pa., Phila. Water Color Club; Hazelton High Sch.; Woodrow Wilson Jr. High Sch. (Phila.); Allentown Art Museum, Print Club at Philadelphia Museum of Art, U. Pa., Toledo Art Museum, Pa. Acad., Reading (Pa.) Mus., Asheville and Hickory (N.C.) Mus. Awarded: bronze medal American Artists Exhibition, Phila., 1924; Jennie Sesnan gold medal Pa. Acad., 1925; picture purchase prize, Springville, Utah, 1933; Fellowship prize Pa. Acad., 1939; hon. mention Phila. Sketch Club, 1939, purchase prize Cape May County (N.J.) Art League, 1940, hon. mention Pa. Soc. Miniature Painters, 1942, hon. mention Print Club of Philadelphia, 1942, the McCarthy Prize, Pennsylvania Society Miniature Painters, 1943, the Dana medal, Pa. Academy of Fine Arts and the Phila. Water Color Club, 1944; the Zabriskie Prize, American Water Color Society, 1945; Purchase Prize, The Buckhill Art Assn., 1945; Ludwig Prize at Audubon Artists Exhibition, 1946; silver medal Da Vinci Alliance Philadelphia, 1950; hon. mention Indiana (Pa.) State Coll., 1951; 1st Prize Woodmere Gallery, 1951; Bronze medal, Nat. Arts club, 1952; Grumbacher Purchase, 1953; Gold Medal, Nat. Arts Club, 1953. Member Philadelphia Art Alliance, Phila. Sketch Club, Germantown Art League, Fellowship of Pennsylvania Academy of Fine Arts, American Artists Professional League, University Club, Phila. Water Color Club, Bucks-Montgomery Press League, Allentown-Bethlehem Art Alliance, Pa.-German Folk Lore Soc., Artists League of Am., Am. Color Print Soc., Nat. Geog. Soc., Am. Water Color Soc., Salmagundi (hon. mem.). Mem. Sellersville Sch. Bd., Sellersville-Perkasie Joint Sch. Bd. Lutheran. Author: Two Hundred Years, an informal history of Pa.-Germans of Bucks County, Pa. Contbg. artist for Curist Publishing Co. Address: Sellersville, Pa. Died July 12, 1956; buried Sellersville Cemetery.

BAUMER, Bertha, librarian. Address: Public Library, Omaha, Neb. Died Aug. 23, 1951.*

BAUR, Bertha E. (Mrs. Jacob Baur) (bour); maiden name Bertha E. Duppler; m. Jacob Baur (died July 19, 1912); 1 dau., Rosemary (Mrs. Bartle Bull). Active in polit., civic and social affairs; candidate for Rep. nomination for Congress, 1926; also candidate for Congress, 9th dist., 1936; Rep. Nat. Committeewoman from Ill.; pres. Woman's Nat. Rep. Club of Chicago. Vic-chmn. Friends of Opera. Clubs: Casino, Saddle and Cycle, Arts (chmn. exec. com.), Woman's, Woman's Athletic. Home: 1511 Astor St., Chgo. Died 1940.*

BAXTER, Batsell, coll. pres.; b. nr. Sherman, Tex., Nov. 17, 1886; s. Francis Price and Laura Etta (Elliott) B.; B.L., Nashville Bible Sch., 1911; B.A., Tex. Christian U., 1917; M.A., Baylor U., 1919; m. Frances Fay Scott, July 12, 1911; 1 son, Batsell Barrett. Ordained ministry Ch. of Christ, 1909; pastor Corsicana, Tex., 1911-12; teacher and dean Thorp Spring (Tex.) Christian Coll., 1912-16; dean Cordell Christian Coll., Okla., 1916-18; science teacher, Abilene Christian Coll. 1919—, pres., 1924—. Democrat. Club: Lions. Home: Abilene, Tex. Died Mar. 7, 1956.

BAXTER, Lionel David MacKenzie, broker; b. Pittsburgh Twp., Ont., Can., Aug. 16, 1889; s. John D. and Nora (Wagner) B.; m. Elsie Middlecott, June 3, 1920; children—Robert MacKenzie, Peter Lionel. Pres. Osler, Hammond & Nanton, Ltd., Winnipeg, Can., Calgary & Edmonton Corp., Osler & Nanton Trust Co., Anglo-Canadian Oils, Ltd., Brandon, Manitoba; dir. Anglo-Canadian Oil Co., Ltd., Calgary, Home Oil Co., Central Manitoba Mines, Ltd., Manitoba Bridge & Iron Works, Ltd., Manitoba Rolling Mill Co., Ltd., Winnipeg, Dominion Bank, Toronto, Guarantee Co. of N.A., Montreal. Served with 1st Canadian Div., 1914-18; advanced to lt. col. Decorated Order of Brit. Empire. Mem. Canadian Legion (pres. Dominion Command). Home: 137 Westgate St., Manitoba, Can. Deceased.

BAXTER, Norman Washington, newspaper correspondent; b. Knoxville, Tenn., April 19, 1891; son of William M. and Mary (Kirkman) B.; graduate Woodberry Forest Sch., Orange, Va., 1909; m. Prue Munger Rust, Nov. 24, 1920; children—Joy, Mary Jane, Norman Kirkman. Began as reporter Nashville (Tenn.), Feb. 10, 1910; with various newspapers, 1911-17; Washington Bur., Phila. Pub. Ledger, 1917-20, London Bur., same, 1920-22; with Washington (D.C.) Post, 1923-31; asst. to dirs. of Reconstruction Finance Corp., 1933-37; pub. relations dir., Distilled Spirits Inst., Inc., 1937-40; asst. to Sec. of Commerce, 1940-45; now Washington corr., The Houston Chronicle. Catholic. Clubs: National Press, Gridiron (Washington). Home: 1314 29th St. N.W. Office: National Press Bldg., Washington. Died Sept. 13, 1952.

BAXTER, Warner, actor; b. Columbus, O., 1891; m. Winifred Bryson. Motion picture star with Fox Film Corp. Has played in, In Old Arizona, Adam Had 4 Sons, 42nd Street, Broadway Bill, One More Spring, Under the Pampas Moon, King of Burlesque, The Prisoner of Shark Island, Wife, Doctor and Nurse, Kidnaped, etc. Home: 911 N. Roxbury Dr., Beverly Hills, Calif. Died May 7, 1951; buried Forest Lawn Meml. Park, Glendale, Calif.

BAY, Charles Ulrick, business executive; b. Rensselaer, New York, September 5, 1888; son of Jens Christopher and Marie (Hauan) B.; ed. high schs. Syracuse, Chicago, Detroit; m. Josephine Holt Perfect, 1942; children—Christopher, Synova, Frederick. Founder and president Bay Company, Bridgeport, Conn., 1915-31 (merged with Parke, Davis & Co., 1931); dir. and chmn. exec. com. First Nat. Bank & Trust Co., Bridgeport, Conn. since 1933; partner A. M. Kidder & Co., mem. N.Y. Stock Exchange, N.Y. City, since 1933, sr. partner since 1940; founder and pres. Bay Petroleum Corp., Denver; dir. Am. Export Lines, N.Y.; dir., chmn. bd. Conn. Ry. Lighting Co. Served as civilian mem. purchase policy adv. com., SOS, War Dept., World War II; Am. ambassador to Norway, 1946-53. Decorated Grand Cross St. Olav, Norway. Episcopalian. Clubs: Yacht, Brook, Bankers, Metropolitan, River (N.Y.C.); Royal Norwegian Yacht (Oslo, Norway) Norwegian; Everglades (Palm Beach). Home: 720 Park Av., N.Y.C. 21. Office: 1 Wall St., N.Y.C. 5. Died Dec. 31, 1955.

BAYARD, Edwin Stanton (bī'ẽrd), agrl. editor; b. Kingston, O., Dec. 13, 1867; s. Samuel Peter and Martha Ellen (Lutz) B.; A.B., Waynesburg Co., 1889, A.M., Litt.D.; m. Mary Virginia Kerr, June 9, 1903 (died Mar. 1944); 1 son, Samuel Preston. Editor in chief, Pa. Farmer, ret. 1950, now editor emeritus. Mem. United States Agrl. Conf., 1921, Nat. Livestock Com., Am. Com. Internat. Inst. of Agr. (Rome); chmn. Allegheny County Farm Bur. Trustee and mem. exec. com. Pa. State Coll. Mem. Am. Aberdeen-Angus Breeders' Assn. (dir.), Pa. Livestock Breeders' Assn. (pres.), East Liberty Chamber of Commerce (pres.), Holland Soc. of New York, Sigma Delta Chi; hon. mem. Am. Vet. Med. Assn., Alpha Zeta, Gamma Sigma Delta, Alpha Gamma Rho. Mem. Pa. N.G. Republican. Presbyn. Mason. Rotarian. Lecturer. Home: University Club, Pittsburgh 13. Office: Highland Bldg., Pitts. 6. Deceased.

BAYDUR, Huseyin Ragip, Turkish diplomat; b. Rhodes, Turkey, Aug. 15, 1891; s. Mehmet Galip and Muneyver (Mehmet) B.; grad. Smyrna Lycee, 1908; LL.B., Faculty of Law, U. Istanbul, 1911. Prof. Turkish lit. Superior Normal Sch., Istanbul, 1911-16; insp. Turkish students in Europe, 1916-19; editor newspaper IFHAM, Istanbul, 1919; editor newspaper ULUS (organ of govt. of Nat. Assembly) and dir. gen. of Press and Information, 1920-21; counsellor to 1st polit. mission of Nat. Govt., Paris, 1921; permanent Charge d'Affaires of the Mission, 1921-24; ambassador to Bucharest, 1924-29, to Moscow, 1929-35, To Rome, 1935-43, to Moscow, 1943-45, to Washington, 1945-48, then to Court of St. James, Eng. Del. to various internat. confs., to U.N. Conf., San Francisco, 1946; chmn. Turkish del. to 2d part of 1st session of U.N. Assembly, 1946. Died Feb. 27, 1955.

BAYER, Lloyd Felch, oil exec.; b. Mt. Vernon, N.Y., Oct. 26, 1893; s. Charles Anthony and Minerva Charlotte (Nemmet) B.; M.E., Stevens Inst. of Tech., Hoboken, N.J., 1914; m. Cora E. Glendenning, May 29, 1919; 1 son, Lloyd Felch. Engr. N.Y. and Queens Electric Light & Power Co., L.I. City, N.Y., 1914-16; chief engr. Tidal Gasoline Co., Tulsa, Okla., 1916-20; mfg. mgr. Tidal Refining Co., 1920-24, v.p. and mgr., 1924-26; v.p. Asso. Oil Co., San Francisco, 1927-36, dir., 1929-36; v.p., dir. Tide Water Asso. Oil Co., San Francisco, 1936-54, sr. vice president and director, 1954—. Honorary trustee San Francisco Boys' Club, Inc. Mem. Soc. Mech. Engrs., Am. Soc. for Testing Materials, Am. Petroleum Inst., Tau Beta Pi. Presbyterian. Mason. Clubs: Newcomen Soc., Rotary (San Francisco); Stock Exchange. Home: 323 Monte Vista Av., Oakland 11, Calif. Office: 79 New Montgomery St., San Francisco 20. Died Sept. 29, 1958.

BAYLES, Theodore Floyd (bā'lēs), theologian; b. West Kortright, N.Y., July 25, 1871; s. John Owen and Martha Brown (Floyd) B.; prep. edn., Stamford (N.Y.) Sem.; A.B., Union Coll., Schenectady, 1895; grad. New Brunswick Theol. Sem., 1898; B.D., Rutgers, 1898, D.D., 1924; m. Mary Bevier, Sept. 17, 1902; children—Marthena, Theodore Bevier. Ordained ministry Ref. Ch. in America, 1898; pastor successively Gardiner, N.Y., Little Falls, Freehold and Bayonne, N.J., and Walden, N.Y., until 1924; prof. practical theology, New Brunswick Theol. Sem., 1924-41, emeritus, 1941—. Mem. Phi Beta Kappa. Republican. Home: 12 Bishop Pl., New Brunswick, N.J. Died Jan. 19, 1952; buried New Platz, N.J.

BAYLEY, William Shirley, geologist; b. Balt., Nov. 10, 1861; s. Robert P. and Emma (Downing) B.; A.B., Johns Hopkins, 1883, fellow, 1885-86, Ph. D., 1886; m. Lucie Jacobs, Mar. 11, 1894; 1 dau., Emily Elizabeth (Mrs. J. Howard Gillen). Prof. geology Colby Coll., 1888-1904; asst. prof. geology U. Ill., 1907-09, asso. prof. mineralogy and economic geology, 1909-13, prof. geology, 1913-31, head dept., 1928-31, retired 1932. Asst. geologist U.S. Geol. Survey, 1887-1908, geologist, 1909-1931; asso. editor Am. Naturalist, 1886-1902; reviewer Neues Jahrbuch für Mineralogie, Berlin, 1890-1908; bus. editor Economic Geology, 1905-43. Fellow A.A.A.S., Geol. Soc. Am. (1st v.p., 1929), Geol. Soc. Washington, Chemische Gesellschaft; mem. Soc. Econ. Geologists, Mineral. Soc. America (pres. 1936), Ill. Acad. Sciences (pres. 1922-23), S.A.R., Phi Beta Kappa, Sigma Xi, Beta Theta Pi. Author: Elementary Crystallography, 1910; Minerals and Rocks, 1915; Descriptive Mineralogy, 1916; Guide to Non-Metallic Mineral Products, 1930; others. Home: Glen Rock, N.J. Died Feb. 13, 1943; buried Urbana, Ill.

BAYLOR, John Roy, educator; b. Albemarle County, Va.; B.A., B.Litt., U. Va., 1872; D.Litt., U. of South, 1923; m. Julia Howard; 1 dau., Eloise B. (wife of Dr. George Martin). Tchr. Mountain Spring Sch., Trinity, Ala., later Miller Manual Labor Sch., Albemarle, Va., until 1888; tchr. sch. for Boys, Savannah, Ga., 2 yrs., later charge Bishop Jackson Sch., Anniston, Ala.; organized Baylor Sch., Chattanooga, Tenn., 1893, and continued as its head. Mem. Phi Beta Kappa. Episcopalian. Author various addresses and pamphlets on Virgil, Lanier, peace, science, etc. Address: The Baylor Sch., Chattanooga, Tenn. Died Aug. 17, 1926.

BAYNE, Howard, banker; b. Belfast, North Ireland, Dec. 8, 1878; s. Samuel Gamble and Emily (Kelsey) B.; came to U.S., 1881, naturalized, 1883; student Berkeley Sch., New York, N.Y., 1890-97; E.E., Columbia, 1901; m. Louise van Beuren, Jan. 10, 1910; children—Elizabeth (Mrs. Imerie de Vegh), Daphne (Mrs. Geoffrey T. Hellman). Technical asst. to Michael I. Pupin of Columbia Univ., during his development of electrical wave math. theories and his loaded coil invention, 1900-02; asst. sec. Security Mobile Oil Co., Beaumont, Tex., 1903-05; treas. Columbia Trust Co., N.Y.C., 1905, sr. v.p. and dir., 1907-24; dir. and mem. finance com. Prudential Ins. Co. of Am., Newark, N.J., 1915-40, chmn. finance com., 1920-40; mem. numerous bondholders protective coms. or R.R., utility and indsl. cos., 1908-33; dir., mem. trust adv. bd. Chase Manhattan Bank; dir., mem. exec. com. Bankers & Shipper Ins. Company, Pacific Fire Company, Jersey Ins. Co., American Reinsurance Co. Chmn. zoning commn., Harding Township, N.J., 1936-37; mem. Bd. of Edn., Harding Township, 1930-36; chmn. rationing bd., Harding Township, 1941-42. Mem. New York Bot. Gardens (bd. mgrs.), N.Y. C. of C., Squadron A Ex-mems. Assn. Clubs: University (N. Y.C.); Morristown (N.J.). Home: New Vernon, N.J. Office: 20 Broad St., N.Y.C. 5. Died Aug. 24, 1958.

BAYNE, Hugh Aiken, lawyer; b. New Orleans, La., Feb. 15, 1870; s. Thomas Levingston and Anna Maria (Gayle) B.; A.B., Yale, 1892; LL.B., Tulane U., 1894, LL.D. (hon.) 1946; m. Helen Cheney, Oct. 8, 1895; children—Helen, Elizabeth C.; m. 2d, Emily Ford, 1919 (died 1937); 1 son, Hugh G. (lt. Air Corps). Admitted to bar, 1894, prac. New Orleans, 1894-98, N.Y. City, 1898-1919; mem. firm Strong & Cadwalader, N.Y. City, 1905-14; mem. legal serivce of Reparations Commn. under treaties of Versailles and St. Germain, 1919-28; served as one of three judges deciding claim of Belgium vs. Austria to Treasure of Order of Golden Fleece and to Tryptich of San Ildenphonse (Rubens), claim of Czecho-Slovakia as successor to Kingdom of Bohemia to 500 works of art taken from Bohemia by Austria between 1616 and 1914; claim of Standard Oil Co. vs. Reparations Commn. to 21 oil tankers of Standard's German subsidiary, appropriated by Reparations Commn. to pay Germany's reparations. Also sole judge of two questions of interpretation of disarmament clauses of Versailles treaty submitted by ambassadors of France, Italy, Great Britain and Japan. Served as major judge advocate, U.S. Army, 1917, in France, J.A., S.O.S., of A.E.F., counsel Prisoners of War Mission, 1918, lt. col., 1919. Decorated Distinguished Service Medal (U.S.), Legion of Honor, Palmiers Universitaire, grade of officers publ. instrn. (France). Clubs: Yale (New York); Skull and Bones (Yale); Graduates (New Haven); Boston (New Orleans). Home: Graduates Club, 155 Elm St., New Haven. Died Dec. 24, 1954; buried Magnolia Cemetery, New Orleans.

BAYNE, Reed Taft (bān), editor, pub.; b. Portland, Conn., Feb. 10, 1885; s. John Strawn and Julia Cook (Taft) B.; grad. high sch., Mendon, Ill; studied law, 1904-07, and ministerial course prescribed by Neb. Congl. Conf., 1907-08; m. Belle Aileen Bennie, Aug. 8, 1918; children—Eleanor Louise and Robert Taft. Ordained ministry Congl. Ch., 1909; successively pastor McCook, Neb., Creston, Ia., Superior, Wis., until 1920; editor Wis. Sunday Times, Superior, 1920-24, Superior Telegram, 1924-25; mng. editor, Duluth (Minn.) News Tribune, 1925-26, editor and pub., 1926-30; pub. Manitowoc (Wis.) Times, 1930-32; editor Manitowoc Herald-Times, 1932-47, publisher, 1947—; vice pres. Manitowoc Newspapers, Incorporated, Two Rivers Reporter, Incorporated. Minnesota Development Company. Moderator Wisconsin Congl. Conf., 1921-22. Mem. Am. Newspaper Pubs. Assn. Republican. Mason (K.T., Shriner). Home: 402 Cleveland Av. Office: 902 Franklin St., Manitowoc, Wis. Died June 7, 1954; buried Manitowoc.

BAYNE, William, investment banker; born East Orange, N.J., June 7, 1890; s. William and Sallie E. (Smith) B.; grad. St. Pauls Sch., Concord, N. H., 1908, Yale, 1911; m. Margaret J. Macgill, Oct. 25, 1919, children—Patricia (Mrs. Nicholas P. Harvey), Carroll (Mrs. William C. Spence), William, Sara Margaret (Mrs. Wayne W. Wall). In advt. dept. Vogue and Vanity Fair, N.Y. City, 1913-16; advt. mgr. New Republic, 1916-17; with Bonbright & Co., Boston, 1949-52, manager New England territory: v.p. and treas. Arthur Perry & Co., Inc., Boston, 1932-45; gen. partner F. S. Moseley & Co., 1945—. Former gov. N.Y. Stock Exchange; former gov. Investment Bankers Am. Mem. Delta Phi. Clubs: Bond (Boston); Piping Rock (Locust Valley, N.Y.); Union Lunch (N.Y. City) Home: Brookville Rd., Brookville, N.Y. Office: 14 Wall St., N.Y.C. Died Oct. 22, 1955.

BAYS, Alfred William, lawyer; b. Rushville, Ill., July 12, 1876; s. Enos William and Elizabeth (Smith) B.; B.S., Knox College, 1901, LL.D. (hon.), 1950; LL.B., Northwestern University, 1904; m. Anna Carnahan, Sept. 1912; children—Catherine Harriet (Mrs. Lawrence Parrish), Marjorie (Mrs. Paul Peter). Lecturer, 1905-09, instr. and asst. prof. commercial law, 1909-12, prof. law, 1912-37, Northwestern U. School of Commerce and Northwestern U. Sch. of Law; also in gen. practice at Chicago; gen. counsel, sec. Abbott Labs., v. chmn. bd., 1947-50. President The Abbott Foundation; trustee Northwestern Univ., Lake Bluff Orphanage, Ravenswood Hospital, Evanston Hospital, La Rabida Jackson Park Sanitarium, Knox College (with H. B. Shattuck) Clara A. Abbott Trust, 1924-39. Republican. Mason. Clubs: University Evanston); Westmoreland Country. Author and Compiler: American Commercial Law Series, 9 vols., 1911-12, 2d edit., 1920-22, 3d edit. (4 vols.), 1935; Business Law, an elementary text in one vol., 1919, 2d edit., 1925; Cases on Commercial Law, 1914, 2d edit., 1923, 3d edit., 1931, 4th edit., 1939. Home: 2330 Ewing Av., Evanston, Ill. Office: Abbott Laboratories, North Chicago, Ill. Died Dec. 22, 1957.

BAYUK, Samuel, business exec.; b. Russia, 1870. Hon. chmn. Bayuk Cigars, Inc., Phila. Mason. Home: 1905 Arrowhead Rd., Richmond, Pa. Office: 9th St. and Columbia Av., Phila. 22. Died Nov. 11, 1954.*

BAZETT, Henry Cuthbert (băz'ĕt), univ. prof.; b. Gravesend, Eng., June 25, 1885; s. Henry and Eliza Ann (Cruickshank) B.; B.A., Wadham Coll., Oxford, U., 1908, B.M., 1910, Bachelor of Surgery, 1910, M.A., (Magdalen Coll.), 1913, M.D., 1920; D.Sc., Univ. of Western Ontario, London, Ont., Can., 1945; student St. Thomas Hosp., London, 1908-12, Harvard, 1912-13; m. Dorothy Rufford Livesey, Mar. 10, 1917; children—Hazel, Donald John. Came to U.S., 1921. Demonstrator physiology, St. Thomas Hosp., 1909-10; demonstrator in pathology and bacteriology, Oxford, 1913-14, Christopher Welch lecturer in clin. physiology, 1919-21; prof. physiology, Univ. of Penn. since 1921, on leave as visiting prof. med. research, in charge aviation med. research, Univ. of Toronto, 1941-43. Served with British Army, 1914-18; with Royal Army Med. Corps, later with med. sect. R.A.F. (3 citations); retired from Reserve with rank of major, 1935. Consultant to mil. planning div. Office Q.M. Gen., Washington, D.C., 1944. Mem. asso. com. on aviation med. research (Can.), on exec. com., 1941-43; mem. subcom. on clothing, com. on Aviation Medicine (U.S.), 1943-45; temporary mem. British Med. Research Council on mission to India, 1944. Radcliffe Travelling fellow Univ. Coll., Oxford, 1912-14; fellow Magdalen Coll., Oxford, 1912-20. Decorated order British Empire, 1919, Mil. Cross; Comdr. British Empire, 1946. Fellow Royal Coll. Surgeons, Coll. Phys. of Phila.; mem. Physiol. Soc., Am., Can. physiol. socs., Sigma Xi, Phi Beta Pi. Mason. Club: British Officers (Phila.). Contbr. of sect. on circulation in Macleod's Physiology and Modern Med., 8th and 9th edits., 1938, 1941; also sects. in other books and sci. papers. Home: 629 Haydock Lane, Haverford, Pa. Office: Medical School, University of Pennsylvania, Phila. Died July 11, 1950; buried Holywell Cemetery, Oxford, Eng.

BEACH, Chester, sculptor; b. San Francisco, May 23, 1881; student, Paris, France, 1904-07. Designer of Monroe-Adams, Lexington-Concord and Hawaiian half dollars, also of the City of Hudson half dollars, 1935. Principal works: Fountain of the Waters and Twelve Signs of the Zodiac, Fine Arts Garden, Cleve.; 3 groups, Panama-Pacific Exhbn.; bronze figure, Barnard Coll. Gymnasium, N.Y.C.; Riders of the Elements fountain, N.Y. World's Fair, 1940; life size marbles Cal. Palace of Legion of Honor, San Francisco, Am. Acad. Arts and Letters, N.Y.C., Herbert Pratt Estate, Glen Cove, L.I., Bklyn. Mus., Cleve. Mus., Met. Mus., Newark Art, Chgo. Art, St. Mark's Ch., N.Y.; bronze figure with marble figures in relief, Am. Tel. & Tel. Bldg., N.Y.C.; also portraitist. Recipient the Julian Acad. medal, 1904; Barnett prize for sculpture, N.A.D., 1907, Watrous gold medal, 1926; silver medal Pan Pacific Exhbn., 1915; 1st prize Nat. Arts Exhbn., 1923; gold medal for sculpture Archtl. League Exhbn., 1924; Potter Palmer gold medal for sculpture, Chgo., 1925; Nat. Arts Club medal and prize, 1926; Numismatic Saltus medal, medallic sculpture, 1946. N.A. Mem. Nat. Sculpture Soc. (pres., 1927-28), Archtl. League N.Y., Am. Numismatic Soc., Nat. Inst. Arts and Letters, Nat. Arts Club. Address: 207 E. 17th St., N.Y.C.; also Star Ridge, Brewster, N.Y. Died Aug. 6, 1956; buried Cold Spring (N.Y.) Cemetery.

BEACH, Joseph Warren, coll. prof.; b. Gloversville, N.Y., Jan. 14, 1880; s. Eugene (M.D.) and Sarah Jessup (Warren) B.; A.B., U. of Minn., 1900; M.A., Harvard, 1902, Ph.D., 1907; m. Elisabeth Northrop, Dec. 7, 1907; children—Northrop, Warren; m. 2d, Dagmar Doneghy, Apr. 22, 1918. Asst. prof. English, 1907-17, asso. prof., 1917-24, prof., 1924-48, University of Minnesota; visiting prof. University of Chicago, summer 1938, Harvard University Summer Sch., 1941; 1948; Salsburg Seminar, 1950; Walker-Ames lecture, U. Wash., 1946; visiting prof. Harvard U., 1949-50, U. Ill., 1950-51, univs. Paris and Strasbourg (Fulbright prof.) 1951-52, Johns Hopkins U., 1952-53; Fulbright lectr. University of Vienna 1954-55. Member Modern Lang. Assn. of America, Beta Theta Pi, Phi Beta Kappa. Author: Sonnets of the Head and Heart, 1903; The Comic Spirit in George Meredith, 1911; (with Arundell Esdaile) Alterations in the Text of George Meredith's Poems, in New York edit., Vol. XXVII, Constable edit., Vol. XXXVI, both 1911; The Method of Henry James, 1918; chapter on Henry James in Cambridge History of American Literature, Vol. III, 1921; The Technique of Thomas Hardy, 1922; Meek Americans, 1925; The Outlook for American Prose, 1926; Glass Mountain (novel), 1930; The Twentieth-Century Novel, 1932; The Concept of Nature in Nineteenth-Century English Poetry, 1936; American Fiction, 1920-1940, 1941. Beginning with Plato Poems, 1944; A Romantic View of Poetry, 1944; Involuntary Witness (poems), 1950; A History of English Literature (with others), 1950; The Making of the Auden Canon, 1957; Obsessive Images, 1958, Ann. Joseph Warren Beach lectureship in his name, U. Minn. Home: 1801 University Av. S.E., Mpls. Died Aug. 13, 1957; buried Lakewood Cemetery, Mpls.

BEACH, King D., clergyman; b. Cass City, Mich.; s. Rev. John R. and Eliza A. (Dopking) B.; A.B., Albion (Mich.) Coll., 1905; D.D., 1921; M.A., U. Pa., 1907; studied Columbia and Union Theol. Sem., 1907-10; m. Myrtle S. Garrett, Mar. 4, 1911; children—Virginia Jane (Mrs. Floyd R. Peterson), John Garrett, Ralph Garrett, King D., Charles Remington. Ordained to Meth. ministry, 1907; mgr. boys' dept. U. Settlement, Phila., 1906-07; served at following pastorates—Trinity Ch., Detroit, Preston Ch., Detroit, First Ch., Grand Rapids, Mich., St. James Ch., Chgo., First Ch., Balt., Trinity Ch., Kansas City, Mo.; pastor 1st Meth. Ch., Jackson, Mich., 1943-50, South Jackson Community Ch., 1950-55, ret. Mem. Ministerial Assn. Rotarian. Author Satellites of Calvary; contbr. of magazine articles. Home: 1109 First St., Jackson, Mich. Died July 3, 1957.

BEACH, R. Clyde, mcht.; b. Ackley, Ia., June 3, 1867; s. Mark M. and Lizzie D. (Devendorf) B.; student pub. schs.; m. Eva E. Bringham, June 28, 1894. Entered mercantile business, Lewiston, Ia., 1894, later investing largely in real estate; purchased, 1907, Idaho Dept. Store, Twin Falls, Ida., later pres.; pres. R. C. Beach Co., dept. store, Lewiston, Dir. Nat. Rivers and Harbors Congress, Pacific N.W. Live Stock Assn. Republican. Clubs: Spokane (Spokane); Commercial (Lewiston and Twin Falls). Address: Lewiston, Idaho. Deceased.

BEACH, S(ylvester) Judd, ophthalmologist; b. Dedham, Mass., Apr. 7, 1879; s. Seth Curtis and Frances Hall (Judd) B.; grad. Phillips Exeter Acad., 1897; A.B., Harvard Coll., 1901, M.D., Harvard U., 1905; m. Louise Harris, Oct. 7, 1909; children—Margaret Judd, Howell Williams (dec.), Edmund Beach. Surgical house officer, Boston City Hosp., 1904-06; house physician, Boston Lying-In Hosp., 1906, (acting) Mass. Eye and Ear Infirmary, 1907; practiced in Augusta, Me., special practice, 1909; mem. staff Augusta Gen. Hosp., Gardner Gen. Hosp.; special practice, Portland, since 1920; consulting ophthalmic surgeon Me. Eye and Ear Infirmary (pres. staff 1946-48); mem. staff local hosps.; guest lecturer graduate courses George Washington, Florida, Virginia and Rochester univs.; mem. council State Dept. of Health, 1916-24. Oculist Medical Advisory Board, World War, 1916-18. Ex-pres. Wayneflete Sch.; sec. Am. Bd. Ophthalmology. vice president Foundation for Vision; member of executive committee, Ophthalmological Study Council. Fellow Am. Coll. Surgeons, Am. Med. Assn. (past chmn. Ophthalmology sect.); mem. Am. Ophthalmol. Soc. (member council, pres. 1944), Am. Acad. Ophthalmology and Otolaryngology (mem. council 1930-35), Soc. for Research in Ophthalmology (mem. commn.), Sigma Alpha Epsilon. Unitarian. Mason. Clubs: Cumberland, Aesculapian (Boston); Portland Rotary (pres. 1932), Fraternity (Portland; Torch of Western Maine (past pres.). Mem. editorial bd., Quarterly Review of Ophthalmology. Lecturer on Refraction. Author: Textbook of Refraction; The Eye and its Diseases (co-author). Home: Cragmoor, Cape Elizabeth, South Portland 7. Office: 704 Congress St., Portland, Me. Died Feb. 10, 1953; buried Augusta, Me.

BEACHAM, Joseph (William), Jr., ret. army officer; b. Bklyn., Apr. 8, 1874; s. Joseph William and Mary (Dovey) B.; LL.B., Cornell U., 1897; distinguished grad. Army School of Line, 1915; grad. Army Staff Coll., 1916, Army War Coll., 1921; m. Bernadett Herman, June, 1925 (died Apr. 14, 1948). Served with U.S. Army, Spanish-American War, 1898, Philippine Insurrection, 1901, World War I, 1918; commd. 2d lt. U.S. Army, 1899, advanced through grades to brig. gen., 1940; instr. Army War Coll., 1921-25; prof. mil. sci. and tactics Cornell U., 1927-32, U. Pa., 1934-38; retired, 1938. Coach, Army football team, 1908-11; mem. Football Rules Com., 1909-14; chmn. Cornell Football Com., 1927-32. Mem. Psi Upsilon. Decorated D.S.M., Silver Star (U.S.); Croix de Guerre and Etoile Noir (France); Order of Redeemer (Greece); Order of Danilo (Montenegro). Presbyn. Clubs: Army and Navy, Chevy Chase (Washington); N.Y. Athletic, Lambs (N.Y.C.). Address: Army and Navy Club, Washington. Died July 1958.

BEACHLEY, Charles E(dward), coal co. exec.; b. Md., 1892; s. William W. and Annie M. Cronise (B.); student Pace Inst., LaSalle Extension U.: m. Ruth E. Baitzell, 1912; children—Vernon B., Ruth I., Charles E., Robert L. With Pa. R.R., 1911-16; with Pittsburgh Consolidation Coal Co., 1916—, asst. sec., 1926, sec., asst. treas. 1927, sec., treas., 1936—. Mason. Republican. Methodist. Club: Downtown. Home: 110 Ordale Blvd., Mt. Lebanon, Pitts. 28. Office: Koppers Bldg., Pitts. 19. Died Aug. 28, 1955.

BEACOM, Thomas H., ry. ofcl.; b. Jones County, Ia.; s. John and Mary (Ryan) B.; student pub. schs. Entered ry. service as timekeeper constrn. gang C.,M.&St.P. Ry., 1884, successively check clk., ticket clk., brakeman, condr., gen. yardmaster, 1884-1902; trainmaster Ia. and Ill. divs. C.,R.I.&P. Ry., 1902-04, successively supt. Okla., St. Louis, Kan., Panhandle, Okla., Mo. divs., 1904-09, gen. supt. 3d dist., 1909-12, asst. gen. mgr. El Reno, Okla., 1912-13, asst. gen. mgr. 1st dist., Des Moines, Ia., 1913-14, gen. mgr. 3d and 2d dists., El Reno, 1914-18, gen. mgr. entire system during fed. control, 1918-20, v.p., gen. mgr., 1920-23; also pres. C.R.I.

&G. Ry. Co., 1914-18; apptd. receiver D.&R.G. Ry. Co., 1923; pres. Joliet Union Sta., 1918-23; pres. 399 Fullerton Pkwy. Bldg. Corp.; v.p. Salt Lake City Union Depot & R.R. Co.; dir. Denver Union Terminal & Ry. Co., Pueblo Union Depot & R.R. Co., St. Louis Terminal Assn. Chmn. transportation com. Nat. Def. Bd., Okla., during World War. Mem. Ry. Guild. Clubs: Midland (Argo); Crystal Lake Country. Office: 220 S. State St., Chgo. Deceased.

BEADLE, Chauncey Delos (bē'dl), botanist; b. St. Catharines, Ont., Can., Aug. 5, 1866; s. Delos White and Harriet Converse (Steele) B.; student Ont. Agrl. Coll., 1884, Cornell U., 1885-86, 1889; m. Margaretta A. Wetzel, Nov. 11, 1891 (died May 11, 1924); m. 2d, Annie Louise (Paget) Rudolph, Mar. 3, 1928 (died June 1, 1941). Dir. Biltmore Herbarium, 1890-1916; supt. landscape dept. Biltmore Estate; sec.-treas. The Biltmore Co.; horticulturist, landscape architect. Democrat. Episcopalian. Contbr. numerous articles pertaining to botany of Southern States. Home: Biltmore, N.C. Died July 4, 1950.

BEAL, Gifford Reynolds, artist; b. N.Y.C., Jan. 24, 1879; s. William Reynolds and Eleanor Louise (Bell) B.; A B., Princeton, 1900; studied art under William M. Chase, and at Art Students' League, New York; m. Maud Ramsdell, May 28, 1908. Prin. works: The Puff of Smoke, Art Inst. Chicago; Mayfair, Albany Boat and Water color Across the Valley, Met. Mus., New York; Freight Yards, Hudson River, Syracuse Mus.; etc. Awarded 3d prize, Worcester Mus., 1903; bronze medal, St. Louis Expn., 1904, Shaw Purchase Prize, Salmagundi Club, 1908; 1st Hallgarten Prize, Nat. Acad. Design, 1910; hon. mention, Art Inst. Chicago, 1912; silver medal, Nat. Arts Club, 1913; Thomas B. Clarke Prize, N.A.D., 1913; 3d medal, Carnegie Inst., 1913; 3d medal, Corcoran Art Gallery, Washington, D.C., 1914; gold medal, Panama-Pacific Internat. Expn., 1915; Mrs. Stuart Duncan water color prize, Newport Art Assn., 1917; Phila. water color prize, Pa. Acad., 1917; gold medal and $1,000 prize, Nat. Arts Club, 1918; gold medal and $300 prize from same, 1925; honorable mention Phila. Arts Club, 1919; $1,500 2d Clark prize; $500 2d Altman prize, Nat. Acad. Design, 1919; Corcoran Silver medal, 1930; $400 Blair prize, Chicago Internat. Water Color Exhbn., 1930; $1,000 1st Altman prize, Nat. Acad. Design, 1930; $300 1st prize, Springfield Art Assn., 1930; $300 Carnegie prize, Nat. Acad. Design, 1932, $1,000 Purchase prize, Century Assn., 1937; silver medal, Paris Expn., 1937; Samuel Saltus medal, 1949, Samuel Morse gold medal, 1953, Nat. Acad. Design; The Art Com. medal, Century Club, 1950; The Edward Palmer Meml. prize Nat. Acad. Design, 1955. Rep. in Arizona State Coll. (Tempe), Washington State College Lehigh University, Met. Mus., New York, Detroit Mus. of Art, Phillips Memorial Gallery (Washington, D.C.), Telfair Mus. (Atlanta, Ga.), Oakland (Calif.) Mus., Harrison Gallery (Los Angeles Mus.), Martin Ryerson Collection (Chicago, Ill.), Yale U., Princeton U., Modern Mus. of Art (New York), Syracuse Mus., Cleveland Mus., Montclair (N.J.) Mus., New York Pub. Library, Newark Mus.; panels Allentown (Pa.) Post Office; panels Interior Dept., Washington, D.C.; mural Princeton U. Nat. Academician, 1914; member American Institute Arts and Letters, Am. Water Color Soc., Archtl. League America, Nat. Soc. Mural Painters. Episcopalian. Clubs: Century, Fencers', Coffee House, Nat. Arts, Lotos. Home: 27 W. 67th St., N.Y.C. Died Feb. 5, 1956.

BEAL, Henry C., mfg. exec.; b. Logansport, Ind., June 7, 1891; s. John H. and Mary Elizabeth (Herr) B.; E.E., Purdue U., 1914, Dr. Engring., 1952; m. Nola B. Hollenback, Sept. 28, 1915; 1 son, Dick Hollenback. Student training course, Hawthorne (Chgo.) Works, Western Electric Co., 1914, supr. methods, drafting and planning, 1915, asst. supt. mfg. planning, 1926, supt. indsl. relations, 1928, supt. operating branch, 1929, asst. works mgr., Kearny, N.Y. Works, 1935, works mgr., 1939, engr. mfr., 1942, dir. and vice pres. mfr., Western Electric Co., 1947; dir. Nassau Smelting and Refining Co., Bell Telephone Labs., Inc. Teletype Corp., Northern Electric Co., Ltd. (Can.), Sandia Corp., Mfrs. Junction Ry. Teletypesetter Corp. Mem. Western Soc. Engrs., Scabbard and Blade, Eta Kappa Nu. Home: 278 Underhill Road, South Orange, N.J. Died Dec. 31, 1959; buried Royal Center, Ind.

BEAL, John M(ann), educator; b. Red Oak, N.C., Apr. 18, 1888; s. John C. and Mary (Edwards) B.; B.S., N.C. State Coll., 1911; M.S., Miss. State Coll., 1913; Ph.D., U. Wis., 1927; m. Anna McBee, June 3, 1914; 1 son, Dr. John Mann. Instr. Miss. State Coll., State Coll., Miss., 1911-13, asst. prof., 1913-15, prof., head dept. botany, 1915-29; Gen. Edn. Bd. fellow John Innes Hort. Inst., London, Eng. and U. Louvain, 1934; vis. prof. botany La. State U., Baton Rouge, summer 1940; asso. prof. U. Chicago, 1929-31, prof., 1931-53, chmn. dept. botany, 1949-53, ret. Former cons. U.S. Dept. Agr. Mem. A.A.A.S., Bot. Soc. Am., Am. Soc. Naturalists, Soc. for Study Evolution, Ill. Acad., Lily Soc., Sigma Xi, Alpha Zeta, Kappa Alpha. Club: Quadrangle. Dept. editor Ency. Brit., 1945-53. Home: Chgo. Died Jan. 16, 1957.

BEAL, Reynolds, artist; b. N.Y., 1867; s. William Reynolds and Eleanor Louise (Bell) B.; mech. engring. course at Cornell; studied under William M. Chase, N.Y., in galleries of Europe, especially at Madrid; m. Helen Higgins, Feb. 16, 1924. Exhibited at Paris Salon and in prin. exhibits in U.S. A.N.A., 1909; mem. Am. Water Color Soc., N.Y. Water Color Club, Phi Kappa Psi. Clubs: Lotos (life), Salmagundi, N.Y.C. Yacht, Nat. Arts (life), Century. Home: 29 Atlantic Av., Rockport, Mass. Died Dec. 18, 1951; buried Rockport, Mass.

BEALE, George William, clergyman; b. Westmoreland County, Va., Aug. 21, 1842; s. Gen. Richard Lee T. and Lucy Maria (Brown) B.; ed. pvt. schs., Fleetwood and Piedmont Acads. and Culpeper Military Inst., So. Bapt. Theol. Sem.; D.D., Wash. and Lee U., 1894; m. Mary A. Bouic, Dec. 3, 1879. Entered C.S.A. Apr. 30, 1861, as pvt. in Co. C, 9th Va. Cav.; advanced to 1st lt.; comd. co. 2 campaigns; was wounded twice, in battles of Reams Station and Hatcher's Run. Ordained Bapt. ministry, Oct. 18, 1868; pastor Machodoc and Pope's Creek, 1868-73, Georgetown, 1874-9, Halifax, Va., 1879-83, Buchanan and Hollins Inst., 1883-94, Heathsville, 1894-05, Richmond and Westmoreland counties, 1905-15. Pres. Gen. Bapt. Assn. Va., 1901, 1902; trustee Richmond Coll., v.p. Va. Bapt. Orphanage, Salem, Va. Democrat. Mem. Soc. of Cincinnati, Va. Bapt. Hist. Soc. (v.p.). Author: History 9th Virginia Cavalry, 1895; A Lieutenant of Cavalry in Lee's Army, 1918. Editor of Semple's History of Virginia Baptists. Home: Hague, Va. Died July 15, 1921.

BEALE, Stephen, seed co. exec.; b. Tunbridge Wells, Eng., Mar. 20, 1903; s. Louis and Mary (Marr) B.; student Manitoba Agrl. Coll., 1920-23; m. Georgia Hinckley, Nov. 27, 1935. With Ferry-Morse Seed Co., Detroit, 1926—, v.p., dir., pres., 1953—. Mem. Am. Seed Trade Assn. (past pres.). Club: Detroit. Home: 1036 Berkshire Rd., Grosse Pointe 30, Mich. Office: P.O. Box 778, Detroit 31. Died Sept. 1958.

BEALER, Alexander Winkler, clergyman; b. Darlington, S.C., Sept. 30, 1860; s. Rev. Geo. B. and Emily (Winkler) B.; grad. Boys' High Sch., Atlanta, 1879; m. Fannie Rudisill, Mar. 15, 1892. Court and polit. reporter Atlanta Journal, 1886-96; oradined Bapt. ministry, 1896; pastor 5th Ch., Atlanta, 1896-99, 1st Ch., Cartersville, Ga., 1899-02, Thomasville, Ga., 1903-09, Murfreesboro, Tenn., 1909-12, Eastman, Ga., 1912-15, Bapt. Tabernacle, Valdosta, Ga., 1915—. Democrat. Home: Valdosta, Ga. Died June 30, 1921.

BEALS, Ralph Albert, librarian; b. Deming, N.M., Mar. 29, 1899; s. Nathan Albert and Alice May (Seeley) B.; A.B., U. of Calif., 1921; M.A., Harvard U., 1925; student U. of Chicago, 1939-40; m. Alice B. Stone, June 12, 1928; 1 dau., Mary Druitt. Sec. to pres., U. of Calif., 1921-23; asst. in English, Harvard U., 1926-28; instr. English, New York U., 1928-33; asst. to dir. Am. Assn. Adult Edn., 1933-39; asst. librarian Pub. Library, Washington, D.C., 1940-42; professor library science and director libraries, Univ. of Chicago, 1942-46. Dean Grad. Library School, 1944-46; dir. New York Public Library, 1946—. Member United States National Commission for UNESCO, 1946-49; Governor's Com. on Library Aid, 1949-50. Served as pvt. in U.S. Army, 1918. Member American Library Assn., Am. Assn. Adult Edn., Bibliog. Soc. America, Inst. graphic Arts, N. Y. Hist. Society, New York Adult Education Council, Phi Beta Kappa. Clubs: Coffee House, Grolier, Century Association, University, Down Town Association. Author of: Aspects of Post-Collegiate Education, 1935; The Literature of Adult Education (with Leon Brody), 1941. Editor: Readings in Description and Narration (with M. E. Barnicle and J. S. Terry), 1930. Editor Jour. of Adult Edn. (with Morse A. Cartwright), 1937-38. Home: 1158 5th Av., N.Y. 29. Office: New York Public Library, N.Y.C. Died Oct. 14, 1954.

BEAM, Walter Irvin, cons. engr.; b. Johnstown, Pa., Aug. 5, 1885; s. Henry F. (M.D.) and Margaret (Irvin) B.; grad. Girard Coll., 1905; D.Eng., Case Inst. Tech.; m. Lela Driver, 1910; children—Mary Margaret (Mrs. John Humphrey Stokoe), John Irvin (USNR). Engring. and construction, Panama Canal, 1905-13; auditor Mack Mfg. Co., Wheeling, W.Va., 1913-17; comptroller U.S. Grain Corp., also dir. finances of Commn. for Relief in Belgium, and European Relief Adminstrn., 1917-21; financial officer and dir. various corps., 1921-27; financial cons., 1927-30; v.p., treas. Farmers Nat. Grain Corp., v.p., treas., dir. and mem. exec. com. The Grain Stabilization Corp., treas. Hall Baker Grain Co., Kansas City, Mo., 1930; later gen. mgr. Case-Moody Corp.; exec. v.p. Cleve. C. of C., 1937-50; cons. engr., 1950—; sec., treas. Inter-American Center Authority, 1951—. Trustee Cleve. Engring. Soc., 1938-41; mem. Soc. Mil. Engrs. Trustee Nat. Air Races, Air Found. Mem. S.A.R., S.R., Soc. Panama Canal (awarded Panama Canal medal). Republican. Presbyn. Mason (32°, Shriner). Author: Masons and Masonry on the Panama Canal, 1913. Home: 650 N.E. 31st St. Office: 14 N.E. First Av., Miami, Fla. Died Sept. 15, 1957; buried Miami, Fla.

BEAMAN, Robert Prentis, banker; b. Norfolk, Va., Dec. 13, 1891; s. Nathaniel and Katherine Lewis (Prentis) B.; grad. Norfolk Acad., 1908; A.B., Washington and Lee U., 1911; m. Salome Lydia Slingluff, Feb. 24, 1923; children—Robert Prentis, Nathaniel III. Began as clk. with Nat. Bank of Commerce, 1911, asst. cashier, 1914-17, cashier, 1919-21, v.p., 1921-26, resigned, 1926; pres. Nat. Bank of Commerce, 1931-42; pres. Commerce Corp., dir. Chesapeake Ferry Corp.; mem. banking and industrial com., 5th Federal Res. Dist. Served in World War as lt. and later capt., U.S. Army, in St. Mihiel and Meusse-Argonne offensives. Mem. Commn. revision of Charter, City of Norfolk, 1933; pres. Norfolk Community Fund, 1940-41; pres. Norfolk-Portsmouth Clearing House Assn.; mem. exec. com. Industrial Commn., Tax Equalization Assn., Hampton Roads Defense Council; mem. Committee of National Credit Association No. 1, Fifth Federal Reserve Dist.; mem. Va. Com. of Deposit Liquidation Com. of Reconstruction Finance Corp.; mem. Tax Com. of Va. State Chamber of Commerce; mem. bd. of dirs. Norfolk Assn. of Commerce; mem. board of management, Navy Y.M.C.A. Selected First Citizen of Norfolk, 1940. Mem. Virginia Bankers Assn. (legislative committee), New York Southern Soc., Va. Hist. Soc., Soc. of Colonial Wars in State of Va., Am. Legion (comdr. Norfolk post, 1926-27), Sigma Alpha Epsilon. Democrat. Episcopalian. Clubs: Norfolk Yacht (Norfolk, Va.); Bankers, Lotos (New York); Surf Club, Princess Anne Country (Virginia Beach, Va.). Home: 5220 Edgewater Dr., Norfolk, Va. Died May 30, 1953; buried Arlington Natl. Cemetery.

BEAMSLEY, Foster Gilman, business exec.; b. Delavan, Wis., Jan. 2, 1890; s. Albert J. and Nora (Foster) B.; student U. Wis., 1912-14; m. Inez Lawrence, June 9, 1915; children—Foster Gilman, Martha Jane (Mrs. George R. Catlett), Jo-Ann (Mrs. John B. Clayton). Dep. nat. bank examiner 9th Fed. Res. Dist., 1914-17; exec. v.p., dir. Duluth Nat. Bank, 1917-30; dir. No. Nat. Bank and No. Trust Co., 1925-30; mem. organizing group, treas., dir. Greyhound Corp., 1926-29; organizer, pres., dir. Transportation Credit Corp., 1930-35; mem. organizing group, financial vice pres. and chmn. exec. com. Nat. City Lines, Inc., Chgo., and subsidiaries, 1936—; dir. Key System Transit Lines, Oakland, California, St. Louis Pub. Co., Ry. Equipment Co., Ltd., subsidiaries. Clubs: Westmoreland Country (Wilmette, Ill.); Mo. Athletic (St. L.) Chgo. Athletic Assn. (Chgo.). Home: 197 Oxford Rd., Kenilworth, Ill. Office: Prudential Bldg., Chgo. 5. Died March 11, 1960. Buried Meml. Park Cemetery.

BEAN, Francis Atherton, flour mill exec.; b. Faribault, Minn., Oct. 1, 1878; s. Francis Atherton and Ellen Jane (Tennant) B.; student State Teachers Coll., Winona, Minn., 1894-97; LL.B., U. of Minn. 1900; m. Bertha Juanita Boynton, Aug. 24, 1907 (dec.); children—(son, died in infancy), Francis Atherton III, Bertha Juanita (Mrs. Harold Von N. Flinsch), John Boynton. With Internat. Milling Co., Minneapolis, Minn., since 1900, chmn. bd. since Jan. 1945. Mem. nat. exec. com. Boy Scouts (awarded silver buffalo). Mem. Am. Bar Assn. Clubs: Encampment Forest Assn., Minneapolis, Minikahda (Minneapolis). Home: 4345 E. Lake Harriet Blvd., Minneapolis 9. Office: McKnight Bldg., Mpls. Died Aug. 1, 1955; buried Mpls.

BEAN, George W., b. Willimantic, Conn., May 29, 1875; s. George E. and Abbie Jane (Foss) B.; student pub. schs. and business coll.; m. 2d, Helen MacGeorge, Sept. 20, 1923. Chief petty officer Signal Corps, USN, Spanish-Am. War; inspecting engr. Isle of Cuba, USPHS, 1900-02; U.S. marine engr., chief engineer's license. Mayor of Port Tampa City, Fla., 1902-06; postmaster Tampa, 1906-15; mem. Tampa City Council, 1916-18; Rep. candidate for Congress, 1912; mem. Rep. Nat. Com. from Fla., 1916-28. Mem. of com. apptd. by President Taft, 1909, to investigate postoffice employment and recommend unified system of work and to investigate and recommend labor saving devices. Washington megr. Am. Gas Assn. for 15 years; now represents utility interests. Clubs: Nat. Press, Nat. Republican. Home: 3406 Q St. N.W. Office: Albee Bldg., Washington. Died Nov. 20, 1950.

BEAR, Harry, dentist; b. Richmond, Va., Nov. 20, 1890; s. Philip and Mary (Meyer) B.; student U. Richmond, Va., 1909-10; D.D.S., Med. Coll. Va. Sch. Dentistry, Richmond, 1913; D.Sc., Temple U., 1945; m. Betty Gellman, June 19, 1917 (dec.); m. 2d, Mrs. Elsa Bluethenthal Strause, Apr. 5, 1941; children—David Morton, Samuel Elmer; instr. metallurgy Med. Coll. Va., 1913-15, asso. in chemistry, 1915-16, prof. exodontia and dental jurisprudence, ethics and economics, 1916-50, dean Sch. of Dentistry, 1929-50. Fellow Am. Coll. Dentists; non-resident fellow N.Y. Acad. Dentistry; mem. Am. (v.p. 1929, trustee 1932-35), Va. (asst. sec. 1916-19, sec. 1919-22, sec.-treas. and editor 1922-24, pres. 1926), dental assns., A.M.A., Am. Soc. Oral Surgeons and Exodontists (treas. 1927, sec. 1928, v.p.,

1929, pres. 1931, sec. 1932-33, sec.-treas. 1933-50), Am. Assn. Dental Schs. (pres. 1940), Richmond (pres. 1917, 1918), N.C. (hon.) dental socs., Internat. Assn. Dental Research, Va. Acad. Science, A.A.A.S., Psi Omega, Omicron Kappa Upsilon. Democrat. Mason (32°). Contbr. dental jours. Home: 906 Westover Rd., Richmond 20. Office: Medical College of Virginia, School of Dentistry, Richmond 19, Va. Died July 30, 1950; buried Richmond.

BEAR, Joseph Ainslie, banker; b. Louisville, May 27, 1878; s. Samuel L. and Hannah (Rosenfield) B.; student pub. schs. N.Y.C., France, Germany, Switzerland; m. Julia Pam, 1947 (dec.); 1 dau., Helen; m. 2d Juliet Beecher, Nov. 3, 1947. Partner J.J. Danzig & Co., 1908-23, Bear, Stearns & Co. since 1923 (both N.Y.C.). Clubs: Harmonie, Bankers. Home: 923 Fifth Av., N.Y.C. 21. Office: 1 Wall St., N.Y.C. 5; also 135 S. LaSalle St., Chgo. 3. Died July 13, 1955.

BEARD, James Randolph, physician; b. Summerville, S.C., Dec. 5, 1903; s. James R. and Hildegarde (Henry) B.; B.S. with honors, Wesleyan U., Middletown, Conn., 1925; M.D., Cornell, 1929; m. Anne Kelsom, June 30, 1931; m. 2d Jean Johnson, March 3, 1945; children—Ina Saxon (adopted), James Randolph. Intern, resident N.Y. Hosp, 1929-31, asst. chief med. clinic, 1935-42; asso. attending physician Bellevue Hosp., 1932-42; internist (cons.) Booth Meml. Hosp., 1939-42; instr. medicine Cornell Med. Coll., 1933-42; lab. cons. Fed. Res. Bank, N.Y. City, since 1939; mem. med. staff Mut. Benefit Life Ins. Co., Newark, since 1946, med. dir. since 1948; member executive council Asso. Life Inc., med. dir., 1954—; mem. Bd. Life Ins. Medicine, 1956—. Trustee Florence Crittenden League; Youth Consultation Service, Newark. Mem. twp. com. Passaic Twp., N.J., 1950-56; police fire commissioner, 1950—, mayor, 1954-56. Comdr. Med. Corps, U.S. N.R. since 1942; active service ETO. Mem. Assn. Life Ins. Med. Dirs. Am. (chmn. com. lab. procedures since 1949), Am. Life Conv. (med. sect.), N.Y. Acad. Medicine, Sigma Nu, Alpha Kappa Kappa, Pi Delta Epsilon. Club: Downtown (Newark). Home: Taff Dr., Millington, N.J. Office: 520 Broad St., Newark 2. Died Apr. 14, 1959, buried Pineview Meml. Gardens, North Augusta, S.C.

BEARD, Joseph Howard, educator, health officer; b. Linden Hill, Md., Jan. 12, 1883; s. Stephen and Mary Amo (Gott) B.; B.A., St. John's Coll., Annapolis, Md., 1902, M.A., 1912; M.D., Johns Hopkins, 1912; m. Mary G. Lee, Feb. 8, 1907; children—Ellen Howard (Mrs. Donald Kibler Harmeson), Charlotte Waters, Joseph Howard, Mary Amo. Engaged in practice of medicine, 1912—; instr. histology and physiology, prof. hygiene and health officer U. Ill. Mem. A.M.A., Am. Pub. Health Assn., Delta Chi. Contbr. numerous articles on health edn. to mags. Home: 1005 S. Race St. Office: Health Service Station, U. Ill., Urbana, Ill. Died Apr. 5, 1950; buried Mt. Hope Cemetery, Urbana.

BEARD, Mary Ritter (Mrs. Charles A. Beard), author; b. Indianapolis, Ind., Aug. 5, 1876; d. Eli Foster and Narcissa (Lockwood) Ritter; Ph.B., DePauw U., 1897; postgraduate work, Columbia; m. Charles A. Beard, Mar. 8, 1900; children—Miriam, William. Travel and study in Europe and Orient. Mem. Kappa Alpha Theta, Phi Beta Kappa. Author: Woman's Work in Municipalities, 1915; A Short History of the American Labor Movement, 1920, revised 1925; On Understanding Women, 1931; Woman as Force in History, 1946, also published in a German translation, 1951. Editor: America Through Women's Eyes, 1933. Co-editor: Laughing Their Way. Author (with husband): American Citizenship, 1914; History of the United States, 1921, revised, 1928; The Rise of American Civilization, 1927; The Making of American Civilization, 1937; America in Midpassage, 1939; The American Spirit: A Study of the Idea of Civilization in the United States, 1942; A Basic History of the United States, 1944. Home: New Milford, Conn. Died Aug. 14, 1958; buried Ferncliff Cemetery, Hartsdale, N.Y.

BEARDSLEY, Frank Grenville, clergyman; b. Ovid, Mich., Nov. 9, 1870; s. Grenville Sterling and Mary Elizabeth (Clark) B.; A.B., Western (now Coe) Coll., Cedar Rapids, Ia., 1894; A.M., Ill. Wesleyan U., 1896, Ph.D., 1897; student Chgo. Theol. Sem. and U. Chgo.; B.D., Oberlin Theol. Sem., 1900; S.T.D., Kansas City U., 1912; m. Mary E. Riddell, Dec. 22, 1896; children—Frank Grenville, Mary Elizabeth, Martha Lydia, Margaret Theodosia, Theodore Sterling, Edith Allene, Whitmore Everett. Ordained Congl. ministry, 1897; pastor in Ia., at Salem, 1897-99, Rock Rapids, 1900-02, Greenwood Ch., Des Moines, 1902-04, Harlan, 1904-08; prof. theology, Talladega (Ala.) Theol. Sem., 1908-09; pastor 1st Ch., Kansas City, Kan., 1909-14, 1st Ch., Keokuk, Ia., 1914-17, 1st Ch., Aurora, Ill., 1917-22, Fountain Park Ch., St. Louis, 1922-31, 1st Ch., Minot, N.D., 1931-42; pastor, 1st Church, Zumbrota, Minn., 1942—. Trustee at large Ill. Congl. Conf., 1917-22; sec. exec. com. Mo. Congl. Conf., 1922-27. Del. Nat. Congl. Council several times. Chaplain Mo. Soc. S.A.R., 1925-28, sec. 1928-29, pres. 1929-30; pres. Camp Jackson Union Soldiers' Monument Assn., 1926-31; chaplain Mo. Dept. Sons of Union Vets. of Civil War, 1926-30, dept. comdr., 1930-31, nat. chaplain, 1933-34; chaplain N.D. Dept. United Spanish War Vets, 1936-47; adv. com. Salvation Army, 1935-43. Mem. Am. Soc. Ch. History, Am. Numismatic Assn., S.A.R., Sons of Vets., Internat. Brotherhood Magicians. Republican. Mason, Odd Fellow. Author: History of American Revivals, 1904 (awarded George Wood prize and gold medal by Am. Tract Soc.); Christian Achievement in America, 1907; The Builders of a Nation, 1921; The Miracles of Jesus, 1926; A Mighty Winner of Souls, 1937; The History of Christianity in America, 1938; Heralds of Salvation, 1939; The Christ of the Ages, or Christianity Attested by Its Historical Effects, 1941; Religious Progress Through Religious Revivals, 1943. Home: Commercial St., Wellfleet, Mass. Died July 31, 1954; buried Geneva, Ill.

BEARDSLEY, Harry M., newspaperman; b. Chanute, Kan., Dec. 27, 1893; s. Albert Lemon and Carrie Alice (Markle) B.; grad. Englewood High Sch., Chicago, 1913; student U. of Chicago; m. Josephine Brandenburg, Mar. 31, 1918; children—Barbara Marguerite (Mrs. R. Mate), Harrison Thompson, Cynthia Jane (Mrs. James Wagner). Reporter, rewrite man, Chicago Journal, 1915-18, rewrite man and Am. Legion editor, 1920; rewrite man Chicago Daily News, 1921-22, real estate editor, 1922-34, rewrite man and columnist, 1934-36, editorial writer since 1936. Radio announcer, sporting and news events, over WMAQ, 1924-32. Served as sergt. inf., United States Army, later in photographic section Signal Corps, Siberia, World War. Member Commissioners Committee on Water Supply, apptd. by commr. pub. works to survey city water dept. and recommend improvements, 1924-25; trustee Wheaton Public Library. Mem. A.L.A., Ill. Library Assn., Sigma Nu. Author: Joseph Smith and His Mormon Empire, 1931. Contbr. to various magazines. Co-author: Kanguk, a Boy of Bering Strait, 1939. Home: 1221 E. Illinois St., Wheaton, Ill. Office: Daily News Plaza, Chgo. Deceased.

BEARDSLEY, William S., governor of Iowa; b. Beacon, Ia., May 13, 1901; s. William and Carrie (Shane) B.; Ph.G., Bowen Inst. of Pharmacy; m. Charlotte E. Manning, Jan. 29, 1919; children—Blaine, Charlotte (Mrs. Doyle E. Stickel), Mary (Mrs. Henry F. Schieg), Dan. Retail drug and jewelry bus., New Virginia, Ia., 1922-38; operator 900-acre farm near New Virginia, Ia., 1938—. Mem. Ia. State Senate, 1932-40, Iowa House of Reps., 1947-48; gov. of Iowa since Jan. 1949. Republican. Methodist. Mason, Odd Fellow. Home: Route 1, New Virginia, Ia. Office: State House, Des Moines, Ia. Died Nov. 21, 1954; buried New Virginia, Ia.

BEASLEY, Rowland Fowler (bēz'lē), editor; b. Wilmington, N.C., Jan. 1871; s. Rev. John J. and Antoinette (Montford) B.; A.B., Wake Forest (N.C.) Coll., 1894; m. Ellie J. Stewart, 1895; children—Mrs. George S. Lee, Jr., Roland F.; m. 2d, Mrs. Clyde D. Powell, 1922. Was founder, 1894, and editor Monroe (N.C.) Jour.; later editor State Jour., Greensboro Telegram; supt. schs. Union County, N.C., 1903-07; founder 1918, and editor Bulletin N.C. State Bd. Charities and Pub. Welfare; commr. public welfare for State N.C., 1917-21; editor Monroe Journal, 1921—. Mem. N.C. Senate, 1903, Ho. of Rep., 1917, 33. Democrat. Baptist. Home: Monroe, N.C. Died June 13, 1953.

BEATTIE, R. Leslie, nickel exec.; b. Haldimand, Ont., Can., May 11, 1891; s. John Irvine and Elizabeth B.; m. A. Edna Allen, Sept. 12, 1922; children—Allan Leslie, Robert Gray, Donald Greer. Joined Canadian Copper Co. (now Internat. Nickel Co. of Can., Ltd.), Copper Cliff, Ont., 1911, works auditor Sudbury dist., gen. asst. to gen. mgr. Canadian operations, 1935-40, asst. v.p., 1940-42, v.p., gen. mgr., 1942—, mem. bd. dirs., 1943—; dir. Internat. Nickel Co., Inc., Toronto Gen. Trusts; dir. Bank of Toronto. Served with Royal Canadian Engrs., World War I. Decorated Mil. Medal (Can.). Mem. Canadian Inst. Mining and Metallurgy, Canadian Legion, BESL. Clubs: Toronto; Granite, Idylyde Golf and Country (Sudbury, Ont.); Port Colborne (Ont.) Golf and Country. Home: 41 Hillholme Rd., Toronto. Office: 25 King St. W., Toronto, Ont. Died June 10, 1953; buried Stayner, Ont., Can.

BEATY, John Yocum, editor, author; b. Finchford, Ia., Dec. 12, 1884; s. David George and Mary (Yocum) B.; student Ia. State Coll., Ames, 1905-08; m. Anna Elizabeth Walkup, Sept. 8, 1910; 1 dau., Roberta Gertrude (Mrs. Justin Leroy Turner). Asso. editor Am. Agriculturist, Springfield, Mass., 1908-11; asst. prof. agrl. journalism, U. Wis., 1911-12; editor Luther Burbank's autobiography, Santa Rosa, Cal., 1912-14; editor Nat. Alfalfa Jour., Sioux Falls, S.D., 1915-17; editor System on the Farm, 1917-20; account exec. Merrill Advt. Agy., Chgo., 1920-22; editor Am. Inst. of Agr., Chgo., 1922-24; book editor Popular Mechanics Press, Chgo., 1924-26; editor Bankers Monthly, Chgo., 1926-50; lectr. trade paper writing Northwestern U., 1950—; spl. lecturer Geneva Lake Sch. of Natural History, Lake Geneva. Mem. Chgo. Acad. Sciences (life), Am. Mus. Natural Hist., Medill Sch. Journalism of Northwestern U. (adv. com.), Nat. Geographic Soc., Am. Nature Assn., School Nature League; co-sponsor and mem. of the Offield-Beaty Ariz. Expdn. of the Chgo. Acad. of Sciences, 1940. Republican. Methodist. Author: Billy Berk, 1930; Spotty, Old Abe, Sunshine Rose, 1931; The Farm in Pictures, Just Dogs, Jolly Life Out of Doos, 1933; Wild Animal Stories and Pictures, Story Pictures of Farm Animals, 1934; How to Understand Banks, 1935; Story Pictures of Farm Work, 1936; Trees, Story Pictures of Our Neighbors, 1937; Story Pictures of Transportation and Communication, Sharp Ears, the Story of a Baby Whale, 1938; Nature Is Stranger than Fiction, 1941; The River Book, 1942; Luther Burbank, Plant Magician, 1943; The Mountain Book, 1944; The Ocean Book, 1946. Contbr. to mags. Home: 476 E. Minnehaha Av., Clermont, Fla.; buried Mt. Emblem Cemetery, Elmhurst, Ill.

BEATY, Richard A. D., clergyman; b. Springfield, Ill., Apr. 13, 1888; s. Doran H. and Rachel (Solomen) B.; grad. student Columbia; grad. Berkeley Divinity Sch., New Haven, 1925; m. Margaret Allin, Oct. 13, 1926. In business until 1920; ordained to ministry of P.E. Ch., 1925; curate St. Peter's Ch.-Chelsea, N.Y.C., 1925-27; rector Grace Ch., City Island, N.Y.C., 1927-33, St. Peter's Ch., Chelsea, 1933—. Sec. Diocesan Conv., Diocese of N.Y., 1934—; asst. sec. House of Bishops, 1940. Trustee of the Berkeley Divinity School, 1936-46. Home: 346 W. 20th St., N.Y.C. 11. Died Feb. 3, 1951.

BEAUDETTE, F(red) R(obert), (bō-dĕt'), veterinarian; b. Wichita, Kan., Apr. 15, 1897; s. Horace Fred and Cassie May (Leach) B.; D.V.M., Kan. State College, 1919, graduate work, 1921-23; D.Sc., Rutgers University, 1951; married Velva Rader, November 15, 1922; children—Robert Rader, John Horace, Thomas Rivers. Instructor bacteriology Kansas State College, 1919-21, asst. prof., 1921-23; asst. prof. poultry pathology Rutgers U., 1923-25, asso. prof. 1925-29, prof., 1929—, chairman dept. animal pathology, 1954—; spl. cons. microbe & immunology study sect., USPHS; corr. mem. academia de Ciencias Medicas, Fisicas y Naturales de la Habana, Sociedad Cubana de Historia Natural Felipe Poey. Received Borden award in poultry sci, 1944; citation, N.J. State Grange, 1948. Received Tom Newman Meml. Award, N.Y. Acad. Sci., 1949; Centennial Award, Mich. State U., 1955; citation, Rutgers Research Council Adv. Bd., 1955. Fellow N.Y. Acad. Sci., 1955; Poultry Sci. Assn.; mem. Am. Veterinary Med. Assn. (asso. editor jour.), Poultry Sci. Assn. (asso. editor Poultry Sci.), Am. Soc. Parasitologists, Am. Microscop. Soc., U.S. Livestock Sanitary Assn., Research Workers of Animal Diseases in N.A., Sigma Xi, Phi Kappa Phi, Gamma Sigma Delta, Alpha Zeta, Phi Delta Theta, Phi Zeta. Republican. Presbyn. Home: 194 College Av. Office: N.J. Agricultural Experiment Station, New Brunswick, N.J. Died: Jan. 17, 1957.

BEAUMONT, Campbell Eben, judge; b. Mayfield, Ky., Aug. 27, 1883; s. Edgar Samuel and May Viola (Wortham) B.; student West Ky. Coll., Mayfield, 1897-1900, University of Kentucky, 1900-02; Bowling Green Business Coll., 1905-06; LL.B., Cumberland U., 1910; m. Lucy Madden Hughes, Dec. 6, 1915; 1 son, Edward Campbell. Admitted to bar, 1912, and began practice at Fresno; deputy dist. atty., Fresno County, 1914-17, asst. dist. atty., 1917; dist. atty., 1918-21; judge Calif. Superior Ct., 1921-39; judge U.S. Dist. Court, Southern Dist. of Calif., since July 1939. Mem. Ky. Nat. Guard, 1904-06. Hon. mem. Calif. Judicial Conf. Pres. Calif. State Judges' Assn., 1932; mem. American Bar Assn., Am. Judicature Society, Sigma Alpha Epsilon, Phi Alpha Delta. Democrat. Presbyn. Mason, K.P. Home: 805 Ashlan Av. Office: Federal Bldg., Fresno, Cal. Died Nov. 19, 1954.

BEAUREGARD, Augustin Toutant (bō'rē-gärd), naval officer; b. San Antonio, Dec. 1, 1885; s. Richard Toutant and Aglae (Phillips) B.; student U.S. Naval Acad., 1903-06, Naval War Coll., Newport, R.I., 1936-37; m. Elizabeth Henry Munford, Nov. 18, 1915; 1 dau., Elizabeth Toutant (wife of Capt. Porter Fryman Bedell, USN). Commd. ensign, USN, 1908, advanced through grades to capt., 1932; commd. rear adm., 1941; naval aide to President-elect Brum of Uruguay on visit to U.S., 1918, Prestes of Brazil on visit to U.S., 1930, Herbert Hoover on South Am. tour, 1928-29; mem. naval mission to Brazil, 1922-27; naval attaché, Paris and Madrid, 1934-36; chief U.S. Naval Mission to Brazil, 1939-41; staff comdr.-in-chief U.S. Pacific Fleet, 1911-12, 16-17; staff comdr. 4th Div. Atlantic Fleet, 1914-15; staff comdr.-in-chief U.S. Fleet, 1932-33; commd. rear admiral, 1941, apptd. naval attache Am. Embassy, Rio de Janeiro, Brazil, 1941; retired because of physical disability, 1942; relieved of all active duty, 1943 while chief of naval mission to Brazil. Decorated Officer Legion of Honor (France); Commemorative Medal of Founding of Republic, Comdr. Order of Naval Merit, Grand Officer of Order of Southern Cross, Army Medal (Brazil); Order Abdon Calderon,

1st class (Ecuador); Victory medal with patrol clasp, World War I, Mexican Campaign Medal, 1914, U.S. Legion of Merit for service of distinguished character in Brazil, Defense ribbon, service in Am. theatre of operations, 1941-43. Club: Army and Navy (Washington). Died Apr. 8, 1951; buried Arlington Nat. Cemetery.

BEAUREGARD, Elie, speaker of Canadian Senate. Address: Parliamentary Bldg., Ottawa, Ont., Can. Deceased.*

BEAVEN, J. C., (bĕv'en), business exec.; b. Burton, Wash., Dec. 13, 1895; s. Samuel William and Lizzie (Baker) B.; grad. Tacoma (Wash.) High Sch., 1913; student McMinnville (Ore.) Coll., 1914-16; m. Helen Wetmore, June 17, 1919; children—Barbara Ann, Virginia Wetmore, Bruce Wetmore. Office clk., Shinola Co., Rochester, N.Y., 1919-21; with F. F. Dalley Corp., Rochester, N.Y., 1921-25; with 2-in-1 Shinola-Bixby Corp., Indianapolis, Ind., 1926-30; with Gold Dust Corp., New York, N.Y., 1930-32; with Hecker-Jones-Jewell Milling Co., New York, N.Y., 1932-38; pres. and dir. Standard Milling Co., Chicago, Ill., since 1938. Enlisted U.S. Signal Corps, Apr. 1916; commd. 2d lt., U.S. Air Force, 1917; served with photographic div. Mem. Millers' Nat. Fedn. (dir.; mem. exec. com.). Trustee U. of Chicago, Bapt. Theol. Union. Pres. bd. trustees Kenilworth Union Ch., mem. bd. govs. Clubs: Indian Hill Golf (Winnetka); Attic (Chicago). Home: 234 Warwick Rd., Kenilworth, Ill. Office: 309 W. Jackson Blvd., Chgo. 6. Died Dec. 8, 1951.

BECH, Georg (bĕk), ret. consul gen. of Denmark; b. Engelsholm, Denmark, Oct. 20, 1875; s. Carl Adolph Rothe and Josepha del Carmen (Petersen) B.; Ph.B., 1894; passed law examination Copenhagen U., 1900; m. Harriet Eleonora Kauffman, Dec. 7, 1901 (dec.); children—Elinor (Mrs. William Schmidt), Gudrun (Mrs. Viggo F. E. Rambusch), Carl Georg, Lennard; m. 2d, Kirsten Havemann, Sept. 8, 1926. Came to U.S., 1900. Began with dock dept. Scandinavian Am. Line, 1901; consular sec., New York, 1904; vice consul, Buenos Aires, 1905; consul, Chgo., 1908; consul gen. New York, 1916-46, ret. Decorated Commander of l'degree of Dannebrog, Silver Cross of Dannebrog (Denmark). Address: Osterled pr. Birkerod, Denmark. Died Feb. 7, 1951; buried Norup, pr. Vejle, Denmark.

BECHDOLT, Frederick Ritchie (bĕk'dōlt), author; b. Mercersburgh, Pa., July 27, 1874; s. Adolph Frederick and Jean (Ritchie) B.; student U. N.D., 1892-95; B.A., U. Wash., 1896; m. Adele Fortier Hale, Dec. 9, 1908. Began as newspaper man, 1899; writer, 1907—. Democrat. Clubs: Family, Press Club (San Francisco). Author: The Hard Rock Man, 1910; When the West Was Young, 1921; Tales of the Old Timers, 1922; Giants of the Old West, 1930; Riders of the San Pedro, 1931; Horse Thief Trail, 1932; The Tree of Death, 1937; Danger on the Border, 1939, Bold Riders out of Santa Fe, 1940; Hot Gold, 1942; Hills of Fear, 1943; Hill Racketeers, 1948. Co-author "9009" (with James Hopper), 1908. Contbr. articles and fiction to mags. Home: Box 5, Carmel, Cal. Died Apr. 12, 1950.

BECHET, Sidney, musician, b. New Orleans, May 14, 1897; s. Homer and Josephine (Mitchel) B.; ed. pub. schs., New Orleans; m. Marilouise Crawford, 1934; m. 2d, Elizabeth Ziegler, 1951; 1 son, Daniel. Began as clarinet player with Bunk Johnson's Eagle Band, 1912-14; with Clarence Williams for tour, 1915-16. Arthur Bruce (Bruce and Bruce Stock Co. as musician and actor), 1916-17, Lawrence Dehé's Band, Chgo., 1917-18, Will Marion Cooks So. Syncopators, for tour of Europe, 1918-19; recording artist for Okeh, N.Y.C., 1923-25; joined Louis Douglas, Black Revue, as featured actor and musician touring France, Belgium, Germany, Hungary, Bulgaria, Greece, Turkey, Egypt, Italy, 1925-27; played in Russia with Benny Peytons band, 1927, with Noble Sissle band, in France, 1928, in U.S.A., 1930-32; leader New Orleans Footwarmers, 1933-34, with Noble Sissle band, 1933-37; leader of various small jazz combinations, 1938—; musician and actor in Broadway production, Hear That Trumpet, 1946; recording artist for Vogue, v.p. King Jazz, Inc., 1945—. Home: Paris, France. Died May 14, 1959.

BECHTEL, Edwin De Turck, lawyer; b. Bechtelsville, Pa., Aug. 19, 1880; s. James and Emma (De Turck) B.; A.B. summa cum laude, Harvard, 1903, A.M., 1904; LL.B., Harvard Law Sch., 1908; m. Louise Hunting Seaman, Feb. 28, 1929. Admitted to N.Y. Bar, 1909; with Carter, Ledyard & Milburn, attys., N.Y.C., 1908—, mem. firm, 1918-48, counsel, 1946—. Trustee and mem. exec. com., Skidmore Coll.; mem. vis. com., dept. of philosophy, Harvard; mem. bd. mgrs. and exec. com., N.Y. Botan. Garden; mem. bd. mgrs. and exec. com., Seamen's Ch. Inst. of N.Y. Mem. Am., N.Y. State and N.Y. County Bar Assns., Assn. Bar of City of N.Y. (hon. chmn. bd.), Horticultural Soc. of N.Y. (chmn. bd.), Huguenat Soc., Phi Beta Kappa. Episcopalian. Clubs: Grolier (council), Century Assn., Harvard of N.Y., Down Town Assn., Faculty of Harvard. Author: Freedom of the Press and L'Association Mensuelle, 1952; Biography & Etchings of Jacques Callot, 1955. Co-author, contbr.: Romance of Fine Prints, 1938; Daumier, Arts et Livres de Provence, 1948; Our Rose Varieties and Their Malmaison Heritage, 1949; Introduction to Vol. IV of Catalog of Frick Art Collection, 1951. Also articles in periodicals. Home: Bedford Four Corners, Mt. Kisco, N.Y. Died July 4, 1957; buried St. Matthew's Cemetery, Bedford, N.Y.

BECHTEL, George M., banker; b. Harrison County, Mo., Apr. 1, 1868; s. J. C. and Matilda (Stecher) B.; ed. pub. schs.; m. Martha Reimers, Oct. 11, 1893; children—Harold R., Esther, Margaret, Marian, Elizabeth. Pres. Geo. M. Bechtel & Co., bankers, First (Bechtel) Trust and Savings Bank, Davenport, 1891-1947, ret.; chmn. bd. Ia. Southern Utilities Co. Republican. Presbyn. Mason (33°). Home: R.F.D. 2, Davenport, Ia. Died Mar. 21, 1952; buried Oakdale Cemetery, Davenport.

BECK, Herbert Wardle, Christian Sci. teacher and practitioner; b. San Francisco; s. Eugene Bogart and Eva Gardner (Smith) B.; grad. Oakland (Calif.) High Sch.; student U. of Calif.; m. Ethel M. Lent-Donaldson, June 17, 1921. With Pacific Coast Borax Co., becoming sec. and dir., also dir. subsidiary corps.; Christian Science practitioner; 1st reader First Ch. of Christ, Scientist, Auburn, Calif.; Chaplain U.S. Army, 1918-19; asst. to mgr. Coms. on Publ. Christian Science Ch., Boston, 1920-26, Com. on Publ. for Northern Calif., 1938-40; mgr. Coms. on Publ., First Ch. of Christ, Scientist, Boston, 1940-42; Christian Sci. lectr. 1942-50, teacher since 1925. Club: Commonwealth of Cal. Contbr. Christian Science periodicals. Home: 1020 San Francisco St., San Francisco. Died Jan. 14, 1954.

BECK, Thomas Hambly, mag. publisher; b. Oakland, Calif., July 24, 1881; s. Walter Francisco and Amy (Simpson) B.; ed. pub. schs.; m. Louie Steven Roy, 1904; 1 dau., Doris Hambly; m. 2d, Dorothy Wright Miller, May 12, 1927 (died 1946); m. 3d, Martha Gallagher. Director of Crowell-Collier Pub. Co.; dir. Met. Life Ins. Co. Trustee Knapp Foundations of N.Y. and N.C.; member board curators Stephens College, Columbia, Mo. Decorated Comdr. Order of British Empire. Home: Wilton, Conn. Office: 640 Fifth Av., N.Y.C. 19. Died Oct. 16, 1951.

BECK, William Hopkins, govt. ofcl., retired; born Washington, D.C., Sept. 8, 1892; s. James Hopkins and Elizabeth Lawton (Morgan) B.; ed. Eastern High Sch., Business High Sch. and Milton Business College (Washington); married Mae Edwards Norwood, October 17, 1923; children—Elizabeth Norwood (Mrs. Hugo G. R. Kenyon), Margaret Houghton (dec.). Served as secretary to Congressman John M. Nelson of Wis., 1910-12; asst. sec. Inst. of Industrial Research, Washington, 1912-15; private sec. to Gilbert Grosvenor, editor Nat. Geog. Soc. Mag., 1915-17; private sec. to Henry White, mem. Am. Commn. to Negotiate Peace, Paris, 1918-19; special asst. to Robert Lansing, sec. of state, 1920; sec. to Bainbridge Colby, Charles E. Hughes, Frank B. Kellogg and Henry L. Stimson, Secretaries of State, 1920-1931; consul gen. at Ottawa, Can., 1931-35, at Oslo, Norway, 1936-39; consul gen. at Hamilton, Bermuda, Mar. 1940-Aug. 1945; consul gen., Southampton, Eng., 1945-50; detailed Dept. of State, Washington 1950-51; chmn. joint dept., ECA claim bd.; retired from foreign service 1951; appt. to staff Nat. Geographic Soc. 1951; asso. sec., gov. Episcopal Eye Ear & Throat Hosp., Washington. Enlisted as private, U.S. Signal Corps, 1917; assigned to Hdqrs. Base Sect. 3, London. Capt. Res. Episcopalian. Home: 2921 Bellevue Terrace, Washington 16. Office: 16th and M Sts. N.W., Washington. Died Mar. 31, 1957; buried Arlington Nat. Cemetery.

BECKER, Benjamin V., lawyer; b. Warsaw, Ind., June 20, 1871; s. Leopold and Caroline (Vogel) B.; ed. pub. schs., Warsaw and Fort Wayne, Ind.; m. Elizabeth Loeb, June 20, 1900; 1 son, John Leonard. Moved to Chicago from Fort Wayne in 1887 and began to read law in the office of Jacob Newman; admitted to Ill. bar, 1892, Supreme Court of United States, 1900; now mem. Levinson, Becker & Peebles (Chicago); dir. Booth Fisheries Corp., Fansteel Metallurgical Corp., North Chgo., Hydro Blast Corp., Chicago, Vascoloy-Ramet Corp., Waukegan, Ill., Westinghouse Air Brake Co. (Wilmerding, Pa.), Webster Electric Co. Racine, Wis., Weiger, Weed and Co., Detroit, Tantalum Defense Plant Corp., North Chicago, etc. Mem. American, Illinois State and Chicago bar assns., Association Bar City of New York, Chicago Hist. Soc., Chicago Acad. of Sciences, Am. Inst. of Mining and Metall. Engrs. Republican. Clubs: Tavern, Standard Club, Lake Shore Country (Chicago); The Wall Street Club, Inc., Wall Street (New York), Home: 179 Lake Shore Dr. Office: 1 N. LaSalle St., Chgo. Died Feb. 5, 1955; buried Rosehill Cemetery, Chgo.

BECKER, Frederic Harry, tannery exec.; b. Freeport, Ill., Aug. 6, 1885; s. Adam and Wilhelmena (Herzog) S.; student pub. schs., Freeport; m. Margaret Fox, Oct. 1, 1904 (dec.); 1 dau., Geraldine Emelyn (Mrs. Edward John Stark). Wholesale jewelry sales, 1904; stock clk. Am. Hide & Leather Co., 1905-06, city salesman, 1906-07, br. office mgr., 1907-13; partner Becker & Berry Co., 1913-17; sales mgr. Ohio Leather Co., 1917—, v.p., gen. mgr., 1927-45, pres., 1945—; dir. First Nat. Bank, Am. Hair & Felt Co., Girard Fed. Savs. & Loan Co. Republican. Mason (Shriner), Elk. Clubs: Youngstown Country, Youngstown. Home: 419 Catalina Av., Youngstown 4. Office: 1052 N. State St., Girard, O. Died July 21, 1954; buried Tod Mausoleum, Tod Cemetery, Youngstown, O.

BECKER, Gustave Louis, pianist, composer; b. Richmond, Tex., May 22, 1861; s. Francis Louis and Maria A. T. (Langhammer) B.; began study of music under father (a bandmaster), and continued in Europe under Moszkowski, Scharwenka, other masters; m. May B. Lamberton, June 20, 1894 (div. 1911); 1 dau., Beatrice L.; m. 2d, Fanny Granger Dow, Feb. 11, 1911 (dec.); children—Valeska Granger and Don Verdi (twins), Richard Quentin. Settled in N.Y.C. 1881; head musical dept. Hasbrouck Inst., Jersey City, 1891-1913; dir. Am. Progressive Piano Sch., 1914—. Gave course in music at Columbia U., summer 1912. Mem. N.Y. Music Tchrs. Assn. (pres. 1911-12), Nat. Music Tchrs. Assn., Piano Tchrs. Congress, Nat. Assn. Am. Composers and Condrs., Asso. Music Tchrs. League (past pres.). Clubs: Andiron, Bohemian (N.Y.C.). Author: The Requisites of Musicianship, 1911; A Graded Course for Piano, 1913; Accuracy in Piano Playing, 1915; Normal Course for Piano Teachers, 1919; also a number of vocal and instrumental compositions. Lecturer on musical subjects; has served as judge of music contests, Nat. Music League, Music Edn. League, Nat. Fed. of Music Clubs, etc. Holder copyright on A Complete Musical Alphabet. Studio: 1050 Amsterdam Av., N.Y.C. 25. Died Feb. 1959.

BECKER, May Lamberton (Mrs. Lamberton-Becker), editor, author; b. N.Y.C., Aug. 26, 1873; d. Ellis Tinkham and Emma Packard (Thurston) Lamberton; student pub. schs., pvt. tchrs.; m. Gustave L. Becker, 1894 (div. 1911); 1 dau., Mrs. Beatrice Lamberton Warde. Began as dramatic and musical critic at 18; lecturer on contemporary lit., 1907—; contbg. editor Literary Review, N.Y. Evening Post, 1915-24; contb. editor Sat. Rev. Lit. (The Reader's Guide) from its foundation, 1924-33; dept. editor Pictorial Review, 1924-25; dept. editor American Girl, 1925-27; now Reader's Guide in Weekly Book Review, N.Y. Herald Tribune, also page of Books for Young People; and book editor The Scholastic. Served as chief Fgn. News Bur., Council Nat. Def., World War I; now selection co-ordinator Books Across the Sea, N.Y. Circle. Recipient Constance Skinner award, 1948. Author: A Reader's Guide Book, 1923; Adventures in Reading, 1927; Golden Tales of Our America, 1929; Books as Windows, 1929; Golden Tales of the Old South, 1930; Golden Tales of New England 1931; Golden Tales of the Prairie States, 1932; Under Twenty, 1932; Golden Tales of the Far West, 1935; First Adventures in Reading, 1936; Choosing Books for Children, 1937; Golden Tales of Canada, 1938; Golden Tales of the Southwest, 1939; Introducing Charles Dickens, 1940 (royalties from which endowed the Charles Dickens ambulance, operating through the Battle of Britain); Growing Up With America; Home Book of Christmas, 1941; Home Book of Laughter, 1948. Home: 114 Morningside Dr. Address: Care N.Y. Herald Tribune, 230 W. 41st St., N.Y.C. Died Apr. 27, 1958.

BECKER, Neal Dow, lawyer, industrialist; b. Cherry Creek, N.Y., Feb. 13, 1883; s. Wm. E. and Eva (Kenyon) B.; LL.B., Cornell U., 1905, A.B., 1906; LL.D., Dickinson Coll., 1948; m. Ivah Smith, June 14, 1909 (dec.); children—Jane (Mrs. G. D. Wever), Marilee (Mrs. A. S. Kellogg); married 2d, Charlotte Dawn Allen, 1954. Practiced N.Y. City 1910-35, mem. Kelley & Becker; pres. Intertype Corp. (mfrs. of typesetting machinery), 1926-52, chmn. since 1952; chmn. Intertype, Ltd. (London, Eng.); mng. dir. Intertype Setzmaschinen G.m.b.H. (Berlin, Germany); trustee, mem. exec. com. Consol. Edison Co. of N.Y.; dir., mem. exec. com. N.Y. Dock Co.; dir. Bank of Manhattan Co., Gen. Baking Co., Avco Mfg. Corp., etc. trustee East River Savings Bank. Trustee Cornell U., 1934—. Trustee Nat. Indsl. Conf. Bd.; mem. Council Fgn. Relations, Nat. Fgn. Trade Council, Assn. Bar City of New York, Soc. of New York Hospital, Delta Chi. Former president Commerce and Industry Assn. of New York, Inc. Clubs: Union, University, Racquet and Tennis, Cornell of New York (ex-pres.); Garden City Golf; American (London); Sunningdale Golf (Eng.), St. Andrews Golf. Home: 340 Park Av., N.Y.C., 22. Died May 16, 1955.

BECKER, Owen Chauncey, lawyer; b. Grosvenors, N.Y., Sept. 29, 1875; s. Stillman G. and Henrietta (Mosher) B.; ed. Cobleskill high sch. (N.Y.), Oneonta State Normal Sch. (N.Y.); B.S., Wesleyan U., 1904; student N.Y. Univ. Law; LL.D., Hartwick College, 1949; m. Vera F. Peck, Sept. 7, 1904; children—Eleanor E. Getman, Henry W., Vera Lucille, Carol C. Jones. Admitted to N.Y. State bar, 1908, and since practiced in Oneonta; admitted to practice U.S. District Court 1913; sr. mem. firm Becker, Plowden-Wardlaw & Leamy; dir., v.p. Citizens Nat. Bank & Trust Co. of Oneonta since 1930. Trustee Wesleyan U.; dir., v.p. Farmers Museum; dir. Nat. Baseball Hall of Fame and Museum, Inc.; trustee

N.Y. State Hist. Assn., Mary Imogene Bassett Hosp., Cooperstown, N.Y., Aurelia Osborn Fox Meml. Hosp., Oneonta, N.Y., and chmn. bd. Welch Thanksgiving Home for Aged, Cooperstown, N.Y. Mem. Chi Psi. Republican. Presbyn. Mason. Clubs: Kiwanis, Oneonta City, Oneonta Country. Home: 42 Elm St. Office: 198 Main St., Oneonta, N.Y. Died June 6, 1954.

BECKETT, Richard Creighton, engr.; b. Millville, N.J., Oct. 6, 1893; s. Bertrand Orris and Luphemia Creighton (McAvoy) B.; B.Sc. in San. Engring., Pa. State Coll., 1916; Certificate of Attendance in Chemistry and Govt., U. Nancy, France, Jan.-July, 1919; m. Sarah Sheppard, Oct. 7, 1922; 1 son, Richard Creighton. Asst. engr. Pa. Dept. of Health, Harrisburg, 1920-21; asst. san. engr., W.Va. Dept. of Health, Charleston, 1921-24; state san. engr. Del. Bd. of Health, Dover, 1924-—. Mem. and sec. State Milk Commn., 1933-35, State Mosquito Control Commn., 1935-39; vice chmn. Commn. Interstate Cooperation, 1936-—; mem. exec. com. Interstate Commn. Del. River Basin, 1936-—; mem. post-war com. on reconstrn., Council of State Govts., gov's. com. post-war reconstruction, State Del. Registered profl. engr., Del. Mem. Am. Water Works Assn., Am. Pub. Health Assn., Am. Fedn. Sewerage Works Assn., New Castle County Regional Planning Commn., Conf. State San. Engrs. Independent. Author: various articles on sanitation and pub. health engring. in profl. mags. and publs. Home: Hazel Rd. Office: Delaware State Board of Health, Dover, Del. Died Dec. 16, 1948; buried Silver Lake Cemetery, Dover.

BECKETT, Thomas Gervus, Jr., investment banker; b. Corsicana, Tex., Feb. 24, 1911; s. Thomas G. and Nannie V. (Horne) B.; B.S., So. Meth. U., 1932; M.B.A., Harvard, 1934; m. Hazael Williams, Nov. 24, 1934; children—Betty Ann, Thomas Gervus 3d. Pres. Beckett-Gilbert & Co., 1934-42; v.p. First Southwest Co., Dallas, 1946-—; pres., dir. Thomas Beckett & Co., Dallas, 1946-—; dir. Century Geophysical Corp., Tulsa., Fritz W. Glitsch & Sons. Served as lt. comdr. USNR, 1942-45. Mem. Investment Bankers Assn. Am. (gov.). Clubs: City, Dallas, Dallas Country, Brook Hollow Golf. Home: 3868 Potomac St. Office: Mercantile Bank Bldg., Dallas. Died Jan. 13, 1956.

BECKMAN, Frederick William, journalist; b. Clayton, Ia., Sept. 5, 1873; s. Herman F. and Louise (Kurdelmeyer) B.; Ph.B., U. Ia., 1897; m. Anna McCullough, June 18, 1901; children—Richard William, Elizabeth Louise. Reporter Council Bluffs Nonpareil, 1898, editor, 1902-03; reporter Sioux City Jour., 1899-1902; mng. editor Des Moines Register-Leader, 1903-09, asso. editor, 1910-11; editor Sunday Mag. Syndicate, 1909-10; prof. journalism, Ia. State Coll., 1911-27; mng. editor Farmer's Wife, 1927-35, editor, 1935-39; editor, pub. Journal, Knoxville, Ia., 1939-50, editor, 1950-—. Named Master Editor-Pub. by Ia. Press Assn., 1944. Army YMCA sec., 1918; mem. Army Ednl. Corps, France and Germany, 1919. Founder, 1924, and chmn. bd. Collegiate Press, Iowa State Coll.; mem. nat. council, Minn. state com. YMCA. Mem. Sigma Delta Chi (hon. pres. 1922), Phi Kappa Phi. Republican. Presbyn. Clubs: Rotary, Knoxville Golf and Country. Co-Author: A Desk Book of Style (with Blair Converse), 7th edit., 1943; Technical Writing for Farm and Home (with same and H. R. O'Brien), 4th rev. edit. 1951. Home: 902 South Roche, Knoxville, Ia. Died July 9, 1957; buried Graceland Cemetery.

BECKMAN, Vincent Henry, lawyer; b. St. Henry, O., Dec. 1, 1879; s. John G. and Catherine (Romer) B.; ed. Miami U. and U. of Cincinnati; LL.B., Cincinnati Law Sch., 1905; m. Irene Gertrude Hummel, Jan. 19, 1915; children—Vincent Henry, Mary Elizabeth (dec.), Paul, Irene Gertrude, John, Robert. Admitted to Ohio bar, 1905, and since practiced at Cincinnati; special atty. State Bank Dept., 1910-14; mem. firm Beckman & Beckman; sec. and dir. Foundation Investment Co., Nat. Theatre Co.; dir., and mem. of the executive com. Eagle-Picher Lead Co.; dir., mem. exec. com. Eagle Picher Mining & Smelting Co., B. Manischewitz Co., dir. Cincinnati Coll. of Music. Member Democratic Exec. Com., Hamilton County, O.; chmn., 1916-26; del. to Democratic Nat. Conv., St. Louis, 1916, New York, 1924, Houston, Tex., 1928, Chicago, 1940, Phila., 1948; nat. presidential elector, 1940, 1948; mem. bd. sinking fund trustees, City of Cincinnati; chairman of the board of Instnl. Visitors, Hamilton Co.; member of board commissioners of sinking fund of Cincinnati School Dist. Mem. Am., Ohio State and Hamilton County bar assns., Cincinnati Lawyers Club, Knights of Columbus. Clubs: Cincinnati, Western Hills Country; West Shore Country (Mich.), Bankers. Home: 535 Purcell Av., Price Hill, Cincinnati. Office: First National Bank Bldg., Cin. Died Nov. 15, 1951.

BEDFORD, F(rederick) H(enry), Jr., business exec.; b. Brooklyn, Sept. 15, 1891; s. Frederick H. and Jennie Van Heusen (Dingee) B.; grad. Poly. Prep. Sch., Brooklyn, 1910; B.S., Amherst Coll., 1914; m. Margaret Stewart, Oct. 13, 1931; 1 dau., Margaret Wright. With mfg. and producing div. Standard Oil Co. of N.J., New York, 1914-15; rep. lubricating dept. in Paris office, Bedford Petroleum Co., 1915-16, organized dept. for mgf. Nujol, New York, 1916, mgr. lubricating and specialties depts., 1919-27, dir. Standard Oil Co., N.J.; organized, president and dir. Stanco Inc., 1927-33; organizer, vice pres. and dir. Standard Oil Co. of Pa., 1928-32; organizer Atlas Supply Co., 1929, and since pres. and dir.; pres. and dir. Standard Alcohol Co., 1932-38; dir. Victaulic Co. of America, 1926-44, Penick & Ford, 1927-44; dir. Ethyl Corp. since 1948. Apptd. chmn. highway transport com. U.S. Council of Internat. C. of C., 1949. Served as 2d lt., U.S. Army, World War I. Decorated Comdr. Legion of Honor (France). Comdr. Order of Crown of Italy. Mem. Am. Petroleum Inst., Am. Legion, Mil. Order World Wars, Chi Phi. Clubs: University, Links, Amherst, Circumnavigators, Knickerbocker, Blind Brook, Cedar Creek, Country Club of Fairfield, Gulf Stream Golf, Pine Valley Golf, U.S. Seniors Golf Assn., India House, Metropolitan, Pacific Union, Turf and Field, Rolling Rock, New York Yacht, Wings, St. Nicholas, St. George's Society of N.Y., Adventurers, 25 Year of Petroleum Industry (gov. eastern area); Pipe Liners; American, Devonshire (London). Made world flight in DC-4 known as Atlas Sky Merchant, 1948; 50,000 miles, crossing equator 6 times, visiting 28 countries on 5 continents, including N.A., S.A., Africa, Asia and Australia, for which awarded Certificate of Performance by Nat. Aero. Assn., 1948; made similar trip to capitals and prin. cities of 11 Central Am. and South Am. countries, 1947, and to 17 European and North African countries, 1949. Home: Shore Rd., Greens Farms, Conn. Office: 30 Rockefeller Plaza, N.Y.C. 20. Died Dec. 3, 1952.*

BEEBE, Katherine, kindergartner; b. Chgo., Jan. 3, 1860; d. Thomas H. and Katherine Beebe; student pvt. schs., Chgo., Highland Park, Ill., Highland Hall Sem.; grad. Chgo. Froebel Tng. Sch. for Kindergartners, 1895. Engaged in kindergarten work, 1884-—. Author: The First School Year, 1895; Home Occupations for Little Children, 1896; Schoolroom Plays, 1898; The Story of Longfellow, 1899; The Story of George Rogers Clark, 1900; Roger and Rose, 1903; A Kindergarten Program, 1904; Kindergarten Activities, 1904; The Home Kindergarten, 1905; (with Nellie F. Kingsley) First Year Nature Reader, 1896. Address: 1404 Asbury Av., Evanston, Ill. Died 1943.

BEEBE, Lewis C., army officer; b. Ia., Dec. 7, 1891; s. Dr. Addison James and Ida Elizabeth (Hamblin) B.; grad. Inf. Sch., 1923, Command and Gen. Staff Sch., 1932, Army War Coll., 1939; m. Dorothy McRae, Dec. 26, 1923; children—William Wallace, John McRae. Commissioned 2d lt., Regular Army, 1917, and advanced through grades to brig. gen., March, 1942. Served as regimental staff officer in 3d div., World War I; instr. Infantry Sch., 1923-26, 1927-30; asst. chief of staff, later dep. chief of staff for Gen. MacArthur on Corregidor; chief of staff for Gen. Wainwright until surrender of U.S. forces in the Philippines, May 6, 1942; Japanese prisoner of war until Aug. 27, 1945; chief of staff for Gen. Wainwright, 1946-47; served in Europe, 1947-50, now retired. Received Distinguished Service Medal, Distinguished Service Cross, French Croix de Guerre, Purple Heart. Mem. Am. Legion (life), Tau Kappa Alpha. Episcopalian. Mason. Address: Faribault, Minn. Died Feb. 17, 1951; buried Arlington Nat. Cemetery.

BEEBE, Royden Eugene Jr., ret. air force officer; b. Ft. Douglas, Utah, July 26, 1908; s. Royden Eugene and Sara (Reid) B.; B.S., U.S. Mil. Acad., 1931; postgrad. Mass. Inst. Tech., 1935; student Nat. War Coll., 1946-49; m. Janet Benedict, Oct. 29, 1932; 1 son, Hugh Grenville. Commd. 2d lt. U.S. Army, 1931, advanced through grades to maj. gen. USAF, 1951; 19th Pursuit Squadron, 1932-35, base operations, Mitchel Field, 1936-39; 9th Bomb Group, 1939-41, operations 3d Air Force, 1941-42; dir. operations Far East Air Force, then chief staff Allied Air Forces S.W. Pacific area, 1942-45; assigned office Sec. Def., 1949-53; dep. chief of staff operations USAF, Europe, 1953-56; mem. strategic survey com. Joint Chiefs of Staff, Washington, 1956-59, ret. Decorated D.S.M.; Comdr. Order Brit. Empire (Eng.). Home: 1676 32d St., Washington 7. Died May 3, 1959; buried Arlington Nat. Cemetery.

BEECH, Walter Herschel, aircraft mfr.; b. Pulaski, Tenn., Jan. 30, 1891; s. Cornelius and Tommy (Hay) B.; m Olive Ann Mellor, 1930; children—Suzanne Mellor, Mary Lynn. Test pilot and gen. mgr. Swallow Airplane Co., 1922-25; pres. and gen. mgr. Travel Air Co., 1925-30; pres. Curtiss-Wright Airplane Sales Co., St. Louis, 1930-32; v.p. Curtiss-Wright Corp., 1930-32; founder Beech Aircraft Co., 1932, pres., dir. and chmn. bd. Beech Aircraft Corp., successors, since 1936. Served as instr. with U.S. Air Corps and doing flight test work, World War I. Mem. Nat. Aeronautics Assn., Inst. Aero. Sciences, Aircraft Industries Assn., Wichita Chamber of Commerce, Quiet Birdmen, Soc. Automotive Engrs., Air Power League, Navy Indsl. Assn. Clubs: Wings, Vet. Pilots, Sportsman Pilots. Home: 48 Mission Road, Eastbrough. Office: Beech Aircraft Corp., Wichita. Died Nov. 29, 1950; buried Old Mission Mausoleum, Wichita.

BEECHLER, Glenn Curtis, lawyer; b. Butler, Ind., June 6, 1881; s. Dr. Curtis Wesley and Mary Wilmina (Phillis) B.; student Ind. U., 1899-1900; A.B., U. Mich., 1904, LL.B., 1906; m. Clare Marie Sullivan, Mar. 21, 1925; 1 dau., Florence Phillis. Admitted to Ind. bar, 1906, practiced in Indianapolis as asso. Messrs. Carson, Thompson & Dowden, 1896-08, in Seattle, 1909-28, N.Y. City, 1929-—; instr. law U. Wash. Law Sch., 1908-10; prof. law John Marshall Coll. Law Sch., Jersey City, 1948-50. Mem. N.Y. Co. Lawyers' Assn., Wash., N.Y. state bars, Supreme Court of U.S., 1932. Democrat. Unitarian. Mason (32°, past master). Author: Beechler on Elections Against Wills—Sect. 18, Decedent Estate Law of New York, 1940. Home and office: 310 W 106th St., N.Y.C. 25. Died Jan. 12, 1954; buried Butler Ind.

BEEK, Alice D. Engley, painter; b. Providence, R.I., June 17, 1867; d. James C. and Mary Elizabeth (Dow) Engley; ed. Miss Ida M. Gardner's School for Girls, Providence; studied art Wheeler Art Sch., R.I. Sch. of Design, with Sydney R. Burleigh (water colorist); acads. Délécluze and Lesar, Paris, and with de Chavannes, L'Hermette, Robert Fleury and Edward Ertz, Paris, and Josef Israels, Holland; m. Anthony Beek, of Kampen, Holland, Sept. 28, 1899; 1 son, Frederic D. Spent 6 yrs. in Paris and 8 yrs. in Holland; exhibited Internat. Exhbn., Paris, 1896, Seattle Expn., 1909, and in London, Eng., Holland and most of the large cities of Europe. Cross of Honor, gold medal and silver medal, Internat. Exhbn., Paris, 1896; Grand Prix, Cross of Honor and gold medal, 1897, her work (water color) being designed as "above competition" at subsequent exhbns.; Grand Prize and gold medal, Seattle Expn., 1909; etc. Mem. Internat. Jury and Commn. of Honor, Paris, since 1897. Mem. Fine Arts Assn., Am. Federation Arts (Washington, D.C.), Nat. League of Am. Pen Women (hon. mem. Seattle br.), Tacoma Fine Arts Assn. (hon. mem.). Republican. Congregationalist. Club: Aloha. Home: 1310 N. 5th St., Tacoma 3. Died Jan. 26, 1951; buried Tacoma Cemetery.

BEELER, Roy Hood, lawyer; b. Powder Springs, Tenn., Feb. 10, 1882; s. Robert Barton and Mattie Jane (Dotson) B.; A.B., Maryville (Tenn.) Coll., 1906; J.D., U. of Chicago, 1910; m. Beulah Hines, June 18, 1913; 1 dau., Frances Elizabeth. Admitted to Tenn. bar, 1911, practiced at Knoxville until Jan. 1927-32, atty. gen. since 1932. Mem. National Assn. Attys. General (pres.). Democrat. Elk. Home: 3604 Hampton Av., Nashville 5. Office: Supreme Court Bldg., Nashville 5. Died Sept. 23, 1954.

BEERBOHM, Sir Max, author; b. London, Eng., Aug. 24, 1872; s. Julius E. and Eliza (Draper) B.; student Charterhouse Sch. and Merton Coll., Oxford U.; m. Florence Kahn, 1910. Author: Works of Max Beerbohn; Zuleika Dobson, An Oxford Love Story, 1912; Seven Men, 1920; And Even Now, 1921; Defence of Cosmetics, 1922; Happy Hypocrite, 1922; Yet Again, 1923; Observations, 1925; Christmas Garland, 2d edit., 1926; Variety of Things, 1928; Works and More, 1930; Around Theatres, 1930; Dreadful Dragon of Hay Hill, 1931. Died May 20, 1956.*

BEERS, Frederick, mfr.; b. New Haven, Dec. 18, 1880; s. Henry Augustin and Mary (Heaotn) B.; prep. edn. Hopkins Grammar Sch., 1895-98; A.B., Yale, 1902; m. Maude Anna Thomas, Dec. 31, 1907 (died 1932); children—Florence Albertine (Mrs. Oliver Hardin Gilbert, dec.), Marjorie Clerc (Mrs. Huber Frye Crippen), Dorothy Heaton (Mrs. Arthur Diehr); m. 2d, Mrs. Dorothy B. Good, June 5, 1934. With Nat. Biscuit Co., bakers, N.Y.C., 1903-—, timekeeper, 1903, student baker, 1903-07, foreman, 1907-13, factory organizer, 1913-21, prodn. mgr., 1921-28, v.p., 1928, pres., 1929-31, now chmn. mfg. com. and v.p. Republican. Clubs: Wyantenuck Country, Yale, Westchester Country. Home: 10 Wildwood Circle, Larchmont, N.Y. Office: 449 W. 14th St., N.Y.C. Died Jan. 16, 1955.

BEESE, Charles William, prof. indsl. engring.; b. Des Moines, Ia., Apr. 2, 1891; s. George and Sarah (McCully) B.; student Des Moines Coll., 1909-11; B.S., Ia. State Coll., 1915, M.E., 1923; m. Ione Johnstone, June 26, 1917; 1 dau., Betty. Instr., Ia. State Coll., 1919-22; prof. and head indsl. engring. dept., Pa. State Coll., 1922-30; indsl. engr., Armstrong Cork Co., 1930-37; prof. indsl. engring., head dept. of gen. engring., dir. war training, dir. div. of tech. insts., asso. dir. engring. extension, dean technical extension division, Purdue University, since 1937. Mem. Engring. Edn. Mission to Japan, 1951; cons. indsl. management edn., Italy, 1952. Served with the U.S. Army 29th Engrs., 1917-19. Member American Society Mechanical Engineers, Am. Society for Engring. Edn., Delta Tau Delta, Tau Beta Pi, Sigma Delta Chi, Phi Kappa Phi, Pi Tau Sigma, Triangle. Republican. Methodist. Mason, Rotarian. Author: Pattern Making, 1928; Cost Accounting, 1947. Home: Route 10. Office: Purdue University, Lafayette, Ind. Died June 29, 1958; buried Grand View Cemetery, West Lafayette, Ind.

BEGEMAN, Louis, educator; b. Evansville, Ind., Mar. 1, 1865; s. Henry and Elizabeth (Schmoll) B.; B.S., U. Mich., 1889, M.S., 1897; Ph.D., U. Chgo., 1910; m. Magdalene Thuman, July 6, 1892 (died 1906); children—Myron Louis, Florence; m. 2d, Mary Whitworth, Aug. 27, 1915 (died Feb.

1957). Prin. schs., Corydon, Ia., 1889-95; prof. physics and chemistry Parsons Coll., Fairfield, Ia., 1905-09; head dept. physics and chemistry Ia. State Tchrs. Coll., 1899-1935, ret. but continued with research in nuclear sci., 1935-57. Mem. A.A.A.S., Central Assn. Sci. and Mathematics, Ia. Acad. Sci., Walt Whitman Club Ia. Sch. Men. Republican. Presbyn. Mason (K.T., Shriner). Author: Principles of Physics, 1908; Every Day Physical Science, 1923. In 1910 determined the charge of an electron, with high degree of accuracy, showing all previous determinations too low. Home: Cedar Falls, Ia. Died May 18, 1958; buried Fairview Cemetery, Cedar Falls.

BEHAN, Joseph C., insurance exec.; b. Albany, N.Y., Mar. 21, 1873; s. Thomas and Winnifred (McManus) B.; ed. pub. sch.; m. Katharin A. Wasserbach, June 24, 1896; children—Louis B., Herbert G. Worked as office and messenger boy, 1888-89; learned stenography and employed by law firm Rosendale & Hessberg, Albany, 1890-93; stenographer Commerce Fire Ins. Co., and D.&H. R.R., 1893-93; stenographer Mass. Mut. Life Ins. Co., (Springfield, Mass.), 1896-1909, supt. of agts., 1909-30, v.p. and dir. 1930-48. Catholic. Club: Colony. Home: 336 Long Hill St., Providence, R.I. Died Dec. 1949.

BEHAN, Warren Palmer, clergyman, ex-coll. pres.; b. Saginaw, Mich., Sept. 21, 1871; s. Edwin Augustus and Ella Adelaide (Palmer) B.; student Beloit (Wis.) Coll., 1890-92; A.B., U. Chgo., 1894, B.D., 1897, Ph D., 1899; LL.D., Ottawa U., 1936; m. Mary Gertrude Wright, Apr. 4, 1899; children—Roger Palmer, Gerald Wright, Fred Hulbert. Ordained to ministry Bapt. Ch., 1898; pastor Wealth Av. Ch., Grand Rapids, Mich., 1898-1905; dir. Bapt. Student's Guild, Ann Arbor, Mich., 1905-07; dir. Bibl. and social studies, YMCA Coll., Chgo., 1907-12; pastor Morgan Park Ch., Chgo., 1911-14; pres. Bapt. Missionary Tng. Sch., Chgo., 1914-19; dir. staff tng. and corr. study Am. Bapt. Publ. Soc., Phila., 1919-22; instr. religious edn. and missions Crozer Theol. Sem., Upland, Pa., 1920-21; head dept. Bible and religious edn. Ottawa (Kan.) U., 1922-37, dean, 1924-36, acting pres., 1931-35; pres. Sioux Falls Coll., 1937-41; interim pastoral work, 1941-50. Mem. S.D. Tchrs. Assn., Beta Theta Pi. Republican. Rotarian. Home: 525 W. Walnut St., Kalamazoo, Mich. Died Dec. 9, 1952; buried Jackson, Mich.

BEHARRELL, Sir George, business exec.; b. York, Eng., Mar. 11, 1873; s. George and Elizabeth (Dalby) B.; student King James' Sch., Almondbury, York, Leeds U.; m. Kate Ripley, Sept. 7, 1898; children—George Edward, Kathleen Mabel, Jacques Ripley, Douglas Wells. Asst. goods mgr. and comml. agt. North Eastern Ry., Eng., 1888-1915; with Ministry of Munitions, 1915; dir. gen. finance and statis. Ministry of Transport, 1919-22; financial advisor Geddes com.; joined Dunlop Rubber Co., Ltd., 1922, became mng. dir., 1923, chmn., 1937, president, 1949. Served as asst. insp. gen. transportation all theatres of war, with rank lt. col., 1916, admiralty anti-submarine campaign, 1917; mem. adv. panel apptd. by prime minister in connection with re-armament program, 1938; chmn. rubber control bd., 1941. Fellow Royal Society Arts, Inst. Motor Industry, Instn. Rubber Industry (pres. 1933-36). Decorated Knight Bachelor, 1919; Distinguished Service Order, several fgn. decorations, Pres. India Rubber Mfrs. Assn., 1926-28, Soc. Motor Mfrs. and Trades, 1927-29, Fedn. British Industries, 1932-33. Mem. Church of England. Home: Barnards, Oakhurst Av., Harpenden, Herts, Eng. Office: St. James's House, St. James's St., London S.W.I. Eng. Died Feb. 20, 1959.

BEHM, Walter Henry John, banker; b. Dayton, O., Apr. 27, 1890; s. George and Emma (Seeger) B.; student night sch.; m. Marie E. Hayes, Oct. 29, 1914; children—Walter George (dec.), Robert Hayes, Mary Elidabeth. Clerk Mutual Home & Savs. Assn., Dayton, O., 1907-08; bookkeeper, teller, cashier, Market Savs. Bank, Dayton, 1909-24; sec. City Trust & Savs. Bank, Dayton, 1924; cashier to dir. and pres., The Winters Nat. Bank & Trust Co. of Dayton, 1924-—; dir. Nat. Cash Register Co., Meade Corp., Dayton Power & Light Co., George Behm & Sons Co., Dayton, The Flexible Co., Loudonville, O., Cin. br., Fed. Reserve Bank of Cleve., 1945-50; mem. Dayton Clearing House Assn. (pres.); Junior Achievement Inc. (treas. and dir.), Dayton. Trustee U. Dayton, Dayton Art Inst. Home: 259 Greenmount Blvd. 9. Office: 40 N. Main St., Dayton 2, O. Died May 21, 1951.

BEHN, Sosthenes, telephone official; St. Thomas, Virgin Is., Jan. 30, 1882; s. William and Louise (Monsanto) B.; ed. St. Thomas, Ajaccio, Corsica. Ste. Barbe, Paris, France; m. Margaret Dunlap; children—Edward John, William Charles, Margaret Cecilia. Chmn. Internat. Tel. & Tel. Corp. (ret.), Internat. Std. Electric Corp.; chmn. bd., pres., Cuban Telephone Co.; pres., dir., Port of Havana Docks Co., Havana Docks Corp., Radio Corp. Cuba, Standard Products Distbg. Co. (Cuba), Internat. Tel. & Tel. Co. (Espana); chmn., dir. Porto Rico Tel. Co., Radio Corp. P.R.; dir., chmn. finance com., Fed. Electric Corp.; dir. Am. Cable & Radio Corp., Capehart Farnsworth Co., The Coolerator Co., Fed. Telecommunications Labs. Inc., Fed. Telephone & Radio Co., Internat. Telecommunications Labs., Inc., Internat. Telephone Bldg. Corp., Kellogg Credit Corp., Kellogg Switchboard & Supply Co., Cia Standard Electric Argentina, Cia de Telefonos de Chile, Standard Electric Corp., P.R., Standard Elektrizitats-Gesellschfat A.G., Standard Electrica, S.A.R.L., Lisbon, Standard Electrica, S.A., Madrid, The Nat. City Bank N.Y. (ret.), L. M. Ericsson Telephone Co. Ltd., Sweden. Del. Rep. nat. conv., 1912; mem. Rep. nat. com., 1912-16. Commd. capt., Signal Corps, U.S. Army, June 19, 1917, later maj. and lt. col.; with A.E.F., France, until Feb. 1919; commanded 232 Field Signal Bn., Chateau Thierry, St Mihiel, Argonne. Awarded D.S.M., Medal of Merit (U.S.); Comdr. Legion d'Honneur (France); Grand Cross Order of Isabela la Catolica of Spain; grand officer Order of St. Gregory. Clubs: Metropolitan (Washington); New York Yacht, Links, Knickerbocker (N.Y.); Union, Country, Yacht, Tennis (Havana). Office: 67 Broad St., N.Y.C. Died June 6, 1957; buried Arlington Nat. Cemetery.

BEHNCKE, David L., 1st pres. Internat. Air Line Pilots Assn., served until July 16, 1951. Address: 6459 S. Albany, Chgo. Died Apr. 14, 1953.

BEHRENS, Charles August, bacteriologist; b. Grand Rapids, Mich., Jan. 5, 1885; s. August Charles and Anna D. (Bornemann) B.; B.S., U. Mich., 1909, M.S., 1910, Ph.D., 1913. Began teaching U. Mich., 1910; prof. bacteriology and san. sci. Purdue U., 1914-—. Commd. 1st lt. San. Corps, U.S. Army, 1918. Fellow Ind. Acad. Sci. (pres. 1923), A.A.A.S., Am. Pub. Health Assn.; hon. mem. Tippecanoe Med. Soc.; mem. Soc. Am. Bacteriologists, Mich. Acad. Sci., Am. Assn. U. Profs., Sigma Xi. Presbyn. Mason (32°). Died June 22, 1950.

BEHYMER, Francis Albert (bē'hi-mer), journalist; b. Miamiville, O., Jan. 27, 1870; s. William S. and Nancy S. (Woodlief) B.; student Ohio grade schs., 1877-92; M. Journalism (hon.), MacMurray Coll., Jacksonville, Ill., 1946; m. Otilie Wilhelmina Meyer, June 23, 1891; children—Weley Francis (dec.), Raymond Woodlief, Ruth Valeria (Mrs. Jean Pierre Ulbright). Reporter, editor and feature writer St. Louis Post-Dispatch, 1888-—. Trustee McKendree Coll., Lebanon, Ill. Home: 617 W. St. Louis St., Lebanon, Ill. Office: 12th and Olive Sts., St. Louis. Died July 15, 1956; buried Lebanon, Ill.

BEINECKE, Walter, ins. exec.; b. N.Y.C., May 4, 1888; s. Bernhard and Johanna (Weigle) B.; student Yale, 1906-08, Williams Coll., 1908-09; m. Katherine Sperry, Feb. 17, 1917; children—Walter, Betsy (Mrs. Carl Shirley). Chmn., chief exec. officer John C. Paige & Co., Inc., N.Y.C.; with Sperry & Hutchinson Co., N.Y.C., 1922-—, chmn. finance com., dir., 1923-—; dir. Austin, Nichols & Co. Mem. Internat. Laws Com. on Bridge. Clubs: Links Golf, Links Club, Sankaty Head Golf, Sankaty Head Beach, Nantucket Yacht (Nantucket, Mass.); Metropolitan, Yale, Williams, Manhattan, Whist, Lawyers (N.Y.C.); Everglades, Old Guard Soc. Palm Beach Golfers Bath & Tennis (Palm Beach, Fla.); Porcupine (Nassua, B.H.); Portland (London). Home: 920 Fifth Av., N.Y.C. Office: 114 Fifth Av., N.Y.C. 11. Died Sept. 3, 1958.

BELCHER, Frank Garrettson, banker; b. Los Angeles, June 30, 1905; s. Frank J., Jr., and Virginia Acheson (Garrettson) B.; B.S., Princeton, 1928; m. Harriet Holbrook, Sept. 20, 1930; children—John Garrettson, Frank Garrettson, David Holbrook, Virginia Carolyn. Dir. J. D. & A. B. Spreckels Cos., San Diego; v.p., dir. First Nat. Trust & Savings Bank, San Diego; maintains Belbrook Stables at Corta Madera Rancho, Cal.; owner Electronic Engring. Assos. Ltd. San Carlos, Cal. Pres. Cal. Pacific Internat. Expn. at San Diego, 1935-36. Dir. Calif. Fish & Game Development Assn., Golden Gate Internat. Expn., San Francisco, Coronado Nat. Horse Show Assn. Chmn. Rep. Nat. Central Com. for No. Cal. USN attache, Venezuela, S.A., 1942; comdr. USN, World War II. Clubs: Bohemian (San Francisco); Cuyamaca (dir.), Coronado Riding (dir.), Marlin of Southern Calif. (founder, dir.); Campus (Princeton); Princeton (New York). Home: 1890 Spindrift Dr., La Jolla, Cal. Died Jan. 12, 1959; buried Fort Rosecrans, San Diego, Cal.

BELCHER, Frank J., Jr., banker, business executive; b. Falls Village, Conn., 1878; graduated New York U., 1901; chairman board of directors First Nat. Trust & Savings Bank, San Diego, Calif.; trustee Calamba Sugar Estate; dir. San Diego Ice and Cold Storage Co., Calif. Ice & Cold Storage Co. Home: Pacific Union Club, San Francisco. Died June 23, 1952.*

BELFORD, John L., priest; b. Brooklyn, N.Y., Oct. 15, 1861; s. Matthew and Rose (Donnelly) B.; A.M., St. Francis Xavier Coll., 1881; student St. Charles Coll., 1881-83; A.B., St. Mary's Sem., Baltimore, 1884, A.M., 1885, D.D., 1922; Ph.D., Fordham, 1925. Ordained to ministry of R.C. Ch., 1888; asst. St. Augustine's Ch., Brooklyn, 1888-93; supt. of schs., Brooklyn, 1893-95; pastor St. Dominic's Ch., Oyster Bay, N.Y., 1895-1900, Sts. Peter and Paul's churches, Brooklyn, 1900-05, Ch. of Nativity, Brooklyn, since 1905. Address: 20 Madison St., Brooklyn 16, N.Y. Died Dec. 12, 1951; buried Holy Cross Cemetery, Brooklyn.

BELGRANO, Frank N., Jr., banker, corp. exec.; former comdr. Am. Legion; b. San Francisco, May 18, 1895; s. Frank N. and Emilia A. (Cavagnaro) B.; grad. high school, Oakland, 1916; m. Margaret Evelyn Biddle, May 16, 1922; children—Margaret and Evelyn (twins), Carla. Began as bank messenger, 1916; became exec. v.p., comptroller United Bank & Trust Co., San Francisco, 1928 (now Bank of Am. N.T. & S.A.); pres. Pacific Nat. Fire Ins. Co., 1930-43; pres. Central Bank, Oakland, Cal. 1943-47; pres. First Nat. Bank, Portland, Ore. 1947-53; chmn., pres. Transamerica Corp., 1953-—. Financial adv. to the U.S. High Commr. to the Philippines, 1945-46. Nat. Comdr. Am. Legion, 1934-35. Enlisted as pvt. U.S. Army, 1917, commd. 2d lt., 1918. Republican. Clubs: Bohemian, Family, Arlington. Home: 1980 Jackson St., San Francisco. Office: Transamerica Corp., 4 Columbus Av., San Francisco 11. Died Nov. 11, 1959.

BELIN, G. d'Andelot, banker, corp. dir.; born Scranton, 1888. Pres., dir. 1st Nat. Bank, Scranton; dir. Scranton Lackawanna Trust Co., Scranton Lace Co., Ames-Baldwin-Wyoming Co., Richwood Stores Co., Elk Lick Coal Co., Cherry River Boom & Lumber Co. Address: Wyoming Av. and Spruce St., Scranton, Pa. Died May 5, 1954; buried Hickory Grove Cemetery, Waverly, Pa.

BELISLE, Hector Louis (bĕl-ēl), educator; b. Worcester, Mass., Oct. 8, 1873; s. Alexander and Marie (Dorval) B.; grad. Classical High Sch., Worcester, 1892; A.B., Harvard, 1896; m. Grace Mildred Potter, June 28, 1905. Tchr. high sch., Lawrence, Mass., 1896-1900; prin. John R. Rollins Grammar Sch., Lawrence, 1900-13; supr. evening schs., Lawrence, 1912-13; supt. schs., Fall River, Mass., 1913-45, ret. Mem. Lawrence Bd. Tchr. Examiners, 1905-13; pres. Bristol County Tchrs.' Assn., 1914-15, Mass. Sch. Masters' Club, 1916-17, N.E. Assn. Sch. Supts., 1931-32, Fall River Rotary Club, 1932-33; sec. Mass. Special Com. on Higher Edn., 1922-24. Trustee Bradford Durfee Textile Sch. Pres. Fall River Council Boy Scouts, 1942-43; pres. Fall River Civic Music Assn., 1942-46. Recipient Silver Beaver award Boy Scouts Am. Mem. Am. Acad. Polit. and Social Sci., Harvard Tchrs. Assn., Franco-Am. Hist. Soc., Mass. Supts'. Assn., N.E.A. Author various papers on history and edn. Address: Fall River, Mass. Died Apr. 23, 1950.

BELK, William Henry, merchant; b. Lancaster County, S.C., June 2, 1862; s. Abel Nelson Washington and Sarah (Walkup) B.; ed. pvt. sch., Sharon, N.C., and high sch., Monroe, N.C.; LL.D., Davidson College, Davidson, N.C.; m. Mary Irwin, June 9, 1915; children—William Henry, Sarah Walkup, John Montgomery, Irwin, Henderson, Thomas Milburn. Began as owner N.Y. Racket Store, Monroe, 1888; now pres. Belk Brothers Co. dept. stores; also dir. various corps. Presbyterian. Mason, K.P. Club: Charlotte Country. Home: 220 Hawthorne Lane. Office: 308 E. 5th St., Charlotte, N.C. Died Feb. 21, 1952; buried Elmwood Cemetery, Charlotte, N.C.

BELKNAP, Charles (bĕl'năp), ret. univ. vice chancellor; b. Oakland, Md., Sept. 6, 1880; s. Charles and Fanny (Wheelwright) B.; student St. Pauls Sch., Concord, N.H., 1897-99; grad. U.S. Naval Acad., 1903; m. Helen M. Rockwood, Oct. 5, 1918. Commd. ensign USN, 1903, resigned, 1919, rank of comdr.; pres. Gen. S.S. Corp., San Francisco, 1919-21; v.p., later pres. Merrimac Chem. Co., Boston, 1921-35; v.p., later pres. Monsanto Chemical Co., St. Louis, 1935-46; vice chancellor Washington U., St. Louis, 1946-51; dir. Wabash R.R., Boatmen's Nat. Bank. Dir., St. Luke's Hosp., St. Louis chpt. A.R.C. Republican. Episcopalian. Clubs: Noonday, Country (St. Louis); University (N.Y.C.). Home: 45 Westmoreland St., St. Louis. Died Dec. 29, 1954.

BELKNAP, Reginald Rowan, naval officer, ret.; b. Malden, Mass., June 26, 1871; s. Rear Adm. George Eugene and Frances Georgiana (Prescott) B.; grad. U.S. Naval Acad., 1891; m. Julia Pomeroy Averill, March 31, 1900; children—Averill (Mrs. Andrew R. Mack), Frances G. (Mrs. Malcolm Edgar), Emilia F. (Mrs. Leonard Cresswell), Mary (Mrs. John Howard), Barberie Ann. Commd. ensign, July, 1893; promoted through grades to capt.; rear adm. by special act Congress for war service, Mar. 3, 1927: retired, 1927. Served in Spanish-American War, Chinese Boxer Campaign and Philippine Insurrection; naval attaché Berlin, 1907-10, Rome and Vienna, 1908-09; Bureau of Navigation, 1902-04, asst. chief, 1912-13, Office of naval operations, planning section, 1917; in charge Am. orgn., Messina earthquake, building dwellings, etc., for 16,000 homeless; war observer, Germany, Aug.-Oct. 1914; naval aide to Ex-President Theodore Roosevelt, special ambassador at funeral Edward VII, 1910; senior officer Santiago de Cuba Insurrection, 1917; invented and patented collapsible anti-submarine net; organized, equipped, trained and commanded U.S. Mine Squadron, personnel, laying 56,500 mines in North Sea, June-Oct. 1918; dir. strategy dept., Naval War Coll., 1921-23; commanded U.S.S. San Francisco, Delaware, Colorado and Naval Training Station, Hampton Roads, Va. Bursar, treas. Gen. Theol. Sem. N.Y.C., 1929-50. Awarded D.S.M. (U.S.); Officer Order Leopold (Belgium), Officer Legion of Honor (France). Exec. chmn. Mass. Bay Tercentenary, 1928; comdr. New York chpt. Mil. Order World War, 1931-35, nat. v.-comdr. in chief, 1933-36, comdr. in chief, 1936-37; comdr. gen. Naval Order, U.S., 1932-37; pres. Naval Academy Grads. Assn. of N.Y., 1934; mem. Nat. Aero. Assn., Loyal Legion of United States (comdr.-in-chief, 1947), Founders and Patriots of America. Episcopalian; warden of Trinity Ch.; mem. bd. mgrs. Seamen's Ch. Inst., N.Y.C.; mgr. Episcopal Gen. Conv., 1934; pres. Am. Ch. Union, 1937; del. to Episcopal Gen. Conv., 1937-49; chmn. Army Day Com., New York, 1934-46; chmn. exec. com., treas., Bundles for America; chmn. of exec. com., Laymen's National Com., 1945-50. Trustee Cathedral of St. John the Divine, 1941-53. Trustee Leake and Watts Childrens Home. Clubs: Yacht, Military-Naval, Union, Century, Church (New York); Army and Navy (Washington); Aero of N.E. (v.p.). Writer on naval subjects. Home: Field Elders, Madison, Conn. Died Mar. 30, 1959; buried Arlington Nat. Cemetery.

BELL, Bernard Iddings, clergyman; born in Dayton, O., Oct. 13, 1886; s. Charles Wright and Vienna Valencia (Iddings) B.; B.A., U. of Chicago, 1907; S.T.B., Western Theol. Sem., Chicago, 1912, D.D. from same, 1921; S.T.D., U. of the South, 1923; Litt.D. from Columbia U., 1929; LL.D., Colorado Coll., 1931; Ped.Doc., U. State of N.Y., 1933; Litt.D., Coe Coll., 1950; Dr. Humane Letters, Ohio Wesleyan, 1952; m. Elizabeth Wood Lee, April 24, 1912; 1 son, Bernard Lee (dec.). Became deacon and priest Episcopal Ch., 1910; vicar St. Christopher's Ch., Oak Park, Ill., 1910-13; dean St. Paul's Cathedral Ch., Fond du Lac, Wis., 1913-18, also examining chaplain to bishop of Fond du Lac; aide to sr. chaplain Great Lakes Naval Training Sta., Oct. 1, 1917-May 1, 1919; warden St. Stephen's Coll., Annandale-on-Hudson, N.Y., 1919-33; prof. religion, Columbia, U., 1930-33; preaching canon St. John's Cathedral, Providence, 1933-46; became canon of Cathedral of SS Peter and Paul, Chgo.; now canon St. James Cathedral Ch., Chgo.; consultant to Bishop of Chicago on education, 1946—. gen. consultant on religion and education, pastor of Episcopalians, University of Chicago, 1948—. William Vaughan Moody lecturer, Univ. of Chicago, 1931; Coleman lecturer, Lafayette Coll., 1935; Yarnall lecturer in English public schs., 1939; Gates lectr. Grinnell Coll., 1941; Merrich lectr. Ohio Wesleyan U., 1952. Mem. Phi Beta Kappa, Kappa Sigma. Mason. Clubs: University, (Chicago, Illinois); Authors' (London). Author: Right and Wrong After the War, 1918; Work of the Church for Men at War, 1919; The Good News, 1921; Post-modernism and Other Essays, 1925; Common Sense in Education, 1928; Beyond Agnosticism—A Book for Tired Mechanists, 1929; Unfashionable Convictions, 1931; The Holy Week, 1933; Men Wanted, 1993; Preface to Religion, 1935; O Men of God! (Bp. of London's Lenten Book), 1936; A Catholic Looks at His World, 1936; In the City of Confusion, 1938; The Priestly Way, 1938; Religion for Living, 1939; Christian Virtues, 1940; Understanding Religion, 1941; Still Shine the Stars, 1941; The Church in Disrepute, 1943; The Altar and the World, 1944; God Is Not Dead, 1945; A Man Can Live, 1946; Crisis in Education, 1949. Editor and contbr.: Affirmations, 1938. Editor: The St. James Lessons in Religion, 1940-45. University and cathedral preacher frequently in England, America and Canada. Address: 70 E. Walton St., Chgo. 11. Died Sept. 5, 1958.

BELL, Bert, football commr.; b. Phila., Pa., Feb. 25, 1894; s. John C. and Fleurette Bell; student, U. of Pa., married, Jan. 4, 1934; children—John Bert, George Upton, Jane. Commr. of Nat. Football League since Jan. 1946. Club: Racquet and Tennis (Phila.). Home: 323 Haverford Av., Narberth, Pa. Office: One Bala Av., Bala-Cynwyd, Pa. Died Oct. 11, 1959.

BELL, Edward August, painter; b. N.Y.C., Dec. 18, 1861; studied art N.A.D.; mem. Art Students' League, 1879; studied, 1881-83, under Von Loefftz at Munich; m. Julia Fitz Overton, Apr. 20, 1903. His pictures are usually symbolic or decorative in theme and carried out by the youthful female figure. Recipient silver medal Royal Acad., Munich; bronze medal, Paris Expn., 1889; 2d Hallgarten prize N.A.D., 1893; silver medal Buffalo Expn., 1901, St. Louis Expn., 1904. A.N.A. Home: Peconic, L.I., N.Y. Died July 4, 1953.

BELL, George Alfred, banker, mfr.; b. Brooklyn, N.Y., Sept. 22, 1878; s. George Alfred and Eliza Corinne (Chandler) B.; C.E., Rensselaer Poly. Inst., 1900); m. Alice R. McCulloch, Mar. 26, 1910; 1 son, John Lewis McCulloch. Chmn. bd. Marion (Ind.) Nat. Bank, Marion National Corp., Bell Fibre Products Corp.; pres. Marion Stove Co., Bell Buildings, Inc., Rutenber Electric Co., Bell Coal Co.; dir. Northwood Realty Co., Price-Hutchins Co. Mem. Marion Assn. Commerce (ex-pres.). Member Sigma Xi, Theta Xi. Republican. Mason, Elk, Moose. Clubs: Columbia (Indianapolis); Mecca, Mechingomesia Country, Marion Hunting (Marion Ind.); Indiana Soc. of Chicago, Union League (Chicago); Klinger Lake (Mich.); Surf, Bath, Com. of 100 (Miami Beach, Fla.); Key Largo Anglers (Key Largo, Fla.). Home: 1116 S. Boots St., Marion, Ind.; also 5743 Collins Av., Miami Beach, Fla. Office: Marion National Bank, Marion, Ind. Died Apr. 19, 1956.

BELL, George Kennedy Allen, bishop; b. Hayling Island, Eng., Feb. 4, 1883; s. James Allen and Sarah Georgina (Megaw) B.; scholar Westminster Sch., 1896-1901, Christ Ch., Oxford, 1901-05, Wells Theol. Coll., 1906-07; B.A. Oxford U., 1905, M.A., 1910, D.D., 1924; D.D., U. Glasgow, 1939, Wycliffe Coll., 1950; Th. D., U. Basle, 1939, U. Göttingen, U. Münster, 1949; LL. D., U. So. Cal., 1945; hon. student on Christ Church, Oxford, Eng., 1952; m. Henrietta Millicent Grace Livingstone, Jan. 8, 1918. Ordained to ministry Ch. of Eng., 1907; curate, Leeds, 1907-10; tutor Christ Ch., Oxford, 1910-14; resident chaplain to archbishop of Canterbury, 1914-24; dean, Canterbury, 1924-29; bishop, Chichester, 1929-58, resigned; select preacher Cambridge U., 1923, 33, 41, 46, 51, Oxford U., 1926-27, 47. Decorated Yugoslav Order of St. Sava; King Haakon of Norway Liberty Cross; Order of Merit (posthumously, German Govt.), 1958. Mem. Council Fgn. Relations (chmn. Ch. of Eng.), World Council Chs. (chmn. central com.). Clubs: Athenaeum (London); Union (Brighton, Eng.). Home: 1 Starr's House The Precincts, Canterbury, Kent, Eng. Died Oct. 3, 1958.

BELL, George L(ewis), assn. exec.; b. Pinos Altos, N.M., Feb. 3, 1888; s. Neil and Susan (Woolfolk) B.; L.B., U. of Calif., 1909; LL.B., Harvard, 1912; m. Rose Von Schmidt, June 1914 (div.); children—Patricia Anne, Gordon W. (dec.); m. Rachel Stice; 1 son, Neil. Asst. prof., Hasting Coll. of Law, U. of Calif., 1913-18; exec. officer and atty. Calif. State Commn. of Immigration and Housing, 1914-18; exec. officer U.S. War Labor Policies Bd., Washington, 1918-19; sole arbitrator men's clothing industry, N.Y. City, 1919-20; cons. in management and indsl. relations, San Francisco, 1920-27; vice pres. and dir., Caterpillar Tractor Co., San Leandro, Calif. and Peoria, Ill., 1927-34; exec. dir. Nat. Men's Clothing Code Authority, N.R.A., N.Y., 1934-35; vice pres. and dir. Am. Clorophyll, Inc., N.Y. City since 1935; chief gen. commodities branch, Bd. Economic Warfare, 1942-43; dir. Pan-Am. branch, and spec. asst. adminstr. Pacific War Theatre; Foreign Econs. Adminstrn. 1943-45; acting dir. Office Internat. Trade, Dept. Commerce, Washington, 1945-49; mem. U.S. Bd. Fgn. Service, 1947-49; chmn. Bd. of Alternates, U.S. Fgn. Trade Zones Bd., 1946-49; comml. attaché and econ. officer American Embassy, Paris, 1949-54; mgmt. consultant, 1954-55; executive vice chairman of committee for a National Trade Policy, 1955-56, president, 1957—. Decorated Officer French Legion of Honor. Club: Cosmos (Washington). Contbr. articles on international trade for trade jours. Home: 5305 Chamberlin Av., Kenwood, Chevy Chase, Md. Offic: 1025 Connecticut Av., Washington 6. Died Oct. 9, 1958.

BELL, John G., exec. v.p. Peoples Drug Stores; b. Union City, Tenn., Jan. 5, 1894; s. John and Margaret L. (Gibbs) B.; student high sch. and pharmacy sch.; m. Anna Belle Elgin, Sept. 17, 1921. With Peoples Drug Stores, Inc., Washington, 1913—, now exec. v.p., dir.; also dir. Am. Security & Trust Co. Pres. Mchts. and Mfrs. Assn., 1943-46. Mem. S.A.R., Friendly Sons of St. Patrick. Kiwanian. Home: 4550 30th St. N.W. Office: 77 P St. N.E., Washington. Died May 26, 1949.

BELL, Joseph B., advt. exec.; b. N.Y.C., July 28, 1900; s. Michael A. and Sara (Sheils) B.; student extension courses in accounting, law, financial mgmt., taxes; m. Edith Margaret Lenihan, Dec. 27, 1924; children—Joan T. (Mrs. John J. Ryan), Denise A. With Ruthrauff & Ryan, Inc., advt., 1928—, asst. treas., 1942-48, v.p., 1948—, treas., 1953—. Chmn. fiscal control group and chmn. planning com. N.Y.U. Mem. Am. Assn. Advt. Agencies (adminstrn. com.). Home: 61 Bronxville Rd., Bronxville 8, N.Y. Office: 405 Lexington Av., N.Y.C. 22. Deceased.

BELL, Kenneth C(arter), banker; b. Sakanjimba Sta., Angola, Africa, Mar. 26, 1895; s. Rev. Wilberforce and Agnes Alberta (Carter) Lee, missionaries, who died during his infancy; adopted parents, Cecil Joseph and Essie L. (Herrington) Bell; brought to U.S., 1897, derivative citizenship; student pub. schs., West Springfield, Mass., Malvern Collegiate Inst., Toronto, 1909-13; B.A., U. of Toronto, 1916; m. Katherine Totman, June 11, 1921; children—Marjorie Louise (Mrs. William H. Chambers), Barbara Blanche. With Chase Nat. Bank of City of N.Y. since 1919, clerk, 1919-25, asst. cashier, 1925-29, 2d vice pres., 1929-42, v.p. since 1942, secretary board of directors, 1947—, vice pres., cashier, 1950—. Member faculty Graduate School of Banking, Rutgers University, 1937-48. Served with Army Y.M.C.A., 1917-18; machinist mate, U.S. Navy, 1918-19. Sec. and dir. The Maple Leaf Fund, Inc., Canadian war relief orgn., 1940-45. Mem. Am. Soc. Corporate Secs. (ex-treas. and dir.), Nat. Assn. Ins. Commrs. (mem. Multiple Line com.), Am. Assn. Univ. Teachers of Ins., Am. Bankers Assn. (past mem. ins. com.), U.S. C. of C. (past mem. ins. com., Risk Research Inst., Inc. (past dir.), Canadian Soc. of N.Y. (dir.; pres. 1949-50). Republican. Presbyterian (trustee). Clubs: University of Toronto (past pres.) (New York); Scarsdale (N.Y.) Golf. Home: 28 Kingston Rd., Scarsdale, N.Y. Office: 18 Pine St., N.Y.C. 5. Died July 3, 1956; buried Maplelawn Cemetery, Fairfield, Me.

BELL, Lawrence Dale, airplane mfr.; b. Mentone, Ind., Apr. 5, 1894; s. Isaac Evans and Harriet (Sarber) B.; student Poly. High Sch., Santa Monica, Cal.; m. Lucille Mainwaring, July 17, 1915. Became shop foreman Glenn L. Martin Co., airplane mfrs., Los Angeles, 1912, later v.p. and gen. mgr.; became gen. sales mgr. Consol. Aircraft Corp., Buffalo, 1928, later v.p. and gen. mgr.; with associates organized Bell Aircraft Corp., 1935; completed airplane, the Airacuda, twin-engine fighting plane mounting 2 cannons, 1937; began making the Airacobra, pursuit plane with 1 cannon, 1939, in mass production for U.S. Army. Pres. Aircraft War Prodn. Council, East Coast, Inc.; pres. Nat. Aircraft War Prodn. Council. Received (with John Stack and Charles E. Yeager) Collier trophy for aid in supersonic flight; chairman board W. J. Schoenberger Co., Cleve., Erie Ins. Co.; dir. Irving Airchute Co., Niagara Share Corp. Mem. Soc. Aeronaut. Sciences, Aero Club of Buffalo (pres. 1932-34), Aircraft Industries Assn. (board govs.) Mason. Clubs: Buffalo, Buffalo Country, Saturn. Home: 925 Delaware Av. Office: Bell Aircraft Corp., P.O. Box 1, Buffalo 5. Died Oct. 20, 1956.

BELL, Ovid, printing; b. Callaway County, Mo., June 10, 1875; s. John P. and Emma Keen (Gilbert) B.; student Westminster Coll., Fulton, Mo., 1893-94; m. Lucy Maud Hall, Sept. 4, 1912; 1 son, Ovid H. (officer Signal Corps, U.S. Army). Sec. to Congressman Richard Parks (Silver Dick) Bland, 1897-99; reporter with Washington bureau, Phila. North American, 1899-1900; editor and owner Fulton (Mo.) Gazette, 1901-27; founder Evening Gazette, 1916; pres. The Ovid Bell Press, Inc., since 1927. Mem. Dem. State Com. of Mo., 1904-08, sec., 1904-06. Pres. Mo. Press Assn., 1913. Mem. Phi Delta Theta. Jeffersonian Democrat. Presbyn. Mason, Rotarian. Author: Short History of Callaway County, Missouri, 1913; Cote sans Dessein, a History (Missouri item), 1930; History First Presbyterian Church, Fulton, Mo., 1948; The Story of the Kingdom of Callaway, 1952. Contributor numerous articles on Missouri history to newspapers and mags. Home: 825 Court St. Office: 1201-05 Bluff St., Fulton, Mo. Died Apr. 3, 1953.

BELL, Ulric, exec., writer; b. Louisville, Ky., Dec. 13, 1891; s. William James and Caroline (Wellington) B.; LL.D., George Washington U., 1935; children—Elidabeth (Peddie), George Ulric, Ulrica; m. Vivian Hall, Jan. 22, 1955. Reporter Louisville Courier-Journal, 1910, city ed., 1919-20, Washington corr., 1921-41; exec. chmn. Fight For Freedom, Inc., 1941; asst. dir. U.S. Office Facts and Figures, Jan.-July 1942; dep. dir. overseas br., O.W.I., 1942-44; exec. v.p. Americans United for World Orgn., 1944-46; executive asst. to pres. 20th Century Fox Film Corp., 1947—; press advisor Cordell Hull, U.S. delegate, 7th International Conf. of Am. States, Montevideo, Uruguay, and during Sec. Hull's tour of S. America, 1933-34. Capt. 83d Inf., 17th Div., at close of World War I. Contbr. to mags. Clubs: Gridiron (pres. 1935), Nat. Press (pres. 1926); Salmagundi. Co-author: Why Korea (motion picture academy award documentary), 1951. Home: 44 West 10th St., N.Y.C. 11. Office: 444 West 56th St., N.Y.C. 19. Died Jan. 1960.

BELL, William Allen, pres. Antioch Coll. since June, 1899; b. Clinton Co., Ind., Jan. 30, 1833; s. Nathaniel and Nancy B.; grad. Antioch Coll., 1860 (A. M., LL.D.); was student at Antioch Coll. under Horace Mann, its 1st pres. Lived at Indianapolis most of life until assuming present position; was prin. high school there. For past 30 yrs. editor and publisher Ind. School Journal (for teachers). Address: Yellow Springs, O. Died Dec. 10, 1906.

BELL, William Brown, mfr., lawyer; b. Stroudsburg, Pa., Feb. 16, 1879; s. Thomas Alsop and Elizabeth (Dunn) B.; A.B., Haverford Coll., 1900; M.A. in Polit. Sci., Columbia, 1901, LL.B., 1903; m. Susan Alsop, Nov. 7, 1903 (died Nov. 4, 1949); 1 dau., Helen Griscom (Mrs. Allen D. Hole, Jr.); m. 2d, Marion Walters, Dec. 2, 1950. Admitted to N.Y. bar, 1903, began practice in N.Y.C.; pres. Am. Cyanamid Co., N.Y.C., 1922—; pres., dir. Davis & Geck, Inc.; v.p., dir. So. Alkali Co., So. Petroleum Corp., So. Minerals Corp., So. Pipe Line Corp.; chmn. bd., dir. So. Chem. Corp., Jefferson Chem. Co.; trustee Guarantee Trust Co. Trustee Haverford Coll., Duke Endowment. Sloan Found.; mem. adv. com. Howard Sch. Pub. Health. Mem. Phi Beta Kappa. Republican. Quaker. Clubs: University, Royale Sporting (Bilbao, Spain). Winner King's Cup, Spanish ocean race, New York to Santander, 1928, with his yacht, Elena. Home: 1115 Fifth Av., N.Y.C. 28. Office: 30 Rockefeller Plaza, N.Y.C. 20. Died Dec. 20, 1950; buried Trenton, N.J.

BELLAMANN, Katherine, author; b. Carthage, Miss.; d. Ephraim Harris and Emma (Williams) Jones; student Miss. schs.; spl. studies N.Y. City, Paris, London; m. Henry Hauer Bellamann, Sept. 3, 1907. Profl. musician, 1907-43; head voice dept. Chicora Coll., Columbia, S.C., 1907-24; singer, tchr. N.Y. City, 1924-44; novelist. Author: My Husband's Friends, 1931; Parris Mitchell of Kings Row (collaborated with late husband), 1948; The Hayvens of Demaret, 1951. Awarded prize sonnet sequence, A Poet Passed This Way, 1949, Unwelcome Spring, 1950; mem. editorial bd. The Pen Woman, 1954—; adv. editor The Lyric, 1954—. Recipient Lyric Sonnet Award, 1953, Alan Swallow Publ. Award, 1954. Mem. Internat. Mark Twain Soc., Bethoven Assn., Author's League Am., Nat. League Am. Pen Women, Miss., Va. poetry socs. Unitarian. Lit. editor The Young Music Lover, 1933. Contbr. lit., mus. mags. Lectr. poetry, novel, 1945-51. Home: 745 S. Prentiss St., Jackson, Miss. Died Nov. 8, 1956; buried Church of Heavenly Rest, N.Y.C.

BELLAMY, F. Wilder, business exec.; b. 1887; grad. Yale, 1909. Sr. partner Dominick & Dominick, N.Y.C.; dir. Bullock Fund. Ltd., Nat. Distillers Products. Home: Katonah, N.Y. Office: 14 Wall St., N.Y.C. 5. Died Oct. 24, 1955. *

BELLAMY, Paul, editor; b. Chicopee Falls, Mass., Dec. 26, 1884; s. Edward and Emma (Sanderson) B.; A.B., Harvard, 1905; Litt.D., Ohio Wesleyan University, 1939; Litt.D., Oberlin Coll., 1941; LL.D., Kent State U.; m. Marguerite Scott Stark, July 7, 1908; children—John (dec.), Richard King, Peter, Joan Marguerite; m. 2d, Mary Jane Mitchell, Nov. 21, 1941. Began as reporter, Springfield (Mass.) Union, 1905; with Cleveland Plain Dealer, 1907-16; v.p. and sec. The Credit Co., Chicago, 1916-18; spl. writer, Cleveland Plain Dealer, 1919, mng. editor, 1920-33, editor, 1933-53, editor emeritus, 1953—. Attended F.A. Central Officers' Training Sch., Camp Zachary Taylor, Ky.; 1st lt. F.A., O.R.C. Pres. Am. Soc. Newspaper Editors, 1933-34; mem. President's com. on Draft Deferment of Federal Employes, 1943. Clubs: Cleveland City; Harvard (New York); Hermit, Union. Home: 13211 Lake Shore Blvd., Bratenahl, O. Office: Plain Dealer Bldg., Cleve. Died Apr. 12, 1956; buried Lakeview Cemetery, Cleve.

BELLATTI, C. Robert (bĕl-lăt'tĭ), editor, pub.; b. Jacksonville, Ill., Dec. 2, 1886; s. Robert M. and Martha (Fitzhugh) B.; B.S., Lincoln (Ill.) Coll., 1908; LL.B., U. of Okla., 1912; m. Edith Skidmore Hoblit, 1908; children—Robert Marsden, Lawrence Fitzhugh, Mary Edith, Alvin Edward (dec.), James Richard. Admitted to Okla. bar, 1912, and began practice at Blackwell; engaged in town development and law practice since 1912; editor and pub. Blackwell Morning Tribune, 1920-40; now publisher Stillwater Daily News-Press; pres. Sta. KSPI. Formerly regent Okla. A. and M. Colls., now mem. indsl. council. Mem. Okla. Civil Def. Council. Formerly mem. Okla. State Bd. Edn., Stillwater Chamber of Commerce (dir.), Sigma Delta Chi, Phi Delta Phi. Dem. Presbyterian. Mason. Clubs: Lions, Country. Home: 2018 W. Sunset Dr. Office: News-Press Bldg., Stillwater, Okla. Died July 22, 1953.

BELLEZZA, Russell G., industrialist; born Norfolk, Va., Sept. 26, 1897; s. Antonio and Lydia (Granbery) E.; B.S., Va. Mil. Inst., 1918, E.E. (post grad.), 1929; B.S. in E.E., Mass. Inst. Tech., 1923, M.S., 1923; m. Marian Thompson; children—Russell Granbery, Marcia Thompson. Asso. prof. and capt., Va. Militia, Va. Mil. Inst., 1919-20; student mgr. street lighting sect., 1926, mgr. of sales cable div., 1929; v.p. in charge of sales Locke, Inc., Balt., 1936, v.p., gen. mgr., 1937, pres., 1939-50, chmn. bd., 1950; v.p. Gen. Cable Corp., N.Y.C., 1950—; asst. adminstr. Bus. and Def. Adminstrn., Dept. Commerce, Washington, 1956-57; asst. to asst. sec. health, edn. and welfare, 1957—. Served as lt., heavy arty., World War I. Mem. Nat. Elec. Mfrs. Assn. Clubs: Siwanoy Country (Bronxville); Mohawk (Schenectady); University (N.Y.C.); Baltimore Country; Corinthian Yacht (Marblehead, Mass.). Home: 3925 Beech Av., Balt. 11. Office: Dept. Health, Edn. and Welfare Bldg., Washington 25. Died Jan. 13, 1958; buried Druid Ridge Cemetery, Balt.

BELLOC, Hilaire, author, poet, historian; b. July 27, 1870; s. Louis Swanton and Bessie Rayner (Parkes) B.; student Oratory Sch., Edgbaston, and Balliol Coll., Oxford U.; Brackenbury history scholar and 1st Class in Honour History Schs., 1895; m. Elodie Agnes Hogan, 1896; 4 children. Served as driver 8th Regt., French Army. Decorated Knight Comdr. with Star, Order of St. Gregory the Great, 1934. Author: Cruise of Nona, 1925; Mr. Petre, 1925; Economics for Young People, 1925; History of England from the Earliest Times to the Beginning of the Present Century, 1925; On Nothing and Kindred Subjects, 1925; Miniatures of French History, 1926; Catholic Church and History, 1926; Highway and Its Vehicles, 1926; Emerald of Catherine the Great, 1926; Napoleon's Campaign of 1812 and the Retreat from Moscow, 1926; Short Talks with the Dead, 1926; Robespierre, 1927; Companion to Mr. Wells' Outline of History, 1927; Towns of Destiny, 1927; Oliver Cromwell, 1928; Haunted House, 1928; Chanty of the Nona, 1928; James the Second, 1928; How the Reformation Happened, 1928; Wandering, 1929; Short History of England, 1929; Shadowed, 1929; Picked Company, 1929; Missing Masterpiece, 1929; Joan of Arc, 1929; Hills and the Sea, 1929; Conversation with an Angel, 1929; Belinda, 1929; Survivals and New Arrivals, 1929; Sonnets and Verse, 1929; Richelieu, 1929; Man Who Shall Make Gold, 1930; Green Overcoat, 1930; Four Men, 1930; Usury, 1931; Six British Battles, 1931; On Translation, 1931; On Something, 1931; Conversation with a Cat, 1931; Avril, 1931; New Cautionary Tales, 1931; Essays of a Catholic Layman in England, 1931; Conversation with an Angel, 1931; Nine Nines or Novenas, 1931; Crammer, Archbishop of Canterbury, 1533-1556, 1931; Question and the Answer, 1932; Napoleon, 1932; Moral Alphabet, 1932; Ladies and Gentlemen, 1932; Question and the Answer, 1932; Charles The First, King of England, 1933; Belinda, 1933; Tactics and Strategy of the Great Duke of Marlborough, 1933; But Soft, We Are Observed, 1933; Shorter History of England, 1934; Cromwell, 1934; William the Conqueror, 1934; Milton, 1935; Selected Essays, 1936; Hedge and the Horse, 1936; First and Last, 1936; Essay on the Restoration of Property, 1936; County of Sussex, 1936; Characters of the Reformation, 1936; Battleground, Syria and Palestine, 1936; Issue, 1937; Essay on the Nature of Contemporary England, 1937; Crusades, 1937; Jews, 3d edit., 1937; Crises of Civilization, 1937; Stories, Essays and Poems, 1938; Return to the Baltic, 1938; Mercy of Allah, 1938; Marie Antoinette, 1938; Louis XIV, 1938; Hedge and the Horse, 1938; Great Heresies, 1938; Economics for Helen, 1938; Charles II, The Last Rally, 1939; Cautionary Verse, 1939; Case of Dr. Coulton, 1938; on Sailing the Sea, 1939; Charles The First, King of England, 1939; Silence of the Sea, and other Essays, 1940; Characters of the Reformation, 1940; Catholic and the War, 1940; On the Place of Gilbert Chesterton in English Letters, 1941; Elizabeth; Creature of Circumstance, 1942. Address: King's Land, Shipley, Horsham, England. Died July 16, 1953.*

BELLOWS, Robert Peabody, architect; b. N.Y. City, Nov. 3, 1877; s. Henry Whitney and Anna H. (Peabody) B.; A.B., Harvard, 1899; study Mass. Inst. Tech., 1901-03; grad. Ecole des Beaux Arts, Paris, 1907; unmarried. Mem. Bellows & Aldrich, 1907-24; alone since 1924. Archtl. adviser to Williamsburg (Va.) Restoration; archtl. adviser, Radcliffe Coll., 1930-31. Awarded Médaille de la Reconnaissance Française (French). Trustee Boston Athenaeum. Fellow American Institute Architects; mem. Boston Soc. Architects (ex-pres.), Boston Archtl. Club (ex-pres.), Soc. Beaux Arts Architects, Société des Architectes Diplômés par le Gouvernement Français; mem. Boston Society of Water Color Painters; archtl. adviser Northeastern U., 1934; chmn. adv. committee Mass. Historic Am. Buildings Survey; mem. exec. com. Architects of New England Exhibit at N.Y. World's Fair, 1939. Trustee Boston Museum of Fine Arts. Mem. Mass. Hist. Soc., N.A.D. (asso.). Unitarian. Clubs: Union, Somerset, Tibonet (Boston). Home: 8 Park St., Boston. Died May 23, 1957.

BELMONT, Morgan, investment banker; b. Hempstead, L.I., N.Y., Mar. 19, 1892; s. August and Elizabeth (Morgan) B.; grad. St. Mark's Sch., 1910; A.B., Harvard, 1914; m. Margaret Andrews, Aug. 14, 1915 (dec. 1945); children—Joan (dec.), Morgan (dec.); m. 2d Helen B. Hildreth, June 4, 1949. Mem. staff August Belmont & Co., 1915, became sr. partner, 1925; now retired. Lt. Air Service, in France and Italy, Feb. 1918-Jan. 1919, World War I; on active duty as major, Air Corps, Army U.S., Oct. 1942-Sept. 1945. Home: East Hampton, L.I., N.Y. Office: 50 Broad St., N.Y.C. Deceased.

BELSTERLING, Charles Starne (bĕl-stẽr'lĭng), counsel and counselor-at-law; b. Phila., May 31, 1874; s. William Franklin and Ida Julia (Sutterle) B.; student Neff College of Philadelphia, Western U. Pa. Law Sch.; m. Florence Fries, June 1, 1898; children—Edna Marion (Mrs. Harold Gilman Dow), Florence Dorothy (Mrs. Sturges Mason Schley), Ruth Martha; m. 2d, Helen Gunter Jackson, May 21, 1931. With A. & P. Roberts Co., Phila., 1892-99; with Am. Bridge Co., 1899-1910; admitted to bar, Pa., 1904, U.S. Supreme Ct., 1917, N.Y., 1917; gen. commerce attorney U.S. Steel Corp., 1914-32, v.p. 1932-42. Member Maritime Commn. Practitioners, Assn. Bar City N.Y., Assn. of Interstate Commerce Practitioners, Am. Iron and Steel Inst., Soc. Colonial Wars State of N.Y., S.R., So. War of 1812, Hist. Soc. of Frankford, Huguenot Soc. of Am., Colonial Soc. of Pa., Pa. Soc. of N.Y., Friends Hist. Soc. Episcopalian. Mason (K.T., Shriner). Clubs: Traffic (hon.), Railroad (N.Y.C.); Traffic (hon.) (Pitts.). Home: 1230 Park Av. Office: 71 Broadway, N.Y.C. 6. Died Dec. 1959.

BELT, Harry H., judge; b. Salem, Ore., Nov. 24, 1883; s. John D. and Nellie (Hacklemen) B.; ed. Dallas Acad. and Ore. State Normal Sch.; m. Martha Paldanius, July 3, 1905; children—Barbara, Myra, George. County sch. supt. Yamhill County, Ore., 1907-10; admitted to Ore. bar, 1910, and began practice at Dallas; judge Circuit Court, 1914-24; elected asso. justice Supreme Court of Ore., 1925; chief justice, Supreme Court, 1945-47. Republican. Episcopalian. Mason, K.P. Home: Salem, Ore. Died Aug. 6, 1950.

BEMENT, Alon, artist, educator; b. Ashfield, Mass., Aug. 15, 1876; s. Emery and Lucy Emma (Williams) B.; diploma Boston Mus. Sch. Fine Arts, 1898, Näas Sloyd Sch., Floda, Sweden, 1899, Académie Julian, Paris, 1900-02, Nat. École des Beaux Arts; m. Katherine Emmet, 1914. Tutor, instr. fine arts Coll. City N.Y., 1902-06; instr., asst. prof. fine arts Tchrs. Coll. Columbia, 1906-19; dir. Md. Inst., 1920-25; dir. Art Center, N.Y.C., 1925-32; dir. Nat. Alliance of Art and Industry, N.Y.C.; dir. League of N.H. Arts and Crafts, 1943-45; dean Traphagen Sch. of Fashion, N.Y.C., 1946—. Exhibited Soc. Am. Artists, N.A.D., Am. Water Color Soc. Author: Figure Construction, 1921; Constructive Design, 1925; American Heritage of Taste. Home: 400 E. 23d St., Peter Cooper Village, N.Y.C. Died Nov. 23, 1954.

BENCHOFF, Howard Johnston, headmaster; b. Rouzerville, Pa., July 15, 1876; s. Loudon Francis and Martha Belle (Johnston) B.; A.B., Franklin and Marshall Coll., 1898, Pd.D., 1922; A.M., Columbia, 1904; m. Kathryn Leona Mahon, Aug. 17, 1904; children—Howard Francis (dec.), Rosalie Keith, Robert Johnston, Kathryn Mahon (dec.), Josephine Harbaugh (dec.); m. 2d, Florence Conant, Sept. 14, 1920. Vice prin. high sch., Chambersburg, Pa., 1898-1900, prin., 1900-03; supt. schs. Breckenridge, Colo., 1904-05; headmaster Massanutten Acad., 1905-55, headmaster emeritus, 1955-58. Pres. Shenandoah Valley, Inc., 1925, Shenandoah Nat. Park Assn., Va. Prep. Sch. Assn., 1938-39; dir. Appalachian Nat. Parks. Republican. Mem. Reformed Ch. in U.S. Mason, Rotarian (1st pres. Woodstock). Lectr. ednl. and religious topics. Home: Woodstock, Va. Died Apr. 7, 1958; buried Woodstock, Va.

BENDER, Harold H(erman), philologist; b. Martinsburg, W.Va., Apr. 20, 1882; s. Isaac Lewis and Margaret Eleanor (Kline) B.; A.B., Lafayette Coll., 1903; Ph.D., Johns Hopkins, 1907; student U. Berlin, 1907-08; Dr. Lithuanian Philology, U. Kaunas, Lithuania, 1922; Litt.D., Lafayette Coll., 1924; m. Amelia Ashcom Hetzel, Sept. 3, 1910; 1 son, John Lewis. Univ. scholar Johns Hopkins, 1904-05, univ. fellow in Sanskrit and comparative philology, 1906-07; instr. modern langs. Princeton, 1909-12, asst. prof., 1912-18, prof. Indo-Germanic philology, 1918, chmn. dept. Oriental langs. and lits., 1927-44, M. Taylor Pyne prof. of Indo-Germanic philology, 1939-50, emeritus from 1950. Clerk of County Ct., Berkeley County, W.Va., 1908; draft registrar, War Dept., Princeton U., 1917; mem. House Inquiry of State Dept., 1918; German expert Dept. of Justice, 1918; Lithuanian translator Port Office Dept., 1917-18; chmn. Near East Relief Fund, Princeton, 1918; cons. lang. expert Mergenthaler Linotype Co. since 1927. Fellow A.A.A.S.; life mem. Am. Philol. Assn., Am. Oriental Soc. (dir. 1923-26, 27-30, 33-36, v.p. 1931-33, 46-47, pres. 1947-48); mem. Com. for Promotion Oriental Research (chmn. 1934-45), Modern Humanities Research Assn. (Eng.), Am. Assn. U. Profs. (mem. council 1923-26), Oriental Club Phila. (pres. 1923-24), Linguistic Soc. Am. (a founder; v.p. 1931, 1936; trustee 1940), Soc. Advancement Scandinavian Study, Internat. Soc. Exptl. Phonetics (London), N.J. Soc. of S.R., St. David's Soc. of N.Y. (life), Phi Beta Kappa, Phi Delta Theta. Mem., former chmn. com. on Indic and Iranian studies Am. Council Learned Socs.; mem. and collaborator Internat. Auxiliary Lang. Assn.; patron and hon. mem. Baltic Am. Soc. Trustee Am. Sch. of Indic and Iranian Studies since 1934; mem. academic com. Baltic U., Hamburg, Germany; mem. adv. bd. Am. Council Learned Socs., 1935-39. Del. Internat. Congress Orientalists, Oxford, Eng., 1928. Decorated Knight of Order of Gediminas, Grand Duke of Lithuania, 1928. Contbr. to Am., European philol. jours., various articles on grammar, syntax, accent and etymology; contbr. to Dictionary of Am. Biography, etc.; writer of etymologies, and spl. editor philology and linguistics, including langs. and tables of langs., Webster's New Internat. Dictionary, 2d edit., 1934. Author: The suffixes "mant" and "vant" in Sanskrit and Avestan, 1910; German Short Stories, 1920; A Lithuanian Etymological Index, 1921; The Home of the Indo-Europeans, 1922; The Selection of Undergraduates, 1926. Home: 7 Chambers Terrace, Princeton, N.J.; (summer) Orient, L.I., N.Y. Died Aug. 16, 1951; buried Princeton, N.J.

BENEDICT, Andrew Bell, univ. adminstr.; b. Nashville, July 21, 1885; s. Andrew Bell and Phoebe Frances (Barrett) B.; Ph.C., Vanderbilt U., 1904, grad. study 1904-05; m. Anne Hillman Scales, Apr. 9, 1913; children—Andrew Bell, Grace Hillman (Mrs. T. F. Paine, Jr.). With Citizens Bank, Seneca, S.C., 1905-06, Nashville Trust Co., 1906-27, 1st v.p., 1922-27; v.p. Ward-Belmont Sch., Nashville, 1927-38, pres., 1938-39; member bd. trustees Vanderbilt U., 1930—, treas., 1932-39, treas.-comptroller, 1939—; dir. Nashville & Decatur R.R. Mem. bd. trustees Joint U. Libraries, Meharry Med. Coll., Nashville, Nashville Sch. Social Work. Mem. Kappa Sigma. Republican. Methodist. Mason. Club: Belle Meade Country

(Nashville). Home: R.F.D. 5, Curtis Woods Lane, Nashville 4. Died May 18, 1953; buried Mt. Olivet Cemetery, Nashville.

BENEDICT, Francis Gano; b. Milwaukee, Wis., Oct. 3, 1870; s. Washington Gano and Harriet Emily (Barrett) B.; A.B., Harvard, 1893; A.M., 1894; Ph.D., U. of Heidelberg, 1895; Sc.D., Wesleyan U., Conn., 1911, U. of Me., 1924; hon. M.D., U. of Wurzburg, 1932; m. Cornelia Golay, July 28, 1897; 1 dau., Elizabeth Harriet. Instr. chemistry, Mass. Coll. Pharmacy, 1892-94; instr. and asso. prof. chemistry, Wesleyan U., 1896-1905, prof., 1905-07; dir. Nutrition Lab. of Carnegie Instn. of Washington, 1907-37. Chemist Storrs Expt. Station, 1896-1900; physiol. chemist of nutrition investigations of U.S. Dept. Agr., 1895-1907. Magician; lecturer, Science and Art of Deception. Fellow Am. Acad. Arts and Sciences, A.A.A.S.; mem. Soc. of Am. Magicians, Am. Chem. Soc., Am. Physiol. Soc., Nat. Acad. Sciences, Am. Philos. Soc., Soc. Royale des Sciences Medicales et Naturelles de Bruxelles, Gessellschaft der Aerzte (Vienna), Kaiserlich Deutsche Akademie der Naturforscher (Halle); corr. mem. Royal Med. Soc. of Budapest, Hungary, 1934. Author: Elementary Organic Analysis, 1900; Chemical Lecture Experiments, 1901. Extensive contbr. of chem. papers, principally on organic and physiol. chemistry to tech. jours. and procs.; also numerous monographs pub. by Carnegie Instn. of Washington. Home: Machiasport, Me. Died May 14, 1957; buried Mt. Auburn Cemetery, Cambridge, Mass.

BENEDICT, Jay Leland, army officer; b. Hastings, Neb., Apr. 14, 1882; s. Fred Jay and Eliza (Calvert) B.; B.S., U.S. Mil. Acad., 1904; hon. grad. Command and Gen. Staff School, 1925; grad. Army War Coll., 1926; m. Dr. Loretta K. Maher, June 14, 1924; 1 dau., Margaret Ann (wife of Capt. Wilbur H. Vinson, Jr., U.S. Army). Private and sergt. Neb. Nat. Guard, 1898-99; commd. 2d lt. inf., U.S. Army, 1904, and advanced through the grades to maj. gen., Oct. 2, 1940; instr. U.S. Mil. Acad., 1908-12 and 1916-17; maj. and lt. col. field arty. and col. inf. during World War I; gen. staff War Dept., 1920-24, and 1926-30; insp. gen. Hawaiian Dept., 1930-34; chief of staff 8th Corps Area, 1937-38; supt. U.S. Mil. Acad., 1938-40; comdg. 4th Army Corps, Nov. 1940-Sept. 1941; comdg. 9th Corps Area, 1941-42; on duty in War Dept., 1942-46; Retd. May 1, 1946. Awarded D.S.M., Legion of Merit. Episcopalian. Clubs: Army and Navy, Army-Navy Country. Home: 4606 Langdrum Lane, Chevy Chase 15, Md. Died Sept. 16, 1953.

BENEDUM, Michael Late, oil operator; b. Bridgeport, W.Va., July 16, 1869; s. Emanuel and Caroline Victoria (Southworth) B.; student pub. schs., Bridgeport; LL.D., Bucknell U., 1940, West. Va. U., 1940, Allegheny Coll., 1941; m. Sarah Nancy Lantz, May 17, 1896 (dec.); 1 son, Claude Worthington (dec.). Asst. gen. mgr. land dept., S. Penn Oil Co., 1889-1900; with J. C. Trees, formed Benedum Trees Oil Co., independent oil operators, employed principally in development of new properties, U.S. Mex., S. Am.; pres. Benedum Trees Oil Co., 1900—, Benedum Trees Co. 1913—; dir. Fidelity Trust Co. Rep. on NRA Planning and Coördinating Com. under oil code, 1933; mem. Bus. Adv. and Planning Council U.S. Dept. Commerce, 1933. Trustee Grove City (Pa.) Coll.; dir. Western Pa. Hosp., Pitts. Trustee Bucknell U., Lewisburg, Pa. Mem. U.S., U. Pa. Bicentennial Commn. by apptmt. President Roosevelt, 1940. Mem. Am. Petroleum Inst., Pitts. C. of C. Democrat. Methodist. Mason. Clubs: Pittsburgh, Pittsburgh Athletic, Duquesne (Pitts.); Longue Vue (Verona, Pa.); Oakmont (Pa.) Country. Home: Woodland Rd. Office: 1506 Benedum-Trees Bldg., Pitts. 22. Died July 30, 1959.

BENET, Christie (bĕn'ĕt), lawyer; b. Abbeville, S.C., Dec. 26, 1879; s. William Christie and Susan (McGowan) B.; A.B., Coll. of Charleston, 1900; B.L., U. of Va., 1902; student U. of S.C., 1897-98, LL.D. (hon.), 1946; m. Alice Van Yeveren Haskell, October 17, 1906; children—Christie (deceased), Alice Van Yeveren (wife of Porcher P. Hopkins). Admitted to S.C. bar, 1903; solicitor 5th Judicial Circuit, S.C., 1908-09; atty. City of Columbia, 1910-12; U.S. senator from S.C. for short term, 1918. Life trustee Clemson Agrl. Coll.; bd. of regents S.C. State Hosp., 1915-47; chmn. Alien Enemy Hearing Bd., Eastern Dist. S.C.; chmn. War Finance Com. for S.C., World War II. Mem. Am., S.C. and Richland County bar assns. (pres. South Carolina Bar Association, 1946-47), Phi Delta Phi, Phi Beta Kappa, Alpha Tau Omega, Omicron Delta Kappa. Democrat. Episcopalian. Clubs: Cosmos, Columbia, Forest Lake Rotary (Columbia). Home: 808 Pickens St. Office: Liberty Life Bldg., Columbia 1, S.C. Died March 30, 1951; buried Elmwood Cemetery, Columbia, S.C.

BENÉT, William Rose, poet, author; b. Fort Hamilton, New York Harbor, Feb. 2, 1886; s. James Walker and Frances Neill (Rose) B.; grad. Albany (N.Y.) Acad., 1904; Ph.B., Sheffield Sci. Sch. (Yale), 1907; M.A. (hon.), Yale, June 1921; Litt.D., Dickinson Coll., Oct. 1933; m. Teresa Frances Thompson, Sept. 3, 1912 (died Jan. 26, 1919); children—James Walker, II, Frances Rosemary (Mrs. Richard S. Dawson), Kathleen Anne (Mrs. George B. Fry); m. 2d, Elinor Wylie, Oct. 5, 1923 (died 1928); m. 3d, Lora Baxter, Mar. 15, 1932 (div. 1937); m. 4th, Marjorie Flack, June 1941. Free lance writer, mostly poetry, 1907-11, reader Century mag., 1911-14, asst. editor, 1914-18. Commd. 2d lt. U.S. Air Service, non-flying, Feb. 28, 1918; hon. disch., Dec. 1918; with Corman Co. (N.Y.) advt. service, Jan.-July 1919; asst. editor The Nation's Business, Washington, 1919-20; asso. editor Lit. Rev. of New York Evening Post, 1920-24; asso. editor Sat. Rev. of lit., 1924-29, now contbg. editor; editor Brewer & Warren, Inc., 1929-30. Mem. Nat. Inst. Arts and Letters (sec.). Club: Elizabethan (Yale U.). Author: (poems) Merchants from Cathay, 1913; The Falconer of God, 1914; The Great White Wall, 1916; The Burglar of the Zodiac, 1918; Perpetual Light (a memorial to T.F.B.), 1919; Moons of Grandeur, 1920; The First Person Singular (novel), 1922; The Flying King of Kurio (story for children), 1926; Wild Goslings, 1927; Man Possessed (poems), 1927; Rip Tide (a novel in verse), 1932; Starry Harness (verse), 1933; Golden Fleece (poems), 1935; With Wings as Eagles: Air Ballads, 1940; The Dust Which Is God (narrative poem), 1941; Day of Deliverance, A Book of Poems in Wartime, 1944; The Stairway of Surprise (verse), 1947. Translator: (with Teresa Benet) The East I Know (by Claudel), 1914. Editor: Poems for Youth, 1923; Fifty Poets—An Auto-Anthology, 1933. Co-editor: (with Canby and Drinkwater) Twentieth Century Poetry, 1930; (with Norman H. Pearson) The Oxford Anthology of Am. Lit., 1938; (with Norman Cousins) The Poetry of Freedom, An Anthology, 1945; Day's End: A Fantasia in One Act; Dock Street Theatre, Charleston, S.C. (nat. Playwriting award, produced May 8, 1939); Adolphus the Adopted Dolphin (children's book, with Marjorie Flack), 1941; Timothy's Angels (Children's book), 1947. Editor The Reader's Encyclopedia, 1948. Teacher and lecturer at Mills Coll., summers, 1936-37. Awarded the Pulitzer prize for poetry, 1942. Home: N.Y.C. Died May 4, 1950.

BENITZ, William Logan, educator; b. Pitts., Oct. 26, 1872; s. Anthony Edward and Emma Jane (Logan) B.; M.E., E.E., Cornell U., 1896; M.M.E., Notre Dame U., 1913; m. Eleanor Matilda Howard, June 12, 1901; children—William Howard, William Logan (dec.), Paul Anthony, Timothy Edward. Began teaching at Notre Dame U., 1896, prof. mech. engring., 1896—; city electrician of South Bend, 1901. K.C. Home: 1341 E. Wayne St. N., South Bend, Ind. Deceased.

BENJAMIN, Raymond, lawyer; b. Vallejo, Calif., Dec. 14, 1872; s. E. M. and Ruth S. (Mahon) B.; Napa (Calif.) Coll., 1887-91; m. Mildred Francis, May 27, 1902 (died June 1938); 1 dau., Barbara; m. 2d, Hazel Weglein, Nov. 14, 1942. Admitted practice Calif., 1893, U.S. Supreme Court, 1915; dist. atty. Napa County, 1902-08; chief dep. atty. gen. of Calif., 1908-19; atty. for state ins. commr., and supt. of banks, 1919-22; represented state in all tax litigation, 1911-24; chmn. Rep. State Com., 1918-22; regional dir. Rep. Nat. Com., 1918-21; spl. asst. to the atty. gen. of U.S., 1921-22; asst. chmn. Rep. Nat. Com., 1918-36; pres. Colmena Oil Co. Mem. Am., Calif. State and San Francisco bar assns., S.A.R., Native Sons of the Golden West. Colonel Twentieth Marines. Episcopalian. Grand Exalted Ruler B.P.O. Elks of the U.S., 1914-16. Mason (Shriner). Clubs: Bohemian (San Francisco); Press (Washington). Author of Corp. License Tax Law of Calif., Syndicalism Law, Alien Land Law, Railroad Regulation Act of 1909, and other Calif. Statutes. Home: Newtown Turnpike, Westport, Conn. Died June 18, 1952; buried Napa, Cal.

BENMOSCHÉ, M(oses) (bĕn-mō-shā), surgeon; b. London, England, Dec. 5, 1883; s. Herman and Jane B.; student St. Mary's Male Acad., Norfolk, Va.; M.D., Med. Coll. of Va., 1904; student Middlesex Hosp. and Coll., London, Eng., 1908-11; m. Simma Guttwoch, 1908; children—Elkanah, Jacob; m. 2d, Gwladys Goodman, August 5, 1943. Instr. in histology, pathology, bacteriology, Medical Coll. of Va., 1904-06; asst. in cancer research, Middlesex Hosp., London, 1908-09; dir. Pathol. Lab., Mobray Hosp., Capetown, S. Africa, 1911-12; dir. Pathol. Lab., Nashua, N.H., 1913-14; practice of surgery, Detroit, Mich., 1915-19; gen. surgery practice and research in cancer, N.Y. City, since 1920; senior in clin. surgery Mt. Sinai Hosp., N.Y. City; certified teacher of anatomy, dept. of anatomy, Middlesex Hosp. Med. Coll., London, Eng. First, with Dr. Frances I. Seymour, to describe the magnification of a fertile human spermatozoon under the electron microscope. Manhattan chmn. City Fusion party, N.Y. City, 1937. Apptd. by gov. of Va. as del. to International Congress on Tuberculosis, Washington, D.C., 1908; chairman, Am. Com. Nat. Sick Fund of Palestine. Hebrew religion. Mason, K.P. (chairman emeritus Grand Lodge com. ritual and instrn.; past supreme regent, Princess of Syracuse). Author: Waifs and Orphans, A Book of Selected Poems; A Surgeon Explains to the Layman, 1940; also monographs on cancer research; also surgical papers on method of reconstructing the internal ring in indirect inguinal hernia. Address: 600 W. 111th St., N.Y.C. Died Sept. 5, 1952.

BENNER, Winthrop Webster, business exec.; b. Mpls., Mar. 25, 1881; s. Webster and Clara Ellen (Hoak) B.; student U. Minn., 1900-03; m. Etta May Fisher, Dec. 21, 1905; 1 dau., Doris May (Mrs. Edwin Jacob Bagnar). Chemist, Oliver Iron Mining Co., 1903-04, Zenith Furnace Co., 1904-07, Atikokan Iron Co., 1907-09; engring. cons., 1909-14; prodn. supt. Firestone Tire and Rubber Co., 1915-26; v.p. Lee Rubber Tire Corp., 1927-41, exec. v.p., 1941-46; pres. Nat. Synthetic Rubber Corp., 1942-48, ret., 1948. Mason. Home: Arcola, Pa. Died June 10, 1950.

BENNET, Robert Ames, author; b. Denver, Feb. 3, 1870; s. Hiram P. and Clara (Ames) B.; student Denver pub. schs. until 1889, Nat. Law Sch., Washington, 1890-91; hon. Master of Letters, U. Colo., 1917; m. Susie A. Housley, June 14, 1893; 1 son, Harold Housley. Admitted to bar, 1892; in practice at Denver, 1892-96, at Port Arthur, Tex., 1897; surveying, 1897-98; city sec. (clerk), city assessor and collector Port Arthur, Tex., 1898-99; surveyor for Bd. of Pub. Works, Denver, 1900-06. Author: Thyra, 1901; For the White Christ, 1905; Into the Primitive, 1908; A Volunteer with Pike, 1909; The Shogun's Daughter, 1910; Out of the Primitive, 1911; Which One?, 1912; Out of the Depths, 1913; The In-Bad Man, 1913; A Missing Key, 1914; The Forest Maiden, 1914; The Quarterbreed, 1915; Brides of Sana, 1915; The Bowl of Baal, 1916; Voyage of the Nantook; The Blond Beast, 1918; Bloom of Cactus, 1920; Waters of Strife, 1921; Hidden Trails, 1922; Tyrrel of the Cow Country, 1923; The Two-Gun Man, 1924; Branded, 1924; The Rough Rider, 1925; The Cattle Baron, 1925; The Boss of the Diamond A, and Go-Getter Gary, 1926; On the Rustler Trail, 1927; Ken The Courageous, 1927; The Tenderfoot, 1928; Sheepman's Gold, 1929; The Border Wolf, 1929; The Roped Wolf, 1931; The Gold Wolf, 1932; Caught in the Wild, 1932; The Hunted Wolf, 1933; Feud of Cattle Kings, 1933; The Texas Man, 1934; Guns on the Rio Grande, 1934; Death Rides the Range, 1935; White Buffalo, 1935; Horsethief Hole, 1936; Man Against Mustang, 1936; Hot Lead, 1937; The Gunfighter, 1938; The Brand Blotters, 1939; Sheepman's Gold, 1939. Home: 5084 Tennyson St., Denver. Died Mar. 11, 1954.

BENNETT, Archibald Synica, marketing research analyst; b. Weyauwega, Wis., Dec. 25, 1877; s. Frank S. and Frances (Baxter) B.; B.S., Lawrence Coll., 1902; grad. work, U. Wis., 1906, Columbia, 1936; m. Clara Eva Gutchow, Dec. 25, 1912; children—Katherine (Mrs. Charles Edgar Strakosch), Jean (Mrs. Edwin Sibley Webster, Jr.). Tchr. mathematics and chemistry various secondary schs., 1902-10; treas., gen. mgr. School Arts Pub. Co., also Bennett Pub. Co., 1910-16 (pioneered children's mag. Something-To-Do, 1914); bus. analyst and sales consultant, N.Y. City, 1916-25; conducted pub. campaign for Oystermen's Com. during diphtheria epidemic, 1925; pub. relations counselor Middle Atlantic Fisheries Assn., 1926; marketing research dir., Geo. L. Dyer Advt. Agy., 1925-27; marketing research consultant for several advt. agys., 1927-30; completed first board survey Frozen Food Industry which became basis for its promotion, 1930-31; helped organize The Grindrod Process Corp., 1931; marketing research dir. Paul Cornell Advt. Agy., N.Y., 1931-33; marketing consultant Reynolds Metal Co., 1935-36; organized cons. and dealer relations div. Wm. J. Burns Internat. Detective Agy. to study nat. marketing problems, 1938; organized A. S. Bennett Assos., marketing research service, 1944. Made a pilot study on packaging, 1944; conducted inventory survey of nat. pool of 2000 part time research interviewers and supervisors, Researching Researchers, Part II, 1948. Mem. Brit. C. of C. Recipient ann. advt. award, 1947. Mem. Am. Marketing Assn., Beta Theta Phi. Republican. Club: Western Universities. Lectr. on topic, The Mind of the Buyer. Author: The Framework of Consumer Thinking Need No Longer be a Mystery, 1945; Marketing Research the "Radar" of the Sales Division, 1945; Some Aspects of Preparing Questionnaires, 1944; 12 Ways to Improve Field Research, 1946; Observations on the So-Called Cheater Problem Among Field Workers, 1948; How to Conduct an Opinion and Attitude Study, 1950. Home: 404 W. 116th St., N.Y.C. 27. Office: 65 E. 55th St., N.Y.C. 17. Died May 24, 1957.

BENNETT, Charles Henry, mfr.; b. Plymouth, Mich., June 27, 1863; s. Lewis Hanchett and Caroline (Baker) B.; student pub. schs. Plymouth; m. Carrie Peck, June 24, 1892. Salesman Daisy Mfg. Co., mfrs. air guns, Plymouth, 1888, later v.p., pres. since 1920; pres. Plymouth Fed. Savs. & Loan Assn., 1910-28, Plymouth United Savs. Bank 1937-52. Mem. finance com. Alma (Mich.) Coll. Presbyn. (bd. trustees). Mason. Clubs: Rotary (Plymouth, Mich.); Athletic, Boat (Detroit). Home: 134 Main St. Office: 101 Union St., Plymouth, Mich. Died Sept. 17, 1956.

BENNETT, Edward, cons. elec. engr.; b. Pitts., Oct. 26, 1876; s. Benjamin and Mary J. (Davis) B.; E.E., Western U. Pa., 1897; m. Ethel Moore, Aug. 16, 1911. Apprentice, Westinghouse Electric & Mfg. Co., 1897-98, research work, 1899; research engr. for George Westinghouse, in development of Nernst lamp, later chief engr. Nernst Lamp Co., 1899-1904;

mem. firm Beebe & Bennett, 1904-05; head electrician Nat. Electric Signaling Co., Washington, 1905-06; with Telluride Power Co., of Utah, 1906-09; with U. Wis., 1909-43, successively, asso. prof. elec. engring. until 1913, prof. 1913-43, chmn. dept., 1918-40, prof. emeritus 1943; cons. engr., 1943-50. Del. Internat. Electrotech. Commn. as rep. Am. Inst. E.E., Paris, France, 1950. Fellow Am. Inst. E.E. (v.p. 1924-26), Inst. Radio Engrs., Am. Phys. Soc.; mem. A.A.A.S., Am. Assn. U. Profs., Soc. for Promotion Engring. Edn. (v.p. 1929-30), Wis. Acad. Sci., History of Philosophy Assn., Acad. Polit. Sci., Sigma Xi, Tau Beta Pi, Eta Kappa Nu, Phi Kappa Phi. Club: University. Author: Introductory Electrodynamics for Engineers, 1926; also numerous bulls. and papers on edn. and engring. Home: 1919 Jefferson St., Madison, Wis. Died Jan. 10, 1951; buried Forest Hill Cemetery, Madison.

BENNETT, Edward Herbert, architect; b. Cheltenham, Eng., May 12, 1874; s. Capt. Edwin C. and Margaret (Callas) B.; grad. Bristol Tech. Coll.; diploma in architecture Ecole des Beaux Arts, Paris, 1900; m. Catherine Jones, Oct. 18, 1913; 1 son, Edward H.; m. 2d, Olive Mary Holden, Jan. 5, 1930. Came to U.S., 1890; began in architect's office, San Francisco, 1892; with George B. Post, N.Y.C., 1½ yrs.; with D. H. Burnham & Co., Chgo., 1904-09; specialized in city planning, 1909—; architect for Chgo. Plan Commn.; planner of Camp Grant, Rockford, Ill., and Camp Henry Knox, Stithton, Ky., cons. archtl. specialist to the sec. of the treasury, chmn. Bd. Architects of U.S. Treasury on Govt. Bldgs., 1927-33; organizer, mem. Bennett, Parsons, Frost & Thomas, changing in 1924 to Bennett, Parsons & Frost, city planners, designers archtl. development of Grant Park, Clarence Buckingham Meml. Fountain, Chgo., deptl. bldgs., Capitol Approach, Washington, D.C. Mem. Archtl. Commn. of Chgo. World's Fair Centennial Celebration, 1933. Decorated Chevalier Legion of Honor (France), 1928. Fellow A.I.A.; mem. City Planning Inst., Soc. Beaux Arts Architects. Episcopalian. Clubs: Century, Chicago, Casino, Onwentsia. Author many city planning reports, including: Plan of San Francisco, 1905; Plan of Chicago, 1909; Plan of Ottawa and Hull, Can., 1915; Plan of Minneapolis, 1917; chapter on Public Buildings and Quasi-Public Buildings in City Planning by John Nolen, 1916; also chapters to City Planning, 1923, and City Planning for Detroit, 1925. As an artist has exhibited oil and water color paintings at Art Inst. of Chicago, Arts Club, New Orleans Mus. of Art, Artists League of Midwest, Lake Forest Acad., 1946, Tryon, N.C., 1947. Held one-man show, Quest Art Galleries, 1940, Mandel Bros. Art Galleries, Chgo., 1949-51. Recipient 1st Premium in oil, 2d in watercolors Piedmont Interstate Fair (amateur sect.), 1952. Home: 89 E. Deerpath, Lake Forest, Ill.; also Long Lane, Tryon, N.C. Office: 80 E. Jackson Blvd., Chgo. Died Oct. 14, 1954; buried Lake Forest, Ill.

BENNETT, Elbert G., banker; b. York, Neb., 1888. Chmn. exec. com. First Security Corp. of Utah, which operates 33 banks in Utah, Ida. and Wyo.; served as mem. Fed. Deposit Ins. Corp. (resigned 1934.). Dir. Denver & Rio Grande R.R.Co., Mountain States Impl. Co., Utah Power and Light Co., Amalgamated Sugar Co. Clubs: Alta (Salt Lake City); Weber, Golf and Country (Ogden); 100,000 Mile; Bankers (New York). Home: 1375 E. 5600 South, Salt Lake City. Died Apr. 1, 1950; buried Ogden, Utah.

BENNETT, Frank Marion, naval officer; b. Marcellus, Mich., May 7, 1857; s. William P. and Lovisa (Brokaw) B.; grad. U.S. Naval Acad., 1879; m. Mary Henderson Eastman, June, 1893. Ensign, USN, 1879, advanced through grades to capt., 1910, now commandant navy yard, Pensacola, Fla. Clubs: Army and Navy (N.Y.C.); Army and Navy (Washington). Author: The Steam Navy of the United States, 1897; The Monitor and the Navy Under Steam, 1900. Contbr. to naval and engring. jours. Home: Cassopolis, Mich. Deceased.

BENNETT, George Allen, coll. dean; b. Water Valley, Miss., Aug. 31, 1904; s. Christopher Columbus and Jonnie Alice (Curtis) B.; A.B., Wabash Coll., 1923; student Louvain (Belgium) U., 1928; M.D., U. Munich, 1937; Sc.D., St. Joseph's Coll., 1951; LL.D., Temple U., 1951; D.Sc., Dickinson Coll., 1955; D.Sc., Grove City College, 1956; married Mary Emily Hennen, 1946; children—George Allen, Thomas B., James C., John Paul. Assistant histol., college of medicine, Baylor University, 1928; teaching fellow anatomy, Harvard Medical School, 1928-30; professor histol., school medicine, Georgetown University, 1930-33, professor anatomy, 1933-34; voluntary asst. dermatology, Munich, 1934-35, anatomy and surgery, 1935-37; mem. faculty Jefferson Med. Coll., Phila., since 1939, prof. since 1948, dean 1950—. Dir. Daniel Baugh Inst. Anatomy. Recipient Am. Acad. Orthopedic Surgery gold medal, 1948. Mem. Am. Anatomy Assn., Phila. Co. Med. Assn. Author: Gesell fur Morphologie und Physiologie. Experimental surgeon. Address: Jefferson Medical College, Phila. 7. Died Feb. 27, 1958.

BENNETT, Henry Garland, college pres.; b. Nevada County, Ark., Dec. 14, 1886; s. Thomas Jefferson and Mary Elizabeth (Bright) B.; A.B., Ouachita Coll., Arkadelphia, Ark., 1907; A.M., U. of Okla., 1924; Ph.D., Columbia University, 1926; LL.B., Ouachita College, 1937; married Vera Connell, January 29, 1913; children—Henry Garland, Phil Connell, Liberty Loven, Mary Lois, Thomas Edwin. Supt. schs., Choctaw County, Okla., 1909-10; supt. schs., Hugo, Okla., 1910-19; pres. Southeastern State Teachers Coll., 1919-28; pres. Okla. Agrl. and Mech. Coll. since 1928. Administrative director State dept., T.C.A., 1951. Democrat. Baptist. Mason (Shriner), Odd Fellow, Rotarian. Author: Coordination of State Institutions for Higher Education in Oklahoma; Trail Breaking; On the High Road; English Literature; American Literature. Home: Stillwater, Okla. Died Dec. 22, 1951.

BENNETT, Ira Elbert, editor, writer; b. Lyons, Ia., Nov. 2, 1868; s. Francis Rodolphus and Marietta (Peck) B.; common and private sch. edn.; Litt.D., Lincoln Meml. U., 1926; m. Mabel Dorman Fyler, Feb. 17, 1896; 1 dau., Amy (Mrs. Claude Langlais). Editor Lower Californian, Ensenada, Mex., 1889-90; city editor Union, San Diego, Cal., 1892-97; Washington corr. San Francisco Chronicle, 1900-05; editorial writer, Washington Post, 1905-08, editor-in-chief, 1908-33; spl. corr. McClure Newspaper Syndicate 1934-38; contbr. to mags.; mng. editor Nat. Republic. Staff cons. Com. on Fgn. Affairs, Ho. of Reps., 1949-51. Decorated by several fgn. govts. Republican. Clubs: Gridiron (pres. 1917), National Press (co-founder). Address: 1614 19th St. N.W., Washington 9. Died Mar. 26, 1957; buried Glenwood Cemetery, Washington.

BENNETT, Irving T(heodore), metals exec.; b. Bridgeport, Conn., July 30, 1900; s. Louis I. and Celeste (Chavell) B.; Ph.B., Yale, 1921, M.S., 1923; m. Irene Beehler, Sept. 29, 1923; children—Irving Theodore, Irene, John Lewis. Vice pres., dir. Revere Copper & Brass Inc., Baltimore, 1943-53, v.p. in charge mfg., 1953, dir., 1951—; chief executive officer General Cable Corp. N.Y., 1953—, chairman board, 1954—; dir. Metal Textile Corp., Roselle, N.J., Metal Textile Corp. Can., Ltd. Member aluminum adv. com. Munitions Bd., 1944-51, Nat. Prodn. Authority, 1951—. Clubs: Baltimore Country, Yale (New York City); Farmington (Charlottesville, Va.). Home: Roland Rd., Ardsley Park, Irvington-on-Hudson, N.Y. Office: Gen. Cable Corp., N.Y.C. 17. Died Oct. 3, 1955.

BENNETT, John, writer, illustrator; b. Chillicothe, O., May 17, 1865; s. John Briscoe Henry and Eliza Jane Trimble (McClintock) B.; student pub. schs., Chillicothe, Art Students' League, N.Y.C.; Litt.D., U. S.C.; m. Susan D. A. Smythe, Apr. 2, 1902; children—Jane McClintock (wife of Forrest Hampton Wells, USN), John Henry van Sweringen (USNR), Susan Adger. Began as newspaper reporter Ross County Register, 1883; editor Chillicothe Daily News, 1885-90. Curator S. C. Hist. Soc., Mus. of Charleston, S.C. Mem. Huguenot Soc. S.C., Hist. Soc. Jefferson County (Va.), Hist. Soc. Ross County (O.), Phi Beta Kappa. Author: Master Skylark, 1897; Barnaby Lee, 1902; Treasure of Peyre Gaillard, 1906; Madame Margot, 1921; The Pigtail of Ah Lee Ben Loo, 1928. Contbr. articles, fiction, illustrations and verse to mags. Home: 37 Legare St., Charleston, S.C. Died Dec. 28, 1956; buried Magnolia Cemetery, Charleston.

BENNETT, John George, bishop; b. Dunnington, Ind., Jan. 20, 1891; s. John Henry and Magdalen M. (Schilling) B.; LL.D., St. Joseph's Coll., Rensselaer, Ind., 1906; student St. Meinrad Sem. Ordained priest Roman Catholic Ch., 1914; bishop of Lafayette, Ind., 1945—. Address: 610 Lingle Av., Lafayette, Ind. Died Nov. 20, 1957; buried St. Mary's Cemetery, Lafayette.

BENNETT, John Newton, coll. dean; b. Branford, Ia., Sept. 5, 1867; s. William Parmenter and Harriet Irene (Blodgett) B.; student Ia. State Coll. Agr. and Mechanic Arts, 1883, 84; A.B., Doane Coll., Crete, Neb., 1890, LL.D., 1919; A.M., U. Neb., 1899; postgrad. U. Wis., summer 1915; m. Florence Whipple, Aug. 12, 1896. Instr. mathematics and sci. Franklin (Neb.) Acad., 1888-93; prin. Chadron (Neb.) Acad., 1893-97; prof. mathematics Doane Coll., 1899-1919, dean of men, 1910-19, pres., 1919-25; dean Drury Coll., Springfield, Mo., 1925-35, ret. to Crete, Neb. Mem. bd. edn. Crete, 1916-18. Trustee, sec. congl. Found. for Edn., 1921—. Ednl. sec. YMCA, Gen. Hdqrs., AEF, in France, 1918-19. Mem. A.A.A.S., N.E.A., Math. Assn. Am. Democrat. Conglist. Home: Crete, Neb. Died July 19, 1948; buried Crete.

BENNETT, Joseph Bentley, ex-congressman; b. Greenup County, Ky., Apr. 21, 1859; s. Benjamin Franklin and Sarah Ann (Snodgrass) B.; ed. Greenup Acad.; m. Annie Louise Mytinger, Aug. 30, 1883. Admitted to bar 1878; began practice, 1880; began mercantile business, 1885, after that practiced occasionally; twice Rep. candidate for county atty.; county judge Greenup County Ky., 1898-1904; mem. 59th to 61st Congresses (1905-11), 9th Ky. Dist.; mem. Rep. State Central Com., 1900—. Mem. Christian (Disciples) Ch. Knigh Templar, Shriner. Address: Greenup, Ky. Died Nov. 1923.

BENNETT, Louis Winston, oil exec.; b. near Custer, Ky., July 11, 1889; s. Hardin Oliver and Amelia (Myers) B.; student Western Ky. State Normal Sch., 1908-09, Bowling Green Bus. U., 1910; m. Carrie Faye Hedgcock, Nov. 20, 1913; children—Louis W., Dwight H. Controller Continental Asphalt & Petroleum Co., Oklahoma City, 1918-24; treas., dir. Josey Oil Co., Tulsa, 1924-30, Sunray Oil Corp., name changed to Sunray Mid-Continent Oil Company, 1930—. C.P.A., Okla. Mem. Tulsa C. of C. (director 1948—), Am. Petroleum Inst., Am. Inst. Accountants, Controllers Inst. Am. Methodist. Clubs: So. Hills Country, Tulsa, (Tulsa). Home: 3219 S. Yorktown, Tulsa 5. Office: P.O. Box 2039, Tulsa 2. Died June 21, 1958; buried Memorial Park Mausoleum, Tulsa.

BENNETT, M(ary) Katharine Jones (Mrs. Fred Smith Bennett), philanthropist; b. Englewood, N.J., Nov. 28, 1864; d. Henry and Winifred (Davies) Jones; A.B., Elmira (N.Y.) Coll., 1885, M.A., 1934; m. Fred Smith Bennet, July 20, 1898. Pres. Woman's Bd. of Home Missions. Presbyn. Ch. U.S.A., 1909-41; pres. Council of Women for Home Missions, 1916-24; pres. Bd. for Christian work in Santo Domingo, 1921-36. Chmn. com. on Indian Wardship of the Home Missions Council, 1939—, (Interdenominational). Ch. Com. for Vol. Service in Defense Areas (Interdenominational). Mem. Assn. U. Women. Home: Englewood, N.J. Died Apr. 15, 1950; buried Brookside Cemetery, Englewood, N.J.

BENNETT, Ralph Culver, lecturer in law, author; born at Evanston, Illinois, March 14, 1878; son of Benjamin and Clara (Culver) B.; B.S., Illinois Wesleyan University, 1902, LL.D. (honorary), 1952; A.B., Yale, 1906, LL.B., 1909, M.A., 1909, D.C.L. 1912, student at Columbia, 1906-08, Harvard, 1910-11, Johns-Hopkins, 1912-13, Univ. of London, 1918-19, Hon. LL.D. and Litt.D., Met. Coll. of Law; m. Emilie Honeyman, May 24, 1939 (dec.). Instr. Roman Law and gen. jurisprudence, Univ. Tex., 1913-14; head prof., acting dean law dept., Univ. Ore., 1914-15; asst. State's atty., Chicago, 1915-17; counsellor-at-law, 1914-30; lecturer on Motion Pictures Law, Univ. S. Calif., 1929-30; author, lecturer since 1930; feature writer, London News of the World, 1932-33; has performed on legitimate stage, also in motion pictures and television. Served as 2d lt. Royal Fusiliers, City of London regt., World War I. Recipient Arthur Twining Hadley Thesis prize and Joseph Parker Roman Law Thesis prize, Yale U., 1912. Mem. Ill. Bar Assn., State Bar Tex., Actors Equity Assn., Screen Actors Guild, Am. Legion, Phi Gamma Delta, Phi Beta Kappa. Clubs: Yale, Harvard, Phi Gamma Delta Graduate (Los Angeles), Altadena Town & Country. Author numerous stories, plays and poems. Address: 1154 Rubio Dr., Altadena, Cal. Died Mar. 28, 1959.

BENNETT, Victor Wilson, marketing consultant and instr.; b. Frostburg, Md., May 19, 1895; s. William Sellman and Frances Susan (Wilson) B.; B. A., Gettysburg Coll., 1917, M.A., 1918; M.A., U. of Pittsburgh, Pa., 1924; Ph.D., U. of Wash., 1937; student U. of Wis., Stanford, and Boston U. Coll. of Bus. Adminstrn.; m. Mary Nell Wright, July 20, 1944 (dec. Sept. 1954); 1 dau., Nellie Susan. Instr. accounting, Boston U., 1919-20; asst. prof. accounting, U. of Pittsburgh, Pa., 1920-23; asso. prof. bus. adminstrn., Emory U., Atlanta, Ga., 1923-24; asst. prof. marketing, U. of Hawaii, 1928-31; asso. prof. and head dept. of marketing, U. of Md., 1939-42; chmn. marketing dept., U. of Miami, Fla., 1946—; accounting and marketing counselor to private firms, 1920—; management counselor Farm Credit Adminstrn., Washington, D.C., 1933-39. Mem. national panel American Arbitration Assn. Served as lt., training Platsburg Barracks, in New York and Troy, N.Y., World War I; maj. U.S. Army, World War II, directing ground training at B-26 Transition Sch., Del Rio, Tex.; personal affairs officer Blackland Army Airfield, Waco, Tex.; dir. counselor training Separation Center, Ellington Field, Houston, Tex. Mem. Advt. Fedn. of Am., Am. Marketing Assn. (past v.p. Washington chpt.; national director), Artus, Am. Legion, Philo Literary Soc. (Gettysburg Coll.), Tau Kappa Alpha, Delta Sigma Phi, Delta Sigma Pi. Dem. Meth. Mason (K.T., Shriner), Elk. Clubs: Rotary, Coral Gables Country, U. Miami Propeller (pres.), Sales Execs. Co-author: Current Economic Policies, 1934; author articles and surveys. Home: 3709 Monserrate St., Coral Gables 34, Fla. Died Mar. 1, 1955; buried Fairview Cemetery, Hubbard City, Tex.

BENNETT, Wendell C(lark), anthropologist; b. Marion, Ind., Aug. 17, 1905; s. William Rainey and Ethel (Clark) B.; Ph.B., U. of Chicago, 1927, A.M., 1929, Ph.D., 1930; m. Hope Ranslow, Oct. 30, 1935; children—Lucy, Martha. Asst. in anthropology, Am. Museum Natural History, 1931-38; asso. prof. anthropology, U. of Wis., 1938-40; asso. prof. of anthropology, Yale, 1940-45, prof. since 1945; specializes in Andean archeology. Exec. secretary Joint Com. Latin Am. Studies, 1942-44. Fellow Royal Anthrop. Inst. Gt. Britain and Ireland (hon.); mem. Am. Anthrop. Assn. (pres. 1952), Soc. Am. Archeology, Beta Theta Pi, Sigma Xi. Club: Cosmos. Author:

The Tarahumara (with R. M. Zingg), 1935; (monographs) Excavations at Tiahuanaco; Excavations in Bolivia; Excavations on the North Coast of Peru; the North Highlands of Peru; Archeological Regions of Colombia; Excavations in the Cuenca region, Ecuador; Northwest Argentine Archaeology; Aneadn Culture History. Home: 176 Linden St., New Haven, Conn. Died Sept. 8, 1953.

BENNION, Adam Samuel, educator, church ofcl.; b. Taylorsville, Utah, Dec. 2, 1886; s. Joseph and Mary Ann (Sharp) B.; A.B., U. Utah, 1908; M.A., Columbia, 1912; student U. Chgo., 1916; Ph.D. U. Cal., 1923; m. Minerva Richards Young, Sept. 14, 1911; children—Phyllis Young (Mrs. Ralph Stohl), Adam Young, Richard Young, Marian Young (Mrs. Wallace Rogers), Edmund Young. Teacher Latter Day Saints High School, 1908-11; tchr. Granite High Sch., 1912-13, prin., 1913-17; asst. prof. English, U. Utah 1917-19; supt. schs. Latter Day Saints, 1919-28; asso. edn. U. Cal., 1922-23; dir. personnel Utah Power & Light Co., 1928-39, asst. to pres., 1934-45, v.p., 1945-53; mem. Council Twelve Apostles, Latter Day Saints, 1953—; prof. edn. summer sessions U. Utah, Brigham Young U., 1925-27. Mem. Am. Acad. Polit. and Social Sci., Nat. Citizens Com. Pub. Schs., Phi Delta Kappa Phi Kappa Phi. Mem. Ch. of Jesus Christ of Latter Day Saints. Author: What It Means to be a Mormon, 1916; Fundamental Problems in Teaching, 1921; Facing Life, 1930; Problems of Youth, 1931; Looking in on Greatness, 1932; The Candle of the Lord, 1958. Home: 1183 Herbert Av. Office: 47 East South Temple St., Salt Lake City. Died Feb. 11, 1958.

BENNITT, Rudolf, educator; b. Springfield, Mass., Dec. 22, 1898; s. Francis Marion and Elizabeth Chandler (Allton) B.; B.S., Boston U., 1920, A.M., 1921; A.M., Ph.D., Harvard, 1923; m. Ruth Eunice Eynon, June 25, 1923; children—Elizabeth Allton, Eleanor Jackson. With Marine Biol. Lab., Woods Hole, Mass., summers 1918-20, 22, instr. in invertebrate zoology, 1925-29; with Bermuda Biol. Sta., summer 1921; asst. prof. zoology DePauw U., 1923-24; with Winona Lake Biol. Sta., Ind. U., summer 1924; instr. in biology Tufts Coll., 1924-27; asso. prof. zoology U. Mo., 1927-37, prof. zoology, 1937-44, William Rucker prof. zoology, 1944—; with Stone Lab., Ohio State U., summer 1930; survey of resident game and furbearers of Mo., under auspices Nat. Park Service, 1934-35. Fellow A.A.A.S.; mem. Am. Soc. Zoologists, Am. Soc. Mammalogists, Ornith. Union (asso.), Wilson Ornith Club, Ecol. Soc. Am., Wildlife Soc. (pres. 1937-38), Phi Beta Kappa, Sigma Xi. Episcopalian. Author: (with Werner O. Nagel) A Survey of the Resident Game and Furbearers of Missouri, 1937; also sci. and miscellaneous papers. Home: 129 Edgewood Av., Columbia, Mo. Died Feb. 2, 1950.

BENOIT-LEVY, Jean, film producer, educator; b. Paris, France, Apr. 25, 1888; s. Fernand and Emelie (Weill) B.-L.; ed. U. Paris; m. Lucy Bloc, Apr. 24, 1920; children—Ginette, Francoise Dargols. Motion picture producer; best known films: La Maternelle, La Mort du Cygne, (Ballerina), (awarded Grand Prix du Cinema at Paris Internat. Expn., 1937); toured as lectr. in Europe before arriving in U.S., 1941; engaged in ednl. work as prof. Ecole Libre des Hautes Etudes, and New School for Social Research (both N.Y.C.); vis. prof. Tchrs. Coll., Columbia U.; dir. French-Am. Bur. of Ednl. Research; lecturer throughout U.S.; now dir. Films and Visual Information Div., U.N. At League of Nations (prior to 1940) served as del. from Com. of Internat. Inst. of Ednl. Cinema and as sec. gen. of French Com. of that inst. Mem. exec. council Film Authors Guild of Soc. of Dramatic Writers; mem. Soc. Dramatic Writers and Composers. Decorated Chevalier de la Legion d'Honneur, Croix de Guerre, Chevalier de l'Ordre de la Sante Publique (France), Chevalier de l'Ordre de Leopold (Belgium). Author: Visual Instruction in the United States (Paris), 1936; Les Grandes Missions du Cinema (Montreal), 1945, (published in U.S. under title) The Art of the Motion Picture, 1946. Contbr. to ednl. mags. and to sci. and professional publs. in U.S. and Europe. Address: 146, Avenue des Champs Elyseés, Paris VIIIe, France. Died Aug. 4, 1959.

BENSLEY, Robert Russell, anatomist; b. Hamilton, Can., Nov. 13, 1867; s. Robert Daniel and Caroline (Vandeleur) B.; A.B., U. Toronto, 1889, M.B., 1892, D.Sc., 1919; m. Cariella May, Sept. 12, 1892; children—Caroline May, Alma Gladys (dec.), Robert Daniel. Asst. demonstrator biology U. Toronto, 1891-98, demonstrator, 1898-1901; asst. prof. anatomy U. Chgo., 1901-05, asso. prof., 1905-07, prof., 1907-33, prof. emeritus, 1933—, research in functions of cellular organs. Editor Internationale Monatschrift für Anatomie und Physiologie, 1912. Mem. Assn. Am. Anatomists (pres. 1918), Alpha Kappa Kappa. Club: Quadrangle. Home: 5447 Ellis Av., Chgo. 15. Died June 11, 1956.

BENSON, Frank Weston, painter; b. Salem, Mass., Mar. 24, 1862; s. George W. and Elizabeth (Poole) B.; tech. edn. in sch., drawing and painting, Mus. Fine Arts, Boston, 1880-83; Julian Acad., Paris, 1883-85; m. Ellen Perry Peirson, Oct. 1888. Instr. drawing and painting Mus. Fine Arts, Boston, 1889-1918. Received medal, Chicago Expn., 1893; Carnegie Inst., Pittsburgh, 1899; 2 prizes, Boston Art Club; 2 prizes, Jordan Gallery, Boston; prize, Cleveland Art Assn.; Shaw Fund prize, Soc. Am. Artists, New York; Clark prize, Hallgarten prize, Nat. Acad. Design; Ellsworth prize, Chicago, and silver medal, Paris Expn., 1900; gold medal, Carnegie Inst., 1903; Lippincott prize, Phila., 1904; 2 gold medals, St. Louis Expn., 1904; gold medal, Phila. Art Club, 1906; silver medal, Corcoran Gallery, Washington, 1907; Potter Palmer medal and prize, Chicago, 1910; Logan prize, Chicago Soc. Etchers, 1918; William A. Clark prize and Corcoran gold medal, Corcoran Gallery, 1919; T. W. Logan gold medal, Chicago, 1922; gold medal Sesquicentennial Expn., Phila., 1926. N.A., 1905; mem. Nat. Inst. Arts and Letters, Ten Am. Painters, etc. Represented in Met. Museum of Art, Corcoran Gallery, Art Inst. Chicago, etc. Home: 14 Chestnut St., Salem, Mass. Died Nov. 14, 1951.

BENSON, George A(aron), editor; b. East Grand Forks, Minn., Nov. 21, 1889; s. William C. and Ella (Brown) B.; student pub. schs. East Grand Forks; m. Helen Routzahn, Aug. 30, 1921 (dec. 1948); 1 son, George Allen; m. 2d, Mildred Augustine Wirt, June 25, 1950. Cub reporter Grand Forks (N.D.) Herald, 1909, mng. editor, 1917-22; asso. editor Fargo (N.D.) Forum, 1922-30; chief Washington bur. Mpls. Jour., 1930-36; mag. writer, 1936-38; editorial writer nat. and internat. affairs Providence Jour., 1938-46; free lance writer, Washington, 1946-48; editor of the editorial page Toledo Times, 1948-53, editor of the Toledo Times, 1953—. Recipient Freedoms Found. editorial award, 1950. Mem. Sigma Delta Chi. Club: Toledo. Columnist various cultural subjects. Occasional contbr. mags. Home: 2704 Middlesex Dr., Toledo. Died Feb. 27, 1959; buried Toledo Meml. Park.

BENSON, Oscar Herman, educator; b. Delhi, Ia., July 8, 1875; s. P. C. and Celia S. (Ortberg) B.; grad. Epworth (Ia.) Sem. and Jr. Coll., 1898; student, various periods, Ia. State Tchrs. Coll., State U. Ia., U. Chgo., Ia. State Coll.; m. Sadie J. Jackson, July 30, 1902; children—Donald Dean, Margaret Irene, Estella Elizabeth. Began as tchr. rural schs., 1894, later village schs. and prin. city schs.; county supt. schs. Wright County, Ia., 1904-10; introduced agr., home econs. and extension teaching, and lectured widely on agrl. subjects before tchrs. insts., farmers' meetings, chautauquas, etc.; with U.S. Dept. Agr., 1910-20, in charge boys' and girls' extension work in agr. and home econs in 33 northern, central and western states; dir. boys' and girls' achievement bur. Eastern States League, Springfield, Mass., 1919-24. Mem. N.E.A., Nat. Assn. Sch. Supts., Nat. Ednl. Conf. for Jr. Extension Teaching (first pres.). Conglist. Author: (with George Herbert Betts) Agriculture, central edit., 1915, gen. edit., 1915, Agriculture and the Farming Business 1915; (sr. author) Food Conservation; Home Management and Home Making. Also series of pamphlets covering 24 topics, on boys' and girls' extension work, and instructions for the one period cold-pack method of home canning (originated and developed the method). Contbr. to two sets of reference books on agr. and child tng. Pres. Home Canners' Assn. Am., 1921-25; writer and Chautauqua lectr. Home: Edgemore, Md. Died Aug. 15, 1951.

BENSON, Reuel A(llen), physician; b. Oakland, Me., Apr. 7, 1878; s. Herbert H. and Sabra (Townsend) B.; B.S., Trinity Coll., 1899; M.D., N.Y. Med. Coll., 1903; m. Ann Dusenberry, Sept. 19, 1940; children—Reuel A., Thomas D. Intern Flower Hosp., 1903-05; pvt. practice as physician, N.Y. City, since 1906; prof. pediatrics and dir. grad. pediatrics N.Y. Med. Coll. since 1940; attending Flower Fifth Av. Hosp.; consultant Met. Hosp. Author: The Camp Counselor, 1951. Contbr. to Long and Goldbergs Social Hygiene, 1938; also articles to pediatric jours. Home: 502 Park Av., N.Y. City 21. Office: 40 E. 61st St., N.Y.C. 21. Died Aug. 7, 1956.

BENT, Erling Sundt, Norwegian diplomat; b. Oslo, Norway, July 16, 1894; s. Didrik Meier and Inga (Sundt) B.; grad. Vestheim Sch., Oslo, (U. Oslo) 1912; diploma in econs. New College, Oxford, 1915; m. Sofie Langerud, Oct. 24, 1928; 1 son, Didrik. Sec. fgn. office, Oslo, 1921, 1924-25, 28-29, 33; attaché Norwegian legation, Lisbon, 1921-22, Paris, 1923; vice consul Norway, Hamburg, 1926-27; sec. Norwegian legation, London and Brussels 1930-32; souschef of protocol, fgn. office, Oslo, 1934-36; vice consul Norway, Montreal, 1936-38; vice consul, Los Angeles, 1938-40, consul, 1941-46; consul gen. Norway, N.Y.C., 1947-52; E.E. and M.P., Rome, 1952-53, Ottawa, Can., 1953-55. Hon. pres. Norwegian Am. C. of C., N.Y.C.; mem. bd. trustees Norwegian Seamen's Ch., Bklyn.; pres. U.S.A. Bd. of Scandinavian Shipping Office, N.Y.C. Decorated Knight 1st class Order St. Olav, St. Olav Medal, Athletics gold medal (Norway); Legion of Honor (France); Comdr. Order of Christ (Portugal); Order of Three Stars (Latvia); Officer Order of North Star (Sweden); Order of Leopold (Belgium); Order Isabela a Catolica (Spain); Order of Merrit (Chile). Lutheran. Clubs: Norske Selskab (Oslo); Leander (Henley, Eng.); Norwegian (Bklyn.); Lawyers (N.Y.C.). Home: Oslo, Norway. Died Apr. 18, 1955.

BENT, Quincy, steel co. exec. (ret.); b. Steelton, Pa., July 28, 1879; s. Luther Stedman and Mary Stearns (Felton) B.; B.A., Williams College, 1901, LL.D., 1953; Engineering Doctor, Lehigh University; married Deborah Norris Brock, January 4, 1910; 1 son, Horace Brock. Began work in steel plant, 1901; supt. Lebanon Furnaces, Pa. Steel Co., 1903-07, mgr. Lebanon Plant, 1907-09; asst. to pres. Md. Steel Co., 1909-16; gen. mgr. Steelton Plant, 1916-18, v.p. 1918-48, Bethlehem Steel Co.; ret. 1948. Trustee Williams Coll. Mem. Am. and British Iron and steel insts., Am. Soc. Mining and Metall. Engrs., Am. Acad. of Polit. and Social Science, Army Ordnance Assn., Alpha Delta Phi. Republican. Episcopalian. Clubs: Philadelphia, Corinthian Yacht (Philadelphia); Eastern Yacht (Boston); Essex Country. Home: Weyhill, R.D. 4, Bethlehem, Pa. Died May 5, 1955; buried St. James The Less, Phila.

BENTLEY, Arthur F(isher), author; born Freeport, Ill., Oct. 16, 1870; s. Charles Frederick and Angeline Alice (Fisher) B.; A.B., Johns Hopkins, 1892, Ph.D., 1895; student, U. of Berlin, 1893-94; m. Anna Harrison, Sept. 18, 1899 (died, Dec. 31, 1924); m. 2d Susan W. Chipman, June 12, 1930 (died Sept. 12, 1942); m. 3d Imogene M. Shaw, May 18, 1946. Fellow A.A.A.S.; mem. Am. Math. Soc., Econometric Soc., Assn. for Symbolic Logic, Philosophy of Sci. Assn., Am. Math. Assn. Author several books, including: The Process of Government, 1908; Relativity in Man and Society, 1926; Linguistic Analysis of Mathematics, 1932; Behavior, Knowledge, Fact, 1935; Knowing and the Known (with John Dewey), 1949; Inquiry into Inquiries, 1954. Home: R.F.D. 2, Paoli, Ind. Died May 21, 1957; buried Grand Island, Neb.

BENTLEY, Cyril Edmund, clergyman, religious dir.; b. Clayton, N.Y., July 11, 1893; s. Rev. Walter E. and Harriott Faye (Chamberlin) B.; student St. Stephen's Coll., Annandale, N.Y., 1911-13; grad. Gen. Theol. Sem., 1916; B.D., Seabury Div. Sch., 1922; m. Edna Frances Braun, July 17, 1916. Rector St. Luke's Ch. and seven asso. missions, Lincolnton, N.C., 1916-21; exec. sec. Diocese of Atlanta (Ga.), founder and editor The Diocesan Record, 1921-25; rector Christ Ch., Macon, Ga., 1925-31; asso. dir. Am. Ch. Inst. for Negroes, N.Y.C., 1931-41, dir., 1941-48; pres. Calhoun (Ala.) Sch., 1941-42; rector St. Paul's Episcopal Ch., Huntington, Conn., 1951-57. Trustee Ft. Valley (Ga.) Coll. Center. Commd. lt. Chaplain Corps, USNR, 1931, on active duty, 1942-46; transferred from Chaplain Corps to Line, 1942; promoted comdr., 1945; served in U.S. and S.W. Pacific; inactive status, 1946—. Decorated Medal of Order of the Sangrael, 1932; Naval Reserve medal, 1943. Mem. Kappa Gamma Chi. Episcopalian. Mason. Author occasional articles. Address: Huntington, Conn. Died Jan. 10, 1957; buried Arlington Nat. Cemetery.

BENTLEY, Gordon Mansir, zoologist, entomologist; b. Great Barrington, Mass., Sept. 23, 1875; s. Charles Harrison and Elvira E. (Mansir) B.; B.S.A., Cornell U., 1900, A.M., 1901; M.S., U. Tenn., 1928; m. Mary Catherine Elmore, June 12, 1912; children—Juanita Louise, Edna Elvira. Prof. botany and zoölogy Union Acad., Belleville, N.Y., 1901-04; instr. entomology N.C. State Coll., Raleigh, 1905; also asst. state entomologist N.C., 1905; instr. in zoölogy and entomology U. Tenn., 1905-08, asso. prof. entomology, 1908-23, prof., 1923-50, head dept. 1926-44, prof. entomology, 1945-50, ret. Sept. 1950; state entomologist and plant pathologist 1909-50, ret.; now cons. entomologist and zoologist. Pres. So. Plant Quarantine Bd., 1929-30, 37-38, 39-44. Fellow A.A.A.S.; mem. N.E.A. Am. Assn. Econ. Entomologists (v.p. 1918-29, 36; pres. plant quarantine and inspection sect. 1925; pres. apiculture sect. 1929), Entomol. Soc. Am. (charter), Tenn. Acad. Sci., Am. Assn. U. Profs., Cotton States Entomologists (sec. 1923-27; pres. 1927), Tenn. State Hort. Society (sec.-treas. 1905-47, life hon. 1948), Tenn. Nurserymen's Assn. (organizer 1905, sec.-treas. 1905-48, hon. sec.-treas. for life), Tenn. Beekeepers Assn. (sec.-treas. 1906-45), Tenn. State Florists Assn. (organizer, 1909; sec. 1909-34), Tenn. Ornithol. Soc., Tenn. and East Tenn. Tchrs. Assns., Am. Rose Soc., Izaak Walton League Am., So. Nurserymens Assn. (hon. life), Sigma Xi, Gamma Alpha, Alpha Zeta, Sigma Nu, Phi Kappa Phi. Presbyn. (elder). Mason (32°, K.T., past comdr.; Shriner, past potentate; Royal Order of Jesters, Red Cross of Constantine, past Sovereign; past Viceroy). Clubs: National Travel, The Cabiri, Square & Compasses, Cornell, University of Tenn. Entomological (founder 1908), Shrine Luncheon (past pres.), Rotary, Knoxville Camera, Biologia, East Tennessee Automobile (dir.). Author: Lectures and Laboratory Guide for Economic Entomology, 1929; Insect Taxonomy, 1929; 120 bulls. on econ. entomology. Contbr. Jour. Econ. Entomology. Editor of Proceedings Tenn. State Hort. Soc., Tenn. Market Bulletin, State Dept. Agr. Reports. Home: Island Home Park, 141 W. Peachtree St. Office: 144 W. Peachtree St., Knoxville 15, Tenn. Died Oct. 8, 1954; buried Highlamb Meml. Cemetery.

BENTLEY, Madison, psychologist; b. Clinton, Ia., June 18, 1870; s. Charles Eugene and Persis Orilla (Freeman) B.; B.S., U. of Neb., 1895 (LL.D., 1935); Ph.D., Cornell U., 1898. Assistant in psychology, instr., asst. prof., Cornell, until 1912; prof. psychology and dir. psychol. labs., U. of Ill., 1912-28; Sage prof. psychology, Cornell, 1928-38; consultant for psychology, Library of Congress, 1938-40, lecturer in psychology, Cornell Univ., 1942-44; chmn. division anthropology and psychology, Nat. Research Council, 1930-31. Capt. Air Service, 1917-18; major, U.S. Army, 1924-34. Fellow A.A.A.S.; mem. Am. Psychol. Assn. (pres. 1925), Phi Beta Kappa, Sigma Xi, and Phi Kappa Psi. Wrote section on History in A Manual of American Literature, 1909; also articles on psychol. subjects in New Internat. Ency., Internat. Year Book, Ency. Americana, United Editors' Ency.; mag. articles. Editor of American Journal Psychology, 1903-51. Author: Studies in Social and General Psychology, 1916; Critical and Experimental Studies in Psychology, 1921; The Field of Psychology, 1924; Studies in Psychology from the University of Illinois, 1925; The New Field of Psychology, Pt. 1, The Psychological Functions and Their Government, 1934; The Problems of Mental Disability in England, 1938; Cornell Studies in Dynasomatic Psychology, 1938; The Theater of Living in Animal Psychology, 1943; Tools and Terms in Recent Researches since 1943; Sanity in the Life Course, 1946; Towards a Psychological History of the Hominids, 1947; Primary Factors in the Government of certain Biomechanical Systems, 1952. Address: 733 Oregon Av., Palo Alto, Cal. Died May 29, 1955.

BENTLEY, William Burdelle, chemist; b. Maple Valley, N.Y., Aug. 8, 1866; s. William Henry and Elizabeth (Cummings) B.; A.B., Harvard, 1889, A.M., 1890, Ph.D., 1898; m. Susan E. Prescott, Dec. 15, 1891 (died 1923); children—William Prescott, Harold Jackson; m. 2d, Henrietta J. Prescott, July 1925 (died May 19, 1956). Asst. in chem. lab. Harvard, 1889-91, U.S. Torpedo Sta., Newport, R.I., summer 1890; adj. and asso. prof. chemistry and physics U. Ark., 1891-1900; prof. chemistry Ohio U., 1900-36, now emeritus. Served as capt. Ordnance Dept., U.S. Army, 1918-19, stationed Watertown (Mass.) Arsenal. Mem. Am. Chem. Soc., A.A.A.S. Mason (K.T.). Home: Athens, O. Died July 14, 1945; buried Athens.

BENTON, Jay Rogers, ins. exec.; b. Somerville, Mass., Oct. 18, 1885; s. Everett Chamberlin and Willena (Rogers) B.; grad. Hopkinson Sch. for Boys, Boston, 1903, and Phillips Acad., Exeter, N.H., 1904; A.B., Harvard, 1908; LL.B., Boston U., 1911; m. Frances Hill, June 16, 1913; children—John Hill, Mary, David, Peter, Nicholas. Admitted to bar, 1911; pub. Belmont Courier, 1914-17; asso. counsel and asst. sec., Mass. Fire & Marine Ins. Co., 1914-18; mem. Mass. Ho. of Reps., 1917-18; asst. atty. gen. of Mass., 1918-23, atty. gen., 1923-27; partner law firm Sherburne, Powers & Needham, 1927-36; v.p. Boston Mutual Life Ins. Co., 1936, pres. since 1937; v.p. and director Waverly (Mass.) Cooperative Bank; dir. Arlington (Mass.) Gas Light Co. Del. Rep. Nat. Conv., 1916. Moderator Town Meetings, Belmont, 1930-40. Trustee Pub. Library, Belmont, since 1940, pub. library, Guildhall, Vt., since 1925; dist. chmn. Boston Community Fund Campaign, 1936; gen. chmn. Boston Salvation Army campaigns, 1936-37; mem. Greater Boston Adv. Com. Salvation Army; mem. Belmont Rep. Town Com. 1906-48; mem. adminstrn. committee South End Boys Club, Boston; dir. Lancaster, N.H., Country Fair; chmn. 5 Liberty Loan campaigns, Belmont. Organized Belmont Mil. Co., 1916; sergt. Co. F, 11th Regt. Inf., Mass. State Guard, 1917-19. Pres. Harvard Exeter Club, 1906-07, N.E. Exeter Alumni Assn., 1934-35, Nat. Exeter Alumni Assn., 1942-44, Belmont Hist. Soc. since 1930, Vt. Assn. of Boston, 1942-44, Beacon Soc., 1940-41, Middlesex Club, 1931-36, B.U. Law Sch. Assn., 1917-18. Charter mem. Am. Law Institute; member Am. Bar Assn. (gen. chmn. conv. 1936), Boston Bar Association, National Assn. Attys. General, Acacia, S.A.R., Pi Eta, Phi Delta Phi. Clubs: Harvard of Belmont (pres. 1938-39), Harvard of Boston, Knockers, Luncheon, Rejuvenators, Republican. Gen. chmn. Greater Boston Development Com., 1944-48. Home: 3 Pequossette Rd., Belmont, Mass.; (summer) Guildhall, Vt. Office: 378 Stuart St., Boston. Died Nov. 3, 1953.

BENTON, John Keith, univ. dean; b. Banks, Ala., May 24, 1896; s. Arthur Franklin and Martha (Frederick) B.; A.B., Birmingham-Southern College, 1923, D.D., 1946; B.D., Yale Univ., 1926; Ph.D., Edinburgh University, 1934; D.D., Southern Methodist University, 1949; m. Lois Cooper, Aug. 6, 1934. Professor of philosophy and religion, Southern Coll., 1926-29; asst. prof. of philosophy and psychology, Drew Univ., 1931-34, asso. prof., 1934-37, prof., 1937-39; visiting prof. of Christian Doctrine, Duke Univ., 1938-39; dean School of Religion, Vanderbilt Univ., since 1939; lecturer in philosophy of religion, Pendle Hill Graduate Center, summer 1937; lecturer Nat. Conf. on Religion and Mental Hygiene, 1937; Jeannette Miriam Goldberg Lectures, Hebrew Union Coll., 1952. Ordained minister, N. Ala. Conf. Meth. Ch., 1933. Served as cadet and pilot, A.S., U.S. Army, 1917-19. Recipient of citation for distinguished service to Christianity, Nat. Council of Chs. 1951. Mem. dept. pastoral services, Nat. Council Churches; assembly of div. of Christian education National Council of Churches; Methodist General Board of Edn. (mem. curriculum com.); mem. U. Christian Mission, mem. survey com. Meth. Theol. Sems., 1947; mem. bd. dirs., Atlanta Seminary Found., 1947—. Fellow of National Council on Religion in Higher Edn. (dir. and chmn. central com., 1935-37); mem. American Association Theological Schools (vice president 1946-48, president 1950-52, member of exec. com., 1940—), Am. Philos. Assn., Am. Acad. of Social and Political Science, Phi Beta Kappa, Pi Gamma Mu, Pi Kappa Alpha. Mason. Club: Faculty. Contbr. Making Religion Effective, 1945. Clinical Pastoral Training, 1945. Mem. adv. council Religion in Life (theol. mag.), 1939-48. Contbr. to relig. jours. Home: 205 Walnut Drive, Nashville 5. Died Aug. 21, 1956; buried Nashville.

BENTON, Mary Lathrop, educator; b. of missionary parents, at Bhamdun, Mt. Lebanon, Syria, Feb. 26, 1864; d. William Austin and Loanza (Goulding) B.; brought to U.S., 1869; A.B., U. Minn., 1885 (Phi Beta Kappa); studied in normal schs. of Blois, Angoulême and Nimes, France, 2½ yrs., 1895-97; studied in Rome and traveled abroad, 1907-08; L.H.D., Smith Coll., 1914; unmarried. Tchr. Mills Coll., Cal., 1893-94; instr., and prof. Latin, Smith Coll., Northampton, Mass., 1897-1914; dean of women, Carleton Coll., Sept. 1914-21. Asst. to pres. and prof. French, Carleton Coll., 1921-25. Conglist. Del. to France, June 1918-Aug. 1919, for Assn. of Am. Colls. as chmn. com. to select French girls for scholarships in Am. colls.; Mar. 1919, went to Lithuania on Y.W.C.A. work with Madam de Gozdawa Turczynowicz (the two first women of the allies to cross Germany after the armistice). Address: 308 Lincoln Av., Palo Alto, Cal. Died 1955.

BENZ, Francis E., publisher; b. St. Paul, May 3, 1899; s. Frank A. and Sophia A. (Junius) B.; A.B., St. Thomas Coll., 1921; S.T.B., Catholic U. Am., 1925; A.M., U. Minn., 1932. Ordained priest, Roman Cath. Ch., 1925; pub. The Catholic Boy for 18 years; co-founder and co-publisher of publications for the Catholic Youth, including The Catholic Miss, The Catholic Student, Mine One, Mine Two, Mine Three, The Little Mine, Escholier Un, Escholier Deux, Escholier Trois. Founder The Knights of the Altar. Mem. Sigma Delta Chi. K. of C., Societas L'Immaculate Conceptione. Club: Minneapolis Athletic. Author: The Red Flame of Sound; (biographies) Pasteur, Knight of the Lab.; On to Suez; Talking Around the Earth; John Barry, Naval Hero. Address: 25 Groveland Terrace, Mpls. 5. Died Apr. 15, 1954.

BENZIGER, August (bĕn'zĭg-er), portrait painter; b. Einsiedeln, Switzerland, Jan. 2, 1867; s. Adelrich and Marie (Koch) B.; student Downside Coll. Eng., in Brussels, Geneva, Munich; art studies Royal Acad., Vienna, Académie Julian and École des Beaux Arts, Paris; m. Gertrude Lytton, July 5, 1898; children—Marie Gertrude Rosa, Helene Henriette (Mrs. Joseph Willimann), Marguerite Marie (Mother Marguerite Benziger). Portrait painter, 1891—; has painted portraits of Presidents McKinley, Roosevelt (Hist. Soc., Chgo.) and Taft, of Popes Leo XIII, Benedict XV, and Pius XI, Pres. Diaz, Mexico, Sir Stuart Knill, lord mayor London, Leon Bourgeois, prime minister of France, Presidents Hauser, Forrer, Deucher and Haab, of Switzerland, J. Pierpont Morgan, Robert S. Brookings (Washington U., St. Louis), Charles F. Brooker, William Bixby, Charles M. Schwab, Cardinals Gibbons, Farley, and O'Connell and Cardinal Bonzano, Apostolic Delegate, Sir Oliver Lodge, Senator Shelby M. Cullom (U.S. Capitol), etc., U.S. and abroad. Comdr. de l'Ordre du Christ; Officier de l'Ordre St. Jacques. Built Grand Hotel and Palace, Brunnen, Switzerland, 1904; offered it to U.S. Govt. during World War I. Clubs: Union Artistique (Paris); Manhattan and Automobile of America (N.Y.C.); Automobile of Switzerland; Automobile of France. Address: 1 E. 66th St., N.Y.C. 21. Died Apr. 13, 1955; buried St. Peters Cemetery, New Brighton, S.I., N.Y.

BERANGER, Clara (Mrs. William C. de Mille), motion picture writer; b. Baltimore; d. Benjamin and Fannie (Kahn) Strouse; B.A., Goucher Coll., 1907; m. 2d, William C. de Mille, Aug. 14, 1928; 1 dau. (by former marriage), Frances Beranger (Mrs. Robert Triest). Staff writer Paramount Picture Corp. and Metro-Goldwyn-Mayer. Member Authors League of America, Society of American Dramatists, Phi Beta Kappa, Phi Beta Kappa Associates. Adapted Dr. Jekyll and Mr. Hyde for screen, also Miss Lulu Bett, Clarence Grumpy, Only 38; writer, The Gilded Lily, The World's Applause, and (play) His Chinese Wife; adaptations and dialogue for talking pictures: The Idle Rich; This Mad World; The Wise Wife; The Social Register; His Double Life; Pagliacci. Contbr. stories and articles to mags., and original stories to screen. Author: (book) You Can Be Happy, 1946; (textbook) Writing for the Screen, 1949; Peace Begins at Home, 1954. Instr. screenwriting, U. of So. Cal., 1945-53. Home: 130 Gillis St., Playa del Rey, Cal. Died Sept. 10, 1956.

BERCH, Samuel Harry, dairy exec.; b. Russia, Dec. 20, 1888; s. Izril and Betty (B); educated in Russia in equivalent of high sch.; m. Rose Chmelnitsky, Jan. 7, 1912; children—Sybil (Mrs. Leo Hartfield), Irene (Mrs. Howard M. London), Vera Leila (Mrs. Milton L. Gunzburg), Beatrice Edith (Mrs. Monte Factor). U.S., 1918, citizen, 1925. Grain merchant, Winnipeg, Can., 1915-18; mfr. dairy products, Seattle, Wash., 1918-25; pres. Western Dairy Products Co., Seattle, Wash., 1925-33; pres. southern div. Western Dairy Products, Inc., Los Angeles, Calif., 1925-33; pres. Arden Farms Co., Wash., Oregon, Calif., over 65 dairy plants, since 1934; pres. The Flexible Vacuum Container Corp. since 1939. Club: Hillcrest Country (Los Angeles). Inventor of flexible vacuum packaging. Home: 9561 Sunset Blvd., Beverly Hills, Calif. Office: 1900 W. Slauson Av., Los Angeles 47, Cal. Died Oct. 29, 1951.

BERDAN, John, corp. dir.; b. Toledo, Mar. 30, 1903; s. Sinclair and Maria C. (Gosline) B.; student U. Mich., 1927; m. Margaret G. Evans, Apr. 30, 1927. Dir. Berdan Co., Toledo, 1944—, Diamond Alkali Co., Marlin Rockwell Corp., Pitts. Gage & Supply Co. Home: 1035 Devon Rd., Pitts. 13. Office: Oliver Bldg., Pitts. Died Nov. 4, 1958.

BERENGER, Victor Henry, diplomat; b. Rugles, Eure, France, Apr. 22, 1867; s. Jules and Marie (Dos) B.; grad. U. Paris, 1892; prizeman de l'Académie Française, 1894, 95; m. Blanche Deschamps (dec.); m. 2d, Genevieve Delzant, 1905 (dec.); m. 3d, Marie Chanut (dec.); m. 4th, Suzanne Beauperthuy. Actively identified with various newspapers from 1892; editor of Matin, 1911-25; senator, 1912-40 (chmn. finance com. 1922-25; chmn. commn. fgn. affairs 1930-40), hon. senator, 1947-52; high commr. for petroleum supplies, 1918-20; ambassador to U.S., 1925-26. Mem. (one of founders) Internat. Diplomatic Acad. from 1929; founder, Chmn. Mediterranean Acad. Officier Légion d'Honneu.; Knight Comdr. British Empire; Grand Officer SS. Maurice et Lazare; Grand Officer Polonia Restituta; Grand Officer of the Lion and the Rising Sun; Officer Order of Isabelle the Catholic; Grand Croxi de St. Sava. Clubs: Metropolitan, Union, University (Washington), Cercle Interallié, Union Interalliée (Paris). Author of various books on hist., econ. and polit. subjects, also poems. Home: Villa l'Escalinada, Av. Primrose, Nice, Alpes Maritimes, France. Died May 17, 1952; buried at Saint Raphael, Var, France.

BERENSON, Bernard, author; b. Lithuania, June 26, 1865; s. Albert Berenson; A.B., Harvard, 1887; Dr. Honoris Causa, Sorbonne, 1955, also University of Florance, 1956; married to Mary Logan Costelloe, December 29, 1900. Author: Italian Painters of the Renaissance; A Sienese Painter of the Franciscan Legend, 1909; Venetian Painting in America—The Fifteenth Century, 1916; Three Essays in Methods, 1917; Essays on Sienese Paintings, 1918; Introductory Essay to the Speculum Humanae Salvationis, 1927; Essays in Medieval Art, 1930. Compiler: Catalog of Italian Paintings Widener Collection: Catalog of Italian Paintings in the Michael Friedsam Collection, 1936; Italian Pictures of Renaissance, 1932; Drawings of Florentine Painters (rev. edit.), 1938. Esthetics and History, 1948; Sketch for a Self-Portrait, 1949; Rumour and Reflection, 1952; Italian Painters of the Renaissance, Caravaggio, Seeing and Knowing, 1953; Piero della Francesca, Arch of Constantine, 1954; Lorenzo Lotto, rev. 1956; Essays in Appreciation, Venetian Paintings of the Renaissance, 1958; One Year's Reading for Fun, also The Passionate Sightseer, 1960. Contributing articles English, French, Italian and German reviews of art, archaeology. Member Am. Acad. Arts and Letters; fgn. mem. Royal Belgian Acad., Royal Norwegian Acad. Office: care American Academy of Arts and Letters, 633 W. 155th St., N.Y.C. Died Oct. 6, 1959.

BEREZOWSKY, Nicolai (bĕ-rĕ-zŏv'skĭ), composer; b. Leningrad, Russia, May 17, 1900; s. Tikon Mihailovitch and Lydia (Nazaroff) B.; grad. Imperial Capella, Juilliard Music Sch., 1927; m. Alice Newman, May 3, 1928 (divorced, Nov. 1947) children—Alexandra, Sergei-Nicolai; m. 2d Mrs. Judith Randal; step-children, Judith E. Randal, Jonathan C. Randal. Came to U.S., 1922, naturalized citizen, 1928. Mem. New York Philharmonic Orchestra, 1922-29; conductor Atwater Kent Radio concerts, 1926-27; asso. with Columbia Broadcasting Co. since 1931; mem. Coolidge String Quartet, 1935-40; guest conductor WOR, WABC, Cincinnati Symphony, Nat. Symphony, Boston Symphony and League of Composers. Works performed by New York Philharmonic, Boston, Phila., Chicago, St. Louis, Cleveland, Rochester Philharmonic, Nat. Symphony of Washington, Nat. Orchestral Assn., etc., also leading chamber music socs. Recipient award, Nat. Acad. of Arts and Letters, 1944; Ditson Fund, Columbia University, 1946-47; prize winner Nat. Broadcasting Co. Contest, Juilliard Publn. Contest, Elizabeth Sprague Coolidge Festival Commn., League of Composers Commn. and Boston Symphony Commn. Exec. dir. League of Composers; mem. bd. govs. Am. Composers Alliance, Internat. Soc. Contemporary Music. mem. Am. Soc. of Composers, Authors and Publishers. Democrat. Mem. Greek Orthodox Catholic Ch. Club:

Bohemians (New York). Address: 544 E. 86th St., N.Y.C. 21. Died Aug. 27, 1953; buried Cutchogue, N.Y.

BERG, Albert Ashton, surgeon; b. N.Y.C., Aug. 10, 1872; s. Moritz and Josephine (Schiff) B.; A.B., Coll. of the City of N.Y., 1894; M.D., Coll. Phys. and Surg., Columbia U., 1891; unmarried. House surgeon, Mount Sinai Hosp., N.Y.C., 1894-96, asso. surgeon, 1899-1912, surgeon, 1912-34, cons. surgeon, 1934-—; cons. surgeon to Hebrew Orphan Asylum, Hebrew Sheltering Orphan Asylum, Barnet Hosp., Paterson, N.J., Monmouth Mem. Hosp., Long Branch, N.J.; dir. surgery Beth Moses Hosp., Brooklyn, N.Y., Montefiore Hosp., N.Y.C. Trustee N.Y. Public Library Mem. bd. visitors, Ray Brook, N.Y. State Hosp. Nat. Regent in surgery, Internat. Coll. of Surgeons (president, 1946-48). Fellow American Medical Association, N.Y. State Med. Assn., American Gastro-enterological Assn., N.Y. Acad. of Medicine, etc. Mem. Am. Bibliophile Soc., English Bibliog. Soc. Fellow (hon.) Surg. Socs. Rome and Piedmont (Italy). Mem. Med. Advisory Bd. during World War. Decorated Third Order of Bolivar of Venezuela. Clubs: Harmonie, Lotos, Grolier (New York, N.Y.). Author: Surgical Diagnosis, 1905. Contbr. numerous articles and monographs to surg. jours. Collector of rare books, manuscripts and letters; presented great library of 50,000 rare volumes, manuscripts and letters of English and Am. lit. to N.Y. Pub. Library and established a trust fund for its maintenance and care. In memory of his brother, Dr. H. W. Berg, donated an Inst. for Research to Mt. Sinai Hosp., New York. Address: 10 E. 73d St., N.Y.C. Died July 1, 1950.

BERG, J(oseph) Frederic, theologian; b. Tübingen, Germany, July 28, 1871; s. Herman C. and Mary J. Bayard (Kirkpatrick) B.; A.B., Rutgers Coll., New Brunswick, N.J., 1892, A.M., 1895, D.D., 1905; grad. Theol. Sem. Ref. Ch. in America, 1895; Ph.D., Columbia, 1896; m. Ruth Tredwell, Nov. 26, 1902. Ordained ministry Dutch Reformed Ch., 1895; pastor Montgomery, N.Y., 1895-1902, Port Richmond, S.I., 1902-11; lecturer on Bibl. theology, 1905-17, prof. N.T. exegesis and Hellenistic Greek, 1911-17, Theol. Sem. Ref. Ch. in America; pastor Ref. Prot. Dutch Ch., Flatbush, N.Y., 1917-45, pastor emeritus since Sept. 1, 1945. President General Synod Reformed Church in America, 1920, Brooklyn Federation of Churches, 1927. Mem. Am. Oriental Soc., Delta Phi, Phi Beta Kappa. Republican. Home: Jan Brunt Manor Rd., East Setauket, N.Y. Died Apr. 4, 1958; buried Presbyterian Church Yard, Setauket.

BERGE, Wendell (bĕrj), lawyer; b. Lincoln, Neb., Apr. 24, 1903; s. George W. and Cora (Ott) B.; A.B., U. of Neb., 1925; LL.B., U. of Mich., 1927; S.J.D., 1930; m. Laura Elizabeth Whelpley, Aug. 18, 1926; children—John Wendell, Douglas James, Asso. with law firm Root, Clark, Buckner & Ballantine, N.Y. City, 1928-30; admitted to Dist. of Columbia bar, 1931; apptd. spl. asst. to atty. gen. of U.S., May 15, 1930, and assigned to staff of Antitrust Div., Dept. of Justice; chief of appellate sect., Antitrust Div., 1935-37, chief trial sect., Apr.-July 1937; 1st asst. to head Antitrust Div., 1937-40; designated acting asst. atty. gen., Dec. 19, 1940; apptd. asst. atty. gen. by President Roosevelt to head Criminal Div., Dept. of Justice, 1941; head of Antitrust Div., 1943-47; resigned as asst. atty. gen., 1947; mem. firm Berge, Fox, Arent & Layne, 1947-—; alternate mem. Temp. Nat. Econ. Com., 1938-41; trustee U. of Neb. Found., Inc. Distinguished Service medal U. Neb., 1942. Member Federal, American, and District of Columbia bar assns., Am. Judicature Soc., Americans for Democratic Action, Acacia, Phi Delta Phi, Delta Sigma Rho. Democrat. Unitarian. Mason. Contributor to Michigan Law Review, Geo. Washington Law Review, Law and Contemporary Problems (Duke U.), Jour. of Criminal Law and Criminology, Federal Probation, Commonweal, Free World, Magazine Digest and Am. Bar Assn. Jour. Author: Cartels: Challenge to a Free World, 1944; Economic Freedom for the West, 1946. Home: 9508 W. Stanhope Rd., Rock Creek Hills, Kensington, Md. Office: Ring Bldg., 1200 18th St., Washington 6. Died Sept. 24, 1955; buried Parklawn, Rockville, Md.

BERGENGREN, Roy Frederick, b. Gloucester, Mass., June 14, 1879; s. Frederick Wilhelm Alexis and Caroline Frances (Boynton) B.; A.B., Dartmouth, 1903; LL.B., Harvard, 1906; m. Gladys Louise Burroughs, Nov. 4, 1912; children—Ruth (dec.), Roy Frederick, Dorothy. Practiced law, Lynn, Mass., 1906-18; commr. of finance, Lynn, 1915-17; mem. Mass. Constl. Conv., 1917-18; exec. sec. Credit Union Nat. Extension Bur. to 1935, mng. dir. Credit Union Nat. Assn., 1935-45. Capt. Ordnance Dept., U.S. Army, 1918-19; finance mgr. of ordnance, Boston dist., 1919. Drafted credit union laws, operative in 41 states and Dist. of Columbia, also federal credit union law. Mem. Chi Phi, Am. Legion. Author: Cooperative Banking, 1923; Credit Coöperation as Adapted to the Needs of the Worker, 1927; Credit Union—A Cooperative Banking Book, 1931; We the People, 1933; Cuna Emerges, 1935; Credit Union North America, 1940; I Speak for Joe Doakes, 1945; Crusade, The Fight for Economic Democracy, 1952. Home: R.F.D. 2, Berlin Rd., Montpelier, Vt. Died Nov. 11, 1955; buried Berlin Cor Cemetery.

BERGER, Meyer, writer, news reporter; b. N.Y. City Sept. 1, 1898; s. Sarah (Waldman) Berger; ed. pub. schs. of Brooklyn; m. Mae Gamsu, Aug. 29, 1926. Office boy N.Y. Morning World, 1911-17, dist. reporter, 1919-22; dist. reporter-rewrite man Standard News Assn., 1922-27; reporter N.Y. Times since 1927, on wartime overseas assignments in Europe, Africa, Pacific, 1942-45; staff The New Yorker, 1938; writer for nat. mags. since 1927. Served as sergt., 106th inf., 27th Div., U.S. Army, overseas, 1917-19. Decorated Purple Heart, Silver star. Conspicuous Service Cross. Awarded Pulitzer prize for local reporting, 1950. Clubs: Silurians, Dutch Treat. Author: The Eight Million, 1942; Men of Maryknoll, 1943; Story of The New York Times, 1951; City on Many Waters, 1955. Office: 229 W. 43 St., N.Y.C. 18. Died Feb. 8, 1959.

BERGH, Louis O., lawyer; b. Bklyn., Nov. 2, 1885; s. Louis DeCoppet and Grace (Bunker) B.; A.B., Yale, 1906; LL.B., St. Lawrence U., 1909; m. Ethel E. Cushing, Sept. 10, 1921 (dec.); m. 2d, Geraldine D. Holden, Nov. 22, 1946. Admitted to N.Y. bar 1910, since practiced in N.Y.C., partner Turnbull & Bergh, 1936-—; asst. dist. atty. N.Y. County, 1913-14; adj. prof. law N.Y.U., 1948-52. Mem. Am. Bar Assn., Assn. Bar City N.Y., Am. Bus. Law Assn., Phi Beta Kappa, Phi Delta Phi, Zeta Psi. Club: Glen Ridge Country. Author: Business Law (with Conyngton), 1948. Home: 10 Crestmont Rd., Montclair, N.J. Office: 111 John St., N.Y.C. 7. Died Nov. 28, 1955; buried Evergreen Cemetery, Bklyn.

BERGMANN, Werner, educator; b. Bielefeld, Germany, Apr. 30, 1904; s. Wilhelm and Caroline (Upmann) B.; student U. of Tübingen, 1924-26; Ph.D., U. of Göttingen, 1928; post doctorate work U. Edinburgh, 1930-31, U. of Heidelberg, 1931, Yale, 1931, M.A. hon., 1947; Guggenheim Fellow, 1954-55; m. Johanna Eberhard, Sept. 8, 1931; children—Barbara Elizabeth, Johannes Dietrich. Came to U.S., 1931, naturalized, 1939. Asst. prof. Yale, 1939-43, asso. prof., 1943-47, prof., 1947-—; Fulbright guest prof. U. Heidelberg, Germany, 1954-55, cons. Bingham Oceanographic Lab., New Haven, 1946-—. Trustee Bermuda Biol. Station, 1950-—. Mem. com. med. research, investigator Office Emergency Mgmt., 1942-45. Mem. Am. Chem. Soc., Soc. Biol. Chemists, Conn. Acad. Arts and Scis. Home: 94 Cottage St., New Haven 11. Died Nov. 2, 1959; buried Grove St. Cemetery.

BERGQUIST, Stanard Gustaf, prof. geology; b. Ironwood, Mich., Aug. 13, 1892; s. Charles John and Ellen Elizabeth (Walquist) B.; A.B., Univ. of Mich., 1915, M.Sc., 1927, Ph.D., 1933; m. Ada Evelyon Whitman, Aug. 6, 1924; 1 dau., Donna Jeanne. Instr. geology, Mich. State Coll., 1916, asst. prof., 1924, asso. prof., 1930, head dept. geology and geography, 1930, prof. geol., 1933, acting head dept. phys. sci., Basic College, 1945-48; head dept. phys. science, 1948-52; member of soil survey, Michigan, summers, 1921, 24, marl survey, Mich. Geol. Survey, summers, 1925-26; geol. Land Econ. Survey, Mich., summers, 1928-33; mem. gov.'s natural gas fact finding com., Mich., 1937; apptd. by gov. to investigate iron mines in Gogebic Co. for State Tax Commn., summer, 1942; field studies in glacial geology for Mich. Geol. Survey, summers, 1935-46; cons. geol. Engrs. Research Assn., 1936-37. Mem. East Lansing Council, 1930-31, East Lansing Bd. of Edn., 1938-44 (pres. 1939-41), East Lansing Charter Revision Commn., 1943; chmn. non-metallic sect. Mich. Minerals Industries Conf., 1942-43. Fellow A.A.A.S., Geol. Soc. of Am.; mem. Mich. Geol. Soc. (bus. mgr., 1936-37, 1940-41), Mich. Acad. of Sciences (pres. 1940), Am. Assn. Univ. Profs., Am. Legion, Sigma Xi, Phi Sigma, Sigma Gamma Epsilon, Phi Kappa Phi. Mem. People's Ch. Mason. Clubs: Inter City Wranglers (pres. 1941-42), Mich. Engineers. Author miscellaneous papers on geology, for sci. jours. Home: 164 Maplewood Dr., East Lansing, Mich. Died Mar. 31, 1956; buried Evergreen Cemetery, Lansing.

BERGSAKER, Anders Johannessen (bĕrgs'ä-kĕr), ch. official; b. near Stavanger, Norway, Jan. 23, 1877; s. Johannes and Martha (Barkve) B.; came to U.S., 1892, naturalized, 1904; A.B., St. Olaf Coll., Northfield, Minn., 1902; C.T., United Ch. Sem., St. Paul, Minn., 1905; attended U. of S.D., 1919-20; D.D., Luther Coll., Decorah, Ia., 1931; LL.D., Augustana Coll., Sioux Falls, S.D., 1931; m. Hulda Mathilda Lunder, July 6, 1911; children—Althea Marie, Elsa Bergliot, Christy Borghild, Alpha Swanhild Hildegard, Arnold Jerome. Ordained ministry Evangelical Luth. Ch., 1905; pastor Slayton, Minn., 1905-10, Dell Rapids, S.D., 1910-18, Elk Point, S.D., 1918-24; stewardship sec. S.D. Dist., Evangelical Lutheran Church, 1924-26; secretary S.D. Home Mission Com., 1917-26; pres. (bishop) S.D. Dist., 1926-31; gen. stewardship sec. since 1931, also gen. sec. Evangelical Lutheran Church since 1934. Director Beloit Orphans Home, 1913-18, Augustana Coll., 1925-31; mem. Com. on Cooperation with other Lutheran Synods; dir. Centennial Campaign of Evangelical Lutheran Church, 1938-45. Director Luther Coll. Emergency Appeal, 1942-44, Boe Meml. Chapel Appeal, 1945-46, membership transfer and contact Dept., since 1943; mem. Commn. on Am. Missions, 1943-45; dir. Lutheran World Action, 1946; del. Evang. Lutheran Ch. to Luth. World Fedn., Lund, Sweden, 1947; mem. commission on American Missions, 1943-45; dir. Lutheran World Action, 1941. Contbr. to church periodicals. Home: 4529 Colfax Av. S. Office: 408 5th Av. S., Mpls. Died Nov. 23, 1951.*

BERKELEY, Randolph Carter, officer U.S. Marine Corps; b. Staunton, Va., Jan. 9, 1875; s. Carter and Lovie Jane (Gilkeson) B.; ed. Potomac Acad., Alexandria, Va.; grad. Marine Corps Field Officers Sch., Quantico, Va., and Army War Coll.; m. Carrie Anna Phillips, Sept. 12, 1906 (died 1907); 1 son, James Phillips (lt. col. U.S. Marine Corps); m. 2d, Bessye Bancroft Russell, Oct. 2, 1911; 1 son, Randolph Carter, Jr. (lt. col., aviator U.S. Marine Corps). Stenographer Richmond and Danville R.R. (now Southern Ry. Co.), 1893, city passenger agent, 1896; 2d lt. Marine Corps, Spanish-Am. War, 1898; through grades to maj. gen., 1939; now retired; shore service in Philippine Islands, Panama, Haiti, Nicaragua, Guam, Cuba; sea service on battleships Oregon and Kentucky and in Chinese waters on river gunboat U.S.S. Helena; pres. Naval Examining Bd., Marine Corps, 1936-39; retired Feb. 1, 1939. Holder of Congressional Medal of Honor, Navy Distinguished Service Medal, Navy Cross, Nicaraguan medals and various campaign badges. Mason. Episcopalian. Club: Army and Navy Country. Home: R.F.D., Beaufort, S.C. Died Jan. 31, 1960; buried Arlington Nat. Cemetery.

BERKEY, Charles Peter (bĕrk'ē), geologist; b. Goshen, Ind., Mar. 25, 1867; s. Peter and Lydia (Stutsman) B.; B.S., U. of Minn., 1892, M.S., 1893, Ph.D., 1897, hon. D.Sc., 1940; hon. Sc.D., Columbia U., 1929; m. Mninie M. Best, Sept. 4, 1894; children—Paul Ainsworth, Virginia Dale. Instr. in geology, U. of Minn., to 1903; tutor, instr. and asst. prof., asso. prof. and prof. geology, Columbia U., 1903-41. A specialist on geology applied to engineering. Employed on state surveys (geol.) of Minn., Wis. and New York; consulting geologist N.Y. Bd. Water Supply, 1906-—; also consulting geologist of the Met. Dist. Water Supply Commn. of Mass., Dept. of Water and Power of Los Angeles; cons. engineer U.S. Reclamation Bureau, Tenn. Valley Authority; petrographer and geologist on many engring. and mining problems; chief geologist Central Asiatic Expdns., Am. Museum Natural History, 1922-—; geologist Port of New York Authority; mem. U.S. Colo. River Bd. Ex-sec. and past pres. Geol. Soc. Am. Fellow A.A.A.S.; mem. N.Y. Acad. Scis. (past pres.), Rochester Acad. Science, Geol. Soc. China, Am. Inst. Mining and Metall. Engrs., Municipal Engrs. City of New York, Am. Soc. Civil Engrs. (hon.), Am. Philos. Soc., Nat. Acad. Sciences, Phi Beta Kappa, Sigma Xi, Tau Beta Pi, Phi Gamma Delta; corr. mem. Geol. Soc. of London. Home: 1076 Cumbermede Rd., Palisade, N.J. Died Aug. 22, 1955.

BERKEY, Peter, corp. exec.; b. St. Paul, Aug. 9, 1885; s. John Addison and Minnesota (De Graff) B.; ed. pub. schs. of St. Paul; m. Clarice K. Stone, Minneapolis, Sept. 10, 1917; children—June, Peter, Jr., John Addison, Andrew De Graff, II. Pres. and treas. Self-Locking Carton Co. (consol. with Shellmar Products Co., 1946, became Gen. Package Corp.), 1910-46, chmn., 1946-55; chmn. Gen. Package div. Diamond Match Co. (became Molded-Packaging div. Diamond Gardner Corp., 1959), 1955-—; dir. The Murray Corp. of Am. bliss & Laughlin, Inc. Rep. Episcopalian. Clubs: Chicago, Saddle and Cycle, Racquet (Chgo.); Glenview Golf (Golf, Ill.); University (St. Paul, Minn.). Home: 936 Lake Shore Dr. Office: 589 E. Illinois St., Chgo. Died July 3, 1959.

BERKSON, Seymour, pub. and author; b. Chgo., Jan. 31, 1905; s. William and Bertha (Bloom) B.; student U. Chgo., 1922-25, hon. fellowship in polit. science; m. Jane Noble Eads, May 16, 1931; 1 dau., Barbara Jane; m. 2d, Eleanor Lambert, Dec. 18, 1936; 1 son, William Craig. Mem. staff Chgo. Herald and Examiner, 1923-31; with Asso. Press, N.Y.C., 1931; joined Universal Service as staff writer, 1931, chief of its bureau in Rome, 1932-34, in Paris, 1934-35; mng. editor Internat. News Service, 1935-45, v.p., gen. mgr., 1945-55; pub. N.Y. Jour.-Am., 1955-—; v.p., dir. Hearst Consol. Publs., Inc. Mem. Internat. Pres. Inst., Silurians, Sigma Delta Chi. Clubs: Overseas Press, Dutch Treat, Downtown Athletic Author: Their Majesties! A Royal Merry-go-Round, 1938; Rise and Fall of Mussolini, 1943. Co-author: The Best I Know, 1941; They Were There, 1941 Contbr. mags. Home: 1060 Fifth Av., N.Y.C. 220 South St., N.Y.C. 15. Died Jan. 4, 1959.

BERL, Eugene Ennalls, Dem. nat. committeeman, lawyer; b. New Orleans, Mar. 2, 1889; s. William and Marie (Waggaman) B.; A.B., Princeton, 1912; LL.B., Harvard, 1915. Admitted to Del. bar, 1915, and since practiced in Wilmington; mem. firm Ward & Gray, and successor firm Berl Potter and Anderson, attys.-at-law, since 1927. City solicitor, Wilmington,

1933-35; nominee for U.S. Senate, 1942; Dem. nat. committeeman since 1948. Served as 1st lt. U.S. Ambulance Service, 1917-18, capt. Claims Service, 1918-19; lt. col. to col. U.S. Army, 1943-46, with Italian Mil. hdqrs., 1943-44, asst. chief of staff G/5 13th Corps. Eng., France, Belgium, Holland and Germany, 1944-45; col. Gen. Staff Corps, 1945-46. Decorated Silver Star medal with two oak leaves, Legion of Merit, Bronze Star medal (U.S.); Croix de Guerre. Mem. Am. and Del. State bar assns. Democrat. Roman Catholic. Clubs: Wilmington, Wilmington Country (Del.); Princeton (N.Y. City); Army and Navy (Wash.). Home: 1303 Market St., Wilmington. Office: Delaware Trust Bldg., Wilmington 28, Del. Died Apr. 1, 1954; buried Cathedral Cemetery, Wilmington, Del.

BERMAN, Oscar, mfr. cotton textiles and work garments; b. Salant, Lithuania, Dec. 23, 1876; s. Charles Meyer and Sophia (Raitz) B.; ed. pub. schs., Lithuania and Cincinnati, O.; m. Cora Frank, Dec. 5, 1900; children—Benjamin, Arnold. Came to U.S., 1893. Began as stock clerk, wholesale men's furnishings, Cincinnati, 1894; traveling salesman, neckwear, 1896-1903; purchased part interest in Laurel Mfg. Co., work garment mfrs., 1903; organizer, 1903, since pres. The Crown Overall Mfg. Co.; pres. Stonewall (Miss.) Cotton Mills, Inc., since 1920; pres. Stonewall Bank, 1924-39; treas. Larned, Carter & Co. (mfrs. "Headlight" overalls); dir. Central Trust Co., Cincinnati. Pres. emeritus Union Made Garment Mfrs. Assn. of Am. (chmn. exec. bd., chmn. nat. wage scale com., 1916-39); chmn. Nat. Joint Com. Prison Labor, 1923-32. Gen. chmn. clothing and textile div. war resources com., Region 10, War Industries Bd., World War; pres. Jewish Community Council of Cincinnati, 1936-40; chmn. Am.-Jewish Joint Distbn. Com. (Ohio region), 1941-43; mem. bd. govs. Hebrew Union Coll. (v.p. 1920); dir. Palestine Economic Corp., Coordinating Com. for Refugees, City Charter Com. of Cincinnati; mem. nat. exec. com. Am. Jewish Congress, Zionist Orgn. America, 1919-20. Mem. Inter-Code Com. of Clothing Code and Cotton Garment Code Authorities, 1934. Mem. Am. Cotton Mfrs. Assn., Internat. Assn. Garment Mfrs. Chamber of Commerce of U.S., Cincinnati Chamber Commerce, Am. Acad. Polit. and Social Science, Am. Oriental Soc., Intercollegiate Menorah Assn., Cincinnati Inst. Fine Arts, Cincinnati Art Mus. Assn., Am. Acad. Jewish Research, Big Brother Assn. Republican. Jewish religion. Mason (Shriner). B'nai B'rith. Clubs: Cincinnati; Congressional Country (Washington). Home: 675 Clinton Springs Av., Cincinnati 29. Office: 3d. Plum and McFarland Sts., Cin. 2. Died Dec. 1, 1951.

BERNARD, Frances Fenton, educator; b. Washington, Dec. 4. 1880; d. Ernest Albert and Mary (Spaulding) Fenton; A.B., Vassar Coll., 1902; fellow in sociology U. Chgo., 1908-10, Ph.D., 1910; m. Luther Lee Bernard, Sept. 16, 1911; 1 dau., Mrs Mary Marjorie Gregor; m. 2d, Edwin A. Park. Tchr. English, Normal Sch., Mankato, Minn., 1903-04; instr. English, Mt. Holyoke Coll., 1904-07, instr. sociology and econs., 1910-11, 17; asst. prof. econs. Wellesley Coll., 1920-21; ednl. sec. Am. Assn. U. Women, 1922-24; dean Smith Coll., Northampton, Mass., 1924-28. Mem. Alpha Zeta Pi, Kappa Delta Pi. Clubs: Nat. Headquarters, University Women (Washington); Vassar (N.Y.C.). Author: Influence of Newspaper Presentations Upon Crime and Other Anti-Social Activity, 1911. Contbr. on ednl. topics. Home: Boston. Died July 21, 1953.

BERNARD, Luther Lee, educator; b. Russell County, Ky., Oct. 29, 1881; s. Hiram Hamilton and Julia Ann (Wilson) B.; B.S., Peirce City (Mo.) Bapt. Coll., 1900, A.B., U. Mo., 1907; Ph.B., U. Chgo., 1910; instr. scis. Peirce City Bapt. Coll., 1901-03; prof. langs. Lamar Coll. (Mo.), 1903-05; fellow in sociology U. Chgo., 1907-10; instr. sociology Western Res. U., 1910-11; prof. history and social scis. U. Fla., 1911-14; prof. sociology U. Mo., 1914-17; asso. prof. and prof. sociology U. Minn., 1917-25; prof. Cornell U., 1925-26; vis. prof. sociology U. Chgo., 4 summers to 1927, professorial lectr. sociology, spring 1927; vis. prof. U. Wash., summers 1928-29, 32, Ore., 1938, 39, Mich., 1940, Cal. (Berkeley), 1942; prof. sociology, Tulane, 1927-28, U. N.C., 1928-29, Washington U., 1929-37, Penn State Coll., 1947-—; Amherst meml. research fellow, 1921-22; Social Sci. Research Council fellow for study soc. scis. in Argentina, 1926-27. Mem. Am. (pres. 1932), The Masaryk (Czechoslovakia) sociol. socs., Inst. Internat. de Soc., Assn. for Hist. Studies (Argentina), Phi Beta Kappa, Phi Kappa Phi, Alpha Pi Zeta (chmn. nat. com. on orgn., 1924-26), Zeta Phi, Alpha Kappa Delta (nat. pres., 1937-47), Alpha Psi Delta. Author: The Teaching of Sociology in the United States, 1909; The Transition to an Objective Standard of Social Control, 1911; Instinct, 1924; Introduction to Social Psychology, 1926; The Development of Methods in Sociology, 1928; Social Control, 1939; Introduction to Sociology, 1942. War and Its Causes, 1944. Joint Author: The Mind and Work, 1914; Introduction to Sociology, 1927; Readings in Sociology, 1927; The Social Sciences, 1927; Modern Scientific Knowledge, 1929; Social Attitudes, 1931; Sociology and the Study of International Relations, 1934; Origins of American Sociology, 1943. Editor: Fields and Methods of Sociology, 1934. Contributor to professional and gen. periodicals in United States, Argentina, China, France, and Mexico. Gen. editor Am. Sociologist; asso. editor Social Forces; mem. editorial bd. Social Science. Home: 608 W. Fairmount Av., State College, Pa. Died Jan. 23, 1951; buried Memorial Park, State College.

BERNARD, Merrill, hydrologist; b. Burlington, Ia., July 25, 1892; ed. N.C. Mil. Acad., 1907; Mil. Coll. of S.C., 1908-10; A. and M. Coll. of Okla., 1911; m. Claudia Turner, Aug. 1, 1914. Engaged in municipal, irrigation and railroad engring. to 1916; civil engring., 1918-20; cons. engr. designing and supervising municipal, drainage and irrigation projects, La., Tex., Central Am., 1929-36; hydrologic specialist for Miss. Valley Com., 1934-36; hydraulic engr. Soil Conservation Service, 1936-37; with U.S. Weather Bureau since 1937, chief River and Flood Div., 1937-39, hydrologic director, 1939-46; chief, climatological and hydrological services, since 1946. Served as 1st lt., U.S. Army, World War I. Mem. American Society Civil Engineers (Norman medalist, 1945), Am. Geophys. Union, Nat. Research Council (v.p. hydrology sect.), Wash. Acad. Sciences; mem. Internat. Union Geodesy and Geophysics (pres. internat. assn. hydrol. 1948), Internat. Meteorol. Orgn. (v.p. hydrol. commn.), Research and Development Bd. (mem. com. on geophys. geog.), Am. Meteorol. Soc. Mem. Am. delegation 220th Anniversary Soviet Acad. Scis., Moscow; mem. Am. Meteorologic Mission to U.S.S.R., 1945. Club: Cosmos (Wash.). Contbr. papers to govt. bulls. and engring. jours. Home: 2205 42d St. N.W., Washington, D.C. Died April 13, 1951.

BERNBAUM, Ernest (bẽrn'boum), educator; b. Bklyn., Feb. 12, 1879; s. Ole Kruse and Dorothea (Christiansen) B.; A.B., Harvard, 1902, A.M., 1905, Ph.D., 1907; m. Ruth Guenther, June 9, 1921. Instr. English, Harvard, 1907-16; prof. English, U. Ill., 1916-45, head of dept., 1925-28, 1944-45, emeritus, 1945-—, chmn. com. on war lecturers, 1917-19. Speaker for League to Enforce Peace, 1922-25. Mem. com. on publs. Am.-Scandinavian Foundn., 1949-—; dir. Amos Fortune Forum, Jaffrey, N.H., 1948-52. Mem. Modern Lang. Assn. Am., Modern Humanities Research Assn., Nat. Council Tchrs. English, Am. Assn. U. Profs. (mem. council 1927-29), Phi Beta Kappa, Phi Kappa Phi, Delta Upsilon. Episcopalian. Clubs: Harvard, English-Speaking Union (Boston); Rotary (Urbana, Ill.); Thorndike (Jaffrey, N.H.). Author: The Mary Carleton Narratives, 1914; The Drama of Sensibility, 1915; The Puritan Pilgrim (poem), 1921. Editor: English Poets of the Eighteenth Century, 1918; Swift's Gulliver's Travels, 1920; Romantic Anthology and Guide Through the Romantic Movement, 5 vols., 1929; The Romantic Period, 1930; Earlier Victorian Period, 1930; Later Victorian Period, 1930; The English Romantic Poets; A Review of Research, 1951. Gen. editor Nelson's Series of College Text Books in English, 1927; gen. editor The Ronald Press Co., 1942-—; cons. editor of publs. of Modern Lang. Assn. America, 1930. Mem. advisory staff College English, 1939-46. Address: Freedom's Haven, Jaffrey Center, N.H. Died Mar. 8, 1958; buried Old Churchyard, Jaffrey Center.

BERNECKER, Edward M., hosp. exec.; b. Seward, Neb., Mar. 13, 1892; s. Oscar Edward and Marie (Goetz) B.; student Walther Coll., St. Louis, M.D., Hahnemann Med. Coll., 1915; L.H.D., N.Y. Med. Coll., 1954, LL.D., Adelphi Coll., 1954; m. Merle Crawford, May 1, 1924; 1 dau., Barbara Ann. Intern Met. Hosp., Welfare Island, N.Y. City, 1915-16, resident surgeon, 1917; deputy med. supt., Met. Hosp., 1920-25, med. supt., 1925-35; med. supt., Kings County Hosp., Brooklyn, N.Y., 1935-37; gen. med. supt., Dept. of Hosps., City of N.Y., 1937-42. commissioner of hosps., 1942-48; adminstr. hospital services New York Univ. and Bellevue Medical Center since Jan. 1949; chief emergency medical service City of N.Y., 1942-45. Served as first lieutenant, M.C., U.S. Army, 1917-19. Mem. Greater N.Y. Hosp. Assn., N.Y. State Hosp. Assn., Am. Hosp. Assn. N.Y. County Med. Soc., Queens County Med. Soc., Med. Soc. State of N.Y.; fellow A.M.A., N.Y. Acad. of Medicine, Am. Coll. of Hosp. Adminstrn. Mason. Mem. Ch. in the Gardens Assn. Home: 10 Holder Pl. Forest Hills, N.Y. Office: University Hospital, 303 E. 20th St., N.Y.C. Died June 27, 1955; buried Maple Grove Cemetery, Horseheads, N.Y.

BERNER, Harry M., business exec.; b. Chgo., 1896; 1 son, Ray H. Formerly exec. v.p. Am. Hosp. Supply Corp., Evanston, Ill., pres., dir., 1954. Pres., dir. Instl. Industries, Inc., Cin.; v.p., dir. Meal Pack Corp., Evanston. Home: 3270 N. Lake Shore Dr., Chgo. Office: 2020 Ridge Av., Evanston, Ill. Died July 31, 1954.

BERNHARD, Alva Douglas, naval officer; b. Pa., Mar. 9, 1886. Commd. ensign, USN, advanced to capt., 1937, rear admiral, 1941; designated naval aviator. Deceased.*

BERNHARD, Joseph, motion picture exec.; b. Phila., May 7, 1889; s. Louis and Clara (Mayer) B.; student pub. schs.; m. Florence Black, Feb. 10, 1919; children—Jack, Maurice, Louis. Began as office boy, 1905; engaged in real estate and banking bus., Phila., 1920-31; joined Warner Brothers Pictures, Inc., N.Y.C., 1930, became gen. mgr. Warner Bros. Theatres and v.p., dir. Warner Bros., Inc.; tech. cons. bur. yards and docks, Navy Dept. World War II; founded Milton Sperling prodn. co. of U.S. Pictures, Inc., resigned as pres., treas., 1947; became pres. Film Classics, 1947, Cinecolor Corp., 1948; produced independently Journey Into Light, Japanese War Bride, Ruby Gentry, 1951; now cons. on mgmt. relations Stanley Warner Film Corp. Recipient Meritorious Civilian Service award from Bureau of Yards and Docks. Home: 30 W. 54th St., N.Y.C. Deceased.*

BERNHEIM, Bertram Moses (bẽrn'hīm), surgeon; b. Paducah, Ky., Feb. 15, 1880; s. Isaac Wolf and Amanda (Uri) B.; A.B., Johns Hopkins, 1901, M.D., 1905; p.-grad. work in Europe, 1906, in U.S., 1907; m. Hilda Marcus, July 26, 1905; children—Minda, Isaac Wolfe, Bertram. Practiced surgery, Baltimore, since 1908, specializing in blood-transfusion, and surg. of the blood vessels; asso. prof. emeritus surg., Johns Hopkins Med. Sch.; visiting surgeon Union Memorial Hosp., Hosp. for Women of Md., Church Home and Infirmary; visiting surgeon Johns Hopkins Hosp. Major, Medical Reserve Corps; member Johns Hopkins Hosp. Base Unit, A.E.F. in France, June 1917-Feb. 1919; received citation in France. Fellow and founder Am. Coll. Surgeons, Am. Bd. Surgery; fellow Am. Med. Assn.; mem. Medico-Chirurg. Faculty of Md. Jewish religion. Author: Surgery of the Vascular System, 1913; Blood Transfusion, Hemorrhage and the Anemias, 1917; Passed as Censored, 1918; Medicine at the Crossroads, 1939; Adventure in Blood Transfusion, 1942; A Surgeon's Domain, 1947 (Norton Award); The Story of The Johns Hopkins, 1948; also numerous articles dealing with surgery. Home: Pikesville 8, Md. Office: 2424 Eutaw Pl., Baltimore 17, Md. Died Nov. 28, 1958; buried Druid Ridge Cemetery, Pikesville, Md.

BERNINGHAUS, Oscar Edmund, artist; b. St. Louis, Mo., Oct. 2, 1874; s. Edmund O. and Augusta P. (Helgenberg) B.; ed. in grammar schs., St. Louis; student, night classes, St. Louis Sch. Fine Arts, otherwise self-taught; engaged in lithography, 1889-94; m. Emilia Miller, 1899 (died 1913); m. 2d, Winnifred Shuler, 1932. Exhibited Nat. Acad. Design, N.Y.; Pa. Acad. Fine Arts, Phila.; Art Inst. Chgo.; Art Mus., St. Louis; San Francisco Expn., 1915; Santa Fe Art Mus.; etc. Awarded Dolph prize, 1907; Bascom prize, 1915; Brown prize (St. Louis Artist's Guild), 1917 (all for figure painting); also participant Chgo. Fine Arts Bldg. prize (Soc. Western Artists), 1913; C. of C. prize, St. Louis, 1918; grand prize, St. Louis Art League, 1920; Artists Guild prize, 1924; Ranger Fund Purchase prize, 1925, and Altman prize, 1926, both N.A.D. Represented in permanent collection City Art Mus., also Branch Library, and pub. schs., St. Louis; five murals, Capitol Bldg., Jefferson City, Mo.; also in permanent collections of City Art Mus., St. Louis, Mo., Fort Worth, Texas, Erie, Pa., San Antonio, Tex.; and numerous pvt. collections; mural in Ft. Scott (Kans.) Fed. Ct. Bldg.; 2 murals in Phoenix (Ariz.) Post Office. Designer of Annual Pageant of the Veiled Prophet, St. Louis. A.N.A., 1926. Hon. mem. St. Louis Artists' Guild, St. Louis Art League, Two by Four Club, Taos (N.M.) Society of Artists. Specializes in life of the Southwest. Home: Taos, N.M. Died Apr. 25, 1952; buried Taos, N.M.

BERNSTEIN, Aline, designer, novelist; b. N.Y.C.; d. Joseph and Rebecca (Goldsmith) Frankau; grad. pub. sch., 1898; m. Theodore Bernstein, Nov. 19, 1902; children—Theodore F., Edla (Mrs. Edla Benjamin). Made many prodns. for N.Y. Theatre, Neighborhood Playhouse, Theatre Guild, Civic Repertory Theatre, Gilbert Miller, Herman Shumlin, Elmer Rice, Playwrights Co., etc.; 2 films for R.K.O., Hollywood, Cal. Mem. Authors League Am., Am. Fedn. Labor. Author: Three Blue Suits; The Journey Down; also many articles on theatrical technic. Deceased.

BERRIEN, Frank Dunn (bĕr'ĭ-ĕn), naval officer; b. Galesburg, Ill., Aug. 17, 1877; s. Leonard Budd and Harriet May (Smith) B.; B.S., U.S. Naval Acad., 1900; grad. U.S. Naval War Coll., 1917; Army War Coll., 1926; m. Mary Elizabeth Whittelsey, Nov. 9, 1907; children—Frank Whittelsey, Mary Elizabeth (Mrs. Harry Hager Lugg). Served on U.S.S. Cincinnati in West Indies in Spanish-Am. War, 1898, Asiatic Station, participating in Philippine Campaign and Boxer War, 1900-04; with Atlantic Fleet on warships Kentucky and Missouri, 1904-07; on staff Rear Adm. C. M. Thomas, on flagships Minnesota and Connecticut, 1907-08; head football coach Naval Acad., 1908-10; comdr. U.S. Destroyer, Trippe, 1910-14; participated in Mexican Campaign, 1914; in charge Naval Magazine, Hingham, Mass., 1914-16; apptd. comdr. U.S. warships Nicholson and Wilkes at Queenstown, Ire., 1917; comdr. U.S. hosp ship, Comfort, 1918; following the armistice became naval post officer at Bordeaux, France, remaining until summer of 1919; chief of staff to comdr. of the Destroyer Force of the Pacific Fleet, 1920; capt. submarine base, New London, Conn., 1921-23; comdr. desrtoyer divs. in Europe, 1923-25; est. and commanded naval unit at Yale Univ.,

1926; qualified as naval observer, Naval Air Sta., Pensacola, Fla., 1928; comdr. U.S. airplane carrier, Lexington, 1928-30; capt. Navy Yard, Washington, 1930; rear admiral, 1935—; on active duty as troop convoy comdr. between San Francisco and South Australia, Mar.-Aug. 1942. Decorated Distinguished Service Medal (U.S.), Order of St. Michael and St. George (Gr. Brit.), Comdr. Order of the Savior (Greece). Mem. Queenstown Assn., Mil. Order World War, Mil. Order of the Dragon, Mill. Order of Carabao; Huguenot Soc., Phi Gamma Delta. Republican. Conglist. Clubs: New York Yacht (N.Y.C.); Army and Navy, Army and Navy Country (Washington). Died Jan. 31, 1951; buried Naval Acad. Cemetery, Annapolis.

BERRY, Charles White, soldier, city ofcl.; b. Greene County, N.Y., Apr. 11, 1871; s. Frank M. and Almira (Horn) B.; M.D., Columbia, 1896; D.P.H. course N.Y.U.; m. Nina La Plante, Dec. 1922; 3 children. Practiced medicine in Bklyn. many yrs.; chmn. N.Y. Fair Price Coal Commn., 1924-25; mem. Reconstrn. Labor Bd. of N.Y., 1919-21; comptroller City of N.Y., 1926—. Served from pvt. to capt. N.Y. N.G., 1903-17, maj. 14th Inf. later 106th Inf., AEF, 1917-18, participated battles at Somme Defensive, Dickebusch Lake, Vierstraat Ridge, Hindenburg Line (Somme offensive), Canal de la Sambre; brig. gen. N.Y. N.G., 1919-23, adj. gen. State N.Y.; comdr. N.Y. N.G., 1923-25. Decorated N.Y. Conspicuous Service Cross; Croix de Guerre with palms (Belgium); Comdr. Order Polonia Restituta; cited for gallantry in action. Democrat. Presbyn. Home: Romer Rd., Dongan Hills, S.I., N.Y. Office: Municipal Bldg., N.Y.C. Died 1941.

BERRY, George Titus, missionary secretary; b. Valatie, N.Y., May 20, 1865; A.B., Princeton, 1887, A.M., 1890; Princeton Theol. Sem., 1889-92. Prof. mathematics Glendale Coll., 1887-89; ordained Presbyn. ministry, 1892; stated supply Second St. Ch., Troy, N.Y., 1892-94. pastor, 1895-1900; asst. sec. Ch. Federation of New York, 1901-04; field sec. Am. McAll Assn., 1905-30; Retired. Home: Longwood Towers, 20 Chapel St., Brookline 46, Mass. Died Nov. 16, 1956; buried Bennington, Vt.

BERRY, Howard, business exec.; b. Hackensack, N.J., Mar. 25, 1886; s. Samuel and Elizabeth (Winton) B.; m. Florence Sparrow, Oct. 4, 1920. In pub. accounting work, 1905-16; auditor Am. Internat. Corp., N.Y.C., 1916-18; gen. auditor Am. Internat. Corp., 1919-21; controller Remington Arms Co., 1921-23; with Mathieson Chem. Corp. now component Olin Mathieson Corp. (formerly Mathieson Alkali Works, Inc.), 1923-51, v.p., treas. and dir. 1930-51, ret.; financial cons., 1951—. Home: 106 S. Harrison St., East Orange, N.J. Died Apr. 27, 1958.

BERRY, Thomas, gov. State of S.D., 1933-37; rancher, Mellette County, S.D. Democrat. Address: H Ranch, Belvidere, S.D. Died Oct. 30, 1951; buried Belvidere.

BERRYMAN, W. A., petroleum exec.; b. Enterprise, Va., Jan. 22, 1892; s. William R. and Bette L. (Warren) B.; ed. pub. schs. of Va.; m. Rebecca Walker, Nov. 21, 1921; 1 dau., Nancy Warren. Auditor Ernst & Ernst, 1918-27; asst. comptroller Standard Steel Car Co., 1927-33; asst. to mng. dir., Gulf European Marketing Interests, Antwerp, Belgium, 1933-39; asst. to v.p., Gulf Oil Corp., 1939-49, v.p. since 1949; v.p. Gulf European Co., Gulf Exploration Co., Gulf Refining Co., Gulf Research & Development Co., Pitts.; dir. Compagnie Nationale Immobiliere S.A., Antwerp, Belgian Gulf Oil Co., S.A., Antwerp, Danish Am. Gulf Oil Co., A.S., Copenhagen, Denmark, Finska Gulf Oil Co., A.B., Helsingfrrd, Finland, Gulf Oil (Gt. Britain) Ltd., London, Eng., Nederlandsche Gulf Olie Maatschappij, N.V., Rotterdam, N.V. Credietvereeniging voor den Handel in Petroleum-prodn., Rotterdam, Olie Handelsvereeniging N.V., Rotterdam, S.A. Espanola de Lubrificantes, Barcelona, Spain, Rimba Rob. Jos. Jecker Minera loel & Benzin A/G, Zurich, United Petroleum Securities Corp., N.Y., Svenska Gulf Oil Co., A.B., Stockholm, Sweden. Mason. Clubs: Antwerp Golf (Antwerp); Pitts. Field, Pitts. Athletic Assn., Duquesne, Fox Chapel Golf (Pitts.). Home: 825 Morewood Av., Pitts. 13. Office: Gulf Bldg., Pitts. 30. Died Aug. 3, 1952.

BERTRAND, Ernest, Canadian govt. ofcl.; b. Plessisville, P.Q., Can., Dec. 15, 1888; s. Georges Onésime and Elise (Savoie) B.; B.A., U. Montreal, 1912, LL.B., 1915; m. Jeannette Marion, May 9, 1920; children—Micheline, Suzanne. Called to bar, Quebec, 1915; crown prosecutor for Montreal, 1919-36; elected to House of Commons, 1935, 40, 45, 49; sworn of Privy Council and appointed Minister of Fisheries, 1942; postmaster general of Can., 1945—. Roman Catholic. Mem. Liberal Party. Clubs: Montreal Reform; Kar-Ha-Kon Hunting and Fishing. Home: 68 Willowdale, Outremont, P.Q., Can. Office: Langevin Block, Ottawa, Ont., Can. Died Oct. 11, 1958.*

BERTRON, Samuel R.; pres., gen. mgr., dir., Houston Lighting & Power Co. Home: 2616 Calumet Dr., Houston 4. Office: 900 Fannin St, Houston 1. Died Oct. 1953.

BESSE, Arthur (bĕs'sē), trade association exec.; b. Bridgeport, Conn., Apr. 13, 1887; s. Lyman Waterman and Henrietta (Segee) B.; B.A. cum laude, Harvard, 1909; m. Eleanor Pass, Feb. 23, 1919; children—Arthur, Richard Waterman, Alden. Asst. mgr. Besse Carpenter & Co., clothiers, Springfield, Mass., 1909-11; real estate management, 1911-13; asst. mgr. Besse-Avery Co., clothiers, Kansas City, Mo., and Besse-Sprague Co., Syracuse, N.Y., 1913-18; treasurer Sherman Welton Co., clothing mfrs., Boston, 1920-22; treas. Besse System Co., chain clothing stores, 1923-26; partner Hale Waters & Co., investment securities, 1926-31; pres. Nat. Assn. Wool Mfrs. and chmn. Code Authority, Wool Textile Industry, under NRA. Mem. Advisory Commission Council of National Defense, 1940. In Chemical Warfare Service, U.S. Army, 1918-20, successively capt., maj. and lt. col.; served as asst. in charge of Gas Defense Div. Dir. Nat. Assn. of Wool Mfrs., Dewey & Almy Chem. Co. Treas. North Am. Yacht Racing Union. Clubs: Union League, Downtown Athletic (New York); Harvard (Boston). Home: 923 Fifth Av. Office: 386 Fourth Av., N.Y.C. Died Nov. 24, 1951.

BESSEY, Ernst Athearn, botanist; b. Ames, Ia., Feb. 20, 1877; s. late Charles Edwin and Lucy (Athearn) B.; B.A., U. Neb., 1896, B.Sc., 1897, A.M., 1898; U. Halle, Germany, 1902-04, Ph.D., 1904; Munich, 1904; m. Edith Carleton Higgins, July 25, 1906; children—Bertha Agnes, William Higgins, Robert John. Bot. collector for N.Y. Bot. Garden in Mont. and Yellowstone Park, 1897, for U.S. Dept. of Agr. in Colo., 1898; asst. in botany Colo. Summer Sch., Colorado Springs, 1894, 95, 96, asst. pathologist, Div. Vegetable Physiology and Pathology, 1899-1901, asst. in charge of seed an dplant introduction, 1901-02, agrl. explorer in Russia, the Caucasus, Turkestan and Algeria, 1902-04, pathologist Bur. of Plant Industry, 1904-05, in charge Subtropical Lab. and Garden of U.S. Dept. Agr. at Miami, Fla., 1906-08; prof. botany and bacteriology, La. State U., 1908-10; prof. botany Mich. State Coll., 1910-45, distinguished prof. botany, 1945-46, retired 1946, acting dean applied science div., 1927-30, dean grad. sch., 1930-44; vis. prof. botany U. Hawaii, 1939-40. Fellow A.A.A.S.; mem. Bot. Soc. Am., Torrey Bot. Club, Am. Phytopath. Soc., Mycol. Soc. Am. (pres. 1941), Mich. Acad. Scis. (pres. 1915-16), Deutsche Botan Gesell, Phi Beta Kappa, Sigma Xi, Alpha Zeta, Phi Kappa Phi, Phi Sigma. Author: Textbook of Mycology, 1935, rev. edit. 1947; with others working on Mich. State U. agrl. dictionary, 1956-57. Home: 213 University Dr., East Lansing, Mich. Died July 17, 1957; buried Deepdale Cemetery, Lansing.

BEST, Alfred M., constrn. exec.; b. Caldwell, N.J., Aug. 31, 1876. Pres., dir. Best Bldg. Co., Inc., N.Y.C.; founder, pres. Alfred M. Best Co., Inc.; chmn. dir. Flitcraft, Inc. Home: 50 Sutton Pl. South, N.Y.C.; also Arcady, Peru, Vt. Office: 75 Fulton St., N.Y.C. Died May 6, 1958; buried Rockland Cemetery, Piermont, N.Y.

BEST, Clarence L., manufacturer. Began as draftsman, later supt., pres. C. L. Best Gas Tractor Co. until merged into Caterpillar Tractor Co. of which is chmn. bd. Address: San Leandro, Cal. Died Sept. 22, 1951.*

BEST, Howard Richard, ednl. adminstr.; b. Neligh, Neb., Aug. 7, 1894; s. Edward T. and May (Gilson) B.; B.A., Yankton Coll., 1917; certificat U. Montpelier, France; M.A., U. Neb., 1929; Ed.D., Columbia, 1939; m. Ruth Beatrice Merrick, Aug. 28, 1920; 1 son, Richard J. (M.D.). Supt. schs., Benedict, Neb., 1921-23, Wagner, S.D., 1923-28, Wayne, Neb., 1928-35, Cranford, N.J., 1935-58. Mem. Met. Sch. Study Council; mem. survey groups, author finance survey, Greenwich, Conn.; chmn. Cranford area Red Cross, 1942-50. Trustee Union Jr. Coll. Served with 342d machine gun battalion, U.S. Army, 1918-19; AEF. Mem. N.J. Athletic Assn. (exec. bd.), Nat. Kindergarten Assn. (pres. 1947-51), Am. Legion, Union County Supts. Round Table, Nat. Assn. Sch. Adminstrs., N.E.A., N.J. Tchrs., Phi Delta Kappa, Kappa Delta Pi. Presbyn. (elder). Clubs: New Jersey Schoolmasters, Kiwanis (past pres.). Author profl. monographs, mag. articles. Address: 130 S. Euclid Av., Pasadena, Cal. Died Aug. 6, 1958; buried Mountain View Cemetery, Pasadena.

BEST, William, v.p., dir. General Cigar Co., Inc., 1917-45, sr. v.p., 1945-49, adviser, 1949—. Dir., treas. The Cigar Inst. of Am.; v.p., chmn. exec. com. Tobacco Mchts. Assn. U.S. Home: 221 Corona Av., Palham, N.Y. Office: 119 W. 40th St., N.Y.C. 18. Died Sept. 21, 1955.

BETHEL, John P., sr. asso. editor Merriam-Webster dictionaries; b. Nassau, Bahamas, Jan. 5, 1904; s. John Alday and Eunice Julia (Johnson) B.; grad. Queen's Coll., Nassau, 1920; B.A., McGill U., 1924; A.M., Harvard, 1925, Ph.D., 1927; m. Eleanor Ruth Hickey, 1931; children—John Peter, Joan Ruth, David James. Came to U.S., 1924, naturalized, 1933. Instr. in English, State Teachers Coll., Buffalo, N.Y., 1927-29; asst. editor Webster's New Internat. Dictionary, second edition, 1930-34; director G. & C. Merriam Company, Springfield, Massachusetts, and general editor Merriam-Webster dictionaries, 1935-52 (Webster's Elementary Dictionary, 1935; Webster's Collegiate Dictionary, Fifth Edition, 1936; Webster's Students Dictionary, 1938; Webster's Dictionary of Synonyms, 1942; Webster's Biographical Dictionary, 1943; Webster's New Collegiate Dictionary, 1949; Webster's Geographical Dictionary, 1949); sr. asso. editor, 1952-58. Episcopalian. Address: 3870 Leafy Way, Coconut Grove, Miami 33, Fla. Died May 28, 1958.

BETHELL, Frank Hartsuff, physician, educator; b. N.Y. City, Apr. 11, 1903; s. Frank Hopkins and Florence (Hartsuff) B.; A.B., Princeton, 1925; grad. study Cambridge (Eng.) U., 1925-27; M.D., Johns Hopkins, 1929; m. Margaret Krieger, Nov. 11, 1930; children—Elaine Hartsuff, David Krieger. Intern, resident M.E. Hosp., Brooklyn, 1929-31; instr. U. Mich., 1931-36, assistant professor, 1936-43, associate professor, 1943-48, professor of internal medicine, 1948—; director of The Thomas Henry Simpson Memorial Inst. for Med. Research. Recipient Henry Russel award by U. Mich., 1939. Fellow A.C.P.; mem. A.M.A., Assn. Am. Physicians, Am. Soc. Clin. Investigation, Am. Soc. Exptl. Pathology, Internat. Hematology Soc., Central Soc. Clin. Research. Home: 409 Lenawee Dr. Office: Thomas Henry Simpson Memorial Inst. Med. Research, Ann Arbor. Died Apr. 21, 1959; buried Churchyard, St. James the Less, Scarsdale, N.Y.

BETHUNE, Mary McLeod, coll. pres. emeritus; born Mayesville, S C.; d. Samuel and Patsy (McIntosh) McLeod; grad. Scotia Sem., Concord, N. C., 1893; student Moody Bible Inst., Chgo., 1893-95; A.M. (hon.), Wilberforce U., 1915; M.S. (hon.), S.C. State Coll., Tuskegee (Ala.) Inst., 1938; LL. D., Lincoln U., Phila., 1935, Howard U., 1942, Atlanta U., 1945, Wiley Coll., Marshall, Tex., 1943; H.H.D., Bennett Coll., Greensboro, N.C., 1945, W. Va. State Coll., 1947, Rollins Coll., Winter Park, Fla., 1949; m. Albertus Bethune, May 1898; 1 son, Albert McLeod, Sr. Instr. Haines Inst., Augusta, Ga., 1895-96, Palatka Mission Sch., Fla., 1899-1903; founder Daytona Norman and Indsl. Sch. for Negro Girls, 1904, now Bethune-Cookman Coll., pres., 1904-42, pres. emeritus, 1942—, pres. adv. bd., 1954-55; a founder, past pres. Central Life Ins. Co.; dir. Negro affairs Nat. Yough Adminstrn., 1936-44. Spl. adviser to Pres. Franklin D. Roosevelt on minority affairs, 1936-44; spl. asst. to Sec. of War for selection candidates for 1st Officers' Candidates Sch. for WACS, 1942. Past pres. Nat. Assn. Colored Women, U.S. br. United Peoples of Africa, Fla. State Fedn. Colored Women's Clubs, Fla. State Tchrs. Assn., Citizens Welfare League Daytona Beach, Assn. Study Negro Life and History; mem. or officer numerous civic and eleemosynary assns., including Fla. Council Human Relations, Am. Med. Edn. Found., Nat. Sharecroppers' Fund, N.A.A.C.P., So. Conf. Ednl. Fund, United Negro Coll. Fund, Fla. State Voters League, Found. African Edn., So. Regional Council, United Council Ch. Women, Council Against Intolerance in Am. Recipient numerous awards and medals including: Spingarn Medal, 1935, Frances Drexel Award, 1937, Thomas Jefferson Award, 1942, Haitian Medal Honor and Merit, 1949, Robert S. Abbott Meml. Award, 1953, Elijah P. Lovejoy medal 1953, Dorie Miller Gold Cup, 1954. Mem. Delta Sigma Theta, Iota Phi Lambda, Lambda Kappa Nu, Phi Delta Kappa (hon. pres.). Democrat. Methodist. Contbr. chpts. and articles to books and mags. Address: 631 Pearl St., Daytona Beach, Fla. Died May 18, 1955; buried adjacent Bethune-Cookman Coll. Campus, Daytona Beach, Fla.

BETTELHEIM, Edwin Summer, J. (bĕt'ĕl-hīm), mil. orgn. executive; b. N.Y.C., Apr. 11, 1887; (desc. Annetje Jans, 1st white girl born on Manhattan Island); s. Edwin Sumner and Emma Ethel (Hutcheson) B.; B.S., Columbia, 1911; LL.B., George Washington U., 1924, LL.M., 1925, A.B., 1926, A.M., 1927; grad. Command and Gen. Staff Sch. (Res.), 1938; m. Dorothy English Caldwell, Oct. 22, 1928. First engaged in constructural engring., later in newspaper work. Served as 2d lt., F.A., U.S. Army, Mexican Border, 1916; 1st lt., 104th and 17th F.A., France, England, Belgium and Germany during World War I; apptd. capt. F.A. Res., 1919, and advanced through grades to col.; past asst. chief of staff Mil. Dist. Washington, ret., 1948; mil. analyst Dept. State; mil. biographer Inter-Am. Mil. Assn.; became asst. chief field forces, Bureau of War Risk Ins., 1919; nat. legislative dir. Vets. Foreign Wars, 1921-31; adj. gen. and exec. officer (treas. gen.) Mil. Order of World Wars since 1931. Mem. Washington Bd. of Trade. Commd. by U.S. Govt. to head expdn. to northern Russia to search for the return to U.S. bodies of Americans lost in Polar Bear Campaign, 1929. Dir. Goodwill Industries, Presidents Com. for Employment Physically Handicapped; trustee Boys Club Am.; mem. council Boy Scouts Am.; mem. Health and Welfare Council Dist. Columbia. Decorated Mexican Border, Victory with bars, German Occupation, Am. Defense and N.Y. State War Service medals, Am. Sector medal, World War II badge and commendation ribbon with palms, Knight Royal Order Scotland, knight chevalier Ordre de la Couronne de Charlemagne I, knight star and ribbon Grand Duke Cyril of Russia, L'Odre St. Anne with crossed swords, Cross and Star Merite

Civique (France); Wojsk Poliskiah, Krzyz Walecz Nosci, Polonia Restituta (Poland); Cruz Merite San Juan Bautista (Puerto Rico); Abdon Calderon 1st Cl. (Ecuador). Mem. Vets. Fgn. Wars (past comdr.), Am. Legion (founder mem.), Mil. Order Fgn. Wars (past comdr. gen.), Res. Officers Assn. (past pres.), Disabled Am. Vets., Fgn. Service Order (grand sec.), Nat. Sojourners (past pres.), Heroes of '76 (past nat. comdr.), Am. Coalition (v.p.), D.C. Bar Assn., St. Andrews Soc., Nat. Council for Friendship with Arab World (treas.), Delta Theta Phi. Episcopalian. Mason (past master, 32°, Shriner, K.T., grand master D.C.; K.C.C.H. past high priest, past Ill. master), Elk, Odd Fellow. Clubs: Old Guard (N.Y.); Army and Navy, Army-Navy Country (member board govs.), University, National Press, Rotary (Washington). Author: Nooks and Corners of Old New York—Memorabilia, 1917; My Experiences in Northern Russia, 1929; Army Mobilization, 1934. Home: 3927 Massachusetts Av. N.W. Office: 1700 I St., Washington 6. Died July 1959.

BETTERS, Paul V(ernon), orgn. exec.; b. Morris, Minn., Apr. 19, 1906; s. Burt Henry and Olivia (Christianson) B.; grad. Pillsbury Acad., Owatonna, Minn., 1921; United States Naval Academy, 1923-24; B.S., Univ. of Minnesota, 1928; M.S., Syracuse University, 1929; graduate study George Washington Univ., 1931; local govt. sch., Selwyn Coll., Cambridge, Eng., summer 1932; m. Myra Graff Keck, June 8, 1929; children—Richard Keck, Judith Keck, Barry Keck, Paula Keck. Fellow and instr. in pub. adminstrn. Sch. of Citizenship and Pub. Affairs, Syracuse Univ., 1929-30; staff New York Commn. on Revision of Pub. Service Laws, State of New York, Albany, New York, 1930; staff The Brookings Instn., Washington, D.C., 1930-32; tech. adv. to Governor of N.C. at Raleigh, 1931; sec. Govtl. Research Assn., Washington, 1931-32; exec. dir., organizer Nat. Inst. Municipal Law Officers, Washington, D.C., 1933-35; exec. dir. The U.S. Conf. of Mayors, Washington, D.C., since 1932; co-founder Nat. Inst. of Governmental Purchasing, Washington, 1945; exec. dir. and founder Nat. Inst. of City and Town Clerks, Washington, 1946. Cons. C.A.A., Office Prodn. Management, Fed. Works Agency, War Assets Adminstrn., U.S. Air Coordinating Com., 1933—; adv. to administrator Civil Works Adminstrn., Washington, 1934-35; liaison officer Pub. Works Adminstrn., 1934-35. Del. U.S. Govt. to Internat. Congress of Local Authorities, London, 1932, Lyon, France, 1934, Paris, France, 1947, The Hague, 1948, Geneva, 1949, Brighton, Eng., 1951, Vienna, 1953; del. Pan-Am. Congress Municipalities, Havana, 1939; del. U.S. cities Helsinki (Finland) Anniversary, 1950; del. U.S. cities Canadian Ann. Confs. of Mayors since 1937; U.S.A.F. Civilian Seminar, Air Univ., Maxwell Field, 1947; dept. of defense Civilian Orientation Conf., 1951. Served as lt. col. assigned to Gen. Staff Corps, U.S. Army, 1942-44. Recipient Citation and Award for Distinguished Service to Am. Cities, U.S. Conf. of Mayors, 1942, 47, 52; distinguished service award, First Nat. Inst. Governmental Purchasing, 1950. Decorated Order Orange-Nassau, The Netherlands, 1948; Knight's Cross, First Class, Royal Order of St. Olaf (Norway) 1950, Star of Italian Solidarity (Italy) 1951, Legion of Honor (France) 1952, City of Rome Medal, 1950, Helsinki Anniversary Medal, 1950. Advisor to U.S. dir. Civilian Def., 1941-42, aide to U.S. Chmn. Permanent Joint Bd. on Def., U.S. and Can., 1940-47; asst. to spl. U.S. Ambassador to Brazil, 1945. Mem. Nat. Aviation Clin., Pres. Conferences on Highway and Fire Safety. Mem. Am. Acad. Polit. and Social Sci., Am. Polit. Sci. Assn., Govtl. Research Assn., Nat. Municipal League, Internat. City Mgrs. Assn., Am. Pub. Welfare Assn., Am. Soc. Planning Ofcls., Nat. Assn. Housing Ofcls., Civil Service Assembly of U.S. and Can., Municipal Finance Officers Assn., Nat. Planning Assn., Urban Land Inst., A.A.A.S., Acad. of Polit. Sci., Internat. Union of Local Authorities (mem. exec. com.), Atty. General's Conf. on Crime, U.S. Fed. Works Agency Constrn. Adv. Council, Am. Society of Public Administration, Nat. Tax Assn., Am. Ordnance Assn., Assn. of U.S. Army, Am. Com. for Internat. Cooperation (vice chmn.), U.S. Bur. Census (adv. com.), Defense Orientation Conf. Assn., Nat. Safety Council. Unitarian. Clubs: Nat. Press, Army and Navy (Wash.); Wings (N.Y.C.). Author: Personnel Classification Board, 1931; U.S. Shipping Bd., 1932; Federal Services to Municipal Governments, 1932; State Centralization in North Carolina, 1932; Recent Federal-City Relations, 1936; City Problems, 1933-50 (ed. annual vols.). You and Your City, 1946; American Cannot Afford Slums, 1947; Government of the People, 1948. Editor: The United States Municipal News since 1933. Contbr. articles, reports and bulls. dealing with municipal affairs, including European Unions of Cities, 1932; Municipal Cooperation in Europe, 1934; Civil Airports in Europe, 1938. Home: Windy Hill, Burnt Mills Hills, Silver Spring, Md. Office: 730 Jackson Pl. N.W., Washington 6. Died May 12, 1956; buried Arlington Nat. Cemetery.

BETTS, Edgar Hayes, mfr.; b. Lansingburg, N.Y., Oct. 23, 1877; s. Edgar Ketchum and Harriet Louise (Gardner) Betts; A.B., Yale University, 1898; L.H.D., Russell Sage College, Troy, N.Y., 1939; m. May Louise Gurley, May 27, 1901 (died Jan. 2, 1941); children—Louise Gurley (Mrs. Samuel S. Stevens), Robert Gurley, Barbara (Mrs. Philip Benson), Edgar Hayes. Joined Earl & Wilson, mfrs. collars and shirts, Troy, 1898, became pres., 1914, corp. dissolved; was pres. Cluett, Peabody & Co., Inc., until July 1929 (resigned); partner Betts & Morris; v.p., treas. W. & L. E. Gurley, mfrs. surveying instruments; v.p. Troy Record; dir. Taylor Truck Co., Troy & Bennington R.R. Co. Mem. Laymen's Fgn. Mission Inquiry. Russell Sage Coll., Brown U.; pres. bd. trustees Emma Willard Sch. Served from pvt. to cpl. Co. A, 2d Ret., N.G. N.Y. Republican. Baptist. Clubs: Troy; Yale (N.Y.C.). Home: The Crossway, Troy, N.Y. Died Mar. 25, 1951; buried Oakwood Cemetery, Troy.

BETTS, George Whitefield, Jr., lawyer; b. Englewood, N.J., Feb. 14, 1871; s. George Whitefield and Margaret E. (Dominick) B.; A.B., Princeton, 1892, postgrad., 1892-93, A.M., 1895; LL.B., N.Y. Law Sch., 1895; m. Mary Howard Hall, Nov. 3, 1903; 1 son, Derick Whitefield. Admitted to N.Y. Bar, 1895, N.J. bar, 1896, counsellor of State of N.J., 1899; asso. firm Convers & Kirlin, N.Y.C., 1895-1900; mem. Hunt, Hill & Betts, 1900—; master in chancery of N.J.; dir. Maritime Assn. Port of N.Y.; dir. Schwarzenbach Huber Co., Clifton Heights Realty Corp., Rodi Corp., Union Apple Co., Thomas & Betts Co., Patrician Piece Dye Wks., Inc., Hudson Service & Storage Co. Past chmn. Bergen County Rep. Com.; past pres., now mem. exec. com. Englewood Rep. Club; chmn. Englewood Municipal Rep. Com. Mem. Grad. Council of Princeton U.; scholarship com. Princeton Alumni Assn. No. N.J. Mem. Maritime Law Assn. U.S. (past pres.), Am., N.J., Bergen County bar assns., N.Y. County Lawyers' Assn., Assn. Bar City N.Y., Whig Hall (Princeton U.). Republican. Episcopalian (sr. warden). Clubs: University, Princeton, Down Town Assn., Downtown Athletic (N.Y.C.); University Club (Washington); Englewood, Knickerbocker Country (Englewood, N.J.); Tiger Inn., Nassau (Princeton U.); Quogue Field, Quogue Beach (Quogue, L.I.). Home: 27 Brayton St., Englewood, N.J.; (summer) Quogue, Long Island, N.Y. Office: 120 Broadway, N.Y.C. 5.; also 1 Engle St., Englewood, N.J. Died Jan. 9, 1959.

BEURY, Charles E. (bĕr'ĭ), educator; b. Shamokin, Pa., Aug. 13, 1879; s. William and Susan M. (Cockill) B.; B.A., Princeton, 1903; LL.B., Harvard, 1906; LL.D., Ursinus Coll., 1926, Lafayette Coll., 1928, U. of Pa., 1931, Princeton U., 1937; A.M., Hahnemann Med. Coll., 1932; D.C.L., Bucknell U., 1938; m. Ella Philson Fischer, June 27, 1906; children—Charles William (deceased), Elizabeth Philson, Marian Fischer, Nancy Lawton (dec.), Barbara, Charles Ezra. Began practice of law at Phila., 1908; associated with William A. Glasgow, Jr., 1908-21; pres. Nat. Bank of North Phila., 1921-28; chmn. bd. Bank of Phila. and Trust Co., 1928-30; pres. Temple University, 1926-41. Director Victory Loan for North Phila.; made trips to Russia and Near East for Near East Relief and Red Cross, 1917, 18, 19. Trustee Welfare Fed. of Phila., Near East Relief; pres. Phila. Forum, 1928-29, 1930-31, 1938, 1939-41; pres. Assn. of Coll. Presidents of Pa., 1934; mem. State Council of Edn. of Pa. since Sept. 1936. Republican. Episcopalian. Clubs: Princeton, University (Phila.). Traveled around the World 4 times. Author: Russia After the Revolution, 1918. Home: 6630 McCallum St., Phila. 19. Died Mar. 9, 1953.

BEVAN, Lynne J(ohn), cons. hydraulic engr.; b. Atlanta, Ill., Dec. 27, 1881; s. John Luther and Armada Sarah (Thomas) B.; B.S., U. of Chicago, 1903; B.S. in mining, U. of Calif., 1905; m. Elizabeth Alexandra Young, Dec. 29, 1914; children—John Alexander, Barbara Louise (Mrs. Jas. A. McGowan). Assistant engineer to John R. Freeman, consulting engineer, 1905-06; assistant engineer and later principal engr. Viele, Blackwell & Buck, cons. hydraulic engrs., 1906-27; cons. engr., specializing in water supply and water power, N.Y. City, since 1928; special lecturer grad. course on water power engring., Polytechnic Inst. Brooklyn, 1934; engring. counsel U.S. Bureau Internal Revenue and to corps. in litigation since 1921. Mem. Town Planning Bd., Montclair, N.J., 1932-38. Mem. American Society of Civil Engineers (chmn. power div. 1929-34), Montclair Soc. Engrs. (pres. 1931-32), Essex County Engring. Soc., Delta Upsilon (nat. pres. 1933-35; nat. treas. 1925-33 and 1935-37), Phi Beta Kappa, Sigma Xi. Republican. Baptist. Mason. Clubs: San Gabriel Country (Calif.); Delta Upsilon (N.Y. City). Compiler of Catalogue of Delta Upsilon, 1917; editor Calif. Jour. of Technology, 1904-05; contbr. articles to tech. jours. Home: 28 Melrose Pl., Montclair, N.J.; (winter) 942 Dale St., Pasadena 5, Cal. Died Jan. 29, 1952.

BEVERIDGE, Frank Stanley, bus. exec.; b. Yarmouth, N.S., Apr. 17, 1879; s. Joseph Henry and Hanna (Vickerv) B.; student Mount Hermon (Mass.) Sch., 1901-04; H.M., Springfield Coll., 1947; LL.D. (hon.), Colgate U.; L.H.D. (hon.), Am. Internat. Coll., Springfield; m. Theresa Burdick, December 21, 1904; children—Evelyn Gertrude (Mrs. Philip Caswell, Jr.), Ruth Margaret (Mrs. Joseph W. Palmer). Photographer's rep. Underwood & Underwood, 1904-09; conducted own bus., 1909-13; asso. Fuller Brush Co., 1913, coll. rep., 1915-16, dist. mgr., 1916-19, div. sales mgr. and sec., 1919, sec. and dir. sales, 1920, v.p. in charge sales, 1921-29; asso. sales mgr. Real Silk Hosiery Mills, 1929-31; founder, Stanley Home Products, Inc., 1931, pres., 1931-51, chmn. bd. since 1951; chmn. bd. Stanley Home Products of Can., Ltd.; dir. Hampden Nat. Bank & Trust Co., Westfield Savs. Bank, Third Nat. Bank & Trust Co., Springfield, Mass. Mem. Westfield Park Commn. Trustee Northfield Schs., Eastern States Exposition, West Springfield, Mass.; corporator American International College; director Y.M.C.A.; formerly president Mt. Hermon Alumni Assn. Recipient Mount Hermon Alumni award; Westfield River Parkway citation; Citation from Pope Pius XII, 1949. Republican. Episcopalian. Mason, Moose. Clubs: Rotary, Colony. Home: 183 Western Av. Office: 42 Arnold St., Westfield, Mass. Died Dec. 4, 1956.

BEVIN, Ernest, British sec. of state for foreign affairs; b. Winsford, Somersetshire, Eng., Mar. 9, 1881. Orphaned at age of 8 yrs., became self-supporting and was associated with various lines of work; sec. West of England Unemployment Union, 1905-09; became founder and sec. Bristol Unemployment Union; union orgn. a life work, 1911—; br. sec. Dockers Union, 1911, later dist. sec., then nat. organizer; mem. exec. com. Transport Workers Fedn. at outbreak of World War I, and served as mem. numerous govt. coms. which organized dock labor and transport service; engaged in amalgamating 45 unions into single body of transport and general workers, 1918-22, later serving as gen. sec.; began building up labor newspaper, Daily Herald, 1920; on leave of absence from union post, became minister of labor and national service, 1940, and being given control of all Brit. labor, created arbitration tribunal, labor supply board, and skilled tng. for unskilled war workers; sec. of state for fgn. affairs, 1945—; represented Great Britain at Potsdam Conf., July 1945, Council of Fgn. Ministers, London, Sept. 1945, Three Power Conf. of Fgn. Ministers, Moscow, Dec. 1945, Security Council, London, Jan. 1946, Council Fgn. Ministers, also Peace Conf., Paris, Apr.-Oct. 1946, 2d meeting UN Gen. Assembly, N.Y.C., 1946. Address: Foreign Office, Downing St., London S.W. 1, Eng. Died Apr. 14, 1951.

BEWER, Julius August (bā'vĕr), theologian; b. Ratingen, Germany, Aug. 28, 1877; s. Julius and Lina (Hevendehl) B.; grad. Royal Gymnasium, Düsseldorf, Germany, 1895; B.D., Union Theol. Sem., New York, 1898; Ph.D., Columbia, 1900; studied univs. of Basel, 1899-1900, Halle, 1900, Berlin, 1900-01; hon. D. Theol. Univ. of Göttingen, 1922; m. Hella Schmidt von Knobelsdorf; 1 son, Henry Julius. Professor of Old Testament language and literature, Oberlin Theological Seminary, 1902-1904; ordained Congl. ministry, 1906; asst. prof. Bibl. philology, 1904-05, asso. prof., 1905-14, prof. O. T. history and theology, 1914-27, Davenport prof. Hebrew and Cognate languages Union Theological Seminary, 1927-45; emeritus prof. since 1945; visiting prof. New Brunswick Theological Seminary, 1945-47. Lecturer on Bibl. lit., Teachers Coll. (Columbia), 1912-28; mem. faculty of philosophy, Columbia U., 1913-45; hon. mem. U. of Göttingen, 1923; Chancellors' lectr. Queens U., Kingston, Ontario. Member Society Bibl. Lit. and Exegesis. Member committee Revision American Standard Bible: Author: A Critical and Exegetical Commentary on the Book of Obadiah and on the Book of Joel, 1911, on the Book of Jonah, 1912, in the International Critical Commentary; Der Text des Buches Ezra, 1921; The Literature of the Old Testament in Its Historical Development, 1922; Ezechiel in Kittel, Biblia Hebraica, 1932; The Book of the Twelve Prophets I, II, 1949; The Book of Isaiah I, II, 1950; The Book of Jeremiah I, II, 1951; The Book of Ezekiel I, II, 1953; also articles in learned jours. Home: 30 Barry Rd., Scarsdale, N.Y. Died Aug. 31, 1953.

BIANCHI, Julio Domingo, diplomat; b. Guatemala City, Feb. 8, 1879; s. Emil C. A. and Waleska (Smout) B.; B.Sc. and Lett., Instituto Nacional de Varones, Guatemala City, 1899; M.D., Facultad de Medicina de Guatemala, 1904; m. Matilde Rosales Alcantára, Feb. 1, 1908. Practiced surgery at Guatemala City; served as prof. anatomy and practice of medicine and therapeutics, and as dean faculty of medicine, U. Guatemala; owned and directed a pvt. hosp. at Guatemala City, 1914-20. A leader and organizer of Unionist Party of Guatemala; E.E. and M.P. from Guatemala to U.S., 1920-22; now in med. practice at Ventura, Cal. Elected del. to Fed. Council of Central America, Nov. 4, 1921. Del. 5th Internat. Sanitary Conf. of Am. Republics; sec. Internat. Pan-Am. Sanitary Bur. Mem. Sociedad de Medicina de Guatemala, Societé Scientiffique du Chili, Gorgas Memorial Inst., etc. Club: Guatemala. Home: Ventura, Cal. Died Apr. 19, 1958.

BIAS, (Bennett) Randolph (bī'ăs), lawyer; b. Hamlin, Lincoln County, W.Va., Dec. 20, 1875; s. Rolan Armstrong and Lucy (Byus) B.; ed. high sch., Marshall Coll. and W.Va. U.; m. Clothilde Gaujot, June 19, 1901; children—Bennett Randolph (dec.), Marie Marguerite (Mrs. Wallace G. Smith, dec.), Ernest Gaujot. Was teacher in public schools, 1894-95; postmaster Williamson, 1897-1909; Republican nominee for Senate, W.Va., 1902; editor Mingo Republican, 1903-04; chmn. Rep. County Com., Mingo County, 1904-08; an organizer Mingo County Bank, 1905; admitted to bar, 1910; mem. Wiles & Bias, 1911-20, Bias & Chafin, 1922-25, now Bias & Bias, del. at large Rep. Nat. Conv., 1924; pres. West Williamson Land Co.; dir. Mountaineer Hotel Corp. Chairman, Mingo Selective Service Bd. 1, 1940-45. Chmn. Four-Minute Men, Mingo County, 1917-19; chmn. Legal Advisory Bd., Mingo County, 1917-18. Voted Man of the Half Century for 1950 by Gavel Club. Mem. Am., West Va. State (pres. 1926), Mingo County bar associations, Am. Law Inst., Nat. Econ. League, Williamson C. of C. (ex-pres.), Phi Kappa Sigma. Episcopalian; lay deputy from W.Va. to Gen. Convs., 1922, 28, 31, 34, 37, 40, 43. Gov. W.Va. Kiwanis Dist., 1927. Club: University. Lecturer on "West Virginia" since 1922. Home: Williamson, W.Va. Died Apr. 12, 1958.

BIBLE, George Albert, banker; b. Hamilton, Ont., Can., July 20, 1878; s. George and Josepha Emma (Eveleigh) B.; student pub. schs. Chgo.; m. Margaret Elizabeth Johnson, Sept. 16, 1904; children—Frances (Mrs. John B. Clow), Robert, Barbara (Mrs. Henry C. Schofield). Gen. passenger dept. Rock Island System, Chgo., Topeka, Kan., Omaha, Neb., Colorado Springs, Colo., 1897-1903, traveling passenger agent, Salt Lake City, 1903-06; cashier Green River (Wyo.) State Bank, 1907-08; cashier Saratoga (Wyo.) State Bank, 1908-09; cashier First Nat. Bank, Rawlins, Wyo., 1909-30, v.p., 1931-37, pres. 1938-49, chmn. bd., 1949-50; pres. Parco (Wyo.) State Bank, 1930-34; dir. Federal Reserve Bank of Kansas City, Mo. (Omaha br.) dist. 10, 1938-47) pres. Sandstone Sheep Co., Pioneer Sheep Co., Rasmussen Sheep Co., Lost Soldier Development Co.; v.p. Cow Creek Sheep Co. County chmn. 2d War Finance Campaign, 1943. Mem. C. of C. Republican. Episcopalian (vestryman). Mason (32°, Shriner), Elk. Club: Lions (past pres.). Home: 715 W. Maple St. Office: First Nat. Bank of Rawlins, Rawlins, Wyo. Died Aug. 22, 1950; buried Rawlins.

BICKELHAUPT, Carroll Owen (bĭk'ĕl-houpt), elec. engineer; b. Roscoe, Dakota Territory, December 15, 1888; s. William George and Ida Emma (Owen) B.; B.S., U. of Wisconsin, 1911, E.E., 1914; D.Eng., South Dakota Sch. of Mines and Tech., 1947; m. Marie Helen Jewett, April 30, 1919; children—Nancy Jewett (Mrs. Joseph Harris), Alice Mary (Mrs. Charles B. Wilson). With Dakota Central Telephone Co., 1904-11; with Am. Telephone & Telegraph Co., 1911-25, toll traffic engr., 1922, comml. engr., 1922-25; v.p. Southern Bell Telephone & Telegraph Co., 1925-30, also dir. and mem. exec. com.; v.p., dir. and mem. exec. com., Cumberland Teleg. & Teleg. Co., 1925-26; asst. v.p. Am. Telep. & Teleg. Co., 1930-41, v.p. 1941-45, v.p. and sec. since 1945; dir. Bell Telephone Securities Co., 1935-37. Maj. Signal Corps, A.U.S. World War I; brig. gen. A.U.S. (dir. communications office chief signal officer, ETO, U.S.A., U.S. Mil. Govt., Germany), World War II; recommd. brig. gen., 1947, ret. 1949. Decorated, Distinguished Service Medal, Legion of Merit, Bronze Star Medal, Army Commendation Ribbon, Armed Forces Res. Medal; (U.S.); Officer, Legion of Honor, Officier d'Academie et de l'instruction Publique, Croix de Guerre with Palm (France); hon. mem. Signal Corps French Army: Commander of Order of Leopold II (Belgium). Diploma of the Medal, Assn. Engr.-Drs. of France, 1947. Fellow Am. Institute Electrical Engrs. (v.p., dir., 1927-29); mem. Am. Engring. Council (v.p. 1933-41, mem. assembly and administrative board); N.Y. Elec. Soc.; del. to meetings of Internat. Cons. Com. on Telephony, Lucerne, Switzerland, 1935, Cairo, Egypt, 1938; tech. observer at meeting of Internat. Cons. Com. on Radio, Bucharest, 1937, and at meeting of Internat. Telecommunications Confs., Cairo, 1938; Am. Soc. Corporate Secs. (dir., past pres.), Armed Forces Communications Assn. (dir., past v.p.), Army Signal Assn., Grant Monument Association of New York (trustee), v.p. N.Y. Soc. Mil. and Naval Ofcrs.; past comdr. N.Y. chapt., Mil. Order of World Wars. Repub. Clubs: University, Downtown Assn. (N.Y.); Army and Navy (Wash., D.C.); Washington (Conn.). Home: 1075 Park Av. Office: 195 Broadway, N.Y.C. Died May 16, 1954; buried Washington, Conn.

BICKETT, Fanny Neal Yarborough, b. Louisburg, N.C., Oct. 11, 1870; d. William Henry and Lucy Mossenburg (David) Yarborough; grad. St. Mary's Sch., Raleigh, N.C., 1889; studied Harvard Summer Sch., N.Y. Chautauqua, U. N.C., U. Chgo., m. Thomas Walter Bickett, Nov. 29, 1898 (died Dec. 28, 1921); children—William Yarborough, Thomas Walter (dec.), Mary Covington (dec.). Active in promotion of pub. health and missionry edn.; in France for YWCA, 1917; chief of Mothers' and Infants' Bur. Pub. Health Dept. of N.C.; chmn. Woman's Interracial Com.; rep. for N.C. of Nat. Prohibition League; pres. Diocesan Auxiliary of Woman's Auxiliary P.E. Ch.; nat. rep. Internat. Com. of P.E. Ch., etc. Trustee Stonewall Jackson Tng. Sch. for Delinquent Boys; chmn. bd. Colored Girls' Reformatory; mem. Com. of 100 Prison Investigation; supt. Pub. Welfare Wake County, N.C., 1924—. Mem. Colonial Dames Am., D.R., Daughters of Confederacy, Auxiliary of Am. Legion, League of Women Voters. Democrat. Clubs: Woman's, Business and Professional Women's. Home: Raleigh, N.C. Died July 1, 1942.

BICKING, Ada Elizabeth, dir. emeritus Arthur Jordan Conservatory of Music, Indianapolis; b. Evansville, Ind.; d. Charles and Anna (Wesseler) Bicking; diploma Am. Inst. Normal Methods (Northwestern U.); B.Ped., Cincinnati Conservatory of Music, 1924; pvt. instrn. in piano under Adelaide Palmer, voice, Helen M. Ames, Nannie C. Love and Leila A. Breed. D. Music (hon.), Evansville (Ind.) College, 1948. Supervisor of music, Vincennes, Ind., 1906-10; teacher Sch. of Edn., Ind. U., summer 1910; head dept. of music, State Teachers Coll., St. Cloud, Minn., 1910-14; supervisor music, Evansville (Ind.) pub. schs., 1914-26; mem. dept. sch. music, Evansville Coll., 1920-24; teacher Ohio State U., summer 1926; state dir. music edn., Mich., 1927-33; mem. faculty Teachers Coll. (Columbia), summers 1931, 32; instr. Nat. Music Camp, Interlochen, Mich., summers 1933-35; head of school music department Arthur Jordan College of Music since 1933, director College, 1935-1945. Mem. N.E.A., Music Educators Nat. Conf. (mem. nat. research council 1937-46; exec. bd. and summer camps com.; sec. nat. conf. at Nashville; hostess Evansville meeting), N. Central Music Educators Conf. (pres. Milwaukee conf.), Nat. Fed. Music Clubs (chmn. music in schs. and colls.), Ind. Fed. Music Clubs (v.p.), Ind. State Teachers Assn. (ex-pres. music sect.), Mich. Teachers Assn., Civic Music Commn. and Art League (Evansville), Evansville Musicians Club (charter mem. and ex-pres.), Lansing (Mich.) Matinee Music Club (hon.), In-and-About Indianapolis Music Supervisors Club (1st v.p.), Nat. Broadcasting Co. (advisory bd.), Coöperative com. of Am. Sch. of Air, Indianapolis Matinee Musicale; hon. mem. Sigma Alpha Iota, Phi Sigma Mu and Eugene Field Soc. Clubs: College (Evansville); Women's City (Detroit). Author: Program Repertoire, 1932. Contbr. to music magazines. Home: 917 Woodsboro, Royal Oak, Mich. Died Feb. 22, 1953; buried Evansville, Ind.

BICKNELL, Lewis Williams, judicial executive; Com.; b. Minneapolis, Dec. 14, 1885; s. George Simpson and Alice Bertha (White) B.; LL.B., U. of Minn., 1907, Admitted to Minn. bar, 1907, S.D. bar, 1908; states atty. Day Co., S.D., 1933-37; chmn. South Dakota Relief Administration, 1933-35, South Dakota Public Welfare Board, 1935-37; member S.D. Judicial Council, 1933—, pres., 1951—. Dem. nominee for gov. S.D., 1940-42; mem. adv. com. S.D. Code, 1937-39; gen. counsel Farm Credit Adminstrn., Omaha, Neb., 1943-48; mem. Dem. Nat. Com., 1948-52; del. Dem. Nat. Conv., 1916-28, 1936. Served as capt. to maj. U.S. Army, 1917-19. Mem. Am. and S.D. bar assns. Club: Minneapolis. Home: 818 1st St. West. Office: Box 615, Webster, S.D. Died Oct. 20, 1953; buried Lakewood Cemetery, Mpls.

BIERER, Andrew Gordon Curtin, Jr. (bĭr'ĕr), lawyer; b. Guthrie, Okla., Dec. 1, 1899; s. Andrew Gregg Curtin and Nancy (Stamper) B.; student University of Wisconsin, 1920; A.B., University of Oklahoma, 1921; LL.B., Harvard, 1925; m. Vinita McDonald, June 29, 1927; children—Andrew Gordon Curtin, III, Alva McDonald. Admitted to Oklahoma bar, 1925, and since practiced in Guthrie; mem. firm Bierer & Moser, 1952—. Mem. Okla. State Bar Commn., later Com. State Bar Examiners, 1927-39; mem. exec. com. Nat. Conf. of Bar Examiners, 1931-41, chmn. 1938, 39). Enlisted Central Machine Gun Officers Training Sch., Camp Hancock, Ga., during World War I; maj., U.S. Army, J.A.G.D.; mem. bd. of review No. 4, Judge Adv. Gen.'s Office, Washington, World War II to Jan. 1946. Pres. State League of Young Democrats of Okla., 1930. Mem. Southwestern Council, U.S. C. of C. Mem. American Bar Assn., Okla. State Bar Assn., Guthrie Bar Assn., Am. Legion (past comdr.), Kappa Sigma. Democrat. Episcopalian. Mason (33°, Shriner). Clubs: Oklahoma, University (Oklahoma City); Harvard of Oklahoma; Guthrie Country. Author of various bar journal articles. Lecturer before professional socs. Home: 800 East Cleveland Av. Office: Bierer Bldg., Guthrie, Okla. Died Aug. 27, 1956; buried Summit View Cemetery, Guthrie, Okla.

BIERER, Andrew Gregg Curtin, lawyer; b. Uniontown, Pa., Oct. 24, 1862; LL.M., Georgetown U., 1886; m. Nannie Stamper, June 26, 1888 (dec. Jan. 19, 1948); children—Louise B. (Mrs. Horace Taylor), A. G. C., Jr. Moved to Hiawatha, Kan., 1865, with father, Col. Everard Bierer, 171st Pa. Vol., and family; practiced law Hiawatha and Garden City, Kan., (city atty.); moved to Guthrie, Okla., at opening of Okla. Terr., Apr. 22, 1889, later city atty.; territorial land and railroad practice; asso. justice Supreme Ct. of Okla., 1894-98; mem. law firms, Bierer & Cotteral to 1894, (John H. Cotteral), Dale & Bierer, 1898-25, (Frank Dale), Bierer & Bierer, 1926-51, (A. G. C., Jr.). Mem. Am., Okla. bar assns., Okla. Hist. Soc. (Roll of Honor). Democrat. Episcopalian. Home: 503 E. Cleveland Av., Guthrie, Okla. Died Feb. 21, 1951.

BIESTERFELD, Chester H., patent lawyer; b. Saginaw, Mich., Oct. 18, 1888; s. Henry and Anna (Roethke) B.; B.S., U. of Mich., 1910; LL.B., Georgetown U., 1915, M.P.L., 1915; m. Mathilde Gerber, Aug. 8, 1917; children—Elaine (Mrs. E. T. Neumann), Doris (Mrs. H. H. Townshend, Jr.), Lenore (Mrs. R. N. McKirahan), Marian (Mrs. Robin White). Engineer and chemist for the Kansas Cement Co., 1910-12; chemist, U.S. Department of Agriculture, 1912-14; examiner for U.S. Patent Office, Washington, D.C., 1914-19; patent atty. U.S. Rubber Co., 1920; pvt. practice patent law, N.Y. City, 1920-26, head patent dept. du Pont Co., Wilmington, Del., since 1926. Served in U.S. Army, 1918. Admitted to D.C. bar, 1915, N.Y. bar, 1922, Del. bar, 1943. Protestant. Author: Book on Patent Law, 1943. Home: 909 Augusta Rd., Wilmington, Del. Died July 10, 1951; buried Lower Brandywine Cemetery, Centerville, Del.

BIGELOW, Archibald Pierce, ret. banker; b. Buda, Ill., Jan. 21, 1868; s. Henry Clay and Lydia (Pierce) B.; student U. Wis., 1884-86; m. Leota Hendeshot, Apr. 17, 1888; 1 dau., Dorothea (Mrs. Marriner A. Browning). Asst. cashier Thayer County Bank, Hebron, 1886; organizer with father Ogden State Bank, 1889, cashier, 1889-1923, pres., 1923-33; v.p. 1st Fed. Savs. & Loan Assn. of Oakland until retirement; pres. Weber River Water Users Assn.; dir. Davis and Weber Counties Canal Co. Recipient nat. gold medal for most outstanding work in presrvation wild life in Western U.S. Pres. Cal. Trap Shooting Assn. Mason (Shriner), Elk, K.P. Club: Bear River (sec.-treas.). Home: 270 Wayne Av., Oakland 6, Cal. Died Dec. 24, 1942; buried Ogden City Cemetery, Ogden, Utah.

BIGELOW, Bruce Macmillan (bĭg'ĕ-lō), univ. vice pres.; b. Norwood, R.I., Aug. 27, 1903; s. Edward David and Ina Fraser (Macmillan) B.; Ph.B., Brown U., 1924, Ph.D., 1930 (Sharpe fellow in history); A.M., Harvard, 1927; Sc.D., R.I. Coll. Pharmacy and Allied Sci., 1954; m. Lois Elizabeth Armstrong, June 14, 1929. Asst. in history, Brown U., 1924 25; instr. English, history, Mass. Inst. Tech., 1926-28; instr. history, Brown U., 1930-35, asst. prof., 1935-43, asso. prof. 1943-47, now prof., dir. of admission, 1932-43, chmn. bd. admission since 1943, asso. dean coll., 1940-43, dean of students, 1943-45, v.p. of univ., 1945—. Mem. corp. Peoples Savs. Bank, Providence Instn. for Savs. Mem. exec. com., trustee Providence Library; program com., trustee Hazen Found.; mem. Walter S. Barr Fellowships Selection Bd.; mem. exec. com., trustee Moses Brown Sch. Mem. bd. dirs. Narragansett Council Boy Scouts Am.; mem. corp. Barker Found., Inc. Mem. R.I. (v.p.), Newport hist. socs., Am. Hist. Assn., R.I. Soc. Colonial Wars, C. of C. (bd. dirs.), Phi Beta Kappa, Phi Sigma Kappa. Clubs: Barnard (v.p.), Quindecim; Art (Providence); Brown (N.Y. and R.I.); Harvard (R.I.). Contbr. articles on history and edn. to various publs. Home: 93 Congdon St., Providence 6. Office: Brown University, Providence 12, R.I. Died Dec. 27, 1954.

BIGELOW, Charles C., machine tool exec.; b. Evansport, O., 1897; pres. and dir. City Auto Stamping Co., Toledo, O., City Machine & Tool Co. Home: 2712 Manitou Dr., Maumee, O. Office: Lint and Dura Avs., Toledo. Died Mar. 31, 1954.

BIGELOW, Florence, educator; b. Natick, Mass., Apr. 23, 1864; d. William Perkins and Martha (Mansfield) Bigelow; A.B., Wellesley Coll., 1885, A.M., 1891. Instr. Wellesley Coll., 1889-93; with Miss. Conant established Walnut Sch. for Girls, Natick, Mass., 1893-1933, pres. bd. trustees, 1925-43. Mem. Wellesley Coll. Alumnae Assn., Am. Assn. U. Women. Conglist. Club: College. Home: 20 Shattuck St., Natick, Mass. Died July 8, 1945.

BIGELOW, Frederick Southgate, editor; b. Boston, Mass., Oct. 23, 1871; s. George Frederick (M.D.) and Rebecca Gertrude (Houghton) B.; student Boston Public Latin School; Mass. Institute Technology, 1890-93; married Mary Beatrice Lowell, June 26, 1915; children—Charles Lowell, Gertrude Ogden, George Frederick. Asso. editor Saturday Evening Post, 1899-1929. Editor and compiler several textbooks and other works. Many years mem. bd. mgrs. Hosps. of Grad. Sch. of Medicine, U. of Pa., and donor of Dr. Chevalier Jackson Bronchoscopic Clinic; mem. advisory council Am. Eugenics Soc. Republican. Episcopalian. Clubs: Franklin Inn, Philobiblon (Phila). One of founders of Phila. Print Club, Le Coin d'Or; mem. Archaeol. Inst. of Am. Contbr. to Saturday Evening Post, Readers Digest, Ladies Home Journal, Esquire, Cosmopolitan, Your Life and other magazines. Home: 303 South Iseminger St., Phila. 7. Died Sept. 28, 1954.

BIGELOW, Herbert Seely, ex-congressman; b. Elkhart, Ind., Jan. 4, 1870; student Oberlin Coll., 1886-91; A.B., Western Reserve, 1894; student Lane Theol. Sem., 1895. Pastor People's Ch., Cincinnati, 53 yrs. pres. 4th Const. Conv., O., 1912; mem. Ohio Ho. of Rep., 1913-14, Cincinnati City Council, 1936, and 1940-41; mem. 75th Congress (1937-38), 2d Ohio Dist. Democrat. Died Nov. 11, 1951.

BIGELOW, Maurice Alpheus (bĭg'ĕ-lō), biologist; b. Milford Center, O., Dec. 8, 1872; s. Alpheus Russell and Hattie (Parthemore) B.; B.S., Ohio Wesleyan U., 1894, LL.D., 1930; M.S., Northwestern U., 1896; Ph.D., Harvard, 1901; Sc.D., Columbia, 1929; m. Anna Neiglick, 1900. Instr. in biology, Ohio Wesleyan U., 1894-95; instr. in zoölogy, Northwestern U., 1896-98; instr. in biology, Teachers Coll., Columbia U., 1899-1903, adj. prof., 1903-07, prof., 1907-39, dir. practical arts, 1914-35, dir. Inst. Practical Science Research, 1934-39, prof. emeritus, 1939—. Founder and editor Nature-Study Review, 1905-10. Fellow A.A.A.S. (see zoöl. sect., 1908-13), Am. Pub. Health Assn.; mem. Am. Soc. Zoölogists, Am. Soc. Naturalists; founder and sec. Am. Nature Study Soc., 1908-10; chmn. exec. com. Am. Social Hygiene Assn., 1925-39; pres. American Eugenics Soc., 1940-45. Educational consultant American Social Hygiene Association and U.S. Pub. Health Service, 1939-45. Author: Early Development of Lepas, 1902; Teaching of Zoölogy in the Secondary School, 1904; Applied Biology (with Anna N. Bigelow), 1911; Introduction to Biology (with wife), 1913; Sex-Education, 1916; Health for Every Day and Health in Home and Neighborhood (with Prof. Jean Broadhurst), 1924; Adolescence, Educational and Hygienic Problems, 1924; also papers in ednl. health and scientific jours. Co-editor Eugenical News, 1942—. Address: R.F.D. 1, Croton-on-Hudson, N.Y. Died Jan. 6, 1955; Rose Hill Cemetery, Chgo.

BIGELOW, Poultney, author; b. New York, N.Y., Sept. 10, 1855; s. John B. (ambassador to France under Lincoln) and Jane Tunis (Poultney) B.; A.B., Yale, 1879, A.M., 1900; Columbia Law Sch., 1882; m. Lilian Pritchard, of Worcestershire, Eng., 1911 (died Dec. 1, 1932). Admitted to bar Supreme Ct., N.Y., 1882. Made first journey around the world in sailing ship, 1875-76; visited shores New Guinea; wrecked on Japan coast; traveled in China, Borneo, Java, Australia, Africa, W.I., Spanish Main, P.I., and Panama; was the first to take a canoe through the Iron Gates of the Danube; studied tropical colonization in nearly every colony of the world. Founder of Outing (1885) as the 1st Am. mag. of amateur sport. Lectured at principal universities on modern history and colonial administration; corr. for London Times during Spanish-Am. War, 1898; was expelled from Russia on account of his political writing, 1892. Hon. member Royal United Service Instn., London, Royal Arty. Instn., Woolwich, Ethological Soc., London; life mem. Royal Geog. Soc., Am. Geog. Soc., N.Y. Hist. Soc., Am. Polit. Science Assn., Army Relief Soc. Clubs: Century (N.Y.); Athenaeum (London); N.Y. Canoe (hon.); chmn. Ends of the Earth Club (N.Y.); Authors' of London (life), Royal Corinthian Yacht of London (life); Cobden of London (hon.); Imperial Yacht of Kiel (life mem. from its foundation and resigned during the war). Hon. prof. Ecole Coloniale, Paris; gold medalist Société Geographique, Lille, France; asso. honorary member Académie des Sciences Coloniales, Paris. Chevalier de la Légion d'Honneur (French). Author: The German Emperor and His Eastern Neighbors; Bismarck; Paddles and Politics Down the Danube; The Borderland of Czar and Kaiser; History of the German Struggle for Liberty, 1806-1848, 4 vols., 1903; White Man's Africa, 1898; Au Pays des Boers (in French), Children of the Nations; Die Volker in Kolonialen Wettstreite; Prussian Memories; Souvenirs de Prusse; Prussianism and Pacificism, 1919; Japan and Her Colonies, 1923; Genseric, 1918; Seventy Summers, 1925; Life of John Bigelow; Life of Attila and His Times. Most of these have been translated into German or French. Clubs: Century (N.Y.); Athenaeum, Pall Mall (London). Home: Bigelow Homestead, Malden-on-Hudson, N.Y. Died May 28, 1954.

BIGELOW, Robert Payne (bĭg'ĕ-lō), zoologist; b. Baldwinsville, N.Y., July 10, 1863; s. Otis and Margaret (Payne) B.; S.B., Harvard U., 1887; Ph.D., Johns Hopkins U., 1892; m. Caroline Evans Chase, Nov. 9, 1911; 1 son, Robert Otis. Instr. biology, Mass. Inst. Tech., 1893-1912, asst. and asso. prof. zoology and parasitology, 1912-22, prof. same, 1922-33, prof. emeritus since 1933, librarian, 1895-1925; librarian Marine Biol. Lab., Woods Hole, 1919-23. Editor Am. Naturalist, 1897-98, Technology Quarterly, 1895-1908. Fellow Am. Acad. Arts and Sciences (corr. sec. 1926-30), A.A.A.S.; mem. Am. Society Naturalists, Assn. Am. Anatomists, History of Sci. Soc. Author of papers on zool. subjects; contbr. series of biol. articles to Reference Handbook of the Medical Sciences, 1900-04 and 1913-17; also author Directions for the Dissection of the Cat, 1925, revised edit., 1935. Contbr. chapters in Sedgwick and Tyler's Short History of Science, revised edit., 1939. Home: 72 Blake Road, Brookline 46, Mass. Died Sept. 6, 1955.

BIGGER, Isaac Alexander, physician; b. Bethel, S.C., June 25, 1893; s. Isaac Alexander and Mary Neel (Johnston) B.; student Erskine Coll., Due West, S.C., 1909-10, Davidson (N.C.) Coll., 1910-11, 1912-13, U. of Va., 1919, M.D., 1919; m. Beatrice Haslam Sept. 9, 1922; children—Dorothy Neel (Mrs. Jack Grober), Barbara Norvelle (Mrs. George W. Reahm), Edith Millicent (Mrs. Claude S. Coleman). Intern U. of Va., 1919-21, resident surgery, 1921-22; instr. surgery U. of Va., 1922-23, asst. prof. surgery, 1923-27; asso. prof. surgery Vanderbilt U., 1927-30; prof. surgery and surgeon-in-chief Med. Coll. of Va. since 1930; mem. deans com. and cons. surgery, McGuire V.A. Hosp., Richmond, since 1946; cons. Portsmouth Naval Hosp. since 1950. Mem. Appeal Bd., State of Va. (Selective Service), 1943-46; mem. subcom. thoracic surgery of coms. on mil. medicine, div. med. sciences, Nat. Research Council, 1941-42. Fellow A. C.S.; mem. Am. Surg. Assn., Am. Cancer Soc. (pres. Va. div., 1945, 1947-48), Am. Assn. Thoracic Surgery (treas., 1937-44, v.p., 1944-45, president, 1946), A.M.A., So. Med. Assn. (chmn. surg. sect., 1935-36), So. Surg. Assn. (pres. 1952-53; rep. on Am. Bd. Surgery 1945-51), Eastern Surg. Soc., So. Soc. Clin. Surgeons, Med. Soc. Va., Richmond Acad. Va. (pres., 1947). Presbyn. Author: Operative Surgery, 2 vols., 1937, new ed., 1940 (with Dr. J. Shelton Horsley). Contbr. articles in med. jours. Home: 709 Shirley Rd., Richmond 25. Office: 1200 E. Broad St., Richmond 19, Va. Died Jan. 27, 1955; buried Hollywood Cemetery, Richmond, Va.

BIGGS, J(ames) Crawford, lawyer; b. Oxford, N.C., Aug. 29, 1872; s. William and Elizabeth Arrington (Cooper) B.; student Horner Mil. Sch., Oxford, 1883-87; Ph.B., summa cum laude, U. N.C., 1893; student U. N.C. Law Sch., 1893, 94; m. Margie Jordan, Feb. 7, 1906; 1 dau., Marjorie. Admitted to N.C. bar, 1894; began practice at Oxford; prof. law, U. of N.C., 1898-1900, Trinity Law Sch., Durham, 1911-12; adjutant N.C. State Guards, 3d Regt., 1894-98; mayor of Oxford 2 terms, 1897, 98; mem. N.C. Ho. of Rep. from Durham County, 1905; Supreme Court reporter, 1905-07; judge Superior Court of N.C., 1907-11; resigned, 1911, and resumed practice at Raleigh, N.C.; special asst. to atty. gen. of U.S., 1917-18, in charge oil litigation against the S.P. R.R. in Cal.; solicitor gen. of U.S., 1933-35; now practicing law in Raleigh, N.C.; special asst. to atty. gen. in charge Northern Pacific Land Grant Case involving 2,800,000 acres, 1935-38; chmn. N.C. Bd. of Elections, 1929-32. Trustee U. N.C., Methodist Orphanage (Raleigh); mem. exec. com. and counselor A.R.C., 1933-35; mem. Federal Bd. of Hospitalization, 1933-35. Mem. Am. Bar Assn. (v.p. representing 4th Fed. Circuit, 1933-34), N.C. State Bar Assn. (pres. 1914-15), Am. Law Inst., N.C. Commn. for Improvement of the Laws, Nat. Conf. Commrs. on Uniform State Laws, Wake County Bar Assn. (pres. 1930), Soc. of Mayflower Descendants, S.A. R., Phi Beta Kappa, Zeta Psi. Democrat. Methodist. Club: Carolina Country (Raleigh). Home: Route 7, Raleigh, N.C. Died Jan. 30, 1960.

BIGHAM, Truman C. (bĭg'ăm), economist; b. Gatesville, Tex., July 4, 1896; s. Madison C. and Lena (Strickland) B.; A.B., Baylor U., 1920; A.M., U. of Chicago, 1925; Ph.D., Leland Stanford U., 1927; m. Leta Laura Leslie, Feb. 22, 1920; 1 son, Truman C. Asst. in econ. Leland Stanford, 1926-27; asso. prof. econ. U. of Ark., 1927-30; prof. econ. U. of Fla. since 1930, dir. grad. offerings College Bus. Administrn.; chmn. grad. sch. Coll. Bus. Administrn., U. of Fla. since 1948. Vis. prof. pub. utilities, U. of Wash., 1935-36. Sec. in charge transportation research Bd. of Investigation and Research, Washington, D.C., 1941-42; cons. to Fla. State Comptroller and Fla. R.R. Commn. Served as master sergt. U.S. Army, 1918-19. Mem. Southern Econ. Assn. (pres. 1937-38), Am. Econ. Assn., Am. Assn. Univ. Profs., Phi Kappa Phi, Beta Gamma Sigma. Awarded Spellman fellowship, U. of Chicago, 1924-25. Editor: Taxation and Public Debt in Florida, 1935; New International Encyclopedia, 1946-47. Author: Principles of Public Utilities (with Eliot Jones), 1931; Transportation: Principles and Problems, 1946. Contbr. to econ. jours. Home: 2309 West Court, Gainesville, Fla. Died Dec. 30, 1952.

BIKRAM, Tribhubana Bir, King of Nepal; b. 1906; succeeded to throne, Dec. 11, 1911. Address: Kathmandu, Nepal. Died Mar. 13, 1955.

BILL, John G., drug. mfr.; b. Marlboro, Mass., 1904; m. Eileen M. Bill; 1 son, Lawrence Bentley. Pres. Merck Sharp & Dohme, div. Merck & Co., Inc. Dir. Jr. Achievement of Del. Valley, Inc., United Fund. Mem. Pa. C. of C. (dir.), Am. Found. for Pharm. Edn. (dir.). Clubs: Union League (Phila.); Drug & Chemical (N.Y.C.). Midday, Oyster Harbors. Home: 454 Windemere Rd., Drexel Park, Pa. Office: 640 N. Broad St., Phila. Died Dec. 1959.

BILL, Raymond, publisher; b. New York, N.Y., Sept. 23, 1896; s. Col. Edward Lyman and Caroline Lee (Raymond) B.; A.B., U. of Wis., 1916; m. Esther E. Kelly, Sept. 1, 1917; children—Jane Raymond, Esther Kelly. Asso. editor Music Trade Review and Talking Machine World, 1916; v.p. and gen. mgr. Edward Lyman Bill, Inc., 1917; pres. Federated Business Publs., Inc., 1927; pres. Sales Management, Inc., publisher, Sales Management Mag. 1928—; chmn., pres. Bill Bros. Pub. Corp., 1933—; pres., dir. Brewster Handcraft Industries, Inc., Executive Publications, Inc.; pres. Business News Service, Inc., treas. Grocer-Graphic, Inc.; v.p. Hetty Corp., Service Public Corp.; dir. Waynesboro Pub. Co., Ahrens Pub. Co., Nat. Business Publications, Inc. Pres., dir. Inst. Bus. Econs.; chmn. exec. com. Nat. Distbrn. Council, U.S. Department of Commerce. Served as aide for information, U.S. Navy, World War. Mem. Nat. Conf. Business Paper Editors (pres. 1937-38), Nat. Fedn. Sales Execs. (pres. 1937-38), S.A.R., National Association of Magazine Publishers (dir.), Am. Legion, Chi Psi, Sigma Delta Chi. Clubs: Bonnie Briar Country (Larchmont, N.Y.); University (New York); St. Augustine (Fla.) Country. Home: 200 Old Church Rd., Greenwich, Conn. Office: 386 Fourth Av., N.Y.C. Died June 13, 1957; buried Lyme, Conn.

BILLIKOPF, Jacob (bĭl'ĭ-kŏpf), social worker; b. Wilna, Russia, June 1, 1883; s. Louis and Glika (Katzenelenbogen) B.; student U. of Richmond, Va., LL.D., 1928; Ph.B., U. of Chicago, 1903; grad. work, same, 1902-04, Sch. of Philanthropy, New York, 1905; m. Ruth Marshall, Feb. 23, 1920 (died Aug. 8, 1936); children—Florence (Mrs. U. Schweitzer), David; m. 2d Esther Freeman, Jan. 8, 1942. Served as superintendent Jewish Settlement, Cincinnati, Ohio, 1904-05; supt. United Jewish Charities, Milwaukee, Wis., 1905-07; supt. of United Jewish Charities, Kansas City, Mo., 1907. Active in orgn. of municipal baths, pub. night schs., free legal aid bureau, remedial loan agency and Kansas City Bd. of Pub. Welfare. Pres. Mo. State Conf. of Charities, 1911-12; served as v.p. Kansas City Bd. of Pardons and Paroles, mem. Kansas City Bd. of Pub. Welfare, and sec. Municipal Recreation Commn. Non-resident lecturer of sociology and economics U. of Mo. Dir. Jewish Ednl. Inst., Kansas City. Pres. Nat. Conf. Jewish Social Workers; exec. dir. campaign to raise $25,000,000 for Jewish war sufferers; formerly exec. dir. Fed. of Jewish Charities, Phila.; impartial chmn., Men's Clothing Industry in N.Y. City and of Ladies' Garment Industry of Philadelphia; vice-pres. Am. Assn. for Old Age Security; chmn. bd., N.Y. Clothing Unemployment Fund; chmn. Com. of One Hundred on Unemployment Relief, Philadelphia, 1930-31; member Pennsylvania State Welfare Commn; formerly mem. bd. of directors, Benjamin Franklin Memorial (Philadelphia); formerly trustee of The Nation; trustee of The Survey mag.; chmn. exec. com. Howard U., Washington, D.C. Mem. advisory com. New School Social Research, 1924-28; pres. Nat. Conf. of Jewish Social Service, 1933-34; apptd. impartial chmn. Govt. Regional Labor Bd. (Phila. area), 1933; exec. dir. Nat. Coordinating Com. for Aid to Refugees and Emigrants coming from Germany; co-dir. Labor Standards Assn. since Jan. 1, 1938. Chairman finance committee Graduate Faculty of Political and Social Science, N.Y. City, Inter-Racial Committee. Awarded citation for "service to community, nation and the world" by University of Chicago Alumni Assn., 1942; Va. Honor Roll of 1942, Richmond (Va.) Times-Dispatch; civilian chmn. Spl. Mil. Clemency Bd. Hon. mem. Phi Beta Kappa, Phi Alpha, Alpha Pi Zeta. Club: National Arts (N.Y. City). Home: 235 S. 15th St. Office: Lewis Tower Bldg., Phila. 2. Died Dec. 31, 1950.

BILLINGSLEY, Allen Loren, advertising; b. Flat Rock, Ind., Oct. 4, 1890; s. Charles Winterrowd and Louie M. Billingsley; A.B., De Pauw U., 1913; m. Alma Lee Mohr, Sept. 6, 1914; children—Henry Edmund, Charles William. Sec. Sidener & Van Riper Advt. Agency, Indianapolis, 1913-18; edn. dir. Nat. City Bank of N.Y., 1918-21; pres. Am. Chamber of Economics, N.Y., 1921-23; with Fuller & Smith & Ross, advt. agency, New York, Cleveland, Chicago, 1923—, pres., 1928—; dir. Ferro Corp., Affiliated Gas Equipment, Inc., Central Nat. Bank, Interchemical Corp., N.Y.C. Dir. Nat. Outdoor Advt. Bur.; trustee Cleve. Better Bus. Bur. (past pres.); chmn. C of C.; trustee St. Luke's Hosp. Assn., Am. High Blood Pressure Assn. Western Reserve U., Cleveland Musical Arts Assn.; past vice chmn. Cleve. Community Fund. Mem. Cleveland Advt. Club (former pres.), Am. Assn. of Advt. Agencies (chmn. 1939, 43); Advt. Affiliation (v.p.), Phi Kappa Psi, Phi Beta Kappa, Sigma Delta Chi. Methodist. Clubs: Pepper Pike, Rotary, Union, Hermit, Mayfield Country (Cleveland); Canadian (New York); Duquesne (Pittsburgh). Contbr. to advt. jours. Home: 2540 Arlington Rd., Cleve. Heights, O. Office: 1501 Euclid Av., Cleve. Died Oct. 7, 1954.

BINDER, Carroll (bind'ĕr), newspaperman; b. Mechanicsburg, Pa., Feb. 20, 1896; s. James Irwin and Emma (Flohr) B.; grad. York (Pa.) Acad.; student University of Pa., 1912-13; A.B., cum laude, Harvard University, 1916, graduate study, 1916-17; married Dorothy Walton, August 24, 1920; children—Carroll (1st lieutenant U.S. Air Force; killed in action over Germany, May 24, 1944), Mary Kelsey (Mrs. Edward Mikkelson), David and Deborah (twins). Began as reporter, later telegraph editor, middlewest and northwest, 1919-22; special writer, Chicago Daily News, 1922-27; specializing on sociological, industrial and political problems; covered the Nicaraguan revolution of 1926-27; corr. in Italy, Chicago Daily News, 1927-29, Soviet Russia, 1929-30, London corr., 1930-31; editorial asst. to publisher and writer of editorials on foreign affairs, 1931-36, foreign editor and dir. foreign service, 1936-44; editorial editor, Minneapolis Tribune, January 1, 1945—. Traveled extensively in Japan and China, 1934; corr. in Europe, 1937, and at Havana Conf. Am. Republics, 1940; visited Australia and New Zealand to study and describe their war efforts, 1941; reported on war from Great Britain and Eire, 1942; investigated and wrote extensively about post-war conditions in

Germany, Austria, France, Great Britain, 1946 and 1950, Japan and Korea, 1947; visited and reported from S.A., 1950. U.S. mem. United Nations subcommn. on freedom of information and of press, 1948-52; U.S. rep. on U.N. com. to draft a conv. on freedom of information, 1951; mem. exec. com. U.S. Nat. Commn. for UNESCO. Freedom Foundation award, 1952, 54; English Speaking Union distinguished award for editorial interpretation, 1953. Mem. Quaker unit of Am. Red Cross, caring for civilian refugees on French front, 1917-19. Mem. Fgn. Policy Assn., Inc., Am. Soc. Newspaper Editors, Nat. Conf. of Editorial Writers. Clubs: Minneapolis, Skylight (Mpls.); Overseas Press (N.Y.C.). Author: The Behavior Research Fund; The New Negro in Chicago; If War Comes to the Pacific. Syndicated articles on foreign affairs, appearing in many publications in U.S. and Latin America; contbr. to mags., in U.S. and abroad. Lecturer and radio commentator. Home: 1627 W. 26th St. Address: 427 Portland Av., S., Minneapolis Tribune, Mpls. Died May 1, 1956; buried Bermudian Cemetery, York Springs, Pa.

BINDER, Rudolph Michael, educator; b. Hetzeldorf, Hungary, Mar. 11, 1865; s. John and Sarah (Orben) B.; came to U.S., 1883; A.B., Harvard, 1893; B.D., U. Chgo., 1897; Gen. Theol. Sem., 1898; student Oxford U., Eng., 1900-01; Ph.D., Columbia, 1903; m. Garnette Faye Brammer, O., 1913; children—James Rudolph, Brammer. Asst. to Dr. William Reed Huntington, Grace P.E. Ch., N.Y.C., 1898-1900, Dr. (later Bishop) David H. Greer, St. Bartholomew's Ch., N.Y.C., 1902-06; tchr. Gen. Theol. Sem., 1901-03; tchr. sociology N.Y.U., 1906—, asst. prof., 1917, prof., 1919, prof. emeritus; spl. investigator Woman and Child Labor, for U.S. Bur. of Labor, 1906-07; asst. editor Ency. Social Reform, 1908. Mem. Am. Sociol. Soc., Am. Econ. Assn., A.A.A.S., Theta Chi, Phi Delta Kappa. Club: Harvard of N.J. Author: Feeling as the Principle of Individuation and Socialization, 1903; Major Social Problems, 1920; Health and Social Progress, 1920; Business and the Professions, 1922; Religion as Man's Completion, 1927; Principles of Sociology, 1928. Editor Social Progress (monthly), 1915-18. Home: Newtown, Pa. Died Oct. 16, 1950.

BINDERUP, Charles Gustav, ex-congressman; b. Horsens, Denmark; s. George Werner and Laurentza (Bjerring) Binderup; brought to U.S. in infancy; self-educated; m. Elena Westengaard, Sept. 18, 1900; children—Margaret (Mrs. Lem Copple), Verna (Mrs. Irvin Nelson), Sylvia (Mrs. Jack Henley). Began as farmer, 1891; became organizer and developer of creameries, salesman, merchant, and real estate dealer, Minden; mem. 74th and 75th Congresses, 4th Neb. Dist. Mem. Danish Brotherhood. Democrat. Presbyn. Club: Commercial. Home: Minden, Neb. Died Aug. 19, 1950.

BINFORD, Lloyd Tilghman, life ins. exec.; b. Duck Hill, Miss., Dec. 16, 1866; s. Colonel James R. and Frances L. (Campbell) B.; student pub. schs.; m. Hattie Horton Nelson, Feb. 6, 1894 (dec.); children—Gladys Lorraine (Mrs. Thomas A. Thrash), Dorothy (dec.), Lloyd Tilghman (dec.), Malvina Elizabeth (Mrs. Edward C. Moon), Frances Campbell (dec.), Margaret Nelson (Mrs. Fred Trexler), Lloyd Tilghman; m. 2d, Jennie May McCallum, Sept. 4, 1937. Began in U.S. Postal Service, 1884; entered life ins. bus. at Jackson, Tenn., 1895, moved to Memphis, 1899; founder and formerly pres. Columbian Mutual Life Ins. Co.; dir. Manhattan Savings Bank & Trust Co., Duck Hill Bank, Fidelity Bank, Hill Bank (Memphis). Pres. Mid South Fair and v.p. C. of C.; pres. Good Fellows Santa Claus Club, Memphis; pres. Monteagle Sunday Sch. Assembly; trustee Union U., Jackson, Tenn., Bapt. Meml. Hosp. Memphis; mem. nat. council YMCA; chmn. Bd. of Theatrical Censors, Memphis. Col. on staffs of 4 govs. of Miss. and 3 govs. of Tenn. Democrat. Baptist. Mason (32°, K.T., Shriner), K.P., Elk., Rotarian. Home: 1723 Peabody Av. Office: Commerce Title Bldg., Memphis. Died Aug. 27, 1956; buried Elmwood Cemetery.

BINGAY, Malcolm Wallace (bin'gā), newspaper editor; b. Sandwich, Ont., Can., Dec. 16, 1884; s. John George and Isabella (McIntyre) B.; brought to U.S. in infancy; ed. grammar sch. (Detroit), Y.M. C.A. night classes, private instruction, and special course, U. of Mich.; hon. D.Litt., Wayne U., 1932; LL.D., Olivet Coll., 1946; m. Sarah Ross, Oct. 28, 1908 (died Oct. 14, 1930); 1 daughter, Sybil Ross (Mrs. Frank P. Gill); m. 2d, Cecelia Fuhrman, Dec. 4, 1931. Began at 17 as reporter Detroit News; sporting editor, 1906-10, city editor, 1910-14; mng. editor, 1914-28; in charge of London Bur. of News, 1928-29; editor dir. Detroit Free Press since May, 1930. Mem. Am. Soc. Newspaper Editors, Newcomen Soc. Baseball Writers' Assn. of Am., Bd. of Commerce, Sigma Delta Chi Frat. (hon.); elected hon. mem. Wayne County Med. Soc., 1933. Episcopalian. Mason. (33 degree). Clubs: Detroit, Detroit Athletic, Detroit Economic, Harmonie Singing Society, Variety. Author "Good Morning" column, feature of Free Press editorial page. Author: Detroit Is My Own Home Town, 1946; Of Me I Sing, 1949. Home: 20383 Sunningdale Park, Grosse Pointe Woods. Office: Detroit Free Press, Detroit. Died Aug. 21, 1953.

BINGHAM, Hiram, explorer, ex-senator; b. Honolulu, H.I., Nov. 19, 1875; s. Rev. Hiram and Minerva Clarissa (Brewster) B.; A.B., Yale, 1898; M.A., U. of Calif., 1900; M.A., Harvard, 1901, Ph.D., 1905; Litt.D., U. of Cuzeo, 1912; m. Alfreda Mitchell, Nov. 20, 1900; children—Woodbridge, Hiram, Alfred Mitchell, Charles Tiffany, Brewster, Mitchell, Jonathan Brewster; m. 2d, Suzanne Carroll Hill, June 28, 1937. Austin teaching fellow in history, Harvard, 1901-02 and 1904-05; preceptor in history and politics, Princeton U., 1905-06; explored Bolivar's route across Venezuela and Colombia, 1906-07; lecturer on South Am. geography and history, Yale, 1907-09, asst. prof. Latin Am. history, 1909-15, prof., 1915-24; Albert Shaw lecturer on diplomatic history, Johns Hopkins, 1910. Del. U.S. Govt. to 1st Pan-Am. Scientific Congress, Santiago de Chile, 1908; explored Spanish trade route, Buenos Aires to Lima, 1908-09; dir. Yale Peruvian Expdn., 1911, discovered ruins of Machu Picchu, located Vitcos, last Inca capital, and made the first ascent of Mt. Coropuna, 21,703 ft.; dir. Peruvian expdns., 1912, 14-15, auspices of Yale U. and Nat. Geog. Soc.; adviser on the South Am. collections in the Yale U. Library; lecturer on South Sea Islands, Naval Training Schools, 1942-43. Alternate, Rep. Conv., Chicago, 1916; del. at large, Cleveland, 1924, Kansas City, 1928, Chicago, 1932, Cleveland, 1936; presdl. elector, 1916; lt. gov. of Conn., 1923-24, elected gov., 1924, resigning Jan. 8, 1925; elected U.S. Senator, Dec. 16, 1924, re-elected for term, 1927-33; mem. President Coolidge's Aircraft Bd. (Morrow Bd.), 1925; chairman American Samoan Commission, 1930; chairman Loyalty Review Board. Director Washington Loan & Trust Co. Capt. 10th Field Arty., Conn. Nat. Guard, 1916; organized U.S. schools of military aeronautics; commd. lt. col., Air Service, Mil. Aeronautics, U.S. Army, Oct. 23, 1917; chief Air Personnel Div., Washington, Nov. 1917-Mar. 1918, and A.E.F., Tours, 1918; comdg. officer Aviation Instrn. Center, Issodoun, France (Allies' largest flying school), Aug.-Dec. 1918. Officer de l'Ordre de l'Etoile Noire (French); Gran Oficial de la Orden del Libertador (Venezuela); Gran Oficial de la Orden "El Sol del Peru" (Peru); awarded Mitre medal of Hispanic Soc.; H. G. Bryant Gold Medal. Fellow Royal Geog. Society; honorary life member National Geog. Society; member Geographic Soc. of Phila., Hispanic Soc. America (hon. president), American Antiquarian Society; honorary member Nat. Acad. Hist. (Bogota); corr. member Lima Geog. Soc., Nat. Acad. Hist. (Caracas, Venezuela). Mem. Sigma Psi. Clubs: Elizabethan, Grad. (New Haven), Century (N.Y.), Metropolitan, Chevy Chase, Alfalfa (Wash.). Author: Journal of an Expedition across Venezuela and Colombia, 1909; Across South America, 1911; Vitcos, the Last Inca Capital, 1912; In the Wonderland of Peru, 1913; The Monroe Doctrine, An Obsolete Shibboleth, 1913; The Future of the Monroe Doctrine, 1920; An Explorer in the Air Service, 1920; Inca Land, 1922; Freedom under the Constitution, 1924; Machu Picchu, 1930; Elihu Yale, Governor, Collector and Benefactor, 1938; Elihu Yale—The American Nabob of Queen Square, 1939; Lost City of the Incas, 1948. Home: 1818 R St., Washington 9. Died June 6, 1956; buried Arlington Nat. Cemetery.

BINGHAM, Norman Williams, lawyer; b. Somerville, Mass., Aug. 12, 1872; s. Norman Williams and Eunice Harriet (Martin) B.; A.B., Harvard, 1895; LL.B., 1898; m. Ethel Prescott Stetson, Feb. 23, 1904; children—Katharine (Mrs. Henry P. Leverich), Elizabeth (Mrs. Thomas Van Orden Urmy), Eleanor (Mrs. Samuel P. Walker), Mary (Mrs. Enno Reimar Hobbing). Admitted to Mass. bar, 1898, since in practice at Boston; sr. partner Bingham, Dana & Gould. Mem. Mass. Com. on Pub. Safety, 1917-18. Mem. Am. (house dels. 1942-44), Mass., Boston (council 1932-38, pres. 1944-45) bar assns. Republican. Unitarian. Clubs: Harvard, Union, Curtis (Boston); Brae Burn Country (West Newton). Grad. treas. athletics, Harvard, 1896-98. Home: 125 Prince St., West Newton, Mass. Office: 1 Federal St., Boston. Died Nov. 12, 1958; buried Mt. Auburn Cemetery, Cambridge, Mass.

BINGHAM, Walter Van Dyke, psychologist; born Swan Lake, Ia., Oct. 20, 1880; s. Lemuel Rothwell and Martha Evarts (Tracy) B.; U. of Kan., 1897-98; B.A., Beloit (Wis.) Coll., 1901, U. of Chicago, 1905-06, U. of Berlin, 1907; M.A., Harvard, 1907; Ph.D., University of Chicago, 1908; Sc.D., Beloit College, 1929, Illinois Wesleyan University, 1950; married Millicent Todd, Dec. 4, 1920. Asso. in psychology, U. of Chicago, 1906-07; instr. ednl. psychology, Teachers Coll. (Columbia), 1908-10; asst. prof. psychology, Dartmouth, 1910-15, also dir. summer session, 1912-15; prof. psychology and head div. of applied psychology, Carnegie Inst. Tech., Pittsburgh, 1915-24; dir. Cooperative Research, same, 1921-24; dir. Personnel Research Fedn., Inc., 1924-34; mem. bd. Psychol. Corp. since 1920 (pres. 1926-28); professorial lecturer in psychology, Stevens Inst. Tech., 1930-40; consultant, Occupational Information Service, U.S. Office of Edn., 1938-39; chief psychologist Adj. Gen's. Office, War Dept., 1940-1947. Exec. sec. com. on classification of personnel in the army, 1917-18; lt. col., Personnel Br. Gen. Staff, U.S. Army, 1918-19. First chmn. Div. of Anthropology and Psychology, Nat. Research Council, 1919-20. Chmn. com. on classification of military personnel, 1949-1946; chmn. bd. on clin. psychol. advisory to the Surgeon Gen., U.S. Army, 1944-47; chmn. council, adv. to dir. personnel and adminstrn. Army Gen. Staff, 1946-48; consultant on personnel policies to Sec. of Defense since 1949. Awarded sec. of war's Emblem for Exceptional Civilian Service, 1944. Hon. corr. British Nat. Inst. Indsl. Psychol.; fellow A.A.A.S. (sec. council 1917); mem. Am. Psychol. Assn. (sec. 1911-14), Am. Assn. Applied Psychol. (pres. 1941); N.Y. State Assn. for Applied Psychology (pres. 1939), Psychometric Soc., Internat. Musical Soc., Sigma Xi, Phi Beta Kappa. Repn. Episcopalian. Clubs: Cosmos (Washington); Century (New York). Author: Studies in Melody, 1910; Aptitudes and Aptitude Testing, 1937, revised 1951. Joint author: Procedures in Employment Psychology, 1926; How to Interview, 1931; Psychology Today, 1932. Cons. editor Jour. of Applied Psychology, Personnel Psychology. Address: 1661 Cresdent Pl., Washington 9. Summer home: Medomak, Me. Died July 7, 1952; buried Arlington Nat. Cemetery.

BINGHAM, William 2d, philanthropist; b. Cleveland, O., July 21, 1879; s. Charles William and Mary (Payne) B.; attended U. Sch., Cleveland, 1898. Dir. of Bingham Associates Fund, a corp. chiefly interested in advancement of medicine; built Joseph H. Pratt Diagnostic Hosp., also Farnsworth Surg. Bldg., affiliated with N.E. Med. Center and Tufts Med. Sch. Boston; owner of Bethel Inn, Bethel, Me.; trustee, Gould Acad., Bethel, Me. Home: Bethel, Me. Died Feb. 17, 1955; buried Cleve.

BINING, Arthur Cecil (bin'ing), educator, author and editor; born at Llanelly, Wales, November 20, 1893; s. Arthur Owen and Jane (Phillips) B.; B.S. (with honors), University of Pennsylvania, 1927; B.D., Crozer Theol. Sem., 1927; A.M., U. of Pa., 1929, Ph.D., 1932; m. Inez Petry, Nov. 26, 1931. Came to U.S., 1911, naturalized citizen, 1922. Clk. in law office, O'Brian & Henderson, Toronto, Can., 1909-11; with U.S. Steel Corp., 1911-12, Jones & Laughlin Steel Corp., Aliquippa, Pa., 1912-22; instr. history, Liberty High Sch., Bethlehem, Pa., 1927-28; asst. instr. history, U. of Pa., 1928-29, instr., 1929-35, assistant professor American history, 1935-44, asso. prof., 1944—; editor D. Van Nostrand Co. Mem. gen. com. Schoolmen's Week, 1937-41. Guggenheim Meml. fellow, 1951-52. Mem. Honourable Soc. of Cymmrodorion, International Mark Twain Society (hon.). Historical Institute of Research, Pa. State Edn. Assn. (pres. U. of Pa. branch, 1937-41), Pa. Hist. Assn. (mem. council since 1934, pres. 1942-45), Am. Industrial Hist. Soc. (mem. council), Am. Hist. Assn., Nat. Council for Social Studies, Middle States Assn. History Teachers (mem. council, 1938-41), Middle States Council for Social Studies (v.p. 1943-45, pres., 1945-46), Social Studies Section of Southeastern Conv. Dist., Pa. State Edn. Assn. (hon. mem. of council), Hist. Soc. of Pa. (life). Am. Assn. for State and Local Hist., Econ. Hist. Assn.; Commn. on Wartime Policy, postwar adv. com., Nat. Council for Social Studies; com. on Archives and Hist. Activities, Commonwealth of Pa. Kappa Phi Kappa, Phi Delta Kappa, Pi Gamma Mu, Delta Theta Chi. Republican. Baptist. Club: Lenape (Philadelphia). Author: British Regulation of the Colonial Iron Industry, 1933; Pennsylvania Iron Manufacture in the Eighteenth Century, 1938; The Rise of American Economic Life, 1943. Co-author: (with D. H. Bining) Teaching the Social Studies in Secondary Schools, 1935, rev., 41, 52; (with W. H. Mohr and R. H. McFeely) Organizing the Social Studies in Secondary Schools, 1911; (with R. F. Nichols), The Role of History, in Education for Citizenship Responsibilities, 1942; (with J. P. Nichols and M. Wolf) History in the High School and Social Studies in the Elementary School, Proceedings of the Middle States Council for the Social Studies, 1944; (with A. C. Howland and R. H. Shryock) This Our World: A Pageant of World History, 1915; (with N. B. Wilkinson and R. L. Brunhouse) Writings in Pennsylvania History: A Bibliography of Secondary Works, 1946; (With A. E. Martin and Morris Wolf) This Our Nation; From Colony to World Leader, 1950; The Teaching of History in the Colleges and Universities of the United States, 1950; A History of the United States, Vol. 1, 1950; (with Philip S. Klein) A History of the United States, Vol II. 1950; The Rise of American Economic Life, rev. edit., 1955; Pennsylvania's Iron and Steel Industry, 1954. Contbr. to Dictionary of American History, history mags. and encys. Editor: The Social Studies, 1937-50, mem. editorial board since 1950; editor: D. Van Nostrand's Social Studies Series: Pa. History 1934-41; Ednl. Outlook, 1939-41. Mem. editorial bd., Pennsylvania History, 1934-1946; Ednl. Outlook, 1939-1946; mem. advisory board, Federal Writers' Project, 1939-42; editor Charles Scribner's Sons' Historical Series for Colleges; Newson's Social Studies Series. Home: 1112 Lindale Av., Drexel Hill, Pa. Died Sept. 30, 1957.

BINNS, Jack, corp. exec.; b. England, 1884; student Sch. of Arts and Sci., Colchester, Eng., 1903; chmn. and treas. and dir., Hazeltine Corp., Washington; pres. and dir. Latour Corp., Hazeltine Research, Inc.; v.p. and treas., Hazeltine Electronics Corp. Home: 333 W. 56th St., N.Y. City. Office: National Press Bldg., Washington. Died Dec. 8, 1959.

BIPPUS, Rupert Frederick, judge; b. Chicago, Feb. 21, 1890; s. Frederick J. and Minnie (Dodd) B.; ed. pub. and high schs., Chicago; LL.B., Chicago-Kent Coll. of Law, 1913, LL.M., 1914; m. Esther M. Erickson, June 1, 1915; 1 dau., Betty Jane. Admitted to Ill. bar, 1913; mem. law firm Bippus, Rose, Burt & Pierce; asst. pros. atty., City of Chicago, 1915-22; atty. for West Park Commrs., Chicago, 1923-24; security commr. State of Ill., 1930-33; adviser to state treas. of Ill. on matters of finance banking and investments, 1942-46; adviser to sec. of state, Ill., 1944-45 former instr. on law of conveyancing, and spl. lectr. on laws and ordinances affecting real property, Chicago Central Coll. of Commerce; former instr. in contract law John Marshall Law Sch. Formerly mem. Nat. Exec. Com.; pres. central states group Nat. Asso. Securities Commrs.; mem. and v.p. Cook Co. Civil Service Commn.; master in chancery Circuit Ct. of Cook County; elected judge Circuit Ct. of Cook County, 1951. Mem. Am., Ill. and Chicago bar assns., Navy League of Am., West Suburban Bar Assn. (past pres.), Phi Sigma Kappa, Phi Alpha Delta. Author: Duties and Legal Liabilities of Bank Directors and Officers, 1928. Home: 319 Lombard Av., Oak Park, Ill. Office: 10 S. LaSalle St., Chgo. 3. Died Sept. 12, 1951; buried Mount Emblem, Elmhurst, Ill.

BIRD, Arthur, composer; b. at Cambridge, Mass., July 23, 1856; s. Horace and Elizabeth (Homer) B.; grad. Belmont High Sch.; studied music, Berlin, under Haupt, Loeschhorn and Urban; m. Wilhelmine Waldmann, at Peterboro, England, Feb. 29, 1888. studied under Liszt; conducted at Milwaukee Musical Festival, 1886; now in Berlin. Composer piano, harmonium, organ works, symphony, carnival, three suites for orchestra, Ballet Bühezahl, opera Daphne. Won Paderewski prize for chamber music, decimet for wind instruments, 1902. Mem. Nat. Inst. Arts and Letters. Address: 33 Wieland St., Charlottenburg, Germany. Died 1923.

BIRD, Charles, psychologist; b. Birkenhead, Eng., Mar. 23, 1893; s. Charles Thomas and Elizabeth Hannah (Carter) B.; B.A., Springfield (Mass.) Coll., 1916; M.A., Clark U., 1917, Ph.D., 1920; m. Dorothy M. Andrew, March 16, 1944; children by previous marriage—Lois Elizabeth, Charles Maurice. Instructor of psychology at the University of Minnesota, 1920-23, asst. prof., 1923-28, asso. prof., 1928-35, prof., 1935—. Served as pfc., 2d Trench Mortar Battery, 2d Div., AEF, 1918-19. Fellow A.A.A.S.; mem. Am., Midwestern psychol. assns., Minn. Acad. Sci., Am. Assn. U., Profs., Sigma Xi., Psi Chi. Democrat. Club: Campus (Mpls.). Author: Effective Study Habits, 1931; Social Psychology, 1940; (with D. M. Bird) Learning More by Effective Study, 1945. Contbr. to psychol. jours. Home: 5836 Knox Av. S., Mpls. 19. Died Jan. 22, 1957; buried Lakewood Cemetery, Mpls.

BIRD, James Pyper, educator; b. Springfield, Mo., Aug. 21, 1871; s. William F. and Elgiva (Barton) B.; A.B., U. Mich., 1893, Ph.D., 1918; grad. work, Sorbonne, U. Madrid; m. Nina Allene Wilber, June 25, 1902; children—Beatrice, James Wilber, Carolyn Elaine, David Barton. Instr. langs. Union U., Jackson, Tenn., 1896-1902; instr. langs. and asst. prof. U. Mich., 1903-15, sec. dept. engring., 1905-15; prof. Romance langs., Carleton Coll., Northfield, Minn., 1915-42, 44; vis. prof. Spanish, Am. U., Washington, 1942-43. Insp. coll. and univ. work, 8th Dist., S.A.T.C., 1918. Decorated Officer de l'Instruction Publique (France). Mem. Modern Lang. Assn. Am., S.A.R., Phi Beta Kappa, Kappa Sigma. Travel condr., lectr. Author: Essentials of French, 1925. Home: Northfield, Minn. Died July 12, 1947.

BIRD, Reginald William, mfg. exec.; b. Brookline, Mass., June 22, 1872; s. William Barnard and Caroline (Crossman) B.; student Hopkinson Sch.; m. Violet Dean Gooderham (dec.); children—John Reginald, Mary Elizabeth (Mrs. William O. Clark), Patricia May (Mrs. W. Prescott Smith); m. 2d, Elizabeth Bowditch (Mrs. Manning Emery), June 9, 1932. Formerly mem. J. A. & W. Bird & Co.; formerly pres., chmn. bd., now dir., mem. exec. com. Flinkote Co.; dir. Exolon Co. Trustee Mass. Found. Pres. Mass. Fedn. Taxpayers Assn. Home: Waveney Farm, Framingham, Mass. Office: 11 Beacon St., Boston. Died Apr. 16, 1959; buried Mt. Auburn Cemetery, Cambridge, Mass.

BIRDSALL, Carl A., banker; b. Thayer County, Neb., June 28, 1892; s. George A. and Jennie (Steinbarger) B.; B.S., University of Chicago, 1916; married Frances Deneen, 1919 (died December 14, 1958). Reporter for Chicago Evening American, 1913-16; began with Continental and Commercial Nat. Bank (Chicago), 1919, asst. cashier, 1923, 2d vice pres., 1927; v.p. Continental Ill. Nat. Bank & Trust Co., 1930, dir., 1947—, pres., 1948—; dir. Elgin, Joliet & Eastern Ry. Trustee Equitable Life Ins. Co. of Des Moines, Ia. Served as capt., Air Service, U.S. Army, 1917-19. Trustee St. Luke's Hosp., Chgo. Zool. Soc. Mem. Phi Kappa Psi. Republican. Presbyn. (trustee). Clubs: Glen View, Chicago, Commercial (Chgo.). Home: 900 N. Michigan Av., Chgo. 11. Office: 231 S. LaSalle St., Chgo. 90. Died Nov. 19, 1956; buried Oak Wood Cemetery, Chgo.

BIRDSEYE, Clarence, processed foods exec.; b. Brooklyn, N.Y., Dec. 9, 1886; s. Clarence Frank and Ada (Underwood) B.; student Amherst, 1910, M.A., 1941; m. Eleanor Gannett, Aug. 21, 1915; children—Kellogg G., Ruth, Eleanor, Henry S. Field naturalist, biol. survey, U.S. Dept. Agr., 1910-12; fur trader, Labrador, 1912-17; U.S. purchasing agent U.S. Housing Corp., 1917-19; asst. to pres. U.S. Fisheries Assn., 1920-22; vice pres. and pres. of companies pioneering in quick freezing dressed seafoods, 1923-29; with Birdseye-Frosted Foods, Inc., and Birdseye Lamps, 1930-34; pres. Birdseye Electric Co., 1935-38; engaged in development of specialized food freezing and dehydrating processes and equipment, 1939—; pres. Process Evaluation & Development Corp., 1955-56. director Cape Ann Nat. Bank, Gloucester, Mass.; consultant to Gen. Foods Corp. Mem. Am. Chem. Soc., Boston Hort. Club, Gloucester Chamber of Commerce, Am. Fisheries Assn., Am. Soc. Refrigerating Engrs., Inst. Food Technologists (chmn. northeast sect. 1945-46), Internat. Assn. Milk Sanitarians, Camp Fire Club. Author numerous papers and talks on food preservation. Granted approximately 250 U.S. and fgn. patents in fields of food preservation and incandescent light. Spent two months on hospital ship with Dr. Wilfred T. Grenfell, assisting in medical care given sick along coast of Labrador. Developed process for making paper pulp from sugar cane "bagasse", straw and other farm residues. Address: Eastern Point Blvd., Gloucester, Mass. Died Oct. 7, 1956.

BIRDWELL, Alton William, emeritus coll. pres.; b. nr. Palestine, Tex., Sept. 18, 1870; s. George Preston and Addie (Kilgore) B.; prep. edn. Summer Hill Select Sch., Omen, Tex.; student summer sessions U. Tex., U. Mo., U. Chgo.; A.M., George Peabody Coll. for Tchrs., 1916; LL.D., Southwestern U., Georgetown, Tex., 1940; m. Maude Margaret Shipe, Sept. 1, 1915; 1 dau., Anne Isabella. Tchr. rural schs., Smith County, Tex., 1892-99; prin. elementary sch., Tyler, Tex., 1899-1903; county supt. schs., Smith County, 1904-06; prin. high sch., Tyler, 1906-09; supt. schs., Troup, Tex., 1909-10; asst. prof. history Southwest Tex. Normal Sch., San Marcos, 1910-11, prof., 1911-22, dean of faculty, 1917-22; pres. Stephen F. Austin State Tchrs. Coll., Nacogdoches, 1922-42, emeritus; tchr. coll. adminstrn. George Peabody Coll. for Tchrs. summers 1927-29. Mem. Am., S.W. hist. assns., N.E.A., Tex. State Tchrs. Assn. (pres.), Phi Delta Kappa. Democrat. Baptist. K.P., Rotarian. Home: Nacogdoches, Tex. Died Oct. 25, 1954; buried Nacogdoches.

BIRGE, Edward Asahel (bûrj), univ. pres. emeritus, zoölogist; b. Troy, N.Y., Sept. 7, 1851; s. Edward White and Ann (Stevens) B.; A.B., Williams Coll., 1873, A.M., 1876, Ph.D., Harvard, 1878; student Leipsic, Germany 1880-81; hon. Sc.D., Western U. of Pa., 1897; LL.D. Williams Coll., 1903, U. Wis., 1915, U. Mo., 1919; Ph.D., Rensselaer Poly. Inst., 1925; m. Anna W. Grant, July 15, 1880 (died Dec. 14, 1919); children—Edward Grant (dec.), Anna Grant. With U. Wis., 1875—, instr. natural history, 1875, prof. zoölogy, 1879-1911, dean Coll. Letters and Sci., 1891-1918, acting-pres. 1900-03, pres., 1918-25, pres. emeritus, 1925—; dir. geol. and natural history survey, Wis., 1897-1919, pres. commrs., 1919-25, in charge of nat. hist. div., 1897—; sec. commrs. of fisheries, Wis., 1895-1915; mem. Bd. Forestry Commrs., Wis., 1905-15; mem. Conservation commn., Wis., 1908-15; dir. Madison Free Library, 1890-1909, pres., 1893-1909. Fellow A.A.A.S.; mem. Wis. Acad. Scis. Arts and Letters (pres. 1890-91, 1918-21), Wis. Hist. Soc., Am. Micros Soc. (pres. 1903), Am. Fisheries Soc. (pres. 1907), Am. Soc. Zoölogists (pres. Central br. 1908-09), Washington Acad. Scis., Am. Soc. Naturalists, Am. Philos. Soc., Ecol. Soc. Am., Acad. Natural Sci., N.Y. Acad. Sci., Sigma Xi, Phi Sigma; senator Phi Beta Kappa, 1904-22, life senator, 1922— (v.p. United chpts. 1913-19, pres. 1919-22). Council award State Med. Soc. of Wis., 1935. Writer on zoölogy and limnology. Home: 2011 Van Hise Av., Madison 5, Wis. Died June 9, 1950; buried Madison.

BIRGE, Edward Bailey, musician; b. Northampton, Mass., June 12, 1868; s. Edward and Cornelia M. (Day) B.; A.B., Brown U., 1891; Mus.B., Yale, 1904; m. Mary Thompson, June 20, 1901. Supervisor music, state normal schs., New Haven and New Britain, Conn., 1896-1901; served as dir. pub. sch. music, Indianapolis, Ind., 1901-21; supt. Am. Inst. Normal Methods, Evanston, Ill., 1911-21; prof. of music, Indiana U., 1921-38, now emeritus prof. music; organist and choir dir. Chmn. Nat. Research Council of Music Edn., 1929. Mem. Music Supervisors' Nat. Conf. (ex-pres.), Music Teachers' Nat. Assn., Ind. Music Teachers' Assn. (pres. 1923), Am. Guild Organists, N.E.A., Delta Upsilon. Conglist. Mason. Organized Peoples Chorus. Indianapolis, 1912, and dir. same until 1921. Clubs: Graduate (New Haven, Conn.); Columbia (Indianapolis). Editor: Silver Song Series No. 7, 1895; Part Songs and Choruses for High Schools, 1908; Supplementary Songs, 1912. Asst. editor Progressive Music Series; editor school music dept. Musician, 1924. Composer of Concert Overture, choruses, etc. Author: History of Public School Music in the United States, 1927. Asso. editor Music Hour Series; asso. editor New Music Horizon Series; chmn. editorial board Music Educators' Journal; chmn. emeritus editorial board Music Educators Journal. Home: 828 E. 3d St., Bloomington, Ind. Died July 16, 1952; buried Florence, Mass.

BIRGE, Julius (bûrj), publisher; b. St. Davids, Pa., Mar. 26, 1909; s. Walter William and MaBelle Claire (Brown) B.; A.B., Harvard, 1931; LL.B., Ind. Law Sch., 1938; m. Evelyn Chambers, Nov. 11, 1938; children—Jonathan Laurance, Evelyn Taggart, Peter Julius. Research asst. J. Walter Thompson Co., 1931-33; admitted to Ind. bar, 1938, practiced in Indpls., 1938-40; with Bobbs-Merrill Co., Inc., Indpls., 1940—, dir., 1945—, sec., 1947—, editor non fiction books, 1950—. Pres. Family Service Association, Indpls., 1950-53; vice president and director Family Service Association of America. Served as pvt. AUS, World War II. Mem. Am., Indpls. bar assns., Indpls. Lawyers Assn., Miss. Valley Hist. Assn., Phi Kappa Sigma, Sigma Delta Kappa. Presbyn. Clubs: Literary, Rotary, Dramatic (Indpls.); Signet (Cambridge, Mass.). Home: 442 Blue Ridge Rd., Indpls. 8. Office: 730 N. Meridian St., Indpls. 7. Died Jan. 29, 1958.

BIRKHEAD, Claude Vivian, lawyer; b. Phoenix, Oregon, May 27, 1880; son of Joseph Chenoweth and Mary Jane (Jennings) B.; student Fort Worth U., 1898-99; hon. LL.D., 1941; m. Lillian Alice Guessaz, Dec. 6, 1905; children—Betty Jane, Mary Ann. Admitted to Tex. bar, 1899, practiced at San Antonio since 1904; sr. mem. Birkhead, Beckmann, Standard, Vance & Wood; apptd. judge 73d Dist., 1910, re-elected 4 yr. term, resigned, 1912; city atty. San Antonio, 1920-21. Counsel San Antonio Dist. Fed. Loan Agency; pres. and gen. counsel, Commercial Cattle Loan Co.; gen. counsel Grayburg Oil Co., San Antonio Ins. Exchange, San Antonio Real Estate Bd.; counsel Nueces Valley Authority; chmn. trustees, general counsel Nix Memorial Hospital; special attorney appointed by Texas Legislature to represent Texas coastal land claims before Congress, 1939. Chairman San Antonio U.S.-Tex. Centennial Com., 1936-37; chmn. Dem. Nat. Campaign Com., Bexar County, Tex., 1936-37; chmn. Fire and Police Civil Service Bd., 1931-36. Col. 131st F.A., U.S. Army, A.E.F., 1917-19; chief of staff, 36th Div., Tex. Nat. Guard, 1919-23; brig. gen., 1923-36; maj. gen. (N.G.U.S.) Army of U.S., comdg. 36th Div. Texas, N.G., 1936; command gen. Camp Bowie, Tex., and 36th Div. Army of U.S., 1940-41; comdg. gen. Internal Security Forces, 3d Service Comd., 1942; retired from active service, June 30, 1942; lt. gen. Tex. State Guard Reserve Corps, comdg. Awarded meritorious service medal (Texas), 1933. Mem. Am., Tex. State and San Antonio bar assns. Fraternal Soc. Law Assn., Internat. Assn. of Ins. Counsel; Founders, Am. Legion; Am. Legion (1st comdr., Dept. of Tex., chmn. bd. trustees of Permanent Fund, 1930-36); Nat. Guard Assn. of U.S. (pres. 1932-33); Military Order of the World War. Democrat. Presbyterian. Mason (K.T.). Club: Ft. Sam Houston Officers'. Home: 4001 N. New Braunfels Av. Address: Majestic Bldg., San Antonio, Tex. Died Nov. 19, 1950; buried Ft. Sam Houston Nat. Cemetery, San Antonio.

BIRKHEAD, Leon Milton, clergyman; b. Winfield, Mo., Apr. 28, 1885; s. Hiram Link and Martha Ann (Trunbull) B.; A.B., McKendree Coll., 1910; student Drew Theol. Sem., 1910-11, Union Theol. Sem. and grad. dept. Columbia, 1911-12; m. Agnes Augusta Schiereck, Sept. 29, 1913; 1 son, Kenneth Milton. Student preacher in Ill., 1904-10; asst. minister Grace M.E. Ch., N.Y.C., 1910-12; asso. minister Maple Av. Ch., St. Louis, 1912-13; pastor Wagner Meml. M.E. Ch., St. Louis, 1913-15, First Unitarian Ch., Wichita, Kan., 1915-17, All Souls Unitarian Ch. (The Liberal Center), Kansas City, Mo., 1917-39; founder, 1937, and since nat. dir. Friends of Democracy. Tech. adviser to Sinclair Lewis during writing of Elmer Gantry, 1926-27. Mason. Author of numerous Little Blue Books, including: Is Elmer Gantry True?; Religious Bunk Over the Radio; Can Man Know God?; President Hoover and Quakerism; The Religion of a Free Man; The Case Against the McCormick-Patterson Press. Offices: Scarritt Bldg., 818 Grand Av., Kansas City, Mo.; and 137 E. 57th St., N.Y.C. 22. Died Dec. 2, 1954.

BIRNEY, (Herman) Hoffman, writer; b. Phila., Apr. 1, 1891; s. Herman Hoffman and Elizabeth Cherrill (Boude) B.; prep. edn., high sch., Durango, Colo., and Phillips Brooks Sch., Phila.; student Dickinson Coll., Carlisle, Pa., 1908-12; m. Marguerite Agnes Bovington, June 14, 1930; 1 son, Herman Hoffman. Served in U.S. Army, with infantry, later Aviation Sec. Signal Corps., Mar. 1917-Nov. 1920 advancing to 2d lt. Air Service. Mem. Phi Delta Theta. Republican. Mason. Author: King of the Mesa, 1927; The Masked Rider, 1928; Steel-dust (juvenile), 1928;

Vigilantes (hist.), 1929; The Canyon of Lost Waters, 1929; Roads to Roam (travel), 1930; The Pinto Pony (juvenile), 1930; Zealots of Zion (hist.), 1931; Two Little Navajos (juvenile), 1931; Kudlu, the Eskimo Boy (juvenile), 1932; Archaeological Sites in Glen Cañon of the Colorado River, 1932; Barrier Ranch (fiction), 1933; Tu'kwi of the Peaceful People (juvenile), 1933; Forgotten Cañon (fiction); Holy Murder—the Story of Porter Rockwell (biography, with Charles Kelly); Grim Journey, 1934; Eagle in the Sun, 1935; The Stranger in Black Butte, 1935; Dead Man's Trail (fiction), 1937; Mountain Chief (juvenile), 1938; Ann Carmeny, 1941; Jason Burr's First Case (under pseudonym of David Kent), 1941; Brothers of Doom, the Story of the Pizarros of Peru, 1942; A Knife is Silent, 1947; The Dice of God, 1956. Contributor to various publs. Jan.-July, 1943, attached to Regional Office, O.W.I., Phila., 1943-47; editor, ammunition and small arms research and development, U.S. Army Ordnance Dept.; editor, rocket research and development, Fort Bliss, Tex., 1947. Home: Huntsville, Ala. Died June 2, 1958.*

BIRNIE, Upton, Jr., army officer; b. Carlisle, Pa., July 7, 1877; s. Upton and Susan Alice (Galt) B.; B.S., U.S. Mil. Acad., 1900; distinguished grad. Inf. and Cav. Sch., 1907; grad. Army Staff Coll., 1908; Army War Coll., 1912, 21; m. Susan Turner Schenck, Apr. 15, 1903; children—Elizabeth Schenck (dec.), Sue Schenck (Mrs. Francis I. Brady), Mrs. Margaret Birnie Capron. Apptd. 2d lt. arty., 1900; advanced through grades to col. F.A. 1929; apptd. maj. gen., chief of field arty., 1934; relieved, 1938; retired with rank of maj. gen., 1938. Decorated D.S.M. (U.S.) Officer Legion of Honor (France); Officer Order of Leopold (Belgium); Officer Order of St. Maurice and St. Lazare (Italy). Presbyn. Home: 1702 Surrey Lane, N.W., Washington 7. Died Oct. 15, 1957; buried Arlington Nat. Cemetery.

BIRTLEY, Robert Lewis, coal operator; b. Scranton, Pa., Dec. 28, 1893; s. Thomas Butler and Hannah (Lewis) B.; grad. Tech. High Sch., Scranton, Pa.; m. Alice Rogers, July 7, 1917; children—Robert L., Carol (Mrs. Kenneth Bayliss), A. Louise. Surveyor, D. & H. Co., Scranton, Pa., 1911-16; pres. and dir. Hammond Coal Co., Girardville, Pa., since 1939, Kohinoor Coal Co., Shenandoah, Pa., since 1941. Operators trustee, anthracite Health and Welfare Fund since 1946; mem. Producers' Adv. Bd., Anthracite Negotiating Com. Served as mem. nat. anthracite distbn. com. Solid Fuels Adminstrn. for War, 1942-46. Mem. Anthracite Operators Assn. (pres., dir.), American Institute of Mining and Metall. Engrs. Republican. Baptist. Clubs: Downtown Athletic (New York); Scranton (Pa.); Scranton Country, (Clarks Summit, Pa.); The Pottsville (Pa.); Ashland (Pa.) Country. Home: 130 Nelson St., Clarks Green, Pa. Office: Hammond Coal Co., Girardville, Pa. Died Aug. 26, 1955.

BISBEE, Spaulding, business exec.; b. Buckfield, Me., 1890; student Hebron Acad., Colby Coll., Boston U. Law Sch. Vice pres., dir., asst. sec., asst. treas. Keyes Fibre Co., Portland, Me. Dir. civil def. Me., 1949-53; mem. Me. bar. Served as maj. World War I; as col., World War II; ret. as brig. gen., 1950. Episcopalian. Mason. Club: Cumberland (Portland). Home: Falmouth Foreside, Portland 99. Office: 465 Congress St., Portland, Me. Died Aug. 29, 1958; buried Evergreen Cemetery, Portland, Me.

BISCOE, Howard Morton, ry. official; b. Westboro, Mass., July 3, 1869; A.B., Yale, 1892. Began as clk. in ticket auditor's office, B.&A. R.R., 1892, and has continued with same rd. consecutively as clk. gen. freight office, and Central Vt. Ry., 1893-96, clk. gen. traffic mgr.'s office, 1896-98, foreign freight agt., also of N.Y.C. & H.R.R.R. at Boston, 1898-1905, gen. freight agt., 1905-10, asst. freight traffic mgr., 1910-11, traffic mgr., 1911-13, v.p. N.Y.C. R.R. in charge B. & A. R.R., 1913-18, federal mgr. B. & A. R.R., 1918-20, v.p., 1920-39, retired July 31, 1939. Home: Waban, Mass. Office: South Station, Boston, Mass. Died Mar. 25, 1951.

BISCOE, Thomas Dwight, educator; b. May 12, 1840; s. Thomas C. and Ellen (Lord) B.; A.B., Amherst Coll., 1865, Walker Inst. Mathematics, 1867-Theol. Sem., 1863-65, U. Halle, 1869-70; LL.D., Marietta Coll.; m. Laura A. Capron, Jan. 12, 1875 (dec.); m. 2d, Ella Shipman, July 13, 1880. Tutor Amherst Coll., 1865, Walker Inst. Mathematics, 1867-69; tchr. Cin., 1871-72; prof. natural scis. Marietta Coll., 1874-1907, emeritus, 1907-30. Address: Marietta, O. Died Feb. 27, 1930.

BISHOP, Arthur Vaughan, educator; b. Riner, Va., Mar. 28, 1883; s. William Millard and Laura Virginia (Lucas) B.; B.S., Va. Poly. Inst., 1906; M.A., U. Va., 1911, Ph.D., 1913; grad. student U. Chgo., summer 1922; m. Ellen P. Hoffman, Sept. 2, 1914. Prin. Blacksburg (Va.) High Sch., 1906-08; instr. Latin, U. Va., 1909-13, mem. Latin faculty, summer schs., 1912-24; prof. Latin and Greek, Hollins (Va.) Coll., 1913-23; prof. Greek and Latin, Georgetown (Ky.) Coll., 1923-28; asso. prof. Latin, Dickinson Coll., Carlisle, Pa., 1928-29, A. J. Clarke prof. Latin lang. and lit., 1929-40, A. J. Clarke prof. classical langs. and lit. class dean, 1940, now prof. emeritus, spl. courses, 1954. YMCA sec. Camp Hancock, Augusta, Ga., summer 1918. Mem. com. Middle Atlantic States, for Evaluating Secondary Schs., 1948; mem. Am. Philol. Assn., Classical Assn. Middle Atlantic States, Pa. State Assn. Classical Tchrs., Phi Beta Kappa, Phi Kappa Phi. Democrat. Presbyn. Rotarian. Home: 223 S. College St., Carlisle, Pa. Died Jan. 6, 1955; buried Ivy Hill Cemetery, Alexandria, Va.

BISHOP, Daniel Sanborn, cartoonist; b. Keokuk, Ia., June 7, 1900; s. Edwin DeForest and Emma Amanda (Sanborn) B.; student Knox Coll., Galesburg, Ill., 1918-19; studied at Acad. Fine Arts, Chgo., 1919-21, Art Inst., Chgo., 1919-21; m. Lucile Juliet Titus, July 3, 1925 (div. Dec. 3, 1937); m. 2d, Florence Leonora Johnstone, Oct. 1, 1938; children—Barbara Ann, Beverly Alden. Began as cartoonist Ore. Journal, Portland, Ore., 1925; instr. cartooning, U. Ore., 1927-28; cartoonist Star-Times, St. Louis, 1929-51; freelance cartoonist, 1951—; pres. TV Art Productions, St. Louis, 1953—. Received Nat. Humane Soc. cartoon award 1927; Nat. Safety cartoon award, 1945. Mem. Portland Symphony, 1925-29. Mem. Artist Guild, Advertising Club, Sigma Delta Chi (pres. 1959). Mason. Home: 4 Berrywood Dr., Glendale, Mo. Died Aug. 22, 1959; buried Oak Hill Cemetery, Kirkwood, Mo.

BISHOP, Eugene Lindsay, M.D., health dir.; b. Nashville, Apr. 3, 1886; s. Eugene Edgar and Elizabeth (Crittenden) B.; M.D., Vanderbilt, 1914; M.P.H., Johns Hopkins, 1923; m. Marie Kerr, Oct. 12, 1916; children—Lindsay Kerr, Eugene Lindsay. Interne, St. Thomas Hosp., Nashville, 1914-15; in gen. practice, Nashville, 1916; field dir., Tenn. State Health Dept., 1916-18, dir. rural sanitation, 1918-22, asst. commr., 1923-24, commr., 1924-35; dir. of health and safety dept., Tenn. Valley Authority, since 1935; asso. prof. preventive medicine, Vanderbilt. Formerly chmn. com. on qualifications State and Territorial Health Officers, and of com. on federal relations, State and Prov. Health Officers (hon. life mem.). Former mem. Nat. Adv. Health Com.; former consultant, Com. for Co-ordination of Health and Welfare Activities of the Federal Govt.; former mem. Advisory Com. to Com. on Research in Med. Economics; mem. bd. scientific directors, 1929-30, 1942-44, elected for 3 yr. term, Jan. 1947. International Health Div., Rockefeller Foundation. Mem. medical advisory bd. United Mine Workers Am. Fellow A.M.A. (sec. preventive and industrial medicine); life mem. Am. Pub. Health Assn. (past pres.; past pres. Southern Br.; former mem. exec. bd. and council); mem. C.A.P. (com. on professional edn.); mem. Am. Soc. Tropical Medicine, A.A.A.S., Southern Med. Assn., Nat. Malarial Soc., Tennessee State Med. Assn., Nashville Academy of Medicine, Alpha Omega Alpha, Alpha Kappa Kappa, Delta Omega. Methodist. Mason. Home: 808 Vine St. Office: 207 Old Post Office Bldg., Chattanooga. Died Feb. 27, 1951; buried Mount Olivet Cemetery, Nashville.

BISHOP, James Robert Thoburn, mfg. exec.; b. Mankato, Kan., Aug. 2, 1896; s. Robert Hamilton and Catherine (Thompson) B.; student U. Prep. Sch., Cleve., 1912-14; B.A., Harvard, 1918, student bus. adminstrn., 1924-25; m. Eleanor Frances Kissick, May 25, 1939; children by previous marraige—Jane Addams (Mrs. John L. Fahey), Mary (Mrs. Michael M. Luther). Fgn. trade dept. Guardian Trust Co., Cleve., 1919-21; securities dept. Union Trust Co., Cleve., 1921-24; printer, pub. Premier Press, Your Garden Pub. Co., Cleve., 1925-33; asst. to pres. Am. Maize Products Co., N.Y. City, 1933-41, v.p. research, 1941-44; v.p. charge Amino Products Div., Internat. Minerals & Chem. Corp. since 1944. Chief grain products sect. food br. W.P.B.; cons. grain products br. U.S. Dept. Agr., 1943-44. Clubs: Bohemian (San Francisco); Sainte Claire, Country (San Jose, Cal.); La Rinconada Golf (Los Gatos, Cal.); Harvard, Chemists, Whitehall Lunch (N.Y.C.); Saddle and Cycle, University (Chgo.); Toledo. Home: 179 E. Lake Shore Dr., Chgo. 11. Office: 20 N. Wacker Dr., Chgo. 6. Died Jan. 23, 1956; buried Lakeview Cemetery, Cleve.

BISHOP, William Warner, librarian; b. Hannibal, Mo., July 20, 1871; s. William Melanchthon and Harriette Anna (Warner) B.; A.B., U. of Mich., 1892 (Phi Beta Kappa), A.M., 1893; fellow Am. Sch. Classical Studies in Rome, 1898-99; Litt.D., Miami U., 1926, New York U., 1927, Columbia, 1930, Catholic U. of America, 1939; LL.D., Oberlin (Ohio) Coll., 1928, U. of Western Ontario, 1932; D.Litt., Nat. U. of Ireland, 1937; LL.D., Ohio Wesleyan, 1937; m. Finie Murfree Burton, June 28, 1905; 1 son, William Warner. Prof. Greek, Mo. Wesleyan Coll., Cameron, Mo., 1893-94; instr. in N.T. and asst. librarian, Garrett Bibl. Inst., Evanston, Ill., 1895-98; librarian and instr. in Latin, Poly. Inst. of Brooklyn, N.Y., 1899-1902; head cataloguer, Princeton U. Library, 1902-04; reference librarian, same, 1904-07; supt. Reading Room, Library of Congress, Washington, D.C., 1907-15; librarian, U. of Mich., 1915-41, emeritus. Chmn. Adv. Group on Coll. Libraries, Carnegie Corp., 1928-34, chmn. Adv. Group on Junior Coll. Libraries, 1935-37, chmn. Advisory Group on Academic Libraries, 1939-43; v.p. Internat. Fed. Library Assn., 1929-31, pres., 1931-36, hon. pres. since 1936; chmn. Bd. on Resources on Am. Libraries, American Library Association, 1936-38; consultant since 1939. Mem. A.L.A. (president 1918-19), Bibliographic Soc. America (pres. 1921-23), Library Assn. of China (hon.); hon. fellow Library Assn. of Great Britain; hon. member Argentine Assn. of Librarians, 1941. Conglist. Clubs: Cosmos (Washington, D.C.); Grolier (N.Y.). Author: Practical Handbook of Modern Library Cataloguing, 2d edit., 1924; The Backs of Books, 1925; Carnegie Corporation and College Libraries, 1938; Checklist of American Copies of S.T.C. Books, 1944, 50. Contbr. numerous articles to library pubs. Home: 1612 Morton Av., Ann Arbor, Mich. Died Feb. 19, 1955; buried Forest Hill Cemetery, Ann Arbor, Mich.

BISSONNETTE, T. Hume, prof. biology; b. Dundas, Ont., Can., June 27, 1885; s. Julien Donald and Annie Isabel (Hume) B.; M.A., Queen's U., Kingston, Can., 1913; Ph.D., U. of Chicago, 1923; m. Julia Irene Powers, Mar. 1, 1924; children—Julien Hume, Donald King. Came to U.S., 1920, naturalized, 1931. Junior master, Galt Coll. Inst., 1906-09; prin. Victoria Pub. Sch., Saskatoon, Can., 1913; science master, biology and chemistry, Regina Coll. Inst., 1914-16; lecturer in biology, Queen's Univ., Can., 1919-20; asst. in zoology, U. of Chicago, 1921-23; instr. in zoology, Y.M.C.A. Coll. of Liberal Arts, Chicago, Ill., 1922-23; prof. biology, Coe Coll., Cedar Rapids, Ia., 1923-25; J. Pierpont Morgan prof. biology and head of dept., Trinity Coll., Hartford, Conn., since 1925; instr. iin marine invertebrate zoology, Marine Biol. Lab., Woods Hole, Mass., 1926-36, in charge of course, 1936-41; research visiting prof., Cambridge U., Eng., 1931-32. Served with C.E.F., 1916-17; 2d lt., Lancashire Fusiliers, B.E.F., 1918-19; wounded and gassed, Harbonnieres, France, 1918; lecturer in botany, Canadian Khaki Coll., Ripon, Yorks, England, 1919. British Board of Education Scholar at U. of Chicago, 1920-21, for war service; head of biology branch, Biarritz Am. Univ. (Army), 1945-46, France; U.S.A.F.L. examiner Höckst, Germany, 1946. Walker Grand prize winner, 1945 for investigations in Photo periodism: for 5 yrs. Fellow A.A.A.S., Ia. Acad. Science; mem. Assn. for Research in Internal Secretions, Am. Soc. Zoologists, Genetics Assn., Genetics Soc., Am. Assn. Univ. Profs. (pres. Trinity chapter 1941), Northeastern Birdbanding Assn., Am. Naturalists, Corp. of Marine Biol. Lab., Nat. Geog. Soc., Gamma Alpha, Sigma Xi. Ind. Republican. Presbyterian. Mason. Lecturer to Conn. Air Raid Wardens' Schs. on prevention and control of panic, 1940-41. Contbr. of over 75 sci. articles in learned publs. Home: 622 Park Rd., West Hartford, Conn. Office: Trinity Coll., Hartford 6, Conn. Died Nov. 30, 1951; buried Stirling, Ont., Can.

BJÖRKMAN, Edwin (August), author; b. Stockholm, Sweden, Oct. 19, 1866; s. Anders August and Johanna Elizabeth (Anderson) B.; ed. South-End Higher Latin Sch., Stockholm; came to America, 1891; m. Lucy Millender, Jan. 25, 1934. Clk., actor, and journalist in Sweden, 1881-91; was editor of the Minnesota Posten, St. Paul, 1892-94; reporter and mus. critic, The Times, Mpls., 1894-97; reporter New York Sun and New York Times, 1897-1905; on editorial staff New York Evening Post, 1906; dept. editor, The World's Work, 1909; editor Modern Drama Series, 1912-15; rep. of Brit. Dept. of Information, in Sweden, 1915-17; dir. Scandinavian bur., Com. on Pub. Information, 1918-19; asso. dir. League of Nations News Bureau, 1920-21; lit. editor Asheville Times, 1926-29. Knight of the Order of the Danneborg, 1919. Scholarship Am. Scandinavian Foundation for literary studies aborad, 1914. Compulsory service term in Swedish Army; mem. 23d Regt., N.Y. Militia, during Spanish-Am. War. Democrat. Club: Pen and Plate. Author: Is There Anything New Under the Sun? 1911; Gleams—A Fragmentary Interpretation of Man and His World, 1912; Voices of Tomorrow, 1913; Scandinavia and the War, 1914; The Cry of Ukraine, 1915; The Soul of a Child (novel), 1922; Gates of Life (novel), 1923; The Search for Atlantis, 1927; The Wings of Azrael (poem), 1934. Translator of Plays by August Strindberg, Björnstjerne Björnson, Hjalmar Bergström, Arthur Schnitzler, Gunnar Heiberg, Fritz von Unruh; novels by Gustaf af Geijerstam, Frank Heller, Harry Soiberg, Olav Duun, etc.; Jesus—A Myth, by Georg Brandes, 1926. State dir. for N.C., Federal Writers Projects, 1935-41. Home: Biltmore, N.C. Died Nov. 16, 1951; buried Riverside Cemetery, Asheville, N.C.

BJÖRNSSON, Sveinn, president of Iceland; b. 1881. Hague Conf. for Codification of Internat. Law, 1930; commn. of Enquiry for European Union, Geneva, 1931; Monetary and Economic Conf., London, 1933; mem. Conf., London, 1933; mem. Conf. on Mesh Regulations and Size Limits for Fish, London, 1937; minister to Denmark, 1920-24, 1926-40; regent of Iceland 3 one-year terms, 1941-43; pres. Republic of Iceland since June, 1944. Address: Bessatadir, Iceland. Died Jan. 25, 1952.

BLACK, Charles E(dmund), ins. exec.; b. New Orleans, Oct. 31, 1896; s. Charles H. and Marie C. (Durel) B.; student pub. schs. of New Orleans; m. Agnes Holder, Aug. 6, 1919. Entered service of Royal-Liverpool Ins. Group in So. dept. of Liverpool & London & Globe Ins. Co., Ltd., 1913; asst. U.S. mgr. Royal Ins. Co., Ltd., Liverpool & London

& Globe Ins. Co., Ltd., since 1946; v.p. Am. & Fgn. Ins. Co., Newark Ins. Co., Queen Ins. Co. America, Star Ins. Co. America since 1946, Virginia Fire & Marine Ins. Co. since Jan. 1953; asst. U.S. mgr. Brit. & Fgn. Marine Ins. Co., Ltd., Thames & Mersey Marine Ins. Co., Ltd., since 1946; dir. Underwriters Adjusting Co., Chicago. Dir N.Y. Bd. Fire Underwriters. Home: Newtown Av., Westport, Conn. Office: 150 William St., N.Y.C. 38. Died June 21, 1954; buried Westport, Conn.

BLACK, Garland C., army officer; b. Dayton, O., Nov. 14, 1894; s. Hiram Craig and Lulu B. (Cone) B.; B.S. in Elec. Engring., U. Mo., 1917; grad. Chem. Warfare Sch., officer course, 1931, Signal Sch., co. officers course, 1933, Command and Gen. Staff Sch., 1937; m. Florence M. Biegler, Aug. 7, 1919; children—Garland C., Marrilyn Jean (wife of Robert G. Bagby USN). Elec. engr. Kansas City Light and Power Co., Kansas City, Mo., 1917; commd. 2d lt., U.S. Army, 1917, advanced through the grades to brig. gen. Decorated Legion of Merit, Bronze Star (U.S.); Chevalier Legion of Honor, Croix de Guerre with palm (France). Mem. Phi Kappa Psi. Address: care The Adjutant General's Office, War Dept., Washington 25. Deceased.

BLACK, George Harold, ret. univ. pres.; b. Georgetown, Ont., Can., June 6, 1873; s. George Washington and Janet (Moore) B.; B.A., with honors, U. Toronto, 1898; postgrad. U. Chgo., 1908; M.A., N.Y. U., 1932, Ph.D., 1933; Litt.D., Rutgers U., 1947; m. Elizabeth Stewart, June 8, 1899; children—Dorothy E. (Bonny), Elizabeth (Wineman), Janet (Gault); m. 2d, Alice Wilmarth, June 1933. Vice pres. Clarksburg (Mo.) Coll., 1898-1900; head sci. dept. State Normal Sch., Cheney, Wash., 1900-03; pres. Idaho State Normal Sch., Lewiston, Ida., 1903-16; pres. Central Washington Coll. of Edn., 1916-31; Div. Gen. Edn., N.Y. U., 1932-35; provost, U. Newark, 1935-40, acting pres. 1940, pres. 1940-46; provost Newark Colls. of Rutgers U. (formerly U. Newark), 1946-47; retired 1947. Pres. Ida. Tchrs. Assn., 1905, Inland Empire Tchrs. Assn., 1915; mem. Wash. State Bd. Edn., 1920, 21, 23—, State Bd. Vocational Edn., 1917—; mem. tech. com. of Joint Com. on Health Problems in Edn. (N.E.A. and A.M.A.), 1922—. Mem. Commonwealth Fund Com. on Investigation of Tchrs. Coll. Curriculum, 1924; chmn. Pacific Coast sub.-div., 1925, del. to Internat. Health Conf., Edinburg, Scotland, 1925, Nat. Assn. Teachers Colls.; first v.p., Am. Assn. Tchrs. Colls., 1926; chmn. Mont. Normal Sch. Commn., 1926. Author of statute creating Ida. Bd. of Edn. Mem. Acad. Polit. Sci., Phi Delta Kappa, Delta Kappa Epsilon. Republican. Presbyn. Clubs: Canadian (N.Y.C.); Exsex, Downtown (Newark), Acad. Political Sci. Home: 165 Laurel Av., Menlo Park, Cal. Died Feb. 24, 1952.

BLACK, Hugh, theologian; b. Rothesay, Buteshire, Scotland, Mar. 26, 1868; ed. Rothesay Acad., Glasgow U., 1883-87, M.A., 1887, Free Church Coll., Glasgow, 1887-91; D.D., Yale, 1908, Princeton, 1911, Glasgow U., 1911; D.Litt. U. Pitts., 1917; m. Edith Margaret Kerr, June 28, 1898; children—Hugh, Margaret Grant, Isobel Stuart, Robert Kerr. Ordained 1891; minister Sherwood Ch., Paisley, Scotland, 1891-96. St. George's United Free Ch., Edinburgh, 1896-1906; came to U.S. 1906; prof. practical theology Union Theol. Sem., N.Y.C., 1906-38; chmn. Montclair com. Brit. War Relief Soc., 1941—. Club: Century (N.Y.C.). Author: The Dream of Youth, 1894; Friendship, 1898; Culture and Restraint, 1900; Work, 1902; The Practice of Self-Culture, 1904; Listening to God (Edinburgh Sermons), 1906; Christ's Service of Love, 1907; The Gift of Influence (University Sermons), 1908; Comford, 1910; Happiness, 1911; Three Dreams, 1912; According to My Gospel (Montclair sermons), 1913; The Open Door, 1914; The New World, 1915; Lest We Forget, 1920; The Adventure of Being Man, 1929; Christ or Caesar, 1938. Address: 109 Lorraine Av., Upper Montclair, N.J. Died Apr. 6, 1953; buried Mt. Hebron Cemetery, Upper Montclair.

BLACK, Hugh S., surgeon; b. Wellford, S.C., Oct. 12, 1892; s. Hugh Ratchford and Mary Louisa Snoddy) B.; A.B., Wofford Coll., 1913; M.D., Jefferson Med. Coll., 1917; m. Iris Burrus, Sept. 29, 1925, (died 1933); m. 2d, Darthey Deene Israel, Nov. 2, 1945. Interne Jefferson Hospital, Philadelphia, Pa., 1918; fellow surgery Mayo Foundation, Rochester, Minn., 1919-23, 1st surg. asst. to Dr. W. E. Sistrunk, 1920-21, 1st surg. asst. to Dr. William J. Mayo, 1921-23; practicing surgeon, Spartanburg, S.C., since 1923, founding and operating with Dr. Hugh R. Black and Dr. Samuel O. Black the Mary Black Clinic Pvt. Hosp., since 1925, surgeon to Wofford Infirmary, Southern Ry., Piedmont & N. Ry., Duke Power Co., vis. surgeon Spartanburg Gen. Hosp., Colored Hosp., Laurens (S.C.) Hosp. visitor and student clinics Europe and S. Am. Fellow Am. Coll. Surgeons; mem. S.E. Surg. Congress, Alumni Assn., Mayo Foundation, Assn. Southern Ry. Surgeons (past pres.), A.M.A., and Southern Med., S. C. State, Tri-State and Spartanburg med. socs., Kappa Sigma, Alpha Kappa Kappa. Democrat. Presbyterian. Club: Piedmont. Contbr. 50 research papers to med. jours. Home: 666 Palmetto St. Office: 392 E. Main St., Spartanburg, S.C. Died May 22, 1950.

BLACK, James Harvey, physician; b. Huntington, W.Va., Mar. 27, 1884; s. John Adam and Mary Nancy (Murphy) B.; student Southwestern U., 1900-02, Coll. of Physicians and Surgeons, Atlanta, 1903-05; M.D., So. Meth. U., Dallas, 1907; m. Alleen Patton, Sept. 4, 1913; children—Emily Anne (Mrs. Armand Garguilo), and Lois (Mrs. Jack W. Crosland, Jr.). Interne St. Paul Hosp., Dallas, 1906-07; pvt. practice of medicine, Dallas, 1907-50, practice limited to allergic diseases, 1937—; prof. bacteriology and pathology, So. Meth. U. Med. Sch., 1907-15, dean, 1914-15; prof. bacteriology and preventive medicine, Baylor U. Med. Sch., 1915-21, prof. preventive medicine, 1921-36, prof. clinical medicine, 1936-43; prof. clin. medicine, Southwestern Med. Coll., Dallas, 1943, now cons. medcine. Diplomate Am. Bd. Internal Medicine. Fellow Am. Acad. Allergy, A.A.A.S., Am. Public Health Assn., Am. Coll. Physicians; mem. Newcomen Soc., Tex. Philos. Soc., A.M.A. (chmn. sect. of pathology and physiology, 1931-32), Am. Soc. Clin. Pathologists (pres. 1929-30), Assn. for the Study of Allergy (pres. 1934-35), N.Y. Acad. Sci., Kappa Alpha. Presbyn. Mason. Clubs: Dallas Town and Gown, Dallas Athletic. Author: Practice of Allergy (with W. T. Vaughan), 1954. Editor, sect. on allergy, Biological Abstracts, 1942—. Formerly mem. editorial bd. Journal of Allergy. Home: 3624 Princeton Av., Dallas 5. Office: 1719 Pacific Av., Dallas 1. Died Nov. 30, 1959; buried Restland Meml. Park, Dallas.

BLACK, Jenny O., pres. Fargo Forum Pub. Co. Address: 101 5th St. N., Fargo, N.D. Died Aug. 16, 1951.

BLACK, John Donald, lawyer; b. Urbana, Ill., Sept. 11, 1872; s. Gen. John Charles and Adaline L. (Griggs) B.; student Columbian U. Law Sch. (now Georgetown U. Law Sch.), Washington, and Harvard Law Sch.; LL.M., John Marshall Law Sch., Chgo., 1948; m. Margaret Horton Potter, Jan. 1, 1902 (dec.); m. 2d, Louise Love Beckwith, 1911 (dec.). Admitted to Ill. bar, 1896; mem. law firm Winston, Strawn, Black & Towner. Mem. Am., Ill. (pres. 1929-30), Chgo. (pres. 1933-34) bar assns., Chgo. Law Inst. (pres. 1931, 1943), Assn. Bar City of N.Y., Art Inst. Chgo. (life), Chgo. Hist. Soc. (life), Chgo. Assn. of Commerce (chmn. exec. com. 1934-35, dir. 1944). Clubs: Chicago, University, Harvard, Mid-Day, Law (past pres.), Saddle and Cycle, Racquet, Legal, Chicago Golf (past pres.). Home: University Club, Chgo. 3. Office: 38 S. Dearborn St., Chgo. 3. Died June 1959.

BLACK, Lloyd Llewellyn, U.S. judge; b. Leavenworth, Kan., Mar. 15, 1889; s. William Wilson and Mollie (Nei) B.; A.B. cum laude U. Wash., 1910, LL.B., 1912; m. Gladys Statler, Apr. 6, 1917; children—William Bryce, David Statler. Admitted to Wash. bar, 1911; asso. with father in firm Black & Black, 1913-32; pros. atty. Snohomish Country, Wash., 1917-19; atty. for Port of Everett, 1923-36; spl. counsel City of Everett, 1916, 20-22; judge Superior Court, Snohomish and Island counties, 1936-39; apptd. U.S. Judge, Western Dist. Wash., 1939, Eastern and Western dists., 1940. Mem. Field Arty. O.T.S., Camp Zachary Taylor, Ky., 1918. Pres. Port Comm. of Port of Everett, 1922-23. Counsel and dir. Snohomish and Island Country chpts. A.R.C., until 1936; pres. adv. bd. Salvation Army, Everett, 1936-39. Mem. Am. Bar Assn., Phi Beta Kappa, Am. Legion (comdr. Earl Faulkner Post, 1929-30). Methodist. Mason, Elk, Eagle, Redman. Clubs: Washington Athletic, Broadmoor Golf (Seattle). Home: 3336 Cascadia. Address: U.S. Court House, Seattle. Died Aug. 23, 1950; buried Acacia Mausoleum, Seattle.

BLACK, Loring M., ex-congressman; b. N.Y.C., May 17, 1886; B.A., Fordham U., 1907, M.A., 1914; m. Beatrice M. Eddy; children—Loring M., Elizabeth Virginia, Jeanne Marie, John Eddy. Admitted to bar, 1909; mem. N.Y. Senate, 1911, 12, 19, 20; mem. 68th to 73d Congresses (1923-35), 5th N.Y. Dist. Democrat. Home: 22 St. Francis Pl., Bklyn. Died May 20, 1956.

BLACK, Robert Lounsbury, lawyer; b. Norwood, O., Sept. 15, 1881; s. Lewis Cass and Abigail (Lounsbury) B.; grad. Phillips Andover Acad., 1899; B.A., Yale, 1903; LL.B., Harvard, 1906; m. Anna McNaughten Smith, Oct. 14, 1916; children—Robert L., Jr., Harrison, Anne McNaughten (dec.), David de Laine, Frances Harrison. Admitted to Ohio bar, 1906; formerly mem. Black & Black, later Black, Swing & Black; has practiced independently since 1919 retired 1953; president Little Miami R.R. Co.; sec. L. B. Harrison Estate, Inc.; counsel and dir. Security Storage Co.; v.p. and trustee L. B. Harrison Hotel. Served as lt., later capt., U.S. Army, 37th Div., Mil. Intelligence, World War; member American Peace Commn. Mission to Germany. Trustee Y. M. Mercantile Library; trustee Veterans Memorial Fund. Extrustee Cincinnati Orphan Asylum; ex-dir. U. of Cincinnati; formerly member rehabilitation Committee Am. Legion. Mem. Am., Ohio State and Cincinnati bar assns., Bar. Assn. City of N.Y. Republican. Episcopalian. Clubs: Queen City, Camargo (Cincinnati); Yale, Grolier (New York). Author: The Little Miami Railroad, 1940; The Cincinnati Orphan Asylum, 1952. Home: Willow Hills Lane, Cin. Office: Blymyer Bldg., Cin. Died Jan. 24, 1954; buried Spring Grove Cemetery, Cin.

BLACK, Ruby Aurora, writer; b. Thornton, Tex., Sept. 14, 1896; d. George W. and Cornelia (Long) Black; student U. Colo.; A.B., U. Texas, 1921; post-grad. U. Wis.; m. Herbert Little, Sept. 17, 1922; 1 dau., Cornelia Jane Herbert Little. Tchr. pub. schs. in Tex., 1914-18; began newspaper work on Thornton (Tex.) Hustler, 1917; mgr. Woman's Nat. Journalistic Register, Chgo., 1921; tchr. journalism U. Wis., 1921-23; labor editor St. Louis Times, 1923; Washington corr., 1926-41, various newspapers; head Ruby A. Black News Bureau, 1928-41; staff corr. United Press, 1933-41; editor-writer Office Inter-American Affairs, 1941-46; mng. editor Equal Rights Mag., 1927-32. Mem. Soc. Women Geographers, Tex. Folk-lore Soc., Phi Beta Kappa, Theta Sigma Phi (editor The Matrix, 1921-29; nat. pres. 1929-31). Club: Women's Nat. Press (pres. 1939-40). Contbr. to mags. Co-editor (with Edwin Rosskam): Washington: Nerve Center, 1939. Author: Eleanor Roosevelt, A Biography, 1940. Home: 2831 15th St. N.W., Washington. Died Dec. 1957.

BLACK, Samuel Duncan, mfr.; b. White Hall, Md., Aug. 2, 1883; s. Samuel Washington and Alice (Duncan) B.; student Balt. Polytech. Inst.; m. Anna Ridgely, Aug. 22, 1903; children—Elizabeth (Mrs. J. F. Apsey), Alice (Mrs. Fielding H. Lewis), Charlotte (Mrs. J. A. Murray), Samuel Duncan. With Roland Telegraphic Co., 1899-1910, successively draftsman, elec. engr., factory supt.; a founder of Black & Decker Mfg. Co., mfrs. portable electric tools, Towson, Md., 1910, pres., 1910—. Presbyn. Club: Baltimore Country. Home: Stevenson Lane. Office: Black & Decker Mfg. Co., Towson, Md. Deceased.

BLACK, Walter Joseph, pub.; b. Brooklyn, May 12, 1893; s. Loring M. and Elizabeth (Mahoney) B.; A.B., Fordham U., 1915, LL.D., 1949; m. Elsie A. Jantzer, Nov. 6, 1918; 1 son, Theodore M. Sec. to Col. G. Harvey, 1916-20; dept. mgr. P. F. Collier & Sons, 1920-23; established own pub. firm Plymouth Pub. Co., N.Y. City, 1923; pres. Walter J. Black, Inc., since 1928, Classics Club since 1941, Detective Book Club since 1942; gen. partner Black's Readers Service Co. since 1949. Roman Catholic. Clubs: Union League, University, Players. Home: 12 Old Sands Light Rd., Sands Point, L.I. Office: Northern Blvd., Flower Hill, Roslyn, L.I., N.Y. Died Apr. 16, 1958.

BLACK, Witherbee, jewelry exec.; b. N.Y.C., 1879; s. Robert C. and Mary Grace (Witherbee) B.; student Princeton, 1901; m. Ethel French, Mar. 7, 1931. Joined Black Starr & Frost-Gorham, Inc. (now Black Starr & Gorham), N.Y.C., 1901, pres., 1912-57; pres. Glorietta Oil Corp. Dir. Fifth Av. Assn., Jewelers Assn. of N.Y., Hundred Year Assn. Clubs: Racquet and Tennis, Leash, Princeton, Westminster Kennel, 24 Karat. Home: 470 Park Av. Office: Fifth Av. corner of 48th St., N.Y.C. Died Aug. 8, 1959; buried Woodlawn, N.Y.C.

BLACKBURN, John Henry, surgeon; b. Woodburn, Ky., Aug. 7, 1876; s. Henry M. and Amanda (Deupree) B.; prep. edn. Franklin High Sch.; M.D., Vanderbilt U., 1899; m. Bess Trousdale Hatcher, May 25, 1904; children—Henry Hatcher, John Deupree. Began practice at Bowling Green, 1900; dir. course post-grad. study for county med. socs., 1907-11, dir. Am. Nat. Bank. Commd. capt. M.C., U.S. Army, 1917, advanced through grades to lt. col., 1918; chief of surg. service Base Hosp. Camp Logan, Tex., 1917-18; chief of surg. service, Base Hosp. No. 86, Mesves Hosp. Center, France; returned to U.S. as regtl. surgeon, 139th F.A.; hon. discharged 1919. Mem. Ky. Bd. Health, 1934—. Fellow A.C.A.; mem. Am. So. med. assns., Ky. (past pres.), Warren County med. socs., S.E. Med. Congress. Democrat. Methodist. Odd Fellow. Clubs: Country, Gun, Kiwanis. Home: 627 E. Main St. Office: 535 10th St., Bowling Green, Ky. Died Feb. 17, 1951.

BLACKBURN, K. Wilde, lawyer; b. W. Belle Vernon, Pa., May 28, 1906; s. James Edward and Emma (Nabors) B.; A.B., Temple U., Phila., 1929; LL.B., U. of Pa., 1932; m. Clara Elizabeth Allen, May 25, 1940; children—James Wilde, Carla Jean. Gen. practice of law, Wilmington, Del., 1933-35; atty. Rural Electrification Adminstrn., Washington, D.C., 1935-41, solicitor's office U.S. Dept. of Agr., 1941-43; atty. solicitor's office, legal work of Commodity Credit Corp. and Farm Security Adminstrn., U.S. Dept. of Agr., 1943-45; asso. solicitor in charge of farm security, U.S. Dept. of Agr., and asso. solicitor in charge of rural electrification, 1945-54, asso. solicitor for agrl. credit, 1954—. Episcopalian. Mason. Home: 4207 S. 36th St., Arlington, Va. Office: Solicitor's Office, U.S. Dept. of Agr., Washington 25. Died Dec. 21, 1954; buried Ivy Hill Cemetery, Alexandria, Va.

BLACKBURN, Merrill Mason, patent lawyer; b. Winneshiek County, Ia., Jan. 7, 1876; s. William and Cynthia Abbie (Converse) B.; Ph.B., Grinnell (Ia.) Coll., 1901; LL.B., M.P.L., Georgetown U., 1914; spl. course in patent law, George Washington U., 1914-15; m. Charlotte Emma Shedd, June 18, 1904; children—Arthur Duncan (dec.), Margaret

Spence (dec.), William Converse Cynthia Elizabeth (dec.). High sch. tchr. and prin., 1901-06; computer Coast and Geodetic Survey, Wasington 1906-08; admitted to practice in D.C., Ia., Ill.; examiner U.S. Patent Office, 1908-19; asso. Parkinson & Lane, Chgo., 1919-24; head of own office in Davenport, Ia., 1924—; patent law counsel for many corps. Mem. Am., Ia. State, Scott County (Ia.) bar assns., Am. Patent Law Assn. Republican. Conglist. Clubs: Rotary (Davenport, Ia.); Scott County Republican. Home: 2519 Pershing Av. Office: Davenport Bank Bldg., Davenport, Ia. Died Dec. 31, 1957; buried Meml. Gardens, Davenport.

BLACKMER, Samuel Howard, justice; b. Bennington, Vt., Mar. 2, 1902; s. Samuel Huling and Fanny Laura (Abbott) B.; A.B., Yale, 1924; LL.B., Harvard, 1927; m. Katrina Roosevelt Schuyler, July 18, 1925; 1 dau., Patricia Ann (Mrs. Roger L. Kellner). Admitted to Vt. bar, 1927; trustee Village of Old Bennington, 1927-38; justice of peace, mem. bd. Civic Authority, Bennington, 1929-38; judge Bennington Municipal Ct., 1929-32; mem. Vt. State Ho. of Reps., 1933-35; states atty., Bennington Co., 1935-37; exec. clk. (personal counsel) to Gov. George D. Aiken, 1937-38; superior judge Vt., 1938-49; asso. justice Vt. Supreme Ct. since 1949. Vice pres., dir. Charles Cooper Indsl. Sch.; trustee Bennington Free Library, Bennington Hist. Mus. and Art Gallery. Mem. Am., Vt. State and Bennington Co. bar assns., Am. Law Inst., Zeta Psi, Delta Sigma Rho. Episcopalian. Mason (33°). Clubs: Bennington, Rotary. Home: 81 Monument Av., Bennington, Vt. Died Dec. 25, 1951; buried Old Bennington Cemetery, Bennington, Vt.

BLACKSTONE, A. E., educator; b. Cumberland, O., July 22, 1886; s. Wilbert T. and Martha J. (Hickman) B.; B.S., Ohio U., Athens, O., 1911; A.M., U. of Pa., 1916; student Ohio State U., 1915, U. of Pa., 1917-22; m. Gladys A. McDowell, Oct. 14, 1911; children—Harold Raymond, Elwin McDowell (1st lt., U.S. Army; killed in action Jan. 25, 1945). Teacher, public schools, Muskingum County, O., 1904-07, Portsmouth (O.) High Sch., 1911-13, Drexel Inst. Day Sch., Philadelphia, 1913-14; prof. of accounting Drexel Evening Sch., 1913-37, Girard Coll. (Phila.), 1914-15, West Philadelphia (Pa.) High Sch., 1915-28; prof. economics, Drexel Inst. Tech., 1928-43, dean Sch. of Bus. Adminstrn. since 1943; also engaged in public accounting, 1917-22, real estate conveyancing, 1922-27. Mem. Phi Kappa Phi, Pi Omega Pi, Alpha Phi Omega. Republican. Protestant. Mason. Home: 121 Walnut Av., Wayne, Pa. Office: 32d and Chestnut Sts., Philadelphia. Died Jan. 30, 1951; buried Washington Meml. Churchyard, Valley Forge, Pa.

BLACKWELL, Hubert Charles Hansard, utility exec.; s. Charles and Emily (Chandler) B.; B.S., Purdue U., D.Eng.; m. Robina E. Cooper, Dec. 22, 1908; children—Gordon C., Hugh G. Construction engr. J. G. White & Co., New York, N.Y., 1904-05; beginning as engr., advanced to vice pres. and gen. mgr. Peoples Light Co., Davenport, Ia., 1906-17; v.p., gen. mgr. and dir. Kansas City (Mo.) Power & Light Co., 1917-24; v.p., gen. mgr. and dir. Union Gas & Electric Co., Cincinnati, O., 1924-26, pres. and dir., 1926-36; president and director Union Light, Heat & Power, Covington, Ky., 1926-45, dir. and chmn. bd. dirs. since 1945; v.p. and dir. Cincinnati, Newport & Covington Ry. Co., 1924-25, pres. and dir., 1928-44; pres., dir. Cincinnati Gas & Electric Co., Cincinnati, O., 1928-45, dir. and chmn. bd. dirs. since 1945; v.p. Columbia Gas & Electric Corp., New York, N.Y., 1930-44, dir., 1936-42; dir. Southern Ohio Savings Bank & Trust Co., Cincinnati. Dir. Purdue Research Foundation, Purdue Univ., LaFayette, Ind., since 1941. Mem. Cincinnati Chamber of Commerce (past dir.; past pres.), Am. Soc. M.E., Am. Inst. E.E., Am. Gas Assn., Edison Electric Inst., Newcomen Soc., Tau Beta Pi, Sigma Nu. Mason, Rotarian. Clubs: Cincinnati Country, Queen City, Cincinnati, University (Cincinnati). Home: 2109 Luray Av., Cincinnati 6. Office: Fourth and Main Sts., Cin. 2. Died Jan. 18, 1955.

BLACKWOOD, Oswald, univ. prof.; b. Clay Center, Kan., Apr. 24, 1888; s. Dr. Thomas and Bella (Watterson) B., A.B., Boston University, 1909; Ph.D., U. of Chicago, 1920; D.Sc. (hon.), Mt. Union, 1944; m. Gertrude Clark, Sept. 18, 1919; 1 d. Gertrude C. (Mrs. W. C. Kelly). Prof. physics Reid Christian Coll. Lucknow, India, 1909-11; instr. physics, U. of Philippines, Manila, 1912-13; asst. prof. physics, U. of Ark., 1919-20; asst. prof. physics, U. of Pittsburgh, 1920-24, asso. prof., 1925-27, prof. since 1927; cons. physicist, Koppers Research Co., Pittsburgh, 1925-32. Fellow A.A.A.S., Am. Physical Soc.; mem. Am. Assn. Physics Teachers, Pittsburgh Physics-Chemistry Teachers Club (pres. 1938-40), Sigma Xi, Beta Theta Pi. Author: Introductory College Physics, 1938; General Physics, 1943. Co-author: Pittsburgh Atomic Physics, 1933; Experimental Physics, 1934; High School Physics, 1950. Home: 251 Lothrop St., Pitts. Died. Mar. 21, 1953.

BLAINE, Mrs. Emmons (Anita McCormick Blaine), philanthropist; b. July 4, 1866; d. Cyrus Hall (inventor of the reaping machine) and Nettie (Fowler) McCormick; m. Emmons Blaine (died June 18, 1892). Founder Sch. Edn., U. Chgo.; mem. Bd. of Edn. several yrs. Home: 101 E. Erie St. Chgo. Died Feb. 12, 1954; buried Graceland Cemetery, Chgo.

BLAIR, Algernon (blâr), contractor; b. Brooklyn, N.Y., Aug. 6, 1873; s. Alexander and Hannah (Farnell) B.; grad. Macon, Ga., high sch., 1888; m. Caroline Livingston Singleton, June 15, 1898 (died 1905); children—Alfred Farnell, Elisabeth (Mrs. Henry Grady Pannell), Carolyn (Mrs. Charles Franklin Voltz); m. 2d, Adele Blue, July 14, 1908. In business as contractor in own name, at Montgomery, Ala., since 1902; has built indsl. and comml. plants, schools and federal pub. bldgs. throughout South, including Camp Sheridan, Montgomery, vets. hosps. at Dawson Springs, Ky., Tuskegee, Ala., Northport, N.Y., Perryville, Md., Roanoke, Va., Gulfport, Miss. and Montgomery, Ala.; post offices, including Beaumont, Tex., Jacksonville, Fla., Key West, Fla., Montgomery, Ala., Lancaster, Pa., Galveston, Austin, Amarillo, Tex., and Kalamazoo, Mich.; Smithfield Court and Central City housing projects, Birmingham, Ala.; also Riverside Heights and Cleveland Courts, Montgomery, Ala., and many other housing projects; airfields, ordnance plants, camps, hospitals, and other facilities War and Navy Depts. since 1940. Dir. First Nat. Bank, Montgomery. Mem. "The Thirteen" of Montgomery (lit. and philos. soc.). Episcopalian. Mason. Clubs: Beauvoir, Rotary Internat. (past dir.). Home: 215 Felder Av., Montgomery 6. Office: First Nat. Bank Bldg., Montgomery 2, Ala. Died Mar. 14, 1952.

BLAIR, David Ellmore, lawyer; b. Salina, Kan., Aug. 16, 1874; s. Edgar W. and Emma A. (McClure) B.; A.B., Kan. Wesleyan U., Salina, Kan., 1896; LL.B., U. of Kan., 1899; m. Mary Eleanor Henley, May 1, 1902; children—Herbert Henley, Mrs. Mabel Emma Gans and Eleanor (Mrs. E. J. O'Keefe). Began practice at Joplin, Missouri, 1899; member law firm Blair and Blair, 1906-08, Blair and Decker, 1900-03, Blair, Decker & Blair, 1903-06; assistant pros. atty., Jasper County, Mo., 1903-04; judge Circuit Court, 25th Judicial Circuit, 1908-17; mem. Pub. Service Com. of Mo., 1917-20; asso. justice, Supreme Court of Mo., 1921-30, chief justice, 1925-26; in practice of law, St. Louis, 1931-34, returned to Joplin, 1934; elected presiding judge Springfield Court of Appeals, Nov. 1940, to fill unexpired term ending Dec. 31, 1944 (only Missourian elected tc all three benches); re-elected to Springfield Court of Appeals November 1944 for 12 yr. term, retired, September 1, 1954. Member of the Jasper County Bar Assn. (pres. 1939), Am. and Mo. State bar assns. Republican. Mason (32°). Home: 1052 S. Fremont Av. Office: Woodruff Bldg., Springfield, Mo. Died Dec. 28, 1954; buried Ozark Meml. Park Cemetery, Joplin, Mo.

BLAIR, Emily Newell, writer, lecturer; b. Joplin, Mo., Jan. 9, 1877; d. James Patton and Anna Cynthia (Gray) Newell; grad. high sch., Carthage, Mo., 1894; student Goucher Coll., Balt., U. Mo.; m. Harry Wallace Blair, Dec. 24, 1900; children—Harriet, James Newell. Press and publicity chmn. in initiative suffrage campaign, Mo., 1914; served as vice chmn. Mo. div. and in charge publicity Woman's com. Council Nat. Defense, Washington; elected mem. Dem. Nat. Com., 1921, 24, vice chmn., 1922, 1st vice chmn., 1924-28. Editor Missouri Women, 1914-15; asso. editor Good Housekeeping Mag. Sec. Woman's Nat. Dem. Club, 1922-26, pres., 1928-29, became hon. v.p. 1929. Mem. bd. trustees Woodrow Wilson Found.; chmn. Consumer's Adv. Bd., NRA, 1933. Clubs: Cosmopolitan (N.Y.C.); Women's Nat. Press. Wrote: History of Women's Committee, Council of National Defense (issued by U.S. Govt.); The Creation of a Home; A Woman of Courage. Home: Alexandria, Va. Died Aug. 2, 1951.

BLAIR, Frank Warrenner, banker; b. Oakland County, Mich., May 13, 1870; s. Henry H. and Sarah (Warrenner) B.; student pub. schs.; LL.D., Olivet (Mich.) Coll., 1928; m. Winifred Johnson, June 24, 1894 (died Apr. 24, 1898); m. 2d, Ellen Ferrier, Nov. 22, 1899. Clk. in drug store, Birmingham, Mich., 1891-99; asst. state accountant, Lansing, 1900-04; state bank examiner, Mich., 1904-06; auditor People's State Bank, Detroit, 1906-08; receiver, Pere Marquette R.R., 1912-15; pres., chmn. bd. Union Trust Co., 1908-32; pres. Union Joint Stock Land Bank of Detroit, 1923-43, now retired; pres. Bagley Bldg. Corp., The Whittier Corp.; v.p. House Financing Corp., Standard Savings and Loan Assn.; dir. Mich. Bell Telephone Co., Republic Gear Co., Nat. Steel Corp., Evans Products Co., others. Vice pres. St. Luke's Hosp.; chmn. bd. trustees Olivet Coll. Ex-pres. Mich. Bankers' Assn. and trust co. sect. Am. Bankers' Assn.; ex-pres. Joint Stock Land Bankers Assn. Mem. Fine Arts Soc. Republican. Episcopalian. Clubs: Detroit, Ingleside, Indianwood Golf and Country, Bankers, Economic. Home: Hickory Farm, Manchester, Mich. Died Apr. 28, 1950; buried Woodlawn Cemetery.

BLAIR, Frederic Howes, clergyman; b. Jacksonville, Fla., Dec. 5, 1887; s. Lemuel P. and Alice S. (Howes) B.; B.A., U. Minn., 1911; S.T.B., Boston U. Sch. Theol., 1916; D.D., U. So. Cal., 1940; m. Josephine Dayton, Dec. 29, 1913 (died Dec. 8, 1940); m. 2d, Helen C. Salzer, May 15, 1943; children—Bonney Richardson, David Dayton, Frederic Draper. Sec. YMCA, U. Denver, 1911-12, U. Minn., 1912-13; ordained minister Meth. Ch., 1916; missionary Japan, 1916-19; supr. religious and welfare work Goodwill Industries, So. So. 1919-24, exec. dir., 1924-50; exec. v.p. Goodwill Industries Am. Inc., 1945—, counsellor, 1950, Western rep., 1951. Home: 752 S. Hudson Av., Pasadena 5, Cal. Office: 342 San Fernando Rd., Los Angeles 31. Died Jan. 21, 1953.

BLAIR, James Carroll, glass mfr.; b. Toledo, O., Jan. 9, 1877; s. Albert Gallatin and Harriette (Ritch) B.; ed. Hiram (O.) Coll., Kenyon Mil. Acad. (Gambier, O.), and U. of Mich.; m. Mary Wright, Oct. 15, 1902. Gen. mgr. A. G. Blair Mining Co. (coal), 1899-1917; v.p. and gen. mgr. Owens Bottle Co., 1917-23; pres. Libbey-Owens-Ford Glass Co., 1923-30. Republican. Presbyterian. Clubs: Toledo, Carranor, Country. Home: 2049 Scottwood Av., Toledo. Died Feb. 1, 1953; buried Woodlawn Cemetery, Toledo.

BLAIR, Vilray Papin, surgeon; b. St. Louis, June 15, 1871; s. Edmund Harrison and Minnie (Papin) B.; A.B., Christian Brothers Coll., 1890, A.M., 1894; M.D., Washington U., 1893; m. Kathryn Lyman Johnson, 1907; children—Kathryn Lyman, Nancy Lucas, Mary Papin (dec.), Vilray Papin, John Bates Johnson. Practiced in St. Louis, 1893-48; prof. emeritus clinical surgery Washington U. Sch. Medicine, oral surgery, School Dentistry; vis. surgeon, Maternity and De Paul hosps.; asso. surgeon Barnes and St. Louis Children's hosps.; in charge plastic and oral surgery section of the head, U.S. Army, 1917-18, chief cons. maxillo-facial surgery, AEF, 1918-19. Fellow A.C.S., Am. Laryngol. Assn., Am. Surg. Assn.; mem. Internat. Surg. Soc., Nat. Inst. Social Sciences, A.M.A., Assn. Am. Anatomists, So., Western surg. assns. Catholic. Clubs: University, St. Louis Country. Home: R.F.D. 1, Florissant, Mo. Office: Metropolitan Bldg., St. Louis. Died Nov. 24, 1955.

BLAIR, Walter Dabney, architect; b. Amelia County, Va., June 14, 1877; s. Lewis Harvie and Alice Wayles (Harrison) B.; student Richmond (Va.) Coll., 1891-93; B.A., U. of Va., 1895, M.A., 1896; B.S., U. of Pa., 1899; grad. École des Beaux Arts, Paris, France, 1902; m. Ethel Gould, May 14, 1907; 1 son, Harrison Westbrook; m. 2d, Elizabeth Hollister Frost, poet, Apr. 16, 1932. Began practice, New York, 1903; professor archtl. design, Cornell U., 1903-04; resumed practice in New York, 1904; architect of Pub. Library Bldg., Charlottesville, Va.; chem. lab., U. of Va.; Stahlman Bldg., Nashville, Tenn.; Edwin Gould Foundation, New York; Warner Library, Tarrytown, N.Y.; 1st Nat. Bank, Montgomery, Ala.; Pensacola (Fla.) Nat. Bank; Empire Bldg., Birmingham, Ala.; etc. Treas. 154 E. 61st St. Corp. Mem. Archtl. Com. of U. of Va. Served with Coast Troops, U.S. Arty., Fortress Monroe, 1918. Fellow Am. Inst. Architects of N.Y. (sec.); mem. Beaux Arts Inst., Architectural League, Phi Beta Kappa, Beta Theta Pi. Home: Tarrytown, N.Y. Office: 154 E. 61st St., N.Y.C. Died Jan. 11, 1953; buried Sleepy Hollow Cemetery, Tarrytown, N.Y.

BLAIR, William Wightman, ophthalmologist; b. Blair, Pa., Nov. 30, 1866; s. George W. and Caroline Snowden (Wightman) B.; student U. Pitts.; M.D., Hahnemann Med. Coll. and Hosp., Phila., 1889; m. Margaret Kennedy Brown, Apr. 16, 1895. Prof. ophthalmology emeritus, Sch. of Medicine, U. Pitts.; cons. exec. surgeon Eye and Ear Hosp.; hon. librarian Lippincott Library. Fellow A.C.S.; mem. A.M.A., Pa., Allegheny County med. socs., Pitts. Acad. Medicine, Am. Acad. Otology and Ophthalmology, Am. Ophthalmol. Soc., Ophthalmol. Soc. United Kingdom, Soc. Biol. Research of U. Pitts. Mason. Clubs: University, Rolling Rock Country, Faculty. Home: Woodland Road. Office: 121 University Pl., Pitts. Died June 12, 1957.

BLAISDELL, James Arnold, coll. pres.; b. Beloit, Wis., Dec. 15, 1867; s. James Joshua and Susan Ann (Allen) B.; A.B., Beloit Coll., 1889, M.A., 1892, D.D., 1910, LL.D., 1956; LL.D., Drury Coll., Occidental Coll., 1923, Pomona Coll., 1928, Colo. Coll., 1930, U. of Cal., 1932; grad. Hartford (Conn). Theol. Sem., 1892; m. Florence Lena Carrier, Dec. 29, 1892 (died July 28, 1940); children—James Brooks, Paul Carrier, Allen Carrier, Barbara (Mrs. Thomas S. Warren); m. 2d, Mrs. Anne Grassie Stickney, Apr. 13, 1943. Ordained Congregational Ch., 1892; pastor, Waukesha, Wis., 1892-96, Olivet, Mich., 1896-1903; prof. bibl. lit., also librarian, Beloit Coll., 1903-10, and pastor 2d Congl. Ch., Beloit; pres. Pomona Coll., Claremont, Calif., 1910-26, during which period initiated plan for group of colls.; transferred to pres. Claremont Coll., center and grad. sch. of group, 1926-36, pres. emeritus 1936—; vice pres. board directors Ultra-Violet Products Company, South Pasadena, California. As member commission American Board Missions, traveled extensively in Japan to study Japanese chs. and ednl. instns., 1918; pres. Inter-America Foundation, 1930-36. Trustee LaVerne College. Formerly chairman of trustees Pacific Colony, Calif. instn, for feeble minded. Initiated orgn. of Western Collegiate Assn. (permanent hon. mem. exec. com.). Mem. Soc. Bibl. Lit. and Exegesis, Nat. and Southwestern acads. of polit. science, Phi Beta Kappa. Clubs: Los Angeles, Claremont University. Pres. of Blaisdell Family Assn. of America (editor Blaisdell Papers). Author: Visions of a Citizen, 1897; also hymns included in Am. hymnals, and numerous addresses and papers. Home: 143 E. 10th St., Claremont, Calif. Died Jan. 29, 1957.

BLAKE, A. Harold, univ. prof., engr.; b. Salt Lake City, Utah, April 3, 1896; s. John Joseph and Bridget (Ryan) B.; B.S. in M.E., U. of Utah, 1920; M.M.E., Cornell U., 1926; m. Lucile Farnsworth, June 8, 1922; children—Robert Harold, William Farnsworth, John Joseph. Instr. mech. engring., U. of Utah, 1920-26, asst. prof., 1926-33, asso. prof., 1933-39, prof. since 1946. Chmn. cubbing commn., Salt Lake Council, Boy Scouts of Am., 1940-42. Served as 2d lt., U.S. Army Inf., 91st Div., 1917-18; maj., U.S. Army Inf., acting adj. gen., with 3d Mil. Area, 1940-41; lt. col., asst. chief of staff G-1, with Hqrs. 9th Corps Area, 1941-42; lt. col., comdg. officer, with W. Va. Ordnance Works, 1942-43; lt. col., dir. engr. maintenance and supply sch., with Corps of Engrs., 1943-45; col. inf. res., 1946-47; col. Ordnance Dept. Res., since 1948. Mem. Am. Soc. M.E., Utah Soc. of Professional Engr., Phi Delta Theta, Tau Beta Pi, Pi Tau Sigma, Theta Tau. Roman Catholic. Co-author: Automotive Manual, 1923. Home: 1618 Yale Av., Salt Lake City 5. Died Oct. 29, 1951; buried Mt. Olive Cemetery, Salt Lake City.

BLAKE, Emily Calvin (Mrs. Walter R. Blake), author; b. Manchester, Eng.; d. Thomas and Margaret (Young) Calvin; student pvt. and high schs.; m. Walter R. Blake; 1 son, Raleigh Calvin. Came to U.S. as a child. Author: Engaged Girl Sketches, 1910; Great Moments in a Woman's Life, 1910; Marcia of the Little Home, 1911; Quaintness of Bobby, 1912; The Promise, 1913; Autobiography of an Impulsive Girl, 1915; Suzanna Stirs the Fire, 1915, London edit., 1918; The Third Weaver, 1929; also numerous short stories in leading mags. Home: Los Angeles. Deceased.

BLAKE, Francis Gilman, M.D., educator; b. Mansfield Valley, Pa., Feb. 22, 1887; s. Francis Clark and Winifred Pamelia (Ballard) B.; A.B., Dartmouth Coll., 1908; M.D., Harvard, 1913; hon. M.A., Yale, 1921; Sc.D., Dartmouth College, 1936; m. Dorothy Dewey, June 1, 1916; children—Francis Gilman, William Dewey, John Ballard. Successively med. interne, asst. resident physician and resident physician Peter Bent Brigham Hosp., Boston, 1913-16; asst. at Hosp. of Rockefeller Inst., New York, 1916-17; asst. prof. medicine, U. of Minn., 1917-19; asso. in medicine, Rockefeller Hosp., New York, 1919-20; asso. mem. Rockefeller Inst., 1920-21; John Slade Ely prof. medicine, Yale School of Medicine, 1921-27, Sterling professor of medicine since 1927, dean 1940-1947. Physician-in-chief, New Haven Hosp., 1921—; sci. dir., med. research and development bd., surg. gen's. office, Dept. of Army, 1952; member board of scientific dirs. Rockefeller Inst., 1924-35; mem. Nat. Research Council, Div. Med. Sciences, 1925-36, chmn. of Div. for term 1933-36. Served as 1st lt., capt. and maj. Med. R.C., U.S. Army, from Jan. 1, 1918; active duty, Feb. 1918-Sept. 1919; consultant to secretary of war and mem. Bd. for Investigation of Epidemic Diseases in U.S. Army since 1941 (pres., 1941-46); mem. Nat. Adv. Health Council, U.S.P.H.S., since 1948; chmn. adv. council, Life Ins. Med. Research Fund, 1946-50; chmn. com. on med. scis., Research and Development Bd., Dept. of Defense, since 1948; mem. exec. council Assn. of Am. Med. Colls., 1932-33; mem. bd. sci. dirs. Yerkes Lab. for Primate Biology 1940-52. Fellow A.C.P. (regent 1939-47, v.p., 1948), mem. Assn. American Physicians (pres., 1949), National Academy Science, American Philos. Society, Am. Acad. Arts and Sciences, American Society for Clinical Investigation (pres. 1931), American Society for Experimental Biology and Medicine, Am. Soc. for Exptl. Pathology, Soc. Am. Bacteriologists, Am. Assn. Immunologists (pres. 1935), Am. Assn. Pathologists and Bacteriologists, Conn. Acad. Arts and Sciences, Harvey Soc., Chi Phi, Phi Rho Sigma, Alpha Omega Alpha, Sigma Xi; A.A.A.S. (v.p. 1946), A.M.A. (chmn. sect. on medicine, 1938). Episcopalian. Clubs: Graduate, New Haven Lawn; Harvard (Boston); Interurban Clinical. Author: (with others) Epidemic Respiratory Disease, 1921; Studies on Exptl. Pneumonia, 1920; Studies on Measles, 1921; Treatment of Scarlet Fever with Anti-Toxin, 1924; Artificial Pneumothorax in Lobar Pneumonia, 1935; Chemo Therapy of Pneumonia, 1939; Penicillin Therapy, 1943; Tsutsugamushi Disease in New Guinea, 1945. Received the Charles V. Chapin Memorial Award, Providence, R.I., 1945; U.S. Typhus Medal, 1945; Medal for Merit, 1945. Home: 1619 19th St., Washington 9. Office: care Surgeon General's Office, Dept. of Army, Washington 25. Died Feb. 1, 1952.

BLAKE, Henry Seavey, publisher; b. Mpls., Feb. 14, 1888; s. Frederick Alden and Harriet Luella (Roberts) B.; student U. Minn., 1907-09; m. Grace Elizabeth Riebeth, Oct. 20, 1909; children—Grace Elizabeth (wife Dr. Homer L. Hiebert), Henry Seavey, David Riebeth. Circulation dir. Capper Publs. Inc., Topeka, 1920-29, pub., mgr., 1929-37, v.p., gen. mgr., 1937-51, pres., pub. since 1951; circulation mgr. Mpls. Tribune, 1909-11, Des Moines Register and Tribune, 1911-13, Houston Post, Winnipeg (Can.) Tribune, St. Paul Pioneer Press and Dispatch; pub. Ohio Farmer, Pa. Farmer, Mich. Farmer; pres. Topeka Broadcasting Co. WIBW and WIBW-TV; pres., dir. Capper, Harman, Slocum, Inc., Cleve. Mem. Topeka Pub. Charities Com.; exec. com. Kan. Council Children; mem. Kan. Juvenile Code Commn. Pres. Capper Found. for Crippled Children; trustee Midwest Research Inst.; Kan. chmn. Boy Scout coordinated campaign. Mem. N.A.M. (dir.), Topeka C. of C. Methodist (mem. ofcl. board, trustee). Mason (Shriner, Scottish Rite). Clubs: Optimist Internat. (1st pres. Topeka br.), High Twelve. Home: 1933 Westwood Dr. Office: Capper Publications, Inc., Topeka, Kan. Died Mar. 10, 1956; buried Topeka, Kan.

BLAKE, Luther Lee, publisher; b. Fayetteville, Tenn.; s. George Washington and Eliza (Hansell) B.; ed. pub. schs.; m. Ray Reed, 1907; children—Mary Eleanor, Willa. Lecturer from 1895-97; stock broker, 1898-1906; founder, 1906, later pres., chmn. bd. Standard Statistics Co., pubs., N.Y.C., now retired. Clubs: Fairfield County Hunt, Fairfield Country. Home: 150 E. 72d St., N.Y.C. Died July 2, 1953.

BLAKE, Maxwell, fgn. service officer; b. Kansas City, Mo., Nov. 15, 1877; s. John Thorn and Annie (Maxwell) B.; student St. John's Mil. Sch., Scarritt Coll., U. Mo.; m. Ruth Maxwell, Sept. 16, 1906. Am. consul at Funchal Madeira, 1906-07, Dunfermline, Scotland, 1907-10; consul gen. at Bogota, Colombia, 1910, Tangier, Morocco, 1910-12; sec. Am. Legation, Tangier, 1912, chargé d'affaires, 1912-17, apptd. diplomatic agt. and consul gen. at Tangier, 1917; Am. mem. Internat. Tax Urbaine for Morocco, 1913; del. Internat. Sanitary Council of Morocco, 1913; rep. on the Internat. Commn. of Pub. Works, Morocco, 1914; mem. internat. commn. Cape Spartel Lighthouse, 1914, pres. Commn., 1920; attached to Am. Commn. to Negotiate Peace, Paris, France, 1918-19; Am. commr., Albania, 1922, commd. E.E. and M.P., 1922; del. Am. High Commn., Turkey, 1923; Am. consul gen., Australia, 1923; Am. diplomatic agt., Tangier, Morocco, 1925-40; retired 1941. Mem. S.A.R., Loyal Legion. Address: State Dept., Washington. Died Jan. 1959.

BLAKE, Monroe Williams, fgn. service officer; b. St. Paul, Jan. 9, 1900; s. Monroe Heath and Mary (Williams) B.; A.B., George Washington U., 1933; m. Regina Olszewski, Nov. 4, 1938. Entered Dept. of State, 1928, clerk, 1928-31, divisional asst., 1934-35; apptd. fgn. service officer, 1935, vice consul, Ciudad Juarez, 1935, Montreal, 1935-36, Warsaw, 1936-39, Basel, 1940-41, Tampico, 1942-43, 2d sec. of Embassy and vice consul Tehran, 1943-46, 2d sec. of embassy and consul Warsaw, 1946-47, 1st sec. of embassy and consul Rome, 1947-51, consul gen. Dakar, 1951-53, Manchester, 1954—. Address: Fgn Mail Rm., U.S. Dept. of State, Washington 25. Died Feb. 6, 1955.

BLAKE, Ralph Mason, educator; b. Greenfield, Mass., July 19, 1889; s. Eugene Berkeley and Elmina Ballou (Mason) B.; A.B., Williams Coll., 1911; M.A., Harvard, 1912, Ph.D., 1915. Instr. phiosophy Princeton, 1915-17; acting prof. philosophy Wells Coll., Aurora, N.Y., 1919; instr., asst. prof., asso. prof., and prof. U. Wash., 1919-30; prof. philosophy Brown, 1930—, also chmn. dept.; vis. prof. U. Chgo., 1927-28, Harvard, 1928-29, Columbia U., 1941. Served in Med. Corps, Camp Funston, Kan., World War I. Mem. Am. Philos. Assn., Am. Assn. U. Profs., Phi Beta Kappa. Unitarian. Contbr. various tech. mags. Home: 20 Aberdeen Rd., Riverside 15, R.I. Died Apr. 15, 1950; buried Greenfield, Mass.

BLAKE, Robert Pierpont, educator; b. San Francisco, Nov. 1, 1886; s. Charles Thompson and Harriet Waters (Stiles) B.; A.B., U. Cal., 1908, LL.D., 1934; A.M., Harvard, 1912, Ph.D., 1916; hon. M.A., Oxford U., Eng., 1924; m. Nadezhda N. Kryzhanovskaya, Jan. 7, 1920; 1 son, Igor Robert. Instr. in ancient history U. Pa., 1912-14; prof. Georgian U., Tiflis, Russia, 1920; with Harvard, 1920—, dir. Univ. Library, 1928-37, prof. history, 1930—, pres. Byzantine Inst., 1948—. Trustee Harvard Yenching Inst. of Chinese Studies; chmn. Am. Council of Learned Socs., 1935-38; exchange prof. U. Sorbonne, 1938. Sr. fellow Dumbarton Oaks Research Library, 1942-43. Mem. Am. Philos. Soc., Am. Acad. Arts and Science (editor 1940), Medieval Acad. Am. Société Asiatique, Soc. Cal. Pioneers, Alpha Delta Phi, Phi Beta Kappa. Clubs: Faculty (Cambridge); Harvard (N.Y.C.). Author: Caesarean Text of Mark (with K. Lake and S. New), 1928; Epiphanius de Gemmis, 1934. Contbr. to Harvard Theol. Rev. and Revue de l'Orient Chrétien (Paris). Home: 40 Appleton St. Address: Harvard University, Cambridge, Mass. Died May 9, 1950; buried North Newport Cemetery, Newport, N.H.

BLAKESLEE, Albert Francis (blāks'lē), botanist; b. Geneseo, N.Y., Nov. 9, 1874; s. Francis Durbin and Augusta Mirenda (Hubbard) B.; A.B., Wesleyan U., Conn., 1896, D.Sc., 1931; A.M., Harvard, 1900, Ph.D., 1904 (Bowdoin medal, 1905); D.Sc., U. of San Marcos (Peru), 1925; D.Sc., U. of Delhi (India), 1947; LL.D., University of Arkansas, 1947; D.Sc., Yale University, 1947; Wesleyan U., 1931, Paris, Sorbonne, France, 1951, Smith Coll., 1952; married to Margaret Dickson Bridges, June 26, 1919 (dec.). Asst. botany Harvard, 1899-1900; instr. botany, Radcliffe Coll., 1900-02; teaching fellow, Harvard, 1901-03; asst. in botany, Summer Sch. of Cold Spring Harbor, L.I., 1901-02; collector in Venezuela for the Cryptogamic Herbarium of Harvard, summer of 1903; investigator in Europe for Carnegie Instn., 1904-06; instr. botany, Harvard, 1906-07; dir. Summer Sch. and prof. botany, Conn. Agrl. Coll., Sept., 1907-14, prof. botany and genetics, 1914-15; resident investigator, Carnegie Sta. for Exptl. Evolution, Cold Spring Harbor, 1912-13, in plant genetics 1915-41, asst. dir. dept., 1923-34, acting dir., 1934-35, dir., 1936-41, asso. in Genetics, Columbia U., 1940-42; William Allan Neilson research professor of botany, Smith College, 1942-43, visiting prof. and dir. Smith College Genetics Experiment Station, 1943—; visiting lecturer at Harvard University, 1948-49. Del. Carnegie Instn. to 3d Pan-Am. Scientific Congress, Lima, 1924-25; del. of A.A.A.S. to Indian Sci. Congress, 1946-48; mem. div. biology and agr., Nat. Research Council, 1931-33; mem. bd. mgrs. N.Y. Bot. Garden, 1933-34, director National Science Fund; trustee Biological Abstracts, 1931-46, president, 1942-46. Awarded A. Cressy Morrison prize, New York Academy Sciences, 1926, 36, also the Henry deJouvenal prize, Palais de la Decouverte, 1938. Honorary fellow, Nat. Institute Scis. of India; fellow A.A.A.S. (sec. Sect. G., 1916-17, v.p. 1918, pres. 1940), Am. Acad. of Arts and Sciences; mem. Am. Philos. Soc., Bot. Soc. America (pres. 1950), Nat. Acad. Sciences, Am. Soc. Naturalists (v.p. 1916; pres. 1930), N.E. Bot. Club, Torrey Bot. Club (asso. editor, 1924—, pres. 1933), The American Genetics Association, Genetic Soc. of America, Am. Eugenics Soc., Assn. for Research in Human Heredity, Human Genetics Society, Society for Study of Development and Growth (pres. 1945-46), Phi Beta Kappa, Phi Sigma, Sigma Xi; asso. mem. Société Royale de Botanique de Belgique, Soc. de Biologie de Paris, Royal Academy of Belgium; corresponding member of Nederlandsche Botanische Vereeniging, Acad. of Natural Sciences of Phila.; foreign mem. Acad. Sciences of Inst. of France, Linnean Soc. (London), Royal Danish Acad. of Science, Royal Physiographical Society of Lund (Sweden); Royal Swedish Acad. Scis., Botan. Soc. India; hon. mem. Soc. Naturalists (Moscow), Mycological Society of Leningrad, Genetics Sooc. of Japan. Author: Sexual Reproduction in the Mucorineae, 1904; New England Trees in Winter (with C. D. Jarvis), 1911, and Trees in Winter (with C. D. Jarvis), 1913. Contbr. to scientific jours. Home: 37 Paradise Rd., Northampton, Mass. Office: Smith College Genetics Experiment Station, Northampton Mass. Died Nov. 16, 1954.

BLAKESLEE, George Hubbard, educator; b. Geneseo, N.Y., Aug. 27, 1871; s. Francis Durbin and Augusta Mirenda (Hubbard) B.; A.B. Wesleyan U., Conn., 1893, L.H.D., 1923; A.M., Harvard, 1900, Ph.D., 1903; universities of Berlin, Leipzig, and Oxford, 1901-03; L.H.D., Williams Coll., 1930; LL.D., Brown U., 1936, Clark U., 1941; D.Eng., Worcester Poly. Inst., 1942; m. Edna Frances Day, Mar. 30, 1910; children—George Day, Frances Hubbard (Mrs. Andrew B. Wardlaw), Edith Augusta (Mrs. William G. Phelps). Instr. history Clark Coll., 1903; now prof. emeritus history and internat. relations Clark U.; also prof. diplomacy and internat. politics, Fletcher School of Law and Diplomacy, 1933-43; editor Journal of Internat. Relations, until 1921. Leader of Round Table, Inst. of Politics, Williamstown, Mass., 1922, 23, 28, 30, and gen. conf., 1925, 26, 29, 31; lectr. Naval War Coll., 1922-42, Army War Coll., 1923-29, 1932; Bennett lectr. Wesleyan U., Conn., 1924, and Weeks vis. prof. govt., 1931-32; lectr. Far Eastern history Harvard, 1926-28, 29; Schouler lectr. Johns Hopkins, 1927; vis. Carnegie prof. internat. relations to univs. in New Zealand, Australia and Japan, 1927. Tech. adviser, Am. del. Conf. on Limitation of Armament, Washington, 1921; officer in Div. Far Eastern Afairs, Dept. of State, 1931-32, cons., 1942-43, officer, 1943-45; spl. asst. to Am. Legation, Peiping, and counselor to Am. member of Lytton Commn., 1932; mem. Am. delegation to the Far Eastern Commission, 1945—; visited Japan with Far Eastern Commission, 1945-46. Mem. confs. Inst. Pacific Relations, Honolulu, 1925-27, Kyoto, Japan, 1929, Virginia Beach, 1939. Lectr. summer schs. U. Hawaii, 1937, Harvard, 1938. Mem. ednl. adv. bd. Fgn. Affairs. Pres. bd. trustees World Peace Found., 1930-46; chmn. Worcester br. Fgn. Policy Assn., 1933-39. Mem. Am. Antiquarian Soc. (sec.), Council Fgn. Relations, Am. Soc. Internat. Law, Phi Beta Kappa. Editor: China and the Far East; Japan and Japanese-American Relations; Recent Developments in China; Latin America; Problems and Lessons of the War; Mexico and the Caribbean. Author: The Recent Foreign Policy of the U.S., 1925; The Pacific Area

—An International Survey, 1929; Conflicts of Policy in the Far East, 1934. Home: 2224 38th St., Washington. Died May 5, 1954.

BLAKESLEE, Howard Walter, newspaper man; b. New Dungeness, Wash., Mar. 21, 1880; s. Jesse Walter and Jennie (Howard) B.; student U. of Mich., 1900-05, hon. M.Sc., 1935; m. Marguerite Fortune, Mar. 19, 1906; children—John Herbert, Merlys, Alton Lauren, Carol; m. 2d, Rosamond Robinson, May 1, 1936; children—Howard W. Jr., Rosamond, Alan Robinson. Began as news writer, 1901; feature writer, Detroit Jour., 1901-02; special sports writer, Chicago and Detroit newspapers, 1903-05; bur. chief, Asso. Press, New Orleans, Atlanta, Dallas, 1906-16, news editor, Chicago, New York, 1916-28, science editor since 1928. Pres. Nat. Assn. of Science Writers, 1936-37. Fellow Am. Inst. of N.Y. City. Co-winner of Pulitzer reporting prize, 1937; received Wilson L Fairbanks award of American Coll. Publicity Assn., Dist. II, 1940, also award for Distinguished Achievement in Interpretation of Higher Edn.; National Headliners Club award for outstanding achievement in journalism, 1940; George Westinghouse Science Writers award, A.A.A.S., 1946; Medal of Sch. of Journalism, Syracuse U., 1946; fellow Sigma Delta Chi, 1950. Republican. Mason. Author: The Atomic Future (book in tabloid form distributed to mem. newspapers by Associated Press), 1946; Atomic Progress, The Hydrogen Race (pub. in Japan), 1951. Home: 5 Longview Rd., Port Washington, L.I., N.Y. Office: 50 Rockefeller Plaza, N.Y.C. Died May 2, 1952; buried Nassau Knolls Cemetery, Port Washington, N.Y.

BLALOCK, Myron Geer (blā'lŏk), ex-Dem. Nat. committeeman; b. Harrison County, Tex., Jan. 3, 1891; s. William Meredith and Willie Henry (Boothe) B.; A.B., U. Tex., 1914, LL.B., 1916; m. Bertha Mary Storey, Aug 22, 1917; children—Mary Dorothy, Myron Geer, Jo Ann. Admitted to Tex. bar, 1916, since practiced at Marshall; mem. own firm, 1919—; now mem. Blalock, Blalock, Lohman & Blalock; at Marshall and Houston; chief justice (by appointment) Tex. Court Civil Appeals, 6th Dist., Texarkana, 1932. Served from capt. to maj. U.S. Army, 1917-19; major Tex. N.G. 1923-38; lt. col. (finance officer) 36th Div. (Tex. N.G.) U.S. Army, 1938-41; col., Hdqrs. A.S.F., Washington, 1941-43; on inactive duty. Mem. Tex. Ho. of Reps., 1913-18. Chmn. Tex. State Dem. Exec. Com., 1934-38; chmn. Dem. Nat. Campaign Com. for Tex., 1936, 40, 44; Dem. Nat. committeeman for Tex. 1940-1948. Mem. State Bar of Tex., Am., Harrison County bar assns., Am. Legion. Methodist. Mason (32°, Shriner). Clubs: Marshall Country, Rotary, Dallas Athletic. Home: 205 E. Merritt St., Marshall, Tex. Died Dec. 28. 1950.

BLANCHARD, Ozro Seth, lawyer; b. Erie, Pa., May 11, 1876; s. Eliphalet A. and Elizabeth (Stapf) B.; LL.B., U. of Mich., 1898; m. Irma Linkey, July 18, 1906; children—Elizabeth Hope (Mrs. Franklin Mecham), Jack Marshall (deceased). Admitted to Iowa bar, 1898, and began practice in Iowa; practice Grants Pass, Ore., since 1905, specializing in mining, corp. and water rights law; pres. First Federal Savings & Loan Assn.; ex-v.p. Redwood Empire Assn. Former mem. exec. com. Dem. State Central Com. Mem. Grants Pass Chamber Commerce (thrice pres.), Ore. State, So. Oregon (ex-pres.) bar assns. Episcopalian. Extensive traveler; has made good will speeches in Japan, China, Australia and other countries of the Orient. Address: Tufts Bldg., Grants Pass, Ore. Died Jan. 23, 1956.

BLANCHET, John Baptiste, clergyman; b. St. Anne, Ill., June 23, 1856; s. Alexis and Marie Leocade (Ouellette) B.; A.B. (with honors), Hobart, 1882, A.M., 1885; attended lectures, Harvard, and Episcopal Theol. Sch., Cambridge; grad. Gen. Theol. Sem., N.Y.C., 1885; D.D., St. John's, Md., 1897; m. Mary Lucretia Cross, June 2, 1884 (dec.); 1 son, John Leon. Deacon, May 29, 1885, priest, Nov. 18, 1885, P.E. Ch.; curate SS. Peter and Paul, Chgo., 1885; then rector various chs. N.Y. Diocese; rector Ch. of Beloved Disciple, Phila. (in absentia), 1909—. Mem. Phi Beta Kappa, Phi Kappa Psi, Am. Acad. Pol. and Soc. Sci. Mason, Odd Fellow. Author: Life and Poems of William Cullen Bryant, 1882; For His Sake, 1902; The Crucifixion, 1904; French Drills, 1904; Good Friday Three-Hour Service, 1906; Holy Noël, 1907; The Sacred Wreath, 1907; Church and Pastoral Card-Record, 1907; O God of Nations (peace hymn), 1909; New Marseillaise, 1918; The Call to the Ideal Life, 1925. Home: Upcohall, Fla. Deceased.

BLANCKE, William Henry (blăn'kē), clergyman, lectr.; b. Dangast, Grand Duchy of Oldenburg, Germany, Jan. 22, 1855; s. Dirck and Maria (Reiners) B.; A.B., Carthage (Ill.) Coll., 1883; studied theol. course Hamma Div. Sch., Springfield, Ohio; D.D., Wittenberg Coll., 1905; m. Mary C. Steinbeck, Oct. 5, 1885 (died Aug. 25, 1943); children—John Henry (dec.), Mary Edna (Mrs. M. E. Redeen), Lillian Edith (Mrs. Bertram P. Holst). Seaman at 15 and sailed before the mast for 3 years; came to U.S., 1873; ordained Evang. Luth. ministry, 1884; pastor Liberty, Ill., 1883-91, St. Paul's Ch., Davenport, Ia., 1891-1916, Newton, Ia., 1918-37; now pastor emeritus. Pres. Evang. Luth. Synod of Ia. 2 terms; trustee Carthage Coll., 1895-1915, 34-45, pres. bd. 10 yrs., mem. exec. com. 1937-40, mem. emeritus 1945—; del. to Nat. Synod many times; mem. Internat. Sunday Sch. Exec. Com., 1892-93; ex-pres. Ia. State Sunday Sch. Assn.; pres. Civic Fed. of Scott County, Ia., 1908-15. Platform dir. Rock River Assembly, Dixon, Ill., 9 yrs.; speaker at Sunday School convs., Chautauqua lecturer, topics: Wild Oats and Other Crops; From Capstain to Pulpit; others. Author: The Sacrament of The Altar. Republican. Home: 1525 First St. N., Newton, Ia. Died July 7, 1951; buried Newton Union Cemetery.

BLAND, Oscar E., judge; b. Greene County, Ind., Nov. 21, 1877; s. Joseph and Arminda (Shipman) B.; student Valparaiso U., Ind. U.; m. Josephine Hanna, June 18, 1902; 1 dau., Hellen Hanna. Admitted to Ind. bar, 1901, practiced at Linton; mem. Ind. Senate, 1907-10; was chmn. finance com. and author 2 cent R.R. fare law, others; Rep. candidate for Congress, 1910, 12, 14; elected 65th to 67th Congresses, 2d Ind. Dist.; judge, U.S. Court of Customs and Patent Appeals, 1923-47; now practicing law. Mem. Friendly Sons of St. Patrick, Sigma Nu, Hon. life mem. Elks. Clubs: Alfalfa, Nat. Press, Columbia Country (Washington). Home: 2950 Macomb St., Washington. Died Aug. 3, 1951; buried Ft. Lincoln Mausoleum, Washington.

BLAND, Richard Howard surety and casualty ins.; b. Balt., Mar. 31, 1880; s. John Randolph and Maria (Harden) B.; prep. edn., University Sch., Balt.; A.B., Harvard, 1902, LL.B., 1905; m. Mary L. Paul, Oct. 25, 1905; children—John Randolph II, Richard Howard J., Frank Paul. Practical law as mem. Bartlett, Poe, Claggett & Bland, Balt., 1905-16; elected v.p., sec. U.S. Fidelity & Guaranty Co., 1916, pres., 1923-32, now chmn.; dir. Consol. Gas, Electric Light & Power Co., Savings Bank of Balt., 1st Nat. Bank, Chesapeake & Potomac Telephone Co. Sec. Draft Bd., Balt. County, World War. Mem. Am. Bar Assn. Democrat. Episcopalian. Clubs: Maryland, Bachelors' Cotillon; Rolling Rd. Golf (Catonsville). Home: Catonsville, Md. Address: U.S. Fidelity & Guaranty Co., Balt. Died May 2, 1959.

BLANDIN, Charles Kenneth (blăn-dīn'); b. Iola, Wis., Apr. 2, 1872; s. Monroe and Eveline (Bennett) B.; ed. pub. schs.; m. Jennie D. Ackerman, June 5, 1892 (died Jan. 29, 1940); 1 son, Monroe (died Jan. 14, 1945). With St. Paul Pioneer Press and St. Paul Dispatch, 1904-27, owner and pub., 1917-27; pres. Blandin Development Co. and subsidiaries, Blandin Paper Co., Blandin Power Co., pres., trustee Charles K. Blandin Found.; trustee F. E. Murphy Estate, Mpls.; pres. First Nat. Bank, Grand Rapids, Minn. Republican. Clubs: Minn., St. Paul Athletic (St. Paul). Home: St. Paul Athletic Club. Office: First Nat. Bank Bldg., St. Paul 1. Died Feb. 9, 1958; buried Grand Rapids, Mich.

BLANDING, Don, author, illustrator; b. Kingfisher, Okla., Nov. 7, 1894; s. Hugh Ross and Ida (Kimble) B.; ed. Lawton (Okla.) High Sch., 1908-12, Art Inst. of Chicago, 1913-15; m. Dorothy Binney Putnam, June 13, 1940 (divorced 1945). Private Infantry U.S. Army, 2d lieut., A.E.F., World War. Corporal, Infantry, 1209th Service Corps Service Unit, Camp Upton, N.Y., 1942-43. Episcopalian. Author and Illustrator: Vagabond's House, 1928; Virgin of Waikiki, 1929; Hula Moons, 1930; Songs of the Seven Senses, 1931; Stowaways in Paradise, 1931; Let Us Dream, 1933; Memory Room, 1935; Pictures of Paradise, 1936; The Rest of the Road, 1937; Drifter's Gold, 1939; Floridays, 1940; Pilot Bails Out, 1943; Today Is Here, 1946; Mostly California, 1948; A Grand Time Living, 1950; Joy is an Inside Job, 1953; Hawaii Says Aloha, 1955; also articles in Asia and travel mags. Address: 1154 N. Ogden Dr., Hollywood 46, Cal. Died June 9, 1957.

BLANDY, William Henry Purnell, naval officer ret., business exec.; b. N.Y.C., June 28, 1890; s. Charles Graham and Elizabeth Harwood (Purnell) B.; student U. Del. (then Delaware Coll.), 1906-09, D.S., 1941; B.S., U.S. Naval Acad., 1913; m. Roberta Hope Amies, May 27, 1914; children—Hope Gilmour (wife of Comdr. John M. Lee, U.S. Navy), William Purnell (lt. (j.g.), U.S. Navy). Commd. ensign, U.S. Navy, 1913, advanced through grades to adm. 1947; chief Bureau of Ordnance, Navy Dept., Feb. 1941-Dec. 1943; comdr. Amphibious Group One, Jan. 1944-July 1945; participated in capture Kwajalein, Saipan, Palau, Iwo Jima and Okinawa; comdr. cruisers and destroyers Pacific Fleet, July-Nov. 1945; dep. Chief of Naval Operations, Special Weapons, Nov. 1945-Dec. 1946, during which period, as comdr. Joint Army-Navy Task Force One, planned and comd. atomic bomb tests at Bikini; comdr. Eighth Fleet in Atlantic, later called Second Task Fleet, Dec. 1946-Feb. 1947; comdr. in chief Atlantic Fleet, 1947-50; comdr. in chief Atlantic (Unified) Command, 1947-50, ret. from active duty, 1950; now dir. Gray Mfg. Co., Perkin-Elmer Corp.; pres. Health Information Found. Sponsor James Forrestal Research Center, Princeton, N.J.; com. pub. policy Inst. War and Peace Studies, Columbia; adv. council N.Y.C. Civil Def. Decorated D.S.M. with 3 gold stars; Grand Officer Order of the So. Cross (Brazil); Comdr. Order of British Empire. Mem. Am. Ordnance Assn. (dir., v.p.), Council on Fgn. Relations, Mil. Order World Wars (hon. life), Naval Order of U.S. (hon. life), Nat. Security Indsl. Assn. (hon.). Clubs: Yacht, University, Dutch Treat, Economic (N.Y.C.); Army and Navy, Army and Navy Country, Chevy Chase (Washington). Home: 277 Park Av., N.Y.C. 17. Office: 420 Lexington Av., N.Y.C. 17. Died Jan. 12, 1954; buried Arlington Nat. Cemetery.

BLANKENHORN, Marion Arthur (blăn'kĕn-hôrn), physician; b. Orrville, O., Nov. 13, 1885; s. Henry and Emma C. (Amstutz) B.; Ph.B., Wooster Coll., 1909; M.D., Western Reserve U., 1914, M.A. in medicine, Grad. Sch., 1920; hon. D.Sc., Wooster Coll., 1939; m. Martha Finley Taggart; children—Martha, Mary Margaret, David Henry. Prof. biology, Buena Vista (Ia.) Coll., 1909-10; resident physician in Lakeside Hosp., Cleveland, Ohio, 1914-17; instr. in medicine, 1919; voluntary asst. Rockefeller Inst. for Med. Research, 1925-26; professor medicine, Western Reserve U., 1929-35; prof. medicine U. Cin., 1935-56, prof. emeritus, 1956—; responsible investigator aviation medicine NRC.; dir. edn. dept. internal medicine Jewish Hosp., Cin., 1957—. Served as capt. M.C., 1917-19; med. cons. 5th Corps Area; med. cons. Surgeon Gen., 1948, Far East Command, 1951, ETO. Fellow A.C.P. (regent v.p.; dir. survey of hosp. standards in internal medicine 1956-57); mem. A.M.A., Assn. Am. Physicians, Am. Soc. Clin. Investigation, Central Soc. Clin. Research, Am. Soc. Exptl. Pathology, Alpha Tau Omega, Nu Sigma Nu, Phi Beta Kappa, Alpha Omega Alpha, Sigma Xi. Home: 6 Rural Lane. Office: Jewish Hosp., Cin. Died Sept. 3, 1957; buried Wooster, O.

BLANKS, Robert Franklin, civil engr.; b. Maplehill, Kan., Sept. 4, 1900; s. Thomas Franklin and Vida Florence (Fairbanks) B.; B.S. in Civil Engring., Kan. State Coll., Manhattan, Kan., 1924, C.E., 1936; D.Sc., Kansas State College, May 1949; married Laura Viola Denman, May 26, 1922; 1 son, Robert Franklin. Municipal engr., Burley, Ida., Jan.-May, 1921; field engring. on location and constrn. Carey (Ida.) Irrigation Project, May-Sept., 1921; sci. and math. instr., Burley (Ida.) High Sch., 1921-22; asst. supt. Burley (Ida.) public schs., 1922-23; instr. in physics, chemistry and math., also athletic coach, Hollister (Ida.) High Sch., 1924-25; asst. supt. and engr. irrigation project, Salmon River Canal Co., Hollister, Ida., 1925-27; instr. in physics, chemistry and math. Hollister High Sch., 1927-28; made hydraulic investigations Am. Falls Reservoir and Basin Water Dist. No. 36, State of Ida., Idaho Falls, May-Oct. 1928; with Office Engring., Fort Hall Irrigation project, U.S. Indian Irrigation Service, Blackfoot, Ida., 1928-29; office and field engring., Columbia Basin Investigations, Washington U.S. Engr. Office, Seattle, Wash., 1929-30; chief, research and geology division U.S. Bur. of Reclamation, Denver, 1930-51. Vice pres., gen. mgr. Great Western Aggregates, Inc.; research cons. Ideal Cement Company. Chairman Reinforced Concrete Research Council Engineering Foundation Winner Thomas Fitch Rowland prize for paper Deterioration of Concrete Dams Due to Alkali-Aggregate Reaction. Mem. Am. Soc. C.E. (chmn. com. on masonry and reinforced concrete), Am. Soc. for Testing Materials, Am. Concrete Inst. (member various coms.; tech. activities com., 1941, chmn., 1945, 46, 47; dir. at large, 1944-45; dir. 6th dist., 1941-42; adv. com., 1945; v.p., 1945, 46, 47, pres. 1948), Highway Research Board, Colorado Society Engrs. (dir. 1951-53, pres. 1955), Sigma Tau, Sigma Xi. Contbr. engring. publs. Patentee materials testing equipment for controlling rate of load application in testing materials. Home: 1062 S. Clayton Way, Dnver 9. Office: Boston Bldg., Denver 2. Died July 14, 1958.

BLANTON, Thomas Lindsay, lawyer, ex-congressman; b. at Houston, Tex., Oct. 25, 1872; LL.B., U. of Tex.; m. May Louise Matthews. Practiced in Cleburne and Albany, Tex., until 1908; judge 42d Jud. Dist. of Tex., 1909-17; mem. 65th Congress (1917-19), 16th Tex. Dist., 66th to 70th Congresses, 71st to 74th Congresses, 17th Tex. Dist.; resumed law practice in Albany, Tex. Democrat. Died Aug. 11, 1957, buried Albany, Tex.

BLASH, Rudolph F., business exec. Chmn. Webster-Chicago Corp., Chgo. Home: Ingleside, Ill. Office: 5610 Bloomingdale Av., Chgo. 39. Died Apr. 2, 1956.

BLATCHFORD, Charles Hammond, lawyer; b. Evanston, Ill., Jan. 2, 1874; s. Eliphalet Wickes and Mary Emily (Williams) B.; grad. Chicago Manual Training Sch., 1891; B.S., Cornell U., 1895; LL.B., Northwestern University, 1897; M.L., Yale, 1898; married Carita Tyler Clark, November 30, 1899 (deceased August 29, 1952); children—Lawrence, Charles Hammond, Huntington, Mary Williams. Mem. firm Smith, Blatchford & Taylor, Chicago, 1898-1910; with Boston & Me. R.R., 1910-13; clerk, 1913—and gen. solicitor Me. Central R.R. and subsidiary cos. 1913-40. Mem. Conn. Naval Reserves, 1898. Mem. Me. State bar assn., Alpha Delta Phi, Phi Delta Phi; fellow Am. Geog. Soc. Republican. Conglist.; pres. Congl. Christian Conf. of Me., 1934-35 and 1941-42. Home: 15 Clifford St., Portland, Me. Died Dec. 2, 1953; buried Forest Hills (Mass.) Cemetery.

BLAUER, William E., business exec.; b. San Jose, Cal., 1879. Mem. exec. and finance com., dir. Pacific Nat. Fire Ins. Co.; mem. exec. com., dir. Bank of Am.; v.p., dir. L. Lions Sons Co., San Jose. Home: Rt. 1, Box 489, Saratoga, Cal. Office: 300 Montgomery St., San Francisco. Died Feb. 1957.

BLEICHER, Clarence E. (blīch'ẽr), automotive exec.; b. Dayton, O., Mar. 25, 1890; s. Martin and Magdalene (Kraft) B.; ed. St. Mary's Parochial Sch., and St. Mary's Inst. (now U. of Dayton); m. Alma D. Keller, July 30, 1913; children—Virginia M. (Mrs. C. S. Motter), Alma J. (Mrs. J. E. Fraser). Apprentice mechanic, Stoddard Dayton automobile plant, Dayton, O., 1907; toolmaker Speedwell Motor Co., 1907-09, Nat. Cash Register Co., 1910-11; asst. foreman in machine-tool and design shop, Carroll Engring. Co., 1917-23; joined Maxwell Motor Car Co., 1923, assigned to line up and follow in all dies for Maxwell Club Sedan and original Chrysler "70" roadster and touring cars, later in charge all tools, asst. master mechanic, Detroit Highland Park plant, 1926; master mechanic Kercheval plant; master mechanic Highland Park, 1928, staff master mechanic, 1930-37; vice pres. and gen. mgr. De Soto Div. of Chrysler Corp., 1937-44, pres. and gen. mgr., 1944, dir. Clubs: Detroit (Mich.) Athletic, Detroit Golf; Grosse Pointe (Mich.) Yacht (dir.). Home: 1009 Yorkshire Rd., Grosse Pointe 30, Mich. Office: Chrysler Corp., De Soto Div., 6000 Wyoming Av., Detroit 31. Died Sept. 23, 1952; buried White Chapel Meml. Cemetery, Birmingham, Mich.

BLENNER, Carle John, painter; b. Richmond, Va., Feb. 1, 1862; s. Burghard Philip and Martha Elizabeth (Bromm) B.; ed. Marburg, Germany, and spl. course, Yale; hon. B.F.A., Yale Art Sch., 1904; 4 yrs. at Julian Acad., Paris; unmarried. Exhibited Paris Salon, 4 times to 1891, Chicago Expn., 1893; current exhbns., N.Y. City, since 1889. Among notable portraits are H.R.H. The Duke of Cambridge, The Marquis of Villalobar of Spain, Sen. Laurence C. Phipps, Prof. Michael I. Pupin, Mme. Nordica, Mme. Lucretia Bori, Mrs. Drexal Dahlgren, Lady Hamilton, granddaughter of The Duke of Cambridge. Awarded medal, Boston, 1891; Hallgarten Prize, Nat. Acad. Design, 1899; bronze medal, St. Louis Expn., 1904; also prize, Springfield Art League and San Antonio (Tex.) Exhbn.; silver medal Charleston, S.C.; medals and prizes at New Haven, Hartford, Conn. Club: Salmagundi. Summer home: Orange, Conn. Studio: 58 W. 57th St., N.Y.C. 19. Died Apr. 12, 1952.

BLESSE, Frederick Arthur, army officer; b. Ill., Nov. 22, 1888; M.D., Hahnemann Coll., 1913; honor grad. Med. Field Service Sch., 1925, Command and Gen. Staff Sch., 1932, Army War Coll., 1936. Commd. 1st lt. Med. Sect., O.R.C., Feb. 1918; on active duty from Apr. 1918; advanced through grades to brig. gen., 1942; served as chief surgeon North Africa Theater of Operations; later surgeon gen. of the Army, ret. 1949; dir. Henrico County Health Dept., Richmond, Va., 1950—. Died June 4, 1954.*

BLEYER, Herman, newspaperman; b. Milw., Mar. 8, 1850; student pub. schs.; m. Isora J. Morehouse, Mar. 8, 1881. Joined Evening Wisconsin as errand boy, 1864, became practical printer in charge composing room for several yrs., mng. editor, 1883-1911, resigned; sec. Milw. Harbor Commn., 1912—, sec. harbor survey work Dept. Pub. Works, Milw., 1912—. Home: 834 Cass St. Office: City Hall, Milw. 2. Died Aug. 19, 1924.

BLIGHT, Reynold E(dward), writer, lecturer; b. Torrington, Devon, Eng., May 19, 1879; s. John and Jane (Pearce) B.; ed. pub. schs.; C.P.A., Calif., 1910; LL.D., Southwestern U., 1927; m. Lydia E. Walters, 1907 (died, 1922); children—Reynold F., Edward M.; m. 2d, Evelyn A. Stackhouse, Sept. 1923. Came to U.S., 1896, naturalized, 1903. Practiced accountancy at N.Y. City, San Francisco and Los Angeles; Sunday morning lecturer, Ch. of the People, 1908-22; mem. Los Angeles City Bd. Edn., 1911-15; instr. Southwestern U., 1913-23, spl. lecturer since 1931; editor Liberal Rev., 1918-19, Masonic Digest, 1921-23 and 1925-33, New Age Mag., Washington, 1923-25, Calif. Certified Public Accountant, 1935-41, Los Angeles Churchman (official organ of Diocese) 1935-43; president, Pierce Insurance Co., vice pres. Pierce Bros. California State Franchise Tax Commr., 1929-31. Mem. Rep. State Central Com., Calif., 1922-23. Pres. Pub. Sch. Protective League of Calif., 1925-26; exec. sec. Southern Calif. Ednl. Assn., 1920-32; sec. Jud. Council Com. on Administration Justice, 1931-32, Citizens Library Council of Calif. Library Assn.; mem. Los Angeles City Bd. of Library Commrs. 1938-48. Mem. Am. Inst. Accountants, International Accountants Soc., Inc. (mem. advisory bd.), Beta Gamma Sigma (hon.), Beta Alpha Psi. Vice pres. Calif. State Bd. Accountancy, 1912-29. Maj. O.R.C. (finance), 1924-39. Episcopalian. Mason (33°, K.T., Red Cross of Constantine, R.O.S., Shriner). field sec. Los Angeles Bodies Scottish Rite, since 1944; mem. of com. on Masonic Information, Grand Lodge of Calif.; mem. Masonic Homes Endowment Fund Bd. since 1936. Clubs: Los Angeles Athletic, Sojourners (ex-pres.)—all Los Angeles; National Press (Washington). Author: What I Believe and Why, 1915; Freemasonry at a Glance, 1928; also numerous articles and pamphlets. Home: 1227 S. Lake St., Los Angeles 6. Office: 1908 Estella St., Los Angeles 15. Died 1951.

BLISS, D. Spencer, former dep. commr. Bureau of Internal Revenue, Washington. Died Apr. 1, 1950.

BLISS, Gilbert Ames, mathematician; b. Chicago, May 9, 1876; s. George Harrison and Mary Maria (Gilbert) B.; B.S., Univ. of Chicago, 1897, M.S., 1898, fellow, 1899-1900, Ph.D., 1900; hon. Sc.D., Univ. of Wis., 1935; student Univ. of Göttingen, 1902-03; m. Helen Hurd, June 15, 1912 (died Dec. 22, 1918); children—Elizabeth, Ames; m. 2d, Olive Hunter, Oct. 12, 1920. Instr. mathematics, Univ. of Minn., 1900-02; associate in mathematics, Univ. of Chicago, 1903-04; asst. prof. mathematics, Univ. of Mo., 1904-05, Princeton, 1905-08; asso. prof. mathematics, 1908-13, prof., 1913-41, chmn. dept. of mathematics since 1927, Martin A. Ryerson distinguished service prof. of mathematics, 1933-41, prof. emeritus 1941, U. of Chicago. Asso. editor Annals of Mathematics, 1906-08. Trans. Am. Math. Soc., 1908-16. Mem. Am. Math. Soc. (pres. 1921-22), Nat. Acad. Sciences, Am. Philos. Soc., Am. Acad. of Arts and Sciences, Sigma Xi, Phi Beta Kappa, Delta Kappa Epsilon. Clubs: Quadrangle, University, Flossmoor Country. Home: Flossmoor, Ill. Died May 8, 1951.

BLISS, James Harris, packing co. exec.; b. Kane Co., Ill., Oct. 13, 1889; s. J. Harris and Grace (Carter) B.; student Northwestern Sch. Commerce, 1911-13; m. Ethel Taylor, Apr. 28, 1915; 1 dau., Patty Taylor (Mrs. J. A. Sizer). Sec.-treas. Siegel-Cooper Co., Chicago, 1916-18; accountant Swift & Co., 1918-22, asst. treas., 1935-45; comptroller Libby, McNeill & Libby, 1922-35; v.p., treas., dir. Swift Internat. Co., Ltd., 1945-50, Internat. Packers, Ltd., since 1950. C.P.A., Ill., 1916. Mem. Am. Inst. Accountants, Ill. Soc. C.P.As. Clubs: Union League, Beverly Country (Chicago) Home: 322 N. East Av., Oak Park, Ill. Office: 135 S. LaSalle St., Chgo. 3. Died July 24, 1952.

BLISS, John Carlton, normal sch. prin.; b. Ovid, N.Y., Apr. 18, 1868; s. John B. and Sarah E. (Warne) B.; A.B., Cornell U., 1889; (hon. Pd.D., State Coll. for Teachers, Albany, N.Y. 1908); m. June MacFerran, of Gouverneur, N.Y., Aug. 14, 1895. Began teaching at Fairfield (N.Y.) Sem., 1889, and continued as teacher, later supt. schs.; insp. State Edn. Dept., Albany, N.Y., 1900-04; in charge teachers' examinations and certification, 1904-08; prin. State Normal Sch., New Paltz, N.Y., 1908-23. Republican. Presbyn. Home: New Paltz, N.Y. Died Jan. 17, 1924; buried Gouverneur, N.Y.

BLISS, Zenas Work, b. Johnston, R.I., Jan. 10, 1867; s. Zenas Randall and Martha Nancy (Work) B.; B.S., Mass. Inst. Tech., 1889; hon. A.M., Brown U., 1916; D.Sc., R.I. State Coll., 1919; m. Lydia Collins Kelly, Oct. 26, 1892; 1 son, Zenas Randall. Engaged in engring. work, 1889-96; mem. R.I. Ho. of Rep., 1903-09, chmn. com. on finance, 1904-09; dep. speaker 1909; lt. gov. of R.I., 1910-12; chmn. State Tax Commn., 1912-35; chmn. Ways and Means Commn., 1935. Chmn. commn. to investigate affairs R.I. County 1918-19; receiver, representing State R.I., R.I. Co., 1921-23; pres. United Electric Rys. Co., 1923, treas., 1928—, also dir.; receiver Interstate Consol. St. Ry. Co.; mem. bd. dirs. Morris Plan Co. of R.I.; dir. Roger Williams Savings Fund and Loan Assn.; receiver Manville Jenckes Co., 1931-33; treas. Woonsocket Rayon Co., 1931-35; treas. Manville Jenckes Corp., 1933-35. A.d.c., rank of col., staff of gov. of R.I., 1905-06. Mem. commn. revising revenue laws R.I., 1909-12, mem. commn. to revise laws on pub. edn., 1920-22. Pres. Nat. Tax Assn., 1921, N.E. Tax Ofcls. Assn., 1920, 35; v.p. bd. mgrs. R.I. State Coll., 1912-35. Mem. bd. trustees William H. Hall Free Public Library, Edgeworth, R.I. Mem. Mil. Order Loyal Legion, Am. Econ. Assn., Am. Polit. Science Assn. Republican. Unitarian. Mason (32°). Clubs: University, Providence Economic (pres. 1926-29), Turks Head, Atlantic Tuna (pres. 1922-25). Home: 238 Armington St., Edgewood, R.I. Office: 171 Westminster St., Providence. Died Jan. 10, 1957; buried Providence.

BLITZ, Anne Dudley, coll. dean; b. Mpls., Jan. 27, 1881; d. Adolph (M.D.) and Anna Dudley (Wickes) Blitz; A.B., U. Minn., 1904 (Phi Beta Kappa); M.A., Columbia, 1914; LL.D., Hobart College, 1933. Tchr. high schs., Minn. and Ida., several yrs.; dean William Smith Coll. (woman's dept., Hobart Coll.), 1915-19; dean of woman U. Kan., 1921-23; dean of women U. Minn., 1923—. Mem. Am. Assn. U. Women, Nat. Assn. Deans Women, N.E.A., Lafayette Cub. Contbr. on pedagog. topics. Home: 523 Ontario St. S.E., Mpls. 14. Died Feb. 18, 1951; buried Lakewood Cemetery, Mpls.

BLIZZARD, Warren Lale, dean; b. McPherson, Kan., Apr. 8, 1888; s. John W. and Zaidee (Leonard) B.; B.S., Kansas State Coll., 1910; m. Alta Handlin. Began as livestock farmer, Reno County, Kan., 1910; asst. animal husbandman, Kan. State Coll., 1911-14; field man Capper Publications, Topeka, Kan., 1914; asst. prof. animal husbandry extension, Ia. State Coll., 1914-15; asst. prof. animal husbandry, Okla. A. & M. Coll., 1915-19, became prof., 1919, head of dept. since 1919, dean agr. and dir. Expt. Station since 1939. Mem. Am. Soc. Animal Production, Nat. Assn. Stallion Enrollment Bds., Phi Kappa Phi, Alpha Zeta, Sigma Nu. Mason (Shriner). Clubs: Saddle and Sirloin (Chicago); Rotary (Stillwater, Okla.). Home: 126 S. Duck St., Stillwater, Okla. Died July 3, 1954.

BLOCH Ernest, composer, conductor; b. Geneva, Switzerland, July 24, 1880; s. Maurice and Sophie (Brunschwig) B.; studied in Geneva, Brussels, Frankfurt-am-Main; awarded degree of D.H.L. from Linfield Coll., 1948; m. Aug. 13, 1904; children—Ivan, Suzanne, Lucienne. Came to U.S., 1916, naturalized, 1924. Condr. symphonic concerts, Lausanne, Neuchatel, Switzerland, 1909-10; teacher and lecturer, Conservatory of Geneva, 1911-15. Mannes Sch., N.Y. City, 1917-19; founder Cleveland Inst. of Music, dir., 1920-25; dir. San Francisco Conservatory, 1925-30; tchr. U. Cal., Berkeley, now prof. emeritus U. Cal. at Berkeley. Recipient award for orchestral music N.Y. Music Critics Circle, 1954. Hon. mem. Accademia di St. Cecilia, Rome; mem. Am. Academy of Arts and Letters (awarded gold medal 1942), Am. Soc. composers, Authors and Publishers. Composer: Symphony in C sharp minor, 1901-02; Hiver-Printemps (symphonic poem), 1904-05; Poemes d'Automme (for voice and orchestra), 1906; Macbeth (opera), 1909; Jewish Cycle (for orchestra), 1912-16; Quartet, 1916; Suite for Viola and Orchestra, 1919; Sonata for Violin and Piano, 1926; Quintet, 1923; Poeme Mystique for violin and piano, 1924; Concerto Grosso for String Orchestra and Piano, 1925; Four Episodes (for chamber orchestra), 1926; America (symphony), 1926; Helvetia (for orchestra), 1928; Jewish Service, 1933; Voice in the Wilderness (for cello and orchestra), 1935; Piano Sonata; Evocations (for orchestra); Concerto for Violin and Orchestra, 1937; Suite Symphonique, 1944; Second String Quartet, 1945; Concerto Symphonique, 1946-48; Scherzo Fantasque, 1948; Concertino, 1950; Rhapsodie Hebraique, 1951; Concerto Grosso No. 2, String Quartet No. 3, Sinfonia Breve, 19552, No. 4, 1953; Symphony (for trombone and orchestra), 1954; Symphony (E flat), 1955; Proclamation (trumpet solo & orchestra), 1955; String Quartet No. 5, 1956; 2 Suites (viello solo), 1956. Address: Agate Beach, Ore. Died July 15, 1959.

BLOCH, Jesse A., tobacco mfr., chmn. bd., dir. Bloch Bros. (Mail Pouch) Tobacco Co.; dir. Wheeling (W Va.) Dollar Savings and Trust Co. Home: Pleasant Valley. Office: 4000 Water St., Wheeling, W.Va. Died Jan. 17, 1951.

BLOCH, Louis, paper mfr.; b. San Francisco, Calif., Aug. 9, 1875; s. Isaac F. and Seline (Kahn) B.; grad. high sch., San Francisco, 1893; student U. of Calif., 1893-94; m. Amelia Davis, Mar. 31, 1901; children—Mrs. Claire Morris, Mrs. Ruth Campbell. Began as employee in paper bag factory, 1894; v.p. and mgr. Crown Columbia Paper Co., 1911-18; pres., 1918-26; Sansac Investment Corp.; v.p. Calif. Montgomery Co.; v.p. and gen. mgr. Crown Willamette Paper Co., 1914-24; pres., 1924-36; mng. dir. Pacific Mills, Ltd., 1914-20; chmn of bd. Crown Zellerbach Corp. since 1928, Pacific Mills, Ltd., since 1920; president Crown-Willamette Paper Company of Texas; director Canadian Crown Willamette Company, Fibreboard Products Company, Pioneer Rubber Mills, Bank of Calif. N.A. (chmn. exec. com.). Dir. Golden Gate Internat. Expn., 1939. Vice chmn. San Francisco Unemployment Stabilization Com.; ex.v.p. San Francisco Chamber of Commerce; director Mount Zion Hospital. Mem. English-Speaking Union. Republican. Jewish religion. Mason. Clubs: Commercial (ex-president), Concordia-Argonaut (dir.), Menlo Circus, Stock Exchange Lunch. Home: 20 Cherry St., San Francisco; (country) Atherton, Calif. Office: 343 Sansome St., San Francisco, Calif. Died June, 1951.

BLOCK, Karl Morgan, clergyman; b. Washington, D.C., Sept. 27, 1886; s. Sigismund Joseph and Joanna Christine (Linder) B.; A.B., George Washington U., 1907; B.D., Theol. Seminary Va., 1910, D.D., 1950; Dr. Systematic Theology, Sch. of the Pacific, 1953; D.D., Roanoke Coll., 1923, University of South, 1935; LL.D., Washington University, 1937; m. Nancy Holliday Shackelford, Oct. 1, 1913 (died Feb. 1945); children—Virginia Randolph, Karl Morgan. Ordained ministry P.E. Ch., 1910; chaplain Woodberry Forest Sch., Orange, Va., 1910-13; rector Grace Ch., Haddonfield, N.J., 1913-17; volunteer chaplain Camp Dix, N.J., 1917-18; rector All Saints' Ch., Norristown, Pa., 1918-20, St. John's Ch., Roanoke, 1920-26, Ch. of St. Michael and St. George, St. Louis, 1926-38; bishop coadjutor, Calif., 1938, bishop since 1941. Trustee St. Luke's Hosp., Mills College. Mem. Delta Tau Delta. Clubs: Commonweath, Pacific Union, University (San Francisco). Democrat. Author: Our Common Life, 1929; The Sword of St. Michael, 1936. Contbr. to Revealing Christ, 1935; The Redeemer, 1937; also to religious jours. Vice chmn. House of Bishops. Home: 1865 Broadway. Address: 1055 Taylor St., San Francisco. Died Sept. 20, 1958.

BLOCK, Leopold E., business executive; b. Jan. 13, 1869, Cincinnati, O.; s. Joseph and Rose (Cahn) B.; ed. public schs. Cincinnati, Ohio, 1875-93; m.

Cora Bloom, June 20, 1900; children—Joseph, Leigh, Babette, Eleanore. Began as accountant and stenographer, 1893; partner, firm of Dreifus Block & Co., 1894-98, gen. mgr. Inland Iron & Forge Co., 1898-1901; president Buffalo (N.Y.) Steel Co., 1900-09. With Inland Steel Co., 1898—, serving as v.p. until 1919, chmn. Bd. 1919-40, chmn. finance com. 1941, dir., 1898—; dir. Inland Steel Container Co., Joseph T. Ryerson & Son, Inc., Buffalo Steel Co., Commonwealth Edison Co., First Nat. Bank of Chgo. Actively identified with civic and charitable movements, especially the Michael Reese Hospital (dir. 1910-40), and Chgo. Mus. Natural History. Mem. Am. Iron and Steel Inst. Clubs: Lake Shore Country, Standard, Mid-Day (Chgo.); Bankers of America (N.Y.C.). Home: 209 E. Lake Shore Dr. Office: 38 S. Dearborn St., Chgo. Died Nov. 11, 1952.

BLOCKER, Daniel James, clergyman, educator; b. Starke, Fla., Oct. 13, 1873; s. Daniel and Ann (Crosby) B.; A.B., Stetson U., 1909, D.D., 1918; A.M., U. Chgo., 1911, B.D., 1912; m. Florence Evelyn Jackson, Aug. 12, 1917; 1 son, Daniel James. Began in constrn. work Fla. rys., later mcht. Jacksonville, Fla.; ordained to Bapt. ministry, 1901; pastor Irving Park Ch., Chgo., 1910-12; prof. psychology and edn. and dean dept. of edn. Stetson U., 1913-21; prof. philosophy and Bible, Coll. of William and Mary, 1921-23, also pastor Bapt. Ch., Williamsburg, Va.; pres. Shorter Coll., Rome, Ga., 1923-25; prof. philosophy Furman U., Greenville, S.C., 1925-30; now head of dept. sociology, William and Mary Coll. Pres. Baptist Young People's Union, Fla., 5 yrs. Mem. Delta Sigma Phi, Delta Theta Chi, Pi Gamma Mu, Omicron Delta Kappa, Phi Beta Kappa. Mason, Odd Fellow. Home: 719 Richmond Rd., Williamsburg, Va. Died Apr. 25, 1957.

BLODGETT, John Wood, lumberman; b. Hersey, Mich., July 26, 1860; s. Delos A. and Jane (Wood) B.; grad. Highland Mil. Acad., Worcester, Mass., 1876; course in business coll.; m. Minnie A. Cumnock, Jan. 16, 1895 (died Oct. 12, 1931); children—Katherine Cumnock (Mrs. Morris Hadley), John W. Actively engaged many yrs. in lumber and timber business and banking; former dir. Fed. Res. Bank Chgo. An organizer Mich.'s 1st Social Welfare Assn., Anti-Tb Soc. Pres. Nat. Lumber Mfrs. Assn., 1922-23. Mem. Rep. Nat. Com., 1900-12. Home: Grand Rapids, Mich. Died Nov. 21, 1951.

BLODGETT, Mabel Louise Fuller, author; b. Bangor, Me., Apr. 8, 1869; d. Ransom Burritt and Louisa S. (White) Fuller; grad. Elmhurst Acad., Providence, R.I.; m. Edward Everett Blodgett, Nov. 17, 1891. Mem. Women's Rep. Club of Mass. Mem. D.A.R., Soc. Mayflower Descendants. Author: The Aspen Shade, 1889; In Poppy Land, 1889; Fairy Tales, 1895; At the Queen's Mercy, 1897; The Giant's Ruby, 1903; When Christmas Came Too Early, 1911. Strange Story of Mr. Dog and Mr. Bear, 1915; The Magic Slippers, 1917; Peas Blossom, 1917. Home: 1180 Beacon St., Brookline, Mass. Died June 1959.

BLOOD, Robert McCutchins, newspaper exec.; b. Boston, Mass., June 12, 1883; s. Robert Allen and Elizabeth Campbell (McCutchins) B.; A.B., Dartmouth, 1906; m. Olive Nickerson, Aug. 2, 1913; children—Mrs. Thomas Ward Miles, Nickerson (killed in service USAAF), Rogers (killed in service USMC). Exec. editor Manchester (N.H.) Union-Leader; mem. bd. incorporators Amoskeag Savings Bank, Manchester, N.H. Recipient Distinguished Service award N.H. Dept. Am. Legion, 1938. Mem. Beta Theta Pi, Dragon Sr. Soc. (Dartmouth). Republican. Conglist. Mason. Home: 498 E. High St. Office: Manchester Union-Leader, 35 Amherst St., Manchester, N.H. Died Aug. 4, 1950; buried New London, N.H.

BLOODWORTH, Andrew Dunn Franklin, city ofcl.; b. Forsyth, Ga., Nov. 25, 1894; s. Oliver Hazzard Bartlow and Leila (Dunn) B.; B.S., Riverside Mil. Acad., 1911; student Ala. Polytechnic Inst., 1911-13; married Virginia May Roop, December 22, 1919; children—Vianne Shelton (Mrs. Walter Gumbel), Vivian Suzanne (Mrs. Stanley Herbert Rice), Dorothy Louise (Mrs. William Orville Yates). Agt. Texas Co., Miami, Fla., 1919-22; pres., gen. mgr. Miami Oil Co., 1922-27; pres. Bloodworth Oil Co., Miami, Fla., 1927-35; asst. city mgr., Miami, 1935-37, 1949-50, city mgr., 1937, 41, 50-51, dir Port Operations, 1942-45, Dept. Yacht Docks, 1945-49, 1951-52. Mem. Kappa Alpha. Presbyn. (trustee). Mason (32°). Home: 1701 S.W. 10 St., Miami 35. Office: Dept. of Yacht Docks, City Yacht Basin. Miami 32, Fla. Died July 20, 1955; buried Woodlawn Park Cemetery, Miami.

BLOOM, Edgar Selden, shipping; b. Bloomsbury, N.J., Dec. 17, 1874; s. Erastus Starner and Mary Taylor (Smith) B.; B.S., U. Pa., 1895, M.E., 1896; m. May Gladys Walace, Oct. 16, 1905; 1 dau., Eleanor Wallace. Constrn. engr. N.Y. Telephone Co., 1896-1906; supt. plant N.Y. & N.J. Telephone Co., 1906-08; gen. supt. plant, Pacific Tel. & Tel. Co., 1909; engr. plant operations Am. Tel. & Tel. Co., 1910-11, v.p., 1922-26; v.p. in charge operations Bell Telephone Co. of Mo., Pioneer Telephone Co. of Okla., S.W. Telephone & Telegraph Co. of Tex., Mo. and Kan. Telephone Co., 1912-13; receiver Central Union Telephone Co., 1914-19; pres. Central Union, Ohio, and Ind. Bell telephone cos. and v.p. Ill. Bell Telephone Co., 1920-21; pres. and dir. Western Electric Co., 1926-39; dir. of purchases, Brit. Purchasing Commn., 1940; pres., dir. Atlantic, Gulf & West Indies S.S. Lines, 1941 (chmn. 1946); dir. Western Electric Co., Inc., Agwi Lines, Inc., N.Y. & Cuba Mail S.S. Co., Nat. Surety Co., Adams Express Co., George A. Fuller Co., Mfrs. Trust Co. of N.Y., Vertientes Canaguey Sugar Co. of Cuba. Mem. Mu Phi Alpha, Delta Upsilon. Republican. Presbyn. Clubs: Commercial (Chgo.); University, Delta Upsilon, Univ. of Pa., Recess, Metropolitan (N.Y.C.); Lake Placid (Lake Placid, N.Y.). Home: 1020 5th Av. Office: Pier 34, North River, N.Y.C. Died Aug. 14, 1955.

BLOSS, James Ramsdell (blōs), physician; b. Ceredo, W.Va., Sept. 5, 1881; s. Hiram Wesley and Carrie Lee (Ramsdell) B.; M.D., U. of Va., 1905; m. Garnett Lucille Coleman, Oct. 17, 1906 (died Feb. 11, 1930); m. 2d, Muessette A. Hollobaugh, July 14, 1932. Interne Chesapeake & Ohio Ry. Hosp., 1905; asst. supt. Huntington State Hosp. for the Insane, 1906-13; practiced at Huntington since 1913; obstetrician in charge of dept., C.&O. Hosp., Huntington; former lecturer on obstetrics for nurses, St. Mary's Hosp., mem. attending staff same (pres. 1934); visiting staff Memorial Hosp., Huntington. Editor W. Virginia Med. Journal, 1916-26, asst. editor, 1926-27, editor, 1927-37, editor emeritus since 1937; former examiner Mental Hygiene Commn., Cabell Co., W. Va. Med. examiner Selective Draft Bd., Huntington, World War I; patron Smithsonian Instn.; founder and sustaining mem. of United States Com. of the World Med. Assn. Diplomate Am. Bd. Obstetrics, Gynecology. F.A.C.S., Acad. Internat. Medicine, A.M.A. (house of delegates, 1920-35; trustee 1935-45; chairman sect. obstetrics and gynecology 1950). Am. Assn. Obstetricians, Gynecologists and Abdominal Surgeons (sec. 1936-47, pres. 1948-49), Am. Psychiatric Assn.; mem W. Va. Obstetric and Gynecol. Soc. (sec.-treas. 1936, pres. 1943), W.Va. State Med. Assn. (pres. 1926; chmn. maternal welfare com.), Southern Med. Assn. (mem. council 1932-38; chmn., 1935; vice chmn. sec. of obstetrics 1935, chmn 1936), Southern Assn. Ry. Surgeons, Chesapeake & Ohio Ry. Surgeons Assn., W.Va. Acad. Science. A.A.A.S., Am. Assn. Ry. Surgeons. Republican. Methodist. Home: 79 Kings Highway. Office: 418 11th St., Huntington, W.Va. Died Apr. 21, 1951; buried Ridgelawn Cemetery, Huntington, W.Va.

BLUCHER, Franz, German govt. ofcl.; b. Essen, Ruhr, Germany, Mar. 24, 1896; s. Franz and Anna Maria (Hegenkamp) B.; student German schs.; LL.D., Free U. Berlin, 1954, Punjab University (Lahore, Pakistan), 1957; married Paula Grosse-Frie, Feb. 9, 1925. Mgr. indsl. firms, 1922-26; mgr. Gemeinnuetziger Wohnungsbau, 1926-35; property custodian underground constrn., also dir. Arbeiterwohnungsbau, 1935-38; dir. banks, 1938-45; chmn. Zonen-Beirat, Brit. Zone, Germany, 1946. member first elected Landtag, North Rhine-Westphalia, 1947-49; mem. Bundestag, 1949—; mem. Econ. Council, 1947; member Bundestag, also federal minister for Marshall Plan, deputy federal chancellor, 1949—; German representative International Ruhr Authority, 1949-51; federal minister for economic cooperation, also deputy federal chancellor, 1953—. Co-founder Free Democratic Party, British Zone, 1945, chairman British Zone, 1945-55, deputy chairman United Free Democratic Party, 1948, chairman, 1949-55; cofounder Free People's Party, 1956. Served with German Army, 1914-20. Decorated Grand Cross Order of Merit, Federal Republic of Germany, Greek Grand Cross Order George I., Grand Cross Order of Merit, Italian Republic, Imperial Iranian Order of Homayun 1st Class; Order of Grosses Goldenes Ehrenzeichen am Bande (Austria); Order Condor de los Andes (Bolivia). Mem. German Group Liberal Internat. (pres. 1947-56). Office: Bad Godesberg-Rhein, Turmstrasse 48, Germany. Died Mar. 26, 1959.

BLUFORD, Ferdinand Douglas, coll. pres.; b. Capahosic, Va., Aug. 4, 1882; s. William Thomas and Alice (Stubbs) B.; student Wayland Acad., Richmond, Va., 1900-04; A.B., Va. Union U., 1908, hon. Pd.D., 1927; Pd.B., Howard U., 1909; student Columbia, 1923; m. Hazel Kirk Diffay, Nov. 24, 1910. Instr. English, Agrl. and Mech. Coll., Normal, Ala., 1909-10; instr. edn., Ky. State Coll., Frankfort, 1910-11; instr. English, St. Paul Normal and Industrial Sch., Lawrenceville, Va., 1911-12; prof. English, Agrl. and Tech. Coll., Greensboro, N.C., 1912-18, dean and v.p., 1918-25, pres. since 1925. Trustee Hayes-Taylor Memorial Y.M.C.A., Richardson Memorial Hosp., Windsor Community Center; mem. exec. com. Nat. War Fund for N. Carolina. Member Southern Regional Education Board, North Carolina Research Society, Assn. Am. Adminstrs., N.E.A., Am. Teachers Assn., Am. Acad. of Political and Social Science, Alpha Phi Alpha. Mason, Elk. Club: Faculty. Home: 1007 Lindsay St., Greensboro, N.C. Died Dec. 21, 1955; buried Piedmont Meml. Cemetery, Greensboro, N.C.

BLUM, Samuel J., educator; b. Salem, N.C., Apr. 2, 1849; s. John David and Amelia (Rothaas) B.; student and tchr. Nazareth (Pa.) Hall Mil. Acad., 1870-79; prepared for ministry under pvt. tutorage of Prof. John C. Brickenstein; D.D., Ursinus Coll., Collegeville, Pa., 1898; m. Louise Schneider (M.D.), Jan. 10, 1882. Ordained Moravian ministry, 1879; pastor 5th Ch., Phila., 1879-92, 1st Ch., York, Pa., 1892-7, prin. Nazareth Hall Mil. Acad., 1897—. Has traveled extensively in Egypt, Palestine, Syria and Greece. Address: Nazareth, Pa. Deceased.

BLUMENSCHEIN, Mary Shepard Greene (Mrs. E. L.), artist; b. N.Y.C.; d. Rufus and Mary Isabel (Shepard) Greene; Adelphi Acad. and Pratt Inst., Brooklyn; studied art under Raphael Collin, Paris, France; m. at Paris, Ernest L. Blumenschein, 1905; children—Ethan Allen (dec.), Helen Greene. Recipient 3d class medal Paris Salon, 1900, gold medal 2d class, 1902; silver medal St. Louis Expn., 1904; Julia Shaw prize, N.A.D., 1915; hon. mention Denver Art Mus., 1934. Represented in Bklyn. Mus. A.N.A., 1913. Address: Taos, N.M. Died May 24, 1958.

BLUMEYER, Arthur Adolphus, banker; b. St. Louis, Dec. 27, 1886; s. Conrad and Elizabeth (Spillman) B.; student pub. schs.; m. Ada Geisel, 1908; children—Ada Jane (Mrs. Sidney G. Holthaus), Mary Ann (Mrs. E. Wayne Weaver), Frank C., Estelle G. (Mrs. Wm. B. Gladney), Susan Antoinette (Mrs. Richard Fitz-Gibbon, Jr.), Arthur Adolphus. Chairman board of directors Bank of St. Louis; president of Industrial Loan Company, General Contract Corp., Washington Fire & Marine Ins. Co.; dir. M.P. R.R. Chmn. St. Louis Housing Authority. Treas. Lindenwood Coll., Nat. Found. Infantile Paralysis, St. Louis and St. Louis County. Presbyn. Home: 40 N. Kingshighway, St. Louis. Office: 901 Washington Av., St. Louis 1. Died June 26, 1959; buried Calvary Cemetery, St. Louis.

BLUNT, Katharine, coll. pres.; b. Phila., Pa., May 28, 1876; d. Stanhope English and Fanny (Smyth) Blunt; A.B., Vassar Coll., 1898; student Mass. Inst. Tech. 1902-03; Ph. D. in Chemistry, U. of Chicago, 1907; LL.D., Wesleyan U., 1936, Mt. Holyoke Coll., 1937, Conn. Coll., 1943. Asst. in chem., Vassar, 1903-05, instr., 1908-13; instr. chem., domestic sci. dept., Pratt Inst., Brooklyn, N.Y., 1907-08; asst. prof. home economics, U. of Chicago, 1913-18, asso. prof., 1918-25, prof. 1925-29, chmn. dept. informally, 1918-25, formally, 1925-29; pres. Conn. Coll. New London, 1929-43 and 1945-46. War work with U.S. Department Agr., Sept.-Dec. 1917, U.S. Food Admin., Jan.-June 1918. Trustee Russell Sage Coll., 1944-50. Formerly mem. Conn. State Bd. Edn., Ocean Beach Park Board (New London, Conn.). Chmn. New London Red Cross War Fund, 1944, 1945. Fellow A.A.A.S.; mem. Am. Home Economics Association (ex-pres.; mem. council), Biochem. Soc., Am. Chem. Soc., Nat. Edn. Assn., Am. Assn. Univ. Women, League of Women Voters (president, New London branch, 1947-51), Omicron Nu, Phi Beta Kappa, Sigma Xi. Clubs: Cosmopolitan (New York); College (Chicago and Boston). Part Author: Food and the War, 1918; Ultra-Violet Light and Vitamin D in Nutrition, 1930. Contbr. to jours. on edn. of women, home economics and biol. chemistry. Address: 38 Glenwood Av., New London, Conn. Died July 29, 1954.

BLY, Robert Stewart, college prof.; b. Deland, Fla., July 15, 1893; s. Egford and Samantha (Sproul) B.; student Stetson Acad., 1908-11; B.S., Stetson U., 1915; A.M., Columbia, 1916; Ph.D., Northwestern U., 1922; m. Otye Brown, Aug. 23, 1928; children—Robert Stewart, Allan Richard. Research chemist Roessler & Hasslacher Chem. Co., 1916-17, Fla. Wood Products Co., 1919; grad. asst. and fellow in chemistry, Northwestern U., 1919-22; research chemist Cutler-Hammer Co., 1922-23; chemist Cook Laboratories, Inc., 1923-24; head of chemistry dept., Fla. Southern Coll., Lakeland, since 1924. Mem. bd. examiners in basic scis., Fla. State, since 1943. Enlisted 30th Engrs., 1917; commd. 2d lt., 1918; hon. disch., 1918. Fellow Am. Inst. Chemists; mem. Am. Chem. Soc. (chmn. Fla. sect. 1929, councilor Fla., sect. 1937, 40), Fla. Acad. Science (Chmn. physical science div., 1944), Sigma Xi, Alpha Chi Sigma, Pi Gamma Mu, Gamma Sigma Epsilon. Author of articles on chemistry. Home: Lakeland, Fla. Died Aug. 24, 1958; buried Oakhill Cemetery, Lakeland, Fla.

BLYTH, Charles R., banker; b. Ashtabula, O., July 31, 1883; s. John S. and Frances G. (Reed) B.; student Roxbury Latin Sch., 1899-1901; B.S., Amherst, 1905; m. Marjorie Ramsay, Oct. 9, 1915 (died Mar. 27, 1923); children—Marjorie Blyth Bell, Barbara Blyth Coghlan; m. 2d, Katherine Ramsay, June 2, 1925; children—Katherine Ramsay, Charles Jr. With Am. Car & Foundry Co., 1906-07. Geo. H. Burr & Co., 1907-09, Louis Sloss & Co., 1910-14. Blyth, Witter & Co. (now Blyth & Co., Inc.), San Francisco, 1914—, pres., 1941—; dir. Crown Zellerbach Corp., Rayonier, Inc., Foster & Kleiser Co. V.p. San Francisco Opera Assn., San Francisco Symphony Assn. Trustee De Young Mus. Leland Stanford U., Palo Alto. Chmn. Liberty Loan drives, No. Cal. World War I. Chmn. San Francisco chpt. A.R.C., 1944-46; chmn. Victory Fund Com. San Francisco Dist.; pres. San Francisco War Chest, 1942, 1943. Trustee, Stanford Research Inst. Republican. Clubs: Recess, River, The Links, Amherst (New York);

Bohemian, Pacific Union, Stock Exchange (San Francisco); Burlingame Country (Burlingame, Cal.); California (Los Angeles). Home: Burlingame, Cal. Office: 2100 Russ Bldg., San Francisco, Cal. Died Aug. 25, 1959.

BLYTHE, Joseph L(ee), former Dem. nat. committeeman; b. Huntersville, N.C., Nov. 8, 1890; s. Richard Samuel and Virginia (Gamble) B.; grad. Huntersville (N.C.) High Sch., 1910; m. Cherrye High, Sept. 14, 1921 (dec. Apr. 1958); children—Martha (Mrs. Harold Richardson), Joseph Lee, Samuel, also Jane C. (Mrs. Claude L. Ives, Jr.). With Bell Telephone Co., 1910-13; entered construction work, 1913-17; in contracting bus., 1919; organized Blythe Bros. Co., 1922, now vice pres.; v.p. Charlotte Equipment Co.; pres. Piedmont Mop Co., 1st Fed. Savings and Loan Corp., Charlotte, N.C. became N.C. State senator, 1938; apptd. Dem. nat. committeeman, June 1947; treas. Dem. Nat. Com., 1948. Served as master engr., sr. grade, Co. B, 105th Engrs., Corps of Engrs., 1917-19. Mem. bd. dirs. Charlotte C. of C.; mem. nat. council Boy Scouts of Am. Mem. Am. Legion, Mecklenburg Hist. Soc. (pres.). Democrat. Home: 2238 Pinewood Circle. Office: 2911 Hutchison Av., Charlotte, N.C. Died Jan. 23, 1949.

BLYTHIN, Edward (bli'thin), judge Ct. Common Pleas; b. Newmarket, N. Wales, Oct. 10, 1884; s. Peter and Elizabeth (Roberts) B.; student elementary sch., Newmarket, Wales, and Rhyl (Wales) Intermediate Sch.; LL.B., Cleve. Law Sch., Baldwin-Wallace Coll., Berea, O., 1916, LL.D., 1941; LL.D., Baldwin-Wallace Coll., 1944; m. Jane Rankin, Apr. 5, 1913; children—Robert, Arthur, Glenn (dec.), Jane (Mrs. Robert Drake), William. Came to U.S., 1906, naturalized, 1911. Bookkeeper with Eng. coal firm, 1904-06, real estate firm, Cleve., 1906-16; engaged in practice of law, Cleve., 1916-41, 42-43; asst. dir. of law, City Cleve., 1935-40, dir., 1940; mayor of Cleve., 1941; financial v.p., sec., office counsel Western Res. U., 1943-48; chmn. bd. Shaker Savs. Assn. Mem. Cleve. Transit Bd., 1943-48; judge, Ct. Common Pleas, Cuyahoga Co., O., 1949—. Mem. bd. trustees Baldwin-Wallace Coll. Mem. Delta Theta Phi. Mason (33°, Shriner). Club: City (ex-pres., Cleve.). Home: 10000 Ridgewood Drive, Parma Heights, Cleve. 30. Office: Court House, Cleve. Died Feb. 14, 1958.

BOARDMAN, Charles Willis, educator; b. Des Moines, Dec. 10, 1885; s. Charles Parsons and Florence Adele (Banker) B.; Ph.B., Grinnell College, 1908; M.A., Columbia, 1925, Ph.D., 1928; m. Exene Taft, Aug. 10, 1910 (dec. Apr. 30, 1931); 1 dau., Anne Ryan (Mrs. Harold E. Quesner); m. 2d Anne Cawley, June 30, 1934. Pub. sch. instr. and prin., Ia., 1909-11; instr. Central High Sch., Mpls., 1911-16, asst. prin., 1916-21; prin. West High School, Mpls., 1922-24; prin. lab. sch. U. Minn., 1924-28, dir. student teaching, 1924-31, asso. prof., 1928-31, prof. edn., 1931-54, emeritus; prof. edn. St. Thomas Coll., St. Paul Coll., 1954—; visiting prof. summer school, U. New Hampshire, 1940, U. Who., 1950, Utah State Agrl. Coll., 1951; writer, cons. Information and Edn. Div. U.S. Armed Forces. Recipient distinguished service award U. Minn., 1959. Mem. Nat., Minn. edn. assns., Nat. Soc. Coll. Tchrs. Edn., Am. Assn. U. Profs., Nat. Assn. Secondary Sch. Prins., Am. Ednl. Research Assn., Nat. Soc. Study Edn., North Central Assn. Colls. and Secondary Schs. (chmn. commn. on secondary schs. 1946-48, pres. 1949-50, sec. since 1951), Phi Delta Kappa. Author: Supervision in Secondary Schs. (with Harl R. Douglass), 1934; Out-of-School Youth in Red Wing, 1945; Democratic Supervision in Secondary Schools (with Harl K. Douglas, R. K. Bent), 1953. Contbr. The Armed Forces and Your Life Plans; also articles profl. jours. Home: 4379 Glenn Pl., Mpls. 24. Office: 106 Burton Hall, U. Minn., Mpls. 14. Died Nov. 23, 1959.

BOARDMAN, Harry Clow, civil engr.; b. Plainfield, Ill., Apr. 29, 1887; s. George Bates and Mary (Clow) B.; B.S., U. Ill., 1910, C.E., 1926; D.Eng. (hon.), S.D. Sch. Mines, 1943; m. Bessie McCumber, May 27, 1923. Draftsman Chgo. Bridge & Iron Co., 1910-16, research engr., 1926—, dir. research, 1945—; engaged automobile tire and accessory bus., Kansas City, Mo., 1919-22; engr., supt. constrn. Internat. Filter Co., Chgo., 1922-24; instr. civil engring. U. Ill., 1924-26. Vice chmn. welding research council Engring. Found., 1949, chmn., 1949-52. Served from pvt. to corpl. N.G., lt. to maj. F.A., U.S. Army, 1917-19. Mem. Am. Welding Soc. (past pres.), Western Soc. Engrs., Am. Soc. C.E., Am. Soc. Metals, A.S.M.E. (chmn. boiler and pressure vessel com.), Am. Soc. Testing Materials, A.A.A.S., Am. Petroleum Inst., Sigma Xi, Tau Beta Pi. Home: 5050 East End Av. Office: 1305 W. 105th St., Chgo. Died Aug. 6, 1956.

BOARMAN, Aleck, judge; b. at Yazoo City, Miss., Dec. 10, 1839; s. I. A. and Martha (Thompson) B.; attended schs. at Shreveport, La., and Ky. Mil. Coll.; m. Frances I. Capen, Nov. 29, 1898. Served from Manassas to Appomattox in C.S.A. in Va. as maj. on staff in the field. Admitted to bar, 1866, and practiced at Shreveport, La.; elected 42d Congress, 1872; judge Dist. Ct. of La., 1876-80; U.S. district judge, Western Dist. of La., 1881—. Republican. Address: Shreveport, La. Died 1916.

BOAS, Ernst Philip (bo'ăs), physician; b. Worcester, Mass., Feb. 4, 1891; s. Franz and Marie (Krackowizer) B.; B.S., Columbia, 1910, M.A., 1912, M.D., 1914; m. Helen T. Sisson, Dec. 25, 1917; children—Donald Philip, Norman Francis, Barbara Gertrud. Instr. in pathology Coll. Phys. and Surg. (Columbia), 1917, instr. in physiology, 1920-21; med. dir. Montefiore Hosp., 1921-29; post-grad. tchr. diseases of the heart Columbia, 1926—, asst. clin. prof. of medicine, 1938-51; cons. physician Mt. Sinai Hosp.; asso. editor Modern Hosp., 1923-29; attending physician Montefiore Hosp., 1929-30; asso. physician Mt. Sinai Hosp. Capt. Med. R.C., 1917-19, chief of med. service Base Hosp. 63, AEF. Chmn. Physicians Forum for Study of Med. Care. Mem. A.M.A., Soc. for Clin. Investigation, Harvey Soc., N.Y. Acad. Med., Am., N.Y. heart assns., Phi Beta Kappa, Alpha Omega Alpha. Democrat. Author: The Challenge of Chronic Diseases (with Nicholas Michelson), 1929; The Heart Rate, 1932; The Unseen Plague Chronic Diseases, 1940; Treatment of the Patient Past Fifty, 1941, 2d edit., 1944, 3d edit., 1947; Coronary Artery Disease, 1949. Writer on diseases of heart and problems of med. care. Home: Nod Hill Rd., Wilton, Conn. Died Mar. 9, 1955.

BOATRIGHT, Byron B(lackburn) (bōt'rit) cons. petroleum engr.; b. Colorado Springs, February 10, 1900; s. William Louis and Minnie Ellen (Stump) B.; E.M., Colo. Sch. of Mines, 1922; Ph.D., U. of Colo., 1936; m. Sylva Dora Kerr, Mar. 10, 1922; children—Barbara Jeanne (Mrs. H. P. Oliver), William Gary (dec.). Flagman survey party, U.S. Gen. Land Office, 1919; rouster, fireman, and tool-dresser Midwest Refining Co., Big Muddy and Salt Creek Fields, Wyo., 1922-25; jr. engr., asst. engr. and later asso. engr. in charge oil and gas leasing div. U.S. Geol. Survey, state of Colo., 1925-26; dist. engr. Panhandle Dist., Marland Oil Co., 1926-28; head petroleum engring. dept. and prof. prodn. engring., Colo. Sch. Mines, 1928-37; cons. petroleum and natural gas engr., Golden, Colo., 1928-37; partner Parker Foran, Knode & Boatright (cons. engrs.), Houston, Tex., 1937-40, Foran, Knode, Boatright & Dixon, 1940-41, Foran, Boatright & Dixon, 1941-45, Boatright & Mitchell (cons. engrs. and geologists), 1945-46; vice pres. and chief engr. Republic Natural Gas Co., Dallas, Tex., 1946-48; 1st vice pres. Conroe Drilling Co., Austin, Tex., 1948-49, dir. 1949; gen. supt. Heep Oil Corp., Austin, Tex. 1948-49; consulting petroleum and natural gas engineer, 1949-53; v.p., gen. mgr., dir. Houston Natural Gas Producing Co., 1953—. Served with reserve force, U.S. Navy, 1918-19; 2d lt. 9th engrs. reserve U.S. Army, 1930-35. Registered engr., Tex. Mem. Am. Inst. Mining and Mech. Engrs., Am. Petroleum Inst., Sigma Xi, Theta Tau, Sigma Phi Epsilon, Blue Key, Kappa Kappa Psi. Republican. Episcopalian. Mason (Shriner). Clubs: Petroleum Engineers (Dallas, Tex.), Houston, Ramada (Houston). Contbr. articles to tech. jours. Home: 11315 Smithdale Rd. Office: Capitol Petroleum Bldg., Houston. Died May 9, 1957; buried Crown Hill, Denver.

BOATWRIGHT, Frederic William (bōt'rit), chancellor; b. White Sulphur Springs, W.Va., Jan. 28, 1868; s. Rev. Reuben Baker and Elizabeth (Woodruff) B.; A.B., A.M., Richmond (Va.) Coll., 1888; student Halle, Leipzig, Paris, 1889-90, 1892; LL.D., Mercer, 1896, Georgetown Coll., 1913, Baylor U., 1920, U. of Richmond, 1946; L.H.D., Med. Coll. of Va., 1945; m. Nellie Moore Thomas, Dec. 23, 1890; children—Frederic (dec.), Evelyn Moore. Prof. modern langs. 1890-1946, president, 1894-1946, University of Richmond, chancellor since 1946. President board of trustees Averett College, Danville, Va.; dir. State-Planter's Bank. Pres. Gen. Assn. of Va. Baptists, 1937-39. Mem. Phi Beta Kappa, Phi Kappa Sigma, Omicron Delta Kappa. Mem. Rotary, Kiwanis. Author: Syllabi French and German Literatures, 1894; Education in Richmond, 1937. Address: University of Richmond P.O., Va. Died Oct. 31, 1951; buried Hollywood Cemetery, Richmond, Va.

BOBB, Clyde S., surgeon; b. Richland Center, Wis., Oct. 28, 1876; s. Martin L. and Mary Jane (Wulfing) B.; grad. S.D. Normal Sch., 1897; M.D., Barnes U. Med. Dept., St. Louis, 1905; m. Emma B. Haynes, 1906; children—Margaret, Eleanor, Edward, Charles. Practiced at Mitchell, S.D., 1905—; mem. firm Drs. Bobb & Bobb. Mem. S.D. Senate, 1914, 15. Mem. Am., S.D., Mitchell Dist. (sec. 5 yrs.), Sioux Valley, So. Minn. med. socs., S.D. Holiness Assn. (pres. 1911—). Republican. Methodist. Woodman. Home: Mitchell, S.D. Died Oct. 16, 1957; buried Graceland Cemetery, Mitchell.

BOBB, Earl Victor, physician; b. Richland Center, Wis., Aug. 2, 1874; s. Martin L. B.; M.D., Northwestern U., 1899; m. Elizabeth Morton, Sept. 25, 1900; children—Phyllis Marie, Dorothy Lillian, Bernard Earl. Began practice at Mitchell, S.D., 1899, specializing eye, ear, nose and throat, San Marino, Cal. Mayor of Mitchell, 1920-24. Mem. A.M.A., S.D. State Med. Assn., Am. Acad. Ophthalmology and Oto-Laryngology, Sioux Valley Eye and Ear Acad. Republican. Methodist. Rotarian. Home: San Marino, Cal. Died Mar. 4, 1939; buried Forest Lawn Cemetery.

BOBBITT, Franklin, educator; b. Southern Ind., Feb. 16, 1876; A.B., Ind. U., 1901; Ph.D., Clark U., 1909; m. Mabel Deiwert. Rural and village tchr., 1893-1902, Philippine Normal Sch., Manila 1902-07; with U. Chgo., 1909-56, prof. edn., 1918-41, prof. emeritus, 1941—; dir. sch. surveys. Specialist in curriculum. Author: What Schools Teach and Might Teach, 1916; The Curriculum, 1918; Curriculum-Making in Los Angeles, 1922; How to Make a Curriculum, 1924; The Curriculum of Modern Education, 1941. Address: Waldron, Ind. Died Mar. 7, 1956; buried Clarksburg, Ind.

BOCOCK, John Holmes, lawyer; b. Hampden-Sidney, Va., Sept. 3, 1890; s. Willis Henry and Bessie (Friend) B.; A.B., U. Ga., 1910; LL.B., U Va, 1915; m Elisabeth Strother Scott, May 3, 1928; children—Bessie (Mrs. Robert Carter), Frederic Scott, Mary Buford. Admitted to Va. bar, 1915, since practiced in Richmond; sr. partner McGuire, Eggleston, Bocock & Woods 1947—; spl. lectr. law U. Va., 1952-55; dir. First & Mchts. Nat. Bank of Richmond, others. Served as 1st lieutenant, United States Army, 1917-19, maj., 1942-45. Decorated Croix de Guerre with palm (France). Mem. Am., Va. State, Richmond bar assns., Phi Beta Kappa. Clubs: Commonwealth (Richmond); Union (N.Y. City). Home: 909 W. Franklin St., Richmond 20. Office: Mutual Bldg., Richmond 19, Va. Died Aug. 14, 1958.

BODE, Boyd Henry (bo'da), educator; b. Ridott, Ill., Oct. 4, 1873; s. Henry and Gertrude (Weinenga) B.; Yankton (S.D.) Coll.; A.B., Penn Coll., 1896; A.B., U. Mich., 1897, LL.D., 1932, Ohio State U., 1948; Ph.D., Cornell, 1900; m. Bernice Ballard, August 20, 1903; children—Hendrik Wade, Eleanor. Asst. in philosophy U. Wis., 1900-02, instr., 1902-06, asst. prof. philosophy, 1906-09; prof. philosophy U. Ill., 1909-21; prof. edn. Ohio State U., 1921-44, prof. emeritus, 1944; vis. prof. Inst. Edn., Cairo, Egypt, 1944-45. Mem. Am., Western (pres. 1913-14) philos. assns., Phi Beta Kappa and Phi Delta Kappa. Author: An Outline of Logic, 1910; Fundamentals of Education, 1921; Modern Educational Theories, 1927; Conflicting Psychologies of Learning, 1929; Democracy As a Way of Life, 1937; Progressive Education at the Crossroads, 1938; How We Learn, 1940. Joint Author: Creative Intelligence, 1917; Ourselves and the World (Lumbley and Bode), 1931; The Educational Frontier, 1933; American Philosophy Today and Tomorrow, 1935. Contbr. on philos. and ednl. subjects to various publs. Home: 727 S.W. 27th St., Gainesville, Fla. Died Mar. 29, 1953; buried Gainesville.

BODELL, Joseph James (bō-dĕl'), investment banker; b. Pawtucket, R.I., Oct. 21, 1881; s. Joseph and Mary Ann (Bullen) B.; ed. under pvt. tutors; m. Marie Christine Cozzens, Oct. 29, 1917; children—Joseph James Jr., Marguerite Ann (Mrs. Gordon L. Wheeler), Jean Bullen (Mrs. Vincent R. Bailey), Mary Sloane (dec.), Stanley Cozzens. Sr. partner Bodell & Co., Providence; director Investors Trust Company; director of American Textile Company., Inc.; dir. The James Hanley Co. Mem. Providence Housing Authority. Mem. Am. Geog. Soc., Bibliophile Soc., R.I. Hist. Soc., Athenaeum. Episcopalian. Mason. Clubs: University, Turks Head, Providence Art (Providence); Wianno, Squantum Association, Rhode Island Country, St. Bernard Fish and Game. Union League (New York). Home: 61 Intervale Rd. Office: 1902 Industrial Trust Bldg., Providence 3, R.I. Died June 30, 1950.

BODENHEIM, Maxwell, author; b. Hermanville, Miss., May 26, 1895; s. Solomon W. and Caroline (Herman) B.; self educated; m. Minna Schein, Nov. 22, 1918. Poetry, essays and poetic plays. Author: Minna and Myself, 1918; Advice, 1920; Introducing Irony, 1922; The Sardonic Arm, 1923; Blackguard, 1923; Crazy Man, 1924; The King of Spain, 1924; Replenishing Jessica, 1925; Against This Age, 1925; Ninth Avenue, 1926; Returning to Emotion, 1927; Georgi May, 1928; King of Spain, 1928; Sixty Seconds, 1929; Bringing Jazz, 1930; Virtuous Girl, 1930; Naked on Roller Skates, 1931; Duke Herring, 1931; Six A.M., 1932; New York Madness, 1932; Run Sheep Run, 1932. Address: care of Liveright Pub. Corp., 386 4th Av., N.Y.C. 16. Died Feb. 7, 1954.

BODINE, Joseph Hall (bō-dēn), prof. zoology; b. Lake Hopatcong, N.J., Sept. 19, 1895; s. Gilbert and Sarah Annie (Hall) B.; A.B., U. of Pa., 1915, Ph.D., 1920; m. Sarah Olivia Heimach, Nov. 19, 1919 (dec. June 1950); 1 son, Joseph Hall; m. 2d, Eunice Willis Beardsley, June 1951. Instr. zoölogy, U. of Pa., 1915-16 and 1920-25, asst. prof., 1925-28, prof., 1928-29; prof. and head dept. zoölogy, U. of Ia., 1929—. Served in Med. Corps, A.E.F., World War. Chmn. scientific advisory com., Biol. Lab., Cold Spring Harbor, N.Y.; mem. exec. com. div. of agr. and biology, 1933-34, vice-chmn. of div., 1934-35, Nat. Research Council; mem. Ia. Basic Sci. Bd., 1935-50; mem. Nat. Research Council Fellowship Bd., 1941. Mem. Atomic Energy Commn. Fellowship Bd.,

1948-—. Director, Iowa Lakeside Laboratory, 1932-—. Fellow A.A.A.S. (sec. sect. F, 1948-51; rep. Am. Physiol. Soc. 1948-49); mem. Am. Assn. Zoologists (v.p. 1933-34, pres. 1947, mem. exec. com. 1948-52), Nat. Acad. Scis., Am. Physiol. Soc., Soc. Exptl. Biol. and Med., Am. Soc. Naturalists (v.p. 1938, pres. 1940), Am. Micro. Soc., Am. Assn. Univ. Profs, Sigma Xi, Gamma Alpha. Mason. Club: Triangle. Mem. editorial bd. Physiol. Zoölogy; asso. editor, Jour. Morphology, Am. Naturalists. Home: Pinehurst, R.R. 2, Iowa City, Ia. Died July 23, 1954; buried Oakland Cemetery, Iowa City.

BODINE, Joseph Lamb, judge; b. Trenton, N.J., Nov. 6, 1883; s. Joseph L. (M.D.) and Frances P. (Davis) B.; A.B., Princeton, 1905; LL.B., Harvard, 1908; m. Gertrude Scudder, Dec. 24, 1918; 1 son, John W. Began practice at Trenton, 1908; U.S. dist. atty., Dist. of N.J., 1919-20; U.S. dist. judge, same dist., 1920-29; justice N.J. Supreme Court, 1929-48; under revised N.J. constitution then became judge N.J. Superior Court; retired Nov. 24, 1948. Trustee Trenton Jr. Coll. Mem. N.J. and Am. bar assns., Am. Law Inst. Democrat. Presbyn. Home: 455 W. State St., Trenton, N.J. Died June 10, 1950; buried Lawrenceville (N.J.) Cemetery.

BODINE, Samuel Louis (bo dine), mem. Rep. Nat. Com.; b. Pittstown, N.J., Jan. 22, 1899; s. Amplius B.C. and Ellen Schenk (Hoagland) B.; student Lafayette Coll.; m. Ida Stryker, July 6, 1932; 1 son, Samuel Tony. Pres. Bodine Lumber Co., Flemington, N.J.; dir. Hunterdon County Nat. Bank. Mayor of Flemington, 2 terms; freeholder Hunterdon County, 2 terms; state senator, N.J., 1943-53, (chmn. appropriations com., pres. of senate); Republican chmn. N.J. State Com.; now mem. Rep. Nat. Com. Vice pres. Hunterdon Med. Center; dir. Prospect Hill Cemetery. Mem. Am. Legion (past post comdr.), Alpha Chi Rho. Mason, Rotarian. Home: Shellbark, Flemington, N.J. Died Sept. 15, 1958; buried Prospect Hill Cemetery, Flemington.

BODINE, William Budd (bō-dēn'), lawyer; b. Balt., May 4, 1869; s. William Budd and Rachel Alice (Allen) B.; A.B., Kenyon Coll., 1890, LL.D., 1936; B.L., U. Pa., 1896. Admitted to Pa. bar, 1896; mem. firm Pepper, Bodine, Stokes & Hamilton (formerly Henry, Pepper, Bodine & Pepper). Mem. Am., Pa., Phila. bar assns., Sharswood Law Club (U. Pa.), Alpha Delta Phi. Club: Rittenhouse (Phila.). Home: Pigeon Run Farm, Charlestown Twp., Chester County, Pa. Office: Land Title Bldg., Phila. 10. Died Nov. 30, 1955.

BODINE, William Warden, bus. exec.; b. Phila., Oct. 18, 1887; s. Samuel T. and Eleanor Gray (Warden) B.; student Episcopal Acad., Phila., and St. Pauls Sch., Concord, N.H.; A.B., Harvard Coll., 1909; LL.B., U. Pa. Law Sch., 1914; m. Angela R. Forney, Apr. 29, 1915. Chmn. bd. Penn Mut. Life Ins. Co. Home: Oakwell, Villanova, Pa. Office: S.E. cor. 6th & Walnut Sts., Phila. 5. Died Sept. 18, 1959; buried West Laurel Hill Cemetery, Bala-Cynwyd, Pa.

BODMAN, Ernest James, investments; b. Warsaw, Ind., Dec. 25, 1875; s. Samuel Luther and Elizabeth (Boyce) B.; educated public schools, Memphis, Tenn.; m. Mary H. Wright, Oct. 26, 1904: children—Samuel W., Anne Caroline (Mrs. John E. Coates). With Union Trust Co., Little Rock, 1904-33, exec. v.p., 1920-33; formerly pres. White & Black River R.R.; dir. San Antonio Southern Railroad (M.P. Lines); investments as E. J. Bodman & Company, Little Rock, Arkansas, since 1933. Major O.R.C., Q.M. Dept. Was chmn. Ark. Profitable Farming Bureau, Ark. Chamber Commerce; chmn. agrl. com. of Ark. Bankers Assn., 1915-33; mem. Agrl. Commn. of Am. Bankers Assn. and U.S. C. of C. One of 5 judges of Internat. Harvester Co. $50,000 scholarship contest for 4-H Clubs, 1931. Former trustee U. Ark. Mem. Little Rock Chamber of Commerce. Episcopalian. Clubs: Little Rock, Oklahoma, Oklahoma City, Civitan (pres., 1931). Author: (brochure) Farm Profits and Education, 1922. Home: 2118 N. Palm St. Office: 305 Center St., Little Rock, Ark. Died Apr. 9, 1958.

BOEING, William Edward (bō'ing); b. Detroit, Mich., Oct. 1, 1881; s. Wilhelm and Marie (Ortman) B.; student Sheffield Scientific Sch. (Yale), 1899-1902; LL.D., State College of Washington, 1947; married Bertha Potter Paschall, Sept. 27, 1921; 1 son, William Edward, Jr. Instructed in flying by Glen L. Martin; founded Boeing Airplane Co., 1916. Awarded Daniel Guggenheim medal for the year 1934, "for successful pioneering and achievement in aircraft manufacturing and air transport." In U.S. Navy, World War; lieutenant (jr. grade) U.S.N.R.F. Retired. King County Airport, Seattle, named Boeing Field, 1928; recipient award for econ. statesmanship Seattle U., 1955. Clubs: Seattle Yacht; Royal Vancouver Yacht; Pacific Union (San Francisco); Chicago (Chicago); California (Los Angeles); Links (N.Y.); Rainier (Seattle). Home: Aldarra Farms, Fall City, Wash. Office: 1411 Fourth Av., Seattle 1. Died Sept. 28, 1956.

BOESCHENSTEIN, Charles (běsh'ěn-stīn), banker, publisher; b. Madison County, Ill., Oct. 27, 1862; ed. Washington Univ.; m. Bertha Whitbread, Nov. 11, 1892; children—Harold, Charles K., Eleanore (Mrs. Frank Godfrey). Pub. Herald, Highland, Ill., 1881-83, Intelligencer, Edwardsville, Ill., 1883-1916; organized Edwardsville Water Co., 1897, vice-pres. and treas. to 1917; dir. Madison County State Bank, 1897-99, Bank of Edwardsville, 1889-1907 (vice president, 1901-02; organized Edwardsville Nat. Bank & Trust Co., 1917, since pres.; dir. National Credit Corp., St. Louis District, Reconstrn. Finance Corp.; mem. Ill. Emergency Relief Commn., 1934-36. Pres. Ill. Press Assn., 1898-99, Edwardsville Pub. Library, 1903-37, Madison Co. Centennial Assn., 1912. Mayor Edwardsville, 1887-89; Dem. State Central Com., 1900-12 (chmn. 1904-12); Dem. Nat. Com., 1912-24; Dem. nominee U.S. Senator, 1913; del. Dem. Convs., 1908-40. Home: Edwardsville, Ill. Died July 3, 1952.

BOETTCHER, Claude Kedzie, business exec.; b. Boulder, Colo., June 10, 1875; s. Charles and Fannie A. (Cowan) B.; grad. Harvard, 1897; m. De Allan McMurtrie, Jan. 29, 1900; 1 son, Charles; m. 2d Edna Case McElveen, Jan. 10, 1920. Partner Boettcher & Co. since 1910; pres. Cement Investors, Inc., Boettcher Realty Co., Boettcher Corp., Brown Palace Hotel, Gen. Securities Co., Ideal Corp.; v.p. or pres. Ideal Cement Co., 1925-52, now chmn. bd.; chairman board of directors American Crystal Sugar Co., Potash Co. of America. Member board trustees chmn. bd. Boettcher Found.; trustee Colo. Mus. Natural History; adv. com. Children's Hosp., Denver. Mem. Pi Eta. Republican. Episcopalian. Clubs: Denver, Country, Cherry Hills Country, Cherry Hills Saddle (Denver); Cooking, Pikes Peak Trails (Colorado Springs, Colo.); Harvard, Racquet, The Brook (N.Y.C.); Everglades, Bath and Tennis, Seminole Golf (Fla.). Home: 400 E. 8th Av. Office: 828 17th St., Denver 2. Died June 9, 1957.

BOETTIGER, John (bŏt'ĭ-ger), newpaper man; b. Chgo., Mar. 25, 1900; s. Adam Charles and Dorothy (Ott) B.; grad. high sch., Chgo., 1918; m. Anna Roosevelt Dall, Jan. 18, 1935. With City News Bur., Chgo., 1921-22, Chgo. Evening American, 1922-23; on staff Chgo. Tribune, 1924-34, asst. Washington corr., 1933-34; asst. to pres. Motion Picture Producers & Distributors of Am., Inc., 1934-36; pub. Seattle Post-Intelligencer, 1936-45; editor, pub. Arizona Times, Phoenix, 1947-48. Served in USN, 1918-19; lt. col. U.S. Army, 1943-45. Decorated Legion of Merit with oak leaf cluster; bronze arrowhead for combat. D-Day landings in Sicily and Italy. Author: Jake Lingle, 1939. Died Oct. 29, 1950.

BOEYNAEMS, Libert Hubert John Louis, bishop; b. Antwerp, Belgium, Aug. 18, 1857; s. John and Leopoldina (Van Opstal) B.; ed. Jesuit Coll., Antwerp, sem. at Mechlin, and Sem. of Missions, Louvain, Belgium; ordained R.C. priest, Sept. 11, 1881. Went to Honolulu, Hawaii, 1881, in charge of missions on Island of Kauai, 1882-95, at Wailuku, Maui, 1895-1902; pro-vicar of mission of Hawaii, 1902-3; apptd. bishop of Zeugma and vicar apostolic of Hawaii, Apr. 6, 1903, consecrated, San Francisco, July 25, 1903. Address: 1183 Fort St., Honolulu, Hawaii. Died May 13, 1926; buried Honolulu.

BOGART, Ernest Ludlow (bō'gärt), educator; b. Yonkers, N.Y., Mar. 16, 1870; s. Richard Walker and Mary (De Angelis) B.; A.B., Princeton, 1890, A.M., 1896; Ph.D., U. Halle, Germany, 1897; m. Stella Marshall, Sept. 15, 1900; children—Eleanor Walker (Mrs. Lewis S. Pilcher, II), Philip Schuyler. Asst. prof. economics and social science Ind. U., 1898-1900; prof. econs. Oberlin Coll., 1900-05; asst. prof. econs. Princeton, 1905-09; prof. econs. U. Ill., 1909-—, head dept., 1920-—; prof. banking and finance Georgetown Sch. Fgn. Service, 1919-20; prof. econs. Claremont Coll., 1929-30, N.Y.U., 1941-46, summers Columbia, 1917, 18, U. Cal., 1924, U. Tex., 1927, U. So. Cal., 1930; mem. Com. on Pub. Information, 1918. In charge commodity studies, bureau of research War Trade Board, 1918; regional economist Fgn. Trade Adviser's Office, Dept. State, 1919-20; adviser on currency and banking to govt. of Persia, 1922-23; mem. adv. com. Nat. Econ. League, 1920-—; chmn. com. on congestion of Port of Havana, 1920; del. Dept. of State to Conv. Fgn. Trade Council, 1920; mem. adv. com. Stable Money Assn., 1929-—; mem. com. on monetary policy U.S. C. of C., 1933; mem. Gov's. Commn. on Unemployment, 1933; mem. Economists' Nat. Monetary Commn., 1934-—; treas. Citizens Conf. on Internat. Econ. Union, 1943. Am. corr. Revue de Science et de Législation financière. Conglist. Mem. Am. Econ. Assn. (v.p. 1918; exec. com. 1929-31; pres. 1931), Am. Assn. U. Profs., Econometric Soc., Econ. History Soc. (trustee 1944-47), Nat. Park Assn., Phi Beta Kappa, Beta Gamma Sigma, Pi Gamma Mu, Delta Sigma Pi, Phi Kappa Epsilon. Clubs: University (exec. com. 1925-28, pres. 1929-30), Century (N.Y.C.); Faculty (Columbia U.), Faculty (N.Y.U.), Andiron (pres. 1945-47). Author: The Finances of the American States, 1897; Housing of Working People of Yonkers, 1898; Economic History of the United States, 1907, 5th edition, 1938; Business Economics, 1910; Financial History of Ohio, 1912; Readings on the Economic History of the United States (with C. M. Thompson), 1915; Centennial History of Illinois (with J. M. Mathews and C. M. Thompson), 1918; Direct and Indirect Costs of the Great World War, 1919; War Costs and Their Financing, 1921; Economic History of Agriculture of U.S., 1923; Internal Improvements in Ohio, 1924; Modern Industry, 1927, revised edit., 1936; Econ. Hist. of the Am. People, 1930, 4th edit., 1947; The Young Plan and Other Papers, 1931; The Water Problem of Southern Calif., 1934; Econ. Hist. of Europe, 1760-1939, 1942; (Italian translation, 1947); Peacham: The Story of a Vermont Hill Town, 1947. Editor: University of Illinois Studies in the Social Sciences; general editor Longman's Economic Series. Home: 25 W. 10th St., N.Y.C. 11. Died Nov. 4, 1958; buried Boston.

BOGART, Humphrey DeForest, actor, producer; b. N.Y.C., December 25, 1899; s. Belmont DeForest and Maud (Humphrey) B.; grad. Trinity Sch., N.Y. City, 1916; student Andover (Mass.) Sch.; m. Lauren Bacall, May 21, 1945; children—Stephen, Leslie. Stage plays: Meet the Wife, Cradle Snatchers, Saturday's Children, Petrified Forest; motion pictures: Petrified Forest, Maltese Falcon, High Sierra, Casablanca, To Have and Have Not, Conflict, The Big Sleep, The African Queen (awarded Oscar for performance), Treasure of the Sierra Madre (most recent) Caine Mutiny, Sabrina, Barefoot Contessa. Served with United States Navy, 1918. Clubs: Players, Coffee House (New York); Los Angeles Yacht; Newport Harbor Yacht; Balboa Yacht; Lakeside Golf. Address: 6363 Wilshire Blvd., Los Angeles. Died Jan. 14, 1957; buried Forest Lawn Meml. Park.

BOGERT, Marston Taylor, chemist; b. Flushing, N.Y., Apr. 18, 1868; s. Henry A. and Mary B. (Lawrence) B.; A.B., Columbia, 1890, Ph.B., 1894, Sc. D., 1929; LL.D., Clark U., 1909; R.N.D., Charles U. (Prague); m. Charlotte E. Hoogland, Sept. 12, 1893; children—Annette B. (Mrs. Frank B. Tallman), Elise B. (Mrs. F. K. Huber). Asst. organic chemistry, 1894-97, tutor, 1897, instr., 1897-1901, adj. prof., 1901-04, prof., 1904-39, emeritus prof. in residence since 1939; mem. Univ. Council, 1909-11, 1916-17, and 1922-29, Columbia; also rep. Columbia U. on bd. trustees N.Y. Coll. of Pharmacy, 1930-36. Lecturer organic chemistry, New York U., 1919-20. Mem. Am. Advisory Com. of Honor 7th Internat. Congress of Applied Chemistry, London, 1909; pres. Organic Sect., 8th Internat. Congress Applied Chemistry, Washington, D.C., and New York, 1912, chmn. com. of presidents of sections of same and v. chmn. exec. com. of same; by invitation of President Roosevelt, mem. of White House Conf. on Conservation of Natural Resources, May 1908; also of the following Conf. with Governors of States and Tys., Washington, D.C., Dec. 1908; mem. Internat. Com. in Honor of Amedeo Avogadro, under patronage of King Victor Emmnaul III of Italy; del. of U.S. Govt. and Nat. Research Council and pres. sect. on chemistry and nat. defense, X. Internat. Congress Chemistry, Rome, 1938; pres. Internat. Union Chemistry, 1938-47. Fellow A.A.A.S., London Chemical Soc., Royal Soc. of Edinburgh (hon.). Member Assn. chimica Italiana, Société Chimique de Paris, Nederland Chem. Ver., Swiss Chemists' Society American Institute Chemists (medalist for 1935-36), Am. Chem. Society (ex-pres.; Nichols medal, 1905; Priestley medal, 1938); hon. mem. Soc. Chem. Industry Eng. (ex-pres.), Chemists Club (ex-pres.), Nat. Acad. Sciences (chmn. chem. sect., 1926-29), Washington Acad. Scis., N.Y. Acad. Scis., Am. Philos. Soc., Am. Acad. Arts and Sciences, Am. Assn. Univ. Profs. (pres. Columbia U. chapter 1932-37), Phi Beta Kappa, Delta Phi, Sigma Xi (councilor 1904; pres. Columbia Chapter, 1906, 1933-37), Phi Lambda Upsilon, Alpha Chi Sigma, Alumni Assn. Graduate Schs., Columbia Unv. (pres. 1935-37; recipient of its Large Scroll 1936); hon. mem. Chemists' Soc. of Poland, Royal Soc. Sciences and Letters (Bohemia), Société de Chimie Industrielle de France (pres. Am. sect. 1920-21); corr. mem. Am. Inst. in Prague. Medalist of Charles U. (Prague) and of the Comensky U. (Bratislava); Comdr. Order of White Lion of Czechoslovakia. Awarded Egleston Medal of Columbia Engineering School Alumni Assn., 1939. First recipient Medal Award, Society of Cosmetic Chemists; Charles Frederick Chandler medalist and lecturer (selection by Columbia U.), 1948. An incorporator of Museums of Peaceful Arts, now New York Museum of Science and Industry, New York, 1915, member board directors since its organization; member national advisory board, Masaryk Institute. In World War I—member executive bd. Nat. Research Council (organizer and 1st chmn. div. of chemistry and chem. technology, with 32 subcoms.); mem. raw materials div. War Industries Bd.; mem. bd. on Gas Warfare; cons. chemist, Bur Mines; mem. scientific staff, Bur. Standards; advisory com. War Trade Bd., advisory bd. materials prodn. div., Signal Corps, War Dept.; consultant Fed. Trade Commn., mil. intelligence div. of Gen. Staff, War Dept., bur. investigation Dept. Justice, postal censorship Post Office Dept., etc. Commd. lt. col. and apptd. chief, Chem. Service Sect., U.S. Army, and asst. dir. Gas Service, Mar. 9, 1918; promoted col., July 13, 1918; served as chief of relations sect., intelligence sect., mem. bd. of review, claims bd. and exec. com. hdqrs. staff of Chem. Warfare Service; mem. standardization sect., purchase branch, Gen. Staff U.S. Army, etc.; hon. disch. May 1, 1919. Apptd. U.S. tariff commr. by President Wilson but declined; consultant in research and development work, Chem. Warfare Service; councillor of Internat. Union Pure and Applied Chemistry, 1926-33 and since 1937; 1st visiting Carnegie prof. of internat. relations to Czechoslovakia, 1927-28; v.p. Nat. Inst. Social Science, 1923-25; collaborator U.S. Dept. Agr., 1926-32 (chmn. advisory bd. to Color Lab. 1926-31); mem. board mgrs. N.Y. Bot. Gardens since 1927; mem. council of advisors, Fed. Union. Inc.; pres. supervisory bd., Am. Year Book Corp. Mem. Referee Bd., Chem. Industries Br., Office of Production, Research and Development, War Production Bd., 1942-45. Mem. Mil. Order Foreign Wars, Mil. Order World War. Asso. editor Jour. Am. Chem. Soc., 1924-30; mem. bd. of editors and editor trustee, Jour. Organic Chemistry since 1937; contbr. Jour. Indsl. Engring. Chemistry, Sience, Jour. Am. Chem. Soc., Jour. Organic Chemistry, etc. Clubs: Megantic Fish and Game, Columbia Men's Faculty, Chemists' (hon.), Century Assn., Holland Soc. of N.Y., St. Nicholas Soc. of N.Y. Home: 1158 5th Av., N.Y.C. 29. Died Mar. 21, 1954; buried Flushing Cemetery, Flushing, L.I., N.Y.

BOGGS, S(amuel) Whittemore, geographer; born Coolidge, Kans., Mar. 3, 1889; s. Crarles F(airman) and Lillian Louise (Whittemore) B.; B.L., Berea (Ky.) Coll., 1909; student Yale U., 1912-13; M.A. Columbia U., 1924; D.Sc. (honorary), Berea College, 1949; married Amy Burt Bridgman, August 16, 1916; children—Mary Lillian, Barbara Bridgman. Private sec. to President Frost, Berea Coll., 1909-12; secretarial work U.P.R.R., Omaha, Neb., 1913-14; secretarial and exec. work Internat. Com. of Y.M.C.A. and other orgns., New York, 1914-19; geog research, map compilation, editor Am. Book Co., etc., 1916-24, including editing maps for World Missionary Atlas, 1921-24; geographer U.S. Dept. of State, 1924—; lecturer on internat. boundaries, Columbia U., summers 1939, 40, 41, and 42; lecturer, Am. Univ., 1945-46. Tech. adviser, U.S. delegation, Conf. for Codification of Internat. Law, The Hague, 1930; ofcl. del. International Geog. Congresses, Cambridge, 1928, Paris, 1931, Warsaw, 1934, Lisbon, 1949, Pan Am. Inst. Geography and History, 3d gen. assembly, Lima, 1941, 4th gen. assembly Caracas, 1946, 1st consultation on geography Rio de Janeiro, 1949, 5th general assembly, Santiago, Chile, 1950, 3d consultation, Washington, 1952, 6th consultation on cartography, Ciudad Trujillo, 1952; member U.S. Geographic Bd., 1924-34, chmn. exec. com., 1927-34, U.S. Bd. on Geog. Names, 1947—, chairman, 1949-51. Fellow A.A.A.S., Royal Geog. Soc.; mem. Assn. Am. Geographers (councillor 1941-42), Am. Soc. Professional Geographers, Am. Council Learned Socs. (sec.-treas. 1942-48, treas., 1948-50), Acad. Polit. Sci., Am. Geophys. Union, Wash. Acad. Sci.; hon. mem. Mexican Soc. Geography and Statistics; corr. mem. Lima Geog. Soc. Presbyn. Clubs: Cosmos (Wash.); Explorers (N.Y.). Author: International Boundries —A Study of Boundary Functions and Problems, 1940; Classification and Cataloging of Maps and Atlases (with Dorothy C. Lewis) 1945. Contbr. to Dist. Am. History and various mags. Home: 4119 Stanford St., Chevy Chase 15, Md. Office: U.S. Dept. of State, Washington 25. Died Sept. 14, 1954.

BOGGS, Sara E., translator; b. Lewistown, Pa., Nov. 27, 1843; d. George and Magdalene Siegrist; student Lewistown pub. schs. and acad.; m. Leander R. Boggs, Mar. 6, 1865 (died Apr. 1904). Translator: Told by the Deaths Head (Jokai), 1902; The Nameless Castle (Jokai), 1898; India and Ceylon (Ernest Haeckel), 1883; Invisible Hands (Zobeltitz), 1894; Little Countess (E. Vely), 1891; The Mistress of Ibichstein (Henkel), 1884; The Hungarian Girl (Mariam Tenger), 1892; others. Author: Sandpeep, 1906. Address: Seal Harbor, Me. Deceased.

BOGIE, Mord M., investment banker; b. Richmond, Mo., July 11, 1903; s. Rector Scholl and Bettie Melvina (Duvall) B.; student U. Wis., 1923; m. Marjorie Ferguson, Sept. 6, 1923; children—Marjorie Dee (Mrs. B. W. Lewis), Betty Lou, Mord. Employed Byllesby & Co., Chgo., 1923-37; treas. Schroder Rockefeller & Co., N.Y.C., 1938, v.p., 1939-40, pres., dir. since 1941; pres., dir. Colonial Utilities Corp., Wilmington, since 1942, Walden (N.Y.) Telephone Co. since 1942, Allied N.H. Gas Co., Portsmouth, N.H., since 1942; v.p., dir. Froedtert Grain & Malting Co., Inc., Milwaukee; chmn. exec. com., dir. Rockwood & Co., Bklyn.; dir. Rootes Motors, Inc.; chmn. Internat. Rys. of Central Am. Mem. Grolier Soc., Council Fgn. Relations, Fgn. Affairs Assn. Clubs: Bond, Recess, Metropolitan (N.Y. City); Ketchaboneck (Westhampton, L.I.); Chicago; Milwaukee Athletic. Home: 200 E. 66th St., N.Y.C. 28. Died July 8, 1952.

BOGUE, Jesse Parker, exec. sec.; b. Athens, Ala., Aug. 16, 1889; s. Parker and Mary Elizabeth (Madison) B.; A.B., De Pauw U., 1914, D.D., 1936; postgrad. Boston U., 1914-15, Garrett Bibl. Inst., summers 1920, 21, 23; m. Adah C. Newhouse, Oct. 4, 1916; children—Mary Elizabeth, Barbara Joy, Jesse Parker. Teacher Ill. Wesleyan U., 1915-16; ordained ministry M.E. Ch., 1916; pastor Linden, Ind., 1916-17; pastor, supt. schs., Bringhurst, Ind., 1919-20; area sec. Ind. M.E. Ch., 1920-22; pastor, Indpls., 1922-25, Knoxville, Tenn., 1925-27, Buffalo, 1927-29; headmaster Troy (N.Y.) Conf. Acad., 1929-30; pres. Green Mountain Jr. Coll., 1931-46; exec. sec. Am. Assn. Jr. Colls., 1946-58; faculty mem. U. Denver, 1947, State U. Ia., 1948, Harvard, 1949-50; vis. prof. higher edn. U. Mich., also cons. State and Am. Assn. Jr. Colls., 1958-59. Mem. Vt. Ho. of Reps., 1945-47. Served as chaplain, 49th Arty. U.S. Army, 1918-19, AEF. Pres. N.E. Jr. Coll. Council, 1938-40. Mem. Am. Assn. Jr. Colls. (v.p., 1942-43), Tau Kappa Alpha. Author: The Community College, 1950. Editor: Am. Jr. Colleges, 1948, 52, 55. Home: 1520 Creal Crescent, Ann Arbor, Mich. Died Feb. 5, 1960; buried Arlington Nat. Cemetery.

BOGUE, Morton Griswold, lawyer; b. Brooklyn, N.Y., Nov. 6, 1880; s. Morton D. and Anna Griswold (Tefft) B.; A.B., Columbia, 1900; student Columbia Law Sch., 1900-03; married. Admitted to N.Y. bar, 1903, and since in practice in N.Y. City; now sr. mem. firm Beekman & Bogue. Special counsel War Finance Corp., 1918-22; spl. counsel Reconstruction Finance Corp., Feb.-May 1932, gen. counsel, May-Dec. 1932. Director American Chain & Cable Co., since 1947. Alumni trustee Columbia U., 1937-43, 1944-45. Mem. Am., N.Y. State (chmn. com. on corp. law, 1935-45) bar assns. Assn. Bar City of N.Y. Pres. U.S. Golf Assn., 1944-46; Delta Psi. Republican. Clubs: Union, St. Anthony, Links, Downtown Assn., Ekwanok Country, Broad Street, Southampton, National Golf Links. Home: 60 E. 67th St., N.Y. City; also Bridgehampton, L.I. Office: 15 Broad St., N.Y.C. Died July 11, 1955.

BOHANNON, Eugene William (bō-hăn'ŏn), educator; b. Boonville, Ind., Oct. 13, 1865; s. George W. and Elizabeth (Wilder) B.; grad. State Normal Sch., Terre Haute, Ind., 1887; A.B., Ind. U., Bloomington, 1890, A.M., 1892; scholar and fellow, Clark U., Worcester, Mass., 1895-98, Ph.D., 1912; m. Mary Agnes Carney, Apr. 18, 1901; children—George Wilder, Mary Elizabeth, Ruth. Prin. of schs., Brownsburg, Ind., 1887-88, Plainfield, Ind., 1889-91; prin. high sch., Pekin, Ill., 1892; supt. schs., Rensselaer, Ind., 1892-95; head of dept. of psychology and pedagogy, State Normal Sch., Mankato, Minn., 1898-1901; pres. State Teachers' Coll., Duluth, 1901-38, pres. emeritus since 1941. Mem. Charter Commn. of City of Duluth. Mem. Minn. State Hist. Soc., A.A.A.S., Phi Gamma Delta. Home: 2323 E. 5th St., Duluth 5, Minn. Died May 9, 1955; buried Boonville, Ind.

BOHN, Charles B.; chmn. bd. Bohn Aluminum & Brass Co.; dir. Mich. Smelting & Refining Co., Capitol Brass Co., Mich. Nat. Bank. Home: 740 Whittier Blvd., Grosse Pointe, Mich. Address: 8162 E. Jefferson, Detroit. Died Apr. 2, 1953.

BOJER, Johan, author; b. Orkedalsoren, Norway, Mar. 6, 1872; s. Hans B. and Johanne (Iversdatter) B.; student Mil. School, Trondheim, Norway, 1890-94; m. Ellen Lange, Nov. 1, 1899; children—Thora (wife of Sculptor Dyre Vaa), Randi (wife of Pastor Odd Godal), Halvard. Previous to taking up writing in 1894 was in business. Decorated Legion of Honor; also decorations from several other countries. Dir. of the New Theatre (Norway). Author: (all translated from the Norwegian) Face of the World, 1919; Great Hunger, 1919; Life, 1920; Treacherous Ground, 1920; Last of the Vikings, 1923; Pilgrimage, 1924; The Prisoner Who Sang, 1924; Imigrants, 1925; New Temple, 1928; Everlasting Struggle, 1931; House and the Sea, 1934; By Day and by Night, 1937; King's Men, 1940. Home: Hvalstad, Oslo, Norway, Died July 3, 1959; buried Lutheran Churchyard, Asker, Norway.

BOKHARI, Ahmed Shah, under-secretary of UN; b. Peshawar, India, Oct. 1, 1898; M.A., Punjab U., Lahore; B.A. and M.A., Cambridge U., Eng. Prof. English lit. Nat. Coll., Lahore, many yrs.; prin. Nat. Govt. Coll., 1947-50; sta. dir., dep. controller broadcasting, dir. gen., All-India Radio, during war yrs.; co-chmn. Commonwealth Broadcasting Conf., London, 1945; attended Internat. High Frequency Broadcasting Conf., Mexico City, 1948; following creation of Pakistan, 1947, served as leader Pakistan delegation India Office partition negotiations, London; rep. Pakistan, 4th Gen. Assembly, U.N., 1949; alternate leader delegation 10th session ECOSOC, 1950; ambassador E. and P., Pakistan permanent representative to UN, 1952-54; under-sec. UN for Pub. Information, 1954—; rep. to Security Council and Disarmament Commn., 1952-53. Recipient Companion of the Order of The Indian Empire. Author numerous publs. in Urdu and Persian; translator (into Urdu) and producer plays by Shakespeare, Shaw, Wilde and other famous playwrights. Address: United Nations, N.Y. Died Dec. 5, 1958.

BOKOR, Margit, opera singer; b. Losonc, Hungary, Apr. 1, 1909; d. Geza Wahl and Malvine (Goldschmiedt) Wahl; piano degree Acad. of Music, Budapest, Hungary, 1928, singing degree, 1929; m. Paul Andrew Goldschmidt; 1 dau., Vera Bokor. Slected for world premier of Richard Straus Opera Arabella, at State Opera, Dresden, 1933; appeared at Vienna State Opera, Salzburg Festivals, 1933-38, Paris Grand Opera, 1939, Rio de Janeiro, 1939, Metropolitan Opera Co., San Francisco Opera Co., Chicago Opera Co., St. Louis Opera Co., Central City Festivals, Montreal Festivals; soloist with New York, Pitts. and other symphony orchestras; has appeared in recitals in more than 50 cities. Home: Hotel Colonial, 51 West 81st St., N.Y.C. 24. Office: Internat. Artists Corp., 420 Madison Av., N.Y.C. 17. Deceased.*

BOLAND, Frank Kells (bō'lănd), surgeon; b. Indianapolis, Ind., May 3, 1875; s. Kells Hewitt and Louise (Bright) B.; A.B.,U. of Ga., 1897, Sc.D., 1926; M.D., Emory U., 1900; studied Johns Hopkins; m. Molly Horsley, Apr. 25, 1905; children—Frank Kells, Joseph Horsley. Resident surgeon St. Joseph's Hosp., Baltimore, 1900-03; practiced at Atlanta since 1903; with Emory U. since 1903, prof. surgery, 1921-30, professor clin. surgery since 1930, prof. surgery, 1942-45; mem. board trustees, 1937-46; prof. anatomy, Emory U. Sch. of Dentistry, 1907-19, prof. physiology, 1919-49; visiting surgeon Grady Municipal Hosp., Emory U. Hosp. Served as lt. col. Med. O.R.C., World War; chief of surg. service, Base Hosp. No. 43 (Emory Unit), Blois, France, 1918-19; apptd. col. Med. Officers Reserve Corps. President Crawford W. Long Memorial Assn.; pres. Atlanta Hist. Soc., 1938-42; chmn. Atlanta Chapter Am. Red Cross, 1938-42; pres. Atlanta chapter, English Speaking Union since 1942. Fellow American College Surgeons, American Surgical Association; mem. A.M.A. (vice chmn. surg. sect. 1930), Southern Med. Assn. (chmn. and sec. surg. sect.; v.p. 1926-27; chmn. council 1934; pres. 1937), Southern Surgical Assn. (v.p. 1926; pres 1934), Am. Assn. for Thoracic Surgery, Amer. Assn. for Traumatic Surgery, Med. Assn. of Ga. (pres. 1925-26), Fulton County Med. Soc. (pres. 1921), U. of Ga. Alumni Soc. (president 1927-28), Emory U. Alumni Assn. (president 1941-42), Southeastern Surg. Congress (pres. 1932-33). Société Internationale de Chirurgie, Chi Phi, Phi Beta Kappa, Phi Beta Kappa Assos., Phi Chi, Omicron Delta Kappa, Alpha Omega Alpha. Citation for "distinguished service" from U. of Ga. Alumni Soc., 1940. Dem. Methodist. Clubs: Rotary, Piedmont Driving. Author: The First Anesthetic, Story of Crawford Long, 1950. Home: 252 Peachtree Circle. Office: 478 Peachtree St., Atlanta. Died Nov. 11, 1953.

BOLAND, John J., steamship co. exec.; b. Buffalo, Sept. 20, 1875; s. Anthony and Winifred (McDonnell) B.; m. Elizabeth McCabe, 1902; children—John, Jr., Elizabeth. Pres. Am. S.S. Co., Buffalo. Democrat. Catholic. Clubs: Buffalo, Buffalo Country. Home: 154 Morris Av. Office: 1016 Marine Trust Bldg., Buffalo, N.Y., and Grand Island, N.Y. Died Oct. 3, 1956; buried Buffalo.

BOLDUAN, Charles Frederick (bŭl'dōō-ăn), health educator; b. Bielefeld, Germany, May 7, 1873; s. William and Juliane (Dreibholz) B.; Ph.G., Coll. of Pharmacy, N.Y.C., 1893; M.D., Coll. Phys. and Surg., Columbia, 1901; student U. Berlin, 1903; m. Adele Jönsson, Sept. 15, 1906; 1 son, Nils W. (M.C. U.S. Army); m. 2d, Herma Engelsdorff, Mar. 1, 1928. Prof. bacteriology and hygiene Fordham U., 1905-08; bacteriologist Dept. of Health, City N.Y., 1904-07; asst. to gen. med. officer Dept. of Health, 1907-13; dir. Bur. Pub. Health Edn., 1913-18; chief, sec. Public Health Edn., USPHS, 1918-21; surgeon USPHS, detailed U.S. consular service, Europe, 1921-28; dir. Bur. of Health Edn., Dept. of Health, N.Y.C., 1928-43; lectr. preventive medicine and hygiene Columbia, 1918-22, Sch. Sociology and Social Service, Fordham, 1928-42. Sec. N.Y. Tb Preventorium for Children. Founder, hon. pres. N.Y., Diabetes Assn. Fellow Am. Pub. Health Assn., N.Y. Acad. Medicine; mem. N.Y. Soc. Med. History; hon. mem. Am. Diabetes Assn. Author: Immune Sera, 5th edit. 1918; Applied Bacteriology for Nurses 8th edit. 1941; Public Health and Hygiene, 3d edit. 1941; Spanish edit. 1943. Translator of Suppression of Tuberculosis, etc., 1905; Serum Diagnosis, 1905; Collected Studies on Immunity, 1906; also scientific papers in medical jours.; numerous statistical stucdies on cancer, heart disease, infant mortality, typhoid fever, etc., hist. studies on health conditions in N.Y. City during 19th century. Editor Bull., N.Y. C. Dept. Health. Address: Northport, L.I., N.Y. Died Apr. 4, 1950.

BOLLINGER, James Wills (bō'lĭn jer), lawyer; b. Geneseo, Ill., Apr. 10, 1867; s. Albert Lester and Emily Diana (Wills) B.; B.A., State U. Ia., 1888, M.A., 1889, LL.B., 1893; m. Mary Elizabeth Gilman, Nov. 1, 1899; children—Susan (dec.), Stephen Albert. In practice of law at Davenport, Ia., 1889-98, 1911—; judge Dist. Court, 7th Ia. Dist., 1898-1911; partner with Judge Donegan of law firm Bollinger & Donegan, 1939—; chmn. bd. Sieg Co. Pres. Davenport Pub. Museum. Mem. Am., Iowa State, Scott County bar assns., Abraham Lincoln Assn. of Springfield, Ill. Phi Kappa Psi. Republican. Club: Treadway Rod and Gun. Home: 425 E. Locust St. Office: Putnam Bldg., Davenport, Ia. Died Jan. 30, 1951.

BOLTON, Charles Knowles (bōl'tŭn), antiquary; b. Cleve., Nov. 14, 1867; s. Charles Edward and

Sarah (Knowles) B.; A.B., Harvard, 1890; m. Ethel Stanwood, June 23, 1897; children—Stanwood Knowles, Geoffrey. Asst. Harvard Library, 1890-93; librarian, Brookline, 1894-98, Boston Athenaeum Library, 1898-1933; instr., asso. prof. Simmons Coll. Works Progress Adminstrn. supr. survey of early Am. portraits in New Eng. and N.Y., 1935-36. Trustee Mus. Fine Arts, 1917-33, Fitchburg Hist. Soc., 1942-44. Mem. Am. Antiquarian Soc., Mass. Hist. Soc., Colonial Soc. of Mass., Navy Hist. Found., Am. Inst. of Heraldry (hon.), Lantern League, Inc. (pres.), Mass. Soc. for Prevention of Cruelty to Animals (v.p.), Soc. for Preservation of New Eng. Antiquities (past pres.), Phi Beta Kappa (hon.). Episcopalian (sr. warden 1912-36). Author: Saskia, the Wife of Rembrandt, 1893; On the Wooing of Martha Pitkin, 1894; The Love Story of Ursula Wolcott, 1895; Brookline, History of a Favored Town, 1897; The Private Soldier Under Washington, 1902; Scotch-Irish Pioneers, 1910; The Elizabeth Whitman Mystery 1912; American Library History, 1911; Christ Church, 1723 (a guide), 1913, new edit., 1923; Portraits of the Founders, Vols. 1 and 2, 1918, Vol. 3, 1926; The Ethics of Librarianship a proposal for a revised code, 1922; Bolton's American Armory, 1927; The Real Founders of New England, 1929; Terra Nova—The Northeast Coast of America, before 1602, 1935; Bolton Families in Ireland, 1937; Workers with Line and Color in New England, 1620-1870, 5 vols. in manuscript (at Boston Athenaeum), 1939-44; a check list of faked and doubtful portraits (at Worcester Art Museum), 1943; Our American Language, 1945. Editor: Letters of Hugh, Earl Percy, from Boston and New York, 1774-76, 1902; The Athenaeum Centenary, 1907; Sarah K. Bolton—Pages from an Intimate Autobiography, 1923. Home: Pound Hill Place, Shirley, Mass. Died May 19, 1950; buried Shirley (Mass.) Centre Cemetery.

BOLTON, Ethel (Stanwood), antiquarian; b. Boston, Mar. 2, 1873; d. Edward and Eliza M. (Topliff) Stanwood; A.B., Wellesley, 1894; m. Charles Knowles Bolton, June 23, 1897; children—Stanwood Knowles, Geoffrey. Registrar Mass. Soc. Colonial Dames, 1913-49; mem. New Eng. Hist. Geneal. Soc.; sec. Shirley Rep. Town Com.; treas. Shirley Girl Scouts. Episcopalian. Clubs: Altrurian of Shirley; Groton Garden, Fitchburg Wellesley; Women's Republican (Boston). Author: The Stanwood Family in America, 1898; Some Descendants of John Moore, 1904; Clement Topliff and His Descendants, 1906; Farm Life a Century Ago, 1909; Shirley Uplands and Intervales, 1914; Wax Portraits and Silhouettes, 1915; American Samplers (with Mrs. E. J. Coe), 1921; Immigrants to New England (1700-1775), 1927; American Wax Portraits, 1929. Editor: Topliff's Travels, 1906; (with Mrs. C. C. Lane) The Smile on the Face of the Tiger (limericks), 1910; The Kelseys of Shirley, 1926. Home: Pound Hill Place, Shirley, Mass. Died Jan. 9, 1954; buried Shirley Centre Town Cemetery, Shirley.

BOLTON, Margaret, teacher of religion; b. Richfield Springs, N.Y., Feb. 12, 1873; d. John and Anne (Lannen) Bolton; grad. State Normal Sch., Albany, N.Y., 1892; courses in English, psychology, and elementary teaching Columbia, 1899-1906, theology Cenacle Convent, N.Y., 1914-16; title of Mother conferred 1921. Tchr. elementary pub. sch., Patchogue, N.Y., 1892; tchr. English, pub. schs., N.Y.C., 1896-1906; model tchr. Tng. Sch. for Tchrs., N.Y.C., 1906-13; asso. prof. of religious teaching Fordham U., 1928-33; method courses in teaching religion Boston Coll., 1931, 32, Loyola U. Chgo., 1931, Tchrs. Coll., Providence, 1932; directress of methods of teaching religion Am. Province of Soc. of Our Lady of the Retreat in the Cenacle. Author: Meditations for God's Loving Children, 1922; History of the Most Wonderful Promise Ever Made, 1924; Spiritual Way Series (4 vols.), 1930; Teachers' Manual, 1930; The Spiritual Way Plan of Teaching Religion, 1931; A Little Child's First Communion, 1931 (enlarged 6 vols., 1935); Foundation Material for Doctrinal Catholic Action, 1937; Way to Achievement (with Mrs. Grace Hart), 1940, 48; Gods Hour in Nursery (pub. post humously). Contbr. to mags. Home: The Cenacle Convent, 628 W. 140th St., N.Y.C. Died Feb. 27, 1943; buried Cenacle Convent, Lake Ron Kon Koma, L.I., N.Y.

BOMAR, Edward Earle (bō-mär), newspaper corr.; b. Aiken, S.C., Nov. 4, 1897; s. Edward Earle and Nancy (Landrum) B.; A.B., Georgetown Coll., Ky., 1919; M.A., Columbia, 1923; m. Mary Rowland Carter, May 26, 1933; children—Mary Rowland, Edward Earle III. Reporter Lexington (Ky.) Herald, 1919-22, Detroit News, 1923-28; on staff Associated Press, Louisville and Baltimore (chief of bur.), 1928-31, chief at Manila, P.I., 1931-35; mem. Washington staff, 1936-42, and since 1946; major to colonel, Army of U.S., 1942-46. Served in U.S. Navy, World War I. Mem. Kappa Alpha. Baptist. Club: National Press (Washington, D.C.). Address: 3055 Foxhall Road N.W., Washington. Died Oct. 27, 1953; buried Arlington Nat. Cemetery.

BONASCHI, Alberto Cinzio (bō-näs'kē), edn. commr.; b. Bergamo, Italy, Feb. 27, 1869; s. Daniele and Gerolama (Rota) B.; grad. Paolo Sarpi Lyceum (Coll.), Bergamo, 1889; Litt.D., Royal Sci.-Lit. Acad. (Univ.), 4 yr. scholarship, Milano, Italy, 1893; Spl. Diploma for History and Geog., 1893; m. Minnie Vivian Kopf, Apr. 8, 1906. Came to U.S., 1898, naturalized, 1906: High sch. tchr., pvt. tutor, lectr. on econ. geog., Philological Assn., Milano, Italy, 1897-98; served as sec., 3d Nat. Geog. Congress, Florence, Italy, 1898; mem. Bd. Examiners, Royal Acad., Milano, Italy, 1897-98; mgr. Italian dept. John C. Seager Trading Co., ship agts. and brokers, N.Y.C., 1900-06, dir.-sec., 1906-09: asst. sec.-editor Italiana C. of C., N.Y.C., 1911-18, sec.-editor, 1919-39, sec. emeritus, 1940—; agt. Transatlantica Italian S.S. Co., 1915, Italian Marine Register, 1912-17; for Italian ships at the Am. Bur. of Shipping, 1917-31. Lectr. Bd. of Edn. on civics and Americanization to fgn. adult classes, 1903-05; tchr. ocean traffic and marine adminstrn., N.Y.C. Coll., 1919-22. Served as ofcl. interpreter for Italian War Debt Funding Mission to U.S., at U.S. Treasury, 1925; mgr. Italian sect. U.S. Govt. com. on pub. information, 1918-19. Mem. Bd. of Edn., City N.Y., 1935-43, v.p., 1942-43; chmn. tchrs. retirement bd., 1935-43; mem. Bd. of Higher Edn., N.Y., 1943—. Mem. Bd. Parole for N.Y.C. Reformatory, 1914-15. Recipient 5 citations and medal from U.S. Treasury for activities in War Savings Bonds campaigns, 1942-45. Charter mem. Assn. of Secs. of Chambers of Fgn. Commerce in U.S. (pres. 1934-36); hon. mem. N.Y. Classical Club; hon. mem. Tiro a Segno (riflemen Assn. affiliated with Natl. Rifle Ass'n. of Am.). Home: 15 Pell St., City Island, N.Y.C. 64, Died Aug. 3, 1948.*

BOND, Charles Sumner, physician; b. Webster, Ind., June 8, 1856; s. Simon and Susan (Harris) B.; attended Earlham and Antioch colls.; student Ohio Med. Coll., 1878; M.D., Bellevue Hosp. Med. Coll., N.Y.U., 1883; B.S., M.S., Earlham, 1887; m. Julia M. Boyd, Sept. 18, 1883; m. 2d, Mrs. Minnie Van Matre, Nov. 16, 1915. In practice, Richmond, Ind., 1883—; coroner Wayne County, Ind., 1884-88; staff Reid Meml. Hosp., 1890-1912; health officer, Richmond, 1906-08; lectr. Ind. Med. Coll., 1905-10. Mem. Assn. Am. Physicians, A.M.A., Ind. (pres. 1895), Miss. Valley (v.p. 1897) med. socs., Ind. Acad. Scis. Mem. Congress on Tb, London, 1901, Washington, 1908. Address: 112 N. 10th St., Richmond, Ind. Died June 16, 1958; buried Earlham Cemetery, Richmond.

BOND, Elizabeth Powell, coll. dean; b. Clinton, N.Y., Jan. 25, 1841; d. Townsend and Catharine (Macy) Powell; student State Normal Sch. (now Coll.), Albany, N.Y.; hon. A.M., Swarthmore, 1897; m. Henry Herrick Bond, May 23, 1872 (died 1881). Dir. physical culture Vassar Coll., 1865-70; dean Swarthmore Coll., 1886-1906, dean emeritus, 1906—. Author: Words by the Way, 1895, 2d series, 1901. Address: 6300 Greene St., Germantown, Pa. Deceased.

BOND, George Hopkins, lawyer; b. Syracuse, N.Y., Aug. 10, 1873; s. William H. and Ida (Hopkins) B.; Ph.B., Syracuse, 1894, Ph.M., LL.B., 1897, LL.D., 1930; m. Florence Cherry Woodford, Jan. 29, 1901; children—Margaret Elizabeth (Mrs. John Dunn Brockway), George H. Began the practice of law at Syracuse, N.Y., 1897; mem. Bond, Schoeneck & King; dist. atty. Onondaga County, N.Y., 1908-14; spl. dep. atty. gen., N.Y., 1915-16; dir. A. E. Nettleton Co., Onondaga Pottery Co., Pass & Seymour, Inc., Marsellus Casket Co., Engelberg Huller Co. (Syracuse). Regent U. State of N.Y. Pres. N.Y. State Assn. Dist. Attys., 1912-13; mem. Am., N.Y. State (pres. 1937-38) bar assns., Soc. Mayflower Descs., S.A.R., Phi Beta Kappa, Delta Kappa Epsilon, Phi Delta Phi. Presbyn. Clubs: University, Onondaga Golf and Country, Century (Syracuse); University (N.Y.C.). Home: 304 Walnut Pl. Office: State Tower Bldg., Syracuse, N.Y. Died May 8, 1954.

BOND, Reford, lawyer; b. Johnsonville, Indian Ty., Aug. 10, 1877; s. James Henry and Adelaide Courtenay (Johnson) B.; prep. edn., Kemper Mil. Coll., Boonville, Mo.; student Roanoke Coll., Salm, Va., and Columbian (now George Washington) U.; LL.B., U. of Mo., 1897; m. Janet Quigley Ware, Nov. 5, 1912; 1 son, Reford. Admitted to Indian Ty. bar, 1899, and has practiced since in Indian Territory, in Oklahoma and in Washington, D.C.; national attorney for the Chickasaw Nation, 1913-21. Mem. Commn. of Review and Revision of Constitution of State of Okla.; pres. State Election Bd.; apptd. as a special justice Supreme Court of Okla.; apptd. chmn. Co-ordinating Board for co-ordinating and unifying system of higher education in Okla.; del. Dem. Nat. Conv., Chicago, 1932. Trustee William H. Murray Ednl. Foundation; chmn. Corp. Commn. of State of Okla., 1934— (re-elected 1936 and 1942). Member Nat. Conf. Petroleum Regulatory Authorities. Oklahoma representative on Inter-State Oil Compact Commission. Mem. American, Okla. State and Grady County bar associations, Kappa Alpha, Phi Delta Phi. Democrat. Mem. Christian Church. Mason (32°, K.T., Shriner), K.P., I.O.O.F. Club: Oklahoma City Golf and Country, Oklahoma, Men's Dinner. Successfully represented Choctaw and Chickasaw Nations in cases involving more than $50,-000,000. Home: 821 N.W. 37th St. Office: State Capitol, Oklahoma City, Okla. Died June 24, 1954; buried Chickasha, Okla.

BOND, Sirus Orestes, coll. pres. emeritus; b. Hackers Creek, W.Va., Aug. 12, 1877; s. Levi Davis and Victoria (Arnold) B.; A.B., Salem (W.Va.) Coll., 1904; A.B., W.Va. U., 1909; A.M., Columbia, 1913, grad. study, 1913-14; Pd.D., Alfred (N.Y.) U., 1924; m. Venie Hagerty, Aug. 9, 1904. Tchr. rural schs., prin. elementary and high schs. until 1914; acting pres. Glenville (W.Va.) State Normal Sch., 1914-15; supr. schs. Shepherdstown Dist., W.Va., prof. edn. Shepherd Coll. State Normal Sch., 1915-19; pres. Salem Coll., 1919-51, pres. emeritus, 1951—; instr. in tchrs. insts., 1913—; mem. firm E. H. Bond & Bro., breeders of pure-bred Hereford cattle, 1901-37; mem. firm Bonds' Greenacres Hereford Farm, 1937—. World v.p. Christian Endeavor, 1923-28; pres. Seventh Day Baptist Gen. Conf., 1925. Mem. N.E.A., Nat. Soc. for Study Edn., W. Va. Edn. Assn. Am. Forestry Assn., Am. Soc. Animal Prodn., W.Va. Livestock Assn. (life), Pi Gamma Mu. Dem. Seventh Day Baptist. Kiwanian. Author: Salem College, Its Past, Present and Future, 1924; Light of the Hills (A history of Salem College from 1888 to 1958). Home: 51 Chestnut St., Salem, W. Va. Died Jan. 11, 1959; buried Brick Church Cemetery, Lost Creek, W.Va.

BOND, William Scott, real estate; b. Chicago, Ill., May 9, 1876; s. William Alonzo and Sarah Barber (Fisher) B.; Ph.B., U. of Chicago, 1897; LL.B., Kent Coll. of Law, Chicago, 1899; m. Maud I. Moore, June 26, 1916. In law offices of Peck, Miller & Starr, 1897-1900; admitted to Ill. bar, 1899; mem. real estate firm William A. Bond & Co., real estate loan reps. of Northwestern Mutual Life Ins. Co., 1912-46; trustee estate L. Z. Leiter; director Pressed Prism Plate Glass Co., Chicago Title & Trust Co., Illinois Bell Telephone Co., Chicago Dock & Canal Co.; mem. bd. trustees Chicago U., 1922-46, now hon. trustee, formerly vice chmn. bd., formerly v.p. U. of Chicago Settlement. Mem. Chicago Real Estate Bd. Republican. Clubs: University, Commercial, Quadrangle. Home: R.F.D. 1, Dundee, Ill. Office: 33 N. La Salle St., Chgo. 2. Died Sept. 10, 1952.

BONNER, Arthur (bŏn'er), clergyman, educator; b. nr. Leicester, Eng., Nov. 29, 1869; s. William and Anne (Hallam) B.; Wesleyan Acad., Wilbraham, Mass., 1888-89; A.B., S.T.B., Boston U., 1908, A.M., 1909, Ph.D., 1911; m. Josephine Chapman Whitaker, Aug. 9, 1892 (dec.); children—Warren A., Willard H. Ordained to M.E. ministry, 1894, served various pastorates in Mass.; pastor Highlands Ch., Lowell, Mass., 1911-12; prof. English and pub. speaking So. U., Greensboro, Ala., 1912-15; pres. Scarritt-Morrisville Coll., Morrisville, Mo., 1915-16; prof. Bibl. lit., asso. prof. English, U. Ala., 1916-18; prof. philosophy, Coll. of the Pacific, 1918-20, prof. English, 1920-33; in pastorate, 1933-38; retired, 1939. Chmn. bd. edn. Pacific Conf. M.E. Ch., South, 1920-23. Dir. and joint organizer Coll. of Pacific Summer School Abroad, 1927-32. Mem. Shakespeare Assn. Am. Mason. Club: City Commons. Author: The Search Eternal, Easter, Sonnet-Elegy, Eight Sonnets at Eighty, Other Occassional Poems, and numerous magazine articles. Address: 2323 Rose St., Berkeley. Cal. Died Sept. 20, 1952.

BONNER, David Findley, clergyman; b. Greenfield, O., Apr. 2, 1842; s. Henry Johnson and Martha (Findley) B.; A.B., Muskingum Coll., 1860, A.M.; grad. Pitts. Theol. Sem., 1865; D.D., Lenox Coll., 1891; m. Mary Elizabeth Smith, Apr. 4, 1865. Ordained ministry U.P. Ch., June 16, 1865; pastor, Knoxville and Monroe, Ia., 1865-66, Knoxville, 1866-70, Caledonia, N.Y., 1871-84; passed into Presbyn. Ch. U.S.A., 1884; pastor Goodwill Ch., Orange County, N.Y., 1884-91, Florida, N.Y., 1891-1903, Marathon, N.Y., 1903-08, Endicott, N.Y., 1908—. Supt. Marion County (Ia.) schs., 1867-88. Life dir. Am. Bible Soc. Republican. Author: Saving the World, 1902; The Psalmody Question, 1908; also various pamphlets on religious topics. Address: Endicott, N.Y. Deceased.

BONNER, Francis A(ugustus), investments, govt. ofcl.; b. Chicago, Ill., May 20, 1885; s. Andrew William and Eleanor C. (Burke) B.; A.B., Harvard, 1907; m. Celestine Louise Horine, Mar. 25, 1913; children—William Andrew, John Francis, Francis Augustus, Jr. With editorial dept. Chicago Evening Post as reporter and subsequently ry. editor and asso. financial editor, 1908-13; asso. dir. Bureau of Railway News and Statistics, Chicago, specializing in railway economics, 1913-18; with Lee, Higginson & Co., in charge of new issue department, Chicago, 1918-32; vice president Blair, Bonner & Co., investment bankers, Chicago, 1934-44; director, Credit Policy Office, O.P.A., 1943-47; cons. to S.E.C. on original amendments to Securities Act. of 1933; special adviser to Securities & Exchange Commission, on regulation of investment banking business, 1938. Chmn. board governors National Association of Securities Dealers, Inc., 1940; past mem. bd. govs. and past chmn. legislation com. Investment Bankers Assn. of America. Clubs: University, Harvard, Tuesday,

Bond, Chgo. Press Vets. Association (Chgo.); Harvard (N.Y.C.); University, Harvard (Washington). Adopted by Blackfeet Indians, Mont., as "Nee-Nay-Nook-Ka" (Chief Elk). Home: 245 Scott Av., Hubbard Woods, Ill.Died 1953.

BONNER, Walter D(aniel), univ. prof.; b. Osceola, Neb., Oct. 27, 1878; s. James Toy and Ida May (Davison) B.; B.S., Neb. Wesleyan U., University Place, Neb., 1906; A.M., Princeton, 1908; Ph. D., U. of Toronto, 1911; m. Grace Gaylord, Sept. 9, 1909; children—James Frederick, Lyman Gaylord, Priscilla (Mrs. Walter James Horton), David Mahlon, Robert Nelson, Walter Daniel, Francis Truesdale. Lecturer in chemistry, Queen's Univ., Kingston, Ont., Can., 1909-11, asst. prof., 1911-15, prof., head dept. chem., Utah U., 1915-46, prof. emeritus, July 1946—. Mem. Am. Chem. Soc., Am. Assn. for Advancement of Science, Phi Beta Kappa, Phi Kappa Phi, Sigma Xi, Alpha Chi Sigma. Author: Qualitative Analysis Without Hydrogen Sulphide (with John R. Lewis), 1935. Home: 1278 E. 13th South St., Salt Lake City 5. Office: University of Utah, Salt Lake City 1. Died Jan. 3, 1956; buried Wasatch Lawn, Salt Lake City.

BONNYMAN, Alexander, industrialist; b. Edinburgh, Scotland, Dec. 8, 1868; s. George and Sarah (Toner) B.; student U. Ky., LL.D. (hon.); m. Frances Berry, Nov. 12, 1906; children—Alex. Jr., Mrs. Margot McKeon, Mrs. Anne B. Atkinson, Gordon. Engring. development of Natural Resources Southeastern U.S., particularly coal mining, Ky., Tenn., Va. (mines now having prodn. capacity of seven million tons annually; pres. Blue Diamond Coal Co., since 1923. Fellow Am. Geog. Soc.; mem. Ky. Soc. Profl. Engrs., (life) Am. Soc. C.E., Acad. Polit. Sci., Am. Inst. Mining and Metall. Engrs., Soc. Am. Mil. Engrs., Am. Ordnance Assn., Am. Acad. Polit. and Social Sci., Scottish Am. Meml. Assn., Assn. Master Knights of Sovereign Mil. Order Malta in U.S.A. Club: Cherokee Country. Home: 2931 Kingston Pike, Knoxville, S.W. Office: Hamilto Bank Bldg., Knoxville 1, Tenn. Died Apr. 15, 1953.

BONOMO, Alfred J. (bŏn'ō mo), prof. and lawyer; b. New Orelans, Apr. 14, 1890; s. Joseph and Josephine (Alt) B.; A.B., Coll. of the Immaculate Conception, New Orleans, 1911; LL.B., Georgetown U., Washington, 1914; A.M., Loyola U., New Orleans, 1915, O.B., 1917, LL.M., 1920, LL.D., 1924; m. Beatrice E. Jung, Mar. 1, 1916; children—Louis F. (dec.), Alfred J. Instr., Georgetown Coll., Washington, 1912-14; mem. faculty Law Sch., Loyola U., New Orleans, 1914-29, prof. radio, script writing, and radio acting, 1940—; director dramatics, 1928-50, dir. ednl. radio show, University Time, 1940—; tchr. television script writing, 1954—; admitted to La. bar, 1915, and practiced law, New Orleans, 1915-28; ednl. dir. radio sta. WWL, New Orleans, since 1940. Mem. Assn. for Edn. by Radio, La. Bar Assn., Blue Key. Democrat. Roman Catholic. Author of radio shows, also several pamphlets on legal subjects. Editor: Saunder's Lectures on the Civil Code of Louisiana. Home: 6301 Freret St., New Orleans 18. Died Dec. 23, 1955; buried Metairie Cemetery, New Orleans.

BONSAL, Stephen (bon'sal), newspaper corr., writer; b Baltimore, Mar 29, 1865; s. Stephen and Frances (Leigh B.; ed. at St. Paul's Sch., Concord, N.H.; also studied Heidelberg, Bonn and Vienna; m. Henrietta Fairfax Morris, Mar. 1900. Was spl. corr. of the New York Herald in the Bulgarian-Servian War, 1885, in Morocco, 1889, Macedonian uprising, 1890, Chino-Japanese War, 1895; traveled through Siberia, 1896; Cuban insurrection, 1897, Spanish-Am. War; China relief expdn., 1900; Samar, Batangas and Mindanao (P.I.) campaigns, 1901; in Venezuela during Matos revolution and blockade by the powers, 1903; upon outbreak of Russo-Japanese War, 1904, traveled for New York Herald 6 months in the Balkans, Albania, Macedonia, Montenegro, etc.; in Russia during the Revolutionary troubles of 1907; visited all the West Indies and parts of S.A., 1908; in Mexico during the Madero revolution, 1910-11, for New York Times. In U.S. diplomatic service as sec. of legation and chargé d'affaires in Peking, Madrid, Tokio and Korea, 1893-97. Apptd. sec. to the governor-gen., P.I., Sept. 1913; commr. Public Utilities, P.I., 1914; spl. mission in Mexico, 1915; with Hindenburg's army on east front, 1915; adviser Am.-Mexican Joint Commn., 1916-17; maj. Nat. Army, 1917, and on duty War Coll., Washington; with A.E.F. in France, 1918; Am. rep. Congress Oppressed Nationalities, Paris, Sept. 1918; lt. col. inf., attached Am. mission to Peace Conf. after armistice; Am. mem. inter-allied mission to Austro-Hungary and Balkan States under General Smuts, and spl. mission to Germany and Bohemia, 1919. Traveled 10,000 miles in Soviet Russia, 1931, and in 1934, across North China and Manchukuo. Clubs: Century, Knickerbocker (New York); Metropolitan (Washington). Frequent contbr. sketches and short stories to mags. Author: Morocco as It Is, 1892; The Real Condition of Cuba, 1897; The Fight for Santiago, 1899; The Golden Horse Shoe, 1900; The American Mediterranean, 1912; Heyday in a Vanished World, 1937; Unfinished Business, Paris-Versailles, 1919 (awarded Pulitzer Prize), 1944; When The French Were Here, 1945; Suitors and Suppliants: The Lesser Nations at Versailles, 1946. Address: 3142 P St. N.W., Washington. Died June 8, 1951.

BOODIN, John Elof (bōōd-dēn'), educator; b. Pjetteryd, Småland, Sweden, Sept. 14, 1869; s. Elias Nelsson and Christina (Magnusson) B.; student Fjellstedt Gymnasium, Upsala, and univs. Colo. and Minn.; A.B., Brown, 1895; A.M., 1896; Ph.D., Harvard, 1899. Instr. in philosophy Brown U., 1896-97; Walker fellow, lectr. Harvard, 1899-1900; prof. philosophy Grinnell Coll., 1900-04, U. Kan., 1904-13, Carleton Coll., 1913-28, U. Cal. at Los Angeles, 1928-39, now emeritus; vis. prof. philosophy U. So. Cal., 1927-28. Visited European universities, including London, Oxford, Cambridge, Paris, and Leipzig, 1920-21. Sec. an dtreas. Western Philos. Assn., 1906-09, pres., 1912-13; pres. Pacific div. Am. Philos. Assn., 1932-33; mem. A.A.A.S., Am. Philos. Assn., Mind Assn., Phi Beta Kappa. Mason. Club: University (Los Angeles). Author: Time and Reality (Psychol. Rev. series), 1904; Truth and Reality, 1911; A Realistic Universe, 1916, revised edit. 1931; Cosmic Evolution, 1925; God, 1934; Three Interpretations of the Universe, 1934; The Social Mind, 1939; Religion of Tomorrow, 1943; A Cosmic Philosophy, 1947. Contbr. to Contemporary American Philosophy, 1930; Religious Realism, 1931; Contemporary American Idealism, 1932; The Philosophy of Bertrand Russell, 1943. Home: University Club, 614 S. Hope St., Los Angeles 14. Deceased.

BOODY, Bertha M., ex-coll. dean; b. Brookline, Mass., Feb. 26, 1877; d. James H. and Mary Wilson (Waterman) B.; A.B., Radcliffe Coll., 1899; Am. Sch. Classical Studies, Rome, 1907-08; A.M., Columbia, 1912. Instr. The Gilman Sch., Cambridge, Mass., 1899-1907, Southwestern State Normal Sch., Pa., 1908-09, Miss Madeira's Sch., Washington, 1909-11; prin. The Charlton Sch., N.Y.C., 1912-14; dean Radcliffe Coll., 1914-20. Conglist. Died Aug. 1943.

BOOK, Dorothy L., social worker, coll. dean; b. Martinsville, Va., Feb. 1, 1903; d. William Henry and Katherine (MacKenzie) Book; A.B., Butler Univ., 1924; spl. courses, N.Y. Sch. Social Work, 1925-32; department psychology, Fordham University Graduate School, 1934-37; LL.D., Boston College, 1953. Case worker, Family Welfare Society, Indianapolis, 1924-25; case worker and asst. dist. sec., Community Service Soc., N.Y. City, 1925-28; dist. sec. Brooklyn Bur. Social Service, 1928-35; instr. Fordham Univ. Sch. of Social Service, 1933-35; field supervisor Dept. Pub. Welfare, Westchester County N.Y., 1935-36; dir. field work Boston Coll. Sch. of Social Work, 1936-40, asst. dean and asso. prof., 1940-43, acting dean, 1943-44, dean and prof. social work since 1944; cons. on social welfare to spl. Commn. on Structure of State Govt., 1950-51. Pres. Mass. Conf. of Social Work, 1946-47; vice chmn., bd. trustees, Mass. Tng. Schs., 1943-48; dir. Boston Greater Community Fund, 1946-49, United Community Services of Met. Boston; Perkins Inst. and Mass. Sch. for the Blind; mem. editorial adv. com. Jour. of Social Case Work (pub. by Family Service Assn. of Am., N.Y.C.), 1943-47. Mem. Commn. on Community Interrelations (N.E. Region), Com. of Catholics for Human Rights, Phi Kappa Phi, Roman Catholic. Club: College (Boston). Contbr. articles to Catholic Charities; contbr. Yearbook(Nat. Probation and Parole Assn.). Rev. editor: Family Budget Counseling, 1944. Home: 222 Beacon St., Boston 15. Office: 126 Newbury St., Boston 16. Died Aug. 9, 1955; buried Hollywood Cemetery, Chestnut Hills, Mass.

BOOKER, George Edward, clergyman; b. Petersburg, Va., Mar. 22, 1872; s. Maj. George Edward and Frances Mary (Eubank) B.; student Coll. of William and Mary, U. Va.; D.D., Randolph-Macon Coll., 1908; m. Anna Parham Howle, Apr. 29, 1896 (died 1933); children—Emma Parham, George Edward III, Nancy Howle. Ordained deacon M.E. Ch., South, 1895, elder, 1897, successively pastor Epworth Ch., Norfolk, Va., Washington St. Ch., Petersburg, Va., Mt. Vernon Ch., Danville, Va., Court St. Ch., Lynchburg, Va., Park Pl. Ch., Norfolk, Va., Monument Ch., Richmond, Va., First Ch., Charlottesville, Va.; presiding elder, Richmond Dist.; mem. 7 successive Gen. Confs., 1914-34; del. to Lausanne (Switzerland) Conf., 1927, Ecumenical Conf., Atlanta, 1932, Sesquicentennial Celebration, Balt., 1933. Trustee Randolph-Macon System of Schs. and Colls.; mem. War Work Commn. of M.E. Ch., South, 1917-18; rep. M.E. denomination at Interdenominational Service. Yorktown Sesquicentennial Celebration, 1931. Mem. Phi Beta Kappa, Kappa Sigma. Democrat. Speaker at various Va. colls. and univs. Address: 1723 Park Av., Richmond, Va. Died Apr. 1, 1951; buried Blandford Cemetery, Petersburg, Va.

BOOLE, Ella Alexander, pres. emeritus World's W. C.T.U.; b. Van Wert, O., July 26, 1858; d. Col. Isaac N. and Rebecca (Alban) Alexander; A.B., Coll. of Wooster, 1878, A.M., 1881, Ph D., 1895, LL.D., 1938; m. Wm. H. Boole, July 3, 1883 (died Feb. 24, 1896). Pres., W.C.T.U. of N.Y., 1897-1903; corr. sec. Woman's Bd. of Home Missions, Presbyn. Ch. in U.S.A., 1903-09; pres. W.C.T.U. State of N.Y., 1909-26; pres. Nat. W.C.T.U., 1925-33; 1st v.p., World's W.C.T.U., 1928-31, pres., 1931-47, pres. emeritus since 1947. Dir. Nat. Kindergarten Assn. since 1937; mem. board of trustees College of Wooster, 1918-26; mem. exec. com. Internat. Temperance Union since 1937. Prohibition candidate for U.S. Senate, 1920. Clubs: Chautauqua Woman's, Nat. Council of Women, Mem. White House Conf. on Children in a Democracy. Mem. Phi Beta Kappa. Address: 377 Parkside Av., Bklyn. 26. Died Mar. 13, 1952; buried Cypress Hills Cemetery, Bklyn.

BOON, Henry George, mfg. exec.; b. Hortonville, Wis., Dec. 9, 1892; s. John Allen and Wilma Esteele (Diener) B.; student Lawrence Coll., Appleton, Wis., 1914; m. Hilda Josephine Vanderloo, Oct. 11, 1919; children—Lois (Mrs. James Femal), John, Richard, Barbara (Mrs. John Hollingsworth). Tech., statis. and prodn. work, Kimberly-Clark Corp., Neenah, Wis., 1914-28, dir., 1938—, vice pres. in charge operations and mem. exec. com., 1945—; dir. Longlac Pulp & Paper Co., Ltd., Terrace Bay, Ont., Can., Upper Can. Timber Co., Ltd., K-C-M Co. Chmn. Outgamie County (Wis.) Red Cross. Mem. Newcomen Soc. Republican. Methodist. Mason, Elk. Clubs: North Shore Country, Riverview Country. Home: Palisades Dr., Menasha, R. 2, Wis. Office: Kimberly-Clark Corp., Neenah, Wis. Died Nov. 10, 1952.

BOOS, Ludwig Charles, rubber exec.; b. Trinidad, B.W.I., May 11, 1903; s. Sir Carl and Lady Edith (Rostant) B.; student Montclair Acad., 1909-18, St. John's Manlius, 1918-23; m. Mary Catherine Boyle, Oct. 16, 1929; 1 dau., Margaret Mary. Joined U.S. Rubber Co. and subsidiaries, 1923, now gen. mgr., U.S. Rubber Co. Internat. Div.; pres., dir. U.S. Rubber Internat. Corp., U.S. Rubber Co. Ltd., Cuba; U.S. Rubber Mexicana, South America; dir. U.S. Rubber International (Great Britain), Ltd., North Brit. Rubber Co., Ltd., U.S. Rubber Co. South Africa, Ltd., U.S. Rubber Internat. (Belgium) Rubber Regenerating Co., Manchester, Eng.; Lastex Yarn and Lactron Thread (Overseas) Ltd., London; Pirelli Lastex Societa, Italo Americana Filo Elastico S.p.A., Milan; U.S. Rubber Internat., S.p.A., Milan. Mem. Nat. Fgn. Trade Council, N.A.M., Rubber Export Assn., Inter-Am. Safety Council. Clubs: Greenwich Country, Metropolitan; Country (Habana, Cuba). Home: Dublin Hill Rd., Greenwich. Conn. Office: 1230 Av. of Americas, N.Y.C. Died Dec. 1959.

BOOTH, Evangeline Cory; b. England, Dec. 25. 1865; d. Gen. William (founder Salvation Army) and Catherine (Mumford) Booth; ed. in London; hon. M.A. Tufts College 1921; LL.D., from Columbia University, 1939; unmarried, Field commissioner of operations of the Salvation Army in London 5 yrs., also prin. Internat. Training Colls.; commanded Salvation Army in Can. 9 yrs.; organized and equipped a party for opening work in the Klondike, 1898; comdr. in chief of Salvation Army in U.S. and its possessions since 1904; elected general of the World Wide Salvation Army, 1934, and residing in London, England; dir. Salvation Army war work, 1914-18; returned to America Dec. 1939 after retiring as internat. leader of the Salvation Army. Awarded D.S.M. (U.S.), 1919; gold medal, Nat. Society of Colonial Dames, for eminent patriotic service, 1928; gold medal Swedish Order of Vasa, 1933; gold medal, Nat. Inst. Social Sciences, for services to humanity, 1933; annual Nat. Humanitarian Award from Variety Clubs of America, 1946. Author and composer of many Salvation Army songs, and of volume, "Songs of the Evangel," 1927. Author: The War Romance of the Salvation Army (with Grace Livingstone Hill), 1919; Love Is All, 1925; Towards a Better World (sermons), 1928; Woman, 1930. Contbr. on religious and social welfare topics. Distinguished as an orator. Address: 120 W. 14th St., N.Y.C. Died July 17, 1950.

BOOTH, George Francis, editor, pub.; b. Hartford, Conn., Nov. 11, 1870; s. William Henry and Eliza (Jackson) Booth; honorary M.A., Williams College, 1939, D.Engring. (hon.), Worcester Poly. Institute, 1940; Dr. Civic Leadership, Clark University, 1945; Dr. of Journalism (hon.), Suffolk University, 1950; Dr. Humane Letters (hon.), Assumption Coll., 1954; married Minnie L. Welles, Nov. 18, 1896; children—Doris Welles (Mrs. Edwin C. Butler), Howard Mason, Robert Welles. Editor and pub., Worcester Telegram, Evening Gazette, Sunday Telegram, Worcester, Mass.; pres. radio station WTAG; director Associated Press 1941-50; vice president and trustee Peoples Savings Bank. Member Mass. State Rationing Board, 1942. Member Metropolitan Water Supply Investigating Commission, 1924-26; delegate to Rep. Nat. Conv., 1924, 1936, 1944; chmn. Mass. delegation to Rep. Nat. Conv., 1932; chmn. Worcester Parks and Playground Commn., 1911-26; first pres. Worcester council Boy Scouts of America, 1911-15. Trustee Worcester Poly. Inst., Worcester Acad., Worcester Art Museum, Memorial Hosp. Mem. New England Daily Newspaper Assn. (ex-pres.), Worcester C. of C. (ex-pres.), Worcester Y.M.C.A. (ex-pres.). Republican. Unitarian. Clubs: Worcester, Economic (ex-pres.), Tatnuck Country Worcester Country (Worcester); Century (N.Y.C.); Nat. Press

(Washington). Home: 64 Beechmont St. Office: 20 Franklin St., Worcester 1, Mass. Died Sept. 1, 1955.

BOOTH, Harold Simmons, chemist; b. Cleve., Jan. 30, 1891; s. Edwin and Lydia Ackley (Simmons) B.; A.B., Adelbert Coll., Western Res. U., 1915, A.M., 1916, Ph.D., Cornell U., 1919; m. Hazel Lavinia Anthony, Dec. 31, 1917; children—Robert (dec.), Marilyn Jane, Elizabeth Lydia. Comml. photographer, 1911-16; instr. chemistry Western Res. U., 1919-24, asst. prof., 1924-30, asso. prof., 1930-37, prof., 1937—; head of dept. of chemistry, Cleveland Coll., 1925—, head of div. of sciences, 1926—, head of div. science and math., 1939—, chmn. summer session div. of chemistry, 1921-42, chmn. dept. chemistry, 1942—, Hurlbut prof. chemistry in univ., 1947. Civilian chemist Cornell Gas Def. Sta., 1917. Dir. Western Reserve sta. USN Research Lab., 1941-44. Fellow Am. Acad. Arts and Sciences; mem. Am. Chem. Soc. (council mem.; hon. chmn. conv. 1943), A.A.A.S., Electrochem. Soc., Phi Beta Kappa, Sigma Xi, Pi Kappa Alpha, Alpha Chi Sigma. Club: Cleveland Author: (with V. R. Damerell) Text on Quantitative Analysis, 1940; (with Donald Ray Marin) Boron Triflourida and its Derivitives, 1949. Editor-in-chief, Inorganic Syntheses, Vol 1; asso. editor, Vol. II, Vol. III. Contbr. profl. jours. Home: R.F.D. 3, Chagrin Falls, O. Office: 10940 Euclid Av., Cleve. Died June 23, 1950; buried Knollwood Cemetery, Mayfield Heights, O.

BOOTH, Willis H., banker; b. Winnemucca, Nev.; s. Levi and Ellen Ann (Bratt) B.; University of California, 1893-97; LL D. (hon.). University of Southern Calif., 1943; m. Chancie Ferris, Jan. 21, 1899; 1 son, Ferris Holyoake. Formerly treas. L. Booth & Sons, machinery, and v.p. Hotpoint Electric Heating Co., both of Los Angeles, Calif.; dir. Edison Gen. Electric Appliance Co. (now Hotpoint, Inc.), Excess Ins. Co. Am., Constitution Reins. Corp., Dividend Shares, Inc., Nat. Retailers Mutual Ins Co., Comml. Solvents Corp., Internat. Bus. Machines Corp., Guaranty Safe Deposit Co., Nation-Wide Securities Co., Inc., Republican primary candidate for U.S. Senate, 1916. Dir. Swedish Chamber Commerce of U.S.A., Argentine-Am. C. of C., Nat. Fgn. Trade Council Am. Arbitration Assn.; hon. pres. Internat. C. of C.; past pres. Los Angeles C. of C., Assoc. C's. of C., Pacific Coast; v.p. Nat. Inst. Soc. Scis. Trustee, National Indsl. Conf. Bd. Appointed by President Coolidge as rep. of U.S. Govt. on Permanent Internat. Commn. for Brazil; apptd. by Gov. Roosevelt as mem. of Special Commn. on Railroad Freight Rates in New York. Decorations: Legion of Honor (France); Order of the Crown of Italy; Order of Restituta (Poland); Golden Sheaf (China); Order of Orange-Nassau (The Netherlands); Knight Royal Order of the North Star (Sweden). Mem. Am. br. Newcomen Soc. of England, Am. Soc. of French Legion of Honor (dir.). Mason (K.T.). Clubs: Sunset (Los Angeles); Metropolitan, Lawyers, The Links, University Pilgrims (New York); American (Paris, France); Deepdale Golf, River. Home: 944 Fifth Av., N.Y.C. 21. Office: 140 Broadway, N.Y.C. Died Feb. 21, 1958; buried Los Angeles.

BOOTHBY, Walter Meredith, medical research; b. Boston, Mass., July 28, 1880; s. Alonzo and Marie Adelaide (Stodder) B.; student Boston U. Sch. of Medicine, 1901-05; A B., Harvard Coll., 1902; M D., Harvard U. Med. Sch., 1906; M.A., Harvard Grad. Sch., 1907; m. Catharine Burns, Nov. 15, 1930; children (by previous marriage)—Gertrude (Mrs. Louis Schulze), Nancy (Mrs. Robert Reinhardt). Interne and house surgeon, Boston City Hosp., 1908-09; practiced surgery in Boston, 1909-16; in charge metabolism and respiration labs., Peter Bent Brigham Hosp., 1913-16; instr. in anatomy, Harvard Med Sch., 1910-16, also lecturer on anesthesia, 1914-16; head of sect. of metabolic research, Mayo Clinic, 1916—; asst. in medicine, Mayo Foundation, 1917-23, asso. prof. in medicine, 1923-26; prof. exptl. metabolism, 1936-48, emeritus professor, 1948—; chmn. Mayo Aero Med. Unit for Research in Aviation Med., 1942-48; guest prof. aviation medicine, Institute of Physiology, University of Lund, Sweden, 1948-50; advisor on research Sch. of Aviation Medicine, prof. physiology, Air U., Randolph Field, U.S. Air Force, Texas, 1950-51; Lovelace Found. for Med. research, 1951—, head of dept of respiratory physiology. Served with A.R.C. Ambulance Hospital, Paris, summer 1915; capt., later major, Med. Corps, U.S. Army, with A.E.F. in France, 22 months; assigned as dir. 1st Corps Gas Sch., Chem. Warfare Service; later instr. Army Med. Sch., Lange, France; at front as chief of surgical team in battles of St. Mihiel and Argonne. President Roosevelt made personal award of Collier Trophy for 1938 to Dr. Walter M. Boothby, and Dr. William Randolph Lovelace II (both of Mayo Foundation), for med. edn. and research, and to Capt. Harry L. Armstrong, M.C., U.S. Army, for mutual contribution to aviation medicine in general and pilot fatigue in particular; certificate of merit, U. Minn., 1949; awarded order Comdr. of North Star by King of Sweden, 1952. Fellow A.C.S., A.C.P.; mem. A.M.A., Am. Physiol. Soc., Am. Soc. Biol. Chemists, American Soc. for Clin. Investigation, Soc. for Exptl. Biology and Medicine, Assn. Am Physicians, Am. Inst. Nutrition, Am. Soc. for Exptl. Pathology, Am. Soc. for Pharmacology and Exptl. Therapy, Am. Soc. Anesthetists, Aero Med. Assn. of U.S., Inst. Aeronautical Sciences, Nat. Aeronautic Assn., Mass. Med. Soc., Alumni Assn. of Mayo Foundation, Minn. State Med. Assn., U.S. Inf. Assn., Sigma Xi. Democrat (liberal). Protestant. Author of 300 sci. papers on respiration, metabolism, thyroid diseases, aviation medicine. Home: 2819 Ridgecrest Dr. Office: Lovelace Found., Albuquerque, N.M. Died July 4, 1953.

BOOTH TUCKER, Frederick St. George de Lautour, ex-comdr. Salvation Army in the U.S.; b. Monghyr, Bengal, India, Mar. 21, 1853; s. William Thornhill Tucker; ed. at Cheltenham Coll., Eng.; m. Emma Moss, d. Gen. Wm. Booth of Salvation Army, 1888 (died Oct. 28, 1903) passed Indian civil service exams., 1874; studied in London until 1876; apptd. to Punjab and held positions of asst. comm'r magistrate, and treas. officer; resigned to join Salvation Army, 1881; inaugurated Salvation Army work in India, 1882; had charge there until 1891; sec. for internat. work, Salvation Army, London, 1891-96, in charge U.S., 1896—. Author: The Life of Catherine Booth, 1892 R3; Life of General William Booth, 1898; In Darkest India and the Way Out; Favorite Songs of the Salvation Army, 1899; Monograph for the Paris Exposition on the Work of the Salvation Army in U.S., 1900. Adopted name of Booth Tucker. Address: 101 Queen Victoria St., London, Eng. Died July 17, 1929.

BOOZ, Edwin George (bōōz), management consultant, engr.; b. Reading, Pa., Sept. 2, 1887; s. Thomas H. and Sarah (Spencer) B.; A.B., Northwestern U., 1912, A.M., 1914; m. Helen M. Hootman, Aug. 9, 1918; children—Donald Robert, Marion Elizabeth McGee. Founder, 1914, and now sr. partner Booz, Allen & Hamilton, management cons., Chicago, N.Y. City, San Francisco, Washington, Minneapolis, Los Angeles; clients include U.S. Gypsum Co., Montgomery Ward & Co., Electric Bond & Share, Western Union Telegraph, University of Chicago, R.C.A., Republic Aviation Corp., General Foods, S.C. Johnson & Son, Inc., Kimberly-Clark, General Mills, Schenley Distillers Corp., Columbia Pictures Corp., Sperry Corp., Standard Oil (Indiana), Inc., Bigelow-Sanford, Island Creek Coal, Weyerhaeuser Timber Company; firm conducts surveys for bus. and instnl. managements. Enlisted as pvt. 333d F.A., U.S. Army, 1917; and commd. lt. after 4 months; 18 months' service as major Inspector General's Dept.; assigned to special staff on bus. orgn., sec. of war. Mem. Assn. Cons. Management Engrs. (past pres.), Alpha Delta Phi. Presbyn. Mason (32°). Clubs: Chicago, Union League, Attic, Executives (Chicago); Glen View Golf (Golf, Ill.); Metropolitan (Washington); University (N.Y. City); Calif. Institute Associates, California (Los Angeles); Tennis, Committee of 25, Thunderbird Country (Palm Springs). Home: 931 Pontiac Rd., Wilmette, Ill. Office: 135 S. LaSalle St., Chgo. Died Oct. 14, 1951.

BORAAS, Julius (bōr'aws), college prof.; b. Goodhue County, Minn., Dec. 7, 1871; s. Johannes J. and Ellen (Hegge) B.; grad. Red Wing Sem., 1890; B.L., U. of Minn., 1895 (Phi Beta Kappa), M.L., 1898, Ph.D., 1917; studied U. of Chicago, summer, 1914; m. Julia Rygh, Nov. 25, 1897; children—Vivian Juliet (Mrs. O. K. Lundeberg), Harold Orlando, Nora Evangeline (Mrs. G. N. Glasoe), Helen Marie (Mrs H. Hoff). Teacher Red Wing Seminary, 1895-99; county supt. schs., Goodhue County, Minn., 1899-1910; prof. edn. and philosophy, St. Olaf Coll., 1910-16, head dept. of edn., 1917-38, became head dept. psychology and edn., 1939, teaching in both fields; emeritus since 1949. Lecturer on school administration and philosophy of education, Univ. of Ia., summers, 1929-32; conductor State Summer Schs., 1911-13; lecturer teachers' insts. Mem. Minn. State Bd. Edn., 1919-37 and 1939-50, pres., 1934-35, 39-40, 49; mem., treas. Bd. of Edn., Northfield, Minn., 1918-39. Mem. Nat. Ednl. Assn., Nat. Soc. Study of Edn., Am. Assn. Univ. Profs., Phi Delta Kappa. Lutheran. Author: Getting Along in Country Schools, 1908; Teaching to Think, 1922; (with Geo. A. Selke) The Administration and Supervision of Rural Schools, 1926; also various articles in English and Norwegian papers and mags. Chapter on "You and the Art of Thinking" in Social Studies, 1935. Home: Northfield, Minn. Died Dec. 4, 1952; buried Northfield, Minn.

BORBER, William, Danish diplomat; b. Copenhagen, Denmark, Nov. 3, 1885; s. Niels Christian and Dorothea Caroline Amalie Ernestine (de Hofman-Schmidth) B.; student, Metropolitanskolen, 1904, A.M. in Polit. Economy, U. Copenhagen, 1911. Sec. Merchants Guild, 1915; mgr. Office Fgn. Trade 1916-19; vice consul, Danish Fgn. Office, 1919-21, sec. commn. regarding comml. treaties, 1919, mem. commn. 1921-26; attached to commn. on reorgn. Danish Fgn. Service, 1920; chief sect. Fgn. Office, 1921; counsellor to Danish Legation, London, 1926-28; permanent del. League of Nations, Geneva, 1928-40, UN, 1947—; E.E. and M.P., 1934, serving in Fgn. Office 1940-47; del. internat. confs. Geneva, 1922, The Hague, 1922, all League of Nations Gen. Assemblies, 1928—, UN Prep. Com., London, 1946, UN Gen. Assembly, London, New York, 1946, N.Y. 1947, 49-51, Paris, 1948, 51-52, rep. on Econ. and Social Council 1948; rep. on Security Council, 1953-54. Address: Ahlmannsalle 23, Copenhagen, Denmark. Died May 14, 1958.

BORCHARD, Edwin (bôr'chärd), prof. of law; b. N.Y. City, Oct. 17, 1884; s. Michaelis and Malwina (Schachne) B.; Coll. City of New York, 1898-1902; LL.B., cum laude, New York Law Sch., 1905; Columbia Coll., and Law Sch., 1905-08, A.B., 1908 (P.B.K.), Ph.D., Columbia, 1913; hon. LL.D., U. of Berlin, 1925, U. of Budapest, 1935; m. Corinne E. Brackett, Jan. 20, 1915; children—Carol Margaret (Mrs. George Spokin), and Alice Gertrude (Mrs. William M. Couch, Jr.). Expert on internat. law to the American Agency, North Atlantic Coast Fisheries Arbitration at The Hague, 1910; law librarian of Congress, Jan. 1911-16, except 1913-14, when served as asst. solicitor Dept. of State; chief counsel for Peru, Tacna-Arica Arbitration; atty. for Nat. City Bank, New York, 1916-17; prof. law, Yale U. Law Sch., since 1917. U.S. tech. adviser Conf. on Codification of Internat. Law, 1930; mem. for U.S. Com. of Experts, Inter-American Codification of Internat. Law. Mem. Internat. Acad. Comparative Law (The Hague); associate, Institut de Droit International. Unitarian. Clubs: Cosmos (Washington); Graduate (New Haven); Yale, Columbia University (N.Y.). Author: Guide to Law and Legal Literature of Germany, 1911; Bibliography of International Law and Continental Law, 1913; The Diplomatic Protection of Citizens Abroad, 1915; Commercial Laws of England, Scotland, Germany and France (with A. J. Wolfe), 1915; Guide to Law and Legal Literature of Argentina, Brazil and Chile, 1917; Declaratory Judgments, 1918, 34 (rev. edit., 1941); Latin-American Commercial Law (with T. Esquivel Obregón), 1920; Convicting the Innocent, 1932; Neutrality for the United States (with W. P. Lage), 1937, 40; American editor and translator Fiore's International Law Codified, 1917. Compiler, Coastal Waters, 1910. Contbr. to American and European legal periodicals. Home: 605 Ridge Rd., Hamden 14, Conn. Died July 22, 1951.

BORDEN, C(harles) Seymour), business exec.; b. Chicago, Ill., Nov. 8, 1880; s. Seymour Skiff and Nelora (Andrews) B.; student Dartmouth Coll., 1901-02; m. Mina Shaw, Oct. 4, 1904; children—Seymour S., Ruth Borden (Mrs. H.S. Embree). With father S. S. Borden, 1902-20; director S. S. Borden Co., 1920-30; pres. and treas. to 1943 when a partnership was formed; sr. partner S. S. Borden Co. (est. 1879), since 1943; sec. and dir. Central Cold Storage Co., since 1918; pres., dir. Chicago Mercantile Exchange, 1946-49, gov. since 1946. Mem. Nat. Poultry, Butter and Egg Assn. (treas., dir. since 1940); dir. Nat. Assn. Commodity Exchanges and Allied Trades, Inc. Club: South Shore Country. Home: 7320 Phillips Av., Chicago 49. Office: 133 S. Water Market, Chgo. Deceased.

BORDEN, Spencer, mfr.; b. Fall River, Mass., Sept. 8, 1872; s. Spencer and Effie A. (Brooks) B.; A.B., Harvard, 1894; m. Sarah H. Ames, June 1, 1901 (now dec.); children—Spencer III (dec.), Blanche Butler (Mrs. Alfred B. Freming), Joan (Mrs. Leonard B. Colt), Ames (dec.), Richard. Pres. Fall River Gas Co., Silver Lake Mills; director Fall River Nat. Bank, Nat. Shawmut Bank (Boston), Flintkote Co., Am. Mutual Liability Ins. Co., Boston Mfrs. Mutual Fire Ins. Co., Mutual Boiler Ins. Co., Sagamore Mfg. Co., Foster Spinning Co., Allied Am. Mutual Ins. Co., Policy Holders Insurance Co. Clubs: Somerset, Harvard, Boston, New York; New York Yacht, Harvard (N.Y.), Porcupine (Nassau, B.W.L.), Agawam Hunt, Hope (Providence). Home: 63 Manning St., Providence; also Union Interallieé, Paris, France. Died Jan. 31, 1957.

BORG, George William, mfr. exec.; b. West Burlington, Ia., Oct. 24, 1887; s. Charles W. and Amelia (Gustafson) B.; student pub. schs.; m. Effie Brown; children—Charlotte, Marshall. Organized with Marshall Beck, Borg & Beck Co., Chicago, mfrs. motor-vehicle clutches, 1913, v.p., 1913-22, pres. 1922; chmn. George W. Borg Corp., Delevan, Wis., Borg-Warner Corp. Served U.S.N.R. Mem. Soc. Automotive Engrs., Motor and Accessories Mfrs. Assn., Chicago Assn. Commerce, Ill. Manufacturers Assn. Club: Lake Shore Athletic (Chicago). Inventor (with Marshall Beck) of disk clutch used in automotive industry. Office: George W. Borg Corp., Delevan, Wis. Died Feb. 21, 1960.

BORGER, Edward M. (bor'ger), petroleum exec.; b. Sewickley, Pa., May 4, 1901; s. William Edward and Alice Annetta (McCune) B.; studied law and business adminstrn., Duquesne U. Admitted to Pa. bar, 1922, U.S. Supreme Court, 1927, and practiced in City of Pittsburgh, 1922-40; counsel and chief counsel, The Peoples Natural Gas Co., N.Y. State Natural Gas Corp., Hope Natural Gas Co., and other natural gas subsidiaries of Standard Oil Co. (N.J.), Pittsburgh, 1935-40; pres., gen. mgr. and dir., Peoples Natural Gas Co.; chmn., dir. N.Y. State Natural Gas Corp.; dir. Consol. Natural Gas Co., N.Y. City, since 1943. Councilman, Borough of Osborne, Pa.; mem. exec. com. Allegheny County Conf. on Community Development. Served in Am. Field Service, North Africa and Italy, 1942-44. Mem. Am. Gas Assn., Am., Allegheny County, and Pa. bar assns., Am. Petroleum Inst., Pa. Soc., Pa. Natural Gas Men's Assn. (dir.), Sewickley Y.M.C.A. (dir.). Presbyn. (trustee). Clubs: Civic (Allegheny County); Duquesne, Allegheny Country, Edgeworth, Shannopin Country (Pittsburgh). Home: 1207 Beaver Rd., Sewickley. Office: Two Gateway Center, Pitts. 22. Died Sept. 20, 1953.

BORGESE, G(iuseppe) A(ntonio) (bôr-jā'sē), author, univ. prof.; b. Polizzi Generosa (Palermo), Nov. 12, 1882; s. Antonio and Rosa (Di Martino) B.; Ph.D., U. of Florence, 1903; m. Maria Freschi, 1908; children—Leonardo, Giovanna; m. 2d, Elisabeth V. Mann, Nov. 23, 1939; children—Angelica, Dominica. Came to United States, 1931, naturalized, 1938. Prof. German literature, University of Rome, 1910-17, University of Milan, 1917-25; professor of aesthetics and history of criticism, University of Milan, 1926-31; head of Press and Propaganda Bur. during Orlando's Premiership, 1917-18; organized Congress and Pact of Rome among nations of Hapsburg Monarchy, Apr. 1918; head of Italian delegation to Interallied Conf., London, Aug. 1918; leader of democratic opinion in Italy for League of Nations and New Europe; opposed Nationalism and Fascism; left Italy, 1931; refused Fascist oath; visiting prof. of Italian culture, U. of Calif., 1931; lecturer at the New School for Social Research, N.Y. City, 1932; Neilson prof. of comparative literature, Smith Coll., 1932-35; prof. of Italian and comparative literature, 1935-36; prof. of Italian literature, U. of Chicago, 1936-48; reinstated at University of Milan, 1948; visiting professor, Political Science, U. of Chicago, Puerto Rico, 1943; sec. Com. to Frame World Constitution since 1945. Dir. monthly magazine, Common Cause, since 1947. Decorated medal for military valor, etc. Honorary mem. Phi Beta Kappa; fellow Am. Academy of Arts and Scis. Author: Poesie, Rubè (English transl., 1923) and many other books of poetry, fiction, criticism, history, philosophy, and politics pub. in Italy; On Dante Criticism, 1936; Goliath, the March of Fascism (first book in English), 1937; The City of Man (in collaboration), 1940; Common Cause, 1943. Foundations of the World Republic, 1953. Contbr. articles Ency. of the Social Sciences, Ency. Britannica, Saturday Review of Literature, Speculum, Atlantic Monthly, The Nation, Life, etc. Home: 5124 Hyde Park Blvd., Chgo. 15. Office: 975 E. 60th St., Chgo. 37. Died Dec. 4, 1952.

BORGMAN, Albert Stephens, prof. English; b. Detroit, Mich., Aug. 20, 1890; s. Martin Grant and Nellie (Harvey) B.; grad. Detroit U. Sch., A.B., U. of Mich., 1911; A.M., Harvard, 1912, Ph.D., 1919; unmarried. Instr. English and German, Norfolk (Va.) Acad., 1914-15; instr. English, N.Y. Univ., 1919-22, asst. prof., 1922-25, asso. prof., 1925-28, prof. since 1928. Served as ensign U.S.N.R.F., 1918. Mem. Phi Beta Kappa. Episcopalian. Clubs: Harvard, Authors (New York); Authors (London). Author: Thomas Shadwell—His Life and Comedies, 1928; The Life and Death of William Mountfort, 1935. Address: New York University, University Heights, N.Y.C. 53. Died Dec. 9, 1954; buried Detroit.

BOROWSKI, Felix (bô-rôf'skĭ), composer; b. Burton, Eng., of Slavonic parentage, Mar. 10, 1872; studied music 1st under private masters; grad. Conservatoire, Cologne, Germany, in violin, pianoforte and composition; lived in London until 1897; m. Edith Frances Grant, Oct. 9, 1897 (died Mar. 22, 1916); children—Olga, Leopold; m. 2d, Elsa Kanne, Aug. 9, 1920. Dir. dept. of composition and lecturer upon musical history, 1897-1916, pres. Chicago Musical Coll., 1916-25 (resigned); supt. Civic Music Association Chicago, 1926-32; professor musicology, Northwestern University, 1937-42, retired. Composer works for orchestra: Three Symphonies: Miracle triomphale, 2 suites: Valse Pathétique; Le Printemps passionné: Ecce Homo; Elegie Symphonique; Peintures, Fantaise-Overture, "Youth" (won $1,000 prize of North Shore Festival Assn., Evanston, Ill., 1923); The Mirror, 1954; tone poem, Semiramis, Requiem for a Child. Allegro de Concert for organ and orchestra, Rhapsody for organ and small orchestra. Overture to a pantomime and Idyll for small orchestra, Chamber music: three string quartets. Piano: Sonate russe; Prelludes; Concerto with orchestra; also smaller works. Violin: Liére Mazur., Schoumka Ukainenne, Aria, 2 iéme Mazur., Adoration, and others. Organ: Suite, 2 Sonatas. Voice: Songs For the stage: Boudour, ballet-pantomime (Chicago Opera Assn., 1919); A Century of the Dance, ballet; satirical opera, Fernando del Nonsentsico. Also critic and writer on musical subjects; musical critic of Chicago Evening Post, 1906; formerly musical editor of Chicago Record-Herald; now musical editor of Chicago Sun-Times and Chgo. musical critic for Christian Sci. Monitor. Mem. Am. Soc. Composers, Authors, Publishers. Author of historical and analytical programmes for the Theodore Thomas Orchestra (now Chicago Symphony Orchestra) 1908—; Ency. of the Symphony, 1949. Co-author: Standard Operas and Standard Concert Guide (with Geo. P. Upton), 1930. Clubs: Tavern, Cliff Dwellers, Arts. Home: 36 Bellevue Pl., Chgo. 11. Office: Chgo. Sun-Times, 211 W. Wacker Dr., Chgo. 6. Died Sept. 6, 1956.

BORST, Guernsey J. (bôrst), educator; b. Seward, N.Y., Nov. 4, 1877; s. Dow V. and Lucy J. (Guernsey) B.; A.B., Cornell U., 1903; Pd.M., N.Y. U., 1909, Pd.D., 1911, Ph.D., 1912; spl. studies, Columbia, 1919-21, A.M., also spl. diplomas in ednl. adminstrn. and as tchr. edn.; m. Alonzella McIntire, Jan. 22, 1913; 1 dau., Alonzella M. Prin. pub. schs., N.Y. and New Eng., until 1913; supt. schs., Danbury, Conn., 1913-20; dean coll. of edn. Valparaiso U., 1920-21; prof. edn., dir. sch. bus. and comml. sci. Skidmore Coll., 1921-46; prof. edn. Syracuse U., summers 1926-27, Rutgers U., summers 1928-42; dean Skidmore Coll. Glens Falls (N.Y.) div., 1946—. Mem. N.E.A., Am. Assn. U. Profs., Am. Assn. Sch. Adminstrs. Pres. Schoolmasters' Round Table, Conn., 1914-16, dir. State Teachers' Assn., Conn., 1918-20. Episcopalian. Mason, Rotarian. Author: Comparative Financial Study of Conn. City School Systems; Experimental Studies in Ednl. Psychology. Home: 32 Laurel Pl., West Caldwell, N.J. Died Sept. 21, 1955.

BOSETTI, Joseph, clergyman; b. Milano, Italy, Jan. 1, 1886; s. Giovanni and Adele (Clavenna) B.; ed., coll. in Switzerland; Ph.D., Propaganda, Rome, Italy, 1904. Came to U.S. 1911, naturalized 1923. Ordained priest, Roman Catholic Church 1908; domestic prelate, 1926—; chancellor and vicar general Diocese of Denver; dir., boys camp, St. Malo, Allens Park, Colo., 1917—; founder and conductor, Denver Grand Opera Co.; producer, operas for Catholic charities; composer, church music; teacher and choir dir. Home and office: 1536 Logan Av., Denver. Died Jan. 22, 1954.

BOSSARD, James Herbert Siward, sociologist; b. Danielsville, Pa., Sept. 29, 1888; s. John Henry and Augusta Minerva (Oplinger) B.; A.B., Muhlenberg Coll., 1909, D.H.L., 1948; M.A., U. of Pa., 1911, Ph.D., 1917; Dorothy M. Lemle, May 14, 1929; children—Barbara, Constance. Prof. history and social science, Muhlenberg Coll. 1911-17; asso. editor, Allentown (Pa.) Morning Call, 1917-18; lecturer on sociology, Lafayette Coll., 1917-18, prof. sociology and economics, 1918, head dept. of economics and govt., 1918-20; asst. prof. sociology, Wharton Sch., U. of Pa., 1920-25, prof. 1925—; prof. of sociology medical school, U. Pa.; William T. Carter Prof. of Child-Development, and dir. William T. Carter Foundation for Child Development, U. of Pennsylvania, 1938—; visiting prof. of sociology and Fellow of Pierson College, Yale University, 1947-48. Taught summers at University of Calif., 1929, 30, 33, 35. Pres. West Phila. Community Conf., 1922-1925. Dir. survey of Northampton County, Pa., for Interch. World Movement, 1919; dir. survey Collegiate Schs. of Business, 1929-31. Director Pa. Com. on Penal Affairs, 1922-41; dir. child welfare div. Pub. Charities Assn. Pa., 1922-44; dir. Univ. Settlement House, 1924-37, Social Service Dept. of U. of Pa. Hosp., Maternal Health Center, 1929-38; pres. Eastern Sociol. Conf., 1934-35; pres. Pa. Birth Control Fedn., 1936-39; mem. Philadelphia Commn. on Federal Housing Projects, Pennsylvania State Probation Commission, 1933. Pres. Parent-Teacher Assn., Lansdowne Friends Sch., 1939-43. Fellow Soc. Research in Child Development; member Am. Acad. Polit. and Social Science, Am. Sociol. Soc. (mem. exec. com.; 2d v.p., 1940; 1st v.p., 1941); Am. Council Learned Societies, Alpha Tau Omega, Pi Gamma Mu. Republican. Episcopalian. Club: The Lenape. Author: Ritual in Family Living, 1950; Toward Family Stability, 1950; Parent and Child: Studies in Family Behavior, 1953; The Large Family System, 1956; One Marriage, Two Faiths, 1957. Co-author: Successful Marriage, 1947; Marriage, The Family, and Parenthood, 1948; Courtship and Marriage, 1953. Part author: Introduction to Sociology, 1952. Spl. editor and co-author: Annals of Am. Acad. Polit. and Soc. Sci. Contbr. articles to mags. Home: 317 Aubrey Rd., Wynnewood, Pa. Died Jan. 29, 1960.

BOST, Ralph Walton (bŏst), chemist; b. Rockwell, N.C., Jan. 5, 1901; s. James Walton and Mary Lee (Miller) B.; A.B., Newberry (S.C.) Coll., 1923; A.M., U. of N.C., 1924, Ph.D., 1928; m. Beulah Christine Cauble, July 12, 1927. Asst. in chemistry, U. of N.C., 1923-24; instr. chemistry, Tulane U. (La.), 1924-26; with U. of N.C. since 1926, instr. chemistry, 1926-28, asst. prof., 1928-34, asso. prof., 1934-37, prof. since 1937, head of chemistry dept. since 1939, also acting dean Sch. of Applied Science, 1933-35. Member American Chemical Society, Chemical Society of London, Elisha Mitchell Scientific Soc., Am. Physical Society, North Carolina Academy of Science, Pi Kappa Delta, Sigma Xi, Kappa Psi, Alpha Chi Sigma. Pres. Chapel Hill (N.C.) Rotary Club, 1935-36. Author: Bibliography of Organic Sulfur Compounds, 1930. Home: 500 E. Rosemary St. Office: Venable Hall, Chapel Hill, N.C. Died Sept. 22, 1951; buried Chapel Hill Cemetery.

BOSTON, Joseph H., artist; b. Bridgeport, Conn.; prin. works Devils Glen and Portrait of Franklin W. Hooper, Bklyn. Inst. Mus., Silver Moonlight, Butler Art Inst., Youngstown, O. Recipient bronze medal Pan-Am. Expn., Buffalo, 1901. A.N.A. Mem. Soc. Am. Artists, Bklyn. Art Club. Clubs: Lotus, Salmagundi (N.Y.C.). Home: 154 W. 57th St., N.Y.C. Deceased.*

BOSTROM, Wollmar Filip (bōō'strûm), Swedish diplomat; b. Tynnelsö Castle, Sweden, June 15, 1878; s. Filip August and Pauline B.; ed. Upsala; m. Gertrud Wennerberg, 1907; 1 dau. Attaché, Paris, 1905; 2d sec. Fgn. Office, Stockholm, 1906, 1st sec., 1908; counselor, London, 1913-18; undersec. of state, 1918-22; apptd. envoyé, 1919; E.E. and M.P. to Spain and Portugal, 1923-26, to U.S., 1926-45, ret. 1945. Former pres. Swedish Tennis Assn. Address: Stockholm, Sweden. Died Nov. 7, 1956; buried Tynneloa.

BOSWELL, Grover Cleveland, educator; b. at Elkton, Tennessee; s. James M. and Fannie (Puckett) B.; student University of Texas, 1925; B.A., East Tex. Teachers Coll., 1926; student Southern Meth. U., 1927; M.A., Simmons U., 1933; LL.D., Texas Wesleyan, 1939; m. Mary Anna Murrell, June 8, 1915; children—Monroe, Helen, Genevieve. Teacher and supt. of various schs., 1914-33; dean McMurry Coll., Abilene, Tex., 1933-36; pres. Weatherford (Tex.) Coll., 1936-41; supt. city schs. and pres. Ranger Coll., 1941-52; gen. land office of Texas, Austin, 1952—. President Weatherford C. of C., 1939, local chapter Am. Red Cross. Dir. N.W. Tex. Meth. Conf. Hist. Commn., West. Tex. Hist. Assn., Tex. So. U.; mem. Central Meth. Conf. Bd. of Education. Delegate Methodist General Conference, Birmingham, Ala., 1938; del. Meth. Uniting Conf., Kansas City, 1939. Mem. Tex. State Teachers Assn. (life). Democrat. Methodist. Mason (Shriner), Odd Fellow, K.P., Elk. Pres. Weatherford Rotary Club, 1941; past pres. Ranger Rotary Club; gov. Rotary Internat., District 186, 1949-50. Address: 1808 Forest Trail, Austin, Tex. Died Sept. 11, 1953; buried Austin, Tex.

BOSWELL, Peyton, Jr., writer, editor; b. Chgo., Sept. 22, 1904; s. Peyton and Bessie (McGee) B.; student Rutgers U.; m. Edna E. Marsh, Sept. 19, 1931; children—Patricia, Peyton. Sport reporter, 1927-29; asso. editor Art Digest, 1929-36; editor, pub. Art Digest, 1936—. Mem. Woodcut Soc., Soc. Miniature Prints. Republican. Club: Salmagundi (N.Y.C.). Author: Modern American Painting (Book-of-Month Club selection), 1939; Henry Varnum Poor, 1941; George Bellows, 1942. Contbr. to Art Digest; Am. Encyclopedia (Painting and Sculpture), 1935-50. Home: 88 Coolidge St., Malverne, N.Y. Office: 116 E. 59th St., N.Y.C. Died June 23, 1950; buried Ringoes, N.J.

BOSWORTH, Arthur Harding, investment banker; b. Denver, Feb. 4, 1886; s. Joab Otis and Leonora (Snyder) B.; Ph.B., Yale, 1908; m. Loula Ferguson, Oct 22, 1912; children—Arthur Ferguson, Elizabeth Ferguson (Mrs. Barry Morey Sullivan). Started investment banking with Wm. E. Sweet & Co., Denver, 1908-13; v.p. Sweet, Causey, Foster & Co., 1913-16; pres., Bosworth, Chanute & Loughridge, 1916-46; chmn. bd. dirs. Bosworth, Sullivan & Co. (consol), 1945—; dir. Daniels & Fisher Stores Co., Pub. Service Co. of Colo., Colo. & So. Ry. Co., No. Okla. Gas Co. Mem. Delta Phi, St. Elmo Club at Yale. Republican. Episcopalian. Mason. Clubs: Denver, Denver Country, University (Denver); Yale (N.Y.C.). Home: 301 High St. Office: 660 17th St., Denver. Died Nov. 1, 1949.

BOSWORTH, Robert Graham, lawyer; b. Denver, Colo., Oct. 11, 1888; s. Joab Otis and Leonora (Snyder) B.; A.B., Princeton U., 1912; LL.B., Harvard, 1915; m. Helen Russell Cauldwell, June 17, 1915; children—Helene, Barbara, Robert Graham. Admitted to Colo. bar, 1916; practiced with firm Pershing, Bosworth, Dick & Dawson, Denver, or its predecessor, since 1915; treas., dir. and atty. Denver Fire Clay Co.; dir. and gen. counsel Northern Okla. Gas Co., Denver Union Stock Yard Co., Daniel & Fisher Stores Co., National Alfalfa Dehydrating and Milling Company, National Chlorophyll and Chemical Company. Commissioned captain, field arty., U.S. Army, Nov. 1917; asst. supervisor of instrn., Am. Arty. Sch., Saumur, France, Apr.-Dec. 1918; comd. 2d Battn., 19th F.A., Luxemburg, Dec. 1918-May 1919; disch., 1919. An original trustees Civic Symphony Soc. Denver; past pres. Denver U. Assos.; state senator, 1939-46; Senate majority floor leader, 1945. Mem. Am., Colorado, Denver bar assns., Cap and Gown (Princeton). Republican. Episcopalian. Clubs: University, Mile High, Denver Country (all Denver). Home: 314 Franklin St. Office: Equitable Bldg., Denver, Colo. Died Sept. 11, 1954.

BOTHE, Walther bōtē), physicist; b. Oranienburg, Germany, Jan. 8, 1891; s. Fredrich and Charlotte (Hartung) B.; Dr.phil., U. Berlin, 1914; m. Barbara Below, July 6, 1920 (dec. 1951); children—Elena (Mrs. Oswald Riedel), Johanna. Lectr. U. Berlin, 1926-29, asst. prof., 1929-30; prof. U. Giessen, 1930-32; prof. U. Heidelberg, 1932—; dir. Physics Inst., Max Planck Inst. Med. Research, Heidelberg, 1934—. Recipient Order Pour le Mérite, peace class, 1952, Planck medal, 1953, Nobel prize in physics (with Max Born), 1954, Grosses Verdienstkeuz Bundesrepublik, 1954. Mem. academies of Heidelberg, Goettingen, Leipiz, Berlin. Home: 6 Im

Baeckerfeld. Office: 29 Jahnstrasse, Heidelberg, West Germany. Died Feb. 8, 1957.

BOTTOM, Raymond Blanton, newspaper pub.; b. Richmond, Va., Sept. 8, 1893; s. Davis and Ella Virginia (Alley) B.; ed. pvt. and pub. schs., Richmond, Va., and various service schs. of U.S. Army; m. Dorothy E. Rouse, July 2, 1925; children—Barbara Agnes (Mrs. Miles D. Forst), Dorothy Evelyn (Mrs. Langdon B. Gilkey), Raymond Blanton. Rodman, instrumentman and chief of surveying party in railroad location and construction, 1911-17; newspaper publisher, 1931—; pres. and business mgr. Daily Press Inc.; president, Southern Colorprint Corporation; pres. Hampton Roads Broadcasting Corp., 1931—; pres. Peninsula Industrial Finance Corporation; director Citizens Marine Jefferson Bank. Member bd. trustees Virginia War Memorial Museum. Commd. 2d lt., promoted 1st lt., Engrs., U.S. Army, 1917; served as 1st lt., later capt., C.A.C., U.S. Army, 1917-31; aerial observer, U.S. Army Air Corps, France and Germany, 1918-19, with 24th and 50th Aero Squadrons; lt. comdr. (D-VS), U.S.N.R., 1942-44. Chmn. Hampton Roads Regional Defense Council, 1940-42. Decorated Victory and Army of Occupation (Germany) medals. Member Military Staff, Governor of Virginia. Member Va. State Chamber of Commerce (director), American Newspaper Publishers Association, Sigma Delta Chi frat. Clubs: James River Country (Newport News); Yacht (Hampton, Va.); Commonwealth (Richmond); National Press (Washington). Home: 103 Powhatan Parkway, Indian River Park, Hampton, Va. Office: 215 25th St., Newport News, Va. Died Oct. 29, 1953; buried Greenlawn Cemetery, Newport News.

BOTTOMLEY, William Lawrence (bŏt'tŭm-lĭ), architect; b. N.Y.C., Feb. 24, 1883; s. John and Susan Amelia (Steers) B.; B.S. in Architecture, Columbia, 1906, Columbia post-grad. scholarship, 1909-10; student Am. Acad. in Rome (McKim Prix de Rome), 1906-09, Ecole des Beaux Arts, 1907-09; m. Harriet Townsend, Aug. 26, 1909; children—Harriet Campbell (Mrs. Shepherd Fitch Smith), Susan Townsend (Mrs. William Nesbit Chambers), Virginia Townsend (Mrs. Campbell Townsend). Began practice as architect, N.Y., 1911; mem. firm Hewitt & Bottomley, architects, 1912-19. Works include: High School, Southampton, N.Y.; High Sch. and auditorium, Portchester, N.Y.; Embassy Club, N.Y.; town house, N.Y. City, and country house, Middleburg, Va., for William Ziegler, Jr.; residences for R. G. Cabell (Richmond, Va.), Warren B. Nash (Goldens Bridge, N.Y.), Amory S. Carhart (Warrenton, Va.). Works: (residences) for General William H. Cocke (Claremont, Va.), Norman de R. Whitehouse (Old Brookville, L.I.), J. Randolph Robinson (Westbury, L.I.), Robert Goelet (Georgetown, S.C.), Elinor M. Ryan (Washington, D.C.), Cornelius J. Rathborne (Westbury, L.I.), Capt. and Mrs. Newton H. White, Jr. (Mitchellville, Md.), Mr. and Mrs. Richard Trimble, Jr. (Westbury, L.I.); town houses for Myron C. Taylor and James C. Warburg; City all and Court House, Plainfield, N.J. Asso. of L. F. Peck; High Sch., Malverne, N.Y. Asso. of J. L. Mills and A. P. Hess. Works: Apt. House, 1049 Park Av., N.Y.C.; asso. J. L. Mills, Hotel Albert, University Place, N.Y.C.; asso. A. P. Hess; Hotel, 10 East 60th St., N.Y.C.; mem. Bottomley, Wagner & White, architects. N.Y.C., 1928—; works: River Club and River House; residences for Mr. and Mrs. Robert Strawbridge, Jr. (Westbury, L.I.), Mrs. W. R. Massie (Greenwood, Va.); Phillips Inn, Andover Acad., Andover, Mass.; Emigration Station, Galveston, Tex. Mayor Village of Old Brookville, L.I., 1928-34; trustee Beaux Arts Inst. Design, 1912-20. Fellow A.I.A., Alumni Asso. Acad. of Rome, Archtl. League, Beaux Arts Soc. Recipient medal of honor, Archtl. League, 1934; Apartment House medal, N.Y. chpt. A.I.A., 1921. Republican. Episcopalian. Author: Spanish Details, 1924. Editor: Great Georgian Houses of America, Vols. 1 and 2, 1933 and 1935. Contbr. to archtl. publs. Home: The Hickory, Glen Head, Long Island, N.Y. Died Feb. 1, 1951.

BOUCHER, Chauncey Samuel (bou'chĕr), educator; b. Chicago, Ill., June 14, 1886; s. Chauncey Watson and Elizabeth (Van Loon) B.; A.B., U. of Michigan, 1909, A.M., 1910, Ph.D., 1914; LL.D., Washington and Jefferson College, 1936, Knox College, 1952; student at Harvard Graduate School, 1911-12; married Ida D'Ooge, June 25, 1913; 1 daughter, Jane Elizabeth. Instr. in history U. Mich., 1910-11, 1913-14; asst. prof. history, Washington U., 1914-19; asso. prof. Am. history, Ohio State U., 1919-20; prof. Am. history, U. of Tex., 1920-23; prof. Am. history, U. of Wis., 1923, 2d semester and summer; prof. Am. history, U. of Chicago, 1923-1935, dean Coll. of Arts, Lit. and Science, 1926-1935; pres. West Virginia U.; 1935-38; chancellor University of Nebraska, 1938-46; Abraham Lincoln lecturer in American Civilization, Knox Coll., 1947-52; retired, 1952; now engaged in writing and lecturing. Vice chairman and member board of review of Commn. on Institutions of Higher Edn., North Central Assn. Colls. and Secondary Schs., 1928-32; trustee of Cooper Foundation since 1940; consultant on higher education, Alabama Educational Survey, 1944-45. Mem. Am. Hist. Assn. (com. on Justin Winsor prize, 1922-26), Miss. Valley Hist. Association (pres., 1920-21), Association of Land-Grant Colleges and Universities (president, 1944-1945), Progressive Education Association's Commission on Relation of Schools and Colleges, 1931-1935, National Society for Study of Education, Society for the Advancement of Edn., Nebraska Schoolmasters Club, Rotary Internat., Phi Beta Kappa, Pi Gamma Mu, Theta Delta Chi; fellow Royal Hist. Soc. Conglist. Author: The Nullification Controversy in S.C., 1916; The Chicago Coll. Plan, 1935, rev. edit., 1940; also 6 monographs on the antebellum history of S.C. and the South, also Correspondence Addressed to John C. Calhoun, 1837-1849. Contbr. on hist. and ednl. subjects to leading periodicals. Asso. editor Miss. Valley Hist. Review, 1921-24. Home: 45 Belvedere Club, Charlevoix, Mich.; also 2016 E. Lee St., Tucson. Died Aug. 13, 1955; buried Charlevoix, Mich.

BOUDIN, Louis B. (bōō'dĭn), lawyer; b. Russia, Feb. 15, 1874; s. Peter and Frome (Feld) B.; came to U.S., 1891; naturalized citizen, 1897; LL.B., N.Y. U., 1896, LL.M., 1897; m. Leah Kanefsky, May 15, 1899; children—Eleanor, Vera (Mrs. Sidney Elliott Cohn); m. 2d, Anna Pavitt, May 1, 1909. Admitted to N.Y. bar, 1898, U.S. bar, 1919; mem. Boudin, Cohn & Glickstein, N.Y.C., 1938—; was candidate for officer of Chief Justice of N.Y. State Court of Appeals, asso. judge and justice Supreme Court, State of N.Y. Mem. Am. Bar Assn., Assn. Bar City N.Y., Nat. Lawyers Guild (dir.), Am. Judicature Soc., N.Y. County Lawyers Assn., Acad. Polit. Sci., Am. O.R.T. Fedn. (chmn. bd. dirs.), Am. Polit. Sci. Assn., Am. Econ. Assn. Mem. Am. Labor Party. Author: The Theoretical System of Karl Marx, 1907; Socialism and War, 1915; Government by Judiciary (2 vols.), 1932. Editor New Review, 1912-15, Ort Economic Review, 1944—. Contbr. law jours. and mags. Home: 200 W. 58th St. Office: 1776 Broadway, N.Y.C. Died May 29, 1952.*

BOULTER, Howard Thornton, editor; b. Omaha, Neb., July 8, 1907; s. Franklin and Helen Thornton (Casey) B.; student San Diego State Coll., 1926-27; m. Kathryn L. Cooper, Dec. 23, 1933; children—Thomas Franklin, Stephen Cooper. Cub reporter Los Angeles Record, 1926; various positions San Diego (Calif.) Union, 1927-43; mng. editor San Diego Eve. Tribune, 1943-51, editor, 1951—. Mem. Asso. Press Mng. Editors Assn., San Diego Chamber of Commerce, Sigma Delta Chi. Republican. Episcopalian. Clubs: San Diego, Kiwanis. Home: 4490 Monroe Av., San Diego 15. Office: Evening Tribune, San Diego 12, Cal. Died Apr. 24, 1953; buried Cypress View, Bronze Room, San Diego.

BOULTER, Thornton, editor San Diego Evening Tribune. Address: San Diego, Cal. Died Apr. 13, 1953.

BOURGOINE, Joseph John, sr. v.p., dir. v.p. Shaw-Walker Co. Home: 9 Northway, Bronxville, N.Y. Office: 405 Lexington Av., N.Y.C. Died May 8, 1955.*

BOURQUIN, George M., ret. judge; b. Warren County, Pa., June 24, 1863; s. Justin and Celestin (Ducray) B.; student pub. schs.; m. Mary M. Ratigan, Sept. 25, 1891. U.S. receiver pub. money, Helena, Mont., 1890-94; admitted to bar, 1894; judge Dist. Ct., Mont., 1905-09; U.S. dist. judge Dist. of Mont., 1912-34; resigned to become Rep. candidate for U.S. Senate. Home: Wilkes-Barre, Pa. Died 1958.

BOURSKAYA, Ina, operatic singer; b. Gitomir, Russia, Sept. 9, 1888; d. Joseph and Teophila (Demlicka) Korzeniowski; ed. Timishid Sch., Gitomir; studied mathematics U. Petrograd; singing in Kieff and Italy; m. W. Bourski, June 1908 (divorced). Début at Kieff, Sept. 1913; Am. début as Carmen, Met. Opera Co., New York, Mar. 1922; with Chgo. Civic Opera Co., 1922; sang in Washington, D.C., Mar. 1924; then with Metropolitan Opera Co. Address: 7040 Yale Av., Chgo., Ill. Died. 1955.*

BOVEY, Charles Cranton (bō'vē), merchant billing; b. of Am. parentage, St. John, N.B., Can., Oct. 25, 1864; s. Charles Argalis and Hannah Caroline (Brooks) B.; grad. Phillips Andover Acad., 1886; B.A., Yale, 1890; m. Kate Estelle Koon, June 14, 1898; children—Martin Koon, Ruth Alden (Mrs. Nathaniel Stevens II), Charles Argalis. Engaged in ry. constrn., 1890; joined Washburn Crosby Co., Mpls., 1891, becoming dir., 1902, v.p., 1914, pres., 1928-29, chmn. bd. until 1935; dir. General Mills, Inc., 1928-52. Trustee William Hood Dunwoody Indsl. Inst., Blake Sch. for Boys (both Mpls), Mpls. Soc. Fine Arts. Mem. Psi Upsilon, Scroll and Key. Republican. Conglist. Clubs: Minneapolis, Skylight, Woodhil Country (Wayzata, Minn.); University (Chgo.). Home: 400 Clifton Av. Office: Gen. Mills Bldg., Mpls. Died July 28, 1955.

BOVIE, William T., teacher, inventor; b. Augusta, Mich., Sept. 11, 1882; s. William and Henrietta (Barnes) B.; A.B., Mich., 1908; A.M., U. of Mo., 1910; Ph.D., Harvard, 1914; Sc.D. (hon.) Albion Coll., 1929; m. Martha Adams, Sept. 15, 1909; 1 son, William Adams. Prof. geology and biology, Antioch Coll., 1906-07; research fellow, Cancer Comm., Harvard U., 1914-20; instr. bacteriol., Harvard U., 1920-21, asst. prof. biophysics, 1920-27; prof. biophysics, Northwestern U., 1927-29; lecturer, social technology, Colby Coll., 1939-48. Awarded John Scott Medal, Franklin Inst., 1928. Mem. Botanical Soc., Physiol. Soc., Physical Soc., Soc. for Cancer Research, Soc. Tropical Medicine, Am. Acad. Arts and Sciences, Am. Chem. Soc. (chmn. biol. sect. 1919-23). Developed pioneer methods for therapeutic use of radio active substances; perfected electric apparatus for bloodless surgery and for prevention of metastasis of cancer cells; inventor various biophysical instruments. Address: 22 Summit St., Fairfield, Me. Died Jan. 1, 1958; buried Maplewood Cemetery, Fairfield, Me.

BOWDITCH, Richard Lyon, steamship exec.; b. Milton, Mass., Oct. 11, 1900; s. Ernest William and Margaret (Swann) B.; student Mass. Inst. Tech., 1923; LL.D., Northeastern U., 1949, Bates Coll., 1954; M.A. (hon.), Marlboro Coll. 1952; m. Mabel Lowell Rantoul, May 11, 1929; children—Richard Lyon, Nathaniel Rantoul, James Lowell. With Logan Co. Coal Corp., Lundale, W.Va., 1923-24; sales dept. C. H. Sprague & Son Co., Boston, 1924—, pres., dir., 1935-54, chmn. bd., 1954—; pres., dir. C. H. Sprague & Son, Ltd., Can., Sprague Steamship Co., Boston; chmn. bd. Imperial Smokeless Coal Corp. (Quinwood, W.Va.), Am. Coal Shipping, Inc., A. H. Bull S.S. Co.; dir. A. H. Bull & Co., Bull-Insular Lines, San Antonio Co., First Nat. Bank Boston, Liberty Mut. Ins. Co., Ludlow Mfg. & Sales Co., New River Co., (Mt. Hope, W.Va), Va. Smelting Co., Sylvania Electric Products Co., Am. Research & Development Corp., Bangor & Arrostrook R.R., Winding Gulf Coals, Inc. With OPS, Washington, 1951. Trustee U.S. Inter-Am. Council; pres. New Eng. Council, 1946-48, chmn. sr. council, 1948-50; mem. civic progress com. City of Boston. Trustee Northeastern U., 1950—; chmn. bd. advisers Fletcher Sch. of Law and Diplomacy; mem. bd. Mass. Inst. Tech., 1941-45; dir. Nat. Coal Policy Conf.; trustee Bates Coll.; mem. bd. advisors Mass. Investors Trust. Served with U.S. Army Engrs. Res., 1922. Mem. Coal Execs. Conf., Transportation Assn. Am. (dir., corp. v.p.), Am. Inst. Mining and Metall. Engrs., Am. Mil. Engrs., Am. Soc. Naval Architects of Marine Engrs., Naval Order U.S., U.S. (pres. 1953-54, chmn. bd. 1954-55, chmn. exec. com. 1955-56, mem. sr. council 1956-59), Internat. (mem. U.S. council) C.'s of C. Club: Commercial (Boston). Home: 31 Fayerweather St., Cambridge, Mass. Office: 10 Post Office Square, Boston. Died July 31, 1959; buried Camden, Me.

BOWDOIN, George E., corp. exec.; b. Balt., Jan. 23, 1898; s. Henry J. and Julia Morris (Murray) B.; student Gilman Sch., Balt., 1910-16; student Princeton, 1920; m. Harriet Sinton, Nov. 20, 1950. Formerly exec. v.p., dir. U. S. Hoffman Machinery Corp., N.Y.C., now pres. Served with 1st div. USMC, PTO; disch. lt. col. Res. Decorated Bronze Star, Silver Star, Gold Star in lieu of 2d Silver Star. Home: 440 Park Av., N.Y.C. 22. Office: 105 4th Av., N. Y.C. 3. Died Mar. 3, 1959.

BOWEN, Albert E., lawyer, church official; b. Henderson Creek, Ida., Oct. 31, 1876; s. David and Annie (Shackleton) B.; A.B., Brigham Young Coll., 1902; traveled in Europe, 1903-05; J.D., Univ. of Chicago, 1911; m. Aletha Reeder, June 1902 (died Apr. 1905); children—Albert R., Robert R.; m. 2d, Emma Lucy Gates, June, 1916. Instr. Brigham Young Coll., 1905, prof. of history, 1906-08; admitted to Utah Bar, 1911, practiced law in Logan and Salt Lake City, 1911-37; Cache County atty., 1913; (mem. of quorum of Twelve Apostles, Church of Jesus Christ of Latter-day Saints since 1937. Pres. Desert News Pub. Co.; dir. Utah State National Bank, Utah-Idaho Sugar Company, National Service Corporation, Utah Pub. Service Corp. Mem. bd. trustees Brigham Young Univ. Mem. Am. Judicature Soc., Order of Coif. Pres. Utah State Bar Assn., 1923-24. Republican. Mormon. Clubs: Salt Lake Country, Timanogas. Home: 255 First Av. Office: 47 E. S. Temple, Salt Lake City. Died July 15, 1953.

BOWEN, Asa Bosworth, physician; b. Eastford, Conn., Apr. 12, 1942; s. Oliver and Betsey Bosworth (Horton) B.; student pub. schs., Conn.; Mexico Acad., Oswego Co., N.Y., 1862-63; M.D., Albany Med. Coll., 1868; m. Minnie Clark, May, 1874. U.S. pension surgeon, 25 yrs.; local surgeon C.&N.-W. Ry., 20 yrs.; pres. Farmers Trust & Savings Bank; v.p. First Nat. Bank. Served USN on man-of-war Neptune, stationed in West Indies, 1864-65. Mem. A.M.A., Ia. State Med. Soc., Am. Assn. Ry. Surgeons. Republican. Mason. Home: Maquoketa, Ia. Deceased.

BOWEN, Edwin Winfield, ducator, writer; born nr. Prince Frederick, Md., Oct. 20, 1866; s. Cephas Henry and Sarah Jane (Simmons) B.; A.B., Randolph-Macon Coll., 1887, A.M., 1889; postgrad. Johns Hopkins, 1889-92, Ph.D., 1892; student U. Leipzig, 1893-94. Prin. Middleburg (Va.) classical Sch., 1887-88; asst. prof. English, U. Mo., 1892-93; prof. Latin, Randolph-Macon Coll., 1894-1950; head of Latin dept., Summer Sch. of South, 1905; traveled in Europe, 1906, 08, 10, during which time wrote a series of letters of travel for the press; elected prof. English, U. of the South, and editor Sewanee Review, 1909, but declined; book reviewer N.Y. Times Saturday Rev., 1903-04; mem. summer faculty, U. Cal., 1912, N.Y.U., 1916, 17, Coll. of William and Mary, 1918, U. Va., 1921; studied in Paris during summer, 1913; dir. Hanover (Va.) Nat. Bank. Mem. Am. Philol. Assn., Modern Lang. Assn. Am., Am. Assn. U. Profs., Classical Assn. Middle West and South, Va. Hist. Soc., Brit. Classical Assn., Phi Beta Kappa; pres. Va. Classical Assn., 1916, 17. Author: Historical Study of the E-Vowel in English, 1893; A History of the O-Vowel in English, 1895; Makers of American Literature, 1907; Questions at Issue in Our English Speech, 1909. Editor: Cicero de Amicitia and de Senectute, 1907; Tacitus' Annals (Career of Germanicus), 1912. Contbr. to Classical jours., Am. and fgn. periodicals, Ency. Americana. Home: Ashland, Va. Died 1953.

BOWEN, Ivan, lawyer; b. Sleepy Eye, Minn., Jan. 28, 1886; s. John Richard and Florence Maria (Gradner) B.; LL.B., Georgetown U., 1911; m. Mildred Muriel Morehart, Apr. 29, 1912; children—Robert M., William M., Mildred E. (Mrs. Lester H. Bolstead), Ivan. Admitted to Minn. bar, 1911; law practiced Mankato, 1913-17, 19-21; mem. Minn. R.R. and Warehouse Commn., 1921-28; partner Bowen & Bowen, Mpls., 1928—; counsel Greyhound Lines; v.p., dir. (ret.) Greyhound Corp.; gen. counsel (ret.) Nat. Assn. Motor Bus Operators. Adv. to employers delegation 24th Conf. Internat. Labor Orgn., Geneva, Switzerland, 1938. Served as capt., F.A., O.R.C., 89th Div., U.S. Army, 1917-19; with Minn. N.G., 1921-40; ret. as col. Recipient Medal of Merit, State of Minn., Mil. Dept., 1940. Mem. Am. (mem. House of Dels., representing sect. pub. utility law), Minn. State bar assns., Am. Legion, Vets. Fgn. Wars. Republican. Presbyn. Mason. Home: Route 4, Excelsior, Minn. Office: 1630 Rand Tower, Mpls. 2. Died Sept. 24, 1959.

BOWEN, John C., cement co. exec.; exec. v.p., and dir., Lehigh Portland Cement Co., Allentown, Pa.; sec. and dir. Pennsylvania Supply Co., Harrisburg, Pa.; dir. Lehigh Valley Trust Co. Trustee Inland Portland Cement Co. Home: Route 1, Macungie, Pa. Office: Young Bldg., Allentown, Pa. Died Jan. 19, 1954.

BOWEN, Louise de Koven (Mrs. Joseph Tilton B.), social worker; b. Chgo., Feb. 26, 1859; d. John and Helen (Hadduck) de Koven; student Dearborn Sem., Chgo.; hon. M.A., Knox Coll., 1922; D.H.L., Tufts, 1926; citizen-fellow Chgo. Inst. of Medicine, 1939; m. Joseph Tilton Bowen, June 1, 1886 (now dec.). Treas. Hull House Assn., Chgo., 1893—, pres., 1935-44, now hon. pres.; pres. Juvenile Protective Assn. 35 yrs., now hon. pres.; v.p. United Charities, 1911-1951; chmn. Woman's Ill. Div. Council Nat. Defense; past mem. Rep. Nat. Com.; pres. Woman's World Fair, Chicago, 1925-27; apptd. Woman Fair Price Commr. for Ill. by Dept. of Justice, 1920; mem. bd., auditor Nat. Am. Woman Suffrage Assn.; v.p. Ill. Equal Suffrage Assn.; pres. Chgo. Equal Suffrage Assn.; del. for U.S. to Internat. Woman Suffrage Alliance in Budapest; established first Boy's Club in Chgo.; del. White House Conf. on Child Health and Protection, under Woodrow Wilson U.S. ofcl. del. Pan-Am. Conf., 1922; mem. com. founding Vis. Nurses of Chgo.; mem. Juvenile Court com. that established Juvenile Court; assisted in foundation of Boys Court and Court of Domestic Relations; pres. Roosevelt Republican Woman's Club several years. Treas. Mt. Desert Island (Me.) Biology Lab.; v.p. Nat. Social Hygiene Assn. of N.Y. Recipient gold medal of Rotarian Club for distinguished service, 1941. Episcopalian. Clubs: Chicago Woman's, Woman's City (hon. pres.), Friday, The Fortnightly, Hull House Woman's (pres. 17 yrs.). Author: Safeguards for City Youth at Work and at Play, 1914; Growing Up With a City, 1926; Speeches, Addresses and Letters of Louise de Koven Bowen, 1938; Baymeath, 1945; Open Windows, 1946; also various brochures and reports on sociol. subjects. Home: 1430 Astor St., Chgo. 10. Died Nov. 9, 1953; buried Graceland Cemetery, Chgo.

BOWEN, Norman Levi, geologist; b. Kingston, Ont., Can., June 21, 1887; s. William Alfred and Elizabeth (McCormick) B.; A.M., Queen's U., 1907, B.S., 1909, LL.D., 1941; Ph.D., Mass. Inst. Tech., 1912; hon. Sc.D., Harvard Tercent; m. Mary Lamont (M.D.), Oct. 3, 1911; 1 dau., Mrs. Jerold Orne. Came to U.S. 1909. Field investigator, Ont. Bur. Mines, 1907-09, Geol. Survey of Can., 1910-11; petrologist, Carnegie Instn., Washington, D.C., 1912-18, and 1920-37; Charles L. Hutchinson distinguished service prof. of petrology U. of Chicago, 1937-47, chmn. dept. geology, 1945-47; prof. mineralogy Queen's U., 1919-20; petrologist Carnegie Instn., Wash., 1947—. Supervisor optical glass production, War Industries Board, World War I. Member Geological Society American (v.p. 1938-45, pres. 1946), Mineral Society Am. (pres. 1937), Mineral. Soc. London, Am. Geophysical Union, Am. Acad. Arts and Sciences, Washington Acad. Sciences, Am. Philos. Soc., Nat. Acad. Sciences, Indian Acad. Sciences (hon.), Kaiserlich deutsch Akademie der Naturforscher (Halle), Soc. Geol. Belgique, Finnish Acad. Sciences, All-Russian Mineral. Soc. Bigsby medalist Geol. Soc. of London, Eng., 1941, Penrose medalist Geol. Soc. of America, 1941. Miller medalist Royal Soc. of Canada, 1943. Clubs: Cosmos (Washington, D.C.); Kingston Yacht. Author: The Evolution of the Igneous Rocks, 1928. Contbr. to Jour. of Geology, Am. Jour. Science, Jour. Physical Chemistry, Bull. Geol. Soc. America, Am. Mineralogist. Jour. Am. Ceramic Soc., Zeitschrift für anoganische Chemie, etc. Joint discoverer of Mullite, the fundamental constituent of fire clay refractories. Prin. petrologist (consultant) U.S. Bur. of Mines, 1942; coordinator research and official investigator for N.D.R.C. contract, Geophysical Lab., 1943. Mem. bd. Natural Resources and Conservation, State of Illinois, 1944-47. Address: 3801 Connecticut Av., Washington 8. Died Sept. 11, 1956.

BOWER, Alexander, artist; b. N.Y.C., Mar. 31, 1875; s. Alexander and Mary Louise (Schwarz) B.; student pub. schs., N.Y.C.; student Pa. Acad. Fine Arts and Sch. Indsl. Art of Pa. Mus., Phila., 1900-06; hon. A.M., Bowdoin, 1938; m. Louise Magee Clark, Sept. 13, 1917. Engaged in indsl. design, mural painting and work in leaded and stained glass, 1900-10; work confined to landscape and marine painting, 1910—. Dir. fine arts, Sesqui-Centennial Internat. Expn., Phila., 1926; dir. Sch. Fine Arts and L.D.M. Sweat Meml. Art Museum, Portland, Me., 1931-51. Chmn. of first Art Commn. of State of Me. Has exhibited at Carnegie Inst., Pitts., Corcoran Gallery, Washington, Art Inst. Chgo., N.A.D., N.Y.C., Pa. Acad. Fine Arts, Phila., etc. Associate Nat. Acad., 1931; mem. Fellowship Pa. Acad. Fine Arts, Phila. Water Color Club, Phila. Sketch Club, Artists Fund Soc., Portland Soc. of Art, Salmagundi Club; hon. asso. mem. Me. chpt. A.I.A. Clubs: Cumberland (Portland); St. Botolph (Boston, Mass.). Home: Arden, Del. Studio: 111 High St., Portland, Me. Died Aug. 6, 1952.

BOWERS, Claude G., historian, found. exec.; b. Hamilton Co., Ind., Nov. 20, 1878; s. Lewis and Juliet B.; ed. pub. schs., pvt. tutors; hon. M.A., Tufts, 1926; LL.D., Notre Dame, 1930; U. of S.C., 1930, U. of N.C., 1931; Litt.D., Holy Cross Coll., 1930; Doctor Honoris Causa Philosophy and Letters, Cath. U. Chile, 1951, U. Ind.; married Sybil McCaslin, November 28, 1911; 1 daughter, Patricia. Editorial writer, Indianapolis Sentinel, 1901-02, Terre Haute Star, 1903-06; editor Ft. Wayne Journal Gazette, 1917-23; editorial writer N.Y. World, 1923-31; polit. columnist N.Y. Journal, 1931-33; ambassador extraordinary and plenipotentiary to Spain, 1933-39; ambassador to Chile, 1939-53; nat. chmn. Woodrow Wilson Birthplace Found., 1954—. Chmn. Am. delegation to 1st United Nations Conf. for Latin-America at Santiago; chmn. Am. delegation to Conf. of Inter-American Institute of Cartography, Geography and History, Santiago, 1950. Candidate for Congress, Terre Haute Dist., 1904-06; del. Dem. Nat. Conv., 1908; chmn. Dem. Nat. Conv., Houston, 1928; also keynote speaker, Nat. Dem. Jackson Day Banquet, Washington, 1928; formerly dir. Ind. Lincoln Memorial Assn.; mem. Ind. Memorial Commn., 1921-23. Apptd. mem. Sesquicentennial and Jefferson Centennial Commn. by President Coolidge, and made sec., 1926; recipient Jefferson medal at formal dedication of Monticello to the nation, July 4, 1926, for work on Jefferson; apptd. mem. commn. to determine the true historical value of Jackson's triumph at New Orleans, by Gov. of Tenn., 1927; hon. pres. Andrew Jackson Soc. created to foster a more just treatment of Jackson in school histories; chmn. of Soc. for Relief of Spanish children in Spanish war; acted as intermediary for the exchange of prisoners. Chmn. Am. delegation to 1st Pan-Am. Housing commn. at Buenos Aires, 1939; initiated first exch. of journalists between S.A. and U.S., 1941; chmn. U.S. delegation Fifth Cong. Inter-Am. Institute of History and Geography at Santiago, 1950. Awarded Order of Freedom by War Dept. for work for hemispheric solidarity, World War II; awarded highest decoration of Chilean Govt., 1950. Member Nat. Inst. Arts and Letters; hon. mem. Childean Acad. History. Clubs: National Press (Washington); Authors (New York); Union, Golf (Santiago). Author: Irish Orators, 1916; Life of J. Worth Kern, 1918; The Party Battles of the Jackson Period, 1922; Jefferson and Hamilton—The Struggle for Democracy in America, 1925; William Maxwell Evarts (in Amer. Secretaries of State and Their Diplomacy), 1928; The Tragic Era—The Revolution After Lincoln, 1929; Jefferson and Civil and Religious Liberty (speeches), 1930; Beveridge and the Progressive Era, 1932; Jefferson in Power—The Death Struggle of the Federalists, 1936; Spanish Adventures of Washington Irving, 1940; The Young Jefferson, 1945; Pierre Vergniaud; Voice of the French Revolution, 1950; My Mission to Spain; Watching the Rehearsal for World War II, 1954; Making Democracy a Reality (lectures), 1954; Chile Through Embassy Windows, 1958; also (brochure) Founders of the Republic (Am. Hist. Assn.). Editor: Diary of Elbridge Gerry, Jr., 1927. Address: 20 W. 84 St., N.Y.C. Died Jan. 21, 1958; buried Highland Lawn Cemetery, Terre Haute, Ind.

BOWERSOCK, Donald Curtis, ins. exec.; b. Wilkinsonville, Mass., Mar. 28, 1899; s. Walter Elliott and Charlotte (Klaus) B.; grad. Brown U., 1920; m. Josephine Evans, Oct. 8, 1925; children—Donald Curtis, Glen Warren. Marine sec. Providence Washington Ins. Co., 1936; sec., 1939; v.p., 1941; v.p. Boston Ins. Co., 1944; pres., dir., 1945—; v.p. Old Colony Ins. Co., 1944, pres., dir., 1945—, Boston Indemnity Co., 1954—; pres. Eastern Underwriters Assn., 1951—. Assoc. of Marine Underwriters. Mem. exec. com., laws com. Nat. Bd. Fire Underwriters; trustee Am. Fgn. Ins. Assn., Provident Instn. Savs.; dir. Am. Bur. Shipping, National Fire Protection Association, Rockland-Atlas National Bank. Pres. Rivers Day Country Sch., 1951-52. Named Ins. Man of Year in New Eng., 1954. Member of the Boston C. of C., U.S. Aviation Underwriters (adv. council), Ins. Execs. Assn., Newcomen Soc. Eng. Clubs: Country (Brookline, Mass.); Bankers of Am. (N.Y. City); Algonquin, Down Town, Brown, Comml. (Boston); Merchants. Home: 135 Edmunds Rd., Wellesley Hills, Mass. Office: 87 Kilby St., Boston 2. Died Nov. 30, 1954.

BOWIE, Clifford Pinckney (bōō'ē) consulting engr.; b. Phillipsburg, Mont., June 28, 1879; s. Clifford Napoleon and Mary Ellen (Irvine) B.; B.S., U. of Calif., 1904, hon. C.E., 1923; m. Alice Frances Jones, June 8, 1906 (died Aug. 10, 1923); 1 dau., Barbara Alice; m. 2d, Nan Mountjoy, June 2, 1928. Asst. engr. to U.S. Reclamation Service, May-Sept. 1903; asst. city engr., Hayward, Calif., May-Dec. 1904; asst. to city engr., San Francisco, Calif., 1904-06; city engr., Chico, Calif., 1906-07, asst. engr., later chief engr. Associated Pipe Line Co., 1907-16; supervising engr. U.S. Bureau Mines Petroleum Sta., San Francisco, 1916-46; consulting engr. since 1946. Served as consulting engineer to United States Fuel Administration, World War. Mem. Am. Inst. Mining and Metall. Engrs. Episcopalian. Clubs: Engineers, Commercial (San Francisco); Hillside, Abracadabra, Lawn Bowling (Berkeley). Wrote bulletins of U.S. Bureau Mines; Construction and Operation of a Single Tube Cracking Furnace for Making Gasloine, 1916; Oil Storage Tanks and Reservoirs, 1918; Extinguishing and Preventing Oil and Gas Fires, 1918; Oil Camp Sanitation, 1921; The Bowie-Gavin Process, 1926; Salvage of Materials in the Oil Industry, 1929; Transportation of Gasoline by Pipe Line, 1932; Hardening of Mud Sheaths in Contact with Oil, and a Suggested Method for Minimizing Their Sealing Effect in Oil Wells, 1937. Contbr. to Nat. Petroleum News, Oil and Gas Jour., etc. Inventions: Bowie-Gavin process, 1920; mud lining oil and gas wells, 1936; oil well formation slotter, 1939; drilling wells through heaving formations, 1940. Address: 2120 Los Angeles Av., Berkeley 7, Cal. Died Apr. 1, 1952.

BOWKER, Horace (bou'kẽr); b. Boston, May 13, 1877; s. William Henry and Charolette Jeanette (Ryder) B.; A.B., Harvard, 1898; m. Adelaide Kent Greene, Oct. 16, 1901 (died Apr. 20, 1938); children—Alice, Horace, Rosamond; m. 2d, Laurence Hewlett Burr, May 12, 1939. Began in fertilizer business, 1899; former pres. Bowker Chem. Co.; former pres. and chmn. bd. Am. Agrl. Chem. Co. Trustee Village of Lawrence. Republican. Episcopalian. Clubs: Harvard (N.Y.C.); Lawrence Beach (Atlantic Beach, L.I.); Rockaway Hunting (Cedarhurst, L.I.). Home: 597 Chauncey Lane, Cedarhurst, L.I., N.Y. Died May 25, 1954; buried Forest Hills, Boston.

BOWLBY, Joel Morgan, corp. exec.; b. Litchfield, Ill., Apr. 26, 1887; s. Joel and Amelia (Smith) B.; grad. So. Ill. U., 1904; LL.D., Xavier U., 1947; m. Alice Fairbairn, Aug. 29 1928 (dec. Dec. 1951); children—Joel Morgan, III, Dudley Churchill; m. 2d, Dorothy S. Horner, December 23, 1953. With Railway Steel-Spring Co., 1904-09; asso. comml. investment banking bus., 1910-12; pub. accountant, 1913-16; with U.S. Liquidation Commn., also chief machine tool sect., office of dir. sales U.S. War Dept., 1920; asso. Barrow, Wade, Guthrie & Co., C.P.A.'s, 1921-41, gen. partner, 1928-41; pres. Eagle-Picher Co., 1941-49, dir., 1941—, chmn. bd., 1949-55. Served as maj. inf., A.E.F., 1917-19. Mem. Am. Inst. Accountants (past mem. council), Ill. Soc. C.P.A.'s (past pres.), Am. Inst. Mining and Metall. Engrs. Episcopalian. Clubs: Queen City (Cin.); Mid Day (Chgo.); Pacific Union (San Francisco); Links (N.Y. City). Office: American Bldg., Cin. 1. Deceased.

BOWLER, James B., congressman; b. Chgo.; student pub., parochial schs. of Chgo.; m. Anastasia V. Sweeney. Mem. Chgo. City Council, 1906-53; commr. compensation City of Chgo., 1923-27, later pub. vehicle license commr.; mem. 83d to 85th Congresses, 7th Ill. Dist. Democrat. Address: House Office Bldg., Washington. Died July 18, 1957.

BOWLER, William Howard, clergyman; b. Seward County, Neb., Sept. 5, 1871; s. Edwin Parker and Caroline (Holden) B.; student pub. schs.; D.D., Linfield Coll., 1924; m. Elma Fulkerson, Apr. 4, 1911; children—William Reginald, Helen Frances. Ordained Bapt. ministry, 1894; pastor Bellevue, Ida., 1894-99, Shoshone, 1900-02; dist. missionary for Ida., 1903-05; evangelist, Ida. and Mont., 1905; supt. home missions, Ida., 1907-13, Ida. and Utah, 1914-17;

exec. sec. Bapt. Laymen's Movement fr the West, 1918; field rep. Gen. Bd. Promotion, No. Bapt. Conv., 1919-24, sec. Bd. of Missionary Coöperation, 1924-34, sec. Council on Finance and Promotion, 1934-49; became asso. sec. Ohio Bapt. Conv., 1940; now retired. Republican. Home: 8545 159th St., Jamaica, N.Y. Died May 7, 1951; buried Brookfield, Mo.

BOWLES, Charles (bōlz), ex-mayor; b. Yale, Mich., Mar. 24, 1884; s. Alfred and Mary (Lutz) B.; grad. Ferris Inst., Big Rapids, Mich., 1904; LL.B., U. of Mich., 1909; m. Ruth Davis, June 1, 1915; 1 dau., Helen Ruth. Admitted to Mich. bar, 1909, and began practice at Detroit; judge Recorder's Court, Detroit, 1926-29; mayor of Detroit, 1930-32; now in practice of law. Clubs: Michigan University, Cadillac Athletic, Optimists, Wayne County Republican, Lake Shore Country. Home: 4261 Fullerton Av. Office: Dime Bank Bldg., Detroit, Mich. Died July 30, 1957.*

BOWLES, Elliott A., drugs exec.; b. Washington, June 29, 1913; s. B. Agee and Caroline P. (Hyatt) B.; B.S., Benjamin Franklin U., 1940; m. June E. Henderson, Jan. 22, 1938; children—Brenda A., Michael H. Vice pres. Whitehall Pharmacal Co., N.Y. City, 1950-55, exec. v.p., 1955-57, pres., 1957—. Episcopalian. Home: 16 Midhurst Rd., Short Hills, N.J. Office: 22 E. 40th St., N.Y.C. 16. Died June 27, 1957; buried Christ Church, Short Hills.

BOWLES, Oliver, mining engr., geologist; b. nr. Lindsay, Ont., Can., Jan. 10, 1877; s. William Henry and Sarah A. (Glaspell) B.; prep. edn. Lindsay Collegiate Inst., Can., 1901-03; B.A., U. Toronto, Can., 1907, M.A., 1908; grad. work U. Mich., U. Minn.; Ph.D., George Washington U., 1922; m. Eva H. Workman, 1908; children—William George, Edgar Oliver. Came to U.S., 1908, naturalized, 1914. Field work, Bureau of Mines, Ont., summers, 1908-10; tchr. geology and mineralogy U. Mich., 1908-09, U. Minn., 1909-14; with State Geol. Survey, Minn., summers 1911-13; temporary geologist U.S. Geol. Survey, parts of 1912-14; quarry technologist, U.S. Bureau Mines, 1914-17, mineral technologist, 1917-23; supervising engr. nonmetallic minerals expt. sta., New Brunswick, N.J., 1923-28, supervising engr. building materials sect., 1928-37, asst. chief nonmetal economics div., 1937-42, chief, 1942-47, retired, 1947; parttime research prof. U. Md., 1948—. Received gold medal from Dept. of Interior for distinguished service in Bureau of Mines; Hardinge award, Am. Inst. Mining and Metall. Engrs. Mem. Am. Inst. Mining and Metall. Engrs., Mineral Soc. Am., Soc. Econ. Geologists, N.Y. Acad. Science, Sigma Xi; hon. mem. Inst. Quarrying of Great Britain. Republican. Christian Scientist. Club: Cosmos (Washington). Author: The Stone Industries; also numerous bulletins, reports and articles in tech. press on stone, slate, lime, cement, asbestos, etc. Adress: 5000 Massachusetts Av., Washington 16. Died Aug. 1, 1958.

BOWLES, Sherman Hoar, publisher The Springfield (Mass.) Republican. Address: 1 Crescent Hill, Springfield, Mass. Died Mar. 3, 1952; buried Springfield Cemetery.

BOWLING, Edgar Simeon (bō'lĭng), dir. P. Lorillard Tobacco Co.; b. Durham County, N.C., Sept. 6, 1875; s. Simeon and Margaret (Bowen) B.; student U. of N.C., 1896; A.B., Trinity Coll. (now Duke U.), 1899; m. Joe Alston Claiborne McIlwaine, Feb. 7, 1912; 1 dau., Joe Claiborne McIlwaine (Mrs. George W. Hebard). Dir. Brit. Am. Tobacco Co., London, Eng., 1917-29; v.p. Brown & Williamson Tobacco Co., 1927-29; dir. Imperial Tobacco Co. of Can., 1919-29, Smith Paper Co., 1917-29, U.S. Foil Co., 1918-36, Am. Bank & Trust Co., Petersburg, Va., 1922-25; dir., v.p. Reynolds Metals Co., 1929-31, Garland S.S. Co. and Stonewall Corp., 1919, 31; dir. P. Lorillard Tobacco Co., 1935—. Mem. Arbitration Bd. of Am. indsl. advisor NRA, 1934. Trustee Duke Meml. and Duke U. Donor Centre Hill Mansion to Petersburg Nat. Battlefield Park. Mem. N.C. Soc. of N.Y. (past pres.), Duke U. Alumni Assn. (pres. 1935), Va. Hist. Soc., Omicron Delta Kappa. Clubs: Bankers, University (N.Y.C.); Scarsdale Golf; Country (Petersburg, Va.). Home: 12 Sunset Av., Bronxville, N.Y. Office: 119 W. 40th St., N.Y.C. Died Apr. 15, 1950; buried Maplewood Cemetery, Durham, N.C.

BOWMAN, Frank Otto, army officer, retired; Mesilla Park, N.M., July 27, 1896; s. Henry D. and Carrie (Otto) B.; B.S., U.S. Military Academy, 1918; grad. Engrs. Sch., basic course and civil engr. course, 1921; m. Lucy Reed Curtis, June 17, 1920; children—Frank Otto, Henry D. II. Commd. 2d lt., Corps of Engrs., U.S.A., 1918, and advanced through grades to maj. gen., 1954; chief engr., II Corps, Jacksonville, Fla., and Eng., 1942; later became engr. European Theater of Operations; engr. Allied Force Hdqrs., England and North African Theater of Operations; engr., 5th Army, 1943, Hdqrs. Service of Supply, North Africa, Apr.-July, 1943; engr. 5th Army, Aug. 1943-45; engr. Yokohma Base, Japan, Oct. 1945; comdg. Ground Forces, Okinawa, May, 1946; asst. chief of staff, G-4, Army Ground Forces, Aug. 1946; comdr. Columbus Gen., Depot, Columbus, O., 1947-49; chief of staff, dep. comdr. Engr. Center, Ft. Belvoir, Va., 1940-53; chief engr. U.S. Army Forces Far East, 1953-55; comdg. gen. Ft. Leonard Wood, Mo., and 6th Armored Div., 1955-56, ret. June 30, 1956. Decorated D.S.M., Legion of Merit with two oak leaf clusters, Purple Heart (U.S.), Comdr. British Empire, Croix de Guerre (French), Comdr. Crown of Italy, Silver Star of Valor (Italy), Military Medal (Brazil), Ulchi Distinguished Mil. Service Medal with Gold Star (Korea). Address: P.O. Box 52, Carmel, Cal.

BOWMAN, George Lynn (bō'mån), lawyer; born near Harrisonburg, Rockingham County, Virginia, Oct. 9, 1874; s. William Harpine and Frances (Hoffman) B.; student Western Coll., Toledo, Ia., 1893-97; studied law, Drake U., Des Moines, Ia., 1898-99; m. Clarissa Potter, Nov. 5, 1903 (died May 19, 1909); m. 2d Lena Odessa Pollard, Oct. 7, 1913 (died Sept. 22, 1931); m. 3d Mary Crosthwait, June 1, 1933 (died Dec. 21, 1938); m. 4th Edna Hoffman, July 25, 1940. Began law practice at Kingfisher, Okla., 1900; county atty., Kingfisher County, 1902-07; del.-at-large, Dem.-Nat. Conv., 1912; del. to Dem. Nat. Conv., 1920, 32, 36, 44, 48; mem. Nat. Com., 1920-24. Pres. bd. trustees Kingfisher Coll.; dir. Okla. Meml. Assn. (past pres.); mem. bd. regents U. of Okla. for 14 yrs. (pres. bd. 1932-36); mem. Okla. State Bar Assn. (pres. 1920); S.A.R.; a supreme officer M.W.A., 1903-36; state foreman Brotherhood Am. Yoemen 12 yrs.; mem. Okla. Fraternal Congress (pres. 1912-14); member board dirs. Okla. Hist. Soc., 1940—; inducted into "Oklahoma Hall of Fame," 1952; member Oklahoma State Senate, 1941-45. Mason. Conglist. Clubs: Rotary (ex-president); Chamber of Commerce (ex-pres.). Home: 410 S. Sixth St. Office: Bowman Bldg., Kingfisher, Okla. Died Aug. 21, 1957; buried Kingfisher (Okla.) Cemetery.

BOWMAN, George T., officer, U.S. Army (ret.); b. Buffalo, June 12, 1869; s. Dennis and Alice (Mills) B.; student Inst. Politics, Williamstown, Mass., 1923; grad. Army War Coll., Washington, 1922; grad. Naval War Coll., Newport, R.I., 1923; m. Lillian Elizabeth Burrows, June 24, 1896 (died Mar. 6, 1946); 1 son, John William (dec.). Cadet, enlisted man, officer 74th regt. N.G., N.Y., 1885-97; capt. 65th N.Y. vol. inf., 1898; lt. 36th U.S. vol. inf., 1899-01; lt. to col. U.S. Cav., 1901-33, brig. gen., (ret.), 1940—; active service, Spanish-Am. War, 1898; P.I., 1899-04; Cuba, Army of Cuban Pacification, 1906-09; Mexican border, Mexico, Punitive Expedition, 1915-16; France, Belgium, Luxemburg, Germany, 1918-19; mem. gen. staff corps, U.S. Army, 1917-21, War Dept. gen. staff, gen. hdqrs., AEF; faculty Army War Coll., 1923-25; chief of staff 62d cav. div., 1927-33. Decoated D.S.M., medals, distinguished marksman, U.S. Army, Spanish-Am. War, Philippine Insurrection, Army of Cuban Pacification, Mexican Punitive Expedition, World War I (battle stars), occupation of Germany); Legion of Honor (France). Mem. Vets. Assn. (74th regt. N.G. N.Y.), Cav. Assn. (Phila.). Clubs: Army and Navy Country (Washington), Fort Monmouth Officers'. Author: Our Military Rifle, 1909; How to Shoot the U.S. Rifle, 1914. Home: Sycamore Av., Shrewsbury, N.J. Died Feb. 14, 1951; buried Arlington Nat. Cemetery.

BOWMAN, Milo Jesse, dean law sch.; b. Madison, Ind., July 1, 1874; s. Milo Judson and Zora A. (Owens) B.; grad. Madison (Ind.) High Sch., 1891; A.B., Hanover (Ind.) Coll., 1896, A.M., 1898, LL. D., 1922; U. Chgo., 1898; LL.B., Indpls. Coll. Law, 1902; m. Martha R. Edwards, June 22, 1897; children—Milo Malcom, John Gillett, Jesse Edwards. Prin. Madison High Sch., 1897-1901; practiced law, Indpls., 1902-06; asst. state law librarian, 1905-07; dean Law Sch., Valparaiso (Ind.) U., 1907—. Mem. Phi Delta Theta; Mason, Odd Fellow, Elk, Woodman. Home: Valparaiso, Ind. Died Jan. 30, 1948.

BOWMAN, Robert Jay, ry. ofcl.; b. Fostoria, O., Apr. 15, 1891; s. Hiram Ellsworth and Nora Sarah (Trone) B.; student pub. schs., Fostoria and Findlay, O.; Dr. Bus. Adminstrn., Bowling Green (O.) State U., 1950; m. Pearl F. Settles, Dec. 19, 1912; 1 dau., Eileen (Mrs. Richard K. Degener). Began as clk. N.Y.C.& St. Louis R.R., 1907, advanced to chief clk. to pres.; asst. to pres. Erie R.R., 1927, asst. v.p., 1928; became v.p. P.M. R.R., 1929, pres., 1942; pres. Chesapeake & Ohio Ry., 1946-48, chmn. exec. com., 1948-57, ret.; dir. Nat. Bank of Detroit, Detroit Fire and Marine Ins. Co. Methodist. Mason. Clubs: Recess, Bloomfield Hills Country (Detroit). Home: The Whittier, 415 Burns Dr., Detroit 14. Office: Gen. Motors Bldg., Detroit 2. Died Jan. 22, 1958.

BOWMAN, Rufus David, clergyman, educator; b. Dayton, Va., Jan. 23, 1899; s. Benjamin F. and Mary Elizabeth (Miller) B.; B.A., Bridgewater (Va.) Coll., 1923, hon. D.D., 1937; B.D., Yale, 1926; student Catholic U. of America, 1937; Ph.D., Northwestern U., 1944; m. Eva Craun, June 16, 1925; children—Mack Daniel, Jane Esther, Judy Margaret. Ordained minister Ch. of the Brethren, 1926; pastor, Roanoke, Va., 1926-29; sec. bd. Christian Edn., Elgin, Ill., 1929-34; pastor, Washington, D.C., 1934-37; pres. Bethany Bibl. Sem., and prof. Practical Theology and Christian Edn. since 1937; mem. bd. dirs. Brethren Pub. House 1935-48 (chmn. 1940-48); mem. Gen. Ednl. Bd. since 1937; chmn. Brethren Adv. Com. on Peace, 1935-40; rep. Church of the Brethren on Fed. Council of Churches; moderator Annual Conf. Ch. of the Brethren, 1940, 47; chmn. Gen. Mission Bd., 1940. Mem. of missions deputation to China and India, 1948-49; chmn. Gen. Brotherhood Bd. Ch. of the Brethren, 1947. Mem. Phi Delta Kappa. Author: The Ch. of the Brethren and War, 1944; Seventy Times Seven, 1945. Lecturer in colleges and assemblies. Home: 837 S. Humphrey Av., Oak Park, Ill. Office: 3435 W. Van Buren St., Chgo. 24. Deceased.

BOYCE, Charles Prevost, investment banker; b. Baltimore, Md., Apr. 7, 1895; s. Frederick Grayson and Rebecca Latimer (Millar) B.; student pub. schs., Baltimore, Baltimore City Coll., Johns Hopkins; m. Caroline Ellicott, Dec. 11, 1920 (div. Feb. 1948); children—Caroline Ellicott, Anne Allen, Charles Prevost, Patricia Ayers; m. 2d, Jacqueline Hurst Johnson, Mar. 2, 1948. Bond salesman, Robert Garrett & Sons, Baltimore, 1916-17 and 1919-20; mem. firm Turner, Boyce & Co., Baltimore, 1920-21; admitted to partnership Stein Bros. (established 1853), 1921, which then became Stein Bros. & Boyce, investment bankers, of which is sr. partner; chmn. of bd. Bayway Terminal Corp.; dir. Blue Ridge Mutual Fund, Ice. Lord Baltimore Hotel; dir. N.Y., N.H. & H. R.R. Co. (mem. exec. com.); former mem. bd. govs., Balt. Stock Exchange. Dir. Md. School for Blind, Baltimore; Served in 1st R O.T.C., Ft. Myer, Va., 1917; 2d. lt., F.A., 80th Div. and later 1st lt., Tank Corps, U.S. Army, with A.E.F., 1917-19. Mem. Investment Bankers Assn. of Am. (former mem. bd. govs.), Soc. Sons of Revolution, Alpha Delta Phi. Democrat. Presbyterian. Clubs: Baltimore Country, Elkridge, Merchants, Baltimore Bond, Maryland, Bachelors Cotillon (Baltimore); Broad St., Racquet and Tennis (N.Y. City); Fishers Island (N.Y.), Louisville Country (Ky.). Home: 911 Poplar Hill Rd. Office: 6 S. Calvert St., Balt. Died Jan. 15, 1955; buried Balt.

BOYCE, Heyward E. (bois), banker; b. Baltimore, Maryland, Apr. 9, 1882; s. Frederick G. and Rebecca (Millar) B.; LL.B., U. of Md., 1902; m. Amabel Lee George, June 28, 1905; children—Heyward E., Rebecca Latimer, John C. G., Elizabeth Lee, Henrietta George. With Wilson, Colston & Co., bankers and brokers, Baltimore, 1898-1908; mem. firm Colston, Boyce & Co., 1908-18; pres. Drovers and Mechanics Nat. Bank, 1921-30; pres., chmn. bd., dir. Md. Trust Co., 1930-49, chmn. bd., dir., 1949—; state chmn. deposit liquidation com. RFC, 1933; pres. Balt. Clearing House, 1948—; trustee Eastern Sugar Assn. (P.R.); dir. Brager-Eisenberg, Inc. (Balt.), Davis Coal & Coke Co., Md. Title & Guarantee Co., Finance Co. of Am., Tower Realty Co. Mem. Md. Hist. Soc. (treas.), Soc. War 1812 (treas.), S.R. (treas.). Presbyn. (chmn. ch. bd. trustees). Clubs: Maryland, Bachelors Cotillon, Baltimore Country (pres.), Merchants, Fishers Island Country (N.Y.), Mountain Lake (Lake Wales, Fla.). Home: 4 Club Rd., Roland Park. Office: Md. Trust Bldg., Balt. Died July 23, 1950; buried Greenmount Cemetery, Balt.

BOYCE, Sir (Harold) Leslie, corporation executive; born Taree, New South Wales, July 9, 1895; son of Charles Macleay and Ethel May Boyce; M.A., Balliol Coll., Oxford U., 1924; m. Maybery Bevan, 1926; children—Richard Leslie, John Leslie, Charles Francis Leslie. Called to bar of Inner Temple, 1922; mem. Brit. Parliament, Conservative Party, for Gloucester, 1929-45; alderman, City of London, 1942-54, sr. sheriff, 1947-48; Lord mayor of London, 1951-52. Chmn., mng. dir. Gloucester Ry. Carriage & Wagon Co., Ltd., William Gardner & Sons, Ltd., Gloucester; chmn. Wagon Repairs, Ltd., Philblack, Ltd., Hatherly Works, Ltd.; dir. various cos. Held office of High Sheriff of Gloucester, 1941-42. Leader United Kingdom Trade Mission to China, 1946. Chmn. exec. com. King George VI Meml. Fund. Created 1st Baronet Knight Comdr. Order Brit. Empire, Knight St. John. Mem. St. John's Ambulance Brigade, 1931—. Mem. Worshipful Company of Loriners (master 1952). Clubs: Carlton, Constnl., Royal Automobile, Australia, City Livery. Home: Badgeworth Hall, nr. Cheltenham, Eng. Died May 30, 1955; buried Holy Trinity Church, Badgeworth.

BOYD, Augusto Samuel, surgeon; b. Rep. of Panama, Aug. 1, 1879; s. Federico and Teodolinda (Briceño) B.; student, Cheltenham (Pa.) Mil. Acad., 1892-93, Columbia Inst., New York, 1893-95; M.D., Coll. of Physicians and Surgeons (Columbia), 1899; m. Raquel de la Guardia, Apr. 17, 1917; children—Augusto Samuel, Dora Raquel. Interne City Hosp., New York, 1899-1901, European Clinics, 1901-03; pvt. practice, New York, 1903-05; chief surgeon Santo Tomas Hosp., Panama, 1905-36; pres. Panama Municipal Council, 1906-08; mem. Panama Congress, 1914-18; pres. Panama Assembly, 1918; vice pres. of Panama Rep., 1936-40, E.E. and M.P. from Panama to U.S., 1936-39; ambassador to the U.S., April 1939-Dec. 1939, when he was called to assume the presidency of the Republic upon the death of President Juan Demóstenes Arosemena and served Arosemena's unexpired term which ended Sept. 30, 1940. Decorated Order of Merit (Ecuador); Order of Vasco

Nuñez de Balboa, Highest Degree (Panama). Pres. Panama-America Chapter of Pan.-Am. Med. Assn.; fellow of Am. Med. Assn., Am. Coll. Surgeons. Address: Panama, Republic of Panama. Died July 17, 1957.

BOYD, Charles Morgan, clergyman, educator; b. Cayce, Miss., Apr. 25, 1875; s. William Baldridge and Frances Ann (Carrington) B.; A.B., A.M., Erskine Coll., Due West, S.C., 1901; B.D., Erskine Theol. Sem., 1902; D.D., Davidson Coll., 1920; m. Ella Jane Lee, Nov. 3, 1904. Ordained ministry Associate Reformed Presbyterian Ch., 1902; pastor, Associate Reformed Ch., Prosperity, S.C., 1902-06, Anderson (S.C.) Ch., 1906-10, First Presbyterian Ch. in U.S., Tuscaloosa, Ala., 1910-31; Westminster Church, Charlotte, N.C., 1931-45; Presbyn. minister to hospitals of Charlotte since 1945; supply preacher Plaza, 1951, Mulberry, 1952, Presbyn. Chs., Charlotte; also prof. church history, U. Ala., 1925-31. Pres. Carolina Spastics Assn., 1948-51; Moderator Synod of Ala., 1920; trustee Gen. Assembly of Presbyn. ch. of U.S. 1933-52, Presbyn. Found. Inc., 1933-52; several times commr. to Gen. Assembly of Presbyn. Ch. in U.S.; chairman Assembly's Permanent Com. on Closer relations and Union with Other Presbyn., Bodies, 1937-38. Trustee Columbia Theol. Sem., Decatur, Ga., 1920-31; chmn. bd. Stillman Inst., Tuscallosa, 1918-31. Democrat. Kiwanian (pres. 1925). Home: 430 Clement Av., Charlotte 4, N.C. Died Feb. 25, 1958.

BOYD, Everett Marion, mng. editor; b. Dayton, O., Aug. 11, 1894; s. Joseph and Anna (Gagel) B.; ed. Dayton pub. schs.; m. Mary Harrington, Nov. 18, 1932; children—Everett, Marianne, Paul. Reporter, sports writer, copyreader, Dayton (O.) Journal, 1912-16; copyreader, asst. telegraph editor Cincinnati Enquirer, 1916-18; asst. telegraph editor, Detroit Free Press, 1919-20; telegraph editor Cincinnati Enquirer, 1921-43, radio editor, 1924-28, mng. editor, 1943-54, exec. editor, 1954-55, v.p., asso. editor, 1955—. Mem. Am. Soc. of Newspaper Editors. Club: Cuvier Press (Cin.). Home: 3417 Erie Av., Cin. 8. Office: Cincinnati Enquirer, 617 Vine St., Cin. 1. Died Jan. 7, 1957; buried Gate of Heaven Cemetery, Cin.

BOYD, Henry W., Jr., shoe mfr. exec.; b. Chicago, June 17, 1908; s. Henry W., Sr., and Olive (Jacoby) B.; M.E., Cornell U., 1931; m. Carolyn Jones, June 9, 1934; children—Henry W., III, Philip H., Ann Caroline. With General Shoe Corp., Nashville, 1931, asst. sec. and treas., 1934-36, sec. and treas., 1936-39, bd. dirs., 1936—, v.p. and treas., 1939-47, pres., 1947—; dir. Am. Nat. Bank (Nashville), Walter Hoving Corp., Tiffany & Co. (N.Y. C.). Mem. Kappa Alpha. Presbyn. (elder). Clubs: Cornell (N.Y.); Belle Meade Country, Blue Grass Country (Nashville). Home: 1304 Chickering Rd. Office: 119 Seventh Av. N., Nashville. Died Feb. 22, 1958.

BOYD, James Ellsworth, educator; b. Muskingum Co., O., Nov. 6, 1863; s. Joseph and Susan (Riley) B.; B.Sc., Ohio State U., 1891; M.S., Cornell U., 1896; m. Emma C. Wells, June 15, 1893; children—Orton Wells, Dorothy May. Asst. in physics, Ohio State U., 1891-95; scholar in physics, Cornell U., 1895; asst. prof. physics Ohio State U., 1896-1901, asso. prof. mathematics, 1901-06, prof. mechanics, 1906-36, emeritus prof., 1936—; asst. U.S. Bur. of Standards, summer 1917. Recipient Lamme engring. medal Ohio State U., 1938. Fellow A.A.A.S.; mem. Am. Soc. M.E., Soc. for Promotion Engring. Edn., Sigma Xi. Republican. Clubs: Faculty, Engineers'. Author: Differential Equations, 1905; Strength of Materials, 1911; Mechanics, 1921; also several tech. papers. Died May 10, 1950.

BOYD, John Frank, ex-congressman; b. Connellsville, Pa., Aug. 8, 1853; s. John and Rebecca B.; student Abingdon (Ill.) Coll., 2 yrs.; studied law; m. Mabel Ayres, 1881. Admitted to Neb. bar; county atty. Antelope County, Neb., 1888-96; judge 9th Jud. Dist., 1900-07; mem. 60th U.S. Congress, 3d Neb. Dist. Republican. Address: Neligh, Neb. Deceased.

BOYD, William Robert, savs. and loan assn. exec.; b. at Lisbon, Ia., May 19, 1864; s. Jasper W. and Elizabeth (Osmond) B.; student Parsons Coll., 1886-87; Ph.B., State U. Ia., 1889, LL.D., 1942; LL.D., Coe Coll. 1935, Parsons Coll., 1944; m. Lou F. Hadley, June 10, 1930. Prin. High sch. Mechanicsville, Ia., 1889-91; editor Tipton (Ia.) Advertiser, 1891-93; editor Cedar Rapids Republican, 1893-99, asso. editor, 1899-1909; pres. Perpetual Savs. & Loan Assn. Chmn. finance com. Ia. State Bd. Edn., the governing body of State U. Ia., Ia. State Coll. Agr. and Mechanics Arts, Ia. State Tchrs. Coll., Ia. State Coll. for the Blind, Ia. Sch. for the Deaf, Tb State Sanatorium. Trustee Cornell Coll., Coe Coll. Republican. Presbyn. Home: 9 Blake Terrace, S.E., Cedar Rapids, Ia. Died Mar. 13, 1950.

BOYD, William Rufus, Jr., banking exec.; b. Fairfield, Tex., Jan. 7, 1885; s. William R. and Lizzie (Self) B.; ed. high sch.; LL.D., St. Bonaventure Coll.; m. Gertrude Watson, May 17, 1906; 1 son, William R., III. Lawyer, Fairfield and Teague, Tex., 1904-08; banker, Eddy, Tex., and Dallas, Tex., 1909-14; oil production, N.M.; farmer and stock raiser in Tex.; with Am. Petroleum Inst. 1920-49, pres. 1941-49, ret. 1949; partner oil firm Boyd, Hardey & Wheelock; chmn. bd. Fairfield (Texas) State Bank. Mem. Tex. State Dem. Exec. Com. Chmn. Petroleum Industry War Council, Wash., 1941-45; nat. dir. President's Rubber Collection Drive, 1942. Decorated Presidential Medal for Merit, Apr. 1946. Democrat. Methodist. Mason (Shriner). Home: Teague. Office: Box 299, Teague, Tex. Died Nov. 1959.

BOYD, William Sprott, mining engr.; b. Sydney, New South Wales, Australia, June 6, 1879; s. Robert Mitchell and Agnes (Brown) B.; B.E., U. Sydney, 1901; m. Helen H. G. McMicking, Sept. 1911; children—Eleanor Sprott, Robert Mitchell Sprott, Wm. Sprott. Mining engr. in Australia until 1905; asst. mine supt. Boston Consol. Mining Co., Bingham, Utah, 1906-10; with Ray Consol. Copper Co., 1910—, mgr., 1919-22, gen. mgr., 1922-30; v.p., mng. dir. Utah Copper Co., Nevada Consol. Copper Co.; v.p. Ray & Gila Valley R.R. Co.; pres. Ray Electric and Telephone Co., 1927-42; v.p. Kennecott Copper Corp., Nev. No. Ry. Co., Gallup-Am. Coal Co., 1942-45; cons. engr. Kennecott Copper Corp., 1945-47, ret. Mem. Am. Inst. Mining and Metall. Engrs., Mining and Metall. Soc. Am. Inst. of Mining and Metallurgy Eng. Episcopalian. Mason. Home: 1721 Manor Dr., Hillsborough, Cal. Office: 625 Market St., San Francisco 5. Died Dec. 30, 1958.

BOYDEN, Albert, lawyer; b. Beverly, Mass., Sept. 19, 1871; s. William C. and Amy L. (Hoag) B., grad. Beverly High Sch., 1887, Roxbury Latin Sch., 1889; A.B., Harvard, 1894, LL.B., 1898. Admitted to Mass. bar, 1898, since practiced in Boston; mem. Boyden, Palfrey, Bradlee & Twombly until 1916; mem. Ropes, Gray, Boyden & Perkins (now Ropes, Gray, Best, Coolidge & Rugg), 1916—. Mem. Mass., Boston bar assns. Unitarian. Mason. Club: Harvard (Boston). Home: 6 Washington St., Beverly, Mass. Office: 50 Federal St., Boston. Died Jan. 14, 1951; buried Beverly.

BOYDEN, Guy Lee, otolaryngologist; b. Brooking, S.D., Feb. 17, 1885; s. Francis and Mary Emaline (Darling) B.; B.S., S.D. State Coll., 1905, D.Sc., 1955; M.D., Northwestern Univ., 1911; m. Zella Thompson, Sept. 26, 1917; children—Mary (Mrs. Wm. C. Lindsell, Jr.), Catherine (Mrs. O. T. Coffelt, Jr.), Thomas (M.D.), Jean (Mrs. Francis L. Hales). Interne Mayo Clinic, 1911-12, resident, 1912-13; gen. practice medicine, Pendleton, Ore., 1913-21; practice limited to otolaryngology, Portland, Ore., 1921—; sr. cons. U.S. Vets. Hosp., Portland, 1948—; mem. faculty, U. Ore. Med. Sch., 1948—, asst. prof. otolaryngology, 1932, asso. prof., 1946, prof. and head dept. otolaryngology, 1946—. Recipient award for distinguished services in ednl. programs Am. Acad. Ophthalmology and Otolaryngology, 1958. Mem. A.M.A., Am., Ore. acads. ophthalmology and otolaryngology, Am. Triologic Society, Pacific Coast Soc. Ophthalmology and Otolaryngology (pres.), Ore., Multnomah County, Portland med. socs., Am. Laryngol. Assn. Contbr. med. jours. Home: 2490 S.W. Arden Rd., Portland 1. Office: 1735 Wheeler St., Portland 12, Ore. Died Sept. 9, 1958; buried Riverview Cemetery, Portland.

BOYER, Charles Clinton, educator; b. Lewiston, Pa., Aug. 6, 1860; s. Joseph and Magdalena (Gunsette) B.; student Kutztown State Normal Sch.; A.M., Muhlenberg Coll., Pa., 1885; course theology Luth. Theol. Sem., and ordained, 1888; Ph.D. cum laude, U. Wooster, 1894; studied psychology Harvard U.; Pd.D., Muhlenberg Coll., 1919; m. Margie Wright, Aug. 7, 1890; 1 son, Carl Wright. Tchr. pub. schs., Paterson, Pa., 1877-78, Lewiston Valley, Pa., 2 yrs., Orwigsburg High Sch., Pa., 2 yrs., Lynnville Acad., Pa., 1 yr.; prof. Latin and Greek, Kutztown State Normal Sch., 1887-89, psychology, 1889-91, pedagogy, 1898-1927, vice prin., 1900-27; pastor Boyertown, Pa., 1891-93. Lutheran. Republican. Author: Concrete Psychology, 1890; Principles and Methods of Teaching, 1899; Waymarks of General History, 1902; Modern Methods for Teachers, 1908; American Boyers, 1915; History of Education, 1919. Home: Kutztown, Pa. Died Aug. 20, 1932; buried Boyer Vault, Fairview Cemetery, Allentown, Pa.

BOYER, Lewis Leonard, ex-congressman; b. on farm nr. Richfield, Ill., May 19, 1886; attended rural schs.; studied civil engring.; m. Effie Proctor; 1 son. County supt. of hwys., Adams County, Ill., 1915-36; mem. 75th Congress (1937-39), 15th Ill. Dist. Democrat. Home: Quincy, Ill. Died Mar. 12, 1949.

BOYER, Pearce Fowler, business exec.; b. Tamaqua, Pa., July 3, 1887; s. Francis Jerome and Mary (Fowler) B.; student law econs. and accounting, night sch. U. Pitts.; m. Hester Boothe, Apr. 28, 1914; children—Willis Boothe, Pearce Fowler, Hester (Mrs. Carl C. Tucker), Robert Jerome. Began with Mellon Nat. Bank, Pitts., 1906; cost accountant, accountant, auditor Am. Bridge Co., subsidiary U.S. Steel Corp., 1907-16; comptroller, treas. Donner Steel Co., Buffalo, 1916-30; co. acquired by Republic Steel Corp., 1930; gen. auditor Republic Steel Corp., 1930, comptroller, 1934, v.p., dir., 1941; dir. Truscon Steel Co. (Youngstown, O.), Susquehanna Ore Co. (Cleve.), Fretz-Moon Tube Co. (Butler, Pa.). Mem. adv. panel to the Army Comptroller. Mem. Am. Iron and Steel Inst., N.A.M., Conrtrollers Inst. Am. Republican. Presbyn. Clubs: Union, Mayfield Country, Pepper Pike Golf (Cleve.). Home: 22550 McCauley Rd., Shaker Heights 22, Ohio. Office: Republic Steel Corp., Republic Bldg., Cleve. 1. Died July 22, 1949; buried Cleve.

BOYES, Kurwin Robert, assn. sec.; b. Providence, Mar. 30, 1896; s. Thomas E. and Mary (MacLeod) B.; student Bryant and Stratton Bus. Coll., Providence, 1916-18; Brown U., Providence, 1919-23; bus. sch., Harvard, 1928; unmarried. Sec. to pres. Providence Gas Co., 1919-23; asst. to mng. dir., Am. Gas Assn., N.Y. City, 1923-26, sec. since 1926. Mem. Am. Mgmt. Assn., Am. Chem. Soc., Am. Trade Assn. Execs. Republican. Baptist. Mason. Club: Brown University (N.Y. City). Home: Five Tudor City Pl., N.Y. City 17 Office: 420 Lexington Av., N.Y. City 17. Died Jan. 30, 1956; buried Providence, R.I.

BOYKIN, Samuel Francis, corp. exec.; b. nr. Portland, Ala., June 15, 1874; s. Samuel Francis and Margaret (Anerum) B.; student pub. schs. Boykin and Camden, S.C.; m. Anne Alexander, Apr. 11, 1899; children—Martha (Mrs. Richard Heber Bennett, Jr.), Francis (Mrs. William Randell Barnett). Bookkeeper A. K. Hawkes, optician, Atlanta, 1891-99; with N. P. Pratt Lab., 1899-1919, pres., 1910-19; treas. The Coca-Cola Co., Atlanta, 1919-20, sec., treas., 1920-34, v.p., treas., 1937-47; pres. Coca-Cola subsidiary, 1934-37; pres., treas. Coca-Cola Internat. Corp., Wilmington, Del., 1947—; dir. Wilmington Trust Co., Artisans Savs. Bank. Trustee Emory U., Martha Berry Schs. Clubs: Ad-City, Piedmont Driving (Atlanta); Country, Rotary (Wilmington). Home: 1300 N. Harrison St., Wilmington, Del. Died July 26, 1953; buried Columbus, Ga.

BOYLAN, John J., bishop of Rockford, Roman Cath. Church; b. New York, N.Y., Oct. 7, 1889; s. Edward Lawrence and Bridget Anne (Morrissey) B.; student La Salle Acad., Providence, R.I., 1904-08; Mt. St. Mary's Coll., Emmetsburg, Md., 1908-10 (hon. A.M., 1917); St. Bernard's Sem., Rochester, N.Y., 1910-15; S.T.B., J.C.L., Cath. Univ., Washington, D.C., 1917; Ph.D., Pontifical Atheneum, Rome, 1923; student summers, Harvard and State U. of Iowa; LL.D., St. Ambrose, 1941; Litt.D., Loras Coll., 1948. Ordained priest, R.C. Ch., 1915; asst. pastor, St. Francis Council Bluffs, Ia., 1917-18; prof. Dowling Coll., Des Moines, 1918-23, pres., 1923-42; diocesan dir. of charities, Des Moines, 1920-23; diocesan supt. of schools, 1924-34; vicar gen. of Des Moines Diocese, 1934-42; staff mem. Mercy Hosp., Des Moines, 1933-36; mem. of summer faculty, Sisters Teachers Coll., Providence, R.I., 1935-42; consecrated bishop of Rockford (Ill), Feb. 17, 1943. Mem. A.A.A.S. Address: 1245 N. Court St., Rockford, Ill. Died July 19, 1953.

BOYLAN, Murtha Joseph, clergyman, educator; b. Cleve., Aug. 28, 1874; s. Terrance and Mary (McAneny) B.; classical studies St. Ignatius Coll., Cleve., 1888-94; joined Soc. of Jesus (Jesuits), 1896; studied in Sem. at Prairie du Chien, Wis., 1896-99, advanced course in science and philosophy, 1899-1902; taught in Jesuit Normal Sch., Brooklyn, O., 1902-06; studied div. St. Ignatius Coll., Valkenberg, Holland, 1906-10; course in asceticism St. Stanislaus Sem., Brooklyn, O., 1910-11. Ordained priest R. C. Ch., 1909; v.p. Campion Coll., Prairie du Chien, Wis., 1911-19; prof. psychology, ethics and pedagogy St. Xavier Coll., Cin., 1919-25; pres. John Carroll U. Cleve., 1925-28; prof. philosophy, history of philosophy, pedagogy, Scripture, ethics Xavier U., Cin., 1928—. Address: Xavier U., Evanston Sta., Cin. 7. Died July 15, 1954; buried Sacred Heart Cemetery, Milford, O.

BOYLE, Charles A., congressman; b. Spring Lake, Mich., Aug. 13, 1907; s. Michael Melvin and Rose (Marsh) B.; Ph.B., Loyola U., Chgo., 1930, J.D., 1933; m. Helen Shaughnessy, Aug. 14, 1940; children—Pat, Mary, Tom, Rose, Irene, Mike, Larry, Cathy. Admitted to Ill. bar, 1934; since practiced in Chgo.; with Boyle, Murphy & Walsh, 1940—; zone atty. FHA, 1937-38; mem. 84th-86th Congress, 12th Ill. Dist.; mem. House Subcommittee on def. and appropriations com. Selected Father of the Year, Mr. Illinois, 1952, 53. Mem. Am., Ill., Chgo. bar assns. Holy Name Soc., Delta Theta Phi. K.C. Clubs: Illinois Democratic, Executive, Edgewater Golf (Chgo.). Home: 1028 W. Loyola Av., Chgo. 26. Office: New House Office Bldg., Washington. Died Nov. 4, 1959.

BOYLE, Hugh Charles (boil), bishop; b. Johnstown, Pa., Oct. 8, 1873; s. Charles and Ann (Keelan) B.; ed. St. Vincent's prep. sch., coll. and sem., Beatty, Pa., 1888-98. Ordained R.C. priest, 1898; asst. St. Aloysius Ch. Wilmerding, Pa., until Jan. 1903; asst. St. Paul's Cathedral and new St. Paul's Cathedral, 1903-09; supt. parish schs., diocese of Pittsburgh, 1909-16; pastor St. Mary Magdalen's Ch., Homestead, Pa., 1916-21; consecrated bishop of Pittsburgh, June 29, 1921. Home: 5078 Warwick Terrace, Pittsburgh 13. Died Dec. 22, 1950; buried St. Mary Cemetery, Pittsburgh.

BOYLE, Walter Fabien, consul general, retired; b. Augusta, Ga., Dec. 14, 1875; s. Thaddeus Walton and Josephine (Wilson) B.; ed. Houghton Inst., and Richmond Acad., Augusta, Ga.; m. Eva Stokes, 1902; 1 dau., Fay Boyle. Served in and under P.O. Dept., 1895-1913; Consular Service, 1914—; consul in Honduras, Mexico and New Zealand; consul gen. at Guatemala City, Guatemala; retired 1941. Address: McLean, Va. Died Feb. 13, 1956; buried Magnolia Cemetery, Augusta, Ga.

BOYNTON, Morrison Russell, clergyman; b. Haverhill, Mass., Oct. 31, 1887; s. Nehemiah and Mary Ella (Wilcox) B.; A.B., Amherst, 1910, D.D., 1930; B.D., Andover (Mass.) Theol. Sem., 1913; S.T.B., Harvard University, 1913; D.D., Chicago Theological Seminary, 1928; married Margaret Whitnell, May 2, 1923; children—Mrs. Mary Margaret MacPherson, Martha Anne Pawle. Ordained to ministry of Congregational Ch., 1913; student pastor Ashland, Mass., 1911-13; asst. minister Clinton Av. Ch., Brooklyn, N.Y., 1913-18; pastor Bryn Mawr Community Ch., Chicago, 1920-36, First Ch., Newton, Mass., 1936—. Served as lieutenant Chaplains' Corps, U.S. Navy, 1918-20. Pres. bd. trustees Andover Theol. Sem.; trustee Jaffna Coll., Ceylon. Mem. Chi Phi. Clubs: Monday, Winthrop. Home: 70 Sumner St., Newton Centre, Mass. Died Sept. 24, 1953.

BOYNTON, Paul L(ewis), educator; b. Llano, Tex., July 24, 1898; s. Edwin Curtis and Alice (Lewis) B.; student Rice Inst., Houston, Tex., 1916-17, Tex. Christian U., 1918-19; B.A., Sam Houston State Teachers Coll., Tex., 1920; M.A., George Peabody Coll. for Teachers, 1923, Ph.D., 1927; m. Juanita Curry, Dec. 25, 1924; children—Edwin Curry, Paulann. Prin. Lufkin (Tex.) High Sch., 1920-21; tchr. and coach Wichita Falls (Tex.) Jr. High Sch., 1921-22; instr. Appalachian State Teachers Coll., N.C., summer of 1922; instr. psychology, U. of Ky., 1923-24, asst. prof., 1924-27, asso. prof., 1927-30, actg. dept. head, 1928-29; prof. psychology, Peabody Coll., Nashville, Tenn., 1930, head of department, 1940; pres. Stephen F. Austin State Coll., Nacogdoches, Tex., since 1942. Chmn. Commn. for Study Mental Hosps. in Tenn., 1936, Adv. Com. of the Coordinated Studies in Edn.; consultant mental hygiene, Tenn. Dept. Institutions, 1938; cons. psychologist Central State Hosp., 1940-42. Mem. Special Commission on Mental Hospital Study, Tenn., 1940. Member N.E.A., Texas Society for Mental Hygiene (pres. 1945-46), Phi Delta Kappa. Mem. Christian Ch. Author: Intelligence, Its Manifestations and Measurement, 1933. Co-author Psychology of Child Development, 1938; also one of collaborators Readings in Psychology, and Educational Psychology; co-author Elementary Educational Psychology, 1946. Editor: Cumberland Education Series. Also author various monographs and contbr. to psychol. and ednl. publs. Home: State College Campus, Nacogdoches, Texas. Died Aug. 6, 1958; buried Nacogdoches.

BOYNTON, William Pingry, educator; b. Weathersfield, Vt., Oct. 28, 1867; s. Cyrus Clark and Gratia Maria (Pingry) B.; grad. Phillips Exeter Acad., 1885; A.B., Dartmouth, 1890, A.M., 1893; Ph.D., Clark U., 1897; Sc.D., U. Ore., 1937; m. Mabel E. Howard, July 21, 1897 (dec. 1946); 1 dau., Mar. Dorothea Boynton Wegner; m. 2d, Mrs. Louise Anderson, Dec. 11, 1950. Scholar and fellow in physics Clark U., 1894-97; mem. faculty U. So. Cal., 1890-93; asst. in physics Dartmouth, 1893-94; instr. physics U. Cal., 1897-1901; tchr. Cogswell Poly. Sch., San Francisco, 1901-02; prof., dean Cal. Coll., East Oakland, 1902-03; asst. prof. physics U. Ore., 1903-06, prof., head dept., 1906-32; prof. physics Ore. State Coll., 1932-37, emeritus, 1937—. Fellow A.A.A.S. Am. Phys. Soc.; mem. Am. Assn. U. Profs., Am. Assn. Physics Tchrs., Phi Beta Kappa, Sigma Xi, Kappa Kappa Kappa, Sigma Pi Sigma, Phi Kappa Phi. Republican. Baptist. Club: University (Claremont, Cal.). Author: Kinetic Theory, 1904; also research articles. Died Mar. 9, 1955; buried Rose Hills Cemetery, Whittier, Cal.

BOYTON, Neil, clergyman, author; b. N.Y. City, Nov. 30, 1884; s. Capt. Paul and Margaret (Connolly) B.; St. Louis U., 1904-05; B.A., Holy Cross Coll., Worcester, Mass., 1908; M.A., Woodstock Coll., 1923. Joined Soc. of Jesus (Jesuits), 1909; teacher St. Joseph High Sch., Phila., Pa., 1914-16; St. Mary's High Sch., Bombay, India, 1916-17, Georgetown Prep. Sch., Garrett Park, Md., 1917-19 and 1923-28, Regis High School, N.Y. City, 1928-31; Loyola School, New York City, 1931-45; assistant pastor, St. Ignatius Loyola Church, New York City, 1945—. Member of the Catholic Writers Guild and the Gallery of Living Catholic Authors. Member of Knights of Columbus. Author: Cobra Island, 1922; Whoopee!, 1923; In God's Country (Short stories), 1923; Where Monkeys Swing, 1924; On the Sands of Coney, 1925; Mangled Hands, 1926; Mississippi's Blackrobe, 1927; Blessed Friend of Youth—Saint John Bosco, 1929; In Xavier Lands (short stores), 1930; Redrobes, 1936; The Mystery of St. Regis, A Yankee Xavier, 1937; Killgloom Park, 1938; Saints for Scouts, 1941; The Silver Fox Patrol, 1944; The Summer Jerry Never Saw, 1945; White Horsemen, 1947; Ex-Cub Fitzie, 1950. Contbr. to Catholic mags. Home: 53 E. 83d N.Y.C. Died Feb. 1, 1956; buried St. Andrew-on-Hudson, Poughkeepsie, N.Y.

BRACE, Donald Clifford, publisher; b. West Winfield, N.Y., Dec. 27, 1881; s. Frank L. and Martha (McDonald) B.; A.B., Columbia, 1904; m. Ida B. Pollock, Dec. 27, 1906; children—Donna McDonald (Mrs. Louis F. Kroeck), Katharine Pollock (Mrs. Robert Cummings). With Henry Holt & Co., pubs., N.Y. City, 1904-19; one of founders Harcourt, Brace & Co., 1919; v.p. and treas., 1919-42; pres. and treas. 1942-48, chmn. bd., 1948-49, ret. Awarded Columbia U. Medal for Excellence, 1950. Mem. Phi Beta Kappa, Sigma Chi. Republican. Clubs: Columbia University, Century (New York); Riverside (Conn.) Yacht. Home: Rockledges, Riverside, Conn. Office: 383 Madison Av., N.Y.C. Died Sept. 20, 1955; buried West Winfield, N.Y.

BRADEN, J. Noble, assn. exec.; b. N.Y.C., Oct. 31, 1892; s. Thomas William and Margaret J. (Armstrong) B.; student pub. schs. N.Y.C.; m. Elizabeth Vogelback, June 12, 1918; 1 son, Richard Noble. Public relations cons. aiding orgn. Arbitration Soc. Am., Inc., 1922, merged with Arbitration Found., Inc. to form Am. Arbitration Assn., 1926, sec., 1926-42, v.p. since 1942; adj. prof. indsl. relations grad. sch. bus. adminstrn., N.Y.U. since 1945; spl. lectr. law sch., Yale, 1946-51. Mem. Am. Trade Assn. Execs., Indsl. Relations Research Assn., N.Y. Soc. Mil. and Naval Officers World Wars. Author: Practice of Commercial Arbitration (with Am. Arbitration Assn. staff), 1928; Code of Arbitration (with Frances Kellor and others), 1931; also articles profl. jours. Lectr. Home: 28 Dorchester Rd., Rockville Centre, L.I., N.Y. Office: 477 Madison Av., N.Y.C. 22. Died Feb. 15, 1957; buried Greenfield Cemetery, Hempstead, N.Y.

BRADEN, James Andrew, author; b. Greene Twp., Trumbull County, O., July 10, 1872; s. James and Miriam (Cory) B.; pub. sch. edn.; m. Rosalie M. Flohr, Aug. 1, 1894 (died 1932); 1 dau., Dorothy A. (Mrs. Edward Cope Smith); m. 2d, Alta L. Taylor, 1940. As advt. mgr. Diamond Rubber Co., Akron, O., became a founding mem. Assn. Nat. Advertisers, 1910; gen. agt. electric rys., 1913-18, then various advt. activities to retirement, 1928. Journalist and author, 1890—. Editor Centennial History of Akron, 1925; mem. Ohio State Archeol. and Hist. Soc., Summit County Hist. Soc. Izaak Walton League Am. Author: Far Past the Frontier, 1902; Connecticut Boys in the Western Reserve, 1903; Captives Three, 1904; The Trail of the Seneca, 1907; The Auto Boys, 1908; The Auto Boys' Outing, 1909; The Auto Boys' Quest, 1910; The Auto Boys' Camp, 1911; The Auto Boys' Big Six, 1913; Little Brother of the Hudson, 1928; The Carved Sea-Chest, 1929; (under publishers' name, Hugh McAllister) Steve Holworth of the Oldham Works, 1930; That Boy at Roaring Brook Farm, 1931. Contbr. to mags. Died June 28, 1954.

BRADFORD, Gerard, engr., ret.; b. N.Y.C., Sept. 13, 1887; s. William and Mary (Chittenden) B.; student U. Vt., 1904-05; B.S., U.S. Naval Acad., 1909, post grad., 1914-15; m. Helen Gartley, July 5, 1917; 1 son, Gerard. Commd. ensign USN, 1909, advancing through grades to lt. comdr., 1917; in submarine service, 1911-14; sea duty in U.S.S. Arizona, San Diego, Louisiana, 1916-18; comdg. officer, naval mine depot, Yorktown, Pa., 1919-22; gunnery officer U.S.S. Pittsburgh, 1922-23; resigned and entered civil life in ins. mgmt., 1924, real estate engring. mgmt., N.Y.C., 1933-40; pres., dir. Witherbee Sherman Corp., 1940, ret. On active duty as comdr. USNR, Washington, 1941-45; placed on retired list, USN, 1943. Decorated Silver Star, World War I. Mem. Am. Inst. Mining and Metall. Engrs., N.Y. Hist. Soc., Sigma Phi. Clubs: University (N.Y.C.); Army and Navy (Washington); University (Hartford), Conn. Home: Bill Hill Rd., Old Lyme, Conn. Died Nov. 5, 1955; buried Arlington Nat. Cemetery.

BRADFORD, Joseph Nelson, architect, educator; b. Coloma, Cal., Apr. 3, 1860; s. Joseph and Rebecca (Pickworth) B.; M.E., Ohio State U., 1883; m. Emma Walter, of Columbus, O., Dec. 30, 1885; children—Grace Bonnet, Florence Bradford. With the Ohio Geol. Survey, summers 1882, 83; engring. dept. Pa. R.R., 1883-85; with Ohio State U., 1885—, successively asst. in mech. engring. and drawing, until 1891, asst. prof. drawing, 1890-93, asso. prof., 1893-99, prof. architecture and drawing, 1899-1906, prof. architecture, 1906—, was also univ. architect, 1911-29. Architect for Emerson McMillan Astron. Obs., Archaeol. and Hist. Mus. Bldg., and over 40 other bldgs. and campus improvements of Ohio State U.; Ohio State Bldg., Jamestown Expn., 1907; etc. Mem. Am. Soc. for Promotion of Engring. Edn., Columbus Soc. Architects, Am. Inst. Architects, Sigma Xi. Republican. Conglist. Club: Faculty. Home: 55 Oakland Av., Columbus, O. Died Dec. 11, 1943.

BRADFORD, Lindsay, banker; b. N.Y.C., Jan. 8, 1892; s. William and Mary (Chittenden) B.; grad. Phillips Acad., Andover, Mass., 1910; A.B., Yale, 1914; LL.D., Colgate U., Hamilton, N.Y., 1939; m. Katharine Walker, Apr. 22, 1922; children—Priscilla (Mrs. Barney Holland), Dorothy Walker (Mrs. John B. Shapleigh, II), Lindsay. Investment banker, Hambleton & Co., N.Y.C., 1915-16, N.Y. Trust Co., 1920-27; with City Bank Farmers Trust Co., 1927-56, dir. 1934-56, pres. 1936-51, chmn. bd., 1951-56, ret., 1956; dir. Mercantile Stores, Phoenix Indemnity Co., Nat. Surety Corp., Burrwood Corp., Hotel Astor, Ritz Carlton Hotel, Delaware & Hudson Co., D. & H. R.R., City Investing Co., Consumers Power Co., El Paso Natural Gas Co. Served as ensign U.S. Navy, 1917-19. Trustee Barnard Coll., Bennington Coll., 1931-46, Russell Sage Found., Community Service Soc., N.Y. Found., trustee Carnegie Inst. of Washington, Phillips Acad., Am. Acad. of Rome. Mem. Century Assn. Clubs: University, Racquet and Tennis, Union, Links, Yale (all N.Y.C.). Home: 215 E. 72d St. Died Oct. 6, 1959.

BRADLEY, Alva, executive; b. Cleveland, O., 1884; student mech. engring., Cornell U., 1903-05, 1907. Chmn. bd. Cleveland Builders Supply Co.; also officer or dir. many other companies. Home: 2114 Elandon Dr. Office: 1276 W. 3d St., Cleve. Deceased.

BRADLEY, Carolyn Gertrude, artist; b. Richmond, Ind.; d. Matthias Herbert and Minnie Lee Anna (Rieser) Bradley; A.B., Earlham Coll., Richmond, Ind.; B.A.E., John Herron Art Sch., Indianapolis; M.F.A., Escuela Universitaria de Bellas Artes, San Miguel Allende, Mexico; studied under Henry B. Snell, William Forsyth, Victor Julius, W. Lester Stevens, George P. Ennis and James R. Hopkins. Teacher in various high schools until 1932; assistant professor dept. of fine arts, Ohio State U., 1932-37, asso. prof., 1937—; specialist in art to Chile, Inter-Am. Ednl. Found., 1946; vis. prof. U. Chile, 1946, U. Costa Rica, 1951; vis. lectr. to Guatamala, Honduras, Costa Rica, Haiti, and Dominican Republic for Internat. Exchange of Persons for Dept. of State. Awards: Clement Studebaker water color prize, Hoosier Salon, Chicago, 1927; Mrs. John N. Carey watercolor prize, Indiana Artists Exhbn., Indianapolis, 1928; purchase prize, Richmond Art Assn., 1928; Vanderpoel water color prize, Nat. Assn. Women Painters and Sculptors, 1929; landscape prize, Richmond Art Assn., 1929; Chamber of Commerce water color prize, Indiana Artits Exhbs., 1931; George A. Zabriskie purchase prize, Am. Water Color Soc., 1934; Margaret Leidy Memorial prize, Nat. Assn. Women Painters and Sculptors, 1934; John T. McCutcheon water color prize, Hoosier Salon, Chicago, 1935; Terre Haute State Normal purchase prize, Hoosier Salon, Chicago, 1935; E. M. Quigg water color prize, Richmond Art Assn., 1935, 37, 42; Clara Chipman Memorial prize, Cincinnati Woman's Art Club, 1938; T. C. Memorial prize, Indiana Artists Club, 1950; etc. Exhibited in Inst. Chileno-Norteamericano de Cultura, Santiago, Chile, 1946, Inst. Guatemalteco-Americano, Inst. Cultural Inter-Am., Honduras, Centro Cultural Costa Ricense N. Am. Concepcion, Chile, Chile, 1946. Mem. Nat. Assn. Women Artists, Washington, Providence watercolor clubs, Cin. Woman's Art Club, Ind. Artists Club, Am., Ohio watercolor socs., Columbus Art League, Nat. League Am. Pen Women. Presbyn. Author: (with F. Meredith, Dietz) Costume and You, 1948; Costume Design, rev. edit., 1954; Western World Costume: An Outline History, 1954. Home: 60 E. Norwich Av., Columbus, O. Died Dec. 8, 1954.

BRADLEY, Cornelius Beach, educator; b. Bangkok, Siam, Nov. 18, 1843; s. Rev. Dan Beach (M.D.) and Emelie (Royce) B.; B.A., Oberlin Coll., 1868, M.A., 1886; B.D., Yale, 1871; m. Mary S. Comings, July 30, 1871. Missionary Am. Missionary Assn. to Siam, 1871-4 (retired because of health); vice prin. Oakland (Cal.) High Sch., 1875-82; instr. English, U. Cal. at Berkeley, 1882-6, asst. prof. English lang. and lit., 1886-89, asso. prof., 1889-94, prof. rhetoric, 1894-1911, prof. emeritus, 1911—. Dir. Berkeley chpt. A.R.C. Apptd. by Nat. Ednl. Council mem. Com. of 10 on Secondary Schools, 1893 (was its secretary and drafted report). Mem. Am. Oriental Soc., Am. Philol. Assn., Cal. Bot. Soc. (corr. sec.), Siam Soc. (hon.). Clubs: Berkeley, Sierra (charter mem.). Editor: Orations and Arguments by English and American Statesmen, 1895; Carlyle's Essay on Burns, 1901; Proceedings of Cal. Acad. Sciences, 1908-13; Half Century among the Siamese and Lao (autobiography of Daniel McGilvary), 1912. Contbr. many essays on scientific, lit. and philol. topics, especially on the origin and history of Siamese alphabetic writing, and on the scientific investigation and plotting of the tone-inflections of speech. Home: 2639 Durant Av., Berkeley 4, Cal. Died Feb. 8, 1936.

BRADLEY, Dwight (Jacques), clergyman; b. Yankton, S.D., Dec. 16, 1889; s. Dan Freeman and Lillian (Jaques) B.; prep. edn. Oberlin (O.) Acad.; student Oberlin Coll., 1908-09, Rollins Coll., Winter Park, Fla., 1909-10, Western Reserve U., 1910-11; A.B., Oberlin, 1912; student Oberlin Theol. Sem., 1912-13; B.D., Pacific Sch. of Religion, Berkeley, Cal., 1915, D.D., 1933; D.D., Colby, 1933, Oberlin, 1935; m. Kathryn Lee Culver, Nov. 21, 1914; children—Margaret Day, William Lee; m. 2d, Elizabeth Ganse Whiting, Mar. 10, 1944. Ordained to ministry Congl. Ch., 1915; asst., Plymouth Ch., Oakland, Cal., 1914-15; minister Highland Ch., Cleve., 1915-17, First Ch., El Paso, Tex., 1917-20, First Ch., Webster Groves,

Mo., 1920-30, First Ch. in Newton, Newton Centre, Mass., 1930-34, Union Ch., Boston, 1934-38; asso. prof. of worship Andover-Newton Theol. Sch., 1933-34, prof. social ethics, 1934-38; dir. council for Social Action of the Congl. Christian Chs. in U.S.A., 1938-43. Acting dir. Christian Commn. for Camp Communities, 1941. Dir. Religious Assos. of Nat. Ctizens Polt. Action Com., 1944-46; cons. personal and group adjustment, lectr., 1946—. With Army YMCA, 1918. Mem. N.Y. Assn. Congl. Chs., Delta Tau Delta. Author: The Recovery of Religion, 1929; Creative Worship, 1930; Fellowship of Prayer, 1932; Adventure Eternal (with Kathryn Culver Bradley), 1937; The Secret Stair, 1937; Highways of the Spirit, 1937; By Faith, 1938; Our Times—What Has the Bible to Say, 1940; Freedom of the Soul, 1943; Your Problem—Can It Be Solved?, 1945. Contbr. to mags. and religious publs. Address: 126 E. 54th St., N.Y.C. 22. Died Dec. 27, 1957.

BRADLEY, James L., army officer (ret.); b. Doniphan, Mo., May 18, 1891; B.S., U.S. Mil. Acad., 1914; grad. Inf. Sch. of Arms, Ft. Sill, 1917, Advanced Course Inf. Sch., Ft. Benning, 1924, Command and Gen. Staff Sch. (honor grad.), 1926, Army War College, 1931. Commd. 2d lt., U.S. Army, 1914, advanced through grades to maj. gen. (temp.), June 20, 1942; with 19th Inf., Vera Cruz, Mex., 1914, 22d Inf., Galveston, Tex., 1915; camp and dist. adjutant, Del Rio, Tex., 1916; with 57th Inf., Camp Travis, Tex., to June 1917, Camp Stanley, Tex., to Oct. 1917; instr. Sch. of Arms, Ft. Sill, 1918; sec. Inf. Sch. of Arms, Camp Benning, 1918-20; with 44th Inf., later 21st Inf., Schofield Barracks, Hawaii, 1920-23; with 4th Inf., Fort Missoula, 1923-24; instr. Inf. Sch., Ft. Benning, 1926-31, Command and Gen. Staff Sch., Ft. Leavenworth, 1932-36; exec. officer 16th Inf., Ft. Jay, 1936-38; with 2d Provisional Brig., Puerto Rico, 1938; comdg. officer 16th Inf., Ft. Jay, 1938; at Hdqrs. 9th Area, San Francisco, 1938-40; asst. chief of staff in charge plans and operations, 4th Army, San Francisco, 1940-41, chief, 1941-42; comdg. gen. 96th. Inf. Div. 1942-46; participated in campaigns of Leyte and Okinawa. Awarded D.S.M., Legion of Merit, Bronze Star. Retired as maj. gen. 1947. Home: 608 West 11th St., Rolla, Mo. Died July 30, 1957; buried Presidio Nat. Cemetery, San Francisco.

BRADLEY, Jay D., clergyman, educator; b. Randolph County, Ala., Aug. 4, 1881; s. William Thomas and Mahala (Knight) B.; Ph.D., D.D., LL.D.; m. Mary Jimmie Stewart, Nov. 10, 1905; children—T. Emory, Mary Kate. Supt. of schs., Rock Mills, Ala., Collinsvile, Ala., Luverne, Ala., Aabama City, Aa, pres. Frankin Collegiate Inst., Franklin, Ga.; pres. Wadley M. and F. Coll.; dean Lanier U.; pres. Webster U., Atlanta, Ga., 1922—; mem. law firm Bradley & Bradley; ordained to ministry Bapt. Ch.; has served as pastor of ch., Luverne, Ala., Fairburn, Ga., Palmetto, Ga., Austell, Ga., Dallas., Ga., Powder Springs, Ga. Vice pres. Lake Odessa (Mich.) Bible Conf. Mem. Nat. Lawyers Guild, U.S., Ga. bar assns., Nat. Assn. Colls. and Univs., Inc. (sec.-treas.). Mason (K.T., Shriner), Order Eastern Star, K.P., Junior Order F.R.G.S., A.Ph.R.S. Formerly editor the Nat. Messenger. Author of over 100 instructor's syllabi in law, theology, science, philosophy, psychology. Home: 1204 Clairmont Av., Decatur, Ga. Office: 7 Peachtree St., Atlanta. Died Mar. 3, 1951.

BRADLEY, Kenneth McPherson, musical educator; b. Campbellsville, Ky., Sept. 27, 1872; s. J. S. and Anna D. (McPherson) B.; ed. Add Ran Coll., Tex., 3 yrs., U. of Wooster, O., 1 yr., U. of Ky., 2 yrs., Cincinnati Coll. of Music, 1 yr., Cincinnati Conservatory, 2 yrs., by pvt. teacher, Paris, France, 1 yr.; hon. Mus.D., Columbia Sch. of Music, 1932; m. Edith Stevens Hosford, May 18, 1936. After finishing sch., organized sch. of music at Waxahachie, Tex., removed sch. 3 yrs. later to Fort Worth, where conducted it 4 yrs.; pres. Bush Conservatory Music, Chicago, 1902-25 and 1931-33; ednl. dir. Juilliard Musical Foundation, New York, 1925-26. Established first Master Sch. of Music in America, 1921 (for exceptionally talented students, tuition free). An organizer and pres. Nat. Assn. of Schs. of Music and Allied Arts. Lecturer, pianist, theorist and instructor. Author: Harmony and Analysis; The Triangle; Theatrical Work in "Progression Series of Music Lessons" of Art Publication Soc. Was first to establish the preceptorial methods in music schs. Chmn. nat. conservatory com. of Soc. Am. Musicians, also of Nat. Music Teachers' Assn.; mem. Soc. Arts and Letters. Founder of free scholarships in Bush Conservatory, for composition, piano, violin and voice students, 1926. Address: 1858 W. 82d St., Los Angeles, Cal. Died Dec. 3, 1954; buried Forest Lawn Meml., Glendale, Cal.

BRADLEY, Otis T(reat), lawyer; b. New Haven, Conn., June 21, 1895; s. Otis Belden and Nellie Lucy (Treat) B.; A.B., Yale, 1915; LL.B., Harvard, 1919; m. Marian B. Alling, Nov. 18, 1926; children—Margaret Osborne, Otis T., Marian A., Edward Michael. Admitted to N.Y. State bar, 1920, and since practiced in N.Y. City, mem. firm of Davis Polk Wardwell Sunderland & Kiendl and predecessor firms since 1930. Dir. F. Kelly Co., Union Fabric Co., Steels & Busks, Ltd. Admitted to U.S. Supreme Court, 1939. Served with Coast Artillery, U.S. Army, 1917-19; commd. 2d lt., 1917, disch. capt., 1919; served in 56th Artillery, C.A.C. in second battle of Marne, Meuse-Argonne campaigns, 1918; Govt. appeal agt., Selective Service. Trustee Union Coll., Bennington Coll., Union Theol. Sem., Southampton Hosp., Buckley Foundation, Chapin-Brearley Exchange, The Chapin Sch., Ltd. Mem. Am. Bar Assn., N.Y. State Bar Assn. (pres., 1950), N.Y. County Lawyers Assn., Assn. Bar City N.Y., N.Y. Hist. Soc. (trustee), Phi Beta Kappa, Zeta Psi. Presbyn. (mem. bd. nat. missions, elder, trustee). Clubs: Nat. Golf Links (Southampton, N.Y.); Grolier, Century, Links, Yale (N.Y. City). Home: 1160 Park Av., N.Y. City 28. Office: 15 Broad St., N.Y. C. 5. Died Nov. 22, 1950.

BRADLEY, Willis W., state legislator; b. Ransomville, N.Y., June 28, 1884; s. Willis W. and Sarah Anne (Johnson) B.; B.Sc., U.S. Naval Acad., 1907; M.Sc., George Washington Univ., 1914; post grad. Ordnance and Gunnery, United States Navy, 1913-15; graduate of the Naval War College, 1938; m. Sue Worthington Cox, Oct. 16, 1907; children—Elizabeth (Mrs. John J. Earle), Sue (Mrs. Bruce McCandless, Anne (Mrs. Wallace H. Brucker), Josephine (Mrs. Guy O. DeYoung). Commd. ensign U.S. Navy, 1907, and advanced through grades to capt., 1933; gov. of Guam, 1929-31; retired, 1946. Mem. of the Congress, 18th District of Calif., 1947-49; mem. assembly, Cal. Legislature, 1952. Mem. board visitors U.S. Naval Academy, 1948. Awarded Congressional Medal of Honor, World War I; Silver Medal from Pope Pius XI; Silver Medal from Italian Red Cross for Messina Earthquake. Mem. Am. Legion, Vets. Fgn. Wars, Am. Vets., Disabled Am. Vets. Army and Navy Union, U.S.A., Mil. Order of Carabao, Naval Order of U.S., American Academy Political and Social Science. Republican. Protestant. Mason (32°, K.T., Shriner). Elk. Moose. National Sojourners (past nat. pres.). Clubs: Army and Navy, Army-Navy Country, Cosmos (Washington, D.C.); University (Long Beach); Propeller of U.S. Home: 284 Argonne Av., Long Beach 3, Cal. Office: State Capitol, Sacramento. Died Aug. 27, 1954; buried Fort Rosecrans Nat. Cemetery, Point-Loma, San Diego, Cal.

BRADSHAW, Charles Sullivan, lawyer; b. Toledo, Ia., Aug. 4, 1871; s. Centenary B. and Mary Ann (Hayzlett) B.; LL.B., Drake U., Des Moines, Ia., 1896; m. Ruth E. Baker, June 28, 1911 (died Nov. 15, 1918); children—Helen Ann (Mrs. B. W. Hotchkiss), Homer Edward, Charles Baker. Admitted Ia. bar and began practice in Des Moines, 1896; successively mem. law firms of Kinne, Hume & Bradshaw, Hume & Bradshaw, Cummins, Hume & Bradshaw; became sr. partner Bradshaw, Fowler, Proctor & Fairgrave; gen. counsel, dir. Ia. Power & Light Co., Des Moines Gas & Electric Co.; counsel Pullman Co. Served as judge 9th Judicial Dist., Ia., 1911-13. Mem. Am. and Ia. State bar assns. Elk. Clubs: Des Moines, Wakonda (Des Moines). Home: 607 Country Club Blvd. Office: Central National Bldg., Des Moines, Ia. Died Mar. 27, 1953.

BRADSHAW, Leslie Havergal, writer, theatrical mgr.; b. Liverpool, Eng.; s. Capt. John (comdr. S.S. Belgenland and commodore of Red Star Line) and Helen (Steel) B.; ed. pvt. schs., Winchester and Southampton, Eng., Cambridge University; m. Isabella Braidwood Dewar Small, March 22, 1947. On editorial staff, Everybody's Mag., 1910-12; sec. to Thomas W. Lawson, Boston, 1912-14; reporter and night rewrite, N.Y. Herald; 1st asst. to Herbert C. Hoover (later President of U.S.) in organizing Food Administration, Washington D.C., 1917; owner and pub. Camp Meade (Md.) Herald and Camp Upton (N.Y.) Despatch, 1917-19; sec. and dir. Ray Verde Copper Co.; pres. Bradshaw Productions, Inc.; producer of dramas, "Chivalry," featuring Violet Heming, Edmund Breese, Mrs. Lionel Barrymore (Doris Rankin), Wallack's Theatre, New York, 1925; "Interference," featuring Alison Bradshaw, Brandon Tynan, Park Theatre, 1927; "The Patriarch," featuring Cecilia Loftus, Ambassador Theatre, 1929; mgr. of B. C. Hilliam ("Flotsam & Jetsam"), Brit. Broadcasting Co. star, England. Financial editor The Elks Magazine, 1923-28; cable supervisor, British Purchasing Commn., N.Y. City 1940-1943. Republican. Clubs: City, National Republican, Newspaper, British, Owls, Society of Silurians, New York Athletic (New York); Old Edwardians (Southampton, Eng.). Author: The Right Sort, 1912, Scientific Developments From The Investor's Viewpoint, 1944; also serials, articles and short stories in mags. Editor, Investment Timing, 1943-48; now editorial consultant to authors and pubs. Address: 1 Bank St., N.Y.C. 14. Died Dec. 28, 1950.

BRADY, John Everett, educator; b. Davidson, N.C., July 22, 1860; s. Rufus Archibald and Martha Jane (Hart) B.; A.B., U. N.C., 1881; post-grad. work univs. of Leipzig, Göttingen, Paris, Athens and Heidelberg, 1882-88, A.M., Ph.D. in Sanskrit, classics and ancient history, Heidelberg, 1888; m. Mary Taylor Seelye, Aug. 20, 1889 (died 1931); m. 2d, Lucille Seelye, 1931 (died Feb. 7, 1934); m. 3d, Annie McGhee Joyner, 1936. Prof. Latin lang. and lit. Smith Coll., Northampton, Mass., 1888-1926, ret. Mem. Am. Philol. Assn. Classical Assn. of N.E. Presbyn. Author: Sound Changes in Modern Greek (in German), 1886; Studies in Quintus Curtius Rufus, 1887; Women in Roman Literature, 1894. Home: Franklinton, N.C. Died Jan. 20, 1941.

BRAGDON, Merritt Caldwell, lawyer; b. Evanston, Ill., Nov. 19, 1892; s. Merritt Caldwell and Elizabeth Wayne (Byerly) B.; A.B., Northwestern, 1913; LL.B. cum laude, Harvard, 1916; m. Miriam Wagner, June 26, 1920; children—Edwin Wagner, Merrit Caldwell, Elizabeth Wayne. Admitted to Ill. bar, 1916, since practiced in Chgo.; mem. Sidley, Austin, Burgess & Smith, and predecessors, 1916—. Served as 1st lt., 331st F.A., U.S. Army, 1917-18. Mem. Am., Ill. State, Chgo. (librarian 1949-52) bar assns., Art Inst. Chgo., Phi Beta Kappa, Beta Theta Pi. Republican. Methodist. Clubs: University, Executives (Chgo.). Home: 1133 Hinman Av., Evanston, Ill. Office: 11 S. LaSalle St., Chgo. 3. Died Jan. 30, 1958.

BRAGG, George Freeman, clergyman; b. Warrenton, N.C., Jan. 25, 1863; s. George Freeman and Mary (Williams) B.; grad. St. Stephens Normal Sch. (colored), Petersburg, Va.; grad. Bishop Payne Div. Sch., Petersburg, 1886; m. Nellie G. Hill, Sept. 20, 1887; children—Harry Graham, Mary H. C., Arthur M., Nellie G. Deacon P.E. Ch., 1887, priest, 1888; rector St. James Ch., Balt., 1891. Gen. sec. Conf. of (P.E.) Ch. Workers (colored) over 30 yrs. Mem. bd. mgrs. House of Reformation for Colored Boys; founder, 1899, v.p. and chaplain Md. Home for Friendless Colored Children. Author: Men of Maryland, 1914; The History of the Afro-American Group of the Episcopal Church, 1922; The Hero of Jerusalem, 1926. Home: 1425 McCulloh St., Balt. Died Mar. 12, 1940.

BRAHENEY, Bernard F., utilities exec.; b. Chgo., Aug. 4, 1892; s. Bernard J. and Catherine (Hoy) B.; student St. Patrick's Comml. Acad. and Bus. Sch.; m. Elizabeth Maguire, Apr. 28, 1928; 1 son, Thomas J. Gen. auditor, v.p. accounting Byllesby Engring. & Management Co., 1920-42; successively account dept. clk., travel auditor, asst. gen. auditor No. States Power Co., 1910-20, v.p., 1942-43, v.p., treas., 1943-47, pres. since 1947. Mem. bd. dirs. Greater Mpls. Safety Council, Glenwood Hills Hosp.; mem. bd. trustees, exec. bd. Keep Minn. Green, Mem. Mpls. C. of C. (dir.), Edison Electric Inst., Central Electric Assn., Minn. Safety Council. Clubs: Minikahda (Minn.); Minneapolis, Minnesota, Athletic (Mpls.). Home: 2701 E. Lake of the Isles. Office: 15 S. 5th St., Mpls. 2. Died Jan. 3, 1954.

BRAINARD, Morgan Bulkeley, life insurance exec.; born Hartford, Conn., Jan. 8, 1879; s. Leverett and Mary Jerusha (Bulkeley) B.; A.B., Yale U., 1900, LL.B., 1903; hon. M.A., Trinity, Hartford, Conn., 1932; LL.D., Bryant Coll., 1953, Wesleyan U., 1954; married Eleanor Stewart Moffat, Apr. 27, 1905; children—Morgan Bulkeley, Charles Edwin, Edward Moffatt, Maxwell Leverett, Constance Morgan. Began with Aetna Life Ins. Co., Hartford, 1905, became pres. 1922, now chmn. bd.; chmn. bd. Aetna Casualty & Surety Co., Standard Fire Ins. Co.; dir. United Aircraft Corp., The Cleveland-Cliffs Iron Co., John P. Maguire & Company, Hartford National Bank & Trust Company, Hartford Steam Boiler Inspection & Insurance Company, Hartford Electric Light Co., Connecticut Power Company, Underwood Corporation. Mem. board directors Hartford Hosp.; trustee Colt Bequest. Republican. Episcopalian. Clubs: Hartford; The Links, Yale (New York). Home: 1090 Prospect Av. Office: 151 Farmington Av., Hartford, Conn. Died Aug. 1957.

BRAINE, Clinton Elgin, Jr. (brān), naval officer, ret.; b. N.Y. City, Dec. 9, 1894; s. Clinton Elgin and Ella Bird (Warburton) B.; B.S., U.S. Naval Acad., 1916; m. Miriam Maude Ellis, Feb. 22, 1919; 1 son, Clinton Ellis. Commd. ensign, U.S. Navy, 1916, and advanced through grades to rear admiral, 1945; duty on battleship, 1916-20; on submarine, 1920-30, staff and cruiser, 1930-38; with Bureau of Ordnance, 1938-41; mem. mission to U.S.S.R., 1941; comd. U.S.S. Memphis, 1941-42; chief of staff 4th Fleet, 1942-45; comdg. Naval Operating Base and Training Station, Newport, R.I.; office of Sec. of Navy, 1946-49, ret. 1949; now asst. to pres. Crucible Steel Co. of Am. Decorated Legion of Merit (3 times), Commendation Medal, World War II, China Defense, Atlantic and European service medals (U.S.), Southern Cross, Naval Medal of Merit, Medal of Merit for Air (Brazil). Clubs: New York Yacht, St. Nicholas, Yale (N.Y. City); Duquesne (Pittsburgh). Home: 108 E. 38th St. Office: 405 Lexington Av., N.Y. City. Now deceased.

BRALLIAR, Floyd Burton, educator, author; b. Richland, Ia., Sept. 11, 1875; s. Washington George and Martha A. (Hornbeak) B.; student Battle Creek (Mich.) Coll.; B.Sc., Walla Walla (Wash.) Coll., 1895; M.S., Emmanuel Missionary Coll., 1919; Ph.D., George Peabody Coll., 1921; m. Ada Conard, of College Place, Wash., 1898 (died 1901); children—Ena Marie (Mrs. Thomas Abernathy) (dec.), Ada Conard (Mrs. William Cheek); m. 2d, Mertie Boynton, 1904 (dec. Mar. 1951); children—Alice Isabelle (wife of Dr. Paul Rolen), Floyd Boynton, John Seward, Max Burton. Began teaching in rural schs., Ia., 1894; prof. of pedagogy, Union Coll., Neb., 1903-04; ednl. supt. Central Union Conf., 7th Day Adventists Church, 1904-06; principal and business mgr. Ia. Industrial Acad., 1905-09; prin. Hillcrest Sch. Farm (for colored agrl. teachers), Nashville, 1909-17; became prof. biology and related science, Nashville Agrl. and Normal Inst., 1917; dean and head dept. of biology, Madison Coll.; scientific breeder of small fruits, also iris and cannas; operates ornamental nursery and plant breeding sta.; first regional v.p. Am. Iris Soc. for the South. Fellow Am. Assn. for Advancement of Science; mem. Ia. and Tenn. State hort. socs., Tenn. Bee-Keeper's Assn. (v.p.), Tenn. State Florists' Assn., Soc. of Am. Florists (lecture bureau), etc. Author: Elo the Eagle, and Other Stories, 1908; Knowing Insects Through Stories, 1918; Knowing Birds Through Stories, 1922; Zip the Coon and Other Stories, 1931; Grape Culture in the South. Editor garden dept. in several daily newspapers. Lectr. for Sch. Assembly Assn. Home: Madison College, Tenn. Died Sept. 5, 1951.

BRANCH, Ernest A., dentist; b. Lumberton, N.C., May 16, 1888; s. John A. and Mary O'Neal (Breece) B.; student Oak Ridge (N.C.) Inst., 1908-10; D.D.S., Atlanta Dental Coll., 1910-13; irregular student N.C. State Coll., 1925-29; m. Marry Emma Parkr, June 14, 1915; children—Mary O'Neal (Mrs. Robert G. B. Bourne), Jacquelyn (Mrs. Robert L. Burrage, Jr.). In pvt. practice of dentistry, Norwood, N.C., 1913-22; mem. vis. staff Forsyth Dental Infirmary for Children, Boston, 1923; pub. health dentist for Wake County, N.C., 1922-27; pvt. practice, children's dentistry, 1927-29; dir. div. of oral hygiene N.C. State Bd. Health, 1929—. Recipient Carl V. Reynolds award N.C. Public Health Assn., 1952. Diplomate Am. Bd. Dental Pub. Health. Fellow Am. Coll. Dentists; mem. N.C. Dental Soc. (pres. 1933-34), Am. Dental Assn., N.C. Pub. Health Assn. (past pres.), Am. Assn. Pub. Health Dentists, Assn. State and Territorial Dental Dirs. (pres. 1950), Phi Omega. Home: 317 Calvin Rd. Office: State Board of Health, Raleigh, N.C. Died Dec. 3, 1958.

BRANCUSI, Constantin, sculptor; b. Pestisani Gorj, Rumania, Feb. 21, 1876; student Sch. Arts and Crafts, Crajova, 1894-98, Ecole des Beaux-Arts, Bucharest, 1898-1902; studied with Antonin Mercie. Participant ann. exhbns. in Paris, 1905-13; one-man shows, Antwerp, 1926, Mowcow, 1928, other European cities and in U.S. at Brummer gallery, 1926; exhibited cubism and abstract art Mus. Modern Art, 1936, sculpture of 20th century, 1952, spl. display, 1952; works represented in Musee National d'Art Moderne, Paris, Tate Gallery, London, Mus. Modern Art, Guggenheim Mus., N.Y.C., Buffalo Fine Arts Acad., Cleve. Mus. Art, Art Inst. of Chgo., Phila. Mus. Art; important works include Bird in Space, Endless Column, Mlle. Pogany. Address: 11 Impasse Ronsin, Paris 15e, France. Died Mar. 16, 1957; buried Montparnasse Cemetery, Paris.

BRAND, Charles L., naval officer; b. Worcester, Mass., Nov. 11, 1887; s. John L. and Annie E. (Butt) B.; B.S., U.S. Naval Acad., 1910; M.S., Mass. Inst. Tech., 1915; m. Helen May Levin, June 17, 1914; 1 dau., Nancy R. Commd. lt. (j.g.), U.S. Navy, 1912, and advanced through the grades to rear admiral, 1942; served as midshipman U.S.S. Georgia, 1910-12; at U.S. Navy Yards, Phila., 1915-20, Puget Sound, Wash., 1920-23, Charleston, S.C., 1923-25, Mare Island, Calif., 1927-31, Puget Sound, 1931-32, Phila., 1936-38; staff of comdr. in chief, Battle Force, 1925-27; head constrn. div., Bureau of Ships, Navy Dept., Washington, D.C., 1932-36; mgr. Navy Yard, Boston, 1938-42; became asst. chief for design and shipbldg., Bur. Ships, Navy Dept., Washington, 1942; retired, 1949. Now representative American President Lines. Awarded Victory medal (World War I), Emergency Medal, 1941; Distinguished Service Medal, Am. Theatre Victory Medal, World War II. Mem. Grad. Bd., Mass. Inst. Tech. Mem. U.S. Soc. Naval Architects (past pres.), Am. Soc. Naval Engrs. Address: 32 Riverbank, Beverly, N.J. Died April 18, 1953.

BRAND, William Henry, investment banker; b. Milw., Sept. 13, 1892; s. Charles S. and Augusta (Traeumer) B.; student pub. schs.; m. Lorraine Mueller, June 21, 1916; 1 dau., Constance (Mrs. James R. Struss). With First Wis. Nat. Bank, 1911-20; pres. Robert W. Baird & Co., Inc., Milw., 1948—; dir. Will Ross, Inc., Interstate Drop Forge Co., Perfex Corp., Mueller Furnace Co. Dir. Children's Hosp.; treas. Columbia Hosp., Milw. Clubs: Milwaukee, Milwaukee Country; University, Lunch (N.Y.C.). Home: 7851 N. Links Circle, Milw. 17. Office: 110 E. Wisconsin Av., Milw. 2. Died Feb. 14, 1957.

BRANDEBERRY, John Benjamin, coll. dean, prof. engring.; b. Newton Falls, O. Dec. 13, 1893; s. John B. and Lydia (Kistler) B.; B.S., Mt. Union Coll., 1913; A.M., Ohio State U., 1915; Ph.D., U. of Mich., 1932; student U. of Chicago, summer 1916; m. Dorothy Kendall, June 25, 1920 (dec.); 1 dau., Barbara B. Morrison; m. 2d, Aubrey Mather, Dec. 15, 1944; children—John Barton, Margaret Louise, Carol Ann. stepchildren—Raymond Louis, Catherine May. Began teaching career as science teacher, Newberry, Mich., 1913-14; assistant professor University of Toledo, 1915-18, asso. prof., 1918-26. Prof. math. and engring. since 1926, dean Coll. Engring. since 1943. Mem. Am. Soc. Testing Materials, O. Soc. Prof. Engrs., Am. Math. Soc., Am. Assn. Univ. Profs., Math. Assn. of Am. (chmn. Mich. sect. 1935, O. sect. 1945, 1946), Am. Soc. Engring. Edn. (chmn. Ohio sect. 1932), Pi Mu Epsilon, Alpha Sigma Phi. Mason (32°, Shriner). Mem. United Brethren Ch. Club: Exchange. Home: 4760 305th St., Toledo 11. Died Sept. 23, 1953; buried Toledo Meml. Park Cemetery.

BRANDEIS, Erich (bran'dis), newspaperman, writer; b. Berlin, Germany; s. Adolph B. and Amelia (Cronheim) B.; A.B., University of Berlin, m. Olga Williamson, 1921. Naturalized citizen, 1927. Reporter San Francisco Examiner, 1913-14; press rep. San Francisco Call, at San Francisco Expn., 1915; feature writer for same paper, 1916-18; contbr. to mags. and syndicates; publicity writer Internat. Magazine Co. (pubs. Cosmopolitan, Good Housekeeping, Harpers' Bazar, etc.), 1922-24. Spl. promotion work for a number of magazines and newspapers among them, King Features Syndicate, Cosmopolitan, Good Housekeeping, New York Times, Current History, Smart Set, Delineator, Adventure, Everybody's, Business Week, System, Life, Forbes, Hearst Newspapers; v.p. Am. Offset Corp., 1935-36; v.p. Americana Corp.; dir. Americana Inst., 1937-38; promotion dir. King Features Syndicate, Inc., Internat. News Service, Internat. News Photos, Central Press Assn., 1938-47. Clubs: Adventurers, Banshees, Nat. Press, Overseas Press Am., Inc. (Washington, D.C.); Sigma Delta Chi. Author: The Successful Physician, 1923 (with Dr. V. C. Thomas); Andrew Jackson, Old Hickory, 1936; Franklin D. Roosevelt, the Man, 1936; also vaudeville playlets, mag. articles, pamphlets and inspirational and business editorials; daily syndicated feature "Looking at Life," appearing in some 150 newspapers. Home: Old Farm Rd., Georgetown, Conn. Office: King Features Syndicate, 235 E. 45th St., N.Y.C. Died Nov. 18, 1954.

BRANDEL, S. W., pres. Marlin-Roswell Corp. Address: 402 Chandler St., Jamestown, N.Y. Died Aug. 30, 1955.

BRANDJORD, Iver Martinson (brănd'yôrd), corporation official; b. Norway, Oct. 18, 1873; s. Martin Iversen and Guri (Ronningen) Brandjord; grad. Lutheran Normal Sch., Madison, Minn., 1897, student U. of N.D., 1900-01; m. Helga Louise Swarstad, June 1, 1910; 1 son, Marcus Allan. Came to U.S., 1893, naturalized citizen, 1900. An organizer, 1910, 1st pres., 1910-11, Ronan (Mont.) State Bank; an organizer, 1911, and now president, The Better Housing Company, Ronan. Auditor Bottineau County, N.D., 1903-09; mem. Mont. Ho. of Rep., 1919-20, 1923-24; commr. state lands and investments, Mont., 1925-37; state adminstr. of pub. welfare, 1937-1941; mem. President Hoover's Commn. on Public Domain, 1930-31. Democrat. Lutheran. Mason. Author of statutes applying amortization plan of payment to all pub. corp. bonds, state land contracts and mortgage loans; author of amendment to Mont. constitution providing for perpetual growth of pub. school permanent fund. Advocate of a supplementary currency based on commodities, home security making the ordinary home exempt from taxation and all claims for debt and The World University of America. Originator of Plan for Interstate Currency for United States of Western Europe. Home: Ronan, Mont. Died July 12, 1950.

BRANDON, Edgar Ewing, educator; born York Springs, Pa., Aug. 9, 1865; s. John Calvin and Mary Braiding (Ewing) B.; A.B., U. of Mich., 1888; A.M., U. of Mo., 1897; studied U. of Paris, 1893-94, and 1901-02, Docteur d'Université, 1904; LL.D., Miami U., 1930; m. Charlotte Taylor, June 11, 1901; m. 2d, Grace Glasgow, Aug. 14, 1929. Latin master, Carthage, Mo., 1889-93, instr. in French, U. of Mich., 1895-96 and 1897-98; fellow in Romance langs., U. of Mo., 1896-97; prof. Romance langs., Miami U., Oxford, O., 1898-31, v.p., 1908-31, dean, 1912-31, acting pres., 1909-10, 1927-28, now emeritus. Dir. Foyer du Soldat, France, 1918-19. Spl. commr. Pan-Am. Union to visit and report on instns. of higher learning in Latin America, 1911-12. Del. to 2d Pan-Am. Scientific Congress, 1915. Mem. Modern Lang. Assn. of America, Phi Beta Kappa, Phi Kappa Tau (pres. 1920-23). Mason. Republican. Presbyterian. Author: Robert Estienne et le dictionnaire français au XVI Siècle, 1904; Latin American Universities, 1912; Précis d'histoire des États-Unis, 1919 (Trans. English, 1919); A Pilgrimage of Liberty, 1944; Lafayette, Guest of the Nation, Vol. I, 1950, II, 1954, III, 1957. Editor: La Tulipe Noire, 1899; Monte Cristo, 1900; Series Lessons for Beginners in French, 1920. Joint editor La petite ville, 1925; Henri III et sa cour, 1926; Turcaret, 1927. Home: 315 E. Church St., Oxford, O. Died June 8, 1957; buried Oxford Cemetery.

BRANDON, Jesse DeWitt, business exec.; b. Frankfort, Ind., May 11, 1891; s. Samuel J. and Savannah (Finney) B.; student pub. schs., Alexandria, Ind.; m. Ethel Rachel Irwin, May 11, 1921; 1 son, Jerry D. Section hand C., C., C. & St. L. R.R., Beech Grove, Ind., 1906-14, gen. foreman, 1914; service engr. Am. Brake Shoe Co., N.Y., 1915-19; service engr. Am. Arch Co., Inc., Canadian ty., hdqrs. Montreal, 1919-23, Chgo., 1923-24, asst. to v.p. 1927, v.p. in charge Chgo. office, 1927-43, v.p. charge entire sales, 1943-47, pres., N.Y.C., 1947—; asst. mgr. Pitts. Steel Co., Chgo., 1924-27. Republican. Clubs: Westchester Country, Uptown, Traffic (N.Y.C.); Chicago, Flossmoor Country, Traffic (Chgo.); Racquet (Phila.); Columbia (Indpls.); Minnesota (St. Paul). Home: 299 Park Av. Office: 60 E. 42d St., N.Y.C. 17. Deceased.

BRANDT, Carl Ludwig, painter; b. nr. Hamburg, Holstein, Germany, Sept. 22, 1831; studied art in prin. galleries in Europe; served in war, 1848-50, between Germany and Denmark; came to U.S., 1852; in Europe, 1865-9, then returned; has painted many noteworthy portraits and other figure pieces and hist. scenes; Nat. Academician, 1872; dir. Telfair Acad. Arts and Sciences, Savannah, Ga., where he spends his winters. Address: Hastings-on-Hudson, N.Y. Died 1905.

BRANDT, John, pres. Land O'Lakes Creameries; b. Forest City, Minn., July 20, 1885; s. Frederic Martin and Henrietta (Post) B.; ed. pub. schs. of Minn.; m. Maude Mary Caswell, Mar. 8, 1908. Pres. Litchfield Creamery Co. (Minn.) since 1910, sec. Litchfield Livestock Shipping Assn. since 1916; pres. Land O' Lakes Creameries, Inc., Minneapolis, since 1921; pres. Nat. Coop. Milk Producers Fedn., Washington, D.C., 1941-49; pres. Dairy Products Marketing Assn., Chicago, Ill., since 1938; dir. 7th Dist., Farm Credit Adminstrn., St. Paul, Minn., since 1935. Mason. Operates 560 acre farm in Meeker County, Minn. Home: 6512 Parkwood Rd., Minneapolis. Address: 2215 Kennedy St. N.E., Mpls. Died Mar. 4, 1953.

BRANGWYN, Sir Frank, artist; b. Bruges, Brussels, May 13, 1867; s. William Curtis and Elenore (Griffith) B.; m. Lucy Ray. Painter in oil, sculptor, furniture designer, muralist, also engaged various other forms of creative art; 1st oil painting accepted by Royal Acad., 1885; works include eight wall panels for Panama-Pacific expn., San Francisco, 1915; other murals in House of Lords, Parliament bldgs., Winnipeg, Can., Mo. State Capitol, RCA Bldg., Rockefeller Center, others; paintings in permanent collections throughout the world; retrospective exhbn. arranged by Brit. Royal Acad., 1952. Recipient numerous honors and awards. Asso. Royal Acad.; v.p. Assn. Architects and Surveyors. Address: The Jointure, Ditching, Sussex, Eng. Died June 11, 1956.*

BRANIFF, Thomas E., airway exec.; b. Salina, Kan., 1883; s. J.A. and Mary Catherine (Baker) B.; student pub. schs., Mo.; LL.D., Okla. City U.; m. Bess Thurman, Oct. 26, 1912. Founder, pres., chmn. bd. dir., Braniff International Airways; pres. T.E. Braniff Co., Dallas, ins.; dir. Kansas City Fire and Marine Ins. Co., Republic Nat. Bank of Dallas. Pres. Braniff Found. Trustee Our Lady of the Lake Coll., San Antonio. Chmn. bd. dirs. Tex. div. Am. Cancer Soc.; dir. Am.-Korean Found.; National Catholic co-chairman National Conference Christians and Jews. Dir. Dallas Grand Opera Assn., World Brotherhood Orgn. in Europe. Chmn. transportation and commerce com. U.S. Inter-Am. Council on Commerce & Prodn. Trustee Inst. Internat. Edn. Mem. Nat. Assn. Mfrs., Internat. C. of C. (U.S. council), U.S. Inter-Am. Council (bd. trustees), Dallas Citizens Council (dir.), Dallas C. of C. (dir.), Dallas Comnty. Chest (dir.), Consquistadores del Cielo. English Speaking Union, Delta Phi Upsilon. Knight Comdr. Order of St. Gregory; Knight of the Order of Holy Sepulchre, Knight Malta; awarded World Brotherhood citn., Nat. Conf. Christians and Jews. Catholic. Clubs: Dallas Critic, Serra, Rotary, Downtown, Notre Dame, Brook Hollow (Dallas); River (Kansas City); Lotus (Okla. City); Burning Tree Country (Washington). Home: 5039 Seneca Dr. Office: Love Field, Dallas 9. Died Jan. 19, 1954.

BRANNAN, William Forrest, pres. Anchor Post Products, Inc.; b. Montpelier, O., Nov. 25, 1893; s. Melvin C. and Emma (Cannon) B.; grad. Bryan High Sch., 1914; student Wooster (O.) Coll., 1914-17; m. Marjorie Case, Aug. 1, 1919; children—Pauline, Robert Russel, Marjorie Marie, Kathrine, Barbara. Began as salesman, 1919, now pres. and dir. Anchor Post Products, Inc., Balt.; dir. Anchor Post Products, Inc. of Cal., Am. Fence Constrn., Black & Decker. Served ensign, pilot Navy Flying Corp., World War I. Democrat. Presbyn. Clubs: Country, Merchants (Balt.); New York Yacht, Gibson Island. Home: Cambridge Arms Apt., Balt. 18. Office: Kane St. and Eastern Av., Balt. 24. Died Dec. 1, 1956; buried Druid Ridge Cemetery, Balt.

BRANSCOMB, John W., bishop; b. Union Springs, Ala., May 11, 1905; s. John Sanford and Ida (Dismukes) B.; ed. Oglethorpe U., Atlanta, Ga., 1922-23; B.Ph., Emory U., Atlanta, 1926, B.D., 1928, D.D. (hon.), 1954; D.D. (hon.), Fla. So. Coll., 1940, LL.D., 1953; LL.D., Bethune-Cookman Coll., 1953; m. Elizabeth Keller, Nov. 28, 1928; children—Betty Joan, John Rufus. Pastor, Boca Grande, Fla., 1928-29, St. Petersburg, Fla., 1929-31, Orlando, Fla., 1931-33, Arcadia, Fla., 1933-36, First Methodist, Tampa, Fla., 1936-44, First Meth. Ch., Orlando, Fla., 1944; elected bishop of The Methodist Church in 1952. Executive sec. Bd. Missions, Fla. Conf. Meth. Ch., 1937-46; del. to Southeastern Jurisdictional Conf., 1940; chmn. Fla. Conf. del. to gen. conf. of Meth. Chs., 1944; exec. sec. Fla. Meth. Centennial, 1944; mem. Gen. Conf. Meth. Ch., 1948; mem. Jurisdictional Conf., Southeastern Methodist Ch., 1948; pres. Southeastern Jurisdictional Board of Missions, 1948-52; mem. Gen. Bd. of Missions; trustee Fla. So. Coll., Weslyan Coll., Macon, Ga., Lake Junaluska Assembly, Bethune-Cookman College; pres. bd. trustees Paine Coll., Augusta, Ga. Exec. sec. Conf. Bd. Missions, Fla. Conf., 1937-52; pres. S.E. Jurisdiction Bd. Missions, 1944-52; sec. Coll. Bishops, S.E. Jurisdiction, Meth. Church. Mem. board directors Tuberculosis Assn., YMCA, Orlando Community Chest. Member Sigma Alpha Epsilon. Clubs: International, Kiwanis, University. Home: 1296 Avondale. Office: 225 E. Duval St., Jacksonville, Fla. Died Jan. 16, 1959.

BRANSON, Edwin Bayer, geologist; b. Belleville, Kan., May 11, 1877; s. John McDowell and Harriet Melviney (Bullen) B.; A.B., A M., U. Kan., 1903; Ph.D., U. Chgo., 1905; m. Grace Muriel Colton, Aug. 24, 1905; children—Carl Colton, Edwin Robert. Instr. in geology Oberlin Coll., 1905-07, asso. prof., 1907-09, prof., 1909-10; prof. geology U. Mo., 1910-—. Served as geologist Mo. Bur. Geology and Mines intermittently, 1914-28; geologist Gypsy Oil Co., parts of 1920-28. Fellow Geol. Soc. Am., Paleontol. Soc. Am., A.A.A.S., Am. Assn. Petroleum Geologists; mem. Mo., St. Louis acads. sci., Phi Beta Kappa, Sigma Xi. Conglist. Author: Geology of Missouri, 1918; Geology and Geography of Middle Eastern Costa Rica; Devonian of Missouri, 1923; Conodonts, 1933; Introduction to Geology, 1935, 2d edit., 1941; The Lower Mississippian of Missouri, 1938; Geology of Missouri, 1945. Contbr. sci. jours. Home: 301 S. Glenwood Av., Columbia, Mo. Died Mar. 12, 1950.*

BRANSON, John William, coll. pres.; b. Laurel County, Ky., Feb. 22, 1888; s. James Garrett and Sarah Catherine (Dees) B.; student Berea Coll., 1912-15; Ph.B., U. Chgo., 1920; M.S., Purdue U., 1927, LL.D., 1952; m. Haidee Sikes, Dec. 23, 1916. Engaged in mfr. of lumber, Ky., 1906-08, live stock business, Ky. and Ga., 1910-12; tchr. pub. schs. of Ga., 1908-10; prin. Sue Bennett Meml. Sch., London, Ky., 1915-17; instr. mathematics Cumberland Coll., 1917-19, Center Coll., 1919-21, Purdue U., 1921-27; head dept. mathematics N.M. State U., 1927-46, acting pres., 1938, 1941-46, 49, dean coll., 1941-49, pres., 1949-—. Mem. War Finance Com., State War Bd., N.M. 1942. Fellow A.A.A.S.; mem. Math. Assn. Am. (pres. SW sect. 1940), Western Interstate Commn. Higher Edn., C. of C. LaCruces. Kiwanian. Author: Plane and Spherical Trigonometry with Tables, 1937. Address: N.M. State U., University Park, N.M. Died Sept. 29, 1957; buried Masonic Cemetery, Las Cruces, N.M.

BRASE, Hagbard (brä'sê), conductor; b. Rada, Sweden, Sept. 25, 1877; s. Johannes and Lydia Caroline (Jungner) B.; student Coll. of Skara, Sweden; grad. Royal Conservatory Music, Stockholm, 1900; Mus.D. honoris causa, Augustana College, 1932; m. Lydia Minna Maria Hernwall, Halmstad, Sweden, 1901; children—Thorborg Lydia, Karin Ingegard, Yngve Hagbard, Sonja Hilda Maria, Minna Edith Ingrid. Came to U.S., 1900, naturalized citizen, 1916. Organist Bethany Oratorio Soc., Lindsborg, Kan., 1900-14, condr. same society, 1915-46; condr. Bethany A Cappella Choir, 1935-46; prof. organ Bethany Coll., 1900-1952, mus. theory since 1900; organist Bethany Luth. Ch., 1921-1943; guest condr. Northwestern Okla. Choral Soc., Enid, 1931-and 1932. Mem. commn. on Lutheran Liturgical Theory and Practice, 1939. Made Knight Royal Order of Vasa (Sweden), 1947. Mem. Phi Mu Alpha. Lutheran. Composer of songs, choruses and compositions, for organ and orchestra. Home: 535 N. 2d St., Lindsborg, Kan. Died Mar. 18, 1953; buried Lindsborg, Kan.

BRASHER, Rex (brā'shēr), ornithologist; b. Brooklyn, N.Y., July 31, 1869; s. Philip Marston and Laura Alida (Bull) B.; grad. St. Francis Coll., Brooklyn, 1884; unmarried. Studied birds, paintings all species in U.S. Mem. Rex Brasher Associates, pubs. Author: Secrets of Friendly Woods, 1926; Birds and Trees of North America (12 vols.), 1934. Contbr. to Compton's Ency., Nature Lovers Library, Outdoor America, Yachting, American Mag., Mentor, Boys' Life, etc. Home: Kent, Conn. Died Feb. 29, 1960.*

BRATTON, Leslie Emmett, naval officer; b. Hastings, Neb., Dec. 8, 1885; s. Alcinas Thomas and Harriet (Stevens) B.; B.S., U.S. Naval Acad., 1907; LL.B., George Washington U., 1915; grad. Naval War Coll., 1928; m. Emeline Kooser Wolf, Mar. 31, 1909; children—Elizabeth (Mrs. Lee C. Ashley), Alice Virginia (Mrs. George S. Writer). Commd. ensign U.S. Navy, 1907, and advanced through the grades to comdr.; retired for physical disability 1930; mgr. of safety for Denver, Colo., 1930-31; v.p. Daly Gen. Ins. Co., Denver, 1931-40; recalled to active duty 1940; promoted to capt., then rear adm.; asst. judge advocate gen. of Navy. Retired, physical disability, 1944. Decorated 1st and 2d World War, and Nicaraguan Campaign medals. Mem. D.C., Colo. bar assns., Phi Delta Phi, Am. Legion, Vets. Foreign Wars. Clubs: Army and Navy, Chevy Chase (Washington); Denver Club, Denver Country Club. Home: 228 Race St., Denver. Died Aug. 2, 1959; buried Arlington Nat. Cemetery.

BRAUFF, Herbert D(avenport), newspaper publisher; b. Chattanooga, Tenn., May 31, 1890; s. William S. and Minnie (Papineaux) B.; student McCallie Sch., Chattanooga, 1907-09, Baylor U. Sch., Chattanooga, 1909-11; m. Laura F. Ellis, July 26, 1924; children—Mary Frances (Mrs. Howard W. Grimes), Dorothy Ann (Mrs. Philip K. Eckman). In newspaper work, Chattanooga Times, 1907-12; reporter Indianapolis Star, 1912-13; reporter and copy reader, Detroit Free Press and Detroit Tribune, 1913-15, New York Press, New York Evening Post, 1915-16; copy reader, Pittsburgh Gazette Times, 1916-20; editor Johnstown Leader, 1920-21; editorial writer, Philadelphia Public Ledger, 1921-23; editor, Reading (Pa.) Tribune, 1923-25; mgr. Altoona (Pa.) Tribune, 1925-28; publisher Vandergrift (Pa.) News since 1928, Wilson (N.C.) Daily Times since 1947, Washington Daily News since 1949 and of The Havelock (N.C.) Progress, 1952-—; director WNCT-TV, Greenville, North Carolina; owner of Nanticoke (Pa.) News, 1930-33. Served as private, 1st class, Sanitary Detach., 107th Artillery, Pa. N.G., 1917-19; overseas service in 4 engagements, 1918. Clubs: Kiwanis (past pres., Vandergrift), Country (Wilson, N.C.). Author: A Saga of America, 1939; Todays' Forgotten Man, 1940; A More Abundant Life, 1942; My 20 Years in Government (dealing with life of James J. Davis), 1942. Home: 601 W. Nash St. Office: The Wilson Daily Times, Wilson, N.C. Died June 15, 1955; buried Chattanooga, Tenn.

BRAUN, Carl Franklin, corp. exec.; b. Oakland, Calif., July 15, 1884; s. Carl August and Leonora (Campbell) B.; A.B., Stanford U., 1907; LL.D. (honorary), Occidental College, 1953; married Winifred Gilbert, Sept. 30, 1909; children—Carl Allan, John Gilbert, Henry August. Pres. C. F. Braun & Co., engrs., 1910-—. Dir. Calif. Inst. of Assos., Cal. Inst. Tech., Friends of Huntington Library, Claremont Men's Coll. Mem. A.S.M.E. (hon.), Sigma Xi, Tau Beta Pi. Clubs: Cal., Annandale, Bolsa Chica, Valley Hunt. Author: Contractual Relations, 1946; Letter Writing in Action, 1947; Fair Thought and Speech, 1947; Management and Leadership, 1948; Corporate Correspondence, 1948; Presentation for Engineers and Industrialists, 1949; Two Hundred Good Books, 1949; Objective Accounting, 1953; Management and Leadership, 1954. Home: 1025 Oak Grove Av., San Marino 9, Cal. Office: Alhambra, Cal. Died Feb. 4, 1954.

BRAUN, Robert, business exec.; b. Norwich, Conn., 1872. Pres. Maine Savings Bank; chmn. bd and dir. Bates Mfg. Co.; dir. New England Public Service Co., Maine Central R.R., Keyes Fibre Co., Oxford Paper Co., Portland Terminal Co., Central Maine Power Co., Public Cervice Co. of New Hampshire, Central Vermont Public Service Corp., Rockland, Rockport Lime Co. Address: 142 Pine St., Portland, Me. Died Nov. 13, 1953.

BRAWLEY, William H., judge; b. Chester, S.C., May 13, 1841; s. Hiram C. and Harriet (Foote) B.; A.B., S.C. Coll., 1860, LL.D., 1905; m. Marion Porter, Apr. 14, 1868. Admitted to bar, 1866; solicitor 6th S.C. Circuit, 1868-74; mem. 52d and 53d U.S. Congresses, resigned 1894; U.S. dist. judge Dist. of S.C., 1894-1911; retired. Mem. S.C. Ho. of Reps., 1880-90. Served in Confederate States Army. Democrat. Clubs: University (N.Y.C.); Metropolitan (Washington). Address: Charleston, S.C. Died 1911.

BRAY, Charles I(seard), educator; b. Huntsville, Ont., Can., July 29, 1882; s. Edward and Charlotte Elder (Breckenridge) B.; B.S.A., U. Toronto, 1904; M.Sc., Miss. State Coll., 1907; Ph.D., U. Ill., 1926; m. Edith Agnes Russell, Aug. 8, 1912 (dec. Mar. 25, 1932); 1 dau., Ruth Elizabeth (Mrs. C. H. Rounds). Dairy herd mgr. Miss. State Coll., 1904-10; asst. prof. animal husbandry Okla. A. and M. Coll., 1910-14; asst. prof. and asso. prof. animal husbandry, Colo. Agr. Coll., 1915-27; prof. animal husbandry La. State U., and sta. animal husbandman, 1927-31, research prof. animal husbandry and sta. animal husbandman in charge research, 1931-—. Fellow A.A.A.S.; mem. Am. Soc. Animal Prodn., Am. Genetic Assn., Alpha Gamma Rho, Alpha Zeta, Pi Gamma Mu. Democrat. Methodist. Mason. Clubs: Block and Bridle, Kiwanis (Baton Rouge). Author: Practical Activities in Animal Husbandry (with G. A. Schmidt), 1928; also agrl. bulletins, agrl. papers. Livestock editor Okla. Farmer Stockman, 1912-14; livestock adviser Western Farm Life, 1921-27. Home: 908 Camelia Av., Baton Route 11. Office: Louisiana State University, Baton Rouge. Deceased.*

BRAY, John Leighton, metallurgist; b. Millbridge, Me., Aug. 11, 1890; s. Charles Ambergh and Vinetta (Cook) B.; B.S. Mass. Inst. of Tech., 1912, Ph.D., 1930; m. Jean Shaw, Aug. 23, 1925; children—Barbara Vilora, John Leighton. Metallurgist, Braden Copper Co., Rancagua, Chile, 1912-15, Consolidated Mining & Smelting Co., Trail, B.C., 1915-16, Black-butte (Ore.) Quicksilver Co., 1916-17, N.Y. & Honduras Mining Co., Honduras, C.A., 1918-20; prof. metallurgy, N.S. Tech. Coll., 1920-21; metallurgist for U.S. Tariff Commn., 1921-23; prof. metallurgy, Purdue U., W. Lafayette, Ind., since 1947, head Sch. Chem. and Metallurgical Engring., 1935-47, prof. metall. engring. since 1947. Served as maj., Ordnance Dept., U.S. Army, World War I. Mem. Am. Inst. Mining and Metall. Engrs., Soc. of Metals, Am. Chem. Soc., Am. Inst. Chem. Engrs., Electrochem. Soc., Inst. of Metals (Eng.), Soc. for Promotion Engrng. Edn., Scabbard and Blade, Sigma Psi, Tau Beta Pi, Phi Lambda Upsilon, Lambda Chi Alpha, Omega Chi Epsilon. Republican. Presbyn. Author: Textbook of Ore Dressing (with R. H. Richards and C. E. Locke), 1925; Principles of Metallurgy, 1930; German Grammar for Chemists, 1937; Introductory Readings in Technical German, 1940; Non Ferrous Production Metallurgy, 1941; Ferrous Production Metallurgy, 1942; Patent Law and Procedure, 1948. Home: 701 N. Chauncey Av., W. Lafayette, Ind. Died Dec. 6, 1952.

BRAY, William L., botanist; b. Burnside, Ill., Sept. 19, 1865; s. William and Martha Ann (Foster) B.; student State Normal Sch., Kirksville, Mo., 1883-85; Cornell U., 1889-91; A.B., Ind. U., 1893; A.M., Lake Forest U., 1894; U. Berlin, 1896-97; Ph.D., U. Chgo., 1898; D.S.C., Syracuse U., 1936; m. Alice Weston, Dec. 28, 1899; children—William Weston, Alice Roberta, Florence. Instr. botany Lake Forest U., 1894-95, adj. prof. biology, 1895; instr. botany U. Tex., 1897-98, adj. prof., 1898-1901, asso. prof., 1902-05, prof., 1905-07; prof. botany Syracuse U., 1907-—, dean grad. sch. 1918-43, retired 1943. Collaborator U.S. Forest Service, 1899-1909; act. dean, N.Y. State Coll. of Forestry, 1911; chief Div. of Forestry, Tex. World's Fair Commn., 1903-04. Fellow A.A.A.S.; mem. Bot. Soc. Am., Ecol. Soc. Am., N.Y. Acad. Sciences, Phi Beta Kappa, Sigma Xi, Phi Kappa Phi. Methodist. Author: Development of Vegetation of N.Y. State, 1915; also several govt. bulls. on Texas forests and various articles on plant distribution and adaptation, in bot. jours. Bray Hall, N.Y. State Coll. Forestry named in his honor, 1933. Address: 863 Ostrom Av., Syracuse, N.Y. Died May 25, 1953.

BRAZER, Clarence Wilson, architect; b. Phila., Mar. 13, 1880; s. Christopher and Julia Wilson (Stackhouse) B.; grad. in architecture Drexel Inst., Phila., 1899, D.S. (hon.), 1942; grad. in town planning, Columbia, studied architecture in Van Pelt Atelier of Society Beaux Arts Architects, N.Y.C., Europe, offices in Phila., also 4 years in N.Y. office of Cass Gilbert; m. Mary Ella Mendenhall, Apr. 25, 1905; 1 son, Wilson M.; m. 2d, Esther Stevens, June 30, 1937; m. 3d, Katharine Webb, June 28, 1946. Began practice at Asbury Park, N.J., 1902; established office N.Y.C., 1905, with br. office at Chester, Pa., 1918-36; mem. firm Brazer & Robb, N.Y.C., 1912-15. Principal works: Delaware County Ct. House, Media, Pa.; Citizens Savings Bank, Fort George Presbyn. Ch., N.Y.C.; War Meml. Bridge, Swarthmore, Pa.; World War Monument, Lansdowne, Pa.; residence of A.K. Ford, Mpls. (A I.A. chapter award for best erected in Minn. 1925-30); Trinity P.E. Ch., Syracuse, N.Y.; Deshong Meml. Mus. and Park, Chester, Pa.; Dunwoody Home for Convalescents, Newton Square, Pa.; St. Paul's P.E. Ch., Kitanning, Pa.; many schs., banks, residences, chs. and pub. bldgs. Designed entire Westinghouse Village for 7,000 population at Essington, Pa. Has restored several important colonial bldgs. Recipient 2d prize for design (later purchased) of Capital of P.R. at San Juan, 1907. Mem. Pa. State Bd. Examiners of Architects, 1919-38 (pres. 1926-31), Nat. Council Archtl. Registration Bds. (pres. 1929-31). Mem. N.Y. chpt. A.I.A., Pa. State Assn. A.I.A. (pres. 1928-30), Archtl. League N.Y., Am. City Planning Inst., Soc. for Preservation New Eng. Antiquities, Hist. Soc. Pa., Delaware County Hist. Soc. (pres. 1927-37), Tri-State Regional Planning Fed. (tech. advisor); Nat. Advisory Council on Sch. Bldgs., Dept. Interior, S.A. R. Welcome Soc. Pa., Am. Philatelic Soc., Essay-Proof Soc. (founder 1943, dir.). Luff award for Research on Bank Note Engravers, 1946; First Award for Research Exhibit U.S. Stamp Essays and Proofs, N.Y., 1947; Nat. Merit Award, 1945. Republican. Mason. Clubs: Collectors' of New York (gov. 1932-43), New York Rotary (historian 1918-32); Chester, Union League of Philadelphia, Pa. Author: U.S. Stamp Essays and Proofs (historical catalogue); Essays for U.S. Adhesive Postage Stamps (cat.; received Eidsness award 1942); Building Code for Chester, Pa.; Course in Architectural Practice for Internat. Corr. Schools; Descriptive Color Dictionary; also many articles in antiques mags. and philatelic mags. Edtor of the Essay-Proof Journal (quarterly). Home: Innerwick, Union St. and Bayside Av., Flushing, N.Y.C. Died May 6, 1956.

BREAZEALE, Phanor, congressman; b. Natchitoches, La., Dec. 29, 1858; ed. private turor; m. July, 15, 1884, Marie Chopin; admitted to La. bar; pres. of bd. of school directors, 1888-91; elected, 1892, dist. pros. atty.; re-elected without opposition, 1896; resigned March 4, 1899; elected mem. constitutional conv., 1898; mem. Congress, 1899-1907, 4th La. dist.; Democrat. Home: Natchitoches, La. Deceased.

BREBNER, John Bartlet, prof. history, author; b. Toronto, Can., May 12, 1895; s. James and Frances Elizabeth (Bartlet) B.; student U. Toronto Schs., 1910-13, U. Toronto, 1913-15; B.A., St. John's Coll., Oxford, Eng., 1920, M.A., B.Litt., Oxford, 1925; Ph.D., Columbia, 1927; Litt.D., Brown U., 1944; LL.D. (honorary), McGill University, 1954; married Adele Mary Rumpf, Mar. 29, 1928; 1 son, Elliot James. Lectr. modern history U. Toronto, 1921-25; instr. history Columbia, 1925-27, asst. prof., 1927-35, asso. prof. 1935-42, prof., 1942-54, Gouverneur Morris prof. history, 1954; Pitt. prof. Am. history and instns., fellow St. Johns Coll., Cambridge, 1954-55. Served in Canadian Army, 1915-18, in British Army, 1918. Engaged in survey of Canadian-American relations by Carnegie Endowment for International Peace, 1932-43. Mem. adv. council U. in Exil, 1935-38. Fellow Royal Hist. Soc.; mem. Economic History Assn., Am., Canadian (pres. 1939-40), hist. assns., Acad. Polit. Science, Canadian Polit. Science Assn.; hon. mem. Nova Scotia Hist. Soc., The New Brunswick Museum. Recipient Edward Blake Scholarship, U. Toronto, 1913; exhibitioner St. John's Coll., 1919; W. A. Dunning fellow Columbia, 1933; J. B. Tyrrell Hist. medal Royal Soc. Canada, 1950. Clubs: Century Assn. (N.Y.C.). Author: New England's Outpost—Acadia Before the Conquest of Canada, 1927; The Explorers of North America, 1492-1806, 1933 (translated into German, 1936); The Neutral Yankees of Nova Scotia—A Marginal Colony During the Revolutionary Years, 1937; The Making of Modern Britain: A Short History, 1943; North Atlantic Triangle—The Interplay of Canada, the U.S. and Great Britain, 1945; Scholarship for Canada, The Function of Graduate Studies, 1945. Co-author: Soviet Russia in the 2d Decade, 1928; Redirectnig Education (2 volumes), 1934, 35; The Mingling of the Canadian and American Peoples, Vol. I, Historical, 1940. Education and the New Age, 1947; Les Explorateurs Célèbres, 1947. Editor: Bibliography of Eng. Lit. and Hist. (brochure), 1930, 2d edit., 1932; Classics of the Western World, 1927, 2d edit., 1934. Associate Current History Mag., 1931-36. Contbr. articles and revs. to encyclopedias, hist. and polit. science publs. Home: 90 Morningside Dr., N.Y.C. 27. Died Nov. 10, 1957; buried Mt. Pleasant, Toronto, Ont., Can.

BRECKENRIDGE, Lester Paige, mech. engr.; b. Meriden, Conn., May 17, 1858; s. Moses Paige and Lucretia L. (Wetherell) B.; Ph.B., Sheffield Sci. Sch. (Yale), 1881; M.A., Yale, 1909; Eng.D., U. Illinois, 1910; m. May Brown, Dec. 19, 1883; children—Blanch F. (Mrs. Henry B. Dirks), Gladys S. (Mrs. Earl D. Finch), May H. (Mrs. D. B. Luckenbill); m. 2d, Susan W. Ford, July 26, 1911. Instr. mech. engring. Lehigh U., 1882-91, except 2 yrs. engaged in engring. work; prof. mech. engring. Mich. Agrl. Coll., 1891-93; prof. mech. engring. U. Ill., 1893-1909, dir. engring. expt. sta., 1905-09; prof. mech. engring. Sheffield Sci. Sch. (Yale) 1909-23, emeritus. Engr. in charge boiler div. U.S. Geol. Survey Fuel Testing Plant, St. Louis, 1904—. Contrived and equipped dynamometer cars, 1897-99; invented automatic recording machine, 1901. Mem. Am. Soc. M.E. (v.p. 1907-09), Soc. Promotion Engring. Edn., Western Soc. Engrs. (v.p. 1905-06), Am. Soc. Heating and Ventilating Engrs. (hon.). Chmn. adv. bd. Super-power Survey, 1920-21; mem. World Power Conf. Author articles in tech. jours., reports, bulls. Home: North Ferrisburg, Vt. Died Aug. 22, 1940; buried Westfield, Mass.

BREED, Charles Blaney, engineer; b. Lynn, Mass., Nov. 28, 1875; s. Charles Otis and Sarah (Guilford) B.; S.B., Mass. Inst. Tech., 1897; married; children—Charles Alfred (by 1st marriage), David Edson and Nancy Eleanor (by 2d marriage). Began with city engring. dept., Lynn, 1894; resident engr., Walden Pond Dam, Lynn; consulting engr. for state commns. on pub. utility projects, also cities and railroads on elimination of grade crossings and transportation econ. problems; prof. r.r. and hwy. transportation, Mass. Inst. Tech., 1906-45, prof. emeritus, 1945—, head dept. civil engring., 1935-45; pres. acad. bd. U.S. Army School. of Mil. Aeronautics, Mass. Inst. Tech., 1917-18; trustee Lynn Five Cents Savings Bank. Mem. Am. Soc. C.E. (ex.-dir.), Am. Railway Engring. Assn., Am. Road Builders' Assn., Boston Soc. C.E. (ex-pres.), N.E. Railroad Club (ex-pres.), Breed Family Assn. (ex-pres.), Chi Epsilon, Sigma Xi, Tau Beta Pi. Rep. Meth. Mason. Clubs: Boston City (ex-pres.), Algonquin, Brae Burn Country (Newton). Author: (with Prof. George L. Hosmer) Principles and Practice of Surveying (vols. I and II), 1906, 1908; also Surveying, 1942; also several brochures on highway transportation economics. Asso. editor American Civil Engineers' Pocketbook, 1911, American Mining Engineers' Handbook, 1913. Home: Harbor Rd., Camden, Me. Died Aug. 9, 1958; buried Mountain View Cemetery, Camden, Me.

BREED, Charles Henry, headmaster; b. Pitts., Mar. 11, 1876; s. Henry Atwood and Cornelia (Bidwell) B.; prep. edn. Shady Side Acad., Pitts.; A.B., Princeton, 1899, A.M., 1902; Ed.D., Lafayette Coll., Easton, Pa., 1928; m. Frances deForest Martin, June 10, 1903; children—Anne Martin (Mrs. Robert Longdon Bentley, Jr.), Elizabeth Leiper, Henry Atwood. Tchr. Latin, Lawrenceville (N.J.) Sch., 1899-1923; organizer Providence (R.I.) Country Day Sch., 1923, headmaster until 1927; headmaster Blair Acad., 1927—. Served as lt. Dept. Justice, U.S., World War I. Mem. Am. Classical League, Classical Assn. of Atlantic States, Headmasters' Club, Phila. Dist. Headmasters' Assn., Phi Beta Kappa. Republican. Presbyn. Clubs: Nassau (Princeton); Princeton, Century (N.Y.C.). Address: 49 South Shore Trail, Sparta, N.J. Died July 30, 1950; buried Princeton (N.J.) Cemetery.

BREED, Robert Stanley, bacteriologist; b. Brooklyn, Pa., Oct. 17, 1877; s. Robert Fitch and Emma Marie (Beers) B.; B.S., Harvard, 1902; student U. Göttingen, 1910, U. Kiel, 1911; m. Louise Miller Helm, Aug. 23, 1899 (died Dec. 13, 1905); 1 dau., Alice Fitch; m. 2d, Emma Margaret Edson, July 2, 1913. Instr. biology U. Colo., 1898-99; asst. in zoology Harvard, 1900-02; prof. biology Allegheny Coll., 1902-13, sec. faculty, 1907-10; bacteriologist N.Y. State Agrl. Expt. Sta., Cornell U., 1913-47, emeritus prof. bacteriology, 1947—. Vice pres. World Dairy Congress, Washington, 1923, London, 1928; del. Berne, 1914, Rome, 1934; permanent sec. Internat. Com. on Bact. Nomenclature, Internat. Assn. Microbiology and Internat. Bot. Congress, 1930—; del 2d Inter-Am. Conf. Agr., Mexico City, 1942. Fellow A.A.A.S. (council 1932-34), Am. Pub. Health Assn. (vice chmn. lab. sect. 1932-33, chmn. 1933-34); mem. Soc. Am. Bacteriologists (pres. 1927), Am. Dairy Sci. Assn., Am. Biol. Soc., Internat. Assn. Milk Sanitarians, Brit. Soc. Applied Bacteriology (corr.), Cuban Soc. Microbiologists, Geneva Hist. Soc. (pres. 1935-42), Phi Beta Kappa, Sigma Xi, Phi Gamma Delta. Presbyn. Clubs: Rotary, University (pres. 1928-30). Author bulls. and articles on biol. subjects, especially milk hygiene and systematic bacteriology. Editor in chief Bergey's Manual Determinative Bacteriology, 1937—; asso. editor Jour. of Bacteriology and of Biol. Abstracts. Address: 6 Sunset Dr., Geneva, N.Y. Died Feb. 10, 1956.

BREED, William Constable, lawyer; b. Malone, N.Y., June 24, 1871; s. Charles Webster and Eweretta Eliza (McVickar) B.; B.A., Amherst, 1893; LL.B., Univ. State of N.Y., 1895; m. Emma Ryder, Sept. 9, 1896; children—William Constable, Alan Ryder; m. 2d, Mrs. Eugenie Stiles. Admitted to bar N.Y.C., 1895; mem. Breed, Abbott & Morgan; dir. Armco Steel Corp., Dictaphone Corp., Nat. Distillers Products Corp. Treas. Am. Citizens Relief Com., London, 1914; chmn. for Greater New York of Am. Red Cross 2d War Fund, 1918; mem. St. Lawrence Waterways Commn. under apptmt. of President Coolidge, 1924; chmn. Disaster Relief Com. for Greater New York of Am. Red Cross; del. Rep. Nat. Conv., 1920, 24. Trustee Amherst Coll., 1918-28. Mem. Commerce and Industry Assn. of New York (dir.), Am. Bar Assn., N.Y. State Bar Assn. (pres. 1928), N.Y. County Lawyers Assn., Assn. Bar City of N.Y., Am. Law Inst., Legal Aid Society (v.p. 1929), Am. Jud. Soc., N.Y. Law Inst., Am. Soc. French Legion of Honor, China Soc. Am., France-America Soc., New England Soc., S.R., United Hosp. Fund (trustee). Episcopalian. Mem. Phi Beta Kappa. Clubs: Broad Street, Church, Downtown Assn., National Republican, Racquet and Tennis, Union League (New York); Union Interalliée (Paris); Piping Rock, Turf and Field. Home: Glen Head, N.Y. Office: 15 Broad St., N.Y. City. Died Dec. 3, 1951; buried St. Paul's Churchyard, Glen Cove, N.Y.

BREEN, Aloysius Andrew, coll. pres.; b. Chgo., Sept. 1, 1867; s. Patrick and Mary (Tehan) B.; student pvt. schs., Chgo., 1886-90, St. Louis U., 1894-7, 1900-03. Joined Soc. of Jesus, 1890; ordained priest Roman Cath. Ch., 1903; prof. English St. Mary's Coll., 1889-90, asst. prefect disciple junior div., 1897-1900, asst. treas., 1904, treas., 1906-07, pres., 1907-14; pres. Rockhurst Coll., Kansas City, Mo., 1914-18; dir. Queen's Work, St. Louis, 1920-26; pres. Regis Coll., Denver, 1926-31; treas. John Carroll U., Cleve., 1931-33, Xavier U., Cin., 1933-52. Address: Xavier U., Cin. Died Jan. 12, 1960.

BREEN, Robert A., assn. exec.; b. London, England, Apr. 19, 1905; s. Thomas George and Adah (Stoneman) B.; came to U.S., naturalized; student Huntington Prep. Sch., 1919-20, Peddie Sch., 1920-22; m. Allyne Haynes, Oct. 9, 1941; 1 stepson, Jack Marshall Jeffus. Began in sales and sales promotion activities, New England; asst. treas., Nat. Fgn. Trade Council, Inc., N.Y.C., 1938-40, asst. sec., 1940-44, sec., 1944—, asst. commr., Gen. World Trade Center, N.Y. World's Fair, 1940; adviser on arrangements and pub. relations to sec. gen., UN Conf. for Orgn. Internat. Peace, San Francisco, 1945; exec. sec., annual Nat. Fgn. Trade convs. Sub-chmn. Red Cross Export-Import Div.; mem. War Bond Drives, Salvation Army, United Service Orgns.; sec. Joint Com. for Fgn. Trade Action, N.Y.C. Mem. Pan.-Am. Soc. of U.S. Editor: Annual Proceedings of National Foreign Trade Conventions, 1945-46, 1947-48. Clubs: Country, Brookville Country (Glen Head, L.I., N.Y.). Home: 1722 Lucille St., Wichita Falls, Tex. Died Sept. 2, 1959; buried Hillcrest Mausoleum, Dallas.

BREESE, William Llywelyn (brēs), mfr., banker; b. Portage, Wis., June 29, 1864; s. Llywelyn and Mary A (Evans) B.; student Ripon (Wis.) Coll., 1880-84; m. Jessie Blackman, 1893 (died 1922); 2 daus., Juliette and Leslyn; m. 2d, Zona Gale, author books and plays, June 12, 1928 (died Dec. 27, 1938). Began active career as partner Van Dusen Lumber Co., Portage, 1886; later mem. Breese, Loomis & Co., mechts., and Grant, Breese & Co., wholesale marble contractors; pres. Portage Knitting Works, 1922—; pres. City Bank of Portage, 1929—. Trustee Ripon Coll. Republican. Presbyn. Mason. Club: Swan Lake Country. Home: 804 MacFarlane Rd. Address: City Bank of Portage, Portage, Wis. Died Oct. 1, 1954; buried Silver Lake Cemetery, Portage.

BREG, W(illiam) Roy, exec. sec. Allied Youth, Inc.; b. St. Paul, Minn., Jan. 31, 1888; s. William Grobe and Martha Elizabeth (Knowland) B.; ed. pub. grade and high schs., Dallas, Tex.; m. Lonnie O. Henry, July 12, 1911; children—Frances Viola (Mrs. Robert D. Marsden), William Roy. Associated with banking and bond business, 1907-15; general agent life insurance company, 1915-16; Texas manager Deming Investment Co., Dallas, 1916-17; general secretary Tex. Christian Endeavor Union, 1917-19; Southwestern sec. Internat. Soc. Christian Endeavor, hdqrs. Dallas, 1919-23; dir. religious edn., City Temple, Dallas, 1923-25; gen. sec. Kan. Christian Endeavor Union, 1925-28; Southern sec. Internat. Soc. Christian Endeavor, hdqrs. Chattanooga and Atlanta, 1928-31; exec. secretary Allied Youth, Inc. since 1931. Trustee Internat. Soc. of Christian Endeavor since 1933; pres. Internat. Christian Endeavor Field Secs., 1919-21. Fellow, first summer session, Yale U., School of Alcohol Studies, 1943. Presbyterian. Contributor Journal of N.E.A., Christian Herald, Christian Science Monitor and other journals; publisher of The Allied Youth. Speaker before 2200 high schools and colleges, to 1,500,000, also before conventions, clubs, etc., on alcohol and other youth problems. Home: 5437 Connecticut Av., Washington 15. Office: Allied Youth Building, 1709 M St. N.W., Washington 6. Died Oct. 31, 1954; buried Dallas.

BREISACH, Paul (brī'sāĸ), condr.; b. Vienna, Austria, June 3, 1896; s. Edward and Dora (Hoenigsvald) B.; studied with Bruno Walter and Heinrich Schenker; m. Susan Herz, Mar. 5, 1919; 1 son, Peter. Condr. Vienna Opera House, 1918; gen. music dir. Mainz, Germany, 1925-30; first condr. Municipal Opera, Berlin, 1930-33; opera concerts and radio appearances throughout Europe; came to U.S. 1939; condr. Met. Opera House, New York, since 1941, Cinn. Summer Opera, since 1945; condr. San Francisco Opera Co., since 1946. Address: 1965 Broadway, N.Y.C. 23. Died Dec. 26, 1952.

BREITUNG, Charles Adelbert (brī'tŭng), gas cons.; b. Toledo, O., Aug. 18, 1892; s. Charles Frederick and Helen (Crane) B.; student Wittenberg Coll., Springfield, Ohio, 1909-10; B.S. in Chem. Engrng., Univ. of Mich., 1917; honorary D.Sc., Laval University, 1945; married Delia Jones, June 17, 1926. Chem. engr. E. N. Breitung & Co., New York, 1919-22; engaged in mining and banking; cons. gas engr. since 1922; asso. with natural gas enterprises in Shreveport, La.; consulting engineer on natural gas pipe lines in Louisiana, Texas, Oklahoma; producer of oil and natural gas. Served with 1st Gas Regiment, United States Army, with A.E.F., 1917-18; (decorated Purple Heart). Grand Cross of Order of the Holy Sepulchre. Knight of Sovereign Military Order of Malta in U.S., Papal Chamberlain of the Cape and Sword. Mem. Inst. Mining and Metall. Engrs., Am. Assn. Petroleum Geologists, Tau Beta Pi, Alpha Chi Sigma. Roman Catholic, K.C. Clubs: Austin (Tex.); University (N.Y.C.). Home: The Ambassador, 407 W. 18th St. Office: Perry-Brooks Bldg., Austin, Tex. Died Apr. 10, 1958; buried Nazareth, Israel.

BREITWIESER, Joseph Valentine (brit'wē-ser), educator; b. Jasper, Ind., Mar. 31, 1884; s. John Conrad and Katherine Elizabeth (Baitz) B.; grad. scientific course Central Normal Coll., Danville, Ind., 1904; A.B., Ind. U., 1907; A.M., 1908; Ph.D., Columbia, 1911; m. Ruth Fowler, Jan. 1910; children—Charles John, Katherine Rebecca, Janice, Joseph Valentine, Roland. Tchr. pub. schs., Tipton County, Ind., 1901-03; asst. in psychol. lab. Ind. U., 1906-07, asst. in psychology and philosophy, 1907-08; asst. in psychology Columbia, 1908-10; asst. prof. psychology and edn. Colo. Coll., 1910-11, prof., 1911-18; asso. prof. edn. U. Cal., 1918-27; prof. edn., dir. grad. div., dir. summer session and dean Sch. of Edn., U. N.D., 1927—; tchr. summers, U. Ill., 1925, U. Wash., 1927. Pres. Lake Agassiz council of Boy Scouts, 1947. Fellow A.A.A.S.; mem. N.D. Edn. Assn. (pres. 1933-35), Am. Psychol. Assn., Am. Genetic Assn., Am. Social Hygiene Assn., Nat. Inst. Social Scinces, Phi Delta Kappa, Sigma Xi. Conglist. Clubs: City Commons of Berkeley (pres.); Rotary (Grand Forks, pres. 1943-44). Author: Attention and Movement to Reactions, 1911; Psychol. Experiments, 1914; Psychol. Advt., 1915; Psychological Effects of Altitude, 1917; Psychological Education,

1925; The Education of the Emotions. Former editor Western Advertising, editor The School of Education Record of U. of N.D. Researcher in psychometry and edn.; pub. lecturer on psychol. and ednl. subjects. Address: Grand Forks, N.D. Died Mar. 7, 1950.

BREMER, George A., ret. ofcl.; b. York, Neb., Feb. 13, 1891; s. John H. C. and Mary (Schrader) B.; student York Coll., 1907-11; m. Delia Conway, Mar. 11, 1914; children—George, Robert. Cashier First Nat. Bank, Jerome, Ida., 1912-15, mortgage and real estate bus., 1916-34; constrn. bus., Boise, Ida., 1937-38; chief underwriter F.H.A., Boise, 1935-36, fed. underwriting supervisor 12 western states, 1939-43, zone commr. 12 central states, 1944-53, ret.; dir. Ida. Power Co., 1915-40. Senator State Ida., 1914-15. Home: 3163 Calle Fresno, Santa Barbara, Cal. Died Jan. 21, 1956.

BREMER, John Lewis (brē'mēr), embryologist; b. N.Y.C., Nov. 3, 1874; s. John Lewis and Mary (Fransworth) B.; A.B., Harvard, 1896, M.D., 1901; post-grad. work, Oxford, 1896-97; m. Mary C. Bigelow, Sept. 29, 1906. Asst. in histology and embryology, 1902, instr., 1903-06, demonstrator in histology, 1906-12, asst. prof., 1912-15, asso. prof., 1915-31, Hersey prof. of anatomy, 1931-41, emeritus 1941—, Harvard University. Fellow American Acad. Arts and Sciences; Mem. Am. Assn. Anatomists, Boston Soc. Natural History. Clubs: Somerset, Harvard. Home: 113 Marlborough St., Boston, Mass. Died Dec. 25, 1959.

BREMER, Otto, banker; b. Seesen, Germany, Oct. 22, 1867; s. Edward and Matilda (Maeder) B.; ed. in Germany. Was in banking business in Germany for 3 yrs.; came to America, 1886; with Nat. German-Am. Bank, St. Paul, 1887-1900; became treas. City of St. Paul, 1900; treas. City of St. Paul, 1900-10; now chmn. bd. Am. Nat. Bank, Jacob Schmidt Brewing Co. Home: 1344 Summit Av. Office: Bremer Arcade, 7th and Robert Sts., St. Paul. Deceased.*

BRENNAN, Andrew James, bishop; b. Towanda, Pa., Dec. 14, 1877; s. James and Ellen (Flood) B.; A.B., Holy Cross Coll., 1900; student St. Bernard Sem., Rochester, N.Y., 1901; D.D., Am. Coll., Rome, 1905. Ordained priest R.C. Ch., Rome, 1904; tchr. Latin and Greek, St. Thomas Coll., Scranton, Pa., 1905-08; chancellor Scranton Diocese, 1908-25; rector St. Peter's Ch., Scranton, 1914-24; auxiliary bishop, Scranton, 1923; rector St. Mary Mt. Carmel Ch., Dunmore, Pa., 1924-26; bishop of Richmond, Va., 1926-45; resigned, Apr. 14, 1945; apptd. Titular Bishop of Telmissus, 1945. Address: De Paul Hospital, Norfolk, Va. Died May 3, 1956; buried St. Joseph's Villa, Richmond, Va.

BRENNAN, Edward James; b. St. Louis, Feb. 12, 1871; s. John and Margaret (Teehen) B.; grad. high sch., 1887; student St. Louis U., 1888-89; m. Elsa C. Bredemeyer, July 7, 1908; children—John Edward, James Arthur. Dep. U.S. marshal, St. Louis, 1894-1903; investigator criminal div. of defective bureau, St. Louis Police Dept., 1903-07; installed finger print system in 1st police dept. in America at St. Louis, 1904; operative U.S. Secret Service Div. of Treasury Dept., 1907-08; trans. to Bur. of Investigation, Dept. of Justice, 1908, and assisted in organizing the present Bur. In charge of investigations of U.S. Dept. of Justice in so-called sugar frauds, New York, 1909, 1910; directed investigation as to interstate transportation of high explosives, Nat. Dynamiting Conspiracy cases, Indpls., 1911-1912 (forty persons convicted, most of whom weere sent to penitentiary); assisted dist. atty. of Los Angeles County, Cal., in preparing cases against Mathew A. Schmidt and Nathan Caplan, indicted for murder growing out of the Times Bldg. explosion, Los Angeles, 1910; div. supt. Bur. of Investigation, Dept. of Justice, at St. Louis, 1912-19, Chgo. div., 1919-21; spl. agent in charge of N.Y. dist., 1921-25, Chgo., 1925; chief spl. agent Special Service Dept. The Pullman Co., 1926—. Has operated through America, also in England, France and Italy. Died Oct. 1, 1954.

BRENNAN, George M., govt. official; b. Chicago, Ill., Feb. 25, 1895; s. James Patrick and Dorothy (Argyle) B.; m. Mamie Farr, Oct. 16, 1934. Engaged in banking business, Denver, later in meat packing and livestock business; with War Finance Corp., Washington, 1923-28, Federal Intermediate Credit Bank, Berkeley, Calif., 1928-32, Reconstruction Finance Corp., Washington, 1932-33; intermediate credit commr., Farm Credit Adminstrn., since July 6, 1933. Democrat. Home: The Westchester, 4000 Cathedral Av. N.W., Washington 16. Office: care Farm Credit Administration, Washington 25. Died Aug. 9, 1952.

BRENNAN, John Francis, steamship co. exec.; b. Wallingford, Conn., Nov. 29, 1893; s. Martin J. and Margaret (Brennan) B.; A.B., Yale, 1915. With U.S. Lines Co. (formerly Internat. Mercantile Marine Co.), N.Y.C., 1919—, passenger traffic mgr., 1936-49, v.p. passenger traffic, 1949—, dir., 1951—; dir. One Broadway Corp. Served from ensign to lt. (j.g.), USNRF, 1917-19; from lt. col. to col., Transportation Corps, AUS, 1942-45. Decorated Legion of Merit. Mem. Propeller Club U.S., Am. Legion. Clubs: Rotary (past dir.), Yale, N.Y. Athletic, Downtown Athletic, Skal (N.Y.C.). Home: 320 Park Av., N. Y.C. 22. Office: 1 Broadway, N.Y.C. 4. Died Feb. 9, 1958; buried St. John's Cemetery, Wallingford, Conn.

BRENNECKE, Cornelius G(odfrey) (brĕn'ĕk-ē), univ. prof.; b. N.Y. City, Aug. 29, 1906; s. Ernest and Anna Elizabeth (Beck) B.; A.B., Columbia, 1926, B.S., 1927, E.E., 1928; Ph.D., New York U., 1936; m. Ruby Julia Kaulbach, June 14, 1935; children—Elizabeth Cornelia, Cornelius Godfrey. Engr., Radio Corp. of Am., and R.C.A. Communications, Inc., N.Y. City, 1928-31; univ. fellow in physics New York U., 1931-33, grad. asst. in physics, 1933-36; instr. in elec. engring. U. of Toledo, 1936-37; asst. prof., 1937-40, asso. prof. elec. engring., 1940-42; asso. prof. elec. engring. Lehigh U., 1942-45; prof. and head dept. elec. engring. N.C. State Coll. since 1945. Consultant various times for Owens-Corning Fiberglas Co., Trojan Powder Co. and others; council Oak Ridge Inst. Nuclear Studies, 1954. Registered engr., Ohio, 1939. Fellow Institute of Radio Engineers since 1951; Fellow Am. Inst. E.E. (chmn. Toledo sect. 1941-42; mgr. Bethlehem dist. Lehigh Valley sect. 1943-45; chmn. N.C. sect. 1948-49; mem. Am. Soc. Engring. Edn. (mem. council 1947-49), N.C. Soc. Engrs., Sigma Xi (pres. N.C. State Coll. chapter, 1947-48), Tau Beta Pi, Eta Kappa Nu, Phi Kappa Phi. Democrat. Mem. United Luth. Ch. Club: Engineers (Raleigh). Contbr. articles to tech. pubs. Musician; organist and choir dir. St. Lucas Ch., Toledo, 1940-42, Grace Luth. Ch., Bethlehem, Pa., 1943-45. Home: 2505 Kenmore Dr., Raleigh, N.C. Died Aug. 2, 1954; buried Montlawn Meml. Park, Raleigh, N.C.

BRENON, Herbert, ret. motion picture producer; b. Dublin, Ireland, Jan. 13, 1880; s. Edward St. John and Frances (Harris) B.; prep. edn. St. Pauls Sch., London, Eng.; student Kings Coll., London U.; m. Helen Oberg, Feb. 18, 1904; 1 son, Cyril. Came to U.S., 1896, naturalized citizen, 1918. Began as call boy Augustin Daly's Theatre, N.Y.C., 1897; actor and stage dir. various cos. until 1909; motion picture dir. and producer, 1909-43, ret. Producer of Ivanhoe; Neptune's Daughter; Daughter of the Gods; War Brides; Peter Pan; A Kiss for Cinderella; Beau Geste (awarded Photoplay gold medal, 1927, as leading film dir. U.S.); Sorrell and Son. Produced in England: The Dominant Sex; The Housemaster; Yellow Sands (with Marie Tempest). Selected by Brit. Govt. to produce the Nat. Propaganda Film, 1917; by newspaper critics of U.S. as world's leading motion picture director, 1928. Democrat. Clubs: Lotos, Lambs (N.Y.C.); Constitutional (London). Home: 6357 La Mirada Av., Hollywood, Cal. Died June 21, 1958; buried Woodlawn Cemetery, N.Y.C.

BRENT, Theodore, shipping exec.; b. Muscatine, Ia., Mar. 30, 1874; s. Theodore Rush and Mary Eliza (Reece) B.; ed. public schools; unmarried. Stenographer, gen. traffic dept., Ft. Scott and Memphis R.R., Kansas City, Mo., 1896-1900; chief clerk to traffic vice pres., St. Louis and San Francisco R.R., 1900-05; asst. to vice pres., Rock Island-Frisco-Chicago and Eastern Illinois System, St. Louis and Chicago, 1910-14; gen. mgr. New Orleans (La.) Joint Traffic Bureau, 1914-16; became mem. 1st U.S. Shipping Bd., 1917; traffic mgr. Federal barge lines, known as Miss. and Warrior River, 1918; one of organizers of Miss. Shipping Co., New Orleans, La., 1918; mgr. Federal Barge Lines, 1920-27; pres. Redwood Steamship Line, operating intercoastal trade between Gulf and Pacific ports, 1928-31, also engaged in econ. research relating to improvements on inland waterways; pres. Coast Transportation Co., since 1932; pres. and dir. International Trade Mart; Miss. Shipping Co., Inc., La. Shipyards, Inc., dir. Hemisphere Internat. Corp. dir. and trustee Hibernia Nat. Bk. in New Orleans. Trustee Alton Ochsner Med. Found., New Orleans, La. Dir. Internat. Ho. (New Orleans), Nat. Fgn. Trade Council (New York), New Orleans Civic Symphony Orchestra of La., Inc., Miss. Valley Assn. (St. Louis, Mo.). Mem. New Orleans Assn. of Commerce, New Orleans Bd. of Trade, Ltd., Propeller Club of U.S. Club: Pickwick (New Orleans); Union League (Chicago). Home: 401 Broadway. Office: Hibernia Bldg., New Orleans. Died June 8, 1953.

BRENTANO, Lowell, editor, author; b. N.Y. City, Apr. 18, 1895; s. Simon and Fredericka (Loewenthal) B.; prep. edn., Friends' Sem., N.Y. City, and pub. schs. Orange, N.J.; A.B., Harvard, 1918; m. Dr. Frances Isabella Hyams, Feb. 12, 1918. Editorial dir. pub. dept., later 1st v.p. Brentano's, Inc., N.Y. City, 1918-33. Associate editor. The American Mercury, 1944; dir. Brentano's Société Anonyme, Paris, since 1946. Member Panel of American Arbitration Association. Mem. Authors League of America, Dramatists' Guild, Phi Beta Kappa, Pi Gamma Mu. Jewish religion. Club: Harvard. Co-Author: (plays) The Spider, 1926; Zeppelin, 1928; Family Affairs, 1929; Danger—Men Working, 1936; (musical) Great Lady, 1937; (novels) The Melody Lingers On, 1934; The Storm Blows Over, 1934; By That Sin Fell the Angels, 1935; Bride of a Thousand Cedars, 1939; co-editor: The Book of the Navy, 1944; Invitation to Travel Series, 1945-48; asso. editor, The Questing Spirit, 1947; author: Ways to Better Hearing, 1945; also many motion pictures. Contbr. to nat. mags. Address: care The Harvard Club, 27 West 44th Street, New York 18, N.Y. Died July 8, 1950.

BRETT, Agnes Baldwin (Mrs. George M. Brett); b. Newark, N.J., Sept. 25, 1876; d. Frederick Wellington and Mary Augusta (Wheeler) Baldwin; A.B., Barnard Coll., 1897; A.M., Columbia, 1900; Am. Sch. Classical Studies at Athens, 1900-02; studied Cabinet des Médailles, Paris, 1912-14; m. George Monroe Brett, 1914; 1 dau., Barbara Jane. Asst. curator, then curator Am. Numismatic Society, 1908-12, formerly asso. curator ancient coins and mem. publ. com.; hon. curator of Greek Coins Museum of Fine Arts, Boston; with U.S. mil. censorship, Post Office, N.Y. City, 1918-19, U.S. Dept. of Justice, N.Y., 1919-20; visiting lecturer archaeology, Columbia, 1936, 1937. Fellow Am. Numismatic Soc.; Royal Numismatic Soc., Eng. Awarded medal of Royal Numismatic Soc. London, 1943; hon. mem. Société Royale de Numismatique de Belgique, Rumanian Numismatic Soc. Republican. Episcopalian. Has specialized in Greek coins and Roman medallions, also in symbols on Greek and Roman coins as related to the ancient religious beliefs; also collector of Babylonian Seal-Cylinders. Author: Coinage of Lampsakos; Electrum, and Silver Coinages of Chios in fifth century, B.C.; Symbolism on Greek Coins; Catalogue of Exhibition of Contemporary Medals, 1910; Catalogue of Exhibitions of American Sculpture, 1922; Contemporary American Sculpture (San Francisco Exhbn.), 1929; Catalogue of Greek Coins, Museum of Fine Arts, Boston, 1955; also articles in professional jours. Home: 12 Middle St., Marblehead, Mass. Died Dec. 26, 1955; buried Harmony Grove, Salem, Mass.

BRETT, Axel, educator; b. Nätjebacka, Sweden, Jan. 31, 1886; s. Johannes and Sofia (Anderson) Brett; B.A., Gustavus Adolphus Coll., 1912; M.A., U. Minn., 1914; student U. Upsala, Sweden, 1914-15; Ph.D., U. Ill., 1923; m. Elsie Helen Retzlaff, Aug. 8, 1918; children—Astrid, Roland James, Elsie Jane. City editor Minn. Stats Tidning, Stm Paul, 1913-14; traveling scholar Am. Scandinavian Found., 1914-15; tchr. Swedish lang. and lit. U. Minn., 1915-16, Central High Sch., Mpls., 1916-18; asst. instr. in philosophy U. Ill., 1918-23; prof. philosophy and psychology, head of dept. U. Tenn., 1923—. Mem. A.A.A.S., So. Soc. for Philosophy and Psychology, Tenn. Acad. Science, Phi Beta Kappa, Phi Kappa Phi, Phi Delta Kappa, Phi Sigma Kappa. Clubs: Irving, Civitan. Home: 3427 Alta Vista Way, Knoxville, Tenn. Died Apr. 9, 1950.

BRETT, Rutherford, judge; b. Mt. Juliet, Tenn., Mar. 21, 1867; s. Alexander and Sophia (Rutland) B.; Carson Coll., 1886-88, Cumberland U., 1888-90; m. Mrs. Gertrude Whitaker Crumpton, June 6, 1893; children—Howard Wayne (dec.), Rutherford Henderson, John Anderson, Rebecca Ward, Gertrude Olivia, Betty (Mrs. Frank J. Ogden), Mary Dale, Edward Carmack and Benjamin Whitaker (dec.) (twins), Thomas Marshall, Robert Williams (dec.). Admitted to Tenn. bar, 1902, removing to Okla. same year; pros. atty. Washita County, Okla., 1907-10, resigned; identified as atty. with nearly every important case in Washita County for 14 yrs.; mem. Supreme Court Commn., Okla., 1915-16; apptd. judge Criminal Court of Appeals, Okla., 1916; apptd. justice Supreme Court of Okla., 1917, for term expiring Jan. 1, 1919; mem. law firm Brett & Brett, Ardmore, Okla., 1919—. Democrat. Baptist. Mason, K.P mem. Modern Woodmen Am., Woodmen of World. Home: Ardmore, Okla. Deceased.

BRETT, Sereno E., army officer; b. Portland, Ore., Oct. 31, 1891; s. James and Clara Marie de Lille (Harvey) B.; B S., Ore. State Coll., 1916; grad. Inf. Sch., 1922, Tank Sch., 1926, Command and Gen. Staff Sch., 1927, Army War Coll., 1934; m. Elizabeth Anderson March, Nov. 5, 1923; children—Elizabeth Ann, James Sereno. Commd. 2d lt. Inf., AUS, 1916, advanced through grades to brig gen. (temp.) 1942; overseas with 1st Div., AEF, 1917; organized and directed 37 mm. Sch., Army Inf. Specialsits Sch., 1917-18; trans. Tank Corps, 1918; instr. in chief Am. Tank Center, Bourg, France, 1918; organized and comd. 327th bn. Tank Corps, 1918; as maj. led first Am. tank attack, 326th bn. St. Mihiel, 1918; comd. 1st Am. Tank Brigade throughout Meuse-Argonne, 1918; returned to U.S., 1919; mem. first transcontinental truck convoy, Washington to San Francisco, 1919; comd. exptl. tank force, Panama Canal Zone, 1923-24; instr. Inf. Sch., 1927-30; exec. officer Mechanized Force, 1930-31; mem. Inf. Bd., 1931-33, 1935-38; fgn. service, Hawaii, 1934-35; instr. Command and Gen. Staff Sch., 1938-40; chief of staff Armored Force, 1940-41; comdg. officer 31st Armored Regiment, 1941, 5th Armored Div., 1942-43; retired, physical disability. Decorated D.S.C., D.S. M. Silver Star with oak leaf cluster (U.S.); Legion of Honor, Croix de Guerre with Palm (France). Mem. Delta Upsilon. Mason. Address: 201 Calle Palo Colorado, Santa Barbara, Cal. Died Sept. 9, 1952.

BRETZ, Julian Pleasant, educator; b. St. Joseph, Mo., Dec. 29, 1876; s. James Polk and Grizelda (Shull) B.; A.B., William Jewell Coll., 1899; Ph D., U. Chgo., 1906. Asst. in history U. Chgo., 1906-07, instr., 1907-08; asst. prof. Am. history Cornell U., 1908-10, prof., 1910-44, prof. emeritus, 1944—. Mem. Phi Beta Kappa, Kappa Alpha (Southern). Home: 111 Kelvin Pl. Address: 111 Kelvin Pl., Ithaca, N.Y. Died June 1951.

BREWER, Charles Edward, ex-coll. pres.; b. Wake Forest, N.C., July 12, 1866; s. John Marchant and Ann Eliza (Wait) B.; B.A., Wake Forest Coll., 1885, M.A., 1886; studied Johns Hopkins, 1887-89; Ph.D., Cornell U., 1900; m. Love Estelle Bell, Oct. 28, 1891; children—Joseph Bell (dec.), Elen Dozier, Ann Eliza, Charles Edward (dec.). Prof. chemistry, Wake Forest Coll., 1889-1915, also dean, 1912-15; pres. Meredith Coll., 1915-39, now pres. emeritus, prof. chemistry. Mem. Bd. Town Commrs., Wake Forest, 1901-15; mem. Southern Assn. Schs. and Colls. Mem. Jr. Order United Am. Mechanics and trusteé Nat. Orphans' homes of same, Tiffin, O., and Lexington, N.C., 1911-35, Nat. Councilor of same, 1931-33. Sec. N.C. Bapt. State Conv., 1908-15. Mem. N.C. Teachers' Assn. (pres 1922) Democrat. Club: Rotary Home: Raleigh, N.C. Died May 1, 1941.

BREWER, James Arthur, advt. exec.; b. Los Angeles, Oct. 23, 1886; s. James Biays and Florence Carlton (Keller) B.; ed. Los Angeles Poly. H.S.; m. Ada Troutman Winslow, July 23, 1921; children—Dyke G., Beverly W. (Mrs. Jewel Emmet Colvin, Jr.), Ada W. (Mrs. Henry Parker Grimshaw), Florence Cathryn (Mrs. George L. (Skip) Allen). With Guaranty Trust & Savings Bank, Los Angeles, California, 1910-17, Seaman Paper Company, N.Y. City, 1920-28; became pres. Brewer-Cantelmo Co., Inc., 1928, now chmn. bd. Served as maj., U.S. Army, 1917-19. Mem. Am. Legion. Mason. Club: Advertising (treas.) (N.Y. City). Contbr. articles on book binding and big game fishing to mags. and newspapers. Home: 49 Highland Av., Montclair, N.J.; also 3819 Cactus Blvd., Tucson. Office: 116 E. 27th St., N.Y.C. Died Mar. 5, 1957.

BREWER, John Marks, educator; b. Antioch, Cal., Oct. 30, 1877; s. Henry Wells and Adeline Deming (Balkam) B.; B.Sc., U. Cal., 1902; A.M., Harvard, 1915, Ph.D., 1916; m Edith Gaddis, June 26, 1909; 1 son, Mark Gaddis (dec.). Tchr. indsl. arts sch., San Francisco, also worker in boys' clubs, settlements and summer camps, later high schs., summer schs., etc., Los Angeles, until 1914, instr. edn. Harvard, 1916-17, 19-20; head dept. edn. Los Angeles State Normal Sch., 1917-19; ednl. dir. S.A.T. C., Los Angeles State Normal School, 1918; asso. prof. edn. U. Cal. at Los Angeles, 1919; asso. prof. edn., grad. sch. edn. Harvard, 1920-44; prof. emeritus, 1944—. Mem. city council, Inglewood, Cal., and introduced first city mgr. on Pacific Coast. Mem. N.E A., Nat. Vocational Guidance Assn., Am. Assn. U. Profs. Pres. First Ch. of Christ, Scientist, 1934-35. Author: Oral English, 1916; The Vocational Guidance Movement, 1918; Education as Guidance, 1932; Occupations, 1936; History of Vocational Guidance, 1942. Co-author: Mental Measurement in Educational and Vocational Guidance, 1925; Case Studies in Educational and Vocational Guidance, 1926; Introductory Business Training, 1940; Cases in the Administration of Guidance, 1929; Newspaper Stories for Group Guidance, 1935; Occupations Today, 1943. Contributor to Encyclopedia Social Sciences, and ednl. jours. Home: 22 Gray Gardens E., Cambridge, Mass.; (summer) Peacham, Vt. Died Aug. 25, 1950.

BREWSTER, Albert Vincent (Mike), journalist; b. Salina, N.Y., Dec. 26, 1881; s. Brainard D. and Frank L. (Godard) B.; student pub. schs., Syracuse, N.Y.; m. Joanna T. Prentiss, Mar. 11, 1912. Reporter Syracuse (N.Y.) Courier, 1898-99; reporter Syracuse Post-Standard, 1900-1911, state editor 1912-13, mgr. circulation, 1914-17, copy reader, 1918-19, asst. city editor, 1919, city editor, 1920-44; mng. editor, 1945-53, ret. Mem. N.Y. State Mng. Editors' Assn., Automotive club of Syracuse and A.A.A.; hon. mem. Patrolmen's Benevolent Assn., Syracuse Firemen's Assn. Republican. Lutheran. Mason. Home: 1010 Euclid Av., Syracuse 10. Office: 300 E. Fayette St., Syracuse 1, N.Y. Died Mar. 2, 1956.

BREWSTER, Edwin Tenney, author; b. Lawrence, Mass., Oct. 11, 1866; s. John Leander and Ada Augusta (Tenney) B.; A.B., Harvard, 1890, A.M., 1891, grad. study in zoölogy, 1893-95; m. Alice S. Rollins, of W. Roxbury, Mass., 1893; children—Ada, William R., James R.; m. 2d, Lilian E. Dodge, of Andover, Mass., 1912. Instr. in sciences, Brewster Free Acad., Wolfeboro, N.H., 1891-93; same, Phillips Acad., Andover, Mass., 1897-1903, 1907-08, 1916-24. Trustee Nute High Sch., Milton, N.H., 1903-22, Brewster Acad., Wolfeboro, N.H., 1934-38. Fellow A.A.A.S.; mem. Am. Eugenics Soc., History of Science Soc. Author: Life of Josiah Dwight Whitney, 1949; Swimming, 1910; The Child's Guide to Living Things, 1911; (with wife) The Nutrition of a Household, 1915; Vocational Guidance for the Professions, 1918; The Understanding of Religion, 1923; What Laymen Want, 1925; Creation—A History of non-Evolutionary Theories, 1927; This Puzzling Planet, 1928. Home: 8 Judson Rd., Andover, Mass. Died March 15, 1960.

BREWSTER, Few, judge; b. Corn Hill, Tex., May 10, 1889; s. Van Buren and America (Seymour) B.; graduate of Howard Payne College, 1909, LL.D.; A.B., U. of Tex., 1913, LL.M., 1916; m. Myra Kilpatrick, Aug. 24, 1918; children—Joan (Mrs. Wade K. Forman), Evelyn (Mrs. Payton V. Anderson), Allen. Admitted to Tex. bar, 1915; gen. practice of law, Temple, Tex., 1916-29; county atty. Bell County, Tex., 1919-22; dist. atty. 27th dist., 1923-28; dist. judge, 1929-41; Judge Commn. of Appeals of Tex., 1941-45; Asso. Justice Supreme Court of Tex., 1945—. Served as 2d lt. Inf., World War I. Chancellor and quiz master, U. of Tex. Law Sch., 1915-16. Mem. Bell-Lampasas Bar Assn. (pres. 1937), Dist. and Appellate Judges of Tex. (pres. 1937-38), Tex. Bar Assn. (sec. 1938-39, v.p. 1939-40), State Bar of Tex. (v.p. 1940, pres. 1940-41). Mem. Am. Legion, Phi Delta Phi. Democrat. Baptist. Mason. Home: 903 W. 17th St. Office: Box 2162, Capitol Station, Austin, Tex. Died Oct. 12, 1957; buried State Cemetery, Austin.

BREWSTER, James Henry, Jr., life ins. exec.; b. Hartford, Conn., June 7, 1882; s. James Henry and Mary Elizabeth (Folts) B.; A.B., Yale, 1904; m. Marguerite Barstow, June 10, 1910; children—Mary Drew (Mrs. W. Malcolm Brady), James Henry III. With Vermilye and Co., bankers, 1904-09; bond mgr. E. B. Smith and Co., 1910-13; partner Rhoades & Co., Bankers, 1913-25; v.p. Aetna Life Ins. Co., 1925-56, treas., 1926-56, ret., dir., 1929—; v.p., treas., dir. Aetna Casualty & Surety Co., Automobile Ins. Co., Standard Fire Ins. Co.; dir. Hartford Nat. Bank & Trust Co., N.J. Zinc Co. (N.Y.), Smyth Mfg. Co., Hartford, Conn.; dir. Emhart Mfg. Co., Scovill Mfg. Co., (Waterbury, Conn.); trustee Soc. for Savs. (Hartford), U.S. Trust Co. (N.Y.). Dir. Hartford Dispensary, Am. Sch. for Deaf; trustee, Horace Bushnell Meml. Assn. Served with Troop B, 1st N.J. Cav. on Mexican Border, 1916. Mem. Soc. Colonial Wars, Psi Upsilon, Wolf's Head. Republican. Conglist. Clubs: Down Town, Union (N.Y.C); Twentieth Century, Farmington Country, Hartford (Hartford, Conn.). Home: 175 Scarborough St. Office: 151 Farmington Av., Hartford, Conn. Died May 4, 1959.

BREWSTER, Walter Stanton; b. Evanston, Ill., Sept. 4, 1872; s. Edward Lester and Mary (Niles) B.; student St. Paul's Sch., Concord, N.H., until June 1891; A.B., Yale, 1895; m. Kate Lancaster, Jan. 24, 1903 (died 1947); children—Sarah (Mrs. Duncan Hodges), Edward Lancaster. Entered service Edward L. Brewster & Co., bankers and brokers, 1896, admitted to the firm, 1899, firm succeeded by Russell, Brewster & Co., 1904, company dissolved, 1938, now retired. Mem. Chgo. Stock Exchange (pres. 1921-22). Trustee, v.p. Art Inst., Chicago. Address: 232 E. Walton St., Chgo. Deceased.

BRICE, Fanny, actress; m. Nicky Arnstein; two children; m. 2d, Billy Rose (div.). Has appeared in Ziegfeld Follies and various other stage productions; now starred on radio program and in motion pictures. Address: care Actors' Equity Assn., 45 W. 47th St., N.Y.C. Died May 29, 1951.*

BRICHER, Alfred Thompson, artist; b. Portsmouth, N.H., Apr. 10, 1837; s. William and Elizabeth (Muir) B.; ed. at Newburyport Acad., Mass.; m. Susie A. Wilder 1868; m. 2nd Alice L. Robinson, 1881. Marine artist, making a specialty of coast and shore views in water and oil colors; asso. Nat. Acad. Design; mem. Am. Water Color Soc. Home: New Dorp, S. I. Studio: 32 Union Sq., E., N.Y. Died 1908.

BRICKELL, Henry Herschel, writer; b. Senatobia, Miss., Sept. 13, 1889; s. Henry Hampton and Lula Johns (Harrison) B.; ed. U. of Miss., 1906-10; m. Norma Long, Mar. 17, 1918. Began as reporter, 1911, copy-reader, 1912; sub-editor, mng. editor and editor various newspapers, 1913-23, lit. editor, 1934-38; editor gen. pub. dept., Henry Holt & Co., N.Y. City, 1928-33; editor of O. Henry Mem. Short Story; lectr. Bowling Rock (N.C.) Summer Sch. of English, Bread Loaf (Vt.) Writers' Conf., U. of N.H. Writers' Conf. Sr. cultural relations officer, U.S. Embassy, Columbia, 1941-44; asst. chief div. cultural cooperation, 1944-46; chief, div. internat. exchange of persons, Dept. of State, 1946-47; cons. Internat. Inst. of Edn., 1947-49; conducted a short story workshop, Ridgefield, Conn., 1951; lectr. state dept. N.Am. Lit., 1951-52; investigated humanities for Rockefeller Found. throughout S.Am., 1952. Awarded Rosenwald and Guggenheim fellowships, 1939, for research and writing. Served as sergt. maj. 1st Regt. Ala. Nat. Guard, Mexican border. Mem. Sigma Upsilon. Author: (translation into Spanish) Cosecha Colombiana, 1943; translated book on Abraham Lincoln by Emeriterio Santovenia, Cuban Historian, 1951. Editor, Writers on Writing, 1949; co-author Our Living Novelist, 1949; co-transl. Ricardo Rajas' El Santo de la Espada, a life of San Martin, 1945. Contbr. Am. lit. survey for Encyclopedia Britannica Yearbook; material to book, What the South Americans Think of Us, 1941. Home: Riedgefield, Conn. Died May 29, 1952; buried Jackson, Miss.

BRICKLEY, Bartholomew A., lawyer; b. Boston, May 7, 1883; s. Patrick J. and Mary T. (Hayes) B.; student Gonzaga Coll., Washington, 1902; Georgetown U., 1904; m. Mary Grace Dolan, Nov. 24, 1909. Admitted to Mass. bar, 1904, practiced law, Boston, principally engaged in corporate practice, 1904—; trustee Internat. Hydro-Electric System. Trustee N.E. Conservatory of Music. Mem. Charitable Irish Soc. Clubs: Union, Algonquin, Clover. Home: 130 Dean Rd., Brookline 46, Mass. Office: 75 Federal St., Boston 10. Died Jan. 18, 1959.

BRICKNER, Barnett Robert, rabbi; b. N.Y.C., Sept. 14, 1892; s. Joseph and Bessie (Furman) B.; B.S., Columbia, 1913, B.S. in Edn., Tchrs. Coll., 1913, M.A. in Edn., 1914, post-grad. work, 1913-15; also studied Tchrs. Inst. of Jewish Theol. Sem., N.Y.C., 1910-15; rabbi Hebrew Union Coll., 1919; Ph.D. in Social Sciences, U. Cin., 1920; m. Rebecca Ena Aaronson, Aug. 10, 1919; children—Joy Marion (Mrs. Samuel Rabinowitz), Rabbi Arthur James Balfour. One of founders of Young Judea Movement, 1910; dir. extension edn. Bur. Jewish Edn., N.Y.C., 1910-15; exec. dir. United Jewish Social Agencies, Cin., 1919-20; rabbi Holy Blossom Synagog, Toronto, Can. (introduced Reform Ritual), 1920-25, Fairmount Temple, Cleve., 1925—. In charge Tng. Sch. for Jewish Welfare Workers in mil. camps in U.S. and abroad, World War I co-founder, 1921, contbg. editor, 1921-25, Canadian Jewish Review; secured permission (with others) of Canadian Govt., 1923, to admit to Canada 5,000 Russian Jewish refugees, stranded in Rumania, and helped to raise funds to settle them there; the Rabbi Brickner Scholarship in Social Service at the U. of Toronto, est. in his honor. Arbitrator for dry cleaning industry, Cleve., 1928-29; leader of movement to oppose ousting of city mgr. from Cleve., 1930; arbitrator between Cleve. Ry. Co. and Street Car Men's Union, 1934, 35; arbitrator Employed Bakers of Cleve., 1935, 36. Chmn. Com. on Army and Navy Religious Activities of Nat. Jewish Welfare Bd., which procures and supervises Jewish chaplains for the armed forces. Exec. chmn. chaplains' com., Central Conf. Am. Rabbis, World War II. Toured Europe and Palestine to study the Jewish situation, Jan.-Mar. 1947. Recipient Naval Citation for meritorious personal service; Medal for Merit by U.S. Govt., 1947. Chmn. Jewish Welfare Fund Com., Cleve. Mem. Central Conf. Am. Rabbis (pres. 1954-56, mem. exec. bd. Social Justice Commn), Nat. Conf. Jewish Social Work, Religious Edn. Assn. Am., Am. Acad. Polit. and Social Science, Fgn. Policy Assn., Jewish Academicans, Zionist Orgn. Am. (former mem. exec. com.), Actions Com. World Zionist Orgn., Nat. Council for Jewish Edn. (exec. bd.), Board Union of Am. Hebrew Congregations (vice chmn.), Jewish Welfare Fedn. Cleve. (v.p.), Bur. Jewish Edn. Cleve., Sigma Alpha Mu. Clubs: Rotary, Professional, Beechmont Country (hon. mem.). Mem. bd. editors History of the Jews in Canada, 1925. Author of History of the Jews of Cincinnati, The God Idea in Light of Modern Thought, Project Method in Jewish Education. Contbr. to mags. Broadcaster weekly addresses and frequently over National Networks. Home: 17800 Parkland Dr. Office: 23737 Fairmount Blvd., Cleve. 21. Died May 14, 1958; buried Cleve.

BRIDGES, Horace James, author, lectr.; b. London, Eng., Aug. 31, 1880; s. James and Mary Elizabeth (Harding) B.; spl. courses London U; D.Litt. (hon.), U. Rochester, 1927; m. Lucy English, June 2, 1906; children—Leonard Horace James, Dorothy Lucy Edith (dec.), rancis Stanton, Horace English. Asso. leader, with Stanton Coit, of West London (Eng.) Ethical Soc., 1905-12; leader Chgo. Ethical Soc., 1913-45, emeritus, 1945—. Ex-pres. Booth House, Chgo. Mem. Unitarian Fellowship. Author: Ethical Movement—Its Principles and Aims, 1911. 2d edit., 1912; Criticisms of Life—Studies in Faith, Hope and Despair, 1915; The Religion of Experience, 1916; Our Fellow Shakespeare, 1916; On Becoming an American, 1919; As I Was Saying, 1923; Jew-Baiting—An Old Evil Newly Camouflaged, 1923; The God of Fundamentalism and Other Studies, 1925; Taking the Name of Science in Vain, 1928; The First Art of Marriage, 1930; Signs of the Times in Religion, 1936; The Emerging Faith, 1937; Humanity on Trial, 1941; Some Applications of Ethical Religion, 1944. Editor: Erasmus in Praise of Folly, 1924. Home: 175 Central Av., Greenport, L.I., N.Y. Died Oct. 7, 1955; buried Greenport.

BRIDGMAN, Grenville Temple, mining engr.; b. Newport, R.I., Aug. 7, 1881; s. William Henry and Ellen (Campbell) B.; grad. Pomfret (Conn.) Sch., 1900; student Yale, 1900-01; B.S., Mass. Inst. Tech., 1909; m. Anita Mailliard, June 3, 1911; children—John Mailliard, Marion Louise, Grenville Temple, Anita Page. Jr. engr. in Peru and Mexico, 1909-10; mgr. Philippine Exploration Co., 1910-11; mgr. Am. Zinc Co. (Tenn.), 1911-14; partner Ashton & Bridgman, engrs., 1914-16; asst. cons. mining engr., Guggenheim Bros., N.Y. City, 1916-24; cons. mining engr. same 1924-40; exec. v.p. Metals Reserve Co., Washington, D.C., 1941-44; deputy surplus property administrator, Washington, D.C., 1944; consulting engr. since 1944. Member Mining and Metallurgical Society America (ex-pres.), Am. Inst. Mining and Metall. Engrs., Delta Upsilon. Republican. Episcopalian.

Mason. Clubs: Yale, Mining (New York); Pacific-Union (San Francisco). Home: 2450 Steiner St. Office: 315 Montgomery St., San Francisco, Cal. Died Nov. 25, 1952.

BRIER, Ernest, pharm. co. exec.; b. Elland, Eng., Sept. 15, 1879; s. Frederick Vickerman and Caroline (Clegg) B.; ed. privately, England; m. Marion Hawks, June 23, 1920; children—Mary Elizabeth (Mrs. Frances A. Goodhue, Jr.), Nancy Fitch (Mrs. Frederick S. Ford, Jr.). Came to U.S., 1920, naturalized, 1929. With Parke Davis & Co., 1904-—, London, 1904-10, Russia, 1910-19, Detroit, 1920-—, v.p., dir., 1939-—. Clubs: Detroit, Country of Detroit. Home: 586 Neff Rd., Grosse Pointe, Mich. Office: Parke Davis & Co., Jos. Campau Av. at the River, Detroit 7. Died Dec. 15, 1950.

BRIGANCE, W(illiam) Norwood, educator, lecturer; b. Olive Branch, Miss., Nov. 17, 1896; s. B(enjamin) Edgar and Rebecca (Joyner) B.; A.B., Univ. of South Dakota, 1916; A.M., U. of Neb., 1920; U. of Chgo., 1921; U. of Wis., 1922; Ph.D., U. of Ia., 1930; m. Jane Martin, Aug. 9, 1922; children—Virginia Joyce (dec.), Shirley Jane (Mrs. J. Roger Oest), High sch. teacher, Dallas, S.D., 1916-17, Hastings, Neb., 1920-21, Proviso (Chgo.), 1921-22; research asst. Neb. Legislative Reference Bur., 1920; prof. speech, Wabash Coll., 1922-36; prof. speech and head of dept. of English, U. of Hawaii, 1936-38 (on leave of absence from Wabash Coll.); again prof. speech, Wabash Coll., 1938-—; mem. summer sch. faculty, U. of Neb., 1923-25, U. of S. Calif., 1932, 1949, U. of Wis., 1940; U. of Hawaii, 1947. Lectr. summer speech confs., U. Ia., 1941, 54, U. of Mich., 1941, 46, 54, La. State U., 1942, U. of Mo., 1946, U. of Wis., 1952. Chmn. adv. com. Alexander Hamilton Bicentennial Commn., 1955-57. Enlisted regular army, 1917, became sgt., later 2d lt. 32d Div.; with AEF, 13 mos. Selected as U.S. Speaker-of-the-year-1951 in ednl., sci. and cultural activities by Tau Kappa Alpha Nat. Bd. of Awards; recipient Order of Merit, Lambda Chi Alpha, 1956, Distinguished Alumnus award Tau Kappa Alpha, 1959, award of merit Nat. Assn. Wabash Men, 1959. Member Speech Assn. of Am. (vice president, 1935, 1945; pres. 1946), Am. Assn. Univ. Profs., Indiana Speech Assn. (pres. 1931), Lambda Chi Alpha, Tau Kappa Alpha (v.p. 1934-39), Phi Beta Kappa Associates, American Legion, and Phi Beta Kappa. Dem. Meth. Clubs: Kiwanis (pres. 1931), Country, Ouiatenon. Author: A Notebook for Beginning Speech (with M. G. Phillips), 1927; The Spoken Word, 1927; Classified Speech Models, 1928; Jeremiah Sullivan Black—a Defender of the Constitution and the Ten Commandments, 1934; Speech (with W. G. Hedde), 1935; Speech Composition, 1937, rev., 1953; Your Everyday Speech, 1937; Speechmaking (with R. K. Immel), 1938; A Drill Manual for Improving Speech (with F. M. Henderson), rev., 1955; American Speech (with W. G. Hedde), 1942, rev., 1955; Speech for Military Service (with R. K. Immel), 1943; Speech Communication, 1947, rev., 1955; Speech: Techniques and Disciplines in a Free Society, 1952; New American Speech, 1957. Editor (for Speech Assn. Am.); A History and Criticism of American Public Address (2 vols.), 1943. Contbr. to various ednl. and literary jours. Editor, Quarterly Journal of Speech, 1942-45. Lecturer on edn., travel and the American scene. Home: 104 W. College St. Address: Wabash College, Crawfordsville, Ind. Died Jan. 30, 1960.

BRIGGS, Elizabeth Darling, librarian; b. North Ridgeville, O., Apr. 13, 1888; dau. Frank William and Edith (Darling) Briggs; A.B., Oberlin (O.) Coll., 1909; certificate Cleveland Pub. Library training class in work with children, 1911; unmarried. Children's librarian, Cleveland Pub. Library, 1911-18, branch librarian 1918-20, head parents and teachers room, 1920-25, head Lewis Carroll room, 1925-27, Sept. 1928-37, acting dir. work with children, Jan.-Sept. 1928, dir. since June 1937; lecturer in edn., Sch. of Edn. Western Reserve U., 1939, lecturer in children's work, Sch. of Library Science, 1921-29, instr. summer 1925, consultant since 1937. Mem. A.L.A. (chmn. sect. for work with children 1934-35; mem. bd. dirs. div. of libraries for children and young people, 1941-47, chmn. constitution com. 1940-45, vice pres. 1944-45, pres. 1945-46; mem. of the council, 1943-47; member of the executive bd., 1946-47; 2d vice president, 1947-48), Ohio Library Association; treasurer Radio Council of Greater Cleveland, 1940-43; mem. children's council of Cleveland Welfare Fedn. since 1945. Republican. Presbyterian. Mem. Library Club of Greater Cleveland and vicinity (pres. 1936-37); Nat. Soc. of New England Women, Council World Affairs. Clubs: Women's City, College (Cleveland); Cleveland-Oberlin Women's (president 1932-33, Altrusa. Editor as chmn. of subcom. on Subject Index to Children's Plays of the A.L.A. bd. on library service to children and young people Subject Index to Children's Plays, 1940. Contbr. to professional jours. Home: 1539 East Blvd., Cleveland 6. Office: Public Library, Cleve. 14. Died July 4, 1953.

BRIGGS, Frank Alonzo, editor; b. Friendship, Wis., Mar. 30, 1872; s. Erastus Thomas and Elmina (Pelton) B.; student Fairfield (Wis.) High Sch., 1889-90, extension courses, special work State Normal Sch., River Falls, Wis., 1892-93, study in law office, Viroqua, Wis., 1895-96; m. Io Cleveland Pascoe, Nov. 10, 1903; 1 dau., Io Elmina (Mrs. Lorenze Godfrey Meier). Mng. editor La Crosse (Wis.) Press, 1898-99; editor Tomah (Wis.) Herald, 1900-01; coml. editor Galveston News, 1903-08, night editor Galveston News, 1908-10; editor Texas Almanac and Industrial Guide, 1910-14; asst. mng. editor Dallas Morning News, 1914-16, mng. editor, 1916-20; editor Farm & Ranch, 1920-46, sr. editor, 1946-58. Past pres. Tex. Agrl. Workers Assn., Southwestern Dairy Assn.; mem. State Com. Farm Secruity Adminstrn. Agr. Editors Assn. of Am., Gov. Economic Commn. Forestry Assn. Episcopalian. Mason. Club: Dallas Agricultural (past pres.). Home: 5442 Mercedes St. Office: Farm & Ranch Bldg., Dallas. Died Sept. 17, 1958; buried Crown Hill, Dallas.

BRIGGS, Frederic Melancthon, surgeon; b. Longwood (Brookline), Mass., Nov. 23, 1857; s. Richard and Mary Frances (Towne) B.; A.B., Harvard, 1879; M.D., Harvard Med. Sch., 1883; studied, Vienna, Austria, 1885-86; m. Grace Stickney Wood, Sept. 26, 1893. Practiced, Boston, 1886-—; apptd. mem. staff, Boston Dispensary, 1886, surgeon, 1888-1912; asst. prof. clin. surgery, 1896-97, prof. 1897-1912, prof. surgery, 1912-14, since emeritus, Tufts Coll. Med. Sch., also sec. of faculty, 1905-14, since emeritus. Democrat. Unitarian. Mem. Am. Med. Assn., Mass. Med. Soc., Boston Med. Library Assn., Mass. Med. Benevolent Soc. (life). Clubs: Harvard (Boston), Pocasset Golf. Home: Pocasset, Mass. Office: 636 Beacon St., Boston. Deceased.

BRIGGS, George Nathaniel, college pres.; b. Tabor, Ia, May 10, 1874; s. Riley W. and Clara E. (Greene) B.; B.Di., Ia. State Teacher's Coll., Cedar Falls, 1893; A.B., State U. of Ia., 1897; grad. student Drake U., and U. of Chicago, also LL.D.; m. Carrie Judd, 1902; children—Dorothy Maud (Mrs. Charles Sandage), Marjorie (Mrs. John Walton), Clara (Mrs. Kenneth Wheeler); m. 2d, Grace Kelley, 1912; children—George, Mary (Mrs. J. H. Gerdes), Roland, Margaret Jane (Mrs. Ben Baker), Philip Homer. Teacher pub. schs., 1893-94; supt. schs., Ia., 1897-1901; div. supt. schs., Philippines, 1901-09; pres. Philippine Normal Sch., 1909-10; spl. rep. Philippine Bur. Edn. in U.S., 1910-14; spl. agt. U.S. Bur. Edn., 1914-15; pres. Graceland Coll., Lamoni, Ia., 1915-—, trustee, 1916-28. Recipient gold medal Panama-Pacific Expn. Mem. A.A.A.S., Am. Polit. Science Assn., Ia. Coll. Pres. Assn. (sec.), N.E.A. Republican. Mem. Reorganized Ch. Latter Day Saints. Address: 1111 N. Howard, Indianola, Ia. Died December 26, 1952; buried Lamoni.

BRIGGS, George Waverley, banker; b. Camden, Ala., Feb. 27, 1883; s. Ritchie Jones and Alice (Burford) B.; student pub. and private schs. San Francisco and Austin and U. Tex.; m. Lorena May Foster, Mar. 20, 1912. Reporter Austin (Tex.) Tribune, 1905, San Antonio Express, 1906-10; mng. editor Austin Statesman, 1910-11; staff corr., Dallas News, 1911; editor Galveston News, 1913-18; mgr. Galveston br. Office of War Trade Board, 1917; asst. mgr. S.W. div. A.R.C., commr. ins. and banking for Tex., 1919-20; v.p., trust officer City Nat. Bank, Dallas, 1920-30, First Nat. Bank, Dallas, 1930-—, hon. sr. trust officer, 1955-—; dir. A. H. Belo Corp. Chmn. Confederate Reunion, Dallas, 1925; chmn. for Tex. of George Washington Bi-Centennial. Pres. Dallas C. of C., 1928-29 (v.p. 1920-27); mem. nat. council U.S. C. of C. (chmn. 1930 and 1939; chmn. Texas State Council, 1941-43); dir. Tex. C. of C., 1920-24; treas. Chinese Famine Relief, Tex. Indsl. Congress, treas. Tex. Div. Nat. Com. on Prisons and Prison Labor; dir. Tex. Tax League, 1922-23; apptd. Penitentiary Commr. for Tex., 1910; mem. Indeterminate Sentence Law Commn. for Tex., 1913; member Texas Civil Judicial Council, 1928-54; chmn. Galveston chpt. A.R.C., 1916-17; Dallas United Charities (dir. 1928-47); vice chmn. for Tex., Nat. Found. Infantile Paralysis, 1938-45, chmn. 1946; v.p., trustee Southwestern Legal Found.; dir. Centennial Central Expn. Corp., Pan-Am. Expn. Decorated King's Medal by George VI for civilian service to Allies, 1946. Mem. English Speaking Union (U.S.) (dir. 1942-48, pres. dallas chpt. 1929-50), Dallas Hist. Soc. (trustee, chmn. exec. com.), Tex. Centennial Commn., Tex. World's Fair commn., Philos. Soc. Tex. (treas., pres. 1940), Am. Bar Assn. (mem. layman's com., judicial sect. 1946, chmn. 1947), Newcomen Soc. Eng. (chmn. Texas committee 1946-54). Democrat. Conglist. Mason (K.T., 33°, I.G. H., Shriner). Clubs: Athletic, City, Critic. Author: The Texas Penitentiaries, 1908; The Housing Problem in Texas, 1911; Digest of Texas Insurance and Banking Laws, 1920. Home: 4439 Fairfax Av. Office: First National Bank, Dallas. Died July 16, 1957; buried Oakwood Cemetery, Austin, Tex.

BRIGGS, Gordon Dobson, lawyer, railroad exec.; b. Pittsfield, Me., Aug. 24, 1912; s. Francis Wayland and Margaret (Goodwin) B.; grad. Hebron Acad., 1929; A.B., Bowdoin Coll., 1933; LL.B., Harvard, 1936; m. Pauline Stearns, June 30, 1934; children—Richard Goodwin, Margaret, Robert Stearns. Admitted to Me. bar, 1936; asst. counsel Bangor Hydro-Electric Co. and subsidiaries and Penobscot Transportation Co., Bangor, Me., 1936-40, gen. counsel, 1940-42; asst. counsel Eastern Corp., South Brewer, Me., 1936-41; asst. gen. counsel, asst. clk. Bangor & Aroostook R.R. Co. and subsidiaries, 1946-50, gen. counsel, clk., 1950-51, v.p., gen. counsel 1951-53, exec. v.p., 1953-—, dir., 1954-—; director Merrill Trust Co. Dir. local Community Chest, 1937-41, pres., 1940; mem. Ho. of Reps., Me. State Legislature, 1941-42. Treas. Good Samaritan Home Assn., Bangor, since 1950. Served with A.U.S., 1942-45; disch. as capt. Mem. Vets. Fgn. Wars, Delta Kappa Epsilon. Mason. Clubs: Tarratine (pres. 1946), Penobscot Valley Country (Bangor, Me.). Home: Box 288 Mounted Route A. Office: 84 Harlow St., Bangor, Me. Died July 1, 1954; buried Mount Hope Cemetery, Bangor, Me.

BRIGGS, John Ely, univ. prof.; b. near Washburn, Ia., July 30, 1890; s. William Jonathan and Anna (McNaughton) B.; A.B., Morningside Coll., 1909-13, M.A., State U. of Ia., 1914, Ph.D., 1916; LL.D., Morningside Coll., 1946; m. Nellie Upham, June 19, 1917; 1 dau., Shirley Ann. Research asst. Ia. State Historical Soc., 1914-16, research asso. 1917-18; asst. prof. State U. of Ia., 1919-26, asso. prof., 1926-37, prof. since 1937; vis. prof. Colo. U., summers 1938, 48, Ohio State U., summer 1947. Mem. Am. Polit. Science Assn. Am. Acad. Polit. and Social Sci., Southern Political Science Assn., Western Political Science Assn., State Historical Soc. of Ia., Political Science Associations 1942-47. Republican. Presbyterian. Club: Kiwanis. Editor: Palimpsest, 1922-45, Iowa State Historical Soc., 1940-43; Author: biography of William Peters Hepburn, 1919; interpretation of Iowa primary in Nat. Municipal Review, Vol. XI, Sept. 1922; History of Social Legislation in Iowa, 1915; History of the Iowa Legislature, 1916; various articles in Iowa Jour. of History and Politics, Political theory "State Rights" in Iowa Law Review, Vol. X, May, 1925, Iowa Old and New, 1939, revised 1948. Home: 336 Beldon Av., Iowa City, Ia. Died Feb. 9, 1952.

BRIGGS, Lucia Russell, educator; b. Cambridge, Mass., Dec. 3, 1887; d. LeBaron Russell and Mary Frances (DeQuedville) Briggs; A.B., Radcliffe Coll., 1909, A.M., 1912; LL.D., Lawrence Coll., 1926; LL.D., Miami U., 1927, Rockford Coll., 1936, U. Wis., 1949, Milwaukee-Downer Coll., 1951. Instructor, Miss McClintock Sch., Boston, 1909-11, Charlton Sch., New York, 1912-14, Oak Park (Ill.) High Sch., Feb.-June 1915, Simmons Coll., Boston, 1915-21; with Comité Franco-Américan pour la Protection des Enfants de la Frontière, Feb.-June 1919; pres. Milwaukee-Downer Coll., 1921-51. Mem. Assn. Am. Colleges (v.p. 1923, 1927, pres. 1928), Assn. Wis. Presidents and Deans (v.p. 1922, pres. 1928), Am. Assn. Univ. Women, North Central Assn. of Colleges and Secondary Schools (v.p. 1936-37; mem. Commn. Higher Education 1926-42), Acad. of Polit. Science, Foreign Policy Assn., Wis. Soc. for Mental Health, Wis. Fedn. Woman's Clubs (1st v.p., 1934-35), English Speaking Union, Inst. Pacific Relations, Phi Beta Kappa (hon.). Trustee Radcliffe Coll., 1935-41. Chmn. Wisconsin Conference on Cause and Cure of War, 1939. Epicopalian. Address: Halfway Pond, Buzzards Bay, R.F.D. 2, Mass. Died Jan. 10, 1960.

BRIGGS, Thomas Roland, educator; b. Huddersfield, England, Sept. 2, 1887; s. Thomas Lynton and Adelaide (Jones) B.; came to U.S., 1888, naturalized, 1918; A.B., Cornell U., 1909, Ph.D., 1913; m. Frances Oliver Ingalls, Aug. 24, 1915; children—Adelaide E., Lynton I., George R., Gifford G. Instr. in chemistry, Worcester (Mass.) Poly. Inst., 1912-14; asst. prof. of physical chemistry, Cornell, 1915-25, prof. of chemistry since 1925; research consultant Edison Storage Battery Div., Thomas A. Edison, Inc., West Orange, N.J., since 1929; consultant to War Dept., 1918; research consultant to various corps. including The Flintkote Co., Reynolds Metals Co. various times. Mem. Am. Chem. Soc., Sigma Xi (pres. chpt., 1921), Phi Kappa Tau, Alpha Chi Sigma. Contbr. articles in field of colloid chemistry, electro-chemistry and phase equilibria in scientific jours. Home: 113 Ithaca Rd., Ithaca, N.Y.; (summer) Marlow, N.H. Died Aug. 9, 1952.

BRIGGS, Walter Owen, mfr.; b. Ypsilanti, Mich., Feb. 27, 1877; s. Rodney Davis and Ada (Warner) B.; LL.D., U. of Detroit, 1927; m. Jane Elizabeth Cameron, Nov. 22, 1904; children—Grace Mary (Mrs. William Dean Robinson), Elizabeth Jane (Mrs. Charles T. Fisher, Jr.), Walter O., Susan Ann (Mrs Everell E. Fisher), Jane Cameron (Mrs. Philip A. Hart, Jr.). With Michigan Central Railroad Company, 1891-1902, advancing to foreman car department; foreman C. H. Little Co., 1902-03; v.p. and gen. mgr. B. F. Everitt Co., 1904-06, pres. and gen. mgr., 1906-08, organizer, 1909, pres. and gen. mgr., 1909-37, and chmn. bd. since 1937, Briggs Mfg. Co., mfrs. automobile bodies, which absorbed the B. F. Everitt Co.; also organized, 1922, Briggs Investment Co., named changed, 1926, to Briggs Commercial & Development Co., of which is pres., gen. mgr. and chmn. bd.; dir. Briggs Motor Bodies, Ltd. (Dagenham, Essex, England); pres. Detroit Baseball Co.

(owner Detroit "Tigers") since 1936. Trustee Am. Found. for the Blind. Commr. City of Detroit Zoöl. Park. Mem. Soc. Automotive Engrs. Republican. Clubs: Detroit, Detroit Athletic, Yacht, Country Club (Detroit) Bloomfield Hills Country, Bloomfield Open Hunt Club; The Players, Cloud, Advertising, Question (New York); Bath, Everglades, Indian Creek (Fla.). Home: 700 Boston Blvd. W. Office: 2121 Trumbull Av., Det. Died Jan. 17, 1952; buried Holy Sepulchre Cemetery.

BRIGGS, William Harlowe, writer, pub.; b. Kalamazoo, Mich., July 22, 1876; s. Henry Clay and Amanda Richmond (Hebard) B.; ed. pub. schs.; m. Berta Nabersberg, June 18, 1913. Established newspapers, The Leaflet, 1891, Ipswich Recorder, 1892, both in S.D.; city editor Rockford (Ill.) Register-Gazette, 1896-1900; editorial work and dramatic criticism on newspapers of Chicago, 1900-04, New York, 1904-07; asso. editor Harper's Weekly, 1907-08; with Harper & Brothers in book dept. since 1908. Mem. Dramatists' Guild. Clubs: Century, Dutch Treat. Author: Behold Thy Wife (produced by Henry W. Savage); The Crosland Comedy; Window Dressing; Blown in the Bottle; By The Dawn's Early Light; Dakota in the Morning, 1942. Home: 49 E. 96th St., New York 28. Address: 49 E. 33d St., N.Y.C. 16. Died July 31, 1952; buried Ferncliff Mausoleum, Ferncliff Cemetery, Westchester County, N.Y.

BRIGHAM, Richard Douglas, banker; b. Oil City, Pa., May 5, 1892; s. Charles Fidelio and Margaret (Jack) B.; student Allegheny Coll., U. Wis.; m. 2d, Mary Elizabeth McNally; children (by previous marriage)—Richard, John. Advt. agt., San Francisco, 1913-15; advt. mgr. Sperry Flour Co., 1915-19; asst. to pres. Anglo Calif. Nat. Bank of San Francisco, 1919-20, asst. v.p., 1920-21, v.p., 1921—, dir., 1924—; director Tide Water Oil Co. Republican. Catholic. Clubs: Bohemian, Olympic, Lakeside Country, Union League, Press, Commercial (San Francisco). Address: 1693 Ridge Rd., Sonoma, Cal. Died Dec. 16, 1957.

BRIGHTMAN, Edgar Sheffield, prof. philosophy; b. Holbrook, Mass., Sept. 20, 1884; s. George Edgar and Mary Charlotte (Sheffield) B.; A.B., Brown U., 1906, A.M., 1908, Litt.D., 1936; S.T.B., Boston U., 1910; Ph.D., 1912; LL.D., Nebraska Wesleyan U., 1929, Ohio Wesleyan U., 1942; studied universities of Berlin and Marburg, Germany, 1910-11; m. Charlotte Hülsen, July 1, 1912 (died May 24, 1915); 1 son, Howard Hülsen; m. 2d, Irma Baker Fall, June 8, 1918; children—Miriam Fall, Robert Sheffield. Asst. in philosophy and Greek, Brown University, 1906-08; professor philosophy and psychology, Nebraska Wesleyan U., 1912-15; asso. prof. ethics and religion, 1915-17, prof. 1917-19, Wesleyan U., Conn.; prof. philosophy, Boston U. Grad. Sch., Sept. 1919—, Borden Parker Bowne prof. philosophy, 1924—, chmn. bd. grad. Sch. 1933-1951; Ingersoll lecturer, Harvard, 1925; lecturer, Lowell Inst., Boston, 1925, 1934; John McTyeire Flowers lecturer, Duke U., 1927; Loud lecturer, U. of Mich., 1937; Swander lecturer, Theol. Sem. of Evangelical and Reformed Church, 1942; Cole lecturer, Vanderbilt U., 1942; Merrick lecturer, Ohio Wesleyan U., 1943; Fondren lectr. So. Meth. U., 1945, Boston U. lectr., 1950-51. Mem. New England Conf. Meth. Church. Mem. Am. Philos. Assn. (pres. Eastern div. 1936), Am. Assn. Univ. Profs., Am. Theol. Soc. (pres. 1933-34), National Assn. Biblical Instructors (pres. 1941-43), Phi Beta Kappa, Kappa Sigma; fellow American Academy of Arts and Sciences; honorary member Kant-Gesellschaft. Clubs: University (Boston); Philosophics Anonymous. Author: The Sources of the Hexateuch, 1918; An Introduction to Philosophy, 1925; rev. edit., 1951; (translated into Chinese, Spanish and Portuguese); Immortality in Post-Kantian Idealism, 1925; Religious Values, 1925; A Philosophy of Ideals, 1928; (Spanish transl.); The Problem of God, 1930; The Finding of God, 1931; Is God a Person?, 1932; Moral Laws, 1933; A Philosophy of Religion, 1940; The Spiritual Life, 1942; Nature and Values, 1945; Person and Reality, 1958. Editor: Proceedings of Sixth International Congress of Philos, 1927. Joint contbr. to various volumes, also to Journal of Philosophy; Philosophical Review, Journal Religion, etc. Home: 42 Braeland Av., Newton Center 59, Mass. Office: 725 Commonwealth Av., Boston 15. Died Feb. 25, 1953.

BRILL, Hascal Russel, judge; b. Phillipsburg, P.Q., Can., Aug. 10, 1846; s. Thomas B. and Sarah (Sager) B.; student Hamline U., 1862-66, LL.D., 1890; student U. Mich., 1866-67; m. Cora A. Gray, 1873; 3 sons, 3 daus. Admitted to bar, 1869; partner Newel & Brill, 1870-74; judge of probate Ramsey County, Minn., 1873-75, Ct. of Common Pleas, 1875-76, Dist. Ct., 2d Jud. Dist., 1876-22. Mem. bd. Hamline U. Many yrs., also past pres. bd. Twice del. Gen. Conf. M.E. Ch, head judiciary com., 1896, mem. commn. on organic law of the ch., 1897. Town of Brill, Barron County, Wis., named for him in 1901. Republican. Methodist (past pres. ofcl. bd.). Home: 471 Laurel Av., St. Paul. Died Mar. 1, 1922; buried St. Paul.

BRILLHART, David H., business exec.; b. Loganville, York County, Pa.; s. David Y. and Mary Alice (Herbst) B.; grad. Juniata Coll., 1902; C.E., Lehigh U., 1906; m. Elizabeth Lehr, Nov. 11, 1922; children—Elizabeth L., Mary I., David W., Andrew L. Chmn. bd. Union Bank & Trust Co., Bethlehem, Pa., Bethlehem Globe Times and Times Publishing Co.; dir. L.V. R.R. Co., Pa. Power & Light Co.; pres., dir. Bethlehem Hotel Corp.; dir., v.p. East Sugar Loaf Coal Co.; trustee, asst. treas. St. Luke's Hosp.; trustee Saucon Valley Country Club, Bethlehem. Recipient honor award Lehigh U. Alumni Assn. Home: Bath Rd. Office: Union Bank & Trust Co., Bethlehem, Pa. Died Dec. 10, 1956.

BRINDLEY, Paul, physician, prof. of pathology; b. Maypearl, Tex., Dec. 27, 1896; s. George Goldthwaite and Mattie (Hanes) B.; student, U. of Tex., Austin, 1918-20; B.S., U. of Tex. Med. Sch., Galveston, 1923, M.D., 1925; m. Anne Mae Ammons, July 2, 1929. With U. of Tex., 1925—, as instr. in pathology, 1925-26, adjunct prof., 1926-27, asso. prof., 1927-29, prof., 1929—; pathologist Med. Br. Hospital, 1929—; cons. in pathology U.S.P.H.S. Hosp., 1931—. Fellow Am. Coll. Physicians, Coll. Am. Pathol., Am. Soc. of Clin. Pathol., 1941; mem. A.A.A.S., A.M.A., Galveston County, Texas and Southern med. socs., Am. Assn. Pathologists and Bacteriologists, Internat. Assn Med. Museums. Baptist. Contbr. articles to med. jours. Home: 4306 Sherman Blvd. Office: Medical School, University of Texas, Galveston, Tex. Died Dec. 28, 1954; buried Galveston Meml. Park, Hitchcock, Tex.

BRININSTOOL, Earl Alonzo (brĭn'ĭn-stōōl), author; b. Warsaw, N.Y., Oct. 11, 1870; s. Jacob James and Ellen (Blossom) B.; ed. pub. schs. and business coll.; m. Estelle R. Owen, Sept. 12, 1893; children—Merrill O., Ellene B. Moved to Los Angeles, 1895; reporter, editorial paragrapher Los Angeles Times, 1900-02; reporter, spl. writer Los Angeles Recod, 1903, Los Angeles Examiner, 1904. Wrote daily column, verse and paragraphs, Los Angeles Express, 1905-14; has been free lance writer, 1915—. Author about 5000 poems on various topics, principally on cowboy and range life. Known for mag. articles and books on the history of the West in connection with the Indian wars and frontier life. Author: (poems). Sonnets of a Telephone Girl, 1902; Trail Dust of a Maverick (cowboy poems), 1914; The Bozeman Trail (with Dr. Grace Raymond Hebard), 2 vols., 1923; A Trooper With Custer (Frontier Series), 1925; Fighting Red Cloud's Warriors, 1926; Campaigning with Custer and the 19th Kansas Volunteer Cavalry (with D. L. Spotts), 1928; Capture and Death of Chief Crazy Horse, 1929; Capt. Benteen's Story of the Custer Fight, 1933; The Dull Knife Outbreak at Fort Robinson, Neb., 1935; Major M. A. Reno Vindicated, 1935; Little Feller (moving picture starring Chic Sale), 1935; The Sioux Ghost Dance War of 1890 in South Dakota, 1951; Troopers With Custer, 1952; Fighting Indian Warriors, 1953. Home: 330 N. Poinsettia Pl., Los Angeles 36. Died July 28, 1957.

BRINK, Francis G., army officer; b. Marathon, N.Y., Aug. 22, 1893; s. Lawrence J. and Martha S. (Sheldon) B.; A.B., Cornell U., 1916; grad. Inf. Sch., basic course, 1921, Command and Gen. Staff Sch., 1936; m. Florence Roos, Aug. 18, 1917; children—Esther Roos, Robert Sheldon, Leilani Tryon. Instr. in physical training, Cornell U., 1916; commd. 2d lt., U.S. Army, 1917, and advanced through the grades to brig. gen.; served through World War I; with 2d Inf. Div., 1919-20; instr. Inf. Sch., 1921-23; with 27th Inf., Hawaii, 1923-28; asst. prof. mil. science and tactics Louisiana State U., 1928-34; with 16th inf., Governor's Island, N.Y., 1937-38, 31st Inf., Philippines, and as force comdr., 1938-41; U.S. Military observer and liaison for War Dept., Singapore, Java and Burma, on Gen. Wavell's staff, 1941-42; in first Java Campaign, 1942; in Hawaii, Aleutians, Alaska, China and Burma operations, 1942-44; chief of operations div. Southeast Asia Command, 1944-45, 1945 to end of war, G-3 Tactical Hdqrs.; U.S. Army Forces, China, 1945-46; China liaison officer to AFPAC, Manila and Tokyo; duty with USAFC, Shanghai and Japan; chief joint adv. staff, A.A.G., Nanking, China, 1946-49; comdg. general O.M.D. 2d Army 1949-50; chief M.A.A.G. Mission, Saigon, Indo China since 1950. Decorated Distinguished Service Medal, Legion of Merit with Oak Leaf Cluster, Commendation Ribbon, Purple Heart. Comdr. Brit. Empire, Order Yun Hui, Order Pao Ting. Author: Divisional Tactics and Adminstrn., Gen. Staff, 1938; Corps, Army Operations, 1938; also several mil. publs. outlining tactics and strategy for operations in Pacific and Asia theaters of operation during World War II. Home: Marathon, N.Y. Address: M.A.A.G., care U.S. Legation, Saigon, Indo China. Died June 24, 1952.

BRINKERHOFF, Robert Moore, cartoonist, illustrator; b. Toledo, May 4, 1880; s. Robert Alexander and Flora (Steuart) B.; student Art Students League, N.Y., 1900-01, Acadamie de la Grand Chaumiere, Paris, France, 1905; m. Edna Patterson, Mar. 3, 1917; 1 son, Robert Huston. Began as cartoonist Toledo Bee, 1898, for Toledo Blade, Cleveland Leader, Cincinnati Post, Evening Mail, New York Evening World, World-Telegram and other newspapers served by United Features Syndicate; created cartoon character, Little Mary Mixup; illustrated humorous stories for mags., also wrote and illustrated children's stories for various publs. Republican. Presbyn. Mem. Soc. of Illustrators (New York). Club: Dutch Treat (N.Y.C.). Author: Little Mary Mixup in Fairyland (also illustrator), 1925. Illustrator of Vagabond Trail, by G. F. Pierrot, 1935 (material gathered on sketching trip around the world, 1931). Home: 50 W. 67th St., N.Y.C.; (summer) Meddybemps, Me. Address: United Features Syndicate, 220 E. 42d St., N.Y.C. Died Feb. 17, 1958.

BRINTON, Willard Cope, cons. engr.; b. West Chester, Pa., Dec. 22, 1880; s. Samuel Lewis and Elizabeth Brinton (Smith) B.; grad. State Normal Sch., West Chester, 1900; S.B., in M.E. cum laude, Lawrence Scientific Sch. (Harvard), 1907; m Laura MacDonald Moses, Apr. 17, 1920. With H. Brinton & Co., Phila., 1900-03; spl. investigations for mgr. works dept. Westinghouse Electric & Mfg. Co., East Pittsburgh, Pa., 1907-10; asst. to v.p. U.S. Motor Co., New York, 1910-12; mech. engr. Bush Terminal Co., New York, 1912-13; consulting practice since 1913, involving work in various parts of the U.S., Europe, Japan and China; pres. and treas. Terminal Engring. Co., Lawrence Safety Brake Co. Mem. Am. Soc. Mech. Engrs., Am. Statis. Assn. (v.p. 1919), Harvard Engineering Society of N.Y. (pres. 1931-32). Clubs: Harvard Club, Harvard-Yale-Princeton, Pittsburgh, Newcomen Society of England, Arctic, Seattle, Washington. Author: Graphic Methods for Presenting Facts, 1914; Graphic Presentation, 1939; and numerous mag. articles. Home: Croton-on-Hudson, N.Y. Office: 36 W. 59th St., N.Y.C. 19. Died Nov. 29, 1957.

BRISTER, Charles James, ry. ofcl.; b. Dayton, O.; s. James Taylor and Mary Eva (Wood) B.; student pub. and comml. schs.; m. Adelaide Lucienne Beecher (died 1937). Began with Big Four Ry., Cin., 1892, occupied several positions, traffic mgr., 1914-20; asst. v.p. N.Y.C. R.R., at Chgo., 1920-30, v.p. in charge frieght traffic, N.Y.C., 1930—; v.p. Pitts. & Lake Erie R.R. Co., Chgo. River & Ind. R.R., Indiana Harbor Belt R.R., Owasco River Ry., Louisville & Jeffersonville Bridge & R.R. Co.; dir. Canadian Pacific Car and Passenger Transfer Co., Hudson River Connecting Ry., Battle Creek & Sturgis Ry., Merchants' Despatch Transportation Corp., N.J. Junction R.R., Northern Refrigerator Line, Inc., Broadway Assn. Chmn. Central Territory Freight Traffic Com., U.S. Ry. Adminstrn., 1918-20. Mem. N.Y. Bd. Trade, Mchts. Assn. N.Y., Nat. Fgn. Trade Council. Clubs: Union League, Recess, Traffic, Railroad (N.Y.C.); Siwanoy Country (Bronxville, N.Y.); Chicago, Traffic (Chgo.). Home: Hotel Biltmore. Office: 466 Lexington Av., N.Y.C. Deceased.

BRISTOL, Arthur E(dward), lawyer; b. N.Y. City, Mar. 5, 1887; s. Edward N. and Minna (Baumgarten) B.; A.B., Amherst Coll., 1909; LL.B., Columbia, 1912; m. Marion Fernald, Nov. 27, 1913; children—Edward F., Ruth (Mrs. Glen M. Robertson), Dorothy (Mrs. Coy N. Cooter). Admitted to N.Y. state bar, 1912. Ill. bar, 1926; mem. law firm, Campbell, Harding, Goodwin & Danforth, N.Y. City, 1937-46; dir. and gen. counsel Union Tank Car Co., 1947, v.p., 1952—. Mem. Am., Ill. and Chicago bar assns., Delta Upsilon. Republican. Conglist. Clubs: University, Traffic (Chicago); Builders. Home: 1109 Forest Av., Wilmette, Ill. Office: 228 N. La Salle St., Chgo. Died May 5, 1954; buried Montclair, N.J.

BRISTOL, Henry P., corp. exec.; b. Clinton, N.Y., 1889; s. William McLaren and Mary Seymour (Lee) B.; A.M., Hamilton Coll., Clinton, N.Y., 1930; m. Gertrude Flesh, June 14, 1928. Chmn. board Bristol-Myers Co. (Del.); dir. Irving Trust Co., Lehigh Valley R.R.; trustee East River Savs. Bank. Trustee Com. Econ. Development, Hamilton Coll. Served as lt., F.A., Mexican Border Service, 1916; maj., F.A., U.S. Army, World War I. Mem. U.S. Council Internat. C. of C. (trustee), Proprietary Assn. (dir.), Sigma Phi. Clubs: Army and Navy, Bay Head Yacht, Bankers, University, Fort Schuyler. Home: 1 Beekman Pl., N.Y.C. 22. Office: 630 Fifth Av., N.Y.C. 20, N.Y. Died Apr. 14, 1959.

BRISTOL, Leverett Dale, health ofcl.; b. Chgo., June 2, 1880; s. Bishop Frank Milton (Meth. Ch.) and Nellie (Frisbie) B.; B.S., Wesleyan U., Middletown, Conn., 1903; M.D., Johns Hopkins, 1907; Dr. P.H., Harvard, 1917; m. Addie Louise Knox, June 27, 1907; children—Corabelle (Mrs. Richard Osborn Rice), Adelaide (Mrs. Livingston Lord Satterthwaite), Leverett Frisbie. Practiced in St. Paul, 1908-13; asso. prof. bacteriology Syracuse U., 1913-14; prof bacteriology U. N.D., and dir. state health labs. 1914-16; fellow and asst. Harvard Med. Sch., 1916-17; state commr. health, Me., 1917-21; prof. preventive medicine and pub. health U. Minn., 1922-23; dir. N.Y. State Health Demonstrations, 1923-29 health dir. Am. Tel. & Tel. Co., 1929-44; exec. dir. Hosp. Council of Greater New York, 1944-45; commr. Me. State Dept. Health and Welfare; 1945-47; cons. on health and indsl. medicine, 1947-48; chief Div. Cancer Control, Pa. Dept. Health, 1948—. Surgeon (maj.) USPHS Res., World War. Mem. Com. on Neighborhood Health Development, New York; bd.

dirs., N.Y. Tb and Health Assn.; mem. N.J. Tb League; past pres. N.J. Health and Sanitary Assn., Montclair (N.J.) Council of Social Agencies, chmn. com. on indsl. diseases, N.J. Health and Welfare Conf. Trustee Wesleyan U., 1919-24. Mem. Am. Med. Assn. (chmn. sect. on preventive medicine 1936-37), Am. Pub. Health Assn. (chmn. sect. indsl. hygiene 1936-37), Nat. Tb Assn., Am. Assn. Indsl. Physicians and Surgeons, Indsl. Health Council; hon. mem. Safety Engrs. of Can., Internat. Soc. Med. Health Officers; mem. Med. Adv. Bd. Am. Mus. of Health, N.Y.; mem. adv. com. on nursing, N.Y. City Dept. of Health; chmn., Joint Adv. Com. on Indusl. Hygiene, N.Y. City Dept. of Health, N.Y. State Dept. of Labor; coop. com. on nutrition in industry, A.M.A.; medical mem. advisory panel on fuel oil rationing, OPA; chmn. Adv. Health Council, U.S. Chamber of Commerce; consultant health and safety, Office Labor Prodn., War Prodn. Bd.; pres. Pub. Health Assn., N.Y. City. Mem. Sigma Xi, Phi Beta Kappa, Alpha Delta Phi, Alpha Kappa Kappa. Republican. Methodist. Rotarian. Contbr. articles on medicine. Author: Industrial Health Service; also chapter on Health of Office Workers in Handbook of Business Administration, 1931; and chapter on Industrial Medicine in the Cyclopedia of Medicine, 1940. Home: 2311 N. Front St. Office: State Dept. of Health, Harrisburg, Pa. Died Feb. 20, 1957; buried Hartford, Conn.

BRITAN, Halbert Hains, educator; b. Bethlehem, Ind. Oct. 8, 1874; s. George Whitney and Mary Arbella (Taylor) B.; A.B., Hanover (Ind.) Coll., 1898, A.M., 1902; Ph.D., Yale, 1902; m. Mary Edith Fisher, Aug. 1, 1907. Prof. philosophy, Bates Coll., 1905—. Mem. Am. Philos. Assn., Phi Gamma Delta. Author: Philosophy of Music, 1911; The Affective Consciousness, 1931. Translator: Spinoza's Descartes' Principles of Philosophy. Contbr. articles to philos. mags. Home: Lewiston, Me. Died Aug. 1945.

BRITTAIN, Marion Luther, coll. pres. emeritus; b. Wilkes Co., Ga., Nov. 11, 1866; s. Jabez Mercer and Ida (Callaway) B.; A.B., Emory Coll., 1886; grad. student U. of Chicago 1898; LL.D., Mercer U., 1919, U. of Ga., 1927, Emory U., 1928; m. Lettie McDonald, Dec. 20, 1889; children—McDonald, Marion Luther, Ida Louise. Princ. of Crew Street Grammar Sch., Atlanta, 1888-90; head dept. of langs., Boys' High Sch., Atlanta, 1890-99; supt. schs., Fulton Co., Ga., 1900-10; state sch. commr. of Ga., 1910; state supt. of schs. of Ga., 1911-22; became pres. Georgia Sch. Tech., 1922. Commd. lt. col. R.O.T.C. by Pres. Wilson, 1922. Internat. judge Fisher Body Guild, 1931-36; mem. bd. visitors U.S. Naval Acad., 1934-39 and 1941; apptd. mem. Prison Bd., Inc., 1935; pres. advisory bd. Techwood Slum Clearance Project of U.S. Govt. Pres. Ga. Teachers' Assn., 1906, Ga. Bapt. Young People's Union, 1902. Winner of Atlanta Constitution's $1,000 prize, 1898. Pres. Southern Ednl. Assn., 1913; pres. Council State Supts. of U.S., 1917. Life mem. N.E.A.; mem. Kappa Alpha, Phi Beta Kappa, Phi Kappa Phi. Democrat. Clubs: Capitol City, The Ten. Author: Introduction to Cæsar, 1900; History and Methods of Sunday School Work, 1901; History of Second Baptist Church of Atlanta, 1905; Blue Book of Stories, 1915; Lessons for Adults, 1922; The Story of Georgia Tech, 1948. Home: 204 North Av., N.W., Atlanta. Died July 1, 1953.

BROADDUS, Bower, U.S. Dist. judge; b. Chillicothe, Mo., May 30, 1888; s. Elbridge J. and Emma (Hollingsworth) B.; student, Univ. of Mo., 1908-09; LL.B., Kan. City Sch. of Law, 1910; m. Harriett Ann Noland, Jan. 31, 1917; children—Bower, Elbridge Sidney, Harriett Ann (Mrs. Jack High). Admitted to Okla. State Bar, 1910, practiced in Muskogee, Okla., 1910-40; police judge, Muskogee, 1912-14; city attorney, Muskogee, 1926-30; mem. Okla. Ho. of Reps., 1933-35, Okla. Senate, 1935-38; apptd. U.S. Dist. Judge, 1940, serving Eastern, Northern and Western dists. of Okla. since 1940. Mem. Okla. Bar Assn., Am. Bar Assn., Pi Alpha Delta, Sigma Alpha Epsilon. Democrat. Baptist. Home: 900 N.W. 39th. Office: 601 Federal Bldg., Oklahoma City. Died Dec. 10, 1949; buried Fairlawn Cemetery, Oklahoma City.

BROADHURST, Edward T., judge; b. Springfield, Mass., Sept. 2, 1879; s. William and Ida F. (Tapley) B.; A.B., Williams Coll., 1901, LL.D., 1955; LL.B., Harvard, 1904; LL.D., Am. Internat. Coll., 1956; m. Bertha Louisa Bassett, Feb. 17, 1917; children—Austin, Edward T. Admitted to Mass. bar, 1904, practiced in Springfield, 1904-23; sr. asso. justice Superior Ct. of Mass., 1923—. Mem. Common Council, Springfield, 1909-15, pres. Council, 1913-15, city solicitor, 1920-21, U.S. commr., 1920-22. Chmn. bd. trustees Am. Internat. Coll. Mem. Phi Beta Kappa, Delta Kappa Epsilon. Republican. Baptist. Club: St. Botolph (Boston). Home: 284 State St., Springfield, Mass. Office: Court House, Boston. Died Dec. 13, 1955; buried Springfield Cemetery.

BROADHURST, George H., dramatist; b. 1866. Author of the plays: What Happened to Jones; Why Smith Left Home; The Wrong Mr. Wright; A Fool and His Money; The Crown Prince; The Duke of Duluth (musical comedy); The Man of the Hour; Bought and Paid For; The Mills of the Gods. Coauthor of musical comedy, Nancy Brown; comedy, That American, etc. Pres. Broadhurst Theatre Co., George Broadhurst Corpn. Club: Lotos. Address: 235 W. 44th St., New York, N.Y. Died Jan. 31, 1952.*

BROADHURST, Jean, educator, author; b. Stockton, N.J., Dec. 9, 1873 : S. Winfield Scott and Mary H. (Butterfoss) B.; B.S., Tchrs. Coll. Columbia, 1903, B.A., 1908; Ph.D., Cornell U., 1914. Tchr. N.J. State Normal Sch., 1903-06; became instr. biology Tchrs. Coll. Columbia U., 1906, asst., 1914, asso. prof., 1920, prof., 1928-39, prof. emeritus of bacteriology, 1939—. Fellow A.A.A.S. Author: Home and Community Hygiene, 1918; Verse for Patriots (with Clara L. Rhodes), 1919; All Through the Day the Mother Goose Way, 1921; How We Resist Disease, 1923; Bacteria in Relation to Man, 1925; Health for Every Day and Health in Home and Neighborhood (with M. A. Bigelow), 1925; The Animal Way, 1928; Microbiology Applied to Nursing (with Leila I. Given), 1929. Home: Hudson View Gardens, W. 183d and Pinehurst Av., N.Y.C. 33. Died Sept. 5, 1954; buried Stockton, N.J.

BROADWATER, J.A.B., corp. exec.; b. Edgefield, S.C., Dec. 16, 1895; s. R.E. and Josephine (Hudson) B.; student pub. schs.; m. Vivian Saunders, June 14, 1923. Treas. Holtsinger Motor Co., Tampa, Fla., 1936-42, Tampa Shipbldg. Co., 1942-49; v.p. Capital Transit Co., Washington, 1949-50, exec. v.p., 1950-51, pres., 1951-56; dir., mem. exec. com. N.Y. Shipbldg. Corp., Camden, N.J.; dir. Glen Echo Park Co., Merritt-Chapman & Scott Corp., Newport Steel Co. (Ky.), Continental Enterprises, Inc. (Jacksonville, Fla.), Devoe & Raynolds, Inc. (N.Y. C.), Scullin Steel Co. Home: 1747 Crestwood Dr. Office: 36th and M Sts., Washington. Died Aug. 1957.

BROCK, Clifford Edward, utilities exec.; b. Bentonville, Ark., June 3, 1893; s. Edward Everett and Florence Belle (Moats) B.; student pub. schs.; m. Iva Viola Kendall, Nov. 25, 1911; 1 dau., Jeanne Frances (Mrs. Stuart E. Bunn). Successively office boy, bookkeeper clk. prodn. dept., supt. gas pipelines, supt. gas prodn. Cities Service Gas Co., 1913-27; mgr. Kay County Gas Co. (subsidiary of Md. Oil Co.), 1927; gen. supt. natural gas div. Kan. Power & Light Co., 1927, mgr. gas, 1937, v.p., dir. 1937—. Mason (K.T., Shriner). Home: 231 W. Prescott Av. Office: Box 59, Salina, Kan. Deceased.

BROCK, Elmer Leslie, lawyer; b. nr. London, Ky., Dec. 15, 1880; s. Daniel R. and Mary (Lucas) B.; student U. Ky., 1901-02; LL.B., U. Denver, 1909; m. Nora Lindon, June 7, 1911; children—Elmer Leslie, Charles L. Admitted to Colo. bar, 1909, began practice at Denver; asst. atty. gen. Colo., 1909-11; practiced at Grand Junction, 1911-12; asso. Smith, Brock & Ferguson, Denver, 1913-23; mem. Smith & Brock, 1923-29; mem. Smith Brock, Akolt & Campbell, 1929-42, now Brock, Akolt & Campbell; formerly gen. counsel and dir. Denver and Salt Lake Ry.; prof. common carriers and public services cos. U. Denver, 1919-34. Mem. Nat. Conf. for Uniform State Laws, 1926-30. Mem. Am., Colo., Denver (pres. 1931-32) bar assns., Phi Delta Phi, Kappa Sigma. Democrat. Baptist. Clubs: Denver, University, Denver Country. Home: 1410 E. 4th Av. Office: Telephone Bldg., Denver. Died Aug. 14, 1949.

BROCK, William Emerson, ex-senator; b. Farmington, N.C., Mar. 14, 1872; s. Richard Emerson and Mary (Howell) B.; student pub. schs.; m. Miriam Acree, 1903; children—William E., Richard Acree. Engaged in farming until 1894; clk. in store, 1896; salesman R. J. Reynolds Tobacco Co., 1896-1909; candy mfr., 1909—; pres. Brock Candy Co.; dir. Provident Life & Accident Ins. Co.; apptd. mem. U.S. Senate by gov. of Tenn. to fill vacancy caused by death of Senator L. D. Tyson, and reelected Nov. 5, 1930, for term 1931-37. Past-pres. C. of C., Chattanooga Mfrs. Assn.; chmn. 1st Liberty Loan drive and mem. exec. com. for all other drives, Chattanooga, World War. Trustee U. Chattanooga, Emory U., Emory and Henry Coll. Democrat. Methodist. Home: 72 North Crest Rd., Chattanooga, Tenn. Died Aug. 5, 1950; buried Forest Hills, Chattanooga.

BROCKWAY, Howard, composer; b. Bklyn., Nov. 22, 1870; s. Leverett E. and Clara (Kingsley) B.; student Bklyn. Poly., but left to study music, 1888; musical studies in Bklyn. with H. O. C. Kortheuer, and 5 yrs. in Berlin, with O. B. Boise (composition), H. Barth (piano); m. Anabel Boise, Feb. 1896; 1 dau., Sylvia; m. 2d, Katharine Engs Bradford, Apr. 17, 1906. Gave concert with Berlin Philharmonic Orchestra of his own works in Berlin, 1895; Boston Symphony Orchestra produced his Sylvan Suite, 1901, and his symphony, 1907. Mem. faculty Peabody Inst., Balt., 1903-09; mem. piano faculty of David Mannes Music Sch., N.Y.C.; mem. faculty Juilliard School of Music, 1925-41. Mem. Nat. Inst. Arts and Letters. Composer: Symphony for grand orchestra, large orchestral works, chamber music, piano composition, choral music, songs for voice and piano. Compiler: Lonesome Tunes, and Twenty Kentucky Mountain Songs. Home: 424 E. 57th St., N.Y.C. Died Feb. 20, 1951.

BRODERICK, Case, ex-congressman, lawyer; b. Grant County, Ind., Sept. 23, 1839; ed. common schs.; m. 1860, Mary A. Ewbank (died 1888). Removed to Kan., 1858, and engaged in farming; probate judge Jackson County, 1868-74; admitted to bar, 1870; county atty., Jackson County, 1876-80; State senator, 1880-84; asso. justice Supreme Ct., Ida., 1884-88, since then lawyer at Holton, Kan.; mem. Congress, 1891-99, 1st Kan. dist.; Republican. Address: Holton, Kan. Deceased.

BRODERICK, Joseph A., banker; b. N.Y.C., Dec. 7, 1881; grad. N.Y.U. Sch. Commerce, Accts. and Finance, 1906. Am. Inst. of Banking, 1908; m. Mary Rose Lyons, Aug. 2, 1916; children—Joseph Lyons, Vincent Lyons, Francis Lyons. With State Trust Co. and Morton Trust Co., N.Y. City, successively as clk., auditor, asst. sec., 1896-1910; bank examiner State of N.Y., 1910-14; chief examiner Federal Res. Bd., 1914-18, sec., 1918-19; v.p. Nat. Bank of Commerce, N.Y. City, 1919-28; supt. of banks State of N.Y., 1929-34; mem. bd. govs. Fed. Res. System, Feb. 1936-Sept. 30, 1937; pres. and trustee East River Savs. Bank, 1937-52; chmn. bd. 1952-57. Member Nat. Assn. Supervisors State Banks (hon.), Am. Inst. Banking (hon.), Alpha Kappa Psi, Phi Alpha Kappa. Club: Bankers (gov.). Home: 200 E. 66th St., N.Y.C. 21. Office: 26 Cortlandt St., N.Y.C. 7. Died Apr. 5, 1959.

BRODRICK, Lynn Rosegrant (brŏd'rĭk), internal revenue collector; b. Marceline, Mo., Feb. 18, 1892; s. Harry Maxwell and Emma Lena (Rosegrant) B.; grad. Marysville High Sch., 1909; m. Elizabeth Jones, Feb. 27, 1923. Business mgr. The Advocate-Democrat, Marysville, Kan., 1912-42; commr. Kan. State Highway Dept., 1932-34; collector of internal revenue, Dist. of Kan., 1940—. Mem. Dem. Nat. Com. for Kan., 1934-42, vice chmn., 1936-40; chmn. Marshall County Dem. Central Com.; chmn. First Dist. Congl. Com. Served as sgt., inf., U.S. Army, World War I. Mem. Nat. Editorial Soc., Am. Legion. Democrat. Presbyn. Mason (Grand master Kan. 1950; past grand high priest Royal Arch of Kan.), Woodman of World, Rotarian. Home: Allis Hotel, Wichita 2. Office: 205 N. 11th St., Marysville, Kan.; also Federal Bldg., Wichita, Kan. Died 1958.

BRODY, Samuel, univ. prof.; b. Garbatchi, nr. Baranowitz, Lithuania (now Poland), Feb. 8, 1890; s. Avram J. and S. Deborah (Malov) B.; A.B., U. of Calif., 1917, A.M. and life teachers certificate, 1919; Ph.D., U. of Chicago, 1928; fellow Guggenheim Foundn. for study in Europe, 1930-31; m. Sophie Edith Dubosky, Aug. 15, 1920; children—Dr. Eugene Bloor, Dr. Arnold Jason. Came to U.S., 1906, naturalized, 1912. Asst. biochemist U. of Calif. Med. Sch., 1919-20; asst. prof. dairy and agrl. chemistry U. of Mo., 1920, asso. prof., 1925, chmn. interdept. com. on growth and metabolism since 1926; chmn. Herman Frasch Foundn. research project in agrl. chemistry Mo. Coll. of Agr., 1929-40, chmn. com. on muscular work in farm animals since 1941, prof. dairy husbandry, 1945, chmn. com. on influence of climatic factors on physiol. reactions and productivity in farm animals since 1946. Served with Air Service, also with development div., C.W.S., U.S. Army, 1918-19. Recipient Borden award, 1950. Fellow A.A.A.S.; mem. Am. Soc. Naturalists, National Research Council (mem. sub-com. on energy metabolism in relation to agr.; sub-com. on standardization), Am. Assn. Univ. Profs., Am. Chem. Soc. (mem. div. biol. chemistry), Am. Soc. Biol. Chemists, Am. Inst. Nutrition, Am. Dairy Sci. Assn., Am. Animal Sci. Prodn., Soc. for Development and Growth, Mo. Hist. Soc., Mo. Acad. Sci., Czechoslovak Acad. Agr., Sigma Xi, Gamma Sigma Delta. Clubs: University, Philosophical (Columbia, Mo.). Author: Bioenergetics and Growth, 1945; also chapters in books and articles in jours. Recipient of several Nat. Research Council grants for nutritional research, 1925-38. Home: 101 Park Hill, Columbia, Mo. Died Aug. 6, 1956.

BROEKMAN, David Hendrines, composer, conductor; born in Leiden, Holland, May 13, 1899; son of Jacob and Bertha (Prins) Broekman; married Faith Jenkins, 1930; children—Melisande, Deetje, Jacqueline, Hendrik Faye. Came to U.S., 1924, naturalized, 1929. Formerly conductor of Royal Opera at The Hague; mem. N.Y. Philharmonic Orchestra, 1924-26; mus. advisor Erpi. also asso. Warner Bros., N.Y.C., 1926-29; mus. dir. Universal Pictures, Hollywood, Cal., 1929-31, Columbia Pictures, 1931-34, CBS, sta. KHJ, 1934-41, U.S. Treasury for bond programs and recordings, 1941-45; mus. dir. Tex. Star Theatre, 1945; prin. conductor Carnegie Pops Concerts, 1946-47; composer original scores Berlin Airlift, Clear and Present Danger, Report on Communism, ABC, 1948-49; panelist TV show Think Fast, ABC, 1948; scoring and conducting Ken Murray TV Show, 1950-52; mus. dir., composer Ford Festival, NBC-TV, 1951, composer-condr. Wide, Wide World, 1955-57; condr. concert series Cooper Union, N.Y.C., 1952-57; music critic. Recipient Alice M. Ditson award, 1954. Author: Shoestring Symphony, 1948. Composer: Manhattan Fairy Tale Suite, Music of David Broekman Series, Jericho, Barbara Allen (opera), The Stranger (opera), The Toledo War (opera), 1st and 2nd Symphonies, Violin Concerto, String Quartet, Concerto (for solo piano, percussion and orchestra), piano sonatas and etudes. Contbr. periodicals. Home: 1215-5th Av., N.Y.C. 29. Died Apr. 1, 1958.

BROENING, William Frederick (brō'nĭng), lawyer; b. Balt., June 2, 1870; s. Henry Jacob and Catherine (Petri) B.; LLB., U. Md., 1898; m. Josephine Marie Grauel, Sept. 6, 1905; children—William F., K. Ethel, E. Calvin (dec.). Practiced law in Balt., 1898—; mem. Robinson & Broening, 1912-18. Mem. City Council, Balt., 1897-99; mem. Ho. of Rep., Md., 1902; state's atty. for Baltimore City, 1911-19; mayor of Balt., 1919-23, 27-31; former chmn. Md. State Indsl. Accident Commn.; city collector and collector of state taxes. Republican. Lutheran. Past supreme gov. Loyal Order of Moose; Md. dir. Moose Vocational Inst., Mooseheart, Ill. Mason, Odd Fellow, K.P., Elk. Office: Municipal Bldg., Balt. Died Oct. 12, 1953.

BROIDY, Edward William, grocery chain exec.; b. N.Y.C., Sept. 27, 1886; s. William A. and Elizabeth (Alperin) B.; student pub. schs.; m. Rena M. Fisher, Apr. 4, 1911. Sec., dir., gen. mgr. The Weisberger Co., dept. store, Richmond, 1915-21; dir., sec. and treas. Thalhimer Bros., Inc., 1921-34; v.p., dir. Allied Stores Corp., N.Y.C., 1934—, also dir. 8 subsidiaries; v.p., dir. Associated Royalty Corp.; pres. Coastal Royalties, Inc. (both Lake Charles, La.). Home: 5433 Alton Rd., Miami Beach 40, Fla. Office: 1140 Broadway, N.Y.C. Died Nov. 9. 1950.

BROKAW, Howard Crosby, retired businessman; b. New York, N.Y., Oct. 26, 1875; s. Isaac Vail and Eloise Elvira (Gould) B.; A.B., Princeton, 1897; m. Edna Goodley Loew, of New York, Nov. 11, 1903. Pres. Brokaw Bros., clothiers, 1913-22, retired. Clubs: University, Union Racquet and Tennis, Piping Rock, Tuxedo, Nat. Golf., N.Y. Yacht. Home: 984 5th Av., New York, N.Y. Died March 19, 1960.

BROKENSHIRE, Charles Digory (bro'ken-shire), clergyman, educator; b. Cin., Jan. 24, 1885; s. Digory and Lucy (Stacey) B.; A.B, Marietta (O.) Coll., 1907, A.M., 1907; B.D., Princeton, 1910, fellow in semitics, 1910-12, 12-13, Procter Semitics fellow of Princeton at U. Heidelberg, Germany, 1913-14; student McGill U., 1928, 29, 31, U. Chgo., 1925, 26, 27, U. Mich.; D.D., Alma (Mich.) Coll., 1937. Ordained to ministry of Presbyn Ch., 1911; pastor Union Ch., Schenectady, 1911; 4th Ref. Ch., Phila., 1912-13, Am. Presbyn. Ch., Frankfurt-Am. Main, Germany, 1914-15, 1st Congl. Ch., Stanton, Mich., 1920-25; prof. Bibl. lit. and religious edn., ancient and modern lang. Alma Coll., 1915-43; prof Bibl. lit., ancient and modern langs. and theology, dean sch. religion Bob Jones Coll. and U., Cleveland, Tenn., and now at Greenville, S.C., 1943—. Mem. A.A.A.S., Am. Soc. U. Profs., Am. Oriental Soc., Soc Bibl. Lit., Am. and Brit. Esperanto socs., Mich. Acad. Sci., Phi Beta Kappa, Pi Gamma Mu, Alma Coll. Honor Soc. Traveled in Europe, 1913-14, Palestine, 1930. Home: Greenville, S.C. Office: The School of Religion, Bob Jones U., Greenville, S.C. Died May 28, 1954; buried Cin.

BROMER, Edward Sheppard, theologian; b. Schwenksville, Pa., Mar. 19, 1869; s. Albert and Catharine (Sheppard) B.; A.B., Ursinus Coll., Collegeville, Pa., 1890, D.D., 1905; B.D., Yale Div. Sch., 1893, grad. fellow, 1893-94; m. Flora Keelor Schwenk, 1890 (died 1941); children—Edna, Henry Earl, Frances Catharine; m. 2d, Lucy Lillian Best, 1944. Ordained to ministry Ref. Ch. in U.S., 1894; pastor successively Orwigsburg, later First Ch., Lebanon, Pa., until 1905; prof. N.T. lang. and exegesis, Ursinus Sch. Theology, 1905-06; pastor First Ch., Greensburg, Pa., 1906-20; prof. practical theology Theol. Sem. Ref. Ch. in U.S., Lancaster, Pa., 1920-39; retired 1939. Mem. Am. Acad. Polit. and Social Sci. (Phila.), Cliosophic Soc. (Lancaster). Mason. Address: 47 Hess Blvd., Lancaster, Pa. Died Nov. 25, 1948; buried Schwenksville, Pa.

BROMER, Ralph Shepherd, physician; b. Schwenksville, Pa., Mar. 21, 1886; s. Albert and Catherine (Schappert) B.; A.B., Yale, 1908; M.D., U. Pa., 1912; m. Alice Rupp, July 6, 1921; children—Ralph Shepherd, Catherine Brandes (Mrs. John Haughton Wrenn). Intern Pa. Hosp., Phila., 1912-14; house officer in orthopedic surgery Children's Hosp., Boston, 1915, roentgenologist, 1921-51; pvt. practice, specialist in radiology, 1915—; radiologist Episcopal Hosp., 1917-32, Bryn Mawr Hosp., Phila., 1932—; cons. roentgenologist, 1951—; prof. clin. radiology grad. sch. medicine U. Pa., 1935—. Served with M.C., U.S. Army, World War I; roentgenologist and adj. Base Hosp. 34, comdg. officer Evacuation Hosp. 36, Nantes, France, 1918-19; disch. as lt. col. Fellow Am. Coll. Radiology; mem. Am. Roentgen Ray Soc. (past pres.), Radiol. Soc. N.A., A.M.A. Home: 318 Millbank Rd. Office: Bryn Mawr Hosp., Bryn Mawr, Pa. Died Sept. 25, 1957.

BROMFIELD, Louis, author; b. Mansfield, O.; s. Charles and Annette Maria (Coulter) B.; student Cornell U., Ohio Northern U., Columbia Univ., hon. B.A., on account of war service; hon. Litt.D., Marshall College, Ohio Northern U.; married Mary Appleton Wood, October, 12, 1921 (dec. Sept. 1952). Served with American Ambulance, attached to French Army, 1917-19. Awarded Croix de Guerre; Legion of Honor, 1939; Societe De Jardins Ouvriers Medal (France); Audubon Soc. Medal; Friends of the Land Medal; Garden Clubs of Am. Medal. Democrat. Protestant. Mem. Inst. Am. Arts and Letters. Dir. U.S. C. of C.; v.p. Friends of the Land. Clubs: Coffee House, Century, Brook. Authors (N.Y.). Author: The Green Bay Tree, 1924; Possession, 1925; Early Autumn (awarded Pulitzer prize, $1,000), 1926; A Good Woman, 1927; The House of Women (play), 1927, 29; The Strange Case of Miss Annie Spragg; Awake and Rehearse; Twenty-four Hours (novel); A Modern Hero (novel); The Farm (novel), 1933; Here Today (one volume four novelettes), 1934; De Luxe (play), 1935; Times Have Changed (play), 1935; The Man Who Had Everything (novel); The Rains Came (novel); also one chapter in "Bobbed Hair," a novel by twenty authors; It Takes All Kinds (novelettes and stories), 1938; England, A Dying Oligarchy (pamphlet), 1938; Night in Bombay (novel), 1939; Wild Is the River (novel), 1941; Until the Day Break (novel), 1942; Mrs. Parkington (novel), 1943; What Became of Anna Bolton, 1944; The World We Live In (stories), 1944; Pleasant Valley (partial autobiography), 1945; A Few Brass Tacks, 1946; Agricultural Economics; The World We Live In (stories) 1946; Kenny (stories) 1947; Colorado (novel) 1947; Malabar Farm, 1948 (partial autobiog.); The Wild Country, 1948 (novel); Out of the Earth, 1950; Mr. Smith, 1951; A New Pattern for a Tired World, 1954; From My Experience: The Pleasures and Miseries of Life on a Farm, 1955; Animals and Other People, 1955; also numerous articles on music, economics, agriculture, internat. politics. Home: Malabar Farm, Lucas, O. Address: care Harper & Brothers, 49 E. 33d St., N.Y.C. 16. Died Mar. 18, 1956; buried Malabar Farm, Lucas, O.

BRONFENBRENNER, Jacques Jacob (brŏn'fĕn-brĕn-ēr), educator; b. Cherson, Russia, Nov. 21, 1883; s. Uria Aaron and Rosalia (Borochovitch) B.; student Imperial New-Russia U., 1903-07; Ph.B., Columbia, 1912; D.P.H., Harvard, 1919; m. Martha Ornstein, Sept., 1913; 1 son, Martin; m. 2d, Alice Klein, Jan. 1921; children—Jack, Alice. Came to U.S., 1909, naturalized, 1914. Asst. Imperial U., Russia, 1905; asst. Pasteur Inst., Paris, 1908-09; fellow and asst. Rockefeller Inst., N.Y.C., 1909-13, asso. mem., 1923-28; dir. research and diagnostic labs. West. Pa. Hosp., Pitts., 1913-17; asst. prof. preventive medicine and hygiene Harvard, 1917-23; prof. and head dept. bacteriology and immunology Washington U., 1928-52, ret. Recipient Pasteur award of Ill. Bacteriologists, 1950. Fellow Am. Pub. Health Assn., A.A.A.S., Am. Coll. Allergists; mem. Soc. Am. Bacteriologists, Am. Assn. Immunologists (pres. 1942-46), Soc. Exptl. Biol. and Medicine, Am. Soc. Exptl. Pathology, Mo. Tb Assn., Harvey Soc. Mem. editorial bd. Jour. of Immunology. Contbr. articles to sci. jours. Home: 5354 Delmar Blvd., St. Louis. Died Aug. 13, 1953.

BRONK, Mitchell, clergyman, writer; b. Manchester, N.Y., Nov. 24, 1862; s. Abram and Cynthia (Brewster) B.; A.B., U. Rochester, 1886, D.D., 1913; studied Union Theol. Sem., 1887-89, univs. Leipzig, Jena, Berlin, Geneva, 1889-91; grad. Crozer Theol. Sem., 1892; A.M., N.Y.U., 1896; m. Marie Wulf, Oct. 15, 1896 (dec.); children—Detlev Wulf, Isabelle. Ordained to Bapt. ministry, 1893; pastor Ascension Ch., N.Y.C., 1893-1900, First Ch., Bayonne, N.J., 1900-1 , Second Ch., Troy, N.Y., 1912-19, First Ch., Stoneham, Mass., 1919-24; editor adult Sunday sch publs. Am. Baptist Publ. Soc., 1924-39, book editor, 1931-40. Mem. Am. Acad. Polit. and Social Science, Soc. Bibl. Lit. and Exegesis, Am. Oriental Soc., Soc. Mayflower Descs., S.A.R., Delta Kappa Epsilon. Mason. Author: Pillars of Gold, 1926; John Bunyan, the Man and the Writer, 1928; Light in the Valley, 1932; Zechariah, in the American Commentary Series, 1935; Manchester Boys, 1937; Discovering My Forty-niner Father, 1943. Contbr. articles, short stories, transls. to newspapers and mags. Home: 6325 Ross St., Germantown, Phila. 44. Died Oct. 31, 1950; buried Phila.

BRONSON, Bennet, mfr.; b. Waterbury, Conn., Dec. 3, 1887; s. J. Hobart and Edith H. (Terry) B.; student Taft Sch., 1899-1904; A.B., Yale, 1909; m. Eleanor C. Lindley, Jan. 20, 1916; children—Lindley (killed in action, Germany, 1945), David Bennet, Edith Terry (Mrs. Edith de Chadenedes). Asso. with Oakville Co., mfrs. metal goods, Waterbury, Conn., since 1909, successively asst. treas., vice pres., pres. and treas.; vice pres. and dir. Scovill Mfg. Co., Waterbury, Conn., since 1923; dir. Colonial Trust Co., Waterbury Savings Bank. Chmn. Naugatuck Valley Indsl. Council. Served as capt., Q.M. Res. Corps, U.S. Army, 1917-19; col. Q.M. Res. Corps, 1942-45. Home: 29 Cliff St. Office: Scovill Mfg. Co., Waterbury, Conn. Died Nov. 23, 1950.

BRONSON, Thomas Bertrand, educator; b. Wyoming, Ia., Dec. 7, 1857; s. Bushnell Knapp and Martha Amelia (Stowe) B.; A.B., U. of Mich., 1881, A.M., 1886, hon. A.M., 1931; studied at U. of Berlin, and at Paris and Rome, 1883, 86, 87, 92, 1900, 11; m. Isabel Harris, 1886 (died 1927); children—Winifred M., Bertrand H.; m. 2d, Louise F. Hazzard, 1931. Teaching since 1876; prof. Michigan Military Academy, 1881-92; head modern language department, Lawrenceville (N.J.) Sch., 1892-1922, asst. headmaster, 1922-28, emeritus since 1928. Established at University of Michigan, annual prize in German, in memory of Professor Calvin Thomas. Mem. Modern Languages Conf. (Washington, 1892), apptd. by "Com. of 10"; mem. N.Y. Conf. Uniform Entrance Requirements Entrance Exam. Bd., 1901-02-03. Mem. Modern Lang. Assn. America (since orgn., 1883). Modern Lang. Assn., Middle States, Md. (exec. council), Beta Theta Pi, Phi Beta Kappa. Rep. Presbyn. Club: Authors' (London). Author: Colloquial German, 1891, and Key, 1891; Everyday French, 1894, Key, 1894. Editor: German Prose and Poetry, 1895; Stories by Grimm, Andersen and Hauff, 1895; Hauff's Karawane, 1895; Coppée's on Rend L'Argent, 1896; Hugo's Scènes de Voyages, 1899; Freytag's Die Journalisten, 1901; Hugo's Sur les Bords du Rhin, 1902. Contbr. to ednl. jours. Address: 2535 Ridge Road, Berkeley 9, Cal. Died Dec. 1, 1948.

BROOKER, John William, education; b. Newport, Ky., May 23, 1899; s. John Robert and Laura (Evans) B.; B.S., Georgetown (Ky.) Coll., 1922, LL.D., 1940; M.A., U. of Mich., 1929; m. Hazel Sherritt, June 21, 1923; 1 dau., Betty Jane. Teacher rural school, Bracken County, Ky., 1917-18; prin. Georgetown (Ky.) High Sch., 1922-23; supt. schs., Cynthiana, Ky., 1923-29; Ky. State dir. school buildings and grounds, 1930-40; Ky. State supt. pub. instrn., 1940-44; dir. pub. relations Ky. Edn. Assn., 1944-48, exec. sec.-treas. since 1948. Mem. Phi Delta Kappa. Home: 2022 Grasmere Dr., Louisville 5. Office: Heyburn Bldg., Louisville 2. Died Aug. 17, 1952; buried Resthaven, Meml. Cemetery, Louisville.

BROOKINGS, Walter DuBois, lumberman; b. Keokuk, Ia., Feb. 28, 1873; s. John Emory and Emma (DuBois) B.; A.B., Harvard, 1895; LL.B., 1898; m. Marian Kinney, Nov. 19, 1909 (died June 3, 1926); children—Robert Somers, Walter DuBois, Henry Nason K., Mary McIntosh; m. 2d, Martha Nutting Brooks, Aug. 27, 1929. Sec. and treas. Brookings Lumber & Box Co., Highland, Calif., 1899-1912, Brookings (Ore.) Timber & Lumber Co., 1912-17, Brookings (Ore.) Land & Town Site Co., 1912-17; v.p. Brookings Commercial Co., 1915-17; investigated pulpwood and forest resources, and paper bag industry in France, Great Britain, Germany and Can., for Union Bag & Paper Corp. of New York City, 1919-20; sec., Miss. Flood Control Com., Nat. Water Power Development Com. Captain, Co. E, 2d Batt., 20th Engrs., A.E.F., Oct. 1917-July 1918; in charge securing timber-lands in the Vosges to supply Am. armies in Eastern France with lumber and timber; maj. 1st Batt., 20th Engrs., July 1918-Feb. 1919; in charge six lumbering operations near Pyrenees. As rep. of Herbert Hoover, took first shipload relief food to Baltic region, landing at Libau, Latvia, Mar. 1919, and remained there until Aug. 1919. Citation A.E.F. "for exceptionally meritorious service"; silver medal (Polish). Mem. Pi Eta, Gamma Delta Psi. Clubs: Cosmos, Harvard, Army and Navy Country (Washington, D.C.). Author: Briefs for Debate (Brookings and Ringwalt), 1896; also numerous articles on problems of natural resources industries. Home: Seminary Hill, Alexandria, Va. Died July 23, 1950.

BROOKINS, Homer De Wilton, editor; b. South Dansville, N.Y., Apr. 27, 1855; s. Thomas Warner and Caroline (Kelley) B.; student Rogersville Union Sem., South Dansville, 1871-75; B.S., U. Rochester, 1880, A.M., 1913; Litt.D., Bucknell U., 1922. Sec. to John H. Deane, N.Y.C., 1880-84; sec. Manhattan Constrn. Co., 1884-87; business mgr. Christian Inquirer (laster The Examiner, now Watchman-Examiner), 1888-95, mem. editorial staff, 1895-1912, asso. and office editor, 1921-35, resigned; asst. treas. Watchman-Examiner Foundation. Mem. Theta Delta Chi. Democrat. Baptist. Home: Bernardsville, N.J. Office: 23 E. 26th St., N.Y.C. Died Apr. 3, 1938; buried Evergreen Cemetery, Basking Ridge, N.J.

BROOKS, Allerton Frank, public utilities; b. Meriden, Conn., Apr. 12, 1890; s. Frank Smith and Alma Alfreda (Miller) B.; Ph.B., Sheffield Scientific Sch., Yale, 1911; m. Mary Ernest Randall, Oct. 1, 1919. Began in engring. dept. Southern New Eng. Telephone Co., New Haven, Conn., 1911, chief engr., 1927-30, v.p. and gen. mgr., 1930-41, now chmn. of bd.; dir. First Nat. Bank & Trust Co., Security Ins. Co., Phoenix Mutual Life Ins. Co., New Haven Savings Bank, Connecticut Public Expenditure Council. Episcopalian. Home: 1191 Ridge Rd., Hamden 14, Conn. Office: 227 Church St., New Haven 6, Conn. Died April 12, 1955.

BROOKS, Arbie Leroy, physician and surgeon; b. Sparta, Wis., Dec. 6, 1889; s. L. A. and Harriet Esther (Campbell) B.; B.S., U. of Wis., 1924; M.D., U. of Colo., 1928; m. Irene Mary Groth, June 7, 1923; children—Robert, Carmen (Mrs. Wayne Taysom), Fern (Mrs. G. C. Heeren), Betty. Intern Henry Ford Hosp., Detroit, 1928-29; teacher in P.I., 1924-26; med. dir. Fisher Body Div. of Gen. Motors, 1929—; mem. staff Pontiac Gen. Hosp. Fellow A. M.A., Am. Assn. Indsl. Physicians and Surgeons; mem. Mich. Med. Soc., Mich. Assn. Indsl. Physicians and Surgeons, Mich., Am. Indsl. hygiene assns., Phi Chi. Club: Industrial Physicians (Detroit). Author articles on profl. subjects. Home: 3720 Erie Dr., Pontiac, Mich.; R. 5, Cass Lake. Office: Fisher Body

Div. of Gen. Motors, 900 Baldwin Av., Pontiac, Mich. Died July 12, 1951.

BROOKS, Charles F., meteorologist; b. St. Paul, Minn., May 2, 1891; s. Morgan and Frona Marie (Brooks) B.; student U. of Ill., 1907-08; A.B., Harvard, 1911, as of 1912, A.M., 1912, Ph.D., 1914; m. Eleanor Merritt Stabler, June 4, 1914; children—Edward Morgan, Margaret, Sylvia, Barbara, Edith Herrick, Norman Herrick, Frona. Research assistant, Blue Hill Observatory, 1912-13; assistant in meteorology and physiography, Harvard, 1913-14; assistant physiography, Radcliffe College, 1914; assistant and collaborator in farm management U.S. Dept. Agr., 1914-18; instr. geography, Yale, 1915-18; instr. meteorology, U.S. Signal Corps Sch. of Meteorology, College St., Tex., World War, May-Nov. 1918; meteorologist U.S. Weather Bur., editing Mo. Weather Review, 1918-21; asso. prof. meteorology and climatology, 1921-26, prof., 1926-32, Clark U., also instr. summers; prof. meteorology and dir., Blue Hill Obs., Harvard, 1931-57, professor of meteorology emeritus, 1957—; visiting prof. University of Chicago, summer, 1939; visiting lecturer, Clark U., summer 1941, U.S. Weather Bur., 1943-44. Meteorologist Cons. for U.S. Weather Bureau, 1948. Expert Climatic Research Div., Q.M. Corps, War Dept.; cons. Nat. Defense Research Com. Pres. Mt. Washington Obs. Mem. internat. commns., Climatol., 1931-45, Snow and Glaciers, 1936-48, Instruments and Methods of Observation 1947-51 (pres. sub-committee on station instruments and methods 1947-53), Clouds and Hydrometeors 1947-53. Fellow A.A.A.S., Royal Meteorol. Society, Am. Geog. Soc.; asso. fellow Inst. Aeronaut. Sciences; mem. Am. Acad. Arts and Sciences, Am. Meteorol. Soc. (organizer, editor 1919-25, 27-36, 39; sec. 1919-54, hon. sec. 1954—), Assn. Am. Geographers (pres. 1947), Am. Geophys. Union (chairman meteorological section 1935-38), Phi Beta Kappa, Sigma Xi. Author: "Why the Weather?" Joint author: Climatology of N. Am. and West Indies (part of a 5 vol. series); Climatic Maps of North America; Eclipse Meteorology; Science from Shipboard; International Cloud Atlas. Home: 1793 Canton Av., Milton 86, Mass. Died Jan. 8, 1958.

BROOKS, C(harles) Wayland, ex-U.S. senator, Rep. nat. committeeman; b. West Bureau Co., Ill., Mar. 8, 1897; s. Rev. Jonas Gardner and Ida Nora (Bickford) B.; prep. edn. Wheaton Coll. Acad.; student U. Ill. until Apr. 1917 (leaving to enlist for war); student law dept., U. Chgo., 1922-23; LL.B., Northwestern U., 1926; m. Gertrude Ackerly, Aug. 26, 1920; 1 son, Russell Ackerly; m. 2d, Mary Thomas Peavey, May 8, 1946; stepchildren—John, Betty Anne. Admitted to Ill. bar, 1926, practiced in Chicago; instr. Ill. law, Northwestern U. Law Sch. Candidate for Congressman at large from Ill., 1934; Rep. nominee for gov. of Ill., at primary election, Apr. 1936; elected U.S. senator to fill unexpired term of late Sen. J. Hamilton Lewis, Nov. 1939; re-elected for full 6 year term, Nov. 3, 1942. Now Rep. nat. committeeman from Illinois. Served with U.S. Marines during World War I; promoted on the field from cpl. to 2d lt. and later promoted 1st lt., wounded 7 times; retired from Army service at age of 21. Awarded D.S.C. (U.S. Army), D.S.C. (U.S. N.); Croix de Guerre (France). Mem. Am., Illinois state, Chicago bar associations, American Legion, Forty and Eight, Purple Heart Association, Army and Navy Legion of Valor, Phi Delta Phi, Delta Sigma Phi. Presbyterian. Mason. Home: 3240 Lake Shore Dr. Office: First National Bank Bldg., Chgo. Died Jan. 14, 1957.

BROOKS, Edward Schroeder, ex-congressman; b. York, Pa., June 14, 1867; s. John H. and Mary A. (Schroeder) B.; student York County Acad., York Collegiate Inst.; m. Emma J. Eimerbrink, 1890; children—Karl S., Mary M. Banker, mfr. steel forgings, and contractors; mem. 66th and 67th Congresses, 20th Pa. Dist.; postmaster of York, 1925-34. Mem. City Council, York, 3 terms; treas. York County, 1903-06. Mem. Rep. State Com., Pa., 1917-18. Life mem. York County Agrl. Soc.; mem. Sons of Vets. Lutheran. Mason, K.P. Home: York, Pa. Died July 12, 1957; buried Prospect Hill Cemetery, York.

BROOKS, Harry Sayer, newspaperman; b. Waverly, N.Y., Aug. 2, 1852; grad. Elmira Free Acad., 1869; learned printing in office Elmira Gazette, becoming one of its editors; founded Telegram 1879, with two partners, whose interests he later bought. Address: Elmira, N.Y. Died 1924.

BROOKS, Joseph Hudson, lawyer; b. Salem, O., Nov. 23, 1845; s. Joseph J. and Judith T. B.; A.B., Yale, 1867; LL.B., Harvard, 1869; m. Henrietta Faber, Sept. 2, 1869. Admitted to bar, 1870; asst. counsel Pa. Lines west of Pitts., 1881-93, gen. counsel, 1893-14. Address: Union Station Pitts. Died Apr. 10, 1914.

BROOKS, Mary Willard (Mrs. Bryant Butler Brooks), b. Washington Court House, O., June 10, 1864; d. Judge Lockhart Dickman and Olive Hester (Clark) Willard; grad. normal dept. Riverside Inst., Lyons, Ia.; m. Bryant Butler Brooks, Mar. 11, 1886; children—Jean Willard (Mrs. Homer Riale Lathrop), Abby Burroughs (Mrs. Russell Henry Nichols), Lena Natrona (Mrs. Marion W. McCleary), Mary Melissa (Mrs. Arthur Leroy Spurlock), Silas Newton. Trustee U. Wyo., 1908-18; mem. Rep. Nat. Com., 1928-37. Mem. D.A.R. Episcopalian. Mem. O.E.S. Clubs: Woman's, Departmental. Home: 1208 S. Wolcott St., Casper, Wyo. Deceased.

BROOKS, Paul David, pub. utilities exec.; b. Knoxville, Tenn., Dec. 6, 1904; s. William Washington and Mary Elizabeth (Atchley) B.; B.S., U. Tenn., 1929; m. Lillie Mary Ray, Sept. 2, 1926; 1 dau., Myra Lou. Mgr., dir. Tenn. Public Service Co., 1933-36, gen. sales mgr., 1936-38; mgr. sales and marketing dept. Ebasco Services, Inc., 1950-53; v.p., dir. Am. Gas & Electric Service Corp., 1954—. Appalachian Electric Power Co., Kingsport Utilities, Inc., Ohio Power Co., Wheeling Electric Co.; v.p. Ind. & Mich. Electric Co., Ky. Power Co. Mem. Edison Electric Inst. N.Y. Presbyn. Club: N.Y. Sales Executives. Home: 136 Highwood Av., Tenafly, N.J. Office: 30 Church St., N.Y.C. 8. Died Oct. 23, 1958.

BROOKS, Robert Nathaniel, bishop; b. Hollis, N.C., May 8, 1888; s. John and Louvenia (Schanck) B.; A.B., Bennett Coll., Greensboro, N.C., 1911; B.D., Gammon Theol. Sem., 1914, D.D., 1925; A.M., Garrett Bibl. Inst., Northwestern U., Evanston, Ill., 1918; student Union Theol. Sem., New York, N.Y., 1925-26, Oxford U. (Eng.), 1931-32; Litt.D., Wiley Coll., Marshall, Tex., 1943; LL.D., Rust Coll., Holly Springs, Miss., 1945; m. Edith Crogman, Sept. 3, 1919. Ordained to ministry, North Carolina Conf., Methodist Episcopal Ch., 1915; sec., bd. of Sunday Schools, Meth. Episcopal Ch., 1918-20; pres. Haven Teachers Coll., Meridian, Miss., 1920-21, Central Alabama Coll., Birmingham, Ala., 1921-22, Samuel Huston Coll., Austin, Tex., 1922-26; prof. church history, Gammon Theol. Sem., Atlanta, Ga., 1926-36; editor, The Central Christian Advocate, New Orleans, La., 1936-44; bishop, Methodist Ch., since 1944. Pres. bd. trustees, Rust Coll., since 1944; Wiley Coll., since 1944, Samuel Huston Coll., since 1944; v.p. bd. trustees Dillard U., since 1945, Bennett Coll., since 1944; mem. bd. edn. Meth. Ch. since 1944 (chmn. com. on Negro edn.); mem. bd. missions and ch. extension, Meth. Ch.; chmn. com. on treasurer's report; mem. Com. Nineteen, Meth. Ch.; pres. College Bishops of Central Jurisdiction, Meth. Ch. Mem. bd. Lay Activities, Meth. Ch.; pres. Meth. Fedn. for Social Action, 1947-49. Elected by Council of Bishops Meth. Ch. to review and appraise Meth. work on continent of Africa, Apr.-Sept. 1947; S. America, June-Sept., auspices Bd. Fgn. Missions, Meth. Ch. Home: 219 South Miro St., New Orleans 19. Office: 631 Baronne St., New Orleans 12. Died Aug. 2, 1953; buried Gulfside Assembly Grounds, Waveland, Miss.

BROOKS, Rodney Joseph, insurance; b. Baltimore, Md., Mar. 4, 1895; s. Joseph White and Flora Isabel (Crouch) B.; student Baltimore Polytech. Inst.; m. Mary Agnes Rodgers, Jan. 16, 1919; children—Rodney Joseph, Frances Rodgers, John Hock, Frank Crouch, Harvey Stone, William Gill, Mary Rodney. Bookkeeper in banking house, then bookkeeper, salesman and mem. firm in ins. agency and brokerage business sr. mem. Tongue, Brooks & Company ins. agents and brokers, Baltimore, since 1920; dir. Fidelity & Deposit Co. of Md.; dir., mem. investment com., Eutaw Savings Bank, dir. Arundel Corp.; dir., mem. exec. com., Finance Co. of Am. Served inf., U. S.A., Apr.-Nov., 1918. Trustee Good Samaritan Hosp., Johns Hopkins U.; pres. St. Vincent de Paul Soc. Democrat. Roman Catholic. K.C. Clubs: Baltimore Country, Maryland, Elkridge (Baltimore, Md.). Home: 920 W. Lake Av. Office: 213 St. Paul Pl., Balt. Died Feb. 23, 1952.

BROOKS, Summer Cushing, biologist; b. Sapporo, Japan, Aug. 17, 1888; s. William Penn and Eva Bancroft (Hall) B.; came to U.S., 1888, citizen by birth; B.S., Univ. of Mass., 1910; Ph.D., Harvard, 1916; m. Matilda Neuffer Moldenhauer, July 14, 1917. Asst. in botany, Mass. Agrl. Expt. Sta., Amherst, Mass., 1910-11; bio-chemist, Research Inst. Nat. Dental Assn., Cleveland, 1916-17; Hanna research fellow, pathology, Western Reserve U., 1917; research fellow tropical medicine, Harvard, 1917-19; asso. prof. physiology and biochemistry, Bryn Mawr Coll., 1919-20; biologist, hygienic lab., U.S. Pub. Health Service, Washington, 1920-26; prof. of physiology Rutgers Univ., 1926-27; prof. of zoology Univ. of Calif. at Berkeley, since 1927. Trustee Marine Biol. Lab., Woods Hole, Mass. Mem. A.A.A.S., Am. Bot. Soc., Am. Physiol. Soc., Am. Chem. Soc., Soc. Exptl. Biol. Medicine, Western Soc. Naturalists (pres. 1933), Phi Beta Kappa, Sigma Xi, Phi Kappa Phi, Phi Sigma Kappa. Club: Cooper Ornithol. (pres. Northern Sect., 1946-48). Author: Permeability of Living Cells (with Matilda M. Brooks), 1941. Contbr. numerous articles to sci. periodicals. Home: 630 Woodmont Av., Berkeley 8, Cal. Died Apr. 23, 1948; buried Woods Hole, Mass.

BROOKS, Walter Rollin, writer; b. Rome, N.Y., Jan. 9, 1886; s. William Walter and Fannie (Stevens) B.; student U. Rochester, 1904-06, N.Y. Homeopathic Med. Coll., N.Y.C., 1906-08; m. Anne Shepard, Jan. 22, 1909 (dec.); m. 2d, Dorothy Carman Collins, Jan. 6, 1953. Asso. editor Outlook, 1928-32; mem. editorial staff New Yorker, 1933, Fiction Parade, 1933-37. Mem. Delta Kappa Epsilon. Author: To and Again, 1927; More To and Again, 1930; Freddy the Detective, 1932; The Story of Freginald, 1936; The Clockwork Twin, 1937; Wiggins for President, 1939; Freddy's Cousin Weedly, 1940; Freddy and the Ignormus, 1941; Freddy and the Perilous Adventure, 1942; Freddy and the Bean Home News, 1943; Freddy and Mr. Camphor, 1944; Freddy and the Popinjay, 1945; Freddy the Pied Piper, 1946 (children's books); Freddy the Magician, 1947; Freddy Goes Camping, 1948; Freddy Plays Football, 1949; Freddy the Cowboy, 1950; Freddy Rides Again, 1951; Freddy the Pilot, 1952; Freddy and the Space Ship, Collected Poems of Freddy the Pig, 1953; Freddy and the Man from Mars, 1954; Freddy and the Basketball Team from Mars, 1955; Freddy and Simon the Dictator, 1956; Freddy and the Flying Saucer Plans, 1957; Freddy and the Dragon, 1958; New York—An Intimate Guide, 1931; Ernestine Takes Over, 1935. Contbr. fiction to mags. Home: Roxbury, Delaware Co., N.Y. Died Aug. 17, 1958.

BROOME, Edwin Cornelius (broom), lawyer, retired educator; b. Central Falls, R.I., Oct. 5, 1874; s. Robert and Margaret (Monkhouse) B.; Ph.B., Brown U., 1897, A.M., 1898, Ed.D., 1927; Ph D Columbia, 1902; Drs. Diploma in Edn., Tchrs. Coll. Columbia, 1902; LL.B., St. Lawrence U., 1907; LL.D., Ursinus Coll., 1925, Juniata Coll., 1934; L.H.D., U. Pa., 1934; Litt.D., R.I. Coll. Edn., 1930; Sc.D., Temple U., 1937; m Grace Wells Rhoads, June 1, 1909; children—Edwin Cornelius, John Rhoads. Tchr. High Sch., Pawtucket, R.I., 1897-98; prin. high sch., Seymour, Conn., 1898-1900; fellow Tchrs. Coll. Columbia, 1900; supt. schs., Rahway, N.J., 1902-06; instr. Adelphi Coll. and supt. elementary dept. Adelphi Acad., 1906-09; lectr. Bklyn. Inst. and for Bklyn. Tchrs. Assn., 1908-09; supt. schs., Mt. Vernon, N.Y., 1909-13, East Orange, N.J., 1913-21, Phila., 1921-38, supt. emeritus, 1938—; lectr. Temple U., 1938-42. Lecturer under N.Y. Bd. Edn., 1902-13; on sch. adminstrn. U. Wis., summer, 1916, Ohio State U., summer 1920. Gen. supr. field work Army Ednl. Corps, AEF, 1918-19. Mem. Nat. Com. on C.M.T.C., 1922; participated in survey N.Y.C. schs., 1924-25; mem. White House Conf. on Child Health and Protection, 1930; dir. Personnel Procurement, U.S.O.-YMCA, 1943. Mem. N.E. A., (chmn. commn. on curriculum dept. of superintendence 1926-29; pres. dept. of superintendence 1931-32), N.Y. State Council of Sch. Supts. (pres. 1912), Pa. State Ednl. Assn. (chmn. tchrs. welfare com. 1929—), Alumni of Tchrs. Coll. (pres. 1915-17), Phi Delta Phi, Phi Delta Kappa, Phi Beta Kappa. Alumni trustee Teachers Coll., 1924-26; bd. dirs. Germantown Symphony Orchestra; mem. Phila. Com. on Public Affairs; mem. Daniel Boone Homestead Commn. Mason. Presbyn. Author: A Historical and Critical Discussion of College Admission Requirements, 1903; Conduct and Citizenship (with Edwin Adams), 1926; Health and Happiness Series (with Dr. S. Weir Newmayer), 1928; Our Democracy (with Edwin W. Adams), 1939. Awarded medal Columbia U. for distinguished service in eudcation, 1932; Good Citizenship medal S.A.R., 1934. Home: 217 E. Sedgwick St., Mt. Airy, Phila. 19. Died Apr. 17, 1950; buried Ivy Hill Cemetery, Phila.

BROPHY, C. Gerald, lawyer; b. Altoona, Pa., Jan. 13, 1898; s. B., Augustine and Anna Marie (Gallagher) B.; A.B., St. Joseph's Coll., Philadelphia, Pa. 1920; A.M., 1922; LL.B., Duquesne U., 1923; m. Alta Fye, June 18, 1931. Admitted to Pa. bar, 1923. Dean, Duquesne U. Sch. of Law since 1940. Mem. Allegheny County, Pa. and Am. bar assns. Home: 200 Fifth Av., Carnegie, Pa. Address: 331 Fourth Av., Pitts. 22. Died Jan. 4, 1956.

BROSMAN, Paul William (brōs'mȧn), judge b. Albion, Illinois, Nov. 9, 1899; s. William Henry and Lida (Leavitt) B.; LL.B., from University of Illinois, 1924; A.B., Indiana University, 1926; J.S.D., Yale University, 1929; m. Katherine Elizabeth Lewis, Aug. 21, 1925; 1 son, Paul William. Mem. of Ill. and La. bars. Instr. business law, Ind. U. Sch. of Commerce and Finance, 1924-25, asst. prof., 1925-26; prof. law, Mercer U., Macon, Ga., 1926-28; Sterling fellow in law, Yale, 1928-29; prof. law, Tulane U., New Orleans, since 1929, W. R. Irby prof. of law 1938-51, asst. dean, 1932-37, dean, 1937-52, prof. of law (on leave of absence) since 1951; mem. summer faculty, various law schs.; now judge U.S. Ct. of Mil. Appeals, Washington. Mem. La. Supreme Ct. Adv. Com. on Integration of Bar, 1940-41; mem. La. Civil Service Commn., 1947-48; mem. Nat. Conf. of Commrs. on Uniform State Laws from La. Served as pvt., S.A.T.C., in United States Army, 1918; served with U.S. Army Air Corps, 1942-45; discharged with rank of lt. col.; now col., Judge Adv. Gen.'s Dept., U.S.A.F. Reserve, Awarded Legion of Merit. Mem. Am. (mem. council sect. legal edn. and admission to bar), La. State (ex-mem. bd. govs.), and New Orleans bar assns., Association American Law Schools, Judge Advocates Assn., American Judicature Society American Law Inst., La. State Law Inst., Am. Acad. Political and Social Science, Order of Coif, Phi Kappa Tau, Phi Alpha Delta, Beta Gamma Sigma, Delta Sigma Rho, Alpha Alpha Alpha, Omicron Delta Kappa. Democrat. Episcopalian. Mason. Clubs: Round Table, Recess, Boston, New Orleans Country (New Orleans); Army and Navy (Washington). Home: 5609 McLean Dr., Bethesda, Md.; also 1776 State St., New Orleans. Office: U.S. Court of Military Appeals Bldg., Washington 25. Died Dec. 21, 1955.

BROUGHTON, Charles Elmer (brou'tŏn), radio exec.; b. Lamartine, Fond du Lac County, Wis., Oct. 22, 1873; s. John and Emma (Cortleyou) B.; ed. pub. and night schs.; m. Emma Born, June 23, 1898; 1 son, Charles Elmer (dec.). Began as apprentice with Fond du Lac Journal, 1884; editorial and free lance writer, 1898-1903; editor and pub. Sheboygan (Wis.) Press, 1907-51, editor emeritus, 1951; exec. v.p., dir. radio sta. WHBL, Inc., 1952, pres. 1953-56, ret.; chmn. bd. Fed. Home Loan Bank, Chgo., 1938-50; Mem. Democratic National Committee, 1932-41; Democratic National Convention, Chicago, 1932; vice chmn. Dem. Nat. Com., Phila., 1936. State chmn. Wis. Defense Savs. Com., 1941; mem. Gov.'s Com. for St. Lawrence Seaway, 1952-53. Appointed col. on staff, gov. of Wis., 1933. Awarded Distinguished Service medal by Salvation Army, 1942. Founder Sheboygan Community Fund, Broughton Conservation award. Dir. Izaak Walton League of Am., Sheboygan Y.M.C.A. (v.p.), Salvation Army. Mason, Odd Fellow, K.P., Elk (pres. Wis. Elks Assn., 1929; hon. founder Elks Nat. Found. 1929; grand esteemed leading knight; chmn. bd. grand trustees, 1945; grand exalted ruler, 1946-47); hon. mem. Sigma Delta Chi. Clubs: Milwaukee Press, Milwaukee Athletic; Nat. Press (Washington, D.C. Home: 315 Erie Av. Office: Foeste Hotel, Sheboygan, Wis. Died Oct. 31, 1956.

BROUGHTON, William S.; b. in Wis., 1874; s. Russell (M.D.) and Julia A. (Smiley) B.; Ph.B., U. of Chicago, 1899; LL.B., George Washington U., 1900. Commr. of Public Debt, Treasury Dept., Washington, D.C., 1919-45; now retired. Member Delta Kappa Epsilon, Phi Delta Phi. Clubs: Sulgrave (asso.), Chevy Chase (Washington). Address: 1819 Q St., Washington 9. Died Jan. 9, 1951; buried Greenwood Cemetery, Brodhead, Wis.

BROWN, A. Luther, textile mfg. exec.; pres., dir. China Grove Cotton Mills; v.p., dir. Cannon Mills Co.; dir. Wiscassett Mills Co. (Albemarle, N.C.), Cabarrus Bank & Trust Co. (Kannapolis, N.C.). Office: Kannapolis, N.C. Died 1955.*

BROWN, Archibald Manning, architect; b. N.Y.C., May 23, 1881; s. Charles Steele and Lucy Nevins (Barnes) B.; grad. Groton Sch., 1899; A.B., Harvard, 1903; diploma Ecole des Beaux Arts, Paris, 1910; m. Helen Parrish, 1903 (died 1932); children—Helen Manning (Mrs. Washington Dodge), Lucy Manning (Mrs. Herbert Barry, Jr.), Archibald Manning, Hope (Mrs. Franklin Olmstead Canfield), Robert Peabody; m. 2d, Eleanor Stockstrom, 1934. Architect, 1911—; mem. firm Peabody, Wilson & Brown, 1911-35; sr. partner Brown, Lawford & Forbes, 1946—; chief architect Harlem River Houses, 1936, Elliott Houses, 1947; architect Children's Museum (part of Brooklyn Mus.), President's House at Dartmouth Coll., residences for Roland Harriman, Adm. Grayson and others. Served as ensign, Class 5 (aviation), USNRF, World War I. Architect mem. Art Commns. of N.Y.C., 3 terms. Former pres. Arcthl. League of N.Y., Art Commn. Assos. Mem. adv. bd. Parsons Sch. of Fine and Applied Arts, New York and Paris. Fellow A.I.A.; mem. N.A.D. Democrat. Episcopalian. Clubs: Racquet and Tennis (past mem. bd. mgrs.) (N.Y.C.); Shinnecock Hills (L.I.) Golf (past pres.); National Golf Links (Southampton, L.I.). Home: 447 E. 57th St. Office: 224 E. 46th St., N.Y.C. 17.*

BROWN, Arthur, Jr., architect; b. Oakland, Cal., May 21, 1874; s. Arthur and Victoria Adelaide (Runton) B.; B.S. in C.E., U. Cal., 1896, LL.D., 1931; grad. Ecole des Beaux Arts, Paris, France, 1901; mem. Inst. de France; m. Jessamine Garrett; children—Victoria, Sylvia. Formerly mem. firm Bakewell & Brown, architects of city halls at San Francisco, Berkeley and Pasadena, Hort. Bldg., Panama-Pacific Internat. Expn., Library Stanford U., etc.; asso. architect Panama-Pacific Internat. Expn. Co., 1912-15; lectr. architecture Harvard, 1918; acting prof. architecture U. Cal., 1918-19; mem. ba. archtl. cons. Treasury Dept., Washington; architect, Dept. of Labor Bldg., Interstate Commerce Bldg., Fed. Office Bldg., Adminstrn. Bldg., U. Cal.; mem. archtl. com. Century of Progress Expn., Chgo., 1933; mem. Archtl. Commn. San Francisco-Oakland Bay Bridge, Comité Permanent International des Architects, Am. Inst. Arts and Letters; chmn. archtl. bd. Golden Gate Internat. Expn., 1939; supervising architect Berkeley Campus, U. Cal.; designed four bldgs. San Francisco Civic Center; cons. to the architect U.S. Capitol, Washington, 1956, 57. Mem. jury for competition for Corregidor-Baton Meml. Monument, 1957. Recipient award of achievement Bldg. Industry Conf. Bd., 1955. Fellow A.I.A.; mem. Societe des Architects Diplomes par le Gouvernement, Am. Acad. Arts and Letters, Nat. Acad. of Design, de l'Academie d'Aix en Provense, Beta Theta Pi, Officer Legion d'Honneur. Clubs: Pacific Union, Bohemian, Burlingame, Faculty (Berkeley); Century (N.Y.C.). Home: Le Verger, 808 Irwin Dr., Burlingame, Cal. Office: 251 Kearny St., San Francisco 8. Died July 7, 1957.

BROWN, Arthur Morton, lawyer; b. Jewett City, Conn., Sept. 24, 1877; s. George Washington and Sarah Frances (Young) B.; student Norwich Free Acad., 1891-94; m. Gertrude E. Sanderson, Oct. 1, 1901; children—Francis Young, Morton Trowbridge. Admitted to Conn. bar, 1901; asso. Solomon Lucas, 1901-06; practiced independently, 1906-15; mem. Brown & James, Norwich, Conn., 1915—; pres. Jewett City Savings Bank; vice chmn. adv. bd. The Hartford-Conn. Trust Co., Thames Branch; v.p. Chelsea Savings Bank; pres. New London Northern R.R.; County Mutual Fire Ins. Co. Served as clerk and treas. Jewett City, 1900; rep. in Conn. Gen. Assembly, 1901-03; rep. in Conn. Constitutional Conv., 1902; mem. state senate, 1903-05; warden of Jewett City, 1914-16; treas. New London County, 1901-24; pros. atty. Town of Griswold, 1903-15; judge of Griswold Town Court, 1915-23; state's atty. New London County 1924-47; mem. Judicial Council of State of Conn., retired. Rep. candidate for gov. Conn., 1936. Mem. Am., Conn. (pres. 1928) bar assns., Eastern Conn. Business Assn., Inc. (Norwich, Conn.). Republican. Baptist. Mason (33°; grand master of Conn., 1923; dep. for Conn. of the Supreme Council, Sovereign Grand Inspectors Gen. of the 33°, Scottish Rite). Clubs: Thames (New London); Arcanum, Commerce Incorporated (Norwich). Home: 51 N. Main St., Jewett City, Conn. Office: 303 Thayer Bldg., Norwich, Conn. Died June 12, 1949; buried Jewett City Cemetery.

BROWN, Arthur Winton, army officer; b. Davenport, Ia., Nov. 9, 1873; s. Samuel Edward and Mary Louise (Davis) B.; ed. pub. schs. Davenport and Hempstead, N.Y.; LL.B., Cornell U., 1897; m. Jessie M. Emery, June 23, 1908; 1 son, Winton. Private, corpl., sergt. Battery A, Utah Arty., May 1898-Aug. 1899; apptd. 2d lt. U.S. Army, Dec. 1899; advanced through grades to col., Dec. 25, 1927; lt. col. judge advocate, N.A. Aug. 5, 1917, col., May 31, 1919, hon. disch., Mar. 21, 1920; apptd. judge advocate gen. with rank of maj. gen., Nov. 30, 1933; retired, Nov. 30, 1937. On legal staff of Tacna-Arica Plebiscitary Commission (Peru-Chile), 1926-27, and of Nat. Board of Elections of Nicaragua (1928-29), American mem. League of Nations Commn. for Administration of the Territory of Leticia (Peru-Chile), 1933-34. Mem. Delta Chi. Episcopalian. Mason. Address: 2221 Bay St. N., St. Petersburg, Fla. Died Jan. 3, 1958; buried Arlington Nat. Cemetery.

BROWN, Baxter Lamont, cons. civil engr.; b. Rush, N.Y., June 20, 1864; s. James Douglas and Mary Ethloyne (Green) B.; student pub. schs., Bklyn.; m. Cora E. Cowgill, Feb. 26, 1889; children—Clarence Cowgill, Alice Mary and Lee Markham (twins), Porter Harris. Location, constrn. and maintenance engr. various rys. until 1901; chief engr. St. Louis Valley Ry., 1901-03; asst. engr. M.P. Ry., 1904; independent practice, St. Louis, 1905—; chief engr. St. Louis, Troy & Eastern R.R., 1907-28, East St. Louis, Columbia & Waterloo Ry., 1910-25; served as cons. engr. City Plan Commn. of St. Louis, Alton & Southern Ry., etc., sole arbitrator on controversies for Vandalia R.R., Frisco R.R., Terminal R.R. Assn. and Mo. Hwy. Dept.; cons. engr., spl. work for City Plan Commn. of Oklahoma City; cons. engr. valuation matters, Ill. Terminal Ry.; spl. service various rys.; engr. (with E. B. Fay) Chain of Rocks-Kingshighway Bridge Co.; pres. Bd. of Pub. Service of City of St. Louis, 1933-41; now cons. engr. Mem. assembly Am. Engring. Council, 1929, 30 and 31; mem. Am. Soc. C.E., Am., St. Louis insts. cons. engrs. Mason. Club: Engineers'. Home: 5660 Kingsbury Av. St. Louis 12. Deceased.

BROWN, Benjamin Henry Inness, lawyer; b. Charleston, S.C., Jan. 12, 1879; s. Benjamin Henry and Sallie (Inness) B.; A.B., Coll. Charleston, 1900; LL.B., Harvard, 1904. Began practice in N.Y. C., 1904; mem. Byrne & Cutcheon until 1918, Hornblower, Miller, Garrison & Potter, 1918-21; Kellogg, Emery, Inness-Brown & Cuthell, 1921-41; counsel to Satterlee & Warfield, 1941-49; retired; gen. counsel S.A.L. Ry., 1916-20; founder Nat. Assn. Owners Ry. Securities. Pres., editor in chief Harvard Law Rev., 1903-04. Mem. Bar Assn. City N.Y. Democrat. Unitarian. Clubs: Union, City Midday, Nat. Arts, Cruising Club of America. Home: 415 Riverside Dr. N.Y.C. 25. Died Feb. 1957.

BROWN, Bernard, dept. store exec.; b. Chicago, May 19, 1908; s. Mandel N. and Lena (Meyer) B.; B.S., Northwestern, 1931, J.D., 1933; m. Ruth Goldblatt, Aug. 26, 1934; children—Stanton Lee, Carol Rita. With Goldblatt Bros., Inc., retail dept. stores, Chicago, since 1935, v.p. since 1943, gen. counsel since 1940, dir. since 1944. Trustee U. of Chicago Cancer Research Found.; mem. adv. com. The Civic Fedn. Mem. Chicago Bar Assn. Home: 2432 N. Deere Park Dr., Highland Park, Ill. Office: 333 S. State St., Chgo. 4. Died Apr. 6, 1951.

BROWN, Caxton, mfr.; b. Brooklyn, N.Y., Mar. 13, 1879; s. Edwin H. and Eugenie M. (Konvalinka) B.; student Poly. Inst., 1892-94, Colombia U., 1896-1900; m. Mabel Josephine Nichols, Apr. 26, 1905; children—Nedra B. (Mrs. Churchill Langhorne), Elaine B. (Mrs. Harvey E. Molé, Jr.). With Weston Electrical Instrument Corp. since 1901, beginning as repairman, chairman, executive com. since 1947; director L. Bamberger & Co., Summit Trust Co. Pres. Union County Park Commn. Mem. Alpha Delta Phi. Republican. Episcopalian. Clubs: Baltusrol Golf (ex-pres.), Galloping Hill Golf (dir.), Pilgrims, Essex, Elec. Mfrs. (treas.). Home: 45 Lenox Rd., Summit, N.J. Office: 614 Frelingbuysen Av., Newark, 5. Died July 25, 1952.

BROWN, Cecil Kenneth, prof. economics; b. Salisbury, N.C., Oct. 24, 1900; s. Pleasant Marion and Caroline Amery (Shelton) B.; A.B., Davidson Coll., 1921, M.A., U. of N.C., 1923, Ph.D., 1927; m. Catherine May Mathews, Aug. 26, 1925 (died Apr. 30, 1927); m. 2d, Evelyn Hill, June 29, 1932; children—Cecil Kenneth, David Shelton, Henry Hill, Margaret Evelyn. Asst. prof. math., Davidson Coll., 1923-25, asso. prof. economics, 1926-29, prof. economics, 1929—, dean of the faculty 1941-53; research asst. Inst. for Research in Social Science, Univ. of N.C., 1925-26, research asso., 1929-30, visiting instr. in economics, summers of 1928, 29, 37, 52. Chmn. Conf. Academic Deans of So. States, 1951. Dir. Piedmont Bank and Trust Co., Cornelius Building and Loan Assn. (Cornelius, N.C.). Chairman Civil Service Board of Mecklenburg County, N.C., 1944-45, 48-49, 54-55; v.p. N.C. Coll. Conference 1948. Mem. Am. Econ. Assn., Phi Delta Theta, Phi Beta Kappa, Omicron Delta Kappa, Sigma Upsilon. Author: A State Movement in Railroad Development, 1928; The State Highway System of North Carolina, 1931; Introduction to Economics, 1941. Presbyterian. Address: Davidson, N.C. Died Jan. 1, 1957; buried Davidson Coll. Cemetery, Davidson, N.C.

BROWN, Charles Harvey, librarian; b. Albany, N.Y., Dec. 23, 1875; s. James H. and Mary E. (Smith) B.; B.A., Wesleyan U., Conn., 1897, M.A., 1899, Litt.D., 1937; N.Y. State Library Sch., 1899-1901; m. Julia W. Heath, Jan. 16, 1909; children—Robert H., Charles H. Asst. Library of Congress, 1901-03; reference librarian John Crerar Library, Chgo., 1903-09; asst. librarian Brooklyn Pub. Library, 1909-19; library specialist U.S. Navy, 1919-22; librarian Iowa State Coll., Ames, 1922-46, emeritus 1946—; vis. bibliographer La. state U., 1949-50; vis. prof. U. of Ill., 1950-51; mem. faculty School of Library Service, Columbia U., summers 1933-38. Pres. Iowa Library Assn., 1928-29; cons. expert on libraries Land Grant Coll. Survey, U.S. Bur. of Edn., 1928-30; pres. Am. Library Assn., 1941-42. Mem. Library Mission to Japan, 1947-48. Mem. A.L.A., Delta Tau Delta, Phi Kappa Phi, etc. Wrote: Report to Iowa State Planning Board on Library Service in Iowa, 1935; also other publs. Home: 317 Lynn Av., Ames, Ia. Died Jan. 19, 1960.

BROWN, Charles Reynolds, clergyman; b. Bethany, W.Va., Oct. 1, 1862; s. Benjamin F. and Sarah J. B.; A.B., Univ. of Ia., 1883, A.M., 1886; S.T.B., Boston U., 1889, S.T.D., 1922; A.M., Yale, 1911, D.D., 1928; D.D., Oberlin, 1912, Brown, 1914; LL.D., Wesleyan Coll., 1915, Boston U., 1937, Mills Coll., 1937; L.H.D., U. of Vt., 1926; m. Alice Tufts, Sept. 23, 1896. Pastor First Congl. Ch., Oakland, Calif., 1896-1911; dean Div. Sch. of Yale U., 1911-28, emeritus dean since 1928. Professional study, Egypt and Palestine, 1897; spl. lecturer on ethics, Leland Stanford Jr. U., 1899-1906; Lyman Beecher lecturer, Yale, 1905-06, 1922-23; spl. lecturer, Cornell, 1909, Columbia, 1911; Earl lecturer Pacific Sch. of Religion, 1924; Ingersoll lecturer on Immortality, Harvard, 1920; John Calvin McNair lecturer U. of N.C., 1926; Fondren lecturer Southern Meth. U., 1936. Moderator Nat. Council Congl. Ch., 1913-15. Mem. Sigma Chi, Phi Beta Kappa. Republican. Mason (32°). Author: The Main Points, 1899; Social Message of the Modern Pulpit, 1906; The Strange Ways of God; The Young Man's Affairs; Faith and Health, 1910; The Modern Man's Religion, 1911; The Latent Energies in Life, 1912; The Quest of Life, 1913; Yale Talks, 1919; The Master's Way, 1919; Living Again, 1920; The Religion of a Layman, 1921; The Greatest Man of the Nineteenth Century, 1921; The Art of Preaching, 1922; Why I Believe in Religion, 1923; What Is Your Name, 1924; Where Do You Live, 1925; Ten Short Stories from the Bible, 1925; These Twelve, 1926; The Making of a Minister, 1927; The Gospel for Main Street, 1929; My Own Yesterdays, 1931; Have We Outgrown Religion?, 1932; They Were Giants, 1934; Finding Ourselves, 1935; The Master's Influence, 1936; Being Made Over, 1939; Dreams Come True, 1944. Home: 233 Edwards St., New Haven 11. Died Nov. 28, 1950; buried Washington, Ia.

BROWN, Charlotte Harding, illustrator; b. Newark, N.J., Aug. 31, 1873; d. Joseph and Charlotte Elizabeth (Matthews) Harding; educated Phila., Pa. Academy of Fine Arts; graduate Phila. School of Design for Women; married James A. Brown, 1905; 1 daughter, Charlotte Adams. Awarded silver medal, Women's Expn., London, 1900, St. Louis Expn., 1904, Panama P.I. Exposition, 1915. Illustrations for Collier's Weekly, Century, Harper's and McClure's mags. Work represented in private collections, Fellowship of the Pa. Acad. Fine Arts, and in Portfolio Am. Artists, Library of Congress, Washington, D.C. Clubs: Plastic, Fellowship, Phila. Water Color. Studio: Smithtown, L.I., N.Y. Died Nov. 1, 1951; buried Smithtown Cemetery, Smithtown, L.I., N.Y.

BROWN, Clarence Montgomery, business exec.; b. New York, N.Y., Dec. 1, 1868; s. Nicholas Francis and Louise Benner (Bell) B.; LL.B., U. of Pa., 1895; m. Luella Conwell, Apr. 2, 1902; children—Howard Benner, Lorna Conwell (Mrs. E. Wayne Haley), Robert Montgomery, Janet Danby (Mrs. William G. Guernsey). Engaged as conveyancer, 1882-95; atty. for corps., 1895-1931; chmn. bd. dirs. Pittsburgh Plate Glass Co., 1931-55, hon. chmn. bd., 1956—; dir. Southern Minerals Corp., Columbia-Southern Chem. Corp., Ins. Co. of N.A., Central-Penn Nat. Bank, Pitcairn Co. Hon. chairman Youth Service, Inc. Phila. Republican. Episcopalian. Clubs: Midday, Duquesne, Union League, Science and Art (Phila.); Seaview Golf (Absecon, N.J.); Cricket, Whitemarsh Valley Golf. Home: Chestnut Hill, Phila. 18. Office: 1616 Walnut St., Phila. 3. Died Feb. 9, 1958; buried West Laurel Hill Cemetery, Montgomery County, Pa.

BROWN, Colvin W., business exec.; b. Burlington, Ill., Dec. 29, 1888; s. Ira J. and Estelle Potter (Wilcox) B.; ed. pub. schs., Elgin, Ill.; m. Pearl M. Sayler, Oct. 21, 1923 (dec.); m. 2d, Regina L. Knott, Nov. 25, 1937. Reporter and city editor, Elgin Daily News, 1906-16; sales mgr. New York Evening Mail Syndicate, 1916; advt. mgr. and dir. advt. and publicity Mutual Film Corp., 1917-20; editor Gaumont News and gen. mgr. Asso. Screen News, 1921; v.p. and mgr. distbn. Thomas H. Ince Corp., 1921-25; v.p. and mgr. fgn. distbn. FBO (now RKO) Pictures, 1925-27; exec. v.p. Pathe Exchange, Inc., 1927-30; gen. mgr. and publisher Motion Picture Herald. 1930-45; dir. Du-Pont-Pathe Film Mfg. Co., 1927-30; dir. and mem. retirement bd. General Aniline & Film Corp. since 1942; dir. Commodore Hotel, Inc., N.Y. City, since 1945. Asst. sec. of Pres's. Exec. Council, 1933-34; consultant publication div., War Dept., 1942; cons. on film allocations Consumers Durable Goods Div., W.P.B., 1943; chmn. Regional Bd. of Review, War Assets Adminstrn., 1946. Home: 50 E. 72d St., N.Y.C. 21. Office: 1600 Broadway, N.Y.C. 19. Died July 8, 1952; buried Elgin, Ill.

BROWN, Cyrus Perrin, banker; b. Providence, Oct. 9, 1868; s. Cyrus Cleveland and Sarah Pierce (Gardiner) B.; student pub. schs.; m. Fannie E. Chadsey, 1890; children—Cyrus P., Edward Cleveland, Adelaide Maybury. Formerly in banking business at Providence; pres. First Nat. Bank, St. Paul, 1917-29; now retired. Clubs: University, Minnesota, Somerset Country, White Bear Yacht (St. Paul); Hope (Providence). Home: Saunderstown, R.I. Died Mar. 27, 1945; buried Elmgrove Cemetery, Allenton, R.I.

BROWN, D(enton) J(acobs), prof. of chemistry; b. Hampton, Pa., Apr. 13, 1882; s. A. David and Anna Mary (Jacobs) B.; A.B., U. of Tex., 1910; Ph.D. Chicago University, 1918; married Sallie Sloan (deceased); 1 son, Denton Sloan (deceased). Instructor chem. Univ. Texas 1914-15, 1917-18; asst. prof. chemistry Agrl. and Mech. Coll. of Tex., 1915-17; asso. prof. chemistry U. of Neb., 1918-27, prof. 1927-50, professor of chemistry emeritus since 1950. Mem. Am. Chemical Society, Am. Assn. Univ. Profs., Phi Beta Kappa, Sigma Xi, Phi Lambda Upsilon, Alpha Chi Sigma, Acacia. Mason (32°). Conductor research in electrochemistry and rates of reaction. Home: 1935 S. 47, Lincoln 6, Neb. Died Oct. 4, 1955; buried Wyuka Cemetery, Lincoln, Neb.

BROWN, Donald C., business exec.; b. Marietta, O.; grad. Marietta College, Pres., dir. and gen. mgr. Mexican Northern Ry., New York, N.Y.; pres. and dir. Fresnillo Co., Towne Securities Corp.; first v.p., Compania Metalurgica Mexicana; v.p., gen. mgr., dir. Tezuitlan Copper Mining & Smelting Co.; v.p., dir. Mexican Lead Co., Mexican Mineral Ry., Montezuma Lead Co., Potosi & Rio Verde Ry. Address: Mexican Northern Railway, 82 Beaver St., N.Y.C. 5. Died Jan. 19, 1954; buried Albuquerque.

BROWN, Downing P., mfg. exec.; b. Portland, Me., June 24, 1887; s. William W. and Lucy (Montague) B.; A.B., Williams Coll., 1908; m. Lucille E. Ewen, Dec. 21, 1922. With Brown Co., Berlin, N.H., since 1908, woods dept., 1908-11, mgr. Canadian mill, 1911-17, asst. mgr. mills, Berlin, N.H., 1919-29, mgr., 1929-32, v.p. in charge sales, 1945—. Home: Glen St., Williamstown, Mass. Office: 150 Causeway St., Boston. Died Apr. 1, 1954; buried Portland, Me.

BROWN, Earl Theodore, physicist; b. Centralia, Wash., Nov. 20, 1890; s. William Chandler and Sarah Ellen (Axtell) B.; B.S., U. Wash., 1918, M.S., 1924; student Stanford, 1928-29, U. Cal., 1929-30; m. Lida Fake, Dec. 25, 1922; children—Nancy Jean, John Theodore. High sch. tchr. and prin., Wash., 1918-19; asso. in physics U. Wash., 1920-21; prof. physics Willamette U., 1921-55. Mem. Am. Assn. Physics Tchrs., Am. Inst. Physics. Republican. Presbyn. Mason. Mem. Men's Garden Club of America. Home: 293 S. 14th St. S.E., Salem, Ore. Died Mar. 3, 1959; buried Belcrest Cemetery, Salem.

BROWN, Edward Eagle, banker; b. Chgo., June 4, 1885; s. Edward Osgood and Helen Gertrude (Eagle) B.; A.B., Harvard, 1905; LL.B., Harvard Law Sch., 1908; m. Phyllis Wyatt, 1913 (died Oct. 6, 1944). Admitted to Ill. bar, 1908; atty. and gen. counsel 1st Nat. Bank of Chgo., 1910-23, v.p., 1923-34, pres., 1934-45, chmn., 1945—; dir., chmn. exec. com., C.,R.I.&P. Ry. Co.; dir. Peoples Gas Light and Coke Co., Inland Steel Co. Mem. bd. trustees U. Chgo., Newberry Library. Mem. Am., Chgo. bar assns., Legal Club, Law Club. Dem. Clubs: Commercial, Chgo., Mid-Day, Chicago Golf, Old Elm (Chgo.). Home: 229 Lake Shore Dr. Office: First Nat. Bank, Chgo. Died Aug. 24, 1959; buried Graceland Cemetery, Chgo.

BROWN, Edward Killoran, prof. of English; b. Toronto, Can., Aug. 12, 1905; s. Edward David and Winifred (Killoran) B.; B.A., U. of Toronto. Can., 1926; Docteur ès letters, U. of Paris, 1935; m. Margaret Deaver, 1936; children—Deaver, Philip. Massey Fellow, U. of Paris, 1926-29; lecturer, later becoming asst. prof. of Eng., U. of Toronto, 1929-35; prof. and head of dept. of English, U. of Manitoba, 1935-37; prof. of English, U. of Toronto, 1938-41; prof. and chmn. of dept. of English, Cornell U., 1941-44; prof. of English, University of Chicago, since 1944; Alexander lecturer, University of Toronto, 1949; secretary to Prime Minister of Canada (Right Hon. W. L. Mackenzie King), 1942. Trustee Newberry Library. Mem. Phi Beta Kappa. Author: Edith Wharton, étude critique, 1935; Studies in the Text of Matthew Arnold's Prose Works, 1935; On Canadian Poetry, 1943; Matthew Arnold: A Study in Conflict, 1948. Translator: Carlyle, by Louis Cazamian, 1932; Le Père Goriat, by Honoré de Balzac, 1946. Editor: Representative Essays of Matthew Arnold, 1936; Victorian Poetry, 1942; At the Long Sault by Archibald Lampman, 1943 (with D. C. Scott); (posthumously) editor: The Selected Poems of Duncan Campbell Scott, 1951; author: Rhythm in the Novel, 1951 (awarded Lorne Pierce Medal by Royal Soc. Canada). Contbr. articles to U. of Toronto Quarterly, Harpers Mag., Yale Review. Address: 4907 Greenwood Av., Chicago 15. Died Mar. 23, 1951; buried Mt. Pleasant Cemetery, Toronto, Can.

BROWN, Edward Norphlet, ry. ofcl.; b. Barbour County, Ala., Mar. 23, 1862; s. E. N. and Frances Elizabeth (Long) B.; A.B. and C. E., Agrl. and Mech. Coll., Auburn, Ala., 1882; m. Frances Thacker Walker, Dec. 2, 1885; children—William Raoul, Mrs. Thacker May Selden, Jr., Minnie Gatra (Mrs. Gatra Brown Moorer). With Athens & Northeastern Ry., Ga., and Richmond & Danville R.R. until 1881; in charge constrn. ry. from Chipley to Greenville, Ga., 1882-83; engr. of maintenance and asst. chief engr. Central R.R. of Ga., 1884-86; went to Mexico, as asst. chief engr. in charge of completing constrn. of main line of old Nat. R.R. of Mexico, 1887, built 352 miles of the line, 1888, opening up a through rate from Am. border to Mexico City, chief engr., 1889-90, gen. supt., 1890-1900, 3d v.p. and gen. mgr., 1900-01, 1st v.p. and gen. mgr., 1901-93; pres. Nat. R.R. of Mexico and Mexico Internat. Ry., 1903-08; pres. Nat. Rys. of Mexico, 1908-14; chmn. bd. St. L-S.F. Ry. Co., 1919-48, ret.; chmn. bd. dirs. C.R.I. &P. Ry. Co. Clubs: City, Mid-day (N.Y.C.). Home: 280 Park Av. Office: 120 Broadway, N.Y.C. Died May 2, 1956; buried Woodlawn Cemetery, N.Y.C.

BROWN, Estelle Aubrey, author; b. Constable, N.Y., d. Nelson and Alta (Hastings) Aubrey; student Franklin Acad., Malone, N.Y.; m. Silas Armstrong, Jr., 1904 (died 1907); m. 2d. Major Harry T. Brown, U.S. Army, 1918 (died 1931). In ednl. work U.S. Indian Service, 1900-18. Author: A Woman of Character (one-act play), 1924; With Trailing Banners (Atlantic Monthly Press novel), 1930; Around Two Worlds, 1938; also short stories and articles in leading mags. Address: 1317 E. Speedway, Tucson. Died Jan. 23, 1958.

BROWN, Fayette, corp. official; b. at Cleveland, O., Aug. 1, 1881; s. Harvey Huntington and Elizabeth Freeman (Hickox) B.; student Univ. Sch., Cleveland, 1892-1900; B.A., Yale, 1904; m. Geraldine Walker, Jan. 18, 1913; children—Fayette, Willard Walker, Barbara, Ralph Hickox, Elizabeth Hickox. Director Interlake Iron Corporation, Interlake S.S. Company, Cleveland Trust Company. Served as 1st lt. Troop A, 1st Ohio Cav., Mexican border, 1916-17; maj. 135th Field Arty., A.E.F., 1918-19. Trustee University Hosps., Lakeview Cemetery Assn. Mem. Psi Upsilon, Scroll and Key at Yale. Republican. Clubs: Union, Kirtland Country (Cleveland); Yale (New York); Graduate (New Haven, Conn.). Home: 2617 Berkshire Rd., Cleveland Heights, O. Office: Union Commerce Bldg., Cleve. 14. Died Jan. 30, 1953.

BROWN, Fletcher, clergyman; b. Guernsey County, O., Aug. 2, 1850; student Central U.; grad. Simpson Coll., 1877, A.M., 1880; B.D., Drew Theol. Sem., 1879. Entered ministry M.E. Ch., 1879, held pastorates at Carlisle, Dunlap, Carson, Adel and Nevada, Ia.; v.p. Simpson Coll., 1887-92, pres., 1892-98; now financial sec. Preachers' Aid Soc. Editor The Educator, 9 yrs. Address: Indianola, Ia. Died 1912.

BROWN, Frank Chilton, clergyman; b. Lewisburg, W.Va., July 4, 1890; s. Frank Chilton and Mary Nelson (Montgomery) B.; A.B. and A.M., Hampden-Sydney Coll., Va., 1909, D.D., 1925; B.D., Union Theol. Sem., Richmond, Va., 1914; student United Free Ch. Coll., Scotland, 1914-15; student U. of Oxford, England, Trinity term, 1935; LL.D., Austin College, 1945; married Mary Oden Hansford, October 27, 1915. Principal Potomac Academy, Romney, W.Va., 1909-11; ordained ministry Presbyn. Ch., U.S., 1914; asst. pastor Henry Drummond Meml. Ch., Glascow, Scotland, 1914-15; pastor First Ch., Logan, W.Va., 1915-20, Breem Meml. Ch., Charleston, W. Va., 1920-36, First Ch., Dallas, Tex., 1926-52; mem. bd. ch. extension since 1950; professor English Bible and pastoral theology, Columbia Theological Seminary, Decatur, Ga., 1952—. Moderator Kanawha Presbytery, 1916, Synod, W.Va., 1930, Dallas Presbytery, 1916, Gen. Assembly of Presbyn. Ch. in U.S., 1940; mem. exec. com. Home Missions Gen. Assembly, Presbyn. Ch., 1939—; mem. bd. trustees Gen. Assembly Presbyn. Ch., U.S., 1928-35. Recipient of Algernon-Sydney Medallion, Hampden-Sydney Coll., 1940. Chmn. com. on Evangelism Gen. Assembly Presbyn. Ch. U.S., 1928-35. Trustee Greenbrier Coll. for Women, 1925-30, Hampden-Sydney College, 1933-35, Davis Stuart Sch. (Synodical orphanage), 1933-35, Austin Presbyterian Theological Seminary, Austin, Tex.; 1944-46; mem. bd. directors, Dallas War Chest, 1944-47; dir., chmn. ch. relations, Dallas Community Chest, 1949; Dallas Boy Scout Council, Freeman Memorial Clinic, trustee Austin College President, Dallas Pastor's Assn., 1947-48; mem. Newcomen Soc., Eugene Field Soc. (hon.), Omicron Delta Kappa, Pi Kappa Alpha. Democrat. Mason. Author: Lost: A Human Soul, 1932. Home: 601 Clifton Rd., N.E., Atlanta. Died July 2, 1955; buried Charleston, W. Va.

BROWN, F(rank) E(merson), chemist, coll. prof.; b. near Cuba, Kan., Feb. 9, 1882; s. Prairie Frank and Marie Elizabeth (Barnhill) B.; A.B. in edn., Kan. State Teacher's Coll., Emporia, 1911, student 1902-10; B.S. in chemistry, Univ. of Chicago, 1912-17, Ph.D. (phys. chemistry), 1918; m. May Maria Holmes, Dec. 25, 1910; children—Frank Emerson, Holmes M.; m. 2d, Louise Jaggard, July 23, 1920; 1 dau., Louise Jaggard. Teacher country schs., Republic County, Kan., 1899-1902, supt. of schs., prin. of high sch., Portis, Kan., 1905-07, Hill City, Kan., 1907-09; supt. of schs., Collinsville, Okla., Jan., 1911-June, 1912; chemistry teacher, night classes, Chicago schs., Y.M.C.A. schs., 1912-18; chemistry teacher Fresno (Calif.) high sch. and jr. coll., spring, 1914; asst. prof. of chemistry, Ia. State Coll., Ames, Feb. 1917, asso. prof., 1918, prof., 1923-52, emeritus, 1952—. Dir. Ia. Acad. Sci., 1956—. Dir. Ia. Sci. Talent Search, 1947—. Recipient Ia. State Coll. Faculty citation for outstanding service, 1956; Sci. Apparatus Makers award in Chem. Edn., Am. Chem. Soc., 1958; Silver Beaver, Boy Scouts Am., 1943. Mem. Am. Chem. Soc. (local section sec., treas., 1918, chmn., 1921, councilor, 1931, 33, 39, and 1945—); chmn. local section officers group, 1940, chmn. Div. of Chem. Edn., 1942; Senate of Chemical Education (chmn. com. on membership affairs 1950-51); Ia. Acad. Sci. (chmn. com. high sch. relations, 1942-50, chmn. com. sci. talent search 1950—; v.p. 1950-51, pres. 1951-52), A.A.A.S., Sigma Xi, Phi Kappa Phi, Alpha Chi Sigma, Phi Lambda Upsilon, Phi Kappa Tau. Presbyterian. Mason. Contbg. ed. Jour. Chem. Edn., 1928-40; editorial bd. Ia. State Coll. Jour. Sci. 1945—. Author: A Short Course in Qualitative Analysis, 1932; Qualitative Analysis Work Book, 1937; contbr. articles on research and teaching of chemistry to chem. jours.; abstractor Chemical Abstracts, 1922—. Home: 138 N. Hyland Av., Ames, Ia. Died Sept. 10, 1959.

BROWN, Franklin Q., pres. Dobbs Ferry Bank, Colony Realty Corp., Newbury Corp.; dir. Lima Locomotive Works, Cuba Grapefruit Co., Ga. & Fla. R.R., Appointed chmn. adv. com. Div. of Finance, U.S. R.R. Adminstrn., 1918. Home: Springhurst, Dobbs Ferry, N.Y. Office: 341 Madison Av., N.Y.C. Died Nov. 6, 1955.

BROWN, Fred Comings, mem. Rep. Nat. Com.; b. Sheldon, Vt., May 9, 1884; s. Dr. Edwin M. and Fannie L. (Comings) B.; grad. Kimball Union Acad., 1905; m. Lucy Holmes, Sept. 16, 1908 (dec.); children—E. Merriman, Frederick H., Carolyn (Mrs. North); m. Reta Chappell, Sept. 19, 1945. Grain mcht., Barton, 1922-50; dir. Enosburg Falls Savs. Bank & Trust Co. since 1935, v.p., 1943-45, pres. since 1945; dir. Missisquoi Pulp & Paper Co. since 1937. Sec., race sec. Orleans Co. Fair, Barton, Vt., 14 yrs.; selectman Town of Barton since 1936; elected mem. State Legislature, 1949; chmn. Rep. State Com., 1952; mem. Rep. Nat. Com. since 1952. Conglist. Home: Main St., Barton, Vt. Died Apr. 4, 1955.

BROWN, Fred Herbert, ex-U.S. senator, lawyer; b. Ossipee, N.H., Apr. 12, 1879; s. Dana J. and Nellie (Allen) B.; student Dartmouth, 1899-1900; studied law in office of James A. Edgerly, Somersworth, N.H.; student Boston U. Sch. Law, 1904-06; m. Edna C. McHarg, May 16, 1925. Admitted to N.H. bar, 1907, practiced with preceptor until his decease, 1908; city solicotor Somersworth, 1910-14; mem. N.H. Constl. Conv., 1912; Dem. presdl. elector, 1912; mayor of Somersworth, 1914-22; US. dist. atty., 1914-22; gov. of N.H., 1923-24; mem. Pub. Service Commn. of N.H., 1925-33; U.S. senator from N.H. for term 1933-39; comptroller gen. of U.S., 1939-40. Mem. N.H. Bar Assn. Mason (K.T.), K.P. Home: 137 N. State St., Concord, N.H. Office: 44 High St., Somersworth, N.H. Died Feb. 3, 1955.*

BROWN, George Granger, educator, cons. engr.; b. N.Y.C., Sept. 3, 1896; s. George Giffins and Emma Lee (Tuttle) B.; B.S., New York U., 1917, Chem. Engr., 1924, Doctor of Engineering (honorary). 1955; M.S.E., U. of Mich., 1922, Ph.D., 1924; m. Dorothy Burrous Martin, Dec. 1, 1917; children—George Martin, Judson Granger, David Malcolm. Engr. and dept. mgr., Aluminum Co. of America, Massena, N.Y., 1917-18; prodn. mgr. Union Special Machine Co., Chicago, 1919-20; cons. engr., mem. chem. engring. staff, U. of Mich., 1920—, prof. 1931—, chmn. dept. chem. and metall. engring. 1942-51. Edward DeMille Campbell Distinguished prof. chem. engring. since 1947, dean coll. engring., chmn. engring. research council 1951—; dir. American Motors Corp.; cons. several corps. With C.W.S., Washington, 1918; director engring. division AEC, 1950. Mem. Am. Inst. Chem. Engrs. (pres. 1944, dir. 1940-42, also the treas., 1953—, chairman edn. com. 1949-54), Am. Soc. Engring. Edn., American Chem. Soc., Detroit Engring. Soc., Psi Upsilon, Phi Beta Kappa, Sigma Xi, Phi Kappa Phi, Tau Beta Pi, Phi Lambda Upsilon, Alpha Chi Sigma, Iota Alpha. Received Vernon Demarell fellowship, 1917; William H. Walker award, American Institute Chemical Engrs., 1939; Hanlon award, Natural Gasoline Assn., 1940. Clubs: Rotary, Golf and Outing (Ann Arbor); Research (U. Mich.); Chemists (N.Y.C.); University (Washington). Author tech. articles and monographs. Home: 1910 Hill St., Ann Arbor. Died Aug. 26, 1957.

BROWN, George Lincoln, coll. pres.; b. Bates County, Mo., Jan. 25, 1869; s. John and Elizabeth (Seaver) B.; B.S., U. Mo., 1892, M.S., 1893; Ph.D., U. Chgo., 1902; LL.D., U. S.D., 1927; m. Winifred Loucks, 1898 (died 1908); children—Cecil Langford, Mrs. Elizabeth Louise Peppers, Mrs. Florence Margaret Bottum; m. 2d, Anna York Loucks, 1910; children—Winifred York Christenson, Charlotte Seaver Morris, George Lincoln, Jr., Gerald Edward. Prof. mathematics S.D. State Coll., 1897-1944, dean of faculty, 1910-44, v.p., 1913-44, dean div. gen. sci., 1924-40, acting pres. various periods, pres., 1940-1941, pres., emeritus, 1944—. Fellow A.A.A.S.; mem. Phi Beta Kappa. Presbyn. Home: Brookings, S.D. Died Aug. 8, 1950; buried Brookings.

BROWN, George Stewart, public relations; b. Buckeye, Ariz., May 21, 1906; s. George P. and Elsa S. (Stewart) B.; A.B., U. of Arizona, 1927; m. Helen Meyer, July 30, 1932; children—Ronny Stewart, Gordon Stewart. Newspaper reporter, Tucson, Ariz., 1925-27, Paris (France) Herald, 1927-29; United Press corr., 1929-39; dir. pub. information Am. Nat. Red Cross, 1939-43, vice chmn. in charge pub. relations, 1943-45; chief public relations officer Allied Commn., Rome, Italy, Jan. 1945; dir. U.S. Information Service in Italy and spl. asst. to Am. ambassador, Oct. 1945; dep. director O.I.C., State Dept., Washington, D.C., Oct. 1946; mgr. pub. relations, Standard Oil Co. of Cal. since 1948. Mem. bd. trustees San Francisco State Coll. Mem. Acad. Polit. Sci., Sigma Chi. Clubs: California (Los Angeles); Press, Union League (San Francisco); National Press (Washington). Home: 3652 Clay St., San Francisco 18. Office: 225 Bush St., San Francisco. Died Apr. 11, 1957.

BROWN, Gilmor, supervising dir. Pasadena Playhouse; b. New Salem, N.D.; s. Orville and Emma Louise (Gilmor) B.; ed. pub. schs.; Litt.D. (hon.), U. So. Cal., 1938. Formerly with Ben Greet Players; as actor toured U.S.; founder, 1917, supervising dir. Pasadena Playhouse; founder, originator studio theatre, Playbox, 1924; supervising dir. dramatics Cal. Inst. Tech., 1927-31. Lectr. on community drama Drama League Inst., Chgo., 1921, Summer Art Colony, Pasadena, 1922-23, U. So. Cal., summers 1923-27; guest star Detroit Symphony Drama, season 1921, Greek Theatre, Berkeley, Cal., 1922, 1941; producer, dir., Lazarus Laughed (Eugene O'Neill), 1928. State supr. Fed. Theatre, 1936-37. Mem. bd. trustees Nat. Theatre Conf. Recipient Arthur Nobel gold medal award Pasadena City Planning Commn., 1926; Officer de l'Instruction Publique (France), 1932; bronze medal Société Les Amites Française, 1936. Author: General Principles of Play Direction (with A. Garwood). Clubs: Fine Arts, Cauldron, Drama League, Browning, Hollywood Bowl, U. Author: (plays) A Soul for Mary Jane (from Dunsany), Take Your Choice; dramatized Cricket on the Hearth, A Christmas Carol. Pres. Nat. Theatre Conf., 1934-40. Corporate mem. Am. Nat. Theatre and Acad. Studio: 39 S. El Molino Av., Pasadena, Cal Died Jan. 1960.

BROWN, Glen David, educator; b. Howard County, Ind., Apr. 3, 1891; s. Grant and Delia Ellen (Stack) B.; A.B., Ind. State Tchrs. Coll., 1916; M.A., Ind. U., 1931; grad. study Johns Hopkins, 1931-34; m. Suzette Lavonne Willcutts, Dec. 24, 1916; children—Mary Ellen (Mrs. C. S. Feagins), Glen David, Joseph Edward. Began teaching career as tchr., later prin. elementary schs. in Ind.; instr. indsl. arts and social scis. West Terre Haute (Ind.) High Sch., part-time 1914-15, prin., 1915-17; tchr., supr. indsl. arts, Muncie, Ind., 1917-18; also civilian instr. C.E. units Purdue; supr. pre-vocational edn., Muncie, 1918-21, dir. vocational edn., 1921-25, asst. supt. schs. charge bus. mgmt. and vocational edn., 1925-31; supr. part-time edn. Balt. City Schs., 1931-33; prin. Boys Advanced Occupation Sch., Balt., 1933-37; prof., head dept. indsl. edn. U. Md., 1937-40, 46—, dir. Balt. div., 1946—; state adminstr. Nat. Youth Adminstrn., 1940-42; part-time supr. trade and indsl. edn., 1942-43, acting state dir. vocational edn. Md. State Dept. Edn., 1943, asst. state dir. vocational edn. state supr. trade and indsl. edn., adult edn., 1944-46, supr. indsl. edn. for adults, 1947-48. Survey study and report, chmn. edn. com. Gov.'s Commn. Problems Affecting the Negro in Md., 1944-45; mem. com. indsl. arts edn. U.S. Office Edn., 1940-42. State dir. Jr. A.R.C. activities, 1917-18; also Presdl. appointee for Ind. on Housing; Md. state adminstr., asst. regional adminstr. Region IV Nat. Youth Adminstrn., 1942-43; Md. state dir. War Prodn. Tng. and War Food Prodn. Tng., 1943-44. Served as instr. tng. in civilian capacity Army Ordnance Sch., Aberdeen Proving Grounds, part-time 1941. Mem. N.E.A. (life), Am. Vocational Assn. (life), Am. Council Indsl. Arts Edn. (charter mem.), Ind., Md. (dir., past pres.) vocational assns., Muncie C. of C. (dir.), Am., Md. (charter mem.) socs. tng. dirs., Am. Assn. Sch. Adminstrs., Nat. Assn. Secondary Sch. Prins., Nat. Pub. Relations Assn., Am. Assn. U. Profs., Nat. Assn. Sch. Bus. Ofcls., Nat. Vocational Guidance Assn., Phi Delta Kappa, Iota Lambda Sigma, Sigma Alpha Epsilon, Phi Kappa Phi. Mason (Shriner). Club: Kiwanis (dist. trustee, past pres.). Author articles profl. publs. Home: 4608 Calvert Rd., College Park, Md. Died Nov. 9, 1957.

BROWN, Harvey H., Jr., business exec.; b. Cleve., Nov. 9, 1892; s. Harvey Huntington and Elizabeth Freeman (Hickox) B.; grad. Taft Sch.; A.B., Yale Coll., 1915; student Mass. Inst. Tech.; m. Edith Findley Gardiner, July 11, 1936; children—Harvey H. III, George Gardiner. Pres., treas. Cleveland Hobbing Machine Co., Cleve., 1943—; dir., 1943; mem. exec. com. Eaton Mfg. Co.; dir. Indsl. Brown Hoist Corp., Enamel Products Co., Brush Boryllium Co. Pres. bd. of trustees Univ. Hosps., Cleve.; trustee Western Res. U., Hawken Sch. Trustee Vis. Nurse Assn., Cleve. Republican. Clubs: Union, Tavern, 50, Kirkand Country (Cleve.); Yale (N.Y.C.); Detroit. Home: 2571 N. Park Blvd., Cleve. 6. Office: 1311 Chardon Rd., Cleve. 17. Deceased.

BROWN, Hilton Ultimus, newspaper dir.; b. Indianapolis, Ind., Feb. 20, 1859; s. Philip Andrew and Julia (Troster) B.; A.B., Butler Univ., Indianapolis, 1880, A.M., 1882, LL.D., 1935; LL.D., Ind. U., 1945; m. Jennie Hannah, Oct. 30, 1883 (died 1939); children—Mark H., Louise (Mrs. J. W. Atherton), Philip (dec.), Mary (Mrs. George O. Stewart), Hilton U. (dec.), Arch. A., Jean (Mrs. Clifford Wagoner), Jessica (Mrs. Floyd R. Mannon), Julia (Mrs. David Konold), Paul V. Served as principal Oaktown (Ind.) Sem., 1880-81; with Indianapolis News, 1881—; successively reporter, city editor, receiver, mng. editor, and gen. mgr., 1901-30; was member bd. now vice pres. The Star-News, Incorporated, Indianapolis; mem. Associated Press for News, 1922—. Ex-president town bd. and sch. board, Irvington; apptd. exec. officer 6th Div. Selective Service Bd., Indianapolis, 1917. Mem. bd. dirs. Butler U., 1885—, pres. bd., 1903-55, emeritus, 1955—; director Christian (Disciples) Board Publication; president of board of Christian Foundation, Butler Foundation and Arthur Jordan Foundation. Member board directors American Newspaper Pubs. Assn., 1903-35. Mem. Indiana Historical Society, Phi Delta Theta (ex-president). Republican. Member Christian Church (life elder). Clubs: Indianapolis Press Club, Indianapolis Literary, Columbia, Portfolio. Author of "Fifty-four Forty or Fight," 1912. Edited letters and verses of his son (who was killed in action, in World War I), entitled, "Hilton U. Brown, Jr., One of Three Brothers in Artillery," 1920; A Book of Memories, 1951. Attended Peace Conf. at Paris and Versailles as corr., and wrote series of letters on battlefields and indsl. conditions in Europe following the war; corr. in Russia, 1926. Elected to Municipal Staff of Honor, 1939. Home: 5087 E. Washington St. Office: The Star-News, Indpls. Died Sept. 20, 1958; buried Crown Hill Cemetery, Indpls.

BROWN, Hiram Staunton, ret. corp. exec.; b. nr. Chestertown, Md., Oct. 3, 1882; s. Hiram and Mary (Hazzard) B.; A.B. magna cum laude, Washington Coll., Chestertown, Md., 1900; m. Mae Roslyn Maltz, Oct. 21, 1908; 1 son, Hiram Staunton. Began as office boy, N.Y. Herald; later with Washington Times; then in Mexico with Mex. Nat. R.R.; for 15 yrs. in pub. utility business with Hodenpyl, Walbridge & Co. and H. D. Walbridge & Co.; pres. U. S. Leather Co., 1924-29; pres. Radio-Keith-Orpheum Corp., 1929-33; officer or dir. various other corps; asst. coordinator of Nat. Def. Purchases, 1940-41; asst. dir. purchases OPM, 1941-42. Lt. col., chief of finance div. of Air Service, World War I; asst. to U.S. Liquidation Commn. in France. Chmn. bd. Washington Coll. Republican. Methodist. Clubs: Westchester Country, Bankers (N.Y.C.). Home: Rye, N.Y.; and Godlington Manor, Chestertown, Md. Died May 4, 1950; buried Chestertown, Md.

BROWN, Holcombe James, consulting engr.; b. New York, N.Y., Dec. 20, 1879; s. Charles Burroughs and Ella (Wyman) B.; grad. St. Paul's Sch., Garden City, N.Y.; student Lawrence Sci. Sch., class of 1902, Harvard, Cambridge, Mass.; m. Marian Russell Prescott, June 14, 1905; children—Marie (dec.), Prescott Holcombe. Employed by U.S. Gypsum Co., Chicago and other cities, 1902-12; v.p., gen. mgr., and dir. Crown Gypsum Co. of Canada, Lythmore, Ont., and Buffalo, N.Y., 1912-14; gen. operating mgr., and dir. Keystone Plaster Co., Chester, Pa., 1914-17; cons. engr. in charge operations, Southern Gypsum Co., North Holston, Va., 1917-20; owner and operator of cons. engring. office in Boston, since 1920; specializes in gypsum mining, mfr. and constrn. of gypsum plants. Sec. Mass. State Bd. for Registration of Professional Engrs. and Land Surveyors; former pres. Engring Societies of New England. Mem. Am. Soc. for Testing Materials (mem. com. C-11 on gypsum), Am. Soc. Mech. Engrs. (mem. com. relations with colls.), Am. Inst. Mining Engrs. (vice pres., dir.), Mining and Metall. Soc. of Am., Harvard Engineering Soc. Home: 174 Valentine St., West Newton 65, Mass. Office: 35 Doane St., Boston 9. Died May 24, 1951.

BROWN, Homer Caffee, army officer; b. Carthage, Mo., Sept. 25, 1893; s. William Henry Samuel and Edna (Caffee) B.; B.S., U.S. Mil. Acad., 1917; grad. Inf. Sch., company officers course, 1924, advanced course, 1930, Command and Gen. Staff Sch., 1934, Army War Coll., 1935, C.W.S., 1935; m. Helen Lahm, Aug. 8, 1917; 1 dau., Elizabeth Caffee (wife Calvin McVeigh Jenkins, USAAC). Commd. 2d lt. U.S. Army, 1917, advanced through grades to brig. gen.; served with 3d Inf., Eagle Pass, Tex., 1917-20, with 21st Inf., Schofield Barracks, Hawaii, 1920-23, with 16th Inf., Governors Island, N.Y., 1930-32; with 9th Inf., Fort Sam Houston, Tex., 1939-40; asst. G-3, Third Army, San Antonio, 1940-41; comdg. officer, 9th Inf., Fort Sam Houston, 1941-45; in S.W. Pacific area 1942-46; G-3, 4th Army, San Antonio, 1946-48, ret. for phys. disability. Mem. Nat. Security League (N.Y.), Press Club (Manlius School), Phi Mu, Scabbard and Blade. Home: 339 Ridgemont Av., San Antonio 2. Address: care The Adjutant General's Office, War Dept., Washington 25. Died Feb. 18, 1950; buried Ft. Sam Houston Nat. Cemetery, San Antonio.

BROWN, Hugh Elmer, clergyman; b. Dayton, Wash., Dec. 25, 1881; s. Hezekiah Newton and Elizabeth Ellen (Carpenter) B.; B.S., Whitman Coll., Walla Walla, Wash., 1904, D.D., 1924; B.D., Yale Div. Sch., 1907; D.D., Chgo. Theol. Sem., 1936; D.S.T., Northwestern U., 1948; 1936; m. Cora Meeker Osborne, Jan. 1, 1907 (dec. Mar. 1, 1952); children—Hugh Osborne, Sumner Churchill. Ordained Congl. ministry, 1907; pastor East Hampton, Conn., 1907-10, Windsor Av. Ch., Hartford, 1911-12, Pilgrim Church, Seattle, 1913-18. 1st Church, Evanston, Ill., 1918, pastor emeritus. Mem. Conn. Prison Commn., 1911-12; theatre censor, Seattle, 1917; YMCA sec. 3d O.T.C., Camp Lewis, Wash., 1918; mgr. Evanston Sunday Afternoon Club. Mem. adv. bd. Chgo. Theol. Sem.; pres. Congl. Bd. of Home Missions, 1936-40; asst. nat. moderator of Gen. Council Congl. Christian Churches, 1936-40; pres. Chgo. Congl. Union; corporate mem. Am. Bd. Fgn. Missions; overseer Whitman Coll., Mem. Phi Beta Kappa. Clubs: University (Evanston); Skokie Golf. Home: 1548 E. 45th St. S., Salt Lake City. Died May 31, 1952.

BROWN, James Dorsey, Jr., investment banker; b. Balt., Nov. 13, 1906; s. James Dorsey and Ella F. (Welsh) B.; student Balt. City Coll., 1923, Johns Hopkins, 1927; m. Sibyl K. Jackson, Oct. 3, 1938; children—James Dorsey III, Sibyl J., Pamela, Sandra. Securities broker and dealer with J. Dorsey Brown & Co., Balt., 1947—. Mem. Phila.-Balt. Stock Exchange (formerly Balt. Stock Exchange). 1933—, v.p., 1938-39, pres., 1946-49, gov., 1937-40, 42-46, 50—. Mem. Soc. Cincinnati, Soc. Colonial Wars, Bachelors Cotillon, Alphi Delta Phi. Clubs: Racquet (Phila.); Green Spring Valley Hunt (Garrison, Md.). Actively promoted federation regional stock exchanges, 1947; organized merger Phila. and Balt. stock exchanges. now Phila.-Balt. Stock Exchange, 1948-49. Home: "The Briars," Owings Mills, Baltimore County, Md. Office: Mercantile Trust Bldg., Balt. 2. Died July 31, 1958.

BROWN, James F., bd. edn. exec.; b. Washington, June 22, 1890; s. James F. and Cora Brown; LL.B., Lake Erie Sch. Law, 1931; m. Virginia A. Beyer, Oct. 15, 1913; children—James F., George E. (AUS). Salesman and estimator Chesapeake Supply Co., Washington, 1907-13; mgr. heating and ventilation dept. Standard Sanitary Mfg. Co., Cleve., 1913-18; asst. purchasing agent, commn. supplies and transportation, commn. of housing, Bd. of Edn., Cleve., 1918-31, dir. schs. and bus. mgr., 1937—; bus. mgr., Bd. of Edn., Elyria, O., 1935-37. Mem. Am. Assn. Sch. Adminstrs., N.E.A., Nat. Assn. Pub. Sch. Bus. Ofcls. and Ohio Affiliates, C. of C., Postwar Planning Council Cleve. Mason, Elk. Home: 11608 Iowa Av. Office: 1380 E. 6th St., Cleve. Died Nov. 2, 1948; buried Lakeview Cemetery, Cleve.

BROWN, James Greenlief, plant pathologist; b. St. Clair, Mich., Nov. 21, 1880; s. George Simeon and Ida Evelyn (Graham) B.; prep. edn. high sch., Marlette, and Ferris Inst., Big Rapids, Mich.; B.S., U. Chgo., 1916, M.S., 1917, Ph.D., 1925; m. Clara May McNeil, June 5, 1912; 1 dau., Imogene (dec.). Tchr. dist. and village schs., Mich., 1897-1903; tchr. sci. Cebu (P.I.) Normal Sch., 1904-06, acting prin., 1906; lab. asst. in botany U. Chgo., 1907-08; research asst. Carnegie Desert Lab., Tucson, 1909-11; instr. in biology U. Ariz., 1909-15, asst. prof. biology, 1916-19, prof. plant pathology Agrl. Coll., and plant pathologist Agrl. Expt. Sta., 1920-52, also head dept. agr., 1922- 6. Fellow A.A.A.S. (mem. council 1941); mem. Am. Soc. Plant Physiologists, Am. Phytopathol. Soc. Bot. Soc. Am., Mycol. Soc. Am., Soc. Am. Bacteriologists, Sigma Xi, Phi Beta Kappa, Phi Kappa Phi. Mason, Kiwanian. Author: Crown Gall on Coniefers; effect of penicillin on crown gall; also various papers on cotton, cactus, and other plant diseases. Built machine used for delinting and surface sterilizing cotton seed with sulphuric acid. Home: 1733 E. 6th St., Tucson. Died Apr. 1, 1954.

BROWN, James Thomas, chief justice, Court of King's Bench, of Saskatchewan; b. Huntingdon, Que., Oct. 22, 1871; s. Samuel and Margaret (White) B.; B.A., McGill U., 1893, hon. LL.D., 1921; m. Alice M. Lewis, 1902; children—Lloyd, Allan L., Wilfrid, Leonard R., Winnifred. Barrister at law, 1896; King's counsel, 1907; practiced law Saskatchewan, 1896-1910; Superior Court judge, 1910-18; chief justice King's Bench, Saskatchewan, since 1918. Served on many commns. and administrative tribunals for Dominion and Provincial govts. Mem. United Church. Address: Court of King's Bench, Regina, Can. Died Apr. 28, 1957.

BROWN, James Wright, editor, pub.; b. Detroit, Oct. 20, 1873; s. James Francis and Janet Garner (Wright) B.; student pub. schs.; m. Sarah Albertina Wilson, Oct. 20, 1898; children—Helen Wilson, James W., Virginia, Charlotte, Robert, George U. (dec.). With Detroit News and Tribune, 1891-95, Chgo. Journal, Chgo. American, Chgo. Tribune, 1895-1903; bus. and gen. mgr. Louisville Herald, 1903-11; gen. mgr. The Fourth Estate, 1911; pres. Editor and Publisher (established 1884; The Journalist, Newspaperdom, Fourth Estate and Advertising have been combined with same), N.Y.C., 1912-52, chmn. bd., 1953—. Recipient gold cross Order of Civil Merit, 1926, Chevalier Legion of Honor, 1928 (France); citation of honor U. Mo., 1935. Pres. John Peter Zenger Meml. Fund, Inc. Mem. Internat. Benjamin Franklin Soc. (pres. 1943-47), Sigma Delta Chi (hon. pres. 1924); hon. life mem. Internat. Circulation Mgrs. Assn.; hon. mem. Co. Newspaper Makers of London. Independent Republican. Presbyn. (elder). Mason. Clubs: Union League, Advertising (pres. 1929-30) (N.Y.C.); National Press (Washington). Home: 234 Valentine Lane, Yonkers, N.Y.; also 24 Cliff Road, Nantucket Island, Mass. Died May 30, 1959; buried Nantucket Island.

BROWN, John Elward, founder and pres. John Brown Schs. of Ark. and Cal.; b. Oskaloosa, Ia., Apr. 2, 1879; s. John F. and Julia A. (Brammer) B.; LL.D., 1937; m. Juanita Arrington Dec. 19, 1900; children—Jean, Helen, Virginia, Mary, Juanita, John E. Pres. Scarritt Collegiate Inst., Neosho, Mo., 1901-03; founder and pres. John Brown U., Siloam Springs, Ark., 1919—, John Brown Acad., Siloam Springs, Ark., 1920—, Brown Mil. Acad. of Ozarks, Sulphur Springs, Ark., 1944—, Brown Mil. Acad., San Diego, Cal., and The Brown Sch. for Girls, Glendora, Cal., 1937—; also founder and pres. Internat. Christian Fellowship; chmn. bd. John Brown Found., owner radio stas. KONE, Tulsa, KUOA and KUOA-FM, Siloam Springs, and KGER, Long Beach, Cal. Served in Spanish-Am. War, 1898. Fellow Nat. Geog. Soc. Methodist. Author of over 40 volumes on ednl. and Bible themes. Address: Siloam Springs, Ark. Died Feb. 12, 1957; buried Oak Hill Cemetery, Siloam Springs.

BROWN, J(ohn) Hammond, author, conservationist; b. Balt., Jan. 18, 1877; s. John Hammond and Georgia Childs (Shipley) B.; student Oakland Acad., Louisa Co., Va., Peddie Sch., Hightstown, N.J., 1897, Richmond Coll., 1898; grad. U. Ky., 1902; m. Margaret Scott Bell, Jan. 18, 1903; children—Druscilla Bell (Mrs. Charles C. Rettberg), Virginia Hammond (Mrs. H. G. Emery), Georgia Shipley (Mrs. R. L. Carmichael). Explorer jungles S. A., Yucatan sector Mexico, W.I., 1898-1903; newspaperman Herald, also Democrat, Lexington, Ky., 1899-1905; columnist Balt. News-Post, Sunday Am., since 1905; writer outdoor subjects since 1907; editor monthly mag. Outdoors Unlimited since 1940. Mem. adv. com. on wild waterfowl U.S. Dept. Interior. Mem. Am. Waterfowl Com. (sec. since 1947), Guardians of the River (founder, exec. dir. 1939), Outdoor Writers Assn. (pres.), Brotherhood Jungle Cock (founder, hon. pres.). Club: Flying Fishermen's (originator, v.p. 1938). Editor (book): Outdoors Unlimited, 1947. Home: 3800 Egerton Rd. Office: 7 St. Paul St., Balt. Died Aug. 13, 1955; buried Woodlawn Cemetery, Balt.

BROWN, John Mackenzie, physician and surgeon; b. London, Ont., Can., Apr. 10, 1878; s. William Linton and Margaret (Mackenzie) B.; M.D., U. Western Ont., 1899; m. Daisy Dunbar Rolls, Dec. 27, 1906 (dec. 1947); children—Donald Mackenzie, Margaret Mackenzie, Barbara Mackenzie (Mrs. Peter Bayne), Gordon Mackenzie; m. 2d, Marion Miller, Mar. 10, 1950. Came to U.S., 1899, naturalized, 1914. Instr. otolaryngology, med. dept. U. Cal., 1909-15; clin. prof. otology, rhinology and laryngology U. So. Cal. Med. Sch., now emeritus prof.; otolaryngologist Children's Hosp., Los Angeles, 1909—, Los Angeles County Hosp., 1932—. Fellow Am. Laryngol., Rhinol. and Otol. Soc. (pres. 1940-41), Am. Laryngol. Assn., Am. Otol. Soc., A.A.A.S., ACS, Am. Acad. Ophthal. Oto-laryng. (pres.). Club: Los Angeles Country. Home: 5342 Russell Av., Los Angeles 27. Office: 1136 W. 6th St., Los Angeles 17. Died 1955.

BROWN, J(ohn) Thompson, director, E. I. du Pont de Nemours Co.; b. Baltimore, Md., June 8, 1882; s. John Willcox and Ellen Turner (Macfarland) Brown; B.S., Virginia Polytechnic Institute 1902; student Cornell University 1902-03; married Ysabel Yolande de Vignier, April 23, 1914; children—John Willcox, Robert Mott, Odile de Vignier (dec.), John Glenn, Mary Turner, Ysabel de Vignier. With E. I. du Pont de Nemours & Co. since 1903, beginning as draftsman and advancing through engring., operating mng. positions, director since 1922, vice pres., 1929-47, member finance committee since 1947. Vice pres. United Community Fund of Northern Delaware. Trustee P.E. Church of Diocese of Delaware, Episcopal Ch. Sch. Foundation, The Delaware Hospital; vice-pres. Del-Mar-Va council, Boy Scouts of America; dir. The Family Soc. Mem. Delta Phi, Omicron Delta Kappa, Phi Kappa Phi. Episcopalian. Clubs: Wilmington, Wilmington Country, Du Pont Country, Rotary (Wilmington). Home: Montchanin, Del. Office: Du Pont Bldg., Wilmington, Del. Died Jan. 31, 1953.

BROWN, Joseph Eckford, lawyer; b. Aberdeen, Miss., Dec. 30, 1905; s. Ernest Elliot and Georgia Wicks (Eckford) B.; LL.B., U. Miss., 1926; m. Agnes Cason, Apr. 17, 1929; children—Joseph Eckford, Agnes Carson. Admitted to Miss. bar, 1926, since practiced in Natchez under own name; pros. atty. Adams County, Natchez, 1927-35; dist. atty. 6th Dist. Miss., Natchez, 1940-47; U.S. atty. So. Dist. Miss., Jackson, 1947—. Mem. Am., Miss. bar assns., Fedn. Ins. Council, Delta Psi. Democrat (Miss. del. nat. conv. 1944). Mason (Shriner). Club: St. Anthony of Miss. (Jackson). Home: 200 St. Charles Av. Office: 331 Market St., Natchez, Miss. Died May 23, 1958.

BROWN, Kenneth Rent, chemist; b. Pendleton, Ind., July 30, 1896; s. Calvin Fletcher and Mary (Rent) B.; A.B., Swarthmore Coll., 1918; m. Rae A. Horrobin, Aug. 21, 1920; children—Kenneth Horrobin, Richard Calvin, Robert Winfield. Chemist Atlas Powder Co., Wilmington, Del., 1918-26, asst. dir. Reynolds exptl. lab., 1926-28, acting dir., 1928-30, dir. research lab., 1930-40, dir. research dept., 1940-51, mem. bd., 1947, v.p., Atlas Powder Co., 1951—. Mem. Am. Chem. Soc. (councilor, 1935). Am. Inst. Chem. Engrs., Am. Inst. Chemists, Soc. Chem. Industry, Electro Chem. Soc., Am. Soc. Testing Materials, Am. Assn. Econ. Entomologists, Phi Beta Kappa, Sigma Xi, Phi Kappa Psi. Republican. Methodist. Clubs: New York Chemists; Philadelphia Engineers, Union League (Phila.). Home: 620 S. High St., West Chester, Pa. Office: Atlas Powder Co., Wilmington 99, Del. Died Mar. 18, 1958; buried Tamaqua, Pa.

BROWN, Lathrop, ex-congressman; b. N.Y.C., Feb. 26, 1883; s. Charles S. and Lucy Nevins (Barnes) B.; A.B., Harvard, 1903 (class of 1904); m. Helen Hooper, Apr. 5, 1911; children—Halla Hooper, Camilla Hooper. Began with Douglas Robinson, Charles S. Brown & Co., real estate, N.Y.C., 1904. Mem. 63rd Congress, 1st N.Y. Dist.; spl. asst. to the sec. of the Interior, Washington, Mar. 1917-Oct. 1918. Enlisted as pvt. Tank Corps, U.S.A. Democrat. Clubs: Union, Racquet and Tennis, Harvard, Down Town, Knickeebocker (N.Y.C.); Metropolitan (Washington, D.C.). Home: Montauk, Long Island, N.Y. Died Nov. 1959.

BROWN, Leigh A., corp. exec.; b. South Apalachin, N.Y., Dec. 19, 1887; s. Frank A. and Jenme (Whittaker) B.; C.E., Cornell U., 1912; m. Fern Barber, Sept. 14, 1914; children—Robert L., Gordon R., Paul W. Chief engr. Iroquois Gas Corp., Buffalo, N.Y., 1917-22, v.p., 1923-33, pres. and dir., 1934-42; pres., dir. Nat. Fuel Gas Co., N.Y.C., 1943-55, ret. as pres., 1955. Republican. Methodist. Rotarian. Home: 245 E. 80th St., N.Y.C. Office: 30 Rockefeller Plaza, N.Y.C. 20. Died Sept. 12, 1959.

BROWN, Lew, producer and songwriter; b. New Haven, Dec. 10, 1894; s. Jacob and Etta (Hirsch) B.; student DeWitt Clinton High Sch., N.Y.C.; married; children—Naomi, Arlene; m. 2d, Catherine Junewich, Nov. 25, 1939. Has written many popular songs; wrote and produced one of first talking pictures, Sunny Side Up; co-author of 21 musical comedies; discovered numerous motion picture stars; pres. Brown and Henderson. Mem. French Soc. of Authors, Composers and Pubs., Am. Legion. Democrat. Author more songs than any other writer in world, including Yes We Have No Bananas, That's Why Darkies Were Born, Beer Barrel Polka, Life Is Just a Bowl of Cherries, Birth of the Blues, and many others. First movie theme song, "Sonny Boy." Home: 100 Socor Rd., Scarsdale, N.Y. Died Feb. 5, 1958.*

BROWN, Lewis H., corp. official; b. Creston, Ia., Feb. 13, 1894; s. Lewis Henry and Arminta (Cole) B.; A.B., State University of Iowa, 1915, hon. LL.D., Temple Univ., 1942, Brown Univ., 1943; Lake Forest College, 1945; D.C.S., hon., N.Y.U., 1950; m. Mary A. Allen, June 24, 1918; children—Rosalind Louise (Mrs. Philip Iglehart), Beatrice Marie (Mrs. William H. Sweney, Jr.), and Mary Barbara (Mrs. C. E. Bayliss Griggs). With Fort Wayne (Ind.) Corrugated Paper Co., 1915-17, Montgomery Ward & Co., 1919-27; asst. to pres. Johns-Manville Corp., 1927-29, pres., 1929-46, chmn. bd. and chief exec. officer, 1946-51; chairman bd. Canadian-Johns-Manville Co., Ltd., Johns-Manville Internat. Corp., Johns-Manville Sales Corp., Johns-Manville Products Corp.; dir. Johns-Manville Corp., American Telephone & Telegraph Co., Federal Reserve Bank of New York; chmn. exec. committee Tax Foundation, Inc.; chairman American Enterprise Assn.; vice chmn. Freedoms Found.; mem. Com. on the Present Danger; dir. Citizens Nat. Com. Attended 1st Officers Training Camp, May 1917; capt. infantry, U.S. Army, Aug. 1917-May 1919, A.E.F., France. Chmn. Noise Abatement Commn., N.Y. City, 1929; mem. Pres'. Emergency Com. for Employment, 1930-31; pres. Asbestos Inst., 1933; mem. Durable Goods Indus. Com., Mar. 1934-Sept. 1935; dir. New York World's Fair, 1939 and 1940; dir. National Industrial Conference Board; member lay council New York Academy Medicine. General chmn. 23rd and 24th Annual Roll Call, and 1940 Citizens War Relief Com., N.Y. Chapter, Am. Red Cross. Received Vermilye medal, 1939, from Franklin Inst. of Pa. for "outstanding contribution in field of industrial management," Medal for Merit, 1946. Member New York Chamber Commerce, Nat. Assn. Manufactors, National Inst. Social Sciences, Phi Alpha Delta, Beta Gamma Sigma. Republican. Clubs: The Links (New York); Round Hill Country (Greenwich, Conn.); Gulf Stream (Del Ray Beach, Florida); Burning Tree Country (Washington); Union League (New York); Chicago; Minnesota (St. Paul); Pacific Union (San Francisco); Rolling Rock (Pittsburgh); Pine Valley Golf (Clementon, N.J.); Blind Brook (Port Chester, N.Y.); National Golf Links (Southampton, N.Y.); Everglades (Palm Beach, Fla.). Author: A Report on Germany, 1947. Home: Deer Park, Greenwich, Conn. Office: 22 E. 40th St., N.Y. City. Died Feb. 26, 1951; buried Putnam Cemetery, Greenwich, Conn.

BROWN, Lloyd Davidson, ret. army officer; b. Sharon, Ga., July 28, 1892; s. Dr. Lawrence Ruffin and Mary A. (Davidson) B.; A.B., U. Ga., 1912; m. Benita Allen, Sept. 10, 1919 (died Dec. 12, 1925); 1 son, Allen Davidson; m. 2d, Katherine Green, July 28, 1928. Commd. 2d lt. U.S. Army, 1917, advanced through grades to maj. gen., 1943, comd. 28th Div., later stationed Fort Benning, Ga.; retired 1948. Mem. Phi Delta Theta, Phi Beta Kappa. Methodist. Home: S. Alexander Av., Washington, Ga. Died Feb. 17, 1950; buried Washington, Ga.

BROWN, Louise Fargo, educator, historian; b. Buffalo; d. Albert Tower and Eva Perry (Fargo) Brown; A.B., Cornell U., 1903, Ph.D., 1909; student London Sch. Econs., 1906-07, U. Geneva, 1907-08, U. Zurich, 1908. Instr. history Wellesley Coll., 1909-14; instr. history Vassar Coll., 1915, asso. prof. history, 1919-34, prof., 1934-44, prof. emeritus, 1944—; dean of women, asso. prof. history U. Nev., 1915-17. Served as sgt. USMC, World War I. Fellow Royal Hist. Soc. London; mem. Am. Hist. Assn., Phi Beta Kappa. Author: Political Activities of the Baptists and Fifth Monarchy Men During the Interregnum, 1911; Freedom of the Seas, 1919; First Earl of Shaftesbury, 1933; Apostle of Democracy: the Life of Lucy Maynard Salmon, 1943; Men and Centuries of European Civilization (with George Barr Carson, Jr.), 1948. Address: Vassar College, Poughkeepsie, N.Y. Died May 1, 1955.

BROWN, Lytle, army officer; b. Nashville, Nov. 22, 1872; s. James Trimble and Jane (Nichol) B.; grad. U.S. Mil. Acad., 1898; B.E., Vanderbilt U., 1893, C.E., 1894; m. Louise Lewis, Dec. 23, 1902; children—Lytle, Eugene Lewis (dec.), Pauline Lewis, Neill Smith, James Trimble, Lewis Castner. Commd. 2d lt. engrs., 1898; promoted through grades to col. N.A., 1917; brig. gen. Nat. Army, 1918; brig. gen. U.S. Army, 1928. Participated in Santiago Campaign; engaged in Battle of San Juan, July 13, 1898; and siege of Santiago; in Philippines, as city engr. Manila, engr. officer Dept. of Northern Luzon, 1900-02; instr., asst. prof. civil and mil. engring. U.S. Mil. Acad., 1903-07; comdr. Co. E, 2d Bn. Engrs., 1907-08; in charge U.S. Engr. Dist., Louisville, 1908-12; comdr. 2d Batn. Engrs., 1912-16, engr. officer Punitive Expdn., Mexico, 1916; in charge U.S. Engr. Dist., Nashville, 1917-18; comdr. 106th Regt. Engrs., engr. officer 31st Div.; apptd. dir. War Plans Div. and pres. Army War Coll., 1918; in charge U.S. Engr. Dist., Florence, Ala., and Chattanooga, Tenn., 1919; in charge constrn. Wilson Dam, Muscle Shoals, Ala., 1919-20; regtl. comdr. 2d Engrs., 1920-21; sr. instr. engring., Gen. Service Schs., Ft. Leavenworth, Kan., 1921-23; dir. Gen. Staff Corr. Sch., 1923-24; dir. and asst. comdt., comdt. General Staff Sch. U.S. Army, 1924-25; comdg. 2d Regt. Engrs., 1925; asst. comdt. Army War Coll., 1926-28; comdg. 19th Brigade, Panama Canal Dept., 1928-29; chief of army engrs., with rank of maj. gen., 1929-33; brig. gen. comdg. Atlantic sector Panama Canal Dept., 1934; maj. gen. comdg. Panama Canal Dept., 1935-36; retired from active service, 1936. Decorated D.S.M. (U.S.); Companion of Bath (Britain); Officer Legion d'Honneur (France). Mem. Nat. Capital Park and Planning Commn., 1932-33; mem. engrs. adv. bd. RFC; mem. Tenn. Conservative Commn., 1939-40; chmn. Gov.'s Adv. Com. on Preparedness; chmn. State Def. Council, 1941; chmn. State Bd. on prevention of stream pollution, state rationing dir., 1942. Home: R.F.D. 5, Franklin, Tenn. Died May 5, 1951.

BROWN, Margaret Wise, author; b. N.Y. City, May 23, 1910; d. Robert Bruce and Maude Margaret (Johnson) Brown; student Château Brilliantmont, Lausanne, Switzerland, 1923-25; student Dana Hall, Wellesley, Mass.; B.A., Hollins (Va.) Coll., 1932. Became mem. studies and publs. dept., Bureau of Ednl. Expts., N.Y. City; editor children's books, William R. Scott, Inc., 1938-41; author under pseudonym, for children and adults. Club: Buckram Beagles (Brookville, L.I., N.Y.). Co-author: Another Here and Now Story Book. Author: The Fish with the Deep Sea Smile; Br'er Rabbit Stories from Uncle Remus; The First Story; When the Wind Blew, 1937; The Children's Year, 1937; The Streamlined Pig, 1938; The Little Pig's Picnic, 1938; Bumblebugs and Elephants, 1938; The Little Fireman, 1938; The Noisy Books, 1939; Punch and Judy, 1940; The Fables of La Fontaine, 1940; The Country Noisy Book, 1941; The Runaway Bunny; The House of a Hundred Windows; The Big Fur Secret; Ssssssh Bang; They All Saw It; The Goodnight Book; The Wonderful Story Book; Horses (under name Golden MacDonald) Big Dog, Little Dog; Red Light—Green Light; Little Lost Lamb; The Little Island; The Man in the Manhole; The Egg Book; Goodnight Moon; The Bad Little Duck-hunter; The Sleep Little Golden Book; The Little Fur Family, Whistle for the Train; The Dark Wood of the Golden Birds: Wait Till the Moon Is Full; Two Little Trains; The Winter Noisy Book; The Golden Egg; The Little Golden Sleepy Book; One Policeman; Two Little Miners; Two Little Firemen; The Little Fisherman; The Little Farmer; Pussywillow. Home: 186 East End Av., New York, N.Y.: also The Only House, Wharfs Quarry, Vinalhaven, Me. Office: 1335 York Av., N.Y.C. Died Nov. 13, 1952.

BROWN, Norriw, ex-senator; b. Maquoketa, Ia., May 2, 1863; s. William Henry Harrison and Eliza Ann (Phelps) B.; B.A., State U. of Ia., 1883, M.A., 1885; admitted to bar, 1884; m. Lula K. Beeler, Nov. 28, 1885 (died Mar. 2, 1925); m. 2d, Ann L. Howland, Feb. 5, 1927 (died Dec. 24, 1939). County atty., Buffalo County, Neb., 1892-96; deputy atty. gen., 1900-04, atty. gen. Neb., 1904-06; U.S. senator, Neb., 1907-13. Rep. Mem. law firm Brown, Crossman, West, Barton & Fitch. Conglist. Mason. Clubs: Omaha, Commercial, Country, Palimpsest, University. Home: Blackstone Hotel. Office: First Nat. Bank Bldg., Omaha, Neb. Died Jan. 25, 1960.*

BROWN, Owsley, distillery exec.; b. Louisville, Feb. 25, 1879; s. George Garvin and Amelia (Owsley) B.; student U. Va.; m. Laura Lee Lyons, Oct. 1905. Practiced law, 1903-04; exec. Brown-Forman Distillers Corp. since 1905, pres., 1917-45, now chmn. bd.; sec., treas., dir. Jefferson Island Salt Co; dir. First Nat. Bank of Louisville, Ky. Trust Co. Chmn. bd. Distilled Spirits Inst. Clubs: Pendennis, Louisville Country, River Valley; Farmington Country (University, Va.). Home: Harrods Creek. Office: 1908 Howard St., Lsvl. Died Oct. 31, 1952.

BROWN, Percy, röntegenologist; b. Cambridge, Mass., Nov. 24, 1875; s. Isaac Henry and Mary Elizabeth (Kennedy) B.; grad. Browne and Nichols Sch., Cambridge, 1893; Lawrence Sci. Sch. (Harvard), 1893-96; M.D., Harvard, 1900; m. Bernice Mayhew, Dec. 7, 1904. Röntgenologist Carney Hosp., 1903-10, St. Elizabeth's Hosp., 1905-11, L.I. Hosp., Boston, 1906-10; cons. röntgenologist Carney Hosp., 1911-13; instr. röntgenology Harvard Med. Sch., 1911-22; röntgenologist to Boston Children's Hosp., Boston Infants' Hosp., 1903-06, 10-22, St. Luke's Hosp., N.Y.C., 1924-29; röntgenologist in chief Western Pa. Hosp., Pitts., 1923. Maj., M.C., U.S. Army, Base Hosp. 5, France, 1917-18. Gold medalist Radiol. Soc. N.A., 1922; Caldwell lectr. Am. Röntgen Ray Soc., 1923. Fellow A.C.P., Am. Coll. Radiology; mem. A.M.A., Mass. Med. Soc., Boston Soc. Med. Sciences, Am. Urol. Soc., Am. Röntgen Ray Soc. (pres. 1911), Röntgen Soc. of London, Deutsche Röntgen Gesellschaft (until 1917), N.Y. Röntgen Soc., Phila. Röntgen Ray Soc. (hon.), Röntgen Ray Soc. New Eng., Boston Sci. Soc., Boston Soc. Natural Hist., Bostonian Soc. Conglist. Clubs: University, Harvard, St. Botolph (Boston); Harvard (N.Y.C.); Aesculapian of Boston (hon.). Author: American Martyrs to Science through the Roentgen Rays, 1935. Co-author of Science of Radiology for Fist Am. Congress of Radiology, Chicago, 1933. Contbr. sci. jours. and author of sundry monographs on subjects dealing with the X-Ray. Home: Egypt (Scituate), Plymouth County, Mass. Died Oct. 8, 1950; buried Martha's Vineyard, Mass.

BROWN, Percy W(hiting), investment broker; b. Concord, Mass., Jan. 21, 1887; s. Charles Edward and Florence Danforth (Whiting) B.; student Milton (Mass.) Acad., 1903-04; A.B., Harvard, 1908; m. Corinne Banks Davis, Mar. 31, 1910 (dec. Oct. 28, 1925), m. 2d, Helen Campbell Hurd, July 5, 1930; children—Roger Hamilton, Edward Randolph. Partner Hornblower & Weeks 1923—, Cleve. office 1924—; dir. Midland Steel Products Co.; mem. bd. govs. N.Y. Stock Exchange, 1942-45. Pres. community fund, Cleve., 1938-40; exec. vice chmn. Ohio War Finance Com., 1943-46. Pres. Cleve. Inst. Music, 1936-38; trustee Case Inst. Tech. Central Officers Tng. Sch., Camp Lee, Va., 1918. Mem. Cleve. C. of C. (pres. 1946-48). Cleve. Orchestra (pres., 1953-55, chmn. bd., 1955-56, chmn. exec. com., 1956—); Concord Antiquarian Society (pres. 1920-24). Home: 2005 Chestnut Hills Dr., Cleve. Heights, O. Office: Union Commerce Bldg., Cleve. Died Dec. 8, 1958; buried Sleepy Hollow Cemetery, Concord, Mass.

BROWN, Raymond Dwight, property development; b. Indpls., June 29, 1886; s. George W. and Mary Jane (Coble) B.; A.B., Wabash Coll., Crawfordsville, Ind., 1908; m. Clara Hyatt, Sept. 16, 1908; children—Betty (Mrs. Clay Johnson Jr.), Raymond, Jean (Mrs. J. W. Hendricks). Retail shoe merchant, Indpls., 1908-16; automotive distbr., 1916-22; property development, 1922—; constructs, leases bldgs. to fed. govtl. agys.; pres., dir. Thorofare Investment Corp., Pentagon Bldg. Corp., R. D. Brown, Inc., Transportation Terminal, Inc., Bapps Corp., Grayburg Oil Co., Managers Discount Corp. Mem. Ind. Soc. of Chgo., Ind. Hist. Soc., Phi Beta Kappa, Phi Gamma Delta. Republican. Presbyn. Clubs: Columbia, Woodstock Country, Athletic (Indpls.). Home: 3025 N. Meridian St., Indpls. 8. Office: 2039 E. Washington St., Indpls. 1. Died Mar. 31, 1959; buried Crown Hill Mausoleum.

BROWN, Rezeau Blanchard, pub. utilities exec; D.Sc. (hon.), U. Wis., 1936. Chmn. bd. San Antonio Pub. Service Co.; pres. Detroit City Gas Co., Am. Light & Traction Co., Grand Rapids Gas Co., Washtenau Gas Co., Muskegon Gas Co., Milwaukee Gas Light Co., Milwaukee Coke & Gas Co., W. Allis Gas Co., Wauwatosa Gas Co., Lakeshore Gas Co., Wis. Eastern Gas Co., Madison Gas & Electric Co.; dir. United Light & Power Co., United Light & Rys. Co., Continental Gas & Electric Co., Am. Light & Traction Co. Home: Arcady, Deer Harbor, Washington. Office: 626 E. Wisconsin Av., Milw. Died May 20, 1952; buried Forest Home Cemetery, Milw.

BROWN, Rollo Walter, author; b. Crooksville, O., Mar. 15, 1880; s. Alexander and Roselba (Search) B.; Litt.B., Ohio Northern U., 1903, A.M., 1904; A.M., Harvard, 1905; Litt.D., Lawrence Coll., 1927, Wabash College, 1932; L.H.D., Marietta College, 1937; LL.D., Ohio Northern University, 1942; m. Ella A. Brocklesby, September 6, 1905. Instructor rhetoric, Wabash Coll., 1905-06, prof. 1906-20; prof. English, Carleton Coll., 1920-23; lecturer on English, Harvard, 1923-24; mem. summer school faculty, Harvard, 1919. While on leave of absence, 1912-13, investigated literary tradition and teaching in écoles and lycées of France. Speaker on Franco-Amer. relations, 1917-18. Corporate mem. Edward MacDowell Assn.; mem. Com. of Authors, Science and Learning in France, 1917. Member Phi Beta Kappa fraternity. Clubs: Harvard Faculty, Boston Authors. Author: The Art of Writing English (with N. W. Barnes), 1913; How the French Boy Learns to Write, 1915; The Creative Spirit—An Inquiry into American Life, 1925; Dean Briggs, 1926; Lonely Americans, 1929; The Firemakers, 1931; Toward Romance, 1932; The Hillikin, 1935; On Writing the Biography of a Modest Man, 1935; As of the Gods, 1937; Next Door to a Poet, 1937; I Travel By Train, 1939; There Must Be a New Song, 1942; Harvard Yard in the Golden Age, 1948; Dr. Howe and the Forsythe Infirmary, 1952; The Hills Are Strong, 1953. Editor the Writer's Art—By Those Who Have Practiced It, 1921. Contributor to numerous magazines and lecturer on current and lit. topics. Home: 52 Garden St., Cambridge, Mass. Died Oct. 13, 1956; buried Mount Auburn Cemetery, Cambridge, Mass.

BROWN, Roy, landscape painter; b. Decatur, Ill., Apr. 7, 1879; s. Charles Henry and Mollie (Ellis) B.; ed. high sch., Decatur studied art at Art Students' League, New York, and Julian Acad., Paris; pupil of Jean Paul Laurens, Réné Ménard and Raffaëlli; m. Grace G. Lockett. Awarded prize and medal Nat. Arts Club, New York; Isador water color prize, Salmagundi Club; Peabody-Baltimore water color prize for group; 2d prize, silver medal, Phila. Art Week; Ranger Fund purchase prize, N.A.D., 1921; Samuel T. Shaw purchase prize ($1,000), 1925; 2d Altman prize for landscape. N.A D., 1926; Salmagundi Club purchase prize, $1,000, 1930; Nat. Arts Club prize for painting, 1936; American Water Color Soc. medal, 1937, 1943; Samuel T. Shaw water color prize Salmagundi Club, 1938. Represented in Metropolitan Museum, New York; Art Institute, Chicago; National Arts Club, New York; Northwestern U. Evanston, Ill.; Art Institute, Milwaukee, Wis.; Art Inst., Decatur, Ill.; Hackley Art Gallery, Muskegon, Mich.; John Herron Art. Inst., Indianapolis, Ind.; Art Inst., Springfield, Ill. N.A., 1926; mem. (life) N.Y. Hist. Society Am. Water Color Soc. (pres. 1939-44, and 1939-49), 1st v.p. Nat. Acad. Design, since Apr. 1949. Member New York Water Color Club, Phila. Water Color Club. Protestant. Clubs: Century, National Arts, Salmagundi (New York). Home: Wilton, N.H. Studio: 33 W. 67th St., N.Y.C. Died May 16, 1956.

BROWN, Samuel Alburtus, physician; b. Newark, Jan. 7, 1874; s. Isaac Payne and Marie (Aldridge) B.; M.D., N.Y.U., 1894, Dr.P.H., 1926; m. Charlotte Cowdrey, June 15, 1898; children—Charlotte Cowdrey, Alberta Hartley. Mem. faculty med. dept. N.Y.U. (formerly U. and Bellevue Hosp. Med. Coll.), 1896-1932, dean, 1915-32, now dean emeritus; cons. physician, Bellevue, New Rochelle Hosp., Meml. Hosp., Long Branch, French Hosp., North Hudson Hosp., Rockaway Hosp., Fitkin Meml. Hosp. Acting chmn. bd. trustees Bellevue Medical Center and N.Y. U. Served as asst. surgeon and surgeon, 12th Regt. Nat. Guard N.Y., 1900-10, lt. col. U.S. Res. Fellow A.C.P.; mem. A.M.A. Med. Soc. State of N.Y., New York County Med. Soc., N.Y. Acad. Medicine (pres. 1924-26), N.Y. Acad. Sciences, S.A.R., Harvey Soc., New York Soc. Mil. and Naval Officers of World War, Am. Legion, Alpha Omega, Phi Gamma Delta, Nu Sigma Nu. Democrat. Episcopalian. Clubs: New York Yacht, Links Golf, Woodmont Rod and Gun, Century. Home: 277 Park Av., N.Y.C.; also Sands Point, L.I., N.Y. Office: 75 55th St., N.Y.C. Died Mar. 16, 1952.

BROWN, Sevellon Ledyard, ret. editor, pub.; b. Washington, Nov. 23, 1886; s. Sevellon Alden and Sally Maynadier (Phelps) B.; student pub. schs.; Litt.D., Bates Coll., 1946 Columbia, 1954; LL.D., Brown U., 1952, R.I. U., 1954; m. Elizabeth Bonney Barry, Apr. 1911; children—Sevellon, III, Barry, Elizabeth Bonney. With Washington bureaus of United Press, N.Y. Morning Sun and N.Y. Herald; chief of Div., Fgn. Intelligence, Dept. of State, 1911, 12; Washington corr. for Providence Journal and other newspapers; editor and pub. Providence Journal and Evening Bulletin; dir. Providence Jour. Co. Mem. adv. council Pulitzer Prize Bd. Served as capt. World War I. Former dir. Am. Soc. Newspaper Editors; ex-chmn. Mng. Editors Assn. of Associated Press; founder and chmn. adv. bd. Am. Press Institute in Columbia U. Clubs: Hope, Agawam Hunt, Art. Home: 92 Prospect St. Office: Journal Bldg., Providence. Died Dec. 28, 1956.

BROWN, Sydney Barlow, educator; b. Pilot Mound, Manitoba, Can., Sept. 2, 1884; s. Robert and Anna Haselden (Unsworth) B.; student Oberlin (O.) Acad., 1901-04; A.B., Oberlin Coll., 1908; A.M., Yale, 1911; student Columbia, 1915-16, Sorbonne, Paris, 1920-21; Docteur d'Université, U. Montpellier, France, 1928; m. Gail Hamilton Ridgway, Sept. 4, 1921. Tchr. Galahad Sch., Hudson, Wis., 1908-10, Boys Collegiate Sch., Pitts., 1911-12, Hallock Sch., Great Barrington, Mass., 1912-15; mem. faculty Bates Coll., Lewiston, Me., 1916-20, prof., head French dept., 1921-26; mem. faculty U. Ariz., 1938—, head French dept., 1937—. Decorated Officier d'Academie, 1938, Chevalier de la Legion d'Honneur, 1949. Mem. bd. Tucson Symphony Orchestra, 1937—. Mem. Am. Assn. U. Profs., Modern Lang. Soc. (Rocky Mountain div.), Nat. Assn. Am. Composers and Condrs., Soc. Ariz. Composers, Tucson Fine Arts Assn., Balzac Soc. America, Phi Kappa Phi, Pi Delta Phi. Conglist. Author: La Peinture des Metiers et des Moeurs Professionnelles dans les Romans de Zola (pub. Montpelier, France). Amateur musician; composer: (songs) Your Song From Paradise, 1927; Love Time Lives for Age, 1928; Footprints, 1937. Amateur artist; works (pastel) exhibited Tucson Fine Arts Assn., 1947-48, 49-50; Boulder City, Nev., 1950. Home: 1025 Mountain Av., Tucson. Died Feb. 9, 1957.

BROWN, Sydney MacGillvary, univ. prof.; b. Marblehead, Mass., Aug. 10, 1895; s. Harrison Clifford and Ella Muriel (MacGillvary) B.; student Boston Latin Sch., 1910-13; B.A., Bowdoin Coll., Brunswick, Me., 1916; B.A., Brasenose Coll., Oxford, Eng., 1921, M.A., B. Litt., 1930; m. Eleanor Blanche Aldridge, June 19, 1919 (divorced 1946); 1 son, Dougtas McGillvary; m. 2d Mary Ellen Callis, Oct., 1946. Asst. prof. European history Lehigh U., 1923-25, asso. prof., 1925-30, prof., 1930-41, prof. history Duquesne U. since 1947. Joined British Royal Air Force, 1916; U.S.N., 1941-45, U.S. Mil. Government, 1945-47. Awarded Distinguished Flying Cross. Mem. Alpha Delta Phi, Phi Beta Kappa. Episcopalian. Author: Medieval Europe, 1932, rev. edit., 1934; England (with E. Wingfield Stratford), 1938; The Royal Pedant, 1939. Contbr. hist. articles. Home: 1214 West Point Av., Pittsburgh. Died Apr. 6, 1952; buried North Catholic Cemetery.

BROWN, Thatcher M., banker; b. N.Y. City, Mar. 8, 1876; son of John Crosby and Mary E. (Adams) B.; graduate Lawrenceville (New Jersey) school, 1893; A.B., Yale, 1897; married Caro Lord Noyes, June 3, 1904 (deceased, March 10, 1947); children—Moreau Delano, Daniel Noyes, Thatcher M. In banking business, 1897—; partner Brown Brothers & Co., 1907-31, Brown Brothers Harriman & Co., 1931-—; chmn. bd. Prudential Ins. Co. Gt. Brt., Hudson Ins. Co.; chmn. local bd. Brt. Gen. Ins. Co. Ltd., Union Assurance Soc., Ltd. of London, Palatine Ins. Co. Ltd. of London; chm. N.Y. local bd. Comml. Union Assurance Co. Ltd. of London; mem. Am. bd. Ocean Accident & Guarantee Corp., Ltd.; mem. Am. investment com. Sun Ins. Office, Ltd.; dir. Centennial Ins. Co., Columbia Casualty Co. of N.Y., Comml. Union Fire Ins. Co.; trustee Atlantic Mutual Indemnity Co., Atlantic Mutual Ins. Co. Trustee Presbyn. Hosp., N.Y.C. Mem. bd. dir. Union Theol. Sem. Mem. Delta Kappa Epsilon, Wolf's Head (Yale). Democrat. Presbyterian. Clubs: Yale, University, Downtown Assn., Century. Home: 139 E. 79th St. Office: 59 Wall St., N.Y.C. 5. Died May 2, 1954.

BROWN, Thomas Richardson, physician; b. Balt., Sept. 11, 1872; s. Thomas R. and Harriet (Carrington) B.; grad. Baltimore City Coll., 1889; A.B., Johns Hopkins, 1892, post-grad work, 1892-93, M.D., 1897; m. Jean McComb Albert, Nov. 27, 1902; 1 dau., Eleanor Albert. Practiced in Balt., 1899—; formerly asso. prof. medicine, Johns Hopkins, now emeritus; attending phys Union Meml. Hosp., Women's Hosp., Ch. Home and Infirmary. Trustee Johns Hopkins U.; chmn. med. adv. bd. Alfred I. du Pont Hosp. of Nemours Found. Democrat. Episcopalian. Mem. A.M.A., Md. Med. and Chirug. Faculty, Alpha Delta Phi, Assn. Am. Physicians, Am. Gastroenterol. Assn., Phi Beta Kappa. Club: Maryland. Home: 14 Whitfield Rd., Guilford, Balt. 10. Died Sept. 26, 1950; buried Greenmount Cemetery, Balt.

BROWN, Walter Franklin, educator; b. Richland, N.Y., Mar. 31, 1891; s. Frank and Ella M. (McClary) B.; grad. Pratt Inst., 1912; grad. study Columbia, summers 1915, 16, 17, 20; M.S., U. Toledo, 1931; m. Ethel C. Chapman, Dec. 24, 1912; children—Thayer A., Stanley C., Eloise C. (Mrs. John M. Hoffman), Joyce C. (Mrs. Jorge M. Fenton). Asst. supt. Merg Engrng. Co., Boston, 1912-13; engring. dept. Watertown (N.Y.) Light & Power Co., 1913-15; tchr. vocational edn., Troy, N.Y., 1915-18; acting prof. physics U. Toledo, 1918-19, asst. prof. elec. engring., 1919-20, asso. prof., 1920-36, prof., head dept. elec. engring., 1936—. Mem. pub. utilities com. Ohio State Bar Assn., 1930-38. Mem. Am. Inst. E.E. (asso. 1926-46), Am. Soc. Engring. Edn., Profl. Engrs. Soc., Phi Kappa Psi, Phi Kappa Phi. Home: 2418 Glenwood, Toledo. Died June 2, 1959.

BROWN, William Adams, Jr., economist; born New York, N.Y., Nov. 14, 1894; s. William Adams and Helen Gilman (Noyes) B.; student Hill Sch., Pottstown, Pa., 1908-12; A.B., Yale U., 1913-17; A.M., Columbia U., 1927, Ph.D., 1929; m. Edith Dunbar Gilman, Sept. 4, 1921; children—Edith Dunbar, Evelyn Adams. Bank clk. Brown Bros. & Co., 1919-26; Cutting traveling fellowship, Columbia U., 1927-28; asst. prof. economics, Brown U., 1928-36, asso. prof., 1936-40, prof. polit. economy, 1940-43; senior staff, Brookings Instn., 1946—. Collaborator Econ., Financial and Transit Dept., League of Nations, 1941, 42; Econ. Studies Div., Dept. of State, 1943-44, Central Secretariat 1944-46; mem. staff Commn. on Fgn. Econ. Policy, 1954; v. chmn., dept. ch. and econ. life Nat. Council of Chs. Mem. Fgn. Policy Assn. (chmn. R.I. branch, 1935-40). Dem. Presbyn. Clubs: Century Assn. (New York); Cosmos (Washington). Author: The International Gold Standard Reinterpreted, 1914-34, 1940; The United States and the Restoration of World Trade, 1949. Address: 1254 31st St., Washington 7. Died Apr. 19, 1957; buried Greenwood, Bklyn.

BROWN, William Averell, lawyer; born Cooperstown, N.Y., Sept. 28, 1885; s. Philip Auld Harrison and Jane Russell Averell (Carter) B.; A.B., Harvard, 1906; LL.B., 1908; m. Mary Alice Warren, May 19, 1927; children—William Averell, Peter Schuyler, James Warren, Mary Alice. Admitted to N.Y. bar, 1909; law clerk, Bowers & Sands, New York, N.Y., 1908-17; lawyer in law dept. U.S. Steel Corp., 1917-18, asst. gen. solicitor, 1918-41, sec. of corp., 1941-52, ret.; mem. law firm Lord & Huntington since 1952. Mem. Assn. Bar City of N.Y., Am. Bar Assn., Am. Iron and Steel Inst. Clubs: Harvard, Century Assn. (New York). Home: 129 E. 95th St. 28. Office: 71 Broadway, N.Y.C. 6. Died Apr. 30, 1953.

BROWN, William O., business exec.; b. Portsmouth, O., March 29, 1876; s. James Anthony and Martha Jane (Martin) B.; grad. Rayen High Sch., Youngstown, O.; m. Alma Marie Maag, Sept. 9, 1903; children—Elizabeth Martha, William James. With U.S. Steel Corp., 1897-1902; bus. mgr. Vindicator, 1902—, treas., 1936—, pres., 1945—; publisher Daily and Sunday Youngstown Vindicator; dir. Youngstown Arc. Engraving Co.; vice pres., dir. WFMJ Broadcasting Co. Life mem. U.S. Revolver Assn., Nat. Rifle Assn. Republican. Methodist. Mason (32°, K.T., Shriner), Elk. Clubs: Youngstown, Youngstown (O.) Country. Home: 302 Boardman Poland Rd., Youngstown 12. Office: Vindicator Bldg., Youngstown 1, O. Died Feb. 23, 1956.

BROWN, William Thayer, business exec.; b. Chgo., Nov. 1, 1895; s. William T. and Mary L. (Spalding) B.; Ph.B., Yale; grad. study Harvard; m. Frances Tener, Nov. 6, 1920; children—William Thayer, Jr. (died in Italy, Nov. 9, 1944), Alex T., Horace S., Jeremy; m. 2d Elizabeth Riggs Barr, Dec. 8, 1945. Vice pres. A.G. Spalding & Bros., Inc., Chicopee, Mass., 1933-52, pres. since 1952; dir. Third Nat. Bank & Trust Co., Springfield, Mass., since 1952. Mem. exec. com. Asso. Industries of Mass. since 1940, v.p. since 1949; dir. Employers Assn. of Western Mass. since 1943, pres., 1947-49. Chmn. Town Plan Commn., Suffield, Conn., 1942-49. Mem. Newcomen Soc. of Eng., Hartford-Springfield Post Am. Ordnance Assn. (dir. since 1952). Republican. Conglist. Home: West Suffield, Conn. Office: care A.G. Spalding & Bros., Inc., Chicopee, Mass. Died Aug. 23, 1953; buried Woodlawn Cemetery, Suffield, Conn.

BROWN, Wilson, naval officer; b. Phila., Pa., 1882; s. Wilson and Sarah Ann (Cochran) B.; student Penn Charter Sch., Phila., 1890; grad. U.S. Naval Acad., 1902; m. Lydia Ballou Chappell, Aug. 4, 1924. Commd. ensign, U.S. Navy, 1902, and advanced through the grades to rear adm., 1936; comdg. training squadron, Scouting Force, U.S.S. New York, 1936-37; supt. U.S. Naval Acad., Annapolis, Md., 1938-41; became vice adm. comdg. Scouting Force, Pacific Fleet, 1941; apptd. aide to President Roosevelt, Feb. 1943; retired Dec. 1944. Episcopalian. Clubs: Army and Navy, Chevy Chase, N.Y. Yacht. Home: Waterford, Conn. Died Jan. 2, 1957.

BROWNE, Belmore, artist; b. New Brighton, S.I., N.Y., June 9, 1880; s. George and Ella (Haskell) B.; ed. pvt. schs.; studied art under William M. Chase and Academy Julian, Paris; married Agnes E. Sibley, October 14, 1913; children—Evelyn, George. Illustrator, 1902-12; began painting, 1913; exhibited Nat. Acad. Design, Pa. Acad., Corcoran Art Gallery (Washington, D.C.), Venice Biennial, etc. Represented in Nat. Gallery (Washington, D.C.), Rochester Mus. of Art, Amherst Coll. Executed dioramas Am. Museum of Natural History, Mus. of Sci., Boston; specialty, mountain landscapes, A.N.A., 1928. Dir. Santa Barbara Sch. of Arts, 1930-34, also San Francisco Mus. of Sci. Capt. Aviation Sect. Signal Corps., World War I; U.S.A.A.F., World War II; Spl. cons. A.A.F. Material Comd., Wright Field, 1942-43; spl. cons. Arctic Training Sch., 1943-45; spl. cons. to Lovat's Scouts (British), Feb.-May, 1944; dir. for Wright Field, Ladd Field, Alaska, 1942-45; consultant 3904th Training Squadron U.S.A.F., 1950-51. Mem. Nat. Court of Honor Boy Scouts of Am. Author: The Conquest of Mt. McKinley, 1913; also other books on Alaskan adventures. Collaborator A.A.F. training manuals. Home: (winter) Ross, Marin County, Calif.; (summer) Seebe, Alberta, Canada. Died May 3, 1954.

BROWNE, Duncan Hodge, clergyman; b. Orange, N.J., Oct. 31, 1879; s. Thomas Prossor and Sarah (Hodge) B.; A.B., Columbia, 1905, post-grad., 1906, hon. S.T.D., 1923; student Gen. Theol. Sem. and Union Theol. Sem., 1905-08; m. Alice Bell Lester, July 12, 1911; children—Lester, Duncan Hodge. Ordained deacon P.E. Ch., 1908, priest, 1909; vicar Bronx Ch. House, N.Y.C., 1908-10; rector Christ Ch., New Brighton, N.Y., 1910-21; dean Saint John's Cathedral, Denver, 1921-24; rector Saint James' Ch., Chgo., 1924-50, ret.; rector St. Peter's, Winanno, 1950-52. Trustee Saint Luke's Hosp. Served as chaplain, capt. with 305th Inf., 77th Div. AEF, France, 1917-19. Decorated for gallantry in action. Mem. Delta Kappa Epsilon. Clubs: University (Chgo.); University, Columbia University (N.Y.C.). Home: 200 E. Delaware Pl., Chgo. 11. Oifice: 666 Rush Av., Chgo. Deceased.*

BROWNE, Edward Tankard, college prof.; b. Northumberland County, Va., Nov. 22, 1894; s. Henry James and Mary Rebecca (Gunn) B.; A.B., U. of Va., 1915, A.M., 1917; Ph.D., U. of Chicago, 1926; m. Catharine Cole Boyd, Sept. 2, 1924; children—Marianne Boyd, Edward T., William Boyd. Instr. in mathematics, U. of Va., 1915-17, Coll. of William and Mary, summer 1919; fellow in math., U. of Chicago, 1919-20; asst. prof. mathematics, Trinity Coll., Hartford, Conn., 1921-22; asst. prof. mathematics, U. of N.C., 1922-26, asso. prof., 1926-32, prof. since 1932. Served with U.S. Army, World War I. Instr. in mathematics, Am. Army Univ., Shrivenham, England, July-Dec., 1945; with Am. army in Germany, Jan.-Feb. 1946. Member American Math. Soc., Math. Assn. of Am. (mem. bd. govs., 1944-45), Elisha Mitchell Sci. Soc. (pres. 1932-33, permanent sec. since 1935), N.C. Acad. Science. Mem. Zeta Psi, Gamma Alpha, Alpha Phi Omega, Phi Beta Kappa, Sigma Xi. Democrat. Methodist. Author: (with J. W. Lasley, Jr.) Introductory Mathematics, 1933; (with E.A. Cameron) College Algebra, 1948, Introduction to the Theory of Determinants and Matrices, 1958; also articles profl. jours. Home: 730 E. Franklin St., Chapel Hill, N.C. Died Mar. 31, 1959; buried New Chapel Hill Cemetery.

BROWNE, George Israel, clergyman; b. Brooklyn, Conn., Mar. 19, 1866; s. George and Katharine Toucey (Camp) B.; B.A., Trinity Coll., Conn., 1888, M.A., 1894; grad. Berkeley Div. Sch., 1891; m. Mary Freeborn Davenport, June 20, 1894. Deacon, 1891, priest, 1892, P.E. Ch.; curate St. John's Ch., Stamford, Conn., 1891-94, rector Trinity Ch., Branford, Conn., 1894-98, St. John's Ch., Bellefonte, Pa., 1898-06, St. Paul's Ch., Harrisburg, 1906-08, St. John's Ch., Lancaster, 1908-20, St. John's Ch., Washington, Conn., 1920-23. Mem. S.R., Penn. Soc., Col. Daniel Putnam Assn. (pres.), Capt. Deliverance Browne Assn., Conn. Soc. Colonial Wars, Delta Kappa Epsilon. Mason (32°, K.T.). Alumni lectr. on pastoral theology, Berkeley Div. Sch., 1916-17. One of editors Social Preparation for the Kingdom of God. Home: Washington, Conn. Died July 29, 1930.

BROWNE, Harry C., C.S. lectr.; b. North Adams, Mass., Aug. 18, 1878; s. Isaac Snell and Elizabeth (Tobin) B.; student pub. schs. North Adams; m. Edith Elizabeth Jacklin, Nov. 7, 1900; 1 dau., Jane Elizabeth. Began as actor, 1900; toured with repertoire companies and later played with stock companies in East and Middle West; began 1909 under mgmt. Klaw and Erlanger, Cohan and Harris, David Belasco, William Harris, Comstock and Gest, Selwyn Bros., Actors Theatre, etc.; radio work with CBS, 1926-31. Became interested in Christian Science in 1910, became practitioner, 1932; served in various capacities 2d Ch., N.Y.C., including first reader, 1933-36; first reader Mother Church, Boston, 1938-41; mem. Bd. of Lectureship 1942-46; pres. Mother Ch., 1948-49; official ch. spokesman on weekly broadcasts, 1946. Served in Santiago Campaign, Spanish Am. War, 1898. Lectured on the war, 1898-99. Mason. Address: 107 Falmouth St., Boston 15. Deceased.

BROWNE, Louis Edgar, foreign trade expert; b. Lynn, Mass., Oct. 20, 1891; s. Edgar Willis and Hattie Westerfield (Adams) B.; ed. U.S. Naval Acad., 1910-12; m. Ouida Risner, May 4, 1920; m. 2d, Eleanor Bode, July 14, 1934; children—Marylou Adams, Virginia Westerfield, Hendrik Adams, Christopher Carter. Began as journalist, 1912; Washington corr. New York Herald, 1913; war corr. Chicago Daily News, New York Globe and Philadelphia Bulletin with Allied Forces in Dardanelles, Suvla Bay, Egypt, India, Mesopotamia, Macedonia; with Servian Army in retreat; with Brit. Forces in France; Holland; Russia, 1917, through Revolution to July 1918; served in U.S.N.R.F., July-Dec. 1918; special corr. Chicago Daily News in Near East, 1919; exec. sec. Am.-Russian Chamber of Commerce 1929-42, 1944-—. Lt. col. on active service with U.S. Army, 1942-43, chief U.S.S.R. Sect., Mil. Intelligence Div., War Dept., Washington. Episcopalian. Mason. Clubs: National Press (Washington, D.C.); Lotos (New York). Author: Economic Handbook of the Soviet Union, 1932; Handbook of the Soviet Union, 1935. Contbr. articles on fgn. trade to jours. Home: Briarcliff Dr., Gainesville, Fla. Office: 245 Fifth Av., N.Y.C. Died Feb. 10, 1951; buried Gainesville, Fla.

BROWNE, Maurice, theatrical dir., dramatist; b. Reading, Eng., Feb. 12, 1881; s. Frederick Herbert and Frances Anna (Neligan) B.; B.A., U. of Cambridge, Eng., 1903, sr. classical scholar, Peterhouse; m. Ellen Van Volkenburg, 1912. Teacher until 1906; founder, 1906, Samurai Press, pub. works of Georgian poets; came to U.S., 1910; founder, with Ellen Van Volkenburg, Chgo. Little Theatre, dir. 1912-1918; engaged in repertory northwest U.S. 1918-26; produced Journey's End, in London, Eng., 1929. Author: Zetétés and other poems, 1905; Epithalamios, 1906; Job (dramatic poem), 1906; Songs of Exile, 1907; The King of the Jews (a tragedy), 1916; also prose publs., The Nature and Function of Poetry, 1908; The Temple of a Living Art, 1913; The New Rhythmic Drama, 1914. Address: London, Eng. Died Jan. 21, 1954.

BROWNE, Ralph Cowan, roentgenologist, inventor; b. Salem, Mass., Nov. 15, 1880; s. Josiah Hill and Katherine (Cowan) B.; grad. high sch., Salem, 1898; m. Mary Belle Moody, Jan. 15, 1908 (died Apr. 1952); m. 2d, Florence May Hart Cox, Nov. 21, 1952. Principally interested in research and invention; now pres. Brown Apparatus Co.; tech. expert L. E. Knott Apparatus Co.; Roentgenologist Salem Hosp. Inventor of elec. system and mechanism adopted by U.S. Govt. in North Sea mine barrage, World War I; inventor Brown portable X-ray apparatus, Brown air-lift mine pump, zincit chalcopyrite detector (used in wireless telegraphy), high resistance transmitters (used in telephony). Republican. Conglist. Home: Salem, Mass. Died Jan. 1, 1960; buried Green Lawn Cemetery.

BROWNE, Robert Bell, educator; b. Oshkosh, Wis., July 15, 1894; s. George Mervin and Addie (Gordon) B.; Ed.B., So. Ill. State Normal U., 1918; M.S., U. Ill., 1929, Ph.D., 1934; m. Frances Fowler, June 19, 1921; children—Robert Bell, Mervin Fowler. Instr. pvt. sch., Burnsville, N.C., 1913-16; prin. high sch., Pittsfield, Ill., 1919-21, supt. schs., 1921-28; prin. high sch., Casey, 1928-29; instr. edn., U. Ill., 1929-31, asst. dean liberal arts, 1931-34, dir. Extension, 1934—, dir. summer session, 1938—, asso. prof. edn. 1940-46, prof. edn., 1946—; dean, univ. extension, summer sessions, 1947—. Mem. Intercollegiate Athletic Conf. 1949—. Served as lt. Inf., U.S. Army, 1918-19. Pres. Urbana Pub. Library Bd.; mem. Ill. State Commn. for Edn. of the Handicapped 1941-52; mem. Ill. State Teachers Examining Bd. 1943—; pres. Nat. Univ. Extension Assn., 1943; mem. Ill. State Library Bd., 1951—. Mem. N.E.A., Ill. Assn. Adult Edn. (pres. 1941), Assn. Summer Deans and Dirs. (pres. 1952), A.A.A.S., Civil War Round Table; Am. Council on Education (del.); Pi Kappa Alpha, Phi Delta Kappa, Phi Eta Sigma, Kappa Delta Pi. Presbyterian. Clubs: Univ. (Urbana); Schoolmasters. Co-author: Workbook in Economic History of the United States, 1932. Home: 812 W. Florida, Urbana, Ill. Died June 6, 1959; buried Oakland Cemetery, Carbondale, Ill.

BROWNE, Waldo Ralph, editor; b. St. Joseph, Mich., Feb. 2, 1876; s. Francis Fisher and Susan Seaman (Brooks) B.; student pub. schs.; m. Susanna Avery Shanklin, June 5, 1915. Asst. editor The Dial, 1900-12, editor, 1912-16; lit. editor The Nation, 1919. Editor and Compiler: Right Reading, 1905; Joys of the Road, 1911; The Rolling Earth (nature-passages selected from writings of Walt Whitman), 1912; Books and the Quiet Life (selections from George Gissing), 1914; Man of the State?, 1919; What's What in the Labor Movement, 1921; Century Library of American Antiques, 1926-34; Barnum's Own Story—the autobiography of P. T. Barnum, 1927. Author: Altgeld of Illinois (biography), 1924; Chronicles of an American Home, 1930. Mem. central eitoral staff Fed. Writers' Project, Works Progress Adminstrn., Washington, 1935-39. Home: Wyoming, N.Y. Died Jan. 1954.

BROWNELL, Francis Herbert, corp. officer; b. Little Compton, R.I., Apr. 21, 1867; s. Frederick Richmond and Anne Dyke (Coggeshall) B.; A.B., Brown U., 1888; student Columbia Law Sch., 1888-90; m. Josephine Noble, Apr. 14, 1894; children—Francis Herbert, Kenneth Cooke. Practiced law, Tacoma, Wash., 1891, Everett, Wash., 1892-1909, Seattle, 1909-16; moved to New York as gen. counsel Am. Smelting & Refining Co., v.p. and gen. counsel 1917, chmn. finance com., 1918—, became 1st v.p. 1920, chmn. bd. and chmn. finance com., 1930—; pres. and chmn. bd. Federal Mining & Smelting Co.; chmn. of bd. dirs. General Cable Corp.; chmn. bd. dirs. Revere Copper & Brass Inc.; dir. and member exec. com. N.P. Ry. Co., Chase Nat. Bank; dir. American Sugar Refining Company. Former president Washington State Bar Association, Everett Chamber Commerce, Everett Hosp. and Everett Library. Mem. of Alpha Delta Phi and Phi Beta Kappa fraternities. Republican. Episcopalian. Clubs: University, Bankers of America, Blind Brook, Round Hill; Rainier (Seattle). Home: Greenwich, Conn. Office: 120 Broadway, N.Y.C. Died Mar. 8, 1954.

BROWNELL, Kenneth C., business exec.; b. Everett, Wash., Mar. 27, 1903; s. Francis H. and Josephine (Noble) B.; grad. Yale, 1925; studnt Harvard Bus. Sch.; m. Elizabeth Hyde, Feb. 12, 1927; children—Kenneth Hyde, Ann, Jonathan Noble. Chmn. Am. Smelting & Refining Co.; dir. Great No. Paper Co., Revere Copper & Brass Co., Gen. Cable Corp., Chase Manhattan Bank, First National Bank of Greenwich. Trustee Rockefeller Institute Medical Research, John Simon Guggenheim Memorial Foundation. Member Phi Beta Kappa, Sigma Xi. Clubs: Bankers, Downtown Association, Yale, Union (N.Y.); Round Hill, Field (Greenwich, Conn.). Home: Greenwich, Conn. Office: 120 Broadway, N.Y.C. Died Aug. 4, 1958.

BROWNING, Grace, social worker; b. Geary, Okla., Dec. 30, 1904; A.B., U. of Okla., 1925; A.M., U. of Chicago, 1934, Ph.D., 1942. Case worker, United Provident Assn., Oklahoma City, Okla., 1925-29, supervisor case work, 1930-33; asso. dir., spl. Placement Bureau for Physically Handicapped, St. Louis County Chapter, Am. Red Cross, 1929-30; instr. Sch. of Social Work, Tulane U., New Orleans, La., 1934-36; asst. in reorgn. of social service div., Okla. Emergency Relief Adminstrn. (on loan), summer 1935; asst. dir., Okla. State Dept. Pub. Welfare, 1936-37; asst. prof., Sch. of Social Service Adminstrn., U. of Chicago, 1937-43; asso. prof. Sch. of Applied Social Sciences, U. Pittsburgh, 1943-45; dir. Div. Social Service and prof. social work, Ind. U. 1945—. Mem. Am. Assn. Social Workers, Mortar Board, Phi Beta Kappa. Author: (with S. P. Breckinridge) The Historical Development of Legislation for Poor Relief in Kansas, 1935; Rural Public Welfare, 1941. Editor: (with E. S. Dixon) Social Case Records: Family Welfare, 1938. Contbr. articles to various periodicals. Address: 122 E. Michigan St., Indpls. Died Feb. 7, 1951; buried Geary, Okla.

BROWNING, McPherson, chmn. bd. Detroit Trust Co.; b. Elkhart, Ind.; s. Henry and Mary (McPherson) B.; ed. U. of Mich.; m. Dorothy Eddy, Oct. 1, 1912; children—McPherson Eddy, Florence Eddy. Successively with McPherson State Bank, Howell, Mich., Nat. Bank of Republic and Griswold Browning Co., Chicago; auditor, bond dept. officer and v.p. Detroit Trust Co., 1907-27, pres., 1927-42, chmn. bd. since 1942; dir. McPherson State Bank. Trustee Harper Hosp. and Children's Fund of Mich. Mem. board directors Detroit Commn. Fund. Clubs: Bankers (past pres.), Detroit (past pres.), Detroit Country; Crosse Pointe, Economic. Home: Howell, Mich. Office: Detroit Trust Co., 201 W. Fort St., Detroit 26. Died 1953.

BROWNING, Miles (Rutherford), ret. naval officer; b. Perth Amboy, N.J., Apr. 10, 1897; s. Oren Fogle and Sarah Louise (Smith) B.; B.S., U.S. Naval Acad., 1917; grad. Naval War Coll., 1936-37; m. Katherine Jane Ejnon, Mar. 30, 1943. Commd. ensign USN, 1917, advanced through grades to rear adm., 1947; served in Atlantic Grand Fleet, World War I; naval aviation, 1924-46; chief of staff, South Pacific Area and Force, 1942-43; comdr. U.S.S. Hornet, 1943-44; air and naval instr. and dir. of naval instrn. Command and Gen. Staff Coll., 1944-46, ret. from active duty, 1947; dir. Md. Civil Def., 1950-52. Decorated D.S.M., Silver Star, Navy Spl. Commendation Ribbon, Army Commendation Ribbon, Presdl. Unit Citation (twice). Contbr. articles on prof. subjects and allied matters to Mil. Rev., Marine Corps Gazette, Sea Power, Jour. of Ednl. Sociology. Home: 3 Elms Farm, Pumpkin Hill Rd., Warner, N.H. Address: care Navy Dept., Washington. Died Sept. 29, 1954.

BRUBAKER, Howard, writer; b. Warsaw, Ind., June 26, 1882; s. John Henry and Harriet (Bly) B.; A.B., Ind. U., Bloomington, 1902; m. Louise Maynard, of N.Y. City, Oct. 7, 1912; m. 2d, Hortense Bass, 1935; 1 son, David B. Financial sec. Univ. Settlement Soc., New York, 1902-05; asst., Bur. Municipal Research, 1906; asso. editor Success Mag., 1907-11; asst. editor Collier's Weekly, New York, 1914-19; contributing editor The Liberator, 1918-24; mng. editor Success, 1922-23; sec. Writers' Publishing Co., 1923—, also with The New Yorker; author column, Of All Things, New Yorker mag., 1925-51. Mem. Beta Theta Pi. Club: Players. Author: Ranny, 1917; White House Blues, 1932. Coined word Dixiecrat. Contbr. short stories and articles to various mags. Home: Green's Farms, Conn. Died Feb. 2, 1957; buried, Greens Farms Cemetery, Green Farms.

BRUCE, Frank M., Sr., pub.; b. Milwaukee, Wis., Dec. 25, 1885; s. William George and Monica (Moehring) B.; B.A., Marquette Univ., 1905, M.A., 1910; B.A., Univ. of Wis., 1906; m. Alma Müeller, Nov. 24, 1910; children—William George, Frank, Alice Mary (Mrs. James Gaunt), Jane, Robert C. Entire career with The Bruce Pub. Co., pubs. ednl. mags., Milwaukee; started as office boy, 1906 and advanced through ranks to pub., sec.-treas. of co. Recipient Alumni award of Merit, Marquette Univ., 1946. Mem. Nat. Sch. Service Inst. (sec.), Internat. Serra (past pres.), Marquette Univ. Alumni Assn. (past pres.), Rural Life Conf. (sec.), St. Vincent de Paul Soc. (met. pres.), Am. Interprofessional Inst., Holy Name Soc., Roman Catholic. K.C. Clubs: Rotary (past pres.), Milwaukee Athletic, University. Home: 1113 S. Third St. Office: 540 W. Milwaukee St., Milw. 1. Died Feb. 22, 1953.*

BRUCE, John Edgar, mfg. exec.; b. Balt., June 4, 1899; s. John Franklyn and Capitola (Shaw) B.; B.A., Harvard, 1920, LL.B., 1924; m. Marian Elizabeth Majesky, Dec. 17, 1937; children—Barbara Ann, Robert David. Asst. gen. counsel Wheeling Steel Corp. 1924—, asst. sec., 1926-34, sec., 1934—; secretary Wheeling Corrugating Co., 1953-58, sec., gen. counsel, 1958—. Mem. Am., W.Va. State, W.Va. Ohio Co. bar assns., Am. Soc. Corporate Secs., Inc. Club: Fort Henry, Wheeling Country. Home: Hubbard Lane. Office: Wheeling Steel Corp., Wheeling, W.Va. Died Aug. 8, 1958.

BRUÉRE, Henry, banker; b. St. Charles, Mo., Jan. 15, 1882; studied Cornell U. 2 yrs.; Ph.B., U. Chgo., 1901; grad. studies Harvard and Columbia; law schs. Harvard and N.Y.U.; LL.D., Hobart Coll.; married Jane Munroe, August 4, 1904; children—Richard Treat, Geoffrey Munroe, Honora (Mrs. Colin McIver), Alison (Mrs. George Carnahan). Dir. boys' clubs welfare work, Boston, 1901-03; dir. McCormick Works, Internat. Harvester Co., welfare work, 1903-05; organizer and dir. Citizen's Betterment Bureau, later Bureau of Municipal Research, New York (made studies of city management, U.S. and Europe; helped introduce budget reforms, N.Y. City and elsewhere), 1907-14; chamberlain, City of New York, in charge of reorganization studies for Mayor's depts., 1914-16; financial adviser Govt. of Mexico, 1917-19; dir. N.Y. State Div., U.S. Employment service, for war emergency, 1918-19; 4th, later 3d v.p. Metropolitan Life Ins. Co., 1923-27; 1st v.p. and treas. Bowery Savings Bank, 1927-31, pres., 1931-49, chmn. bd., chief exec. officer, 1949-52, hon. chmn. bd. dirs., 1952—; mem. N.Y. adv. com. RFC, 1932-39; bd. reorgn. mgrs. C.&N.W. Ry., 1945. Spl. asst. to Pres. of U.S. in coordination of activities, 1933; dir. N.Y. World Fair, 1939; mem. N.Y. U.S. Savs. Bond Com. during war period; mem. Moore com. on constitutional Tax and Debt Limits and City-Sch. Fiscal Relations, 1949-51; mem. gov's. commn. on School Buildings, 1950-51; hon. v.p. Budget Commn., N.Y. C.; chmn. Mayor's adv. com. for better housing. Mem. Winter Park Long Term Planning Bd., 1957—. Mem. personnel com. and nat. council Boy Scouts Am., 1927-56; hon. trustee N.Y. Pub. Library; trustee, treas. Inst. Pub. Adminstrn., trustee Gramercy Park, N.Y.; trustee Valerie Home, Inc., 1916—, treas., 1931-55. Recipient gold medal, Nat. Inst. Social Scis.; distinguished service N.Y.C.; medal New York Citizens Budget Commission; honorary Phi Beta Kappa. President Nat. medal, U. Chgo.; citation Sec. Treasury, Mayor of Municipal League, 1951-53. Clubs: University, Players, Century, Pilgrims; University: (Winter Park, Fla.). Author of handbooks on municipal and business adminstrn. Home: 890 Georgia Av., Winter Park, Fla. Died Feb. 17, 1958.

BRUES, Charles Thomas (brōōz), zoölogist; b. Wheeling, W.Va., June 20, 1879; s. Charles Thomas and Ada (Mossie) B.; B.S., University of Texas, 1901, M.S., 1902; studied Columbia University, 1903-04; A.M., Harvard Univ., 1942; m. Beirne Barrett, June 16, 1904; children—Austin Moore, Alice Mossie. Fellow in zoölogy, Columbia, 1903-04; spl. field agt., U.S. Dept. Agr., 1904-05; curator invertebrate zoölogy, Milwaukee (Wis.) Pub. Mus., 1905-09; instr. in econ. entomology, 1909-12, asst. prof., 1912-26, associate professor, 1926-35, professor entomology 1935-45, professor emeritus, 1946—. Harvard; associate curator insects, Museum Comparative Zoology. Biological research West Indies, 1910, 12, 1926-27; Dutch East Indies, 1937; Philippines, 1949. Member National Research Council, 1917-19. Fellow Am. Acad. Arts and Sciences, A.A.A.S., Entomol. Soc. America (pres. 1929); mem. Am. Assn. Econ. Entomologists, Cambridge Entomol. Club, Am. Soc. of Naturalists Boston Soc. of Natural Hist., Chicago Acad. Sci. (hon.), Florida Academy Science, Florida Entomological Soc. (honorary), Sigma Xi. Club: Harvard Faculty. Author: (with A. L. Melander) A Key to the Families of North Amer. Insects, 1915, Insects and Human Welfare, 1920 (2d ed., 1947); Classification of Insects (with A. L. Melander), 1931. Insect Dietary; An Account of the Food Habits of Insects, 1945. Editor of Psyche (jour. of entomology) 1909—. Author several hundred articles in scientific jours., mainly on insects. Address: Biological Laboratories, Harvard Univ., Cambridge 38, Mass. Died July 22, 1955; buried Mount Auburn Cemetery, Cambridge.

BRUINS, John H., fgn. diplomatic service; b. May 5, 1896; s. William H. and Henrietta (Teroller) B.; A.B., Hamilton Coll., 1918; m. Dorothy Irene Dangremond, Aug. 14, 1926; children—William H., Barton. Financial, credit investigator, 1919-23; entered State Dept. Fgn. Service, 1923; vice consul, Riga, Latvia, 1924-26; Singapore, 1926-29; consul, Southampton, 1929-31; Hamburg, 1931-33; Danzig, 1934; Prague, 1935-39; Hong Kong, 1939-41; on duty in State Dept., 1942-44; first sec. to Am. Embassy near Govt. of Czechoslovakia in London, 1944-45, counselor of Am. Embassy, Praha, Czechoslovakia, 1946-48; at National War Coll., Wash., 1948-49; counselor Am. embassy, London, 1949-50, counselor American legation, Beirut, Lebanon, since 1951. Served as 2d lt., U.S. Army mil. intelligence div., 1918-19. Life fellow Am. Geog. Soc. Mem. Lambda Chi Alpha. Presbyn. Clubs: Royal Hong Kong Golf; Cosmos (Washington); Allies (London). Address: American Embassy, Beirut, Lebanon. Died Dec. 26, 1954; buried Arlington Nat. Cemetery.

BRUMBAUGH, Roy Talmage, clergyman; b. Pipersville, Pa., Apr. 15, 1890; s. Simon Smucker and Elizabeth (Moyer) B.; student Lehigh U., 1908-09; B.S., Gettysburg (Pa.) Coll., 1912, D.D., 1930; grad. study U. Pa., summer 1914, U. Ill., summer 1915; grad. Princeton Theol. Sem., 1919; m. Margaret Valentine, Jan. 24, 1911; children—Margaret Elizabeth, Katherine Adele, Ruth Valentine, Roy Talmage. Tchr. Friends Sch., Wilmington, Del., 1912-13, high sch., Trenton, N.J., 1913-16; ordained to ministry Presbyn. Ch., 1919; pastor successively at Atlanta, Ga., Coatesville, Pa., Phila., 1920-30; pastor First Ch., Tacoma, Wash., 1930-35, Independent Bible Ch., Tacoma, 1935-41, Bible Presbyn. Ch., Tacoma, 1941—. Moderator Presbytery of Chattanooga, 1923, Chester, Pa., 1927, Olympia, Wash., 1933-34; moderator Presbytery Pacific N.W. of Bible Presbyn. Ch. of Am., 1940-41, 51-52. Dir. Ind. Bd. for Presbyn. Fgn. Missions, Faith Theol. Sem., Summer Bible Sch. Assn., 1933-48; pres. Ind. Fundamental Chs. Am., 1938; mem. sponsoring com. Am. Council Christian Chs. Coms. Nat. Missions and Young People of the Bible Presbyn. Ch. Am., 1944-52. Chaplain, Wash. State Guard Res., 1940-42. Moderator Bible Presbyn.

Synod, 1947-48; rep. Internat. Council Christian Chs. round the World flight, 1950. Mem. S.A.R., Phi Gamma Delta. Author: The Faith That Wins, 1929, also 13 booklets, 1930-34; Nations in Commotion, 1934; Daniel and the Latter Days, 1935; Booklets for Christian Workmen, 1947; of evangelical papers, 1937-39; God Tells Us, 1939-40. Contbr. to religious mags. and newspapers. Bible conf. and radio speaker. Weekly religious articles in Tacoma Times, 1930-34, and 1942-40, page on Christian Thinking, Western Railway Rev. 1943-47; Is the End Near, 1945; contbr. Christian Beacon. Home: 1728 N. Fife St., Tacoma 6. Died Jan. 3, 1957.

BRUMM, Charles Napoleon, ex-congressman; b. Pottsville, Pa., June 9, 1838; s. George R. and Salome (Gernholt) B.; student Pa. Coll., Gettysburg; m. Virginia James, Apr. 7, 1862. Served 3 mos. pvt. and lt., and 3 yrs. as 1st lt. 76th Pa. Vols., and asst. q.-m. and a.-d.-c. on staff of Gens. Barton and Pennypacker. Admitted to bar, 1871, and since practiced Minersville, Pa. Elected to Congress, 1878, but counted out; mem. 47th to 50th Congresses (1881-89), 54th, 55th (1895-99), 59th Congress for unexpired term (1906-07), of George R. Patterson, deceased, and 60th Congress (1907-09), 12th Pa. Dist.; resigned, Jan., 1909; county judge, 1909—. Republican. Mem. Loyal Legion, G.A.R. Address: Minersville, Pa. Deceased.

BRUMM, John Lewis (brum), educator; b. Flint, Mich., Aug. 13, 1878; s. Lewis and Louise (Baltz) B.; A.B., U. Mich., 1904, A.M., 1906, postgrad., 1906-08; m. Clara Louise Moffett, Sept. 18, 1908; children—John Moffett, Phyllis Louise, Jean Carol. Instr. rhetoric U. Mich., 1905-11, asst. prof. rhetoric, 1911-18, asso. prof., 1918-21, prof. journalism, 1924-48, head dept. journalism, 1924-48, ret., prof. emeritus, 1948, lectr. extension service; editor Cass City (Mich.) Chronicle, summers 1902-03. Organizer, 1918, permanent sec. U. Press Club of Mich.; co-organizer Mich. Interscholastic Press Assn., 1925; dir. Jr. Class plays, 1915-24, Sr. Class plays, 1920-24. Mem. Am. Assn. U. Profs., Am. Assn. Tchrs. Journalism, Am. Acad. Polit.. nd Social Sci., Phi Kappa, Phi, Sigma Delta Chi, Phi Kappa Sigma. Ind. Republican. Methodist. Club: University. Author: (plays) The Strait-Jacket, Scrambled Ego, The Mayor's Husband, What Grandmothers Know, Why Print That?, Editors Are Also People, Puppets, Sundown. Editor: Manual of English Composition, 1918; Educational Problems in College and University, 1921. Editor The Alumnus, 1918-19. Home: 1419 S. University Av., Ann Arbor, Mich. Died Aug. 16, 1958.

BRUNAUER, Esther Caukin, specialist in internat. affairs; b. Jackson, Cal., July 7, 1901; d. Ray O. and Grace Elizabeth (Blackwell) Caukin; A.B., Mills Coll., 1924; A.M., Stanford, 1925, Ph.D., 1927; studnt Geneva Sch. Internat. Studies, summer 1928, U. of Berlin, 1933; m. Stephen Brunauer, July 8, 1931; children— Kathryn, Elizabeth. Sec. internat. relations and asso. in internat. edn. Am. Assn. Univ. Women, 1927-44; specialist in internat. orgn. affairs Dept. of State, 1944-46; asst. sec. Am. group Dumbarton Oaks Conversations, 1944; tech. expert U.S. del. UN Conf. on Internat. Orgn., San Francisco, 1945, U.S. del. UNESCO Constituent Conf., London, 1945; apptd. U.S. rep. on preparatory commn. UNESCO, with rank of minister,. 1946; sr. adviser U.S. delegation, 1st Gen. Conf. UNESCO, Paris; cons. UNESCO relations staff, Dept. of State, Washington, now asst. dir.; adviser, U.S. del. to 1st, 2nd and 3d Gen. Confs. UNESCO, Paris, Mexico and Beirut. Fellow Oberleander Trust (Germany), Carl Schurz Found., 1933-34; chmn. nat. defense commn. Nat. Com. on Cause and Cure of War, 1936-41; 1st vice chmn. Women's Action Com. for Victory and Lasting Peace, 1943-44; one of founders Com. to Defend America by Aiding the Allies, also mem. adv. policy com.; chmn. D.C. chpt. Commn. to Study Orgn. of Peace, 1943-44. Women's Nat. Press Assn. Award for pub. service in field of internat. relations, Apr. 1947. Regional trustee Mills Coll. Mem. Amer. Assn. Univ. Women, Am. Polit. Sci. Assn., Phi Beta Kappa, Phi Delta Gamma (hon.). Author numerous study guides, pamphlets and articls on internat. affairs; speaker on radio. Home: 3417 Quebec St. N.W., Washington 16. Office: Dept. of State, Washington 25. Died June 26, 1959.

BRUNDIDGE, Oscar Dean, lawyer; b. Wills Point; Tex., June 10, 1886; s. Brown H. and Nancy E. (Flowers) B.; student Baylor U., 1904-05; studied law under pvt. tutors; m. Reba Raines, Sept. 16, 1917; children—Lt. Billy D. (dec.), Robert L., Nancy (Mrs. H. C. Garrett). Admitted to Tex. bar, 1910, and since practiced in Dallas, Tex.; mem. firm Burgess, Burgess, Chrestman, Brundidge, 1918-35, Chrestman, Brundidge, Fountain, Elliot & Bateman, 1935-51, Brundidge, Fountain, Elliott & Bateman, 1951—; vice pres. and dir. Reliance Life Ins. Co.; chmn. bd. and gen. counsel Great Am. Reserve Ins. Co. Served as 1st lt., U.S. Army, 1917-19; retired as lt. col., U.S. Army Res., 1939. Mem. Dallas City Council, 1943-47; mem. adv. bd. for registrants, 1941-43, adv. com. U.S. Bur. Census; chmn. health and accident ins. com. Am. Bar Assn., 1944-45; mem. Tex., Dallas, bar assns., Internat. Assn. Ins. Counsel, Am. Counsel Assn., Nat. Conf. Commrs. on Uniform State Laws, Mil. Order World War (pres. Dallas chpt. 1940). Member Am. Life Convention; president, Round Table International, 1928; comdr. John W. Low post Am. Legion 1941. Clubs: Dallas Round Table, Lions. Democrat. Author: Digest of Life Insurance Laws of Texas, 1940; Digest of Insurance Laws of Texas, 1940-46; Total Disability in Health Insurance, 1941. Editor: Legal Spotlight in Best's Life Ins. News, 1942—. Home: 727 Wilson St., Lancaster, Tex. Office: 2902 Maple Av., Dallas. Died July 8, 1956; buried Hillcrest Mausoleum, Dallas.

BRUNKER, Albert Ridgely, business exec.; b. Phila., Jan. 7, 1883; s. Robert J. and Edith Mary (Henry) B.; ed. Germantown Friends' Sch., Phila.; B.S., U. Pa., 1903; m. Margaret Gaylord, Dec. 15, 1923; m. 2d, Edith Henry, June 10, 1935. Served as mining engr. throughout the west for Harrison Bros. & Co., Inc., Phila., 1903-08, also as sales mgr.; gen. sales mgr. in N.Y.C., Pitts., Chgo., for Am. Steel Foundaries, 1908-12; pres. Liquid Carbonic Co., Chgo., 1912-24, chmn. bd., 1926; pres. Pyramid Paint Co., Phila., 1910—; pres. and dir. Compania Minera de Isla de Pinos, S.A., Havana, Cuba; pres. Atlantic Steel Castings Co., Chester, Pa., 1915-20, A.R. Brunker & Co., Phila., 1912-19, Pittsburgh Metall. Co., Niagara Falls, N.Y., 1937-41; pres. Overarm Machine Co., 1941-45, Miner-Edgar Chem. Co., 1929-33, Universal Materials, Inc., 1948—; v.p. Ky. Lumber Co., Louisville, Ky., v.p., treas., 1912-27; v.p. Evans Lead Co., Charleston, West Virginia, 1923-30; v.p., Menasha Printing and Carbon Company, 1923-30; dir. Isle of Pines Mining Co., Ltd. (Can.), Marland Oil & Refiring Co., Continental Oil Co., Am. Protein Co. (Boston), Osterhaut Elec. Corp.; chmn. bd. Brunker, Jones & Page, Inc. (engrs.), Chgo., Canteen Food Service, Inc. Chief, chem. div. War Industries Bd., World War I. Mem. Rep. Nat. Com. of Ill. Life trustee U. Pa.; bd. corporators Womans Medical College Pa. dir. Chgo. Crime Commn.; chmn. Civic Safety Com. (Chgo.). Member Sigma Xi, Phi Beta Kappa, Delta Tau Delta. Mason (32°, Shriner). Clubs: University (Phila.); University, Onwentsia, Campfire, Executives, Commonwealth (Chgo.); U. Pa., (N.Y.C.). Home: Deerpath Inn, Lake Forest, Ill. Office: 111 W. Washington St., Chgo. Died Dec. 1959.

BRUNO, Frank J(ohn) (brōō'nô), prof. applied sociology; b. Florence, Italy, June 1, 1874; s. Jerolomo and Zippora Elizabeth (Menchini) B.; brought by parents to U.S., 1876; A.B., Williams Coll., 1899; S.T.B., Yale University, 1902; LL.D., Washington University, 1946; graduate study, Hartford (Conn.) Theol. Sem., 1905-06, New York Sch. of Social Work, 1908, Columbia, 1913-15; m. Susan Grey L. Topham, May 28, 1902 (died May 17, 1950); 1 son, John Grey; m. 2d Joanna C. Colcord, Nov. 24, 1950. Ordained ministry Congl. Ch., 1902; asst. pastor Waterbury, Conn., 1902-04; pastor South Congl. Ch., Granby, Conn., 1904-05, South Congl. Ch., Pueblo, Colo., 1905-07; gen. agt. Associated Charities, Colorado Springs, Colo., 1907-11; supt. Charity Orgn. Soc., N.Y. City, 1911-14; gen. sec. Associated Charities (later Family Welfare Assn.), Minneapolis, Minn., 1914-25; also lecturer, 1915-25, professorial lecturer, 1919-25, acting chmn. dept. sociology and social work, 1919-22, U. of Minn.; prof. applied sociology and head dept. social work, Washington U., 1925-45; in British Mus. and London Sch. of Economics, 1933-34. Pres. Minn. Conf. of Social Work, 1916-17, Mo. Assn. for Social Welfare, 1938-39. Mem. Am. Sociol. Soc.; American Assn. Social Workers (pres. 1927, 29, 42; mem. exec. com.), Internat. Assn. Schs. of Social Work (exec. com.), Internat. Conf. of Social Work (chmn. Am. sect. 1934-38), Nat. Tuberculosis Assn. (bd. dirs. 1941-43), Nat. Soc. Crippled Children (bd. dirs. 1945), Am. Assn. Sch. of Social Work (bd. dirs. since 1940), Am. Social Hygiene Assn., Nat. Conf. of Social Work (pres. 1932-33), Family Welfare Assn. America. Club: University. Author: The Theory of Social Work, 1936; Trends in Social Work, 1946. Contbr. to Encyclopedia Britannica, The Survey, Social Science Abstracts, The Family, Social Work Year Book. Cons. editor Social Science Abstracts, Encyclopedia of Social Sciences. Home: 413 Ulen Dr., Lebanon, Ind. Died Aug. 7, 1955.

BRUSH, Katharine (Katharine Ingham Brush), author; born Middletown, Connecticut; dau. Charles Samuel and Clara Louise (Northrop) Ingham; ed. Centenary Collegiate Inst., Hackettstown, N.J., 1913-18; m. Thomas Stewart Brush, June 26, 1920 (deceased); 1 son, Thomas Stewart; married 2d, Hubert Charles Winans, Oct. 2, 1929 (divorced). Mem. of staff Boston Traveler, Boston, Massachusetts, 1918-20; began writing fiction, 1923. Episcopalian. Author: Glitter, 1926; Little Sins, 1927; Night Club (short stories), 1929; Young Man of Manhattan, 1930; Red-Headed Woman, 1931; Other Women (short stories), 1932; Don't Ever Leave Me, 1935; This Is On Me, 1940; You Go Your Way, 1941; The Boy From Maine, 1942; Out of My Mind, 1943; This Man and This Woman, 1944. Contbr. to Cosmopolitan, Good Housekeeping, King Features Syndicate, etc. Home: 320 Park Av., N.Y.C. 22. Died June 10, 1952.

BRUYN, Charles DeWitt, former corp. exec.; b. Kingston, N.Y.; m. Jane Teller (dec. 1959); two daus. Formerly with B. H. Howell, Son & Co.; pres. then chmn. bd., Nat. Sugar Refining Co., 1940-44, ret.; trustee Atlantic Mut. Ins. Co. Served in Food Adminstrn., World War I. Home: 116 Walnut St., N.Y.C. Died May 7, 1959.

BRYAN, Adolphus Jerome, educator; b. Lebanon, Tenn., Aug. 3, 1900; s. Harden Rufus and Etta (Sherrill) B.; A.B., Vanderbilt U., 1924, A.M., 1925; Ph.D., Harvard, 1936; m. Lucile McDearman, Sept. 1, 1920. Teacher in pub. schs. and high sch. prin., 1920-23; instr. in English, U. of Tenn., 1925; instr. La. State U., 1926-28, asst. prof., 1928-31, asso. prof., 1931-36, prof. English, 1936—. Mem. Modern Lang. Assn., S. Central Modern Lang. Assn., Am. Assn. Univ. Profs. Democrat. Mem. Ch. of Christ. Author: (with Percy Marks) The College Writer, 1945; (with Harry Shaw) A Complete Course in Freshman English, 1945. Home: Route 2, Baton Rouge. Died July 22, 1951; buried Bethlehem Cemetery, Lebanon, Tenn.

BRYAN, Claude S., dean vet. medicine; b. Bedminster, Pa., June 5, 1908; s. Amos and Anne (Stever) B.; B.S., Pa. State Coll., 1930; M.S., Mich. State Coll., 1932, Ph.D., 1937, D.V.M., 1942; m. Jean Lenore Miller, June 9, 1933; children—Marjorie Ann, Nelda Jane. Grad. asst. bacteriology and pub. health Mich. State Coll., 1930-31, instr. bacteriology and pub. health, 1931-41, asst. prof. bacteriology and pub. health, 1941-42, asso. prof., 1942-43, prof. bacteriology and pub. health, 1943-44, prof. and head dept. surgery and medicine, 1944-49, dean of vet. medicine since 1947. Mem. Am. Vet. Med. Assn., U.S. Livestock San. Assn., Am. Pub. Health Assn., Conf. Research Workers of N.A., Internat. Assn. Milk and Food Sanitarians, A.A.A.S., Am. Dairy Sci. Assn. Author: Dairy Bacteriology and Public Health; contbg. author Bovine Mastitis; also author numerous articles. Home: 525 M.A.C. Av., East Lansing, Mich. Died July 30, 1951; buried Lansing, Mich.

BRYAN, Ernest Rowlett, writer, lecturer; b. Bath, N.Y., Aug. 14, 1906; s. Daniel Beach and Anna Rowlett (Aulls) B.; A.B., Syracuse U., 1929; student Harvard, 1930; A.M., George Washington U., 1933; student N.Y.U., 1934; Litt.D., Whitworth Coll., 1949; Ph.D., Am. U., 1952; m. Mildred Seymour Gott, September 15, 1932; one daughter, Carol Norris (Mrs. Jack A. Veerman). Field secretary of the World Peace Foundation, 1929-31. ednl. sec., 1934-36; asst. dir., publs. Div., Nat. Edn. Assn., 1931-34; forum lecturer U.S. Office of Edn. Pub. Forms, 1936-37; exec. sec. Nat. Council for Adult Civic Edn. 1938; special writer U.S. Pub. Health Service, 1938-42; chief of div. of information and publications, National Archives, Mar. 1942 to 1943; became lecturer on pub. relations, American U., 1942; mem. bd. dirs. Pierce, Hedrick & Sherwood, Inc., financial counselors; dir., sec. Eastland Gardens, Inc., 1952—; contbg. editor The Christian Endeavor World, Columbia, Ohio; general secretary, Internat. Soc. Christian Endeavor, 1947-49, pres., 1949—. Lt. (j.g.) U.S. Naval Reserve, 1943-44, lieut., 1944-45; lieut. commander, Jan.-Sept., 1946; head of project supervision, Motion Picture and Training Films Prodn., Navy Dept., 1946—. Mem. testing and training com., Research and Development Bd., Nat. Military Establishment. Trustee Internat. Soc. Christian Endeavor. Mem. N.E.A., Am. Legion, Zeta Psi, Phi Kappa Alpha, Pi Gamma Mu, Pi Delta Epsilon, Janus. Clubs: Town Hall (New York); Boston City (Boston); National Press Club (Washington). Author: America Turns to Social Security, 1938; Between Mountain Ridge and Surging Sea, 1952. Contbr. to journals. Home: 3829 Cathedral Avenue, N.W., Washington 16; and 114 E. William St., Bath, N.Y. Address: The Christian Endeavor World, 1221 E. Broad St., Columbus 5, O. Died Dec. 17, 1954; buried Rock Creek Cemetery, Washington.

BRYAN, Henry Francis, naval officer; b. Cin., May 3, 1865; grad. U.S.N. Acad., 1887. Ensign, July 1, 1889; lt. jr. grade, June 19, 1897; lt., Mar. 3, 1899; lt. comdr., June 16, 1905; comdr., July 1, 1909; capt., July 1, 1913; promoted temporary rank rear adm., Aug. 1918. Served on Newark, Spanish-Am. War, 1898; on Alabama, 1903-06; Office of Neaval Intlligence, Navy Dept., 1906-07; at Naval Acad., 1907-10; exec. officer Vermont, 1910-11; comdr. Prairie, 1911-12; duty Office of Naval Intelligence, 1912-14; comd. Kansas, 1914-16; at Naval War Coll., Newport, R.I., 1916-17; apptd. chief of staff 2d Naval Dist., Mar. 23, 1917. Address: Navy Dept., Washington. Died Mar. 19, 1944.

BRYAN, James Wesley, ex-congressman; b. Lake Charles, La., Mar. 11, 1874; s. James Wesley and Delia K. (Singleton) B.; B.A., Baylor U., 1895; B.A., Yale 1897; m. Lorena Kearse, Mar. 26, 1899; children—James Wesley, Merlaine, Billie. Admitted to La. bar, 1898; moved to Wash., 1905; city atty. Bremerton, 1907, 11; mem. Wash. Senate, 1908-12; mem. 63d Congress from Wash. at large; pros. atty.

Kitsap County, 1924-28. Progressive, 1913-15, later Republican. Club: Yale (Seattle). Office: Harrison Bldg., Bremerton, Wash. Died Aug. 26, 1956; buried Bremerton.

BRYAN, James William, ex-govt. ofcl.; b. Nashville, Nov. 25, 1882; s. Malachi Thomas and Maria (Campbell) B.; student pvt. and pub. schs., Nashvill, Spring Hill (Tenn.) Acad.; student Vanderbilt U., 1901-03; m. Blanche Overdeer, Dec. 11, 1915. Spl. reporter Courier Journal, Louisville, 1900; mng. editor, Cumberland Telephone Journal, Cumberland Tel. & Tel. Co., Nashville, 1903-05; reporter, specialty writer and contbr. to various mags. and newspapers, including Nashville American, Atlanta Georgian, Nashville Tennessean, 1905-11; publisher, Nashville, Tenn., 1911-13; asst. eitor Nat. Waterways Mag., pub. by Rivers and Harbors Congress, Washington, 1913-15; publisher Washington, Balt., Phila. and Lancaster (Pa.), 1915-22; engaged in promotion and finance, 1922-31, including creating and financing Nat. Press Bldg. and Congressional Country Club, Washington; in field and lecture work Nat. Highways Users Conf., Washington, 1931-35; asst. to sec. of treasury and chief information sect. U.S. Savings (War) Bonds, Treasury Dept., Washington, 1935-41; became asst. to sec. commerce, Washington, 1941; now retired. Mem. Pres. Wilson's War Adv. Com., Herbert Hoover's War Food Com., Liberty Loan and Red Cross citizens' coms., during World War I. Mem. inter-agency publs. com. O.W.I. interdepartmental war savings bond com. Treasury Dept. (both Washington, D.C.). Mem. alt., or del. from D.C. to Dem. nat. convs., 1920-35. Mem. Phi Delta Theta. Club: National Press (Washington). Author: The Art of Photo Engraving, 1914; Woodrow Wilson's Aministration and Achievements (with Frank B. Lord), 1919; (monograph) Memorial to Ulysses S. Grant, 1920. Formerly asst. editor of Art and Archeology, monthly mag. pub. by Archeol. Inst. of America. Home: 3038 Dunbarton Av., Washington 7. Died 1952.

BRYAN, Kirk, geologist; b. Albuquerque, N.M., July 22, 1888; s. Richard W. D. and Susie Hunter (Patten) B.; A.B., U. of N.M., 1909; A.B., Yale U., 1910, Ph.D., in absentia, 1920; A.M. (honorary), Harvard, 1942; D.Sc. (honorary), U. of N.M., 1947; m. Mary Catherine MacArthur, July 11, 1923; children—Richard Conger, Mary Catherine, Kirk, Margaret Stuart. Entered service U.S. Geol. Survey, 1912, as geologic aid and advanced successively through grades to senior geologist, 1927; instr. geology, Yale U., 1914-17; lecturer physiography, Harvard, 1926-27, asst. prof., 1927-30, asso. prof., 1930-43, prof. since 1943. Served as pvt., then 2d lieut., engrs., geol. sec. in chief engr's. office, U.S. Army, 1918-19, with A.E.F. in France. Fellow Am. Assn. for Advancement of Science (v.p. and chmn. Sect. E, 1939), Geol. Soc. of America (vice-pres. 1948), mem. Am. Acad. (council 1935-38), Assn. Am. Geographers (council 1935-38), Soc. Am. Military Engrs., Am. Geographical Soc., Am. Geophys. Union, Boston Geol. Soc. (pres. 1936), Geol. Soc. Wash., Northwest Scientific Assn., Sigma Xi, Pi Kappa Alpha. Spl. assignments—geologist Columbia Basin Project, 1923; Nat. Geo. Soc., Chaco Canyon Expdn., 1923-25; geologist Middle Rio Grande Conservancy Dist., 1927, 34, 35; geologist for Mexican Govt., San Juan Project. Democrat. Clubs: Economy (pres. 1942-43), Faculty (Cambridge). Address: 5 Scott St., Cambridge, Mass. Died Aug. 22, 1950; buried Albuquerque, N.M.

BRYAN, L. R., Jr., vice chmn. bd., chmn. exec. com.; b. Quintana, Tex., Aug. 17, 1892; m. Katherine McGown; children—L. R. III, Hoyd, Stephen Austin. dir. Bank of the Southwest, Houston; dir. Fort Worth & Denver Ry. (Fort Worth). Houston Br. Fed. Res. Bank of Dallas. Pres. area found., Boy Scouts Am. Trustee Houston Symphony Soc. Endowment Fund. Trustee San Jacinto Mus. of History Assn. (pres.). Served as maj., U.S Army, World War I. Mem. Tex. Philos. Soc., Newcomen Soc., Sons Republic of Tex., Tex., Gulf Hist. Assns. Episcopalian. Knight San Jacinto. Home: 3315 Ella Lee Lane. Office: Bank of the South West, Houston. Died Jan. 30, 1959; buried Houston.

BRYAN, William Lowe, educator; b. nr. Bloomington, Ind., Nov. 11, 1860; s. Rev. John and Eliza Jane (Philips) B.; A.B., Ind. U., 1884, A.M., 1886, LL.D., 1937; Berlin, 1886-87, Paris and Würzburg, 1900-01; Ph.D., Clark U., 1892; LL.D., Ill. Coll., 1904, Hanover Coll., 1908, U. Notre Dame, 1917, U. Mich., 1918, U. Pitts., 1922, Clark U., 1930, Evansville Coll., 1937, Wabash Coll., 1938; L.H.D. Ohio U., 1932; m. Charlotte A. Lowe, July 13, 1889. Instr. Greek Ind. U., 1884-85, prof. philosophy, 1885-1902, v.p. 1893-1902, pres., 1902-37, pres. emeritus, 1937—. Trustee Carnegie Foundation for Advancement of Teaching, 1910-38. Fellow A.A.A.S.; mem. Am. Psychol. Assn. (pres. 1903), Phi Beta Kappa. Author: (with wife) Plato the Teacher, Selections from Plato (edited with notes and introduction), 1897; The Republic of Plato, with Studies for Teachers (with wife), 1898; The Spirit of Indiana, 1917; Paradise, 1927; The President's Column, 1934; Farewells, 1938; Wars of Families of Minds, 1940; The Psychology of Learning a Life Occupation (with Ernst Hiram Lindley and Noble Harter), 1941; Last Words, 1951. Contbr. Johnson's Ency., psychol. jours., etc. Address: University Campus, Bloomington, Ind. Died Nov. 21, 1955; buried Crown Hill Cemetery, Indpls.

BRYANT, Eliot H., naval officer ret.; b. Rusheville, Ill., Aug. 21, 1896; s. James Reeves and Jennie Elizabeth (Moriarity) B.; B.S., U.S. Naval Acad., 1918; M.S., Columbia, 1927; m. Miriam H. Hawkins, Oct. 30, 1937. Commd. ensign, USN Acad., 1918; and advanced through grades to v. adm.; student Submarine Sch., New London, 1918; duty in various submarines, 1918-30; asst. naval attache, Berlin and other prin. embassies of Europe, 1930-33; staff comdr. Submarines U.S. Fleet, 1933-35; gunnery officer U.S.S. Northampton, 1935-37; on duty Bu. Engring. Submarine Design, Navy Dept., 1937-39; student Sr. War Coll., Newport, R.I., 1939-40, comd. gun boat U.S.S. Asheville in S. China Patrol, 1940; comd. div. of submarines in the Asiatic Fleet, 1940-42; duty Bur. Ships, submarine design, Navy Dept., 1943; comd. squadron submarines, 1943; chief of staff to Comdr. Submarines 7th Fleet, 1944-45; comd. U.S.S. Chicago, 1945; pres. Bd. Review, Discharges and Dismissals, Navy Dept., Washington, D.C., to April 1946; comdr. Cruiser Div. Two, May 1947; now vice adm., retired. Decorated D.S.M., Legion of Merit, Navy Unit commendation, Letter of Commendation ribbon, Army Distinguished Unit badge, Victory medal, American Defense Service medal, Fleet clasp, Asiatic-Pacific Area Campaign medal with 2 stars, World War II Victory medal, Philippine Defense with 1 star, Philippine Liberation, and Submarine Combat Insignia pin. Presbyn. Club: Annapolis Yacht. Home: Cider Jug Farm, Annapolis, Md. Died Oct. 16, 1955; buried U.S. Naval Acad. Cemetery, Annapolis.

BRYANT, Louise Stevens; b. Paris, France, of Am. parents, Sept. 19, 1885; d. Charles E. and Miriam Collins (Nicholson) Stevens; A.B., Smith Coll., 1908; Ph.D., Dept. Med. Sciences, U. Pa., 1914; m. 1909. With dept. of physiology Am. Mus. Natural History, 1908-09; with div. edn. and statistics Russell Sage Found., 1909-11; in charge social service dept. Psychol. Clinic, U. Pa., 1911-14; instr. psychology Pa. Sch. for Social Service and Health, 1914-17; also in charge dept. statistics and records Municipal Court of Phila., 1914-18; with statistics br. Chief of Staff, U.S. Army, and Statistical Bureau, War Industries Board, Washington, 1918-19; survey of nutrition of sch. children, Washington; nat. ednl. and publ. sec. Girl Scouts, Inc., 1919-23; sec. Publs and Research Com. on Dispensary Development of United Hosp. Fund, 1923-27; dir., exec. sec. Nat. Com. on Maternal Health, 1927-35; organized, directed and edited pioneer med. study and publ. program in field of human fertility; asso. with Mabel E. Todd in preparation of text on structural hygiene, 1936-37; with art dept. in charge circulating exhbns. Am. Assn. U. Women, 1938-52. Fellow A.A.A.S., N.Y. Acad. Medicine (asso.); mem. Alumnae Assn. Smith Coll., Am. Civil Liberties Union. Unitarian. Author: School Feeding—Its Organization and Practice at Home and Abroad, 1913; Better Doctoring—Less Dependency, 1927; Medical Aspects of Human Fertility, 1932; also numerous articles on applied psychology, maternal health, etc. Editor and Co-Author: (with M. M. Davis) Clinics, Hospitals and Health Centers, 1927; Control of Conception—An Illustrated Medical Manual (with R. L. Dickinson), 1931. As attorney-in-fact for Havelock Ellis, arranged for new edition of his seven-volume work, "Studies in the Psychology of Sex," pub. 1935. Home: 1589 Midland Av., Bronxville 8, N.Y. Died Aug. 29, 1956; buried Ferncliff, Hartsdale, N.Y.

BRYANT, Randolph, lawyer, judge; b. Sherman, Tex., May 2, 1893; s. David E. and Arizona (Thompson) B.; B.A., Christian Brothers Coll., St. Louis, 1913; LL.B., U. Tex., 1916; m. Julia Hoard, Apr. 27, 1918; children—William Randolph, Randolph, David Thompson. Admitted to Texas bar, 1916; practiced with Head, Dillard, Smith, Maxey & Head, Sherman, Tex., 1919-22; U.S. dist. atty., Eastern Dist. Tex., 1922-31, dist. judge, 1931—. With Machine Gun Co. on border service, 2d Texas Inf., 1916-17; student 1st O.T.C., Leon Springs, Tex., 1917; commd. 1st lt. F.A., 1917; assigned to 133d F.A. 36th Div., AEF, 1918-19; with 17th Corps, 2d French Army, at Verdun; hon. disch., 1919. Mem. Am., Tex. bar assns., Phi Delta Theta. Home: 1204 S. Crockett St. Office: Federal Bldg., Sherman, Tex. Died Apr. 24, 1951.

BRYANT, W(illiam) Sohier, physician; b. Boston, May 15, 1861; s. Henry and Elizabeth Brimmer (Sohier) B.; ed. pvt. schs. at home and abroad, St. Paul's Sch., pvt. tutors; A.B., cum laude, Harvard, 1884, A.M., M.D., 1888; m. Martha Lyman Cox, 1887 (dec.); children—Mrs. Mary Cleveland Blanchard, Elizabeth Sohier, Mrs. Alice de Vermandois Frank (dec.), Julia Cox, Gladys de Brion, William Sohier (dec.). Began practice in Boston; was aural surgeon Boston Dispensary; asst. in anatomy and otology, Harvard; sr. asst. surgeon Mass. Charitable Eye and Ear Infirmary; in N.Y., 1903; was adj. prof. dept. diseases of ear, New York Post-Grad. Med. Sch. and Hosp.; cons. otolaryngologist Manhattan State Hosp.; sr. asst. surgeon aural dept., N.Y. Eye and Ear Infirmary; instr. otology Coll. Phys. and Surg. (Columbia); clin. asst. dept. otology Vanderbilt Clinic; asst. surgeon St. Bartholomew's Clinic; clinical instr. and attending surgeon, otol. dept., Cornell U. Med. Sch.; physician in class of nose, throat and ear diseases, Presbyn. Hosp. Dispensary. Mem. Mass. N.G., 1881-98; asst. surgeon 1st Mass. Regt., Heavy Arty., Spanish-Am. War; maj. and brigade surgeon U.S.V. Served with Maj. Gen. Fitzhugh Lee in 7th Army Corps and occupation of Cuba until May 1899, then surgeon, 2 yrs., Battery A, Mass. N.G.; became member of Medical Reserve Corps, 1911; served in World War, 1917, major Medical R.C., with British Army, contract surgeon in charge Royal Victoria Hosp., otolaryngologist British Red Cross Hosp., at Netley, Hants, England; later with French Army, voluntere et benevol, Hospital Auxiliere 49, Orleans, France, at Am. Red Cross Mil. Hosp. 3, Paris, 1918; lt. col. Med. Corps U.S.; dir. med. affairs and del. Emelia Dist., Am. Red Cross in Italy; col. Med. O.R.C., later col. Inactive Res. Awarded Grand Cross Order of St. John of Jerusalem. Fellow Am. Coll. Surgeons, Boylston Med. Soc.; mem. Boston Med. Library Assn., Mass. Med. Soc., Mass. Benevolent Medical Soc., A.M.A. (chairman sect. laryngology and otology), Am. Otol. Society, Med. Soc. State of N.Y., Med. Soc. County N.Y., Am. Board. Otolaryngology, Am. Laryngol., Rhinol. and Otol. Soc., Assn. Mil. Surgeons of U.S., Naval and Mil. Order of Spanish-Am. War, N.E. Historic Geneal. Soc., Am. Legion, Nat. Rifle Assn., St. Nichols Soc., British Legion, British Great War Vets. of Am., Vets. of Fgn. Wars of U.S. Fedn. of French Veterans, Mass. Soc. of the Cincinnati, N.Y. Soc. Mil. and Naval Officers of World War, S.A.R., Boston Soc. Natural Hist., Soc. Mayflower Descendents, Res. Officers Assn. of U.S., Loyal Legion, United Spanish War Vets., Sons of the Revolution, Soc. Colonial Wars, Sojourner, N.Y. Genealogical and Biog. Soc., Military Order World War, Mil. Order Foreign Wars, American Soc. French Legion of Honor, Military Intelligence Res. Soc., Mass. Bay in New England (gov.), Am. Vets. Assn.; Vet. Corps Artillery N.Y., Mil. Soc. War of 1812. Delta Kappa Epsilon. Zeta Psi. Decorated Chevalier Legion of Honor (French); Officer Crown of Italy; Grand Cross of the Order of St. Johns the Baptist. Episcopalian. Mason (K.T., 32°, Shriner). Clubs: Harvard (New York City), Century (New York); Porcellian (Cambridge, Mass.). Author: Anatomy and Physiology of the Ear, and Tests of Hearing (in Burnett's System of Diseases of the Ear, Nose and Throat), 1893; Ear Section, Knight and Bryant's med. publs. Rowed as No. 7 and stroke, Varsity, 1884. Address: 30 E. 40th St., N.Y.C. Deceased.

BRYN, Helmer Halvorsen, Norwegian diplomat; b. Norway, Sept. 23, 1865; s. Halvor and Inger Margarethe (Larsen) B.; student U. Christiania; m. Laura Grilstad, Feb. 14, 1893. E.E. and M.P. from Norway to U.S., 1910—. Address: Legation of Norway, Washington. Died May 28, 1933.

BRYSON, Gladys (Eugenia), sociologist; b. Carlisle, Ky., Apr. 2, 1894; s. Homer Buell and Minnie Noble (Mann) Bryson; A.B., Georgetown (Ky.) Coll., 1918; A.M., U. of Calif., 1927, Ph.D., 1930; Sterling fellow, Yale, 1927-28. Nat. student sec. Y.W.C.A., 1919-25; teaching fellow, dept. of sociology and social institutions, U. of Calif., 1925-27, mem. staff Internat. House, 1930-31; asst. prof. sociology Smith Coll., 1931-34, asso. prof., 1934-40, prof., 1940—, chmn. dept. of sociology, 1945—, chairman of the division of social scis., 1948—. Mem. Am. Sociol. Soc., Am. Acad. Polit. and Social Scis., A.A.A.S., Am. Assn. Univ. Profs., Am. Assn. Univ. Women, Eastern Sociol. Soc. (pres. 1946-47), League Women Voters. Author: Man and Society; The Scottish Inquiry of the 18th Century, 1945. Contbr. articles to social sci. jours. Home: Lawrence House, Northampton, Mass. Died Dec. 18, 1952; buried Cynthiana, Ky.

BRYSON, Joseph Raleigh (brī'sŭn), congressman; b. Brevard, N.C., Jan. 18, 1893; s. Robert L. and Mattie (Allison) B.; A.B., Furman U., Greenville, S.C., 1917; LL.B., U. of S.C., 1920; LL.D. (honorary), Bob Jones University, 1948; married Ruth Rucker, Aug. 5, 1920; children—Joe Bob, Ruth, Billy, David, Judy. Mem. S.C. State Lgislature, 1921-24, State Sen., 1929-32; mem. 76th-82d Congresses (1939-53), 4th S.C. Dist. Served in U.S. Army, during World War; disch. as 2d lt. Mem. Jr. Order United Mechanics, Woodmen of the World, Redmen. Dem. Baptist. Mason (32°, Shriner), Odd Fellow. Home: 402 Bennett St. Office; Federal Bldg., Greenville, S.C. Died Mar. 10, 1953; buried Woodlawn Meml. Park, Greenville.

BRYSON, Lyman (Lloyd), writer; b. Valentine, Neb., July 12, 1888; s. George E. and Nancy Melissa (Hayes) B.; A.B., U. Mich., 1910, A.M., 1915; LL.D., Occidental, 1943; Litt.D., Moravian College, 1949, Drexel Inst., 1954; L.H.D., Jewish Theol. Sem. Am., 1950, Columbia, 1954; m. Hope Mersereau, Oct. 4, 1912 (died Mar. 23, 1944); 1 son, Vernon; m. 2d., Katherine McGrattan, May 11, 1945. Mem. editorial staff, Omaha Daily Bee, 1907-11, Omaha Daily News, 1911-12; Detroit Evening News, 1912-13; instr. and asst. prof. rhetoric and journalism, U. of Mich., 1913-17. In service Am. Red Cross, Washington hdqrs., 1918-19, Paris, 1919-20, League of Red Cross Socs., 1920-24. Traveler and lecturer on Junior Red Cross, America, Europe and Asia; extension lecturer, U. of Calif., 1925-32; asso. dir. San Diego Mus., 1928, dir., 1929-30; exec. dir. Calif. Assn. for Adult Edn., 1929-32; dir. U. of Calif. Summer Sch. in Adult Edn., 1931, 1932; lecturer Sch. of Am. Research, Alburquerque, N.M., 1931; visiting prof. of edn. Tchrs. Coll. (Columbia), 1934-35, prof. edn., 1935-53. Chief Bur. Special Operations O.W.I., 1942. Adult Education Forum leader, Des Moines, Ia. Pub. Schs., 1932-34; counsellor on pub. affairs, C.B.S.; dir. CBS program, Invitation to Learning. Fellow A.A.A.S.; mem. Am. Assn. Adult Edn. (pres. 1944), Inst. for Intercultural Studies (pres.), Conference on Science, Philosophy and Religion (hon. pres.), Phi Beta Kappa, Sigma Delta Chi, Kappa Delta Pi, Phi Delta Kappa. Clubs: Century, Coffee House, Dutch Treat, Columbia Faculty. Author: Smoky Roses (verse), 1916; The Grasshopper (prize play produced Arts and Crafts Theatre, Detroit), 1917; Adult Education, 1936; Which Way America?, 1939; The New Prometheus, 1941; Working for Democracy (with Kerry Smith); Science and Freedom, 1946-47; Communications of Ideas, 1948; Science and Freedom, 1947; The Next America, 1952; The Drive Toward Reason, 1954. Editor The People's Library. Contbr. short stories to mags. Winner of Nelson C. Field poetry prize, U. Mich., 1909. Home: 450 River Dr. Address: 485 Madison Av., N.Y.C. 22. Died Nov. 1959.

BUCHANAN, Daniel Houston, economist; b. Beloit, Kan., Nov. 29, 1883; s. Thomas Ramsay and Alda Jane (Leslie) B.; Litt.B., Sterling Coll., 1909; A.B., Colo. Coll., 1911; Ph.D., Harvard, 1931, D. Sc., Kiogisuku U., Tokyo, 1928; m. Eula A. Spencer, Aug. 21, 1913; children—Daniel Houston, Edna Spencer (Mrs. T. B. Craver). Prof. econs. Keiogiguku U., 1914-25; research asso. in econ. history Harvard, 1926-28, instr. and tutor, 1928-31; asso. prof. George Washington U., 1931-34; prof. Fisk U., 1934-35; prof. econs. U. N.C., 1935—; vis. prof. econs. Civil Affairs Tng. Sch., U. Chgo., 1943-44. Adviser on Far Eastern Econ. Affairs, Dept. of State, Washington, 1944-45. Mem. Asiatic Soc. Japan (librarian), Econ. History Soc. Eng., Econ. History Soc. U.S., Am., So. econ. assns. Presbyn. Author: The Development of Capitalist Enterprise in India, 1934; Historical Approach to Rent and Price Theory (Readings in Distribution of Wealth and Income), 1946. Mng. editor: Southern Econ. Jour., 1943-45. Home: 301 N. 8th St., Sterling, Kan. Died Feb. 16, 1959; buried Sterling.

BUCHANAN, Ella, sculptor; b. Preston, Kan.; d. John Calder and Catherine (Bergey) Buchanan; student pub. schs., Springfield, Ill.; studied sculpture under Charles J. Mulligan, Art Inst. Chgo., 1908-11; library course Kansas City, Mo. Librarian, Public Library, Pittsburg, Kan., 1902-08; asst. instr. in sculpture, Art Inst. Chgo., 1911-15; settled in Los Angeles, 1915; v.p. Sculptors' Guild of So. Cal.; also mem. College Art Assn. Am. Exhibited at Art Inst. Chgo., San Diego Expn., Cal. Art Club, San Francisco Nat. Sculpture Expn. Principal works: The Suffragist Arousing Her Sisters; White Slavery; End of the Strike; Fragment from the Bread Line; The Desert Man; Out of the Trenches; Altar of the Nations; Gen. Pershing; Theodore Roosevelt; The Young Lincoln; Martha Baker Monument, Chgo.; bust of Woodrow Wilson; Dancer and Drinking Fountain, Barnsdall Park, Los Angeles; for Alter Ego, Long Beach Pacific Expn.; 2d award for Mormon Monument (Utah); 1st award for Nefka, Ebell Spring Exhibit; hon. mention for Lot's Wife, San Diego Expn., 1929; prize for The Prodigal Son (Los Angeles Fair); Eleanor Roosevelt (statuette) award, 1940, Ebell Salon Exhibit. Home: Los Angeles. Died July 1951.

BUCHANAN, Frank, ex-congressman; b. McKeesport, Pa., Dec. 1, 1902; s. Thomas and Mary (Campbell) B.; B.S., U. Pitts., 1925; m. Vera Daerr, Jan. 4, 1929; children—twins, Joan and Jane. Former mem. U.S. Congress, 33d Dist. Pa. Mem. Am. Econ. Assn., Phi Gamma Delta. Democrat. Elk, Eagle, Moose. Home: 1121 Washington St., McKeesport, Pa. Died Apr. 27, 1951; buried Mt. Vernon Cemetery, McKeesport, Pa.

BUCHANAN, James L., banker; vice pres., The First Nat. Bank of Chicago; dir. Triangle Publs., Inc., Rhinelander Paper Co. Dir. Cath. Charities of Chgo. Home: 180 E. Delaware St., Chgo. 11. Office: 38 Dearborn St., Chgo. 90. Died Dec. 27, 1955; buried All Saints Cemetery, Chgo.

BUCHANAN, James William (bŭkăn'ăn), prof. zoölogy; b. Basil, O., Jan. 30, 1888; s. James Wilson and Almeda (Jenkins) B.; B.S., Ohio U., Athens, O., 1913; student U. of London, Eng., 1919; Ph.D., U. of Chicago, 1921; m. Pearle Oliver, July 20, 1918; children—James O., William Ervine. Began as teacher, 1906; asso. prof. of biology, U. of Miss., 1913-15; fellow in zoölogy, U. of Chicago, 1915-16; instr. in zoölogy, N.Y. Univ., 1916-17; senior instructor 3d Army Post Schools, Coblenz, Germany, 1919; instr. and asst. prof. biology, Yale, 1921-30; asso. prof. zoölogy, Northwestern U., 1930-33, prof., 1933-49, chmn. dept., 1940-49; Morrison prof. zoölogy, 1945-49; acting dean, Coll. Liberal Arts, 1945-46. Hancock prof. zool., dir. research Hancock Found., U. So. Calif., since 1949. Served as 1st lt. inf., U.S. Army, with A.E.F., W.W.; maj. U.S. Inf. Reserve Fellow A.A.A.S. (sec., Sect. F., 1940-48), mem. American Soc. Zoölogists, Am. Physiol. Soc., Am. Nature Assn., Chicago Acad. of Science (hon. life mem.), Phi Beta Kappa, Sigma Xi, Sigma Pi, Gamma Alpha. Mason. Address: Hancock Found., U. of So. Calif., L.A. 7. Died June 27, 1952; buried Inglewood Cemetery, Inglewood, Los Angeles County, Cal.

BUCHANAN, John P., farmer, ex-gov. Tenn.; b. Tenn., 1847; student pub. schs. Always a farmer; mem. exery Dem. State Conv., 1875—; mem. Tenn. Ho. of Reps., 1887-91; gov. Tenn., 1891-93. First pres. State Farmers' Alliance, 1888, when that body, the Agrl. Wheel and the Farmer's and Laborers' Union combined, 1889, became pres. of new orgn. Address: Murfreesboro, Tenn. Died May 14, 1930; buried Evergreen Cemetery, Murfreesboro.

BUCHANAN, Kenneth B., bus. exec.; b. Ft. Thomas, Ky., 1895; pres., treas. and dir., Sanborn Map Co., N.Y. City. Home: 24 Winslow Rd., White Plains, N.Y. Office: Ten Cedar St., N.Y.C. 5. Died Apr. 7, 1956.

BUCHANAN, Leonard Brown, electrical engr.; b. Woburn, Mass., Mar. 2, 1873; s. George and Olive Jane (Lowell) B.; grad. Woburn High Sch., 1889; B.S., Mass. Inst. Tech., 1893; m. Ethel Louise Winn, Oct. 21, 1913; children—Elizabeth Olive (dec.), Lowell Winn, Ruth Miriam (Mrs. George Lenart). With Stone & Webster, Inc., since 1893, as elec. and chem. engr., and in charge of lab. and research work; identified particularly with indusl. enterprises of the firm since 1899; chmn. bd. of Chicago, Wilmington & Franklin Coal Co.; dir. Stone & Webster Realty Corporation; director of the Woburn Cooperative Bank. Trustee of the Woburn Five Cents Savings Bank. Trustee Woburn Pub. Library, Choate Memorial Hosp. Clubs: Down Town, Massachusetts Fire Chiefs' (Boston). Home: 10 Bennett St., Woburn, Mass.; (summer) Rockport, Mass. Office: 49 Federal St., Boston 7, Mass. Died Nov. 9, 1955; buried Woburn, Mass.

BUCHANAN, Norman Sharpe, economist; b. Goderich, Ont., Can., Aug. 31, 1905; s. Walter Alexander and Mabel (McKenzie) B.; A.B., U. of Toronto, 1927; A.M., Cornell U., 1929, Ph.D., 1931; m. Marjory Chadwick, 1948; children (by previous marriage)—Sheila Jane, Leigh. Came to U.S., 1927, naturalized 1938. Instr. econ. Cornell U., 1927-30; asst. prof. econ. Colgate U., 1930-36; asst. prof. econ. U. Cal., 1936-39, asso. prof. 1939-45, prof., 1945-47, 50-55, asso. dir. for the Social Sciences, Rockefeller 1947-50, dir. 1955—; vis. asso. prof. econ. Columbia, 1943-44. Travelling European fellowship Social Sci. Research Council, 1939-40. Fellow Inst. for Advanced Study, Princeton, N.J., 1945-46. Member of American Philosophical Society, Royal Econ. Soc., Am. Econ. Assn., Phi Delta Theta, Beta Gamma Sigma. Author: Economics of Corporate Enterprise, 1940; International Investment and Domestic Welfare, 1945; Rebuilding the World Economy (with F. A. Lutz) (20th Century Fund) 1947; Approaches to Economic Development (with H. S. Ellis), 1955 Contbr. articles on econ. to prof. jours. Office: 49 W. 49th St., N.Y.C. Died Apr. 25, 1958.

BUCHANAN, Thomas C(halmers), lawyer, govt. official; b. Beaver, Pa., Nov. 12, 1895; s. John McFarren and Jane (Mitchell) B.; A.B., Washington and Jefferson Coll., 1917; student U. of Pittsburgh Law Sch., 1920-21; m. Juliet Bradford, June 10, 1925; children—Thomas Chalmers, III, Juliet Sophia, John Bradford. Admitted to Pa. bar, 1922, and practiced in Beaver, 1922-48; secretary for the Department of Forest and Waters, Conservation Dept., Commonwealth of Pa., 1935-36; commr. Pub. Service Commn. of Pa., 1936-37; commr. Pa. Public Utility Commn., 1937-45; commr. Fed. Power Commn. 1948-53, chmn. 1952-53, resigned. Mem. Am. Legion. Am., Pa. and Beaver County (pres., 1955-56) bar assns. Democrat. Presbyn. Home: 701 Corporation St. Office: 334 Insurance St., Beaver, Pa. Died Apr. 10, 1958; buried Mill Creek Cemetery, Hookstown, Pa.

BUCHANAN, Mrs. Vera Daerr, congresswoman; b. Wilson, Pa., July 20, 1902; d. John and Jennie (Leasure) Daerr; student pub. schs. Duquesne, Pa.; m. Frank Buchanan, Jan. 4, 1929 (dec. Apr. 27, 1951); children—Joan (Mrs. William M. Cavalacante), Jane (Mrs. John E. Thomas, Jr.). Elected to fill unexpired term of late husband as mem. 82d Congress, 33d Pa. Dist.; mem. 83d and 84th Congresses, 30th Pa. Dist. Democrat. Home: 1121 Washington St., McKeesport, Pa. Office: House Office Bldg., Washington 25. Died Nov. 26, 1955.

BUCHANAN, William Asbury, Canadian govt. ofcl.; b. Fraserville, Ont., Can., July 2, 1876; s. Rev. William and Mary (Pendrie) B.; student pub. schs. Ont. m. Alma Maude Freeman, 1903; children—Donald W., Hugh P. Served on editorial staff of Peterborough Review, 1892-98; news editor Toronto Telegram, 1898-1903; mng. dir. St. Thomas Jour., 1903-05; established Lethbridge Herald in Alberta, as weekly in 1905, as daily in 1907; now pres., mng. dir. Lethbridge Herald Co., Ltd.; organized pioneer legislative library, Edmonton, 1907; elected to Alberta Legislative Assembly for Lethbridge, 1909; apptd. mem. of govt. of Alberta, 1910; elected to House of Commons, 1911, 17; summoned to Senate of Can., 1925, now a senator; pres. The Canadian Press, 1944-46. Mem. internat. bd. YMCA; gen. council Boy Scouts Assn. Can. Mem. Lethbridge Bd. Trade (hon. pres.), Canadian Geog. Soc. (v.p.), St. John Ambulance Assn. (Alberta br.), Blood Indians of Alberta (hon. Chief), Venerable Order Hosp. of St. John of Jerusalem (officer). Clubs: Chinook, Lethbridge Country; Ottawa Country. Mem. Liberal Party United Church of Can. Home: 1404 4th Av. S. Office: The Lethbridge Herald, 323 6th St., Lethbridge, Alberta, Can. Died July 11, 1954.

BUCHBINDER, Jacob Richter, surgeon; b. Chgo., Ill., Aug. 11, 1887; s. Henry and Lola (Richter) B.; A.B., Northwestern U., 1907, M.D., 1911; m. Hazel Felman, Sept. 1917; children—Jane, Robert F. Interne Cook Co. Hosp., 1911-13; asso. attending surgeon Wesley Memorial Hosp., 1913-29; clinical asst. and asso. in surgery, Northwestern U. Med. Sch., 1913-25, asst. prof. of surgery, 1925-29, asso. prof., 1929—; attending surgeon Cook Co. Hosp., 1925, Passavant Memorial Hosp., 1929. Served in Med. Corps U.S. Army during World War. Fellow Am. Coll. Surgeons; mem. Am. Med. Assn., Ill. State and Chicago med. socs., Chicago Surg. Soc., Western Surg. Assn., Alpha Omega Alpha, Sigma Xi. Home: 70 E. Walton Pl., Chicago. Died Sept. 17, 1947.

BUCHHOLZ, Heinrich Ewald (Ezekiel Cheever) (bŭk'hōlz), writer, pub.; b. Balt., Jan. 19, 1879; s. Heinrich and Emily (Wattenschidt) B.; student pub. and pvt. schs.; m. Nellie Gascoyne, June 6, 1905; children—Nellie G. (Mrs. Jack Langford), Eleanor L. Mgr. Internat. Lit. Syndicate, 1899-1905; financial editor Balt. Evening Herald, 1905-06; spl. contbr. Balt. Sun, 1906—; editor Mchts. and Mfrs. Jour., 1909-18; owner, editor of Atlantic Ednl. Jour., 1911-18; editor Ezekiel Cheever's Sch. Issues, 1921—; pres. Warwick & York, Inc.; mng. editor Jour. of Ednl. Psychology; editor Ednl. Adminstrn. and Supervision. Mng. editor Men of Mark in Maryland, 1906; editor Md. subjects in Students' Reference Library, 1908. Mem. N.E.A. Author: The Civil War, 1905; Governors of Maryland, 1906; Reconstruction, 1906; The Crown of the Chesapeake, 1907; Of What Use Are Common People?, 1923; U.S.—A Second Study in Democracy, 1926; Fads and Fallacies in Present-Day Education, 1931. Editor: Edgar Allan Poe—A Centenary Tribute, 1910; W.& Y. Course of Study Series, 1917—. Contbr. to periodicals and newspapers under pen name of Ezekiel Cheever. With Md. State Dept. of Edn. program of vocational tng. of war production workers, 1941-45; trainee follow-up survey, U.S. Office of Edn., 1942-45. Home: 2634 N. Calvert St., Balt. 18. Office: 10 E. Centre St., Balt. 2. Died July 25, 1955.

BUCHHOLZ, John Theodore, botanist; b. Polk County, Neb., July 14, 1888; s. Conrad C. and Christine (Weber) B.; B.S., Ia. Wesleyan Coll., 1909; A.B., State U. of Ia., 1909; M.S., U. of Chicago, 1914, fellow, 1916-17, Ph.D., 1917; studied Ia. Lakeside Lab. and Cold Spring Harbor, N.Y.; m. Olive Peterson, Aug. 15, 1912; children—Olive Miriam, Christine, Ruth Elizabeth. Instr. biology, 1909-11, head science dept., 1911-18, Ark. State Normal Sch., Conway; prof. biology, West Tex. State Normal Coll., Canyon City, 1918-19; prof. botany and head of dept., U. of Ark., 1919-26; prof. botany, U. of Tex., 1926-29; prof. botany, U. of Ill., since 1929, head dept., 1938-42. Visiting investigator Carnegie Instn. dept. of genetics, Cold Spring Harbor, summers, 1921-41. Fellow A.A.A.S. (sec. sect. G, 1937-40, v.p., chmn. 1942); mem. Bot. Soc. America (pres. 1941), Am. Soc. Naturalists, Genetics Soc. of America, Am. Assn. Univ. Profs., Torrey Bot. Club, Calif. Bot. Soc., Sigma Xi. Contbr. on botanical subjects—morphology and embryology of conifers; on the genetics of Datura, especially the role of pollen-tube growth in the heredity of polyploids, on plants with extra chromosomes and genes affecting pollen-tube growth. Clubs: University and Dial (Urbana); Chaos (Chicago). Address: 706 S. Coler Av., Urbana, Ill. Died July 1, 1951; buried Mt. Hope Cemetery, Urbana.

BUCK, Beaumont Bonaparte, ret. army officer; b. Mayhew, Miss., Jan. 16, 1860; s. J. G. H. and Martha S. (Garner) B.; grad. U.S. Mil. Acad., 1885, Army War Coll., 1909; m. Susanne Long, of Memphis, Tenn., Dec. 30, 1908. Commd. 2d lt. 16th Inf., June 14, 1885; 1st lt. 19th Inf., May 4, 1892; trans. to 16th Inf., Aug. 12, 1892; maj. 2d Tex. Inf., May 13, 1898; hon. mustered out vols., Nov. 9, 1898; capt. U.S.A., Mar. 2, 1899; maj. 13th Inf., June 25, 1908; trans. to 16th Inf., Nov. 7, 1908; adj. gen., July 13, 1910; assigned to 13th Inf., July 2, 1912; lt. col. inf., Apr. 28, 1914; assigned to 9th Inf., July 16, 1914; col., July 1, 1916; brig. gen. N.A., Aug. 5, 1917; maj. gen., Aug. 8, 1918. Comdt. cadets, U. of Mo., 1889-92, Baylor U., Waco, Tex., 1893-4; distinguished marksman, 1893; at Austin and Dallas, Tex., and Miami and Jacksonville, Fla., 1898; duty in Philippines, 1899-1902, 1906, 1911-14; on Mexican border, 1914; duty Mass. N.G., 1915-17.

Comd. 28th Inf., 1st Div. A.E.F., June 12, 1917, 2d Inf. Brig., 1st Div., Aug. 5, 1917, 3d Div. (regulars), Aug. 8, 1918, 34th Div., Oct. 17, 1918. Participated in the first all-Am. (Cantigny) offensive, May 28-29, 1918, and Aisne-Marne, St. Mihiel and Meuse-Argonne offensives; returned to U.S., Nov. 15, 1918; comdr. Camp McArthur, Dec. 20, 1918, Camp Meade, Md., Mar. 1919, Laredo dist., Mexican border, May 1919-Mar. 1920; assigned to 20th Inf., Ft. Crook, Neb., Apr. 13, 1920; at Camp Travis, Tex., Aug. 15, 1921; assigned acting chief of staff, 90th Div. Organized Reserves, at San Antonio, Tex., Aug. 15, 1921. Awarded D.S.C. (U.S.); Chevalier and Comdr. Legion of Honor, and Croix de Guerre with two palms (French); Italian War Cross. Address: San Antonio. Died Feb. 10, 1950.

BUCK, Carl Darling, philologist; b. Orland, Me., Oct. 2, 1866; s. Edward and Emeline (Darling) B.; A.B., Yale, 1886, Ph.D., 1889; mem. Am. Sch. Classical Studies, Athens, 1887-89; studied in Leipzig, 1889-92; hon. Ph.D., U. Athens, Greece, 1912; Litt. D., Princeton, 1935; m. Clarinda Darling Swazey, Sept. 10, 1889; children—Carl Edward, Howard Swazey, Clarinda Darling. Asst. prof. Sanskrit and Indo-European comparative philology U. Chgo., 1892-94, asso. prof., 1894-1900, prof., 1900-03, prof. and head dept., 1903-33, Martin A. Ryerson distinguished service prof., 1930-33, prof. emeritus, 1933—; ann. prof. Am. Sch. Classical Studies, Athens, 1923-24. Mem. Am. Philos. Soc., Am. Acad. Arts and Sciences, Am. Philol. Assn. (pres. 1915-16), Am. Linguistic Soc. (pres. 1927, 37), Phi Beta Kappa, Delta Kappa Epsilon. Author: Vocalismus der oskischen Sprache Leipzig, 1892; Hale-Buck Latin Grammar (with William G. Hale), 1903; Grammar of Oscan and Umbrian, 1904; Sketch of the Linguistic Conditions in Chicago, 1903; Introduction to the Study of the Greek Dialects, 1909, rev. edit., 1955; Comparative Grammar of Greek and Latin, 1933; Reserve Index of Greek Nouns and Adjectives (with W. Petersen), 1945; Dictionary of Selected Synonyms in the Principal Indo-European Languages, 1949. Contbr. to philol. jours. Mem. bd. editors Classical Philology. Club: Quadrangle. Home: 5609 Kenwood Av., Chgo. 37. Died Feb. 8, 1955.

BUCK, Carl E(dward), health official; b. Leipzig, Germany (of Am. parentage), Oct. 12, 1891; s. Carl Darling and Clarinda Darling (Swazey) B.; student Hotchkiss Sch., Lakeville, Conn., 1907; B.S., Dartmouth Coll., 1914; student Harvard and Mass. Inst. Tech. School Pub. Health, 1914-15; Dr.P.H., U. of Michigan School of Pub. Health, 1922; m. Anne Lee Simms, Apr. 12, 1920; children—Carl Edward, William Gilmore Simms; m. 2d, Lucile Kisor, Feb. 19, 1932. Mem. Typhus Fever Commn. to Balkans, 1915-16; health commr., Oak Park, Ill., 1916-17; liaison officer, Am. Red Cross and Calif. State Dept. Pub. Health; staff mem. on malarial control, Internat. Health Bd. of Rockefeller Foundation; dir. school health service Detroit Dept. Health, 1922-23, epidemiologist and secretary, 1923-24, deputy commissioner and executive officer 1924-30; field director American Public Health Association, New York, 1931-48, Univ. Michigan School of Public Health, since 1948. Lecturer (at various times) on public health adminstrn., Wayne U., U. of Mich., U. of Minn. Served as 2d lt., pilot, U.S. Army Air Corps, 1917-19. Decorated Order of St. Sava, 3d class, Serbia; recipient Sedgwick Meml. Medal, American Public Health Association, 1953. Member American Public Health Association Michigan. Public Health Assn. (ex-pres.), Delta Kappa Epsilon, Casque and Gauntlet. Clubs: Dartmouth of Detroit (ex-pres.); Dartmouth of N.Y. Editors: Weekly Health Review, Detroit, 1927-30. Since 1932 has made and pub. health studies of Ariz., N.Mex., Okla., Mich., Fla., Calif., Alaska, Manitoba, N.Y. City, Chicago, Los Angeles County, Calif., Kansas City, Mo., Providence, Charlotte, Greensboro, N.C., Houston, Tex., Hartford, Conn., Colo., Ida., Wyo., Boston, Phila. Home: 1402 Washington Heights, Ann Arbor, Mich. Died Nov. 21, 1953.

BUCK, Harold Winthrop, elec. engr.; b. N.Y.C., May 7, 1873; s. Albert Henry and Laura S. (Abbott) B.; Ph.B., Yale, 1894; E. E., Columbia Sch. Mines, 1895; m. Charlotte R. Porter, 1902; children—Winthrop Porter, Gurdon; m. 2d, Mary Perry, 1941. Entered Schenectady works General Electric Co., 1895, student, later asst. engr.; elec. engr. Niagara Falls Power Co. from 1900; now retired. Took out several patents for mech. and elec. devices, a process for making corundum in an elec. furnace. Fellow Am. Inst. E.E. (pres. 1916-17); mem. Franklin Inst., Engring. Inst. Can. Home: 3 E. 71st St., N.Y.C. Died Aug. 5, 1958; buried Putnam Cemetery, Greenwich, Conn.

BUCK, Peter Henry, ethnologist; b. Urenui, Taranaki, New Zealand, Aug. 15, 1880; s. William Henry and Nga-Rongo B.; student Te Aute Coll., New Zealand, 1896-98; M.B., Otago Med. Sch., U. of New Zealand, 1904, Ch.B., 1904, M.D., 1910; M.A., Yale, 1936; D.Sc., U. of New Zealand, 1937; D.Sc., U. of Rochester, 1939; m. Margaret Wilson, Aug. 14, 1905. Came to U.S., 1927. Med. officer of health, New Zealand, 1905-08; mem. Parliament, New Zealand, 1904-14; dir. Maori hygiene, New Zealand, 1919-27; ethnologist, Bishop Museum, Honolulu, 1927-32, 1934-36; visiting prof., Yale U., 1932-34; dir. Bishop Mus. and prof. anthropol., Yale, 1936-48; pres. bd. trustees, Bernice P. Bishop Museum, since 1948. Maj., World War, with New Zealand forces (services in Gallipoli, France, Belgium), 1914-19. Received D.S.O., 1914-15 Star, and other British war and victory medals. Decorated Knight Comdr. St. Michael and St. George. Received Hector medal (anthropology, N.Z.), Rivers Memorial medal (Royal Anthrop, Inst., London). Fellow Royal Soc. of New Zealand, Royal Anthrop. Inst., A.A.A.S.; mem. Am. Anthrop. Assn., Polynesian Soc., Sigma Xi (Yale). Author (under Maori name of Te Rangi Hiroa): Evolution of Maori Clothing, 1926; Material Culture of the Cook Islands, 1927; Samoan Material Culture, 1930; Ethnology of Tongareva, 1932; Ethnology of Manihiki and Rakahanga, 1932; Mangaian Society, 1934; Ethnology of Mangareva, 1938; Vikings of the Sunrise, 1938; Anthropology and Religion, 1939; Arts and Crafts of Cook Islands, 1943; Introduction to Polynesian Anthropology, 1945; The Coming of the Maori, 1948. Contbr. to Jour. of Polynesian Soc. Home: 144 Judd St. Address: Bishop Museum, Honolulu 17, Hawaii. Died Dec. 1, 1951.

BUCK, Philo Melvin, Jr., college prof., writer; b. Morristown, N.J., Feb. 18, 1877; A.M., Harvard, 1900; Litt.D., Ohio Wesleyan Univ., 1935; m. Aletheia Hall, Aug. 27, 1902; children—Edward MacMillan, Carolyn Laura (Mrs. William Harvey Reeves). Instr. English, Ohio Wesleyan U., 1898-99, high schs., St. Louis, 1900-10; head dept. English, William McKinley High Sch., St. Louis, 1904-10; asso. prof. rhetoric, 1910-12, prof. rhetoric, 1912-19, dean Coll. of Arts and Sciences, 1919-24, chmn. dept. of comparative lit., 1924-26, U. of Neb.; chmn. dept. comparative lit., U. of Wis., emeritus prof. comparative lit., U. Wis., since 1947; spl. services prof. comparative lit., 1947-49. Lecturer on comparative lit., Utah State Coll., summer 1948. Exchange prof. Baroda Coll., U. of Bombay, India; lecturer on American lit. in other Indian universities, 1922-23; lecturer U. of Utah, summer, 1931, U. of Southern Calif., summer, 1935; Syracuse U., 1947, Utah State Coll., 1948; traveled in the Orient, especially India, 1931, 1938-39. Capt.; adj. gen.'s dept., 34th Div., U.S. Army, 1917-18; in charge publ. section Military Intelligence Division, Gen. Staff, 1918-19. Asso. editor Midwest Quarterly to 1917. Mem. Modern Lang. Assn. America, Inst. Litt. et Artistique, Paris, France, Alpha Tau Omega, Phi Beta Kappa, Phi Kappa Phi, Sigma Delta Chi. Clubs: University, Blackhawk Country. Author: The Art of Composition (with William Schuyler), 1907; Social Forces in Modern Literature, 1913; Milton on Liberty, 1926; Literary Criticism—A Study of Values in Literature, 1929; The Golden Thread, 1931; An Anthology of World Literature, 1934, rev. edit., 1940. Contbr. to Goethe Centenary, Univ. of Wis., 1933; The World's Great Age, 1936; Directions in Contemporary Literature, 1941. Editor various texts; contbr. to mags. and publs. Home: 1852 Summit Av., Madison, Wis. Died Dec. 9, 1950.

BUCK, Richard Sutton, civil engr.; b. Georgetown, Ky., Nov. 21, 1864; s. Richard Sutton and Juliana Scott (Randolph) B.; student U. of Miss., 1883; C.E., Rensselaer Poly. Inst., 1887; m. Laura Beverly Miller, June 30, 1890 (died Mar. 1, 1934); children—Richard Sutton, Horace Miller; m. 2d, Judith Marshall Fishburn, Jan. 25, 1936 (died July 16, 1942). Served with engineer and quartermaster corps, U.S. Army, 1887-90; manager Carney Phosphate Co., Florida, 1890-92; bridge design, New York City, 1893-95; in charge construction Niagara Falls and Clifton Arch Bridge and Niagara Ry. Arch Bridge, across Niagara River, 1895-98; chief engr. Lewiston and Queenstown Bridge, 1898-99, Manhattan and Queensboro bridges, 1899-1902, Dominion Bridge of Canada, 1902-04; cons. engr. in charge constrn. Manhattan and Queensboro bridges, 1904-07; mem. Sanderson & Porter, N.Y. City, 1907-12; again chief engr. Dominion Bridge Co., 1912-14; engr. of way and structures New York Rys. Co., 1914-17; maj. 11th Engrs., U.S. Army, with A.E.F. in France, 1917-18; valuation engr. and cons. parctice since 1919; served as adviser to legal counsel Brooklyn City R.R., in suit involving $13,000,000; with others reported on projected bridge 9 miles long across San Francisco Bay. Awarded D.S.O. (British) for services on Somme and Arras fronts. Mem. Am. Soc. C.E., Soc. Mil. Engrs., Engring. Inst. of Can. Awarded Rowland prize, Am. Soc. C.E., 1899. Democrat. Clubs: Brooklyn Engineers (past pres.); Cosmos (Washington, D.C.). Home: 2123 R St. N.W., Washington. Died Aug. 1, 1951.

BUCK, Walter Albert, naval officer; b. Oskaloosa, Kan., June 4, 1895; s. Walter and Anna (Gramse) B.; B.S., Kansas State Coll., 1913, M.S., 1916; M.B.A., Grad. Sch. Bus. Adminstrn., Harvard, 1924; m. Mildred Ann Reed, Sept. 4, 1920; children—Walter James, John Addison. Commd. ensign, U.S. Navy, 1917, and advanced through the grades to rear adm.; retired March, 1948. Chief Bur. Supplies and Accounts, and Paymaster Gen. of the Navy, 1946-48; pres. Radiomarine Corp. of Am., Mar.-Dec. 1948; operating v.p. RCA Victor Div., 1949-50, v.p. and gen. mgr. since 1950; dir. RCA, Radiomarine Corp. of Am. Decorated World War I medal with Mine-Laying Clasp, Nat. Defense Medal with A, Am. Theater Medal, Legion of Merit (2 times). Mem. Sigma Tau, Scabbard and Blade. Clubs: New York Yacht (N.Y.); Army and Navy, Army-Navy Country (Washington). Home: 514 E. Lancaster Av., Wynnewood, Pa. Office: RCA Victor, Camden, N.J. Died June 12, 1955.

BUCKENDALE, L. Ray, business exec.; b. Detroit, Mich., Apr. 19, 1892; s. Adolph and Margaret Esther (Ryan) B.; B.Engring., U. of Mich., 1916; unmarried. Employed by The Timken-Detroit Axle Co., Detroit, Mich., 1911-16, engr. at plant No. 3, 1916-17, engr., 1919-36, vice pres. in charge engring., 1936—. Served as capt. Ordnance, U.S. Army, 1917-19. Mem. Soc. Automotive Engrs. (pres.), Engring. Soc. Dtroit, Army Ordnance Assn. Club: Detroit Yacht. Home: 14530 Harbor Av., Detroit 15. Office: 100-400 Clark Av., Detroit 32. Died Apr. 1952.*

BUCKLAND, Albert William James, publishing exec.; b. Burks Falls, Ont., Apr. 5, 1900; s. Rev. Caleb Henry and Ellen Mary (McTear) B.; student Ont. Agrl. Coll., 1919-22, U. Western Ont., 1922-23, Princeton, 1932; m. Alberta Lillian Sharpe, Nov. 3, 1923; 1 dau., Barbara Mary (Mrs. George Warren Chisholm). Reporter The Telegram, 1925-32, news editor, 1932-48, mng. editor, 1948-52, became pres., editor in chief, 1952; dir. Telegram Pub. Co., Ltd., Toronto, from 1950, now pres. and editor-in-chief. Club: University (Toronto). Home: 473 Oriole Pkwy. Office: 233 Bay St., Toronto, Ont., Can. Died Jan. 1960.

BUCKLAND, Edward Grant, ry. official; b. Buffalo, Dec. 31, 1866; s. Andrew J. and Julia A. (Turner) B.; B.A., Washburn Coll., Topeka, Kan., 1887, LL.D., 1921; LL.B., Yale, 1889, M.A., 1895, LL.D., 1937; m. Sally Tyler Clark, June 21, 1898; children—Charles Clark, Julia Turner (Mrs. Harrison Fuller), Susan Lord (Mrs. Arthur Milliken), Chester Parsons. In general practice of law New Haven, Connecticut, 1889-98; instr. and asst. prof. of law, Yale, 1889-98; atty., 1898-1906, v.p., 1907-14, v.p. and gen. counsel, 1914-18, pres., 1918-20, v.p. and gen. counsel, 1920-24, v.p. in charge of law, finance and corporate relations, 1914-28, dir., 1918-41, chmn. bd., 1929-47, N.Y., N.H.&H. R.R. Co. and affiliated cos.; officer or dir. various other corps. Seaman, ensign, lt. (j.g.), lt.-comdr., and comdr. Naval Batt., C.N.G., 1893-98; lt. col. Home Guard, Conn., 1917-20. Rep. Episcopalian. Mem. Conn. Acad. Science, Phi Delta Phi, Phi Beta Kappa. Mason. Clubs: Yale (New York); Graduate, Lawn, Country, Quinnipiack (New Haven). Home: 254 Prospect St. Office: 71 Meadow St., New Haven. Died Mar. 30, 1953; buried Grove St. Cemetery, New Haven.

BUCKLER, Richard Thompson, ex-congressman; b. Coles County, Ill., Oct. 27, 1865; s. John and Harriet (Davis) B.; student pub. schs.; m. Addie Ball, Nov. 27, 1890; chilren—Ruth Naomi (dec.), Eva May (Mrs. Robert E. Scobie), Jack, Adeline LaFerne (Mrs. Dewey John Kiewel), Mary Marie (Mrs. Elery Storholm), Maxine Elliott. Began as farmer, 1885; owner, operator of farm, Polk County, Minn., 1904—. Dir. Red River Valley Livestock Assn., Crookston, Minn.; pres. Crookston Unit of Farmers Union, Ednl. and Coop. Union Am.; mem. Polk County unit, Am. Farm Bur.; state chmn. Farmer-Labor party, 1924; senator, Polk County, 1915-19, 23-27, 31-33; mem. 74th to 77th Congresses, 9th Minn. Dist. Farmer-Laborite. Baptist. Eagle. Home: R.F.D., Crookston, Minn. Deceased.

BUCKLER, William Hepburn, archeologist; b. of Am. parents, Paris, France, Feb. 1, 1867; s. Thomas Hepburn (M.D.) and Eliza (Ridgely) B.; M.A., Trinity Coll. (Cambridge U., Eng.), 1890; LL.B., Cambridge U., 1891; studied Law Dept., U. of Md., 1893-94 (prizeman, 1894, for thesis on Instalment Sales); M.A., Oxford, 1925, D.Litt., 1937; LL D., Aberdeen, 1935, Johns Hopkins, 1940; m. Georgina Grenfell Walrond, May 25, 1892; children—Lucy Ridgely (Mrs. Vivian Seymer), Barbara Isabel (Mrs. Charles Wrinch). Practiced law, Baltimore, Md., 1894-1902; sec. emergency com. after Baltimore, fire, Feb. 1904; sec. U.S. special embassy to King's wedding, Spain, 1906; sec. U.S. Legation Madrid, Spain, 1907-09; mem. staff Am. Expdn. to Sardis, Asia Minor, 1910-14; special agent Dept. of State, Embassy, London, 1914-18; attached Am. Comm. to Negotiate Peace, Paris, June-Dec. 1919; made journeys in Asia Minor, 1924, 26, 30, 33; asso. All Souls Coll., Oxford, Eng., 1924-25. Mem. bd. trustees Johns Hopkins U., 1904-12. Member council American Society for Archeological Research in Asia Minor; v.p. Society for Hellenic Studies, Society for Roman Studies; fellow British Academy. Wrote: History of Contract in Roman Law (Yorke Prize, Cambridge), 1894; Relation of Roman Law to Other Historical Sciences (Vol. II, Proc. Internat. Congress Arts and Sciences, St. Louis), 1904; Chapter VI, in Hollander and Barnett's Studies in American Trade Unionism, 1906; Chapter XXII in Ripley's Railway Problems, 1907; Lydian Inscriptions, 1924; Sardis-Greek and Latin Inscriptions (with David M. Robinson), 1932; Monuments of Western Phrygia, etc. (with W. M. Calder, C. M. Cox and K. Guthrie), 1933, 1939. Residence: 1 Bardwell Rd., Oxford, Eng. Died Mar. 2, 1952.

BUCKLEY, Edwin M., investment banker; m. Lucy Kidder. Senior mem. Spencer, Trask & Co. Mem. exec. com. Near East Foundtion; trustee Bd. Fgn. Missions of Presbyn. Ch.; mem. bd. trustees The Northfield Schs.; dir. Union Theological Sem. Clubs: Metropolitan, Midday, Downtown. Home: 817 Fifth Av. Office: 25 Broad St., N.Y.C. 4. Died June 20, 1949; buried Brookside Cemetery, Englewood, N.J.

BUCKLEY, Harry D(ouglas), corp. exec.; b. St. L., Feb. 24, 1889; s. Frank W and Margaret (Endres) B.; student pub. schs. St.L.; m. Florence McElvain, Apr. 24, 1918. Mgr. Garrick & Columbia Theatres, St.L., 1911-17; sales mgr. United Artists Corp., K.C., Mo. and L.A.. 1919-23, v.p., dir. 1926-46; gen. mgr. Douglas Fairbanks Pictures Corp., 1923-26; v.p., gen. mgr. United Artists Theatre Circuit, Inc., 1927-34, Corp., Penn Fed. Enterprises, Inc., Lsvl. Operating v.p., 1946—, dir., 1927—; v.p., dir. United Artists Theatre Circuit, Inc., Biddle Realty Co., 1620 Broadway Co., Inc., Lowes United Artists Columbus Corp. Home: 1160 Park Av., N.Y.C. Died June 2, 1955.

BUCKLEY, James V., ex-congressman; b. Lansing, Ill., May 15, 1892; ed. pub. schs., Saginaw County, Mich.; m. Claire M. Mercier; children—Vincent J., Donald Charles, Quentin D. Engaged in real estate and bldg. bus. for more than 20 yrs., Calumet region, Cook County, Ill.; mem. 81st Congress (1949-51), 4th Illinois Dist. Pres. Local 714, U.A.W., C.I.O. K.C. Democrat. Home: 111 Memorial Dr., Calumet City, Ill. Died July 30, 1954; buried Calvary Cemetery, Gary, Ind.

BUCKLEY, Leo Jerome, union ofcl.; b. Lewiston, Me., Feb. 4, 1899; s. Michael Horace and Margaret (Moriarty) B.; student pub. schs.; m. Elizabeth Ray, Apr. 18, 1940; 1 son, Thomas. Vice pres. N.Y. Stereotypers Union, 1932-38; pres. Internat. Stereotypers & Electrotypers Union, 1939—. Served on newspaper commn. War Labor Bd., also printing div. W.P.B.; mem. industry div. no. 49 Wage and Hour Bd. Mem. Internat. Allied Printing Trades Assn. (chmn. bd. govs.). Roman Catholic. Home: 2812 Harrington Av., N.Y.C. 61. Office: 475 5th Av., N.Y.C. 17. Died June 10, 1956; buried Gate of Heaven Cemetery.

BUCKLEY, Oliver Ellsworth, research engr.; b. Sloan, Ia., Aug. 8, 1887; s. William Doubleday and Sarah Elizabeth (Jeffrey) B.; B.S., Grinnell Coll., 1909, D.Sc., 1936; Ph.D., Cornell, 1914; D.Sc., Columbia U., 1948; D. Eng., Case Inst. Tech., 1948; m. Clara Lane, Oct. 14, 1914; children—Katherine Lane (Mrs. R. G. Nuckolls), William Douglas, Barbara (Mrs. Frederick B. Wolf), Juliet Georgiana (Mrs. Patrick Alsup). Instr., Grinnell (Ia.) Coll., 1909, Cornell, 1910-14; with the research department Western Electric Co., 1914-25; with Bell Telephone Labs., 1925-52, asst. dir. research, 1927-33, dir. of research, 1933-36, exec. v.p., 1936-40, pres. 1940-51, chmn. bd., 1951-52, dir., 1940-55; dir. Summit Trust Company. Mem. bd. of Edn. of South Orange-Maplewood, N.J., 1938-50, pres., 1948-50. Trustee Jackson Memorial Lab., Thomas A. Edison Foundation. Served as major, Signal Corps, A.E.F., World War I, in charge research section Div. Research and Inspection, Signal Corps, Paris; mem. communications and guided missiles divisions Nat. Defense Research Com., World War II. Medal for Merit. Chmn. sci. adv. com. O.D.M. 1951-52, Bd. Multiple Sclerosis Soc. Member gen. adv. com. AEC, 1948-54; mem. Army Ordnance sci. adv. com., 1951-55. Fellow Am. Phys. Society, Am. Acad. Arts and Scis., Am. Inst. E.E. (Edison medal 1954), Acoustical Soc. Am.; mem. Nat. Acad. Scis., Am. Philosophical Society (v.p.1954-57), Franklin Institute, Engineering Foundation Board (chmn. 1939-42), National Inventors Council, Sigma Xi, Phi Beta Kappa, Phi Kappa Phi. Clubs: Century (N.Y.C.); Cosmos (Washington). Home: 13 Fairview Terrace, Maplewood, N.J. Died Dec. 1959.

BUCKMAN, C. B., ex-congressman; b. nr. Newton, Pa., 1851; s. William and Jane E. B.; student pub. schs.; m. Emma C. Harvey, 1876. Engaged in farming and lumbering until 1901; mem. Minn. Ho. of Reps., 1881, mem. State Senate, 12 yrs.; mem. U.S. Congress, 6th Minn. Dist., 1903-07. Republican. Address: Little Falls, Minn. Died Mar. 1, 1917; buried Little Falls.

BUCKNER, Chester Arthur, farm mgr.; b. nr. Ottumwa, Ia., Jan. 28, 1885; s. Stephen Andrew and Ida Demeris (Barker) B.; A.B., University of Iowa, 1909, A.M., 1911; Ph.D., Columbia, 1918; LL.D., U. of Pittsburgh, 1943; m. Neva Grace Starrett, April 25, 1911. Fellow in education, University of Iowa, 1913-14, Columbia, 1916-17; teacher of mathematics, high sch., Clinton, Ia., 1909-10; head dept. of English, high sch., Manila, P.I., 1911-13; asst. prof. of edn., U. of Kan., 1914-16; asst. to dir., Lincoln Sch. of Teachers Coll., Columbia, 1917-19; dir. bureau of sch. service, U. of Kan., 1919-20; prof. secondary edn. and head dept., U. of Pittsburgh, 1920-43, dir. teacher apptmt. bureau, 1922-23, chairman Sch. of Edn., 1st semester, 1924-25, dir. high sch. practice teaching, 1929-31, head div. of professional edn., 1932-35. Lecturer in edn., summers, Cornell, 1919, 27, U. of Wis., 1924, U. of Southern Calif., 1931. Mem. adv. com. study secondary and higher edn. in Pa., Carnegie Found., 1928-32. Chmn. Western Pa. Edn. Conf., 1930-43; chmn. Committee for Revision of Pa. State Course of Study in High School English, 1935-37; mem. bd. dirs., dir. research Farinco Products, Inc., 1952—. Trustee, Parsons College, 1944-47. Fellow A.A.A.S.; mem. N.E.A. (dept. secondary sch. principals), Am. Assn. Sch. Principals, Am. Assn. U. Profs., Nat. Soc. Coll. Tchrs. Edn. (mem. exec. com. 1927-30), Nat. Soc. Study Edn., Am. Ednl. Research Assn., Phi Delta Kappa, Kappa Phi Kappa, Acacia. Methodist. Mason. Clubs: Elks, Abracadabra, Wit and Wisdom, Pennsylvania Schoolmen's, Faculty. Author: Educational Diagnosis of Individual Pupils; also collaborator sch. surveys. Home: R.F.D. 4, Fairfield, Ia. Died June 28, 1958; buried Highland Center, Ia.

BUCKNER, David Ernest, life ins. exec.; b. Pittsboro, N.C., Dec. 9, 1894; s. John Murphy and Dillie Gay (McBane) B.; A.B., Wake Forest Coll., 1917; grad. study Genoble U., France, 1919; m. Wylanta McKay, June 30, 1925; children—David E., John Herbert. Supt. schs., Siler City, N.C., 1917-18; instr. mathematics N.C. State Coll. Agr. and Engring., 1919-23; with Jefferson Standard Life Ins. Co., Greenboro, N.C., 1923—, beginning as clk., successively asst. actuary, asso. actuary, v.p., actuary, 1943—. Served as cpl. U.S. Army, 1918-19. Fellow Soc. of Actuaries. Baptist. Mason (Shriner). Home: 303 W. Greenway N. Office: Jefferson Standard Life Insurance Co., Greensboro, N.C. Died July 6, 1956; buried Forest Lawn Cemetery, Greensboro.

BUCKNER, Walter Coleman, clergyman; b. Macedonia, Ia., Jan. 9, 1883; s. Rev. John W. and Cora Estelle (Willard) B.; prep. edn., high schs., Scranton, Ia., and Hiawatha, Kan.; student Baker U., 1900-03; D.D., Coll. of the Pacific, 1936, U. Southern California, 1940; LL.D., Baker University, 1942; m. Eva Harriet Wright, July 30, 1908; children—Theodore John (deceased), Gladys (Mrs. Nicholas Bondoc), Louise (Mrs. Leon Eakes), Walter Coleman. Ordained ministry M.E. Church, 1908; pastor Dinuba, California, 1908, Corcoran, 1909-10, Tulare, 1911-17, Pomona, 1917-21, Pasadena, 1921-24; supt. Pasadena dist., M.E. Ch., 1924-30; pastor First M.E. Ch., Fresno, Calif., 1930-36; dist. supt. Long Beach District, 1936-38, Los Angeles Dist., 1938-42; pastor First Meth. Ch., Santa Ana, Calif., 1942-44; Vermont Square Meth. Ch., Los Angeles, 1944-46; co-pastor First Meth. Ch., Glendale, 1946-51; minister of adminstrn. First Meth. Ch., Pasadena, 1951—. Mem. North Am. Bd. for Study of Religion in Higher Edn.; hon.-trustee U. Religious Conf. at U. of Calif. at Los Angeles; mem. nat. panel of arbitrators, Am. Arbitration Association; Com. on Judiciary, Gen. Conf., 1936; del. to Gen. Conf. M.E. Ch., 1932, 36; del. Uniting Conf., Kansas City (mem. com. on judiciary), 1939; member Judicial Council, Methodist Church, 1939—; trustee Southern California Conference Methodist Church (pres. of board); trustee. Methodist. Hosp., Pasadena Council of Churches. Mem. Delta Tau Delta, Pi Gamma Mu. Mason. Contbr. to Christian Advocate, Zion's Herald, Religious Edn., and other religious and sociol. periodicals. Address: 429 N. Kenwood Av., Gelndale, Cal. Died Sept. 12, 1953; buried Mountain View Cemetery, Pasadena, Cal.

BUCKY, Philip Barnett, cons. engr., educator; b. Chgo., June 27, 1899; s. David and Libby (Gradford) B.; B.S., U. Ill., 1921; E.M., Pa. State Coll., 1926. Field experience in all capacities from mucker to supt. in coal and metal mines, 1917-23; asst. prof., Pa. State Coll. and cons. engr., 1923-29; prof., sch. of mines Columbia, 1929—, exec. officer, 1946-52; cons. engr. on mining methods, and spl. problems in all mineral fields requiring bulk extraction and spl. knowledge of ground behavior, various companies and U.S. Govt. Served as carpenter mate USN, 1918; capt., A.R.C., 1918. Holder W. Va. Mine foreman's certificate, 1921. Mem. Am. Inst. Mining and Metall. Engrs. (chmn. mining methods com., vice chmn. papers and publs.), Mining and Metall. Soc., Am. Phys. Soc., A.A.A.S., Soc. Exptl. Stress Analysis, Soc. Promotion Engring. Edn., Sigma Xi, Tau Beta Pi, Sigma Gamma Epsilon. Clubs: Nanhook Yacht, University (Columbia). Author: Mining by Block Caving, 1945. Contbr. to Peeles Mining Engineers Handbook, 1941. Contbr. tech. jours. Patentee on ground support, mining methods and fragmentation. Home: 17 N. Chatsworth Av., Larchmont, N.Y. Office: Sch. of Mines, Columbia U., N.Y.C. 27. Died Aug. 8, 1957.

BUDD, Charles Henry, banker; b. Niagara County, N.Y., Mar. 21, 1848; s. Andrew Spickerman and Mary (Penoyer) B.; grad. bus. dept. Genesee Wesleyan Sem., Lima, N.Y.; LL.B., U. Mich., 1872; m. Carrie Eastman, 1877 (died 1881); 2d, Nellie C. Moyer, 1889. Practiced law in Montevideo, 1872-76, then in St. Paul, returning about 1878 to Montevideo; entered partnership of Moyer Bos. in pvt. bankers, pres. Chippewa County Bank, 1888-03, and its successor, Chippewa County State Bank, 1908-13; organizer, 1914, pres. Montevideo State Bank; mgr., treas. Montevideo Improvement Co. County atty. Chippewa County, 1872, 74-76; judge of probate, 1872-3; McKinley presdl. elector for Minn., 1896. Organizer and many yrs. sec., treas. Montevideo Library Assn. Trustee Windom Coll., Montevideo. Dir., treas. Montevideo Independent Sch. Dist. No. 1. Progressive. Methodist. Odd Fellow (past grand master Minn.; past grand rep. Sovereign Grand Lodge). Address: Montevideo, Minn. Died Dec. 24, 1929.

BUDER, Gustavus Adolphus (bú-der), lawyer; b. Cairo, Ill., Jan. 7, 1871; s. William and Susette B.; LL.B., Washington U., 1892; m. Lydia D. Feuerbacher, June 6, 1899 (died Aug. 27, 1930); 1 son, Gustavus Adolphus. Admitted to bar, 1892; since practiced law in St. Louis; sr. mem. G.A. Buder. Son & Assos. Pres. Arc. Realty Co., Arcadia Realty Co., Pontiac Realty Co., Arcadia Refining Co., Arcadia Royalty Company; president, director Lyiade Investment Trust; dir., atty. Scruggs, Vandevoort-Barney, Inc., Burroughs Adding Machine Company, Packard Motor Car Company of Missouri, Selden-Breck Constn. Co., Arcarea Reserve Co., Miss. Served as pvt. Battery A, 1st Mo. Vol. Arty., Spanish-Am. War; participated in Puerto Rican expdn., 1898. Decorated Medal of Order of Leopold II (Belgium) for services, 1914-18. Incorporator, former v.p., hon. dir., life mem., Municipal Theater Assn.; mem. St. Louis Pub. Library Bd., St. Louis Park and Playground Assn. (v.p.), Am., Mo., Ill., St. Louis bar assns.; mem. Spanish-Am. War Vets., Vets. Fgn. Wars, Mo. Press Assn. (former pres.), Am. Press Assn. (former pres.), St. Louis Law Library (life mem.). Republican. Unitarian. Clubs: Rotary, Bankers of Am., New St. Louis, Advertising, Mo. Athletic, St. Louis Automobile (St. Louis); Detroit. Home: 3137 Longfellow Blvd. Office: Buder Bldg., St. Lous, Mo. Died Apr. 14, 1954.

BUDGE, Alfred, judge; b. Providence, Utah, Feb. 24, 1868; s. William and Eliza (Pritchert) B.; ed. Provo and Logan acads., Utah; LL.B., U. of Mich., 1892, hon. M.A., 1919; LL.D., Univ. of Idaho, 1942; m. Ella Hoge, July 5, 1894; children—Alfred H., Drew S., Ina E., Ora A., Walter L., Bruce C., Hamer H., Belva A., Ella L. (dec.). District attorney, 5th Judicial District of Ida., 1894-98; county atty., Bear Lake County, Ida., 1898-1902; dist. judge, 5th Jud. Dist., 1902-14; justice Supreme Court of Ida., since 1914 (chief justice, 1917, 23, 29, 33, 34, 41, 47). Instr. law sales, law dept., Northwestern U., summer, 1923; resident instr., law dept. U. of Ida. Independent. Home: 1418 Warm Springs Av., Boise, Ida. Died Jan. 25, 1951; buried Cloverdale Meml. Cemetery, Boise.

BUDGE, Ross A(ddison), banker; b. Pocatello, Ida., May 18, 1910; s. Jesse Robert Stratford and Grace Elizabeth (Hoff) B.; A.B. summa cum laude, Univ. Utah, 1930; M.B.A. cum laude, Harvard, 1932; m. Janet Elizabeth Majors, Oct. 31, 1936; children—Melinda, Alexander Majors, Daphne. Member treas. dept., Allied Chemical & Dye Corp., N.Y. City, 1932-35; securities analyst, Pacific Mutual Life Ins. Co., Los Angeles, 1935-37; securities analyst, The Nat. City Bank of New York, 1937-40, asst. cashier, 1940-44, asst. vice pres., 1944-47, vice pres. since 1947. Treas. and mem. exec. com., The History Committee, Inc., a non-profit orgn. to record the history of Am. Chem. industry since 1944. Club: Siwanoy Country, Bronxville, N.Y. Office: 55 Wall St., N.Y. City 15. Home: 32 Grove Lane, Bronxville 8, N.Y. Died Oct. 4, 1950.

BUDINGTON, Robert Allyn, zoölogist; b. Leyden, Mass., Oct. 22, 1872; s. Stephen Buckland and Ereda (Baker) B.; B.A., Williams Coll., 1896, M.A., 1899, Sc.D., 1929; studied Columbia, 1899-1903; m. Mabel Frances Stone, Dec. 27, 1906; children—Robert Allyn, William Stone. Instr. science and mathematics Dow Acad., Franconia, N.H., 1896-98; asst. in biology Williams Coll., 1898-99; asst. demonstrator physiology Coll. Phys. and Surg. Columbia, 1900-02; instr. physiology and zoölogy Mt. Hermon (Mass.) Sch., 1903-05; instr. biology Wesleyan U., Conn., 1905-08; asso. prof. zoölogy Oberlin Coll., 1908-13, prof. zoölogy, 1913-40, prof. emeritus, 1940—, head dept., 1913-36 instr. invertebrate morphology instr. Marine Biological Lab., Woods Hole, Mass., 1902-10, instr. embryology, 1912-19. Fellow A.A.A.S.; mem. Am. Soc. Zoölogists, Am. Naturalists, Ohio Acad. Science. Conglist. Author: (with H. W. Conn) Advanced Physiology and Hygiene, 1909; Physiology and Human Life, 1927. Contbr. to Am. Jour. Physiology, Biol. Bulletin, School and Society, etc. Home: Winter Park, Fla. Died Oct. 23, 1954.

BUDLONG, Frederick Grandy, bishop; b. Camden, N.Y., July 10, 1881; s. Rev. Frank Dorr and Sarah Elizabeth Hale (Grandy) B.; grad. Shattuck Mil. Sch., Faribault, Minn., 1900; A.B., Hobart Coll., Geneva, N.Y., 1904; grad. Gen. Theol. Sem., N.Y. City, 1907; special courses at Columbia; S.T.D., Hobart, 1920; D.D., U. of Pittsburgh, 1921; S.T.D., Gen. Theol. Sem., 1932; D.D., Berkeley Div. Sch., 1932; D.D., Trinity College, Conn., 1932; married Mary Elizabeth Corbett, April 30, 1910 (died June 12, 1946); one son, Harrison Montgomery; m. 2d,

Kathleen Faulconer (Kelly), Nov. 18, 1947. Deacon and priest, Protestant Episcopal Church, 1907; curate St. John the Evangelist Ch., St. Paul, Minn., 1907-09; rector Christ Ch., St. Paul, 1909-12, Christ Ch., Winnetka, Ill., 1912-16, St. Peter's Ch., Chicago, 1916-21; 1st prin. Diocesan Sch. of Religious Instr., at Chicago, 1915; rector Ch. of the Ascension, Pittsburgh, Pa., 1921-25, Christ Ch., Greenwich, Conn., 1925-1931; consecrated bishop-coadjutor of Conn., Dec. 16, 1931; became bishop of Conn., Jan. 28, 1934, ret. 1951. Del. from Minnesota 1st Peace Congress, Chicago, 1910; dean of St. Paul, 1912; lecturer Western Theol. Sem., 1912-20, Berkeley Divinity Sch. since 1941. President of Province of New England, since 1947. Mem. Nat. Council of the Episcopal Ch., 1942. Mem. Soc. Colonial Wars, Society Mayflower Descendants, Phi Beta Kappa, Sigma Phi. Republican. Mason. Clubs: Duquesne (Pittsburgh); Graduates (New Haven); Yale (New York). Home: 745 Farmington Av., West Hartford 7, Conn. Died Sept. 25, 1953; buried Clinton, N.Y.

BUEHR, Karl Albert, artist; b. Feuerbach, Stuttgart, Germany; s. Frederick K. and Fredericka (Doh) B.; grad. with honor Art Inst. Chgo., 1894; m. Mary G. Hess, June 28, 1899; children—Mary Kathleen, George Frederick, Lydia Avery (dec.). Gold medal Colorosse Art Sch., 1901; bronze medal, St. Louis Expn., 1904; hon. mention, Paris Salon, 1910; silver medal, Chgo. Soc. Artists, 1914; silver medal, San Francisco Expn., 1915; Logan prize and Butler prize, 1918, Art Inst. Chgo.; silver medal, Peoria Soc. of Allied Arts, 1920; Harry Frank prize, Chgo. Art Inst., 1920; Norman Wait Harris prize, 1922; Municipal Art Club prize, 1925; William Thompson prize, Chgo., 1926; Bux. Men's Art Club prize, 1926; Chgo. Galleries Assn. $1,000 prize, 1931; James Patten prize, Evanston, Ill., 1933; Women's Club prize, Evanston, 1933. First prize, Evanston Woman's Club, 1945. Mem. 1st Ill. Cav., Spanish-Am. War, 1898. Represented in Hist. Mus. of Des Moines, Ia., John H. Vanderpool Art Assn., Chgo., Hamilton Club, Chgo., Northwestern U., Evanston, Ill., U. Chgo., Bethany Coll., W.Va., Frances Willard Meml. House, Evanston. Asso. of Nat. Acad.; mem. Chgo., Galleries Assn. Club: Cliff Dwellers, Home: 1738 Jarvis Av. Office: 509 S. Wabash Av., Chgo. Died 1952.*

BUEHRING, Paul Henry (bū'rĭng), clergyman; b. Elkhorn, Wis., July 5, 1880; s. Rev. Henry William and Dorothea (Wiedenroth) B.; student Wartburg Acad., Waverly, Ia., 1893-94; A.B., Wartburg Coll., Clinton, Ia., 1898; student Wartburg Sem., Dubuque, Ia., 1898-99; grad. Luth. Sem., Columbus, O., 1905; A.M., U. Chgo., summer 1923; B.D., Augustana Sem., Rock Island, Ill., 1927; D.D., Capital U., Columbus, 1929; unmarried. Ordained Luth. ministry, 1905; pastor Zion Luth. Ch., St. Marys, O., 1905-11; prin. Hebron (Neb.) Acad., 1911-19; prof. theology Lutheran Sem., Columbus, 1919-27, prof. hist. theology, 1927—, dean, 1936-46, emeritus, 1946—. Chmn. Bd. Fgn. Missions Am. Luth. Ch.; mem. Commn. on Luth. Church-Fellowship, 1935-46. Mem. Am. Soc. Ch. History. Author: Christian Ethics (with Dr. M. Reu), 1935; The Spirit of the American Lutheran Church, 1940. Editor: Mission Studies, 1931. Home: 758 Francis Av., Columbus 9, O. Died Aug. 16, 1958.

BUEL, Walker Showers (bū'ĕl), newspaperman; b. Springfield, O., Jan. 15, 1890; s. Jesse Allen and Frances (Showers) B.; student Buchtel Coll. (now U. Akron), Akron, O., 1907-10, Western Res. U., 1910-11; m. Sakie E. Prout, June 23, 1917; children—Walker Prout, Meredith Showers. With Cleveland Plain Dealer, 1912—, polit. writer, 1914-17; state legislative corr. Plain Dealer, Columbus, 1917-19, Washington corr. for Plain Dealer, 1919—, asso. editor, 1934—. Mem. Delta Kappa Epsilon (pres. Washington Alumni Assn. 1925-26). Methodist. Mason. Clubs: Gridiron (pres. 1932), Alfalfa, Nat. Press (Washington); Chevy Chase (Chevy Chase, Md.); City (Cleve.). Home: 3815 Gramercy St., Washington 16. Office: Albee Bldg., Washington 5. Died May 23, 1957.

BUESSER, Frederick G. (bē'sēr), physician, educator; b. Troy, N.Y., Apr. 27, 1881; s. Gustavus D. and Nellie (Conners) B.; student U. Vt., 1901-04; M.D., Wayne U., 1905; postgrad. N.Y.C., Chgo., Rochester, Minn., Paris, Lyon and Dijon, France; m. Lela Carpenter, Mar. 1, 1915; children—Frederick G., William Carpenter (dec.), Elizabeth L. (Mrs. John F. Pfender), Anthony Carpenter. With Harper Hosp., Detroit, 1905—, vol. asst., out-patient dept. of internal medicine, 1905-07, asst. physician, 1908-10, attending physician, 1910-19, physician dept. internal medicine, 1919-22, sr. physician, 1923-45, cons. physician, 1945—; vis. physician Detroit Tb. Sanatorium; cons. physician City of Detroit Receiving Hosp., Charles Godwin Jennings Hosp.; with Wayne U. Coll. Medicine, 1905—, instr. clin. medicine, 1905-07, asst. prof., 1908-19, asso. prof. gastro-enterology, 1919-35, now prof. clin. medicine; former chmn. faculty adv. council; lecturer, Postgrad. Sch. Medicine, U. Mich. Mem. Continuation Sch. of Medicine, Wayne County; mem. State Com. on Med. Procurement and Assignment; mem. med. adv. bd. 1, Mich. Served from lt. to maj. M.C., AEF and BEF, 1917-19. Diplomate Am. Bd. Internal Medicine. Fellow A.C.P., Detroit Acad. Medicine (ex-pres.); mem. A. M.A., Mich., Wayne County med. socs., Assn. Mil. Surgeons, Delta Mu, Nu Sigma Nu, Alpha Omega Alpha (hon.). Republican. Episcopalian. Clubs: Detroit Golf, Detroit Athletic. Home: 921 Taylor Av. Office: 1553 Woodward Av., Detroit. Died July 1, 1950.

BUFFUM, Hugh Straight, educator; b. Lineville, Ia., Apr. 15, 1877; s. Erwin Soloman and Narcissa Evaline (Sullivan) B.; student Parsons Coll., Fairfield, Ia., 1897-99; B.A., State U. Ia., 1901, M.A., 1902, B.D., 1904, Ph.D., 1906; m. Hazel May Price, June 25, 1913; children—Thomas Erwin, Hugh Price. Supt. schs., Lamoni, Ia, 1902-04; tchr. Ia. City Acad., 1904-06; instr. edn. State U. Ia., 1906-07; prof. edn. Cornell Coll., 1907-08; prof. ednl. theory State Normal Sch., Valley City, N.D., 1908-11; supt. tng. sch. No. State Normal Sch., Marquette, Mich., 1911-12; prof. edn. and psychology Parsons Coll., 1913-14; prof. edn. Ia. State Tchrs. Coll., 1914-18, now prof. emeritus. Mem. Area Bd. Boy Scouts Am. Fellow Iowa Acad. Sci.; mem. S.A.R., Soc. Mayflower Descs. (state elder), Ia. Ornithologists Union, Phi Beta Kappa, Phi Delta Kappa. Mason. Presbyn. Radio broadcaster, Station KXEL, 4 years. Wrote: (brochure) Federal and State Aid to Education in Iowa, 1906. Home: 2300 Franklin St., Cedar Falls, Ia. Died Oct. 17, 1959.

BUGAN, Thomas Gregory, lawyer; b. Chicago, Dec. 29, 1898; s. George and Antoinette (Kruzic) G.; student DePaul U.; LL.B., John Marshall Law Sch.; m. Violet Leona Newman, Mar. 8, 1946; children—Gregory Stephen, Russell Joseph. Admitted to Ill. bar, 1931; asst. state's atty., Cook Co., 1933-40; atty. Ill. Tax Commn. and Ill. Dept. Revenue, 1941-46; pvt. practice of law, Chicago, 1946—. Mem. Am. (com. on taxation), Ill. (com. on taxation) and Chicago (com. on inquiries) bar assns., Nat. Tax Assn. Club: Chicago Traffic, South Shore Country. Author: When Does Title Pass. Home: 9810 Oakley Av., Chgo. 43. Office: One N. LaSalle St., Chgo. 43. Died Sept. 5, 1955; buried Mt. Hope Cemetery, Chgo.

BUGBEE, Benjamin C., cons. engr.; b. Waukesha, Wis., May 21, 1879; s. Vanness Harris and Jeannette (Soence) B.; ed. pub. schs. of Waukesha; m. Edith Allene Puffer, June 20, 1898; children—Virginia H., George P., Benjamin C., Arthur L. Mech. engr. power plant, constrn. supt., asst. chief engr., Wis. Electric Power Co., 1900-18; asso. Chas. A. Cahill & Sons, cons. engrs., 1920-29; sole owner Charles A. Cahill & Sons, cons. engrs. (all at Milwaukee) since 1940; vice pres. and dir. Waukesha Nat. Bank since 1934; pres. and dir. Indsl. Bldg. & Loan Co. since 1933; dir. Gen. Malleable Grey Iron & Aluminum Corp., Waukesha Motor Co. Mem. Engrs. Soc. of Milwaukee. Republican. Methodist (trustee and treas.). Mason (K.T.). Club: Merrill Hills Country. Home: 117 East Av. N., Waukesha, Wis. Office: 724 E. Mason St., Milw. Deceased.

BUGBEE, Percy Isaac, sch. adminstr.; b. Colton, N.Y., 1858; s. John F. and Clementina P. (Gates) B.; B.A., St. Lawrence U., 1879, M.A., 1882, D.Sc., 1898; m. Ida M. Farnes, 1893. Prin. State Normal Sch., Oneonta, N.Y., 1898-1933. Pres. N.Y. tchrs. Assn., 1912. Mem. Phi Beta Kappa. Republican. Universalist. Home: 18 Walnut St., Oneonta, N.Y. Died May 15, 1935; buried Glenwood Cemetery, Oneonta.

BUHL, Lawrence D. (būl), mfr.; student U. of Mich.; m. Cora S. Peck. Pres. Buhl Land Co.; dir. Buhl Sons Company, Parke Davis & Co., Detroit. Served in World War. Clubs: University, Yondotega, Detroit, Detroit Boat, Country, Bloomfield Hills Country, Grosse Point. Home: 249 Lake Shore Rd., Grosse Pointe Farms 36, Mich. Address: 1612 Buhl Bldg., Detroit 26. Died Mar. 3, 1956.

BUIST, Harold J(ohn), business exec.; b. Cardiff, Wales, Sept. 4, 1897; s. James J. and Alicia (Murphy) B.; C.P.A., Ind., 1926; m. Nelle Perry, June 25, 1927; 1 dau., Janet. Came to U.S., 1921, naturalized, 1927. Pub. accountant for George B. Buist & Co., Fort Wayne, Ind., 1921-29; asso. Allied Mills, Inc., 1929, sec. Chgo. 1932-33, sec.-treas., 1933-41, exec. v.p., 1941-45, pres. and chmn. bd., 1945—. Served in Brit. Army and Royal Air Force, World War I. Clubs: Skokie Country, Glencoe. Home: 145 Sheridan Rd. N., Winnetka, Ill. Office: Board of Trade Bldg., Chgo. Died Nov. 8, 1957; buried All Saints Cemetery, Des Plaines, Ill.

BUKOFZER, Manfred F., music educator and musicologist; b. Oldenburg, Ger., March 27, 1910; s. Lion and Elizabeth (Schulmann) B.; ed. Stern Conservatory, Hochschule für Music (Hindemith), Berlin; stu. Univs. of Heidelberg, Berlin; Ph.D., Basle Univ., Switzerland, 1936; m. Ilse Kaemmerer, May 20, 1939. Came to U.S., 1939, naturalized, 1945. Lecturer, Volkshochschule of Basle Univ. (Switzerland), 1937; guest lecturer, Basle Univ., Cambridge, Oxford, Warburg Inst., 1938-39; lecturer in music, Western Reserve Univ., Cleveland, 1940; asst. prof. of music, Univ. of Calif., Berkeley, 1941, asso. prof., 1944, prof., 1946; teacher Univ. of Chicago, Columbia Univ. Participant Internat. Congresses of musicology Barcelona, 1936, N.Y., 1939, conf. on scholarship and research in the Arts, Princeton Bicentennial, 1947. Walker-Ames prof. music, U. of Wash., Seattle, winter 1949. Mem. Internat. Soc. Musicol., Am. Musicol. Soc., Mediaeval Acad. of Am., American Society for Aesthetics. Author: Geschichte des Englischen Diskants, 1936; Sumer is icumen in, A Revision, 1944; The Music of the Laudes in Kantorowicz; Laudes Regia, 1946; Music in the Maroque Era, 1947; Studies in Medieval and Renaissance Music, 1950; Coperario, Rules how to Compose, 1952; John Dunstable, Complete Works, 1953. Contbr. numerous articles to musical magazines. Home: 1072 Keeler Av., Berkeley 8, Cal. Died Dec. 7, 1955.

BUKOWSKI, Peter Ivan, banker; b. Chicago, Feb 1, 1894; s. Vincent and Frances (Sienkowski) B.; m. Gertrude Edna Hall, June 28, 1919; children—Richard Peter (lost at sea), Robert Hall, Edith Frances (Gauger). With merchandising and cataloging depts. Montgomery Ward & Co., 1912-16; indoctrination with Dept. Commerce, Washington, then assigned as asst. comml. attache Am. Embassy, Petrograd Russia, 1916-17, asst. mil. attache, also rep. in N Russia for Hoover Relief Orgn. for Eastern Europe and A.R.C., 1917-19; with several Chicago banks in various capacities from examiner to pres., 1920-32 asst. mgr., later mgr. Chicago loan agy. R.F.C., 1933-45; pres. Cosmopolitan Nat. Bank Chicago, 1945 51, since 1952; dep. adminstr. R.F.C., Washington 1951; dir. C. E. Niehoff & Co., Avondale Savs. & Loan Assn. Mem. Am. Legion. Republican. Clubs Bankers, Lake Shore (Chgo.). Home: 5706 N.W Circle Av., Chgo. 31. Office: 801 N. Clark St. Chgo. 10. Died July 7, 1956; buried Desplaines. Ill.

BULKELEY, William E. A., retired ins. exec.; b Hartford, Conn., 1868; s. William H. and Emma (Gurney) B.; student Trinity Coll., 1890; m. Alys M. Harper, Jan. 14, 1911. Vice pres. Aetna Life Ins. Co., 1923-47, now retired. Life trustee Trinity Coll. Mem. Delta Psi. Mason. Home: 11 Sycamore Rd., Hartford, Conn. Died Apr. 1, 1950.

BULL, E. Myron, steamship exec.; b. Cranford, N.J., Mar. 31, 1904; s. Ernest Miller and Edith (Upham) B.; A.B., Cornell U., 1926; LL.B., Yale, 1929; m. Frances Patten, Apr. 23, 1931; children—E. Myron, Frances. Admitted to N.Y. State bar, 1929; asso. with firm Hughes, Schurman & Dwight, N.Y. City, 1929-37; partner Dwight, Harris, Koegel & Caskey, 1937-41; dir., v.p., gen. counsel A. H. Bull Steamship Co., 1933-41, pres. and dir. since 1941; A. H. Bull & Co., Bull Insular Line, Baltimore Insular Line, Bull Steamship Line, Forty West St. Realty Corp., Ericsson Line; dir. Corn Exchange Bank Trust Co., Centennial Ins. Co.; trustee Irving Savs. Bank, Atlantic Mut. Ins. Co. Mem. Am. com. Lloyd's Register of Shipping; dir. Maritime Assn., Port of N.Y.; mem. bd. mgrs. Am. Bur. Shipping. Mem. N.Y. Produce Exchange, Fed., N.Y. State bar assns. Commerce and Industry Assn. of N.Y. (dir.). Clubs: India Mem. House, Tuxedo, Racquet and Tennis, City Midday. Home: Tuxedo Park, N.Y. Office: 115 Broad St., N.Y.C. 4. Died June 4, 1953.

BULL, Ludlow (Seguine), Egyptologist; b. N.Y. City, Jan. 10, 1886; s. Dr. Charles Stedman and Mary Eunice (Kingsbury) B.; grad. Pomfret (Conn.) Sch., 1903; A.B., Yale, 1907; LL.B., Harvard, 1910; Ph.D., U. of Chicago, 1922; m. Katharine Davis Exton, Nov. 25, 1924; children—Frederick Kingsbury, 2d, Roger Ludlow, Agnes Davis. Admitted to N.Y. bar, 1911, and practiced in N.Y. City, 1910-15; fellow in Semitics, U. of Chicago, 1920-22; mem. Oriental Inst., U. of Chicago, expeditions to Egypt, Mesopotamia, Syria, 1919-20, Egypt, 1923; asst. curator Egyptian Dept., Met. Museum, N.Y. City, 1922-28, asso. curator, 1928—; lecturer in Egyptology, Yale, 1925-36, research asso. with rank of prof., 1936—; curator Yale Egyptian Collection, 1925—. Asso. fellow Davenport Coll. Served as pvt. Med. Corps, U.S. Army with Yale Mobile Hosp., A.E.F., 1917-18, 1st lt. San. Corps, A.E.F., 1918-19. Trustee Pomfret Sch. (pres. Alumni Assn., 1942-45), Kingsley Trust Assn. (New Haven), 1936-38 (adv. com., 1941—); trustee, Am. Schs. Oreintal Research (Jerusalem and Baghdad). Mem. Com. Mediterranean Antiquities, Am. Council Learned Socs., 1930-36. Fellow Am. Geog. Soc.; mem. Am. Oriental Soc. (del. to centenary Royal Asiatic Soc. 1923; rec. sec. 1925-36; v.p. 1938-39; pres. 1939-40), Archeol. Inst. Am. (executive com. N.Y. soc.), Society Bibl. Lit., Egypt Exploration Soc. (London), trustee Cathedral St. John the Divine, N.Y., 1943—, Youth Consultation Service (N.Y.), Am. Research Center in Egypt, Antiquarian and Landmarks Society of Connecticut, Palestine Exploration Soc. (Jerusalem) Soc. Egyptol. Reine Elisabeth (Brussells), Scroll and Kay (Yale), Psi Upsilon, Ind. Republican. Episcopalian. Clubs: Century, Church (past pres.), University (N.Y. City); Lawn (New Haven); Litchfield (Conn.) Country (former pres.) Author: The Rhind Mathematical Papyrus, Vol. II (with A. B. Chace, and H. P. Manning), 1929; Inscriptions at Deir el Hagar, in H. E. Winlock, Ed Dakhleh Oasis, 1936. Editor of 6 vols. Publications of the Egyptian Expedition and 6 vols. Publications of the Egyptian Dept., Metropolitan Museum, N.Y. City. Mem. editorial board Metropolitan Museum Studies, 1928-34. Contbr. articles to professional jours. Home: Litchfield, Conn. Office: care Metropolitan Museum, N.Y.C. 28. Died July 1, 1954; buried Litchfield, Conn.

BULLARD, Edward Payson, Jr. (bo͝ol'lȧrd), mfg. exec.; b. Columbus, O., July 10, 1872; s. Edward Payson and Alice Martha (Camp) B.; grad. Williston Sem., 1891; student Amherst, 1891-92; m. Mary E. Deacon, Aug. 17, 1897; children—Jean, Edward Payson III. With Bridgeport Machine Tool Co., which later became Bullard Machine Tool Co. and finally Bullard Co., successively asst. supt., v.p. and pres.; pres. Bullard Engring. Co., 1916-18; dir. First Nat. Bank of Bridgeport; trustee of the Bridgeport People's Savings Bank. Inventor of the Mult-Au-Matic for which awarded Howard N. Potts medal of Franklin Inst., 1920; medal Am. Soc. M.E., 1937. Citation for modern pioneering N.A.M., 1941. Mem. Am. Soc. M.E. Republican. Presbyn. Clubs: Brooklawn Country, Pine Orchard. Home: 829 Verna Hill Rd., Fairfield, Conn. Office: Bullard Co., 286 Canfield Av., Bridgeport, Conn. Died June 26, 1953.*

BULLARD, F(rederic) Lauriston, editor, author; b. Wauseon, O., May 13, 1866; s. Frederic Lauriston and Helen Maria (Ballard) B.; B.A., Wooster (O.) Coll., 1891, M.A., 1894, D.Litt., 1930; B.D. magna cum laude, Yale, 1903; LL.D., R.I. State Coll., 1929; Litt.D., Northeastern U., 1934; m. Clara Elizabeth Keil; children—Edward Lauriston (dec.), Frederic Keil, Helen Dorothea (wife of Col. Paul E. Zuver), Robert Paul, Clara Elizabeth (Mrs. William G. Millane). In ministry Presbyn. and Congl. chs., 10 yrs.; newspaper work, 1907—, mostly with the Boston Herald, Sunday editor, 1915-19, chief editorial writer, 1919-43. Winner Pulitzer editorial prize for 1926. Author: Historic Summer Haunts, 1913; Famous War Correspondents, 1914; Tad and His Father, 1915; A Few Appropriate Remarks—The Gettysburg Address, 1944. Editor: The Diary of a Public Man, 1945; Abraham Lincoln and The Widow Bixby, 1946, numerous Lincoln Monographs. Contributor numerous mag. articles and editorials. Mem. Massachusetts Historical Soc., Mil. Hist. Soc. of Mass., Phi Beta Kappa. Awarded diploma of honor for distinguished contbns. to the study of Abraham Lincoln, by Lincoln Meml. U., 1941. Home: 141 Walton Park, Melrose Highlands 76, Mass. Died Aug. 1952.

BULLARD, James Atkins, educator; b. Parsippany, N.J., Feb. 23, 1887; s. Charles Bulkley and Minnie Woolsey (Atkins) B.; B.A., Williams Coll., 1908; Ph.D., Clark U., 1914; m. Augusta Bates Benedict, Sept. 9, 1911; 1 dau., Jane (wife of Dr. Gordon M. Meade). Asst. prof. mathematics U.S. Naval Acad., 1918-20, associate prof., 1920-27, prof., 1927-28; prof. mathematics, U. Vt., 1928-54, prof. emeritus, 1954—. chmn., 1942-54. Home: 216 S. Willard St., Burlington, Vt. Died Apr. 10, 1959; buried Parsippany, N.J.

BULLENE, Egbert Frank, ret. army officer; b. Salinas, Cal., Jan. 25, 1895; s. Alfred Frank and Lida (Hatch) B.; Columbia Prep. Sch., 1913-14, B.S., U.S. Naval Acad., 1917, Army Indspl. Coll., 1928, Chem. Warfare Corps, line and staff course, 1926, field officers course, 1933, Command and Gen. Staff Sch., 1937, Army War Coll., 1940; m. Lois Esther Salsman, Sept. 29, 1919; 1 son, Roger. Commd. 2d lt. 1917, advanced throuh grades to maj. gen., 1951; bn. comdr., 4th Div., World War I; spl. detail in North China when Japanese came over the Great Wall for first time in 1933; served in F.A., Cav., and Corps; instr. at Command and Gen. Staff Sch., 1937-39; comd. joint Am.-British secret Army-Navy project overseas, 1944; in European and Pacific Theatres, 1945; mem. mil. commn. which tried and convicted Gen. Yamashita; comd. Army Chem. Center, Md., 1946-50; chief chem. officer of the Army, ret. 1954. Decorated Legion of Merit, Bronze Star, Purple Heart, Commendation Ribbon, Victory Medal with four clasps. Mason. Address: P.O. Box 2968, Carmel, Cal. Died Feb. 21, 1958; buried Nat. Cemetery of the Presidio of San Francisco.

BULLIET, Clarence Joseph (bo͝ol'ĕt), art and drama critic; b. Corydon, Ind., Mar. 16, 1883; s. Paul Constantine and Sarah Jane (Marsh) B.; A.B., Indiana U., 1905; m. Katherine Adams, Oct. 22, 1905 (dec. May 21, 1946); 1 son, Leander Jackson; m. 2d Catherine Girdler, Dec. 22, 1949. Writer, Louisville Herald. 1905; with Indianapolis Star, 1906-12; press representative of Robert B. Mantell, 1912-19; news editor Louisville Herald, 1920-23; art and drama critic Chicago Evening Post, 1924-32; art critic Chicago Daily News since 1932, motion picture critic 1939-42, music critic, 1941-48; contributing critic, Art Digest, since 1946; instructor in art history and art philosophy, Grad. Sch., Claremont Colls., Claremont, Calif., summers 1939, 40, 41, 50. A worker for Belgian Relief, in U.S. and Can., summer 1916. Founding mem. Internat. Assn. Art Critics, Paris, 1948. Fellow Royal Society of Arts, London; mem. Indiana Soc. of Chicago, Chicago Press Veterans Assn., Phi Beta Kappa. Author: Robert Mantell's Romance, 1918; Apples and Madonnas, 1927 (chosen as the representative book on Modern Art for White House library), Venus Castina, 1928; The Courtezan Olympia, 1930; Art Masterpieces of the World's Fair, 1933, 34; The Significant Moderns, 1936; Masterpieces of Italian Art, 1939; French Art from David to Matisse, 1941; How Grand Opera Came to Chicago, 1942; Art Treasures from Vienna, 1950; The Story of Lent in Art Masterpieces, 1951. Home: 1730 Oxford St., Rockford, Ill. Address: Chicago Daily News, Chgo. Died Oct. 20, 1952; buried New Albany, Ind.

BULLITT, William Marshall, lawyer; b. Louisville, Ky., Mar. 4, 1873; s. Thomas Walker and Annie P. (Logan) B.; B.S., Princeton, 1894; LL.B., U. Louisville, 1895; m. Nora Iasigi, May 31, 1913; children—Thomas Walker, Nora Iasigi (Mrs. Eugene W. Leake, Jr.), Barbara (Mrs. Lowry Watkins). Practiced at Louisville, 1894-57; sr. mem. Bullitt, Dawson & Tarrant. Solicitor-gen., U.S., 1912-13; Rep. nominee for U.S. Senate, 1914. Dir. gen. counsel, Citizens Fidelity Bank and Trust Co., 1907-57; trustee Am. Surety Co., N.Y.; trustee, mem. exec. com., ins. and agy. com. Mutual Life Ins. Co. N.Y. Trustee Carnegie Endowment for Internat. Peace. Del. at large Rep. Nat. Conv., Chgo., 1908 (mem. com. on resolutions), and 1916; chmn. Bd. of Pub. Safety of Louisville, 1907-09. Maj. and deputy commr. for France of Am. Red Cross, 1918-19. Special counsel for U.S. Shipping Bd. and U.S. Shipping Bd. Emergency Fleet Corp., 1921-22; spl. asst. to atty. gen. of U.S. in Atlantic Corp. litigation, 1924-25; argued over 50 cases in Supreme Court of United States, including constitutionality of anti-removal statutes, the "War time" Prohibition Act, 18th Amendment, Frazier-Lemke Act, Fed. Farm Loan Act, income taxation of Federal judicial salaries, Fed. taxation of State bonds and municipal securities, Federal estate taxation of proceeds of life ins. policies, constitutionality of state statutes of various states, Rehabilitation Act of Cal., etc.; mem. vis. com. on mathematics Harvard. Fellow Pierpont Morgan Library; mem. S.A.R., Soc. Colonial Wars, Assn. Bar City N.Y., Am., Ky., Louisvill bar assns., Am. Math. Soc., Math. Assn. America, Amateur Astron. Assn., Am. Law Inst., N.Y. State C. of C. Clubs: Union, Down Town Association, National Republican (N.Y.C.); Metropolitan (Washington); Faculty of Harvard U. (Cambridge, Mass.); Pendennis, Country, Arts, Filson (Louisville). Author: The Relation of the Individual Policyholder to the Assets of a Mutual Life Insurance Company; The Supreme Court of the U.S. and Unconstitutional Legislation; Accidental Means; Distribution of Divisible Surplus in the Light of Present Economic Conditions, 1938. Editor of Bullitt's Civil and criminal Codes of Kentucky, 1899, 1902. Home: Oxmoor, Route 6, Louisville 7. Office: Kentucky Home Life Bldg., Louisville 2. Died Oct. 3, 1957; buried Oxmoor Cemetery.

BULLOCK, Harry Elmer, coal mine operator; b. Whitley County, Ky., May 4, 1884; s. Edward Henry and Elizabeth (Foley) B.; student Williamsburg (Ky.) Acad., 1900-02, U. Ky., 1928-29; A.B., Lincoln Meml. U., 1904, Litt.D., 1928; m. Miranda Owens, Sept. 16, 1908; children—Ruth (Mrs. E. Paul Reed), Harry E., Virginia (Mrs. Caywood C. Thomson), Evan. Chemist, U.S. Steel Corp., 1906; author and accountant Trosper Coal Co., 1907, pres. and mgr., 1907-09; mgr. Poteau Coal & Mining Co. and Poteau, Ft. Smith & Western Ry., 1910; pres. Ky. Jewel Coal Co., 1911—, Ky. Block Coal Co., 1915—; v.p. Midland Mining Co., 1916—; also pres. Carrs Fork Coal Co., 1918-25. State chmn. Ky. Red Cross during World War I. Served as co-dir. Ky. Relief Commn., 1932-33; chmn. State-Wide Welfare Com.; Ky. rep. Pres.' Orgn. on Unemployment Relief; pres. So. area Goodwill Industries of Am.; exec. sec. Ky. state com. A.R.C., 1933, attached to disaster staff Louisville div., Ohio River Flood, 1937; mem. Lexington Municipal Housing Commn., 1938-42; chmn. bd. trustees Union Coll., Barbourville, Ky., 1938—; dir. Lincoln Meml. U., Union Coll. Pres. Lexington Flying Service, 1941—; mem. Ky. Aeronautical Commn., 1942-46 (chmn. 1944-46). Mem. Am. Inst. Mining and Metall. Engrs., Pi Gamma Delta. Republican. Methodist. Mason (Shriner). Home: Pisgah Pike, Versailles, Ky. Died Apr. 1948.*

BULLOCK, Theodore (Tunison), economist; b. Iowa City, Ia., Aug. 16, 1889; s. Motier Acklin and Catherine (Tunison) B.; A.B., U. Neb., 1911, A.M., 1914; m. Ruth Brownell, June 19, 1917; children—Catherine Louise (Mrs. Wm. McConnell), Mary Bigelow (Mrs. V. Paul Henneman). Instr. econs. U. Neb., 1916-19, asst. prof., 1919-24, asso. prof., econs. and bus. law, 1924-37, prof., 1937—, charge placements for Coll. Bus. Adminstrn., 1921—. Mem. Am. Econ. Assn., Polit. Sci. Assn., C. of C., Beta Gamma Sigma, Alpha Kappa Psi. Republican. Conglist. Clubs: Kiwanis, Candlelight. Specializes in trust problems and land economics. Home: 2420R, Lincoln, Neb. Died Sept. 22, 1953; buried Wyuka Cemetery, Lincoln.

BULOVA, Arde, chmn. bd. Bulova Watch Co. Address: Bulova Park, Flushing 70, N.Y. Died Mar. 18, 1958; buried Woodlawn Cemetery, N.Y.

BULOW, William John, ex-senator; b. Moscow, O., Jan. 13, 1869; s. Joseph and Elizabeth (Ebendorf) B.; LL.B., U. of Mich., 1893; m. Katherine Reedy, Nov. 25, 1898 (died Sept. 17, 1918); children—Maurine, Wm. J., Kathleen; m. 2d, Mrs. Sarah Farrand, Oct. 13, 1922. Began practice at Beresford, 1898. Mayor of Beresford, 1912-13; city atty., Beresford, 1902-12 and 1913-27; county judge, Union County, S.Dak., 1918; gov. of S.Dak., 1927-31; mem. U.S. Senate, 1931-43. Dem. Home: Beresford, S.Dak. Died Feb. 26, 1960.

BULWINKLE, Alfred Lee, ex-congressman; b. Charleston, S.C., Apr. 21, 1883; s. Herman and Frances (McKean) B.; student law dept., U. N.C., 1903-04; D.C.L., Lenoir-Rhyne Coll., 1941; m. Bessie Lewis, 1911; children—Frances (Mrs. E. Grainger Williams), Alfred Lewis (U.S. Army). Admitted to N.C. bar, 1904; pros. atty., Gastonia, 1913-16. Mem. 67th to 70th and 72d to 81st Congresses, 11th N.C. Dist. Mem. Joint Congl. Policy Bd.; del. Internat. Aviation Conf., 1944; U.S. adviser Internat. Civil Aviation Orgn. Conf., Montreal, Can., and Geneva, Switzerland, 1947. Capt. Inf., N.C.N.G., 1909-17; maj. comdg. 2d bn., 113th F.A., 30th Div., AEF, 1917-19. Mem. exec. bd. United Lutheran Ch. in America. Mem. N.C. State Bar Assn. Democrat. Lutheran. Mason, Elk. Home: Gastonia, N.C. Died Aug. 31, 1950.

BUNCE, Arthur C., economist; born Manchester, Eng., Jan. 11, 1901; s. Arthur and Elizabeth (Fitton) B.; B.S., U. of Saskatchewan, 1925; M.S., U. of Wis., 1935, Ph.D., 1937; m. Beatrice Mitchell, Aug. 11, 1926; children—Arthur Thomas, Bayne Richard. Naturalized U.S. citizen, 1941. Attended summer sch. of League of Nations, Geneva, Switzerland, 1925; staff of Pickering Coll., Ont., Can., 1927-28; studied folk high schs. and rural reconstrn. work, Denmark and India, 1928; organized adult agrl. edn. for Internat. Y.M.C.A., Korea, 1928-34; asso. prof. economics Ia. State Coll., 1937-43; economist of bd. of govs. Fed. Res. System, 1944-45; dept. of state econ. adviser to Lt. Gen. Hodge in Korea, Feb. 4, 1946, U.S. commissioner on U.S.-U.S.S.R. Joint Commn., 1946 and 1947, with personal rank of minister of U.S.A.; appointed chief of E.C.A. special mission to Korea Sept. 24, 1948, appointed chief of the United States special technical and economic mission to Thailand, 1950; aptd. chief Far Eastern sect. Fed. Res. Bd., Aug. 1951. Author: Eonomic Nationalism and the Farmer, 1938; Economics of Soil Conservation, 1942; also of bulls. and articles in various publs. Awarded Governor General's gold medal, U. of Saskatchewan, 1926. Home: R.R. 2, Annandale, Va. Office: Federal Reserve Board, Washington 25. Died May 27, 1953.

BUNIN, Ivan Alekseevich, author; b. Voronej, Russia, 1870; s. Alexei and Ludmila (Chubarova) B.; m. Vera Muromtseva, 1922. Received Nobel prize for literature, 1933. Mem. Christian Orthodox Church. Author: Gentleman from San Francisco, 1941; other books and short stories published in Russia and France. Address: 1 rue Jacques Offenbach, Paris 16, France. Died Nov. 8, 1953; buried Ste. Genevieve-Des-Bois, near Paris.

BUNKER, Charles Waite Orville, naval officer; b. Viroqua, Ia., Feb. 23, 1882; s. Charles Fremont and Isola B. (Bassore) B.; B.Sc., U. Neb., 1901; M.D., Cornell U., 1950; m. Eleanor G. Caldwell, Nov. 12, 1910; children—Garrett, Eleanor L. Asst. Cornell U. Med. Coll., 1901-05; intern Bellevue Hosp., N.Y. C., 1905-07; commd. lt. (j.g.) USN, 1907, advanced through grades to rear adm., 1938; med. officer, 1907-44; retired with rank of rear adm. M.C., 1944. Fellow A.C.S.; mem. A.M.A., Omega Upsilon Phi. Clubs: Garden City (L.I.) Golf; New York Yacht, University (N.Y.C.); Burning Tree (gov.), Army-Navy, Army and Navy Country (Washington). Home: 5312 Moorland Lane, Bethesda 14, Md. Died Sept. 1958.

BUNNELL, Charles Ernest, (bŭn-nĕl'), emeritus univ. pres.; b. Dimock, Pa., Jan. 12, 1878; s. Lyman Walton and Ruth Naomi (Tingley) B.; A.B., Bucknell U., 1900, A.M., 1902, LL.D., 1925; m. Mary Anna Kline, July 24, 1901; 1 dau., Jean. Arrived in Alaska, as tchr. in Indiana schs., under U.S. Bur. Edn., 1900; prin. pub. schs., Valdez, 4 yrs.; admitted to bar, 1908, practiced at Valdez; judge U.S. Dist. Ct., 4th Jud. Div. by apptmt. of President Wilson, 1915-21; 1st pres. Alaska Agrl. Coll. and Sch. of Mines (now U. Alaska), 1922-35, pres. U. Alaska 1935-49, emeritus, 1949—. Dem. candidate for del. to Congress, 1914. Life Mem. Pioneers of Alaska; mem. Arctic Brotherhood, Phi Beta Kappa. Episcopalian. Mason, Elk. Home: College, Alaska. Died Nov. 1, 1956.

BUNNELL, Edward Horace (bŭn-nĕl'), vice-pres. Assn. Am. Railroads; b. Trinidad, Colo., Feb. 17, 1882; s. Thomas Luther and Lucy (Smith) B.; grad. Trinidad Business Coll., 1900; student Washington U. (evenings), 1925-26; m. Mary Elizabeth Hagenbuch, Sept. 30, 1929; 1 dau. (by previous marriage), Ruth Geraldine (Mrs. H. A. Baker). Clerk and mgr. N. W. Fisher Mercantile Co., 1895-1900; car clk. and timekeeper mech. dept. A.,T.&S.F. Ry., 1900-03, clk.

and chief clk. accounting dept., 1903-04, spl. accountant and chief clk. to auditor of disbursements, 1904-10, auditor of disbursements, 1910-19; gen. auditor St. Louis-San Francisco Ry. Co., 1919-22, comptroller, 1922-32, chief accounting officer, 1932-34; became comptroller Muscle Shoals, Birmingham & Pensacola R.R., 1925; v.p. of finance, accounting, taxation and valuation dept., Assn. Am. Railroads since Dec. 1934. Mem. bd. dirs. Travelers Aid Soc. of Washington, D.C. Club: Columbia Country (Washington). Contbr. to publs. of Nat. Assn. Credit Men, r.r. publs., etc. Home: 3133 Conn. Av. N.W. Office: Transportation Bldg., 17th and H Sts., N.W., Washington. Died Nov. 19, 1953.

BUNTING, George Avery, business exec.; b. Bishopville, Md., Apr. 3, 1870; s. Lemuel W. H. and Jane (Long) B.; A.B., Washington Coll., Md., 1891; A.M., 1893; Ph.G., U. Md. Sch. of Pharmacy, 1899; hon. D.Sc., Washington Coll., 1937; m. Nellie Bowen, Dec. 18, 1901; children—Dorothy, George Lloyd. Engaged as prin. pub. schs., Bishopville, Md., 1891-93; prin. Odessa (Del.) Acad., 1894-96; propr. Bunting's Drug Store, Baltimore, Md., 1902-22; incorporated Noxzema Chemical Co., 1917, pres. 1917-49, now chmn. bd.; also chmn. bd. Noxzema Chem. Co. of Canada (Toronto, Canada). Served as regt. sergt. Md. N.G., 1899-1900. Mem. Md. Bd. Pharmacy, 1922-34. Mem. Balt. C. of C.; dir. Nat. Marine Bank, Balt.; mem. bd. govs. Washington Coll., Chestertown. Mem. Am. Chem. Soc., Am. Pharm. Assn. Nat. Assn. Retail Druggists, Md. Pharm. Assn. (pres. 1915-16), Md. Acad. Sciences, Baltimore Veteran Druggists (pres. 1997), S.A.R., Eastern Shore Soc., mem. Alpha Psi Circle Omicron Delta Kappa, Washington Coll. (hon.). Independent Republican. Unitarian. Mason. (Scottish Rite, 32°, Shriner). Clubs: Baltimore Country, University, Kiwanis. Home: 4412 N. Charles St., Balt. 18. Office: 32d and Falls Cliff Rd., Balt. 11. Died Jan. 1, 1960.

BURBANK, Harold Hitchings, economist; b. Moore's Mills, N.B., Can., July 3, 1887; s. Henry Johnson and Sarah Abagail (Smith) B.; parents citizens of U.S.; A.B., Dartmouth, 1909, A.M., 1910; Ph.D., Harvard, 1915; m. Alice M. Eaton, June 10, 1914. Instr. Dartmouth 1910-11; instr. Harvard, 1912-19, asst. prof. econs., 1919-23, asso. prof. econs., 1923-27, prof. econs., 1927—, David A. Wells prof. polit. economy, 1931—, chmn. dept. economics, 1927-38; chmn. bd. of tutots in history, govt. and economics, Harvard, 1916-46, chmn. div. of history, govt. and economics, 1942-46; chmn. dept. economics, 1942—, mem. faculty of Littauer Sch. of Pub. Administration. Mem. Am. Acad. Arts and Sciences, Colonial Soc. Home: 41 Fresh Pond Lane, Cambridge, Mass. Died Feb. 6, 1951; buried Mount Auburn Cemetery, Cambridge.

BURBANK, Mortimer Lincoln, chmn. bd. The Outlet Co.; b. Providence, Feb. 23, 1878; s. Charles H. and Louisa (Gregory) B.; student Taunton (Mass.) High Sch., 1893-97; m. Gretchen Kinnicutt, Oct. 27, 1904; children—Calef Mortimer, Doris Kinnicutt (Mrs. Robert D. Parker), Lawrence Abner. Bookkeeper at Taunton, Mass., 1897-1901; office and shipping clk. Am. Enamel Co., Providence, 1901-03: in continuous employ The Outlet Co., Providence, 1903-—, became sec., treas., dir., 1925, then pres., later pres., treas. and dir., pres. and dir., now chmn. bd.; pres., treas., dir. Samuels Realty Co. 1939-50; dir. Insl. Trust Co.; trustee Citizens Savings Bank, 1943—. Mem. S.A.R. Republican. Conglist. Clubs: R.I. Historical, Town Criers of R.I., Squantum. Turks Head. Home: 123 Waterman St., Providence 6. Office: 176 Weybosset St., Providence 2. Died Dec. 14, 1956.

BURCH, Charles Bell, ins. exec.; b. Auburn, Me., Mar. 8, 1891; s. William Mark and Lizzie (Decker) B.; B.S. in Ciivil Engring., Norwich U., 1913; grad. student U. Mich., 1921; m. Jane M. Bell, June 1, 1916 (dec.); children—William Mark, Donald C. Walter T. Engr. City of Greenfield, Mass., 1913, U.S. Engrs. Ohio River, 1914-15. H. Koppers Co., Pitts., 1916-17, Pitman-Brown Co., Salem, Mass., 1917; with Mich. Mutual Liability Co., Detroit, 1921-—, v.p., 1956—. Served as capt. constrn. div. U.S. Army, 1918-20. Mem. Sigma Nu. Clubs: Detroit Athletic, Detroit Yacht. Home: 35 Sylvan Av., Pleasant Ridge, Mich. Office: 26 W. Adams Av., Detroit 26. Died Sept. 20, 1959; buried Roseland Park Cemetery, Detroit.

BURCH, Frank Earl, ophthalmologist; b. Menomonie, Wis., Mar. 27, 1876; s. Newell and Susan (Paris) B.; M.D., U. Minn., 1897; m. Katharine Jackson, Dec. 30, 1901 (dec.); children—Edward Paris, Katharine (Mrs. Glen Taylor). In general practice, Glencoe, Minn., 1898-1904, specializing in ophthalmology, 1904—; asso. prof. ophthalmology U. Minn., 1920-26, prof. and chief of dept., 1926—, prof. emeritus, 1944. Served as maj. M.C., U.S. Army, 1918-19; comdr. Base Hospital, Camp Dodge, World War I. Fellow A.C.S.; mem. Am., Minn. med. assns., Minn. Acad. Medicine (pres. 1927), Minn. Acad. Ophthalmology (pres. 1919), Am. Acad. Ophthalmology and Oto-Laryngology (pres. 1936), Ramsey County Med. Soc. (pres. 1920), Am. Ophthalmologic Soc., Phi Gamma Delta, Nu Sigma Nu. Presbyn. Club: Minnesota. Contbr. sci. articles to jours. Home: 754 Linwood Place. Office: 424 Hamm Bldg., St. Paul. Died June 30, 1957.

BURCH, Guy Irving, population analyst; b. Clayton, N.M., May 24, 1899; s. Fred Irving and Minnie Boone (Boggs) B.; ed. Culver Military Acad., 1914-16, Pawling Sch., 1917-18, Cavalry Officers Training Sch., Leon Springs, Tex., 1918, Columbia U., 1919-23. 25; m. A. Wilhelmine Taylor, June 24, 1920; children—Sally Ann, Caroline Sue. Founder and dir. Population Reference Bur. since 1929; contributing editor Eugenics, 1931; mem. Council on Population Policy, 1935-36; supplied Joint Army and Navy Selective Service Com. with age group data for original draft bill, 1940; chmn. Population-Resources Roundtable, 1947, U.S. Eastern Table Tennis Championships, 1944. Served with U.S. Army as private 35th Inf., World War I. Fellow Population Assn. of Am., 1931-35 (charter and organizing mem.); mem. Am. Eugenics Soc. (dir. 1932-47, sec. 1933-36), mem. D.C. Table Tennis Assn. (pres. 1944-45), S.A.R., Phi Delta Theta. Author: Population Roads to Peace or War (with E. Pendell), 1945, rev. edit. Human Breeding and Survival, 1947. Editor: Human Facts in Science, 1935-36; Population Bulletin since 1940. Contbr. articles to mags. Home: 142 South Columbus St., Arlington, Va. Office: 1507 M St. N.W., Washington 5. Died Jan. 13, 1951.

BURCH, Thomas Granville, ex-congressman; b. Henry County, Va., July 3, 1869; s. John W. and Sarah Fannie B.; ed. pub. schs.; m. Mary Anson, Apr. 22, 1903. Identified with banking business at Martinsville; chmn. bd. Piedmont Trustee Bank; dir. Bassett Industries, Inc. U.S. marshal, Western Dist. Va., 1914-21; apptd. mem. Commn. to Simplify and Reorganize State Govt. of Va., 1927; mem. State Transportation and Pub. Utility Adv. Commn., 1929; mem. State Bd. Edn., 1930, 31; mem. 72d to 77th Congresses, 5th Va. Dist. Democrat. Episcopalian. Mason (Shriner), Odd Fellow, K.P., Elk, Red Man, Kiwanian. Home: 303 Church St., Martinsville, Va. Died Mar. 20, 1951.

BURCHILL, Thomas F., ex-congressman; b. N.Y., Aug. 3, 1882; student St. Francis Xavier and Niagara univs.; married, 1906; 5 children. Auctioneer and appraiser, 1903—. Mem. N.Y. Legislature, 1919-24, State Senate, 1924-38; mem. 78th Congress, 15th N.Y. Dist. Democrat. Mem. Friendly Sons of St. Patrick, Elk, K.C. Home: 347 W. 21st St., N.Y.C. Died Mar. 26, 1955.*

BURDGE, Howard Griffith, educator; b. Cin., Oct. 13, 1873; s. William Melville and Ellen M. (Griffith) B.; student Bloomsburg, (Pa.) Normal Sch.; A.B., Allegheny Coll., 1900; A.M., Columbia, 1920, Ph. D., 1922; m. Maude Delamater, June 28, 1898; 1 dau., Beatrice; m. 2d, Edith Maize, June 14, 1930; m. 3d, Elmira G. Scovel. Prin. Chamberlain Inst., Randolph, N.Y., 1900-03; prin. high sch. Ellicottville, N.Y., 1903-07; supt. schs., Wellsville, N.Y., 1907-18; dir. research and vocational tng. N.Y. State Mil. Tng. Commn., 1918-21; asst. dir. Ednl. Finance Induqiry, under auspices Am. Council Edn., 1922-23; prin. State Normal Sch., Fredonia, N.Y., 1922-28; with editorial dept. Eastman Teaching Films, Inc., Rochester, N.Y., 1928—. Chief ednl. adviser 2d Army, AEF, Toul, France, 1918-19. Mem. N.E.A., Phi Beta Kappa, Phi Delta Kappa, Kappa Delta Pi, Kappa Phi Kappa, Pi Gamma Mu. Unitarian. Mason, Kiwanian. Author: Our Boys, 1921; Burdge, Sprong, Griffith and Goltry genealogies, 1935; (with David Eugene Smith) New York State Arithmetic Series, 1925, Smith-Burdge Arithmetic eries, 1926. Home: Pine-Brook Lodge, Conway, N.H. Died Nov. 4, 1957.

BURDICK, Charles Baker, engr.; b. Chgo., Mar. 6, 1874; s. William Richard and Mary (Dewey) B.; B.S. in municipal and sanitary engring., U. Ill., 1895; m. Mabel Taylor, Oct. 8, 1909 (died 1935); children—Mary, Janet. Served as asst. to present partner and others, and resident engr. on several water works and sewerage projects for municipalities, 1895-1902, in gen. practice of engring., 1902—; mem. Alvord & Burdick, 1902-22, Alvord, Burdick & Howson, 1927—; designer and cons. engr. of works for water supply, sewerage, flood relief, etc., for many cities including Milw., Louisville, Denver and Des Moines, also project for numerous corps. Supervising engr. Camp Grant, Rockford, Camp Las Casas, San Juan, P.R. and Picric Acid Plant, Little Rock, Ark., World War I. Mem. Am. Soc. C.E., Am. Water Works Assn., Western Soc. Engrs. (past pres.), Ill. Soc. Engrs. (past pres.), Sigma Chi. Clubs: Engineers', University, La Grange Country. Author: Relief from Floods, 1918. Home: 419 S. Waiola Av., La Grange, Ill. Office: 20 N. Wacker Dr., Chgo. Died Feb. 17, 1955.

BURDICK, Willard DeLure, clergyman; b. Utica, Wis., Aug. 28, 1863; s. Russell Dighton and Luransa (Champlin) B.; B.A., Milton (Wis.) Coll., 1890, M.A., 1893; B.D., U. Chgo., 1893; D.D., Salem (W.Va.) Coll., 1918; m. I. Genette West, Apr. 18, 1892; children—William Dighton, Marjorie Janette, Russell Willard. Ordained to ministry Seventh Day Bapt. Ch., 1893; pastor successively Jackson Center, O., Nile, N.Y., and Farina, Ill., until 1914; evangelist Am. Sabbath Tract Soc., 1915-24, also pastor Dunellen, N.J., 1918-24; corr. sec. Am. Sabbath Tract Soc., 1922-28; gen. sec. Seventh Day Bapt. Denomination, 1924-29; pastor Rockville, R.I., 1929-38; now retired. Mem. adv. bd. Milton Coll.; pres. Seventh Day Bapt. Gen. Conf., 1931, Seventh Day Bapt. Missionary Soc., 1932-38. Republican. Home: Milton, Wis. Died June 28, 1948; buried Milton.

BUREAU, E(rnest) A(dolphe), educator, elec. engr.; b. La Chapelle aux Naux, France, June 11, 1886; s. Florent Joseph and Hortense Ernestine (Rivry) B.; brought to U.S., 1890; Ph.B., Ottawa (Kan.) U., 1906; student U. Chgo., summers 1908, 09; B.S. in Elec. Engring., Purdue U., 1915, E.E., 1916; student Armour Tech. Sch., summer 1940. Cal. Inst. Tech., 1940-41; m. Isabel Cook, Aug. 3, 1909; children—Elise Adele (Mrs. Garni Moretti), J. Jeanne. Prof. elec. engring., 1918-52, head dept. Coll. Engring., U. Ky., 1942-52, ret. Mem. Am. Inst. E.E., Am. Soc. Engring. Edn., Am., Ky. socs. profl. engrs., Am. Assn. U. Profs., Ky. Acad. Sci, Tau Beta Pi, Eta Kappa Nu, Sigma Xi, Phi Sigma Kappa, Triangle. Mem. Ch. of Disciples of Christ. Home: 201 State St., Lexington, Ky. Died July 13, 1954; buried Lexington Cemetery.

BURG, Alfred William, mfg. exec.; b. Allegheny, Pa., 1880; exec. v.p., dir. Torrington (Maine) Co.; treas., dir. First Federal Savings & Loan Assn. of Torrington; dir. Torrington Nat. Bank & Trust Co., Hendey Machine Co. Mason (Shriner). Home: 27 Forest St. Office: 59 Field St., Torrington, Conn. Died Oct. 10, 1956.

BURGAN, John, newspaperman, author; born Vintondale, Pa., Mar. 25, 1913; s. John Lewis and Anne (Davidson) B.; A.B., U. of Pittsburgh, 1934; m. Wanda Smith, Dec. 2, 1939. Newspaper reporting and pub. relations, Rochester, N.Y., 1934-41; publicity, Albany, N.Y., 1941; mng. editor Ventura (Calif.) County Star-Free Press, 1949-50, asst. editor since Dec. 1950. Author: Even My Own Brother, 1942; Two Per Cent Fear, 1947; The Long Discovery, 1950; Martin Butterfield, 1950. Contbr. short stories, nonfiction to Sat. Eve. Post, Colliers, Harpers, since 1946. Served with U.S. Navy, 1942-46, P.T.O., 1943-45; disch. to res. as lt. Mem. C. of C., Concert Series Assn. (pres.). Democrat. Presbyn. Club: Rotary (Ventura). Home: 2020 Vista del Mar Dr. Office: 567 E. Santa Clara St., Ventura, Cal. Died Apr. 6, 1951; buried Ventura, Cal.

BURGEE, Joseph Zeno, architect; b. St. Louis, Dec. 30, 1897; s. Henry J. and Ellen (Kelly) B.; student U. Ill., 1916-17; m. Helen Dooley, Oct. 5, 1929; children—Joseph Zeno, John Henry, Nancy Ellen. Supt. constrn. Holabird & Root, Chgo., 1927-40, resident engr., project mgr., 1940-41, resident partner, project engr., 1942-44; partner Holabird, Root & Burgee since 1945. Spl. advisor O.P.M., W.P.B., Washington, 1941-42. Chmn. heavy rescue com. Civil Def. Corps. Trustee U. Chgo. Cancer Research Found.; life mem. Notre Dame Found.; dir. United Cath. Charities. Served with 1st Ill. Cav., Mexican Border, 1916; 1st lt. 58th F.A. brigade. 33d Div., World War I. Mem. Ill. C. of C. (dir.), Chgo. Assn. Commerce, Chgo. Nat. History Mus., Art Inst. Chgo. (life), Am. Soc. Profl. Engrs., U. Illinois Alumni Assn. (life), A.I.A., Am. Soc. Mil. Engrs., Am. Soc. C.E., Western Soc. Engrs., Nat. Council Archtl. Registration Bds. Clubs: Rotary, Chicago Athletic Assn., Tavern, South Shore Country. Home: 1430 N. Lake Shore Dr., Chgo. Office: 180 N. Wabash Av., Chgo. 1; also 270 Park Av., N.Y.C. Died Jan. 5, 1956; buried Holy Sepulchre Cemetery, Chgo.

BURGER, Kathryn Reynolds (Mrs. John D. Burger), pharm. and cosmetics mfr.; b. Chicago, Ill.; daughter of Richard J. and Catherine (Kurtz) Reynolds; ed. high school, also business course and beauty course; m. John D. Burger, June 12, 1918 (dec.). Participated (with husband) in development Kaywoodie Co. (pipes) and Civic Briar Pipe Co. (Eng.), also designer leather items for latter company; sold cos. to Consol. Grocers Corp., Dec. 28, 1950; engaged in advertising and designing Dura-Gloss lines, Lorr Labs., Inc., Paterson, N.J., 1939; pres. of Lorr Laboratories, Inc., 1943-54; created, developed and packaged cosmetic lines, Milkmaid Cosmetics, 1941, originating concept of utilizing farm products (pasteurized milk and cream) in cosmetics. Mgr. of small village, Burgerville, Bouchette, Que., Can., 1943-52. Mem. Compagnons de Rabelais. Clubs: River, Regency ; Maidstone (East Hampton, L.I., N.Y.); Everglades, Bath and Tennis. Home: Waldorf Astoria Towers, Park Av. and 50th St., N.Y.C. Died Feb. 6, 1958.

BURGESS, Albert Franklin (bûr'jĕs), entomologist; b. Rockland, Mass., Oct. 2, 1873; s. Emory and Mary (Lewis) B.; B.S., Mass. Agrl. Coll., 1895, M.S., 1897; m. Mary E. Dwight, June 20, 1904; children—Emory D., Albert F. Asst. entomologist, Mass. State Bd. Agr., 1895-99; asst. in entomology, U. of Ill., 1899-1900; asst. insp. 1900-02, chief insp. of nurseries and orchards, 1902-07, Ohio Dept. Agr.; expert in charge of breeding experiments, Bur. of

Entomology, U.S. Dept. of Agr., 1907-43, in charge of preventing spread of the gypsy moth for same bureau, 1913-28; principal entomologist of U.S. Plant Quarantine and Control Adminstrn., 1928-34; principal entomologist U.S. Bur. of Entomology and Plant Quarantine, 1933-43, ret. Asso. editor Journal of Economic Entomology, 1908-10, business mgr., 1910-24, 1931-32. Published 5 annual reports and 9 bulls. on nursery and orchard inspection, numerous bulls. issued by U.S. Bur. of Entomology and many scientific articles on entomol. subjects. Fellow A.A.A.S., Entomol. Soc. America; mem Am. Assn. Econ. Entomologists (sec., 1903, 1906-23 and 1930-31; 1st v p., 1904; pres., 1924), Washington Entomol. Soc., Entomol. Soc. of France, Am. Assn. Hort. Inspectors (past pres.), Cambridge Entomol. Club (past pres.), Nat. Shade Conf. (chmn. 1931), Phi Sigma Kappa, Sigma Xi. Republican. Mason. Club: Cosmos (Washington). Home: 24 Franklin St., Greenfield, Mass. Died Feb. 23, 1953.

BURGESS, (Frank) Gelett, author, illustrator; b. Boston, Jan. 30, 1866; s. Thomas H. and Caroline (Brooks) B ; B S., Mass. Inst. Tech., 1887; m. Estelle Loomis, 1914 (died October 11, 1947). Began as draughtsman with South Pacific Railway, 1887-90; instr. topographical drawing, University of Calif., 1891-94; designer, 1894-95, and asso. editor The Wave; editor "Lark," 1890-97; asso. editor "Ridgeway's," 1906. Club: Bohemian (Calif.). Author: Vivette, 1897; The Lively City o' Ligg, 1898; Goops and How to Be Them, 1900; A. Gage of Youth, 1901; Burgess Nonsense Book, 1901; Romance of the Commonplace, 1902; More Goops, 1903; The Picaroons (with Will Irwin), 1903; The Reign of Queen Isyl (with same), 1903; The Rubaiyat of Omar Cayenne, 1904; A Little Sister of Destiny, 1906; Are You a Bromide?, 1907; The White Cat, 1907; The Heart Line, 1907; The Maxims of Methuselah, 1907; Blue Goops and Red, 1909; Lady Méchante, 1909; Find the Woman, The Cave Man (play), 1911; The Master of Mysteries, 1912; The Goop Directory, 1913; The Maxims of Noah, 1913; Love in a Hurry, 1913; Burgess Unabridged, 1914; The Goop Encyclopædia, 1915; Romance of the Commonplace (enlarged), 1916; War, the Creator, 1916; Mrs. Hope's Husband, 1917; Ain't Angie Awful!, 1919; Have You an Educated Heart?, 1923; Why Men Hate Women, 1927; The Bromide and Other Theories, 1933; Two O'Clock Courage, 1934; Too Good Looking, 1936; Look Eleven Years Younger, 1937; Short Words are Words of Might, 1939; Ladies in Boxes, 1942; New Goops, 1951; also short stories and articles for English and Am. mags. Lecturer. Home: Carmel, Cal. Died Sept. 18, 1951; buried Monterey, Cal.

BURGESS, George Heckman, cons. engr.; b. Oshkosh, Wis., June 19, 1874; s. Frederick and Anna A. (Heckman) B.; B.S., in C.E., U. of Wis., 1895; m. Harriet Painter Van Trump, Oct. 10, 1899; children—George Van Trump, Louise (Mrs. Russell F. Passano), Frederick. Engr. Edge Moor Bridge Works, 1895-96; began as rodman Pa. R.R., 1896; asst. bridge insp., 1895-96, bridge insp., 1898-1901, asst. engr., Pitts., 1901-05; asst. engr Erie R.R., N.Y.C., 1905-06, engr. terminal improvement, 1906-08, prin. asst. engr., 1908-09; chief engr.' Del. & Hudson Company and subsidiary companies, 1909-13; chmn. valuation com., Del. & Hudson R.R., 1913-25; with Coverdale and Colpitts, cons. engrs. since 1925, partner since Jan. 1928. Pres. Tenn., Ala. & Ga. Ry., 1929-45, director since 1945. Republican. Episcopalian. Member American Society, Civil Engineers, American Ry. Engring. Assn., Engring. Inst. of Canada, Am. Inst. Cons. Engrs. Clubs: Engineers', University, Downtown Association, Metropolitan, Down Town Athletic (N.Y.). Home: 51 5th Av., N.Y. City 3. Office: 120 Wall St., N.Y.C. 5. Died Mar. 1, 1957.

BURGESS, May Ayres, educator; b. Newton Highlands, Mass., May 17, 1888; d. Milan Church and Georgiana (Gall) Ayres; graduate Normal Department, U. of Puerto Rico, 1905; B.S., Simmons Coll., Boston. 1911; Ph.D., Columbia, 1920; m. Warren Randolph Burgess, May 17, 1917; children—Leonard Randolph, Julian Ayres. With Dept. of Edn. of Russell Sage Foundation, 1913-14 and 1919, 20, U.S. Food Administration, Washington, D.C., 1917, statistics branch Gen. Staff, War Dept., 1917-18; dir. Joint Statistics Bureau of Com. on Dispensary Development, N.Y. City, 1923-26; dir. Com. on Grading of Nursing Schs., N.Y. City, 1926-34. Mem. N.E.A., Am. Statis. Assn., Am. Public Health Assn., (honorary) National League of Nursing Education. Club: Cosmopolitan. Author: (with L. P. Ayres) Health Work in the Pub. Schs., 1915; (with same) Sch. Buildings and Equipment, 1915; (with others) Healthful Schools—How to Build, Equip, and Maintain Them, 1918; The Measurement of Silent Reading, 1921; Nurses, Patients and Pocketbooks, 1928; Results of the First Grading Study of Nursing Schools, 1930-31; Results of Second Grading of Nursing Schools in the U.S. (monographs), 1923; Nursing Schools Today and Tomorrow (final report of com. on the grading of nursing schools), 1934; Height Charts for Boys and Girls, 1937. Also various repts. and scale for measuring ability in silent reading. Home: Jackson Av., Hastings-on-Hudson, N.Y. Died July 15, 1953; buried Mount Hope (N.Y.) Cemetery.

BURGESS, Roy Howard, Jr., transportation exec.; b. Chicago, Nov. 15, 1910; s. Roy Howard and Genevieve (Malkin) B.; student U. Ill., 1927, Walton Sch. Commerce, 1941-42, College Advanced Traffic, 1944; m. Evelyn Baumgartner, Oct. 17, 1936; children—Fred Martin, Mary Dianne. With Internat. Forwarding Co. since 1928, dir. since 1945, pres. since 1951; pres. and dir Internat. Expediters, Inc., since 1951; admitted to practice before Interstate Commerce Commn., 1945. Mem. bd. govs. Freight Forwarder Inst. Mem. traffic advisory bd. La Salle Extension U. Mem. Assn. Interstate Commerce Commn. Practitioners, Nat. Freight Traffic Assn. Clubs: Traffic, Transportation, Executives, Lake Shore, Butterfield Country, International. Author: Freight Transportation Selling, 1950. Home: 691 Wingate Rd., Glenn Ellyn, Ill. Office: 200 Illinois St., Chgo. 11. Died Dec. 12, 1954.

BURGIN, Henry T. (bûr'gin), army officer; b. North Middletown, Ky., Oct. 9, 1882; s. Perry and Sithey Hedges (Gaitskill) B.; grad. U.S. Mil. Acad., 1905; distinguished grad. Coast Arty. Sch., Ft. Monroe, Va., 1908; honor grad. Sch. of the Line, Command and Gen. Staff Sch., 1921; grad. staff class, Command and Gen. Staff, 1922; grad. Army War Coll., 1923; m. Winona Elizabeth Derby, Nov. 7, 1911. Commd. 2d lt. Arty. Corps, U.S. Army, 1905, and advanced through the grades to maj. gen. Oct. 1940; served as major and lt. colonel, div. ordnance officer, 41st Div., with A.E.F. in France, Dec. 1917-Mar. 1918, and then acting chief of staff of Am. troops on Italian Front; has served at harbor defenses of Puget Sound, San Francisco and San Diego and field arty. at Ft. Sam Houston and duty at Ft. Monroe; foreign service at harbor defenses of Manila and Subic Bays, P.I., and on Gen. Staff, Hawaiian Div.; 3 tours of duty at Washington, D.C., including acting chief of C.A.; comdg. 9th C.A. Dist., June 1937-Aug. 1941; promoted maj. gen., Oct. 1, 1940; in command seacoast and anti-aircraft artillery troops, Hawaiian Dept. August 1941 to June 1944; command Central Pacific Base Command, July 1944-Oct. 1945; retired as major gen., Aug. 1946. Decorated Legion of Merit, Distinguished Service Medal; Fatigue de guerra, Chevalier de St. Maurice et Lazarus (Italy); Victory Medal, Purple Heart, Am. Defense Service Medal, Asiatic Pacific Campaign Medal (U.S.). Home: 537 Hassayampa Dr. Address: 537 N. Hassayampa Dr., Prescott, Ariz. Died July 31, 1958; buried U.S. Mil. Acad., West Point, N.Y.

BURGISS, William Wesley (bûr'jis), realtor; b. Greenville, S.C., Aug. 12, 1863; s. Nicholas Franklin and Mary Evelyn (Gilreath) B.; student Capt. Patrick's Mil. Sch., Greenville; m. Margaret Henrietta Bailey, Sept. 14, 1887; children—Walter Westmoreland (dec.), Victor Franklin (dec.), Milton Bailey (dec.), William Hamlin (dec.), Harold Dean, Margaret Evelyn (Mrs. Shuman B. Gerald). Mcht., cotton mill builder, operator and pres. (built Victor Mills and Franklin Cotton Mills, Greer, S.C.) and real estate operator, Greenville, 1890-—. Donor of more than $1,000,000 to W. W. Burgiss Charities, Inc., now chmn. bd. dirs.; dir. Emma Moss Booth Meml. Hosp., Greenville; donor Shriners Hosp. for Crippled Children, Greenville. Presbyn. Home: 111 Williams St. Office: 2 W. Coffee St., Greenville, S.C. Deceased.*

BURKE, Arthur Devries, author, dairy technologist; b. Wheeling, W.Va., Jan. 1893; s. Thomas Carrol and Anna (Little) B.; B.S., U. Wis., 1916; M.S., Ohio State U , 1920, grad. student, 1927-28; m. Marguerite Outcalt, Feb. 1, 1921. Dairy inspr. Huntington, W.Va., 1916-17; instr. dairy dept. Ohio State U., 1919-20; asst. prof. of dairying Okla. A. and M. Coll., 1920-22, asso. prof., 1922-29; prof. and head dairy dept. Ala. Poly. Inst., 1929-46. Mem. adv. council Sealtest, Inc., 1935-48. Served as 2d and 1st lt., C.A.C., U.S. Army, 1917-19. County chmn. A.R.C., 1940-47; apptd. welfare chmn. Lee County Defense Council, 1941; chmn. Campus Defense Council, Ala. Poly. Inst., 1942. Mem. Am. Dairy Science Assn. (former sec., v.p. and pres. so. sect.), Internat. Assn. Ice Cream Mfrs. (mem. statis. research com. 1939-47), Ala. Dairy Products Assn. (former pres., v.p., sec.; now exec. sec.), Am. Legion (comdr. Stillwater, Okla., 1925, Auburn, Ala., 1935), Alpha Gamma Rho, Gamma Sigma Delta. Democrat. Presbyn. (elder). Club: Auburn Kiwanis (pres. 1939; lt. gov. Ala. 1940). Author: Practical Ice Cream Making, 1933 revised 1945; Practical Dairy Tests, 1935; Practical Manufacture of Cultured Milks and Kindred Products, 1938. Tech. editor for Milk Dealer, 1920-—; Ice Cream Review, 1929-—. Contbr. tech. jours. Home: Annalue Farm, Auburn, Ala. Died Aug. 16, 1950.

BURKE, George James, lawyer; b. Northfield Twp., Washtenaw County, Mich., Dec. 5, 1885; s. Anthony and Ellen (Dealy) B.; LL.B., U. of Mich., 1907; m. Edna J. Fritts, Dec. 29, 1910; children—Katherine E. (dec.), George J., H. William, Dorothy A., Martin J. Practiced at Ann Arbor, Mich., since 1907; pros. atty. of Washtenaw County, 1911-15; mem. Crime Commn. of Mich., 1933-35; state dir. for Mich. of Federal Housing Adminstrn., 1934; vice chmn. Detroit Regional Labor Bd., 1934 35; chmn. State Civil Service Commn., 1937-38 and 1941-43; pres. Citizens Mutual Auto. Ins. Co. (Howell, Mich.); counsel and dir. Ann Arbor Trust Company, Ann Arbor Bank (Ann Arbor), Mich. Life Ins. Co. (Detroit); pres. Argus, Inc.; dir. King Seeley Corporation. Member advisory com. on rules of criminal procedure, Supreme Court of United States, since 1941; general counsel and legal advisor Office of Price Administration, Washington, D.C., 1943; judge Am. Mil. Ct., Nurnberg, Germany, 1947-48; mem. com. to adv. an Ednl. System of Mich., 1948. Member Michigan State Troops, Co. 74, 1917-18; hon. discharged as corpl. Mem. Washtenaw County Bar Assn. (pres. 1931). Democrat. K.C. Clubs: Ann Arbor, University of Michigan Union, Detroit Athletic, Lansing Press. Home: 626 Oxford Rd. Office: Ann Arbor Trust Bldg., Ann Arbor, Mich. Died Oct. 3, 1950; buried Ann Arbor, Mich.

BURKE, Haslett Platt, judge; b. Monona County, Ia., Apr. 28, 1874; s. John Thomas and Clara Jane (Hardy) B.; pub. schs., Harlan, Ia.; m. Rose M. Sanner, Mar. 16, 1904. Admitted to Ia. bar, 1896, and moved to Colo. same yr.; clerk Dist. Court, Logan County, Colo., 1901-03; dist. judge 13th Jud. Dist., 1907-19; judge Supreme Court, Colo., 1919-39, chief justice, 1927, 37-38, reelected, 1938 for 10 yr. term, retired, 1949; lectr. on constl. law Denver U. Law Sch., 1926-33. Chmn. bd. arbitration between Western railways and Brotherhood of Locomotive Firemen, 1927. Pres. bd. trustees Clayton Coll. for Orphan Boys, Denver, 1925-29; chmn. adv. bd. Denver Orphans' Home. Tendered appointment as U.S. senator by Gov. Carr, Dec. 1941; declined. Served as cpl. 12th Co., U.S. Vol. Signal Corps, Spanish-Am. War. Mem. Am., Colo. bar assns., Phi Alpha Delta, Acacia. Republican. Mason (33°, grand cross insp. gen. Colo., grand master Colo. 1920-21), Red Man. Many pub. addresses on legal and hist. subjects. Home: 3500 E. 7th Av. Address: 1370 Grant St., Denver 3. Died Oct. 4, 1957.

BURKE, John Woolfolk, ophthalmologist; b. Alexandria, Va., Oct. 7, 1884; s. Julian Thompson and Esther Dashiell B.; M.D., U. Va., 1906; m. Elizabeth Atkinson, Nov. 26, 1912 (dec. Aug. 1946); children—Elizabeth, John Woolfolk, Eda (dec.), Margaret Mayo; m. 2d, Olive Patten, June 21, 1955. Practiced at Washington, 1910-—; professor ophthalmology, Georgetown U. Sch. Medicine, 1925-30. Served as maj. Med. R.C., U.S. Army, 1917-19. Mem. A.M.A., Am. Ophthal. Soc., D.C. Med. Soc. Episcopalian. Clubs: Metropolitan, Chevy Chase. Home: 2311 Tracy Pl. Office: 1740 M St. N.W., Washington. Died Oct. 5, 1959.

BURKE, Michael E., ex-congressman; b. Beaver Dam, Wis., Oct. 15, 1863; grad. Wayland Acad., Beaver Dam, 1884; law student U. Wis., 1886-87. Admitted to bar, 1888, since in practice at Beaver Dam. Mem. Wis. Ho. of Rep., 1890-94, Wis. Senate, 1894-98; city atty., 1893-1908; mayor, 1908-10; mem. 62d Congress, 6th Wis. Dist., 63d Congress, 2d Dist. Del. Dem. Nat. Conv., St. Louis, 1904. Address: Beaver Dam, Wis. Deceased.

BURKE, Patrick H., lawyer, banker; b. Shenandoah, Pa., 1877; s. Edward J. and Margaret (L'Velle) B.; student pub. schs. and law offices; m. Anna C. Watson, 1906; children—John F., Joseph W., Edmond F., Eileen (Mrs. J. Raymond McGill). Pres., dir. Miners Nat. Bank, Shenandoah, 1917-—; dir. Phila. & Reading Coal & Iron Co., Shen Penn Prod. Co., Wadesville Prodn. Co. Dir. A.R.C., Good Samaritan Hosp., Boys Scouts Am. Mem. C. of C. (dir.), Am., Pa. bar assns., Am. Legion. Republican. Catholic. Elk. Club: Fountain Springs Country. Home: 214 W. Oak St. Office: Burke Bldg., Shenandoah, Pa. Died Aug. 30, 1957.

BURKE, Thomas Henry, ex-congressman; b. Toledo, O., May 6, 1904; s. William and Mary (Hayde) B.; ed. St. Patrick's Elementary Sch. and St. John's Coll., Toledo, O.; m. Lucille Elizabeth Smith, Oct. 22, 1927; children—Geraldine (Mrs. Dwight Whiting), Thomas A., Jacqueline, Patrick, Kathleen. Recording sec. Local 12, United Automobile Workers —C.I.O., 1 yr., financial sec., 6 yrs., v.p., 5 yrs.; exec. sec. Toledo Indsl. Union Council, CIO, 4 yrs.; mem. Ohio Ho. of Reps., 1941-42, mem. Toledo City Council, 1944-48; vice mayor, Toledo, 1948; mem. 81st Congress (1949-51), 9th Ohio Dist. Served with U.S. Navy, 4 yrs., Naval Fleet Res., 12 yrs. Democrat. Roman Catholic. Knight of Equity, Moose, Eagle. Mem. Local 12, UAW-CIO. Home: 620 South St., Toledo 9, O. Died Sept. 12, 1959.

BURKE, Victor, educator; b. Kent, Wash., Mar. 12, 1882; s. Harry and Sarah Eugenia (Jones) B.; A.B., Stanford, 1907, A.M., 1908, Ph.D., 1911; grad. study Columbia, 1910; m. Georgiana B. Spooner, Oct. 19, 1912. Instr. in bacteriology Stanford, 1918-21; asst. prof. bacteriology Wash. State Coll., 1921-23, asso. prof., 1923-25, prof. and head dept., 1925-49, retired 1949. Mem. Soc. Am. Bacteriologists, Sigma Xi, Phi Kappa Phi. Democrat. Author: The Cyclogasteridae, 1930; also many articles in field of bacteriology. Bacteriol. editor Webster's New Internat. Dictionary. Contbr. research articles to tech.

publs. Home: 15401 Ma Srones Hill Rd., Saratoga, Cal. Died Oct. 7, 1958; buried Oak Hill Meml. Park.

BURKE, Webster H., lawyer, ret. coll. pres.; b. Chgo., May 10, 1881; s. Edmund W. and Myra G. (Webster) B.; A.B., Northwestern U., 1902; LL.B., Chgo.-Kent Coll. Law, 1903, LL.M., 1907; m. Charlotte Thompson, June 23, 1904; children—Edmund Webster, Dorothy (dec.). Admitted to Ill. bar, 1903; mem. Burke, James & Burke; officer and mem. faculty Chgo.-Kent Coll. Law, 1904-56, dean, 1920-49, pres., 1918-56. Mem. Am., Ill., Chgo. bar assns., Art Inst. Chgo., Am., Ill., Chgo. hist. socs., Delta Upsilon, Phi Delta Phi. Republican. Methodist. Club: Union League. Home: 838 Sheridan Rd., Evanston, Ill. Office: 100 N. La Salle St., Chgo. 2. Died July 1958; buried Graceland Cemetery.*

BURKET, Harlan Fessenden, lawyer; b. Findlay, O., May 15, 1860; s. Jacob F. and Pamy D. (Walters) B.; grad. Oberlin Coll., 1882, Ph.B., 1890, A.M., 1891; m. Augusta Dukes, Jan. 16, 1895; 1 son, Jacob F. Admitted to bar, 1887, since practicing at Findaly, O.; now mem. Burket & Burket; pres. Am. Nat. Bank of Findlay; pros. atty., Hancock County, Ohio, 1891-94. Vice pres. Ohio Rep. League, 1889-91; mem. Am., Ohio State (pres. 1913-14) bar assns., Ohio Archeol. and Hist. Soc., Old North West Geneal. Soc., S.A.R. Del. Universal Congress Lawyers and Jurists, St. Louis, 1904. Lutheran. Republican. Home: Findlay, O. Deceased.*

BURLINGAME, C. Charles, psychiatrist, univ. prof.; b. Rockford, Ill., Oct. 27, 1885; s. Charles Henry Camlin and Ella S. F. (Dagwell) B.; ed. in public schs., Rockford, Ill., and private tutors; M.D., Ill. Gen. Med. Coll., Chicago, 1908; m. Ruth Beardsley Parsons, Dec. 31, 1912. Asst. phys. Westboro (Mass.) State Hosp., 1908-12; med. dir., asst. supt. and actg. supt. Fergus Falls (Minn.) State Hosp., 1912-15; industrial psychiatrist, Cheney Bros., Manchester, Conn., 1915-17 and 1919-21; exec. officer joint adminstrv. bd. Columbia U.-Presbyn. Hosp. Med. Center, N.Y. City, 1921-28; exec. v.p. Presbyn. Hosp., N.Y. City, 1923-25; in private psychiatric practice, N.Y. City, 1925-31; hosp. cons. govt. of Uruguay and other S. Am. and European countries since 1925; psychiatrist in chief Inst. of Living, 1931-50; asso. in psychiatry Columbia since 1932; cons. in psychiatry U.S. Vets. Hosp., Newington, Conn., since 1931, Neurol. Inst., N.Y. City, 1932-39 (now mem. courtesy staff); attending psychiatrist Vanderbilt Clinic, N.Y. City, 1932-34, asso. attending psychiatrist since 1934; attending neuro-psychiatrist Vet. Home & Hosp. Commn., Conn.; cons. in psychiatry St. Francis Hosp., Hartford, Conn., since 1933; cons. in psychiatry Charlotte Hungerford Hosp., Torrington, Conn., since 1934; clin. prof. psychiatry and mental hygiene, Yale, 1936-38; cons. Hosp. St. Raphael, New Haven, since 1943; cons. psychiatry Hartford Hosp., 1945; cons. psychiatry and neurology, Meriden Hosp.; sr. psychiatry U.S. Vets Hosp., Northampton; cons. psychiatry to sec. war (Insp. Gen. Office, Gen. Staff, U.S. Army), 1944-45. Chmn. Adv. Bd. in Am. of The Am. Hosp. in Paris Served as 1st lt., capt., maj. and lt. col., U.S. Army Med. Corps, A.E.F.; dir. Med. and Surg. Sec. Dept. Mil. Affairs, Bureau Hosp Adminstrn., Med. and Surg. Dept. Am. Red Cross in France. Diplomate Am. Bd. Psychiatry and Neurology. Mem. Am. Coll. Physicians, Am. Psychiatric Assn. (former v.p. bd. dirs. Research Council on Problems of Alcohol, mem. sci. bd., mem. com. pub. edn.), N.Y. Acad. Medicine (chmn. Salmon com. for psychiatry and mental hygiene, mem. sect. neurology and psychiatry), Am. Soc. of Research Psychosomatic Problems (former chmn. com. indsl. medicine). Am. Psychiatric Found. (chmn. sci. com.; dir.), Southern Psychiatric Assn., A.M.A., Am. Med. Editors and Authors Assn., Assn. Research in Nervous and Mental Diseases, Assn. Study Internal Secretions, N.Y. Psychiatric Assn., N.Y. Neurol. Soc., N.Y. Soc. Clin. Psychiatry, N.E. Soc. Psychiatry. Conn. Soc. Psychiatry, N.Y. State Med. Soc., N.Y. Co. Med. Soc., Conn. Soc. Mental Hygiene (v.p. 1938-40), Hartford County Medical Society, Hartford Med. Soc. (pres. 1947), Conn. State Med. Soc. (pres. elect 1950-51, adv. com. Vets. Adminstrn., com. national legislation, trustee bldg. fund, chairman com. pub. relations), Central Neuro-Psychiatric Hosp. Assn., Pan-Am. Med. Assn., Nat. Assn. Mfrs. (chmn. sub-com. psychiatry), Nat. Conf. Bd. Phys. and Surgs. in Industry. N.E. Conf. Indsl. Phys. and Surg., State Bd. Edn., Sociedad Cubana de Neurologia y Psiquiatria, Am. Soc. French Legion of Honor. Am. Legion, Council Fgn. Relations. Psi Upsilon Rho. Awarded Gold Medal of Honor, Officer Legion of Honor (France). Order University of Palms (French Academy), Officer Order St. George and Notre Dame de Mont Carmel (France), National Eagle (Poland), Revolution Medal (Czechoslovakia), Citation for conspicuous and meritorious service with A.E.F. (U.S.). Mem. Commn. to Study Conn. Laws and Facilities pertaining to the Prevention, Treatment and Care of Mental Diseases and Defects and Allied Problems. Commn. to Survey the Human Resources of Conn. Chmn. Com. for Formulating Standards for School Psychologists, Conn. State Bd. of Edn. Clubs: Union, Yale, Columbia University, Columbia University Faculty, Vidonian (New York); Sleepy Hollow Country (Scarborough-on-Hudson); Hartford, Hartford Golf, Twentieth Century (Hartford); Bohemian (San Francisco); 100,000 Mile; Grad. (Yale). Editor: Digest of Neurology and Psychiatry; asso. editor: Am. Jour. Psychiatry. Home: 11 Fernwood Rd., West Hartford, Conn.; and 610 Park Av., N.Y., N.Y. Office: 610 Park Av., New York 21, N.Y.; and 459 Marlborough St., Boston. Died July 22, 1950; buried Fairview Cemetery, West Hartford, Conn.

BURLINGHAM, Charles C(ulp), lawyer; b. Plainfield, N.J., Aug. 31, 1858; s. Aaron Hale (D.D.) and Emma (Starr) B.; A.B., Harvard, 1879; LL.B., Columbia, 1891; LL.D., Williams, 1931, Columbia, 1933, Harvard, 1934; m. Louisa W. Lawrence, Sept. 29, 1883 (died Dec. 7, 1937); children—Charles, Anne Hoe, Robert (dec.). Admitted to bar, 1881; counsel Burlingham, Hupper and Kennedy. Mem. Am., N.Y. State bar assns., Assn. Bar City of N.Y. (pres. 1929-31), N.Y. County Law Assn., Am. Law Inst., Internat. Law Assn., Maritime Law Assn. of U.S., Comité Maritime Internate.; former pres. N.Y. Bd. of Edn., N.Y. Welfare Council, Harvard Alumni Assn., Columbia Law School Alumni Assn. Democrat. Sr. warden St. George's Episcopal Ch. Clubs: Century, Harvard. Home: 860 Park Av. Office: 26 Broadway, N.Y.C. Died June 6, 1959.

BURNELL, Edward John, mfg. exec.; b. Tondu, Wales, Apr. 7, 1888; s. William Henry and Alice (Jenkins) B.; student Moravian Prep. Sch., Bethlehem, Pa., 1906-08, Lehigh U., Bethlehem, 1908-10; m. Margaretta Elizabeth Good, Feb. 21, 1911; children—Edward John, Phyllis (Mrs. G. R. Tucker). With Link-Belt Co. since 1913, engring. draftsman, 1913-15, squad engr., 1915-17, dist. engr., Pittsburgh, 1917-20, dist. mgr., Boston, 1920-27, dist. mgr. Pittsburgh, 1927-29, gen. sales mgr., Chicago, 1929-36, vice pres. and gen. mgr., Chicago, 1936-43, vice pres. in charge of company sales since 1944; dir. Link-Belt Co. (Chicago), Pacific Div. Mem. Chem. Corps. Adv. Bd. Dir. Am. Mining Congress, Foundry Equipment Mfrs. Assn.; past pres. Conveyor Equipment Mfrs. Assn.; past pres. Lehigh U. Alumni Club (Chicago); dir. Y.M.C.A. (Hyde Park, Chicago); mem. Newcomen Soc., Sigma Nu. Episcopalian. Clubs: University, Economic, Executives; Midlothian Country (pres. 1931-43); Sunset Ridge Country (Winnetka). Home: 566 Ash St., Winnetka, Ill. Office: Bell Bldg., 307 N. Michigan Av., Chgo. 1. Died July 23, 1949.

BURNELL, Max Ronald, surgeon; b. Metamora, Mich., Oct. 6, 1893; s. Byron and Blanche (Hollenbeck) B.; student Albion Coll., 1912-14; M.D., U. Mich., 1918; m. Mary Catherine Yeakle, Mar. 9, 1927. Instr. L.I. Coll. Hosp., 1918-21; med. advisor Clara Elizabeth Fund, 1938-50; med. dir. AC Spark Plug Div., 1931-49; chief staff Women's Hosp. (all at Flint, Mich.), 1945-48; med. dir. Gen. Motors Corp., Detroit, 1949—. Advisor U. Mich. Social Sci. Research Project. Med. advisor, Nat. Assn. Mfrs. Mem. bd. gov. U. Mich. Inst. Indsl. Health, 1950-52; chmn. Mich. Indsl. Health Com. Recieved Wm. S. Knudsen Award, 1951-52. Fellow A.C.S., Am. Assn. Indsl. Physicians and Surgeons; mem. Sigma Chi, Nu Sigma Nu. Clubs: Golf, City (Flint); Detroit, Recess (Detroit). Contributor articles to medical journals. Home: 3301 Westwood Pkwy., Flint, Mich. Office: 3044 Grand Blvd., Detroit 2. Died Sept. 19, 1959.

BURNET, W. Everit, stock broker; b. East Orange, N.J., Jan. 15, 1875; s. Robert and Sarah (Kershaw) B.; grad. East Orange High Sch.; m. Eloise Maxwell Nichols, Oct. 10, 1901; 1 dau., Mrs. Elinore Burnet Cummins. Began wtih Alexandre & Burnet, members N.Y. Stock Exchange, 1912, firm merged with Strong, Sturgis & Co. (which originally started 1869 as Capron, Strong & Co.) 1920, company being known as W.E. Burnet & Co., 1927—, now sr. partner of co.; dir. South Porto Rico Sugar Co., Central Romana Corp., N.Y. City. Republican. Christian Scientist. Clubs: Union League, Downtown Assn., Economic, St. Andrew's Soc.; Essex County Country (West Orange, N.J.); Lake Placid Club (Lake Placid, N.Y.). Home: 32 Brookside Rd., West Orange, N.J. Office: 11 Wall St., N.Y.C. 5. Died May 20, 1954.

BURNS, Allen Tibbals, social service; b. Haverhill, Mass., Aug. 29, 1876; s. William Treat and Ella Louise (Marsh) B.; A.B., U. Chgo., 1897, postgrad. 1899-1903; m. Jessie G. Wadsworth, July 20, 1911; children—Scott W., Janet W.; m. 2d, Florence M. Seder, Nov. 6, 1937. YMCA sec., 1903-07; dean Chgo. Sch. Civics and Philanthropy, 1907-09; sec. Pitts. Civic Commn., 1909-14; dir. Cleve. Found., 1914-18; dir. studies on methods of Americanization, Carnegie Corp., 1918-21; chmn. labor adjustment bd. Rochester Clothing Industry, 1921-22; exec. dir. Nat. Information Bureau of N.Y.C., 1922-25; exec. v.p. Community Chests and Councils, Inc., N.Y.C., 1926-42, cons., 1943, ret.; exec. dir. Moblzn. for Human Needs, 1931-41; vice chmn. Citizens Com. on Displaced Persons, 1947. Mem. exec. com. Chgo. Municipal Voters' League, 1907-09; mem. Chgo. Housing Com., 1909; sec. Pitts. Charter Com., 1911; trustee Cleve. Welfare Fedn., 1914-17. Dir. America's Making, Inc., Nat. Conf. Social Work (pres. 1921). Home: East Lansing, Mich.; (winter) Ft. Myers, Fla. Died Feb. 9, 1953.

BURNS, Andrew J., pub. co. exec.; b. N.Y. City, Nov. 11, 1873; s. Michael and Catherine (McKenna) B.; student pub. schs. N.Y. City; m. Emma Hoenninger, Oct. 5, 1898; 1 dau., Anne M. Brislin. Clk. Nat. Ry. Publ. Co., N.Y. City, 1889-99, chief clk., 1899-1915, asst. mgr., v.p., 1915-27, pres. since 1927; chmn. bd., pres. Ry. Equipment & Publ. Co., N.Y. City since 1939. Club: Traffic (N.Y. City). Home: 150 Greenway Terrace, Forest Hills, L.I. Office: 424 W. 33 St., N.Y.C. 1. Died Nov. 13, 1958.

BURNS, Bob, actor; b. Greenwood, Ark., Aug. 2, 1890; s. William Robert and Emma (Needham) B.; student U. of Ark.; m. Elizabeth Fisher, Sept. 1921 (now dec.); 1 son, Robert; m. 2d, Harriet Foster, May 31, 1937; children—Barbara Ann, William, Stephen. Began professional career on vaudeville stage, 1911; now identified with motion pictures and radio programs. Served as sergt. U.S. Marine Corps. Episcopalian. Mason. Inventor of Bazooka (musical instrument). Home: Canoga Park, Cal. Died Feb. 2, 1956; buired Forest Lawn Meml. Park, Glendale, Cal.

BURNS, Dennis Francis, educator; b. Chgo., Aug. 31, 1889;s. Michael and Mary (Byrne) B.; student St. Ignatius Coll., Chgo., 1907-08, St. Stanislaus Sem., Mo., 1908-12; A.B., St. Louis U., 1914, A.M., 1915, graduate study, 1920-22; studied Colegio de Javier, Burgos, Spain, 1922-24, Maison de la Colombiere, France, 1924-25; Ph.D., S.T.D., Gregorian U., 1931. Joined Soc. of Jesus, 1908; instr. St. Louis U. High Sch., 1915-20; prof. philosophy Loyola U.; Chgo., 1925-26, 33-34, regent law sch., prof. jurisprudence, 1934-35, prof. theology, 1954—; prof. sacramental theology Mundelein Sem., 1926-27; prof. fundamental theology St. Louis U., 1927-31; prof. philosophy John Carroll U., Cleve., 1931-33, 40-44; pres. Xavier U., Cin., 1935-40; dir. laymen's retreats, 1944-46; prof. philosophy and religion U. Detroit, 1946-54. Mem. Am. Cath. Philos. Assn., St. Thomas Aquinas Acad. Extra curricular lectr. on religion, philosophy and social science, also writer of essays. Address: Loyola U., 6525 Sheridan Rd., Chgo. 26. Died Sept. 9, 1957; buried All Saints Cemetery, Des Plaines, Ill.

BURNS, Edward H(arold), sports writer; born Frankfort, Ind., Jan. 17, 1891; s. Edward H. and Flora (Donaldson) B.Sr.; A.B., Wabash Coll., 1913. Reporter Frankfort Daily News (father's paper), 1906-11, Crawfordsville (Ind.) Jour., 1911, Crawfordsville Review, 1912-13; gen. assignment reporter Chicago Herald, 1914-15; city editor, Joliet (Ill.) Herald-News, 1916; reporter, Chicago Examiner, 1917, Chicago Tribune, 1918, federal bldg. and prohibition reporter, 1919-26, sports writer, 1926—; Chicago corr. and columnist, Sporting News, 1927—, regularly assigned to Maj. League baseball, Big Ten Football, Nat. League Hockey, etc. Served in United States Army, 1918. Official scorer, World Series, 1945, 48. Chairman baseball's "Most Valuable Player" com., 1948. Mem. Am. Legion, Baseball Writers Assn. of Am. (nat. pres., 1948), Sigma Chi. Republican. Reprints in various sports anthologies including: Headlining America, 1939; Sports Extra, 1945. Contbr. to Sport and Baseballl mag. Home: 212 S. Maple Av., Oak Park, Ill. Office: Sports Dept., Chgo. Tribune, Chgo. Died Jan. 27, 1955; buried Rosehill Cemetery, Chgo.

BURNS, Elmer Ellsworth, author; b. Monroe County, Ia., Feb. 22, 1868; s. Aaron William and Martha Ann (Prather) B.; B.S., Simpson Coll., 1894; post-grad. U. Chgo., 1894-95, 98-99; m. Harriet Thompson, June 23, 1898. Tchr., Indianola, 1895; tchr. of physics Joseph Medill High Sch., Chgo., 1904-38, ret. Mem. Epsilon Sigma. Methodist. Author: The Story of Great Inventions, 1910; also a series of tech. books. Editorial writer The World Book. Home: 3515 Home Av., Berwyn, Ill. Died Feb. 13, 1956; buried Mt. Auburn Cemetery, Berwyn.

BURNS, George Plumer, botanist; b. Maroa, Ill., Oct. 30, 1871; s. George William and Emily Harriet (Mouser) B.; grad. Ill. State Normal U., 1891; B.S., Ohio Wesleyan U., 1898, A.M.; Ph.D., U. Munich, 1900; m. Annette May Hollington, June 30, 1898. Instr. in botany Ohio Wesleyan U., 1897; instr. botany, later asst. prof. and jr. prof., and dir. Bot. Gardens, U. Mich., 1900-10; prof. botany U. Vt., 1910—, head dept., 1910-44, prof. emeritus, 1944—. Mem. Vt. (pres.), N.E. bot. clubs, Bot. Soc. Am., Ecol. Soc. Am. Phi Delta Theta, Sigma Xi, Phi Beta Kappa. Republican. Methodist. Contbr. articles to bot. jours. on forest ecology. Address: 453 S. Willard, Burlington, Vt. Died 1953.

BURNS, John Joseph, lawyer; b. Cambridge, Mass., May 1, 1901; s. John Joseph and Mary (Kelleher) B.; A.B., Boston Coll., Newton, Mass., 1921, LL.D., 1935; LL.B., Harvard, 1925, S.J.D., 1926; LL.D., Loyola University, 1936; m. Alice Blake, June 14, 1930; children— John Joseph, Daniel Blake, Robert Emmett, Alice Terese, Brian Patrick, Ellen Moira, Michael. Admitted to Mass. bar, 1926; practiced in Boston with Gaston, Snow, Saltonstall & Hunt, 1926-28; prof. law, Harvard, 1928-31; asso. justice Superior Court of Mass., 1931-34; gen. counsel Securities and

Exchange Commn., Washington, D.C., 1934-37; special counsel, U.S. Maritime Commn., 1937; partner in law firms Burns, Blake & Rich of Boston, and Burns, Currie, Rich, & Rice; dir. W. R. Grace & Co., United Corp., Catholic. Home: 89 Fletcher Rd., Belmont, Mass. Office: 10 Post Office Square, Boston, Mass.; and 40 Wall St., N.Y.C. Died May 11, 1957.

BURNS, Kevin, physicist; b. Pleasant Ridge, N. B., Can., Mar. 1, 1881; s. John and Gertrude (Campbell) B.; brought to U.S., 1885; A.B., U. of Minn., 1903, Ph.D., 1910; studied in Europe, 1911, 12; hon. D.Sc., St. Bonaventure College, 1947; married Hazel Bunney, 1911 (died 1917); 1 son, Kevin; m. 2d, Ruth Buchanan, 1926 (dec. 1957); children—John Buchanan, George Campbell. Asst. at Lick Obs., Cal., 1904-07, U. of Minn., 1907-10; Martin Kellogg fellow, Lick Obs., residence in Europe, 1911-12; asst. physicist, Bur. of Standards, Washington, 1913-17, asso., 1917, physicist, 1917-19; astronomer, Allegheny Obs., Pitts., 1920-51, asst. dir., 1930-51. Mem. Sigma Xi, Philos. Soc. Washington, A.A.A.S., A.A.S. (treas. 1941-47), Internat. Astron. Union, Unitarian. Has specialized in spectroscopy, pioneer in spectrochemical analysis; measured standard wavelengths; determined stellar velocities and distances. Home: 3444 Delaware Av. Address: Allegheny Observatory, Pitts. 14. Died Apr. 30, 1958.

BURNS, Lee, architect; b. Bloomfield, Ind., Apr. 19, 1872; s. Harrison and Mary Constance (Smydth) B.; student Butler U.; m. Anna Ray Herzsch, June 5, 1907; children—Betty Lee (Mrs. Daniel W. Layman, Jr.), David Vawter. Began practice at Indpls., 1910; mem. Burns & Burns. Work of firm includes: bldgs. at Ind. U., Butler U., a number of schools and other pub. bldgs., and many country and town houses such as those of Chandler Werbe, Walter C. Marmon, Arthur E. Osborn, Albert Rabb, Herbert M. Woollen, Wm. Ross Teel. Firm awarded gold medal Ind. Soc. Architects, 1928. Served as pvt. Ind. Vol. Inf., Spanish-Am. War. Trustee Butler U. Mem. bd. dirs. John Herron Art Inst. Mem. Geo. Rogers Clark Meml. Commn., James Whitcomb Riley Meml. Assn.; mem. Ind. Soc. Architects (past pres.), A.I.A., Ind. Hist. Soc. (chmn. exec. com.), Soc. Indiana Pioneers, Art Assn. Indpls., S.A.R. Democrat. Clubs: Rotary, Players (charter mem.), Woodstock, Contemporary, Portfolio, Indianapolis Literary. Author: The National Road in Indiana, 1919; Indianapolis, the Old Town and the New, 1923; Life in Old Vincennes, 1929; Early Architects and Builders in Indiana, 1935. Home: 4205 Washington Blvd. Office: 333 N. Pennsylvania St., Indpls. Died Jan. 8, 1957.

BURNS, Owen McIntosh, judge; b. Danville, Ill., Sept. 6, 1892; s. William Charles and Jennie (McIntosh) B.; A.B., U. Ill., 1916, LL.B., 1921; m. Marion Foster, 1930; children—William, Franklin, Jeanne. In gen. practice of law in fed. and state cts. of Ill. and Pa., 1921-49; U.S. atty., May 1947-Oct. 1949; judge U.S. Dist. Ct. for Western Dist. of Pa. since 1949. Served as capt., inf., U.S. Army, World War I. Mem. Alpha Epsilon, Phi Delta Phi. Home: 1815 Plymouth St. Office: U.S. Court House Bldg., Erie, Pa. Died Oct. 26, 1952.

BURNS, P(ercy) P(ratt), college dean, prof.; b. Jemison, Ala., June 7, 1884; s. Rev. Amaziah Erasmus and Ella Isadora (Deramus) B.; A.B., summa cum laude, Howard Coll., Birmingham, Ala., 1904; grad. student Univ. of Chicago, summer 1913; A.M., Harvard, 1920; Litt.D., (hon.), Mercer Univ., 1928; m. Effie Salena Sheppard, June 26, 1912. Teacher, English and Latin, South Carolina Co-Educational Institute, Edgefield, South Carolina, 1904-11; acting professor of English, Howard College, Birmingham, Alabama, 1911-12, professor of English and head of dept. since 1912, commandant of cadets, 1911-12, registrar, 1918-20, dean of students, 1920-21, dean of coll. since 1921. Member education commn. So. Baptist Convention. Mem. Assn. Am. Univ. Profs., Coll. English Assn., Nat. Council Teachers of English, Conf. of Academic Deans, Assn. Ala. Colls. (past pres.), Ala. Edn. Assn. (mem. exec. com. dept. of English), Assn. of Coll. English Teachers of Alabama (treas.), Kappa Phi Kappa, Omicron Delta Kappa. Democrat. Baptist (deacon). Mason. Club: Executives. Chmn. bd. dirs. The Alabama Baptist (denominational weekly) since 1945. Lecturer and author of reviews and critical essays. Home: 208 Pinetree Lane, Roebuck Court, Birmingham 6. Died June 4, 1957; buried Elmwood Cemetery.

BURR, Alexander George, judge; b. Pitrodie, Perthshire, Scotland, Feb. 25, 1871; s. Rev. Alexander and Mary (MacLachlan) B.; brought by parents to U.S., 1883; LL.B., U. Mich., 1894, hon. LL.M., 1934; LL.D., U. N.D., 1938; m. Josephine Roberta Carothers, June 7, 1900 (died 1915); children—Alexander Carothers, Mary Margaretta (wife of Rev. Kenneth E. Wells), Robert MacLachlan (dec.), Roberta Cameron. Admitted to N.D. bar, 1894, began practice at Bottineau; states atty., Bottineau County, N.D., 1895-97, 1901-05; judge Dist. Court, N.D., 1908-26; judge, Supreme Court, N.D., 1926-41. Trustee Jamestown (N.D.) Coll., 1907—. Mem. Am. Soc. Internat. Law, N.D. Bar Assn. Democrat. Presbyn.; moderator Synod of N.D., 1904; mem. permanent judicial commn., Gen. Assembly Presbyn. Ch., 1924-26. Clubs: Kiwanis, Country. Author: Apostle Paul and the Roman Law, 1927. Home: Rugby, N.D. Chambers: Bismarck, N.D. Died Feb. 8, 1951.*

BURR, Borden, lawyer; b. Talladega, Ala., Nov. 2, 1876; s. William H. and Sarah C. (Borden) B.; student Webb Sch., Bellbuckle, Tenn., 1892-93; A.B., University of Alabama, 1896, LL.D., 1942; LL.B., Washington and Lee University, 1898; m. Mamie Camp, 1899; 1 son, William H.; m. 2d, Nell Forman, 1907; 1 son, Samuel H. Admitted to Alabama bar, 1898, and began practice of law at Talladega, Ala.; Birmingham, Ala., since 1909; mem. Percy Benners & Burr, 1909-29, Benners, Burr, McKamy & Forman, 1929-43, Benners, Burr, Stockely & McKarny, since July 1943; pres. Rockhouse Land Co.; dir., asst. gen. counsel All States Life Ins. Co. With Y.M.C.A. 4 months in France, 1918. Delegate Democratic National Convention, 1904; delegate at large Dem. Nat. Conv., 1912, 24, 28; chmn. Dem. State Campaign Com. Chamn. Ala. State Assn. Y.M.C.A., 1914-18. Trustee Louisville (Kentucky) Presbyterian Theol. Sem. Past pres. Ala. State Bar Assn.; mem. Univ. of Ala. Alumni Assn. (pres. 1915-18), Am. Bar Assn., Am. Law Inst., Am. Judicature Soc., Sigma Nu (past regent, now trustee), Phi Beta Kappa, Omicron Delta Kappa. Democrat. Presbyterian. Clubs: Kiwanis, Country, Traffic and Transportation, The Club, The Lawyers. Home: 9 Honeysuckle Lane. Office: Brown-Marx Bldg., Birmingham, Ala. Died Aug. 4, 1952.

BURR, Charles Walts, neurologist; b. Phila., Nov. 16, 1861; s. D. Ridgway and Hannah (Walts) B.; B.S., U. Pa., 1883, M.D., 1886, D.Sc., 1933. Neurologist Phila. Gen. Hosp., 1896-1931, psychiatrist, 1931-40; prof. mental diseases U. Pa., 1901-31, prof. emeritus, 1931—; physician to Orthopaedic Hosp. and Infirmary for Nervous Diseases, 1911-40. Pres. Am. Neurol. Assn., 1908, Phila. Psychiatric Soc., 1909, 10, Phila. Neurol Soc., Pathol. Soc. Phila. Fellow Coll. Physicians of Phila.; mem. A.M.A. Phi Beta Kappa. Address: 1527 Pine St., Phila. Died Feb. 19, 1944; buried Soc. of Friends Cemetery, Phila.

BURR, Edward, army officer; b. Boonville, Mo., May 19, 1859; s. William E. and Harriette Holly (Brand) B.; student Washington U., 1874-8; grad. U.S. Mil. Acad., 1882; m. Katherine Green, June 24, 1886. Commd. 2d lt. U.S. Engrs., 1882 advanced through grades to lt. col. 1898; hon. mustered out of vol. service, 1899; maj., 1903, lt.-col., 1908, col., 1912, birg. gen. N.A., 1917. Apptd. comdr. 166th F.A. Brig., 91st Div., 1918. Mem. Am. Soc. C.E. Clubs: Army and Navy, Chevy Chase. Address: War Dept., Washington. Died Apr. 15, 1952.

BURR, Hudson C., newspaperman; b. Plainfield, N.J.; s. Samuel D.V. and Evelyn (Hart) B.; B.S. in Elec. Engring., Brown U.; m. Cornelia Fill, 1914 (dec.); m. 2d, Marie Ware, 1932. Successively asst. comml. engr. Westinghouse Co., illuminating engring. The Holophane Engring. Co., asst. advt. mgr. The Metal Industry, advt. mgr. Transportation World, mgr. Cellokay Mfr. Corp.; interested C.S., 1913, class instrn., 1915, first reader br. ch., 1919-22; registered C.S. practitioner, 1941; joined Christian Science Monitor Staff, 1926, acting mgr. N.Y. advt. office, asst. advt. mgr. in Boston, mgr. nat. advt. pub. agent Mary Baker Eddy; trustee C.S. Pub. Soc., 1942—. Served as office, Signal R.C., A.S., 1917-18. Mem. Phi Gamma Delta. Clubs: Brown University, Boston Yacht, Eastern Yacht (Boston). Mason (32°, K.T.). Home: Longwood Towers, Brookline, Mass. Office: 1 Norway St., Boston. Died Apr. 19, 1949.

BURRAGE, Guy Hamilton, naval officer; b. Lowell, Mass., June 14, 1867; s. Hamilton and Mary How (Davis) B.; grad. U.S. Naval Acad., 1887; m. Mary Rickets Graham, Sept. 4, 1894. Commd. ensign USN, 1880, advanced through grades to vice adm., 1942; served in U.S.S. Wheeling uring Spanish-Am. War; exec. officer U.S.S. Chattanooga, 1905-07, U.S.S. Connecticut, 1910; comd. U.S.S. Albatross, 1910-12; comdt. midshipman U.S.Naval Acad., 1912-15; comd. U.S.S. Nebraska, 1915-19; comdt. Navy Yard, Norfolk, Va., 1919; comdt. naval forces in Europe, 1926-28; comdt. 5th Naval Dist. and Naval Operating Base, Norfolk, Va., 1928-31; retired 1931. Home: 719 Yarmouth St., Norfolk, Va. Died June 16, 1954; buried Congressional Cemetery, Washington.

BURRELL, George Arthur, chem. engr.; b. Cleve., Jan. 23, 1882; s. Alexander A. and Jane (Penny) B.; student Ohio State U., 1902-04, Chem. E., 1918; Sc.D., Wesleyan U., 1919; m. Mary L. Schafer, 1906; 1 dau., Dorothy May; m. 2d, Naomi L. Schafer, June 16, 1914. Chemist U.S. Geol. Survey, 1904-08; in charge research work, gas mine gas, and natural gas and gasoline investigations, U.S. Bureau Mines, Pitts., 1908-16; cons. engr. petroleum and natural gas work, 1916-43; asst. to dir. Bureau of Mines, 1917; col. U.S. Army, in charge all research work, C.W.S., 1917-18; located supply of helium gas in Tex. and initiated the govt. helium program. Decorated D.S.M. (U.S. Army). During 1919-20 had charge constrn. of refineries for the Island and Raritan Refining Cos. (N.Y.C.), was pres. Island Refining Co. and v.p., gen. mgr. Raritan Refining Co.; pres. Burrell Corp., 1923-52, became chmn. bd.; pres. Atlantic States Gas Co., 1936-54; v.p. Commonwealth Gas Corp., 1942-54; retained by Russian govt. to modernize natural gas industry, 1930-31. Inventor Burrell gas detector, Burrell gas analysis apparatus; co-inventor Burrell-Oberfell process of extracting gasoline from natural gas by charcoal methods; designed and built many natural gasoline refineries. Recipient Lamme medal for achievements in engring. Ohio State U., 1935; Hanlon award, Nat. Gasoline Assn. Am., 1948. Mem. Am. Petroleum Inst., Am. Chem. Soc., Am. Inst. Chem. Engrs., Am. Inst. Chemists, Tau Beta Pi, Sigma Xi. Clubs: Uptown, Westchester Country (N.Y.C.). Author: Handbook of Gasoline, 1917; Recovery of Gasoline from Natural Gas, 1925; An American Engineer Looks at Russia, 1932; and also many papers and govt. publs. on gas, gasoline, petroleum and allied subjects. Home: 101 W. 57th St., N.Y.C. Died Aug. 16, 1957.

BURRELL, H(erbert) Cayford, geologist; b. Boston, Dec. 26, 1903; s. Herbert Leslie and Caroline White (Cayford) B.; student Middlesex Sch., Concord, Mass., 1915-21; S.B., Harvard, 1928, A.M., geologist, Zinc Corp., Ltd., Broken Hill, N.S.W., 1929, Ph.D., 1946; student U. of Wis., 1932-33; m. Mary Josephine Runkel, July 25, 1929; children—Frederick R., Patricia R. Geologist Cerro de Pasco Copper Corp., Morococha, Peru, 1929-32; 1st resident Australia, 1934-37; with Central Geog. Survey, 1937-39; lab. research on Broken Hill ores Harvard, 1939-42; with coordinator Interam. Affairs, Bd. Econ. Warfare, and Fgn. Econ. Adminstrn. in connection with development of operations and purchase manganese ores for U.S. Govt., 1942-45; staff geologist Oliver Iron Mining Co. (U.S. Steel Corp. subsidiary) in cos. exploration for iron ore in Venezuela, 1946-49; trans. to raw materials dept. U.S. Steel Corp. of Del., Pittsburgh. 1949, since served as geologist; mgr. raw materials development, Columbia-Geneva Steel Div., U.S. Steel. Mem. Am. Inst. Mining and Metall. Engrs., Mining and Metall. Soc. Am. Author: Geology of the Broken Hill Ore Deposit, Broken Hill, N.S.W., Australia (with J. K. Gustafson, M. D. Garretty), 1950. Home: 424 Golden Gate Av., Belvedere, Calif. Office: 235 Montgomery St., San Francisco. Died Nov. 9, 1953; buried Harmony Grove, Salem, Mass.

BURRELL, John Angus, author, educator; b. Marysville, Mont., Apr. 9, 1890; s. Alexander Telfer and Abigail Mary (Kiersted) B.; student Chgo. Latin Sch., 1904-05, Berkeley (Cal.), High Sch., 1905-06, Teton County High Sch., Chateau, Mont., 1906-09; A.B., U. Wis., 1914; grad. study Columbia, 1920-24. Prof. English, Columbia 1952—. Served as ensign USN, World War I. Mem. Chi Psi. Episcopalian. Author: History of Adult Education in Columbia University, 1954. Co-author (with Dorothy Brewster); Dead Reckonings in Fiction, 1924; Adventure or Experience, 1930; Modern Fiction, 1934; Outline Modern World Fiction, 1951. Editor (with Bennett A. Cerf): Bedside Book of Famous American Stories, 1936; Anthology of Famous American Stories, 1953. Address: 200 W. 108th St., N.Y.C. 25. Died June 1, 1957; buried Choteau, Mont.

BURRILL, Stanley Stinton, lawyer; b. Akron, Ia., June 13, 1902; s. William Wesley and Ella Elsie (Stinton) B.; B.S.C., State U. Ia., 1924, J. D., 1926; m. Anne Elizabeth (Lucas) Stimpson, May 19, 1953; children by previous marriage—Louise (Mrs. James E. Ebeling), Karen C. Admitted to Ia. bar, 1926, Cal. bar, 1927; practice of law, 1927—; partner Hill, Farrer & Burrill, Los Angeles; pres. Sunset Ry. Fellow Am. Coll. Trial Lawyers; mem. Am., Los Angeles bar assns., State Bar Cal., Order of Coif, Phi Delta Phi, Alpha Sigma Phi. Mason. Club: Jonathan (Los Angeles). Home: 6007 W. 6th St., Los Angeles 36. Office: 411 W. 5th St., Los Angeles 13. Mar. 2, 1957.

BURRITT, Bailey Barton (bûr'ĭt), social worker, b. Monroe County, N.Y., May 31, 1878; s. Melville C. and Miranda H. (Horton) B.; A.B., U. or Rochester, 1902; A.M., Columbia University, 1903; LL.D., University of Rochester, 1945; m. Ruth H. Dennis, May 1909; children—Phyllis, Alan, Hazel, Bailey Barton, Alice, Ruth. Asst. sec. State Charities Aid Assn., N.Y. City, 1908-13; sec. Com. on Criminal Courts, Charity Orgn. Soc., N.Y. City, 1911-13; dir. Dept. Social Welfare, N.Y. Assn. for Improving Condition of the Poor, 1913-14; gen. dir. same, 1914-39; chairman, executive council, Community Service Soc., 1939-44 (mem. board trustees); exec. sec. Health Maintenance Com., 1944—; exec. dir. Nat. Health Council, 1947-48; mem. bd. dirs. Judson Health Center, Health Council of Greater of N.Y.; mem. exec. com. N.Y. Tuberculosis and Health Assn.; chmn. exec. com. American Social Hygiene Association. Appointed captain American Red Cross, July 1918; served as director and organized Home Service, American Red Cross in France, July 1, 1918-January 1, 1919. Member economic advisory committee President Harding's Conf. on Unemployment, 1921; mem. Westchester County Gov. Commn., 1923-24, which prepared new charter; mem. President Hoover's Com. on Child Health and Protection; member President Roosevelt's White House Conference on Children in a Democracy, 1939-40; member Mayor La Guardia's Commn. on Merging Emergency Relief Bureau with the Dept. of Pub. Welfare. Mem. Am. Acad. Polit. and Social Science, Nat. Conf. Social Work, Theta Chi, Phi Beta Kappa. Baptist. Club: Nat. Arts (New York). Home: 16 Prospect Dr., Yonkers 5, N.Y. Office: 105 E. 22d St., N.Y.C. 10. Died June 18, 1954.

BURROUGHS, George W., clergyman; b. Louisville, Miss., Nov. 3, 1889; s. Columbus Judson and Lou Cretia (Baine) B.; A.B., Bethel Coll., McKenzie, Tenn., 1914; A.M., Vanderbilt U., 1919; B.D., 1923; m. Opal Margaret Pratt, May 11, 1915; children—George W., Thomas Pratt, Judson Bayne. Ordained to ministry Cumberland Presbyn. Ch., pastor, Chattanooga, Tenn., 1920-25, Arrington St. Church, Nashville, 1933-43; prof. practical theology Sch. of Religion, Vanderbilt U., 1930—. Mem. bd. edn. Cumberland Presbyn. Ch., 1920-25, bd. ch. edn., 1938-39, pres. bd. publ., 1940-43; moderator Cumberland Presbyn. Gen. Assembly, 1941-42. Contbr. church periodicals. Address: 2207 Highland Av., Nashville. Died Dec. 6, 1950; buried Mount Olivet Cemetery, McKenzie, Tenn.

BURROW, Trigant (bûr-rō), phylobiologist, psychiatrist; b. Norfolk, Va., Sept. 7, 1875; s. John W. and Anastasia (Devereux) B.; prep. edn., St. Francis Xavier's Acad., N.Y.C., pvt. schs.; A.B., Fordham, 1895; M.D., U. Va., 1899, Ph.D., Johns Hopkins, 1909; grad. studies U. Va., Munich, Vienna, Johns Hopkins and Zurich, 1900-10; m. Emily Sherwood Bryan, Aug. 9, 1904; children—John D. (dec.) Emily Sherwood, (Mrs. Hans Syz). Demonstrator in biology U. Va., 1899-1900; asst. physician U. Frauenklinik, Munich, 1900; asst. in exptl. psychology Johns Hopkins, 1906-09, in clin. psychiatry Johns Hopkins Hosp., 1911-27; practice and research in psychiatry and psychoanalysis, 1911-23, social psychiatry and the group method of anlaysis, 1923-28; research in phylopathology, or in the modifications of behavior induced through adjusting the organism's internal tensional patterns; also to instrumental recording of these physiological changes, 1928—; sci. dir. The Lifwynn Foundation for Lab. Research in Analytic and Social Psychiatry, Westport, Conn., 1927—. Participant in 2d Internat. Symposium on Feelings and Emotions. Moosehart, Ill., 1948. Mem. A.M.A., A.A.A.S., Med. and Chirurg. Faculty of Md., Am. Psychopath. Assn., Am. Psychiatric Assn., Am. Psychol. Assn., Am. Anthropol. Soc., Human Genetics Soc. Am., N.Y. Acad. Scis., So. Soc. for Philosophy and Psychology, Phi Beta Kappa, Phi Delta Theta. Author: The Social Basis of Consciousness, 1927; The Structure of Insanity, 1932; The Biology of Human Conflict, 1937; The Neurosis of Man-An Introduction to a Science of Human Behavior, 1949; (pub. posthumously) Science and Man's Behavior, The Contribution of Phylobiology, 1953, A Search for Man's Sanity, The Selected Letters of Trigant Burrow, 1958; also articles in field of medicine, exptl. psychology, psychoanalysis, individual and social psychiatry and phylopathology. Home: S. Morningside Dr., Greens Farms, Conn. Office: 77 Park Av., N.Y.C. 16; also Lifwynn Foundation, 52 S. Morningside Dr., Westport, Conn. Died May 24, 1950.

BURROWES, Alonzo (Lon) Moore, newspaper editor; B. Higginsville, Mo., Dec. 11, 1887; s. Evans Barkalow and Teresa (Moore) B.; student Sedalia (Mo.) High Sch., 1899-1901, St. Joseph's Novitiate, Burkettsville, O., 1901-02, St. Joseph's Coll., Rensselaer, Ind., 1902-03; unmarried. Began as newspaper reporter, Sedalia Democrat, 1905; then with Sedalia Capital and St. Louis Times; became copy editor St. Louis Post-Dispatch; then with St. Louis Globe-Democrat, successively as reporter, rewrite man, copy editor, telegraph editor, night editor, chief of copy desk, asst. mng. editor and now mng. editor. Roman Catholic. Home: Melbourne Hotel, Grand and Lindell Blvds. Office: 1133 Franklin Av., St. Louis. Died Aug. 1953.

BURROWS, Warren Booth, lawyer; b. Groton, Conn., Sept. 14, 1877; s. Calvin and Lucy Agnes (Booth) B.; LL.B., U. of Mich., 1904; m. Emily Avery Copp, of Groton, Jan. 22, 1916; children—Belton Allyn, Warren Avery, Calvin. Admitted to Conn. bar, 1905, and began practice at New London; mem. Conn. Ho. of Rep., 1925, Conn. State Senate, 1927; mem. commn. to revise Conn. statutes, 1927; judge U.S. Dist. Ct., Conn., 1928-30; atty. gen. of Conn., 1931-35; now retired. Republican. Baptist. Mason, Odd Fellow. Club: Graduate (New Haven). Home: 70 Fort Hill Rd., Poquonock Bridge, Conn. Died Dec. 8, 1952; buried Burrows Cemetery, Poquonock Bridge.

BURROWS, William Russell, pub. utilities exec.; b. Lynn, Mass., May 20, 1872; s. William Albert and Sarah (Russell) B.; student Mass. Inst. Tech.; m. Helen Liese, 1899; children—William Russell, Alan Liese, Helen Frances (Mrs. Philip H. Reagan). Began as unskilled worker; invented labor saving machinery for lamp mfr. for 10 yrs.;later in various exec. positions and mgr., Edison Lamp Works; v.p. in charge mfg. Gen. Electric Co., Schenectady, N.Y., 1927-44, ret., in charge labor relations and cost reductions. Clubs: Essex County Golf, Mohawk Golf (Schenectady). Home: 378 Oakwood Av., Orange, N.J. Office: 1 River Rd., Schenectady, N.Y. Died Mar. 2, 1955.

BURSLEY, Joseph Aldrich (bûrs'lê), educator, corp. exec.; b. Fort Wayne, Ind., June 14, 1877; s. Gilbert Everett and Ellen Rebecca (Aldrich) B.; student U. Mich., 1895-97, 98-99, Cornell U., 1897-98; B.S. in Mech. Engring., U. Mich., 1899; m. Marguerite Knowlton, Apr. 8, 1908 (dec.); children—Anne Knowlton (dec.), Joseph Aldrich (dec.), Jerome Knowlton (dec.), Anne Bursley Steed, Rebecca Bursley Winder, Margery Bursley Angst. Apprentice Pa. Co., Ft. Wayne, 1899-1902; merc. bus., 1902-04; instr. mech. engring., 1904-09; asst. prof. U. Mich., 1909-11, jr. and asso. prof., 1911-47, prof. 1917-47, also dean students 1921-47, emeritus prof. and dean, 1947—; pres. Double A Products Co., Manchester, Mich., 1936—. Mem. common Council, Fort Wayne, 1903-04, and Common Council, Ann Arbor, Mich., 1925-29. Ednl. adviser Nat. Interfraternity Conf., 1939-46. Served as maj. and lt. col. Ordnance Dept., U.S. Army, World War I; organizer and C. O. Army Stores Course, U. Mich., 1917; chief of instrn. sect., Ordnance Dept., Washington, 1918; chief of plant sect. Detroit Dist. Ordnance Office, 1918-19; chief Detroit Dist. Salvage Bd., 1919-20. Col. O.R.C., U.S. Army. Mem. Am. Soc. M.E., Engring. Soc. Detroit, Soc. for Promotion Engring.Edn., Am. Ordnance Assn., S.A.R., Mass. Soc. Mayflower Descs., Tau Beta Pi, Pi Delta Epsilon, Phi Kappa Phi, Phi Eta Sigma. Republican. Episcopalian. Mason (32°). Clubs: University, Ann Arbor Golf. Author: (with John R. Allen) Heat Engines, 1910, 14, 25, 31, 41. Home: 2107 Hill St., Ann Arbor, Mich. Died Sept. 4, 1950.

BURT, Clayton Raymond, corp. exec.; b. Lynn, Mass., Dec. 17, 1874; s. Byron S. and Laura M. (Miner) B.; student St. Johnsbury (Vt.) Acad.; m. Charlotte E. Wells. With Brown &Sharpe Mfg. Co., Providence, as apprentice, later in exec. capacity, 1892-1905; gen. supt. Barber Colman Co., Rockford, Ill., 1905-13; charge munitions plants, Toronto, 1913-19; pres. New Process Gear Co., Syracuse, N.Y., 1919-23; gen. mgr., later v.p. and pres. Pratt & Whitney Co., Hartford, Conn., 1924-36; pres. Niles-Bement-Pond Co. and gen. mgr. Pratt & Whitney div., 1936-43, chmn. bd. 1943-48; pres., gen. mgr. Potter & Johnston Co., 1948—; dir. Silex Co., Arrow-Hart & Hegeman Electric Co., Fenn Mfg. Co. (Hartford) Shepard Niles Crane & Hoist Corp. (Montous Falls, N.Y.), Plume and Atwood Mfg. Co. (Waterbury, Conn.); trustee Hartford-Conn. Trust Co., West Hartford Trust Co. Trustee YMCA, Saint Johnsbury Academy. Mem. Nat. Machine Tool Builders Assn. (past pres.), N.A.M. (dir.), Mfrs. Assn. Conn. (dir.), Mfrs. Assn. Hartford County (mem. bd. govs.), U.S., Conn., Hartford C.'s of C., Am. Soc. M.E., Am. Soc.. Metals, Soc. Mil.. Engrs., Am. Standards Assn., Soc. Automotive Engrs., Am. Soc. Tool Engrs., Hartford Engring. Soc., Nat. Aeronautic Assn., Am. Ordnance Assn. (life mem.), Air Power League (charter mem.). Clubs: Hartford, Hartford Golf, Hartford Canoe, Cuntry Club of Farmington (bd. dirs.) (Hartford); Union League, Railroad Machinery, Economic (N.Y.C.); Union (Cleveland), Detroit Athletic (Detroit); Quinnipiack (New Haven); Wannamoisett (R.I.). Home: 57 Ridgewood Rd., West Hartford, Conn. Office: Potter & Johnston Co., Pawtucket, R.I. Died Oct. 21, 1957.

BURT, (Maxwell) Struthers, author; b. Baltimore, Md., Oct. 18, 1882; s. Horace Brooke and Hester Ann (Jones) B.; A.B., Princeton, 1904; studied Merton Coll., Oxford, England, 1906; LL.D., University of North Carolina; married Katharine Newlin (author), Feb. 9, 1913; children—Nathaniel, Julia Bleecker. Began as reporter, Phila. Times, later instr. English, Princeton; ranching Wyoming, 1908—; pres. Bar B. C. Ranch Co. until 1937. Served as pvt. Air Service, U.S. Army, 1918. Chevalier Order of White Rose (Finland). Elector, Hall of Fame. Mem. Am. Inst. Arts and Letters. Episcopalian. Clubs: Cap and Gown (Princeton); Coffee House, Princeton (New York); Rittenhouse, Franklin Inn, Art Alliance (Phila.). Author: In the High Hills, 1914; John O'May and Other Stories, 1918; Songs and Portraits (verse), 1921; Chance Encounters, 1921; The Interpreter's House, 1924; The Diary of a Dude Wrangler, 1924; When I Grow Up to Middle Age (verse), 1925; The Delectable Mountains, 1926; They Could Not Sleep, 1928; The Other Side, 1929; Festival, 1931; Entertaining the Islanders, 1933; Escape from America, 1936; Powder River, 1938; Along These Streets, 1941; War Songs, 1942; Philadelphia: Holy Experiment, 1945. Home: Three Rivers Ranch, Moran P.O. Wyo.; (winter) "Hibernia," Southern Pines, N.C. Died Aug. 29, 1954; buried Jackson, Wyo.

BURTON, Hiram Rodney, physician, ex-congressman; b. Lewes, Del., Nov. 13, 1842; s. Joshua S. and Ruth Hunn (Rodney) B.; student St. Peter's Acad., Lewes; M.D., U. Pa., 1868; m. Margaret Virginia Rawlins, June 19, 1877 (died May 1897). Practiced medicine at Frankford, Del., 1868-72, Lewes, Del., 1872—; now sr. mem. firm, Burton & Chappelear; dir. Lewes Nat. Bank, Md., Del. & Va. R.R.; mem. bd. mgrs. Farmers' Mut. Ins. Co. of Del. Deputy collector of customs, Lewes, 1876-88; acting asst. surgeon, U.S. Marine Hosp. Service, 1890-94; mem. bd. med. examiners of Del., 1895-99. Rep. candidate for State senator, 5th Dist., Sussex County, 1898; mem. 59th and 60th Congresses, Del.-at-large. Del. Rep. convs., 1896, 1900; del. Rep. Nat. Conv., 1908; trustee State Hosp. for Insane. Mem. Del. State Med. Soc. (v.p.), A.M.A., Soc. Colonial Wars. Episcopalian. Address: Lewes, Del. Deceased.

BURTON, Jean, editor, author; b. Abernethy, Saskatchewan, Can.; d. John and Helen Jane (Turnbull) Burton; student St. Alban's Coll., Prince Albert, Saskatchewan, and U. of Saskatchewan; B.A., U. of Brit. Columbia; M.A., U. of Alberta. Became mem. editorial com. Canadian Forum, Toronto, 1929; mem. editorial bd. Canadian Mercury, Montreal, 1929; asso. editor New Frontier, Toronto, 1936. Author: Sir Richard Burton's Wife, 1941; Heyday of a Wizard, 1944; Garibaldi, 1945; Katharine Felton, 1947; Lydia Pinkham Is Her Name, 1949. Co-author: Elisabeth Ney, 1943. Contbr. to Canadian Forum, Canadian Mercury, New Frontier, Atlantic Monthly, etc. Home: 2235 Durant Av., Berkeley. Died Jan. 18, 1952.

BURTON, Oliver Milton, business exec.; b. Geneva, Ill., Mar. 18, 1877; s. John and Elizabeth Lucy (Long) B.; student pub. schs. of Chicago; m. Anna J. Tatham, Oct. 20, 1909. Began business career with father in 1896; in 1899 became sec. and treas. J. Burton Co.; in 1907 organized and became pres. Dixie Cotton Felt Mattress Co.; chairman board Burton-Dixie Corpn., Chicago. Mem. bd. govs. Am. Furniture Mart. Trustee, v.p. Glenwood Sch. for Boys. Mem. Nat. Council Defense during World War I. Mem. adv. com. dairy sci., U. Ill. Pres. Ill. Guernsey Breeders Assn. Breeder of fine Guernsey cattle. Clubs: Chicago, Old Elm; Wausaukee (Wis.); Grand Island Lodge (Bath, Ill.). Home: Conway Road and Burton Lane, Lake Forest, Ill. Office: 2024 S. Racine Av., Chgo. Deceased.

BURTON-OPITZ, Russell, physician, physiologist; b. Ft. Wayne, Ind., Oct. 25, 1875; s. Charles and Anna B.; M.D., Rush Med. Coll., 1895; S.B., U. Chgo., 1897, post-grad. work, 1897-98, S.M., 1902, Ph.D., 1905; post-grad. U. Vienna, 1898; m. Jeanette Jonassen, 1909 (dec. 1930); 1 dau., Arlyn; m. 2d, Elizabeth Elliot Phillips Cordts, 1932. Asst. in physiology U. Breslau, 1898-1901; investigator Marine Biol. Sta., Naples, 1901; asst. in physiology Harvard, 1901-02; asst. Columbia, 1902-03, instr., 1903-04, adj. prof., 1904-10, asso. prof. physiology, 1909-23, head dept. of physilogy, 1909-11, lectr. in physiology, 1923—; cons. physician Cumberland Hosp.; cons. diseases of heart Lenox Hill, Englewood, North Hudson, Holy Name, Christ, Hackensack hosps. (all N.Y.C.). Fellow A.A.A.S.; mem. A.M.A., Am. Physiol. Soc., Soc. Exptl. Medicine and Biology, Am. Soc. Naturalists, Deutsche Physiol. Gesellschaft, Am. Soc. Biol. Chemists, Medical Soc. State N.Y., New York County Med. Soc., Am. Soc. Pharm. and Exptl. Therapy, N.Y. Cardiol. Soc. (pres.), Sigma Xi, Alpha Omega Alpha (pres.). Contbr. to Am. and fgn. physiol. and med. jours. Author: Text Book of Physiology, 1920; Advanced Lessons in Practical Physiology, 1920; Elementary Manual of Physiology. Home: 218 Bridle Way, Palisade, N.J. Died Nov. 18, 1954.

BURTT, Wilson Bryant, army officer; b. Hinsdale, Ill., Jan. 1, 1875; s. George H. and Ellen M. (Keyes) B.; grad. U.S. Mil. Acad., 1899; honor grad. Army Sch. of the Line, 1911; grad. Army Staff Coll., 1912. Commd. 2d lt. Inf., 1899, advanced through grades to birg. gen. Nat. Army, 1918; with regt. at Havana, Cuba, Mar.-Sept., 1899, in Philippines, 1900-03, 07-10; instr. Ky. State U., 1904-07; instr. N.G. Cal., 1913-15; observer, German armies in the field, 1914-15, in Mexico, 1916; with AEF in France as asst. chief Air Service and chief of staff, 5th Army Corps, 1917-19, served in Vosges sector, St. Mihiel offensive, Meuse-Argonne offensive; appt. instr. Gen. Staff Coll., 1919. Decorated D.S. M. (U.S.); Croix de Guerre with Palm, and Legion of Honor (French); Order of St. Michael and St. George (British); Order of the Crown (Italian). Mason (Shriner), Elk. Address: Care War Dept., Washington. Died Mar. 21, 1957.

BUSCH, Adolf Georg Wilhelm, violinist, composer; b. Siegen, Westphalia, Aug. 8, 1891; s. Wilhelm and Henrietta (Schmidt) B.; studied under Fritz Steinbach, Willy Hess (violin), Bram Eldering, U. of Cologne; under Hugo Grueters (composition) at Bonn; hon. Dr. Music, U. of Edinburgh, 1933; m. Frieda Grueters, May 15, 1913; 1 dau., Irene (Mrs. Rudolf Serkin); married 2d Dr. Hedgwig Vischer, Sept. 1, 1947; children—Nicholas, Thomas. Swiss citizen since 1935; came to U.S., 1939, naturalized in 1949. Made debut as concert violinist at age of 18; concert-master, Konzertverein, Vienna, 1912; head of violin dept. Berlin Hochschule, 1918. Formed famous string quartet, 1912; also formed chamber music orchestra in Basle, 1935; soloist throughout Europe;

toured Europe, Egypt and Palestine after introduction of the Jewish Laws, refusing to concertize in Germany after 1933; visited U.S. as soloist in concerts conducted by Arturo Toscanini, 1931; with Rudolf Serkin played recitals of piano and violin sonatas all over the world; re-established Busch Chamber Music Orchestra, 1941, since toured U.S. Composer of choral, orchestral, vocal, sacred, organ and chamber music, sonatas, violin solos and violin duets. Home: R.F.D. 3, Brattleboro, Vt. Died June 9, 1952.

BUSCH, Fritz, orchestra condr.; b. Siegen, Westphalia, Germany, Mar. 13, 1890; s. Wilhelm and Henriette (Schmidt) B.; student Conservatory of Music, Cologne, Germany; Dr. honoris causa, U. of Edinburgh Scotland; m. Margareta Boettcher, Aug. 29, 1911; children—Hans Peter, Eta Ruth, Gisela. Orchestra condr., Bad Pyrmont, 1910-12, Axi-la-Chapelle, 1912-18; generalmusikdirektor, Stuttgart, Germany, 1918-22, Dresden (Germany) Staatsoper, 1922-33; condr. Glyndebourne Opera, Eng., 1934-39, Danish State's Radio, 1933-40, and 1946-50, Teatro Colon, Buenos Aires, Argentina, 1933-44, Metropolitan Opera, N.Y. City, since 1945; made guest appearances throughout the world. Mem. Royal Acad. of Musik, Stockholm, Sweden. Decorated Comdr. Pour le Merite, Chile. Home: 370 W. 245th St., Riverdale, N.Y. City 63. Office: Metropolitan Opera, Broadway, N.Y.C. Died Sept. 14, 1951; buried Germany.

BUSCH, Joseph Francis, bishop; b. Red Wing, Minn., Apr. 18, 1866; s. Frederick and Anna M. (Weimar) B.; ed. at Inssbruck, Austria, and at Catholic U., Washington, D.C. Ordained priest R.C. Ch., July 28, 1889; served as sec. to Archbishop Ireland, and asst. pastor at Cathedral and at St. Mary's Ch., St. Paul; successively pastor South St. Paul, St. Lawrence's Parish (Minneapolis), and Le Sueur, Minn.; and dir. Diocesan Mission Band, St. Paul, until 1910; consecrated bishop of Lead, S.D., May 19, 1910; apptd. bishop of St. Cloud, Minn., Jan. 19, 1915. Home: 214 Third Av., S. St. Cloud, Minn. Died May 31, 1953.

BUSEY, Paul Graham (bū'sē), banker; b. Urbana, Ill., Oct. 5, 1881; s. Matthew Wales and Katherine Wheeler (Richards) B.; student U. of Ill., 1898-1902, Art Inst., Chicago, 1903-04, Art Acad., Chicago, 1904; m. Blanche Black, June 25, 1909 (divorced); children—Patricia Blanche (Mrs. Wade Ambrose), Matthew Wales. With Busey State Bank, Urbana, Ill., since 1905, bookkeeper, 1905-10, teller, 1911-17, asst. cashier, 1917-20, v.p., 1920-32, pres. 1932-45; pres. Busey First National Bank since 1945; director Commercial Bldg. & Loan Assn.; author and owner Busey Fraternity Accounting System. Dir. Urbana Bd. of Edn.; v.p. and regional chmn. Ill. State School Bd. Assn.; dir. Urbana Assn. of Commerce (treas.); mem. Urbana Pub. Library Board. Mem. Ill. Bankers Assn., Am. Bankers Assn., Soc. of Cincinnati of State of Va. Republican. Episcopalian. Mason. Clubs: Union League (Chicago); Champaign County Country (Champaign, Ill.); Urbana Country, Rotary (Urbana). Contbr. to business mags. Home: 1301 S. Busey Av. Office: 201 W. Main St., Urbana, Ill. Died Sept. 24, 1950; buried Woodlawn Cemetery, Urbana.

BUSEY, Samuel Thompson, ex-army officer, ex-congressman; b. Greencastle, Ind., Nov. 16, 1835; s. Matthew Wales and Elizabeth (Bush) B.; student Urbana pub. schs.; m. Mary E. Bowen, Dec. 25, 1877. Was sgt. and 1st lt. Urbana Zouaves, 1861-62; town collector, Urbana, Ill., 1862; commd. 2d lt. in recruiting service Union Army, 1862, advanced through col., 1863; led regt. in assault on Ft. Blakeley, Ala., Apr. 9, 1865, was bvtd. brig.-gen. on request of Maj.-Gen. C. C. Andrews and Gen. U. S. Grant, and called by his comrades "The Hero of Fort Blakeley." Mayor and pres. bd. edn., Urbana, 1880-9; organized and conducted Busey's Bank, 1867-88; mem. 52d U.S. Congress. Gold Democrat. Address: Urbana, Ill. Died Apr. 1910; buried Woodlawn Cemetery, Urbana.

BUSH, Alvin Ray, congressman; b. Clearfield County, Pa., July 4, 1893; ed. public schools; m. Lucinda M. Bush; children—Shirley L., Alvin C. Pres., gen. mgr. Williamsport Transportation Co.; dir. Lowry Electric Co., Williamsport Yellow Cab Co.; breeder Guernsey cattle. Mem. 82d Congress, 15th Pa. Dist., 83d-86th Congresses, 17th Pa. Dist. Served overseas with 541st Motor Truck Co., World War I. Dir. Muncy Valley Hosp. Mem. Pa. Guernsey Breeders Assn., Am. Legion, 40 and 8. Republican. Methodist. Mason. Address: Wyno Farms, R.D. 2, Muncy, Pa. Died Nov. 5, 1959.

BUSH, Benjamin Jay, clergyman; b. Jenison, Mich., May 21, 1883; s. Jacob P. and Margaret (Haminger) B.; A.B., Hope Coll., Holland, Mich., 1906, A.M., 1909; grad. New Brunswick Theol. Sem., 1909; D.D., Centre Coll., Danville, Ky., 1917; m. Mae Julia Van Drezer, Aug. 26, 1909 (died May 25, 1938); children—Marguerite Enid, Jay Luman, Robert Phillips; m. 2d, Mrs. Mary Coke Murdoch, November 14, 1942. Ordained to the ministry of the Reformed Church in U.S.A., 1909; pastor New Paltz, N.Y., 1909-13, Reformed Ch., West Hoboken, N.J., 1913-16, Second Presbyn. Ch., Lexington, Ky., 1916-17, Westminster Presbyn. Ch., Detroit, 1927-45. Spl. lectr. on contemporary European history Macalester Coll., 1940-50. Interim minister Madison Co. Larger Parish, North Carolina, 1949, 1st Presbyn. Ch., St. Joseph, Mo., 1951. Spl. areal rep. World Council Chs., Holland, Belgium, Czechoslovakia, Hungary, Spain, Portugal; mem. Busey Inst. Com., 1944-45; mem. reorgn. com. Reformed Presbyterian Alliance, also member executive committee. Chairman U.P. Commn. Christian Education in Kentucky, 1925-27; moderator Synod of Ky., 1925-26, Synod of Mich., 1935. Mem. Governor's Mich. Labor Mediation Bd., 1937. Member Mayor's Interracial Com. of Detroit. Mem. Detroit Civilian Defense Com. Chmn. Greater Detroit Intercultural Interracial Fellowship. Trustee Louisville Theological Seminary, member American Seminar Com.; member Board Nat. Missions, Presbyn. Ch., U.S.A. (exec. com.). Pres. Detroit Council of Churches, 1942-43. Vice pres. the Presbyterian (publn.). Rep. Presbyterian. Ch. in U.S.A. in Europe, for reconstrn. and inter-church aid, 1945-49; chmn. scholarship com., World Council of Churches. Home: 62 Fairway Dr., Beverly Hills, Asheville, N.C. Died Nov. 25, 1957.

BUSH, Leonard T., advertising agent; b. England, Apr. 26, 1891; s. Edmund and Eleanor Jane (Turner) B.; came to U.S., 1898, naturalized, 1918; grad. Pierce Bus. Sch., Philadelphia, Pa., 1909; student New York U., 1915-16; m. Mary Ellen Down, Apr. 5, 1916 (died Jan. 20, 1920); children—Ellen Jean (Mrs. Ralph F. Anthony), R. Elizabeth (adopted); m. 2d, Edith L. Fleu, June 22, 1921. Copy boy, Phila. (Pa.) Bulletin, 1906; in advt. dept., C. J. Heppe & Son, music store, Phila., Pa., 1907-11; sec. to George Wharton Pepper, lawyer, 1911-13; with Compton Advt., Inc., and predecessor cos., since 1919, Blackman-Ross Co., 1919-21, The Blackman Co., 1921-35, Blackman Advt., Inc., 1935-36, firm name Compton Advt. Inc. since 1937, head of media dept., 1919-35, sec. and treas., 1935-36, dir. since 1936, vice president, secretary and treasurer, 1937-46, vice president, secretary, since 1947; treasurer and director The Compton Advertising, Inc. (an Ohio corporation). Served with Bureau of Yards and Docks, U.S. Navy, Washington, D.C., 1918. Mason (Shriner). Club: Pine Valley (N.J.) Golf. Home: Swamp Road, Rushland, Pa. Office: 630 Fifth Av., N.Y.C. 20. Deceased.

BUSHNELL, Charles Joseph (bo͝osh'nĕl), sociologist; b. Des Moines, Ia., May 1, 1875; s. Joseph Platt and Agnes O. (Tubbs) B.; Ph.B., U. Chgo., 1898, Ph.D., 1901, grad. work, 1908-09; m. Olga Lenore Hewitt, June 29, 1905. Prof. social sci. Albany (Ore.) Coll., 1901-03, Heidelberg U., Tiffin, O., 1903-07, Trinity U., Waxahachie, Tex., 1907-08, Okla. Agrl. and Mech. Coll., Stillwater, 1909-10; prof. sociology Lawrence Coll., Appleton, Wis., 1910-13; pres. Pacific U., Forest Grove, Ore., 1913-17; prof. social sci. Pa. Mil. Coll., Chester, 1917-18; Chautauqua lectr. for govt., 1918; now prof. sociology U. Toledo. Assisted in organizing charity work in Chgo. while student in univ., 1894-1901, in establishing ednl. and playground systems in various cities, summers 1906-11; mem. Toledo Met. Housing Authority. Mem. Am., Ohio (pres. 1927-28) sociol. socs., Am. Assn. Social Workers, Toledo Open Forum, Nat. Assn. Housing Ofcls., Am. Assn. U. Profs., Toledo Social Hygiene Council, Toledo Fgn. Policy Assn. (mem. council), Toledo Council of Churches, Family Welfare Council, Pi Gamma Mu (nat. treas.). Mason. Republican. Conglist. Author: Changing Patterns of Human Progress; Current Social Problems; Social Progress and Social Trends. Pub. lecturer. Home: 2130 Wyndhurst Rd., Toledo, O. Died Apr. 16, 1950.*

BUSHONG, Robert Grey (bo͝osh-ông'), lawyer; b. Reading, Pa., June 10, 1883; s. Jacob and Lillie (Roberts) B.; A.B., Yale, 1903; LL.B., Columbia, 1906; m. Helen Bowman, July 20, 1919; 1 dau., Sarah. Admitted to Pa. bar Sept. 23, 1906, and began practice at Reading. Mem. Pa. Ho. of Rep., 1909; pres. judge Orphans Court of Berks County, 1914-15; del. Rep. Nat. Conv., 1916, 24; mem. 70th Congress (1927-29), 14th Pa. District. Republican. Episcopalian. Mason. Author: Pennsylvania Land Law, 3 vols., 1938. Home: Sinking Spring, R.F.D. 2. Office: 24 N. 6th St., Reading, Pa. Died. Apr. 6, 1951; buried Charles Evans Cemetery, Reading.

BUSSER, Ralph Cox, (bŭs'ẽr), consul, lawyer; b. York, Pa., Jan. 3, 1875; s. William F. and Mary C. (Cox) B.; LL.B., U. Pa., 1899; m. Bertice S. Bates, 1902; children—Ralph C., Harold B., William F., John H. Practiced law at Phila. until 1909; Am. consul, Erfurt, Germany, 1909-13, Trieste, Austria, 1913-17, Almeria, Spain, 1917, Bergen Norway, 1917-19 Trieste, Italy, 1919-20, Corunna, Spain, 1920-22 Plymouth, Eng., 1922-26, Cardiff, Wales, 1926-30, Leipzig, Germany, 1930-40; retired from the Foreign Service, 1940; now practicing law in Phila. Mem. Am. Soc. Internat. Law, Phila. Law Acad., Am. Bar Assn., Lawyers Club of Phila., Am. Acad. Polit. and Social Science. Author: The German System of Industrial Schooling, 1913; Ordeal of the Press in Its Struggle For Freedom, 1954. Home: 42 Carpenter Lane, Germantown, Phila. 19. Address: Morris Bldg., Phila. 2. Died Mar. 6, 1955.

BUSSOM, Thomas Wainwright (bŭs-sŏm'), prof. Romance langs.; b. Reading, Pa., Mar. 11, 1889; s. William Elwood and Mary Elizabeth (Ray) B.; A.B., Amherst, 1912; grad. study, Johns Hopkins, 1912-13; Ph.D., U. of Minn., 1920; A.M., Wesleyan U., 1924; unmarried. Instr. in Romance langs., Amherst, 1913-14, Trinity Coll., Hartford, Conn., 1914-17, U. of Minn., 1919-20; asso. prof. Romance langs., Wesleyan U., 1920-23, prof. since 1923; dir. Honors College, Wesleyan U. since 1937. Served with U.S. N.R.F., advancing to lt. j.g., 1917-19. Mem. Modern Lang. Assn. America, Phi Beta Kappa, Delta Kappa Epsilon. Democrat. Episcopalian. Author: The Life and Dramatic Works of Pradon, 1922. Editor: Daudet's Fromont jeune et Risler aîné, 1937. Contbr. articles to lang. jours. Address: 77 Peach St., Middletown, Conn. Died Nov. 1951.

BUTLER, Arthur Pierce, educator; b. Boston, Apr. 21, 1866; s. Edward Knowles and Frances Elizabeth Lewis (Pierce) B.; A.B., Harvard, 1888; m. Lydia Raguet Farnham, Aug. 9, 1906; children—Arthur Pierce, Edwin Farnham. With Boston Woven Hose & Rubber Co., 1888-94, mgr. San Francisco and Chgo. brs., 1889-94; in Europe, 1894-96; asso. prin. and headmaster Morristown (N.J.) Sch., 1898-26, ret. Mem. Schoolmasters' Assn. N.Y.C., Head Masters' Assn., History Tchrs. Assn. of Middle States and Md., Nat. Econ. League (council for Md.), Delta Kappa Epsilon, Alpha Delta Phi. Unitarian. Clubs: Harvard (N.Y.C. and Boston). Home: Fernald Point Rd., Southwest Harbor, Me. Died Dec. 24, 1953.

BUTLER, Charles, architect; b. Scarsdale, N.Y., Oct. 14, 1870; s. Benjamin Franklin and Ellen Grenville (Parker) B.; A.B., Columbia, 1891, Litt.D., 1930; govt. diploma in architecture, École des Beaux Arts, Paris, 1897; Sc.D., Renssalaer Poly. Inst., 1931; m. Elizabeth Van Nostrand Marvin, Feb. 10, 1917. Began practice, N.Y. City, 1899; asso. with Cary S. Rodman until his death, 1911; asso. with others under title Robert D. Kohn, Charles Butler and assos.; designed Children's Hosp. at Johns Hopkins Hosp., 1909; new bldg. for Dept. of Interior, Washington, 1915; camp hosp., at Camp McClellan, Ala., 1918; permanent mil. hosp. for French Ministry of War, at Issy-les-Moulineaux, France; Nurses Home, Semi-Private Pavilion, Mt. Sinai Hosp., N.Y.; Temple Emanu-El, N.Y.; Chronic Disease Hosp., Welfare Island, N.Y. (with York and Sawyer), 1937-39. Was attached to French Ministry of War, as expert in hosp. constrn., 1915-16. Past pres. State Bd. Examiners of Architects; collaborator for Bd. Design, N.Y. World's Fair, 1939. Fellow A.I.A. (past pres. N.Y. chpt., dir.); mem. Société des Architectes Diplomés par le Gouvernment Français, Chevalier de la Legion d'Honneur. Democrat. Unitarian. Clubs: Century, (N.Y.C.); Interallié, Paris. Authors: Hospital Planning (with Addison Erdman), 1946. Home: 133 E. 39th St. Office: 56 W. 45th St., N.Y.C. Died 1953.

BUTLER, Charles Thompson, lawyer; b. Oregon, Mo., Apr. 30, 1884; s. Dr. John Thomas and Margaret (Thompson) B.; Ph.B., U. of Miss., 1905; A.M., U. of Mo., 1908, LL.B., cum laude, 1908; m. Annie W. Gilbert, Jan. 21, 1914; children—Laura G. (Mrs. Weston Bourret), Charles Thompson. Admitted to Miss. bar, 1907, Tex. bar, 1909, Calif. bar, 1921; practiced at Beaumont, Tex., 1909-20 and 1928—, New York (legal dept. The Texas Co.), 1922, Los Angeles, 1923-27; formerly atty. for S.P. Lines, Kansas City Southern Ry., The Texas Co. and various oil, gas and utility corps.; now atty. for Missouri Pacific Lines, Sun Oil Co.; formerly v.p. and attorney Nona Mills Co., Nona Mills Co., Ltd. Mem. Beaumont City Council and City Commn., 1930-32. Chmn. Beaumont Community Chest, Beaumont Open Forum, 1931. Mem. Am. Bar Assn. (com. on internat. legal war problems, 1943), Tex. State Bar (former dir.), Calif. State Bar, U.S. Supreme Court Bar, Jefferson County Bar Assn., Am. Judicature Society, Beaumont Chamber of Commerce (former director), Delta Psi, Phi Delta Phi, Order of the Coif. Standing Master in civil cases U.S. District Court, Eastern Dist. of Texas, Beaumont Div., 1940—. Methodist. Mason (Shriner). Home: Crosby Hotel. Office: Lynn Bldg., Beaumont, Tex. Died Feb. 20, 1954; buried Brookhaven, Miss.

BUTLER, Dan B(ernard), mayor; b. Ottawa, Ill., Jan. 18, 1879; s. Joseph and Nancy (Kinnally) B.; student Holy Family Sch., 1887-92, Cerighton U., 1892-98. Accountant, Pacific Express Co., Omaha, 1900-02; bookkeeper for county clk., Omaha, 1902-06; city clk., Omaha, 1906-12; mem. City Commn., charge of finance, fire, police and street maintenance depts., 1912-27; coal business, 1927-30; with State Banking and Ind. depts., 1930-33; finance commr. and mayor of Omaha, 1936-45. Mem. C. of C. Democrat. Catholic. Elk (past exalted ruler), Eagle. Club: Field. Home: 3169 Farnam St., Omaha. Neb. Died Mar. 14, 1953.*

BUTLER, Edmond Borgia, lawyer; b. New York, N.Y., Oct. 10, 1896; s. Edmond J. and Catherine (Quigley) B.; A.B. cum laude, Fordham Coll., 1916; A.M., Fordham U., 1917, LL.B. summa cum laude, 1920, LL.D., 1950, stud. N.Y.U. Grad. Sch. Bus.

Adminstrn., 1920-21; m. Marie Adele O'Connell, Sept. 8, 1928. Admitted to bar N.Y., practiced alone 1945-46; in partnership with Gerald B. Weldon, Edward T. Galloway, Joseph E. Swierzbinski, 1946-53, partner of Joseph E. Swierzbinski, 1953—; became lecturer in law, trusts and future interests Fordham U., 1923, later became asso. prof. law, trusts, future interests and real and personal property, professor of law 1935—. Referee in examination of accounts of coms. of incompetents, under presiding justice of Appellate Div., First Dept. of Supreme Ct., State of N.Y., 1927-45. Chmn. N.Y.C. Housing Authority, 1942-47; member of the Mayor's Com. on Unity, City of N.Y.; N.Y. City Commn. on Temporary Care of Children since 1947; member bd. govs. Nat. Housing Officials; mem. state commn. to celebrate anniversary of founding Supreme Ct. of State of N.Y. Mem. St. Vincent de Paul Soc. (pres. Sup. Council). Asst. sec. N.Y. State com. to investigate defects in the law and its adminstrn., 1923-25. Mem. Bar Assn. of City of N.Y. (com. on Domestic Relations Ct., com. on Real Property), N.Y. State chmn. com. to cooperate with Law Revision Commn.; committee on state legislation) and Bronx County bar associations, Forham Alumni Association (past pres.). National Catholic Alumni Assn. (past pres., chmn. nat. exec. com.). Clubs: Manhattan, Catholic (New York). Editor: Case Book on Trusts, 1930, 1931. Home: 3240 Henry Hudson Parkway, New York 63. Office: 50 E. 42d St., N.Y.C. 17. Died Mar. 21, 1956.

BUTLER, Edward Hubert, editor, pub.; b. Buffalo, N.Y., June 19, 1883; s. Edward H. and Mary Elizabeth (Barber) B.; prep. edn., Nichols Sch., Buffalo, 1897-99, Hill Sch., 1899-1903; A.B., Yale University 1907; married Kate Maddux Robinson; 1 daughter, Kate Robinson (Mrs. James H. Righter). Succeeded father as editor and publisher Buffalo Evening News, 1914, now editor, pub., pres. Buffalo Evening News, Inc. Pres. Am. Newspaper Pubs. Assn., 1928-29; v.p. Asso. Press, 1924-26; dir. Asso. Press (1940-50), Metropolitan Life Ins. Co., Am. Airlines; mem. N.Y. State Pubs. Assn. Mem. Saratoga Springs Commn., and Saratoga Springs Authority. Dir. Buffalo Museum of Natural Sciences; dir. and life member, Buffalo Fine Arts Academy. Mem. Delta Kappa Epsilon. Republican. Presbyterian. Clubs: Buffalo, Saturn, Buffalo Athletic, Buffalo Country; Yale (New York). Home: 672 Delaware Av. Office: 216 Main St., Buffalo. Died Feb. 19, 1956; buried Forest Lawn Cemetery, Buffalo.

BUTLER, Harold Lancaster, musician; b. Silver City, Ida., June 18, 1874; s. Gilbert Lancaster and Frances (Gilpin) B.; A.B., Valparaiso (Ind.) U., 1895, LL.B., 1896; grad. Gottschalk Lyric Sch., Chgo., 1897; studied with Sauvage (N.Y.C.), Blasco (Milan), Dubulle (Paris); m. Florence Higgins, May 23, 1898; 1 dau., Florence Vale. Dir. music dept. Valparaiso U., 1899-1903; dir. vocal dept., Syracuse U., 1903-05, 07-15; dean sch. fine arts U. Kan., 1915-23; dean College of Fine Arts, Syracuse U., 1923-46, dean emeritus, 1946—. Prin. basso Castle Sq. Opera Co., 1897-99, sang in 16 grand operas. Mem. Music Tchrs. Nat. Assn. (pres. 1926-28), Am. Acad. Tchrs. Singing, Nat. Assn. Pres.' State Music Tchrs.' Assn., Nat. Assn. Schs. Music and Allied Arts (pres. 1928-31). Republican. Episcopalian. Mason (32°), Rotarian. Has given over 500 recitals in N.Y.and Middle West. Home: 622 James St., Syracuse, N.Y. Died Aug. 22, 1957.

BUTLER, Henry Varnum, naval officer; b. Peterson, N.J., Mar. 9, 1874; grad. U.S. Naval Acad., 1895. Promoted through grades to vice adm., 1935; former comdr. Aircraft Squadrons, U.S. Battle Fleet; former comdt. and supt. Naval Gun Factory, Navy Yard, Washington; former comdt. Navy Yard, Charleston, S.C., and 6th, 7th and 8th Naval Dists. Retired Apr. 1, 1938. Died Aug. 6, 1957.

BUTLER, Hugh Alfred, U.S. senator; b. Missouri Valley, Ia., Feb. 28, 1878; s. Harvey Gibson and Ida (Wills) B. student Doane Acad., 1896; B.S., Doane Coll., 1900, LL.D., 1940; m. Fay Johnson, Feb. 5, 1903 (dec.); children—Lawrence Hugh (dec.), Robert Johnson (dec.). Became engr. C.,B.&Q. R.R., 1900, grain miller at Curtis, Neb., 1908-13; Crete Mills, 1913-18; former Butler-Welsh Grain Co., Omaha, Neb., 1918, of which was sr. partner; dir. Neb. Consol. Mills, Sheridan (Wyo.) Flour Mills, Inc. Mem. Rep. Nat. Com. from Neb. 1936; U.S. senator from Neb., 1941—. Mem. Omaha Bd. of Edn.; chairman bd. Doane Coll. Pres. Grain and Feed Dealers Nat. Assn., 1929-30; mem. bd. Rotary Internat., 1935-36. Republican. Conglist. Mason, I.O.O.F., M.W.A. Clubs: Omaha, Omaha Country, Omaha Athletic. Home: Omaha Athletic Club, Omaha, Neb. Office: Senate Office Bldg., Washington. Died July 1, 1954; buried Forest Lawn Cemetery, Omaha.

BUTLER, Jerome Ambrose, newspaperman; b. Ruskin, Tenn., July 20, 1899; s. John Albin and Anne (Ennis) B.; student University of Missouri, 1922-24; married Francelia McWilliams, July 4, 1939; one daughter, Annie (Mrs. John Wandell). With Chicago Tribune, 1925; St. Louis Globe-Democrat, 1926-28; Chicago Daily News, 1929-30; financial editor, later city editor Chicago Journal of Commerce, 1930-35, New York Herald Tribune, 1936; Herald Tribune's European edit. in Paris, 1936-40, city editor Paris Herald Tribune, 1939-40; city editor New York News, 1940, New York Sun, 1941; news editor Aviation News Mag., 1943-45; Washington bur. mgr., Chicago Journal of Commerce and corr. for London Mirror, 1945-46; Washington corr. Hearst Newspapers since 1946. Served in 1st World War with 6th regt., U.S. Marine. Awarded Purple Heart. Mem. Overseas Writers, White House Corr. Assn., Sigma Phi Sigma. Presbyterian. Club: National Press (Washington). Home: 2012 N. Oakland St., Arlington, Va. Office: 607 Times-Herald Bldg., Washington. Died May 30, 1949; buried Arlington Nat. Cemetery.

BUTLER, Joe Beaty, civil engring.; b. Omega, Okla., May 11, 1895; s. George Henry and Bessie May (Gordon) B.; B.S. in C.E., Okla. A. and M. Coll., 1915, B.S. in Edn., 1924; M.S. in C.E., Mo. Sch. of Mines, 1924, Civil Engineer, 1922; married Jessie Ethel Eyler, November 23, 1919; 1 daughter, Betty Jo (Mrs. J. R. Snowden). Engineering asst. railroad maintenance and valuation surveys in Middle West, 1915-17; highway survey and constrn., 1919-20; with dept. of civil engring., Mo. Sch. of Mines, since 1920, prof. and head of dept. since 1931; surveyor Phelps County, Mo., 1921-25; supervisor South Mo. County and Highway Planning and Mapping Studies, 1934-40. Served as lt. 109th Engrs., U.S. Army, 1917-19; with A.E.F., 10 months. Sec. Phelps County (Mo.) Defense Council, 1942-43. Mem. Am. Soc. Civil Engrs., Am. Rd. Builders Assn. (div. dir., v.p.), Am. Soc. for Engring. Edn. Missouri Soc. Professional Engrs. (pres. 1937), Nat. Soc. Profl. Engrs. (nat. dir.), Chi Epsilon, Theta Tau (hon.), Kappa Delta Pi, Phi Kappa Phi. Mason. Methodist (Rolla dist. lay leader). Clubs: Engineers (St. Louis); Lions (Rolla, Mo.). Author of bulletins: contributor to tech. jours. Home: 305 W. 9th St., Rolla, Mo. Died Mar. 27, 1955, buried Rolla, Mo.

BUTLER, John Cornelius, ex-congressman; b. Buffalo, July 2, 1887; married; 3 sons. Electrical supt. Marine A. Elevator, Buffalo; em. 77th-80th, and 82d Congresses, 44th N.Y. Dist. Republican. Home: Buffalo. Died Aug. 13, 1953.

BUTLER, John Winchel Spencer, lawyer; b. Burghill, O., Mar. 31, 1876; s. John Edward and Electa Louesa (DeWolf) B.; B.L., U. of Calif., 1901, M.L., 1902; m. Mattie E. White, July 20, 1899 (died May 17, 1934); children—Jack California, Mattie Myrtle (Mrs. Russell Alexander Harris); m. 2d, Mattie Eleana Richards, Jan. 30, 1937. Admitted to Calif. bar, 1902, and since practiced in Sacramento; senior partner of Butler and Reckers; assistant district atty., Sacramento County, 1907-08. Mem. bd. dirs. Sutter Hosp., Calif. Museum Assn. Mem. Am. and Sacramento bar assns., Calif. State Bar Assn. (pres. 1922-23), Golden Bear Soc. of U. of Calif., Kappa Alpha (Southern), Phi Delta Phi. Republican. Mem. Christian Church. Mason (Shriner; potentate Ben Ali Temple 1938), Odd Fellow. Home: 1114 39th St. (16). Office: Capitol Nat. Bank Bldg., Sacramento 14. Died Mar. 14, 1951.

BUTLER, Pierce, educator, clergyman; b. Clarendon Hills, Ill., Dec. 19, 1886; s. John Pierce and Eva Content (Whipple) B.; A.B., Dickinson Coll., Carlisle, Pennsylvania, 1906, A.M., 1910; Litt.D., 1944; graduate study Columbia and Union Theological Seminary; B.D., Hartford (Conn.) Theological Seminary, 1910, research fellow, 1910-12, Ph.D., 1912; married Ruth Lapham, June 29, 1926. Priest, P.E. Ch., 1940; reference asst. Newberry Library, 1916, head of book selection, 1917-19, custodian Wing Foundation in Typog. History, 1919-31; lecturer on history of printing and biblog. method. U. of Chicago, 1928-31, professor library history since 1931; assistant St. Paul's Church, Chicago, 1938-44. Member American Library Institute, Gutenberg Gesellschaft (Germany), Alpha Chi Rho. Episcopalian. Mason. Clubs: University, Caxton, Cliff Dwellers, Quadrangle. Author: Check List of Fifteenth Century Books, 1933; The Will of Nicolas Jensen, 1928; Introduction to Library Science, 1933; The Origin of Printing in Europe, 1940; The Reference Function of the Library, 1943. Books and Libraries in Wartime, 1944. Member editorial board The Library Quarterly. Home: 5807 Dorchester Av. Address: Grad. Library School, U. of Chicago, Chgo. Died Mar. 28, 1953.

BUTLER, Pierce, emeritus prof.; b. New Orleans, Jan. 18, 1873; s. James Pierce and Mary Louisa (Harrison) B.; A.B., Tulane U., 1892, A.M., 1894, LL.D., 1942; spl. student French philology, Sorbonne, 1894-95; Ph.D., Johns Hopkins, 1899, fellow in English, 1897-99; m. Cora Waldo, June 25, 1902; children—Virginia Waldo, Pierce, Mary Frances. Instr. and fellow in English and history, 1892-94, prof. English 1906-38, dean grad. faculty, 1913-18, dean H. Sophie Newcomb Meml. Coll., Tulane U., until 1938, now dean emeritus. Mem. Am. Hist. Assn., Modern Lang. Assn. Am., Simplified Spelling Bd., La. Hist. Soc., Phi Beta Kappa (ex-pres. Alpha of La.), Delta Tau Delta. Club: Round Table. Author: Legenda Aurea—Légende-Dorée, 1899; Life of Judah P. Benjamin, 1906; Women of Medieval France, 1907; Analytical Questions on Shakespearian Plays, 1936; The Unhurried Years, 1948; Laurel Hill and Later, 1954. Compiler: Materials for the Life of Shakespeare, 1930. Also contributor articles to Library of Southern Literature, Great American Lawyers, The South in the Building of the Nation, Sewanee Rev. Home: Laurel Hill, Natchez, Miss. Died Jan. 16, 1955.

BUTLER, Pierce, lawyer; b. St. Paul, Mar. 17, 1893; s. Pierce and Anna M. (Cronin) B.; Litt.B., Princeton, 1914; LL.B., Harvard, 1917; m. Hilda Vallandingham, Aug. 24, 1917; children—Pierce 3d, Maeve (Mrs. Robert H. Beck), Deirdre (Mrs. Jean Pellotier), Michael V. Admitted to Minn. bar, 1920, since practiced in St. Paul, as partner Doherty, Rumble, Butler & Mitchell; officer Leo Butler Co., Butler Ore Co. Served as lt., U.S. Army, 1917-19; lt. col., Minn. State Guard, 1951—. Home: 1600 Edgcumbe Rd., St. Paul 5. Office: First Nat. Bank Bldg., St. Paul 1. Died Mar. 26, 1957.

BUTLER, Ralph, otolaryngologist; b. Loag, Pa.; s. James and Rachel M. (James) B.; B.E., West Chester State Normal Sch. (now West Chester Tchrs. Coll.), 1893; M.D., U. Pa., 1900; studied diseases of ear, nose and throat, Vienna, 1901-02, Berlin, 2 mos., 1906; m. Ida Shaw, Dec. 18, 1905. Resident St. Joseph's Hosp., Phila., 1900-01; asst. aural surgeon U. Pa., 1902-06, instr. in otology, 1907-16, asst. prof. otology, 1916-24, prof. laryngology and vice dean of otolaryngology, grad. school of medicine, 1918-46, emeritus prof. laryngology, 1946—; prof. diseases of nose and throat Phila. Polyclinic and Coll. for Graduates in Medicine, 1912-18; cons. otolaryngology Lankenau Hosp., Drexel Home and Women's Hosp. of Phila. Fellow A.C.S.; mem. A.M.A., Am. Otol. Soc., Am. Laryngol. Assn., Am. Laryngol., Rhinol and Otol. Soc., Med. Soc. State Pa., Phila. County Med. Soc., Phila. Med. Club, Alpha Kappa Kappa. Republican. Presbyn. Mason. Address: 1930 Chestnut St., Phila. 3. Died Apr. 1954.

BUTLER, Robert, business executive; born in St. Louis, Missouri, July 16, 1897; s. Walter Butler; ed. St. Thomas Coll.; Dartmouth; U. of Minn.; LL.D., Villanova College, Duquesne Univ., Universidad de Santo Tomas de Villanueva (Havana, Cuba); m. Margaret Porter; children—Margaret Porter (Mrs. William Mitsch), Walter, Mary Helen (Mrs. Raymond J. Higgins), Catherine Jean (Mrs. Joseph F. Ringland). Engr. Java, Dutch East Indies; organized Walter Butler Co.; pres. Walter Butler Co., Walter Butler Constrn. Co., Walter Butler Bldg. Co., Inc., Walter Butler Shipbuilders, Incorporated, Builders Trust Company; member board directors American National Bank; built chem. warfare plant, Huntsville, Ala., and second largest Naval training station in U.S., at Farragut, Ida.; constructed oceangoing cargo vessels and frigates, Superior, Wis., and Duluth, Minn.; brought the Dionne quintuplets to Superior to christen five cargo vessels, 1943; state finance dir. for Dem. Nat. Com., 1944. Apptd. first United States ambassador to Australia, July 1946; A.E. and P., to Cuba, 1948. Commissioned capt., Philippine Army, 1916; lt., U.S. Army, 1918; dep. gov. and tribal war justice, Mati Davao, Philippine Islands. Trustee Coll. of St. Catherine. Mem. Am. Soc. Naval Architects and Marine Engrs., Delta Kappa Epsilon. Clubs: Minnesota, Athletic (St. Paul); Kitchi Gama (Duluth); Athletic (Spokane); White Bear Yacht; Metropolitan (N.Y.C.). Home: Stonehome Peninsula, White Bear Lake. Office: Minnesota Bldg., St. Paul 1. Died Sept. 15, 1955.

BUTLER, Rush Clark, lawyer; b. Northwood, Ia., Aug. 27, 1871; s. Lindley S. and Julia (Pickering) B.; Ph.B., Ia. State U., 1893; m. Isabelle Crilly, June 6, 1901; children—Rush C., Crilly, Milburn. Admitted to bar, 1894; successively member Cassoday & Butler; Cassoday, Butler, Lamb & Foster; Butler, Foster, Pope & Ballard; Butler, Pope, Ballard & Elting, Washington, ret. 1936. Retained by Interstate Commerce Commission, 1908-14, to represent public interest in investigation of relations between coal carrying roads and coal operators under the terms of Tillman-Gillespie joint resolution of Congress; gen. counsel Nat. War-Savings Com., Washington, 1917-18; general counsel Am. Coll. of Surgeons. Awarded Certificate of Accomplishment, State U. of Ia., 1947, Pres. Trade and Commerce Bar Assn., 1929-36; mem. Am. and Chicago bar assns., Ill. State Bar Assn. (pres., 1927-28), Northwestern University Associate, State Univ. of Ia. Alumni Assn. (pres. 1935-37), Beta Theta Pi, Phi Delta Phi; charter mem. Com. of Fifteen. Life mem. Art Inst., Field Mus., Chicago Hist. Soc. (all of Chicago). Republican. Conglist. Mason. Clubs: Industrial (pres. 1927-28), Law, Commercial (Chicago). Author: (with Cornelius Lynde) The Federal Trade Commission and the Regulation of Business Laws, 1915. Home: 7257 Hollywood Bl. Hollywood, Cal. Died Jan. 12, 1953; buried Forest Lawn Cemetery, Hollywood.

BUTMAN, Arthur Benjamin, foreign trade expert; b. Yonkers, N.Y., Oct. 31, 1865; s. Capt. Benjamin R. and Jane Millis (Hamlin) B.; ed. pub. and pvt. schs.; m. Desdemona Simonds, Dec. 31, 1891. Commercial agt. Dept. of Commerce, investigating industrial and trade conditions throughout the world, 1906-13; mgr. foreign trade dept. Hide and Leather (mag.) Boston, 1915-18; called to Washington, to organize a division in Dept. of Commerce for collection of data as to supplies of certain commodities for the Army and Navy, 1918; apptd. by Secretary Hoover, chief of shoe and leather mfrs.' div., Dept. of Commerce, 1921, retired 1933. Mem. S.A.R. Republican. Episcopalian. Mason (K.T.). Home: Maplehurst Inn, Antrim, N.H. Died Oct. 28, 1955; buried Hartford, Vt.

BUTTERWORTH, Charles Fred, business exec.; b. Lowell, Mass., Feb. 22, 1868; s. Hugh and Charlotte Elizabeth (Wilkins) B.; student pub. and pvt. schs.; m. Bessie Frances Bailey, June 13, 1894; children—Jeanne (Mrs. Irvin G. Ammen), Helen. Became auditor Draper Co. (afterward Draper Corp.), 1902, advanced to dir. and asst. treas., 1916, treas., 1929, v.p., 1938, chmn. bd., 1940, retired, 1951. Moderator, Town Meeting of Hopedale, 1930-50; commr. Hopedale Trust Funds; trustee and treas. Hopedale Community House. Chmn. Republican town com. of Hopedale, many yrs. Mason, Odd Fellow, K.P. Home: 49 Hopedale St. Office: care Draper Corp., Hopedale, Mass. Died Apr. 8, 1959; buried Pine Grove Cemetery, Milford, Mass.

BUTTERWORTH, G(eorge) Forrest, lawyer; b. N.Y.C., Feb. 26, 1892; s. George F. and Alice (Crawford) B.; grad. Browning Sch., 1908; A.B. magna cum laude, Columbia, 1913, LL.B., 1916; m. Isabel I. Baird, Oct. 4, 1916 (dec. Mar. 1919); children—George Forrest 3d, Isabel (Mrs. Silliman); m. 2d, Eva Horner, Apr. 2, 1921; 1 s. John F. Admitted to N.Y. bar, 1916; asso. Bowers & Sands, 1916-17; staff Cadwalader, Wickersham & Taft, 1917-18, 19-21, partner, 1921—; trustee U.S. Trust Co. N.Y. Sec., dir. Fedn. Protestant Welfare Agencies, Inc., 1942—; trustee Hobart Coll., Gen. Theol. Sem.; sec. Brookgreen Gardens, 1937—. Served with U.S. Army, 1918-19. Episcopalian (chancellor Prot. Episcopal Diocese N.Y.). Home: Hilltop Pl., Rye, N.Y. Office: 14 Wall St., N.Y.C. 5. Died Apr. 18, 1956.

BUTTS, Charles, geologist; b. Portville, N.Y., Sept. 18, 1863; s. William Othello and Eliza Jane (Southworth) B.; B.S., Alfred (N.Y.) U., 1899; M.S., 1900; D.Sc., U. Ala., 1927; m. Mellye Arledge, Nov. 1903; m. 2d, Ella Virginia Rickles Pearson, Nov. 30, 1909. Field asst., U.S. Geol. Survey, 1900; asst. to N.Y. state paleontologist, 1900-01; asst. geologist, U.S. Geol. Survey, 1901-09, paleontologist, 1909-12, geologist, 1912-33, retired; geologist Va. Geol. Survey, 1933, 37. Mem. Geol. Soc. Am., Geol. Soc. Washington, Washington Acad. Sciences. Republican. Presbyn. Contbr. to geol. periodicals. Home: 1808 Kenyon St. N.W. Washington. Died Oct. 4, 1946.

BUTTS, Edmund Luther, ret. army officer; b. Stillwater, Minn., Aug. 15, 1868; s. Edmund Gregory and Amelia Augusta (White) B.; B.S., U.S. Mil. Acad., 1890; m. Lilian Stafford Hatié, Jan. 9, 1900. Commd. 2d lt., inf., U.S. Army, 1890, advanced through grades to brig. gen., 1940; retired, 1932; spl. instr. phys. tng. throughout army, 1893-96; comd. 30th Inf., 3d Div., AEF France, to Aug. 1, 1918, 7th Inf., 3d Div., Aug.-Oct. 1918; participated in 6 major campaigns, including St. Mihiel, Meuse-Argonne and 2d Battle of Marne. Decorated D.S.C. (U.S.); Croix de Guerre with palm (Fracnce); 30th Inf. cited by Gen. Petain as sustaining principal shock of German attack, July 15, 1918, and regtl. flag received decoration of Croix de Guerre with palm; flag also awarded legend Rock of the Marn, July 14-18, 1918, authorized by Pres. Truman, 1948. Illustrated phys. tng. of soldiers, mus. drill, etc., at 1st mil. tournament, Madison Sq. Garden, N.Y. City. Became sr. instr. Minn. N.G. St. Paul, 1921. Author: Manual of Physical Training for the United States Army, 1897; The Key Point of the Marne, 1930. Home: 1800 Broadway, San Francisco 9. Died June 6, 1950; buried Presidio Nat. Cemetery, Presidio of San Francisco.

BUTZ, Reuben Jacob, lawyer, banker; b. Butzdale, Lehigh County, Pa., Jan. 13, 1867; s. Reuben D. and Mary A. Butz; A.B., Muhlenburg Coll., Allentown, 1887, A.M., 1890; LL.D., Franklin and Marshall Coll., 1924; LL.D., Muhlenburg College, 1938; married Mary E. Schindel, July 1, 1897 (died Sept. 27, 1908); m. 2d, D. Florence Horn, June 11, 1914 (died Aug. 22, 1941); children—Mary S. (Mrs. Mary Butz Leister), Ruth (Mrs. Ruth Butz Dent). Admitted to the Pa. bar, 1889, practicing at Allentown; mem. Butz, Hudders, Tallman & Rupp; former pres. Allentown National Bank. Chmn. Liberty Loan Drive, Lehigh County, World War. Pres. bd. trustees Muhlenberg Coll., 1913-50; ex-pres. bd. Cedar Crest Coll., Allentown, Pa.; past pres. bd. trustees Allentown Hosp.; mem. bd. of trustees Theol. Sem. of Reformed Church at Lancaster, Pa. Mem. Allentown C. of C. (first pres.), Phi Gamma Delta. Republican. Mem. Reformed Ch. in U.S. Mason (32°), Elk. Clubs: Livingston, Lehigh Country. Home: 1629 Hamilton St. Office: Allentown Nat. Bank Bldg., Allentown, Pa. Died Dec. 10, 1957.

BUWALDA, John Peter (bōō-wŏl-dȧ), prof. geology; b. Zeeland, Mich., Dec. 16, 1886; s. Peter John and Eva (Takoma) B.; B.S., U. of Calif., 1912, Ph. D., 1915; m. Irma Wann, Aug. 17, 1917; children—Peter John, May, William John, Robert John. Instr. in geology, U. of Calif., 1915-17; asst. prof. geology, Yale U., 1917-21; asso. prof., U. of Calif., 1921-25, prof., 1925-26, dean of summer sessions, 1923-26; prof. geology and head of div. geol. sciences, Calif. Inst. Tech., 1926-47, prof. geology, 1954—. Research asso., Carnegie Instn.; Professor of Geol. Cal. Inst. Tech. 1947-54, mem. federal bd. expert advisers on Yosemit Nat. Park. Mem. A.A.A.S., Geol. Soc. America, Seismological Soc. America dir.), Am. Assn. Petroleum Geologists, Am. Assn. Univ. Profs., Sigma Alpha Epsilon, Sigma Xi, Theta Tau, Gamma Alpha. Republican. Club: Faculty (Calif. Inst. Tech.). Home: 2103 San Pasqual St., Pasadena 10, Cal. Died Aug. 19, 1954.

BUYS, John L., coll. prof.; b. Sodus Point, N.Y., Nov. 18, 1897; s. William Henry and Lillian Mary (Dutcher) B.; B.S. Cornell U., 1919, M.S., 1921, Ph.D., 1922; m. Kathryn Slingerland, Sept. 9, 1922 (died Sept. 17, 1935); children—Marilyn Jean, Norman Slingerland, Janice Kathryn; m. 2d, Doris Louise Fonda, Sept. 7, 1940; 1 dau., Lauren Marie. Asst. in entomology Cornell U. 1919-21, instr. 1921-22, instr. in nature study summer sch., 1922-24; asst. prof. biology U. of Akron, 1922-23; prof. biology and head dept. St. Lawrence U., Canton, N.Y., since 1923. Served as pvt. U.S. Army, Sept.-Dec., 1918. Fellow Entomol. Soc. of Am.; mem. Beta Beta Beta, Alpha Gamma Rho, Sigma Xi. Universalist. Author: The Cicadellidee of the Vicinity of Ithaca, N.Y., 1924; Leafhoppers of Mt. Marcy and Mt. Mac Intyre, Essex County, N.Y., 1931. Home: 10 Hillside Rd., Canton, N.Y. Died May 24, 1955, buried Canton, N.Y.

BUZZNELL, Reginald W., army officer; apptd. brig. gen. Inf., Aug. 1942. Address: Camp Blanding, Fla. Died Jan. 23, 1959.*

BYOIR, Carl (bī'oir), pub. relations counsel; b. Des. Moines, Ia., June 24, 1888; s. Benjamin and Minna (Gunyan) B.; A.B., U. of Ia., LL.B., Columbia; m. Grace Lancaster, Dec. 7, 1921. Reporter, Iowa State Register, 1903-05; city editor Waterloo (Ia.) Times-Tribune, 1905-06; largely instrumental in introducing the Montessori System in America, 1912; pres. House of Childhood, Inc., 1912; with Morgan Shepard founded John Martin's Book for Children, 1913; circulation mgr. The Cosmopolitan (mag.), 1916; asso. chmn. Committee U.S. Govt. on Public Information, 1917-18; chmn. bd. American Gear Co. of Ill., 1918-26; chmn. bd. Am. Gear Co. of Mass., 1926-27; pres. Carl Byoir and Asso., Inc. 1930-46, chmn. bd. since 1946; elected dir. Schenley Distillers Corp.,1948; chmn. bd., dir. Bus. Orgn., Inc.; v.p., dir. Bymart, Inc. Director The Exchange National Bank of Chicago. Dir. United Action Campaign for Am. Legion, A.F.L., and Assn. of Nat. Advertisers, 1932. Gen. dir. of the birthday ball for the president, 1934, 35, 36, 37. Lt. col. U.S. Army Reserve. Decorated Chevalier Order of the Crown of Italy. Clubs: Advertising (New York); Army & Navy (Washington). Died Feb. 3, 1957.

BYRD, Richard Evelyn, explorer, naval officer (ret.); b. Winchester, Va., Oct. 25, 1888; s. Richard Evelyn and Eleanor Bolling (Flood) B.; ed. Shenandoah Valley Mil. Acad., Va. Mil. Inst. and U. of Va.; grad. U.S. Naval Acad., 1912; m. Marie D. Ames, of Boston, Mass., Jan. 20, 1915. Ensign U.S. Navy, 1912; advanced through grades to lt. comdr.; ret. Mar. 15, 1916; promoted to grade of comdr. after north polar flight, 1926; promoted to rank of rear adm., 1930. Entered Aviation Service Aug. 1917; comdr. U.S. Air Forces of Can., July 1918, until Armistice; comdr. aviation unit of Navy-MacMillan Polar Expdn., June-Oct. 1925; made flight in aeroplane with Floyd Bennett over North Pole and back to base at Kings Bay, Spitzbergen, May 9, 1926, covering distance of 1,360 miles in 15½ hours; made trans-Atlantic flight with 3 companions, from New York to France, distance of 4,200 miles, flight lasting 42 hours, June 29-July 1, 1927; flew over South Pole, Nov. 29, 1929; made 1st expdn. to Antarctic, 1928-30, 2d expdn., 1933-May 10, 1935; on both expdns. made important discoveries, among them being Edsel Ford Mountains and Marie Byrd Land; spent 5 mos. of winter night alone at scientific work in shadow of South Pole. In 1939 was made commander of United States Antarctic Service, an expedition sent to the Antarctic by Government; made four noteworthy flights resulting in discovery of five new mountain ranges, five islands, more than 100,000 square miles of area, a large peninsula, and 700 miles of hitherto unknown stretches of antarctic coast. During World War II served with Fleet Admiral King in Washington and Fleet Admiral Nimitz in Pacific; overseas 4 times (3 times in Pacific, once, Western front in Europe); cited 4 times; apptd. commanding officer U.S. Navy Antarctic Expdn., 1946. Advisor Dept. Defense, Polar defense and strategy. Holds 18 honorary degrees from colleges and universities. Presented by President Coolidge with Hubbard gold medal, June 23, 1926, "for valor in exploration"; awarded Congressional Medal of Honor, 1926, Special Congressional Medals (1930, 37 and 46), Congressional Life Saving Medal of Honor, Navy D.S. M., Navy Cross, Navy Flying Cross. Patron's medal of Royal Geog. Soc. (British, 1931), and gold medal Reale Societa Geografica (Italy, 1931); Elisha Kent Kane medal of Phila. Geog. Soc.; Langley medal of aerodromics of Smithsonian Instn., David Livingstone Centenary medal by Am. Geog. Soc., D.S.M. of State of N.Y. presented by Gov. Franklin D. Roosevelt; also 65 other medals; received from President Roosevelt (September 1940) gold star in recognition of services as commander of U.S. Antarctic Service Expedition, 1939-41; 22 citations from Navy Dept.; twice awarded Legion of Merit medal and special citation for service in Pacific, World War II; decorations by Portuguese and Rumanian govts.; also Officer Legion of Honor and Comdr. Legion of Honor (France) Medal, Order of Christopher Columbus, Santo Domingo; Grand Lodge Medal for Distinguished Achievement; Loczy Medal, Hungarian Geog. Society; Vega Medal, Swedish Geog. Society Mem. Phi Beta Kappa, Kappa Alpha, and about 200 other orgns. Episcopalian. Clubs: Century, Explorers (New York); Chevy Chase (Washington); Tavern, University, Somerset, Union Boat, Engineers', Country (Boston); Dedham Polo and Country. Author: Skyward, 1928; Little America, 1930; Discovery, 1935; Exploring with Byrd; Alone, 1938. Address: 9 Brimmer St., Boston. Died Mar. 11, 1957.

BYRNE, Christopher Edward, bishop; b. Byrnesville, Jefferson County, Mo., Apr. 21, 1867; s. Patrick and Rose (Byrne) B.; A.B., St. Mary's (Kan.) Coll., 1886, A.M., 1896; studied philosophy and theology, St. Mary's Sem., Balt. Ordained priest R.C. Ch., Sept. 23, 1891; s. asst. priest St. Bridget's Ch., St. Louis, 1891-97; pastor Sacred Heart Ch., Columbia, Mo., 1897-99, St. Joseph's Ch., Edina, Mo., 1899-1910, Holy Name Ch., St. Louis, 1911-18; named bishop of Galveston, July 18, 1918, consecrated Nov. 10, 1918. Home: 1402 Av. J., Galveston, Tex. Died Apr. 1, 1950; buried Calvary Cemetery, Galveston.

BYRNE, Sister Marie José, college pres.; b. New York, N.Y., Aug. 13, 1876; d. George Philip and Louise Abigail (Kingsland) Byrne; A.B., Coll. of St. Elizabeth, Convent, N.J., 1902; A.M., Columbia, 1909, Ph.D., 1915; mem. Sisters of Charity. Instr. Greek and Latin, Coll. of St. Elizabeth, 1902-05 and 1906-08, prof. Latin and Greek, 1910-21, dean 1921-40, pres. since 1940. Mem. Am. Assn. of Univ. Women, National Education Association, Classical League, Classical Association of Atlantic States. Translator: Considerations on Eternity (from Latin), 1920. Author: Prolegomena to an Edition of Decimus Magnus Ausonius, 1916. Address: College of St. Elizabeth, Convent Station, N.J. Died Nov. 11, 1951; buried Holy Family Cemetery, Convent, N.J.

BYRNE, William Thomas, congressman; b. Town of Florida, Montgomery County, N.Y., Mar. 6, 1876; LL.B., Albany Law Sch., 1904. Admitted to N.Y. bar 1904, practicing in Albany; mem. N.Y. State Senate, 1923-37; mem. 75th to 78th Congresses (1937-45), 28th N.Y. Dist.; mem. 79th to 82d Congresses (1945-53), 32d N.Y. Dist. (State having been reapportioned). Democrat. Home: Loudonville. Office: 11 N. Pearl St., Albany, N. Y.Died Jan. 27, 1952, buried St. Johns Lutheran Cemetery, Colonie, N.Y.

BYRNES, Ralph Leonidas, physician; b. Walcott, Ia., Mar. 30, 1878; s. Thomas (M.D.) and Jennie (Allen) B.; B.Sc., State U. Ia., 1902, M.Sc. and M.D., 1906; studied Harvard, 1911; spl. work in bacteriology, New Haven, 1918, in pulmonary tb, Yale Army Med. Sch.; m. Edith Whitney Merritt, Oct. 6, 1908. Hosp. service, 1906-08; practice at Avoca, Ia., 1908-10; at Pottenger's Sanatorium, Monrovia, Cal., 1910; prof. bacteriology and pathology U. Utah, dir. State Bd. Health and Lab., 1911-15; prof. pathology, bacteriology and clin. microscopy U. So. Cal., 1915-16; prof. diseases of the chest Coll. Med. Evangelists, Los Angeles, 1919-23; estab. first endocrine and mental hygiene clinic, Belvedere Health Center, Los Angeles County Health Dept., 1930. Commd. 2st lt. Med. R.C., 1912; 1st lt. Utah N.G. 1912-15; capt. and maj. various mil. camps in U.S., 1917-19; camp surgeon and pres. Bd. Tb Examiners, 1917-19; returned to pvt. practice, 1919. Diplomate Am. Bd. Internal Medicine. Mem. A.M.A., Cal., Los Angeles County med. socs., Am. Pub. Health Assn., A.C.P, Los Angeles Acad. Criminology (dir. and chmn. com., 1924), S.A.R., Am. Legion (chmn. and dir. Service Bur., 1928—, comdr. Allied Post 302, 1927; finance officer, 1928—), Pi Kappa Alpha, Phi Beta Pi. Republican. Episcopalian. Mason (K.T., Shriner). Clubs: Los Angeles Athletic, Am. Legion Luncheon. Optimist (bd. govs.). Home: 3706 W. 4th St. Address: Box 5846 Metropolitan Station, Los Angeles. Died Feb. 16, 1943; buried Family Plot, Walcott, Ia.

BYRON, Joseph Wilson, army officer; b. Fort Meade, S.D., June 3, 1892; s. Joseph Charles and Jane Frances (Wilson) B.; student Phillips Exeter Acad., 1909-10; B.S., U.S. Mil. Acad., 1914; m. Susanne Rice, Apr. 14, 1917; children—Jane Wilson (Mrs. Vernon N. Simmons, Jr.), Susanne (Mrs. Frank Kent Bradford), Joseph Rice, Edmund Rice (deceased), Sedgwick Rice. Commd. 2d lt., U.S. Army, and served, 1914-19; with W. D. Byron & Sons, tanners, Williamsport, Md., 1919-42, as asst. treas., 1922-24, v.p. and gen. mgr., 1924-28, pres., 1928-42; v.p., chmn. exec. com. Hagerstown Shoe &

Legging Co.; resigned to re-enter the Army; was chief Army Exchange Service; maj. gen. dir., Special Services Division; inactive duty, June 23, 1946; recommd. maj. gen. O.R.C., Feb. 27, 1947; pres. First Fed. Savings & Loan Assn. Industry advisor, NRA, 1933; sect. chief (dollar-a-year man), Office Production Management and WPB, 1941-42. Trustee Y.M.C.A.; dir. pres. Pub. Health Assn.; v.p. Boy Scout Council (Silver Beaver award); past president Hagerstown Rotary Club. Republican. Presbyterian. Clubs: Army and Navy, Chevy Chase (Washington). Home: 760 Preston Rd., Hagerstown, Md. Died Apr. 12, 1951; buried Rose Hill Cemetery.

C

CABELL, James Branch (kăb'ĕl), author; b. Richmond, Va., Apr. 14, 1879; s. Robert Gamble and Anne (Branch) C.; A.B., William and Mary, 1898; m. Priscilla Bradley Shepherd, Nov. 8, 1913 (dec.); 1 son, Ballard Hartwell; m. 2d Margaret Waller Freeman, June 15, 1950. Instr. French and Greek, William and Mary, 1896-97; worked in pressroom Richmond (Va.) Times, 1898; on staff N.Y. Herald, 1899-1901; on staff Richmond (Va.) News, 1901; engaged in coal-mining in state of W. Virginia, 1911-13; genealogist Va. S.R., 1919-20; historian Va. Soc. Colonial Wars, 1916-29, Va. Soc. S.A.R., 1917-23; pres. Va. Writers' Club, 1918-21; editor The Reviewer, 1921· editor Va. War History Commn., 1919-26; editor The Am. Spectator, 1932-35. Mem. First Families of Va., Soc. of the Cincinnati, Kappa Alpha (So.), Phi Beta Kappa. Episcopalian. Author: The Eagel's Shadow, 1904; The Line of Love, 1905; Gallantry, 1907; The Cords of Vanity, 1909; Chivalry, 1909; The Soul of Melicent (reissued as Domnei), 1913; The Rivet in Grandfather's Neck, 1915; The Certain Hour, 1916; From the Hidden Way, 1916; The Cream of the Jest, 1917; Beyond Life, 1919; Jurgen, 1919; The Judging of Jurgen, 1920; Figures of Earth, 1921; The Jewel Merchants, 1921; Joseph Hergesheimer, 1921; The Lineage of Lichfield, 1922; The High Place, 1923; Straws and Prayer-Books, 1924; The Silver Stallion, 1926; The Music from Behind the Moon, 1926; Something About Eve, 1927; Ballades from the Hidden Way, 1928; The White Robe, 1928; The Way of Ecben, 1929; Sonnets from Antan, 1929; Townsend of Lichfield, 1930; Some of Us, 1930; Between Dawn and Sunrise (with John Macy), 1930; These Restless Heads, 1932; Special Delivery, 1933; Smirt, 1934; Ladies and Gentlemen, 1934; Smith, 1935; Preface to the Past, 1936; Smire, 1937; The Nightmare Has Triplets, 1937; Of Ellen Glasgow, An Inscribed Portrait (with Ellen Glasgow), 1938; The King Was in His Counting House 1938; Hamlet Had an Uncle, 1940; The First Gentleman of America, 1942; The St. Johns (with A. J. Hanna), 1943; There Were Two Pirates, 1946; Let Me Lie, 1947; Witch-Woman, 1948; The Devil's Own Dear Son, 1949; Quiet Please, 1952; As I Remember It, published 1955; genealogical publications include: Branchiana, a Record of the Branch Family in Virginia, 1907; Branch of Abingdon, a Record of the Branch Family in England, 1911; The Majors and Their Marriages, 1915. Home: 3201 Monument Av., Richmond 21, Va.; (summer) Poynton Lodge, Ophelia, Va. Died May 5, 1958.

CABELL, Royal Eubank, ex-commr. internal revenue; b. Inglewood, Nelson County, Va., Mar. 12, 1878; s. Patrick Henry and Bettie Willis (Eubank) C.; A.B., Roanoke Coll., 1897; A.M., Princeton, 1898; student law U. Va.; LL.B., Richmond Coll., 1902; LL.D., Northwestern U., 1943; m. Lillian Hoge Lorraine, Nov. 12, 1908; children—Charles L. William, Lillian, Royal Eubank Jr. Member law firm Cabell & Cabell, 1902; postmaster Richmond, Va., 1906-09; U.S. commr. internal revenue, 1909-13; resumed law practice at Richmond. Dist. elector Roosevelt-Fairbanks ticket; del.-at-large Rep. Nat. Conv., Chgo., 1912. Mem. Phi Delta Theta, Theta Nu Epsilon, Phi Beta Kappa, Soc. of the Cincinnati in State of Va. Clubs: Metropolitan, University (Washington); Business Men's Deep Run Hunt. Home: 3412 Hawthorn Av. Office: Mutual Bldg., Richmond, Va. Died Sept. 8, 1950.

CABELL, Wymond, stock broker; b. Richmond, Va., Apr. 2, 1898; s. Henry Landon and Adah (Wymond) C.; grad. Woodberry Forest Sch., 1915; student U. of Va., 1915-18; m. Margaret Palmer Miller; children—Wymond, Landon. Employed by Branch, Cabell & Co., mem. New York stock exchange, Richmond, Va., 1919-20, partner, 1920-36, senior partner since 1936. Served with U.S. Navy, World War I. Pres. Assn. of Stock Exchange Firms 1944-1946; mem. bd. governors Assn. of Stock Exchange Firms 1941-1948, New York Stock Exchange 1942-1948. Treas. Soc. of the Cincinnati in State of Va. Clubs: Commonwealth (Richmond); River (N.Y.). Home: Tuckahoe Apts., Richmond 21. Office: 814 E. Main St., Richmond, Va. Died Feb. 14, 1956, Hollwood Cemetery, Richmond, Va.

CABLE, John Ray, college prof.; b. Freeman, Mo., March 5, 1891; s. Charley Chauncey and Dora Ann (George) C.; student William Jewell Coll., Liberty, Missouri, 1909-12; A.B., U. of Mo., 1913; B.S. in Edn., 1913; student U. of Wisconsin, summer 1913; A.M., U. of Chicago, 1917; Garth Fellow in Econ., Columbia, 1920, Ph.D., 1923; m. Alma Steele, January 6, 1916; children—John Charles, Dorothy Ann. Asst. cashier, Interstate Bank, Drexel, Mo., 1915-16; grad. asst. in economics, U. of Mo., 1916-17; asst. prof. economics, U. of Okla., 1917-23; asso. prof. finance and banking, Washington U., St. Louis, Mo., 1923-44; pres. Mo. Valley Coll., Marshall, 1944-48; prof., head dept. econ., John B. Stetson U., Fla., since Sept. 1948, Carnegie research grant, 1950; visiting professor economics University of Utah, summer 1925; cons. econ., St. Louis Clearing House Assn., 1943. Fellow Am. Geog. Soc.; mem. Am. Econ. Assn., Acad. Polit. Science, Arthus, Acacia, Beta Gamma Sigma, Phi Delta Kappa, Pi Gamma Mu, Alpha Pi Zeta. Democrat. Presbyterian. Mason. Club: University (St. Louis, Mo.). Author of The Bank of the State of Missouri; Survey Bank Taxation. Contbr. numerous articles and revs. to various publs. Home: 614 Cherokee St., DeLand, Fla. Died Dec. 2, 1951; buried Harrisonville, Mo.

CABOT, Francis Higginson; b. Staten Island, N.Y., Feb. 13, 1895; s. Francis Higginson and Maud (Bonner) C.; student Groton Sch., 1907-13; A.B., Harvard, 1917; m. Currie Duke Mathews, Apr. 18, 1921; children—Mary Currie, Francis Higginson. Clerk and asst. sec. with Am. Internat. Corp., 1918-23; v.p. Stone & Webster, 1923-35; pres. Gen. Pub. Service Corp., 1934-35, chmn. of bd., 1935-42; dir. Gen. Pub. Service Corp., 1943. Served as lt. (j.g.) U.S. Navy, 1918; with Office of Prodn. Management and War Prodn. Bd., Jan. 1941-Sept. 1943; dir. Commodities Bur., Jan. 1943—; asst. dep. dir. gen. for Industry Divs., Feb.-Apr. 1943. Episcopalian. Clubs: Knickerbocker, Century Assn. (N.Y.C.). Home: North, Mathews County, Va. Died Feb. 4, 1956; buried Ware Church, Gloucester, Va.

CABOT, Stephen Perkins, educator; b. Brookline, Mass., Sept. 20, 1869; s. Francis and Mary Louisa (Higginson) C.; A.B., Harvard, 1892; hon. M.A., Brown U., 1921; unmarried. Teacher Miss Pierce's Sch., Brookline, 1900-01; teacher French and German, St. George's Sch., Middletown, R.I., 1901-17, headmaster, 1917-26; exec. regent Avon (Conn.) Old Farms, chancellor, 1928-30. Pres. Judge Baker Guidance Center, 1932-47; dir. Community Recreation Service of Boston, 1931-47, pres., 1937-47; v.p. Family Welfare Soc. of Boston, 1930-39, pres., 1939-45; dir. Burroughs Newsboy Found., Boston, 1935-43; pres. New England Modern Language Assn., 1912-13. Mem. Headmasters' Assn., Motion Picture Research Council (New Eng. chmn. 1934-35; hon. v.p. since 1935), N.E.A., Mass. Civic League (v.p.). Unitarian. Clubs: Harvard (Boston). Author: Secondary Education in Germany, France, England and Denmark, 1930. Home: 112 Pinckney St., Boston. Died Dec. 11, 1951; buried Walnut Hill Cemetery, Brookline, Mass.

CADDELL, Albert D(avid), engr.; b. Toronto, Can., May 20, 1888; s. Walter William and Christine Margaret (Jack) C.; ed. pub. and collegiate schs. and Toronto Tech. Coll.; m. Helen Margaret Remy, Dec. 28, 1916; children—Jack Remy, William David, Helen Margaret Ligman. Came to U.S., 1912, naturalized, 1923. Works mgr. North American Watch Co., Mansfield, O., 1916-26; exec. sec. Mfrs. Club, also sec.-mgr. Chamber of Commerce and sec., treas. Mfrs. Assn. Central Ohio, 1927-34; exec. sec. and spl. rep., Div. Safety and Hygiene, Indsl. Commn. of Ohio, 1934-41; dir. safety Curtis-Wrigtht Airplane Div., Columbus, O., 1941-44; exec. sec. Am. Soc. Safety Engrs. since 1944; former mem. Ohio Indsl. Council; former dir. Mansfield Ohio Y.M.C.A. Mem. President's Conf. on Indsl. Safety. Registered professional engr., Ill. Evangelical Lutheran. Mason. Club: Rotary (past pres.). Editor: Engineering for Safety. Home: 2440 W. Estes Av., Chicago 45. Office: American Society of Safety Engineers, 20 N. Wacker Dr., Chgo. 6. Died Jan. 3, 1952.

CADE, Cassius Marcellus, banker; b. Noble County, O., Aug. 4, 1856; s. Samuel and Emeline (Rowe) C.; ed. Lebanon and Holbrooke Normal schs., Ohio; m. Lizzie Hartz, Nov. 28, 1899. Taught sch. in Ohio, 1872-80; sec. and treas. So. Kan. Townsite Co., Coldwater, 1884-87; real estate bus., Kingfisher, Okla. Ty., 1889-95; with Choctaw, Okla. & Gulf R.R., 1895-98; cashier State Nat. Bank, Shawnee, Okla., 1898-1923; v.p. Cimarron Valley Bank, Bank of Meeker; dir. First Nat. Bank (Geary, Okla.), Bank of Earlboro (Okla.). First county clk. Kingfisher County, 1889-91; first mayor, Coldwater, Kan., 1885; chmn. Rep. State Com., Okla., 1902-04; Okla. mem. Rep. Nat. Com., 1904-12; mem. Okla. State Bd. of Pub. Affairs, 1931-35; retired. Made mem. Okla. Hall of Fame, 1939. Catholic. K.P., Elk, Eagle. Club: Country. Home: 831 East Drive, Oklahoma City. Died Dec. 14, 1953; buried Rose Hill Cemetery, Oklahoma City.

CADEK, Ottokar T(heodore) (chä'dĕk), musician; b. Chattanooga, Tenn., Feb. 20, 1897; s. Joseph O. and Marguerite (Girard) C.; Artist diploma, Conservatory of Music, Zurich, Switzerland, 1916; B.M., Birmingham Conservatory of Music, 1944; m. Sara Hitchcock, Mar. 26, 1924; 1 dau., Jerrie. Made debut in Chicago, 1917; first violinist New York String Quartet, 1919-33, New York Chamber Music Soc., 1925-33; asso. condr. and concertmaster Birmingham Civic Symphony Orchestra, 1933-42; prof. of music U. of Ala. since 1943, also condr. Univ. Symphony Orchestra; dir. Cadek Conservatory of Music, Chattanooga, 1927-45; head of violin dept. and condr. Nat. Music Camp, Interlochen, Mich., summers, 1946-55; first violinist University Alabama String Quartet. Has made 2 transcontinental tours, appearing in concerts in large cities of U.S. Organized Birmingham Chamber Music Soc., 1936; dir. Chamber Music Festivals, 1938, 39, 40. Served as corpl., U.S. Army, 1918. Winner violin competition, Hug Bros., Zurich, 1914; presented Stradivarious violin for service to chamber music, 1948. Mem. Am. Assn. Univ. Profs., Music Teachers Nat. Assn., Am. String Teachers Assn. (mem. commn. on research). Unitarian. Contbr. articles in field to mus. periodicals. Home: 32 Guild's Wood, Tuscaloosa, Ala. Office: Univ. of Alabama. University, Ala. Died July 25, 1956; buried Mount Olivet Cemetery, Nashville.

CAFFEE, Robert Henderson, printer; b. Cincinnati, 1902; s. Albert H. and Mary A. (Veazey) C.; B.S., Carnegie Inst. Tech.; m. Doris Hunter, Oct. 17, 1931; children—R. Hunter, Peter K. Began as messenger U.S. Treasury Dept.; later telephone page, House of Reps.; salesman and sales mgr. various Pittsburgh printing firms, 1930-42; gen. mgr. William G. Johnston Co., 1942, pres. since 1943; dir. Manchester Savings Bank & Trust Co. Mem. Nat. Assn. Mfrs. (mem. indsl. problems com.), Printing Industry Am., Inc. (a founder 1945; pres. 1950-51), Soc. Advancement Management (past chmn. Pittsburgh adv. com.), Nat. Indsl. Advertisers Assn., Research and Engring. Council of Graphic Arts Industry, Advt. Council Pittsburgh (past dir.), Printing Industry of Pittsburgh (a founder, past v.p.), Indsl. Advt. Council of Pittsburgh, Sigma Nu. Presbyn. Clubs: Advertising, Sales Executives, Athletic Association (Pittsburgh). Speaker on business management topics before printing, advt. and other business groups. Home: 230 Parkway Drive, Pitts. 28. Office: 1130 Ridge Av., Pitts. 12. Died Apr. 13, 1957.

CAFFEY, Francis Gordon, judge; b. Gordonsville, Ala., Oct. 28, 1868; s. Dr. Hugh William and Alabama (Gordon) C.; A.M., Howard Coll., 1887, LL.D., 1919; A.B., Harvard, 1891, A.M., 1892; LL.D., Columbia, 1946; student Harvard Law Sch., 1892-94. Practiced, Montgomery, Ala., 1894-1902, becoming mem. Tompkins & Troy, later Watts, Troy & Caffey; became partner John C. Breckinridge, later firm of Clarke, Breckinridge & Caffey, N.Y.C., 1902; solicitor U.S. Dept. Agr., 1913-17; U.S. atty. for So. Dist. of N.Y., 1917-21; mem. Bouvier, Caffey & Beale, 1921-29; U.S. dist. judge So. Dist. N.Y., 1929-47. Mem. bd. visitors U.S. Mil. Acad., 1899; judge adv. gen. on staffs of Govs. Samford and Jelks, Ala., 1900-02. Trustee Nat. Child Labor Com. Served as lt. col. 3d Ala. Inf., Spanish-Am. War. Democrat. Baptist. Clubs: Harvard (N.Y. C.); Harvard (Boston). Home: Verbena, Ala. Died Dept. 20, 1951; buried Verbena.

CAHAN, Abraham, author; b. Vilna, Russia, July 7, 1860; s. Shachno and Sarah C.; grad. Teachers' Inst., Vilna; m. Anna Braunstein of Kieff, Russia, 1887. Came to U.S. 1882; edited weekly newspaper and monthly mag. in Yiddish. Editor-in-chief Jewish Daily Forward. Contbr. to leading Am. periodicals since 1887. Author: Yekl, A Tale of the New York Ghetto; The Imported Bridegroom and Other Stories; White Terror and the Red, 1905; Raphael Naarizoch (in Yiddish), 1907; The Rise of David Levinsky; Bletter von Mein Leben, (autobiography; 5 vols., in Yiddish). Address: 175 E. Broadway, N.Y. City. Died Aug. 31, 1951; buried Mount Carmel Cemetery (Workmen's Circle Plot), Brooklyn.

CAHILL, George Francis (kā'hĭl), urologist; b. New Haven, Jan. 1, 1890; s. Thomas J. and Margaret A. (McMahon) C.; M.D., Yale, 1911; Sc.D., Columbia, 1956; m. Eva Marian Wagner, Oct. 16, 1916; children—Margaret Frances (Mrs. H. Thomas McGrath), Marian Elizabeth (Mrs. Gordon Page Guthrie), George Francis. Pathol. med., surgical interne Bellevue Hosp., N.Y.C., 1911-14; surg. resident N.Y. Post-Grad. Hosp., 1914; instr. surgery N.Y.U., 1915-22; instr., asst. prof., asso. prof. urology N.Y. Post-Grad. Hosp., 1915-28, Columbia, 1919-39, prof. urology, dir. Squier Urol. Clinic, 1939-55, emeritus prof., 1955—; head dept. urology Coll. Phys. and Surg. Columbia, also exec. officer Columbia-Presbyn. Med. Center until 1955; cons. urologist Presbyn. Hosp. and Vnderbilt Clinic; cons. surgeon Willard Parker Hosp.; cons. urologist at Babies and Yonkers Gen., Francis Delafield hosps.; pres. med. bd. Presbyn. Hosp., 1946-49. Commd. 1st lt. 1917, capt. 1917-18. Med. R.C.; British 3rd Army, 1917, French Army, 1918, comdg. officer Base Hosp. 119, AEF, France, 1918-19. Mem. spl. adv. com. U.S. VA, 1946-52. Recipient gold medal A.M.A., 1947, Trimble medal, 1948. Fellow A.C.S. (gov.), N.Y. Acad. Sciences, A.A.A.S.; mem. Am. Bd. Urology (pres. 1953-54, trustee), A.M.A., Am. Urol. Assn. (pres. 1952-53), Am. Assn. Genito-Urinary Surgeons, Internat. Soc. of Urology (pres. 9th congress, N.Y.C. 1952), Harvey Society, Acad. Medicine (N.Y.), N.Y. Urol. and Surg. Soc., Soc. of Clin. Urology (pres. 1947-

48), Phi Rho Sigma. Clubs: Yale (N.Y.C.); Metropolitan, Camp Fire of America. Contbr. med. publs. on urol. surgery, adrenals, cancer. Home: Campbell Rd., Suffern, Rockland County, N.Y. Office: 121 E. 60th St., N.Y.C. 22. Died July 25, 1959.

CAHN, Bertram Joseph, chmn. bd. and pres. B. Kuppenheimer & Co., Inc.; b. Chgo., Nov. 10, 1875; s. Joseph and Miriam (Schwab) C.; A.B., Yale, 1896; LL.B., Northwestern U.. 1899; m. Irma B. Kuppenheimer, November 5, 1907; children—Betty (Mrs. J. Robert Cohler), Anabel (Mrs. Lester E. Frankenstein). Admitted to Ill. bar, 1899; practiced in Chgo., 1899-1913; asso. B. Kuppenheimer & Co., Inc., 1913-—, sec., treas., 1917-21, v.p., 1921-27, pres., 1932-—, chmn. bd., 1927-—; mem. adv. bd. Lumbermen's Mutual Casualty Co. Life trustee Northwestern U.; past pres., trustee Chgo. Ethical Soc.; past pres., dir. Chicago Crime Commn., Civic Fedn.; past chmn. Board of Advisors Unemployment Compensation, State of Ill.; past chmn., dir. Chgo. Area Project; formerly industry mem. War Labor Bd., 6th Region; dir. Citizens Assn. Chgo.; chmn. commn. for rehabilitation House of Correction; mem. bd. Salvation Army; dir. Chgo. Assn. Commerce and Industry. Trustee Chgo. Hort. Soc. Dir. Ill. Mfrs. Assn., Asso. Employers of Ill.; past chmn. Research Council for Econ. Security; chmn. bd. Ill. Div. Am. Cancer Soc. Mem. Ill., Chgo. bar assns. Clubs: Midday, City, Economic, Standard, Yale, Commercial (Chgo.). Home: 270 S. Western Av., Lake Forest, Ill. Office: 3040 W. Lake St., Chgo. 12. Died Aug. 11, 1959; buried Rosehill Cemetery, Chgo.

CAINE, John Thomas, III, stock show mgr.; b. Logan, Utah, June 4, 1882; s. John Thomas and Kathinka (Ballif) C.; B.S., in Animal Husbandry, Agrl. Coll. Utah, 1903, M.S.A., Ia. State Coll. Agr. and Mechanic Arts, 1905; m. Jean Crookstone, July 10, 1912; children—Margaret Jean, John Thomas, Robert Preston. Instr., asst. prof. and prof. in charge dept. animal husbandry Utah Agrl. Coll., 1906-16, dir. extension div., 1916-20; with comml. livestock work, 1920-25; chief of Packers and Stockyards Adminstrn., U.S. Dept. Agr., Washington, 1925-27; with Internat. Live Stock Show of Chgo., 1927-43; gen. mgr. Nat. Western Stock Show, Denver, 1943-—. Mem. Am. Assn. Animal Prodn., Nat. Live Stock Assn., Nat. Wool Growers Assn., Phi Kappa Phi, Gamma Sigma Delta. Democrat. Clubs: Men's (Logan); Timpanogos (Salt Lake City); Saddle and Sirloin (Chgo.). Co-Author: Western Agriculture. Home: Denver. Deceased.

CAINE, Milton A., mining exec.; b. Saginaw, Mich., Aug. 26, 1882; s. George A. and Julia (Fradd) C.; student Mich. Agrl. Coll. (now Mich. State Coll.) 2 yrs.; B.S., E.M., Mich. Coll. of Mining and Tech. 1905; m. Elisabeth Dodds, Oct. 28, 1908; children—Milton Dodds, Sara Julia, Robert Norman. Exec. v.p., dir. Tenn. Corp.; v.p., dir. Tenn. Copper Corp.; v.p. Miami Copper Co.; dir. S.A. Gold and Platinum Co., Gen. Development Co. Mem. Am. Inst. Mining and Metall. Engrs., Tau Beta Pi. Republican. Presbyn. Clubs: Bankers (N.Y. C.); Wykagyl, Tennis (New Rochelle). Home: 150 Valley Rd., New Rochelle, N.Y. Office: 61 Broadway, N.Y.C. 6. Died Dec. 25, 1955.*

CAIRNS, Alexander, clergyman, lecturer; b. Belfast, Ireland, Oct. 7, 1871; s. James and Mary Jane (McMullan) C.; brought to U.S., 1873; Ph.B., Adrian (Mich.) Coll., 1897, B.D., 1899, M.A., 1909, LL.D., 1926; m. Mary Annie Obee, Aug. 12, 1897; children—Ruth Esther, Grace Annie, John Alexander, Mary Margaret, William Morris. Ordained ministry, 1897; tchr. in Japan, 1897-1901; pastor in U.S., 1901-06; lecturer, 1907-20, 26-—; pastor High Street Presbyn. Ch., Newark, 1920-25; columnist, 1927-29; pastor of Community Presbyn. Ch., Bloomfield, N.J., 1933-42; now retired. Mem. N.J. Audubon Soc., Sigma Alpha Epsilon. Mason. Has lectured in every state of U.S. and throughout Canada. Guest preacher in Ireland, 1934, 37. Titles of lectures: The Man Worth While; The Man of Galilee; Why God Loves the Irish; The Bishop of D—; Lincoln the Liberator; Savonarola, etc. Home: Richmond, Me. Died Oct. 5, 1957.

CAIRNS, W(illiam) D(eWeese), educator; b. Troy, O., Nov. 2, 1871; s. Samuel Alexander and Mary Brook (Gunn) C.; prep. edn., high sch., Troy, 1885-89; A.B., Ohio Wesleyan U., 1892; A.B., Harvard, 1897, A.M., 1898; Ph.D., U. Göttingen, Germany, 1907; m. Iva Crofoot, Aug. 25, 1898 (dec. Nov. 2, 1926); children—Mary Catherine, Robert William; m. 2d, Bertha Noble Pope, June 17, 1930. Instr. mathematics, high sch., Troy, O., 1894-96, Calumet, Mich., 1898-99; instr. mathematics, Oberlin Coll., 1899-1904; asso. prof., 1904-20, prof., 1920-39, emeritus, 1939-—. Mem. Math. Assn. Am. (sec.-treas., 1915-—), A.A.A.S., Am. Math. Soc., Nat. Council Tchrs. of Mathematics, N.E.A., Phi Beta Kappa, Alpha Tau Omega. Republican. Conglist. Original investigations in integral equations, in binomial theorem as applied to probability, math. analysis, investigation of preparation for univ. mathematics. Home: Oberlin, O. Died July 15, 1955.

CALDER, Curtis Ernest, corp. officer; b. Winfield, Kan., May 15, 1890; s. Christopher and Sophia MacIntosh Calder; ed. high sch.; m. Bennie Marie Glanton, Oct. 13, 1914; children—Curtis Ernest, Jr., Gordon Samuel, Norman Bruce, Benjamin Glanton (dec.). Various positions in public utilities, 1906-13; sec. Tex. Power & Light Co., 1913-17, v.p., 1917-21, pres., 1921-27; president Dallas Power and Light Co., Texas Electric Service Co., 1921-27; pres. American & Foreign Power Co., Inc., N.Y. City, 1927-44; chmn. Electric Bond and Share Company, 1944-52, chairman executive committee, 1952-—; vice chairman Ebasco Services, Inc.; dir. Am. Bank Note Co., Devon Securities Corp., Am. & Fgn. Power Co., Inc., Canadera, Ltd., Fed. Ins. Co., Vigilant Ins. Co., Lehman Corp , Nat. City Bank, Cathay Ins. Co., Metropolitan Opera Assn., U.S. and International Securities Corp., U.S. and Fgn. Securities Corp. Comdr. Order Merit (Ecuador), Gran Oficial, Orden de Cristobal Colon (Dominican Republic). Chmn. Community Chest, Dallas, Tex., 1923-24; public gov. N.Y. Stock Exchange, 1939-41; director general of the W.P.B., 1943. Member of the Saint Andrews Society. Presbyterian. Mason. Clubs: Metropolitan, St. Nicholas, Recess, Sleepy Hollow Country (Tarrytown). Home: 4 Hampshire Circle, Bronxville, N.Y. Office: 2 Rector St., N.Y.C. 6. Died Apr. 2, 1955; buried Kensico Cemetery, Valhalla, N.Y.

CALDWELL, Benjamin Palmer, chemist; b. New Orleans, Apr. 2, 1875; s. Dr. John Williamson and Mary Howe (Palmer) C.; A.B., Tulane U., 1893, B.E., 1895, Ch.E., 1896; Ph.D., Johns Hopkins, 1901; m. Helen Mercer Wright, Dec. 23, 1902; children—Benjamin Palmer, Hamilton Mercer Wright (dec.). Fellow Tulane U., 1893-95, successively instr. in chemistry, asst. prof., asso. prof., prof. gen. and theoretical chemistry, 1895-1916; absent on leave as fellow in chemistry, Johns Hopkins, 1899-1901; visited France, Germany, and Eng., 1901, examining chem. ednl. facilities; prof. chemistry Oglethorpe U., Atlanta, 1916-19; prof. analytical chemistry Bklyn. Poly. Inst., 1919-27, prof. physical chemistry, 1927-45, emeritus prof. physical chemistry, 1945-—. Fellow A.A.A.S., New Orleans Acad. Sciences; mem. Am. Chem. Soc. (charter mem. and ex-pres. La. sect.), Phi Beta Kappa (charter mem. and ex-pres. Alpha of La.), Phi Lambda Upsilon, Sigma Xi. Democrat. Presbyn. Home: 1725 Gen. Pershing St., New Orleans 15. Died Sept. 21, 1950.

CALDWELL, Bert Wilmer, hosp. cons.; b. Effingham, Ill., Feb. 20, 1875; s. Henry D. and Ann Mary C.; A.B., Austin Coll., Effingham, Ill., 1894; M.D., Barnes Med. Coll., St. Louis, 1898; m. Georgia Hanson, Jan. 26, 1894; 1 son, Henry Hanson. Began practice of medicine at St. Louis, 1898; with Isthmian Canal Commn., in charge Santo-Tomas and other hosps., Republic of Panama, during building of Panama Canal, 1905-15; mem. Rockefeller-Red Cross Commn. to the Balkans, 1915; attached to Am. Embassy in Berlin, as commr. to insp. Allied prison camps, Germany, 1916; supt. Allegheny Gen. Hosp., Pitts., 1916-17; in charge 8th dist. USPHS, Chgo., 1919; mem. Yellow Fever Commn., Rockefeller Found. in Mexico, in charge Gulf Coast from Tampico to Yucatan, 1920-22; supt. University Hosp., State U. Ia., 1922-25; supt. Tampa (Fla.) Municipal Hosp., 1925-27; exec. sec. Am. Hosp. Assn., 1927-43. Served in Spanish-Am. War; col. Med. Dept., U.S. Army, World War I. Republican. Presbyn. Mason. Editor: Hospitals, 1936-42. Home: Rockton, Ill. Died July 1951.

CALDWELL, Daniel Templeton, clergyman; b. Huntersville, N.C., June 27, 1892; s. John Smiley and Anna (Brown) C.; A.B., Davidson (N.C.) Coll., 1914; B.D., Union Theol. Sem., Richmond, Va., 1917, Th.D., 1933; S.T.B., Princeton Theol. Sem., 1918; student Princeton U., 1917-18; D.D., Hampden-Sydney Coll., 1935; m. Cora Belle Sloan, Sept. 10, 1918; children—Daniel Templeton, Mary Ruth. Ordained to ministry Presbyn. Ch., 1917; pastor Immanuel Presbyn. Ch., Wilmington, N.C., 1918-25, Second Presbyn. Ch., Petersburg, Va., 1925-41; dir. Defense Service Council, Presbyn. Ch. in U.S., 1941-47; dir. of Christian education synod of North Carolina Presbyn. Ch., U.S., 1947-51; supply pastor, Morehead Presbyterian Church, Morehead City, N.C., 1951. Chmn. board trustees Gen. Assembly's Training Sch., Richmond, Va.; moderator, Synod of Va., 1941. Mem. Friar Club (Princeton Theol. Sem.). Republican. Mason. Club: Petersburg (Va.) Rotary (pres. 1937), Country (Va.). Author: Bible Teaching in Cooperation with Public Schools, 1936; also They Answered the Call, published in 1952. Home: 1400-A Whilden Pl. Office: Watson Bldg., Greensboro, N.C. Died Jan. 29, 1952; buried Thyatira Presbyn. Church Cemetery, Salisbury, N.C.

CALDWELL, Francis Cary, educator; b. Ithaca, N.Y., Dec. 25, 1868; s. George Chapman and Rebecca Stanly (Wilmarth) C.; A.B., Cornell U., 1890, M.E. in Elec. Engring., 1891; Nat. Polytechnicum, Zürich, Switzerland, 1892-93; m. Louise Taft, Orton, July 12, 1900; children—Anne Davenport (wife of Dr. W. A. Kramer, dec.), Edward Orton (dec.). With Thomson-Houston Electric Co., 1891-92; asst. prof. elec. engring. Ohio State U., 1893-97, asso. prof., 1897-1901, prof., 1901-39, prof. emeritus, 1939-—; dir. Ranco, Inc.; engr. Div. of Vehicle Lighting of Bur. of Motor Vehicles, Ohio; lectr. on illumination, Inst. of Technology, Prague, Czechoslovakia, 1924-25; hon. curator Collection of Applied Electricity, Ohio State Museum, 1931-—. Trustee Antioch Coll., Yellow Springs, O., 1923-34. U.S. rep. on pub. lighting, Internat. Commn. on Illumination, 1935-—. Registered profl. engr., Ohio. Fellow Am. Inst. E.E.; mem. Ohio Traffic Safety Council, Illuminating Engring. Soc. (dir. 1921-24), Soc. for Promotion Engring. Edn., Tau Beta Pi, Sigma Xi, Phi Beta Kappa, Theta Xi, Eta Kappa Nu. Republican. Unitarian. Clubs: Faculty (Ohio State University), Engineers. Author: Notes and Questions for the Dynamo Laboratory, 1900; Electrical Engineering Problems, 1904-13; Electrical Engineering Test Sheets, 1911; Modern Lighting, 1930. Editor: Technical Letters on Industrial Lighting, 1919. Contributing editor E.M.F. Electrical Year Book, 1922-26; General Engineering Handbook, 1931-40; Pender's Handbook for Electrical Engineers, 1935. Home: 206 16th Av., Columbus, O. Died July 21, 1953.

CALDWELL, Fred T., public utilities exec.; b. Bloomfield, Iowa, 1883; grad. Ia. State Coll., 1903. Vice pres. and dir. Internat. Telephone & Telegraph Corp.; vice chairman, Internat. Standard Electric Corp., Federal Telephone and Radio Corp.; exec. v.p. and dir. Internat. Telephone & Telegraph Corp. (Espana), Compania Telefonica Nacional De Espana, Madrid; v.p. and dir. Standard Electrica S. A. Madrid; dir. Compania Radio Aerea Maritina Espanola, Madrid; Sociedad Anonima Radio Argentina, Buenos Aires; Standard Electrica Lisbon. Home: 770 Park Av., N.Y. 21. Address: International Telephone & Telegraph Corp., 67 Broad St., N.Y.C. Died Dec. 21, 1951.

CALDWELL, Hugh Milton, ex-mayor Seattle; b. Knoxville, Tenn., June 7, 1881; s. Thomas M. and Jane (Kearsley) C.; LL.B., Nat. U. Law Sch., Washington, 1903, LL.M., 1904; m. Sarah Smith Howard, Oct. 21, 1903; children—Eleanor Washington, Jane Kearsley, Anne Howard, Hugh Milton; m. 2d, Lois McCrea, Nov. 26, 1937. Began practice law at Seattle, 1905; mem. Caldwell & Riddell, 1908-13, Wright, Kelleher & Caldwell, 1913-16; later in practice, Santa Barbara; chief dep. pros. atty. King County, Wash., 1911-12; corp. counse City of Seattle, 1916-18 (resigned); elected mayor of Seattle, 1920. Pvt. 3d Rgt., N.G. Wash.; commd. capt. M.I. Div. U.S. Army, 1918; trans. as maj. Judge Adv. Dept.; served at Camp Lewis, Wash. Mem. Am., Cal. bar assns., Phi Sigma Kappa, Am. Legion. Republican. Episcopalian. Mason (32°, K.T., Shriner, past imperial potentate N.A.). Clubs: University; Jonathan (Los Angeles). Citrus grower. Home: San Clemente, Cal. Deceased.

CALDWELL, John Handly, milling co. exec.; b. Liberty, Mo.; s. John Calhoun and Winifred Davis (Cobb) C.; grad. Haymes Acad., Excelsior Springs, Mo.; m. Sarah Inez Kinley (dec. Mar. 21, 1951); children—John Handly, Winifred (Mrs. Crasher); m. 2d, Mary Lewers Latshaw, Dec. 31, 1953. Vice pres. Ralston-Purina, 1928-46; chmn. bd. Hoosier Soybean Mills, Inc., Marion, Ind. Mem. Chgo. Bd. Trade, 1928-46; pres. St. Louis Mchts. Exchange, 1929; bd. arbiters Nat. Arbitration Com., 1946-—. Exec. v.p. Associated Fund, Inc.; trustee Drake U., 1936-53. Mem. Nat. Grain and Feed Dealers Assn. (past v.p.). Home: 4605 Lindell Blvd. Office: Merchants Exchange Bldg., St. Louis. Died Nov. 18, 1954.

CALDWELL, Louis Goldsborough, lawyer; b. Oak Park, Ill., Sept. 25, 1891; s. John Davis and Susan (Cook) C.; A.B., Amherst Coll., 1913; M.A., LL.B., Northwestern U., 1916; m. Irene Buysse, Oct. 31, 1921; dau., Barbara Suzanne. Admitted to Ill. bar, 1916; mem. Kirkland, Fleming, Green, Martin & Ellis, Apr. 1919-July 1928, and since Feb. 1929; in charge Washington office as resident partner since Sept. 1930; gen. counsel Fed. Radio Commn., July 1, 1928-Feb. 23, 1929. Lecturer Northwestern U., 1916 and 1919-28. Enlisted in Am. Field Service, 1917; enlisted in Foreign Legion, French Army, 1918, promoted to 2d lt., 1919. Awarded Croix de Guerre (France), 1918. Alumni trustee Amherst Coll., 1928-39; mem. Am. Bar Assn. (chmn. com. radio law 1928-29, chmn. com. communications 1929-33; mem. spl. com. administrative law 1933-36; chmn. 1933-35; mem. Washington com.), Fed. Communications Bar Assn. (pres. 1936-37, mem. exec. com., 1937-40), D.C. Bar Assn. (chmn. com. on administrative practice, 1938-41; chmn. administrative law section 1943-44), Assn. Interstate Commerce Practitioners, Am. Law Inst., Inst. of Radio Engineers, Phi Beta Kappa, Order of Coif, Delta Upsilon, Phi Delta Phi. Conglist. Clubs: National Press, Metropolitan (Washington, D.C.); Tavern (Chicago). Editor Jour. Radio Law, 1931-32. Home: 2900 Cleveland Av. N.W. Office: 800 World Center Bldg., Washington 6. Died Dec. 11, 1951; buried Tecumseh, Mich.

CALDWELL, Robert Breckenridge, lawyer; b. Vandalia, Mo., Jan. 5, 1882; s. Samuel Kincaid and Mary Kate (Flowerree) C.; B.A., U. of Mo., 1903, LL.B., 1907; m. Eula McCune, Oct. 3, 1908; children—Robert Breckenridge, Catherine. Admitted to Mo. bar, 1907, and since engaged in practice of law; mem. Caldwell, Downing, Garrity & Eastin, Kansas

City, Mo.; chmn. and agent Fed. Res. Bank of Kansas City, Mo., Dist 10, 1938-53; dir., chmn. bd. Cook Paint & Varnish Co.; dir. Gustin-Bacon Mfg. Co., Standard Steel Works, C.J. Patterson Co., and others. Trustee under will of William Rockhill Nelson, deceased. Mem. Am., Kansas City, Mo. State bar assns., Kansas City Lawyers Assn., Kappa Sigma, Phi Delta Phi, Phi Beta Kappa, Order of Coif. Formerly mem. Mo. State Bd. of Law Examiners. Democrat. Clubs: University, Kansas City, Mission Hills, Country (Kansas City, Mo.). Home: 1215 W. 57th St. Terrace. Office: 1000 Fed. Reserve Bank Bldg., Kansas City, Mo. Died Sept. 3, 1956; buried Forest Hill Cemetery.

CALDWELL, Robert J., cotton mcht., mfr., banker; b. Louisville, May 12, 1875; s. John Armour and Margaret W. (Cook) C.; grad. Polytechnic Inst. of Brooklyn; LL.D., Rollins Coll., 1927; m. Jean B. Holmes, Apr. 25, 1913 (dec.); children—Tracy Fairfax, Jean (Mrs. William M. von Hubler). Began as salesman in cotton house; established R. J. Caldwell Co. and Connecticut Mills Co., 1910, Canadian Conn. Cotton Mills, R. J. Caldwell, Ltd., and Conn. Cottons Co., 1913; retired from active business; formerly dir. of many corps. and of Seaboard Nat. Bank; mem. council of Profit Sharing Industries, Akron. Veteran of the 1st Cavalry, Nat. Guard of N.Y. During World War financed airplane investigation which resulted in reorganization of Air Service. Was chmn. com. on industrial relations of Nat. Rep. Adv. Com. on Policies and Platform, also of indsl. relations com. of Nat. Rep. Club; spl. industrial commr. to Europe for U.S. Govt., 1919; guest of French Govt., 1919, in behalf of rehabilitation of devastated area; spl. economic commr. for U.S. Govt. to Great Britain, Czechoslovakia and Belgium, 1920, and was awarded honorary diploma Masarykova Akademia Prace, Prague, 1923; presented to the City of Prague in 1928, the first statue erected in Czechoslovakia, of President Masaryk. Served as first Am. del. to Fedn. of League of Nations Socs., Vienna, 1923; accomplished financial mission, 1923, to Czechoslovakia and Hungary, resulting in 1st internat. loan to Hungary through League of Nations; del. Internat. Y.M.C.A. Boys' Conf., Austria, 1923; organizer and chmn. Exec. Com. of Russian Refugee Relief Soc. of America; exec. vice chmn. Mayor La Guardia's com. for completing Czechoslovak Pavilion at New York Worlds Fair; dir. of the Save the Children Fedn., Am. Friends of Lithuania, Baltic Am. Soc. Mem. com. Religious Minorities of Ch. Peace Union; mem. Council on Fgn. Relations; mem. Am. Com. of Internat. Labor Office of Geneva and Montreal; mem. France-America Soc., English Speaking Union, Pilgrims, Acad. Polit. Sciences, Am. Soc. Legion of Honor, St. George's Soc. of N.Y. Decorated twice by Old Russian Red Cross, 1st and 2d class; also recipient of Cross of the Holy Sepulchre from the Patriarch of Jerusalem; Order of the White Rose (Finland); Order of Grand Duke Gedyminus (Lithuania); Order of Comdr. of White Lion (Czechoslovakia); decorated by King of Montenegro; Chevalier Legion of Honor (France); Palmes d'Or of Order of Crown, League of Honor (Belgium). Episcopalian. Clubs: Overseas Press, Church (New York); Seawanhaka-Corinthian Yacht; University (Winter Park); Economic. Author: Industrial Democracy; Coming Events Cast Their Shadows Before; Paramount Issue; also writer of many articles. Delivered addresses at Yale, Columbia and Rollins Colls. Home: 439 E. 51st St., N.Y.C. 22. Died Dec. 21, 1951; buried Rosedale Cemetery, Orange, N.J.

CALDWELL, Stephen Adolphus, univ. dean, univ. prof.; b. Bienville, La., Mar. 1, 1889; s. J.D. and Cordelia (Whitney) C.; student U. of Richmond, 1907-10; A.B., La. State U., 1925; A.M., U. of Tex., 1927, Ph.D., 1934; m. Grace Martin, June 1, 1929; children—Stephen Adolphus, Elaine Caldwell Brown. Prin., Ringgold High School, 1911-14; prin. Amite City High Sch., 1914-15; supt. Morehouse Parish schs., 1915-22; asso. prof. La. Tech., 1922-26; instr. U. of Tex., 1931-34; dean Northeast Jr. Coll., Monroe, La., 1936-37; asst. prof. La. State U., 1934-36, prof., 1937-44, dean jr. div. 1944—. Chmn. Istrouma Area Boy Scouts of Am. (recipient Beaver Award); mem. bd. dirs. Community Chest, Baton Rouge, La. Mem. So. Econ. Assn., La. Coll. Conf., La. Acad. Sci., S.W. Social Science Assn. (pres. 1948-49) Club: Lions (dist gov.). Author: A Banking History of Louisiana, 1935; Social Science; Economics and government, 1937; (bulletin) The Trade Territory of New Orleans, 1936; (bulletin) Economic Development of the Shreveport Trade Area, 1943. Contbr. articles to law, business and social sci. jours. Home: 1487 Steele Blvd., Baton Rouge. Died Apr. 16, 1956; buried Roselawn Cemetery, Baton Rouge.

CALDWELL, William, educator; b. Edinburgh, Scotland, Nov. 10, 1863; student Stewart's Instn. (Classical sch.), Edinburgh; M.A., Edinburgh U., 1884, 1st class honors in phiolsophy, 1886, Dr. Mental and Moral Sci., Bruce of Grangehill scholar and medallist, 1886, Sir William Hamilton fellow in mental philsophy, 1887, Shaw fellow in mental philosophy, 1889; postgrad. Germany, Paris, Eng., 1887-91; m. Atha Haydock. Asst. prof. logic and metaphysics U. Edinburgh, 1887-88; govt. examiner in philosophy U. St. Andrews, 1889-92; called to Sage Sch. of Philosophy, Cornell U., 1891, U. Chgo., 1892; prof. moral and social philosophy Northwestern U., 1894-1903; prof. moral philosophy McGill U., 1903—. Mem. Am. Psychol. Assn., Am. Philos. Soc. Author: Schopenhauer's System in its Philosophical Significance (substance of Shaw Fellowship Lectures given at Edinburgh U., 1893)—imported by Scribner's from Blackwood's. Contbr. to leading reviews and jours. on philosophy, ethics and sociology. Address: Montreal, Can. Deceased.

CALHANE, Daniel Francis, educator, cons.; b. Bradford, Mass., Aug. 19, 1869; A.B., Harvard, 1894, A.M., 1896, Ph.D., 1904; m. Luette E. Richmond, Sept. 8, 1906. With Worcester Poly. Inst., 1903-36, as instr., asst. prof. and prof. indsl. and applied electro-chemistry, prof. emeritus, 1936—; now engaged in pvt. research and cons. work. Fellow A.A.A.S.; mem. Electrochem. Soc. Inventor of small type electric furnace for high temperatures. Author of papers on pure and applied chemistry. Address: 32 Berkmans St., Worcester, Mass. Died Sept. 20, 1951.

CALHERN, Louis, actor; b. Bklyn., Feb. 19, 1896; s. Eugene Adolph and Hubertina (Friese) Vogt; student pub. schs. of St. Louis; m. Ilka Chase (div.); m. 2d, Julia Hoyt (div.); m. 3d, Natalie Schafer (div.); m. 4th, Marianne Stewart, Nov. 25, 1946 (div. 1955). With Prospect Stock Co., Bronx, N.Y., 1912; played with George M. Cohan, Song and Dance Man, 1923; in Cobra, 1924; with Lauretta Taylor, In A Garden, 1925; with Emily Stevens, Medda Gabler; with Ethel Barrymore, The Love Duel, 1929; Dinner at Eight, 1933; Golden Boy, London, 1938; Life with Father, 1940; Jacobowsky and The Colonel, Theatre Guild, 1944; The Magnificent Yankee, 1946. Appeared in motion pictures, Notorious, Arch of Triumph, High Society. Served in France with 143d field arty., 40th div. as sgt. World War I. Recipient Donaldson award Delia Austria medal, Barter Theatre award for best New York performance, season 1945-46. Clubs: Players, Lambs (N.Y.C.). Died May 1956.*

CALHOUN, Byron E., hotel exec.; b. Chgo., Oct. 4, 1902; s. Edward N. and Stella M. (Wilson) C.; student Cornell; m. Lucille Peters, June 4, 1934; children—Carole, Byron E., Caren. Auditor Western Exchange Bank, Kansas City, Mo., 1918-19; mgr. Hotel Bellerive, Kansas City, 1920-22, Hotel Lowery, St. Paul, 1923-27, Hotel Muehlebach, Kansas City, 1934, Hotel St. Paul, 1934-42; owner Hotel Radisson, Mpls.; pres. Intercontinental Hotels Corp., Hotel Weylin Corp., N.Y.C., also dir. Mem. Minn. Hotel Assn. (past pres.), Mpls., Northwestern hotel assns. Clubs: Greenwich (Conn.) Country; Lafayette (Mpls.); N.Y. Athletic, Cloud (N.Y.C.). Address: 130 East End Av., N.Y.C. Died Sept. 4, 1957; buried Greenwich, Conn.

CALHOUN, Fred Harvey Hall, geologist; b. Auburn, N.Y., June 27, 1873; s. John Hamilton and Ellen (Hall) C.; B.S., U. Chgo., 1898, Ph.D., 1902; m. Grace B. Ward, June 9, 1904; children—John Ward, Fred. Asst. in geol. dept. U. Chgo., 1899-1902; asst. prof. geology and physics Ill. Coll., 1902-04; prof. geology and mineralogy Clemson (S.C.) Coll., 1904—, also dir. agrl. dept., 1915-33, dean sch. chemistry and geology, 1933-50; cons. geologist S.A.L. R.R.; asst. geologist U.S. Geol. Survey, 1903-15; geologist U. Colo., summer, 1903, 05, 09, U. Chgo., summer, 1907, U. Mich., summer 1911, U. Ia., summers 1914, 15. Fellow Geol. Soc. Am., A.A. A.S.; mem. S.C. Acad. Science (pres.), Phi Delta Theta, Alpha Nu, Alpha Chi Sigma, Phi Kappa Phi. Episcopalian. Rotarian. Author of geol. monographs. Home: Clemson, S.C. Died May 2, 1959; buried Churchyard St. Paul's, Pendleton, S.C.

CALL, S(amuel) Leigh, publisher; b. Springfield, Ill., Mar. 31, 1872; s. James J. and Elizabeth Frances C.; ed. high sch. and bus. coll.; m. Mary Bradish; 1 dau., Mary Leigh. Ed. and co-pub. Ill. State Journal, Springfield, 1923-28; joint owner Journal Printing Co. since 1928, now pres.; dir. Springfield Marine Bank; v.p. Springfield Stockyards Co. Exec. sec. to Lt. Gov. John G. Oglesby, 1909-13, 1917-21. Home: 931 S. 4th St., Springfield, Ill. Died Nov. 19, 1952.

CALLAGHAN, Alfred (kal'ă hăn), municipal ofcl.; b. San Antonio, Mar. 30, 1890; s. Bryan and Adele (Guilbeau) C.; B.S., St. Louis Coll. (later, St. Mary's U.), San Antonio, 1910; m. Anna Cadena, Sept. 17, 1947. Utility clerk Internat. & Great Northern R.R. 1912; deputy tax collector, Bexar County, San Antonio, 1914-18, city of San Antonio, 1919-21; with Park Dept., 1921-27; Corp. Ct., San Antonio, 1927-39; taxation commr., San Antonio, 1943-47, became mayor, 1947; with Office of Coonty Clk., 1959—. Mem. C. of C. Democrat. Roman Catholic. Home: 3720 W. Commerce St., San Antonio 7. Office: City Hall, San Antonio 5. Died Feb. 16, 1959; buried Fort Sam Houston Nat. Cemetery.

CALLAGHAN, Stephen, judge; b. Lebanon, Mo., Oct. 3, 1876; s. William Henry and Lucy (Fulbright) C.; grad. University Acad., Columbia, Mo., 1896; LL.B., N.Y. Law Sch., 1898; m. Ethel Van Dien, Nov. 28, 1905. Admitted to N.Y. bar, 1898; mem. Bd. of Aldermen, N.Y.C., 1910-11; justice Municipal Court, 1912-15; apptd. by gov. as justice Supreme Court of N.Y., May 5, 1915, and elected for term, 1915-29; Republican. Episcopalian. Mem. Brooklyn Bar Assn., Brooklyn C. of C. Mason. Clubs: Lawyers, Hamilton, Montauk. Home: 584 4th St., Brooklyn, N.Y. Died Oct. 1952.

CALLAHAN, Donald A., lawyer; b. Galena, Ill., Sept. 8, 1876; s. Thomas and Mary Jennings (Rowe) C.; studied law in office of W. T. Hodson, Galena, 1898-1902; m. Agnes Kelly, May 10, 1905; 1 dau., Mary (Mrs. George W. Zeller). Admitted to bar of Ill., 1902, Ida., 1919; tchr. in Ill., 1898-99; practiced law Galena, Ill., 1902-13, Chgo., 1913-19; gen. practice law Wallace, Ida., 1919—; mem. Ida. Ho. of Reps., 1921-23, State Senate, 1923-33; dir. and pres. Callahan Consolidated Mines, Inc., Wallace, Ida., 1937—. Served as chmn. OPA, Shoshone County, Ida., World War II. Mem. Am. Mining Congress (dir., v.p.). Republican. Roman Catholic. K.C. (past state dep. Ida.), Elk, Rotarian. (past pres.). Home: 221 Cedar St. Office: Gyde-Taylor Bldg., Wallace, Ida. Died Oct. 26, 1951.

CALLAHAN, John, supt. schs. emeritus; b. Goldens Bridge, N.Y., Dec. 16, 1865; s. M. J. and Johanna (Walsh) C.; ed. high sch., Prescott, Wis., and by pvt. study; received unlimited state certificate for Wis., 1894; LL.D., U. Wis., 1950; m. Minnie A. Powers, Sept. 12, 1889; children—Gertrude Leona, Alice Beatrice, Julia Tormey. Tchr. rural schs. until 1889; ward prin. schs., Crookston, Minn., 1889-90; supervising prin., Glenwood City, Wis., 1890-98, New Richmond, 1898-1901; supt. schs., Menasha, Wis., 1901-18; state dir. vocational edn., Wis., 1918-21; Wis. state supt. schs., 1921-50, state supt. schs. emeritus, 1950—. Chief State School Officers. Mem. N.E.A., Wis. Assn. Sch. Adminstrs., Wis. Edn. Assn., Am. Vocational Assn., Wis. Anti Tb Assn. (past pres., mem. sr. council). Clubs: Rotary (Madison); City (Milw.); Elks (Menasha). Home: 402 S. Owen Dr. Office: State Capitol, Madison, Wis. Died May 10, 1956; buried Clayfield, near Ellsworth, Wis.

CALLANAN, Edward A., rubber co. exec.; b. Springfield, Mass., 1889; grad. Mass. Inst. Tech., 1914. Pres., dir. Brown Rubber Co., Inc., Lafayette, Inc. Home: 625 Ridgewood Dr., West Lafayette, Ind. Office: Box 1000, Lafayette, Ind. Died Apr. 14, 1956.

CALLAWAY, Ely Reeves, Sr., cotton mfr.; b. La Grange, Ga., June 5, 1880; s. Abner Reeves and Mary Wilburn (Ely) C.; attended high school and business dept. Valparaiso (Ind.) U.; m. Loula Walker, Oct. 21, 1908; children—Bessie Walker, Mary (Mrs. M. R. Waters), Loula (Mrs. B. P. Albright), Ely Reeves, Jr. Vice pres., gen. mgr. Callaway's Dept. Store, LaGrange, 1910-18; pres. LaGrange Nat. Bank and LaGrange Savings Bank, 1919-28; became treas. Callaway Mills, Inc., N.Y. City, 1922, vice president of Callaway Mills Co., LaGrange, Ga. until retirement, December 1, 1953. Owner of Highlands Hereford Farm, La Grange. Dir. of various Liberty Loan drives during World War I, Troup County, Ga.; state dir. Ga. United War Work campaign, 1918; associate administrator War Finance Committee and chairman, 9th District War Finance Com., World War II; chmn. Troup Co. Nat. War Fund, Ga., World War II. Trustee LaGrange Coll., Troup Farmers Found., LaGrange. Mem. Nat. Assn. Credit Men (chmn. Textile Com. 1914). Mem. nat. council, Boy Scouts of America, and chairman for Georgia, 1921, honorary member National Council, 1954; awarded Silver Beaver, 1943; committeeman Roosevelt Memorial Assn. of Ga., 1919; asso. dir. Bapt. Seventy-five Million Campaign for Ga., 1919; v.p. Ga. Bapt. Conv., 1934; pres. Salvation Army Advisory Bd., La-Grange, Ga., 1932; dir., past v.p. Ga. State Y.M. C.A.; trustee Ga. Bapt. Orphan's Home, Hapeville, Ga. (v.p. 1937). Democrat. Baptist. Clubs: Rotary (pres. 1938), Highland Country. Home: 1201 Vernon Rd., LaGrange, Ga. Died Nov. 5, 1956; buried La-Grange.

CALLAWAY, Llewellyn Link ret. justice; b. Tuscola, Ill., Dec. 15, 1868; s. James Edmund and Mary Elizabeth (Link) C.; student pvt. and pub. schs., Virginia City, Mont., and Hamilton Sch., Phila.; student U. Mich., 1886-87, LL.B., 1891; m. Ellen N. Badger, Dec. 12, 1894; children—Miriam (Mrs. Sam D. Goza, Jr.), James E. (dec.), Llewellyn L., Mary Elizabeth (Mrs. Gordon Doering). Practiced at White Sulphur Springs, Mont., 1891-94, Virginia City, 1894-1903; county atty. Madison County, Mont., 1894-98; mayor of Virginia City, 3 terms; Supreme Court commr. of Mont., 1903-04; judge 5th Jud. Dist. of Mont., 1905-13 (tried many important cases, especially water suits); chmn. Mont. Conservation Commn., 1908-09; chmn. Bd. Law Examiners of Mont., 1917-22; acting chmn. Legal Adv. Bd., Cascade County, Mont., and four-minute speaker, World War; apptd. chief justice Mont. Supreme Court to fill vacancy caused by death of Theodore Brantly, 1922, chief justice, 1922-35; retired. Mem. Mont. Geog. Bd., Am., Mont. (past pres.), Cascade County (past pres. bar assns.). Republican. Mason (33°; past grand master Mont.; past grand high priest, past grand comdr.; mem. supreme council So. Jurisdiction U.S., insp. gen. in Mont.), Elk. Pres. Great Falls Commercial Club, 1922. Home: 427 Lawrence St., Helena, Mont. Died Aug. 6, 1951.

CALLAWAY, Merrel Price, banker; b. Mitchell County, Ga., Nov. 26, 1872; s. James and Nellie (Furlow) C.; LL.B., Mercer U., Macon, Ga., 1897; m. Annie Crutchfield, 1901 (died 1908); 1 son, William Crutchfield; m. 2d, Henrietta Etheridge, Sept. 16, 1911 (died 1942); children—James Etheridge (deceased), Henrietta Drewry, Mary Irwin; m. 3d Hazelhurst Plant McCaw, December 1949. Connected with fire insurance business at Macon, Georgia, 1898; admitted to Ga. bar, and practiced at Macon, 1901-10; spl. counsel for r.r. cos. before Interstate Commerce Commn., Washington, D.C.; pres. Continental Trust Co. and v.p. Fourth Nat. Bank, Macon, 1918-19; v.p. Guaranty Trust Co. of New York, 1919-42; trustee Central of Ga. Ry. Co., 1942-48, chmn. bd., 1948-53, hon. chmn. and advisor bd. dirs., 1953—, dir. also dir. Ocean Steamship Co. of Savannah, Citizens & Southern Nat. Bank of Savannah. Pres. trust div. Am. Bankers Assn., 1 yr.; an organizer and pres. 2 yrs. Corporate Fiduciaries Assn. N.Y. Hon. fellow Met. Mus. Art, N.Y.; mem. Phi Delta Theta. Episcopalian. Clubs: Union (N.Y.); Chevy Chase (Washington); Oglethorpe (Savannah). Address: Savannah, Ga. Died June 16, 1957.

CALLEN, Alfred Copeland (kăl'lĕn), mining engr.; b. Pen Argyl, Pa., July 17, 1888; s. Benjamin Tucker and Jennie (Fear) C.; E.M., Lehigh U., 1909, M.S., 1911; m. Ida C. Saylor, Apr. 9, 1912; children—Katharine Edna, Martha Saylor, Alfred Copeland. Instr. physics, Lehigh Univ., 1909-10, mining engring, 1910-11; mgr. Pottstown (Pa.) Machine Co., 1911-14; instr. mining engring., U. of Ill., 1914-16, asso., 1916-17; prof. mining engring. and dir. mining extension, W.Va. U., 1917-24; prof. mining engring. and head of dept., U. of Ill., 1924-39; prof. mining engring., Lehigh U., since 1939, dean Coll. of Engring., 1939-45. Editor: Coal Mine Management, Chicago, 1922-29. Gov. Ill.-E. Iowa Kiwanis Dist., 1930; trustee Kiwanis Internat., 1932-36, pres., 1936-37. Mem. Am. Inst. Mining and Metall. Engrs. (chmn. mineral industry education division 1944), Mining and Metallurgical Society of America, Illinois Mining Inst. (pres. 1930), American Soc. Engring. Edn. (member of council 1941-44), Theta Delta Chi, Tau Beta Pi, Sigma Xi, Omicron Delta Kappa, Pi Tau Sigma. Republican. Methodist. Mason (K.T., 33°). Author: various engring. and ednl. bulletins and articles. Home: 820 Beverly Av., Bethlehem, Pa. Died July 30, 1951; buried Nisky Hill Cemetery, Bethlehem.

CALLENDER, Harold, newspaper corr.; b. Kansas City, Kan., Sept. 29, 1892; s. Edward Russell and Marie Louise (Cable) C. student univs. of Kan., N.Y. and the Sorbonne, Paris; m. Bessie Stough. Corr. N.Y. Times, Europe, 1926-40, S.A., 1941, Washington, 1942-43, Algiers, North Africa, 1943, Paris, 1944—. Decorated Legion of Honor, 1947; recipient Overseas Press Club of America's award for best press reporting from abroad of foreign affairs, 1949. Mem. Anglo-Am. Pess Assn. of Paris (pres. 1957). Club: Travellers (Paris). Author: A Preface to Peace, 1944; Fun Tomorrow, 1953. Address: New York Times, 37 rue Caumartin, Paris, IXme, France. Died Oct. 8, 1959.

CALLENDER, Sherman D., ret. judge; b. Hartsgrove, Ashtabula County, O., Mar. 18, 1869; s. Robert F. and Lois (Winslow) C.; grad. New Lyme (O.) Inst., 1891; Ph.B., Oberlin (O.) Coll., 1895; LL.B., Ohio State U., 1898; m. Sylvia Cornell, Apr. 23, 1904; children—Alice, Lois Winslow, Sylvia Elizabeth. Practiced law at Detroit, 1899-1930; judge Recorders Court, Detroit, 1930-35; circuit Court judge, 3d Judicial Dist., Mich., 1936-48, ret. 1948; sec. Vinton Corp. Mem. Detroit Charter Commn., 1918; mem. Mich. Ho. of Reps., 1925-27; chmn. Mich. Code of Criminal Procedure. Mem. Am., ich., Detroit bar assns., Detroit Bd. Commerce, Mich. Soc. S.A.R. Republican. Conglist. Mason (32°, Shriner). Clubs: Detroit Athletic, Detroit Boat, Detroit Golf, Exchange, Ingleside. Home: 831 Edison Av. Office: Dime Bank Bldg., Detroit. Died Oct. 15, 1952.

CALLVERT, Ronald Glenn, (kăl'vĕrt), newspaper editor; b. Adel, Ia., Sept. 24, 1873; s. Stephen Alexander and Rachel Barns (Berger) C.; ed. high schs., Des Moines and Sheldon, Ia.; m. Kathryn Shotwell Andrews, May 10, 1909; 1 son, Ronald Shotwell. Began as printer, Bellingham (Wash.) Reveille, later reporter, editor, 1900-01; sec. Bd. of State Land Commrs., Olympia, Wash., 1901-05; reporter, later city editor Los Angeles (Calf.) Record, 1906-07; newspaper corr. Olympia, 1907-09; asst. mng. editor Oregonian, Portland, Ore., 1909-28, mng. editor, 1928-31, asso. editor, 1931-51. Awarded Pulitzer prize for distinguished editorial writing during 1938. Republican. Protestant. Home: 5646 Chelsea Av., La Jolla, Cal. Died Feb. 14, 1955; buried San Diego, Cal.

CAMACHO, Manual Avila (kä-ma'chō), ex-pres. of Mexico; b. Teziutlan, Puebla, Mexico, Apr. 24, 1897; s. Manuel Avila Castilla and Euprosia Camacho de Avila; educated in accounting; m. Soledad Orozco, 1920; 1 adopted son, Eulogio. Fought as 2d lt. in the forces against Huerta, 1914; advanced in Mexican Army to gen.; cited for his efforts in defense of Moralia, 1924; served as chief of staff, Ministry War and Navy, under President Rodriguez; led in suppression of revolt of Cedillo, 1938; apptd. sec. nat. defense, but resigned, 1939, to campaign for nomination for presidency; nominated by party sympathetic to labor and elected, July 1940, for term 1940-46; declared war on Japan following attack on U.S. Played on polo team which won 3d place 1936 Olympics. Address: Mexico City, Mexico. Died Oct. 13, 1955.

CAMERON, Charles Conrad, ry. official; b. St. Louis, Mo., Aug. 4, 1869; ed. pub. and high schs., St. Louis; m. Mary Louise Cahoon, Aug. 1, 1894; children—Charles Conrad (dec.), Alan Bruce, John Donald. Began with Wabash, St. Louis & Pacific Ry. (now Wabash Ry. Co.), 1882; with Ill. Central System, 1894—, asst. gen. freight agt., 1899-1903, gen. freight agt. and coal traffic mgr., 1903-25, asst. freight traffic mgr., 1925-28, freight traffic mgr., 1928-31, gen. traffic mgr. June 1, 1931, v.p., 1931-39, retired. Mem. Com. on Ry. Transportation, U. of Ill. Mem. Beta Gamma Sigma. Conglist. Mason (Shriner). Club: Chicago Traffic. Home: 1643 E. 56th St., Chicago, Ill. Died 1951.

CAMERON, Edwin J(ohn), dir. research lab.; b. Cambridge, Mass., Sept. 17, 1895; s. John J. and Annie (Ellis) C.; B.S., Mass. Inst. Tech., 1920; Ph.D., George Washington U., 1927; m. Dorothy Ellouise Pray, Sept. 21, 1921; 1 son, John Pray. Bacteriologist Comml. Solvents Corp., Terre Haute, Ind., 1920-23; Nat. Canners Assn., Washington, 1923-36, asst. dir. research lab., 1936-39, dir. research lab., 1939-55, dir. all research labs., 1955—. Served with M.C., U.S. Army, A.E.F., World War I. Mem. Soc. Am. Bacteriol., The American Chemical Society Institute of Food Technologists. Club: Cosmos. Contbr. articles on thermophilic bacteria, sources of thermophilic bacteria and relations to canned food spoilage; thermophilic contamination of beet and cane sugar. Home: 2651 16th St., N.W., Washington 9. Office: 1133 20th St., Washington 6. Died Mar. 21, 1955; buried Arlington Nat. Cemetery.

CAMERON, Frank Kenneth, chemistry; b. Baltimore, Md., Feb. 2, 1869; s. Maj. John Malcolm and Elizabeth (Fitz-Patrick) C.; A.B., Johns Hopkins, 1891; Ph.D., 1894; m. Katherine Boyle, Sept. 14, 1899 (died Nov. 25, 1903); m. 2d, Virginia B. Newton, Oct. 6, 1908 (dec. Nov. 15, 1954); children—Francis, Katherine. Research fellow and instr. chemistry, Cornell U., 1894-95; asso. prof. chemistry, Catholic U. of America, 1895-97; research asst. and instr. in physical chemistry, Cornell U., 1897-98; expert, U.S. Dept. Agr., 1898; chemist to Div. of Soils, U.S. Dept. Agr., 1899; in charge Lab. of Soil Chemistry, U S. Dept. Agr., 1899-1915; prof. chemistry, U of North Carolina, 1926-46, emeritus professor 1946—; cons. practice. Awarded Herty medal, 1939. Roman Catholic. Mem. various sci. socs., including A.A.A.S., Am. Chem. Soc., Soc. Electrochemistry, Elisha Mitchell Sci. Soc.; mem. S.A.R. K.C. Clubs: Cosmos (Washington); University, Alta (Salt Lake City). Author: Les Constituants Mineraux des Solutions des Sols (with James M. Bell), 1907; The Soil Solution, 1911; also over 200 research papers. Asst. editor Zeitschrift Kolloide Chemistry, 1910-14, Jour. Phys. Chemistry, 1910-23, 31-33, Jour. Indsl. and Engring. Chemistry, 1912-21. Home: 47 Maxwell Rd., Glen Lennox, Chapel Hill, N.C. Died Aug. 18, 1958; buried Old Chapel Hill Cemetery.

CAMERON, George Toland, newspaper pub.; b. Red Bluff, Calif., Mar. 16, 1873; s. James Strong and Augusta (Gerke) C.; ed. Cogswell Polytech. Sch., San Francisco; m. Helen Margaret de Young, Nov. 30, 1908. Organizer, 1905, Pacific Oil Transportation Co., builders of pipe line from Coalinga to Monterey, Calif.; built pipe line from Bakesfield to Port Costa, Calif., for Associated Oil Co.; pres. Santa Cruz Portland Cement Co. since 1908; organizer and president, 1911, Universal Oil Co.; publisher San Francisco Chronicle and pres. Chronicle Pub. Co. since 1925; trustee Cypress Lawn Cemetery Assn. Republican. Clubs: Bohemian, San Francisco Golf and Country, Burlingame Country, Pacific Union. Home: Burlingame, Calif. Office: Chronicle Bldg., San Francisco. Died Oct. 3, 1955.

CAMERON, Gordon Wyatt, bus. exec.; b. Brooklyn, Nov. 9, 1895; s. William Freeland and Jessie Ray (Wyatt) C.; A.B., Williams Coll., 1916; m. Mary Windsor Crane, July 24, 1920; children—Gordon Crane, Mary Windsor (Mrs. Sherwood B. Stockwell). With Aluminum Co. of Am., 1916—, co. assignments Chile, Argentina, Brazil, Albany, N.Y., Indianapolis, Pittsburgh, N.Y. City and San Francisco, 1919-24, mgr. Boston office, 1924-43, chief coordinator def. plants constrn., Pittsburgh, 1941-43, treas., 1943—, v.p., 1952—; dir. Aluminum Goods Mfg. Co. Davo Corp.; trustee Equitable Life Ins. Co. of Ia. Mem. bd. dirs. Eye and Ear Hosp., Pittsburgh; vice chmn., mem. bd. dirs. Pittsburgh chpt. A.R.C. Served as 1st lt., inf., World War I, 13 mos., A.E.F., France. Mem. Phi Sigma Kappa. Clubs: Duquesne, Fox Chapel Golf, Pittsburgh Golf (Pittsburgh); Rolling Rock (Ligonier, Pa.); Williams (New York). Home: 5023 Frew St., Pittsburgh 13. Office: Alcoa Bldg., Pitts. 19. Died Apr. 29, 1955; buried Allegheny Cemetery, Pitts.

CAMERON, Ralph Henry, ex-senator; b. Southport, Me., Oct. 21, 1863; s. Henry and Abigail Ann (Jones) C.; student pub. and high schs.; m. Ida May Spaulding, Nov. 25, 1895. Interested in various copper and silver mines and power projects in Ariz.; locator and builder of the Bright Angel Trail into the Grand Canyon of the Colo., in Ariz.; sheriff of Coconino Co., Ariz., 1891-92, 1894-98; chmn. bd. supervisors, Coconino Co., 1 term; del. 61st Congress, from Ariz.; owing to the admission of Ariz. to statehood, his term of office extended until the President's proclamation, Jan. 1912; candidate for U.S. Senate, Dec. 1911; mem. U.S. Senate, term 1921-27. Republican. Methodist. Home: Phoenix, Ariz. Died Feb. 12, 1953.*

CAMERON, William John, b. Hamilton, Ont., Dec. 29, 1878; hon. LL.D., Alma (Mich.) and Washington and Jefferson colls.; m. Eleanor Maude Clough, 1901; 4 children. Lived in Detroit, 1887-46; on editorial staff The Detroit News, 1903-18; with Ford Motor Co., 1918-46, editor The Dearborn Independent, ret.; pastor Lakeside Unity Temple, Oakland, Cal. Home: Oakland, Cal. Died Aug. 1, 1955.

CAMERON, William McC., first vice chmn. and dir. Celanese Corp. of America; dir. Canadian Celanese, Ltd., Am. British Chemical Supplies, Am. Analine Co., Celanese Celluloid Corp. Home: Ritz Towers, 57th St. and Park Av. Office: 180 Madison Av., N.Y. C. Died Oct. 1950.

CAMMACK, Edmund Ernest, corp. exec.; b. Spalding, Eng., Dec. 7, 1881; student Bedford Modern Sch., Eng.; m. Zelie Kirkby, Feb. 12, 1910; 1 adopted son, Christopher. Came to U.S., 1910. Clerk, London County Banking Co., 1900-03, Nat. Bank of South Africa, Johannesburg, 1903-05; clk., later actuary African Life Assurance Soc., Ltd., Johannesburg, 1905-10; actuarial asst. Aetna Life Ins. Co., 1910-15, asso. actuary, 1915-22, actuary, 1922-24, v.p., actuary, 1924—, dir., 1947—; v.p., dir. Standard Fire Ins. Co., Aetna Casualty and Surety Co. Fellow Actuarial Soc. Am., Am. Inst. Actuaries, Casualty Actuarial Soc. Clubs: Hartford, Hartford Golf, Metropolitan. Home: 40 Mohawk Dr., West Hartford, Conn. Office: 151 Farmington Av., Hartford 15, Conn. Died Dec. 17, 1958.

CAMMACK, James William (kăm-măk), judge; b. Owenton, Ky., Mar. 10, 1902; s. James W. and Nellie (Allen) C.; LL.B., University of Kentucky, 1924, M.A., 1929, Ph.D., 1937, LL.D. (honorary), 1955; student University of Chicago, 1929-30, Peabody Coll. for Teachers, 1932; m. Sarah Gilmour, Feb. 17, 1927. Admitted to Ky. bar, 1924, and began practice in Owenton; taught school part time until 1930; with State Dept. of Edn., 1930-34; state dir. N.R.A., 1935; mem. Pub. Service Commn., 1935-38; mem. Court of Appeals, Sept. 1938—, chief justice Court of Appeals, Jan. 1951-Jan. 1953. Member Ky. Bar Assn., Am. Bar Assn., Am. Acad. Polit. and Social Sci., Am. Judicature Soc., Delta Chi. Dem. Presbyterian. Mason. Home: Owenton, Ky. Office: Court of Appeals, Frankfort, Ky. Died July 30, 1958; buried Lexington Cemetery.

CAMP, Albert Sidney, congressman; b. Coweta County, Ga., July 26, 1892; s. William Walker and Ella (Leigh) C.; B.L., U. of Ga., 1915; student Edinburgh (Scotland) U., 1919; m. Sarah Farmer, Nov. 19, 1925; children—Albert Sidney, Molly Farmer, (Mrs. W. E. Davis). Admitted to Ga. bar, June 1915, and began practice in Newnan; asst. U.S. atty., Northern Dist. of Ga., 1934-39. Elected mem. 76th Congress (1939-41), 4th Georgia District, re-elected 78th-83rd Congresses. Chmn. of Coweta County Democratic Exec. Committee 1915-20. Served with Headquarters Detachment, 82d Div. U.S. Army, 1917-19; with A.E.F. Mem. Ga. Bar Assn., Am. Legion (comdr. Ga. Dept. 1933-34). Democrat. Methodist. Mason (Shriner). Clubs: Newnan Kiwanis (pres. 1930), Newnan Country. Home: Newnan, Ga. Office: House Office Bldg., Washington. Died July 24, 1954; buried Newnan, Ga.

CAMPAU, Francis Denis (kăm'pō), lawyer; b. Grand Rapids, Mich., Sept. 8, 1880; s. Andrew Sylvestre and Mary Elizabeth (Blackwell) C.; Ph.B., U. of Chicago, 1903; LL.B., Harvard, 1905; m. Ethel Laurens Dunn, Aug. 2, 1909; 1 dau., Jacqueline Denise (dec.). Practiced, Grand Rapids, 1905—. Pioneer in establishing state workman's compensation and employers liability laws; also cases on unfair trade before FTC. Mem. Mich. State Bar Assn., Am. Bar Assn., Grand Rapids Bar Assn., Psi Upsilon. Republican. Catholic. Home: 56 Packard Av. S.E., Grand Rapids, Mich. Died July 3, 1958; buried Oakhill Cemetery, Grand Rapids.

CAMPBELL, Arthur Griffith, army officer; b. Lexington, Va., Nov. 15, 1884; s. John Hammond and Mattie (Steele) C.; B.S., Va. Mil. Inst., 1906; grad. Coast Arty. Sch., 1915 (advanced course 1923), Command and Gen. Staff Sch., 1924, Army War Coll., 1928; m. Virginia Roberts, Feb. 19, 1921. Comdt. Hoge

Meml. Mil. Acad., 1906; asst. prof. Va. Mil. Inst., 1907; commd. 2d lt. CAC, 1908, promoted through grades to brig. gen., 1940; command and staff duties with arty. of AEF, 1917-18; mem. War Dept. Gen. Staff, 1918-21; asst. chief of staff, 6th Corps Area, 1928-32, 8th Corps Area, 1939-40; retired as brig. gen., 1944. Decorated Chevalier Legion of Honor, France, 1920. Mem. Kappa Alpha. Presbyn. Mason. Club: Army and Navy (Washington). Home: Fort Adams Newport, R.I. Address: care Adjutant General, U.S. Army, Washington 25. Died Jan. 25, 1957.

CAMPBELL, Bruce Alexander (kăm'-ĕl), lawyer; b. Albion, Ill., Oct. 28, 1879; s. Joseph McCown and Amabel (Thompson) C.; A.B., U. of Ill., 1900; private study in law office; m. Beulah Wilson Campbell, June 19, 1906; 1 son, Joseph Bruce. Admitted to Ill. bar, 1901, practiced at Albion, Ill., until 1905, and since practiced at East St. Louis, Ill.; mem Kramer, Kramer & Campbell, 1905-31, Kramer, Campbell, Costello & Wiechert, 1931-53, retired; director Churchill Downs, Incorporated Village attorney of Albion, 1903-04; mem. Ill. Ho. of Rep., 1904-06; del. Dem. Nat. convs. 1912, 24, 28, 32, 36, 40, 44, 48, 52; chmn. Dem. State Conv., 1922, 26, 30, 32, 44; chmn. Dem. State Managing Com., 1932, 44; chmn. Dem. State Central Committee of Illinois, 1934-38; chmn. Illinois State Commn. for Physically Handicapped Children, 1934-35, chairman Illinois Elks Assn. Crippled Children's Clinic since 1927; candidate for Dem. nomination for gov. of Ill., 1932. Del. and pres. Ill. Conv. for ratification of amendment repealing 18th Amendment, 1933. Recipient of award from Northwestern Univ. Mem. Am. Law Inst. since orgn.; mem. Am. Ill. State (pres. 1922-23, sr. counselor 1951), East St. Louis (pres. 1912) bar assns., Sigma Alpha Epsilon, Phi Beta Kappa, Phi Delta Phi. Democrat. Mason (Shriner). Mem. Modern Woodmen. Elk; president Illinois Elks Association, 1911-12; Grand Exalter Ruler, 1918-19; mem. Elks War Relief Com., 1918-21, Nat. Hdqrs. Com., 1921-31; vice-chmn. Nat. Memorial and Publs. Com., 1931-37, chmn. since Feb. 1937. Clubs: East St. Louis Rotary (pres. 1927-28). Home: 7630 N. 5th Av., Phoenix. Died Sept. 29, 1955; buried Mount Hope Cemetery, Belleville, Ill.

CAMPBELL, Chandler, marine corps officer; b. Wheeling, W.Va., Feb. 10, 1880. Apptd. 2d lt. USMC, 1900, and advanced through grades to col., 1932; ret. from active duty, 1936; brevetted with rank of brig. gen., 1942; participated Philippine campaign, 1902, Nicaraguan campaign, 1912, Haitian campaign, 1915, Dominican campaign, 1916; comd. 10th Marine Regt., 1918. Died Oct. 28, 1956; buried Nat. Cemetery, Arlington, Va.

CAMPBELL, Charles L., pub. utility exec.; b. St. John, New Brunswick, Can., July 11, 1877; s. Charles and Elizabeth Brown (Partelow) C.; ed. pub. and private schs. in Canada; m. Ruth Mayhew Miller, June 24, 1905; children—James Gardner, Ruth Elizabeth. Came to U.S., 1901, naturalized, 1915. Office boy C.P. Ry., Can., 1894; chmn. finance com. Conn. Light & Power Co.; trustee Conn. Bank & Trust Co.; director Conn. Mutual Life Ins. Co., Gray Mfg. Co. Trustee Tax Foundation; director of Connecticut State Chamber of Commerce; chmn. Conn. Pub. Expenditure Council; trustee Nat. Indsl. Conf. Bd. Republican. Episcopalian. Clubs: Hartford, 20th Century. (Hartford). Home: 777 Prospect Av., West Hartford, Conn. Office: Selden St., Berlin, Conn. Died July 8, 1956.

CAMPBELL, Charles Sherman, banker; b. Portage Twp., Kalamazoo County, Mich., Nov. 24, 1863; s. Hugh and Mary (Gilmore) C.; grad. high sch., Schoolcraft, Mich., 1884; m. Caroline M. Taylor, Apr. 5, 1904; 1 dau., Mary Elizabeth. Teacher, rural schs., Mich., 1885-89; began in banking with Nesbit & Miller, Schoolcraft, 1889; with Mich. Nat. Bank (consol. with 1st Nat. Bank, 1912), since 1890, pres. since 1905; chmn. bd. 1st Nat. Bank & Trust Co., Kalamazoo, Mich.; treas. Kalamazoo Vegetable Parchment Co.; dir. Kalamazoo Paper Company, Fidelity Building & Loan Company, Kalamazoo Stove Co., Saniwax Paper Co. Trustee Kalamazoo Coll., Bronson M.E. Hosp. Presbyterian. Clubs: Park, Kalamazoo Country (Kalamazoo). Home: 1520 Whites Rd. Office: 108 E. Michigan Av., Kalamazoo, Mich. Died Jan. 27, 1953.

CAMPBELL, Charles S(outter), mfg. exec.; born Cedar Rapids, Ia., Aug. 2, 1887; s. James R. and Helen A. (Strong) C.; A.B., Yale, 1909, B.D., 1917; m. Mary Lathrop Abbe, June 15, 1910; children—Charles Soutter, William Patrick, Robert Abbe, Mary, Anne, Joan. With J. B. Williams Co., Glastonbury, Conn., since 1937, pres. and treas. since 1949; pres. Durham-Enders Razor Corp., Mystic, Conn., since 1930. Clubs: University (N.Y.); Lawn, Graduates (New Haven); Yeamans Hall (Charleston), Hartford, University (Hartford). Home: 12 St. Ronan Terrace, New Haven 11. Office: The J.B. Williams Co., Glastonbury, Conn.; also Durham-Enders Razor Corp., Mystic, Conn. Died Sept. 21, 1954.

CAMPBELL, Delwin Morton, veterinary editor and publisher; b. Topeka, Kan., Jan. 19, 1880; s. Newton Josephus and Mary Jean (Mitchell) C.; student Kansas State Normal Coll., 1897-98; Kan. State Agrl. Coll., 1903-05; D.V.M., Kansas City Vet. Coll., 1907; m. Gertrude Elma Hole, May 1, 1907; children—Eloise Belle (Mrs. Harner Selvidge), Dorothea Gertrude (Mrs. Joseph Calvin Sides), Delwin Morton, Jr. Editor, Vet. Medicine, 1908-49, consulting editor since 1949. Col. Veterinary Corps, U.S. Army, 1941-44. Mem. Am. Vet. Med. Assn., Am. Pub. Health Assn., A.A.A.S., Assn. Mil. Surgs. U.S. Democrat. Author: Colics of the Horse, 1945; Veterinary Account Book, 1917; Veterinary Service in Wartime, 1942; Army Veterinary Service, 1944. Co-author: Veterinary Military History of the United States (2 vols.), 1935; vet. sect. The Americana Annual since 1946. Address: 7632 S. Crandon Av., Chicago 49. Died Mar. 27, 1952; buried Arlington Nat. Cemetery.

CAMPBELL, Douglas Houghton (kăm'bĕl), botanist; b. Detroit, Dec. 16, 1859; s. James Valentine and Cornelia (Hotchkiss) C.; Ph.M., U. of Mich., 1882, Ph.D., 1886, LL.D., 1932; studied in Bonn, Tübingen and Berlin, 1886-88; unmarried. Instr. in biology, Detroit High Sch., 1882-86; prof. botany, Ind. U., 1888-91, Leland Stanford U., 1891-1925, prof. emeritus since 1925. Mem. Nat. Acad. Sciences, Am. Philos. Soc.; fellow Am. Acad. Arts and Sciences, Royal Soc. Edinburgh; foreign mem. Linnaean Soc.; mem. various other socs., Am. and European. Clubs: University (San Francisco); Authors' (London). Author: Elements of Structural and Systematic Botany, 1890; Structure and Development of Mosses and Ferns, 1895, 3d edit., 1918. Lectures on Evolution of Plants, 1899; A University Text Book of Botany, 1902, 2d edit., 1907; Plant Life and Evolution, 1911; Outline of Plant Geography, 1926; Evolution of the Land Plants, 1940. Also many monographs and other scientific papers. Address: Box 943, Stanford University, Cal. Died Feb. 23, 1953.

CAMPBELL, Edmund Schureman, prof. of art and architecture; b. Freehold, N.J., Oct. 28, 1884; s. James Wall Schureman and Mary (Valentine) C.; student Stevens Prep. Sch., 1902; B.S., Mass. Inst. Tech., 1906, M.S., 1907; student Ecole des Beaux Arts, Paris, 1911-12; m. Catharine McEnerny, 1918; children—James Schureman, Thomas Banta, Peter Bruce. Mem. faculty Carnegie Inst. Tech., Pitts., 1907-14, in charge dept. of architecture, Armour Inst. Tech., Chgo., 1914-24; dean Beaux Arts Inst. of Design, N.Y.C., 1924-27; in charge sch. of architecture, prof. of art and architecture and curator Museum of Fine Arts, U. Va., 1927—. Formerly mem. Fine Arts Com. and State Exam. Bd. for Architects, Va.; mem. Williamsburg Adv. Bd. of Architects. Mem. Water Color Soc., Va. Soc. Architects, Aztec Soc. Club: Farmington Country. Home: Mount Fair Farm, Mt. Fair, Va. Died May 9, 1950.

CAMPBELL, Eldridge, surgeon; b. Alderson, W. Va., Dec. 21, 1901; s. Eldridge H. and Bessie (Spessard) C.; B.S., U. Va., 1923; B.A. (Rhodes Scholar), Balliol Coll., Oxford U., 1925; M.D., Johns Hopkins, 1927; m. Eleanor Brown, July 2, 1930; children—Elizabeth Spessard, Jean McComb, Thomas Richardson Brown. Intern, asst. resident, resident surgery and neurological surgery Johns Hopkins Hospital, 1927-34; faculty Albany Med. Coll., 1934—, prof. surgery, 1946—; practice neurological surgery, Albany, 1934—; surgeon-in-chief Albany Hosp., 1946—. Served as col. M.C., U.S. Army, 1942-46, unit dir., surgeon in chief 33rd Gen. Hosp., acting neurosurg. cons. M.T.O.; neurosurg. cons. Surgeon Gen., Japan, Korea, 1952. Decorated Legion of Merit. Diplomate Am. Bd. Surgery, Am. Bd. Neurol. Surgery. Fellow A.C.S., mem. Am. Surg. Assn., Am. Neurological Assn., Harvey Cushing Soc., Halsted Surg. Soc., So. Surg. Soc., Excelsior Surg. Soc., Soc. U. Med. Cons. in World War II, Soc. Neurological Surgeons, Soc. Univ. Surgeons, Internat. Soc. Surgeons. Clubs: Schuyler Meadows (Loudonville); Ft. Orange (Albany). Home: Old Niskayuna Rd., Loudonville. Office: Albany Hospital, Albany, N.Y. Died Feb. 15, 1956; buried Albany Rural Cemetery.

CAMPBELL, Gabriel, educator, philosopher; b. Dalrymple, Scotland, Aug. 19, 1838; s. Robert and Anne (Muir) C.; B.Pd., Mich. Normal Coll., 1861, M.Pd., 1892; A.B., U. Mich., 1865, A.M., 1868; B.D., Chgo. Theol. Sem., 1868; post-grad. U. Berlin, 1870-72; D.D., Dartmouth, 1886; m. Louis T. McMahon, Sept. 20, 1865. Ordained to ministry Congl. Ch., 1868; prof. philosophy U. Minn., 1867-81, declined presidencey, 1868, v.p., 1872-81; prof. philosophy Bowdoin Coll., 1881-83; prof. philosophy Dartmouth, 1883-1910, prof. emeritus, 1910-23; declined presidency Western Res. U., 1889. Vice pres. philos. sect. Chgo. Expn., 1893; mem. exec. com. Internat. Assn. Arts, Paris, 1897; chmn. Am. com. on the Fichte Centenary at U. Berlin, 1910. Served as capt. Co. E, 17th Mich. Inf., Civil War. Mem. Philos. Soc. Berlin, Am. Philos. Assn., Loyal Legion, G.A. R. (post comdr.). Author: New German Course, 1868; also numerous pamphlets on philosophy. Address: Hanover, N.H. Died Oct. 18, 1923; buried Hanover.

CAMPBELL, George Ashley, telephone research engr.; b. Hastings, Minn., Nov. 27, 1870; s. Cassius Samuel and Lydia Lorraine (Ashley) C.; B.S., Mass. Inst. Tech., 1891; A.B., Harvard, 1892, A.M., 1893, Ph.D., 1901; studied Göttingen, Vienna and Paris; m. Caroline Gillis Sawyer, 1913; children—Alexander Hovey (dec.), Ashley Sawyer. With Am. Tel. & Tel. Co., 1897-1934; with Bell Telephone Labs., 1934-35. Mem. Am. Acad. Arts and Sciences, Math. Soc., Math. Assn. America, Physical Soc., A.A.A.S. Distinguished Service medal, Inst. Radio Engrs., 1936; Elliott Cresson medal, Franklin Inst., 1939. Edison medal, Am. Inst. of Elec. Engrs., 1940. Pioneering research in connection with loading, crosstalk, 4-wire repeater circuits, sidetone reduction, electric wave filters, inductive interference, antenna arrays, maximum output networks, Fourier integrals and electrical units. Author: Collected Papers, 1937. Republican. Conglist. Home: Upper Montclair, N.J. Died Nov. 10, 1954; buried Easthampton, Mass.

CAMPBELL, Harold Demy (kăm'ĕl), marine corps officer; b. Middlesex, Vt., Mar. 30, 1895; s. Eugene Ellsworth and Bertha (Denny) C.; C.E., Norwich University, 1917; graduate Air Corps Tactical Sch., 1929, Marine Corps Schools, 1935; student Senior Officers Course (British), England, 1942; married Mildred Fairbanks Shattuck, Mar. 10, 1898; children—Marilyn Denise, Harold Denny, Nancy Jean (dec.). Commd. 2d lt., U.S. Marine Corps, 1917. and advacned through the grades to maj. gen., 1946; served overseas 27 months during World War I; became marine aviator, 1921; chief aviation section Marine Corps Schs., 1931-35; air officer Fleet Marine Force. 1935-39; Am. adviser to Lord Louis Mountbatten, 1942-43; served in Central, South and Western Pacific areas, 1943-45, comdg. 4th Marine Air Wing, later 2d Marine Air Wing and as island comdr., Peleliu; comdg. gen. Marine Corps Air Bases and 9th Wing; 1st island comdr., Peleliu, Western Carolines, Western Pacific. Decorated Purple Heart, Legion of Merit, Navy-Marine Corps Medal, 11 campaign ribbons. Awarded Schiff Trophy for world's record of greatest number of hours in air as pilot without accident, 1926. Member Quiet Birdmen, Am. Legion, Marine Corps League, Phi Kappa Delta, Sigma Nu (life). Author: Employment of Marine Corps Aviation in Landing Operations, Employment of Marine Corps Aviation in Small Wars, and Flying over Nicaragua (syndicated mga. article). Home: 90 S. Main St., Waterbury, Vt. Address: care Marine Corps Headquarters, Washington 25. Died Dec. 29, 1955; buried Arlington Nat. Cemetery.

CAMPBELL, John Bayard Taylor, newspaper editor; b. San Francisco, Calif., Apr. 19, 1880; s. Alexander and Ruth Ellen (Taylor) C.; student U. of Calif., 1898-99; m. Florence Fish, Oct. 4, 1909; children—John Bayard Taylor, Alexander. Reporter San Francisco Chronicle, 1899; editor Tucson (Ariz.) Citizen, 1907-11; city editor Los Angeles Herald, 1911-16; news editor, Los Angeles Evening Herald, 1916-33; managing editor Los Angeles Evening Herald Express, 1933-54, advisory editor Los Angeles Herald-Express, 1954—. Clubs: Los Angeles Athletic, Del Mar, Pacific Coast, Hollywood Athletic. Member Sigma Delta Chi. Author: Whence Came These Women, 1907; Rose of Los Angeles, 1929. Wrote many motion picture scenarios including Heartbeats produced by David Wark Griffith. Home: 540 N. June St., Los Angeles; (country) Campbell's Crag, Topango Canyon, Cal. Office: Los Angeles Herald-Express, Los Angeles. Died July 27, 1956; buried Rosedale Cemetery.

CAMPBELL, J(ohn) W(illiam), financer; born Brooklyn, Oct. 27, 1886; s. John and Wilhemina (Van Loon) C.; ed. pub. schs. of Brooklyn; m. Rosalind Danhauser, March 8, 1921. President, director Phoenix Campbell Corporation. Clubs: Metropolitan, Lotos (N.Y.C.); Blind Brook (Portchester, N.Y.); Everglades (Palm Beach, Fla.); Farmington Country (Charlottesville, Va.). Home: Westchester Country (Rye, N.Y.). Office: 15 Vanderbilt Av., N.Y.C. 17. Deceased.

CAMPBELL, Johnston B., ex-commerce commr.; b. Stillwater, Minn., Aug. 5, 1868; s. Hugh and Lucinda (Fee) C.; LL.B., U. Minn., 1890; m. Martha Shearer, Sept. 13, 1893. Began practice at Duluth, Minn., 1890; moved to Moorhead, Minn., 1897, Spokane, Wash., 1903; founded Spokane Mchts. Assn., 1903, atty. in freight rate litigation which extended over many yrs. and was decided in favor of Spokane in 1918. Mem. Portland Dist. Freight Traffic Conv. of the Ry. Adminstrn. during World War I. Mem. U.S. ICC, 1921-30, chmn. 1928-30; practice of law until retirement, 1950. Republican. Presbyn. Mason (32°, Shriner). Club: Cosmos. Home: Spokane, Wash. Died Nov. 5, 1953.

CAMPBELL, Leon (kămp'bĕl), astronomer; b. Cambridge, Mass., Jan. 20, 1881; s. William J. and Leonora (Rawding) C.; student pub. schs., Cambridge, and spl. instrn. Harvard Obs.; m. Fredrica J. Thompson, June 15, 1905; children—Leon, Florence May, Malcolm Fredric, Ruth Evelyn, Eleanor Beatrice. Asst. at Harvard Obs., 1899-1911, in charge of Arequipa (Peru) sta., 1911-15, variable star investigator, and astronomer, 1915—; instr. in astronomy Harvard, 1928, Pickering Meml. astronomer, 1931—. Assists in extension of research among amateur astronomers. Mem. Am. Astron. Soc., Am. Assn. Variable Star Observers (pres. 1919-22), Internat. Astron. Union, Lima Geog. Soc. (hon.). Contbr. to annals of Harvard Obs. and astron. mags.; coauthor, the Story of Variable Stars, 1941. Died May 10, 1951.

CAMPBELL, LeRoy Brotzman (kăm'bĕl), dir. Warren Conservatory of Music; b. Jasper, N.Y., Apr. 30, 1873; s. Frank Elbert and Celestia Eliza (Brotzman) C.; B.E., Central State Tchrs. Coll., Lock Haven, Pa., 1892; student Oberlin (O.) Coll., 1892-96; grad. Leipzig (Germany) Royal Conservatory Music (honor and scholarship student), 1900; Mus.D., Grove City (Pa.) Coll., 1925; studied in music normals in Paris, London, Leipzig, Vienna and Munich; m. Nellie Belle Baker, June 9, 1910. Began as dir. music dept. State Tchrs. Coll., Fredericksburg, Va., 1896; founded Warren (Pa.) Conservatory of Music, 1906, and has since been its director; has conducted 20 summer tours to Europe, 12 being mus. normals or pilgrimages; made a one year trip around the world for the purpose of musical and ednl. research; ednl. dir. Progressive Series Coll. European Summer Teachers' Normals. Fellow Am. Geog. Soc.; mem. Music Tchrs. Nat. Assn. (life), Soc. Arts and Scis. Am., Am. Matthay Assn. (v.p.), Warren Acad. Sciences (pres. 1918). Democrat; nominated candidate for state representative, 1937. Methodist. Rotarian. Author: The True Function of Relaxation in Piano Playing, Velocity Plus, 1922; The Unusual in London and Vicinity, 1935; also brochures on piano playing, ear training and Gothic architecture, and about 40 pub. mus. compositions. Contbr. articles to mus. publs.; has had 5 prize essays in same. Has given mus. and other lectures in 32 states and several foreign countries, including China and India. Served as judge for 114 contestants at Paris Conservatory, 1933, and again in 1937; made extensive tour as judge Nat. Piano Playing Tournament of America, 1938-51. Conducted musical appreciation tour, for Univ. Travel bur., 1948. Home: 600 5th Av., Warren, Pa. Died Oct. 5, 1958.

CAMPBELL, Wallace, business exec.; b. Chgo., Nov. 28, 1878; s. Wallace and Josephine (Lorrain) C.; student pub. schs., Wheaton, Ill.; m. Mary Bushnell Hazard, Jan. 1, 1916; children—Wallace, Margaret (Mrs. Andrew Staley), Jane (Mrs. Barton P. Smith), Hugh D. Mem. comml. dept. Chgo. and Ill. Bell Telephone Co., 1897-1914; became chief clerk The Solvay Process Co., Syracuse, N.Y., 1915, v.p., 1919, v.p. Canadian subsidiary, Brunner, Mond, Canada, Ltd., Montreal, 1922-28, v.p. Solvay Sales Corp., N.Y.C., 1928-29; partner Sturges, Chaffee & Hazard, Providence, 1929-—; dir. Allied Chem. and Dye Corp., R.I. Hosp. Trust Co., Hellenic Hydro Elec. and Metall. Corp. Mem. R.I. state senate, 1933-34. Mem. Newcomen Soc. Republican. Conglist. Clubs: Hope, Art. Home: Peace Dale, R.I. Office: Industrial Trust Bldg., Providence. Died Apr. 4, 1950.

CAMPBELL, Walter Stanley (Stanley Vestal), educator, writer; b. Severy, Kan., Aug. 15, 1887; s. Walter Mallory and Isabella Louise (Wood) Vestal; grad. Southwestern State Normal Sch., Weatherford, Okla., 1908; Rhodes Scholar, Merton Coll., Oxford U., 1908-11, B.A. and M.A., honors in Sch. Eng. Language and Literature, 1911; married Isabel Jones, Dec. 26, 1917; children—Malory, Dorothy. Instr., Male High Sch., Louisville, Ky., 1911-14; research among Indians, 1914-15; instr. in English, U. of Oklahoma, 1915-17, assistant professor of English, 1919-28, associate professor, 1928-39, professor and director of courses in professional writing since 1939, research professor, 1947. Fellow Guggenheim Memorial Foundation, 1930-31, Rockefeller Foundation, 1946. Served as captain, field artillery, United States Army, 1917-19. Director Assn. Am. Rhodes Scholars. Mem. Modern Lang. Assn., Soc. Am. Historians, Oklahoma Hall of Fame, Kappa Alpha (Southern), Phi Beta Kappa. Episcopalian. Author: (under name Stanley Vestal) Fandango, Ballads of the Old West, 1927; Kit Carson, the Happy Warrior of the Old West, 1928; Happy Hunting Grounds, 1928; Dobe Walls, 1929; Sitting Bull, 1932; Warpath, 1933; The Wine Room Murder, 1935; New Sources of Indian History, 1934; Mountain Men, 1937; Revolt on the Border, 1938; Professional Writing, 1938; The Old Santa Fe Trail, 1939; Writing Magazine Fiction, 1940; King of the Fur Traders, 1940; Short Grass Country, 1941; Bigfoot Wallace, 1942; Writing Non-fiction, 1944; The Missouri, 1945; Jim Bridger, 1946; Warpath and Council Fire, 1948; Writing Advice and Devices, 1950; Queen of Cowtowns: Dodge City, 1952; Joe Meek, 1952; The Book Lover's Southwest, 1955; Sitting Bull, 1957. Editor: Early Days Among the Cheyenne and Arapahoe Indians by John H. Seger, 1934; Wah-to-Yah and the Taos Trail by L. H. Garrard, 1937; The Oregon Trail by Francis Parkman, 1927. Contbr. to mags. Address: University of Oklahoma, Norman, Okla. Died Dec. 1957.

CAMPOS, Maria E. (Miss), Dem. nat. committeewoman; b. July 6, 1891. Address: P.O. Box 1590, San Juan 7, Puerto Rico. Died Dec. 6, 1951; buried Meml. Cemetery, San Juan, Puerto Rico.

CAMROSE, 1st Viscount of Hackwood Park (William Ewert Berry), chmn. and editor in chief, The Daily Telegraph of London; b. Merthry Tydfil, South Wales, June 23, 1879; s. Alderman John Mathias and Mary Ann Berry; educated privately; Dr. of Laws (hon.), Bristol; m. Mary Agnes Corns, 1905; children—Mary Cecilia (wife of Major R. McNair Scott), J. Seymour, W. Michael, Sheila (wife of The Rt. Hon. The Earl of Birkenhead), Molly Patricia (m. Baron Sherwood), Rodney Mathias, Julian, Diana Phyllis (wife of W. P. Macauley). Founder Advertising World, 1901; editor in chief Sunday Times, 1915-37; chmn. Allied Newspapers (now (Kemsley Newspapers), 1924-37; prin. adviser, Ministry of Information, 1939; chmn. and editor in chief, The Daily Telegraph of London since 1928; chmn. The Amalgamated Press, Ltd., since 1926. Deputy lt., County of Southampton, 1941. Created Baronet, 1921, 1st Baron Camrose of Long Cross, 1929, 1st Viscount Camrose of Hackwood Park, 1941. Author: British Newspapers and Their Controllers, 1948. Clubs: The Royal Yacht Squadron (vice commodore), Carlton, Athenaeum, Turf. (London). Home: Hackwood Park, Basingstoke, Hampshire, England; and 2d Carlton House Terr., London, S.W. 1. Office: The Daily Telegraph, Fleet St., London, E.C. 4, Eng. Died June 15, 1954.

CAMSELL, Charles, Canadian govt. ofcl.; b. Fort Liard, N.W. Ty., Can., Feb. 8, 1876; s. Julian Stewart and Sarah (Foulds) C.; student St. Johns Coll., Queen's U., Kingston, Ont., Harvard, Mass. Inst. Tech.; B.A., Manitoba U.; LL.D., Queen's 1922, Alberta, 1929, Manitoba U., 1936; m. Isabel Doucie Thomas, Oct. 26, 1905; children—Charles Stewart Mackintosh, Isabel D. (Mrs. T. G. Mayburry), Phyllis Dora (wife of Dr. M. O. Klotz). Engaged in travel explorations, 1894-1902; geologist Canadian Northern Ry. Co., 1903; joined Geol. Survey, 1904, took charge of B.C. office, 1918; apptd. dep. minister of mines, 1920, dep. minister of mines and resources, 1936, the commr. Northwest Territories, ret.; now commr. Fed. Dist. Commn., Ottawa. Rep. Can. Imperial Confs., London and Ottawa, also at Empire Mining and Metall. Congress, S. Africa, 1930, World Power Confs., Berlin and Washington. Chmn. Canadian sect. World Power Conf.; dir. Canadian sect. North Pacific Planning Project; mem. Internat. Niagara Bd. Decorated Companion St. Michael and St. George, 1935; recipient Murchison grant Royal Geog. Soc., 1922; Founders medal, 1946; Gold medal Inst. Mining and Metallurgy London, 1930; Fellow St. John's Coll. Fellow Geol. Soc. of Am. (v.p. 1937), Royal Soc. Can. (pres. 1930), Can. Geog. Soc. (pres. 1928-41, hon. mem.); mem. Can. Inst. Mining and Metallurgy (pres. 1948). Engring. Inst. Can. (pres. 1932), Am. Inst. of Mining and Metall. Engrs. (hon.). Clubs: Rideau, Royal Ottawa Golf (Ottawa). Author: Son of the North. Home: 240 Mariposa Av., Rockcliffe Park, Ottawa, Can. Died Dec. 19, 1958.

CAMUS, Albert, (kämüs) author; b. Mondovi, Algiers; Nov. 7, 1913; Bachelier, Licencié ès Lettres (philosophie), diplome d'Etudes Supérieures de Philosophe, U. Algiers. Journalist in Algiers; editor in chief Combat, 1944-45. A dir. Librarie Gallimard. Recipient Nobel prize in lit., 1957. Author numerous works, including: L'Envers et l'Endroit (essays); Le Minotaure ou La Halle d'Oran; L'Etranger (pub. U.S. 1955); Le Myth de Sisyphe (pub. U.S. 1955); Lettres a un ami allemande; La Peste; L'Homme revolté (essay); Plusieurs piéces de Theatre; Le Malentendu; Les Justes (play); Fall (play) pub. in U.S. 1957; Exile and the Kingdom, 1958. Address: 29 rue Madame, Paris 6°, France. Died Jan. 4, 1960.*

CANADA, John William, editor; b. Summerfield, N.C., Dec. 14, 1871; s. William and Elizabeth (Strader) C.; A.B., U. N.C., 1896, grad. work, 1896-1900; m. Verona Keener, Jan. 13, 1910; 1 dau., Jane Verona. Engaged in ind. newspaper work, 1900-05, weekly and spl. corr., Tex., 1905-11; editor, pub. Southland Farmer, 1911-26; organizer Nat. Farm Loan Assns., 1917, sec.-treas. 1917-35; organizer Houston Agrl. Credit Corp., 1923, sec.-mgr., 1923-35; editor The Milk Producer (dairy jour.), 1936-—; organizer Milk Producers Fed. Credit Union, 1936, since pres. Dir. Houston Agrl. Credit Corp., 1923, Port City Packinghouse, Port City Stockyards. Mem. Phi Beta Kappa. Democrat. Methodist. Author: Life at Eighty, a biography, Memories and Comments by a Tarheel in Texas, 1952; Dr. Seaman A. Knapp, shows a nation a New Farm Life, 1957; Andrew Jackson—The Fourteenth Amendment Then and Now, 1957. Breeder of registered Jersey cattle; began direct shipment of gardenias by mail, 1929. Home: 324 San Jacinto, La Porte, Tex. Died Feb. 1, 1958.

CANDLER, Charles Howard, co. dir.; b. Atlanta Dec. 2, 1878; s. Asa G. and Lucy E. (Howard) C.; A.B., Emory U., 1898, LL.D., 1942; student Atlanta Coll. Phys. & Surg., 1898-1900, Univ. and Bellevue Hosp. Med. Coll., 1900-01; m. Flora H. Glenn, Dec. 3, 1903; children—Charles Howard, Catherine (wife of Dr. William C. Warren, Jr.), Louisa (Mrs. Alfred T. Eldredge). Dir. Coca-Cola Co., Trust Co. of Ga., Atlantic Steel Co., Atlantic Co., Nat. Mfrs. & Stores Corp. Chmn. bd. trustees Emory U.; trustee Atlanta Music Festival Assn., Inc. Mem. Phi Beta Kappa, Kappa Alpha, Phi Alpha, Sigma, Omicron Delta Kappa. Methodist. Rotarian. Author: Asa Griggs Candler. a biography, 1950. Home: 980 Briarcliff Rd. N.E., Atlanta 6. Office: Candler Bldg., Atlanta 3. Died Oct. 1, 1957; buried West View Cemetery, Atlanta.

CANN, Norman D., lawyer; born at Cohasset, Massachusetts, Dec. 9, 1898; s. Joseph Murray and Abbie (Wentworth) C.; B.C.S., Southeastern U., Washington, D.C., 1925; LL.B., Atlanta (Ga.) Law Sch., 1928; m. Jane McCurdy, Jan. 7, 1922; children—Dorothy Jane (wife of Maj. William A. Cromartie), Gloria Wentworth (Mrs. J. H. Rains). Internal revenue agent, Atlanta, Georgia, 1925-28, asst. revenue agent in charge, 1928-38, head of Pacific Div. tech. staff, San Francisco, Calif., 1938, New York Div. tech. staff, New York, N.Y., 1939, asst. commr., Washington, D.C., 1940-44, dep. commr. 1944-—. Admitted to Ga. bar, 1928; C.P.A., Ga., 1928. Served as sgt., Co. A, 344th Bn., Tank Corps. A.E.F., World War I. Decorated Purple Heart. Mem. Am. Inst. Accountants, Ga. Soc. C.P.A.'s, Delta Theta Phi, Phi Phi Pi, Am. Legion. Author spl. articles on taxation. Home: 10 Vernon Terrace, Alexandria, Va. Office: 425 13th St., Washington 4. Died Mar. 17, 1956.

CANNON, A. Benson, physician; b. Wilcox County, Ala., Nov. 10, 1888; s. Edmund Rashe and Pencye (Bigger) C.; LL.D., Erskine Coll., S.C., 1909; M.D., Tulane U., 1913; student U. of Vienna, 1924-25; m. Eleanor Moore Reid, Nov. 9, 1916; 1 dau., Cynthia. Interne Presbyn. Hosp., New York City, 1913-16; asst. dermatologist in office Dr. John A. Fordyce, 1916; prof. dermatology, Coll. of Phys. and Surgs., Columbia Univ.; dir. dept. dermatology, City Hosp.; consultant Woman's, New York Neurological, St. Mary's, Nassau County and Sharon hosps., Vassar Hosp. (Poughkeepsie, N.Y.). Trustee Erskine Coll. Mem. A.M.A., Am. Acad. of Dermatology and Syphilology, New York Dermatol. Soc., New York Acad. of Medicine, Vienna Dermatol. Soc. (hon. mem.), Clin. Research Soc., Sigma Alpha Epsilon, Alpha Kappa Kappa. Clubs: Millbrook Hunt; Rapahanock Hunt (Va.); New Canaan Golf. Contbr. articles to med. jours. Home: 1160 Park Av. Address: 371 Park Av., N.Y.C. Died Nov. 27, 1950; buried Millbrook, N.Y.

CANNON, James III, educator; b. Farmville, Va., Nov. 30, 1892; s. (Bishop) James, Jr., and Lura Virginia (Bennett) C.; student Webb Sch., Bell Buckle, Tenn., 1907-10; A.B., Trinity Coll. (now Duke U.), 1914; A.M., Princeton, 1917; Th.B., Th.M., Princeton Sem., 1925; D.D. Birmingham-Southern Coll., 1938; LL.D., Kentucky Wesleyan College, 1956; m. Margaret Wagner Faw, Dec. 22, 1920; children—James IV (dec.), Walter Faw. Editor Richmond Virginian and business mgr. Christian Advocate, Richmond, 1914-15; ordained ministry M.E. Ch., S., 1917; asst. prof. Bibl. lit., Trinity Coll., N.C., 1919-21, prof. also of missions, 1921-26; Ivey prof. history of religion and missions, Divinity Sch., Duke U., 1926-—, dean Duke U. Div. Sch., 1951-58, dean emeritus, 1958-—. Army Y.M.C.A., worker, U.S., France, Italy, 1917-18; chaplain 1st lt. A.E.F., 1918-19; senior chaplain 1st division. Decorated Croix de Guerre (France), 1919. Mem. Phi Beta Kappa (senate 1953-58), Sigma Chi. Author: (with H. E. Spence) A Guide to Study of English Bible. 1926; History of Southern Methodist Missions, 1926. Adv. editor The Muslim World, 1947-55. Home: 803 Lancaster Av., Durham, N.C. Died Mar. 1960.

CANNON, John Kenneth, U.S.A.F. officer; b. Salt Lake City, Mar. 9, 1892; s. John M. and Margaret (Peart) C.; student Utah State Coll., 1910-14, Air Corps Tactical Sch., 1935-36, Command and Gen. Staff Sch., 1936-37; m. LaVon Bennion, June 16, 1922; children—Joan, Marion, Margaret. Commd. 2d lt., U.S. Army, 1917; promoted through grades to general. October 29, 1951; rated command pilot, command observer; chief U.S. Mil. Mission to Argentina, June 1938-Oct., 1941; with American Army abroad; chief of staff, 1st Air Force, Mitchel Field; comdg. gen. 1st Intercepter Command, Feb.-Sept., 1942; comd. 12th Air Support Comd. in support of Western Task Force during invasion French Morocco, North Africa; organized Air Training Command Mediterranean Theatre of Operations; dep. comdr. Mediterranean Allied Tactical Air Force for Sicilian Campaign and Invasion of Southern Italy; assumed comd. U.S. 12th Air Force and Mediterranean Allied Tactical Air Force, 1943; air comdr.-in-chief, All Allied Air Forces in Mediterranean and European Theatre, 1945. Comd. Air Training Command, 1946-48; comdr-in-chief U.S. Air Forces in Europe, 1948-51; now in command Tactical Air Command. Sigma Chi. Address: U.S.A.F., Air Adjutant General's Office, Washington. Died Jan. 12, 1955.

CANNON, Martin L., cotton textile exec.; b. Concord, N.C., Mar. 25, 1885; s. James William and Mary Ella (Bost) C.; ed. Va. Mil. Inst. and U. of N.C.; m. Ohla H. Brown, Sept. 2, 1909; children—Martin L., James G., Frances Ann (Mrs. John R. Hersey). Sec. and treas., later pres., Imperial Cotton Mills, 1909-27; pres. Social Circle Cotton Mills, 1915-46; dir. Cannon Mills Co., Wiscasset Mills, Am. Trust Co., Jefferson Standard Life Ins. Co. Chmn. Mecklenburg County (N.C.) Defense Council, World War II. Mem. N.Y. Southern Soc., Sigma Alpha Epsilon.

Presbyterian. Mason. Clubs: Charlotte City, Charlotte Country; Twenty-Nine (New York). Home: 400 Hermitage Rd. Office: Liberty Life Bldg., Charlotte 2, N.C. Deceased.

CANNON, Raymond J., ex-congressman; b. Ironwood, Mich., Aug. 26, 1894; both parents died shortly after his birth; grad. Minocqua High Sch.; student Marquette U. Law Sch. Earned way through sch. by playing professional baseball; admitted to Wis. bar, 1914, since in practice at Milw.; represented Joe Jackson in action for damages for breach of contract against Chgo. White Sox which resulted in verdict awarding damages of $19,000; was legal adviser to Jack Dempsey for 10 years. Candidate for judge of Wis. Supreme Court; mem. 73d and 75th Congresses, 4th Wis. Dist. Democrat. Died Nov. 25, 1951.

CANTOR, Nathaniel, sociologist, criminals; b. Nov. 26, 1898, Indianapolis, Ind.; B.A., Columbia University, 1921, Ph.D., 1925; LL.B., U. Buffalo, 1929; awarded scholarship in philosophy, Columbia Univ., 1921, fellow Social Science Research Council, 1932-33. Has done special work in causes of crime, treatment of offenders, European development in crime research, social work and the correctional field, mental hygiene and education; asso. prof. Univ. of Buffalo, 1928-32, prof. since 1932, chmn. dept. since 1942; visiting professor Columbia University, 1951-52; vis. prof. education U. Cal. at Los Angeles, 1957; consultant U.S. Foreign Operations Adminstrn. for European Productivity Agency, 1954-55. Member Am. Prison Association, American Sociol. Society, N.Y. State Bar. Author: Crime, Criminals and Criminal Justice, 1932; Crime, 1935; Crime and Society, 1939; The Dynamics of Learning, 1943; Employee Counseling: A New Approach to Industrial Psychology, 1945; Learning Through Discussion, 1951; The Teaching-Learning Process, 1953, others; also slide-film series Human Relations for Industry. Contbr. sociol., psychiat. and criminal jours. of U.S. and abroad. Home: 67 Endicott Dr., Buffalo. Died Dec. 5, 1957.

CANTWELL, Robert Murray, educator; b. St. Louis, Mo., Feb. 7, 1899; s. John England and Letitia Marie (Green) C.; A.B., St. Louis U., 1920, M.A., 1922; m. Zita Marie Doyle, Aug. 20, 1928; children—Mary Zita, Robert Murray, William Francis, John Christopher. Teacher St. Louis (Mo.) Univ. High Sch., 1920-24; pub. accountant and lecturer, St. Louis U., 1926—; certified pub. accountant, State of Mo., 1938; asst. prof. accounting, St. Louis U., 1937-43, asso. prof., 1943—, dean sch. of commerce and finance, 1943-48. Mem. bd. dirs. St. Louis C. of C., 1944-47. Mem. Mo. Soc. Certified Pub. Accountants, Am. Accounting Assn., Cath. Econ. Assn., Pi Mu Epsilon, Delta Sigma Pi. Home: 5149 Westminster Pl. Office: 3674 Lindell Blvd., St. Louis 8. Died June 10, 1954; buried Calvary Cemetery, St. Louis.

CAPARO, Jose Angel (kă-pă-rō'), univ. prof.; b. Cuzco, Peru, Nov. 2, 1888; s. Mariano Placido and Cecilia (Perez) C.; came to U.S., 1904; C.E., U. of Notre Dame, 1908, M.S. in E.E., 1909, M.E., Ph. D., 1913; Sc.D., U. of St. Anthony, Peru, 1910; M.A., U. of Chicago, 1919; m. Elizabeth Ella Kocsis, June 9, 1921; children—Edward Paul, Joseph Francis. Instr. mathematics, U. of Notre Dame, 1908-10; prof. chemistry and anthropology, U. of St. Anthony, 1910-11; instr. physics and mathematics, U. of Notre Dame, 1912-13, acting head dept. elec. engring., 1913-18, head of dept., 1919-39, professor of electrical engineering, 1939-43, professor emeritus, 1946—; engineer, Ind. and Mich. Elec. Co., 1923-25; with Ind. Bell Telephone Co., 1927-29. Peruvian del. from U. of St. Anthony, Cuzco, Peru, S.A., to 8th Internat. Congress of Applied Chemistry, 1912, to the 2d Pan-Am. Scientific Congress, 1915. Served as war instr. and asst. dept. elec. engring., Carnegie Inst., 1918. Fellow Am. Inst. E.E.; charter mem. Math. Assn. Am. Democrat. Catholic. Author: Desire for Gold and Conquest, 1953. Writer of elec. articles. Home: 1024 Leeper Blvd., South Bend 17, Ind. Died July 12, 1954; buried Cedar Grove Cemetery, Notre Dame, Ind.

CAPEK, Thomas (chăp'ĕk), banker, lawyer; b. Czechoslovakia, Dec. 6, 1861; s. John and Katherine (Capek) C.; LL.B., U. Mich., 1888; spl. lit. course Columbia, 1889; m. Anna Vostrovsky, 1894; 1 son, Thomas. Came to U.S., 1880, naturalized citizen 1886. Practiced law in Omaha, Neb., 1890-91, N.Y. C., 1895-1910; mem. Neb. Ho. of Rep. ,1890-91; v.p. Bank of Europe, N.Y.C. 1910-12, pres. 1912-32. Mem. Czechoslovak Geneal. Soc. in Prague, Royal Czech Learned Soc., Czechoslovak Emigration Inst. (life); hon. mem. Nat. Slavonic Soc. Recipient Czechoslovak Revolutionary medal. Democrat. Unitarian. Club: Authors. Author: Memoirs of Czech Immigrants to America, 1889; The Slovaks of Hungary, 1906; Fifth Years of Czech Printing in America, 1911; Bohemia under Hapsburg Misrule, 1915; Bohemia (Czech) Bibliography (with wife), 1915; Czechs and Slovaks in American Bankings (with son), 1920; The Czechs (Bohemians) in America, 1920; Jan V. Capek (biography), 1921; The Czech (Bohemian) community of New York, 1922; From New York to Prague and Return, 1922; Our America, 1926; Augustine Herrman, Founder of Bohemia Manor in Maryland, 1930; My America (autobiography), 1935; Our Americans (with wife), 1940; Charlotte Garrigue Masaryk (biography, with wife), 1940; Ancestry of Frederick Philipse. First Lord of Philipse Manor in Yonkers, N.Y. ,1939; Czechs and Slovaks in U.S. Census, 1939; Vistors from Bohemia and Moravia to the U.S., 1848-1939, 1940; Am. Czechs in Public Office, 1940; The First Czech Society in America 1850-1950, 1950. Home: 3553 82nd St., Jackson Heights, N.Y. Died Mar. 28, 1950; inurned Greenwood Crematory, Brooklyn, N.Y.

CAPEN, Oliver Bronson, publisher; b. Binghamton, N.Y., June 28, 1878; s. Rev. James Winchell and Leonora Sophia (Colt) C.; A.B., Hobart Coll., Geneva, N.Y., 1902; A.M., Columbia, 1903; m. Noreen Sheridan Hayes, Dec. 14, 1926. With Doubleday, Page & Co., 1903-07, Crowell Pub. Co., 1907-15; sec. and treas. Popular Science Pub. Co., pubs. Popular Science Monthly, 1915-24, pres., treas. and gen. mgr., 1924-30, dir. since 1930; sec. and dir. McCall Corp., pubs., 1917-27, dir. since 1927. Trustee Hobart, William Smith colls. Mem. Phi Beta Kappa, Kappa Alpha. Republican. Episcopalian. Clubs: University, Bedford Golf and Tennis. Author: Country Homes of Famous Americans, 1904. Home: Bedford, N.Y. Died May 2, 1953; buried St. Mathew's Cemetery, Bedford, N.Y.

CAPEN, Samuel Paul, educator; b. Somerville, Mass., Mar. 21, 1878; s. Elmer Hewett and Mary Leavitt (Edwards) C.; A.B., Tufts Coll., 1898, A.M., 1898; A.M., Harvard, 1900; Ph.D., U. of Pa., 1902; U. of Leipzig (on leave of absence from U. of Pa.), 1901-02; LL.D., Lafayette, 1920, U. of Chicago, 1932, Univ. of Pa., 1933, McMaster U., 1938, Syracuse Univ., 1944, Alfred University, 1946, Colgate Univ., 1949; D.C.L., Univ. of Buffalo, 1950; L.H.D., Tufts, 1921, Hobart, 1925; Sc.D., George Washington U., 1927; Litt.D., Clark U., 1937; Univ. of Rennes, France, Dr. Honoris Causa, 1948; m. Grace Duncan Wright, Mar. 25, 1908; 1 dau., Mary Capen Davis. Instr., asst. prof. and prof. modern languages, Clark College, 1902-11; prof. German Clark Coll., 1911-14; lecturer on ednl. administration, Clark U., 1911-14; pres. Worcester Pub. Edn. Assn., 1908-11; mem. Worcester Sch. Bd., 1908-14; specialist in higher edn. in U.S. Bur. of Edn., 1914-19; dir. Am. Council on Edn., 1919-22; chancellor U. of Buffalo, 1922-50, emeritus. Exec. sec. coms. on edn. of Council of Nat. Defense, 1917; mem. Advisory Bd. of War Dept., com. on edn. and spl. training, 1918-19; mem. advisory com. of ednl. bur. of Y.M.C.A., 1918; mem. div. of ednl. relations of Nat. Research Council, 1922-30, chairman, 1930-33; mem. Commn. on Med. Edn., 1925-32; mem. Nat. Advisory Com. on Education, 1929-31; sec. Ednl. Research Com. of Commonwealth Fund, 1920-27; pres. Assn. of Urban Universities, 1922-23; chmn. exec. com. Am. Council on Edn., 1923-24; chmn. Com. on Administrative Units of Commonwealth Fund, 1923-27; asso. dir. Regents Inquiry into Character and Cost of Public Edn. in State of N.Y., 1935-38; mem. Alien Enemy Hearing Board for Western New York, 1941-45; v.p. in America of British Society for Experiment and Research in Education, 1919-22; trustee Am. Univ. Union in Europe, 1919-22; Tufts Coll., Carnegie Found. for Advancement of Teaching, 1935-50, Bennington Coll., 1940-42. Decorated Royal Order St. Sava., 4th class (Serbian). 1919. Mem. Nat. Inst. of Social Sciences, N.E.A., A.A.A.S., Soc. for Advancement of Edn., Delta Phi Alpha, Phi Delta Kappa, Beta Gamma Sigma, Theta Delta Chi, Phi Beta Kappa, Phi Kappa Phi and Alpha Omega Alpha fraternities. Unitarian. Clubs: Cosmos, University (Washington); Chevy Chase (Maryland); Harvard, Century, University (New York); Saturn, Harvard, Buffalo (Buffalo). Author Opportunities for Foreign Students at Colleges and Universities in the United States, 1915; Resources and Standards of Colleges of Arts and Sciences, 1918; The Management of Universities, 1953; also bulls. and articles. Editor: Lessing's Nathan der Weise, 1914. Editor of Educational Record, 1920-22. Has participated in numerous surveys of ednl. instns. and systems. Home: 42 Linwood Av., Buffalo 9. Died June 22, 1956.

CAPPER, Arthur, ex-senator; b. Garnett, Kan., July 14, 1865; s. Herbert and Isabella (McGrew) C.; grad. high sch., Garnett, 1884; m. Florence Crawford, 1892 (now dec.). Began as compositor, Topeka Daily Capital, 1884; successively reporter, city editor, Washington corr., of the Topeka Daily Capital, pub. and proprietor since 1892; also publisher and proprietor of Capper's Weekly, Kansas Farmer, Household Magazine, Capper's Farmer, Missouri Ruralist, Ohio Farmer, Pennsylvania Farmer, Mich. Farmer, Topeka Daily Capital, Kansas City Kansan; owner radio sta. WIBW, Topeka and KCKN, Kansas City, Kan. Candidate Rep. nom. for gov. of Kan., 1911; elected gov. of Kan., terms 1915-19; U.S. senator, 1919-49. Mem. senate coms., Fgn. Relations, Chmn. com. Agr., Dist. Columbia; mem. Nat. bd. Am. Red Cross, 4-H Clubs; mem. Nat. Council Boy Scouts of America. Mason (Shriner), Odd Fellow, Elk, Workman. Clubs: Topeka, Country; Press (Washington, D.C.). Home: Topeka. Died Dec. 19, 1951; buried Topeka Cemetery.

CAPPS, Edward, univ. prof.; b. Jacksonville, Ill., Dec. 21, 1866; s. Stephen Reid and Rhoda S. (Tomlin) C.; A.B., Ill. Coll., 1887, LL.D., 1911; Ph.D., Yale, 1891; studied in Athens and Halle, 1903-05; Litt.D., Oberlin, 1923, U. of Mich., 1931, Oxford, 1946; L.H.D., Harvard, 1924; LL.D., U. of Athens, 1937 (Centenary); m. Grace Alexander, July 20, 1892 (now dec.); children—Rhoda (dec.), Priscilla, Edward, Alexander. Tutor in Latin, Yale, 1890-92; prof. Greek lang. and lit. U. Chgo., 1892-1907; prof. classics Princeton, 1907-36, now emeritus; lectr. Inst. of Advanced Study, 1936-41. Trustee and chmn. mng. com. Am. Sch. of Classical Studies at Athens, Greece, 1918-38; chmn. Commn. for Excavation of the Agora of Ancient Athens; chmn. trustees Athens (Greece) Coll.; trustee Near East Found., Athens Coll.; lectr. on the Grek Thatre, Harvard, 1903; Turnbull lecturer on poetry Johns Hopkins, 1917; American editor Loeb Classical Library, editor-in-chief . Chgo., Decennial Publications (29 vols.); mng. editor Classical Philology, 1906-07. Dir. div. Humanities, Rockefeller Found. and Gen. Edn. Bd., 1929-30. Pres. Classical Assn. Middle West and South, 1907-08, Am. Philol. Assn., 1914-15, Am. Assn. Univ. Profs., 1920. Served as A.R.C. commr. to Greece, 1918-19, with rank of lt. col.; E.E. and M.P. to Greece, 1920-21. Decorated Golden Cross Knight Comdr. Order of Redeemer, by King Alexander of Greece, 1919; Comdr. Order of the Phoenix, by King George II. Fellow Am. Acad. Arts and Scis.; mem. Am. Philos. Soc., Archeol. Soc. Athens (hon.), Phi Beta Kappa. Clubs: Century (N.Y.); Nassau (Princeton). Author: From Homer to Theocritus, 1902; Four Plays of Menander, 1910; the Greek Stage According to the Extant Dramas; The Chorus in the Later Greek Drama; The Introduction of Commedy into the City Dionysia; Chronological Studies in the Greek Tragic and Comic Poets; Epigraphical Problems in the History of Attic Comedy; The Plot and Text of Menander's Epitrepotes; Greek Comedy in the Columbia University Lectures on Greek Literatur, 1911. Also sundry other articles in classical philology. Home: 42 Mercer St., Princeton, N.J. Died Aug. 21, 1950; buried Jacksonville, Ill.

CAPRON, Charles Alexander, lawyer; b. Walden, N.Y., Dec. 7, 1886; s. Cyrus Kemper and Frances Alvira (Littlefield) C.; LL.B., N.Y. Law Sch., 1910; m. Margaret Eleanor Mosher, Aug. 24, 1915 (dec. June 17, 1946); children—William Mosher, Frances Margaret (Mrs. Gilbert Irvine Smith). Admitted to N.Y. bar, 1910, since practiced in N.Y.C.; asso. Turner, Rolston & Horan, mem. successor firms Geller, Rolston & Blanc, 1918-27, Taylor, Blanc, Capron & Marsh, 1927-32, Mitchell, Capron, Marsh, Angulo & Cooney since 1932. Mem. Montclair Housing Authority, 1938-40; mem. planning bd., Montclair, since 1940, chmn. since 1944; mem. development bd., Montclair, since 1945. Mem. bd. trustees Montclair Community Chest, 1930-41; mem. bd. N.J. Symphony Orchestra since 1950; chmn. Montclair com. N.J. Symphony Orchestra, 1945-52. Mem. Montclair Assn. (exec. com. 1937-44), Montclair Art Assn. (bd. trustees 1932-35), League Nations Assn. N.J. (pres. 1930 34), Am. Assn. U.N. (bd. trustees N.J. br. since 1943), Am. Bar Assn. (mem. council real property, probate trust law div. 1950-52; v.p. trust law 1951-52), N.Y. State Bar Assn., Assn. Bar City N.Y., N.Y. County Lawyers Assn. (dir. 1939-45, mem. jud. com. since 1939, chmn. com. surrogates ct. 1940-52). Episcopalian (warden, St. James, Upper Montclair; mem. standing com. Diocese of Newark; bd. trustees since founding 1941, pres. 1948-49, Laymen's Movement for a Christian World; trustee Wainwright House, Inc.). Clubs: Down Town Assn. (N.Y.C.); Upper Montclair (N.J.) Country. Home: 41 Bradford Av., Upper Montclair, N.J. Office: 20 Exchange Pl., N.Y.C. 5. Died Feb. 3, 1955.

CAPSTAFF, John George, color photography authority; b. Gateshead-on-Tyne, Eng., Feb. 24, 1879; s. John Squire and Elizabeth (Hogg) C.; ed. Heaton Sch. oof Science and Art and Armstrong Coll., Durham; m. Alice Grace Wallace, of Newcastle-on-Tyne, Sept. 23, 1912; children—Phyllis Mary, Elizabeth. Came to U.S., 1913; engaged in research in photography with Eastman Kodak Co., Rochester, N.Y., 1913—; pioneered in 16 millimeter motion pictures; responsible for application of the reversal process to motion pictures; holds many photographic patents; authority on color photography. Recipient Modern Pioneer award, 1940; Progress medal of Soc. Motion Picture Engrs., 1944; hon. fellowship Royal Photographic Soc., 1944; recipient Progress Medal of Royal Photog. Soc. Great Britain, 1947; hon. fellowship Photographic Soc. of Am., 1950. Home: 5151 Roxbury Rd., San Diego 16, Cal. Died Jan. 31, 1960.

CARAWAY, Hattie Wyatt, former U.S. senator; b. Bakerville, Tenn., Feb. 1, 1878; d. Willia mCarroll and Lucy Mildred (Burch) Wyatt; A.B., Dickson (Tenn.) Normal Coll., 1896; m. Thaddeus H. Caraway, Feb. 5, 1902 (died ov. 6, 1931); children—Paul Wyatt, Forrest, Robert Easley (dec.). Apptd. by Gov. Harvey Parnell as U.S. senator to fill unexpired term of husband, and elected spl. election, Jan. 12, 1933, trm expiring Mar. 1933, reelected for terms expiring 1939 and 1945. Apptd. mem. of U.S. Employees Compensation Comm. Democrat. Methodist. Home: Jonesboro, Ark.; and Methodist Bldg., Washington. Died Dec. 21, 1950.

CARDEN, Edward Walter, pres. Bank of Hawaii; b. Honolulu, Hawaii, Oct. 21, 1892; s. John Joseph and Anna Diane (Woodward) C.; grad. McKinley High Sch., Honolulu, 1910; student U. Cal., 1911-15; m. Hazel Hunt Vinton, Aug. 10, 1918; 1 dau., Barbara Vinton (Mrs. Welwyn F. Dallam, Jr.). With Bank of Hawaii, 1915—, beginning as jr. clerk, pres., 1937-55, vice chmn. bd. dirs., 1956, ret. 1956; dir. Love's Biscuit & Bread Co., Ltd .Served as 1st lt. Inf., World War I. Formerly mem. Bd. of Edn. and Bd. of Prison Dirs. and Bd. of Health. Mem. Sigma Chi. Clubs: Oahu Country, Waialae Country (Honolulu). Home: El Mirasol Hotel, Santa Barbara, Cal. Died June 29, 1957.

CARDWELL, James R., inventor, industrialist; b. Concord, Va., Oct. 27, 1873; s. Charles W. and Dolly Ming (Franklyn) C.; m. Zouella Durbin, Mar. 14, 1904; children—Dorothy (Mrs. Kenneth Knickerbocker), Virginia Ann (Mrs. Reinhardt). Began as office boy Am. Cotton Oil Co., 1893, became master car builder, 1898; organized Cardwell Mfg. Co., 1905, Union Draft Gear Co., 1909 (reorganized as Cardwell-Westinghouse Co., 1930, of which is now chmn.); organizer Acme Visible Records Co.; v.p. and dir. Diamond T. Motor Car Co.; dir. Allied Mills Co., Domestic Credit Co. Developed improved r.r. brake shoe, draft gear. Home: 365 Oak Knoll Rd., Barrington, Ill. Office: 332 S. Michigan Av., Chgo. Died Dec. 8, 1957.

CAREW, John F., judge, ex-congressman; b. Williamsburgh (Brooklyn), N.Y., Apr. 16, 1876; s. Michael H. and Ellen T. C.; A.B., Columbia, 1893; LL.B. Columbia U. Sch. of Law, 1896; m. Mary O'Brien, 1903 (died 1949); children—John F., James F., Magner, Mary, Blanche. Admitted to N.Y. bar, 1897; mem. N.Y. Assembly, 1904; mem. 63d to 71st Congresses (1913-31), 18th N.Y. Dist.; apptd. justice N.Y. Supreme Court, Dec. 24, 1929, elected to same office for term 1931-45. Democrat. Address: 141 S. Park Av., Rockville Centre, L.I., N.Y. Died Apr. 13, 1951.*

CAREY, Archibald, Christian Science lecturer; b. Eastlake, Mich., July 22, 1884; s. Henry Westonrae and May Mumford (Ransom) C.; A.B., U. of Mich., 1905, LL.B., 1907; C.S.B., Mass. Metaphysical Coll., Boston, 1931; LL.D., Principia College, 1952; m. Margery Allen, June 30, 1924; children—Sallie B. Cunningham, Philip, Allen, Archibald, Margery May Goodale. Member of law firm, Carey, Armstrong and Weadock, specializing in corporation law, 1909-29; practitioner, teacher of Christian Science since 1931; mem. bd. of lectureship First Church of Christ, Scientist, Boston, since 1946, lecturing in N. Am., S. Am., Europe and Africa. Vice chmn. bd. trustees Principia Coll. of Liberal Arts, Elsah, Ill.; trustee Principia Sch., St. Louis, Mo.; chmn. Christian Sci. Bd. Lectureship, 1956-57; pres. and mem. bd. trustees, Ill. Philanthropic and Ednl. Found. Formerly first reader and chmn. bd. dirs. First Church of Christ Scientist, Detroit; mem. bd. trustees Grosse Pointe Country Day Sch., Detroit Tuberculosis Sanatorium; treas. Chamber Music Soc. of Detroit. Served with U.S.N.R. Republican. Club: Detroit. Contbr. numerous articles on Christian Science to periodicals. Home: 501 Washington Rd., Grosse Pointe, Mich.; (summer) Brookhurst, Karlin, Mich. Office: Book Tower, Detroit 26. Died Feb. 19, 1957.

CAREY, Charles Emerson, paper exec.; b. Hutchinson, Kan., July 9, 1893; s. Emerson and Anna May (Puterbaugh) C.; grad. Cornell Univ., 1915; married; children—Charles E., James D., Mrs. Constance C. Alaire. Pres., dir. Central Fibre Products Co., Inc., Chgo., Inland Paper Box Co., Denver, C. F. Downey Box Co., North Kansas City, Mo., Am. Folding Box Co., St. Louis; v.p., dir. Carey Salt Co., Emerson Carey Investment Corp., Hutchinson & No. Ry. (all Hutchinson), Nat . Assn. Egg Case and Egg Case Filler Mfrs., Chgo., Continental Paper Products Co., Denver; dir. Chippewa-Pameroy Co., (Chgo.), Drillers Gas. Co. (Wichita, Kan.). Mem. Nat. Paperboard Assn. (dir.), Sigma Alpha Epsilon. Republican. Home: 15 W. 20th St., Hutchinson, Kan. Office: Central Fibre Products Co., Inc., 111 W. Washington St., Chgo. Died July 9, 1954.

CAREY, Hampson, steel exec.; b. Salem, O., Nov. 25, 1896; s. James Robertson and Caroline (Hampson) C.; student Phillips Andover Acad.; Yale; m. Claudia Shepard Heard, June 7, 1920; children—Catharine (Mrs. James H. Murdock), James Robertson, Carolyn Louise. With Jones and Laughlin Steel Corp., Pittsburg, 1920-51, mgr. collections, 1937-42, asst. treas., 1942-48, treas., 1948-51, mem. bd. dirs.; asst. treas. Pittsburgh Parking Authority. Served with 135th F.A., Battery A, 37th Div., U.S. Army, France, World War I. Mem. C. of C., Civic League of Mt. Lebanon. Presbyn. (trustee). Clubs: Farmington (Charlottesville, Va.); Midas, Duquesne, Harvard-Yale-Princeton St. Clair Country (Pittsburgh). Home: 1515 Mohican Dr., Pittsburgh 28. Died July 13, 1951.

CAREY, William Francis, contractor, engr.; b. Hoosick Falls, N.Y., Sept. 14, 1878; s. William and Catherine (Ryan) C.; ed. schools, Hoosick Falls; m. Ocean K. Daily, Oct. 29, 1904; children—Francesca, William Francis. Partner various contracting concerns engaged in building railways for Chinese Govt., financed by Am. Internat. Corp. of New York; gen. supt. of excavation during bldg. of Panama Canal; built railroad in Bolivia from Cochabamba to Santa Cruz; sanitary commr., N.Y.C., 1936-45; engaged in cement rock mining in Brazil and Argentina; pres. Carey, Baxter & Kennedy, Inc., Siems Carey Ry. & Canal Co.; v.p., The China Corp.; dir. Curtis-Wright Corp., Lone Star Cement Corp.; mem. exec. com. Lone Star Cement Corp. Member Defense Commn., Washington, as spcial advisor on construction of army, marine and aviation cantonments, World War II. Catholic. Clubs: Bankers, Engineers, Grand Street Boys Assn.; Hoosick Falls (N.Y.) Country; Bay Shore Yacht; Scranton (Pa.) Club; Split Rock (White Haven, Pa.). Home: 100 S. Montgomery Av., Bay Shore, L.I., N.Y. Office: Hotel Biltmore; also 342 Madison Av., N.Y.C. Died Feb. 22, 1951.

CARL, Melvin Latshaw, banker; b. Linfield, Pa., Sept. 14, 1906; s. Henry Clayton and Harriet (Latshaw) C.; student Pa. State Coll., 1922-24; m. Mildred H. Funkey, Nov. 11, 1925; children—Richard L., Judith A. With Royersford Trust Co., 1924-32, Pa. Dept. Banking, 1932-41; with Montgomery Trust Co. (now Montgomery County Bank & Trust Co.), Norristown, Pa., 1941—, now pres.; dir. Taylor Fibre Co., McCarter Iron Works, Dill Co. (all Norristown). Dir. Montgomery Hosp., Norristown. Home: 1742 Williams Way. Office: Main and Swede Sts., Norristown, Pa. Died June 6, 1959.

CARLES, Arthur B., artist. Former instr. Pa. Acad. Fine Arts; works on exhibition t Pa. Acad. Fine Arts, Pa. Museum of Art, San Francisco Museum of Art, Art Inst. of Chgo. Recipient ippincott prize, 1917; Temple medal, 1930; J. Henry Scheidt Meml. prize, 1939. Died June 19, 1952.*

CARLETON, Guy, army officer; b. Austin, Tex., Sept. 9, 1857; s. William and Elizabeth Carleton; grad. U.S. Mil. Acad., 1881, Army War Coll., 1909; m. Cora B. Arthur, June 20, 1883. Commd. 2d lt. 2d Cav., June 11, 1881; 1st lt., 1888; capt. 10th Cav., 1898; q.-m., 1901; assigned to 13th Cav., 1905; maj. 4th Cav., 1906; lt. col. cav., 1912; assigned to 3d Cav., 1912; col. of cav., 1915; brig. gen., N.A., 1917; maj. gen., 1918. Was at Forts McGinnis and Custer, Mont., and Sherman, Ida., 1881-90; at Fts. Walla Walla, Wash., Ft. Lowell, Ariz., and Ft. Wingate, N.M., 1890-95; on recruiting duty and at Ft. Riley, Kan., 1895-98; comd. troop Montauk Pt., N.Y., Huntsville, Ala., and San Antonio, 1898-99; comd. Dist. of Campechuela, Cuba, 1899, Manzanillo, and Bayamo, Cuba, 1899-1900; in Philippines, 1901-03, 07; duty Gen. Staff and dir. Army War Coll., 1909-12; insp. gen. Philippine Dept., 1916-17; comdr. 159th Depot Brigade, Camp Taylor, Louisville, Ky., 1917; apptd. comdr. Provisional Depot for Corps and Army Troops, Camp Wadsworth, Spartanburg, S.C., 1917. Retired as col. regular army, 1921. Mem. Order of Carabao. Democrat. Episcopalian. Odd Fellow. Clubs: Army and Navy (Washington and Manila). Home: San Antonio. Died Jan. 8, 1946.

CARLEY, W. F., pres. Post Publishing Co. Address: 250 Washington St., Boston. Died Sept. 7, 1954.*

CARLIN, Walter Jeffreys, lawyer; b. Brooklyn, N.Y.; s. Joseph and Margaret (Driscoll) C.; LL.B., N.Y. Law Sch., 1904; LL.D., St. John's U., St. Mary's Coll., 1936, Fordham U., 1939, St. Lawrence U., 1940; m. Jeannette King, Nov. 8, 1911 (dec.); 1 dau., Marjorie Jean. Admitted N.Y. bar, 1904; chmn. bd. Lafayette Nat. Bank of Brooklyn; president Lafayette Safe Deposit Co.; director Namm's, Inc., 35 Park West Corporation. Served as pvt. N.Y.N.G. and promoted through grades to colonel, 1899-1901, 1903-21; lt. colonel, Judge Advocate Gen.'s dept., United States Army Reserves, 1922-37. Decorated Chevalier of the Legion of Honor; Cavaliere Order of the Crown of Italy; Officer of the Acad. (France); Officer Order of Crown of Belgium; Caballero, Orden del Merito Juan Pablo Duarte (Dominican Republic); Caballero, Orden de Cristobal Colon (Dominican Republic), Shell of the Holy Land, Master Knight, Sovereign Military Order of Malta; Knight, Grand Cross, Equestrian Order of Holy Sepulchre, Knight of St. Gregory The Great. Member of New York City Milk Commission, 1913, N.Y.C. Commn. on Plan and Survey, 1926, N.Y.C. Board of Education, 1933-39; chmn. Appeal Bd. No. 11, Selective Service, 1940-47; pres. National Catholic Community Service of Brooklyn and L.I., 1941—; mem. exec. com., War Com., Bar of City of N.Y., 1942-46. Member American, N.Y. State, City bar assns., Brooklyn Bar Assn. (ex-trustee), Soc. Med Jurisprudence (past pres.), N.P. Soc. Mil. and Naval Officers World Wars, C. of C. (dir.), Phi Kappa Psi. Democrat. Catholic. K.C. Clubs: Montauk, Cathedral (Bklyn.); Lawyers (N.Y.C.). Home: 11 Fifth Av. Office: 37 Wall St., N.Y.C. Died Apr. 24, 1958; buried Holy Cross Cemetery, Bklyn.

CARLISLE, Chester Lee (kär'lil), physician, psychiatrist; b. Columbus, O., July 18, 1876; s. Isaac Burson and Lauretta Stedman (Gee) C.; student Ohio State U., 1894-95; M.D., Western Reserve U., 1898; m. Hallie Elizabeth Haberman, Apr. 15, 1903; one daughter, Corabell (Mrs. E. E. Corbett). Interne Charity Hospital of Cleveland, Ohio, 1898-99; medical officer Manhattan State Hosp., New York, 1901-04; med. ofcr. Willard State Hosp., New York, 1904-11, Kings Park State Hosp., L.I., N.Y., 1911-17; chief div. of mental defect and delinquency, N.Y. State Bd. of Charities, 1917-20; with U.S. Pub. Health Service, 1920-21; with Vets. Adminstrn. since 1921, clin. dir., Palo Alto, Calif., 1934-46; ret. 1946. Capt., M.C., U.S. Army, 1918-19. Mem. Assn. Mil. Surgeons, Am. Psychiatric Assn., Assn. Research Human Heredity, N.Y. Soc. Clin. Psychiatry, N.Y. Neurol. Soc., A.A.A.S., Assn. for Research in Nervous and Mental Diseases, Nat. Com. for Mental Hygiene, Mil. Order of World War (past comdr. San Francisco Chapter), Am. Legion, Mil. Order Fgn. Wars, Delta Tau Delta. Episcopalian. Mason. Club: Waverly (Palo Alto). Author: Causes of Dependency, 1918; Oregon State Survey of Mental Defect, Delinquency and Dependency, 1920. Contbr. articles to med. jours. Home: 500 N. California Av., Palo Alto, Cal. Died Apr. 29, 1952; buried Marion, O.

CARLISLE, Clifton Hugh, banker; b. Cortland, O., 1869; s. William J. and Jane (McCort) C.; A.B., Harlem Coll., 1891; married; children—Donald Cook, Frank Kenneth, Supt. of schools in Ohio, 1891-1901; engaged in mercantile business, 1901-08; with Goodyear Tire and Rubber Co., Akron, O., 1908-10; with Goodyear Tire and Rubber Co. of Can., Ltd., since 1910, successively as gen. mgr., sec.-treas., vice pres., pres., chmn. finance com. and dir.; chmn. bd. The Dominion Bank, Toronto, Canada; director Canadian General Investments, Limited, Montreal Trust Company. Clubs: National, Lambton Golf and Country. Home: "Browside," Forest Hill Village, Toronto. Office: King and Yonge Sts., Toronto, Can. Died July, 1952.

CARLISLE, G(eorge) Lister, Jr., engr.; b. N.Y. City, Sept. 15, 1877; s. George Lister and Mary Swift (Coffin) C.; Harvard Sch., New York City; B.S. in Mech. Engring. Yale, 1900; m. Leila Laughlin, Feb. 28, 1915. Entered mining work on design of Experimental breaker, Auchincloss mine, Pa., 1900-02, in charge of erection of breaker; in gold-mining, partner Pres. H. S. Zalaya, Nicaragua 1905-10; mining, U.S., 1910-16; mem. Carlisle-Clark African expdn., Am. Museum of Natural History, N.Y. City, 1928; contbr. completed lion group to museum for Roosevelt African Hall, Trustee, Berry Coll., Rome, Ga.; mem. bd. Am. Geog. Soc., Nat. Audubon Soc., N.Y. City. Mem. Yale Engring. Assn., Am. Inst. Mining and Metall. Engrs. Rep. Conglist. Clubs: Century, Yale, Explorers (New York); Captains, Wharf Rats (Nantucket, Mass.). Home: Norfolk, Conn. Died Dec. 22, 1954.

CARLSON, Anton Julius, physiologist; b. Bohuslän, Sweden, Jan. 29, 1875; s. Carl and Hedwig (Anderson) Jacobson; A.B., Augustana Coll., 1889, A.M., 1899; Ph.D., Stanford U., 1903; honorary degrees of M.D., LL.D., Sc.D. from 8 univs. and colls.; m. Esther Shegren, Sept. 26, 1905; children—Robert Bernard, Alice Esther, Alvin Julius. Came to U.S., 1891. Research asso. Carnegie Instn., 1903-04; asso., asst. prof., prof. and chmn. dept. of physiology, U. of Chicago, 1904-40, now Frank P. Hixon Distinguished Service prof. emeritus. Consultant U.S. Food and Drug Adminstrn., U.S.P.H.S.; lecturer in China under auspices of Rockefeller Found., 1935; with Am. relief expedition in Europe, 1918-19; mem. Internat. Congresses of Physiology in Vienna, 1909, Groningen, 1913, Edinburgh, 1923, Stockholm, 1927, Boston, 1930, Leningrad and Moscow, 1935, Copenhagen, 1950, Montreal, 1953; member medical and research committees of the National Foundation of Infantile Paralysis. Served O.S.R.D. Lt. colonel, Med. Corps, U.S. Army, 1917-19. Awarded Distinguished Service Gold Medal (A.M.A.), Distinguished Service Citation (Minn. Med. Assn.); voted Humanist of Year, 1953. Fellow A.A.A.S. (past pres.); pres. Nat. Soc. for Med. Research, Research Council on Problems of Alcohol, Chicago Com. on Alcoholism; past pres. Am. Biol. Soc., Am. Physiol. Soc., Fedn. of Am. Socs. for Exptl. Biology, Inst. of Medicine, Am. Assn. Univ. Profs.; mem. American Gerontological Society (president), Nat. Acad. Sci., National Research Council, A.M.A. Am. Inst. Nutrition, Am. Inst. Chemists, etc.; mem. biological and med. socs. of France, Germany, Sweden, China and Argentina. Author (books): Control of Hunger in Health and Disease; The Machinery of the Body; also some 200 research reports. Contbr. to Am. and German jours. on physiological subjects. Home: 5228 Greenwood Av., Chgo. 15. Died Sept. 2, 1956.

CARLSON, Clarence Erick, ret. banker; b. Wheaton, Ill., Sept. 28, 1892; s. Charles and Elin Carlson; student Sch. of Commerce, Northwestern U.,

1918; m. Stella J. Johnson, June 2, 1917; children—Clarence E., Ward S., Mrs. Joy C. Dutton. With First Nat. Bank Chicago, 1912-57, v.p., 1944-57, ret. Mem. Chgo. Mercantile Exchange (gov.). Republican. Methodist. Mason (past master). Clubs: Chicago Athletic Association; Brookwood Country (Addison, Ill.). Home: Route 2, Box 904, Mack Rd., West Chicago, Ill. Office: 38 S. Dearborn St., Chgo. Died Apr. 28, 1958; buried Wheaton Cemetery.

CARLTON, A(rthur) C(lifford), engr., museum dir.; b. Balt., Aug. 24, 1895; s. William Arthur and Dovie (Hutton) C.; S.B., Mass. Inst. Tech., 1917; m. Mabel Caldwell Jones, May 28, 1919. Engr. Chile Exploration Co., Chuquicamata, Chile, 1920-22; dept. supt., gen. supt. Balt. Copper Smelting & Rolling Co., 1923-31; curator fuels, metals and chemistry Mus. Sci. and Industry, Chgo., 1932-41; civilian engr. Ordnance Dept., Chgo. Ordnance Dist., 1942-46; exec. dir. mus. Franklin Inst., Phila., since 1946. Served as 2d lt. to capt. Inf., U.S. Army, 1917-19. Mem. Am. Ordnance Assn., Radnor-Ithan-St. Davids Civic Assn., Phi Kappa Sigma. Home: Radnor, Pa. Office: Franklin Institute, Parkway and 20th St., Phila. 3. Died Nov. 12, 1958; buried Chapel Cemetery, Valley Forge, Pa.

CARLTON, Clarence Clay, automotive exec.; b. Akron, O., May 17, 1882; s. Wallace L. and Ella M. (Tinker) C.; ed. Buchtel Coll.; A.B., U. of Akron, 1904; U. of Mich. Law, 1905; U. of Chicago, 1906; m. Anna L. Durling, Aug. 8, 1906 (died 1937); children—Janet Ann (dec), James C., Thomas R.; m. 2d Emily Russell, Feb. 6, 1939. Served as superintendent of schools at Mantua, O., 1904-08, Medina, O., 1908-12; elected superintendent of schools, Elyria, O., 1912; resigned same year to become sec. to pres. Firestone Tire & Rubber Co., Akron; held various positions with Firestone until June 1917; sales manager Prudden Wheel Co., Lansing, Mich., 1917-20; sec. Motor Wheel Corp. since 1920, vice pres. and secretary since 1938. Director and v.p. Automotive Council for War Production; chmn. automotive parts advisory com., Automotive Division, W.P.B. and O.P.A. Managing dir. Automotive Com. for Air Defense, 1940; mem. Mich. War Council. Organized Lansing Safety Council, 1940, and served as 1st pres.; state chmn. Com. for Econ. Development. Pres. Automotive Parts and Equipment Mfrs., Inc., 1934-41, now director; dir. N.A.M., Mich. Mfrs. Assn.; mem. Soc. Automotive Engrs.; pres. and dir. Tire and Rim Assn., 1914-15, and 1932-34. Mason (32°). Clubs: Detroit Athletic, Recess, Economic (Detroit); Lansing City Press, Economic, Country (Lansing). Home: 136 Oakland Dr., East Lansing, Mich. Office: 735 E. Saginaw St., Lansing 3, Mich. Died June 9, 1951; buried Deepdale Cemetery, Lansing.

CARLTON, Newcomb, exec. (ret.); b. Elizabeth, N.J., Feb. 19, 1869; s. William James and Helen (Newcomb) C.; M.E., Stevens Inst., 1890; A.M., Harvard, 1917; LL.D., Colgate U., 1930; m. Josephine Winslow Smith, Oct. 31, 1906; 1 son, Winslow. Practiced as mech. engr., Buffalo, 1891-99; dir. of works Pan-Am. Expn., 1899-1902; v.p. Bell Tel. Co. of Buffalo, 1902-04; v.p. Westinghouse Elec. & Mfg. Co., 1904; mng. dir. Brit. Westinghouse Elec. & Mfg. Co., London, 1905-10; v.p. Western Union Tel. & Tel. Co., 1910-14, pres., 1914-33, chmn. bd., June 1933-May 1943, hon. chmn., 1943-49. Life trustee Am. Acad. in Rome. Grand officer Crown of Italy. Mem. Am. Soc. French Legion of Honor, Newcomen Soc. Clubs: Harvard, Century. Home: 10 Gracie Sq. Office: 120 Wall St., N.Y.C. 5. Died Mar. 12, 1953.

CARLTON, Richard Paul, mining and mfg. exec.; b. Mpls., Dec. 20, 1893; s. Pier August and Mathilde (Hartman) C.; grad. U. Minn., 1921; m. Florence Alice Nuwash, July 20, 1921; children—Dorothy (Mrs. Henri G. Foussard), Joyce (Mrs. Thomas S. Hartzell), Jean (Mrs. W. N. Whitaker). Joined Minn. Mining & Mfg. Co., St. Paul, 1921, pres., 1949—. Mem. Sigma Nu. Clubs: Minnesota, Town and Country, White Bear Yacht, St. Paul Athletic, Somerset (St. Paul); Indian Creek (Miami Beach, Fla.); Union League (Chgo.). Home: 1142 Summit Av., St. Paul 5. Died June 17, 1953; buried Lakewood Cemetery, Mpls.

CARMAN, Albert Pruden, physicist; b. Woodbury, N.J., July 1861; s. Rev. Thomas C. and Phebe C. (Pruden) C.; A.B., Princeton, 1883, A.M., 1885, D.Sc., 1886; m. Maude W. Straight, June 21, 1900. Fellow and tutor physics and mathematics Princeton, 1883-87; student Berlin, 1887-89; prof. physics and elec. engring. Purdue, 1889-92; Leland Stanford Jr. U., 1892-96; prof. physics and head of dept. U. Ill., 1896-1929, ret. Mem. Am. Physical Soc. Contbr. to tech. jours. Home: 910 W. California Av., Urbana, Ill. Died Feb. 10, 1946; buried Forest Home Cemetery, Oak Park, Ill.

CARMICHAEL, Archibald Hill (kär'mĭ-k'l), ex-congressman; b. Sylvan Grove, Ala., June 17, 1864; s. Jesse Malcolm and Amanda (Smith) C.; A.B., U. Ala., 1886; m. Annie Sugg, Jan. 21, 1889 (died 1920); children—Jesse Malcolm, Charles Elmore, Archibald Hill, Herbert, Paul Ligon (dec.). Admitted to Ala. bar, 1886, practicing at Tuscumbia; solicitor Dist. Court of Ala., 8th Jud. Circuit, 1890-94; speaker Ala. Ho. of Reps., 1906, 15; mem. Ala. Senate, 1918; mem. 73d and 74th Congresses, 8th Ala. Dist. Dir. First Nat. Bank (Tuscumbia). Pres. pro tem bd. trustees U. Ala.; mem. State Bd. Edn., Tuscumbia Bd. Edn.; mem. State Constl. Conv., 1901. Del. at large Dem. Nat. convs., 1916, 28, 32. Mem. Phi Beta Kappa, Sigma Nu. Democrat. Methodist. Mason (32°), K.P., Maccabee. Home: 802 E. 6th St., Tuscumbia, Ala. Died July 15, 1948.

CARMICHAEL, Omer (kär'mi-kl), educator; b. Hollins, Ala., Mar. 7, 1893; s. William Colin and Lucy (Wilson) C.; A.B., U. Ala., 1914; A.M., Columbia, 1924, Harvard, 1957, Yale, 1957; L.H.D., Dartmouth, 1957; LL.D., Univ. Kentucky, 1957; m. Elnora Reed Blanchard, Oct. 9, 1926; children—Shirley Ann, Donald Monroe, Carol Elizabeth. Rural sch. tchr. Tallapoosa Co., Ala., 1911-12; tchr. high sch, Selma, Ala., 1914-16, prin., 1916-19, supt. schs., 1920-26; supt. schools Talladega, 1919-20, Tampa, Fla., 1926-30, Lynchburg, Va., 1932-45, Louisville, Ky., 1945—; tchr. (summers), Alabama Coll., 1922, U. Fla., 1928, 29, 31, U. Ala., 1932, 48, Duke U., 1932, 36, 37, U. Louisville, 1949. Trustee Lynchburg Coll., Presbyn. Orphans Home. Active civic affairs serving on bds. of Boy Scouts, Y.M.C.A., Community Chest, C. of C., fgn. relations coms., Mental Hygiene Clinic, Nat. Conf. Christians and Jews, etc. Recipient Fiorella H. LaGuardia award, 1957; Brotherhood award Nat. Conf. Christians and Jews, 1958. Mem. Am. Assn. Sch. Adminstrs. (mem. adv. and exec. coms.; rep. to Am. Council on Edn. and chmn. 1946 Yearbook commn., v.p., 1954-55), Nat. Soc. Study Edn., Am. Acad. Polit. and Social Sci., N.E.A. (life), Ala. (pres.), Fla., Va. and Ky. state ednl. assns., Southern Assn. Colls. and Sec. Schs., Ky. Assn. Colls. and Secondary Schs. (pres.), Phi Beta Kappa, Phi Delta Kappa, Kappa Delta Pi. Presbyn. (elder, moderator Montgomery Presbytery, Synod Va., 1940; commr. Gen. Assembly, 1944, 57). Mason. Club: Rotary (past pres. Selma & Lynchburg). Author: The Louisville Story (with Weldon James). Assisted in surveys of public schs. of Watertown, Mass., Fort Worth, Tex., Richmond, Va. and Chgo. Home: 2316 Saratoga Dr., Louisville 5. Office: 506 W. Hill St., Louisville 8. Died Jan. 1960.

CARMODY, John, judge; b. Granville, Wis., Jan. 6, 1854; s. John and Mary (Purcell) C.; high sch. edn.; m. Anna Madden, July 12, 1886. Admitted to bar, 1880; practiced at Waseca, 1880-05; city justice and judge Municipal Ct., Waseca; moved to Hillsboro, N.D., 1885; city atty. and mayor, Hillsboro; state's atty. Traill County, N.D.; apptd. asso. justice Supreme Ct. of N.D., 1909, for an unexpired term ending, 1910. Democrat. Roman Catholic. Pres. N.D. State Bar Assn. Home: Hillsboro, N.D. Address: Bismarck, N.D. Died 1920.

CARMODY, Martin Henry, lawyer; b. Grand Rapids, Mich., s. Martin and Anastacia (Murphy) C.; Ph.B., U. of Mich., 1899, LL.B., 1901; LL.D., 1939; LL.D., University of Notre Dame, 1932; married Frances G. Brady, January 25, 1911; 1 daughter, Mary Louise (Mrs. Maurice L. Nee). Admitted to Michigan bar, 1901, and began practice at Grand Rapids. Mem. Am., Mich. State and Grand Rapids bar assns. Decorated Knight of St. Gregory the Great, 1920, and Grand Cross, same order, 1929; Comdr. French Order of Morocco, 1920; Chevalier Legion of Honor (France), 1920; Golden Rose of Tepeyac (Mexico), 1931; Secret Chamberlain to His Holiness Pope Pius XI, 1931; Silver Buffalo (Boy Scouts of Am.), 1932. Republican. Mem. Knights of Columbus (Supreme Knight 1927-39; Supreme dir. Boy Activities since 1939). Mem. Ancient Order of Hibernians, Elks, Moose. Clubs: University, Peninsular, Blythefield Country, Catholic Club (New York). Home: 553 Madison Av. S.E. Office: 918-924 Michigan Trust Bldg., Grand Rapids, Mich. Died Dec. 9, 1950.

CARMONA, Antonio Oscar de Fragoso, pres. of Portugal; elected 1926, reelected, 1928, 35, 39, 42. Address: Lisbon, Portugal. Died Apr. 18, 1951.*

CARNEGIE, Dale (kär-nā-gĭ), lecturer, author, columnist; b. Maryville, Mo., Nov. 24, 1888; s. James William and Amanda Elizabeth (Harbison) C.; State Teachers Coll., Warrensburg, Mo., 1904-08, Am. Acad. Dramatic Arts, 1911, N.Y.U. Sch. of Journalism, 1914; Columbia Sch. of Journalism, 1913; B.C.S. Balt. Sch. of Commerce and Finance, 1916-17; Litt. D., Md. Coll. for Women, 1936, U. Tampa, 1949; LL.D., Lincoln Coll., 1951; m. Dorthy Vanderpool, Nov. 5, 1944; 1 dau., Donna Dale. Has conducted courses in effective speaking and applied psychology, in U.S., Europe, 1912-45; lectured in Can., U.S. and British Isles, on "With Allenby in Palestine and Lawrence in Arabia," 1919-20; impresario for Lowell Thomas and Sir Ross Smith, 1921-22; traveled in Europe, Africa and Arctic regions, 1923-25; has done research on career of Abraham Lincoln. Radio broadcasts include: Maltex Hour, 1933-35; Getting Ahead, 1937-38; How to Win Friends and Influence People, 1938; How to Get Ahead, 1941; Little Known Facts About Well Known People, 1943-45. Fellow Royal Geographical Society, 1921. Writes daily syndicated newspaper column. Author: Public Speaking and Influencing Men in Business, 1926; Lincoln the Unknown, 1932; Little Known Facts About Well Known People, 1934; How to Win Friends and Influence People, 1936; Five Minute Biographies, 1937; Biographical Roundup, 1945; How to Stop Worrying and Start Living, 1948. Home: 27 Wendover Rd., Forest Hills, N.Y. Office: 15 W. 46th St., N.Y.C. Died Nov. 1, 1955; buried Belton, Mo.

CARNEGIE, Hattie, couturiere; b. Vienna, 1889; brought to U.S. as child; ed. pub. schs. of N.Y. City; m. 3d, John Zanft. Established (with partner), Carnegie—Ladies Hatter, 1909; firm was incorporated, 1913, became sole owner of the firm and later established Hattie Carnegie, Inc. Address: 42 E. 49th St., N.Y.C. Died Feb. 22, 1956.

CARNES, Cecil, author, war correspondent; b. Fairview, O., Sept. 11, 1909; s. Sidney Grant and Lyda (Dugan) C.; Sc.B. in Journalism, Ohio State U., 1932; m. Elizabeth Dew, March 27, 1934; children—Conrad, George, Calland. Staff writer, N.Y. World Telegram, 1932-41; staff writer radio program, We, the People, 1941-43; war corr. for Saturday Evening Post. Producer, The Washington Story, Memo to America, Am. Broadcasting Co.; television dir. ECA, 1950; in Europe as mag. writer-historian for ECA/OSR, Paris, 1950-52. A founding mem. Citizens for Eisenhower and Nixon (chief speakers bur., also charge radio, television for Eisenhower campaign, 1952). Mem. Sigma Delta Chi. Author: John L. Lewis, 1935; Jimmy Hare, News Photographer, 1940; Mexican Masquerade, 1942; Last Man Off Wake Island, 1943; American Guerrilla, 1943; Secret Mission Submarine, 1944; You Must Go to Mexico, 1946; (with Fred Carnes) Down the Pan-American Highway, 1946; You Must See Canada, 1948. Produced movie A Lesson from Korea, 1950. Contbr. to nat. mags. Home: Border Villas, North Laredo, Tex. Died Feb. 12, 1953.

CARPENDER, Arthur S., naval officer (retired); b. New Brunswick, N.J., Oct. 24, 1884; s. John N. and Annie S. (Kemp) C.; student St. Paul's Sch., Concord; Rutgers Prep. Sch.; grad. U.S. Naval Acad., 1908; grad. sr. course, Naval War Coll.; completed course in submarine instrn., 1922; m. Helena B. Neilson, Apr. 30, 1912. Commd. ensign, U.S. Navy, 1910, advanced through grades to rear adm., 1941, temporary vice adm., 1942, retired as adm., 1946; comd. U.S.S. Fanning; staff commander U.S. Naval Forces, Europe, World War I; comdr. destroyers, U.S. Atlantic Fleet, later comdr. S.W. Pacific Force; comdt. 9th Naval Dist., World War II; U.S. Navy dir. pub. relations. Supt. Admiral Farragut Academies, Pine Beach, N.J., and St. Petersburg, Fla., since 1948. Decorated D.S.M., Legion of Merit with gold star, Army D.S.M., Distinguished Service Order; Comdr. Mil. Div., Order British Empire, Order Orange-Nassau with Swords (Netherlands). Mem. Navy League of U.S. (v.p.). Clubs: Army and Navy (Washington); Chevy Chase (Md.); New York Yacht. Home: Riverside Dr., Pine Beach, N.J. Address: Admiral Farragut Academy, Pine Beach, N.J. Died Jan. 10, 1960.

CARPENTER, Arthur DeVere, lecturer, writer; b. Napoli, N.Y., Sept. 13, 1866; s. Charles and Harriet A. (Palmer) C.; student Colgate U., 1886-90; grad. Crozer Theol. Sem., Chester, Pa., 1893; m. Grace Murdock, June 18, 1890; children—DeVere Weston, Elizabeth Barker (Mrs. E. V. D. Corput), Charles Sherwood, Arthur Bernarr, Helene Byington (Mrs. A. R. Van Sant), Harry Murdock. Ordained Baptist ministry, 1893; pastor Dover, Del., Plattsburgh, N.Y., and Durango and Denver, until 1904; state evangelist for Wash., 1904-07; supt. city missions, Seattle, 1907-11; editor, pub. Church Life, 1911-15; astronomical lecturer, 1915-16, chautauqua lecturer until 1935, now school, club and college lecturer; delivered 140 lectures in New Zealand, winter of 1919-20; lecture tour in Australia, Tasmania, and New Zealand, summer 1924. Mem. Internat. Lyceum and Chautauqua Assn., Delta Upsilon. Lectures: The Energy of the Universe; The New Astronomy; Worlds in the Making; The Immanence of God; Man and Meteorology; Other Worlds Than Ours; Old Mother Earth; Sensational Adventures in Astronomy; etc. Contbr. syndicated paragraphs to newspapers under title of Star Lore, 1929-31; also numerous current science feature articles to young people's publs. Home: 400 Boylston Av. N., Seattle 2. Died Aug. 4, 1958.

CARPENTER, Arthur Howe, metallurgist; b. Georgetown, Clear Creek County, Colo., Oct. 19, 1877; s. Franklin Reuben and Annette Fuller (Howe) C.; freshman class, Ohio U., 1894, A.M., 1914; student Northwestern U., 2 yrs.; m. Margaret Lucile, d. Dafydd J. Evans, June 5, 1901; children—Franklin Dafydd, Margaret Annette (Mrs. D. M. Dutton), Mary Elizabeth (Mrs. S. L. McCarthy). Assayer and research chemist, 1894-96, assistant supt. Deadwood and Delaware Smelting & Refining Co., Deadwood, S.D., 1898-99; jr. partner firm of Carpenter & Carpenter, Denver, 1900; supt. Clear Creek Mining & Reduction Co., Golden, Colo., 1901-03; research work, Calumet, Mich., 1904; gen. mgr. Takilma (Ore.) Mining & Smelting Co., 1905; chief chemist, Am. Smelting & Refining Co., Leadville and Denver, Colo., 1906-08; research work, etc., 1909; prospecting, Nev., 1910-11; research metallurgist, Am. Vanadium Co.,

1912-18; gen. mgr. Colo. Vanadium Corp., 1918-20; asst. prof. metallurgy, Armour Inst. Tech. (Ill. Inst. Technology), Chicago, 1920-28, became associate prof., 1929, head metallurgy division; lecturer geology, astronomy, meteorology; emeritus professor since November 1, 1944. Staff consultant, metallurgy, Armour Research Foundation; cons. practice. Fellow A.A.A.S.; mem. Am. Inst. Mining and Metall. Engrs., Ill. Acad. Science, Am. Soc. Testing Materials, Soc. Promotion Engring. Edn., Astron. Soc. of Pacific, Am. Assn. of Variable Star Observers, Chicago Astron. Soc. (dir. 1935-37, 1939-45), Soc. Amateur Telescope Makers of Chicago (pres.), Phi Lambda Upsilon, Alpha Chi Sigma, Pi Gamma Mu, Delta Tau Delta, S.A.R. Republican. Episcopalian. Mason. Contbr. mining and metall. publs. Inventor methods of covering pipe with lead. Made 20½ telescope used by Elgin Obs. for daily Arcturus ceremony at Century of Progress Expn., Chicago, 1933 and 1934. This telescope was made as a memorial to Dr. Franklin R. Carpenter and D. J. Evans, and presented to Ohio Univ., Athens, O. Club: Faculty. Home: 365 S. 5th Av., Middleport, O. Died Mar. 20, 1956; buried West Union St. Cemetery, Athens, O.

CARPENTER, Delph E., lawyer, agriculturist; b. near Greeley, Colo., May 13, 1877; s. Leroy S. and Martha Allen (Bennett) C.; student lit. dept. of Denver, 1896-97, law dept., 1897-99, LL.B., 1899; LL.D., from U. of Colorado, 1927; m. Michaela, d. Capt. M. J. Hogarty, U.S. Army, June 5, 1901; children—Michaela Hogarty, Donald Alfred, Sarah Hogarty, Martha Patricia. Engaged in gen. practice until 1908, since in irrigation and interstate river practice; counsel in original proceeding in case of Wyo. vs. Colo., 1910-19, involving appropriation of waters of the Laramie River; managing and dir. counsel for Colo. in South Platte litigation between Neb. and Colo.; spl. counsel for Colo. in Republican River litigation between Neb. and Colo.; counsel for Colo. in interstate boundary, New Mexico vs. Colo., 1919-25; mem. Colo. Senate, 1908-12 (chmn. com. interstate water investigations, 1909-11); spl. asst. atty. gen. of Colo., in charge interstate water litigation, 1918; spl. envoy gov. of Colo. to gov. of New Mexico to arrange submission La Plata River interstate water controversy to interstate compact commn.; originator program exercise treaty powers of states in interstate river controversies; drew legislation, 1920-21, enacted by Calif., Colo., Nev., N.M., Ariz., Utah and Wyo., providing for formulation by interstate treaty commn. of compact between the seven states respecting the future use and disposition of waters of the Colorado River and tributaries, and prepared congressional legislation providing for a nat. representative on same commn.; apptd. interstate compact commr. for Colo., 1921, to serve on interstate treaty commns. respecting settlement of future use and disposition of Colo., La Plata, Ark., S. Platte and Laramie rivers; spl. counsel for Colo. for reargument Laramie River and Republican River cases before U.S. Supreme Court, 1921-22; concluded Colorado River compact, 1922, also La Plata River compact (Colo. and N.M.); apptd., 1923, treaty commr. Colo., use and disposition waters of Rio Grande, Arkansas, S. Platte and N. Platte rivers; concluded compact bet. Colo. and Neb. in waters S. Platte; reappointed, 1925, counsel for Colo., Rio Grande controversy with N.M., Tex. and U.S.; in charge of all interstate river controversies for Colo., 1923-27; commr. for Colo. at conf. of governors and commrs. of Colorado River states at Denver, Aug. and Sept. 1927; concluded compact between Colo., N.M. and Tex., respecting waters of the Rio Grande River, 1929; engaged in negotiations respecting North Platte and Colorado rivers, and in miscellaneous interstate river work, 1928-31; counsel for Colo. in suit of Ariz. vs. Calif., et al., before U.S. Supreme Court, 1930-31; commr. for Colo., North Platte River compact negotiations (Colo. and Wyo.), 1931-32. Awarded University Recognition medal, U. of Colo., 1923, "for distinguished public service." Reclaimed by irrigation about 400 acres of arid land in Weld County, Colo.; breeder of registered shorthorn cattle. Mem. Am., Colo. and Weld County bar assns., Beta Theta Pi; hon. mem. Colo. Soc. C.E. Republican. Methodist. Mason. Home: 1112 Tenth St., Greeley, Colo. Died Feb. 27, 1951; buried Linn Grove Cemetery, Greeley, Colo.

CARPENTER, H(iram) Beach, business exec. and gen. counsel; b. Rockford, Ill., Apr. 19, 1892; s. Murray M. and Martha (Beach) C.; A.B., U. of Mich., 1914; LL.B., Columbia, 1917; m. Liana La Pointe, Oct. 15, 1919; children—Liana Louise (Mrs. Frederick M. Adams), Elizabeth Ann (Mrs. Charles Robert Jones), Robert Beach. Served in United States Naval Reserve Force, 1917-19. Assistant legislative counsel, U.S. Senate, 1919-20; with Am. Sugar Refining Co., N.Y. City, since 1920, gen. counsel, 1929-41, vice-pres., 1941-53, president, 1953-54, vice chairman of the board, 1954——; director since 1948, mem. exec. com. since 1951; dir. Spreckles Sugar Co., Equitable Life Assurance Soc. of U.S., Scarsdale (N.Y.) Village Bd. of Trustees, 1942-45, mayor, 1945-47. Former dir.-at-large U. Mich. Alumni Assn. (Alumni Service Medal, 1950). Democrat. Clubs: Scarsdale Golf, Scarsdale Town; U. Mich. (N.Y.C.). Home: 45 Popham Rd., Scarsdale, N.Y. Office: 120 Wall St., N.Y.C. Died Sept. 27, 1955.

CARPENTER, J. Henry, church exec.; b. Auburn, N.Y., Jan. 7, 1893; s. Edward Rush and Mary E. (Parker) C.; A.B., Colgate U., 1917; M.R.E., Boston U., 1924; Ed.D., New York U., 1937; ordained Presbytery of Brooklyn-Nassau, 1933; m. Erma Mary Hall, July 20, 1917; children—James David (dec.), Jean Caroline (dec.), Erma Elizabeth, Mary Bertha. Supt. Madison County Ch. and Bible Sch. Assn., 1910-17; war work sec., Y.M.C.A., 1917; sec. Nassau-Suffolk Y.M.C.A., 1918; Religious Edn. Dept., Inter-Church World Movement, 1919; mgr. Internat. Council of Religious Edn. Camp, N.H., 1919-27; dir. religious edn., Central M.E. Ch., Brockton, Mass, and West Roxbury, Mass., 1920-23; dir. Albany div., Council of Religious Edn., 1924-25; dir. religious edn., Brooklyn Fedn. of Churches, 1926-32; instr., New York U., 1930-36; exec. sec. Brooklyn Ch. and Mission Fedn. since 1932; exec. sec. Brooklyn Bible Soc., 1936-1948; exec. sec. Brooklyn div. of Protestant Council, 1946. Sec. Joint Com. on Urban Ch.; mem. bd. mgrs. central dept. field adminstrn. Nat. Council Chs. of Christ in U.S.A., mem. fgn., home missions, Christian edn. divs., mem. Mayor's Adv. Com. for the Aged. Went to China as adviser on cooperative movement, 1942. Am. Com. in Aid of Chinese Indsl. Cooperative (chmn. 1941-43). Pres. Brooklyn Council for Social Planning, 1949-51; bd. dirs. Welfare Council, City of N.Y., 1949. Mem. Brooklyn com. on Racial Unity; trustee Keuka Coll.; hon. mem. Mayor's Com. for commemoration of Golden Anniversary of City of N.Y.; dir. Nat. Council for Permanent Fair Employment Practices Com. Mem. North Am. Administrative Com. of World Council of Christian Edn., Descs. Am. Revolution, Greater N.Y. Interfaith Com., Internat. Assn. Daily Vacation Bible Schools. Welfare Council N.Y. City, Christian Cooperative Fellowship in N. America (pres.), Assn. of Exec. Secs., (pres. 1938-39), Cooperative League of U.S.A. (chmn. tour com.). Assn. Council Secretaries (pres. 1946), East and West Assn. (mem. advisory com.), Presbyterian Fellowship for Peace (mem. exec. com.), treas. National Conference on Church and War, 1949, Kappa Delta Phi, Theta Phi. N.Y. corr. Christian Century since 1939. Author: Peace Through Coperation 1944; pamphlets on coperatives and the church. Home: 610 E. 38th St. Office: 252 Fulton St., Bklyn. Died June 16, 1954; buried Oakwood Cemetery, Chittenango, N.Y.

CARPENTER, John Alden, composer; b. Park Ridge, Ill., Feb. 28, 1876; s. George B. and Elizabeth Curtis (Greene) C.; A.B., Harvard, 1897, hon. A.M. 1922; studied music under Bernard Ziehn and Sir Edward Elgar; m. Rue Winterbotham, Nov. 20, 1900 (died 1931); m. 2d, Ellen Waller Borden, Jan. 31, 1933. Began with Geo. B. Carpenter & Co., mill. ry., ship supplies, 1897, v.p., 1909-36. Dir. Ill. Children's Home and Aid Soc. Republican. Conglist. Clubs: University, Saddle and Cycle. Composer: (with wife) When Little Boys Sing, 1904; (with wife) Improving Songs with Anxious Children, 1907; Sonata (for violin and piano), 1912; Gitanjali (song offerings), 1913; Adventures in a Perambulator (suite for orchestra), 1914; Concertino (for orchestra and piano), 1915; Symphony, performed 1st at Norfolk Festival, June, 1917; The Birthday of the Infanta, a ballet-pantomime prod. by Chicago Opera Co., season of 1919-20; (ballet) Skyscrapers, prod. by Metropolitan Opera Co., New York, 1926, and by State Opera, Munich, Germany, 1928; Song of Faith, chorus and orchestra, prod. Washington Bi-Centennial, 1932; Patterns, Piano and Orchestra, prod. Boston Symphony Orchestra, 1932; Sea Drift, symphonic poem prod. by Chicago Symphony Orchestra, Nov., 1933; Danza (for orchestra), 1935; Concerto for Violin and Orchestra, 1938; Symphony for 50th Anniversary of Chicago Symphony Orchestra, 1940; Symphony No. II, first performance by N.Y. Philharmonic Symphony Orchestra, 1942; The Seven Ages, symphonic suite, first performance by N.Y. Philharmonic Symphony Orchestra, 1945; also numerous published songs. Decorated Legion of Honor (France), 1921. Home: 999 Lake Shore Drive, Chgo. 11. Died Apr. 26, 1951; buried Beverly, Mass.

CARPENTER, William Seal, prof. politics; b. near Wilmington, Del., Jan. 28, 1890; s. Harry Fisher and Sarah Gawthrop (Seal) C.; B.S., U. of Pa., 1911, A.M., 1912; Ph.D., Princeton, 1914; studied London (Eng.) Sch. of Economics and Polit. Science, 1919; m. Alice Myrtle Getchell, Aug. 7, 1924; 1 dau., Jane. Instr. in polit. science, U. of Wis., 1914-17; instr., asst. prof. and asso. prof. politics, Princeton, 1920-30, prof., 1930——, chmn. dept., 1935-46. Served with A.E.F., 1918-19. Mem. adv. research council Bureau of Prohibition, 1931; research asso. Princeton Local Govt. Survey, 1935——; mem. N.J. State Planning Bd. 1937-44; mem. bd. mgrs., Friends' Home for Children, Phila., 1937——; mem. N.J. Commn. on Postwar Econ. Welfare, 1943. Pres. N.J. State Civil Service Commn., 1944-51. Mem. Am. Polit. Sci. Assn., Am. Soc. Planning Ofcls., S.R., Kappa Alpha. Mem. Soc. of Friends. Clubs: Princeton (N.Y.C.); Nassau (Princeton). Author: Judicial Tenure in the United States, 1918; Democracy and Representation, 1925; Development of American Political Thought, 1930; (with Paul T. Stafford) State and Local Government in the United States, 1936; Problems in Service Levels, 1940; The Unfinished Business of Civil Service Reform, 1952; Foundations of Modern Jurisprudence, 1958. Editor: Locke's Two Treatises of Civil Government, 1924; (with Paul T. Stafford) Readings in Early Legal Institutions, 1932. Contbr. articles and revs. in fields of law and politics. Home: 52 Hartley Av., Princeton, N.J., and Greenville, Me. Died Nov. 9, 1957; buried China, Me.

CARR, Arthur R., dean engring.; b. Whitehall, Mich., Apr. 9, 1893; s. Harrison Burdette and Susie E. (Stearns) C.; B.Pd., Mich. State Normal Coll., Ypsilanti, 1914, A.B., 1915; B.S. in Engring., U. of Mich., 1920, M.S. in Engring., 1921, Ph.D., 1934; LL.D., Eastern Mich. Coll., 1956; m. Edith Ilone Smith, July 14, 1917. Supt. of schs., Stockbridge, Mich., 1915-18; instr. chem. engring., U. of Mich., 1920-24; asst. prof. chemistry, Coll. of City of Detroit, 1924-29, prof. of chem. engring. and head of dept. of engring., 1929-33; dean coll. engring., Wayne U., Detroit, 1933——; pres. Wayne Engineering Research Institute; assistant in survey of clays and shales of Mich., Mich. Geol. Survey, 1923; engr. in charge of inflation of Dirigible ZMC-2, Grosse Isle, Mich., 1929; chem. engr. in charge research, Shakespeare Co., Kalamazoo, 1929-30. Served with Engineer Reserve Corps as instr. S.A.T.C., U. of Mich., 1918. Mem. Municipal Utilities Com., Detroit, 1937; dir. engring. defense training, Wayne U. Mem. Am. Chem. Soc., Mich. Engring. Soc., Am. Soc. for Engring. Edn., Nat. Soc. Profl. Engrs., Am. Soc. Testing Materials, Engring. Soc. of Detroit, Sigma Rho Tau, Tau Beta Pi, Alpha Chi Sigma, Phi Lambda Upsilon, Mu Sigma Pi. Mason. Author: Fuels and Their Utilization (with C. W. Selheimer), 1940. Home: 25320 Waycross, R.D. 3, Birmingham, Mich. Office: Wayne U., Bd. of Edn., Detroit 1. Died June 12, 1956; buried Marshall, Mich.

CARR, Charlotte, b. Dayton, O., May 3, 1890; d. Joseph Henry and Edith (Carver) Carr; A.B., Vassar Coll., 1915; M.A., MacMurray College, Jacksonville, Ill., 1938; L.H.D., U. Pa., 1939; unmarried. Personnel mgr., 1921-23; asst. dir. Bur. of Women and Industry, N.Y. Dept. of Labor, 1923-25; dir. Bur. Women and Children, Pa. Dept. of Labor, 1925-29, sec. labor and industry, 1930-34; exec. dir. Emergency Relief Bur., N.Y.C., 1935-37; dir. of Hull House, Chgo., 1937-43; asst. to vice chmn. War Manpower Commn., 1943-45; dir. Citizens Com. on Children, N.Y.C., 1945-53, ret. Mem. Nat. Women's Trade Union League, League of Women Voters. Episcopalian. Home: 31 W. 11th St., N.Y.C. 11. Died Aug. 8, 1957; Greenwich, Conn.

CARR, Gene, illustrator, cartoonist; b. N.Y.C., Jan. 7, 1881; s. Charles and Sarah (Cox) C.; ed. pub. schs.; never studied art; m. Helen Stilwell, Aug. 22, 1906 (divorced); 1 dau., Cleanthe; m. 2d, Helen Adams Breadner, Aug. 5, 1937; 1 son, Michael Breadner. Employed on the N.Y. Recorder, 1894, later on the N.Y. Herald, Phila. Times, N.Y. Evening Journal and N.Y. World. Creator of humorous series, Lady Bountiful, Phyllis the Servant Girl, Romeo the Dog, All the Comforts of Home, The Prodigal Son, Father, Willie Wise, Stepbrothers, Flirting Flora, Reddy and Caruso, Metropolitan Movies (in the Morning World); Little Nell, Just Humans, McClures Syndicate, King Features; This and That, George Mathew Adams Syndicate. Contbr. to Sat. Eve. Post, Colliers, Liberty, Am. Mag. Redbook, American Legion, Boys Life, This Week. Address: Walpole, N.H. Died Dec. 9, 1959.

CARR, George Wallace, ret. architect; b. Milw., Mar. 19, 1879; s. Henry Moore and Sarah (Burke) C.; student Art Inst., Chgo., also Armour Inst., 1898-1900; student engring., France, Belgium, Italy, 1901-03; m. Helen Demerest Taylor, May 3, 1905 (dec. 1940); children—Janet Taylor, Wallace Taylor; m. 2d, Caryl Cody Pfanstiehl, Mar. 18, 1943. Draftsman Crane & Barkhausen, Milw., 1900; draftsman, later chief of staff Pond & Pond, Chgo., 1901-14; with George C. Nimmons, 1914-16, partner in charge plan, design, layout Carr & Wright, Inc. (formerly Nimmons, Carr & Wright, now Dunlap & Edgar), architects and engrs. Chgo., 1919-52; ret.; asst. to dir. Holston Ordnance Works, Tenn. Eastman Corp., Kingsport, Tenn., 1942-43. Mem. Met. Housing Council, Chgo.; mem. Highland Park Zoning Bd. Served with constrn. div. U.S. Army, 1916-19. Fellow A.I.A. Episcopalian. Clubs: Cliff Dwellers, Tavern (Chgo.). Home: 721 W. 11th St., Claremont, Cal. Died Mar. 24, 1958; buried Milw.

CARR, Harry C., banker; born in St. Louis, Missouri, October 13, 1886; son Harry C. and Alice (Zimmerman) C.; student Columbia Univ.; m. Anstes Turner, May 24, 1911; children—Harry C., Anstes Valle; married 2d, Mrs. Katherine Gilbert. Started as draftsman Elliott Frog & Switch Co., St. Louis, 1905; manager eastern railroad supply dept. Simmons Hardware Co., 1912-15; dist. mgr., asst. to pres., export mgr., Sun Oil Co. 1915-28; managing dir. European properties, Gulf Oil Co., 1928-32; dir., treas., v.p., Bayuk Cigar, 1933-41; pres. First National Bank of Phila., 1941-51, chmn. of the bd. since 1951; director Atlantic Refining Co., Fire Assn. of Philadelphia, Reliance Ins. Co., Curtis Publishing Co.; member board of trustees

Penn Mutual Life Ins. Co. Clubs: Racquet, Union League, Rittenhouse (Phila.); Gulph Mils Golf; Links (New York). Home: Montrose Av., Rosemont, Pa. Office: 15th and Walnut St., Phila. Died Feb. 20, 1955.

CARR, Harvey, psychologist; b. Morris, Ill., 1873; s. Hamilton and Bell (Garden) C.; student DePauw U., 1893-95; B.Sc., U. Colo., 1901, M.Sc., 1902; Ph.D., U. Chgo., 1905; m. Antoinette Cox, Dec. 30, 1908; children—Frances Garden, Laurence Hamilton, Virginia Thurston. Instr. psychology Pratt Inst., Bklyn., 1906-08; asst. prof. psychology U. Chgo., 1908-16, asso. prof., 1916-23, prof., 1923-38, chmn. of dept., 1926-38, prof. emeritus, 1938—. Adv. editor Journal of Gen. Psychology; coöperating editor Comp. Psychology Monographs. Mem. Am. Psychol. Assn. (pres. 1926), Sigma Xi, Sigma Nu. Club: Quadrangle. Author: Textbook of Psychology, 1925; An Introduction to Space Perception, 1935. Contributor on comparative psychology, visual speace perception, ednl. theory, etc. Home: Culver, Ind. Died June 27, 1954.

CARR, James O., lawyer; b. Manchester, N.H., Aug. 24, 1872; s. James R. and Catharine L. (Danforth) C.; ed. Manchester High Sch.; m. Sara E. Appel, Dec. 18, 1895. Admitted to N.Y. bar, 1899, began practice at Schenectady; v.p., dir. Westexas Oil & Royalty Corp. of Fort Worth, Tex.; dir. Allegheny Ludium Steel Corp. and predecessor firm, 1918—. Republican. Mason. Clubs: Duquesne, Pittsburgh Athletic Assn., Oakmont Country. Address: Oliver Bldg., Pitts. Died May 23, 1949.

CARR, John Wesley, educator; b. Lawrence County, Ind., Dec. 13, 1859; s. James Newton and Laura E. (Stallings) C.; A.B., Indiana U., 1885, A.M. from same univ., 1890; grad. study, Columbia, 1908-09; Ph.D., New York U., 1913; m. Rachel Ashcraft, Oct 7, 1878 (died Apr. 27, 1927); children—Anna Louise (dec.), Charles Edmund (dec.), Harry Ashcraft, Frank Clyde; m. 2d, Mary Willia Moss, Apr. 21, 1928 (died September 18, 1948). Teacher rural schools, Greene County, Indiana, 1877-81; principal high school, Bloomington, Indiana, 1885-87, Muncie, 1887-90; supt. public schools, Anderson, Indiana, 1890-1905, Dayton, O., 1905-08, Bayonne, N.J., 1909-16; prin. Friends' Central Sch., Phila., 1916-18; in War Camp Community Service, Boston, Mass., Norfolk, Va., and Charleston, S.C., World War; dir. Div. of Hygiene, Ednl. Dept., Ky., 1920-22; state supervisor high schs. of Ky., 1922-23; organizer and first pres. Murray (Ky.) State Teachers Coll., 1923-26, dean, 1926-33, pres. and dean, 1933-36, dean 1936-40, president emeritus since 1940; historian, Murray State College. Life member N.E.A. (president Dept. Superintendence 1906). Democrat. Methodist. Author: Taxation and Teachers' Salaries in Indiana, 1904; A System of School Support—New Jersey, 1913; Course in Physical Education for the Common Schools of Kentucky, 1920. Home: Murray, Kentucky. Died Feb. 18, 1960.

CARR, Ralph L., ex-gov. Colo.; b. Rosita, Colo., Dec. 11, 1887; s. William Frank and Mattie (Kimberlin) C.; grad. high sch., Cripple Creek, Colo., 1905; A.B., U. Colo., 1910, LL.B., 1912 ;m. Gretchen Fowler, Feb. 1, 913; children—Robert Frank, Cynthia Joan; m. 2d, Mrs. Eleanor Farrall Howe, Mar. 3, 1948. Admitted to Colo. bar, 1912, began practice at Victor; mgr. Victor Daily Record, 1912-13; editor Trinidad (Colo) Picketwire, 1915-17; in practice at Antonito and Denver; county atty. Conejos County, Colo., 1922-29; asst. atty. gen. of Colo., 1927-29; U.S. dist. atty., Colo., 1929-33; gov. of Colo., 1939-43. Mem. Hoover Commn. on Reorgn. Exec. Branch of Govt. Legal adviser to Colorado Interstate River Commr., on Rio Grande Compact, 1928-29, 1934-35, 1937-38. Mem. bd. regents, U. Colo., 1945—. Mem. U.S. C. of C. (dir., chmn. natural resources com.), Am., Colo., Denver bar assns., Order of Coif, Delta Tau Delta, Phi Delta Phi. Republican. Christian Scientist. Mason. Norlin medal for distinguished achievement in practice of legal profession, U. Colo., 1933. Home: Denver. Office: Symes Bldg., Denver. Died Sept. 22, 1950.

CARR, Wooda Nicholas, ex-congressman; b. Pittsburgh, Feb. 6, 1871; s. John D. and Amanda M. (Cook) C.; A.B., Monongahela Coll., Pa., 1891; m. Julia M. Kisinger, Oct. 21, 1903. Became editor Uniontown, Pa., News, 1892, later of Uniontown Democrat; admitted to bar, 1895; associated with brother as Carr & Carr, 1908—. Chmn. Dem. Central Com., Fayette Co., Pa., 1901-03; mem. 63d Congress (1913-15), 23d Pa. Dist. Presbyn. Mason, K.T., A.A.S.R. Address: Uniontown, Pa. Died June 29, 1953.

CARRÉ, Jean Marie, educator; b. Maubert-Fontaine, France, Mar. 7, 1887; s. Leon and Marie (Thilges) C.; Baccalauareat et Licenses, Lycee Henri IV, 1905; Docteur es Lettres, U. Strasbourg, 1920; m. Paulette Joubin, June 29, 1920; children—Denyse, Marielle, Alain. Prof. various European schs. and univs., prof. Columbia, 1922-23, Stanford, 1926, Middlebury Coll., 1929, U. Cairo, Egypt, 1929-33; prof. Sorbonne, until 1956. Decorated Croix de Guerre, Legion of Honor (France). Hon. mem. Am. Acad. Arts Letters and Scis. Author: Histoire d'une division de couverture, 1920; Goethe eu Angleterre, 1920; Les Ardennes et leurs ecrivains, 1922; La vie aventureuse de Jean Arthur Rimbaud, 1925; Michelet et Son temps 1925; Images d' Amerique, 1927; La viede Goethe, 1927; Les deux Rimband, 1928; La vie de Robert Louis Stevenson, 1929; Les lettres de la vie littéraire d' Arthur Rimbaud, 1931; Voyageurs et Ecrivains français en Egypte, 2 vols. 1933; Le voyage in Egypte d' Eugene Fromentin. 1935; Promenades dans trois continents, 1935; Les Ecrivains français et le mirage allemand, 1947; Autour de Verlaipe et de Rimbaud, 1949. Home: 1 Place du Pantheon, Paris V, France. Died Jan. 3, 1958.

CARRIER, Willis Haviland, mech. engr.; born Angola, N.Y., Nov. 26, 1876; s. Duane Williams and Elizabeth (Haviland) C.; grad. high schs. Angola and Buffalo; M.E., Cornell U., 1901; Dr. Engring., Lehigh U., 1935; D.Sc., Alfred University, Alfred, N.Y., 1942; m. Edith Claire Seymour, 1902 (died 1912); m. 2d, Jennie Tifft Martin, 1913 (died 1939); m. 3d, Elizabeth Marsh Wise, 1941. Engr. Buffalo Forge Co., 1901-06, chief engr., 1906-15; cons. engr., 1915—; pres. Carrier Engring. Corp., 1915-31, chairman bd. Carrier Corp., 1931-43, chmn. emeritus, 1948—. Member American Society Mechanical Engineers, American Soc. Refrigerating Engrs. (pres 1927), Am. Soc. Heating and Ventilating Engrs. (pres. 1931), Sigma Xi. Republican. Presbyterian. Clubs: Engineers, Cornell (New York); Century, Bellevue Country, Onondaga Country (Syracuse). Author: Fan Engineering, 1914; Modern Heating, Ventilating and Air Conditioning (with others); also various scientific papers before American Society M.E. and Am. Soc. Refrigerating Engrs., among them, in 1911, a paper entitled "Rational Psychometric Formulae," presenting the theory and practical data on which the art of air conditioning has been founded. Home: 2570 Valley Drive. Office: care Carrier Corp., Syracuse, N.Y. Died Oct. 7, 1950; buried Forest Lawn Cemetery, Buffalo.

CARRINGTON, Elaine, writer; b. New York, N.Y.; d. Theodore Sterne and Mary Louise (Henriques) S.; ed. St. Agatha's Sch., New York; Columbia U.; m. George Dart Carrington, March 23, 1920; children—Patricia, Robert Bruce. Writer of several radio serials, "Pepper Young's Family," "When a Girl Marries," "Rosemary," producer of The Carrington Playhouse; author; "All Things Considered" (collection published short stories); "Nightstick," a play from which the moving picture, "Alibi," was made. Episcopalian. Clubs: Civitas, Pen and Brush. Home: 17 West 54th St., New York, (summer) Shepherd Hill, Bridgehampton, L.I. Office: 2 E. 54th St., N.Y.C. Died May 4, 1958.

CARRINGTON, FitzRoy, curator; b. Surbiton, Surrey, Eng., Nov. 6, 1869; s. Robert Charles and Sarah Jane (Pewtress) C.; student Bute House, Petersham, Eng., Victoria Coll., Jersey, Channel Islands; M.A., Dickinson Coll., June 11, 1913; m. Charlotte Austen Singleton, Feb. 24, 1897; children—Harold Keppel, Phyllis Charlotte, Elizabeth Curtis, Sidney. Came to U.S., 1886. Formerly with Frederick Keppel & Co., N.Y.C.; curator dept. prints Mus. Fine Arts, Boston; lectr. on history and principles of engraving Harvard; dir. Children's Art Centre, Boston, and of Children's Art Centre of U. Settlement, N.Y.C. Author: Engravers and Etchers (Scammon lectures Art Inst. Chgo.), 1917. Compiler and editor: Prints and Their Makers, 1916; The Queen's Garland, The King's Lyrics, The Pilgrim's Staff, others. Editor of The Print Collectors' Quar. Club: Authors' (London). Address: West Main St., Niantic, Conn. Died Dec. 31, 1954; buried Stonington, Conn.

CARRIS, Lewis Herbert, welfare worker; b. Tyre, N.Y., Dec. 2, 1869; s. Eliphalet J. and Sarah (Van Wickle) C.; student Union Coll., Schenectady, N.Y., 1889-91, Harvard, 1895-96; B.L., Hobart Coll., 1898, LL.D., 1933; A.M., Columbia, 1913; m. Helen M. Storer, 1920. Tchr., prin. schs., Savannah, Apalachin, Union Springs and Wolcott (all N.Y.), until 1904; supt. schs., Freeport, N.Y., 1904-06; city sch. prin. Newark, 1906-12; county supt. schs., Essex County N.J., 1912-13; asst. commr. edn. N.J., 1913-17; with Federal Bd. for Vocational Edn., Washington, 1917-22; asst. dir. for industrial edn., 1917-19, field rep., 1919-20, asst. dir. for industrial rehabilitation, 1920-21, and administrative head, 1921-22; field sec. Nat. Soc. for Prevention of Blindness, 1922-23, mng. dir., 1923-38, gen. dir., 1939-40, dir. emeritus, 1940—; v.p. Nat. Health Council, 1929-33; vice chmn. N.Y. State Commn. for Blind, 1926-35; U.S. corr. Internat. Assn. for Prevention of Blindness, 1929-45. Recipient Leslie Dana gold medal, 1942. Mem. N.E.A., Delta Phi. Presbyn. Mason. Clubs: Town Hall, Sidney Golf and Country. Home: Bainbridge, N.Y. Office: 1790 Broadway, N. Y.C. Died Mar. 20, 1950; buried Bainbridge, N.Y.

CARROLL, James F., newspaper editor; b. Troy, N.Y., Apr. 15, 1890; s. Thomas B. and Catherine H. (Bruce) C.; A.B., Williams Coll., 1913; m. Isabel Minshall, 1923 (dec. 1926); 1 dau., Helen. Reporter, spl. writer, Sunday editor, city editor Springfield (Mass.) Republican, 1916-20; editorial writer, later editor editorial page Sioux City Tribune, 1920-24; editor editorial pages Worcester (Mass.) Telegram and Eve. Gazette, 1924-42; editor editorial page Dayton (Ohio) Journal Herald since 1943. Mem. American Society of Newspaper Editors, Sigma Delta Chi, Delta Upsilon. Clubs: Rotary, Engrs. (Dayton, O.). Home: Biltmore Hotel, Dayton. Office: The Journal Herald, Dayton 2, O. Died Apr. 8, 1957.

CARROLL, John, artist; b. Wichita, Kan., Aug. 14, 1892; s. Frank and Veda (Peck) C.; prep. edn., Mark Hopkins Art Acad., San Francisco, and under Frank Duveneck, Cin.; student U. Cal., 1913-15; married. Prof. painting, Art Students' League, N.Y. C., 1926; prof. painting, Soc. of Arts and Crafts, Detroit, 1930-44; prof. painting, Art Students League, N.Y.C., 1944—. Rep. in Pa. Acad. of Fine Arts, Phila.; Los Angeles Mus. Fine Arts; Harrison Gallery, Los Angeles; Indpls. Inst. of Art; Omaha Mus. of Art; Detroit Mus. Art; Whitney Mus. Art, N.Y.C., Toledo Mus. of Art; Newark Mus. of Art; Montclair (N.J.) Mus., Mus. of Honolulu, Nat. Acad., IBM, Met. Mus. Art Students League, Ency. Brit., N.Y.C., Wadsworth Atheneum, Hartford, Conn., New Britain (Conn.) Mus., others. Awards: Purchase prize, Pa. Acad. Fine Arts, 1922; first prize, Pan Am. Exhbn., Los Angeles, 1925; Norman Waite Harris silver medal, Art Inst. Chicago, 1927; first lithographic prize, 1929, and gold medal for painting, San Francisco, 1930; gold medal, Detroit Mus. of Art, 1936; Altman prize, Nat. Acad., 1949; Altman prize, Allied Artists, 1954. John Simon Guggenheim fellow, 1927. Served as ensign U.S. Navy 2 yrs., World War I. N.A. Club: Century Assn. (N.Y.C.). Home: East Chatham, N.Y. Studio: 152 W. 57th St., N.Y.C. Died Nov. 7, 1959.

CARROLL, Joseph Francis, univ. prof.; b. County Wicklow, Ireland, July 31, 1892; s. Joseph and Rosanna (Golding) C.; student Mungret Coll., Limerick, 1907-10, St. Stanislaus Coll., Tullamore, 1910-11; A.B., St. Andrew-on-Hudson, Poughkeepsie, N.Y., 1914; A.M., Woodstock (Md.) Coll., 1917; student Catholic theology, Ignatiuskolleg, Valkenburg, Limburg, Holland, 1922-26, Kanisiuskolleg, bei Baexem, Exaten, Roermund, Holland, 1926-27; (specialized in physics, chemistry and mathematics) U. of Munich, 1927-29; Ph.D., U. of Bonn, 1932. Came to U.S., 1911, naturalized, 1939. Entered Society of Jesus, 1910; ordained priest, 1924; asst. prof. physics, Regis Coll., Denver, Colo., 1917-20; asst. prof. physics, Marquette U., Milwaukee, Wis., 1920-22, head of physics dept. since 1932. Fellow A.A.A.S., Indsl. X-ray Soc.; mem. Am. Physical Soc., Am. Assn., Spectrographers. Address: Marquette University, Milw. 3. Died Dec. 12, 1955.

CARROLL, Paul Thomas, army officer; b. Woonsocket, R.I., Apr. 6, 1910; s. Peter Christopher and Cora (McLaughlin) C.; student R.I. State Coll., 1928-29; B.S., U.S. Mil. Acad., 1933; student Inf. Sch., 1939, Armed Forces Staff Coll., 1948, Nat. War Coll., 1952-53; m. Ruth Cooper; children—Paul Thomas, Robert Cooper, David Warriner. Commd. 2d lt. U.S. Army, 1933, advanced to brigadier general, 1953; unit comdr. 5th inf. div., 1941-44; mem. War Dept. Gen. Staff, 1944-48; instr. Command and Gen. Staff Coll., 1949, Army War Coll., 1950; mil. asst. Supreme Allied Comdr. Europe, 1951-52; mil. liaison officer The White House, 1953—, staff sec., 1954—. Home: 7405 Alaska Av. N.W., Washington. Died Sept. 17, 1954; buried Arlington Nat. Cemetery.

CARROLL, Philip A(costa), lawyer; b. Baltimore, May 10, 1879; s. John Lee and Mary Carter (Thompson) C.; student Stonyhurst, Lancashire, Eng., 1897; A.B., Harvard, 1902, LL.B., 1905; m. Nina Ryan, Aug. 16, 1923; children—Phillip, John, Lee, Mary Carter. Admitted to Md. bar, 1906; asso. with office Brown & Brune, Baltimore, 1905-07. Cary & Robinson, N.Y. City, 1907-10; partner Cary & Carroll, 1910-19, Shearman & Sterling (now Shearman & Sterling & Wright), 1919—; dir. Royal Typewriter Co. Commd. capt., Air Service, A.E.F., 1917-19; disch. with rank of lt. col., 1919. Recipient Legion of Honor. Mem. Assn. Bar City of N.Y., N.Y. County Lawyers Assn., Am. and N.Y. State bar assns. Democrat. Roman Catholic. Clubs: Knickerbocker, Racquet and Tennis, Links. ome: 33 E. 70th St., N.Y. City 21. Office: 20 Exchange Pl., N.Y.C. 5. Died July 8, 1957; buried Doughoregan Manor, Howard County, Md.

CARROLL, Richard Augustine, editor; b. Cambridge, Mass., Oct. 27, 1898; s. Valentine and Brigit (O'Reilly) C.; student pvt. schs.; m. Eva V. Howell, July 24, 1924; children—Nancy Carroll (wife of Raymond King, U.S. Army), Richard Scott. Writer novels, screen plays, short stories, 1920; with Gold Medal Books, Fawcett Publs., 1950—, exec. editor, 1951-54, editor-in-chief, 1954—. Served as maj., Signal Corps, AUS, World War II. Clubs: Lambs, Dutch Treat, Artists and Writers (N.Y.C.). Home: Cos Cob, Conn. Office: 67 W. 44th St., N.Y.C. 18. Died Mar. 11, 1959; buried Putnam Cemetery, Greenwich, Conn.

CARROLL, Robert Paris, psychologist; b. nr. Ringgold, Ga., Mar. 11, 1886; s. Thompson Benjamin and Sarah Christian Tennessee (Paris) C.;

student U. of Chattanooga, 1909-10, Emory and Henry Acad., 1910-11; A.B., Emory and Henry Coll., 1914; student Va. Poly. Inst. and U. of Va., 1917, Toulouse U., France, 1919; M.A., Teachers Coll., Columbia, 920, student summer 1921, 1921-22, Ph.D., 1927; m. Ruby Sinclair Houghton, Aug. 12, 1914; children—Raymond Edward, Sarah Katherine, Ruth Elizabeth. Teacher, pub. schs., Ga., 1905-10, Va., 1911-12, 1914-18; head of dept. psychology and edn., Sullins Coll., Bristol, Va., 1920-21, Emory and Henry Coll. and Martha Washington Coll., 1922-23; instr. in psychology, Teachers Coll., Syracuse U., 1923-24, asso. prof. 1924-32. Teacher of edn. and psychology, Coll. William and Mary, summer 1920, U. of Tenn., summers, 1928, 31, U. of Md., summer, 1932; field service, teacher training extension, Pa. State Coll., Sept. 1932—; dir. Inst. of Research in Edn. and Character, 1929—. Served as 1st lt. and chaplain 79th Div., 304th Field Hosp., U.S.A., 1918-19. Law Preservation Party candidate for gov. of N.Y., 1930. Mem. N.E.A., Am. Psychol. Assn., Am. Assn. Univ. Profs., Phi Delta Kappa, Kappa Phi Kappa, Phi Kappa Phi. Methodist. Author: A Drill Book in Methods of Computation in Educational Measurements, 1926; An Experimental Study of Comprehension in Reading, 1926; Fundamentals in the Technique of Educational Measurements, 1928. Contbr. to School and Society, Jour. of Ednl. Research, Jour. of Edn., Jour. Exptl. Psychology, Jour. of Ednl. Psychology, etc. Club: Rotary. Home: 1211 Pennsylvania Av., Warren, Pa. Died Mar. 28, 1954.

CARROLL, Robert Sproul, psychiatrist; b. Cooperstown, Pa., Feb. 18, 1869; s. Jonathan Edward and Margaret Jane (Sproul) C.; student Denison U., Granville, O., 1885-86; M.D., Marion Sims Coll. of Medicine (St. Louis U.), 1893; M.D., Rush Med. Coll. (U. of Chicago), 1897; m. 2d, Grace Stewart Potter (pianist), Feb. 28, 1918; children (1st marriage)—Mrs. Heloise Handcock, Donald Frederic (major in U.S. Army). Practiced medicine at Calvert, Tex., 1893-1902; associate superintendent Marysville (Ohio) Sanatorium, 1902-04; established Dr. Carroll's Sanitarium, Inc., Asheville, N.C., 1904, title changed 1912 to Highland Hosp., Inc. (hosp. donated to psychiatric dept. Duke U., 1939; retired as pres. and med. dir., 1946). Lecturer in psychiatry, Sch. Med., Duke U. Fellow Am. Psychiat. Assn., Assn. for Research in Nervous and Mental Disease, Assn. for Study of Internal Secretions, Southern Soc. Philosophy, Internat. Assn. Philosophy, A.A.A.S., Am. Eugenics Soc., Am. Ethnol. Soc., Eugenical Research Assn., Nat. Econ. League, Am. Museum Natural History, Assn. for Research in Human Heredity, N.Y. Acad. Sciences. Republican. Presbyn. Author: The Mastery of Nervousness, 1917; The Soul in Suffering, 1919; Our Nervous Friends, 1919; Old at 40 or Young at 60, 1920; The Grille Gate, 1922; Aseptic Meningitis in Combating the Praecox Problem, 1923; What Price Alcohol, 1941. Home: 400 Midland Drive, Asheville, N.C. Died June 26, 1949; buried Lakeview Cemetery, Cleveland.

CARRUTHERS, John Franklin Bruce, educator; b. Fort Scott, Kan., Aug. 31, 1889; s. James B. and Anna (Wood) C.; A.B., Princeton, 1912, A.M., 1917; grad. Princeton Theol. Sem., 1917; D.D., Lafayette Coll., Easton, Pa., 1924; post grad. study U. of Geneva (Switzerland), Boston U., U. of So. Cal., Princeton, Harvard, U. of Pa.; m. Mabel Grandin, July 9, 1919; children—John, Jane, Priscilla, Polly. Ordained to ministry of Presbyterian Ch., 1918; minister's asst. First Presbyn. Ch., Baltimore, 1912-14, Ch. of the Covenant (now Nat. Presbyn. Ch.), Washington, D.C., 1917-18; chaplain, Manson prof. and head of Bible dept. Lafayette Coll., 1919-24; prof. religious edn. Occidental Coll., Los Angeles, 1924-26, lectr. on archeology, 1926-28; lectr. archeology U. of Calif. extension faculty, 1927-28; research asst. to pres. U. of Southern Calif. and sec. univ. institute of arts and sciences, also asst. to chancellor U. of Internat. Relations, Los Angeles, 1930-35; chaplain Nat. Presbyn. Ch., Washington, 1943; founder and dean Los Angeles Intercollegiate Sch. Religious Edn. and Social Service. Served as chmn. bd. Am. Sch. for Girls, Damascus; mem. bd. trustees Am. Coll., Teheran; mem. faculty League of Nations Union Sch., Geneva; mem. overseer bd. Calif. Coll. of China. Served as chaplain U.S.S. Oklahoma, World War I; became head chaplain morale, edn. and recreation 6th Div. Bureau of Nav., 1919; chaplain War Dept. pub. relations orientation lecturer for army camp instrs.; chaplain-adj. 1st Aero Squadron, Camp Hopkins, World War II. On spl. missions to Russia, 1926, 1930; made survey for bd. govs. Near East Relief (N.Y. office) of postwar problems in Syria, Greece, Iraq, Lebanon and Turkey. Founder United Nations Chaplains League, 1945, Mil. Order Chaplains of United Nations, 1946; pres. Jap. Problem League of West Coast; organizing founder and 1st pres. Town Hall, Inc.; chmn. Nat. Small Bus. Research Bureau, Am. Religious Radio Assn.; chaplain Nat. Com. Christian Leadership; connected with many other sectional and national orgns. Mem. Am. Assn. Univ. Profs., Acad. Polit. Science, Soc. Bibl. Literature and Exegesis, A.A.A.S., Phi Kappa Phi, Pi Gamma Mu. Democrat. Asso. editor of Who's Who in New Deal. Clubs: Princeton (New York); Nassau, Dial (Princeton); Cosmos (Washington); Valley Hunt (Pasadena). Home: 1015 Prospect Blvd., Pasadena, Calif; (summer) Camp Tidioute, Vancouver Island, Sproat Lake P.O., Can. Died Jan. 1960.*

CARSON, Charles Averette, lawyer; b. Kissimmee, Fla., Apr. 26, 1891; s. Charles and Annie (Bryan) C.; A.B., Colorado Coll., 1913; m. Carrie Burger, Jan. 5, 1914; children—Elizabeth (Mrs. Don Frederickson), Caroline (Mrs. Howard E. Boice), Jean (Mrs. T. E. Arnold), Charles Averette III, Inez (Mrs. Derrell Manley). Admitted to bar, 1923; deputy county attorney, Maricopa County, Arizona, 1925-27; city attorney, Phoenix, 1930-32; special assistant attorney general for Ariz. and counsel Ariz. Colo. River Commn., 1933-35; mem. firm Cunningham, Carson, Messinger & Carson; special atty. Dept. of Justice, 1942-46. Mem. Ariz. Alien Enemy Hearing Bd., 1941-46, Ariz. Bd. Bar Examiners, 1933; former mem. Maricopa Co., Ariz. State Dem. exec. coms.; mem. bd. trustees, Sch. Dist. No. 1, Maricopa Co. (Phoenix pub. schs.), 1933-42; atty., Colo. River Commn. of Arizona, 1942-45; spl. atty. for State of Ariz. on Colo. River matters, since 1945; chief counsel Ariz. Interstate Stream Commn., since 1948. Mem. Am. Bar Assn., State Bar of Ariz. (pres. 1933-35, gov. 1933-47), S.A.R. (past pres. Ariz. Soc.), Beta Theta Pi, Phi Beta Kappa. Democrat. Episcopalian (chancellor Episcopal Ch. in Ariz. since 1939). Club: Arizona (Phoenix). Office: Title and Trust Bldg., Phoenix. Died Jan. 14, 1952.

CARSON, Frank L(ee), banker; b. Ashland, Kan., June 23, 1890; s. Cale W. and Martha (Congleton) C.; grad. high sch., Ashland, 1909; A.B., U. of Kan., 1913; m. Carrie May Price, Nov. 12, 1917; children—Mary Martha Kellogg, Virginia Lee Garver, Frances Price Aitchison, Caroline Curtis, Frank Lee, John Congleton. With 1st Nat. Bank, Wichita, Kan., 1914, cahsier, 1918-28, president, 1928-44, chmn. bd. since 1944; cashier First National Bank, Hansford, Texas, 1916-18; director Wichita Perpetual Building & Loan Co., Central States Fire Ins. Co., Kan. Gas and Electric Co. Mem. Delta Upsilon. Democrat. Presbyn. Mason (32°). Clubs: Whchita. Wichita Country. Home: 55 Mission Rd., Eastborough, Wichita. Office: 1st National Bank, 105 N. Main St., Wichita. Died Mar. 4, 1952.

CARSON, John Miller, army officer; b. Phila., June 26, 1864; s. Capt. John Miller and Annie L. (Miller) C.; B.Sc., U.S. Mil. Acad., 1885; m. Margaret Forster Sumner, Dec. 14, 1887, 1 dau., Margaret Sumner (Mrs. Henry C. Holt). Commd. 2d lt. 5th Cav., 1885, promoted through grades to brig. gen. (temp.), 1918; brig. gen. Q.M. Corps, 1920; retired after 40 yrs. service, 1922; adj. U.S. Mil. Acad., 1890-95; adj. 5th Cav., 1895-97; q.m. at hdqrs. U.S. troops in P.R. 1898; asst. to chief q.m. Dept. of P.R. 1898-99, in Philippines, 1899; duty Office Q.M. Gen., 1900-03; q.m. and disbursing officer and officer in charge of constrn., U.S. Mil. Acad., 1903-11; constrn. q.m., Corregidor Island, P.I., 1911-14; asst. to depot q.m., N.Y.C., 1914-16, depot q.m., 1916-17 gen. supt., Army Trans. Service, N.Y.C., 1917; chief q.m., Line Communications, AEF, France, 1917-18, dep. chief q.m., 1918-19, acting chief q.m., 1919; spl. duty Office Q.M. Gen., Washington, 1919; zone supply officer, N.Y.C., 1919-20; asst. q.m. gen., 1920-22. Decorated D.S.M.; Spanish-Am. War; Occupation of Purto Rico; Phillippine Insurrection; World War medals; Comdr. Legion of Honor, France; Polonia Restituta, Class IV, Poland. Mem. Loyal Legion, Soc. Foreign Wars, Mil. Order of World Wars. Address: Chandler Farms, Pomfret, Conn. Died Jan. 18, 1956; buried U.S. Mil. Acad. Cemetery, West Point, N.Y.

CARSON, Joseph Kirtley, Jr., lawyer, state senator; born McKinney, Kentucky, December 19, 1891; son of Joseph Kelly and Sallie Elizabeth Adeline (Johnson) C.; Bachelor of Laws, University of Ore., 1917; hon. LL.D., Univ. of Portland (Ore.), 1942; m. Hazel Irene Jenkins, March 26, 1926 (died 1928); m. 2d, Myrtle Cradick, June 19, 1937; children—Joan Cradick, Lucian Joseph. Admitted to Ore. bar, 1917, U.S. Supreme Ct., 1936; gen. practice of law, Portland; commr. U.S. Maritime Commn., 1947-50. Mayor of City of Portland, Ore., 1933-41; now Oregon state senator. Served in the United States Army, 1917-19; colonel O.R.C.; served in World War II, 1942-46. Deocrations: Bronze Star Medal; St. Olav's Medal (Norway); Order Orange-Nassau (Netherlands); Order Leopold II (Belgium); Military Medal (Czechoslovakia). Democrat. Episcopalian. Mem. Ore. Bar Assn., Delta Theta Pi. Mason. Maccabees, Woodmen. Clubs: University, Multinomah, Aero, Arlington (Portland); Army and Navy, Nat. Press (Washington); Columbia Edgewater Country (Portland). Home: 7119 N. Fowler Av. Office: Yeon Bldg., Portland, Ore. Died Dec. 20, 1956.

CARSON, Luella Clay, educator; b. Portland, Ore., Mar. 12, 1856; d. John Crosthwaite and Elizabeth (Talbot) C.; Carson; grad. St. Helen's Hall, Portland, 1877; state diploma, Ore., 1888, Life diploma, 1890; student Boston Sch. Expression, Harvard, univs. of Chgo., Cal., Cambridge, Eng., summers 1888-1902, Columbia, 1916-17; A.M. (hon.), U. Ore., 1894, LL.D., 1909; A.M. (hon.), Pacific U., 1894, Litt.D., 1909; Litt.D., Mills Coll., 1925. Preceptress Taulatin Acad. and Pacific U., 1880-85; vice prin. Couch Sch., Portland, 1886-88; prof. rhetoric and elecution U. Ore., 1888-95, rhetoric and Eng. lit., 1895-1903, rhetoric and Am. lit., 1903-09, dean of women, 1895-1909; pres. Mills Coll., 1909-14; dean of women and mem. English dept. Drury Coll., 1917-19; mem. English dept. Milw.-Downer Coll., 1919-20; acting head English dept. Yankton (S.D.) Coll., 1920-21. Mem. Am. Assn. U. Women, Modern Lang. Assn. Am., Pacific Coast, Ore. hist. assns., Nat. Inst. Social Scis., A.A.A.S., Religious Edn. Assn. Conglist. Author: Public School Libraries and a Reference Library for Teachers of English, 1903; Hand Book of English Composition, 1907, rev. 1919. Home: Porter Hall, Claremont, Cal. Deceased.

CARSON, Robert, architect; b. Macon, Ill., July 19, 1906; s. Robert and Katherine (Irose) C.; B. Arch., U. Pa., 1928. Designer, Raymond Hood, N.Y. City, 1929-34, Wallace K. Harrison, 1934-39; partner Carson & Lundin, architects, N.Y. City, resident architect Rockefeller Center, 1939-57, works include Esso Bldg., Rockefeller Center, Sinclair Oil Bldg., 666 Fifth Av. Bldg., 1st Nat. City Bank (all N.Y.C.), First Nat. Bldg., Tulsa, others. Recipient award, Fifth Av. Assn., 1950, 52, 54, 56, 58. Fellow A.I.A. (v.p. N.Y. chpt., 1958-59), Archtl. League N.Y., Nat. Inst. Archtl. Edn. (trustee 1947-50), Phi Gamma Delta. Club: University. Home: 165 E. 66th St., N.Y.C.; also Sagaponak, N.Y. Office: 425 Park Av., N.Y.C. 22. Died Mar. 1, 1960.

CARSTARPHEN, Frederick Charles, cons. engr.; b. Denver, Apr. 1, 1881; E.M., Colo. Sch. Mines, 1905, D.Eng., 1932; m. Kate Fullerton, June 23, 1908 (dec.); children—Catherine, Elizabeth (dec.), Charles Frederick, Florence, Marion. Began as newsboy Denver Post, 1897; Post "kite expert," flying kites in western cities and from top of Pike's Peak, 1900-01; field engr. constrn. of water systems, Golden, Colo., 1904; U.S. dep. surveyor, 1905; engr. Colo. Portland Cement Co., 1906-07; mem. Hewitt-Carstarphen Co., cons. engrs., 1906-08; mem. Western Engring. Constrn. Co., 1908-09; mgr. Vulcan Sulphur Co., 1909, Gilsonite Co. of America, 1910-12; U.S. mineral surveyor, 1910-14; mining engr. Spring Canon Coal Co., 1913; chief aerial tramway engr. Am. Steel & Wire Co., Trenton, N.J., 1913-23; v.p. and chief engr. Mfrs. Selling Co., Trenton, 1923-26; has served as cons. for U.S. Smelting, Mining & Refining Co., Pittsburgh Coal Co., U.S. Bur. of Reclamation, Westinghouse Electric & Mfg. Co., Hardie Tynes Co., Consol. Steel Co., Nacional Comision de Irrigacion, Mex., Reconstruction Finance Corp., Moffat Tunnel Commn., Mosquito Mines Corp., V. Z. Reed Mines, Babcock & Wilcox Co., for city of Denver on Cherry Creek flood control, Tenderfoot Mining Co., Mollie Kathleen Project (Cripple Creek, Colo.), Strong Leasing & Mining Co. (Victor, Colo.), Squaw Gulch Gold Mining Co., Golden Star Mining Co. (Cripple Creek), Pacific Gas & Electric Co. (San Francisco), Morrison-Utah-Winston-Lawler Co., Contractors Seminole Dam (Wyoming), Aguilar Mines (South America), etc.; designed ski-tow at Denver's Winter Park, Colorado. Built telpher systems at the powder plants, during World War; now mem. commn. on Aerial Tramways, and cons. engr. for Engr. Bd., U.S. Army, Ft. Belvoir, Va. Fellow A.A.A.S.; mem. Am. Soc. C.E. (Wellington award, 1929; ex pres. Colo. sect.), Am. Inst. Mining Engrs., Colo. Soc. Engrs. (past pres.), Engrs. Club of Trenton (past pres.), Tau Beta Pi, Kappa Sigma. Mason (Shriner). Author of brochures and articles on tech. engring. subjects. Special lecturer at Denver University on Mechanics and Strength of Materials, 1943. Home: 721 Marion St., Denver. Died 1942.*

CARTER, Amon Giles, newspaper pub.; b. Crafton, Tex., Dec. 11, 1879; s. William and Josephine (Ream) C.; ed. pub. schs.; m.; children—Beatrice (Mrs. Hugo Speck), Amon G., Jr., Olive Ruth (Mrs. J. Lee Johnson, III). Began as newsboy; now pres., pub. Fort Worth (Tex.) Star-Telegram (morning, evening Sun). Democrat. Clubs: Ft. Worth (pres. 35 yrs.), Ft. Worth Boat, Colonial Golf, Rivercrest Country (Ft. Worth); Advertising, Metropolitan (New York); Alfalfa (Washington). Home: Rivercrest Addition. Office: Star-Telegram Bldg., Fort Worth, Tex. Died June 23, 1955; buried Greenwood Cemetery, Fort Worth.

CARTER, Clifton Carroll, ret. army officer, educator; b. Lexington, Ky., July 12, 1876; s. John Hubbell and Judith Ann (Coons) C.; grad. U.S. Mil. Acad., 1899, Coast Arty. Sch., 1903, Sch. of Submarine Defense, 1907; B.S. in E.E. Mass. Inst. Tech., 1909; m. Mai Angevine Coleman, Oct. 1, 1902; children—Clifton Coleman, Marshall Sylvester. Commd. 2d lt. arty., 1899, advanced through grades to col. Arty. Corps, 1921; chief ordnance officer and chief signal officer, Dept. of Havana, Cuba, 1899-1901; various stations in U.S., 1902-11; mem. Gen. Staff Corps, chief of staff, Dept. of Hawaii, at Honolulu, 1911-12; pres. Coast Arty. Bd., 1913; adj. U.S. Mil. Acad., 1914-17, prof. natural and experimental philosophy, 1917-40; ret.; promoted to brig. gen. ret.,

1948. Spl. observer in France, 1918. Mem. Society for Promotion of Engring. Edn., Institute of Aeronautical Sciences. Medals: Spanish-American War, Army of Cuban Occupation, Victory Medal (service in France). Author: Simple Aerodynamics and the Airplane. Home: 3133 Connecticut Av., Washington 8. Died Sept. 20, 1950; buried Arlington Nat. Cemetery.

CARTER, DeWitt, ins. exec., gen. contractor; b. Atlanta, Apr. 13, 1892; s. DeWitt and Emma (Couch) C.; student Wallace Univ. Sch., 1912-15; m. Frances Kirkpatrick, May 29, 1920; children—Jane Emma, Frances Mildred (Mrs. Thomas Wardlaw Steele). Vice pres. Caldwell and Co., 1919-30; pres. Nashville Securities Co., 1931-48; v.p. Foster & Creighton Co., Nashville, 1948—; chmn. bd. Am. United Life Ins. Co., 1948—. Mem. Council Fgn. Relations (Nashville com.). Methodist. Clubs: Zodiac, Belle Meade, Cumberland (Nashville); Indianapolis Athletic. Home: 4810 Franklin Rd., Nashville 4. Office: First Am. Nat. Bank Bldg., Nashville 3 Died Jan. 17, 1957; buried Woodlawn Meml. Park, Nashville.

CARTER, Edward Clark, educator; b. Lawrence, Mass., June 9, 1878; s. Clark and Emma Henrietta (Pease) Carter; preparatory education high school Lawrence and Phillips Academy, Andover, Mass.; A.B., Harvard, 1900; married Alice Olin Draper, August 5, 1908; children—William Draper, Edward Clark (dec.), John Alden, Ruth Dana. Graduate sec., Phillips Brooks House, Harvard, 1900-02; sec. Nat. Y.M.C.A., India, Calcutta, 1902-08, 1911-17; sec. N. Am. Student Movement, 1908-11; chief sec. Y.M. C.A., A.E.F., Paris, 1917-19; fgn. sec. Brit. Y.M. C.A., London, 1920-22; sec. The Inquiry, N.Y.C., 1922-30, chairman, 1930-33. Secretary of American Inst. Pacific Relations, 1926-33, exec. vice chmn. 1946-48; sec. general of the Inst., 1933-46; pres. Russian Relief, 1941-50; dir. United Service to China; Consultant, United Nations Econ. Commn. for Asia and the Far East, Shanghai, China, Mar.-June 1948; provost New School for Social Research, 1949-50, dir. internat. studies. 1950-51. Member of Delta Upsilon. Decorated Officer Order of British Empire; Officer Legion of Honor (France); Order of Crown of Siam; Kaiser-i-hind gold medal (India); Order of the Red Banner of Labor (U.S.S.R.). Club: Century. Home: 215 E. 72d St. N.Y.C. 21; (summer) Sunset Farm, Lee, Mass. Died Nov. 9, 1954.

CARTER, Edwin Farnham, telephone co. exec.; b. Farmington, Mo., May 24, 1877; s. William and Maria (McIlvaine) C.; grad. St. Louis Manual Tng. Sch., 1895; student Washington U., 1898-1900; m. Mary Ida Bull, May 12, 1906; children—Edwin Follett (dec.), Jesse McIlvaine, Mary Clem. Began as inspector with Bell Telephone Co. of Mo., 1900, comml. mgr., 1910; bus. mgr. Eames & Young, architects, St. Louis, 1911-13; comml. engr. Southwestern Bell Telephone Co., 1913-17, gen. mgr. Kan. div., 1917-19, gen. mgr. Tex. div., 1919-21, gen. comml. mgr. of co., 1921-26, v.p., Apr.-Aug. 1926; pres. Ohio Bell Telephone Co., 1926-30; v.p. Am. Tel. & Tel. Co., 1930-37. Mem. Phi Delta Theta. Republican. Home: Darien, Conn. Died Jan. 24, 1956.

CARTER, Ernest Trow, musician; b. Orange, N.J., Sept. 3, 1866; s. Aaron and Sarah Swift (Trow) C.; A.B., Princeton, 1888; M.A., Columbia, 1889; LL.B., Columbia, 1934 (as of 1890); Mus.D., Princeton, 1932; student of mus. composition, Berlin, 1894-98; m. Laura Hoe, Sept. 29, 1891; children—Laura Hoe (Mrs. Charles Harold Fahy), Roger Ernest, Elizabeth Woodbridge (Mrs. Edward Lambert Richards). In practice of law at N.Y. City, 1891-92; tchr. music Thacher Sch., Ojai, Cal. 1892-94; organist and choirmaster, Am. Ch., Berlin, 1897-98; lectr. on music, organist and choirmaster, Princeton, 1899-1904, since in New York as composer and dir. Member Citizen's Union of New York, Phi Beta Kappa. Clubs: University, Princeton, Players, Century, The Bohemians. Composer of operas: The White Bird, produced Chicago, 1924; Osnabrück, Germany, 1927; New York, 1937; Riverside, Calif., 1939; The Blonde Donna, New York, 1931; Redlands, Calif., 1937, 1949; Riverside, Calif., 1941. Address: Wallack Point Stamford, Conn. Died June 20, 1953; buried Woodlawn Cemetery, N.Y.C.

CARTER, Fred G., hospital administrator and consultant; b. Richland County, Wisconsin, February 28, 1888; s. Alonzo Theodore and Sarah J. (Hamilton) C.; A.B., University of Wisconsin, 1911, post-graduate work, 1915-18; M.D., Johns Hopkins, 1920; m. Ima Watterson, Nov. 17, 1923; 1 dau., Barbara. Athletic dir. La Crosse (Wis.) High Sch., 1911-12, La Crosse State Teachers Coll., 1912-15, Colo. Sch. of Mines, Golden, 1916-17; surg. internship Johns Hopkins Hosp., 1920-21; surg. resident Ancker Hosp., St. Paul, 1921-22, med. resident, 1922-23, asst. supt., 1923-24, supt., 1924-35; adminstr. Christ Hosp. Cincinnati, 1935-39, St. Luke's Hosp., Cleve., 1939-53, v.p. charge of development, 1953-55, cons., 1955—. Served in U.S. Army, 1917-18, World War. Chmn. Joint Advisory Com. of the three nat. hosp. assns., 1938-40. Fellow Am. Coll. of Hosp. Adminstrn. (pres. 1935-36; mem. board of regents, 1946-49; mem. Am. Hosp. Assn. (pres. 1939-40; mem. Council on Administrative Practice, 1938-40, Council on Govt. Relations, 1942-47; Award of Merit, 1952); Minnesota Hospital Assn. (president 1932-33), Ohio Hosp. Assn. (pres. 1938-39), Med. Supts'. Club, Alpha Omega Alpha, Sigma Nu, Mem. editorial bd. Modern Hospital. Contbr. to professional jours. Originator numerous innovations in hosp. design, equipment, and procedure. Home: 18800 Shaker Blvd., Cleve. 22. Died Feb. 19, 1956; buried Lakeview Cemetery, Cleve.

CARTER, Fred Mason, ret. pres. Nat. Lead Co.; b. Beardstown, Ill., Dec. 20, 1868; s. Eliphalet Stephen and Ellen Elizabeth (Carter) C.; ed. high sch., Mendota, Ill.; m. Mabel Claire Robinson, of Bath, N.Y., July 24, 1893. With Warder, Bushnell & Glessner Co., Chgo., 1887-96, Milw. Harvester Co., 1896-98, Carter White Lead Co., Chgo., 1898-1906; with Nat. Lead Co., N.Y.C., 1906-38, pres., 1933-38; retired. Republican. Episcopalian. Clubs: Bohemian (San Francisco); La Rinconada Golf (Los Gatos, Calif.); Saratoga Men's (Saratoga, Calif.). Home: Los Gatos, Cal. Deceased.

CARTER, Gale H., shipping exec.; b. Harrow on Hill, Eng., Mar. 9, 1865, of Am. parents; s. Dr. H. Skelton and Florence (Russell) C.; student M. W. Lyons Collegiate Inst., Woodbridge Sch. Columbia, 1893-97; m. Marian Thomas, Jan. 25, 1902 (died 1937); m. 2d, Emma M. Dilliard, Mar. 8, 1941. Employed W. R. Grace & Co., importers and exporters, 1897, served in various positions, becoming v.p., 1921, also dir.; pres. Pacific Mail S.S. Co., 1922-25; pres. Grace Line, Inc., Atlantic and Pacific S S. Co., New Orleans and S. Am. S.S. Co.; v.p. Panama Mail S.S. Co.; was also dir. Grace Nat. Bank, Mutual Protection and Indemnity Assn.; now retired. Served in USN, during Spanish-Am. War. Mem. Alpha Delta Phi. Episcopalian. Clubs: Columbia University (N.Y.C.), Pacific Union (San Francisco). Home: 42 Shore Rd., Old Greenwich, Conn. Deceased.

CARTER, George, editor; b. Smyrna, Del., July 31, 1865; s. John and Mary Hurd (Spratt) C.; ed. elementary pub. schs. and business coll.; m. Susie Etta Wyatt, 1886; m. 2d, Ann B. Foard, June 19, 1895; children—Mildred Lee (Mrs. J. Bayard Briggs), F(rancis) Bayard, G(eorge) Gray (the two sons held Rhodes scholarships at same time). Worked at printer's trade; local editor Del. Farm and Home; editorial staff New York newspaper 14 yrs.; served as reporter, city editor, and editor Wilmington Journal-Every Evening, editor emeritus, 1939—. Mem. Del. Com. of Defense, World War. Past pres. Delmarvia Press Assn.; pres. Goodwill Industries. Republican. Episcopalian. Mason (K.T.). Clubs: Torch, Church, The Senate. Home: Cedarbrook, Smyrna, Del. Died Oct. 23, 1948.

CARTER, George Milton, adj. gen., Me.; b. Washburn, Me., June 11, 1894; s. Calvin D. and Faustina A. (Dickinson) C.; A.B., in Edn., Univ. of Me., 1918; A.M., Columbia, 1939; Honorary LL.D., University of Maine, 1948; maried Myrtle Ruby Stairs, Aug. 16, 1917; children—G. Milton, W. Berkeley. Teacher Secondary Washburn High Sch., 1920-21; supt. schs. Union No. 122, Washburn, 1921-23, No. 124, Caribou, Me., 1923-41. Served in R.O.T.C., Univ. of Me., 1914-17, C.M.T.C.; Plattsburg, N.Y., 1917; commd. 2d lt. inf., transferred to arty., Sept. 1917; left for fgn. service, Sept. 1917; served as officer 102d F.A., 26th Div. and as instr. Saumur arty. sch., France, 6 mos.; returned to U.S.A. with 102d F.A., Apr. 1919; commd. capt. F.A., Me. Nat. Guard, 1931; comdg. officer Battery B, 152d F.A., Me. Nat. Guard. 1931-40; apptd. adj. gen. State of Me., 1941, became maj. gen., 1954, also state dir. selective service, 1948. Recipient Distinguished medal, N.G. Assn. U.S., 1955. Member Mathematics Teachers Assn., 1920-47; N.E.A. (life); Me. Teachers Assn. (treas. 1925-27, pres. 1938-39), Kappa Phi Kappa. Republican. Methodist. Home: 41 School St. Office: State House, Augusta, Me. Died Sept. 11, 1958.

CARTER, Henry Holland, prof. English; b. Brecksville, O., Aug. 16, 1884; s. Elwyn Leyton and Amanda Jane (Snow) C.; Grad. Oberlin Acad., 1903; A.B., Oberlin Coll., 1907; M.A., Yale, 1908; Ph.D., 1914; student U. of Berlin, summer 1912; m. Ella Charlton Fulton, Aug. 10, 1910; children—Jane Elizabeth, Mary Snow, Margaret Gray, Bertha Anne. Asst. prof. English, Miami U., Oxford O., 1908-11; same, Carleton Coll., Northfield, Minn., 1914-17, prof., 1917-21; prof. English and head of dept., Miami U., 1921-22; prof. English, Ind. U., since 1922, head of dept., 1923-41. Mem. Modern Lang. Assn. America, Phi Beta Kappa. Episcopalian. Editor: Ben Jonson's Every Man in His Humor, 1921; English in Action (with J. C. Tressler), 1937; Remedial Exercises in English Composition (with Stith Thompson), 1937; A Reader for Writers (with Frank Davidson), 1938, revised edition, 1947; Grammar and Practice Leaves for Writing, Forms A and B (with W. Edson Richmond), 1948. Home: 1305 Maxwell Lane, Bloomington, Ind. Died Dec. 3, 1952; buried Richfield, O.

CARTER, Horace A., manufacturer; b. Needham Heights, Mass., Jan. 6, 1869; s. William and Martha (Lee) C.; ed. public Schools and Comers Commercial Coll., Boston; Sc.D. (hon.), Boston U., 1945; m. Bertha Louise Manson, Dec. 23, 1891 (died 1946); children—Raymond Manson (dec.), Manson Hildreth (dec.), Horace Ronald, Lyndall Frederic; m. 2d, Emily B. Tilden, 1947. Treasurer William Carter Co., Needham Heights, 1902—, v.p., exec. v.p., 1944-54, pres., treas., 1954—; chmn. bd. dirs. Needham Nat. Bank (Mass.). Mem. Needham Sch. Com., 1900-12, chmn., 1908-11; trustee Boston Deaconess Hosp., Boston U.; mem. Exec. Gov.'s Council of Mass., 2 yrs.; pres. Ancient and Honorable Co. of Mass. Mem. Mass. C. of C. (pres.). Mason (32°, Shriner), Odd Fellow. Clubs: Brae Burn (Newton, Mass.); Algonquin (Boston). Home: 790 Highland Av., Needham Heights, Mass. Office: Carter's Underwear, Boston. Died May 2, 1959.

CARTER, Hubert Lazell, wholesale paper mcht.; b. West Newton, Mass., Nov. 30, 1877; s. James Richard and Carrie (Giles) C.; A.B., Harvard, 1898; m. Edith H. Adams, June 7, 1906; children—James Richard, Elfriede, Hubert Adams, Sylvia. In paper business, 1898—; sec. N.E. Paper Merchants Assn., 1909-16, pres. 1925-26; pres. Boston Paper Trade Assn., 1928-30; v.p., treas. Carter, Rice & Co. Corp., Boston, to 1946; retired; dir. Nashua Gummed & Coated Paper Co. Alderman Newton, Mass., 1917-22. Republican. Episcopalian. Clubs: The Country, Brae Burn Country, Tuesday (Newton); Harvard (Boston). Home: 170 Otis St., Newtonville 60, Mass. Office: 50 Congress St., Boston 9. Died Jan. 15, 1956; buried Mt. Auburn Cemetery, Cambridge, Mass.

CARTER, Jesse Washington, judge; b. Carrville, Calif., Dec. 19, 1888; s. Asa Manning and Josephine Amanda (Sweet) C.; LL.B., Golden Gate Law Coll., San Francisco, California, 1913, LL.D., (honorary). 1956; married to Tiny Elva Gish, August 7, 1910; children—Oliver Jesse, Harlan Field, and Marian Rose (Mrs. Silvio Eugene Bui); m. 2d, Thelma H. Williams, February 9, 1941; married 3d, Jean Woodward, April 18, 1952. Admitted to California bar, 1913; practiced in San Francisco, 1913-14, Redding, 1914-39; dist. atty., Shasta County, 1919-27; city atty., Mt. Shasta, 1927-39, Redding, 1937-39; atty. Bd. Dental Examiners of Calif., 1924-32; apptd. associate justice, Supreme Court of Calif., Sept. 12, 1939. Del. to Dem. Nat. Conv., 1932; mem. Calif State Senate, 1939. Mem. bd. govs. State Bar of Cal., 1927-33. Mem. jury awards panel Freedoms Found., 1957. Hon. fellow Am. Coll. Trial Lawyers, 1953. Mem. Am. Law Inst., Shasta County, San Francisco and Am. bar assns., Phi Delta Phi. Mason. Clubs: Rotary (Redding); Sutter (Sacramento). Home: Oak Knoll Dr., Sleepy Hollow., San Anselmo, Cal. Died Mar. 15, 1959; buried Mt. Tamalpais Cemetery, San Rafael, Cal.

CARTER, Leyton E(lwin), dir. Cleveland Foundation; b. N. Royalton, O., Aug. 31, 1892; s. Elwin Leyton and Amanda Jane (Snow) C.; A.B., Oberlin Coll., 1914; grad. work, Columbia, 1914-17; L.H.D. (hon.), Western Reserve University, 1949; married Catherine Fifield Burtt, Aug. 22, 1916; children—Sara Jane, Leyton Elwin, Mary Catherine. Instr. Western Res. U., 1917-19; asst. sec. Civic League, Cleveland, O., 1919-20; dir. Municipal Research Bur., Cleveland, O., 1920-28, Cleveland Foundation since 1928; instr. Am. govt. and econ., Fenn Coll. since 1920. Lecturer in municipal govt., Western Res. U., 1938-39, govt. courses Cleveland Coll., 1942-43. Exec. sec. joint legislative com. on economy and taxation, Ohio Gen. Assembly, 1925-26. Sec. regional govt. com. of 400. Cuyahoga County, 1928-30; member of board trustees Cleveland Welfare Federation (chmn. Tremont area committee 1936-38, mem. planning and research coms.); mem. bd. dirs. Cleveland Adult Edn. Assn., 1930-36; mem. pub. finance and taxation com. Cleveland Chamber of Commerce, 1930-37; chmn. conf. com. on urban problems U.S. Chamber of Commerce, since 1942; mem. bd. dirs. Cleveland Child Health Assn., 1937-42, Mus. Sch. Settlement 1930-37; vice chmn. Ohio Sch. Survey Comm., 1932-33, Cuyahoga County White House Conf. Com., 1932-33; mem. central bd. mgrs. Y.M.C.A., 1932-36 (member bd. trustees, 1936-44)); member Citizens Charter Com., 1934-37; trustee Fenn Coll. since 1934, Oberlin Coll. since 1936; chmn. Cleveland Housing Com., 1933-38; mem. bd. trustees Fgn. Affairs Council, 1935-37; sec. Citizens Sch. Survey Com., 1935; charter mem. and vice chmn. Regional Assn. Cleveland since 1936; chmn. occupational planning com. Greater Cleveland, 1941, 1943; charter mem. postwar planning council of Greater Cleveland, 1943-46 (chmn. on pub. finance and taxation, mem. bd. trustees and exec. com.); treas. Cleveland Neighborhood Conservation Project, 1941-46; chmn. Children's Council, Cleveland Welfare Fedn., 1947; chmn. Inventory Study Com., Welfare Fedn., 1948; chmn. finance Nat. Com. on Founds. and Trusts for Community Welfare; president Ohio Citizens Council on Health, Welfare, 1949-52; chmn. Highway Finance Com., Cleveland Automobile Club, 1948. Distinguished Service award Cleveland Community Chest, 1951. Contbr. various articles to mags. Home: 17116 Shaker Blvd., Shaker Heights, O. Office: 1338 Terminal Tower, Cleve. 13. Died Nov. 16, 1953.

CARTER, Nathan A., Sr., transportation exec.; b. Sardis, Miss., 1885; m. Julienne Maxey; children—Nathan Alexander, Maxey (Mrs. W. D. Evans). Vice pres. Fruehauf Trailer Co., gen mgr. Fruehauf-Carter div.; v.p. Arkansas Bus & Truck Assn.; dir. Tenn. Motor Transport Assn. Clubs: Rotary (Memphis); Executive; Newcomen. Hoome: 4276 Montrose Dr. Office: 587 Hernando St., Memphis. Died Feb. 21, 1958; buried Memphis.

CARTER, Randall Albert, bishop; b. Fort Valley, Ga., Jan. 1, 1867; s. Tobias and Grace (Chivers) C.; student Allen U., 1880-84; LL.D., 1926; A.B., Paine Coll., Augusta, Ga., 1891, A.M., 1900, D.D., 1901; m. Janie S. Hooks Apr. 22, 1891 (dec.); 1 dau., Mrs. Grace Carter Cole. Ordained to ministry Colored M.E. Ch., 1887; pastor Butler St. Sta., Atlanta, Ga., 1892, Barnesville Sta., 1893-94; presiding elder, 1894-98 and 1903-14; sec. Epworth League, 1898-1903; bishop Colored M.E. Church since May 1914. Mem. Committee on Episcopacy of Gen. Conf. 20 yrs.; fraternal del. to Gen. Conf. M.E. Ch., Chicago, 1900, Kansas City, 1928, Atlantic City, 1932; del. Ecumenical Council of Methodism, London, 1901, Toronto, Can., 1921; mem. exec. com. Federal Council of Chs. of Christ in America; mem. Counselling Com. of Y.M.C.A.; mem. exec. com. Assn. for Study of Negro Life and History, Nat. Geog. Soc., Acad. of Polit. Science; fellow Am. Geog. Soc. Republican. Mason, K.P. Author: Morning Meditations and Other Selections, 1917; Feeding Among the Lilies; Canned Laughter, 1923; Brief Study of the Hebrew Prophets, 1937; Gathered Fragments, 1939. Home: 4408 Vincennes Av., Chgo. 15. Died Feb. 6, 1954.

CARTER, Raymond Lanson, univ. dean; b. Ellisston, O., July 6, 1886; s. John Harrison and Lavona M. (Veon) C.; ed. Valparaiso U., 1903, Chicago Med. Coll., 1907-08, Ohio Northern U., 1913-14, U. of Toledo, 1917-21 (B.S., A.M.), Ohio State U., 1923-29 (Ph.D.); m. Rose A. Gerner, Aug. 18, 1910; children—Lanson David (dec.), Donald Raymond, Rosemary, Lois Ann. Teacher, rural schools, 1901-05; prin. high school, asst. county supt. and village school supt., 1908-23; asst. prof. of edn., U. of Toledo, 1923-27; div. curriculum research, Cuyahoga, Cleveland, 1927-29; prof. of edn., U. of Toledo, 1929—, dir. of Jr. Coll., 1931—, dean of adminstrn., 1935—; acting pres., 1946-48. Mem. N.E.A. (dept. of supts.), Phi Delta Kappa. Club: Toledo Torch (sec. and treas.). Home: 2427 Middlesex Dr., Toledo. Died Oct. 16, 1950; buried Lakeview Cemetery, Port Clinton, O.

CARTER, Russell Gordon, author; b. Trenton, N.J., Jan. 1, 1892; s. John Rogers and Alice Virginia (Hughes) C.; S.B., Harvard, 1916; m. Florence Diehl, Dec. 29, 1917; children—Virginia Gordon, Catherine Juliette. With publicity dept. Dem. Nat. Com., 1916; reporter Hartford Daily Courant, 1917; editorial staff Youth's Companion, 1919-25; editor of The Beacon, 1925, Boston Center for Adult Edn. 1943-56. Enlisted United States Army, Sept. 22, 1917; promoted 2d and 1st lt. inf.; served in France 13 mos.; participated in Aisne-Marne offensive, Oise-Aisne, Meuse-Argonne; cited by comdg. gen. 32d Div.; awarded the Silver Star medal "for gallantry in action"; in Germany with Army of Occupation. Mem. exec. com., Com. for a Jewish Army. Mem. Pro-Palestine Fedn., Am. Palestine Committee, Am. League for a Free Palestine, Friends of the Universal Jewish Encyclopedia, American Resettlement Com., China's Children, France Forever, Pi Gamma Mu. Club: Boston Authors. Author: Bob Hanson, Tenderfoot (with R. H. Bowles), 1921; Bob Hanson, Scout, 1921; Bob Hanson, First Class Scout, 1922; Bob Hanson, Eagle Scout, 1923; A Patriot Lad of Old Boston, 1923; A Patriot Lad of Old Philadelphia, 1924; Red Gilbert's Flying Circus, 1924; A Patriot Lad of Old Salem, 1925; Red Gilbert's Floating Menagerie, 1926; A Patriot Lad of Old Trenton, 1926; A Patriot Lad of Old Cape Cod, 1927; The Glory of Peggy Harrison (with Harford Powel, Jr.), 1927; The White Plume of Navarre, 1927; A Patriot Lad of Old Long Island, 1928; The Giant's House (with Harford Powel, Jr.), 1928; A Patriot Lad of Old Saratoga, 1929; Three Points of Honor, 1929 (Boys' Life prize of $4,000 as the best story based on the Boy Scout oath and law); The King's Spurs, 1930; A Patriot Lad of Old Rhode Island, 1930; Yellow Jacket, 1931; The Singing Dog, 1931; His Own Star, 1931; A Patriot Lad of Old Maine, 1932; Good Luck, Lieutenant!, 1932; A Patriot Lad of Old New Hampshire, 1933; The Crimson Cutlass, 1933; City of Adventure, 1934; A Patriot Lad of Old Connecticut, 1935; Shaggy—The Horse from Wyoming, 1935 (awarded first prize of $500, Julia Ellsworth Ford Foundation contest for best juvenile literature in 1935); A Patriot Lad of Old West Point, 1936; The Golden Galleon, 1936; Brothers of the Frontier, 1938; The 101st Field Artillery, A.E.F., 1917-1919, 1940; Teen-Age Historical Stories, 1948; Teen-Age Animal Stories, 1949; Mr. Whatley Enjoys Himself, 1954. Contbr. fiction to Messenger of the Sacred Heart, other Cath. mags. Recipient Jr. book award certificate Boys Clubs Am., 1950. Home: 14 Blackstone Terrace, Newton 58, Mass. Died May 7, 1957.

CARTER, Steven V., congressman; b. Carterville, Utah, Oct. 8, 1915; s. Joseph T. and Effie Mae (Stevens) C.; A.B., State U. Ia., 1937, J.D., 1939; m. Mabel Lucille Ketchum, Jan. 1, 1937; children—Steven Anthony, Charles Leon. Admitted to Ia. bar, 1939, since practiced in Leon; county atty. Decatur County, 1941-43; city atty. Leon, 1950; mem. 86th Congress, 4th Dist. Ia. Exec. bd. So. Ia. area Boy Scouts Am.; active Community Chest. Served as lt. (j.g.) USNR, World War II. Recipient Presdl. unit citation. Mem. Vets. Fgn. Wars. Am. Legion. Mem. Reorganized Ch. of Jesus Christ of Latter-day Saints. Mason; mem. Order Eastern Star. Club: Lions. Home: 910 Church St., Leon, Ia. Office: New House Office Bldg., Washington. Died Nov. 4, 1959; buried Leon Cemetery, Leon, Ia.

CARTER, William Francis, lawyer; b. Farmington, Mo., Oct. 30, 1867; s. William and Maria (McIlvaine) C.; prep. edn., Smith Acad., St. Louis; LL.B., U. of Mich., 1890; m. Grace Thoroughman, Nov. 15, 1893; children—Emmet T., Martha W. Henson. Admitted to Mo. bar, 1890, and began practice at Farmington; moved to St. Louis, 1892; director Coca-Cola Bottling Company, Industrial Bank & Trust Co. President Board of Education, St. Louis, 1919-20; pres. Chamber of Commerce, 1919-21. Home: 625 S. Skinker St. Office: 418 Olive St., St. Louis. Died Jan. 19, 1951; buried Oak Grove Mausoleum, St. Louis County, Mo.

CARTER, William Henry, business exec.; b. Needham, Mass., June 15, 1864; s. William and Martha (Lee) C.; student pub. schs.; m. Addie M. Taylor, June 1, 1893 (dec.); m. 2d, Hazel M. Goodwin, June 28, 1941. With William Carter Co., Needham Heights, since 1878, pres. since 1918. Mem. Mass. Legislature, 1906, U.S. Congress, 1914-18. Republican. Methodist. Mason (Shriner), Odd Fellow. Home: 112 Greendale Av. Office: 963 Highland Av., Needham Heights, Mass. Died Apr. 23, 1955; buried Needham (Mass.) Cemetery.

CARTY, Donald Joseph (kär'tĭ), educator; born Methuen, Mass., June 27, 1908; s. William Joseph and Nora Agnes (Whatmore) C.; student Boston Coll., 1925-26; B.L.I., Emerson Coll., Boston, 1930; student Harvard, summer 1930; A.M. in speech, Marquette U., 1934; A.M. in education, Columbia, 1938; Ph.D., Fordham Univ., 1947; student N.Y. Univ., summer 1948; unmarried. Instr. in speech, St. Edward's U., 1930-31; lecturer in speech, Boston Coll., 1934; instr. in speech, Augustinian Acad., Staten Island, 1941; instr. in English, Horace Mann Sch. for Boys, Teachers Coll., Columbia, 1944-45; visiting asst. prof. of English, Coll. of Mt. St. Vincent, N.Y. City, 1943; asst. prof. of English, U.S. Army, Specialized Training Program, Manhattan Coll., N.Y. City, 1943-44; field supervisor. Engring., Sci. and Management War Training Program, 1941-45, head dept. of speech, dir. of drama, since 1934; dir. Manhattan College Players since 1934, Manhattan College Experimental Theatre since 1948. Drama consultant; tournament adviser, Hearst Nat. Tournament of Orators, N.Y., Mem. Am. Assn. Univ. Profs., Speech Assn. of Am. Republican (mem. Nat. Rep. Club, N.Y. City). Roman Catholic. K.C. Club: Columbia Univ. (N.Y. City). Home: 34½ Van Corlear Pl., N.Y.C. 63. Office: Manhattan College, N.Y.C. 71. Died Aug. 22, 1954; buried St. Mary's Roman Catholic Cemetery.

CARUANA, George J., titular archbishop; b. Malta, Apr. 23, 1882; s. Amabile and Mary Carmen (Sammut) C.; grad. St. Ignatius Coll., Malta, 1900; Capranica Coll. and Gregorian U., Rome, grad. from latter, 1906. Ordained priest R.C. Ch., 1905; apptd. sec. to apostolic delegate, Manila, P.I., 1907; settled in U.S., 1910, naturalized citizen, 1915; asst. to Our Lady of Mercy Ch., Brooklyn, N.Y., 1910-14; pastor St. Leo's Ch., Corona, N.Y., 1914-21; sec. to Cardinal Dougherty, Phila., 1921; nominated bishop of Puerto Rico, Aug. 5, 1921, consecrated Oct. 28, 1921. Served as lt. chaplain U.S.A., Canal Zone, Aug. 10, 1918-Aug. 19, 1919; promoted to the titular Archdiocese of Sebasta and apolstolic administrator of Guatemala, C.A., 1925; apptd. apostolic del. to Mexico, 1925; apptd. apostolic del. of the Antilles, 1926; internuncio of Haiti, 1927, apostolic nuncio of Cuba, 1935. Home: Nunciatura Apostolica, Vedado, Habana, Cuba. Died Mar. 26, 1950.

CARVER, George, educator, author; b. Cin., Dec. 19, 1888; s. Robert Dieuaide and Elizabeth Darby (McGraw) C.; student U. Ala. and U. Chgo.; A.B., Miami U., 1916; m. Eva Schultz, July 23, 1919; 1 son, Robert Bradley. Instr. in English, Pa. State Coll., 1916-18, State U. Ia., 1919-23, asso. in English, 1923-24; lecturer in English, U. Pitts., 1924-26, asst. prof. English, 1926-27, asso. prof., 1927—. Served with AEF, 1918-19. Mem. Modern Lang. Assn. Am., Phi Kappa Sigma. Catholic. Author: The Catholic Tradition in English Literature, 1926; Points of Style, 1928; Essays and Essayists, 1929. Co-Author: Writing and Rewriting, 1923; minumum Essentials of Good Writing, 1924. Co-Editor: Representative Catholic Essays, 1926; The Stream of English Literature, 1930; Periodical Essays of the Eighteenth Century, 1930. Address: U. Pitts., Pitts. Died Oct. 29, 1949; buried Chgo.

CARVER, John Stuart, educator; b. Boston, Feb. 14, 1892; s. John Franklin and Kate (Wade) C.; B.S., U. of Mass., 1913; m. Marth Jane Buck, Oct. 1, 1921; children—John Stuart, Edward Samuel, Donald Stanley. Head of poultry dept. Essex County School, Mass., 1915-18; extension specialist, U. Me., 1918-21, ednl. dir. Norfolk Vet. Training Schol, Mass., 1921-23; chmn. poultry dept. and prof. poultry husbandry, State Coll. of Wash., 1923—; acting dir. Wash. Agrl. Expt. Stas., 1956-57. Fellow Poultry Sci., 1951; received Poultry Sci. Teaching award for 1949. Mem. Sigma Xi, Phi Kappa Phi, Alpha Zeta. Author many bulls. on poultry mgmt. and nutrition. Contbr. sci. articles in agrl. pubis. Home: 406 Howard St., Pullman, Wash. Died Aug. 31, 1957; buried Pullman, Wash.

CARVER, Walter Lexor, engr.; b. Cleve., Oct. 16, 1889; s. Loren D. and Margaret (Jacob) C.; ed. pub. schs., spl. lab. and research work; m. Marie MacDonald, Dec. 10, 1914. Apprentice Nat. Screw & Tack Co., Cleve., 1908-10; with engring. dept. Peerless Motor Car Co., 1910-13; chief engr. and supt. production Wallis Tractor Co., Cleve. and Racine, Wis., 1913-16; fgn. countries, 1916-17; supt. production; etc., Moline (Ill.) Plow Co., 1917-20; chief engr. tractor dept. Midwest Engine Co., Indpls., 1920; gen. mgr. Antigo (Wis.) Tractor Corp., 1921-22; v.p., treas. T. B. Funk Co., Indpls., 1922—. Traveled widely throughout the world; tech. work in Petrograd, Russia, 1916-17; automotive work with Russian Army, at Riga front, 1917; made first tech. tests of tractor haulage of arty. for U.S. Govt. Mem. Soc. Automotive Engrs. Unitarian. Address: 39 Fifth Av., N.Y.C. Died Apr. 12, 1958.

CARVER, Williard, chiropractic educator; b. Maysville, Ia., July 14, 1866; s. John Waterman and Eliza Maria (Nutting) C.; student Oskaloosa (Ia.) Coll., 1884-87; LL.B., Ia. Coll. Law (Drake U.), Des Moines, 1891; grad. Parker Sch. of Chiropractic, Ottumwa, Ia., 1906; m. Mary Ellen Stutsman, Nov. 4, 1919; 1 son, Ronald Lovelock. Practiced law and conducted a bank at Barnes City, Ia., 1892-94; practiced at Ocheyedan, Ia., 1894-98, Oskaloosa, Ia., 1898-1905; founder and pres. Carver Chiropractic Coll., Oklahoma City, 1906, Carver Chiropractic Inst., N.Y.C. (founded 1919), and Carver Chiropractic U., Denver, 1923; aso. Chiropractic Research U., Washington. Mem. Internat. Assn. Chiropractic Schs. and Colls. (pres.), Nat. Naturopathic Assn. (v.p.), Nat. drugless Practitioners' Assn. (v.p.), Am. Chiropractic Assn. (nat. advisory bd.); mem. bd. govs. Internat. Chiropractic Congress. Author: Carver's Chiropractic Analysis, 1909, 2d edit., 1915; 3d edit., vols. 1 and 2, 1921, 22; Applied Psychology, 1914; Rough Nuggets, 1917; Psycho-Bio-Physiology, 1919; Carver's Scientific Catechism, 1924. Address: 520 N.W. 9th St., Oklahoma City 3. Died Dec. 23, 1943; buried Fairlawn Cemetery, Oklahoma City.

CARVILLE, E. P., ex-senator; b. Mound Valley, Nev.; s. Edward and Emily Ellen (Porcher) C.; student Notre Dame U.; m. Irma M. Callahan, Aug., 1910; children—Edward, Richard llen, Robert Thomas. Admitted to Nev. bar; has been dist. atty., Elko County, Nev., dist. judge Elko County, and U.S. dist. atty. of Nev.; gov. of Nev., 1943-45; apptd. U.S. senator to fill unexpired term, Aug. 1945. World. Address: 1127 Gordon Av., Reno, Nev. Died June 27, 1956; buried Nevada Meml. Park. Mausoleum.

CARY, Edward Henry (kâr'i), surgeon; b. Union Springs, Ala., Feb. 28, 1872; s. Joseph Milton and Lucy Janette (Powell) C.; pre. edn., Union Springs Acad. and night sch., N.Y. City; M.D., Bellevue Hosp. Med. Coll. (New York U.), 1898; LL.D., Baylor U., 1916; m. Georgie Fonda Schneider, Apr. 19, 1911; children—Georgie, Edward Henry, Florence, Jenette (dec.), Catherine. Interne, Bellvue Hosp., 1898-99, N.Y. Ey and Ear Infirmary, 1899-1901; prof. ophthalmology and otolaryngology and head of dept., Baylor University, 1902-43, dean of Medical School, 1902-22, chairman department surgery, 1921-29; chairman faculty, Med. Sch., 1909-29; chmn. staff, Baylor Hosp., 1909-29; prof. emeritus of ophthalmology, Southwestern Med Sch., U. of Tex.; chmn. adv. bd., sch. and hosp., 1909-29; now pres. Group Hosp. Service, Inc., Group Med. and S?g. Service; pres. Cary-Schneider Investment Co.; dir. Republic Nat. Bank. Recipient Linz Award for 1945. Pres. and chmn. exec. bd. National Physicians Com.; pres. Kesller Plan Assn. Chmn. dist. bd. med. examiners, Dallas, World War; organized Baylor Med. Unit which served in France during World War. Mem. Appeal Board of Selective Service Dist. No. 7. Pres. Southwestern Med Foundation, Philos. Soc. of Tex. (past pres.); president Dallas Historical Society. Fellow Am. College Surgeons; mem. Am. Med. Assn. (trustee 1925-29; pres. 1932-33), Amer. Laryngol., Rhinol. and Otol. Soc., Southern Med. Assn. (ex-pres.), Texas State Med. Soc. (ex-pres.), Dallas County Med. Soc. (ex-pres.), Tex. Ophthal. and Otolaryngol. Soc. (ex-pres.), Am. Acad. of Ophthalmology and Otolaryngology, mem. council), Phi Alpha Sigma, Alpha Omega Alpha, Soc. Colonial Wars, Mason (32°, Shriner). Clubs: Critic, Dallas

Athletic, Brookhollow, Dallas Golf and Country. Home: 4712 Lakeside Drive, Dallas 5. Office: Medical Arts Bldg., Dallas. Died Dec. 11, 1953; buried Hillcrest Mausoleum, Dallas.

CARY, Guy, lawyer; b. N.Y.C., Nov. 14, 1879; s. Clarence and Elisabeth Miller (Potter) C.; A.B., Harvard, 1902, LL.B., 1904; m. Cynthia Roche Burden, July 24, 1922; children—Guy Fairfax, Cynthia. Admitted to N.Y. bar, 1905; now mem. firm Shearman & Sterling & Wright; dir. Air Reduction Co., Ala. Great So. R.R., Celanese Corp. Am., City Investing Co., Home Ins. Co., Nat. City Bank of N.Y., Nat. City Safe Deposit Co., Pa. Dixie Cement Corp., So. Ry. Co. Office: 20 Exchange Pl., N.Y.C. 5. Died Aug. 27, 1950.

CARY, Joyce, author; b. Londonderry, Ireland, Dec. 7, 1888; s. Arthur Pitt and Charlotte (Joyce) C.; M.A., Trinity, Oxford University, 1912; D.L., University of Edinburgh, 1953; married Gertrude Margaret Ogilvie, June 1, 1916; children—Arthur Lucius Michael, Peter Joyce, Tristram Ogilvie, George. Joined Irish Coop. movement, 1912, Nigerian Polit. Service, 1913, Borgu, 1917. Served with Montenegrin btn. and Brit. Red Cross, Balkan War, 1912-13; with Nigeria Regt. Cameroons Campaign, 1915-16. Author: Aissa Saved, 1932; An American Visitor, 1933; The African Witch, 1936; Castle Corner, 1938; Mister Johnson, 1939; Power in Men, 1939; Charley Is My Darling, 1940; A House of Children, 1941; Herself Surprised, 1941; The Case for African Freedom, 1941; To Be a Pilgrim, 1942; Process of Real Freedom, 1943; The Horse's Mouth, 1944; Marching Soldier, 1945; Britain and West Africa, 1946; The Moonlight, 1946; A Fearful Joy, 1949; Prisoner of Grace, 1952; Except the Lord, 1953; Not Honour More, 1955; Art and Reality, 1957; The Captive and the Free, 1959. Home: 12 Parks Rd., Oxford, Eng. Died Mar. 29, 1957; buried Oxford, Eng.

CASADY, Thomas (kăs'å-dĭ), bishop; b. Des Moines, Ia., June 6, 1881; s. Simon and Sarah Conarroe (Griffiths) C.; B.A., State U. Ia., 1902; student Gen. Theol. Sem., N.Y.C., 1903-06; m. Frances Le Baron Kasson, June 27, 1906; children—Phineas McCray, Simon, Thomas, Jr., France Le Baron, Richard Robbins, George McFarland (dec.). Deacon, 1906, priest, 1907, P.E. Ch.; rector successively St. Mary's Ch., Oelwein, Ia., St. Mark's Ch., Des Moines, Ch. of the Ascension, Pueblo, Colo., until 1920, All Saints Ch., Omaha, until 1927; bishop of Okla., 1927—; elected pres. of the Province of the Southwest, Amarillo, Tex., 1944. Mem. Sigma Chi. Democrat. Mason. Home: 608 E. 18th St. Office: P.O. Box 1098, Oklahoma City. Died Sept. 9, 1958.

CASE, George Sessions, mech. engr., mfr.; b. Interlaken, N.Y., Oct. 16, 1882; s. Frank Castle and Fannie (Sessions) C.; B.S., Case Sch. Applied Science, 1904, M.E., 1927; m. Amey Ellen Hall, Dec. 4, 1906; children—Geo. S., Barbara Jane. With Lamson & Sessions Co., since 1904, became factory mgr., 1912, treas., 1921, v.p., 1926, pres., 1929, chmn. of bd., 1938; dir. Peck, Stow & Wilcox Co., Baker-Raulang Co., Johnston & Jennings Co., The Lamson & Sessions Co., J. Hungerford Smith Co. Maj. Chem. Warfare Service, 1918; stationed at Edgewood Arsenal and Washington. Mem. Am. Soc. M.E., Cleveland Engring. Soc., Soc. Automotive Engrs., Phi Delta Theta, Tau Beta Pi. Republican. Presbyn. Clubs: Union, Mayfield Country. Home: 17414 S. Woodland Rd., Shaker Heights 20, O. Office: 1971 W. 85th St., Cleveland 2. Died Oct. 11, 1950; buried Lakeview Cemetery, Cleveland.

CASE, Rolland Webster, ret. army officer; b. Manchester, Mich., May 26, 1882; s. Clarence Webster and Dora (Robison) C.; B.S., U.S. Mil. Acad., 1905; attended Ordnance Sch. of Tech., 1912-13, Command and Gen. Staff Sch., 1922-23, Army War Coll., 1928-29; m. Jessie Tucker, July 17 (dec.); 1 dau., Lucy Imogene (Mrs. Clyde Wendelken, Jr.); m. 2d, Mary Gertrude King, Aug. 18, 1933. Commd. 2d lt., Inf., U.S. Army, 1905, 1st lt., Ordnance, 1909, 1st lt., Inf., 1911; was capt., Ordnance, 1911-13; commd. capt. Inf., 1916; served as maj. (temp.), 1917-18; commd., maj., Inf., 1920; transferred to Ordnance Dept., 1920; commd. lt. col., Ordnance, 1929, col., 1935, brig. gen. (temp.) 1940; retired 1944; dir. research, Coll. of Engring., N.Y.U., 1944-48, ret. Mem. Army Ordnance Assn. Republican. Episcopalian. Mason. Clubs: Army and Navy, Army and Navy Country (Washington); Engineers (N.Y.C.). Home: Washington. Died Dec. 16, 1957.

CASEMENT, Dan Dillon, live stock raiser; b. Painesville, O., July 13, 1868; s. John Stephen and Frances Marion (Jennings) C.; student Western Reserve Acad., Hudson, O., 1884-86; A.B., Princeton, 1890; A.M., Columbia, 1891; m. Olivia Thornburgh, of Washington, D.C., Dec. 1, 1897; children—Mary Eliza (Mrs. Harold A. Furlong), Frances Jennings (Mrs. Geoffrey Landesman), John Stephen. Began as range cow hand, 1891; ran range cattle, western Colo., and operated farm in Kansas, 1891-96; worked on constrn. Ferrocaril al Pacifico, Costa Rica, Central America, 1896-1903; farming and ranching since 1903. Commd. capt. field arty., Ft. Sheridan Training Camp, 1917; served in A.E.F. in France, Jan. 1918-Jan. 1919. Trustee Lake Erie Coll., Painesville, O., since 1909; pres. Farmers' Independence Council of America since 1935. Mem. Am. Nat. Live Stock Assn., Kansas Live Stock Assn. Republican. Clubs: Princeton (New York); El Paso (Colorado Springs, Colo.). Wrote regularly for Breeder's Gazette many yrs. and served as corr. editor same, 1920-26. Contbr. to numerous mags. Home: Manhattan, Kan. Died Mar. 7, 1953; buried Painesville, O.

CASER, Ettore, painter; b. Venice, 1880; s. Antonio and Ernesta (Berti) C.; art edn., Acad. in Venice. Came to U.S., 1909. Served in Italian Army, World War; awarded Croce di Guerra (Italy). A.N.A., 1932; mem. Salmagundi Club. Home and Studio: 1931 Broadway, N.Y.C. Died 1944.*

CASEY, Lee, newspaper man; b. Goshen, N.Y., Aug. 20, 1889; s. Sam L. and Blanche (Murray) C.; attended St. George's School, Newport, R.I., and U. of the South, Sewanee, Tenn.; m. Geraldine Croft, 1924 (died 1946). With Kansas City Star, 1908-12, Chicago Examiner, 1915-16; with Rocky Mountain News, 1912-15, 16—, now asso. editor. Died Jan. 29, 1951.

CASEY, Robert Pierce, coll. dean; b. Dorchester, Mass., Dec. 8, 1897; s. Peter Julius and Lucy Curtis (Howe) C.; student Boston Latin Sch., 1911-15; A.B., Harvard, 1918, S.T.B., 1922; Ph.D., U. of Cambridge, Eng., 1924, B.D., 1951; Fellow in Greek palaeography, 1924; fellow of Grad. Sch. U. Cin., later asst., asso. prof. and prof. history and philosophy of religion, 1924-33; prof. and head dept. Bibl. lit. and history of religion, Brown University, 1934-50; fellow and lecturer divinity, Sidney Sussex College, Cambridge, England, 1950, now fellow, dean, also lecturer in theology. Member of the advisory bd. Studies and Documents. Mem. paleographical expdn., Mt. Athos and Patmos, 1925; archaeological expdn., Lake Van, 1938. Ordained to priesthood, Episcopal Ch., 1940. Served as pvt., Inf., U.S. Army, 1918. Mem. Am. Acad. Arts and Sciences, Am. Assn. of Teachers of Slavic Languages (R.I. chmn.), Phi Beta Kappa. Hon. mem. III Mexican Med. Congress. Episcopalian. Author: Serapion of Thmuis; Against the Manichees, 1931; Clement of Alexandria: Excerpta ex Theodoto, 1934; Religion in Russia, 1946; Early Russian Monasticism, 1953. Address: Sidney Sussex College, Cambridge, Eng. Died Apr. 5, 1959; buried St. Guile's Cemetery, Cambridge, Eng.

CASEY, William Joseph, banker; b. Balt., Nov. 10, 1871; s. Thomas J. and Margaret (D'Oyley) C.; educated St. Vincents Parochial Sch., Calvert Hall Coll., LL.D., Loyola Coll., Balt., married Mary Creswell Twiname, 1899 (died April 1934); m. 2d, Catherine Gwinnette Doughty, Oct. 1936. Chairman of board, chairman exec. com. Maryland Trust Co.; mem. exec. com. Balt. Gas & Electric Co.; dir. Provident Savings Bank. Chmn. Commn. on Governmental Efficiency and Economy (1931-47), a fact finding and planning body in municipal and state govt.; also devised and directed plan sponsored by similar organization which reorganized administrative methods of Baltimore, 1923-27. Trustee of various civic enterprises. Awarded Meritorious Achievement Medallion, Advt. Club of Balt.; Md. Inst. Gold Medal of Honor, 1948; Balt. Assn. Commerce citation, 1947; Mayor and Bd. of Estimates Silver award, 1947; Calvert Hall Coll. Citizenship Gold Medal, 1952; Md. Merit award, Hibernian Soc., 1953; Am. Nat. Red Cross Twenty Yr. Service award, 1958; named Cath. Man of Year, Nat. Conf. Christians and Jews, 1958. Home: 3811 Canterbury Rd. Office: Calvert and Redwood Sts., Balt. Died Mar. 23, 1959; buried Druid Ridge Cemetery.

CASH, Albert D(enis), lawyer; b. Cincinnati, Aug. 21, 1897; s. Denis F. and Margaret (Heister) C.; A.B., Xavier U., 1916; LL.B., U. Cincinnati, 1920; m. Esther Boehnlein, June 30, 1926 (dec. 1940); children—Denis F., Albert D., Kathleen, Robert; m. 2d Elizabeth Cassatt Reid, Fed. 1, 1947; 1 stepson, Alfred C. Reid. Served with F.B.I., 1917; admitted to Ohio bar, 1920, since practiced Cincinnati, mem. Dolle, O'Donnell & Cash. Mem. Cincinnati City Council since 1938, mayor Cincinnati, 1948-51. Served with F.A., Central Officers Tng. Service, 1918. Mem. Am., Ohio, Cincinnati bar assns., Nat. Municipal League (exec. bd.). Home: 3773 Erie Av., Cin. 8. Office: Carew Tower, Cin. 2. Died Aug. 2, 1952.

CASH, William Thomas, librarian; b. Lamont, Fla., July 23, 1878; s. Benjamin Franklin and Susan (Mixon) C.; ed. pub. schs. of Taylor Co., Fla.; m. Gracie Lou Wentworth, Jan. 18, 1912; children—Laura Louise (Mrs. S. J. Pajcic), Alma Fleta (dec.), William Thomas and Alton Horace (twins), Alwyn Clymer, Erma Clarice (Mrs. Norman R. Hurd), Reginald LeMoyne, John Wellborn. Farm hand, 1892-97; teacher pub. schs., Taylor Co., 1897-1920; instr. history, (summer sch.) Fla. State Coll. for Women, 1917-20. Mem. Fla. Course of Study Commn., 1918; mem. Fla. Ho. of Reps., 1909, 15, 17, State Senate, 1918-20; county supt. of pub. instrn., Taylor Co., Fla., Jan. 1921-1925; editor Perry (Fla.) Herald, 1925-28; librarian, Fla. State Library, Tallahassee since April 1927. Mem. Nat. Assn. State Libraries, Fla. Hist. Soc., Fla. Acad. of Scis., Fla. Library Assn., Tallahassee Hist. Soc., Southeastern Library Association, Colonial Research Foundation, Historical Association Southern Florida. Democrat. Methodist. Club: Rotary. Author: History of the Democratic Party in Florida, 1936; Story of Florida (history of state) 4 vols., 1938; foreword to Florida Becomes à State, 1945. Contbr. Dictionary of American History, 1940. Home: 231 Lafayette Circle. Office: New Supreme Court Bldg., Tallahassee, Fla. Died July 8, 1951.*

CASHEN, Thomas Cecil, ret. labor ofcl.; b. South Thompson, O., Sept. 15, 1879; s. John and Sarah (McKee) C.; student pub. schs. Cleve.; m. Marie Burhenne, Sept. 7, 1905; 1 dau., Mae Cashen (Mrs. David R. Kelly). Began as locomotive fireman L.S. &M.S., 1899, yard service, 1906-13; in grocery and meat business, 1902-06; v.p. Switchmen's Union North America, 1918-21, internat. pres., 1921-47. Dir Labor Coop. Ednl. and Pub. Soc., Washington; chmn. Ry. Labor Execs. Assn. (Washington). Democrat. Catholic. Home: 9006 Keating Av., Skokie, Ill. Died Mar. 1959.*

CASHMAN, Earl William, ret. elec. distbg. exec.; b. Waseca, Minn., Feb. 14, 1891; s. James and Jeanette (Campbell) C.; student Highland Park Coll., U. Minn.; m. Emeline Cashman, Oct. 19, 1918. With Graybar Electric Co., 1913-55, ret. as v.p., dir., mem. exec. com., 1955. Home: 540 Park Av., N.Y.C. Died Aug. 3, 1959; buried St. Mary's Cemetery, Mpls.

CASON, Hulsey (kā'sŭn), psychologist; b. Lexington, Ga., Feb. 21, 1893; s. Emory Hugh and Jessie (Jones) C.; A.B., Mercer U., 1913; A.M., Columbia, 1920, Ph.D., 1922; m. Eloise May Boeker, Sept. 6, 1923; children—Roger Lee, Jean; m. 2d Marion Conrad, Aug. 30, 1939; 1 son, Emory Conrad. Asst. prof. psychology, Syracuse U., 1923-26, U. of Rochester, 1926-27, prof. psychology, 1927-30; prof. psychology, U. of Wis., 1930-40, U. of Miami since 1948; summers lecturer in psychology, U. of N.C., 1923, Columbia, 1927, 29, U. of Wis., 1930; research psychologist, U.S.P.H.S., 1940-48. Served as 1st lt., Inf., 7th Div. Regular Army, 1917-19, Mexican Border and A.E.F. in France. Diplomate in Clin. Psychology, Am. Bd. of Examiners in Professional Psychology, 1948. Fellow Am. Psychol. Assn., A.A.A.S.; mem. Am. Assn. U. Profs., Southern Soc. for Philosophy and Psychology, Midwestern Psychol. Assn., Fla. Psychol. Assn., Fla. Acad. Scis., Sigma Xi, Phi Delta Kappa, Psi Chi. Unitarian. Club: Country (Coral Gables). Author: Conditioned Pupillary and Eyelid Reactions, 1922; Laws of Exercise and Effect, 1924; Common Annoyances, 1930; Pleasant and Unpleasant Activities, 1932; Nightmare Dream, 1935; Psychopathic Personality, 1942; Concept and Symptoms of the Psychopath, 1948 (also in Spanish, 1950, 51). Mem. editorial bd. Jour. of Psychology since 1935. Genealogist. Home: 619 Anastasia Av., Coral Gables, Fla. Died May 1, 1950; buried Warren, Ga.

CASS, Charles Anderson, ret. paper mfg. exec.; b. Allegheny, Pa., Nov. 20, 1880; s. Joseph Kerr and Sarah Margaret (Anderson) C.; prep. edn. Lawrenceville Sch.; A.B., Princeton, 1902; m. 2d, Agnes Droop; children—Mary (Mrs. Frank S. Goodwin), Joseph Kerr III. With W.Va. Pulp & Paper Co., 1902—, asst. treas., 1908-09, sec., 1909-47, dir., 1927—, retired from active participation in bus., 1947. Presbyn. Clubs: University, Racquet and Tennis, Princeton (N.Y.C.); Nassau (Princeton); Neaman's Hall (Lenox(Mass.). Home: 120 East End Av., N.Y.C. Died Apr. 1958.

CASSELMAN, Arthur Vale, church official; b. Minerva, O., July 20, 1874; s. Rev. Amos and Louisa Carrie (Leyde) C.; grad. Wichita (Kan.) Acad., 1892; A.B., Heidelberg Coll., 1895, D.D., 1923; B.D., Heidelberg Theological Seminary, 1898; Litt.D., Catawba College, 1942; m. Nima Hodsdon Drake, July 26, 1905; 1 daughter, Louise Climena. Ordained ministry Reformed Ch. in U.S., 1898; pastor Grace Ch., Columbiana, O., 1898-1902; field sec. Bd. of Foreign Missions, Ref. Ch., 1902-05; pastor Calvary Ch., Reading, Pa., 1906-21; sec. of missionary edn., Bds. of Home and Fgn. Missions, Ref. Ch., 1922-32; asso. sec. Bd. of Foreign Missions, 1932-33; sec., Dec. 1933-41; executive secretary, Board of International Missions, Evang. and Ref. Church, 1941-44; emeritus, 1944. Grad. Chaplain's Training Sch., Camp Taylor, Ky., 1918; successively chaplain Camp Hill, Newport News, Va., transport S.S. Lutitia, Base Hosp. No. 46, Landernau, France. Made world tour of missionary visitation and exploration, 1922-23; gen. dir. motion-picture photographic expdn. to Asia under auspices of Inter-church World Movement, 1919-20; ednl. deputation to Bagdad, 1926; visit to mission fields, China and Japan, 1935. Republican. Author: Making America Christian, 1931; The Winnebago Finds a Friend, 1932 and 1944; Into All the World, 1934; The End of the Beginning, 1936; Red and Black and Gold, 1940; Unto the Progress of the Gospel, 1942; A Mission in the Heart of China, 1952; It Happened in Hunan, 1953. Home: 731 N. Fourth St., Reading, Pa. Office: Schaff Bldg., 1505 Race St., Phila. Died May 1, 1957.

CASSIDY, James E., bishop; ordained ministry R.C. Ch., Sept. 8, 1898; consecrated bishop, May 27, 1930; apptd. bishop of Fall River, Mass., July 28, 1934, as successor to Bishop Daniel F. Feehan, who died July 19, 1934. Address: 394 Highlan Av., Fall River, Mass. Died May 17, 1951.*

CASSIDY, M(ichael) Joseph, govt. ofcl.; b. Macon, Ga., Mar. 29, 1893; s. Patrick John and Mary Ann (Campbell) C.; A.B., Spring Hill Coll., 1914; C.E., Cath. U., 1917. Cons. engr. Elroy G. Smith Co., Augusta, Ga., 1921-37; constrn. supervision Zone V, Fed. Housing Adminstrn., L.A., 1938-42, asst. zone commr. Zone V, Washington, 1943-46, zone commr., 1947-55, executive officer regional liaison, 1955—. Served as lt., 20th C.E., France, World War I; supervision rehabilitation engr. troops after Armistice, 1918-20. Club: Columbia Country (Chevy Chase, Md.). Home: 6640 Hillandale Rd., Bethesda, Md. Office: 811 Vermont Av., Washington 11. Died Dec. 17, 1957.

CASSILL, Harold E., editor; b. Des Moines, Ia., Jan. 31, 1897; s. William Wright and Alice (Barnes) C.; student of Monmouth (Ill.) Coll., 1916-18; m. Margaret McQuiston, June 29, 1932; 1 dau., Dorothy Ann. Began newspaper work on Monmouth, Ill., Daily Review, 1917; reporter Spokane Daily Chronicle, 1918-22, editorial writer and city editor, 1923-41, managing editor, 1941-47; assistant general manager Spokesman-Review and Spokane Daily Chronicle, 1947-50, gen. mgr. since 1950. Mem. bd. dirs. Spokane Co. chpt., Am. Red Cross; Spokane Community Concert Assn.; Spokane Philharmonic Orchestra; Inland Empire Council of Camp Fire Girls; mem. C. of C. (v.p.), Bur. Advt., Am. Newspaper Pubs. Assn. (dir.), Agrl. Pubs. Assn. (dir.), Am. Soc. Newspaper Editors, Sigma Delta Chi. Conglist. Club: Spokane. Home: E. 609 13th Av., Spokane 3. Office: Review Building, Spokane 10, Wash. Died Aug. 2, 1957; buried Greenwood Cemetery, Spokane, Wash.

CASSINGHAM, John W., ex-congressman; b. Coshocton, O., June 22, 1840; s. George F. and Elizabeth C.; student pub. schs. of Coshocton; m. Caroline Lamberson, Nov. 5, 1863. Dep. county treas., 1957-68, county auditor, 1880-87, filled several minor offices; in merc. bus. and coal mining until 1880, since in coal mining; also paper mfr. until 1893; mem. U.S. Congress, 17th Ohio Dist., 1901-05; pres. Commercial Nat. Bank. Del. Dem. Nat. Conv., Chgo., 1896. Democrat. Home: Coshocton, O. Deceased.

CASTAÑEDA, Carlos Eduardo (käs tän yä'thä), educator, historian; b. Camargo, Mexico, Nov. 11, 1896; s. Timoteo and Elise (Leroux) C.; brought to U.S., 1908; A.B., U. of Tex., 1921, A.M., 1923, Ph.D., 1932; LL.D., University of St. Edwards, 1941; LL.D. Catholic University of America, 1952; studied univs. of Mexico and Havana and College of William and Mary; m. Elisa Rios, Dec. 27, 1921; children—Irma Gloria (dec.), Consuelo, Rose Mary. Teacher, Beaumont (Texas) High School, 1921; teacher Spanish, Brackenridge High School, San Antonio, 1922-23; asso. professor Spanish, College of William and Mary, Va., 1923-27; with U. Tex., 1927—, librarian Latin Am. library, 1923-46, associate professor history, 1939-46, prof. history, 1946—, mem. exec. council Inst. Latin Am. Studies, asso. editor The Americas; on leave 1943-45 with Fair Employment Practices Committee, becoming regional director, 1945; prof. history Univ. Mexico, summers, 1925, 26; teacher, summers, Our Lady of Lake Coll., San Antonio, 1928-34, U.N.M., 1937, 38, U. Tex., 1932, 33, 35, Cath. U. Am., 1939. Decorated Knight Comdr. Order Isabella la Catôlica (Spain), Knight Comdr. Order Holy Sepulchre of Jerusalem; Knight of Malta, Soverign Order of St. John of Jerusalem Knights of Malta. Fellow Texas Historical Association; member American Hist. Assn., Am. Catholic Hist. Assn. (pres. American Catholic History Association (president 1939), Am. Catholic Library Assn., Philos. Soc. of Tex., Southwestern Com. Latin-Am. Culture (sec.-treas.), Cath. Assn. for Internat. Peace, Phi Beta Kappa, Omicron Delta Kappa, Phi Alpha Theta; hon. mem. Sociedad Mexicana de Geografia y Estadistica Institut Historique et Heraldique de France, Ateneo Nacional de Ciencias y Artes de Mexico, Hispanic Soc. of America, Centro de Estudios Historicos de Buenos Aires; Sociedad Chihuahuense de Estudios Historicos; Academia Mexicana de la Historia, Texas Inst. of Letters, Academia de Historia de Guatemala. Acad. Am. Franciscan History, Historiog. Tex., K.C. Hist. Commn.; corr. mem. Acad. de la Historia, Acad. de Ceiencias Politicas (Venezuela). Clubs: University Faculty, Fortnightly (Austin); Social Science. Author: The Mexican Side of the Texan Revolution, 1928; Three Manuscript Maps of Texas by Stephen F. Austin, 1930; The Finding of Texas, 1936; The Winning of Texas, 1936; A Report on the Spanish Archives in San Antonio, Tex., 1937; The Missions at Work, 1938; The Passing of the Missions, 1939; Guide to Latin-American Manuscripts in Texas Library, 1939; End of the Spanish Regime in Texas, 1942; The Land of Middle America, 1947; The Fight for Liberty, 1948. Co-author: History of Latin America for Schools; The Church in Texas, 1938-48; Guide to the Manuel E Gondra Collection of Mss. in the University of Texas, 1951; El Proceso del General Scott por sus relaciones con el General Santa Anna, 1949; Pan Americanism and World Peace, 1954; Mexico in Manuscripts, 1955. Translator: History of Texas, 1673-1779 (by Fray Juan Augustin Morfi), 2 vols. 1935. Compiler: Early Texas Album (with F. C. Chabot), 1929. Edited: Dialogues of Cervantes de Salazar, 1954; The Church in The Southwest, 1953; Historia de Todos los Colegios de la Ciudad de Mexico hasta 1780, por Felix Osores, 1930; La Guerra de Reformasegun el Archivo del General Doblado, 1932. Contbr. to historical reviews. Home: 301 W. 37th St., University Station, Austin, Tex. Died Apr. 3, 1958; buried Mt. Calvary Cemetery, Austin.

CASTIGLIONI, Arturo (cas-tiyō-ne), physician, prof. med. history; b. Trieste, Italy, Apr. 10, 1874; s. Victor and Enrichetta (Bolaffio) C.; M.D., Vienna Univ., 1896; m. Marcella Sanguinetti, Apr. 26, 1903; children—Laura Luzzatto, Victor F. Came mto os., 1939, naturalized 1946. Clin. asst. Vienna, 1896-98; head sanitary service, Lloyd Triestino, 1899-1918, of Italian Line, 1918-36; prof. history medicine, U. Padua, 1922-38; mem. high council Pub. Health, Rome, 1922-29; prof. U. for Foreigners, Perugia, 1934-38; lecturer, history medicine, Univs. of Sao Paulo, Rio de Janeiro, Buenos Aires, Santiago, Chile, 1930; Hideyo-Noguchi lecturer, Johns Hopkins, Balt., 1933; research asso. and lecturer, history medicine Yale, 1939, prof. 1943-47, ret. Pres. N.Y. Soc. Med. History, 1942-44; lecturer oreign area courses, m. officers, Yale, 1941-42, Felow N.Y. Acad. Med.; hon. mem. Royal Soc. Medicine (London), Academia Nacional de Medicina (Buenos Aires, Gesellschaft der Aerzte (Vienna), Am. Assn. Hist. Medicine (Baltimore); hon. mem. Med. Hist. Soc. of São Paulo, Buenos Aires, Lima (Peru); Acad. Medicine (Genoa). Author: Il Volto de Ippocrate, 1925; Storia della Medicina, 1927 (3d edit., 1949), Italian Med. 1932; History of Tuberculosis, 1933; The Renaissance of Medicine in Italy, 1934; L'orto della Sanita, 1934; Adventures of the Mind, 1946, first pub. in Italy as Incantesimo e Magia. Contbr. articles and essays to English, Italian, French, Dutch, Sanpanish, German and Am. med. jours. Home: Via di Villa Grazioli 1, Rome, Italy. Died Jan. 21, 1952; buried Milano.

CASTILLO NAJERA, Francisco, diplomate; b. Durango, Mexico; s. Romualdo Castillo and Rosa (Najera) C.; A.B., Instituto Juárez, Durango, 1904; M.D., Facultad Nacional de Medicina, Mexico City, 1912, surgeon, 1913; m. Eugenia Dávila, Mar. 14, 1917; children—Francisco, Rosa Eugenia, Luis, Guillermo. Began as physician, 1913; dir. mil. hosps., Leon y Torreón, 1915-18, Juárez Hosp., Mexico City, 1918-20, Med. Mil. Sch. of Mexico, 1920; minister from exico to China, 1922-24; minister to Belgium, 1927-30; minister to Holland, 1930-32; minister to France, 1932-35; became ambassador from Mexico to U.S., 1935; now chmn. Mexican delegation to U Decorated orders: Sol del Peru, Merito (of Chile), Order of Crown of Belgium, Order of Orange of Nassau, Grand Officer Legion of Honor (France), Grand Officer Republic of Spain. Author: The Campaign Against Yellow Fever in Mexico, 1923; and of various books in Spanish. Address: care United Nations, 610 Fifth Av., N.Y.C. Died Dec. 20, 1954.*

CASTLE, Eugene Winston, films exec.; b. San Francisco, Apr. 9, 1897; s. Albert Ernest and Virginia (Winston) C.; ed. public schs. (San Francisco), High Sch. of Commerce, and Bates Acad.; LL.D., Defiance (O.) Coll., 1944; m. Mildred Kuhnheim, Nov. 19, 1937. Began as reporter and newsreel cameraman, 1915; Western rep. nat. newsreel, Gaumont-Mutual Weekly, 1916-17, Pacific Coast ed., 1919-21; founder and first editor, Pacific Coast edition Fox News, 1922-23; founder of Castle Films, 1924. Served with U.S. Marine Corps, 1917-18; awarded good conduct medal. Mem. Am. Legion. Republican. Roman Cath. Clubs: Bohemian (San Francisco); Motion Picture Pioneers, Overseas Press (N.Y.C.). Pioneer in prodn. and internat. distbn. 8mm and 16mm motion pictures for home libraries and use of pub. instns. Author: Billions, Blunders and Baloney; The Great Giveaway, 1957. Contbg. editor American Mercury mag. Home: 875 Fifth Av., N.Y.C. 21. Office: 30 Rockefeller Plaza, N.Y.C. Died Feb. 1960.

CASTLEMAN, Francis Lee, Jr., univ. dean; born Trenton, N.J., July 11, 1902; s. Francis Lee and Jessie Maude (Platt) C.; student Episcopal Acad., Phila., 1917-21; A.B., Lehigh U., 1925, C.E., 1926; M.S., U. Pa., 1937, M.S., 1932, D.Sc., 1935; student Mass. Inst. Tech., summer 1940; m. Mary M. Steinberger, Sept. 15, 1934. Jr. engr., Am. Bridge Co., 1926-28, asst. engr. of erection, 1929-31, engring. dept., 1931-33, asst. engr., 1934-35; design engr., Percival M. Sax Consultant, 1928, Pa. R.R. Co., 1928-29; asst. and asso. prof. structural engring., Vanderbilt U., 1935-42; prof. and head, dept. civil engring., U. Conn., 1942-46, dean, sch. engring. and prof. civil engring., since 1946, dir. Engring. Expt. Sta. since 1946. Mem. Conn. State Bd. Registration profl. engrs. and land surveyors since 1947, chmn. 1951-53; mem. bldg. code adv. com., State Conn. Mem. Am. Soc. C.E. (Conn. sect., pres., 1948), Soc. Exptl. Stress Analysis, Am. Soc. for Engring. Edn., Conn. Soc. C.E., Tau Beta Pi, Chi Epsilon, Pi Mu Epsilon, Sigma Pi Sigma, Sigma Chi. Episcopalian. Club: Hartford Engineers. Contbr. articles in civil and engring. jours. Home: Whitney Rd., Storrs, Conn. Died Dec. 30, 1954; buried Berryville, Va.

CASTLEMAN, Virginia Carter, author; b. Gaston, N.C., Aug. 26, 1864; d. Rev. Robert A. and Mary (Lee) C.; grad. Herndon Sem., Va. (pvt. sch. founded by the mother), 1883, Edgeworth Sch., Balt., 1884, Drexel Inst. Library Sch., 1899. Organizer Herndon Library, 1899-1900; dir. music, Herndan (Va.) Sem. Mem. D.A.R. Author: A Child of the Covenant, 1893; Roger of Fairfield, 1906; Pocahontas—a dramatic poem, and Miscellaneous Poems, 1907; Betweenwhiles, 1919. Writes musical articles for The Etude. Mem. Internat. Literary Assn. Home: Herndon, Va. Deceased.

CASTO, C. Everett, former pres. and dir. Ward Baking Co.; b. Rockport, W.Va., 1883; grad. W.Va. U., 1905; m. Elizabeth Grant; children—Mrs. Florence C. Dotson, Mrs. Jean C. Warhol, Dale. Mason. Home: 35-51 80th St., Jackson Heights, N.Y. Died Apr. 8, 1958; buried Parkersburg, W.Va.

CASWELL, Albert Edward, physicist; b. Winnipeg, Manitoba, Can., May 24, 1884; s. John J. and Patience Ethel (Smith) C.; student U. of Manitoba, Winnipeg, Manitoba, 1903-05; A.B., Stanford U., 1908, Ph.D., 1911; m Mary Constance Edwards, July 3, 1912; children—John Edwards, Miriam Esther (Mrs. Ford L. Danner), also Dwight Allan, Randall Smith. Came to U.S., 1905, naturalized, 1916. Instr. in physics, Purdue U., Lafayette, Ind., 1911-13; instr. in physics, U. of Ore., Eugene, Ore., 1913-15, asst. prof., 1915-17, prof., 1917-32, prof. physics and head of physics department, 1934-49, professor emeritus, 1949—; on leave of absence to act as staff mem. Radiation Lab., Mass. Inst. Tech., 1942-45; nat. research fellow in physics, Princeton Univ., 1919-20; prof. physics, Ore. State Coll., Corvallis, Ore., 1932-34. Trustee Westminster Foundation of Ore., 1921—; 1st v.p. Ore. Council of Churches, 1938-42, 1945-46. Mem. Am. Assn. Physics Teachers, Am. Phys. Soc., Am. Astron. Soc., A.A.A.S., Am. Assn. Univ. Profs., Sigma Xi, Sigma Pi Sigma, Pi Mu Epsilon. Club: Kiwanis (Eugene, Ore.). Author: Experimental Physics, 1928; Outline of Physics, 1928, rev. edit., 1938; International Critical Tables (wrote section on thermoelectricity), 1929. Contbr. Physical Review and other scientific jours. Home: 1960 Unviersity St., Eugene, Ore. Died June 18, 1954.

CATES, Junius Sidney (kāts), agrl. journalism; b. Graham, N.C., Aug. 10, 1877; s. Henry Manley and Mary Elizabeth (Bradshaw) C.; B.Agr., N.C. State Coll., Raleigh, 1902, M.Agr., 1904, D.Agr., 1939; grad. student Cornell U., 1904-05; Ph.D., Am. U., Washington, 1916; hon. D.Agr., U. of N.C., 1939; m. Theodosia Dutrow, Oct. 17, 1908; 1 dau., Rosanna Elizabeth. Asst. to N.C. state chemist, 1902-04; scientist U.S. Dept. Agr., in charge weed and tillage investigations, 1905-12; editor in chief Southern Planter, Richmond, Va., 1912-14; exec. Office of Farm Mgmt., U.S. Dept. Agr. 1914-19; staff writer Country Gentleman, Phila., 1919—; also contbr. to various mags. Made discoveries leading to simplified control methods for troublesome Am. weeds; developed principle that weeds alone make tillage necessary. Mem. A.A.A.S., Am. Soc. Agronomy, Kappa Sigma, Alpha Zeta, Phi Kappa Phi. Club: Chevy Chase. Home: 4305 Lorcom Lane, Arlington, Va. Died Oct. 18, 1949; buried Phillip Chapel, Graham, N.C.

CATES, Louis Shattuck, mining engr.; b. Boston, Dec. 20, 1881; s. Edwin Wallace and Emily Allen (Johnson) C.; S.B., Mass. Inst. Tech., 1902; Dr. Engring. (hon.), Mich. Coll. Mining and Technology, 1936; D.Sc., U. Ariz., 1946; D.Sc. (hon.) Columbia, 1947; m. 3d, Ethel Chesbrough Lewis, May 12, 1951. Mine operator in Mexico, 1902; asst. to pres. Nat. Steel & Wire Co., N.Y., 1903-04; in charge of construction and development, at Bingham Canyon, Utah, for Boston Consolidated Mining Co., 1904-08, gen. mgr., 1909; with Ray (Ariz.) Consol. Copper Co., 1910-22; asst. gen. mgr. Utah Copper Co., 1919-22, gen. mgr., 1922-30, also v.p., 1923-30; asst. gen. mgr. Bingham & Garfield Ry. Co., 1919-22, gen. mgr., 1922-30, also vice pres., 1923-30; pres. Phelps Dodge Corp., copper, 1930-47, chmn. bd., 1947—; dir. of Phelps Dodge Copper Products Corp., Long Island R.R. Co., Phelps Dodge Refining Corp., Niagara Fire Ins. Co., So. Peru Copper Corp. Mem. div. of engring. and indsl. research, Nat. Research Council, 1939-41. Developed system making it economically possible, by underground methods, to mine low grade prophyry ores. Decorated Comdr. Order of the Crown (Belgium); Knight Order of the Condor of the Andes (Bolivia); Chevalier of the Legion of Honor (France). Awarded Saunders Gold Medal by Am. Inst. Mining and Metall. Engr., 1939; Gold Medal by Mining and Metall. Soc. Am., 1956; Knight Comdr. Agrl. & Indsl. Order Merit, Cuba, 1957. Mem. Corp. Mass. Inst. Tech. (life). Engr., 1939. Mem. Corp. Mass. Inst. Tech., 1933-1938.

V.p., dir. Copper and Brass Research Assn., 1931-32; mem. Am. Mining Congress (pres. 1925), Mining and Metall. Soc. of Am. (pres. 1931), Am. Inst. Mining and Metall. Engrs. (v.p. 1934-37, dir. 1919-21, 1931-34, 1936-39, pres. 1946), Nat. Inst. Social Scis. (life), Soc. Mayflower Descs., Gen. Soc. Colonial Wars, The Pilgrims of the U.S., S.A.R., Chi Phi. Republican. Episcopalian. Mason (32° Shriner). Clubs: India House, The Links, The Brook, Pinnacle, University (N.Y.C.); Piping Rock (Locust Valley, N.Y.). Home: 950 Fifth Av. N.Y.C. 21. Office: 300 Park Av., N.Y.C. 22. Died Oct. 29, 1959.

CATHCART, Stanley H(olman) kath'kart), geologist; b. Millerstown, Pa., Aug. 20, 1889; s. Thomas Preston and Linda (Holman) C.; B.S., Pa. State Coll., 1912, M.S., 1916; grad. study Yale, 1917-18, 19-20; m. Iva Louise Waterbury, Oct. 20, 1921. Asst. geologist, geologist U.S. Geol. Survey, 1918-25; geologist U.S. Geol. Survey, 1918-25; geologist Standard Oil Co. N.J., 1925-30, Socony Vacuum Oil Co., 1937-41, Tex. Oil Co., 1943-47, Pa. Geol. Survey, 1930-37, advanced geologist, 1941-43, state geologist since 1947. Mem. Geol. Soc. Am., Am. Assn. Petroleum Geologists, Engring. Soc. Pa., Appalachian, Pittsburgh geol. socs., Sigma Xi. Mason. Clubs: Torch, Rotary (Harrisburg, Pa.). Home: 3113 N. Front St. Office: Pa. Geological Survey, Harrisburg, Pa. Died Mar. 19, 1953; buried Liverpool, Pa.

CATLIN, Theron Ephron, congressman; b. St. Louis, 1878; s. Daniel and Justina G. (Kayser) C.; A.B., Harvard, 1899, LL.B., 1902; unmarried. Admitted to bar, 1903, practice at St. Louis, 1904—. Mem. Mo. Ho. of Rep., 1907-9; mem. 62d Congress (1911-13), 11th Mo. Dist.; Republican. Home: 21 Vandeventer Pl. Office: 319 N. 4th St., St. Louis. Died March, 1960.

CAULDWELL, Oscar Ray, marine corps officer (ret.); b. Rockville, Ind., Aug. 14, 1892; s. John Monroe and Christina (Ward) C.; student Wabash Coll., 1910-12; B.S., U.S. Naval Acad., 1916; student Purdue U., 1947-48; m. Margaret MacFarland Brown, July 19, 1924; children—Nancy (Mrs. D. C. Fisher), Sara (Mrs. Marco Ambrosini) (deceased). Commissioned 2d lt. USMC, 1916, advanced through grades to maj. gen., 1946; served in France, World War I (wounded in action); comdr. 3d regt., World War II; asst. div. comdr. Bougainville campaign, 1943; ret. from active duty, 1946. Mem. Alpha Gamma Rho. Presbyn. Home: Avon Old Farms, Avon, Conn. Died Sept. 1959.

CAULLERY, Maurice Jules Gaston Corneille, biologist; b. Bergues, Nord, France, sept. 5, 1868; s. Jules and Uranie (Godbille) C.; ed. Lycée de Douai, Ecole Normale Superieure; m. Sabine Hubert, Nov. 3, 1900; children—Solange (Mrs. L. Godard), Michel, Denise (Mrs. D. Van Den Berghe), Francine (Mrs. V. Elisséef). Lectr., Faculté des Sciences, Université de Lyon, 1896-1900; prof. Faculté des Sciences de Marseille 1900-03; prof. Facultédes Sciences de Paris, 1909-40; chair of evolution of present organisms. Decorated Commandeur De La Legion d'Honneur. Mem. Academie des Sciences; fgn. mem. Royal Soc. London, Royal Soc. Edinburgh, Royal Acad. Belgium, Am. Acad. Scis. (Boston), N.Y. Acad. of Scis., Philos. Soc. Phila., Linnaeus Soc. London, and other sci. orgns. Author numerous publs. in field. Home: 6 rue Mizon, Paris XV. Office: Laboritoire d'Evolution des Etres Oganisés, 106 Blvd. Raspail, Paris VI, France. Died July 13, 1958.

CAVALLARO, Joseph B(runo), lawyer; b. Bklyn., Nov. 27, 1903; s. Anthony and Josephine (Cafarella) C.; student Coll. City N.Y., 1920-22; LL.B., Fordham U., 1926; LL.M., Bklyn. Law Sch., 1927; LL.D., St. John's U., 1951; m. Linda Permegiani, Aug. 22, 1925; children—Loretta, Joseph Bruno, Richard, John, Peter James. Admitted to N.Y. bar, 1927; with Wingate and Cullen, Bklyn., 1923—, mem. firm, 1943—. Mem. bd. higher edn., N.Y.C., 1946—, chmn., 1952—; nat. adv. com. Am. Relief for Italy, Inc.; former co-chmn. Borough of Bklyn. Nat. Conf. Christians and Jews; mem. Am. Christian Palestine Com.; mem. Bklyn. council Boy Scouts Am.; borough vice chmn. Greater N.Y. Fund Orgn.; chmn. Youth Counsel Bur.; mem. nat. bd. Am. Com. Italian Migration. Treas., former pres. Nocturnal Adoration Soc. Bklyn., 1937—; mem. Bishop's Lay Com. for Charities, 1933—; dir. St. Manresa House of Retreats, 1951—; counsel Immaculate Conception Day Nursery, Bklyn., 1952—; dir. Bklyn. Cath. Interacial Council, 1953—. Trustee Indsl. Home for the Blind, Bklyn., Bklyn. Cancer Com., Inc., dir. Bklyn. Philharmonia. Recipient numerous honors and awards for civic and religious activities. Knight Comdr. Order of the Holy Sepulchre, 1954. Mem. Bklyn., N.Y. State bar assns., Italian Hist. Soc. (trustee), Bklyn. C. of C., Am. Judicature Soc., Am.-Italy Soc., Inc., Bklyn. Cancer Soc., Acad. Polit. Sci., Cath. Lawyers Guild Bklyn. (trustee), Soc. St. Vincent de Paul. K.C. Clubs: Catholic (N.Y.C.); Rotary, Management, Lawyers, Democratic (Bklyn.). Address: 2260 Benson Av., Bklyn. 14. Died Aug. 22, 1957; buried Holy Cross Cemetery.

CAVE, Edward Powell, merchant; b. Hopkinsville, Ky., Nov. 26, 1880; s. Robert Clifton and Fannie (Daniel) C.; grad. Central High Sch., St. Louis; m. Ralpha Eugiena Moll, June 17, 1909; children—Ralph Clifton, Edna Daniel, Eleanore Moll. With Ely & Walker Dry Goods Co., St. Louis, 1898—, v.p. and mdse. mgr., 1922-30, pres., 1930—, now chmn. bd.; dir. 1st Nat. Bank in St. Louis, Burlington Industries; San Francisco dir. Walton N. Moore Dry Goods Co. Democrat. Club: Bellerive Country. Home: Spoede Rd., Creve Coeur, Mo. Office: 1520 Washington St., St. Louis. Died Aug. 28, 1957.

CAVE, H(arry) W(infield), coll. prof., dairy husbandman; b. Fayette, Ia., Apr. 30, 1890; s. Benjamin Austin and Serena Arvilla (Cowles) C.; B.S.A., Ia. State Coll., 1914; M.S., Kans. State Coll., 1916; m. Anita Lucille Meltzer, Dec. 25, 1917; children—Douglas Austin, Elizabeth Ann (Mrs. Walter S. Bryde), Robert Harry. Fieldman, Golden Valley Dairy Co., Kansas City, Mo., 1916; asst. prof. dairy extension W.Va. Univ., 1916-18; asst. prof. dairy husbandry Kan. State Coll., 1918-20, asso. prof., 1920-26, prof., 1926-39; prof. of dairying and head dept. dairying Oklahoma A. and M. Coll., 1939-50. Research fellow Kan. State Coll., 1914-16; hon. fellow U. of Wis., 1930-31. Coach of 4 intercoll. dairy cattle judging teams winning national championships. Ofcl. type classification judge Am. Jersey Cattle Club since 1942; official judge Holstein-Friesian Assn. of Am.; judge state and regional dairy cattle shows. Fellow A.A.A.S.; mem. Am. Dairy Sci. Assn. (pres. 1940-41), Am. Dairy Assn. (mem. exec. com.), Okla. Holstein Breeders Assn. (vice pres.), Okla. Jersey Cattle Club (sec.), Stillwater C. of C., Phi Kappa Phi, Sigma Xi, Alpha Zeta, Gamma Sigma Delta, Phi Sigma, Sigma Phi Epsilon. Republican. Presbyterian. Mason. Club: Lions (dir. 1946-47). Author: Visible Dairy Herd Book System (with F. W. Atkeson), 1937. Contbr. articles to sci. bulls. and jours. Home: 1719 W. Third Av., Stillwater, Okla. Died June 23, 1953.

CAYWOOD, Roland Blanchard, pres. H. D. Lee Co.; b. New Hartford, Ia., Aug. 24, 1890; s. Wilbur and May (Hughes) C.; A.B., Coll. of Emporia (Kan.), 1909; m. Edith Helen Rittgers, June 29, 1915; children—Roland Wade, Frank Rittgers, Donald Wilson. With H. D. Lee Company, Kansas City, since 1910, vice president and gen. mgr. since 1935; president, Eloesser-Heynemann Co., San Francisco. Mem. Nat.-Am. Wholesale Grocers Assn. (pres., 1943-44), chmn. board, 1945-46; mem., v.p., Nat. Assn. Mfrs. Mo. Valley Wholesale Grocers Assn. (pres. 1936-37, chmn. bd. 1938, 39, 40, 41); dir. City Nat. Bank and Trust Co., Kansas City Chamber of Commerce. Mason. Clubs: Kansas City, Mission Hills Country (Kansas City, Mo.). Home: 5101 Ward Parkway. Office: 117 W. 20th St., Kansas City, Mo. Died Jan. 7, 1952; buried Kansas City.

CECIL, Charles Purcell, naval officer; b. Sept. 4, 1893; entered U.S. Navy, 1912, and advanced through the grades to rear adm., 1943. Decorated Navy Cross (twice). Address: Navy Dept., Washington 25. Deceased.

CECIL of Chelwood, Viscount (Edgar Algernon Robert Gascoyne) writer, govt. ofcl.; b. Eng., Sept. 14, 1864; student Eton College and Univ. Coll. Oxford U.; LL.D., Cambridge, Edinburgh, Manchester, Liverpool, St. Andrews, Aberdeen, Princeton, Columbia and Athens univs.; m. Lady Eleanor Lambton. Admitted to the bar, 1887; mem. Parliament from Marylebone East (Conservative), 1906-10, Hutchin Div. of Hertfordshire, 1911-23; parliamentary undersec. of state for foreign affairs, 1915-16; minister of blockade, 1916-18; became asst. sec. of state for foreign affairs, 1918; served as mem. Brit. delegation at Paris Peace Conf., 1919; lord privy seal, 1923-24; chancellor Duchy of Lancaster, 1924-27. Awarded Woodrow Wilson peace prize, 1924, Nobel Peace Prize, 1937. President League of Nations Union and International Federation of League of Nations Society. Chancellor, Birmingham University, 1918-44. Mem. Privy Council, King's Council. Author: A Great Experiment, 1941, (autobiography); All the Way (autobiography), 1948. Home: Chelwood Gate, Haywards Heath, Sussex. Office: 25 Charles St., Berkeley Square, London, W. 1, Eng. Died Nov. 24, 1958.

CECIL, James McCosh, advt. exec.; b. Selma, Ala., June 2, 1891; s. Russell and Alma (Miller) C.; student, McGuire's Univ. Sch.; A.B., Hampden-Sydney Coll., Va., 1910; m. Alston Drake, April 13, 1914; children—James McCosh, Amanda Alston (Mrs. Charles J. Schuster), Mary Drake (Mrs. Jack Major); m. 2d, Tamara Matoussevitch Scott, June 21, 1945; m. 3d Edythe Walker Denker, June 14, 1949; 1 son, Charles Granville. President Cecil and Presbrey, Incorporated, advertising agency, N.Y. City, since 1939; dir. Childs Co., Aklon Corp. Nat. councilor, U.S. C. of C., 1939-42; chmn., N.Y. Council of Advt. Agents, 1931; dir., Am. Assn. of Advt. Agencies, 1932; vice pres., Netherland-American Foundation; pres. National Hospital for Speech Disorders, Arthritis & Rheumatism Foundation, New York State; director, member exec. com. Nat. Civil Service League; mem. council N.Y.U.; trustee N.Y.U. Bellevue Med. Center; dir. Inst. for Psychotherapy, Music Research Found.; vice president Travelers Aid Soc.; gen. chmn. Greater N.Y. Red cross Fund, 1947-48. Decorated Officer Order of Orange and Nassau (Netherlands). Mem. S.A.R., Pilgrims. Republican. Presbyterian. Clubs: Racquet and Tennis, Piping Rock, The Brook, Links Golf. Home: Horseshoe Rd., Mill Neck, L.I., N.Y. Office: 247 Park Av., N.Y.C. 17. Died Sept. 17, 1954; buried Hollywood Cemetery, Richmond, Va.

CECIL, Lamar, judge; b. Houston, Nov. 2, 1902; s. Lamar Hallum and Anna Mae (Fisher) C.; B.A., Rice Inst., 1923; LL.B., U. Tex., 1927; m. Mary Reed, September 15, 1930; children—Lamar, Grayson (Mrs. Robert Ewing Clemons), Reed Hallum. Admitted to Tex. bar, 1927, practiced in Beaumont, 1927-54 with firms Duff & Cecil and Cecil Keith & Mehaffy; U.S. judge Eastern Dist. of Tex. 1954—. Counsel, Tex. Eisenhower delegation Rep Nat. Conv., Chgo., 1952. Fellow Am. Coll. Trial Lawyers; mem. Am., Jefferson County (past pres.) bar assns., State Bar Tex. Episcopalian. Home: 2495 Broadway. Office: P.O. Box 231, Beaumont, Tex. Died Feb. 14, 1958; buried Beaumont.

CERF, Edward Owen, editor; b. Chgo., Mar. 27 1918; s. Barry and Emily (Owen) C.; B.A., Princeton, 1940; m. Jane Lauren Pipes, Aug. 13. 1946; 1 son, Barry John. Reporter Oregon Daily Journal, 19?9; contbg. editor Time, Inc., N.Y.C., 1940, sr. editor 1951-58; asst. mng. editor Life mag., 1958-59, editor, 1959—. Served from pvt. to maj. US MC, 1941-46; ret. as col. Res. Office: 9 Rockefeller Plaza, N.Y.C. 20. Died May 6, 1959.

CÉSPEDES Y ORTIZ, Carlos Miguel (sĕs'pĕ-des), Cuban lawyer; b. Ciudad de Cárdenas, Cuba, July 6, 1881; s. Miguel de Céspedes y Coffigny and Eloísa Ortiz y Coffigny; law degree U. Havana, 1904; m. Margarita Johanet y Montalvo; 3 daughters. Sec. of pub. works under Pres. Machada, 1925; sec. of justice, 1929; sec. pub. instrn., 1930; senator from Camaguey, 1931, Matanzas, 1948. Died June 8, 1955.

CHACE, George Hart, ins. exec.; b. Middleboro, Mass., Aug. 13, 1883; s. Franklin Stuart and Frances Lavinia (Hart) C.; student Harvard, class of 1906; m. Florence Corinne Brelsford, Sept. 7, 1921 (died 1936); m. 2d, Ruth Bowers Duy, Dec. 4, 1937 (died 1938); m. 3d Ethel Rake de Beck, Aug. 2, 1941. With Prudential Ins. Co. of America, Newark, 1905—, clerk, 1905-09, asst. div. mgr., 1909-18, div. mgr., 1918-22, sec. to pres., 1922-27, asst. sec., 1927-36, 2d v.p., 1936-38, v.p., 1938-48, retired, Sept. 1 1948. Republican. Clubs: Canoe Brook Country (Summit, N.J.). Home: 149 Tennyson Dr., Short Hills, N.J. Office: 755-69 Broad St., Newark 1. Died June 10, 1957; buried Restland Meml. Park.

CHACE, Malcolmn Greene, corp. ofcl.; b. Central Falls, R.I., 1875; grad. Sheffield Sci. Sch., Yale, 1896; m. Elizabeth Edwards, Apr. 15, 1903 (died 1947); children—Malcolm Greene, Arnold Buffum, Eliot, Jane, Elizabeth C.; m. 2d, Mrs. Kathleen Dunster. Dir. Berkshire Fine Spinning Associates, Phenix Nat. Bank, Chase Nat. Bank, Seaborard Oil Co. of Del., Mathieson Alkali Works, International Paper Co. Home: One Sutton Place South, N.Y.C.; (summer) Hyannis, Mass. Died July 16, 1955.*

CHADWICK, Charles, author; b. Brooklyn, N.Y., Nov. 19, 1874; s. Charles Noyes and Alice Ann (Caruth) C.; father the founder and commr. of the Catskill aqueduct for N.Y. City; grad. Froebel Acad.; Adelphi Acad., 1893; A.B., Yale, 1897; LL.B., New York Law Sch., 1899; m. Grace Southard Nugent, Aug. 31, 1925. Admitted to N.Y. bar, 1899, and began practice in N.Y. City; dep. asst. dist. atty., under Wm. T. Jerome, 1902-06; asst. corp. counsel under Mayor McClellan, 1908-09. Spl. writer on football for New York World 1899-1909, articles syndicated to Chicago Tribune and other papers. Mem. Assn. Bar City of New York, Conn. State Bar Assn., Authors' League America and Authors' Guild, Psi Upsilon. Republican. Conglist. Author: The Cactus (novel), 1925; The Moving House of Foscaldo (novel), 1926; also short stories in Century, Ladies' Home Journal, Everybody's and other mags. Extension lecturer Harvard U. and Colls. of Greater Boston since 1932, also Mass. State Extension since 1942. Home: 21 Union St., Charlestown, Mass.; and Old Lyme, Conn. Died Sept. 28, 1953; buried Duck River Cemetery, Old Lyme, Conn.

CHADWICK, George Halcott, geologist; b. Catskill, N.Y., May 27, 1876; s. Nathaniel Kimball and Celia Serena (Halcott) C.; Ph.B., U. Rochester, 1904, M.S., 1907; hon. Sc.D., St. Lawrence U., 1940; m. Bertha Elisabeth Ellwanger, Feb. 22, 1908 (died Mar. 22, 1937); children—Elizabeth Ellwanger, George Halcott; m. 2d, Irene Brugger, Sept. 30, 1944. With Ward's Natural Sci. Establishment, 1896-1906, N.Y. State Museum, 1906-07, St. Lawrence U., 1907-14, U. Rochester, 1914-23, Empire Gas & Fuel Co., Okla., 1923-25, Williams Coll., 1925-26, Vassar, 1929, U. Newark, 1943-44, The Natural Sci. Assn. of the Catskills, Inc., 1944—; surveys: N.Y. State, Pa. Topographic and Geologic, 1926-31, Cities Service Group, 1930-31, Nat. Park Service, 1935-37. Fellow Geol. Soc. Am.; mem. Alpha Delta Phi, Phi Beta Kappa, Sigma Xi. Republican. Episcopalian. Contbr. on Devonian Stratigraphy, geology of Mount Desert

Island, Me. Address: The Natural Science Assn. of the Catskills, Inc., Box 165, Catskill, N.Y. Died Aug. 1953.

CHAFEE, Zechariah, Jr. (chāf'fē), prof. law; b. Providence, R.I., Dec. 7, 1885; s. Zechariah and Mary Dexter (Sharpe) C.; A.B., Brown U., 1907; LL.B., Harvard, 1913; LL.D., St. John's U. (Bklyn), 1936, Brown U., 1937, U. Chicago, 1953; D.C. L., Boston U., 1941; Litt.D., Colby College, Waterville, Maine, 1944; m. Bess Frank Searle, July 20, 1912; children—Zechariah III, Robert S. (dec.), Anne C. Brien, Ellen C. Tillinghast. With Builders Iron Foundry, Providence, 1907-10, mem. bd. dirs., 1914—; in practice with Tillinghast & Collins, Providence, 1913-16; assistant professor law, Harvard, 1916-19, professor, 1919-1956, University professor, 1950-56, Lowell Institute Lecturer, 1956-57. Syndic Harvard University Press, 1936-46; consultant to Nat. Commn. on Law Observance and Enforcement (part author of report on lawlessness in law enforcement, 1931), 1929-31. Fellow Brown Univ. Mem. Am. Bar Assn. (sub-com. drafting Fed. Interpleader Act of 1936, Bill of Rights Com.) Freedom of Press Commn., 1943-47; mem. U.N. subcommn. on Freedom of Information and the Press 1947-48; U.S. del. to U.N. Conf., Geneva, 1948; mem. Am. Philos. Soc., Colonial Soc. of Mass., Am. Acad. Arts and Sci., Mass. Hist. Soc., Alpha Delta Phi, Phi Beta Kappa. Episcopalian. Clubs: Harvard (Boston); Tavern, Century (New York). Author: Freedom of Speech, 1920; Chapter on Law in Civilization in the United States, 1922, America Now, 1938; The Inquiring Mind, 1928; Cases on Equitable Remedies, 1939; State House vs. Pent House—Legal Problems of the R.I. Race Track Row, 1937; The Constitutional Convention That Never Met (2 parts), 1938, 1939; Free Speech in the United States, 1941; Weathering the Panic of '73, 1942; Reissued Notes on Bills and Notes, 1943; Government and Mass Communications, 1947; Some Problems of Equity, 1950; Documents on Fundamental Human Rights, 1951; How Human Rights got into the Constitution, 1952; Freedom of Speech and Press, 1955; The Blessings of Liberty, published 1956. Part Author: Cases on Equity (Chafee, Simpson and Maloney), 1934. second edition 1946; Return to Freedom, 1944. Editor: Brannan's Negotiable Instruments Law (4th edit.), 1926. Wrote legal intro. to Suffolk Co. Court Records (1671-80), 1933. Home: 987 Memorial Dr. Office: Langdell Hall, Cambridge 38, Mass. Died Feb. 8, 1957; buried Swan Point Cemetery, Providence.

CHAFER, Lewis Sperry (chāf'fēr), clergyman, educator; b. Rock Creek, Ashtabula County, O., Feb. 27, 1871; s. Thomas Franklin and Lois Lomira (Sperry) C.; prep. edn., New Lyme (O.) Acad., 1885-88; student Oberlin Coll. and Conservatory of Music, 1889-92; completed ministerial studies under Rev. Frank E. Fitch, D.D., 1900; D.D., Wheaton (Ill.) Coll., 1926; Litt.D., Dallas Theol. Sem., 1942; Th.D. (honoris causa), Faculte Libré de Theologie Protestante, Aix-en-Provence, France, 1946; m. Ella Loraine Case, Apr. 22, 1896. Ordained Presbyn. ministry, 1900; traveling evangelist, 1900-14; Bible lecturer, 1914-24; founder, 1924, and since pres. and professor systematic theology, Dallas (Texas) Theological Seminary. Republican. Author: Satan, 1909; True Evangelism, 1911; The Kingdom in History and Prophecy, 1915; Salvation, 1916; He That Is Spiritual, 1918; Grace, 1922; Major Bible Themes, 1926; The Ephesian Letter, 1935; Systematic Theology, 1947 (8 vols.); also numerous pamphlets. Contbr. to religious jours.; editor Bibliotheca Sacra. Home: 4208 Edmondson Av., Dallas. Died Aug. 22, 1952; buried Hillcrest Cemetery, Dallas.

CHALIFOUR, Joseph Onésime, business exec.; b. Quebec City, P.Q., Can., May 1, 1889; s. Onésime and Léa (Clouter) C.; student Comml. Acad. Que., St.-Dunston's Coll., Ecole Hautes Etudes Montreal Laval U.; m. Juliette Bolduc, Feb. 15, 1916; children—Madeline (Mrs. René Nadeau), Jacques Raymond, Paul, Pierre, Denise (Mrs. Gerard Nadeau), Marc, Jean-Robert, André. Mgr. O. Chalifour Engring. Co., 1912-18; pres., gen. mgr. O. Chalifour, Inc., 1918—; pres. L'Action Sociale Ltée Editors (of daily newspaper L'Action Catholique), 1936-40, 1950—, v.p., 1940-50. Hon. pres. Camp Ecole Lac Trois-Saumons 1918—. Recipient Merite Diocésain (silver medal), 1946, Churchwarlen of St.-Charles-Garnier. Mem. Canadian Mfrs. Assn. (pres. Que. br. 1924-25). Assn. des Merchands de Bois de la P.Q. (pres. 1925-26), Que. Builders Exchange (dir.). Instinct Canadian Centre des Patrons Société St.-Jean-Baptiste (legislative com. 1949-50), Canadian Lumbermen Assn. Mem. Comité Central de L'Action Sociale Catholique. Club: Merchands de Bois de Quebec. Home: 1185 Ploermel. Office: 580 Prince Edward. Quebec City, Que., Can. Died July 13, 1956; buried Belmont Cemetery, Quebec City.

CHALKLEY, Otway H., chmn. Philip Morris & Co. With Am. Tobacco until 1911; then with P. Lorillard Co., later buyer of tobacco in Turkey and mgr. in China of Tobacco Products Export Co.; returned to U.S. and became treas. Philip Morris & Co., now chmn. Address: 119 5th Av., N.Y.C. Died Mar. 1956.*

CHALMERS, Gordon Keith, college pres.; b. Waukesha, Wis., Feb. 7, 1904; s. William Everett (D.D.) and Mary Dunklee (Maynard) C.; A.B., Brown University, 1925; B.A., Oxford, Eng., 1928, M.A., 1934; M.A., Ph.D., Harvard U., 1933; LL.D., Hobart Coll., Geneva, N.Y., 1938; Litt D., Rockford Coll., 1941, Brown U., 1946, Notre Dame U., 1953; L.H.D., Ripon College, 1945; married Roberta Teale Swartz, September 3, 1929; children—Geoffrey Teale, Ann Maynard, John Putnam, Stephen E. Instr. in English, Mount Holyoke College, 1929-33, assistant professor, 1933; president Rockford College, 1934-37, Kenyon Coll., 1937—; cons. U.S.A.A.F., 1942-44; v.p. Franco-Am. Audio-Visual Distbn. Center, 1948-53, pres., 1953—; member national com. Fulbright awards, 1951; chmn. school and college study of admission with advanced standing since 1951. Mem. Modern Lang. Assn. of Am. Oxford Soc., Newcomen Soc. of Eng., Assn. of Am. Colls. (mem. commn. on liberal edn., past chmn.), Am. Council on Edn. (chmn. problems and policies com.), Coll. English Association (president 1949-50, director since 1950), North Central Assn. (v. chmn. commn. on colls. and univs., bd. of review, 1952-54), Ohio Coll. Assn. (pres. 1943-45), Mediæval Acad. of America, Am. Association of Rhodes Scholars, American Academy of Arts and Sciences, Phi Delta Theta, Phi Beta Kappa, Delta Sigma Rho, Sphinx. Episcopalian. Clubs: University (N.Y. City); Union (Cleveland), Cosmos (Washington). Author: The Republic and the Person, a Discussion of Necessities in Modern American Education, 1952; editor American Oxonian, 1946-49; also articles and essays on edn. and on 17th Century thought and letters. Home: Cromwell House, Gambier, O. Died May 8, 1956; buried Mount Auburn Cemetery, Cambridge, Mass.

CHALMERS, Henry, economist; b. New York, N.Y., June 28, 1892; s. Isidor C. and Sarah (Abrams) C.; A.B., Cornell U., 1914, A.M., 1914; Ph.D., Brookings Grad. Sch. of Economics, Washington, D.C., 1928; m. Sallie Kittner, Sept. 2, 1923; children—Judith Lynn, David Mark. Asst. to export manager Bear Mill Mfg. Co., 1912-13; statistician N.Y. State Dept. of Health, 1914-18; spl. expert U.S. Tariff Commn., 1918-21; chief div. foreign tariffs, Dept. of Commerce, 1921-41; adviser on commercial policy since 1941. On special missions, to Japan for investigation of industrial and competitive conditions, 1919-20, to Europe, for survey of post-war tariff situation, 1923, to Mexico for trade negotiations, 1947, Morocco, 1949. Mem. Am. delegations, Internat. Customs Conf., Geneva, 1923, World Economic Conf., London, 1933, 9th Pan Am. Conf., Bogata, 1948, and numerous other internat. confs., 1923—. Served for short time as pvt. with 39th Inf., U.S.A., World War I. Mem. Am. Econ. Assn., Am. Acad. Polit. and Social Science, Phi Beta Kappa, Tau Epsilon Phi. Mason. Club: Cosmos. Author: Japanese Cotton Industry and Trade, 1921; European Tariff Policies Since the War, 1924; Preparing Shipments to Latin America, 1928; The Depression and Foreign Trade Barriers, 1934; World Trade Policies: The Changing Panorama, 1920-53. Contbr. The Economic World Today, 1933; American Economic Problems, 1943; Economic Problems of Latin America, 1944. Contbr. articles on tariffs to Encyclopedia Britannica. Home: 5335 43rd St., Washington 15. Office: Dept. of Commerce, Washington. Died June 4, 1958; buried King David Cemetery, Nat. Meml. Park, Falls Church, Va.

CHAMBELLAN, Rene Paul (chăm'bĕl-lăn), sculptor; b. West Hoboken, N.J.; s. Pierre and Louise (Finiel) C.; student New York U., 1912-14, Beaux Arts Inst. of Design, 1914-17, Ecole Julian, Paris, 1918-19; m. Suzanne Houillon, Mar. 11, 1919; children—Rene, Suzanne, Madeleine. Instr. in sculpture, New York U.; sculpture for Yale U., Northwestern U., Lafayette and Cornell colls., Rockefeller Center (New York), State office buildings (New York and Buffalo), Buffalo City Hall, Scottish Rite Temple (Scranton, Pa.), Radiator and News Bldgs. (New York City), Worcester (Mass.) Memorial Auditorium, Chicago Tribune Bldg., Engineers Memorial (Louvain Clock Tower, Belgium), Court House (Nashville, Tenn.), State Bldg., Nashvile, Tenn., large group for N.Y. World's Fair; Criminal Courts Bldg., N.Y. City; large sculpture relief for Airlines Terminal, N.Y. City; Ellett Memorial, Richmond, Va.; Reynolds Flight Memorial, Ga.; Hamilton Memorial; war memorials for New Life Ins. Co., Am. Tobaco Co.; mausoleums for Healy, Berret, C. D. Ryan, Medill McCormick; war monument for Detroit Mich. Midland County; Children's Shrine, Masonic Temple, Alexandria, Va. Served as sergeant, 11th Engrs., U.S. Army, in France, 1917-19. Home: Grantwood, N.J. Died Nov. 29, 1955.

CHAMBERLAIN, Allen (chām'bĕr-lĭn), writer; b. Boston, May 2, 1867; s. Augustine Jason and Hannah Augusta (Allen) C.; ed. Boston Latin Sch.; m. Grace Melbourne Inman, May 21, 1890; 1 son, Francis. Began as spl. writer for Boston Herald, 1889, later reporter, Boston Post, Boston Transcript; free lance writer, 1895—. A founder, 1898, and first sec. Mass. Forest and Park Assn.; chmn. Mass. State Geog. Com., 1926-32; mem. Soc. for Protection N.H. Forests, Mass. Trustees of Pub. Reservations, Am. Forestry Assn. (ex-v.p.); asso. mem. Soc. Am. Foresters. Unitarian. Club: Appalachian Mountain (ex-pres.). Author: Vacation Tramps in New England Highlands, 1919; Beacon Hill—Its Ancient Pastures and Early Mansions, 1925; The Annals of the Grand Monadnock, 1936; Pigeon Cove—Its Early Settlers and Their Farms, 1940; also Hist. Maps of Grand Monadnock Mountain (N.H.), Cape Ann (Mass.), etc. Home: Rockport, Mass. Deceased.

CHAMBERLAIN, Dwight Lincoln, banker; b. New Haven, Conn., Sept. 12, 1877; s. Louis Kettle and Ellen (Lewis) C.; ed. Boardman High Sch.; m. Charlotte Hemingway Fabrique, Nov. 1916 (died 1918); 1 dau., Lois; m. 2d, Esther Hosking Lane, Nov. 1925 (dec. 1950); children—Dwight, Rosalie. Asst. supt., Bradstreet Co., 1900-17; credit mgr. Yale Nat. Bank, 1917-18, this bank merged with First Nat. Bank and Trust Co., New Haven, Conn., 1918, v.p., 1923-44, pres., 1944-55, chmn. 1955—, dir. 1923—. Mem. bd. trustees Conn. Pub. Expenditure Council, Inc.; treas. New Haven Taxpayers Research Council, Inc.; dist. v.p. New Haven Co.-Conn. C. of C., Inc. Clubs: Quinnipiack, New Haven Country, Conn. State Srs. Golf Assn. (trustee). Home: 29 Wilton Rd., Hamden, Conn. Office: 42 Church St., New Haven. Died Nov. 30, 1955.

CHAMBERLAIN, Glenn R., utilities exec.; b. Grand Rapids, Mich., Nov. 23, 1877; s. Newton L. and Esther Jane (Stiles) C.; student pub. schs.; m. Lena Celeste Mannel, Sept. 12, 1905 (dec.); children—Wallace Mannel, Glenn R., Barbara Jane (Mrs. Hoffius). Timekeeper, office mgr. Grand Rapids Gas Light Co., 1897-1905, sec., comml. mgr., 1905, pres., gen. mgr. until 1938 when Co. merged with Mich. Consol. Gas Co., Detroit, now 1st v.p.; pres., gen. mgr. Kent County Gas Co. since 1927 (merged with Grand Rapids Gas Light Co., 1936); pres. Am. Mich. Pipe Line Co.; pres., gen. mgr. Am. Prodn. Co. (cos. merged with Mich. Consol., 1938); dir. Mich.-Wis. Pipe Line Co.; pres., dir. Austin Field Pipe Line Co.; v.p. Am. Light & Traction Co., 1949; pres., dir. Milw. Gas Light Co.; exec. v.p., dir. Milw. Solvay Coke Co. Past dir. Assn. Commerce, Community Chest. Mem. Am. Gas Assn. (past sec., treas., v.p., pres.), Mich. Gas Assn. (life), Soc. Colonial Wars, Soc. Mayflower Descendants (life.). Mason (32°, Shriner). Clubs: Peninsular, Kent Country, Green Ridge Country, Rotary, Milwaukee. Home: Hillcrest Acres, Comstock Park, Mich. Deceased.

CHAMBERLAIN, Herbert Marvin, banker; b. Salt Lake City, Utah, June 20, 1878; s. John Marvin and Louise (Rawlings) C.; educated Salt Lake City Schs.; m. Gertrude Anstee, Oct. 25, 1899; 1 son, Marvin George; m. 2d, Jo I. Smart, Sept. 16, 1935. Began as messenger Walker Bank, 1897; exec. v.p. Walker Bank & Trust Co.; pres. Wasatch Holding Co.; mem. State Depository Bd. Pres. Utah Bankers Association, 1931-32; mem. Am. Bankers Assn. (pres. state bank div., 1936-37; now mem. exec. com.), Utah Mfrs. Assn. (dir.); mem. bd. govs. C. of C. (Salt Lake City). Mason (32°, K.T., Shriner). Clubs: Rotary, Alta, Country. Home: 1321 Yale Av. Office: Walker Bank & Trust Co., Salt Lake City, Utah. Died Dec. 5, 1951.*

CHAMBERLAIN, John M(ynderse), ex-govt. ofcl.; b. Elyria, O., June 14, 1904; s. George and Etta Catherine (Mynderse) C.; student U. Mich., 1926-27; m. Alice Albertine Barton, Feb. 6, 1932; 1 dau., Ann Carolyn. Radio, refrigeration, sales and service, 1924-29; design, project engr. Waco Aircraft Co., Troy, O., 1929-36; aero. engr. Bur. Air Commerce, Washington, 1936-38; aero. engr. Civil Aero. Authority, 1938-42; asst. dir. safety bur. Civil Aero. Bd., 1942-48, dir. bur. safety regulation, 1948-57; asso. dir. regulations, bureau of safety, 1957, ret. Mem. Am. Radio Relay League. Episcopalian. Mason. Licensed radio amateur, comml. pilot. Home: 2256 Constitution Blvd., Sarasota, Fla. Died Mar. 6, 1959.

CHAMBERLAIN, Joseph Perkins, prof. law; b. Cleveland, O., Oct. 1, 1873; s. Robert Linton and Ellen Steele (Perkins) C.; grad. Belmont (Calif.) Sch., 1892; student Harvard 1 yr., U. of Calif., 1 yr.; grad. Hastings Law Sch., 1898; Ph.D., Columbia, 1923, LL.D., 1929; LL.D., Western Reserve U., 1938, U. of Calif. 1948; M.A., Oxford U., 1939; m. Elizabeth Stillman, Nov. 9, 1905. Admitted to Calif. bar, 1902, and practiced at San Francisco until 1905; lecturer in law, Sch. of Jurisprudence, Univ. of Calif., 1907-08; mem. legislative drafting research fund, Columbia U., since 1909, dir. since 1919, prof. pub. law 1923-50; professor emeritus of public law since July 1950. Counsel N.Y. Charter Commission, 1935-36; mem. High Commn. for Refugees Coming from Germany, 1933-35; chmn. American Council Voluntary Agencies for Foreign Service since 1943. George Eastman professor, Oxford University, 1939-40; assistant to sec. of treasury, 1940; chmn. Am. Council of Voluntary Agencies for Fgn. Service, 1943-50, hon. chmn., 1951; mem. adv. com. on voluntary foreign aid, dept. of state, since 1949; director Equitable Life Assurance Society of U.S. since 1923. Trustee Emigrant Industrial Savings Bank of New York since 1942. Trustee Western Reserve Univ., Cleveland, O. Chmn. Am. Council of Learned Socs., 1926-27; member American Philosophical Soc., American Academy of Arts and Sciences, Chi Phi. Republican. Clubs: Century, City, Nat. Arts (New York); Cosmos (Washington); Waterbury. Author: Regime of the International Rivers, Danube and Rhine, 1923; Legislative Processes—National and State, 1936. Co-Author of Index-Digest of State Constitutions, 1915, The Judicial Function in Federal Administrative Agencies, 1942; writer numerous articles on legislation and internat. relations. Home: 8 Sutton Square, N.Y. City 22. Died May 21, 1951.

CHAMBERLIN, Henry Harmon, author; b. Worcester, Mass., Aug. 6, 1873; s. William Wigglesworth and Elizabeth Ferguson (Paine) C.; A.B., Harvard, 1895, A.M., 1896; m. Armida Theresa Zoraide Moja, June 1, 1907; 1 son, Harmon Paine (senior lt., U.S. N.R.). Dir. Nat. Security League, chmn. Worcester br. same; chmn. Worcester Com. Italian War Relief Fund, World War I. Mem. National Assn. for Constitutional Govt., Am. Poetry Assn. (pres. emeritus), Poetry Soc. of America, Italy-America Soc. Hon. pres. Loggia Colombo-Mazzini 168 Ordine Figli d'Italia in America. Decorated Cavaliere della Corona d'Italia. Republican. Unitarian. Clubs: Harvard, Omar Khayyam of America (pres. 1934 and 1935), Authors (Boston); Pacific, Nantucket Yacht (Mass.). Secretary Worcester branch Constitutional Liberty League of Massachusetts. Author: The Age of Ivory, 1904; Poems, 1911; The Master Knot, 1923; Sir Aldengar, 1927; Late Spring (translation of Theocritus), 1936; Last Flowers (transl. of Bion and Moschus), 1937; Horace Talks (transl. Horace's Satires), 1940; also essays and lectures on literary subjects, principally the classics. Contbr. numerous articles to daily press on preparedness, universal mil. training, etc., also poems. Home: 22 May St., Worcester, Mass. Died July 10, 1951; buried Rural Cemetery, Worcester, Mass.

CHAMBERLIN, Joseph Hanson, educator; b. Beloit, Wis., Nov. 2, 1846; s. John and Cecilia (Gill) C.; A.B., Beloit Coll., 1872, A.M., 1875; postgrad. Yale, U. Leipzig, 1879-81; Litt.D., Marietta Coll., 1895, Western U. Pa., 1897; m. Lilla Celia Redington, July 6, 1876. Prin. common schs. of Lancaster, Wis., and Black River Falls, Wis.; in charge Latin Dept. Carleton Coll., 1874-76; prof. Latin and modern langs. Marietta Coll., 1881-95, Latin and English, 1895-1907, English, 1907-16, emeritus prof., 1916-32, dean, 1894-1909, acting pres., 1896-1900. Address: Marietta, O. Died Apr. 6, 1932.

CHAMBERS, Charles Carroll, foundry exec.; b. Galena, Ill., July 2, 1888; s. Mathew Robert and Mary Josephine (Smith) C.; grad. Culver Mil. Academy, 1908, U. Wis., 1912; m. Marjorie Graham, Dec. 25, 1917; children—Marjorie Ann (Mrs. Joe W. Beckham), Charles Carroll. Instr., English, mil., athletics, Culver (Ind.) Mil. Acad., 1912-13; salesman E. F. Houserman Co., Cleveland, 1915-20, sales mgr., 1920-22; treas., v.p. Wrought Iron Range Co., St. Louis, 1932-36; vice-pres., general mgr. So. Malleable Iron Co., East St. Louis, Ill., 1935-38; pres., gen. mgr. Tex. Foundries, Inc., Lufkin, Tex., 1939—, Sec. dir. Culver Ednl. Found. 1930-53, v.p. 1953. Served as lt. col., U.S. Army, 1916-19; col. Gen. Staff, War Dept., Washington, 1922; col., chief staff 37th Div., Ohio N.G., 1920-23; now col., inf. retired. Decorated D.S.C., Silver Star, Purple Heart (U.S.); Belgian War Cross; French Cross of War. Mem. Vets. Fgn. Wars, Am. Legion, S.A.R., Am. Foundrymans Assn., Nat. Assn. Mfrs., Malleable Founders Soc. (dir., pres. 1951-52), U.S. C. of C., Tex. Mfrs. Assn. (dir. 1954-55), Texas Bur. For Econ. Understanding (dir. 1953-55), Phi Gamma Delta (field sec., 1913-15), Sigma Delta Chi. Mason (Scottish Rite, Shriner), Episcopalian. Clubs: Houston, Ramada, Petroleum, Coromado (Houston); Army & Navy (Washington); Lufkin, Lufkin Country. Home: 1017 Grove St. Office: Texas Foundries, Inc., Box 180, Lufkin, Tex. Died Mar. 15, 1958; buried Garden of Memories, Lufkin.

CHAMBERS, I(saiah) Mench, clergyman; b. Miffinburg, Pa., May 22, 1865; s. William W. and Elva Caroline (Mench) C.; A.B., Lafayette Coll., 1889, A.M., 1892, D.D., 1913; grad. Union Theol. Sem., N.Y.C., 1892; m. Anna W. Weaver, June 1, 1892. While at coll. took charge of small chapel at East Stroudsburg, Pa., and remained a supply 3½ yrs. and built $10,000 ch. before graduation; ordained Presbyn. ministry, 1892; pastor First Ch., Merchantville, N.J., 1902—. Inaugurated, 1907, The Syndicate of Love, an orgn. now reaching around the world, for the distbn. through personal letters the "hopeword" for the sorrowful and discouraged. Mem. Presbyn. Ministers' Assn. Phila.; moderator synod of N.J., 1912-13. Author: At the Beautiful Gate (poems), 1895; Reuben, the Builder, 1900; Harold Payson, 1901; The Modern Devil, 1903; Satan or Christ, 1911. Address: Merchantville, N.J. Died 1922.

CHAMBERS, Othniel Robert, psychologist; born Jasper, Ind., Apr. 19, 1894; s. John Wesley and Annie Elzora (Turman) C.; A.B., A.M., Ind. U., 1922; Ph.D., O. State U., 1926; m. Gladys Dawson, Aug. 12, 1919; children—Martha Elizabeth (Mrs. Allard Smith), Othniel R. Teaching asst., psychol. lab., Ind. U., 1921-22; instr. Ind. State Normal Sch., Terre Haute, summer 1922; grad. teaching asst., O. State U., 1922-23; instr. in psychology, 1923-26; prof. psychology, Southwest State Tchrs. Coll., California, Pa., summer 1926, U. of Tex., 1926-29, Ore. State Coll. since 1929, head dept. psychology since 1934. Served as comdg. officer, 117th Am. Train, 42nd div., U.S. Army, 1917-19. Mem. Am. Psychology Assn., A.A.A.S., Sigma Xi, Kappa Delta Rho. Mason. Home: 408 N. 8th St., Corvallis, Ore. Died Feb. 21, 1951.

CHAMBERS, Robert, biologist; b. Erzerum, Turkey, October 23, 1881; s. Rev. Robert and Elizabeth (Lawson) C. (both Canadians); B.A., Robert College, Constantinople, Turkey, 1900; M.A., Queens University, Kingston, Canada, 1902, hon. LL.D., 1944; Ph.D., University of Munich, Germany, 1908; research student, Columbia, 1911-12; m. Bertha Inez Smith, June 15, 1910; children—Robert, killed in action, Pacific, December, 1941, William Nesbit, Edward Lucas, Bradford; married 2d, Eloise Parkhurst, December 3, 1954. With A.B.C.F.M. in Turkey until 1909; lecturer in biology, Toronto University, 1909-11; assistant professor histology, Univ. of Cincinnati, 1912-15; instructor anatomy, Cornell Univ. Med. Coll., N.Y. City, 1915-19, asst. prof., 1919-23, prof. microscopic anatomy, 1923-28; research prof. of biology, Washington Sq. Coll. (N.Y. U.), 1928-48, prof. emeritus continuing research through Nat. Inst. Health grant. Trustee Marine Biol. Corp., Woods Hole, Biological Lab., Cold Spring Harbor. Naturalized citizen of U S. Fellow A.A.A.S.; mem. Marine Biol. Lab., Am. Soc. Zoölogists (pres. 1948-49), Am. Soc. Naturalists, Am. Assn. Anatomists (v.p. 1939), Am. Assn. Cancer Research, Soc. Exptl. Biology and Medicine, Harvey Soc. (pres. 1944-45, 1945-46), Union Am. Biol. Soc. (pres. since 1946), British Biol. Corp., Am. Physiol. Soc., Am. Soc. Bot., Soc. Gen. Physiology; asso. fellow N.Y. Acad. Med. N.Y. Acad. Scis., fgn. corr. mem. Nat. Acad. Med., France. Investigations, summers, Marine Biol. Lab., Woods Hole; has made investigations in cytology and on phys. nature of protoplasm and the constituents of the living cell by means of an instrument devised for dissecting and injecting living cells under highest magnification of compound microscope, cellular physiology, cancer in tissue culture, and of blood capillary circulation in traumatic shock. Awarded Traill medal Linnean Society, London, for researches on physical nature of protoplasm, 1925, and John Scott medal by City of Philadelphia, "for invention of devices for microdissection of living cells,' 1925. Contributor to Encyclopedia Britannica, also numerous research articles to American and European journals. Co-editor of "Protoplasma" (journal). Home: Woods Hole, Mass. Office: New York University, N.Y. City 3. Died July 22, 1957.

CHAMBERS, Robert Augustus, lawyer; b. N.Y. City, Oct. 10, 1894; s. Robert and Josephine Blanche (Singer) C.; A.B., Yale, 1917; student Magdalen Coll., Oxford, 1919; LL.B., Columbia, 1924; m. Jean Boalt Wheeler, June 28, 1928; children—Lillian Marsh (Mrs. Bohn C. Lindemann), Ridgeley White, Robert Augustus, Jr., John Wheeler. Admitted to New York bar, 1925; with firm of Willcox, Hunt & Swiger, N.Y. City, 1927-28; partner in firm Willcox, Swiger & Chambers (now Swiger, Chambers, Kelley & Harrigan), N.Y. City since 1928; dir. Time, Inc., and various small cos. Trustee and 2d vice pres. Allen-Stevenson Sch. of N.Y.; trustee Northern Westchester Hosp., Mt. Kisco, N.Y.; alternate del. Rep. Nat. Conv., Kansas City, 1928; trustee, asst. sec. and counsel, Boys' Club of N.Y., Inc.; treas. Washington Square Home for Friendless Girls. Served in C.A. C. as 2d and 1st lt., 74th Regt. Heavy Railway Arty., U.S. 2d Army, World War I. Mem. Mil. Order of Foreign Wars, Am. Vets. Assn., S.R., Am. Bar Assn., Assn. Bar City of N.Y., Westchester County Bar Assn., N.Y. State C. of C. Republican. Episcopalian. Mason (32°). Clubs: Church, Down Town, Metropolitan, Metropolitan Opera, Union League, University, Uptown, Yale (New York); Lake Placid; Blind Brook; Bedford Golf and Tennis; Chevy Chase (Washington); New Haven Lawn, Graduate (New Haven, Conn.); Union Interalliée of Paris. Home: Katonah's Wood, Katonah, N.Y. Office: 60 E. 42d St., N.Y.C. 17. Died 1951.

CHAMBERS, William, naval officer; b. Phila., Aug. 25, 1884; M.D., Jefferson Med. Coll., 1907; grad. Naval War Coll. Senior Course; post-grad. course in aviation medicine (flight surgeon); grad. Naval Med. Sch., Gen. Course; rear admiral Med. Dept., Sept. 1942; med. officer in command; later vice adm., comdr. Naval Med. Center, Bethesda. Address: Naval Medical School, Navy Dept., Washington. Deceased.

CHAMBERS, William Earl, army officer; b. Chicago, Ill., Feb. 9, 1892; s. William Henry and Charlotte (Stilson) C.; B.S., U.S. Mil. Acad., 1916; graduate Infantry Sch., 1922; distinguished grad. Command and Gen. Staff Sch., 1926; grad. Army War Coll., 1934; Air Corps Tactical Sch., 1937; m. Aline Ingram, Dec. 11, 1920; children—William E., Margaret Aline (wife of Hiram W. Rainey, Jr.); married 2d Thekla Glenn Harshberger, Sept. 14, 1950. Commd. 2d lt., U.S. Army, June 12, 1912, promoted through grades to brig. gen., June 20, 1942. Decorated Distinguished Service Medal, Legion of Merit, Philippine Distinguished Service Star. Mem. Mass. Soc. of Cincininati, S.A.R., Tau Kappa Epsilon. Address: P.O. Box 563, Ithaca. Died Feb. 11, 1952; buried West Point, N.Y.

CHAMBLIN, Walter Williams Jr., business exec.; b. Leesburg, Va., July 16, 1898; s. Walter and Jennie Hamilton (Lynch) C.; A.B., Ohio State U., 1922; m. Bess E. Miller, May 29, 1933. Clerk Loudon Nat. Bank, Leesburg, Va., 1917; news reporter, Columbus (O.) Dispatch, 1917; sports and gen. news reporter, asst. dir. advt. promotion dept. Ohio State Jour., 1919-22; reporter Cleveland Plain Dealer, 1922-23; with Washington Bur. Asso. Press, 1923-25, chief house staff, 1925-28, mem. staff covering Rep. and Dem. nat. convs., 1928, Al Smith campaign, 1928, night editor, Washington Bur., 1928-29, day editor, 1929-30; mem. passenger and freight traffic development dept., C.&O. Ry. and P.M. R.R., Washington, 1930-37; dir., managing dir., Nat. Indsl. Council, Washington, 1938-40; exec. dir. Nat. Assn. Mfrs., Washington, 1940-45, vice pres. in charge all governmental relations, since 1945. Chief q.m. U.S.N.R. Aviation Detachment, World War I. Mem. Washington Bd. Trade, Army Ordnance Assn. (Washington), Acad. Polit. Sci., Sigma Delta Chi, Phi Kappa Psi. Protestant Episcopalian. Clubs: National Press, Capitol Hill (Washington); Columbia Country (Chevy Chase, Md.). Home: 3700 Massachusetts Av., N.W., 16. Office: 918 Sixteenth St., Washington 6. Died Sept. 23, 1955; buried Leesburg, Va.

CHAMOT, Emile Monnin (shă-mō), sanitary chemist, microscopist; b. Buffalo, Mar. 4, 1868; s. Christopher Peter and Eugenie (Monnin) Chamot; B.S. in Chemistry, Cornell U., 1891, Ph.D., 1897; studied U. Nancy (France), 1897, Tech. Hochschule, Braunschweig (Germany) and Polytechnicum (Delft, Holland), 1898; m. Cora Ellen Genung, June 1897. Began as asst. in chemistry Cornell U., 1890, became prof. chem. microscopy and sanitary chemistry, 1910, now retired; Am. exchange prof. to France, 1924-25. Expert on questions dealing with purity and pruification of water and industrial microscopy. Mem. Am. Chem. Society, Am. Acad. Arts and Sciences, Sigma Xi, Alpha Chi Sigma. Author: Analysis of Water for Household and Municipal Purposes (with H. W. Redfield), 1911; Elementary Chemical Microscopy, 1915; Handbook of Chemical Microscpy (with C. W. Mason), 1930; also many papers on sanitary chemistry, microscpy, etc. Home: 927 E. State St., Ithaca, N.Y. Deceased.

CHAMPION, John B., clergyman, educator; b. Prince Edward Island, Can., June 18, 1868; s. James W. and Margaret J. (Brooks) C.; grad. Prince of Wales Coll., 1885; B.A., U. of New Brunswick, 1900; M.A., Acadia U., 1903; B.D., Colgate Div. Sch., 1903; Th.D., Eastern Bapt. Theol. Sem., 1928; m. Emma J. Dunbar, Sept. 16, 1891 (died May 7, 1932); children—Una May (wife of Dr. Stanton G. Nichols), Gladys Mabel (wife of Dr. W. H. Bueermann), William D., Ralph L., C. Belle (Mrs. W. Hutton Granville), John C., Elaine C. (Mrs. Maurice Reed Entwistle); m. 2d, Edith M. Webster, May 15, 1935; 2 sons, Benjamin W., David C. Came to U.S., 1900, naturalized, 1923. Ordained Bapt. ministry, 1893; pastor at Geneva, N.Y., Calvary Ch., Brantford, Ont., Roxborough, Pa., McMinnville, Ore., White Plains, New York until 1925; prof. Christian doctrine, Eastern Baptist Theological Seminary, Philadelphia, 1925—, retired in 1941. Author: The Living Atonement, 1910; (monograph) The Virgin's Son, 1924; More Than Atonement, 1927; Why Modernism Must Fail, 1932; Sovereignty and Grace, 1933; Personality and The Trinity, 1935; Inspiration Explains Itself, 1938; The Heart of the New Testament, 1941. Home: 4012 Primrose Rd., Torresdale, Phila. Died Jan. 18, 1948; buried Lawnview Cemetery, Rockledge, Pa.

CHANCE, Edwin Mickley, pres. United Engineers and Constructors, Inc.; b. Phila., Pa., Jan. 13, 1885; s. Henry Martyn and Lillie E. (Mickley) C.; grad. DeLancey Sch., 1903; B.S. in Chemistry, U. of Pa., 1907; m. Eleanor Kent, Jan. 11, 1909 (died Nov. 21, 1940); children—Henry Martyn II, Britton. Assaying and mining in Nev., 1907-09; chemist and engr. Phila. & Reading Coal & Iron Co., Pottsville, Pa., 1909-13; cons. practice, Wilkes-Barre, 1913-17; engring. mgr. Day & Zimmerman, Inc., Phila., 1919-25; v.p. Day & Zimmerman, Inc., 1925-28; pres. Day & Zimmerman Engring. & Constrn. Co., Inc., 1928; v.p. United Engrs. & Constructors, Inc., 1928-31, pres., 1931—; pres. Dwight P. Robinson & Co., Inc., U.G.I. Contracting Co. Served as capt. to lt. col. Ordnance Dept., Chem. Warfare Service, U.S. Army, in charge design, construction and operation of poison gas, shell filling plant, Edgewood Arsenal, 1917-18; with A.E.F., 1918. Trustee and mem. ex. bd. U. of Pa., chmn. bd. grad. edn. and research member bd. (U. of Pa.), trustee Henry Phipps Inst. (U. of Pa.). Mem. Acad. Natural Science (Phila.), Franklin Inst., Army Ordnance Assn. Awarded Edward Longstreth medal of merit, Franklin Institute. Clubs: Midday, Racquet (Philadelphia); New York Yacht, Mantoloking Yacht, Cruising Club of America, Sportsmen's Club of America. Contbr. tech. publs.; chem. and metall. inventions. Home: Ocean Av., Mantoloking, N.J. Office: 1401 Arch St., Phila. 5. Died Nov. 26, 1954.

CHANDLER, Albert Edward, lawyer; b. San Francisco, Sept. 28, 1872; s. William Sylvester and Catherine Agnes (Comerford) C.; B.S., U. Calif., 1896; m. Maud Laura Grover, Oct. 14, 1903; children—Edward Grover, Dorothy Maud (Mrs. Louis Bonin Longare). State engr. State Nev., 1903-05; mem. Calif. State Water Commn., 1915-19; admitted to Calif. bar, 1919, and since practiced in San Francisco, specializing in water-right matters; spl. counsel, San Francisco, Los Angeles, Pasadena and Vallejo, Calif. Mem. Big C Soc., Golden Bear, Psi Upsilon. Clubs: Faculty, University, Engineers, Commonwealth (San Francisco). Home: 2619 Benvenue Av., Berkeley 4, Cal. Office: Balboa Bldg., San Fracncisco 5. Died Jan. 29, 1954.

CHANDLER, Asa Crawford, biologist; b. Newark, Feb. 19, 1891; s. Frank Thomas and Augusta (Jappé) C.; A.B., Cornell, 1911; M.S., U. Cal., 1912, Ph. D., 1914; m. Belle Clarke, June 1, 1914 (dec.); 1 dau., Dorothy Belle; m. 2d, Ina Henrietta Sands, July 9, 1921 (dec.); children—Frank Sands, Emily Alice; m. 3d, Mrs. Lillie Moore Laughlin, Dec. 23, 1944. Grad. asst. zoöl. dept. U. Cal., 1911-14; instr. zoölogy, later asst. prof., Oregon State Agrl. Coll., 1914-18; instr. biology Rice Inst., Houston, 1919-24; charge bookworm research lab. Sch. Tropical Medicine, Calcutta, India, 1924-27; prof. biology Rice Inst., 1927—, also spl. cons. USPHS, 1942-47. Served as 2d lt. San. Corps, U.S. Army, 1918-19. Fellow A.A.A.S.; mem. Am. Soc. Parasitologists, Am. Soc. Tropical Medicine and Hygiene, Am. Micros. Soc., Am. Soc. Naturalists, Sigma Xi. Republican. Author: Animal Parasites and Human Disease, 1918; Anthelmintics and Their Uses (with R. N. Chopra), 1928; Hookworm Disease, 1929; Introduction to Parasitology, 9th edit. 1955; The Eater's Digest, 1941. Made helminthological survey of India, 1924-27. Home: 6315 Vanderbilt Av., Houston 5. Office: Rice Inst., Houston 1. Died Aug. 23, 1958.

CHANDLER, Fremont Augustus, orthopedic surgeon; b. Chicago, Ill., Nov. 29, 1893; s. Fremont E. and Mary (Saxe) C.; B.S., U. of Wis., 1916; M.D., Coll. Phys. and Surg. (Columbia), 1919; m. Eleanor Cromwell, Feb. 9, 1924; children—Stuart, Stephen Cromwell. Resident Sloane Hosp. for Women, N.Y. City, 1919; interne Hartford (Conn.) Hosp., 1919-20; resident surgeon, Grenfell Hosp., St. Anthony, Newfoundland, 1920-21; resident N.Y. Orthopedic Dispensary and Hosp., 1921-24. Began practice of orthopedic surgery in Chicago, 1924; senior attending orthopedic surgeon St. Luke's Hosp.; prof. Orthopedic Surgery U. of Ill. Mem. Med. Corps, U.S. Army, 1917-18; lt. (s.g.) U.S.N.M.R.C., 1928-38. Fellow A.C.S., Internat. Coll. Surgeons (hon.); pres. Am. Bd. Orthopedic Surgery, Inc., 1940-41 (sec., 1934-40); mem. Central Surg. Soc., A.M.A., (sec. sect. orthopedic surgery, 1932-35, vice chmn., 1935-36, chmn., 1936-37), Am. Assn. for Study and Control of Rheumatic Diseases (charter mem.), Am. Acad. Orthopedic Soc., Ill. State and Chicago med. socs., Chicago Orthopedic Soc. (past pres.), Clin. Orthopedic Soc. (pres., 1940-41), Soc. Med. History of Chgo., Inst. Medicine of Chgo., Am. Orthopaedic Assn. (past pres.), Internat. Soc. Orthopaeidic Surgery and Traumatology, Sigma Sigma, Delta Upsilon, Phi Beta Pi, Alpha Omega Alpha, Sigma Xi. Republican. Episcopalian. Club: University, Asso. editor Lewis-Walters Surgery, Jour. Bone and Joint Surgery. Home: 1350 N. State St. Office: 6 N. Michigan Av., Chgo. Died Dec. 24, 1954.

CHANDLER, Raymond Thornton, writer; b. Chicago; s. Maurice B. and Florence Dart (Thornton) C.; student Dulwich Coll., London; privately in France and Germany; m. Pearl Hurlburg, Feb. 8, 1924 (dec.). Began as contbr. of verse, essays, book reviews and special articles to daily and weekly papers, London, Eng., 1909; following World War I, entered business career in U.S., becoming officer in various independent oil corporations; began writing fiction as contbr. to magazines, 1933. Served with Canadian Expeditionary Force and with R.A.F. during World War I. Clubs: Garrick (London); Mystery Writers of Am. Author (books): The Big Sleep, 1939; Farewell, My Lovely, 1940; The High Window, 1942; The Lady in the Lake, 1943; Red Wind, 1946; Spanish Blood, 1946; The Little Sister, 1949; The Simple Art of Murder, 1950; The Long Goodbye, 1954; Playback, 1958. Address: La Jolla, Cal. Died Mar. 26, 1959.

CHANDLER, Thomas Alberter, ex-congressman; b. Ind. Ty., July 26, 1871; s. Burges G. and Annie (Gunter) C.; grad. Worcester Acad., Vinita, Ind. Ty., 1888; student Drury Coll., Springfield, Mo.; m. Marie Louise Wainwright, of Fayetteville, Ark., Oct. 23, 1894; children—Norma, Collis P. Oil producer, farmer, real estate bus.; admitted to bar, 1907; apptd. Cherokee revenue collector, 1891; Cherokee town sit commr., 1895; dep. clk. U.S. Court for Northern Dist. of Ind. Ty., 1900-07; mem. 1st Bd. of Pub. Affairs for State of Okla., 1909-10; del. Rep. Nat. Conv., Chgo., 1908; mem. 65th and 67th Congresses, 1st Okla. Dist. Methodist. Mason (32°, K.T.), K.P., Elk. Home: Vinita, Okla. Died June 22, 1953; buried Vinita, Okla.

CHANDOR, Douglas (shän-dôr′), portrait painter; b. Woldingham, Surrey, Eng., Aug. 20, 1897; s. Jack Arthur and Lucy May (Newton) C.; ed. Radley Coll., Berkshire, Eng., 1910-1914; art edn., Slade Sch., London, 1918-20; m. Pamela Trelawney, 1920 (divorced 1932); 1 dau., Jill Trelawney; m. 2d, Ina Kuteman Hill, Apr. 17, 1934. Came to U.S., 1926. Served with 1st Life Guards, Brit. Army, 1914-18; disabled and disch. as 1st lt. Lovat Scouts. Portrait painter since 1919. First exhibited Royal Acad. London, 1922. Works: Prince of Wales, 1921, 1926; Prime Ministers of Brit. Empire, 1923; Queen of Rumania, 1926; President Hoover, Vice President Curtis and entire cabinet, 1929; President Roosevelt (State Capitol, Austin, Tex.), 1935; Trustees of Duke U. Endowment Fund, 1931; Governor Richie of Md., 1930; Mrs. Duke Biddle and Family (New York), 1930; Mrs. E. T. Stotesbury, Mr. and Mrs. Atwater Kent and Family (Phila.), 1927; Gov. Cameron Morrison and Family (N.C.), Dwight Davis, Gov. Gen. of Philippines (War Dept.), Andrew Mellon, 1929, G. B. Dealey, Dallas, 1938; Mrs. Elliott Roosevelt (Fort Worth, Texas), 1940; Mrs. James Roosevelt (New York), 1940; Hon. Sam Rayburn (Hall of Congress, Washington, D.C., and State Capitol, Austin, Tex.); Charles Roeser, 1941; William R. Boyd, Jr., 1945; President Franklin D. Roosevelt, 1945; Winston Churchill, 1946; Mrs. Winston Churchill, 1946; Everett De Golyer, 1947; Michael L. Benedum, 1948; Bernard M. Baruch, 1948; Gen. Hanford McNider, 1949; Mrs. Eleanor Rodsevelt; ex-gov. James E. Cox and over 200 other portraits of Americans prominent in social and polit. life. Club: Union (New York). Home: Waldorf Towers, New York, N.Y.; "White Shadows," Weatherford, Tex. Died Jan. 13, 1953.*

CHANEY, John Crawford, ex-congressman; b. Columbiana Co., O., Feb. 1, 1854; s. James and Nancy (Crawford) C.; grad. Ascension Sem. Sullivan, Ind., 1874; LL.B., U. of Cincinnati, 1882; m. Ella Saucerman, of Sullivan, Dec. 25, 1876. Admitted to bar, 1883, and since in practice at Sullivan. Chmn. Co. Rep. Com., and mem. State Central Com., 1884-85; presdl. elector, 1888; asst. to U.S. atty.-gen., 1889-93; candidate for Congress, 2d Ind. Dist., 1904; mem. 59th and 60th Congresses (1905-09), 2d Ind. Dist. Presbyterian. Address: Sullivan, Ind.

CHANEY, Morris J., banker; b. Ogle County, Ill., Oct. 1, 1858; s. Osborn and Amanda (Rice) C.; grad. high sch., Rockford, Ill.; m. Helen McEarline, Nov. 19, 1886. Organized Bank of Wakonda, S.D., 1893, Citizens Bank & Trust Co., Vermillion, S.D., 1914, later became acting pres. both instns., now retired. Mem. S.D. Ho. of Rep., sessions 1903-09 (speaker, 1907-09). Republican. Conglist. Mason (K.T.), Odd Fellow, K.P. Home: Vermillion, S.D. Died 1941.

CHANLER, Margaret (Mrs. Winthrop Chanler), author; b. Rome, Italy, Aug. 6, 1862; d. Luther and Louisa Cutler (Ward) Terry; privately ed.; diploma in music from St. Cecilia Conservatory, Rome; D.Litt., Nazareth Coll., Rochester, N.Y.; m. Winthrop Chanler, Dec. 16, 1886; children—Laura Astor (Mrs. Lawrence Grant White), John Winthrop (dec.) Beatrice (Mrs. Pierre Francis Allegaert), Hester Marion (Mrs. Edward Motley Pickman), Marion Winthrop (dec.), Gabrielle (Mrs. Porter Ralph Chandler), Hubert Winthrop, Theodore Ward. Came to U.S., 1886. Roman Catholic. Clubs: Colony (N.Y.C.); Genesee Valley (Rochester, N.Y.). Author: Roman Spring, 1934; Autumn in the Valley, 1936. Translator of G. von Le Fort's Hymns to the Church, 1937. Home: Sweet Briar Farm, Geneseo, N.Y. Died Dec. 18, 1952; buried St. Mary's Cemetery, Geneseo.

CHANNING, George, Christian Science lectr.; b. Providence, Nov. 21, 1888; s. George and Clara (Channing) Stucker; A.B., Brown U., 1911; student law school Yale, 1911-12; C.S.B., Mass. Metaphysical Coll., 1934; m. Adelaude Glaser, Mar. 16, 1918; 1 dau., Carol (Mrs. Alexander Carson). Reporter Providence Journal, 1913-16, Detroit Free Press, 1916-18, Detroit Journal, 1919-20; city editor, Seattle Star, 1921-23; advt. rep. Christian Science Monitor, San Francisco, 1923-25; 1st reader, Fifth Ch. C.S., San Francisco, 1926-29; C.S. com. on publ. for Northern Calif., San Francisco, 1932-38; Christian Science teacher San Francisco, 1934, lecturer, 1938-41, 1945-49, 1953—; 1st reader, Mother Ch., Boston, 1941-42; trustee C.S. Pub. Soc. 1942-44; editor C.S. religious publs., 1949-50, mgr. coms. on publ. C.S. Ch., 1950-52. Served as corpl. U.S. Army, 1918-19. Mem. Kappa Sigma. Mason (32°). Clubs: Rotary (Sausalito); University, Commonwealth (San Francisco). Home: 244 Curry Lane, Sausalito, Cal. Office: 291 Geary St., San Francisco 2. Died May 29, 1957.

CHAPIN, Edward Whitman, lawyer; b. (Willimansett) Chicopee, Mass., Aug. 23, 1840; s. Whitman and Theodocia (McKinstry) C.; A.B., Amherst, 1863; m. Mary L. Beebe, May 16, 1866. Admitted to Mass. bar 1865; pres. Farr Alpaca Co., mfrs. worsted goods, Holyoke, Mass.; v.p. Mechanics' Savings Bank; dir. Holyoke & Westerfield R.R. Co.; judge of Holyoke Police Ct., 1898—. Mem. bd. trustees Mt. Holyoke Coll. (ex-pres.); dir. Holyoke Pub. Library, Holyoke City Hosp. Republican. Conglist. Mason. Clubs: Bay State, Holyoke Golf, Literary. Home: 181 Elm St. Office: 362 Dwight St., Holyoke, Mass. Died May 6, 1924.

CHAPIN, Edward Young, banker; b. Petersburg, Ky., Oct. 8, 1865; s. William Henry and Mary (Kelley) C.; LL.B., U. of Cincinnati, 1886; m. Elise Hutcheson, Apr. 30, 1890. Studied law in office of John G. Carlisle and began practice of same, at Covington, Ky., 1886; moved to Chattanooga, Tenn., 1887; founder, 1894, and pres. the Administration & Trust Co.; asso. 1912. with H. S. Probasco in founding the American Trust & Banking Company, of which is chairman of board; president Chattanooga Steam Laundry, Star Laundry; sec. United Hosiery Mills, Crystal Springs Bleachery; dir. Title Guaranty & Trust Co. (mem. exec. com.), Little Theatre, East Tennessee Iron & Coal Company; vice-president Tennessee Stove Works. President Frye Institute; treas. and mem. bd. Chattanooga Tuberculosis Sanatorium. Democrat. Mason (K.T.). Clubs: Mountain City, Chattanooga Golf and Country, Fairyland Golf and Country. Author: A Harvesting of Green Fields (novel); numerous booklets describing fiduciary service of trust cos. Home: 24 Bluff View, Chattanooga; (summer) Signal Mountain, Tenn. Address: American Nat. Bank & Trust Co., Chattanooga, Tenn. Died Mar. 7, 1954; buried Forest Hill Cemetery, Chattanooga, Tenn.

CHAPIN, Fred H., pres. and chmn. bd. Nat. Acme Co.; chmn. bd. Ohio Forge & Machine Co.; pres. and trustee A. M. McGregor Home for Old Folks, Cleveland, Ohio; director Cleveland Trust Company, White Motor Company, Oliver Corporation, Eaton Manufacturing Company, Land Title Guarantee & Trust Co. Trustee Holden Arboretum. Cleve. Found. Home: 2065 Hanover Rd., Cleveland Heights, O. Office: E. 131st and Coit Rd., Cleve. Died Aug. 5, 1958; buried Knollwood Cemetery, Mayfield Heights, O.

CHAPIN, William Wallace, editor, publisher; born Phila.; s. William and Emily C.; ed. Quaker Sch. and University Pa.; m. Dorothy Roberts, Nov. 4, 1926; one daughter, Catherine Chapin Parsons. Was the pub., owner Chgo. Herald, Chgo. Inter-Ocean, Seattle Post-Intelligencer, San Franciso Morning Call, Oakland Enquirer, Newark Star and Eagle; later owner, pub. Sacramento Union; now owner and pub. San Francisco Argonaut (oldest publ. on Pacific Coast); pres. The Muhlenberg Corp. Charter mem. Associate Press. Trustee Carnegie Endowment for International Peace, 1939—. Served as militia officer 4 years. Mem. Newcomen Soc. Am. Republican. Episcopalian. Clubs: Burlingame (Cal.); Bohemian, Olympic (San Francisco); Bankers (N.Y.C.); Seattle Tennis (Seattle, Wash.; hon. member). Home: 2108 Washington St. Office: 544 Market St., San Francisco. Died Nov. 7, 1957.

CHAPLIN, John Howard, mfr.; b. Dec. 4, 1893; s. Wilfred S. and Helen (McAllaster) C.; ed. Phillips Andover and Yale; m. Shirley Ingraham; children—John Howard and Jill. With Veeder-Root, Inc., Hartford, Conn., since 1917, became v.p., 1932, now pres., dir. since 1931; dir. Holo Krome Screw Corp., Bristol Brass Corp., Conn. Bank & Trust Co., Am. Hardware Corp., E. Ingraham Co., Travelers Ins. Co., Travelers Indemnity Co., Travelers Fire Ins. Co., Charter Oak Fire Ins. Co. Club: Hartford. Home: 241 S. Main, W. Hartford, Conn. Office: Garden and Sargeant Sts., Hartford, Conn. Died Aug. 1958.

CHAPLIN, William Edwards, editor; b. Omaha, Neb., Feb. 25, 1860; s. Edwards Hastings and Helen Constance (Stillman) C.; student pub. schs.; LL.D., U. Wyo., 1940; m. Erminnie May Ralston, Feb. 14, 1882; children—Thomas Edwards, Mazie. Asso. "Bill" Nye in publ. of Laramie Daily Boomerang and owner of half interest in the paper after Nye left Wyo.; founder, 1890, Laramie Republican, and its editor until 1920. Mem. City Council, Laramie, 1885-89; mem. Wyoming Constnl. Conv., 1889; mayor of Laramie, 1894; register U.S. Land Office, Cheyenne, Wyo., 1898-1915; sec. of state of Wyo., 1919-23. Republican. Served 20 yrs. as rep. Grand Lodge K. of P. to Supreme Lodge. Clubs: Cheyenne, Young Men's Literary. Home: 5502 Woodman Av., Van Nuys, Cal. Died Jan. 9, 1948.

CHAPMAN, Arthur, jurist; b. Portland, Me., Aug. 6, 1873; s. Albion Keith Parris and Elizabeth Maria (Foss) C.; A.B., Bowdoin Coll., 1894; LL.B., 1944; law student, 1898-1900; m. Agnes Sleeth Fairbrother, May 23, 1905; children—Richard Sleeth, Arthur. Teacher, 1895-98; admitted to Me. bar, 1900; mem. Portland Common Council, 1900-02, pres. 1902, bd. of aldermen, 1902-03; assistant United States Attorney, 1905-16; United States commissioner, 1917-25; justice Superior Court, State of Maine, 1925-42; justice Supreme Judiciary Court, Maine. 1942-45, active retired justice, 1945—. Chmn. Southern Portland Planning Bd., 1946—. Trustee Peabody Law Sch. Mem. Cumberland County and Me. State bar assns., Theta Delta Chi. Mason. Clubs: Bowdoin, Middle Temple, Fraternity, Rotary Internat. (Portland, Me.). Home: 25 Channel Rd., South Portland, Me. Address: 142 Federal St., Portland, Me. Died Jan. 5, 1959.

CHAPMAN, Charles Hiram, univ. pres.; b. Portage City, Wis., Oct. 28, 1869; grad. Oshkosh (Wis.) Normal Sch., 1888; grad. Johns Hopkins U., 1889. Ph.D., 1891. Former pres. U. Ore., Eugene. Address: Eugene, Ore. Deceased.

CHAPMAN, Clowry, b. Fort Scott, Kan., July 28, 1871; s. Wilson Shannon and Florence (Littlejohn) C.; LL.B., U. Mich., 1894, Emeritus degree (52d year), 1946; m. Louise Dewey, Nov. 8, 1899 (died July 17, 1927); 1 dau., Ruth; m. 2d, Mrs. Charlotte Davies Ireland, June 9, 1928 (deceased Nov. 1958). Admitted to bar, Mich. and Ill., 1894, N.Y., 1912; partner L. G. Richardson, general counsel Central Union Telephone Co., 1900. Served as trade mark and goodwill counsel, as exec. with advt. agy., factory and periodicals. Co-designer nat. Made in U.S.A. trade mark; created Water Level Route and globe design trade mark Rock Island States of America. With Alfred McCann, Sr., was pioneer in advertising-vigiliance work. Formerly lectured on telephones and telegraphs, Northwestern U. Law Sch., also lectured for Alexandr Hamilton Inst. and Internat. Corr. Schs. Author: The Education of the Negro, 1893; Public Policy, 1894; Conditions in Deeds and Devises, 1896; Legalized Wrong, The Trial of Jesus, 1899; The Law of Advertising and Sales That Develop Good Will, 2 vols., 1908; Insuring Markets, 1917; The Law on Advertising, 1929; Trade Marks, 1930; How Advertisments Defeat Their Own Ends, 1931; Washington's Secret of 1782, 1937; What Keeps Business Going, 1938; Advertising for Moderns, 1941; Ad-News Continuities (war period), 1943; Advertising, 1947; Telegraph and Telephone, 1947; The Man Who Carried the Message to Garcia, 1947; He Also Knew Lincoln, 1947; Washington—Before His 26th Year, 1946. Address: 189 E. 64th St., N.Y.C. Died Mar. 27, 1950.

CHAPMAN, David Carpenter, wholesale druggist; b. Knoxville, Tenn., Aug. 9, 1876; s. John Ellis and Alice (Young) C.; ed. U. Tenn.; m. Sue Johnston, Nov. 4, 1911. Pres. Chapman Drug Co., Chapman Realty Co.; v.p. Home Bldg. & Loan Assn. Served as 2d lt., U.S. Vols., Spanish-Am. War; col., Tenn. N.G., 1917-18. Dir. Nat. Conf. on State Parks. Mem. Tenn. Acad. Science, Great Smoky Mountains Conservation Assn. (pres.), Am. Civic Assn., Am. Forestry Assn., Sigma Alpha Epsilon; hon. mem. Tenn. Soc. N.Y. Mason. Club: East Tenn. Automobile (dir.). Largely responsible for establishment of the Great Smoky Mountains Nat. Park, in Tenn. and N.C. Home: Route 3. Office: 516 State St., Knoxville, Tenn. Died July 26, 1944.

CHAPMAN, E(dmond) B(eaubien), newspaperman; b. Maple Hill, Kan., June 19, 1884; s. William Wray and Mary Florence (Beaubien) C.; student pub. schs., Maple Hill; m. Alberta Louise Sams, Apr. 14, 1910; children—Edmond Beaubien, William Sams. Staff various midwest newspapers, including Topeka (Kan.) Capital, Ark. Gazette, Little Rock, St.L. Globe Democrat, Sioux City (Ia.) Tribune, 1905-18; mng. editor Salina (Kan.) Jour., 1907-08; agrl., feature writer K.C. (Mo.) Star, 1918-28; columnist, editorial writer Topeka State Jour., 1928-40, since 1952, mng. editor, 1940-52. Mem. Kan. State Editorial Assn. (pres. 1934), Topeka C. of C., Sigma Delta Chi. Republican. Mem. Christian Ch. Mason (Shriner). Clubs: Press, Rotary (Topeka); Press (K.C.). Home: 817 W. 10th. Office: 121 W. 8th St., Topeka, Kan. Died Oct. 11, 1954; buried Maple Hill, Kan.

CHAPMAN, Edward Mortimer, ret. clergyman, author; b. Old Saybrook, Conn., Sept. 27, 1862; s. Robert and Maria Green (Shepard) C.; A.B., Yale, 1884, B.D., 1890; m. Isabel Northrop, June 28, 1894 (died 1920); children—Edward Northrop, Lucia Tully (Mrs. T. Dudley Goord); m. 2d, Louise Wadsworth Jones, Dec. 22, 1923. Ordained Congl. ministry, 1890; pastor Rochester, N.H., 1890-92; asso. pastor Central Ch., Worcester, Mass., 1892-99; pastor North Ch., St. Johnsbury, Vt., 1900-05; acting pastor First Church, Detroit, 1905; pastor Old Lyme, Conn., 1907-15. Del. Am. Commn. on Agrl. Cooperation in Europe, 1913. Lecturer Bibl. lit., Conn. Coll. for Women, 1917-28. Chmn. New London Chapter Am. Red Cross, World War. Mem. Soc. Colonial Wars, Phi Beta Kappa. Clubs: Century (New York); Winthrop (Boston). Author: The Dynamic of Christianity, 1904; English Literature in Account with Religion, 1910; Companions of the Way, 1918; A Modernist and His Rreed, 1926; New England Village Life, 1937. Occasional contbr. essays and reviews to mags. Home: Old Saybrook, Conn. Deceased.

CHAPMAN, Elbridge Gerry, army officer; b. Denver, Nov. 20, 1895; s. Elbridge Gerry and Florence Fairfield (Lake) C.; A.B., U. Colo., 1917, LL.B., 1920; student New Coll., Oxford U., Eng., 1919, Law Sch., Northwestern U., 1923-24; m. Margaret Elene, June 8, 1927; 1 child, Craig. Commd. 2d lt. Inf., U.S. Army, 1917, advanced through grades to maj. gen. (temp.), 1943; legal staff Gov. Gen., P.I., 1932-35; Command and Gen. Staff Sch., 1938; comdg. gen. Airbonre Command, 1942-—. Decorated D.S.C., Silver Star with oak leaf cluster, Purple Heart. Mem. Phi Gamma Delta. Mason. Home: Denver. Address: Hdqrs. 13th Airborne Div., Camp Mackall, N.C. Died July 6, 1954.*

CHAPMAN, Harry Powell, editor; b. Portsmouth, Va., Nov. 26, 1888; s. James Harry and Elizabeth (Thompson) C.; A.B., Roanoke Coll., 1908, A.M., 1909; m. Josephine Mann Koehler, Oct. 4, 1913; children—Harry Powell, Jr. (naval aviator, lt., killed in Pacific area, Oct. 1943), Sophie Ann (Mrs. James Lewis Ingles). Reporter, Lynchburg News, 1910; reporter, sports writer, city editor, Roanoke Times, 1910-13; news editor Savannah Morning News, 1913-15; editor Roanoke Times since 1915; news commentator radio sta. WSLS, Roanoke, 1943-47; lecturer in journalism, Roanoke Coll., 1924-26; prin. Cedar Bluff (Va.) High Sch., 1909-10; dir. Comas Cigarette Machine Co., Salem, Va. Pres. Roanoke Chamber of Commerce 1945, nat. councilor 1946, dir. 1945-46; mem. U.S., Va. State and Roanoke chambers of commerce, Democrat. Episcopalian. Kiwanian (pres. 1934; lt. gov. Capital dist. 1936). Clubs: Shenandoah (Roanoke); National Press (Washington). Home: Edgehill, Roanoke. Office: Times-World Corp., Roanoke, Va. Died June 1, 1952; buried East Hill Cemetery, Salem, Va.

CHAPMAN, Horace L., banker; b. Alleghany County, N.Y., July 10, 1837; s. Samuel, Jr., and Betsey E. (Leete) C.; student pub. schs. Allehany County; m. Frances Benton, Sept. 24, 1868. Studied law in office Oscar F. Moore; admitted to bar, 1865, never practiced; bought interest in pvt. banking firm which became Kinney & Chapman, 1863; established banking house in Jackson, O., 1865, which became 1st Nat. Bank in 1870, since served as pres.; engaged in iron and coal bus. in Jackson County, 25 yrs.; pres. Chapman Coal Co.; dir. Glove Iron Co. (Jackson, O.), Chapman Mining Co. (Moxohala, O.). 1st lt. of Portsmouth (O.) City Troop, 1861-65. Dem. nominee for gov. Ohio, 1897; del. nat. conv. Kansas City, 1900. Clubs: Columbus, Columbus Country. Home: Columbus, O. Died 1917.

CHAPMAN, Ira T., supt. schs.; b. Lima, O., June 26, 1874; s. John Henry and Eliza Ann (Berry) C.; A.B., Ohio Wesleyan U., 1903; A.B., A.M., Harvard, 1905; grad. student Clark U., Worcester, Mass., 1908-10, Columbia U., 1912-17; m. Bertha Agnes Law, June 11, 1906; 1 dau., Eleanor Willis (Mrs. Richard D. Gerould). Tchr. rural schs., village high sch., 1892-1900; supt. Huntington (Mass.) Dist., 1905-07, Milbury Oxford Dist., 1907-12; supt. schs., Norwalk, Conn., 1912-17, New Brunswick, N.J., 1917-23, Elizabeth, N.J., 1923-—. Trustee Elizabeth Pub. Library. Mem. N.E.A., Am. Assn. Sch. Adminstrs., Horace Mann League, Nat. Soc. Study of Edn., N.J. State Tchrs. Assn., N.J. Council of Edn., N.J. School-Masters' Club. Republican. Methodist. Mason. Clubs: Harvard of N.J., Scholia (Columbia U.), Kiwanis. Home: 30 Hillside Rd. Address: 417 S. Broad St., Elizabeth, N.J. Died Aug. 1957.

CHAPMAN, John A. corp. exec.; b. Chgo., June 29, 1873; s. John E. and Mary C. (Adams) C.; grad. St. Paul's School; Princeton U., 1895; m. Eleanor T. Stickney, Oct. 24, 1908. With Fraser & Chalmers, 1893; Chgo. Tel. Co., 1895; McCormick Harvesting Co., 1898; McCormick Estate office, 1905; William A. Read & Co., 1917; pres. Chapman, Grannis & Co., 1922-30; v.p. Bartlett, Knight & Co., Chicago, 1930-40; now with William Blair & Co.; dir. Internat. Harvester Co., A. C. McClurg & Co. Clubs: Chicago, University; Onwentsia. Home: Lake Forest, Ill. Office: 135 S. La Salle St., Chgo. Died Jan. 12, 1960.

CHAPMAN, Judson W(illiam), editor; b. Anderson, S.C., July 5, 1900; s. Dr. James Davis and Janie (Weston) C.; ed. Furman Fitting Sch., 1911-15, and Furman Univ., 1915-17; m. Zena Haselton, July 11, 1919; children—Paul Haselton, Judson William, George Weston. Newspaper carrier, Greenville (S.C.) Piedmont, 1911, reporter, 1916-22; copy desk, St. Louis (Mo.) Post-Dispatch, 1922; city editor, Greenville News, 1924-25, mng. editor, 1926-27; editor, Greenville Piedmont, 1928-48; v.p. and editorial director of the Greenville News-Piedmont Company (publisher of the Piedmont and the News), since 1936. Served U.S. Army, 1918-19. Mem. S.C. Press Assn. (pres., 1943-44), Furman Univ. Alumni Assn. (dir.), Am. Soc. Newspaper Editors, Asso. Press, Am. Legion. Democrat. Baptist. Clubs: Rotary (pres., 1944), Greenville Country, Poinsett (Greenville); Biltmore Forest Country (Biltmore, N. C.). Home: Poinsett Hotel. Office: Greenville News-Piedmont Co., Greenville, S.C. Died Aug. 7, 1951.

CHAPMAN, Lila May, librarian; b. Dadeville, Ala.; d. Abner Thomas and Mary Virginia (Mitchell) Chapman; A.B., Wesleyan Coll., Macon, Ga.; B.L.S., Emory U. Library Sch., 1906; unmarried. Library organizer, 1906; librarian, Carnegie Library, Corsicana, Tex., 1907-08; librarian Birmingham Pub. Library, 1909-13, vice dir., 1914-25; dir. city and county library system, Birmingham Library, 1926-47. Trustee Wesleyan Coll., Ga., 1933-36. Member A.L.A. since 1907; mem. Southeastern Library Assn. (v.p. 1937-38), Ala. Library Assn. (asso. bd. mem., past pres.), Phi Mu (nat. 1st v.p. 1931-34, nat. librarian since 1934; distinguished service citation, 1952), Birmingham Hist. Soc., Macon Art Assn., Am. Assn. U. Women, So. States Art League (bd. govs. since 1937); asso. mem. Am., Chgo. socs. etchers. Episcopalian. Democrat. Clubs: Birmingham Art, Macon Study. Contbr. to Aglaia of Phi Mu; articles to library publs. Home: 1580 Oglethorpe St., Macon, Ga. Died Oct. 22, 1953.

CHAPMAN, Paul Wilber, educator; b. Brookfield, Mo., Feb. 10, 1891; s. George Wolcott and Henrietta (Wilber) C.; B.S.A. and B.S. Edn., U. of Missouri, 1914; M.S., U. of Georgia, 1931; D.Sc., Clemson College, 1937; m. Elizabeth Lewis, Aug. 10, 1916; children—Carolyn, Paul Wilber. Teacher pub. schs., Macon, Mo., 1915-16; supt. schs., Queen City, Mo., 1916-17, New London, Mo., 1917-19; Mo. state supervisor of agrl. edn., 1919-20; prof. rural journalism, Ga. State Coll. Agr., since 1920; Ga. state supervisor agrl. edn. since 1920; state dir. Ga. State Bd. Vocational Edn. since 1925; dean State Coll. of Agr., Univ. of Georgia, since 1934; consultant U.S. Office of Edn., occupational information and guidance service; consultant Agrl. Commn. Am. Bankers Assn.; mem. bd. dirs. American Foundation for Agriculture. Mem. Nat. Advisory Com. on Edn. Mem. N.E.A. (pres. dept. vocational edn. 1928), Am. Vocational Assn. (pres. 1930), Nat. Assn. State Dirs. of Vocational Edn. (pres. 1929), Pi Kappa Alpha, Alpha Zeta, Omicron Delta Kappa, Phi Kappa Phi fraternities. Democrat. Presbyterian. Mason. Club: Athens Rotary (pres.). Author: Farm Crops, 1925; Pleasant and Profitable Farming (with L. M. Sheffer), 1928; The Green Hand (novel), 1932; The Young Man in Farming (with A. K. Getman), 1933; Livestock Farming (with L. M. Sheffer), 1936; Occupational Guidance, 1937; Southern Crops (with Roy Thomas), 1938; Successful Farming, 1939; Round the World with Cotton, Better Farm Living, Better Rural Communities, Better Rural Careers, Farming Opportunities (all 1941), Victory Barnyard, 1943; The Home Flock, 1943. Editor: Live Stock and Poultry, 1926; Horticulture, 1926; Southern Forestry, 1938; Conservation Efficient Farm Management, 1948. Dept. editor The Progressive Farmer. Contbr. articles to tech. publs. of American Resources, 1940; Food Processing, 1942; Home: 163 W. View Dr., Athens, Ga. Died Apr. 28, 1953; buried Oconee Hill Cemetery, Athens, Ga.

CHAPMAN, Roy H., judge; b. Lake Butler, Fla., July 15, 1885; s. William Washington and Addie Mary (Owenby) C.; ed. East Fla. Sem., 1902-05, U. of Fla., 1905-06, John B. Stetson U., 1906-08 (LL.B.); m. Edith L. Lanier, June 17, 1930. Admitted to Fla. bar and practiced in Lake City; mem. firm Cone & Chapman, 25 years; served as county atty., city atty.; justice Supreme Court of Fla., chief justice since Jan. 9, 1945. Has served as del. Dem. Nat. Conv.; chmn. Dem. Congl. Dist. Com.; mem. Bd. Law Examiners, 1925-31. Democrat. Baptist. Mason (K.T., Shriner). Club: Rotary. Home: 1117 Myers Park Dr. Office: Supreme Court Bldg., Tallahassee, Fla. Died Aug. 9, 1952; buried Lake Butler, Fla.

CHAPMAN, Virgil Munday, senator; born at Simpson County, Ky., March 15, 1895; son of James Virgil and Lily (Munday) C.; LL.B., U. Ky., 1918 (jr. and sr. honor prizes); m. Mary Adams Talbott, June 12, 1920; 1 dau. Elizabeth Grimes (Mrs. Francis J. Danforth, Jr.). Editor in chief Ky. Law Journal, 1917-18; admitted to Ky. bar, 1917, practiced at Irvine, Ky., firm of Miller & Chapman, 1918-20; mem. Franklin, Talbott & Chapman, Lexington, 1920-25. City atty., Irvine, 1918-20; mem. 69th, 70th and 72d Congresses, 7th Ky. Dist., 73d Congress at large, 74th to 80th Congresses, 6th Ky. Dist. United States senator, Kentucky, 1948-—. Democratic campaign speaker, active in orgn. cooperative marketing by tobacco growers; mem. Ho. Com. Interstate and Fgn. Commerce. Chmn. of exec. committee Dem. Nat. Congressional Com. Mem. Am., Ky. State, Bourbon, Fayette County bar assns., S.C.V., Morgan's Men's Assn., Alpha Delta Sigma, Phi Alpha Delta, Tau Kappa Alpha, Order of the Coif, Scabbard and Blade. Mem. Disciples of Christ Ch. Mason (Shriner), Odd Fellow, Elk. Clubs: Nat. Press, Jefferson Islands (Washington); Lexington (Lexington, Ky.). Home: Paris, Ky. Died Mar. 8, 1951.

CHAPPELL, Edward A(lan) (chăp-el), pub. exec.; b. Mukwonago, Wis., Nov. 14, 1886; s. William and Caroline (Slack) C.; student Wheaton Coll., 1904-05; A.B., Lake Forest Coll., 1909; m. Edith Burge, Oct. 10, 1914 English instr., Wis. and Ia. high schs., 1909-13; advt. mgr., Ia. City (Ia.) Press-Citizen, 1913-28, bus. mgr., 1928-35; pub., Chillicothe (O.) Scioto Gazette, 1935,-39, Poughkeepsie (N.Y.) Sunday Courier, 1939-41, Poughkeepsie New Yorker, 1941-52, ret.; treas., dir. Poughkeepsie Newspapers, Inc., 1941-52, v.p., dir., 1952-—; v.p. dir. Speidel Newspapers Inc., 1952-—, Visalia (Cal.) Newspapers Inc., 1948-—; treas., dir. WGNY Broadcasting Co., Inc., 1939-—. Trustee, Vassar Bros. Hosp., Poughkeepsie. Mem. Ia. State Hist. Soc., Poughkeepsie C. of C. Republican. Presbyn. Mason. Elk. Clubs: National Press (Washington), University, Amriat, Dutchess Golf and Country (Poughkeepsie). Home: 16105 Ridge Crest Av., Los Gatos, Cal. Died Nov. 30, 1955; buried Oakland Cemetery, Iowa City, Ia.

CHAPPELL, Edwin B., editor; b. Tenn., Dec. 27, 1853; s. William B. and Elizabeth (Whitaker) C.; B.A., Vanderbilt U., 1879; D.D., Central Coll., 1892; m. Jennie D. Headee, June 17, 1880. Ordained M.E. Ch., S., ministry, 1883; pastor, La Grange, Tex., 1882-84, San Antonio, 1884-88, Austin, 1888-91, La Fayette Park and Cook Av. chs., St. Louis, 1891-98, West End and McKendree chs., Nashville, 1898-1906; Sunday Sch. editor M.E. Ch., S., 1906-30; spl. writer for Meth. Pub. House, Nashville, 1930—. Trustee Emory U., Paine College (Augusta, Ga.). Mem. Phi Beta Kappa. Author: Studies in the Life of John Wesley; Building the Kingdom; The Church and Its Sacraments; Evangelism in the Sunday School; Recent Development of Religious Education in the Methodist Episcopal Church, South. Address: 810 Broadway, Nashville. Died July 29, 1936.

CHAPPELL, George Shepard (pseud. Walter E. Traprock), author, architect; b. New London, Conn., Jan. 2, 1878; s. Alfred Hebbard and Adelaide Estelle (Shepard) C.; B.A., Yale, 1899; student Ecole des Beaux Arts, Paris, 1900; m. Amy Wentworth Beard, Oct. 4, 1905. Mem. Am. Inst. Architects, Soc. Beaux Arts Architects, Delta Kappa Epsilon. Republican. Clubs: Yale, University. Author: Rollo in Society, 1921; The Cruise of the Kawa, 1921; My Northern Exposure, 1922; Sarah of the Sahara, 1923; The Restaurants of New York, 1925; The Younger Married Set, 1926; Through the Alimentary Canal With Gun and Camera, 1930; The Saloon in the Home (with Ridgely Hunt), 1930; Dr. Traprock's Memory Book, 1931; The Gardener's Friend and Other Pests (with Ridgely Hunt), 1931; Evil Through the Ages, 1932; Shoal Water, 1933; Animals Arise!!!, 1935; also many articles in mags. Home: Toll Gate, Bantam, Conn. Office: 101 Park Av., N.Y.C. Died Nov. 1946.

CHAPPEL, James Edward, newspaper editor and pub.; b. Cadiz, Ky., Nov. 23, 1885; s. John Jefferson and Ida (Cooper) C.; A.B., South Kentucky Coll., 1903; student Vanderbilt U., 1904-07; Litt.D., Birmingham-Southern Coll., 1937; m. Corinne Warren Sedberry, Nov. 21, 1908; children—Sara Corinne (Mrs. Walter Puckett, Jr.), Mary (Mrs. Clare Barclift). Reporter Nashville Am., 1907-10; state news editor Birmingham News, 1910-11, city editor, 1911-15, mng. editor, 1915-22, asst. to publisher, 1922-36; pres., gen. mgr. Birmingham News Company, 1936-53, pres. and editor, 1953—; mem. exec. com. and dir. Security Comml. Bank. Mem. bd. dirs. The Associated Press, 1943-52. Served in Ky. Nat. Guard as adjutant, 1903-05. Mem. Pres. Roosevelt's Com. on Farm Tenancy, 1936. Mem. bd. trustees Vanderbilt U., 1938; mem. bd. dirs. Jefferson county chapter, Am. Red Cross. Member Birmingham Chamber Comm. (dir. 1931-37), Southern Newspaper Pub. Assn. (pres. 1936, chmn. bd. 1937-38, treasurer 1939-47), Am. Newspaper Publishers Assn. (spl. standing com. 1942-45, 1952-54), Am. Soc. Newspaper Editor, Sigma Alpha Epsilon, Omicron Delta Kappa. Democrat. Presbyn. Club: Kiwanis (ex-pres.). Industry mem. newspaper pub. industry commn., Nat. War Labor Bd., 1943-45. Home: Town House, 8th Av. and 20th St. Office: 2200 4th Av., Birmingham 2, Ala. Died Jan. 29, 1960; buried Elmwood Cemetery, B'ham, Ala.

CHAPPLE, Joe (Joseph) Mitchell (chăp'l), editor; b. La Porte City, Ia., July 18, 1867; s. William and Louisa (Mitchell) C.; ed. Cornell Coll., Ia., (hon. A.M., same, 1904; LL.D., Lincoln Memorial U., 1915); m. Annie F Ryder, Nov. 23, 1886 (deceased); m. 2d, L. Evangeline White, May 15, 1941. At 16 edited paper in Grand Rapids, N.D., and later became editor and propr. of the Ashland Daily Press; in newspaper work, Chicago, Washington and New York until 1897; took charge of The Bostonian, 1897, changing name to The National Magazine, of which has since been editor and publisher; editor and pub. of Reader's Rapid Review. Author: (novels) The Minor Chord, 1895; Boss Bart, Politician, 1896; Mark Hanna, 1903; Heart Throbs, 1906; The Panama Canal, 1907; The Happy Habit, 1908; Heart Songs, 1909; Little Helps, 1910; History Making, 1911; Heart Letters, 1912; Heart Chord, 1915; C'est le Guerre, We'll Stick, 1918; A Top o' the World, 1922; Harding the Man, 1923; Vivid Spain, 1927; To Bagdad and Back, 1928; Favored Florida, 1928; Favorite Heart Throbs of Famous People, 1929; Our Jim (a biography), 1929; Face to Face with Our Presidents, 1930; Holiday Moods of the Year, 1933; Chapel Bells, 1934; Mother O'Mine, 1935; Treasure Chest of Memories, 1937; Heart Songs, 1938; Willkie and American Unity, 1940. Producer Heart Throb motion picture series, "My Old Sweetheart," "Annabel Lee." Known as after dinner speaker and has also done extensive work on the Chautauqua platform and lyceum bureaus. His lectures "Flashlights of Famous People," "Confessions of an Optimist," "On the Wings of Tomorrow" and "The Great Personality Parade" are counted as keynotes of widely extended experiences and travels and heart to heart chats with over 7,000 celebrities in 21 countries; radio series, "Face to Face with our Presidents," given on nationwide broadcast; radio program series over NBC, "Personalities Whom I Have Met," 1946. Home: 29 Jefferson St., Winthrop, Mass. Office: 900 Statler Building, Boston. Died Apr. 17, 1950; buried Roselawn Cemetery, Champaign, Ill.

CHARBONNEAU, Joseph, archbishop and metropolitan of Montreal, Quebec; ordained June 1916; 1st bishop of Hearst, Ontario, June 1939; titular archbishop of Amorio and coadjutor with right of succession to archbishop of Montreal, May 1940; succeeded to the See, Aug. 1940. Address: Archbishop's Palace, 987 Lagauchetiere West, Montreal, P.Q., Can. Died Nov. 19, 1959.*

CHARLES, Dorothy, editor, librarian; b. Wichita, July 11, 1906; d. John Wesley and Mabel Grace (Munns) Charles; A.B., Ia. State Tchrs. Coll., 1927; Library certificate, U. Wis., 1928; A.M., U. Mich., 1931. Asst. cataloger Milw. Pub. Library, 1928-30, Ind. State Library, 1931-32; head cataloger Osterhout Free Library, Wilkes-Barré, Pa., 1932-35; asst. cataloger library U. So. Cal., 1936-38, asst. prof. library sci., 1937-39, U. Denver, summer 1938; instr. grad. library sch. U. Chgo., 1943-46; editor Bibliog. Index, N.Y.C., 1939-43, International Index since 1947. Del. Library Assn. Conf., London, 1950. Mem. Council Nat. Library Assns., 1949-50, 53-54. Mem. A.L.A. (council mem. 1951-52, 54-55; dir. div. cataloging and classification, 1948-49, 51-52, pres. div., 1953-54), N.Y. Regional Group Catalogers and Classifiers (pres. 1950-51) Kappa Delta Pi. Meth. Club: Library. Contbr. profl. publs. Office: H. W. Wilson Co., 950 University Av., N.Y.C. 52. Died Sept. 2, 1956.

CHARLES, William Barclay, ex-congressman; b. Glasgow, Scotland, Apr. 3, 1862; ed. pvt. and high schs.; came to U.S., 1884; m. Eleanor Rhodes of Marietta, O. Settled in Amsterdam, N.Y., 1886; dealer in cotton, mill supplies, etc.; dir. Amsterdam First National Bank, Farmers National Bank of Amsterdam; mem. N.Y. Assembly, 1904, 5, 6; mem. 64th Congress (1915-17), 30th N.Y. Dist. Republican. Episcopalian. Mason. Mem. Nat. Assn. Mfrs. Home: Amsterdam, N.Y. Died Nov. 25, 1950; buried Green Hill Cemetery.

CHARLTON, Clyde B., lawyer, mfg. exec.; born Rolfe, Ia., Jan. 10, 1899; s. James Henry and Franc Lenore (Beam) C.; A.B., State U. Ia., 1921; LL.B., J.D., 1923; m. Grace Orcutt, June 12, 1926; children—Ann, Clyde Henry. Admitted to Ia. bar, 1923, since practiced in Des Moines, mem. firm Brody, Charlton, Parker & Roberts and predecessor firms since 1929; specialized in trial work, 1925-45, corporate, tax and bus. adv. practice since 1935; gen. counsel and dir. Wood Bros., Inc., 1935-47, v.p. and dir. Ia. Paint Mfg. Co. since 1933; v.p. and dir. Ia. Guarantee, Inc., since 1938; pres. and dir Orcutt Hybrid Corn Co., 1940-46. Mem. 42nd Gen. Assembly of Ia., 1926. Mem. Am. and Ia. bar assns., "I" Club, Alumni Assn. State U. Ia. (pres. 1935), Order of Coif, Sigma Nu, Phi Delta Phi. Republican (del. nat. conv., 1932). Mason. Clubs: The Law, Des Moines, Wakonda. Home: 5241 Woodland Av., Des Moines. Died Oct. 29, 1951.

CHARLTON, Joseph W(illiam), educator; b. Oberlin, Ohio, Feb. 26, 1892; s. John Walton and Sarah Jane (Race) C.; A.B., Oberlin Coll., 1914, A.M., 1916; Ph.D., U. Chgo., 1938; m. Maude Emily Clements, Aug. 22, 1921. Statistician White Motor Co., Cleve., 1920-24; instr. U. Chgo., 1926-27; asst. prof. economics Grinnell (Ia.) Coll., 1927-29, asso. prof., 1929-47, prof. econs., 1947—, chmn. econs. dept., 1956-57. Pres. Mid-West Collegiate Athletic Conf., 1948-49. Dir. Poweskiek County chapter A.R.C., 1948—. Served as 1st lt., 7th Inf., 3rd div., U.S. Army, 1917-18; sr. instr., automatic weapons sect., Second Corps Sch., Chatillon-sur-Seine, France, 1918-19. Mem. Am., Mid-West econ. assns., Phi Beta Kappa. Republican. Conglist. Author: History of Banking in Illinois, 1863—, 1939. Home: 1407 Elm St., Grinnell, Ia. Died Jan. 31, 1957; buried Woodlawn Cemetery, Elyria, O.

CHARSKE, F. W. (chär'skē), ry. official; b. Hempstead, Tex., Jan. 26, 1881; student Agrl. and Mech. Coll. of Tex. Began, 1901, as clk. office of auditor of passenger accounts, Tex. lines of S.P. Co., Houston, Tex.; with N.Y., Tex. & Mexican Ry. and Gulf, Western Tex. & Pacific Ry., 1901-03; chief clk. passenger accounting dept. La. Lines of S.P. Co., at New Orleans, 1903-10; asst to auditor passenger accounts Pacific System, same co., San Francisco, 1910-11; spl. accountant staff of controller U.P. and S. P. systems, at New York, 1911-14, auditor freight accounts U.P. R.R., at Omaha, 1914-17; auditor, Ore. S.L. RR., at Salt Lake City, 1917-18; gen. accountant U.P. System, at New York, Aug.-Dec. 1918, asst. to pres., 1918-20, controller, 1920-24, v.p., controller, 1924-27, and now chmn. exec. com. Home: Darien, Conn. Office: 120 Broadway, N.Y.C. Died May 3, 1953.

CHARTERS, Werrett Wallace, educator; b. Hartford, Ont., Can., Oct. 24, 1875; s. Alexander Maxwell and Mary Ann (Mealley) C.; A.B., McMaster U., 1898, LL.D., 1923; grad. Ontario Normal Coll., 1899; B.Pd., Toronto U., 1901; Ph.M., University of Chicago, 1903, Ph.D., 1904; LL.D., Muskingum Coll., 1942; married Jessie Blount Allen, Dec. 21, 1907; children—Mrs. Margaret Allen Lyon, Mrs. Jessie Aileen House, Mrs. Jean Ferguson Graham, Werrett Wallace, Jr. Began as teacher rural school, Rockford, Ont., 1894, 1895; principal Model School, Hamilton, Canada, 1899-Dec. 1901; principal Elementary Sch., supervisor of practice teaching, etc., State Normal Sch., Winona, Minn., 1904-07; prof. theory of teaching, 1907-17, dean sch. of edn., 1910-17, U. of Mo.; prof. edn., U. of Ill., 1917-19, also dean Sch. of Edn., 1918-19; prof. edn. and dir. research bureau for retail training, Carnegie Inst. of Tech., 1919-23; prof. edn., 1923-25, dean Grad. Sch., 1924-25, also dir. Research Bur. for Retail Training, U. of Pittsburgh; prof. edn., U. of Chicago, 1925-28; dir. Bur. Edn. Research, Ohio State U., 1928-42, emeritus since 1942; research dir. Stephens Coll. 1920-50, emeritus since 1950. Dir. Bur. Training, War Manpower commn., 1942-43. Baptist. Rotary. Chmn. bd. trustees. Bd. of Edn. Northern Baptist Conv. Mem. N.E.A., Coll. Teachers of Edn., Nat. Soc. Study of Edn., Edn. Research Assn., Sigma Alpha Epsilon, Phi Delta Kappa, Kappa Delta Pi (laureate). Author: Method of Teaching, 1910; Teaching the Common Branches, 1913; Curriculum Construction, 1923; The Teaching of Ideals, 1927, etc. Co-author: Personal Leadership in Industry, 1925; Commonwealth Teacher Training Study, 1929, etc. Writer of numerous bulls., articles and repts. on tech. phases of edn. Home: Pine Croft, Maple City, Mich. Died Mar. 8, 1952; buried Hagersville, Ont., Can.

CHASE, Cleveland King, prof. Latin; b. Lyons, Ia., Nov. 30, 1871; s. Rev. Prof. Frederick Augustus and Julia (Spence) C.; A.B., Oberlin, 1891, A.M., 1896; hon. fellow in Latin, U. of Chicago, 1893-94, grad. scholar, 1894-95, fellow, 1895-96; Göttingen U., 1899-1900; Am. Sch. Classical Studies, Rome, 1900-01; Litt.D., Colgate U., Hamilton, N.Y., 1919; m. Helen Younger, of Santa Cruz, Calif., June 23, 1902; children—Cleveland Bruce, John Waddell, Frederic Peter Spence. Instr. in Latin, Oberlin, 1896-99; asst. prof. Latin, State U. of Ia., 1901-02; prof. Latin, Earlham Coll., Ind., 1902-11; prof. Latin, Hamilton Coll., since 1911, mem. advisory council Am. Sch. Classical Studies in Rome (sec. 1926-30). Mem. Am. Legion, Archaeol. Inst. America (life), Am. Philol. Assn., Classical Assn. of Middle West and South, Classical Assn. of Atlantic States, Phi Beta Kappa. Home: Clinton, N.Y. Died Nov. 27, 1951; buried St. Mary's Cemetery, Clinton.

CHASE, Edna Woolman, editor; b. Asbury Park, N.J., Mar. 14, 1877; d. Franklyn and Laura (Woolman) Alloway; ed. pub. and pvt. schs. and under tutors; married; 1 dau., Ilka. Entire career with Vogue, became editor in chief, 1914, now chmn. editorial bd. Awarded Legion of Honr (France). Home: Died Mar. 20, 1957; Locust Valley, N.Y.

CHASE, George Henry, archaeologist; b. Lynn, Mass., June 13, 1874; s. Amos Breed and Sarah Augusta (Chase) C.; A.B., Harvard University, 1896, A.M., 1897, Ph.D., 1900, LL.D., 1947; studied Am. Sch. Classical Studies at Athens, 1896-98; L.H.D., Oberlin Coll., 1935; Litt.D., Boston Univ., 1939; m. Freedrica Mark, June 20, 1908; children—Thomas King (dec.), Richard Breed. Master in Greek and Latin, St. Mark's Sch., 1900-01; instr. Greek and Latin, Harvard, 1901-03, tutor in Greek, 1903-04, instr. classical archaeology, 1904-06, asst. prof., 1906-16, John E. Hudson prof. archaeology, 1916-45, dean grad. sch. of arts and sciences, 1925-39, dean Harvard Univ., 1939-45, prof. emeritus since 1945; acting curator, Dept. Classical Art, Museum Fine Arts, Boston, since 1945. Asso. editor Am. Jour. of Archaeology since 1910. Fellow Am. Acad. Arts and Sciences; mem. Archaeol. Inst. America, Am. Philol. Assn., Am. Philos. Soc. (Phila.), Numismatic and Antiquarian Soc. of Phila., German Archaeological Soc., Delta Upsilon. Universalist. Mem. Phi Beta Kappa. Club: Harvard (Boston). Author: The Loeb Collection of Arretine Pottery, 1908; Greek and Roman Sculpture in American Collections, 1924; (with C. R. Post) A History of Sculpture, 1924. Compiler: Catalogue of Arretine Pottery in the Museum of Fine Arts, Boston, 1916. Editor Harper's Fine Arts Series. Contbr. numerous articles to Harvard Studies in Classical Philology, etc. Home: 1 Bryant St., Cambridge 38. Office: Museum of Fine Arts, Boston. Died Feb. 2, 1952.

CHASE, Harry Woodburn, educator; b. Groveland, Mass., Apr. 11, 1883; s. Charles Merrill and Agnes (Woodburn) C.; A.B., Dartmouth, 1904, A.M., 1908; Ph.D., Clark U., 1910; LL.D., Lenoir Coll. and Wake Forest Coll., 1920, U. of Ga., 1923, Dartmouth, 1925, U. of N.C., 1930, U. of Mich., 1932, Lafayette, 1934; Dr. of Humanities, Rollins Coll., 1931; Litt.D., Columbia, 1934; m. Lucetta Crum, Dec. 26, 1910; children—Elizabeth Woodburn (Mrs. Marion Foy Stone), Carl Carter. Dir. clinic for sub-normal children, Clark U., 1909-10; prof. psychology, U. of N.C., 1910-18; acting dean coll. of liberal arts, 1918-19, chmn. faculty, Jan.-June 1919, pres., 1919-30; pres. University of Ill., 1930-33; chancellor, New York University, 1933-51, chancellor emeritus since 1951. Trustee Russell Sage Foundation. Mem. bd. of dirs. Metropolitan Opera Assn.; trustee Town Hall, N.Y. Pub Library. Decorated Officer Southern Cross (Brazil); Chevalier, French Legion of Honor; Officier de la Couronne de Chene, Luxembourg; King Christian X Medal of Liberation, Denmark; Annual Gold Medal Award, New York Academy Pub. Edn., 1948. Mem. N.Y. Acad. Pub. Edn. (past pres.), Phi Beta Kappa, Sigma Xi, Sigma Nu. Episcopalian; mem. Trinity Ch. Vestry (N.Y.). Clubs: University, Century, Lotos (hon. pres.), Lawyers (N.Y.C.). Address: 986 S. Osprey, Sarasota, Fla. Died Apr. 20, 1955; buried Sarasota, Fla.

CHASE, Irving Hall, mfr., banker; b. Waterbury, Conn., May 13, 1858; s. Augustus Sabin and Martha Clark (Starkweather) C.; prep. edn., high sch., Waterbury, Gunnery Sch., Washington, Conn., Phillips Andover Acad., A.B., Yale, 1880; m. Elizabeth Hosmer Kellogg, Feb. 28, 1889; children—Marjorie Starkweather, Eleanor Kellogg, Lucia Hosmer, Elizabeth Irving, Dorothy Mather. Chmn. bd. Waterbury Nat. Bank; pres. Morris Plan Bank of Waterbury, Lake County Groves Corporation; director U.S. Time Co., Waterbury Buckle Co., Waterbury Savings Bank. Mem. Conn. Senate, 1907-08, 09-10. Dir. Gaylord Farm Assn.; trustee St. Margaret's Sch., Conn. Junior Republic. Republican. Conglist. Clubs: Waterbury; Point Judith Country (gov.). Home: 63 Prospect St., Waterbury, Conn. Died Mar. 14, 1951.

CHASE, James Mitchell, ex-congressman; b. Glen richey, Pa., Ded. 19, 1891; s. John M. and Jane T. (Phillips) C.; grad. high sch., Clearfield, Pa., 1911; LL.B., Dickinson Sch. Law, Carlisle, Pa., 1916; m. Elise Lake, Oct. 6, 1920; 1 son, Henry Hughes. Admitted to Pa. bar, 1919, began practice at Clearfield; mem. 70th, 71st and 72d Congresses, 23d Pa. Dist. Served in U.S. Air Service, 1917-19. Comdr. Am. Legion, Dept. of Pa., 1924-25. Republican. Baptist. Home: Clearfield, Pa. Died Jan. 1, 1945; buried Clearfield.

CHASE, Mrs. Lewis (Pearl-Adell), writer, lecturer; b. Plainville, N.Y., Aug. 4, 1872; d. John Buck and Helen Hopkinson (Betts) Rowell; ed. pvt. schs., Chicago, Baldwinsville (N.Y.) Acad. and under tutors; married; 1 dau., Frances Hopkinson Chase Hollis. Asst. lit. editor, Louisville (Ky.) Courier-Journal, 1907-08; lived in Bordeaux, France, 1909-10, London, 1911-15; conducted parties of Austrian and German women and children to their native countries after outbreak of European War, 1914-15, returning with British subjects to London; lecture tour, America, 1916; in charge canteen work in one of mil. hdqrs. of A.E.F. in France, 1917-18; maintained privately supported "open house" for soldiers in Paris, 1919; resided India, 1920; Peking, China, 1921-43; interned by Japanese, repatriated on Gripsholm, Dec. 1943. Fellow Royal Geog. Soc. Author: A Vagabond Voyage Through Brittany, 1915. Contbr. prose and light verse to Brit. and Am. periodicals. Address: Hotel Tudor, 304 E. 42d St., N.Y.C. 17. Died Oct. 4, 1955.

CHASE, Stanley Perkins, coll. prof.; b. Portland, Me., Apr. 14, 1884; s. Charles Henry and Maria Belford (Johnson) C.; A.B., Bowdoin Coll., Brunswick, Me., 1905; A.M., Harvard, 1906, Ph.D., 1911; m. Helen Johnson, June 21, 1912. Asst. in English, Harvard Coll., 1906-07; instr. English lit., Northwestern U., 1907-09; instr. English, Union Coll., Schenectady, N.Y., 1911-12, asst. prof., 1912-19, asso. prof., 1919-25; prof. English lit. Bowdoin Coll., 1925-26, Henry Leland Chapman prof. English lit. since 1926, vis. prof., spring 1925; teacher Syracuse U., summer 1921. Awarded Bowdoin prize for grads. in div. of modern languages by Harvard U., 1910. Mem. Modern Lang. Assn. of Am., Am. Assn. Univ. Profs. (foundation mem.), Shakespeare Assn. of Am., Mediaeval Acad. Am., Delta Kappa Epsilon, Phi Beta Kappa (sec. Bowdoin chpt. 1925-48; pres. 1948, senator united chpts. 1946-52). Democrat. Episcopalian. Co-editor: (with eight pupils) The Pearl (Bowdoin edit.), 1932. Author: The Pearl: the fourteenth century English poem rendered in modern verse, 1932. Contbr. to symposium Humanism and Am. (editor N. Foerster), 1930. Home: 256 Maine St., Brunswick, Me. Died Jan. 21, 1951; buried Pine Grove Cemetery, Brunswick.

CHATHAM, (Richard) Thurmond, congressman; b. Elkin, N.C., Aug. 16, 1896; s. Hugh Gwyn and Martha Lenoir (Thurmond) C.; student, U. of N.C. and Yale; m. Lucy Hodgin Hanes, Oct. 29, 1919 (died July 1950); children—Hugh Gwyn II, Richard Thurmond; m. 2d Patricia Firestone Coyner, Nov. 16, 1950; 1 son, Walter Firestone. Began in mills of Chatham Mfg. Co., 1919, advancing to position as pres., chmn. bd., now ret.; owner-operator Klondike Farm, Elkin, N.C.; mem. 81st to 84th U.S. Congresses, from 5th N.C. Dist. Served with U.S. Navy, 1917-19 and 1942-45. Decorated Bronze Star Medal, Sec. of Navy's Commendation Medal, Am. Theater and European Theater ribbons, Asiatic Theater ribbon with 3 battle stars, World War I and Victory ribbons (U.S.), Royal Order of Nassau with swords (Netherlands). Mem. State Bd. of Conservation and Development. Trustee U. of N.C. mem. bd. dirs. Meth. Children's Home (Winston-Salem); dir. Hugh Chatham Memorial Hosp., Elkin. Past pres. N.C. Dairymen's Assn. Mem. Farm Bureau. Democrat. Mem. Nat. Grange. Home: Elkin, N.C. Died Feb. 5, 1957.

CHATTERTON, Fenimore, ex-gov. Wyo.; b. Oswego, N.Y., July 21, 1860; s. German H. and Ama (Mazuzan) C.; prep. edn. Columbian Coll., Washington; LL.B., U. Mich., 1892; LL.D., U. Wyo.; m. Stella Wayland, Oct. 15, 1900; children—Eleanor, Constance. Post trader Ft. Steele, Wyo., 1883-88; mem. firm Hugus & Chatterton, bankers and gen. mdse., Ft. Steele and Saratoga, Wyo., 1878-88; county judge, county treas. Carbon County, Wyo., 1888-90; admitted to bar, 1891; built Saratoga and Encampment Ry.; pres. Wyo. State Ry.; dir. 1st Nat. Bank, Rawlins, Wyo.; mem. and atty. Pub. Service Commn., Wyo. Bd. Equalization, 1927-33; resumed practice, Cheyenne, 1933, now ret. and engaged in writing. Chmn Rep. State Com., 1893-94. Mem. Am. Bar Assn. Episcopalian. Mason (33°, grand master Wyo. 1895-95, grand comdr. K.T. 1902-03, master Kadesh 1907-08). Originator many irrigation projects and constructor canals reclaiming 500,000 acres. Home: Arvada, Colo. Died May 9, 1958; buried Lakeview Cemetery, Cheyenne, Wyo.

CHEATHAM, John Henry, textile mfr.; b. Greenwood, S.C., July 6, 1882; s. R. G. and Sallie M. (Spikes) C.; student Furman U., 1900-03; m. Jayne Jackson, Jan. 20, 1909; children—John M., Robert W., Virginia, John H., Richard B. Bookkeeper Easley (S.C.) Cotton Mills, 1903-15; pres., treas. Dundee Mills, Inc., since 1918, Hartwell Mills, Rushton Cotton Mills, Lowell Bleachery South; dir. State Bank. Dir., treas. Textile Inst. Tech.; trustee, treas. Ga. Baptist Found., Inc. Mem. Ga. Cotton Mfrs. Assn. (pres. 1935-36), American Cotton Manufacturers Association (president 1938-39). Democrat. Baptist. K.P., Modern Woodmen. Clubs: Rotary, Country. Home: 728 Macon Rd., Griffin, Ga. Died Feb. 17, 1950.

CHEEK, F(rank) J(acobs), Jr., coll. prof.; born Paris, Ky., Aug. 25, 1893; s. Rev. F. J. and Elizabeth Ann (Ingels) C.; A.B., Centre Coll. of Ky., 1914; C.E., Rensselaer Poly Inst., 1919; S.M., Mass. Inst. Tech., 1933; m. Martha A. Butt, Aug. 26, 1924; 1 dau., Martha R. High sch. teacher mathematics, 1914-15; office mgr. state agency Northwestern Mutual Life Ins. Co., 1915-16; constrn. engr. and field supt. Turner Constrn. Co., N.Y. City, 1919-22; operated own office, 1922-23; asso. prof. Kan. State Coll., 1923-37; prof. hydraulic and sanitary engring. U. of Ky., 1937-59. Consultant in Engring. Curricula Central U. of Venezuela; mem. State Bd. of Examiners for Waterworks Operators; mem. State Bd. of Examiners for Sanitary Engrs.; nat. vice chmn. Engring. College Magazines, Associated, 1948-49, national chairman, 1949-51. Member American Soc. C.E., Am. Soc. Engring. Edn., Ky. Soc. Professional Engrs., Sigma Chi, Alpha Rho Chi, Sigma Xi, Tau Beta Pi. Registered profl. engr., Ky. Democrat. Presbyn. Home: 1492 Tates Creek Rd., Lexington 5, Ky. Died Apr. 23, 1959.

CHEEVER, David (chē'vẽr), surgeon, educator; b. Boston, June 25, 1876; s. David Williams and Anne Caroline (Nichols) C.; A.B., Harvard, 1897; M.D., 1901; m. Jane Welles Sargent, June 8, 1907; children—David, Francis Sargent, Charles Ezekiel, Daniel Sargent, Jane Hunnewell. Began practice at Boston, 1901; asst. surgeon, Boston City Hosp., 1905-12; surgeon Peter Bent Brigham Hosp., 1913-39, emeritus, 1939—; asst. and demonstrator in anatomy, Harvard Med. Sch., 1903-13, asst. prof. surg. anatomy, 1913-22, asso. prof. surgery, 1922-39, emeritus, 1939—. Lieut. col. BEF, chief surgeon Base Hosp. 22, in charge Harvard Surg. Unit, 1915-16. Recalled to duty as acting surgeon in chief of Peter Bent Bingham Hosp., 1942. Overseer Harvard U., 1939—; pres. Boston Medical Library, 1941—. Bevan lectr. Chgo. Surg. Soc., 1939; Balfour lectr. U. Toronto, Canada, 1941. Fellow Am. Acad. Arts and Sciences, Société Internationale de Chirurgie; (hon.) Royal Soc. Medicine (London, Eng.); mem. Am. Surg. Assn. (pres. 1940), Soc. Clin. Surgery, A.M.A., New Eng. Surg. Soc. (pres.), Inter-Urban Surg. Soc., Mass. Med. Soc., Mass. Hist. Soc., Sigma Xi, Alpha Omega Alpha. Republican. Unitarian. Contbr. articles and monographs on surg. subjects. Address: 193 Marlboro St., Boston. Died Aug. 13, 1955; buried Mount Auburn Cemetery, Cambridge, Mass.

CHENERY, Winthrop Holt, educator, librarian; b. Belmont, Mass., Mar. 8, 1872; s. Winthrop Louis and Ruth Baldwin (Holt) C.; S.B., Mass. Inst. Tech., 1896; .B., Harvard, 1897, A.M., 1898, Ph.D., 1904; unmarried. Instr. in Spanish, U. of Mich., 1901-04; instr., 1905-07, asst. prof. Spanish and Italian, 1907-14, asso. prof. Romanic langs., 1914-20, librarian, 1912-19, Washington U., St. Louis; chief Dept. of Spl. Libraries, Boston Pub. Library, 1920-27; librarian Washington U., 1927-38. Address: 516 E. Andover Dr., Burbank, Cal. Died Oct. 18, 1953.

CHENEY, Archibald Myron, lawyer; b. Fairview, Utah, Dec. 10, 1880; s. William Wells and Agnes (Anderson) C.; Brigham Young U., 1903; LL.B., Georgetown U., 1909; m. Clara Allen, Sept. 30, 1908; children—Arch Allen, Inez Beth, Barbara Claire. Admitted to Utah bar, 1909, and since practiced law in Salt Lake City; mem. law firm Cheney, Marr, Wilkins & Cannon and predecessor firms since 1909; spl. asst. to atty. gen. as hearing officer under Selective Service. Mem. Am. and Utah bar assns. Clubs: Alta, Country. Home: 105 E. South Temple St. Office: Continental National Bank Bldg., Salt Lake City 1. Died Nov. 19, 1951.

CHENEY, Charles Baldwin, journalist; b. Ft. Madison, Ia., June 29, 1872; s. Rev. Joseph Warren and Lavinia Rachel (Baldwin) C.; A.B., Simpson Coll., 1894; m. Lora M. Allen, Feb. 23, 1899 (dec.); m. 2d, Mabel V. Fitzgerald (dec.); 1 dau., Margaret Virginia (Mrs. R. Marlow Sargent). Reporter, later asst. editor Mpls. Times, 1894-98; sec. to mayor of Mpls., 1899-1900; polit. editor Mpls. Journal, 1901-36, asso. editor, 1936-39; columnist on Mpls. Tribune, 1939-46. Mem. Sigma Alpha Epsilon. Republican. Methodist. Club: Six O'Clock. Author: Minnesota Politics. Home: 510 Groveland Av., Mpls. Died June 13, 1955.

CHENEY, Harold Clark, publisher; b. New Haven, June 19, 1877; s. Benjamin H. and Sarah Jane (Austin) C.; prep. edn. Hopkins Grammar Sch., New Haven; A.B., Yale, 1899; m. Gertrude Lucile Stebbing, Oct. 12, 1915; children—Sara Austin (Mrs. Duncan B. Farnsworth), Elizabeth Lord (Mrs. W. J. Widhelm). Vice pres., dir. and mgr. ednl. dept. Charles Scribner's Sons, pubs., N.Y.C. Mem. nat. adv. com. New York World's Fair, 1939-40. Trustee, The Bishop and Trustee Corp. of P.E. Ch., Diocese of Chgo. Mem. Chgo. Assn. of Commerce (chmn. Ill. com. 1932; chmn. ways and means com. 1933-34), Am. Hist. Assn., Soc. of Colonial Wars. Republican. Episcopalian (vestryman). Mason. Clubs: Chicago Athletic Assn., Barrington Country (pres. 1940-41), Yale, Psi Upsilon; Rotary (pres. 1928-29); University (N.Y.). Home: Barrington, Ill. Office: 600 W. Van Buren St., Chgo. Died July 15, 1957; buried Evergreen Cemetery, Barrington, Ill.

CHENEY, Howell, silk mfr.; b. Hartford, Conn., Jan. 1, 1870; s. Frank W. and Mary (Bushnell) C.; A.B., Yale, 1892, M.A., 1898; m. Anne Kimberly Bunce, Oct. 27, 1898 (died 1931); children—Anne Kimberly (dec.), Laura, Helen, David H., Kimberly, Timothy, Mary Bushnell, Emily. Mfr., South Manchester, Conn., 1893-1935; dir., sec. Cheny Brothers, 1925-35; trustee Manchester Savings Bank, 1900-05. Chmn. School Com., South Manchester, 1898-1939; chmn. High School Com., Manchester, 1927-1933; mem. State Bd. Edn., 1909-19; mem. Yale Corp., 1914-38; trustee Mt. Holyoke Coll., 1912-26, 1930-40, Am. Sch. for the Deaf, 1913, Hartford Retreat for the Insane, 1912-15, 35—, Nat. Child Labor Com., 1914. Pres. Mfrs. Assn. of Hartford County, 1922-25; dir. N.A.M., 1912-15, Nat. C. of C., 1914-16; state dir. Nat. War Savings Com., 1918-19; trustee Milton Acad., 1919-29; chmn. bd. trustees Hartford Jr. Coll., 1939—; trustee Manchester Meml. Hosp. Apptd. mem. adv. council, chmn. industrial unit adv. council NRA, July 1, 1935; sec., treas. Conn. Economic Council, 1936—. Mem. Bd. Appeals SSS, 1941-45. Mem. Am. Acad. Polit. and Social Science, Psi Upsilon, Skull and Bones (Yale). Republican. Conglist. Club: Graduate (New Haven). Home: 110 Forest St., Manchester. Office: 34 State St., Hartford, Conn. Died Aug. 23, 1957; buried Manchester, Conn.

CHENEY, Monroe George (chē'nē), petroleum geologist; b. Franklinville, N.Y., Sept. 1893; s. Monroe George and Annie Naomi (Button) C.; B.S., Cornell U., 1916; student Royal Sch. of Mines, London, Eng., 1919; m. Margaret Booth, June 8, 1918; children—Monroe George, Harris Graham. Geologist, various business interests, 1916-17; cons. geologist and pres. Anzac Oil Corp., Coleman, Tex., since 1919. Served with U.S. Army, 1917-19; 111th Engrs., 36th Div., 1918-19. Fellow Geol. Soc. Am., A.A.A.S.; mem. Am. Assn. Petroleum Geologists, (sec.-treas., 1934; pres. 1945), Soc. Econ. Geologists, Am. Inst. Mining and Metall. Engrs., Soc. Explor. Geophysicists, Am. Geog. Soc., Am. Geophysical Union, Am. Petroleum Inst., Sigma Phi Epsilon. Contributor numerous articles on geology and oil developments to tech. jours. Home: 1015 W. Walnut St. Office: State Bank Bldg., Coleman, Tex. Died Sept. 28, 1952; buried Overall lease, near Coleman, Tex.

CHENNAULT, Claire Lee (shen'nawlt), airline exec., ret. army officer; b. Commerce, Tex., Sept. 6, 1893; s. John S. and Jessie (Lee) C.; grad. La. State Normal Coll., La. State U.; m. Nell Thompson, Dec. 25, 1911 (div. 1946); children—John S., Max T., Jessie Nell (Mrs. A. R. Lee), Charles L., Pat. T., David W., Robert K., Rosemary L. (Mrs. Norman H. Marten); m. 2d, Anna Chan, Dec. 2, 1947; 2 daus. Claire, Cynthia. Pub. sch. teacher, La., 1908-13; commd. 1st lt. Inf., U.S. Army, trans. to Aviation Sect., Signal Corps, 1917; flight training, 1918; Mexican Border Patrol, 1919-23, Hawaiian Pursuit Squadron, 1923-26, instr. Brooks Field, 1926-30, spl. aviation training, 1930-31, mem. U.S. Army Pursuit Development Bd. 1931-36, leader Air Corps Exhbn. Group, 1932-36, retired 1937; adv. to Chaing Kai-shek, 1937-41; leader Flying Tigers; recalled to active duty and promoted to brig. gen., 1942, organized and comd. China Air Task Force, 1942, activated 14th Air Force and comd. 1943-45;

maj. gen., 1943, retired 1945; organized CNRRA Air Transport, pres., dir., 1946-48; pres., dir. Civil Air Transport, Inc., 1948-50, chmn., dir., 1950-55; chmn., dir. Asiatic Aviation Co., Ltd., CAT, Inc., 1955—; dir. Chinese Air Transport, Ltd. Decorated D.S.M. Army and Navy, Air Medal, D.F.C., D.F.C. Cluster, Air Medal Cluster, D.S.M. Cluster) Chinese Long Sword, Chinese Cloud and Banner Fifty Class, Blue Sky and White Sun, Chinese Cloud and Banner Second Class, Chinese Army, Navy and Air Force Medal; Comdr. British Empire; Croix de Guerre with Palm, Legion of Honor; Chevalier Polonia Restituta. Mem. Am. Legion, V.F.W. Mason. Protestant. Clubs: American, Columbia Country, Shanghai Amateur Baseball (pres., 1948) (all China). Author: Role of Defensive Pursuit, 1933; Way of a Fighter, 1948; also numerous mil. texts and articles. Home: 12 Uri Chang, Taipeh, Formosa. Office: 801-918 16th St., Washington. Died July 1958.

CHERRY, Robert Gregg, ex-gov. N.C.; b. York County, S.C., Oct. 17, 1891; s. LaFayette and Harriet E. (Davis) C.; A.B., Duke U., 1914; m. Mildred Stafford, June 28, 1921. Admitted to bar, 1914, and since engaged in practice of law, Gastonia, N.C.; mayor of Gastonia, 1919-23; representative, N.C. Gen. Assembly, 1931-40, speaker of house, 1937; state senator, 1941-43; gov. of N.C., 1945-49; resumed practice of law Gastonia, N.C., 1949. Served as capt., Co. A, Machine Gun Battalion, 30th Div., U.S. Army, 1918-19; overseas, 1918-19; maj., 120th N.C. Nat. Guard, 1920-23. Mem. bd. trustees Duke U. Mem. Gaston County, N.C. (vice pres. 1934-35) and Am. bar assns., Sons of Confederate Vets., Am. Legion (state comdr. 1928-29). Democrat. Methodist. Mason (K.T.), Knight of Pythias, Knight of Khorassan, Red Man, Odd Fellow, Elk. Home: 212 W. Ninth Av., Gastonia, N.C. Died June 25, 1957; buried Mausoleum, Gaston Meml. Park, Gastonia.

CHERRY, Wilbur Harkness, prof. law; b. Toledo, O., Nov. 28, 1887; s. William (M.D.) and Kate (Lenderson) C.; B.A., McGill U., 1907; LL.B., Columbia U., 1910; unmarried. Admitted to bars of N.Y., 1910, Minn., 1912; associated with law firm Esselstyn & Haughwout, N.Y. City, 1910-11; practiced law, Minneapolis, 1912-25; instr. law, U. of Minn., 1914-17, prof. law, part time, 1917-25, full time since 1925. Sec. Minn. Crime Commn., 1926-27; member U.S. Supreme Court Advisory Com. on Rules of Civil Procedure since 1935; adviser, Code of Evidence, Am. Law Inst., 1939-42; compliance commr., War Production Board, 1942-46. Mem. Am. Bar Association (house of delegates 1939). Minn. State Bar Assn. (mem. drafting Com. for Minn. Business Corp. Act, 1933; drafting com. for Probate Code, 1935; mem. bd. govs. 1926-43), Assn. of Am. Law Schools (pres. 1939), Minneapolis Legal Aid Society (pres. since 1947), Phi Delta Phi. Independent Republican. Clubs: Campus, Minneapolis Athletic. Home: Minneapolis Athletic Club, Minneapolis. Died Feb. 21, 1950.

CHERWELL, 1st Baron, of Oxford (Frederick Alexander Lindemann) (chär'wĕl), Brit. govt. ofcl.; b. Sidholme, Sidmouth, Devon, Eng.; s. A. F. Lindemann; student Blair Lodge, Darmstadt, U. Paris; Ph. D., Berlin U. Prof. exptl. philosophy and fellow Wadham Coll. since 1919; student Christ Ch. since 1921; personal asst. to Prime Minister, 1940; paymaster-gen., 1942-45, 1951-53; mem. United Kingdom Atomic Energy Authority. Created Baron Cherwell of Oxford, 1941. privy councillor, 1943; Companion of Honour, 1953. Served as exptl. pilot, dir. phys. lab. R.A.F., 1914-18. Fellow Royal Soc. Author articles profl. publs. Home: Christ Church, Oxford. Office: Clarendon Laboratory, Oxford, Eng. Died July 2, 1957.

CHESLEY, Albert Justus, health ofcl.; b. Mpls., Sept. 12, 1877; s. Clarence Percival and Aline Kilbourne (Goodale) C.; M.D., U. Minn., 1907; m. Placida Gardner (M.D.), Feb. 13, 1920; 1 dau., Emma Louise. With Minn. Bd. Health 1902— successively in lab. service epidemiologist, dir. dv. epidemiology, dr. dv. preventable diseases, 1902-21, sec., exec. officer state bd., 1921—; became prof. pub. health, dept. preventive medicine U. Minn., 1925, ret. as clin. prof. emeritus. Pres. Conf. of State and Provincial Health Authorities of N.A., 1924, sec., 1927-45, Arthur T. McCormack award, 1950. Mem. bd. sci. dir., internat. health div. Rockefeller Found. Served with 13th Minn. Vol. Inf., Spanish-Am. War; pub. health expert to A.R.C. Commn. to France, also chief of staff, to Poland, later commr. to Poland, 1918-20. Decorated War with Spain, Philippine Insurrection campaign medals, 8th Army Corps Congl. Medal for Philippine Service (U.S.); Medaille de la Reconnaissance Francaise 3d classe (France); three decorations from Polish govt.; recipient Distinguished service medal Minn. Med. Assn., 1948; Outstanding Achievement award U. Minn., 1951; Achievement in Human Tb Control award Minn. Pub. Health Conf., 1951; Sedgwick Meml. medal Am. Pub. Health Assn., 1955. Diplomate Am. Bd. Preventive Medicine and Pub. Health. Fellow Am. Coll. Preventive Medicine, Royal San. Inst. Gt. Britain (hon.); life mem. Am. (pres. 1930), Canadian (hon.) pub. health assns., Am. Social Hygiene Assn. (hon.); mem. Am., Minn., Hennepin County med. assns., Assn. Mil. Surgeons U.S., Am. Epidemiology Soc., Am. Assn. Pathologists and Bacteriologists, Vets. Fgn. Wars, Nu Sigma Nu. Mason. Home: 11 River Terrace St., Mpls. Died Oct. 17, 1955; buried Fort Snelling Nat. Cemetery, Mpls.

CHESTER, Hawley Thomas, ins. exec.; b. Cleve., Feb. 9, 1889; s. Rev. Carlos Tracy and Helen (Hawley) C.; student U. Pa., 1910; m. Lillian Lowenherz, June 16, 1917; children—Hawley Thomas, Peter Tracy (killed in action 1944). With Insurance Co. of North America until 1925; partner Chubb & Son, 1925—; v.p. Federal Ins. Co., Raritan Twp., 1928—, dir., 1948—; v.p., dir. Vigilant Ins. Co., N.Y.C., 1939—; dir. Cia. de Seguros Federal de Cuba, 1941—, pres., 1945—; dir. Premium Credit Corp., Underwriters Salvage Co., Pennroad Corp. Trustee Peabody Home, N.Y.C., 1938—. Mem. Inland Marine Underwriters Assn. (pres. 1940-41), Bd. Underwrietrs N.Y. (pres. 1937-39), Am. Inst. Marine Underwriters (pres. 1934-36), Assn. Average Adjusters of U.S. (chmn. 1944-45). Clubs: Down Town Assn., India House, Drug and Chemical, Union, The Leash (N.Y.C.); Wee Burn Country (Darien, Conn.). Home: 1120 Fifth Av., N.Y.C.; also Darien, Conn. Office: 90 John St., N.Y.C. Deceased.

CHEVALIER, John B., financial exec.; b. Providence, Jan. 31, 1887; s. Charles N. and Elizabeth Ada (Waterhouse) C.; A.B., Harvard, 1908, A.M., 1909; m. Louisa Howard, Jan. 1, 1921; children—Harold Fine, Charlotte. Engaged in business, Bombay, India, 1909-12, Shanghai, China, 1912-17; banking N.Y.C. and abroad, 1920-34; sec. Am. Asiatic Assn., India House, N.Y.C., 1928—. Red Cross worker at VA Center, Bath, N.Y., 1953. Treas. Am. Econ. Mission to the Far East, 1935. Nat. councillor C. of C. of U.S., 1928—. Trustee Nat. Council of Am. Importers, 1928—. Mem. Federal grand jury, N.Y.C. Mem. administrative council Am. Arbitration Assn.; mem. N.Y. adv. council, Yenching U., Peiping, China; mem. Aero. C. of C. (Washington); mem. Far East com. of N.Y. World's Fair, 1939, India Relief, New York, 1945; trustee Asia Inst., N.Y.C., Moro School, Jolo, P.I. Served as aviator with AEF, France, 1917-19. Mem. 1st Res. Aero Squadron (N.Y.). Mem. Nat. Ski Assn. Republican. Episcopalian. Clubs: Harvard, India House (N.Y.C.); Rowing, Tiffin (Shanghai, China); Bombay (India) Gymkhana; Appalachian Mountain (Boston). Home: 27 W. 44th St. Office: India House, 1 Hanover Square, N.Y.C. 4. Died Sept. 14, 1955.

CHEVALIER, Stuart, lawyer; b. Louisville, Aug. 31, 1879; s. William Plumer and America (Joyce) C.; A.B., King Coll., Bristol, Tenn., 1898, LL.D., 1928; LL.B., Washington and Lee U., 1903; m. Elizabeth Pickett, Oct. 17, 1936. Admitted to Ky. bar, 1904; prof. law Washington and Lee U., 1903-04; asst. city atty. Louisville, 1913-18; prof. Jefferson Sch. Law, Louisville, 1913-18; asst. chief counsel, later chief counsel U.S. Housing Corp., Dept. of Labor, Washington, 1918-19; spl. atty. Bur. Internal Revenue, Washington, 1919-20; partner Miller and Chevalier, N.Y.C. and Washington, specializing in fed. taxation, 1920—. Chmn. Los Angeles County chpt. Nat. Found. for Infantile Paralysis. Mem. bd. trustees Occidental Coll.; mem. bd. Southwest Mus., Am. Assn. for UN, Cal. Ednl. Found. Mem. Kappa Sigma, Phi Beta Kappa Assos. Democrat. Presbyn. Author: A Window on Broadway, 1936; War's End and After, 1943; The World Charter and the Road to Peace, 1946; The U.N.—Its First Six Years, 1952; The Universal Declaration of Human Rights, etc., 1952; also articles published in Vital Speeches. Home: 1065 Charles St., Pasadena 3, Cal. Died July 2, 1956; buried Mountain View Cemetery, Pasadena.

CHEVERTON, Cecil Frank (shĕv'ĕr-tŭn), coll. prof.; b. Rich Hill, Mo., Feb. 1, 1889; s. Frank Henry and Isabelle (Greening) C.; A.B., Drake U., 1914, A.M., 1915, B.S.L., 1916, D.D., 1939; student Columbia and Union Theol. Sem., 1916-17; Ph.D., Boston U., 1918; also D.D. from Pacific School of Religion, 1940; m. Olive Vivian Pope, Sept. 1, 1923; children—Jeanne Alice, Richard Dean, David Pope, Martha Loraine. Professor religious education and Bible, Eureka Coll., Eureka, Illinois, 1918-20; prof. religious education and Bible, Calif. Christian Coll. (now Chapman Coll.), Los Angeles, Calif., 1920-29, pres., Aug. 1930-42; professor, Old Testament, Brite Coll. of the Bible (grad. sem. Texas Christian U.), 1943-47, chairman Undergrad. Sch. Religion, Texas Christian U., since 1947. Mem. Phi Beta Kappa. Member of Disciples of Christ Church. Author: When Kings and Prophets Held the Stage, 1930; Old Testament for New Students, 1951; also author of Sunday school lesson material, "The Bible and Social Living," 1941. "Social Teachings of the Bible," 1928. Home: 2621 University Drive, Fort Worth, Tex. Died Aug. 3, 1953.

CHEW, Samuel Claggett, coll. prof.; b. Balt., Aug. 31, 1888; s. Samuel C. and Agnes Robb (Marshall) C.; grad. Boys' Latin Sch., Balt., 1906; A.B., Johns Hopkins, 1909 (winner Tocqueville medal), Ph.D., 1913, Litt.D. (hon.), 1950; m. Lucy Evans, Dec. 21, 1918. Master, Gilman Country Sch., Balt., 1909-10; fellow, Johns Hopkins, 1910-12; sr. master, the Hotchkiss Sch., Salisbury, Conn., 1913-14; asso., 1914-16, asso. prof., 1916-20, prof. English lit., Bryn Mawr College, 1920-54, professor emeritus, 1954—, vis. prof., 1957—; spl. lectr. Johns Hopkins, 1921, U. Chgo., 1923, Western Reserve U., 1927-29, 1941, Pierpont Morgan Library, 1942, Harvard, 1946, Alexander lecturer, U. Toronto, 1946, lecturer, Claremont Grad. Sch., 1949, vis. prof., 1955-57; vis. lectr. Pomona Coll., 1954-55; research asso. Henry E. Huntington Library, 1943-44. Democrat. Episcopalian. Mem. Modern Lang. Assn., Am. Philos. Soc., Soc. Am. Historians, Phi Beta Kappa. Author: The Dramas of Lord Byron, 1915; Thomas Hardy—Poet and Novelist, 1921, enlarged edit., 1928; Byron in England—His Fame and After-Fame, 1924; Swinburne, 1929; The Crescent and the Rose —Islam and England During the Renaissance, 1937; The Virtues Reconciled: An Iconographical Study, 1947; Fruit Among the Leaves, 1950. Co-author: A Literary History of England, 1948; The Chief Romantic Poets, 1950. Editor works including: Byron, 1936; Tennyson, 1941. Contbr. articles and revs. to periodicals. Home: 603 Woodleave Rd., Bryn Mawr, Pa. Died Jan. 15, 1960.

CHICKERING, Allen Lawrence, lawyer; b. Oakland, Calif., Sept. 20, 1877; s. William Henry and Caroline Amelia (Clapp) C.; A.B., U. of Calif., 1898, LL.B., 1901; law study, Harvard, 1898-1900; m. Alma H. Sherman, May 19, 1903; children—Mary C. (Mrs. Harold R. Erdman), Allen L., William W. (dec.), Sherman, William H. (Killed in action, Lingayen Gulf, P.I. Jan. 6, 1945). In practice of law at San Francisco since 1901; mem. Chickering & Gregory; v.p. San Diego Gas & Electric Co.; dir.; mem. exec. com. Pacific Gas & Electric Co., Pacific Telephone & Telegraph Co., So. Pacific Co.; dir. Caterpillar Tractor Co., Schmidt Lithograph Co., Founders Insurance Company, Riverside Cement Company. Chmn. bd. of trustees Rancho Santa Ana Botanic Garden; mem. bd. of fellows Claremont (Cal.) College. Mem. gen. exec. bd. all Liberty Loan drives, 12th Fed. Reserve Dist., World War. Trustee Hastings Coll. of Law, San Francisco. Mem. Am. Bar Assn., San Francisco Bar Assn., Assn. Bar City New York, Cal. Hist. Soc. (dir.), Delta Kappa Epsilon, Phi Delta Phi. Republican. Conglist. Clubs: Pacific Union (San Francisco); North Fork Association (Placer County, Calif.) Harvard, Lawyers (New York). Home: 11 Sierra Av., Piedmont 11, Calif. Office: 111 Sutter St., San Francisco 4. Died Jan. 6, 1958; buried Mt. View Cemetery, Oakland, Cal.

CHICKERING, William Elbridge, ret. army officer; b. Smithville, N.J., Jan. 8, 1895; s. Charles Holland and Margaret Turner (Reick) C.; B.S., U. Pa., 1916; m. Frances Sladen Bradley, Apr. 2, 1921; children—William Elbridge, Jr., Elizabeth Sladen (Mrs. John Swinton King), John Bradley. Commd. 2d lt. Inf., 1917, advanced through the grades to brig. gen., 1944; retired, 1946; v.p. Internat. Group, Am. Machine & Foundry Co. Awarded Legion of Merit (with Oak Leaf Cluster), Silver Star, Purple Heart; Order of the British Empire; Czechoslovak War Cross, 1939. Mem. Sigma Alpha Epsilon. Clubs: University (N.Y.C.); Army and Navy (Washington). Home: Island Heights, N.J.; also 314 E. 41 St., N.Y.C. 17. Died Mar. 2, 1959; buried Arlington Nat. Cemetery.

CHIDESTER, John Young, editor; b. Williamsport, Pa., Sept. 3, 1881; s. Francis LeRoy and Georgetta (Schuck) C.; grad. high sch., Williamsport, 1900; m. Rachel Estella Neece, Oct. 2, 1902; children—Louis Oren, John Young. Began as reporter on Gazette and Bulletin, Williamsport, 1900, later with The Sun, Grit and as mng. editor of The News; became connected with Pittsburgh Press, 1913, mng. editor, 1922-24, editor, 1924-29; became pub. Daily News Standard, Uniontown, Pa., 1933; now retired. Democrat. Presyn. Mason (Shriner). Home: 312 Morgantown St., Uniontown, Pa. Died Sept. 2, 1948; buried Oak Lawn Cemetery, Uniontown.

CHIDSEY, Thomas McKeen, judge; b. Easton, Pa., Jan. 26, 1884; s. Andrew Dwight and Emily Stewart (McKeen) C.; A.B., Lafayette Coll., 1904, LL.D., 1948; LL.B., U. Pa., 1907; m. Ellen Lea, Nov. 14, 1913; children—Louise Lea (Mrs. Donald F. Torrey, Jr.), Ellen Lea (Mrs. James S. Eckels). Admitted to Pa. bar, 1908; practiced various cos. Pa., N.Y., N.J. fed. cts., 1908-47; atty. gen. Commonwealth of Pa., 1947-50; apptd. by Gov. James H. Duff asso. justice Supreme Ct. of Pa., 1950, elected justice, 1951. Rep. candidate for judge (Northampton Co.), 1923, 1939. Mem. Am., Pa. State bar assns., Phi Delta Phi, Phi Kappa Psi. Episcopalian. Home: 107 E. Wayne Av. Office: Drake Bldg., Easton, Pa. Died Apr. 19, 1958; buried Easton.

CHIFLEY, The Rt. Hon. Joseph Benedict, prime minister Australia; b. Bathurst, New South Wales, Sept. 22, 1885; s. Patrick and Mary Anne (Corrigan) C.; student Patrician Brothers' High Sch., Bathurst; m. Elizabeth MacKenzie, June 6, 1914. Elected mem. Australian Ho. of Reps., 1928, 40, 43, 46; mem. joint Parliamentary com. on public accoun 1929-30; minister for defence, 1931-32; treas., 1941—; minister for post-war reconstruction, 1942-45; acting prime minister April-July, 1945; prime minister, 1945—; mem. Royal Commn. on monetary and banking systems, 1935-36; dir. labor supply and regulations Munitions Dept., 1940; mem. Capital Issues Bd., 1940, mem. Bd. of Inquiry, 1941; gov. Internat. Bank for Reconstrn., Internat. Monetary Fund, 1948—; privy councilor, 1945. Home: 10 Busby Street, Bathurst, New South Wales, Australia. Office: Parliament House, Canberra, A.C.T., Australia. Died June 1951.

CHILD, Charles Manning, biologist; b. Ypsilanti, Mich., Feb. 2, 1869; s. Charles Chauncey and Mary Elizabeth (Manning) C.; Ph.B., Wesleyan U., Conn., 1890, M.S., 1892, hon. D.Sc., 1928; Ph.D., U. Leipzig, Germany 1894; m. Lydia Van Meter Aug. 15 1899; 1 dau. Jeannette Manning. Grad. asst. Wesleyan U., 1890-92; Naples Zoöl. Sta., 1894 and 1902; asst. in zoölogy U. Chgo., 1895-96, successively asso. instr., asst. prof., asso. prof., and prof., 1916-34, prof. emeritu, 1934—; vis. prof. Duke, 1930; Rockefeller Found. vis. prof., Tohoku Imperial U., Sendai, Japan, 1930-31; now lecturer in biology Stanford. Fellow A.A.A.S.; mem. Acad. Scis., Am. Soc. Zoölogists, Am. Naturalists, Am. Physiol. Soc., Am. Assn. Anatomists, Linneau Soc. London (fgn. mem.), Société Royale Zoologique de Belgique (hon.), Phi Beta Kappa. Author: Die physiologische Isolation von Teilen des Organismus (Leipzig), 1911; Senescence and Rejuvenescence, 1915; Individuality in Organisms, 1915; The Orgin and Development of the Nervous Systm from a Physiological Viewpoint, 1921; Physiological Foundations of Behavior, 1924; Patterns and Problems of Development, 1941; also numerous articles giving results of researches, in Am. and European mags. Home: 571 Kingsley Av., Palo Alto, Cal. Died Dec. 19, 1954; buried Greenmount Cemetery, Balt.

CHILD, Katherine Blake, art educator; b. Boston, Apr. 8, 1867; d. Linus and Helen (Barnes) Child; student pub. schs., Boston and Dana Hall, Wellesley, Mass.; studied art at South Kensington Mus., Eng.; pupil of Louis F. Day, in Euorpe, and C. Howard Walker, Boston. Founder, 1910, Child-Walker Sch. of Fine Arts, Inc. (Boston), Child Walker Sch. of Design, Stuart Sch. (a Junior Coll. of the Arts), and Stuart Club (residence for girls); dir. Graudate House (Florence, Italy). Mem. Am. Fedn. Arts, Am. Assn. Museums, Soc. of Arts and Crafts (Boston). Clubs: Woman's City (Boston); Cosmopolitan (N.Y.C.); Lyceum (Paris). Home: 8 Via del Ronco, Florence, Italy. Address: 102 Fenway, Boston. Deceased.

CHILDS, C(harles) Frederick, investment banker; b. Brattleboro, Vt., Nov. 22, 1875; s. Walter Henry and Clara Maria (Davis) C.; B.A., Yale, 1899; m. Edith Harris Newell, Dec. 31, 1900 (died 1952); children—Madeleine C. Pullman, Claire C. McBride, Frederick Newell. Rep. bond dealers in Boston, 1900-03; moved to Chicago, 1904; mgr. western office of Fisk & Robinson, bankers, N.Y., until 1910; mgr. bond dept. Continental & Comml. Trust & Savings, Bank of Chicago, 1910-11; pres. C. F. Childs & Co., Specialists in United States government bonds, 1911-28 and since 1930. Founder Manufacturers Credit Co.; co-founder Investment Bankers Association of America; chmn. Com. of Data compiling First Liberty Loan circulars, chmn. of Organization Com. for sales in State of Ind. Vice-pres. Am. Trust Co. and Am. Nat. Co., San Francisco. Supervisor of Foreign Branch Offices C. F. Childs and Co.-Am. Nat. Co. in London, Paris, Berlin, Amsterdam. Founder and pres. Childs Securities Corp. Author of bulletins "Concerning Economics and U.S. Government Bonds," also a Book concerning U.S. Govt. Securities. Alderman, Lake Forest, Ill., 1908-09, Mayor 1910-11. Republican. Episcopalian. Clubs: Chgo., Onwentsia, Yale, Shoreacres, Attic (Chgo.); Yale, Metropolitan (N.Y.C.). Home: Lake Forest, Ill. Office: 141 W. Jackson Blvd., Chgo. Died Mar. 14, 1955; buried Lake Forest.

CHILDS, Eversley, mfr.; b. Bklyn., Feb. 5, 1867; s. William Henry Harrison and Maria (Eversley) C.; student Polytechnic Inst., Bklyn.; m. Mary Shubrick, Eversley, William Henry Harrison. Began as office boy, Mica Roofing Co., 1884; chmn. and dir. the Bon Ami Co.; dir. Technicolor, Inc., Technicolor Motion Picture Corp. Republican. Presbyn. Clubs: Union League, India House, New York Athletic (N.Y.C.). Home: 710 Park Av., N.Y.C. 21; (summer) Setauket, L.I., N.Y. Office: 17 Battery Place, N.Y.C. 4. Died Dec. 20, 1953.

CHILDS, Frank Hall, law author; b. Findlay, O., Feb. 16, 1859; s. Judge Nathaniel Emmes and Emily (Hall) C.; ed. normal sch.; LL.B., Kent Coll. of Law, Chicago, 1893; m. Amy Hunt, Feb. 18, 1886 (died Oct. 2, 1928). Began in Govt. Printing Office, Washington, D.C., 1878, later in pension office and ry. mail service; began practice of law at Chicago, 1893; teacher various law schools. Mem. Am. and Ill. State bar associations. Republican. Moved to Calif. 1925. Author: Childs on Suretyship and Guaranty, 1907; Childs on Personal Property, 1914; American Business Law (4 volumes), 1918; Where and How to Find the Law, 1923; Elements of Business Law, 1930; also various brochures and articles. Editor: Ewell on Fixtures (2d edit.), 1905. Home: 15218 Friends St., Pacific Palisades, Cal. Died July 6, 1954; buried Woodlawn Cemetery, Santa Monica, Cal.

CHILDS, Geoffrey Stafford, business exec.; b. Media, Pa., July 29, 1892; s. Walter Cameron and Edith (Smith) C.; B.C.S., New York U., 1912; m. Olivia Hughes Waelchli, June 15, 1915; children—Elizabeth, Muriel (Mrs. Leon S. Rhodes), Walter Cameron, 2d, Virginia (Mrs. Hugh H. Gyllenhaal), Geoffrey Stafford, Jr., Alan. Office mgr. Alexander Hamilton Inst., N.Y. City, 1913-26; exec. v.p. Pitcairn Aviation, Inc., Phila., 1926-29; exec. v.p. Autogiro Co. of America, Phila., 1929-34; v.p. Michigan Sugar Co., Saginaw, Mich., since 1934, pres. since 1940; dir. 2d Nat. Bank & Trust Co., Saginaw. Vice pres. U.S. Beet Sugar Assn.; pres. Farmers and Mfrs. Beet Sugar Assn.; dir. Mich. Welfare League. Republican. Swedenborgian. Clubs: Detroit, Saginaw, Saginaw Country, Rotary (pres. 1946-47); Huntingdon Valey Country (Phila.). Author: Office Management, 1924; numerous pamphlets on beet sugar industry. Home: 903 S. Michigan. Office: 2d Nat. Bank Bldg., Saginaw, Mich. Died Dec. 6, 1957; buried Saginaw, Mich.

CHILTON, William Edwin, Jr., publisher; b. Charleston, W.Va., Dec. 2, 1893; s. William Edwin and Mary Louise (Tarr) C.; B.A., Yale, 1917; m. Louise Burt Schoonmaker, June 20, 1920 (died June 1928); children—William Edwin III, Mary Carroll. Pres. Daily Gazette Co., 1922—; mng. editor Charleston Gazette, 1924—. Served as ensign naval aviation, World War I. Mem. Am. Legion, 40 and 8 Soc., Delta Kappa Epsilon. Democrat. Elk. Clubs: Nat. Press, Delta Kappa Epsilon (N.Y.C.); Kanawha Country; Metropolitan (Washington). Home: Charleston, W.Va. Died Sept. 21, 1950.

CHINDBLOM, Carl Richard, lawyer; b. Chicago, Ill., Dec. 21, 1870; s. Carl P. and Christine C.; A.B., Augustana Coll., Rock Island, Ill., 1890; LL.B., Kent Coll. of Law, Chicago, 1898; hon. A.M., Bethany Coll., Kan., 1905; hon. LL.D., Augustana Coll., 1939; m. Christine Nilsson, Apr. 27, 1907; children—Richard Nelson, Ruth Christine (Mrs. Wendell H. Carlson). Teacher Martin Luther Coll., Chicago, 1893-96; admitted to Ill. bar, 1900; atty. Ill. State Board of Health, 1906; mem. Board County Commrs, Cook County, Illinois, 1907-10; county atty., 1912-14; master in chancery, Circuit Ct. of Cook County, 1916-19; mem. Ho. of Reps., 66th to 72d Congress (1919-33), 10th Ill. Dist.; referee in bankruptcy, U.S. Dist. Court, Northern Dist. of Ill., Eastern Div., 1934-42. Republican. Lutheran. Life mem. Am., Ill., Chgo. bar assns.; mem. Am. Judicature Soc. Life member; Chicago Art Institute; American Scandinavian Foundation; American-Swedish Historical Foundation; Swedish Colonial Soc.; Augustana Hist. Soc.; John Ericsson Republican League of Ill. (former pres.); chmn., John Ericsson Memorial (monument) Com., Wash., D.C., 1926. Decorated Comdr., Royal Order of Vasa (Sweden), 1934, Royal Delaware Tercentenary Medal (Sweden), 1938; Royal Swedish-Am. Pioneer Centennial Medal, 1948. Mason. Club: Swedish (Chgo.). Home: 5735 N. Campbell Av., Chgo. 45. Office: 105 W. Madison St., Chgo. 2. Died Sept. 12, 1956.

CHINLUND, Edwin F., corp. exec.; b. Chgo., Nov. 28, 1890; s. Charles Gustav and Wilhelmina Charlotte (Nelson) C.; ed. pub. schs., Chgo., student Northwestern U., 1908-16; m. Lillian Barbara Otto, July 9, 1908; children—Edwin Christian, Harold Charles; m. 2d, Helen Alice Brown, Mar. 19, 1925; children—Thomas Joseph, Stephen James, Edith Helen. Began as jr. accountant, Chicago Railway Co., 1907; C.P.A., Arthur Andersen & Co., Chgo. and N.Y.C., 1918-25, partner, 1925; comptroller Internat. Telephone & Telegraph Corp., 1925-32, v.p. comptroller and dir., 1932-37; partner, Arthur Andersen & Co., N.Y.C. 1937-39; pres. Postal Telegraph, Inc. and Postal Telegraph-Cable Co., 1939-42; v.p. R. H. Macy & Co., Inc. (dir. and mem. exec. com.) since 1942; treas., 1945-57, dir., mem. exec. com., chmn. finance com., cons., 1957—; chmn. Scandinavian Airlines, Inc.; dir. Gen. Pub. Utilities Corp., Gen. Telephone Corp., Western Union Telegraph Co. Dir. Public Health Research Inst. of City N.Y., Jackson Lab. Assn., Hudson Guild, Roosevelt Hosp.; chmn. com. for Modern Courts, Inc., New York, C.P.A., Ill. Mem. Am. Inst. Accountants, Controllers Institute of Am. Clubs: Blind Brook (Port Chester, N.Y.); Century Assn., Union League (N.Y.C.); Vineyard Haven (Mass.) Yacht. Home: 45 Gramercy Park North. Office: 151 W. 34th St., N.Y.C. Died Jan. 1960.

CHINN, Armstrong, railroad official; b. Dallas, Tex., Sept. 26, 1894; s. William Yates and Kate (Armstrong) C.; B.S. and C. E., Va. Poly. Inst., 1916; m. Edith E. Shumadine, Apr. 6, 1920; children—Armstrong, Edith Elizabeth wife of Dr. D. Scott Sears). Instrumentman, C.,B.&Q. R.R., 1916-17 and 1919-22, asst. engr., 1923, div. engr. and roadmaster, 1923-25, asst. roadmaster, 1925-26, asst. dist. engr., maintenance of way, 1926-27, dist. engr., maintenance of way, 1927, dist. engr., maintenance of way, and supervisor work equipment, 1927-29; chief engr., The Alton Railroad, 1929-43, gen. mgr., 1943-45, chief exec. officer 1945-46; pres. Terminal R.R. Assn. of St. Louis since 1946. Served as 2d lieutenant F.A., A.E.F., France, 1918-19. Mem. Am. Ry. Engring. Assn., (past pres.), Roadmasters and Maintenance of Way Assn. of Am., Am. Ry. Bridge and Bldg. Assn. Clubs: Western Railway; Maintenance of Way, Union League (Chgo.); Missouri Athletic, Bellerive Country, Noonday (St. Louis). Home: 4399 McPherson Av., St. Louis 8. Office: Union Sta., St. Louis 3. Died Aug. 27, 1958; buried Norfolk, Va.

CHINN, C(lement) B(ell), banker; b. Frankfort, Ky., Aug. 11, 1891; s. Dr. Clement B. and Jennie (Markham) C.; student Centre Coll., Danville, Ky., 1907-08, U. of Chicago, summer 1916; m. Dorothy Adamson, Mar. 26, 1938. Mem. sanitary dept., Isthmian Canal Commn., Ancon, C.Z., 1910-13; mem. Red Cross Sanitary Commn. to Serbia. 1915; pres. Belcher Oil Co., Miami, Fla., since 1945, dir. since 1924; pres. First Nat. Bank of Miami 1948-52. vice chairman of the board of directors since 1952. Served as capt. Sanitary Corps, 84th div., U.S. Army, 1917-19; Hosp. Centre, Limoges, Bassens, Camp Four, France. Mem. Miami C. of C. (dir.). Democrat. Presbyterian. Clubs: Bath (Miami Beach); Riviera Country (Coral Gables, Fla.). Home: 2601 Hornando, Coral Gables 34. Died Aug. 22, 1953; buried Woodlawn Cemetery, Miami, Fla.

CHIPMAN, Norris Bowie, fgn. service officer; b Washington, June 28, 1901; s. George Bowie and Gertrude (Norris) C.; A.B., Dartmouth, 1925; Russian diploma, Sch. Oriental Langs., Paris, France, 1933; m. Fanny Bunand Sevastos, June 20, 1935; 1 dau., Claudette. Entered fgn. service U.S. Dept. State, 1928, Russian lang. officer, Riga, 1929-30, 1933-34; with Div. Eastern European Affairs, Dept. State, 1934-36, research for territorial studies, 1942-44; head econ. research sect., Moscow, 1936-39; consul and 2d sec., Cairo, 1940-42; polit. reporter Embassy, Paris, 1944-50; 1st sec., Rome, Italy, 1950, counselor polit. sect., 1950; chief internal German affairs div., Office of Polit. Affairs, Office of U.S High Commr. for Germany; 1st sec. Am. Embassy, London to 1957; dep. chief of mission, counselor of embassy, Belgrade, Yugoslavia, 1957—. Clubs: Chevy Chase (Md.); Union (Paris, France). Home: 5 Puskinova, Belgrade. Office: Am. Embassy, Belgrade, Yugoslavia. Died Aug. 7, 1957.

CHISHOLM, Hugh J(oseph), paper mfr.; b. Portland, Me., Apr. 17, 1886; s. Hugh J. and Henrietta (Mason) C.; A.B., Yale, 1908; LL.B., Harvard, 1911; LL.D., U. Me., Bowdoin Coll.; m. Sara C. Hardenbergh, June 25, 1910; children—Hugh Joseph, Mrs. Barbara Cole, William H. Chmn. bd. Oxford Paper Co. and allied cos.; chmn. Nashwaak Pulp & Paper Co.; dir. Maine Central Railroad Co., Grace National Bank. Republican. Clubs: Union League, Yale, Racquet & Tennis, Blind Brook Golf, Links, Leash. Home: Portland, Me. Office: 230 Park Av., N.Y.C. Died Dec. 1959.

CHISHOLM, Sir Joseph Andrew, chief justice of Nova Scotia; b. St. Andrews, Antigonish, N.S., Jan. 9, 1863; s. William and Flora (Mackintosh) C.; ed. St. Francis Xavier U., Antigonish, N.S., 1879-83 (B.A., M.A., hon. LL.D.), Dalhousie U., Halifax, 1884-86 (LL.B., hon. LL.D.); hon. D.C.L., King's U.; m. Frances Alice Affleck, Nov. 1891 (now deceased); children—Mary Patricia Flora (wife of W. F. Mackinnon, M.D.), Frances Alice Marjorie (widow of J. N. Lyons, M.D.), Gwendolyn Agnes (deceased), Katherine Smith, Ellen Mary (wife of Prof. W. R. Maxwell). Began as barrister, 1886; King's counsel, 1907; alderman, City of Halifax, 1907-08, mayor, 1909-12; justice Supreme Court of N.S., 1916-31, chief justice since 1931; served as administrator of N.S. on several occasions in the absence of the lieut. gov. Honors: Knight Bachelor, 1935. Roman Catholic. Club: Halifax (Halifax, N.S.). Edited, Speeches and Letters of Joseph Howe, 1900. Home: 22 Carleton St. Office: Supreme Court of Nova Scotia, Halifax, N.S. Died Jan. 22, 1950; buried Halifax.

CHRISMAN, Arthur Bowie, author; b. nr. White Post, Va., July 16, 1889; s. Isaac Arthur and Mary Louisa (Bryarly) C.; student elec. engring. Va. Poly. Inst., 1906-08. Sch. teacher 2 yrs., also draftsman, farmer, movie extra, lecturer and story teller. Episcopalian. Author: Shen of the Sea (winner John Newbery Medal of A.L.A. for most distinguished lit. for children, 1925), 1925; The Wind That Wouldn't Blow, 1927; Treasures Long Hidden, 1941. Home: Fox, Ark. Died 1953.

CHRISTENSEN, Bernard Victor (krĭs' tĕn-sĕn), college dean; b. Westfield, Wis., Apr. 15, 1885; s. Gunder and Wilhelmina (Detert) C.; Ph.B., U. of Wis., 1917, M.S., 1925, Ph.D., 1927; student U. of Minn., summer 1914; m. Maude M. Scott, June 28, 1911; 1 dau., Phyllis Ann. Rural sch. teacher, Marquette County, Wis., 1905-06; prin. State Graded Sch., Modena, Wis., 1906-08; prin. high sch., Prentice, Wis., 1909-11, Friendship, Wis., 1911-13, Baldwin, Wis., 1913-16; supt. pub. sch., Arcadia, Wis., 1917-19, Augusta, Wis., 1919-23; instr. pharmacy, U. of Wis., 1924-27; prof. pharmacognosy and pharmacology, U. of Fla., 1927-39; dir. Sch. of Pharmacy, U. of Fla., 1933-39; dean coll. of pharmacy, Ohio State U., 1939—. Mem. U.S. Pharmacopocia Revision Com., chmn. sub-com. on volatile oils, 1931-

50; A.A.C.P. rep. Am. Council on Pharmaceutical Edn. Awarded Ebert prize by Am. Pharm. Assn., 1939. Fellow A.A.A.S.; mem. Am. Pharm. Assn. (pres. 1941-42; mem. council, 1941—), American Foundation Pharmacy Edn. (mem. bd. dirs., 1943-48), American Assn. Colleges of Pharmacy (chmn. exec. committee 1943-48, president 1949-50), Ohio State Pharm. Assn., Plant Science Seminar (pres. 1931), Sigma Xi, Rho Chi, Gamma Alpha, Phi Sigma, Beta Phi Sigma. Democrat. Conglist. Mason, Eastern Star. Home: 2230 Abington Rd., Columbus 8. Address: College of Pharmacy, Ohio State University, Columbus 10, O. Died Sept. 13, 1956; buried Wausau, Wis.

CHRISTENSEN, John Cornelius, expert accountant; b. Randolph, Kan., Aug. 18, 1874; s. Niels and Christina Elizabeth (Johnson) C.; B.S., Kan. State Agrl. Coll., 1894; U. of Kan., 1897-98; m. Alice Victoria Ipsen, Jan. 1, 1914. County treas., Riley County, Kan., 1903-07; bank cashier, Leonardville, Kan., 1908-09; dep. bank commr. of Kan., 1909-11; financial sec. Kan. State Agricultural Coll., 1911-13; assistant secretary U. of Michigan, 1914-31, controller of univ., 1931-44, controller emeritus since 1945. Appointed by Carnegie Corporation as financial expert for survey of Carnegie Institute Tech. and Carnegie Inst. Fine Arts, Mus. and Library, 1921; apptd. by U.S. Bur. of Edn. for higher edn. surveys in Kan. and Mass., 1922; apptd. by Gen. Edn. Bd. for coll. accounting surveys, 1923-32; mem. Nat. Com. on Standard Reports for Instns. of Higher Edn. and one of editors of final report of Com., 1935; mem. finance advisory service Am. Council on Edn. Chmn. Nat. Com. for preparation Manual on University Business Organization and Administration. Mem. Phi Kappa Phi. Presbyterian. Clubs: University (Ann Arbor); Rotary. Author of various addresses pub. in pamphlets. Asso. editor Journal of Higher Education. Home: 2127 Woodside Rd., Ann Arbor, Mich. Died Sept. 30, 1952; buried Manhattan, Kan.

CHRISTENSEN, Niels Anton, engr.; b. Toerring, Denmark, Aug. 16, 1865; s. Christian and Anne Marie (Nielsen) Jensen; apprentice in shipbuilding and marine engring.; grad. Tech. Inst. Copenhagen; m. Mathielde Thomesen, Aug. 19, 1894; 1 dau., Esther Marie (Mrs. Charles Jacob Young). Came to U.S. 1891, naturalized citizen. Successively in charge machinery for waterworks of Calcutta, India, then charge refining nitrate of soda, Chile; asso. with Fraser-Chalmers, machinery mfrs., 1892-93; asst. to supt., chief engr. Edward P. Allis Co., Milw., 1894-96; founded Christensen Engring. Co., for mfr. air brakes on cable cars, 1896, with company until 1903. Active during World War I, World War II developing special hydraulic and compressed air equipment for aircraft. Royal Danish vice-consul, Ohio, 1928—. Decorated Denmark Victory Medal, King Christian X. Republican. Episcopalian. Mason (32°). Club: Mayfield Country (Cleve.). Owns over 200 patents. Address: 1719 Sheridan Rd., S. Euclid, O. Died Oct. 1952; buried Van Hornesville, N.Y.

CHRISTIAN, Henry Asbury, physician (ret.); b. Lynchburg, Va., Feb. 17, 1876; lineal descendant of Thomas Christian, who patented land in Virginia, Jan. 15, 1657; s. Camillus and Mary Elizabeth (Davis) C.; A.B., A.M., Randolph-Macon Coll., 1895, LL.D., 1923; M.D., Johns Hopkins, 1900; A.M., Harvard, 1903; hon. Sc.D., Jefferson Med. Coll., 1928, U. of Mich., 1938; LL.D., Western Reserve U., 1931, U. of Western Ontario, 1938; m. Elizabeth Sears Seabury (Mayflower desc.), June 30, 1921. Asst. pathologist, 1900-02, asst. visiting pathologist, 1902-05, Boston City Hosp.; asst. pathologist Children's Hosp., 1903-07; instr. pathology, Harvard, 1903-05, theory and practice of physic, 1905-07, asst. prof., 1907-08, dean Faculty of Medicine and Med Sch., 1907-12, Hersey prof., 1908-39, emeritus since 1939, recalled to active teaching, 1942-46; clin. prof. medicine, Tufts Coll. Med. Sch., 1943-46; dean Faculty of Medicine and Medical School, Boston, Massachusetts, 1908-12; asst. visiting physician Long Island Hosp., 1905; phys.-in-chief Carney Hosp., 1907-12, and to Peter Bent Brigham Hosp., 1910-39, emeritus since 1939; visiting physician, Beth Israel Hospital, Boston, 1942-46. Major Med. Reserve Corps, U.S. Army, 1918-21; commd. but not called to service in World War I. Resident chmn. division medical scis., Nat. Research Council, Oct. 1, 1919-Oct. 1, 1920. Awarded D.S.M. by A.M.A., 1947. Fellow Am. Acad. Arts and Scis., Am. Coll. Phys.; hon. fellow Royal Coll. Phys. (Can.); mem. Assn. Am. Phys. (pres. 1935), Am. Assn. Pathologists and Bacteriologists, A. M.A., Am. Soc. for Clin. Investigation (pres. 1919), A.A.A.S., Boston Med. Library Assn., Mass. Med. Soc., Am. Soc. Exptl. Pathology, Am. Assn. Univ. Profs., Interstate Post Grad. Med. Assn. of North America (president 1931), Sigma Chi, Phi Beta Kappa (asso.), Alpha Omega Alpha, Sigma Xi fraternities; corresponding mem. Medico-Chirurgical Society (Edinburgh), Wien Gesellsch. f. inner. Med. und Kinderheilkunde, Sociedad de Medecina Interna de Buenos Aires. Clubs: Thursday Evening, Examiner, Somerset, Harvard, St. Botolph (Boston); Century (N.Y. City); Country (Brookline). Author: Diagnosis and Treatment of Heart Disease; Principles and Practice of Medicine (4 editions); Bright's Disease; Purpuras; Non-valvular Heart Disease; also papers on pathological and clinical med. subjects. Editor (for Oxford University Press) Oxford Medicine and Oxford Monographs. Home: Longwood Towers, 20 Chapel St., Brookline 46, Mass. Died Aug. 24, 1951; buried Mt. Auburn Cemetery, Cambridge, Mass.

CHRISTIANS, William F(lorian), educator; b. Victor, Colo., Oct. 2, 1903; s. Ward and Flora (Peak) C.; Ph.B., U. Chgo., 1925, M.S., 1932, Ph.D., 1938; Am. Field fellow, U. Grenoble, France, 1926-27; m. Magdalene Schäffer, June 23, 1927; 1 dau., Dagny Schäffer (Mrs. Anthony J. Tarell, Jr.). With accident acturial dept. Travelers Ins. Co., Hartford, Conn., 1927-28; asst. traveling auditor Internat. Harvester Co., Chgo., 1929-31; instr. geography Syracuse U., 1932-33; fellow dept. geography U. Chgo., 1933-34; instr. U. Pa., 1934-39, asst. prof., 1939-44, asso. prof., 1944-54, prof., 1954—. Wage analyst Wage Adminstrn. Agy., 1942-45; geographer OSS, China, 1945-46. Served as lt. col. AUS, 1949, now lt. col. Res. Mem. Assn. Am. Geographers, Sigma Xi, Lambda Chi Alpha. Author: Economic Geography of South America (with R. H. Whitbeck and F. E. Williams), 1940. Contbr.: Global Geograph, 1944, India, Pakistan and Ceylon, 1951; World Political Geography, 1956; Ency. Americana, Ency. Brit. Home: 311 Overhill Rd., Wayne, Pa. Office: U. Pa., Phila. 4. Died Mar. 13, 1956; buried Valley Forge Gardens, King of Prussia, Pa.

CHRISTIANSEN, F. Melius, director of music; b. Eidsvold, Norway, Apr. 1, 1871; s. Anders and Oleane Wilhelmine (Johnsen) C.; came to U.S., 1889; grad. Northwestern Conservatory of Music, 1891; studied Royal Conservatory of Music, Leipzig, Germany, 1897-1899, 1906-07; D.Mus. (hon.), Oberlin College, 1929, Muhlenberg College, also University of Minn., 1937; m. Edith Signora Lindem, July 14, 1897 (died 1949); children—Jacobi Melius, Olaf Christian, Paul Joseph Anders, Elsa Margret. Dir. Sch. of Music, St. Olaf Coll., Northfield, Minn., 1903-43. Decorated Knight Order of St. Olaf, Class I, by King of Norway. Lutheran. Founder and dir. St. Olaf Luth. Choir. Author: Practical Modulation, 1916. Composer: Reformation Cantat, 1917; The Prodigal Son (Cantata), 1918; St. Olaf Choir Series (8 vols.), 1920. Asso. Editor: Lutheran Hymnary, 1913; 50 Famous Hymns for Ladies' Voices, 1914. Founder Christiansen Choral Sch., 1934. Home: Northfield, Minn. Died June 1, 1955; buried Oak Lawn Cemetery, Northfield.

CHRISTIANSON, Adolph Marcus, judge; b. Brummundalen, Norway, Aug. 11, 1877; s. Christian M. and Eline C.; brought to U.S., 1882; student pub. schs.; m. Edith Baldwin, May 14, 1906; children—Ruth Edith, Adolph Marcus. Admitted to N.D. bar, 1900; state's atty. McHenry County, N.D., 1901-05; justice Supreme Court of N.D., 1915-45, chief justice in turn, chief justice, 1945, 4 yr. term. Mem. nat. council, pres. Mo. Valley area council Boy Scouts Am.; pres. Bismarck Community Chest, 17 yrs. Adminstr. Federal Civil Works Adminstrn., 1933-34; chmn. State Emergency Relief Com., 1933-34; state adminstr. Fed. Emergency Relief Adminstrn., 1934. Republican. Mason (33°, K.T.). Died Feb. 11, 1954.

CHRISTIANSON, Theodore, jurist; b. Dawson, Minn., June 4, 1913; s. Theodore and Ruth E. (Donaldson) C.; B.L., U. Minn., 1935, LL.B., 1937; m. Dorothy Joyce Ovrom, June 3, 1939; children—Sally Joyce, Theodore Arthur. Admitted to Minn. bar, 1937; asso. Cummins, Cummins, Christianson & Hammond, St. Paul, 1937-44, mem. firm 1946-50; asso. justice Supreme Ct. Minn., since 1950. Treas. Minn. chpt. Am.-Scandinavian Found. Served as lt. (j.g.) U.S.N.R., World War II. Mem. Am., Minn. State bar assns., Am. Legion, Minn. Alumni Association, Minn. Law Alumni Assn. (pres.), Phi Delta Phi. Clubs: Kiwanis Athletic (St. Paul); Informal. Home: 1338 Hillcrest Av. St. Paul 5. Office: State Capitol, St. Paul 1. Died Sept. 19, 1955.

CHRISTIE, Arthur Carlisle, physician, radiologist; b. W. Sunbury, Butler County, Pa., Dec. 29, 1879; s. Milton Hughes and Harriet Josephine (Rhodes) C.; grad. high sch., Corry, Pa., 1898; M.D., Cleveland Coll. Physicians and Surgeons (medical department Ohio Wesleyan University), 1904; M.S., Ohio Wesleyan, 1919; D.Sc., The American University, 1942; grad. Army Med. Sch., Washington, D.C., 1907; m. Maude Irene Hopkins, June 1, 1904; children—Mrs. Geneva Irene Morris, Carlisle Van Dyke, Milton Arthur, Harriet Inez Beck. Practiced Clymer, N.Y., 1904-06; joined Med. Corps., U.S. Army, 1906; served in Philippines, 1907-10, Columbus (O.) Barracks, 1910-12; prof. operative surgery and Roentgenology, Army Med. Sch., Washington, D.C., 1912-16; resigned as capt.; in World War as maj., lt. col. and col. M.C.; gen. charge X-ray work for Army, 1917-Aug. 1918; apptd. sr. consultant in Roentgenology, A.E.F. in France, Sept. 1918; hon. discharged, Feb. 1919; col. M.R.C. Formerly prof. of radiology George Washington U. Med. Coll. Mem. firm Drs. Groover, Christie & Merritt, specializing in Roentgenology; formely prof. clinical radiology, Georgetown Univ. Med. School; consultant U.S. Public Health Service. Mem. special advisory group Veterans Administration; consultant in radiology Walter Reed General Hosp. Pres. Fifth Internat. Congress of Radiology, Chicago, 1937; chmn. com. on Radiology, Natl. Research Council; hon. consultant U.S. Army Medical Library. Hon. fellow British Faculty of Radiologists, 1950. Mem. editorial bd. Am. Jour. Roentology and Radium Therapy. Fellow Am. Med. Assn., Am. Coll. of Physicians, International College Surgeons; member Am. Roentgen Ray Soc. (pres.). Radiol. Soc. N.A.. Am Coll. Radiology (pres.), Med. Society of D.C. (president). Republican. Methodist. Mason (32°). Club: Army and Navy, Rotary. Author: Manual of X-ray Technique, 1913, 17; Roentgen Diagnosis and Therapy, 1924; Economic Problems of Medicine, 1935. Home: Crescent City, Fla. Office: 1835 I St. N.W., Washington 6. Died June 22, 1956.

CHRISTIE, R. E., v.p., dir. Crucible Steel Co Am.; dir. Trent Tube Co., Snyder Mining Co. Home: 85 Wykakyl Terrace, New Rochelle, N.Y. Office: Crucible Steel Co. of America, 405 Lexington Av., N.Y.C. Died June 27, 1956.

CHRISTOPHER, George H., congressman; b. nr. Butler, Mo., Dec. 9, 1888; grad. pub. schs. of Bates Co.; grad. Hill's Bus. Coll., Sedalia, 1907; married; seven sons and two daughters; owner 975 acre farm, Amoret, Mo. Mem. 81st Congress (1949-51), 6th Mo. Dist., 84th to 85th Congresses, 4th Dist. Democrat. Mason (Shriner), Odd Fellow. Home: Rte 3, Butler, Mo. Office: House Office Bldg., Washington. Died Jan. 23, 1957; buried Oak Hill Cemetery, Butler, Mo.

CHRISTOPHER, George T., automobile mfg. exec.; b. Terre Haute, Ind., Oct. 2, 1887; s. William H. and Rose (Creel) C.; B.S., Rose Polytech. Inst., 1911; m. Marie L. Morrison, Apr. 13, 1914. With Westinghouse Electric & Mfg. Co., 1911-13, beginning as shop apprentice; supt. of production Standard Wheel Co., 1913-16; v.p. in charge mfg. Delco-Remy Electric Co., 1918-27; chief inspector Oldsmobile Motor Car Co., 1927-30; v.p. in charge mfg. Pontiac Motor Car Co., 1930-32, Buick Motor Co., 1932-34; with Packard Motor Car Co., 1934—, pres., gen. mgr., 1942—. Served as 1st lt. Ordnance Dept., U.S. Army, 1916-18. Home: R.F.D. 1, Tipp City, O. Died June 7, 1954; buried Meml. Park Cemetery, Dayton, O.

CHRISTOPHERSON, Charles Andrew (krĭs-tŏf'ĕr-sŭn), lawyer; b. Amherst, Fillmore County, Minn., July 23, 1871; s. Knudt and Julia (Nelson) C.; ed. business coll. and normal sch., Sioux Falls, S.D.; m. Abbie M. Deyoe, Nov. 30, 1897; 1 son, Charles A. Admitted to S.D. bar, 1893, and since practiced at Sioux Falls; chmn. Union Savings Bank, Sioux Falls. Member Board of Edn., Sioux Falls, 10 yrs. (pres. 3 yrs.); elected mem. House of Rep., S.D., 1912, reelected, 1914 (speaker); mem. 66th to 72d Congresses (1919-33), 1st S.D. Dist. Republican. Conglist. Mason (past grand comdr. Commandery S.D.; past potentate A.A.O.N.M.S.); past exalted ruler Elks; past noble grand I.O.O.F.; K.P. Clubs: Minnehaha, Country (Sioux Falls). Home: 1000 S. Phillips Av. Office: Amherst Bldg., Sioux Falls, S.D. Died Nov. 2, 1951; buried Woodlawn Cemetery, Sioux Falls.

CHRISTY, Howard Chandler, illustrator; b. Morgan County, O., Jan. 10, 1873; s. F. M. Christy; ed. at Duncan Falls, O.; m. Mrs. Nancy May Palmer, Aug. 14, 1919; 1 dau., Natalie Chandler. Went East, 1893; since then on New York illustrated periodicals; went to Cuba with 2d U.S. regulars and "Rough Riders"; saw the fighting before Santiago; his letters and illustrations pub. in Scribner's Mag., Harper's Mag., Collier's Weekly and by R. H. Russell, pub. Illustrating serials in Cosmopolitan and Hearst's mags. since 1910; also 3 books for James Whitcomb Riley and 3 of his own books, and others. Medals, Paris Expn., Chicago Expn., Nat. Acad. Design; received honorable mention Buffalo Exposition, etc.; received special medal Society for Sanity in Art, 1941. Renewed portrait painting, 1920, and painted portraits of Will H. Hays, George Harvey, Post Wheeler (counselor Am. Embassy, London), President Warren G. Harding (for U.S.S. Leviathan), President and Mrs. Coolidge, Charles E. Hughes, Senator Coleman du Pont, Bishop Joseph Glass, Mr. and Mrs. E. L. Doheny, Premier Mussolini, Crown Prince Humbert of Italy, Prince Phillip of Hesse, Vice Pres. Garner, William B. Bankhead, Henry T. Rainey, Amelia Earhart, Capt. Eddie Rickenbacker, Alben Barkley, Senator and Mrs. Claude Pepper, Mary Roberts Rinehart, Will Rogers (memorial at Claremore, Okla.), Mrs. Will Rogers, Hon. James A. Farley, Hon. George B. Cortelyou, Comdr. and Mrs. Colvin, U.S.N., Mrs. Hobart Cole-Ramsey, Miss Marjorie Souby, Hon. Henry Steagall, Maj. Gen. James C. Magee, Brig. Gen. L. C. Fairbank, Lt. Comdr. John D. Bulkeley, U.S.N., Hon. S. E. Cox, Edward Bond, Mrs. Donald Munson, Mr. and Mrs. Judson Blount, Hon. Edgar B. Dunlop, Mrs. Dave H. Morris, Brig. Gen. R. K. Robertson, Hon. Kent E. Keller, Mrs. Marjorie O'Boyle, Mrs. Richard Alcott, Mrs. Gordon Johnson, Comdr. and Mrs. P. K. Leberman, U.S.N., Mr. David Knott, Mr. and Mrs. Paul Spencer Clapp, Mrs. Tom Girdler, Col. Arthur Herrington, Miss Anne Pitts, Hon. Chas. Edison, Fritz Kreisler, Sen. George Radcliff, and others; painted "Signing the Constitution," large historical painting in Capitol, Washington, D.C., signers of United Nations Charter, at San Francisco; completed for Capitol Bldg., State of Ohio, Gen. Anthony Wayne's Treaty with Indians at Greenville, O., Opening Northwest Territory; painted portrait Lt. Gen. Raymond McLain (Okla. Hist. Soc.), portraits Hon. Herbert Hoover, Col. Louis Johnson, Mrs. Louis Johnson, James Ferrell, Hon. Sol Bloom, Mary Baker Eddy, Judge and Mrs. Harry Vodrey, Chief Justice Carrington T. Marshall, Mr. and Mrs. Edward Pool, Gene Autry, Thomas Gillcrease, Miss Descygne Gillcrease, Mrs. Rosamond Dodge, Miss Marylen Jones, Mr. and Mrs. Ned Hackett, Francis Cardinal Spellman, Dr. Norman Vincent Peal, Oley Speaks, Richard Goodwin, Postmaster Albert Goldman, Postmaster Thomas Patton, Mrs. Herbert Northrup, Wm. Randolph Hearst, Mrs. Floyd Odlum, Dr. Chas. Lee Smith, Fred Waring, Mrs. Dudley Ingraham, Sylvia Kress, David Knott, Mrs. Agustus Wedell, Walter Teagle, Jr., Mrs. Fred Temple, Mrs. W. J. Alford, Miss Braniff, Edward Barber, Mrs. Joseph M. Bryan, Mrs. Smith Davis, Mrs. Patrick J. Hurley, John D. Ewing, Joseph Callen, Mrs. Grant Mason, Hon. Edith Nourse Rogers; 2 paintings for Stephen Foster memorial museum, "Life of Thomas A. Edison" (capital bldg., Columbus, O.); posters. Home: 1 W. 67th St., N.Y.C. Died Mar. 4, 1952.

CHRISTY, William C., army officer; b. Ariz., Nov. 25, 1885; B.S., U.S. Mil. Acad., 1907; grad. Cav. Sch., 1924; honor grad. Command and Gen. Staff Sch., 1925; grad. Army War Coll., 1928; commd. 2d lt. Cav., 1907, advanced through grades to brig. gen., 1943; served on Gen. Staff Corps, 1928-32, 35-39, 42—. Address: A.P.O. 830, care Postmaster, New Orleans. Died Jan. 31, 1957.*

CHRYSLER, Jack Forker, investment exec.; b. Bellevue, Pa., Jan. 7, 1912; s. Walter Percy and Della Viola (Forker) C.; student Cheshire (Conn.) Acad., 1933; m. Edith Backus, Nov. 26, 1941; children—Helen F., Jack Forker. Apprentice tng., mechanics and engring. Chrysler Corp., Detroit, 1934-37, now dir.; mem. accounting dept. New Gear Process Co., Syracuse, N.Y., 1938; v.p., dir. W. P. Chrysler Bldg. Corp., N.Y.C., 1939-53; dir. Air Express Internat. Corp., Vision, Inc., Electronics Corp. Am. Mem. Am., N.Y. stock exchanges. Trustee Dickinson Sch. Law, N.Y. Med. Coll. of Flower and Fifth Av. Hosp., L.I. U. Served from lt. (j.g.) to lt. USN, 1942-44. Mem. Am. Arbitration Assn. (dir.). Home: 72 E. 71st St., N.Y.C. 21. Office: 405 Lexington Av., N.Y.C. 17. Died Nov. 7, 1958.

CHRYST, Robert D(unn), newspaper editor; b. Syracuse, N.Y., Nov. 8, 1890; s. Mathew J. and Ellen (Dunn) C.; student pub. schs.; m. Katherine E. Sullivan, June 4, 1928; children—Joan Ellen (Mrs. William Charlson), Helen Ann, Carol Catherine, Robert Dunn, Mary Kathleen. Reporter Syracuse Herald, 1908-17, 19-22, asst. city editor, 1916-17, city editor, 1922-46; mng. editor Syracuse Herald Jour., Sunday Herald Am., 1946—. Served s 1st lt. Inf., U.S. Army, 1917-21. Mem. Syracuse Liederkranz Soc., Syracuse C. of C. Roman Catholic. Clubs: Bellevue Golf and Country. Syracuse Yacht. Home: 218 Strathmore Dr., Syracuse 4. Office: 220 Herald Pl., Syracuse 2, N.Y. Died Oct. 10, 1956; buried Syracuse, N.Y.

CHRYSTIE, Thomas Ludlow (krĭst-ē), lawyer; b. N.Y. City, Feb. 25, 1872; s. T. M. Ludlow (M.D.) and Julia A. (Ross) C.; A.B., Columbia, 1892; LL.B., New York Law Sch., 1893; m. Sallie Hooper Morrow, Sept. 29, 1896 (died Feb. 19, 1927); children—Elizabeth Ludlow (Mrs. Ralph Polk Manny), Thomas Witter, Frances Nicholson; m. 2d, Virginia F. Stevenson, May 29, 1929; 1 dau., Julia Ross. Admitted to N.Y. bar, 1894, and since practiced in N.Y City; transfer tax appraiser, New York County, 1911-12; asst. atty. for N.Y. State comptroller, 1912; special assistant attorney general for Conn., 1934, for Mass., 1937. Secretary Citizens Com. of 9 on reorganization of New York Police Force, 1905-06. Trustee Columbia U., 1920-26. Mem. Am. Bar Assn., Am. Law Inst., N.Y. State Bar Assn., New York County Lawyers' Assn., Assn. Bar City of New York, Soc. Colonial Wars, Soc. of the Cincinnati, St. Nicholas Soc., Columbia Coll. Alumni Assn. (ex-pres.), The Pilgrims, Phi Gamma Delta. Democrat. Episcopalian. Mason. Clubs: University, Down Town Assn., Columbia Univ., Phi Gamma Delta Club (ex-pres.), Columbia Varsity "C" Club (ex-pres.), Apawamis. Author: Chrystie on Inheritance Tax, 1914. Home: 580 Park Av., N.Y.C. 21. Office: 15 Broad St., N.Y.C. 5. Died Aug. 14, 1954; buried Woodlawn Cemetery, New Windsor on Hudson, Orange County, N.Y.

CHRYSTIE, Thomas Witter lawyer; b. N.Y.C., Aug. 23, 1902; s. T. Ludlow and Sallie H. (Morrow) C.; student Taft Sch., 1917-20; A.B., Columbia, 1924, LL.B., 1926; m. Helen Duell, June 30, 1927; children—Mabel Halliwell, Thomas Ludlow, II. instr. law Am. Inst. Banking, 1926-29; admitted to N.Y. bar, 1927, since practiced in N.Y.C.; mem. Chrystie & Chrystie, 1932-52, Webster Sheffield & Chrystie since 1952; dir. Woodmont Corp., Detroit. Dir. Soc. for Promoting Gospel Among Seamen Port of New York. Trustee of Columbia University, Taft Sch., Watertown, Conn., 1947-52; chmn. Columbia Coll., Council 1953-54. Mem. Assn. Bar City of N.Y. (exec com. 1950-54), Am. Law Inst., Am. N.Y. State bar assns., N.Y. Law Inst. (sec. since 1952), N.Y. Co. Lawyers Assn., Nat. Tax Assn., Soc. Cincinnati, St. Nicholas Soc., Pilgrims Assn. Columbia Coll. Alumni Assn. (pres. 1949-51), Assn. Alumni Columbia Law Sch. (past treas.), Phi Gamma Delta, Phi Delta Phi. Democrat. Episcopalian. Clubs: Downtown Assn., Columbia U. (past sec.), Century, Shenorock Shore (Rye, N.Y.). Contbr. articles profl. pubs. Home: 343 E. 84th St., N.Y.C. Office: 40 Wall St., N.Y.C. 5. Died Feb. 21, 1956.

CHUBB, Chester Niles, pub. utilities; b. Lawrence, Mass., Aug. 19, 1878; s. Harry Niles and Clara (Taylor) C.; B.S., Mass. Inst. of Tech., 1901; m. Edith Moses, 1907; 1 son, Niles. With United Gas Improvement Co., of Philadelphia, 1902-17, United Light & Power Co., 1917-25; pres. Iowa-Neb. Light & Power Co., 1925-29; represented Am. utility syndicate in Europe, 1929-31; exec. vice-pres. Am. Light & Traction Co., 1931-35, v.p. and dir., 1935-42; pres. and dir. San Antonio Pub. Service Co., 1935-42, dir., 1942-48; pres. United Light & Rys. Co. and Continental Gas & Elec. Co. since 1948. Life mem. Union Interalliée, Paris. Episcopalian. Clubs: San Antonio Country. Home: 308 Torcido Dr., San Antonio 2. Office: Banker's Bldg., Chgo. Died Feb. 9, 1951.

CHUBB, Lewis Warrington, research dir.; b. Fort Yates, N.D., Oct. 22, 1882; s. Col. Charles St. John and Sarah L. (Eaton) C.; high school, Columbus, O.; M.E. in Elec. Engring., Ohio State U., 1905; Sc.D., Allegheny Coll., 1933; D.Sc., U. of Pittsburgh, 1933; m. Mary Porter Everson, Mar. 28, 1910 (died 1919); children—Lewis Warrington, John Everson, Morris Wistar; m. 2d, Ora Lee (Dias) McGregor, May 10, 1926; 1 dau., Vivian McGregor. With Westinghouse Elec. & Mfg. Co., 1905-30; engring. apprentice, 1905-06; in research and development magnetic materials, 1906-18, in charge research sect.; with elec. development sect., materials and process engring. dept., 1916-20; mgr. radio engring. department, 1920-30; asst. v.p. in charge engring. RCA Victor Co., Camden, N.J., Jan.-June 1930; dir. Westinghouse Research Labs., East Pittsburgh, 1930-48. Mem. spl. uranium com. Nat. Acad. Scis., 1941-42; mem. spl. planning bd. on atomic energy Office Sci. Research and Development, 1941-42, consultant to dir. (O.S.R.D.), 1941-43. Awarded John Fritz medal for 1947. Fellow Am. Inst. E.E., Inst. Radio Engrs.; mem. O. State U. Research Found. (bd. dirs.), Phys. Soc., Sigma Xi, Tau Beta Pi. Republican. Episcopalian. Clubs: University, Edgewood Country. Awarded between 100 and 200 patents as result of elec., mech. and chem. researches; Lamme medal, Ohio State U., 1934. Contbr. many articles and papers. Home: "Sunnytop," Churchill Road, Pitts. 35. Died Apr. 2, 1952; buried Allegheny Cemetery, Pitts.

CHURCH, Angelica Schuyler, artist and sculptor; b. Briarcliff, N.Y., Apr. 11, 1877; d. Benjamin Silliman and Mary (Van Wyck) C.; student Brearley Sch., N.Y. Sch. of Applied Design for Women, 1901-05; also studied under Beard, Chase and Alphonse Mucha, of Paris. Painter and modeler of figures, 1905—; supr. modeling and sculpture, Finch-Lenox Sch., N.Y.C., 1916-20; best known figures are On Duty and The Rescue, mounted police groups, purchased by Andrew Carnegie for the N.Y. Police Dept., life size figure of Christ in Calvary Ch., N.Y., Our Lady of Peace and Spirit of the Dutch Pioneer. Recipient Audubon Soc. silver medal and Internat. Flower Show sweepstake gold medal, 1921. Conducts courses for teachers of art; makes facsimile copies of paintings; painter of miniatures. Active in Red Cross and War Camp Community work, World War I. Mem. Mus. French Art (life), Ossing Hist. Soc. Republican. Episcopalian. Home: 23 Dale Av., Ossining, N.Y. Died May 5, 1954.

CHURCH, Benjamin Butler, social worker; b. Boston, Dec. 23, 1883; s. Titus and Maria (Mingo) C.; A.B., Livingstone Coll., Salisbury, N.C.; m. Grace Peters, Dec. 23, 1907. Teacher, State Indsl. Sch., Bordentown, N.J., 1907-11, Livingstone Coll., 1911-17; with war work council YMCA, 1917-19; with nat. staff Nat. Recreation Assn. (New York), 1919-21; teacher Livingstone Coll., 1921-26; dir. South Side Boys' Club, Chgo., 1926—. Served as mem. draft bd. during World War II. Recipient Keystone bronze medal from Boys' Clubs of America, for distinguished service, 1949. Pres. Boys' Club Assn. Chgo. Mem. Omega Psi Phi. Republican. Deceased.

CHURCH, Denver Samuel, ex-congressman; b. Folsome, Cal., Dec. 11, 1866; s. Emeory J. and Katherine (Rutan) C.; A.B., Healdsburgh Coll., Cal., 1885; m. Louise Derrick, Dec. 30, 1889. Admitted to Cal. bar, 1893; dist. atty. Fresno County, 1907-13 (resigned); mem. 63d to 65th Congresses, 7th Cal. Dist., 73d Congress, 9th Cal. Dist. Democrat. Address: Fresno, Cal. Died Feb. 22, 1952.

CHURCH, John Huston, army officer; b. Pa., June 28, 1892; s. William and Elizabeth (Kime) C.; grad. Bucknell Acad., Lewisburg, Pa., 1910; student N.Y.U., 1915-17; grad. Inf. Sch., 1921, Command and Gen. Staff Sch., 1937; m. Jean Haller, Sept. 1, 1922; 1 dau., Martha J. Commd. 2d lt., inf. U.S. Army, 1917, advancing through grades to maj. gen.; comdr. 24th Div., Korea, 1950; comdr. Inf. Center, Ft. Benning, Ga., 1951-52. Decorated D.S.C., Silver Star, Legion of Merit, Purple Heart with 2 clusters. Office: care Dept. of the Army, Washington 25. Died Nov. 3, 1953.*

CHURCHILL, Everett Avery, educator; b. Hanover, Mass., Dec. 2, 1892; s. Edward Thomas and Edith Forest (Mann) C.; grad. Bridgewater (Mass.) State Normal Sch., 1914; A.B., magna cum laude, Wesleyan U., Conn., 1917; post-grad. work, Boston U., Harvard; Ed.M., Harvard, 1921, Ed.D., 1924; m. Lucy Isabel Hutchinson, Mar. 23, 1918; 1 son, Byron Everett. Prin. high sch., Bowdoinham, Me., 1913-14, North Dartmouth, 1914-16; instr., Huntington Sch., 1919-20; dean Northeastern U. Sch. of Law, Boston, 1920-35; and dir. Schs. of Law, Commerce and Finance, and Business Adminstrn., same, 1922-25; now v.p. Northeastern Univ. Student Plattsburg, O.T.C., May-Aug. 1917; 2d lt., 1st lt. and capt., Camp Devens, Mass.; hon. disch. June 24, 1914. Mem. Sch. Com. Town of Belmont, term 1931-34, chmn., 1933-34; mem. Warrant Com. and Unemployment Relief Com., Belmont, 1933-34; pres. Belmont Relief Soc., 1935-42; mem. Northeastern U. Corp. since 1937, and mem. of bd. trustees since 1941, sec. since 1943; chmn. Babson Inst. Survey Com., 1937. Mem. Bd. Immigration and Americanization, Mass., 1939-45. Mem. New England Association Colls. and Secondary Schools, Nat. Edn. Assn., American Association for Adult Edn., 6th International Congress of Philosophy, Am. Acad. Polit. and Social Science, Soc. for Advancement of Edn., Inc., A.A.A.S., Phi Beta Kappa, Phi Delta Kappa, Kappa Delta Phi. Republican. Methodist. Mason. Club: Commons. Editor: Instruments of Social Progress, 1938; Education for Defense, 1940. Home: 32 Fernald Dr., Cambridge, Mass. Office: 360 Huntington Av., Boston, Mass. Died Dec. 29, 1959.

CHUTE, Charles Lionel (chūt), social economist; born at Saugus, Massachusetts, August 4, 1882; s. Rev. Edward L. and Julia Hawes (Cleaveland) C.; A.B., Oberlin Coll., 1904; A.M., Columbia, 1910; grad. New York Sch. Social Work, 1910; m. Audrey Smith Chute, Aug. 3, 1915; children—Eloise, Alfred Lionel. Special agent of the National Child Labor Com., N.Y. City, 1910-12; sec. Pa. Child Labor Assn., Phila., 1912-13; sec. N.Y. State Probation Commn., Albany, N.Y., 1913-21; exec. dir. Nat. Probation and Parole Assn., N.Y. City, 1921-48, hon. v.p. and mem. bd. trustees since 1948; sec. Interprofl. Commn. on Marriage and Div. Laws; mem. U.N. sub-com. on Probation; bd. dirs. Am. League to Abolish Capital Punishment. Mem. Am. Assn. of Soc. Workers, Am. Prison Assn., Town Hall Club. Author of chapters in "Probation and Criminal Justice," "Probation Year Book" Crime, Courts and Probation (with Marjorie Bell), 1956; and numerous reports and mag. articles. Home: Mountain Lakes, N.J. Office: 1790 Broadway, N.Y.C. 19. Died Sept. 25, 1953; buried Newburyport, Mass.

CLAGUE, Frank, ex-congressman; b. nr. Warrensville, O.; s. Philip and Catherine (Brew) C.; ed. State Normal Sch., Mankato, Minn.; m. Stella Porter, Apr. 25, 1895. Teacher pub. schs. 4 yrs.; admitted to Minn. bar, 1891; pros. atty. Redwood Co., Minn., 1895-1903; mem. Minn. Ho. of Rep., 1903-07 (speaker, 1905); mem. Minn. Senate, 1907-15; judge Dist. Court, 9th Jud. Dist. of Minn., term 1918-Jan. 1, 1925 (resigned); mem. 67th to 72d Congresses (1921-33), 2d Minn. Dist. Republican. Episcopalian. Mason (32°, K.T., Shriner), Od Fellow, Elk. Home: Redwood Falls, Minn. Died Mar. 25, 1952.*

CLAIR, Edward L., business exec.; born Washington, Pa., Jan. 20, 1894; s. John J. and Elizabeth (Foley) C.; student Duquesne U., Pittsburgh, 1910; B.S., Carnegie Inst. Tech., Pittsburgh, 1914; m. Anne Catherine Gilday, Nov. 9, 1920; children—John E. (dec.), Mrs. Mary Patricia Johnson. Employe Interlake Iron Corp., and predecessor company, Cleveland, in operation of blast furnace and by-product coke ovens, 1920, pres. since 1949; also pres. Olga Coal Co. since 1949. Mem. Am. Inst. of Mining and Metall. Engrs., Am. Iron and Steel Inst. Republican. Roman Catholic. K.C. Home: 19101 S. Moreland Blvd., Shaker Heights 22, O. Office: Union Commerce Bldg., Cleveland 14. Died June, 1951.

CLANCY, Frank J., newspaper exec.; b. Elmira, N.Y., Jan. 15, 1891; s. James and Alice (Coleman) C.; student Union Coll., Schenectady, 1908-10; m. Margaret Sullivan, Sept. 21, 1921 (dec. Feb. 1951). Reporter, copy editor, legislative corr., Buffalo Express, 1913-23, bus. mgr., 1923-26, dir., sec., 1923-26; dir., sec. Buffalo Courier-Express, 1926-41, bus. mgr., 1941-43, gen. mgr., treas., 1943-48, v.p., 1949-55, chmn. bd., 1956—; treas. radio sta. WEBR, Niagara Photo Engraving Co. Mem. Am. Newspaper Publishers Assn., Sigma Delta Chi. Republican. Catholic. Club: Buffalo Country. Home: 675 Delaware Av., Buffalo 2. Office: 785 Main St., Buffalo 5. Died Dec. 11, 1958.

CLAPP, Clyde Alvin, ophthalmologist; b. Chatham, O., May 29, 1880; s. Alvin Rice and Martha Maria (Talbot) C.; ed. pub. schs., Ohio, 1886-98; M.D.,

Baltimore Med. Coll., 1902; m. Lilian A. Dickason, June 25, 1905 (died 1914); children—Roger Alvin, Clyde Melville; m. 2d, Ellen L. Richardson, Aug. 7, 1928. Began practice in Baltimore, 1902; specialized in ophthalmology since 1905; asso. professor ophthalmology, Baltimore, Med. Coll., 1910-13; asso. in ophthalmology, U. of Md., 1913-20, asso. prof., 1920-22, professor of ophthalmology; demonstrator in ophthalmology, Johns Hopkins U., 1922-23, associate prof., 1923-48, now emeritus associate professor of ophthalmology; surgeon Baltimore Eye and Ear Hospital since 1918; ophthalmologist St. Vincent's Infant Asylum. Member A.M.A., American Ophthal. Soc., Am. Coll. Surgeons, Baltimore City Med. Soc., Ophthal. Soc. United Kingdom. Republican. Presbyterian. Club: Baltimore Country. Author: Cataract-Etiology and Treatment, 1934. Contbr. tech. articles on original research. Home: 300 E. Cold Spring Lane. Office: 513 N. Charles St., Baltimore, Md. Died April 9, 1955.

CLAPP, Paul Spencer, elec. engr.; b. Toledo, Ia., July 29, 1890; s. Samuel E. and Nellie (Morse) C.; B.S. in E.E., Ia. State Coll., 1913, E.E., from same coll., 1923; m. Rosalind Wainwright, June 24, 1932; children—Paul, Rosalind, Julia Ann. With the Western Electric Co. at Chicago and New York, engring. research, engr. on first transcontinental telephone line, also on early transoceanic telephone experiments, 1913-17; assistant purchasing agent Allied Machinery Corporation, Feb.-Sept. 1917; with International Western Electric Co., 1918-19; managing director Nat. Electric Light Assn., 1926-32; v.p. Columbia Gas and Electric Corp., 1932-42; v.p. Ohio Fuel Gas Co., 1942—, Cincinnati Gas & Elec. Co., 1942—; mem. bd. Columbia Engring. Corp., v.p. since 1945. Sec. St. Lawrence Commn. of U.S., 1924-26, Second Nat. Radio Conf., 1925. Commissioned 1st lieut. Signal Corps, U.S. Army, 1917, later captain; served in U.S. and France; with Peace Commission, Paris, and Am. Relief Administration in Central Europe and Russia, returning to U.S., 1923; spl. asst. to Herbert Hoover, Secretary of Commerce, 1923-26; retired colonel Engineers Corps, 1949. Decorated by Roumanian Govt., 1919. Awarded Anson Marstin medal for achievement in engineering, Iowa State Coll., 1945. Received Alumni Merit Award, Iowa State Coll., 1948. Member Am. Inst. E.E., Edison Electric Inst., Nat. Assn. Mfrs., Tau Beta-Pi, Delta Upsilon. Republican. Protestant. Clubs: University, Recess (New York); Manhasset Bay Yacht (Washington). Address: 123 E. 78th St., N.Y.C. Died Dec. 5, 1953; buried Arlington Nat. Cemetery.

CLAPP, Philip Greeley, musician; b. Boston, Mass., Aug. 4, 1888; s. Henry Lincoln and Florence Sue (Greeley) C.; A.B., Harvard, 1908, A.M., 1909, Ph.D., 1911; m. Gladys Elizabeth Chamberlain, Dec. 26, 1919 (divorced 1929); m. 2d, Mildred Ethel Wright, July 21 1934 divorced on June 9, 1951). Instructor of music at Harvard, 1911-12, Middlesex Sch., 1912-14; dir. music, Dartmouth, 1915-18; band leader, A.E.F., 1918; prof. and dir. music, State U. of Ia., since 1919; dir. extension Juilliard Sch. of Music, 1927-28. Guest prof. U. of Calif., Berkeley, summers, 1926, 29, Los Angeles, summer, 1927; guest condr., Am. Orchestral Assn., 1929. Member Harvard, Musical Assn., Phi Beta Kappa. Composer: Norge (tone poem), produced Boston Symphony Orchestra, 1909; In Summer (prelude), produced St. Louis Symphony Orchestra, 1914, also by Minneapolis Symphony Orchestra, 1925, and Chicago Symphony Orchestra, 1928; Symphony in E minor, Boston Symphony Orchestra, 1914; Symphony in E flat major, Boston Symphony Orchestra, 1917; Symphony in A major, Peoples Symphony Orchestra of Boston, 1931; Symphony in E major, Waterloo (Ia.) Symphony Orchestra, 1933; Overture to a Comedy, Cleveland Philharmonic, 1940, St. Louis Symphony Orchestra, 1943; An Academic Diversion, Eastman-Rochester Symphony, 1942; A Chant of Darkness (text by Helen Keller), for chorus and orchestra, 1935 and 1947; The Taming of the Shrew (opera), 1948; The Flaming Brand (opera), 1950; published compositions: Brass Sextet, Woodwind Quintet and Trombone Quartet; (part songs) Remembrance, The Quiet Hour, Lenore; (anthem) O Gladsome Light. Contbr. to Boston Evening Transcript, Musical Quarterly, etc. Received Bruckner Medal of Honor, 1940, Mahler Medal of Honor, 1942, both awarded by Bruckner Soc. of America. Home: 430 S. Summit St., Iowa City, Ia. Died Apr. 9, 1954.

CLARK, Albert Montgomery, judge; b. Lawson, Mo., Mar. 4, 1879; s. Robert James and Sally Ann (Moore) C.; student coll. at Lawson, Mo., 1896-98; LL.B., Vanderbilt U., 1900; m. Bessie Zimmerman, Jan. 28, 1906; children—Irma Fay (Mrs. David E. Harrison), Ida Ann (Mrs. Powell B. McHaney), Jean Elizabeth (Mrs. Bernard J. Galbreath). Admitted to Mo. bar, 1900, began practice at Richmond, Mo.; pros. atty., 1913-16; mem. State Legislature, 1917-20; state senator, 1931-38; judge Supreme Court of Mo., 1939—; dir. Richmond Savings & Loan Assn. Pres. Richmond, Mo., Sch. Bd., 1922-35. Mem. Mo. Constl. Conv., 1922-23; chmn. Mo. Commn. to Chgo. World's Fair, 1933-34. N.Y. and San Francisco World's fairs, 1939. Mem. Pi Kappa Alpha, Delta Theta Phi. Democrat. Methodist. Mason, Odd Fellow. Clubs: Rotary (Richmond, Mo.); Country (Jefferson City, Mo.). Address: Supreme Court Bldg., Jefferson City, Mo. Died June 9, 1950; buried Lawson, Mo.

CLARK, Alfred Edward, lawyer; b. Ont., Can., Aug. 17, 1873; s. John and Mary Jane (Caldwell) C.; ed. pub. schs. Minn.; m. Dehlia E. Wagner, Mar. 1918. Practiced law, Mankato, Minn., 1897-1905; located in Portland, Ore., 1906; chmn Charter Commn. City of Portland, 1911; mem. commn. apptd. 1911 to revise judicial system of Oregon and modes of pleading and procedure; mem. Portland Civil Service Commn., 1913-15. Mem. Am. and Ore. State bar assns. Commd. maj. asst. judge adv. gen., U.S. Army, Sept. 1917; hon. disch., Aug. 1919, with rank of col. Apptd. rep. War Dept., Sept. 1919, to sit with Imperial Munitions Bd. in adjusting war claims and contracts between U.S. and Can. Clubs: University, Aero (Portland); Nat. Republican (New York). Author articles and monographs on internat. and constl. law. Home: Portland, Ore. Office: Yeon Bldg., Portland, Ore. Died Jan. 30, 1951; buried Riverview Cemetery, Portland, Ore.

CLARK, Allan, sculptor; b. Missoula, Mont., June 8, 1896; s. Harry Percival and Bess (Harrison) C.; student Stadium High Sch. and Puget Sound Coll., Tacoma, Art Inst. Chgo., Art Students League, N.Y.C.; m. Joy Cassidy, June 26, 1936. Began as sculptor, 1917; worked with stone and terra cotta; became instr. Beaux-Arts Inst. of Design, N.Y.C.; traveled in Japan, Korea, China to study Oriental art, 1924-27; visited the cave chapels, Turkestan, for Fogg Museum and made drawings for the museum; has applied the Oriental technique to wood carving. Works include portrait bust of Madam Galli-Curci; figure of Nakamura Gonjiro (Honolulu Acad. Art); wood carving of Maria of Cochiti (Seattle Art Museum); bust of James Russell Lowell (Hall of Fame); bust of Klah, Navajo medicine man (Mus. of Navajo Ceremonial Arts); Study for a Garden Pool, Whitney Museum; Mei-Kwei Met. Mus., N.Y.C. Recipient Rosenwald Meml. prize Grand Central Art Galleries, 1930. Mem. Nat. Inst. Arts and Letters. Address: Jacona Ranch, Santa Fe, N.M. Died Apr. 17, 1950.

CLARK, Allan Jay, metallurgical engr.; b. Jersey City, N.J., Apr. 12, 1874; s. Bernard Stearns and Adele (Shiffer) C.; grad. Berkeley Sch., New York, 1891; E.M., Sch. of Mines (Columbia), 1896; hon. Dr. Engring., S.D. Sch. of Mines, 1940; m. Jane Parfrey, Oct. 2, 1901; children—Elizabeth Adele, Bernard Stearns, Marian Louise. Engr. with Tenn. Coal, Iron & R.R. Co., 1896; metallurgist with Homestake Mining Co., 1897-1927, chief metallurgist since 1907; cons. practice; retired, 1943. State chmn. for S.D., Naval Cons. Bd., 1915. Mem. Am. Inst. Mining and Metall. Engrs., Alpha Delta Phi. Republican. Episcopalian. Contbr. papers on metall. of gold; awarded Consol. Goldfields medal, Instn. Mining and Metallurgy (London), for paper "Metallurgy of the Homestake Ores," of which was co-author. Home: Spearfish, S.D. Died March 23, 1950; buried Rosehill Cemetery, Spearfish, S.D.

CLARK, Alva Benson, elec. engr.; b. Clay Center, O., Feb. 15, 1890; s. George Frederick and Nellie Judith (McIntyre) C.; B.E.E., U. of Mich., 1911; m. Anna C. Harper, Nov. 25, 1920 (now dec.); children—Judith H., Patricia H. (dec.); m. 2d, Helen Kerstetter, Aug. 13, 1938. Elec. engr. Am. Telephone & Telegraph Company, 1911-34; with Bell Telephone Laboratories since 1934, as director of transmission development, 1935-40, director of systems development, 1940-44, vice pres. since 1944. Delegate to Comité Consultatif International Telephonique and Internat. Electro-Tech. Commn. meetings, Belgium and Scandinavia, 1930. Consultant, or member of various divisions, Office Scientific Research and Development, 1941-45; became expert cons. to sec. war, 1944; dir. research and development, Nat. Security Agency, 1954—. Cited as Distinguished Alumnus by U. of Mich., 1941. Fellow Am. Inst. Elec. Engrs., Acoustical Soc. America; senior member of the Institute of Radio Engineers; mem. Tau Beta Pi, Sigma Xi. Clubs: Downtown Athletic, Michigan Alumni (N.Y. City). Author of several pub. papers; holds 44 patents on elec. communication devices. Home: 4301 Massachusetts Av., N.W., Washington. Office: Washington. Died Nov. 14, 1955.

CLARK, Anson Luman, eclectic physician-surgeon; b. Clarksburg, Mass., Oct. 12, 1836; s. Thomas Skeels C.; A.B., Lombard U., 1958, A.M., 1868; grad. Eclectic Med. Inst., Cin., 1861; m. P. J. Lemon, Aug. 20, 1859; m. 2d, Mary F. Dunton, Jan. 22, 1871. Mem. ho. reps., 27th Gen. Assembly, Ill. Pres. bd. trustees Bennett Coll. of Eclectic Medicine and Surgery, Chgo., 1872-1905, prof. diseases of women and obstetrics, 1868-1905. Pres. bd. edn., Elgin, Ill., 1890. Served as 1st asst. surgeon, 127th Ill. vol. inf., 1862-65. Republican. Author: Clark's Diseases of Women, 1878. Home: 106 Spring St. Office: YMCA Bldg., Elgin, Ill. Deceased.

CLARK, Arthur Elwood, business exec.; b. Milford, Conn., Aug. 13, 1871; s. William B. and Mary Hall (Roberts) C.; student Yale Bus. Coll.; m. Grace E. Sackett, June 24, 1898; 1 dau. Madeline (Mrs. J. Lawrence Pond). Entered service of N.Y., N.H.&H. R.R., 1890, asst. sec., 1908-10, sec. 1910-43, retired, 1943, dir., 1937—. Republican. Conglist. Club: New Haven Country, Quinnipack, New Haven Railroad. Home: 19 Old Hartford Turnpike, Hamden, Conn. Died Nov. 6, 1950.

CLARK, Arthur Henry, publisher, mfr.; b. London, Eng., Dec. 20, 1868; s. Joseph and Sophia (Hart) C.; ed. pvt. schs. and Oxford U.; m. Elizabeth J. Baveystock, 1892 (divorced); children—Ethel B., Robert B., Elizabeth B.; m. 2d, Fannie Z. Bell, 1910; children—Mary A., Arthur H., Jr., Wallace B. Came to U.S., 1888, naturalized citizen, 1895. Apprenticed to Henry Sotheran & Co., London, 1885; with A. C. McClurg & Co., Chicago, 1888-91; dir. The Burrows Bros. Co., Cleveland, O., 1892-1901; founder, 1902, and pres. The Arthur H. Clark Co., pubs.; pres. The Cleveland Worm & Gear Co., 1920-28; pres. Cleveland Laboratory Co., 1922-37; founder and pres. Cleveland Inst. of Aviation, 1928-34. Dir., Pacific Southwest Academy. Member American Historical Association, Ill. State Hist. Soc., Western Reserve Hist. Soc., Am. Oriental Soc., Hakluyt Soc., Champlain Society, Am. Polit. and Social Science Assn., Miss. Valley Hist. Soc., Calif. Hist. Soc., Fellow Am. Geog. Soc., Pi Gamma Mu, etc. Mem. C. of C. Republican. Presbyn. Mason. Clubs: Athletic, Rowfant, Lions, Nat. Town and Country, Canadian Campfire. Author: Style and General Format for Publications, 1910; Bibliography of the Publications of the Rowfant Club, 1925; Bibliography of Books on History of States, Counties, etc., of U.S., 1928. Pub. Jesuit Relations and Allied Documents, 73 vols.; The Philippine Islands and Dutch East Indies, 1493-1898, 55 vols.; Documentary History of American Industrial Society, 11 vols.; Early Western Travel Series, 32 vols., and others. Home: 1644 Hill Drive, Los Angeles 41. Office: 1264 S. Central Av., Glendale 4, Cal. Died May 15, 1951; Mountain View Mausoleum, Pasadena, Cal.

CLARK, Austin Hobart, biologist; b. Wellesley, Mass., Dec. 17, 1880; s. Theodore Minot and Jeanette (French) C.; grad. high sch., Newton, Mass., 1899; A.B., Harvard, 1903, grad. study, 1904; m. Mary Wendell Upham, Mar. 6, 1906 (died Dec 28, 1931); children—Austin Bryant Jackson, Sarah Wendell, Hugh Upham, Anne Bradstreet, Mary Holmes; m. 2, Leila Gay Forbes, Sept. 23, 1933. Organizer of expedition to Margarita Island, Venezuela, 1901; in zoöl. research, Lesser Antilles, 1903-05; acting chief of scientific staff of U.S. Fisheries S.S. Albatross, 1906-07; mem. staff Smithsonian Inst., 1908-50, ret. dir. press service, A.A.A.S.; press. relations ofcr. 8th Pan-Am. Sci. Congress, 1940; pub. relations ofcr. Centennial Celebration, A.A.A.S., 1948; vice-chmn. Am. Geophys. Union; pres. Washington Acad. of Sciences; pres. Entomological Society of Washington; member long range planning com. Va. Acad of Science; mem. exec. com. and long range planning com. Southern Association of Science and Industry; member advisory board Virginia Fisheries Laboratory; research work in oceanography, marine biology, ornithology and entomology; served as aide-de-camp to the Prince of Monaco 1921. Exec. com., bd. trustees Nat. Parks Assn.; exec. com., bd. govs. Nature Conservancy. Fellow Royal Geog. Soc. Decorated Knight of Order of Dannebrog (Denmark). Club: Cosmos. Author: Animals of Land and Sea, 1925; Nature Narratives, Vol. I, 1929, Vol. II, 1931; The New Evolution, 1930; Animals Alive, 1948; also monographs and bulletins and about 600 scientific articles in English, French, Italian, German and Russian. Home: 1818 Wyoming Av. N.W., Washington 9, D.C. Died Oct. 28, 1954, buried Mt. Auburn Cemetery, Cambridge, Mass.

CLARK, (Charles) Badger, author; b. Albia, Ia., Jan. 1, 1883; s. Charles Badger and Mary Ellen (Cleaver) C.; student Dakota Wesleyan U., hon. D.Litt., 1923. Methodist. Author: Sun and Saddle Leather (verse), 1915; Grass Grown Trails (verse), 1917; Sun and Saddle Leather, including Grass Grown Trails and New Poems, 1920; Spike (fiction), 1923; Sky Lines and Wood Smoke (verse), 1935. Mem. Phi Beta Kappa. Poet laureate of S.D. Home: Legion Lake, Custer, S.D. Died Sept. 26, 1957; buried Hot Springs, S.D.

CLARK, Barrett H., author, editor; b. Toronto, Can., Aug. 26, 1890; s. S. H. and Anna M. (Fralick) C.; student U. Chgo., 1908-09, 1911-12, U. Paris, 1910; m. Cecile Matilda Smith, Aug. 28, 1916; children—Nancy, Molly, Barrett. Actor and asst. stage mgr., with Mrs. Fiske, 1912-13; instr. in drama, Chautauqua, N.Y., 1909-17; lit. editor Samuel French, pub., N.Y.C., 1918-36; exec. dir. Dramatists Play Service, N.Y.C., 1936—. Mem. bd. dirs. Drama League America, 1915-26; dramatic editor Drama Magazine. Was dramatic dir. Camp Humphreys, World War. Mem. Delta Upsilon. Club: Town Hall. Author: The Continental Drama of Today, 1914; British and American Drama of Today, 1915; Contemporary French Dramatists, 1915; How to Produce Amateur Plays, 1917-25; A Study of the Modern Drama, 1925; Eugene O'Neill, 1926 (revised, 1947); Oedipus of Pollyanna, 1927; Professor Clark, a Memoir, 1928; Speak the Speech, 1930; An Hour of American Drama, 1930; Eugene O'Neill Bibliography (with R. Sanborn), 1931; also author: Intimate Portraits,

1951. Co-editor (with Geo. Freedley) and contbr. to A History of Modern Drama, 1947. Editor: World's Best Plays (58 volumes), 1915-26; Walter Prichard Eaton's Plays and Players, 1916; Masterpieces of Modern Spanish Drama, 1917; European Theories of the Drama, 1918; Jurgen and the Censor, 1919; Representative One Act Plays by British and Irish Authors, 1921; co-editor: Great Short Stories of the World, 1925; Appleton Play-Book, 1926; Great Short Novels of World, 1927; Great Short Biographies of World, 1928; The American Scene (part author), 1930; World Drama, 1932; A World of Stories for Children (in collaboration), 1940: Favorite American Plays of the 19th Century, 1942. Translator and editor: Hervieu's The Labyrinth, 1913; Three Modern Plays from the French, 1914; Four Plays of the Free Theater, 1914; Four Plays of Emile Augier, 1915; Three Plays of Donnay, 1916; Sardou's Patrie! 1915; Hyacinthe-Loyson's Apostle, and Curel's False Saint, 1916; Brieux's Artists' Families, 1918; Two Belgian Plays by Vanzype, 1917; The Fourteenth of July and Danton, and The People's Theater (by Romain Rolland), 1918; (in collaboration) The Judge, and The Story of a Novel and Other Stories (by Maxim Gorky), 1925. Editor America's Lost Plays, 20 vols.; co-editor: One-Act Plays, 1929; Favorite American Plays of 19th Century, 1943; Nine Modern American Plays, 1951. Home: 818 Pleasantville Rd., Briarcliff Manor, N.Y. Office: care Dramatists Play Service, 14 E. 38th St., N.Y.C. Died Aug. 5, 1953.

CLARK, Bennett Champ, judge; born Bowling Green, Mo., Jan. 8, 1890; s. Champ and Genevieve (Bennett) C.; A.B., U. of Mo., 1913; LL.B., George Washington U., 1914; LL.D., Marshall Coll., Bethany Coll., Washington and Lee U., U. of Missouri; m. Miriam Marsh, Oct. 2, 1922 (dec. 1943); children—Champ, Wilbur Marsh, Kimball; married 2d, Violet Heming, Oct. 6, 1945. Parliamentarian U.S. House of Rep., 1913-17; admitted to Mo. bar, 1914; in practice at St. Louis since 1919. Commissioned capt. U.S. Res., Aug. 1917; lt. col. 6th Mo. Inf., Aug.-Sept. 1917; lt. col. 140th U.S. Inf., Sept. 1917-Sept. 1918; col. Gen. Staff, 1919. Elected U.S. senator from Mo. for term ending Jan. 3, 1939; apptd. senator to fill unexpired term of Harry B. Hawes, Feb. 3, 1933; re-elected senator for term ending January 3, 1945; associate justice of the United States Court of Appeals, District of Columbia, since 1945. Past nat. comdr. Am. Legion; past comdr. 35th Div. Vets. Assn.; ex-pres. Nat. Guard Assn. of U.S.; mem. Order of the Coif, Phi Beta Kappa, Delta Tau Delta, Phi Delta Phi, Delta Sigma Rho. Democrat. Presbyterian. Mason, Odd Fellow. Club: Chevy Chase (Washington). Author: John Quincy Adams, "Old Man Eloquent," 1932. Compiler: Constitution Manual and Digest of Practice U.S. House of Representatives, 1913, 14, 15, 16, Joint author: Social Studies, 1934. Home: St. Louis County, Mo. Address: U.S. Court of Appeals, Washington. Died July 13, 1954; buried Arlington Nat. Cemetery.

CLARK, Bobby (Robert Edwin Clark), actor; born Springfield, O., June 16, 1888; s. Victor B. and Alice Marilla (Sneed) C.; ed. in public schs.; m. Angele Gaignat, Sept. 28, 1923. Actor in minstrel shows and Sells-Floto Circus, 1905; with Ringling Bros. Circus, 1906-11; appeared in vaudeville, 1912-16; in burlesque, 1916-21; in reviews (Broadway), 1922-24; in musical shows, 1925-40; with Theatre Guild (The Rivals), 1941-48; in musical shows since 1949. Mem. Actor's Guild. Episcopal Actors Guild, Authors League, Actors Fund of America. Episcopalian. Clubs: Lambs, Players. Author of numerous vaudeville sketches, review sketches, motion picture shorts; also adaptation of Moliere's "Le Bourgeois Gentilhomme," and new version of Victor Herbert's "Sweethearts." Home: 101 W. 55th St., N.Y.C. Died Feb. 12, 1960.

CLARK, Bonnell Wetmore, ret. v.p. Westinghouse Electric & Mfg. Co.; b. Gagetown, N.B., Can., Aug. 1, 1883; s. Dewitt C. and Maude (Wetmore) C.; student U. Mich.; m. Katherine E. Orchard, Nov. 15, 1905; children—Joanne, Katherine, Virginia. With Robertson Cataract Electric Co., 1906; sales mgr. Gould Storage Battery Co., 1916; with Westinghouse Electric Supply Co., 1925—, gen. mgr., 1929, v.p., 1932, pres. 1937-41; v.p. Westinghouse Electric & Mfg. Co., 1941—. Home: William Penn Hotel. Office: Union Bank Bldg., Pitts. Died Mar. 3, 1955.

CLARK, Cameron, architect; b. Holyoke, Mass., Mar. 24, 1887; s. Edward and Ellen (Phillips) C.; Rotch traveling scholar, Europe, 1912-14; student Mass. Inst. Tech., 1910, Am. Acad., Rome, Italy, 1912; m. Agnes Selkirk, 1921; children—Cameron, Cordelia Perine. Designed instnl., civic bldgs., N.Y., Conn., also residential constrn., Pa., N.Y., Mass., N.J., Conn., Virgin Islands; asso. architect Clark & Arms, 1915-18; pvt. practice since 1918; cons. architect Borough of Manhattan, 1943-45, East River and Harlem River drives, Battery Park Unverpass; designed model homes for Good Housekeeping, Ladies Home Jour., House Beautiful mags. Mem. adv. planning bd. Borough Manhattan, 1943-45; chmn. postwar planning council, Fairfield, Conn., 1946-48, chmn. citizens adv. planning bd., 1949-51; dir. Greenfield Hill Improvement Soc., 1949-52; dir. Fairfield Co. Planning Assn., 1949-53. Served with camouflage sect. U.S.N., World War I. Fellow A.I.A.; mem. Municipal Art Soc. (dir.). Alumni Am. Acad. Rome (treas.). Clubs: Archtl. League N.Y.; Pequot Yacht, Country of Fairfield, Fairfield County Hunt. Home: Merwin's Lane, Southport, Conn. Office: 101 Park Av., N.Y.C. 17: also St. Thomas, Virgin Islands. Died Mar. 23, 1957; Oaklawn Cemetery, Fairfield Conn.

CLARK, Chester Frederic, coll. dean; b. Fitchburg, Mass., 1899; s. Henry Disbrow and Sophia Abbott (Peirce) C.; student Mass. Agrl. Coll., 1919-21, U.S. Coll. Vet. Surgeons, 1924-25; D.V.M., Mich. State Coll., 1929; m. Muriel Hoover, July 1, 1930; children—John Hoover, Marjorie Elizabeth, Andrew Abbott. Faculty dept. animal pathology Mich. State Coll., 1929-46, head dept. surgery and medicine, 1949-51, dean sch. vet. medicine, 1951—; state vet., Mich., 1946-49. Mem. Audubon Soc., Am., Mich. State vet. med. assns., Phi Zeta, Sigma Psi. Clubs: Kiwanis, Hiawatha Sportsman's. Home: 1101 Burcham St., East Lansing, Mich. Died July 28, 1957; buried Evergreen Cemetery, Lansing, Mich.

CLARK, Clifford Pease, educator; b. Ludlow, Mass., Feb. 13, 1872; s. William Pease and Lydia Ann (Edson) C.; student Wilbraham (Mass.) Acad., 1888-91; A.B., Wesleyan U., Middletown, Conn., 1895-96; Ph.D., Princeton, 1910; m. Louise Jane Earle, Sept. 7, 1898; 1 dau., Carita Louise (Mrs. Samuel Spafford Ackerly). Instr. in Greek and Latin, West Newton (Mass.) English and Classical Sch., 1896-97; prof. classical langs. Fairmount Coll., Wichita, Kan., 1897-1907; dean of academic dept. Drury Coll., Springfield, Mo., 1907-09; instr. in classics Dartmouth, 1910-16, asst. prof., 1916-19; founder, 1919, dir. and pres. bd. trustees, Clark School Found., Hanover, N.H.; dir. Dartmouth Nat. Bank. Mem. N.E. Classical Assn., Phi Beta Kappa, Psi Upsilon. Rep. Conglist. Clubs: Graduate, Hanover Golf. Home: 16 Ocean Ridge, Hanover, N.H. Died June 4, 1953.

CLARK, Cyrus J., med. officer; b. Carmel, Ind., Nov. 16, 1900; s. Cyrus J. and Ella L. (Hershey) C.; m. Edith Lakey, Sept. 29, 1929; children—Cyrus J., III, Kenton Eric, Patricia Ellen. Began career as physician; chief med. staff, Indianapolis City Hosp., clinical prof. cardiology, Ind. U. Sch. Med. (chmn. dept. post grad. edn.). Col. M.C., A.U.S.; comdg. officer, 32d Gen. Hosp., World War II. Home: 1501 E. 38th St. Office: 6325 Guilford Av., Indpls. Died Jan. 22, 1953; buried Summit Lawn, Westifeld, Ind.

CLARK, Dan Elbert, educator; b. Ogden, Ia., July 25, 1884; s. Elbert C. and Ada T. (Hitchcock) C.; student Morningside Coll., 1903-04; A.B., State U. Ia., 1907, Ph.D., 1910; m. Abigail E. White, July 5, 1911; children—Dan Elbert, Joyce A. Mem. faculty U. Ia., 1909-18; asso. editor State Hist. Soc. Ia., 1908-18; service with A.R.C., 1918-21; with U. Ore., 1921—, now prof. of history, also dir. of summer sessions, 1926-47, head dept. history, 1940—. Mem. Am. Hist. Assn. (pres. Pacific Coast br., 1931), Ia., Ore. (dir.) hist. socs., Phi Beta Kappa. Republican. Conglist. Author: History of Senatorial Elections in Iowa, 1912; Government of Iowa, 1915; Samuel Jordan Kirkwood, 1917; The West in American History, 1937. Contbr. to hist. jours. Mem. bd. editors Pacific Northwest Quar. Home: 1981 Moss St., Eugene, Ore. Died 1956.

CLARK, D(avid) Worth, ex-senator; b. Idaho Falls, Ida., Apr. 2, 1902; s. David Worth and Nellie (Kelleher) C.; A.B., Notre Dame U., Ind., 1922; LL.B., Harvard, 1925; m. Virgil Irwin Clark, June 26, 1926; children—Nancy Lee, Helen Noel, Dorothy Dee. Practiced in Pocatello, Ida., 1926-33; asst. atty. gen. of Ida., 1933-35; mem. 74th and 75th Congresses, 2d Ida. Dist.; mem. U.S. Senate from Ida., 1939-45. Democrat. Address: Los Angeles. Died June 19, 1955.

CLARK, Edward L(eonidas), coll. pres.; b. Summertown, Tenn., May 29, 1892; s. Samuel Leonidas and Linda Catherine (Shaw) C.; A.B., Moores Hill (now Evansville) Coll., Evansville, Ind., 1914; student U. of Chicago, 1916-17, Columbia, summer 1919; A. M., U. of Ore., 1932; LL.D., Willamette U., 1935; m. Ferne Olga Gildersleeve, Oct. 17, 1918; children—Ferne Elizabeth (Mrs. Sam Fry), Edward Leonidas, Charles Willard. High school teacher, 1913-14; book salesman, 1914-15; clerk Central Y.M.C.A. schools, Chicago, 1915-16, prin. evening school, 1916-19; dean Sch. of Business, Ore. Inst. Tech. (now Multnomah Coll.), 1919-26, pres., 1926—. Pres. Portland Council of Churches, 1937-39, now trustee and mem. bd. mgrs.; chairman local com. for National Christian Mission, 1940-41; mem. Gen. Board of Evangelism, Meth. Ch.; lay del. to Western Jurisdictional Conf., Meth. Ch., 1940, 44; conf. lay leader Ore. Meth. Conf., 1942-48. Chmn. Meth. Minister's Pension Fund Campaign, Ore. Annual Conf.; mem. Commn. on Ch. Union of the Meth. Ch. Chmn. bd. dirs. Portland Fed. Savs. and Loan Assn. Mem. N E.A., Phi Delta Kappa. Republican. Clubs: University Rotary, City (corr. sec., 1936-37) (Portland). Home: 5853 S.W. Terwilliger Blvd., Portland 1. Office: 819 S.W 6th Av., Portland 4, Ore. Died Mar. 25, 1952.

CLARK, Emily (Mrs. Edwin Swift Balch), writer; d. William Meade and Nancy (Tapscott) Clark; ed. Virginia Randolph Ellett Sch., Richmond, Va.; m. Edwin Swift Balach, Nov. 1, 1924 (dec.). Writer on Richmond Evening Journal, 1919-20, Richmond News Leader, 1920-23; founder and one of editors of The Reviewer (Richmond). The first modern lit. rev. in the South, 1921-25. Episcopalian. Mem. Colonial Dames of America. Author: Stuffed Peacocks, 1927; Innocence Abroad, 1931. Contbr. to mags. and New York Herald Tribune. Home: 1634 Spruce St., Philadelphia, Pa. Died July 2, 1953.

CLARK, Emory W., retired banker; b. Detroit, 1868; ed. grammar and high schs.; married; children—Elizbeth (Mrs. Walbridge S. Taft), Martha (Mrs. Serge Daniloff), William Reeve. Became identified with banking business, 1902; formerly chmn. bd. First Nat. Bank in Detroit; dir. Mich. Bell Telephone Co.; trustee Mutual Life Ins. Co. of N.Y. Mem. Detroit Bd. Commerce, Mich. Soc. Colonial Wars. Clubs: Yondotega, Detroit, Detroit Boat, Bloomfield Hills Country, Grosse Pointe Country, Boone and Crockett. Home: 635 Lake Shore Rd., Grosse Pointe Shores 30, Mich. Office: Nat. Bank Bldg., Detroit 26. Died Apr. 29, 1958.

CLARK, Frank Hodges, ret. naval officer; b. in Mass., Dec. 18, 1871; grad. U.S. Naval Acad., 1893. Commd. ensign USN, 1893, advanced through grades to rear adm., 1927; apptd. comdr. Destroyer Squadrons, Scouting Fleet, 1927; then head of Fleet Tng. Div.; became mem. Gen. Bd. USN, 1933, chmn., 1934; retired, 1936. Address: 45-2126 Connecticut Av., Washington 8. Deceased.

CLARK, Frank Sylvester; b. Middletown, Conn., Mar. 7, 1868; s. Benjamin Franklin and Fanny J. (Dean) C.; captured by the Sioux Indians while crossing the plains, 1872; found by father 4 yrs. later but spent most of time to manhood with the Indians; ed. pub. schs. and under pvt. tutors; m. Hattie L. Forsha, May 19, 1887 (dec.); children—Benjamin Franklin (dec.), Lewis Quincy. Chief engr. Central Ind. Insane Hosp., 1891-93; elec. engr. C.,C.C.& St.L., R.R., 1893-97; 2d lt. U.S. Vol. Engrs., 1898; promoted to 1st lt., 1899, at Mariano, Cuba, and placed in command of Co. A, with brevet rank of capt.; hon. discharged, 1899; asst. mgr. Standard Oil Co., 1900-07; asst. to pres. and asst. gen. mgr. U.S. Cement Co., Bedford, Ind., 1908-09; gen. mgr. Continental Portland Cement Co., 1910; now pres. Frank S. Clark & Co., real estate and ins., Indpls.; treas. U.S. Mail Box Co.; chmn. finance com. Excelsior Investment Co.; pres. Ashland Saving and Loan Assn., First Federal Savings & Loan Assn. Admitted to Indiana bar, 1914. Mem. city Council, Indianapolis, 1895-99. Treas. Nat. Dem. League of Clubs of U.S. Mem. Western Soc. Engrs., S.A.R., Mil. Order Foreign Wars, Vets. Foreign Wars (chmn. council), U.S. Vol. Assn. (pres.), Spanish-Am. War Vets. Assn. Mason (32°), K.P., Elk. Clubs: Indiana Democratic, Independent Athletic. Made col. and retired by act of Ind. State Legislature, 1936, and made commandant Ind. State Soldiers Home, LaFayette, Dec. 1936, also v.p. bd. trustees, 1932-36. Home: 2701 Boca Ciega Drive, St. Petersburg, Fla. Died July 14, 1958; buried Indpls.

CLARK, George Halford, corp. ofcl.; b. Rochester, N.Y., Oct. 14, 1860; s. Brackett H. and Lucretia (Bowker) C.; student pub. schs.; m. Adele D. Hathaway, Dec. 11, 1900 (died Sept. 1944); children—Brackett H., Halford R., Donald R. Started in barrel-stave mfg. business with father, later asso. B. H. Clark & Sons; organized The Cochrane-Bly Co.; dir. Eastman Kodak Co., Genesee Valley Trust Co. Dir. Rochester Inst. Technology (treas.), Eastman Dental Dispensary. Republican. Mason (Shriner). Clubs: Genesee Valley, Rochester, Rochester Yacht. Home: 630 Rock Beach Rd., Rochester 12, Office: 31 Exchange St., Rochester 4, N.Y. Died Feb. 1956.

CLARK, George J., pres. The Third Nat. Bank and Trust Co., 1391 Main St., Springfield, Mass. Died Dec. 26, 1949.*

CLARK, Harold Benjamin, ret. investment banker; b. New Rochelle, N.Y., Dec. 8, 1878; s. Benjamin Stephen and Mary Jane (Conklin) C.; B.S., Harvard, 1901; m. Dorothy Q. Pardee, Jan. 12, 1907. Entered employ of Moffat & White, bankers, 1901; five years later admitted to general partnership, firm name changed to White, Weld & Co., 1910; dir. Am. Chicle Co., Pardee & Curtin Lumber Co., Trinity Petroleum Co., Capital Airlines. Served as lt. col. C.W.S., AEF, World War I. Mem. bd. trustees Five Points House, Am. Museum of Natural History. Mem. Down Town Assn. Clubs: Harvard, Racquet and Tennis, Boone and Crockett; gov. Laurentian (Canada). Home: Apple Hill, New Canaan, Conn. Office: 40 Wall St., N.Y.C. 5. Died Oct. 28, 1956.

CLARK, Harold Johnson, lawyer; b. Syracuse, N.Y., June 12, 1891; s. J. Scott and Carrie (Johnson) C.; B.S., Northwestern U., 1913, LL.B., 1915; m. Helen Hale, Nov. 9, 1915; children—Donald Hale, Catherine Arnold. Admitted to Ill. bar, 1915;

associated in practice with Manierre & Pratt, Chicago, 1915-17, Cutting, Moore & Sidley, 1917-21; mem. firm of Hamlin, Clark & Pierson, 1921-24; mem. Zimmerman and Clark, 1924-29; personal trust officer, Central Trust Co. of Ill., 1929-32; trust officer City Nat. Bank & Trust Co., 1932-35; gen. practice of law, 1935—; partner law firm of Ogren & Clark, 1936-52; practiced law alone, 1952-58. Rep. candidate for Circuit Court judge, 1941. Mem. Ill. Res. Militia, 1917-18; 2d lt. Field Arty., U.S.A., 1918; lt. F.A. Reserve, 1918-33. Trustee Northwestern U. Mem. Am., Ill State and Chicago bar assns., Beta Theta Pi, Phi Delta Phi, Phi Beta Kappa. Order of the Coif. Republican. Conglist. Clubs: Law, Union League (Chicago); Glen View Golf. Home: 1630 Ashland Av., Evanston, Ill. Office: 231 S. La Salle St., Chgo. Died Aug. 8, 1958; buried Meml. Park, Evanston.

CLARK, Harry Camp, lawyer; b. Bay City, Mich., June 8, 1883; s. Heman E. and Melissa C. (Heath) C.; grad. Derby (Vt.) Acad., 1901; C.E., U. Vt., 1907; m. Georgia L. Kessinger, June 6, 1911. Admitted to Cal. bar, 1915, began practice at San Diego; mayor of San Diego, 1927-31. Served as 2d lt., later capt. U.S. Army, 1917-19. Mem. Am., Cal., San Diego (pres. 1927) bar assns., Am. Legion, Vets. Fgn. Wars (past comdr.), Fine Arts Soc. San Diego, Kappa Sigma. Republican. 1st Church of Christ, Scientist. Mason. Club: Cuyamaca (San Diego). Home: 4252 Witherby St. Office: San Diego Trust and Savings Bldg., San Diego, Cal. Died Dec. 27, 1950; buried Fort Rosecrans Nat. Cemetery, San Diego.

CLARK, Harry Henderson, educator, lecturer; b. Winchester, Tenn., Aug. 6, 1880; s. Rufus Anthony and Ellen Elizabeth (Henderson) C.; Winchester Normal Sch., 1898; B.A., Yale, 1903, M.A., 1915; grad. student Peabody, 1922-25; LL.D., Lincoln Memorial U., 1917; m. Alice Montmorency Falkland, Aug. 3, 1907. Prof. English and pedagogy Winchester Normal Sch., 1907-09; supt. schs., Somerville, Tenn., and prin. Fayette County High Sch., 1909-11; prof. English and psychology State Normal Sch., Murfreesboro, Tenn., 1911-12; prof. secondary edn. U. Tenn., 1912-21; supr. lectures, Summer Sch. of the South, 1915-19; ednl. sec. Tenn. Bapt. Conv., 1921-25; head dept. edn. Furman U., 1925-30, was also dean summer sch.; pres. Judson Coll., Marion, Ala., 1930-31; supt. of schools, Knoxville, Tenn., 1931—. Chmn. So. Bapt. Edn. Commn. Mem. S.C. Tchrs.' Assn. (pres. 1929-30), Zeta Psi, Phi Kappa Phi, Phi Beta Kappa (Yale). Democrat. Baptist. Mason (K.T.). Home: Columbia, S.C. Died Feb. 5, 1952.

CLARK, Henry A., first vice pres. and dir. The Cuban-American Sugar Co.; b. New York, N.Y., 1865. Home: 45-10 Kissena Blvd., Flushing 20, L.I., N.Y. Office: The Cuban-American Sugar Co., 347 Madison Av., N.Y.C. Died Oct. 29, 1951.

CLARK, Herma N., columnist, monologist; b. Princeton, Ill.; d. Maj. Atherton and Jerusha (Whitmarsh) Clark; ed. Princeton and Oberlin Coll. Chgo. corr. Town and Country, 1917-25; writer "When Chicago Was Young" column, Chicago Tribune since 1929. Mem. Soc. of Midland Authors. Republican. Presbyn. Club: The Cordon. Author books including: The Elegant Eighties; Keys for Happiness, 1949; (play) America Versus Mary X. Public (with Alice McClanaham); Port of Chicago (with Alice Gerstenberg). Home: 4950 N. Ashland Blvd., Chgo. 40. Address: Tribune Tower, 435 N. Michigan Av., Chgo. Died Nov. 1959.

CLARK, Horatio David, trade assn. exec.; b. Massena, N.Y., Sept. 7, 1894; s. Joseph Henry and Helen (Donaghue) C.; B.S., Colgate U., 1919; m. Florence Stubbs, Dec. 31, 1921; children—Mary (Mrs. Davis G. Johnson), Catherine (Mrs. William F. Burns), Helen (Mrs. Robert E. Coffey). Exec. sec. Toy Fair C. of C., N.Y.C., 1921-31; asst. sec. Toy Mfrs. of the U.S.A., Inc., 1921-44, sec., 1944—. Mem. Am. Trade Assn. Execs. (dir.), Trade Assn. Execs. in N.Y.C. (past pres.), Am. Legion (past comdr.), Phi Kappa Psi. Republican. Mason. Home: 418 Cliff Rd., Sewaren, N.J. Office: 200 Fifth Av., N.Y.C. 10. Died Apr. 17, 1957; buried Massena, N.Y.

CLARK, John Arvine, engring. exec.; b. Syracuse, N.Y., May 22, 1889; s. George Arvine and Margaret (Flanigan) C.; M.E., Cornell U., 1910; m. Ivel L. Martin, June 7, 1934. Student engr. Westinghouse Machine, Pitts., 1910-12; engr. Hope Natural Gas Co., Clarksburg, W.Va., 1912-50, pres., 1950-52, chmn. bd., 1953, dir., 1946—; dir. River Gas Co., Mariteta, O., 1947—; Consolidated Nat. Gas Co., N.Y.C., 1952—. Served as 2d lt. U.S. Army, Engrs. Corp., 1918-19. Mem. Am. Gas Assn., Newcomen Soc. Home: 600 E. Main St. Office: 445 W. Main St., Clarksburg, W.Va. died Aug. 8, 1954.

CLARK, John Robert, judge; b. Louisville, Colo., Dec. 19, 1888; s. James M. and Jane Ann (Carlton) C.; LL.B., U. Colo., 1911; m. Alice Charlotte Boyle, June 25, 1913; children—Jane Adelaide (Mrs. Robert P. Craig), Carlton Boyle (dec.), Mariam Lenore (Mrs. Jesse Robert Bennett), Alice Maybelle (Mrs. Irvin E. Hixson), Roberta Ann (Mrs. William Kenneth Johnson). Admitted to Colo. bar, 1911; with McMullin & Sternberg, Grand Junction, Colo., 1911-12; own law office, Meeker, Colo., 1912-37; city atty., Meeker, 1913-36; judge Dist. Ct., 9th Jud. Dist. of Colo., 1936-42, 42-48, 48-51; apptd. justice Supreme Ct. of Colo., by Gov., 1951, elected for 10 yr. term, Nov. 1952. Mem. Am., Ninth Jud. Dist., Colo. State (pres. 1943-44) bar assns., Am. Judicature Soc. Republican. Episcopalian. Mason (hon. 33°, grand master 1944-45). Home: 1135 Grant St., Denver 3. Office: 250 State Capitol, Denver 2. Died May 14, 1956; buried Meeker, Colo.

CLARK, Keith, writer, educator; b. St. Peter, Minn., June 4, 1879; d. Edward and Agnes Anne Shields (Bean) Clark; B.A., Hamline U., 1898; M.A., U. of Minn., 1922; Ph.D., Columbia Univ., 1931. Editorial writer St. Paul Dispatch Pioneer-Press and writer spl. column, "From the Watch Tower," 1905-17; dir. pub., Y.W.C.A. in France, 1918-20; editor Women's Bur., Dept. of Labor, Washington, D.C., 1920-21; asst. prof. history and polit. science, Carleton Coll., 1923-31, asso. prof., 1931, asso. prof. polit. science, 1931-42. Visiting professor, Kobe College, Nishinomiya, Japan, 1st semester, 1938; lecturer in Japanese cities. Mem. Inst. of Politics, Williamstown, Mass., 1921-25. Del. to Nat. Council of French Women, Strassbourg, 1919; mem. Carnegie party of Am. Profs. in Europe, 1926. Mem. Am. Soc. Internat. Law, Am. Polit. Sci. Assn., Minn. Hist. Assn., League Women Voters, Am Assn. Univ. Women, Women's Overseas Service League. Author: The Spell of Spain, 1913; The Spell of Scotland, 1916; International Communications, 1931. Contbr. to Nat. Dict. American History. Home: Northfield, Minn. Deceased.

CLARK, Melville, harpist, merchant; b. Syracuse, N.Y., September 12, 1883; s. George Waldo and Lillie L. (Becker) C.; ed. high sch. and business coll., Syracuse U.; m. Dorothy Speich, pianist, Jan. 8, 1921. children—Melville Jr., Dorothy E., Timothy. In music business, Syracuse, since 1899; pres., Clark Music Co.; invented improvements "which have made possible a perfect portable harp; developed improved method of pedaling concert harp; mfr. Wurlitzer Concert Harp. Played over 6000 concerts in principal cities in the United States, Canada and England; engaged by the Bd. of Edn. of Syracuse to deliver a series of lecture concerts on "Musical Appreciation," which were attended by 15,000 persons. First temp. pres., National Assn. Harpists, Inc.; sec. 12 years of Central N.Y. Music Festival Assn.; founder Syracuse Symphony Orchestra. Gave several concerts for President Woodrow Wilson; also gave concert for President and Mrs. Franklin D. Roosevelt at White House, 1935. Broadcasting, NBC, with Helen Jepson, Columbia, Mutual, WFBL (harp programs). Received silver medal, Turin, Italy, 1911; Good Citizenship Medal awarded by Am. Legion, 1935. Perfected plan for aero-stations presented to the war departments of both U.S. and Great Britain for distributing literature. Perfected and developed the Melville Clerk nylon harp string; invented a harp of plastic and nylon impervious to weather. Adv. bd. Nat. Assn. of Music Merchants; mem. Nat. Press Bur., Syracuse C. of C., Jr. C. of C. (hon.), Inventor's Congress, Phi Mu Alpha; hon. mem. Vets. Foreign Wars. Clubs: Technology, Rotary (dir. and 1st v.p. Syracuse club), Kiwanis (ex-pres.); Advertising and Business Men's Club (Syracuse). Mason (Scottish Rite). Author: How to Play the Harp, 1945; Audiotricity, 1946; Singing Strings. Invented aero-station, used by British Govt. during World War I. Presented Am. Regina Music Box to Princess Elizabeth. Home: Drovers Tavern Farms, R. 2. Cazenovia, N.Y. Office: Clark Music Bldg., 416-420 Salina St., Syracuse, N.Y. Died Dec. 11, 1953; buried Morningside Cemetery, Syracuse, N.Y.

CLARK, Myron H., management counsel, govt. ofcl.; b. Bedford, Mass., July 25, 1881; s. Charles Henry and Abbie (Davis) C.; S.B. Mass. Inst. Tech. 1903; m. Augusta Farnum, Oct. 7, 1909; children—Eugene Whittredge, Philip Farnum. Chemist Boston Rubber Shoe Co., Malden, Mass., 1903-07, supt., 1907-14; gen. mgr. footwear factories U.S. Rubber Co., 1914-27; gen. planning mgr. Johns Manville Corp., 1927-29; asst. to pres. Crucible Steel Co., 1929-31; v.p. Reading (Pa.) Iron Co., 1931-35; mgr. Myron Clark & Assos., Boston, 1927—; dir. Labor Management Inst., U. Conn., 1946-52; now dir. productivity and tech. assistanc div. Mut. Security Agy.; cons. management eng . European Productivity. Mem. Am. Management Assn., A.A.A.S., Soc. Advancement Management (pres.), Am. Arbitration Assn. (panel mem.), A.S.M.E., Am. Acad. Polit. and Social Sci., Soc. Advancement Edn. Republican. Conglist. Mason (K.T., 32°). Clubs: Univ. (Boston); Univ. (N.Y. C.). Home: 30 Chestnut St., Andover, Mass. Office: 258 Park Sq. Bldg., Boston. Died Aug. 30, 1953; buried Bedford, Mass.

CLARK, Ray Henry, ret. army officer; b. Gueydan, La., Sept. 19, 1896; B.S. in Elec. Engring., U. So. Cal., 1918; grad. Air Service Primary Flying Sch., 1922. Advanced Flying Sch., bombardment course, 1922, AC Tactical Sch., 1940. Served as 1st lt. (temporary) Air Service, 1918; commd. 2d lt. to brig. gen., 1944; AC tech. supr. Fairfield (O.) Air Depot, 1940-42; became Air Force tech. supr., office of dir. of tech. inspection, Hdqrs. AAF, Washington, 1942; tech. supr. Tenth Air Force, New Delhi, India, 1942-43; commd. air base, CBI Theater of Operations, 1943, became air inspector for the theater Oct. 1943, ret. 1953; chmn. bd. Golden Spread Securities, Inc., investment firm, 1953—. Address: Amarillo, Tex. Died Oct. 27, 1955.

CLARK, Reed Paige, fgn. service officer; b. Londonderry, N.H., Aug. 19, 1878; s. William and Alice Whitney (McIntire) C.; A.B., Columbia (now George Washington) U., 1898, A.M., LL.B., 1901; m. Jeanne Marie Bertrand, Nov. 12, 1928; 1 son, Reed Paige. Instr. in French, Columbian Sci. Sch., 1898-1901, in German, Nat. Park Seminary, Md., 1899-1900, in modern langs. Columbian U., 1900-01; pvt. sec. to U.S. Senator Burnham of N.H., and clk. to various senate coms., 1901-11; admitted to N.H. bar, 1907; gen. receiver Liberian Customs, 1911-16; exec. sec. N.H. Fuel Adminstrn., 1917 (3 mos.); agt. of N.Y. comml. house at Accra, Gold Coast, 1918-19; entered Consular Service, 1919; consul at Loanda, Angola, 1919-24, Port Elizabeth, Union of So. Africa, 1924-25, Mexico City, 1925-26; commd. diplomatic sec., 1926; chargé d'affaires at Monrovia, Liberia, 1926-27; consul at Mexico City, 1927-28, at Guadalajara, Mex., 1928-29, at Santo Domingo, 1929-30, at Belgrade, Yugoslavia, 1930-36; first sec. at Vienna, 1936-37; consul at Victoria, B.C., 1937-43, retired. Republican. Mason. Club: University (Washington). Home: Stonehenge, Londonderry, N. H. Address: Dept. of State, Washington. Died Sept. 5, 1958.

CLARK, Robert Thomas, Jr., educator; b. Nashville, July 27, 1906; s. Robert Thomas and Elizabeth (Frame) C.; B.A., Vanderbilt U., 1927, M.A., 1928; student U. Leipzig, 1928-29; Ph.D., Stanford, 1932; m. Lucy E. Austin, Dec. 19, 1936. Instr. German, Vanderbilt U., 1929-31; acting instr. Stanford, 1931-32; instr. Duke U., 1932-34; asst. prof. La. State U., 1933-35, asso. prof., 1935-42, prof., head dept., 1942-45; prof. Germanic langs. U. Tex., 1945-53; prof. German U. Cal. at Berkeley, 1953—, chmn. dept., 1954—. Mem. Modern Lang. Assn., Linguistic Soc. Am., Philol. Assn. Pacific Coast, Phi Beta Kappa. Author: Herder, His Life and Thought, 1955. Contbr. profl. jours. Home: 2661 Cedar St., Berkeley 8, Cal. Died May 27, 1957; buried Nashville.

CLARK, Roe Sidney, machinery exec.; b. Granville, Mass., Sept. 25, 1887; s. Sidney A. and Carrie (Smith) C.; student pub. schs.; m. Sarah Hosmer, June 1, 1910. With Johnson's Bookstore, 1901-04, 09-10, Chapman Valva Mfg. Co., 1905-06, 08, Walworth Mfg. Co., 1907, Electric Goods Mfg. Co., 1912-15; retail bus., 1911-12; joined Package Machinery Co., Springfield, Mass., 1916, became treas., sec., 1931, v.p., treas., 1938, pres., 1952—; chmn. bd. Reed-Prentice Corp., Worcester, Mass.; sec., dir. Bay State Thread Works; chmn. exec. com., member bd. directors Cheney Bigelow Wires Works; mem. bd. trustees Palmer Savs. Bank; dir. L. S. Starrett Tool Co., Athol, Mass. Trustee Bay Path Jr. Coll.; bd. govs. Western New Eng. Coll.; v.p., dir. Goodwill Industries; pres., mem. exec. com. Asso. Industries of Mass.; trustee, chmn. investment com. Hitchcock Acad.; incorporator Springfield (Mass.) Hosp.; trustee Wing Meml. Hosp.; dir. Mass. div. Am. Cancer Soc., Hampden Co. Tb. Assn. Mem. Western Mass. Employers Assn. (past pres.), Nat. Metal Trade Assn. (past pres. Western Mass. br., past dir., treas.), Y.M.C.A. (pres., dir.), Western Mass. Credit Men's Assn. (past pres.), Mass. C. of C. (dir.), Controllers Inst. Am., Am. Management Assn. Mason (Shriner). Clubs: Colony, University, Rotary Springfield, Mass. Home: 406 Longhill Street, Springfield, Mass. Office: care Package Machinery Co., Springfield, Mass. Died Dec. 22, 1955; buried Hillcrest Park Cemetery.

CLARK, Roland Eugene, banker; b. Houlton, Me., July 3, 1879; s. Michael McGuirk and Henrietta (Braden) C.; A.B., Bowdoin College, 1901, M.A. (hon.), 1952; LL.B., Georgetown U., 1904; m. Gladys Goodin Tingle, Feb. 14, 1941. Admitted to Me. bar, 1905; pvt. sec. to Congressman Llewellyn Powers, 1901-05; practiced law Houlton, 1905-17; v.p. charge trust dept. Fidelity Trust Co., Portland, Me., 1919-33, Nat. Bank Commerce, Portland since 1933. Trustee Portland Pub. Library; mem. bd. trustees, treas. Bowdoin Coll. since 1949, mem. bd. overseers, 1939-49. Served as 2d lt. to maj. 1st Inf. Div., U.S. Army, 1917-19, asst. div. adj. 1st Inf. Div., asst. adj. gen. 1st Army, A.E.F. Pres. trust div. Am. Bankers Assn., 1939. Mem. Psi Upsilon. Republican. Conglist. Club: Cumberland (Portland). Home: 15 Clifford St., Portland 4. Office: National Bank of Commerce, Portland, Me. Died Nov. 1, 1958.

CLARK, Rollin M., ins. exec.; b. Camden, N.J., Mar. 15, 1899; s. Austin M. and Grace (Roper) C.; C.; B.S. in Mech. Engring., U. Pa., 1920; LL.B., George Washington U., 1929; m. Helen E. Corsette, June 30, 1927; children—Shirley Grace, Janet Dorothy, Linda Ann. Ins. insp., 1920-23; ins. dept., later asst. mgr. C. of C. of U.S., Washington,

1923-29; ins. editor U.S. Daily, 1929-33; dep. supt. of ins., later first dep. State of N.Y., 1933-37; asst. comptroller Continental Casualty Co., 1937-38, comptroller, 1938-39, v.p., comptroller, 1939-40, v.p., sec., 1940-44, first v.p., sec., 1944—, dir., 1938—; first v.p., sec., dir. Continental Assurance Co.; v.p., dir. Transportation Ins. Co., Nat. Casualty Co. Mem. Sigma Xi, Tau Beta Pi, Theta Chi, Phi Delta Phi. Presbyn. Mason (32°, Shriner). Club: Sunset Ridge Country. Home: 614 Thornwood Lane, Northfield, Ill. Office: 310 S. Michigan Av., Chgo. Died Sept. 16, 1950.

CLARK, Samuel Wesley, lawyer; b. Platteville; Wis., Dec. 28, 1872; s. Samuel P. and Lizzie D. (Huntington) C.; grad. normal course Redfield Coll., 1894; studied law in office of Senator Thomas Sterling, Redfield; m. Daisy G. Labrie, Feb. 7, 1900 (died Nov. 26, 1915); children—Sterling H. and Stanton L. (twins), Elmer Alfred; m. 2d, Essie Eggler, Aug. 14, 1919; 1 child, Mavis. Mem. firm Sterling & Clark, Redfield; state's atty., Spink County, S.D., 1900-04; atty. gen. of S.D., 1906-10; U.S. dist. atty. Dist. of S.D., 1921-26. Established constitutionality of anti-discrimination laws in case of State of S.D. vs. Central Lumber Co., 1912. Mem. Am., S.D. State (pres. 1929-30) bar assns. Republican. Conglist. Mason, Kiwanian. Home: 916 E. 2d St., Redfield, S.D. Died Jan. 5, 1949; buried Redfield.

CLARK, Sheldon, oil exec.; b. Chicago; ed. U. Col. Chmn. bd. Sinclair Oil Corp.; v.p. Sinclair Refining Co.; dir. 1st Nat. Bank, East Chicago, Omnibus Corp., Chicago Motor Coach Corp., Union Nat. Bank, Indiana Harbor, Richfield Oil Corp., Sinclair Oil Co. Mem. Chicago Plan Commn. Adv. gov., Chicago Stock Exchange; chmn. Illinois State Athletic Commn. Hon. pres. (past nat. pres.) Navy League U.S.; vice chmn. Joint Army and Navy Com. on Welfare and Recreation (Wash., D.C.). Commodore Yachtman's Assn. Am., Nat. Petroleum Assn. (dir.), Western Petroleum Refiners, Delta Tau Delta, Delta Chi. Mem. Nat. exec. bd. Boy Scouts Am. (chmn. exec. com. Region 7). Clubs: University, Chicago, Saddle and Cycle, Barrington Hills, La Jolla (Cal.) C.C., Chicago Yacht. Home: 1301 N. State St., Chgo. Died Aug. 15, 1952.

CLARK, Stephen Cutter, bishop; b. Pasadena, Cal., Aug. 6, 1892; s. Stephen Cutter and Grace Miller (Greene) C.; student Classical Sch. for Boys, Pasadena, 1898-1910, Occidental Coll., Los Angeles, 1910-13; A.B., U. Cal. at Berkeley, 1914; student Gen. Theol. Sem., N.Y.C., 1914-15; B.D., Episcopal Theol. Sch., Cambridge, Mass., 1917; D.D. (hon.), Occidental Coll., Los Angeles, 1945; m. Helen Marcia Moodey, June 21, 1917; children—Stephen Cutter, Helen Eveleth (Mrs. Robert E. Patterson), John Moodey, Anne Miller (Mrs. Robert Henry Tarr). Ordained to ministry P.E. Ch., 1917; minister St. Lukes Ch., Park City, Utah, 1917-18; rector St. Paul's Ch., Pomona, Cal., 1918-27, St. Mark's Ch., Pasadena, 1927-46; bishop of the missionary dist. of Utah, 1946—. Pres. bd. dirs. St. Mark's Hosp., Rowland Hall Sch. for Girls (Salt Lake City); pres. Corp. of the Missionary Dist. of Utah; trustee Westminister Coll. (Salt Lake City); dir. Salt Lake City Community Chest; sec. Diocese of Los Angeles, 1930-46; pres. Pasadena Council of Social Agencies, 1941-44; pres. Pasadena Pastor's Union, 1944-45. Democrat. Clubs: The Twenty (Los Angeles); Alta (Salt Lake City). Author: The Diocese of Los Angeles, Brief History, 1945. Editor: Los Angeles Churchman, 1930-35; Los Angeles Edition of Forth, 1943-46. Home: 233 First Av., Salt Lake City 3. Office: 55 B St., Salt Lake City 3. Died Nov. 30, 1950.

CLARK, Theodore, business exec.; b. Spokane, Wash., June 28, 1895; s. Francis Lewis and Winifred (Wiard) C.; A.B., Harvard, 1917; m. Dorothy Ayer, Nov. 3, 1917; children—Dorothy W. (Mrs. William F. Auer), Theodore Lewis. Mech. supt. Eastern Mfg. Co., Bangor, Me., 1917, 1918-25; with Kendall Co., Boston, 1925—, v.p., dir., 1948— ;trustee Milton Savings Bank. Served as 1st lt. C.W.S., 1917-18. Clubs: Union (Boston); Hoosic (Milton). Home: 147 Canton Av., Milton 87, Mass. Office: 140 Federal St., Boston 10. Died Nov. 3, 1949.

CLARK, Thomas Curtis, author; b. Vincennes, Ind., Jan. 8, 1877; s. Thomas Jefferson and Emma Rose (Jennings) C.; A.B., Ind. U., 1899; studied U. of Chicago, 1901-02; m. Hazel P. Davis, June 1910; 1 son, Robert Earle. Editor with Christian Bd. of Publn., St. Louis, 1907-11; editorial staff The Christian Century, Chicago, 1912-48; editor 20th Century Quarterly; asso. editor The Pulpit; mem. publ. firm Willett, Clark & Co., 1927-48. Mem. Poetry Soc. America, Soc. Midland Authors, Hyman Soc. America. Member of Church of Disciples of Christ. Author: Poems and Songs, 1909; Friendly Town, 1915; Love Off to the War and Other Poems, 1918; Lincoln and Others, 1923; It Shall Not Be Again and Other Poems, 1931; Abraham Lincoln—Thirty Poems, 1934; Home Roads and Far Horizons—Songs and Sonnets, 1935; Fifty Lincoln Poems, 1943; God's Dreams and Other Poems, 1944; (oratorios, with Bethuel Gross) Seven Voices at Christmas, Holy Week Litany, Christmas Litany, Litany of Peace. Compiler: The New Patriotism (with E. A. Gillespie), 1927; A Child's Thought of God (with E. A. Gillespie) 1927; Quotable Poems (with E. A. Gillespie), Volume 1, 1928, Vol. 2, 1931; Poems of Justice, 1929; The Master of Men, Poems About Jesus, 1930; Poems for Special Days and Occasions, 1930; The Golden Book of Faith, 1931; One Hundred Poems of Peace (with W. E. Garrison), 1934; One Hundred Poems of Immortality (with W. E. Garrison), 1935; Golden Book of Religious Verse, 1937; One Thousand Quotable Poems, 1937; Enduring Poems for Daily Needs, 1937; Poems for Life, 1941; Three Hundred Favorite Poems, 1945; Today Is Mine: An Anthology of Daily Devotion, 1949; Poems for the Great Days (with R. E. Clark), 1948; Christ in Poetry, An Anthology (with Hazel D. Clark), 1951; The Golden Book of Immortality, 1954. Contbr. to anthologies. Syndicate writer, composer, hymn writer; won first prize in nation-wide contest of Hymn Soc. of America, 1945. Wrote Crusade hymn for Nat. Crusade for a Christian World, 1947. Home: 242 Marshall Av., Bellwood, Ill. Died Dec. 7, 1954.

CLARK, Victor Selden, economist; b. Portageville, N.Y., June 12, 1868; s. Maj. Selden N. and Helen E. (Davis) C.; Litt.B., U. Minn., 1890; hon. fellow, U. Chgo.; student Göttingen and Berne univs., 1892-93; fellow Columbia, 1897-98, Ph.D., 1900. High sch. prin. and supt. in Minn., 1893-97; supt. pub. instrn. and pres. Insular Bd. of Edn. of P.R. under mil. govt.; engaged in investigating foreign and insular labor conditions for U.S. Govt., 1902-09; in charge of census of Hawaii, 1910; commr. of immigration, labor and statistics T.H., 1910-13; in charge of the division of manufactures and economic history Carnegie Instn., Washington; editor The Living Age, Boston, 1920-28; dir. Brookings Instn. Survey of P.R., 1918-29; cons. in economics, Library of Congress, 1929-40. Editor: The Colloquies of Erasmus (Latin), 1895; Eutropius' Historia Romana (Latin), 1897. Author: The Labor Movement in Australasia, 1906; History of Manufactures in the United States, 1915, 29; Puerto Rico and Its Problems (with others), 1930; (bulletins) Teachers' Manual, 1900; Studies in the Latin of the Middle Ages and the Renaissance, 1900; education in Puerto Rico; Labor Conditions in Cuba, 1902; Labor Conditions in Hawaii, 1903, 05, 10, 15; Labor Condtiions in New Zealand, 1904; Labor Conditions in Australia, 1905; Labor Conditions in the Philippines, 1905; Labor Conditions in Java, 1905; Labor Conditions in Mexico, 1908; The Canadian Industrial Disputes Act, 1908, 09; Women and Children Wage Earners in Great Britain, 1908; Employment Conditions in Train-Yard Service Under 8-Hour Law, 1917; What is Money?, 1934. Fellow Royal Econ. Soc.; mem. Beta Theta Pi Fraternity. Clubs: Cosmos (Washington); Century (N.Y.C.). Economic consultant, Library of Congress. Home: 3930 Connecticut Av., Washington. Deceased.

CLARK, Walter Ernest, univ. pres. emeritus; b. Definance, O., June 9, 1873; s. Lemen Taylor and Martha Ann (Robinson) C.; A.B., Ohio Wesleyan U., 1896, A.M., 1898, LL.D., 1918; Ph.D., Columbia, 1903; LL.D., U. Nev., 1938; m. Euphemia Murray Abrams, June 6, 1908; children—Walter Van Tilburg, Euphemia Murray, David Greer, Miriam Ladd. Instr. mathematics Ohio Wesleyan U., 1896-99; instr. econs. and politics, Coll. City N.Y., 1901, prof., head dept. polit. sci., 1907-17; pres. U. Nev., 1917-38, emeritus 1938—. Resident and settlement worker Greenwich House, N.Y.C. 1903-08; lecturer, Pub. Evening Lecture System, 1905-17; lectured weekly on economics at Nat. City Bank and at N.Y. chpt. Am. Inst. Banking, 1915-17; extension lectr. econs. to N.Y.C. pub. sch. teachers, 1911-17. Decorated Chevalier Legion of Honor (France). Pres. Nat. Assn. State Univs., 1931-32. Sergeant signal corps, Co. K, 4th Ohio N.G., 1893-97. Mem. Am. Econ. Assn., A.A.A.S., N.E.A., Phi Kappa Phi, Phi Delta Theta, Phi Beta Kappa. Mason. Club: Rotary. Author: Josiah Tucker, Economist, 1903; The Cost of Living, 1915; The Trust Problem (with J. W. Jenks), 1917, revised edit., 1929; also many mag. and ency. articles, etc. Address: 524 Cheney St., Reno. Died May 1, 1955.

CLARK, William, judge; b. Newark, N.J., Feb. 1, 1891; s. J. William and Margaretta (Cameron) C.; grad. Newark Acad., 1904; grad. St. Mark's Sch., 1908; B.A., Harvard, 1911, M.A., 1912, LL.B., 1915; m. Marjorie Blair, Sept. 20, 1913 (div. 1947); children—Anne, John William, Blair; married 2d, Sonia Tomara, Oct. 4, 1947. Admitted to N.J. bar, 1916, counsellor at law, 1920; mem. Lindabury Depue & Faulks, 1920-23; apptd. judge N.J. Court of Errors and Appeals, 1923; judge U.S. Dist. Court, N.J., 1925-38; judge U.S. Circuit Court of Appeals for the Third Circuit, July 5, 1938—. Apptd. legal cons. to Gen. Lucius Clay, U.S. Military Government in Germany, Jan. 1948; apptd. chief judge, Mil. Govt. Courts of Germany, Sept. 1948; chief justice high commn. courts, Germany, 1949-54. Entered First R.O.T.C., Ft. Meyer, Va., May 1917; commd. 2d lt., Aug. 1917, and assigned to 314th F.A.; 1st lt., Jan. 1918; capt. Sept. 1918; oversea service 1 yr.; silver star citation "for gallantry in action"; maj., F.A., O.R.C; received Certificate of Graduation from Business and Professional Men's Company at Plattsburgh Barracks, New York, Aug. 3, 1940; entered U.S. Army, March 24, 1942, with rank of lt. col.; served overseas, Pacific and European theatres, North Africa, Sicily, Italy, Normandy and Belgium; promoted to col. Wounded. Decorated Comdr. British Empire. Trustee of New Jersey Historical Society, and New Jersey Museum Assn. Member Am., N.J. and Essex County bar assns., Assn. Bar City of New York, Am. Law Inst., Am. Soc. Internat. Law, Am. Acad. Polit. Science. Republican. Presbyterian. Home: 12 Battle Rd., Princeton, N.J. Died Oct. 10, 1957; buried Arlington Nat. Cemetery.

CLARK, W(illiam) A(lexander) Graham, textile expert; b. Raleigh, N.C., Aug. 14, 1879; s. Judge Walter (chief justice of N.C.) and Susan Washington (Graham) C.; B.S., 1897, M.E., 1899, Agrl. and Mech. Coll., Raleigh, N.C.; M.E., Cornell U., 1900; m. Pearl Chadwick Heck, Dec. 6, 1911; children—Margaret Heck (Mrs. Guy Edwin Crampton, Jr.), Graham Montrose. Treasurer, general manager of cotton mills, 1900-06; commercial agt., Dept. Commerce and Labor, investigating markets abroad for Am. cotton mill products and the methods of foreign competitors, Aug. 1906-Dec. 31, 1910, visiting over three-fourths of the countries of the world; textile expert to Tariff Bd., Jan. 1, 1911-12; commercial agt. of Dept. of Commerce, Nov. 1912-June 1917; chief of textile div., United States Tariff Commission, 1917-49, ret. Democrat. Baptist. Club: Cosmos. Author: Clark's Weave Room Calculations; also many pamphlets concerning fgn. markets for Am. cotton goods, cotton textiles in foreign countries, embroidery and lace mfg., cotton goods trade of Latin America, etc. Home: 3712 Morrison St., Washington 15. Died Jan. 24, 1953.

CLARK, William Clifford, govt. official; b. Martintown, Ont., Can., Apr. 18, 1889; s. George Ellis and Catherine (Urquhart) C.; M.A., Queen's Univ., Kingston, Ont., 1910; A.M., Harvard, 1915; LL.D., Queen's Univ., 1935; m. Margaret Hilda Smith, Sept. 16, 1916; children—George Clifford, Eleanor Urquhart (Mrs. D. A. McGinnis), Margaret Catherine (Mrs. D. Johnston), Kenneth Skelton. Lectr., asst. prof., asso. prof. and prof. of econ. and dir. of courses in commerce and adminstrn., Queen's Univ., 1915-23; employed in investment banking, Chicago and New York City, 1923-31; prof. of commerce and dir. of courses in commerce and adminstrn., Queen's Univ., 1931-32; financial advisor, Can. govt., Ottawa, Imperial Conf., 1932; Dep. Minister of Finance and Sec. to Treasury Bd., Can. govt., Ottawa, since Nov., 1932; financial advisor Can. govt. World Monetary and Econ. Conf., London, 1933; mem. bd. dirs. and exec. com., Bank of Canada, Central Mortgage & Housing Corp. and Indsl. Development Bank; member Fgn. Exchange Control Bd., Can. Farm Loan Bd. Trustee Queen's Univ. Decorated Companion of the Order of St. Michael and St. George, 1935. Mem. American Economic Assn., Am. Statistical Assn., Canadian Econ. and Political Science Assn., Royal Economic Society. Clubs: Rideau, Five Lakes Fishing (Ottawa). Author: The Skyscraper, 1929; chapter on Construction Industry in Persons, Foster and Hettinger's The Problem of Business Forecasting, 1929; chapter on the Construction Industry in Warshow's Representative American Industries, 1930. Contbr. articles on economic and financial subjects to various periodicals. Home: 555 Maple Lane, Rockcliffe Park. Office: Deputy Minister of Finance, Confederation Bldg., Ottawa, Ont., Can. Died Dec. 27, 1952.

CLARK, William Irving, physician; b. N.Y. City, Apr. 12, 1879; s. William Irving and Isabel (Robins) C.; Princeton U., 1896-98; A.B., Columbia, 1900; M.D., Coll. Phys. and Surg. (Columbia), 1904; m. Elizabeth H. Pratt, June 23, 1906; children—Katharine Irving (Mrs. Vincent Morgan), William Irving. Interne Roosevelt Hosp., 1904-06; surgeon out-patient dept., Memorial and Worcester City hosps., 1908-17; asst. surgeon Memorial Hosp., 1918-27; consultant in indsl. surgery, 1927—; instr. in indsl. medicine, Harvard Univ., 1919-31, asst. prof., 1931-45; clin. prof., 1940-45; retired; chief surg. to Norton Co., grinding wheels and grinding machines, 1911-48, dir. of personnel, 1919-47, retired 1948; now medical consultant to Norton Co. Shattuck lecturer, Mass. Med. Soc., 1930; chmn. Harvard Advisory Com. on Prison Hygiene. Lt. Am. Red Cross, overseas, 1917-18; capt. M.C., U.S. Army, 1918-19. Mem. President's Housing Com., Com. on Cost of Med. Care; chmn. advisory com. on healthful working conditions, Nat. Association Mfrs. vice president board of trustees Memorial Hospital, 1951—; trustee of Worcester Art Museum. Fellow American College Surgeons, American Academy of Arts and Sciences. Mem. A.M.A., Mass. Med. Soc.; dir. asso. Hosp. Service (ret.); N.E. Surg. Soc., Worcester Fire Soc., St. Wulstan Soc., Am. Antiquarian Soc. Republican. Episcopalian. Clubs: Worcester, Tatnuck Country. Author: Health Service in Industry, 1922; Industrial Medicine, 1935; also sections on indsl. medicine in Oxford Loose Leaf Medicine and Nelson Loose Leaf Medicine. Contbr. to Jour. Am. Med. Assn., Jour. Industrial Hygiene, etc. Home: 5 Marston Way, Worcester 9, Mass. Died Apr. 5, 1958; buried Rural Cemetery, Worcester.

CLARK, William Walker judge; b. Elgin, Ill., Feb. 14, 1858; s. De Marcus and Mary Ella (Walker) C.; A.B., Hamilton College, 1878, LL.D., 1912; m. Hattie M. Hill, Sept. 18, 1879. Began practice at Wayland, N.Y., 1879; dist. atty. Steuben County, 1893-1902; judge Steuben County Court, 1902-06; asso. justice Supreme Court of N.Y., 7th dist., 1906-34; pres. 1st Nat. Bank, Wayland. Republican. Home: Wayland, N.Y. Died 1949.

CLARK, Winfred Newcomb, pub. utility exec.; b. Paxton, Ill., Oct. 13, 1876; s. Abram L. and Sarah E. (Foster) C.; student of U. of Ill., 1894-96; B.Sc. in E.E., Colo. Sch. of Mines, 1898; m. Mary Ward, Apr. 15, 1903; children—Muriel (Mrs. James Gittinger), Helen Louise (Mrs. Geo. Ashby), Winfred Ward. Asst. engr. Colo. Telephone Co., 1898; elec. engr. Silver Lake Mines Co., 1898-99; operating engr. La Bella Mill Water & Power Co., 1899-1900; constr. and operation of Pikes Peak Power Co. and successor companies, 1900-12; pres. Southern Colo. Power Co. (successor to Pikes Peak Power Co.), 1931-51, ret.; registered C.E., State of Colo. Rocky Mt. Elec. Assn. award, 1935. Chmn. Pueblo Co. Relief Assn., 1932-33. Mem. Am. Inst. E.E., Pueblo Engrs. Soc., Colo. Engring. Soc., Am. Mining Congress. Republican. Episcopalian. Mason, Shriner, K. of P., Elk. Clubs: Rotary, Pueblo Golf and Country. Home: 2201 Greenwood. Office: Southern Colorado Power Co., Pueblo, Colo. Died July 19, 1952.

CLARKE, Caspar William, banking exec.; b. Seattle, Wash., June 13, 1892; s. Charles Henry and Frankie (Anderson) C.; B.A., Williams Coll., 1915; m. Virginia Cook, Nov. 8, 1920 (dec.); children—Dorothy Jane, Virginia Frankie; m. 2d, Catherine Collins, Jan. 15, 1929; children—Charles H., Caspar Collins. Asso. with Union Savings & Trust Co., 1915-24; cashier Nat. Bank of Commerce, 1924-29; v.p. Pacific Nat. Bank of Seattle, 1931-38, exec. v.p. 1938-47; chmn. bd., 1947—; dir. Ore. Mesabi Corp., San Juan Fishing & Packing Co. (Seattle). Served as 1st lt., 63d Coast Arty. Corps, A.E.F., 1917-19. Advisory com. Seattle Agency of RFC, exec. com. Seattle Community Chest. Mem. bd. overseers Whitman Coll., Walla Walla, Wash. Mem. Phi Delta Theta. Republican. Episcopalian. Clubs: Seattle Gof (pres. 1940-41). University, Rainier (pres. 1946-47), Washington Athletic (Seattle). Home: The Highlands, Seattle 77. Office: Second and Madison Sts., Seattle, Wash. Died June 23, 1949.

CLARKE, Charles S., ry. ofcl.; b. Frederick, Md., July 16, 1863; s. James C. and Susannah (Schaffer) C.; ed. Soule U., New Orleans; married. Held various positions on I.C. R.R., 1879-90; div. supt., 1890-99, gen. supt., 1899-1902, gen. mgr., 1902-04, M. & O. R.R.; 1st v.-p. Mo. P. Ry, 1904-11; pres. Am. Refrigerator Transit Co., until 1911; dir. St. Louis, Iron Mountain & Southern Ry. Mem. Am. Ry. Assn., Am. Ry. Guild, Am. Geog. Soc., Am. Assn. of Maintenance of Way. Clubs: Maryland Soc. (N.Y. C.); Calumet (Chgo.); Athelston, Mobile Yacht (Mobile), Noonday, Mercantile, Traffic, St. Louis, Bellerive (St. Louis). Address: Hotel Jefferson, St. Louis. Died Nov. 12, 1920.

CLARKE, David Roland, lawyer; b. Ashland, Ill., Jan. 8, 1892; s. Dan Bezeliel and Ammelia Jeannette (Burdick) C.; prep. edn. Whipple Acad., Jacksonville, Ill.; A.B., U. Ill., 1914; LL.B., Harvard, 1917; m. Zada Rowena Walker, Dec. 27, 1915; children—Zada Rowena, Martha Jeannette (Mrs. J. David McJunkin), Davida (Mrs. Alfred W. Maddock). Admitted to Ill. bar, 1917, and began practice at Chicago; mem. firm Fyffe & Clarke since 1921, sr. mem. since 1931; gen. counsel assns. and exhbns.; dir. Walker Estates, Inc.; breeder Holstein-Freesian cattle, Union, Ill. Mem. Am., Ill., Chgo. bar assns., Chicago Law Inst., Chi Psi. Democrat. Clubs: Law, Legal, University of Chicago. Author addresses, papers and pamphlets dealing with current legal and legislative subjects. Home: 160 Cary Av., Highland Park, Ill. Office: 208 S. LaSalle St., Chgo. 4. Deceased.

CLARKE, Donald Henderson, author; b. South Hadley, Mass., Aug. 24, 1887; s. Louis Henry (M.D.) and Georgiana Irene (Henderson) C.; student Harvard, 1904-06, 1909-11; m. Gladys Weber, Sept. 1, 1929. Formerly newspaper writer, New York World, N.Y. Times, N.Y. Am. Author: In the Reign of Rothstein, 1929; Louis Beretti, 1929; The Autobiography of Frank Tarbeaux, 1930; Millie, 1930; Impatient Virgin, 1931; Young and Healthy, 1931; Baby Face (serial), 1931; The Chastity of Gloria Boyd, 1932; John Bartel, Jr., 1932; Female, 1933; Lady Ann, 1934; Kelly, 1935; Regards to Broadway, 1935; Alabam', 1935; Confidential, 1936; That Mrs. Renney, 1937; Housekeeper's Daughter, 1938; Murderer's Holiday, 1940; Lady Named Lou, 1941; Joe and Jennie, 1949; Man of the World, 1951. Address: care Vanguard Press, 424 Madison Av., N.Y.C. 17. Died Mar. 29, 1958.

CLARKE, Harley Lyman, pub. utilities and indsl. exec.; b. Richmond, Mich., Dec. 1, 1882; s. William DeGraff (M.D.) and Emma (Cummings) C.; student lit. law dept. U. Mich., 1900-02; m. Hildur Freeman, 1905; children—John W., Hermona L. Officer or dir. various pub. utility and indsl. cos.; founder Utilities Power & Light Corp. Founder Shakespeare repertory Soc. for Visual Edn., Chgo. Republican. Mason (32°, K.T., Shriner). Home: 21 S. George St., Mt. Prospect, Ill. Died June 3, 1955.

CLARKE, Horace Donald, naval officer; b. May 15, 1892; entered USN, 1911, and advanced through the grades to commodore, 1945. Address: Navy Dept., Washington 25. Died May 10, 1957.

CLARKE, Ida Clyde (Mrs. Thomas H. Clarke), author; b. Meridian, Miss., Mar. 24, 1878; d. Charles William and Annie (Campbell) Gallaher; ed. under pvt. tutors; m. Thomas H. Clarke, Jan. 14, 1900 (died 1911); children—Beverly L., Charles Haden. Mem. editorial staff Nashville Tennesseean until 1909; mng. editor Taylor-Trotwood Mag., 1910; mem. staff Nashville Banner, 1910-13; editor Southern Missionary News Bur., 1913-16; contbg. editor Pictorial Review, 1916-27; now instr. in journalism U. Miami (Fal.). A pioneer worker for woman suffrage in Tenn.; was 1st pres. Business Woman's Equal Suffrage League, Nashville. Clubs: National Arts, Pen and Brush, Woman's Press, Women's City, P.E.N., Town Hall, Am. Women's Assn., Wall Street Woman's (hon.), Sigma Theta Phi (hon.), Dixie Club of New York (hon.), etc. Author: Record No. 33; American Women and The World War; The Little Democracy; Uncle Sam Needs a Wife; Tomorrow's Americans (with Aberdeen Alonzo Bowden), 1930; Men That Wouldn't Stay Dead, 1936. Editor and Compiler: Women of 1923; Women of 1924; Women of Today, 1926. Address: 34 Whittredge Rd., Summit, N.J. Died Aug. 27, 1956.

CLARKE, William Francis, lawyer; born Duluth, Minn., Mar. 23, 1894; s. Thomas and Margaret (Burke) C.; Ph.B., De Paul U., 1916, J.D., from same univ., 1917; m. 2d, Mary Hartnett, Nov. 25, 1944. Instructor, Metropolitan Business College, Elgin, Ill., 1913-14, De La Salle Institute, Chicago, 1914-15, De Paul Acad., 1915-18; dean of De Paul Univ. Coll. of Commerce, 1918-25; dean of De Paul Coll. of Law, 1925-49; in private practice of law in Chicago, 1949—; sec. and treas. De Paul Educational Aid Society. Member board directors Lawson Y.M.C.A. Mem. American, Illinois State and Chicago bar assns., Delta Theta Phi, Delta Sigma Pi, Pi Gamma Mu, Blue Key. Democrat. Mem. Knights of Columbus, Elks. Clubs: Executives, City, Author: Folly of Bigotry; The Soul of the Law. Address: 1244 W. Elmdale Av., Chgo. Died Jan. 18, 1955; buried All Saints Cemetery.

CLARKSON, Edward Everett, business exec.; b. Ogdensburg, N.Y., Mar. 25, 1864; s. George W. and Mary (Spears) C.; student pub. schs., Ogdensburg, Syracuse, N.Y.; m. Flora W. Walker, Jan. 1888; 1 dau., Marion Agnes (Mrs. Ralph Nading Hill). Partner dept. store Barlow, Clarkson & Co., Burlington, Vt., 1887-89, Huntress & Clarkson, 1889-1901; propr. E. E. Clarkson & Co., 1901-32; dir. Howard Nat. Bank & Trust Co., 1926-53, v.p., 1927-29, pres., 1929-48, chmn., 1948-53; v.p., treas. Abernethy, Clarkson, Wright, Inc., 1932-51; v.p., dir. E. B. & A. C. Whiting Co., Burlington; dir. Hotel Vermont, Champlain Transportation Co., Burlington Spool & Bobbin Co., O. L. Hinds & Co., Crystal Confectionary Co.; trustee Burlington Savings Bank. Trustee Mary Fletcher Hosp., Burlington. Clubs: Burlington Country (founder), Ethan Allen (Burlington). Home: 227 S. Willard St., Burlington, Vt. Died Mar. 1953.

CLARKSON, Edward Rycroft, business exec.; b. Panal, Eng., Sept. 1, 1886; s. Robert W. and Eleanor M. Rycroft; grad. Liverpool Coll., 1907; married Eunice Tomlinson, Apr. 15, 1914; children—Margaret (Mrs. A. S. McQueen, Jr.), William R. (M.D.), Eleanor (Mrs. Clyde S. Rine), Nancy (Mrs. R. L. Kress). Sec., treas. Male Attire, Ltd., Montreal, Can., 1907-14; comptroller West India Electric Co., Ltd., Kingston, Jamaica, B.W.I., 1915-16; auditor Peat, Marwick Mitchell & Co., New York, 1916-18, mgr. Pittsburgh branch, 1918-21; controller Kaufmann Dept. Stores, Inc., 1921, treas., dir., 1925-46; v.p. The May Dept. Stores Co., Pittsburgh, since 1946; dir. Pittsburgh Credit Bureau, Telephone Answering Service, Inc., Service Engraving Co., English-Speaking Union, Allegheny Broadcasting Co.; treas. Civic Light Opera Assn. of Greater Pittsburgh; asst. treas. Service Engraving Co. Trustee Olivet Coll. Mem. Controllers Inst. of Am., Controllers Congress of Nat. Retail Dry Goods Assn., Pittsburgh C. of C., Pa. C. of C., Am. Arbitration Soc., Civic Club of Allegheny County, Church Club of Diocese of Pittsburgh, Fgn. Policy Assn. Mason (Shriner). Club: Duquesne. Home: 554 Briar Cliff Rd., Pittsburgh 21. Office: 400 Fifth Av., Pitts. 19. Died Feb. 2, 1952.

CLARKSON, Ralph, painter; b. Amesbury, Mass., Aug. 3, 1861; s. Joseph T. and Susan M. (Watson) C.; ed. high sch., Amesbury, Mass.; studied art, Boston Art Mus., until 1884; Julian Acad. under Lefébvre and Boulanger, 1884-87; m. Fanny Rose Calhoun, Jan. 15, 1890. Exhibited in Salon of 1887; returned to N.Y., where painted portraits; in 1892 again went abroad, spending part of the time in Italy; returned to Am., 1895, and settled in Chgo., 1896. Pres. Municipal Art Commn., Chgo., State Art Commn.; mem. Am. art jury, Paris Expn., 1900; mem. art jury and internat. jury of award, St. Louis Expn., 1904; mem. internat. jury, San Francisco Expn., 1915. Instr. and governing mem. Art Inst. Chgo., A.N.A., 1911; a founder Friends of Am. Art; mem. adv. com. Tiffany Found. (N.Y.); mem. Nat. Inst. Arts and Letters, Portrait Painters, N.Y. Water Color Soc. Summer Home: Oregon, Ill. Studio: 410 S. Michigan Av., Chgo. Died 1942.

CLARSON, James Willis, Jr. (klär'sŭn), educator; b. Baltimore, Md., Jan. 13, 1879; s. James Willis and Mary Jane (Van Alstine) C.; grad. Baltimore City Coll., 1899; student Harvard, 1908, home study div. U. of Chicago, 1910-12; B.S., Ia. State Coll., 1918; A.M., U. of Chicago, 1922, Ph.D., 1928; m. Agnes Gertrude Mahone, Nov. 23, 1904. Teacher, village sch., Williston, Md., 1900-01; prin. rural high schs., Caroline County, Md., 1901-03; prin. and teacher, elementary and prep. schs., Baltimore, 1903-09; prin. private normal sch., Howell, Mo., 1909-10; supt. schs., Ia., 1910-17; also dir. teacher-training, 1914-17; also instr. in edn., Ia. State Coll., summer 1915; part-time instr. in edn., same coll., 1917-18; instr., Mo. State Normal Sch., summer 1918; prof. edn. and teacher training, N.M. Coll. Agr. and Mech. Arts, 1918-21; acting state supervisor agrl. edn., N.M., part-time, 1920-21; prof. secondary edn., U. of Ariz., since 1921, dean coll. of edn. since 1927, also dean of the summer session since 1927; prof. edn., U. of Chicago, summers 1921-28. Member of Arizona Education Association (ex-pres.), National Edn. Assn. (dir. 1935), Am. Assn. School Adminstrs., Nat. Soc. for Study Edn., Phi Delta Kappa, Pi Gamma Mu (gov. Ariz. province), Phi Kappa Phi (ex-pres.). Episcopalian. Mason (K.T.). Club: Kiwanis (ex-pres.). Home: 2143 E. 4th St., Tucson. Died June 9, 1950; buried Druid Ridge Cemetery, Baltimore.

CLATWORTHY, Fred Payne, landscape photographer; b. Dayton, O., Aug. 30, 1875; s. Rev. Frederick, D.D., and Emma C. (Payne) C.; student Colgate, Denison, Stetson univs.; LL.B., Chgo. Coll. of Law, 1898; m. Mabel Leonard, Oct. 12, 1911; children—Fred Payne, Helen Margaret, Barbara Louise. Began in photography Chgo., 1900; specialized in natural color photography and in projecting natural color pictures of western U.S. and fgn. countries before large audiences; supplied illustrations for World's Work, Outlook, Nat. Geog. Mag., etc. Mayor Estes Park, Colo., 1919. Mem. Denver Art Assn., Pictorial Photographers Am., Beta Theta Pi, Alpha Phi, Colo. Mountain Club; Lions (hon. mem.) (Riverside, Cal.); Rotary (Estes Park). Republican. Baptist. Home: (summer) Estes Park, Colo.; (winter) 698 W. Ramon Rd., Palm Springs, Cal. Died July 18, 1953; buried Ft. Collins, Colo.

CLAUDEL, Paul, French diplomat, author, playwright; b. Villeneuve-sur-Fère, Aisne, France, Aug. 6, 1868; s. Louis Prosper and Louise (Cerveaux) C.; grad. Ecole des Sciences Politiques, Licencié en Droit; m. Reine Sainte Marie Perrin, of Lyons, France, Mar. 15, 1906; children—Marie, Pierre, Reine, Henri, Reneé. Apptd. vice consul of France, N.Y.C., 1893; consul, Boston, 1894, Shanghai, China, 1895; minister, Rio de Janeiro, 1916, Copenhagen, 1919; ambassador at Tokyo, 1921; A.E. and M.P. to U.S. 1927-33, to Belgium, 1933-35; ret., 1935, to devote entire time to writing. Recipient Grand Cross Legion of Honor (France). Mem. Academie Francaise. Author of numerous books, verse, plays, including: (plays) L'Echange, 1893; The Book of Christopher Columbus, 1930; (verse) Poèmes de Guerre; (books best known in U.S. through published translations): The East I Know, 1914; The Tidings Brought to Mary, 1916; Selected Poems, The Satin Slipper, The Eye Listens, Correspondence of Paul Claudel and André Gide (1899-1926), Joan at the Stake (which furnished libretto for Arthur Honegger oratorio). Home: Paris, France. Died Feb. 23, 1955.

CLAUSEN, Roy Elwood, univ. prof.; b. Randall, Ia., Aug. 21, 1891; s. Jens and Mathilda (Christianson) C.; B.S., Okla. Agrl. and Mech. Coll., 1910; B.S., U. of Calif., 1912, Ph.D., 1914; m. Mae Winifred Falls, July 19, 1916; 1 son, Roy Elwood. Instr. genetics, U. of Calif., 1914-16, asst. prof., 1916-24, associate prof., 1924-28, prof., 1928—; special duties at the Los Alamos Sci. Lab., Manhattan Dist., 1944-45. Served in U.S. Army, 1917-19. Fellow for special study in cytogenetics. International Education Bd., Stockholm Högskolan, 1926-27; travel fellow for inspection of genetics instns. in northwestern Europe, May-Sept. 1927; spl. consultant in genetics Hawaiian Agrl. Expt. Station and expt. stations of Hawaiian Sugar Planters Assn. and Pineapple Producer Cooperative Assn., May-June 1941; faculty research lecturer U. Cal. at Berkeley, 1954. Mem. Nat. Acad. Science, A.A.A.S. (v.p.; chmn. exec. com. Pacific Div. 1935-44, pres. 1947-48; mem. exec. com. 1940-44), Bot. Soc. America, Am. Genetic Assn., Genetics Society of America (vice president 1952; president 1953), merican Soc. Naturalists, Am. Assn. Univ. Profs., Western Soc. Naturalists, Alpha Zeta, Phi Sigma, Sigma Xi, Phi Kappa Phi. Sec.-gen. 6th Pacific Science Congress, 1939. Democrat. Clubs: Faculty (Berkeley). Author: Genetics in Relation to Agriculture (with E. B. Babcock), 1918, 2d edit., 1927. Contbr. articles to scientific jours. Home: 1885 San

Juan Av., Berkeley 7, Cal. Died Aug. 21, 1956; buried Golden Gate Nat. Cemetery, San Bruno, Cal.

CLAUSEN, Samuel Wolcott, pediatrician; b. Canaseraga, N.Y., Oct. 17, 1888; s. Charles J. and Sarah Gardner (Wolcott) C.; A.B., Williams Coll., 1910; student Princeton U., 1910-11; M.D., Johns Hopkins U., 1915; m. Ethel Marjorie Luce, Oct. 15, 1927. Interne Harriet Lane Home, Baltimore, 1915-16; asst. resident physician Johns Hopkins Hosp., 1916-17; instr. and asso. in pediatrics, Washington U. Sch. of Medicine, St. Louis, 1917-24; prof. pediatrics and pediatrician-in-chief, U. of Rochester Sch. of Medicine and Strong Memorial Hosp., Rochester, N.Y., since 1924; mem. med. staff Rochester Convalescent Hosp. for Children; research work in problems of nutrition with spl. reference to vitamins. Mem. A.A.A.S., Am. Pediatric Soc., Am. Acad. Pediatrics, A.M.A., Am. Chem. Soc., Rochester Acad. Medicine, Soc. for Exptl. Biology and Medicine, Central N.Y. Pediatric Club, Sigma Xi, Alpha Omega Alpha. Episcopalian. Contbr. articles to med. and chem. jours. Home: Route 1, Pittsford, N.Y. Office: 260 Crittenden Blvd., Rochester, N.Y. Died Dec. 29, 1952.

CLAUSON, Clinton Amos, gov. of Me.; b. Mitchell, Ia., Mar. 28, 1895; s. Albert and Belle (Bergerude) C.; grad. Palmer Sch. Chiropractic, Davenport, Ia., 1919; m. Ellen J. Kelleher, Dec. 25, 1919; children—Marjorie Ann (wife of Dr. William A. Chasse), Cornelius K. Practicing chiropractor, Waterville, Me., 1919-32; city treas., Waterville, 1930-31; collector internal revenue Dist. of Me., 1933-52; wholesaler, retailer in oil, Fairfield, Me., 1952-59; mayor, Waterville, 1956-57; gov. of Me., 1959—. Mem. bd. incorporators Waterville Savs. Bank; adv. bd. Depositors Trust Co. Adminstr. for Me., War Bond Sales Program, 1941-43. Served with U.S. Amry, World War I. Mem. Am. Legion (finance com. Me.), Newcomen Soc. N.A. Mason, Odd Fellow. Home: Blaine House. Office: State House, Augusta, Me. Died Dec. 30, 1959.

CLAUSON, J(ames) Earl, writer; b. Troy, N.Y., Aug. 13, 1873; s. Walter B. and Julia (Wilson) C.; student Amherst Coll.; m. Bertha V. Stickney, June 17, 1903; 1 son, James Wilson. Newspaper work, Albany, N.Y., Worcester, Mass., Providence, R.I., etc.; Sunday editor Providence Jour., 1905-10; editorial staff Frank A. Munsey Co. mags., 1910-11; asst. mng. editor N.Y. World, 1921-31. Mem. Delta Kappa Epsilon, Providence Art Club. Author: Cranston, A Historical Sketch, 1904; These Plantations, 1937. Editor: The Dog's Book of Verse, 1916. Home: Wickford, R.I. Died June 24, 1937; buried Jacksonville, Vt.

CLAWSON, Clinton Dudley, mfg. exec.; b. Hamilton, O., Apr. 6, 1902; s. James Clarence and Grace (Hendry) C.; student Ohio State U., 1925; m. Helena Knapp, Aug. 17, 1927; children—Martha Roseberry, Stephen Whiting, William Everett, Daniel Evans; m. 2d, Ingeburg Bartels, Dec. 4, 1954. With Ferro Corp., 1931—, pres., 1947—. Recipient distinguished alumnus award Ohio State U., 1956. Mem. Council on World Affairs, C. of C., Newcomen Soc., Phi Delta Theta. Clubs: City, Acacia Country, Cleveland Athletic (Cleve.); Metropolitan (N.Y.C.). Address: 4150 E. 56th St., Cleve. 5. Died Jan. 4, 1958.

CLAWSON, Marion Don, coll. pres.; b. Clay City, Ill., Feb. 10, 1900; s. Ellis Henry and Shaba (Bissey) C.; ed. Clay City and Harter-Stanford Township High Sch.; student St. Louis (Mo.) U., 1922-25; D.D.S., Washington U., 1926; m. Rue G. Stanford, Sept. 4, 1926; 1 dau., Carolyn Maureen. Engaged in gen. practice of dentistry, Bonne Terre, Mo., 1926-28, in dental survey, England, 1928-29; in pvt. practice, St. Louis, 1929; prof. operative dentistry, Am. Univ. of Beirut, Syria, 1930-34, dir. dental education, 1932-34; dir. dental health services, Iraq Petroleum Co., Haifa, Palestine, 1934-41, chief dental surgeon (company service), Kirkuk Hosp., Kirkuk, Iraq, 1936-41; mem. hosp. staff Am. Univ., Beirut, 1930-34; visiting clinician St. Joseph U., Beirut, also Syrian U., Damascus, Syria, 1934-41; prof. dentistry, Meharry Med. Coll., Nashville, since 1942, dir. dental edn. since 1942, pres. of college since Jan. 1945. Dir. dental service, Manhattan Project for Atomic Research, Oak Ridge, Tenn., 1943-45. Enlisted as hospital apprentice, U.S. Navy, 1920, discharged as pharmacist mate 2d class, 1922. Mem. bd. trustees Fisk Univ., Meharry Med. Coll. Received Pierre Fauchard award for contributions to international dentistry, 1945. Mem. A.M.A., Am. Dental Soc. of Europe, Am. (com. on internat. relations) and Mo. dental assns., Palestine Dental Soc., Acad. Odontology (Buenos Aires), Internat. Dental Fedn., Internat. Commn. Oral Hygiene, Union of Drs. of Dental Surgery of Syria and Lebanon, Internat. Coll. Dentistry, pres. coll.-at-large, 1947, pres. U.S. sect. Internat. Coll., 1947; regent 29th Dist. Internat. Coll. (Turkey, Syria, Lebanon, Iran, Iraq, Palestine, Trans-Jordan, Cyprus), 1931-41; Office Strategic Services U.S. Govt., Arab Section, 1946; mem. Council of Fgn. Relations, Fedn. Dentaire Internat. (Geneva, Switzerland), Delta Sigma Delta, Omicron Kappa Upsilon, Kappa Pi. Clubs: Nashville, Executives, Zodiac, Rotary International (Nashville). Contributor to science publications, United States and abroad. Home: 209 W. Vanderbilt Dr., Oak Ridge, Tenn. Died Dec. 17, 1951; buried Mt. Zion Cemetery, Clay City, Ill.

CLAXTON, Mary Hannah Johnson (Mrs. Philander P. Claxton), b. Nashville; d. George S. and Hannah Iredel (Payne) Johnson; library course U. Chgo.; m. Philander Priestley Claxton, Apr. 23, 1912; children—Phil P., Mary Payne. Active in creating pub. library movement, Nashville, and head of Carnegie Library 10 yrs.; promoted Free State Library Commn. in Tenn.; organized first system in the South for supplying and sending books to the pub. schs. by pub. library; active in promoting rural libraries in rural schs. Mem. Auxiliary Com. of U.S. Pan.-Am. Scientific Congress, League of Am. Pen Women, Nat. Council of Women, Nat. Congress of Mothers, A.L.A., D.A.R., U.D.C., others. Episcopalian. Clubs: College Women's, Washington, Ala. Univ. Women's. Home: Clarksville, Tenn. Died July 17, 1955.

CLAXTON, Philander Priestley, educator; b. Bedford County, Tenn., Sept. 28, 1862; s. Joshua Calvin and Anne Elizabeth (Jones) C.; A.B., U. Tenn., 1882, A.M., 1887; postgrad. Johns Hopkins, 1884-85; student edn. and schs. Germany, 1885-86; visited schs. Europe, 1897, 1925, 30; Litt.D., Bates Coll., 1906; LL.D., Western Res. U., 1912, U. N.C., 1914, Allegheny Coll., 1915, U. Md., 1921; m. Varina S. Moore, Dec. 1885 (died 1891); 1 dau., Claire; m. 2d, Anne Elizabeth Porter, Sept. 1894 (died 1905); children—Henel Elizabeth, Calvin Porter, Anne Elizabeth, Robert Edward (dec.); m. 3d, Mary Hannah Johnson, Apr. 23, 1912; children—Philander Priestley, Mary Payne. Supt. schs., Kinston, N.C., 1883-84, Wilson, 1886-87, Asheville, 1887-93; prof. pedagogy, German, 1893-96, prof. pedagogy and dir. Practice and Observation Sch., N.C. State Norman and Indsl. Coll., 1896-1902; prof. of edn. U. Tenn., 1902-11, prof. secondary edn. and insp. high schs., 1906-11; U.S. commr. of edn., 1911-21; provost U. Ala., 1921-23; supt. schs., Tulsa, 1923-29; pres. Austin Peay Normal School, Clarksville, Tenn., 1930-46, pres. emeritus, 1946—. Was editor N.C. Journal of Edn. 1897-1901, Atlantic Ednl. Journal, 1901-03; mem. So. Ednl. Bd., chief bureau of investigation and information, 1902-03; supt. Summer Sch. of South, 1902-11; mem. Rockefeller Sanitary Commn.; dir. Moral Edn. Bd. Mem. council N.E.A.; sec., pres. So. Ednl. Assn.; dir. Playground Assn. Am.; chmn. exec. com. Nat. Story Tellers' League; v.p. Am. Sch. Peace League; mem. Study Edn., A.A.A.S., League for Enforcement Peace; chmn. Nat. Student Forum on Paris Pact, 1929-38. Mem. Phi Beta Kappa, Phi Delta Kappa. Democrat. Methodist. Club: Cosmos. Author: (with James McGinniss) Effective English, 1917, Effective English, Junior, 1921; also many addresses and published articles on edn. Home: Clarksville, Tenn. Died Jan. 1957; buried Knoxville, Tenn.

CLAY, Ryburn Glover, banker; b. Marietta, Ga., Jan. 20, 1891; s. Alexander Stephens and Frances (White) C.; wife, Helen N.; children—Zaida Willis, Ryburn Glover. Began as banker, 1907; pres. Clay Moore, Inc.; former pres. Fulton Nat. Bank, Atlanta, Ga.; former dir. Federal Reserve Bank of Atlanta (6 years); mem. advisory board Federal Reserve System; former pres. Southeastern Pipe Line Co.; v.p Claymore, Inc.; treas. Maxwell Constrn. Co.; director Colonial Stores, Southeastern Greyhound Lines, Randall Bros. Former dir. Georgia State Highway Dept. Trustee Scottish Rite Hospital, Young Harris Coll.; mem. adv. bd. Salvation Army, and Polio Funds; dir. Atlanta Art Assn.; mem. Chamber of Commerce; chmn. Jackson Day Dinner, 1941; former mem. Stone Mountain Memorial Assn.; former chmn. Dem. Finance Com. of Ga. Democrat. Episcopalian. Clubs: Capital City (dir.), Piedmont Driving, Atlanta Athletic (Atlanta); Bankers (New York). Home: 21 Cherokee Road, Atlanta. Died Dec. 10, 1955; buried Westview Cemetery, Atlanta.

CLAYBORN, John Henry, bishop African Meth. Episcopal Ch. Served as a chaplain Rep. Nat. Conv., 1952. Address: 1800 Marshall St., Little Rock, Ark. Died June 17, 1954.

CLAYPOOL, Harold K., ex-congressman; b. Bainbridge, O., June 2, 1886; s. Horatio C. and Elizabeth L. (Kile) C.; studied Ohio State U.; m. Frances C. Helfrich, May 1, 1909; 1 son, Forest C. E. (dec.). Pub., Hunter and Trader Mag.; mem. 75th-77th Congresses, 11th Ohio Dist. Democrat. Presbyn. Elk, Eagle. Club: Chillicothe. Home: Chillicothe, O. Died Aug. 2, 1958; buried Grandview Cemetery, Chillicothe, O.

CLAYTON, Ernest, banker; b. Waterloo, Lancashire, Eng., July 8, 1889; s. William and Sarah (Ratcliffe) C.; ed. pub. schs.; m. Maude Angell Burton, Oct. 15, 1919; children—Alden Gould, Eleanor Angell. Came to U.S., 1890, father naturalized, 1896. Messenger Indsl. Trust Co., 1906, asst. treas., 1924, treas., 1929, v.p., treas., 1931, pres., 1941, chmn. bd., 1953—; dir. Newport Trust Co., Newport, R.I., Scott Testers, Inc., Hope Webbing Co., Pawtucket, R.I. Trustee R.I. Pub. Expenditures Council. Served with A.E.F. Clubs: Hope, Agawam Hunt, University, Providence Art, British Empire, Turk's Head. Home: 165 Taber Av. Office: 111 Westminster St., Providence, R.I. Died Dec. 26, 1955; buried Swan Point.

CLAYTON, William Brasher, elec. mfg. co. exec.; b. Bklyn., Apr. 7, 1888; s. Col. B. T. and Louise (Marston) C.; B.S., Ala. Poly. Inst., 1905; m. Bess Sheppard, Apr. 24, 1948. With Gen. Electric Co. 1905-53, dept. mgr., Dallas, 1914-39, dist. mgr., 1939-53, v.p. (comml.), 1942-53, mem. president's staff, 1945-53, ret.; v.p. Gen. Electric Realty Corp. Pres. Tex. A. and M. Research Found., 1946—. Chmn. Dallas Co. U.S. savs. bonds div. Mem. bd. Canterbury House Student Center So. Meth. U., 1953—. Served as capt. U.S. Army, World War I. Mem. Am. Legion (ex-comdr. Electric post), C. of C. Episcopalian. Mason (32°). Clubs: Electric (past pres.), Kiwanis, Dallas Country, Downtown (Dallas). Author: Testing Electric Apparatus (with Jas. D. Craig). Home: 3719 Mockingbird Lane, Dallas 5. Office: 1801 N. Lamar St., Dallas 2; also 650 17th St., Denver 2. Died July 31, 1957.

CLEARY, Daniel Francis, govt. ofcl.; b. Chicago, June 4, 1910; s. Daniel Francis and Anna Margaret (Early) C.; A.B., Loyola, 1934, J.D., 1937; m. Gertrude Scanlan, Apr. 10, 1937; children—Mary Denise, Ann Deirdre, Daniel F. Admitted to Ill. State bar, Dec. 1937, practice of law, Chicago, 1937-42; mem. firm Garvey, Cleary & Doyle; retraining splist. Dept. of Labor, Washington, 1945-46; sr. atty. Vets. Adminstrn., Washington, 1946-49; chmn. War Claims Commn. since 1949. Served as 1st lt., capt. and maj., U.S.A.A.F., 1942-45; disch. to A.A.F. Res. as maj. Mem. Chicago bar assn., Am. Legion, Disabled Am. Vets., Internat. Brotherhood Elec. Workers (A.F. of L.). Democrat. Roman Catholic. Club: National Press (Washington). Home: 3735 Oliver St., Washington 15. Office: Tariff Bldg., Washington 25. Died Dec. 5, 1953; buried Arlington Nat. Cemetery.

CLEARY, George J., life ins. exec.; b. Kearney, Neb., Oct. 16, 1896; s. James A. and Bridget T. (Hurley) C.; student Neb. State Tchrs. Coll.; LL.B., Creighton University, 1918; m. Dorothy L. Cleary, May 1, 1923; children—John E., Margaret A. Admitted to the Nebraska bar; attorney for the Mut. Benefit Health & Accident Assn., 1920-49, v.p., 1936-49, dir., 1940-49; atty. United Benefit Life Ins. Co., Omaha, 1926-49, became pres., dir., 1949, now chmn. exec. com. Served in USN, 1918-19. Mem. Am., Neb., Omaha bar assns., Delta Theta Phi. K.C. Home: 100 S. 90th St., Omaha. Office: 3316 Farnam St., Omaha 3, Neb. Died Oct. 11, 1955; buried Calvary Cemetery, Omaha, Neb.

CLEAVELAND, Harry Hayes, Jr., realty exec.; b. Rock Island, Ill., Aug. 29, 1898; s. Harry Hayes and Olive (Cox) C.; grad. Knox Coll., 1920; grad. study Harvard, 1920-21; m. Fay Booth, Sept. 6, 1922; 1 son, Harry Hayes. Partner H. H. Cleaveland Agy., Rock Island, 1921—; v.p. Bituminous Casualty Corp., 1936-45, pres., 1945—, Ft. Armstrong Co., Oheda Realty Trust; v.p. Blackhawk Fed. Savings & Loan Assn.; dir. Rock Island Bank & Trust Co. Trustee Knox Coll. Served as 2d lt., inf., U.S. Army, 1918. Mem. Ins. Fedn. Ill. (v.p.), Phi Delta Theta. Republican. Presbyn. Elk. Mason. Clubs: Davenport (Ia.); Union League (Chicago); Arsenal Golf (Rock Island). Home: 54 Hawthorne Rd. Office: 320 18th St., Rock Island, Ill. Died Nov. 10, 1952.

CLEAVINGER, John Simeon (klĕv'ĭn-jĕr), library service; b. Springfield, Ill., Dec. 3, 1880; s. Robert Thomas and Emma (Bearce) C.; A.B., U. of Ill., 1909, B.L.S., 1910; m. Cora W. Todd, Feb. 15, 1919; 1 dau., Martha Bearce (Mrs. P. E. McCaskie). Librarian Jackson (Mich.) Pub. Library, 1910-19; tchr. U. Ill. Library Sch., 1919-23; librarian Pub. Library, Saginaw, Mich., 1923-26; asso. prof. Columbia U. Sch. of Library Service, 1926-46; ret., 1946. Librarian, Camp Custer, Mich., 1917-18. Mem. A.L.A., Alpha Tau Omega, Phi Beta Kappa. Nonpartisan. Episcopalian. Club: Faculty. Author: Library Personnel and Training Agencies in Michigan, 1940. Home: 106 Morningside Drive, N.Y.C. Died Dec. 30, 1954; buried Oak Ridge Cemetery, Springfield, Ill.

CLEE, Frederick Raymond, clergyman; b. Worcester, Mass., Oct. 25, 1897; s. rederick and Margaret (Kelley) C.; A.B., Clark U., 1917, Litt.D., 1941; R.D., Union Theol. Sem., N.Y.C., 1922; D.D., Rutgers U., 1927; m. Ethel Stevens, Sept. 7, 1922; children—Robert Stevens, Jane Margaret. Ordained to ministry Presbyn. Ch., 1922; minister Good Shepherd Ch., N.Y.C., 1922-27, Old Bergen Ch., Reformed Ch. in Am., Jersey City (founded 1660), 1927-43; minister First Ch. in Albany (Reformed), 1943—; dir. Domestic Mission Bd., Reformed Ch. in America; pres. Gen. Synod of Reformed Ch. in America, 1936-37. Served in Am. Field Service with French Army, 1917, in U.S. Army, with AEF, 1918. Pres. Kiwanis Club of Jersey City, 1939. Home: 22 Stonehenge Lane, Albany, N.Y. Died Apr. 11, 1951.

CLEGG, Lee Milton, business cons.; b. Providence, R.I., July 16, 1897; s. Robert Ingham and Emma (Poole) C.; B.S., Case Institute Technology, 1918; married Albertine Helen Ahrens, September 27, 1930; children—Lee M., Donna Jeannette (Mrs. John W.

Moffly, IV), Michael Ahrens. With Thompson Ramo Wooldridge, Inc. (formerly Thompson Products, Inc.), Cleve., 1919—, successively sales mgr., v.p., dir., now consultant; director National Malleable & Steel Castings Co., Cleveland, O.; dir. Automotive Parts Manufacturers Association, Detroit. Served as 2d lieut., Field Artillery, World War I. Trustee Case Inst. of Tech. (Cleveland). Member Case Alumni Assn. (pres. 1938-39), Cleveland C. of C., Cleveland Engring. Soc., Soc. Automotive Engrs., Phi Kappa Psi. Mason (32°). Clubs: Union (Cleveland); Country, Pepper Pike (Chagrin Falls, O.); Detroit (Mich.) Athletic; Gatineau Fish & Game (Point Comfort, P.Q.). Home: 13705 Shaker Blvd. Office: 23555 Euclid Av., Cleveland 17, O. Died Jan. 5, 1960.

CLEGHORN, Sarah Norcliffe, author; b. Norfolk, Va., Feb. 4, 1876; d. John Dalton and Sarah Chestnut (Hawley) C.; grad. Burr and Burton Sem., Manchester, Vt., 1895; student Radcliffe Coll., 1895-96. Pacifist, socialist, anti-vivisectionist. Author: A Turnpike Lady, 1907; The Spinster, 1916; Fellow Captains (with Dorothy Canfield Fisher); 1916; Portraits and Protests, 1917; Three Score, 1936; The Seamless Robe, 1945. Contbr. poems and ballads to mag. Home: Stapeley Hall, 6300 Green St., Phila 44. Died Apr. 4, 1959; buried Chestnut Hill Friends Burial Ground, Plymouth Meetings, Pa.

CLELAND, John Scott (klēl'ánd), coll. dean; b. Coin, Ia., July 23, 1887; s. John Wilson and Elizabeth (Scott) C.; A.B., Muskingum Coll., 1908; A.M., Princeton, 1909; Ph.D., U. of Pittsburgh, 1914; m. Margaret Hardy Brown, July 26, 1917 (died 1936); m. 2d, Eva Margaret Hanna, 1941; children—Robert Scott, John Wilson, Wallace Brown. Associate professor in economics, Dickinson College, Carlisle, Pa., 1914-15; prof. economics, Carroll Coll., Waukesha, Wis., 1915-17 and 1919; asso. prof. economics, U. of Ky., 1920-21; dean Muskingum Coll., 1920-27, Monmouth Coll. since 1927. Served in U.S. army camps as 1st lt. F.A., U.S. Army, 1917-19. Mem. Am. Econ. Assn. United Presbyn. Home: Monmouth, Ill. Died Dec. 7, 1951.

CLELAND, Robert Glass, educator; b. Shelbyville, Ky., Feb. 19, 1885; s. Robert Wickliffe and Sallie Steele (Glass) C.; grad. Occidental Acad., Los Angeles, 1903; A.B., Occidental Coll., 1907, Litt.D., 1942; A.B., Princeton, 1909, Ph.D., 1912; LL.D., Coe Coll., Cedar Rapids, Ia., 1941; m. Muriel Guy Stewart, 1913 (died 1943); children—Robert Stewart, George Horace. With Occidental Coll., Los Angeles, 1912-43, incumbent of Norman Bridge chair of Hispanic-Am. relations, formerly v.p. and dean of faculty; research asso. Huntington Library, 1937-3 mem. permanent research staff 1943—. Mem. Doheny Research Found. for Study of Mexico, 1917-18. Mem. Am. Hist. Assn. (pres. Pacific Coast br. 1924-25), So. Cal. Hist. Soc. (pres.), Phi Beta Kappa, Tau Kappa Alpha, Phi Gamma Delta. Democrat. Presbyn. Clubs: Sunset, Twilight. Author: Mexican Year Book (1920-21), 1922, also (1922-24); History of California, The American Period, 1922; One Hundred Years of the Monroe Doctrine, 1923; Ca fornia Pathfinders, 1928; The History of Occidental College, 1887-1937, 1937; The Place Called Sespe, 1940; The Cattle on a Thousand Hills, 1941; From Wilderness to Empire, 1944; California Pageant, 1946; California In Our Time, 1947; This Reckless Breed of Men, 1950; El Molino Viejo, 1950. Co-editor: Knopf's Western America Series. Contbr. articles on Mexico to Atlantic Monthly etc. Address: Huntington Library, San Marino 9, Cal. Died Sept. 3, 1957.

CLEMENS, James Ross (klĕm'ĕns), pediatries; b. St. Louis, Sept. 19, 1866; s. Bryan Mullanphy and Mary Ross (Warfield) C.; licentiate in medicine and surgery, Apothecaries Soc., London, 1900; studied St. Thomas, London hosps.; admitted by exam. mem. Royal Coll. Surg., licentiate Royal Coll. Phys.; m. Katherine Boland, 1899; children—Mary Muriel, Cyril Coniston. Prof. pediatrics St. Louis U., 1908—; dean Med. Dept. Creighton U., Omaha, Neb., 1916-18. Maj. Med. Corps, U.S. Army. Mem. A.M.A., Mo. State Med. Assn., St. Thomas Pediatric Soc., James Boswell Club, Chgo. (hon.). Winner prize for play offered by One-Act-Play Theatre, London, Eng., 1935; 2d prize Oxford U. Press play writing competition for plays suitable for English schs., 1937. Elected mem. Dramatists' Alliance of Stanford U., 1940. Represented in "Poetry and Its Appreciation" (by Untermeyer and Davidson), 1934. Contbr. articles to Am. and Eng. Mags. Catholic. Home: 37 Gray Av., Webster Groves, Mo. Died July 18, 1948; buried Calvary Cemetery, St. Louis.

CLEMENT, Allan Montgomery, stocks, bonds, etc.; b. Chgo., Oct. 31, 1869; s. Austin and Sarah (Montgomery) C.; grad. Chicago Manual Training Sch., 1886; m. Grace Groves, 1894; children—Austin Arthur, Franklin Groves. Began business career in 1886 and was in the house of Clement, Bane & Co. for 15 yrs.; partner Raymond Pynchon & Co., stock brokers, 3 yrs.; then partner in Lester, Kneeland & Co., 1 yr., which firm after the death of Mr. Lester, was succeeded by Kneeland, Clement & Curtis, and in Jan. 1907, became Clement, Curtis & Co., ret., 1942; with E. F. Hutton & Co., 1942-49, merged with Clement, Curtis & Co., July 1949. Republican. Clubs: Chicago Athletic, Glenview. Home: 209 Lake Shore Dr. Office: 141 W. Jackson Blvd., Chgo. Died Apr. 7, 1953; buried Rosehill Cemetery, Chgo.

CLEMENT, William Tardy, marine officer; b. Lynchburg, Va., Sept. 27, 1894; s. William Joseph and Mary Elizabeth (Frees) C.; B.S., Va. Mil. Inst., 1914; widower; children—John Cristy, David Alexander, Nancy Carrington; married 2d, Mrs. Ethel G. Mathiesen; 1 son, Robert Andrew Mathiesen. Commissioned 2d lieutenant, United States Marine Corps, 1917, and advanced through grades to lt. gen., 1944; expeditionary duty, Republic of Haiti, 1917-19; duty at Quantico, Va., 1919-23; with Am. Legation Guard, Peking, China, 1923-25; duty at San Diego, Calif., 1925-27 and 1929-30; expeditionary duty, Shanghai, China, 1927-29; comdr. marine detachment, U.S.S. West Virginia, 1930-32; Naval Ammunition Depot Guard, Bremerton, Wash., 1932-34; student and instr., Marine Corps Sch., Quantico, Va., 1934-38; comdr. 1st bn., 5th Marines, 1938-40; fleet marine officer for U.S. Asiatic Fleet aboard U.S.S. Augusta and U.S.S. Houston, 1940-41; at outbreak of war, joined 4th Marines and served throughout Bataan; escaped from Bataan, 1942, and returned to U.S.; mem. staff of comdr., U.S. Naval Forces in Europe, 1942-43; asst. comdr. and comdr. Marine Corp Schs., Quantico, Va., 1943-44; asst. div. comdr., 6th Marine Div., during seizure of Okinawa Shima, Ryukyu Islands and later during occupation of Tsingtao, China, 1944-45; comdr. 3d Fleet Landing Force in initial landings and occupation at Yokusuka Naval and Air Base, Japan, 1945; comdg. gen. 3d Marine Brigade (formerly 6th Div.) Tsingtao area, June 1946; returned to U.S., Sept. 1946; pres. Naval Retiring Bd., 1947-49; dir. Marine Corps Reserve, April 1947, Hdqrs. M.C.; comdg. gen. Marine Corps Recruit Depot, San Diego, Cal., 1949-52. Awarded Navy Cross for service on Bataan, Legion of Merit for Okinawa, 2d Legion of Merit, occupation of Japan, 3d Legion of Merit services in China, U.S. Army Presdl. Citation for Bataan, Bronze Star Medal, U.S. Navy Presdl. Citation, World War I Medal with star, Haitian Campaign Medal, Marine Corps Expeditionary Medal with two stars, Yangtze Campaign Medal, China Service Medal, Asiatic-Pacific Theatre Ribbon with three stars, European Theatre Ribbon, U.S. Theatre Ribbon, Philippine Defense Medal (U.S.), Medal and Diploma of Special Collar Order of Yun Hui, Pao Ting Medal (China); Commander Order of Orange (Nassau). Home: 6120 Avenida Cresta, La Jolla, Cal. Died Oct. 17, 1955; buried Arlington Nat. Cemetery.

CLEMENTS, George P., counselor agr., conservation; b. Dumfries, N.B., Can., Nov. 12, 1867; s. Frederick William dePyster and Mary Anna (Jones) C.; came to U.S., 1881; M.D., U. of Nebraska, 1896; LL.D., University of California, 1944; m. Esther W. Hoag, May 25, 1898; 1 dau., Catherine Emily (Mrs. John Clifford Argue). In passenger dept. C.,B.&Q. R.R., 1886-89; with Armour & Co., Armour & Cudahy and Cudahy Packing Co., 1890-92; in gen. med. and surg. practice, Clarkson and Albion, Neb., 1896-1900; owner and operator of pureblood stock farm, 1897-99; engaged in gen. and exptl. agr., Riverside, Calif., 1900-18; organizer, 1918, and mgr. agrl. dept. Los Angeles (Calif.) Chamber of Commerce, 1918-39, counselor on agr. and conservation, 1939-47. Chmn. City Council, Clarkson, Neb., 1897-98; dep. state health commr., Neb., 1897-99; coroner, Colfax County, Neb., 1898. Decorated Chevalier du Merite Agricole (France), 1933; selective service medal, U.S. Congress, World War II. Dir. Los Angeles Co. Farm Bur., Calif. Jr. Republic; mem. Calif. State Land Use Planning Com., 1941—; mem. adv. com. on land utilization for State Planning Bd.; mem. Soil Conservation Service Regional Bd.; mem. Appeal Bd. No. 10, Selective Service; mem. S.W. Museum, Museum Hill Com. Fellow (1940) Pacific Geog. Soc. (dir., v.p. and treas., 1921-31); mem. Los Angeles Tb and Health Assn. (dir. and sec. 1921-37, Fellow, 1940—), State Assn. County Agrl. Commrs. (hon.), Southern California Consevration Assn. (dir.). Sigma Xi. Democrat. Episcopalian. Mason. Clubs: University, Andreas Canyon (pres. 1922-39, dir. since 1939). Contbr. articles and papers on agrl. economics. Home: 4805 Alta Canada Road, La Canada, Calif. Office: Chamber of Commerce, Los Angeles 15. Died Aug. 7, 1958; buried Forest Lawn, Glendale, Cal.

CLEPHANE, Walter Collins (klē-făn'), lawyer; b. West Haven, Conn., July 17, 1867; s. Lewis and Annie M. (Collins) C.; LL.B., George Washington U., 1889, LL.M., 1890, LL.D., 1932; m. Nellie Mathilda Walker, Jan. 20, 1896; children—Beatrice A. (dec.), Douglas W., John W. Clerk wholesale store, N.Y., 1884; court stenog. Washington 1889—; mem. Clephane Latimer & Hall; became prof. law, George Washington U., 1897, now emeritus; dir., mem. exec. com. Nat. Savings & Trust Co.; mem. Nat. Ry. Labor Panel and many ry. arbitration and presdl. emergency boards. Judge adv. U.S. Army, 1918-20; later col. judge adv., O.R.C. Ex-pres. bd. trustees Indsl. Home Sch., D.C. Mem. Am., D.C. bar assns., Columbia Hist. Soc., Order of Coif, Phi Delta Phi, Kappa Alpha. Republican. Presbyn. Clubs: Cosmos (Washington); hevy Chase (Md.). Author: Clephane on Organization and Management of Business Corps., 1905; Clephane on Equity Pleading and Practice, 1926. Home: 6000 Connecticut Av., Chevy Chase 15, Md. Office: Investment Bldg., Washington 5. Died Aug. 15, 1951; buried Arlington Nat. Cemetery.

CLEVELAND, Frank Ernest, architect; b. Richmond, P.Q., Can., Nov. 11, 1877; s. William Thompson and Emma (Foster) C.; student architecture in Europe, 1900-04; m. Beulah I. Barker, Apr. 5, 1904; children—William Templeton, Foster Barker. Came to U.S., 1878, naturalized, 1898. With Cram and Ferguson, architects, Boston, as designer of ecclesiastical bldg. and furnishings; Baptistry of Cathedral of St. John the Divine, N.Y.C., East Liberty Presbyn. Ch., Pitts., St. James Ch., N.Y.C., furnishings of St. Vincent's Ch., Los Angeles, and others, 1904—. Recipient gold medal for design and draftsmanship by Architectural League of New York, 1903. Master craftsman Boston Soc. of Arts and Crafts. Fellow A.I.A.; mem. St. Augustine Hist. Soc. and Inst. Sci., Bostonian Soc. Republican. Episcopalian. Home: 177 Summit Av., Wollaston (Quincy), Mass. Office: 248 Boylston St., Boston. July 30, 1950; buried Blue Hill Cemetery, Braintree, Mass.

CLEVELAND, Paul W(illiams), s. Festus W. and Edith C. (Williams) C.; LL.B., Northwestern U.; m. Mary L. Spring; 1 dau., Cynthia (Mrs. Graham Fairbank). Financial consultant; director and chmn. finance com. Am. Stamping Co., Cleveland; dir. Beatrice Foods Co., Inc. Mem. Sigma Chi, Phi Delta Phi. Republican. Clubs: Caxton, Tavern, University. Home: 682 Lincoln Av., Winnetka, Ill. Died July 17, 1952.

CLEVERLEY, Frank(lin) T(homas) (clĕv-ĕr-lē), Red Cross exec.; b. Norwalk, Conn., Feb. 4, 1903; s. Abraham Blanch and Bertha May (Crockett) C.; student, N.Y.U., 1920-25; m. Mary Foster Underwood, Apr. 9, 1925; 1 dau., Mary Winslow. Administrative asst. to dean, grad. sch. of bus., N.Y.U., 1923-25; officer mgr., Conn. Light and Power Co., 1926-29; bus. rep., Cape and Vineyard Electric Co., Hyannis, Mass., 1929-37; co-owner and mgr., High Brewster Inn, 1931-42; club dir., exec. asst. to del., dep. commr., commr., A.R.C., Mediterranean theater of operations, 1943-47; adminstr. of fgn. operations, A.R.C., 1947—. Selectman, assessor and chmn., Bd. of Welfare, Brewster, Mass., 1938-44; pres., Cape Cod Rep. Club, 1940-41; dir. Chatham (Mass.) Dramatic Guild, 1930-37. Served as capt., Mass. militia, 1942-43. Decorated by Danish Red Cross for service in World War II. Mem. Theta Chi, Delta Phi Epsilon. Republican. Protestant. Home: 3308 Valley Dr., Alexandria, Va. Office: American National Red Cross, Washington 13. Died Aug. 18, 1952; buried "Little Red," Flint Hill, Va.

CLIFFORD, Harry Ellsworth, elec. engr.; b. Lowell, Mass., Apr. 21, 1866; s. Raeburn Gilman and Helen Rebecca (Hodgdon) C.; S.B., Mass. Inst. Tech., 1886, S.D. (hon.), 1937; grad. student, Harvard, 3 yrs.; m. Harriet Briggs Rogers, June 24, 1896; 1 dau., Gretchen. Asst. prof. theoretical physics, 1895-1902, asso. prof. theoretical electricity, 1902-04, prof. theoretical and applied electricity, 1904-09, Mass. Inst. Tech.; became Gordon McKay prof. elect. engring., Grad. Sch. Applied Sci. (Harvard), 1909, now emeritus, became dean Harvard Engring. Sch., 1930, now emeritus; cons. practice prof. Post Grad. Sch., U.S. Naval Acad., 1913-15, mem. Bd. Visitors; mem. adv. bd., U.S. Coast Guard, 1933—; cons. editor, McGraw-Hill Book Co., 1910—. Fellow Am. Acad. Arts Scis., A.A.A.S., Am. Inst. E.E. (past chmn. Boston br.; mem. Edison medal com.); Illuminating Engring. Soc.; mem. Nat. Electric Light Assn. (past chmn. N.E. br.), Am. Electric Ry. Assn., Circolo Matematico di Palermo, Tau Beta Pi, Sigma Xi, etc. Republican. Unitarian. Clubs: University, Harvard (Boston); Brae Burn Country. Home: Newton Center, Mass. Died 1952.

CLIFFORD, John David, judge; b. Lewiston, Me., May 15, 1887; s. John Dumas and Katherine (Sullivan) C.; A.B., Bowdoin Coll., 1910, LL.D., 1952; B.L., Georgetown U. Law Sch., 1913; LL.D., Portland Law School, 1952; m. Lucille Smith, July 14, 1915; children—Jeanne Louise, John D., 3d. Admitted to Me. bar, 1913; later to bar Supreme Court of D.C. and Dist. Court of U.S. for Me.; mem. firm Clifford & Clifford, Lewiston, 1914—; mem. Me. State Legislature, 1915-16; U.S. atty. for Me. 1933-47; apptd. judge of U.S. Dist. Ct. for Me., March 1947. Gov. Huntington Sch., Boston. Mem. Am., Me. State and Androscoggin County bar assns., Alpha Delta Phi. Democrat. Catholic. K.C., Grange. Clubs: Rotary, Cumberland (Portland, Me.). Home: 16 Ware St., Lewiston, Me. Office: Fed. Court House, Portland, Me. Died Nov. 18, 1956; buried Lewiston.

CLIFTON, John Leroy, educator; b. Etna, O., June 13, 1881; grad. high sch., Etna, 1898; B.S., Ohio U., 1913; Ph.D., Ohio State U. Began as tchr. rural schs., Licking County, O., 1898; supt. schs., Homer, O., 1903-07, Mendon, O., 1907-11; exam. dept., Ohio State Dept. Edn., 1911-13; asst. state supt. schs., 1913-15; asst. prof. Ohio State U.,

1915-17, prof., 1917-27; state supt. pub. instr., dir. edn., Ohio, 1927-31; prof. sch. adminstrn., Ohio State U., 1931—. Author numerous ednl. books and articles. Home: 207 15th Av., Columbus, O. Died Apr. 24, 1943; buried Union Cemetery, Columbus, O.

CLIFTON, Louis, dir. univ. extension; b. Scott County, Ky., Feb. 22, 1887; s. James Harrison and Susan (Jackson) C.; student Eastern State Normal Sch., 1908-10; A.B., U. Ky., 1925, A.M., 1929; student U. Cin., 1925-26, Columbia, 1930; m. Sarah Ellen Ward, Dec. 27, 1913; 1 dau., Dorothy Eloise. Prin. Ky. grade and high schs., 1908-26; joined Extension Dept., U. Ky., 1926, acting dir. 1934-35, director, 1935—, became associate dean college of adult and extension education, now associate dean emeritus. Member N.E.A., Kentucky Edn. Assn., Phi Delta Kappa, Kappa Delta Pi, Mason. Club: Kiwanis (Lexington). Home: 125 State St., Lexington, Ky. Died Nov. 3, 1957; buried Lexington (Ky.) Cemetery.

CLINE, Isaac Monroe, meteorologist; b. Madisonville, Tenn., Oct. 13, 1861; s. Jacob Leander and Mary Isabel (Wilson) C.; A.B., Hiwassee College, Tenn., 1882, A.M., 1885; M.D., U. of Ark., 1885; Ph.D., Texas Christian U., 1896; hon. Sc.D., Tulane U., 1934; m. Cora M. Ballew, Mar. 17, 1887 (died Sept. 8, 1900); children—Allie May (wife of Ernest E. B. Drake), Rosemary (Mrs. Vora Williams), Esther Ballew (Mrs. Albert Allen Jones). Entered U.S. Weather Service (then Signal Corps, U.S.A.), July 7, 1882; asst. observer, Little Rock, Ark., 1883-85; in charge of observation sta., Abilene, Tex., 1885-89, Galveston, Tex., 1889-91; local forecaster and sect. dir. Tex. Sect. Climatol. Service, Weather Bur. of U.S. Dept. of Agr., 1891-1901; at New Orleans, 1901-35, in charge forecast center embracing Tex., Okla., Ark. and La.; also in charge coöperation between Mexican Weather Service and U.S. Weather Bur.; prin. meteorologist U.S. Weather Bur., retired Dec. 31, 1935. Instr. climatology, U. of Tex., 1897-1901. Fellow Am. Meteorol. Soc. (pres. 1934-35), New Orleans Acad. of Sciences (pres. 1934-35), Am. Geog. Soc., A.A.A.S.; mem. Nat. Inst. Social Sciences, Pi Gamma Mu. Del. 2d Pan-Am. Scientific Congress, Washington, 1915; mem. Union Goedesique et Geophysique, Commission pour l'Etude des Raz de Maree. Hon. curator of paintings, Louisiana State Museum. Conglist. Club: Nat. Arts (New York). Author of many bulls. and published articles on climate of the Southwest, its effect on health and on agr., "Summer Hot Winds on the Great Plains," "Relation of Storm Tides to the Center and Movement of Tropical Hurricanes" (a contbn. to the knowledge and forecasting of hurricanes), "Tropical Cyclones" (Introducing the integration method for the first time in study of storms, and presenting new conclusions which define and describe cyclone characteristics), 1926; Storms, Floods and Sunshine (giving important and interesting happenings in the United States Weather Service during its first sixty years), 1945 revised third edition, part I, Memoirs; part II Characteristics of Tropical Cyclones. In Mississippi flood of 1927 issued flood warnings predicting area and depth 2 weeks in advance of arrival of flood and for this work was commended by President Hoover, and presented by Southern Pacific Co. with bronze tablet eugolizing work. Has made a spl. study of art and has brought together a notable collection of American paintings and antique oriental bronzes. Bronze bust placed permanently in the Isaac Delgado Museum of Art by citizens of New Orleans. Address: 29 Farnham Pl., New Orleans 20. Died Aug. 3, 1955; buried Metairie Cemetery.

CLINE, Robert Alexander, banker; b. Cin., May 11, 1894; s. Thomas and Anna (Kearns) C.; student Kenyon Coll., 1916; m. Martha Kunkel, Feb. 22, 1930; 1 son, Robert Alexander. Pres. Robert A. Cline, Inc., 1925—; pres. Cline & Co.; chmn. Lincoln Nat. Bank (consol. into Fifth Third Union Trust Co.), 1943-55, vice chmn., 1955-57, chmn. bd. 1957—; dir. Cambridge Tile Mfg. Co., Bexley Constrn. Co., Cline Ins. Agy., Inc., Prodn. Machine Tool Co. Mem. Met. Housing Authority. Dir. Boys Club of Cin., Inc., Community Chest Cin., Hamilton County, O., 1951-54; chmn. U.S. Savs. Bonds Drive, Hamilton County, O., 1951-53; sec. Cin. Bur. Govtl. Research; vice chmn. Citizens United for Community Progress 1950; chmn. adv. council Naval Affairs, Cin., v.p., dir. Cin. C. of C. Trustee Bethesda Hosp. Mem. Cin. Real Estate Bd. (pres. 1932), Soc. Indsl. Realtors, Inst. Real Estate Mgmt., Am. Bankers Assn., Cin. Music Festival Soc., Am. Inst. Banking, Mus. Natural History, Better Bus. Bur. (dir.), Delta Kappa Epsilon, Omega Tau Rho. Clubs: Bankers; Camargo; Cincinnati Country; University; Queen City; Recess. Home: 2564 Handasyde Av., Cin. 8. Office: Fifth Third Union Trust Co., 4th and Walnut Sts., Cin. 2. Died Nov. 20, 1958; buried Gate of Heaven Cemetery, Cin.

CLINNIN, John V., lawyer; b. Huntley, Ill., Apr. 5, 1876; s. James Gregory and Jane (Dougherty) C.; LL.B., Chgo. Kent Coll. Law, 1908-11; married; children—Muriel, John V. Chief dep. recorder Cook County, 1903-13; asst. corp. counsel City of Chgo., 1915-16; 1st asst. U.S. Dist. Atty., 1921-22; chmn. Ill. Athletic Commn., 1929-31; mem. Ill. Civil Service Commn., 1932—. Enlisted 1st Ill. Inf., 1894; served in Santiago de Cuba campaign during Spanish-American War; col. comdg. 130th Inf., AEF, 1918, retired with rank brig. gen., 1922; major gen. comdg. Ill. Res. Militia, 1940, retired 1943. Decorated D.S.M., Silver Star, Purple Heart; recipient citations Gen. Barry, Gen. Pershing, Gen. George Bell, Jr. Comdr. Columbia Camp U.S. War Vets., Ill. branch Soc. of Army of Santiago de Cuba, North Shore Post Am. Legion, 1920-21; sr. vice comdr. Am. Legion Dept. Ill., 1923-24; nat. comdr. Disabled Am. Veterans, 1926-27; comdr. Chipilly Post, Am. Legion, 1928-29. Republican. Home: 332 Washington Av., Wilmette, Ill. Office: 11 S. La Salle St., Chgo. Died Sept. 16, 1955.

CLOAK, Frank Valentine Centennial, bishop; b. Phila., Feb. 14, 1876; s. John Henry and Sarah Jane (Adair) C.; ed. Ref. Episcopal Prep. Sch., 1894-95, Ref. Episcopal Sem., 1895-98, D.D., 1916; m. Harriet A. White, July 6, 1899 (dec. June 1946); children—Harriet Emma (Mrs. John T. Werhel), Frank Theodore. Ordained to ministry Ref. Episcopal Ch., 1898; rector Saint John's Ch., Chillicothe, Ill., 1899-1904, Ch. Redeemer, Detroit, 1904-07, Emmanuel Ch., Phila., 1907-26; taught in Phila. High Schs., 1912-25; rector Christ Meml. Ch., Phila., 1926—; presiding bishop Ref. Episcopal Ch., 1937-48; now ret. bishop in jurisdiction Synod, Chgo. Sec. bd. trustees Ref. Episcopal Theol. Sem., 1915-17. Mem. Phila. Ministerial Assn. (past pres.). Home: 8220 Cedarbrook St., Phila. Died Oct. 2, 1953.

CLOPPER, Edward Nicholas, social worker; b. Cincinnati, O., Jan. 1, 1879; s. Edward Nicholas, Sr., and Mary Caroline (McClintock) C.; B.S., Bethany Coll., W.Va., 1897; A.M., U. of Cinn., 1910, Ph.D., 1912; m. Grace Moser (dec. Mar. 1959); children—Rhoda (Mrs. George F. Hubbard), Josephine (dec.), Cornelius Jansen lt. comdr., U.S.N.R. Teacher McKinley Agricultural School, Ponce, P.R., 1901-03; supt. schs. Dist. of San Juan, 1903-04; prin. Central High Sch. of Porto Rico, 1904-07; gen. supt. schs. of Porto Rico, 1907-08; Ohio Valley sec. National Child Labor Committee, 1908-12; trustee, Experimental Study of Children, Cincinnati, 1910-26; superintendent, Cincinnati House of Refuge for Children, 1912-13; field secretary National Child Labor Committee, 1913-21; prepared New York State legislative measures on child welfare for Gov. Miller, 1921-22; secretary Council of Social Agencies, Cincinnati, 1922-25; exec. sec. Pittsburgh Fedn. of Social Agencies, 1925-33; prof. sociology, U. of Cincinnati, in charge of grad. training for Pub. Welfare Administrn., 1933-38; chmn. Ohio Child Welfare Planning Com., 1938-40; prof. social administration, Ohio State U., 1942-45; asso. editor of quarterly of Hist. and Philos. Soc. of O. since 1951. Lectr. on social sci., U. Cin. 1923-25, U. Pitts., 1930-33; chmn. of Dept. of Social Service for Episcopal Diocese of Southern Ohio, 1925. Delegate 1st Pan-American Child Welfare Congress, Buenos Aires, 1916, and secretary of U.S. Committee for 2d Congress, Montevideo, 1919; U.S. Government delegate to 4th Congress, Santiago, Chile, 1924. Director child welfare surveys in Okla. for Univ. of Okla., 1917, in Mich. for Mich. Child Welfare Comm., 1917, in Ala. for U. of Ala., 1918; in Ky. for State Bd. of Health and Ky. Child Labor Assn., 1919; in Tenn. for Tenn. Child Welfare Comm., 1920; in W.Va., 1921 Mem. Beta Theta Pi. Republican. Episcopalian. Club: MacDowell Society (Cincinnati). Author: Plan de Estudios para las Escuelas Rurales de Puerto Rico, 1904; Facts of Porto Rican History, 1905; (with C.A. Perry) Course of Study for Graded Schools of Porto Rico, 1906; Child Labor in City Streets, 1912; Sixty-second Annual Report of Cincinnati House of Refuge, 1912; Society and the Child, 1929; Child Welfare in Ohio, 1939; An American Family, 1950. Editor: Child Welfare in Okla., 1917; Child Welfare in Ala., 1918; Child Welfare in Ky., 1919; Child Welfare in Tenn., 1920; Rural Child Welfare, 1921; also various reports on child labor and children's codes, 1908-21. Contbr. to Ency. Americana. Home: 4254 Spring Grove Av., Cincinnati 23. Summer home: Ellsworth, Me. Died Nov. 30, 1953; buried Spring Grove Cemetery, Cinn.

CLOSE, Lewis Raymond, ret. corp. exec.; b. Dec. 18, 1881; s. Lewis Gile and Alice (Foster) C.; student George Washington U.; m. Lide Packer, Aug. 8, 1910. With B.&O. R.R. Co., 1899-1902, Clairton (Pa.) Steel Co., 1902-03, Pa. R.R., 1903-07; traveling auditor Southern Ry., 1907-09; examiner ICC, 1909-16; comptroller for M. A. Hanna Co., Cleve., 1916-28; with following corps, 1928-53, pres., 1932-53, Lehigh Valley Coal Corp., Lehigh Valley Coal Sales Co., Lehigh Valley Coal Co. Republican. Mason. Clubs: Bankers (N.Y.C.); Westmoreland (Wilkes-Barre, Pa.), Midday (Phila.). Home: Redding Ridge, Conn. Died Sept. 1957.

CLOUD, William Woodward, b. Balt.; s. Daniel and Maria Louisa (Woodward) C.; Balt. City Coll., Poly. Inst.; law sch. U. Md.; m. Frances Dashiell, June 7, 1899. Jr. clerk Md. Savs. Bank, 1885, advanced through various positions, becoming pres., 1908-11; organized State Bank of Md., 1911, pres. 1911-17; pres. Taxicab Co., Yellow Cab Co.; formerly dir. Equitable Trust Co., Calvert Mortgage Co. (Balt.). Hon. pres. Nat. Assn. Taxicab Owners; formerly gen. chmn. Balt. Safety Council. Chmn. Ednl. Commn. Nat. Conf. Street and Highway Safety; mem. transportation and communication com., U.S. C. of C.; mem. Gov's. Commn. for Revising Motor Vehicles Laws of Md.; chmn. adv. com. Conv. and Visitors Bur.; v.p., dir. Balt. Assn. Commerce. Democrat. Episcopalian. Clubs: Maryland, Merchants, Baltimore Country, Automobile of Md. (dir.). Ret. from active bus., 1946. Home: Rusty Rocks, 7 Club Rd., Roland Park, Balt. 10. Died Nov. 11, 1957.

CLOUGH, Charles C., banker. Adminstrv. v.p. Manufacturers Trust Co., N.Y. City; v.p. and dir. Manufacturers Safe Deposit Co.; treas. and dir. Hotel New Yorker, 261 Fifth Av. Corp.; treas. Central Liquidating Corp.; dir. Hobson Miller Paper Co. Home: 174 Brixton Rd., Garden City, N.Y. Office: 55 Broad St., N.Y.C. Died Mar. 16, 1954; buried Cypress Hill Abbey.

CLOUGH, Francis Edgar, surgeon; b. LaCrosse, Wis., Feb. 9, 1878; s. Edgar E. and Mary (Howe) C.; student Boston U., 1896-98; M.D., Rush Med. Coll., Chgo., 1902; m. Louise J. Handke, Nov. 15, 1905; 1 son, William James. Chief surgeon Homestake Mining Co., Lead, S.D., 1918—; trained the champion "first aid" mining team of U.S., 1915. Pres. S.D. Bd. Health and Med. Examiners, 1927; formerly health officer, Lead. Capt. M.C., U.S. Army, World War I; was asst. chief of fracture service Camp Grant, Ill. Fellow A.C.S.; mem. A.M.A., Am. Assn. Ry. Surgeons, Am. Am. Assn. Indsl. Surgeons, S.D. Med. Soc. (ex-pres.), Western Surg. Soc., Beta Theta Pi. Republican. Methodist. Mason (32°, Shriner). Home: Lead, S.D. Died Mar. 1953.

CLOUGH, Frank C., editorial cons.; b. Conway Springs, Kan., Sept. 4, 1900; s. James Fowler and Isabelle (Wilson) C.; student Coll. of Emporia, 1920-21, Kan. State Tchrs. Coll., Emporia, 1921-23; m. Gladis Rice, Feb. 4, 1928; 1 son, James Rice. Coll. reporter Emporia Gazette, 1920; reporter Kansas City Star, 1924-25; reporter Emporia Gazette, 1925-28, city editor, 1928-29, mng. editor, 1929-42; editor bus. publs., N.Y. City, 1944-45; editorial dir. Speidel Newspapers, Inc. (nat. group of 8 daily newspapers), Palo Alto, Cal., 1945-57, editorial consultant, 1957—. Assistant director of the press div., U.S. Office Censorship, Washington, 1942-44. Mem. Pulitzer Prize juries, 1950, 51. Trustee William Allen White Found., William Allen White Sch. Journalism, University of Kansas. Mem. Nat. Assn. Asso. Press Mng. Editors (dir. 1939-40), Am. Soc. Newspaper Editors, Sigma Delta Chi. Republican. Clubs: Rotary (pres., 1941, Emporia); National Press (Washington); Press and Union League (San Francisco); Palo Alto Chamber of Commerce. Author: William Allen White of Emporia, 1941. Address: 507 E. Valerio St., Santa Barbara, Cal. Deceased.

CLOUGH, George Hatch, corp. exec.; b. Exeter, N.H., May 28, 1876; s. Albert Hatch and Zetta (Currier) C.; student pub. schs.; m. Grace B. Parker, June 14, 1899; 1 son, Robert Morrill. Pres. The Russell Co., Sutton's Mills; treas., dir. Mt. Tom Sulphite Pulp Co.; dir. Am. Enka Corp., Boston Woven Hose & Rubber Co., Liberty Mut. Ins. Co., Mechanicville Coal & Supply Co., Nat. Shawmut Bank, Shawmut Corp., United Mut. Fire Ins. Co., Boston Mut. Fire Ins. Co.; trustee Shawmut Bank Investment Trust. Club: University. Died Oct. 1948.

CLOUGH, Raphael Floyd, (kluf), lawyer, dir.; b. Sioux Rapids, Ia., May 10, 1886; s. Fred and Sophia (Pancoast) C.; student Ia. State Tchrs. Coll., 1907; A.B., U. Ia., 1911, LL.B., 1913, J.D., 1925; m. Ruth Ellison, June 15, 1916; children—Barbara (Mrs. Robert R. Spargo), Ray Ellison. Admitted to Ia. bar, 1913, since practiced, Mason City; dir. Pioneer Fed. Savings & Loan Assn., Mason City. Mem. legal staff Fgn. Econ. Adminstrn., Washington, 1943-44; mem. bd. dirs. Mason City Ind. Sch. Dist., 1945-51. Republican alt. del. Nat. conv., Kansas City, Mo., 1928, del., Chgo., 1932, presidential elector at large, 1940, past chmn. Cerro Gordo Co. central com. Mem. Am., Ia. (gov., pres.), Cerro Gordo Co. (past pres.), 12th Jud. Dist. (past pres.) bar assns., Phi Alpha Delta. Conglist. Mason, Elks (past exalted ruler). Clubs: Country, Euchre and Cycle. Home: 1432 N. Hampshire Av. Office: Brick & Tile Bldg., Mason City, Ia. Died Dec. 7, 1957; buried Ellmwood Cemetery.

CLOUGH, S. DeWitt (klŭf), ret. lab. executive; b. Chgo., June 30, 1879; s. Walter and Salina (Wells) C.; student pub. schs.; LL.D. Knox Coll., 1941; m. Rachel M. Clough; 1 son, Sherman. Joined Abbott Labs. as advertising mgr., 1903, sec., 1915, dir. 1915—, v.p., 1927, pres., 1933-46, chmn. bd., mem. exec. com., 1946, now hon. chmn. bd. and cons. Hon. dir. Crerar Library (Chgo.) v.p. Am. Heart Assn. (awarded Gold Heart 1954); mng. dir. Chgo. Heart Assoc., 10 years, now chmn. bd. dirs. awarded gold Oscar, 1956. Mem. penicillin producers adv. com. pharm. mfrs. adv. com. WPB. Pres. Advt. Assn. Chgo., 1914-16. Mem. Am. Drug. Mfrs.

Assn. (exec. com.), Northwestern U. Assos. Club: Union League (Chgo.). Author: Backbone, and Every Day Courage. Home: 1367 N. State St., Chgo. 10. Died Jan. 1960.

CLOUGH-LEIGHTER, Henry (kluf' lī-tĕr), music editor, composer, organist; b. Washington, May 13, 1874; s. James Henry and Sarah Katherine (Humphries) Leighter; student pvt. schs., Columbian (now George Washington) U., 1887-89; pupil of Dr. J. Humfrey Anger, Trinity U., Toronto. Organist St. Michael's and All Angels' Ch., Washington, at age 15; organist and choir master Ch. of the Ephiphany and the Jewish Synagogue, Washington, 1892-99, Grace Ch., Providence, 1899-1900; instr. theory of music Howe Sch. of Music, Boston, 1900-01; editorial staff Oliver Ditson Co., Boston, 1901-08; became tech. editor Boston Music Co., 1921; now editor-in-chief E. C. Schirmer Music Co., Boston. Composer many art-songs, cycles, cantatas and large choral works with organ or orchestra accompaniments, including The Christ of the Andes, a symphonic ode for chorus and orchestra; piano compositions and many organ transcriptions. Editor musical, pedagogical and tech. works. Address: 45 Grand View Av., Wollaston 70, Mass. Died Sept. 15, 1956; buried Mt. Wollaston Cemetery, Quincy, Mass.

CLOW, James Beach, mfg. exec.; b. Chicago, Nov. 18, 1903; s. James Culbertson and Pearl Genevieve (Libby) C.; student Hotchkiss Sch., Lakeville, Conn., 1918-22; Ph.B., Yale, 1926; m. Edith Louise Newcomet, Feb. 15, 1930; children—Nancy Newcomet, James Culbertson. With J. B. Clow & Sons since 1927, began as clerk, dir. since 1928, asst. sec., 1929-36, asst. treas., 1931-36, sec., 1936-42, v.p. since 1940; pres. Eddy Value Co.; pres. Iowa Value Co. (subsidiaries). Served as lt. comdr., U.S.N.R., 1942-45. Dir. Welfare Council of Metropolitan Chicago; trustee, St. Luke's Hosp. Mem. Zeta Psi. Republican. Clubs: Chicago, Racquet, Tavern (Chicago); Shoreacres, Onwentsia (Lake Forest). Home: 1550 N. Green Bay Rd., Lake Forest, Ill. Office: 201 N. Talman Av., Chgo. 12. Died May 5, 1953.

CLOW, Kent Sarver, mfg.; b. Chicago, Ill., Apr. 4, 1888; s. William Ellsworth and Margaret (Sarver) C.; ed. Yale, 1910; m. Eleanor Corwith Hamill, June 1, 1915 (dec. 1920); 1 dau. Elsie; m. 2d, Frances Reid Jones, Feb. 15, 1922; children—Frances Reid. Kent S., William E., II. Pres. and dir. James B. Clow & Sons, Chicago, Ill.; pres. and dir. Eddy Valve Co., Waterford, N.Y., Iowa Valve Co., Oskaloosa. Ia.; dir. First Nat. Bank, Lake Forest, Ill. President United Charities, 1933, 1934 (past director); director Lake Forest Hosp. Assn. Clubs: Chicago (sec.), Casino, Commercial, Onwentsia, Shoreacres, Racquet, Old Elm. Home: 900 N. Green Bay Road, Lake Forest. Office: 201 N. Talman Av., Chgo. Died Dec. 14, 1952; buried Lake Forest (Ill.) Cemetery.

CLOW, William Ellsworth, Jr., mfr.; b. Chicago, Ill., Apr. 5, 1886; s. William Ellsworth and Margaret A. (Sarver) C.; grad. University School, Chicago, 1903; B.A., Yale, 1907; m. Isabelle Mann, Oct. 3, 1908 (died 1939); children—Beatrice Clow Laflin, Mary Melville (Mrs. Mario Braggiotti); m. 2d, Mrs. Nadyne McNeill Traer, Dec. 30, 1939. With James B. Clow & Sons, mfrs. waterworks plumbing, heating supplies, since Sept. 1907; advanced to pres., now chmn. bd. dirs. Served as ensign U.S. Navy, 1917-18. Mem. Scroll and Key (Yale). Clubs: Chicago, Onwentsia, Shoreacres, Old Elm, Casino. Home: Lake Forest, Ill. Office: 201 N. Talman Av., Chgo. 12. Died Aug. 6, 1953.

CLOWES, George Henry Alexander (kloos), research dir.; b. Ipswich, Eng., Aug. 27, 1877; s. Josiah Pratt and Ellen (Seppings) C.; student Royal Coll. Sci., London, Göttingen U., Berlin U., Pasteur Inst. (Paris); Ph.D., Göttingen, 1899; D.Sc. (hon.), Butler U., 1931; LL.D., Wabash Coll., 1938; m. Edith Whitehill Hinkel, June 1910; children—Alexander Temple (dec.), George H. A., Allen Whitehill. Came to U.S., 1900, naturalized citizen abt. 1921. With Eli Lilly & Co., mfg. chemists, Indpls., 1918—, dir. research lab., Indpls., Woods Hole, Mass., 1920-46. Pres., chmn. bd. Indpls. Symphony Orchestra, 1939—; v.p., dir. John Herron Art Mus., 1933—. Recipient Banting Medal, 1947. Served Chem. Warfare Service, World War I. Mem. Am. Chem. Soc., Soc. for Exptl. Biology and Medicine, Bio-Chem. Soc., Cancer Assn., Immunologists and Pathologists, Chem. Soc. (Eng.). Republican. Episcopalian. Clubs: Indianapolis Athletic, Indianapolis University; Woodstock; Meridian Hills Country; Cosmos (Washington); Woods Hole Golf. Research in cancer; coöperated in development of insulin, liver extract, penicillin, etc. Home: 3744 Spring Hollow Rd., Golden Hill, Indpls. Office: Lilly Research Labs., Indpls. Died Aug. 25, 1958; buried Ch. Messiah, Woods Hole, Mass.

CLUETT, E(rnest) Harold (kloo'ĕt), mfr. ex-congressman; b. in Troy, N.Y.; July 13, 1874; s. of George Bywater and Amanda Rockwell (Fisher) C.; grad. of Albany (N.Y.) Acad., 1892; B.A., Williams, 1896; studied Oxford U., Eng.; m. Margaret Robertson Gorham, Oct. 10, 1899 (died Sept. 16, 1944); m. 2d, Catharine ReQua Johnson, Sept. 14, 1946; children—3 sons, 3 daughters. Treas. Cluett, Peabody & Co., 1900-16, v.p., 1916-29, chmn. bd., 1929-37; dir. Nat. City Bank. Mem. 75th to 77th Congresses, 29th N.Y. Dist. Chief industrial sect. Watervliet Arsenal, 1918; spl. mission to France for YMCA, 1918; mem. National War Work Council. V.p. Troy Boys Club, Samaritan Hosp. Presdl. elector for Taft, 1912, Hughes, 1916. Trustee Orphan Asylum. Mem. C. of C. (pres. 1917, 18), Am. Ordnance Assn., Delta Psi. Republican candidate for U.S. Senate, N.Y. State, 1934. Clubs: Republican (N.Y.C.); Troy, Troy Country (former pres.). Home: Pinewood, Troy, N.Y. Died Feb. 4, 1954; buried Oakwoods Cemetery, Troy.

CLUTE, Willard Nelson, author; b. Painted Post, N.Y., Feb. 26, 1869; s. George N. and Ruth (Wright) C.; student U. Chgo.; m. Ida Martin, Dec. 22, 1897; 1 dau., Beulah Katharine. Asst. curator bot. dept. Columbia, 1897; curator N.Y. Bot. Garden, 1898-99; instr. biology Joliet (Ill.) High Sch., 1903-10; instr. botany Curtis High Sch., Chgo., 1910-11; tchr. biology, Flower Tech. High Sch. for Girls, Chgo., 1911-28; instr. botany and dir. Bot. Garden, 1938-41. Founder, pub. Plant World, Bryologist, Fern Bulletin, Am. Botanist, also editor last two. Founder Am. Fern Soc. (hon. mem.), Binghamton Acad. Sciences, Joliet Bot. Club (dir.). Fellow A.A.A.S.; mem. Am. Genetic Assn., Soc. Midland Authors, Ill. State Acad. Science (pres. 1927). Author: A Flora of the Upper Susquehanna Valley, 1898; Our Ferns in Their Haunts, 1901; The Fern Collector's Guide, 1902; The Fern Allies of North America, 1905; Laboratory Botany for the High School, 1909; Agronomy for High Schools, 1912; Laboratory Manual and Notebook in Botany, 1913; Experimental General Science, 1917; American Plant Names, 1923; Practical Botany, 1924; Useful Plants of the World, 1927; Botanical Essays, 1929; Common Names of Plants, 1931; Swamp and Dune, 1931; Off the Record, 1935; Our Ferns, Their Haunts, Habits and Folklore, 1938; A Second Book of Plant Names, 1930. Home: 5257 Hinesley Av., Indpls. 8. Died Mar. 7, 1950.

CLUVERIUS, Wat Tyler (klū-vē'rĭ-ŭs), naval officer, coll. pres.; b. New Orleans, La., Dec. 25, 1874; s. Wat Tyler and Martha Lewis (Manning) C.; grad. U.S. Naval Acad., 1896; m. Hannah Walker Sampson, Apr. 5, 1900 (died Jan. 20, 1938); children—Elisabeth Sampson, Martha. Wat Tyler. Commd. ensign U.S. Navy, 1898; promoted through grades to rear adm., May 30, 1928. Participated in West Indian, Philippine and Mexican campaigns and with Mining Squadron, in North Sea, World War; later apptd. comdt. Navy Yard, Norfolk, Va.; commanded second div. of battleships, U.S. Fleet; chief of staff U.S. Fleet; comdr. fourth cruiser div., U.S. Fleet; comdt. 9th Naval Dist.; comdr. base force, U.S. Fleet; comdt. 4th Naval Dist., Phila.; retired, Jan. 2, 1939; now president Worcester (Mass.) Poly Institute, Worcester Chapter American Red Cross. Mem. Worcester Council of Boy Scouts; trustee Worcester Academy; dir. Worcester Community Chest. Naval Bd. Prodn. awards. World War II. Member United States Naval Inst., Am. Soc. Naval Engrs., American Society for Engineering Education. Am. Assn. for Advancement of Science, Hampton Roads Chemist Club, American Society Mechanical Engineers, American Antiquarian Society, Worcester Engring. Society, Newcomen Society of England (American Branch), National Aeronautical Society, Engring. Society of Western Mass., Navy League of U.S., Naval Order of the U.S., Military Order of World War, United Spanish War Vets., Mil. Order Fgn. Wars. Phi Delta Theta (past president), Sigma Xi. Episcopalian. Clubs: Army and Navy (Washington): Army and Navy (Chicago); Army and Navy (New Orleans); Worcester; Engineers (Phila.); Rotary, Lions. Home: 1 Drury Lane, Worcester 5, Mass. Died Oct. 28, 1952; buried Arlington Nat. Cemetery.

COALE, Griffith Baily, mural artist; b. Baltimore. May 21, 1890; s. William Ellis and Mary Ella (Baily) C.; grad. Md. Inst., Baltimore, 1911; studied painting in Munich, Paris, Italy, Spain, 4 yrs.; m. Elizabeth A. van A. Manning, May 18, 1933; children—Robert Duncan Gordon, Elizabeth. Painter in Baltimore, 7 yrs., N.Y. City, 1922—; completed numerous murals, portraits and decorative paintings; best known decorations: Mfrs. Trust Co., Pub. Nat. Bank (formerly Lee Higginson & Co.), City Farmers Trust Co., Dry Dock Savs. Instn., Railroad Bldg. and Crosley Bldg. (N.Y. Worlds Fair), Home Office of Met. Life Ins. Co., Columbia U. Library (commemorative painting of visit of King and Queen of Eng., to Columbia U., 1939), New Criminal Ct. Bldg., N.Y. Athletic Club, Brooklyn Borough Gas Co., Half Moon Hotel (all N.Y. City); Library of S.S. America; 2 balancing mural paintings Bancroft Hall. U.S. Naval Acad.; large painting Va. State Capitol (studies for painting owned by Mariners' Mus., Newport News, Va.); official portraits, Johns Hopkins U., and other univs., colls., schs., bus. instns. and pvt. commns. Exhibited in all contemporary Am. annual exhbns., in spl. exhbns. Nat. Gallery, London; Carnegie Inst., Pittsburgh; Met. Mus Art, N.Y. City; Salon des Artists Française, Paris. Had one-man show, N.Y. City. Chmn. exhbn. com. Whitney Mus., N.Y. City. Served as marine camoufleur U.S. Shipping Bd., 1917-18; commd. lt. comdr., U.S.N R., 1941; assigned as combat artist for the Navy; promoted comdr., 1946; retired, 1947. Past president National Society Mural Painters; secretary board trustees Marine Museum of City of New York; secretary Ship Model Soc. of N.Y.; member editorial adv. bd. Am. Neptune. Trustee Marine Hist. Assn., Mystic, Conn.; pres. Stonington (Conn.) Hist. Soc.; mem. Soc. Nautical Research (Greenwich, Eng.), Authors Guild, P.E.N. Club, Coffee House Club; hon life mem. N.Y. Commandery Naval Order of U.S. Episcopalian. Author: North Atlantic Patrol (with 17 reproductions of paintings done in Newfoundland and Iceland by author), 1942; Victory at Midway (with 18 reproductions of paintings made at Pearl Harbor and Midway), 1944; book of Egypt, Holy Land, Southeast Asia Command, and Indian and Pacific oceans (in prep.); also book, Arrival First English Settlers, Jamestown, Island, May 13, 1607. Address: 73 Water St., Stonington, Conn. Died Aug. 20, 1950.

COATE, Roland Eli, architect; b. Richmond, Ind., Dec. 5, 1890; s. John M. and Emma (Williams) C.; student Earlham Coll., 1908-10; A.B., Cornell U., 1914; m. Gladys Robinson, June 2, 1928; children—William B., Sussanah, Roland Eli. Began as architect in 1915; in private practice, 1922—. Served as 1st lt., A.S., 1917-19; with A.E.F. 17 months. Fellow A.I.A.; mem. Tau Beta Pi. Home: 1685 LaVista Pl., Pasadena 3, Cal. Died Oct. 17, 1958; buried San Gabriel (Cal.) Cemetery.

COATES, Charles F., certified pub. acct.; b. Meriden, Conn., Oct. 8, 1889; s. Charles E. and Emma Ruby (Golden) C.; student pub. schs. Meriden; m. Claire Erlick, May 4, 1936; 1 son, William Mills (by former marriage). Gen. partner Hadfield, Rothwell, Soule & Coates, C.P.A.'s, Hartford, Conn., since 1922; dir. Nicoll Talcott Corp., Silent Glow Oil Burner Corp. Mem. Am. Inst. Accts. (past council mem.), Conn. Soc. C.P.A.'s (past pres.), Conn. State Bd. Accountancy (past pres.), Conn. State (dir.), Hartford (past pres.) C.'s of C., Am. Soc. C.P.A.'s (past v.p.), Conn. Development Commn. (chmn.). Republican. Methodist. Mason (32°, Shriner, past potentate). Clubs: Auto (pres.), Hartford, Wampanoag Country, Canoe, Twentieth Century. Home: 89 Cliffmore Rd., West Hartford, Conn. Office: 750 Main St., Hartford 3, Conn. Died Sept. 12, 1957.

COATES, Eric, composer; b. Hucknall, Nottinghamshire, Eng., Aug. 27, 1886; s. William Harrison and Mary Jane Gwynne (Blower) C.; student Royal Acad. of Music, London (scholarship), 1906, fellowship, 1922; m. Phyllis Marguerite Black, Feb. 3, 1913; 1 son, Austin. Toured South Africa with Hambourg String Quartet, 1908; conducted broadcasts of compositions for BBC, 1922—, Stockholm, 1936, Copenhagen, Oslo, Stockholm, Hilversum, 1938, Copenhagen, N.Y. (CBS), 1946; appeared as composer-conductor at many English Festivals. Rep. British music at Interim Congress at Internat. Confederation of Composers and Authors, Washington, 1946. Dir. Performing Right Soc., Ltd., London, and mem. exec. com. Composers' Guild. Works for orchestra include: Miniature Suite, 1911, Countryside Suite, 1914, Summer Days Suite, 1919, Joyous Youth Suite and Merrymakers Overture, 1922, Phantasy, The Selfish Giant, 1925, Phantasy, The Three Bears, 1926, Four Ways Suite, 1927, Phantasy, Cinderella, 1929, From Meadow to Mayfair Suite, 1931, Concert Valse, Dancing Nights, 1931, Ballet, The Jester at the Wedding, 1932, The London Suite, 1933, The Three Men Suite, 1935, Song of Loyalty (for the late King George V's Jubilee), 1935, London Again Suite, 1936, Saxo Rhapsody for alto saxophone and orchestra, 1936, Springtime Suite, 1937, Ballet, The Enchanted Garden, 1938, Four Centuries Suite, 1942, The Three Elizabeths Suite (dedicated by permission to Her Majesty the Queen), 1944; Impression of a Princess; several orchestral marches and many songs. Mem. Brit. Light Music Assn. (pres.). Home: 63 Berkeley Court, Baker St., London, N.W. 1, Eng. Died Dec. 21, 1957.

COBB, Bernard C., ret. pub. utilities exec.; b. Boston, Aug. 13, 1870; s. Sanford H. and Mary E. (Capen) C.; ed. Phillips Andover Acad.; m. Caroline D. Ellis, Nov. 19, 1901; children—Margaret E. (Mrs. William J. Ryan), Mary K. (Mrs. Carl F. Muller), Alby C. (Mrs. Peter J. Reidy), Alice E. (Mrs. Charles G. Quinlan). With Pa. R.R. Co., Grand Rapids, Mich., 1889-95, Grand Rapids Gas Light Co., 1895-98; gen. supt. Detroit City Gas Co., 1898-1901; v.p., gen. mgr. Saginaw-Bay City Ry. Co., 1901-06; mem. firm Hodenpyl, Walbridge & Co., New York, 1906-11; v.p. Hodenpyl, Hardy & Co., 1911-28; chmn. bd. Commonwealth & Southern Corp., 1930-33; now retired. Home: Altamont, N.Y. Died Sept. 30, 1957; buried Kensico Cemetery, Valhalla, N.Y.

COBB, Bertha Browning, author; b. Waltham, Mass., Oct. 23, 1867; d. Phineas Laurence and Elizabeth Howard (Miles) Barnes; grad. Boston Normal Sch., 1884; m. Ernest Cobb, June 29, 1904. Tchr. pub. schs., Waltham, Boston, 1885-1904. Mem. N.E.

Woman's Press Assn. Tchr. story-telling in Perry Tng. Sch., Boston, 1943, 44, 45. Unitarian. Club: Woman's. Joint Author (with husband): Around the World with Father Time, 1909; Metcalf Readers (primer, first and second readers), 1909; Busy Builders' Book, 1911; Arlo, 1915; Clematis, 1918; Anita. 1920; Pathways of European Peoples, 1923; Who Knows (puzzle stories), 1924; Allspice, 1925; Dan's Boy, 1926; Pennie, 1927; André, 1930; One Foot on the Ground—A Plea for Common Sense in Education, 1933; Robin (novel for children, with E. Cobb). 1933; The Mind's Eye, 1941. Home: Newton Upper Falls, Mass. Deceased.

COBB, Candler, lawyer; b. Chicago, Apr. 18, 1887; s. Henry Ives and Emma Martin (Smith) C.; A.B., Harvard, 1907; reading, Oxford (Eng.) Univ., 1907-08; LL.B., New York Law Sch., 1910; m. Beatrice Carpenter, Dec. 20, 1910; children—Beatrice (Mrs. Alexander Loudon), Florence C. (Mrs. Thomas B. Husband). Admitted to New York, Federal bars, 1911; in practice, N.Y. City, 1911—; asst. U.S. Atty. for Southern Dist. of N.Y., 1917-19; comml. attaché Am. Embassy, London, 1921-23, liaison attaché on Settlement Brit. War Debt, 1922; gen. practice of law in Europe, 1932-40; mem. local draft bd., Selective Service System, N.Y. City, 1940-42, N.Y. City dir., Selective Service System, 1946—; mem. N.Y. State War Finance Com. and down-State chmn., Seventh War Loan, 1943-45; dir. Holland-Am. Mchts. Corp., Kreutoll Realization Corp., Nat. Varnished Products Corp. Served as maj., U.S.A., 1942-43, adminstr., N.Y. City Selective Service Hdqrs. Awarded Army Commendation Ribbon, N.Y. State Conspicuous Service Cross, Congl. Selective Service Medal; officer, Order of the Orange-Nassau (Netherlands). President and trustee, Gilbert A. Robertson Home, 1941—; trustee, Protestant Epis. chs., Rome and Florence, Italy, Nice and Paris, France; mem. vestry, Am. Pro-Cathedral, Paris, 1937-46; mem. bd. and finance com., Fresh Air Assn. of St. John; chmn. exec. com., dir. Fedn. of Protestant Welfare Agencies. Mem. Am. C. of C. of France (sec., 1st v.p., 1936-38), Mil. Order of World Wars, N.Y. Soc. of Mil. and Naval Officers. Clubs: India House, Union, Harvard (N.Y.C.); Marlborough (London); Harvard of France (pres. 1938-40). Home: 49 E. 86th St. Office: 20 Exchange Pl., N.Y.C. 5. Died May 24, 1955.

COBB, James A., lawyer; b. Arcadia, La., Jan. 29, 1876; student Straight U., New Orleans, Fisk U., Nashville; LL.M., Howard U., 1900, Pd.B., 1902. Admitted to bar of D.C., 1901; spl. asst. U.S. atty., 1907-15; del. Rep. Nat. Conv., Chgo., 1920, alternate del., Cleve., 1924. Judge Municipal Ct., Washington, 1926-35; resumed practice of law as head of firm, Cobb, Howard & Hayes. Former prof. constitutional law, vice dean, Howard U. Law Sch. Mem. Citizens' Efficiency Com., to revamp and codify the laws of D.C.; mem. George Washington Bicentennial Commn. (incorporated by act of Congress 1932); mem. Washington Housing Assn., chmn. legal com. Mem. D.C. Appeals Bd. for Selective Service. Trustee Pub. Library; mem. Commrs. Traffic Adv. Com. Mem. Nat. Bar Assn. Criminal Justice Assn., Am. Acad. of Polit. and Social Sci., Nat. Econ. League, Am. Geog. Soc., Sigma Pi Phi. Club: Nat. Country (chmn. exec. com.). Home: 1732 S St. N.W. Office: 613 F St. N.W., Washington. Died Oct. 14, 1958.

COBB, James Shepard, chmn. bd. and dir. Abercrombie & Fitch Co.; b. Florence, Mass., July 1, 1869; s. E. G. and Esther M. (Redfield) C.; student Amherst Coll.; m. Helen Fitch, Aug. 20, 1915. Vice pres. Library Bureau, 1910; v.p. Abercrombie & Fitch Co., N.Y.C. 1912-28, became pres. 1928, now chmn. bd. Dir. Fifth Avenue Assn. Clubs: University (N.Y.C.); University (Chgo.). Home: 440 Park Av. Office: 45th St. and Madison Av., N.Y.C. Deceased.*

COBLENTZ, Edmond David (kō'blĕnts), editorial cons.; b. San Francisco, Sept. 30, 1882; s. Samuel and Henriette (Kramer) C.; student U. Cal.; married; 1 dau., Denise. Began as newspaper reporter, 1900; city editor San Francisco Examiner, 1907-13; mng. editor San Francisco Call-Post, 1913-15, San Francisco Examiner, 1919-25, pub., 1925-27; editor N.Y. American, 1927-37, becoming Sunday editor N.Y. Journal and American, 1937; editorial cons. West Coast Hearst Newspapers; pub. San Francisco Call-Bulletin, 1940-50; editorial cons. West Coast Hearst Newspapers, 1950—. Club: Family (San Francisco). Home: P.O. Box 37, Sonoma, Cal. Died Apr. 16, 1959; buried Home of Peace Meml. Park, Colma, Cal.

COBO, Albert E(ugene) (kō'bō), govt. ofcl.; b. Detroit, Oct. 2, 1893; s. August and Elizabeth (Byrn) C.; student The Bus. Inst., Detroit, 1912-13, Alexander Hamilton Inst., 1920-22; m. Ethel Ruby Christie, June 3, 1914; children—Elaine Elizabeth (Mrs. Paul H. Hurst), Jean (Mrs. John S. Collman). Office boy Detroit Copper & Brass Rolling Mills, 1910-12; operator retail candy and ice cream stores, Detroit, 1912-18; mem. sales dept. Sunstrand Co., 1918-22; nat. br. mgr. Burroughs Adding Machine Co., 1923-33; with city govt. Detroit, 1933—, dep. city treas. and dir. finance, 1933-35, city treas., 1935-49, mayor, 1949—. Mem. President's Civil Defense Advisory Council. Mem. Am. Municipal Assn. (pres.). Congl. Mason (Shriner), Elk. Clubs: Optimist, Economic (Detroit). Home: 16873 Huntington Dr., Detroit 19. Offcie: City Hall, Detroit 26. Died Sept. 12, 1957; buried Woodlawn Cemetery, Detroit.

COBURN, Frederick William, editor, writer; b. Nashua, N.H., Aug. 6, 1870; s. Frank and Susan (Whitney) C.; A.B., Harvard, 1891; student Art Students' League of Washington, 1892-94, N.Y.C., 1894-96; m. Grace Alice Denton, Sept. 16, 1895; children—Selena Varnum, Eric Denton. Instr. classics and English, Friends Sch., Weshington, 1891-94, Rugby Acad., N.Y.C., 1894-95, Ethical Culture Schs., 1895-1900; asso. editor School Journal, N.Y.C., 1899-1901; editorial asst. Prang Ednl. No., Boston, 1902; writer and editor Publicity Bur., Boston, 1903-13; art editor, also art critic Boston Herald, 1903—; asso. editor Lowell Courier-Citizen, 1918—. Author: History of Lowell, Mass. (3 vols.), 1920. Compiler: Business Encyclopedia and Legal Adviser (5 vols.), 1912. Editor Bulletin of N.E. Conservatory of Music. Contbr. on art to Boston Sunday Herald. Home: 722 E. Merrimack St., Lowell, Mass. Died Dec. 16, 1953; buried Winchester, Mass.

COCHEL, Wilber Andrew (kŏch'ĕl), editor; b. Tipton, Mo., Aug. 7, 1877; s. William Henry and Charlotte (Calvin) C.; A.B., U. Mo., 1897, B.S., 1905, LL.D., 1931; m. Caroline Fahnestock, Oct. 1, 1908. Animal husbandman, Purdue U., 1905-09; prof. animal husbandry Pa. State Coll., 1909-12, Kan. State Agrl. Coll., 1912-18; southwestern rep. Shorthorn Breeders' Assn., 1918-25; editor Weekly Kansas City Star, 1925-46; agrl. adv. Kansas City Star 1946-48. Former pres. Am. Soc. Animal Prodn. Trustee Andrew Drumm Inst., Independence, Mo.; dir. St. Luke's Hosp., Kansas City; trustee Farm Found., Chgo. Fellow Am. Acad. Sci.; mem. Alpha Zeta, Phi Beta Phi, Sigma Delta Chi. Democrat. Episcpalian. Mason (32°). Clubs: University, Kansas City Country. Author of numerous ednl. bulls., series of spl. articles on Russian travels and conditions, 1930. Home: R.F.D. 4, Parkville, Mo. Died May 5, 1955.

COCHRAN, Archelaus M., farmer; b. Columbia, Tenn., Sept. 25, 1938; s. W. M. and Nancy J. C.; student Dallas pub. schs.; attended med. coll. U. La., 1859-60; m. Laura A. Knight, Feb. 22, 1886 (dec.); m. 2d, Mary A. Collins, Jan. 11, 1871. Capt. in Civil war, 1862; mem. Tex. Legislature, 1866; postmaster Dallas, 1879; chmn. Rep. State Exec. Com. for Tex., 1881; div. collector Internal Revenue, dist. Tex., 1883; Rep. nominee for gov. Tex., 1886; canvassed Tex. and Ga. against prohibtion, 1887; commr. World's Columbian Expn. for Tex., 1890; canvassed Chicago and Cook Co., Ill., for Republicans, 1891; Republican nominee for Congress, 1901, for Legislature, 1905. Republican. Address: Dallas, Tex. Deceased.

COCHRAN, Henry Jessup, banking; b. Mendham, N.J., Apr. 8, 1879; s. Rev. I. W. and Annie (Carter) C.; A.B., Princeton, 1900; m. Nannette R. Pierce, Apr. 12, 1904; children—Katharine (Mrs. P. A. Chamberlain), Homer P., Henry J., Bradford. Statistician for the American Locomotive Company of New York, 1901-07; with Suffern & Son, certified public accountants, 1907-10; partner Patterson & Cochran, accountants, New York, 1910-12; v.p. Astor Trust Co., 1912-17; v.p. Bankers Trust Co., 1917-29, president 1929-31, vice chmn. board, 1931-37, vice chmn. trust investment com., 1937-38; pres. Franklin Savings Bank, 1938-50, chmn. bd. since 1950; dir. and mem. finance com. Am. Smelting & Refining Co.; dir. American Enka Corporation, National Biscuit Co., Bankers Trust Co. Trustee emeritus Princeton Univ. Republican. Presbyterian. Clubs: Princeton, Union League, Down Town (New York); Nassau (Princeton); Lake Placid (N.Y.); Plainfield (N.J.) Country. Home: 1341 Prospect Av., Plainfield, N.J. Office: 656 8th Av., N.Y.C. 18. Died Sept. 10, 1952.

COCHRAN, Thomas Cunningham, former congressman; b. Sandy Creek Twp., Mercer County, Pa., Nov. 30, 1877; s. Wilson Henry and Elizabeth Eve (Robinson) C.; grad. high sch., Mercer, Pa., 1896; A.B., Westminster Coll., New Wilmington, Pa., 1901, LL.D., 1937; studied law in father's office: m. Olive Belle Pierson, Aug. 15, 1906; children—Wilson Henry, Charles Edward, Cornelia Elizabeth, Olive Amanda, Thomas Cunningham. Admitted to Pa. bar, 1903, and began practice at Mercer; dist. atty. Mercer County, 1906-09; solicitor Mercer County, 1920-27; mem. 70th to 73d Congresses (1927-35), 20th Pa. Dist. (nominated for 1st term by Rep., Dem., Socialist and Prohibition parties); sr. mem. law firm Cochran and Cochran, Mercer, Pa. Member board of directors of Lone Star Gas Co. Del. from U.S. Congress to Conference of Interparliamentary Union, Paris, 1927, Berlin, 1928, Geneva, 1929, London, 1930, Istanbul (Constantinople), 1934; observer, conference Oslo, Norway, 1939, Istanbul, 1951, Interparliamentary Union, Washington, 1953. Trustee Westminster Coll.; dir. Am. Peace Soc. Mem. Am., Pa. and Mercer County bar assns., Am. Acad. Polit. and Social Sci., Acad. Polit. Sci., Am. Judicature Soc., U. Mich. Lawyers Club, Sigma Phi Epsilon. Republican. Presbyn. Mason (32°). Clubs: Wanango Country, Greenville Country, Rotary, Duquesne (Pitts.). Home: Mercer, Pa. Died Dec. 10, 1957; buried Mercer Citizens Cemetery.

COCHRANE, Edward Lull, ret. naval officer; b. Mare Island, Cal., Mar. 18, 1892; s. Brig. Gen. Henry Clay (U.S. Marine Corps) and Elizabeth (Lull) C.; student U. Pa., 1909-10; S.B. (with distinction), U.S. Naval Acad., 1914; post grad., 1916; M.S., Mass. Inst. Tech., 1920; at U.S. Naval War Coll., 1939; LL.D., Hahnemann Med. Coll., 1943; E.D. (hon.), Poly. Inst. Bklyn., 1946; Stevens Inst. Tech., 1954; Sc.D. (hon.), Tufts Coll., 1950; m. Charlotte Osgood Wilson, June 3, 1916; children—Richard Lull (comdr. United States Navy), Edward Lull, Jr. (lt., U.S.N.). Command ensign U.S. Navy, 1914, and advanced through the grades to vice admiral, 1942; on U.S.S. Rhode Island, 1914-16; selected for post-grad. in naval constrn., 1915; assigned Phila. Navy Yards, 1917; in charge of constrn. of 2 battle cruisers, 1920-24; Bur. Constrn. and Repair, Navy Dept., 1924-29; submarine and general design; tech. adviser Internat. Conf. Safety of Life at Sea, London, 1929; in charge of design and constrn. submarines, Navy Yard, Portsmouth, N.H., 1929-33; Force constrn. staff, comdr. Scouting Force, U.S. Fleet, 1933-35; New Design Bur. Constrn. and Repair, Navy Dept., 1935-39; Bur. of Ships, Navy Dept., as hull asst. to head design div., 1939-40. also head preliminary design branch, 1941-42; asst. naval attaché, Am. Embassy, London, 1940; chief of Bur. of Ships, Nov., 1942-Nov., 1946; chief Material Div., Navy Dept., 1946-47, ret.; professor of naval construction, head dept. of naval architecture and marine engring., Mass. Inst. Tech., 1947-50; chmn. Fed. Maritime Board and Maritime Adminstr. Dept. of Commerce, 1950-52; dean engring. Mass. Inst. Tech., 1952-54, v.p. indsl. and governmental relations, 1954—. Awarded Mexican campaign medal, 1915; Victory medal World War I; Nat. Def. medal, 1944, Am. Def. medal, Asiatic-Pacific campaign medal, Am. Theatre medal, Victory medal, World War II; David W. Taylor medal for notable achievement in naval architecture and marine engring., 1945; Knight Comdr. Mil. Div., Order British Empire, Navy Distinguished Service Medal. Mem. Soc. Naval Architects and Marine Engrs., Am. Soc. Naval Engrs., British Inst. Marine Engrs., British Instn. Naval Architect, U.S. Naval Inst., Nat. Acad. Scis., Am. Acad. Arts and Scis., United Seaman's Service (pres. 1954), Am. br. Newcomen Soc. Eng. Clubs: Army and Navy, Chevy Chase (Washington); Country (Brookline, Mass.); Army and Navy Country (Arlington, Va.); University (N.Y.C.). Home: 2 Larchwood Dr., Cambridge 38, Mass. Died Nov. 14, 1959; buried Arlington Nat. Cemetery.

COCHRANE, Edward W., sports editor; b. Rome, Mich., July 22, 1894; s. Henry F. and Coral McKee (Wray) C.; student Kalamazoo Coll., 1910-13; m. Roberta Martin, June 24, 1931. Sports editor Kansas City Journal, 1914-36, Chicago Herald-American, 1937-42; sports dir., syndicated sports columnist, King Features Syndicate, 1942-44; owner and operator stock farm in California. Services often used for many civic enterprises. Mem. Baseball Writers' Assn. of America, Chicago Athletic Assn., Illinois Athletic Club, golf clubs (16) Chicago District, Sigma Delta Chi. Home: Carmel-by-the-Sea, Cal. Died Aug. 8, 1954; buried Forest Lawn, Meml. Park, Glendale, Cal.

COCKCROFT, James, publisher; b. N.Y.C., Sept. 2, 1842; s. James M. and Lucretia M. (Voorhies) C.; m. Alida T. Ketcham. Originator, 1887; encyclopaedic system of law books; pres. Edward Thompson Co. Author: American and English Encyclopaedia of Law, 1887; Encyclopaedia of Pleading and Practice, 1895; Encyclopaedia of Forms and Precedence, 1895. Address: Northport, L.I., N.Y. Deceased.

COCKE, Matty L., educator; b. Hollins, Va., Oct. 9, 1855; d. Charles Lewis and Susanna Virginia (Pleasants) C.; grad. Hollins Coll., 1874; LL.D., Roanoke Coll., 1926. Instr. mathematics, 1877-83, librarian, registrar, 1885-1900, pres. Hollins Coll., 1901-33, pres. emeritus, 1933—. Democrat. Baptist. Home: Hollins College, Va. Died Aug. 15, 1936.

COCKSHUTT, Henry, former lt. gov. of Ont., industrialist; b. Brantford, Can., July 8, 1868; s. Ignatius and Elizabeth (Foster) C.; ed. Brantford pub., high schs.; LL.C., U. of Toronto, U. of Western Ont.; m. Isabelle Rolls, June 28, 1895; children—Margaret, Katharine. With Cockshutt Plow Co. Ltd., 1884—, sec.-treas., 1888, mng. dir., 1893, pres., 1911-21; 1922-34; mayor of Brantford, 1899-1900; apptd. lt. gov. Ont., 1921, retired, 1927. Pres. Bd. of Trade, 1898; pres. Can. Mfrs. Assn., 1906; chmn. Cockshutt Plow Co. Ltd., Brantford, Ont., Frost & Wood Co. Ltd., Smith's Falls, Ont., Gypsum Lime & Alabastine (Can.), Ltd., Cockshutt Moulded Aircraft Ltd.; dir. Bank of Montreal, Que., Royal Trust Co., Montreal, Canadian Pacific Ry., Lake Erie & Northern Ry. Co., Bell Tel. Co., Can., Internat. Nickel Co. of Can., Ltd., The Guarantee Co. of N. Am.; mem. Can. Adv. Bd., Sun Ins. Office Ltd. Canadian v.p. Dir. Barnardo's Homes; gov. Victorian Order of Nurses for Can.; chancellor, U. of Western Ont.; gov. Trinity Coll., Toronto, Ont.; v.p., Upper Can. Bible Soc. Organized 215th Batt., 1916, lt. col. in command; ret. from active duty, 1926, with title Hon. Col. Clubs: Brantford, National, York, Toronto Golf (Toronto), Mount Royal (Montreal), Manitoba (Winnipeg), Rideau (Ottawa). Address: Brantford, Ont., Can. Died 1949.*

CODY, Henry John, univ. pres., clergyman; b. Embro, Ont., Can., Dec. 6, 1868; s. E. John and Louisa (Torrance) C.; student Galt Collegiate Inst., 1881-85; B.A., U. Coll., U. Toronto, 1889, M.A., 1890; student Wycliffe Theol. Coll., 1892-94; D.C.L., Bishop's Coll.; D.D., Queen's, King's, Trinity, Emmanuel, Knox, Wycliffe colls.; LL.D., Toronto, Manitoba, Alberta, Western, McMaster, McGill, Brown, Glasgow, B.C. univs., Rockford Coll.; m. Florence L. Clarke, Aug. 1894 (died 1932); 1 son, Henry Maurice (dec.); m. 2d, Barbara Blackstock, Dec. 1933. Began as teacher of classics, Ridley Coll., St. Catharines, 1889; ordained, 1893; prof. div. Wycliffe Coll., U. Toronto, 1893-14; rector St. Paul's Ch., Toronto, 1899-1932; archdeacon of York, 1909-20; minister of edn. Province of Ont., 1918-20; gov. U. Toronto, 1917-—, chmn. bd. govs., 1923-32, pres. 1932-45, chancellor, 1944-1947. Mem. legislative assembly of Ontario, 1918-20, also minister of edn. Fellow Royal Soc. of Can., Royal Soc. of Arts (Eng.), Am. Geog. Soc.; trustee Royal Ontario Museum, Ridley College, Haverqal College. Served as lt. col., hon. chaplain Queen's Own Rifles of Canada; overseas World War I; hon. col. O.T.C., U. Toronto; pres. Boy Scouts Assn. Can., 1944. Decorated Companion of Order of St. Michael and St. George, Chevalier of Legion of Honor (France); Order of Golden Grain (China); Efficiency Decoration; Medal of St. Olaf (Norway). Clubs: York (Toronto), University (N.Y.C.). Progressive Conservative. Mem. Anglican Ch. Author: Josiah Wood Lectures on Citizenship. Contbr. to Reconstruction in Canada, 1943; also contbr. articles to mags. Home: 6 Dale Av., Toronto, Ont., Can. Died Apr. 27, 1951.

CODY, (Alpheus) Sherwin, author; b. Cody's Mills, Mich., 1868; s. Aldus and Eliza Ann (Patrick) C.; A.B., Amherst Coll., 1889; m. Marian T. Hurley, 1896; 1 son, Morrill. Ednl. director Sherwin Cody Sch. of English; originator Nat. Bus. Ability Tests. Mem. Phi Beta Kappa, Phi Delta Theta. Author: The Art of Short Story Writing, 1894; How to Write Fiction, 1895; In the Heart of the Hills (novel), 1896; Four Famous Americans, 2 vols., 1899; The World's Best Series, 4 vols. (compilations), 1902, 1903, 1904, 1905; The Art of Writing and Speaking the English Language, 4 vols., 1903; The Best Tales of Poe, and the Best Poems and Essays of Poe, 1903; Story Writing and Journalism, 1905; Dictionary of Errors, 1905; How to read and What to Read, 1905; The Cody System—Business Correspondence and Advertisement Writing for Business Men, 1904, 1906; Success in Letter Writing, 1906; The Nutshell Library, 12 vols. (compilation), 1907; How to Do Business by Letter, 1908; How to Do Business by Letter and Advertising, 1911; (spl. Brit. edit., also translated into French, German, Italian, Spanish, Portuguese); Literary Composition, 1912; Business Practice Up to Date, 1913; How to Deal with Human Nature in Business, 1915; 100% Speller, 1915; 100% Self-Correcting Course in English, 1918; Commercial Tests and How to Use Them, 1919; Business Ability Development Course, 1923; Fundamentals of Business (with W. M. Jackson), 1923; Poe—Man, Poet, and Creative Thinker, 1924; Habit-Forming Language Practice, 1930; The New Art of Writing and Speaking the English Language, 6 vols., 1933, same in 1 vol., 1938. Pocket Cyclopedia of Good English, 1940; Coaching Children in English, 1944; Good English Quick Reference Book, 1944; An Evening with Poe, 1949; An Evening with Mark Twain, 1949; Letters: Writing to Get People to Do Things, 1950; Greatest Stories—and How they were Written, 1950. Address: care Morrill Cody, U. S. Information Service, 1776 Pennsylvania Av., N.W., Washington. Died Apr. 4, 1959.

COE, Charles Francis, author, lawyer; b. Buffalo, Nov. 25, 1890; s. Francis Ulysses and Anna Gertrude (Ostrander) C.; student pub. schs., pvt. tutors; m. 2d, Ruth Bernice Ensign; children—Alan C., Betty. Practicing atty. Palm Beach, Fla.; sr. partner Coe, Richardson and Broberg; counsel Milam, McIlvaine, Carroll and Walters; v.p., gen. counsel, Motion Picture Producers and Distbrs. Am., Inc., 1940-43. Trustee U. Fla., Endowment Fund. Chmn. pub. relations com. Fla. State Bar Assn., 1938-39. Writer spl. articles on crime; regarded as outstanding penologist and criminologist. Winner Freedom Found. best editorial, 1949, 50, 51. Mason. Clubs: Lotos (pres. 1935-36), Lambs, Coffee House, Hudson River Country (N.Y.); Old Guard Society Palm Beach (pres. 1942-43) Sailfish Club (pres. 1934-36), Seminole Golf Club (gov. 1941-49), Everglades (Palm Beach), Tuscawilla Club (West Palm Beach). Author: Me . . . Gangster, 1927; The River Pirate, 1927; Swag, 1928; Hooch, 1928; Triumph, 1929; Votes, 1930; About 2 A.M.; In This Corner (with Jack Dempsey); Pay Off; The Other Half; Show Down, Vigilanti; Repeal; Ransom; G.-Man, 1935; Lifer; Knockout; Rendezvous at Arms; Salvated Paradise; Law and the Profits, 1940; Never A Dull Moment, 1944; Pressure, 1951; Ashes, 1952. Contributor to the Saturday Evening Post. Editor and publisher Palm Beach Post, Palm Beach Times, Palm Beach Post-Times (Sunday). Home: Palm Beach, Fla. Died Dec. 28, 1956.

COE, Fred Joiner, banker; b. North Ridge, Niagara County, N.Y., Nov. 7, 1870; s. Bradford E. and Mary (Joiner) C.; grad. high sch., Niagara Falls, N.Y., 1885; m. Bessie Barnes Low, Oct. 12, 1897; children—James Low, Donald Low. Began in banking business at Niagara Falls, N.Y., 1893; president Power City Trust Co., 1923-45; retired; pres. Mountain View Development Co.; chmn. Niagara Falls Hotel Corp.; director Spirella International Incorporated, Old Fort Niagara Association, Incorporated, Fort Niagara, New York; trustee Niagara County Savings Bank. President Niagara Falls Chamber of Commerce, 1927-29 and 1932-33. Mem. Society Colonial Wars, S.A.R. Republican. Presbyterian. Clubs: Niagara, Niagara Falls Country; Gatineau Fish and Game (Quebec); Youngstown (N.Y.) Yacht. Home: 331 Buffalo Av., Niagara Falls, N.Y. Died Dec. 7, 1951; buried Oakwood Cemetery, Niagara Falls, N.Y.

COE, George Albert, educator; b. Monroe Co., N.Y., Mar. 26, 1862; s. Rev. George W. and Harriet (Van Voorhis) C.; A.B., U. of Rochester, 1884, A.M., 1888; S.T.B., Boston U., 1887, Ph.D., 1891; student U. of Berlin, 1890-91; LL.D., U. of Rochester, 1909; m. Sadie E. Knowland, of Alameda, Calif., Sept. 3, 1888. Prof. U. of So. Cal., 1888-90; acting prof. philosophy, 1891-93; John Evans prof. philosophy, 1893-1909, Northwestern U., Evanston, Ill.; prof. religious educaiton, Union Theol. Sem., 1909-22; same, Teachers Coll., 1922-—. Mem. Religious Edn. Assn. America (pres., 1909-10), Am. Philos. Assn., Am. Psychol. Assn. Author: The Spiritual Life-Studies in the Science of Religion, 1900; The Religion of a Mature Mind, 1902; Education in Religion and Morals, 1904; Psychology of Religion, 1916; A Social Theory of Religious Education, 1917; Law and Freedom in the School, 1923; What Ails Our Youth? 1924. Contbr. to philos. and theol. mags. Home: 509 W. 121st St., New York, N.Y. Died Nov. 9, 1951.

COE, William Robertson; born Worcestershire, England, June 8, 1869; son Frederick Augustus and Margaret (Robertson) C.; ed. Albion Acad., Cardiff, Wales; LL.D., U. of Wyo., 1948; M.A., Yale, 1949; m. Jeanie H. Falligant, Sept. 7, 1893 (died 1898); m. 2d, Mai Huttleston Rogers, June 4, 1900 (died 1924); children—William Rogers, Robert Douglas, Henry Huttleston Rogers, Natalia Mai (Countess Leonardo Vitetti); m. 3d, Caroline Graham Slaughter, Dec. 4, 1926. Came to United States, 1883, naturalized, 1900. With ins. firm of Johnson & Higgins, Phila., 1884-93, transferred to New York office and mgr, adjusting dept., 1893-1902, dir. 1902-10, pres., 1910-16, chmn. bd., 1916-43; dir. and chmn. exec. com. bd. dirs. Virginian Ry. Co.; dir. Loup Creek Colliery Co., Wyo. Land Co. Mem. Average Adjusters Assn. since 1890 (chmn. 1900), Am. Antiquarian Soc. Republican. Episcopalian. Clubs: Metropolitan, Cloud, Turf and Field, Pilgrims, River (New York); Southside Sportsmen's, Piping Rock (L.I.). Author: General Average in U.S. Endowed Chair of Am. Studies program, Yale, 1950. Home: Planting Fields, Oyster Bay, L.I., N.Y.; also River House, 435 E. 52d St., N.Y.C. Office: Chrysler Bldg., N.Y.C. Died Mar. 14, 1955.

COEN, John Ralph, lawyer; b. Ottumwa, Ia., Aug. 14, 1885; s. Winfield S. and Martha E. (Harbison) C.; student Kan. State U., 1909-11; m. Adrian Saunders, Dec. 23, 1917. Admitted to practice before Kan., Colo. bars, 1911; practiced at Sterling, Colo., 1911-34. Denver, 1934-—. Chmn. Rep. Central Com. of Colo., 1924-32. Regent Colo. State U., 1920-22. Mem. Phi Delta Phi. Republican. Presbyn. Elk (grand exalted ruler 1931-32, trustee Elks Nat. Found.). Chmn. Rep. State Central Com., 1924-32. Mason. Club: Denver. Home: 1745 Leyden St. Office: 301 Equitable Bldg., Denver. Died Nov. 20, 1954.

COES, Harold Vinton (kōz), engr., mfr.; b. Hyde Park, Mass., June 21, 1883; s. Zorester Bennett and Alice (Miller) C.; prep. edn., Northeast. Manual Tng. Sch., Phila.; B.S. Mech. Engring., Mass. Inst. Tech., 1906; m. Agnes Wickfield Day, June 5, 1909; children—Kent Day, Harold Vinton. Mech. engr. Liquid Carbonic Cho., Chgo., 1908-11; indsl. engr. Lockwood, Greene and Co., Chgo. and Boston, 1911-14; v.p., mgr. Sentinel Mfg. Co., New Haven, Conn., 1914-16; indsl. engr. Gunn, Richard & Co., engrs., N.Y., 1916-18, Ford, Bacon & Davis, Inc., 1918-24, gen. mgr. Platt Iron Works, Dayton, O., for same; v.p., gen. mgr. Belden Mfg. Co., mfrs. elec. wire, cables, etc., Chgo., 1924-28; v.p. Ford, Bacon & Davis, Inc., N.Y., 1928-37, partner 1937-48, dir., 1943; ret. exec. v.p., dir. Vulcan Iron Works, Wilkes-Barre, Pa., 1934; past pres. United Engring. Trustees, Inc., dir. Easy Washing Machine Corp., Syracuse, N.Y. Mem. adv. council, Coll. Engring., Princeton, Indsl. Engring. Dept., Columbia; Civilian asst. in operation and adminstrn. munition plants in U.S., Can., World War. Cons. engr. Planning and Development Dept., Govt. of India for Ford, Bacon & Davis, 1945-46. Chmn. finance com. Engrs. Nat. Hoover Com. Fellow Am. Soc. M.E. (past pres.); Inst. Mgmt. (past pres.); mem. Soc. Advancement of Mgmt., Am. Mgmt. Assn. (chmn. exec. com.), Indsl. Marketing Execs. Assn., Assn. Cons. Mgmt. Engrs. (past pres.), Montclair Soc. Engrs., Army Ordnance Assn., Newcomen Soc. of England, St. Andrews Soc. (hon.), Pi Tau Sigma. Republican. Unitarian. Club: Engineers (N.Y.C.). Author: Production Control (Alex. Hamilton Inst.). Asso. editor Handbook of Business Administration, also of Cost and Production Handbook. Home: 18 Braemore Rd., Upper Montclair, N.J. Office: 39 Broadway, N.Y.C. Died Dec. 4, 1958; buried Mount Hebron Cemetery, Upper Montclair, N.J.

COFFEE, Rudolph Isaac, rabbi; b. Oakland, Cal., July 24, 1878; s. Michael Harris and Rosa (Abrahamson) C.; A.B., Columbia, 1900; rabbi, Jewish Theol. Sem. America, New York, 1904; Ph.D., U. of Pittsburgh, 1908; m. Doris Hirshfeld, Nov. 6, 1910 (died 1916); children—Roger H., Marian L.; m. 2d, Mrs. Minnie Z. Jaffa, 1925. Asst. in edn., Teachers Coll. (Columbia), 1900-03; organized religious work in Y.M.H.A., N.Y., and in charge of same, 1900-03; actg. supt. and supt. Hebrew Orphan Asylum, New York, 1903-05; rabbi "Tree of Life" Congregation, Pittsburgh, 1906-15; dir. social service dept. Independent Order of B'nai B'rith, Chicago, 1915-17; rabbi Temple Judea, Chicago, 1917-20, Collingwood Av. Temple, Toledo, 1920-21, Temple Sinai, Oakland, Cal., 1921-33. Mem. State Bd. Charities and Corrections, 1924-31; chaplain California Assembly, 1925-26; sec. San Francisco Conf. of Christians and Jews, 1934-40; pres. Temple of Religion, Golden Gate Internat. Expn., 1937-—, vice pres. Cal. Prison Assn., 1940-—; also v.p. Interfaith Com. for Aid to the Democracies, 1941-—; pres. Nat. Chaplains Association, 1942-43; Jewish chaplain California State Prisons, 1941-—; Jewish chaplain San Francisco Fire Dept., 1946-—. Chairman Travelers Aid Society, Oakland, 1921-26. Editorial writer The Sentinel, Chicago, 1918-23; editor Jewish Times, San Francisco, 1922-24; editorial writer, Emanu El, San Francisco, 1928-32. Pres. Jewish Com. for Personal Service in State Instns., 1923-42, hon. pres., 1942-—. Author: Hebrew Cosmology, 1908; Israel's Contribution to America, 1910; Temple Judea Manual, 1919. Home: 2400 Buchanan St., San Francisco. Died May 10, 1955; buried Emanu-El Mausoleum, San Francisco.

COFFEY, Edward Hope, writer; b. New Briton, S.I., N.Y., July 14, 1896; s. Edward Hope and Annie Stetson (Develin) C.; A.B., Princeton, 1920; m. Dorothy Irving Stewart, July 19, 1923 (died 1954); 1 son, Edward Hope, III. Copywriter, Barton, Durstine & Osborn, advt. agts., N.Y.C., 1920-25; column condr., N.Y. Herald Tribune, 1925-30 (substituted for Don Marquis during latter's vacations, 1923, 24). Served as seaman, 2d class, U.S.N.R., later with Naval Aviation Sect. (lighter than air), as chief q.m., student officer, World War; qualified baloon pilot. Lived in Cannes, France, 1931-39. Commd. capt., Signal Corps, Army of the U.S., maj., 1943; lt. col., 1944; inactive O.R.C., 1946-—. Recipient Legion of Merit; Christopher award, 1955. Princeton Campus Club, Authors' Guild, Am. Vets. Com. Author (under pen name Edward Hope): Alice in the Delighted States, 1928; Manhattan Cocktail, 1929; She Loves Me Not, 1933, dramatized by Howard Lindsay, motion picture version made, 1934; Calm Yourself!, 1934 (filmed); Marry the Girl, 1935 (filmed); Ask Me No Questions, 1936 (pub. in U.S. as Let X Equal Marjorie, 1938); Spanish Omelet, 1937. Contbr. under pen name to various mags. Home: 9442 Sierra Mar Pl., Los Angeles 46. Office: care Harold Ober, 40 E. 49th St., N.Y.C. Died Feb. 23, 1958.

COFFEY, Harry K., ins., aircraft exec.; b. Guthrie, Ky., Nov. 9, 1895; s. Robert Harrison and Eva Amorette (Chalkley) C.; student pub. schs., Hemet, Cal.; extension courses U. Cal., Northwestern Sch. Bus.; Aviation Sch., 1914; m. Elma V. Van Wey; children—Howard K., Colin V. With H.D. Lee Merc. Co., 1916-19; joined Mt. Benefit Health & Accident Assn. and United Benefit Life Ins. Co. of Omaha, 1920, gen. agt. for Ore., Wash., Ida., and Alaska since 1925; pres. Columbia Aircraft, Flightcraft Inc. Pilot since 1914; made flight to Point Barraow, Alaska, to establish meml. for Will Rogers and Wiley Post. Served as machine gun officer O.T.S., 1916; nat. co-ordinating officer U.S.A.F. Civilian Air Patrol, since 1941. Pres. Nat. Aero. Assn., Mgrs. Assn. Club: Aero of Oregon. (pres.). Home: 1850 N. Shore Rd., Oswego, Ore. Office: Nat. Aeronautic Assn., 1025 Connecticut Av., Washington 6 ; also 1001 S.W. 10th Av., Portland 5, Ore. Died June 15, 1954; buried Lincoln Meml. Park, Portland, Ore.

COFFEY, John Will, army officer; b. N.Y.C., Jan. 12, 1897; B.S., U.S. Mil. Acad., 1917; grad Ordnance Sch., 1923; Command and Gen. Staff Sch., 1933; AC Tactical Sch., 1939; Army War Coll., 1940. Commd. 2d lt. CAC, 1917; transferred to Ordnance and advanced through the grades to brig. gen., 1943; prof. ordnance U.S. Mil. Acad. Address: Ordnance Dept., Indianatown Gap, Pa. Deceased; buried Mil. Cemetery, West Point, N.Y.

COFFEY, Robert Lewis, Jr., ex-congressman; b. Chattanooga, Tenn., Oct. 21, 1918; s. Robert Lewis and Curry Ethel (Brindley) C.; student, U. Pitts., 1935-38, Pa. State Coll., 1938-39, AC Advanced Flying Sch., 1939-40, Command and Gen. Staff Coll., 1943; m. E. Eileen Mercado-Parra, Oct. 15, 1942; children—Robert Lewis, Eileen Maria, David Mario. Coal miner, track worker, shot firer, motorman, in coal mines, 3 yrs.; mining engr., coal inspector, 1 yr. mil. air attaché, U.S. Embassy, Chile, 1946-48; mem. 81st Congress, 26th Dist., Pa. Served from 2d lt. to col. USAF, 9 yrs.; active as col. in USAF Res. Decorated Distinguished Flying Cross, (3 times), Air Medal (26 times), Purple Heart, Bronze Star, Chilean Order of Merit. Mem. Am. Legion, Am. Vets., Vets. Foreign Wars, Officers Reserve Assn., Air Reserve Assn., Air Force Assn. Democrat. Elk. Clubs: Army and Navy; North Fork Country. Home: 2036 Franklin St., Johnstown, Pa.; also 920 F Sligo Creek Pkwy., Silver Spring, Md. Office: House Office Bldg., Washington. Died April 21, 1949; buried Arlington Nat. Cemetery.

COFFEY, Walter Castella, univ. pres.; b. Hartsville, Ind., Feb. 1, 1876; s. Calvin Allen and Josephine (Simmonds) C.; Hartsville Coll., 1892-93; and Franklin Coll., Ind., 1897-98, 1900-01; Ind. U., 1899; B.S., U. Ill. 1906, M.S., 1909; LL.D., Hamline U., 1927; D.Sc., Franklin (Ind.) Coll., 1943; U. Minn., 1946; m. Jennie Crislor Lardner, August 14, 1907; children—Lardner Allen, Walter Calvin. Instr. animal husbandry, 1906-07; asso. 1907-11; asst. prof., 1911-13, prof. sheep and meat, 1913-21, U. Ill.; dean Dept. Agr., U. Minn., 1921-41; acting pres., 1941, pres. 1941-45, pres. emeritus 1945—. Chmn. Bd. and Federal Reserve Agent and Class C dir. Federal Reserve Bank Mpls., 1938-45. Dir. International Live Stock Exposition. Pres. Dairy Council of Twin Cities. Trustee of Hamline U.; mem. at large of the Minneapolis Area Council and Nat. Rural Scouting Com. Boy Scouts of America. Distinguished Service award, Am. Farm Bureau Federation, 1942. Mem. Minn. Hort. Soc. (honorary life), Minn. State Agrl. Soc. (honorary life), Minn. Hist. Soc., St. Paul Assn. of Commerce, Sigma Alpha Epsilon (awarded achievement medal, 1944), Alpha Zeta, Phi Kappa Phi, Sigma Xi, Gamma Sigma Delta. Mason. Methodist. Clubs: Campus (University of Minnesota); Rotary, Informal (St. Paul). Author: Productive Sheep Husbandry, 1918, revised 1929. Co-Author: Live Stock Enterprises, 1928. Home: 1803 N Pascal Av., St. Paul 13. Died Jan. 31, 1957.

COFFIN, Henry Sloane, clergyman, author; b. N.Y.C., Jan. 5, 1877; s. Edmund and Euphemia (Sloane) C.; B.A., Yale, 1897, M.A., 1900; studied New Coll., Edinburgh, 1897-99, U. Marburg, 1899, Th.D., 1930; B.D., Union Theol. Sem., 1900; D.D., N.Y. U., 1906, Yale, 1915, Harvard, 1922, Princeton, Columbia, 1925, Glasgow U., 1926, Union Coll., 1928; Episcopal Theol. Sem., 1935, LL.D., Amherst Coll., St. Andrews U., 1934, Wabash, 1932, 1934, Hamilton Coll., 1938; D.D., Bowdoin, 1944; Litt.D., Coll. of Ozarks, 1931, Western Res. U., 1937; S.T.D., Jewish Theol. Sem, 1937; D.Theol., Marburg, 1930; Faculte Libre de Theologie Protestante, Paris, 1938; m. Dorothy Prentice Eells, Sept. 6, 1906; children—Ruth P. Nash, David D. Ordained to Presbyn. ministry, 1900; pastor Bedford Park Ch., N.Y.C., 1900-05, Madison Av., Ch., 1905-26, asso. prof. practical theology Union Theol. Sem., 1904-26; pres. Union Theol. Sem., 1926-45; moderator Presbyn. Ch. in U.S.A., 1943-44. Joseph Cook lectr. in China and India, 1946-47. Annual preacher, Yale, Princeton, etc. Mem. Bd. of Nat. Missions Presbyn. Ch.; dir. Ch. Extension Com. of Presbytery of New York (Inc.). Trustee Robert College, Constantinople, 1905-48; fellow Corp. Yale, 1921-45. Member Delta Kappa Epsilon, Phi Beta Kappa, Skull and Bones, Chi Alpha. Club: Century. Author: The Creed of Jesus, 1907. Social Aspects of the Cross, 1911; The Christian and the Church, 1912; University Sermons, 1914; The Ten Commandments, 1915; Christian Convictions, 1915; In a Day of Social Rebuilding (Lyman Beecher Lectures at Yale), 1918; A More Christian Industrial Order, 1920; What Is There in Religion?, 1922; Portraits of Jesus Christ, 1926; What to Preach (Warrack lectures), 1926; The Meaning of the Cross, 1931; What Men Are Asking—Some Current Questions in Religion, 1933; God's Turn, 1934; Religion Yesterday and Today, 1940; The Public Worship of God, 1946; God Confronts Man in History, 1947; A Half Century of Union Theol. Sem., 1954. Co-author: Some Social Aspects of the Gospel, 1912; Church and State in the Modern World, 1937; The Ministry, 1949; Isaiah in Interpreter's Bible. Co-editor: Hymns of the Kingdom, 1910. Home: Coombe-Pine, Lakeville, Conn. Died Nov. 25, 1954; buried Sleepy Hollow Cemetery, Tarrytown, N.Y.

COFFIN, Howard Aldridge, ex-congressman; b. Middleboro, Mass., June 11, 1877; s. George Henry and Jane Clifford (Guild) C.; A.B., Brown U., 1901; m. Abbie Sweetland Ghodey, Oct. 4, 1904 (deceased, December 28, 1945); children—Richard Guild, Carolyn (wife of lieutenant Frederick C. Nash, U.S.N.), Dean Fiske, Gail (wife of Duncan Edmands, United States Coast Guard); m. 2d Marie Thraikill Brown, June 18, 1949. Teacher Friends School, Providence, Rhode Island, 1901; representative Ginn & Co., book publishers, 1901-11; controller, Warren Motor Car Co., Detroit, Mich., 1911-13; mgr., Firestone Tire and Rubber Co. (for Mich.), 1913-18; sec., Detroit Pressed Steel Co., 1918-21; asst. to pres., Cadillac Motor Car Co., Detroit, 1921-25, vice pres., later pres. White Star Refining Co., 1925-33; gen. mgr. Socony-Vacuum Oil Co., Inc. (purchaser White Star Refining Co.), Michigan-Ohio div., since 1933. Mem. 80th Congress (1947-49), 13th Michigan Dist. Vice chmn. appeal bd. No. 1, Selective Service, Mich. Trustee First Liquidating Corp., Detroit, Mich. Trustee Grace Hosp. (Detroit), Brown U. Detroit Coll. of Law. Member executive com. United War Chest Mem. bd. Detroit Young Men's Christian Assn., Nat. Council Y.M.C.A. (New York); mem. Internat. Board Y.M.C.A. (New York). Clubs: Detroit Athletic (past dir.), Rotary (past dir.; past pres.), Detroit Golf (past dir.), Economic (dir.) (Detroit); Burning Tree Golf, Columbia Country, University (Washington). Home: 2500 Que St., N.W., Washington also Greenbank, R.F.D., Potomac, Md. Died Feb. 28, 1956; buried Detroit, Mich.

COFFIN, Marie T(hrailkill) Brown (Mrs. Howard Aldridge Coffin), mem. Rep. Nat. Com.; b. Columbus, O.; d. Marshall E. and Laura (Haughn) Thrailkill; student Western Coll. for Women, 1910; A.B., Ohio State U., 1913; m. Hon. Thaddeus Harold Brown, Nov. 10, 1915 (dec. 1941); 1 son, Thaddeus H. Brown; m. 2d Hon. Howard Aldreidge Coffin, June 28, 1949 (dec. 1956). Columnist, Washington in War. Columbus (O.) Evening Dispatch, 1941-42; head Washington bur. columnist Behind the Scenes, Dayton (O.) Journal-Herald, 1947-49; spl. feature writer Washington staff N.A. Newspaper Alliance, Inc., 1949—; mem. Senate Press Gallery, 1947-51. Apptd. 1st chmn. Ohio Day in Washington, 1943; mem. Nat. Home and Hospitality Com. for Servicemen, 1951. Mem. Rep. Nat. Com. for D.C., 1948—, chmn. women's finance com., 1944-51, mem. strategy and territorial com., 1948-49, site and date com. Nat. Conv., 1952. Vice chmn. Dewey-Warren D.C. campaign com., 1948; mem. bd. govs. Rep. League Women of D.C., 1951; vice chmn., co-founder rep. Women's Orgns. of Ohio, 1931-33; v.p. D.C. Rep. Club, 1951-52; co-chmn. Nat. Rep. Women's Speakers Task Force, 1951-52; head Women's Div., Eisenhower-Nixon campaign, D.C., 1952; mem. arrangements com. Rep. Nat. Conv., 1952; vice chmn. exec. com. Inauguration Pres. Eisenhower and Vice Pres. Nixon, 1953; co-chmn. Inaugural Ball, 1953; Official mem. Rep. D.C. Delegation San Francisco Conv., 1956; chmn. Women's Div. Eisenhower-Nixon campaign, D.C., 1956; vice chmn. exec. com. Inaurgural Com., D.C.; Inauguration Ofcl. Hostess, chmn. hostesses and hospitality com. Inauguration Pres. Eisenhower, 1957; v. chmn. govs. reception inauguation chmn. distinguished guest reception, Pan-Am. Union Bldg. Inauguration, 1956-57; mem. Alexander Hamilton Commn. Chmn. Damon Runyon Meml. Cancer Fund; dir. Washington unit Am. Women Voluntary Services; mem. bd. Columbus (O.) Children's Hosp., 1922-32; bd. trustees George Washington U. Hosp., 1948-51. Mem. UN Forum (vice chmn. exec. com.), Matrix Soc., Ohio Soc. Washington (bd. govs. 1932), Columbus Founders Soc. (1st sec. 1918-24), Theta Sigma Phi. Presbyn. Clubs: American Newspaper Women's, Capitol Hill (bd. govs.) (Washington). Home: 2500 Q St., Washington 7. Died Aug. 18, 1959.

COFFIN, Oscar Jackson, ret. univ. dean, journalist; b. Moore County, N.C., Feb. 4, 1887; s. Alexander Horney and Ida Elizabeth (Moring) C.; A.B., U. N.C., 1909; m. Gertrude Wilson, Sept. 5, 1912; 1 son, Edwin Wilson. Tchr. pub. schs., 1909-10; reporter Winston-Salem (N.C.) Journal, 1911; news editor Charlotte Observer, 1912-16; city editor Raleigh Times, 1916-18, editor, 1918-26; columnist Greensboro Daily News, 1926—; prof. journalism U. N.C., 1926-56, dean sch. of journalism, 1950-55, Democrat. Methodist. Home: 16 Dixie Trail, Raleigh, N.C. Died Oct. 29, 1956; buried Old Cemetery, Chapel Hill, N.C.

COFFIN, Robert Peter Tristram; b. Brunswick, Me., Mar. 18, 1892; s. James William and Alice Mary (Coombs) C.; A.B., summa cum laude, Bowdoin, 1915, Litt.D., 1930; A.M., Princeton, 1916; Rhodes scholar from Me. to Trinity Coll., Oxford U., Eng., 1916-17, 1919-21, B.A., Oxford, 1920, B.Litt., 1921; Litt.D., U. of Me. (commencement speaker), 1937; married Ruth Neal Phillip, Jan 22, 1918 (died Apr. 5, 1947); children—Mary-Alice, Margaret Rollins, Robert Peter Tristram, Richard Neal. Henry W. Longfellow scholar, Princeton, 1915-16; with Wells College, Aurora, New York, 1921-34, instructor in English until 1922, asst. professor, associate professor and professor, 1922-34, Anna Adams Piutti professor of English, 1928-34; Pierce professor English, Bowdoin College, since 1934; lecturer Columbia U., summer, 1937 and 1938, University of New Hampshire, summers, since 1938; book review and poetry editor of Yankee, 1937-?9 teacher at Corpus Christi Fine Arts Colony, 1948-53; inaugurated George Elliston Professorship of poetry U. Cin., 1951; Class of 1898 lectr. Haverford Coll., 1953; Fulbright spl. lectr. on Am. lit. and civilization U. Athens, Greece, 1953-54. Largely responsible at Wells College for founding and carrying on the Oxford idea of honor work in English lit.; year's leave of absence to study honor system at Oxford University, England, 1928-29. Student Oxford Univ. O.T.C., 1917; 2d O.T.C., Plattsburg, N.Y., and Ft. Monroe, Va.; 2d lt. C.A.C., U.S. Army, 1917; member 72d Arty. Regt., A.E.F., 1918-19; hon. disch. Jan 1919. Fellow of American Academy of Arts and Sciences; mem. Modern Lang. Assn. America, Internat. P.E.N., Poetry Soc., America, Soc. of Am. Historians, Rochester (N.Y.) Poetry Soc., Authors, Newcomen Soc. (American Branch), Phi Beta Kappa, Zeta Psi. Republican. Congregationalist. Clubs: Authors, Nat. Arts (hon. life). Author: Christchurch, (verse), 1924; Book of Crowns and Cottages (essays), 1925; Dew and Bronze (verse), 1927; Golden Falcon (verse), 1929; An Attic Room (essays), 1929; Laud, Storm Center of Stuart England (biography), 1930; The Dukes of Buckingham (biography), 1931; Portrait of an American (biography), 1931; The Yoke of Thunder (verse), 1932; Ballads of Square-Toed Americans (verse), 1933; Lost Paradise (autobiography), 1934; Strange Holiness (verse), 1935; Red Sky in the Morning (novel), 1935; John Dawn (novel), 1936; Saltwater Farm (verse), 1937; Kennebec: Cradle of Americans (Rivers of America series; historical), 1937; New Poetry of New England (Turnbull Lectures, Johns Hopkins U.), 1938; Maine Ballads (verse), 1938; Collected Poems (verse), 1939; Captain Abby and Captain John (biography), 1939; Thomas-Thomas-Ancil-Thomas (novel), 1941; There Will Be Bread and Love (verse), 1942; The Substance That Is Poetry (Patten Lectures, Indiana U.), 1942; Book of Uncles (essays), 1942; Primer for America (verse), 1943; Mainstays of Maine (essays), 1944; Poems for a Son with Wings (verse), 1945; People Behave Like Ballads (verse), 1946; Yankee Coast (essays), 1947; Collected Poems new enlarged edit., 1948; The Third Hunger and The Poem Aloud (lectures), 1949; Coast Calendar (essays), 1949; One-Horse Farm (verse), 1949; Maine Doings (essays), 1950; Apples by Ocean (verse), 1950; On the Green Carpet (Elliston Lectures U. Cin.), 1951; Sir Isaac Coffin, Admiral and Prophet (Newcomen address), 1951; New England: Life in America (history-geography), 1951. Compiler: A Book of Seventeenth Century Prose and Seventeenth Century Prose and Poetry (with A. M. Witherspoon). 1929, 46. Phi Beta Kappa poet Harvard Commencement, 1932; Katherine Lee Bates poet Wellesley Coll., 1927, 31, 36, 43; Phi Beta Kappa poet Colby College, 1935, Tufts Coll., 1936, Hamilton Coll., 1937, U. Va., 1936, Boston U., 1939, Bates Coll., 1941, Fla. State College for Women, 1945, Randolph-Macon Coll., 1945, U. Rochester, 1945, Bucknell University, 1945; Percy Graeme Turnbull Meml. lecturer Johns Hopkins, 1938; Pattion Found. lectr. Ind. U., 1941, Samuel Harris lectr. on Literature and Life, The Third Hunger, Bangor Theological Seminary, 1945; gave Centennial address Baylor U., 1945; Cole lectr. Wheaton Coll., 1945; speaker Eighth Literature Festival, Coker Coll.; lectr. Seminary, 1945, Pacific Sch. of Religion, 1948, 49; spl. lecturer Washington University, Peabody Coll., Univ. Cal., Mills Coll., U. N.M., Tex. State Coll. for Women, S.W. Texas State Coll., Okla. Coll. for Women, Huntington Coll., J. B. Stetson U., U. Fla., U. Ga., Wesleyan Coll., Madison College, 1948, So. Lt. Festival at Delta Coll. (Miss.), 1948; teacher Corpus Christi Fine Arts Colony, 1949-51, U. Fla., summer 1947. Subject of Robert P. Tristram Coffin Day, Bowdoin College, 1948; recipient of gold medal as national honor poet, 1935; golden rose, New England Poetry Society, 1936; Pulitzer prize for poetry (Strange Holiness), 1936. Elected mem. Nat. Inst. of Arts and Letters, 1946. Contbr.: Dictionary Am. Biography, to Dictionary of Am. History, also articles, verse and illustrations to publs. of U.S. and England. Home: 44 Harpswell St., Brunswick, Me. Died Jan. 20, 1955.

COFFMAN, George Raleigh, ret. prof.; b. Ancona, Ill., Oct. 22, 1880; s. Joseph Samuel and Catherine (Grim) C.; A.B., Drake U., Des Moines, Ia., 1903; A.M., Harvard, 1909; Ph.D., U. of Chicago, 1913; m. Bertha Reed, Nov. 24, 1909. Asst. in Greek, Drake U., 1901-03; English teacher, high sch., Moulton and Des Moines, Ia., 1903-06; asst. in English, Bradley Poly. Inst., 1906-08; instr. in English, Washington U., 1909-11; asst. prof. English, U. of Mont., 1913-14, prof. 1914-19, chmn. English dept., 1916-19; prof. English, Grinnell Coll., 1919-23, also chmn. dept.; exchange lecturer, Harvard, 1923-24; prof. English, Coll. Practical Arts and Letters, Boston U., 1924-30, head English department, 1926-30; head English dept. U.N. Car., 1930-45; Kenan prof. English 1930-51, emeritus 1951. Lectr. in English lit., Wellesley Coll., 1928-30. Guggenheim Research Fellow 1952-53. Fellow Mediaeval Acad. Am. (president 1945-48), American Academy of Arts and Sciences; mem. Modern Language Association, Modern Humanities Research Assn., Phi Beta Kappa. Club: Faculty (Cambridge). Author: A New Theory Concerning the Origin of the Miracle Play, 1914. Articles and reviews in modern lang. periodicals. Editor: A Book of Modern Plays, 1925; Five Significant English Plays, 1930. Editor: Studies in Philology, 1930-50.

Adv. asst. English Lit., Directory of Am. Scholars for Am. Council Learned Socs., 1942. Home: 26 Hollis St., Newton 58, Mass. Died Jan. 25, 1958; buried Newton (Mass.) Cemetery.

COGGESHALL, Arthur Sterry (cŏgs'awl), paleontologist; b. Bridgeport, Conn., July 17, 1873; s. Sterry Israel and Harriet Ellen (Jeffries) C.; ed. pub. schs., New Haven, Conn.; D.Sc. (hon.), Occidental Coll., 1950; m. Jennie Louise Smith, Apr. 24, 1895; children—Ethyl Adele (Mrs. Elmer P. Kuhn), Mildred Olive (Mrs. Benedict Kristoff), Hazel Eloise (Mrs. Rigby Pogmore); m. 2d, Adelaide Arneson, Oct. 28, 1946. With Am. Mus. Natural History, N. Y.C., 1896-99, curator pub. edn. and preparator-in-chief dept. of paleontology, Carnegie Mus., Pitts., 1899-1929; designed and perfected cast steel method of mounting large Dinosaurus, 1904; dir. St. Paul Inst., St. Paul, Minn., 1929-31; chief Ill. State Mus., Springfield, 1931-37; dir. Santa Barbara (Cal.) Mus. Natural History, 1937—. Specialized work, Dinosaurs, Brit. Mus. Natural History Br., 1905; Natural History Mus., Jardin des Plantes, Paris, France, 1901; Mus. Fur Nature Künde, Berlin, Ger., 1908; Royal Mus. Natural Hist., Vienna, Austria, 1909; Museo Geologico, Bologna, Italy, 1909; Imperial Mus., St. Petersburg, Russia, 1911; Nat. Mus. of Argentina, La Plata, Argentina, 1912; National Mus. of Spain, Madrid, Spain, 1913. Protestant. Officer de l'Instruction Publique de France, 1908; Francis Joseph Order of Merit with Golden Crown, Austria, 1909; Cavaliere della Corona d'Italian, 1909; Order of St. Anne, Russia, 1910; Caballero de la Orden civil de Alfonso XII, Spain, 1914; Caballero de la Real Orden de Isabel la Catolica, Spain, 1914. Mem. forest adv. com., sec., Western Mus.' Conf. Fellow A.A. A.S.; mem. council Am. Assn. Mus'. Lectr. natural history subjects and travels; instr. U. Cal. Nature Sch. Home: 653 Mission Canyon Rd., Santa Barbara, Cal. Died Aug. 13, 1958.

COGSHALL, Wilbur Adelman, prof. astronomy; b. Mendon, Mich., Feb. 8, 1874; s. Wilbur I. and Martha (Leavitt) C.; B.S., Albion (Mich.) Coll., 1895; studied U. Chgo., Yerkes Obs.; A.M., Ind. U., 1902; m. Harriet Bayliss, Jan. 21, 1899; children—Wilbur Bayliss, Sarah Louise, Frederick John. Prof. astronomy Ind. U. Mem. Am. Astron. Soc., Ind. Acad. Science, Sigma Xi, Alpha Tau Omega. Methodist. Has specialized in astro-photography. Home: Rockford, Ill. Died Oct. 5, 1951; buried nr. Flagstaff, Ariz.

COGSWELL, Ledyard, Jr.; b. Albany, N.Y., May 13, 1878; s. Ledyard and Cornelia (McClure) C.; grad. Albany Acad., 1895; A.B., Yale, 1899; student Harvard Law Sch., 1899-1901; m. Dorothy Treat Arnold, Feb. 1, 1921; children—Dorothy Arnold (Mrs. Lee P. Stack, Jr.), Arnold, Cornelia Ledyard. Messenger N.Y. State Bank, Albany, 1901, asst. cashier, 1905-10, v.p., 1910-22, pres., 1922-28; chmn. bd. Pittsburgh Tube Co.; pres. Albany Lumber & Planing Mill Co.; dir. Albany Insurance Co.; trustee Albany Savings Bank. Capt. Q.M.C., U.S. Army, 1917-18, maj., 1918; col. U.S. Res., chief of Buffalo Ordnance Dist., 1923-39. Pres., trustee Albany Inst. of History and Art. Mem. Delta Kappa Epsilon. Republican. Presbyterian. Clubs: Fort Orange, University. Albany Country, Schuyler Meadows (Albany); University, Yale (New York). Home: Loudonville, Albany Co., N.Y. Office: 75 State St., Albany 7, N.Y. Died July 30, 1954.

COHEN, A. Broderick (kō'ĕn), educator; b. New York, N.Y., Aug. 26, 1884; s. Isidore and Mathilde (Broderick) C.; A.B., Columbia, 1906, A.M., 1909; Bachelor's and Master's diplomas in secondary edn., Teachers Coll., Columbia; m. Beatrice Levin; children—Jefferson, Rowland, Helen. Teacher and adminstr. in high schs., 1906-24; prin. Vacation High Sch., N.Y., 1920-24; prof. and dir. school of general studies and summer session, Hunter Coll., 1925-52, now emeritus prof. also chmn. com. on graduate study; public relations counselor and ednl. cons., from 1952. Leader successful movement to introduce sabbatical year plan into N.Y.C. public school system 1918-25. President Eastern Assn. for Extension Edn., 1931-32, mem. exec. committee 1932-33; mem. N.Y. Adult Edn. Council, Bklyn. Jewish Social Service Bur. (past v.p.), formerly chairman educators division Brooklyn Federation Jewish Charities. President N.Y. Acad. Pub. Edn., 1936-38, chmn. com. on membership, mem. exec. com.; chmn. educators div. Boy Scouts Campaign Com. for N.Y.C., from 1937; mem. at large Brooklyn Council Boy Scouts Found. Greater N.Y., from 1939; chmn. college div. Joint Distbn. Committee, 1937; formerly mem. exec. com. S. Parkes Cadman Memorial Committee; mem. Scholars and Educators of Semi-Centennial Com., Jewish Theological Sem., 1937; mem. L.I. Tercentenary Com., 1936; member Bklyn. Citizens Com. of 15, N.Y. World's Fair, 1939-40. Del. of Hunter College to Nat. Association Urban Univs., from 1926; chmn. Com. of Presidents of N.Y.C. Ednl. Assns., N E.A. Meeting, 1938; chairman college and univ. committee of N.Y.-Bklyn. Fedn. Campaign, 1938; executive vice chmn. Com. of 100, organized to complete the Brooklyn Central Library Building; past chmn. Com. on Brooklyn Branch Libraries; past chairman Commission on International Cultural Relations of Association of American Colleges; member bd. trustees Brooklyn Child Guidance Clinic; mem. adv. council of China Institute in America; member Assn. U. Evening Colls.; 1st vice chmn. and mem. bd. Save the Children Federation. Fellow American Geog. Society; mem. N.E.A., Am. Assn. Sch. Adminstrs., Am. Assn. Adult Edn., Acad. of Polit. Science, Acad. Polit. and Social Science, Schoolmasters Assn. of N.Y. and Vicinity, N.Y. Soc. for Exptl. Study of Education, N.Y. Vocational Guidance Association, World Assn. Adult Education, Bronx Boro-Wide Teachers Assn. (hon.), formerly mem. Brooklyn C. of C. (chmn. com. on central library bldg.), School Gardens Assn. (hon.), Shakespeare Assn. of America, Sigma Tau Delta (hon.); former vice chmn. Council on Adult Edn. for the Foreign-Born; Lexington School for the Deaf, member of Board and Chairman of the School Com. Democrat. Mason. Club: Brooklyn Rotarian. Home: 2215 Newkirk Av., Bklyn. 26. Office: Hunter College, 695 Park Av., N.Y.C. Died Feb. 27, 1956.

COHEN, Alfred Morton, lawyer; b. Cincinnati, Oct. 19, 1859; s. Morton S. and Phebe (Phillips) C.; ed. pub. schs., Cincinnati; LL.B., Cincinnati Law Sch., 1880; Doctor of Hebrew Law, Hebrew Union Coll., 1929; m. Millie Phillips, June 19, 1889; children—Ruth (wife of Dr. Louis L. Mann), Hannah (Mrs. Sylvan Z. Rothschild), Philip A. Sr. mem. Cohen, and Baron; chmn. bd. People's Bank & Savings Co. Ex-mem. City Council, Cincinnati; mem. State senate, 2 terms, 1897-1900; Dem. and Independent Rep. candidate for mayor of Cincinnati, 1900, pres. Ohio electoral coll., 1913, 1933, 1937 and 1941 and mem., 1917; Ohio rep. Conf. Commn. of Uniform State Laws, Montreal, Aug. 1913; Democrat. Hon. Internat. pres. B'nai B'rith; hon. chmn. bd. govs. Hebrew Union Coll. Club: Cincinnati. Home: 3557 Reading Rd. (Avondale). Office: Ingalls Bldg., 6 E. 4th St., Cincinnati, O. Died Mar. 9, 1949.

COHEN, Archie H., govt. ofcl.; b. Phila., Oct. 16, 1889; s. Frank Morris and Minnie (Glickman) C.; LL.B., John Marshall Law Sch., 1914, LL.D., 1954; m. Rose Ida Samuel, June 24, 1913; children—Nathan M., Ruth E. (Mrs. Robert I. Hyman). Admitted to Ill. bar, 1915; practiced in Chgo., 1915-53; prof. law Loyola U., Chgo., 1927-33; master in chancery Circuit Ct. Cook County, Ill., 1927-33; lectr. bankruptcy law John Marshall Law Sch., Chgo.; referee bankruptcy U.S. Dist. Ct., No. Dist. of Ill., Eastern Div., 1934-44; mem. bd. review Gen. Services Adminstrn., 1953—. Mem. Am., Ill., Chgo., Fed. bar assns., Decalogue Soc. Lawyers (past pres.), Tau Delta Phi. Elk (past exalted ruler); mem. B'nai B'rith. Editor Referees' Jour., 1949—. Home: Hotel Windsor Park, Washington 8. Office: Gen. Services Bldg., Washington 25. Deceased.

COHEN, Barnett, biochemist, bacteriologist; born Rogachev, Russia, Feb. 16, 1891; s. Louis and Rose (Goedelberg) C.; brought to U.S., 1893, naturalized, 1900; student Townsend Harris Hall, N.Y. City, 1904-07; B.S., Coll. City of N.Y., 1911; Ph.D., Yale, 1921. Asst. chem. bacteriologist, City of Savannah, Ga., 1915-16; chemist, hygienic lab. U.S. P.H.S., Washington, 1920-28; asso. prof. physiol. chemistry Johns Hopkins since 1928. Ofcl. investigator Office Scientific Research and Development, 1941-45. Served as 2d lt., U.S. Army, 1918. Mem. A.A. A.S., Am. Chem. Soc., Am. Pub. Health Assn., Soc. Biol. Chemists, Soc. Am. Bacteriologists (pres. 1950, archivist since 1935). Club: Cosmos (Washington). Author: The Leeuwenhoek Letter—A Translation, 1937. Editor: Bacteriological Reviews since foundation 1937. Home: 10 W. Read St., Balt. 1. Died Oct. 22, 1952; buried Linden Hill Cemetery of Central Synagogue, Queens, N.Y.

COHEN, Benjamin A., ex-under sec. U.N.; born Concepcion, Chile, Mar. 18, 1896; s. Alberto and Rebecca (Gallerstein) C.; ed. English Sch., Lota, Chile, Ph.B., Univ. Chile, Santiago; M.S., magna cum laude, Georgetown U.; LL.D., Am. U., 1948, Ithaca Coll., 1952; L.H.D., U. Fla.,1950; m. 2d, Rita Jane Mayer, Feb. 1, 1948; children—Benjamin Carlos, Paz, Roland David; 1 son (by previous marriage), Luis. Engaged as reporter and editor of several Chilean papers, contributor and editor of magazines, specializing in foreign affairs, 11 years; division associate National Library of Chile, 5 years; press attache Chilean Embassy Centennial of Brazil, 1922; under-secretary to 5th Pan-Am. Conf., Chile, 1923; sec., Chilean Defense Commn. at Tacna-Arica Arbitration, 1923-24; 2d sec. Chilean Embassy to U.S. and representing Chile at various Pan-Am. confs. in U.S., 1924-27; chargé d'affaires, Washington, D.C., 1933; minister resident and chief diplomatic dept., Chilean Fgn. Office, and del. to various Pan-Am. confs., 1936-39; ambassador to Bolivia, 1939-45, to Venezuela, 1945; exec. secretariat, exec. com. of Preparatory Commn. U.N. (chief of sects. 8 and 10); chief, information planning sect.; secretariat, first assembly UN, London, 1946; later asst. sec.-gen. in charge dept. pub. information, UN; under-secretary UN charge trusteeship and information non-selfgoverning territories, 1955-59. Decorated Commander Order of Merit (Ecuador), Order Juan Manuel de Cespedes (Cuba), Order of the Aztec Eagle (Mexico), Order of Leopold (Belgium), Crown of Italy, Red Cross (Ger.), Honor and Merit (Haiti), Merit for Teachers (Bolivia); Quetzal (Guatemala); Grand Officer; The Sun (Peru), Southern Cross (Brazil), San Sava (Yugoslavia), Grand Cross; Leopold II (Belgium); Condor of the Andes (Bolivia), Vasco Nunez de Balboa (Panama), One World Statesmanship Award, 1950. Fellow American Geographic Soc. (New York City), Chilean Society History and Geography (Santiago), Chilean Bibliographical Society (Santiago), Acad. Polit. Science (N.Y. City), Am. Acad. Polit. and Social Science, Chilean Inst. High Internat. Studies (Santiago); mem. Am. Inst. Internat. Law, Am. Soc. International Law (Washington), Internat. Law Assn. (London), Chilean Commn. for Codification of Internat. Law, corr. mem. Bolivian Acad. of History (La Paz), Acad. of Arts (Athens, Greece). Clubs: Overseas Press; Union (Santiago, Chile); Rockefeller Center Luncheon, Fgn. Press (hon. mem.). Home: 77 Park Av., N.Y. City 16. Office: care United Nations, N.Y. City. Died March, 1960.

COHEN, Felix S., lawyer; b. New York, N.Y., July 3, 1907; s. Morris Raphael and Mary (Ryshpan) C.; A.B., Coll. of City of N.Y., 1926; A.M., Harvard, 1927, Ph.D., 1929; LL.B., Columbia, 1931; m. Lucy Kramer, Sept. 22, 1931; children—Gene Maura, Karen Ann. Sec. to Justice of Supreme Court of New York, 1931-32; admitted to N.Y. bar, 1932, D.C., 1948; private practice, 1932-33 and since 1948; Washington partner in firm Riegelman, Strasser, Schmurz and Spiegelberg since 1952; lecturer on legal philosophy, New Sch. for Social Research, 1932-33; asst. solicitor U.S. Dept. of Interior 1933-43; member board of appeals, Dept. of Interior, 1936-48, chairman 1940-1948; special assistant to Atty. Gen., 1939; chief Indian Law Survey, U.S. Dept. of Justice, 1939-40; asso. solicitor, U.S. Dept. of the Interior, Washington, D.C., 1943-1948; visiting lecturer (professor), Yale Law Sch. since 1946 and at City College of New York since 1948. Mem. American Philosophical Assn., Inst. of Living Law (research consultant), Inst. of Ethnic Affairs (dir.), Phi Beta Kappa, Lambda Mu. Jewish religion. Author: Ethical Systems and Legal Ideals, 1933; Handbook of Federal Indian Law, 1941; Combating Totalitarian Propaganda: A Legal Appraisal, 1944; Readings in Jurisprudence and Legal Philosophy (with Morris R. Cohen), 1951. Contbr. articles, book revs., to professional and nat. mags., law jours. Home: 2827 Hurst Terrace N W., Washington; also Lake Clear Junction, N.Y. Office: 1700 K St., Washington 6; also 120 Broadway, N.Y.C. Died Oct. 19, 1953; buried King David Park, Falls Church, Va.

COHEN, Henry, rabbi; b. London, Eng., Apr. 7, 1863; s. David and Josephine C.; ed. Jews Hosp., Lower Norwood, London; Jews' Coll. Evening Classes; Dr. Hebrew Law, Hebrew Union Coll., Cincinnati, 1924; D.D. honoris causa, Jewish Inst. Religion, 1939; LL.D., honoris causa, Texas Christian Univ., 1948; m. Mollie Levy, Mar. 6, 1889; children—Ruth (died 1934; formerly wife of Rabbi E. Frisch), Harry. Ordained rabbi, 1884; pastor Kingston, Jamaica, 1884-85, Woodville, Miss., 1885-88, Galveston, 1888-1950, now rabbi emeritus; elected for life in 1903. Pres. gentlemen's com., Lasker Home for Homeless Children, Galveston; former mem. advisory bd. Hebrew Union Coll.; mem. Am. Friends of the Hebrew Univ.; hon. v.p. Jewish Publ. Soc. America; former mem. exec. com. Union of Am. Hebrew Congregations; mem. council of direction Immigrant Publ. Soc. N.Y.; supervisor dist. 18, dept. of synagogue school extension, Union Am. Hebrew Congregations; mem. exec. council Am. Jewish Hist. Soc.; former pres. Tex. Hist. Soc., Galveston; hon. pres. Texas Creative Community; mem. adv. council Library of Southern Literature (Atlanta, Ga.), B'nai B'rith; mem. exec. com. Jewish Immigrants Information Bur.; one of 100 mems. of The Peoples Lobby of U.S.; mem. advisory board Galveston Community Chest, 1925-27; apptd. by Gov. Dan Moody of Texas, mem. Texas Prison Board, 1927; 1st pres. and mem. bd. Am. Red Cross, Galveston; a founder and mem. bd. Galveston Open Forum (ex-pres.); mem. administrative com. Jewish Agency for Palestine, 1936 and 1937, exec. mem. 1939; hon. vice-chmn. United Palestine Appeal for 1936 and 1937; co-chancellor Texas Kallah, 1936; elected dep. mem. Administrative Com. of Jewish Agency, Zurich, 1937; hon. vice chmn. United Palestine Appeal, 1943; mem. bd. dirs. American Council for Judaism, 1944; apptd. by Gov. James V. Allred of Texas, chmn. advisory com. Southwestern States Probation and Parole Conf., 1936; mem. Galveston County Parole Bd. since 1937; mem. Commn. on Internat. Justice and Goodwill, Fed. Council of Chs.; mem. exec. bd. Boy Scouts Bay Area Council, Galveston; v.p. Adoue Seamen's Bethel; mem. exec. council of Galveston United Charities; mem. Tex. State Recovery Bd. under NRA; mem. Com. of 1,000 of China's Children Fund, 1939; mem. advisory com. Tex. Commn. Inter-racial Cooperation, 1938; local worker Jewish Immigrants' Information Bur., 1907-14; hon. life mem. Leo N. Leir Memorial Hosp., Hot Springs, Ark. Received Certificate of Merit, Am. Nat. Red Cross. Hon. life mem. Central Conf. of Am. Rabbis; mem. Am. Oriental Soc.; v.p.

Philos. Soc. of Tex., 1936; mem. exec. council Am. Jewish Hist. Soc., 1892; hon. v.p. Jewish Publ. Soc.; v.p. Tex. Folklore Soc.; mem. Internat. Soc. Theta Pi, hon. mem. Zeta Beta Tau. Democrat. Club: Judeans (New York). Compiler: Talmudic Sayings, 1894, 2d edit., 1910. Prayer in Bible and Talmud (transl. from German), 1894 (2d edit.), 1910; Hygiene and Medicine of the Talmud, 1901. Author of many pamphlets on Bibl. and hist. subjects. Wrote brochure, One Hundred Years of Jewry in Texas. Contbr. to Jewish Ency., Universal Jewish Ency., 1 volume of Jewish Ency. Delivered baccalaureate address, Hebrew Union Coll., 1916; commencement address, Med. Coll. U. of Tex., June 1927; baccalaureate sermon, U. of Texas, 1928. The Henry Cohen Community House erected in Galveston, 1928, to commemorate 40 years of continuous community service. Took charge of U.S. refugees from Mexico (Congress sending him $75,000 for distbn.), 1912. Author of Jewish Chaplain Navy Bill signed by President Wilson. Lecturer on prison problems. Received medal and ribbon from Vets. of Foreign Wars (Galveston), 1941, for outstanding citizenship, service bar from Washington Hdqrs. Am. Red Cross, 1942, for 26 consecutive years membership. Address, 1920 Broadway, Galveston, Tex. Died June 12, 1952.

COHEN, Julius Henry, lawyer; b. Brooklyn, Sept. 26, 1873; s. Henry and Elizabeth (Wolf) C.; LL.B., New York U., 1896; m. Ida Strasburger, July 20, 1900. Admitted to N.Y. bar, 1897, and since practiced in N.Y. City; atty. for Transit Reform Com. of 100, 1900-05; asso. in prosecution of charges against Dist. Atty. Asa Bird Gardiner, in investigating Dept. of Street Cleaning; counsel for mfrs. in cloak strike, 1910; in "protocol" experiment, 1913; special counsel for Pub. Service Commn. in street car strike, 1916; special dep. atty. gen. in Port of N.Y.-N.J. Harbor Case, 1917; and counsel for Chamber of Commerce of State of N.Y. and Merchants' Assn.; counsel and sec. War Bd. for the Port of New York, World War; counsel N.Y.-N.J. Port and Harbor Development Commn., 1917-21; gen. counsel Port of New York Authority, 1921-42, special atty. gen. in cases involving constitutionality of New York Emergency Housing Laws, etc.; vice chmn. and gen. counsel St. Lawrence Power Commn., 1931; v.-chmn. Citizens' Union, 1919-21 (chmn. legislative com. of same, 1902-13); mem. bd. of dirs. American Arbitration Assn. Mem. Am. Bar Assn., N.Y. State Bar Assn. (chmn. Com. on Unlawful Practice of the Law), Assn. Bar City of N.Y., N.Y. County Lawyers' Assn. Mem. Soc. Ethical Culture. Clubs: City, Metropolis Country. Author: Law and Order in Industry, 1916; The Law—Business or Profession, 1916; The League to Enforce Industrial Peace, 1917; Commercial Arbitration and the Law, 1918; American Labor Policy, 1919; They Builded Better Than They Knew, 1946. Home: 59 Hillcrest Av., White Plains, N.Y. Office: 20 Pine St., N.Y. City 5. Died Oct. 4, 1950.

COHEN, Octavus Roy, author; b. Charleston, S.C., June 26, 1891; s. Octavus and Rebecca (Ottolengui) C.; Porter Mil. Acad., Charleston, class of 1908; B.S., Clemson Coll., class of 1911; Litt.D., Birmingham-Southern Coll., 1927; m. Inez Lopez, Oct. 6, 1914; 1 son, Octavus Roy. Civ. engr. with Tenn. Coal, Iron & R.R. Co., 1909-10; with editorial depts. Birmingham (Ala.) Ledger, Charleston (S.C.) News and Courier, Bayonne (N.J.) Times and Newark (N.J.) Morning Star, 1910-12; admitted to S.C. bar, 1913, and practiced 2 yrs.; devoted time to writing since 1915. Lieutenant United States Naval Reserve, 1930-40. Member Authors' League of America, American Dramatists, Council of Authors' Guild, Omicron Delta Kappa and Gamma Alpha Mu fraternities; hon. v.p. U.S. Table Tennis Assn. Clubs: Athletic, Artists and Writers Golf Assn.; Authors' Club (N.Y. City). Author: The Other Woman (with J. U. Giesy), 1917; The Crimson Alibi, 1919; Polished Ebony, 1919; Gray Dusk, 1920; Come Seven, 1920; Six Seconds of Darkness, 1921; Highley Colored, 1921; Midnight, 1922; Assorted Chocolates, 1922; Jim Hanvey, Detective, 1923; Dark Days and Black Knights, 1923; Sunclouds, 1924; Bigger and Blacker, 1925; The Iron Chalice, 1925; Black and Blue, 1926; The Outer Gate, 1927; Detours, 1927; The Other Tomorrow, 1927; The Light Shines Through, 1928; Florian Slappey Goes Abroad, 1928; Spring Tide, 1928; The Valley of Olympus, 1929; The May Day Mystery, 1929; Epic Peters, Pullman Porter, 1930; The Backstage Mystery, 1930; Lilies of the Alley, 1931; Cameos, 1931; Star of Earth, 1932; Carbon Copies, 1933; The Townsend Murder Mystery, 1933; Scarlet Woman, 1934; Transient Lady, 1934; Scrambled Yeggs, 1934; Black to Nature, 1935; With Benefit of Clergy, 1935; Child of Evil, 1936; I Love You Again, 1937; East of Broadway, 1938; Florian Slappey, 1938; Strange Honeymoon, 1939; Romance in Crimson, 1940; Kid Tinsel, 1941; Lady in Armor, 1941; Masquerade in Miami, 1942; Sound of Revelry, 1943; Romance in the First Degree, 1943; Danger in Paradise, 1944; Love Has No Alibi, 1945; Dangerous Lady, 1946; Don't Ever Love Me, 1947; My Love Wears Black; More Beautiful than Murder, 1948; A Bullet for My Love, 1950; The Corpse that Walked, 1951; Lost Lady, 1952; Borrasca, 1953; Love Can be Dangerous, 1955; also author of plays including: The Crimson Alibi (with George Broadhurst), 1919; The Scourge, 1920; Come Seven, 1920; Shadows, 1920; Every Saturday Night, 1921; Alias Mrs. Wallace, 1928. Contbr. series of Negro stories to Saturday Evening Post since 1918; also author of motion pictures, radio and television programs. Contributed short stories and serials to Colliers and other mags. Home: 11986 Foxboro Dr., Los Angeles 49. Died Jan. 6, 1959; buried Forest Lawn Meml. Park, Glendale, Cal.

COHN, Alfred Einstein (kōn), physician; b. N.Y. City, Apr. 16, 1879; s. Abraham and Maimie (Einstein) C.; A.B., Columbia, 1900; M.D., Coll. Physicians and Surgeons (Columbia), 1904, D. Sc. (hon.), 1940; studied U. of Freiburg, U. of Vienna and Univ. Coll., London; m. Ruth Walker Price, Apr. 24, 1911. In practice in N.Y. City, 1909-11; with Rockefeller Inst. for Med. Research since 1911, mem. since 1920, mem. emeritus since 1944. Lt. Col. M.C., U.S. Army, cons. in cardio vascular diseases, 1918; served in France. Mem. bd. of govs. N.Y. Tuberculosis and Health Assn., 1925-45; chmn. of com. on research N.Y. Heart Assn., 1921-48 (mem. advisory commn. on research 1946-48); councillor to VA, Washington, 1921-46; member executive committee group on adult edn. Carnegie Corp., 1924-26; member Lasker Found., 1928-40; mem. China Med. Board, 1934-45; mem. Com. on Library, 1934-41; member bd. of editors Bulletin of N.Y. Acad. of Medicine; mem. Am. Com. on Refugee Scholars, Writers and Artists (treas. from 1945); mem. med. bd. Irvington House, Irvington-on-Hudson, 1930-45; chairman subcom. on heart diseases and rheumatic fever, N.Y. World's Fair, 1937-40. Mem. exec. committee Internat. Student Service, 1934-42; mem. bd. directors, sec.-treas. Student Service of America, Incorporated, 1943-47; member Club for Research on Ageing, from 1939; vice pres. Com. for Nat. Morale, 1940-42, chmn. exec. com., 1942-49; chmn. science com. Research Council of Dept. of Hosps., New York, 1935-51, treas., 1943-51. Spl. adviser Board of Economic Warfare, 1942-44; mem. Health Com. Office of Foreign Relief and Rehabilitation Operations, 1943-44; bd. dirs. Iranian Inst. and Sch. Asiatic Studies, 1944-49, pres., 1947-49; bd. dirs. Sydenham Inst., 1947-48; member health committee American Jewish Joint Distribution Committee since 1944; Council on Foreign Relations since 1946. Visiting prof. medicine, Union Med. Coll., Peking, China spring of 1925. Fellow N.Y. Academy of Medicine; mem. Am. Soc. Pharmacology and Experimental Therapeutics, Am. Assn. Hist. Medicine, Assn. Am. Phys., Am. Assn. Anatomists, Am. Physiol. Soc., Am. Assn. Pathol. and Bacteriol., Am. Soc. Clin. Investigation, Am. Med. Assn., Botanical Soc. of Am. (physiol. sect.), Hist. of Science Soc., Harvey Soc. (pres. 1930), Internat. Assn. Geographical Pathology, New York Academy of Sciences, Soc. for Experimental Biology and Medicine (councillor 1929-33), A.A.A.S., Am. Assn. Adult Edn., Am. Soc. for Research in Psychosomatic Medicine, N.Y. Scientists Assn. since 1945, Am. Assn. on Indian Affairs, 1945-47. Author: Medicine, Science and Art, 1931; Minerva's Progress, 1946; No Retreat from Reason, 1948; The Burden of Diseases in the United States (with Claire Lingg), 1950; also about 180 med. investigations. Home: 200 E. 66th St., N.Y.C. 21. Died July 20, 1957.

COHN, Edwin Joseph, prof. biological chemistry; b. New York, N.Y., Dec. 17, 1892; s. Abraham and Maimie (Einstein) Cohn; student Amherst Coll., 1910-13; B.S., U. of Chicago, 1914, Ph.D., 1917; grad. student, Harvard, 1915-17, M.A., (hon.) Harvard 1943, D.S. (hon.), Amherst Coll., 1944; D.S. (hon.), Columbia, 1945, D.S. (hon.), Harvard, 1945; M.D. (hon.) Geneva, 1946, Berne, 1947; m. Marianne Brettauer, July 30, 1917 (deceased); children—Edwin J., Alfred; m. 2d, Rebekah Higginson, June 15, 1948. Nat. Research council fellow in chemistry, 1919-22, studied at Carlsberg Laboratory, Copenhagen and Cambridge U., Eng.; asst. prof. physical chemistry, Harvard, 1922-28, asso. prof., 1928-35; prof. biol. chemistry and head of dept. of physical chemistry, Harvard Med. Sch., 1935-49, Higgins University professor Harvard, since 1949; chairman of division medical sciences, 1936-49; dir. U. Lab. of Physical Chemistry related to med. and pub. health, Harvard, since 1949; chairman department biophys. chemistry since 1950. Served as first lieutenant Sanitary Corps, United States Army, 1918-19; honorary consultant to the Medical Dept. of the Navy since 1942. Received Alvarenga prize, Coll. of Phys. of Phila., 1942. Passano Award for distinguished service to American Clin. Medicine, 1945; John Scott Medal, Phila., 1946; John Phillips Memorial Medal, Am. College of Physicians, 1946; Theodore William Richards Medal from Am. Coll. Physicians, 1948; Medal of Science, Free University of Belgium, 1947; Medal of Merit, U.S. Govt., 1948 French Legion Honor, 1952. Silliman lectr. Yale, 1946; Am. Swiss Found. lectr., 1947; Belgian Am. Ednl. Found. lectr., 1947; Julius Streglitz meml. lectr., A.C.S., 1949. Fellow A.A.A.S., Am. Acad. Arts and Sci, N.Y. Acad. Sci.; mem. Nat. Acad. Sci., Am. Philos. Soc., Am. Chem. Soc. Am. Soc. Biol. Chem., Am. Physiol. Soc., Sigma Xi. Contbr. articles on chem. of natural products and systems, liver fractions, plasma fractions, physical chem. of proteins, blood, and other tissues, to professional journals. Author: (with J. T. Edsall) Proteins, Amino Acids and Peptides, 1943; Research in Medical Sciences, March of Medicine, 1946. Clubs: Harvard, St. Botolph (Boston); Faculty (Cambridge). Home: 183 Brattle St., Cambridge, Mass. Died Oct. 1, 1953.

COHN, Harry, motion picture exec.; b. New York, N.Y., July 23, 1891; s. Joseph and Bella (Hudesman) C.; ed. pub. schs.; m. Joan Perry, July 31, 1941; 2 s., John, Harrison. Actor, 1898-1913; creator motion pictures in songs; organized Jack and Harry Cohn Motion Pictures, CBS Film Sales Corp., Columbia Pictures Corp.; vice pres. Columbia Pictures Corp., 1932, pres. since 1932. Office: 1438 N. Gower St. Hollywood 28, Cal. Died Feb. 27, 1958.

COHN, Jack, motion picture exec.; b. N.Y. City, Oct. 27, 1889. In advt. agy. field, 1902-08; in lab. work with Carl Laemmle's Independent Motion Picture Co. (Imp), later becoming editor and producer Universal Weekly, early newsreel with staff cameramen at key points, and in charge Imp studio prodn., N.Y. City, 5 yrs.; introduced animated cartoons; also instrumental in prodn. Laemmle (Universal) early successes; formed own producing Co., 1919; with Harry Cohn and Joe Brandt formed C.B.C. Pictures, which became Columbia Pictures Corp., 1924, now exec. v.p. Mem. Picture Pioneers (initiated formation of orgn. and became 1st pres., 1939); became chmn. arts and sports com. U.S.O., 1942. Address: 729 7th Av., N.Y.C. 19. Died Dec. 10, 1956.

COHN, Joseph Hoffman, clergyman; b. Austria-Hungary, Mar. 27, 1886; s. Leopold and Rose (Hoffman) C.; attended Adelphi Coll., Brooklyn; Moody Bible Inst., Chicago; private tutoring in Jewish and Hebrew literature; D.D., Los Angeles Bapt. Sem., 1937; m. Josephine Stone, May 1916; children—Cordelia Stone, Joseph Hoffman Jr., Huntley Stone. Joined father, Leopold Cohn, former rabbi, in work of Williamsburg Mission to the Jews, 1907; he expanded it into what is now known as the Am. Bd. of Missions to the Jews (dir.); dean, founder, Jewish Missionary Institute N.Y.; instrumental in producing Am. Transl. of New Testament into Yiddish when Nazis had destroyed all existing editions and plates, 1941; traveled in Europe and Palestine in the interest of refugee work abroad and in establishing fgn. stations of Am. Bd. Missions to Jews. Trustee Williamsburg Mission to Jews; organized and directed N.Y. Congress on Prophecy, conf. of Bible students, N.Y. City, 1942. Editor: The Chosen People, 1935; Shepherd of Israel, 1935. Author: Passover Trilogy, 1934; The Chosen People Question Box, 1936; Will the Church Escape the Tribulation, 1936; I Have Loved Jacob, 1948; Beginning at Jerusalem, 1948; How to Win the Jews to Christ (correspondence course); Pleroma; etc. Founder of "The Chosen People" radio broadcast. Home: Hotel Beacon. Office: 236 W. 72d St., N.Y.C. Died Oct. 5, 1953.

COHN, Ralph Morris, motion picture distbr., TV producer; b. N.Y.C., May 1, 1914; s. Jack and Jeanette (Lesser) C.; B.A., Cornell U., 1934; m. Doris Huffam, Oct. 21, 1952; 1 dau. (by previous marriage), Jan Marcia. Asst. producer Columbia Pictures, 1935-36, producer, 1936-41, v.p., 1958—; exec. producer Darmour Prodns., 1941-43; partner Triangle Prodns., 1945-47; formed Screen Gems, Inc., TV subsidiary Columbia Pictures, 1949, gen. mgr., 1949-52, v.p., gen. mgr., 1953-58, pres., 1958—, also dir. Served with Signal Corps, AUS, World War II. Home: Pinebrook Rd., Bedford, N.Y. Office: 711 Fifth Av., N.Y.C. 19. Died Aug. 1, 1959.

COHN, Saul, pres. City Stores Co.; b. New York, N.Y., Aug. 26, 1885; s. Isidor and Bessie (Sussman) C.; m. Sadie L. Sive, Mar. 8, 1908; 1 son, Leonard Henry. Private law practice, 1907-29; vice president, dir. Maison Blanche Co., New Orleans, B. Lowenstein & Bros., Inc., Memphis, Tenn., Loveman, Joseph & Loeb, Birmingham, Ala., Kaufman Strauss Co., Inc., Louisville, Ky., Richard Store Co., Miami, Fla.; pres. and dir. City Stores Co., Phila., City Stores Mercantile Co., Inc., N.Y. City; dir., chmn. exec. committee, R. H. White Corporation, Boston; Oppenheim Collins & Co., Inc., N.Y. City; dir., mem. exec., investment coms., U.S. Trust Co., Newark, N.J.; dir., mem. exec. com. Bankers Bond & Mortgage Guaranty Co., Phila., U.S. Mortgage & Title Guaranty Co., Newark, N.J., U.S. Realty & Improvement Co., Bankers Securities Corp., Phila., Loft Candy Corp., N.Y.; director Lit Bros., Phila., Wise, Smith and Company, Hartford, Swern and Company, Trenton, N.J. Dir. Yeshiva College, New York City; former pres. Nat. Retail Dry Goods Assn. Clubs: Empire State, Kiwanis, National Democratic (N.Y. City), Carteret Book (Newark, N.J.). Home: 67 S. Munn Av., E. Orange, N.J. Office: 132 W. 31st St., N.Y.C. 1. Died 1954.

COIL, Everett Johnston, economist; b. Mexico, Mo., Aug. 30, 1907; s. Paul Everett and Floy (Johnston) C.; A.B., William Jewell Coll., 1928; M.B.A., Harvard, 1930; student, Columbia, 1931; m. Mary Beaton, Jan. 1, 1941; children—Ann D., Paul. Asst. prof. econs. U. Me. 1930; instr. econs. Columbia, 1931; asso. Dr. H. S. Person, cons. bus.

mgmt., N.Y.C., 1932-33; asso. economist Nat. Resources Com., 1934-35; economist Rural Electrification Adminstrn., 1936-37; exec. dir. Nat. Planning Assn., 1937—. Mem. Am. Econ. Assn., Am. Soc. Planning Ofcls., Am. Soc. Pub. Adminstrn., A.A.A.S. Democrat. Baptist. Clubs: Cosmos (Washington); Harvard (N.Y.C.). Author: Little Waters (with Harlow S. Person), 1935; Rural Electric Cooperatives in Europe, 1937; Democracies Must Also Plan, 1939; War and Our Latin American Trade Policy, 1939. Work includes gen. supervision of published writings relating to research studies of Nat. Planning Assn. Home: 1306 24th St. South, Arlington, Va. Office: 800 21st St., Washington 6. Died Oct. 12, 1950.

COKENOWER, James W., physician, surgeon; b. nr. Shelbyville, Ill., Aug. 13, 1851; A.M., Westfield (Ill.) Coll., 1871; grad. Coll. Phys. & Surg., Keokuk, Ia., 1877, Ky. Sch. Medicine, Louisville, 1881; m. Katie E. Stalford, 1890. Practiced medicine, Des Moines, 1881—; former surgeon, Benedict Home, orthopedic surgeon, Ia. Children's Home; mem. attending med. and surg. staff Mercy Hosp.; examiner for several life ins. cos., etc. Mem. A.M.A., Western Gynecol. and Surg. Assn. Editor: Transactions Iowa State Med. Soc. Home: 1002 Forest Av. Office: 6th and Walnut Sts., Des Moines. Deceased.

COKER, William Chambers, botanist; b. Hartsville, S.C., Oct. 24, 1872; s. James Lide and Susan Armstrong (Stout) C.; B.S., S.C. Coll., Columbia, S.C., 1894; Ph.D., Johns Hopkins, 1901; studied at Bonn, Germany, 1901-02; LL.D., U. of S.C., 1925; D.Sc., U. of N.C., 1947; m. Louise Venable, Oct. 28, 1934. With Atlantic Nat. Bank, Wilmington, North Carolina, 1894-97; teacher summer school, Brooklyn Inst. Arts and Sciences, Cold Spring Harbor, L.I., 1900; asso. prof. botany, U. of N.C., 1902-07, prof., 1907-20, Kenan professor botany, 1920-44; Kanan Research professor botany, 1944-45, emeritus since 1945; also director Coker Arboretum. Chief of botanical staff of Bahama expedition of the Geographical Society of Baltimore, 1903. Fellow A.A.A.S.; mem. Bot. Soc. Am. (chmn. Southeastern sect.), Am. Soc. Naturalists, Am. Mycological Soc., Elisha Mitchell Scientific Soc., N.C. Acad. Sciences, American Forestry Assn., N.C. Forestry Assn., Chi Psi, Phi Beta Kappa, Sigma Xi. Democrat. Editor Journal, Elisha Mitchell Scientific Soc., 1904-45; chmn. bd. Univ. N.C. Press, 1936-43; pres. Highlands Biol. Laboratory, 1933-44, honorary president since 1944; honorary curator of botany, Charleston Museum, 1943-53; trustee, Brookgreen Gardens, S.C., 1944-1947. Author: Vegetation of the Bahama Islands, 1905; The Plant Life of Hartsville, S.C., 1912; The Trees of North Carolina (with H. R. Totten), 1916; The Saprolegniaceae, 1923; The Clavarias of the United States and Canada, 1923; The Gasteromycetes of the Eastern United States and Canada (with J. N. Couch), 1928; Trees of the Southeastern States (with H. R. Totten), 1934; The Boletaceae of North Carolina (with A. H. Beers). 1943; The Stipitate Hydnums of the Eastern United States (with A. H. Beers), 1951. Contbr. numerous articles on morphological botany, particularly on the gymnosperms and fungi. Home: Chapel Hill, N.C. Died June 27, 1953; buried Chapel Hill.

COLAW, John Marvin, tchr.; b. Crabbotton, nr. Monterey, Va., Mar. 16, 1860; s. Cornelius and Mary E. (Newman) C.; A.B., Dickinson Coll., Pa., 1882, A.M. 1885; 1 yr. in law sch. U. Va; m. Josie M. Judy, Oct. 21, 1886 (died Nov. 28, 1893); 2d, Lizzie J. Gibson, Sept. 4, 1895. Practiced law 8 yrs. and was commonwealth's atty. for Highland County, Va.; except period of law practice has been in sch. work, 1886—; prin. Monterey High Sch.; asso. editor Am. Math. Monthly, 8 yrs. Mem. Am. Math. Soc. Contbr. to math. jours. Joint Author: (Colaw & Ellwood's) Primary Arithmetic, 1900; Advanced Arithmetic, 1900; Teacher's Manual, 1901; School Algebra, 1903; Geometry; (Colaw & Duke's) Intermediate Arithmetic, 1906; Practical Arithmetic, 1906; Elementary Arithmetic, 1907; Teachers' Handbook, 1909; Elementary Algebra, 1911; Key to Algebra, 1911. Address: Monterey, Va. Died Feb. 26, 1940.

COLBERN, William H., army officer; b. Mo., June 26, 1895; grad. F.A. Sch., 1924, Cav. Sch., 1925, Polish Cav. Sch., 1932, Command and Gen. Staff Sch., 1937; commd. 2d lt. Inf., 1917; transferred to F.A. as capt., 1923, advanced through grades to brig. gen., 1942; served on Gen. Staff Corps, 1939-40. Address: Field Artillery, Fort McClellan, Ala. Died Apr. 30, 1959.*

COLBURN, Albert E., army officer; brig. gen., May 1942. Address: Camp Hulen, Tex. Deceased.*

COLBURN, Allan Philip, educator; b. Madison, Wis., June 8, 1904; s. Willis Paul and Jane (Grimm) C.; student Marquette U., Milwaukee, 1922-24; B.S., U. of Wis., 1926, M.S., 1927, Ph.D., 1929; m. Evelyn Safford, Nov. 21, 1931; children—Judith, Willis, Carolyn. Research chem. engr., DuPont Co., Wilmington, Del., 1929-38; asso. prof. chem. engring., U. of Del., 1938-41, prof. since 1941, asst. to the pres., 1947-50, acting pres., Apr.-Nov. 1950, provost since 1950, chmn. engring. expt. sta. since 1947; cons. chem. engr. since 1941; sec. Haskell Research Found., Inc., since 1949. Cons. to Research and Development Bd., Dept. of Defense, since 1948. Recipient Walker award, Am. Inst. Chem. Engrs., 1936, Profl. Progress award, 1948. Dir. Del. chpt. Am. Red Cross since 1946. Mem. Am. Inst. Chem. Engrs. (dir., 1944-47, chmn. awards com., 1946 47, 1951), N.E A., Am. Soc. Engring. Edn. (chmn. grad. studies div. 1952, chmn. ednl. methods div. 1953), Am. Soc. M.E. (chmn. heat transfer div., 1948), Am. Chem. Soc., A.A.A.S., Sigma Phi Epsilon, Tau Beta Pi, Sigma Xi, Phi Lambda Upsilon, Phi Kappa Phi. Home: 49 Winslow Rd., Newark, Del. Died Feb. 6, 1955.

COLBURN, Burnham Standish (kōl'bûrn), banker; b. Detroit, Dec. 10, 1872; s. William Cullen and Mary Augusta (Standish) C.; B.S., in C.E., U. Mich., 1896; m. Elizabeth Grosvenor Pierce, Nov. 21, 1900; children—William Cullen (dec.), Elizabeth G. (Mrs. E. Wrayford Willmer), Burnham Standish, Evelyn (Mrs. F. H. Fentener Van Vlissingen, Jr.), Mary Louise (Mrs. J. Frazier Glenn, Jr.). Draftsman, Detroit Bridge & Iron Works, 1896; resident engr. Victoria Jubilee Bridge, Montreal, 1898; one of organizers Canadian Bridge Co., 1900, sec.-treas. until 1911; v.p. Peoples State Bank, Detroit, 1911-13; asst. in orgn. Biltmore Estate Co. (treas.) and development of Biltmore Forest since 1920; chmn. bd. First Nat. Bank & Trust Co. Field dir. A.R.C., Pensacola, Fla., World War. Pres. bd. trustees Asheville Sch. Mem. Nat. Soc. Mayflower Descendants, Psi Upsilon. Repub. Presbyn. Clubs: Pen and Plate (Asheville); Biltmore Forest Country. Home: Biltmore Forest, Biltmore, N.C. Office: First Nat. Bank & Trust Co., Asheville, N.C. Died Dec. 26, 1959.

COLBY, Bainbridge (kōl'bĭ), lawyer; b. St. Louis, Dec. 22, 1869; s. John Peck and Frances (Bainbridge) C.; A.B., Williams Coll., Mass.; 1890; Columbia Law Sch., 1 year; LL.B., N.Y. Law Sch.; LL.D. and other hon. degrees from various instns.; m. Mrs. Joseph N. Ely, 1929. Practiced, N.Y.C., 1892—; represented Samuel L. Clements ("Mark Twain") in settlement of affairs of his publishing house, Charles L. Webster & Co.; one of counsel of interests which brought about reforms in Equitable Life Assurance Soc.; counsel in Northern Securities litigation; counsel for Truesdale investigating com. Mut. Life Ins. Co. Mem. N.Y. Assembly, 29th Dist., 1901-02. Actively identified with candidacy of Theodore Roosevelt for presdl. nomination, 1912, and in charge of contests to seat Roosevelt delegates in Rep. Nat. Conv., Chicago, 1912; one of founders Prog. Nat. Party and del. Prog. Nat. Conv., Chicago, 1912; Progressive party nominee for U.S. senator, 1914, 16. Commr. U.S. Shipping Bd., and mem. U.S. Shipping Bd. Emergency Fleet Corp., 1917-19. Mem. Am. Mission to Inter-Allied Conf. at Paris, Nov. 1917. Sec. of state in cabinet of President Wilson, Mar. 22, 1920-Mar. 4, 1921; partner of Woodrow Wilson in practice of law, 1921-23. Apptd. as counsel for Joint Com. of N.Y. State Legislature in investigation of Pub. Service Commn. and Pub. Utilities, 1916; special asst. to atty. gen. of U.S. as counsel to the Govt. in proceedings for enforcement of Anti-Trust Law; of counsel for the Am. newspapers, 1933-34, in the issue with the federal administration on the freedom of the press, and in resistance to the effort of the NRA to subject the press to revocable licenses under the code system. Trustee Colby Coll. Member Am. Bar Assn., Assn. Bar City of N.Y., Civil Service Reform Assn., Mo. Soc. N.Y. (pres.), Phi Beta Kappa. Clubs: University, Metropolitan, Manhattan, Squadron A Veterans (N.Y.C.); Metropolitan (Washington); Chevy Chase (Md.) Country. Author: The Close of Woodrow Wilson's Administration and the Final Years. Home: 920 5th Av. Office: 111 Broadway, N.Y.C. Died Apr. 11, 1950.

COLCORD, Bradford C(laude), iron exec.; born Instanter, Pa., Mar. 14, 1897; s. Dr. Amos Watson and Eva (Bradford) C.; B.S., U. of Mich., 1922; m. Elizabeth Phillips, December 29, 1928; children—Nancy Averill (Mrs. Donald Robert Tucker), Bradford Phillips. Superintendent blast furnaces Crucible Steel Co., Midland, Pa., 1926-30, St. Louis Gas & Coke Corp., Granite City, Ill., 1930-33, Sloss-Sheffield Steel & Iron Co., Birmingham, 1933-35, Woodward (Ala.) Iron Co., 1935-36; asst. gen. supt. Nat. Tube Co., McKeesport, Pa., 1936-39, gen. supt. 1939-42; asst. v.p. operations Nat. Tube Co., Pittsburgh, 1942-46, gen. supt. Lorain, O., 1946-48; pres. Woodward Iron Co. since 1948, dir. since 1948; dir. Continental Gin Co. since 1951, Birmingham Fire Ins. Co. since 1952. Served as ensign, U.S. Navy, 1918. Dir. Community Chest. Mem. adv. bd. Birmingham Ordnance Dist.; exec. com., Com. of 100, Birmingham. Dir., v.p. Birmingham Civic Symphony. Mem. Mayflower Soc., Am. Ord. Assn. (dir. local chpt.), Nat. Assn. Mfrs. (dir.), Am. Iron & Steel Inst., Assn. Iron & Steel Engrs., Am. Inst. Mining & Metall. Engrs., Am. Foundrymen's Soc., Eastern States Blast Furnace & Coke Assn., S.A.R., Newcomen Soc., Ala. Min. Inst. (dir.), Ala. Hist. Soc., Asso. Industries Ala. (dir.), Kappa Sigma. Presbyn. Clubs: Rotary, Mountain Brook, Country (Birmingham); Union (Cleveland); Duquesne (Pittsburgh). Home: 4227 Altamont Road, Birmingham 9. Office: Woodward, Ala. Died Aug. 16, 1953.

COLCORD, Frank Forest, cons. engr.; b. Boston, Nov. 12, 1877; s. Benjamin F. and Ada I. (Reed) C.; S.B., Mass. Inst. Tech., 1898. Asst. to supt. Chgo. & Aurora Smelting Refining Co., 1898-1900; chief chemist Am. Smelting & Refining Co., Perth Amboy, N.J., 1900-08; chief clerk U.S. Metals Refining Co., Carteret, N.Y., 1908-10; asst. to v.p. U.S. Smelting Refining & Mining Co., N.Y.C., 1910-38, v.p., mgr. metal sales, 1938-47, now dir. Apptd. mem. primary lead producers industry adv. com. and mem. silver producers industry adv. com., W.P.A., 1942. Mem. Mining and Metall. Soc. Am., Am. Inst. Mining and Metall. Engrs., Electrochem, Soc. Mason. Club: Lawyers (N.Y.C.). Contbr. tech. articles profl. jours. Home: 2595 Devonport Rd., San Marino, Cal. Died Mar. 21, 1952.

COLDREN, Philip (kōl'drĕn), newspaper editor; b. Stella, Neb., Aug. 16, 1882; s. Eleazer Maine and Mary Ann (Andrews) C.; student Washburn Coll., Topeka, Kan., 1901-04; m. Lela Irene McLellan, June 20, 1904 (died June 21, 1905); m. 2d, Louise Wallace, Dec. 19, 1909. Owner and pub. Granite (Okla.) Enterprise, 1904-06; reporter Oklahoma City newspapers, 1907-11; editor Joplin (Mo.) Globe since 1912, and Joplin News-Herald since 1922. Trustee Joplin Carnegie Library, 1920-50, pres. bd., 1927, and 1935-50. Mem. Ozark Press Assn. (ex-pres.). Mem. Community Ch. Clubs: Joplin, Kiwanis, Twin Hills Country. Home: Olivia Apts., P.O. Box 210, Joplin, Mo. Died Dec. 12, 1955.

COLE, George Douglas Howard, educator, author; b. Cambridge, Eng., Sept. 25, 1889; s. George and Jessie (Knowles) C.; student St. Paul's Sch., London, 1902-08; B.A., Balliol Coll., Oxford U., 1912, M.A., 1915; m. Margaret Isabel Postgate, Aug. 18, 1918; children—Janet Elizabeth, Anne Rachel, Humphrey John Douglas. Research fellow, Magdalen Coll., Oxford U., 1912; deputy prof. philosophy, Durham U., 1913-14; fellow Magdalen Coll. until 1919; head research dept. Amalgamated Engrs., 1915-18; Labour Party, 1918-21; staff tutor London U., 1921-25; reader in economics Oxford U. and fellow of Univ. Coll., Oxford U., 1925-44; fellow Nuffield Coll., 1940-44; chmn. Social Reconstruction Survey, Oxford U., 1940-44; sub-warden Nuffield College, 1942-43; Chichele prof. social and polit. theory, Oxford U., and fellow of All Souls Coll., Oxford, 1944-57; hon. fellow University Coll., Oxford, 1945—. Chmn. Fabian Soc., 1939-46, 48-50, pres. 1952—; mem. bd. Inst. Social History. Fellow Royal Economic Society, Royal Statistical Society. Member Labour party. Club: Detection (London). Author of many books on economic, social and political questions of which the following are among the more recent: Of Persons and Periods, 1938; British Trade Unionism Today, 1938; The Common People (with R. W. Postgate), rev. 1947; Socialism in Evolution, 1938; A Plan for Democratic Britain, 1939; Chartist Portraits, 1941; Europe, Russia and the Future, 1941; Great Britain in the post-war world, 1942; Fabian Socialism, 1943; Full Employment, 1943; Money, Present & Future, 1944; Bldg. & Planning, 1945; Samuel Butler, 1947; History of Labour Party. Meaning of Marxism, 1948; World in Transition, 1949; Essays in Social Theory, 1950; Socialist Economics, 1949; (with wife, about 30 detective stories, of which following are the more recent): Big Business Murder, 1935; Dr. Tancred Begins, 1935; Scandal at School, 1936; Last Will and Testament, 1936; The Brothers Sackville, 1936; Disgrace to the College, 1937; The Missing Aunt, 1937; Mrs. Warrender's Profession, 1938; Off with Her Head, 1938; Double Blackmail, 1939; Greek Tragedy, 1938; Wilson and Some Others, 1940; Murder in the Munition Works, 1940; Counterpoint Murder, 1941; Knife in the Dark, 1941; Toper's End, 1942; Death of a Bride, 1945; also author of various hist. works, including A Short History of the British Working Class Movement, Lives of William Cobbett and Robert Owen, and A Century of British Cooperation, 1945; A Short History of the British Working-Class Movement (1789-1947), 1948; A History of the Labour Party from 1914 (1948); The Meaning of Marxism, 1948; World in Transition (U.S.A. only), 1949; Introduction to Economic History 1750-1950, 1952; Socialist Thought, I: The Forerunners 1789-1850, 1953; Socialist Thought, II: Marxism and Anarchism, 1848-1890, 1954, III: The Second International, 1889-1914, 1955; IV: Communism and Social Democracy, 1914-31, 1956; V: Socialism and Facism, 1931-9, 1960; An Introduction to Trade Unionism, 1953; Money, Trade and Investment, 1954; The Post-War Condition of Britain, 1956; The Case for Industrial Partnership, 1957. Home: 107 Oakwood Court, Kensington, London, W. 14, Eng. also All Souls College, Oxford, Eng. Died Jan. 14, 1959.

COLE, Glen Walker, glass mfg.; b. Corning, N.Y., May 14, 1895; s. C. Glen and Harriet Ellen (Walker) C.; A.B., Cornell U., 1918; m. Eleanor Wickam Houghton, June 2, 1920; children—Phyllis (dec.), Adelaide, Sidney T., Eleanor Houghton. Lab. asst., Corning Glass Works, Corning, N.Y., 1919-20, with prodn. dept. at Wellsboro (Pa.) plant, 1920-21, asst. plant supt., 1921-22, in charge scheduling of manufacture, Corning (N.Y.) plant, 1922-30, prodn. mgr., 1930-36, v.p. in charge prodn., 1936-38, v.p., dir., asst. general manager, 1938-41; president, 1941-46, vice chairman board of directors, 1946. Served as 1st lt., Co. D, 308th Machine Gun Bn., 78th Div., U.S. Army, World War I. Dir. and v.p. Pittsburgh-Corning Corporation; vice chairman board of directors of Corning Glass Works of Canada, Limited; director Corhart Refractories Company, Dow Corning Corp. Received Gen. Hdqrs. Citation and Divisional Citation for bravery World War I. Mem. Kappa Alpha. Clubs: University, Knickerbocker (New York); Corning (N.Y.) Country; Thendara Country, Adirondack League (Old Forge, N.Y.). Home: 33 E. 3d St. Office: Corning Glass Works, Corning, N.Y. Died Oct. 18, 1955.

COLE, Harry Outen, constrn. engr.; b. Morgantown, W.Va., Apr. 3, 1874; s. Minrod and Sarah Jane (Lough) C.; B.Sc. in Civil Engring., W.Va. U., 1898; m. Mabel Wilson, June 12, 1901 (died 1921); 1 dau., Catherine; m. 2d, Margaret Buchanan, Feb. 14, 1929. Draftsman, estimator and designer of steel work until 1903; with V. G. Bogue, N.Y.C., as asst. engr. bridges, also cons. engineer rys. and bridge engr. Mexican projects; apptd. asst. engr. in charge designs Pacific Div. Isthmian Canal, 1908, later resident engr. and div. engr. until completion of canal; mem. Cole Bros., Balt. until 1916; asst., later constrn. engr. Braden Copper Co. and Chile Exploration Co., hdqrs. N.Y.C.; pres. Cole Bros. Constrn. Co., Morgantown, 1921—; sec., dir. Morgantown Hotel Co. Mem. Am. Soc. C.E., Phi Kappa Sigma. Republican. Presbyn. Mason (K.T., Shriner), Elk. Kiwanian. Home: Morgantown, W.Va. Died Feb. 13, 1950.

COLE, Howard Ellsworth, oil operator; b. Cleve., Feb. 13, 1873; s. Elijah and Mary (Owen) C.; ed. high sch. and business college. Began in office of Standard Oil Co. of Cleveland, O., later asst. to v.p. same co.; gen. mgr. Waters Pierce Oil Co. in Mexico, later gen. mgr. Standard Oil Co. of N.Y. for Japan and Korea, residing in Yokohama; returned to N.Y. City as dir. Standard Oil Co. of N.Y., retired sr. v.p., 1931; dir. Chase Bank. Mem. Am. Asiatic Assn., Fgn. Trade Council Am., Met. Museum, China Soc. of Am., Persian Soc., Ohio Soc. of New York, Am. Mus. Natural History, Pilgrims of U.S., Am. Geog. Soc., Bibliophile Soc. Mason. Clubs: Town Hall, Metropolitan, India House (N.Y.C.); Thatch House (London, England); Sleepy Hollow Country; York Harbor Reading Room, York Golf and Tennis. Home: York Harbor, Me. Died Apr. 27, 1950; buried Kensico Cemetery, Valhalla, N.Y.

COLE, Lewis Gregory, roentgenologist; b. Lake Mahopac, N.Y., May 21, 1874; s. Joseph G. and Lucina (Cole) C.; M.D., Coll. Phys. and Surg. Columbia, 1898; m. Marion E. Herring, Apr. 3, 1901. Practiced in N.Y.C., 1898—; prof. roentgenology Cornell U. Med. Coll., 1913-21; roentgenologist French Hosp., N.Y.C.; cons. roentgenologist Meml. Hosp., Fifth Av., French and Lawrence hosps. Commd. maj. Med. R.C., 1917. Mem. Am. Roentgen Ray Soc. (pres. 1916-17), Radiol. Soc. N.A., Phila Roentgen Ray Soc., A.M.A., N.Y. State Med. Soc., Clin. Congress of Surgeons of N.A., N.Y. Acad. Medicine. Conglist. Progressive Republican. Office: 36 E. 61st St., N.Y.C. Died Oct. 15, 1954.*

COLE, Ralph R(ussell), business exec.; b. Rockford, Ill., May 4, 1900; s. Allen K. and Ada E. (Griswold) C.; student Drake U., Des Moines, Ia., 1918-22; m. Doris L. Beldin, Sept. 25, 1925 (dec. 1932); children—John A., Carol J.; m. 2d, Esther P. Peltier, May 19, 1934. Sec. Consol. Water Power & Paper Co., 1942-51, now vice president, treas., dir.; v.p., dir. Consoweld Corp.; treas., director Consol. Water Power Co., 1942—; treas., dir. Newaygo Timber Co., Ltd., 1946; sec., dir. DuBay Cranberry Co., 1945; dir., v.p., Mead Realty Co., Wisconsin Rapids, Wis., 1955. Mason. Clubs: Elk, Rotary, Bulls Eye Country. Home: Ridgewood Trail, Wisconsin Rapids, Wis. Office: Wisconsin Rapids, Wis. Died Mar. 19, 1958.

COLE, Rossetter Gleason, musician; b. on farm nr. Clyde, Mich., Feb. 5, 1866; s. Henry Walcott and Mary Charlotte (Gleason) C.; Ph.B., Univ. of Mich., 1888, hon. A.M., 1913; Mus.D., Grinnell Coll., 1927; m. Fannie Louise Gwinner, Aug. 6, 1896 (died Aug. 16, 1936); taught English, German and Latin in high schs., 1888-90; studied composition and organ in Berlin, 1890-92; there by competitive exam. won a 3 yrs.' scholarship in the Royal Master School for Composition, under Max Bruch. Dir. sch. of music and prof. music, Ripon (Wis.) Coll., 1892-94; prof. music, Grinnell (Iowa) Coll., 1894-1901; teacher, Chicago, 1902-07; editor of Good Music, 1903-07; prof. music and dir. Sch. of Music, U. of Wis., 1907-09; pvt. teacher, Chicago, since 1909. Dir. theory dept., Cosmopolitan Sch. of Music, Chicago, since 1915, dean since 1935. Prof. (in charge) music, Columbia University, New York City, summer sessions 1908-39; v.p. for Iowa, 1897-1900, pres. 1903, 09, 10, Music Teachers' Nat. Assn.; dean Ill. Chapter, Am. Guild Organists, 1912-14 and 1929-31. Mem. Soc. Am. Musicians (pres. 1939-1941), Phi Beta Kappa. Club: Cliff Dwellers. Composer: The Passing of Summer (lyrical cantata), 1902; Hiawatha's Wooing, 1904; King Robert of Sicily, 1906; Ballade for 'cello and orchestra, 1907; Fantaisie Symphonique and Rhapsody for organ, 1912, 14; Legend, for piano, 1916; The Broken Troth (cantata for women's voices), 1917; sonata for piano and violin, 1917; Pierrot Wounded (melodrama), 1917; The Rock of Liberty (a Pilgrim ode), 1920; Symphonic Prelude, for orchestra in MS. (first perf. Chicago Symphony Orchestra, 1916); overture Pioneer, for orchestra (first perf. Chicago Sym. Orchestra, 1919), "Heroic Piece" for orchestra and organ (first perf. by Chicago Sym. Orchestra, Feb. 11, 1924); "The Maypole Lovers" (3-act opera), 1919-31 (awarded David Bispham Memorial Medal, 1934); Orchestral Suite No. 1 from same (first perf. Chicago Sym. Orchestra, Jan. 9-10, 1936), also Suite No. 2 from same; "Rhapsody" for orchestra; and about 90 other published compositions for voice, piano, organ, chorus and orchestra. Author: Choral and Church Music, Vol. VI in The Art of Music series, 1917. Home: care Greak Lakes Foundation, R.R. No. 2, Libertyville, Ill. Died May 18, 1952; buried Forrest Hill Cemetery, Ann Arbor.

COLE, William Purrington, Jr., judge, ex-congressman; b. Towson, Md., May 11, 1889; s. William Purrington and Ida Estelle (Stocksdale) C.; B.C.E., Md. Agrl. Coll. (now U. Md.), 1910; studied Law Sch., U. Md., 1911-12; m. Edith Moore Cole, June 27, 1918; 1 son, William Purrington III (killed in action, Europe, Sept. 11, 1944). Admitted to Md. bar, 1912; gen. practice at Towson, Md.; m. 70th, 72d to 77 Congresses, 2d Md. Dist.; resigned to accept appt. as judge U.S. Customs Ct.; now judge U.S. Ct. of Customs and Patent Appeals. Commd. 1st lt. 316th Inf., 79th Div., U.S. Army, 1917; in 3 battles in France; promoted capt. 1918. Mem. Am. Md., Balt. County bar assns., Phi Kappa Sigma. Democrat. Episcopalian. Home: 100 W. University Pkwy., Balt. 10, Office: Internal Revenue Bldg., 10th and Constitution Av., Washington. Died Sept. 22, 1957.

COLE, Wilson Giffin, clergyman, educator; b. Homestead, Pa., Apr. 29, 1884; s. Aaron Whitman and Mary (Moran) C.; diploma, Beaver Coll. Acad., Pa., 1905; A.B., Allegheny Coll., Meadville, Pa., 1909; A.M. from U. of Pittsburgh, 1925; S.T.B., Boston U. Sch. of Theology, 1928; D.D., Allegheny Coll., 1929; m. Margaret Richards, Apr. 18, 1911; 1 dau., Claire Rodkey (Mrs. Harold C. Hancock). Pastor Spencer M.E. Ch., Pittsburgh, 1912-16, First Ch., Wilmerding, Pa., 1916-20, New Brighton, Pa., 1920-22, Oakland Ch., Pittsburgh, and dir. Wesley Foundation, Pittsburgh, 1922-25; pastor Grant Av. Ch., Denver, 1925-31; also prof. homiletics, Iliff Sch. of Theology, Denver, 1928-31; pastor Janes M.E. Ch., Brooklyn, N.Y., 1931-36, University Meth. Ch., Syracuse, 1936-50, now emeritus. Mem. exec. com. bd. trustees U. of Denver; chmn. Com. on Restating Standards for the Modern Family. Mem. Phi Delta Theta, Phi Delta Kappa, Pi Lambda Mu and Theta Chi Beta fraternities. Mason (32°). Clubs: The Wranglers, Friends of Reading, Social Literary, Current Events, Kiwanis Club. Writer of The Luxury of Religion, The Hill Far Away, The Leadership of Lincoln, Talking to Yourself, Signs of Splendor, The Audience Answers Back, The Creation of the Future, etc. Contbr. to religious jours. Home: 1108 E. Genesee St., Syracuse 10, N.Y. Died Sept. 8, 1954.

COLEMAN, Claude C., neurol. surgeon; b. Caroline County, Va., July 21, 1879; s. Henry Frank and Jane (Patrick) C.; student William and Mary Coll., 1894-97, D.Sc. (honorary), 1948; M.D., Med. Coll. of Va., 1903, D.Sc., 1950; student at the New York Polyclinic Postgraduate Med. Sch., 1906; m. Julia Langhorne Cone, Apr. 28, 1917; children—Anne Putney, Julia Langhorne, Claude C., Jane Patrick; m. 2d, Ruth Threadcraft Putney, June 16, 1931; married 3d Constance Cardoza, Dec. 30, 1948. Began practice at Richmond, 1910; prof. principles of surgery, Med. Coll. of Va., 1912-13, prof. neurol. surgery, 1924-51, consultant in neurol. surgery, 1951—; clinical prof. neurol. surgery, University of Va., 1937-1941. Served as maj. Med. Corps, U.S. Army, during World War; dir. Sch. of Brain Surgery, U.S. Army, Ft. Oglethorpe, 1918; civilian consultant in neurol. surgery to surgeon general, World War II; neurosurgical consultant Special Medical Advisory Board Veterans' Administration. Member board of visitors Coll. of William and Mary. Fellow Am. Coll. Surgeons; mem. Soc. Neurol. Surgeons (pres. 1926). Southern Surgical Assn., A.M.A., Kappa Alpha, Phi Beta Kappa. Democrat. Clubs: Country Club of Va.; Gloucester Country. Author: Medical Department U.S. Army in the World War, vol. 2 (with others), 1924; section on the nervous system in Horsley and Bigger's Operative Surgery, 4th edit., 1937; sect. on Peripheral Nerves in Bancroft's Surgery, 1945. Contbr. surgical articles to jours. Home: 5115 Cary St. Rd. Office: 1200 E. Broad St., Richmond, Va. Died Jan. 9, 1953; buried Hollywood Cemetery, Richmond, Va.

COLEMAN, Cyril, lawyer; b. Meriden, Conn., Sept. 1, 1902; s. John L. and Dora A. (Cosgrove) C.; A.B., Harvard, 1924, LL.B., 1927; m. Katherine Alexander, June 4, 1931; children—Mary, John, Marcia, Dora. Admitted to Conn. bar, 1927, since practiced in Hartford, asso. with Day, Berry & Howard since 1927, partner since 1930. Mem. Police Commn., City of Hartford, 1934-35, Met. Dist. Commn., 1940-47, Park Bd., 1944-47, Charter Commn., 1945-47; mem. jud. council State of Conn., 1948-51, 1956—. Mayor of Hartford, 1947-51. Mem. Am. (state del. to Ho. of Dels., 1948-51, bd. govs., 1951-54), Conn. State, Hartford Co. (pres. 1952-53) bar assns. Clubs: Univ., Hartford (Hartford); Graduates (New Haven). Home: 777 Prospect Av., West Hartford, Conn. Office: 750 Main St., Hartford 3, Conn. Died Sept. 20, 1958; buried Mt. St. Benedict Cemetery, Hartford, Conn.

COLEMAN, D'Alton Corry, ret. chmn. bd., pres. C.P. Ry. Co.; b. Carleton Place, Ont., July 9, 1879; s. James and Mary Jane (Doherty) C.; ed. Arnprior (Ont.) Collegiate Inst.; hon. LL.D., U. Manitoba, 1932; D.C.L., Bishops U., 1937; m. Anna Grant, Feb. 21, 1906 (died Aug. 24, 1920); children—James Alexander, Rowan Corry; m. 2d, Florence Mary Lynch, Oct. 28, 1922. Private sec. to George A. Cox, Toronto, 1897; editor Belleville Daily Intelligencer, 1898; with C.P. Ry. Co. 1899-47, successively pvt. sec., chief clerk, accountant, at Winnipeg, Cranbrook, B.C., North Bay, Ont., supt. Kootenay Div., Nelson, B.C., 1907-08, Vancouver, B.C., 1908; supt. car service, Winnipeg, 1908, gen. supt., Winnipeg, 1912-13, Calgary, 1913-15; asst. gen. mgr., Winnipeg, 1915-18; v.p. Western Lines, Winnipeg, 1918-34; v.p., dir. co., 1934-42, pres., 1942-47, also dir., ret. 1947; dir. Odeon Theatres, Met. Life Ins. Co.; mem. Canadian com. Hudson's Bay Co., Empire Trust Co. Trustee Bishop's U.; gov. Montreal Gen. Hosp., Royal Victoria Hosp., McGill U., Notre Dame Hosp. Montreal Festivals; v.p. Boys Farm and Training Sch.; mem. Canadian Com., Hudson's Bay Co.; mem. Canadian gen. council Boy Scouts of Can. Decorated Knight of Grace and mem. Commandery Council, Order of St. John of Jerusalem; hon. pres. Navy League of Can.; past pres. Assn. Canadian Clubs; past pres. and life mem. of Canadian Club of Winnipeg; past chmn. bd. govs. U. Manitoba; dir. Can. Arena Co.; v.p. Can. Hockey Club. Clubs: Mount Royal, St. James's, Forest and Stream (Montreal, Canada); Rideau (Ottawa); Manitoba (Winnipeg); Ranchmen's (Calgary); Vancouver (Vancouver); Century Assn. (N.Y.). Home: 3940 Cote des Neiges Road, Montreal, Can. Died Oct. 17, 1956.

COLEMAN, George William, impartial arbitrator; b. Boston, June 16, 1867; s. George and Mary (Carville) C.; grad. (Franklin medal) English High Sch., Boston, 1885; hon. A.M., Colby Coll., 1911; LL.D., Wake Forest and Franklin colls., 1922; m. Alice Blanchard Merriam, June 30, 1891. Asst. editor Jour. Edn., 1886-89; shipwrecked on voyage to Buenos Aires, S.A., as corr. various jours.; bus. mgr. New England Mag., 1890-92; pub. house organ, Walker-Stetson-Sawyer Co., wholesale dry goods, Boston; advt. mgr. The Golden Rule (now Christian Endeavor World), 1893-1905; pub. Chrisian Endeavor World, 1905-10; dir. publicity W. H. McElwain Co., 1910-15; chmn. Open Forum Speakers' Bureau; pres. Babson Inst., Wellesley Hills, Mass., 1921-35, pres. emeritus, 1935—; pres. Webber College, Babson Park, Fla., 1930-39, pres. emeritus, 1939—; dir. George B. Graff Co., Boston. Dir. Edward A. Filene Good Will Fund; trustee Howard U., Washington. Ipartial arbitrator Men's Clothing Trade, Boston Region. Mem. Boston City Council, 1914-17 (pres. 1915); del.-at-large Rep. Nat. Conv., 1912, Mass. Constl. Conv., 1917. Pres. and host of series of annual sociol. confs., meeting at Sagamore Beach, June 1907-17; orginator and dir. of Sunday Evening Ford Hall Forum, begun at Boston, spring of 1908, under auspices of Boston Bapt. Social Union. Vice pres. N.E. Bapt. Hosp.; pres. Pilgrim Publicity Assn., 1909-11; pres. Asso. Advt. Clubs Am., 1911-13. Pres. No. Bapt. Conv., 1917-18. Chmn. Mass. Ind. Voters' Assn. Clubs: Advertising (N.Y.C.); Twentieth Century, Advertising, Boston Bapt. Social Union, Puddingstone. Author: Searchlights, 1909; The People's Prayers, 1914; Democracy in the Making, 1915; This Business of Living (short essays), 1936. Home: 90 The Fenway. Address: Little Bldg., Boston. Died July 31, 1950; buried Foret Hills Cemetery, Jamaica Plain, Mass.

COLEMAN, John Strider, business exec.; b. Charlestown, W.Va., Oct. 12, 1897; s. Charles Nelson and Nellie (Strider) C.; ed. pub. and pvt. schs., Charlestown, W.Va. and Washington, D.C.; LL.B., Georgetown University, 1924; LL.D., University Detroit, 1952, Bethany Coll., 1953, Wayne U., 1953; B.Sc., Cleary Coll., 1955; m. Elsie Hudson, Jan. 15, 1921; 1 son, John Hudson. Salesman Washington br. Burroughs Adding Machine Co., now named Burroughs Corporation, 1920-24, government department 1924-30, asst. br. mgr. city of Washington, 1930-34, spl. rep., 1934-37, div. mgr., Detroit, Mich., 1934-39, asst. to vice pres., Detroit, 1939-42, exec. asst., 1942-44, vice pres. and dir., 1944-46, pres. and dir. since 1946, mem. exec. com. since 1947. Dir. Fruehauf Trailer Company, Michigan Bell Telephone Company, Am. Optical Co., Am. Motors Corp., Nat.

Bank Det., Std. Accident Ins. Co.; past chmn. Fed Res. Bank of Chgo. Mem. adv. bd. U.S. P.O. Dept.; mem. bd. Nat. Indsl. Conf. Bd.; trustee Com. Econ. Development. Dir. United Found. Met. Detroit; dir. Com. for Nat. Trade Policy. Served as ordnance sgt. U.S. Army A.E.F., 1917-18. Decorated Officer, French Legion of Honor, 1954; Officers Cross, Order of Merit, Federal Republic of Germany), 1956; Knight Commander, Order British Empire, 1957. Member of the U.S. (president 1956-57), C. of C. (trustee U.S. council), Army Ordnance Assn., Engring. Soc. of Detroit, Gamma Eta Gamma. Republican. Episcopalian. Mason. Clubs: Economic, Detroit, Detroit Athletic. Recess (Detroit); University, Brook (N.Y.C.). Home: 700 Seward Av., Detroit 2. Office: 6071 2d Av., Detroit 32. Died Apr. 13, 1958; buried Arlington Nat. Cemetery.

COLEMAN, Philip Frantz, banker; b. Norristown, Pa., Jan. 1, 1893; s. Philip E. and Mary (Frantz) C.; grad. Germantown Acad., 1910; m. Edith R. Soden, Mar. 6, 1920; children—Warren P., Philip Frantz, John S., Robert L. Sr. v.p. First Pennsylvania Banking & Trust Co., Phila.; dir. H. W. Butterworth & Sons Co., Beck Engraving Co., Inc., Struthers-Dunn, Inc. Mem. Pennsylvania Soc. Club: Union League (Phila.). Home: Kenilworth, Alden Park, Phila. 44. Office: First Pennsylvania Banking & Trust Co., 15th and Chestnut Sts., Phila. 44. Died Nov. 1956.

COLEMAN, Sydney Haines, social service; b. Bellona, N.Y., Aug. 31, 1886; s. William H. and Hannah (Potts) C.; grad. Penn Yan (N.Y.) Acad., 1904; Ph.B., Syracuse U., 1910; m. Marion McGhee, June 17, 1914 (died 1919); m. 2d, Sarah Williams, Aug. 23, 1920; children—Ruth Straigh, James Robert. Gen. mgr. Erie County Soc. for Prevention Cruelty to Animals, 1910-13; field sec. Am. Humane Assn. and editor Nat. Humane Review, 1913-20; organizer, 1920, mgr. until 1921, Pub. and Indsl. Safety Council, Buffalo, N.Y.; dir. State Bureau Rehabilitation, Western N.Y., 1921-22; mgr. safety bureau, Buffalo C. of C., 1922-24; gen. mgr. Am. Humane Assn., 1924-27; pres., 1927-46; editor Humane Rev., 1924-46; exec. v.p. Am. Soc. for Prevention of Cruelty to Animals, 1931-51. Pres. Am. Fondouk Maintenance Com.; pres. Yonkers Council Boy Scouts, 1944-47; v.p. N.Y. State Humane Assn. Mem. Delta Tau Delta, Sinfonia. Republican. Methodist. Mason. Clubs: Syracuse University (N.Y.C.). Rotary. Author: Humane Society Leaders of America, 1924; also many brochures on child and animal protection. Home: 2835 Polk St., Hollywood, Fla. Died Mar. 23, 1955; buried Bellona, N.Y.

COLEMAN, William Coffin, mfr.; b. Chatham, N.Y., May 21, 1870; s. Robert Russell and Julia M. (Coffin) C.; grad. Kan. State Tchrs. Coll., Emporia, 1893; spl. student Ottawa (Kan.) U., 1893-94; studied law U. Kan., 1897-98; m. Fanny Sheldon, Jan. 1, 1901; children—Robert Sheldon, Clarence William. Began 1901, at Wichita, Kan., as salesman for gasoline lamps, improved same and entered mfg. field as Coleman Lamp & Stove Co., of which is pres.; city commr. Wichita, 1921-25; mayor of Wichita, 1923-24. Pres. No. Bapt. Conv., 1927; dir. YMCA. Republican. Clubs: Wichita Country, Rotary. Home: Hillcrest Homes. Office: 240 N. St. Francis Av., Wichita, Kan. Died Nov. 2, 1957; buried Old Mission Mausoleum, Wichita.

COLEMAN, William Henry, educator; b. Auburn, Neb., Apr. 12, 1888; s. Henry John and Helena (Johnson) C.; A.B., Neb. Wesleyan U., 1909, A.M., U. of Neb., 1916; Ph.D., Columbia, 1931; m. Viola Georgianna Horrum, Aug. 19, 1909; children—Geraldine Helene, George Willard. Supt. schs. Hardy, Neb., 1909-10, Ogallala, Neb., 1910-12, Bertrand, Neb., 1912-16, Crawford, Neb., 1916-22, Rawlins, Wyoming, 1924-26, Mesa, Ariz., 1931-34; head dept. of edn. and psychology, Shurtleff Coll., Alton, Ill., 1934-38, acting president, 1938-39, dean and registrar, 1939-41; senior specialist on sch. facilities, U.S. Office of Edn., Washington, D.C., 1941-44; chief edn. specialist, Fed. Works Agency since 1944. Chief ednl. officer U.S. Office of Education since 1946; spl. mission to Tokyo, Japan and Wiesbaden, Germany to train school administrators, 1949-50. Member Academy Science, Am. Assn. School Adminstrs., Phi Delta Kappa. Methodist. Mason (Shriner), Eastern Star. Author: Critique of Spelling Vocabulary Investigation, 1931; Learning to Spell (with others), 1931; articles in Yearbook of School and University, Patent on device for teaching music, 1945, 46. Home: 1900 F St. N.W., Washington 6. Office: Fed Sec. Agency, U.S.O.E., Washington 25. Died Dec. 2, 1952.

COLETTE (Sidonie Gabrielle) (pseudonym Colette Willy), author; b. Saint Sauveur-en-Puisaye, Burgundy, Jan. 28, 1873; d. Jules Joseph and Sidonie (Sanday) Colette; m. Henry Gauthier-Villars, 1893 (div. 1906); m. 2d, Henry de Jouvenel, 1910 (div. 1924); m. 3d, Maurice Goudeket, 1935. Pres. Acad. Goncourt. Decorated Grand Officier Legion of Honor. Author numerous essays, plays, short stories and novels among which are: (translated into English) Chéri; The Last of Chéri; Gigi; Julie de Carneilhan; Chance Acquaintances, Creatures Great and Small; Creature Conservations; Other Creatures; Creature Comfort; Claudine at School; Claudine in Paris; The Vagabond; Ripening Seed; Mitsou; Music-Hall Sidelights; My Mother's House; Sido. Address: care Farrar, Straus and Cudahy, Inc., 101 Fifth Av., N.Y.C.; also 9 rue de Beaujolais, Paris Ier, France. Died Aug. 3, 1954. Buried Paris, France.

COLGATE, Henry A.; b. West Orange, N.J., 1890; s. Richard Morse and Margaret Cabel (Auchincloss) C.; A.B., Yale, 1913; m. Jeannette Pruyn, June 28, 1919; m. 2d, Linda Wallace, Oct. 11, 1930; m. 3d, Denise Smith, May 28. 1954 (div. 1957). Partner Wood, Struthers Co.; dir. Colgate-Palmolive-Peet Co., Internat. Paper Co. Trustee Colgate U.; pres. The Seeing-Eye; trustee Boys Club of N.Y. Clubs: Yale University, University, Downtown Assn., River, Links. Piping Rock. Home: N.Y.C. Office: 30 Wall St., N.Y.C. Died Oct. 16, 1957.

COLLENS, Charles, architect; b. N.Y.C., Oct. 14, 1873; s. Charles Terry and Mary Abbely (Wood) C.; B.A., Yale, 1896; student Ecole des Beaux Arts, Paris; m. Margaret Winsor, May 20, 1903; children—Margaret Lyman, Charles Terry, Linda. Sr. mem. firm Allen, Collens & Willis, Boston; architect bldgs. Union Theol. Sem., N.Y.C., Meml. Chapel, Williams Coll., library, art bldgs. Vassar Coll., library Ohio State U., library and chapel Mt. Holyoke Coll., Newton City Hall, Andover Theol. Sem., Cambridge, Mass., Park Av. Bapt. Ch., N.Y.C., Hartford Theol. Sem., Riverside Ch., N.Y.C., Cloister Mus., N.Y. C., and others. Fellow A.I.A.; mem. Boston Soc. Architects, Nat. Acad. Design, Beaux Arts Soc., Phi Beta Kappa, Psi Upsilon. Clubs: St. Botolph (Boston); Brookline (Mass.) Country, Yale (N.Y.C.). Office: 20 Newberry St., Boston 16. Died Sept. 18, 1956.

COLLET, John Caskie (kŏl'lĕt), federal judge; b. Keytesville, Mo., May 25, 1898; s. James Anderson and Mary Elizabeth (Miller) C.; prep. edn. Mo. pub. schools; student Westminster College, 1914-17; LL.D., Westminster College, 1945; married Hazel E. Bozworth, November 9, 1921; children—William Anderson, John Caskie. Admitted to Mo. bar, 1902; served as city atty., later prosecuting atty., Chariton County, 1925-29; asst. counsel Mo. State Highway Dept., 1930-33; chmn. Mo. Pub. Service Commn., 1933-35; apptd. to Mo. Supreme Court, 1935, elected for 10 year term, 1936; apptd. judge U.S. Dist. Court of Mo., 1937; appointed a judge of U.S. Court of Appeals, Eighth Judicial Circuit by Pres. Truman, April 1947. Acted as stabilization administrator, O.W. M.R., Oct. 1, 1945-Feb. 25, 1946; cons. in White House Office, 1947-52. Served in U.S. A.S., 1917-18. Mem. Am., Mo. State bar assns., Phi Delta Phi, Order of the Coif, Kappa Alpha. Democrat. Baptist. Mason. Clubs: The Kansas City, Kiwanis. Home: 9631 State Line, Kansas City, Mo. Died Dec. 5, 1955; buried Forest Hills, Kansas City, Mo.

COLLIE, George Lucius, geologist; b. Delavan, Wis., Aug. 11, 1857; s. Joseph and Ann Elizabeth (Foote) C.; B.S., Beloit Coll., 1881; A.M., Harvard, 1891, Ph.D., 1893; m. Katharine E. Burrows of Chicago, Mar. 26, 1896 (dec.); children—Helen Tannisse (dec.), Kenneth Gordon. Asst. prin. and prin. Delavan High Sch., 1885-90; Morgan fellow, Harvard, 1891-92; prof. geology, 1892-1923, prof. of anthropology, 1923-31, curator of Logan Museum of Archaeology, 1893-1931, dean 1899-1931, acting pres., 1902-03 and 1905-08, Beloit Coll., also dir. Logan Mus. Sch. for Prehistoric Research, Les Eyzies, France, and Tebersa, Algeria; Asst. Wis. Geol. Survey, 1898. Fellow Geol. Soc. of America, A.A.A.S.; mem. Am. Anthrop. Assn., Phi Beta Kappa. Traveled around the world, 1910-11, on geol. trip covering 40,000 miles. Writer on geol. and ednl. topics. Y.M. C.A. sec., overseas service with A.E.F. in France and Eng., 1918-19. Engaged in research for early man in France and Algeria, 1926-28. Home: Beloit, Wis. Died Dec. 28, 1954; buried Spring Grove Cemetery, Delavan, Wis.

COLLIER, Edward Augustus, clergyman, author; b. N.Y.C., Nov. 21, 1835; s. Ezra and Mary Shaw (Atwood) C.; A.B., N.Y. U., 1857, A.M., 1860, D.D., 1884; student Princeton Theol. Sem., 1860; m. Isabella G. James, Aug. 1, 1861. Licensed by Presbytery of Nassau, 1859; ordained by Presbytery, North River, 1860; acting pastor, Congl. Ch., Saugerties, N.Y., 1860-61, Presbyn. Ch., Amenia, N.Y., 1861-64; pastor Ref. Protestant Dutch Ch., Kinderhook, N.Y., 1864-1907, since pastor emeritus. Republican. Mem. Psi Upsilon, Phi Beta Kappa. Author: Lyrics from the Psalter, 1907; A History of Old Kinderhook, 1914; also many metrical versions of Psalms, etc. Home: Kinderhood, N.Y. Died Dec. 20, 1920; buried Kinderhood Reformed Ch. Cemetery.

COLLIER, Harry D., oil company exec.; b. San Francisco, Calif., Mar. 29, 1876; s. William Hoyle and Annie (Winston) C.; m. Ella May Killen, Dec. 9, 1903. With Standard Oil Co. of Calif. since 1903, dir. since 1924, v.p., 1931-40, pres., 1940-45, chmn. bd., 1945-49, chmn. finance com., 1950-51, dir. 1924-56; dir. Crocker-Anglo Nat. Bank, Matson Navigation Co. Clubs: Stock Exchange, Bohemian, Pacific-Union (San Francisco); Burlingame Country Burlingame); California (Los Angeles); Rainier (Seattle); Links, Pinnacle, Twenty Nine (N.Y.C.). Home: 2790 Green St., San Francisco 23. Office: Russ Bldg., San Francisco 4. Died Jan. 30, 1959; buried Cypress Lawn, Colma, Cal.

COLLIER, John Howard, chmn. Crane Co.; b. Chicago, Ill., Sept. 22, 1884; s. Frank Howard and Fannie Gibbs (Brown) C.; student Purdue U., 1901-03, Master of Industry, 1942; m. Virginia MacMakin, Oct. 18, 1919; children—Joan, MacMakin. With Crane Co., 1903— becoming supt., 1906; mgr., 1912-17, gen. mgr., 1917-29; resided abroad with headquarters London and Paris, as chmn. of the bd., Crane Ltd., Eng., and pres. Cie Crane, France, 1929-33; v.p. Crane Co., 1933-41, pres., 1941-46; dir. Crane, Ltd., Canada, Trenton Potteries Co., Canadian Potteries Co., Ltd., Warren King, Ltd., Port Hope Sanitary Mfg. Co., Ltd., Crane Co. of Minn., Crane-O'Fallon Co. Former trustee Ill. Inst. Tech. Episcopalian. Clubs: Chicago, University, Tavern, Casino, Art (Chgo.); Old Elm; University (Bridgeport, Conn.); Fairfield (Conn.) Beach. Home: Greenfield Hill, Fairfield, Conn. Died July 27, 1955.

COLLIER, William Miller, diplomat, lawyer; b. Lodi, N.Y., Nov. 11, 1867; s. Rev. Isaac Henry and Frances Mary (Miller) C.; A.B., Hamilton Coll., 1889, A.M., 1892; LL.D. (hon.), George Washington U., 1916; Hamilton Coll., 1918; New York U., 1920; Syracuse U., 1920; L.H.D., Hobart Coll., 1920; D.C.L., Wesleyan, 1920; Litt.D., Washington and Jefferson, 1921; equivalent degrees, Nat. U. of Chile, 1921; Catholic U. of Chile, 1928; U. of Arequipa, Peru, 1927; m. Frances Beardsley Ross, Sept. 13. 1893. Admitted to N.Y. bar, 1892, gen. practice of law, Auburn, N.Y., 1892-1903; referee in bankruptcy, 1898-99; N.Y. State Civil Service Commr., 1899-1903, pres. of commn., 1901-03; spl. asst. U.S. Atty. Gen. to enforce anti-trust laws, 1903-04; Am. Minister to Spain, 1905-09; in spl. practice internat. law, U.S. and Europe, 1910-16; pres. George Washington U., 1917-21; ambassador to Chile, 1921-28; since then has devoted time to travel and study, making 3 round-the-world trips. Awarded Grand Cross of Isabella the Catholic (Spain), 1916; Order of the Crown of Siam, 1921; Grand Cross Order of Merit, Chile, 1930; Order of the Grand Condor, Bolivia, 1927; Grand Cross of the Order of the Liberator, Venezuela, 1928. Hon. citizen of La Paz, Bolivia; Cuczo, Arequipa, Puño, Julliaca, Peru. Mem. Holland Soc. of N.Y., Phi Beta Kappa, Chi Psi. Clubs: University (N.Y.); Chevy Chase. Author: The Trusts; What Can We Do with Them—What Can They Do for Us?, 1900; Collier on Civil Service Law, 1901; Collier on Bankruptcy, 1898; At the Court of His Catholic Majesty, 1912; (with Señor Feliu) La Primera Mission de los Estados Unidos en Chile (in Spanish). 1924. Home: 2 Hamilton Av., Auburn, N.Y. Office: care of Nat. Bank, Auburn, N.Y. Died Apr. 15, 1956; buried Fort Hill Cemetery, Auburn.

COLLINGS, Clyde Wilson (kŏl'lĭngs), urological surgeon; b. Vancouver, Wash., Feb. 28, 1892; s. Dellbert A. and Emma May (McCafferty) C.; student U. Wash., 1913-15; M.D., Ore. U., 1919; m. Martha Monigle, 1944; 1 son, Anthony; children by previous marriage—Clyde Wilson, Amzell Iona. Urological interne and resident urologist Bellevue Hosp., N.Y. C., 1919-21, asst. attending urologist, 1921-36; sr. instr. of urologic surgery and chief of urologic clinic N.Y.U. Med. Coll., 1921-36; asst. vis. urologist St. Vincent Hosp., 1921-26; cons. urologist St. Joseph's Hosp., Far Rockaway, L.I., 1921—; founder mem. med. staff Doctors Hosp., 1929—; sr. surgeon attending staff Los Angeles County Gen. Hosp.; asso. prof. surgery (urology) Sch. Medicine, Coll. Med. Evangelists; chief urologic clinic and sr. surgeon attending urologic staff White Meml. Hosp. Served with USN Med. Dept., World War I, lt. comdr., World War II. Fellow Royal Society Medicine Eng., A.C.S.; mem. A.M.A., N.Y. state and county med. socs., N.Y. Acad. Medicine, Cal., Los Angeles County med. socs., Am., French urol. assns., Delta Tau Delta. Republican. Episcopalian. Clubs: Midwick Polo, Santa Barbara Polo, U.S. Polo Assn. Contbr. to med. jours. of U.S., England and France. Inventor of radio electric knife for transurethral surgery, 1923; devised the first operation with the cutting high frequency current and knife electrode through the urethroscope, 1923. Home: Collingswood, Encino, Cal. Office: 1930 Wilshire Blvd., Los Angeles. Died July 4, 1952; buried Inglewood Park Cemetery, Inglewood, Cal.

COLLINGS, Howard Paxton, physician; b. Rockville, Ind., Jan. 30, 1865; s. Spotsard and Rebecca (Mattox) C.; grad. Central Normal Coll., Danville, Ind., 1888; M.D., Bellevue Hosp. Med. Coll., N.Y., 1891; interne St. Vincent's Hosp., N.Y., 1891-92; m. Jessie Snyder, Oct. 3, 1892. In practice at Hot Springs, Ark., 1892—; mem. bd. govs., vis. physician St. Joseph's Hosp. Fellow A.C.S.; mem. A.M. A., Ark., State, Hot Springs (ex-pres.) med. socs., Med. Assn. of Southwest, etc. Del. to 17th Internat. Med. Congress, London, 1913. Mason (K.T.). Democrat. Episcopalian. Home: 130 Cedar St. Office: Medical Arts Bldg., Hot Springs, Ark. Deceased.*

COLLINGWOOD, G(eorge) Harris, forester; born Fayetteville, Ark., May 27, 1890; s. Charles Barnard and Harriet (Thomas) C.; B.S., Mich. State U., 1911; student U. of Munich, Germany, 1913-14; M. A., U. of Mich., 1917; m. Jean Cummings, Sept. 1, 1916; children—Charles Cummings, Thomas Peeke, Eloise (Mrs. Baxter C. Prescott), Jean (Mrs. John H. Spelman), Rebecca Cummings (Mrs. James P. McHale), George Harris. Engaged as forest ranger Apache National Forest, 1911-15; assistant extension prof. forestry, Cornell, 1916-23, extension forester, U.S. Dept. Agr., 1923-28; forester, Am. Forestry Assn., 1928-40; chief forester, Nat. Lumber Mfrs. Assn. 1940-46; dir. office of forest products. Nat. Housing Agency (all at Washington), 1946, asst. dir. forest products, div., Office Housing Expediter, 1947; research dir. on agrl. activities, Hoover Commn., 1948; forestry cons., C. of C. of U.S., 1949; analyst in conservation and natural resources Legislative Reference Service, Library of Congress, 1949-—, head natural resources sect., 1958-—. Consultant to secretary of agriculture for evaluation of insect and plant disease control programs, 1951-52. Recepient Mich. State College Alumni Award, 1954; Conservation and Distinguished Service awards, American Forestry Association, 1956. Fellow American Association for the Advancement Sci., member Society American Foresters, Am. Forestry Assn. (hon. v.p. 1955). Republican. Conglist. Clubs: Cosmos, Torch. Author: The Production of Maple Syrup and Sugar in New York State Cornell Extension Bull., 1928; Farm Forestry Extension, U.S.D.A. Bull., 1925; Knowing Your Trees, 1937; Forestry Manual for Chambers of Commerce, 1949. Contbr. numerous articles to mags. and jours. Home: 2853 Ontario Rd., Washington 9. Office: Library of Congress, Washington 25. Died Apr. 2, 1958; buried Centreville, Mich.

COLLINS, Francis Arnold, author; b. Newark, June 6, 1873; s. Francis Asbury and Virginia Handy (Miller) C.; grad. Manual Tng. Sch., Phila., 1894; student U. Pa., Class 1898; m. Rose C. Voordhees, Sept. 28, 1899; 1 son, Arnold Miller. On reportorial staff N.Y. Evening Sun, 1899-1900; asst. Sunday editor N.Y. Herald, 1901-08. Clubs: Town Hall (N.Y. C.); The Authors (London, Eng.). Author: The Boy's Book of Model Aeroplanes, 1910; The Second Boy's Book of Model Aeroplanes, 1911; The Wireless Man, 1912; The Camera Man, 1916; The Air Man, 1917; The Fighting Engineers, 1918; Naval Heroes of Today, 1918; Sentinels Along Our Coast, 1922; Mountain Climbing, 1923; Our Harbors and Inland Waterways; Romance of Park Avenue. Contbr. to periodicals. Address: 250 Park Av., N.Y.C. Died 1957.

COLLINS, Frank Shipley, botanist; b. Charlestown, Mass., Feb. 6, 1848; s. Joshua Cobb and Elizabeth Ann (Carter) C.; grad. high sch., Malden (Mass.), 1863; A.M., Tufts 1910; m. Anna Lendrum Holmes, Oct. 18, 1875. In commercial pursuits 1864-1912. Has been a student of botany many yrs. Asso. Univ. Mus. Harvard U. Fellow Am. Acad. Arts and Sciences; mem. Boston Soc. Natural History, Mass. Hort. Soc., N.E. Bot. Club (ex-pres.), A.A. A.S., Bot. Soc. America; corr. mem. Torrey Bot. Club: Author: Flora of Middlesex County, 1888; The Green Algae of North America, in Tufts College Studies, 1908-18; Phyotheca Boreali-Americana, 1894-1919 (subscription). Contbr. to bot. jours. Home: North Eastham, Mass. Died May 25, 1920.

COLLINS, Frederick Lewis, author; b. Lawrence, Mass., Mar. 23, 1882; s. Lewis Peter and Lovina Ellen (Hawes) C.; student Phillips Andover Acad., A.B., Harvard, 1903; m. Elizabeth Paine, Apr. 27, 1904; children—Barbara (died 1909), Marjory; m. 2d, Barbara Maclaren. Sec. Crowell Pub. Co., 1905-10; editor Woman's Home Companion, 1906-10; pres. McClure Publications, Inc., 1911-20; editor McClure's Mag., 1913-20. Served in War Dept. (ordnance), Treasury Dept. (war risk ins.), Interior Dept. (Americanization), 1917-18, and abroad, 1919; corr. Am. Commn. to Negotiate Peace, Paris, 1919. Pres. Periodical Publishers' Assn. Am., 1920-21. Clubs: Union League, American Yacht, Manursing Island, West Side Tennis. Author: This King Business, 1923; Our American Kings, 1924; Travel Charts and Travel Chats, 1926; American Travel Charts and Travel Chats, 1928; The Christmas Trail, 1928; Vacation Travel Charts and Travel Chats, 1930; Glamorous Sinners, 1932; Consolidated Gas Company of New York—A History, 1934; The F.B.I. in Peace and War, 1943; The Romance of Stainless Steel, 1943; Homicide Squad, 1944; Money Town, 1946. Contbr. to mags. Address: West Falmouth, Mass. Died July 25, 1950.

COLLINS, Harold Moorman, consular service; b. Lynchburg, Va., June 27, 1894; s. Lewis Preston and Ella Bolling (Moorman) C.; B.A., Washington and Lee U., 1914; studied law and journalism, Columbia, 1917; m. Mary Shields Procter, Mar. 5, 1918; 1 son, Lewis Preston. Commd. provisional 2d lt. 2d Cav., U.S. Army, 1917; temp. 1st lt., 1918-19; overseas service 1918-19. Vice consul at Dublin, Irish Free State, 1921-25; consul, Dublin, 1925-26, Nantes, France, 1926-—. Mem. Sigma Alpha Epsilon. Baptist. Home: Marion, Va. Died Sept. 20, 1942.

COLLINS, John Martin, editor; b. Topeka, Kan., May 24, 1892; s. Edward Patrick and Anna (Horan) C.; ed. pub. schs. of Winfield, Kan.; m. Jess Fremont Wagner, Aug. 18, 1916; 1 son, John M. Mem. news staff Winfield Free Press and Winfield Courier, 1913-15; with news staff Topeka Daily Capital, 1915, city editor, 1916; mem. staff Kansas City Star, 1917-18, Weekly Kansas City Star, 1919-25, asso. editor, 1925-46, editor since Mar. 1946. Vice pres. Am. Royal Livestock and Horse Show since 1948. Selected by Am. Assn. Agrl. Coll. Editors at Cornell, 1949, as winner of annual Rueben Brigham Memorial award as farm paper editor who has done most to further cause of agrl. edn.; designated as Hon. Am. Farmer by Future Farmers of Am. Mem. Kansas City C. of C. (chmn. agrl. promotion com.), Sigma Delta Chi. K.C. 4°). Clubs: Serra, Press (charter mem., organizer). Home 5737 Central St., Kansas City 2. Office: Kansas City Star, K.C. 17, Mo. Died May 22, 1952; buried Mt. Calvary Cemetery, Topeka.

COLLINS, Joseph Martin, beverage mfr.; b. Cartersville, Ga., July 29, 1907; s. Charles Lewis and Mittie (Middlebrooks) C.; LL.B., U. Ga., 1929; student exec. program Columbia, 1953; m. Hermione Barksdale, Jan. 31, 1935; children—Barksdale, Josephine, Dorsey. Admitted to Ga. bar, 1929, Ill., 1946; sales dept. Coca-Cola Co., 1935-37, asso. counsel, 1938-43, v.p., 1956-—, gen. counsel bottling subsidiaries, 1944-52, exec. coms., dir., 1946-58, chmn., 1956-—. Staff RFC subsidiaries, T.H., 1943-44. Mem. Am., Ga., Ill. bar assns. Clubs: Piedmont Driving (Atlanta); Saddle and Cycle (Chgo.). Home: 12 Lake Av., Bronxville, N.Y. Office: 515 Madison Av., N.Y.C. 22. Died Sept. 19, 1957.

COLLINS, Vivian, army officer; brig. gen., 1942. Address: Selective Service, St. Augustine, Fla. Died Aug. 22, 1955.*

COLLINS, Whitley Charles, aircraft mfg. exec.; b. Des Moines, Ia., Apr. 28, 1898; s. Anthony James and Catherine (Whitley) C.; B.S., Wharton Sch. of Banking and Finance, U. Pa., 1921; m. Amelia Rogg, Sept. 19, 1936; children—Rogg, Whitley. With new bus. dept., Continental Ill. Nat. Bank & Trust, Chgo., 1921-29; v.p., gen. mgr. Lockheed Aircraft, 1929-30; credit mgr. Security First Nat. Bank, Los Angeles, 1931; chmn. Collins-Powell Co., 1932-—; v.p., dir. Elastic Stop Nut Corp., Union, N.J., 1939-45; pres., chief exec. officer Northrop Aircraft, Inc., Hawthorne, Cal., 1954-—; pres. Radioplane Co., Van Nuys, Cal., 1940-57; chmn. bd. Holga Metal Products Co., Van Nuys, Cal., 1951-58. Chmn. Hollywood Bowl Assn.; trustee Cal. Institute of Technology, Claremont Men's College. Served as sgt., F.A., U.S. Army, World War I. Mem. Delta Tau Delta. Clubs: Los Angeles Country, Bel-Air Bay, California, Beach (Los Angeles). Home: 1010 N. Roxbury Dr., Beverly Hills, Cal. Office: 1001 E. Broadway, Hawthorne, Cal. Died May 12, 1959.

COLLINS, William (Olin), educator; b. Douglas Co., Ga., Feb. 23, 1891; s. Francis Marion and Laura Ann (Peacock) C.; grad., Agrl. and Mining Sch., Monroe, Ga., 1911; B.S.A., U. Ga., 1916; m. Harriet Brandon Lawson, Oct. 31, 1931. Farm mgr., Newton Co., Ga., 1912; instr. in agrl. chemistry, U. Ga., 1916, adj. prof., 1917-18, asso. prof., 1919-26, prof., 1926-32, asso. prof. soil survey, 1932-35, prof. of soils, 1935-48, head of dept. of agronomy, 1938-—. Served with C.W.S., AUS, 1918. Fellow, Ga. Acad. of Sci.; mem. Am. Soc. of Agronomy, Soil Sci. Soc. of Am., A.A.A.S., Soil Conservation Soc. of Am., Friends of the Land, Blue Key, Aghon, Gridiron, Sphinx, Alpha Zeta, Alpha Gamma Rho. Democrat. Methodist. Co-author: Soils and Crops, 1941. Home: 132 Ridgewood Pl., Athens, Ga. Died Dec. 17, 1952.

COLLINS, William Henry, astronomer; b. Peekskill, N.Y., Oct. 22, 1859; s. William B. and Mary (Griffen) C.; B.S., Harverford Coll., Pa., 1881, A.M., 1892; m. Julia Cope, May 22, 1894. Dir. Haverford Coll. Astron. Observatory, 1892-1904; prefect Haverford Coll., 1897-1919. Author: Proceedings of Haverford College Observatory, 1892-1904. Home: Haverford, Pa. Died 1939.

COLMAN, Ronald (kōl'mȧn), motion pictures; b. Richmond, Surrey, Eng., Feb. 9, 1891; s. Charles and Marjory Read (Fraser) C.; m. Thelma Ray, Sept. 18, 1919 (divorced); m. 2d, Benita Hume, Oct. 1938; 1 dau., Juliet. Served with London Scottish Inf., 1909-12; in World War with the original British Expeditionary Force, 1914. Came to U.S. in 1920; has filled leading roles in "The White Sister"; "Romola"; "The Dark Angel"; "Lady Windermere's Fan"; "Kiki"; "Her Sister from Paris"; "Beau Gete"; "The Magic Flame"; "The Night of Love"; "The Winning of Barbara Worth"; "Leatherface"; "The Rescue"; "Bulldog Drummond"; "Devil May Care"; "The Unholy Garden"; "Arrowsmith"; "Raffles"; "Under Two Flags"; "Clive of India"; "The Man Who Broke the Bank at Monte Carlo"; "A Tale of Two Cities"; "Lost Horizon"; "Prisoner of Zenda"; "If I Were King"; "The Light That Failed"; "The Talk of the Town"; "Random Harvest," "Kismet", "Late George Apley", "A Double Life," "Champagne for Caeser," (radio) Halls of Ivy, 1950-52, also TV program, Halls of Ivy, 1954-55. Received Academy Award for best actor, 1947; Foreign Correspondents Award, 1947; George Eastman House award, 1955. Home: San Ysidro Ranch, Montecito, Santa Barbara, Cal. Died May 18, 1958; buried Santa Barbara.

COLMORE, Charles Blayney (kŏl'mōr), bishop; b. Victoria, Tenn., Mar. 31, 1879; s. Robert Lionel and Priscilla Diana (Addenbrooke) C.; B.A., U. of South, 1898, M.A., 1900, B.D., 1903, D.D., 1914; m. Sarah Rogers Palmer, Nov. 18, 1903; children—Henry Perrine, Charlotte Knight, Sarah Addenbrooke, Robert Lionel, Charles Blayney, Margaret Priscilla, John Palmer. Ordained deacon P.E. Ch., 1903, priest, 1904; in charge at Pulaski, Tenn., 1903-05; rector Cathedral Parish, Havana, Cuba, 1905-13; consecrated bishop P.E. Ch. in P.R., 1913; retired from active duty, 1947. Mem. Alpha Tau Omega. Democrat. Club: University. Address: Box 1031, Winter Park, Fla. Died June 28, 1950; buried Winter Park.

COLNON, Aaron (kōl'nŏn), corp. exec.; b. Chgo., Nov. 14, 1894; s. John E. and Helen M. (Neems) C.; A.B., Loyola U., 1914; LL.B., Northwestern U., 1917; m. Marion C. Lydon, Apr. 25, 1925; children—John E., Helen M., Jane A., Peter A., Thomas A. Began as office asst. John E. Colnon & Co., 1914; exec. v.p. Chgo. Trust Co., 1930-31; pres. John E. Colnon & Co., 1931-—; pres. Fort Dearborn Mortgage Co., 1933-—; sec., dir. 208 S. La Salle St. Corp.; chmn. Great Lakes Dredge & Dock Co.; formerly trustee C., R.I.&Pacific Ry. Served as 1st lt. F.A., U.S. Army, 1917-19. Mem. Am. Bar Assn. Roman Catholic. Clubs: Chicago, Chicago Athletic, South Shore Country. Home: 6909 Cregier Av. Office: 208 S. La Salle St., Chgo. Died Nov. 13, 1950.

COLPITTS, Walter William (kōl'pĭts), consulting engr.; b. Moncton, N.B., Can., Sept. 17, 1874; s. Henry Herbert and Lucy Anne (Bissett) C.; B.Sc., McGill U., Montreal, 1899 (valedictorian; winner Brit. Assn. medal), M.Sc., 1901, LL.D., 1921; m. Florence Rossington, Oct. 15, 1907; children—Lucy Anne, Jeremy Rossington. Came to U.S., 1901, naturalized citizen, 1921. Began as office boy to chief engr. of Intercolonial Ry., 1891; served as draftsman, rodman and instrumentman on r.r. surveys; chief clk. to Sir Thomas Shaughnessy, pres. Canadian Pacific Ry., 1899-1900; transferred to constrn. dept., 1900-01; engaged in r.r. constrn., irrigation and power projects in Southwestern States and Mexico, 1901-13; mem. Coverdale & Colpitts, cons. engrs., New York, since 1913; dir. of the Bank of New York, Pepsi-Cola Co., The Budd Co., Carriers & General Corp., Celotex Corp.; trustee Bank of N.Y. Gov., McGill Univ. Mem. Am. Inst. Cons. Engrs., Am. Soc. C.E., Am. Ry. Engring. Assn., Engring. Inst. of Can., Alpha Delta Phi. Republican. Methodist. Clubs: Lawyers, Canadian (ex-pres.), Recess, Economic (New York); Nassau, Tiger Inn (Princeton); Chicago; Faculty (Montreal). Home: 75 Cleveland Lane, Princeton, N.J., (summer) Big Moose, N.Y. Office: 120 Wall St., N.Y.C. Died Dec. 23, 1951.

COLT, Harris Dunscomb, lawyer; b. N.Y.C., Mar. 19, 1861; s. Harris and Catherine (Dunscomb) C.; A.B., Yale, 1884; LL.B., Columbia, 1886; m. Elizabeth H. Bowne, Dec. 19, 1894 (dec. 1929); 1 son, H. Dunscomb. Admitted to N.Y. bar, 1886, since practiced in N.Y.C.; sr. mem. Curtis Mallet-Prevost Colt & Mosle. Mem. N.Y. State, N.Y.C. bar assns., Soc. Colonial Wars, Mayflower Descs., S.R. Clubs: Century, University, Downtown, Grolier, Yale. Home: 2 E. 70th St., N.Y.C. 21. Office: 63 Wall St., N.Y. C. 5. Died Sept. 27, 1959.

COLTON, Elizabeth Sweetser, Orientalist; b. Amherst, Mass.; d. Aaron Merrick and Z. Elizabeth (Gould) C.; grad. Am. Inst. of Sacred Lit., with certificate in all courses of Assyrian, Arabic, Hebrew langs.; 2 yrs. of supplementary work (inscriptions in Assyrian, Arabic classics) with Prof. F. K. Sanders, Yale, 1893-95; spl. student Radcliffe Coll., in Arabic, Sanskrit, Pali, 1904-05, U. of Berlin, 1905-06, taking courses in Arabic, Syriac, Assyrian, Sanskrit, Pali and Avestan; studied in India, 1906-08 (Sanskrit and Persian). Early prepared for concert stage in Paris and Munich, but gave up mus. career to be head of vocal music dept. at Miss Porter's Sch., Farmington, Conn., for 14 yrs.; has studied 54 langs. carefully, 20 critically, and speaks 6 langs. fluently. Lecturer on Oriental subjects. Mem. Am. Oriental Soc., Soc. of Bibl. Archaeology (London), Royal Asiatic Soc. of Great Britain and Ireland. Congregationalist. Address: 23 Park St., Easthampton, Mass. Died June 7, 1927.

COLTON, Ferry Barrows, writer, editor; b. Montpelier, Vt., Jan. 6, 1903; s. Willard Chapin and Elizabeth Barrows (Peck) C.; A.B., Amherst Coll., 1926; m. Charlotte L. Whiteford, Sept. 25, 1943; children—Elizabeth Craig, Robert George. Editorial worker, feature writer Springfield (Mass.) Daily & Sunday Republican, 1926-30; feature writer A.P., N. Y. City, 1930-31, asst. sci. editor, Washington, 1931-35; mem. editorial staff Nat. Geog. Mag., 1935-—, asst. editor, 1951-—. Fellow A.A.A.S.; mem. Nat. Assn. Sci Writers (pres. 1949), Delta Tau Delta, Kappa Theta. Conglist. Clubs: Nat. Press, Cosmos (Washington). Mem. of Nat. Geog. Soc., U.S. A.A.F., solar eclipse expedition to Brazil, 1947. Contbr. articles in Nat. Geog. Mag., Scientific Monthly. Home: 5416 32d St. N.W., Washington 15. Office: Nat. Geog. Mag., Washington 6. Died Aug. 10, 1954; buried Green Mount Cemetery, Montpelier, Vt.

COLUM, Mary M. (Mrs. Padraic Colum) (kŏl'ŭm), writer; b. Ireland; d. Charles and Maria (Gunning) Maguire; grad. of Nat. U. of Ireland, also Dominican Coll., Dublin; Pensionnat Sacre Coeur, Vaals, Holland; m. Padraic Colum, writer, of Dublin, 1912. Came to U.S., 1914. Lit. critic of The Forum and Century Mag.; apptd. guest prof. comparative lit. Columbia U., 1952. Contbr. Dial, Scribner's, New Republic, Saturday Review, Yale Review, etc. Awarded Guggenheim fellowship in lit. criticism, 1930, 38; John Ryder Randall gold medal by Georgetown Univ., for distinction in literature, 1934; $500 award for lit. criticism, Am. Inst. Arts and Letters, 1941. Mem. Nat. Inst. Arts and Letters. Author: From These Roots, 1937; Life and the Dream, 1947. Home: 415 Central Park W., N.Y.C. Died Oct. 22, 1957.

COLVER, Benton Noble, otolaryngologist; b. Wellington, O., June 3, 1880; s. Byron Henry and Josephine L. (Noble) C.; A.B., Albion (Mich.) Coll., 1914; M.D., Am. Med. Missionary Coll., 1904, U. Pa., 1911; m. Agnes Grace Kellogg, July 14, 1908; children—William Kellogg, Nancy, Yost. Res. phys. Nat. Cash Register Plant, Dayton, O., 1904-05; pathologist Battle Creek (Mich.) Sanitarium, 1905-10, chief dept. otolaryngology, 1911-29, prof. otolaryngology, faculty Coll. Med. Evangelists Los Angeles, since 1929; head dept. otolaryngology White Meml. Hosp. since 1929. Served with M.C., U.S. Army, World War I. Fellow A.C.S.; mem. A.M.A., Am. Acad. Ophthalmology and Otolaryngology, Am. Laryngol., Rhinol., Otol. Soc., Royal Soc. Medicine (Eng.), Southwestern Mich. Triol. Soc., Calif. State Med. Soc., Los Angeles Co. Med. Soc., Los Angeles Soc. Ophthalmology and Otolaryngology, Detroit Soc. Otolaryngology, Phila. Otol. Soc. (charter mem.), Seventh Day Adventist. Contbr. articles med. jours. Home: 1650 Melrood Dr. Offices: 1509 Wilson Av., Glendale 7, Cal. Deceased.

COLVIN, Addison Beecher, state ofcl.; b. Glens Falls, N.Y., 1858; ed. Glens Falls Acad.; m. Marie Louise Hees, 1882. Became a printer; editor Glens Falls Messenger and Glens Falls Daily Times; pres. Glens Falls Trust Co., Glens Falls Gas Co.; officer in numerous corps. Treas. State N.Y., 1893—. Pres. N.Y. State Republican League of Clubs. Address: Glens Falls, N.Y. Deceased.

COLVIN, Allan DeWitt, pub. utilities exec.; b. Troy, N.Y., Nov. 26, 1883; s. Henry and Alice D. (Hastings) C.; C.E., Rensselaer Poly. Inst., 1906; m. Lena H. Marshall, Oct. 27, 1917; 1 son, Henry M. Asst. to Dr. William M. Robb, cons. engr., Troy, 1906-07; asst. supt. elec. dept. Troy Gas Co., 1907-09; asst. in physics and elec. engring. Rensselaer Poly. Inst., 1909-11; asst. to gen. mgr. and asst. gen. mgr. Hartford Electric Light Co., 1911-21, gen. mgr., 1921-29; exec. v.p., dir. Conn. Power Co., 1929, now pres.; incorporator Savs. Bank of New London; dir. Hartford Elec. Light Co., Union Bank and Trust Co. (New London). Trustee Public Library of New London; life trustee Rensselaer Poly. Inst. Profl. engr. Conn. Mem. Am. Inst. E.E., Conn. Soc. C.E., Rensselaer Soc. Engrs., Sigma Xi, Tau Beta Pi. Clubs: Thames, Country (New London); University (Hartford). Home: 8 Nathan Hale St. Office: 31 Union St., New London, Conn. Died Mar. 11, 1950; buried Troy, N.Y.

COLVIN, D(avid) Leigh, prohibitionist; b. S. Charleston, O., Jan. 28, 1880; s. David Taylor and Maria (Larkin) C.; student Am. Temperance U., Harriman, Tenn.; A.B., Ohio Wesleyan U., 1900; studied U. Cal., U. Chgo.; Ph.D., Columbia, 1913; m. Mamie White, Sept. 19, 1906 (dec. 1955); 1 dau., Virginia (Pierson). Pres. Intercoll. Prohibition Assn., 1899-1908 and 1912-20; v.p. Nat. Temperance Council, 1913-23; v.p. World Prohibition Federation, 1918-34, treas. 1934-48; pres. Nat. Temperance and Prohibition Council, 1936-37, Internat. Reform Fedn. (Washington), 1937—; exec. sec. Prohibition Nat. Campaign Com., 1916; sec. Com. of 60 on Nat. Prohibition, 1916-20; sec. Nat. Legislative Conf., 1917-25; treas. United Com. on War Temperance Activities in Army and Navy, 1917-20; a speaker of Flying Squadron in campaign for law enforcement, 1921-24; Prohibition nominee U.S. Senate, N.Y. State, 1916; mayor N.Y.C., 1917; v.p. U.S., 1920; Pres. U.S., 1936. Served as speaker to men in promotion of patriotism, World War, rank of captain U.S. Army, Nat. legislative supt. Flying Squadron Found., 1923-24. Washington editor Nat. Enquirer, Indpls., 1923-24; sec. United Com. for Prohibition Enforcement, 1924-33; chmn. Prohibition Nat. Com., 1926-32; mem. Nat. Conf. of Orgns. Supporting 18th Amendment (v.p.); mem. Prohibition Bd. of Strategy, 1931; sec. Nat. Temperance Council; nominee of Law Preservation Party for U.S. Senate, 1932; treas. Nat. Prohibition Emergency Com., 1933; speaker, leader The New Crusade for Nat. Prohibition. President World Prohibition Fedn. (London). 1948. Methodist. Mem. Alpha Tau Omega. Author: Bicameral Principle in the New York Legislature, 1913; Prohibition in the United States, 1926. Contbr. numerous articles on Prohibition. Has spoken in over 400 Am., European univs. and colls.; traveled 27,000 miles campaigning as nominee of prohibition party for Pres. of U.S., 1936. Home: 62 Crestwood Av., Yonkers, N.Y. Died Sept. 7, 1959.

COLVIN, H(oward) Milton (kŏl'vĭn), lawyer; b. Bourbon, Ind., Sept. 7, 1886; s. John Wesley and Violet May (Croco) C.; A.B., U. of Wash., 1910; LL.B., Yale, 1912, J.S.D., 1926; attended l'Académie de Droit Internat., The Hague, summers 1931, 32; m. Katharine Ostrander, Feb. 4, 1922; children—Milton, Katharine, John Tower. Supervisor of schs., P.I., 1906-08; instr. Spanish, U. Wash., 1910; admitted to Okla. bar, 1912, practice at Tulsa, 1912-15; acting head of dept. social scis., asst. prof. law, U. of Ariz., 1915-16; acting chancellor, Coll. City of El Paso (Tex.), 1916-17; asso. field dir., dept. mil. relief, Am. Red Cross, 1917-20; editor Arizona (monthly mag.), 1920; asst. prof. law, State U. of Mont., 1921-22, prof., 1922-27; prof. law, Tulane U., 1927-34; lectr. on U.S. and Latin Am. relations, Inst. of Foreign Affairs, Earlham Coll., 1934; lectr. on comparative law, Cath. U. of Am., 1934-37; counsel Fed. Emergency Relief Adminstrn., 1934-37; spl. counsel Resettlement Adminstrn., 1935-36; counsel U.S. Works Progress Adminstrn., 1936-39; chief legal research section, U.S. Housing Authority, 1939-41; spl. asst. gen. counsel, Fed. Works Agy. 1941-42; chief, mutual ownership war housing, legal sect., of rural housing, legal sect., Fed. Pub. Housing Authority, 1942-43; sec., and legal counsel, Def. Homes Corp., 1943-48; mem. Pres. Loyalty Bd. for Pub. Housing, 1948—; field counsel Pub. Housing Adminstrn., 1949—; prof. Internat. Law, Washington and Lee U., 1951-56. Del. Internat. Congress of Univs., Havana, Cuba, 1930; chmn. Com. Internat. Law Sources, Assn. Am. Law Schs., 1931-32; chmn. Consumers Council of Nat. Emergency Council, New Orleans, New Orleans Parish, 1934; mem. Nat. Civil Service Reform League. Mem. Am. Bar Assn. (chmn. com. on comparative laws of housing, 1938-40), Fed. Bar Assn. (chmn. com. on cooperation with Inter-Am. Bar Assn., 1944-46. Riccobono Seminar of Roman Law Am., Am. Soc. Internat. Law, chmn. com. on coordination of Inter-Am. law), League of Nations Assn. (nat. adv. com., 1925-45), UN League of Lawyers (pres.), Order of Coif, Phi Delta Phi; dir. thirty years survey crim. cts. of New Orleans for Pres'. Research Com. on Social Trends, 1931-32; mem. bd. dirs. Internat. Assn. of Lawyers (Vienna); v.p. Am. Assn. Auditeurs de l'Académie de Droit Internat. (The Hague), 1934-37; adjoint sec.-gen. Internat. Congress of Comparative Law, The Hague, 1932; mem. 8th Am. Sci. Congress, 1940. Mason. Author: Path of Civil Law in the United States (Paris), 1933; "Casus Belli" (treatise in Ency. Social Sciences, Vol. III), 1935; Roman and Civil Law Elements in the Sources of the Law of the United States (Vol. III, Studi In Memoria De Aldo Albertoni, pub. Milan, Italy), 1935; "Participation of the United States of America with the Latin American Republics in the Common Heritage of Roman and Civil Law" (Vol. X, Eighth American Scientific Congress, pub. by U.S. State Department, Washington), 1943. Contbr. to legal journals in U.S. and articles in Spanish to law reviews in Paraguay, Cuba, Spain. Club: Yale (Washington). Home: 103 McDowell St., Lexington, Va. Office: 900 N. Lombardy St., Richmond, Va. Died Aug. 28, 1956; buried Stonewall Jackson Cemetery, Lexington, Va.

COLVIN, Mamie White (Mrs. D. Leigh Colvin), (kŏl'vĭn), ex-national president W.C.T.U.; b. Westview, O., June 12, 1883; d. Rev. Levi and Mary Belle (Hudelson) White; A.B., Wheaton (Ill.) College, 1905; student Columbia University, 1906-07, and 1909-10; Doctor of Art of Oratory, Staley College of the Spoken Word, Boston, Massachusetts, 1937; LL.D., Houghton College, June 1946, Wheaton Coll., 1947; L.H.D., Southwestern U., 1948; m. D. Leigh Colvin, September 19, 1906; 1 dau., Virginia Leigh (Pierson). Winner of silver, gold, grand gold, diamond and grand diamond medals in national oratorical contest; winner of coll., state (Ill.), interstate and nat. intercollegiate oratorical prizes in contests of Intercollegiate Prohibition Assn., 1904. Pres. N.Y. County of W.C.T.U., 1916-21, state v.p., 1921-26, state pres., 1926-44; v.p. Nat. W.C.T.U., 1933-44, pres., 1944—; 1st vice pres. World's W.C.T.U., 1950—; pres. Prohibition Trust Fund Assn., 1932—; 1st v.p. Nat. Temperance & Prohibition Council, 1949-51. Prohibition candidate for Congress (spl. election), 1918, for lt. gov., 1918, for mem. of Assembly, 1923. Del. Quadrennial Gen. Conf., M.E. Ch., Columbus, Ohio, 1936; del. to gen. conference of Methodist Ch., 1948. Member D.A.R., League of Women Voters, Wheaton Coll. Scholastic Honor Soc., Nat. Council of Women (bd. dirs.). Mem. Business and Professional Women's Club. Attended Yale Sch. of Alcohol Studies, summer, 1944. Methodist. Editor in chief, Union Signal (official organ Nat. W.C.T.U.). Contbr. to temperance periodicals. Home: 1885 Overbrook Av., Clearwater, Fla. Died Oct. 30, 1955; buried Westfield, Ind.

COLYER, Douglas, officer British air force; b. Gravesend, Kent, Eng., Mar. 1, 1893; s. Henry Charles and Charlotte (Hill) C.; B.A., St. Catharine's Coll., Cambridge U., 1922. Became 2d lt., Lincolnshire Regt., 1915; transferred to Royal Flying Corps, 1916; served in France and Palestine, 1915-18; student Royal Air Force Staff Coll., 1929; air adviser to Latvian Govt., 1930-31; air attaché, British embassy, Paris, France, 1936-40; dir. gen. of personal services British Air Ministry, 1940; air officer comdg. No. 15 Group, Coastal Command, 1942; asst. chief of air staff (policy), 1943-44; head Royal Air Force delegation, British Joint Staff Mission, Washington, D.C., 1944—. Decorated Companion of Bath, Distinguished Flying Cross (British), Officer Legion of Honor (France), Order of Polonia Restituta, 2d class (Poland). Clubs: Boodle's (London); Army and Navy (Washington). Address: British Joint Staff Mission, Public Health Bldg., Washington, D.C. Died Sept. 11, 1956.

COMBS, George W. newspaper corr.; b. Clay County, Ky., Dec. 30, 1877; s. Tinsley and Mary (Burns) C.; ed. Agrl. and Mech. Coll. (now U. of Kentucky) and Sue Bennett Memorial Sch., London, Ky.; m. Margaret Lyttle, Aug. 21, 1901 (dec.); children—Ethel (Mrs. William G. Biederman), Leila Margaret (Mrs. Claude W. Leathers), Maj. W. Edgar, U.S.M.C., Leonora Y. (Mrs. Joseph H. Green). Became Washington corr. Baltimore Sun, 1908, now ret. Club: National Press (treas. 1943—, chmn. bd. govs. 1936, Washington). Home: 6239-33d St. N.W., Washington. Died Dec. 5, 1958; buried Fort Lincoln Cemetery, Washington.

COMBS, J. M. (kōmz), ex-congressman, judge; b. Center, Tex., July 7, 1889; s. Frank and May (Beck) C. Admitted to Tex. bar; engaged in gen. law practice, 1918-23, 25-33, 43-45; dist. judge 75th Judicial Dist. of Tex., 1923-25; justice Appellate Court, 1933-43; mem. 79th to 82d Congresses, 2d Tex. Dist. Democrat. Home: 2250 Ashley St., Beaumont, Tex. Died Aug. 22, 1953.*

COMBS, James Horton, business exec.; b. nr. Mt. Sterling, Ky., Aug. 28, 1880; s. Alfred and Esther (Horton) C.; student U. Ky., 1897-1900; m. Edna Rubel, Sept. 21, 1904 (dec. 1944); children—Nancy (dec.), Esther. Treas. Combs Lumber Co., 1902, v.p., 1920-46, pres., 1946—; v.p., gen. mgr. Fayette Home Telephone Co., Lexington, Ky., 1925-27; exec. v.p. Ashland (Ky.) Home Telephone Co., 1927-28; dir. First Nat. Bank & Trust Co. of Lexington, Lexington Water Co., Ashland Oil and Refining Co. Mem. bd. trustees Julius Marks Sanitoria. Served as food adminstrn. Lexington, Fayetee County, World War I; first Fed. prohibition dir. for Ky. Mem. C. of C., Kappa Alpha. Presbyn. (deacon). Clubs: Lexington Country, Idle Hour Country, Lexington, Tom Combs (polit.). Home: Wellington Arms. Office: 439 E. Main St., Lexington, Ky. Deceased.*

COMBS, Morgan Lafayette, coll. pres.; b. Honaker, Va.; s. Lafayette and Emily Frances (Thompson) C.; A.B., U. Richmond, LL.D., 1952; A.M., U. Chgo.; Ed.M., Harvard, Ed.D.; student at Univ. of Berlin, summer 1935; married Eulalia Hilliard; children—Morgan LaFayette (dec.), Robert Hilliard; Teacher and prin. in pub. and pvt. schs.; supt. of schs., Buchanan County, Va., 1917-22; state supervisor of secondary edn., Va., 1922-26; prof. secondary edn., Boston U., 1926-27; state dir. of ednl. research and surveys, Va., 1927-29; pres. Mary Washington Coll. of Univ. of Virginia, 1929—. Prof. of edn., Coll. of William and Mary, summer, 1927, George Washington U., summer, 1928. Trustee Bluefield (Va.) Coll., 1920-40; mem. bd. of trustees, Fork Union Mil. Acad.; v.p. Va. Assn. Colleges and Universities, 1935; dir. Coop. Edn. Assn. of Va., 1923-35; chmn. Va. Com. on Secondary Schs. Southern Assn. Colls. and Secondary Schs., 1922-26; mem. Nat. Com. on Administration of Teacher Training; delegate to World Federation of Education Associations, Dublin, Ireland, 1933, 53; mem. Citizen's Com. for Reorgn. Exec. Br. Govt.; mem. panel Indsl. and Labor Relations. Mem. legal adv. bd. Selective Service, Buchanan County, 1917-18; director War Savings, Buchanan County, 1917; in mil. service, 1918. Mem. American Association of School Administrators, N.E.A., Va. Social Science Assn., Interracial Commn., Phi Beta Kappa, Tau Kappa Alpha, Phi Delta Kappa, Alpha Phi Sigma, Am. Legion. Mem. bd. dirs. Fredericksburg, Va., Chamber of Commerce, 1924-41. Democrat. Baptist. Clubs: Chamber of Commerce, Young Democrats, Kiwanis (bd. dirs. 1930-33), Mansfield Hall Country. Wrote: Efficiency in Relation to Size of High Schools, 1928. Contbr. to Jour. of Edn., High Sch. Quart., Sch. Rev. Apptd. one of 5 Am. educators forming commn. to study ednl. systems of Germany and Austria, and traveled and studied in Europe, summer 1935, under auspices Carl Schurz Memorial Foundation for development of cultural relations between U.S. and German-speaking countries. Home: Fredericksburg, Va. Died October 25, 1955; buried family plot in Oak Hill Cemetery, Fredericksburg.

COMEAUX, C(harles) Stewart, mfg. exec.; b. Bayou Goula, La., Dec. 6, 1889; s. C. Lucas and Lillie Lee (Winfree) C.; student La. State U., law sch., 1911; m. Margaret S. Gregory, Oct. 16, 1915. Entered trade assn. work, 1912; formed Inst. of Makers of Explosives, 1913, served as exec. sec., treas. to 1952, now adv.; organizer Sporting Arms & Ammunition Mfrs. Inst., N.Y.C., 1926, served exec. sec.-treas. to 1952, now adv. Treas. Wildlife Mgmt. Inst. (Washington), 1946—; pres. N.Y. post Am. Ordnance Assn., 1948-50, nat. dir. 1950—; spl. asst. to Chief Ordnance, U.S. Army 1942-44. Mem. Hon. Ordnance Res. (retired with Army Commendation and Oak Leaf Cluster), Mil. Order World Wars, Am. Legion, Res. Officers Assn. of U.S., Nat. Rifle Assn. (life mem.), Outdoor Writers Assn., Alumni Fedn. (La. State U.). Episcopalian. Mason (32°, K.T.). Clubs: Army and Navy (Washington); Larchmont (N.Y.) University; Winged Foot Golf (Mamarouek, N.Y.). Home: Coronado, Oklawaha, Fla. Office: 250 E. 43d St., N.Y.C. 17. Died Dec. 1954.

COMEY, Arthur Coleman (kō'mē), city planner, regional planner and landscape architect; b. Somerville, Mass., Sept. 6, 1886; s. Arthur Messinger and Kate (Coleman) Comey; A.B., cum laude, Harvard, 1907; Harvard Sch. of Landscape Architecture, 1904-07; m. Eugenia Louise Jackson, Oct. 2, 1915; children—Katherine, Richard Jackson; m. 2d, Janet I. Mowry, June 26, 1930; married third, Elizabeth G. Pattee, July 25, 1950; m. 4th, Janet Mowry, Jan. 24, 1954. Supt. parks, Dixon, Ill., 1908, Utica, N.Y., 1909-10; city planner Milwaukee County, Wis., 1910, St. Paul, 1911; cons., from 1912; zoning dir. Boston City Planning Bd., 1922-24; lectr. Harvard Sch. of Landscape Architecture, 1928-29; asst. prof. Harvard Sch. City Planning, 1930-36; asso. prof. Harvard Dept. of Regional Planning, 1937-40. Cons., Houston, Tex.; Dover, N.J.; Detroit; Milw.; Birmingham, Mich.; Manchester, N.H.; Portland, Me.; Meriden, Conn.; also to Boston and other N.E. cities; UN Hdqrs. Commn.; T.V.A. Recipient 1st prize in Richmond (Cal.) competition. Member Mass. Homestead Com., 1913-19. Town planner, U.S. Housing Corp., 1918-19, World War. Fellow Am. Soc. Landscape Architects; mem. Am. Inst. of Planners (ex-gov.), Am. Soc. C.E., Boston Soc. Landscape Architects (pres.), Am. Inst. Cons. Engrs., Mass. Fed. Planning Bds., Am. Planning and Civic Association, Mass. Governor's Com. on Open Spaces, Trustees of Public Reservations, President's Conf. on Home Building and Home Ownership. Consultant, Nat. Resources Planning Board, 1934-43 (mem. urbanism committee, local planning com.), Maine State Planning Bd., Mass. State Planning Bd., New England Regional Planning Commission. Clubs: Harvard Faculty, Appalachian Mountain, Chocorua Mountain (ex-v.p.), Harvard Mountaineering, Ski Club of Great Britain, Harvard Ski Club. Author: Houston—Tentative Plans, 1913; Regional Planning Theory, 1923; Transition Zoning (Harvard City Planning Studies, V.), 1933; State and National Planning Classification (with K. McNamara), 1937; Planned Communities (with M. Wehrly), 1940; Integration of the New England Regional Plan, 1942; Sudbury Valley Regional Planning (with Howard M. Turner), 1950. Editor: City and Regional Planning Papers, by A. Bettman (Harvard City Planning Studies, XIII), 1946. Asso. editor: Nat. Municipal Rev., 1927-32. Home: Kittery Point, Me. Died Jan. 26, 1954.

COMFORT, Frank J., lawyer; b. Mason City, Ia., May 30, 1890; s. Thomas Francis and Ellen (Powers) C.; student Iowa State College, 1908-09, University of Iowa, 1909-13; LL.B., Drake University, 1913; married Marie Anna Bittorf, August 17, 1921; children—Elizabeth Ellen, Frank Bittorf. Admitted to Iowa bar, 1913; law clerk, Cummings, Hume & Bradshaw, Des Moines, Ia., 1913-14; law clerk Fidelity and Casualty Ins. Co., N.Y. City, 1914, claim examiner in Des Moines, 1914-15; U.S. referee in bankruptcy, Southern Dist. of Iowa, 1915-30; gen. practice of law, Des Moines, since 1916; sr. partner with George P. Comfort, 1920-38; mem. Comfort, Comfort & Irish since 1938; pres. Des Moines Bldg. Co.; dir. and counsel Ins. Plan Savings & Loan Assn. Served in O.T.C., Camp Pike, July-Nov. 1918. Member Iowa State Law Examining Board. Dem. Nat. committeeman, 1940-44; Democratic presidential elector, Iowa, 1944; del. Dem. Nat. Convs., 1932-40; del.-at-large, Dem. National Conv., Phila., 1948. Mem. Polk County, Iowa State and Am. bar assns., Kappa Sigma, Knight of Columbus. Clubs: Wakonda, Des Moines (both of Des Moines). Home: 4230 Lowell Dr. Office: 1120 Savings & Loan Bldg., Des Moines 9, Ia. Died Nov. 1, 1955; buried Glendale Cemetery, Des Moines, Ia.

COMFORT, Mandred Whitset, physician; b. Hillsboro, Tex., June 10, 1895; s. Edgar Whitset and Eulah (Stoud) C.; A.B., Austin Coll., 1916, LL.D., 1954; M.D., Univ. of Tex., 1921; M.S. in Neurology, Univ. of Minn., 1926; m. Aurelia Jones, Mar. 14, 1931. Teacher Sterling City, Tex., 1916-17; adj. prof. of anatomy, Univ. of Tex., 1921-23; fellow Mayo Foundation, Rochester, Minn., 1923; apptd. asso. in medicine The Mayo Clinic, July 1, 1928, prof. of medicine The Mayo Foundation Grad. Sch., 1946—; cons. physician St. Mary's Hosp., 1928—; cons. Nat. Cancer Inst., 1946-50, and 1952—. Member board of governors The Mayo Clinic. Diplomate American Bd. Internal Medicine. Fellow A.M.A., A.C.P., mem. Assn. Am. Physicians, Am. Gastro-Enterological Assn. (pres. 1957), Southern Minn. Med. Assn., Central Soc. for Clin. Research, Minn. Soc. Internal Med., Alumni Assn. of Mayo Foundation, Sigma Xi, Alpha Kappa Kappa, Alpha Omega Alpha. Presbyterian. Contbr. numerous articles on gastroenterology br. of internal medicine to professional jours. Home: 701 Ninth Av. S.W. Office: 102-110 Second Av. S.W., Rochester, Minn. Died Aug. 7, 1957; buried Hillcrest Meml. Park, Dallas.

COMFORT, William Wistar, coll. pres.; b. Germantown, Pa., May 27, 1874; s. Howard and Susan Foulke (Wistar) C.; A.B., Haverford Coll., 1894, LL.D., 1940; A.B., Harvard, 1895, A.M., 1896, Ph.D., 1902; Litt.D., U. Pa., 1917; LL.D., U. Md., 1918, Lake Forest U., 1925; m. Mary Lawton Fales, 1902. Instr. Romance langs. Haverford Coll., 1897-98, instr. and asso. prof., 1901-09, pres., 1917-40; travel and study in Europe, 1898-1901; prof. Romance langs. and lits., head dept. Cornell U., 1909-17. Mem. Modern Lang. Assn. Am. Mem. Soc. of Friends. Author: French Prose Composition, 1908; The Choice of a College, 1925; Just Among Friends, 1941; Stephen Grellet: A Biography, 1942; William Penn: A Tercentenary Estimate, 1944; Quakers in the Modern World, 1949. Editor: Calderon's La Vida es sueno, 1904; Les Maitres de la critique litteraire au dixneuvieme siecle, 1909; Characters Types in the old French Chansons de Geste, 1906; Rivarol's L'Universalite de la Langue Francasie, 1919. Translator: The Quest of the Holy Grail (translated from the Old French), 1926; The Clermont Assizes—Abbe Flechier's Memoires sur les Grand Jours d'Auverque, 1937. Contbr. Am. and European mags. Home: Haverford, Pa. Died Dec. 24, 1955; buried Haverford Friends Meeting, Haverford, Pa.

COMPTON, Karl Taylor, physicist; b. Wooster, O., Sept. 14, 1887; s. Elias and Otelia (Augspurger) C.; Ph.B., Coll. of Wooster, 1908, M.S., 1909, D.Sc., 1923; Ph.D., Princeton, 1912, D.Sc., 1930; D.Sc., Lehigh U., 1927, Stevens Inst. Tech., 1931, Clarkson Coll., 1932, Boston U., 1932, Columbia, 1940, N.Y.U., 1946, W.Va. U., 1948, Cambridge U., 1952, Israel Inst. Tech., 1954; LL.D., Harvard, 1930, U. Wis., 1934, Middlebury Coll., 1936, Williams Coll., 1936, Johns Hopkins, 1937, Franklin and Marshall Coll., 1937, Northeastern U., 1938, St. Lawrence U., 1939, U. Cal., 1941, Northwestern U., 1942, Tufts Coll., 1943, Norwich U., 1944, Coll. of William and Mary, 1947, Rollins Coll., 1949; D. Eng., Bklyn. Poly. Inst., 1930, Case Sch. Applied Sci., 1931, Rutgers U., 1941, Worcester Poly. Inst., 1946; Dr. Applied Sci., Ecole Polytechnique, Montreal, 1944; L.H.D., U. Hawaii, 1947; Dr. Tech., Finnish Inst. Tech., 1949; m. Rowena Rayman (dec.); 1 dau., Mary Evelyn (Mrs. Russell Alderman) m. 2d, Margaret Hutchinson; children—Jean Corrin (Mrs. C. W. Boyes), Charles Arthur. Instr. chemistry Coll. Wooster, 1909-10; instr. physics Reed Coll., Portland, Ore., 1913-15; asst. prof. physics Princeton, 1915-19, prof., 1919-30, chmn. dept. physics, 1929-30; pres. Mass. Inst. Tech., 1930-48, chmn. of cor., 1948-54. Trustee Am. Optical Co., 1952-54; dir. Fed. Res. Bank Boston, 1951-54. Gen. Foods Corp., 1952-54, Gen. Motors Corp., 1952-54, High Voltage Engring. Corp., 1950-54, John Hancock Mut. Life Ins. Co., 1948-54, McGraw-Hill Pub. Co., 1949-54, Research Corp. of N.Y., 1933-53, Tracerlab, 1948-54. Served as aero engr., Signal Corps, U.S. Army, 1917; asso. sci. attache Am. Embassy, Paris, 1918. Chmn. research and development bd. Nat. Mil. Establishment, 1948-49; cons. physicist Dept. Agr. and Gen. Electric Co., 1924-30; mem. vis. com. U.S. Bur. Standards, 1931-41; mem. bus. adv. and planning council Dept. Commerce, 1933-36; mem. adv. com. U.S. Weather Bur., 1935-48; mem. Adv. Com. on Research for Railroads, 1935-36; mem. War Resources Bd., 1938-40; mem. nat. defense research com. Office Sci. Research and Development, 1940-47, chief Office of Field Service, 1943-45, dir. Pacific br., 1945; mem. Sci. Intelligence Mission to Japan, 1945; mem. Baruch Rubber Survey Com., 1942; chmn. U.S. Radar Mission to U.K., 1943; spl. rep. sec. war in S.W. Pacific Area, 1943-44; mem. Secs. War and Navy Com. on Postwar Research, 1944; mem. sec. war's spl. adv. com. on atomic bomb, 1945; chmn. Research Bd. Nat. Security, 1945-46, Joint Chiefs of Staff Evaluation Bd. on Atomic Bomb Tests, 1946, Research and Development Bd., 1948-49, New Eng. Com. on Atomic Energy, 1954, President's Adv. Commn. on Universal Tng., 1946-47; mem. Naval Research Adv. Com., 1946-48, War Dept. Research Adv. Panel, 1946-48, Nat. Security Tng. Commn., 1951-54. Trustee Edison Found., 1946-53, Ford Found., 1946-51, Meml. Found. Neuro-Endocrine Research, 1932-47, New Eng. Indsl. Research Found., 1941-48, Nutrition Found., Inc. (chmn. bd. trustees 1941-54), Rockefeller Found. and Gen. Edn. Bd., 1940-53 (exec. com. 1941-42, nominating com. 1941-44), Sloan Found., 1942-54, Sloan-Kettering Inst., 1947-54, Brookings Inst., 1940-50, Norwich U., 1935-50, Princeton (charter 1952-54), Western Coll., Oxford, O., 1947-49, Population Council, 1953-54; mem. adv. bd. Bartol Research Found., 1927-36, Watumull Found., 1944-54; chmn. governing bd. Am. Inst. Physics, 1931-36; chmn. com. on engring. schs. E.C.P.D., 1932-39; chmn. Sci. Adv. Bd., 1933-35. Chmn. adv. com. sci. research Nat. Assn. Mfrs., 1937-41; mem. Mass. Commn. on Stabilization of Employment, 1931-33; dir. Boston C. of C., 1932-33; chmn. instns. div. Boston Community Fund, 1938-39; chmn. new products com. New Eng. Council, 1939-41. Cons. Brit. Parliamentary and Sci. Com., 1954. Pilgrim Trust lectr. Royal Soc. London, 1943. Fellow Am. Phys. Soc. (councillor; v.p. 1925-27; pres. 1927-29), Optical Soc. of Am.; mem. A.A.A.S. (pres. 1935-36; exec. com. 1931-40), Am. Philos. Soc., Am. Chem. Soc., Franklin Inst., Am. Inst. E.E., Am. Soc. M.E., Inst. Aero. Scis., Am. Acad. Arts and Scis., Am. Inst. N.Y., Am. Soc. Engring. Edn. (v.p 1937; pres 1938-39), Phi Beta Kappa, Sigma Xi, Alpha Tau Omega, Tau Beta Pi. Recipient Rumford medal Am. Acad. Arts and Scis., 1931, Medal for Merit, 1946, Washington Award, 1947, Marcellus Hartley medal Nat. Acad. Sci., 1947, Lamme medal Am. Soc. Engring. Edn., 1949, Col. Thacher E. Nelson award Advt. Club Boston, 1949, William Procter prize for sci. achievement Sci. Research Soc. of Am., 1950, Hoover medal Founder Engring. Socs., 1951, Joseph Priestley award Dickinson Coll., 1954; Hon. Comdr. Order Brit. Empire, 1948; Comdr. Royal Norwegian Order St. Olav, 1948; French Legion of Honor, 1951. Presbyn. Clubs: Tavern, Algonquin, Union, University (Boston); University (N.Y.C.); Cosmos (Washington). Home: 100 Memorial Dr., Cambridge, Mass. Died June 22, 1954.

COMPTON, Richard J., dir. Compton Advertising Inc.; b. St. Louis, Aug. 19, 1891; s. Richard J. and Cornelia (Letcher) C.; ed. pub. schs., St. Louis; m. Margaret Deacon, Feb. 22, 1916; dir. Lamb & Robinson, London. Served as 2d lt. field arty., U.S. Army, World War Gov. Am. Assn. Advt. Agencies. Republican. Episcopalian. Clubs: Racquet and Tennis, India House, River, Pilgrims (New York); Woodway (Glendale, Conn.); New Canaan (Conn.) Country; Ballast Reef (Darien, Conn.); Racquet, Queen City (Cincinnati); Dutchess Valley Shooting and Fishing; American Chesapeake; Rancho Santa Fe Golf. Home: Rancho Sante Fe, Calif. Office: 630 5th Av., N.Y. City 20. Died Feb. 6, 1951; buried Oak Hill Cemetery, Kirkwood, Mo.

COMPTON, Walter (legal name Walter A. Knobloch), bus. exec.; b. Charleston, S.C., Oct. 9, 1912; s. John W. and Aline V. (Rugheimer) K.; A.B., Roanoke Coll., Salem, Va., 1934; m. Frances M. Miller, July 22, 1940; children—John William II, Frances Aline, Frederica Maree. Began bus. career as editor Charleston (S.C.) County Record; instr. English, Roanoke Coll., Salem, Va., 1934-35; radio announcer-newscaster, stations WCSC (Charleston, S.C.), WIS (Columbia, S.C.), 1936; program dir. sta. WFBC (Greenville, S.C.), 1936-37; news editor, chief of special events, sta. WOL (Washington, D.C.), also MBS White House announcer, since 1937; originator of radio program, Double or Nothing, 1940, master of ceremonies, 1940-43; creator of program Background for News; became a pioneer television daily news commentator, 1947; gen. mgr. television sta. WTTG, Washington, D.C. (DuMont network). Mem. Radio Corrs. Assn., Kappa Alpha, Alpha Psi Omega, Blue Key. Address: 12th and E. Sts., Washington, D.C. Died Dec. 9, 1959.

COMPTON, William Randolph, banker; b. Lockport, N.Y., June 27, 1866; s. James Robinson and Frances Hope (Lewis) C.; ed. pub. schs.; m. Caroline Louise Parker, of Dayton, O., Sept. 24, 1889; children—Randolph, William Randolph, Frances Hope. Began at 18 as clk. with Tootle & Hosea Co., wholesale dry goods, St. Joseph, Mo.; in banking business on own account, at Arlington, Kan., 1886-88; in banking at Macon, Mo., 1888-98; removed to St. Louis, 1908; pres. William R. Compton Co., investment bankers; apptd. receiver Kansas City Joint Stock Land Bank, 1927. Democrat. Presbyn. Mason (32°, K.T., Shriner). Address: 200 E. 66th St., N.Y.C. Died July 1957.

COMSTOCK, A(lexander) Barr, lawyer; b. Detroit, Mich., Oct. 29, 1886; s. Ezra Young and Nellie Preston (Barr) C.; student Boston Latin Sch., 1901-04; A.B., Harvard, 1908, LL.B., 1910; married Dorothy Dewey, Dec. 7, 1916 (deceased January 24, 1953); children—Alexander Barr, Dorothy Dewey. Admitted to Massachusetts bar, 1910; with legal department Boston Elevated Railway Co., 1910-12; practiced law, in Boston, 1912-42; mem. firm Goodwin, Parker, Raymond & Comstock, 1921-39; in Dept. of State, 1943-44; spl. asst. to atty. gen. assigned tax div., Dept. of Justice, since 1944. Now or formerly dir. of many business corps., including Comstock & Wescott, Incorporated. Capt. gas defense div., Chemical Warfare Service, U.S. Army, World War I; hon. discharge, 1918. Delegate to President's Smaller Business Conference, 1937. Formerly town meeting member, Brookline and Dedham. Formerly dir. City Missionary Society of Boston. Member Foreign Policy Assn. (mem. of council, Mass. br.), Mass. Br. League of Nations Assn. (dir. former chmn., exec. com.), Boston Citizens Com. for World Court (mem.

exec. com.), Mass. Br. of League to Enforce Peace (ex-chmn. com. on state orgn.), Institute on World Orgn. (co-chmn.), Am., Mass., Boston and Federal bar assns., Am. Soc. Internat. Law, Acad. of Polit. Science, Am. Legion. Episcopalian. Clubs: Cosmos, Harvard (Washington), Harvard (Boston). Contbr. various periodicals. Home: 1911 R St. N.W. Office: care Dept. Justice, Washington. Died Mar. 31, 1956.

COMSTOCK, Alzada, college prof.; b. Waterford, Conn., Nov. 23, 1888; d. Leolin Alison and Lucy Ella (Tefft) Comstock; grad. Williams Memorial Inst., 1906; A.B., Mt. Holyoke Coll., 1910, grad. work, 1911; student Chicago Sch. Civics and Philanthropy, 1911-12; A.M., Columbia, 1920, Ph.D., 1921; grad. work London Sch. Econ., 1919-20, Sorbonne, 1929; unmarried. Asst. in psychology Mt. Holyoke Coll., 1910-11, instr. econ., 1913-18, asst. prof. econ., 1918-27, prof. econ. since 1927. Asso. in econ. Barnard Coll., 1921-22. Contbg. editor Current History, also contbr. to New International Year Book, since 1943. Awarded Guggenheim fellowship, Geneva, Switz., and Hungary, 1926-27. Chmn. com. on internat. relations Am. Assn. U. Women, 1939-45; mem. fellowship com. Internat. Fedn. Univ. Women, 1942-46; mem. Am. Econ. Assn., Royal Economic Assn. Nat. Tax Assn., Phi Beta Kappa. Eighteen European trips. Author: State Taxation of Personal Incomes, 1921; Taxation in the Modern State, 1929. Contbr. many articles to professional publs. Home: 28 Silver St. Office: Mount Holyoke College, South Hadley, Mass. Died Jan. 15, 1960.

COMSTOCK, Sarah, author; b. Athens, Pa.; d. Walter and Louise Shipman (Saltmarsh) Comstock; A.B., Stanford. First work as spl. writer, San Francisco periodicals; short stories and articles in Harper's, Century, Outlook, North Am. Review, World's Work, Good Housekeeping, Ladies' Home Journal, etc.; serial novels in Woman's Home Companion; series of articles, The Western Farmer's Wife, The Mormon Woman, and The Western Woman Voter, in Collier's; The American Girl of Today, in Good Housekeeping, etc.; articles on the American scene in Harper's, and popular psychology articles in various magazines. Formerly editor dept. "Woman Today" in Collier's. Club: Town Hall. Author: The Soddy, 1912; Old Roads from the Heart of New York, 1915; The Valley of Vision, 1919; The Daughter of Helen Kent, 1921; Speak to the Earth, 1927; Roads to the Revolution, 1928; The Moon Is Made of Green Cheese, 1929. Address: 30 Charlton St., New York 14, N.Y. Died Jan. 20, 1960.

CONARD, Frederick Underwood, mfg. exec.; b. Bklyn., Dec. 17, 1891; s. George Powell and Helen Mary (Underwood) C.; M.E., Stevens Inst. Tech., 1915; m. Julia Ellmaker Hand, Sept. 12. 1917; children—Frederick Underwood, George Powell II, John Hand, Waller MacNiven. Various positions textile mfg., Bklyn., 1915-16; with Pub. Service Gas Co., Newark, N.J., 1916-17; with Underwood Corp. (formerly Underwood Typewriter Co.) since 1919, works mgr., 1929-38, v.p. since 1938; pres., dir. Niles-Bement-Pond Co. since 1947; dir. Ry. Equipment & Pub. Co., N.Y.C., Dime Savings Bank, Hartford, Hartford Gas Co., Smyth Mfg. Co., Phoenix State Bank & Trust Co. Chmn. bd. edn. West Hartford. Trustee Fairfield State Hosp. Served with A.E.F., U. S. Army, 1917-19. Mem. Nat. Assn. Mfrs., Hartford Co. Mfrs. Assn., S.R., Army Ordnance Assn., Soc. Am. Mil. Engrs., Reserve Officers Assn., Am. Legion, Newcomen Soc., Chi Phi. Republican. Conglist. Mason. Clubs: University, (Bridgeport, Conn., N.Y. City), Union League (Chicago), Hartford Golf, Hartford; Essex Yacht, Dauntless (Essex, Conn.). Home: 167 Steele Rd., West Hartford 7. Office: Charter Oak Blvd., West Hartford 1, Conn. Died Mar. 14, 1954.

CONAWAY, Charles Herman (kŏn'a-wā), farmer; b. Arlington, Ind., Apr. 22, 1885; s. Henry Lonso and Marian Josephine (Beckner) C.; student Marion Normal Coll., State Normal Sch., Terre Haute, Ind.; LL.B., Hamilton Coll. of Law, Chgo.; m. Ruby McCormick, Dec. 31, 1908; children—Opal Marie, Wallace Bernard, Margaret Josephine, Earl Rodney. Farmer in N.D., 1910—; twp. clk., pres. sch., twp. bd. Sec.-treas. Farmers Grain Dealers Assn. of N.D., 1930—. Farmers Nat. Grain Dealers Assn., 1932—; dir., sec. St. Joe Co-op Elevator Co.; gen. chmn. Northwest Shippers Adv. Bd. (Mpls.), chmn. County Dept. Adjustment Bd. Mem. Nat. Traffic Assn. Clubs: Kiwanis, City Commercial. Methodist. Elk. Lectr., editor. Address: Fargo, N.D. Died Aug. 25, 1958.

CONCANNON, Charles Cuthbert (kŏn'kăn'ŭn), chemist; b. Boston, Mar. 13. 1889; s. John Stephen and Gertrude (Kavanagh) C.; grad. Boston Latin Sch.; A.B., Harvard, 1911. Asso. with Dr. Jokichi Takamine, Japanese sci. and philanthropist, to 1922; chief of Chem. Div., Bur. Foreign and Domestic Commerce, U.S. Dept. of Commerce, 1922—, in charge of export licensing chemicals, 1948—. Chmn. Am. delegation 10th Internat. Congress of Chemistry, Rome, 1938; on leave from U.S. govt. as advisor to Chilean govt., 1943-44; advisor to Peruvian govt., 1945. Mem. Am. Inst. Chemists, Am. Chem. Soc., Am. Marketing Soc., Soc. for the Advancement of Mgmt. Clubs: University, Harvard (pres. 1951-52) (Washington); Harvard, Chemists (N.Y.C.); Harvard (Boston). Widely known as lectr., writer on econs., comml. development of chem. industry. Contbr. many articles on chem. topics. Home: 1200 16th St. N.W. Office: Dept. of Commerce, Washington. Died 1957.

CONCHESO, Aurelio Fernandez, Cuban diplomat; b. Sancti-Spiritus, Santa Clara, Cuba; student La Salle Coll.; Dr. Civil and Pub. Law, U. Havana; diplomas internat. and penal law, univs. Rome and Berlin; m. Zoila R. Mulet; children—Aurelio Enrique, Maria Teresa, Carlos Felipe. Former prof. penal law U. Havana; represented Cuba various internat. convs., including 18th Assembly League of Nations, Disarmament Commn., Geneva, others; sec. of justice during Five Mem. Govt. of Cuba, 1933; rep. Cuba in Germany as E.E. and M.P., 1934-38; sec. of edn., 1938-39; sec. of the presidency under Govt. of Gen. Batista, 1939-40; ambassador of Cuba to U.S., 1940-44; 53—; minister plenipotentiary to USSR, 1943; former magistrate Supreme Ct. of Cuba. Cuban rep. 2d Conf. Fgn. Ministers, Rio de Janeiro, 1943. Decorated Grand Cross Nat. Order of Merit Carlos Manuel de Cespedes; Grand Cross Cuban Red Cross; Order of Cadiz. Catholic. Author: To Liberty through Culture, 1939; also Reform in Penal Law; Essay on Criminal Policy; Literary Essay on Marti; other sci. publs. Address: Office of Cuban Embassy, 2630 16th St., Washington. Died Nov. 10, 1955.

CONDO, Gus S., lawyer; b. Lafayette, Ind., July 1, 1874; s. Samuel S. and Sarah Ann (Pottorf) C.; ed. pub. schs., Spencerian Business Coll. (Cleve.), Sprague Corr. Sch. of Law (Detroit); m. Nelle Kiley, June 30, 1902; 1 dau., Anne Agnes. Admitted to Ind. bar, 1895, since practiced at Marion; sr. partner law firm Condo & Caine; city atty. Marion, 1899; county atty. Grant County, 1904-06; mem. Ind. Ho. of Reps., 1904-09; dir. Marion Nat. Bank (Marion), Consol. Finance Corp. (Indpls.). Pres. Marion Assn. Commerce, 1918-21; dir. Marion Community Chest, Grant County Tuberculosis Assn., Izaak Walton League Am.; mem. Am.; Ind. State, Grant County bar assns. Republican. Catholic. Elk. Clubs: Mecca, Meshingomesia (Marion); Columbia (Indpls.). Home: 110 Wabash Av. Office: Marion Nat. Bank Bldg., Marion, Ind. Died 1957.*

CONDON, Herbert Thomas, dean; b. The Dalles, Ore., Mar. 17, 1870; s. Thomas and Cornelia (Holt) C.; B.S., U. of Ore., 1892; LL.B., U. of Mich., 1894; m. Maude Wilkins, Mar. 8, 1899; children—Harold Thomas, Robert Wilkins, Donald Francis, Jean Goltra (Mrs. Floyd M. Stanley), Herbert Thomas, Jr. Practice law, Eugene, Ore., 1894-96; newspaper work, 1897; registrar and comptroller, Ore. Agrl. Coll., Corvallis, 1897, U. of Idaho, 1898-1903; registrar and comptroller, U. of Wash., 1903-30, dean of men, 1930-40, dean of students, 1940-49, sec. bd. regents since 1919. Mem. Phi Gamma Delta. Republican. Conglist. Club: Kiwanis. Home: 1305 E. 43d St., Seattle 5, Wash. Died June 28, 1952.

CONE, Herman, textile co. exec.; b. 1895, N.Y. C.; Doctor of Textile Science (hon.), 1953; m. Louise Wolf; children—Herman, Alan. Pres. Cone Mills Corp., 1938—, chmn. bd., 1950—. Mem. joint civilian orientation conf. U.S. Dept. Defense, 1953. Named Man of Year, Phi Psi, N.C. State Coll., 1952. Address: Greensboro, N.C. Died Dec. 10, 1955.*

CONGER, Abraham Benjamin, judge; b. near Ty Ty, Ga., July 14, 1887; s. Abraham Benjamin and Elizabeth (Young) C.; student Norman Junior Coll., Norman Park, Ga. 1906; A.B., Mercer U., 1911, LL.B., 1912; m. Margaret Onys Willis, May 19, 1915; children—Margaret Elizabeth, Abraham Benjamin, Jr., James Willis, Leonard Hodges. Admitted to Ga. bar, 1912, and since practiced in Bainbridge, Ga. Gen. counsel Ga., Fla. & Ala. Ry. Co., 1925-27; dist. counsel S.A.L. Ry. Co., 1928—; dist. counsel Ga. Power & Light Co., 1933—; U.S. Dist. Judge, 1949—. Mem. Ga. Ho. of Reps. 1915-16; mayor of Bainbridge, 1922-23; trustee Bainbridge public schs., 1918-38. Served on Dem. Dist. Com., 1943-47; chmn. Bd. of Appeals, Fifth Dist. Selective Service for duration of war. Recipient citation from Pres. Wilson as 4-minute speaker; citation from Pres. Truman, for service with Selective Service System. Mem. Bainbridge C. of C., Albany Circuit Bar Assn. (pres.), Ga. Bar Assn. Am. Bar Assn ; Phi Delta Theta. Democrat. Baptist (deacon). Mason (Shriner). Clubs: Country; Rotary; Lynn Haven; Sportsman's. Home: E. Shotwell St., Bainbridge, Ga. Died Dec. 9, 1953; buried Oak City Cemetery, Bainbridge.

CONKEY, Henry Phillips, ex-pres. W. B. Conkey Co.; b. Chicago, Apr. 26, 1885; s. Walter B. and Kate (Phillips) C.; student U. of Chicago, 1903-05; m. Celia Sherwood, Jan. 7, 1925. Entered employ of W. B. Conkey Co., printers, binders, book mfrs., Chicago, 1905, v.p., 1919-23, pres., 1923-49, pres. and treas. since 1928; now advisor and cons. Rand McNally & Co., Chicago; asso. dir. Lumbermens Mut. Casualty Co. and mem. adv. bd. Ill. Mfrs. Div.; dir. Book Mfrs. Inst. (pres. 1944-46), Ind. Mfg. Assn.; past pres. Employing Bookbinders Assn. of America; mem. bd. dirs. Franklin Assn., Chicago; mem. Nat. Panel Arbitrators, Am. Arbitration Assn. Dir. Am. Red Cross, Washington, D.C., World War, 1918. Member Chicago Hist. Soc., Chicago Natural Hist. Mus. (life), Ill. Soc. Sons of Am. Revolution, Am. Inst. Graphic Arts, Delta Kappa Epsilon (Delta Delta Chapter). Republican. Episcopalian. Clubs: Chicago, University, South Shore Country (Chicago). Home: Greenway Farm, Middleburg, Va. Died Feb. 10, 1953; buried Rose Hill Cemetery, Chgo.

CONKLIN, Clifford Tremaine, agrl. editor; b. Struthers, O., July 18, 1890; s. William and Isabelle (Bidwell) C.; B.S., Ohio State U., 1916; m. Ora B. Kistler, June 3, 1913; children—Clifford Tremaine, Richard Kistler, Martha Jeanne. Engaged in county extension work, 1916-17; asst. prof. animal husbandry Ohio State U., 1917-25; exec. sec. Nat. Ayrshire Breeders' Assn., also editor Nat. Ayrshire Digest, 1925-52, ret. 1952. Mem. bd. Rutland (Vt.) Hosp.; bd. dirs. Brandin Free Pub. Library. Named to Hall of Fame, Dept. Animal Husbandry Ohio State U.; recipient Distinguished Service award Ayrshire Breeders Assn., 1951; honored by Dairy Shrine Club. Mem. Am. Soc. Animal Prodn., Am. Dairy Sci. Assn., Agrl. Soc. Methodist. Mason. Clubs: Saddle and Sirloin (pres.), La Boheme. Created head test plan; instituted approved sire and dam program, type classification plan. Home: 14 High St., Brandon, Vt. Died Apr. 6, 1956; buried Pinehill Cemetery, Brandon, Vt.

CONKLIN, Edwin Grant, biologist; b. Waldo, O., Nov. 24, 1863; s. Dr. Abram V. and Maria (Hull) C.; S.B., Ohio Wesleyan U., 1885, A.B., 1886; A.M., 1889; Ph.D., Johns Hopkins, 1891; hon. Sc.D., U. Pa., 1908, Ohio Wesleyan U., 1910, Yale, 1930; LL.D., Western Reserve U., 1925, Johns Hopkins, 1940, U. Pa., 1943, Princeton, 1945; m. Belle Adkinson, June 13, 1889 (died Mar. 7, 1940); children—Paul, Mary (Mrs. Samuel Masland, dec.), Isabel. Prof. biology Ohio Wesleyan, 1891-94; prof. zoölogy Northwestern, 1894-96, U. Pa., 1896-1908; prof. biology Princeton, 1908-33, emeritus, 1933—, spl. lecturer in biology. Trustee Woods Hole Lab., 1897—, also Woods Hole Oceanographic Instn.; pres. Bermuda Biol. Station, 1926-36. Fellow A.A.A.S. (pres. 1936), Am. Acad. Arts and Sciences; mem. Nat. Acad. Scis., Am. Soc. Zoölogists (pres. 1899), Assn. Am. Anatomists, Am. Soc. Naturalists (pres. 1912), Am. Philos. Soc. (sec. 1900-08, v.p., 1932-42, exec. officer, 1936-42, pres. 1942-45, 48—), Phila. Acad. Natural Sciences (v.p. 1901—), Phi Beta Kappa, Sigma Xi; mem. adv. bd. Wistar Institute; pres. Science Service, 1936-45; foreign mem. Royal Soc. of Edinburgh, Zoölogy Societé of London, Societé Belge de Biologie, Academie Royale de Belgique (1948), Societé Royale de Sci. Md. et Naturelle de Bruxelles, Königlich, Böhmische Gesellschaft der Wissenschaften. Lecturer; Harvey Soc., 1913; Harris Foundation, Northwestern, 1914; Hale Lectures, Nat. Acad. Sci., 1917; NcNair Lectures, U. N.C., 1920; Lowell Inst., 1922; Rice Inst. 1923; Sedgwick Meml., 1929; Potter Meml., Jefferson Med. Coll., 1930; Penrose Meml., Am. Philos. Soc., 1934; Milton Acad. War Meml., 1935; Barnwell Address, 1938; Sharp Lectures, Rice Inst., 1941. Co-editor Biological Bulletin, Journal of Experimental Zoölogy, Genetics. Author: Heredity and Environment; Mechanism of Evolution; Direction of Human Evolution; Synopsis of General Morphology; Future of Evolution; Revolt Against Darwinism; Science and the Faith of the Modern; Embryology and Evolution; Problems of Development; Biology and Democracy; Freedom and Responsibility; What Is Man?; Man, Real and Ideal; and about 200 other works on heredity, development, education, etc. Recipient of John J. Carty gold medal and award, 1942-43; Nat. Inst. Social Science gold medal, 1943. Home: 139 Broadmead, Princeton, N.J. Died Nov. 21, 1952.

CONKLING, Grace (Walcott) Hazard (Mrs. Roscoe Platt Conkling), author; b. N.Y.C., Feb. 7, 1878; d. Christopher Grant and Frances (Post) Hazard; B.L., Smith Coll., 1899; student Harvard Summer Sch., 1899; studied music, langs., U. of Heidelberg, 1902-03, Paris, 1903-04; m. Roscoe Platt Conkling, Sept. 18, 1905; children—Elsa, Hilda. Tutor S. Woodstock, Conn., 1899-1901; tchr. English, Latin, Greek, Graham Sch., N.Y.C., 1901-02; tchr. English, Smith Coll., 1914—, now prof. Mem. Poetry Soc. Am., N.E. Poetry Soc., P.E.N., Phi Beta Kappa. Clubs: Authors' (Boston); Women's University (N. Y.C.). Author: Afternoons of April, 1915; Wilderness Songs, 1920; Imagination and Children's Reading, 1922; Ship's Log and Other Poems, 1924; Flying Fish—a Book of Songs and Sonnets, 1926; Witch and Other Poems, 1929. Contbr. poems to Century, Atlantic Monthly, Yale Rev., Poetry, Harper's, etc. Lectr. on contemporary poetry and its lit. Home: 31 Maynard Rd., Northampton, Mass. Died Nov. 15, 1958; buried Florida, N.Y.

CONKLING, Roscoe Powers, state supreme court justice; b. Carrollton, Mo., May 3, 1889; s. Virgil and Alpha (Powers) C.; LL.B., U. Mo., 1912; LL. D., William Jewell Coll., Liberty, Mo., 1954; m Mildred Scott, Nov. 24, 1914; children—Corrie (Mrs. John W. Province), Hazel (Mrs. Clayton E. Smith).

Admitted to Mo. bar, 1912; practiced law, Kansas City, Mo., 1912-24, St. Joseph, 1924-46; judge Supreme Ct. of Mo., 1947—, chief justice, 1953—. Spl. commr. Supreme Ct., 1943; mem. bd. Mo. State Law Examiners, 1926-30. Mem. bd curators Stephens Coll., Columbia, Mo. Served with F.A., U.S. Army, 1918. Mem. Am. Bar Assn., Am. Legion, Am. Law Inst., Mo. Jud. Conf., Conf. Chief Justices, Beta Theta Pi, Phi Alpha Delta. Baptist. Mason. Home: 1008 Fairmount Ct. Office: Supreme Court Bldg., Jefferson City, Mo. Died Oct. 28, 1954.

CONLEN, William J(ames), lawyer; b. nr. Madison, N.J., Mar. 1, 1878; s. John H. and Mary (Butler) C.; LL.B., U. Pa., 1901; m. Jean C. O'Neill, Sept. 29, 1929 (died Dec. 1947); m. 2d, Helen Fahy, June 1948. Admitted to Pa. bar, 1901, since practiced in Phila.; head firms Conlen, Brinton & Acker, then Conlen, Acker, Manning & Brown, now Conlen, La Brum & Beechwood; v.p. Union Petroleum S.S. Co., 1915-18; past dir. Union Petroleum Co., Wirt Electric Speciality Co. Chmn., mem. various War coms., World War I. Mem. Internat. Law Assn. (past pres. Am. br.), Am. Soc. Internat. Law, Am. and Pa. bar assns., Merion Civic Assn. (past pres.), N.J. Soc. Pa. (past pres.). Club: Lincoln (past pres.). Author: Philadelphians Abroad, 1905; Vignettes of Mexico, 1937; also articles in law mags. Amateur painter; pictures exhibited at the Phila. Art Club, Union League and through the medium of television. Home: 819 Pennstone Rd., Bryn Mawr, Pa. Office: Packard Bldg., Phila. Died Apr. 12, 1956.

CONLEY, Edgar Thomas, army officer; b. "Green Ridge," Fairland, Md., Apr. 12, 1874; s. Charles William and Martha Ellen (Larrick) C.; student Lehigh U., 1892-93; grad. U.S. Mil. Acad., 1897; m. Clare Madeline Geary, Dec. 7, 1904; children—Edgar Thomas, Mary (wife of Capt. Thomas Morgan Wathington, Jr.), Reginald Geary. Commd. 2d. lt. inf., June 11, 1897; promoted through grades to brig. gen., 1933. Served in Santiago Campaign in Cuba, 1898; in Philippine Insurrection, 1899-1901; in charge prisoners of war div. Office of Provost Marshall Gen., A.E.F., 1919; maj. gen., The Adjutant Gen., 1935-38, retired, Apr. 30, 1938. Awarded Silver Star medal "for gallantry in action against Spanish forces at Santiago"; D.S.M. "for exceptionally meritorious and distinguished services A.E.F." Episcopalian. Author: Riflemen's Score Book for Krag and Springfield, 1906; Field Equipment Manual for Officers and Men of 30th Infantry, 1916; Training in Bayonet Fighting, 1916. Home: R.F.D. 2, Silver Spring, Md. Died Aug. 20, 1956.*

CONLEY, Elmo Hansford, lawyer; b. Lexington, Ky., Nov. 25, 1896; s. Walter Green and May (Crabtree) C.; student U.S. Naval Acad.; A.B., Pomona Coll., 1917; LL.B., Harvard, 1922; m. Madeleine Kimball, Oct.18 , 1924; children—Madeleine Kimball, Thayer. Admitted to Cal. bar, since practiced in L.A., asso. Gibson, Dunn & Crutcher, 1922-29, partner since 1929; dir. Pacific Mut. Life Ins. Co., Security-First Nat. Bank of Los Angeles, Redondo Improvement Co., Newport News Land Co., Los Angeles Transit Lines, Purex Corp., Huntington Land & Improvement Co., Inglewood Park Cemetery Co., Rodeo Land & Water Co. Chmn. aviation tax panel, 1941-45; spl. adv. committee, joint com. on taxation U.S. Congress. Trustee, vice chmn. Henry E. Hunting Library and Art Gallery; trustee management com. Collis P. and Howard Huntington Meml. Hosp.; trustee Pomona Coll. Served with U.S.N., 1917-22. Mem. Am., Cal., L.A. bar assns. Clubs: Cal. (pres. 1944-46), San Gabriel Country (pres. 1941-44), Chaparral (pres. 1947), Twilight. Contbr. articles law jours. Home: 1550 Hillcrest Av., Pasadena 5, Cal. Office: 634 S. Spring St., Los Angeles 14. Died Feb. 5, 1957.

CONLEY, George J., osteopathic surgeon; b. Paxton, Ill., Dec. 3, 1872; s. John T. and Ruth (McMurtry) C.; student Purdue U., 1891-93; D.O., Nat. Sch. of Osteopathy, at Kansas City, Mo., 1901; M.D., Eclectic Med. U., Kansas City, Mo., 1902; post grad. work Kansas Coll. of Osteopathy and Surgery, 1919; m. Laura Burdick, 1899 (died 1901); 1 dau., Virginia Maurine (Mrs. James E. Finney); m. 2d, Lucy J. Fincknaur, 1905 (died 1921); m. 3d, Rowena Smith, July 28, 1933. Practiced in Kansas City, 1901—; founded Lakeside Hosp. and pres., 1923—; pres. bd. of control, Kansas City Coll. of Osteopathy and Surgery, 1916—, now emeritus; founder S.W. Osteopathic San., Blackwell, Okla., 1914, pres., 1914—. Fellow Am. Coll. Osteopathic Surgeons; mem. Am. Osteopathic Assn. (trustee 1931; v.p. 1933-34; pres. 1934-35), Mo. State Osteopathic Assn. (pres. 1915). Democrat. Club: Kansas City. Contbr. profl. jours. Home: Briar Cliff Hills, North Kansas City, Mo. Office: 116 W. 47th St., Kansas City 2, Mo. Died Feb. 23, 1950.

CONLEY, William Maxwell; b. at Maxwell Creek, Mariposa County, Calif., July 17, 1866; ed. common schs.; m. Emma Bedesen, July 19, 1893; children—Philip, Matthew. Moved to Merced, 1873; taught sch., 1885-89; chief dep. assessor, 1889-90; admitted to bar by Supreme Court, 1891; moved to Madera, 1892, assisted in co. div. before legislature, 1892-93; judge Superior Ct. of Calif., 1893-1921; resigned to enter practice of law; now sr. mem. Conley, Conley and Conley. Candidate for asso. justice Supreme Court, 1898; received complimentary vote of Dem. minority for U.S. senator, 1899; candidate for Congress, 6th Calif. Dist., 1904; for chief justice of Supreme Court, 1914; del. at large Dem. National Conv., 1908; candidate for Dem. presdl. elector, 1924. Senior past grand pres. Native Sons of the Golden West, 1898. Retired. Home: 718 Carmen Av., Fresno, Cal. Died Mar. 7, 1954.

CONN, Donald Deans; b. Woburn, Mass., May 24, 1894; s. George Chester and Harriet (Deans) C.; C.E., U. of Mich., m. Louise Trask, June 2, 1917; children—Louis, George. In traffic dept. Pere Marquette Ry.; later traffic mgr. Shevlin, Carpenter & Clarke Co., Minneapolis; chief of transportation div. Joint Commn. U.S. Congress, 1921-22; chmn. Northwest Governors' Coal Commn. (coal strike), 1923; asst. federal fuel administrator, June-Oct. 1923; mgr. car service div. Am. Ry. Assn., Washington, D.C., 1923-27; mng. dir. Calif. Vineyardists Assn., and Associated Calif. Fruit Industries, 1927-34; exec. v.p., Transportation Assn. of America, 1934-54; Mem. Am. Assn. Freight Traffic Officers. Clubs: Union League (Chicago); Phi Gamma Delta, Traffic Club (New York). Home: 930 Judson St., Evanston, Ill. Office: 6 N. Michigan Av., Chgo. 2. Died Aug. 13, 1954; buried Lakewood Cemetery, Mpls.

CONNELL, George Boyce (kŏn-nĕl'), univ. adminstr.; b. Douglasville, Ga., Feb. 1, 1905; s. Hance Hewlette and Nannie (Cobb) C.; A.B., Mercer U., 1924, A.M., 1930; LL.D. (honorary), Howard College, 1954; married Doris Collier, Dec. 28, 1929; 1 son, Hewlette Collier. Athletic coach 6th Dist. A. and M. Sch., Barnesville, Ga., 1925-27; athletic coach, v.p., Piedmont Jr. Coll., Waycross, Ga., 1927-28; v.p. and dean, Gordon Military College, Barnesville, 1928-46; v.p. Mercer U., 1946-53, pres. 1953—. Mem. commn. on liberal edn. Am. Assn. Colls., 1957—; chmn. Ga. com. Rhodes Scholarship Trust, 1957, 58; mem. So. Bapt Education Commission. Served as mem. Ga. State Counsel on Vets. Edn., 1943-48. Mem. Ga. Assn. Colls. (pres. 1954-55), Assn. So. Bapt. Colls. and Secondary Schs. (pres. 1956), Ga. Found. for Ind. Colls., Inc. (pres.), Am. Assn. UN, Dixie Athletic Conf. (pres., 1950), Ga. Edn. Assn. (pres. dept. of higher edn. 1948-50), Kappa Phi Kappa, Phi Eta Sigma. Baptist. Rotarian (past pres.). Home: 1309 Adams St., Macon, Ga. Died Apr. 21, 1959; buried Penfield, Ga.

CONNELLEY, Earl John, govt. ofcl.; b. Columbus, O., Jan. 31, 1892; s. John and Anna Elizabeth (Bowers) C.; m. Grace Muzzio, June 30, 1920; 1 son, Earl John. Successively spl. agt., spl. agt. in charge, insp. F.B.I., Dept. of Justice, 1920-40, asst. dir., 1940—. Served as pvt. and 1st lt., U.S. Army, 1917-19, with 314 Field Signal Bn., 89th Div., as officer in charge Army Signal Supply Depot, Ft. Wood, N.Y. Harbor and Army Base, Bklyn. Roman Catholic. Home: 506 E. Fourth St., Cin. 2. Office: care F.B.I., Washington 25. Died July 20, 1957; buried Gate of Heaven Cemetery, Cin.

CONNELY, Emmett Francis, investment banker; b. Adrian, Mich., June 13, 1891; s. Michael Joseph and Kathryn Louise (Hurley) C.; A.B., U. Mich., 1915; m. Harriet Louise Cullom, Oct. 29, 1919; children—Richard Day, Cullom, Molly. Clerk Montgomery Ward Co., Chgo., 1915; prodn. dept., Hudson Motor Car Co., 1916-17, 1919-20; salesman and sales mgr. Detroit Trust Co., 1920-27; v.p., 1927-30; v.p. First Detroit Co., 1930-31, pres., 1931-33; pres. First of Michigan Corp., 1933-43, chmn. bd., 1943-49; dir. Am. Seal-Kap Corp., Chicago Ry. Equipment Supply Corp., Briggs Mfg. Co., Nat. Rubber Machinery Co. Abingdon Potteries. Chairman Detroit A.R.C. 1946-47; dir. Jr. Achievement, Inc. (mem. exec. com.). Served as capt. 10th F.A., 3d Division, U.S. Army, 1918-19; with A.E.F., 9 months; major, 182d F.A., Michigan Nat. Guard, 1920-24; colonel, U.S. Army, 1942-45. Trustee Village of Grosse Pointe Farms, 1932-39. Mem. Advisory bd. U. Detroit; trustee United Found., Greater Detroit Hosp. Fund, 1948-49; trustee Turtle Bay Music School New York; mem. exec. com. Committee for United Europe. Mem. of the Investment Bankers Assn. Am. (gov. 1936-39, pres. 1939-41), Sigma Phi. Roman Catholic. Clubs Detroit, Country of Detroit; Yondotega; The Links, Bond, University of Michigan (N.Y.C.); Eastward-Ho Country (Chatham, Mass.). Author Let Business Roll Its Own, 1940. Home: 133 E. 80th St., N.Y.C. 21. Office: 25 Broad St., N.Y.C. 4. Died Feb. 2, 1960.

CONNER, Lewis Atterbury, physician; b. New Albany, Ind., Jan. 17, 1867; s. Charles Horace and Katharine Boudinot (Atterbury) C.; Ph.B., Sheffield Sci. Sch., Yale, 1887; M.D., Coll. Phys. and Surg., Columbia, 1890; m. Emma Witt Harris, Nov. 27, 1900 (died Sept. 14, 1921); children—Katharine Atterbury, William Harris, Edith Harris, Sylvia Colt; m. 2d, Laila Ann Coston, Sept. 27, 1923; 1 dau., Ann Atterbury. Attending physician N.Y. Hosp., 1905-32, cons. physician, 1932—; prof. medicine Cornell U. Med. Coll., 1916-32, prof. clin. medicine 1932 until ret. Col. U.S. Army M.C., 1918-19; brig. gen. Med. R.C., 1920. Fellow N.Y. Acad. Medicine; mem. Assn. Am. Physicians, A.M.A. Editor Am. Heart Journal, 1925-38. Club: University (N.Y.C.). Address: Niantic, Conn. Died Dec. 5, 1950.

CONNER, Martin Sennett ("Mike Conner"), ex-gov. Miss., lawyer; b. Hattiesburg, Miss., Aug. 31; 1891; s. Oscar Weir and Holly Gertrude (Sennett) C.; B.S., U. Miss., 1910, LL.B., 1912; LL.B. cum laude, Yale, 1913; m. Alma Penn. Graham, Dec. 15, 1921; 1 dau., Rachel. Began practice at Seminary, Miss., 1913; speaker Miss. Ho. of Rep., 1916-24; gov. of Miss., term 1932-36; now mem. Conner & Nobles; S.E. Conf. commr. athletics, 1940-48. Mem. Kappa Alpha (Southern), Phi Alpha Delta. Democrat. Methodist. Mason (Shriner, K.C.C.H.). Home: 1535 N. State St. Address: Box 1370, Jackson, Miss. Died Sept. 16, 1950.

CONNERS, William James, Jr., publisher; b. Buffalo, Sept. 22, 1895; s. William James and Mary Alice (Jordan) C.; prep. edn. Nichols Sch., Buffalo, 1908-13, Harstrom Sch., Norwalk, Conn., 1914; A.B. honoris causa, Yale, 1918; m. Corinne H. Tilford, Oct. 23, 1917; children—William James III, Rita Corinne, Sally Ann. Publisher and pres. Courier-Express, Buffalo, 1919—; chmn. bd. Great Lakes Transit Corp.; pres. Frontier Contracting Co., George W. Jenings Co.; pres., dir. Frontier Warehouse Co., Inc.; dir. Marine Trust Co.; chmn. bd., dir. WEBR, Inc., Buffalo. Served as lt. (j.g.) Naval Aviation, USN, World War; entered USNR, 1936, commd. lt. comdr. on active duty 1941-45; apptd. capt., assigned to inactive duty, 1945. Mem. Alpha Delta Phi. Catholic. Clubs: Buffalo, Saturn, Buffalo Country, Anglo American Fish and Game. Home: 1140 Delaware Av. Office: Courier-Express, Buffalo. Died Feb. 3, 1951; buried Holy Cross Cemetery, Lackawanna, N.Y.

CONNOLLY, James Brendan, author; b. South Boston, Mass.; s. John and Ann (O'Donnell) C.; m. Elizabeth Frances Hurley, Sept. 28, 1904; 1 dau., Brenda. Clerk, insp. and surveyor with U.S. Engr. Corps at Savannah, Ga., 1892-95; won 1st Olympic championship of modern times at Athens, 1896; served with 9th Mass. Inf., U.S. Vols., 1898; and was at siege of Santiago; served in U.S. Navy, 1907-08. Prog. candidate for Congress, 1912. Mem. Nat. Inst. of Arts and Letters, Army of Santiago de Cuba; hon. mem. Gloucester Master Mariners. Author: Out of Gloucester, 1902; The Seiners, 1904; Deep Sea's Toll, 1905; Crested Seas, 1907; An Olympic Victor, 1908; Open Water, 1910; Wide Courses, 1911; Sonnie Boy's People, 1913; The Trawler, 1914; Head Winds, 1916; Running Free, 1917; The U-Boat Hunters, 1918; Hiker Joy, 1920; Tide Rips, 1922; Steel Decks, 1925; Coaster Captain, 1927; Book of the Gloucester Fishermen, 1927; Gloucestermen, 1930; Navy Men, 1939; The Port of Gloucester, 1940; Canton Captain, 1942; Master Mariner; Life and Voyages of Amasa Delano, 1943; Sea-Borne: Thirty Years Avoyaging, 1944. Winner Collier's short story competition, 1914. Corr. for Scribner's Magazine in Europe, 1901, for Harper's Mag. in Arctic Ocean, 1902, for Collier's in Mexico, 1914, and in European waters, 1917, 18. Commr. (in Ireland) for American Com. for Relief in Ireland, 1921. Home: 9 Braemore Road, Boston. Died Jan. 20, 1957.*

CONNOLLY, James J., ex-congressman; b. Phila., Pa., Sept. 24, 1881; s. William John and Sarah A. (Harrigan) C.; ed. Catholic High Sch.; m. Mary A. Morrissey, Sept. 30, 1908. Mem. 67th to 73d Congresses (1921-35), 5th Pa. Dist. Republican. Catholic. Home: 9537 Banes St., Philadelphia, Pa. Died Dec. 10, 1952.*

CONNOLLY, Robert Emmet, railroad exec.; b. N.Y.C., Aug. 11, 1884; s. Bernard R. and Mary A. (O'Donnell) C.; student N.Y.U., Fordham U. Sch. Law; m. May T. Kane, June 27, 1908; children—Mary, Richard, Catherine. Treas. Ill. Central System, 1918—, sec., v.p., 1934—; sec. dir. Ill. Central R.R. Co., Chicago, St. Louis & New Orleans R.R. Co., Valley Corp., R.R. Credit Corp. Clubs: Faculty (N.Y.U.), Downtown Athletic, Catholic (N.Y.C.); Chicago. Home: Braeburn Rd., Flossmoor, Ill. Office: 135 E. 11th Pl., Chgo. 5. Died Oct. 12, 1950.*

CONNOR, Louis George, agrl. economist; b. Annandale, Va., Apr. 13, 1883; s. William S. and Emmaline (Mercer) C.; B.S., Wesleyan U., Conn., 1910, M.S., 1913; M.S. in Agriculture, Cornell U., 1912; Ph. D., George Washington University, 1917; m. Ethel Keats, March 29, 1930. Connected with the Department of Agriculture, Washington, D.C., many yrs.; principal commodity specialist, U.S. Tariff Commn., 1921-50 (ret.). Served in A.E.F., World War I, in G2 at G.H.Q. and 1st Army Hdqrs.; consultant various war agencies, World War II. Member Farm Economics Assn., Agrl. History Soc. Independent Republican. Methodist. Author of many technical articles. Home: 5299 MacArthur Blvd., Washington 16. Deceased.

CONOVER, Elbert Moore (kŏn'ō-vẽr), clergyman; b. Harrisonville, N.J.; s. Samuel S. and Atlantic (Moore) C.; direct desc. of Wolfert Gerretse Van Kovenhoven, who came from Amersfoort, Holland, in

1630; Dickinson Prep. Sch., Carlisle, Pa., 1902-04, Dickinson Coll., 1904; B.D., Theol. Sem. Drew U., 1913; private study of architecture in Europe, 1926 and 1932; Sc.D. Dickinson Coll., 1948; m. Ethel Holdcraft, June 23, 1908 (Dec. July, 1952); children—Paul H., Theodore E. Joined N.J. Conf. M.E. Ch., 1910; pastor Haleyville, Wall; Thorofare, Millville, all in N.J.; org. inter-church work, 1916-17; pastor Wenonah, N.J., 1917-19; asst. sec. dept. of war emergency and reconstruction, M.E. Ch., 1919-20, exec. sec., 1920-24; dir. Bur. of Architecture M.E. Ch., 1924-34; sec. Assn. Depts. of Ch. Architecture, 1924-34, director Interdenominational Bur. of Architecture since 1934; sec. N. Am. Conf. on Church Architecture, 1932-40; president, 1940-45, secretary since 1945; member committee on worship, and member committee on church school administration, Nat. Council of Chs. Organizer Social Service Commn., N.J. Conf. M.E. Ch. (sec. 1914-36); mem. Com. on Religious Work in Canal Zone since 1941; mem. Christian Commn. on work in camp and defense areas. Technical adviser to jury Alumni of Am. Acad. of Rome Competition, 1942-43. Author: Building the House of God (required study of all candidates for ministry in M.E. Ch). 1928, also monographs Building a Seven Day a Week Church. The Church School Building, Leadership in Church Building, Rebuilding Town and Country Church; Building for Christian Education, 1940; Planning the Small Church, 1944; Planning for Worship, 1945; Planning Church Buildings, 1946; Church Building Finance, 1946; The Church Building Guide, 1947, 1948; Church School and Parish House Building, 1948; The Church Builder, 1949. Contbr. to The Church Looks Ahead; chapter on The Church Building in "Church Attendance." Contbr. to religious and architectural journals. Lecturer on religious arts and church adminstrn. Home: Office: 300 4th Av., N.Y. City 10. Died Nov. 17, 1952.

CONOVER, Harvey, publisher; b. Chicago, Ill., Nov. 24, 1892; s. Lawrence P. and Isabelle (Storer) C.; student Mercersburg Acad. and U. of Wis.; m. Dorothy Jobson, June 23, 1920; children—Dorothy Ann, Frances, Harvey, Lawrence. With A. W. Shaw Co., Chicago, 1919-21; western mgr., v.p. and later Mast Publications, Inc., 1928, since pres., treas.; dir. pres., Engring. Mag. Co., 1921-27; founder Conover Anchor Post Products, Inc., Indsl. Directories, Inc., Yachting Pub. Corp. Served with Am. Ambulance for French Armies, 1916, six mos.; U.S. Air Service, 1st lt. pilot, 90th Aero Sqdn., participating in St. Mihiel, Argonne offensives. Awarded Army Citation, Distinguished Service Cross, Croix de Guerre, Aero Club Medal of Honor, Purple Heart. Visited Britain at request of Donald Nelson, chmn. W.P.B., and Oliver Littleton, Brit. Minister Prodn., Feb.-April, 1943; visited S.W. Pacific war theatre for Bur. Aeronautics of U.S. Navy, Dec.-Feb. 1945; mission to Germany at invitation of U.S. Air Force to study Berlin Airlift Operations, 1948. Member Holland Soc., Nat. Aeronautics Assn., Beta Theta Pi. Clubs: New York Yacht, Larchmont Yacht, Cruising of America, Essex Yacht, Press, Off Soundings; Royal Ocean Racing (Eng.); Royal Swedish Yacht. Contbr. indsl. and business publs. Home: Edgewater Point, Mamaroneck, N.Y. Office: 205 E. 42d St., N.Y.C. Died Jan. 1958.

CONRAD, Casper Hauzer, Jr., army officer (ret.); b. Columbus, O., Sept. 26, 1872; s. Casper H. and Ella (Coton) C.; B.S., U.S. Mil. Acad., 1895; grad. Mtd. Service Sch., 1st yr. course, 1916; hon. grad. Sch. of the Line, 1920; B.S., U. of Ill., 1922; grad. Army War Coll., 1923; m. Eva M. Shacklette, Nov. 28, 1923. Commd. 2d lt. Cav., 1895; advanced through grades to col., 1920; served as col. inf., N.A., 1917-19; brig. gen. regular army, 1928. Served in Cuba, 1898-1901; Philippines, 1901-02; St. Louis Expn., 1904-05; Philippines, 1905-08; Tex., Mexican border, 1908-09; organized, comd. 360th Inf., 90th Div., 1917-18; mem. War Dept. Gen. Staff, 1918-19; Germany comdg. Advance Embarkation Sect., comdg. Base Sect. 1, St. Nazaire, France, 1919; Philippines, 1924-25, Washington, 1926-28; comdr, Ft. Shieridan, Ill., and 12th Inf. Brig., 1929-30; comdr. 23d Inf. Brig. (Philippine Scouts), 1930-31; comdr. Fort William McKinley and Philippine Div., 1931-33, 4th Inf. Brigade, Ft. Francis E. Warren, Wyo., 1933-35, 3d Div., Ft. Lewis, Wash., 1935-36; ret., 1936. Decorated D.S.M., 1920. Mem. Soc. Indian Wars. Episcopalian. Home: 477 Burr Road, San Antonio 9. Deceased.

CONRAD, Charles (kŏn'ärd), naval officer; b. Washington, Mar. 3, 1875; s. William and Adelaide (Zimmerman) C.; grad. Rockville (Md.) Acad., 1892; M.E., Cornell, 1896; m. Dora E. Allen, May 3, 1898 (dec. 1949); children—Adelaide Zimmerman (Mrs. Kenneth Gordon), Dorothy Allen (Mrs. Theodore G. Haff), Charlotte Allen (Mrs. Maurice K. Brady), Mary Waters Allen (Mrs. Elmer M. Jackson), Barbara Allen (lieut. WAVES), Charles Allen (lieut. comdr. USN); m. 2d, Mrs. Margaret F. Eaton, Jan. 18, 1952. Began as ensign Supply Corps U.S. Navy, May 26, 1898, advanced through grades to rear adm., 1936; served 9 years on various battleships, 8 years as disbursing or supply officer at various navy yards, 5 years in Bur. of Supplies and Accounts, Washington, Philippines, 1901-04, fiscal officer at Vera Cruz, Mexico, 1914; adminstr. of customs and financial adviser, Republic of Haiti, 1915-16; under instruction at Naval War Coll., Newport, R.I., 1917; U.S. Shipping Bd., 1919-20; spl. asst. Dir. Budget, 1922-25; gen. insp. Supply Corps, East Coast, 1928-32, Paymaster Gen., chief Bur. Supplies and Accounts, Navy Dept., 1935-39; ret., 1939. Apptd. by exec. order, chmn. Interdepartmental War Savs. Bond Com., Apr. 16, 1941. Dir. Nat. Savs. & Trust Co., Washington. Awarded campaign badges for Spanish-Am. War, Mexican, Haitian and San Dominican services, and World War I, World War II, Legion of Merit. Clubs: Army and Navy, Chevy Chase. Home: 2311 Connecticut Av. Address: Navy Dept., Washington. Died June 19, 1954.

CONRAD, Charles Wearne, consulting engr.; b. Fennimore, Wis., May 28, 1887; s. Anthony Lee and Anne (Wearne) C.; E E., U. of Tex., 1909; m. Flora D. Tandy, June 3, 1913; children—Charles Tandy, Anthony Lee, II. Mgr. Canadian Water, Light & Power Co., Canadian, Tex., 1909-13; asst. elec. engr., Chicago Assn. Commerce, 1913-15; elec. engr. Eddystone (Pa.) Rifle Plant, Midvale Steel & Ordnance Co., 1915-16, plant engr., 1916-19; supt. Eddystone Rifle Storage Arsenal, U.S. Ordnance Dept., 1919-20; plant engr., 1922-35, Bird & Son, Inc., paper and bldg. products, East Walpole, Mass., 1920-30, gen. supt., 1930-35, v.p., 1935-46; pres. Conrad & Young, Inc. since Feb. 1946, name now changed to Conrad & Son, Inc. Member Engring. Socs. of New Eng., Am. Soc. M.E., Plant Engrs. Club (hon.), Boston, Delta Tau Delta. Republican. Home: 808 Washington St., Walpole, Mass. Office: 33 Union St., East Walpole, Mass. Died Oct. 24, 1957; buried Maple Grove Cemetery, Walpole, Mass.

CONRAD, Cuthbert Powell, utility exec.; b. Osceola, Mo., Jan. 28, 1893; s. Cuthbert Powell and Sara Eugenia (Harris) C.; B.S., U. of Wis., 1915, C.E., 1916; m. Beatrice Carroll Tabor, Apr. 17, 1920. Instr. hydraulic engring., U. of Wis., 1916-17; jr. partner, Mead & Seastone, cons. hydraulic engrs., Madison, Wis., 1921-24; chief hydraulic engr., Brazilian Traction Co., Rio de Janeiro and São Paulo, 1925-40; pres. Ia.-Ill. Gas and Electric Co., Davenport, Ia., 1946-54, chmn., 1954——. Served in Civil Engring. Corps, USN, 1917-20 and 1940-46, retiring to inactive duty with the rank of commodore, April, 1946. Awarded Legion of Merit, World War II. Member American Society of Civil Engineers, Tau Beta Pi. Clubs: Army and Navy, Army and Navy Country (Washington); Davenport, Davenport Country, Outing (Davenport, Iowa); Rock Island (Ill.) Arsenal Golf, Short Hills Country (Moline); Blackhawk Hiking (Davenport, Rock Island, Moline). Home: 11 Edgehill Terrace, Davenport, Iowa. Office: 206 E. 2d St., Davenport, Ia. Died Jan. 24, 1956; buried Arlington Nat. Cemetery.

CONRAD, Nicholas John, chmn. bd. S. & C. Electric Company; born Port Washington, Wisconsin, Mar. 21, 1883; son of Christopher and Katherine (Hoefer) C.; B.S. in electrical engineering, University of Wisconsin, 1905; m. Irene Billups, Sept. 10, 1910; children—John Robert, Jane. With Commonwealth Edison Co., Chicago, 1905-17, in charge testing and starting engring. of generating stations; co-founder, sec., treas., and gen. mgr. Schweitzer & Conrad, Inc., mfrs. high voltage elec. equipment, 1910-30; not active in management, 1930-45; acquired all stock 1945 and resumed mngmnt. as pres.; chmn. bd. 1952; name of co. changed to S & C Electric Co. Chmn. Suburban Div., chmn. Work Relief Project of Cook Co. Emergency Relief Fund, 1932, 33; chmn. country towns div. U.S.O., 1942; chmn. Chicago adv. com. Naval Officer Procurement, 1942; Chicago dist. mgr. W.P.B., 1943; mem. Selective Service, Cook Co. Appeal Bd., 1943-47; industry panel mem., W.L.B., 1943-46; trustee Village of Winnetka, 1943-46. Fellow Am. Inst. E.E.; mem. Western Soc. Engrs. Inventor high voltage elec. protective and switching equipment. Republican. Clubs: Union Lague (Chicago) (pres. 1937-39); Indian Hill. Founder America Wake Up Crusade, Union League Club of Chicago, 1937; conducted crusade, 1937-41. Home: 1099 Pelham Rd., Winnetka, Ill. Office: 4435 Ravenswood Av., Chgo. 40. Died Sept. 18, 1956; buried All Saint's Cemetery, Des Plaines, Ill.

CONROW, Wilford Seymour (kŏn'rō), portrait painter; b. South Orange, N.J., June 14, 1880; s. William Edward and Anna Malcolm (Hanford) C.; Poly. Inst. Bklyn., 1895-96; B.S., Princeton, 1901; art studies N.Y. Sch. of Art, 1901-02; under J. Hambridge, 1916; in Paris with J. P. Laurens, Henri Moriset and P. Tudor-Hart, and at École des Beaux Arts, 1911-14; m. Mrs. Lyra Beach Mallet, Nov. 2, 1911. Sec. Conrow Brothers, Inc., wholesale paper, N.Y., 1902-10. Portraits in Hickory (N.C.) Mus. of Art, Sheldon Swope Art Gallery, Terre Haute, Ind., Mint Mus., Charlotte, N.C., Columbus (Ga.) Mus. Arts and Crafts, U. Tenn. Coll. Medicine, Poly. Inst. Bklyn., U. Ga., Princeton, Yale, Purdue, Emory univs., Tchrs. Coll. Columbia, Union Theol. Sem.; Vassar Coll.; U. Ill.; Central High Sch., Charlotte, N.C.; Bklyn. Mus.; High Mus., Atlanta; Ohio Valley Gen. Hosp., Wheeling, W.Va.; L.I. Coll. Hosp., Bklyn.; Mountainside Hosp., Montclair, N.J.; Fifth Av. Hosp., N.Y.C.; Highsmith Hosp., Fayetteville, N.Y.; Cosmos Club, Washington; Governor's Room, State Capitol, Trenton, N.J.; Superior Court, Charlotte and Goldsboro, N.C.; Internat. Com. Room, Y.M.C.A., N.Y.C.; N.Y. Hist. Soc.; 369th Regt. Armory, N.Y. N.G.; George Washington Life Ins. Co., Charleston, W.Va.; Utica (New York) Mut-Ins. Co.; Bklyn Savs. Bank; Kanwha Trust Co. and First Nat. Bank, Charleston, W.Va.; Woodward (Ala.) Iron Co.; Office of Postmaster Gen., Washington. Exhibited: Salon Nat. des Beaux Arts, Paris; Nat. Gallery of Art and Corcoran Biennial, Washington; Nat. Acad. Design; Pa. Acad.; U. of Georgia; High Mus. of Art, Atlanta; Mint Mus., Charlotte, N.C. Student 1st Plattsburgh R.O.T.C., May-Aug., 1917; 1st lt. Co. A, 40th Engrs. (camouflage); with A.E.F., Jan., 1918-Jan., 1919; in charge Central Camouflage Works, later chief instr. camouflage sect. Army Engr. Sch. Citation from C.I.C. Mem. Allied Artists of America (v.p. 1948-52), American Artists Profl. League (nat. sec. 1928-50, 1st national v p. 1950-52), Audubon Artists, Municipal Art Society, Fine Arts Federation of N.Y., Am. Veterans Soc. of Artists, Inc., N.Y. Soc. Mil. and Naval Officers World Wars (life mem.), S. R., Andiron Club of N.Y.C., Phi Beta Kappa, Kappa Pi, hon. 1945. Clubs: Century, Salmagundi, Princeton (N.Y. C.). Author: Accent in Art of the Great Chalice of Antioch, 1923; Wiliam Henry Goodyear, an Appreciation, 1923; (with Dr. G. A. Eisen), Portraits of Washington, Sculpture (Vol. III), 1932; Studies in the Symmetry of Man, 1935, 37. Editor and pub. Old Nassau (Princeton), 1905. Home and studio 222 W. 59th St., N.Y.C. 19; (summer) Bryn Avon, Hendersonville, R. 4, N.C. Died Nov. 24, 1957.

CONROY, Peter Joseph, educator; b. Watervliet, N.Y., Oct. 26, 1894; s. William Patrick and Mary Ellen (Birmingham) C.; Diploma, Fordham Prep. Sch., 1915; Ph.G., Fordham Coll. Pharm., 1917; B.S., Fordham U., 1926, M.S., 1927, Ph.D., 1929; A.M., Columbia, 1940; student, New York U. and Bellevue Hosp. Med. Coll., 1921-23; m. Marguerite E. Schoenstadt, May 13, 1919; 1 dau., Marguerite Ellen. Mem. faculty Fordham U., 1924——; lecturer chemistry and gen. sci., Fordham Sch. Edn., 1924-44; prof. of chemistry and head dept. Fordham U. Coll. Pharmacy, 1927——; asst. prof. pharmacology, N.Y. Med. Coll., 1929-30. Lecturer food and nutrition, A.R.C., Crestwood, N.Y., 1942-43. Awarded Alumni medal, 1917; Bene Merenti medal (20 yr. service and achievement), 1945. Fellow A.A.A.S., Am. Inst. Chemists, Am. Geog. Soc.; mem. Am. Chem. Soc., Am. Pharm. Assn. (also N.Y. br.), German Apothecary Soc., N.Y. Acad. Sci., N.Y. State Pharm. Assn., Westchester Pharm. Assn. (hon. life mem.). Cons. pharm. chem. editor, Pharm. editor, Chain Store Age, 1942-47. Home: 410 Scarsdale Rd., Crestwood, P.O. Tuckahoe 7, N.Y. Office: Fordham Univ., Fordham 58, N.Y.C. Died June 17, 1955; buried Holy Mount Cemetery, Eastchester, N.Y.

CONROY, Thomas Francis, newspaper writer; b. New York, N.Y., July 4, 1897; s. Eugene Sherman and Augusta (Anderson) C.; student Columbia, 1916; m. Bessie Weisman, June 3, 1923; 1 son. Harold. Writer Brooklyn Eagle, 1916, Paper Trade Journal, New York, N.Y., 1917, Trade News Service, N.Y., 1918, Fairchild Pubs., 1918; joined N.Y. Times, 1922, asst. bus. news editor. Candidate officer F.A., U.S. Army, 1918. Mem. World Trade Writers Assn. Republican. Home: 302 96th St., Bklyn. 9. Office: 229 W. 43d St., N.Y.C. 18. Died May 15, 1953; buried Restland Meml. Park, East Hanover, N.J.

CONSTANTINE, Earl Gladstone, trade assn. exec.; b. Varna, Bulgaria, Aug. 5, 1885; s. Trico and F. Dora (Keeste) C.; prep. edn. Robert Coll., Istanbul, Turkey, 1898-1901, Cleveland High Sch., St. Paul, Minn., 1902; A.B., U. of Minn., 1902-06. Instr. of French, Spanish and European history, Spokane (Wash.) High Sch., 1907-10; sec. Associated Industries of the Inland Empire, Spokane, 1910-13; mng. dir. Federated Industries of Wash., Seattle, 1914-15; sec. Nat. Industrial Council, N.Y. City, 1916-25; exec. dir. Nat. Assn. of Mfrs., N.Y. City, 1921-25; treas. Sales Management (mag.) and dir. Federated Business Pubs., N.Y. City, 1926-29; special rep. Ulen & Co., Bogota, Colombia, 1929-31; exec. dir. Hosiery Code Authority, N.R.A., 1933-35; member Consumer Goods Adv. Com., N.R.A., 1934-35; mng. dir. Nat. Assn. of Hosiery Mfrs., N.Y. City, 1932-37, pres. since 1938; mem. Adv. Council on Fed. Reports Bur. of Budget since 1942, chmn., 1947-49. Trustee Am. Coll. of Sofia, Bulgaria, 1940; dir. U.S. Textile Research Inst., 1940-46; Trade and Industry Law Institute; Hosiery Exposition, Inc. Member Am. Trade Assn. Execs. (dir. 1935-40; pres. 1939-40). Trade Assn. Execs. in N.Y. (sec., 1938-39; pres., 1939-40). Clubs: Bonnie Briar Country of Larchmont, N.Y. (sec., 1926; pres., 1927-28, 1932-36); Empire State, Union League (N.Y. City). Frequent speaker on economic and business subjects. Contbr. articles on bus. and econ. subjects to trade jours. and newspapers. Home: 108 E. 38th St. Office: 468 4th Av., N.Y.C. Died Jan. 3, 1952.

CONVERSE, Harry Pollard, editor; b. Louisville, Ky., Aug. 20, 1876; s. F. Bartlett and Ellen Elizabeth (Pollard) C.; A.B., Princeton, 1899; m. Helen Mary Austin, June 16, 1917; 1 dau., Marys A. Newspaper work, 1899-1907; mng. editor Christian Observer since 1907; this paper founded, 1813, and under management since 1827 of 3 direct generations of Converse family. Democrat. Presbyterian. Clubs: Pierian, Louisville Country. Home: 44 Castlewood. Office: 412 S. 3d St., Louisville, Ky. Died Feb. 29, 1960.

CONVERSE, Myron Frederick, pres. Worcester Five Cents Savings Bank; b. Worcester, Mass., Nov. 27, 1876; s. Frederick Samuel and Mary Chapin (Bond) C.; ed. pub. schs., Worcester; m. Anna Woodbury Shattuck, Oct. 15, 1932. With Worcester Five Cents Savings Bank since May 14, 1894, successively clk., clk. of corp., asst. treas., treas., v.p. and pres. since June 28, 1927; v.p. Worcester Mutual Fire Ins. Co.; dir. Mechanics Nat. Bank, State Mutual Life Assurance Co., Norwich & Worcester R.R. Trustee Beckers Junior College Bus. Adminstrn.; dir. Worcester Hahnemann Hospital; pres. Mutual Savings Central Fund, Inc.; trustee Worcester County Mechanics Assn., Worcester County Retirement Bd., Rural Cemetery, Worcester Natural History Soc. (ex-pres.), Worcester Y.M.C.A. Member Worcester County Horticultural Soc. (past president), Savings Bank Association of Mass. (ex-pres.), Mass. Bankers Assn. (ex-pres.), Mass. Savings Bank Officers' Club (ex-pres.), Nat. Assn. of Mutual Savings Banks (ex-pres.). Republican. Baptist. Mason (33°); I.O.O.F. Clubs: Rotary (ex-pres.), Worcester, Economic (ex-pres.), Bohemians, Inc., Tatnuck Country, Worcester Country. Ex-chmn. local bd. No. 165, Selective Service System. Ex-pres. Savings Div., Am. Bankers Assn. Home: 412 Lincoln St. Office: 316 Main St., Worcester 8, Mass. Died Nov. 12, 1950; buried Worcester Rural Cemetery.

CONWAY, Carle Cotter, corp. exec.; b. Oak Park, Ill., Dec. 19, 1877; s. Edwin Stapleton and Sarah Judson (Rogers) C.; B.S., Yale, 1899; m. 2d, Helen Patricia Flynn, June 29, 1940. Formerly pres., chmn. bd. Continental Can Co., Inc., now chmn. exec. com.; chmn. exec. com., Reading Co. Trustee Nat. Found. for Infantile Paralysis; dir. Boys' Clubs of Am. Clubs: University, Yale, Links Blind Brook, Cloud (N.Y.C.); Piping Rock, Rolling Rock, Lake Placid. Home: 1 Sutton Pl. S. Office: 100 E. 42d St., N.Y.C. Died Aug. 19, 1959.

CONWAY, (Daniel) Walter, judge; b. Sioux Falls, S.D., Nov. 13, 1898; s. Daniel J. and Jennie Frances (Conness) C.; Ph.B., Creighton U., Omaha, Neb., 1921, LL.B., 1924; m. Ann G. English, Apr. 27, 1927; children—Jane Frances, Ann Marie and Mary Louise (twins), Constance Margaret, Daniel Joseph. Admitted to Neb., S.D. bar, 1924; mem. law firm Conway, Feyder & Conway, Sioux Falls, 1926-33. Deputy state's atty., Minnehaha County; 1929, 30; asst. city atty., Sioux Falls, 1931, 32; atty. gen. State of S.D., 1933-37; became state counsel for Home Owners' Loan Corporation, 1937; judge of the Municipal Court, 1942—. Served as private U.S. Army, October 13, 1918-Dec. 13, 1918. Mem. Am., S.D. bar assns., Am. Legion, 40 and 8. Democrat. Catholic. K.C. Home: 924 W. 4th St. Office: City Hall, Sioux Falls, S.D. Died Oct. 11, 1956.

COOK, Albert Samuel, ret. state supt. schs.; b. Greencastle, Pa., Jan. 12, 1873; s. Samuel Hassler and Nannie A. (Fahrney) C.; grad. Cumberland Valley State Normal Sch., Shippensburg, Pa., 1889; Gettysburg, Coll., 1892-93; A.B. cum laude, Princeton, 1895, A.M., 1906; post grad. 1 yr. in edn. Tchrs. Coll. Columbia, 1904-08; Litt.D., Western Md. Coll., 1923, St. Johns Coll., Annapolis, Md., 1923, U. Md., 1924; LL.D., Gettysburg Coll., 1937; m. Helen J. Earnshaw, Dec. 27, 1898; children—Earnshaw, Catherine Norris, Albert S. Tchr. country sch., 1889-91; prin. Bel Air (Md.) Acad. and Graded Sch., 1895-98; prin. Franklin High Sch., Reistertown, Md., 1898-1900; supt. Baltimore County Schs., 1900-20: supt. of schools Md., 1920-42. Mem. N.E.A., Nat. Soc. for Study Edn., Ednl. Soc., Balt., State Tchrs. Assn. (pres. 1908), Pa. Beta, Phi Delta Theta, Kappa Delta Pi. Democrat. Episcopalian. Clubs: Maryland, Chesapeake (Balt.); Elkridge. Home: Towson, Md. Died Mar. 10, 1952.*

COOK, Charles R., chmn. bd., dir. Cook Paint & Varnish Co.; b. Lindley, Mo., 1884; grad. Cornell U., 1907. Home: 1405 Dumford Circle, Kansas City, Mo. Office: P.O. Box 389, Kansas City 10, Mo. Died Apr. 2, 1949.

COOK, Chester Aquila, real estate exec.; b. Woonsocket, R.I., Apr. 30, 1870; s. Ira B. and Ida Lucy (Capron) C.; A.B., Brown U., 1891; LL.B., Harvard, 1894; m. Martha F. Richardson, Oct. 2, 1895; children—Everett R., Helen Mary (Mrs. W. I. Aitken); m. 2d, Florence Amanda Spiehler, Jan. 18, 1928. Managed properties of George B. Cook, 1894-98, Ira B. Cook, father, 1898-1910; co-trustee with brother, Raymond C. Cook of Ira B. Cook Properties, 1910-49; dir. Lake Shore Nat. Bank (Chgo.), 1928-49; dir. Booth Fisheries Co., Aquila Inc., Omaha. Bd. of dirs. of Evanston Hosp., YMCA. Mem. Northwestern U. Assos., Citizen's Bd. U. Chgo., Delta Phi, Phi Beta Kappa. Republican. Universalist. Clubs: Glenn View (Golf, Ill.); University (Chgo.); University (Evanston, Ill.). Home: 2520 A St., Lincoln, Neb. Died July 31, 1953; buried Rose Hill Cemetery, Chgo.

COOK, Frederic White, ex-sec. of state for Mass.; b. Somerville, Mass., May 2, 1873; s. Sanford R. and Harriet F. (Dassance) C.; student Somerville pub. schs. 1979-91; m. Kathleen Russell, of Brooklyn, N.Y., Dec. 19, 1905. Filled various positions in city govt. of Somerville, Mass., 1892-1900, asst. city clk., 1900-05; city clk., 1905-20; sec. of the Commonwealth of Mass. 1921-48. Trustee Charlestown Five Cents Svaings Bank, Somerville Hosp. Republican. Unitarian. Mason. Home: Somerville and Plymouth, Mass. Died Nov. 16, 1951.

COOK, Grant L(yle), lawyer; b. Brant, Mich., July 8, 1894; s. Theodore A. and Edna A. (Jennings) C.; student Alma Coll.; LL.B., U. of Mich., 1917; m. Rhea Newton, Apr. 5, 1925; 1 dau., Rhea (Mrs. Ralph E. Oberlin, Jr.). Chmn. bd. and dir. L. A. Young Spring & Wire Corp., Detroit; dir. Detroit Gasket & Mfg. Co., Dearborn Motors Corp., Leonard Refineries Inc., Motor Valve & Mfg. Co., Leonard Pipe Line Co., Good Roads Machinery Co., Am. Electric Switch Corp., Fuller-Johnson Corp., Frankenmuth Brewing Co.; senior member law firm Cook, Beake, Miller, Wrock & Cross, Detroit. Trustee Alma (Mich.) Coll. Mem. Mich., Detroit and Am. bar assns., Gamma Eta Gamma. Republican. Presbyterian. Clubs: Lawyers (U. of Mich.); Economic, Detroit Athletic, Detroit, Recess, The Players, Detroit Boat, Universiy of Michigan (mem. bd. govs.), (Detroit); Red Run Golf (Royal Oak, Mich.); Beach Grove Golf (Tecumseh, Ont.). Home: 160 Touraine Rd., Grosse Pointe Farms 30, Mich. Office: Penobscot Bldg., Detroit 26. Died Nov. 24, 1953; buried, Woodlawn Cemetery, Detroit.

COOK, Irving Winthrop, banker; b. Provincetown, Mass., Mar. 26, 1876; s. Joseph Winthrop and Mary A. (Smith) C.; grad. high sch., Provincetown, 1894; m. Carrie D. Knowles, June 14, 1899; children—Georgia K. (Mrs. Hugh S. Ferguson), Hilda (Mrs. Joseph H. Swift, Jr.), Barbara (Mrs. Richard A. Henry), Katharine (Mrs. Kempton S. Howland). Began with First Nat. Bank, Hyannis, Mass., 1894. Assistant cashier, 1897-1902, cashier, 1902-12, pres., 1912-16; pres. Hyannis Trust Co., 1916-19; president First Nat. Bank, New Bedford, 1919-41, chmn. bd. 1941— (bank now named First Safe Deposit Nat. Bank New Bedford). Trustee St. Luke's Hospital (New Bedford); mem. Am. Bankers Assn. (ex-pres. nat. bank div.). Republican. Universalist. Mason. Club: Wamsutta (ex-pres.). Home: 254 Hawthorn St. Office: 1st Nat. Bank, New Bedford, Mass. Deceased.

COOK, John, wire mfr.; b. Bklyn., Feb. 28, 1889; s. George and Elvira (Johnson) C.; M.E., Stevens Inst. Tech., 1911; m. Elizabeth Ransom, June 10, 1916; children—John R., Doris (Mrs. Norman Trosby), Paul M., Mary E. (Mrs. John W. McKean). Pres., dir. Cornish Wire Co., N.Y.C., 1920—, Cook Mfg. Co., Paterson, N.J., 1935—; dir. Warren Wire Co. N.J. Served as 1st lt. U.S. Army, 1917-18. Patentee in field. Home: 146 S. Irving St., Ridgewood, N.J. Office: Cornish Wire Co., 50 Church St., N.Y.C. 7. Died Sept. 17, 1955.

COOK, Melville Thurston, botanist; b. Coffeen, Ill., Sept. 20, 1869; s. William Harvey (M.D.) and Elizabeth Frances (Robinson) C.; student, DePauw U., 1888-89, 91-93, A.M., 1902; A.B., Leland Stanford Jr. U., 1894; Marine Biol. Lab., Woods Hole, Mass., 1896, 1899, 1900; U. Chgo., summers, 1897, 1898; Ohio State Lab., Sandusky, summers, 1902, 1903; Ph.D., Ohio State U., 1904; hon. Sc.D., U. P.R., 1940, DePauw U., 1940; fellow New York Bot. Garden, 1906-07; m. Dora Reavill, Sept. 8, 1897; children—Harvey Reavill, Harold Thurston, Elizabeth (Mrs. Harry A. Ross). Prin. high sch. Vandalia, Ill., 1894-95; instr. in biology De Pauw U., 1895-97, prof. 1897-1904; chief dept. plant pathology and econ. entomology Estacion Central Agronomica, Santiago de las Vegas, Cuba, 1904-06; plant pathologist Del. Agrl. Expt. Sta., Newark, 1907-11; state plant pathologist of N.J., and prof. plant pathology Rutgers Coll., 1911-23; plant pathologist N.J. Agrl. Expt. Sta., 1911-23, Insular Expt. Station, Rio Piedras, P.R., 1923-40, retired 1940; vis. prof. botany La. State U., 1944—; editor Journal of Dept. Agr. of P.R., 1928-40, research lectr. sch. tropical medicine, 1926. Lecturer on embryology, Central Coll. Phys. and Surg., Indpls., 1902-03; on comparative anatomy Med. Coll. Ind., 1903-04. Fellow A.A.A.S., (v.p. 1921, sec. bot. sect. 1918-20, chmn. of sect. 1921), Ind. Acad. Sci., Bot. Soc. Am.; mem. Am. Phytopathol. Soc. (v.p. 1916, pres. 1917), Ecol. Soc. Am., Am. Assn. Econ. Entomologists, Entomol. Soc. Am., Ind. Acad. Sciences, N.J. Science Teachers' Assn. (pres. 1920-22), S.A.R., Delta Upsilon, Sigma Xi, Phi Beta Kappa, Pi Gamma Mu, Gamma Sigma Delta. Mason (32°, K.T., Shriner, grand sr. warden P.R., 1929). Author: Diseases of Tropical Plants, 1912; Applied Economic Botany, 1919; College Botany, 1920; Los Enfermedades de las Plantas Economica de las Antillas, 1939; Los virosis de las plantas, 1943; Viruses and Virus Diseases of Plant, 1947. Contbr. to bot. jours. Home: care Mrs. Harry A. Ross, 1045 Via Tranquila, Santa Barbara, Cal. Died Aug. 11, 1952.

COOK, Orator Fuller, Jr., botanist; b. Clyde, N.Y., May 28, 1867; s. Orator Fuller and Eliza (Hookway) C.; Ph.B., Syracuse U., 1890, hon. D. Sc., 1930; m. Alice Carter, Oct. 11, 1892. In charge dept. biology, Syracuse U., 1890-91; made (1891-97) extended visits to Liberia for exploration and investigation as agt. N.Y. State Colonization Soc.; prof. natural sciences in Liberia Coll., 1891-97, pres. same, 1896-97; secured extensive collection of plants and animals now under investigation in U.S. Nat. Mus.; custodian and asst. curator U.S. Nat. Mus., 1898—. Spl. agt. in charge plant importation, U.S. Dept. of Agr., 1898-1900, in charge of investigation in tropical agr., 1900—, visiting P.R., Guatemala, Mexico, Costa Rica, etc.; prof. botany, George Washington U., 1904. Author of various articles and reports on Liberia and Africa colonization, P.R., tropical agr., botany, zoölogy, evolution, history of cultivated plants, especially on breeding, acclimatization, and cultural improvement of cotton and rubber plants, also on classification of palms and millipeds. As botanist representing U.S. Dept. Agr. with Bingham expdn. to Peru under auspices of Nat. Geog. Soc. and Yale U., Mar.-Sept. 1915, investigating plants used by the Incas; expdn. to Haiti summer of 1917 on agrl. exploration and study for improvement of agricultural conditions. Expdn. to China for study of agrl. conditions, summer of 1919; Carnegie Instn. expdn. to Central America to study ancient Maya civilization, 1922; expdns. to Haiti, Panama, Mexico, Colombia, and Ecuador, to investigate native cottons and sources of rubber, 1923-31; botanist in charge palm classification, Fairchild Tropical Garden, Cocoanut Grove, Fla., 1937. Home: Lanham, Md. Died Apr. 23, 1949.

COOK, Vernon, lawyer; b. Balt., Feb. 4, 1870; s. Henry F. and Catherine E. (Jarboe) C.; A.B., Johns Hopkins, 1890; LL.B., U. Md., 1892; m. Jessie R. Kellinger, Feb. 2, 1898; children—Marjorie, Vernon, Jr. Admitted to Md. bar, 1892, since engaged in gen. practice of law, Balt.; mem. Gans & Haman, 1901-14, Cook, Chesnut & Markell, 1914-31, Cook & Markell, 1931—; dir. Emerson Drug Co., Md. Glass Corp., Citro Chem. Co., Independent Ice Co. Mem. Commn. to Revise Balt. City Charter, 1945. Mem. Am., Md., Balt. bar assns. Republican. Club: University. Home: 4 E. Highfield Rd. Office: First Nat. Bank Bldg., Balt. Died May 3, 1954.

COOK, Waldo Lincoln, newspaper editor; b. Woonsocket, R.I., Feb. 19, 1865; s. William N. and Rhoby (Sherburne) C.; grad. Tufts College, Mass., 1887 (A.B., extra ordinem, 1893; A.M., causa honoris, 1921); m. Elizabeth S. Friend, May 9, 1893; 1 son, Sherburne Friend. On Springfield Republican since Apr. 1888; became editorial writer, 1896, and chief editorial writer, 1911, editor since 1922, now ret. Mem. Phi Beta Kappa. Home: 18 Dorchester St., Springfield, Mass. Died Sept. 16, 1951; buried Springfield, Mass.

COOK, William Cassius, state supt. schs.; b. Windom, W.Va., Nov. 21, 1882; s. William Henry Harrison and Mary Jane (Cooper) C.; A.B., Concord State Normal Sch., Athens, W.Va.; grad. study U. W.Va.; m. Lulu Stewart, 1907; children—Eunice Stewart, William Cassius. Tchr. rural schs., W.Va., until 1907; county supt., McDowell County, W.Va., 1909-25; dist. supt., Browns Creek Dist., McDowell County, 1926-29; state supt. free schs., W.Va., 1929—. Mem. W.Va. State Bd. Edn., 1919—; pres. Southern W.Va. Tchrs. Round Table; pres. State Edn. Assn., W.Va., 1925. Mem. Acad. Sci., Kappa Delta Pi. Republican. Baptist. Mason, Elk. Kiwanian. Author: Status of Education in West Virginia; Problems in School Finance. Home: Welch, W.V.a. Office: Dept. of Education, Charleston, W.Va. Died Dec. 10, 1947.

COOKE, Flora Juliette, educator; b. Bainbridge, O.; d. Sumner and Rosetta (Ellis) Hannum; adopted daughter of Charles E. and Luella (Miller) Cooke; ed. pub. and high schs., Youngstown, O., Chgo. Normal Sch. and U. of Chgo. Extension; unmarried. Teacher Chgo. Normal Sch. and Chgo. Inst., under Francis W. Parker, 1891-1900; prin. Francis W. Parker Sch. 1901-1934; trustee 1934-48. Mem. N.E.A., Nat. Soc. for Scientific Study of Edn., Northern Ill. Teachers' Assn., Audubon Soc., Polit. Equality League, Acad. Science. Methodist. Author: Nature Myths, 1895. Contbr. on ednl. subjects. Home: 616 York Pl. Address: 530 Arlington Pl. Chgo. Died Feb. 1953.

COOKE, Harold Groves, coll. pres.; b. Scatterwood, S.D., June 12, 1890; s. John Bunyan and Loucinda Jane (Groves) C.; A.B., Southwestern U., Georgetown, Tex., 1911, D.D., 1943; B.D., Southern Meth. U., Dallas, Tex., 1920; LL.D. (hon.), Oklahoma City University, 1952; m. Erie Kimbell, Sept. 2, 1914; children—Laura Lee (Mrs. Eschol Hudnall), Harold Groves, John Bunyan, Charles James, Myra Lou. Admitted to Tex. bar, 1912; ordained to Meth. ministry, 1913; pastor in Meth. Ch., 1913-38; prof. of homiletics and City Ch. Orgn. and Adminstrn.,

Southern Meth. U., 1928-30; dist. supt. in Meth. Ch., 1939-42; pres. McMurry Coll., Abilene, Tex., since 1942. Mason (32°, Scottish Rite, Shriner). Clubs: Lions (Tulsa, Okla., pres., 1920-22); Rotary (Abilene, Tex.), Kiwanis (Knoxville, Tenn.). Author: The Paris Plan, Treatise on Church Finance. Home: 2350 Cooke St.; Abilene, Tex. Died Mar. 16, 1958.

COOKE, Helen Temple, educator; b. Rutland, Vt., Apr. 13, 1865; d. Edmund Foster and Mary Ann (Bardwell) Cooke; ed. Rutland pub. schs. Conducted a pvt. sch. in Rutland, 1882-94; spl. student, Wellesley Coll., 1894-99; prin. Dana Hall Sch., 1899—; prin. of "Tenacre," a sch. for younger girls est. in Wellesley, Mass., 1910, Pine Manor est. 1911, now a Junior College including the Dana Hall Grad. Sch. of Music, est. 1925. Address: Wellesley, Mass. Died Apr. 12, 1955; buried Walpole N.H.

COOKE, Henry D., naval officer, ret.; b. Washington, Sept. 21, 1879; s. Henry David and Anna Howell (Dodge) C.; grad. U.S. Naval Acad., 1903; m. Elinor Talbot, Jan. 4, 1921. Midshipman U.S. Naval Acad., 1899; became dir. physical tng. U.S. Naval Acad. 1930, become comdt., 1931, ret.; commd. rear adm. USN, 1939, ret.; resumed active duty 1941. Recipient Bronze Star medal. Mem. S.A.R. Clubs: Army and Navy (Washington); New York Yacht (N.Y.C.). Address: 41 Round Hill Rd., Roslyn, L.I., N.Y. Died July 6, 1958.*

COOKE, James Francis, editor, exec.; b. Bay City, Mich., Nov. 14, 1875; s. George and Caroline (Johnson) C.; ed. under many teachers, America and Europe; hon. Mus. Doc., Ohio Northern U., 1919, Capitol U., 1927, Cincinnati Conservatory, 1929, U. of Pa., 1930; LL.D., Ohio Northern U., 1925, Usinus Coll., 1927; L.H.D., Bethany Coll., 1931; Ed.D., Coll. of Emporia, 1938; LL.D., University of Michigan, 1938; Litt.D., College of Ozarks, 1940; Doctor Fine Arts, Grinnell Coll., 1950; Mus.D., Butler U., 1951; Dr. Journalism, Hastings Coll., 1951; A.F.D., Houghton Coll., 1955; m. Betsy Eleanor Beckwith, 1899 (dec. 1954); 1 son, Francis Sherman, Tchr. piano and voice, organist and conductor, New York and Brooklyn, many yrs.; was asst. to Prof. Franklin W. Hooper at Brooklyn Inst. Arts and Sciences; visited numerous Europeaan musical conservatories and American colleges to study teaching systems; wrote regularly in German and French for European publications; public speaker on humanistic, business and artistic subjects (addresses also in French, German and Italian); editor Etude, the music magazine, Philadelphia, 1907-50, now editor emeritus; president Theodore Presser Company, Phila., 1925-36, John Church Co., 1930-36, Oliver Ditson Co., Inc., 1931-36. Pres. Presser Found., 1918-56, now president emeritus; president Philadelphia Music Teachers' Assn., 1910-27, Writeabout Club, 1916-17, Drama League of Phila., 1917. "Four-Minute Man," 1917. Pres. Henry Labarre Jayne Memorial Fund; pres. Chestnut St. Business Men's Assn., 1938-54; mem. bd. dirs. Mus. Fund Soc. Mem. Pres. Eisenhower's People-to-People Partnership. Decorated Chevalier Legion of Honor (France), 1930. Mem. Franco-Am. Inst. of Sci. (v.p.), Societa pro Cultura Italiano, Sons of the Revolution, Mus. Teachers Nat. Assn. (hon. life), Phi Mu Alpha Sinfonia (hon.). Clubs: Rotary, Union League, Penn Club, Art Alliance. Author: Standard History of Music, 1909; Mastering the Scales and Arpeggios, 1913; Great Pianists on Piano Playing, 1914; Musical Playlets for Children; Music Masters, Old and New; Great Singers on the Art of Singing, 1921; Great Men and Famous Musicians, 1925; Young Folks' Picture History of Music, 1925; Light, More Light, 1925, enlarged edit., 1941; Musical Travelogues, 1934; Street of the Little Candles, 1937; How to Memorize Music, 1947; The Fabulous Dr. Franklin, 1956; A Historical Musical Pilgrimage, 1958; Memoirs-Friends Everywhere, 1958; also pub. poems, short stories, songs, numerous pianoforte pieces and plays (4 plays produced professionally). Home: 38 Llanberris Road, Bala-Cynwyd, Pa. Office: 1717 Sansom St., Philadelphia 3, Pa. Died Mar. 3, 1960.

COOKE, Joseph Platt, bus. exec.; b. Oakland, Calif., Nov. 19, 1896; s. Joseph Platt and Maud (Baldwin) C.; student Hotchkiss Sch., Lakeville, Conn., 1913-16, Yale, 1916-17 and 1919-20, Harvard, 1920-21; m. Alice Hastings, June 17, 1920; children—Elise (Mrs. Frederick Wm. Pratt, Jr.), Joseph Platt. With Alexander & Baldwin, Ltd., Honolulu, Hawaii, since 1921, beginning as stock transfer clerk, later sec., treas., and asst. mgr., 1938-43, gen. mgr., 1943, pres., 1946-48, now chmn. bd.; dir., treas. Baldwin Packers, Ltd., Pacific Plant Products, Ltd.; vice pres., dir. East Maui Irrigation Co., Ltd., Haleakala Pineapple Co., Ltd. Hawaiian Comml. and Sugar Co., Ltd.; pres. Kahuku Plantation Co., Kauai Electric Co., Ltd., Kauai Pineapple Co., Ltd., Kauai Terminal, Ltd., McBryde Sugar Co., Ltd.; dir. The Hawaiian Trust Co., Ltd. Mem. Psi Upsilon. Clubs: Pacific of Hawaii, Outrigger (Honolulu). Home: 4433 Kahala Av. Office: 822 Bishop St., Honolulu) 1, Hawaii. Died June 8, 1953.

COOKE, Juan Isaac, diplomat; b. Buenos Aires, Argentina, July 29, 1895; s. Guillermo William and Maria Aurelia (Luciani) C.; M.L., Nat. U. La Plata, 1918; m. Elvira Lenzi, Feb. 7, 1919; children—John William, Carlos Federico, Jorge Felix. Mem. editorial staff, La Epoca, 1916-22; mem. acad. council, sch. legal and social scis. U. La Plata, 1920-24, asst. prof. constnl. law, 1926-30; undersec. of govt. Province of Buenos Aires, 1922-23, nat. rep., 1938-43, minister of fgn. affairs and worship, 1945-46; editor-owner, daily El Plata, 1935; prof. Argentine and comparative constnl. law, sch. law and social scis. U. Buenos Aires, 1947, prof. constnl. history, 1953, mem. inst. of polit., constnl. and adminstrv. law; ambassador of Argentina to Brazil, 1947-54; ambassador, permanent rep. of Argentina to UN, 1954—, pres. ECOSOC, 1954—. Mem. commn. of Argentine Congressmen who visited the U.S.A. on invitation of Dept. of State and Ho. of Reps., 1941; del. of Argentina to Inter-Am. Legal Com. of Rio de Janeiro, 1952; pres. Argentine delegation to 5th session of Econ. Commn. for Latin Am., 1953. Decorated Grand Cross Orden al Merito (Chile), Orden del Sol (Peru), Orden Nacional del Merito (Paraguay), Orden Crucero del Sud (Brazil), Orden Eloy Alfaro. Author: Curso de Sociedades Comerciales (with Dr. Luis Horacio Sommariva), 1917; La Compensación en el Derecho Comercial Argentino, 1922; Bienes Reservables, 1923; Política Argentina, 1927; Por la Verdad del Sufragio, 1939; Hay Que Argentinizar la Patagonia, 1939; En Defensa de las Instituciones y de la Soberanía Argentina, 1939; La Nueva Ley de Amnistía, 1940; Represión Legal del Fraude, 1941; Hacia la Unidad Política y Económica de la Nación, 1941; Consejo de Defensa Nacional, 1941; Jurisdicción de la Nación sobre Tierras Adquiridas en las Provincias, 1942; also collected speeches, and ofcl. documents. Home: 480 Park Av., N.Y.C. Office: Argentine Permanent Delegation to UN, 720 Fifth Av., N.Y.C. 19. Died June 23, 1957.

COOKE, Morris Llewellyn, consulting engr. in management; b. Carlisle, Pa., May 11, 1872; s. William Harvey (M.D.) and Elizabeth Richmond (Marsden) C.; M.E., Lehigh U., 1895, Sc.D., 1922; m. Eleanor Bushnell Davis, June 16, 1900. Reporter on Phila. Press, Denver News and Evening Telegram (New York), 1890-94; served apprenticeship in Cramp's Shipyard, Phila., later journeyman machinist at Southwark Foundry; engr. for Acetylene Co., Washington, D.C., 1896-97; asst. engr. U.S. Navy during Spanish-Am. War; engaged in commercial orgn. work, 1899-1905; consulting engr., 1905-11; dir. Dept. Pub. Works, Phila., 1911-15; chmn. storage sect. War Industries Bd. of Council Nat. Defense and mem. Depot Bd. U.S. Army, 1917; exec. asst. to chmn. U.S. Shipping Bd., 1918. Made study of collegiate administrative methods in U.S. and Can. for Carnegie Foundation, 1910; dir. Giant Power Survey Pa., 1923; chmn. Miss. Valley Com. of Pub. Works Adminstrn., 1933; dir. water resources sect. of Nat. Resources Bd., 1934; adminstr. Rural Electrification Adminstrn., 1935-37; chmn. Great Plains Com., 1936-37; tech. cons. Labor Div., Office of Production Management, 1940-41; U.S. expert adjudication Mexican oil dispute, head Am. Tech. Mission to Brazil, 1942. Trustee of Power Authority, State of New York, 1928-33; member Com. to Survey Patent System, 1946-47; chmn. President's Water Resources Policy Commn., 1950-51. Co-chmn. Com. for an Effective Fgn. Aid Program. Fellow A.A.A.S.; fellow Am. Soc. Mech. Engrs. (council 1915); mem. Taylor Soc. (pres. 1927), Franklin Inst., Delta Phi, Sigma Xi; hon. mem. Masaryk Acad. (Prague), Czechoslovak Order of the White Lion, Order Aztec Eagle (Mexico), Legion od Honor (France). Democrat. Episcopalian. Clubs: Engineers (N.Y.C.); Engineers (Philadelphia, Pa.); Cosmos (Washington, D.C.). Author: Academic and Industrial Efficiency, 1910; Snapping Cords,1915; Our Cities Awake, 1918; (with Philip Murray) Organized Labor and Production, 1940; Brazil on the March, 1944. Editor: Public Utility Regulation, 1922; What Electricity Costs, 1933. Homes: St. Georges Rd., Phila. 19; also New Hope, Pa. Died Mar. 5, 1960.

COOKE, Richard Dickson, lawyer; b. Norfolk, Va., Apr. 29, 1880; s. Merritt Todd and Mary (Dickson) C.; Norfolk Acad., Pantops Acad., LL.B., U. Va., 1902; m. Fannie Webb Royster, Apr. 15, 1909; children—Sheppard Royster, Mary Dickson (Mrs. John P. Edmondson), Richard Dickson. Admitted to Va., bar, 1902; mem. Willcox, Cooke & Willcox, Norfolk, 1902—; dir. Nat. Bank Commerce, Norfolk, F. S. Royster Guano Co. Pres. Norfolk Community Fund, 1931-32, United War Fund, 1941-43. Mem. council City Norfolk, 1946-50, mayor, 1946-49. Mem. com. mgmt. Naval Y.M.C.A., 1939—; trustee Mary Baldwin Coll., 1940—. Recipient 1942 Distinguished Service medal, Cosmopolitan Club. Mem. Am., Va. State, Norfolk and Portsmouth (pres. 1946-47) bar assns., Sigma Chi. Presbyn. Clubs: Rotary, Virginia, Yacht and Country (Norfolk); Princess Anne Country (Virginia Beach, Va.). Home: 517 Warren Crescent. Office: Bank of Commerce Bldg., Norfolk, Va. Died Oct. 10, 1958; buried Elmwood Cemetery, Norfolk, Va.

COOKE, Robert Locke, educator; b. Brockton, Mass., Oct. 21, 1889; s. William Henry and Ada (Locke) C.; B.S., U. Cal., 1911, M.A., 1930, Ed.D., 1932; m. Olive Montgomery, June 8, 1918; children—Robert Montgomery, Alma Rose, Weldon John. Grad. asst. engring. physics U. Cal., 1911-12; instr. Cal. Sch. Mech. Arts, 1912-16; instr. sci. high sch., Yolo Co., Cal., 1916-19, Merced, Cal., 1922-24, Crockett, Cal., 1928-35; asso. prof. edn. Wheaton (Ill.) Coll., 1935-40, prof., 1941—, chmn. dept. edn., 1945—. Mem. Phi Delta Kappa. Republican. Author: Philosophy, Education and Certainty, 1940. Contbr. profl. publs. Editorial counselor, The Book of Life, twenty first edit. Home: 310 Scott St., Wheaton, Ill. Died July 23, 1955; buried Wheaton Cemetery.

COOKE, Thornton, banker; b. South Sodus, N.Y., Dec. 22, 1873; s. Sidney Granger and Helen Maria (Thornton) C.; A.B., U. of Kan., 1893; A.M., Harvard, 1897; m. Emily Darlington Hulme, Oct. 15, 1898; children—Sidney Merritt, Martha Darlington (dec.), Laure Payon Morse. Asst. cashier, later cashier Bank of Herington (Kan.), 1893-96, 1897-1902; asst. treas. Fidelity Trust Co., Kansas City, Mo., 1902-06, treas., 1906-11, v.p., 1911-16; pres. Midwest Nat. Bank, Kansas City, 1916-18; with Capital Issues Committee, Washington, D.C., 1918-19; pres. Columbia National Bank, Kansas City, 1919-46; chmn. bd., 1947-50, retired, 1950; trustee, Flour Mills of America, Incorporated, 1939-41. City attorney Herington, 1896; mayor, 1900. President Kansas City Clearing House Assn., 1930-32 and 1946-48; member adv. committee Reconstruction Finance Corp., Kansas City Office. Mem. Am. Bankers Assn. (chmn. com. on taxation 1924-32); Mo. Bankers Assn. (pres. 1916-17), Phi Beta Kappa, Beta Gamma Sigma, Phi Delta Theta. Democrat. Unitarian. Clubs: University, Kansas City Country, Harvard. Editor: Survey of Bank Taxation in United States (4 editions), 1925-31. Contributor to Harvard Quarterly Journal of Economics, Banking, Am. Economic Review, London Economist, Nation's Business, Atlantic Monthly. Home: 5012 Summit St. Office: 921 Walnut St., Kansas City 13, Mo. Died Feb. 25, 1952; buried Mount Moriah Cemetery, Kansas City, Mo.

COOLBAUGH, Melville Fuller (kōōl'baw), coll. pres. emeritus; b. Coolbaugh, Pa., Feb. 8, 1877; s. John and Abbie (Woodward) C.; B.S., Colorado Coll., 1902, LL.D., 1925; M.A., Columbia, 1905; LL.D., U. Colo., 1927; spl. research work Mass. Inst. Technology, 1914-15; m. Osie Frances Smith, Nov. 17, 1905; children—John, Franklin, Lois May Hinkley, David Fogg. Instr. chemistry Colo. Coll., 1902-04; asst. in chemistry Columbia, 1904-05; prof. chemistry, S.D. State Sch. of Mines, 1906-14; asst. prof. chemistry Case Sch. Applied Science, Cleve., 1915-17; prof. chemistry Colo. Sch. Mines, 1917-18; with C.W.S., U.S. Army, World War, June-Dec., 1918; private research, 1919; dir. metall. research for Metals Exploration Co., Denver, 1919-25; pres. Colo. Sch. of Mines, 1925-46, pres. emeritus, 1946—. Inventions in ore roasting, hydro and electro metallurgy; sec. Colo. Geol. Survey; mem. Colo. Planning Commn., 1934-45; mem. State Mineral Resources Bd.; regional rep., Region 11, Engring., Science and Management War Training; mem. Pres. Truman's Com. of 19 on Fgn. Aid, 1947. Mem. Am. Chem. Soc., Am. Electro-Chem. Soc., Am. Inst. Mining and Metall. Engrs., Colo. Mining Assn., Colo.-Wyo. Acad. Science, Mining and Metall. Soc. of America, Sigma Gamma Epsilon, Sigma Xi. Mason. Clubs: Teknik, Schoolmasters, Mile High, University (Denver); Kiwanis (Golden). Home: Golden, Colo. Died Sept. 9, 1950.

COOLEY, Robert Lawrence, educator; b. Village of Waubeka, Town of Fredonia, Wis., May 3, 1869; s. Charles Festus and Helen M. (English) C.; grad. Oshkosh Normal Sch., 1894; M.A., U. of Wis., 1924; D.Sc., Stout Inst., Menomonie, Wis., 1925; m. Carrie S. Ide, Sept. 1, 1898; children—Katharine Ide, Margaret Ide. Rural sch. tchr., later prin. high sch., Oconto, Wis., supt. schs., Oconto, 1895-1903; grammar sch. prin., Milw., 1903-12; inaugurated Milw. Vocational Sch., 1912, under part-time law of Wis., retired, 1939. In charge educational work of Q.M. T.C., near Jacksonville, Fla., by request of Col. Goethals, 1918; called to Washington, to assist in ednl. work of the Motor Transport Corps until Armistice; mem. Nat. Adv. Com. on Edn., 1929; mem. adv. com. Nat. Survey of Secondary Edn., 1929. Mem. N.E.A., Am. Vocational Assn. (pres. 1928, 29), Wis. Tchrs. Assn. (pres. 1928). Republican. Mason, K.P., Kiwanian. Clubs: Professional Men's, City. Home: Waubeka, Wisconsin. Office: 1015 N. 6th St., Milw. Died May 19, 1944; buried Union Cemetery, Waubeka, Town of Fredonia, Wis.

COOLEY, Thomas Ross, naval officer; b. Grass Valley, Calif., June 26, 1893; s. Thomas Ross and Mary Adelaide (Cota) C.; B.S., U.S. Naval Acad., 1917; m. Adelaide Prescott Morris, Apr. 21, 1919; children—Adelaide Morris (Mrs. Hal W. Smith), Mary Lawrence. Commd. ensign U.S. Navy, 1917, advanced through grades to rear adm., Mar. 20, 1943; served at sea and shore stations, Europe, Orient, Central and South Am., U.S.; mem. faculty U.S. naval Acad., 1922-24-27-29-37-40; comdg. officer U.S.S. Almaak, Washington and battleship div., 1941-42, 44-47; dir., officer personnel, U.S. Navy

Dept., 1942-44; comdr. U.S. Naval Base, Newport, R.I., since 1947. Served World Wars I and II. Awarded Legion of Merit, Victory medals (both world wars), various campaign and service medals and ribbons, Medal of Merit (Nicaragua). Mem. U.S. Naval Inst., U.S. Naval Acad. Alumni Assn. Roman Catholic. Clubs: Army-Navy (Washington), Acme Gun, Pacific Fleet. Home: Grass Valley, Calif. Office: Quarters A, U.S. Naval Base, Newport, R.I. Died Nov. 1959.*

COOLIDGE, Amory, cotton mfr.; b. Boston, 1895; grad. Harvard, 1917. Exec. v.p., dir. Pepperell Mfg. Co.; dir. Scott & Williams, Inc. Served as officer USN, World War I. Clubs: Eastern Yacht, Myopia Hunt, Essex County, Tennis and Racquet. Home: Dedham, Mass. Office: 160 State St., Boston. Died Apr. 2, 1952.*

COOLIDGE, Arthur William, lawyer; b. Woodfords, Me., Oct. 13, 1881; s. Merrit B. and Lucy Greenwood (French) C.; student Westbrook Sem., Deering, Me.; A.B., Tufts Coll., Mass., 1903, A.M., 1945; LL.B., Harvard, 1906; m. Mabel F. Tilton, Dec. 15, 1910; children—Dorothy B. (Mrs. Eugene R. Cox), Robert Tilton, Arthur William. Admitted to Mass. bar 1906, and since practiced law in Boston; mem. Mass. legislature, 1937-40; mem. Mass. senate, 1941-46, pres. of senate, 1945-46; lt.-gov. of Mass., 1947-48; Rep. candidate for governor of Mass. primary 1950. Served on Massachusetts State Guard, Finance Commn. of Norwood, Mass.; mem. sch. com., Reading, Mass.; dir. Washingtonian Hosp., Mass. Tuberculosis League. Mem. Mass., Middlesex, and Am. bar assns., Ancient and Hon. Artillery Co. of Boston, Mayflower Descendants, Theta Delta Chi, Republican. Unitarian. Mason (grand master Mass., 1944). Home: 210 Summer Av., Reading, Mass. Office: 68 Devonshire St., Boston 9. Died Jan. 22, 1952; buried Forest Glen Cemetery, Reading, Mass.

COOLIDGE, Elizabeth Sprague ((ko͞ol'ĭj), music patron; b. Chicago, Ill.; d. Albert Arnold and Nancy Ann (Atwood) Sprague; hon. A.M., Mt. Holyoke Coll., 1926; Litt.D., Smith College, 1927; A.M., Yale, 1927, Mills College, 1928; LL.D., U. of Calif., 1933; Mus.D., Pomona Coll., 1938; m. Dr. Frederic Shurtleff Coolidge, Nov. 12, 1891 (now dec.); 1 son, Albert Sprague. Donor Auditorium, Library of Congress; South Mountain Temple of Chamber Music, Pittsfield, Mass.; Sprague Memorial Hall, Yale Univ.; Pension Fund, Chicago Orchestra; Crippled Children's Home, Pittsfield, Mass.; Coolidge Foundation, Washington, D.C. Decorated Legion of Honor (France); Order of Leopold (Belgium), Order of the Crown (Belgium); awarded Cobbett medal of London; hon. citizen of Frankfort with medal. Clubs: Colony, Cosmopolitan (New York); Chilton (Boston); Friday, Fortnightly, Arts (Chicago); Sulgrave (Washington, D.C.); Wednesday Morning, Country (Pittsfield, Mass.); American Women's (Paris and London). Home: Hotel Continental, Cambridge, Mass. Died Nov. 4, 1953.

COOLIDGE, George Greer, mfr.; b. Plainfield, N.J. Jan. 25, 1885; s. Henry and Carrie Louise (Wright) C.; Ph.B., Yale U., 1904; m. Ethel Van Kirk Byram, Oct. 22, 1910; 1 dau., Elizabeth Coolidge Ebbert. With Lackawanna R.R. Shops, Scranton, Pa. 1904-06; Westinghouse Air Brake Co. Shops Wilmerding, Pa. 1906-07; v.p. dir. Harbison-Walker Refractories Co. 1933-—; dir. Fidelity Trust Co., Blow Knox Co.; vice pres. Dollar Savings Bank, Pittsburgh. Member Asso. Charities (past pres.), Community Fund (dir.), Am. Iron & Steel Inst., Engrs. Soc. of Western Pa., Family Soc. of Allegheny County. Trustee U. of Pittsburgh; dir. Municipal Planning Assn., Child Guidance Clinic. Republican. Episcopalian (Sr. Warden). Home: 5440 Aylesboro Av., Pitts. Died Nov. 2, 1954; buried Allegheny Cemetery, Pitts.

COOLIDGE, Grace Goodhue (Mrs. Calvin Coolidge); b. Burlington, Vt., Jan. 3, 1879; d. Andrew Issachar and Lemira (Barrett) Goodhue; Ph.B., U. of Vt., 1902, LL.D., 1929; LL.D., Boston U., 1924, George Washington U., 1929, Smith Coll., 1929; m. Calvin Coolidge, 29th President of U.S., October 4, 1905 (died Jan. 5, 1933); children—John, Calvin (dec.). Taught sch. at Clarke Sch. for the Deaf, Northampton, Mass., 1902-05. Mem. Hoover-Curtis Eastern Campaign Com., 1932. Trustee Mercersburg Acad., resigned from bd. regents, 1945. Chmn. bd. corp., Clarke Sch. for the Deaf, Northampton, Mass. Republican. Congregationalist. Home: Northampton, Mass. Died July 8, 1957; buried Plymouth, Vt.

COOLIDGE, Julian Lowell, educator; b. Brookline, Mass., Sept. 28, 1873; s. Joseph Randolph and Julia (Gardner) C.; A.B., Harvard, 1895, LL.D., 1940; B.Sc., Oxford, 1897; Ph.D., U. Bonn, Prussia, 1904; D.Sc., Lehigh U., 1938; m. Theresa Reynolds, Jan. 17, 1901; children—Jane Revere, Julian Gardner, Archibald Cary, Margaret Wendell, Elizabeth Peabody, Rachel Revere, John Phillips, Theresa Reynolds. Teacher mathematics Groton (Mass.) School, 1897-99; instr. mathematics Harvard, 1900, assistant prof., 1908, prof., 1918-40, prof. emeritus, 1940-—. Served as major, U.S. Army, 1917-19; liaison officer attached to French Gen. Staff, Paris, 1918-19. Decorated Cross Legion of Honor, Officer and Officer de l'Instruction Publique, France, 1919. Fellow American Acad. Arts and Sciences; mem. Am. Math. Soc. (past v.p.), Math. Assn. Am. (pres. 1925), Assn. Math. Teachers in N.E. (past pres.), Phi Beta Kappa. Club: Harvard (Boston). Author: Elements of Non-Euclidean Geometry, 1909; Treatise on the Circle and the Sphere, 1916; Geometry of the Complex Domain, 1924; Introduction to Mathematical Probability, 1925; Algebraic Plane Curves, 1931; History of Geometrical Methods, 1940; History of the Conic Sections, 1943. Home: 27 Fayerweather St., Cambridge 38, Mass. Died Mar. 5, 1954.

COOLIDGE, Lawrence, lawyer and trustee; b. Boston, Jan. 17, 1905; s. Harold Jefferson and Edith (Lawrence) C.; student Longwood Day Sch., Brookline, Mass., 1912-17, Groton (Mass.) Sch., 1917-22, U. of Ariz., 1922-23; A.B. cum laude, Harvard, 1927, LL.B., 1931; m. Victoria S. Tytus, Jan. 16, 1932; children—Robert Tytus, Lawrence, Nathaniel Silsbee. Asst. dean, Harvard Coll., 1928-29; admitted to Mass. bar, 1931; asso. firm Loring, Coolidge, Nobel & Boyd, 1931-34; partner, 1934-37; partner Gaston, Snow, Rice & Boyd, 1937 and since Dec. 1945. dir. Nat. Shawmut Bank, Boston. Trustee Western Real Estate Trust, University Associates, Suffolk Savings Bank for Seamen, and others. Served with U.S.N.R. (active duty), 1942-45; separated with rank of comdr., Dec. 1945. Awarded 7 campaign stars, commendation ribbon. Trustee Peabody Museum of Salem (Mass.), Boston Floating Hosp., Church Home Soc. (pres.). Overseer Harvard U. Trustee of Donations of Protestant Episcopal Ch. Republican. Presbyterian. Clubs: Somerset, Myopia, Tavern, Union Boat, Harvard (Boston); Harvard (New York). Editor and pub. Thoughts on Thomas Jefferson by Thomas Jefferson Coolidge, 1936. Home: Main St., Hamilton, Mass. Office: 82 Devonshire St., Boston. Died Jan. 3, 1950; buried Hamilton Cemetery.

COOLIDGE, T(homas) Jefferson, banker; s. T. Jefferson and Clara (Amory) C.; A.B., Harvard, 1915; children—Thomas Jefferson, Catherine, J. Linzee. Apptd. special asst. to Sec. of Treasury Morgenthau, in charge fiscal affairs, Mar. 1934, under-sec. of the Treasury, 1934-36; dir., mem. exec. com. United Fruit Co.; dir. Old Colony Trust Co., Boston Edison Co., N.E. Mutual Life Insurance Co., First National Bank of Boston. Trustee Isabella Stewart Gardner Mus., Mus. of Fine Arts, Peter Bent Brigham Hospital; trustee and treasurer of the Humane Soc. of Mass. Mem. Phi Beta Kappa. Clubs: Somerset, Tavern (Boston); The Brook (New York); Myopia Hunt, The Country (Brookline). Home: Coolidge Point, Magnolia, Mass. Office: 80 Federal St., Boston. Died Aug. 6, 1959.

COON, Jesse Drake, lawyer; b. St. Cloud, Minn., Oct. 11, 1885; s. Ruene Runyan and Eva (Huntington) C.; student Grand Island (Neb.) Coll., 1905-07; A.B., Sioux Falls (S.D.) Coll., 1909; Ph.B., U. of Chicago, 1915, J.D., 1915; m. Hilda Miller, Nov. 25, 1915; 1 dau., Nan Alice (wife of Lt. Harry Evans Allen Nord, U.S. Navy). Admitted to bar, 1913, engaged in practice of law, 1913-—; mem. firm Coon and Coon, Sioux Falls, S.D., 1915-—; counsel Senate Com. on D.C., 1953-—. Served as state's attorney, 1925-26; South Dakota Republican state chmn., 1938-40, Willkie state chmn., 1940. Trustee Sioux Valley Hosp. Dir. bd. Sioux Falls Coll.; dir. Carnegie Free Pub. Library. Pres. Minnehaha County bar assn., 1942; nat. counsel Pi Kappa Delta, 1920-40. Cosmopolitan Club Medalist. 1952. Mason (Shriner), K.P. Pub. sepaker on govt. by the people. Home: 1401 South Duluth Av. Office: 125 S. Main Av., Sioux Falls. S.D. Died Sept. 29, 1954; buried Hills of Rest, Sioux Falls.

COONEY, Charles Edwin, lawyer; b. Syracuse, N.Y., Aug. 14, 1873; s. Patrick D. and Rose (Carberry) C.; A.B., Syracuse U., 1897, LL.B., 1899; m. Josephine Wathen, Apr. 25, 1907 (dec.); m. 2d, Josephine Quinn, Nov. 29, 1922; children—Margaret Rose (Mrs. W. Wallace R. Hughes), Charles E. Admitted to N.Y. bar, 1889; mem. firm Costello, Cooney & Fearon, Syracuse. Mem. Phi Delta Theta, Phi Delta Phi, Phi Kappa Alpha. Home: 3566 E. Genesee St., Syracuse 3. Office: University Bldg., Syracuse 2, N.Y. Died June 30, 1958.

COONRADT, Arthur C., (ko͞on'räd), prof. mech. engring.; b. Rockford, Ill., Aug. 12, 1887; s. Arthur R. and Carrie B. (Chapin) C.; A.B. in Mech. Engring., Stanford, 1909; Aero. Engr., N.Y.U., 1928; m. Ann Rock, Apr. 17, 1911; 1 son, Frederic C. Power plant designer Portland Electric Power Co., 1911-19; sales mgr. Grays Harbor Ry. and Light Co., 1919; dist. rep. Lidgerwood Mfg. Co., Seattle, 1920-24; power plant designer Stone & Webster Co., Seattle, 1924; instr. in mech. engring., Ore. State Coll., 1925-27; asst. prof. mech. engring., N.Y.U., later prof. Mem. Tau Beta Phi, Iota Alpha. Club: Gnome (Cal. Inst. Tech.). Home: 2120 W. 93d St., Los Angeles 47. Died Aug. 8, 1949.

COONS, Albert, retail exec.; b. Du Bois, Pa., Nov. 11, 1890; s. Cosmar P. and Theresa (Schwarz) C.; student Central High Sch., Phila., 1905-08, Alexander Hamilton Inst., 1911; m. May Lisette Bochroch, Jan. 14, 1920; 1 son, Albert. Leather goods mfr. and jobber, Coons Bros., Phila., 1907-10; with Louis Samler, dept. store, Lebanon, Pa., 1910-18, gen. mgr., 1919-29, part owner, 1919-29; dir. mem. exec. com. and merchandise counsellor for 14 stores, Hahn Dept. Stores, New York, since 1933; dir. and v.p. in charge of 16 stores, Allied Stores Corp., New York, since 1934; now pres., dir. Lebanon County Trust Co.; dir. Lebanon Steel Foundry. Served as sgt. 1st class, AEF, 1918-19. Director Pa. Retailers Assn.; dir. A.R.C. (Lebanon County (Pa.) chapter), Good Samaritan Hosp., Lebanon Library Assn. Republican. Jewish religion. Clubs: Lebanon Country, Kiwanis (Lebanon). Home: 300 Hathaway Park, Lebanon, Pa. Office: 401 5th Av., N.Y.C. Died Aug. 25, 1959.

COOPER, Alfred Duff (see Norwich, Viscount)

COOPER, Bryant Syms, univ. prof.; b. Nashville, Sept. 24, 1903; s. Wade Hampton and Carolyn Baber (Binkley) C.; A.B., Vanderbilt U., 1925, A.M., 1926, Ph.D., 1934; student U. of Munich, 1932, Harvard, 1933; m. Antionette Preutt, Feb. 5, 1925 (div. 1944); 1 dau., Nanette (dec.); m. 2d, Anne Cannon, Dec. 18, 1945; step-children—Winifred (Mrs. George P. Dance), Elizabeth (Mrs. Hugh L. Sawyer) MacGowan. Instr. English, Oberlin Coll., 1926, George Peabody Coll. for Teachers, 1927, instr. philosophy Vanderbilt U., 1927-31; prof. humanities U. of Fla., 1946-—. Dir. Executives Club. Mem. Am. Philos. Assn., So. Assn. for Philosophy and Psychology, South Atlantic Modern Lang. Assn., English-Speaking Union, Am. Assn. Univ. Profs., S.A.R., Delta Kappa Epsilon. Episcopalian. Clubs: University, Vanderbilt (Washington); Harvard, Country (Gainesville, Fla.). Home: 110 N.W. 21st St., Gainesville, Fla.; also 2126 Connecticut Av., Washington. Died July 12, 1952; buried Rock Creek Cemetery, Washington.

COOPER, Charles Phillips, educator; b. Hamilton, N.Y., Jan. 16, 1866; s. Theron (D.D.) and Mary A. (White) C.; A.B., Wesleyan U., Conn., 1888, A.M., 1891; Litt.D., Syracuse U., 1920; m. Olive Sprague, July 5, 1899 (dec.); 1 son, Theron (dec.). Reporter Hartford (Conn.) Evening Post, 1888-89; sucessively reporter, city editor, asst. mgn. editor and mng. editor New York Evening Sun, 1889-1913; staff New York Times, 1913-19; mem. faculty sch. journalism Columbia, 1919-40, prof. emeritus, 1940-—. Mem. Delta Kappa Epsilon. Republican. Mason. Contbr. to various publs. Home: 476 E. 18th St., Bklyn. Died Oct 30, 1950.

COOPER, Drury W., lawyer; b. New Brunswick, N.J.; s. Jacob and Mary D. (Linn) C.; A.B., Rutgers Coll., 1892, LL.D., 1952; LL.B., New York Law Sch., 1894; m. Esther Stevenson Nicholas, 1898; children—Esther Nicholas, Drury W., Mary Linn, Elizabeth W., Jacob, John N., Theodore W., Richard Lawlor. Admitted to N.Y. bar, 1894, practiced since, N.Y. City, specializing in patent law; member Cooper, Byrne, Dunham, Keith & Dearborn; dir. Internat. Business Machines Co., Republic Steel Co. Mayor, New Brunswick, N.J., 1906-07. Trustee Rutgers U. Mem. Am. Bar Assn., Am. Law Inst., N.Y. Co. Lawyers Assn., New York Law Inst., Assn. Bar City New York, N.Y. State Bar Assn., N.Y. Patent Law Assn., S.A.R., Phi Beta Kappa, Delta Phi. Republican. Congregationalist. Clubs: University, Downtown. Home: 30 Parkhurst Pl., Montclair, N.J. Office: 233 Broadway, N.Y.C. Died Sept. 10, 1957; buried Mt. Hebron Cemetery, Montclair, N.J.

COOPER, Edward, ex-congressman; b. Treverton, Pa., Feb. 26, 1873; s. John and Maria (Padbury) C.; B.L., Washington and Lee U., 1893; m. Francis Douglass Smith, Oct. 5, 1895; children—Edward (dec.), Frances Douglass. Began coal bus. with father; dir. Mill Creek, Coaldale, McDowell, Crystal, cos., Pocahontas Consol. Co., Bramwell Accident Ins. Co., Flat Top Fuel Co. Mem. Town Council, Bramwel, 8 yrs.; del. Rep. Nat. Conv., Chgo., 1912 (voted for Roosevelt); mem. 64th and 65th Congresses, 5th W.Va. Dist. Mason (K.T.). Clubs: Shenandoah (Roanoke, Va.), Bluefield Country. Home: Bramwell, W.Va. Died Mar. 2, 1928; buried Hollywood Cemetery, Richmond, Va.

COOPER, George, chmn. bd. Brown & Williamson Tobacco Co.; dir. Brit.-Am. Tobacco Co. Home: Sunderland Rd., Richmond, Va. Office: 1600 W. Hill St., Louisville. Died July 27, 1959; buried Hollywood Cemetery, Richmond, Va.

COOPER, George Franklin, naval officer; b. Americus, Ga., Sept. 26, 1864; s. George Franklin and Cornelia Irene (Staley) C.; grad. U.S. Naval Acad., 1886; m. Louise Lowell, June 5, 1894. Commd. ensign, June, 1888; jr. lt., 1897; lt., 1899; lt.-comdr., 1905; comdr., 1909; capt., 1913. On board Vandalia, in the Pacific, 1886-88; on Boston, in Atlantic, 1888-89, Kearsarge, 1889-91; asst. in electricity at Navy Yard, N.Y.C., 1891-92; insp. electricity, Bath (Me.) Iron Works, 1892-94; on Raleigh, in Atlantic, 1894-99; served U.S. Naval Acad., 1897-99; on Baltimore in Philippines, 1899; on duty Nautical Sch., Manila, 1899-1900; on Monadnock in Philippines and China, 1900-02; U.S. Naval Acad., 1902-04; navigator Denver, N.A. Sta., 1904-05; exec. officer Des Moines, N. Atlantic Sta., 1905-06; exec. officer Indiana, 1906-07; at hydrographic office, Washington, 1907-09; on board Rhode Island, Atlantic Fleet, as exec. officer, June-Dec., 1909; comd. Celtic, Atlantic Fleet,

1909-10; comd. Marietta, Central Am. waters, 1910-11; in charge elec. class Navy Yard, N.Y.C., 1911-12; hydrographer Bur. of Navigation, Washington, 1912-14; comd. Louisiana, Atlantic Fleet, 1914-16. U.S. commr. to Internat. Conf. on Safety of Life at Sea, London, 1913-14; Naval War Coll., 1916-17; 4th Naval Dist., Phila., 1917-19; comdg. U.S.S. Kaiserin Auguste Victoria, 1919; comdt. 8th Naval Dist. and Naval Sta., New Orleans, 1919—. Baptist. Mem. Mil. Order Carabao. Clubs: Chevy Chase, Army and Navy (Washington). Home: Americus, Ga. Died May 6, 1953.

COOPER, Henry Elliott, ret. banker; b. Pawtucket, R.I., Aug. 21, 1873; s. George and Margaret (McCutcheon) C.; A.B., Brown U., 1895; student Harvard Law Sch., 1895-96; m. Catharine Clark, Aug. 11, 1917; 1 stepson, James Wilson. In employ of Nicholson File Co., Providence, 1896-1901; stock and bond broker, Wall St., N.Y.C., 1901-07; mem. John D. Rockefeller's Personal staff, 1907-12; v.p. Equitable Trust Co., N.Y.C., 1912-30, Chase Nat. Bank of City of N.Y., 1930-32; pres. Harriman Nat. Bank & Trust Co., 1932-33; ret. Mem. Phi Beta Kappa, Alpha Delta Phi. Clubs: Union, University, Recess. Home: 960 Park Av., N.Y.C. Died July 3, 1958.

COOPER, Homer Eber, coll. pres.; b. nr. Auburn, W.Va., Jan. 29, 1877; s. Charles Slavens and Mary Jane (Hall) C.; grad. Glenville (W.Va.) State Normal Sch., 1902; A.B., W.Va. U., 1907; A.M., Columbia, 1916, Ph.D., 1924; m. Clara Frances Chassell, Dec. 31, 1922; children—Homer Chassell, Olin Chassell. Rural sch. tchr., 3 yrs., village sch. prin., 3 yrs.; supt. schs., Point Peasant, W.Va., 1907-11, Bluefield, W.Va., 1911-15; head extramural instrn. dept. U. Pitts., 1917-21; supt. Md. Casualty Co. Tng. Sch., 1922-24; dean Eastern Ky. State Tchrs. Coll., Richmond, 1924-31; research asso. Inst. Sch. Experimentation, Tchrs. Coll., Columbia, 1931-32; dir. practice teaching Westminster Coll., New Wilmington, Pa., 1934-35; dean West Liberty (W.Va.) State Tchrs. Coll., 1935-39; pres. Blue Ridge Coll., New Windsor, Md., 1939-42; lectr. economics University Maryland, 1942-43; asst. professor econ. and geog., ordnance research College Engineering, Univ. Delaware, 1944-45. Director of W.Va. Nature Assn.; mem. arboretum com. Oglebay Park, Wheeling, W.Va.; mem. Carroll Co. (Md.) dist. com. Boy Scouts Am. Mem. Am. Assn. U. Profs., Am. Acad. Polit. and Social Sci., Phi Delta Kappa. Presbyn. Club: Kiwanis. Author: Cost of Training Teachers, 1924; Prospectus of Freedom Coll., 1952; Education for a Free Society, 1957. Contbr. ednl. jours. Home: Berea, Ky. Died Jan. 21, 1953; buried Richmond (Ky.) Cemetery.

COOPER, Jere, congressman; b. Dyer County, Tenn., July 20, 1893; s. Joseph W. and Viola May (Cooper) C.; LL.B., Cumberland U., 1915; unmarried. Admitted to Tenn. bar, 1915, and began practice at Dyersburg; city atty., Dyersburg, 8 yrs., 1920-28; mem. 71st-82d Congresses, 9th Tenn. Dist., 83d-85th Congresses, 8th District. Enlisted in Tennessee National Guard, 1917; commissioned 1st lieutenant, June 23, 1917; transferred with company to Co. K, 119th Inf., 30th Div., U.S. Army, and served with A.E.F.; capt., July 9, 1918;; served abt. 1 yr. with Am. Expeditionary Forces; hon. discharged, Apr. 2, 1919. Elected state comdr., Tenn., Am. Legion, 1921, and mem. Nat. Exec. Com., 1922; mem. Kappa Sigma. Democrat. Mem. Cumberland Presbyn. Ch. Mason (K.T., Shriner). Maccabee. Home: Dyersburg, Tenn. Died Dec. 18, 1957.

COOPER, John Montgomery, anthropologist; b. Rockville, Md., Oct. 28, 1881; s. James Joseph and Emma Lillie (Tolou) C.; student Calvert Hall, Baltimore, Md., 1888-97, St. Charles Coll., Md., 1897-99; Ph.D., American Coll., Rome, Italy, 1902, S.T.D., 1905. Asst. pastor St. Matthew's Ch., Washington, D.C., 1905-18; instr. Catholic U. of America, 1909-23, asso. prof., 1923-28, prof. of anthropology since 1928. In charge camp and community activities, Nat. Catholic War Council, 1918-20. Pres. Anthrop. Soc. of Washington, 1930-32; pres. American Anthrop. Assn. 1940; sec. and treas. Catholic Anthrop. Conf. since 1926; v.p. Am. Folklore Soc., 1943. Fellow A.A.A.S.; mem. Washington Acad. Sciences. Awarded Mendel medal, 1939. Author: Analytical and Critical Bibliography of Tribes of Tierra del Fuego, 1917; Birth Control, 1923; Play Fair, 1923; Content of Advanced Religion Course, 1924; Religion Outlines for Colleges (4 vols.), 1924-30; Children's Institutions, 1931; Northern Algonquian Supreme Being, 1934; Snares and Deadfalls of Northern Algonquians, 1938; Temporal Sequence and Marginal Cultures, 1941. Editor of Primitive Man. Address: Catholic University of America, Washington. Died May 22, 1949; buried Rock Creek Cemetery, Washington.

COOPER, Lane, univ. prof.; b. New Brunswick, N.J., Dec. 14, 1875; s. Jacob and Mary (Linn) C.; A.B., Rutgers Coll., 1896; studied Columbia; M.A., Yale, 1898; studied univs. of Berlin and Leipzig; Ph.D., Leipzig, 1901; studied College de France, Paris, 1902; hon. Litt.D., Rutgers, 1921; H.L.D., Wesleyan 1943; unmarried. Instr. Coll. of St. James (preparatory school), Md., 1898-99, instructor English, 1902-06, asst. prof., 1906-15, prof. English lang. and literature, 1915-41, John Wendell Anderson professor of same, Cornell U., 1941-43, professor emeritus since 1943. Mem. Modern Lang Assn. of Am. (exec. com.), Concordance Society (exec. com.), Phi Beta Kappa (pres. N.Y. Theta Chapter, 1910-11), Delta Phi; v.p., Class of '96, Rutgers U., since 1946; pres. Research Club, Cornell U., 1932-33. Author and Editor: The Prose Poetry of Thomas De Quincey, 1902; Theories of Style, 1907; Literature for Engineers, 1909; (with others) A Manual of American Literature, 1909; A Concordance to the Poems of William Wordsworth, 1911; The Function of the Leader in Scholarship, 1911; Aristotle on the Art of Poetry, 1913 (rev. edit., 1947); Methods and Aims in the Study of Literature, 1915 (rev. edit., 1940); A Concordance of the Works of Horace, 1916; Louis Agassiz as a Teacher, 1917 (rev. edit., 1945); The Greek Genius and Its Influence, 1917; George Meredith, An Essay on Comdey, 1918; Two Views of Education, 1922; An Aristotelian Theory of Comedy, 1922; A Concordance of the Latin, Greek, and Italian Poems of John Milton, 1923; The Poetics of Artistotle, Its Meaning and Influence, 1923; A Concordance of Boethius, 1928; (with Alfred Gudeman) A Bibliography of the Poetics of Aristotle, 1928; The Rhetoric of Aristotle, 1931; Aristotle, Galileo, and the Tower of Pisa, 1935; Evolution and Repentance, 1935; Plato—Phaedrus, Ion, Gorgias, Symposium, and Selections from the Republic and Laws, 1937; Aristotelian Papers, 1939; Plato on the Trial and Death of Socrates—Euthyphro, Apology, Crito, Phaedo, 1941; Fifteen Greek Plays, 1943; Experiments in Education, 1943. Contbr. to philol. and other periodicals; one of the editors of Cornell Studies in English. Was prof. elect, Smith Coll., 1915, U. Mich., 1927; acting asso. prof., summer term, U. Ill., 1914; acting prof., summer quarter, Stanford U., 1918, summer session, U. Cal., 1919. Address: Goldwin Smith Hall, Ithaca, N.Y. Died Nov. 27, 1959; buried Evergreen Cemetery, New Brunswick, N.J.

COOPER, Myers Y(oung), banker, realtor, home builder; b. St. Louisville, O., Nov. 25, 1873; s. Lemuel Young and Ann (Greenlee) C.; student Lebanon (O.) Normal U., 1891-93; LL.D., Lincoln Meml. U., Tenn., 1923, Wilmington (O.) Coll., 1926, Baldwin-Wallace, Bethany (W.Va.); Muskingum colls., 1929, St. Xavier (Cin.), Ohio Wesleyan Univs. 1929, Ohio, Miami, Wilberforce univs., 1930; m. Martha Kinney, Dec. 15, 1897; children—Raymond Kinney, Martha Ann (Mrs. Mills Judy), Real estate, home builder, 1896—; with Norwood-Hyde Park Bank & Trust Co., 1903—, pres., 1903-54, now chmn.; organizer Myers Y. Cooper Co., Cin., 1928, chmn., 1929-55; gov. Ohio, 1929-31; pres. Raymond Realty Co., Hyde Park Lumber Co., Standard Castings Co., Westwood Planing Mill Co.; dir., chmn. exec. com. Farmers Fertilizer Co., Columbus, O. Del. Rep. Nat. Conv., 1920—, del.-at-large, 1930—, vice chmn. delegations, 1948-52; mem. Hamilton Co. Rep. Exec. Com. Vice pres. Bethesda Hosp.; trustee, mem. bd. Hiram Coll.; trustee Lincoln Meml. U.; mem. Hoover Found., Save the Children Fedn. Received Golden Deeds award Exchange Club, 1954; honor award Goodwill Industries. Mem. Ohio Fair Mgrs. Assn. (hon. pres.), Nat. Assn. Real Estate Bds., Hamilton Co. Agrl. Soc. (pres.), S.A.R., Mayflower Soc. Mem. Disciples of Christ Ch. (chmn. bd.). Clubs: National Exchange (exec. com., past nat. pres.); Cincinnati, Queen City, Republican, Cuvier Press (Cin.); Committee of 100 (dir. Miami, Fla.). Home: 3030 Erie Av., Cin. 8. Office: Fifth Third Bank Bldg., Cin. 2; also 1004 Cotorro Av., Coral Gables, Fla. Died Dec. 6, 1958; buried Spring Grove, Cin.

COOPER, Richard Watson, educator; b. Cheswold, Kent County, Del., Dec. 22, 1866; s. Richard M. and Susan (Jefferson) C.; grad. (highest honors), Dickinson Sem., Williamsport, Pa., 1887; A.B., cum laude, Wesleyan U., Conn., 1890, D.D., 1909; Litt.D., Hamline U., 1909; m. Emma White, June 29, 1892; children—Richard White, Harry P., Hermann, Edwin J., William Paul, Dorothy. Librarian, Wesleyan U., 1890-91; head dept. of English, Wesleyan Acad., Wilbraham, Mass., 1891-99; prof. English lit., Hamline U., St. Paul, 1899-1909; Minn. state lecturer in English, 1901-04; lecturer in English drama, U. of Minn., 1906-07; pres. Upper Iowa U., 1909-16; exec. sec., Council of Ch. Bds. of Edn., 1916-17; sec. Assn. of Am. Colls., 1915-18; with A.E.F., France, Apr. 1918-Aug. 1919, mem. Ednl. Corps, registrar, A.E.F. Univ., Beaune, France; decorated Officer d'Académie (palms), May 1919; dir. Bur. of Edn., Service Citizens of Del., 1919-27. Lecturer; clergyman. Mem. N.E.A., Psi Upsilon, etc. Mason (32°). Edited and issued from Dijon, France, The Registrar and The Catalogue of the A.E.F. University, 1919. Wrote: Better Attendance in Delaware Schools, 1922; (with Hermann Cooper) Negro School Attendance in Delaware, 1923; The One Teacher School—A Study in Attendance, 1925. Address: R.D. 3, Newark, Del.; (summer) Cable, Wis. Died Apr. 15, 1954.

COOPER, Robert Archer, U.S. judge; b. Laurens County, S.C., June 12, 1874; s. Henry Addison and Elizabeth Archer (Jones) C.; student Jones High Sch., Abbeville County (now Greenwood County), S.C.; LL.D., Polytechnic Inst., San German P.R., 1947; m. Mamie Machen, Mar. 22, 1899 (died June 22, 1914); 1 dau., Elizabeth; m. 2d, Dorcas Calmes, Nov. 15, 1917; 1 son, Robert A. Admitted to S.C. bar, 1898, began practice at Laurens; magistrate, Laurens, 1899-1900; mem. S.C. Ho. of Rep. 2 terms, 1900-04; elected solicitor 8th Jud. Circuit, S.C., 1905, reëlected, 1908, 12; gov. of S.C., 2 terms, 1919-22. Mem. Federal Farm Loan Bd., 1922-27; designated as farm loan commr., July 3, 1923; asst. to chmn. Exec. Com. of Dem. Nat. Com., 1929-32; U.S. dist. judge Dist. of P.R. 1934-47; now ret. Baptist. Mason (grand master of S.C., 1915-17; potentate Charleston, S.C., 1915). Address: Ottaray Hotel, Greenville, S.C. Died Aug. 7, 1953.

COOPER, Wyllis, radio and television writer and producer; b. Pekin, Ill., Jan. 26, 1899; s. Charles E. and Margaret L. (Oswald) C.; grad. Pekin High Sch., 1916; m. Emily Beveridge, Sept. 14, 1929. Advt. writer 1919-29; radio writer, 1929—; motion picture writer, 1936-39; continuity editor CBS, Central Div., 1930-32, NBC, Central Div., 1933-36. Originated radio dramatic series Lights Out, 1933, writing and directing it until 1936; Empire Builders, 1929-30, Immortal Dramas, 1934; Hollywood Hotel, 1938-39; Good Neighbors, 1941; Spirit of '41, 1941; Spirit of 1942, 1942; Quiet Please, 1948-49. Expert cons. Office Sec. of War, 1942; writer-producer The Army Hour, War Dept. ofcl. weekly radio broadcast; dir. program development NBC, 1943; TV producer-writer-director: Escape, Stage Thirteen (CBS); Volume One (ABC), 1950-51; TV cons. Served as sgt. U.S. Cav., Mexican Border, 1916; with Signal Corps, 1917-19, with AEF, 1918-19; capt. 31st Inf., Ill. Nat. Guard, 1923-27, Cavalry Res., 1928-33. Democrat. Mason. Club: Lambs (N.Y.C.). Home: R.D., Glen Gardner, N.J. Died June 22, 1955; buried Lower Valley Cemetery, Califon, N.J.

COOVER, Melanchthon, theologian; b. Johnstown, Pa., Mar. 26, 1861; s. Jacob and Ann Margaret (Lindsay-Teeter) C.; A.B., Pa. Coll., 1887, A.M., 1890; grad. Luth. Theol. Sem., Gettysburg, Pa., 1890; D.D., Franklin and Marshall Coll., 1905; LL.D., Gettysburg Coll., 1923; m. Lucy May Moses, Sept. 3, 1891; children—Donald Bruce, Margaret (wife of Rev. Howard R. Gold). Ordained to Luth. ministry, 1890; pastor St. Paul's Ch., Ardmore, Pa., 1890-1901, Christ Ch., Gettysburg, 1901-04; prof. English Bible, chaplain Gettysburg Coll., 1904-05; prof. N.T. exegesis and ecclesiastical history Luth. Theol. Sem., Gettysburg, 1905-16, prof. N.T. lang., lit., theology, 1916-26, emeritus. Mem. bd. Luth. Pub. Soc., Gen. Synod, 1908-15, of Am. Sect. Internat. Sunday Sch. Lesson Com., 1908-14. Mem. Soc. Bibl. Lit. and Exegesis, Phi Beta Kappa, Phi Gamma Delta. Author: Quest and Query (verse), 1923; (booklets) Tempted Messiah, and Peter's Confession and Keys, 1909; also Liturgies of Sunday School (in Ency. of S.S. and Religious Edn.). Home: Gettysburg, Pa. Died Nov 21. 1955; buried Gettysburg, Pa.

COPE, Gilbert, genealogist; b. nr. West Chester, Pa., Aug. 17, 1840; s. Joseph and Eliza (Gilbert) C.; student Friends' schs.; m. Anna Garrett, Feb. 5, 1880. Compiler Futhey & Cope's History of Chester County, Pa., and of genealogies of Cope family, 1861 (now being revised), Browns of Nottingham, Dutton, Sharpless, Darlington, Smedley, Baily, Hood and Dunwood families; editor of Kirk Genealogy, 1912; visited England with wife, 1905, 1907, and copied several volumes of the early Friends' records for Geneal. Soc. of Pa. Mem. Hist. and Geneal. socs. of Pa.; corr. mem. N.E. Hist. Geneal. Soc., 1861—, and of N.Y. Geneal. and Biog. Soc.; sec. Chester County Hist. Soc., etc. Prohibitionist. Mem. Soc. of Friends. Address: Box 71, West Chester, Pa. Died Dec. 17, 1928; buried Oakland Friends Cemetery.

COPE, Robert S., corp. official; b. Savannah, Ga., July 23, 1870; s. James E. and Harriet S. (Thompson) C.; ed. pub. schs.; m. Mary L. Lovell, Nov. 23, 1898; children—John L., Emily D. (wife of Dr. Wallace W. Fennell), Mary L. (Mrs. James Reeves Sweat), Alfred L., Ansley, and James E. Began as clerk, 1888-92; sec.-treas. of Peace River Phosphate Mining Co., 1892-1904; v.p. and gen. mgr. Barker Chem. Co., 1905-30; pres. Reliance Fertilizer Co. since 1910; dir. Citizens & Southern Nat. Bank; Macon, Dublin & Savannah R.R. Served in Savannah Vol. Guards, 1891-99. Mem. C. of C. Presbyn. (chmn. bd. trustees). Home: 1719 Abercorn St. Office: 106 Bay St. E., Savannah, Ga. Died June 19, 1952; buried Bonaventure Cemetery, Savannah.

COPELAND, Charles Townsend, prof. English; b. Calais, Me., Apr. 27, 1860; s. H. C. and Sarah (Lowell) C.; A.B. cum laude, Harvard, 1882; 1 yr. Harvard Law Sch.; Litt.D., Bowdoin Coll., 1920; unmarried. Lecturer on English lit., 1893-1910, asst. prof. English, 1910-17, asso. prof., 1917-25, Boylston prof. of rhetoric and oratory, Harvard, 1925-28, emeritus since 1928. Lecturer in Lowell Inst., univ. exten. courses in English lit., 1907-27. Fellow Am. Acad. of Arts and Sciences. Independent in politics. Author: Life of Edwin Booth (Beacon Biographies), 1901; Freshman English and Theme Correcting in Harvard College (with H. M. Rideout) 1901. Editor: Letters of Thomas Carlyle to His Youngest Sister (with introductory essay), 1899; Tennyson's The Princess (with H. M. Rideout), 1899; Representative Biographies (with F. W. C. Hersey), 1909; Selections from Wordsworth, Byron, Shelley, and Keats, in Gateway Series (with H. M. Rideout), 1909; The Copeland Reader (anthology of verse and prose), 1926; Anthology of Translations, 1934. Club: Harvard (N.Y.). Mem. Phi Beta Kappa (hon.). Trustee State Library of Mass.; hon. life mem. Harvard Union. Address: 5 Concord Av., Cambridge, Mass. Died July 24, 1952; buried Calais, Me.

COPELAND, Edward Rivers, lawyer; b. Lawrence Co., Ala., Feb. 1, 1879; s. William Baker and Mary Olivia (Henry) C.; student So. U., 1896-98, U. Ala., 1900; LL.B., Birmingham-So. Coll., 1922; m. Isabelle Rose McDonald, Aug. 22, 1941; 1 son, Edward Rivers. Admitted to Ala. bar, 1920, Fla. bar, 1925, since practiced in Miami Beach; mem. Copeland, Therrel & Baisden since 1943. Mem. local bd. 4 S.S.S., 1942-45, mem. bds. 46 and chmn. 169 Dade Co., Fla. since 1948; Mem. Am. Judicature Soc., Comml. Law League, Am., Fla. State, Dade Co., Miami Beach bar assns., Kappa Alpha. Methodist. Club: Kiwanis (Miami Beach). Home: 4951 Cherokee Av., Miami Beach 40. Office: Miami Beach First National Bank Bldg., P.O. Box 558, Miami Beach 39, Fla. Died May 18, 1952.

COPELAND, Lennie Phoebe, mathematician; b. Brewer, Me., Mar. 30, 1881; d. Lemuel and Emma (Stinchfield) Copeland; B.S., U. Me., 1904, Sc.D., 1948; M.A., Wellesley Coll., 1911; Ph.D., U. Pa., 1913. Instr. math. Wellesley Coll., 1913-20, prof., 1920-36, emeritus prof., 1946—. Pres. New Eng. Assn. Tchrs. Mathematics, 1925-27. Counselor in natural history Appalachian Mountain Club. Mem. A.A.A.S., Am. Math Soc., Math Assn. Am., Phi Beta Kappa, Sigma Xi. Contbr. profl. jours. Home: 1190 8th St. N., St. Petersburg, Fla. Died Jan. 11, 1951; buried Bangor, Me.

COPELAND, Oren S., ex-congressman; b. Huron, S.D., Mar. 16, 1887; s. Samuel R. and Josephine D. (French) C.; student U. of Neb., 1904-07; m. Iva C. Young, Mar. 16, 1916; 1 son, Richard Ellis. Salesman Lincoln Gas Co., 1907-08; in advt. dept. Star Pub. Co., 1909-10, coal and oil salesman, 1910-28; owner Copeland Fuel Co., 1928—; v.p. Lincoln Benefit Life Ins. Co. Commr. pub. safety, Lincoln, Neb., 2 yrs.; mayor, Lincoln, 4 yrs.; mem. 77th Congress, 1st Neb. Dist. Republican. Mem. 1st Christian Ch. Mason (Shriner), K.P. Club: Optimist Internat. Home: 2700 F St. Office: 941 N. 14th St., Lincoln, Neb. Died Apr. 9, 1958.

COPELAND, William Franklin, educator; b. Tappan, O., Aug. 16, 1872; s. William D. and Clarissa B. C.; Ph.B., Ohio U., 1902, Ph.M., 1903, Ph.D., 1907; m. Helen Reinherr, Sept. 14, 1905. Asst. in biology and geology Ohio U., 1902-05, botany, 1907, prof. elementary sci., 1907-10, prof. agr., 1910—. Mem. A.A.A.S., Am. Soc. Naturalists, Nature Study Soc., Am. Forestry Assn., Ohio Acad. Science. Home: Athens, O. Died Feb. 13, 1950.

COPPIN, Levi J., bishop; b. Fredericktown, Md., Dec. 24, 1848; s. John and Jane C.; grad. P.E. Div. Sch., Phila., 1887; D.D., Wilberforce, 1899; m. Fannie M. Jackson, 1881 (dec.); m. 2d, M. E. Thompson, M.D., 1914. Ordained A.M.E. ministry, 1877; pastor city missions in Phila. and later various chs., Phila. and Balt.; editor A.M.E. Ch. Review, 1888-96; bishop A.M.E. Ch., 1900—; resident bishop, S. Africa, with residence in Cape Town, 1900-04. Author: The Relation of Baptized Children to the Church; Key to Scriptural Interpretation; Observations of Men and Things in South Africa; Fifty-two Sermon Syllabi; Unwritten History. Home: 1913 Bainbridge St., Phila. 46. Died June 25, 1924.

COPPINI, Pompeo (kōp-pē'nē), sculptor and painter; b. Moglia, Mantua, Italy, May 19, 1870; s. Giovanni and Leandra (Raffa) C.; became student in course in civil engineering but dropped it to engage in study of art; graduate with highest honors, Accademia di Belle Arti, Florence, Italy, 1889; honorary Doctor of Fine Arts, Baylor Univ. (Tex.), 1940; m. Elisa De Barbieri, Feb. 27, 1897 (dec. Dec. 1957). Came to U.S., 1896; naturalized U.S., 1902. Prof., head, fine arts dept., Trinity University, Texas, 1943; executed 45 pub. monuments in various cities, including many portrait statues; most natable: State of George Washington, Mexico City; equestrian statue, Gen. J. H. Morgan, Lexington, Ky.; U.S. Senator John H. Reagan monument, Palestine, Texas; equestrian statue, Terry's Ranger, Austin, Tex.; Falkenberg monument, Denver, Colo.; Gen. J. C. Root monument, Memphis, Tenn.; Stephen F. Austin statue, Austin, Tex.; Joanna Troutman statue, Austin, Tex.; Gen. Sam Houston meml., Huntsville, Tex.. statue of Gen. Sul Ross, A. & M. Coll., Coll. Station, Tex.; statue U.S. Senator James P. Clarke of Ark., Statuary Hall, Washington, D.C.; Hon. James D. Richardson statue, Dallas, Tex.; Confederate Memorial to "The Last Stand," Victoria, Tex.; Confederate Memorial Fountain, Corpus Christi, Tex.; cowboy equestrian group, Ballinger, Tex.; war memorial fountain, U. of Tex., the gift of late Maj. George W. Littlefield; allegorical bronze doors, Scottish Rite Cathedral, San Antonio; John Ball's group, Grand Rapids, Mich.; George Washington statue, Portland, Ore; Oscar Hammerstein statue for Hammerstein Theatre, N.Y. City; Philip Schuyler Malcolm statue, Portland, Ore.; pediment, San Antonio (Tex.) Express Pub. Co. Bldg.; $100,000 cenotaph, "Heroes of the Alamo," San Antonio, Tex.; Baylor Memorial, Baylor U., Waco, Tex.; designed Am. Legion Tex. Centennial half-dollar; 6 bronze statues, Hall of Tex. Heroes, Centennial Exhbn., Dallas, 1936—Gen. Sam Houston, Stephen F. Austin, Mirabeau Lamar, William Travis, J. W. Fannin and Thomas J. Rusk; Hon. Albert Steves Memorial, Wittie Art Museum, San Antonio; heroic portrait bust of Geo. B. Cortelyou for Consol. Edison Co., N.Y., Inc.; bronze statue Dr. J. Frank Norris, (Fort Worth); Young Genius of Music for Anna Hertsberg Music Memorial Bldg., George W. Brackenridge Memorial (all San Antonio); heroic marble statue meml. fountain, Martyrs of War, Moglia-Mantova, Italy; bronze portrait of Dr. Harry Fishburne Estill, Library of Sam Houston, Huntsville, Tex. Bronze heroic bust George Storch, library Trinity U.; 10 foot statue of George Washington for mall U. Tex., Austin, 1954. Rep. by collection of 44 of his original works, Baylor U., Waco, Tex. Executed number of portraits and landscape paintings. Awarded grand premium and gold medal for bust of Maj. Gen. Ulysses Grant MacAlexander, Bologna-Italy Exhbn., 1931. Allegorical Memorial, Sunset Meml. Park, San Antonio; decorated posthumously Star of Italian Solidarity. Lived in N.Y., 1896-1901, San Antonio, Tex., 1901-16, Chicago, 1916-22, New York 1922, retired to San Antonio, 1935. Charter mem. Scientific Soc. of San Antonio, Tex. Hon. mem. Westchester County Coin Club, San Antonio Rotary (hon.). Author: Autobiography, From Dawn to Sunset. Decorated Comdr. Crown of Italy; made hon. citizen of Italy, 1951. Founder and president emeritus Coppini Acad. Fine Arts, San Antonio. Mason (32°, K.T. Shriner). Home and studio: 115 Melrose Pl., San Antonio 12. Died Sept. 26, 1957; buried Sunset Meml. Park, San Antonio.

COPPRIDGE, William Maurice, physician, urologist; b. Danville, Va., July 24, 1893; s. William David and Mary Ellen (Ferguson) C.; student St. Mary's Coll., 1911; student U. of N.C., 1913-16; M.D., Jefferson Med. Coll., Phila., 1918; m. Ferrie Patterson Choate, July 2, 1919; children—Alton James, James Wendell Ligon (adopted). Asst. prof. pathology U. of N.C., 1919; dir. labs., urologist Watts Hosp., Durham, N.C., 1920, chief of staff in urology, 1920—; clin. prof. urology U. of N.C. Med. Sch., 1952—; mem. bd. med. examiners State of N.C., 1938-44. Mem. Med. R.C., U.S. Army, World War I; chief med. services Office of Civilian Defense; mem. N.C. Com. for procurement and assignment of physicians in armed forces, World War II. Mem. commn. to study needs of med. edn. in N.C., 1937-38, 44-45; mem. 1st med. care commn. of N.C., 1945—. Diplomate Am. Bd. Urology. Fellow A.C.S.; mem. Durham-Orange Counties Med. Soc. (pres. 1925, 46), Med. Soc. of State of N.C. (pres. 1946-47), So. Med. Assn. (mem. exec. com. 1941-46), Am. Urol. Assn., Southeastern Branch Am. Urol. Assn. (pres. 1944-46), Tri-State Med. Soc., A.M.A., N.C. Urol. Assn., N.Y. Acad. Sci. Democrat. Presbyn. Clubs: Hope Valley Country, Durham Pistol (Durham). Home: 1024 W. Forest Hills Blvd. Office: 111 Corcoran St., Durham, N.C. Died Aug. 1959.

CORBETT, Harvey Wiley, architect; b. San Francisco, Jan. 8, 1873; s. Samuel James (M.D.) and Elizabeth Jane (Wiley) C. (M.D.); B.Sc., U. of Calif., 1895, hon. LL.D., 1930; grad. Ecole des Beaux Arts, Paris, 1900; hon. Master of Architecture, Liverpool U., 1925; hon. Litt.D., Columbia, 1929; m. Gail Sherman, June 28, 1905; children—Jean. John Maxwell. Lecturer in architecture at Columbia; mem. adv. bd. sch. of Architecture Princeton; former architect mem. Fine Arts Commission State of N.Y. and built Maryland Institute, Springfield (Mass.) Municipal Group, N.Y. School Applied Design for Women, Bush Terminal Office Bldg. (New York), Bush House, London, Holy Innocents Ch. (Brooklyn), George Washington Masonic Nat. Memorial (Alexandria, Va.), Hotel No. 1 Fifth Ave., Roerich Museum (New York), Bushnell Memorial Hall (Hartford, Conn.). Chmn. Archtl. Commn., Chicago World's Fair Centennial Celebration, 1933; asso. architect New Office Bldg. Met. Life Ins. Co. and Rockefeller Center, New York; Brooklyn Coll. Group, Brooklyn; chief architect Amsterdam Houses, N.Y. City; asso. architect, Sigmund Stern Dormitory, Univ. Calif.; New Criminal Courts Bldg. Jail, N.Y. City. N.A. Recipient American Award, American Found.; fellow A.I.A., Royal Inst. British Architects; mem. Société Beaux Arts Architects (ex-pres.), Société des Architects Diplomés par le Government Francais (ex-pres.), Architectural League New York (ex-pres.), Nat. Sculpture Soc., Am. Fed. Arts, Archaeol. Inst. America, N.Y. Building Congress, Phi Gamma Delta, Sigma Xi. Clubs: Rockefeller Center Luncheon, Faculty of Columbia, Quail, Town Hall; Architects (London); National Arts (pres.). Home: 160 W. 85th St. Office: 1270 Av. of the Americas, N.Y.C. Died Apr. 21, 1954.

CORBETT, Henry L., investments; b. Portland, Ore., July 29, 1881; s. Henry Jagger and Helen (Ladd) C.; grad. Portland Acad.; A.B., Harvard, 1903; m. Gretchen Hoyt, June 3, 1908. Began career as bank clerk, First Nat. Bank, Portland, Ore., 1903; pres. Corbett Investment Co., 1926—; mem. exec. com. So. Pacific Co. Republican. Presbyterian. Home: 300 S.W. Tryon Hill Rd., Portland 1. Office: 1011 Corbett Bldg., Portland 4, Ore. Died Apr. 22, 1957; buried Riverview Cemetery.

CORBETT, Jim, author, army officer; b. Naini Tal, India, July 25, 1875; s. Christopher William and Mary Jane (Prusha) C.; educated in pvt. schs.; unmarried. Awarded Volunteer Decoration, Kaiser I-Hind 1st Class, Order of British Empire, Companion Indian Empire. Mem. Natural History Soc. (New York), Assn. for Preservation of Wild Life in United Provinces (hon. sec.), Soc. for Preservation of Fauna of Empire. Mem. Conservative Party. Mem. Ch. of England. Author: The Man-Eaters of Kumaon, 1945; The Man-Eating Leopard of Rudraprayag, 1947; My India, 1952; Jungle Lore, 1953; The Temple Tiger, 1954; Tree Tops, 1955. Address: Nyeri, Kenya, British East Africa. Died Apr. 19, 1955.

CORBETT, Laurence Jay, cons. elec. engr.; b. Saratoga, Cal., May 19, 1877; s. John Jay and Margaret Anne (Johnstone) C.; U. Ida., 1896-1900; B.S. in Elec. Engring., U. Cal., 1902; post-grad., Union Coll., Schenectady, 1903; m. Laura Gertrude Arthur, June 12, 1906; children—Ethel Jane, Arthur J., John Laurence. Successively with Gen. Electric Co., Schenectady, 1902-03, Union Iron Works, San Francisco, 1904, Spokane & Inland Empire (elec.) Ry., Spokane, Wash., 1905, Washington Water Power Co., Spokane, 1905-06; cons. practice, Spokane, 1906-11; head dept. elec. engring. U. Ida., 1911-18; asso. prof. mech. engring. U. Cal., 1920; engr. Pacific Gas & Electric Co. (hydro-electric and transmission div.), 1920-35, and on Pacific Coast and nat. tech. coms.; cons. elec. engr. and writer, 1935-42; engring. plan approval sect. U.S. Maritime Commn., Oakland, Cal., 1942-47, in charge deck machinery. Mem. Bd. Examiners of Architects, State of Ida., 1917-18; with Fed. Bd. for Vocational Edn., 1919. Served as capt. C.E., U.S. Army; commd. col. Engr. Res., 1931-41. Fellow A.A.A.S; mem. Am. Inst. E.E. (life), Pacific Coast Elec. Assn., Astron. Soc., Pacific Soc., Am. Mil. Engrs. (past pres. San Francisco post), Reserve Officers Assn. (pres. East Bay chpt. Cal. Dept. 1941; pres. bd. trustees for the duration). Mason (32°). Club: National Writers. Author: Inductive Coordination, 1936. Contbr. to tech. press and to soc. proceedings on insulation of long transmission spans, inductive coordination, etc. Home: 1010 Shattuck Av., Berkeley 7, Cal. Died May 3, 1951.

CORBIN, Horace Kellogg, banker; b. Elizabeth, N.J., Apr. 25, 1887; s. William H. and Clementine (Kellogg) C.; student Hill Sch., 1902-04; Litt.B., Princeton U., 1908; m. Hannah Stockton, May 25, 1912 (dec. July, 1953). Engring. contractor, 1911-17; v.p., dir. Fidelity Union Trust Co., 1929-40, pres., 1940-55, chmn., 1955—; pres. Motor Finance Corp., Newark, 1921-39, now dir.; dir. L. Bamberger & Co., Prudential Ins. Co., Wallace & Tiernan, Inc., Public Service Electric & Gas Co. of N.J. Commr. Port of New York Authority. Trustee of Princeton. Served as 1st lt. Q.M.C., U.S. Army, 1918-19. Home: Llewellyn Park, West Orange, N.J. Office: 755 Broad St., Newark 1. Died Feb. 5, 1960.

CORBIN, John, author; b. Chgo., May 2. 1870: s. Calvin Rich and Caroline Elizabeth (Fairfield) C.; A.B., Harvard, 1892, A.M., 1893; a year's residence Balliol Coll., Oxford; m. Amy Foster, 1899. Asst. instr. English composition Harvard, 1895-1907; asst. editor Harper's Mag., 1897-1900; dramatic critic Harper's Weekly, 1899-1900; editorial staff Ency. Brit., 1900-02; dramatic critic N.Y. Times, 1902, N.Y. Sun, 1905-07; literary mgr. New Theatre, N.Y. C., 1908-10; sec. The Drama Soc., N.Y.C., 1913-16; produced The Tempest on a reconstruction of Shakespeare's stage, 1916; dramatic critic N.Y. Times, 1917-19, editorial writer, 1919-26. Club: University. Author: The Elizabethan Hamlet, 1895; Schoolboy Life in England—an American view, 1898; An American at Oxford, 1902; A New Portrait of Shakespeare, 1903; The First Loves of Perilla, 1903; The Cave Man, 1907; Which College for the Boy, 1908; Husband and the Forbidden Guests, 1910; The Edge, 1915; The Return of the Middle Class, 1922; The Unknown Washington, 1930; Two Frontiers of Freedom, 1940. Contbr. stories and articles on edn., the drama and pub. affairs to mags. Home: Crow Ledge, Cross River, N.Y. Died Aug. 30, 1959.

CORBIN, William Lee, college professor, librarian; b. Athens, Pa., Jan. 8, 1872; s. John LeRoy and Delette Emma (Cook) C.; student Homer (N.Y.) Acad.; A.B. cum laude, Amherst, 1896; M.A., Yale, 1900; Austin scholar in English, Harvard, 1910-11; spl. student in English, Oxford U., England, 1911-12; married Ethel Christina Olin, December 15, 1904 (died September 9, 1941). Principal Union School, Canaseraga, N.Y., 1897-99; librarian Norfolk (Conn.) Library, 1899-1902; head of English dept. Cascadilla Sch., Ithaca, N.Y., 1902-04; instr. in English, Wells

Coll., 1904-06; asso. prof., 1906-20; prof. English, Rollins Coll., 1920-21, Boston U., 1921-24; librarian Smithsonian Instn. and custodian Smithsonian deposit Library of Congress, 1924-42, retired for age, Jan. 31, 1942; spl. asst. Smithsonian Archives, 1942-43; also prof. English, Boston U., summers, 1925-26; lecturer on English lit. and composition, American U., 1926-32. Mem. A.A.A.S., American Assn. Univ. Professors, Poetry Soc. America, Shakespeare Assn. America, Shakespeare Soc. Washington, A.L.A., D.C. Library Assn., Delta Upsilon. Republican. Conglist. Clubs: Cosmos, Yale, Harvard. Contbr. abt. 40 articles on Am. authors to 11th edit. Ency. Britannica; also contbr. to other books and various mags., including The Century, The Amherst Graduates' Quarterly; lecturer on lit. and ednl. subjects. Address: 3020 Tilden St. N.W., Washington 8. Died Sept. 18, 1952; buried Rock Creek Cemetery, Washington.

CORBUS, Budd Clarke (kôr'bŭs), surgeon; b. La Salle, Ill., July 22, 1876; s. Dr. Josephus R. and Sarah (Angle) C.; M.D., Coll. Phys. and Surg., Chicago, 1901; m. Gertrude Pitkin, Dec. 15, 1903 (died July 1915); 1 son, Budd Clarke; m. 2d, Ruth Bent, Dec. 22, 1917; children—William Godfrey, Josephus R. Mem. house staff Alexian Brothers' Hosp., 1902-03; practiced Chgo. since 1903; now in research cancer with H. T. Davis, Northwestern U. Certified by American Board of Urology. Fellow American College Surgeons; mem. A.M.A., Am. Urol. Assn., Chicago Med. Soc., Chicago Urol. Soc. Republican. Conglist. Author: Diathermy in Genito-Urinary Diseases with Special Reference to Cancer (with V. J. O'Conor), 1925. Collaborator Cabot's American Textbook on Urology, History of Urology. Contbr. to med. jours. Home: 1415 Grove St., Evanston, Ill. Died Nov. 6, 1954; buried Graceland Cemetery, Chgo.

CORCORAN, Thomas J(oseph), printer; b. Syracuse, N.Y., Sept. 13, 1896; s. James and Johanna (Bradshaw) C.; grad. Travis Prep. Sch., Syracuse, 1917; m. Virginia Weis, Oct. 12, 1921; children—Mary (Mrs. Vincent Moffet), Eileen (Mrs. J. Warren McGee), Edward, Paul, Johanna (Sister Thomas Marie), Thomas, Virginia, Arthur, William, Raymond. Apprentice printer Syracuse Herald, 1912; pres., treas. Peerless Press, Inc., N.Y., since 1929; pres., dir. 1st Fed. Savings & Loan Assn., Syracuse, since 1948. Pres. Syracuse Typographical Union No. 55, 1921-22, sec.-treas., 1924-28; pres. Syracuse Fedn. Labor, 1924-25; asst. indsl. commr. N.Y. State Dept. Labor, 1940-43, area dir. War Manpower Commn., 1943-46. Mayor, City of Syracuse, 1950-53. Served as petty officer, U.S. Navy, World War I. Mem. bd. dirs. Am. Red Cross, Group Hosp., St. Joseph's Hosp., Catholic Charities. Dir. Soc. Prevention Cruelty to Animals, Onondaga Health Assn. Mem. Am. Legion, C. of C., Citizens Found., Onondaga Hist. Assn. Ancient Order Hibernians. K.C. Home: 190 Robineau Rd., Syracuse 4. Office: 1112 E. Fayette St., Syracuse 10, N.Y. Died Jan. 10, 1956.

CORDES, Frank (kŏrds), ret. chmn. bd. Blaw-Knox Co., b. Lewistown, Pa., Oct. 7, 1870; s. Joseph R. and Martha Catherine (Fichthorn) C.; student pub. schs. of Pa.; m. Ethel T. Lomax, July 5, 1899; children—Catherine (Mrs. Arthur Kline), Margaret Hilda (Mrs. Howard S. Philips), Ethel Gertrude, Frances Christinana. Chemist Carnegie Steel Co., Braddock, Pa., 1888-95; metallurgist, later mgr. roll foundaries Lincoln Foundry Co. (later merged with United Engring. & Foundry Co.), 1895-1912; pres. Best Mfg. Co., Pitts., 1913-14; pres. Hubbard Steel Foundry Co., East Chicago, Ind., 1914-19; mgr. plant Wheeling (W.Va.) Mold and Foundry Co., 1922-27; pres. Lewis Foundry and Machine Co., 1927-29; v.p. Blaw-Knox Co., Pitts., 1929-36, pres., 1936-37, chmn. bd., 1937-46, ret.; also pres. Lewis Foundry and Machine Co., Union Steel Casting Co.; dir. Pitts. Rolls Corp., Nat. Alloy Co. Holder of several patents on appliances used in steel industry. Mem. Am. Iron and Steel Inst. Republican. Mason. Clubs: Metropolitan, Longue vue Country; Castalia (O.) Trout Fishing. Home: 211 Lytton Av., Pitts.; also (summers) Catawba Cliffs, O. Office: Farmers Bank Bldg., Pitts. Died Oct. 20, 1952.*

CORDOVA, Gabriel (kôr'dō-vä), business exec.; b. Mexico City, Mexico, Sept. 8, 1891; s. Mariano and Angela (Sola) C.; B.A., Instituto de Ciencias, Aquascalientes, Mexico, 1908; grad. study U. Mich., 1918. U. Detroit, 1919; m. Anita Lea Faust, Nov. 30, 1922 (dec.); children—Adriana (Mrs. George H. Freeman), Ralph; m. 2d Helen C. Crawford, May 23, 1932. Came to U.S., 1915. Various exec. positions Nat. Rys. of Mexico, 1908-15; with Maxwell Motor Co., 1915-19;asst. dir. fgn. sales Wahl Co., 1920-25; Latin Am. mgr. Reed, Tilley & Co., 1925-29; Northeast sales Gen. Paint Corp., 1930-32; exec. sec. Mexican C. of C. of U.S., Inc., N.Y. City, since 1933. Home: 11 Pine St., Port Washington, L.I. Office: 60 Wall St., N.Y.C. 5. Died May 13, 1953.

COREY, Herbert (kor'ī), newspaper man; b. Toledo, Ohio, June 28, 1872; s. Abel M. and Minnie S. (Herbert) C.; ed. pub. schs.; m. Carolyn Koehl, Nov. 30, 1901. Formerly cowboy, stage driver, and sheep herder in Colo. and Wyo.; connected with various western newspapers, until 1900; became corr. Cincinnati Enquirer, 1900, later traveling corr. and New York corr., Cincinnati Times-Star; traveling corr. Associated Newspapers, 1912-30; war corr. throughout the war in Europe and with A.E.F. in France, and contbd. letters from Germany, England, France, Italy, Serbia, and others. Author: The Truth About Hoover; Farewell, Mr. Gangster; Submarine; The Army Means Business, etc. Clubs: Nat. Press, Overseas Writers (president two terms), Authors, Palaver (Washington). Contbg. editor, Nation's Business. Contbr. to mags. and periodicals. Home: 4712 Blagden Av. N.W., Washington. Died Dec. 28, 1954.

CORI, Gerty Theresa, biochemist; b. Prague, Austria, Aug. 15, 1896; d. Otto and Martha (Neustadt) Radnitz; grad. Realgymnasium of Tetschen, Czechoslovakia, 1914; M.D., German U. Prague Med. Sch., 1920, Sc.D., Boston U., 1948, Smith Coll., 1949, Yale, 1951, Columbia University, 1954; married Carl F. Cori, August 5, 1920; 1 son, C. Thomas. Came to the United States, 1922, naturalized, 1928. Asst., Children's Hosp., Vienna, 1920-22; asst. biochemist State Inst. for Study of Malignant Diseases, Buffalo, 1922-31; research asso. Washington U. Med. Sch., 1931-47, prof. biol. chemistry, 1947—. Mem. adv. bd. Nat. Sci. Found. Recipient Midwest award Am. Chem. Soc., 1946; Squibb award in endocrinology, 1947; Nobel prize in medicine and physiology, 1947; Garvan medal, 1948; Sugar research prize National Academy Sciences, 1950; Borden award of the Association Medical Colleges. Mem. Nat. Acad. Sci., Am. Philos. Soc., Am. Soc. Biol. Chemists, Harvey Society, American Chemical Soc., Sigma Xi. Condr. research in carbohydrate metabolism and enzymes. Home: 1080 N. Berry Rd., Webster Groves 19, Mo. Office: Washington Univ. Med. Sch., St. Louis 10. Died Oct. 26, 1957.

CORK, James M., physicist; b. Yale, Mich., July 9, 1894; s. George M. and Jennie (Lee) C.; B.S., University of Michigan, 1916, M.S., 1917, Ph.D., 1921; married to Laurie Kaufmann, 1918; children—Janet Lee (wife of Doctor John C. Wahr), James A. Asst. physicist U.S. Bur. Standards, 1919; asst. prof. physics, Penn. State College, 1919-20; instr. physics, U. of Mich., 1920-25, asst. prof. 1926-31, asso. prof. 1932-37, prof. since 1937; exchange prof., Victoria U., Manchester, Eng., 1926-27; consultant Argonne National Laboratory, 1950—. Served as lieut. Signal Corps, U.S. Army, 1918. Mem. National Defense Research Com., 1942-45. Fellow Am. Physical Society, A.A.A.S.; member Washington Philos. Soc., Sigma Xi, Gamma Alpha. Author: Pyrometry (with W. P. Wood), 1927, 1941; Heat, 1933, 1942; Radioactivity and Nuclear Physics, 1946, 1957. Contbr. articles to tech. jours. on heat, X-rays and radioactivity. Home: 2034 Day St., Ann Arbor, Mich. Died Nov. 27, 1957; buried Forest Hills Cemetery, Ann Arbor.

CORLE. Edwin (korl), author; b. Wildwood, N.J., May 7, 1906; s. Samuel E. and Marie (Dever) C.; A.B., U. Cal., 1928; grad. student Yale, 1928-30; m. Jean Armstrong, Sept. 23, 1944; 1 dau., Jean Recipient silver medal award from Commonwealth Club of San Francisco for novel People on the Earth, 1938; Guggenheim fellowship for creative writing, 1941-42. Author: Mojave, 1934; Fig Tree John, 1935, spl. edit. 1955; People On the Earth, 1937, spl. edit. 1950; Burro Alley, 1938, spl. edit. 1946; Solitaire, 1940; Desert Country, 1941; Coarse Gold, 1942, spl. edit. 1952; Listen Bright Angel 1946 rev. edit. retitled The Story of the Grand Canyon, 1951; Three Ways to Mecca, 1947; John Studebaker: An American Dream, 1948; The Royal Highway, 1950; In Winter Light, 1949; The Gila: River of the Southwest, 1951; Billy the Kid, 1953. Contbr. articles and stories to Holiday, Atlantic Monthly, Harpers, Yale Rev., New Yorker, Scribner's, others. Club: Players (N.Y.C.). Home: Hope Ranch, Santa Barbara, Cal. Died June 11, 1956; buried Santa Barbara Cemetery.

CORLETT, George Milton, lawyer; b. Richardson County, Neb., Nov. 7. 1884; s. Charles Milton and Mary Eliza (Stafford) C.; student U. of Colo., 1901-03; LL.B., U. of Neb., 1904; m. Martha Jean Rupert, Apr. 5, 1905; children—Charles Rupert (lt. col., Marine Corps Res.), Veva Hattie (Mrs. Lonnie Pippin), Vera Mary (Mrs. Hugh Winter). County supt. of schs., Rio Grande County, Colo., 1905-06; admitted to Colo. bar, 1905, and since practiced in Monte Vista; specializes in irrigation law; senior mem. Corlett & Corlett; pres. Production Credit Assn., Monte Vista. Served as maj. 65th Inf., U.S. Army, during World War; later lt. col. O.R.C. Mayor, City of Monte Vista, 1919-21; lt. gov. of Colo., 1927-31. Received Congressional Certificate of Merit, 1946. Mem. Nat. Com. Production Credit Assn. representing Colo., Kan., Okla. and N.M. Mem. bd. dirs. Monte Vista Community Co. Mem. Am. Bar Assn., also Colo. Bar Assn. (exec. com.), San Luis Valley Bar Assn., Colo. Sheriffs and Peace Officers Association (hon.), Alpha Tau Omega; asso. mem. Colo. Soc. Civil Engrs. Republican. Mem. Christian Ch. Mason (32°, Shriner), Odd Fellow. Clubs: The Denver, Rotary (hon.). Address: Monte Vista, Colo. Died Feb. 16, 1955; buried Monte Vista.

CORLISS, Guy Carleton Haynes, judge; b. Poughkeepsie, N.Y., July 4, 1858; s. Cyrus K. and Clarinda M. C.; grad. high sch., 1873; m. Effia V. Edson, June 6, 1883. Removed to Grand Forks, Dakota Ty., 1886; chief justice Supreme Ct. of N.D., 1889-98; 1st dean N.D. Law Sch., U. of N.D., 1899-1902, prof. of law, 1902-12. Address: Portland, Ore. Died Nov. 24, 1937; buried Portland.

CORNELIUS, Adam E(dward) (kôr-nēl'yŭs), steamship operator; b. Buffalo, N.Y., June 25, 1882; s. Jacob and Philippina (Reiner) C.; grad. High Sch., Buffalo; m. Emma Reiser, Jan. 22, 1910; children—Adam Edward, Ruth, Esther, Elizabeth Jane. Began as clerk and stenographer in steamship brokerage office, 1901; bcame partner with John L. Boland in Boland & Cornelius, vessel brokers, 1904; started buying ships for Boland & Cornelius fleet, 1906, now incorporated in Am. Steamship Co.; chmn. bd. same, 1915—; dir. Marine Trust Co. of Buffalo, Grain Handling Corp., Lake Carriers Assn. Republican. Lutheran. Clubs: Buffalo, Buffalo Athletic, Transportation. Address: 133 W. Grimsby, Kenmore, N.Y. Died Dec. 10, 1953; buried Buffalo.

CORNELIUS, Martin Phelps, lawyer, ins. exec.; b. Saguache, Col., Feb. 14, 1883; s. Charles S. and Eugenia C. (Hamilton) C.; ed. U. Chicago; LL.B., Kent Coll. Law; m. Mary A. Hazzard, June 3, 1911. with Continental Casualty Co., Chicago since 1909, asst. gen. atty., 1910-11, gen. atty., 1917-21, v.p., dir. 1921-30, 1st v.p., 1930-37, pres. 1937-44, gen. atty., 1944-51, sr. consultant, dir., 1951-52; di. Continental Assurance Co., 1924-52. Home: 400 N. Scoville Av., Oak Park, Ill. Died July 8, 1952.

CORNELIUS, Willard M., chmn. bd. Parker Rust Proof Co.; b. Adrian, Mich., 1884; s. J. D. H. and Lurette (Moore) C.; LL.B., Univ. of Mich., 1906; m. Ingeborg K. Hawkins, July 19, 1934. Practiced law, 1906-15; with Parker Rust Proof Co. since 1916, dir. since 1917, became pres., 1930, chmn. bd. since 1945; chmn. of the bd. Hardie Manufacturing Company; dir. Detroit Bank & Trust Co., Lenawee County Savings Bank, Bank Lenawee County, Udylite Corp., Bagley Bldg. Corp. Mem. Alpha Tau Omega. Clubs: Detroit Athletic, Detroit, Detroit Golf; Surf (Miami, Fla.). Home: 18114 Parkside Av Office: Milwaukee at Dubois St., Detroit. Died Dec. 18, 1957.

CORNELL, William Bouck, univ. prof.; b. Bouck's Island, Fultonham, Schoharie County, N.Y., July 14. 1883; s. Charles Ezra and Katharine Lawyer (Bouck) C.; M.E., Cornell U., 1907; m. Emily Adelaide Lebengood, Nov. 19, 1913; 1 son, William Ezra. Instr. in engring., Cornell U., 1907-08; asst. to engr. in charge constrn. of hydro-electric power developments in Ida. and Utah with Tellurdie Power Co.; underground cable engr. Am. Telephone & Telegraph Co.; sales engr. Niles-Bement-Pond Co.; sales engr. Acheson Graphite Co. and sec. and gen. mgr. of affiliated co.; prodn. engr. Willys-Overland Co.; prof. management and chmn. dept. of management and industrial relations, New York Unviersity, 1921—. Licensed professional engineer State of N.Y. Life member board trustees of Cornell Universtiy. Member of advisory board of Internat. Accountants Society, Inc., Alexander Hamilton Institute, Inc.; mem. Am. Soc. Mech. Engrs., Inst. of Management, Am. Management Assn., Nat. Panel of Arbitrators of Am. Arbitration Assn., Alpha Tau Omega, Alpha Kappa Psi, Theta Nu Epsilon, Delta Mu Delta, Sphinx Head, Beta Gamma Sigma. Republican. Episcopalian. Mason. Clubs: Cornell (New York and Essex County, N.J.). Editor: The Development of American Industries—Their Economic Significance, 1932, rev., 1941. Author: Office Administration (with G. S. Childs), 1924; Syllabus of Industrial Organization and Management, Principles and Practice, 1925 (translated into Czechoslovakian at the request of the Masaryk Akad. of Labor of Czechoslovakia); Fundamentals of Business Organization and Management, 1927; Industrial Organization and Management, 1928; Business Organization, 1930, rev., 1947, 48; Business Organization and Practice, 1936; Organization and Management in Industry and Business, 1936, rev., 1947, 1957. Home: 197 Grove St., Montclair, N.J. Died Nov. 22, 1957; buried Ithaca, N.Y.

CORNMAN, Daniel, army officer; b. Carlisle, Pa., Feb. 8. 1852; s. Ephraim and Barbara (Shrom) C.; grad. high sch., Carlisle, 1869, U.S. Mil. Acad., 1873; m. Julia E. Leighton, Oct. 8, 1877. Second lt. 21st Inf., 1873, 1st lt., 1877, capt., 1888, maj., 1899, lt.-col. 24th Inf., 1901, col. 7th Inf., 1903. retired 1915. Served in Nez Percé Shoshone and Sioux Indian campaigns, and Spanish-Am. War and Philippine insurrection. Democrat. Episcopalian. Mason. Address: care Adjutant General U.S.A., Washington. Died Feb. 5, 1924.

CORNWELL, John J., ex-governor; b. Ritchie County, W.Va., July 11, 1867; s. Jacob H. and Mary E. (Taylor) C.; student Shepherd Coll., Shepherdstown, W.Va., 1888, and W.Va. Univ., Morgantown, 1889-90; LL.D., W.Va. Univ., U. of Md., U. of Vt.; m. Edna Brady, June 30, 1891; children—John J. (dec.); Mrs. Eugene E. Ailes. Prin. owner The Hampshire Review since 1890, editor; lawyer; financed and built Hampshire Southern R.R. (40 miles long); pres. Bank of Romney; consulting counsel B.&O. R.R. Co. Delegate Democratic National conventions in 1896, 1912, 24, 32, 40; mem. W.Va. Senate, 1896-1906; Dem. nominee for gov. of W.Va., 1904; elected gov., term 1917-21 (only Dem. elected). Mason, Odd Fellow, Elk. Author: Knock-about Notes, 1915; A Mountain Trail, 1939. Home: Romney, W.Va. Died Sept. 8, 1953.

CORRIGAN, Emmett, advertising; b. Saranac, N.Y., Aug. 4, 1891; s. Owen and Rose (Murtagh) C.; grad. Plattsburgh (N.Y.) High Sch., 1910, Plattsburgh State Normal Sch., 1915; m. Barbara Koehl, October 29, 1918; children—Claire Rose (Mrs. Floyd Carlisle, Jr.), 1st Lt. Emmett Thomas (killed in action, Germany, World War II), Barbara Genevieve. Prin. Altona, N.Y., Union Sch., 1911-13; entered advertising agency of Rudolph Guenther, Inc., 1915, and since with this firm and successor firms; now chmn. bd. dirs. Albert Frank-Guenther Law, Inc.; has specialized in advertising for banks, investment houses, insurance companies. Served with United States Army, with A.E.F., northern Russia, 1918-19. Dir. Am. Finds of Norway. Mem. N.Y. State War Finance Com., during World War II. Catholic. Clubs: Bankers, Metropolitan (New York City); Manhasset Bay Yacht (Port Washington, N.Y.). Home: 5 Meadow Woods Rd., Great Neck, L.I., N.Y. Office: 131 Cedar St., N.Y.C. Died Oct. 21, 1950.

CORRIGAN, John, fgn. service officer; b. Atlanta, July 25, 1878; s. John Augustus and Ellen (Lynan) C.; student pub. schs., 1885-96, bus. coll., 1896-97; spl. summer course in econs. and langs., U. of Paris, 1919; m. Irene E. Hand, Dec. 29, 1907; 1 son, Judson Hand; m. 2d, Violet Beament Beresford, Dec. 7, 1927. Reporter Atlanta Constitution, 1900-06, Washington corr., 1907-17; vice consul, Havre, France, 1919, consul, 1920-22; consul, Cherbourg, 1922-25, Dublin, Ireland, 1925, Izmir, Turkey, 1926-29, Venice, Italy, 1930-36, Durban, Union of S. Africa 1936—. Served as capt. U.S. Army with AEF, 1917-19. Democrat. Clubs: Nat. Press, Racquet (Washington). Home: Atlanta, Ga. Address: American Consulate, Durban (Natal), Union of South Africa. Died Aug. 1959.*

CORRIGAN, Walter Dickson, Sr., lawyer; b. Almond, Wis., Dec. 28, 1875; s. James E. and Hellen (Dickson) C.; student Iowa State Coll., 1893-95; LL.B., Drake U., Des Moines, Ia., 1896, LL.M., 1904; m. Jessie A. Donaldson (died 1925); children —Helen F. (Mrs. William J. Iekel), Jessie E. (Mrs. A. C. Pegis), Thomas M., Walter Dickson (grandson, adopted as son); m. 2d, Libby Miller, 1926. Admitted to Wis. bar, 1897, and practiced in Waupaca, 1897, Plainfield, 1897-1905, Milwaukee, since 1905; dist. atty. Waushara County, 1899-1901; asst. attorney general of Wisconsin, 1903-05; general attorney and solicitor Wis. Central Ry., 1907-09; specializes in trial and appellate court work; vice pres. dir. and gen. counsel Gladstone (Mich.) Amusement Co.; gen. counsel, Layton Park State Bank, Cedarburg Mutual Fire Ins. Co., Wis. Jewelers Assn., Milwaukee Jewelers Guild, Inc. Mem. Milwaukee Co. (past pres.), Wis. State and Am. bar assns., Ozaukee Co. Bar Assn. (past pres.); hon. mem. Bar Assn. 7th Judicial Circuit of Wis. Mason (32°), Elk. Author: History of Town of MeQuon. Contbr. to law publs. Home: The Homestead Orchard, R. 2, Cedarburg, Wis. Office: Plankinton Bldg., 161 W. Wisconsin Av., Milw. 3. Died Nov. 20, 1951.

CORT, Stewart J., steel exec.; b. Bethlehem, Pa., Mar. 16, 1881; s. Joseph Turney and Martha Henderson (Shaw) C.; Met.E., Lehigh U., 1906, Eng. D., 1948; m. Carolyn Mvrtilla Schreiner, June 14, 1910; children—Stewart Shaw, Carol. Joined Carnegie Steel in open hearth dept. Duquesne works, 1906, asst. supt., steel div., 1909; with Bethlehem Steel Co., 1916—, successively supt. steel div. Cambria plant (formerly Cambria Steel Co.), supt. steel div., supt. Saucon div., gen. mgr. Sparrows Point plant, v.p. charge steel div. operations, 1947-58, retired as vice pres., January 1, 1958, dir., 1947—. Mem. Am. Iron and Steel Inst., Am. Inst. Mining Engrs., Brit. Iron and Steel Inst. Club: Saucon Valley Country. Home: 2875 N. Main St. Office: 701 E. 3d St., Bethlehem, Pa. Died Sept. 23, 1958.

CORTILET, Michael P. (kor'tȧ-lĕt), bus. exec.; b. Chicago, Jan. 31, 1896; s. Angelo and Domenica (Parisi) C.; ed. pub. schs.; m. Hazel Jackson, Jan. 8, 1916. Clerk Western Electric Co., 1911-16; with Am. Can Co. since 1916, sales dept., 1921, Chicago sales mgr., 1935-47, mgr. sales Central div., 1947-50, v.p. Central div. since Apr. 1950. Clubs: Chicago Athletic, South Shore Country, Flossmoor Country.‡ Athletic, South Shore Country, Flossmoor Country. Deceased.

CORUM, Martene Windsor (Bill), reporter; b. Speed, Mo., July 29, 1894; s. Robert Wyan and Vida Celia (Henderson) C.; student Westworth Mil. Acad., Lexington, Mo., 1914-15; A.B., U. of Mo., 1917; Litt.B., Columbia, 1920; m. Elaine Kolle, Sept. 1, 1925; 1 son, Robert Strange. Sports writer N.Y. Times, 1921-25; sports columnist N.Y. Journal-American, 1925—. War corr. N.Y. Jour.-Am. and Internat. News in European theater, 1945. Sports announcer Gillette Safety Razor's Cavalcade of Sports, 1941—. Served as chmn. various sports coms. of A.R.C., Heart Fund, Boy Scouts Am., others; pres. Churchill Downs race track. Served as enlisted man, Mexican Border 1916; lt. to maj., 101st Inf., 26th Div., U.S. Army, 1917-19; participated in four major actions in France. Decorated 3 Silver Stars, Purple Heart. Mem. Am. Legion (present at foundation in Paris, 1918), baseball, boxing, and N.Y. Turf Writers assns. Democrat. Baptist. Clubs: Columbia, Racquet and Tennis. Contbr. on sports to Ency. Britannica, mags. and television; also to sports and newspaper anthologies, including Anthology of Sports, Great Reporters. Home: Park Lane Hotel. Office: 20 South St., N.Y. C. Died Dec. 1958.*

CORWIN, Arthur Frank, business exec.; b. Baiting Hollow, L.I., N.Y., Jan. 7, 1877; s. Josiah Frank and Jane Amanda (Norton) C.; grad. Norwich Free Acad., 1896; grad. Sheffield Scientific School, Yale, 1899; m. Claudia Howell Thomas, June 29, 1904 (died May 28, 1941); children—Gwendolyn Belle (Mrs. Frederick G. Frost Jr.). Apprentice, S. Penn Oil Co. in oil producing fields, Mannington, W.Va., 1899-1906, dir. and gen. supt., S. Penn Oil Co., Pittsburgh, 1906-11; dir. and mgr., Penn-Mex Fuel Co. Pittsburgh, 1911-15; dir. and pres., The Carter Oil Co., (Standard Oil, N.J., subsidiary), N.Y. City, 1915-26; dir. Standard Oil Co. of New York, 1926-32, and dir. Socony-Vacuum Oil Co., Inc. (successor to Standard Oil Co. of N.Y.) and mem. exec. com. since 1933, vice pres. since 1934; dir. and vice pres. of S. Am. Gulf Oil Co., N.Y. City, 1936-45; pres. and chmn. bd., Colombia Petroleum Co., New York, 1936-45; ret. 1945. Trustee, Village of Bronxville, N.Y., 1919-22, pres., 1922-23, mem. planning commn., 1924-26. Dir. Am. Bur. of Med. Aid to China, 1945-48; Westchester County Council of Social Agencies, White Plains, N.Y., since 1946. Mem. Am. Petroleum Inst. (past dir.), Public Health Nursing Assn., Delta Psi. Republican. Protestant. Clubs: India House, Yale (N.Y. City); St. Andrews Golf (Hastings-on-Hudson); Dorset (Vt.) Field; Ekwanok Country (Manchester, Vt.); Highland Park Fla. (Lake Wales, Fla.). Home: 29 Elm Lane, Bronxville 8, N.Y. Office: 26 Broadway, N.Y.C. 4. Died Mar. 13, 1957; buried Kensico Cemetery.

CORWIN, Charles Edward, clergyman; b. Millstone, N.J., Sept. 7, 1868; s. Edward Tanjore (q.v.) and Mary Esther (Kipp) C.; A.B., Rutgers U., 1892, A.M. (hon.), 1907; B.D., New Brunswick Theol. Sem., 1895; m. Ellen Gibb Kingsley, June 15, 1898. Ordained to ministry Ref. Ch. in America, 1895; pastor North Branch, N.J., 1907—. Mem. Phi Beta Kappa. Author: Onesimus, Christ's Freedman, 1903. Contbr. to religious revs. and jours. Address: North Branch, N.J. Died June 8, 1958.

COSGROVE, John Phillips, business exec.; born Jersey City, N.J., May 17, 1897; s. Wallace Marks and Mary Alice (Tripp) C.; ed. N.J. Mil. Acad., 1912-16; Stevens Inst. of Tech., 1916-17; m. Marie Fischer, June 17, 1922; children—John Clifford, Marjorie Allison. Machinist, Am. Radiator & Standard Sanitary Corp., 1918-20, machine shop foreman, 1920-21, export salesman, 1921-29, export mgr., 1929-36, overseas rep., Europe, 1936-46, vice pres., dir., 1946-51, exec. v.p., dir., 1951. Dir. Ideal Boilers & Radiators, Ltd., London; Compagnie Nationale des Radiateurs (National Radiator Co.), Paris; Anderson, Meyer & Co., Ltd. N.Y. City. Clubs: Engrs., Metropolitan (N.Y. City); American (London); American (Paris). Address: P.O. Box 208, Locust, N.J. Died Dec. 13, 1951; buried Bloomfield Cemetery, Bloomfield, N.J.

COSGROVE, Terence Byrne, lawyer; b. Marseilles, Ill., Aug. 5, 1881; s. Terry Anthony and Sarah Elizabeth (Byrne) C.; B.A., St. Viator's Coll., 1904, M.A., 1906; LL.B., Notre Dame U., 1906, LL.D., 1938; M.L., Yale, 1907. Admitted to Ill. bar, 1907, Calif. bar, 1911; instr. law sch. U. Ill., 1907-10; city atty., San Diego, Calif., 1913-19; practicing lawyer, Los Angeles, since 1920; sr. partner Cosgrove, Cramer, Diether & Rindge; dir. Times-Mirror Co., Citizens Nat. Trust & Savings Bank of Los Angeles, Michael J. Connel Charities, Ltd. Lay trustee U. Notre Dame; trustee Michael J. Connell Found. Mem. Am., Calif. State, Los Angeles bar assns., Knights of Malta, Knight Comdr. St. Gregory. Home: California Club, 538 S. Flower St., Los Angeles 17. Office: 458 S. Spring St., Los Angeles 13. Died June 20, 1956; buried Seneca, Ill.

COSTELLO, J. F., v.p. Joseph Hoover & Sons Co., Phila. Home: 7494 N. Tulpehocken St., Phila. 38. Office: 49th and Market Sts., Phila. 39. Deceased.

COSTELLO, Lou (Louis Francis Cristillo), film and radio comedian; b. Paterson, N.J., Mar. 6, 1908; s. Sebastion and Helen (Rege) C.; ed. pub. schs. of N.J.; m. Anne Battler, Jan. 20, 1934; children—Patricia, Carole Lou, Christine. Laborer and extra at Metro-Goldwyn-Mayer Studios, Culver City, Calif., 1930; stunt man; began acting career at the Empress Theatre, St. Joseph, Mo., as Dutch dialect comedian; with Minsky Burlesque Co., New York, 1932; on Kate Smith radio hour, 1938-40; in Streets of Paris, mus. comedy on Broadway, 1939-40; has appeared since 1940 in "One Night in the Tropics," "Buck Privates," "In the Navy," "Hold That Ghost," "Ride 'em, Cowboy," "Keep 'em Flying," "Rio Rita," "Pardon My Ice," "In Society," "Here Come The Coeds," "The Naughty Nineties," "Lost In A Harem," "Abbott and Costello in Hollywood", Abbott and Costello Meet the Mummy, 1955. Awarded State of N.J. Distinguished Service Gold Medal by Passaic County Am. Legion, 1941. Elk. Clubs: Masquers (Hollywood, Calif., pres.); Lambs (New York). Address: 8533 Sunset Blvd., Los Angeles 46. Died Mar. 3, 1959.

COSTELLO, Louis B(artlett), publisher; b. Wells, Me., Sept. 14, 1876; s. Nicholas H. and Annie (Hill) C.; A.B., Bates Coll., 1898, LL.D., 1952; m. Sadie M. Brackett, Feb. 14, 1900; children—Louise (Mrs. Elis J. Wickman), Russell. With Lewiston Daily Sun, 1898-1926; treas., sec., gen. mgr., dir., Sun Corp. (pubs. of Daily Sun and Evening Jour.), 1926-45, pres. and treas., since 1945. Trustee, Bates Coll., Lewiston, since 1916 (mem., exec. com., finance com. and bldg. and grounds com.); Androscoggin Co. Savings Bank (past pres.). Mem. Asso. Press, Am. Newspaper Pubs. Assn., Me. Daily Newspaper Assn. (past pres.). Baptist. Mason (K.T.). Home: 45 Campus Av. Office: 104 Park St., Lewiston, Me. Died May 6, 1959; buried Riverside Cemetery, Lewiston.

COTE, Alcide, Canadian govt. ofcl.; b. St. Johns, Que., Can., May 19, 1903; s. Trefflé and Eléanor (Hébert) C.; B.A., B.L., St. Johns Classical Coll., LL.B., U. Montreal, 1928. Admitted to Quebec bar, 1928; King's Counsel, 1943. Mayor, City of St. Johns, 1945-49; elected rep. St. Johns-Iberville-Napierville, House of Commons, 1945, 1949, 1953; postmaster gen. of Canada, Ottawa, 1952—. Del. Canadian Fedn. Mayors and Municipalities, Internat. Union of Cities, The Hague, Netherlands, 1948; chmn. Les Semaine Soc. du Canada, St. Johns, 1942. Vice chmn. Canadian delegation to UN, 1953. Member St. Johns-Iberville Jr. Bd. Trade (founder, pres., 1936-38), St. Vincent de Paul Soc. (chmn. particular council, St. Johns), Que Province Fedn. Jr. Bds. Trade (mem. senate, 1948), Canad'an Bar Assn., Rural Bar Assn. Province Que. (dir.), Bd. Trade. Roman Catholic. Liberal. K.C. Clubs: Kinsmen, St. Johns Yacht (past commodore). Home: St. Jean, Que. Address: Postmaster General's Office, Ottawa, Ont., Can. Died Aug. 7, 1955; buried Catholic Cemetery, St. Johns, Que., Can.

COTHRAN, Perrin Chiles, insurance exec.; b. Chiles Crossroads (Millway), S.C., Feb. 22, 1886; s. Capt. (CSA) Wade Elephare and Sara (Chiles) C.; B.S., C.E. Clemson Coll., S.C., 1904; m. Annie Wilson Howe, Dec. 31, 1910 (divorced 1916); 1 dau., Josephine (Mrs. Samuel Wilson); m. 2d, Ruth Galbraith, Sept. 18, 1941; children—Perrin Galbraith, Robert Chiles. Asst. resident engr., Carolina, Clinchfield & Ohio R.R., Clinchport, Va., 1904-06; resident engr. Va. Pocahontas Coal Co., Coalwood, W.Va., 1906-08; resident engr. N.&S. Ry., Raleigh, N.C., 1908-10; spl. agt. N.C. Home Ins. Co., Raleigh, N.C., 1910-12, Conn. Fire Ins. Co., Richmond, Va., 1912-17; mgr. Am. Fgn. Ins. Assn. of east coast, S.A., Rio de Janeiro, Brazil, 1919-27; spl. agt. Phoenix Ins. Co., Phila., 1927-28; sec. Phoenix Ins. Co., Hartford, Conn., 1928-35; vice pres. and sec. Phoenix-Conn. group of ins. cos.; dir. Phoenix Ins. Co., Conn. Fire Ins. Co.; pres. and dir. Stock Co. Assn., Washington, D.C.; vice pres. and dir. Reliance Ins. Co., Montreal, Can., dir. First Nat. Bank of Hartford, since 1941. Mem. governing com. New York Fire Ins.: Rating Orgn., New York City, governing com. Md. Rating Bur., Baltimore, Md., bd. of govs. Middle Dept. Assn. of Fire Underwriters, Phila., Pa. Served as capt., major and lt. col. of engrs., 195rh engrs., 30th Am. div., III corps, U.S. Army, IV British Army, A.E.F.; col. res. corps engrs., comdg. officer 301st engrs., 76th div., U.S. Army; trans. inactive res., 1940. Mem. bd. of finance, City of Hartford, 1937-44. Democrat. Mason. Clubs: Bankers (New York City); Dauntless (Essex, Conn.); Hartford, Hartford Golf (Hartford, Conn.). Home: 11 Woodside Circle. Office: 30 Trinity St., Hartford, Conn. Died Dec. 23, 1959.*

COTTER, Charles F., gen. mgr. Home Owners Loan Corp. Address: 1626 K St., Washington. Deceased.*

COTTER, John F(rancis), lawyer; b. Detroit, July 14, 1879; s. Maurice and Mary (Roche) C.; A.B., U. of Mich., 1902; LL.B., Detroit Coll. of Law, 1904; m. 2d, Helen Erlach, Jan. 31, 1931. Admitted to Mich. bar, 1904, and practiced in Detroit, 1904-11; joined The Studebaker Corp., South Bend, Ind., 1911 became gen. atty., 1915, became dir., 1935; now retired. Home: 1839 N. Wilber St., South Bend 28, Ind. Died Dec. 17, 1957.

COTTER, William Edward, lawyer; b. Chicago, Mar. 21, 1893; s. Patrick and Helen (Fitzgerald) C.; LL.B., U. Notre Dame, 1913; D.C.S., Holy Cross Coll., 1950; LL.D. (honorary), St. Michael's College, 1954, St. Mary's College, Notre Dame, Ind., 1956; married Evarista Brady, June 7, 1916; children—Evarista Ruth (Kane), William Edward II, Mary Camille (Millard). Counsel Union Carbide and Carbon Corp. since 1917; dir. John Price Jones Co., Inc., Jones & Berkeley, Pricejon Corporation. Cofounder, sec.-treas. Cath. Actors Guild Am., 1914-17; sec.-treas. So. Traffic Assn., 1920-22; treas. Am. Meml. Devastated War Area of France, 1923-24; dir. Amateur Cinema League, from 1928; mem. Cardinal's

Com., Cath. Charities, from 1930; treas. Internat. Acetylene Assn., 1931-32; sponsor, mem. Child Welfare Assn. of Am., 1935; dir., v.p. Broad St. Hosp., 1935-38; pres. Nat. Notre Dame Alumni Assn., 1937-38; mem. Social Service Com. for Venezuela, 1938-39; mem. bd. of council Fordham U., from 1939; mem. nat. adv. com. N.Y. Worlds Fair, Inc., 1939-40; dir. Downtown Hosp., 1939-42; chmn. Selective Service Board, New Rochelle, N.Y., 1940-45; dir. Occupational Research Found., from 1941; mem. exec. com., dir. United China Relief (Fellowship of Wisteria), 1941-42; mem. exec. com. Navy Relief, 1942; executive vice chmn. commerce and industry div. U.S.O., 1942, Nat. War Fund, 1943; chmn. chemical div. A.R.C., yearly, 1943-45, 50-52; dir. commerce and industry div., 3-6th War Loans, 1943-45; mem. executive com. War Finance Com., State of N.Y., 1943-45; chmn. N.Y. County, 7th War Loan, 1944; chairman Greater N.Y. Victory Loan, 1945; mem. N.Y. State adv. com. U.S. Savings Bonds Div., from 1946; dir. United Negro College Fund (chmn. for N.Y. 1946-47, nat. chmn. 1948, member national council from 1948); dir., co-founder Family Theatre of the Air; general vice chmn. N.Y.U.-Bellevue Med. Center Fund, from 1948; member Lay Com. for Financing Med. Care, 1948-49; mem. nat. planning com. and exec. vice chmn. of campaign Am. Heart Assn., 1948-49; chmn. steering com., trustee, sec. Nat. Fund for Med. Edn., from 1949; vice chmn. of Greater N.Y. campaign Arthritis and Rheumatism Found., yearly, 1949-53; mem. adv. bd. Albertus Magnus College, New Haven, from 1950; mem. bd. of dirs. Citizens Com. for Hoover Report, from 1949; mem. adv. com. on Graduate School Bus. Adminstrn., and Sch. of Commerce, Accounts and Finance, N.Y.U., from 1950; mem. commerce and industry council of Nat. Urban League, from 1950; dir. United Cerebral Palsy Assns., Inc., from 1951; member Internat. Soc. Welfare of Cripples, from 1951; mem. adv. bd. Xavier U., from 1951; bd. dirs. Nat. Soc. for Prevention of Blindness; mem. spl. gifts com. and chmn. chem. div. N.Y.C. Cancer Com.; mem. bd. of council N.Y.U., from 1952, trustee of Law Center Found., from 1952; trustee Town Hall, Inc., from 1952; mem. board Cath. Youth Orgn., from 1952; v.p. Lincoln ednl. Found., from 1952; dir. Goodwill Industries N.Y., from 1952; pres. adv. bd. St. Mary's Coll., Notre Dame, Ind., from 1952; dir. of Westchester Heart Assn., from 1952; chmn. board of trustees St. Agnes Hospital, White Plains, New York, from 1952. Mem. Inst. Social Scis., Acad. Polit. Sci., English-Speaking Union Friendly Sons of St. Patrick, Am. Irish Hist. Soc. Mem. Mil. Order of Malta in U.S. (Knight Sovereign); Knight Comdr. Order of Holy Sepulchre of Jerusalem (Papal). Clubs: Union League, University, Economic (N.Y. City); Scarsdale Golf; Westchester Country. Home: 1 Beekman Pl., N.Y.C. 22. Died Aug. 1957.

COTTIS, George W., surgeon; b. Guelph, Ont., Mar. 18, 1880; s. Charles and Jessie (Mimmack) C.; M.D., Cornell, 1904; m. Eliza A. Fancher, 1906; children—Marcia, Ralph. Intern Bellevue Hosp., N.Y.C., 1904-05; capt. Royal Army M.C., 1917-18; private surgery practice, Jamestown, N.Y., 1918—; chief Emergency Med. Service, Jamestown, 1942; chief of surg. staff Jamestown Gen. Hosp., 1941-42; mem. Governor's N.Y. State Health Commn., 1930-32. Diplomate Am. Bd. of Surgery. Fellow A.C.S.; mem. A.M.A., N.Y. State Med. Soc. (trustee 1933-41; vice-speaker 1928-32; pres. 1942), Western N.Y. Surg. Assn. Republican. Contbr. articles on goiter, gastric surgery, peritonitis, etc., to jours. Died Oct. 20, 1950.

COTTON, William Edwin, supt. expt. station; b. Oskaloosa, Ia., Sept. 17, 1866; s. George E. and Mary M. (Binns) C.; D.V.M., George Washington U., 1911; m. Grace E. Caskey, Sept. 20, 1898 (died Sept. 11, 1928); children—Cornelia Marie, Edwin Rowland, John Caskey. Asst. Bur. Animal Industry, U.S. Dept. Agr., 1893-94, expert asst., 1894-1910, asst. supt. expt. station (now Animal Disease Sta.), Beltsville, Md., 1910-28, supt. 1928-37; prof. of infectious diseases, Vet. Coll., Ala. Poly. Inst., Auburn, Ala.; retired, 1948. Mem. Am. Veterinary Med. Assn. (first v.p., 1933-34, mem. exec. com., 1939-44), Internat. Vet. Congress, U.S. Livestock Sanitary Assn., Research workers in animal diseases in N. Am. (pres. 1931-32); fellow A.A.A.S. Presbyterian. Contbr. repts. and bulletins, U.S. Dept. Agr. Research in animal diseases, tuberculosis, infectious abortion, etc. Recipient Borden award for research in dairy cattle diseases, 1946. Home: Brockwood, Wilson Lane, Bethesda, Md. Died Sept. 7, 1951; buried Rockville Union Cemetery, Rockville, Md.

COTTON, William H., portrait painter; b. Newport, R.I., July 22, 1880; s. William Henry and Elizabeth (Hazard) C.; studied Cowles Art Sch., Boston, under Andreas Anderson and Joseph De Camp, also Académie Julian, Paris, under Jean Paul Laurens; m. Georgia Dvorak, Sept. 29, 1914 (deceased, 1949); m. 2d, Mildred Massey LaPorte, 1950. Has exhibited at N.A.D., New York; Corcoran Art Gallery, Washington; Art Inst. Chicago; Pa. Acad. Fine Arts; St. Louis Art Mus.; Carnegie Inst., Pittsburgh, etc. Hon. mention, Phila. Art Club, 1905; 1st Hallgarten prize, N.A.D., 1907; 1st medal, Dallas, Tex., 1909; Purchase prize, Boston Art Club, 1916; 1st Lewis prize for caricature, Phila. Water Color Soc., 1926. Caricaturist Vanity Fair, 1931-36; The New Yorker Mag., 1932—. Mural paintings in the Capitol, Apollo, Times Square, Selwyn theatres of New York; represented in the exhbn. of Am. artists at Luxembourg Museum, at the invitation of the French Govt. Asso. Nat. Acad.; a founder Nat. Assn. Portrait Painters; mem. Newport Art Assn. Home: Stockton, N.J. Died Jan. 5, 1958.

COTTRELL, Donald C(lark), mfr.; b. Westerly, R.I., Aug. 17, 1892; s. Calvert Byron, Jr., and Agnes (Clark) C.; grad. St. Mark's Sch., 1911; A.B., Harvard, 1915; m. Lois Lee Page, May 22, 1920; children—Janet Page (Mrs. James P. Balding, Jr.), Donald C., Mary Lee (Mrs. Kenneth W. Jacobs, Jr.). With The Cottrell Co. and predecessor, Pawcatuck, Conn., 1915-20, 32—, v.p. charge Milw. factory, 1936-49, pres., dir., 1949—; with United Drug Co., Boston, also Sanderson & Porter, Guaranty Co. N.Y., 1920-32; dir. Washington Trust Co. (Westerly). Mem. Pawcatuck Bd. Trade. Vice pres. Stonington Welfare League, 1955—; treas. Stonington Village Improvement Assn., 1955—. Trustee Westerly Hosp., 1950—, Pequot-sepos Wildlife Sanctuary, 1950-55, Westerly Library Assn., 1952—. Served as capt. U.S. Army, 1917-19. Mem. Nat. Printing Equipment Assn. (dir.), Mfrs. Assn. Conn. (dir.), A.I.M. (asso.), Pawcatuck Bd. Trade. Clubs: Harvard (N.Y.C.); University (Milw.); Misquamicut (Watch Hill, R.I.). Home: North Rd., Stonington, Conn. Office: 86 Mechanic St., Pawcatuck, Conn. Died Sept. 16, 1956.

COTTRELL, Edwin Angell (kŏt-rĕl), professor emeritus; b. Newport, R.I., Dec. 14, 1881; s. Robert Clarke and Annie Johnson (Southwick) C.; grad. Williston Sem., Easthampton, Mass., 1901; student Brown U., B.A., Swarthmore Coll., 1907; M.A., Harvard, 1913; m. Louise Wright Hornor, Sept. 9, 1908. Instr. poilt. science, Pa. State Coll., 1907-11, asst. registrar, 1909-11; asst. in govt., Harvard, 1911-15, lecturer in polit. science, Wellesley, 1912-17, Brown U., 1915-16; prof. polit. science and dir. Bur. Governmental Research, Ohio State U., 1917-19; prof. polit. science Stanford, 1919—, exec. head of department, 1927-45, dean School of Social Sciences, 1931-45, lecturer on government Harvard, summer, 1913, spring, 1922, U. of Wash., summer, 1924, Am. Univ., 1932-33, U. Calif. Los Angeles, summer, 1935, at Berkeley, summer, 1936,dean Western Sch. for Comml. Orgn. Secs., 1920-24. Sec. Boston Budget Commn., 1915; asst. sec. Boston Chamber Commerce, 1916; with U.S. Bur Efficiency, 1918. Mem. City Council, Palo Alto, 1923-29; mayor Palo Alto, 1924-25; mem. Calif. Com. County Home Rule, 1931, Calif. Commn. Taxation and Costs of Govt., 1936-41. Mem. Bd. Public Works (chmn. personnel bd., 1947). Dir. Pub. Service Program, Calif. Nat. Youth Adminstrn., 1941-43. Pub. mem. Panel Nat. War Labor Bd., 10th Region, 1943. Vice-pres. Calif. Merit System League, 1941-43. Pres. Western Governmental Research Assn., 1943-46; cons. on local govt., Haynes Foundation, Los Angeles, 1947—. Member Federal Loyalty Review Board, 1949—. Trustee San Francisco Bur. Govt. Research. Mem. Am. Polit. Science Assn. (exec. council; 2d v.p. 1929; 1st v.p. 1938), Nat. Municipal League (exec. council), Am. Soc. Public Adminstrn., Internat. City Mgrs. Assn., Am. Assn. Univ. Profs., Phi Delta Theta. Mason. Clubs: Chit Chat. Commonwealth; Town Hall, University (Los Angeles). Home: 316 N. Rossmore Av., Los Angeles 4. Office: Haynes Foundation, 601 S. Hill St., Los Angeles. Died Feb. 10, 1953; buried Palo Alto, Cal.

COTTRELL, Mary James (kŏt'trĕl), newspaper corr.; b. Huntsville, Tenn., Apr. 24, 1899; d. Judge Henry Clay and Bettie Jane (Walker) James; grad. Harriman (Tenn.) High School, 1917; student Milligan (Tenn.) Coll., 1918-19; special courses U. of Tenn.; m. Jesse Samuel Cottrell, Oct. 15, 1938 (now deceased). Teacher of social science, city schs., Knoxville, Tenn., 1922-38; associated with Jesse S. Cottrell News Bureau, 1938-44, continuing operation of news bureau following death of husband, serving as Washngton correspondent for Nashville (Tenn.) Banner, Charlotte (N.C.) Observer, Greenville (S.C.) News, Schenectady (New York) Union Star, Troy (N.Y.) Times Record, Manchester (New Hampshire) Union-Leader, Wilmington (N. C.), Star News, Madison (Wis.) State Journal, Green Bay (Wis.) Press Gazette, LaCrosse (Wis.) Tribune, Appleton (Wis.) Post Crescent. Pres. Knoxville (Tenn.) Business and Professional Women's Club, 1936-37. Mem. White House Corrs. Assn., Congressional Press Galleries, Mrs. Roosevelt's Press Conf. Assn., Delta Kappa Gamma. Club: Womens National Press, United Nations (Washington). Home: 2509 N. Powhatan St., Arlington, Va. Office: National Press Bldg., Washington 4. Died Nov. 29, 1952.

COUCH, Herbert Newell, educator; b. Laurel, Ont., Can., Dec. 4, 1899; s. Isaac and Sarah Jane (Richardson) C.; A.B., Victoria Coll., U. of Toronto, 1924; A.M., Johns Hopkins, 1926, Ph.D., 1927; A.M. ad eundem, Brown U., 1945; m. Eunice Burr Stebbins, May 12, 1928; one daughter, Eunice Burr (Mrs. William H. Claflin). Came to the United States in 1924, naturalized, 1937. Asso. in classics and curator of Classical Museum, U. of Ill., 1928-30; asst. prof. of classics, Brown U., 1930-38, asso. prof., 1938-45, prof. of classics since 1945, chmn., dept. of classics, since 1948, sec. faculty since 1951. Mem. Am. Philol. Assn., Classical Assn. of New England. Author Classical Civilization: Greece, 1940; Beauty and Parting, 1945; Cicero on the Art of Growing Old, 1959. Contbr. translations and articles to classical periodicals. Home: 17 Arlington Av., Providence 6. Died June 6, 1959; buried Swan Point Cemetery, Providence.

COUDERT, Frederic René (kōō-dâr'), lawyer; b. New York, Feb. 11, 1871; s. late Frederic René and Elizabeth (McCredy) C.; A.B., Columbia, 1890, A. M., 1891, Ph.D., 1894; m. Alice Tracy Wilmerding, May 1897; children—Frederic René, Benjamin Tracy, Ferdinand Wilmerding, Alexis Carrel. Admitted to bar, 1892, and since in practice at New York; mem. law firm Coudert Bros. 1895—; spl. asst. atty. gen. of U.S., 1913-14; was legal adviser to the British Embassy, 1915-20; pres. Chapultepec Land Improvement Co. Trustee Columbia U. Served as 1st lt. comdg. Troop A, N.Y. Vol. Cav., 1898. Pres. Nat. Highways Protective Soc., 1912-14. Hon. mem. of Internat. Olympic Com. for the U.S. Mem. Am. Bar Assn., Assn. Bar City of N.Y., de l'institut de Droit Internat., etc.; hon. mem. N.Y. State Soc. of the Cincinnati; govt. del. Universal Congress Lawyers and Jurists, St. Louis, 1904. Hon. pres. France-Am. Soc.; Pilgrims of the U.S. (v.p.); Officier d'Instruction publique, Commander Legion d'Honneur (France), Officer Crown of Belgium. President American Society International Law, 1942-46; member Phi Beta Kappa. Clubs: Century, Manhattan, University, Fencers (hon. pres.), Seawanhaka, Piping Rock, Down Town, Union (New York); Metropolitan (Washington, D.C.); Union Interalliée, Travellers (Paris). Author: Certainty and Justice, 1913; A Half Century of International Problems—A Lawyer's Views, 1954; numerous articles on law and internat. relations. Home: 124 E. 56th St., N.Y. City; also Oyster Bay, L.I. Office: 488 Madison Av., N.Y.C. 22. Died Apr. 1, 1955.

COUGHLIN, Clarence Dennis, ex-congressman; b. Kingston, Pa., July 27, 1883; s. James Martin and Mary (Welter) C.; student Wesleyan Coll., Conn., 1901-03; A.B., Harvard, 1906; m. Helen Barring, June 27, 1910. Tchr. of lit. and history, high schs., Fairview and Wilkes-Barre, 1906-10; admitted to Pa. bar, 1910, since practiced in Luzerne County; apptd. to Luzerne bench, 1925, elected to full term, by the largest Republican majority ever polled up to that time in the county, 1927, failing health toward the close of his term prevented his renomination. Treas. Wilkes-Barre Can Co., W. B. Bartels & Sons Co. (Wilkes-Barre), Diamond Land Improvement Co. (Scranton, Pa.). Mem. 67th Congress. Chmn. Rep. Party of Luzerne County, 3 terms; mem. Rep. State Com., 1916-18. Methodist. Mason (Shriner), Elk. Club: Westmoreland. Home: 29 River St., Wilkes-Barre, Pa. Died Dec. 15, 1946; buried Mt. Greenwood Cemetery, Trucksville, Pa.

COUGHLIN, Timothy J., clergyman, coll. dean; b. Bayonne, N.J., May 22, 1893; s. Timothy and Mary Ann (Maloney) C.; A.B., Seton Hall Coll., South Orange, N.J., 1916; A.M., Immaculate Conception Sem., South Orange, 1918. Entered Society of Jesus, 1924; ordained priest Roman Catholic Ch., 1920. Tchr. history, St. Joseph's Coll., Phila., 1926, 36; regent Hudson Coll., Jersey City, 1936-41; pres. Canisius Coll., Buffalo, 1941; now dean, Hudson Coll. Mem. bd. dirs. Buffalo, Museum of Science; mem. Nat. Cath. and Jesuit ednl. assns. Address: 2652 Hudson Blvd., Jersey City 6. Died Feb. 13, 1951.

COULSTON, Melvin Herbert, lawyer; b. West Bingham, Pa., Aug. 28, 1877; s. Joseph and Martha I. (Daniels) C.; A.B., Cornell U., 1902; m. Clemency J. King, June 3, 1903; 1 dau., Jeseamine (Mrs. Harvey W. Neville). Asst. examiner U.S. Patent Office, Feb. 1902, held various positions, 1902-21; asst. counsel Eastern R.R. Assn., 1921-27, gen. counsel, 1927-36; counsel Eastern Sect., Patent Div. of Assn. Am. Railroads, 1936-47. Home: Genesee, Pa. Died May 15, 1952; buried Genesee Cemetery.

COULTER, Charles M. (kōl'tẽr), clergyman; b. Crooksville, Ohio, November 16, 1897; son Charles C. and Margaret (Watts) Coulter; A.B., Ohio Wesleyan University, 1921, D.D., 1936; S.T.B., Boston University School of Theology, 1924; married Mary K. Lovell, June 16, 1921; children—Margaret Celeste (Mrs. Sauerhoff), Mary Jo (Mrs. Brower). Licensed as local preacher, 1915; circuit in Morgan County, O., 1916-17, Jacksontown, O., 1917-20, Jerome, O., 1920-21; pastor Meth. Ch., Hull, Mass., 1921-24; university pastor. Ohio State U., King Av. Meth. Ch., Columbus, O., 1924-25; pastor Morgan Memorial Meth. Ch., 1924-26, pastor First Meth. Ch. and dir. of Wesley Foundation, Athens, O., 1926-34; dist. supt., Dayton (O.) Dist. of Meth. Ch., 1934-37; pastor, North Broadway Meth. Ch., Columbus, O.,

1937-44, Hyde Park Community Meth. Ch., Cincinnati, 1944-48; First Meth. Ch., Oak Park, Ill., 1948-53, Epworth Methodist Ch., Toledo, 1953—. Trustee Ohio Wesleyan U.; mem. bd. trustees Methodist Church, Wesley Foundation of Ohio; del. Gen. Conf. Meth. Ch., 1936, 40, 44, 48, Jurisdictional Conf. Meth. Ch., 1940-44, 48; mem. bd. Home for Aged of Meth. Ch., Cincinnati. Mem. Ohio Council of Churches, Fed. Council of Churches of Christ in Am., Ohio Area Council of Meth. Ch. (bd. mem.; v.p.); vice chmn. Chicago Area Student Commn. Meth. Ch. Served with S.A.T.C., World War I. Mem. Am. Legion (chaplain Ohio Dept. 1942), Phi Mu Delta. Mason. Clubs: Rotary (Athens, O.); Kiwanis (Columbus, O.); Cooperative (Dayton, O.); Clergy, Cosmic and X (Cincinnati); Rotary (Oak Park, Ill.); Kiwanis, Torch (Toledo). Address: 2339 Middlesex Dr., Toledo. Died Apr. 5, 1956; buried Crooksville, O.

COULTER, John Lee, economist and statistician; b. Mallory, Minn., Apr. 16, 1881; s. John and Catherine (McVeety) C.; A.B., U. of N.Dak., 1904, A.M., 1905, LL.D., 1922; studied law, 1904-05; Ph.D., U. of Wis., 1908, studied U. of Minn., Ia. State Coll.; Doctor of Sci. (hon.), N. Dakota A. and M., 1950; m. Phoebe Everett Frost, Sept. 23, 1911; children—John Lee, Kirkley Schley, David Creswell. Instr. Ia. State Coll., 1907, U. of Wis., 1907-08, U. of Minn., 1908-09; asst. prof. economics, U. of Minn., 1909-10; spl. agent Minn. Board of Health, 1909-10; expert spl. agent U.S. Census Bureau, 1910-12, in charge of Div. of Agr., 1912-14; prof. rural economics, Knapp Sch. of Country Life, Nashville, Tenn., 1914-15; dean W.Va. Coll. Agr. and dir. Expt. Sta., 1915-21; pres. N.D. A. and M. Coll., 1921-29; became chief economist and chmn. advisory bd. U.S. Tariff Commn., 1929, mem. commn., 1930-34; mem. U.S. Com. for Reciprocity Information, 1934-35; lecturer George Washington U., 1910-13, Summer School of the South, 1910, 11. Mem. and sec. U.S. Com. and Am. Com. sent to Europe to investigate rural credit and cooperation. Formerly mem. editorial staff Quarterly Jour. of Am. Statis. Assn. and Am. Econ. Review. Mem. W.Va. State Council Defense, 1917-18; expert for Nat. Exports Council, 1917, War Industries Bd., 1918; maj., A.S.A.P., 1918; with Army Overseas Ednl. Commn., 6 months, 1918-19. Prog. Republican. Presbyterian. Mason. Fellow Am. Statis. Assn.; mem. Am. Econ. Assn., Am. Polit. Science Assn., Am. Assn. Labor Legislation, Am. Assn. of Agrl. Colls. and Expt. Stas. (v.p. 1917 and 1927), Farm Economics Assn., Nat. Econ. League, Phi Beta Kappa, Phi Beta Kappa Associates (pres. Washington chpt.). Club: Cosmos (Washington, D.C.). Author: Economic History of Red River Valley of the North, 1910; Cooperation Among Farmers, 1911; Postwar Fiscal Problems and Policies, 1945; also author numerous bulletins, reports and articles. Lecturer and cons. economist. Home: 2100 S St. N.W. Office: Investment Bldg., Washington 5. Died Apr. 16, 1959; buried Arlington (Va.) Cemetery.

COULTER, Merle Crowe, educator; b. Lake Forest, Ill., June 13, 1894; s. John Merle and Georgianna Margaret (Gaylord) C.; B.S., U. Chgo., 1914, Ph.D., 1919; m. Prudence Lettie Wood, Sept. 30, 1918; children—Prudence M. (Mrs. Ambrose Richardson), John Merle. Asst. biology Williams Coll., 1914-15; asso. botany U. Chgo., 1917-18, instr., 1918-21, asst. prof., 1921-27, asso. prof., 1927-31, prof., 1931—, asso. dean div. biol. sci., 1948—. Home: 5447 Woodlawn Av., Chgo. 15. Died Mar. 17, 1958; buried Warsaw, Ind.

COUNTRYMAN, Gratia Alta, librarian; b. Hastings, Minn., Nov. 29, 1866; d. L. N. and Alta (Chamberlain) Countryman; B.S., U. Minn., 1889, A.M. (hon.), 1932; unmarried. Became connected with Minneapolis Public Library, 1899, librarian, 1904-36, librarian emeritus, 1936—. Rec. sec. Minn. Library Commn., 1899-1918; del. of A.L.A. to 2d Internat. Library and Bibliog. Congress, Madrid, Spain, 1935. Fellow Am. Library Inst.; mem. A.L.A. (pres. 1933-34), Minn. Library Assn., Mpls. Council Adult Edn. (pres. 1929-32), Minn. Hist. Soc. (life mem. and dir.). Twin City Library Club, Mpls. Soc. Fine Arts, Am. Pen Women, Am. Assn. U. Women, Delta Kappa Gamma, Phi Beta Kappa, Delta Gamma. Clubs: Woman's, College Women's Business Women's (pres. 1919-21). Address: 2502 E. Superior, Duluth, Minn. Died July 26, 1953.

COUNTWAY, Francis A., ret. soap and glycerine mfr.; b. Boston, Sept. 2, 1876; s. David L. and Ada M. (Reid) C.; ed. high sch., Somerville, Mass.; unmarried. Began with Lever Brothers Co., Cambridge, Mass., 1898, gen. mgr. and treas., 1912-13, pres., 1913-46, ret.; dir. Harvard Trust Co. (Cambridge), Philippine Refining Corp. (N.Y.C.), Assn. of Am. Soap and Glycerine Producers. Inc. (N.Y.C., pres. 1938-41). Mem. Soap and Glycerine Industry Adv. Com., Washington. Mem. adv. com. Cambridge Hosp. Republican. Episcopalian. Clubs: Algonquin, Union, Badminton and Tennis, University, Brae Burn Country, Brookline Country, Kittansett and the Westchester Country. Home: 20 Chapel St., Longwood, Brookline, Mass.; (summer) Marion, Mass. Office: 50 Memorial Drive, Cambridge, Mass. Died Sept. 19, 1955; buried Mt. Auburn Cemetery, Cambridge.

COURCHESNE, Georges (kōō-shĕn), archbishop; b. Pierreville, Québec, Can., Sept. 13, 1880; s. Alexandre and Celina (Bazin) C.; A.B., Laval Univ., 1900; Ph.D., Montréal Univ., 1929, Doctor of Pedagogy, Doctor of Letters, 1949; graduate study, Univ. of Rome, 1908-10, Fribourg, Switzerland, 1910-11. Instr., Coll. of Nicolet, 1904-08, prof. of rhetoric, 1911-17, principal, of Normal Sch., of Nicolet, 1919-28; prof. pedagogy at Laval Univ., Québec, 1919-28; bishop of Rimouski, 1928-46, archbishop, since 1946. Awarded the Medal of Mérite Scolaire, from supt. of pub. instr., 1945; Médaille de l'Ordre de la Fidélité française, 1948. Mem. of the Catholic Com. of the Counsel of Pub. Edn. (province of Québec), since 1928. Roman Catholic. Author: Nos Humanitiés, 1927; Pastoral, 5 vols., 1928-50. Contbr. to French language reviews. Home: Archbishop's House, Rimouski, Que. Can. Died Nov. 14, 1950; buried Rimouski Cemetery.

COURSEY, Oscar William, author; b. Forreston, Ill., Apr. 10, 1873; s. David Franklin and Maletha (Mullen) C.; grad. Sch. Commerce, Dak. Wesleyan U., 1893, D.Litt., 1924; m. Julia B. Nolt, Oct. 21, 1896; children—Oliver D. (dec.), Dwight H., Una M. (dec.), Lawton, Lloyd (dec.), William (dec.). Teacher in rural sch., S.D., 1891; sergt. 1st S.D. Inf., in Philippines, 1898-99; capt., later maj., S.D. N.G., 1902-05; county supt. schs., Davison Co., S.D., 1901-04; traveling salesman, 1905-31; postmaster of Mitchell, South Dakota, 1932-36. Mason. Odd Fellow; mem. Sons of Veterans and United Spanish War Veterans, Veterans of Foreign Wars. Republican. Methodist. Author: History and Geography of the Philippine Islands, 1903; School Law Digest, 1905; Who's Who in South Dakota, Vols. I-V, 1913-25: The Philippines and the Filipinos, 1914; The Woman With a Stone Heart (novel), 1915; Biography of General Beadle, 1914; Biography of Senator Kittredge, 1915: Just a Friend, 1919; Three Jewish Martyrs, 1922; Wild Bill, 1924; Shorts (short stories), 2 vols., 1925, 29; Beautiful Black Hills, 1926; Where the Sod Shanty Stood (with V. D. Boyles), 1926; Dakota Literature, 1928; That Lonely Jew, 1929; History of Dakota Wesleyan University for Fifty Years, 1935; Pioneering in Dakota, 1937. Compiler: Ethical Selections, 1914; Literature of South Dakota, 1916; Winning Orations, 2 vols., 1917, 25. Contbr. to various mags.; lecturer. Home: Mitchell, S.D. Deceased.

COURTS, Malon Clay, investment banker; b. Clarkesville, Tenn., Apr. 10, 1908; s. Richard Winn and Mary (McPherson) C.; A.B., U. Ga., 1929; m. Vaughn Nixon, Sept. 16, 1931; children—Elaine, Richard. Partner Courts & Co. since 1933; mem. N.Y., New Orleans cotton exchanges, N.Y. Produce, N.Y. Cocoa exchanges, N.Y. Coffee and Sugar Exchange, Inc., Commodity Exhcnage, Inc., N.Y.C., Chgo. Bd. Trade; asso. mem. N.Y. Curb Exchange; dir. Atlantic Realty Co., Genuine Part Co., Economy Auto Stores. Co-chairman fund campaign Atlanta chpt. A.R.C., 1947; co-chmn. Atlanta Community Fund, 1952; chmn. Citizens Parks Adv. Com. Mem. bd. trustees Westminster Schs., Atlanta. Served as lt. comdr. USNR, aide Adm. Louis E. Denfeld, 1943-45. Mem. Chi Phi. Episcopalian. Clubs: Rotary, Nine O'Clocks, Piedmont Driving, Capital City, Peachtree Golf (Atlanta). Home: 146 W. Wesley Rd. N.W., Atlanta. Office: 11 Marietta St. N.W., Atlanta 1. Died June 29, 1957; buried Westview Cemetery, Atlanta.

COUSINS, Arthur George, newspaper exec.; born Braunton, Devon, Eng., 1882; s. Harry Cousins; ed. City School, London; m. Kate Riches. Chairman Odhams Press, Ltd., Daily Herald Ltd. Chmn. adv. com. Oxfordshire War Agrl. Com. Home: Bix Manor Farm, near Henley-on-Thames. Office: 93 Long Acre, London W. C. 2, Eng. Died Sept., 1949.

COUSLEY, Stanley W., oil company exec., b. N.Y.C., Sept. 8, 1887; s. Andrew and Margaret (Mathews) C.; ed. pub. schs., Phila.; tutored in law; m. Helen Grace Brinser, May 16, 1925; children—Patricia Ann, Stanley W., Jr. Admitted to bar of Pa., 1912; clerk Fidelity-Phila. Trust Co., 1902-12; trust adminstr., 1912-20; asst. sec., 1920-21, sec., 1921-26, asst. vice pres., 1926-29, v.p., 1929-45, sr. v.p., 1945-47; dir., pres., 1947-52, retired; president Murphy Oil Co. Pa.; chairman of the board Murphy Oil Co. Oklahoma director Beneficial Saving Fund Soc., Murphy Oil Co., Fidelity-Phila. Trust Co., Botfield Refractories Co. Served as 1st lt. in 30th Div., World War I. Mem. Phila. Bar Assn., Am. Legion. Republican. Clubs: Merion Cricket, Midday, Union League (Phila.). Home: 1120 Springmill Rd., Villanova, Pa. Office: 123 S. Broad St., Phila. 9. Died May 4, 1958.

COUZENS, Frank, ex-mayor Detroit; b. Detroit, Feb. 28, 1902; s. James (U.S. senator) and Margaret Ann (Manning) C.; student Newman Sch., Hackensack, N.J.; m. Margaret Lang, Oct. 19, 1922; children—Frank, Margaret, James, Mary, Barbara, Homer, George. Started as builder, 1922; commr. City Plan Commn., 1927-28. Dept. of Street Rys., Detroit, 1929, 30, 31; elected pres. Detroit Common Council, 1932, acting mayor, 1933; resigned, and elected mayor, Nov. 1933, for term 1934-36, reëlected, 1936, term, 1936-38. Chmn. bd. Wabeek State Bank of Detroit; pres. Wabeek Corp. Served from maj. to lt. col. U.S. Army, 1942-43. Home: 610 Longfellow Av., Detroit. Died Oct. 31, 1950.

COVARRUBIAS, Miguel (kō-värr-ōō'bē-äs), artist; b. Mexico City, Mexico; s. Jose Covarrubias and Elena (Ducland) Acosti; student pub. schs., Mexico City; m. Rosemonde Cowan, 1930. Began as caricaturist for Mexican newspapers; went to New York on scholarship of Mexican Govt., 1923; became caricaturist New York papers and Vanity Fair; lived in China, Java and Bali, 2 yrs.; now painter in New York and Mexico. Author: ThePrince of Wales and Other Famous Americans, 1925; Negro Drawings, 1927; Island of Bali, 1937. Home: Zamora 36, Mexico, D.F., Mexico. Died Feb. 4, 1957; buried Mexico City.

COVEY, Arthur Sinclair (kō'vē), artist; b. Bloomington, Ill., June 13, 1877; s. Byron and Emmeline (Edwards) C.; ed. Southwestern Coll., Winfield, Kan.; art edn., Art Inst. Chgo., Royal Acad. Munich, Germany; m. Mary Sale, 1908 (died 1917); children—Margaret Sale, Laird Fortune; m. 2d, Lois Lenski, 1921; 1 son, Stephen. Specializes in murals. Awarded gold medal of honor, Archtl. League of New York, 1925; bronze medal, Panama-Pacific Expn., 1915. Murals: Wichita (Kan.) City Library; vestibule Adminstrn. Bldg., Kohler, Wis.; Norton Hall decorations, Worcester, Mass.; frieze in Land Plane Bldg., LaGuardia Field, N.Y.C.; ceiling for Squibb Building, N.Y.C.; John Brown Memorial, Torrington, Conn.; exterior decorations, Contemporary Arts Bldg., N.Y. World's Fair, 1939. Nat. Academician; mem. Soc. Mural Painters (ex-pres.), Archtl. League N.Y. (ex-v.p.). Club: Salmagundi (N.Y.C.). Home: R.F.D. 2, Torrington, Conn.; also 201 Lake Blvd., Tarpon Springs, Fla. Died Feb. 1960.

COVINGTON, Harry Stockdell, banker; born Long Lick, Ky., Feb. 11, 1892; s. David and Hannah Elizabeth (Stockdell) C.; student Transylvania Coll., 1909-11, U. of Ky., 1911-12, Ga. Sch. Tech., 1918, Air Ground Sch., 1918; m. Irene Elizabeth Mitzell, Jan. 7, 1919. Began as clerk Third Nat. Bank, Lexington, Ky., 1912; asst. receiver Ambridge (Pa.) Nat. Bank, 1914; bank examiner Louisville (Ky.) Clearing House Assn., 1914; chief clerk and auditor Metropolitan Trust Co., N.Y. City, 1916; asst. to pres. Universal Leaf Tobacco Co., New York, 1919; asst. cashier Fort Dearborn Nat. Bank, Chicago, 1920; pres. and dir. North Shore Trust & Savings Bank, Chicago, 1922; exec. vice pres. and dir. Nat. Bank of Commerce, later Guardian Nat. Bank of Commerce, Detroit, 1923; voting trustee, dir. and v.p. U.S. Sugar Corp., Clewiston, Fla., 1932; v.p. and dir. Salem Brass & Iron Foundry Co., Bridgeton, N.J., 1934; pres. and dir. North American Corp., Cleveland, and subsidiaries, 1936; entered govt. service, 1942, mem., later chmn. Price Adjustment Bd., Cincinnati, 1946, vice chmn. Army Price Adjustment Bd., 1949; mem. War Contracts Price Adjustment Bd.; vice chmn. and mem. Army Renegotiation Div., Armed Services Renegotiation Bd., 1949. Served as 2d lt., Army Air Force, 1917; machine gun, bombing and aerial combat instr., 1917-18. Mem. Assn. Reserve City Bankers (past pres.), Army Ordnance Assn. Awarded Dept. of Army Medal for Exceptional Civilian Service; Army Service Forces Commendation for Meritorious Service; Army Service Forces Ordnance Dept. Certificate of Commendation. Home: 28 W. Kirke St., Chevy Chase 15, Md. Office: The Pentagon, Washington. Died May 9, 1950.*

COWAN, Frank Augustus, communications engr.; b. Escatawpa, Ala., Aug. 30, 1898; s. James T. and Annie Ellen (Adamson) C.; B.S. in Elec. Engring., Ga. Inst. Tech., 1919; m. Dorothy L. Bush, July 3, 1942. With Am. Tel. & Tel. Co., 1920—, successively spl. services engr., div. transmission engr., asst. dir. operations, asst. dir. operations long lines, 1950—. Served as lt. comdr. USNR, 1942-49. Recipient Lamme Gold Medal, Am. Inst. E.E., 1953. Fellow Am. Inst. E.E. (chmn. communications group N.Y. sect. 1944-45), Inst. Radio Engrs. Home: 44 E. 67th St., N.Y.C. 21. Office: 32 Av. of Americas, N.Y.C. 13. Died June 21, 1957.

COWAN, James Raymo, mfg. exec.; b. White Plains, N.Y., Mar. 24, 1890; s. James Kent and Capitola Jane (Eggleston) C.; student N.Y. Univ., 1907-08; m. Virginia Luty, Nov. 19, 1927. Engring. asst., Catskill Aquaduct, White Plains, N. Y., 1908-13, Barge Canal, N.Y. City, 1913-15, New York Subways, 1915-17; engr., The Foundation Co., N.Y. City, 1917-20, cost engr., 1920-22, supt. constrn., 1922-30; mgr., Ross Republic Marble Corp., Knoxville, Tenn., 1930-41, pres., 1938-41; pres., The Ga. Marble Co., 1941-55, chmn. bd. 1955, director, 1941—; pres. and director Alabama Limestone Company; director Atlanta Transit Co., Dawson Timber Development Co. Mem. Nat. Assn. Mfrs. (past dir.), Associated Industries of Ga. (past dir., v.p.). Mason. Club: Capital City (Atlanta). Home: 904 Church St., Marietta. Office: Tate, Ga. Died Apr. 3, 1955; buried Sewickley Valley Cemetery, Sewickley, Pa.

COWARD, Thomas Ridgway, publisher; b. New York, N.Y., Aug. 5, 1896; s. Edward Fales and Mabel

(Ridgway) C.; prep. edn. Groton Sch., 1909-15; student Yale, 1915-18; m. Marian S. White, Sept. 23 1925 (divorced Aug. 1941); children—Jenifer Gregg, Elena Susanna; m. 2d, Elisabeth Goldbeck, 1943. Special assistant Department of State, 1918-20; mgr. N.Y. office of Yale Univ. Press, 1920-22; editor Bobbs-Merrill Co., pubs., 1922-27; pres. Coward-McCann, Inc., since 1927; dir. G. P. Putnam's Sons, Promenade Publications. Member Beta Theta Pi, Wolf's Head. Democrat. Episcopalian. Clubs: Century, Yale, Tavern, Southampton; (New York); St. Botolph (Boston). Contbr. to lit. mags. National squash tennis champion, 1922. Home: 420 E. 50th St. Office: 210 Madison Av., N.Y.C. 16. Died Jan. 11, 1957; buried Bristol, R.I.

COWL, Jane (maiden name Cowles) (koul), actress; b. Boston, Dec. 14, 1884; d. Charles A. and Grace Cowles; student Erasmus Hall, Bklyn., 1902-04, Columbia, 1904-06; m. A. E. Klauber, 1908. Appeared in small roles with David Belasco Co., Republic Theatre, New York; début as Fanny Perry in Is Matrimony a Failure?, 1909; with stock co., Hudson Theatre, 2 seasons; next appeared in The Upstart and The Gamblers, Maxine Elliott's Theatre, 1911; starred successively in Within the Law, Common Clay, Lilac Time, Information Please, up to 1919; Smilin' Through, 1920-22; appeared as Juliet in Romeo and Juliet, Henry Miller's Theatre, New York, 1923; starred in Pelleas and Melisande and Anthony and Cleopatra, 1923; in Noel Coward's Easy Virtue, playing in U.S. and Eng., 1925-26; in The Road to Rome, 1927-28; in Rain from Heaven, 1934, First Lady, 1935-36, Merchant of Yonkers, 1939, Old Acquaintance, 1940-41. Co-Author: (plays, with Jane Murfin) Daybreak; Information Please; Liac Time. Appeared in two last named in New York and throughout U.S. care Coudert Bros., 2 Rector St., N.Y.C. Died June 22, 1950.

COWLES, Edward Spencer, neurologist, psychiatrist; b. Williamsburg, Va., Sept. 22, 1889; s. John Bertram and Harriet (Spencer) C.; student William and Mary Coll.; M.D., U. Coll. Medicine, Richmond, Va., 1907; post-grad. work Harvard Med. Sch.; m. Florence Jaquith (dec.); children—Virginia, Mary; m. 2d, Mme. Nona de Mohrenschildt, dau. the late Hon. William Gibbs McAdoo, Aug. 1927; m. 3d, Lorraine Posey. Dir. Psychopathic Sanitarium, Portsmouth, N.H., 1910-16; head dept. psychopathology N.Y. Poly. Medical School and Hosp., 1916-17; head war examining bd., N.Y.C. 1918; dir. Park Av. Hosp., N.Y.C., 1916—; dir. Body and Mind Foundation, Inc., N.Y.C., formerly med. mem. Joint Commn. to Investigate Healing for the P.E. Ch. of America. Fellow A.A.A.S. Popularized psychiatry with masses of people through lectures and mag. articles. Author: Industrial Education, 1918; Psychopathology, 1918; Religion and Medicine in the Church, 1925; New Aspects of Chronic Alcoholism, 1937; A New Approach to the Pathology and Treatment of the Psychoneurosis and of the Melancholia Mania Psychosis, 1939; Don't Be Afraid, 1941; Alcoholism Can be Cured, 1950; Conquest of Fatigue and Fear, 1954. Address: 591 Park Av., N.Y.C. 21. Died Nov. 16, 1954.

COWLES, Frederic Albert (kou'lĕs), musical dir.; b. Columbus, Ky., Nov. 26, 1881; s. Wilbur Fisk and Elizabeth (McGee) C.; ed. Louisville, N.Y.C., Chgo., under pvt. teachers, and short period of study in Europe; m. Charlotte Haile, June 17, 1924. A founder and dir. Louisville Conservatory of Music; condr. Louisville Civic Chorus; dir. Crescent Hill Woman's Club Chorus; organist 4th Av. Presbyn. Ch. State chmn. Nat. Guild Piano Tchrs. Asso. Am. Guild Organists; mem. Ky. Music Tchrs. Assn. (pres. 1922). Republican. Episcopalian. Home: Weissinger-Gaulbert Apts., Louisville. Died Nov. 24, 1949.

COWLES, John Henry (kōlz), Masonic ofcl.; born Edmonson County, Ky., Aug. 22, 1863; s. Joseph and Martha Ann (Mitchell) C.; student Cumberland U., Lebanon, Tenn., and business coll.; hon. LL.D., George Washington U., Cumberland U.; Litt.D., William Jewell Coll. Formerly in wholesale mercantile business, Louisville; head John H. Cowles & Co., brass founders; mem. Standard Printing Co., The Pyne Co., Martin & Cowles, Globe Bldg. & Lcan Co. Sovereign grand comdr. Supreme Council 33° (mother council of the world), A.A.S.R., Southern Jurisdiction of the U.S.A.; Master Mason since 1888. Decorated Star of Rumania; Comdr. Crown of Rumania; Order Nishan Iftikhar (Tunisia); National Order "Al Merito" of Ecuador. Capt. 1st Ky. Vol. Inf., Spanish-Am. War, 1898. Col. staff Gov. Sampson of Ky.; admiral staff Gov. Laffoon; lt. col. staff Gov. Sholtz of Fla. Clubs: Metropolitan Police Boys, National Press, Army and Navy (Washington); Chevy Chase; Filson (Ky.). Address: 1733 16th St., Washington 9. Died June 18, 1954; buried Crypt, House of the Temple, Washington.

COWLES, LeRoy Eugene, univ. pres. emeritus; b. Chester, Utah, Apr. 13, 1880; s. William Henry and Sarepta Evelyn (Judkins) C.; student Weber Acad. (Ogden), 1900-03; Ph.B., U. Chgo., 1910, A.M., 1913; postgrad. U. Cal., 1920-21, Ph.D., 1926; m. Cecelia Etta Brown, Mar. 3, 1904; children—Leon LeRoy, Harper Brown, Willis Howard, Etta Lugene (Mrs. Raymond H. Hawkins), Calvin David. Tchr. pub. schs., Heber City, Utah, 1903-05; instr. Weber Acad. 1905-08 10-13; prin. Carbon County High Sch. Price, Utah, 1913-14; asst. prof. edn. U. Utah, 1915-17, asso. prof. edn., 1917-19, prof. edn., 1919-20, prof., head dept. of ednl. adminstrn., 1921-41, dean of lower div., 1932-41, pres., 1941-46; teaching fellow U. Cal., 1920-21, guest prof., summer 1947; guest prof., acting head dept. secondary edn. U. N.M., 1947-48; dir. secondary edn. Utah dept. pub. instrn., 1949-50. Ex-officio mem. bd. of regents U. Utah, 1941-46. Missionary, eastern states, Ch. Latter-day Saints, 1898-1900. Mem. N.E.A. (life), Am. Assn. Sch. Adminstrs., Utah Edn., Assn., Utah State Tchrs.' Retirement Bd. (pres. 1935-41), Utah Soc. S.A.R., Phi Delta Kappa, Phi Kappa Phi. Club: Salt Lake City Exchange. Author: Utah Educational Program of 1919, 1926; Provo School System (with Dr. L. John Nuttall), 1929; Building Needs and Transportation Program, Carbon School District, Utah, (with Dr. L. John Nuttall) 1929; Organization and Administration of Education in Utah, 1934, revised edit. 1946; University of Utah and World War II, 1949. Home: 124 University St. Address: University of Utah, Salt Lake City 2. Died Jan. 2, 1957.

COWLEY, Matthew, lawyer, ch. ofcl.; b. Preston, Ida., Aug. 2, 1897; s. Matthias Foss and Abbie (Hyde) C.; student U. of Utah, 1919-21; LL.B., George Washington U., 1924; m. Elva Eleanor Taylor, July 13, 1922; children—Eleanor Jewell (Mrs. Val J. Sheffield), Duncan Meha. Admitted to Utah Bar, 1926, practice, Salt Lake City, 1925-38; ordained apostle, Ch. Jesus Christ Latter-Day Saints, 1945, missionary, New Zealand, 1914-19; pres. New Zealand Mission, 1938-45; mem. Council Twelve Apostles 1945—; pres. Missions Pacific and Orient, Ch. Jesus Christ Latter-Day Saints, 1946-50. Dep. co. atty., Salt Lake Co., 1926-28, co. atty., 1930-33. Mem. bd. trustees Brigham Young U. Mem. Polynesian Soc., Sigma Chi. Home: 28 N. State St. Office: 47 East South Temple St., Salt Lake City. Died Dec. 13, 1953.

COX, Daniel Hargate, naval architect; b. N.Y.C., Mar. 13, 1872; s. Townsend and Anne H. (Townsend) C.; grad. U.S. Naval Acad., 1894, Royal Naval Coll., Greenwich, Eng., 1898; m.Frances L. Buckler, Apr. 3, 1903. Resigned from Navy as naval constr., 1902; sec.-treas. Soc. Naval Architects and Marine Engrs., 1910-33. Mgr. ship constrn. U.S. Shipping Bd. Emergency Fleet Corp., 1917-18. Clubs: Down Town, Cedarhurst Yacht. Home: Lawrence, L.I., N.Y. Office: 11 Broadway, N.Y.C. 4. Died Sept. 1, 1955.

COX, Edward Eugene, congressmen; born Mitchell County, Ga., Apr. 3, 1880; s. Stephen Edward and Mary (Williams) C.; LL.B., Mercer U., 1902; m. Roberta Patterson, Jan. 19, 1902 (died 1916); children—Lamar Patterson, Mary Bennet; m. 2d, Grace Hill, Aug. 5, 1918; 1 dau., Gene. Admitted to Ga. bar, 1902, and began practice at Camilla; apptd. judge Superior Court of Albany Circuit, 1912, and later elected to same office; resigned to become candidate for Congress, 1916 (defeated); mem. 69th to 82d Congresses (1925-53), 2d Ga. Dist. Mem. Sigma Alpha Epsilon. Democrat. Baptist. Mason, K. P., Elk. Home: Camilla, Ga. Died Dec. 24, 1952; buried Camilla.

COX, Forrest Dale, pub. relations exec.; b. Orange Co., Ind., Feb. 3, 1902; s. Henry and Nancy (Grimes) C.; A.B., Ind. U., 1924; m. Helen Middlehurst, Oct. 1, 1927; 1 dau., Alice Jane. Instr. journalism Ind. U., 1924-25; state editor Miami (Fla.) Herald, 1925-27; mem. editorial staff, bus. columnist Cleveland Plain Dealer, 1927-37; instr. Fenn College, Cleve., 1933-37; pub. relations dir. Internat. Harvester Co. since 1938. Trustee Village of Hinsdale, 1945-49, pres., 1949-53; vice president of board managers Y.M.C.A., Chicago; president of the board of trustees Provident Hosp. Mem. Automobile Mfrs. Assn. (chmn. motor truck pub. relations com. since 1938), Phi Beta Kappa, Sigma Delta Chi, Phi Delta Theta. Mason. Clubs: Univ., Execs. (Chgo.). Home: 206 N. Monroe St., Hinsdale, Ill. Office: 180 N. Michigan Av., Chgo. 1. Died May 14, 1958.

COX, Guy Wilbur, chmn. John Hancock Mutual Life Ins. Co.; b. Manchester, N.H., Jan. 19, 1871; s. Charles Edson and Evelyn Mary (Randall) C.; A.B., Dartmouth, 1893, A.M., 1896; LL.B. magna cum laude, Boston U., 1896; L.H.D., Syracuse U., 1943; LL.D., Boston U., 1943; m. Edith M. Paine, Oct. 17, 1925. In gen. practice of law at Boston, 1896-1923, but chiefly as counsel for life ins. cos. and pub. utility corps.; chmn. John Hancock Mut. Life Ins. Co.; dir. First Nat. Bank of Boston. Mem. bd. of trustees of Boston University (chmn.); mem. City Council, Boston, 1902, Mass. Ho. of Rep., 1903-04, Senate, 1906-07; chmn. Mass. Commn. on Taxation, 1907; mem. Mass. Constl. Conv., 1917-19. Republican. Conglist. Clubs: Algonquin, University, Brookline Country. Home: Hotel Vendome. Office: 197 Clarendon St. Boston. Died Dec. 9, 1955; buried Pittsfield, N.H.

COX, Jacob Dolson, manufacturer; b. Cleveland, O., November 1, 1881; s. Jacob Dolson and Ellen Atwood (Prentiss) C.; A.B., Williams Coll., 1903; m. Phyllis Graves, Nov. 23, 1937. Began as mechanic Cleveland Twist Drill Company, 1903; in logging and lumber business, Tacoma, Wash., and Vancouver, B.C., 1909-10; returned to Cleveland Twist Drill Co., 1910, 3d v.p., 1912-19, pres. and gen. mgr. since 1919; dir. Cleveland Trust Co. Pres. Nat. Metal Trades Assn., 1932-33; dir. Asso. Industries (ex-pres.); trustee St. Luke's Hosp., Lake View Cemetery Assn., Western Reserve Hist. Soc., Y.M.C.A., Fenn Coll., Case Inst. Technology, (Cleveland). Mem. Cleveland Chamber Commerce, Cleveland Engring. Soc., Phi Beta Kappa, Chi Psi. Republican. Episcopalian. Clubs: Union (ex-dir.), University, Kirtland Country (Cleveland); Williams (New York); Stage Harbor Yacht, Monomoy Yacht (Chatham, Mass.). Author: Economic Basis of Fair Wages, 1927. Home: 10401 Lake Shore Blvd., Cleveland 8. Office: 1242 E. 49th St., Cleve. 14. Died Feb. 16, 1953.

COX, James C., ret. chmn. bd., dir. Wm. Wrigley Jr. Co., Chgo.; chmn. bd., dir. Nat. Blvd. Bank; dir. Fifteen Hundred Lake Shore Drive Bldg. Corp. Home: 1500 Lake Shore Dr. Office: 410 N. Michigan Av., Chgo. Died July 1957.

COX, James M(iddleton), ex-gov. Ohio; b. Jacksonburg, O., Mar. 31, 1870; s. Gilbert and Eliza A., C.; pub. and high sch. edn.; m. Margaretta Blair, Sept. 15, 1917. Raised on farm; worked printer's office; taught country sch.; became newspaper reporter and connected in editorial capacity with Cincinnati Enquirer; bought the Dayton Daily News, 1898, Sprngfield Press-Republic, 1905, forming The News League of Ohio; bought the Miami Metropolis, Miami, Fla., Canton News, Ohio, 1923 (sold Canton News 1930), Springfield (O.) Sun, 1928, Atlanta Jour., 1939, Dayton (O.) Jour. Herald, 1948, Atlanta Constitution, 1950. Mem. 61st, 62d Congs. (1909-13), 3d Ohio Dist.; gov. of Ohio, 1913-15, 17-19, 19-21; Dem. nominee for Pres. of U.S., 1920. Vice chmn. Am. delegation to World Monetary and Econ. Conf., London, and pres. of its Monetary Commn., 1933. Episcopalian. Author: Journey Through My Years, 1946. Home: Trailsend, Dayton, O. Office: Dayton Daily News, Dayton, O. Died July 15, 1957.

COX, Raymond Benjamin, banker; b. Easton, Md., Aug. 30, 1883; s. Benjamin P. and Susie E. (Mason) C.; ed. public schools; m. Ethel Baker, Oct. 25, 1913; 1 son, Raymond Benjamin. Began with Mfrs. Nat. Bank, Baltimore, 1902; auditor First Nat. Bank, Baltimore, 1910; asst. cashier Fourth Nat. Bank, New York, 1912; v.p. Webster and Atlas Nat. Bank of Boston, 1914; pres., 1920—; trustee Warren Instn. for Savings. Pres. Baltimore chapter Am. Inst. Banking, 1909, pres. nat. assn., 1911; pres. Mass. Nat. Bank Assn., 1927; pres. Boston Clearing House Assn., 1947. Mem. Boston C. of C. (dir.). Episcopalian. Clubs: Cohasset Golf, Algonquin (pres.) (Boston). Home: Forest Av., Cohasset, Mass.; also 490 Commonwealth Av., Boston. Office: 199 Washington St., Boston, Mass. Died June 27, 1948.

COX, William Stakely, educator; b. Searcy, Ark., June 12, 1861; s. Ichabod Frank and Mary C. (Stakely) C.; B.C. Eng., Ala. Agrl. and Mech. Coll., 1884; B.Arch., Cornell U., 1886. With Cox Coll., 1887—, now president Cox College and Conservatory, and Atlanta Conservatory of Music. Also extensively engaged in farming. 1st lt. La Grange Light Guard, 6 yrs. Baptist. Home: College Park, Ga. Died Nov. 11, 1938.

COXE, Alfred Conkling, jurist; b. Utica, N.Y., May 7, 1880; s. U.S. Circuit Judge Alfred Conkling and Maryette A. (Doolittle) C.; grad. St. Paul's Sch., Concord, N.H., 1897; A.B., Yale, 1901; student Cornell U. Law Sch., 1901-03 (Class of 1904); m. Helen P. Emery, Oct. 11, 1913; children—Alfred Conkling, John, Samuel Hanson. Admitted to N.Y. bar, 1903, and began practice at Utica as mem. Matteson De Angelis & Coxe; removed to N.Y.C., 1905, asso. in practice with Boardman, Platt & Soley and successors, O'Brien, Boardman, Platt & Dunning, O'Brien, Boardman, Platt & Littleton; then practiced alone and as mem. firm Tomlinson, Coxe & Tomlinson; apptd. U.S. dist. judge So. Dist. of N.Y., May 7, 1929. Mem. Assn. Bar City of Ne wYork, Alpha Delta Phi. Republican (former pres. N.Y. Young Republican Club). Presbyn. Clubs: University, Lawyers, Nat. Republican. Home: 211 East 61st St. Address: U.S. Court House, Foley Square, N.Y.C. Died Dec. 21, 1957.*

COXEY, Jacob S(echier) (kŏks'ē), ex-mayor; b. Selinsgrove, Pa., April 16, 1854; s. Thomas and Mary (Sechler) C.; ed. pub. schs., Danville, Pa.; m. Caroline Ammerman, Oct. 1874 (divorced); children—Jesse A. (dec.), Mary, Horace L., Albert H. (dec.); m. 2d, Henrietta Jones, Sept. 1890; children—Jacob S., Legal Tender (dec.), David N., Ruth Patricia. Began as stationary engr. in rolling mills, Danville, later in scrap iron business; actively identified with silica sandstone quarrying, 1881-1929. Leader of bands of unemployed to Washington, 1894 and 1914, petitioning Congress to enact a law to furnish money without interest to all communities for employment of unemployed on pub. improvements and needs. Populist candidate for Congress, 1894. for gov. of Ohio, 1895 and 1897; independent candidate for U.S. Senator, 1916, for Congress; candidate for nomination for Congress, Rep. primaries, 1928 and 1930; mayor of Massillon (Republican), 1931-33; candidate for President of U.S., on Farmer-Labor ticket, 1932, 36; carried State of Ohio for President in preferential (Republican) primaries, 1932; candidate for U.S. Senate from Ohio, Rep. primaries, 1934; candidate for Congress on Lemke ticket, 1936. Author: Coxey's Own Story, 1914. Editor and publisher, The Human vs. Gold-Standard; The Truth About Money Weights and Measures. Spoke from steps of capitol, Washington, on 50th anniversary of unemployment march (1944); appeared before banking and currency com. of U.S. Senate to speak on proposed monetary plan, 1946. Home: 121 2d St., Massillon, O. Died May 16, 1951; buried Massillon Cemetery.

COY, (Albert) Wayne, radio, TV exec.; b. Shelby County, Ind., Nov. 23, 1903; s. Albert Roscoe and Lillian Monell (Nation) C.; A.B., Franklin (Ind.) Coll., 1926, Litt.D., 1947; Mus.D., Cin. Coll. Music, 1948; m. Grace Elizabeth Cady, Sept. 6, 1927; children—Stephen Cady, Philip Wayne (dec.), Albert Wayne. Began as reporter, 1919; city editor Franklin (Ind.) Star, as 1926-30; editor and pub. Delphi (Ind.) Citizen, 1930-33; under sec.to gov. of Ind. and sec. Gov.'s Commn. on Unemployment Relief, 1933-34; dir. Gov.'s Com. on Unemployment Relief and adminstr. Ind. State Welfare Dept., 1934-37; Ind. state adminstr. WPA, 1935-37; regional adminstr. WPA, 1935-36; administrative asst. to U.S. High Commr. to P.I., 1937-39; asst. adminstr. Fed. Security Agency, 1939-41; special asst. to the President and liaison officer, Office for Emergency Management, 1941-43; asst. dir. Bureau of the Budget (Executive Office of the President), 1942-44; asst. to pub. Washington (D.C.) Post, and dir. sta. WINX and WINX-FM, 1944-47; chmn. FCC, 1947-52; cons. Time, Inc., 1952-57; co-owner with Time, Inc., and pres. Albuquerque Broadcasting Co. (KOB-KOB-TV), 1957; pres. Twin State Broadcasting Co. (WFBM, WFBM-TV, Indpls., and WTCN, WTCN-TV, Mpls.), 1957—. Served as 2d lt. Q.M. C., Ind. N.G., 1934-40; mem. adv. com. on Selective Service, 1940; member Joint Army and Navy Welfare and Recreation Bd. Mem. Acad. Polit. Sci., Phi Delta Theta, Sigma Delta Chi. Democrat. Baptist. Mason. Home: 8002 N. Broadway, Indpls. 20. Died Sept. 24, 1957; buried Franklin, Ind.

COYKENDALL, Frederick (koi'kĕn-dawl), pres. Cornell Steamboat Co.; b. Kingston, N.Y., Nov. 23, 1872; s. Samuel Decker and Mary Augusta (Cornell) C.; A.B., Columbia, 1895, A.M. and C.E., 1897; LL.D., Hamilton Coll., 1940; m. Mary Beach Warrin, Oct. 14, 1897; 1 dau., Ursula (Mrs. Frank Fish Walker). Sec. Cornell Steamboat Co., 1897-1900, mgr., 1900-13, pres. since 1913; dir. University Patents, Inc.; formerly managing dir. and secretary Columbia U. Press, now pres.; chmn. bd. trustees Columbia U.; trustee New York State Historical Association. Fellow A.A.A.S.; mem. American Institute Graphic Art, Founders and Patriots of America, St. Nicholas Soc., The Holland Society, Phi Beta Kappa, Delta Kappa Epsilon. Awarded '89 gold medal for achievement, Columbia, 1926. Republican. Clubs: Union, Century, University, Grolier, Down Town, Columbia University, Coffee House. Author: A Note on the Monk, 1935. Contbr. to Bibliographical Jour. Compiler: Arthur Rackham, A List of Books Illustrated by Him, 1922. Home: 1 W. 72d St. Office: 716 12th Av., N.Y.C. Died Nov. 19, 1954.

COZENS, Frederick Warren (kŭz'ĕnz), univ. prof., writer on physical education; b. Portland, Ore., Nov. 19, 1890; s. Frederick and Caroline Elizabeth (Beharrell) C.; student U. of Ore., 1909-11; A.B., U. of Calif., 1915, A.M., 1918; Ph.D., U. of Ore., 1928; m. Helen Kerron, Aug. 10, 1916 (dec. Dec. 1953); children—Frederick Kerron, James. Teaching fellow in phys. edn., U. of Calif., 1915-16, instr., 1916-19; asst. prof. phys. edn., U. of Calif. at Los Angeles, 1919-29; asso. prof., 1929-34, prof., 1934—, dean Coll. of Applied Arts, 1939-42; prof. and dir. physical edn., Berkeley, 1942—. Instr. Sch. of Mil. Aeronautics, Berkeley, 1917-19. Awarded Ling medal by Ling Foundation, Los Angeles, Medal of Merit from Minister of Social Welfare and Pub. Health of Czecho-Slovak Republic, 1939. Fellow Am. Phys. Edn. Assn.; mem. Am. Assn. U. Profs., Am. Acad. Phys. Edn. (pres. 1949-50), Am. Assn. Health, Phys. Edn. and Recreation (pres. 1938-39), Am. Student Health Assn. (v.p. Pacific Coast sect., 1938-39), Southern California Football Association (president 1938), Acacia and of Sigma Xi, Phi Delta Kappa, Phi Epsilon Kappa frats. Methodist. Mason. Author: Tests and Measurements in Physical Education (with J. F. Bovard), 1930, 2nd edit., 1938; 3d edit., 1949 (with J. F. Bovard and E. P. Hagman); Problem Manual in Physical Edn. Measurements, 1932; Introduction to Physical Education (with E. W. Nixon), 1934, 4th edit., 1952; Achievement Scales in Physical Education Activities for Boys and Girls (with N. P. Neilson), 1934; Physical Education Achievement Scales for Boys in Secondary Schools (with M. H. Trieb and N. P. Neilson), 1936; Achievement Scales in Physical Education for College Men, 1936, Achievement Scales in Physical Education for College Women (with H. Cubberley and N. P. Neilson), 1937; Sports in American Life (with F. S. Stump?), 1953; also four monographs on phys. edn. Contbr. articles to phys. edn. jours. Home: 1004½ Cragmont Av., Berkeley 8, Cal. Died Jan. 2, 1954.

CRABBE, George William, past gen. supt. Anti-Saloon League Am.; b. Range Township, Madison Co., O., June 1, 1875; s. John William and Ellen (Minshall) C.; student De Pauw U., and Ohio Wesleyan U.; hon., A.M., Western Md. Coll., 1921; LL.D., Ohio Northern Univ., 1942; m. Maude Foster, June 20, 1900; married 2d, Anne M. Dickhaut, June 7, 1950. Became teacher public schools, Ohio, 1892; clerk, Courts of Madison County, 1900-06; admitted to Ohio bar, 1906; atty. Ohio Anti-Saloon League, 1906-13; atty. and supt. W.Va. Anti-Saloon League, 1913-17; atty. and supt. Md.-Del. Anti-Saloon League since 1917; gen. sec. Anti-Saloon League Am., 1940-48; now emeritus. Editor Md.-Del. edit. Issue. Mem. Gen. Conf. M.E. Ch., 1924, 28, 32, 36, 40, 44, 48; mem. Uniting Conf. of Meth. Chs.; chmn. of com. which wrote declaration of M.E. Ch. stand on liquor question, 1924 and 28. Republican. Odd Fellow. Club: Optimist. Home: 2901 Mt. Holly St., Baltimore. Died Sept. 4, 1951; buried Oak Hill Cemetery, London, O.

CRABTREE, Harold Roy, mfr.; b. Montreal, Can., Mar. 2, 1918; s. Harold and Louisa (Stafford) C.; B.Sc., McGill U., 1938; m. Caroline Ruth Hanna, Nov. 17, 1945; children—Sandra, Harold, Stafford. Vice pres., gen. mgr., dir. Woods Mfg. Co., Ltd., St. Lambert, Que., 1952-56, pres., 1956—; became pres., dir. Pyramid Paper Products, Ltd. and subsidiaries, 1948; pres., mng. dir., Wabasso Cotton Co., Ltd. and subsidiaries, 1955, also dir.; chmn. bd. Fraser Companies, Limited; dir. Bank of Montreal, Montreal Trust Co., Howard Smith Paper Mills, Ltd., Alliance Paper Mills, Ltd., Don Valley Paper Co., Ltd., Dennaconna Paper Co., Ltd., Paton Mfg. Co., Ltd., R.&H. Bearings Co., Ltd., Fraser Cos., Ltd. and subsidiaries, Renold Chains Can., Ltd., Woods-Dryden Paper Bags, Ltd., Prairie Bag Co., Cellucord Co. of Can., Ltd., MacGregor Paper & Bag Co., St. Maurice Valley Cototn, Ltd., St. Maurice Warehousing, Ltd., Occidental Fire Ins. Co., Ltd. Mem. Cotton Inst. Can. (pres.), Primary Textiles Inst. (pres.), Canadian C. of C. (vice chmn. exec. council), Canadian Mfrs. Assn. (chmn. Montreal br.). Home: 615 Belmont Av., Westmount 6, Que. Office: 1235 McGill College Av., Montreal 2, Que., Can. Died Feb. 18, 1956.

CRAFT, E. A., railroad exec.; b. Danville, Ill., Sept. 11, 1893; s. William Henry and Emma J. (Westmen) C.; m. Kathryne Mershon, Sept. 26, 1923; children—Cynthia (Mrs. James T. Holland), Alan. Successively chmn., rodman, instrumentman asst. engr., Chgo. and Eastern Ill. R.R., 1909-17; asst. supt. and asst. to engr. maintenance of way, Southern Pacific Lines in Texas and Louisiana, 1920, asst. to chief engr. and engr. maintenance of way, 1920-39, asst. to exec. v.p., 1939-43, v.p., 1944, exec. v.p. since Apr. 1945; exec. v.p. Texas and New Orleans R.R. Co.; pres., dir. So. Pacific Bldg. Co., Rio Bravo Oil Co., S.P. Terminal Co., Tex. Town Lot Co.; director Southern Pacific Transport Co., Union Terminal Company, Dallas, Texas National Bank, Houston C. of C., Texas Research League. Served with U.S. Army, 1917-19, World War I; 1st lt. later capt., Engr. Corps.; major, Transportation Corps, A.E.F. Decorated Purple Heart. Trustee, Texas A. & M. College Research Found., Texas Econ. Ednl. Council. Mem. Texas Soc. Profl. Engrs., Am. Railway Engrs. Assn., Am. Wood Preserving Assn., Newcomen Soc. of England, Sigma Alpha Epsilon. Clubs: Engineers, Country, Ramada (Houston); Boston (New Orleans). Address: 5219 Bayard Lane, Houston. Died Dec. 20, 1954.

CRAIG, Austin, historian; b. Eddytown, N.Y., Feb. 22, 1872; s. Austin (D.D.) and Adelaide (Churchill) C.; student Cornell and U. Rochester, 1891-93; B.L., Pacific U., 1894, A.M., 1911, Litt. D., 1929; completed doctoral courses and theses academically approved and later pub., but for political or religious reasons the following degrees were not taken: Dr. in Humanities, Rizal U., 1912; D.Litt., Imperial Japanese U., Tokyo, 1922; Dr. Philosophy and Literature, Royal and Pontifical U. of St. Tomas de Manila, 1923; Dr. Civil Law, Northern Colls., P.I., 1924. County sch. supt., Washington County, Ore., 1895-98; admitted to Ore. bar, 1898; practiced corp. law in Ore. until 1904, then entered P.I. Civil Service, 1912; organized social sci. depts. and headed history dept. with final title of Rizal research prof., U. of Philippines, 1919-22; prof. hist., dean grad. studies, U. Manila, 1922-27; lectr., 1931-32; back to U.S., 1935. On revisiting Manila, 1937, was made the second Am. hon. mem. of Cabelleros de Rizal in pub. ceremony at Rizal mausoleum. Pres. Far Eastern Soc., S.A.R., 1918-39. Cal. Soc. Mayflower Descendants. Officially adopted son of Rizal Province and made hon. citizen of municipality of Dapitan, Mindanao. Republican. Conglist. Mason (32°, K.T., K.C.C.H.). Clubs: Shrine, Elks (Minneapolis). Author and editor of 3½ foot bookshelf of Orientalia and Philippiniana (some of the volumes in Japanese, Spanish and French). Author: (theses) Life and Labors of Jose Rizal, 1912; Oriental History for Philippine Islands, 1933; Philippines and Filipinos, of Yesterday, 1934; Back ground of Constitution of Philippine Islands, 4 vols., 1935-37. Home: 1800 Summit Av., Mpls. 5; and Manila, P.I. Died Feb. 11, 1949.

CRAIG, Charles Franklin (krāg), army officer, author; b. Danbury, Conn., July 4, 1872; s. William Edward and Maria Hamlin (Payne) C.; M.D., Yale, 1894, hon. M.A., 1914; D.Sc., Tulane U., 1945; m. Lilian Osmun, July 7, 1893; children—Marjorie Lilian, Edward Arthur. Acting asst. Surgeon U.S. Army, 1898-1903; advanced through grades from 1st lt. to col. M.C., 1918; pathologist and bacteriologist Sternberg U.S. Army Gen. Hosp., Chickamauga Park, Ga., 1898, Simpson Gen. Hosp., Fortress Monroe, Va., 1898-99, Camp Columbia Hosp., Havana, 1899, U.S. Army Gen. Hosp., Presidio, Cal., 1899-1905, Div. Hosp., Manila, 1906; mem. U.S. Army Bd. for Study of Tropical Diseases, Manila, 1906-07; lab. Ft. Leavenworth, Kan., 1907-109; attending surgeon, N. Y.C., 1909; asst. curator Army Med. Museum, 1909-13, curator, 1919-20; asst. prof. bacteriology and clin. diagnosis Army Med. Sch., Washington, 1909-13, prof. bacteriology, parasitology and preventive medicine, also dir. labs., 1920-22, comdt. and dir. clin. pathology and preventive medicine, 1926-30; asso. prof. bacteriology, med. dept. George Washington U., 1910-11; comdg. officer Central Dept. Lab. U.S. Army, Ft. Leavenworth, 1913-16, Dept. Lab. No. 2, So. Dept., El Paso, Tex., 1916-17, Ft.Leavenworth, 1917-18; organized and comd. Yale Army Lab. Sch., 1918-19; med. insp. Hawaiian Dept., 1922-26; asst. comdt. Army Med. Center, Washington, 1930-31; prof. tropical medicine and dir. dept., sch. medicine Tulane U., 1931-38, emeritus prof. tropical medicine, 1939—. Asso. editor Am. Jour. Parasitology; editor Am. Jour. Tropical Medicine, etc. Fellow A.C.S., A.C.P., Assn. Mil. Surgeons U.S. (life), A.M.A., Am. Pub. Health Assn.; mem. Am. Soc. Tropical Medicine (pres. 1914-15), Royal Soc. Tropical Medicine and Hygiene, Conn. Med. Soc., Wash. Acad. Sciences, Internat. Leprosy Assn., Soc. Tropical Medicine and Hygiene of Egypt, Internat. Soc. Tropical Medicine (sec. div. research), Am. Soc. Parasitologists (pres. 1934-35), Am. Acad. Tropical Medicine (pres. 1935), Bexar County (Tex.) Med. Soc. (hon.), Am. Soc. Clin. Pathologists. Recipient gold medal Am. Acad. Tropical Med., 1943, Founder's medal Assn. Mil. Surg., 1948. Mem. Alpha Omega Alpha, Sigma Xi, Nu Sigma Nu; pres. Yale Med. Alumni Assn., 1910-11. Decorated D.S.M., 1922. Club: Army and Navy Country (Washington). Author: The AEstivo-Autumnal Malarial Fevers, 1901; The Malarial Fevers, Haemoglobinuric Fever and the Blood Protozoa of Man, 1909; The Parasitic Amoebae of Man, 1911; The Wassermann Test, 1918, 21; A Manual of the Parasitic Protozoa of Man, 1925; Amebiasis and Amebic Dysentery, 1935; Clinical Parasitology (with Faust), 1937; The Laboratory Diagnosis of Protozoan Diseases, 1941; The Etiology, Diagnosis and Treatment of Amebiasis, 1944. Also wrote chapters in Osler's Modern Medicine, 1907, 14, in Hare's Mod. Treatment, 1911; Oxford medicine and Oxford Tropical Medicines, 1919; Musser's Internal Medicine, 1932; Brennemann's Pediatrics, 1935; Riemann's Treatment in General Medicine, 1939; Barr's Modern Medical Therapy in General Practice, 1940; Blumr's Therapeutics of Internal Diseases, 1941. Clinical Tropical Medicine, Bercovitz. Home: 225 Henderson St., San Antonio. Died Dec. 9, 1950; buried Ft. Sam Houston Cemetery.

CRAIG, Clarence Tucker, clergyman, educator; b. Benton Harbor, Mich., June 7, 1895; s. Alfred Edwin and Clara (Tucker) C., A.B., Morningside Coll., Sioux City, Ia., 1915; S.T.B., Boston U., 1919, Ph.D. from same U., 1924; D.Litt., Boston U., 1947; M.A., Yale Univ., 1946; grad. study Harvard U., 1919-20, Basel U., Switzerland, 1920, U. of Berlin, 1921-22; D.D., Evansville (Indiana) College, 1927, University of Glasgow (Scotland), 1951; married Rena Catherine Stebbins, Sept. 4, 1925; children—John Tucker, Peter Stebbins, Martha Alden, Michael Alden. Teacher, Anglo-Chinese Coll., Foochow, China, 1915-16. Ordained to ministry of M.E. Church, 1918; pastor, Walpole, Mass., 1918-19; asso. Trinity M.E. Church., Evansville, Indiana, 1921, pastor Clifton M.E. Church, Cincinnati, 1922-26, Simpson M.E. Ch., Brooklyn, N.Y., 1926-28; prof. N.T. lang. and lit., Oberlin (O.) Grad. Sch. Theology, 1928-46; ednl. rep. for Revised Standard Version, 1946; prof. New Testament Yale Divinity Sch., 1946-49, dean, Drew Theological Sem., since Sept. 1949. Teacher Garrett Biblical Institute, summers 1931, 34, 49, Union (N.Y.) summers 1942, 45, 47. Mem. bd. mgrs. Am. Bible Soc., Nanking Theol. Sch. Chmn. adv. com. First Assembly World Council Chs. Mem. Am. Standard Bible Translation Committee, mem. Commn. on Ritual and Orders of Worship, Meth. Ch., 1940-48; mem. Soc. of Bibl. Lit. and Exegesis, Nat. Assn. Bibl. Instrs. Editor: The Nature of the Church, 1945; The Challenge of Our

Culture, 1946; Christian World Mission, 1946. Author: The Christian's Personal Religion, 1925; Jesus in Our Teaching, 1931; We Have an Altar, 1934; The Study of the New Testament, 1939; The Beginning of Christianity, 1943; One God, One World, 1943; The One Church, 1951. Contbr. to New Testament Studies, 1942; Introduction to the Revised Standard Version, 1946; Christian World Mission, 1946; The Universal Church in God's Design, 1948; also to various religious publs. Mem. editorial bd., Religion in Life; asso. editor Ecumenical Rev. Home: Drew Forest, Madison, N.J. Died Aug. 20, 1953.

CRAIG, Daniel Frank, army officer; b. Mahaska Co., Ia., Oct. 3, 1875; s. Samuel C.; grad. Mounted Service Sch., 1910; distinguished grad. Army Sch. of the Line, 1912; graduate Army Staff College, 1916; graduate General Staff Coll., 1921; m. Florence Elizabeth Burt, May 19, 1906. Commd. 1st lt. 20th Kan. Inf., May 10, 1898; capt., May 9, 1899; hon. disch., July 12, 1899; capt. 36th U.S. Inf., July 5, 1899; hon. mustered out, Mar. 16, 1901; commd. 2d lt. Arty. Corps, May 8, 1901; 1st lt., July 28, 1903; capt., Jan. 25, 1907; assigned to 4th Field Arty., June 6, 1907; maj., May 15, 1917; col. N.A., Aug. 5, 1917; brig. gen. (temp.), Oct. 1, 1918. Served in Philippines, 1898-1901, and 1904-07; at Vera Cruz, Apr. 26-Nov. 26, 1914; with Punitive Expdn., Mexico, May 21-Dec. 1, 1916; detailed as mem. Gen. Staff Corps, Nov. 15, 1916; chief of staff, 12th Div., Dec. 4, 1916-Mar. 24, 1917; asst. chief of staff Southern Dept., Mar. 25-Apr. 6, 1917; with War Coll. Div. Gen. Staff, Washington, D.C., Apr.-Aug., 1917; arrived in France Aug. 5, 1918; comdr. 302d Regt. Field Arty., 151st Brigade, F.A., 76th Div., until Oct. 15, 1918; assigned as comdr. 157th F.A. Brigade, Oct. 21, 1918, 158th F.A. Brigade, Mar. 11, 1919, 5th F.A. Brigade, Apr. 15, 1919, 2d F.A. Brigade, Jan. 24, 1919. Presented with Silver plaque by Republic of France while a brigade comdr.; awarded D.S.M., "for exceptionally meritorious and distinguished services." Mason (K.T., Shriner). Episcopalian. Home: Garnett, Kan. Address: Care the Adjutant General, U.S. Army, Washington, D.C. Died Apr. 17, 1929.

CRAIG, Edward Chilton, lawyer; b. Mattoon, Ill., Apr. 7, 1872; s. James Wesley and Mary (Chilton) C.; B.Litt., U. Ill., 1893; studied Harvard Law Sch., 1894-95; LL.D., Southwestern, of Memphis; m. Fannie Ione Dilley, Nov. 9, 1899; children—George M., Donald C. Admitted to Ill. bar, 1896, began practice as partner of father at Mattoon; practiced at Mattoon until 1923; gen. atty. I.C. R.R. Co., Chgo., 1923-29, gen. solicitor, 1929-33, gen. counsel, 1933-42, retired. Mem. Am., Ill., Chgo. bar assns., Phi Beta Kappa, Phi Delta Phi. Democrat. Episcopalian. Clubs: University, Traffic, South Shore Country. Home: 2373 E. 70th St., Chgo. Deceased.

CRAIG, George M., banker; b. Washington County, Ark., Sept. 17, 1862; s. James T. and Elizabeth C.; ed. common schs.; m. Jane A. Taliaferro, Sept. 14, 1886 (dec.); children—Bennette (Mrs. E. B. Germain), Louise (Mrs. E. V. Henry), George T. (dec.). Gen. merchandise business, Bentonville, Ark., 1884-95; with Guardian Trust Co., Kansas City, Mo., 1896-98; mgr. Port Arthur (Tex.) Land & Townsite Co., 1898-1901; pres. 1st Nat. Bank, Port Arthur, 1900-11; pres. Merchants Nat. Bank, 1911—. Home: 1953 Lake Shore Drive, Box 999, Port Arthur, Tex. Died June 10, 1950; buried Magnolia Cemetery, Beaumont, Tex.

CRAIG, Oscar John, educator; b. Madison, Ind., Apr. 18, 1846; s. Miles W. and Mary S.C.; A.B., DePauw U., 1881, A.M., 1884; Ph.D., U. Wooster, 1889; m. Narcissa Gasaway, Aug. 20, 1875. Supt. city schs., Sullivan, Ind., 1880-83; prin. prep. dept. Purdue U., 1883-87, prof. polit. economy and history, 1887-95; pres. U. Mont., 1895-1908. Contbr. to mags. Address: Missoula, Mont. Died Mar. 5, 1911.

CRAIG, Winchell McKendree, neurosurg; b. Washington Ct. House, O., Apr. 27, 1892; s. Thomas Henry and Eliza Orlena (Pine) C.; student Culver Mil. Acad., 1911; A.B., O. Wesleyan U., 1915; D.Sc., 1937; M.D., Johns Hopkins Med. Sch., 1919; M.S. in surgery, U. Minn., 1930; m. Jean Katherine Fitzgerald, Feb. 16, 1928; children—Winchell McKendree, James Stewart, Jean Mary Patricia, Graham Fitzgerald. Resident surg., St. Agnes Hosp., Baltimore, 1919-21. Fellow Mayo Foundation, Grad. Sch. Univ. of Minn., 1921-24, instr., 1925, professor neurosurgery, 1937; senior cons. Surgery Mayo Clinic, 1946—; neurological surgeon, cons., Mayo Clinic, St. Mary's Hospital, Methodist Hospital. Served as commander, capt. and rear adm., M.C., U.S.N.R., chief surgeon, U.S. Naval Hosp., Corona, Calif., 1941-42; chief surg. Nat. Naval Med. Center, Bethesda, Md., 1942-45; dir. Grad. Training Program. Bur. Med. and Surg., Washington, D.C., 1945-46; res. cons. to Surg. Gen. U.S. Navy; cons. VA. Trustee Ohio Wesleyan U. Awarded Legion of Merit, Naval Res. Medal, Bronze Star. Fellow A.M.A., Am. Coll. of Surgeons; mem. Italian Soc. Neurosurgery (hon.), Neurosurgery of French Language (honorary), Am. Surgical Assn., Am. Neurol. Assn., Western Surg. Assn., Southern Surg. Assn., Minn. Soc. of Neurology and Psychiatry, Internat. Surg. Soc., Central Neuropsy. Assn., Society Neurological Surgeons, Central Society Clinical Research, Harvey Cushing Society, Am. Acad. Neurol. Surgery (hon.), Johns Hopkins Alumnae Assn., Minn. Surg. Soc., Internat. Neurol. Assn., Am. Legion, Association of Military Surgeons of the United States (pres. 1953), Res. Officers Assn., Sigma Xi, Beta Theta Pi, Phi Beta Pi. Clubs: University (Rochester, Minn.); Golf and Country (Rochester, Minn.); Ohio Society of New York. Author 300 med. papers and chapters in monographs or systems of medicine. Editorial bd. Journal of Neurosurgery. Home: 828 Eighth St. S.W. Address: care Mayo Clinic, Rochester, Minn. Died Feb. 12, 1960.

CRAIGHEAD, Edwin Boone, univ. pres.; b. Ham's Prairie, Mo., Mar. 3, 1861; A.M., Central Coll., 1883; post-grad. studies, Vanderbilt U., 1884-86; Leipzig and Paris, 1886-88; LL.D., U. Mo., 1898; D.C.L., U. of South, 1907; m. Kate Johnson, Aug. 6, 1889. Prof. Greek, Wofford Coll., S.C., 1890-93; pres. Clemson (S.C.) Coll. (S.C. Agr. and Mech. Co.), 1893-97, Central Coll., Fayette, Mo., 1897-1901, Mo. State Normal Sch., 1901-04, Tulane U., 1904-12, U. Mont., 1912-15; commr. edn., N.D., 1915-17. Editor New Southwest, Missoula, Mont., 1917. Mem. bd. Carnegie Found. for Advancement of Teaching, 1904-15. Mem. Am. bd. Hibbert Jour., Oxford, Eng. Fellow A.A.A.S. Address: Missoula, Mont. Died Oct. 22, 1920.

CRAIGIE, (Sir) William Alexander, lexicographer, educator; b. Dundee, Scotland, Aug. 13, 1867; s. James and Christina (Gow) C.; M.A., U. St. Andrews, 1888; B.A., U. Oxford, 1893, M.A., 1902; LL.D., St. Andrews, 1907, D.Litt., Calcutta, 1921, U. Oxford, 1928, Cambridge U., 1928, U. Mich., 1929, U. Wis., 1932, D.Phil., U. Iceland, 1946; m. Jessie Kinmond Hutchen, June 28, 1897 (died Feb. 10, 1947). Lectr. in Latin, U. St. Andrews, 1893-97; apptd. co-editor Oxford Dictionary, 1901; lectr. Scandinavian langs. U. Oxford, 1905-16, prof. Anglo-Saxon, 1916-25; fellow Oriel Coll.; Oxford, 1917-25; prof. English, U. Chgo., 1925-36, now emeritus. Mem. Brit. Acad., Philol. Soc. (London), Modern Lang. Assn. Am., Icelandic Soc. of Letters, others. Home: Ridgehurst, Christmas Common, Watlington, Oxon., Eng. Died Sept. 2, 1957.

CRAM, Ralph Warren, retired editor; b. Zanesville, O., June 19, 1869; s. Charles Warren and Clarissa (Deming) C.; ed. pub. schs.; m. Mabel LaVenture, Dec. 27, 1892 (died Jan. 9, 1948); children—Eloise Blaine, Margaret Mason (Mrs. Frank W. Siemen), Mary Deming (Mrs. Miles Max Miller), Ralph LaVenture (dec.). With Davenport Democrat since 1883, editor 1908-40 (retired); chmn. bd. Morris Plan Co.; pres. Davenport Artillery Holding Co. Advisor for Ia., Dept. Commerce Works Progress Adminstrn. Airport program, 1933-34. Former trustee Scott Co. Pub. Hosp.; dir. Upper Miss. Waterway Association. Member Chamber of Commerce (Davenport). Signer charter National Aeronautic Association, 1922 (v.p.). Democrat. Presbyterian. Clubs: Contemporary, Kiwanis, National Press. Editor of Scott County (Ia.) History of War Activities. Author of various pamphlets and mag. articles on aeronautics, including "Soloing at 62," from his own flying experience. Flew on all but first of Nat. Air Tours, 1925-31. Home: 2226 Adams St. Address: The Democrat, Davenport, Ia. Died May 8, 1952; buried Oakdale Cemetery, Davenport.

CRAM, William Everett, author, farmer; b. Hampton Falls, N.H., June 27, 1871; s. Rev. William Augustine and Sarah Elizabeth (Blake) C.; m. Esther L. Sanborn, June 30, 1909; children—Margaret L., Joseph L. Author: Little Beasts of Field and Wood, 1900; American Animals (with Witmer Stone), 1902; More Little Beasts of Field and Wood, 1912; Time and Change, 1927. Contbr. to sci. and lit. mags. Home: Hampton Falls, N.H. Died July 8, 1947.

CRAM, Wingate Franklin, ry. exec.; b. Bangor, Me., Dec. 4, 1887; s. Franklin Webster and Martha Cook (Wingate) C.; prep. edn. Phillips Andover Acad.; A.B., Harvard, 1900; student Columbia Law Sch.; m. Anna E. Sabin, June 20, 1905; children—Cynthia, Sibyl C. Fulenwider. With Bangor & Aroostook R.R., 1901—, successively president's asst., 1901-09, clerk of corp., 1909-17, treas., 1917-36, pres., 1936-48, chmn. bd., 1948—; pres., dir. Van Buren Bridge Co., No. Telegraph Co., Bangor Investment Co. Clubs: Harvard, Knickerbocker, Whist (N.Y.C.); Penobscot Valley Country, Tarratine, Conduskeag Canoe (Bangor). Home: 41 Broadway. Office: 84 Harlow St., Bangor, Me. Died Oct. 4, 1952.

CRAMER, Kenneth Frank, army officer; b. Gloversville, N.Y., Oct. 3, 1894; s. Frank Henry and Stella Sophia (Brown) C.; Litt.B., Princeton U., 1916, M.A., 1917 (Boudinot fellow in Am. history, 1916-17); grad. Command and Gen. Staff Sch., 1938, Inf. Sch. (Spl. Div. Officers' Class), 1942; m. Ruth Rose Fuller, Jan. 3, 1920; children—Margaret Fuller Van Pelt, Dorothy Ruth Van Pelt. Teacher, Newark and Woodbridge (N.J.) High Sch., 1919-20; wholesale coal business, 1920—; v.p. Harnden-Cramer Coal Co., Inc., 1923-27; pres. K. F. Cramer Coal Co., Inc., 1927-52. Acting adj. gen., State of Conn., Jan.-Mar. 1939; asst. adj. gen., State of Conn., 1939-50. Commd. 2d lt. Inf. O.R.C., Aug. 1917, promoted 1st lt., Oct. 1918; hon. discharged June 4, 1919; commd. 1st lt. Inf. Res., Feb. 1922, maj., May 1931, capt. 43d Tank Co., Conn. Nat. Guard, May 1931, col. 169th Inf., Nov. 1940, inducted into U.S. Army, Feb. 24, 1941, promoted to brig. gen., Aug. 17, 1942; major gen., comdg. 43d Inf. Div., July 12, 1946; recalled to active duty as comdg. gen. 43d Div., 1950; comdg. gen. So. Area Command, 1952—. Member War Department General Staff Committee on National Guard and Reserve Policy. Chief N.G. Bur., 1947-50. Member Connecticut House of Reps., 1929-33, Conn. Senate, 1933-37; sec. Conn. delegation, Rep. Nat. Conv., 1936. Awarded Silver Star with 3 Oak Leaf Clusters, Legion of Merit, Bronze Star, Air Medal, Army Commendation Ribbon, Purple Heart, Victory medal (3 bars), Army Occupation (Germany, Japan), Asiatic-Pacific Theatre with bronze arrowhead and 3 stars; Am. Theatre, Victory Medal, World War II, Inter-Allied Victory Medal (French), Philippine Liberation Medals with 3 stars, American Defense Medal. Member Wethersfield Board of Education, 1927-37, Met. District Commission for Hartford County, 1929—, Veterans Home Building Commission, 1931-37; secretary Commn. to reorganize the State Govt., 1935-37, State Library Com., 1937—; mem. Charter Oak Council, Boy Scouts of America, 1927-36. Mem. Phi Beta Kappa Assos., Conn. Hist. Soc., Wethersfield Hist. Soc., Am. Legion (dept. comdr. 1927; nat. exec. com. 1932-33; nat. coms. on constitution and by-laws, legislation and nat. defense), Mil. Order of Purple Heart (dept. comdr.), 78th Div. Vets. Assn., 24th Div. Veterans Assn., (pres.) U.S. Infantry Assn., Conn. National Guard Assn., Reserve Officers Assn. (president Hartford Chapter and dept. v.p.), Soc. Mayflower Descendants, S.A.R., Gen. Soc. War of 1812, Sons Union Vets. of Civil War (camp comdr., chmn. council-in-chief), Wethersfield Business Men's and Civic Assn., Princeton Alumni Assn. of Conn. Valley (v.p.), Phi Beta Kappa. Republican. Conglist. Mason (32° Shriner). Clubs: Nat. Sojourners, Princeton Gateway, Hartford Rotary. Recalled to active duty U.S. Army, Sept. 5, 1950. Address: 75 Center St., Wethersfield, Conn. Died Feb. 20, 1954; buried Arlington Nat. Cemetery.

CRAMER, Sterling B., banker; b. Hiawatha, Kan., Aug. 19, 1881. With the Fifth Third Union Trust Co., Cin., 1933—, now 1st v.p. and dir.; dir. Robbins and Myers, Inc., Springfield, O., Gruen Watch Co. Clubs: Cincinnati Country, Queen City. Home: Queen City Club, 331 E. 4th St., Cin. 2. Office: Fourth and Walnut Sts., Cin. 1. Died May 25, 1955.

CRAMER, Stuart Warren, Jr., ret. army officer, business exec.; b. Charlotte, N.C., Jan. 28, 1892; s. Stuart Warren and Bertha Hobart (Berry) C.; student, Univ. of N.C., 1907-08, Phila. Textile Sch., 1921-22; B.S., U.S. Mil. Acad., 1913; m. Julia Baxter Scott, Nov. 3, 1923; children—Stuart Warren, John Scott. Commd. 2d lt. U.S. Army, 1913, and advanced through grades to maj., June 7, 1918; mil. career as cav. officer in Mexican campaign, 1915, and World War I; instr., U.S. Mil. Acad., 1917; a.d.c. to aide to pres. elect of Brazil, 1919; general staff corps librarian, Army War Coll., 1919-21; ret. from regular Army, Nov. 20, 1922; with Cramerton Mills, Inc. and Cramerton Mills Co., 1922-46, pres., 1939-46; spl. asst. to chmn., Munitions Bd., Washington, 1947, dep. chmn., 1948—; president John M. Scott & Co., Charlotte, N.C., Linville Resorts, Inc., Linville, North Carolina; director Wachovia Bank & Trust Co., Charlotte News Publishing Company. Chairman Gaston County Republican Exec. Com., 1928, N.C. finance chmn., 1940; mem. N.C. Park Commn., 1929-33; N.C. state chmn., Nat. Indsl. Information Com.; mem. Cotton Mill Industry Com. and Combed Cotton Fabrics Industry Adv. Com., W.P.B., 1943-45, Cotton Weavers' Industry Adv. Com., O.P.A., 1943-45. Mem. exec. com., Nat. Assn. Mfrs., 1942-44, nat. v.p. in charge of Washington contacts and dir., 1944, also chmn. Govt. War Orgn. sub-com., Dir. Cotton Textile Inst. (also mem. exec. com.), Am. Cotton Mfrs. Assn. (1st v.p., 1944; rep. on tour of inspection of Frech textile industries, 1925), N.C. Textile Found. Awarded citation by adj. gen. for service at Santa Anita during Mexican campaign, 1915, campaign medal for service in France, War Cross (Czechoslovakia). Mem. So. Combed Yarn Spinners Assn. (pres. 1940-41). Republican (del. nat. conv. 1944). Episcopalian. Clubs: Charlotte (N.C.) Country, Augusta (Ga.) Nat. Golf (N.J.), Univ., Chevy Chase, Army Navy (Washington), Racquet and Tennis (New York). Home: (winter) 200 Hermitage Rd., Myers Park, Charlotte; also Palm Shadows, Mountain Lake Club, Lake Wale, Fla.; (summer) Cloudcroft, Linville, N.C. Office: 1618 Johnston Bldg., Charlotte, N.C. Died Jan. 6, 1957.

CRAMPTON, Albert M., judge; b. Moline, Ill., Jan. 7, 1900; LL.B., Cornell, 1922; spl. courses, Harvard Law Sch. Admitted to bar, 1923; practiced law, Moline, 1923-31 and 1943-48; judge City Court, 1931-43; judge Supreme Ct. of Ill., 1948—, chief justice, 1953. Mem. bd. edn., Moline, 1944-47. Past pres. Rock Island County Bar Assn. Mem. Am. Legion. Home: Moline, Ill. Died Mar. 13, 1953; buried Riverside Cemetery, Moline, Ill.

CRAMPTON, Guy Chester, educator; b. Mobile, Ala., Sept. 21, 1881; s. Orson L. (Dr.) and Cleffey B.; (de la Tourette) C.; A.B., Princeton, 1904; A.M., Cornell U., 1950; grad. study Freiburg and Munich; Ph.D., U. Berlin, 1908; M S., Harvard, 1920; unmarried. Asst. in biology Princeton, 1908-10; prof. zoölogy and entomology Clemson (S.C.) Agrl. Coll., 1910-11; asso. prof. entomology, U. Mass., Amherst, 1911-15, prof. 1915-47, ret. Fellow A.A. A.S.; mem. Entomological Soc. Am., Entomol. Soc. France, Phi Beta Kappa, Sigma Xi, Phi Kappa Phi, Gamma Alpha, Sigma Alpha Epsilon. Republican. Presbyn. Research in comparative morphology throughout the Class Insecta; the evolution of insects and related arthropods; lines of descent in insectan orders, etc. Home: Fernald Hall, Amherst, Mass. Died Oct. 31, 1951; buried Pine Crest, Mobile, Ala.

CRAMPTON, Henry Edward, zoölogist; b. N.Y.C., Jan. 5, 1875; s. Henry Edward (M.D.) and Dorcas Matilda (Miller) C.; student Coll. City of N.Y., 1889-92; A.B., Columbia, 1893, Ph.D., 1899; m. Marion M. Tully, Oct. 27, 1896. Asst. in biology Columbia, 1893-95; instr. Mass. Inst. Tech.; 1895-96; fellow, lecturer, tutor, and instr. in zoölogy Columbia, 1896-1901, adj. prof., 1901-04, prof., 1904-43, emeritus prof., 1943-—; instr. embryology Marine Biol. Lab., Woods Hole, Mass., 1895-1902; in charge of embryology, Cold Spring Harbor, 1903-06; asso. Carnegie Inst.; curator invertebrate zoölogy Am. Mus. Natural History, 1909-20; asso. Bishop Museum, Honolulu. Scientific expdns. Islands of South Pacific Ocean, 1906, 07, 08, 09, British Guiana and interior of Brazil, 1911; expdns. to Bahamas, 1912, Porto Rico, 1913-14, 14-15, South Seas, 1919, Western Pacific, Asia, Malaysia, Australia, 1920-21, South Seas, 1923-24, South Seas and Asia, 1928-29, Hawaiian Islands, 1929, 30, 31, 35; research asso., Am. Mus. Natural History, 1943-—. Former sec. treas. Eugenics Soc. U.S. Fellow N.Y. Acad. Sciences (ex-v.p., rec. sec., pres. and corr. sec.), A.A.A.S., Washington Acad. Scis.; mem. Am. Soc. Naturalists (v.p., 1921), Am. Soc. Zoölogists (v.p. 1911), Theta Delta Chi, Sigma Xi, Phi Beta Kappa. Clubs: Century, Explorers (v.p. 1926-30) (N.Y.C.). Author: The Doctrine of Evolution, 1911; also various monographs on evolution, embryology, exptl. zoölogy and travel. Home: 315 W. 106th St., Died Feb. 26, 1956.

CRANDALL, Albert Rogers, educator; b. Little Genesee, N.Y., Sept. 16, 1840; s. Jarius and Julia A. (Wells) C. (Puritan stock); prep. edn. Alfred (N.Y.) Acad.; A.M., Ph.D., Milton (Wis.) Coll.; student natural sci. Mus. Comparative Zoology, Harvard, 5 yrs.; m. Ellen A. Saunders, Feb. 16, 1874. Pvt. and sgt. N.Y. Guard, 1861; 1st lt. 40th Wis. Inf. Vols., 1863; asst. Ky. Geol. Survey under Prof. N. S. Shaler, 1873, later John R. Procter, until 1891; prof. natural history Ky. State Coll., 1875-93, Alfred U., 1895-1903; prof. natural history Milton Coll., 1903-20, prof. emeritus, 1920-—. Has written numerous reports of geology of Ky.; also addresses and papers on phases of modern edn. Address: Milton, Wis. Died Jan. 12, 1926; buried Milton.

CRANDALL, Arthur Fitz James, newspaper man; b. Easton, Washington Co., N.Y., Aug. 11, 1854; s. Henry Sargent and Mary Carmichael (Mills) C.; student Cornell, class of 1877, Art Students' League, 1880-81; m. Marion Stevens, of Orwell, Vt., Jan. 1, 1892; children—Helen Russell, Marion Lansing. News editor New York Evening Post, 1891-1924; retired with pension after purchase of Post by Curtis Pub. Co. Republican. Home: Briarcliff Manor, N.Y. Died Sept. 27, 1951; buried Orwell (Vt.) Cemetery.

CRANE, Arthur Griswold, state official; b. Davenport Center, N.Y., Sept. 1, 1877; s. Edward Payson and Mary Ward (Griswold) C.; B.S., Carleton Coll., 1902; studied U. Wis., summers, 1908, 09; A.M., Tchrs. Coll. Columbia, 1918; Ph.D., Columbia, 1920; LL.D., U. Wyo., 1946; m. Lura May DeArment, Aug. 23, 1904; children—Paul, Mary. Supt. schs., Minto, N.D., 1902-05; prin. Fergus County High Sch., Lewistown, Mont., 1905-07; supt. schs., Jamestown, N.D., 1907-12; pres. State Normal Sch., Minot, N.D., 1912-20 (built and organized this sch.); prin. State Normal Sch., Edinboro, Pa., 1920-22; pres. U. Wyo., 1922-41; sec. of state, Wyo., 1947-—, acting gov., 1949-51. Maj., San. Corps, office Surg. Gen., Washington, 1918-19; dir. ednl. sect. div., rehabilitation disabled soldiers and sailors. Chmn. Nat. Com. on Edn. by Radio, 1936-41; mem. Nat. Ry. Labor Panel, 1944-—. Mem. N.E.A., N.D. Edn. Assn., Nat. Assn. State Univs. (pres. 1939), Phi Beta Kappa, Delta Sigma Rho, Phi Delta Kappa. Presbyn. Mason. Author: History of Physical Reconstruction, in official Medical History of the World War. Joint editor courses of study for use in army hosps. Home: 3221 Dey Av. Office: Capitol Bldg., Cheyenne, Wyo. Died Aug. 11, 1955; buried Beth El Cemetery, Cheyenne.

CRANE, Charles Howard, architect; b. Hartford, Conn., Aug. 13, 1885; s. Charles E. and Virginia (Hagen) C.; student pub. and high schs., Hartford; m. Freda Heinz, Sept. 14, 1905; 1 son, Charles Lyman. Began active career as draughtsman in Hartford, 1904; went to Detroit, 1905; employed in offices of Albert Kahn and Smith, Hinchman and Grylls, 1905-09; in practice on own account making specialty of theatres, 1909-—; in London, Eng., 1934-—, building Earl's Court, permanent exhbn. bldgs. Home: 5 Halkin Pl., Belgrave Square, London, Eng. Office: 112 Madison St., Detroit; also 7, Buckingham Gate, London S.W. 1, Eng. Died Aug. 14, 1952.

CRANE, Charles Richard, II, plumbing fixture mfg. exec.; b. Lake Geneva, Wis., Aug. 7, 1892; s. Herbert Prentice and Jessie (Doolittle) C.; student Oxford Sch., Univ. Sch., Chgo., Lawrenceville (N.J.) Sch.; m. Margery Baker, June 22, 1916; children—Robert Baker, Richard Clement. Apprentice molder in foundry Crane Co., 1908-12, supt. of garage, 1912-16, asst. gen. supt. mfg. depts., 1916-22, asst. to v.p. charge mfg., 1922-25, asst. v.p charge sales, 1925-30, v.p. sales dept., 1930-35, v.p. charge European Operations, 1935-45, dir., 1921-35, since 1946; v.p. supervising exec. policy of British subsidiary, Crane, Ltd., since 1945, dir. since 1931; dir. Trenton Potteries Co., Maxwell Bros. Co. Mem. Army Ordnance Assn. Clubs: Chicago Athletic, Tavern (Chgo); Twenty Nine Inc. (N.Y.C.); Bohemian (San Francisco); Glen View (Golf, Ill.). Office: 836 Michigan Av., Chgo. 5. Died May 7, 1954.

CRANE, Clinton Hoadley, corp. executive; b. Englewood, N.J., Jan. 30, 1873; s. Jonathan H. and Elizabeth (Hoadley) C.; A.B., Harvard, 1894; U. of Glasgow, Scotland, 1897-98; Sc.D., Colo. School of Mines; D.Eng., Missouri U.; m. Rebecca Riggs, Apr. 23, 1900; 1 daughter, Rebecca Eddison. With William Cramp & Sons, ship builders, Phila., 2 yrs.; mem. Tarns, Lemoine & Carne, 1909-13; pres. St. Joseph Lead Co., 1913-47, chmn., 1947-57, trustee; v.p. Mo.-Ill. R.R. Co. Pres. Lead Industries Assn., 1928-47. Mem. Society Naval Architects and Marine Engineers, American Institute Mining and Metall. Engineers. Mining and Metall. Society of America. Clubs: Harvard, New York Yacht, Seawanahaka Yacht, Down Town, Century (New York) Tarratine Yacht (Me.). Home: 876 Park Av., N.Y.C. Died Dec. 1, 1958.

CRANE, Cyrus, lawyer; b. Suffield, Conn., Oct. 4, 1866; s. James P. and Cyrena M. (Sykes) C.; A.B., U. of Kan., 1887; m. Josephine E. Hutchings, November 12, 1891; children—Helen C. (Mrs. E. W. Bennison), Cyrus. Aditted to Mo. bar, 1890; mem. firm Lathrop, Morrow, Fox & Moore, 1898-1928, Lathrop, Crane, Reynolds, Sawyer & Mersereau, 1928-45, Lathrop, Crane, Sawyer, Woodson & Righter, 1945-—; dir. Farm & Home Savings & Loan Assn., H. T. Poindexter & Sons Mdse. Co.; atty. in Mo. and Ia. for A.T.&S.F. Ry. and in Mo. and Kan. for K.C.S. Ry. Presdl. elector, 1908; Republican candidate for mayor of Kansas City, 1918. Chmn. bar com. of U.S. Dist. Court for Western Dist. of Mo. Mem. Am., Mo. (ex-pres.), Kansas City (ex-pres.) bar assns., Lawyers' Assn. Kansas City, Phi Kappa Psi, Phi Beta Kappa, Phi Alpha Delta (hon.), S.R. (ex-pres. Kansas City chapter), Order of Coif (hon.). Unitarian (chmn. bd. trustees). Clubs: Professional Men's (ex-pres.), University. Home: 3519 Holmes St. Office: Land Bank Bldg., Kansas City 9, Mo. Died Feb. 5, 1951; buried Lawrence, Kan.

CRANE, G(rauley) Stewart, mfr.; b. Port Huron, Mich., Dec. 31, 1887; s. George H. and Lucy Ellen (Stewart) C.; B.S., U. Mich., 1910; m. Rosalie H. Garson, Nov. 25, 1916; children—Charlotte Anne (Mrs. Charles G. Sims), Mary Ellen (Mrs. Clinton L. Rossiter, III). Pres., dir. Cutler-Hammer, Inc., 1945-—; dir. Marshall and Ilsley Bank (Milw.) Dir. Columbia Hosp., Milw.; mem. Community Welfare Council of Milwaukee County (ex-chmn. bd. dirs., dir.). Republican. Episcopalian. Clubs: Milwaukee, Milwaukee Athletic, Milwaukee Country, University (Milw.); Lake Shore (Chgo.). Home: 7624 N. Beach Dr., Milw. 11. Office: 315 N. 12th St., Milw. 1. Died Sept. 28, 1957; buried Forest Home Cemetery, Milw.

CRANE, Jefferson Davis, airline exec.; born Gulfport, Miss., Oct. 23, 1908; s. Jefferson Davis and Carolyn Elizabeth (Elliott) C.; grad. Pascagoula (Miss.) High Sch., 1927; m. Nell B. Quinn, Sept. 1, 1932; children—Elsie Rhea, Carolyn Ann, John Daniel, Charles Edward. Mechanic, Gates Flying Circus, Teterboro, N.J., 1928-29, with Wright Aero Corp., Paterson, N.J., 1929-32; transport pilot Lennox Bros. Flying Sch., West Haven, Conn., 1932-37; mechanic Delta Airlines, Atlanta, 1937-39; supt. overhaul Nat. Airlines, Inc., Miami, 1939-41, supt. maintenance, 1941-45, vice pres. maintenance and engrng., 1945-48; engring., inspection and planning since 1948. Democrat. Methodist. Home: 2261 S.W. 60th Av., Coral Gables, Fla. Office: National Airlines, Inc., Miami, Fla. Died Jan. 20, 1952; buried Pascagoula, Miss.

CRANE, John Alden, army officer; b. St. George, Md., Dec. 2, 1885; s. Charles Thomas and Annie Louisa (Levering) C.; A.B., Johns Hopkins, 1907; grad. Army War Coll., 1928; m. Mary McKim, Oct. 21, 1908; children—Alden McKim, Mary McKim, Lizetta Violet. Commd. 2d lt., U.S. Army, 1908, and advanced through grades to major gen., 1943; served in P.I., 1908-10, 19-21; with 1st div. in France, 1917-18; mil. attaché to Turkey and Bulgaria, 1932-36; stationed at Ft. Bragg, N.C., 1940-—. Decorated Distinguished Service Cross, Silver Star, Purple Heart, French Croix de Guerre with palm. Officer Legion of Honor, Comdr. Order of the Sword (Sweden). Comdr. Order of St. Alexander (Bulgaria). Mem. Alpha Delta Phi. Mason. Clubs: Army Navy Country (Washington); Army and Navy (Manila). Home: Garrison, Md. Died Nov. 3, 1951.

CRANE, Raymond E(lmer), business exec.; b. Oakland, Cal., Aug. 11, 1881; s. Charles W. and Sarah Elizabeth (Merritt) C.; student pub. schs. Oakland; m. Ellen Fearn, 1905; children—Radford, David, Robert. Founder Eljer Co., Ford City, Pa., pres. since 1910; pres. Nat. San. Co., Salem, O., since 1929, Rimersburg Coal Co., Rimersburg, Pa.; dir. Textron, Inc., Providence. Mem. Nat. Assn. Mfrs., U.S., Pa. C's of C. Republican. Methodist. Clubs: Rotary; Surf, Committee of One Hundred, Key Largo Anglers (Miami Beach, Fla.). Home: R.F.D. 3, Kittanning, Pa.; also Bal Harbour, Fla. Office: Eljer Co., Ford City, Pa. Died Oct. 3, 1954.

CRANE, William G(arrett), coll. prof.; b. Hawarden, Ia., March 12, 1897; s. Eli Hall and Phidelia Woodrow (Darling) C.; A.B., State Univ. Ia., 1919, M.A., 1920, U. of Paris (Sorbonne), 1928-29; summers U. of Grenoble, 1926, U. of Dijon, 1928, U. of Wisconsin, 1927, 1933; Ph.D., Columbia, 1937; m. Phyllis E. Drinkwater, Aug. 16, 1938. In foreign dept., Nat. City Bank of New York, 1920-22. Roberts fellow, Columbia U., 1922-24, Roberts traveling fellow, 1924-25; instr. English, U. of Cincinnati, 1925-28; field service fellow for French univs., 1928-29, research in Bodleian Library, Oxford, 1929-31, tutor English, 1931-34, instr. 1935-37, asst. prof. 1938-44, asso. prof., 1945-48, prof., 1949, City Coll., New York; chmn. dept. English, 1945-50; research in Bodleian Library, Oxford, 1949-50. Armed Services Rep., 1942-43, Armed Forces Rep. and Vets. Counselor, 1941-46. Served as 2d lt., Field Arty., World War I. Guggenheim Fellow, 1956-57. Fellow A.A.A.S., Am. Geog. Soc.; mem. Internat. Assn. U. Profs. English, Acad. Polit. Sci., Am. Acad. Polit. and Social Sci., Am.-Italy Soc., American Friends of Greece, English Assn. (London), Modern Lang. Assn., Modern Humanities Research Assn. (London), Nat. Council Tchrs. of English, N.Y. Council Tchrs. of College English, English Assn., Malone Society Oxford, Luttrell Soc., Phi Beta Kappa. Clubs: Lotos (New York). Author: (in collaboration) Models and Values, 1928; Wit and Rhetoric in the Renaissance 1937; American Literature in the College Curriculum, 1948; Twelve Hundred Years, 1948, 49; How to Think and Write, 1950. Editor: Lord Berner's trans. of Diego de San Pedro's "Carcel de Amor," 1950; Henry Peacham's Garden of Eloquence, 1954. Home: 680 Riverside Dr., N.Y.C. Died Feb. 18, 1960.

CRAVEN, Leslie, lawyer; b. Helena, Mont.; s. Arthur J. and Emily (Kerr) C.; A.B., Stanford, 1909, J.D., 1911; fellow Harvard Law Sch., 1909-10; m. Nov. 26, 1921; children—Elizabeth Page, Frances Louise, Don. Admitted to Ore. bar, 1912, practiced at Portland until 1916; asst. counsel Presidents' Conf. Com. (valuation orgn. of rys.), Chgo., 1916-18, counsel, 1919-32; prof. law Duke, 1932-34; mem. research staff Joseph B. Eastman, Federal Coördinator of Transportation, 1933-34, counsel, 1934-36; mem. Willkie, Owen, Farr, Gallagher & Walton, 1938-—; rep. rys. in O'Fallon r.r. valuation case, 1927-29. Commd. 2d lt. F.A., U.S. Army Camp Taylor, 1918. Mem. Am. Bar Assn., Am. Law Inst., Phi Beta Kappa, Order of the Coif. Clubs: Recess, University (N.C.); American Yacht (Rye, N.Y.). Home: Brooklands 4, Bronxville, N.Y. Address: 15 Broad St., N.Y.C. Deceased.

CRAVEN, Thomas Tingey, naval officer ret.; b. Vallejo, Cal., July 8, 1873; s. Henry S. and Eugenie (Von Klinkofstrom) C.; B.S., U.S. Naval Acad., 1896; student (later mem. of staff), U.S. Naval War Coll., 1915; m. Antoinette Merritt, July 25, 1901; children—Thomas Tingey, Ann Craven de Kay, Olga Craven Thurber. Commd. ensign USN, 1896, advanced through grades to vice adm., 1935; with Gen. Bd. of Navy, 1911; dir. target practice and engring. competitions, Washington, 1912; comdr. U.S.S. Sacramento, 1916-17; head U.S. Naval Aviation, France, 1917-18; dir. Naval Aviation, USN Dept., 1919, laid ground work for establishment of Bur. of Aeronautics; dir. naval communications U.S. Navy Dept., 1927-28; promoted rear adm., 1928; chief coördinator Fed. govt. under Pres. Hoover, 1931-33; comdr. battleships, 1935; retired from active duty, 1937; supt. N.Y. State Maritime Acad., 1938-39. U.S. del. to internat. congress for regulation of communications, Washington, 1927. Decorated campaign medals for service in West Indies, P.I., Mexico China; Sampson medal, Navy D.S.M. (U.S.); Double Dragon (China); Legion of Honor (France); War Cross and Victory medal (Italy), Polish Cross.

Home: 187 Newton St., Weston, Mass. Died Apr. 5, 1950; buried Greenwood Cemetery, Bklyn.

CRAVER, Harrison Warwick (krā'vẽr), librarian; b. Owaneco, Ill., Aug. 10, 1875; s. Harrison Eugene and Caroline Ernestine (Weirauch) C.; B S., in chemistry, Rose Poly. Inst., 1895, hon. Sc.D., 1933; m. Adelaide Nevins Martin, June 17, 1902. Chemist various steel cos., Leechburg and Pittsburgh, Pa., and Graham, Va., 1896-99; technology librarian, Carnegie Library of Pittsburgh, 1900-02; asst. supt. Allegheny Iron & Steel Co., Brackenridge, Pa., 1902; technology librarian, 1903-08, librarian, 1908-17, Carnegie Library of Pittsburgh; director, 1917-45; consulting librarian, Engineering Societies Library, New York City, since 1946. Republican. Episcopalian. Member of Pa. Free Library Commn., 1909-17, A.L.A. (councilor, 1909-17, and since 1924; exec. bd., 1913-17; chmn. bd. of edn., 1928-31; pres. 1937-38), Newcomen Soc., History of Science Soc.; fellow A.A.A.S., N.Y. Library Club (pres. 1921-22); pres. Keystone State Library Assn., 1908-09. Club: Engineers. Home: 3333 N. Charles St., Balt. 18. Died July 27, 1951; buried Princeton (N.J.) Cemetery.

CRAWFORD, Charles, army officer; b. Coshocton, O.; s. Thomas and Margaret (Parkhill) C.; grad. U.S. Mil. Acad., 1889; Army War Coll., 1912; m. Miss E. M. Miller (dec. 1919). Commd. 2d lt. 10th Inf., 1889; promoted through grades to col. inf., 1917; brig. gen. N.A., 1918; retired, 1919. Mil. police duty, Oklahoma City, 1889-90; assisted U.S. Commn. dealing with Indian tribes, 1890, Iowas, Sac and Foxes, Shawnees, Kickapoos, Cheyenne and Arapahoes; organized Apache Indian Co., 10th Inf., 1891-92; participated in battle of San Juan Hill, Cuba, 1898, in which his captain in official report commented on his fearlessness under fire; in various fights and skirmishes in P.I., 1890-1902; instr. Inf. and Cav. Sch. and Staff Coll., Ft. Leavenworth, 1903-07; in P.I., 1909-11; on Gen. Staff, 1913-16; in Canal Zone, 1916-17; commd. 6th Brig., 3d Div., AEF in 2d Battle of Marne, July 15, 1918, and in advance north and on Vesle River, Aug. 1918. Author: Six Months with Sixth Brigade; Re-Stating Economic Theory. Presbyn. Home: Paola, Kan. Died Dec. 28, 1945; buried Paola.

CRAWFORD, Charles Wallace, ret. govt. ofcl; b. Lorena, Tex., July 21, 1888; s. John Tilly and Alice Lee (Clark) C.; B.S., Okla. A. and M. Coll., 1909, M.S., 1916; m. Relia Brewer, Jan. 3, 1915; children—Alice Florence (Mrs. J. Prescott Blount), John Justin. Asst. chemist Okla. Agrl. Expt. Sta., instr. in chemistry Okla. A. and M. Coll., 1909-10; asst. Wash. State chemist and instr. in chemistry Wash. State Coll., Pullman, 1910-11; chemist Internat. Refining Co., Cushing, Okla., 1916-17; asst. chemist Bur. of Chemistry (later became Food and Drug Adminstrn.), U.S. Dept. Agr. Chgo., New Orleans, Washington, D.C. 1917-54, trans. with Food and Drug Adminstrn. to Federal Security Agency, 1940; asso. commr. Food and Drugs, 1945-48; dep. commr. Food and Drugs, 1948-51, commr., 1951-54, ret. Mem. Assn. of Food and Drug Officials of the U.S., A.A.A.S. Home: 762 Summit Av., Mill Valley, Cal. Died Sept. 15, 1957; buried Angeles Garden, Mount Tamalpaes Cemetery, San Rafael, Cal.

CRAWFORD, David A., chmn. bd. Michiana Products Corp.; b. St. Louis, Mo., Apr. 1, 1879; s. Robera L. and Frances E. (Webb) C.; A.B., U. Wis., 1905, LL.D., 1940; m. Grace M. Williamson, Oct. 1, 1925; children—David A. (dec.), Elizabeth (Mrs. N. E. Duval), Edward W. Instructor University of Wisconsin, 1905-07; employed by American Car and Foundry Company, 1907, continuing 9 yrs.; v.p. and treas. Haskell & Barker Car Co., Inc., 1916-22; v.p. The Pullman Co., 1922-24; pres. Pullman Car & Mfg. Corp., car builders, Chicago, 1924-28; exec. v.p. The Pullman Co., 1928-29, pres., 1929-47, chmn. finance com., 1950-52; v.p. Pullman, Inc., 1927-29, became pres., 1929, now dir.; chmn. bd. Michiana Products Corp., Michigan City, Ind.; dir. Am. Tel. & Tel., Armour & Company, Continental Illinois National Bank & Trust Company, Chgo. Trustee Wisconsin Alumni Research Found. Mem. Phi Beta Kappa. Clubs: Chicago, University, Glen View. The Links (N.Y.); Bohemian (San Francisco). Home: Mountain Lake, Lake Wales, Fla. Office: 79 E. Adams St., Chgo. 3. Died July 22, 1957.

CRAWFORD, Fred Lewis, ex-congressman; b. Dublin, Tex., May 5, 1888; s. William Carroll and Mary Jane (Rape) C.; edn. grade schs., and business coll., Tex.; student polit. economy, extension course, U. Mich., 1925-26; m. Clara Belle Lyons, May 1910 (died 1927); m. 2d, Elizabeth Ann Jones, Nov. 1932; 1 son, William Douglas. Began as apprentice with English firm accountants, 1914; in accounting field 1915-17; engaged in building, financing and operating beet sugar mills in various sects. of U.S., 1917-35; mem. 74th to 82d Congresses, 8th Mich. Dist., mem. house insular affairs com.; atty., Washington, 1953—; dir. Refiners Transport & Terminal Corp., Mich. Nat. Bank, Petroleum Transit Corp. Republican. Methodist. Elk. Died Apr. 13, 1957.

CRAWFORD, Harry J(ames), lawyer; b. Richmond, O., Dec. 3, 1871; s. Abel Jones and Mary (Hammond) C.; A.B., Ohio Wesleyan U., 1897; LL.B., Western Res. U., 1898; m. Jemima H. Brandebury, June 14, 1899; children—Hammond, Henry James, Jane (Mrs. Laurent Torno), Martha Hamilton. Admitted to Ohio bar, 1898, since practiced in Cleveland; with Webster, Angell & Cook, 1898-1901, Brewer, Cook & McGowan, 1901-02; asso. Squire, Sanders & Dempsey, 1902-13, partner since 1913; dir. Cleveland Ry. Co., Ohio Goodyear Securities Co., Petrequin Paper Co., Wellman Engring. Co. Foreman Cuyahoga Co. Grand Jury, 1951; pres. Shaker Heights Sch. Bd., 1916-22. Mem. Am., Ohio State, Cleveland (pres. 1937-38) bar assns., Sigma Chi, Phi Delta Phi. Mason (32°). Clubs: Union Mayfield Country, Mid-Day, Skating (Cleveland). Home: 13980 South Park Blvd., Shaker Heights 20, O. Office: Union Commerce Bldg., Cleve. 14. Died Apr. 25, 1954; buried Lakeview Cemetery, Cleve.

CRAWFORD, Harry Jennings, banker, oil producer; b. Emlenton, Pa., Jan. 19, 1867; s. Samuel Washington and Jane C.; student Emlenton pub. schs.; m. Elizabeth Hafele; children—Elizabeth Louise, Katherine Jane. Began as foreman South Penn Oil Co., 1888; supt. Pa. Fuel Supply Co., 1890; v.p. Emlenton Water Co.; pres. First National Bank of Emlenton, Oil City National Bank; v.p., chmn. bd. Mountain Fuel Supply Co.; chmn. bd. Quaker State Oil Refining Corp., Reno Oil Co., Jas. B. Berry Sons Co., Enterprise Oil Co., Crawford & Gregory, Union Heat & Light Co., Grove City, Pa., Slippery Rock (Pa.) Heat & Light Co., Talon, Inc.; dir. Lone Star Gas Co., Columbia Gas & Electric Corp. (N.Y.C.), Manufacturers Light and Heat Co. (Pitts.), Devonian Oil Co. (Tulsa). Lightning Fastener Co. of Ont. (Can.). Trustee Grove City Coll. (v.p.). Republican (del. nat. conv. 1932). Presbyn. Mason (33°). Clubs: Oil City, Wanango Country (Oil City). Presented high sch. bldg. to Emlenton, adminstrn. bldg. to Grove City Coll., home for Assn. Blind, Venango Co. Home: Emlenton, Pa. Died Nov. 3, 1953; buried Emlenton Cemetery.

CRAWFORD, John M(cLenaghan), mfr.; b. Limavady, County Derry, Ireland, Oct. 16, 1867; s. Joseph and Eliza Jane (McLenaghan) C.; ed. schs. of Limavady, Ireland, and Bradford, Pa.; m. Elizabeth McAllister, Dec. 6, 1910 (died Oct. 27, 1956); children—Emma Elizabeth (Mrs. B. F. Harris, III), John McAllister. Came to U.S., 1883, naturalized, 1889. Shipping clerk, Bradford, Pa., 1884-93; with William Forgie, Washington, Pa., 1893-97; founded Parkersburg (W.Va.) Rig and Reel Co., mfrs. oil field equipment, 1897, sec.-treas., pres., 1897-33, chmn. bd., 1933—; pres. North Fork Oil Co. (Ill.), Okla. producing & Refining Co., N.Y. Quartet Oil Co., Hillside Oil Co., Homaokla Oil Co. (Okla.). Mem. City Council, Parkersburg, 1900-01; col. governor's staff, W.Va., 1900-12; pres. Parkersburg Board of Commerce, 1920-24; dir. Chesapeake and Potomac Telephone Co., Consolidated Natural Gas Co. Dir. C. of C. of U.S., 1921-27; mem. W.Va. Tax Commn., 1926-27, State Bd. of Edn., 1933-35; dir. Am. Peace Soc.; v.p. Ohio Valley Improvement Assn.; trustee Asheville (N.C.) Sch. Recipient S.R. medal for outstanding citizenship. Am. Petroleum Inst. (dir.). Episcopalian. Mason (33°, K.T.). Clubs: Bankers (N.Y.C.); Parkersburg Country. Home: 1601 Market St. Office: 620 Depot St., Parkersburg, W.Va. Died Oct. 20, 1950; buried Crawford Mausoleum, Mt. Olivet Cemetery, Parkersburg.

CRAWFORD, Leonidas Wakefield, college prof.; b. Fayettevile, N.C., Dec. 23, 1877; s. Leonidas Wakefield and Mary Anna (Pullen) C.; grad. Trinity High Sch., Durham, N.C.; B.A., Trinity Coll. (Duke U.), 1898; M.A., Columbia, 1903; Ph.D., Northwestern U., 1922; m. Helen May Meredith, Dec. 23, 1908; 1 son, Meredith Pullen. Instr. in English, Rutherford (N.C.) Coll., 1900-02, Poly. Inst., Brooklyn, 1905-06; tutor Coll. City of New York, 1907-08; prof. English, Sweetbrier (Va.) Coll., 1909-11; prof. English and dean Emory and Henry Coll., Emory, Va., 1911-18; prof. religious edn., George Peabody Coll., since 1920, prof. English, 1937-46, emeritus since 1946. Mem. faculty Columbia U., summers 1915-39; dir. religious edn., West End Meth. Ch., Nashville, 1922-37. Mem. Phi Beta Kappa, Kappa Delta Pi, Internat. Soc. Theta Pi. Author: Vocations Within the Church, 1920. Co-editor: Studies in Religious Education, 1931. Home: 3619 Sperry Rd., Nashville, Tenn. Address: Geo Peabody Coll. for Teachers, Nashvile. Died Dec. 10, 1952; buried Mount Olivet Cemetery, Nashville.

CRAWFORD, Ralph Dixon, geologist; b. nr. Peotone, Ill., Mar. 7, 1873; s. Ralph and Nancy Elizabeth (Cotes) C.; prep. edn. No. Ind. Normal Sch.; B.A., U. Colo., 1905, M.A., 1907; Ph.D., Yale, 1913; m. Theophania Huntington, Sept. 5, 1907. Tchr. pub. schs., Ill., Tex., Colo. until 1902; with U. Colo., 1904—, successively as asst. in geology, 1904-07, instr., 1907-08, asst. prof., 1908-14, prof. mineralogy and petrology, 1914—. Field asst. U.S. Geol. Survey, summer 1906; asst. Colo. Geol. Survey, 1907-09, geologist, 1909-25. Fellow A.A.A.S., Mineral Soc. Am., Geol. Soc. Am.; mem. Am. Assn. Univ. Profs., Sigma Xi. Republican. Conglist. Wrote (bulls.): Geology and Ore Deposits of Monarch and Tomichi Districts, Colo., 1913; Geology and Ore Deposits of Gold Brick Dist., Colo. (with P. G. Worcester), 1916; Geology and Ore Deposits of Red Cliff District, Colo. (with Russell Gibson), 1925. Home: 1050 Tenth St., Boulder, Colo. Died Mar. 7, 1950.

CRAWFORD, Russell Tracy, astronomer; b. Davis, Calif., Mar. 26, 1876; s. Frederick Gustavus and Mary Lanette (Foster) C.; B.S., U. of Calif., 1897, Ph.D., 1901; studied U. of Berlin, winter semester, 1911; m. Mary Crooke McCleave, Oct. 20, 1902 (died Apr. 21, 1903); m. 2d, Helen Alice Young, May 22, 1913. Mem. examining force U.S. Civ. Service Commn., 1902-03; with University of Calif. since 1903, instr. in astronomy until 1906, asst. prof., 1906-10, asso. prof., 1910-19, prof., 1919-46, emeritus since 1946; chairman of dept., 1938-41, since 1942. Dir. Students Observatory, 1939-46, dir. emeritus since 1946. Mem. Bd. of Edn., Berkeley, 1906-09. Maj. Air Service, U.S. Army, 1918-19. Fellow A.A.A.S.; mem. Astron. Soc. Am., Astron. Soc. Pacific (pres. 1914), Astronomische Gesellschaft, Phi Beta Kappa, Sigma Xi. Investigated the orbits of many comets and two satellites; computed general perturbations of several asteroids. Club: Faculty (Berkeley). Author: The Determination of Orbits of Comets and Asteroids. Editor: Cajori's Newton's Principia, A Revision of Motte's Translation. Home: 2740 Hillegass Av., Berkeley 5, Cal. Died Dec. 21, 1958.

CRAWLEY, Clyde B(rocks), physicist, educator; b. Hopkinsville, Ky., July 3, 1907; s. Thomas Bacon and Wilmoth (Pace) C.; student Transylvania Coll., 1927-28; A.B., U. Ky., 1930, M.S., 1931; Ph.D., Cal. Inst. Tech. (fellow, 1931-34), 1934; m. Urah Betty Divine, Dec. 31, 1928; 1 dau., Judith Fay. Prof. and head dept. of physics and mathematic Blue Mountain (Miss.) Coll., 1934-35; asst. prof. physics U. Ala., 1934-41, asso. prof., 1941-43; asso. prof. physics U. Ky., 1943-46, prof., 1946—. Mem. Am. Phys. Soc. (also Southeastern sect.), Am. Assn. Physics Tchrs., Am. Assn. U. Profs., So. Assn. Sci. and Industry, Ky. Assn. Physic Tchrs., Sigma Xi, Phi Beta Kappa, Sigma Pi Sigma, Pi Mu Epsilon. Mem. Christian Ch. Home: 170 Cherokee Park, Lexington 10, Ky. Died Oct. 26, 1949.

CREAGER, Marvin H. (krā'gẽr), newspaperman; b. Grand Haven, Mich., Feb. 4, 1882; s. Marvin H. and Mary (Swenson) C.; A.B., U. of Kan., 1904; m. Helen A. Adler, Dec. 27, 1910; children—Mary Louise, Eunice Elizabeth, Joanne. Began as reporter and sporting editor Kansas City (Mo.) World, 1901-05; telegraph editor Kansas City Post, 1906; night telegraph editor Kansas City Star, 1906-09, night city editor, 1909-11, spl. writer, 1911, telegraph editor, 1912-16, Washington corr., 1916-17, literary and Sunday editor, 1917-20; mng. editor Milwaukee (Wis.) Journal, 1920-38, pres. and editor, 1938-43; v.p. and editorial advisor, 1943—. Sec. Am. Soc. of Newspaper Editors, 1926-30, pres., 1936-37. Mem. Phi Kappa Psi, Sigma Delta Chi. Conglist. Home: 4827 N. Lake Drive. Office: The Journal, Milw. Died Dec. 4, 1954.

CREAGER, Rentfro Banton, lawyer; b. Waco, Tex., Mar. 11, 1877; s. Francis Asbury Warwick and Katherine (Rentfro) C.; B.Sc., Southwestern U., 1898, LL.D., 1930; LL.B., U. Tex., 1900; m. Alice Terrell, Feb. 3, 1904; children—Katharyn N. (widow of Carlisle Williams), Elizabeth Alice (widow of Lt. Col. Wayne J. Dunn), Frances (wife of Lt. Col. John W. Darrah, Jr.), Rentfro Banton. Began practice at Brownsville, Tex., 1900; collector of customs, Brazos de Santiago Dist., under Presidents Roosevelt and Taft; pres. Illind Oil Corp., Evansville, Ind. Republican nominee for gov. Texas, 1916; del. at large, Rep. Nat. Conv., 1916, 20, 24, 28, 32, 36, 40, 44; floor mgr. for nomination of Robert A. Taft, 1940; elected chmn. Rep. State Com., Tex., 1921; mem. Rep. Nat. Com., 1923—, mem. exec. com. nat. com., 1928. Mem. Ex. Com. of Nat. Com., 1928—. Tendered appointment as ambassador to Mexico by President Coolidge, Dec. 1923, but declined; had also declined appointment to same office by President Harding. Mem. Am. Bar Assn., Phi Delta Theta, Theta Nu Epsilon. Episcopalian. Mason (32°, K.T., Shriner), Elk. Club: Brownsville Country. Home: 1238 E. Elizabeth. Office: First National Bank Bldg., Brownsville, Tex. Died Oct. 28, 1950; buried Brownsville.

CREAGER, William Pitcher, civil engr.; b. Balt., Sept. 21, 1878; s. Noble Harwood and Mary (Neal) C.; C.E., Rensselaer Poly. Inst., 1901; m. Margaret Burns, Apr. 9, 1904; 1 dau., Elizabeth Mary. Provincial supr. Philippine Govt., 1901-04; designer N.Y. State Barge Canal, 1904-06; draughtsman to chief hydraulic engr. J. G. White Engring. Corp., 1906-22; v.p. and chief engr. Power Corp. of N.Y. and other corps, 1922-31; cons. engr., 1931—. Lt. col. U.S. Army, retired. Mem. Buffalo War Council; dep. comdr. Buffalo Office Civilian Protection; former trustee Rensselaer Poly. Inst.; mem. adv. engring. council, Princeton U. Mem. Am. Soc. C.E., Am. Inst. Cons. Engrs., Theta Xi, Sigma Xi. Clubs: Wanakah Country, Saturn. Author: Engineering for Masonry Dams, 1917; La Construction des Grands Barroges en Amerique, 1923; Hydro Electric Handbook (with others), 1927; Engineering for Dams (with others), 1942; also chapter in Handbook for Electrical Engineers and Structural Engineers Handbook Library. Handbook for Mechanical Engineers. Contbr. many articles to sci. mags. Home: Sheraton Hotel. Office: Electric Bldg., Buffalo. Deceased.

CRECRAFT, Earl Willis (krā'krăft), educator; b. Brookville, Ind., Jan. 27, 1886; s. Albert Newton and Mary (Tyner) C.; Ph.B., Franklin (Ind.) Coll., 1907, LL.D., 1934; A.M., Columbia, 1911, Ph.D., 1915; m. Lucy Ann Guthrie, Aug. 19, 1914; children—Lucy Anne (dec.), Jane Willis, Richard Guthrie, William Albert, Susan. Prin. high sch., Shelbyville, Ind., 1908-10; instr. politics Columbia, 1912-13; instr., lectr. govt. N.Y.U., 1913-19; also head social science dept., high sch., Bayonne, N.J., 1914-19; prof. polit. science U. Akron, 1919-38; dean Coll. Liberal Arts and prof. polit. science, Kent State U., 1938-47; vis. prof., summers, Syracuse U., 1932, Cornell U., 1933. Asst. sec. Honest Ballot Assn. N.Y.C., 1913; sec. Hudson County (N.J.) Citizens Fedn., 1913-14; mem. staff Bur. Municipal Research (Akron), 1920; spl. lectr. on citizenship Ohio State Dept. of Americanization, 1922. Mem. Advisory Council on Radio in Edn. Mem. Am. Polit. Science Assn., Am. Hist. Assn. (asso. mem. Commn. on Social Studies in the Schs.), Nat. Municipal League, Am. Acad. Polit. and Social Science, Am. Soc. Internat. Law, Am. Assn. U. Profs., Kent C. of C., Internat. Assn. Torch Clubs, Omicron Delta Kappa, Phi Delta Theta. Presbyterian. Mason (K.T., 32°, Shriner). Clubs: Rotary, Akron City. Author: Government of Hudson County, N.J., 1915; Government and Business, 1928; Freedom of the Seas, 1935. Home: 626 Park Av., Kent, O. Died Mar. 30, 1950; buried Kent.

CREECH, John W., banker; b. Lee County, Va., Nov. 24, 1849; s. Jonathan and Martha (Morris) C.; ed. common sch. edn.; married. Engaged in r.r. bldg. for more than 25 yrs., as mem. Creech & Lee, Creech, Lee & Crane, and Winston Bros. & Co.; also bred and reared standard bred trotting horses; pres. Bank of Herington. Mem. Kan. Ho. of Rep. 2 terms (chmn. Com. on Ways and Means); candidate for lt.-gov. of Kan., 1910; Republican. Mem. Christian (Disciples) Ch. Mason (32°), K.T. Home: Herington, Kan. Deceased.

CREEDEN, Daniel W., pres. Libby, McNeill & Libby; b. Brockton, Mass., Dec. 31, 1891; s. Michael and Catherine H. (Buckley) C.; A.B., Harvard, 1913. Began with Swift & Co., 1913; gen. mgr. John P. Squire Co., 1921, v.p., 1930; v.p. Swift & Co., 1934; pres. Libby, McNeill & Libby since 1940. Home: 7100 South Shore Drive. Office: Union Stock Yards, Chgo. Died July 29, 1953.

CREEL, George, author; b. Lafayette County, Mo., Dec. 1, 1876; s. Henry Clay and Virginia (Fackler) C.; educated in public schools; married Blanche Bates, Nov. 28, 1912 (died December 25, 1941); children—Frances Virginia, George Bates; married 2d, Alice May Rosseter, March 24, 1943. Editor Kansas City Independent, 1899-1909, Denver Post, 1909-10, Rocky Mountain News, 1911-13; chairman Committee on Public Information, by apptmt. of Pres. Wilson, Apr. 14, 1917-Mar. 1919. Chmn. San Francisco Regional Labor Bd., 1933; chmn. Nat. Advisory Bd., Works Progress Adminstn., 1935. Apptd. U.S. commr. Golden Gate Internat. Exposition by President Roosevelt, 1939. Past pres. Authors League Fund. Dem. Clubs: Dutch Treat, Metropolitan (New York); Bohemian, (San Francisco); Press, University (Washington). Author: Quatrains of Christ, 1907; Children in Bondage (with Edwin Markham and B. B. Lindsey), 1913; Wilson and the Issues, 1916; Ireland's Fight for Freedom, 1919; How We Advertised America, 1920; The War, the World and Wilson, 1920; Uncle Henry, 1923; The People Next Door, 1926; Sons of the Eagle, 1927; Sam Houston, 1928; Tom Paine—Liberty Bell, 1931; War Criminals, 1944; Rebel at Large, 1947; Russia's Race for Asia, 1949. White House Physician (collaborator). Contbr. to mags. Home: Bohemian Club, San Francisco, Cal. Died Oct. 3, 1953; buried Mt. Washington Cemetery, Kansas City, Mo.

CREELMAN, Harlan, theologian; b. Maitland, N.S., Nov. 15, 1864; s. Rev. William and Nancy (Cox) C.; student U. N.B., Fredericton; grad. Normal Sch., Castine, Me., 1885; B.D., Yale, 1889, Ph.D., 1894; hon. M.A., Yale, 1908; D.D., Temple U., 1916; m. Josephine Thorp Rice, June 15, 1892 (died Sept. 17, 1940); m. 2d, Helen Walbridge Creelman, Aug. 30, 1941. Ordained Congl. ministry, 1889; pastor Worthington, Mass., 1889-93; instr. Bibl. lit., Yale, 1893-99; Miner prof. Hebrew, cognate langs. and Bibl. lit., Congl. Coll. (McGill U.), Montreal, Can., 1899-1908; prof. Hebrew lang. and lit., Auburn Theol. Sem., 1908-38, prof. emeritus, 1938-—. In charge O.T. work at various times, 1899-1908, at Wesleyan and Presbyn. (Theol.) colls., Montreal, and Semitic work at McGill; mem. revision com. of The 1911 Bible, Mem. Soc. Bibl. lit. and Exegesis Religious Edn. Assn., Fed. Council of Chs. of Christ in Am., League of Nations Assn., The Osborne Assn., Inc. Author: An Introduction to the Old Testament, Chronologically Arranged, 1917, 1927. Contbr. to theol. publs. Home: Ashmore Lodge, Worthington, Mass. Died May 26, 1950; buried Worthington.

CREIGHTON, William J. (krā't'n), architect; b. Los Angeles, Calif., July 31, 1892; s. William St. Clair and Lilly Grace (Vaccaro) C.; student, Los Angeles Polytechnic, 1907-11; B.S. in Architecture, U. of Pa., 1915, M.S., 1917; student Sch. of Aeronautical Engring., Mass. Inst. Tech., 1918; m. Alice Townley Smyth, June 12, 1920; children—William Smyth, Suzanne Meade, Edward Telfair, Alice Townley. Registered architect in New York, New Jersey, Connecticut, Pennsylvania, Virginia and Dist. of Columbia. Designer in office of McKim, Mead & White, New York, 1920-27; partner, La Farge, Clark & Creighton, N.Y., 1927-30; pvt. practice, William J. Creighton, 1930-45; with Toombs & Creighton 1945-48; pvt. practice, 1949-—; architects 6th Dist. Fed. Reserve Bank, Georgia Warm Springs Foundation, Fulton County Adminstrn. Bldg., Rich's, Inc. Dept. Store; designed building for New York Geneal. and Biological Society; designed residence for Garrard Winston, New York; estates for John Hay Whitney (Va.), Philip G. Cole (Harrytown, N.Y.), Henry Pratt (Bristol, Pa.), Theodore Montague (Greenwich, Conn.); architect for Atlanta Pub. Library; architect for Fulton Co. Adminstrn. Building. Served as 1st lt., R.M.A. Pilot, U.S. Army, World War I. Awarded medals, archtl. projects, Beaux Arts Inst. Mem. Mayor's Com. of Architects of New York, planning bd. Township of New Castle, Westchester County, New York. Mem. Am. Arbitration Soc., Am. Inst. of Architects (pres. Ga. chapter), Beaux Arts Inst. of Design, Phi Gamma Delta. Club: Athletic (Atlanta). Home: R. 3, Windy Hill Rd., Marietta, Ga. Office: 1205 Spring St. N.W., Atlanta. Died July 17, 1955.

CREIM, Ben Wilton (krīm), elec. engr.; b. Chicago, Sept. 19, 1898; s. Nathan B. and Ida (Belovitch) C.; student Los Angeles Poly. Jr. Coll., 1916, George Washington U., 1917, 1918; m. Mardel Bernadine Brinkmann, Mar. 24, 1923; children—Donald Henry, Audrey Jane (Mrs. Arthur T. Sturgess). Elec. engr. Bur. Power & Light, Los Angeles, 1919-27; chief elec. engr. Modesto (Calif.) Irrigation Dist., 1927-35; regional engr. Rural Electrification Adminstrn., Washington, 1936-39; asst. chief engr. Bonneville Power Adminstrn., Portland, Ore., 1939-42; regional power mgr. Bur. Reclamation, Sacramento, 1945-50; adminstr. Southeastern Power Adminstrn., Dept. Interior, Elberton, Ga. since 1950. Served as machinist mate 1st class, U.S.N.R., World War I, comdr. II. Fellow Am. Inst. E.E.; mem. Am. Legion, 40 et 8. Home: 130 Lake Forest Dr. Office: Southeastern Power Administration, Elberton, Ga. Died Feb. 4, 1952; buried Arlington Nat. Cemetery.

CRENSHAW, James Llewellyn, educator; b. Dermott, Ark., July 10, 1887; s. John T. and Anna (Crawford) C.; A.B., Centre Coll., 1907, A.M., 1908; Ph.D., Princeton, 1911; m. Louise F. Hodges, June 30, 1923. Asst. chemist Geophys. Lab., Washington, 1910-15; mem. faculty Bryn Mawr (Pa.) Coll. since 1915, prof. chemistry since 1924. Mem. Am. Chem. Soc., A.A.A.S., Franklin Inst., Electro Chem. Soc., French Chem. Soc., Sigma Xi. Contbr. articles in chem. jours. Home: 118 Merion Av., Bryn Mawr, Pa. Died Nov. 22, 1950.

CRESS, George Clifford, clergyman; b. Cin., Aug. 25, 1873; s. Joseph Porter and Abigail (Crary) C.; prep. edn., high sch.; grad. Div. Sch. U. Chgo., 1906; D.D., Grand Island Coll., 1927; m. Amanda Witter Zook, Mar. 29, 1906; children—Gladys Alora and Vera Allene. Ordained to ministry, 1898; missionary in Central Africa, 1899-1900; student pastor Chgo., 1901-06; pastor successively Evanston, Wyo., Colorado City, Colo., and Lewistown, Mont., until 1914; state supt. Mont. Bapt. Conv., 1915-24, also sec. Mont. Home Mission Council of 9 denominations, 1919-24; field editor The Baptist, Chgo., 1924-27; field rep. No. Bapt. Conv., Bd. Missionary Cooperation, 1927-30; became asso. sec. Ministers and Missionaries Benefit Bd. of No. Bapt. Conv., 1930, retired 1945. Mem. Bapt. Bd. of Promotion, 1919-24, that raised over $60,000,000 for denomination philanthropies; widely known as lecturer on popular subjects. Republican. Mason (32°). Recipient Carnegie medal and $1,000 for saving life from drowning, 1915. Home: 646 E. Lincoln Av., Mt. Vernon, N.Y. Office: 152 Madison Av., N.Y.C. Died Jan. 26, 1951; buried Ferncliff Cemetery, Hartsdale, N.Y.

CRESS, George Oscar, army officer; b. Warsaw, Ill., Sept. 18, 1862; s. George and Mary E. C.; grad. U.S. Mil. Acad., 1884, Army War Coll., 1911; m. Dora Scott Dean, May 26, 1886. Commd. 2d lt. Cav., U.S. Army, 1884, advanced through grades to brig. gen. (temp.), 1918; prof. mil. sci. and tactics Knox Coll., Galesburg, Ill., 1889-93; duty Yellowstone Nat. Park, 1897-98; in Philippines, with Gen. Lawton, 1899-1900; constructing q.m. at Ft. Riley, Kan., 1900-04; prof. mil. sci. and tactics Mich. Mil. Acad., Orchard Lake, Mich., 1904-08; duty Insp. General's Dept., 1916-18; organized 49th F.A., 1918; in charge militia affairs So. Dept., 1919; apptd. comdr. Columbus Barracks, Oct. 6, 1919. Address: War Dept., Washington. Died May 8, 1954.

CRESSLER, Isabel Bonbrake, educator; b. Chambersburg, Pa., Apr. 10, 1872; d. Charles Henry and Elizabeth Sager (Jones) Cressler; A.B., Wilson Coll., Chambersburg, 1895; grad. study Cornell U., summer, 1902. Prin. Latin Sch., Chambersburg, 1897-1903; tchr. mathematics Wilson Coll., 1903-05; prin. Roman Sch. for Girls, Rome, Italy, 1905-09; co-prin. Elmhurst Sch., Connersville, Ind., 1909-26, Stoneleigh Sch. for Girls, Rye Beach, N.H., 1926-30, Stoneleigh-Prospect Hill Sch., Greenfield, Mass., 1930-—. Home: Greenfield, Mass. Deceased.

CRESSY, Warren Francis (krĕs'sē), lawyer; b. Oxford, Conn., July 5, 1878; s. Anson Fiske and Mary J. (Hill) C.; LL.B., Yale Law Sch., 1905; m. May L. Butler, June 29, 1908 (dec. Apr. 16, 1947); 1 son, Warren F.; m. 2d Ruth E. Butler, July 1, 1949. Admitted to Conn. bar, 1905, began practice of law; mem. Cressy, Bartram, Melvin & Sherwood since 1929; dir. Stamford Savings Bank, Stamford Trust Co.; chmn. of bd. Stamford Savings Bank. Pres. Alfred W. Dater Council, Boy Scouts of America, 1941-47. Mem. Nat. Council, Boy Scouts Am. Mem. Common Council, City of Stamford, 1914-16, Bd. of Edn., 1925-34, director Nat. Conf. Bar Examiners (chmn. 1946-47); dir. Am. Judicature Soc., 1939-42; dir. Danbury Meth. Home for the Aged; mem. Conn. War Council Legal Com., 1942-43. Pres. Stamford Scholarship Foundation. Member Judicial Council, State of Connecticut. Director Stamford Mus. Mem. Am. Bar Assn. (House of Del., 1936-40; Conn. chmn. com. on administrative law). Assn. Bar City N.Y., Am. Law Inst., Am. Counsel Assn. (director), Conn. State Bar Assn. (pres. 1940-42), State Bar Examining Committee, 1933-50; chairman of commission on revision Appellate Procedure Supreme Court, 1949-50; chairman Fairfield County Bar Library Com., Stamford C. of C. (pres. 1931-33, treasurer 1936-43. Republican. Methodist. Clubs: (New York); University (Bridgeport); Graduates of Yale U., Rotary. Home: 84 St. George Av. Office: 300 Main St., Stamford, Conn. Died Mar. 11, 1952; buried Lakeview Cemetery, New Canaan, Conn.

CRESWELL, Edward J(ohnson), lawyer, labor relations dir.; b. Cleve., Oct. 22, 1905; s. Elmer E. and Sue (Westhafer) C.; B.S., Harvard, 1926; LL.B., Western Res. U., 1931; m. Marian Stucky, Aug. 3, 1934; children—John Ellsworth, Joyce Elizabeth. Admitted to Ohio bar, 1932; practicing lawyer, Cleve., 1932-34; asst. state counsel HOLC, 1934-37; counsel Glenn L. Martin Co., Balt., 1943-50, counsel, dir. labor relations, 1950-—; rep. aircraft industry before various U.S. Congl. coms. Washington and regional atty. NLRB, 1939-43. Mem. Kappa Sigma. Club: Harvard (Balt. and Cleve.). Author: Special Assessments in Municipal Government, 1926; also articles in legal publs. Home: 118 Edgewood Rd., Towson 4, Md. Office: Glenn L. Martin Co., Balt. 3. Died Sept. 22, 1957.

CREW, Henry, physicist; b. Richmond, O., June 4, 1859; s. Wm. Henry and Deborah A. C.; A.B., Princeton, 1882; Ph.D., Johns Hopkins, 1887; m. Helen C. Coale, July 17, 1890; children—Alice H., Mildred, William H. Instr. physics, Haverford Coll., 1888-91; astronomer Lick Obs., 1891-92; prof. physics, Northwestern U., 1892-1930; chief of div. of basic sciences, Century of Progress Expn., Chicago, since 1930. Collaborator Astrophysical Journal, 1892-1942. Del. Congress of Physicists, Paris, 1900; mem. Nat. Acad. Sciences, Am. Physical Soc. (pres. 1909), Ill. Acad. Sciences (pres. 1912), Am. Philos. Soc., Am. Assn. Univ. Profs. (pres. 1929-30), History of Science Soc. (pres. 1930); fellow Am. Acad. Arts and Sciences, Phi Beta Kappa. Recipient of Oersted medal of Am. Assn. Physics Teacher, 1941. Author: Principles of Mechanics, 1908; General Physics, 1908; Rise of Modern Physics, 1928. Translator of Maurolycus' Optics, 1940. Contbr. to scientific jours. Clubs: University (Chicago and Evanston); Westmoreland Golf. Home: 620 Liberty Pl., Evanston, Ill. Died Feb. 17, 1953; buried Wilmington, O.

CRILE, Austin Daniel (kril), b. Chile, O., Apr. 25, 1870; s. Michael and Margaret (Deeds) C.; student Scio (O.) Coll., 1887-89; B.D., Luth. Theol. Sem., Chgo., 1894; post-grad. U. Chgo. Div. Sch., 1901-03; Ph.D., Tusculum Coll., Greeneville, Tenn., 1919; m. Winifred Augusta Wood, June 12, 1890; children—Dennis Rider Wood, Herman Revere, Winifred Lucile Bertha, Florence Evylin Alberta. Began as tchr. at 17; financial sec. Luth. Theol. Sem., Chgo., 1894-97, securing endowment and erecting the sem. bldg.; ordained Luth. ministry, 1894; pastor Wicker Park Ch., Chgo., 1897-1910 (ch. growing from mission ch. to largest Evang. Luth. Ch. in Chgo.); resigned and located at Roswell, N.M.; est. the Manse Stock Farm and Orchard; chmn. and mgr. N.M. Live Stock and Products Expn., Roswell, N M., 1914-16; pres. N.M. Coll. Agr. and Mechanics Arts, 1917-19; farm and ranch prop., 1933-41. Commr. of Pub. Lands for N.M., 1929-—; pres. Pecos Valley Artesian Conservancy Dist.; loan corr. Federal Land Bank, Wichita, Kan. Dir. Pecos Valley Compress Co. Chaplain N.M. Mil. Inst., Roswell; mem. N.M. State Bd. of Edn., 1917-19; mem. N.M. State Fair Commn., 1917-19; mem. Pecos Valley Cotton Growers; pres. Roswell C. of C.; regent

Eastern N.M. Normal Sch. Republican. Clubs: Rotary and Kiwanis (hon. mem.). Home: Roswell, N.M. Died Oct. 30, 1954; buried Roswell.

CRILLEY, A(lbert) Cyril, govt. official; born Waynesbo.o, Pa., Jan. 26, 1902; s. Albert Bahner and Sue Alice (Myers) C.; bachelor of fgn. service, Georgetown U., 1926; m. Edna G. Burrows, June 27, 1928; children—Anthony Cyril, Joan Burrows. Commercial intelligence div., Bur. of Fgn. and Domestic Commerce, 1926-30; trade commr., comml. attache, Latin Am. Republics, 1930-37; European rep., New Yo k exporter-importer, 1937-39; dist. mgr., Dept. of Commerce, Puerto Rico, Virgin Islands, 1940-42; rep., Bd. of Econ. Warfare, Puerto Rico, 1940-42; with Office of Fgn. Service, U.S. Dept. of State, since 1945, chief, div. of Fgn. Reporting Services, since 1947. U.S. Navy del., Fgn. Service Officer's Conf., Havana, 1941; rep., Consular Conf., Ottawa, 1947, Mexico City, 1948; assigned to Point IV Program Tech. Coop. Adminstrn. Served with U.S. Navy, 1942-45. Awarded Commendation ribbon (Navy), Naval Reserve medal. Mem. Am. Fgn. Service Assn. of Dept. of State. Home: 6120 Offutt Rd., Chevy Chase, Md. Office: T.C.A., Dept. of State, Washington. Died Dec. 22, 1951; buried Arlington Nat. Cemetery.

CRIPPS, Sir Stafford, chancellor exchequer; b. London, Eng., Apr. 24, 1889; s. Lord Parmoor and Theresa (Potter) C.; student Winchester Coll., 1901-07, University Coll., London, 1908-11; m. Isobel Swithinbank, July 11, 1911; children—John Stafford, Isobel Diana, Anne Theresa, Enid Margaret. Called to the bar, 1913; solicitor general, 1930; British ambassador, Moscow, 1940-42; Privy Councillor, 1941; mem. War Cabinet as Lord Privy Seal and leader House of Commons, 1942; special mission to India, 1942; minister aircraft prodn., Nov. 1942-May 1945; pres. Bd. of Trade, 1945-47; chancellor of the exchequer, 1947-50, F.R.S. Decorated Companion of Honor, 1951. Author: Cripps on Compensation; Church and Clergy; Why This Socialism?; Democracy Up-to-Date; Towards Christian Democracy; Democracy Alive; God in Our Work. Home: Frith Hill, Far Oakridge, nr. Stroud, Glos., Eng. Died Apr. 20, 1952.

CRISCUOLO, Luigi, financier and publicist; b. Salerno, Italy, Mar. 25, 1887; s. Antonio and Maria Rosa (Saporiti) C.; father of the ancient baronial family of the Patriciates of Amalfi and Naples; student pub. schs.; brought to U.S., 1889. Financial statistician, Redmond & Co., bankers, N.Y.C., 1911-18; financial editor The Independent, 1915-20; was sec. U.S. Railroad Adminstrn. Adv. Com. on Finance; with Merrill, Lynch & Co., N.Y.C., 1910-35; chmn. protective com. First Mortgage Bondholders of Midland Bldg., Chgo., mem. protective com. Dayton Biltmore Hotel Land Trust Certificates; chmn. protective com. Debenture Bondholders of Bond Electric Corp., also Panhandle Producing & Refining Co. Common Stockholders; mem. Ind. Noteholders Com. of McCallum Hosiery Co.; mem. Elected Com. for First Mortgage Bondholders of N.Y., Westchester & Boston Ry. Co.; mem. Preferred Stockholders' com. of Schulte Retail Stores Corp. (N.J.), 1936-41; chmn. bd. dirs. Merchants Nat. Properties, Inc., 1937-50; pres., dir. Midland Building Corp., Chgo., 1938-48; ex-div. sec. and treas. Mernat Trading Co., Inc. (N.Y.); ex-dir. McCrory Stores Corp., Atlas Stores Corp., Chain Store Shareowners, Inc., H. Milgrim & Bros., Inc. (N.Y. City); A. Hollander & Son, Inc., 1929-44. Chmn. Am. Italian Congress, 1946. Organizer, chmn. Italian Divs. Liberty Loan Com., Nat. War Savings Com., New York, 1917-19; mem. Greater Italy Dollar Loan Com., 1920. Trustee, v.p. The Marconi Meml. Found., Inc., 1937; mem. Nat. Com. of America Spanish Relief Fund; mem. commn. on citizenship Cath. U. Am. Mem. Civil Legion of U.S., Old Italy-America Soc. (founder 1917-18), Royal Italian Geog. Soc., Am. Irish Hist. Soc. (life), Sociedad de Geografia y Estadistica de Mexico; hon. mem. and gold medalist Italian Acad. Sciences and Letters (Genoa); corr. mem. Biographic Inst. of Vienna, Pontifical "Academia Tiberina" of Rome, Collegio Araldico Romano (Roman Coll. of Heralds); hon. mem. Soc. Acad. Histoire Internat. (Paris), Società Luigi Camoens (Naples), Sociedad Hispano-Am. de Heraldica y Genealogia (Mexico), Soc. Siciliana di Storia Patria (Palermo); hon. pres. Monarchial Party of Sicily, Italy, 1948. Diploma from Dante Alighieri Soc. of Italy for 25 yrs. service for Italian culture, 1937; fellow Andhra Research U., Jeypore, India, 1939. Received an illuminated parchment from the citizens of Ravello, Italy, signed by the Archbishop of Amalfi, the public authorities, the nobility, clergy and populace attesting to his services in raising funds for the restoration of the famous XIII Cathedral of St. Pantaleone, 1933. Del. in U.S. of Montenegrin "loyalist government" (headquarters Rome) of which the late Queen Milena was regent (1921-24); founder and chmn. Jan. 1924, Com. for Montenegrin Independence; founder and chmn. Am. League for Italy, 1935; chmn. Council of Americans of Italian Origin; chmn. Am. Bill of Rights Day Assn. (N.Y.). Grand Master Equestrian Amalfitan Order of St. Andrew Apostle (Archdiocese of Amalfi, Italy); pres. Amalfi Relief Fund, New York (for support of 400 children in orphanages, Amalfi and vicinity). Decorated Medal of Legionnaires of Fiume; Chevalier Order of Crown of Italy, 1921; Grand Cordon Order of Danilo I (Montenegro), 1922; Grand Cross of Montenegrin Red Cross, 1922; Grand Officer and mem. Am. Nat. Council Order of Grand Officer and mem. Am. Nat. Council Order of Holy Sepulchre (Vatican); Knight Order N.S. de la Mercede (Spain); Knight Constantinian Order of St. George (House of Bourbon, Naples and Sicily); Cross of Loreto and Lateran Cross (Vitican); Grand Cross Order of St. Lazare; Grand Crosses; Order San Domingo de Guzman; Imperial Nemagnic Constantinian Order St. Stephen; Order St. Hubert of Lorraine and Bar (Europe) (Lt. Gen. in the U.S.); Santa Brigida di Svezia (Naples); Universalis Meriti (France); Legion of Honor of the Immaculate Conception (Sicily), Grand Cross Order of San Juan Bautista Puerto Rico, 1947. Awarded Silver Medal of Royal Italian Geog. Soc., 1948; Silver Jubilee Medal, Soc. de Salvare, Romania, 1948; pres. société Internat. de l'Ordre de Danilo I. Mem. Orders and Medals Society Am., Italian Hist. Soc. Am. (hon.), Unione Lavoratori Italiani all' Estero (Trieste) (hon.). Roman Catholic. Author: The Italo-American Entente, 1925; Montenegro's Right to Live, 1928; also many pamphlets on Italian-American finances, Balkan affairs and chain store finance; publisher The Rubicon, (monthly review of public affairs), 1941—; writer of column for the Italian lang. newspapers in U.S. Home: 12 E. 87th St., N.Y.C. 28. Office: 50 Broadway, N.Y.C. 4. Deceased.

CRISPIN, M(ordecai) Jackson, banker; b. Berwick, Pa., May 13, 1875; s. Benjamin Franklin and Margaret (Jackson) C.; A.B., Princeton, 1896; m. Marie Brockway, June 7, 1900 (died 1907); 1 dau., Elizabeth Brockway (Countess Tripcovich); m. 2d, Erma Marchant, Apr. 3, 1916 (div.); m. 3d, Andree Detrez, Sept. 23, 1931; 1 dau., Jacqueline Marguerite. In employ First Nat. Bank, Berwick, Pa., 1896; with Jackson & Woodin Mfg. Co., Berwick, 1897-99, and successor Am. Car & Foundry Co., 1899-1901; gen. mgr. and treas. U.S. Metal & Mfg. Co., N.Y.C., 1901-16; then with N.Y. office Am. Car & Foundry Co. until retirement, 1920; dir. First National Bank of Berwick, Pa., 1903—, pres., 1909—. Pres. bd. trustees Crispin Cemetery (private) Phila., 1924—, (City Council surrounded it with Holme-Crispin Park, 1928); trustee State Teachers Coll., Bloomsburg, Pa., 1940-44; mem. com. and in charge research to compile and complete Falaise Roll of seigneurs of William the Conqueror, 1930-38; later edited and published the Roll. Decorated Officer of Acad., 1931; Chevalier of Legion of Honor (France), 1937. Served as gen. chmn. Sesquicentennial Com., Berwick, Pa.; Berwick-on-Tweed, Eng., named Crispin Road after him, 1936. Long active in local civic affairs; donated to Berwick High School the Crispin Meml. athletic field, 1929; donated ground for Berwick Hosp. and Nurses Home; officially cited by Dept. Pa. of Am. Legion for distinguished services, 1938. Chmn. War Savings staff Victory Loan Com. and U.S.O. (Berwick); Columbia County chmn. War Finance Com. for all war loan drives. Mem. Council Swedish Colonial Soc., Vet. Corps Arty. State of New York, Soc. 1812. Mem. Soc. Colonial Wars, S.A.R., Am. Soc. French Legion of Honor (Pa. dir.). Recipient silver medal by Am. Car & Foundry Co. for services in World War. Republican (del. Nat. Rep. Conv. 1916). Episcopalian. Mason (32°). Clubs: Berwick (Pa.) Golf; Valley Country (Hazelton, Pa.); Westmoreland (Wilkes-Barre, Pa.); Racquet (Phila.); University, Bankers (New York City); American (Paris). Author: Falaise Roll, Recording Prominent Companions of William, Duke of Normandy, at the Conquest of England, 1938; Captain William Crispin; Crispin's of Kingston-on-Hull; Thomas Holme Tercentenary. Presented stained glass window to St. Nicholas Church, Carrickfergus, Ireland, commemorating burial in the chancel of Capt. William Crispin's father, another Capt. William Crispin. Mem. Acad. of Rouen. Author: The Crispen Cemetery. Home: Berwick, Pa. Died July 2, 1953; buried Mausoleum, Pine Grove Cemetery, Berwick.

CRISS, Clair C(arlton), ins. exec.; b. Sac City, Ia., Apr. 10, 1879; s. James Louis and Villa (Wodell) C.; M.D., Creighton U., 1912; m. Mabel L. Chambers, Dec. 1, 1901. Pvt. practice of medicine, Omaha; treas. and gen. mgr., Mutual Benefit Health and Accident Assn., Omaha, 1910-33, president, 1933-49, chmn. bd. since 1949; pres. United Benefit Life Ins. Co., 1926-49, chmn. bd. since 1949; pres. United Benefit Fire Ins. Co. since 1946. Recipient Distinguished. Citizen award from Omaha C. of C., 1944. Mem. Internat. Claim Assn., U.S. and Omaha C. of C., Health and Accident Underwriters Conf., A.M.A., Neb. Med. Assn.; Ak-Sar-Ben. Elk. Club: Omaha Athletic. Home: 216 Fairacres Rd., Omaha 3. Office: 3316 Farnam St., Omaha, Neb. Died Mar. 9, 1952.

CRITCHLOW, Francis B. (kritch'lō), lawyer, special asst. atty. gen.; b. Salt Lake City, Utah, June 12, 1888; s. Edward B. and Mary W. Critchlow; A.B., Princeton U., 1910; m. Marie A. Bacon, Jan. 1, 1920; children—Francis B., John B. Admitted to Utah bar, 1912, and since in practice at Salt Lake City; mem. firm Critchlow and Critchlow; special asst. atty. gen. of U.S. since 1934. Club: University (Salt Lake City). Home: 348 South Citrus Av., Los Angeles, Calif. Office: Continental Bank Bldg., Salt Lake City, Utah; Federal Bldg., L.A. Died June 28, 1951.

CRITTENDEN, Eugene Casson, physicist; b. Oswayo, Pa., Dec. 19, 1880; s. Shuble Edgar and Ida Viola (Rowlee) C.; grad. Mansfield (Pa.) State Normal Sch., 1898; A.B., Cornell U., 1905; D.Sc. (hon.) Case Sch. Applied Sci., 1946; m. Norma Snyder, May 10, 1910; children—Marjorie, Eugene. Instr. physics Cornell U., 1905-09; physicist, various grades Nat. Bur. Standards, Washington, 1909—, chief div. of electricity, 1921-46, asst. dir. bur., 1933-46, asso. dir., 1946-50; retired; specialized in surveys of measurement and use of light, adminstrn. research, testing work in electricity. Official del. from U.S. to Internat. Commn. on Illumination, Geneva, 1924, Saranac Inn, 1928, Great Britain, 1931, Holland, 1939. V.p. Internat. Commn., 1939-48; pres. U.S. Nat. Com. of Internat. Electrotech. Commn., 1939-46. Mem. Internat. Com. on Weights and Measures, 1946—, chmn. Standards Council, dir. Am. Standards Assn., 1939-48. Recipient Illum. Engring. Soc. medal, 1946. Mem. Am. Inst. E E., Am. Physical Soc., Optical Soc. Am. (pres. 1932-33), Illum. Engring. Soc. of U.S. (pres. 1925), Illuminating Engring. Soc. of Great Britain, A.A.A.S., Washington Acad. Scis. (pres. 1940), Philos. Soc. Washington (pres. 1922), Gamma Alpha, Sigma Xi, Phi Beta Kappa Unitarian. Club: Cosmos. Home: 1715 Lanier Pl. N.W., Washington 9. Died March 28, 1956.

CROCE, Benedetto (krō'chā), philosopher; b. Pescasseroli, Province of Aquila, Feb. 25, 1866; ed. U. of Rome; m. Adele Rossi, 1914; children—Elena, Alda, Silvia, Lidia. Named Italian Senator for life, 1910. Minister of Edn., 1920-21; minister without Portfolio, 1943-44. Founded Italian Institute for Historical Studies, Naples, Italy, 1947. Author: Philosophy of Spirit, 1917; Theory and History of Historiography, 1933; History of Europe in the Nineteenth Century, 1933; Defense of Poetry, 1933; Recenti Controversie Intorno All unita Della Storia d' Italia, 1936; Freedom—Its Meaning (with others), 1940; History as the Story of Liberty, 1941. Editor of La Critica, 1903-44. Address: Trinita Maggiore, 12 Naples, Italy. Died Nov. 20, 1952.

CROCKARD, Frank Hearne, iron mfr.; b. Wheeling, W.Va., Oct. 29, 1873; s. William and Eliza Ann (Anderson) C.; ed. Lehigh U. and Mich. Coll. of Mines, Houghton; m. Elizabeth Handlan Mendel, Dec. 1898; 1 son, Francis Hearne. Asst. mgr., later mgr., Riverside Works Nat. Tube Co., Wheeling, W.Va., 1899-1906; v.p. Tenn. Coal, Iron & R.R. Co. (subsidiary U.S. Steel Corp.), 1906-17, in charge of operations and the work of rebuilding and extensions, in coal and ore mines, the By-Products Coke Plant, blast furnaces, steel works and community houses; pres. Nova Scotia Steel & Coal Co., New Glasgow and North Sydney, N.S., 1917-18, supplying shrapnel, heavy projectiles, railroad cars and steel ships, to Canadian and English armies; ex-pres. Woodward Iron Co., largest producer Southern merchant pig iron; cons. engr.; asst. dep. dir. steel br. WPB, Washington. Mem. adv. bd. Birmingham Ordnance Dist.; lt. col. Specialist Reserve, U.S. Army. Dir. Ala. Museum. Fellow A.A.A.S.; Am. Soc. C.E., Am. Inst. Mining and Metall. Engrs. (dir.), Ala. Mining Inst. (bd. of govs.), Am. Iron and Steel Inst., Brit. Iron and Steel Inst., Beta Theta Pi. Episcopalian. Clubs: Country, Mt. Brook (Birmingham, Ala.); Lotos (New York). Home: 2238 Highland Av., Birmingham, Ala. Died Mar. 2, 1955.*

CROCKER, Stuart Miller, public utilities; b. Cambridge, Mass., May 26, 1898; s. John Franklin and Martha Avice (Earl) C.; S.B., Harvard, 1921; m. Helen Carrère Barbour, July 1, 1947. Solicitor, commercial div., Radio Corp. of America, 1920-21; asst. to chmn. bd. Gen. Electric Co., 1922-27; v.p., treas. United Electric Securities Co., 1928-29; v.p. Internat. Gen. Electric Co., Inc., 1930-43; asst. to exec. v.p. Gen. Electric Co., 1938-39, v.p., 1940-43; pres., dir. and chmn. exec. com. The Columbia Gas System, Inc., 1943-51, now chmn., chief exec. officer, chmn. exec. com.; chmn., dir. Columbia Gas System Service Corp.; dir. Guaranty Trust Co. N.Y., Amere Gas Utilities Co., Atlantic Seaboard Corp., Central Ky. Natural Gas Co., Cumberland and Allegheney Gas Co., Home Gas Co., Keystone Gas Co., Inc., Mfrs. Light and Heat Co., Natural Gas Co. of W.Va., Ohio Fuel Gas Co., Preston Oil Co., Va. Gas Distbn. Corp., Va. Gas Transmission Corp., United Fuel Gas Co. Dir. A.R.C., (N.Y. chpt.), Nat. Information Bur. Served with North Sea Mine Force, U.S.N., 1917-18. Vice chmn. U.S. Nat. Com. World Power Conf. Sec. Am. delegation 1st Com. of Experts, apptd. by Reparations Commission during formation of Dawes Plan, 1924; sec. Am. delegation 2d com. of experts, apptd. by Reparations Commn., which drafted Young Plan, 1929. Vice chmn. Citizens Family Welfare Com., N.Y.C., 1933; vice chmn. and exec. dir. United Hosp. Campaign, 1935, chmn., 1936, member citizens com., 1937-43; mem. council, 1943—; exec. vice chmn. A.R.C. War Fund of Greater N.Y., 1942, mem. adv. com. 1943-46. Mem. Greater N.Y. Fund (members council), 1947—. Trustee, chmn. exec.

com. Roosevelt Hosp.; trustee Colgate U., Milton Acad., N.Y. Trade School. Mem. Acad. Polit. Sci., Am. Geog. Soc., Am. Mus. Natural History, Bibliophile Soc., Council Fgn. Relations, Nat. Inst. Social Sciences, Newcomen Soc. Eng. (Am. br.), Pilgrims of U.S., New Eng. Soc., North Sea Mine Force, Am. Gas Assn., C. of C. State of N.Y., Nat. Industrial Conf. Bd., Nat. Petroleum Council, Utilities Publication Com. Republican. Clubs: Harvard, Links, Madison Square Garden, Metropolitan, University, Economic (dir.) (N.Y.C.); Links Golf, Nat. Golf Links of Am., Southside Sportsmen's (L.I.); Duquesne, Rolling Rock (Pitts.); 1925 F St. (Washington); Eastward-Ho Country, Chatham Beach, Monomoy Yacht (Chatham, Mass.). Home: Suffolk Lane, East Islip, L.I., N.Y.; also "Mill Hill," Chatham, Cape Cod, Mass. Office: 120 E. 41st St., N.Y.C. 17. Died Sept. 3, 1956; buried Quaker Burying Ground, South Yarmouth, Mass.

CROFTS, Frederick Sharer, book pub.; b. Hudson, N.Y., Jan. 10, 1883; s. Clarence Livingston and Julia Maria Caldwell Parkhurst C.; A.B., Cornell U., 1905; Litt.D., Union Coll., Schenectady, N.Y., 1939; m. Margaret Livingston Lee, June 17, 1920. Salesman with The Century Co., 1905-10, mgr. edn. dept., 1910-18; mgr. ednl. dept. Harper & Brothers, 1919-24; founded F. S. Crofts & Co., Oct. 1924, since pres. and dir.; vice pres. and dir. Appleton-Century Crofts, Inc.; dir. Cornell Univ. Press, Comstock Publishing Co., Querido, Inc. Served as field dir. Am. Red Cross, 1918-19. Mem. Am. Hist. Assn., Am. Political Sci. Assn., Modern Lang. Assn., N.E.A., A.L.A., Sons of the Revolution. Republican. Episcopalian. Mason. Clubs: Century, The Players (New York); Nassau (Princeton); Graduates (New Haven); University (Madison, Wis.); University (Urbana, Ill.). Home: Hunting Ridge Road, Stamford, Conn. Office: 35 W. 32 St., N.Y. City. Died Sept. 16, 1951; buried St. James Church, Hyde Park, N.Y.

CROMELIN, Paul Bowen, lawyer; b. Washington, Jan. 30, 1890; s. William H. and Mattie J. (Selby) C.; LL.B., Georgetown U., 1912, L.L.M., M.L.D., 1913; m. Ruth Rice Sniffin, June 26, 1918; children—Jean (Mrs. Robert A. Meyers), Carol (Mrs. John H. Cragoe), Paul Bowen. Admitted to D.C. bar, 1912; practiced Washington; mem. Cromelin & Townsend, and predecessors, since 1919; asst. U.S. atty., D.C., 1919-21; gen. counsel Masonic and Eastern Star Home of D.C., Methodist Home of D.C. since 1922; v.p., dir. ABC Theatre, Inc., Silcrome, Inc. director Acacia Mutual Life Insurance Co., J. Frank Kelly, Inc., Law Reporter Printing Co. Mem. com. admissions and grievances U.S. Dist. Ct. for D.C.; mem. 4th regional area U.S. Loyalty Bd. Trustee Am. U., Friendly Sons of St. Patrick, D.C. Soc. for Crippled Children; chmn. bd. trustees Sibley Meml. Hosp. Served as capt. A.C., U.S. Army, 1917-18. Mem. Bar Assn. of D.C. (pres., 1942-43), Am. Bar Assn., Am. Law Inst., Barristers (pres., 1924), Washington Bd. Trade (past dir.), Soc. Natives, Am. Legion, Georgetown U. Alumni, Nat. Sojourners, Sigma Nu Phi. Methodist. Mason (33°, K.T., Shriner; master, 1920, grand master, 1937, chmn. jurisprudence com., Grand Lodge, F.A.A.M., Scottish Rite Bodies, D.C.), O.E.S. (grand patron, D.C., 1932), Royal Order of Scotland, Red Cross of Constantine, Royal Order Jesters. Clubs: Nat. Press, Rotary, Vinson, Congl. Country, Les Amis d'Escoffier. (Washington). Home: The Berkshire Apts., Washington. Office: 1366 National Press Bldg., Washington 4. Died May 14, 1956; buried Congressional Cemetery, Washington.

CROMPTON, George (crŏmp'tŭn); b. Worcester, Mass., June 7, 1872; s. George and Mary Christina (Pratt) C.; grad. Worcester Acad., 1891; A.B., Harvard, 1895; m. Alice Hastings, Apr. 11, 1896; children—George, Davis Hastings. Began with Crompton Loom Works, 1895; became pres. and treas. Crompton Associates, real estate, 1896; treas. Crompton & Knowles Loom Works, 1897-1900; mem. firm Crompton-Thayer Loom Co., 1903-07; treas. Reed-Prentice Co., 1912-16; v.p. and mem. bd. of investment People's Savings Bank of Worcester; dir. Crompton & Knowles Loom Works. Vice pres. St. Vincent's Hosp.; trustee Rural Cemetery. Mem. Econ. History Assn., Am. Antiquarian Soc., Am. Econ. Assn., Foreign Policy Assn., Acad. Polit. Science, Worcester Hist. Soc., Newcomen Society, Pi Gamma Mu. Republican. Catholic. Clubs: Worcester, Tatnuck, Worcester Fire Soc. (Worcester); Somerset, Harvard (Boston). Author: The Tariff—An Interpretation of Bewildering Problem; The Crompton Loom. Home: 74 William St., Worcester 9. Office: 340 Main St., Worcester 8, Mass. Died Nov. 16, 1953.

CROMWELL, Emma Guy (Mrs. William Cromwell), parliamentarian, ex-treas. of Ky.; b. Franklin, Ky.; d. Ashley and Alice Milliken (Quesenberry) Guy; grad. Howard Female Coll., Gallatin, Tenn.; studied U. of Mich., Western Normal Coll. (Bowling Green, Ky.), and at Chautauqua, N.Y.; m. William Cromwell, June 1, 1897 (dec. 1909). Elected state librarian of Ky., 1896; enrolling clerk, Ky. Ho. of Reps., 1916-18; parliamentarian Ky. Senate and Ho. of Reps., 1922; tchr. parliamentary law and parliamentarian various convs.; sec. state of Ky., 1924-27; state treas. of Ky., 1927-31; state park dir. of Ky. 4 years; apptd. state librarian and dir. of Library and Archives, Sept. 2, 1937. Mem. Bd. of Edn., Frankfort. Mem. D.A.R., U.D.C., Penwomen's League (Washington), Am. Auxiliary. Mem. Missionary Soc. of M.E. Church. Democrat. Clubs: Garden, Women's (Frankfort). Compiler: Compendium of Parliamentary Law, 1918; Citizenship (manual), 1920; Woman in Politics, 1939. Home: 627 State St. Address: Frankfort, Ky. Died July, 1952.

CROMWELL, Lincoln, banking; b. New York, N.Y., May 20, 1865; s. James William and Elizabeth Stuart (Henderson) C.; student Brooklyn Poly. Inst., 1879-82; A.B., Columbia, 1886, A.M., 1887, LL.B., 1889; prize fellow in science, 1886-89; m. Mabel Wheeler Smith, Oct. 30, 1895; children—Jarvis, Eleanor (wife of Dr. Fremont A. Chandler), Margaret, Elizabeth Mary (died June 16, 1925). Admitted to N.Y. bar, 1889; salesman for William Iselin & Co., commn. mchts., 1889-97, partner since 1897; chmn. of bd. William Iselin & Co., Inc., since 1931; dir. Iselin-Jefferson Co. and other corps.; trustee Bowery Savs. Bank, Bank of New York and 5th Av. Bank. Mem. bd. mgrs. St. Luke's Hosp.; pres. Phi Beta Kappa Assos., 1946-47, now dir.; commr. Municipal Art Commission of New York, 1944-47; vice pres. of N.Y. chapter Am.-Scandinavian Foundation; v.p. Citizen's Union of New York; dir. Legal Aid Soc. of New York, Grenfell Assn. America. Successively vestryman, treas., sr. warden Grace P.E. Ch., 1917-35. Chmn. of Mayor's Commn. on Revision N.Y. Teachers' Salaries, 1926-27; chmn. com. which arranged the contract between N.Y. City and U.S. Treasury to demolish old postoffice and build new federal courthouse and postoffice; mem. Governor's Commn. on Defaulted Guaranteed Mortgages, 1934-36; Governor's emergency scrip committee, 1932. With Council of National Defense and Quartermaster's Department, 1917-18, and sect. chief War Industries Bd., 1918. Awarded Columbia U. Service medal, 1936. Mem. The Pilgrims, Council on Fgn. Relations, Phi Beta Kappa (N.Y. Alumni pres. 1910), Delta Kappa Epsilon. Republican. Episcopalian. Clubs: Century, Racquet and Tennis, City, Merchants (New York); Authors' (London). Home: 711 Park Av. Office: 357 4th Av., N.Y.C. Died Feb. 8, 1952.

CRONIN, Edward Joseph, state ofcl.; b. Chelsea, Mass., Feb. 25, 1912; s. Joseph and Alice (Martin) C.; LL.B., Northeastern U., 1939. Admitted to Mass. bar, 1948; elected sec. commonwealth, Commonwealth of Mass., 1948, re-elected, 1950, 1952. Mem. Criminal Investigation Div. Agts. Assn. (exec. sec.), 63d Inf. Div. Assn. (past pres.), Am., Mass. bar assns., Mass. Chiefs Police Assn. (hon.), Am. Legion, Amvets, Vets. Fgn. Wars, Disabled Am. Vets, Hibernians, Mass. City Clks., Assn. State Secs., Nat. Lancers, Ancient and Honorable Arty. Co. Elk. K.C. Home: 61 Cook Av., Chelsea 50, Mass. Office: 18 Tremont St., Boston. Died Nov. 25, 1958.

CRONIN, John William, physician; b. Springfield, O., June 15, 1905; s. John James and May (Commins) C.; A.B., Miami Univ., Oxford, O., 1928, D.Sc., 1955; M.B., Univ. of Cincinnati, 1932, M.D., 1933; certificate of psychiatric training, U. of Colo., 1937, F.A.C.S., 1941; m. Virginia Dunkle, June 19, 1937; children—Virginia May, John William. Intern U.S. Marine Hosp., Stapleton, Staten Island, N.Y., 1932; practiced with U.S.P.H.S., 1933—, commd. regular corps, 1935, and promoted through grades to med. dir., 1947, served at U.S. Penitentiary, Lewisburg, Pa., 1933-35, U.S. Quarantine St., Miami, Fla., 1935-36, U.S. Marine Hosp., Seattle, Wash., 1936, U.S. Coast Guard Cutter Northland, Bering Sea and Arctic Ocean Patrol Force, 1936; instr. neurology and psychiatry, U. of Colo. Schs. of Medicine and Nursing, 1937; chief surgeon, U.S.P.H.S. Hosp., Lexington, Ky., 1937-40; chief medical officer U.S. Penitentiary, Leavenworth, Kan., 1940-41, instr. Cushing Memorial Hosp. Sch. of Nursing, Leavenworth, 1940-41, chief med. officer, Fed. Reformatory, El Reno, Okla., 1941-43, exec. med. officer, U.S. Coast Guard training sta., Brooklyn, N.Y. and U.S. Maritime Service training sta., Sheepshead Bay, N.Y., 1943-44, asst. chief Hosp. Dir. U.S. P.H.S. hdqrs., 1944, Med. officer in charge U.S. P.H.S. Dispensary, Washington, 1944-47, Chief, Fed. Employees Health Div., 1947-49, chief Div. Hosp. and Med. Facilities, 1949-56, chief Bur. Med. Services, 1956—. Diplomate American Bd. Preventive Medicine and Pub. Health. Fellow Am. Pub. Health Assn., A.C.S., A.M.A., Am. Coll. Preventive Medicine, Am. Psychiatric Assn.; mem. D.C. Med. Soc., Soc. Med. Assn., Med. Correctional Assn., Am. Assn. Indsl. Physicians and Surgeons, Mil. Surgeons Assn., Am. Public Health Assn., Am. Assn. Pub. Health physicians (trustee), Delta Kappa Epsilon, Alpha Kappa Kappa, Phi Sigma. Christian. Club: Cosmos (Washington). Contbr. articles to med. jours. Home: 5528 Trent St., Chevy Chase 15, Md. Office: U.S. Public Health Service Headquarters, Washington. Died Mar. 26, 1958; buried Arlington Nat. Cemetery.

CRONIN, Timothy T. (krō'nĭn), lawyer; b. Chicago, Ill., June 27, 1884; s. Timothy and Mary (Swanson) C.; ed. Milwaukee Normal Sch.; Ph.B., U. of Wisconsin, 1909, LL.B., 1913; m. Maud F. Clohisy, Nov. 9, 1916; children—Catherine M. Timothy J. Began career as attorney, 1913; U.S. atty. for Eastern Dist. of Wis., 1944—. Served with U.S. Army, World War I. Mem. Wis. State and Federal bar assns., Am. Legion (40 and 8), Phi Delta Phi. Rotarian, Knights of Columbus. Home: 28 Woodland Lane, Oconomowoc, Wis. Office: Federal Bldg., Milw. Died Sept. 20, 1955; buried St. Jeromes Cemetery, Oconomowoc, Wis.

CROOK, Jere Lawrence, surgeon; b. Henderson, Tenn., Mar. 10, 1874; s. Joseph Alexander (M.D.) and Martha Cooper (Cawthon) C.; M.A., Union U., Jackson, Tennessee, 1892; M.D., Vanderbilt University, 1894; LL.D., Union University, 1943; married Jennie J. Jones, Apr. 21, 1898 (died July 16, 1902); children—Senter Cawthon, Jere Lawrence; m. 2d, Millian Cooke Green, June 17, 1914; children—Lt. Joseph Alexander Crook, U.S.N., killed in service Aug. 16, 1942, William Grant, Nancy Green, Martha Cawthon, Angus McDonald Green. Interne City and County Hospital, Sacramento, Calif., 1894-95; practiced at Jackson, Tenn., since 1895; founder, 1908, with father, The Crook Sanitorium, Inc., now pres.; also serving as mem. surgical staffs various railways; chmn. med. adv. bd. of 6 counties World War I, and capt., S.A.T.C. unit, Union University; specialist in surgery U.S. Vets.' Bur. Trustee Union U.; ex-pres. Jackson Y.M.C.A. Fellow A.M.A., American College of Surgeons; mem. Southern Med. Assn. (pres. 1920-21), Tenn. State Med. Assn. (ex-pres.), Midsouth Post Graduate Medical Assembly, West Tennessee and Madison County medical socities (past president of each), American Association of Railway Surgeons (past pres.). Chmn. com. which wrote Constn. of Southern Med. Assn., 1906. Democrat. Baptist. Odd Fellow, Elk, K.P.; mem. W.O.W. Clubs: Jackson Rotary (ex-pres.), Jackson Country. Home: 1210 N. Highland Av. Office: The Crook Sanatorium, Jackson, Tenn. Died Oct. 31, 1953.

CROPLEY, Charles Elmore, fed. judicial officer; b. Georgetwon, D.C., July 28, 1894; s. Charles Barlow and Grace Willson (Elmore) C.; ed. by private tutors; m. Roma Wornall, Feb. 4, 1928; 1 dau., Louise Woodbridge. Page U.S. Supreme Ct., 1907, asst. clerk, 1913, served in all grades to additional dep., 1921, dep. clerk, 1927, clerk, sec. of all Supreme Ct. Memorial Meetings, since 1927; in binding div. Library of Congress, 1911; Smithsonian deposit, 1912, periodical div., 1912; agency corr. Southeastern div. Contl. Casualty Co., 1913; legal research and transcription for various states, fgn. govts., law firms; contbr. to bar assns. libraries; contbr. and editorial work for legal pub. cos., newspapers. Trustee Gunston Hall Corp., 1942; dir. Family Service Assn., 1941. Mem. Am. Judicature Soc. Episcopalian. Club: Chevy Chase (Md.). Collaborator with author: Robertson's Appelate Practice and Procedure in the Supreme Ct., U.S., 1928, (revised edition with forms, 1929). Home: 2900 Connecticut Av., Washington 8. Office: Supreme Court of the U.S., Washington 13. Died June 17, 1952; buried Oak Hill Cemetery, Washington.

CROSBY, Charles Noel, ex-congressman; b. Cherry Valley, O., Sept. 29, 1876; s. Hiram William and Fanny (Spellman) C.; student New Lyme (Ohio) Inst., 1889-93; B.S., Western Reserve U., 1896; student Allegheny Coll., 1896-97; m. Isabelle Fetterman, of Cherry Valley, O., 1901; children—Fanny, Theodore, Jean, Penelope (Mrs. R. A. Donaldson), Virginia, Charles N., Ronald, John, Ann. Organizer, 1901, National Silo & Lumber Co. (later merged into International Silo Co.), pres. and gen. mgr., 1901-33; bought control of Bunday Lumber Co., 1927. Owner and operator of 2 farms in Pa. and Ohio. Mem. 73d to 75th Congresses (1933-39), 29th Pa. Dist. Mem. Linesville and Meadville Sch. Bds., 1920-29; pres. Meadville C. of C., 1922-24. Mem. Beta Theta Pi. Democrat. Presbyn. Club: Iroquois. Home: Hyattstown, Md. Deceased.

CROSBY, Edwin Stanislau, corp. exec.; b. Bordentown, N.J., Nov. 13, 1887; s. John and Mary (Fitzpatrick) C.; M.E., Cornell, 1910; m. Iva Blanchard, Oct. 10, 1914; 1 son, James Blanchard. Chemist Internat. Harvester Co., Chgo., 1910-12; asst. sales mgr. DeLaval Steam Turbine Co., Trenton, N.J., 1912-17; v.p. in charge sales, dir. Celite Co., N.Y.C., 1920-28; pres. Johns-Manville Internat. Corp., N.Y. C., 1928—, Johns-Manville Boley, Ltd., Buenos Aires, Argentina, 1931—, Johns-Manville S.A., Belgium, 1931—; mng. dir. Johns-Manville Co., Ltd., Eng., 1930—; v.p. Canadian Johns-Manville Co., Ltd., Toronto; dir. Asbestos de Mexico, S.A., Roclaine, France. Dir. Societe des Dalles et Produits Amianetes, France, Societe Anonymeoour le Fabrication de Materiaux de Construction, Belgium, Fabrica Argentina de Materiales de Construccion, S.A., Argentina. Mem. Am. Soc. M.E. Roman Catholic. Clubs: Engineers, Cornell University (N.Y.C.); Baltusrol Gold (Springfield, N.J.). Home: 7 Washington Park, Maplewood, N.J. Office: 22 E. 40th St., N.Y.C. 16. Died May, 1958.

CROSBY, Harley N., judge; b. Parish, N.Y., June 25, 1873; s. Solomon H. and Celia Ann (Nutting) C.; B.L., Cornell, 1896, LL.B., 1897; LL.D., Syracuse U., 1944; m. Helen Inez Howe, Nov. 30, 1899;

children—Barbara C., Margaret I. Began law practice 1898; supervisor Town of Ellicott, Chautauqua County, N.Y., 1904-06; surrogate, same county, 1906-21; justice, Supreme Court of N.Y., 1922-28, asso. justice, appellate div., 4th dept., 1929-39; presiding justice, 1940-43; retired. Chmn. draft bd. World War I. Mem. Delta Chi. Republican. Mason. Club: University (Jamestown, N.Y.). Home: 1 Hough St., Falconer, N.Y. Died Apr. 26, 1955.

CROSBY, H(arold) E(llsworth), business exec.; b. Maryville, Mo., Jan. 22, 1899; s. Ullyses Grant and Jenny Lind (Pike) C.; B.S. in Archtl. Engring., Ia. State Coll., 1922; m. Lydia Clara Ferber, Dec. 27, 1924. Vice pres. constrn. div. and dir. G. C. Murphy Co.; v.p. and dir. Mack Realty Co. Served as 2d lt., F.A., U.S. Army, World War I, lt. col., Corps of Engrs., and Gen. Staff, World War II. Mem. bd. trustees, chmn. bldg. com. McKeesport Hosp.; dir., chmn. bldg. com. McKeesport YMCA. Mem. Am. Inst. Architects, Alpha Tau Omega, McKeesport, C. of C., Am. Legion. Mason (Shriner). Club: Youghiogheny Country (McKeesport). Home: 1512 Manor Av. Office: 531 Fifth Av., McKeesport, Pa. Died Jan. 12, 1958.

CROSIER, Edwin Neil, business exec.; b. McKeesport, Pa., Jan. 23, 1910; s. Fred Holston and Mae (Runyeon) C.; student Robert Morris Sch. Bus., Pitts., 1934; m. Rose Seddon, Jan. 10, 1931; children—Carol Rose, Penny Lee. With Price Waterhouse & Co., Pitts., 1930-49, jr. accountant to prin. of firm; sec., treas. Sharon Steel Corp., 1949—; dir. Carpentertown Coal & Coke Co., Pitts., Joanne Coal Co., Pitts., Steel Trucking, Inc., Dearborn, Mich., Mallory-Sharon Titanium Corp., Niles, O. Mem. Pa. Inst. C.P.A.'s, Am. Inst. Accountants, Am. Society Corporate Secs., Am. Iron and Steel Inst. Mason (32°). Home: 932 Hazen Rd., Sharpsville, Pa. Office: Sharon Steel Corp., Sharon, Pa. Died Sept. 22, 1956.

CROSKEY, John Welsh (krôs'kē), ophthalmologist; b. Phila., Pa., Jan. 26, 1858; s. Henry and Ann (Dunnohew) C.; student Swarthmore Coll., 1886-87; M.D., Medico-Chirurg. Coll., Phila., 1889 (gold medalist); certificate of proficiency, Phila. Sch. of Anatomy, 1889; m. Elisabeth Estes Browning, Dec. 15, 1880 (dec.); children—Henry B., Elisabeth B. (Mrs. L.E. Bailey, dec.), Marion L., John Welsh Croskey, Jr. (dec.), m. 2d, Marie Lanche Bretschneider, January 21, 1939; two stepsons, Gordon Bretschneider, Louis Lanche Bretschneider. Began as chief assistant to surgical clinic, Medico-Chirurgical Coll., 1889, later lecturer on minor and operative surgery; assistant surgeon to Wills Hospital, 1891-97; surgeon same, 1897-1902; appointed consulting ophthalmic surgeon to George Nugent Home for Baptists, 1899; ophthalmic surgeon to Philadelphia Gen. Hosp., apptd. 1900, cons. surgeon, apptd. 1925; also lecturer to training Sch. for Nurses; ophthalmic surgeon to Samaritan Hosp., Annie M. Warner Hosp., 1902-05; prof. ophthalmology, laryngology and otology, Temple U., 1902-05, etc.; acting assistant surgeon, United State Public Health Service; now retired; ophthalmologist Home of the Merciful Saviour for Crippled Children. Formerly editor and owner International Medical Magazine, and editor Medico-Chirurg. Jour. Fellow Am. Acad. Ophthalmology and Oto-Laryngology, A.M.A.; mem. Med. Soc. State of Pa., Phila. County Med. Soc. (sec. bd. of censors), W. Phila. Med. Assn. (ex-pres.), Hist. Soc. Pa., Valley Forge Historical Society, Fort Washington Historical Society, Academy Natural Science of Phila., Am. Med. Authors Assn., Colonial Soc. America, S.R., Gen. Alumni U. of Pa., Medical Alumni U. of Pa., Alumni Assn. Medico-Chirurg. Coll. (ex-pres.), Navy League (life), St. George Soc., St. Andrews Soc., Dickens Fellowship. Republican. Mason. Clubs: Kiwanis, Paxon Hollow Golf, Overbrook Golf, Merion Cricket, Golfers Association of Medical Society State of Pa. (ex-pres.), Am. Med. Golfing (ex-pres.), Penn Club (dir.). Author: Dictionary of Ophthalmic Terms, 1907; History of Blockley; Anatomy and Physiology of the Eye and Its Appendages; Historical Catalogue of the St. Andrews Society. Home: Fort Washington, R.F.D. No. 1, Ambler, Pa. Died July 30, 1951.

CROSS, Arthur Chester, educator; b. Mecosta, Mich., Sept. 3, 1884; s. Edward A. and Catherine Rachael (Harrison) C.; student Western State Normal Sch., Kalamazoo, 1909-11; A.B., U. Mich., 1916, A.M., 1917; m. Gertrude E. Ryan, Aug. 8, 1921; children—Arthur Douglas, Richard John. Tchr. Aberdeen (S.D.) High Sch., 1916; prof. history and principal U. Wyo. Tng. High Sch., 1917-20; prof. history Kirksville (Mo.) State Tchrs. Coll., 1921; supt. schs., Greybull, Wyo., 1922; sec. Bur. Community Orgn., U. Colo., 1923-30, state high sch. visitor, chmn. state com. on secondary edn. for North Central Assn., asst. prof. edn., 1930-37, asso. prof. edn., 1937—, asst. dir. extension div., 1931-37, mem. exec. com., 1935-37, mem. Com. of Seven, 1941-42, mem. adminstrv. com., 1942, North Central Assn.; asso. prof. edn. U. Hawaii, Honolulu, summer session, 1940; acting dir. extension div. U. Colo., 1943-46, dir. extension div., 1946-51. Chmn. State Com. for Revision of Standards for Accrediting Nurses' Tng. Schs., 1935; chmn. adv. com. State Board Nurse Examiners, 1938—; chmn. Gov's. Adv. Com. Edn., and Tng. Vets., 1945—. Served as pvt. inf. U.S. Army, 1918. Dir. Colo. Mental Hygiene Society, 1930-33, Colo. Tb Assn., 1929—, Assn., Colo. Prison Assn., 1930—; pres. Colo. State-Wide Health Agencies, 1926-28; pres. Boulder County Tb Assn., 1924-28, dir., 1939—; v.p. Colo. Edn. Assn., 1949., pres., 1949-50; mem. com. on use of evaluation criteria N. Central Assn. Secondary Schs. Mem. Schoolmasters Assn., Kappa Delta Pi (counsellor 1942), Phi Delta Kappa. Democrat. Clubs: Rotary, Colorado Schoolmasters (pres. 1942-43). Home: 764 13th St., Boulder, Colo. Died Apr. 12, 1951; buried Green Mountain Cemetery, Boulder.

CROSS, Hardy, civil engr.; born in Nansemond County, Va., Feb. 10, 1885; s. Thomas Hardy and Eleanor Elizabeth (Wright) C.; B.A., Hampden-Sydney Coll., 1902, B.S., 1903, hon. Sc.D., 1934; B.S. in C.E. from Mass. Inst. of Tech., 1908; M.C.E., Harvard, 1911; hon. M.A., Yale Univ., 1937; hon. D.Eng., Lehigh Univ., 1937; m. Edythe Hopwood Fenner, Sept. 5, 1921. Instr. in English, Hampden-Sydney Coll., 1902-03; instr. in English and mathematics, Norfolk Acad., 1903-06; engr. bridge dept. M.P. Ry., 1908-10; asst. prof. civ. engring., Brown U., 1911-18; gen. practice structural engring., 1918-21; prof. structural engring., Univ. of Ill., 1921-37; became prof. civil engineering Yale, 1937, former head dept., now prof. emeritus Strathcoma. Mem. Am. Soc. C.E., (awarded Norman medal, 1933), Am. Ry. Engring. Assn., Am. Concrete Inst. (awarded Wason medal 1936), Western Soc. Engrs., Conn. Soc. Civil Engineers, Am. Soc. Engring. Edn., Royal Society Arts, American Institute Consulting Engineers (awarded Lamme medal, 1944), Am. Acad. Arts and Sciences, Kappa Alpha, Sigma Xi, Tau Beta Pi, Sigma Tau, Chi Epsilon, Omicron Delta Kappa. Democrat. Mason. Author: Continuous Frames of Reinforced Concrete (with N. D. Morgan), 1932; also bulls. and tech. articles. Home: 207-78th St., Virginia Beach, Va. Died Feb. 11, 1959.

CROSS, Harold L., lawyer, educator; b. N.Y.C., July 8, 1890; s. Charles A., and Jennie (Lown) C.; LL.B., Cornell, 1911; LL.D., U. Me., 1950; m. Elaine Foster, June 19, 1915; children—Harold L. (killed in action in Germany), Malcolm A., Schuyler F. Atty. Sackett, Chapman, Brown & Cross, 1916-37; prof. journalism Columbia, 1937-50, asso. dean 1949-50; dean Grad. Sch. of Journalism, Chungking, China, 1943-44; counsel Brown Cross and Hamilton. Recipient Peter Zenger award U. Ariz., 1958. Mem. Am. Soc. Newspaper Editors, Cornell Law Assn., Kappa Sigma, Phi Delta Phi, Sigma Delta Chi (Distinguished Achievements Fellow). Republican. Presbyn. Mason, Rotarian. Author: The Peoples Right to Know, 1953; also editorials, articles on newspaper law. Home: East Boothbay, Me. Office: 154 Nassau St., N.Y.C. Died Aug. 9, 1959; buried Pluckemin, N.J.

CROSS, Harry Parsons, lawyer; b. Wakefield, R.I., Sept. 29, 1873; s. Elisha Watson and Frances Cooper (Wright) C.; graduate St. Paul's Sch., 1892; A.B., Yale, 1896; LL.B., Harvard, 1900; m. Lorania Carrington King, 1896 (dec. 1904); children—Lorania (Mrs. Ronald M. Scott), Frances King (Mrs. Philip H. Cruikshank), Harry King; m. 2d Virginia Gammell, 1906 (div.); children—Hope Gammell (Mrs. Hope Gammell Curtis), Virginia (Mrs. Carlton R. Mabley, Jr.), Elisa Anthony Hoppin (Mrs. Curtis B. Brooks); m. 3d Lucile Lawson Atwood, 1929. Admitted to R.I. bar, 1901, Circuit Ct. U.S., 1902, Supreme Ct. U.S., 1909; 2d asst. atty. gen. R.I., 1907-12, 1st asst. atty. gen., 1913; mem. Greenough, Easton & Cross, 1912-29, Greenough, Lyman & Cross since 1929; sec. Hopelands Co.; dir., mem. exec. com. Indsl. Trust Co., Providence, bd. mgrs. Westerly; dir. Calumet & Hecla Consol. Copper Co., Providence Jour. Co., R.I. Tool Co. Chmn. senate redistricting com. R.I. State Legislature, 1925; chmn. state commn. for re-apportionment legislative dists. R.I. 1928; chmn. R.I. State House Commn., 1933-39; incorporator, sec. Providence Govtl. Research Bur., 1932-43; sec. R.I. Pub. Expenditure Council, 1943-50. Chmn. Republican State Conv., 1906, 18; del.-at-large Rep. Conv., Chgo., 1916; R.I. rep. auxiliary com. Pres. Taft Inaugural Ball, 1909; state chmn. Pres. Roosevelt Meml. Campaign, 1919. Pres., trustee, incorporator Lincoln Sch., 1912; pres. R.I. Soc. Prevention Cruelty Children, 1924-35, hon. chmn. bd. dirs. since 1935; mem. bd. trustees, executive com. Roger Williams Gen. Hosp. Mem. Gen. Soc. Colonial Wars (past historian gen., lt. gov. gen.; v. gov. gen. since 1951, council mem. since 1945), S.A.R., Newcomen Soc. Eng., Am., R. I. State bar assns., Eng. Speaking Union (dir. R. I.), Psi Upsilon. Epis. Mason. Clubs: Somerset (Boston); Graduates, Elihu (New Haven); Knickerbocker, Yale (N.Y.C.); Rolling Rock (Pitts.); Clambake, Reading Room (Newport, R.I.); Squantum (past pres.), Providence Art, Hope, Anawan, Agawam Hunt (Providence). Home: Watch Hill. Office: 15 Westminster St., Providence. Died Mar. 12, 1955.

CROSS, John Walter, architect; b. S. Orange, N.J., Feb. 24, 1878; s. Richard James and Matilda (Redmond) C.; A.B., Yale, 1900; student Sch. of Mines (Columbia), 1900-02; grad. Ecole Nationale et Speciale des Beaux Arts, Paris, 1907; m. Lily Lee Page, Aug. 17, 1908 (died 1920); children—John Walter, Howard Page; m. 2d, Katherine Hoyt (Mather), June 2, 1932. Was associated with his brother Eliot Cross, firm of Cross & Cross, New York, 1907-42; organized firm of Cross and Son, Jan., 1946; firm architects City Bank Farmers Trust Co. Bldg., Radio Bldg., Stone & Webster Bldg., N.Y. City, Guaranty Trust Bldgs., 5th Av. and 44th St., N.Y. City, and Place de la Concorde, Paris, France, the Douglas Elliman Bldg., Church of Notre Dame, Chickering Bldg., Postum Bldg., Barclay Hotel, Harriman Bldg., Lee Higginson & Co. Bldg., Gen. Electric Bldg., Union & New Haven Trust Co. Bldg., Walter Camp Memorial, New Haven, U.S. Post Office, Jamaica, L.I., Federal Office Bldg., New York, Links Club, Hangar Club, Aetna Life Ins. Bldg., New York, Tiffany & Co. Bldg., New York. Chief architect U.S. Housing Corp., Dept. of Labor, 1918. Mem. Art Commn. of N.Y. City, 1926-29; mem. Nat. Commn. Fine Arts, Washington, 1928-32. Decorated Order of Polonia Restituta (Poland). Fellow A.I.A. (medal of honor N.Y. section, 1925), Arch. League N.Y.; mem. Nat. Inst. of Arts and Letters, Beaux Arts Institute Design, Society des Architectes Diplôme par le Gouvernement (Paris). Republican. Clubs: Century, Links Golf, National Golf, Racquet and Tennis, Coffee House, Links. Home: 960 Fifth Av. Office: 505 Park Av., N.Y. City. Died July 25, 1951.

CROSS, William Campbell, business exec.; b. Chgo., Jan. 24, 1887; s. Austin J. and Mary D. (Bell) C.; student pub. schs. Chicago; m. Leonora Beatrice Kirner, Jan. 11, 1912. Began as plant clk. Carnation Co., Los angeles, 1907, successively purchasing agt., plant supt., asst. gen. supt., asst. eastern mgr., gen. supt., v.p., dir., now ret. Mason. Clubs: Union League (Chgo.); Country (Los Angeles). Home: 117 N. Glenroy Av., Los Angeles 49. Office: 5045 Wilshire Blvd., Los Angeles 36. Died Nov. 1959.

CROSSEN, George Edward, coll. dean; b. St. Paul, Minn., July 21, 1905; s. William and Ellen Agnes (Burke) C.; B.S., Univ. of Minn., 1933, M.S., 1937, Ph.D., 1940; m. Eleanor Ruth Curry, Sept. 22, 1934; 1 son, George William. Instructor pharmacy, College of Pharmacy, University of Minnesota, 1933-41, asst. prof., 1941-42; dean and prof. of pharmacy Drake Univ., 1942-45; dean and prof. of pharmacy Ore. State Coll., Corvallis, since 1945; tech. consultant since 1941; dir. analytical lab. Ore. Bd. of Pharmacy since 1945. Mem. Am. Pharm. Assn. (chmn. pract. sect., 1944-46; pres. North Pacific br., 1947-49), Am. Assn. College Pharmacists (exec. com. 1948-49), Am. Chem. Soc., A.A.A.S., Minn., Ia. and Ore. pharm. assns., C. of C., Rho Chi (exec. com. 1947-52), Kappa Psi (1st grand vice regent 1947-49), Sigma Xi, Phi Lambda Upsilon. Republican. Roman Catholic. Elk, K.C., Kiwanian. Author: Laboratory Manual of Inorganic Pharmaceutical Chemistry (with C. H. Rogers), 1941; Pharmaceutical Preparations (with Karl J. Goldner), 1942; The Art of Compounding (with Justin L. Powers), 1942. Mem. Revision Com., U.S. Pharmacopeia, 1950-60. Home: 1260 Spring Lane, Corvallis, Ore. Died June 28, 1958.

CROSSEN, Harry Sturgeon (krôs's'n), gynecologist; b. Centerville, Ia., Feb. 2, 1869; s. James and Sarah Affinity (Sturgeon) C.; M.D., Washington U., 1892; m. Mary Frances Wright, Mar. 28, 1895; children—Theodore Wright, Ruth Victoria (wife of Dr. Henry Spence Brookes, Jr.), Robert James, Virginia Mabel (Mrs. Charles McEwen Avery, Jr.), David Frederic. Intern, later asst. supt. St. Louis (Mo.) City Hosp., 1892-95; supt. and surgeon in charge St. Louis Female Hospital, 1895-99; began private practice, St. Louis, 1899; instructor in gynecology, Washington U., 1901-21, prof. clin. gynecology, 1921-35, professor emeritus since 1935; gynecologist, Barnes Hospital, St. Luke's Hospital, St. Louis Maternity Hospital. Served as captain, later major Medical Corps, U.S. Army, in France, 1917-19. Trustee Pilgrim Congregational Church, St. Louis. Fellow A.M.A.; mem. Mo. State Med. Assn., Am. Gynecol. Society, St. Louis Gynecological Society. Club: University. Author: Diseases of Women, 1907; Operative Gynecology, 1915; Gynecology for Nurses, 1927; Synopsis of Gynecology, 1931; Foreign Bodies Left in Abdomen, 1940. Home: 37 Algonquinwood, Webster Groves, Mo. Office: University Club Bldg., St. Louis. Died Mar. 10, 1951; buried Oak Grove Cemetery, St. Louis.

CROSSER, Robert, ex-congressman; b. Holytown, Lanarkshire, Scotland, June 7, 1874; s. James and Barbara C.; brought to America, 1881; A.B., Kenyon Coll., 1897, M.C.L., 1929, LL.D., 1942; student Columbia U. Law Sch., 1897-98 (part of yr.), LL.B., Cincinnati Law Sch., 1901; m. Isabelle D. Hogg, Apr. 18, 1906; children—Justine Crosser Sweeny (deceased), Barbara Crosser Sweeny, Robert, James (deceased). Engaged in practice of law, Cleveland, O., 1901-30; prof. law of torts Baldwin-Wallace Law Sch., Cleveland, 1904; mem. Ohio Ho. of Reps., 1911-12; mem. 4th Constl. Conv., 1912; mem. 63d Congress (1913-15), Ohio at large; and 64th, 65th, and 68th to 83d Congresses (1915-19 and 1923-55), 21st Ohio Dist. Recipient Aztec Eagle, Mex. Pres. Nat. Popular Govt. League; mem. Am. Acad. Polit.

& Social Sci., Acad. Polit. Sci., Alpha Delta Phi. Democrat. Mem. Phi Delta Phi. Home: 10311 Ramona Blvd., S.E., Cleve. 4. Died June 3, 1957.

CROSSETT, Edward C(lark), lumber co. exec.; b. Davenport, Ia., Aug. 7, 1882; s. Edward Savage and Harmony E. (Clark) C.; A.B., Amherst Coll., 1905; married Elisabeth A. Rankin, January 2 1909. Pres. and director Crossett Timber Company, Wauna, Ore., 1908, Crossett Western Co., 1923, chmn. bd., 1936; pres. and dir. Fordyce (Ark.) Lumber Co., 1911, chmn. bd., 1950; v.p. and dir. Crossett (Ark.) Lumber Co., Cossett Timber & Development Co., Bastrop, La., 1906, pres., 1935, chmn. bd. 1950—; chmn. bd. The Crossett Company, 1953—. Director bur. chpt. prodn. A.R.C., 1917-18, dir. dept. development, nat. hdqrs., 1919. Fellow Royal Photog. Soc. (London), Photog. Soc. America; member Phi Beta Kappa, Delta Kappa Epsilon. Mason. Clubs: Chicago, University, Racquet (Chicago); New York Yacht. Home: 1517 Lombardy Rd., Pasadena 5, Cal. Office: 80 E. Jackson Blvd., Chicago 4; also Crossett Lumber Co., Crossett, Ark. Died July 30, 1955.

CROSSFIELD, Richard Henry, educator, clergyman; b. Lawrenceburg, Ky., Oct. 22, 1868; s. Richard H. and Elizabeth (Jackson) C.; A.B., Ky. U. (now Transylvania Coll.), 1889; grad. The Coll. of the Bible, Lexington, Ky., 1892; M.A., Ph.D., U. of Wooster, 1900; LL.D., Georgetown Coll., 1915, U. of Ky., 1917, Transylvania, 1930; m. Annie Ritchie Terry, Feb. 5, 1895; children—Dorothy, Terry. Ordained minister of Disciples of Christ, 1894, pastor Glasgow, later Owensboro, Ky., 17 yrs.; pres. Transylvania Coll., 13 yrs.; pres. Coll. of the Bible, 8½ yrs.; pres. William Woods Coll., Fulton, Mo., 3 yrs.; pastor First Christian Ch., Norfolk, Va., 1924-27, First Christian Ch., Birmingham, Ala., 1927-37. President Transylvania Coll., Lexington, Ky., 1938-39, pres. emeritus since 1939. Mem. Bd of Edn. of Disciples of Christ; mem. Birmingham Sunday School Council, Pension Fund of Disciples of Christ. Mem. American Acad. of Polit. and Social Science. Clubs: Internat. Kiwanis, Country, Clergy, Theta Phi. Author: The Christian Principles of Sociology and Their Application to Present-Day Problems; Pilgrimages of a Parson. Contbr. to mags. Lecturer and traveler. Home: 212 The Ridgely, Birmingham, Ala. Died July 30, 1951.*

CROSSLEY, Robert J(erome), banker; b. Carbondale, Pa.; Dec. 4, 1902; s. Robert Giddings and Anna Elizabeth (Young) C.; m. Myrtle Amelia Engdall, Sept. 23, 1925; 1 son, Robert Jerome. With 1st Nat. Bank, Chicago, 1928—, v.p., 1947—. Mem. Am. Inst. of Banking (past dir., Chgo. chapter), Grad. Sch. of Banking (permanent pres., class, 1943), Robert Morris Associates (past pres., Chgo. chapter, past nat. director), Chgo. Assn. of Credit Men. Republican. Methodist. Clubs: Bankers (Chicago), Union League, Executives (Chicago) Flossmoor Country. Home: 1360 Lake Shore Dr., Chgo. Office: 38 South Dearborn St., Chgo. Died March 18, 1960.

CROTHERS, Bronson, physician; b. Elmira, N.Y., July 10, 1884; s. Samuel McChord and Louise (Bronson) C.; A.B., Harvard, 1905, M.D., 1910; m. Alice Ames, Dec. 24, 1917; 1 son, Charles Gordon. Intern Mass. Gen. Hosp., 1910-11; intern Children's Hosp., Boston, 1911, faculty, mem. staff, 1920—; sr. cons. neurology Children's Med. Center, 1952—; asst. neurology Harvard Med. Sch., 1920-21, instr. neurology, asst. pediatrics, 1924-27, instr. pediatrics, 1927-30, instr. neurology, 1927-29, asst. prof. pediatrics, 1929-44, clin. prof. pediatrics, 1944-52, emeritus, 1952—. Served as maj., M.C., U.S. Army, 1918-19. Mem. Am. Pediatric Soc. (past pres.), Am. Neurol. Assn., Am. Acad. Pediatrics, Am. Acad. Neurology; asso. mem. Brit. Pediatric Assn. Home: 81 Raymond St., Cambridge, Mass. Died July 17, 1959.

CROTHERS, George Edward (krŭth′ẽrz), lawyer; b. Wapello, Louisa County, Ia., May 27, 1870; s. John and Margaret Jane (Fair) C.; mother a sister of late Senator James G. Fair; lived on Ia. farms until 13, then moved to San José, Calif.; A.B., Stanford, 1895, A.M., 1896; m. Elizabeth, d. of late W. H. Mills, of San Francisco, Mar. 23, 1911 (died Aug. 18, 1920). One of attys. of record for the Fair trustees during protracted litigation, 1899-1902; had personal charge of forgery branch of Fair estate litigation. Jointly with brother wrote and caused to be passed by legislature, 1899, and by people, 1900, amendment to State Constn. enabling the correction of defects in the organization and grants of Stanford U. and the perfecting of its title; also several acts of legislature to same end; represented Mrs. Stanford and trustees in amendment, confirmation and legal construction of Univ. Grants, and during closing years of her life was sole trustee of property valued at several million dollars which Mrs. Stanford provided should go to the univ. through him upon her death. Apptd. judge Superior Court, San Francisco, Aug. 12, 1913; elected to succeed himself, Nov. 3, 1915; retired from bench, 1921, and resumed practice. First alumni trustee Stanford, 1902-12 (sec., asst. treas., mgr., bd. trustees, 1902-08); one of 5 trustees Stanford Kindergarten Trust; hon. trustee San Francisco Boys' Club, Inc. Donor of Crothers Hall, a dormitory for advanced law students, also installed in the dormitory a law library of about 6000 books, at Stanford, 1948, also Crothers Meml. Hall, dormitory for engring. students, in honor of mother, 1953. Pres. Gen. Alumni Assn. Stanford, 1899-1900 and 1913-14; mem. Am. Hist. Assn., Cal. Hist. Soc., Am. Law Inst., Am. Polit. Sci. Assn., Nat. Municipal League, Seismol. Soc. Am., Sigma Nu, Phi Delta Phi, Schoolmasters' Club of Calif. Chmn. Independent Republicans, San Francisco, 1909-12, and Rep. County Com., 1912-13. Episcopalian. Clubs: University, Pacific Union, Monterey Peninsula, Menlo Country, Commercial, Stanford Faculty, Press, Commonwealth. Author: (booklets): Outline of the Founding of the Leland Stanford Junior University; The Educational Ideals of Jane Lathrop Stanford. Home: 1000 California St., San Francisco 6. Office: 315 Montgomery St., San Francisco 4. Died May 16, 1957.

CROTHERS, Rachel, playwright; b. Bloomington, Ill., 1871; d. Dr. Eli Kirk and Marie Louise (de Pew) Crothers; grad. Ill. State Normal Sch., Normal, Ill., 1892. Mem. Soc. Am. Dramatists, Authors' Leagut America, P.E.N. Founder, and pres. Stage Women's War Relief. Clubs: Colony (charter mem.), Cosmopolitan, Town Hall. Author: (plays) The Three of Us; The Coming of Mrs. Patrick; Myself Bettina; A Man's World; Young Wisdom; Ourselves; The Heart of Paddy-Whack; Old Lady 31; Upon Upon a Time; Mother Carty's Chickens; A Little Journey; 39 East; He and She; Nice People; Everyday; Mary the 3rd; Expressing Willie; A Lady's Virtue; Venus; Let Us Be Gay, 1929; As Husbands Go, 1931; When Ladies Meet, 1932; Susan and God, 1937. Directs production of own plays. Received the National Achievement award Chi Omega, 1939. Founder and pres. of the Am. Theatre Wing, War Service, Inc., 1942. Home: Redding, Conn. Died July 5, 1958.

CROTTI, André, surgeon; b. 1873; grad. U. of Lausanne, Switzerland, 1902; M.D., Starling-Ohio Med. Coll., Columbus, O., 1908; former prof. clin. surgery, Ohio State U., Coll. of Medicine; mem. staff Grant Hosp., Children's Hosp., Mt. Carmel Hosp. Regarded as a leading authority on goiter. Fellow Am. Coll. Surgeons; past pres. Internat. Coll. Surgeons; mem. A.M.A. and other med. socs. Home: 1592 E. Broad St. Office: 1 S. 4th St., Columbus, O. Died Jan. 31, 1958.

CROUCH, Austin, clergyman; b. Carrollton, Mo., July 13, 1870; s. Elbert Hildebrand and Adelaide (Newell) C.; A.B., Baylor U., 1899, D.D., 1920; student So. Bapt. Theol. Sem., Louisville, 1899-1900; A.M., Howard Coll., Birmingham, Ala., 1906; D.D., Carson-Newman Coll., Jefferson City, Tenn., 1916, Union U., Jackson, Tenn., 1916; m. Arianna Hill, 1895 (dec. 1900); m. 2d, Myrtle Oldham, 1911 (dec. Mar. 1946). Paid way through schools by preaching in Texas and Ky.; ordained ministry So. Bapt. Ch., 1893; pastor successively Corinth, Miss., Woodlawn Ch., Birmingham, Gaston Av. Ch., Dallas, First Ch., Murfreesboro, Tenn., First Ch., Jonesboro, Ark., until 1922; supt. dept. of church extension Bapt. Home Mission Bd., 1922-23; again pastor First Ch., Murfreesboro, 1923-27; exec. sec. exec. com. So. Bapt. Conv., 1927-46, retired as exec. sec. emeritus. Democrat. Author: The Plan of Salvation, 1924. Home: Sutherland Av., Nashville 5. Office: 127 9th Av., N. Nashville 4. Died Aug. 28, 1957.

CROUCH, Charles T., pres. and dir. Sibley, Lindsay & Curr Co., 250 Main St. E., Rochester 4, N.Y. Died June 13, 1949.

CROUCH, Leonard Callender, judge; b. Kingston, N.Y., July 30, 1866; s. Henry Gage and Almira L. (Callender) C.; Ph.B., Cornell U., 1889; student Cornell U. Coll. of Law, 1 yr.; LL.D., Syracuse U.; m. Annie Laura Paine, Oct. 8, 1895; children—Margaret Paine, Helen Bothwell, Henry Callender, Paul Austin, Charlotte Hope. Admitted to N.Y. bar, 1891; practiced, Kingston, N.Y., 1891-92, Syracuse, 1892-13; apptd. justice State Supreme Court of N.Y. to fill vacancy, May 1913, elected for terms 1913-41; apptd. to appellate div., 1923, to Court of Appeals of New York, 1932, and elected, 1934 for full term, retired, Dec. 31, 1936; official referee Court of Appeals, 1937—. Democrat. Home: 747 Comstock Av. Office: 412 Court House, Syracuse, N.Y. Died July 3, 1953.

CROW, Charles Augustus, ex-congressman; b. Sikeston, Mo., Mar. 31, 1873; s. James Levi and Amanda (Rodden) C.; ed. pub. schs.; m. Mary Brown, Nov. 22, 1893 (dec. June 10, 1909); m. 2d, Emma Gardner, Oct. 27, 1910. Lived on farm until 23, Bernie, Mo., 1896-1901, Caruthersville, 1901—; postmaster, Caruthersville, 1901-02, mem. 61st Congress (1909-11), 14th Mo. Dist. Republican. Address: Caruthersville, Mo. Died Mar. 1938.

CROW, Orin Faison, educator; b. West Springs, Spartanburg County, S.C., Mar. 9, 1896; s. Henry and Mary (West) C.; A.B., U. of S.C., 1917; A.M., George Peabody Coll. for Teachers, 1925, Ph.D., 1931; m. Innis Cuttino, Sept. 2, 1919; children—Dorothy, Mary (Mrs. J. R. Anderson). Principal high school, Hartsville, South Carolina, 1919-24; prof. edn., University of S.C., since 1925, acting dir. extension, 1925-26, dean of Sch. of Edn., 1930-53, dean faculty, 1953—, dir. summer sch. 1946-53; instr. summers Winthrop College, Rock Hill, S.C., 1924, George Peabody Coll. for Teachers, 1928. Editor South Carolina Education, 1925-26. Served as 2d lt. F.A., U.S. Army, with A.E.F., World War I; col. F.A., World War II. Vice-pres. National Association Colleges and Depts. of Education, 1935-36; pres. Assn. of Deans of Edn. in Univs. and Land Grant Colleges of South, 1947; chmn. S.C. State Com. on Secondary Schs. of Southern Assn., 1946-52; mem. exec. com., 1951-53. Mem. English-Speaking Union (president Columbia branch 1952-53), A.A.A.S., N.E.A., National Society College Teachers of Edn., Phi Beta Kappa, Phi Delta Kappa, Kappa Phi Kappa (mem. nat. council 1934-36), Kappa Delta Pi, Sigma Phi Epsilon. Democrat. Baptist. Mason. Clubs: Kosmos, Wardlaw, Forum, Kiwanis (gov. Carolinas dist. 1950; mem. internat. bd. trustees 1951-53). Author: The Selection of Teachers in South Carolina; The Control of the University of South Carolina, 1801-1926. Co-author history of Columbia (S.C.). Founder 1935 and editor, 1935-40, S.C. High School Literary Yearbook. Editor: (also wrote introduction) Loyalty to Facts: The Educational Writings of Patterson Wardlaw, 1949. Rep. of Masonic Grand Lodge of S.C. to Grand Lodge of Italy. Home: 810 Sumter St., Columbia, S.C. Died Sept. 20, 1955; buried Greenlawn Meml. Park, Columbia, S.C.

CROW, Randolph Fairfax, cotton seed oil exec.; b. Wilmington, N.C., Nov. 15, 1877; s. John E. and Emily Polk (Davis) C.; ed. in pvt. schs., Wilmington; unmarried. Established South Texas Cotton Oil Co., 1910, chmn. bd. since 1930; dir. Wesson Oil & Snowdrift Co., Reed Roller Bit Co. Mem. bd. dirs. Houston Child Guidance Clinic, 1939, DePelchin Faith Home and Negro Child Center since 1939. Asst. Fed. Food Adminstr. for Tex., 1917-18; chmn. Inst. of Shortening Mfrs. Mem. Tex. Cotton Seed Crushers Assn. (pres. 1920-21), Nat. Cotton Seed Crushers Assn. (prs. 1924). Home: 1116 Hawthorne, Houston 6. Office: P.O. Box, Houston 1. Died Feb. 9, 1952.

CROWDER, John Batte, coll. dean; b. Jarratt, Va., May 14, 1904; s. Charles Phillip and Courtney (Batte) C.; A.B., U. Richmond, 1925; pvt. study piano, Richmond, Va., 1922-25, Vienna, 1925-28; A.M., Eastman Sch. Music, 1938; m. Jane Elizabeth Chapple, Mar. 10, 1934; children—Courtney, Lou. Prof. music Mont. State U., 1929-51, dean sch. music, 1939-51; dean Coll. Fine Arts, dir. Sch. Music U. Ariz., 1951—. Mem. Music Tchrs. Nat. Assn. (pres. 1952-53, exec. com., 1945—), Nat. Assn. Schs. Music. Contbr. articles edn., music mags. Home: 2925 Toledo Pl., Tucson. Died Oct. 12, 1957; buried Evergreen Cemetery, Tucson.

CROWE, R. L., dean; b. Dyer County, Tenn., Nov. 27, 1887; s. Bennett Dillie and Emma Lee (Kirkpatrick) C.; student Jackson Mil. Acad., 1903-08; Ph.C., Ohio State U., 1910; student U. of Tenn., Coll. of Medicine, 1910-14; m. Mary Margaret McEwen, Sept. 1912; children—Norma Latta (wife of Dr. Harold G. Barker), Helen Louise (wife of Dr. L. B. Snapp II). Began as teacher, 1912; dean Sch. of Pharmacy, U. of Tenn. Commd. maj. Old N.G. of Mo. Mem. Alpha Kappa Kappa, Phi Delta Chi (nat. pres.), Rho Chi (hon.). Home: 1700 N. Parkway Av., Memphis. Deceased.

CROWELL, Bowman Corning, pathologist; b. Yarmouth, N.S., Can., Jan. 10, 1879; s. Samuel Atwood and Mary Edna (Corning) C.; A.B., McGill U., 1900, M.D. and C.M., 1904; D.Sc., Marietta Coll., 1949; m. Frances Everett Horton, Apr. 25, 1909 (died Mar. 9, 1935); m. 2d, Frances Beatrice Henry, June 24, 1937. Resident pathologist, later interne, N.Y. City Hosp., 1904-07; instr. in pathology New York U. and Bellevue Med. Coll., 1907-11; also pathologist, Bellevue Hosp., 1908-11; pathologist, Bur. Science, Manila, P.I., 1911-15; asso. prof. pathology and bacteriology, and chief of dept., U. of Philippines, 1912-14, prof. and chief of dept., 1914-18, dir. Grad. Sch. Tropical Medicine and Pub. Health, 1916-18; chief of service, pathol. dept., Oswaldo Cruz Inst., Rio de Janeiro, Brazil, 1918-22; prof. pathology, Med. Coll. State of S.C., 1922-23, Jefferson Med. Coll., Phila., Pa., 1923-26; also pathologist and dir. labs., Jefferson Hosp., 1923-26; visiting pathologist, Phila. Gen. Hosp., 1923-26; asso. dir. and dir. clin. research, Am. Coll. Surgeons, Chgo., 1926-49, asso. dir. emeritus, 1949; lectr. in pathology, Northwestern U. Med. Sch., 1927—; mem. Nat. Malaria Com. Dir. Gorgas Meml. Inst., Washington; mem. bd. Am. Cancer Society. Recipient 1st ann. award Am. Cancer Soc., 1949. Mem. Internat. Assn. Med. Museums, Ill., Chgo. med. socs., Chgo. Pathol. Soc., A.A.A.S., Am. Assn. for Cancer Research, Am. Soc. Clin. Pathol. (hon.), Inst. of Medicine Chgo., Brazilian Acad. of Medicine (hon.), Chgo. Acad. of Sciences, Phi Delta Theta, Nu Sigma Nu. Republican. Presbyn. Clubs: Chicago Literary, University. Office: 40 E. Erie St., Chgo. 11. Died Apr. 26, 1951; buried Vancouver, B.C.

CROWELL, Lester Avant, Sr., surgeon; b. Lincoln County, N.C., Oct. 17, 1867; s. Dr. Eli and Martha Beatrice (Lowrance) C.; M.D., Baltimore Md. Coll., 1892; m. Mary Jane Hull, Sept. 12, 1894; children—Gordon (dec.), Mary Beatrice (Mrs. T. C. Abernathy), Corinne (Mrs. J. W. Schenck), Lester Avant,

Frank. Physician, Lincolnton, N.C., since 1890; pres.-treas. Gordon Crowell Memorial Hosp. Mem. Bd. Med. Examiners of N.C., 1920-26. Dir. Western Insane Asylum, Morganton, N.C. Fellow Am. Coll. Surgeons; mem. A.M.A., N.C. Med. Soc. (pres. 1929-30), Southern Med. and Surgery Soc. Methodist. Contbr. to med. jours. Home: 415 S. Aspen St., Lincolnton, N.C. Died May 29, 1952.

CROWELL, Merle, editor, publicist; b. North Newport, Me., Dec. 28, 1888; s. Wilson Daniel and Lydia (Coburn) C.; grad. Coburn Classical Inst., Waterville, Me., 1906; student Colby Coll., Waterville, Me., 1906-07; Litt.D., from same coll.; m. Mary Brewer Leonard, Sept. 3, 1921; children—Robert Norman, Gordon; m. 2d, Dorothy Carman, Jan. 1, 1931 (dec. Nov. 1953); m. 3d, Neeley Reyburn, Apr. 23, 1955. Reporter New York Evening Sun, 1911-15; asso. editor and staff writer American Mag., 1915-23, editor in chief, 1923-29; senior editor, The Reader's Digest, 1944; magazine writer and publicist since 1929. Enrolled in R.O.T.C., Plattsburg, N.Y., May 12, 1917; 2d lt., Aug. 1917; capt., May 1918; hon. disch. with rank of maj., May 1919. Dir. of Public Relations, Rockefeller Center, Inc., 1931-44. Alumni trustee Colby Coll., 2 terms, 1937-43. Mem. New England Soc. (life), Delta Kappa Epsilon. Protestant. Clubs: Nat. Press, Dutch Treat. Home: Cherry St., Katonah, N.Y. Office address: The Reader's Digest, Inc., Pleasantville, N.Y. Died Aug. 14, 1956; buried St. Mathews Churchyard.

CROWLEY, Charles Francis, football coach; b. Cambridge, Mass., Apr. 1888; s. Jeremiah and Mary (Collins) C.; grad. Cambridge Latin Sch.; student Harvard, 1907-10; LL.B., U. of Notre Dame, 1913; m. M. T. Williams, 1917; children—Mary Williams, Jean Frances. Football coach at Dallas, 1914-17, Harvard, 1921-22; became head football coach, Columbia, 1924. Served as capt. inf., U.S. Army, 1917-19. Clubs: Harvard (Boston), Notre Dame. Football specialist for New York Times. Home: 610 Huron Av., Cambridge, Mass. Died Oct. 3, 1954.

CROWLEY, Patrick Edward, ry. official; b. Cattaraugus, N.Y., Aug. 25, 1864; s. Dennis and Helen (Mulcahy) C.; LL.D., U. Notre Dame, 1929; m. Caroline Nichols, June 10, 1891; children—Charles E., Norman L., Eleanor S., Caroline S. Successively messenger, telegraph operator, station agt. and train dispatcher, Erie R.R. Co., 1878-89; train dispatcher N.Y.C.&H.R. R.R. Co., Mar. 1, 1889, and consecutively train master, div. supt., asst. gen. supt., gen. supt., asst. gen. mgr., and gen. mgr., same rd., Apr. 15, 1912-Jan. 1, 1915, asst. v.p., Jan. 1, 1915-Sept. 15, 1916, v.p., Sept. 15, 1916; federal mgr. Central N.Y. Southern R.R., Lake Erie & Pittsburgh R.R., N.Y.C. R.R. during period of Govt. control; v.p. Mar. 1, 1920, N.Y.C. R.R., Ottawa & N.Y. Ry., St. Lawrence & Adirondack Ry., Raquette Lake Ry., Fulton Chain Ry.; pres. retired; trustee Emigrant Industrial Savings Bank; dir. Reading Co., Western Union Telegraph Co. Catholic. Clubs: Transportation, Union League, Siwanoy Country. Home: 186 Cottage Av., Mt. Vernon, N.Y. Office: 230 Park Av., N.Y.C. Died Oct. 1, 1953; buried Gate of Heaven Cemetery, Valhalla, N.Y.

CROWLEY, Xavier, coll. ofcl., clergyman; b. Jersey City, May 25, 1906; s. Philip B. and Catharine (Maguire) C.; B.A., St. Francis Coll., 1935, M.A., 1936; LL.D., Villanova U., 1956. Pub. relations St. Francis College, 1936-38, president, 1953-56, executive director of development, 1956—; ordained priest Roman Cath. Ch., 1938; founder, dir. T.O.R. Franciscan Mission Band, 1939-53; preacher of retreats, clergy and nuns in U.S., retreats and missions to laity. Del. from Pa., White House Conf. on Edn., 1955. Trustee St. Francis Coll., 1940-45, 53-56, 56-59, Steubenville Coll., 53-56, 56-59. Mem. Delta Epsilon Sigma (founder). Contbr. to sacerdotal jours. Address: St. Francis Coll., Loretto, Pa. Died June 16, 1958.

CROWTHER, Frank (krou'thēr), ex-congressman; b. Liverpool, Eng., July 10, 1870; s. Samuel and Mary Ellen (Powell) C.; student Mass. Inst. Tech., 1888; D.M.D., Harvard Dental Sch., 1898; m. Miss Mary E. Lydiard, May 24, 1893 (died Sept. 2, 1910); m. 2d, Laura K. Eitelman, June 1, 1913 (died July 31, 1917); m. 3d, Mrs. James M. Young, June 1921. Practiced dentistry at Boston, Mass., 1898; moved to Perth Amboy, N.J., 1901, to Schenectady, N.Y., 1912; mem. N.J. House of Assembly, 1905-06; mem. Middlesex County (N.J.) Tax Bd., 1906-09; pres. Common Council, Schenectady, 1917; mem. 66th to 77th Congresses (1919-43), 30th N.Y. Dist. Retired Jan. 3, 1943. Republican. Presbyterian. Past Grand Master I.O.O.F. of N.J.; Past Exalted Ruler B.P.O.E., Perth Amboy; Mason, K.P. Clubs: Republican, Masonic. Home: 2225 Greenwood, Pueblo, Colo. Died July 20, 1955; buried Roselawn Cemetery, Pueblo.

CROZIER, W(illiam) J(ohn), univ. prof.; b. N.Y. City, Aug. 28, 1892; s. William George and Bessie (MacKay) C.; Townsend Harris Hall, 1905-08; B.S., Coll. City of New York, 1912; A.M., Harvard, 1914, Ph.D., 1915; Frederick Sheldon, travelling fellow, 1915-18; m. Blanche Maude Benjamin, June 25, 1915; children—Priscilla, Ruth; m. 2d, Louise Baylis Hoagland, June 2, 1934; 1 dau., Mary Louise. Resident naturalist Bermuda Biol. Station for Research, 1915-18; asst. prof. physiology, Coll. of Medicine, U. of Illinois, 1918-19, of zoölogy, U. of Chicago, 1919-20; prof. zoölogy, Rutgers, 1920-25; asso. prof. gen. physiology, Harvard U., 1925-27, prof. since 1927, research prof. since 1934, Lowell lecturer, 1934, also dir. Lab. of Gen. Physiology to 1934. Visiting lecturer Belgian universities, C.R.B. Foundation, 1934; Roscoff, Banyuls, Naples, 1934-35. Received Townsend Harris Alumni Medal, Coll. of City of N.Y., 1942. Operations analyst, U.S. Army Air forces, 1944-45. Co-editor Journal of Gen. Physiology; mem. editorial bd. Journal of Gen. Psychology, and Monograph on exptl. biology. Fellow Am. Acad. Arts and Sciences; mem. Am. Soc. Naturalists, Am. Physiol. Soc., Phi Beta Kappa, Sigma Xi. Home: 18 Woodbine Rd., Belmont, Mass. Died Nov. 2, 1955.

CRUIKSHANK, Margaret (Mrs. Ernest Cruikshank), educator; b. Hillsboro, N.C.; d. Halcott Pride and Olive (Echols) Jones; B.S., Columbia, 1911; A.M., Duke, 1937; m. Ernest Cruikshank, June 17, 1911; children—Ernest, Mary Pride, Olive. Pres. Columbia (Tenn.) Inst., 1922-32; prin. St. Mary's Sch., Raleigh, N.C., 1932-45. Mem. Am. Assn. U. Women. Democrat. Episcopalian. Address: St. Mary's School, Raleigh, N.C. Died Dec. 26, 1955; buried Oakwood, Raleigh, N.C.

CRUIKSHANK, R(obert) J(ames) (krŏŏk'shănk), author, journalist; b. London, Eng., Apr. 19, 1898; s. Robert James and Ellen (Bachelor) C.; ed. privately; m. Margaret Adele MacKnight, July 27, 1939; children—Victoria Margaret, Caroline Mary. Am. corr. London Daily News, Washington and New York, 1928-35; editor London Star, 1936-41; dir. Am. div. British Ministry of Information, London, 1941-45; dep. dir.-gen. Brit. Information Services in U.S., 1941-42; dir. The Daily News, Ltd., London, since 1945; editor New Chronicle, 1948-54. U.K. del. subcommn. on Freedom of Information of Human Rights Commn. of U.N., New York, 1947. Decorated Companion of St. Michael and St. George. Author: The Double Quest, 1936; Roaring Century, 1945; The Liberal Party, 1949; Charles Dickens and Early Victorian England, 1949; The Moods of London, 1951. Home: 198 W. Hill, Putney, London. Office: Daily News, Ltd., London E. C. 4, Eng. Died May 14, 1956; buried Putney Vale Cemetery, London, Eng.

CRUM, Bartley Cavanaugh, lawyer, pub. b. Sacramento, Cal., Nov. 28, 1900; s. James Henry and Emma (Cavanaugh) C.; A.B., U. Cal., 1922, J.D., 1924; D.H.L. (honorary), Hebrew Union Coll., 1951; m. Gertrude Bosworth, October 8, 1929; children—Patricia, Bartley. Admitted to Cal. bar, 1924, and practiced in San Francisco; asso. John Francis Neylan, 1924-38, became asso. Philip S. Ehrlich, 1938; pres. radio sta. KYA, San Francisco, 1946, KLAC, L.A., 1946; admitted to N.Y. bar, 1949, partner in law firm Hays, Podell, Algase, Crum & Feuer, N.Y.C., special counsel President's Committee on Fair Employment Practices, 1942; mem. Anglo Am. Com. on Inquiry on Palestine, 1946; cons. Am. Delegation U.N., San Francisco, 1945. Mem. Kappa Alpha. Republican. Roman Catholic. Clubs: Bohemian, Press, Commonwealth, (San Francisco). Author: Behind the Silken Curtain, 1947. Contbr. articles to mags. Home: 165 E. 80th St. Office: 39 Broadway, N.Y.C. Died Dec. 1959.

CRUM, Roy W(inchester), civil engr.; b. Galesburg, Ill., Apr. 9, 1885; s. George and Elizabeth (Martin) C.; B.C.E., Ia. State Coll., 1907, C.E., 1914; m. 1st Nina Bates (dec.), 1909; children—George Winchester, Josephine Elizabeth; m. 2d, Bertha Gates Roberts, 1924. With engr. corps, Pa. R.R., parts of 1906, 07, 10; instr., asst. prof., asso. prof., Ia. State Coll., 1907-19; Engr. Materials and Tests, Ia. State Highway Commn., 1919-28; dir. Highway Research Bd., NRC, 1928—. S.A.T.C., 1918. Mem. Am. Soc. C.E. (pres., Ia. sect., 1926, pres. D.C. sect., 1944, chmn., Highway Div., 1932-1941; director, 1946-49), American Concrete Institute (chairman Standards committee, 1931-44; president, 1944), American Society for Testing Materials (chmn. com. on Concrete and Concrete Aggregates, 1932-38, chmn. com. on Road Materials, 1929-30), Ia. Engring. Soc. (pres. 1922), A.A.A.S. (fellow), Sigma Xi, Tau Beta Pi, Phi Kappa Phi, Alpha Tau Omega. Congregationalist. Mason (K.T., Shriner). Clubs: Cosmos, Engineers (Washington). Editor: Annual Proceedings Highway Research Bd., 1928—, Highway Research Abstracts, 1931—. Received Ia. State Coll. Alumni Merit Award, 1947, Marston Medal, 1948. Home: Ashton, Md. Office: 2101 Constitution Av., Washington. Died May 13, 1951; buried Ames, Ia.

CRUMBINE, Samuel Jay, physician; b. Emlenton, Pa., Sept. 17, 1862; s. Samuel Jacob and Sarah (Mull) Krumbine; student Soldiers Orphan Sch., Mercer, Pa., 1870-78; Cincinnati Coll. Medicine and Surgery, 1889; m. Katherine Zuercher, Sept. 17, 1890; children—Warren Jay, Violet Ruth (Mrs. C. F. Chrisman). Pvt. practice medicine, Spearville, Kan., and Dodge City, Kan., 1885-1904, Topeka, 1904-07; mem. Kan. State Bd. Health, Topeka, 1899-1904, sec. and exec. officer, 1904-23; sec. and exec. officer Am. Child Health Assn., N.Y.C., 1923-25, Gen. Exec., 1925 until liquidation, 1936 when ret. Voluntary child health consultant, Save the Children Fedn, 1938—. Coroner, Ford County, Kan., 1898-1902. Served as sec., U.S. Examining Bd. for Pensions, 1894-1904; sent by Pres. Hoover to study health of children in Puerto Rico, 1930-31; pres. State and Provincial Bds. of Health, 1913-14. Served as med. mem., State Bd. Appeals, Topeka, World War I. Grand med. examiner, A.O.U.W. of Kan., 1901-03. Hon. life mem. Kan. Public Health Assn. 1946. Fellow Am. Public Health Assn. Organized Kan. Soc. for Study and Prevention of T.B., 1908 and served as pres., 1908-10. Republican. Presbyterian. Mason (past master, past high priest, past prelate; past patron, O.E.S., life mem. 1946). Author: Kron-Crumbine Graded Lessons Physiology and Hygiene (with Wm. Kron), 1912; The Most Nearly Perfect Food (with Dr. J. A. Tobey), 1935; Frontier Doctor, autobiography, 1948. Home: 35-37 78 St., Jackson Heights, N.Y. Died July 12, 1954.

CRUMLEY, Thomas, clergyman, author; b. Cin., Mar. 27, 1872; s. Thomas and Mary (Campbell) C.; student Notre Dame U., Ind., and Catholic U., Washington. Ordained priest R.C. Ch., 1897; mem. faculty Notre Dame U., 1898—, prof. of logic, 1906—. Author: Logic, 1926. Home: Notre Dame, Ind. Died Mar. 6, 1954; buried Community Cemetery, Notre Dame.

CRUMP, Edward Hull, ex-congressman; b. nr. Holly Springs, Miss.; pub. schs. edn.; m. Bessie Byrd McLean; children—Edward, Robert, John. Formerly head of E. H. Crump Buggy Mfg. Co.; elected mem. Bd. Pub. Works, Memphis, 1905; fire and police commr., 1907; elected Mayor of Memphis 3 times to 1916; again elected Mayor in 1939; county trustee (treas.) 4 times, 1916-24; del. Dem. State Conv., 1902-04; Dem. Nat. Conv., Baltimore, 1912, New York (del. at large), 1924, Houston, 1928, del. Chicago, 1932, 40, 44, Phila., 1936; became member Dem. State Com. Tenn., 1926; mem. 72d and 73d Congresses (1931-35), 10th Tenn. District; Dem. Nat. Committeeman for Tenn.; pres. E. H. Crump & Co., investments, banking, real estate, insurance, manufacturing and farming; nat. advisory committeeman for Tenn. for NY. World's Fair, 1939; mem. Sesquicentennial Phila. Com., 1925. Regent Smithsonian Instn. Home: 1962 Peabody Av. Office: North Memphis Savings Bank Bldg., Memphis. Died Oct. 16, 1954; buried Elmwood Cemetery, Memphis.

CRUSINBERRY, William Alfred, educator; b. Woodford County, Ill., Nov. 19, 1850; s. James C.; grad. Lenox Coll., 1877, Oskaloosa, A.M., 1880; m. Clara Herrick, June 13, 1889. Prof. mathematics and astronomy Lenox Coll., 1877-85; prin. schs., Floyd, Ia., 1885-87; prof. mathematics and astronomy Garfield U., Wichita, Kan., 1887-90; prof. mathematics and astronomy Drake U., 1890-1900. prof. astronomy, 1900-02, introduced astronomy and raised subscriptions for installing telescope; prin. High Sch., 1902-21, retired then taught part time at Drake U. and tutored until death. Address: 1010 26th St., Des Moines Ia. Died Jan. 11, 1929; buried Glendale Cemetery, Des Moines.

CRUTCHFIELD, James Stapleton; b. Goshen, Ky., July 3, 1874; s. Albert and Harriet (Mayo) C.; ed. pub. and high schs., Louisville, Ky.; m. Alice Pilkington, June 7, 1900 (dec.); children—Margaret (Mrs. A. T. Roy), Harriet (Mrs. John K. Orndorff), Catharine (Mrs. E. P. Swatek, Jr.), James Stapleton, Albin Pilkington, George Wythe (dec.), Robert Woolfolk, Alice Pilkington (Mrs. H. C. Wadsworth), Grace Pilkington (Mrs. L. A. Christensen). Began in Florida as buyer and seller of fruits and vegetables, 1892; moved to Pittsburgh, Pennsylvania, 1896, and established firm Crutchfield and Woolfolk, commn. mchts.; organizer, 1919, Am. Fruit Growers, Inc., chmn. bd. dirs. Deerfield Groves Co. (Wabasso, Fla.), William Penn Bank of Commerce; president Union Fruit Action Co. Served as vice administrator and member executive council Federal Food Administration, 1917-18, vice dir. food supply dept. Com. of Pub. Safety of Pa. Formerly dir. U.S. and Pittsburgh chambers of commerce; v. chmn. Economis Policy Com. Trustee Western Theol. Sem., Grove City College, Y.M.C.A. of Pittsburgh. Director Laymen's Movement for a Christian World, United Bd. for Christian Colleges in China; chmn. bd. trustees Pine Mountain (Ky.) Settlement Sch. Presbyterian. Clubs: Duquesne (Pittsburgh); Pennsylvania Society (N.Y. City). Home: Beaver Rd., Sewickley, Pa. Address: Pa. Lines Produce Terminal, 21st and Smallman Sts., Pitts. 22. Died Apr. 15, 1954.

CUBBINS, William Robert, surgeon; b. Memphis, Aug. 6, 1874; s. John and Miriam (Windiate) C.; Hanover (Ind.) Coll., 1891-92; B.S., Centre Coll., Ky., 1896; M.D., Northwestern U., 1900; m. Cora Hott Brindley, Sept. 18, 1901; children—Lawrence B., William Robert; m. 2d, Mary O'Connor, May 6, 1946. Interne, Cook County (Ill.) Hosp., 1900-02; asst. prof. surgery, 1910-18, asso. prof., 1918-36, Northwestern U. Med. Sch.; prof. surgery Loyola U., 1936-46; prof. surgery, Post-Grad. Med. Sch., 1905-21; surgeon Post-Grad. Hosp.; Chief surg. staff Cook County Hosp., 12 years, resigned 1946; now prof.

surgery, U. S.D. Mem. sr. surg. staff St. Lukes Hosp., Chgo. Chief surg. service, Base Hosp., Camp Beauregard, Mar. 1-July 5, 1918, and of Evacuation Hosp. No. 22, A.E.F., 1918-19. Fellow Am. Coll. of Surgeons (gov.); mem. A.M.A., Chgo. Med. Soc., Chgo. Surg. Soc. (pres. 1929, 30), Chgo. Pathol. Soc., Western Surgery Soc., Northwestern U. Med. Sch. Alumni Assn. (pres. 1915-16), Cook County Alumni Assn. (sec. 1912-15; pres. 1915-16), Phi Delta Theta, Nu Sigma Nu. Clubs: University, Country. An editor of Surgery, Gynecology and Obstetrics. Contbr. numerous articles to surg. publs. Home: Dundee, Ill. Office: 104 S. Michigan Av., Chgo. Died Nov. 15, 1959; buried Graceland Cemetery, Chgo.

CUDDIHY, Herbert Lester, publisher; b. N.Y.C., Oct. 12, 1896; s. Robert J. and Emma (Bennett) C.; grad. Lawrenceville Sch., 1913; student Princeton, 1917; m. Julia Murray, July 31, 1918. With Funk & Wagnalls, N.Y.C., 1918—, sales mgr., 1925-40, gen. mgr. and pres., 1940-46, chmn. bd., 1946—, dir., 1938—. Clubs: Players, Dutch Treat, Coffee House. Home: 1088 Park Av. Office: 153 E. 24 St., N.Y.C. Died July 5, 1953.

CUDDY, Warren N., lawyer; b. Abingdon, Md., Oct. 11, 1886; s. George Lawson and Sarah N. (James) C.; A.B., U. Puget Sound, Wash., 1911; m. Lucy Hon, Aug. 16, 1916; children—David Warren, Daniel Hon. Admitted to Wash. bar, 1912; clk. U.S. Dist. Court, Alaska, 1921-28; U.S. atty. 3d Dist. of Alaska, 1928-33; now in practice of law. Republican. Mason. Home: Anchorage, Alaska. Died Sept. 9, 1951.*

CULBERTSON, Albert L., ret. army officer; b. Ill., 1884; commd. 2d lt., Inf., Ill. Nat. Guard, Oct. 1904; advanced to capt. 1913; commd. capt. Fed. Service, 1917, maj. Reserve and Nat. Guard, 1919; col. and lt. col., 1922; brig. gen. of the line, 1940; Fed. service 1941, in command 66th Inf. Brigade, 33d div., Camp Forrest, Tenn., ret. 1945. Decorated Purple Heart, World War I. Address: Delavan, Ill. Died 1956.*

CULBERTSON, Ely, author, lecturer, bridge, authority; born in Poyana de Vervilao, Roumania, July 22, 1891; son of Almon Elias (an American citizen) and Xenia (Rogoznaia) Culbertson; educated in Geneva University and L'Ecole des Sciences Economiques et Politiques, Paris; m. June 11, 1923, Josephine Murphy (author and lecturer on bridge; writer of syndicated articles for 200 newspapers; asso. editor Bridge World Magazine); children—Joyce-Nadja, Ely Bruce; m. 2d, Dorothy Renata Baehne, Jan. 1947; 1 son, Alexander. Writer on lit. and sociology, 1916; president The Bridge World, Incorporated, December 1929—. Kem Playing Card Company, 1937-39; editor The Bridge World Magazine, N.Y.C. Chairman of Am. coöperative committee on laws of contract bridge; mem. S.A.R., Am. Acad. of Polit. and Social Sciences, American Civil Liberties Union, Academy Political Science. Founder, president, The World Fedn., Inc.; chairman Citizens Com., U. N. Reform, Inc. Mem. Greek Orthodox Ch. Clubs: Whist (chmn. coöp. com. N.Y.C.). Author: Contract Bridge Blue Book, 1930; The Strange Lives of One Man, 1940; (mystery play) The Queen Twice Guarded; The World Federation Plan, 1942; Total Peace, 1943; Must We Fight Russia?, 1946; Culbertson on Canasta, 1949; Culbertson's Hoyle, 1950; Culbertson Point-Count Bidding, 1952; Contract Bridge Complete, 1954; Culbertson's Self-Teacher, 1954. Contbr. to mags. on internat. politics and mass psychology. Home: Brattleboro, Vt. Office: 171 W. 57th St., N.Y.C. Died Dec. 27, 1955; buried Brattleboro.

CULLEN, Hugh Roy, oil exec.; b. Denton County, Texas, July 3, 1881; s. Cicero and Louise (Beck) C.; D.Sc. U. Pitts., 1936; LL.D., U. Houston, 1947, Baylor U., 1945; m. Lillie Cranz, Dec. 29, 1903; children—Roy Gustav (dec.), Lillie Cranz (Mrs. Paul Portanova), Agnes Louise (Mrs. Isaac Arnold), Margaret Ruth (Mrs. Douglas Marshall), Wilhelmina Daisy (Mrs. Corbin J. Robertson). Began as a rep. Houston cotton factor, Texas and La.; became owner, operator cotton bus., Houston and Okla.; also dealt in real estate and became active in oil bus., Texas, 1918; pres. Quintana Petroleum Corp., Houston. State finance chmn., v.p. Texas World Fair Commn., 1939; mem. Golden Gate Internat. Expn., 1939; dir. Boy Scouts Am.; mem. adv. bd. Air Scouts Am.; dir. Oil World Expn. (Tulsa); v.p. Petroleum Assn. Am. Trustee Museum Fine Arts; chmn. bd. of Regents, University of Houston; former chmn. bd. Houston Symphony Soc. Awarded Distinguished Service award by Mid-Continent Oil and Gas Assn.; Good Citizenship medal by Texas Soc. of S.A.R.; Nat. Citizenship award by Vets. Fgn. Wars; Citizenship medal by Dept. Texas Vets. Fgn. Wars U.S.; various citations for outstanding contributions in producing oil and aiding in War Bond drives by War Dept. and Treasury. Mem. Am. Hosp. Assn. (hon.), Sons Republic Texas, Huguenot Soc. S.C., Musicians Protective Assn. of A.F. of L. (hon., local 64), Acad. Polit. Sci., Phi Chi (hon.). Clubs: Country, Houston, Bayou, River Oaks Country (Houston). Home: 1620 River Oaks Blvd., Houston 6. Office: 1710 First City Nat. Bank Bldg., Houston 2. Died July 4, 1957.

CULLEN, Thomas Stephen, surgeon; b. Bridgewater, Ontario, Nov. 20, 1868; s. Rev. Thomas and Mary (Greene) C.; ed. Collegiate Institute, Toronto; M.B., U. of Toronto, 1890, also LL.D.; hon. D.Sc., Temple U. Specialist in abdominal surgery; formerly prof. gynecology, Johns Hopkins U., now prof. emeritus; visiting gynecologist, Johns Hopkins Hosp. Honorary member La Societa Italiana Ostetricia Ginecologia, Rome; corr. mem. Gesellschaft für Geburtshülfe, Leipzig; corr. mem. Gynecol. Soc. of München; hon. fellow Edinburgh Obstet. Soc.; pres. Southern Surg. and Gynecol. Assn., 1916; Med. and Chirurg. Faculty of Md., 1927. Trustee and pres. of Enoch Pratt Library, Baltimore; trustee American Medical Association, 1929-41; chairman Chesapeake Bay Authority, Public Works District 10, 1933-34. Member Phi Beta Kappa. Author: Cancer of the Uterus, 1900; Adenomyoma des Uterus, Verlag von August Hirschwald, 1903; Adenomyoma of the Uterus, 1908; Myomata of the Uterus (with Howard A. Kelly), 1909; Embryology, Anatomy and Diseases of the Umbilicus Together with Diseases of the Urachus, 1916; Henry Mills Hurd, 1920; Early Medicine in Maryland, 1927; also wrote Accessory Lobes of the Liver for Archives of Surgery. Contbr. to med. jours. on gynecol., pathology and abdominal surgery. Editor of 2 vols. on gynecology, Lewis System of Surgery, 1928. Home: 20 E. Eager St., Balt. Died Mar. 4, 1953; buried Easton, Md.

CULLIMORE, Allan Reginald, educator; b. Jacksonville, Ill., Mar. 2, 1884; s. Thomas McIntyre and Mary Pearce (Joy) C.; B.S. in C.E., Mass. Inst. of Tech., 1907; Sc.D., from the University of Newark, 1941; D.Eng., Stevens Inst. Tech., Rutgers University, 1948; D.Eng., Newark College of Engineering, 1948; married Edith Van Alst, March 25, 1912. Draughtsman Am. Bridge Co., 1906-08; asst. supt. of constrn. City of St. Louis, Mo., 1909-12; dean Coll. of Industrial Science, Toledo, O., 1912-16; dean of engring., Delaware Coll., 1916-19; dean Newark Coll. of Engring., 1919-27, pres., 1920-49, chmn. dept. of management and personnel since 1949. Major Sanitary Corps, U.S. Army, 1918-19. Del. to Constitution Conv., N.J., 1947. Dir. Ednl. Survey State of N.J., 1948. Mem. Loyalty Review Bd., U.S. Civil Service, Area 14. Mem. visiting com. Dept. Civil Engring., M.I.T., 1946-50. Chmn. Com. on Student Development, E.C.P.D., 1946-50. Recipient Lamme Award in Engring. Edn., 1951. Mem. Am. Soc. of M.E., Am. Soc. Engring. Edn., Am. Soc. C.E., Beta Theta Pi, Tau Beta Pi, Phi Kappa Phi. Presbyn. Clubs: Down Town, Engineers (N.Y.), Rotary (hon.). Home: 158 Garfield Pl., South Orange, N.J. Died Sept. 20, 1956; buried Fairmont Mausoleum, Newark.

CULLINAN, Craig Francis, oil prodn. exec.; b. Washington, Pa., Oct. 25, 1894; s. Joseph Stephen and Lucie (Halm) C.; Ph.B., Yale, 1917; D.Sc., Southwestern U., 1948; m. Lucia Edith Phillips, Nov. 15, 1919; children—Craig Francis, Joseph Stephen II. Supt. Galena-Signal Oil Co. (of Tex.), 1919-20; pres. Am. Petroleum Co. (of Tex.), 1920-26; v.p. Am. Republics Corp. (holding corp., owning stock in many oil producing and mfg. cos.), 1926-28, pres., 1928-32; pres. Am. Petroleum Co., 1932-36; pres. Am. Republics Corp., 1936—. Chmn. bd. dirs The Tex. State U. for Negroes. Served in U.S. Navy, Apr. 1917-Dec. 1918. Home: 6 Longfellow Lane, Shadyside, Houston. Office: Petroleum Bldg., Houston. Died Aug. 14, 1950; buried Houston.

CULLINAN, Edith Phillips (Mrs. Craig Francis Cullinan), b. N.Y.C. Dec. 22, 1895; d. Wendell Christopher and Lucia Maria (Taggart) Phillips; ed. Merrill van Laer Sch., N.Y.C.; m. Craig Frances Cullinan, Nov. 15, 1919; children—Craig Francis, Jr. (USNR), Joseph Stephen II. Served with Motor Corps of Am., 1917-18; supr. Aircraft Warning Service, 1942-43. Mem. bd. mgrs. Am. Hearing Society; member Jr. League of Houston (Tex.); engaged in various other civic and charitable interests. Home: 6 Longfellow Lane, Houston 5. Died Nov. 30, 1949.

CULVER, Bernard Mott, insurance; b. Sandwich, Illinois; son of James Henry and Harriett (Stewart) Culver; Ph.B., Grinnell College; m. Erne Constans; one son, Donald S. Assistant manager Scottish Union & National Insurance Co., 1907-17; vice-pres. Niagara Fire Insurance Co., 1917-29, president, 1932-46; pres., 1932-46 of Continental Ins. Co., Fidelity Phenix Fire Ins. Co., Am. Eagle Fire Ins. Co., Fidelity & Casualty Co.; chmn. bd. of all cos. since June, 1946; chmn. bd. Sanborn Map Co.; trustee Central Hanover Bank & Trust Co.; dir. Home Life Ins. Co., Shell Union Oil Corporation. Republican. Clubs: Down Town, Union, Drug and Chemical, Arcola Country. Home: 988 5th Av., New York, N.Y. Office: 80 Maiden Lane, N.Y.C. Died July 19, 1951.

CULVER, Bertram Beach, mfg. exec.; b. St. Louis, June 14, 1875; s. Henry Harrison and Emily J. (Hand) C.; ed. pub. schs. St. Louis and Smith Acad.; student Washington U.; m. Edna May Lammert, Feb. 11, 1907 (dec. Nov. 6, 1956); children—Bertram Beach, Henry Harrison. Started with Wrought Iron Range Co., St. Louis, 1893, pres., 1911— dir. First Nat. Bank in St. Louis. Chmn. Culver Ednl. Found. which operates Culver Mil. Acad. Republican. Presbyn. Mason (33). Home: R.F.D. 1, Creve Coeur, Mo. Office: 5661 Natural Bridge Av., St. Louis 20. Died Dec. 1959.

CULVER, Montgomery Morton, educator; b. McClure, O., Aug. 31, 1891; s. Walter Scott and Lovina (Beatty) C.; A.B., Definance Coll., 1922; A.M., Ohio State U., 1924; Ph.D., U. Pitts., 1927; m. Kathryn M. Harman, Apr. 6, 1918; children—Phyllis Jeanne, Montgomery Morton. Tchr. Damascus twp. pub. sch., 1909-17, 1919-23; asst. in mathematics, Ohio State U., 1923-24; mem. dept. math. U. Pitts., 1924—, prof., 1934—. Served as sgt. Q.M.C., 1917-19, with AEF, 1918-19. Mem. Am. Math. Soc., S.A.R. Home: 219 Lehigh St., Edgewood, Pa. Office: Univ. of Pittsburgh, Pitts. Died Nov. 2, 1950; buried Hockman Cemetery, McClure, O.

CUMBERLAND, William Wilson, economist; b. La Verne, Calif., Jan. 2, 1890; s. Julian Fee and Clara Euphemia (Huggins) C.; A.B., Occidental Coll., Los Angeles, Calif., 1912; A.M., Columbia, 1913; Ph.D., Princeton, 1916; LL.D. (honorary), Occidental College, 1937. Union College, 1953; married Edith Griffith Osmond, Sept. 14, 1916; children—Mary Catherine, Julian Osmond, William Wilson, Helen Edith. Supt. Chrystie Street House, N.Y.C., 1914; instr., asst. prof., asso. prof. and chief div. of research in agrl. economics, U. of Minn., 1916-19; leave of absence, 1917-19; research asso., U. of Calif. and Doheny Research Foundation, 1917-18; trade expert War Trade Bd., Washington, D.C., 1918; economic expert with Reparation and Financial commns., Am. Commn. to Negotiate Peace, Paris, France, 1919; financial expert Am. Mil. Mission to Armenia (Harbord Commn.), 1919; financial expert with U.S. High Commn., Am. Embassy, Constantinople, Turkey, 1919-20; asst. foreign trade adviser and foreign trade adviser, Dept. of State, Washington, D.C., 1920-21; financial commr. and supt. gen. of customs, Republic of Peru, 1921-23; gov. Reserve Bank of Peru, 1923-24; financial adviser, gen. receiver of Republic of Haiti, 1924-27; financial expert for Dept. of State, in Nicaragua, 1927-28; partner Wellington and Co., firm mem. New York Stock Exchange, 1928-45; partner Ladenburg, Thalmann & Co., Mem. N.Y. Stock Exchange and investment banker, since 1945; dir. St. Louis Southwestern R.R., Alliance Realty Co., Chemetals Corp., Robert Gair Co., Inc., Am. Zinc, Lead and Smelting Co. Economist with NRA, Wash., 1933. Am. del. to Conference on German Long-Term Debts, Berlin, 1934; economic consultant United Nations Conference on International Orgn., San Francisco, 1945. Economists Nat. Com. on Monetary Policy. Mem. Acad. Polit. Science, Am. Acad. Polit. and Social Sci., Fgn. Policy Assn., Pan-Am. Soc., Am. Econ. Assn., N.Y. Soc. of Security Analysts, Am. Statis. Assn. (pres. New York Chapter, 1938-39), Phi Beta Kappa, Pilgrims. Author: Cooperative Marketing, 1918; Nicaragua—An Economic and Financial Survey, 1928; The American Individual Enterprise System (co-author) 2 Vols., 1946. Club: Downtown Athletic. Home: 349 Booth Av., Englewood, N.J. Office: 25 Broad St. N.Y.C. 4. Died Feb. 20, 1955; buried Forest Lawn Cemetery, Los Angeles.

CUMMER, Clyde Lottridge, dermatologist; b. Cadillac, Mich., Feb. 23, 1882; s. Robert James (M.D.) and Abbie A. (Stone) C.; Ph.B., Adelbert Coll. (Western Reserve U.), 1904; M.D., Western Reserve U., 1907; m. Marienne Dix North, Feb. 25, 1915; children—Robert North, Katharine Anne (Mrs. H. Lansing Vail, Jr.). With School of Medicine, Western Reserve University, 1909-46, successively as teacher and associate professor of clin. pathology, asst. clinical prof. in dermatology and syphilology; visiting dermatologist Charity Hospital; graduate study, dermatology department Vanderbilt Clinic and College Physician and Surgeon, N.Y. City, 1924-25. Mem. Med. Advisory Bd. No. 7, Selective Service, U.S. Army, World War I and Bd. of Appeals No. 8, Selective Service 1942-47, appeal bd. N. Fed. Judicial Dist. Ohio, 1951-52; hon. consultant U.S. Army Med. Library 1942-46. Received Distinguished Service award, Acad. of Medicine of Cleveland, 1942. Mem. Am. Dermatol. Assn., Am. Med. Assn. (mem. council on sci. assembly 1937-47; mem. House of Dels., 1932-33, 1934-43; chmn. sect. on dermatology and syphilology, 1944-46; mem. War Participation Com., 1942-45), American Academy Dermatology and Syphilology (treas. 1938-46, pres. 1947-48), Ohio State Med. Assn. (pres. 1933-34; chmn. com. on education, 1936-43; Cleveland Dermatological Society (pres. 1929), Acad. Medicine of Cleveland (pres. 1923), Cleveland Medical Library Assn. (chmn. bd. 1929-37; sec. com. for building Allen Meml. Library Bldg. 1923-26; pres. 1940-41; chmn. Pub. Health Council State of Ohio, 1939-40; mem. S.A.R., Beta Theta Pi, Nu Sigma Nu, Phi Beta Kappa, Sigma Xi, Alpha Omega Alpha. Republican. Episcopalian. Author: Cummer Memoranda (geneal. record), 1912; Manual of Clin. Lab. Methods, 1922, 26, 31. Contributor to Blakiston's New Gould Medical Dictionary, 1949. Contbr. to med. lit. and med. history. Home: 19201 Van Aken Blvd., Shaker Heights, Cleve. 22

(summer) Indian River, Mich. Office: Hanna Bldg., Cleve. 15. Died June 7, 1958; buried Lake View Cemetery, Cleve.

CUMMINGS, Homer Stillé, former atty. gen. of U.S.; b. Chicago, Ill., Apr. 30, 1870; s. Uriah C. and Audie (Schuyler Stillé) C.; Ph.B., Yale, 1891, LL.B., 1893; LL.D., Rollins Coll., 1934; LL.D., Lake Forest U., 1934; LL.D., Oglethorpe U., 1934; D.H.L., Lincoln Memorial U., 1935; LL.D., John Marshall Coll. of Law, 1935; LL.D., Pa. Military College, 1938; Trustee George Washington University; m. Cecilia Waterbury, April 2, 1929 (died Aug. 9, 1939); m. Julia M. Alter, dau. Mr. and Mrs. Frank W. Alter, of Chicago, July 13, 1942. Admitted to Conn. bar, 1893, practiced at Stamford until Mar. 4, 1933 and since Jan. 2, 1939; as counsel to firm Cummings & Lockwood, Stamford, and mem. firm Cummings, Stanley, Truitt & Cross, D.C.; mem. bars of New York and District of Columbia; admitted to practice in Supreme Court of United States and large number of federal district courts; mayor of Stamford, 3 terms, 1900-01, 1901-02 and 1904-06, corp. counsel. 1908-12. Del. at large Dem. Nat. Convs., 1900, 04, 24, 32, 36, 40, 44; Presidential Elector, 40, 44; member Democrat National Committee, 1900-25 (resigned), vice chmn., 1913-19, chmn., Feb. 26, 1919-July 1920. Candidate for Congress, Conn. at large, 1902, for U.S. senator, 1916; temporary chmn. Dem. Nat. Conv., San Francisco, and delivered keynote speech, 1920; chairman committee on resolutions, Democratic National Convention, New York, 1924; a floor leader for Gov. Franklin D. Roosevelt, Chicago, 1932; state's atty. for Fairfield County, Conn., July 1, 1914-Nov. 1, 1924 (resigned); former dir. First Stamford Nat. Bank; pres. Mayors' Assn. of Conn., 1902-03, Stamford Board of Trade, 1903-09; mem. Conn. State Council of Defense, 1917; chmn. Com. on State Prison Conditions, 1930. Tendered apptmt. as gov.-gen. of P.I., Feb. 1933; atty. gen. of U.S. in Cabinet of President Roosevelt, Mar. 4, 1933-Jan. 2, 1939 (resigned); del. at large, Democratic National Conv., 1948. Fellow of Institute of Judicial Administration. Author and sponsor of many reforms in United States Department of Justice and Federal Judicial System, including new rules of civil procedure, creation of administrative office for federal courts, and juvenile delinquency act; extended and improved prison system, established Alcatraz; called nat. Conf. on Crime; secured legislation extending authority of Fed. Bur. Investigation, and widening scope of Federal power in matter of kidnapping and inter-state crime; made authoritative survey of release procedures, Federal and State. Argued Gold Clause cases in Supreme Court. Chosen by Argentina and Chile to arbitrate Beagle Channel Islands controversy, 1938. Mem. Am. Bar Assn., 1909—; mem. Am. Judicature Soc. (v.p.), Am. Law Inst., Am. Soc. Internat. Law. Mason, Odd Fellow, Elk, Eagle. Mem. First Congl. Church, Stamford, Conn. Clubs: National Democratic (New York), Metropolitan, National Press, Burning Tree, Kenwood Golf and Country (Washington, D.C.). Author: Liberty Under Law and Administration, 1934; Federal Justice (with Carl McFarland), 1937; We Can Prevent Crime, 1937; The Tired Sea, 1939. Home: 4308 Forest Lane N.W. Address: 1625 K St. N.W., Washington. Died Sept. 10, 1956.

CUMMINGS, Joe Brown, lawyer; b. McMinnville, Tenn., June 26, 1913; s. Joseph Sumner and Mary Cynthia (Ramsey) C.; A.B., Cumberland U., Lebanon, Tenn., LL.B., 1934; m. Agnes McDaniel, Oct. 9, 1934; children—Linda Blair, Cynthia Smartt. Admitted to Tenn. bar, 1934, and since practiced in Nashville; mem. Williams, Cummings & West; municipal judge Nashville, 1941-43. Mem. exec. com. Nat. Safety Council, 1942-43. Mem. Am., Tenn., Nashville bar assns., Assn. Interstate Commerce Commn. Practitioners, Sigma Alpha Epsilon, Blue Key. Presbyn. Home: 112 Mockingbird Rd., Nashville 5. Office: Stahlman Bldg., Nashville 3. Deceased.

CUMMINS, Joseph Michael, army officer; b. St. Louis, Mo., July 21, 1881; s. Hugh and Anastatia (Nary) C.; A.B., St. Louis U., 1901; honor grad. Army Sch. of the Line, 1922; grad. Gen. Staff Sch., 1923, Army War Coll., 1927; Sc.D. (hon.), Clemson Coll., 1942; m. Eileen Hart Davis (dau. of Brig. Gen. T. F. Davis, U. S. Army), Jan. 12, 1910; children—Joseph Michael (killed in action), Thomas Davis (dec.), Eileen Hart, Robert Hugh (dec.), Kathleen Nary. Commd. 2d lt., U.S. Army, 1903, and advanced through grades to brig. gen., 1938, maj. gen., 1940; instr. Gen. Service Schs., 1923-26; mem. Gen. Staff, War Dept., 1930-34; dir. Inf. Bd., 1934-36; dir. War Plans Div., Army War Coll., 1936-38; comdg. 18th Brig., Boston, 1938-39; comdg. gen. Atlantic Sector Panama Canal Dept., 1939; comdg. 5th Div., 1940, 6th Corps Area, 1941; retired 1942. Roman Catholic. Address: Dunedin, Fla. Died Oct. 16, 1959; buried Arlington Nat. Cemetery.

CUMMINS, Robert Rankin, railroad exec.; b. Marion, Ala., Sept. 30, 1884; s. Anthony and Rebecca (Rankin) C.; B.S., U. Ala., 1907; m. Cleo Brown, June 28, 1909; 1 dau., Elizabeth (Mrs. E. B. Wulbern). With Central of Ga. Ry. Co., 1909—, successively asst. engr., track supr., div. engr., trainmaster, div. supt., engr. maintenance of way, asst. gen. mgr., gen. mgr., 1909-42, v.p. gen. mgr., 1942—; pres., dir. Sylvania Central Ry. Co., Albany Terminal Co., Macon Terminal Co., Chatham Terminal Co., Central of Ga. Motor Transport Co.; v.p., dir. Birmingham Terminal Co., Atlanta Terminal Co., Macon Terminal Co. Served overseas as 1st lt. Engr. Corps U.S. Army, 1917-18. Mem. Am. Ry. Engring. Assn., Phi Kappa Sigma. Democrat. Presbyn. Mason. Clubs: Oglethorpe, Savannah Golf, Newcomen Soc. Home: 110 W. Gaston St., Savannah, Ga. Office: care Central of Georgia Ry. Co., Savannah, Ga. Died Feb. 26, 1952.

CUMMINS, William Taylor, physician; b. Media, Pa., May 17, 1879; s. Joseph Grubb and Sarah Jane (Otley) C.; grad. Biol. Dept., U. of Pa., 1902, M.D., Med. Dept., 1902; m. Josephine Widdicombe, Sept. 9, 1908 (died 1932); m. 2d, Laura E. Anderson, Sept. 28, 1938. Asst. demonstrator of pathology, U. of Pa., 1902-11; demonstrator of pathology, Woman's Med. Sch., Phila., Pa., 1907-10; physician Henry Phipps Inst., Phila., 1907-10; bacteriologist, Dept. of Health, N.Y. City, 1911; dir. labs., Southern Pacific Gen. Hosp., San Francisco, Calif., since 1911. Mem. A.M.A., Am. Assn. Pathologists and Bacteriologists, Am. Soc. Clin. Pathologists, Alpha Kappa Kappa. Republican. Presbyterian. Clubs: Commonwealth, Olympic. Author: Syllabus of General Pathology, 1908; Syllabus of Special Pathology, 1909. Home: 217 25th Av. Office: 1400 Fell St., San Francisco. Died May 5, 1953.

CUNINGGIM, Jesse Lee (kŭn'ĭng-gĭm), clergyman; b. Lenoir Inst., N.C., Mar. 21, 1870; s. William Henry and Louisa (Hardy) C.; A.B., U. N.C., 1891; B.D., Vanderbilt U., 1895; U. Chgo., 1898-1902; D.D., So. Meth. U., 1922, Duke, 1936; m. Maud L. Merrimon, June 29, 1910; children—Augustus Merrimon, Margaret Louise. Dir. Corr. Sch. of M.E. Ch., S., 1902-14; sec. Dept. of Ministerial Supply and Tng., M.E. Ch., S., 1910-14; prof. Bibl. dept. Vanderbilt U., 1902-15; presiding elder Durham dist., N.C., 1915; pastor Elizabeth City, N.C., 1915-17; prof. religious edn. So. Meth. U., 1917-21; pres. Scarritt Bible and Tng. Sch., Kansas City, Mo., 1921-24; pres. Scarritt Coll. for Christian Workers, Nashville, Tenn., 1924-43, pres. emeritus, 1943—. Mem. Phi Beta Kappa. Author: (booklets) A Plan for Better Religious Instruction in the Southern Methodist Church, 1901; The Organized Adult Bible Class, 1908; The Making of a Ministry, 1909; Sunday School Organization and Management (book with Eric M. North); The Family of God, 1948. Address: Sterling Court, Apt. C, 3, Nashville. Died Nov. 25, 1950; buried Mt. Olivet Cemetery, Nashville.

CUNNINGHAM, Augustine Joseph, mfr.; b. Rochester, N.Y., May 17, 1878; s. Joseph Thomas and Ellen Nora (Keogh) C.; pvtly. ed.; unmarried. Began in mfr. of automobiles, 1900; pres. James Cunningham Son & Co., Inc., mfr. electronic switches. Republican. Roman Catholic. Clubs: Rochester Country, Genesee Valley. Home: 1000 East Av. Office: 33 Litchfield St., Rochester 8, N.Y. Died July 31, 1957; buried Holy Sepulchre Cemetery, Rochester, N.Y.

CUNNINGHAM, Cornelius Carman, educator; born Weehawken, N.J., Nov. 9, 1890; s. John Henry and Ellen Jane (Abrams) C.; student Colgate Univ., 1911-13; A.B. summa cum laude, Beloit (Wis.) Coll., 1915; M.A., Northwestern U., 1924; Ph.D., State U. of Ia., 1936; m. Bernice Anna Fry, Aug. 10, 1919 (divorced); children—Lew Sarett, Joseph Conrad; m. 2d, Josephine Cuvier Dresden, Oct. 7, 1933; children—Carman, Bessie Marie, Cornelius Dresden. Began as professor, Yankton (South Dakota) College, 1915; assistant professor English, Berea (Kentucky) College, 1916-17; instructor English, Univ. of Wis., 1920; prof. pub. speaking, Wabash Coll., Crawfordsville, Ind., 1920-22; asst. prof. of pub. speaking, Univ. of Ariz., 1923-24; prof. of pub. speaking and chmn. dept. of English, N.C. State Coll., Raleigh, 1924-29; prof. pub. speaking, Northwestern U., 1929-42, prof. lit. interpretation, 1942-47; now prof., Dept. of Speech Arts, San Diego (California) State College; instructor in functional speaking for senior naval officers, 11th District, 1947-52. Sergeant maj., U.S. Army, during World War; with A.E.F., France, wounded in Argonne, Oct. 1918. Mem. Nat. Assn. Teachers of Speech, 1925-47 (past vice-pres.; chairman nat. committee on interpretation 1942-45); mem. Nat. Travel Club, Phi Beta Kappa, Delta Sigma Rho, Pi Kappa Belta (gov. South Atlantic Province, 1924-29), Tau Kappa Epsilon. Cons. on pronunciation Webster's Internat. Dictionary, 2d edit. Platform experience in polit. campaigns; preacher, lecturer and interpretative reader of drama. Author: Literature As a Fine Art, 1941; Making Words Come Alive, 1951; Making Words Win for You, 1953; (with Mary G. G. Brainard) Campaigns of the 146th Regiment, N.Y. State Volunteers, 1915. Contbr. to profl. jours. Co-editor, Studies in American Public Address, 1943. Has succesfully coached student debaters, trained debating teams and has been coach of winners in 9 nat. oratorical contests, 16 interstate contests, etc. Home: 5691 Lindo Paseo, San Diego 15, Cal. Died Sept. 15, 1958.

CUNNINGHAM, Edwin Sheddan, consular service; b. East Tenn., July 6, 1868; s. Maj. Ben and Jane A. (Sheddan) C.; A.B., Maryville Coll., 1889, LL.D., 1932; LL.B., U. of Mich., 1893, M.A., 1938; m. Elizabeth Rhoda Israel, Nov. 14, 1911 (died 1934). Admitted to bar, Mich. and Tenn., 1893; practiced at Maryville, Tenn., as mem. Cates & Cunningham, 2 yrs.; admitted to U.S. Court for China, 1916. Am. consul at Aden, Arabia, 1898-1901, at Bergen, Norway, 1901-06, at Durban, Natal, S. Africa, 1906-10, at Bombay, India, 1910-12; consul-gen. at Singapore, Straits Settlements, 1912-14, at Hankow, China, 1914-19, at Shanghai, China, 1919-35; retired Dec. 1935; now devoting time to study of current Far Eastern affairs. Designated, 1920, by colleagues to represent consular body on bd. of Governor's Gen. Hosp., and in 1921 on Pilot Bd., resigning latter position to accept invitation to join Court of Consuls and became senior consul May, 1926. Served as chairman of various consular body units in negotiation with the Chinese authorities concerning local matters, notably the rendition of the Mixed Court, Extra-Settlement Road question, Trade Marks, etc.; chmn. Joint Commn. to implement the Sino-Japanese agreement of May 5, 1932; by executive order of Mar. 3, 1933, retained on active duty for period not in excess of 5 years from July 6, 1933; retired, Dec. 1935. Awarded Wen Fu Decoration, 3d Class, 1922; The Red Cravat with White and Blue Border of Order of Jade, 1936. Mem. American Red Cross. Presbyterian. Clubs: Rotary, Am. Univ. of China, Shanghai Golf, Shanghai Race, Internat. Race, and life mem. American, Shanghai, Columbia Country. Home: 306 Cunningham St., Maryville, Tenn. Died Jan. 20, 1953; buried Grandview Cemetery, Maryville, Tenn.

CUNNINGHAM, Eugene, writer; b. Helena, Ark., Nov. 29, 1896; s. Ira Eugene and Istarena Adkins (Stradley) C.; ed. pub. schs., Dallas and Ft. Worth, Tex., and by pvt. instrn., 1903-11; m. Mary Emilstein, Dec. 1, 1921; children—Mary Carolyn, Jean, Cleve. Traveled in Central America writing articles for Wide World Mag., London, and U.S. mags. and newspapers, 1919. Servde in U.S. Navy, 1914-19, in Mexican Campaign and during first World War; in Naval Reserve until 1923; in Naval Intelligence, 1941. Author: Gypsying Through Central America, 1922; Regulation Guy, 1922; Trail to Apacaz, 1924; Riders of the Night, 1932; Buckaroo, 1933; Triggernometry, a Gallery of Gunfighters, 1933; Daimond River Man, 1934; Texas Sheriff, 1934; Trail of the Macaw, 1935; Redshirts of Destiny, 1935; Quick Triggers, 1935; Pistol Passport, 1936; Whistling Lead, 1936; Ranger Way, 1937; Texas Triggers, 1938; Gun Bulldogger, 1939; Red Range, 1939; Spiderweb Trail, 1940; Gunfighters All, 1941; Buscadero Trail, 1951; Gunsight Chance, 1951; Riding Gun, 1951; and Outlaw Justice, Border Guns, Bravo Trail under pseudonym of Leigh Carder; Deep Soundings under pseudonym Alan Corby. Editor: Buckboard Days (Poe); Apache Days—And after (Cruse); Neustro Pueblo (Seewerker-Owens). Contbr. to anthologies and to leading mags. Home: 120 Sutro Heights Av., San Francisco 21. Died Oct. 18, 1957.

CUNNINGHAM, George William, lawyer; b. Liberty Center, Ia., Jan. 11, 1898; s. William Arthur and Hallie (Nash) C.; student Coll. of Emporia, Kan., 1916-19; B.S., Kan. State Tchrs. Coll., 1920; LL.B., La Salle Extension U., 1926; m. Rachel Amalia Scott, Aug. 24, 1919; children—Leda Arlen (Mrs. Ralph Howell Jones), Elizabeth Jean (Mrs. William Mitchell Ayers). Admitted to Okla. bar, 1925, Mo., 1940; with Skelly Oil Co., 1924-33, atty., 1929-33; atty. Shell Oil Co., 1933-37, gen. atty., asst. sec., 1937—; lectr. oil and gas law, U.S., Can. Pres. Tulsa Family and Children's Service, 1948-51, dir.; dir. Tulsa Garden Center, 1952—, pres., 1952-55. Mem. Am., Okla., Mo. bar assns., Am. Judicature Soc., Mid-Continent Oil and Gas Assn. (exec. com., chmn. legal com. Okla.-Kan. div. 1941—), Ky. Oil and Gas Assn., Am. Petroleum Inst. Natural Gasoline Assn. Am., C. of C. Presbyn. (elder). Mason. Club: Tulsa. Home: 1731 E. 30th St., Tulsa 5. Office: Mayo Bldg., Tulsa 2. Died Jan. 7, 1958; buried Tulsa.

CUNNINGHAM, Holly Estil, author, lecturer, educator; b. Jackson County, W.Va., Jan. 13, 1883; s. Nathan Decatur and Sarah Ann (Shafer) C.; A.B., Lebanon (O.) Coll., 1908, LL.B., 1910; student U. of Cincinnati; Ph.D., U. of Chicago, 1918; m. Lelia Jane Morris, 1905. Began teaching in pub. schs. of W.Va.; pres. and prof. philosophy Lebanon (O.) Coll., 1914-17; prof. and head dept. philosophy U. of Okla., 1917-23; prof. and head dept. W.Va. U., 1923-29; prof. and dir. summer session Atlantic U., 1930-32, also trustee and sec. of univ.; pres. Alfred Holbrook Coll., 1932-40; pres. Edison Coll. 1941-50; prof. philosophy Asbury Coll., Wilmore, Ky., since 1950. Chairman Lee County Red Cross, 1945-46. Lecturer Asso. Clubs, Inc., 1949. Mem. A.A.A.S., Southern Soc. for Philosophy and Psychology, Am. Philos. Assn. (Western and Eastern branches), Am. Assn. Univ. Profs., W. Va. Acad. Sciences, Southwestern Polit. Sci. Assn., Acacia, Kappa Delta Phi, Phi Delta Kappa. Baptist. Mason (32°), Odd Fellow, Rotarian. Author: Types of Logical Theory, 1918; An Introduction to Philosophy, 1920; Textbook of Logic, 1924; Fundamental Concepts in the Physical Sciences, 1927; The New Deal in Education, 1932; New Concepts in Education, 1935; A Program of Education, 1937; Education and the Concept of Utility, 1939; Modern Science and Ancient Morality, 1947; An Introduction to Philosophy, revised, 1949; Adventures in Philosophy, Vol. 8, 1951. Home: 108 Bellevue St., Wilmore, Ky. Died Jan. 23, 1952; buried Asbury College Plot, Wilmore, Ky.

CUNNINGHAM, John Ferguson, educator; b. Afton, Ia., Feb. 4, 1877; s. Robert Henry and Virginia Ross (Loy) C.; B.S., Ohio State U., 1897, M.S., 1899; m. Edna Mumper, Oct. 30, 1907; children—John F., Richard M. Instr. in horticulture and forestry, Ohio State U., 1898-99; editor Ohio Farmer, Cleveland, O., 1899-1922; pres. editor, Wisconsin Agriculturist and Farmer, Racine, Wis., 1922-29; pub. Fla. Grower, 1932-40, dean College of Agr., Ohio State U., 1932-47. War food commr., World War I. Trustee Ohio State U. 8 yrs. (chmn. 2 yrs.); mem. bd. of control Ohio Agrl. Expt. Sta. several years., O. Wildlife Research Station since 1936; dir. O. State Univ. Research Foundation since 1937; member of Board of Appeal, State of Ohio since 1950; chmn. Ohio Farm Chemurgic Commn.; chmn. Ohio Soil Conservation Com.; member Ohio State Fair Relocation Committee. Fellow A.A.A.S., Ohio Acad. of Science; mem. Am. Agricultural Editorial Assn. (pres.), Am. Forestry Assn., Phi Gamma Delta, Sigma Xi, Alpha Zeta (co-founder), Gamma Sigma Delta. Republican. Presbyterian. Mason. Clubs: Rotary (ex-pres.), Faculty; Kit-Kat. Home: 1991 Suffolk Rd., Columbus, O. Died Apr. 28, 1953.

CUNNINGHAM, Warren W(ardlaw), lawyer; b. Elizabeth, N.J., Oct. 11, 1885; s. Charles Eugene and Annie (Warren) C.; student Memphis U. Sch., 1899-1901, Princeton Prep. Sch., 1901-02; A.B., Princeton, 1906; LL.B., N.Y. Law Sch., 1909; m. Lucy Pinckney Elliott, Apr. 8, 1918; children—Esther Elliott (Mrs. Robert P. Shay), Charles. Admitted to Bar, N.Y. State, 1909, since practiced in N.Y.C., mem. Hall, Cunningham & Haywood and predecessor firms, 1913—; chmn. bd. dirs. Art Metal Constrn. Co., Jamestown, N.Y., 1945—; dir. Am. Maize-Products Co., The County Trust Co., Speer Carbon Co., Trojan Powder Co. Served as mayor, Village of Scarsdale, N.Y., 1927-29. Chmn. Westchester County Tax Commn., 1939-45. Mem. Am., N.Y. State, City of N.Y. bar assns. Republican. Presbyn. Clubs: University Union League, Princeton, St. Andrew's Golf, Am. Yacht. Home: 16 Autenrieth Rd., Scarsdale. Office: 41 E. 42nd St., N.Y.C. 17. Died Nov. 10, 1953; buried St. James the Less, Scarsdale, N.Y.

CURLEE, Francis M., lawyer; b. Corinth, Miss., Feb. 1, 1877; s. William Peyton and Mary Elizabeth (Boone) C.; LL.B., U. Miss., 1902; children—Francis M. Curlee (dec.), Shelby Hammond III. Admitted to Miss. bar, 1902, and began practice at Corinth; moved to St. Louis and began practice there, 1905. Pres. Curlee Clothing Co. Served from capt. to lt. col., F.A., U.S. Army, 1917-19. Mem. Am., Mo. (pres. 1920-21), St. Louis bar assns., Delta Psi. Democrat. Mason. Club: Glen Echo Country. Home: Defiance, Mo.; also 5724 Chamberlain Av., St. Louis. Office: 1001 Washington Av., St. Louis 1. Died Mar. 1958.

CURLEY, James Michael, mayor, ex-congressman; b. Boston, Nov. 20, 1874; s. Michael and Sarah (Clancy) C.; student pub. grammar and high sch., Boston; LL.D., Suffolk Law Sch., 1935; m. Mary E. Herlihy, June 27, 1906; m. 2d, Mrs. Gertrude M. Dennis, Jan. 7, 1937. Real estate and ins. bus., Boston, 1902—; mem. Curley Bros.; trustee Hibernia Savings Bank (pres. 1919-38); Curley Luck Gold Mining Co. Mem. Boston Common Council, 1900-01; mem. Mass. Ho. of Reps., 1902, 03; Bd. Aldermen, 1904-09; City Council, 1910-11; mem. 62d and 63d Congresses, 12th Dist.; resigned, Feb. 2, 1914, after assuming office as mayor of Boston; reëlected for terms 1922-26, 30-34; gov. Mass., 1935-37; mem. 78th and 79th Congresses, 11th Mass. Dist.; elected mayor of Boston, 1945, for term ending 1950. Decorated Order Rising Sun (Japan); Order of St. Sophia (Serbia); Order of the Commander of Crown of Italy; recipient of medal of Gratitude (France). Mem. Boston C. of C., Ancient and Hon. Arty. Co. Democrat. Elk, K.C. Clubs: Catholic of New York; Mayors' of U.S.; Mayors' of Mass.; University. Home: 350 Jamaica Way, Boston. Died Nov. 12, 1958.

CURLEY, William A., newspaper editor; b. N.Y. City; m. Mary Grace, Mar. 9, 1937. Began as office boy for advt. agt.; bicycle writer, N.Y. Recorder, until its demise; advt. dir. Wolf-Am. Bicycle Co.; with Hearst Orgn. since 1898; sports writer, N.Y. Evening Jour., 1898; successively sports editor, Sunday and news editor, N.Y. Am., mng. editor Los Angeles Herald, 1911-13, San Francisco Call, 1913-14, editor Chicago Am., 1914-27; editor N.Y. Jour. since 1927; asst. editor-in-chief Hearst Consol. Publs. 1942—. Home: Smithridge Rd. New Canaan, Conn. Office: New York Journal-American, 210 South St., N.Y.C. Died Oct. 23, 1955; buried Holy Cross Cemetery, Bklyn.

CURRAN, Thomas Jerome, lawyer, former state ofcl.; b. N.Y.C., Nov. 28, 1898; s. Danial J. and Margaret Mary (Connors) C.; A.B., Fordham Coll., 1920; LL.B., Fordham U., 1923, LL.D., 1946; J.S.D., St. Johns U., 1935; LL.D., Manhattan College, 1948; m. Margaret Frances Farley, June 26, 1926; children—Paul Jerome, John Daniel. Admitted to N.Y. bar, 1924; mem. firm Curran and Stim, N.Y.C.; asst. U.S. atty. So. Dist. of N.Y. 1928-31; alderman, 10th Aldermanic Dist., N.Y. County, 1934-37; sec. of state for N.Y., 1943—. Minority leader, Bd. of Aldermen, N.Y.C., 1934-37; del. N.Y. State Constl. Conv., 1938; exec. mem. Rep. orgn. 10th Assembly Dist. (now 1st Assembly Dist.), 1936—, exec. mem., 1945—; chmn. Rep. exec. com., New York County, 1940—; pres. N.Y. County Rep. Com., 1940—; pres. Nat. Rep. Club, 1942-43. Dir. Lawyers Mortgage and Title Co. Served in U.S. Army, June-Dec. 1918; commd. 2d lt., Sept. 1918; served from 2d lt. to capt., 69th Inf., N.Y. N.G., 1919-22. Mem. Am. Legion, 40 and 8, Mil. Order Fgn. Wars, Friendly Sons of St. Patrick, Soc. of Am. Wars, Delta Theta Phi. Roman Catholic. K.C. Clubs: Manhattan, Nat. Republican, N.Y. Young Republican, 1st Assembly Dist. Republican, Downtown Athletic, Tough. Home: 25 Bank St. Address: 29 Broadway, N.Y.C. Died July 29, 1958; buried Calvary Cemetery, L.I.

CURREY, Brownlee Own, investment banker; b. Nashville, Tenn., Oct. 22, 1900; s. Robert Brownlee and Elizabeth (Norton) C.; student Montgomery Bell Acad., Nashville, 1919; A.B., Vanderbilt, 1923; m. Frances Hampton, Nov. 2, 1926; children—Brownlee, Margaret. Br. mgr., Fourth and First Nat. Bank, Nashville, 1921-25; mgr., 1926-30; organized Equitable Securities Corp., Nashville, Dec. 1930 and since served as pres. of co. with brs. in N.Y. City, Hartford, Connecticut, Atlanta, Birmingham, Knoxville, Greensboro, Memphis, Jackson, Miss., New Orleans and Dallas; pres. and dir. Cherokee Corp. since 1947; vice pres. and dir. So. Assn. of Sci. and Industry, Inc., since 1947. Dir., Moore-Handley Hardware Co., Inc., Nashville Gas and Heating Co., Tenn. Natural Gas Lines, Inc., Transcontinental Bus. System, Inc., United Transit Co., West Ky. Coal Company Farm and Ranch Pub. Co., Ward-Belmont Sch., Inc., West Meade Farms, Inc. Mem. board commrs. Watkins Institute, Nashville. Trustee So. Research Inst. (chmn. bd.) Univ. Nashville including Montgomery Bell Acad.; Vanderbilt Univ. (mem. athletic com.); mem. bd. Tax Foundation, Inc., Boy Scouts of Am. (dir. and mem. exec. bd. Middle Tenn. area), mem. Newcomen Soc., So. Soc., Tenn. Taxpayers' Assn. (dir. and mem. exec. com.); Phi Delta Theta. Episcopalian (mem. bd. endowment corp.). Clubs: The Links; Belle Meade Golf and Country, Nashville; Nat. Golf (mem. bd. govs.), Augusta, Ga.; Farmington Country, Charlottesville, Va.; Links. Home: Lynwood Blvd., Nashville 5. Office: 322 Union St., Nashville 3. Died Feb. 21, 1952.

CURRIE, John S., pres., dir. Robinson & Co.; b. Carbonear, Newfoundland. Pres. St. Johns News; vice chmn. Broadcasting Corp. of Newfoundland. Mason. Home: Winter Place, St. Johns. Office: Robinson & Co., St. Johns, Newfoundland, Canada. Died Dec. 14, 1956.*

CURRY, John F., b. Anghantrea, County Fermanagh, Ireland, Nov. 23, 1873; s. Michael and Ann J. (McManus) Curry; brought with parents to New York City in infancy; educated public schools; LL.D. from Mount St. Mary's College, Md., 1930; m. Mary Frances McKiernan, June 14, 1906; children—Veronica, John Francis, Francis Richard, Robert Emmet, Bernard. Began with Western Union Telegraph Co., later with Union Stock Yard & Market Co.; head of John F. Curry Agency, Inc. (insurance), 1910—. Apptd. financial clk. under city paymaster, 1899; mem. N.Y. Assembly 2 terms, 1903, 04; mem. exec. com. Tammany Hall, 1905-29; commr. of records, surrogate's court, 1911-29; head of Tammany Hall, Apr. 1929-Apr. 1934; sachem Tammany Soc. K.C. Mem. Elks, Red Men, Ancient Order of Hibernians, Lakeville Golf, Paumonok Golf. Home: 1010 Fifth Av., New York, N.Y. Died, Apr. 25, 1957.

CURRY, Michael John, ret. ry. ofcl.; b. Syarcuse, N.Y., Sept. 30, 1879; s. Michael and Margaret (Monahan) C.; student Syracuse High Sch., 1892-96, Henley Business Coll., Syracuse, 1896-97; m. Margaret H. Miller, June 26, 1917; children—John M., Vincent J. Successively with N.Y.C. R.R., C.,R.I.&P. Ry. and El Paso & South Western Ry. as clk., sect. to chmn., gen. agt. and asst. to pres., 1898-1925; asst. to exec. v.p. S.P. Co., 1925-27; v.p. and asst. sec.-treas W.P. R.R. Co. and sec.-treas. W.P. R.R. Corp., 1927-48, ret. Catholic. Home: 10 Perth Av., New Rochelle, N.Y. Died July 20, 1954.*

CURRY, Peter H., chmn. bd. dirs. South Penn Oil Co. Home: 905 Maryland Av. Office: Chamber of Commerce Bldg., Pitts. Died Jan. 26, 1959.*

CURTIS, A(rthur) J(ohn) R(amage), business exec.; b. Chgo., Apr. 21, 1887; s. John Crosby and Marion (Ramage) C.; A.A., Lewis Inst.; 1908, M.E., 1910; m. Estelle Mildred Scherling, 1913; children—Arthur Rudolph, Herbert John, Jane Elizabeth. Lab. technician Universal Portland Cement Co., 1909, asst. engr., 1910-16; dir. of extension Portland Cement Assn., 1916-20, mgr. Cement Products Bur., 1920-27, asst. to gen. mgr. 1927-46, sec. Accident Prevention Com., 1927—, asst. sec. and safety dir., 1947—. Insp. mil. concrete schs., World War I; sec. Nat. Conf. on Concrete House Construction, 1920; sec., cement sect. Nat. Safety Council, 1927-43, mem. exec. bd., 1943-46, bd. of dirs., 1946—; charter mem. Indsl. Hygiene Found.; mem. President's Conf. on Indsl. Safety, 1948; mem. bd. mgrs. Lewis Inst., 1940; trustee Ill. Inst. Tech. and Armour Research Found., 1940—. Awarded Joseph A. Holmes Safety Assn. medal and certificate of honor, U.S. Bur. of Mines, 1947. Mem. Am. Soc. Agrl. Engrs. (pres. 1922), Am. Indsl. Hygiene Assn. Republican. Presbyn. Club: Union League (Chgo.). Author of numerous papers, reports and articles on bldg. subjects, accident prevention and indsl. hygiene. Home: 934 Bonnie Brae, River Forest, Ill. Office: 33 W. Grand Av., Chgo. Died Nov. 10, 1956; buried Forest Home Cemetery, Forest Park, Ill.

CURTIS, Charles Gordon, inventor; b. Boston, Apr. 20, 1860; s. George Ticknor and Louise A., C.; C.E., Columbia, 1881, M.S., 1907; LL.B., N.Y. Law Sch., 1883. Patent lawyer, 8 yrs.; organized C. & C. Electric Motor Co., the first to make electric motors and electric fans; organized Curtis Electric Mfg. Co., of which was pres.; invented and developed the Curtis Steam turbine; sold steam turbine rights to Gen. Electric Co.; introduced turbine of own design into British, Japanese, German and U.S. Navies. Recipient Count Rumford Gold and Silver medals Am. Soc. of Arts and Sciences. Republican. Invented Curtis Scavenging System for 2-cycle engines. Home: University Club. 1 W. 54th St., N.Y.C. Died Mar. 10, 1953; buried Westchester, N.Y.

CURTIS, Charles Pelham, lawyer; b. Boston, May 8, 1891; s. Charles Pelham and Ellen Amory (Anderson) C.; student Groton Sch., 1904-10, Ecole des Sciences Politiques, Paris, 1913-14; A.B., Harvard, 1914; LL.B., Harvard, 1917; m. Edith G. Roelker, July 17, 1914; children—Sarah C. (Mrs. Lewis Iselin), Anita D. (Mrs. Anita McClellan), Charles P., Jr., William Roelker, Richard Cary, II, (killed in A.A.F., Italy, January 1945); married 2d. Frances W. Prentice, February 27, 1936. Admitted to Mass. bar, 1919; with firm of Choate, Hall & Stewart, 1919-21, partner since 1932; special assistant U.S. atty., Mass., 1922-23; mem. Curtis & Curtis, 1925-32; trustee Century Shares Trust; dir. Incorporated Investors, Inc. Income Fund; pres. Dumaines; dir. Nat. Bank Nicaragua, 1937-38; special asst. to under sec. of state, 1941. Member Mass. Constitutional Conveniton, 1917. Mem. Harvard Corp., 1924-35. Lecturer in government Harvard, 1928, in sociology, 1932. Mem. Soc. of Fellows (senior fellow), 1933-36. Served in U.S. Navy, on U.S.S.S. Duncan, 1917-19, World War. Mem. Am. Acad. Arts and Scis., Am. Law Inst.; mem. council Survey Legal Procession Fellow Am. Bar Foundn. Am.; mem. Mass., Boston, Fed., N.Y.C. bar assns., Phi Beta Kappa. Author: Hunting in Africa, East, and West (with Richard C. Curtis), 1925; Introduction to Pareto (with George C. Homans), 1934; The Practical Cogitator (with Ferris Greenslet), 1945; Lions Under the Throne, 1947; It's Your Law, 1954; The Modern Prudent Investor, 1955; The Oppenheimer Case, 1955; A Commonplace Book, 1957. Clubs: Tavern, Somerset, Century, Saturday, Examiner, Pocellian. Home: 18 Mount Vernon St., Boston 8. Office: 30 State St., Boston 9. Died Dec. 1959.

CURTIS, Constance, artist; b. Washington; d. Dr. Edward and Augusta Lawler (Stacey) Curtis; pupil Art Students' League, New York, and William M. Chase. Exhibited Paris Exposition, 1900, St. Louis Exposition, 1904, Sesque-centennial International Exposition, 1926, New York World's Fair, 1940. Awarded first prize National Association Women Artists, 1922, for picture, "At the Italian Booth"; hon. mention, Stockbridge Art Assn., 1933, for picture, "Gardenias and Satin"; awarded 1st prize, Nat. Assn. of Women Artists, Black and White Exhbn., 1935, for drawing, "Portrait Sketch." awarded the Grumbacher prize at the exhibition of the New York Chapter of the Am. Artist's Professional League, Nov. 1944 for painting: "Woman in Gray." Mem. Art Students League, Allied Artists of America, Cosmopolitan Club, Nat. Soc. Colonial Dames, The Citizens Union, Assn. Women Artists. Home and Studio: 125 E. 91st St., New York 28, N.Y. Died Nov. 26, 1959.

CURTIS, Eugene Judson, business exec.; b. Clinton, Ia., July 26, 1884; s. George Martin and Ettie (Lewis) C.; student Phillips Andover; B.A., Yale, 1909; m. Ardelle Jones, Nov. 16, 1910 (died 1939); children—Frances C. Brackett, Virginia C. Fenn, Eugene J. Jr., Charles F. II; m. 2d, Margaret De Lescaille, Aug. 17, 1945. Bus. mgr. Yale Daily News, 1909; mfr. Curtis woodwork in all capacities, 1909—; v.p., gen. mgr. Curtis Bros. & Co., Clinton, Ia., 1915-21; exec. v.p. Curtis Cos., Inc., 1921-47, pres., 1947—; pres., dir. McCloud River R.R. Co., San Francisco; dir., sec. Bald Mountain Mining Co., Trojan, S.D. Served as dir. and mem. exec. com. Lumber Code Authority, chmn. stock millwork adv. com. OPA; mem. com. W.P.A. Chmn. bd. trustees

Clinton YMCA; pres., dir. Clinton Coliseum Co. Served as pres. Clinton Bd. of Edn. Trustee First Presbyn. Ch., Clinton. Home: Hillcrest. Office: Curtis Cos., Inc., Clinton, Ia. Died Feb. 28, 1951; buried Clinton.

CURTIS, George Lewis, woodwork mfr.; b. Clinton, Ia., Aug. 23, 1878; s. George Martin and Etta (Lewis) C.; grad. Williston Sem., Easthampton, Mass., 1898; student Yale, 1898-99; m. Frances Wilcox, May 16, 1900 (dec.); children—Elizabeth Wilcox (Mrs. Henry Waldo Murphy), George Martin, Louise (Mrs. Thomas Chalmers Curtis); m. 2d, Alice E. Holmes, Nov. 27, 1935. Began as mfr. of woodwork, Clinton, 1899; pres. Curtis Cos., Inc. 1911-47, Chmn. bd. since 1947; president G. L. Curtis Company, Clinton; director Malco Refineries, Inc., Roswell, New Mexico, City National Bank of Clinton, McCloud River Lbr. Co. Chmn. War Service Com. of mill work industry, World War I. Trustee Y.W.C.A., Jane Lamb Memorial Hosp. Republican. Presbyterian. Mason. Clubs: Clinton Country (Clinton); Chicago (Chicago); Tucson Country (Tucson). Home: Hillcrest, Clinton, Ia. Died Mar. 17, 1956; buried Springdale Cemetery, Clinton, Ia.

CURTIS, Gerald Beckwith, educator; b. Bethlehem, Conn., Feb. 22, 1882; s. Frederick Smillie and Ida Jewell (Whiting) C.; student Curtis Sch. (Brookfield Center), Horace Mann Sch., N.Y.C.; B.S., Columbia, 1906; m. Martha Charnley Atwater Lewis, June 23, 1909; children—Sarah Lewis, Frederick Whiting, Florence Elizabeth (dec.), Deborah Atwater. Mech. engr. De La Vergne Machine Co., N.Y.C., 1906-07, Worthington Pump Co., 1907; with Curtis School for Young Boys, Brookfield Center, Conn., 1907—, owner and prin., 1935—. Served as 1st lt. inf., Conn. Home Guard, 1917-18. Chmn. Rep. Town Com., 1916-20; grand juror Town of Brookfield, 1930—; mem. Congl. Laymen's Adv. Com. of Conn., 1934—. Trustee Danbury Hosp., 1930—, mem. bd. mgrs., 1935—; dir. Fairfield County Planning Assn. Mem. Conn. Schoolmasters' Assn., Secondary Edn. Bd., Columbia Engring. Soc., Beta Theta Pi. Republican. Conglist. Clubs: Columbia (New York); Rotary (Danbury, Conn.); and others. Home: Brookfield Center, Conn. Died June 5, 1956; buried Oak Cliff Cemetery, Derby, Conn.

CURTIS, Harvey Lincoln, physicist; b. Mason, Mich., Dec. 14, 1875; s. Wm. Howell and Sarah Bowen (Ormsby) C.; Ph.B., U. Mich., 1900, A.M., 1903, Ph.D., 1910; m. Anna Puffer, Aug. 26, 1903; children—Roger W., Howard J., Alvin G. (dec.), Norma L., Mildred A. Asst. in phys. lab. U. Mich., 1902-03; instr. physics Mich. State Agrl. Coll., 1903-07; with Bur. of Standards, Washington, successively asst. physicist, 1907-13, asso. physicist, 1913-18, physicist, 1918-24, sr. physicist, 1924-28, prin. physicist, 1928-46; retired 1947. Recipient Joint Army and Navy Cert. of Appreciation, 1948. Fellow Am. Physical Soc., A.A.A.S., Am. Inst. E.E. (chmn. Washington, sect. 1935); mem. Washington Acad. Scis. (pres. 1942), Washington Philos. Soc. (pres. 1931), Am. Soc. for Testing Materials, Am. Optical Soc., Phi Beta Kappa; mem. Internat. Electrical Congress, Paris, France, 1933. Methodist. Club: Cosmos. Author: Electrical Measurements; also scientific papers of Bur. of Standards and articles in technical journals. Home: 6816 Delaware St., Chevy Chase 15, Md. Died Apr. 17, 1956; buried Rock Creek Cemetery, Washington.

CURTIS, Henry Stoddard, lecturer, author; b. Olivet, Mich., Feb. 9, 1870; s. Samuel and Mary Ann (Stoddard) C.; A.B., Olivet (Mich.) Coll., 1894; A.B., Yale, 1895; Ph.D., Clark U., 1898; m. Charlotte Doremus Scudder, of Winchester, Mass., Nov. 25, 1902; children—Henry Stoddard, Bessie Scudder, Elnora Charlotte. Asst. dir., dir. and gen. dir., playgrounds, N.Y.C., 3 summers, 1898-1901; made trip to Germany and England to study playgrounds; supr. playgrounds, D.C., 1905-09; dir. hygiene and phys. tng. Mo., 1923-30; dir. recreation survey U. Mich., 1930—. Mem. Columbia U. Ednl. Survey to Panama, 1931; organizer, 1906, and later sec., v.p. Playground Assn. Am.; sec. Nat. Child Welfare Conf., 1910; exec. sec. The Huron-Clinton Parkway Com.; has conducted playground revivals in 15 cities and lectured at many univs., normal schs., insts. Mem. N.E.A., Play Assn. of Am., Progressive. Conglist. Author: Play and Recreation in the Open Country, 1914; Education Through Play, 1915; Practical Conduct of Play, 1915; The Play Movement and Its Significance, 1917; Recreation for Teachers. Formerly YMCA phys. dir. and lecturer in France; later supervisor farmers' inst. for intermediate sect., AEF U., Beaume, France. Home: 1100 Hill St., Ann Arbor, Mich. Died Jan. 8, 1954; buried Arborcrest Cemetery, Ann Arbor.

CURTIS, James Freeman, lawyer; b. Manchester, Mass., Aug. 16, 1878; s. Greely Stevenson and Harriot (Appleton) C.; A.B., Harvard, 1899, LL.B., 1903; m. Nov. 26, 1912, Laura Beatrice Merriam; children—Laura Elizabeth, James F., Frazier, Pauline; m. 2d, Eleanor Munroe Green, Sept. 25, 1938. With firm of Storey, Thorndike, Palmer & Thayer, Boston, 1903-06; asst. atty.-gen. of Mass., 1906-09; asst. dist. atty., Suffolk County, Mass., Mar.-Nov., 1909; asst. sec. of treasury, Nov. 26, 1909-July 31, 1913; counsel and dep. gov. Fed. Reserve Bank of New York, 1914-19: mem. Denison & Curtis, 1919-21, Curtis, Fosdick & Belknap, 1921-36, Curtis, Belknap & Webb, 1937-39, Curtis & Belknap, 1940-47; counsel to Patterson, Belknap & Webb since 1947. Unitarian. Clubs: Tavern, Harvard (Boston); Harvard, Racquet and Tennis, Century Assn., Coffee House, Down Town Assn., Piping Rock (New York). Intercollegiate golf champion, 1898. Home: Roslyn, N.Y. Office: 1 Wall St., N.Y.C. Died Nov. 25, 1952; buried Roslyn, N.Y.

CURTIS, John Talbot, lawyer; b. Stratford, Conn., Aug. 15, 1900; s. Howard Junior and Ellen Virginia (Talbot) C.; student Army and Navy Prep. Sch., 1917-18; B.S., U.S. Mil. Acad., 1920; LL.B., Yale, 1926; m. Isobel Ramsay Buckley, Nov. 5, 1928; children—Charles Buckley, Clare Howard (Mrs. Charles P. Rimmer, Jr.), Mary Talbot. Admitted to Conn. bar, 1926, N.Y. bar, 1928; practicing lawyer, Bridgeport, Conn., 1926-27, and since 1933, N.Y. City, 1928-32; legal staff R.F.C., Washington, 1932-33; mem. Curtis & Gerety; dir. Southport Savs. Bank, Pepperidge Farm, Inc., Southport Area Association, J. Pedersen Manufacturing Company. Past president Pequot Library Assn. Southport; trustee Bridgeport Protestant Orphan Asylum. Served as 1st lt. Inf., U. S. Army, 1920-22; col., dir. procurement, Boston Q.M. Depot, 1942-45; base q.m. Base K. Leyte, P.I., 1945. Mem. Am., Conn. State and Bridgeport bar assns. Clubs: Army and Navy (Washington); University (Bridgeport); Country (Fairfield, Conn.); Pequot Yacht (Southport); Fairfield County Hunt (Westport, Conn.). Home: 174 Old South Rd., Southport. Office: 955 Main St., Bridgeport 3, Conn. Died May 21, 1958.

CURTIS, Melville Goss, mfr. textiles; b. Olean, N.Y., Aug. 21, 1875; s. Rev. Henry M. (D.D.) and Evelyn Cramer (Goss) C.; A.B., Yale, 1897; m. Emma Warren, May 24, 1909; children—Evelyn Goss (Mrs. James Houston Young), Katherine Wilson (Mrs. Theodore H. Vetterlein, Jr.). Asso. with Collins & Aikman Corp., mfrs. textiles, Phila., entering employ in 1897, chmn. bd., 1929—. Republican. Presbyn. Clubs: Union League, Racquet, Philadelphia Country (Phila.). Home: 120 Llanberris Rd., Bala-Cynwyd, Pa. Office: 51st and Parkside Av., Phila. Died May 23, 1950.

CURTIS, Richard Cary, lawyer; b. Boston, May 25, 1894; s. Charles P. and Ellen Amory (Anderson) C.; student Groton Sch., 1906-12; A.B., Harvard, 1916, LL.B., 1921; m. Anita D. Grosvenor, Aug. 9, 1917. Admitted to Mass. bar, 1921; mem. firm Curtis & Curtis, 1923-32; partner Choate, Hall & Stewart, 1932—; dir. New Eng. Tel. & Tel. Co., Fiduciary Trust Co., Chain Store Investment Corp., Fifty Associates; trustee Boston Personal Property Trust. Lt. (j.g.) submarine service, USN, 1918-19. Trustee, asst. treas. and v.p. Boston Museum of Fine Arts; mem. corp. Peter Bent Brigham Hosp. Mem. Am., Mass., Boston bar assns., Boston Legal Aid Soc. (dir.), Phi Beta Kappa. Clubs: Somerset, Tavern (Boston); Brookline Country, Essex County. Author: Hunting in Africa East and West (with Charles P. Curtis, Jr.), 1925. Home: 215 Warren St., Brookline, Mass. Died Jan. 20, 1951; buried Mt. Auburn, Cambridge, Mass.

CURTISS, David Raymond, mathematician) b. Derby, Conn., Jan. 12, 1878; s. Hamilton Burton and Emily Wheeler (Curtis) C.; A.B., U. Cal., 1899, A.M., 1901; Ph.D., Harvard, 1903, traveling fellow, 1903-04; studied École Normale Supérieure, Paris France; m. Sigrid Eckman, June 25, 1907 (dec. Apr. 1941); children—John Hamilton, Margaret Eckman, Alice Judson; m. 2d, Ruth C. Kneen, July 23, 1943. Instr. mathematics Yale, 1904-05; asst. prof. mathematics Northwestern U., 1905-07, asso. prof., 1907-09, prof., 1909-43, prof. emeritus, 1943—; lectr. mathematics Harvard, 1920-21. Fellow A.A.A.S. (vice-pres. sect. A, 1921); mem. Am. Math. Soc. (council, and vice-pres.), Math. Assn. America (pres.), Société Mathématique de France, Circolo Mathematico di Palermo, Delta Tau Delta, Phi Beta Kappa, Sigma Xi. Author: Analytic Functions, 1926; (with E. J. Moulton) Trigonometry, 1927, High School Trigonometry, 1928, Analytic Geometry, 1930, Brief Course in Trigonometry, 1940, Essentials of Trigonometry, 1942, Essentials of Analytic Geometry, 1947. Contbr. to math. jours. Editor Trans. Am. Math. Soc., 1913-19, also Bulletin Am. Math. Soc. and Carus Monographs. Home: 1249 Montery A St., Redlands, Cal. Died Apr. 28, 1953.

CURTISS, William Hanford, glass mfg. exec.; b, Olean, N.Y., Jan. 15, 1884; s. William O. and Ella (Hanford) C.; A.B., Williams Coll., 1906; m. Emily Frost, Sept. 11, 1915; children—William Hanford, Jr., Ruth (Mrs. John Elliot Leggat). Employed in sales, shipping and spare parts depts. Walter A. Wood Mowing & Reaping Machine Co., 1907-20; asst. to pres. Corning Glass Works, 1920-29, v.p., 1929-53, sec., 1936-53, dir. 1937—, exec. com., 1946—, hon. v.p., 1954—; pres. The Corning Museum of Glass 1952—; dir. Corning Fibre Box Corp., Corhart Refractories Co. Served from capt. to lt. col. U.S. Army, 1916-19. Awarded Croix de Guerre. Dir. and mem. Steuben Area Council, Boy Scouts of Am. and mem. Region 2 exec. com. Pres. bd. trustees Corning Pub. Library, 1929-35. Clubs: Corning Country, University, Williams, St. Anthony (New York). Home: 148 E. 5th St. Office: Corning Glass Works, Corning, N.Y. Died Jan. 1960.

CURTISS, William John, journalist; b. Rochester, N.Y., July 16, 1873; s. Jay C. D. and Frances Marion (Sheffer) C.; grad. Rochester Free Acad., 1892; A. B., Cornell U., 1896; m. Mary Isabel Smith, Apr. 24, 1897; 1 dau., Marion (Mrs. Joseph G. Stanton). Asso. editor Cornell Daily Sun, 1895, editor-in-chief, 1896; reporter, later market editor New York Commercial, 1898-1902; asst. city editor, later night editor New York Jour. of Commerce, 1903-06; New York mgr. Commercial Telegram Bureauz, 1907-11; Am. financial corr. London Times, 1912-16; Am. business mgr. Commercial Telegram Bureaux, 1907-11; Am. fi- York Commercial, 1921-22; in charge public utility news Wall Street Jour., 1922-26; in charge publicity G. L. Ohrstrom & Co., Inc., N.Y.C., 1926—; Am. corr. London Economist, 1920-24. Mem. C. of C. of State of N.Y., Kappa Sigma, Quill and Dagger. Republican. Episcopalian. Contbr. to Financial Digest, Water Works Engring. and other mags. Mem. staff Bradstreet's. Home: 41 N. Fullerton Av., Montclair, N.J. Office: 44 Wall St., N.Y.C. Died Feb. 10, 1947; buried Linden, N.J.

CUSHING, Harry Alonzo, lawyer; b. Lynn, Mass., Sept. 15, 1870; s. Alvin Matthew and Elizabeth (Pearsons) C.; A.B., Amherst, 1891; A.M., Columbia, 1894, Ph.D., 1896, LL.B., 1901; m. Elizabeth Newton, Sept. 16, 1899. Admitted to bar, 1901, and since in practice at N.Y.C.; lectr., tutor history Columbia, 1895-1900, lectr. history and constl. law, 1901-03, prof. law, 1907-09. Mem. Assn. Bar City N.Y.; sec. N.E. Society of N.Y., 1908-42. Club: Century. Author: History of the Transition from Provincial to Commonwealth Government in Massachusetts, 1896; voting Trusts, a Chapter in Modern Corporate History, 1915, 27. Editor: The Writings of Samuel Adams (4 vols.), 1904-08. Home: Norfolk, Conn. Died Sept. 6, 1955; buried Holyoke, Mass.

CUSHING, John E., ret. transportation exec.; b. San Rafael, Cal., Nov. 20, 1887; s. Sidney B. and Grace N. (Eldridge) C.; A.B., Stanford, 1908; m. Grace Isabel Beaver, Aug. 21, 1915. Began with Bates & Chesebrough, 1909-12; W. R. Grace & Co., 1912-16, Williams, Dimond & Co., N.Y., 1916-17; in Army Transport Service, N.Y., 1917-19; with U.S. Shipping Bd., Washington, 1919-20; partner Williams, Dimond & Co., 1921-23; with Am. Hawaiian S.S. Co. 1923, v.p., 1925, pres., 1938-47; pres. Matson Navigation Co., 1947-50, retired; dir. Pacific Mfg. Co. (Santa Clara), Bank of California, N.A., Pacific Tel. & Tel. Co., Matson Navigation Co., Firemans Fund Ins. Co. (all San Francisco); trustee Stanford U. With War Shipping Adminstrn., 1942, Pacific coast dir. Feb.-June, 1942, asst. dep. adminstr. ship operations, Washington, 1942-43, asst. dep. adminstr. Pacific Area, San Francisco, 1943-45. Club: Pacific Union. Home: 2525 Webster St. Office: 215 Market St., San Francisco. Died Apr. 22, 1956.

CUSHING, Stephen S., judge; b. Nashua, N.H., Mar. 20, 1884; s. George R. and Catherine (Moran) C.; B.S., Dartmouth, 1906; A.M., Middlebury Coll., 1916; LL.D., Norwich U., 1933; m. Bessie L. Morton, June 19, 1912; 1 son, Morton L. Admitted to Vt. bar, 1909; city atty., St. Albans, Vt., 1912-15; states atty. Franklin County, Vt., 1915-17; legislative draftsman State Vt., 1921-31; sec. Vt. Tax Commn., 1929-31; mem., chmn. Pub. Service Commn., 1931-38; superior judge, 1938-49, chief superior judge, 1949-52; asso. justice State Vt. 1952-53. Served as capt., mil. aid to gov., Inf., U.S. Army, World War I. Mem. Am., Vt. bar assns., Am. Legion, 40 et 8, Mil. Order Fgn. Wars. Mason. Home: 61 Bank St., St. Albans, Vt. Died Sept. 23, 1957.

CUSHMAN, Arlon Vannevar, patent lawyer; born Amherst, Mass., Jan. 17, 1869; s. Marshall B. and Josephine (Bassett) C.; grad. Amherst Coll., 1890; LL.B., L.M., L.M.P., George Washington U., 1893; m. Maude Michael, Sept. 28, 1898; 1 son, William Michael. Admitted to D.C. bar, 1892, and practiced Washington, 1893-1950; a founder and sr. partner firm Cushman, Darby & Cushman specialists in patent law. Mem. Am. Patent Law Assn. (past v.p.), Am. and D.C. bar assns., Soc. Mayflower Descendants, S.A.R., Phi Delta Phi. Clubs: Cosmos, Metropolitan (Washington); Chevy Chase (Md.). Home: 2402 Wyoming Av., Washington 8. Office: American Security Bldg., Washington 5. Died Nov. 5, 1950.

CUSHMAN, Frank, industrial edn.; b. Boston, July 15, 1879; s. Frank and Carrie E. (Prince) C.; student Mass. Inst. Tech., Jr. Coll. of Kansas City, Mo., U. Kan.; m. Susan Abbie Wood, Oct. 5, 1901; children—Alice Wadsworth (Mrs. Wm. G. Eliot 3d), Robert Wood. Asst. instr. Mass. Inst. Tech., 1898-1901; tchr., later vice prin. Manual Tr. High Sch., Kansas City, Mo., 1901-13; head mechanic arts Northeast High Sch., Kansas City, 1914; head vocational dept. Central High Sch., Kansas City, 1915; head sch., Mechanic Arts, Kansas City Poly. Inst., 1916-18; in charge war tng. work, Kansas City pub. schs., 1917-18; asst. prin. Night High Sch., Kansas

City, 1915-18; civilian engr. U.S. Govt. Service, Langley Field, Va., summer 1918; fed. agt. indsl. edn. W. Central States, 1918-19, E. Central, 1919-20, N. Atlantic, 1920-22; prin. Lathrop Trade Sch., Kansas City, Mo., part of 1920; chief of Indsl. Edn. Service under U.S. Office of Edn., Washington, 1922-38; cons. vocational edn., 1938—; with Los Angeles Bd. of Edn., school year, 1926-27. Served as lt. comdr. USNR. Unitarian. Mason. Author: Mathematics and the Machinist's Job, 1926; Foremanship and Supervision, 1927, 2d edit., 1938; also articles and papers in ednl. and tech. mags. Home: 4217 38th St. N.W. Office: Dept. of Interior, Office of Education, Washington. Died June 1953.

CUSTIS, Marvin A(shdowne), business executive; born in Washington, D.C., November 11, 1866; the son of Lemuel Wheeler and Elizabeth E. (Ashdowne) C.; grad. Hahnemann Med. Coll.; m. Frances Henshaw Baden, Jan. 21, 1896; 1 dau., Eleanor Parke. Practicing physician until 1925; with Perpetual Bldg. Assn., Washington, 1914—, dir. and trustee, 1914, auditing com., 1917, treas., 1923, pres., 1935, chmn. bd., exec. com., 1947—; mem. Fidelity Investment Co., 1927—, v.p., 1927-30, pres., 1930-45. Mem. Washington Bd. of Trade, Washington Bldg. Congress, Washington Real Estate Bd., Soc. Residential Appraisors, A.M.A., Am. Inst. Homeopathy, Med. Soc. D.C., U.S. Power Squadrons, Am. Rose Soc. Mason (K.T., Shriner); mem. Order of Eastern Star, Improved Order of Red Men. Club: Reciprocity (life mem.). Home: 626 E. Capitol St. Office: 11th and E Sts. N.W., Washington. Died June 3, 1956; buried Congressional Cemetery, Washington.

CUTHRELL, Hugh H(amlin) (cŭthrell') pub. utility exec.; b. Winston-Salem, N.C., Dec. 5, 1892; s. Claude Francis and Lezetta D. C.; student Wake Forest Coll.; A.B., U. N.C., 1915; m. Faith Baldwin, Nov. 6, 1920. Constrn. engr. South P.R. Sugar Co., 1921; engr. distbn. Kings Co. Lighting Co., Bklyn., 1922-27; with Bklyn. Union Gas Co. since 1927, vice president, 1936-51, pres. since Sept. 1951, chmn. of the board since August, 1952; trustee, mem. exec. com. City Savs. Bank. Mem. gas industries adv. council U.S. Dept. of Interior, chmn. N.Y. State Utilities Exec. Conf., 1952. Mem. d. dirs. A.R.C., chmn. blood donor com.; president of L.I. Coll. Hosp.; mem. lay adv. bd., Kings Co. Hosp.; 1st Panel Sheriff's Jury. Recipient Charles A. Munroe award, 1932. Mem. Society of Gas Lighting, Guild of Gas Managers, N.Y. Soc. Mil., Naval Officers, World Wars, Bklyn. Inst. Arts, Scis., Salvation Army Assn., N.Y. Am. Gas Assn. (pres. 1949-50), Am. Mngmt. Assn., Instn. Gas Engrs. (hon.), Soc. Gas Lighting (pres. 1949-50), Assn. Technique del l'Industrie du Gaz en France (hon.). Brooklyn (dir.), Queensborough C.'s of C. Clubs: Kiwanis (pres. 1942), Bklyn. (v.p., bd. dirs.), Engrs. (bd. management) (N.Y.C.); Garden City Golf; Pine Valley Golf. Home: Rt. 2, Weed Av., Norwalk, Conn. Office: 176 Remsen St., Bklyn. 2. Died Aug. 31, 1953; buried Lakeview Cemetery, New Canaan, Conn.

CUTLER, Anna Alice, educator; b. New Haven, Conn., Jan. 24, 1864; d. Evarts and Ellen Louisa (Knight) Cutler; A.B., Smith Coll., 1885, A.M., 1889; Ph.D., Yale, 1896. In charge dept. of philosophy, Rockford (Ill.) Coll., 1892-93; instr. logic, Smith Coll., 1893-95, English, 1897-99, philosophy, 1899-1902, asso. prof., 1902-05, prof., 1905-30, Smith Coll. Mem. Am. Philos. Assn. Conglist. Address: 407 Whitney Av., New Haven, Conn. Died 1957.

CUTLER, Bertram, corporation official; b. Staten Island, N.Y., Sept. 17, 1880; s. William Henry and Annie (Standring) C.; student Westerleigh Collegiate Inst., Westerleigh, S.I., 1895-1900, Packard Business College, N.Y. City, 1900-02; m. Edith Mae Coyne, Nov. 9, 1904; 1 son, Bertram Standring. Associated in confidential capacity with John D. Rockefeller, later John D. Rockefeller, Jr. since 1902; dir. Morristown Trust Co., Merchants Fire Assurance Corp.; trustee Equitable Life Assurance Soc. Conglist. Clubs: Morris County Golf, Morristown; Rockefeller Center Luncheon. Home: New Vernon Rd., Green Village, N.J. Office: 30 Rockefeller Plaza, N.Y.C. Died Feb. 14, 1952.

CUTLER, Condict Walker, Jr., surgeon; b. Morristown, N.J., Aug. 9, 1888; s. Condict Walker and Cora (Carpenter) C.; B.S., Columbia, 1910, M.D., 1912; unmarried. Interne Roosevelt Hosp. 1913-15, asst. surg., 1927-32, asso. surg., 1932-38, attending surgeon, 1948-53, cons. surgeon, 1953—, sec. med. bd., 1948-53; resident gynecologist Sloane Hosp. for Women, 1915-16; attending surg. Lincoln Hosp., 1929-31; dir. surgery Goldwater Meml. Hosp., 1939-53; pres. med. bd. 1949-51, cons. surgeon, 1953—; dir. surgery Morristown (N.J.) Meml. Hosp., 1952-54, consulting surgeon, 1954—; consulting surgeon and trustee N.Y. Dispensary, 1932-48; Rockland State Hosp., since 1943; instr. surgery, Columbia, 1920-28, asso. prof. clin. surgery 1947, prof. clin. surgery, 1947-54; chief Emergency Med. Service, Manhattan Nat. Office of Civilian Defense, 1941-43; surg., mem. cons. bd. and chmn. procurement and assignment service, New York, War Manpower Commn., 1940-43; pvt. practice, N.Y.C. since 1916. Served as 1st Lt. M.C., U.S. Army, A.E.F., 1918-19; Lt. Col. M.C., U.S. Army, 1943-44, Col., 1945-46; surg. consultant, 1st Service Command. Received Legion of Merit, 1946. Presidential citation, 1943, Congressional Medal for Meritorious Service, 1946, Columbia Medal for Excellence 1944, Alumni medal, 1946. Trustee Columbia, 1940-43, 1949-51, N.Y. Acad. Medicine, 1941— (chairman committee on medical education, 1945-47, chairman section of surgery, 1935-36); member joint administrator board Columbia-Presbyn. Med. Center, 1949-51. Fellow A.C.S.; mem. Am. Surg. Assn., Internat. Surg. Assn., N.Y. Acad. Medicine, Society Consultants to Armed Forces, American Assn. Surg. of the Hand (president, 1950), A.M.A., Med. Soc. of County of New York (treas., 1947-52), Am. Legion (past comdr. Columbia U. post), Mil. Order Fgn. Wars, Asso. Alumni Columbia College (pres., 1938-40); asso. Alumni Coll. Physicians and Surgeons (pres. 1950). Republican. Methodist. Club: University of New York City. Author: The Hand: Its Diseases and Disabilities, 1941. Co-author: History of Roosevelt Hospital, 1956. Contbr. numerous monographs and articles to med. publs. Home: 225 Central Park West, N.Y.C. 24. Office: 630 Park Av., N.Y.C. 21. Died July 6, 1958.

CUTLER, George Chalmers, trustee; b. Brookline, Mass., May 8, 1891; s. George C. and Mary (Wilson) C.; A.B., Harvard, 1913, LL.B., 1916; m. Susan Margaret Stackpole, July 5, 1916; children—George C., Diana, Mary, Susan Margaret. Partner, Herrick, Smith, Donald & Farley, Boston, 1923-24, Edward B. Smith & Co., N.Y.C.; 1925-29; instr. Harvard Law Sch., 1930; v.p. Guaranty Trust Co., N.Y.C., 1930-35; pres., chmn. bd. Safe Deposit & Trust Co., Balt., 1935-45; chmn. exec. com. Inc. Investors, Boston; dir. Atlantic Coast Line R.R., Dun & Bradstreet, Louisville & Nashville R.R., Parker Corp. Trustee, Children's Hosp., Boston Lying-In, St. Timothy's Sch. Served as lt. (j.g.) USN(T), World War I. Home: 100 Village Av., Dedham, Mass. Office: 200 Berkeley St., Boston. Died April 21, 1956.

CUTLER, Henry Edwin, lawyer; b. Creston, Ind., May 18, 1879; s. Leslie G. and Flora V. C.; student pub. schs., Crown Point, Ind.; pvt. study in offices of practicing attys. and Chicago Title & Trust Co.; m. Henrietta Marquardt, 1904; children—Mary Lucile, Paul W., Henry Edwin, John Alden, Jeanne E., Thomas Grant. Admitted to Ill. bar, 1906, and since in practice, specializing in municipal bonds and securities law; mem. Chapman, Cutler & Parker, 1918-27, Chapman & Cutler, 1927—. Mem. Am., Ill., Chgo. bar assns., S.A.R. Mason. Club: Union League. Home: 407 Central Av., Wilmette, Ill.; (country) Cutler Farms, Creston, Ind. Office: Harris Trust Bldg., Chgo. Died July 8, 1959.

CUTLER, James Elbert, univ. prof.; b. Princeville, Ill., Jan. 24, 1876; s. Frank W. and Antonaiah (Hoag) C.; B.A., U. Colo., 1900, LL.D., 1934; Ph.D. Yale, 1903; m. Carolena D. Sperry, June 25, 1903 (dec. Feb. 1945), m. 2d, Ida May Devine, Aug. 28, 1946. Instr. Eng. & civil govt., State Prep. Sch. of Colo., 1899-1900; instr. polit. economy, Yale, 1903-04; instr. economics, Wellesley Coll., 1904-06; asst. prof. polit. economy, U. of Mich., 1906-07; asso. prof. sociology, 1907-10, prof. sociology, 1910-46, prof. emeritus, 1946—; dean Sch. Applied Social Scis., 1916-41, Western Reserve U. Maj. AUS, office of Chief of Staff, 1918-19. Mem. Am. Acad. Polit. and Social Sci., Am. Sociol. Soc., Nat. Conf. of Social Welfare, Am. Assn. of University Profs., Nat. Assn. Social Workers, Phi Gamma Delta, etc. Club: City. Author: Lynch Law, 1905; A Study in Professional Education at Western Reserve University—the School of Applied Social Sciences, 1916-30 (with M. R. Davie), 1930. Contbr. to revs., etc. Home: 20201 North Park Blvd., Cleve. 18. Died Oct. 29, 1959.

CUTLER, John W., investment banker; b. Bangor, Me., May 12, 1887; s. George C. and Mary (Wilson) C.; A.B., Harvard, 1909; m. Rosalind Fish, Oct. 22, 1910; children—Susan K. (Mrs. Richard C. Aldrich), John W., Patricia R. (Mrs. Robert L. Fowler), Peter S., Judith B. (Mrs. Jackson J. Shinkle). Partner, Smith, Barney & Co. and predecessor firm Edward B. Smith & Co., also Guaranty Co. of N.Y., 1920—; dir. Internat. Tel. & Tel. Corp., The Hoover Co., Youngstown Steel Door Co., N.Y. Air Brake Co., A. E. Staley Mfg. Co. Clubs: Harvard, Links, Recess (N.Y.C.); Tennis and Racquet (Boston); National Golf Links (Southampton); Highlands Country (Garrison). Home: 133 E. 80th St., N.Y.C. 21. Office: 14 Wall St., N.Y.C. 5. Died Mar. 18, 1950.

CUTLER, William Frye, ret. mfr.; b. Washington, Mar. 5, 1888; s. Otis Henderson and Mary Albertine (Straut) C.; student, Hill Sch., Pa., 1906; student Sheffield Sci. Sch. (Yale) 1906-08; m. Mildred C. Connor, May 10, 1930. Spl. apprentice Pennsylvania R.R., 1909-11; asst. to pres. Am. Brake Shoe & Foundry Co., 1913, v.p., 1921-54; with Hale & Kilburn Corp., 1914; v.p. Southern Wheel Co., 1914-18, pres., 1918-54; pres. Southern Wheel div., and v.p. Am. Brakeblok Div. (Am. Brake Shoe & Foundry Co.); dir. N.J.&N.Y. R.R., Am. Brake Shoe Co.; trustee N.Y. Trust Co. Dir. Assn. Mfrs. Chilled Car Wheels. Mem. Squadron A. Cav., N.Y. N.G., Mexican Border Service, 1916. Mem. Aztec Soc., Chi Phi. Republican. Episcopalian. Clubs: Yale, Deepdale Country, Links. Home: 277 Park Av. Office: 230 Park Av., N.Y.C. Died Apr. 6, 1957; buried Airmont Cemetery, Suffern, N.Y.

CUTTER, Victor Macomber, corp. officer; b. Dracut, Mass., Sept. 2, 1881; s. Charles Howe and Annie G. (Macomber) C.; prep. edn., Lowell High Sch.; B.L., Dartmouth, 1903; M.C.S., Tuck Sch. of Administration and Finance (Dartmouth), 1904; A.M., Dartmouth, 1933; m. Florence de Jongh, Apr. 5, 1913; children—Victor Macomber, Thelma, Donald de Jongh. Began in fruit business in Costa Rica, 1904; dir. New Eng. Mutual Life Ins. Co., New Eng. Telephone & Telegraph Co. Mem. Caribbean Com. U.S. Shipping Bd., World War. Life mem. Corp. Mass. Inst. Tech.; life trustee Dartmouth Coll.; Colby Jr. Coll. Mem. Phi Beta Kappa. Republican. Conglist. Clubs: University, Union (Boston); Dartmouth (New York). Home: 68 Beacon St., Boston 8. Died Dec. 25, 1952.

D

DAGGETT, Robert Frost, architect; b. Indianapolis, Ind., Mar. 13, 1875; s. Robert Platt and Caroline (Frost) D.; B.S., U. of Pa., 1896; grad. Ecole des Beaux Arts, Paris, 1901; m. Lizette Lothian, Oct. 30, 1901; children—James Lothian, Robert Frost. Began practice at Indpls., 1901; architect for Indpls. Athletic Club, James Whitcomb Riley Hosp. for Children, LaRue D. Carter Meml. Hosp., Community Hosp. Indpls., bldg. for Ind. U. Med. Center, Eli Lilly & Co., Indpls. Chamber of Commerce Building, buildings for Indiana, DePauw, Purdue, and Butler universities, churches and public schools. Served as capt. U.S. Engrs., World War I; col. Coast Arty. Res. Fellow A.I.A.; mem. Alpha Tau Omega. Republican. Mason. Home: 4904 Washington Blvd. Office: 567 W. Westfield Blvd., Indpls. Died. Sept. 6, 1955.

DAGGETT, Stuart, educator; b. Milw., Mar. 2, 1881; s. George and Marion Chapin (Stuart) D.; A.B., Harvard, 1903, A.M., 1904, Ph.D., 1906; m. Constance Dorothea de RondenPos, May 19, 1910; children—Carlos Ormsby (dec.), Stuart, Marion. Instr. Harvard, 1906-09; asst. prof. ry. econs. U. Cal., 1909-14, prof. transportation, 1917—, dean Coll. of Commerce, 1920-27, Faculty Research lectr., 1951. Mem. War Industries Bd., Div. of Planning and Statistics, 1918; expert for Presdl. Com. on Coordination of Rail and Water Facilities, 1924; Pacific Coast arbitrator, Longshoreman and Waterfront Employers, 1944. Mem. Am. Econ. Assn., Sigma Alpha Epsilon. Pacific Railway Club. Unitarian. Author: Railroad Reorganization, 1908; History of the Southern Pacific, 1922; Principles of Inland Transportation, 1928, 34, 41, 55; Railroad Consolidation West of the Mississippi River, 1933; The Structure of Transcontinental Railroad Rates, 1947. Home: 1427 Hawthorne Terrace, Berkeley, Cal. Died Dec. 22, 1954; buried Mountain View Cemetery, Oakland, Cal.

DAHL, Gerhard Melvin, ret. transit corp. exec.; b. Ft. Howard, Wis., June 8, 1876; s. Rev. Theodore H. and Lena (Gjertsen) D.; LL.B., U. Wis., 1896, M.A., 1921; m. Georgeanna Cate, June 5, 1900 (died 1949); m. 2d, Mrs. Mary E. Dahl. Practiced law in Wis., 1899-1906, Ohio, 1906-10; was city atty. Waupaca; dist. atty. Portage County, 1902-06; street r.r. commr., Cleve., 1910-12; moved to N.Y., 1912; v.p. Electric Bond & Share Co., 1912-17; v.p. Chase Nat. Bank, 1917-23; partner Hayden-Stone & Co., 1923-24; chmn. bd. Bklyn. Manhattan Transit Corp., 1924-43; dir. Miller Marine. Decorated Order of the Rising Sun, 3d Class, by Emperor of Japan, 1921. Republican. Mem. Theta Delta Chi. Clubs: Racquet and Tennis, Metropolitan, Union League (N.Y.C.). Home: 920 Fifth Av., N.Y.C. Died Dec. 29, 1953.

DAHL, Myrtle Hooper (dawl), educator; b. Valley City, N.D., Feb. 27, 1887; d. William Harrison and Julia Anna (Roach) Hooper; student Hutchinson (Minn.) High Sch.; graduate State College, Mankato, Minnesota, MacPhail School Music Minneapolis, Minnesota; married Paul O. Dahl, Sept. 17, 1930. Teacher elementary grades, Northfield, Minn., 1907-09; teacher of music, grades, Lidgerwood, N.D., 1909-11, Davenport, Wash., 1911-12; teacher elementary grades, Minneapolis, Minn., since 1912. Mem. Governors Commission on Youth, 1945-49. Member N.E.A. (pres. 1941-42; also mem. exec. com. junior past president, member board of trustees; formerly president Dept. Classroom Teachers); mem. Minn. Edn. Assn. (past president mem. exec. bd.; chmn. legislative com.; past pres. Dept. Classroom Teachers), Minneapolis Classroom Teachers Assn. (past pres.), Minneapolis Div. of Minn. Edn. Assn. (past pres.), State Fedn. Business and Professional Women's Clubs (chmn. edn. com.; parliamentarian), Minneapolis Business and Professional Women's Clubs (past pres.), Delta Kappa Gamma. Contbr. to 10th Yearbook, Dept. of Classroom Teachers, N.E.A. Home: Box 227, R.F.D. 3, Mound, Minn. Died Mar. 18, 1952; buried Hutchinson, Minn.

DAHLBERG, Bror Gustave, corp. exec.; b. Christianstadt, Sweden, Jan. 21, 1881; s. Adolph Frederick and Alma (Luning) D.; brought to U.S., 1889; m. 2d, Gilda Krieger, May 16, 1932; children—Alma, Craig. Elevator pilot advancing to assistant to general freight agent N.P. and G.N. rys., 1894-1912; in furniture bus., 1912-13; traffic and r.r. rate counselor, 1913-16; v.p. Minn. & Ont. Paper Co., Internat. Lumber Co., Minn., Dakota & Western R.R. Co., Ont. & Minn. Power Co., 1914-21; organizer Celotex Corp., 1921, pres., chmn. bd., dir., 1921-46, chmn. bd., 1946-50, dir., gen. adviser to the bd., 1950-—; organizer Celotex, Ltd. (London), 1926, chmn. bd., 1926-51; organizer, pres., chmn. bd., dir. South Shore Oil & Development Co. 1927-—: organizer, chmn. bd. dir. The South Coast Corp., 1924-50, dir., 1950-—; organizer Shore Exploration Co., 1950, since dir., chmn. bd.; organizer, pres., dir. The So. Sugar Co. (now U.S. Sugar Co.), 1926-33; dir., chmn. bd. Sloane-Blabon Corp., 1935-44. Mem. Chgo. Zool. Soc., Nat. Inst. Social Sci., Am. Soc. Planning Appeals, U.S. C. of C., Art Inst. Chgo. Republican. Clubs: Mid-Day (Chgo.); Metropolitan (N.Y.C.); New Orleans Country; Bohemian (San Francisco); Everglades (Palm Beach, Fla.). Home: 4537 Collins Av., Miami Beach, Fla. Office: 4537 Collins Av., Miami Beach, Fla.; also 120 S. LaSalle St., Chgo. Died Feb. 20, 1954.

DAHLE, Herman B., ex-congressman; b. Perry, Wis., Mar. 30, 1855; ed. Wis. State U.; m. Annie Kittleson, 1877. Established firm of O. B. Dahle & Son, Mt. Vernon, Wis., Aug., 1877, lived there 10 yrs., moved to Mt. Horeb Spring, 1888; mem. Dahle Bros., Mt. Horeb, Wis., 1891, and is senior partner Mount Horeb Bank; mem. 56th-57th Congresses: 2d Wis. dist. Republican. Home: Mount Horeb, Wis. Died Apr. 25, 1920.

DAHLGREEN, Charles W., painter, etcher; b. Chicago, Ill., Sept. 8, 1864; s. Charles and Karoline (Klanroth) D.; ed. pub. schs.; studied art in Chicago and abroad; m. Augusta Rentrop, July 4, 1888; children—Margurete and Grant R. Exhibited in Salon, Paris, France, 1910, and other European cities; awarded 1st prize in still life, Düsseldorf, 1888; 1st prize, Art Students' League, Chicago, 1908; hon. mention Panama P.I. Expn., 1915; Julius Rosenwald and Clyde N. Carr prize, Art Inst. Chicago, 1919; Municipal Art League $500 purchase prize, 1920; 1st prize in landscape, Hoosier Salon, 1925; Chicago Gallery purchase prize, 1926, 28; Cary $200 award, 1928; F. C. Ball purchase prize $1,200, 1931; J. F. Brower $200 prize, Chicago Art Inst., 1933; Cunningham etching prize, Hoosier Salon, 1935. One of his etchings exhibited at Century of Progress Expn., Chicago, 1934, chosen for tour of leading museums of U.S. Represented in Congressional Library, Washington, N.Y. Public Library, Hackley Art Gallery, Muskegon, Mich., Smithsonian Instn., Vanderpool Memorial Gallery, Chicago. Mem. Painters and Sculptors of Chicago, Chicago Soc. Etchers, Oak Park Art League, Union Internationale des Beaux Arts et des Lettres, Chicago Galleries Assn. Exhibited at Carnegie Inst., 1941. Republican. Unitarian. Home: 409 N. Cuyler Av., Oak Park, Ill. Died June 19, 1955.

DAIGNEAU, Ralph H. (dān-yo), business exec.; b. St. Paul, May 4, 1891; s. F. Emerson and Alice (Merrick) D.; ed. pub. schs. of Minn.; m. Nell R. Zuehlke, Apr. 3, 1918. With Geo. A. Hormel & Co., Austin, Minn., since 1908, became dir., 1928, vice pres., 1929, vice pres. and dir. sales since 1946. Consultant, O.P.A., 1942-43; mem. corn policy com., War Food Administrn., 1943; sr. marketing specialist, War Meat Bd., 1943-45. Mem. Am. Legion, 40 and 8, Izaak Walton League. Elk. Home: 600 Fairview. Office: Austin, Minn. Died Sept. 18, 1955.

DAINE Robert, corp. exec.; b. Paris, France, Jan. 2, 1895; s. Georges and Jeanne (Corniquet de Lottre) D.; student Institut Catholique d' Arts et Metiers de Lille, Ecole Superieure de Mecanique et d'Electricite de Paris; grad. Elec. Mech. Engr.; m Agnes Ford, Dec. 17, 1924 (div.); 1 son, Robert Armand; m. 2d, Isabelle Gwynn Pugh, Nov. 5, 1950. Came to U.S., 1922. Pres. Compagnie des Bateau Alseroix, 1919-20; secretaire gen. Credit Central Paris, 1920-21; pres., dir. The Teleregister Corp., 1928 —, chmn. bd., 1954—, also mem exec. com.; dir. Trans-Lux Corp., Trans-Lux Movie Ticker Corp., Trans-Lux Crispo Corp. Served as capt. Frency Air Corps, 1915-18; sec. technique de l'aeronautique War Ministry, 1918-19. Decorated Chevalier de la Legion d'Honneur, Croix de Guerre (4 citations): Cavaliere della Corona d' Italia, Merito di Guerra; Mil. Cross (Eng.). others. Clubs: Metropolitan, Bankers (N.Y. C.). Home: Briscoe Rd., New Canaan, Conn. Office: 445 Fairfield Av., Stamford, Conn. Died Apr. 8, 1957: buried New Canaan, Conn.

DAKIN, Henry Drysdale (dā'kin), ret. research chemist; b. London, Eng., Mar. 12, 1880; s. Thomas Burns and Sophia (Stevens) D.; B.Sc., Victoria U., Manchester, Eng., 1901; D.Sc., U. Leeds, 1907, LL.D., 1936; Ph.D. (hon.), U. Heidelberg; Sc D., Yale; m. Susan Dows Herter, July 1916 (died 1951). Demonstrator in chemistry U. Leeds, 1901-02; research worker Lister Inst. Preventive Medicine, successively at London and Heidelberg, 1901-05, and Herter Lab., N.Y.C., 1905-20; sci. adviser to Merck Inst. Therapeutic Research; dir. Merck & Co. Fellow Royal Soc. Eng.; mem. Soc. Exptl. Biology, Inst. Chemistry of Great Britain and Ireland, London Chem. Soc., others. Decorated Chevalier Legion of Honor; recipient Philip A. Conne medal by Chemists' Club, Davy medal by The Royal Soc. (Eng.). Author: Oxidation and Reductions in the Animal Body, 1912; Handbook of Chemical Antiseptics (with E. K. Dunham), 1917. Editor Jour. Biol. Chemistry, 1911-31. Home: Scarborough-on-Hudson, N.Y. Died Feb. 10, 1952.

DALE, Albert Ennis, newspaper editor; b. Whitehall, N.Y., Nov. 4, 1890; s. Frederick S. and Ida Amanda (Ennis) D.; student pub. schs. Albany, N.Y.; m. Coralyn A. Phillips, Feb. 17, 1938; children—Albert Ennis, William Grover. Gen. reporter, city editor, polit. editor Albany (N.Y.) Knickerbocker-Press, 1912-18; reporter, night editor Asso. Press, Albany, 1911; legislative corr. N.Y. Sun, 1918-19, N.Y. Evening Mail, 1920-22; city editor, mng. editor Albany Evening News, 1922-29; mng. editor Detroit Times, 1929-30, Wis. News, Milwaukee, 1931-32; news editor N.Y. Evening Jour., 1932; editor Detroit Times, 1932-36, Pittsburgh Sun-Telegraph, 1936-37, Chicago Am., 1938-39, Times Herald, Washington, 1940; dir. pub. relations N.B.C., N.Y. City, 1941-45; publicity, pub. relations various bus. and profl. people, 1945-51; editor Sun-Telegraph, Pittsburgh, 1951-54; with Allied Public Relations Associates, N.Y.C., 1954-—. Dir. public relations Greater N.Y. Fund, 1940-41, U.S.O. campaign, 1945-47; dep. dir. N.Y. State Mil. Census, 1917-18; also publicity dir. N.Y. State Def. Council; commr. Albany Port, 1925-28. Mason. Clubs: Nat. Press (Washington); Silurians (N.Y. City). Home: Washington Well Farm, Skillman, N.J.; also 100 Prestley Rd., Bridgeville, Pa. Office: 787 Fifth Av., N.Y.C. Died Nov. 21, 1954; buried Troy, N.Y.

DALEY, Robert Morris, physician; b. Chatham, N.Y., July 22, 1874; s. William Champlin and Katherine Experience (Bailey) D.; student Cornell Univ., 1891-93; M.D., Columbia, 1896; m. Marie Elizabeth Kain, Nov. 10, 1900 (dec. May 1918); children—Marie Elizabeth (Mrs. William S. Ballenger, Jr.); m. 2d, Anne Russell, May 16, 1925. Interne Bellevue Hosp., N.Y. City, 1896-98; practice med. N.Y. City, since 1899; clinical asst. nervous diseases, Cornell Med. Sch., 1899-1900; asst. med. dir. The Equitable Life Assurance Soc., New York, 1911-16, asso. med. dir., 1916-36, med. dir. since 1936. Served as 1st lt. and asst. surgeon 69th Vol. Inf., Spanish-Am. War; capt. and asst. surgeon 69th N.Y. Nat. Guard, 1899-1900. Awarded Certificate cum laude, New York State License Bd., 1898. Mem. Assn. Life Ins. Med. Dirs. (pres. 1928-30, served on many life ins. med. coms.). Republican. Presbyterian. Home: Southold, L.I., N.Y. Office: 393 7th Av., N.Y. City 1. Died June 3, 1950; buried Presbyn. Cemetery, Southold, L.I., N.Y.

DALLA VALLE, Joseph Maria, educator; b. N.Y. C., Mar. 7, 1906; s. Henry J. and Maria C. (Campiotti) Dalla V.; B.S., Harvard, 1927, M.S., 1928, ScD., 1930. Cons. engr., Cleve., 1930-32; field and research engr. USPHS, Washington, 1933-41; cons. engr., N.Y.C., 1941-48; faculty Ga. Inst. Tech., 1948-—, asso. prof., 1948-49, prof. chem. engring., 1950-54. regents prof., 1954-—. Fulbright lecturer Med. Sch., U. Milan, 1953-54. Mem. bd. dir. Oak Ridge Inst. Nuclear Studies, 1955. Author: Micromeritics, 1943; The Industrial Environment, 1948; Fine Particle Measurements (with Clyde Orr, Jr.). Contbr. articles profl. publs. Office: Georgia Institute of Technology, Atlanta. Died June 1, 1958; buried Dalton, Ga.

DALLAS, Charles Donald, ret. corp. exec.; b. Hamilton, Ont., Can., Oct. 24, 1881; s. Andrew Chisholm and Lucy (Flack) D.; grad. Armour Sci. Acad., 1902; hon. D. Engring., Ill. Inst. Tech., 1941; m. Harriet Louise Hughes, Oct. 30, 1909; children—Hughes, Harriet Louise, Mary Walford. Office boy, later salesman Am. Brass Co., Chgo., 1902-06; asso. father in 1906 in orgn. of the Dallas Brass & Copper Co., of which he was pres., treas., and dir. until merger of five large brass and copper cos. into the Revere Copper & Brass, Inc., N.Y.C., of which he was pres., dir. 1947, chmn. bd. dirs. 1947-51, retired; dir. General Cable Co., Am. Smelting & Refining Co. Gov. Copper and Brass Research Assn. Trustee Hadley Corr. Sch. for the Blind, Am. Heritage Found. and Jr. Achievement, Inc. Mason. Clubs: Commonwealth, Commercial (Chgo.); The Seigniory (Que.); University, Bedford Golf and Tennis, Waccabuc Country (N.Y.C.); Newcomen Soc. of Eng.; Royal Canadian Yacht (Toronto). Author: You and Your Money; The Spirit of Paul Revere and articles and pamphlets. Home: 8306 Sanderling Rd., Sarasota, Fla.; also Mt. Holly Rd., Katonah, N.Y. Died Apr. 11, 1959; buried St. Mathews Ch., Bedford, N.Y.

DALLMANN, (Charles Frederick) William, clergyman; b. Germany, Dec. 22, 1862; s. William and Fredericke (Neumann) D.; brought to U.S., 1868; A.B., Concordia Coll., Ft. Wayne, Ind.; grad. Concordia Theol. Sem., St. Louis; D.D., 1926; m. Louise Bertram, Sept. 11, 1887; children—Lucy (dec.), Wm. (dec.), Clara, Walther, Paul, Dorothy, Bertram. Ordained Luth. ministry, 1886; founded chs. Baltimore, Washington, N.Y. City, Brooklyn, Boston, Milwaukee and Sheboygan; pastor in Milwaukee; now pastor emeritus; has served as editor The Lutheran Witness. V.p., Synod of Mo., Ohio, and other States, 1926-30. Republican. Author: The Ten Commandments, 1893; The Lord's Prayer, 1907; Portraits of Jesus, 1909; Follow Jesus, 1911; Jesus, 1914; Life of Luther, 1917; The Christian, 1918; Luther the Liberator, 1919; Great Religious Americans, 1921; The Titles of the Christians, 1926; The Battle of the Bible, 1927; Paul, 1929; Peter, 1930; How Peter Became Pope, 1931; John, 1931; Why Not Episcopal?, 1933. Co-editor Evang. Luth. Hymn Book, Evang. Luth. S.S. Hymnal; Christmas Hymns, 1935; Easter Bells, 1937; He Is Risen, 1938; What Is Lutheranism?, 1938; Jesus Appeared, 1939; Kate Luther, 1941; Short Stories by Jesus, 1943; My Life, 1945; The Lutheran Lord's Supper in the Episcopal Church, 1948; The Organization of the Missouri Synod, 1949; Robert Burns; Patrick Hamilton; William Tyndale; Miles Cloverdale; John Hus; The Midnight Lion; Paul Gerhardt; Martin Luther, rev. edit., 1951. Home: 215 S. Elmwood Av., Oak Park, Ill. Died Feb. 2, 1952; buried Wanderer's Rest Cemetery, Milw.

DALY, Brenton L., railway exec.; b. Charlottetown, Prince Edward Island, Mar. 14, 1884; s. James C. and Emely E. (Doucette) D.; student pub. schs.; m. Nina L. Ault, Feb. 5, 1907; children—Dulcie Maud, June Vivian. With Canadian Nat. Rys. 1903-—, as brakeman, condr., gen. chmn., supervisory dir., 1936-—. Mem. Order Ry. Condrs. K.C. Club: Canadian Ry. Home: 33 Elmwood Av., Senneville. Office: 360 McGill St., Montreal, Que., Can. Died May 31, 1956.

DALY, Carroll John, novelist; b. Yonkers, N.Y., Sept. 14, 1889; s. Joseph F. and Mary L. (Brennan) D.; student Yonkers High Sch., De La Salle Inst. and Am. Acad. Dramatic Arts, N.Y.C.; m. Margaret G. Blakley, Dec. 11, 1913; 1 son, John Russell. Began as theater mgr.; owned and operated theaters in Atlantic City and Asbury Park, N.J., and Arverne and Yonkers, N.Y.; writer detective stories, 1922-—. Author: White Circle, 1926; Snarl of the Beast, 1927; Man in the Shadows, 1928; Hidden Hand, 1929; Tag Murders, 1930; Tainted Power, 1931; Third Murderer, 1931; Amateur Murderer, 1933; Murder Won't Wait, 1933; Murder From the East, 1935; Mystery of Smoking Gun, 1936; Mr. Strang, 1936; Emperor of Evil, 1937; Race Williams Cuts In, 1939; Better Corpses, 1940; Ready to Burn, 1941; Satan Laughs, 1942; Dead Men Do Tell, 1942; Satan Strikes, 1943; Sign of the Rat, 1943; Mr. Sinister, 1944; One More To Die, 1944; This Corpse On Me, 1945; This Corpse on Me, 1946; Bury Me in the Same Grave, 1947; Murder After Midnight, 1948; Murder at Our House, 1949; Murder in the Mind, 1950; Don't Eat With the Dead, 1950; Strange Case of Alta May, 1951; Cousin Oliver, 1952; Importance of Being Ernie, 1952; Lantern in the Mind, 1953; The Children's Gun, 1953; Murder for a Stuffed Shirt, 1954. Contbr. fiction to mags. Hon. mem. Santa Monica Writers Club. Home: 2470½ Florencita Dr., Montrose, Cal. Died Jan. 16, 1958.

DALY, Edward James, judge; b. Hartford, Conn., Mar. 29, 1892; s. James Richard and Catherine (Deegan) D.; LL.B., Cornell University, 1914; LL.D., St. Bonaventure U.; married Viola Shea; children—Betty Ann (Mrs. Theodore T. Horton), Edward James, Mary Lou (Mother Mary Anthony). Admitted to Conn. bar, 1915 and practiced in Hartford until 1937; partner Forward & Daly; assistant U.S. district attorney for Connecticut, 1922; attorney gen. State of Conn. until 1937; judge Conn. Superior Court, 1937-54; associate justice Connecticut Supreme Court of Errors, 1954-58, chief justice, 1958-—; judge in war crimes trials, Nurnberg, Germany, 1947-48. Served as lt. A.S., Signal Corps. U.S. Army, World War I. Mem. Am. (v.p. 1935-36), Conn. State, Hartford Co. bar assns., Sigma Alpha Epsilon. Roman Catholic. Elk. Club: Hartford Golf. Home: 48 Woodland Park. Office: Supreme Ct. of Errors, P.O. Box 1350, Hartford, Conn. Died July 20, 1959; buried Mt. St. Benedict Cemetery, Hartford, Conn.

DALY, Reginald Aldworth, educator; b. Napanee, Ont., May 19, 1871; s. Edward and Jane Maria (Jeffers) D.; A.B., Victoria U., Toronto, 1891; A.M., Harvard, 1893, Ph.D., 1896, Sc.D. (hon.), 1942; studied Heidelberg 1897-98, Paris, France, 1898; Sc.D. (hon.) U. Toronto, 1923, U. Chgo., 1941; m. Louise P. Haskell, June 3, 1903; 1 son, Reginald Aldworth (dec.). Geologist for Can., internat. boundary sruveys, 1901-07; prof. phys. geology Mass. Inst. Tech., 1907-12; Sturgis-Hooper prof. geology Harvard, 1912-42, emeritus Sturgis-Hooper prof. geology, 1942-—. Fellow Am. Acad. Arts and Scis., Geol. Soc. Am. (pres. 1932), Royal Soc. Edinburgh (hon.); mem. Am. Philos. Soc., Phila. Acad. Natural Sci. Nat. Acad. Scis., Seismol. Soc. Am., Am. Geophys. Union, Geol. Soc. South Africa; hon. mem. Norwegian Acad., Russian Acad., Swedish Acad., Mineral Soc. of Leningrad, Glasgow, Edinburgh. Stockholm, Belgium geol. socs.; fgn. mem.

Geol. Soc. London; fgn. corr. Acad. Sci. France. Author: Geology of the North American Cordillera at the 49th Parallel of Latitude (3 vols.); Igneous Rocks and Their Origin, 1914; Our Mobile Earth, 1926; Igneous Rocks and the Depths of the Earth, 1933; The Changing World of the Ice Age, 1934; Architecture of the Earth, 1938; Strength and Structure of the Earth 1940; The Floor of the Ocean, 1942. Asso. editor Am. Jour. Science. Home: 23 Hawthorn St., Cambridge 38, Mass. Died Sept. 19, 1957; buried Elmwood Cemetery, Columbia, S.C.

DAMIANOV, Georgi, chief of state of Bulgaria; chmn. Presidium of Bulgarian Grand Nat. Assembly; mem. Politburo of the Bulgarian Communist Party. Office: The Presidium, Sofia, Bulgaria. Died Nov. 1958.*

DAMMANN, Theodore, b. Milw., Nov. 4, 1869; s. Rev. William and Emma D.; student Concordia Coll.; m. Alma Ulbricht, July 30, 1896; children—Ruth (Mrs. Harry H. Effler), Mildred (Mrs. G. Park Singer). Pres. Wis. Conservatory of Music, 1911-—; pres. Dammann Realty Co.; dir. Sterling Bldg. & Loan Assn. Treas. Milwaukee County 6 yrs.; sec. State of Wis., 1927-39. Trustee Luth. Altenheim Assn., Wis.; mem. Am. Luther Assn. Progressive Republican. Club: Milwaukee Athletic. Home: 4130 N. Newhall St., Shorewood, Wis. Office: 2758 N. Teutonia Av., Milw. Died Jan. 16, 1946; buried Forest Home Cemetery, Milw.

DAMON, Ralph Shepard, aviation official; b. Franklin, New Hampshire, July 6, 1897; s. William Cotton and Effie (Ives) D.; A.B. cum laude, Harvard, 1918; D.Eng., Clarkson College of Technology, 1941; m. Harriet Dudley Holcombe, Oct. 14, 1922; children—Priscilla Loomis, Barbara Ives, William Alden, Edmund Holcombe. Began as milwright asst. G. Elias & Co., Buffalo, N.Y., 1920; served in various capacities with Curtiss Aeroplane & Motor Co. and affiliated companies, 1922-35, ending as pres., 1935; developed Curtiss-Wright "Condor" comml. transport, 1933; v.p. in charge operations Am. Airlines, 1936-41, v.p. and gen. mgr., 1943-45, pres., 1945-49; president Republic Aviation Corporation, 1941-43; pres. and dir. TWA, Inc. since Jan. 1949; dir. L.I. Trust Co., Goodyear Tire & Rubber Co., Veeder Root Co., Strategic Materials Co., Sheraton Corp., N.Y. Telephone Co., N.Y. Trust Co., Guardian Life Insurance Co., Bankers Securities Corp. Mem. Nat. Adv. Com. Aeros. Trustee Clarkson College Technology. Served as flying cadet, Air Corps, U.S. Army, 1918-19, reserve officer, 1918-23. Mem. Institute of Aeronautical Sciences, Soc. Automotive Engrs., A.S.M.E., Alpha Sigma Phi. Presbyn. Mason. Clubs: Harvard, Wings, Links (N.Y.C.); Kansas City (Mo.). Home: 88 Eleventh St., Garden City, N.Y. Office: 380 Madison Av., N.Y.C. 17. Died Jan. 4, 1956.

DAMON, Robert Hosken, bus. exec.; b. Mt. Vernon, Ill., Sept. 6, 1902; s. William Henry and Erie Jane (Palmer) D.; B.A., U. Wis., 1924, LL.B., 1926; m. Margarite Cunningham, June 11, 1923 (dec.); children—Norma Louise Myers, Melody Holtatz, Robert John; m. 2d, Thelma E. Donop, Sept. 19, 1955; one daughter, Donna Ileen. Admitted to the Wisconsin bar, 1926, the Illinois bar, 1927; engaged in practice of law, Chgo., 1926-38; mem. of Damon, Hayes, Hoban & Shaheen and predecessor firms, 1934-—; pres., chmn. bd. Johnson Fare Box Co., 1934-—; chmn. bd., pres. Bowser, Inc., Fort Wayne, Ind., S. F. Bowser Co., Ltd., Hamilton, Can., Eagle Lock & Screw Co., Terryville, Conn., Briggs Filtration Co., Bethesda, Md., Gudeman Co., Chgo., Nat. Sci. Labs., Inc., Wash., Bowser Internat., Inc., N.Y.C., Process Filters, Inc., Buffalo, N.Y., Parking Corp. Am., Chgo.; chmn. bd. Airport Fueling Systems, Inc., Washington, Coin Auditing Systems, N.Y., Petinco Systems, Chgo., Visible Cash Controls, Chgo., N.S.L. Electronics, Limited, Canada. Mem. Am., Chgo., Ill., Wis. bar assns., Phi Alpha Delta. Clubs: Chicago Athletic, Midday (Chgo.); Fort Wayne (Ind.) Country; Metropolitan (N.Y.C.); Seigniory (Quebec). Home: 2130 Lincoln Park W., Chgo. 14; also Countryside Lake, Mundelein, Ill. Office: 33 N. La Salle St., Chgo. 2. Died Jan. 1960.

DAMON, Samuel Mills, minister of finance under late Hawaiian Republic; b. Honolulu, Mar. 13, 1845; s. Rev. Samuel C. and Julia (Mills) D.; ed. in Honolulu; m. H. M. Baldwin, Sept. 5, 1872. Has held many positons of trust under Hawaiian govt.; banker, 1871-—; sr. mem. banking house of Bishop & Co., now dir. Mem. Soc. Beaux Arts, Paris, Royal Soc. of Arts, London; decorated order Golden Treasure, Japan; Knight Order Christ, Portugal; Victoria Jubilee medal. Owner of the celebrated Moanalua gardens, near Honolulu. Address: Honolulu, Hawaii. Died July 1, 1924.

DAMROSCH, Walter Johannes (dăm'rŏsh), conductor; b. Breslau, Prussia, Jan. 30, 1862; s. Dr. Leopold and Helene (von Heimburg) D.; musical edn. under his father and Rischbieter, Urspruch and Hans von Bülow; hon. Mus.D., Columbia Univ., 1914; hon. Mus.D., Princeton U., 1929; Dartmouth, U. of Me., New York U., Washington and Jefferson Coll., N.Y. State U., Brown Univ., U. of Pa. Came to U.S. with father, 1871; m. Margaret, d. late James G. Blaine, May 17, 1890; children—Alice, Gretchen, Polly, Anita. Became conductor Newark (N.J.) Harmonic Soc., 1881; on death of father, 1885, became asst. condr. and dir. German Opera Co. and succeeded him as mus. dir. Oratorio and Symphony socs., which, 1896, rendered for 1st time in United States, Wagner's Parsifal in concert form; delivered series of lecture-recitals beginning in United States, 1890; founded Damrosch Opera Company for production of Wagner in 1894; toured the United States in original opera, The Scarlet Letter, 1894; Wagner's Ring of Nibelingen, Tristan and Isolde, etc., 1896; devoted exclusively to the New York Symphony Orchestra which he organized into a permanent orchestra, 1903; resigned as dir., 1927; musical counsel for Nat. Broadcasting Co., 1928-47; founder and conductor orchestral radio concerts for public schools and colleges, 1928-42. President American Academy Arts and Letters, 1940-48; member National Inst. Art and Letters (pres. 1937). Composer: Manila Te Deum (prod. New York, Dec. 1898, and Philadelphia, 1899); Cyrano, opera in 4 acts, prod. Met. Opera, New York, Feb. 1913; wrote and directed new version of "Cyrano," 1939, produced in concert form by Philharmonic-Symphony Society, Feb. 20 and 21, 1941; incidental music to Medea, and Iphigenia in Aulis by Euripides (prod. Greek Theatre, Berkeley, Calif., Aug. 1915); Electra by Sophocles, performed New York, Feb. 6, 1917; An Abraham Lincoln Song (for orchestra, chorus and baritone solo, first performed Met. Opera House in Apr., 1936, at a Music Appreciation Hour broadcast), 1935; Death and General Putnam (for baritone solo), 1936; The Man Without a Country (opera in 2 acts, world premiere Met. Opera House, May 12, 1937), 1936; The Opera Cloak (opera in 1 act, produced by The New Opera Company), 1942; composed the ballad "Dunkirk," for baritone, male chorus and orchestra, 1943. Club: Century. By request of General Pershing, reformed the bands of A.E.F. and founded a school for its bandmasters at General Headquarters, Chaumont, France, under eminent French instrs., 1918; founder and condr. orchestral radio concerts for pub. schs. and colls. Address: 168 E. 71st St., N.Y. City. Died Dec. 22, 1950.

DANA, Henry Wadsworth Longfellow, writer lectr.; b. Boston, Jan. 26, 1881; s. Richard Henry III and Edith (Longfellow) D.; A.B., Harvard, 1903, A.M., 1904, Ph.D., 1910. Tchr. St. Paul's Sch., Concord, N.H., 1903-04, Thacher Sch., Ojai, Cal., 1904-06; asst. in comparative lit. Harvard, 1908-10; lecturer d'Anglais, U. Paris (Sorbonne), 1910-12; instr. comparative lit. Columbia, 1912-17, asst. prof., 1917; lectr. New Sch. for Social Research, N.Y., 1921-32, Cambridge (Mass.) Sch. of the Drama, 1930-32. Trustee Washington Allston Fund, Boston. Mem. Modern Lang. Assn. Am., Cambridge Hist. Soc. Club: Harvard Faculty (Cambridge). Author: The Six Centuries Since Dante, 1926; Opinions and Attitudes in the Twentieth Century: Shaw in Moscow, 1934; The Theatre in a Changing Europe: Development of Soviet Drama, 1937; Handbook on Soviet Drama, 1938; The Craigie House: The Coming of Longfellow, 1939; The Dana Saga, 1941; Longfellow and Dickens; The Story of a Trans-Atlantic Friendship, 1943; Drama in Wartime Russia, 1943; History of the Modern Drama: Russia, 1947; The Origin and Development of Longfellow's "Evangeline" 1947; The Longfellow House; History and Guide, 1948. Editor: Seven Soviet Plays, 1946; Two Years Before the Mast, 1946. Contbr. to periodicals, including Old-Time New England, Theatre Arts, The American Mercury, Soviet Russia Today, New Masses, Proceedings of Cambridge Hist. Soc. Lived in Soviet Union, 1927-28, 31, 32, 34, 35. Home: 105 Brattle St., Cambridge, Mass. Died Apr. 26, 1950; buried Mt. Auburn Cemetery, Cambridge.

DANA, James Dwight, lawyer; b. New Haven, Conn., Feb. 20, 1889; s. Edward S. and Caroline (Bristol) D.; student Hopkins Grammar Sch., New Haven, 1902-05, Thacher Sch., Ojai, Calif., 1906-07; A.B., Yale, 1911; LL.B., Harvard U., 1915; m. Anna English, Oct. 6, 1917. Admitted to Conn. bar, 1915; with firm Bristol & White, 1915-20, mem. firm, 1920-34; mem. firm Wiggin & Dana since 1934; trustee New Haven Savings Bank; dir. Union & New Haven Trust Co., United Illuminating Company, Kerite Company, Capewell Manufacturing Co., The C. S. Mersick & Co., Malleable Iron Fittings Co. Trustee Sheffield Scientific Sch., Hopkins Grammar Sch.; dir. Grace-New Haven Community Hosp. Asso. fellow Calhoun Coll., Yale. Member Am. and Conn. bar assns., New Haven County Bar Assn., Alpha Delta Phi, Scroll and Key (Yale). Republican. Clubs: Graduate, New Haven Country, New Haven Lawn, Quinnipiack (New Haven); Yale (New York). Home: 30 Hillhouse Av. Office: 205 Church St., New Haven, Conn. Died Dec. 2, 1954; buried Grove St. Cemetery, New Haven.

DANCER, H. M., chmn. Dancer-Fitzgerald-Sample. Inc., advt. agy. Address: 347 Madison Av., N.Y.C. 17. Deceased.*

DANFORTH, George Jonathan, lawyer; b. Meeme, Manitowoc County, Wis., Nov. 21, 1875; s. Quincy A. and Gertrude (Silbernagel) D.; grad. Oshkosh (Wis.) State Normal Sch., 1900; LL.B., U. of Wis., 1903; m. Nora I. Tollefson, Aug. 21, 1907; children—George Jonathan, Edward A., Marit G., Elinor. Admitted to S. Dak. bar, 1903, and since practiced at Sioux Falls; now mem. firm Danforth & Danforth; chmn. Bd. Policyholders Nat. Life Insurance Co. of Sioux Falls (name changed to National Reserve Life Ins. Co. of Sioux Falls and Topeka); pres. of Home Savings Assn. of Sioux Falls. State's atty. Minnehaha County, 1910-11; referee in bankruptcy, 1915-16; mem. State Senate, 1919-21 (chmn. judiciary com.); mem. Bd. of Health, Sioux Falls, 1919-24; commissioner at large S.D. State Bar, also pres. Trustee-sec.-treas. Pub. Library, Sioux Falls, 1907-09. Mem. Am. Bar Assn., S. Dak. State Bar Assn., Minehaha County Bar Assn. (ex-pres.), Sioux Falls Chamber Commerce. Republican. Conglist. Mason. Clubs: Kiwanis, Knife and Fork. Home: 531 South Euclid Av. Office: Boyce-Greeley Bldg., Sioux Falls, S.D. Died Mar. 30, 1952; buried Woodlawn Cemetery, Sioux Falls.

DANFORTH, William H., miller; b. Charleston, Mo., Sept. 10, 1870; s. Albert Hampton and Rebecca (Lynn) D.; M.E., Washington University, 1892; LL.D. (honorary), Berea (Kentucky) College; m. Adda Bush, Oct. 24, 1894; children—Dorothy (Mrs. Randolph P. Compton), Donald. Founder, 1893, now chmn. bd. Ralston Purina Co., mills at St. Louis, Kansas City, Minneapolis, Buffalo, Nashville, Fort Worth, Battle Creek, Mich., Bloomington, Ill., Davenport, Ia., Wichita, Kan., Denver, St. Johnsbury, Vt., Lafayette, Ind., Pocatello, Ida., Lubbock, Tex., Richmond, Ind., Wilmington, Del., Circleville, Ohio, Charlotte, N.C., Iowa Falls, Iowa, Omaha, Neb., Tampa and Miami, Fla., Los Angeles, Oakland, Stockton, Visalia, Calif., Macon, Georgia, Montreal, Canada, Woodstock, Canada. Amarillo, Tex., Delmar, Del., Spokane, Wash., Jackson, Miss.; dir. First National Bank, St. Louis Union Trust Company, N.Y. Life Ins. Co. Ill. Terminal R.R. Mem. Bus. Adv. Council, U.S. Dept. of Commerce. Dir. Y.M.C.A., Third Div., A.E.F., 1918. Trustee Berea (Ky.) Coll.; dir. Washington U. Mem. Am. Youth Found. (pres.). Danforth Found. (pres.). Nat. Christmas Carols Assn. of St. Louis (pres.), Phi Delta Theta. Republican. Conglist. Clubs: Noonday, Bogy Country. Author of "Russia Under the Hammer and Sickle"; "Random Ramblings in India"; "Fight"; "Growth"; "Action"; "Power"; "I Dare You": "Around the World." Home: 17 Kingsbury Pl. Office: 835 S. 8th St., St. Louis. Died Dec. 24, 1955.

DANIEL, Lewis C., A.N.A.; b. N.Y. City, Oct. 23, 1901; s. Abraham and Carrie (Falk) D.; ed. N.Y. City public schools; student Nat. Acad. of Design; studied privately with Harry Wickey; m. Hildreth Alexander, 1945; 1 s., Jonathan. Formerly teacher Cooper Union, N.Y. City, for 4 yrs. Mem. Soc. Am. Etchers. Awarded 3 fellowships at MacDowell Colony; Eyre medal for prints, Pa. Acad. Fine Arts, represented in collections of Whitney Museum, Pa. Acad. Fine Arts, Cooper Union Library, N.Y., Pub. Library; Library of Congress; also in Fifty Prints of the Year, 1927, 28, 29; 100 Prints of Year, Soc. of Am. Etchers, 1937-40; one-man show of paintings, Assn. Am. Artists, N.Y. City, 1940, Seligman Gallery, 1943, Babcock Galleries, 1946, 48 and 52, Limited edition of etchings for Song of the Open Road by Walt Whitman. Commissioned to illustrate Leaves of Grass, selected by Book of the Month Club as dividend book, 1940. Interpreted Brahms Symphony No. 1 for Capehart collection; painted Seige of Stalingrad for Office of War Information, picture now hanging in Russian Embassy, Washington. Awarded $200 Phila. water-color prize, Oct. 29, 1944; Paintings of the Year, 1947; Nat. Acad. prize for etching, 1949; Audubon Artists award, 1950; Art Dirs. Club award of distinctive merit, 1953. A.N.A. elect. Home: 801 Riverside Drive. Studio: 65 W. 56th St., N.Y.C. Died July 8, 1952.

DANIEL, Robert Norman, educator; b. Gravel Hill, Va., Nov. 30, 1888; s. John Robert and Florence Lillian (Hall) D.; prep. edn. Fork Union (Va.) Mil. Acad., 1903-04; A.B., U. Richmond, 1907, A.M., 1908; Ph.M., U. Chgo., 1911; D. Litt., Georgetown (Ky.) Coll., 1942; LL.D., Furman U., 1948; m. Frances Evelyn Pack, June 24, 1914; children—Frances Evelyn, Robert Norman, Elizabeth Sanderson, Charles Pack. Instr. in Latin and German, Fork Union Mil. Acad., 1908-09; asso. prof. English, Furman U., 1911-14; prof. Eng., Georgetown (Ky.) Coll., 1914-20; prof. English, Furman U., 1920-—, dean, 1922-48, dean emeritus, 1948, Mem. Modern Lang. Assn., S. Atlantic Modern Lang. Assn., S.E. Coll. English Assn., Club of Thirty-Nine, Phi Beta Kappa, Pi Kappa Phi. Democrat. Baptist. Author: Furman University, 1951. Home: 311 University Ridge, Greenville, S.C. Died Sept. 20, 1956; buried Springwood Cemetery, Greenville.

DANIELS, Benjamin, business exec., b. N.Y. City, Aug. 15, 1898; s. Louis and Rose (Weinzweig) D.; m. Gertrude Bloom, Nov. 25, 1917; one dau. Doris Pearl. Joined A. S. Beck Shoe Co., 1915, vice pres., gen. mgr., 1926, became pres., 1945, now dir.; pres. Daniels Shoe Corp., Lowell, Mass., 1947, Ciro Realty Corp., Capri Realty Corp., Ciro Hosiery Co.; partner Triad Hosiery Co., Romona Hosiery Mills, Inc., Amherst Hosiery, Clio Hosiery, Laurel Hosiery, Marbill

Hosiery; chmn. bd. Am. Sun Petroleum Corp., Daniels Oil Co.; dir. Sanson Hosiery Mills, Inc. Address: 480 Park Av., N.Y.C. 22. Died July 3, 1957; buried Ferncliff Cemetery, Hartsdale, N.Y.

DANIELS, Francis Cummings, govt. ofcl.; b. Marquette, Mich., Apr. 19, 1896; s. Martin and Elizabeth (Cole) D.; student No. State Normal Sch., Marquette, 1915-17; tchrs. certificate, U. Chgo., 1917; m. Elizabeth Cullity, June 23, 1927. Prin. Covington (Mich.) Sch., 1917-18; with Bowser Pump Co., 1919, Larrowe Milling Co., 1920-24; salesman Empire Grain & Elevator Co., 1924-36; sales mgr., gen. mgr. Coop. Feed Dealers, Inc., Binghampton, N.Y., 1936-54; cons., adviser adminstr. Commodity Stblzn. Service, Dept. Agr., 1954—, gen. sales mgr., 1955—, also v.p. Commodity Credit Corp., 1955—. Dir. Nat. Grain and Feed Dealers, Washington. Mason (Shriner). Home: 41 Crary Av., Binghampton, N.Y.; also 2801 Quebec St., Quebec House, North, Washington 8. Office: Commodity Credit Corp., Dept. of Agr., Washington 25. Died Mar. 24, 1959.

DANIELS, Henry H.; bishop. The Protestant Episcopal Church, Helena, ret. Address: 9 Kohrs Block, Helena, Mont. Died Mar. 5, 1958.

DANIELS, John, writer, editor, lecturer; b. Ridgeway, Ia., May 11, 1881; s. John and Olive Erskine (Baker) D.; A.B., Harvard, 1903 as of 1904, A.M., 1904; m. Caroline Dornbach, June 30, 1909 (dec. 1945); children—Whitman, Lincoln, John. Engaged since 1904 in research, writing, organization and adminstrn., having largely to do with Am. democracy and internat. co-operation; nat. sec. English-Speaking Union of the United States, 1921-35; made a field study of American cooperatives, 1937. Editor: The Popular Educator (1940). Mem. nat. panel arbitrators Am. Arbitration Assn. Mem. Indsl. Relations Research Assn., Common Council for Am. Unity, Am. Council for the Community, Nat. Urban League, Whitman Soc. of America. Coop. League of U.S.A., India League of Am., World Alliance for Internat. Friendship through Religion. Met. Museum Art, United World Federalists, Phi Beta Kappa. Author: Outline of Economics, 1908; In Freedom's Birthplace (a study of the Negro in U.S.), 1914; America Via the Neighborhood (Carnegie Corp. Americanization series), 1920; Cooperation: An American Way, 1938; also magazine articles. Currently engaged in research, writing and lecturing with labor mgt. relations as a leading interest. Home: 403 W. 115th St., N.Y. 25. Died Feb. 17, 1953.

DANIELSON, Clarence Hagbart, army officer; b. Lead, S.D., Aug. 7, 1889; s. Ole and Hannah (Berg) D.; B.S., U.S. Military Acad., 1913, Command and General Staff School, 1930-32, Army War College, 1937-38; National War College, 1946; married Edith May Baird, December 2, 1914; children—Ole, Willis. Commissioned 2d lieut., Infantry, 1913, and advanced through the grades to maj. gen., 1944; Mexican border service, 1913-17; Mexican Punitive Expdn., 1916; Hawaiian Dept., Honolulu, T.H., 1917-18; Insp. Gen. Dept., Camp Custer, Mich., Camp Grant, Ill., Washington, D.C., 1918-19; Adj. Gen. Dept., 1923; Adj. Gen. Office (both Washington, D.C.),1920-23,1926-30, 1933-36; adj. gen. Harbor Defenses, Manila, Subic Bays, Ft. Mills, Corregidor, P.I., 1923-25; asst. adj. gen. 2d Army Corps Area, 1925-26; Adj. Gen. Office, Washington, 1926-30; asst. adj. gen., Hawaiian Div., Schofield Barracks, T.H., 1932-33; Adj. Gen. Office, Washington, D.C., 1933-36; Gen. Staff Corps, War Dept. Gen. Staff, 1936-37; adj. gen., U.S. Military Acad., 1938-41; adj. gen., 1st Army, Governors Island, N.Y., 1941-42; appt. dir. Officer Procurement Service, 1942; comdg. gen. Seventh Service Comd., Jan. 1944; retired, Oct. 1946. Decorations: Legion of Merit with Oak Leaf Cluster; Army Commendation Ribbon; D.S.M.; Estrella Abdon de Calderon, 1st Class (Ecuador). Mason. Clubs: Army-Navy, Columbia Country (Washington); Army-Navy (Arlington, Va.). Home: 3202 Riverview Blvd. W., Bradenton, Fla. Office: c/o Adjutant Gen. Army, Washington. Died May, 22, 1952; buried U.S.M.A., West Point, N.Y.

DANIELSON, Jacques, pianist; b. Moscow, Russia, July 23, 1875; s. Samuel and Anna (Brook) D.; ed. Moscow Conservatory of Music; m. Fannie Hurst, 1915. Came to U.S., 1892; prof. piano, N.Y. Coll. Music, 1895-10; asst. to Rafael Joseffy, pianist, Steinway Hall, N.Y.C. 1910—. Club: Bohemian Musicians' (N.Y.C.). Home: 665 Lexington Av., N.Y. C. Died Mar. 3, 1952.

DANIELSON, Reuben Gustaf, banking exec.; b. Chgo., Oct. 12, 1884; s. Frank G. and Mathilda H. (Alzen) D.; student Lake View High Sch., Chgo. Bus. Coll.; m. Rose C. Froehde, July 3, 1915. Clerk First Nat. Bank, 1903; later stenographer and clk. Continental Nat. Bank; continued as clerk following consolidated with Commercial Nat. Bank to form Continental & Commercial Nat. Bank, 1910, became mgr. of transit dept., asst. cashier, 1918, cashier, 1920, retained position as cashier when the Continental & Commercial Nat. Bank and the Continental & Commercial Trust & Savings Bank merged in 1927 to form the Continental Nat. Bank and Trust Co.; elected cashier in 1929 of the Continental Ill. Bank and Trust Company (a consolidation of the Continental Nat. Bank and Trust Co. and Ill. Merchants Trust Co.), v.p. and cashier, 1932-49, v.p., 1949—, 1949—. Mason. Clubs: Union League (Chgo.); Evanston Golf. Home: 1410 Lincoln St., Evanston, Ill. Died Apr. 15, 1950; buried Rosehill Cemetery, Chgo.

DANIELSON, Richard Ely, editor; b. Brooklyn, Conn., Nov. 7, 1885; s. William H. and Alice Hart (Robinson) D.; grad. William Penn Charter Sch., Phila., 1903; B.A., Yale, 1907, M.A., 1910; m. Barbara Deering, Nov. 5, 1910; children—Richard Ely, James Deering, Marion Deering. Editor Boston Independent, 1924-28; pres. Sportsman Pub. Co.; editor The Sportsman, 1927-37; president Atlantic Monthly Co. and asso. editor The Atlantic Monthly, 1940. Pres. bd. trustees Groton Community Hosp., 1952—. Commd. major, AUS, April 28, 1942; Gen. Staff Corps with troops, June 1942; lt. col., 1943. With Am. Red Cross, French Army in France, 1917-18; commd. 1st lieut. Infantry, U.S. Army, April 12, 1918; capt. Feb. 15, 1919; intelligence officer at Nantes till Dec. 1918; intelligence officer, Bordeaux, asst. chief of staff G2, for Base Sect. No. 2 until June 1919. Decorated Order of Black Star. Republican. Episcopalian. Clubs: Somerset, Tennis and Racquet, Tavern (Boston); Knickerbocker, (New York); M.F.H. Groton Hunt Club, 1922-36. Author: Martha Doyle and other Sporting Memories, 1938. Home: Groton, Mass., and 301 Berkeley St., Boston. Office: 8 Arlington St., Boston. Died May 23, 1957; buried Groton (Mass.) Cemetery.

DANNREUTHER, Walter T. (dän-roi'tĕr), gynecologist; b. Buffalo, May 27, 1885; s. Gustav and Nellie M. (Taylor) D.; prep. edn., DeWitt Clinton High Sch.; M.D., Long Island Coll. Hosp. (awarded Dudley Medal), 1906; m. Anna Rogers Tower, Oct. 26, 1911. House surgeon Jersey City (N.J.) Hosp., 1906-07; began practice, N.Y.C., 1907; prof. gynecology and dir. dept., New York Post-Grad. Med. Sch. (Columbia U.), 1925-48; prof. obstetrics and gynecology, Post-Grad. Med. School, N.Y.U., 1948-50, professor emeritus since 1950; cons. various hosps. Awarded Alumni Achievement medal L.I. Coll. Hosp., 1949. Pres. Am. Bd. Obstetrics and Gynecology, 1930-55. Served as capt. O.R.C. Fellow Am. Coll. Surgeons (bd. govs.), hon. fellow N.E. Obstet. and Gynecol. Soc., Central Assn. of Obstetricians and Gynecologists, Royal Obstet. and Gynecol. Soc. of Belgium, South Atlantic Assn. of Obstetricians and Gynecologists, Pittsburgh Obstetrical and Gynecology Society; mem. A.M.A., Am. Assoc. of Obstetricals and Gynecologicals (pres. 1932), Am. Gynecol. Society (president 1951), N.Y. Acad. Med., N.Y. Obstet. Soc., N.Y. Medico-Surg. Soc. (pres. 1925), N.Y. Co. Med. Soc. (pres. 1934), etc. Episcopalian. Mason (32°, K.T., Shriner). Clubs: New York Athletic (N.Y.C.); Greenock Country (Lee, Mass.). Revised Medical Gynecology, by Samuel W. Bandler, 1922. Contbr. to Urinary Analysis and Diagnosis; also contbr. many articles to med. jours. Home and office: 580 Park Av., N.Y.C. 21. Died Jan. 1960.

D'ANTONI, Salvador (dän-tō-nē), ret. chmn. bd., pres. Standard Fruit & Steamship Corp. Office: 944 St. Charles Av., New Orleans. Died Jan. 3, 1957.

da PONTE, Lorenzo Brooke (dá-pōn-tā), lawyer; b. Galveston, Tex., Apr. 23, 1878; s. Harry and Gertrude (Hay) da P.; student U. Tex. Law Sch., 1899-1900; m. Helen Mims, Feb. 13, 1904 (died Oct. 30, 1934); children—Helen (Mrs. Edward E. Neale), Bernice (Mrs. Charles W. Adams), Durant; m. 2d, Edna L. Moore, Nov. 9, 1938. Admitted to Tex. bar, 1902, practiced in Beaumont, 1902-08, Tacoma, Wash., 1908-10; asso. with N. P. Ry., 1910—, asst. div. counsel, Tacoma, 1910-29, Western counsel, Seattle, 1929-37, gen. counsel, St. Paul, 1937—. Republican. Clubs: Minnesota, St. Paul Athletic (St. Paul). Home: 436 Holly Av. Office: Northern Pacific Bldg., St. Paul. Died Nov. 26, 1950.

DARBY, Ada Claire (där'bĭ), author; b. St. Joseph, Mo., Dec. 31, 1883; d. Charles Hammond and Ada (Leonard) D.; grad. Central High Sch., St. Joseph, 1901. Literary editor St. Joseph News-Press, 1916-24; writer of book reviews and short stories for women's mags. Mem. Mo. Writers Guild. Author: Pinafores and Pantalettes, 1927; Skip-Come-A-Lou, 1928; "Scally' Alden, 1929; Hickory Goody, 1930; Sometimes Jenny Wren, 1931; Gay Soeurette, 1933; Keturah Came 'Round the Horn, 1935; Peace Pipes at Portage, 1938; "Show Me," Missouri, 1938; Yonder The Golden Gate, 1939; Columbine Susan, 1940; On The Santa Fe Trail (with Hallie Hall Violette), 1940; Look Away, Dixie Land!, 1941; Jump Lively, Jeff, 1942; (collaborator) Children of the U.S.A., 1946; Island Girl, 1951. Lecturer. Home: 2719 Oliver St., St. Joseph, Mo. Died Dec. 23, 1953; buried Mount Nora Cemetery, St. Joseph, Mo.

DARBY, John Frederick, petroleum exec.; b. Odell, Ill., Aug. 31, 1872; s. Thomas Jared and Mary (Blakesley) D.; LL.D., Grinnell (Ia.) College, 1895; grad. work, U. of Chicago; student Chicago Coll. of Law (Lake Forest U.) 2 yrs.; m. Marine Poole, May 11, 1923. Began as high sch. teacher, 1895; located in Muskogee, Okla., 1903; engaged in real estate business, farm loans and banking, later producing refining and marketing oil; dir., Darby & Rothwell, Inc.; director Commercial National Bank of Muskogee, Okla., Oklahoma Natural Gas Co.; partner Lynde, & Darby, Tulsa, Okla. Chairman, Oklahoma Commn. on Conciliation and Cooperation, World War I. Mem. Okla. State Bd. of Agr., 1911-15, Mid-Continent Oil & Gas Assn. (pres. 1919-20); chmn. Okla. Production Com. (petroleum code under NRA); mem. Okla. Advisory Com. R.F.C.; mem. Am. Relief Assn. Trustee Grinnell College. Decorated: Order of the White Cross, Finland. Chmn. Okla. delegation to Rep. Nat. Conv., 1932; del. to Rep. Nat. Conv., 1944. Mem. Phi Beta Kappa, Phi Beta Kappa Associates. Episcopalian; vestryman Grace Church, Muskogee, Okla. Clubs: Tulsa, Southern Hills Country (Tulsa); Town and Country (Muskogee); Kansas City (Mo.); Broadmoor Golf, Cheyenne Mountain Country (Colorado Springs, Colo.). Home: 402 N. 17th St., Muskogee, Okla., and Chandler, Ariz. Office: Philtower, Tulsa 3. Died Feb. 27, 1953; buried Tulsa.

DARBY, William Lambert, clergyman; b. Evansville, Ind., Nov. 29, 1875; s. Rev. William Johnson and Mary Belle (Lambert) D.; prep. edn., high sch., and Montgomery Bell Acad., Nashville; A.B., Cumberland U., 1895, B.D., 1898, LL.D., 1930; B.D., Union Theol. Sem., 1907; studied Columbia, 2 yrs.; D.D., Coll. of the Ozarks, 1912; m. Edith Holland, 1904; children—Marjorie Phelps (dec.), Bertha Louise, Paul Holland; m. 2d, Mrs. Florence H. Wiber, 1917. Ordained Presbyn. ministry, 1898; pastor Kirksville, Mo., 1898-1906, Astoria, N.Y.C., 1906-10, Clarksville, Ark., 1910-14; state supt. Home Missions, Ala., 1914-18; YMCA war work sec., 1918-29; dir., lectr. Radcliffe Chautauqua, 1920, 21; field sec. James Millikin U., 1921, 22; exec. sec. Fedn. Chs., Washington, 1922-40, also Washington sec. Fed. Council Chs. and sec. Gen. Com. on Army and Navy Chaplains, 1925-32. Pres. Washington City Bible Soc., 1940-45; sec. Nat. Capital Dist., Am. Bible Soc., 1945-48. Pres. Christian Endeavor Union, Mo. and Ark., each 2 yrs. Mem. Kappa Sigma. Republican. Mason. Home: 919 Pickering St., Ogdensburg, N.Y. Died Mar. 26, 1951; buried Washington.

DARLINGTON, Frederick, cons. engr., mfg. exec.; b. Lincoln University, Pa., Apr. 23, 1867; s. Franklin and Mary (Jackson) D.; B.S., Pa. State Coll., 1886; m. Josephine Sanford, Sept. 16, 1890; children—Mrs. Josephine Stanley, Mrs. Helen McCandless. With Am. Bridge Co., 1888-89, Hunt & Clap Chem. Lab., Pitts., 1890, Westinghouse Electric Co., Pitts., 1891; with United Electric Light & Power Co. and Brush Illuminating Co., N.Y.C., 1892-98; engring. and scientific investigations with William Stanley, Great Barrington, Mass., 1898-1903; with Westinghouse Electric & Mfg. Co., 1905-12, cons. engr., 1914-17, 23—, also asst. to v.p., 1923—; v.p. and mgr. Ala. Power Co., 1913; chief of power sect. of War Industries Bd., Washington, 1918. Republican. Fellow Am. Inst. E.E. Clubs: Union League, Lawyers (N.Y.C.). Home: Great Barrington, Mass.; and 38 E. 37th St., N.Y.C. Office: 150 Broadway, N.Y.C. Died Oct. 27, 1943.

DARLINGTON, Henry (Vane Bearns), ret. clergyman; advt. exec.; b. Bklyn., June 9, 1889; s. Bishop James Henry and Ella L. (Bearns) D.; student Dickinson Coll., 1907, D.D., 1927; A.B., Columbia U., 1910; grad. Gen. Theol. Sem., 1913; grad. student Columbia; D.D., Greek Sem. of St. Athanasius, 1923; married Dorothy Stone-Smith, Nov. 24, 1920; children—Peter (USAFR), Henry (USNR), Deacon, 1913, priest, 1914, P.E. Church; curate St. Thomas' Church, New York, 1913-14; missionary in charge three chs. and founded Mission Serepta, 1914-15; rector St. Barnabas Ch., Newark, 1915-22, Ch. of the Heavenly Rest, N.Y., 1922-25, Ch. of the Heavenly Rest and Chapel of Beloved Disciple, 1925-50. Headmaster, Day School, Church of the Heavenly Rest, 1929-50; acct. exec. Necrgaard, Miller & Co., N.Y.C., 1951-54; limited partner Hill, Darlington & Co., N.Y.C., 1955—. Pioneer Ministry Spiritual Healing, and held regular services in the Parish, 1935-50. Organized, built and operated Turnpike Bridge Co., Delaware, N.J., 1914-26. Commd. 1st lt. chaplain N.A., Feb. 18, 1918; chaplain Coast Defense, East N.Y.; chaplain 50th C.A.C., 1st Army, A.E.F., France; hon. discharged, Feb. 1919; commd. capt. chaplain, N.Y. Nat. Guard, Feb. 28, 1924; assigned junior chaplain 44th Inf. Div. N.J. Nat. Guard, 1924; promoted chaplain major, June 12, 1933, advanced to senior chaplain; transferred to chaplain major 27th Div. N.Y. Nat. Guard; resigned, Sept. 1940; recommd. sr. chaplain lt. col., Hdqrs. N.Y. Guard, Nov. 1940; promoted col., Jan. 1945; permanent chaplain, association ex-members of Squadron A; transferred back to N.Y. Nat. Guard, promoted brig. gen., Oct. 1949; now on state reserve list. Chmn. Protestant Council's Commission in Ministry to Veterans and Service Personnel. Chaplain general S.A.R., 1938-41, also various posts Am. Legion. Dir. N.Y. Co. Red Cross, 1949—; mem. N.Y. Co. Red Cross blood bank, 1950—; mem. veterans com., N.Y. Welfare Council. Decorated Officer Order of George I of Greece; received 10 and 15 Year medal New York National Guard, 10 and 15 yr. medal Squadron A, 10 yr. medal N.J. Nat. Guard. Formerly trustee Bard College, 1925-40; trustee The Protestant-

Episcopal School. Member Society Colonial Wars, Sons Revolution, Society of Cincinnati (chaplain Rhode Island Soc.), Huguenot Soc., Pilgrims, Mil. Order Foreign Wars (chaplain gen., 1951), Mil. Order World Wars (chaplain, 1947), Mil. Chaplains Assn. U.S.A. (pres. 1952), S.A.R., N.Y. Chapter Mil. and Naval Officers World War, St. Nicholas Soc., Sojourners, St. Andrews Soc., Phi Delta Theta. Mason (32°, K.T., Shriner grand chaplain, N.Y.). Clubs: Union, Columbia U. Author of many pamphlets, sermons and the like. Address: 2 E. 93rd St., N.Y.C. 28. Died Dec. 20, 1955; buried Woodlawn Cemetery.

DARLINGTON, Urban Valentine W., bishop; b. Shelby County, Ky., Aug. 3, 1870; s. James Henderson and Kitty (Pemberton) D.; student Ky. Wesleyan Coll., 1889-95 (D.D.); m. Virginia Bourne, Feb. 12, 1913. Ordained ministry M.E. Ch., S., 1896; pastor Washington, Ky., 1896-1900, Millersburg, 1900, Covington, 1901-05, Parkersburg, W.Va., 1905-09, Huntington, 1909-13; sec. of edn. Western Va. Conf., 1914, 16; presidg. edler, 1915; pres. Morris Harvey Coll., Barboursville, W.Va., 1917-18; bishop Methodist Ch., 1918——. Pres. bd. trustees Paine Coll., Augusta, Ga.; trustee Emiry U., Atlanta, Ga. Democrat. Member Ecumenical Methodist Conf., 1911, 1921. Home: Huntington, W.Va. Died Oct. 1, 1954; buried Frankfort, Ky.

DARR, Edward A(ustin), business exec.; b. Baltimore, Md., July 23, 1890; s. William H. and Mary Elizabeth (Coffman) D.; student McDonogh (Md.) Sch., 1900-02; LL.B., Univ. of Md., 1913; m. Frances Payne, Jan. 1919 (died 1920), 1 son, Edward; m. 2d, Ruth Ely, Nov. 1924 (dec. 1958); children—Drusilla, Deborah, Mary, David, Cicely. Admitted to Md. Bar, 1913; mgr. sales dept., R. J. Reynolds Tobacco Co., Winston-Salem, N.C., since 1938, mem. bd. dirs., 1938——, v.p., 1946-52, pres., 1952-57, vice chmn. board, chmn. exec. com., 1957——. Mem. Reynolds Park Recreation Commn., Winston-Salem, 1935-45. Served U.S. Marine Corps, 1918. Mem. N.C. Archaeological Soc., Wachovia Hist. Soc., Am. Legion, Nat. Sales Execs., C. of C. Democrat. Protestant. Clubs: Twin City, Forsyth Country, Old Town, Rotary (Winston-Salem); Metropolitan, Athletic, Economic (N.Y.C.). Home: 1067 E. Kent Rd. Office: R. J. Reynolds Tobacco Co., Winston-Salem, N.C. Died Oct. 8, 1958.

DARRAH, Thomas W(alter), army officer; b. Marquette, Kan., July 11, 1873; s. Samuel Jones and Mary (Temperly) D.; grad. U.S. Mil. Acad., 1895, Army Sch. of the Line, 1920, Gen. Staff Sch., 1921, Army War Coll., 1923; m. Rose Wood, Apr. 19, 1899; children—Marion Maxwell (Mrs. Warren D. Brewster), Jean West (Mrs. Woodlief Thomas). Commd. 2d lt. inf., U.S. Army, 1895, advanced through grades to brig. gen., 1931; with subsistence dept. U.S. Army, 1901-05; instr. dept. chemistry U.S. Mil. Acad., 1907-11; sr. regtl. instr. O.T.C., Fort Benjamin Harrison, Ind., 1917; participated in Champagne-Marne Defensive, Aisne-Marne, Oise-Aisne and Meuse-Argonne offensives, World War: chief of staff, 4th Corps Area, 1924-26; comd. 34th Inf., U.S. Army, 1926-28: chief to staff, 3d Corps Area, 1928-31; comdg. Pacific sector Panama Canal Dept., 1932-34; retired, 1937. Decorated two Silver Star Medals for gallantry in action, Santiago, Cuba, Legaspi, Luzon, P.I. Home: 122 E. 82d St., N.Y.C. Died Jan. 21, 1955; buried Arlington Nat. Cemetery.

DARST, Joseph Miltenberger, city ofcl.; b. St. Louis, Mar. 18, 1889; s. Joseph C. and Annie (Miltenberger) D.; student St. Louis U., 1913; m. Lucille Rose, Feb. 12, 1930. Vice pres. Jos. Darst Realty Co., St. Louis, 1918-30, pres., 1930—— (name changed to Jos. M. Darst and Assos., 1941). Dir. pub. welfare City of St. Louis, 1933-41; dir. Fed. Housing Authority, Eastern Dist. Mo., 1947-48; mayor City of St. Louis, 1949-53. Served as lt., 35th div. U.S. Army, 1917-18. Mem. Urban League of St. Louis (dir.), St. Louis Real Estate Bd., 35th Div. Assn., Am. Legion, C. of C. Democrat (chmn. Truman-Barkley Club of Mo., 1948, supervising campaign). Clubs: Co-operative, Key, Columbian, Missouri Athletic. Home: 4943 Lindell Blvd., St. Louis 8. Office: City Hall, St. Louis 3. Died June 8, 1953.

DAS, Taraknath (tȧs), author, publicist, educator; b. nr. Calcutta, India, June 15, 1884; s. Kali Mohon and Biraj Mohini (Bose) D.; edn. in India, Norwich U., Vt.; A.B., U. of Wash., 1910, A.M., 1911 (Fellow in Polit. Sci. and Economics); student U. Calif., U. of Berlin, Columbia U.; Ph.D., Georgetown U., 1924; Ph.D. (hon.), University of Munich, 1954; married Mary Keatinge Morse, 1924. Came to U.S., 1906, naturalized citizen, 1914. Special lecturer on Far Eastern Affairs, Catholic Univ. of America, Washington, D.C., 1934-35; spl. lecturer history and internat. relations, Coll. of the City of N.Y. 1936-47, internat. relations, U. of Md., summers, 1937 and 1938. Mem. faculty New England Institute of Internat. Relations, Wellesley College; Inst. of Internat. Relations, Bryn Mawr College; Inst. of Internat. Relations, Cornell U., summer, 1941; lecturer, Dept. of Polit. Science, Queens College, Flushing, N.Y., 1941; Watumull Foundation Special Lecturer on Oriental History and World Politics, Catholic University of America, Washington, D.C., 1944-45: Watumill Foundation visiting prof., Inst. Public Affairs and Regional Studies, N.Y. U., 1945-48; adjunct prof. public affairs, New York U., since 1948. Lecturer, dept. history, Columbia U., N.Y. City, since 1947; mem. faculty. Inst. Pub. Affairs, U. Va., 1950, Inst. Internat. Affairs, U. Wyo., 1951, U. Denver, 1951, Columbia, summer 1953, U. Hawaii, summer 1952, 54, U. So. Cal. Los Angeles, summer 1955, Brooklyn Coll., 1956; Watermull Found. travelling fellow, lectr. univs. of India, Japan, Israel and Germany, 1952-53. Founder, sec., treas., dir. Taraknath Das Found., Inc., 1930——. Fellow Am., Geog. Soc., A.A.A.S.; mem. Am. Soc. Internat. Law, Am. German Cultural Cooperation Com., Am. Acad. Polit. and Social Sci. Acad. Polit. Sci, Am. Hist. Assn. Hindu religion. Author: Is Japan a Menace to Asia?, 1917; India in World Politics, 1923; Sovereign Rights of Indian Princes, 1924; British Expansion in Tibet, 1927; Revolution in Inden (German), 1930; How Orient and Occident Can be Correlated 1931; Indien in der Weltpolitik, 1932; Religious, Social and Political Ideals of Rabindranath Tagore, 1933; Foreign Policies of Preisdent Franklin D. Roosevelt, 1934; La Questione del Pacifico vista da un Oreintale (Italian), 1934; Foreign Policy in the Far East, 1936; Essays on World Politics (Bengalee), 1937; Diplomatic Struggle Among Great Powers for Mastery of the Far East (Japanese), 1939; Asia's Part in War and Peace, 1942; The War Comes to India, 1942; Requisites for Better Understanding Between East and West, 1945; Status of Hyderabad Before and After the British Rule in India, 1949. Editor: Am. India Feature & News Service; contbr. Mod. Rev., Calcutta. Selected for Hall of Fame, N.Y. World's Fair, 1940. Home: Hotel Ansonia, Broadway and 73d St., N.Y.C. 23. Died Dec. 22, 1958.

D'ASCENZO, Nicola (däs-sĕn'tsō), artist; b. Torricella, Peligna, Italy, Sept. 25, 1871; s. Giacinto and Mary Joseph (Italiana) D'A.; came to U.S., 1882; ed. Pa. Acad. Fine Arts, Phila.; Pa. Museum and Sch. Industrial Art, New York Sch. of Design Scoula Libera, Rome, Italy; m. Myrtle Goodwin, June 12, 1894; 1 son, Nicola Goodwin. Proprietor The D'Ascenzo Studios, makers of stained glass, murals, mosaics. Phila. Prin. works: historical windows, Washington Memorial Chapel, Valley Forge, Pa.; clerestory windows, Mercersburg (Pa.) Acad.; chapel windows Georgetown Prep. Sch., Garrett Park, Md.; windows Folger-Shakespeare Library of Washington, D.C.; windows and Stations of the Cross, Ch. of the Holy Child, Phila.; great west window, Princeton U. Chapel; windows for Riverside Bapt. Ch. (New York), St. James P.E. Ch. (Bristol, Pa.), Unitarian Ch. (Phila.), and Fidelity Phila. Bldg. (Phila.); window in Chapel of the Holy Spirit, Nat. Cathedral, Washington, D.C.; clerestory and aisle windows in Labor and Press Bays, Cathedral of St. John the Divine, N.Y. City; clerestory and front windows, St. Andrew's R.C. Ch., N.Y. City; windows, St. Stephen's R.C. Ch., Arlington, N.J., and First Presbyn. Ch., Atlanta, Ga.; all windows, First Presbyn. Ch., Birmingham, Ala.; all windows and chancel mosaics; Independent Presbyn. Ch., Birmingham, Ala.; mausoleum windows. Forest Lawn Memorial Park, Glendale, California. Awarded gold medal, Archtl. League of New York, 1925; gold medal, T-square Club, 1897-98; gold medal Alumni Assn. of Pa. Museum and Sch. of Industrial Art; gold medal, Pa. Arts and Sciences Soc.; medalist Columbian Exposition: chosen by Russell Sage Foundation for Wall of Fame, Am. Common, World's Fair, N.Y. City, 1940. Member Archtl. League New York, Soc. Mural Decorators, Science and Art Club of Germantown, Pa. Arts and Sciences Soc., Drexel Inst. (spl. com. on art), Pa. Museum and Sch. Industrial Art (instrn. com.); hon. mem. Am. Inst. Architects. Former sec. State Art Jury, Pa. Mem. Bd. of Public Edn., City of Phila.; pres. Phila. Sketch Club. Home: 425 W. Price St. Office: 1604 Summer St., Phila. 3. Died Apr. 13, 1954; buried Valley Forge Cemetery.

DASCH, George (dăsh), musician; b. Cin., May 14. 1887; s. George and Margaret (Job) D.; diploma Coll. of Music, Cin., 1895, Mus. D. (hon.) 1945; m. Louise Garben, Sept. 26, 1906; children—Henry (dec.), Elizabeth Margaret, Dorothy Louise (Mrs. Dudley Powers), Charlotte (dec.). Mem. Cin. Symphony Orchestra, 1895-98; joined Theodore Thomas Orchestra, Chgo., 1898, and continued with same and its successor, Chgo. Symphony Orchestra until 1923; asst. condr. Chgo. Civic Orchestra, under Frederick A. Stock, 4 yrs. condr. Little Symphony Orchestra of Chgo., 1921——; first violinist George Dasch String Quartet; condr. Northwestern U. Symphony Orchestra, 1928-45; resigned from Northwestern Sch. Music, 1945; now mem. faculty, music dept. of Evansville Coll. Condr. Chgo. Business Men's Orchestra, Evansville (Ind.) Philharmonic Orchestra. Mason. Collaborator, with Frederick A. Stock and Osbourne McConathy, Symphony Series of Programs for School and Community Orchestra. Home: 2230 Henley St., Glenview, Ill. Died Apr. 12, 1955; buried Graceland Cemetery, Chgo.

DASHIELL, Paul Joseph, naval officer; b. Annapolis, Md., July 16, 1867; s. Julius Matthias and Mary Thornton (Voss) D.; A.B., Johns Hopkins, 1887, Ph.D., 1891. Instr. in organic chemistry Lehigh U., 2 yrs.; prof. chemistry U.S. Naval Acad., 1892-1906, prof. mathematics 1906——, now capt. USN. Football ofcl., 1894-1904; mem. Football Rules Com. Member Phi Kappa Psi, Phi Beta Kappa. Clubs: Maryland (Balt.); Army and Navy (Washington). Address: Annapolis, Md. Died July 6, 1937; buried U.S. Naval Acad. Cemetery, Annapolis.

DATTNER, Bernhard, neuropsychiatrist; b. Ustron, Silesia, Austria, July 7, 1887; s. Adolf and Anna (Hechter) D.; Jur. D., U. of Vienna, 1911; M.D., 1919; m. Margaret Friedrich, Jan. 14, 1939. Came to U.S., 1938, naturalized, 1943. Cons. U.N. World Health Orgn. since 1950; N.Y. State Dept. of Health, Albany, since 1949; cons. in neurology U.S.P.H.S., Marine Hosp., Staten Island and Ellis Island since 1948; special cons., U.S.P.H.S., Washington, since 1946; asso. clin. prof. of neurol., N.Y. Univ. Sch. of Med., 1943-47; asst. clin prof. of neurol., Coll. Phys. and Surg., Columbia, 1945-47; acting attending neurologist, Goldwater Meml. Hosp., N.Y. City, since 1946, Bronx Hosp. since 1942; attending neurologist, Montefiore Hosp. since 1945; asso. visiting neuropsychiatrist Bellevue Hosp. since 1943. Diplomate Am. Bd. Psychiatry and Neurology; fellow N.Y. Acad. Medicine, Am. Neurol. Soc., N.Y. Neurol. Soc., Mexican Soc. Neurology and Psychiatry (hon.); corr. mem. Vienna Med. Soc., Vienna Neuro-psychiatric Soc. Author: Moderne Therapie der Neurosyphilis, (Vienna, Austria), 1933; Management of Neurosyphilis, 1944. Home: 235 22d St., N.Y. City 10. Office: 133 58th St., N.Y.C. 22. Died Aug. 11, 1952.

DAUBIN, Freeland Allen, naval officer; b. Lamar, Mo., Feb. 6, 1886; s. Crittenden Clay and Ella Nettie (Bowen) D.; grad. U.S. Naval Acad., 1909; m. Elizabeth Virginia Scott, June 3, 1912; children—Freeland Allen, Elizabeth Bowen, William Scott, Scott Crittenden. Commd. ensign, USN, 1909, advancing through the grades to rear adm., 1941; served in battleships, destroyers and submarines; comdr. submarines Atlantic, 1942-44; comdt. Navy Yard, New York, 1944——. Decorated Distinguished Service Medal. Home: Quarters "B," Navy Yard. Office: Navy Yard, N.Y. Died Oct. 24, 1959; buried Fort Rosecrans Nat. Cemetery, San Diego, Cal.

DAUGHERTY, Edgar Fay (daw'hĕr-tē), clergyman; b. Franklin, Ind., June 26, 1874; s. Roll C. and Elizabeth A. Daugherty; A.B., Franklin (Ind.) Coll., 1898, D.D., 1938; A.M., Butler Coll., 1901; B.D., Yale, 1902; D.D., Ind. Sch. of Religion, 1925; m. Martha E. Myers, Oct. 8, 1902; children—Carlos Wynn, Dorothy Melba. Ordained Disciples of Christ ministry, 1902; pastor, Danville, Ind., 1902-04, Wabash, Ind., 1904-10, Vincennes, Ind., 1910-18, 1st Christian Ch., Los Angeles, 1918-25; pastor Jackson St. Christian Ch., Muncie, Ind., 1925-48, pastor emeritus, 1948——; lectr. Pres. Ind. Conv. Disciples of Christ, 1929-30. Mem. Sigma Alpha Epsilon. Republican. Mason. K.T. Author: A Hoosier Parson, his Boosts and Bumps, 1951; (monographs) The Point of Honor, Democracy's Vindication, The Contribution of the Disciples, Mobilization—Its Content and Issues; At the Seventieth Milestone. Home: Stone Crest, 3205 W. Jackson St., Muncie, Ind. Died Mar. 16, 1957.

DAUGHERTY, Harry Kerr, lawyer; b. Mercer County, Pa., Dec. 28, 1868; s. William Watson and Mary (Kerr) D.; student Grove City Coll.; m. Mabel A. Gould, Sept. 6, 1899; children—Mrs. Helen Gould Murray, Haywood H. Admitted to bar, 1895; 1st lt. 15th Pa. Regt., Spanish-Am. War; mustered out at Ahens, Ga., 1899; mem. Pa. Ho. of Reps., 1901, 1903; apptd. asst. atty. for defense of claims before Spanish Treaty Claims Commn., Wash., spent 6 mos. in investigation and taking testimony in Cuba, 1906; mem. Spanish Treaty Claims Comm., Washington, 1907-12. Arbitrator in controversy bet. N.Y. Central and Nickel Plate rys. and Brotherhood of Telegraphers. Del. Rep. Nat. Conv., 1916, 20. Borough solicitor Grove City Borough, 1913-26; dep. atty. gen. of Pa., 1917-20; asst. solicitor of U.S. Treasury, 1926——. Methodist. Home: Grove City, Pa. Died Nov. 24, 1945.

DAUGHTERS, Freeman, prof. and dean of school of edn.; b. Lawrenceburg, Ind., Feb. 13, 1873; s. William Turpen and Sarah Elmira (Heaton) D.; A.B., Kan. Normal Coll., Ft. Scott, Kan., 1896; grad. Phila. Div. Sch., 1899; S.T.B., 1903; M.A., Columbia U., 1915; Ed.D., Intermountain Union Coll., 1933; unmarried. Began teaching, Bronson, Kan., 1893; social work, Phila., 1896-99; deacon, P.E. Ch., 1899; priest, 1900; rector Wallace, Ida., and Shamokin, Pa., 1899-1906; withdrew from ministry 1907; engaged in newspaper work 1906-09; prin. high sch., Sandpoint, Ida., 1909-14; prof. of edn., U. of Montana, 1915-43, chmn. dept. edn., 1915-30, dir. summer session, 1921-24, dean school of edn., 1930-42. Republican. Candidate for sec. of state, Ida., 1912, defeated with rest of ticket. Dir. Mont. Conf. on Edn. Problems, 1932-40; chmn. of com. on revision of standards for higher institutions of Northwest Assn., 1938-39;

member State Bd. of Edn. Examiners, 1919-40; chmn. Commn. on Higher Edn. of Northwest Assn., 1940-43. Mem. many professional orgns. Co-author: Ann Boleyn, 1913. Retired. Home: 2020 Douglas St., Forest Grove, Ore. Died Sept. 3, 1951; buried Forest Grove (Ore.) Cemetery.

DAVEE, Henry A., school supt.; b. Martinsville, Ind., July 29, 1872; s. Zachariah L. and Elvira (King) D.; student Kan. Normal Coll., Fort Scott; grad. Mont. State Normal Coll., Dillon, 1902; Ph.B., U. Wis., 1906; m. Mabel Flinders, Dec. 24, 1902. Began teaching in the rural schs. of Bourbon County, Kan., later prin. graded schs.; organized high sch. at Chinook, Mont., 1899; supt. schs., Hoquiam, Wash., 1903-04, Roseburg, Ore., 1906-07, Lewistown, Mont., 1907-13; state supt. schs., Mont., 1913-17; supt. Tng. Sch., River Falls, Wis., 1917—. Democrat. Methodist. Mason. Address: 421 E. Elm, River Falls, Wis. Died June 26, 1955.

DAVELER, Erle Victor (dăv'lĕr), corp. exec.; b. Denver, Dec. 31, 1885; s. John S. and Vicca M. (Smith) D.; B.S., U. Cal., 1907, Met.E., 1918, LL.D., 1947; m. Reby Mettam Bartley, June 1, 1912 (died Aug. 11, 1947); m. 2d, Lola Bullard, Oct. 27, 1949 Metall. work, Tonopah, Nev., 1907-09; research Utah Copper Co., 1909-11; asst. supt. mills Ray Consol. Copper Co., 1911-13; supt. mills and asst. mgr. Alaska Gold Mines, 1913-18; successively supt., gen. supt. and gen. mgr. Butte & Superior Co., 1918-30; v.p., treas., dir. Nev. Consol. Copper Corp., Utah Copper Co., Bingham & Garfield R.R., Ray & Gila Valley R.R., Gallup Am. Coal Co., Nev. No. R.R., 1930-43; v.p., dir. Am. Zinc., Lead & Smelting Co., 1943; pres., dir. Mesabi Iron Co., 1953—; chmn. exec. com. Lone Star Cement Corp.; dir. Cuban Atlantic Sugar Co., Granite City Steel Co., Texas Gulf Sulphur Co.; trustee shareholders Trust of Boston; dir. Minerals Benefication, Inc., Guardian Life Ins. Co. Trustee Charles Hayden Found., Stevens Inst. Tech. Mem. Mont. Bd. Edn., 1928-39. Mem. Am. Inst. Mining and Metall. Engrs., Mining and Metall. Soc. (past pres.). Republican. Episcopalian. Mason. Clubs: The Recess, Mining, University (N.Y.C.); Sleepy Hollow Country. Home: 988 Fifth Av. Office: 420 Lexington Av., N.Y.C. Died Nov. 11, 1957; buried Gate of Heaven Cemetery, Valhalla, N.Y.

DAVENPORT, Frederick M(organ), adminstr., ex-congressman; b. Salem, Mass., Aug. 27, 1866; David and Annie L. (Green) D.; A.B., Wesleyan U., Conn., 1889, LL.D., 1915; Ph.D., Columbia, 1905; LL.D., Hamilton Coll., 1933, Ohio Wesleyan U., 1939, Middlebury Coll., 1943. U. So. Cal., 1950, Syracuse U., 1952; m. Edith Jefferson Andrus, Jan. 2, 1899; children—Frederick Morgan, Margaret Dyckman (Mrs. Ernest S. Griffith), Winthrop, Barbara (Mrs. Karl E. Stromsem). Prof. law and politics Hamilton Coll., 1904-29; mem. 69th to 72d Congresses, 33d N.Y. Dist. Mem. N.Y. Senate, 1909, 10; Progressive nominee for lt. gov. N.Y., 1912, for gov., 1914; mem. N.Y. Senate, 1919-25. Pres. Nat. Inst. Pub. Affairs, Washington; chmn. Fed. Personnel Council of U.S. Govt. Trustee Pub. Adminstrn. Clearing House, Chgo., Wesleyan U., N. Am. Holding Corp. Recipient Stockberger award Soc. Personnel Adminstrn., 1950; Theodore Roosevelt D.S.M., 1951. Mem. Am. Polit. Sci. Assn., Phi Beta Kappa Assos. Republican. Clubs: Union League (N.Y.C.); Ft. Schuyler, Yahnundasis (Utica). Home: 8000 Parkside Lane N.W., Washington 12. Office: 1626 K St. N.W., Washington 25. Died Dec. 26, 1956; buried Woodlawn Cemetery, N.Y.C.

DAVENPORT, Russell (Wheeler); inst. dir., b. S. Bethlehem, Pa., July 12, 1899; s. Russell W. and Cornelia Whipple (Farnum) D.; grad. Thacher Sch.; Ojai, Calif., 1917; A.B., Yale 1923; LL.D., Albright Coll., Reading, Pa.; m. Marcia Gluck (d. Alma Gluck). May 13, 1929 (divorced, 1946); 1 d., Cornelia Whipple, 1 step-daughter, Patricia Clarke; married 2d, Natalie Potter Ladd, October 25, 1952; stepchildren—Mary Sargent and Olivia Ladd. Mem. editorial staff Time 1923-24; reporter Spokesman Review, Spokane, Wash., 1924-25; editorial staff Fortune, 1930-37, mng. editor, 1937-40; chairman bd. of editors, 1941. Coordinator pre-convention campaign to nominate Wendell Willkie, 1940; personal rep. Republican candidate campaign of 1940, and chief of candidate research staff; chief editorial writer, Life Mag., 1942-44; cons. pub. officer Columbia Broadcasting System, to 1947; in charge explt. dept., Time, Inc., July 1947-May 1948; editor Life Round Tables, 1948-51; dir. Inst. for Creative Research, Inc., since Dec. 1951. Private 1st class U.S. Army with A.E.F., 1917-19. Awarded Croix de Guerre (France), Purple Heart. War corr., Germany, Austria, 1945. Mem. Psi Upsilon. Episcopalian. Club: University. Century (N.Y.C.). Author: Through Traffic, 1929; My Country (poem), 1944; The Dignity of Man, 1954; U.S.A. Permanent Revolution. Contbr. verse to mags. Address: 541 E. 72d St., N.Y.C. 21. Died Apr. 19, 1954.

DAVEY, Wheeler P(edlar), physics and chemistry; b. Cleve., Mar. 19, 1886; s. Thomas George and Myra Eliza (Christian) D.; A.B., Western Reserve U., 1906; M.S., Pa. State Coll., 1911; grad. study U. Chgo., summers, 1909, 10, 11; Huntingdon fellow, Cornell U., 1912-13, Ph.D., 1914; m. Laura L. Gunn, Aug. 28, 1912; children—Myra Ellen, George Thomas, Ruth Barton, Mary Louise. Tchr. physics and chemistry, Central Inst., Cleve., 1906-08; high sch., Mansfield, O., 1908-09; instr. in physics, Pa. State Coll., 1909-11; asst. in physics, Cornell U., 1911-12, instr. in physics, 1913-14; research physicist research lab. Gen. Electric Co., Schenectady, N.Y., 1914-25; prof. physical chemistry and prof. indsl. research, Pa. State Coll., 1926-31; research prof. physics and chemistry, 1931-49. research prof. emeritus 1949—. Chmn. Schenectady (New York) Civil Service Commn. 1916-17. Lecturer on X-rays and crystal structure, Union U., 1920-26; lecturer in physics dept., Grad. Sch., Pa. State Coll., summers, 1922, 23, 24; lecturer on crystal structure, U. of Mich., summer, 1925; Thurston lectr., Am. Soc. M.E., 1928. Mem. elect. insulation com. N.R.C., 1928-41, chmn. physics sub-com., 1935-40. Mem. optics sub-com., Chicago Century of Progress Expn.; mem. Am. Inst. Physics Council of Applied Physics, 1935-38. Mem. editorial bd. Jour. of Chemical Physics, 1933. Award of merit, Am. Soc. Testing Materials, 1952. Fellow Am. Phys. Soc., Inst. of Physics (London); mem. governing bd. Am. Inst. of Physics, 1931-33 and 1937-41; Am. Soc. Testing Materials, Am. Soc. for Metals, Soc. Rheology (pres. 1930-33; asso. editor, 1933-36, editor, 1936-41), Sigma Xi, Phi Lambda Upsilon, Sigma Pi Sigma chmn. placement bd., 1934-45), Alpha Pi Mu, Acacia. Mem. joint com. (A.S.T.M., I.P. and American Chrystallographic Society) on chemical analysis by X-ray diffraction methods, 1940—, chairman, 1940-56. Republican. Presbyn. Mason. Contributor to Fairbanks' Laboratory Investigation of Ores, 1928. Author: A Study of Crystal Structure, 1934; also articles on X-rays, cyrstal structure, automatic X-ray diffraction apparatus, criterions for the rating of physics departments, planning new physics buildings. Home: Glennland Bldg., State College, Pa. Died Oct. 12, 1959; buried Diamond Grove Cemetery, Jacksonville, Ill.

DAVIDOW, H(arry) M., retail exec.; b. Troy, N.Y., Nov. 19, 1900; s. Aaron David and Hinda Elena (Nartow) D.; student pub. schs.; m. Pebble Melton, Sept. 11, 1946; 1 son, Harry M. First exec. v.p., gen. mgr. Washington area, dir. The Hecht Co.; Washington area; dir. Bank of Commerce & Savings. Dir. D.C. chpt. A.R.C., D.C. Soc. for Crippled Children, Hebrew Home for Aged. Mem. Better Bus. Bur. Clubs: Woodmont Country; Circus Saints and Sinners; Advertising (Washington). Home: 2500 Q St. N.W. Office: F. St. at 7th St. N.W., Washington. Deceased.

DAVIDSON, J. Brownlee, prof. agrl. engring.; b. Douglas, Neb., Feb. 15, 1880; s. James H. and Margaret Jane (Dickson) D.; B.S., M.E., U. of Neb., 1904, A.E., 1914, Dr. Engring., 1931; m. Jennie Baldridge, June 14, 1906; children—Margaret Elizabeth, Ethel Brownlee, James Vincent (dec.), Helen Mary (dec.). Instr. farm mechanics, U. of Neb., 1904-05; asst. prof. and profl. agrl. engring., Ia. State Coll. Agr. and Mechanic Arts, 1905-15; prof. agrl. engring., U. of Calif., 1915-19, Ia. State Coll. Agr. and Mechanics Arts, 1919-56. Dir. Survey of Research in Mech. Farm Equipment for U.S. Dept. Agr. (on leave), 1926; mem. Am. Com. on Colonization, Russia (on leav), 1929; cons. farm equipment mfrs.; Hon. mem. Am. Soc. Agrl. Engrs. (chmn. com. History); life mem. Am. Soc. Engring. Edn., Ia. Engring. Soc.; "Estranger" mem. Swedish Royal Agrl. Soc.; mem. Sigma Xi, Phi Kappa Phi, Gamma Sigma Delta, Sigma Tau (nat. pres.), Tau Beta Pi, Zlpha Zeta; Assn. of College Honor Societies (mem. council). Congregationalist. Author: Farm Machinery and Farm Motors, 1908; Agricultural Engineering, 1913; Agricultural Machinery, 1931; (with others) A Study of Extension Service, 1933; Report of an Inquiry into Changes in Quality Values of Farm Machines, 1933; farm equipment consultant, War Production Board, 1943; United Nations Relief and Rehabilitation Adminstrn., 1944. Chmn. Com. on Agricultural Engineering, Ministry of Agriculture and Forestry, China (on leave, 1946-48). Recipient of Cyrus Hall McCormick medal for achievement in engring. of agr., 1933. Club: Rotary. Address: 1601 E. 14th Av., Denver. Died May 8, 1957; buried College Cemetery, Ames, Ia.

DAVIDSON, James Edward, public utilities; b. Flint, Mich., Nov. 10, 1879; s. Wilbur Fisk and Margareta Page (Turner) D.; grad. Detroit Business Univ.; m. Edith L. Stokes, Apr. 15, 1903; children—Dorothy Burnham Coleman, James Edward, John Stokes. Supt. Port Huron (Mich.) Light & Power Co., 1899-1905; apptd. mgr. Consol. Lighting Co., Montpelier, Vt., 1905, later pres. and gen. mgr.; v.p., gen. mgr. Pacific Power & Light Co., Portland, Ore., 1910-17; v.p., gen. mgr. Neb. Power Co., Omaha, 1917-28, pres., 1928-46; gen. mgr. Omaha Pub. Power Dist. since 1946; vice pres., gen. mgr., Citizens Power & Light Co., Council Bluffs, Ia., 1917-36; dir. Chicago Great Western Railway, Occidental Bldg. & Loan Assn., Union Stock Yards Co. of Omaha, South Omaha Terminal R.R. Co. Pres. Nat. Electric Light Assn., 1925-26, served as chmn. comml. nat. sect., pres. Vt., N.E., Northwest and Neb. divs. and mem. pub. policy com.; chmn. Lighting Ednl. Com. which sponsored Internat. Better Home Lighting Contest, 1924-25; chmn. exec. com. Electric Refrigeration Bur., 1931-33; vice pres., trustee and mem. advisory com. Edison Electric Inst.; pres. Assn. Edison Illuminating Companies, 1936-38; mem. bd. trustees, Midwest Research Inst.; pres. bd. of regents Municipal Univ. of Omaha, 1930-36; trustee Father Flanagan's Boys' Home. Chmn. bd. of trustees, Omaha Safety Council. Exec. dir. Omaha Civilian Defense Council, 1941-45. Elected Omaha's 1st citizen, 1929; cited for outstanding civic service by Vets. of Fgn. Wars, 1942. Mem. of the Newcomen Soc. of England, Greater Omaha Assn. (chmn. 1928-38), Omaha Ad-Sell, Sojourners (hon.), Joseph Warren Camp, Heroes of '76. Gov. Knights of Ak Sar Ben (pres. 1939-48), King XXIX, 1923. Episcopalian (vestryman, Trinity Cathedral). Mason (Shriner, Past-Potentate Tangier Temple). Clubs: Omaha, Omaha Country, Rotary, Omaha Field, Omaha Athletic, Stock Yards 400 Club. Author: numerous papers and pamphlets on electrical topics. Home: 109 S. 53d St. Office: Electric Bldg., Omaha 2. Died Nov. 12, 1949: buried Port Huron, Mich.

DAVIDSON, James Hamilton, lawyer; b. Burlington, O., Jan. 25, 1839; s. James and Mary Frances (Combs) D.; A.B., Ohio Wesleyan, 1861, A.M., 1864; m. Abigail Ashley Lamb, July 1, 1861. Enlisted pvt. Co. B, 14th Ky. Inf., 1861; promoted 1st lt. and capt.; promoted maj. 49th Ky. Inf., 1863; col. 122d U.S. C.T., 1864; hon. discharged, 1866; lt. U.S.A., 1866; declined. In fall of 1864 was pres. mil. bd. to examine all applicants for commns. in U.S.C.T. at Lexington, Ky., and was asst. supt. of orgn. of colored troops in Ky. Removed to St. Paul, 1866; city editor Daily Press (now Pioneer Press) until 1870; admitted to bar, 1867; gen. counsel N. Western Union Packet Co., 1870, and later Keokuk No. Line Packet Co. and other corps. until 1885; practiced law, Chgo., 1895-1906; returned to St. Paul, 1906. Platform lectr., debater, camp-fire talker. Chmn. Minn. State Waterways Commn., 1910-11. Republican. Methodist. Mem. G.A.R., Loyal Legion. Address: Pioneer Bldg., St. Paul. Deceased.

DAVIDSON, Jo, sculptor; b. N. Y. City, Mar. 30, 1883; s. Jacob S. and Haya (Getzoff) D.; pupil of George de Forest Brush, Hermon A. McNeil. Art Students' League and of Ecole des Beaux Arts, Paris; m. Yvonne de Kerstrat, 1909 (died 1934); children (sons), Yvon Jacques and Jean Michel; m. 2d, Florence Gertrude Lucius, 1941. Prin. works: President Woodrow Wilson and bust of Anatole France, in Luxembourg Mus., Paris; "The Dance," Neighborhood Playhouse, New York; Dr. Abram Jacobi, Mount Sinai Hosp., New York; John Purroy Mitchel Memorial, Columbia U., New York; colossal bust of John D. Rockefeller, Standard Oil Bldg., New York; colossal bust of Adolf Zukor, Paramount Bldg., New York; heroic statue in marble of late Senator Robert M. La Follette, Rotunda of the Capitol, Washington, D.C.; Walt Whitman Bear-Mountain-Harriman State Bank, N.Y. State; Dorothy Thompson, Sinclair Lewis, Sir James Barrie, James Joyce, George Bernard Shaw, H. G. Wells, Arnold Bennett, etc. Marshal Foch, General Pershing and Marshal Joffre, Musée des Invalides, Paris; also portrait-busts of Clemenceau, Myron TT. Herrick, Nicholas Murray Butler, Andrew W. Mellon, Rabindranath Tagore, Zangwill, Lord Northcliffe, Chickerin, Chaliapin; statue of Will Rogers, Claremore, Okla., and The Capitol, Washington, D.C.; busts of President Franklin D. Roosevelt, Vice-President Henry A. Wallace, Senator George W. Norris, Helen Keller, Madame Chiang Kai-Shek, Van Wyck Brooks, Chas. Dana Gibson, Hermon A. McNeil, Presidents of South American republics; bas-relief of Andrew W. Mellon, National Gallery of Art, Washington, D.C.; Ernie Pyle, Univ. of Indiana. Mem. Nat. Sculpture Society, Institute of Arts and Letters, Academy of Design. Clubs: Century, Coffee House, Dutch Treat. Overseas Press, Lotos. Home: 323 E. 58 St., New York; and 6 Rue Leconte de Lisle, Paris, France. Died Jan. 2, 1952.

DAVIDSON, Levette Jay, educator; b. Eureka, Ill., May 16, 1894; s. Edwin Jay and Charity Ella (Munsel) D.; A.B., Eureka Coll., 1915; A.M., U. Ill., 1916, Harvard, 1917; Ph D., U. Mich., 1922; m. Mary Louise Camp, Mar. 31, 1918; children—Rachel Jane, Roscoe Levette. Instr. English, Northwestern U., 1917-18, Mich. State Coll., 1919-21, asst. English, U. Mich., 1921-22; asso. prof. English, U. Denver, 1922-29, prof., 1929—, chmn. dept., 1940—, acting chancellor, 1953; dir. Western Folklore Conf., mem. editorial staff Western Folklore, 1947—. Sgt. AUS, 1918-19. Mem. Am. Assn. U. Profs., Modern Lang. Assn., Coll. English Assn. (v.p. 1954, dir. 1955), Denver Posse Westerners (sheriff 1950), Am. Dialect Soc. (v.p. 1953), State Hist. Soc. Colo. (dir.), Colo. Authors League (pres. 1949), Am. Folklore Soc. (council mem.), Phi Beta Kappa. Author: Literature of Rocky Mountain West, Rocky Mountain Tales, Literary Experience. A Guide to American Folklore, Poems of the Old West. Contbr. articles lit. publs. Home: 2262 S. University Blvd., Denver. Died May 14, 1957; buried Fairmount Cemetery, Denver.

DAVIDSON, Lyal Ament, navy officer; b. Muscatine, Ia., Dec. 2, 1886; s. Joseph Trimble and Judith

(Ament) D.; B.S., U.S. Naval Acad., 1910, M.S., Columbia, 1917; m. Carolyn Gwathmey, June 3, 1916; children—William Gwathmey, Judith Ament, Carolyn Tayloe. Commd. ensign 1911 and advanced through grades to rear adm. 1941; comdr. 9th Destroyer Div., U.S. Fleet, 1934-36; comdg. officer U.S.S. Relief, 1938-39, U.S.S. Omaha, 1939-40; comdr. Cruiser Div. 8, U.S. Atlantic Fleet; comdr. cruisers Atlantic Fleet; Task Force comdr. assaults on French Morocco, Sicily, Italy and Southern France; retired with rank of vice adm., 1946. Prof. naval science and tactics U. Mich., 1940-41, U.S. Naval War Coll., 1942. Decorated D.S.M. with gold star, Legion of Merit with gold star, Mexican Service Medal, Victory Medal, 2d Nicaraguan Campaign Medal, Am. Def. Service Medal, European-African, Middle Eastern Area Campaign Medal (U.S.); Companion Mil. Order of the Bath (British), mentioned in dispatches (Eng.), Officer Legion of Honor, Croix de Guerre with palm (French). Mem. U.S. Naval Inst., Am. Soc. Naval Engrs., Quarterdeck Soc. (Univ. Mich.). Clubs: Rotary, Army and Navy (Washington), University (Michigan). Home: 2909 34th St., Washington 8. Died Dec. 29, 1950; buried Arlington Nat. Cemetery.

DAVIDSON, Maurice P., lawyer; b. New York, Sept. 14, 1879; s. Philip and Rebecca Davidson; ed. City Coll., LL.B., New York Law Sch., 1900; m. Blanche Reinheimer, May 3, 1903; children—Robert M., John F., Alfred E., Harold P., Frank P. Admitted to N.Y. bar, 1901; mem. firm, Davidson and Mann and predecessor firms, 1903; lectr. politics and econs. Mem. com. on Fed. Power Coordination in N.Y.C., 1935; chmn. bd. engrs. to design and build power plant for N.Y.C., 1935; commr. Dept. Water Supply Gas and Electricity, 1934-36; pres. Electronized Chem. Corp.; v.p. Sanib Corp. Mem. bd. trustees Power Authority of State N.Y., 1939; N.Y. State del. to Nat. Rivers and Harbors Congress, 1941. Chmn finance committee Russian Relief, Inc., 1944-46. Chairman of the Enemy Alien Hearing Board, No. 5, Southern Dist. of N.Y., 1942-45; counsel to Vol. Land Corps, Inc., exec. vice chmn. Progressive Nat. Com. Supporting Franklin D. Roosevelt in 1936; chmn. N.Y. State Independent Voters Com. for Roosevelt and Wallace, 1940; pres. Soc. of Friends of Mexico; dir., chairman law com., N.Y. Com. Atomic Information. Major comdg. 2d Batt., 10th Regt., New York Police Res., 1917-18; capt. (Judge Adv. General), A.U.S., December 2, 1924-29; major (Judge Adv. General's staff), N.Y. Guard, 1943. Founder and chmn. City Fusion Party, 1933-34. Mem. New York City, Am., and N.Y. State bar assns., N.Y. County Lawyers, Comml. Law League of America (past pres.), Citizens Union. Mason. Clubs: City (New York), National Democratic. Organization chmn. New York War and Peace Mem. Com., 1946-47. Home: 355 Riverside Dr., N.Y.C. 25. Office: Chanin Bldg., 122 E. 42d St., N.Y.C. 17. Died July 16, 1956; buried Linden Hill Cemetery, Bklyn.

DAVIDSON, Victor H., typewriter mfg. exec. Exec. v.p., mem. exec. com., director Smith-Corona, Inc., Syracuse, N.Y.; vice president of L. C. Smith & Corona Typewriters of Can. Home: 407 Sedgewick Dr., Syracuse. Office: 701 E. Washington St., Syracuse 1, N.Y. Deceased.

DAVIDSON, William Andrew, mfg. co. exec.; b. St. Thomas, Ont., Can , Nov. 30, 1884; s. William and Martha (Kennedy) D.; B.E.E., U. Mich., 1912; m. Emma Alice Reede, Jan. 1, 1913. Came to U.S., 1908, naturalized, 1937. Engr. The Singer, Mfg. Co., South Bend, Ind., 1912-16, Elizabeth, N.J., 1916-20, works mgr., St. Johns, P.Q., 1920-23, asst. v.p., N.Y.C., 1923-47, v.p., 1947-54, ret.; pres. Diehl Mfg. Co., Finderne, N.J., 1948-—; dir. Singer Mfg. Co., Diehl Mfg. Co., Poinsette umber & Mfg. Co., Bourne & Co. Mem. Tau Beta Pi. Republican. Presbyn. Clubs: Echo Lake Country; University of Michigan (N.Y.C.). Home: 2 Woodmere Dr., Summit, N.J. Office: 149 Broadway, N.Y.C. Died July 25, 1957; buried Westport, Conn.

DAVIES, Arthur Powell, clergyman, author; born Birkenhead, Eng., June 5, 1902; s. Arthur and Martha (Powell) D.; B.D., Richmond Coll., U. of London, 1925; D.D., Meadville College, 1947; L.H.D., Howard University, 1955; married Muriel Avenbury Hannah, Dec. 28, 1927; children—Gwendolyn, Bronwen. Came to U.S., 1928, naturalized citizen, 1935. Meth. ministry, 1925-33; Unitarian since 1933; pastor, Ilford, London, 1925-28, Portland, Me., 1929-32, Summit, N.J., 1933-44; pastor All Souls Church, Washington, D.C., since 1944. Chmn. Emergency Conf. on Civilian Control of Atomic Energy; pres. Food for Freedom, 1946-47. Mem. bd. trustees Meadville Theol. Sch., U. Chgo.; bd. dirs. Unitarian Service Com. Club: Cosmos. Author: American Destiny, 1942; The Faith of An Unrepentant Liberal, 1946; America's Real Religion, 1948; Man's Vast Future, 1951; The Temptation To Be Good, 1952; The Urge to Persecute, 1953; The Language of the Heart, 1955; The Meaning of the Dead Sea Scrolls, 1956; The Ten Commandments, 1956; The First Christian, 1957. Contbr. to mags. Speaker on current affairs. Home: 3818 Jenifer St., N.W., Washington. Died Sept. 26, 1957; buried Washington.

DAVIES, Harry William, banker; b. White Plains, N.Y., Oct. 30, 1896; s. Edward P. and Mary (Scharrer) D.; student Pace Inst.; m. Ruth M. Heath, May 6, 1917; children—Ruth H., Robert S. Successively Deputy Commr. of Finance, White Plains, N.Y.; partner Hurdman & Cranston, N.Y. City; v.p. and comptroller L. C. Smith & Corona Typewriters, Inc., Syracuse, N.Y., now dir. and chmn. finance com.; chmn. bd. Marine Midland Trust Co. of Central N.Y. Syracuse; dir., chmn. finance com. Easy Washing Machine Corp. Dir., past pres. C. of C.; treas. Onondaga Co. War Service Meml., Inc.; mem. Syracuse Meml. Hosp. Men's Assn., Inc., N.Y. State Banking Board; C.P.A., New York State. Republican. Episcopalian. Clubs: Century, Kiwanis, Onondaga Golf and Country (Syracuse); Bankers, Union League (N.Y. City). Home: 57 Ely Drive, Fayetteville, N.Y. Office: 344 S. Warren St., Syracuse, N.Y. Died Dec. 5, 1956.

DAVIES, Joseph Edward, lawyer, diplomat, author; b. Watertown, Wis., Nov. 29, 1876; s. Edward and Rahel (Paynter) D.; A.B., Univ. of Wis., 1898, LL.B., 1901, LL.D., 1941; Ph.D., Presbyterian Coll. of S.C., 1937; Ph.D., U. of Brussels, 1939; LL.D., Indiana Univ., 1942; D.Litt., Rollins Coll., Fla., 1944; D.Sc., Clarkson Coll. of Tech., 1945; LL.D., Univ. of Wales, Cardiff, 1946; m. Emlen Knight, Sept. 10, 1902; children—Eleanor (Mrs. Millard Tydings), Rahel (Mrs. E. Fontaine Broun), Emlen Knight (Mrs. Robert L. Grosjean). Admitted to Wis. bar, 1901; practice, Wis., 1902-13, Washington, 1918-36, resumed practice, 1941; state's atty., 1902-06; past sec. and Wis. mem. Dem. Nat. Com.; chmn. western hdqrs. Dem. campaign, Chicago, 1912; commr. Corp. U.S., 1913-15; ex-officio mem. War Industries Bd.; chmn. Fed. Trade Commn., 1915-16; nominated candidate U.S. Senate, Mar. 1918; econ. adviser to Pres. Wilson at Versailles Conf., 1918; counsel for govt. of Mexico, 1920; counsel for govt. of Peru in arbitration proceedings before Pres. of U.S. in Tacna Arica controversy with Chile; also served as counsel govts. U.S., Holland, Greece, Dominican Republic; counsel for taxpayers in Ford Stock Valuation Tax Case, 1924-27; counsel for claimant in arbitration U.S. and Egypt in Salem Case; counsel to Pres. Republic of Santo Domingo in refinancing external loan, 1932-36; ambassador U.S. to U.S.S.R., 1936-38; ambassador from U.S. to Belgium and minister to Luxembourg, 1938-39; spl. envoy of Pres. Roosevelt with rank of ambassador to confer with Marshal Stalin, May-June 1943; spl. envoy of Pres. Truman with rank of ambassador to confer with Prime Minister Churchill, June 1945; spl. adviser to Pres. Truman and Sec. of State Byrnes, with rank of ambassador, to Potsdam Conf., July-Aug. 1945; apptd. spl. asst. to Sec. of State Hull, in charge War Emergency Problems and Policies, 1939-41. Vice chmn. Dem. Nat. Com., 1936; chmn. Pres. Roosevelt's Inaugural Com., 1941, 1945; chmn. the President's War Relief Control Bd., 1942-46. Awarded Medal for Merit (Highest civilian decoration of U.S.), 1946; also decorations of the highest order by govts. of Greece, Belgium, Yugoslavia Luxembourg, Santo Domingo, U.S.S.R., France, Chile, Peru, and Panama, United States. Mem. Phi Beta Kappa, Delta Upsilon, Sigma Delta Chi. Vice pres. Hon. Soc. of Cymmrodorion for the Encouragement of Art, Lit. and Sci. of Wales (London, Eng.). Conglist. Clubs: Metropolitan, Chevy Chase (Washington); Burning Tree Golf (Bethesda, Md.); Metropolitan, (N.Y.C.); Everglades, Bath and Tennis, Palm Beach Country (Palm Beach, Fla.); Gulf Stream (Delray, Fla.). Author: Mission to Moscow, 1941; Reports on Lumber, Fertilizer, Oil, Farm Machinery, Industries, Taxation of Corporations, Conflict of State Laws in the United States as to Corporations and Trust Laws, and Unfair Competition; contbr. to various periodicals, 1913-47. Home: Tregaron, 3029 Klingle Rd. Office: 1000 Vermont Av. N.W., Washington. Died May 9, 1958; buried Cathedral St. Peter and St. Paul (Nat. Cathedral), Washington.

DAVILA, Carlos, journalist, Chilean diplomat; b. Los Angeles, Chile, Sept. 16, 1887; s. Luis and Amelia (Espinosa) D.; grad. U. of Santiago, Chile, 1907; LL.D., Columbia, 1928, U. So. Cal., 1929; m. Francis Adams, Mar. 11, 1950; children—Luz and Paz Davila, Adeline Adams. Newspaper work El Mercurio, Chile, 1914-17; founder and dir., La Nacion, 1917-27, Los Tiempos, 1925-27; founder of Hoy (mag.), 1932; Chilean ambassador to U.S., 1927-31; provisional pres. of Chile, 1932; visiting prof. of Internat. Law, auspices of Carnegie Endowment for Internat. Peace, North Carolina Univ., 1933; dir., Consol. Gas Utilities Corp., Okla. City, since 1945, Editors Press Service, Inc., N.Y. City, since 1933; weekly columnist for chain of So. Am. newspapers, 1944-—; sec.-gen. Organization of American States, 1954-—. Council mem., U.N.R.R.A., 1943-46; Chilean rep., Inter-Am. Financial and Econ. Adv. Com., 1940, and author of Davila Plan creating the Inter-Am. Development Com., Jan. 1940; mem. Econ. and Social Council of U.N., Lake Success, 1946. Awarded Cabot prize, Columbia U. Sch. of Journalism, 1941. Author: We of the Americas, 1949. Contbr. various essays on politics and economics to mags., newspapers and other publs. Home: 201 18th St. Office: Pan American Union, Washington 6. Died Oct. 19, 1955; buried Santiago, Chile.

DAVIS, Alton Frank, industrial exec.; b. Diamond, O., Oct. 24, 1889; s. Frank J. and Hattie (Hiser) D.; student Mt. Union Coll., 1907-09; M.E., Ohio State U., 1914; D.Sc. (honorary), Mount Union College, 1951; m. Carrie Spring, Nov. 16, 1921; 1 dau., Mary Jane. Engring. dept., City of Alliance, O., 1909-11; with Lincoln Electric Co., Cleveland, since 1914, became v.p., 1928, v.p. and sec., 1938, now sr. v.p. Sec. James F. Lincoln Arc Welding Found. (created to stimulate progress of arc welding, 1937); sec. The Lincoln Electric Found.; member of the board trustees Euclid-Glenville Hosp.; trustee Cleveland Hosp. Service Assn.; trustee Cleveland Gen. YMCA. Mem. Am. Welding Soc., (Miller Medal 1954), Soc. Promotion Engring. Edn., C. of C., A.S. Mech. Engrs., Soc. M.E., Am. Society for Metals, National Alumni Association Ohio State University (past president), Sigma Alpha Epsilon, Eta Kappa Nu. Republican. Presbyterian. Clubs: Canterbury Country, Union, Mid-Day, Mayfield Country, City, Rowfant; Faculty (Ohio, State U.); National Press (Washington). Publisher: The Stablizer, Lessons in Arc Welding, Simple Blue Print Reading, Procedure Handbook of Arc Welding Design and Practice. Editor: Designing for Arc Welding. Also publisher of Foundation books: Arc Welding in Design Manufacture and Construction; Design for Arc Welding; Studies in Arc Welding; Maintenance Arc Welding; Welding Helps for Farmers; Arc Welding Lessons for School and Farm Shop; Welded Deck Highway Bridges. Created Welding Library at Ohio State U. 1942 (now largest collection of books, papers, magazines, articles and original material on welding. Named Industrial Advertising Man of the Year of 1950. Home: 22075 Shaker Blvd., Shaker Heights 22. Office: 22801 St. Clair Av., Cleve. 17. Died May 25, 1959.

DAVIS, Andrew Jay, ins. exec.; b. Pittsburgh, Pa., Sept. 13, 1887; s. Wilmer M. and Julia B. (Minehart) D.; B.S., Maple Inst., Concordville, Pa., 1908; LL. B., U. of Pa., 1911; m. Anne Pennock Bishop, Oct. 10, 1911; children—J. Bishop, Andrew Jay. Admitted to Pa. bar, 1911; lawyer, Provident Mutual Life Ins. Co., Phila., 1912-18, asst. gen. counsel, 1918, gen. counsel, 1918-23, v.p. and gen. counsel, 1923-31, vice president, 1931-53, retired, director, 1931-—; director Central Penn National Bank. Mem. Assn. of Life Ins. Counsel, Law Assn. of Phila., Order of the Coif. Clubs: Union League (Phila.); Aronimink Golf (Newtown Square, Pa.). Home: Boxwood Farm, Providence Rd., Media, Pa. Office: Market at 46th St., Phila. 39. Died Jan. 3, 1956; buried Arlington Cemetery, Drexel Hill, Pa.

DAVIS, Arthur Kyle, college pres.; b. Petersburg, Va., July 16, 1867; s. Williams Thomas and Caroline Virginia (Robinson) D.; A.B., Randolph-Macon Coll., 1887, A.M., 1888; Litt.D., Hampden-Sydney Coll., 1927; m. Lucy Pryor McIlwaine, Nov. 12, 1890; children—Mrs. Lucy McIlwaine Jones, Caroline Robinson (Mrs. John B. Young), Arthur Kyle Jr. Pres. So. Coll. (Junior), Petersburg, 1889-1942. Founder, and lecturer 2 yrs., Shakespeare Club. Twice pres. Va. Assn. Colls. and Schs. for Girls; mem. Am. Hist. Assn., Va. Hist. Soc., Archael. Inst. Am., Am. Assn. Jr. Colls., So. Assn. Colls. and Schs., Assn. Va. Colls., Va. Classical Assn., Va. Social Science Assn., So. Sociol. Congress, Nat. Economic League, Sons Confed. Vets. (A. P. Hill Camp), Phi Beta Kappa, Pi Gamma Mu, Kappa Alpha. Episcopalian. Clubs: Commonwealth (Richmond); Country (Petersburg); Authors' (London). Author: Three Centuries of an Old Virginia Town; Education in Virginia; Virginia and the Methodists; Virginia's War History; Plans and Personnel; Outline for City or County War History; Editor of Quarterly Supplements, Calendars and Reports in Va. Hist. Mag. Dist. dir. for Southside Va., Potomac div. Am. Red Cross; chmn. Va. War History Commn. Editor of Virginias of Distinguished Service in the World War; Virginia War History in Newspaper Clippings; Virginia War Letters, Diaries and Editorials; Virginia War Agencies, Selective Service and Volunteers; Virginia Organizations in the War; Virginia Communities in War Time. Home: 214 S. Sycamore St., Petersburg, Va. Address: Box 1151, University Sta., Charlottesville, Va. Died July 9, 1953.

DAVIS, Benson Willis, prof., coll. adminstr.; b. Clyde, N.C., Nov. 22, 1907; s. Thomas Benjamin and Celia (Keith) D.; A.B., U. of N.C., 1929, A.M., 1936, Ph.D., 1938; postdoctoral student, Columbia, 1947; m. Mary Payne, Nov. 30, 1933. Teacher, coach athletics, N.C. high schs., 1929-35; instr. Latin, U. of N.C., 1935-37, teaching fellow, 1937-38; prof. classical langs., John B. Stetson U., 1938-41, dean of the univ., 1940-41; prof. English, Greek, philosophy, 1945-—, dean of men, 1946-52, head department philosophy, 1952-—; dean Meredith College, 1941-45. Carnegie Research grant, 1947, 49. Member Southern Soc. Philosophy and Psychology, American Academy Political and Social Sciences, Classical Assn., Fla. Edn. Assn., Classical Assn. of Middle West and South, Fla. Philos. Soc. (founder, 1st pres.), Pi Kappa Phi. Democrat. Baptist. Kiwanian. Author: book revs., articles. Home: Daytona Rd., DeLand, Fla. Died Mar. 30, 1959; buried Oakdale Cemetery, Deland, Fla.

DAVIS, Bergen, physicist; b. White House, N.J., Mar. 31, 1869; s. John and Catherine Marie (Dilts) D.; B.S., Rutgers, 1896, Sc.D. (hon.), 1929; A.M., Columbia, 1900, Ph.D., 1901, Sc.D. (hon.) 1929; studied Gottingen 1901-02, Cambridge, 1902-03; m. Matie Pearl Clark, 1922. Instr. physics Columbia, 1903-09, adjunct professor, 1909-13, associate professor, 1913-1918, professor of physics, 1918-39, professor emeritus, 1939—. Awarded medal and prize of Research Corporation 1929. Fellow A.A.A.S. (v.p. sect. B 1932), Am. Phys. Soc., Am. Optical Soc.; mem. Nat. Acad. Scis., Sigma Xi, Delta Upsilon. Mem. Reformed Dutch Ch. Author of numerious articles and papers. Home: 44 Morningside Dr., N.Y.C. 25. Died June 30, 1958; buried Dutch Reformed Cemetery, Readington, N.J.

DAVIS, Bradley Moore, botanist; b. Chgo., Nov. 19, 1871; s. Charles Wilder and Emma Frances (Moore) D.; A.B., Stanford, 1892; A.B., Harvard, 1893, A.M., 1894, Ph.D., 1895; research at Bonn, 1898, Naples, 1904; m. Annie Elizabeth Paret, Sept. 22, 1908; 1 dau., Margery French (Mrs. Allen M. Boyden). Asst. in botany, U. Chgo., 1895, asso. in botany, 1896-98, instr. botany, 1898-1902, asst. prof. plant morphology, 1902-06. head dept. botany Marine Biol. Lab., Woods Hole, 1897-1906, in charge of bot. sec., biol. survey Woods Hole, Bur. of Fisheries, 1903-09; asst. prof. botany U. Pa., 1911-14, prof., 1914-19; prof. botany U. Mich., 1919-42, prof. emeritus, 1942—. Editor statis. div. U.S. Food Adminstrn., 1918. Chmn. Ann Arbor Com. to Defend America, 1940-44. Asso. editor Genetics. Fellow Am. Acad. Arts and Scis.; mem. Am. Philos. Soc. (sec. 1918-19), Bot. Soc. America, Am. Soc. Naturalists (sec., 1913-19, pres. 1921), Am. Genetic Assn., A.A.A.S., Mich. Acad. Science, N.E. Bot. Club, Am. Assn. U. Profs.; Loyal Legion. Club: Chicago Literary. Co-author: Principles of Botany, 1906; Laboratory and Field Manual of Botany (with Joseph Y. Bergen), 1907. Also writer of many papers on plant cytology and plant genetics. Home: 2814 S W. Labbe Av., Portland 1, Ore. Died Mar. 13, 1957.

DAVIS, Calvin Olin, educator; b. Macomb, Mich., Feb. 5, 1871; s. Calvin and Roselia (Phillips) D.; A.B., U. Mich., 1895, A.M., 1904; postgrad. U. Chicago, summer 1905; Ph.D., Harvard, 1910; married to Winifred Ellen Mack, December 27, 1904 (deceased September 1953); 1 daughter, Mary Helen (Mrs. John Holt). Tchr. high sch., South Bend, 1895-1905, prin., 1905; asso. prof. and prof. edn. U Mich., 1905-41, insp. of high schs., 1905-12. sec. faculty sch. of edn., 1921-41, sec. sch. edn., 1927-41, now prof. emeritus of edn., lect. extension dept. Mem. sch. survey staffs, N.Y.C., 1912, Grand Rapids, 1915, Flint, 1922, Va. State, 1927; summer tchr. U. Chgo., 1920, Stanford, 1922, U. Va., 1941. Nat. chmn. Tercentenary Celebration Planning Com. on Establishment of Secondary Schs. in America, 1929-35. Mem. N.E A., Nat. Soc. Sci. Study Edn., Soc. Coll. Tchrs. Edn., N. Central Assn. Colls. and Secondary Schs. (sec. commn. on secondary schs. 1914-25), Mich. State Tchrs. Assn., Mich. Schoolmasters' Club, Phi Delta Kappa, Phi Beta Kappa. Republican. Conglist. Clubs: University, Rotary (pres. 1922-23), Golf and Outing. Author: (with others) High School Education, 1912; High School Courses of Study, 1914; A Guide to Methods and Observation in History, 1914 (with others) The Modern High School, 1914; Public Secondary Education, 1917; The Six-three-three Plan of Administration of Schools, 1917; Junior High School Education, 1924; (with E. E. Lewis) Problems of the Junior High School, 1925; Our Secondary Schools, 1925; Our Evolving High School Cirriculum, 1927; History of the N. Central Association of Colleges and Secondary Schools, 1944; History of the First Congregational Church in Ann Arbor, 1947; History of the Ann Arbor Rotary Club, 1947. Editor: Part 1, North Central Association Proc., 1918-25; also editor North Central Association Quarterly Mag., 1926-41. Asso. editor Clearing House. Home: 1030 Martin Pl., Ann Arbor, Mich. Died June 22, 1954; buried Ann Arbor.

DAVIS, Cameron Josiah, clergyman; b. Watkins, N.Y., Dec. 13, 1873; s. Frederick and Frances (Hewette) D.; B.A., Trinity Coll., Conn., 1894; M.A., 1897, D.D., 1923; B.D., Gen. Theol. Sem., 1897, S.T.D., 1930; D.D., Hobart Coll.; m. Elizabeth Sacker, Aug. 8, 1900; children—Elizabeth (Mrs Harold A. Jones), Frances (Mrs. A. A. Chambers). Deacon, 1897, priest, 1898, P.E. Ch.; curate Trinity Ch., Buffalo, 1897, rector, 1901; consecrated bishop co-adjutor of Western New York, 1929, bishop, 1931-47, retired 1947. Mem. standing com. Diocese of Western N.Y. many yrs.; dep. Gen. Conv. P.E. Ch., 1922-25, 28; chmn. joint commn. on Holy Matrimony, 1940-46. Pres. ch. pension fund Church Life Ins. Co. Mem. Phi Beta Kappa, Delta Kappa Epsilon. Republican. Clubs: Buffalo, Saturn, Country. Author: Talks on the Episcopal Ch. Home: 371 Delaware Av., Buffalo. N.Y. Deceased.

DAVIS, Carl Braden, surgeon; b. Chgo., Oct. 9, 1877; s. Dr. Charles Gilbert and Isabella (Braden) D.; A.B., U. Chgo., 1900, M.D., Rush Med. Coll., 1903; m. Elsie Florence Booth, Dec. 10, 1907 (died June 5, 1933); m. 2d, Virginia Winslow Smith, Feb. 1945. Practiced in Chgo., 1903—; clin. prof. surgery Rush Med. Coll.; attending surgeon Presbyn. Hosp. Fellow A.C.S., Am. Surg. Assn., Soc. Clin. Surgery; mem. A.M.A., Chgo. Med. Soc. Clubs: University, Glenview Country. Home: 156 Chestnut St., Winnetka, Ill. Office: Peoples Gas Bldg., Chgo. Died Dec. 11, 1950.

DAVIS, Cecil Clark, artist; b. Chgo., July 1877; d. John Marshall Clark and Mary Louise (Qua) Clark; ed. pvt. schs. Chgo. and Farmington, Conn.; m. Richard Harding Davis, May 1899. Portrait painter. Recipient gold medal, Salon, Rio de Janeiro, 1920; gold medal Phila. Arts Club, 1925; portrait prize Nat. Assn. Women Painters and Sculptors, 1926; popular prize Newport Art Assn., 1932; also portrait prize Art Inst. Chgo. Mem. Nat. Assn. Women Painters and Sculptors, Am. Women's Assn. Club: Arts (Chgo.). Home and Studio: Marion, Mass.; also Santa Barbara, Cal. Died Sept. 12, 1955; buried Marion, Mass.

DAVIS, Charles Strout, manufacturer; b. Terre Haute, Indiana, February 2, 1877; s. Daniel Nicholds and Margaret Deith (Hyde) D.; B.A., Harvard, 1889; m. Florence Grace Johnson, November 17, 1904; children—Johnson Strout, Florence Isabel (Mrs. John Drum), Charles Strout. Mem. editorial staff New York Times, 1899-1900; coal miner and jobber, western Ind., 1901-07; sec.-treas., gen. mgr. Glascock Bros. Mfg. Co., Muncie, 1907-18, now chmn. bd.; chmn. bd. Borg-Warner Corp., Chgo., 1928, president, 1929-50, now chairman of the board; dir. City Nat. Bank & Trust Co., Morse Chain Co. (Ithaca, N.Y.). Director and hon. vice pres. Nat. Assn. Mfrs.; member advisory bd. Ill. Manufacturers Association. Former pres. Social Bur. of Muncie; mem. Ill. Post-War Planning Commn.; trustee Ill. Inst. Tech., Armour Research Found., Chicago Mus. Coll. Mem. Chicago Hist. Soc., Phi Kappa Psi, Pi Eta. Republican. Episcopalian. Mason (32°, K.T.). Clubs: Chicago, Racquet, Casino, Union League, Glenview Golf; Columbia (Indianapolis); Northport Point (Michigan) Yacht, Northport Point Country, Bath and Tennis, Everglades, Gulf Stream Golf, Four Arts (Palm Beach, Fla.). Home: 1500 Lake Shore Drive, Chicago; also 8 South Lake Trail, Palm Beach, Fla.; and Northport Point, Mich. Office: 310 S. Michigan Av., Chgo. Died July 2, 1954; buried Beech Grove Cemetery, Muncie, Ind.

DAVIS, Clinton Wildes, packing exec.; b. Portland, Me., June 2, 1888; s. Walter G. and Mary Howard (Wildes) D.; student St. Paul's Sch., Concord, N.H., 1904-07; A.B., Yale, 1911; m. Mary L. d'Este, June 24, 1911. Partner Portland Packing Co., 1912—, pres. and treas., 1932—; dir. First Portland National Bank, New England Tel. & Tel. Co.; trustee Maine Savings Bank. Mem. Soc. of Colonial Wars. Clubs: Cumberland, Portland Yacht; Yale, Union (Boston); University (N.Y.C.). Home: 22 Chadwick St., Portland 4. Office: 433 Congress St., Portland 3, Me. Died Oct. 15, 1958.

DAVIS, David John, pathologist, coll. dean emeritus; b. Racine, Wis., Aug. 9, 1875; s. David W. and Catharine (Jones) D.; B.S., U. Wis., 1898; M.D., Rush Med. Coll., 1904; Ph.D., U. Chgo., 1905; studied univs. of Vienna and Freiburg; m. Myra H. Jones, July 27, 1908; children—Dorland Jones, Edward David. Practiced in Chgo., 1904—; prof. pathology U. Ill., 1914-43, dean of med. sch., 1925-43, prof. emeritus, dean emeritus, 1943—. Pres. bd. dirs. Chgo. Municipal Tb Sanatorium, 1946; Dir. Chgo. Inst. Medicine. Mem. A.M.A., Ill. Med. Soc. (permanent historian 1946—). Soc. Am. Bacteriologists, Am. Assn. Pathologists and Bacteriologists, Am. Assn. Pathologists and Bacteriologists, Chgo. Pathol. Soc., Sigma Xi, Phi Beta Kappa, Alpha Omega Alpha. Republican. Conglist. Clubs: University, Crystal Downs. Contbr. about 150 papers, chiefly in Jour. Infectious Diseases and Jour. A.M.A., on infection with influenza bacilli, streptococci, sporotricha and med. edn. Home: 721 Elmwood Av., Wilmette, Ill. Died Dec. 20, 1954.

DAVIS, Donald Derby, paper co. exec.; b. Wyoming, Ill., Sept. 19, 1888; s. Francis Heflin and Adeline (Scott) D.; student U. Mich., 1907-11; m. Grace Gerhauser, June 12, 1915; children—Margaret (Mrs. Arthur E. Larkin, Jr.), Davis Larkin, Donald Derby, Mary Adeline (Mrs. David Pierson). Engr. and accountant Detroit Trust Co., 1911-15; factory mgr. Hale & Kilbourne Co., Phila., 1915-17; exec. sec. Milling Div., U.S. Food Adminstrn., 1917; with Liberty Nat. Bank, N.Y.C., 1918-20, N.Y. Trust Co., 1920-22; sec., treas. and v.p. Washburn Crosby Co., Mpls., 1922-28; successively treas., v.p. Gen. Mills, Inc., Mpls., 1928-34; pres. Gen. Mills, Inc., and associate companies, 1934-42; vice chmn. WPB, Washington, 1942-44; exec. v.p. Minnesota & Ontario Paper Co., 1944-45, pres., 1945—; dir. First Nat. Bank, Munsingwear Corp. (Mpls.), Hoist & Derrick Co. (St. Paul). Maj., U.S. Arir Service, 1917-18. Mem. Mpls. C. of C., Mpls. Civic Council, Northwestern Hospital Assn. (chmn. adv. com.), Community War Chest (pres.). Episcopalian. Clubs: Minneapolis, Bohemian, Woodhill Country; Chicago; Bankers, Links (N.Y.C.). Home: Ferndale, Wayzata 5, Minn. Office: Baker Arcade Bldg., Mpls. 2. Died June 7, 1950.

DAVIS, Donald W(alton), educator; b. Frazer, Pa., Feb. 25, 1882; s. William Harmar and Mary (Charles (Siddall) D.; grad. West Chester (Pa.) State Normal Sch., 1900; A.B., Harvard, 1905, Ph.D., 1913; m. Katherine Myrl Bressler, Sept. 7, 1907; children—Mary Eleanor (Mrs. Donald T. Ries), Donald Walton, Virginia Myrl (Mrs. Robert J. Faulconer). Asst. in zoölogy U. Cal., 1905-06; prof. biology Sweet Briar (Va.) Coll., 1907-09; grad. student in zoölogy, Harvard, and instr. zoölogy, Radcliff, Coll., 1909-12; asst. prof. zoölogy Clark Coll., 1912-14; prof. biology De Pauw U., 1914-16, Coll. of William and Mary, 1946—, also head dept. Served as 1st lt. inf., assigned to 1st Pioneer Inf., 1918-19; apptd. capt. Cav. Res., 1920. Fellow A.A.A.S.; mem. Bot. Soc. Am., Genetics Soc. Am., Va. Acad. Sci. (pres. 1927-28), Am. Assn. U. Profs. (council mem. 1941-46), Sigma Xi, Phi Beta Kappa, Omicron Delta Kappa. Episcopalian. Home: 349 Scotland St., Williamsburg, Va. Died June 30, 1950; buried Williamsburg, Va.

DAVIS, E. Asbury, merchant; b. Somerset County, Md., Aug. 24, 1870; s. Francis A. and Sallie (Long) D.; Baltimore City Coll., 1885; m. Jennie Conradt, Oct. 20, 1892; children—Francis A., Allan C., Hamilton C., Clara A., Virginia. Partner F. A. Davis & Sons, and Washington Tobacco Co. Pres. U.S. Fidelity & Guarantee Co.; v.p. Old Dominion Tobacco Co. Home: Warrington Apts., Balt. Office: 119 S. Howard St., Balt. Died Mar. 15, 1955.

DAVIS, Edward C. P., lawyer; b. Battle Creek, Mich., Nov. 29, 1898; s. Arthur Walter and Nellie (Barber) D.; A.B., U. Mich., 1920, J.D., 1922; m. Deborah F. Young, May 31, 1924. Admitted to Mich. bar, 1922, and since practiced in Detroit; partner Dickinson, Wright, Davis, McKean & Cudlip, 1929—; dir. Gar Wood Industries, Inc., Douglas & Lomason Company, United Metal Craft Corporation. Member American, Michigan State and Detroit bar assns. (mem. coms.), Order of Coif, Delta Chi. Clubs: Detroit, Country of Detroit. Home: 890 Lake Shore Rd., Grosse Pointe Shores, Mich. Office: National Bank Bldg., Detroit 26. Died Oct. 26, 1957.

DAVIS, Edward Everett, educator; b. Williamsburg, Mo., Mar. 11, 1881; s. Robert Augustus (g.s. of Daniel Boone) and Martha Caroline (Ogan) D.; B.Litt., John Tarleton Coll., Stephenville, Tex., 1906; B.A., U. of Tex., 1913, M.A., 1917; m. Mertie Helen Higgins, Aug. 27, 1924. Teacher rural schs. several yrs.; research specialist in rural edn., extension dept. U. of Tex., 1914-23; prof. edn., State Teachers Coll., Huntington, W.Va., summer, 1922; prof. edn. Ohio State U., summer, 1923; prof. and dir. edn., Stephen F. Austin State Teachers Coll., Nacogdoches, Tex., 1923-25; dean N. Tex. Agrl. Coll., Arlington, Tex., 1925-46; dean emeritus and prof. government, North Texas Agricultural College, since Sept. 1945. Mem. Phi Delta Kappa. Democrat. Baptist. Club: Rotary. Author: The Twentieth Century Rural School, 1920; Good Citizenship, 1926; The White Scourge, 1939; also various bulls. on rural edn. and rural schs. Home: 1316 W. Park Row, Arlington, Tex. Died Dec. 13, 1950; buried Rose Hill, Arlington.

DAVIS, Elmer (Holmes), writer; b. Aurora Ind., Jan. 13. 1890; s. Elam Holmes and Louise (Severin) D.; A.B., Franklin Coll., 1910, A.M., 1911; awarded Rhodes scholarship, Queen's Coll., Oxford U., Eng., B.A., 1912; honoray Litt.D., Franklin College, 1931, Franklin and Marshall College, 1941, Swarthmore College, 1954; L.H.D., Wabash College, 1942; LL.D. (honorary), St. Lawrence University, 1946; married Florence MacMillan, February 5, 1917; children—Robert Lloyd, Carolyn Anne. Teacher, Franklin (Ind.) High School, 1909-10, editorial staff Adventure, 1913-14; on staff of New York Times, 1914-24. News analyst, Columbia Broadcasting System, 1939-42. Dir. O.W.I., U.S. Govt., 1942-45. Received Medal for Merit; Decorated Dutch Order Orange-Nassau, Order White Lion. News analyst, Am. Broadcasting Co., 1945-56. Mem. Council, Authors League Am., 1926-46 (pres., 1939-41). Mem. Phi Delta Theta. Club: Century (N.Y.). Author: (essays) But We Were Born Free, 1954; Two Minutes Till Midnight, 1955; various novels. Home: 1661 Crescent Pl., Washington. Died May 18, 1958.

DAVIS, Frank Garfield, prof. edn.; b. Saginaw, Mich., Aug. 16, 1884; s. Levi Herbert and Iris Ramona (Winegarden) D.; student Clarion (Pa.) State Normal Sch., 1901-03, Kan. Wesleyan University, 1905-06; Ph.B., summa cum laude, Bucknell University, 1911; M.A., Columbia, 1924; Ph.D., New York U., 1930; m. Bess Estelle Carnall, Feb. 6, 1915; children—Carol Lee, Margaret Louise, Frank Alan. Teacher rural schs., 1902-03; prin. grade schs., 1903-05; and 1906-08; supt. schs., Valdez, Alaska, 1911-17, Auburn, Wash., 1917-18; prin. jr. high sch., Cleveland, O., 1918-24; prof. edn. and head of dept., Bucknell U., 1924—, dir. Demonstration Sch., 1925-41, also dir. summer sch. and extension work, 1935-

43, dir. of admissions, 1943-46, alumni sec., 1943-50. Mem. N.E.A., Pa. State Education Assn. (pres. 1927 and 1934; sec.-treas., coll. teachers of edn. sect.; chmn. commn. on professional ethics), Nat. Dept. Secondary Sch. Prins. (mem. planning com.; chmn. research com.; regional coordinator Pa. Branch), Assn. Liberal Arts Colls. of Pa. for Advancement of Teaching (sec., treas., pres., 1940-41); chmn. counseling com. Nat. Vocational Guidance Assn., 1941-44; chmn. certification com., 1946-47; pres. Central Pa. br., 1939-40, 1946-48. Mem. Am. Assn. Sch. Adminstrs., Am. Assn. Univ. Profs., Phi Delta Kappa, Kappa Phi Kappa. American Assn. of School Administrators, Phi Delta Kappa, Kappa Phi Kappa. Baptist. Mason. Author: Guidance for Youth (with wife), 1928, new edit., 1937; A Course in Supervised Teaching, 1933; Guidance Practices in 124 Pennsylvania Secondary Schs.; Guidance Program for Hesse, 1948; Guidance Manual for Principals, 1949; co-author and editor: Pupil Personnel Service, 1948; Guidance Handbook for Teachers, 1949. Contbr. to professional publs. Home: 140 S. Front St., Lewisburg, Pa. Died Oct. 21, 1957; buried Lewisburg Cemetery.

DAVIS, Frank Parker, lawyer; b. Mount Pleasant, D.C., Sept. 16, 1870; s. Benjamin Parker and Maria Jessephine (Swett) D.; LL.B., Columbian U. (now George Washington U.), 1896, Master Patent Laws, 1897; m. Edith Amanda Kelly, Oct. 28, 1903; children—Frank Parker, Amanda Bernice (Mrs. Henry Austin Pickard), Fitzroy, Edith Maria (dec.) and Edward Albert (twins). Admitted to D.C. bar, 1896, and practiced in Washington, 1896-99, Boston, 1899-1902, Dayton, O., 1902-06, in Chicago since 1906; counsel to firm Davis, Lindsey, Hibben & Noyes, Chicago, since 1947; Rector, Hibben & Davis, 1906-10, Hibben, Davis & Macauley, 1910-34, Davis, Macauley May, Lindsey & Smith, 1934-36, Davis, Lindsey, Smith & Shonts, 1936-47. Dir. Burroughs Adding Machine Co. since 1925. Mem. citizens defense corps, Evanston Defense Council, heading div. staff corps air raid control centre, World War II. Member Am. Patent Law Assn., Patent Law Assn. of Chicago (past pres.), Am. Bar Assn., Phi Delta Phi. Republican. Episcopalian. Clubs: Glen View (Ill.) Golf; The Evanston; The Detroit. Home: 1117 Sheridan Rd., Evanston, Ill. Office: McCormick Bldg., Chicago 4. Died Sept. 25, 1958.

DAVIS, George H., engineer; born Oswego, N.Y., 1863; son Samuel A. and Esther T. (Parks) D.; grad. Oswego State Teachers College, 1885; M.E., Cornell U., 1892; m. Katherine McGrath, 1898; children—Philip McGrath, Putnam. Design, constrn. and management mills and pub. utilities, Baltimore and New York, 1892-95; partner and dir. Ford, Bacon & Davis, Inc., New Orleans, New York and San Francisco, 1895-1941; engaged with partners in design, constrn. and management various pub. utilities, railways and indsl. plants, New Orleans, San Francisco and other southern and western cities, 1895-1907, including resurveys and reconstruction of San Francisco because of the earthquake and fire of 1906; vice-pres. and mgr. Am. Cities Railway & Light Co., 1907-11; pres. Am. Cities Co., 1911-13; design, constrn. and reconstruction various terminals, railways, warehouses, harbor structures, etc., New Orleans, Mobile and Galveston, 1914-18; preparation of a report to the secretary of war on the strategic seclusion and mil. strength of the New Orleans area for airplane, army and naval bases and operating terminals, 1918; Supervision of production Platt Iron Works, Dayton, O., of army tanks for A.E.F., 1918; supervision of construction New Orleans Army Supply Base, 1918-19; dir. Atlantic Aircraft Corp., 1925-27, Fokker Aircraft Corporation, 1927-30; active in development and manufacture of airplane engines; general engineering practice and capital management since 1921. Member American Society Mech. Engrs., American Society Civil Engrs., Louisiana Engring. Soc. Clubs: University, Engineers', Cornell, City Midday, Boston Club (New Orleans). Home: 6 Guion Lane, Larchmont, N.Y. Office: 20 Exchange Pl., N.Y.C. 5. Died May 1957.

DAVIS, George Harvey, grain dealer; b. Amboy, Ill., Apr. 7, 1876; s. James Blair and Sarah Frances (Wheat) D.; ed. pub. schs. of Kansas City and Kansas City (Mo.) Business Coll.; m. Elizabeth Otterman, Oct. 26, 1899. Began as clerk, 1891; mgr. br. grain office, 1896-98; in grain business on own account in Kansas City, 1898—; organized Davis-Noland-Merrill Grain Co., Kansas City, 1923, pres., 1923—; chmn. Mo. State Highway Commn. 1942-46; chairman code authority, grain exchange United States, N.R.A., 1934-35; director First National Bank Kansas City. Pres. Kan. City Board Trade, 1912. Pres. Chamber of Commerce of U.S., 1937, 38; pres. Am. Royal Live Stock Show, Kan. City, 1938-40. Presbyterian. Mason (Shriner). Clubs: Kansas City, Mission Hills Golf, Kansas City Country (Kansas City); Chicago Club (Chicago); Metropolitan (Wash.). Home: The Walnuts, 5049 Wornall Rd. Office: Board of Trade Bldg., Kansas City, Mo. Died May 5, 1955; buried Mount Washington Cemetery, Kansas City, Mo.

DAVIS, Graham Lee, hosp. adminstr.; b. Woodville, N.C., Apr. 15, 1893; s. Dr. Judson J. and Mary Elizabeth (White) D.; student Wake Forest (N.C.) Coll., Jan.-June 1915, Univ. of N.C., 1916-17, George Washington Univ., 1919-21, New York Univ., 1923-25; m. Anne-Marie Ferre, Sept. 6, 1921; children—Miquette, John Pierre. Asst. to dir. hosp. sect., The Duke Endowment, Charlotte, N.C., 1924-39; dir. div. of hosps., W. K. Kellogg Foundation, Battle Creek, Mich., 1940-51, on leave as director of National Commission on Financing Hosp. Care, 1951-53, cons. 1953-56; dir. Onslow Meml. Hosp., Jacksonville, North Carolina, 1956—. Served as sergt. and 2d lt. Army Air Corps, France, 1917-19. Hon. fellow, Am. College Hosp. Adminstrs., 1947. Fellow Am. Public Health Assn.; mem. Am. Assn. Hosp. Consultants, Am. Hosp. Assn. (chmn. com. on accounting and statistics, 1938-41, chmn. council on adminstrn. practice, 1941-43, chmn. com. on postwar planning for orgn. hosp. care commn. to make nat. study of hosp. resources and needs, 1942-46, pres. 1947. A.M.A. (committee post war medical service since 1942); mem. joint com. Am. Hosp. Assn. and Am. Pub. Health Assn., 1946; mem. Mich. Hosp. Assn. (pres. 1941-42), mem. Fed. Hosp. Council, 1946-49; mem. exec. com. Nat. Health Assembly, 1948; Health facilities and services study of British Columbia, 1946, Inter-Am. Hosp. Assn., Am. Statis. Assn. Republican. Baptist. Editor Southern Hospitals, 1934-39. Contbr. numerous articles to med. and hosp. jours. Address: Onslow Meml. Hosp., Jacksonville, N.C. Died July 4, 1958.

DAVIS, Hal Strange, business exec.; b. Honey Cote, Tex., Aug. 11, 1900; s. Thomas Hugh and Linnie Almeda (Strange) D.; student U. Ark., 1918, U. of Tex., 1920-23; m. Barbara Hoff Sterzl, Nov. 2, 1935; children—Hal S., Thomas Lloyd, Mrs. Barbara Lynne Walsh, Valerie Ann; m. 2d, Myrtle E. Van Wart, May 8, 1954. Trainee S. H. Kress & Co., N.Y.C., 1924, asst. mgr., 1925, mgr. Galveston (Tex.) store, 1926-27, Tulsa store, 1928-31, Northeastern dist. mgr., N.Y.C., 1932-40, regional mgr., 1940-43, dir., 1941—, v.p., store orgn., 1943-52, exec. v.p., 1952-54; pres. dir. Candle Craft Inc. Newark, N.J. 1957—. Mem. Limited Price Variety Stores Assn., Circus Saints and Sinners. Republican. Methodist. Mason (Shriner). Club: Baltusrol Golf. Home: 52 Martindale Rd., Short Hills, N.J. Retired 1954. Died June 10, 1959; buried Texarkana, Ark.

DAVIS, Harry Lyman, ex-gov. Ohio, ins. exec.; b. Cleve., Jan. 25, 1878; s. Evan H. and Barbara D.; student pub. schs., Cleve., night bus. coll.; m. Lucy V. Fegan, July 16, 1902; 1 son, Harry L. Began at 13 in rolling mills, Newburgh, O.; later solicitor for Bell Telephone Co.; v.p., gen. mgr. Davis Telephone Adjustment Co.; treas. City of Cleve., 1910-11; nat. organizer Loyal Order of Moose, 1912; with Davis & Farley, gen. ins., 1913-15; mayor of Cleve., 1916-20, 34-35; gov. of Ohio, 1921-23; now pres. The Harry L. Davis Co., Gen. ins.; former pres. Ohio Trust Co., Cleve. Republican. Baptist. Home: 3105 S. Moreland Blvd. Office: Terminal Tower, Cleve. Died May 21, 1950; buried Lakeview Cemetery, Cleve.

DAVIS, Harvey Nathaniel, mech. engr.; b. Providence, R.I., June 6, 1881; s. Nathaniel French and Lydia Martin (Bellows) D.; A.B., Brown U., 1901, A.M., 1902; A.M., Harvard, 1903, Ph.D., 1906; Sc.D., Brown U., 1928, Northeastern Univ., 1938, Columbia Univ., 1940; LL.D., Rutgers, 1928; E.D., Stevens Institute of Technology, 1948; D.Eng., New York University, 1936, Rose Polytechnic Institute, 1938, Rensselaer Polytechnic Institute, 1949; m. Suzanne C. Haskell, June 28, 1911 (died Jan. 1, 1919); children—Suzanne, Louisa Frederika; m. 2d, Alice M. Rohde, Sept. 20, 1920 (died Aug. 22, 1933); children—Marian, Nathaniel; m. 3d, Helen Clarkson Miller, Feb. 8, 1935. Instr. mathematics, Brown Univ., 1901-02; inst. physics, 1904-10, asst. prof., 1910-19, prof. mech. engring., 1919-28, Harvard; became pres. Stevens Inst. Tech., 1928, retired, 1951. Dir. Office Production Research and Development of War Production Bd. Nov. 1942-June 1944. Engr. in turbine dept., Gen. Electric Co., 1917-18; aeronautical mech. engr. A.S., 1918-22; cons. engr. Franklin Ry. Supply Co., 1920-27, United States Bureau of Mines, 1921-25, also Air Reduction Company, 1922-25. Regent Smithsonian Inst. since 1938; trustee Blair Acad. Stevens-Hoboken Acad. Fellow Am. Acad. Arts and Sciences, American Phys. Society, A.A.A.S., American Soc. M.E. (pres. 1937-38); mem. Am. Math. Soc. (life), Franklin Inst. (hon.), The Instn. of M.E.; (London), Am. Philos. Soc., Newcomen Soc., Washington Acad. Sciences, American Association for Adult Education, also Phi Beta Kappa, Sigma Xi, Tau Beta Pi, Delta Phi. Conglist. Clubs: Cosmos (Washington), Brown University (president, 1935), Harvard, Century (New York). Author: (with L. S. Marks) Steam Tables and Diagrams, 1908; with N. Henry Black) Practical Physics for High Schools, 1913; Elementary Practical Physics, 1938. Home: Hoxie House, Castle Point, Hoboken, N.J. Died Dec. 3, 1952.

DAVIS, Hassoldt, explorer and writer; b. Boston, Mass., July 3, 1907; s. Albert Milton and Lucille (Hassoldt) D.; student Harvard 2½ years (class of 1929); divorced. Spent year among South Pacific Islands, 1929-30; subsequently worked with Andre Roosevelt on moving picture of Bali named "Goona-Goona"; returned to South Seas for 2 more yrs.; writer and photographer with Denis-Roosevelt Asiatic Expdn., 1939, driving up Burma Road into China and later visiting Kingdom of Nepal; made collection of ethnological data on Nepal and comprehensive photographs of country. During 1947-48, led expedition sponsored by UNESCO and French Government to explore Tumac Humac Mountains of French Guiana and to film nomadic Indians; led ethnal. expdn. to Ivory Coast of Africa, 1949-50. Joined Free French Forces, 1941, serving in Tchad, Lybia, Tunisia, Italy, France and Indo-China campaigns, 1941-46. Awarded Croix de Guerre (twice), Award of Legion of Honor (France). Mem. Royal Geog. Soc. Australia, Cercle de la France d'Outre Mer. Club: Explorers (N.Y. City). Author: Islands Under the Wind, 1933; Save Me the Sun, 1939; Land of the Eye, 1940; Nepal, Land of Mystery, 1942; The Fighting Family Paux, 1943; Half Past When, 1945; Feu d'Afrique, 1946; The Jungle and the Damned, 1952; Sorcerers' Village (film), 1955 (book) 1955; World Without a Roof, 1957; Bonjour Hangover, Captain Billy's Magic, 1959. Home: 2 W. 67th St., N.Y.C. 23. Died Sept. 10, 1959; buried Lincolnville (Me.) Cemetery.

DAVIS, James Thomas, coll. dean; b. Heard County, Ga., May 2, 1880; s. Walter Jonathan and Elizabeth (Smith) D.; grad. North Tex. Normal Sch., 1904; A.B., U. Tex., 1918, A.M., 1921; B.S., A. and M. Coll. Tex., 1920; LL.D., Howard Payne Coll., 1926; m. Uta Willson, eb. 23, 1906; children—Thomas Willson, James William, Dorothy Uta. Tchr. rural schs., Tex., 1899-1902; tchr. Latin, Honey Grove High Sch., 1904-05; prin. Navasota (Tex.) High Sch., 1905-07; supt. schs. Grimes County, Tex., 1907-10, Navasota, 1910-19; dean John Tarleton Agrl. Coll., 1919-45, dean emeritus, 1945—. Pres. 1940-42, and life dir. West Tex. C. of C.; dir. Stephenville C. of C. Hon. mem. Boy Scouts of Am.; hon. Lone Star Former of Future Farmers of America. Mem. So. Assn. Colls. and Secondary Schs. (pres. 1935-36), Am. Assn. Jr. Colls. (pres. 1928-29, exec. com. 1928-43), Mid-Tex. Tchrs. Assn. (pres. 1921-22; mem. bd. dirs. 1924-30), Tex. Assn. Jr. Colls. (pres. 1928), N.E.A. (life), Tex. Tchrs. Assn. (life), Tex. Baby Chick Assn., Kappa Delta Pi, Alpha Tau Alpha. Democrat. Baptist. Mason. Club: Lions (past pres.; del. to Internat. 1924). Author: Common Words—How to Spell Them, 1918. Contbr. to ednl. jours. Home: 1191 W. Jones, Stephenville, Tex. Died May 12, 1950; buried Stephenville.

DAVIS, Jesse Buttrick, educator; b. Chgo., Mar. 2, 1871; s. Simon L. and Sarah W. (Buttrick) D; A.B., Colgate, 1895, A.M., 1911, Litt.D., 1922; A.M., U. Mich., 1916; m. Lillian B. Drewery, Sept. 2, 1879; children—Lillian Purmort, Kenneth Drewery, Aileen Buttrick. Tchr. Central High Sch., Detroit, 1895-1907; prin. Central High Sch., Grand Rapids, 1907-20; dir. vocational guidance, Grand Rapids, 1912-20; pres. Grand Rapids Jr. Coll., 1914-20; supr. secondary edn. conn., 1920-24; professor secondary edn. Boston U., 1924—, dean sch. edn., 1935-42, adminstrv. asst., 1942-51. Lectr. on vocational guidance, summer session U. Mich., 1914, U. Minn., 1915; dir. Jr. Placement Service, U.S. Dept. Labor, 1917-18; instr. secondary edn., Tchrs. Coll. Columbia, summer session 1919; lectr. secondary edn. Grad. Sch. Edn., Yale, 1921-24, Harvard Grad. Sch., summer 1923, Grad. Sch. Edn., Harvard, 1924-32. Chmn. bd. dirs. Huntington Av. br. YMCA, 1944-48. Mem. Nat. Vocational Guidance Assn. (pres. 1914-16), N.E.A. Dept. Secondary Sch. Prins. (pres. 1917), Mayflower Soc., Phi Beta Kappa, Delta Upsilon, Phi Delta Kappa; Mem. exec. com. Coöperative Study of Secondary School Standards, 1935—. Mason. Clubs: University; Mass. Schoolmasters (pres. 1939); Neighbors (Newton Center, Mass.). Author: Vocational and Moral Guidance, 1914; The Saga of a Schoolmaster. Lectr. ednl. problems; cons. sch. surveys and planning of sch. bldgs. Home: 18 Hazelton Rd., Newton Center 59, Mass. Died Nov. 2, 1955; buried Newton Cemetery, Newton Center.

DAVIS, John William, lawyer; b. Clarksburg, W. Va., Apr. 13, 1873; s. John J. and Anna (Kennedy) D.; A.B., Washington and Lee U., Va., 1892, LL. B., 1895, LL.D., 1915; LL.D., U. of W.Va., 1919, U. of Birmingham, Eng., 1919, U. of Glasgow, 1920, Union U., N.Y., 1921, Yale, 1921, Dartmouth, 1923, Brown U., 1923, Princeton, 1924, Oberlin, 1947, N.Y. U., 1951, D.C.L., Oxford U. (Eng.), 1950, Columbia, 1953, Hofstra Coll., 1953; m. Julia T. McDonald, June 20, 1899 (died Aug. 17, 1900); 1 dau., Julia McDonald; m. 2d, Ellen G. Bassel, January 2, 1912 (died July 13, 1943). Admitted to bar, 1895; assistant professor law, Washington and Lee University, 1896-97; in practice, Clarksburg, 1897-1913; mem. Davis Polk, Wardwell Gardiner & Reed, N.Y. City, 1921—, now David Polk, Wardwell Sunderland & Kiendl; mem. West Virginia Ho. of Dels., 1899; Dem. candidate for presdl. elector at large, 1900; del. Dem. Nat. Conventions, 1904-32; elected to 62d and 63d Congresses (1911-15), 1st W.Va. Dist.; resigned from Congress to become solicitor gen. of U.S., Aug. 30, 1913; solicitor gen. to 1918; ambassador extraordinary and plenipotentiary to Great

Britain, 1918-21. Counselor American Red Cross, 1913-18. Mem. Am. delegation for conf. with Germans on treatment and exchange of prisoners of war, Berne, Switzerland, Sept. 1918. Dem. candidate for President, 1924. Hon. bencher of the Middle Temple (Eng.). Pres. Am. Bar Assn., 1922; pres. W.Va. Bar Assn., 1906; pres. Assn. Bar City of New York, 1931-1932; mem. Phi Kappa Psi, Phi Beta Kappa, G.B.E. (British). Mason (33°). Clubs: Metropolitan, National Press, Lawyers (Washington, D.C.), Century, University, Recess, Down Town, Piping Rock Creek, Links. Home: Locust Valley, L.I., N.Y. Office: 15 Broad St., N.Y.C. Died Mar. 24, 1955.

DAVIS, LeCompte, lawyer; b. Mercer County, Ky., May 1, 1864; s. Henry Clay and Josephine (Le Compte) D.; B.L., Centre Coll., Danville, Ky., 1887; m. Edythe Gilman, Apr. 18, 1908. Admitted to Ky. bar, 1887; since in practice at Los Angeles; asst. dist. atty. Los Angeles County. 1893-95; assisted in defense McNamara dynamiting cases, also in defense of Clarence Darrow, accused of bribery in said cases, also defended Harry New. Mem. Am., Los Angeles County bar assns. Democrat. Clubs: National Arts (N.Y.C.); Gamut Press, Jonathan. Home: 2755 Raymond Av., Los Angeles. Deceased.

DAVIS, Manton, lawyer; b. Mayfield, Ky., July 15, 1876; s. Robert Thomas and Sarah Elizabeth (Jenkins) D.; student West Ky. Coll.; LL.B., U. Va., 1901; m. Mary Kent, Jan. 1918 (dec.); children—Olivia (Mrs. Randolph Brown), Mary (Mrs. Harold Scott, Jr.); m. 2d, Anne Long, 1948. Admitted to Mo. bar, 1901, practiced in St. Louis until 1917; asst. gen. atty. RCA, 1923-25, rep. in China, 1925-26, gen. atty., 1927-34, also v.p., 1929-41, v.p., counsel, 1934-41, ret.; dir. RCA Communications, Cuba Transatlantic Radio Corp. Served as capt. 354th Inf., 89th Div., AUS, in France and Germany, 1917-19; major, officer in charge civil affairs, Coblenz, Germany, 1919; American legal adviser Inter Allied Rhineland High Commn., 1919-23; lt. col. J.A.G. Reserve. Mem. Am. Bar Assn., Phi Beta Kappa, Phi Delta Phi, Kappa Alpha. Democrat. Clubs: Sunset Golf (St. Petersburg); Fishers Island (N.Y.C.) Country. Home: 2410 Coffee Pot Dr., St. Petersburg, Fla.; (summer) Fishers Island, N.Y. Died July 1957; buried Mayfield, Ky.

DAVIS, Manvel H., lawyer; b. Greensburg, Kan., Apr. 7, 1891; s. John W. and Isabel N. (Hogan) D.; grad. Culver (Ind.) Mil. Acad, 1910; A.B., Yale, 1915; LL.B., Harvard, 1920; m. Genevieve Marcell, Feb. 13, 1933; children—John M., Louis M., Richard M. Admitted to Mo. bar, 1920, since practiced in Kansas City, mem. Davis, Thomson, Van Dyke & Fairchild, 1946—; dir., mem. exec. com. Central Surety & Ins. Corp. Mem. Mo. Ho. of Reps., 1924-28; Mo. Senate, 1928-32; Rep. nominee for U.S. Senate, 1940 (defeated by Harry S. Truman); gen. chmn. Mo. for Eisenhower; del. Chgo. Nat. Conv., mem. credentials com. Veteran World War I and II. Mem. Am., Mo. bar assns., Phi Gamma Delta. Republican. Presbyn. Clubs: Kansas City, Kansas City Country, University. Home: 1233 W. 63d Terrace, Kansas City 5. Office: Commerce Bldg., Kansas City 6, Mo. Died Feb. 10, 1959; buried Forest Hill Cemetery.

DAVIS, Mary Gould, author, editor; b. Bangor, Me., Feb. 13, 1882; d. Owen Warren and Abigail (Gould) D.; student pub. schs. Joined staff N.Y. Pub. Library, 1910, supr. story telling dept., 1922-44, ret.; editor and compiler, 1922—; young peoples book editor Sat. Rev. Lit., 1944-53; author, 1931—; lectr., 1932—. Mem. A.L.A. Club: Town Hall (N.Y.C.). Author: A Baker's Dozen, 1928; The Truce of the Wolf, 1931; The Handsome Donkey, 1933; Sandy's Kingdom, 1935; With Cap and Bells, 1935; Three Golden Oranges, 1936; Wakaina and the Clayman, 1946; Randolph Caldecott: An Appreciation, 1946. Editor of Childrens Books, Saturday Review of Lit. Compiler: The Girls' Book of Verse, 1933. Home: 207 W. 106th St., N.Y.C. 25. Died Apr. 15, 1956.*

DAVIS, Monnett Bain, U.S. ambassador; b. Greencastle, Ind., Aug. 13, 1893; s. Henry Thomas and Minerva Rockwell (Bain) D.; A.B., U. of Colo., 1917; m. Pearl Evangeline Erhart, Dec. 22, 1917; 1 son, Thomas Monnett. Am. consul at Port Elizabeth, S. Africa, 1921-23, at Saltillo, Mexico, 1924; assigned to Dept. of State, Washington, D.C., 1925-28, chief Visa Office, 1928; fgn. service inspector, 1929-33; consul general Stockholm, 1933-34, Shanghai, China, 1935-36, Singapore, 1936-37, Buenos Aires, 1938-41; first sec. of embassy, Buenos Aires, 1940-41; chief Div. of Foreign Service Administration, Dept. of State, 1941-43; dep. dir. Office of Fgn. Service, Dept. of State, Washington, D.C., 1944; dir., 1945; minister to Denmark, 1945; career minister, counsellor of embassy and consul general, Shanghai, China, 1946; rep. U.S. Econ. Commn. for Asia and the Far East (UN), 1947; ambassador to Panama, 1948; apptd. A.E. and P. to Israel since Feb. 1951. Served as 2d lt. U.S. Army, 1918; 1st lt. O.R.C., 1919-20. Mem. Sigma Phi Epsilon. Mason. Club: Metropolitan (Washington). Address: care Office Near East Affairs, Dept. of State, Washington 25. Died Dec. 26, 1953.

DAVIS, Nathan Smith, physician; b. Chgo., June 25, 1889; s. Nathan Smith (M.D.) and Jessie Bradley (Hopkins) D.; prep. edn. Univ. Sch for Boys, Chgo.; A.B., Harvard, 1910; M.D., Rush Med. Coll., 1913; m. Cordelia Fairbank Carpenter, July 6, 1923; children—Nathan Smith, Graham, Stephen Fairbank, Alden Carpenter. Asst., asso. medicine Rush Med. Coll., 1915-20; asso. medicine Northwestern U. Med. Sch., 1921-28, asst. prof. medicine, 1928-53, asso. professor, 1953-55, associate professor medicine emeritus, 1955—. Member Ill. State Planning Commn., 1933 41; treas., trustee Nat. Physicians Com. for Extension Med. Service, 1939-41. Served as 1st lt. M.C., Ill. N.G., 1916; capt. M.C., U.S. Army, 1917-19. Fellow Acad. Internat. Medicine (president 1945-46, secretary 1947—), A.C.P.; mem. American Medical Writers Association, American Society, Study Arteriosclerosis, Am. Gerontological Soc., Am. Geriatric Soc., Am. Chgo. heart assns., Central Soc. Clin. Research, A.M.A., Ill. State Med. Soc., Chgo. Med. Soc. (sec. 1929-31, pres. 1939-40), Soc. Internal Medicine Chgo., Inst. Medicine Chgo., Chgo. Society Med. History, Miss. Valley Med. Soc., Am. Therapeutic Soc., Chgo. Acad. Sci. (pres. 1938), A. A.A.S., Art Inst. Chgo., Field Mus. Natural History, Chgo. Geog. Soc., Nu Sigma Nu. Episcopalian. Clubs: Commonwealth, Harvard. Home: 259 Ridge Ave., Winnetka, Ill. Office: 700 N. Michigan Av., Chgo. 11. Died Apr. 20, 1956; buried Rosehill Cemetery, Chgo.

DAVIS, Newton Eads, ch. ofcl.; b. Dublin, O., Nov. 24, 1876; s. Joseph Watts and Mary (Butt) D.; A.B., Ohio Wesleyan U., 1900, A.M., 1901; B.D., Drew Theol. Sem., 1904; studied Columbia and N.Y. univs.; D.D., Ohio Wesleyan U., 1937; m. Florence Belle Hiffner, June 21, 1900. Ordained M.E. ministry, 1906; pastor West Orange, N.J., 1903-04, Nevada, O., 1904-07, Barberton, 1907-11, Lorrain, 1911-13, Ulrichville, 1904-15; financial sec., St. Luke's Hosp., Cleve., 1915-20; exec. sec. Bd. of Hosps. and Homes of M.E. Ch., 1920-24; same Bd. of Hosps., Homes and Deaconess work of M.E. Ch. (now Meth. Ch.), 1924—; promotional dir. Lakeside Found., Lakeside, O., 1941; pastor Meth. Ch., Ashley, Ohio, 1943; pastor Nankin, Ohio Federated Ch., 1944-45; interim minister, Royal Poinciana Chapel, Palm Beach, 1947; minister Federated Ch., Savannah, Ohio, 1948. Sec. Bd. Home Missions N.E. Ohio Conf., 14 yrs.; mem. council of bds. of benevolence of M.E. Ch. Pres. Am. Protestant Hosp. Assn., 1925-26; mem. World Service Commn., 1924-40; apptd. counselor in Promotion and Finance, June 1941, dir. promotion and finance for philanthropic instns. and chs. 1943; minister Kilbourne, Ohio, Methodist Ch., 1946-47. Mem. Sigma Alpha Epsilon. Republican. Author: Methodist Philanthropy: The Four Horsemen of the American Revolution, 1949; A Philanthropic Promoter on Wheels (autobiography), 1949. Address: 268 Sherman, Ashland, O. Died Apr. 3, 1959; buried Ashland, O.

DAVIS, Owen, dramatic author; b. Portland, Me., Jan. 29, 1874; s. Owen Warren and Abbie (Gould) D.; ed. U. of Tenn. and Harvard; m. Elizabeth Drury Breyer. Commenced his career as a dramatic author with Through the Breakers, 1898; his earlier efforts consisted of sensational melodramas, My Lady Nell, 1911, Lola, 1911, An Every Day Man, 1912, The Family Cupboard, 1913, Beggars on Horseback, 1914, Sinners, 1915, Mile-a-Minute Kendal, 1916, Any House, 1916, The Scrap of Paper, 1917, The Arabian Nights, 1918; since that date has written For Ever After, 1918, The Flaming Soul, 1919, Those Who Walk in Darkness, 1919, Peggy, Behave, 1919, At 9:45, 1919, The Alibi, 1919, Opportunity, 1921, The Haunted House, 1921, Up the Ladder, 1922, The Bronx Express, 1922; Dreams for Sale, 1922, The World We Live In (adapted from The Insect Play), 1922, Icebound, 1923, Home Fires, 1923, Lazybone, 1924, Find the Woman, Peacocks, 1924. Easy Come, Easy Go, Beware of Widows, 1925; The Donovan Affair, The Great Gatsby (from a novel), Sandalwood (with Fulton Oursler), Gentle Grafters, The Phantom Ship (from the German), The Man Who Forgot (with S. N. Behrman), 1926, The Triumphant Bachelor, 1927, Carry On, To-Night at Twelve, 1928; Spring Is Here, 1929, The Ninth Guest, 1930, Just to Remind You, 1931, The Harbor Light, 1932, A Saturday Night, 1933, Jezebel, 1933, Too Many Boats, 1934, Spring Freshet, 1934, Virginia (with Laurence Stallings), 1937, Let's Never Change, 1938, Family Honeymoon (adaptation), Mr. and Mrs. North, 1941. The Snark Was a Boojum, 1943, No Way Out, 1944; is said to have written 300 melodramas; his play, "Icebound", gained the Pulitzer Prize, 1923. Died Oct. 13, 1956.

DAVIS, Pierpont, architect; b. Baltimore, Md., Dec. 27, 1884; s. Francis Earlougher and Annie Legate (Swindell) D.; student Baltimore City Coll., 1 yr., Md. Inst. Art and Design, 3 yrs.; m. Gertrude Alberta Churchill, Nov. 17, 1909; children—Gabrielle Churchill (wife comdr. William James Kuehn, U.S. N.R.), Althea Churchill (wife of Dr. Hugo Lucic, capt. U.S.N.R.). In architectural practice since 1910; mem. firm Pierpont and Walter S. Davis since 1916; sec. O. H. Churchill Co., Laurel Av. Corp.; an architect of Pentagon Bldg., Washington; 1 of 5 architects Los Angeles County General Hospital, Hall of Justice, Los Angeles County Museum; President Library of Architecture and Allied Arts; member Municipal Art Commn., City of Los Angeles. Award of Distinguished Honor in Architecture, So. Cal. Chap. A.I.A. for St. John's Episcopal Church of Los Angeles. Fellow A.I.A. Clubs: California, Los Angeles Country, Los Angeles Yacht. Home: 500 S. Rossmore Av., Los Angeles, Cal. Died July 15, 1953.

DAVIS, Ralph Waldo, bus. exec.; b. Crawfordsville, Ind., Sept. 5, 1895; s. Joseph Lindsay and Frances (Hall) D.; Ph.B., U. Chgo., 1916; m. Geraldine Scott, Nov. 14, 1923; children—Scott, Elizabeth. With Atlas Cement Co., 1917; partner Paul H. Davis & Co., 1919-53, Ralph W. Davis & Co., 1953—; dir. Burgess-Norton Mfg. Co., John J. Nesbitt, Inc., Wells-Gardner & Co., Seismograph Service Corp., Northern Ill. Corp.; chmn. bd. govs. Chgo. Stock Exchange, 1945-46. Gov. Midwest Stock Exchange. Served with Am. Expeditionary Forces, World War I, 1917-19. Mem. S.A.R., Am. Legion. Republican. Episcopalian. Clubs: Chicago Athletic, Chicago; Mill Reef (Antigua, B.W.I.); Geneva Golf. Mem. bd. alderman, Geneva, 1931-38. Home: 321 Franklin St., Geneva, Ill. Office: 180 W. Adams St., Chgo. Died Jan. 30, 1960.

DAVIS, Richard J., Christian Science lecturer and teacher; s. James H. and Emily E. (Simmons) D.; student U. of Chicago, 1904-07; m. Kathryn Buell Carter, Jan. 8, 1927. Instr. Iowa Coll., Grinnell, Ia., 1907-08; actor in various Shakespearan cos., 2 yrs.; staff Christian Science Monitor, 8 yrs.; 1st reader, Fifth Ch. of Christ, Scientist, Chicago, 3 yrs.; apptd. to Christian Science Bd. of Lectureship of the First Church of Christ, Scientist, Boston, 1924, Massachusetts Metaphysical College, 1937; apptd. teacher Mass. Metaphys. Coll., 1949; apptd. editor The Christian Science Journal, Sentinel and Heralds, 1950. Apptd. 1st Christian Scientist chaplain, USN, 1918, served 2½ yrs. Mem. Delta Upsilon. Mason. Address: 58 Domingo Av., Berkeley Cal. Died Feb. 23, 1956.

DAVIS, Robert McNair, educator; b. Marshall, Mo., Aug. 3, 1884; s. Robert and Mary (Fletcher) D.; A.B., Harvard, 1905; Harvard Law Sch., 1905-07, S.J.D., 1928; J.D., U. Chgo., 1908; grad. study Yale Law School, 1927; m. Elizabeth Birchard, Dec. 28, 1905 (dec.); 1 son, William Birchard; m. 2d, Janis Patchen, June 28, 1944; children—Diana Janis, Malcolm McNair, Lisa Claire. With West Pub. co., St. Paul, 1908-10; admitted to Ore. bar, 1910, and began practice at Portland; prof. law U. Ariz., 1916-21, also dean of men, 1920-21; prof. law U. Cal., 1921-23; dean of law sch. U. Ida., 1923-29; research fellow Harvard Law Sch., 1927-28; dean of law sch. U. Kan., 1929-34, prof. of law, 1929-57, prof. law emeritus, 1957—. Mem. Am. (mem. gen. council 1926-29), Kan. State bar assns., Am. Acad. Polit. and Social Science, Am. Soc. Internat. Law, Fgn. Policy Assn., Am. Assn. U. Profs., Lawrence C. of C., Order of The Coif, Phi Kappa Phi, Delta Sigma Rho, Phi Alpha Delta, Kappa Alpha. Presbyn. Clubs: University, Rotary, Country. Contbr. to law reviews. Home: 1208 W. Cedar Ht., Arlington, Tex. Died June 22, 1959.

DAVIS, Roger Wolcott, lawyer; b. Hartford, Conn., Jan. 8, 1890; s. Frederick Wendell and Mary (Taintor) D.; student Mass. Inst. Tech., 1908-09; Ph.B., Yale, 1911, LL.B., 1913; m. Helen Louise Merriam, Jan. 27, 1917; children—Roger Wolcott, Merriam, Wendell. Admitted to Conn. bar, 1913, since practiced in Hartford; sr. partner Davis, Lee, Howard & Wright, 1939—; dir. Morris Plan Bank of Hartford. Alderman, City of Hartford; judge Windsor Town Ct. Pres. Travelers Aid Soc.; trustee, pres. Windsor Library Assn. Mem. Conn. Humane Soc., Am., Conn., Hartford bar assns., Windsor Hist. Soc. (pres.), Hartford Coll. Law (pres.), Hartford Coll. Ins. (v.p.), Soc. Mayflower Descs. Conn. (gov.), Delta Kappa Epsilon, Phi Delta Phi. Republican. Conglist. Clubs: Windsor Garden; Technology of Hartford (pres.), Hartford Engineers, University. Home: 390 Broad St., Windsor, Conn. Office: 101 Lafayette St., Hartford 6, Conn. Died Apr. 13, 1959.

DAVIS, Rowland Lucius, judge; b. Dryden, N.Y., July 10, 1871; s. Lucius and Harriet L. (Francis) D.; grad. State Normal Sch., Cortland, N.Y., 1896; LL.B., Cornell U., 1897; m. Iva A. Yager, June 15, 1905; children—Rowland L., Harriett Iva., Margaret Esther (dec.). Practiced law in Cortland, 1897-1915; apptd. justice Supreme Court of N.Y., 6th Dist., Aug. 3, 1915, and elected, 2 terms, 1916-41; designated by gov. to sit in the Appellate Div., 4th Dept., Rochester, N.Y., 1921, to Appellate Div., 3d Dept., Albany, 1927, to Appellate Div., 2d Dept., Bklyn., 1931, ret. 1939; retired as justice of Supreme Ct., 1941. Pres. Cornell Law Assn., 1931-32. Republican. Home: 30 Madison St., Cortland, N.Y. Died Feb. 1, 1954; buried Cortland.

DAVIS, Roy, educator (retired); b. Rotterdam, Holland, Jan. 7, 1876; s. Matthew John and Lillie F. D.; B.A., Dalhousie University, Halifax, Nova Scotia, 1899, M.A., 1900; M.A., Harvard University, 1902; Litt.D., Acadia University, 1930; m. Jessie V. Makin, June 25, 1910. Came to U.S., 1901. Head of English dept., high sch., Pawtucket, R.I., 1904-08; master in English, Mechanic Arts High Sch.,

Boston, 1908-15; prof. and head of English dept., 1916-42, asst. dean, 1919, College of Business Administration, Boston University, acting dean, 1928. Lecturer King's Coll. (London), 1937; lecturer Grad. Div. Boston University, 1941. Honorary Mexican vice consul Chmn. N.W.L.B. Adv. Panel on Wages for N.E., 1944. Pres. Am. Bus. Writers Assn. Ex-pres. N.E. Assn. of Teachers of English; mem. Phi Delta Kappa, Beta Gamma Sigma. Rep. Presbyn. Mason. Clubs: St. Botolph, Canadian (pres., 1945-46), Marshfield Country. Author: (with C. H. Lingham) Business English and Correspondence, 1914; Business Practice, 1916; Stories of the Day's Work (with F. G. Getchell), 1918; Practical Exercises in English, 1919; Business English, 1920; Advanced Exercises in English, 1924; Business Letter-Writing (with C. H. Lingham), 1925; English in School and Out (with W. H. Cunningham), 1929; Tests in English; Junior Exercises in English (2 volumes); Modern Business English, 1933; Write and Speak Better (with Wm. G. Hoffman), 1937; (brochure) Flying Rumors, etc. Editor: Everyday English, 1938; Business Writing (with C. C. Parkhurst), 1940; Americans at Work, 1941; Business English Work Book, 1941. Better Letters, 1945 (with H. R. Rasely; As in a Glass, 1946; Speaking and Writing (with W. G. Hoffman), 1949; James Anerthee, 1950; English Composition (with C. Chandler Parkhurst), 1950. Home: Marshfield Mass.; also 145 Bay State Rd., Boston. Died Feb. 26, 1953, buried Riverside Cemetery, Pawtucket, R.I.

DAVIS, T(heodore) Lawrence, educator; b. Penacook, N.H., Apr. 3, 1891; s. Homer Mackenzie and Juliette (Thurber) D.; studied Coll. of Liberal Arts, Boston Univ.; first grad. Coll. Bus. Adminstrn., Boston U., B B.A., 1915, M.B.A., 1917; S.C.D., Kansas Wesleyan U., 1923; LL.D., U. of N.H., 1927; Ed.D., Am. Internat. College, 1937; m. Pauline Louise Gagnon, August 1, 1921 (died November 20, 1946), 1 son, Theodore Lawrence. With Merchants National Bank, Manchester, New Hampshire, 1909-13; with Boston University since 1913; organizer, director Boston U. War Emergency Courses, 1917; secretary University Council, Boston University, since 1919; educational founder Coll. of Practical Arts and Letters, Boston U., dean since 1919. Mem. Beta Gamma Sigma. Decorated Legion of Honor (French Govt.), 1935. Ednl. consultant, and author of various reports pertaining to coll. adminstrn. Chosen by Mrs. Larz Anderson, 1937, to develop Anderson Meml. Centre, Boston U., in memory of her husband. Founded Lancaster Institute, 1945, pres. since 1945. Home: 275 Goddard Av., Brookline 46, Mass. Office: 27 Garrison St., Boston 16; and Lancaster Inst., George Hill Rd., Lancaster, Mass. Died Oct. 16, 1953; buried Forest Hills Cemetery, Jamaica Plain, Mass.

DAVIS, Thomas Jefferson, banker; b. Tazewell, Va.; s. M. G. B. and Nancy M. (Davis) Davis; B.S., Bethany (W.Va.) Coll., LL.D., 1934; m Jane Brown, Nov. 26, 1903; children—James Brown, Virginia Nancy, Thomas Jefferson, Laurence Laird. Began as clk., Catlettsburg (Ky.) Nat. Bank, 1889; one of organizers and cashier, 2nd Nat. Bank, Ashland, Ky, Bank of Ashland and 1st Nat. Bank, Louisa, Ky.; asst. cashier, later cashier, 5th Nat. Bank, Cincinnati, Ohio, 1892-1902; cashier and v.p. 1st Nat. Bk., Cincinnati, 1902-29; chmn. bd., 1929-34, pres., 1934-44; mem. of exec. com. since Sept. 1944; v.p. Bank of Athens (O.); dir. Union Central Life Ins. Co. (mem. exec. com.), Cincinnati Gas and Electric Co., U.S. Printing & Lithograph Co. Chmn. Liberty Loan Com., Cincinnati, World War. Trustee Ohio U.; mem. bd. trustees and treas. Christ Hosp., Cincinnati. Decorated Order of Leopold (Belgium), 1918. Republican. Episcopalian. Clubs: Queen City, Commonwealth, Commercial, Optimist, Camargo Country. Home: n.e. cor. Given & Shawnee Run Rd., Cincinnati 27. Office: First National Bank Bldg., Cin. 2. Died Jan. 8, 1952; buried Cin.

DAVIS, Thomas Latham, banker; b. Omaha, Neb., Feb. 21, 1882; s. Frederick Henry and Nellie Stockbridge (Clarkson) D.; grad. St. Paul's Sch., Concord, N.H., 1900; B.A., Yale, 1904; m. Bess Brady, Oct. 30, 1907; children—John Frederick, Elizabeth Ann (Mrs. John R. Lauritzen). With First Nat. Bank, Omaha, since 1904, pres. since 1934, chmn. since 1947. Mem. Delta Kappa Epsilon. Republican. Episcopalian. Clubs: Omaha, Minnesouri Angling. Home: 3628 Jackson St. Office: First National Bank, Omaha, Neb. Died Jan. 27, 1955.

DAVIS, Thomas Walker, lawyer; b. Wilmington, May 27, 1876; s. Junius and Mary Orme (Walker) D.; ed. Cape Fear Acad., Wilmington, and Univ. of N.C.; m. Anna MacKay Peck, Nov. 14, 1905. Began as clk. in office of gen. supt. Atlantic Coast Line R.R. Co., Wilmington, 1893, successively passenger rate clk., freight rate clk., chief rate clk., until 1899; admitted to N.C. bar, 1900; local counsel, Atlantic Coast Line R.R. Co., 1901-12, div. counsel, 1912-20, asst. gen. counsel, 1920-22, gen. solicitor 1922-49; mem: Davis & Davis, 1901-16, Rountree, Davis & Carr, 1916-17, Rountree & Davis, 1917-20, Davis & Poisson, 1928-30; mem. bd. of dirs. Tide Water Power Co. Served as sergt. maj. U.S. Vols., Spanish-Am. War; maj. J.A.G. Dept., U.S. Army, World War I; lt. col. O.R.C. Mem. Am. Bar Assn. (member gen. council, 1925-27, com. on commerce, 1926-27, 1931-34; executive committee 1928-30), N.C. State Bar (sec., treas., 1906-20; president 1920); Am. Inst. of Law, Am. Legion, N.C. Hist. Assn., State Lit. and Hist. Assn., N.C. Folk-Lore Soc. Democrat. Episcopalian. Clubs: Cape Fear, Cape Fear Country, L'Arioso German, Surf. Home: 1709 Market St. Office: Insurance Bldg.. Wilmington, N.C. Died Dec. 31, 1951.

DAVIS, Tom J. (Thomas Jefferson), former pres. Rotary Internat., lawyer; b. Weir City, Kan., Jan. 30, 1888; s. Richard H. and Margaret Jane (Duff) D.; LL.B., U. Mich., 1912; LL.D., Linfield Coll., McMinnville, Ore., Jamestown (N.D.) Coll.; m. Hester Christen, July 8, 1914; children—Hester Margaret Peggy, Thomas Jefferson, Shirley Virginia. Admitted to Mont. bar, 1912, since practiced in Butte; dir. recreation YMCA, in Spruce Prodn. Div., U.S. Army, 1918; acting prof. law U. Mont., 1923; dir. Work Projects Adminstrn., western Mont., 1936; mem. bd. Northwestern Mut. Fire Assn., Northwest Casualty Co., Tahoma Finance Co., Martin Agy., Seattle; mem. exec. bd. Mont. Sch. Mines. Joined Butte Rotary club, 1915, v.p., 1917-18, pres., 1920-21, dist. gov. Utah, Ida., Mont., 1921-22, v.p. 3d Internat., 1924-25, pres. Rotary Internat., 1941-42; del. to many Internat. convs.; speaker numerous dist. confs. Cons. to U.S. delegation (Rotary nominee) San Francisco Charter meeting, 1945; state chmn. U.S.O.; chmn. Salvation Army Adv. Bd., Butte; dir. Butte Boy Scout Council; acting indsl. sec. Internat. Com. of YMCA in relation to industries to Pacific Cosst; pres. Butte YMCA, Northwest Soc. Crippled Children, Mont. Soc. for Crippled Children; formerly v.p. Fgn. Mission Soc. of No. Bapt. Conv. Mem. Am., Mont. (past pres.), Silver Bow Co. (past pres.) bar assns., C. of C. (dir.), Phi Sigma Kappa, Alpha Kappa Psi (hon.). Mason (Shriner). Clubs: Rotary, Town, Country, Executives (past pres.). Home: 2700 Floral Blvd., Butte, Mont. Died Oct. 22, 1953; buried Butte.

DAVIS, William Church, army officer (ret.); b. nr. McGraw, N.Y., May 11, 1866; s. Samuel and Roxana (Brown) D.; ed. State Normal Sch., Cortland, N.Y., 1881-85; B.S., U.S. Mil. Acad., 1890; grad. U.S. Arty. Sch., 1894-96, U.S. Sch. Submarine Defense, 1903-04; m Margaret Turner Schenck, Sept. 9, 1896; children—Margaret Brown, William Schenck, Samuel. Commd. 2d lt. U.S. Army, 1890, advanced through grades to maj. gen., 1942; ret. 1921. Served in U.S. Army, U.S. Vols. and O.R.C., in P.I., Europe, and U.S.; prof. mil. science Colo. State Agr. Coll., 1896-97; depot Q.M., Baltimore, 1898-99; in charge of Army Transport Service, Manila, 1899-1900; in command, Forts Revere and Strong, Boston Harbor, 1908-09, Fort Rosecrans, San Diego, Calif., 1913-14, Fort Barrancas, Pensacola, Fla., 1915-17; general staff, 1910-11, 20-21; in command artillery brigades 31 and 32 Europe, 1918-19, Decorated: D.S.M.; Spanish War; Filipino Insurrection; Victory (with 3 clasps); cited, in order of comdg. gen. 5th U.S. Army Corps, for service in Meuse-Argonne, France, 918. Hon. mem. bd. of dirs.. A.R. C., Berkeley, Cal. Mem. Am. Legion, S.A.R. Republican. Home: 2440 Oregon St., Berkeley 5, Cal. Died Sept. 23, 1958; buried Presidio Cemetery, San Francisco.

DAVIS, William Francis, Jr., drugs; b. Arlington, Mass., Oct. 17, 1909; s. William Francis and Jessica (Golan) D.; B.S. Boston U., 1931, LL.B. cum laude, 1933, LL.D., 1950; m. Marion Livingston, Nov. 20, 1936 (dec.); children—William F., Scott L. Asso. Gaston, Snow, Saltonstall and Hunt, 1933-35; gen. counsel, Rexall Drug Co., 1936, vice pres., 1940, dir. since 1941. Senior partner, law firm of Adams, Duque, Davis & Hazeltine, Los Angeles, since January 1949. Trustee Massachusetts Memorial Hospital Member Beacon Soc., Delta Sigma Rho, Gamma Eta Gamma. Conglist. Clubs: Winchester Country, University, California. Home: 740 S. Amalfi Drive, Pacific Palisades, Calif. Office: 523 W. 6th St., Los Angeles. Died June 14, 1951; Newton (Mass.) Cemetery.

DAVIS, William Hersey, clergyman, educator; b. Norfolk County, Va., Jan. 20, 1887; s. Quinton Clarence and Sarah Elizabeth (Davis) D.; B.A. (Tanner Greek medalist), University Richmond, 1912, M.A., 1913, D.D., 1931; Th.M., So. Baptist Theological Seminary, Louisville, 1917, Th.D., 1919; research study, Berlin and Oxford, 1926-27; D.D. Furman University, 1929, Georgetown Coll., 1947, m. Mabel Lee Sewell, Sept. 26, 1912; 1 son, William Hersey. Ordained ministry Bapt. Ch., 1918; pastor First Ch., North Vernon, Ind., Deer Park Ch., Louisville, Finchville, Ky., until 1925; prof. N.T. interpretation So. Bapt. Theol. Sem., 1920-—, dir. Library, 1930-—. Mem. Am. Philol. Assn., Soc. Bibl. Lit. and Exegesis, Sigma Phi Epsilon and Phi Beta Kappa. Democrat. Clubs: The Quindecim, The Ten. Author: A Beginner's Grammar of the Greek New Testament, 1924. Co-author: A New Short Grammar of the Greek Testament (with A. T. Robertson), 1931; Greek Papyri of the First Century, 1933; A Source Book of Interbiblical History (with E. A. McDowell). Home: 1012 Cherokee Rd., Louisville. Died Sept. 5, 1950.

DAVIS, William Philip, corp. ofcl.; b. Moss Point, Miss., Nov. 30, 1897; s. Philip M. and Evelyn (Ikerd) D.; B.S., Miss. State Coll., 1918; m. May Herring, June 14, 1922; children—William Philip, Mrs. Adair D. Cannon. With Internat. Paper Co., southeastern states, 1919-42, charge paper converting operations, N.Y.C., 1943-49; pres., gen. mggr., dir. Potlatch Forests, Inc., Lewiston, Ida., 1949-—; pres. Twin Feather Mills, Inc. (Kamiah, Ida.), Wash., Ida. & Mont. R.R. Home: 629 10th St. Offie: Potlatch Forests, Inc., Lewiston, Ida. Died Mar. 18, 1958; buried Moss Point, Miss.

DAVISON, George Willets, banker; b. Rockville Centre, L.I., N.Y., Mar. 25, 1872; s. Robert A. and Emeline (Sealey) D.; Wilbraham Acad., Mass.; B.A., Wesleyan U., Conn, 1892; LL B., New York U., 1894; LL.D., Dickinson Coll., Carlisle, Pa., 1912; LL.D., Williams College, 1932, New York University, 1946; married Harriet R. Baldwin, April 24, 1895. Practiced law, 1894-1912; vice pres. Central Trust Company of New York, 1912-18; vice pres. Central Union Trust Co. of New York, 1918-19, pres., 1919; pres. The Hanover Bank, N.Y. City, 1929-33, chairman board, 1933-39, hon. chmn. since Jan 1939; dir. Fed. Reserve Bank of N.Y., 1933-38; chmn. bd. N.J., Ind. & Ill. R.R.; director N.Y. Clearing House Building Company, Fidelity & Casualty Company, Virginia Ry., Ann Arbor R.R., United Fruit Co., Union Carbide & Carbon Corp., Chrysler Corp., Continental Ins. Co. Asst. district attorney Queens County, N.Y., 1887-99, district attorney 1899; member and secretary commission to revise charter of Greater New York, 1900; chairman commission making study of banking laws of N.Y., 1929; chmn. advisory com. for N.Y. Loan Agency of RFC, Feb. 11, 1932-Apr. 17, 1933; mem. Fed. Advisory Council to represent 2d Fed. Reserve Dist., Jan., 1933-May, 1933; chmn. Clearing House Com., 1932-33; pres. N.Y. Clearing House Assn., 1933-35. Decorated Chevalier Legion of Honor (France), 1932. Mem. board trustees Wesleyan Univ. Mem. N.Y. State Bar Assn., Alpha Delta Phi, Phi Delta Phi, Beta Gamma Sigma, Phi Beta Kappa. Republican. Methodist. Clubs: University, Grolier. Home: Greenwich, Conn. Office: 70 Broadway, N.Y.C. 15. Died June 16, 1953.

DAVISON, Thomas Callahan, surgeon; b. Woodville, Ga., Nov. 13, 1883; s. Charles C. and Elizabeth (Callahan) D.; M.D., Emory U., Atlanta, 1906; m. Lucile Goodwin, Apr. 15, 1931; children—Betty, Margaret. Intern Ga. Bapt. Hosp., 1906-07; practiced Atlanta, 1907-—; chief surg. service, Grady Hosp., 1928-40, chief staff, cons., 1940-53; pres., founder, Sheffield Cancer Clinic, 1934, attending, cons. surgeon, 1937-—; chief staff, chief surg. service, Ga. Bapt. Hosp., 1940-—; asso. prof. clin. surgery, Emory U. Med. Sch. Served as col., U.S. Army M.C., World War I. Diplomate Am. Bd. Surgeons (mem. founders group), Am. Bd. Thoracic Surgery, Fellow A.C.S., Internat. Coll. Surgeons; mem. Fulton Co. Med. Soc. (pres. 1931), Med. Assn. Ga., So. Surgeons Assn., Southeastern Surgeons Congress (founder 1929; pres. 1939), A.M.A., Am. Goitre Assn. (pres. 1950), Am. Assn. Thoracic Surgeons, Am. Legion, Phi Chi. Club: Piedmont Driving. Contbr. over 100 articles to med. jours. Home: 25 Valley Rd. N.W. Office: 478 Peachtree St. N.E., Atlanta. Died Sept. 17, 1953; buried Westview Cemetery, Atlanta.

DAVISSON, Clinton Joseph, physicist; b. Bloomington, Ill., Oct. 22, 1881; s. Joseph and Mary (Calvert) D.; B.S., U. of Chicago, 1908; Ph.D., Princeton Univ., 1911; D.Sc. (hon.), Purdue Univ., 1937, Princeton, 1938; Dr. (hon.), Lyon, 1939, D.Sc. (hon.), Colby, 1940; m. Charlotte Sara Richardson Aug. 4, 1911; children—Clinton Owen Calvert, James Willans, Elizabeth Mary Dixon, Richard Joseph. Instr. in physics, Carnegie Inst. Tech., 1911-17; mem. tech. staff Bell Telephone labs. (formerly engineering dept. Western Electric Co.), 1917-46; visiting prof. of physics, U. of Va., 1947-49; member editorial board Physical Review. Mem. Nat. Research Council. Became hon. life mem. N.Y. Acad. Sciences, 1942. Fellow A.A.A.S. (chmn. sect. B 1933), Am. Phys. Soc., Optical Soc. America; mem. Nat. Acad. Scis., Am. Philos. Soc., Am. Acad. Arts and Scis., Franklin Inst., Am. Inst., Sigma Xi, Phi Beta Kappa. Awarded Comstock prize ($2,300), Nat. Acad. Sciences, 1928, for "most important research in electricity, magnetism and radiant energy made in N.A., during the past 5 years"; Elliot Cresson medal, 1931; Hughes medal, Royal Soc. London, 1935; Nobel prize for physics, 1937; Alumni medal U. of Chicago, 1941. Discoverer (with Dr. L. H. Germer) of diffraction of electrons by crystals, 1927. Republican. Contbr. on scientific subjects. Home: 2605 Jefferson Park Circle, Charlottesville, Va. Died Feb. 1, 1958.

DAWES, Beman Gates (dawz), ex-congressman; b. Marietta, O., Jan. 14, 1870; s. Gen. Rufus R. and Mary Beman (Gates) D.; bro. of Charles Gates, Rufus Cutler and Henry M. Dawes; student Marietta Acad. and Coll., 1886-90; m. Bertie Burr, Oct. 3, 1894. Mem. exec. com. Pure Oil Co., pres., 1914-—, bd. chmn., 1924-—; mem. 59th and 60th Congresses,

15th Ohio Dist. Founder of Dawes Arboretum, Licking County, O. Republican. Home: R.F.D., No. 5, Newark, O. Office: Pure Oil Co., Columbus, O. Died May 15, 1953.

DAWES, Charles Gates, former ambassador, ex-vice-pres. of U.S.; b. Marietta, O., Aug. 27, 1865; s. Gen. Rufus R. and Mary Beman (Gates) D.; A.B., Marietta Coll., 1884, A.M., 1887; LL.B., Cincinnati Law Sch., 1886; m. Caro D. Blymyer, Jan. 24, 1889; children—Rufus Fearing (deceased), Mrs. Carolyn Ericson, Dana McCutcheon, and Virginia (Mrs. Richard T. Cragg). Admitted to bar of state of Nebraska, 1886; in practice of law at Lincoln, Neb., 1887-94; interested in gas and electric business at various places. Was executive of McKinley movement in Ill., resulting in McKinley instructions at Springfield Conv., 1896; mem. exec. com. of Rep. Nat. Conv. in campaign of 1896; comptroller of the currency, 1897-1901; organized Central Trust Co. of Ill., Chicago, 1902, of which he was pres., 1902-21, chmn. bd., 1921-25, hon. chmn. bd., 1930-31; hon. chmn. bd. Central Republic Bank & Trust Co., 1931-32; chmn. bd. City Nat. Bank & Trust Co. since Oct. 6, 1932. Commd. maj. engrs., U.S. Army, June 1917; lt. col., July 1917; col., Jan. 1918; brig. gen., Oct. 1918. Arrived in France, July 1917, as lt. col. ry. engrs.; apptd. to administrative staff of comdr. in chief of A.E.F., Sept. 1917, and served as chmn. Gen. Purchasing Bd., and gen. purchasing agt. A.E.F.; later mem. Military Bd. of Allies Supply, mem. Liquidation Commn. of A.E.F. and mem. Liquidation Bd. of War Dept.; resigned from Army, 1919, and returned to U.S., Aug. 1919. Decorated D.S.M. (U.S.); Companion of the Bath (British); Comdr. of SS. Maurice and Lazarus (Italian); Order of Leopold (Belgium), 1919; Comdr. Légion d'Honneur (French), 1919. Apptd. 1st dir. U.S. Bur. of the Budget, 1921; apptd., 1923, by Reparations Commn., as pres. com. to investigate possibilities of German budget, resulting in the "Dawes Plan." which was put into effect Sept. 1, 1924; nominated by Rep. Nat. Conv. for vice-pres. of U.S., and elected Nov. 1924, for term 1925-29; A.E. and M.P. from U.S. to Great Britain, 1929-32; pres. Reconstruction Finance Corp. (controlling $2,000,000,000 of credits), 1932. Awarded the Nobel Peace prize for 1925 jointly with Sir Austen Chamberlain, British foreign secretary, and turned over his share of the prize to endowment of Walter Hines Page School of Internat. Relations. Chmn. Econ. Commn. of Am. Experts visiting Santo Domingo, 1929; chmn. finance com. "Chicago World's Fair 1933" since 1929. Clubs: Chicago, Commercial, Union League, University, Onwentsia, Glenview, Evanston Country. Author: The Banking System of the United States, 1892; Essays and Speeches, 1915; A Journal of the Great War, 1921; The First Year of the Budget of the United States, 1923; Notes as Vice-President, 1935; How Long Prosperity, 1937; A Journal of Reparations, 1939; Journal as Ambassador to Great Britain, 1939; A Journal of the McKinley Years, 1950. Home: 225 Greenwood Blvd., Evanston, Ill. Office: 208 South La Salle St., Chicago 4. Died Apr. 23, 1951.

DAWES, Henry May; b. Marietta, O., Apr. 22, 1877; s. Rufus R. and Mary Beman (Gates) D.; A.B., Marietta (Ohio) Coll., 1896, also LL.D. from same college; brother of Charles G., Rufus C. and Beman G. Dawes; m. Helen Curtis, Apr. 5, 1905; children—Curtis, Mary G. Schulz. Settled at Chicago, 1907. Formerly pres. Southwestern Gas & Electric Co., and v.p. Dawes Bros.; pres. Pure Oil Co., Dec. 1, 1924-47; chmn. exec. com. since April 1947; dir. City Nat. Bank & Trust Co., Pure Oil Co. Comptroller of the currency, by appointment of Presidents Harding and Coolidge, May 1, 1923-Dec. 1924 (resigned); mem. Federal Reserve Bd. Dir. Am. Petroleum Inst. (past v.p.); member Petroleum Industry War Council; mem. Chemical Warfare Service adv. bd., Nat. Petroleum Council. Mem. Delta Upsilon. Republican. Presbyterian. Clubs: University, Chicago, Economic, Glenview Golf (Chicago); Old Elm (Fort Sheridan, Ill.; Biltmore Forest Country (Biltmore, N.C.). Home: 101 Greenleaf St., Evanston, Ill. Office: 35 E. Wacker Drive, Chgo. 1. Died Sept. 29, 1952.

DAWES, James William, ex-gov. Neb.; b. McConnelsville, O., Jan. 8, 1845; s. Dr. Edward M. and Caroline (Dana) D.; acad. edn. Admitted to Wis. bar, 1871; located in Neb., 1871; mem. Neb. Constl. Conv., 1875; mem. Neb. Senate, 1877; chmn. State Central Com., 1876-82; mem. Rep. Nat. Com., 4 yrs.; del. Rep. Nat. Conv., 1880; gov. of Neb., 1883-87. Trustee Doane Coll., 1875. Address: Crete, Neb. Deceased.

DAWES, William Ruggles, banker; b. Ripon, Wis., Oct. 5, 1862; s. Hector and Jane (Ruggles) D.; A.B., Ripon Coll., 1884; m. Margaret Booker, 1885. With Spink Co. Bank, Redfield, S.D., 1884-89; sec. Lincoln Coal Co., Dawes Business Block Co., Lincoln, Neb., 1890-98; cashier Chicago Postoffice, 1898-1902; cashier Central Trust Co. of Ill., 1902-19, v.p., 1911-31; pres. North Side State Savings Bank, 1909-20; v.p. Mechanics & Traders State Bank, 1912-22; dir. Market Traders State Bank, 1923-25; dir. Addressograph-Multigraph Corp., 1926-46; pres. Miss. Valley Assn., 1928-31; pres. Chicago Regional Port Commn., 1930; pres. Central Ill. Securities Corp., 1932-35, chmn. of bd., 1935-39, pres., 1939-45; chmn. of the bd. since 1946. Trustee Ripon Coll. since 1907, chmn. bd., 1937-48. Mem. Chicago Assn. Commerce (pres. 1924-28); dir. Chamber of Commerce of U.S., 1930-36. Republican. Conglist. Clubs: University, Commercial. Home: 190 E. Pearson St. Office: 135 S. La Salle St., Chicago. Died Sept. 21, 1951.

DAY, Charles Ivan; b. Damariscotta, Me., Jan. 23, 1882; s. George Oliver and Charlotte M. (Hodgkins) D.; B.S., U. of Me., 1904; M.E. Cornell U., 1905; m. Isabelle Merry Chapman, Apr. 30, 1908; 1 son, Laurence Chapman. Lieut. U.S. Revenue Cutter Service, 1905-07; chief engr. Fla. East Coast Hotel Co., 1907-13; v.p. and gen. mgr. Southern Utilities Corp., Jacksonville, Fla., 1913-19; with W. & L. E. Gurley Co., mfrs. of Engring. and surveying instruments, since 1919, gen. mgr., now pres.; pres. Am. Tool & Machine Co. since 1928; dir. Troy Prudential Assn. Mem. Troy C. of C. (pres. 1932). Trustee of Russell Sage College, Samaritan Hosp.; treas. of Knickerbocker Playgrounds. Mem. Am. Soc. Mech. Engrs., Am. Soc. Civil Engrs., Alpha Tau Omega. Baptist. Mason. Clubs: Engineers (New York); Troy, Rotary, Country (Troy). Home: 7 Whitman Court. Office: 514 Fulton St., Troy, N.Y. Died June 22, 1950; buried Hillside Cemetery, Damariscotta, Me.

DAY, Edmund Ezra, University president emeritus; born at Manchester, New Hampshire, December 7, 1883; son of Ezra Alonzo and Louise Moulton (Nelson) D.; S.B., Dartmouth, 1905, A.M., 1906; Ph.D., Harvard, 1909; LL.D., U. of Vt., 1931, Syracuse U., U. of Pa., Dartmouth, Harvard, 1937; New York U., 1942; St. Lawrence U., U. of Cincinnati, 1943; Coll. of William and Mary, 1945; U. of North Carolina, Union Coll., U. of Buffalo, 1946, Princeton, 1947, U. of Mich., 1949; L.H.D., Hobart Coll., 1947; m. Emily Sophia Emerson, June 5, 1912; children—Emerson, Caroline Louise (Mrs. Frederick C. Copeland), Martha Elizabeth, David Allen. Instr. econs., Dartmouth, 1907-10; successively instr., asst. prof. and prof. economics, Harvard, 1910-23; with U. of Mich., 1923-28, prof. economics and dean Sch. of Business Adminstrn., 1923-27; on leave with Laura Spelman Rockefeller Memorial, 1927-28; with Rockefeller Foundation, 1928-37, as dir. for the social sciences; with Gen. Edn. Board, 1930-37, as dir. for gen. edn.; pres. Cornell University 1937-49, president emeritus since February 1950, chancellor, 1949-50; member Ednl. Policies Commn., 1937-45; president Assn. Land-Grant Colls. and Univs., 1942-43; pres. World Student Service Fund, 1945-46; class C dir. of Fed. Res. Bank of N.Y., 1938-42; dir. Nat. Bur. of Econ. Research, 1939-44; councillor Nat. Indsl. Conf. Bd. since 1939; chairman, American Council on Education, 1943; pres. New York State Citizens Council, 1948-49. Trustee Tuskegee Institute since 1939. Statistician, div. of planning and statistics, U.S. Shipping Bd., 7 mos., 1918-19, dir., same div., June-Aug. 1919; statistician central bur. of planning and statistics, War Industries Bd., Sept.-Dec. 1918; U.S. rep. on Preparatory Commn. of Experts for World Monetary and Economic Conf., 1932-33. Mem. Am. Econ. Assn., Am. Statis. Assn. (pres. 1927), Royal Econ. Soc. (British), Phi Beta Kappa, Theta Delta Chi. Conglist. Author: Index of Physical Production, 1920; Statistical Analysis, 1925; The Growth of Manufacturers (with W. Thomas), 1928; The Defense of Freedom, 1941. Home: Brook Haven, Highgate Rd., Ithaca, N.Y. Died March 23, 1951; buried Sage Chapel, Cornell U., Ithaca, N.Y.

DAY, Florence Roberts, educator, social work; b. Chgo., July 21, 1898; student Lake Erie Coll., 1916-18; A.B., U. Wis., 1920; M.S., Western Res. U., 1924. Dist. sec. Asso. Charities, Cleve., 1924-27; prof. social case work Western Res. U., 1927-43; prof., organizer grad. sch. applied social science U. Denver, 1931, dir. sch. for social work, Smith Coll., 1943-56, ret. Sec. Great Lakes region, Family Welfare Assn. Am., 1937-38; leader Family Welfare Assn. Am. Inst. in southern, western, middle Atlantic regions; leader inst. under auspices State Welfare Conf. in N.Y., Mich., Ill., O., Colo. Mem. Family Service Assn., Nat., Internat. confs. social work, Am. Assn. Social Workers, Alpha Phi. Presbyn. Home: 73 Woodlawn Av., Northampton, Mass. Died Aug. 15, 1957; buried Lake View Cemetery, Cleve.

DAY, Frank Parker, educator; b. Shubenacadie, N.S., Can., May 9, 1881; s. George Frederick and Keziah (Hardwick) D.; B.A., Mount Allison U., Sackville, N.B., 1903, LL.D., 1927; B.A., Oxford U., 1907, M.A., 1909; grad. study U. Berlin; Litt. D., N.Y. U., 1929; m Mabel Eliza Killam, 1910; 1 son, Donald Frank. Prof. English, U. N.B., 1909-12; prof. English, Carnegie Inst. Tech., 1912-14, dean of freshmen and dir., 1919-26; prof. English, Swarthmore, 1926-28; pres. Union Coll., Schenectady, 1929-1933. Served as maj., later lt. col. Canadian Inf., 1914-19. Clubs: Mohawk (Schenectady); Century (N.Y.C.); Twenty Club (Oxford). Author: River of Strangers (novel), 1926; Autobiography of a Fisherman, 1927; Rockbound, 1928; John Paul's Rock, 1930. Home: Lake Annis, N.S., Can. Died 1950; buried Yarmouth, N.S.

DAY, George Parmly, publisher; b. Sept. 4, 1876; s. Clarence Shepard and Lavinia Elizabeth (Stockwel) D.; A.B., Yale, 1897, hon. M.A., 1910; hon. M.A., Princeton, 1922; LL.D., Colgate U., 1933; LL.D., Lake Erie Coll., 1946; m. Wilhelmine Octavia Johnson, Oct. 11, 1902. An organizer Yale Pub. Assn., 1907; founder Yale U. Press, 1908, pres. and treas., 1908-44, now chmn. bd.; treas. Yale, 1910-42. Decorated Royal Order North Star, Knight, by King Gustav V., Sweden, 1939. Mem. Psi Upsilon, Scroll and Key (Yale). Republican. Episcopalian. Clubs: Yale, Century (N.Y.C.); Graduate, Elizabethan (New Haven). Home: 313 Saint Ronan St., New Haven 11. Office: Box 1729, New Haven. Died Oct. 1959.

DAY, Herbert James, newspaper pub.; b. Sioux Falls, S.D., Nov. 16, 1889; s. Charles M. and Annie L. (Davenport) D.; A.B., U. Mo., 1911; M.D., U. Minn., 1915; m Mary E. Bandy, June 3, 1916. Pres. Argus-Leader Co., Sioux Falls; dir. Cadkar, Inc. Home: 1129 Alta Vista Dr., South Vista, Cal. Office: Argus-Leader, Sioux Falls, S.D. Died Apr. 4, 1954.

DAY, William A., pres. Federal Reserve Bank of San Francisco. Address: Sansome and Sacramento Sts., San Francisco. Died May 26, 1951.*

DAYTON, John Havens, ret. naval officer; b. Rock Island, Ill., Feb. 3, 1869; s. Frederick Lord and Almira (Olds) D.; grad. U.S. Naval Acad., 1890; m. Nancy Maupin Reed, Apr. 14, 1896. Commd. ensign USN, 1892, advanced through grades to vice adm., 1928; served on Mangrove, Spanish-Am. War, 1898, Iowa, 1904-05; duty U.S. Naval Acad., 1905-08; navigator, Charleston, 1908-10; capt. of yard, Naval Sta., Cavite, P.I., 1910-11; duty Gen. Bd., Navy Dept., 1911; aide to Admiral of the Navy, 1911; comd. Naval Tng. Sta., Newport, R.I., 1911-13; comd. Saratoga, 1913-15; asst. to Bur. of Navigation, Navy Dept., 1915-16; apptd. comdr. receiving ship and Naval Training Sta., Norfolk, Va., 1916; comdg. Michigan, 1918, Arizona, 1918-20; comdt. Washington Navy Yard, 1920-23; comdr. spl. service squadron, 1923-25; comdt. Navy Yard, Mare Island, 1925-28; comdr. U.S. Naval Forces, Europe, 1928-29; retired, 1930. Clubs: Army and Navy, New York Yacht. Home: Jamestown, R.I. Died Sept. 7, 1953.

DAYTON, Lewis Seeley, newspaper editor; b. Marlboro, N.Y., Jan. 19, 1894; s. Eldorous and Katherine (Lyons) D.; grad. Kingston (N.Y.) Acad., 1912; m. Irene Estelle Rice, Mar. 15, 1920. Staff writer and editorial desk Yonkers (N.Y.) News, 1913-17; editorial desk Elizabeth (N.J.) Daily Jour., 1917-21, Newark Sunday Call, 1921-22; city editor, mng. editor Yonkers Statesman, 1923-24; editorial desk New York Evening Journal, 1924-25; staff and desk Asso. Press, N.Y.C., 1925-27; mng. editor Yonkers Herald-Statesman, 1925-35, editor, 1935-38, vice pres., 1938-45; pres. and mng. dir. Research Digest Assos., N.Y. C., 1945-48. Chief planning sect. Dept. of State (N.Y. Office), World War II. Dir. Boy Scouts Am.; mem. Charter Revision Commn. on Yonkers, Com. of 12 for Yonkers. Mem. N.Y. Soc. Newspaper Editors, Am. Soc. Newspaper Editors, Asso. Dailies of N.Y. State. Rotarian. Home: 10 The Crossway, Yonkers, N.Y. Died June 25, 1950.

DAYTON, Roy, business exec.; b. Tawas, Mich., Jan. 13, 1883; s. James Orson and Elizabeth Anna (Smith) D.; student North Tonawanda (N.Y.) High Sch., 1898-1901, Ithaca (N.Y.) Conservatory of Music, 1902-03; m. Florence Ethel Evans, Sept. 14, 1909; 1 dau., Eleanor Elizabeth. Reporter, Rochester (N.Y.) Times, 1905, city editor, 1906; editor, Daily News (North Tonawanda, N.Y.), 1906-08; newswriter and contbr. to periodicals, 1909-15, sec., Trudeau Sch. Tuberculosis, and Edward L. Trudeau Foundation, 1916—; asst. sec., bd. of trustees, Trudeau Sanitoirum, 1936—. Controller, Trudeau Found., 1947-49; registrar Trudeau Sch. Tuberculosis. Mem. bd. of trustees, and sec., Saranac Lab. for Study of Tuberculosis, bd. of dirs., Saranac Lake Study and Craft Guild. Republican. Elk. Clubs: Osler Saranac Lake (pres., 1932-34). Home: 7 Academy St. Office: 6 Church St., Saranac Lake, N.Y. Died Dec. 25, 1955.

DAYTON, William A(dams), forest ecologist; b. N.Y.C., Dec. 14, 1885; s. William Adams (M.D.) and Emma (Samson) D.; grad. Irving Inst. (now Irving Sch. for Boys), Tarrytown, N.Y., 1901; B.A., Williams Coll., 1905, M.A., 1908; corr. courses, U. Chgo.; student U.S. Dept. Agr. Postgrad. Sch.; m. Helen Rollins, Aug. 18, 1918; children—William Adams, 3d, Elva Samson (Mrs. Merrill F. Aukland), Orlo Hazen. Variously employed as teacher, clerk, farmer, stenographer to 1906; Office of 2d Asst. Postmaster Gen., Washington, 1906-10; with U.S Forest Service, 1910-55, beginning as plant ecologist, in charge range forage investigations, 1911-55, principal dendrologist, 1942-55, retired, now adviser. Rep. U.S. Dept. Agr. on Editorial Com. on Standardized Plant Names, 1939; chmn. tree name com. U.S. Forest Service; del. to Internat. Union Protection of Nature, Lake Success, N.Y., 1949; del. 7th International Bot. Congress, Stockholm, 1950; sec., chmn. 6th Internat. Grassland Congress, State Coll., Pa., 1952; mem. com. of Fullbright fellowships NRC, 1949-51. Recipient gold medal by Mass. Hort. Soc., 1940; distinguished service gold medal, U.S. Dept. Agr.,

1955. Fellow A.A.A.S. (mem. of council 1945); mem. Am. Forestry Assn., Am. Genetic Assn., Am. Fern Soc., Internat. Assn. Plant Taxonomy, Am. Nature Assn., Am. Soc. Plant Taxonomists, Biol. Soc. Washington, Bot. Soc. Am., Bot. Soc. Washington, Cal. Bot Soc., Ecol. Soc. Am. (charter mem.; rep. on bd. govs. Am. Inst. Biol. Sci., 1948-58), Internat. Dendrology Union, Am. Soc. Range Mgt., N.E. Bot. Club, Soc. Am. Foresters (sec.-treas. Wash. sect. 1933-36; chmn. 1940-41), So. Appalachian Bot. Club, So. Cal. Acad. Sciences, Wildlife Soc. (charter mem.), Torrey Botanical Club, Washington Acad. Sci. (v.p. 1938-52). Baptist. Club: Cosmos (Washington). Author: Notes On National Forest Range Plants, Part I, Grasses (with W. R. Chapline), 1914; Important Western Browse Plants, 1931; Range Plant Handbook (with others), 1937; Rev. Edition of Standardized Plant Names (with H. P. Kelsey and others), 1942; The Forests of Costa Rica (with others), 1943. Contbr. articles to jours. and bulletins. Home: 4818 24th St. N., Arlington, Va. Died Oct. 20, 1958; buried Nat. Meml. Park.

DEAL, Herbert L., telephone executive; b. Kent, Mich., Oct. 9, 1906; s. Clarence E. and Estella May (Mac Diarmid) D.; A.B., U. Ore., 1928; m. Kathryn Kirk, Oct. 12, 1929; 1 dau., Barbara L. With Bell Telephone Co. of Nev., 1951-53, v.p., dir., 1953; v.p., gen. mgr., Pacific Tel. & Tel. Co., 1951-53; asst. v.p. Am. Tel. & Tel. Co., 1953—. Mem. Phi Beta Kappa, Sigma Alpha Epsilon. Home: Countryside Dr., Summit, N.J. Died May 11, 1955.

DEAN, Arthur Lyman, ex-coll. pres., corp. exec.; b. Southwick, Mass., Oct. 1, 1878; s. William Kendrick and Nellie May (Rogers) D.; A.B., Harvard, 1900; Ph.D., Yale, 1902; m. Leora Elvena Parmlee, Aug. 11, 1904; children—Sylvia, Lyman Arnold, Pierson Goddard. Asst. instr., Sheffield Sci. Sch. (Yale), 1902-03; instr. plant physiology, Yale, 1903-07, instr. indsl. chemistry, 1908-09, asst. prof., 1909-14; with A.D. Little, chemist and engr., Boston, 1907-08; pres. U. Hawaii, 1914-27; dir. Experiment Sta. of Assn. of Hawaiian Pineapple Canners; pres. Alexander and Baldwin Co. Research asst. Carnegie Instn., 1904-05; chief, sec. of wood chemistry U.S Forestry Service, 1905-07. Mem. A.A.A.S., Am. Chem. Soc., Sigma Xi, Kappa Gamma Chi, Phi Sigma Kappa. Republican. Club: University (Honolulu). Developed process for refinement chaumoogra oil for use in treatment leprosy. Home: Honolulu, Hawaii. Died June 1952.

DEAN, Ben, former pres. Kiwanis International; formerly city editor Grand Rapids (Mich.) Herald; now engaged in advt. business. Past pres. Kiwanis Internat., elected 1944. Mem. exec. com. Grand Rapids C. of C.; past pres. East Grand Rapids, Bd. of Edn.; former chmn. Grand Rapids chpt. A.R.C. Baptist. Author of book on furniture styles; contbr. to mags. Home: 559 Locust St. S.E., Grand Rapids 6, Mich. Died Jan. 21, 1956; buried Rosedale Meml. Park, Grand Rapids.

DEAN, Gordon Evans, investment banker; b. Seattle Dec. 28, 1905; s. John Marvin and Beatrice Alice (Fisken) D.; A.B., U. of Redlands, Calif., 1927, LL.D., 1950; J.D., U. of So. Calif., 1930; LL.M., Duke U. Law Sch., Durham, N.C., 1932; m. Adelaide Williamson, Aug. 9, 1930 (div.); children—Martha, Franklin Evans; married 2d, Mary Benton Gore, December 19, 1953; children—Deborah, and Gordon Gore. Law clerk Meserve, Mumper, Hughs and Robertson, Los Angeles, 1927-28; admitted to Calif. bar, 1930, N.C. bar, 1931, U.S. Supreme Court, 1935; instr. in law and asst. to dean of Law Sch., Duke U., 1930-34; spl. atty. criminal div., U.S. Dept. of Justice, 1934-36, chief sect. of criminal appeals, 1936-37; spl. exec. asst. to U.S. atty. gen. in charge all public relations, 1937-39 and Jan. to June, 1940; special asst. to U.S. atty. gen. in anti-trust litigation, 1939; partner McMahon, Dean & Gallagher, Washington, D.C., June 1940-May 1945. Officer, U.S. N.R., 1943-45. Asst. to Justice Robert H. Jackson in trial of leading Nazi war criminals, Nuremberg, Germany, May 1945-February 1946. Prof. criminal law U. of So. Calif. Law Sch., 1946-49; apptd. mem. A.E.C., May 1949, chmn., 1950-53; mem. Lehman Bros., investment bankers, N.Y.C., since 1953; chmn. bd. Nuclear Science and Engineering Corporation; sr. v.p., dir. Gen. Dynamics Corp., 1955—; dir. Fruehauf Trailer Co., Callahan Zinc-Lead Co. (N.Y.C.). Mem. Com. to Draft Rules of Criminal Procedure for U.S. Cts., 1941; mem. Western States Loyalty Board, 1949—. Decorated Medal of Freedom, 1946, Commander Order of Leopold, 1954. Member American Bar Association, Kappa Sigma Sigma, Phi Delta Phi, Pi Kappa Delta, Order of Co'f. Democrat. Baptist. Clubs: Burning Tree Country, Cosmos (Washington); University (N.Y.C.). Author: Report on the Atom, 1953. Contbr. jours. Office: 1 William St., N.Y.C. Died Aug. 15, 1958.

DEAN, Howard B., aviation exec.; b. N.Y.C., Feb. 28, 1897; s. Herbert H. and Marion (Brush) D.; grad. Taft Sch., 1915; Ph.B., Yale, 1918; m. Maria Cook, Apr. 10, 1920; children—Howard B., Marianne, Nancy. Mem. bond dept. Guaranty Trust Co. N.Y.C., 1919-21; partner Struthers & Dean, 1921-42; v.p., dir. Pan Am. Airways, also Pan Am. Grace Airways, 1943—. Gov. Assn. Stock Exchange Firms, 1934-42; gov. N.Y. Stock Exchange, 1937-42. Served as 1st lt. F.A., U.S. Army, 1918. Clubs: Union, Cloud, Links, St. Atnhony, Nat. Golf Links Am., Maidstone (East Hampton, L.I.). Home: 400 Park Av., N.Y.C. Office: 135 E. 42d St., N.Y.C. Died Mar. 21, 1950; buried Sag Harbor, L.I., N.Y.

DEAN, Richard Doggett, educator, engr.; b. Nesbitt, Miss., Sept. 10, 1884; s. Thomas Jefferson and Eliza Francis (Doggett) D.; student Randall U. Sch., Hernando, Miss., 1900-04; B.S., Miss. State, 1908, post grad. in elec. engring., 1909; D.D.S., U. of Tenn., 1922, M.D., 1931; m. Marguerite Gladys Taylor, Sept. 5, 1914. Inspector Municipal Elec. Testing Labs., Seattle, 1909-12; dir., 1912-18; active practice dentistry, Memphis, 1922-24, student instr. U. of Tenn. Coll. Dentistry, 1922, prof. applied dental physics, metall. and materials, 1922-24, prof. surgery and pathol., chief div. oral medicine and surgery since 1924, dean Coll. of Dentistry since 1941. Served in S.A.T.C., U.S. Army, 1918. Expert cons. Army Service Forces, 1944. Assos. and alumni of Univ. of Tenn. presented to U. of Tenn. the likenesses of Dr. Dean and of his wife, Dr. Marguerite Dean, done in oils, which are hanging on the walls of new dental bldg., 1948; colleagues founded the Richard Doggett Dean and Marguerite Taylor Dean hon. Odontol. Soc., Dec. 6, 1948. Mem. Am., Tenn. dental assns., Internat. Assn. Dental Research, Ninth Dist. Dental Soc., Omicron Kappa Epsilon, Alpha Omega Alpha, Delta Sigma Delta. Research and investigation (with wife) in physical properties of dental materials, bacteriol., serol. and immunogenic studies on Vincent's Infection, bacteriophage as a therapeutic measure in treatment of dental pulps, etc. Contbr. articles to profl., sci. jours. Home: R. 1, Box 39, Lake Cormorant, Miss. Office: 847 Monroe Av., Coll. of Dentistry, University of Tenn., Memphis 3. Died Aug. 29, 1950.

DEAR, J(oseph) Albert, newspaperman; b. Jersey City, Jan. 16, 1899; s. Joseph Albert and Julia A. (Reid) D.; student Stevens Prep. Sch., Princeton; Ph.B., U. Chgo., 1919; m. Mary W. Eddy, 1921 (dec. 1923); 1 son, Joseph Albert IV; m. 2d, Ella Cyrene Bakke, 1926; children— David R., Ralph C., Bryan B. (dec.), Walter M. II. Advt. solicitor, reporter Chgo. Daily News, 1919; reporter Omaha Daily News, Omaha World-Herald, 1920; reporter, circulation mgr., editor Jersey Jour., Jersey City, 1921-51; pres. Dear Publication & Radio, Inc., Jersey City, 1946—. Served as 2d lt. inf. U.S. Army, World War I. Presbyn. Home: 88 Bentley Av., Jersey City 4. Office: 40 Journal Sq., Jersey City 6. Died Sept. 19, 1959; buried Valleau Cemetery, Ridgewood, N.J.

DEARBORN, Walter Fenno, educator; b. Marblehead, Mass., July 19, 1878; s. Josiah Weare and Martha Mehitable (Dinsmore) D.; A.B., Wesleyan U., Conn., 1900, A.M., 1903; Ph.D., Columbia, 1905; studied univs. of Gottingen, Heidelberg and Munich; M.D., Munich, 1913; A.M., Harvoard, 1941; m. Ellen Kedean, Sept. 24, 1917; children—Elaine, Natalie. Instr. asst. prof. edn. U. Wis., 1905-09; asso. prof. edn. U. Chgo., 1909-12; asst. prof. Harvard, 1912-17, prof., 1917-47, emeritus prof., 1947—; prof. psychology and edn. and dir. psycho-ednl. clinic Lesley Coll., 1947—. Trustee Mass. State Infirmary, 1913-32, Walter E. Fernald State Sch., 1942—; dir. Psycho-Ednl. Clinic. Fellow Am. Acad. Arts and Sciences; Asso. Fellow Mass. Med. Society, 1943; hon. mem. Hungarian Soc. of Edn.; mem. Phi Beta Kappa, Phi Nu Theta, Sigma Xi. Author: (monograph) Psychology of Reading, 1906; Dearborn Group Tests of Intelligence, 1920; Intelligence Tests—Their Significance for School and Society, 1928; Growth of Public School Children, 1938. Co-author: Predicting the Child's Development, 1941; Reading and Visual Fatigue, 1947. Home: 79 Fresh Pond Parkway, Cambridge 38, Mass. Died June 21, 1955.

DEARDORFF, Neva Ruth (dĕr'dorf), social worker; b. Hagerstown, Ind., Feb. 11, 1887; d. Daniel W. and Sarah Elizabeth (Teetor) Deardorff; A.B., U. Mich., 1908, M.A. (hon.), 1933; Ph.D., U. Pa., 1911. With Bur. Municipal Research, Phila., 1912-14, chief of div. vital statistics Bur. Health, Phila., 1914-16; asst. dir. Phila. Bur. of Municipal Research, 1916-18; nat. hdqrs. staff A.R.C., 1918-21; asso. prof. social economy, grad. sch. Bryn Mawr Coll., 1921-24; asso. editor The Survey, 1922-24; exec. sec. children's Commn. of Pa., 1924-27; dir. Research Bureau, Welfare Council of New York, 1927-38, 41-46; asst. exec. dir. Welfare Council, 1940-46; dir. of statistics and research Health Insurance Plan of Greater N.Y., 1946-57; non-resident lectr. U. Chgo., 1935-38. President Child Welfare League of America, 1925-27; mem. exec. com. Nat. Conf. Social Work, 1926-29, 3d v.p., 1947-48; trustee White Williams Found., 1921-29; chmn. city planning com. Citizens Union; chmn. N.Y.C. Com. on Fed. Censuses; mem. bd. dirs. Citizens' Com. on Children, Health Ins. Plan of Greater New York. Mem. Research Com., Am. Statis. Assn. (v.p. 1940), Phi Beta Kappa. Mem. Congl. Christian Ch. Mem. Engring. Woman's Club. Author: English Trade to the Baltic During the Reign of Elizabeth, 1911; Child Welfare Conditions and Resources in Seven Pennsylvania Counties, 1927; co-author, The Hospital Discharge Study, 1942-43. Contbr. to social science and social welfare periodicals. Home: 52 Gramercy Park. Office: Health Insurance Plan of Greater New York, 425 Av. of the Americas, N.Y.C. Died Aug. 21, 1958; buried Hagerstown, Ind.

DEARING, William Prentice, educator; b. Pike County, Ind., Sept. 30, 1874; s. John Bizzrel Thomas and Bettie Ann (Selby) D.; A.B., Oakland City (Ind.) Coll., 1894, theol. dept. same, 2 yrs.; U. Chgo., 1 yr.; LL.D., Franklin (Ind.) Coll., 1921; D.D., No. Bapt. Theol. Sem., Chgo., 1930, Hillsdale (Mich.) College, 1936; LL.D., Oakland City College, 1945; m. May Cockrum, Jan. 1, 1896 (died June 8, 1943); children—Mazo, William Cockrum; m. 2d, Mary M. Murray, Oct. 12, 1944. Dean Oakland City College, 1895-1903, pres., 1903-46, pres. emeritus, 1946—. Ordained to ministry Bapt. Ch. at 19; lectr. before tchrs.' insts.; widely known as chautauqua and commencement speaker. Past pres. State Library and Hist. Bd.; pres. Ind. State Tchrs. Assn., 1925-26; v.p. State Schoolmen's Club. Republican. Kiwanian. Home: 1400 S. Washington, Kokomo, Ind. Died Dec. 15, 1958.

DEASY, John Francis (dézĭ), ry. ofcl.; b. Hammorton, Pa., Mar. 25, 1882; s. Daniel J. and Mary (Ford) D.; student Phila. Textile Sch., Brown Prep. Sch.; law study, 4 yrs.; m. Lillian C. Kershaw, June 29, 1912; children—Nelson Scott (dec.), John Kershaw. Began as telegraph operator with Pa. R.R., 1901, clk. and operator, 1903-05, clerical work, yards and stas., 1905-07, acting extra agt., Amboy div., 1908-10, acting terminal and shipping agt., Amboy div., 1910-12, extra and supervising agt., Trenton div., 1912-17, asst. freight claim agt., 1917-18, supt. stas. and transfers lines E. of Pitts., 1918-20, asst. chief freight transportation, 1920-27, chief, 1927-28, asst. v.p. of operation, 1928-31, regional v.p., central region, 1931-33, v.p. in charge operation, 1933-47, v.p., asst. to pres., 1947—. Republican. Presbyn. Mason. Clubs: Duquesne (Pitts.); Union League (Phila.); Merion Golf (Haverford, Pa.); Rolling Rock (Ligonier, Pa.). Home: Rosemont, Pa. Office: Broad St. Station Bldg., Phila. Died Dec. 28, 1953.

DeBARDELEBEN, Henry Ticknor, coal mining; b. Prattville, Ala., Jan. 2, 1874; s. Henry Fairchild and Ellen (Pratt) D.; B.A., Ala. Poly. Inst., 1892; grad. Eastman Bus. Coll., Poughkeepsie, N.Y., 1892; m. Lulie Thomas, Apr. 1896 (died 1910); m. 2d, Donie Drane, Apr. 1911. Supt. Alice Furnace div.of Tenn. Coal, Iron & R.R. Co., 1894-95, Watts Iron & Steel Syndicate, 1895-96, Gracie-Woodward Iron Co., 1896, Woodward Iron Co., 1897-98, Red River Furnace Co., 1899-1904; mgr. Bon Air Coal & Iron Co., 1904-07; v.p., gen. mgr. Woodstock Iron & Steel Corp., 1907-09; pres. Russelville Iron Ore & Metal Co., 1909-10; v.p. Ala. Fuel & Iron Co., Birmingham, 1909—; pres. De Bardeleben Coal Corp., 1923-47, chmn. bd., 1947; v.p. Ala. Fuel & Iron Co., Nat. Coal Assn.; dir. Ala. Coals, Inc. Apptd. July 1918, by U.S. R.R. Adminstrn. as mgr. Warrior River Sect., Miss.-Warrior River Service, continued as mgr. under War Dept. until 1922. Adviser Solid Fuels Adminstrn. for War, 1942-47. Mem. Kappa Alpha. Republican. Episcopalian. Home: 1929 21st Av. S. Office: 1007 Southern Ry. Bldg., Birmingham, Ala. Died Nov. 2, 1948.*

de BEAUMONT, Guerin Jean Michel du Boscq (gîrĕn de bō-mōn), diplomat; b. Airel (Manche), France, Aug. 29, 1896; s. Gaston du Boscq and Cecile (Chevalier) de B.; B.L., St. Louis de Gonzague, Paris, 1906, B.A., 1913; Licencie es Lettres (M.A.) Sorbonne, Paris, 1915; Licencie en droit (M.L.) Faculté de Droit de Paris, 1921. Attaché to Rhineland Commn., 1919; avocat a la Cour de Paris (barrister at law at the Paris bar), 1924; sec. at Conf. of Barrister, 1925-26; sec. Free French Delegation in Washington, 1942; agent gen., N.Y.C., of the French Com. of Nat. Liberation, 1943; consul gen. of France, 1945—; Minister Plentipotentiary in charge of Consulate Gen., 1946—. Municipal Counsellor of Airel, Manche (France). Served as ensign French Navy, 1917-19; lt. (j.g.), 1939-40; lt. (s.g.), Free French Navy, 1942. Decorated Cooix de Guerre, Chevalier Legion of Honor, Medal of the French Resistance (France). Club: Knickerbocker. Home: 34 rue de Lubeck, Paris. Office: French Ministry of Foreign Affairs. Died Oct. 13, 1955.

DEBEVOISE, Thomas (McElrath) (dĕ-bĕ-vwois'), lawyer; b. N.Y. City, Apr. 2, 1874; s. George W. and Katherine Price (McElrath) D.; A.B., Yale, 1895; LL.B., N.Y. Law Sch., 1897; m. Anne Farnam Whitney, Dec. 6, 1898; children—Eli Whitney, Katherine Price. Admitted to N.Y. bar, 1897, and began practice at N.Y.C. Mem. N.Y. State Bar Assn., Bar City N.Y., Alpha Delta Phi. Republican. Episcopalian. Clubs: Yale, University, Century, Union, Rockefeller Center Lunch (New York); Morristown, Morris County Golf. Home: Green Village, N.J. Office: 30 Rockefeller Plaza, N.Y.C. Died Dec. 20, 1958.

DeBISSCHOP, Frank J., mfr.; b. Bayonne City, N.J., Jan. 12, 1879; s. Andrew and Quilimina (Lamal) DeB.; student pub. schs., Southington, Conn.; m. Ida Mae Spender, Aug. 7, 1901; 1 dau., Lois (dec.).

Foreman Waterbury Clock Co., 1900-04, B & B Co., 1904-08; supt. Rome Brass & Copper Co., 1908-09; pres., central mgr., Rome Hollow Wire & Tube Co., 1909-24; pres. United Wire & Supply Corp., Providence, 1925—. Dir. A.R.C.; dir., trustee YMCA. Clubs: Aero, Navy League. Home: 296 Oaklawn Av., Cranston 9, R.I. Office: 1497 Elmwood Av., Providence 7. Died Mar. 7, 1955.

DeBOARD, Elmer H., railway exec.; b. Norris City, Ill., Nov. 30, 1892; s. Benjamin Franklin and Mary Elizabeth (DeLapp) DeB.; student LaSalle Extension U.; m. Mae Booth, Oct. 29, 1913; children—Elmer B., Gordon A., Jacob M., Richard E. Clk., agt. B. & O. R.R., 1913-16. with gen. traffic office, Cin., 1916-20; traffic mgr. Chevrolet Motor Co,. Atlanta, 1920-21; clk. Det., Tol. & Ironton R.R., 1921-23, chief clk., 1923-24, gen. freight agt., 1925-30, traffic mgr., 1930-47, v.p. traffic since 1947. Republican. Presbyn. Mason (Shriner). Clubs: Traffic, Grosse Ile Golf and Country, Recess. Home: 45 Massachusetts, Highland Park, Mich. Office: 4921 Calhoun, Dearborn, Mich. Died July 8, 1953; buried Acacia Park, Birmingham, Mich.

De BOST, William Ludlam (dĕ-bō); b. N.Y.C., Apr. 24, 1870. Chmn. Union Dime Savings Bank, N.Y.C.; dir. Met. Life Ins. Co., Home Ins. Co., Cruikshank Co., N.Y. Telephone Co., Bankers Trust Co., Cobel Royalties, Inc. Trustee Grant Monument Assn. Former pres. Sailors Snug Harbor, C. of C. State of N.Y. Clubs: Down Town Assn., Union, Metropolitan, Union League, Long Island Country. Home: 155 E. 72d St. Office: Av. of the Americas and 40th St., N.Y.C. Died Jan. 18, 1951; buried Woodlawn Cemetery, N.Y.C.

DeBUYS, Laurence Richard (de-boo-ez'), pediatrician; b. New Orleans, Nov. 12, 1878; s. James and Stella (Rathbone) DeB.; B.S., Tulane U., 1899, M.D., 1904; post grad. work in pediatrics Harvard, 1907, 08; clinics in Germany, Austria, England, France; m. Miriam Duggan, June 14, 1904; children—Laurence Richard, William Eno, Herbert Fowler, John Forester, Henry Duggan. Intern Charity Hosp., 1902-04; practiced medicine, Houma, La., 1904-07, New Orleans, 1907—, practice limited to pediatrics 1910—; hchief of clinic, dept. of gynecology and obstetrics and clin. asst., dept. of pediatrics Tulane U., 1907-08, asso. prof. pediatrics, 1912-17, clin. prof., 1917-19, asst. prof. pediatrics post grad. sch. medicine, 1912-17, prof. of pediatrics, 1919-29; chief pediatric staff New Orleans Presbyn. Hosp., 1910-11; vis. pediatrist Charity Hosp. of La., 1907-22, chief of staff in pediatrics, 1919-22; mem. staff Touro Infirmary 1910—, chief of pediatric dept., 1919-39, cons. pediatrician, 1939—, chmn. exec. com. med. staff, 1937-38, prof. pediatrics nurses Tng. Sch., 1924-34; physician in charge Jewish Childrens Home, 1925-36, Isadore Newman Sch., 1925-36; cons. pediatrics U S. Marine Hosp., 1931-34; chmn. pediatric div. Emergency Med. Service, OCD, 1942; sec. La. State Com. on Nat. Defense Med. Sect., and mem. Vol. Med. Service Corps, World War I. Mem. White House Conf. on Child Health, 1929; mem. follow-up com., 1929-31. Mem. Court of Honor, Boy Scouts Am., 1918-21. Diplomate Am. Bd. Pediatrics. Fellow A.C.P. (bd. govs. 1925-26), Am. Acad. Pediatrics (emeritus); mem. La. Pediatric Soc. (organizer and pres. 1924-28), So. Med. Assn. (hon.) (chmn. pediatrics sect. 1925), A.M.A. (hon., chmn. sect. diseases of children 1917-18), Assn. Am. Med. Colls., Am. Child Health Assn. (charter mem.; mem. bd. dirs. 1923-29), Abraham Jacoby Mem. Fund of A. M.A. (an organizer, chmn. com. 1923-24), Archivos Americanos de Medicina (corr. editor), Pan. Am. Med. Assn. (v.p. pediatrics sect. 1933), Orleans Parish Med. Soc. (hon.) (v.p. 1911-14), La. Med. Soc. (hon.) (sec. 1912-15; sec.-treas. 1915-19; chmn. many coms.), Assn. Am. Tchrs. of Diseases of Children (pres. 1916-17). Milk Commn. New Orleans Pure Milk Society (pres. 1931-35). Child Welfare Association, Alumni Assn. Tulane U. (member executive committee 1913-15),American Assn. Med Milk Commrs. (councillor 1918-23; pres. 1919-20), Assn. for Study of Internal Secretions (councillor 1916-31), Am. Child Health Assn. (emeritus), Am. Pediatric Soc. (v.p. 1930-31; now emeritus), Assn. Study Internal Secretions (life); hon. mem. Dallas So. Clin. Soc., Tri-State Dist. Med. Assn., Lafourche Valley Med. Soc.; Alpha Omega Alpha, Alpha Tau Omega, Theta Nu Epsilon, Phi Chi Med. Fraternity (charter mem.). Del. to Conf. on Maternity and Child Welfare, London, 1928; 2d Internat. Pediatric Congress, Stockholm, 1930, Rome, 1936; Internat. Hygiene Congress, Germany, 1930. Mem. bd. dirs. New Orleans Golf Assn., 1933—, v.p., 1939-40, pres., 1941-42, 42-43 (one of 3 hon. life members). Democrat. Roman Catholic. Clubs: New Orleans Country (chmn. tournament com. 1935) La Kennel (pres. 1943-1944). Contributor chpts. Abt's Pediatrics, Feer's Pediatrics. Member editorial board American Journal Diseases of Children, 1926-39; mem. cons. staff Archives of Pediatrics, 1919-26; collaboratorAmerican Jour. of Syphilis, 1916-23. Contbr. numerous articles to med. jours. Pioneer in use of motion pictures in medicine, demonstrating peristaltic waves by motion pictures, 1913. Address: 1417 Delachaise St., New Orleans. Died June 20, 1957; buried Metaire Cemetery, New Orleans.

DE CAMP, John A., supt. schools; b. Tuscarora, N.Y., Jan. 20, 1872; s. Charles and Eliza (Northway) D.; grad. State Normal and Training Sch., Geneseo, N.Y., 1891; A.B., Williams Coll., 1900, M.A., 1906; Pd.D. (hon.), Hamilton Coll., Clinton, N.Y., 1936; m. Sara W. Sears, Aug. 18, 1910; children—Hilda, John A. Teacher and prin. schs., N.Y. and Mass., 1899-1910; supt. pub. schs., Little Falls, N.Y., 1910-17, Utica, N.Y., 1917—. Presbyterian. Home: 115 Clinton Pl. Office: 13 Elizabeth St., Utica, N.Y. Died Mar. 3, 1953; buried Williamstown, Mass.

DECKER, Alonzo Galloway, mfg. exec.; b. Balt., Jan. 16, 1884; s. Alonzo and Mary (Galloway) D.; ed. pub. school; m. Fanny Dugan Fox 1907; children—Alonzo Galloway, Jane Travers (Mrs. Carl-Heinrich Asmis), Virginia Lamdin. With S. Duncan Black founded Black & Decker Mfg. Co., electric tools and motors, Towson, Md., 1910, now pres.; dir., chmn. exec. com., pres. Indsl. Corp. Balt.; pres., dir. Black & Decker Mfg. Co., Ltd., Can.; dir. Md. Trust Co. Pres. and dir. Hosp. for Consumptives of Md. Home: Stevenson Lane, Towson 4, Md. Office: Towson 4, Md. Died Mar. 18, 1956.

DECKER, Charles Elijah, prof. paleontology; b. Dixon, Ill., Sept. 27, 1868; s. Henry and Emogene (Bunnell) D.; A.B., Northwestern U., 1906; A.M., U. Chgo., 1908, Ph.D., 1917; hon. D.Sc., Oklahoma City U., 1935; m. Gertrude Monlux, May 31, 1900 (died Jan. 31, 1954); m. 2d, Mrs. Ethelyn Wolfard, Sept. 30, 1955. Tchr. Allegheny Coll., 1909-16; instr. in geology U. Okla., 1916-17, asst. prof., 1917-19, asso. prof., 1919-25, prof. paleontology, 1925-43, research prof. emeritus of paleontology, 1943—; also taught geology, summers, U. Ill., Cornell U., Colo. State Tchrs. Coll., and 1 semester Northwestern U. Mem. Silurian Com. NRC. Fellow A.A.A.S., Geol. Soc. Am., Paleontol. Soc., Okla. Acad. Science (pres. 1 yr.); mem. Soc. Economic Paleontology and Mineralogy, Sigma Gamma Epsilon (nat. sec. 6 yrs., nat. pres. 8 yrs.), Sigma Xi; hon. mem. Am. Assn. Petroleum Geologists (sec.-treas. 7 yrs.), Alpha of Omega chpt. Phi Beta Kappa, 1927. Author: Minor Folds, 1920; Lists of Characteristic Fossils, 1925; Physical Characteristics of the Arbuckle Limestone (with C. A. Merritt), 1928; Stratigraphy and Physical Characteristics of the Simpson Group (with C. A. Merritt and R. W. Harris), 1931; Two Lower Paleozoic Groups, Okla., 1939; Timbered Hills and Arbuckle Groups, Arbuckle and Wichita Mountains, Okla., 1939; Stratigraphic significance of graptolites of Athens shale, 1952; Upper Cambrian graptolites from Virginia and Tennessee (with I. B. Gold), 1958; What higher magnification is doing for the study of graphtolites (with N. R. Hassinger), 1958; numerous graptolite papers; also various tech. brochures, articles. Home: 508 Chautauqua Av., Norman, Okla. Died Aug. 23, 1958; buried Dixon, Ill.

DECKER, Edward William, banker; b. Austin, Minn., Aug. 24, 1869; s. Jacob S. and Mary Ann H. (Smith) D.; grad. high sch., Austin, 1887; m. Susie May Spaulding, Feb. 24, 1892. Began as messenger Northwestern Nat. Bank, Mpls., 1887, cashier, 1900-03, v.p., gen. mgr., 1903-12, pres., 1912-34, ret.; asst. cashier and cashier Met. Bank, 1895-1900; also pres. Minn. Loan & Trust Co., 1910-18, chmn. 1918; dir. Northwestern Nat. Life Ins. Co. of Mpls. Mem. Minn. Soc. of N.Y. Republican. Conglist. Mason. Clubs: Minneapolis, Twin City Bankers'. Home: 510 Groveland Av. Office: Northwestern Bank Bldg., Mpls. Died Nov. 3, 1956.

DECKER, Floyd F(iske), mathematician; b. Denison, Tex., Mar. 23, 1881; s. Alonzo Wertz and Hannah Lucretia (Amos) D.; A.B., Syracuse U., 1901, A.M., 1905, Ph.D., 1910; m. Mary Makepeace, Aug. 30, 1910; children—Elizabeth Carol (Mrs. Burton B. Corwin), Robert Makepeace. Instr. in mathematics Syracuse U., 1904-10, asst. prof., 1910-14, asso. prof., 1914-17, prof., 1917—, dir. extension sch., 1919-30. Fellow A.A.A.S.; mem. Am. Math. Soc., Math. Assn. Am., Am. Assn. U. Profs., Sigma Xi, Phi Beta Kappa, Phi Kappa Phi, Pi Mu Epsilon. Republican. Methodist. Author: Symmetric Functions, 1910; Second Year Algebra, 1922. Contbr. to math. jours. Home: 312 Marshall St., Syracuse 10, N.Y. Died Nov. 28, 1949; buried Oakwood Cemetery, Syracuse.

DEEMER, Elias, ex-congressman; b. Bucks County, Pa., Jan. 3, 1838; common sch. edn.; enlisted July, 1861, as pvt. Co. E, 104th Pa. vols.; discharged May, 1862, for disabilities resulting from injuries received in line of duty. Removed to Williamsport, Pa., 1868, where he has since resided; pres. common council, 1888-90; lumber mfr.; pres. Williamsport Nat. Bank, 1894—. Mem. G. A. R. Mem. Congress, 16th Pa. dist., 1901-03, 15th dist., 1903-07; Republican. Home: Williamsport, Pa. Died 1918.

DEEN, Joshua Lee, coll. dean; b. Minneota, Minn., Nov. 15, 1896; s. William Henry and Tilla Regina (Dahl) D.; student St. Olaf Coll., Northfield, Minn., 1914-16; B.S., U. Minn., 1927; M.F., Yale, 1929, Ph.D., 1931; m. Leila Ruth Doherty, June 3, 1918. Bank clerk, 1917-18, 19-21, cashier, 1921-22; comml. traveler, 1922-25; instr. in forestry Yale, 1931-33; asst. prof. forestry Pa. State Coll., 1933-36, asso. prof., 1936-38; dean of forestry and range mgmt. Colo. A. and M. Coll., Fort Collins, 1938—, dean of faculty, 1946—. Served in U.S. Army 1918. Mem. Soc. Forestry in Suomi, Soc. Am. Foresters, Am., Colo. forestry assns., Ecol. Soc. Am., Wildlife Soc., Sigma Xi, Tau Phi Delta, Xi Sigma Pi. Club: Am. Legion (Fort Collins), Elk, Rotary. Home: 1413 S. College, Fort Collins, Colo. Died Apr. 24, 1951; buried Colo. State U. Forest, Pingrie Park, Colo.

DEEPING, Werwick, author; b. Southend, Essex, Eng.; s. George Davidson and Marianne (Warwick) D.; B.A., M.A., and M.B., Trinity Coll., Cambridge Eng., m. Maude Phyllis Merrill. Author: Sorrell and Son, 1928; Old Pybus, 1928; Woman's War, 1929; Ropers Row, 1929; Bertrand of Brittany, 1929; Apples of Gold, 1929: Exile, 1930; Bridge of Desire, 1931; Old Wine and New, 1932; Eyes of Love, 1933; Two Black Sheep, 1933; Valour, 1934; Seven Men Came Back, 1934; Man on the White Horse, 1934; White Gate, 1935; Stories of Love, Courage and Compassion, 1935; Golden Cord, 1935; No Hero—This, 1936; Marriage by Conquest, 1936; Woman at the Door, 1937; These White Hands, 1937; Blind Man's Year, 1937; Malice of Men, 1938; Folly Island, 1939; Bluewater, 1939; Shield of Love, 1940; Red Saint, 1940; Man Who Went Back, 1940; Joan of the Tower, 1941; Dark House, 1941; Corn in Egypt, 1941; I Live Again, 1942; Slade, 1943; Over Germany-Over Spain, 1944; Reprieve, 1945; The Impudence of Youth, 1946; Langhing House, 1947. Address: Eastlands, Weybridge, Surrey, Eng. Died Apr. 20, 1950.

DEESZ, Louis A(spell) (dēz), dean of engring.; b. Denver, May 22, 1888; s. Louis Phillip and Lucy (Soper) D.; student Colo. Coll., 1907-11; B.S., Carnegie Inst. Tech., 1922, E.E., 1936; m. Henrietta Davis, Aug. 13, 1913; children—Lucy Ann (Mrs. Duncan Huebner); m. 2d, Myrtle May Robbins, May 28, 1939. Elec. engr. Colo. Light & Power Co., Cripple Creek, 1912; supt. of transmission Fed. Light & Power Co., Trinidad, Colo., 1913; constrn. engr. Federal Light & Power, Deming, N.M., 1914; asst. chief engr. Intermountain Ry. Light & Power Co., Colo. Springs, Colo., 1915-16; asst. elec. supt. Colo. Fuel & Iron Co., Pueblo, 1917-19; gen. engr. Westinghouse Elec. Corp., 1919-22; engr. of tests Colo. Fuel & Iron Co., 1922-30; cons. engr. Freyn Engring. Co., Chgo., assigned to "Energocenter" and "Stalproect" Moscow and Siberia, USSR, 1930-33; lecturer on engring. U. Moscow, Russia, 1931; chief dist. combustion engr. Republic Steel Corp., Youngstown dist., 1933-42; instr. in physics and math. Deming (N.M.) High Sch., 1913-14; prof. elec. engring., Youngstown (Ohio) Coll., 1939—, dean of night sch., 1940, dean Wm. Raven Sch. of Engring., 1942—. Chmn. Rockefeller Com. on Edn., Pueblo, Colo., 1925-30; mem. Mahoning Valley Indsl. Council River Survey, Youngstown, 1936-42. Served as 1st lt., 120th Constrn. Corps, U.S. Army, 1918. Decorated Udarnick of the USSR, 1932. Registered engr., Colo. Mem. Nat. Soc. Profl. and Registered Engrs., Am. Soc. Engring. Edn., Am. Inst. E.E., Kappa Sigma, Mu Pi Epsilon. Republican. Methodist. Mason (32°, Shriner). Author articles on electrical precipitation, combustion engring., and rotating elec. machinery. Home: 21 East Avondale Av., Youngstown 5, O. Died Apr. 19, 1950; buried Forest Lawn Cemetery, Youngstown.

DEETZ, Charles Henry, cartographic engr.; b. Sellersville, Pa., Apr. 10, 1864; s. Thomas Berger and Caroline (Nase) D.; Phillips Exeter Acad., 1885; student civil engring. (geodetic course). Mass. Inst. Tech., 1885-88; m. Clarissa Hannah Wilson, Dec. 7, 1892. Field worker with U.S. Coast and Geod. Survey in Ala. and Fla., 1888, also served in Eastern States; assigned to cartographic work in preparation nautical charts; specializes in map projections; U.S. Coast and Geodetic Survey for Army War Service, revising publs. on map. projection and cartography, 1942-43, ret. Mem. Philos. Soc. Washington, Am. Numis. Assn. Author: Lambert Conformal Conic Projection, 1918; Lambert Projection Tables for France, with Conversion Tables, for the use of the Army, 1918; (with Oscar S. Adams) Elements of Map Projection, with applications to map and chart construction, 1921, revised edit., 1944; Cartography, a review and guide for the construction and use of maps and charts, 1936; revised edition, 1943. Contbr. cartographic articles to sci. and tech. publs. Home: 2504 Cliffbourne Pl. N.W., Washington 9. Died Mar. 1946.*

DEFOE, Harry Joseph, shipbuilding; b. Bay City, Mich., Sept. 2, 1875; s. Joseph and Lucy Ann (Covey) D.; grad. West Bay City (Mich.) High Sch.; m. Verna Herric Lusk, Aug. 15, 1900 (dec., 1913); m. Maude Ethel Currey, July 15, 1916; children—Thomas Joseph, William Martin, Lucy Helen. Began as school teacher; engaged in shipbuilding since 1905; mng. partner Defoe Shipbuilding Co. (Defoe Boat & Motor Works) since 1905. Began boat building by construction of wooden boats to 80 ft. in length, shipped chiefly in knockdown form; during World War I established steel shipyard (now conducted as Defoe Shipbuilding Co.); in 1940, when tremendous expansion of U.S. govt. shipbuilding required conservation of both manpower and space, devised "bottom up and rollover" construction, by which method steel hulls of ships between 300 and 400 ft. long were built bottom up on building forms, then rolled over to upright position by means of two wheels, or hoops, which encircled the hull and rested on heavy steel tracks; this made possible vast savings in manhours, and almost all downhand welding, which proved to average twice as fast as overhead welding and gave better results; firm has built a large number of vessels for the U.S. Navy, and has been awarded Navy E Mem. Soc. Naval Architects and Marine Engrs., Engring. Soc. of Detroit, Propellor Club of U.S., Newcomen Soc. of Eng. Mason. Clubs: India House (New York); Yacht (Detroit); Saginaw (Mich); Country, Boat, Rotary International (Bay City). Recipient President's Certificate of Merit, 1947. Home: 1412 Center Av., Bay City, Mich. Died Mar. 21. 1957; buried Elm Lawn Cemetery, Bay City. Mich.

de FOREST, Henry Lockwood, b. Plainfield, N.J., 1875; grad. Yale, 1897. Vice pres., dir. Hackensack Water Co., Spring Valley Water Works & Supply Co., dir. Pratt Read & Co., Inc., trustee Provident Loan Soc.; partner De Forest, Elder & Mubeany. Home: 955 Hillside Av., Plainfield, N.J. Office: 20 Exchange Pl., N.Y.C. 5. Died Mar. 18, 1954; buried Cold Spring Harbor, L.I., N.Y.

deFOREST, Johnston, lawyer; b. Plainfield, N.J., Sept. 5, 1873; s. Robert W. and Emily (Johnston) deF.; grad. Phillips Acad., Andover, Mass., 1892; A.B., Yale, 1896; LL.B., Columbia, 1899; m. Natalie Coffin, Oct. 6, 1903 (dec.); m. 2d, Mary E. Ogden, Sept, 9, 1911; 1 dau., Priscilla Mary (Mrs. Douglas Williams). Admitted to New York bar, 1899; practiced law, New York, N.Y., since 1899; engaged in real estate; director Dolphin Jute Mills, Niagara Fire Insurance Company, Tide Water Associated Oil Company. Trustee, Presbyn. Hosp., Community Service Soc., Phipps Houses, Inc., Russell Sage Foundation (assistant secretary). Dir. Regional Plan Assn., Inc. Mem. Assn. Bar, City of N.Y., N.Y. State Bar Assn. Clubs: University Century, Seawanhaka Corinthian Yacht, New York Yacht, Down Town Assn., Yale, Huguenot Society (New York). Home: Shore Road, Cold Spring Harbor, N.Y. Office: 20 Exchange Pl., N.Y.C. Died Nov. 25, 1952.

DEFREES, Joseph Rollie (dĕ-frēz'), naval officer, ret.; b. Smithboro, Ill., June 12, 1876; s. Newton Talmage and Anna Maria (Johnson) D.; grad. U.S. Naval Acad., 1900; m. Bernice Fairbanks, May 29, 1913; children—Helen Fairbanks (wife of Lt. J. J. Tomanichal, USN), Joseph Rollie (killed in action, World War II). Commd. ensign USN, 1902, advanced through grades to rear adm., 1933. During World War Comdr. of U.S. transport; then comdr. Submarine Force, Atlantic Fleet, later Asiatic Fleet; comdr. Torpedo Sta., Newport, R.I., for some time; later chief of staff Scouting Force; then comdt. Navy Yard, Washington, and comdr., Submarine Force, U.S. Fleet; dir. Shore Establishments div. UN; later comdt. 11th Naval Inspector of naval material, Los Angeles, 1941-45; now retired. Decorated Navy Cross, Spanish Campaign Badge, Victory Medal. Clubs: Army and Navy (Washington); Chevy Chase. Home: 143 S. Orange Grove Av., Pasadena, Cal. Died Aug. 1958.

de GASPERI, Alcide (dĕ-gäs'pĕr-ē), ex-premeir Italy; b. Pieve Tesino, Italy, Apr. 3, 1881; s. Amadeo and Maria (Morandini) de G.; laureate in philology and philosophy, U. of Vienna, 1905; m. Francesca Romani, June 14, 1922; children—Maria Romana, Lucia, Cecilia, Paola. Mgr. Il Nuovo Trentino, 1904; parliamentary rep. of Trento in Austrian Parliament, 1911; pres. Congress for Partito Populare, 1921; Christian Democrat dep. in Italian Parliament; sentenced to 4 yrs. imprisonment for anti-fascist activities, 1926; engaged in underground activities during German occupation, 1944; minister without portfolio in first Italian democratic govt. after liberation of Rome; fgn. minister in present Italian cabinet and previous cabinets, since Dec. 1944; Italian premier, since 1945-July 1953. Author: I tempi e gli uomini che prepararono la Rerum Novarum, 1946 and other sociol. and polit. publs. Contbr. articles to Italian newspapers. Home: Via Bonifacio VIII° n. 21, Rome, Italy. Died Aug. 19, 1954; buried St. Lorenzo Church, Rome, Italy.

DE GOGORZA, Emilio Eduardo, baritone singer; b. Bklyn., May 29, 1874; s. Julio Antonio Gomez and Maria Francisca Navarrete Y. (Romay) de G.; was taken abroad at age of 2 mos.; ed. Ecole Monge, Paris, France, and Baylis House, Salt Hill, Slough, Berks, Eng.; m. Emma Eames, operatic soprano, July 13, 1911. Began as boy soprano in Eng.; debut in New York with Madame Sembrich's Co., Met. Opera House, 1897; soloist with leading orchestras and musical festivals, and has made many transcontinental tours as concert and recital artist; repertoire includes classic and folk songs, and solos from operas, in English, Spanish, French, Italian and German. Republican. Roman Catholic. Home: Bath, Me. Died May 1949.

DE GOLYER, E(verette) L(ee) (dĕ-gōl'yẽr), geologist, oil producer; b. Greensburg, Kan., Oct. 9, 1886; s. John William and N. Kagy (Huddle) De G.; A.B., U. of Okla., 1911; hon. D.Sc., Colo. Sch. of Mines, 1925, Southern Methodist University, 1945, Tulane University, 1954; LL.D., Trinity College, 1947, Princeton, 1949, U. Mexico, 1951, Washington U., 1952; m. Nell Virginia Goodrich, June 10, 1910; children—Nell Virginia, Dorothy Margaret, Cecelia Jeanne, Everette Lee. With U.S. Geol. Survey, 1906-09; geologist and chief geologist Mexican Eagle Oil Co., 1909-14; cons. practice, 1914-19; v.p. and gen. mgr., 1919-26, pres. and gen. mgr. 1926-29, chmn. bd., 1929-32, Amerada Corp., Amerada Petroleum Corp. and Amerada Refining Corp.; v.p. and gen. mgr. Geophys. Research Corp.; pres. Atlatl Royalty Corp., 1932—; pres. Felmont Corp., 1934-39; sr. mem. DeGolyer & McNaughton, 1936—. Asst. dep. petroleum adminstr. for war, Washington, 1941-43; head Petroleum Adminstrn. for War mission to Mexico, 1942; head Dept. Interior Petroleum Reserves Corp. mission to Middle East, 1943-44; tech. adviser N.R.A. oil code, 1933; mem. Nat. Petroleum Council, 1946—; mem. U.S. Mil. Petroleum Adv. Bd., 1947—; mem. adv. com. on raw materials U.S. Atomic Energy Commn., 1947—; mem. U.S. adv. com. Am. participation Internat. Sci. Conf. on Conservation and Utilization of Resources, 1948—; mem. adv. bd. Nat. Security Resources Bd., 1948—; cons. War Dept. and Bur. Mines Survey of Coal, Oil Shale and Natural Gas Reserves, 1948—. Aldred lecturer Mass. Inst. Tech., 1929; Cyrus Fogg Brackett lecturer Princeton, 1929, Lewis Clark Vanuxem lecturer, 1941. Anthony F. Lucas medalist, 1941, John Fritz medalist, 1942; Sidney Powers gold medal from the American Association of Petroleum Geologists, 1950; received a distinguished service citation University of Oklahoma, 1948. Fellow Geol. Soc. Am., A.A.A.S., N.Y. Acad. Scis., Brit. Inst. of Petroleum, Am. Geog. Soc.; mem. Am. Assn. Petroleum Geologists (pres. 1925; hon. mem. 1945), Am. Inst. Mining and Metall. Engrs. (pres. 1927; became hon. mem. 1952), Nat. Academy of Sciences, Am. Petroleum Inst. (dir. 1935—), Am. Geophys. Union, Instituto Sudamericano del Petroleo, Soc. Econ. Geologists, Soc. Exploration Geologists, Soc. Exploration Geophysicists (hon. 1930), Pan Am. Inst. Mining Engring. and Geology (U.S. sect.), Dallas Mus. Fine Arts (pres., 1948—), Phi Beta Kappa, Sigma Xi, Tau Beta Pi, Kappa Alpha, Pi Epsilon, Sigma Gamma Epsilon, Pi Gamma Mu. Conglist. Mason. Clubs: Bankers, Engineers, University, Mining, Grolier (New York); Cosmos (Washington); Houston (Tex.); Brook Hollow Country, Dallas Country, Petroleum, Thirteen (Dallas); Zamorano (Los Angeles). Chmn. editorial bd. Sat. Rev. Lit., 1948—. Asso. editor New Colophon, Southwest Rev. Home: 8525 Garland Rd. Office: 5625 Daniels Av., Dallas. Died Dec. 14, 1956.

DE GOLYER, Robert Seeley, architect; b. Chicago, Ill., June 9. 1876; s. Nelson and Laura DeG.; ed. pub. and high schs., Evanston, Ill.; student Yale U., 1 yr.; B.S. in Architecture, Mass. Inst. Tech., 1898; m. Eleanor V. Harris, 1911. Began practice, Chicago, 1899; served as designer for John H. Parkinson, Los Angeles, 1902-05; in charge office of Marshall & Fox, Chicago, 1905-15; founder and pres. Robert S. de Golyer & Co., 1915-35; Robert S. De Golyer & Waler T. Stockton, 1935-43; Robert S. de Golyer since 1945. Prin. works: 1242 Lake Shore Drive Apts., Hotel Ambassador East, The Brockton, and many other bldgs. in Chicago and western cities. Chief architect Federal Housing Project, Julia C. Lathrop Homes, Chicago; asst. architect Pentagon Bldg., Washington, D.C. Served as capt. Construction Div., U.S. Army, World War; Construction Div., Quartermaster Corps, U.S. Army, 1941; Engr. Corps, U.S. Army, 1942, Defense Plant Corp., 1943-45. Fellow Am. Inst. Architects. Methodist. Clubs: Lake Zurich Country. Home: 125 Kedzie St., Evanston, Ill. Died Oct. 11, 1952.

DE GRAEFF, Dr. A. C. D., Netherland diplomat; b. The Hague, Holland, Aug. 7, 1872; LL.D., U. Leyden, 1894; m. C. A. van der Wyck, Mar. 25, 1897. In colonial service of Netherlands, 1895-1918; minister to Tokyo, Japan, 1920-22; E.E. and M.P. to U.S. from Netherlands, 1923—. Decorated Knight Netherlands Lion; Officer Order of Orange Nassau; Grand Cross Holy Treasure (Japanese); Grand Cross of the Crown (Roumanian); Comdr. Order of Cambodge (French). Protestant. Club: Metropolitan. Address: 15th and Euclid Sts., Washington. Died 1957.

DEISS, Charles F(rederick) (dīs), geologist; b. Covington, Ky., Mar. 18, 1903; s. Charles Fred and Anna Dorothea (Reinhart) D.; A.B., Miami Univ., 1925; Ph.D., Univ. of Mich., 1928; m. Minnette Blanch Davison, Jan. 22, 1929. Asst. prof. geology Mont. State Univ., Missoula, Mont., 1928-30, asso. prof., 1930-36, prof. 1936-42, dir. of library 1937-40; consultant Mont. Power Co., 1940-41; asst. geologist U.S. Geol. Survey, hdqrs., Missoula, Mont., 1940-41, geologist since 1942, in charge exploration for dolomite in western U.S., 1942-45, and for phosphate in Ida., 1944-45; prof. and chmn. dept. geology Ind. Univ. and State Geologist of Ind. since Sept. 1945. Mem. Geol. Soc. Am., Paleontological Soc., A.A.A.S., Am. Inst. Mining, Metall. and Petroleum Engrs., Am. Association of Petroleum Geologists, Soc. Econ. Geologists, Ind. Acad. Sci., Assn. Am. State Geologists (pres. 1954), Sigma Xi, Sigma Gamma Epsilon, Delta Upsilon. Author sci. bulls. Contbr. articles on geologic subjects to various jours. Address: Owen Hall, Indiana University, Bloomington, Ind. Died June 13, 1959; buried Bloomington, Ind.

DEITRICK, Frederick Simpson, ex-congressman; b. New Brighton, Pa., Apr. 9, 1875; A.B., Geneva Coll., Beaver Falls, Pa., 1895; LL.B., Harvard U., 1898. Practiced in Boston, 1898—; mem. Mass. Ho. of Rep. 3 terms; mem. 63d Congress, 8th Mass. Dist. Democrat. Home: Cambridge, Mass. Office: 84 State St., Boston. Died Apr. 1948.

DE JESÚS, Angel Román (dā-hā-sōōs'), judge; b. Ciales, Puerto Rico, Aug. 9, 1891; s. Miguel and Lastenia (Sánchez) deJ.; LL.B., Cornell U., 1913; m. Rosa Sanjuan, July 4, 1915; children—José Angel, Angel Rafael. Admitted to Puerto Rico bar, Nov. 17, 1913; judge Municipal Court, Juana Diaz, 1915-16, Coamo, 1916-17, San Juan, 1917-18; apptd. acting registrar of property, San Juan, 1926; referee in bankruptcy, 1928-30; judge Dist. Court of San Juan, 1930-37; asso. justice Supreme Court of P.R., 1938-48, chief justice since 1948. Mem. Am. and Puerto Rican bar assns., Ateneo Puertorriqueño. Democrat. Roman Catholic Clubs: Casino de Puerto Rico (San Juan). Home: 711 Concordia St., Miramar, P.R. Address: Box 1385, San Juan, P.R. Died Apr. 30, 1951.

de JURENEV, Nicholas, public utility exec.; b. nr. city of Ekaterinoslav, Russia, Dec. 22, 1904; s. Boris Alexasder and Helen (von Bark) de J.; came to U.S., 1924, naturalized, 1931; M.C.S., Dartmouth, 1926; m. Barbara Zimmer, Mar. 11, 1932; 1 dau., Nicole Helen. Asst. to v.p., Foreign Dept., Chatham Phenix Nat. Bank & Trust Co., N.Y. City, 1926-29; asst. mgr., Paris office, Lee, Higginson & Co., 1929-32; mgr. Haskins & Sells, C P A's, N.Y. City, 1932-45; comptroller Am. & Fgn. Power Co., Inc., N.Y. City, 1945—, Ebasco Internat. Corp. N.Y. City, 1945—; v.p. and dir. Cuban Elec. Co., Mexican Elec. Co., Northern Mexico Power & Development Co., Ltd., Cordoba Light & Power Co. and Central Mexico Light and Power Co., 1947-49; v.p., Argentine Elec. Cos., Brazilian Elec. Power Co., Shanghai Power Co., S. Am. Power Co., Havana Elec. & Utilities Co., 1949-50; dir. Pernambuco Tramways & Power Co., Ltd., Rio Grandense Light and Power Syndicate, Ltd., So. Brazil Elec. Co., Ltd., Ecuador Elec. Co., Guanajuato Power & Elec. Co., Michoacan Power Co., Puebla Tramway, Light & Power Co., Vera Cruz Electric Light, Power and Traction, Ltd. C.P. A., N.Y. State, 1937. Clubs: Ox Ridge Hunt (gov. Darien, Conn.); Fairfield Hunt (Westport, Conn.); Downtown Athletic (N.Y. City). Home: Apple Tree Lane, Norwalk, Conn. Office: 200 E. 66th St., N.Y.C. 21. Died Apr. 28, 1954; buried Roslyn Cemetery, Roslyn, N.Y.

De KLEINE, William, physician; b. Jamestown, Mich., Nov. 28, 1877; s. Hilbert and Alice (Kremers) DeK.; A.B., Hope College, 1902; hon. D.Sc., 1937; M.D., Northwestern Univ., 1906; M.Sc., U. of Mich. Sch. of Pub. Health, 1915; grad. student Mass. Inst. Tech., summer 1924; m. Lottie Maria Hoyt, June 28, 1906; 1 son, Edwin Hoyt (M.D.). Practiced medicine, Grand Haven, Mich., 1906-14; dir. Mich. Tuberculosis Survey Campaign (state-wide clinical survey), State Bd. of Health, 1915-17; health officer (full time), Flint, Mich., 1917-22, Saginaw, Mich., 1922-25; dir. child health demonstrations, Mansfield, O. (conducted by Am. Child Health Assn.), Fargo, N.D., and Salem, Ore. (conducted by Commonwealth Fund of New York), and organized full-time health dept. in each city, 1925-28; became asso. with Am. Red Cross during Miss. flood, 1927, med. director Am. Red Cross, 1928-42; participated in all major disasters as organizer med. relief activities; in pvt. practice of internal medicine (spl. interest in nutritional therapy). 1942-43; state commissioner of health, Mich., 1944-47; engaged in private practice of medicine, 1947-56; now retired. Formerly president Mich. Tuberculosis Assn., Mich. Pub. Health Assn.; formerly mem. bd. dirs. Nat. Tuberculosis Assn. Fellow Am. Pub. Health Assn., A.M.A.; mem. Ingham County (Mich.) Med. Soc., Southern Med. Assn. Presbyn. Contbr. to med. and health jours. Pioneer in field of pub. health and traveling tuberculosis clinics and nutrition in clinical medicine. Address: 90 Concord Dr., Buffalo 15. Died Sept. 20, 1957; buried Forest Grove (Mich.) Cemetery.

de KOVEN, Anna Farwell, author; b. Chicago, Nov. 19, 1862; d. Senator Charles Benjamin and Mary Evelyn (Smith) Farwell; A.B., Lake Forest U., 1880; m. Reginald de Koven, the composer, May 1, 1884 (died Jan. 16, 1920); 1 dau., Ethel LeRoy (Mrs. H. Kierstede Hudson). Author: Translation of an Iceland Fisherman (Pierre Loti), 1889; A Saw-Dust Doll, 1894; By the Waters of Babylon, 1901; By the Waters of Babylon, 1904; Life and Letters of John Paul Jones, 1913; Les Comtes de Gruyére (in French), 1914, (in English), 1916; A Cloud of Witnesses, 1920; A Primer of Citizenship, 1923; Horace Walpole and Madame du Deffand, 1929. Contbr. of prose and poetry to periodicals. Home: 1025 Park

Av., N.Y.C. Died Jan. 12, 1953; buried Woodlawn Cemetery. N.Y.

DE LA BARRE, Cecil Franzen (dĕl'ȧ-bȧr), educator; b. Amherst, Neb., July 5, 1900; s. Charles Lander and Emelia Amanda (Franzen) De La B.; B.S., Va. Poly. Inst., 1926, M.S., 1931; Ed.D., Columbia Univ.; m. Elva Maude Hedly, June 25, 1927. Engaged in practice of engineering, 1926-29; research fellow Virginia Poly. Inst., 1929, successively instr., asst. professor, associate professor, 1929-46, professor since 1946. Treasurer National Wildlife Federation, 1936-39; chmn. Va. Conservation Edn. Council, 1937-44, sec. 1940-44; pres. Va. Wildlife Fedn., 1937-40; pres. Va. Assn. of Izaak Walton League Chapters, 1940, 43 (sec. since 1945); dir. edn., Va. Commn. Game and Inland Fisheries, 1940-41. Served in U.S. Navy, 1917-19, 1941-45, now comdr. U.S.N.R. Mem. A.A.A.S., Virginia Acad. of Science, Phi Delta Kappa, Kappa Delta Pi, Am. Legion, Izaak Walton League (nat. dir. 1952), Phi Sigma. Democrat. Mason. Club: Rotary. Contbr. articles to profl. jours. and outdoor magazines; editor Virginia Wildlife, 1937-41; lecturer on conservation. Chmn. com. on resource management So. Assn. Sci. and Industry, 1947-50. Home: Hillcrest Dr., Blacksburg, Va. Died Sept. 10, 1952; buried Westview Cemetery, Blacksburg.

DELAFIELD, Lewis Livingston, lawyer; b. N.Y. City, Oct. 27, 1886; s. Lewis Livingston and Charlotte H. (Wyeth) D.; A.B. cum laude, Harvard, 1908, LL.B., cum laude, 1911; m. Ruth Manierre, Oct. 1, 1921; children—Lewis L., Ruth D. (Mrs. Clarkson N. Potter); m. 2d, Elsa Ringletaube, June 14, 1956. Admitted to N.Y. State bar, 1912, and since practiced in N.Y. City; mem. firm Hawkins, Delafield & Wood. Trustee Roosevelt Hosp. (sec. bd., 1930—). Pres. Indian Mt. Sch., Lakeville, Conn., 1929-42. Mem. Govs. Com. on Sch. Finance and Adminstrn. (Friedsam com., 1925-26, Burlingham com., 1933). Mem. govs. adv. com. on Constrn. of N.Y. State Thruway, 1950. Permanent mem. Selective Service Legal Adv. Bd., N.Y. City, 1917-18; chmn. Selective Service Local Bd., Nassau Co., N.Y., 1940-46, mem. local bd., 1950-52. Chmn. Nassau Emergency Work Bur., 1933-34. Mem. Nassau Co. Bd. Pub. Welfare, 1938—; dir. Five Towns Community Chest (pres. 1941-44, 48-50); mem. exec. com. Five Towns Community Council; pres. Nassau Co. Policy Boy Clubs, 1945-50. Mem. Am., N.Y. State, Nassau Co. and N.Y. City bar assns., Harvard Law Sch. Assn. of N.Y. City (pres. 1944-45). Clubs: Union (N.Y. City); Rockaway Hunting (Cedarhurst, L.I.); Cedarhurst Yacht (Lawrence, L.I.). Home: 137 Piermont Rd., Hewlett Bay Park, L.I., N.Y. Office: 67 Wall St., N.Y.C. 5. Died Aug. 18, 1957; buried Wood Lawn Cemetery.

DE LA MARE, Walter (John) (dé-lȧ-mâr'), author; b. 1873; hon. degrees from univs. of Cambridge, St. Andrews of Bristol, London; Hon. Fellow Keble Coll., Oxford. Club: Athenaeum. Author: Songs of Childhood, 1902; Henry Brocken, 1904; Poems, 1906; The Three Mulla-Mulgars; The Return, 1910; The Listeners and Other Poems; A Child's Day, 1912; Peacock Pie, 1913; Motley and Other Poems, 1918; Flora, 1919; The Veil and Other Poems; Crossings, a Play; Memoirs of a Midget, 1921; Down-adown-Derry, 1922; The Riddle, and other Stories; Come Hither, 1923; new edition, 1928; Ding Dong Bell, 1924; Broomsticks and Other Tales, 1925; The Connoisseur, and other Stories, 1926; Told Again; Stuff and Nonsense, 1927; Stories from the Bible, 1929; Desert Islands; On the Edge, short stories; Poems for Children, 1930; Lewis Carroll, 1932; The Fleeting and other Poems, 1933; The Lord Fish, and other Stories, 1933; Early One Morning, 1935; The Wind Blows Over, 1936; This Year, Next Year, 1937; Memory, and other Poems, 1938; Behold, This Dreamer, 1939; Pleasures and Speculations, 1940; Bells and Grass, 1941; Collected Poems, 1942; Love, 1943; Collected Rhymes and Verses, 1944; The Burning Glass, 1945; The Traveller, 1946; Collected Tales, 1949; Winged Chariots and Other Poems, 1951; Private View, 1953; O Lonely England, 1953; Selected Poems, 1954. Address: care Athenaeum Club, Pall Mall, London, Eng. Died June 22, 1956; buried St. Paul's Cathedral, London, Eng.

DELAMARTER, Eric, organist, conductor; b. Lansing, Mich., Feb. 18, 1880; s. Rev. Louis and Mary Elizabeth (Baker) D.; ed. Kalamazoo (Mich.) High Sch., Albion Coll.; hon. Mus.D., Wooster (Ohio) Coll., 1931; profl. study under Wilhelm Middelschulte and Mary Wood Chase, Chicago; with Charles Marie Widor and Alexandre Guilmant, Paris, France, 1900-02; m. Rubee B. Wilson, Apr. 18, 1906; children—Jeanne, Marjorie; m. 2d, Alice Young Maine, June 9, 1925. Organist and choirmaster, New England Congl. Ch., Chicago, 1900-12; later organist 1st Ch. of Christ, Scientist; organist and choirmaster 4th Presbyn. Ch., 1914-36; mem. faculty, Olivet (Mich.) Coll., 1904-05, Chicago Mus. Coll., 1909-10; prof. U. of Mo., Ohio State U., U. of Tex., in the 1940's; music critic, Chicago Record-Herald, Tribune, and Inter Ocean, 1901-14; apptd. conductor Mus. Art Soc., Chicago, 1911-13; asso. condr. Chicago Symphony Orchestra, 1918-36. Member Sigma Chi. Author compositions for organ, etc. Address: care Northern Trust Co., Chicago. Died 1953.*

DE LAND, Charles Edmund, lawyer; b. Kirkland Tp., Oneida County, N.Y., Jan. 6, 1854; s. La Fayette and Delia (Gage) D.; ed. Whitestown (N.Y.) Sem.; read law at Galesburg, Ill. Admitted to Ill. bar, 1878; practiced at Galesburg, 1878-83, at Pierre, S.D., 1883—. Dir. State Hist. Soc. of S.D.; mem. State Bar Assn. S.D.; hon. mem. Mo. Hist. Soc. Author: Annotated Statues of Trial Practice and Appellate Procedure for the Dakotas, 1896; Annotated Rules of Supreme Courts of South and North Dakotas, 1896; Annotated Incorporation Laws of South Dakota, 1900, 1903, 1907; Aborigines of South Dakota; Historical Notes on Military and Trading Posts of the Northwest; The Verendrye Expeditions; Thoughts Afield; Tragedy of the White Medicine; The Mis-Trials of Jesus; The Psychic Trio; Black Mount of Gold; Renewed From Without; Papers on Our Internal and International Waterways. Contbr. of papers in Central Law Journal, St. Louis. Republican. Home: Pierre, S.D. Deceased.

DELANDER, N. Paul, banker; b. St. Paul, Jan. 10, 1890; s. S. N. and Betsey Delander; student pub. schs. of St. Paul; m. Mildred C. Neuenschwander, Nov. 6, 1919; children—Marian Louise, Jane Audrey. Clerk, Merchants Nat. Bank, St. Paul, 1906-18; mem. bond dept. Merchants Trust Co., 1918-23, v.p., 1923-29; v.p. First Securities Corp., 1929-32; v.p. First Nat. Bank of St. Paul, 1932—, sr. v.p., 1948—; pres., dir. First State Bank, 1938—; dir. Midland S.S. Line, Inc., Anchor Casualty Co., First Trust Co., Stott Briquet Co., Queen City Ins. Co., First Service Corp. Mem. bd. dirs. St. Paul Community Chest, Tozer Found., Inc.; trustee Hazelden Found., Children's Hosp., St. Paul. Republican. Mason (Shriner). Clubs: Minnesota, Athletic, Town and Country (St. Paul). Home: 277 Woodlawn Av., St. Paul 5. Office: First Nat. Bank of St. Paul, St. Paul 1. Died Feb. 22. 1948.

DELANEY, Sadie Peterson, librarian; b. Rochester, N.Y., Feb. 26, 1889; d. James and Julia Frances (Hawkins) Johnson; student Coll. City N.Y., 1920; library tng. N.Y. Pub. Library, 1919-21; L.H. D., Atlanta U., 1950; m. Edward Louis Peterson, 1906 (div. 1921); 1 daughter, Grace Hooks; married Rudicel A. Delaney, April 28, 1928. Librarian New York Public Library System, 1920-23; organized hosp. library Tuskegee (Ala.) VA Hosp., 1924, since served as chief librarian; organized work with blind, 1930; instr. courses for hosp. librarians, 1940-48; vol. work with blind of Ala., 1930—; with Library Congress Com. on Blind, 1931-48. Pioneer, authority in bibliotherapy for mental patients. Elected one of Prin. Women of Am., London, Eng., 1930; Woman of the Year by Iota Phi Lambda, 1948, by Zeta Phi Beta, 1949; recipient Am. Legion award for meritorious service to vets., 1949; Nat. Urban League award as Woman of the Year, 1950; citation Book Trolley Hosp. Library Guild, London, Eng., 1950, Outlook for the Blind, 1950; nat. award Nat. Council of Colored Women's Club, Harvard U., 1952; VA top award for outstanding contbns. in field; cited by S.E. Library Assn., N.Y. Post, Boston Glove, Washington Post Herald, My Day column by Mrs. Eleanor Roosevelt; posthumous award exceptional service citation A.L.A., Assn. Hosp. and Instn. Libraries, 1958. Mem. N.A.A.C.P., Nat. Council Colored Women, A.L.A. (councilor hosp. libraries 1946-51), Guild Hosp. Libraries London, Urban League, S.E. Library Assn., Tuskeggee Mental Hygiene Assn., Tuskegee Civic Assn., Book Lovers Guild (chmn. Tuskegee Inst.), Iota Phi Lambda (Founder, hon. pres.). Democrat. Episcopalian. Clubs: Woman's (Tuskegee Inst.); Woman's Civic (Poughkeepsie, N.Y.); Philatelic (a founder, Tuskegee). Contbr. to library, med., ednl. publs. Pioneered in utilizing reading materials in rehabililitation of boys and girls, rehabilitation and cure of mental patients and in development of techniques for teaching the blind to read. Collector antique china, philatelist, mumismatist. Life's work presented to U.S. Congress and cited by Congl. Record, 1957. Address: P.O. Box 162, Tuskegee, Ala. Died May 4, 1958; buried Greenwood Cemetery, Tuskegee.

DELANO, Frederic Adrian (dĕl' ȧ-nō), retired; b. at Hong Kong, China, Sept. 10, 1863; s. Warren and Catherine Robbins (Lyman) D. (both natives of Mass.); lived most of boyhood at Newburgh, N.Y.; A.B., Harvard, 1885; married Matilda A. Peasley, November 22, 1888 (deceased, 1943); children—Mrs. Alexander G. Grant (dec.), Mrs. J. L. Houghteling. Began railway service with the C., B.&Q., Railroad Company, with engineering party in Colorado, Aug. 1, 1885; entered Aurora (Ill.) shops, same road, Oct. 1, 1885, as apprentice machinist; apptd. temporarily acting engr. of tests at Aurora, Apr. 1887; placed in charge bur. rail inspn. at Chicago, July 1, 1887; asst. to 2d v.p. at Chicago, Apr. 1889; supt. freight terminals at Chicago, July 1890; supt. motive power at Chicago, Feb. 1, 1899; gen. mgr. at Chicago, C., B.&Q. R.R., July 1, 1901-Jan. 10, 1905. Pres. Wheeling & Lake Erie R.R. Co., Wabash-Pittsburgh Terminal Ry. Co., May 1, 1905-08; 1st v.p. Wabash R.R., May 1, Oct. 5, 1905; pres., Oct. 5, 1905-Dec. 1911, and one of receivers, Dec. 1911-Dec. 1913; pres. C., I. & L. (Monon) Ry. Co., Dec. 1913-Aug. 10, 1914. Mem. Federal Reserve Bd., for 6-yr. term, and designated as vice-gov. for 2 years; resigned, June 1918, to enter army. Commd. maj. Engr. Corps, July 17, 1918; assigned to staff of Gen. Atterbury, dir. gen. of transportation at Tours, France; promoted lt. col. Trans. Corps and apptd. deputy dir. transporation at Paris, Oct. 26, 1918; promoted col., Trans. Corps, May 2, 1919; hon. disch., Oct. 25, 1919; commd. col. Engr. R.C., Jan. 1, 1920. Awarded D.S.M. for service in France, Sept. 9, 1921; Legion of Honor (France), 1919; Order of Sheng Li (Victory) from Chinese govt., 1948. Appointed receiver by Supreme Court of U.S. in Red River Boundary Case, Okla. vs. Texas, U.S. intervenor. Chmn. Internat. Commn. League of Nations on inquiry into the production of opium in Persia and the possible substitution of other crops or industries. Formerly regent Smithsonian Instn. Chmn. Nat. Capital Park and Planning Commn. of Washington; retired Aug. 1942 after 18 years service. Formerly chmn. Nat. Resources Planning Bd., 1934-43; now retired. Chairman emeritus Am. Planning and Civic Assn. Clubs: University (Chicago); Metropolitan, Cosmos (Washington, D.C.). Home: 2400 16th St., Washington. Died Mar. 28, 1953; buried Fairhaven, Mass.

DELANO, William Adams, architect; b. N.Y.C., Jan. 21, 1874; s. Eugene and Susan Magoun (Adams) D.; A.B., Yale, 1895, B.F.A., 1908, M.A., 1939; diploma École des Beaux Arts, Paris, 1903; m. Louisa Potter, May 23, 1907; 1 son, Richard Potter. Prof. design Columbia, 1903-10; mem. Delano & Aldrich, 1903-50, ret. as sr. partner, now adv. architect; apptd. archtl. cons. to Commn. on Renovation of White House, 1949; firm designed Knickerbocker, Colony, India House, Brook and Union Clubs, N.Y. C., new Am. Embassy, Paris, new Post Office building, Japanese Embassy, Washington, D.C., La Guardia Field, N.Y., Air Terminals for Pan-Am. Airways, Miami and Midway, Guam and Wake Islands, also many public and office bldgs., university and school bldgs., private homes. Firm won competition for enlargement of facilities, U.S. Military Acad., West Point, N.Y., 1945. Prof. design, Columbia, 1903-10. Mem. Nat. Commn. Fine Arts, 1924-28; mem. Nat. Capital Park and Planning Commn. 1929-46; trustee N.Y. Public Library, N.Y. Orthopedic Dispensary and Hospital, Governors (India House). Mem. Board of Design (N.Y. World's Fair, 1939). Pres. Art Commn. of City of N.Y. Vice pres. Grenfell Assn. of Am. Horticultural Soc. of N.Y. Decorated Officier Legion of Honor (France). Academician Nat. Acad. Design; fellow A.I.A. (Gold medalist 1953); mem. Nat. Inst. Arts and Letters (Gold medalist 1940), Am. Acad. of Arts and Letters, Beaux Arts Soc. (pres. 1927-29); corr. mem. Academie des Beaux Arts, Institut de France. Clubs: Architectural League of N.Y., Century (v.p. 1947-49, hon. mem. 1956), Knickerbocker, Coffee House, India House, Brook (N.Y.C.); Piping Rock (L.I.). Home: 131 E. 36th St., N.Y.C. Died Jan. 1960.

de LAUBENFELS, Max W., zoologist; b. Mt. Pleasant, Ia., May 9, 1894; s. Harry J. and Hattie M. (Walker) de L.; A.B., Oberlin Coll., 1916; A.M., Stanford U., 1926, Ph.D., 1929; also studies U. Cal., Art Inst. Chgo., several European univs.; m. Beth Jones, Aug. 10, 1921; children—Peter Max, Leroy Arthur, David John, Allan Neal, Marilyn Beth. Business in Chgo., 1916-21; instr. Oberlin Coll., 1927, Pasadena City Coll., 1928-47; prof. zoology U. Hawaii, 1947-50, Ore. State Coll., 1950—; research for 10 univs. (incl. fgn.); for govt. agencies incl. Bur. Fish, Office Naval Research, Nat. Research Council, State Fla., various biol. stas., museums and pvt. corps., others. Fellow A.A.A.S.; mem. many sci. socs. Conglist. Mason. Author 50 sci. articles incl. 7 monographs on Porifera; also textbooks. Home: 200 Allen Lane, Corvallis, Ore. Died Feb. 4, 1958; buried Corvallis.

DELK, Edward Buehler, architect; b. Schoharie, N.Y., Sept. 21, 1885; s. Edwin Heyl (D.D.) and Ella R. L. (Buehler) D.; descendant of Roger Delk of Virginia, 1647; grad. Mercersburg (Pa.) Academy, 1903; B.S. in Architecture, U. of Pa., 1907; grad. study U. of London, 1919; m. Jane Willis Townsend, 1936. Began practice at Philadelphia, 1913; moved to Kansas City, Mo., 1920; cons. architect, J. C. Nichols Investment Co.; pvt. practice since 1924. Prin. works: Tulsa Museum of Art, Theodore Gary residence, Macon, Mo.; Villa Philmonte, Cimarron, N.M.; Bartlesville Country Club; John H. Kane residences, Bartlesville, Okla.; co-architect; Philtower Bldg., Tulsa; Kansas City Country Coub; residences of Vernon Foster, Frank Phillips, Bartesville, Okla.; Municipal Starlight Theatre (summer opera), Kansas City, 1944; architect (with Jo Davidson, sculptor), William Allen White Memorial, Emporia, 1945, (with Tracy Wood), Union Nat. Bank Bldg., Kansas City, 1950. Co-architect Kan. U. WW II Campanile Carillon. 1st lt., Air Service, A.E.F., U.S. Army, 1917-19. Mem. Am. Inst. Architect, Archtl. League Kansas City, Archtl. T Square Club of Philadelphia (ex-pres.), Kappa Sigma. Awarded $1,000 prize Kansas

City Liberty Memorial Competition, 1922; honor award medal, Kansas City Chapter Am. Inst. Architects, 1930, 35, 36. Republican. Lutheran. Clubs: Pennsylvania, Art (Phila); Country (Kansas City). Home: 5320 Belleview. Office: Park Board, City Hall, Kansas City, Mo. Died Sept., 1956.

DELUCA, Giuseppe, baritone; b. Rome, Italy, Dec. 25, 1876; s. Nicola and Lucia (De Filippi) D.; ed. Tech. Inst., Rome; grad. Royal Acad. of St. Cecelia, Rome, 1897; m. Olimpia Fierro, 1903 (dec.). Debut as Valentin, in Faust, at Piacenza, Italy, 1897; spent 8 seasons at La Scale Theatre, Milan, and appeared in capitals of Europe; Am. début as Figaro, in Barber of Seville, at Met. Opera House, New York, Nov. 25, 1915, achieving immediate popularity; sings prin. rôles in Rigoletto, Barbiere, Don Giovanni, Otello, Don Carlos, Ernani, Dammnation of Faust, Don Pasquale, Hamlet, Trannhäuser, Parsifal, Pagliacci, Favorita, etc. Roman Catholic. Decorated Comdr. Order of the Crown (Italy), Order of Christ (Portugal), Order of Carol I of Roumania. Died Aug. 26, 1950.*

DEMAREST, William Henry Steele (dĕm'ă-rĕst), clergyman, educator; b. Hudson, N.Y., May 12, 1863; s. David D. and Catharine L. (Nevius) D.; A.B., Rutgers, 1883, A.M., 1886; grad. New Brunswick (N.J.) Theol. Sem., 1888; D.D., Rutgers, 1901, New York Univ., 1916; LL.D., Columbia Univ., 1910, Union Coll., Schenectady, N.Y., 1911, U. of Pittsburgh, 1912; Rutgers University, 1941; unmarried. Ordained Ref. Ch. in America ministry, 1888; pastor, Walden, N.Y., 1888-97, Catskill, N.Y., 1897-1901; prof. church history New Brunswick Theol. Sem., 1901-06; pres. Rutgers Coll., 1905-24; pres. New Brunswick Theol. Sem., 1925-35, emeritus, 1935-—. Trustee Rutgers University. Pres. board dirs. Ref. Ch. in Am., 1937-44, pres. Gen. Synod of Ref. Ch. in Am., 1909; v.p. Huguenot Soc. of Am. (chaplain N.J. Society); member Holland Society, Phi Beta Kappa, Delta Phi. Author: History of Rutgers College, 1924; Notes on the Constitution of the Reformed Church in America, 1928. Compiler: Tercentenary Studies of the Reformed Church in America, 1928; New Brunswick (1680-1930), 1932; Demarest Family Genealogy, 1938-—. Clubs: University (New York), New Brunswick History (pres.). Home: 542 George St., New Brunswick, N.J. Died June 23, 1956, buried Elmwood Cemetery, New Brunswick.

deMARTINO, Nobile Giacomo, diplomat; b. Berne, Switzerland, Sept. 7, 1868; s. Renato and Countess E. (de Wirsen) de M.; grad. Inst. Social Sciences, Florence, Italy, 1889; married. In diplomatic service 1891-—; served in varius capacities at Berlin, Constantinople, Cairo, Berne; apptd. sec. gen. Ministry Fgn. Affairs, 1913; Ambassador at Berlin, 1920, London, 1921-23, Tokio, 1923-24; A., E.&P. to U.S. 1925-—. Catholic. Address: Rome, Italy. Died June 29, 1957.

DEMBY, V., E(dward) Thomas, bishop; b. Wilmington, Feb. 13, 1869; s. Thomas and Mary F. Demby; student Howard High Sch. Eddy Ander Pvt. School, Wilmington, Inst. of Colored Youth, Phila., Centenary Bible Inst. (now Morgan State Coll. Md.), Lincoln U., and pvt. work in Latin, Greek and philosophy; student Howard U., 1892-93; B.D., Wilberforce, 1893; S.T.D., U. of Chicago, 1894; grad. Matthew's Hall, Denver, Colo., 1896; spl. work in Hebrew and cognate langs., also in philosophy and psychology; D.D., Paul Quinn Col. Waco Tex. 1919; Litt.D., Selma U., 1925; Mus.B., Oskaloosa Coll., 1925, LL.D., 1926; LL.D., Wilberforce, 1929, L.H.D. 1941; m. Pollie Alston-Sherrill, 1899 (died Nov. 1, 1809); m. 2d, Antoinette Martina Ricks, Sept. 17, 1902; 1 son, Thomas Benjamin (dec.). Was teacher in Delaware, Texas, British America and Tenn.; prin. and dir. of a corr. school of theology, 1893-94; vice prin. Hoffman Hall. Nashville. Tenn., 1899; deacon, 1898, priest, 1899, P.E. Ch.; rector St. Paul's Ch., Mason, Tenn., 1899-1900, St. Augustine's Ch., Kansas City, Mo., 1900-02, St. Michael's Ch., Cairo, Ill., 1903, St. Peter's Parish, Key West, Fla., 1903-07, Emmanuel Ch., Memphis, Tenn., 1907-15; apptd. archdeacon, 1912; organized The Guild of One More Soul, 1915; suffragan bishop of colored race in Ark. and other dioceses in Province of the Southwest, 1918-39; first colored bishop of Am. Ch., with jurisdiction, in U.S. Was dean and prof. physical science and philosophy, Paul Quinn Coll.; conducted as pvt. acad. in Denver; reestablished Hoffman-St. Mary's Indsl. Inst., Mason, Tenn., prin., 1912-18; asso. mem. Forward Movement Commn.; mem. Joint Commn. on Negro Work. Mem. Social Soc., Am. Humane Assn., Race Relation Com., Am. Assn. for Advancement of Colored People, So. Conf. for Human Welfare, Church Union, Church Hist. Soc., Am. Acad. Polit. and Social Science, Pi Gamma Mu, Sigma Pi Phi. Democrat. Mason (32°). Mem. I.B.P.O. Elks of the World. Formerly asst. to the late Bishop Thomas F. Gailor, Diocese of Tenn., and the late Bishop James Matthew Maxon for Colored Work. Author: the Mission of the Protestant Episcopal Church in the Province of the Southwest, 1938. Was editor of 3 ch. papers. Established Christ Ch. Parochial and Industrial Sch., Forrest City, Ark. special fields of endeavors are youth movement, religious education and race relations; also preaching and teaching missions; retired, Feb. 1, 1939; served the Church of the Holy Cross, Pittsburgh, Pa., 1942-43. Guest speaker Interracial and Internat. Service, Detroit 1946. Address: 10519 Englewood Av., Cleve. 8. Died Oct. 14, 1957.

de MENASCE, Jacques (dĕ mê-näsh), composer, concert pianist; b. Bad Ischl, Austria, Aug. 19, 1905; s. Baron Henri and Charlotte (Gerson) de M.; diploma with honors Schotten Gymnasium and Music Acad., Vienna; studied piano with Emil von Sauer and Paul Weingarten, composition with Joseph Marx. Paul Pisk, Alban Berg; m. Georgette Frank. Came to U.S., 1941, naturalized, 1947. Toured European cities, soloist European radio; with symphony orchestras of Vienna, Budapest, Rotterdam, Geneva, Zurich, Luxemburg, others; recitals, N.Y.C., also Chgo.; rep. on program Festival of Internat. Soc. Contemporary Music, Berkeley, Cal., 1942; European concert tours, 1947-49; with Am. Music Festival, Columbia U., 1949, Société des Concerts, Paris, 1949, and appearances throughout U.S. Compositions include: Piano Concerto No. 2, 1939; Divertimento for Piano and Strings, 1940; Violin and Piano Sonata, 1940; Sonatina No. 2 for Piano, 1942; Five Fingerprints (piano), 1943; Perpetuum Mobile (piano), 1944; Hebrew Melodies, 1945; Sonatina No. 3 for Piano, 1946; Status Quo (ballet), 1947; Lecho Dodi (choral), 1947; Little Suite for Piano, 1950; Outre Nuit, 1952; Two Letters from Children, 1953; Sonata for Viola and Piano, 1955; Concerto for Violin and Viola, 1959; others. Decorated Legion of Honor (France). Member American Society of French Legion of Honor. Clubs: Lotos, Bohemians (N.Y.C.). Contributor profl. publs. Address: 300 E. 57th St., N.Y.C. Died Jan. 1960.

de MILLE, Cecil Blount (de-mil), motion picture producer; b. Ashfield, Mass., Aug. 12, 1881; s. Henry Churchill and Mathilda Beatrice (Samuel) de Mille; student Pa. Mil. Acad., Chester, Pa., Am. Acad. Dramatic Arts, N.Y.C.; A.F.D., U. So. Cal.; Litt.D., Pa. Mil. Acad., Brigham Young U., Baylor U., Temple U.; m. Constance Adams, Aug. 16, 1902; children—Cecilia Hoyt (Mrs. Joseph Harper), Katherine Lester (Mrs. Anthony Quinn), John Blount, Richard deMille. Organized Mercury Aviation Co., pioneer comml. aviation co. to carry passengers on regular flights, Hollywood, 1918, pres., 1918-23; playwright and theatrical producer, 10 yrs.; identified with motion picture bus., 1913-—; with Samuel Goldwyn and Jesse L. Lasky founded the Jesse L. Lasky Feature Play Co., 1913, became dir. gen., co. merged in 1918 to become Famous Players-Lasky, and in 1927 to the present Paramount Pictures Corp.; in 1924 established DeMille Pictures Corp.; joined Metro-Goldwyn-Mayer as producer-dir., 1928, returned to Paramount as ind. producer, 1932; producer Lux Radio Theatre of the Air, 1936-45; v.p. and chmn. motion picture loans Comml. Nat. Trust & Savs. Bank of Los Angeles (later Bank of Am.). Pres. DeMille Found. for Polit. Freedom. Pres. Motion Picture Relief Fund; chmn. motion picture div. Community Chest of Los Angeles; mem. bd. Acad. Motion Peture Arts and Scis.; council Motion Picture Orgns.; 3 times pres. Assn. Motion Picture Producers. Former chmn. Red Cross Blood Donor drive for motion picture and radio industries; chief cons. on motion pictures to U.S. Information Agy.; chmn. Los Angeles Am. Cancer Soc. Decorated Order of Holy Sepulchre (Jerusalem); Order of Orange-Nassau (Holland); Companion Order of White Elephant (Thailand); Grand Order of Republic of Italy; Chevalier Legion of Honor (France); recipient numerous citations and awards for civic service, and accomplishments in motion picture prodn.; several schs. named in his honor. Mem. Am. Legion, S.A.R., German League of Human Rights (hon.), Screen Dirs.' Guild (hon.). Mason (Shriner). Clubs: Lambs, Wings. Producer 70 pictures, most outstanding being: Carmen, The Cheat, 1915; Joan the Woman, 1916; The Whispering Chorus, 1917; Male and Female, 1919; Manslaughter, 1922; The Ten Commandments, 1923; The Volga Boatman, 1925; The King of Kings, 1926; Dynamite, 1929; The Sign of the Cross, 1932; Cleopatra, 1934 The Crusades, 1935; The Plainsman, 1936; The Buccaneer, 1937; Union Pacific, 1938; Northwest Mounted Police, 1940; Reap the Wild Wind, 1941; The Story of Dr. Wassell, 1943; Unconquered, 1946; Samson and Delilah, 1949; The Greatest Show on Earth, 1952; The Ten Commandments, 1956. Home: 2000 de Mille Dr. Office: Paramount Studios, Hollywood 28, Cal. Died Jan. 21, 1959; buried Hollywood Memorial Park.

de MILLE, William Churchill, playwright; born Washington. N.C., July 25, 1878; s. Henry Churchill and Beatrice (Samuel) de M.; A.B., Columbia, 1900; spl. work, 1901-02; diploma Am. Acad. Dramatic Arts, New York. 1901; Litt.D. (hon.), U. Southern California, 1953; m. Anna A. George, Mar. 30, 1903; children—Agnes George, Margaret George; m. 2d, Clara Beranger, Aug. 14, 1928. Engaged in writing plays since 1900; formerly directing at Paramount, Long Island; prof. drama U. So. Cal., 1941-53, now prof. emeritus. Jeffersonian Democrat. Episcopalian. Clubs: New York Athletic, Holland Soc. (New York City); Tuna of Catalina Island (past president). Author (plays) "Strongheart"; "The Warrens of Va."; "The Land of the Free"; "The Woman"; (book), The Forest Ring, 1914; Hollywood Saga (book), 1939. Co-author: "The Genius"; "The Royal Mounted'"; "Classmates." Contributor to magazines. Lecturer. Now prof. of drama, Univ. of Southern Cal. Address: Playa del Rey, Cal. Died Mar. 5, 1955.

DEMING, Harold S., lawyer; b. Brooklyn, N.Y., Sept. 13, 1883; s. Horace E. and Caroline S. (Springsteed) D.; ed. Phillips Acad., Andover; A.B., Harvard, 1905, LL.B., 1908; m. Katherine Burritt, Apr. 23, 1913; children—MacDonald, Barbara, Quentin, Angus. Admitted to N.Y. State bar, 1908; mem. law firm Haight, Deming, Gardner, Poor Havens, N.Y. City, since 1918; asst. U.S. Atty., So. Dist. of N.Y., 1908-10; dep. asst. dist. atty., N.Y. Co., 1910-12; asso. counsel Curran Alderman Com., 1912. Decorated Knight Royal Order North Star (Sweden). Mem. N.Y. Bar Assn., Phi Beta Kappa, Delta Upsilon. Knight Comdr. Order St. Olaf, Norway. Clubs: Harvard, India House, Century. Home: South Mountain Rd., New City, N.Y. Office: 80 Broad St., N.Y.C. 4. Died Mar. 7, 1954.

DEMING, Thomas Harlan, newspaper editor; b. Mt. Olivet, Ky., Apr. 28, 1874; s. Judge Osmer Sage and Leona (Rigg) Deming; ed. public sch., and Alleghany Coll. Meadville, Pa.; unmarried. Began as reporter Warren (O.) Tribune Chronicle, 1896, editor since 1902. Methodist. Home: Reeves Apts. Office: Tribune Bldg., Warren, O. Died Apr. 9, 1949.

DEMPSEY, Edward Joseph (dĕmp'sê), lawyer; b. Town of Merton, Waukesha County, Wis., Mar. 18. 1878; s. Edward Louis and Ann (Mountain) D.; student State Teachers Coll., Oshkosh, Wis., 1898-1901; law study, U. of Wis., 1904-06, U. of Chicago, summer 1905; LL.D., U. Wis., 1945; married Sadie A. Hearn, June 26, 1907 (dec. Nov. 15, 1952); children—John Edward, Joseph Francis, George Raymond (killed in action June 28, 1944). Principal of the Frentz School, Oshkosh, 1901-04; admitted to Wis. bar, 1907, and practiced since at Oshkosh; mem. Bouck, Hilton, Dempsey & Magnusen; sec. and dir. Nicolet Paper Corp.; dir. Employers Mut. Fire Ins. Co.; dir. Employers Mutual Liability Ins. Company of Wis., Wis. Bankshares Co., Title Guaranty Co. of Wis., Milprint, Inc., First Nat. Bank (Oshkosh); chmn. bd. and dir. Riverside Paper Corp.; dir. and sec. Green Bay and Miss. Canal Co.; dir. Naber & Co., First Wisconsin Trust Co., First Wis. Nat. Bank, Universal Foundry Company; director Oshkosh Motor Truck, Inc., (Wisconsin). Bergstrom Paper Co. Mem. bd. trustees and gen. counsel Lawrence Coll. of Appleton, Wis.; mem. bd. regents Wis. Teachers Coll., 1914-46, pres. bd., 1924-46. Pres. Bd. Bar Commrs. Wis., 1940-49; trustee Oshkosh Found.; mem. Wis. State Bd. of Edn., 1917-23. Mem. Am. Bar Assn., Wis. Bar Assn. (pres. 1928-29), Phi Alpha Delta. Dem. Mem. Knights of Columbus. Clubs: Rotary, Candlelight, Oshkosh Country. Home: 189 E. Irving St. Office: First Nat. Bank Bldg., Oshkosh, Wis. Died July 24, 1956.

DEMPSEY, John J., ex-gov., congressman; b. Whitehaven, Pa., June 22, 1879; student pub. schs. Pa.; married; 3 children. Railroad work at age of 13; was v.p. Brooklyn Rapid Transit Co.; v.p. Continental Oil & Asphalt Co., 1919-20; independent oil operator, 1920-28; president of the United States Asphalt Corporation. Mem. 74th to 76th Congresses (1935-41), N.M. at large; mem. U.S. Maritime Commn.; apptd. under sec. of Interior, 1941; took office as gov. of New Mexico, Jan. 1, 1943; inaugurated second term, Jan. 1945; mem. 82d-85th U.S. Congresses, N.M. at large. Home: Santa Fe. N.M. Office: House Office Bldg., Washington. Died Mar. 11, 1958; buried Santa Fe, N.M.

DEMPSEY, John Stanley, pres. Buda Co.; b. Buda, Ill., June 14, 1891; s. Watson Charles and Alice May (Wilson) D.; student U. Ill., 1910; m. Lyda L. Huling, Sept. 16, 1916; children—Robert Clark (maj. USAAC, killed in action, July 9, 1943), George Huling. With Buda Co., 1911-—, successively clk., chief bookkeeper, office mgr., asst. treas., treas. and sec. and treas., 1911-39, pres., treas., 1939-—. Republican. Episcopalian (sr. warden). Club: Chicago Athletic (Chgo.); Flossmoor Country. Home: Brassie Av., Flossmoor, Ill. Office: The Buda Co., Harvey, Ill. Died Aug. 17, 1950.

DENARI, Andrew F(rank) (dĕnârê), business exec.; b. Bklyn., Nov. 19, 1905; s. Eugene and Mary (Rebasti) D.; student pub. schs.; m. Mary Gombas, Jan. 29, 1938; children—Carol Anne, Eileen Mary, Gregory Andrew, Sandra Lois. With Pa. Coal Co., 1919-30; with Pittston Co., N.Y.C., 1930-—, v.p., 1943-55, exec. v.p., 1955-56, pres., 1956-—, officer and dir. affiliates and subsidiaries; Bakes & Williams Inc., Sheridan-Wyoming Coal Co., Globe Fuel Products, Inc., Pittston Clinchfield Coal Sales Corp., Metropolitan Petroleum Corp., Lillybrook Coal Co., Davis-Clinchfield Export Coal Co., Pittston Marine Corp., U.S. Trucking Corp.; dir. Chemway Corp. Republican. Roman Catholic. Clubs: Cloud, Economic. Home: 487 Park Av., Manhasset, L.I. Office: 250 Park Av., N.Y.C. 17. Died May 2, 1958; buried Holy Rood Cemetery, Westbury, L.I., N.Y.

DENDRAMIS, Vassili, Greek diplomat; b. Athens, Greece, May 1883; LL.D., U. Athens, Journalist, 1903-07; sec. Press Bur. of Fgn. Ministry, 1907-10; attaché Ministry of Fgn. Affairs, 1910-12; vice consul, successively, Albania, Smyrna and Constantinople, 1912-14; sec. Greek legation, Bucharest, 1914-19; acting consul gen., successively, Berne, Trieste and Milan, 1920-22; permanent rep. of Greek govt., League of Nations, Geneva, 1923-27; minister at Sofia, 1928-32; dir. Press Bureau of Ministry of Fgn. Affairs, 1932; minister at Cairo, 1933-36; minister simultaneously to Argentina, Brazil, Chile and Uruguay, 1936-45; minister for press and information, 1946; apptd. permanent rep. of Greece to UN, with rank of ambassador, 1946; ambassador to U.S. and minister (simultaneously) to Mexico, Cuba, Columbia and Panama, 1947. Address: Royal Greek Embassy, Washington 8. Died May 9, 1956.

DENE, Shafto Henry Monckton, advt. exec.; b. Plattsburg, N.Y., Feb. 18, 1898; s. Robert Monckton and Charlotte C. (Cole) D.; student U. Chgo., 1920; m. Marjorie Ruth Hartzell, Jan. 3, 1927; 1 son, Jeffrey Abbott. From salesman to asst. sales mgr. Armour & Co., 1919-26; copywriter Erwin, Wasey & Co., Chgo. and N.Y.C., 1926-35; with Kudner Agy., Inc., N.Y.C., 1935—, sr. v.p., mem. exec. com., dir. and copy chief, 1950—. Served with Marine Bombing Wing, AEF, 1918. Mem. Am. Legion (charter), First Marine Aviation Force Vets. Assn. Mason. Clubs: Mount Kisco (N.Y.) Country; Recess (Detroit); Campfire of Am. (Millwood, N.Y.). Author: Songs in Silhouette, 1926; Trail Blazing in the Skies, 1943. Home: 245 Bedford Rd., Chappaqua, N.Y. Office: 575 Madison Av., N.Y.C. 22. Died Apr. 15, 1956.

DENECHAUD, Charles Isidore (dĕn'ĕ-shō) lawyer; b. New Orleans, La., Jan. 3, 1879; s. Edward Francis and Juanita (Del Trigo) D.; student Jesuits Coll., New Orleans; LL.B., Tulane U. Law Sch., 1901; LL.D., Loyola U., 1924; m. Rose M. Stafford, Oct. 30, 1907; children—Rosemary E., Kathleen F., Charles I., Margaret S. Practiced in New Orleans since 1901; former prof. civil law Loyola U., New Orleans; pres. Barcom, Inc.; dir. Nat. Am. Bank, Am. Safe Deposit Co., Inc., New Orleans Roosevelt Corp., New Orleans Hosp. Service Assn., New Orleans chpt. A.R.C. (hon. life mem.); chmn. bd. advisers Hotel Dieu and Xavier U. (New Orleans); trustee Cath. U. Am. (Washington); mem. bd. advisers Loyola U. (New Orleans). Mem. sch. bd. (Catholic), Diocese of New Orleans; mem. bd. commrs. New Orleans City Park; dir. Delgado Museum of Art, Marquette Assn. for Higher Edn., Internat. Trade Mart, New Orleans League for Better Hearing, Art Assn. of New Orleans, Internat. House Am. Hosp. Assn. (hon.); mem. New Orleans Assn. Commerce. Overseas commr. Nat. Catholic War Council of U.S., Paris, 1918-20. Created Knight of St. Gregory the Great by Pope Pius XI, 1924; Chamberlain of the Cape and Sword by Pope Pius XI, 1938. Past dist. deputy Knight of Columbus; past Grand Knight of Marquette Council, K.C. Pres. Fedn. Cath. Socs. of La., 1908-12; nat. pres. Am. Fedn. Cath. Socs., 1912-14 (declined 3d term); pres. Jesuit Alumni Assn., 1916-18; mem. Am., La. State, New Orleans bar assns., Blue Key. Contbd. article The Catholics of the South, in The Catholic Builders of the Nation (1923). Clubs: Pickwick, New Orleans Country. Home: Roosevelt Hotel. Office: Am. Bank Bldg., New Orleans 12. Died Oct. 21, 1956.

DeNEEFE, Robert, comptroller, Gulf-Mobile & Northern R.R to 1940, v.p. and comptroller, 1940—. Address: 105 Bienville Av., Mobile, Ala. Died Oct. 19, 1956; buried Pine Crest Cemetery, Mobile.

DENHAM, Robert Newton, lawyer; b. St. Louis, Mo., Oct. 23, 1885; s. Robert Newton and Sarah (Compton) D.; LL.B., U. of Mo., 1907; LL.M., U. of Mich., 1908; m. Mabel Hunt, Mar. 11, 1910 (divorced); 1 d., Marjorie (Mrs. E. C. Moerschel); m. 2d, Lyda Sells, June 16, 1920 (dec.); 1 d., Bobbie Mae; m. 3d, Christine Cameron Ross, May 29, 1934; children—Helen Cameron, Robert Newton. General practice of law, Yakima, Wash., 1910-14, Seattle, Wash., 1914-17; spl. reorganization service, Irving Nat. Bank, N.Y. City, 1920-29; on staff and by spl. assignments; reorganized Coral Gables, Inc., Fla., 1929-30; spl. office counsellor, Eldridge & Co., N.Y. City, 1930-33; spl. counsel to Comptroller of Currency, Washington, D.C., reorgn. of closed banks, 1933-34; trial examiner, Nat. Labor Relations Bd., 1938-47; private practice, Washington, D.C., counsellor on reorganization and govt. departmental business, 1934-37. Apptd. gen. counsel N.L.R.B. under Labor Management Relations Act, Aug. 1947, resigned Sept. 1950; pvt. practice law, Washington; pres. Fed. Trial Examiner Conf., Washington, D.C. Served as 2d lt., U.S. Air Service, 1917-19, World War I. Republican. Club: Early Bird Breakfast, National Press (Washington); Kenwood Golf and Country (Bethesda, Md.). Home: 4307 Bradley Lane, Chevy Chase, Md. Office: 1025 Connecticut Av., Washington 6. Died June 18, 1954; buried Arlington Nat. Cemetery.

DENIOUS, Jess C. (dĕn'yŭs), newspaper editor; b. Mogadore, O., July 14, 1879; s. Oliver and Martha (Moore) D.; Drake U., 1901-02; A.B., Baker U., 1905; m. Juliet Pettijohn, June 30, 1915; children—Martha Elizabeth, Jess C. Reporter Ottawa (Kan.) Herald, 1905-06; part owner Erie (Kan.) Record, 1906-09; editorial writer Wichita (Kan.) Beacon, 1909-10; editor Dodge City (Kan.) Globe since 1910, owner, 1910-53; pres. Globe Pub. Co., 1930—; pres. Dodge City Broadcasting Co.; dir. Victory Life Ins. Co. Western Light & Telephone Co., Grain Products, Inc., Preferred Fire Ins. Co. Del. to Republican Nat. Conv., 1924; sec. Kan. Rep. State Com., 1926-28; elected to Kan. State Senate, 1932, 36; elected lt. gov. Kan., 1942-44; mem. 1st Legislative Council established by Kan. Legislature, 1933. Chmn. Gov's. Commn. for Reorgn. State Govt., 1950; dir. Kansas Children's Service League, Member American Newspaper Pubs. Assn., Associated Press, Nat. Editorial Assn., Kan. Press Assn., Kan. State Chamber Commerce (dir.), Kan. Authors Club, Kappa Sigma. Presbyterian. Mason (32°, K.T., Shriner). Clubs: Topeka Press; Dodge City Country; Kansas City. Home: 1109 First Av. Office: 705 Second Av., Dodge City, Kan. Died Dec. 1, 1953; buried Maple Grove Cemetery, Dodge City, Kan.

DENIOUS, Wilbur Franklin, lawyer; b. Mogadore, O.; s. Oliver and Martha M. (Moore) D.; Ph.B., Baker U., 1898, LL.D., 1940; LL.B., U. Denver, 1902; m. Edith J. Boughton, Sept. 27, 1905 (died 1922); children—Dayton, George Boughton, Emma Jean (Mrs. Wilson M. Patterson), Wilbur F., Martha Muriel (Mrs. Joe V. Hawn); m. 2d, Mrs. Sherman P. Saunders, Sept. 25, 1939. Admitted to Colo. bar, 1902, since practiced in Denver; practiced alone, 1902-05, 20—; mem. firm Dayton & Denious, 1905-20; v.p., dir. Gates Rubber Co.; dir. Internat. Trust Co., and other cos. Chmn. Bd. Examiners of Colo. for Admission to the Bar, 1922—; trustee U. Denver. Mem. Am., Colo. (pres. 1937-38), Denver (pres. 1920-22) bar assns., Phi Delta Phi, Kappa Sigma (past nat. pres.). Republican. Mason. Clubs: Denver, Denver Press, Denver Country, Denver Athletic, Cactus, Mile High (Denver). Home: 2101 E. 7th Av. Office: Equitable Bldg., Denver 2. Died Oct. 10, 1957.

DENMAN, William, judge; b. San Francisco, Nov. 7, 1872; s. James and Helen Virginia (Jordan) D.; B. Litt., University of California, 1894, LL.D., 1944; LL.B., Harvard Law School, 1897; m. Leslie Van Ness, April 4, 1905. Admitted to bar, 1898; in general practice of law many years; assistant professor of law and lecturer Hastings College of Law and University of California, 1902-06. Chmn. of com. apptd. by mayor of San Francisco to report on causes of municipal corruption in San Francisco, and drafted report, 1908-10; organized state-wide movement for non-partisan election of judges, 1908, which obtained enactment of law, 1911; drafted non-partisan majority election law, now part of San Francisco charter, and campaigned for its passage. Chmn. U.S. Shipping Bd. and pres. Emergency Fleet Corp., also rep. of U.S. in shipping negotiations with Balfour World War Mission, 1917; federal receiver Coos Bay Lumber Co., 1919-22, chmn. bd., 1922-25; U.S. circuit judge 9th Circuit since 1935, chief judge, 1948. Author plan (1936) in part inc. in court enlargement bill of 1937 for separation of administration of lower Federal Courts from Dept. of Justice, for creation of court administrator and 50 additional judges (including 20 judges at large) for staffing of Federal Courts so their judges from time of commencement should press litigation to final decision. Mem. San Francisco Bar Assn. (trustee 1904-06, gov. 1911-19), Calif. State and Am. bar assns., Am. Judicature Soc., Phi Beta Kappa. Clubs: Commonwealth, Pacific Union, Bohemian, Sierra (charter member). Home: 2790 Green St. Address: 316 Post Office Bldg., San Francisco 1. Died Mar. 9, 1959.

DENNETT, Carl Pullen (dĕn'nĕt), b. Bangor, Me., July 14, 1874; s. Charles H. and Emma (Pullen) D.; student U. of Me. Law Sch., 1895-96; m. Marie Griffin, Sept. 9, 1905; children—Anne Bulen, Priscilla Alden. Brokers clk., N.Y. City, 1893; bank clk., 1894; partner Pearl & Dennett, brokers, 1895-1910; financial v.p., dir. and mem. exec. com. Griffin Wheel Co., 1910-14, trustee representing controlling interest, 1914-19; trustee various estates, etc., since 1919; pres. General Capital Co., 1929-43; pres., dir. Capital Mgrs., Inc.; mem. indsl. adv. com. First Fed. Res. Dist.; dir. N.Y. Central System, Florence Stove Company, John Hancock Mutual Life Ins. Company, First Nat. Bank (Boston), Capital Managers, Inc., United-Car Fastener Corp. Vice-chmn. Am. Red Cross Commn. to Switzerland, 1918-19. Vice chmn. industrial adv. com. of First Fed. Res. Dist. Republican. Mason. Clubs: Algonquin, Tennis and Racquet (Boston); The Country (Brookline); Essex County (Manchester, Mass.); Metropolitan, Recess (New York); Bohemian (San Francisco), Bath and Tennis, Gulf Stream Golf, Everglades (Palm Beach, Fla.). Author: Prisoners of the Great War, 1919; That Reminds Me, 1948. Home: 88 Clyde St., Chestnut Hill, Mass. Office: 45 Milk St., Boston 9. Died Nov. 17, 1955.

DENNETT, Edward Power, clergyman, editor; b. Keokuk, Ia., Jan. 6, 1863; s. Wesley Wing and Anna Hamilton (Power) D.; A.B., Coll. Pacific, 1882, D.D., 1904; S.T.B., Boston U. Sch. Theology, 1886; m. Alice E. Evans, 1891; 1 dau., Edith Evans. Ordained M.E. ministry, 1886; pastorates in Stockton, San Francisco, Alameda, Berkeley, Cal.; dist. supt. Oakland Dist., 1911-14; editor Cal. Christian Advocate, 1924-1932. Mem. Commn. on Unification with M.E. Ch., S. Mem. Gen. Conf. M.E. Ch. 7 times to 1924. Mem. exec. com. Cal. Anti-Saloon League. Mem. Phi Kappa Psi. Republican. Author: The Christian Program, 1905. Home: 859 Indian Rock Av., Berkeley, Cal. Died Jan. 27, 1947; buried Mountain View Cemetery, Oakland, Cal.

DENNIS, Fred L., clergyman; b. Shelby County, Ind., Nov. 21, 1890; s. John William and Sarah (Youngs) D.; A.B., Ind. Central Coll., 1916, D.D., 1927; B.D., United Theological Seminary, Dayton, Ohio, 1919; LL.D., Otterbein College, 1947; married Anna Maude Sullivan, December 20, 1911; children—Othella Gertrude (Mrs. Leslie C. Poling), Ruby (Mrs. John F. Finney), Fred, Janet (Mrs. Robert M. Eisendrath, Jr.), Martha (Mrs. C. W. Vertrees), Joanne Ruth (Mrs. C. W. Leedy). Ordained to the ministry of Ch. of U.B. (Evangelical United Brethren since union Nov. 1946), 1915; held student pastorates through coll. and sem.; pastor in Dayton, O., 1919-26 and 1929-41; supt. Miami (Ohio) Conf. United Brethren Ch., 1926-29; bishop, 1941—. Past pres. Ind. Council Churches. Address: 2019 Harvard Blvd., Dayton 6, O. Died Jan. 28, 1958; buried Memorial Park, Dayton.

DENNIS, Gabriel Lafayette, govt. ofcl.; b. Monrovia, Liberia, Sept. 24, 1896; s. Wilmot Eugene and Johnette Louise (Crusoe) D.; student Coll. of W. Africa, Monrovia, Mulgrove Coll., Liverpool, Eng., Syracuse (N.Y.), U.; LL.D., Coll. of Emporia (Kansas); m. Thelma T. Reeves, Feb. 29, 1940; (divorced 1950); children—John Lafayette, Wilmot Lafayette. Cadet and clerk, Dept. State of Liberia, 1914-16; sec. Liberian Plenary Commn. to U.S. under Pres. C. D. B. King; sec. of treasury, 1932-40; mem. Liberian del. League of Nations, 1932; chmn. Liberian del., U.N. Conf. on Food and Agr., Va., U.S., 1943; mem. U.N. Interim Commn. on Food and Agrl., Washington, chmn. Liberian delegation UNRRA, Atlantic City, 1943-44; sec. State of Liberia, 1944; asso. chmn. Liberian del., U.N. Conf. on Internat. Peace and Security, San Francisco, 1945; prin. del. U.N. Orgn. Gen. Assembly, London, Jan.-Feb. 1946, chmn. Liberian del., U.N. Gen. Assembly, Lake Success, 1947; consul for Belgium to Liberia, 1922-44; del. of Liberia to 50th Anniversary of Foundn. of Protestant Mission in Belgian Congo, 1928; chmn. Liberian del. to San Francisco Treaty of Peace with Japan Conf., Sept. 1951; mng. dir. Liberian Entertainments Co.; real estate and plantation owner; dir. The Liberia Co., Liberian Fishery and Cold Storage Industry, Monrovia. Mem. Bank of Liberia, Ltd.; lectr. world geography and physics. Trustee Tubman Tchrs. Coll., Monrovia; pres. bd. trustees Coll. of W. Africa; pres. bd. mgrs., Booker T. Washington Agrl. and Indsl. Inst., Kakota, Liberia; mem. bd. trustees Y.M.C.A., Liberia. Decorated by many orders of Liberia and Europe. Mem. Internat. Diplomatic Acad., Geneva, Switzerland; Royal African Soc. (London; life mem.); Liberian Amusements and Arts Assn., United Races of Am., State of Calif. (mem. bd. govs.). Methodist: lay leader, vice chmn. bd. stewards, Meth. Ch., Monrovia; pres. bd. ch. Missions and Extensions in Liberia; lay del., to Gen. Conf., Atlantic City, 1932, Columbus, O., 1936, of Liberia to Internat. Missionary Council, Madras, India, 1938, 39. Club: Saturday Afternoon (Monrovia). Address: 96 Broad St., Monrovia, Liberia. Died June 23, 1954.

DENNIS, Lindley Hoag, vocational educator; b. Dover, N.H., Dec. 12, 1880; s. William Brown and Leah Helen (Goodwin) D.; grad. State Tchrs. Coll., Bloomsburg, Pa., 1899; student Cornell U., summer 1906; B.S., Pa. State Coll., 1912; A.M., Columbia U., 1933; m. Geraldine Gearhart Conner, June 23, 1904 (dec.); 1 son, Lindley Henry; m. 2d, Dorothy E. Arrison, Nov. 30, 1940. With Pa. Dept. Pub. Instrn., 1912-33, successively expert asst. in agrl. edn., state dir. vocational edn., 1920-33, dep. state supt. pub. instrn., 1925-33; asst. state supt. pub. instrn. Mich., 1933-34; exec. sec. Am. Vocational Assn., 1934-51; cons. vocational edn., 1951—; cons. State Dept. and Fgn. Operations Adminstrn., 1953-54. Mem. N.E.A., Pa. State Ednl. Assn., Nat. (pres. 1924-25), Pa. (past pres.) socs. vocational edn., Gen. Alumni Assn. Pa. State Coll., Phi Kappa Phi, Phi Delta Kappa, Alpha Zeta (nat. governing bd. 42 years, high treas., gen. sec. 1955), Iota Lambda Sigma. Republican. Presbyn. Mason (32°, Shriner). Home: 6108 Western Av., Chevy Chase, Md. Died Aug. 5, 1955; buried Trevorton, Pa.

DENNIS, Samuel K., lawyer; b. Worcester County, Md., Sept. 28, 1874; s. Samuel K. and Sally Handy (Crisfield) D.; prep. edn. Blair Acad., Blairstown, N.J.; LL.B., U. Md., 1903; LL.D., Washington Coll., Chesterton, Md., 1931; Litt.D., Loyola Coll., Balt., 1938; m. Helen Gordon Moore, June 1, 1911. Sec. to gov. of Md., 1900-04; practiced in Balt., 1904—; U.S. atty. Dist. of Md., 1915-20; chief judge Supreme Bench of Balt., 1928-44, resigned; prof. equity jurisprudence U. Balt. Law Sch.; dir. Eutaw Savings Bank, Fidelity Trust Co., Fidelity & Deposit Co. Was dir., sec., sec.-treas. and pres. Md. Tb. Sanatorium for 23 yrs.; chmn. Balt. chpt. A.R.C. Mem. Md.

Ho. of Dels., 1904. Mem. Am., Md. (pres.), Balt. bar assns., Md. Hist. Soc. (v.p.). Democrat. Presbyn. Club: Maryland. Home: 100 Ridgewood Rd., Roland Park, Md. Address: Davison Chem. Bldg., Balt. Died Jan. 11, 1953.

DENNISON, Clare, dir., Sch. Nursing, U. Rochester; b. Nova Scotia, Can., July 21, 1891; d. Lewis Palmer and Florence (Calkin) Dennison; came to U.S., 1915, naturalized 1930; student Acacia Villa Sem., Nova Scotia, Can., 1906-10; student nurse, Mass. Gen. Hosp. Sch. Nursing, Boston, 1915-18, B.S., Columbia, 1931. Clinical instr. in medicine, Mass. Gen. Hosp. Sch. Nursing, 1918-20, asst. supt. nursing, 1921-28; dir. Sch. Nursing, U. Rochester, 1931—. Mem. Nat. League of Nursing Edn., Am. Nurses Assn. Home: 260 Crittenden Blvd. Office: Strong Meml. Hosp., U. Rochester, Rochester, N.Y. Died Feb. 1954.

DENNISON, Ethan Allen, architect; b. Summit, N.J., Apr. 4, 1881; s. Charles Melville and Emma (McFarlan) D.; grad. Erasmus Hall, Brooklyn, 1897; studied Godfrey Architectural Prep. Sch., Paris, Ecole des Beaux Arts, 1899-1905 (awarded 3 medals); m. Elizabeth Pugh, Nov. 5, 1913; children—Ethan Allen, Jr., Charles Pugh, Ann; m. 2d, Hanni Buchi, 1 dau., Janet. Began in office of Trowbridge and Livingston, N.Y., 1905; practiced alone, 1907-10; mem. Dennison & Hirons, 1910-29; head of Ethan Allen Dennison & Assos. since 1929. Active in planning numerous buildings, including Hartford National Bank, Phoenix National Bank, Society for Savings of Hartford, Dept. Stores for Sage Allen Co. and for Wise-Smith Co., Hartford, Bridgeport Trust Company, Liberty Title and Trust Co. (Phila.), Corn Exchange Bank (N.Y.), U.S. Nat. Bank (Johnstown, Pa.), Hdqrs. of State Bank, N.Y., now Mfg. Trust Co., Peoples Trust Co., Brooklyn, now Nat. City Bank, Fed. Trust Co., Newark, N.J., and 60 other bank buildings; Sports Building (U.S. Military Acad.), important stations Pennsylvania R.R.; chosen in competition one of architects on housing program in New York and was one of group to plan $20,000,000 Fort Green project, Brooklyn; won Rockland Co. Ct. House Competition, 1928, Williamsburg Dime Savings Bank competition, 1924. Awarded Medal of Honor, Soc. of Diploma Architecte, France, Legion of Honor, French Govt. Mem. S.A.R., Archl. League (N.Y. City), Beaux Arts Soc. of N.Y., Am. Soc. of French Legion of Honor. Chmn. Red Cross drive for N.Y. architects, 1933-39. Clubs: Century (N.Y.), Apawamis, Mansuring Island (Rye), Charleston (Charleston, S.C.). Artist in water colors. Home: Middle Haddam, Conn.; Ravenwood Plantation, Walterboro, S.C. Office: 40 E. 49th St., N.Y.C. Died Oct. 8, 1954.

DENNISON, Henry Strugis, pres. Dennison Mfg. Co.; b. Boston, Mar. 4, 1877; s. Henry B. and Emma J. (Stanley) D.; A.B., Harvard, 1899; Sc.D., U. Pa., 1927; D.B.A., U. Mich., 1929; m. Mary Tyler Thurber, Feb. 12, 1901 (died Mar. 31, 1936); m. 2d, Gertrude B. Petri, Oct. 11, 1944. Pres. Dennison Mfg. Co., Framingham, Mass., 1917—; dep. chmn. Fed. Res. and dir. Federal Reserve Bank of Boston, 1937-45. Asst. dir. Central Bureau of Planning and Statistics, Washington, World War I; exdir. service relations U.S. Post Office Dept.; mem. Prres. Wilson's Indsl. Conf., 1919, Pres. Harding's Unemployment Conf., 1921; mem. Bus. Adv. and Planning Council of U.S. Dept. of Commerce, 1933; apptd. mem. Nat. Labor Bd., 1934; chmn. Indsl. Adv. Bd. under NRA, 1934; mem. Nat. Resources Planning Board, 1935-43, Nat. Manpower Council, 1951-52. Mem. Am. Acad. Arts and Sciences. Trustee, The Twentieth Century Fund, N.Y.C. Club: Harvard (Boston). Author: Organization Engineering, 1931; (with others) Profit Sharing and Stock Ownership for Employees, 1926; Toward Full Employment, 1938; Modern Competition and Business Policy, 1938. Home: Framingham, Mass. Died Mar. 29, 1952.

DENNISON, Jackson Belden, univ. prof., economist; b. Onslow, Ia., April 5, 1891; s. John and Matilda (Campbell) D.; A.B., Lenox Coll., Hopkinton, Ia., 1912; A.M., U. Wis., 1915, grad. student, 1919-21; grad. student, U. Minn., 1915-17; m. Mildred Rothhaar, June 20, 1923; children—John, Ellen, Margaret. Instr., Hamline U., St. Paul, Minn., 1915-17; instr., U. Wis., 1921-22; asst. prof. economics, Miami U., 1921-22, asso. prof. economics and bus., 1922-37, prof. bus., 1937-39, prof. finance since 1939; dir. Bureau of Bus. Research, since 1939; research asso. Cincinnati Bureau of Govtl. Research, 1931, 1945-46; dir. Oxford Nat. Bank. Served in F.A., U.S. Army, WW I with A.E.F. Mem. Am. Statis. Assn., Am. Finance Assn., Tau Kappa Alpha, Delta Sigma Pi, Beta Gamma Sigma. Mason (32°). Home: 327 E. Vine St., Oxford, O. Died Dec. 27, 1959.

DENNY, George Hutcheson, univ. chancellor; b. Hanover County, Va., Dec. 3, 1870; s. Rev. George H. and Charlotte M. (Wright) D.; A.B., Hampden-Sydney Coll., 1891, A.M., 1892; Ph.D., U. of Va., 1896; LL.D., Furman U., S.C., 1903, Washington Coll., Md., 1905, Tulane, 1912, Washington and Lee U., 1913, U. of Alabama, 1937; D.C.L., U. of the South 1914; m. Janie Junkin, d. Givens B. Strickler, June 1, 1899. Tutor, Hampden-Sydney Coll., 1891-92; taught at Pantops Acad., Charlottesville, 1892-96; prof. Latin and German, Hampden-Sydney Coll., 1896-99; prof. Latin, Sept. 1899-1911, acting pres., 1901-02, pres., June 1902-Dec. 1911, Washington and Lee U. (recalled as president 1929, declined); president University of Alabama, 1912-37, became chancellor, 1937, recalled as president, 1942, again chancellor, 1943. Chairman, Virginia Education Commission, 1944-45. Pres. Southern Assn. of Colls. and Prep. Schs., 1905, Coöp. Edn. Assn. Va., 1903-12; trustee Carnegie Foundation for Advancement of Teaching, 1905—; chmn. Rhodes Scholarship Com. for Ala., 1912-37; chmn. Va. State Bd. of Charities and Corrections, 1908-11; pres. Alabama State Board of Arbitration, 1912-16; member Alabama Centenary Commission; director of University of Alabama Million Dollar Campaign. Dir. Rockbridge (Va.) Nat. Bank; dir. Ala. Museum of Natural History. Mem. Ala. Edn. Assn. (life), Soc. Promotion Engring. Education, S.A.R., Eugene Field Society (honorary life membership), Phi Beta Kappa (senator of united chapters, 1932-38), Omicron Delta Kappa, Sigma Chi, Phi Eta Sigma, Blue Key; mem. Am. branch Newcomen Society of England; mem. advisory com. Soc. of Nat. Reserve Corps, U.S. 1913-18; exec. com. Nat. Assn. State Univs., 1914-15; mem. Coll. of Electors of Hall of Fame, 1940, 44, 45, 50. Head cottonseed industry div. of U.S. Food Adminstrn., Washington, 1917-18; apptd. by President Hoover mem. nat. commn. to study relations of fed. govt. to education, 1929; pres. Assn. of American Separated State Univs., 1929; pres. National Assn. State Universities, 1931. Mem. Southern Univ. Conference; mem. Southeastern Conf. (athletic); mem. Nat. Council Boy Scouts of America, 1935—. Named by popular vote, 1925, "the most distinguished professional leader of Alabama," Ala. Hall of Fame. Acclaimed First Citizen of Ala., Birmingham, Nov. 1946. Awarded Civitan key for outstanding service. Democrat. Presbyn. Rotarian. Clubs: Country (Tuscaloosa, Ala.); Fortnightly (Lexington, Va.). Author: The Subjunctive Sequence After Adjective and Substantive Predicates and Phrases, 1896. Contbr. to Library of Southern Literature, The South in the Building of the Nation, and articles in various encys. and mags. Home: University, Ala.; (summer) Lexington, Va. Office: University, Ala. Died Apr. 2, 1955; Stonewall Jackson Meml. Cemetery, Lexington, Va.

DENNY, George Vernon, Jr., ednl. exec., broadcaster; b. Washington, N.C., Aug. 29, 1899; s. George Vernon and Carrie Ricks (Cobb) D.; B.S., in commerce, U. N.C., 1922; LL.D., Temple U., 1940, Ithaca Coll., 1951; m. Mary Traill Yellott, June 12, 1924 (div. 1943); children—Mildren Nelson Horton, George Vernon III, Mary Virginia; m. 2d, Jeanne Sarasy, Apr. 2, 1944. Instr. dramatic production, U. of N.C., 1924-26; actor, 1926-27; mgr. W.B. Feakins, Inc., 1927-28; dir. Inst. Arts and Scis., Columbia U., 1928-30; asso. dir. League of Polit. Edn., 1931-37; pres. The Town Hall, Inc., N.Y. City, 1937-51; founder America's Town Meeting of the Air, 1935, moderator, 1935-52, organized and conducted broadcasts on round the world mission; founder Covered Bridge Shopping Area, 1954; organized Internat. Seminars, Inc., now pres., 1958, conducted seminars in 7 S.A. countries. Mem. N.W. Conn. Assn. (pres.). Clubs: Pi Kappa Phi, University. Editor (book) Faith for Today. Writer mag. articles. Address: West Cornwall, Conn. Died Nov. 11, 1959.

DENNY, Robert H., life ins. exec.; b. Plymouth, Ill., Oct. 17, 1897; s. Robert Alexander and Ella Henrietta (Marsh) D.; student Central State Normal, 1914-17; m. Ida J. Cross, June 18, 1926. Agt., later supervisor, dist. mgr. Mut. Benefit Life Ins. Co., N.Y. City, 1919-29; asso. state agt. Nat. Life Ins. Co., Cleveland, 1929-36; gen. agt. N.Y. City, State Mut. Life Assurance Co. of Worcester, Mass., 1936, dir. agencies, 1939-43, supt. agencies, 1943-46, v.p., supt. agencies since 1946. Served as pvt. to lt., A.E.F., U.S. Army, World War I. Mem. Worcester Life Underwriters Assn., Am. Legion. Clubs: Worcester, Worcester Country, Economic, Rotary, University (Worcester). Home: 77-1 Park Av., Worcester 5. Office: 340 Main St., Worcester 8, Mass. Died Dec. 3, 1956; buried Hudson Falls, N.Y.

De NORMANDIE, Robert L(aurent), obstetrician; b. Portsmouth, N.H., Aug. 24, 1876; s. James and Emily (Jones) DeN.; grad. Roxbury Latin Sch., 1894; A.B., Harvard, 1898, M.D., 1902; m. Alice W. Brown, Apr. 18, 1906; children—James, Alice, Ellen. Engaged in practice of medicine, Boston, 1902—. Diplomate Am. Bd. of Obstetrics and Gynecology. Fellow A.C.S.; mem. A.M.A., Mass. Med. Soc., Boston Obstet. Soc., Am. Assn. Obstetricians, Gynecologists and Abdominal Surgeons. Clubs: Union, Harvard, Aesculapian. Author: Case Histories in Obstetrics, 1914. Contbr. med. jours. Home: Lincoln, Mass. Died Apr. 20, 1953.

DENSMORE, Frances; b. Red Wing, Minn., May 21, 1867; d. Benjamin and Sarah (Greenland) Densmore; studied piano, organ and harmony Oberlin Conservatory Music, 1884-86; piano with Carl Baermann, Boston, and counterpoin twith Prof. John K. Paine, Harvard, 1889-90; piano with Leopold Godowsky, 1898; A.M. (hon.), Oberlin Coll., 1924; Litt.D., Macalester Coll., 1950. Began studying music of Am. Indians, 1893; made spl. researches in Am. Indian music for the Bur. of Am. Ethnology, 1907—; collaborator Bur. of Am. Ethnology, Smithsonian Instn., 1926—; made survey of music of Indians in Gulf States for NRC, 1932-33; research on Indian music for the S.W., Museum, Los Angeles, 1935-37, asso. in anthothology, 1950; worked for James Jerome Hill Reference Library, St. Paul, writing description of water-color drawings of N.A. Indians (by Seth Eastman) in Library, 1940; cons. Nat. Archives, on Smithsonian-Densmore Collection of sound-recordings of Am. Indian music 1941-43, spl. work in connection with the collection for Library of Congress, 1948—; cons. Nat. Com. on Folk Arts of U.S. Made survey of Indians in Mich. for U. Mich., 1945. Mem. 19th, 20th, 25th Internat. Congresses of Americanists. Mem. nat. com. Nat. Folk Festival, 1933—. Recipient award Nat. Assn. Am. Composers and Condrs. for service to American music, 1940-41. Fellow A.A.A.S.; mem. Nat. Assn. for Am. Composers and Conductors, Soc. Women Geographers (exec. council, 1933-42), Minn. Hist. Soc. (life), Minn. Archeol. Soc. (hon.), Sigma Alpha Iota (hon.), Thursday Musical (hon. Mpls.). Republican. Episcopalian. Author: Chippewa Music; Chippewa Music II; Teton Sioux Music; Northern Ute Music; Mandan and Hidatsa Music; Poems from from Sioux and Chippewa Songs; Indian Action Songs; The American Indians and Their Music; Handbook of the Collection of Musical Instruments in the United States National Museum; Music of the Tule Indians of Panama; Chippewa Customs; Uses of Plants by the Chippewa Indians; Papago Music; Pawnee Music; Menominee Music; Yuman and Yaqui Music, Cheyenne and Arapaho Music; Music of Santo Domingo Pueblo, New Mexico; Nootka and Quileute Music; Choctaw Music; Music of the Indians of British Columbia; A Search for Songs Among the Chitimacha Indians in Louisiana; Bibliography 1901-46; numerous contbsn. to The American Anthropologists and other sci. jours. Home: 729 W. 4th St., Red Wing, Minn. Died June 5, 1957.

DENSMORE, John B., lawyer; b. Waterloo, Ia., Nov. 25, 1877; s. John F. and Catherine (McDonald) D.; prep. edn. high sch., Waterloo; LL.B., Ind. Law Coll., 1909; m. Mary Elizabeth Kennedy, Sept. 23, 1903. Electrician Bell Telephone Co., various stas. in Ia. to 1902; with Mine Workers' Jour., Indpls., 1904-09; practiced law, Polson, Mont., 1909-13; 1st judge Municipal Court, Polson, and brought about commn. form of govt. there; solicitor Dept. of Labor, 1913-18; apptd. dir. gen. U.S. Employment Service, 1918. Democrat. Catholic. Club: University (Washington). Home: 2813 Woodley Rd. N. W. Office: National Met. Bk. Bldg., Washington. Died July 29, 1937.

DENT, Hawthorne K., insurance exec.; b. Portland, Ore., Oct. 29, 1880; s. William and Alma (Kingsbury) D.; ed. Hill Military Acad., Portland, Ore., 1899; m. Dorothy Lindley, June 9, 1926 (dec. 1952); m. 2d, Ethel M. Hofius, Aug. 6, 1954. Founder, pres., dir. General Ins. Co. of America, 1923-52, chmn. bd. dir. since 1952; chmn. bd., dir. Gen. Casualty Co. of Am., First Nat. Ins. Co. of Am., Gen. America Corporation, SAFECO Insurance Company of America. Chairman Seattle Community Fund Campaign, 1929, 30. Mem. Seattle C. of C., S.A.C. Clubs: Rainier, Seattle Golf, Seattle Yacht. Home: 1500 42d Av. N. Office: General Insurance Bldg., Seattle. Died Jan. 1958.

DENTON, Minna Caroline, home economist; b. Baxter Springs, Kan., Jan. 16, 1873; d. Lucius Gary and Caroline Antoinette (Hubbard) D.; B.A., U. Mich., 1900, M.A., 1901; Ph.D., U. Chgo., 1918. Tchr. pub. schs., Ft. Smith, Ark., 1891-98; lab. asst., bot. labs., U. Mich., 1900-01; instr. biology and sanitation, Milw.-Downer Coll., 1901-06; instr., later prof. physiology and sanitation, and prof. domestic science, Lewis Inst., Chgo., 1906-14; hon. fellow in home economics, U. Chgo., 1908; instr. same, summer session, 1913; prof. home economics, Ohio State U., 1914-16; fellow in physiology, U. Chgo., 1916-17, Ellen H. Richards fellow, 1917-18; with U.S. Dept. Agr. as asst. chief Office of Home Economics, and nutrition chemist Bur. Home Economics, 1918-25; prof. and head home economics dept., George Washington U., 1925-29; prof. household science, U. Cal., summer, 1925, U. Wash., summer, 1928; cons. to mfrs., 1929—. Pres. D.C. Home Economics Assn. 1922-24. Mem. Am. Chem. Soc., Am. Home Economics Assn., Sigma Xi. Home: Ft. Smith, Ark. Died Jan. 20, 1958; buried Oak Cemtery, Ft. Smith.

DENVER, Matthew Rombach, ex-congressman; b. Wilmington, O., Dec. 21, 1870; s. Gen. James W. and Louise C. (Rombach) D.; A.B., Georgetown U., 1892; m. Veda Slack, Oct. 24, 1900; 1 dau., Virginia (Mrs. Williams). Pres. Clinton County Nat. Bank & Trust Co.; pres. Irwin Augur Bit Co. Pres. Ohio Bankers Assn., 1918-19. Del. Dem. Nat. Conv., 1896, del. at large, 5 times since 1908, mem. Dem. State Exec. Com., 1896-1904, 1926-30, Dem. State

Central Com., 1905-08; mem. 60th, 61st, 62d Congresses (1907-13), 6th Ohio Dist. Home: Wilmington, O. Died May 13, 1954.

DEPEW, Claude Ira (dê-pū'), lawyer; b. Mill Grove, Mercer County, Mo., Jan. 6, 1893; s. Levi Jacob and Nettie May (Flowers) D.; grad. Gem City Business Coll., Quincy, Ill., 1909; LL.B., Hamilton Coll. of Law (extension course), 1918; m. Frances Anne Bell, Nov. 4, 1914; children—Mary Frances (Mrs. Guy Reeder Campbell, Jr.), Mina Margaret (Mrs. John Henry Bush), Nancy Jane (Mrs. Marshall Bingham), Spencer Long, Jeanette Anne (Mrs. J. Ronald Bevers). Secretary of the Fred Harvey System, 1910-11; government clerk, P.I., and spl. agt. Philippine Customs Service, 1911-14; with U.S. Dept. of Agr. and Forest Service, 1914-16; extension sec., N.M. Coll. of Agr. and Mechanic Arts and editor N.M. Farm Courier, 1916-17; admitted to Kan. bar, 1919, and since in practice of law at Wichita; partner Depew, Stanley, Weigand, Hook & Curfman since 1920; dir. The Wichita Corp. (Western League Ball Club); dir. gen. counsel Ranson-Davidson Investment Co.; dir. Southern Supply Co. Mem. Am. and Kan. State (president 1954-55) bar assns., Wichita Bar Assn. (pres., 1938-39). Del. first Inter-American Bar Conf., Havana, 1941 and Third Conf., Mexico City, 1944. Republican. Mason. Elk (past exalted ruler, Wichita Lodge). Club: Wichita (Wichita). Home: 441 Morningside Dr., Wichita, Kan. Office: 830 First Nat. Bank Bldg., Wichita, Kan. Died May 15, 1956; buried Wichita Park Cemetery.

DE PRIEST, Oscar, ex-congressman; b. Florence, Ala., 1871; family moved to Kansas, 1878; ed. pub. schs. and business dept. Salina Normal Sch. Painter and decorator by trade; real estate business, Chgo.; county commr. Cook County, Ill., 2 terms; alderman, Chgo., 1915-17, 1943-47; del. Rep. Nat. Conv., 1928, 32, 36; mem. 71st-73d Congresses (1929-35), 1st Ill. Dist.; mem. Cook County Rep. Central Com., 1928-48, vice chmn., 1932-36. Mason (32°, Shriner), mem. Order of Eastern Star, Elk. Home: Chgo. Died May 12, 1951; buried Graceland Cemetery, Chgo.

DERBIGNY, Irving A. (dûr'bĭ-nĭ), coll. adminstr.; b. New Orleans, La., Mar. 27, 1900; s. Charles A. and Julia (Mallo) D.; A.B., Talladega (Ala.) Coll., 1921; A.M., Cornell U., 1925; Ph.D., Columbia, 1932; A.M., U. of Minn., 1939; m. Maurice Ethelred Newsome, Aug. 29, 1928; 1 dau., Mary Carolyn. Instr. in science, Va. State Coll., 1921; prof. of chemistry, Talledega Coll., 1932-36; dean instr. Tuskegee Inst., 1936-49, v.p. since 1949. Mem. N.E.A., Assn. Deans and Registrars, Am. Teachers Assn., Alpha Phi Alpha, Alpha Kappa Mu (formerly nat. pres.), Sigma Xi, Phi Lambda Upsilon. Mason. Author: Survey of General Chemistry, 1934; General Education in the Negro College, 1946. Contbr. research articles to Jour. of Higher Edn., Univ. Adminstrn. Quar., Jour. of Negro Edn., School and Society, Quar. Rev. of Higher Edn. Among Negroes. Home: 2803 Oak Av., Newport News, Va. Office: P.O. Box 186, Tuskegee Institute, Ala. Died Dec. 10, 1957; buried Newport News, Va.

DERBY, George McClellan, colonel U.S. Army; b. at sea, Nov. 1, 1856; s. Capt. George H. Derby, U.S.A. and Mary A. (Coons) D.; ed. pvt. schs. Paris, Dresden and Lausanne, Switzerland, 1865-71; Washington U., St. Louis, 1872-73, Symonds Acad. Sing Sing, N.Y., 1873-74; grad. U.S. Mil. Acad., 1878, U.S. Engrs. Sch. of Application, 1881; m. Clara Matteson McGinnis, Nov. 6, 1878; m. 2d, Bessie Kidder, Apr. 4, 1904; children—George Townsend (U.S.A.), Roger Barton (U.S.A.), Hollis Hasket, Elizabeth Crowninshield. 2d lt. Engr. Corps, 1878; 1st lt., 1881; capt., 1888; maj., 1898; lt. col. chief engr. U.S.V., May 9, 1898; hon. discharged, May 12, 1899; lt. col. engrs., U.S.A., 1906. On duty with battalion of engrs. U.S.A., 1878-81; asst. to Gen. John Newton in local charge of works at Hell Gate, E. River, and other river and harbor work in N.Y. and N.J., 1881-89; instr. practical mil. engring., U.S. Mil. Acad., 1889-93, and was mem. Academic Bd., U.S. Mil. Acad.; asst. to engr. commr., D.C., 1893-94; in charge 4th dist. Miss. River improvement, 1894-1902; chief engr. 5th Army Corps in Cuba during Santiago campaign, and chief engr. 2d Army Corps, 1898; in charge Louisville and Portland canal and other river and harbor work, Louisville, Ky., 1902-03; in charge reservoirs at headwaters of Miss. River, etc., Minn., 1903-06; retired at own request after 33 yrs. service, June 7, 1907. On active duty in charge 4ht dist. Miss. River improvement, 1917-19; promoted col. U.S.A., 1919. Cited for gallantry in action. Fellow A.A.A.S.; mem. Am. Soc. of Civil Engrs. Active in civic and social work in New Orleans, 1899-1921, serving on Parking Commn. and other commns.; was pres. La. S.P.C.C.; for 10 yrs. pres. of La. S.P.C.A.; dir. New Orleans Charity Orgn. Soc., La. Free Kindergarten Assn., Home for Homeless Men, etc. Club: Round Table (New Orleans). Home: 1015 S. Carrollton Av., New Orleans. Died Oct. 1948.

DERICKSON, Samuel Hoffman, prof. biology; b. Perry County, Pa., Apr. 9, 1879; s. Henry Benner and Lizzie Naomi (Hoffman) D.; student Lebanon Valley Acad., 1897-98; B.S., Lebanon Valley Coll., 1902, M.S., also hon. D.Sc., 1925; student Johns Hopkins U., 1903 and 1910; also student biol. labs., Cold Spring Harbor, N.Y. and Bermuda Islands; m. Jennie Vallerchamp, June 28, 1905; children—George Vallerchamp, Mary Elizabeth (dec.). Actg. prof. of biology Lebanon Valley College, 1903, professor 1907-50, emeritus professor of biology since 1950, actg. pres., 1912, treas. and trustee since 1918. Fellow A.A.A.S.; mem. Bot. Soc. of America, Am. Fern Soc., Pa. Acad. Science (pres.), Am. Soc. Zoölogists (asso.), Torrey Botanical Club, Am. Assn. Univ. Profs. Republican. Mem. United Brethern Ch. Mason (paast master). Address: 473 E. Main St., Annville, Pa. Died Nov. 27, 1951; buried Mt. Annville Cemetery, Annville.

DERN, John, lawyer; b. Salt Lake City, July 26, 1903; s. George H. and Lottie (Brown) D.; B.S., U. Pa., 1924, LL.B., 1927; m. Jean MacLeish, Sept. 20, 1930; children—John, Bruce MacLeish, Jean Elizabeth. Admitted to N.Y. bar, 1927, Ill. bar, 1930; mem. Sidley Austin Burgess & Smith, 1929—, partner, 1935—; gen. counsel, dir. Am. Natural Gas Co.; dir. Carson Pirie Scott & Co , Burgess Battery Co., Burgess Cellulose Co., Mich. Consol. Gas Co., Milw. Gas Light Co., Milw. Solvay Coke Co., Mich.-Wis. Pipe Line Co., Am. La. Pipe Line Co. Trustee U. Pa. Mem. Am., Ill., Chgo. bar associations. Clubs: Cliff Dwellers, Chicago, Union League (Chgo.); Kansas City, Indian Hill, Old Elm. Home: 94 Mary St., Winnetka, Ill. Office: 11 S. La Salle St., Chgo. Died May 22, 1958; buried Memorial Park Cemetery, Evanston, Ill.

DE ROSE, Peter (dê-rōz), composer; b. N.Y. City; s. Anthony and Armelina (Agresti) de R.; ed. N.Y. City pub. schs.; m. May Singhi Breen, Dec. 1929. Began as stock boy with Schirmer Music Co. while still in school and began composing at this time; mem. piano, ukulele and harmony singing team, Breen ("The Ukulele Lady") and De Rose, "Sweethearts of the Air," Nat. Broadcasting Corp., 1923-39. Composer: (waltzes) Tiger Rose, When Your Hair Has Turned to Silver, Somewhere in Old Wyoming; (songs) Muddy Water, Somebody Loves You, Have You Ever Been Lonely?, Wagon Wheels, Rain, Oregon Trail, Deep Purple, Lilacs in the Rain, The Moon Fell in the River, Somewhere, I Hear America Singing; (piano solos) Deep Purple (also vocal edit.), Royal Blue, American Waltz; (vocals) I Heard a Forest Praying, Seabees, Moon Light Mood, Twenty-four Hours of Sunshine, Who do you Know in Heaven?, A Marshmallow World, No Range to Ride. Member A.S.C.A.P., S.P.A. Address: 190 Riverside Dr., N.Y.C. 24. Died Apr. 23, 1953.

DE ROSSET, William Lord, bus. exec.; b. Wilmington, N.C., Oct. 27, 1832; s. Armand John and Eliza Jane (Lord) DeR.; ed. St. Timothy's School and St. James Coll., Md.; student U. N.C.; m. E. S. Nash, June 10, 1863. Worked at machinist trade Lawrence, Mass.; in mercantile bus. Wilmington, N.C., 1852-61; col. 3d N.C. inf., C. S. A.; since the war in business pursuits; maj.-gen. comdg. N.C. div., United Confederate Vets., 1895-1900. Address: Wilmington, N.C. Died Aug. 14, 1910.

DERWENT, Clarence (dĕr'wĕnt), actor, dir.; b. London, Eng., Mar. 23, 1884; s. Charles and Alice (Falk) D.; student St. Pauls, London, 1898-1902. Came to U.S., 1916. Played on London stage with Sir Herbert Tree, Granville Barker, etc., 1908-16, with Sir Frank Benson's Shakespearian Co., London, 1904-08; 1st engagement in U.S. with Grace George in Shaw's Major Barbara, N.Y.C., 1916; played leading parts with Otis Skinner, Margaret Anglin, Laurette Taylor, Katharine Cornell, Lunt and Fontanne, etc. Dir. following plays on Broadway: Rebecca, 1944; Mademoiselle, 1932; Brittle Heavan, 1934. Pres. Actors Equity Assn., chmn. Exptl. Theatre Bd.; mem. bd. Am. Nat. Theatre and Am. Theatre Wing. Mem. Ethical Soc. Club: Lambs. Home: 325 W. 45th St. N.Y.C. Office: Actors Equity Assn., 45 W. 47th St., N.Y.C. Died Aug. 6, 1959.*

DERY, D(esiderius) Geofge (dĕr'ĭ), ret. silk mfr.; b. Baja, Austria; s. Maxmilian G. and Joan (Latinov) D.; grad. Vienna Textile Acad., 1884; A.B., St. Mary's Acad., Vienna, 1885; m. Helen Meszaros, Nov. 21, 1891 (dec.); children—Joan (dec.), George M., Charles F., Helen. Came to America, 1887; supt. silk mills in New York, 1888-92; began mfg. in own name, at Paterson, N.J., 1892; built silk mill in Pa., at Catasauqua, 1897; owner of 42 factories in N.J., Pa., Mass. and Va., retired 1936; active in abstract scientific work. Mem. Silk Assn. Am. (dir.), N.A.M., A.A.A.S., Met. Mus. Art. Republican. Lutheran. Clubs: Republican, Manhattan, Aldine, Engineers', Army and Navy (N.Y. C.); Manufacturers' (Phila.); Hamilton (Paterson, N.J.); etc. Author: Under the Big Dipper, 1916; Jean Kressley, 1919. Home: Catasauqua, Pa. Deceased.

DESMOND, Thomas Henry, land architect, engr.; b. Hyde Park, Boston, Dec. 19, 1884; s. John Jerome and Margaret (Conway) D.; student Roxbury (Mass.) Latin Sch., Roxbury, 1897-99; diploma in horticulture, Conn. Agrl. Coll., 1906; B.S.A., Cornell, 1908; student landscape architecture in Europe, 1913; m. Olive Antoinette Eddy, June 1, 1910; children—John E., Thomas C., Robert C., Philip D., Elizabeth (Mrs. Dana A. Keil), MacChesney, James M., Sylvia E. (Mrs. Austin M. Sheldon). Draftsman, superintendent construction, designer, office chief, Townsend & Fleming, landscape architects, Buffalo, N.Y., 1908-13; independent practice landscape architect, Hartford, Conn., 1913-18; dist., town planner, U.S. Housing Corp., Washington, 1918; pvt. practice, Simsbury, Conn., 1919-28; pres., treas., Thomas H. Desmond, Inc., Simsbury, Conn., 1928—; inspector C.C.C. State Park Development in New England and asst. regional officer, regional 1, Nat. Park Service, 1934-37; supt. landscape constrn. Pentagon Bldg., U.S. War Dept., Washington, 1942-43; planning cons. Conn. State Park and Forest Commn. 1943—; supt. Conn. State Parks 1948-49; president Town and City Planning, New Haven, Conn. Sec. Simsbury Development Co. Important works: Willow Brook Park, New Britain, Conn., estates F. B. Rentschler, Geo. J. Mead, etc., U.S. Coast Guard Acad., New London, Conn., U. Conn. campus; developed plans for Westminster Sch., Taft Sch., Conn. Masonic Home, etc. Registered engr. and land surveyor, Conn. Mem. Pres. Hoover's conf. on small home bldg. and ownership (collaborator report on Home Grounds planning), 1932. Fellow Am. Soc. Landscape Architects (vice pres. 1942-49; trustee); mem. American Arbitration Assn. (mem. nat. panel arbitrators 1941—; bd. edn., Town of Simsbury, Conn., 1924-28, chmn. town plan commn., 1928-34, mem. zoning bd. appeals, 1940—, Am. Planning and Civic Assn., Conn. Soc. C.E., Conn. Hort. Soc., Conn. Forest and Park Assn., Wilderness Soc., Eta Lambda Sigma. Republican. Conglist. Mason (grand master, grand lodge of Conn., 1939-40, bd. mgrs. Masonic Charity Found. Conn., 1939—), co-founder, Philosophic Lodge of Research, 1941. Office: One Drake Hill Rd., Simsbury, Conn. Died May 20, 1950; buried Simsbury (Conn.) Center Cemetery.

DESPARD, Clement L., marine ins. broker; b. N.Y.C., July 14, 1884; s. Clement L. and Carolina R. (Bates) D.; S.B., Harvard, 1908; m. Jessie van Rensselaer Bond, Nov. 3, 1923. Engaged in marine insurance, and average adjuster; chmn. Despard & Co., N.Y.C.; v.p. Ben Grosvenor Corp., Pomfort, Conn.; dir. L. W. Minford & Co., Overlakes Corp. Dir. Ins. Brokers Assn. State N.Y. Ins. Fedn. N.Y., Inc., Soc. of N.Y., Inc.; mem. exec. com. Seaman's Church Inst. Former trustee Pomfret Sch.; trustee Rumson Country Day Sch. Vestryman St. George's Ch., Rumson, N.J. Clubs: The Brook, Racquet and Tennis, Down Town Assn., Harvard, Seabright Lawn Tennis and Cricket (gov.), Seabright Beach (gov.); Rumson Country (pres.). Home: Rumson, N.J. Office: 1 Cedar St., N.Y.C. Died Oct. 10, 1957.

D'ESPOSITO, Joshua (dĕs-pô-sē'tō), cons. civil engr.; b. Sorrento, Italy, July 30, 1878; s. Antonino and Louisa Marie (di Pontecorvo; D'E.; student Royal Nautical Inst., Sorrento; hon. Eng. D., Ill. Inst. Tech., 1941; m. Katherine Von Olnhausen, Aug. 18, 1908; children—Louise, Joshua, Julian. Came to U.S., 1898, naturalized citizen, 1907. Began as draftsman Pa. R.R. Co., 1904, advanced to asst. to chief engr., 1913, in charge Chgo. terminal developments, 1913; asst. mgr. Emergency Fleet Corp., U.S. Shipping Bd., Washington, 1917-19; returned to Chgo., 1919, in charge Union Station project until completed, 1925; in pvt. practice, 1927—; apptd. state engr. Pub. Works Adminstrn., 1933; project engr. Sanitary Dist. Chgo., 1934. Mem. commn. and federal project engr. Chgo. Subway, cons. engr. subway, also Chgo. Plan Commn. Mem. Am. Soc. C.E., Am. Ry. Engring. Assn., Western Soc. Engrs. Independent Republican. Clubs: Union League, Engineers Exmoor Country. Home: 2744 Ridge Av., Evanston, Ill. Office: 20 N. Wacker Drive, Chgo. Died Nov. 16, 1954; buried All Saints Cemetery, Des Plaines, Ill.

DESPRES, Maurice Samuel, merchant; b. Chgo., Feb. 3, 1901; s. Isaac and Hattie (Samuel) D.; extension student Columbia, 1919-24; m. Margaret Lovat-Ellis, Nov. 10, 1930; 1 dau., Pamela Harriet. Partner Despres-Jacobs, 1923-31; pres. Dale Distbg. Co., Inc., since 1931, mng. dir. Electronic Research Supply Agy., 1942-45; chmn. bd. dirs. Dale-Conn., Inc., New Haven, since 1936; pres. Dale-New Jersey, Inc., Newark, since 1944; dir. Admiral Corp., Chgo., Section Seven Corp., San Francisco. Served tank corps. U.S. Army, World War I. Mem. N.Y. Heart Assn., Police Athletic League Yonkers (dir.) Club: Nat. Democratic; Harmonie. Home: 35 E. 76th St., N.Y.C. Office: 40 E. 32d St., N.Y.C. 16. Died May 2, 1954.

DESSAR, Louis Paul, artist; b. Indpls., Jan. 22, 1867; s. Joseph B. D.; student Coll. City of N.Y.; pupil of Nat. Acad. Design, N.Y.C.; M.E. Bouguereau and Tony Robert Fleury, Paris, and Ecole des Beaux Arts, Paris; m. Elizabeth Coombe, Sept. 3, 1891. Awarded 3d Class medal, Paris Salon, 1891; medal, Chgo. Expn., 1893, picture bought by French govt., 1893; mention Carnegie Inst., 1897; first Hallgarten prize, Nat. Acad. Design, 1900, N.A., 1906. Represented in Nat. Gallery, Washington, Omaha and St. Louis galleries and Metropolitan Mus. Art, N.Y.C. Home: Old Lyme, Conn. Died Feb. 1952.

DESSION, George Hathaway, educator; b. Brooklyn, Dec. 17, 1905; s. Alphonse and Nellie Louise (Piguet) D.; A.B., Cornell, 1926, A.M., 1927, LL. B., Yale, 1930, M.A. (hon.), 1938; m. Anna Margaret James, Sept. 10, 1932. Admitted to Conn. bar, 1930, N.Y. State bar, 1932; mem. law faculty, Yale, since 1931, with faculties of psychiatry and pub. health since 1935, Lines prof. of law since 1938; fellow Social Science Research Council, 1933-34; fellow John Simon Guggenheim Meml. Found., 1951-52; spl. asst. to atty. gen. of U.S. (anti-trust and criminal div.), 1938-43, special counsel campaign expenditures investigation com., U.S. House of Rep., 1944-45; atty., U.S. Securities and Exchange Commn. (protective com. study), 1934-35; intermittent legal assignments U.S. Government, 1934-45; director of crisis and disaster study, Rand Corp., 1948-49. Legal cons. to the Forensic Com. of the Group for the Advancement Psychiatry, 1950. Mem. U.S. Supreme Court Adv. Com. on rules of criminal procedure, 1941-46; spl. Enemy Alien Hearing Board (Ft. Howard), 1942-43; asso. director Correctional Instns. Survey. Conn. Commn. on the Orgn. of State Depts., 1949-50; consultant on law enforcement agencies, Conn. Commn. on the Reorganization of State Depts., 1935; del. representing Yale and Internat. Soc. of Criminology to 2d Internat. Congress on Criminology, Paris, 1950, also to 12th Internat. Penal and Penitentiary Congress, The Hague, 1950; cons. to Commonwealth of Puerto Rico, 1953-54. Trustee Fairfield State Hospital. Member Bars of U.S. Dist. Courts for Connecticut and the Eastern Dist. of Ky.; mem. Internat. Soc. of Criminology (rep. assn. as consultant to economic and social counsel, U.N., 1950), Am. Soc. Pub. Adminstrn., Acad. Polit. Sci., Policy Science Found. (sec.-treas. and dir.), Conn. Joint Com. of State Mental Hosps. (vice chmn.), Conn. Govs. Com. for Study and Prevention of Sex Crimes (chmn.), Conn. State Bar Assn. (mem. com. on criminal law), Conn. Soc. for Mental Hygiene (dir. 1945-46), New Haven Co. Bar Assn., Delta Sigma Rho, Delta Theta Phi. Author: Criminal Law Adminstrn. and Public Order, 1947. Mng. editor Yale Law Journal, 1929-30. Contbr. articles in legal periodicals. Home: 470 Whitney Av., New Haven 11. Died June 19, 1955.

De SYLVA, George Gard (Buddy) (dĕ-sĭl'vă), theatrical and motion picture producer; b. N.Y.C., Jan. 27, 1896; s. Aloysius and Georgetta (Gard) De S.; student U. So. Cal., 1915-16; m. Marie Wallace, Apr. 11, 1925. Began as song writer, 1918, writing lyrics and librettos for musical shows; formed De Sylva, Brown and Henderson, Inc., music pub. co., 1927; producer motion pictures and musical comedies, 1929—; exec. in charge of production Paramount Studios, Hollywood Cal., 1941-44; pres. B. G. De Sylva Theatrical Enterprises, N.Y.C., 1939—; pres. B. G. De Sylva Productions, Inc.; chmn. bd. Capitol Records, Inc. Mem. Phi Nu Delta (now Theta Xi). Club: Lambs (N.Y.C.). Wrote lyrics and librettos for: Ziegfeld Follies, George White's Scandals, Queen High, Good News, Follow Through, Hold Everything, Three Cheers, Flying High, Sinbad, Big Boy, etc. Produced motion pictures: Sunnyside Up, Just Imagine, Little Colonel, Littlest Rebel, Captain January, Poor Little Rich Girl, Rage of Paris, Bachelor Mother. Produced musical comedies: Take a Chance, 1933, DuBarry Was a Lady, 1939, Louisiana Purchase, 1940, Panama Hattie, 1940. Home: 444 N. Faring Rd., Los Angeles. Office: 551 5th Av., N.Y.C. Died July 11, 1950.

DETMER, Julian Francis, merchant, importer; b. Cleveland, O., Dec. 4, 1865; s. Henry and Josephine (Kleine) D.; ed. pub. and pvt. schs., Cincinnati, O.; m. Esther Marie Downey, June 10, 1896 (died 1924); children—Esther Marie (Mrs. William Baden), Eugene Julian Vincent, Jerome Vincent. Woolen merchant and importer since 1885; founder firm Detmer & Moore (later Detmer & Richter), 1885; founder, 1888, and pres. Detmer Woolen Co., Columbus, O. (branches 11 U.S. cities), and Detmer, Bruner & Mason, Inc.; now president Detmer Securities Corp.; dir. County Trust Co., White Plains; propr. Detmer Nurseries, Tarrytown, N.Y. Patron of Metropolitan Opera Co.; mem. Metropolitan Opera Guild. Mem. Nat. Inst. Social Sciences, Am. Criterion Soc., League for Polit. Edn., Audubon Soc., N.Y. State Chamber Commerce, Westchester Co. Chamber Commerce, Met. Mus. Art, Brooklyn Bot. Gardens, Am. Mus. Natural History, Mus. City of New York, Acad. Polit. Science, N.Y. Zool. Soc., New York Bot. Gardens, Ohio Soc. New York, Am. Acad. Polit. and Social Science, Am. Fed. of Arts, Nat. Alliance of Arts and Industry, Am. Forestry Assn., Nat. Probation Assn., Internat. Benjamin Franklin Soc., Am. Scenic and Hist. Soc., Tarrytown Hort. Soc., Hudson River Conservation Society. Republican. Clubs: Metropolitan, Skytop, Sleepy Hollow Country, Everglades. Winner first prizes with products of pvt. tree nursery, Grand Central Palace, 1920, also many other first prizes. Home: Tarrytown-on-Hudson, N.Y. Died Nov. 26, 1958; buried Kensico Cemetery.

DE TRÉVILLE, Yvonne, coloratura; b. Galveston, Tex., Aug. 25, 1881; father French, mother American; mus. edn. under Mme. Marchesi, Paris, being the youngest mem. of her class; unmarried. Début in grand opera, and created La Boheme in English, N.Y. C. at 16; soon after appeared in rôle of Lakmé at Opera Comique, Paris; prima donna; Stockholm Royal Opera, and St. Petersburg Symphony Concerts, 1903-4; Cairo Khedivial Opera, and St. Petersburg Imperial Opera, 1904-5; Bucharest Nat., Berlin, Budapest Royal, Nice Municipal, Nice Casino Municipal operas, 1905-6; Theatre de la Monnaie, Brussels, Nice Casino Municipal, Nice Municipal, Budapest Royal operas, Vienna Philharmonic Orchestral concerts, and Munich, Kaim Orchestral Concert and created rôle of Errisiñola (opera by Louis Lombard, q.v.) at Trevano Castle, Switzerland, 1906-7; Theatre de la Monnaie, Brussels, Nice Casino, Nice Municipal, Cologne Royal Opera, 1907-8; Theatre de la Monnaie, Brussels, and Vienna Imperial and Royal Opera, 1908-9; Vienna Imperial and Royal and Budapest Royal operas, 1909-10; made concert and operatic tour of Germany, Austria, Hungary, Poland, and Roumania, 1910-11. Decorated by H. M. King Carol of Roumania with the Order of Bene Merito of the 1st Class. Sang Ophelia in the gala performance of Ambroise Thomas centenary celebrations in France, summer 1911; operatic tour of Germany, Austria, and Russia, winter of 1911; returned to Brussels as Prima Donna of royal opera at Royal Theatre de la Monnaie, 1912-13; appeared in concert, America, 1913-14, in U.S., Can., Mexico, 1915-17. Sings in English, French, Italian, German, Roumanian, Hungarian, Swedish, Danish and Russian. Home: 68 Rue de l'Aurore, Brussels, Belgium. Died Jan. 25, 1954.

DETWEILER, George H., lawyer; born Schuylkill Haven, Pa., June 25, 1883; s. Peter Christman and Luzetta, Rebecca (Horn) D.; prep. edn. Temple Sch., Phila., 1903-05; LL.B., Temple U., 1907-11; m. Eleanore Gambel Middleton, Jan. 25, 1908; children—Sylvia Eleanore (dec.), Robert Aaron. Clerk of P.&R. Ry., Reading, Pa., 1901-02, Phila., 1903, stenographer Pullman Co. Phila., 1903-13; admitted to Pa. bar, 1912; in practice, Phila., 1913—. Chmn. exec. com. Meth. Book Room, Phila., 1945—. Mem. Pa. State Occupational Diseases Compensation Commn., 1935, 36, 37; mem. com. to select new pres. for Temple U., 1941. Mem. Am., Pa. (chmn. com. on workmen's compensation law 1933-41, 44-50), Phila bar assns., Internat. Assn. Ins. Counsel, Fedn. Ins. Counsel, Gen. Alumni Temple U. (pres. 1940-41). Republican. Methodist. Mason (32°; past dist. dep. grand master Pa.; chmn. grand lodge com. on lectures, charged with formulating plan for Masonic edn. in Pa., 1943-48). Clubs: Union League, Lawyers, Caveat, Constitutional (Phila.). Home: 550 Review Rd., Swarthmore, Pa.; also 210 E. Atlantic Blvd., Ocean City, N.J. Office: Lewis Tower, Phila. 2. Died Mar. 7, 1953.

DETWILER, Samuel Randall, prof. anatomy; b. Ironbridge, Pa., Feb. 17, 1890; s. Isaiah H. and Mary (Hallman) D.; student Ursinus Coll., Collegeville, Pa., 1910-12; Ph.B., Yale U., 1914, A.M., 1916, Ph.D., 1918, hon. M.S., 1931; m. Gladys I. Hood, July, 1942; children (previous marriage)—Samuel Randall (dec.), Ross Harrison. Asst. Instr. biology, Yale, 1914-17, instr. in anatomy, 1917-20; asso., Peking (China) Union Med. Coll., 1920-23; asst. prof. zoölogy, Harvard, 1923-26, asso. prof., 1926-27; prof. anatomy and exec. officer of dept., Columbia, 1927—. Served as physiologist (civilian basis), U.S. C.W.S., 1917-18. Mem. Am. Assn. Anatomists (mem. exec. com. 1930-34, v.p. 1952-54, pres. 1954-56), Am. Physicians Art Assn., N.Y. Acad. Scis., Am. Naturalists, Am. Neurol. Assn., Soc. Exptl. Biology and Medn., Am. Acad. Arts and Sciences, Nat. Acad. Sciences, Harvey Soc., Am. Philos. Soc., Sigma Xi, Gamma Alpha, Nu Sigma Nu, Omicron Kappa Upsilon. Author: Neuroembryology, 1936; Vertebrate Photoreceptor, 1943. Mem. editorial bds.: Exptl. Biology, monograph series; Jour. Exptl. Zoology; Columbia Biol. series. Mem. adv. board of Human Biology. Contbr. to Jour. Exptl. Zoology, Jour. Comparative Neurology, Proc. Soc. Exptl. Biology and Medicine, Am. Jour. Anatomy, Anat. Record and other journals. Home: 160 Cabrini Blvd., New York 33. Office: 630 W. 168th St., N. Y.C. 22. Died May 2, 1957.

DETWILER, W(illiam) Frank, mfr.; b. Bedford, County, Pa., Oct. 14, 1880. Formerly exec. v.p. and gen. mgr., Allegheny Steel Co., elected pres., 1937; on merger with Ludlum Steel Co., chmn. bd. Allegheny Ludlum Steel Corp., 1938. Home: 1305 N. Highland Av., Pitts. Office: Brackenridge, Pa. Died Sept. 5, 1950.*

DETWILLER, Frederick Knecht (dĕt'wil-ler), artist; b. Easton, Pa., Dec. 31, 1882; s. John J. (M.D.) and Arabella (Knecht) D.; Ph.B., Lafayette Coll., 1904; L.H.D., 1945; LL.B., N.Y. Law Sch., 1906; admitted bar, in N.Y. State, 1906; studied art, architecture and painting Columbia U., Ecole des Beaux Arts (Paris), Art Student's League (N.Y.C.), Royal Inst. di Belle Art (Florence, Italy), École Americaine des Beaux Arts (Fontainebleau, France); m. Emelyne Lewis Gatch, Mar. 20, 1930. Exhibited in Salon, Paris, 1914; Whitney Museum of Am. Arts; Nat. Acad. Design, N.Y.; Art Inst. Chgo., Pa. Acad. Fine Arts; Corcoran Gallery, Washington, D.C.; Brooklyn Inst. Arts and Sciences; Adler Planetarium Astron. Museum, Chicago; Am. Museum Natural History, New York; Architectural League of N.Y.; U.S. Nat. Museum Smithsonian Instn., Washington, D.C.; exhibited prints, America in War, Artists for Victory, U.S. tour of museums, 1944-46. Awarded Shaw prize for etching, Salmagundi Club, 1920; print prize, Lotos Club, N.Y. City, 1940; medal Society Beaux Arts Architects, N.Y., 1910; medal of honor, Allied Artists America, 1941. Pennell purchase prize, Library of Congress exhibition, 1944. Represented in Lyman Allyn Mus., New London, Conn.; Mus. Fine Arts, U. Ga., Athens, Ga.; Lehigh Co. Hist. Soc., Allentown, Pa., Brooklyn Mus.; Cincinnati Art Mus.; Bennington (Vt.) Mus.; Art Center, Gallup, N.M.; Am-Museum of Natural History, New York; Peabody Museum, Salem, Mass.; Conn. State Library, Hartford; Farnsworth Art Museum, Wellesley College, Mass.; Lafayette Col., Easton, Pa.; Vanderpoel Memorial Art Gallery, Chicago; Museum of City of N.Y.; Bibliothéque Nationale and Musee Carnavalet, Paris; Library of Congress; Div. of Graphic Arts and Div. of History, U.S. Nat. Museum, Smithsonian Instn., Washington; Imperial War Museum, British Museum and Victoria and Albert Museum, London; Print Div., N.Y. Pub. Library; Internat. Y.M.C.A. Coll., Springfield, Mass; Print Div., Pub. Library, Newark, N.J.; Cabinet des Estampes, Bibliothéque Royal de Belgique, Brussels; Prentkabinet, Ryks Museum, Amsterdam; Walker Art Museum, Bowdoin Coll., Brunswick, Me.; Fogg Art Museum, Harvard U.; New York Hist. Society; Hayden Planetarium, N.Y. City; Borough Hall, Hellertown, Pa.; Naval Museum, U.S. Naval Acad., Annapolis, Md.; Old State House and Old Senate Chamber, Annapolis; City Museum, Vancouver, B.C., Canada; Pub. Archives of Canada, Ottawa; Metropolitan Museum of Art, New York. Appointed artists in residence, Lafayette Coll., Pa., 1948. Trustee Artists Fellowship, associate Nat. Acad., 1939; mem. Am. Water Color Soc., Salons of America (director 1922-25), Allied Artists of America (pres. 1943-45), Audubon Artists (dir.), Phila. Soc. of Etchers, Soc. Independent Artists (dir. 1925-34), Soc of Am. Etchers, Brooklyn Water Color Club, Conn. Acad. Fine Arts, Brooklyn Soc. Artists, Fine Arts Fedn. of New York, Am. Veterans Society Artists, American Color Print Society, The Artists of Carnegie Hall, Inc. (pres. 1933-36 and 1938-39), Carolina Art Assn., Southern Print Makers, Pa. Society S.R., Am. Friends of Lafayette (exec. council 1942-48), Art Students League (N.Y.). Chicago Soc. Etchers, Zeta Psi. Decorated Knight of the Holy Sepulchre, Greek Orthodox Church, May 1930. Clubs: Lotos, N.Y. Water Color, Salmagundi (pres. 1944-46). Originator of Frederick K. Detwiller System of Graphic Art Education—a traveling exhbn. used by schs. and colls., 1929—. Home: 41 McCartney St., Easton, Pa. Studio (summer) New Harbor, Me. Died Sept. 20, 1953.

DEUEL, Alanson Chase, newspaper and radio exec.; b. E. Hamburg, N.Y., Oct. 10, 1874; s. Israel and Mary Emeline (Chase) D.; ed. pub. schs., Hamburg and Buffalo, N.Y.; m. May Brock, Feb. 22, 1912 (dec. Dec. 30, 1930); m. 2d Helen Langmuir, Mar. 2, 1935. Joined Niagara Falls Gazette Pub. Co., Nov. 1895, pres. and pub., 1905—; pres., radio sta. WHLD; chmn. bd., Power City Trust Co.; v.p., Niagara Falls Hotel Corp.; dir. Maine Trust Co. of Western N.Y. Past pres. Travelers Aid Soc., Niagara Falls; mem. Niagara Frontier State Park Commn., Niagara Frontier Authority; dir. of Niagara Falls Memorial Hospital. Clubs: Niagara City, Niagara Falls Country (Niagara Falls), Bath and Tennis, Everglades, Old Guard (Palm Beach). Home: Mountain View Dr., Lewiston, N.Y.; (winter) 920 S. Ocean Bl., Palm Beach, Fla. Office: 308 Niagara St., Niagara Falls, N.Y. Died Oct. 19, 1954; buried Riverdale Cemetery, Lewiston, N.Y.

DEUEL, Harry James, Jr., college dean; b. St. Paul, Minn., Oct. 15, 1897; s. Harry James and Myrtle Lillian (Mouser) Deuel; A.B., Carleton College, 1918; Ph.D., Yale University, 1923; married Grace Antoinette Cutting, July 16, 1924. Chemists aid, later junior chemist, office home econ.., U.S. Dept. Agriculture, 1917-20; instr. dept. physiology med. sch., Cornell U., 1923-27, asst. prof., 1927-28; prof. physiology med. sch., U. of Md., 1928-29; prof. biochemistry med. sch., U. of S. Calif. since 1929, dean of graduate school, 1949—; Fulbright lecturer, Dunn Nutritional Laboratory, Cambridge, England, 1955-56. Member of food, and nutrition adv. com. Cal. State Disaster Council. Served in Students' Army Training Corps, 1918. Vice chmn., city and county food and nutrition com., Los Angeles. Mem. Am. Soc. Biol. Chemists, Am. Physiol. Soc., American Inst. Nutrition (received Borden award, 1949), Soc. of Experimental Biology and Medicine (chmn. Southern Calif. sect. 1941-42), Biochem. Soc. (London), Am. Chem. Soc., Harvey Soc., A.A.A.S., Am. Oil Chemists Assn., Assn. Study Internal Secretions, Sigma Xi (chmn. of U. of S. Calif. chapter, 1939-41), Phi Kappa Phi (pres. U. of S. Calif. chapter, 1945-46.). Phi Lambda Upsilon, Phi Beta Pi. Author: the Lipids. Vol. I. Chemistry, Interscience, 1951; Vol. II. Biochemistry. Interscinece, 1954. Mem. and dir. Annual Reviews, Inc., 1946—, pres.

1953—; asso. editor, Am. Jour. Physiol., Circulation Research; contbr. 250 articles to sci. publs. Home: 365 W. Bellevue Dr., Pssadena 2, Cal. Office: 3518 University Av., Los Angeles 7. Died Apr. 17, 1956; buried Olive Wood Cemetery, Riverside, Cal.

DEUTSCH, Alcuin Henry (doich), clergyman, educator; b. Valla, Hungary (now Wallern, Burgenland), Feb. 13, 1877; s. Joseph and Anna (Schneider) D.; brought to U.S., 1881; B.A., St. John's U., Collegeville, Minn., 1898; studied philosophy and theology Collegio San Anselmo, Rome, Italy, Ph.D., 1903. Joined Benedictine Fathers (O.S.B.), 1896; ordained priest R.C. Ch., 1902; asst. pastor St. Joseph's Ch., Mpls., 1914-16; prof. philosophy, St. John's U., 1903-14 prof. moral theology, 1916-22, pres., 1922—; elected abbot St. John's Abbey, 1921. Address: St. John's Abbey, Collegeville, Minn. Died May 12, 1951; buried St. John's Abbey Cemetery.

DEUTSCH, Monroe Emanuel, univ. provost; b. San Francisco, Calif., Aug. 17, 1879; s. Michael and Ida (Lilienfeld) D.; B.A., U. of Calif., 1902, M.A., 1903, Ph.D., 1911; LL.D., St. Mary's College, 1933, U. of Santa Clara, 1935, Occidental College, 1936, Mills College, 1937; University of California, 1948; married Alice Lois Feder, August 30, 1906. Teacher Mission High Sch., San Francisco, Calif., 1903-04; head of classical dept. high sch., Berkeley, Calif., 1904-07; asst. in Greek, U. of Calif., 1907-08, asst. in Latin, 1908-09, instr., 1909-14; asst. prof. Latin, 1914-19, asso. prof., 1919-22, prof. since 1922, also dean Coll. of Letters and Science, 1922-30, v.p. and dean, 1930-31, v.p. and provost, 1931-47, emeritus 1947, dean summer session, Los Angeles, 1918-20; prof. Latin, summer session, U. of Chgo., 1926. Studied in Europe, 1912-13, 1926-27. Apptd. annual prof., Am. Acad. in Rome, for 1931-32, resigned, 1930. Pres. Berkeley Community Chest, 1937-38; trustee Mills College, 1943-53; pres. Western Coll. Assn., 1949-50. Originated plan for Benjamin Ide Wheeler medal bestowed for distinguished service on citizen of Berkeley, 1927, awarded same, 1939; distinguished alumnus award, Cal. Alumni Assn., 1948. Mem. commn on needs of Cal., in higher edn., 1947-48. Pres. World Affairs Council of N. Cal., 1947-51. Mem. adv. bd. San Francisco State Coll., 1949-51; cons. Santa Barbara Public Library, 1951-52; pres. Rosenberg Foundation, 1940-50; vice pres. World Student Service Fund, 1943, 44. Mem. Philological Assn. Pacific Coast (pres. 1921-22), Classical Assn. Pacific States (pres. 1921-22), Am. Philo. Assn., Am. Assn. Univ. Profs., Am. Assn. for the United Nations, Delta Upsilon, Phi Beta Kappa (president Calif. chapter 1924-26, 1940-41), Golden Bear. Decorated Chevalier of the Legion of Honor (France); Commander Order of Merit (Chile); King Christian X Medal of Liberation (Denmark). Democrat. Jewish religion. Clubs: Faculty, Commonwealth (v.p. 1941-42, pres. 1943-44), Rotary (pres. Berkeley Club 1927-28; hon. mem. 1936—); Channel City of Santa Barbara. Writings deal with life of Julius Caesar and with Suetonius. Editor: The Abundant Life (by Benjamin Ide Wheeler), 1926. Author: Our Legacy of Religious Freedom, 1941; The Letter and the Spirit, 1943; The College from Within, 1952. Home: Hotel Clift, San Francisco. Died Oct. 21, 1955.

DEVER, Paul Andrew (děv ěr), ex-gov. Mass.; b. Boston, Jan. 15, 1903; s. Joseph Patrick and Anna Amelia (McAlevy) D.; LL.B. cum laude, Boston U., 1926. Admitted to Mass. bar, 1926, since in practice at Boston; rep. to the Gen. Ct. of Mass., 1928-34; atty. gen. Mass., 1935-41; lectr. sch. law Boston U., 1941-42; gov. Mass., 1949-53. Comdr. USNR, 1942—. Mem. Ancient and Honorable Arty. Co. Mem. Am., Boston, Cambridge bar assns., Woolsack Soc., Phi Delta Phi. Democrat. Catholic. K.C. Home: 86 Buckingham St., Cambridge, Mass. Died Apr. 11, 1958.

DEVIN, William Augustus (děv'ĭn), judge; b. Oxford, N.C., July 12, 1871; s. Robert I. (clergyman) and Mary (Transou) D.; student Horner Mil. Sch., 1883-88, Wake Forest Coll., 1888-91, LL.D., 1952; U. N.C., 1892-94; hon. LL.D. from U. of North Carolina; m. Virginia Bernard, Nov. 29, 1899; 1 son, William Augustus. Admitted to N.C. bar and practiced at Oxford, N.C., 1899-1913; in partnership with Judge A. W. Graham, Oxford, 1903-13; was mayor of Oxford, 1903-09; mem. North Carolina General Assembly, 1911 and 1913; judge of North Carolina Superior Court, 1913-35; justice Supreme Court of N.C. 1935-51, chief justice, 1951-54, emergency justice of the court 1954—; chairman Judicial Council, N.C. Major in N.C. Nat. Guard, Mem. N.C. State Dem. Exec. Com. Mem. N.C. Bar Assn., N.C. State Bar, Inc., Am. Judicature Soc., Kappa Alpha. Phi Delta Phi, Gimghoul. Democrat. Baptist. Mason. Clubs: Monogram (U. of N.C.); Carolina Country; Torch Club. Home: Oxford, N.C. Address: N.C. Supreme Court, Raleigh, N.C. Died Feb. 18, 1959; buried Oxford, N.C.

DEVINY, John Joseph (děv'ĭ-nĭ), govt. ofcl.; b. Washington, June 19, 1882; s. Edward and Johanna (Sullivan) D.; student Gonzaga High School, Washington, Josephinum Coll., Columbus, O.; LL.B., Washington (D.C.) Coll. Law, 1919; m. Edith V. Potts, July 12, 1906; 1 dau., Katherine E. (Mrs. Louis G. Carrico). Asst. dir. U.S. Bur. Engraving and Printing, Washington, 1924-26; dir. research and publicity Miller Saw-Trimmer Co., Pitts., 1926-28; exec. v.p. United Typothetae of Am., Chgo. and Washington, 1928-35; one of original execs. U.S. Social Security Bd., asst. dir. Bur. of Old Age and Survivors Ins., then mem. of appeals council, Washington, 1935-41; dep. pub. printer U.S. Govt. Printing Office, Washington, 1941—; cons. to Govt. of Czechoslovakia on matters related to engraving and printing, 1925; exec. dir. Code Authority, NRA with jurisdiction over 12,000 printing plants in U.S.; apptd. Pub. Printer of U.S. by Pres., 1948. Recipient medal from U.S. Govt. for supervision prodn. Liberty Bonds during World War I. Mem. Am. Trade Assn. Execs. (mem. nat. bd. dirs. 1932-34), Internat. Assn. Printing House Craftsmen (a founder of Craftsmen's movement in N. Am. 1st treas. internat. assn. 1919, pres. 1922-23, 26-27), Washington Bd. Trade. Mem. bar Supreme Court and Court Appeals, D.C. Roman Catholic. Elk, Modern Woodman. Clubs: National Press, Washington Printing House Craftsmen. Writer and speaker throughout U.S. and Can. on econ., indsl. and managerial subjects connected with the graphic arts. Home: 3571 Brandywine St., Washington 8. Office: U.S. Govt. Printing Office. North Capitol and H. Sts., Washington 25. Died Feb. 10, 1955.*

De VLIEG, Ray Albert, corp. exec.; b. Grand Rapids, Mich., July 13, 1888; s. Jerry A. and Mary (Van Der Dyke) De V.; ed. pub. schs., Detroit; m. Edna May Kreitzer, Nov. 2, 1935; children—Robert L., Eugene L. Gen. works mgr. Chrysler Corp., Detroit, 1922-30; vice pres. Reo Motor Car Co., Lansing, 1930-36; vice president in charge of manufacturing Nash-Kelvinator Corporation, Detroit, Michigan, 1936-55. Republican. Clubs: Golf, Old Athletic (Detroit); Athletic (Milwaukee). Home: 19460 Cumberland Way, Detroit 32. Office: 14250 Plymouth Rd., Detroit 32. Deceased.

DEVLIN, Thomas Francis, physician; b. Phila., Jan. 20, 1869; s. Thomas and Helen (Sanford) D.; A.B., LaSall Coll., Phila., 1887; student Georgetown U., 1887-88; M.D., U. Pa., 1891, post grad., 1891-92; m. Stella Hill, May 29, 1905; children—Thomas Francis, John Joseph. Physician, Phila., 1892—; asso. with St. Mary's Hosp.; staff mem. Misericordia Hosp., Archbishop Ryan Meml. for Deaf-mutes; pediatrist; pioneer in endocrinology as applied to children. Dir. and partner with wife, Marydell Sch. for physically and mentally retarded children. Republican. Catholic. Home: Manor Av., Langhorne, Pa. Died June 30, 1952.

DEVOE, Alan (dē-vō), author, naturalist; b. Montclair, New Jersey, Oct. 13, 1909; s. William Beck and Edith Guy (Taylor) D.; student Montclair High Sch., 1923-27, Columbia U., 1927-30; m. Mary Sheridan Berry, June 14, 1932. Author monthly department, "Down to Earth," American Mercury, 1937—; asso. editor The Writer; contributing editor Audubon Mag., Am. Mercury; spl. contbr., editorial cons. natural history Reader's Digest. Sponsor, Defenders of Furbearers, Washington. Author: Phudd Hill, 1937; Down to Earth, 1940; Lives Around Us, 1942; Mind in Nature (monograph), 1946; Speaking of Animals, 1947; This Fascinating Animal World, 1951; Our Animal Neighbors (with Mary Berry Devoe), 1953. Contributor to Atlantic Monthly, Country Gentleman, The Land, Nature Magazine, etc. Lectr. radio and television. Home: Phudd Hill, Hillsdale, N.Y. Died Aug. 17, 1955; buried Mt. Hebron Cemetery, Montclair, N.J.

DEVOE, Robert W., lawyer; b. Lebanon, Neb., Feb. 7, 1882; s. Elmore E. and Sarah (Casement) D.; LL.B., U. Neb., 1909; m. Maud Sovern, May 18, 1904; children—Melba D. (Mrs. Chauncey E. Barney), Robert D. Admitted to Neb. bar, 1909; Cheyenne County atty., 1910-14; mem. law firm Peterson & Devoe, Lincoln, Neb., 1914—; atty. Bankers Life Ins. Co. of Neb., 1915—; gen. counsel Neb. Nat. Life Ins. Co. Federal food adminstr., Lincoln Neb., 1917-18. Republican candidate for atty. gen. of Neb., 1916; chmn. Rep. State Central Com., 1919-20; commr. Uniform State Laws, 1923-27. Regent U. Neb., 1936-54, pres. bd. 1941, 46, 50, 54. Mem. Nat. Assn. Governing Bds. State Univs. (pres. 1943), Internat. Assn. Ins. Counsel, Am., Neb. (pres. 1928), Lincoln bar assns., U. Neb. Found., State Public Works Com., Theta Kappa Nu (now Order of Coif), Delta Chi, Delta Theta Phi, Innocents. Mason (33°, Shriner). Clubs: University, Lincoln Country. Editor: Neb. Law Bull., 1924-38 (also contbr. articles to bar sect.). Home: 2945 Georgian Ct. Office: Bankers Life Bldg., Lincoln, Neb. Died Nov. 30, 1957.

DEVOE, William Beck, lawyer; b. N.Y. City, Sept. 6, 1884; s. Charles and Anne Elizabeth (Beck) D.; A.B., Columbia, 1906; LL.B., New York Law Sch., 1908; m. Edith Guy Taylor, Oct. 6, 1908; 1 son, Alan Taylor. Admitted to N.Y. bar, 1908, to U.S. Supreme Court bar, 1924; law clk. in office Geo. D. Beattys, 1908-11; asst. to Abram I. Elkus, 1911-13; partner of Carl L. Schurz, 1913-24; gen. counsel Hamburg-Am. Line, 1924-40; sec. and dir. N.J. Machine Corp., 1918-40, Oceanic Service Corp., 1924-40, United Am. Lines, 1926-40; counsel for German shipping companies in internat. arbitration U.S. and Germany to settle war claims, 1928-30; retired from practice, 1940. Author: Corporation Almanac, 1919; Where and How, a Manual of Corporate Procedure (8th edit.), 1928. Contbr. articles on legal and financial topics to periodicals. Home: 300 E. 57th St., N.Y. City 22. Died June 10, 1951; buried Mt. Hebron Cemetery, Upper Montclair, N.Y.

DEVOR, Donald Smith, corp. exec.; b. Ft. Loudon, Pa., Jan. 24, 1889; s. John Henderson and Adeline Beatrice (Smith) D.; grad. Pa. State Coll., 1909; m. Esther Campbell, Oct. 30, 1911; children—Donald Smith, Adeline Beatrice (Mrs. Philip E. Penberthy), Richard Campbell. Joined Houdaille-Hershey Corp., Detroit, 1934, v.p., dir. since 1938. Served as maj., Q.M.C., U.S. Army, World War I. Clubs: Detroit, Detroit Golf, Athletic, Recess (Detroit). Home 850 Harcourt Rd., Grosse Pointe Park 30, Mich. Office: Fisher Bldg., Detroit 2. Deceased.

DeVOSS, James Clarence (dě vôss), coll. dean; b. nr. Creighton, Neb, Sept. 29, 1884; s. James T. and Ina Ruth (Brown) DeV.; A.B., U. Colo., 1911, A. M., 1912; Ph.D., Stanford, 1924; m. Alice O. Fisher, Aug. 28, 1912; 1 dau., Alice Jean (Mrs. H. C. Davis). Asso. prof. psychol., asst. dir. research Kan. State Tchrs. Coll., 1914-18; faculty San Jose State Coll. since 1922, prof. psychology, dir. bur. research, 1923-27, dean upper div., 1927-48, dean profl. edn., 1948-51, exec. dean, 1951-54; vis. prof. U. Cal., summers 1924-27, U. So. Cal, 1928-38, Northwestern U., summer 1937. Fellow A.A.A.S.; mem. Am. Coll. Personnel Assn., Am. Ednl. Research Assn., Am. Psychol. Assn., Am. Vocational Guidance Assn., Cal. Tchrs. Assn., Mental Hygiene Soc., N.E.A., Nat. Soc. Study Edn., No. Cal. Ednl. Research Assn. (sec. treas. 1922-24, pres. 1925-26), Sigma Xi, Phi Beta Kappa, Phi Delta Kappa, Kappa Delta Pi. Kiwanian. Author: Educational Tests and Measurements (with W. S. Monroe and F. J. Kelly), 1917-24: The Educational Achievement of Gifted Children (with L. M. Terman), 1924; Educational Psychology (with Monroe, Reagan), 1930. Home: 5336 Greenside Dr., San Jose, Cal. Died Apr. 24, 1956.

De VOTO, Bernard Augustine (dē-fō'tō), writer; b. Ogden, Utah, Jan. 11, 1897; s. Florian Bernard and Rhoda (Dye) De V.; A.B., Harvard, 1920 (as of 1918); Litt.D., Middlebury Coll., 1937, Kenyon Coll., 1942; University of Colorado, 1948, Northeastern U., 1948; married Helen Avis MacVicar, June 30, 1923; children—Gordon King, Mark Bernard. Instructor and assistant professor of English, Northwestern University, 1922-27; instructor and tutor, 1929-34, lecturer, 1934-36, Harvard. Served as 2d lt. inf., U.S. Army, 1917-18. Mem. adv. bd. for Nat. Parks. Awarded Pulitzer Prize for history; Bancroft Prize: also National Book award for non-fiction. 1953. Mem. Nat. Inst. Arts and Letters, Phi Beta Kappa. Clubs: Century, Harvard (N.Y.). Author: The Crooked Mile, 1924; The Chariot of Fire, 1926; The House of Sun-Goes-Down, 1928; (in collaboration) The Taming of the Frontier (history), 1925; The Writer's Handbook (text book), 1927; Mark Twain's America, 1932; We Accept with Pleasure. 1934; Forays and Rebuttals, 1936; Minority Report, 1940; Mark Twain at Work, 1942; The Year of Decision: 1846 (History), 1943; The Lietrary Fallacy, 1944: Mountain Time, 1947; Across the Wide Missouri, 1947; The World of fiction, 1950; The House, 1951; The Course of Empire, 1952; The Easy Chair, 1955. Editor Life and Adventures of James P. Beckwourth, 1930; Mark Twain in Eruption, 1940; The Journals of Lewis and Clark, 1953. Contributor of Stories, Articles, historical essays, reviews to magazines. General editor Americana Deserta; editor Harvard Graduates' Magazine, 1930-32. Editor of The Easy Chair, Harper's Magazine, 1935—, The Saturday Review of Literature, 1936-38; mem. editorial board New England Quarterly, 1942—. Address: 8 Berkeley St., Cambridge, Mass. Died. Nov. 13, 1955; buried The Lolo Nat. Forest, Ida.

DEWEY, Charles Almon (dū'ĭ), judge; b. Washington, Ia., Sept. 11, 1877; s. Almon Ralph and Sarah (Rousseau) D.; grad. Oberlin (O.) Acad., 1897; student Oberlin Coll., 1897-98; LL.B., State U. Ia., 1901; m. Jessie Irene Laffer, Sept. 1, 1910; 1 son, Almon Rousseau. Admitted to Ia. bar, 1901, began practice at Washington, Ia.; city atty., Washington, 1905-09; county atty. Washington County, 1909-15; dist. judge, Ia., 1918-28; judge U.S. Dist. Ct., So. Dist. Ia., 1928—. Served as cpl. U.S. Vols., Spanish-Am. War. Mem. Delta Tau Delta. Republican. Methodist. Mason; Grand Master of Masons in Iowa, 1929-30. Clubs: Rotary, Prairie, Des Moines. Retired. Home: 3007 Grand Av., Des Moines, Ia. Died Mar. 2, 1958; buried Washington, Ia.

DEWEY, James F., strike mediator; b. Locust Dale, Pa., Feb. 12, 1887; s. James and Ellen (Wilson) D.; ed. pub. and teachers training schs.; hon. LL.D., Wayne Univ., Michigan; m. Mae Dorothy Canfield, June 30, 1909; children—James F., Kathryn (Mrs. Harold G. Simms), Thomas C. Telegrapher Phila. & Reading R.R., 1907-08; auditor Phila. & Reading Coal & Iron Co., 1908-09; pub. school teacher, 1909-10; with Pa. R.R., 1911-19; mem. Pa. State Mediation Bd., 1919-22; spl. asst. U.S. sec. of labor and mem.

U.S. Com. of Conciliation since 1922. Labor relations counsel for numerous national corps.; has been active as mediator in many large strikes of U.S. since 1922; apptd. on bds. and commns. by Presidents Harding, Coolidge, Hoover and Roosevelt. Special mediator, settled Gen. Motors strike, 1946; referee U.A.W. and Briggs Body Co., Detroit. Received Meritorious Citation from Army and Navy, World Wars I and II. Mem. Nat. Assn. Pub. Labor Officials. Republican. Catholic. K.C. Home: 401 E. 19th St., Chester, Pa. Office: Dept. of Labor, Washington. Died Aug. 1950.

DEWEY, James F., woolen mfr.; b. Montpelier, Vt., Mar. 7, 1883; s. William T. and Alice E. (French) D.; grad. Montpelier (Vt.) High Sch., 1900; student Worcester (Mass.) Acad., 1900-01; grad. Lowell (Mass.) Textile Inst., 1904; M.S. (hon.) Norwich U., Northfield, Vt., 1920; m. Emily S. Dewey, Oct. 16, 1909; children—William T., Anna (Mrs. Edward J. Hughes). Supt. A. G. Dewey Co., Quechee, Vermont, 1904, president and treas. 1930-54; treas. The Dewey Corp.; trustee Green Mountain Mut. Fire Ins. Co., pres. Woodstock Electric Co.; state senator, 1929-31. Mem. Vt. War Labor Bd., 1916-18. Treas. Rep. State Com., 1918-40, chmn., 1940-44; Rep. nat. committeeman 1944-52. Vermont chmn. Nat. Foundation Infantile Paralysis. Trustee Norwich U., Worcester Acad. Dir. and vice pres. Nat. Association of Woolen Mfrs.; hon. v.p. for life Associated Industries of Vermont. Mason (Shriner), Elk. Rotarian. Clubs: Dragon Senior Society (Dartmouth Coll.); Metropolitan, New York Athletic; Lakota Trout (pres.) (Woodstock, Vt.). Home: Quechee, Vt. Died Feb. 7, 1956; buried Quechee, Vt.

DEWEY, John, univ. prof.; b. Burlington, Vt., Oct. 20, 1859; s. Archibald S. and Lucina A. (Rich) D.; A.B., U. of Vt., 1879, LL.D., 1910; Ph.D., Johns Hopkins U., 1884; LL.D., U. of Wis., 1904, Peking Nat. U., 1920, U. of Paris, 1930; D.Sc., U. of Pa., 1946; Ph.D., Oslo Univ., 1946; m. Alice Chipman, July 28, 1886; children—Fred'k A., Evelyn, Morris (dec.), Lucy A., Gordon (dec.), Jane U., Sabino L. (adopted); married 2d, Mrs. Roberta Grant, Dec. 11, 1946; children (adopted)—John, Jr. and Adienne. Instructor and asst. prof. philosophy, University of Mich., 1884-88; prof. philosophy, U. of Minn., 1888-89, U. of Mich., 1889-94; prof. and head dept. philosophy, 1894-1904, dir. Sch. of Edn., 1902-04, U. of Chicago; prof. philosophy since 1904, Columbia U., now emeritus. Mem. Nat. Acad. of Sciences, American Psychol. Assn. (pres. 1899-1900), Am. Philos. Soc. (pres. 1905-06); corr. mem. L'Institut de France. Clubs: Century. Author: Psychology, 1886; Leibnitz, 1888; Critical Theory of Ethics, 1894; Study 1894; School and Society, 1899; Studies in Logical Theory, 1903; How We Think, 1909; Influence of Darwin on Philosophy, and Other Essays, 1910; German Philosophy and Politics, 1915, rev. edit., 1942; Democracy and Education, 1916; Reconstruction in Philosophy, 1920; Human Nature and Conduct, 1922; Experience and Nature, 1925; The Public and Its Problems, 1927; The Quest for Certainty, 1929; Art as Experience, 1934; A Common Faith, 1934; Liberalism and Social Action, 1935; Logic: The Theory of Inquiry, 1938; Culture and Freedom, 1939; Education Today; Problems of Man, 1946; Knowing and the Known (with Arthur Bently), 1949. Home: 1158 Fifth Av., N.Y.C. Died June 2, 1952.

de WINDT, Delano, ret. headmaster; b. Chgo., Oct. 30, 1892; s. Heyliger Adams and Bertha Williams (Mandell) de W.; student Harvard, 1911-12; grad. Williams Coll., 1915; m. Ruth Church, June 17, 1916; children—Ruth (Mrs. A. R. Hoxton, Jr.), Mary (Mrs. William Archer Speers), Edward Mandell, Ann (Mrs. Frederick R. Schroeder, Jr.). Employee Morse Twist Drill & Machine Co., New Bedford, Mass., 1916; treas. Monument Mills, Housatonic, Mass., 1919-34; with Gramatan Nat. Bank & Trust Co., Bronxville, N.Y., 1934-36; with Berkshire Sch., Sheffield, Mass., 1936—, headmaster, 1943-51, ret.; former dir. Nat. Mahaiwe Bank, Great Barrington, Mass. Formerly treas. Fairview Hosp. Served with USNRF, 1916-18. Mem. Alpha Delta Phi. Club: Wyantenuck Country (Great Barrington). Home: Castle Hill Av., Great Barrington, Mass. Died Nov. 19, 1953.

DE WOLF, Frank Walbridge, geologist; b. Vail, Ia, Mar. 22, 1881; s. John Horton and Carrie M. (Tempest) D.; S.B., U. Chgo., 1903, post-grad., 1903-04; m. Fanny Davis, Dec. 26, 1904; children—John Walbridge, Eleanor, Robert Williams, Frank Tempest. Geologic aid and asst. geologist U.S. Geol. Survey, Washington, 1904-08; asst. state geologist, Ill., 1908-09; acting dir. Ill. Geol. Survey, 1909-11, dir. 1911-23. Asst. dir. U.S. Bur. of Mines, 1917-18; mem. com. on geology and paleontology and chmn. sub-com. on geology of cantonments NRC, 1917, div. of states relations, 1919-23; chief geologist Humphreys Corp., 1923-27; v.p., and gen. mgr. La. Land and Exploration Co., oil producers, 1927-31; head of dept. geology U. Ill., 1931-46, emeritus, 1946—; cons. on petroleum geology. Fellow Geol. Soc. Am. Soc. Econ. Geologists; mem. Am. Inst. Mining Engrs., Am. Assn. Petroleum Geologists (ex-v.p.), Ill. State Acad. Science (ex-pres.), Phi Delta Theta, Sigma Xi. Conglist. Clubs: University, Urbana Golf and Country, Kiwanis. Home: 601 W. Delaware Av., Urbana, Ill. Died Sept. 16, 1957.

DEXTER, Robert Cloutman, sociologist; b. Shelburne, N.S., Can., Oct. 1, 1887; s. William and Willamina (Snow) Dexter; A.B., Brown U., 1912, A.M., 1917; postgrad. Harvard, 1913; Ph.D., Clark U., 1923; m. Elisabeth Williams Anthony, June 12, 1914; children—Lewis Anthony, Harriet Angell (Mrs. P. W. Pennington). Dist. sec. for Providence (R.I.) Charity Orgn. Soc., 1912-13; agt. Mass. Soc. for Prevention of Cruelty to Children, 1913-15; gen. sec. Montreal Charity Orgn. Soc., 1915-18; with mil. relief dept. A.R.C., 1918-19; maj., 1919; gen. sec. Atlanta (Ga.) Charity Orgn. Soc., 1919-21; instr. sociology Clark U., 1922-23; prof. social and polit. sci. Skidmore Coll., Saratoga Springs, N.Y., 1923-27; dir. depts. social and fgn. relations Am. Unitarian Assn., Boston, 1927-40; exec. dir. Unitarian Service Com., 1940-44; relief work in Czechoslovakia, 1938, in Portugal, 1941-44; attache Am. Embassy, Lisbon, 1944; European rep. Church Peace Union, 1945-46; gen. sec. World Alliance for Friendship through the Churches, 1946-48; dir. World Affairs Council of R.I., 1948—; chmn. exec. com. World Fedn. UN Assns., 1946—. Mem. Am. Assn. Social Workers, Delta Upsilon. Democrat. Unitarian. Club: Union (Boston). Author: Social Adjjustment, 1927; The Minister and Family Troubles, 1931. Home: Belmont, Mass. Office: Arcade Bldg., Providence. Died Oct. 11, 1955.

DEXTER, Robert E., architect; b. England, Dec. 5, 1855; s. Robert Edward and Sarah Anne (Doyle) D.; ed. Birmingham (England) Sch. of Art; came to U.S., 1883, naturalized 1893; m. Mary Reeve, May 14, 1895. Architect, Dayton, O., 1888. Draughtsman in offices in Boston, Chicago and New York, 1883-88; practice in Dayton, O., 1888-1918; retired. Fellow A.I.A. (emeritus). Home: 341 Lighthouse Av., Pacific Grove, Cal. Died July 19, 1953.

DE YO, Anna Marden (dê-yō), corr. sec. Nat. W.C.T.U.; b. Glasgow, Ill., Oct. 18, 1868; d. Henry and Mary (Lindsay) Marden; student high sch., Roodhouse, Ill., 1881-85, U. Cal., summer, 1918; m. Palmer George De Yo, Mary 27, 1885; children—Mae Lucile (Mrs. Stuart S. Smith), Ena Lenore (Mrs. Cuyler H. Leonard), Olive Irene (Mrs. Arthur Graff). Organizer and lectr. W.C.T.U., Cal., 1911-14, corr. sec., 1914-27; corr. sec. Nat. W.C.T.U., 1927-42; active in W.C.T.U. of Fresno City and County, Cal., 1942-53. Vice-pres. Women's Legislative Council, Cal., 1916-18; sec. Women's Com. of 5,000, Cal., 1922-27. Mem. League of Women Voters, Bus. and Profl. Womens Club. Republican. Methodist. Clubs: Republican (Evanston); Western Women's (San Francisco). Home: San Francisco. Office: 1730 Chicago Av., Evanston, Ill. Died Mar. 4, 1953.

DEYO, C. W., business exec.; b. New Platz, N.Y., 1880. Chmn. bd. dirs. F. W. Woolworth Co.; dir. Woolco Realty Corp. Home: Ponus Ridge, Conn. Office: 233 Broadway, N.Y. City 7. Died Dec. 18, 1953.

DeYOUNG, Harry Anthony, artist; b. Chgo., Aug. 5, 1893; s. Adrian and Gertrude (De Young) DeY.; student Art Inst. Chgo., U. Ill.; pupil of F. de Forest Schook, John W. Norton, Edward Lake, Fabians Kelly; m. Mabelle G. Murdoch, Dec. 26, 1917; 1 dau., Anita-Amelia. Landscape and mural artist, portrait painter, lecturer and teacher, 1919—; asst. instr. Bailey's Harbor (Wis.) Summer Sch., 1922; dir. Glenwood (Ill.) Sch. of Landscape Painting, 1923-24; dir. Midwest Summer Sch. of Art, 1925-29; instr. at. Acad. of Art, 1927-28; pvt. art classes and painting camps in Tex., 1928—. Dir. Sol Ross State Teacher's College summer art colony, Alpine, Texas, 1940—. Represented in Moore Collection, Los Angeles; Harold Swift Collection, Chicago; Chicago Pub. Sch. Collection; Fenger High Sch., Chicago; Hammond (Ind.) High Sch.; Lincoln High School, Milwaukee, Wis.; and other high schools; also in Witte Museum, San Antonio and the Alamo; murals in St. Anthony Hotel, San Antonio, and Corpus Christi (Tex.) Museum. Honor student Art Inst. Chicago, 1917; awarded 2d prize Art Students League, 1917; Fine Arts Bldg. prize, 1925; hon. mention Art Inst. Chicago, 1925; members prize, Chicago Galleries Assn., 1927; hon. mention in Davis Competition, San Antonio, 1929. Served as Sergt. Q.M.C., U.S. Army, World War. Mem. Texas Federated Art Assn.; charter mem. Soc. of Tex. Artists; hon. mem. Lower Rio Grande Valley Art League; Corpus Christ Art Guild; mem. Corpus Christi Art Assn. Home: Boerne, Tex.; (summer) Sol Ross College, Alphine, Tex. Studio: 509 7th St., San Antonio. Died Jan. 15, 1956.

d'HUMY, Fernand Emile, business exec.; dir. Western Union Telegraph Co., dir. and v.p. Ramp Bldgs. Corp., New York. Registered professional engr., N.Y. State Fellow Am. Inst. Elec. Engrs., Inst. Radio Engrs. Author biographical books. Home: 50 Smith St., Chappaqua, N.Y. Office: 60 Hudson St., N.Y.C. 13. Died Dec. 22, 1955.

DICK, Albert Blake, Jr., business exec.; b. Chgo., Feb. 11, 1894; s. Albert Blake and Mary Henrietta (Mathews) D.; B.A., Yale, 1915; m. Helen Aldrich, Apr. 21, 1917; children—Albert B. Dick III, Helen (Mrs. Beckwith R. Bronson). With A. B. Dick Co., mfrs. office equipment and supplies, 1915—, started as salesman, clerk, v.p., treas., 1919-34, pres., treas., 1934-47, chmn. bd. dirs., 1947—; dir. A. B. Dick Co., Marshall Field & Co., No. Trust Co., Commonwealth Edison Co., No. Ill. Gas Co., First Nat. Bank of Lake Forest; former mem. bd. dir. N.Y. Central R.R., Mich. Central R.R., Frank G. Hough Co., Libertyville, Ill. Trustee Presbyn. Hosp., Chgo., Lake Forest Hosp., John and Mary R. Markle Found., N.Y.C., Chgo. Natural History Mus.; former trustee Shedd Aquarium, Chgo., John Crerar Library, Chgo., 1st State Pawners Soc. Former mayor, alderman, Lake Forest, Ill. Served from 2d class seaman, USN, to ensign, USNR, World War I. Mem. Chgo. Hist. Soc., Art Inst. Chgo., Delta Kappa Epsilon. Republican. Presbyn. Clubs: Commercial, Chicago, Attic (Chgo.); Onwentsia (Lake Forest); The Links (N.Y.C.); The Royal Bermuda Yacht (Hamilton, Bermuda). Home: 975 N. Lake Rd., Lake Forest, Ill. Office: 5700 W. Touhy Av., Niles, Ill. Died Oct. 24, 1954.

DICK, Henry Kissinger, educator; b. Reading, Pa., Oct. 4, 1886; s. Henry A. and Mary A. (Kissinger) D.; A.B., Princeton, 1909; A.M., Harvard, 1910. Instr. English Western Res. U., 1911-14; mem. faculty Columbia, 1919-52, prof. English, 1950-52. Served with M.C., U.S. Army, 1917-19. Mem. 1st Ref. Ch., Reading, Pa. Club: Berkshire Country (Reading, Pa.). Home: 800 N. 3d St., Reading, Pa. Died June 14, 1953; buried Schwartzwald Cemetery, Jacksonwald, Pa.

DICK, William Henry, lumberman, pres. Miss. River Flood Control Assn.; b. Rock Island, Ill., Feb. 19, 1872; s. Christian Daniel and Naomi Estill (Shinn) D.; student W. W. Daggett's Business Coll., Oshkosh, Wis.; m. Susa Isabelle Blackwood, June 29, 1898; children—Helen Mae (Mrs. Rubin G. Davis), Marjorie (Mrs. Ernest H. Atkins), Naomi (Mrs. Joe W. Davis). Bookkeeper, Meiklejohn & Hatten Lumber Co., Manawa, 1890-97; sec.-mgr., Hatten Lumber Co., New London, Wis., 1897-1907; v.p. Tallahatchie Lumber Co., Phillipp, Miss., 1907-29; pres. Delta Mercantile Co., 1912-20; pres. Planters Bank, Phillipp, 1922. Pres. Southern Alluvial Land Assn., 1921-26, Miss. River Flood Control Assn. since 1921, Nat. Drainage Assn., 1927-33; chmn. Nat. Conf. on Water Resources. Originated the idea and directed efforts which resulted in passage by Congress of amendment to R.F.C. Act, enabling drainage, irrigation and levee districts to borrow funds from R.F.C. to refinance outstanding bonds. This resulted in a saving of over two hundred million dollars to rural land owners. Republican. Presbyterian. Mason (Shriner). Leader of the Levee Bds. of Miss. River in securing passage through the Nat. Congress of Flood Control Bills of 1922-23, 28. Address: 2714 Terrace Drive, Tampa, Fla. Died Jan. 11, 1951; buried Myrtle Hill Cemetery, Tampa.

DICK, William K., corp. official; b. Brooklyn, N.Y., May 28, 1888; s. John Henry and Julia (Mollenhauer) D.; ed. Pomfret (Conn.) Sch., and pvt. tutors; m. 2d, Virginia Montez Conner, Dec. 24, 1941; children—Direxa V., Will K.; (by previous marriage) William F., John H. Pres. and dir. Dick Securities Corp.; dir. and chmn. exec. com. St. Regis Paper Co.; dir. and mem. exec. com. Nat. Sugar Refining Co.; dir. Best Foods Inc., Eastern States Corp., Irving Trust Co., Norwood & St. Lawrence R.R. Co., St. Regis Paper Co. of Canada, Ltd., St. Regis Timber Company, Limited. Trustee Boys Club of New York, South Side Hospital. Mason. Clubs: Racquet and Tennis, Down Town Assn., Turf and Field, Southside Sportsmen's (New York), National Golf, Brook, Holland Lodge; N.Y. Yacht, Seminole Golf. Home: Allen Winden Farm, Islip, L.I., N.Y. Office: 115 Broadway, N.Y.C. Died Sept. 5, 1953.

DICKEN, Clinton Orr, confectionery mfg. exec.; b. Syracuse, Neb., Nov. 19, 1885; s. William S. and Alice J. (Robinson) D.; B.S., Ore. State Coll., Corvallis, 1907; A.B., U. Chgo., 1913; m. Emily Rodgers, Aug. 13, 1914 (dec. 1930); 1 son, James Rodgers (U.S.N. lost at sea, 1944); m. 2d Roxana Cate Rodgers, June 24, 1932; stepchildren—Jean (Mrs. Harold Drysdale), Emily (Mrs. David E. Davis). Registered pharmacist, Portland, Ore., 1907; partner drug bus., Portland, 1908-11; chemist E. J. Brach & Sons, Chgo., 1913-16, purchasing agt., 1916-26, gen. factory mgr., 1926-28, became v.p., 1928, gen. mgr., 1947, mem. bd. dirs., 1948, exec. v.p., 1951. Clubs: University (Chgo.); Golf (Hinsdale). Home: 736 S. Park Av., Hinsdale, Ill. Office: 4656 W. Kinzie St., Chgo. 44. Died Apr. 7, 1957.

DICKER, Samuel Byron, mayor, lawyer; b. N.Y. City, Apr. 4, 1889; s. Moritz and Rose (Weinberg) D.; A.B., Cornell U., 1911; LL.B., Harvard Law Sch., 1923; unmarried. Jr. statistician State Dept. of Labor, Albany, N.Y., 1911-12, sr. statistician, 1913-14, chief Div. of Labor Statistics, 1915-20; admitted to New York State bar, 1924; partner Reilly, Dicker, McLouth & Lines, Rochester, New York; director Rochester & Genesee Valley R.R. Councilman, Rochester since 1936; mayor Rochester 1939—. Mem. N.Y. State and Rochester bar assns., Phi Beta Kappa. Rep. Jewish religion. Elk (treas. Rochester Lodge No. 24). Clubs: Cornell, Harvard (Rochester). Home: 150 Westminster Rd. Office: 1150 Lincoln Alliance Bldg., Rochester, N.Y. Died Feb. 9, 1960.

DICKERSON, Luther L., formerly librarian Indianapolis Public Library. Address: Oklahoma City. Died March 24, 1957; buried Bethany, Okla.

DICKERSON, Robert Carl, business exec.; b. Richmond, Tex., July 11, 1884; s. James Jones and Fannie (Norris) D.; student Univ. of Tex., 1901, Univ. of the South, 1902, 1903; m. Camille Searcy, Sept. 15, 1920; children—Robert Carl, James Searcy, Richard Searcy. Exec. v.p., sec. Am. Cotton Shippers Assn. since 1924. Democrat. Presbyterian. Home: 1930 Peabody Av., Memphis, Tenn. Office: P.O. Box 1022, Memphis 1. Died Apr. 4, 1953.

DICKINSON, Edward, author, musician; b. W. Springfield, Mass., Oct. 10, 1853; s. Henry and Angeline (Dunham) D.; A.B., Amherst, 1876, A.M., 1881; studied music in Boston, later in Berlin, including lectrs. U. Berlin, 1885-86, 1888-89, 1892-93; Litt.D., Oberlin, 1911; m. Jennie M. Kellogg, Oct. 4, 1882. Organist, Springfield Mass., 1872-78; organist, tchr. music, Elmira, N.Y., 1879-85; dir. music, Elmira Coll., 1883-92; prof. history and criticism of music, Oberlin Coll. and Conservatory, 1893-1922 (now emeritus). Author: Music in the History of the Western Church, 1902; The Study of the History of Music, 1905; The Education of a Music Lover, 1911; Music and the Higher Education, 1915; The Spirit of Music, 1925. Compiler The Students Book of Inspirations, 1919. Home: Oberlin, O. Died Jan. 25, 1946; buried Westwood Cemetery, Oberlin, O.

DICKINSON, Helena Adell (Mrs. Clarence Dickinson), author; b. Port Elmsley, Ont., Can., Dec. 5, 1875; d. Benson S. and Harriet (Millar) Snyder; M.A., Queen's U., Kingston, Can., 1895; Ph.D., Heidelberg U., Germany, 1901; Mus.D. (hon.), Cedar Crest Coll., 1949; m. Clarence Dickinson, June 15, 1904. Lecturer on liturgics and history of art, Union Theol. Sem., N.Y. Mem. Am. Guild of Organists, Hymn. Society of America, Am. Federation of Music Clubs (hon. member). Presbyn. Author: A Study of Henry D. Thoreau, 1902; Metrical Translations of 150 Ancient Carols, 1930; German Masters of Art, 1914; (with husband) Excursions in Musical History, 1917; A Book of Antiphons, 1919; The Troubadours and Their Music, 1920; A Nativity Play in Ancient Christmas Carols, 1919; The Technique and Art of Organ Playing, 1921; A Choirmaster's Guide, 1923; A Treasury of Worship, 1926; Metrical Translations of 50 Ancient Carols, 1935; The Choir Loft and The Pulpit, 1943; Metrical Translations of 50 Ancient Motets and Carols, 1948, also from German 22 Early Amermoranian Anthenus. Home: 7 Gracie Square, N.Y.C. 28; also Cornwall-on-Hudson, N.Y. Died Aug. 25, 1957; buried Prospect Hill Cemetery, Caldwell, N.J.

DICKINSON, John, lawyer; b. Greensboro, Md., February 24, 1894; s. Willard and Caroline (Schnauffer) D.; A.B., Johns Hopkins, 1913; A.M., Princeton, 1915, Gordon Macdonald fellow, 1915-16, Charlotte Elizabeth Procter fellow, 1916-17, Ph.D., 1919; LL.B., Harvard, 1921; LL.D., Tusculum Coll., 1929, Dickinson, 1934, Johns Hopkins, 1948; m. Lula Martin McIver (Scott), June 1, 1938. Lecturer on history, Amherst Coll., 1918-19; tutor in div. history, govt. and economics, Harvard, 1919-21; clk., law office John C. Hammond, Northampton, Mass., summers, 1920, 21; law clk., McAdoo, Cotton & Franklin, N.Y. City, 1921-22; in practice with Hon. William G. McAdoo, Los Angeles, Calif., 1922-25; lecturer on govt., Harvard and Radcliffe Coll., 1924-27; asst. prof. politics, Princeton, 1927-29; prof. law, U. of Pa., 1929-48; asst. sec. of Commerce, 1933-35; chairman U.S. Central Statistical Board, 1934-35; asst. U.S. Atty. General, 1935-37; gen. solicitor of the Pennsylvania Railroad, 1937-41, gen. counsel of same, 1941-46; vice president, gen. counsel since 1946. Economist, United States War Trade Bd., 1917; 1st lt., U.S. Army, attached to Gen. Staff, 1917-18. Trustee Md. Agrl. Society for Eastern Shore. Fellow Am. Acad. Arts and Sciences; mem. Am. Philos. Soc., Am. Polit. Science Assn., Council on Fgn. Relations, Am. Law Inst., Am. Bar Assn., Pa. Bar Association and Phi Beta Kappa. Democrat. Episcopalian. Clubs: Philadelphia, Franklin Inn (Phila.); Century (New York); Met. (Washington, D.C.). Author: The Building of an Army, 1922; Administrative Justice and the Supremacy of Law, 1927; Hold Fast the Middle Way, 1935. Co-author: Report on the Cloak and Suit Industry of New York City, 1925. Editor and translator: The Statesman's Book of John of Salisbury, 1927. Contbr. to Am. Polit. Science Rev., Polit. Science Quarterly, Speculum, Am. Jour. Internat. Law, Dictionary Am. Biography, etc. Home: "Crosiadore," Trappe, Md. Address: 1740 Broad St. Station Bldg., Phila. Died Apr. 9, 1952; buried Spring Hill Cemetery, Easton, Md.

DICKINSON, Robert Latou, gynecologist; b. Jersey City, N.J., Feb. 21, 1861; s. Horace and Jeannette (Latou) D.; ed. Poly. Inst. Brooklyn and in Switzerland and Germany; M.D., L.I. Coll. Hosp., 1882; m. Sarah Truslow, May 7, 1890 (dec.); children—Margaret (dec.), Dorothy (wife of Prof. George B. Barbour), Jean (wife of Truman Squire Potter, M.D.). Former gynecologist and obstetrician, Brooklyn Hospital; former prof., L.I. Coll. Hosp.; asst. chief, med. sec. Nat. Council Defense, Washington, 1917; lt.-col., med. adviser and mem. Gen. Staff, Washington, 1918-19; on mission to China for Public Health Service, 1919, Near East, 1926. Fellow of A.C.S. (dir.); member American Assn. Marriage Counsellors, Am. Assn. for the Study of Sterility, Am. Gynecol. Soc. (ex-pres.), N.Y. Academy Medicine, N.Y. Obstetrical Society (ex-pres.), Brooklyn, Chicago and British gynecol. socs., Am. Gynecol. Club (ex-pres.), Am. Geog. Soc.; sec. Nat. Com. on Maternal Health, 1923-37 (hon. chmn. since 1937); senior vice pres. Planned Parenthood Federation since 1939; pres. Euthanasia Soc. since 1946; member National Sculpture Society. Awards received: Long Island Med. Coll. Alumni Assn., 1944; Am. Phys. Edn. Assn., 1945; A. and M. Lasker (for research), 1946. Democrat. Clubs: Century, Town Hall, Hamilton, Cosmos. Author: (booklet) Palisades Guide, 1921; New York Walk Book (with others), 1923, 39, 50; A Thousand Marriages, 1931; Control of Conception, 1931-38; Atlas of Human Sex Anatomy, 1933; The Single Woman, Her Sex Education, 1933; co-author Sex Variants, 1941; Birth Atlas, 1941; Techniques of Conception Control, 1941; Human Sterilization, 1950; also 200 researches and reports on obstetrics, diseases of women, hosp. orgn. and sex problems. Co-editor of American Text Book of Obstetrics, 1895. Illustrator of own writings. Sculpture (with A. Belskie) of Birth Series for N.Y. World's Fair, 1939; pelvic teaching models, 1941-47. Home: 360 E. 50th St. Office: 2 E. 103d St., N.Y. City 29. Died Nov. 30, 1950.

DICK-READ, Grantly, physician, author; b. Beccles, Suffolk, Eng., Jan. 26, 1890; s. Robert John and Fanny Maria (Sayer) D.; student Bishop's Stortford Coll., Hertfordshire; B.A. with honors, St. John's Coll., Cambridge, 1911, M.B., B.Ch., 1916, M.A., 1916, M.D., 1920; m. Dorothea Cannon, Apr. 7, 1920; m. 2d, Jessica Bennett, Apr. 10, 1952. House physician London Hosp., 1911-14, resident accoucheur, 1918-22; demonstrator pathology Cambridge U., 1918-20; pvt. practice of medicine, Eastbourne, Eng., 1922-23, Woking and Harley St., 1926-48, Johannesburg, South Africa, 1949-53; retired from active practice, 1953; lectr., writer, 1953—; lectr. Maternity Center Assn. N.Y., French Acad. Medicine. Paris, 1947, Ireland, Scotland, Wales, Am., English univs., South Africa, 1948, German Swiss, French Italian univs., 1957. Captain, Royal Army Medical Corps, 1914-18. Mem. Royal Coll. Surgeons, Royal Coll. Physicians. Mason. Author: Natural Childbirth, 1933; Childbirth Without Fear, 1944; Birth of a Child, 1947; Introduction to Motherhood, 1951; No Time for Fear, 1955; Antenatal Illustrated, 1955. Contbr. sci. articles profl. publs. Home: Heronby, Beech Rd., The Avenue, Wroxham, Norwich, Eng. Office: care Barclay's Bank, Ltd., East St., Chichester, Sussex, Eng. Died June, 1959; buried Eaton, Norwich.

DICKSON, Edward Augustus, editor, pub.; b. Sheboygan, Wis., Aug. 29, 1879; s. William H. and Gurie (Iverson) D.; B.L., University of California, 1901; LL.D. (honorary) Moravian College, Bethlehem, Pa.; m. Wilhelmina de Wolff, December 26, 1907. In Japan, 1901-02; engaged in newspaper work since 1903; Washington corr., 1910-12; editor and owner Los Angeles Evening Express, 1919-31. Commissioner Los Angeles Dept. Water and Power. Pres. Western Federal Savings and Loan Assn. Decorated Officier de l'Instruction Publique (France) and Knight of the Order of the Crown of Italy for "distinguished service in the field of journalism and education." Del. to Rep. Nat. Conv., 1932; mem. Rep. State Central Com. of Calif., 1918-22. Mem. Calif. State Council of Defense, 1917-18; chmn. Los Angeles Centennial Commission. vice pres. California Direct Legislative League. Mem. board directors of Olympic Games Assn. Chmn. board Regents U. of Cal. Mem. bd. L.A. Library Bd. Mem. Nat. Com. for Goethe Bicentennial. Mem. Hist. Soc. So. Calif. (pres.), Phi Delta Theta; pres. Lincoln Club. Republican. Methodist. Clubs: California, Sunset. Home: 425 S. Windsor Blvd. Office: 600 S. Hill St., Los Angeles 5. Died Feb. 22, 1956; buried Forest Lawn Meml. Park, Glendale, Cal.

DICKSON, Frank Stoddard, adj. gen., ex-congressman, tchr.; b. Hillsboro, Ill., Oct. 6, 1876; s. Prof. J. M. and Illinois (Stoddard) D.; grad. pub. schs., 1891, county sch., 1892, Decatur (Ill.) High Sch., 1896; m. Theresa Dixon Scott, Jan. 20, 1903; children—Dorothy Lambur, Mrs. Heaton Buckley. Enlisted pvt. Co. I, 4th Ill. Vol. Inf. in Spanish-Am. War; saw service in Cuba; was successively regimental commissary and q. m.; now capt. q. m., 4th Inf., I. N. G. Engaged as tchr., 1903—. Republican; mem. Congress, 23d Ill. dist., 1905-07; adj. gen. Ill., 1910-12. Methodist. Club: Hamilton (Chgo.). Address: Ramsey, Ill. Died Feb. 24, 1953.

DICKSON, Leonard Eugene, prof. mathematics; b. Independence, Iowa, Jan. 22, 1874; s. Campbell and Lucy (Tracy) D.; B.S., Univ. of Tex., 1893, M.A., 1894; Ph.D., U. of Chicago, 1896; student U. of Leipzig, Germany, 1896, U. of Paris, France, 1897; hon. D.Sc., Harvard, 1936, Princeton, 1941; m. Susan Davis, Dec. 30, 1902; children—Campbell, Eleanor (Mrs. Harlow Higinbotham). Instr., U. of Calif., 1897; prof. mathematics, U. of Chicago, 1900—; editor, Am. Math. Monthly, 1902-08, Trans. Am. Math. Soc., 1910-16. Corr. de l'Académie de l'Institut de France. Mem. Nat. Acad. of Science, Phi Beta Kappa, Sigma Chi. Home: Quadrangle Club, 57th and Univ. Av. Office: Univ. of Chicago, Chgo. Died Jan. 17, 1954; buried Cleburne, Tex.

DICKSON, Robert Barnes, corp. exec.; b. Streator, Ill., Jan. 13, 1883; s. Gavin and Elizabeth (Logan) D.; student pub. schs., Galva, Ill.; m. Ellen Katherine Kellogg, Oct. 6, 1915; children—James Kellogg, Dorothy Dickson Anderson. Bookkeeper Kewanee (Ill.) Boiler Corp., 1905-07, successively salesman, branch manager sales manager, 1907-30, president, 1930—; dir. Am. Radiator & Standard San. Corp. (N.Y.C.). Republican. Conglist. Mason (32°, Shriner), Elk. Club: Midland Country (Kewanee). Home: 145 E. Division St., Kewanee, Ill. Died Apr. 9, 1950; buried Kewanee, Ill.

DICKSTEIN, Samuel, justice; b. Lithuania, Feb. 5, 1885; s. Rev. Israel and Slata B. (Gordon) D.; brought to U.S. at age of 3; New York Law Sch., 1903-06. Admitted to N.Y. bar, 1908; spl. dep. atty. gen., State of N.Y., 1911-12, 1913-14; mem. Bd. of Aldermen, N.Y. City, 1917; mem. N.Y. Ho. of Rep., 1919-22; mem. 68th to 79th Congresses (1923-47), 12th N.Y. Dist.; chmn. Immigration and Naturalization Com. since 1931. Author of many housing laws, kosher laws of N.Y. State. Mem. and vice chmn. of Spl. Com. to investigate un-American activities; elected Justice Supreme Court, N.Y. State, 1st Dist., Nov. 1945, for term, 1946-55. Mem. N.Y. City Bar Assn., American Bar Assn., N.Y. Criminal bar assn., New York County Lawyers' Assn.; hon. mem. Vets. Foreign Wars. Democrat. Mason (Shriner), Elk. Home: 450 West End Av. Office: 60 Center St., N.Y.C. 7. Died Apr. 22, 1954.

DIDUSCH, James Francis (dē-dōōsh), medical artist; b. Baltimore, Md., June 17, 1890; s. Joseph Martin and Katherine (Rena) D.; student Md. Institute School Mechanical Arts, 1904-08, Maryland Institute School Fine Arts, 1908-11, Dept. of Art as Applied to Medicine, Johns Hopkins, 1910-13; m. Therese Marie Eder, July 1, 1915; children—George James, Anne Therese (Mrs. Hans Schuler, Jr.), Joseph Martin. Artist on staff dept. embryology, Carnegie Instn. of Washington, 1913-40; asso. prof. art as applied to medicine, Johns Hopkins, Med. Sch. 1940-43; mem. staff dept. embryology Carnegie Instn. of Washington since 1943. Mem. Johns Hopkins Med. Soc., Md. Inst. Sch. of Fine Arts Alumni Assn. Illustrator: Surgery of Blood Vascular System (Bertram Bernheim), 1913; Operative Gynecology (Richard W. TeLinde), 1945; chapter on embryology, Encyclopedea Brittanica; Vol. 32, Contributions to Embryology, Carnegie Instn. of Washington. Yearly publs. Dept. Embryology, Carnegie Instn. Washington, 1913-40. Translated and revised treatise on development of human mesonephres by Jujior Shikinami. 1926. Home: 1001 E. Biddle St., Baltimore 2. Office: 1902 E. Madison St., Balt. Died Mar. 16, 1955.

DIECKMANN, William Joseph, univ. prof., born Belleville, Ill , Oct. 20, 1897; s. August Conrad and Mary (Rieder) D.; ed. McKendry Coll.; B.S., Wash. Univ., 1920, M.D., 1922; m. Katherine Morrison, May 1, 1918; 1 dau., Dorothy Jean. Interne and resident, obstetrical service, Barnes Hosp., Washington Univ. Sch. Medicine, 1922-24; instr., dept. obstetrics, 1924-28, asst. prof. obstetrics, 1928-29, asso. prof. obstetrics and gynecology 1929-31, staff, Barnes Hosp., 1924-31, St. Louis Maternity Hosp., 1927-31; asso. prof. obstetrics and gynecology, Univ. of Chicago, 1931-42, Mary Campau Ryerson prof., 1942—; chmn. Dept. Obstetrics and Gynecology and chief of service, Chgo. Lying-in Hosp. 1942-54; attending gynecologist, Albert Merritt Billings Memorial Hosp. Pres. Chicago Gynecological Soc., 1944-45. Mem. A.M.A., Am. Bd. Obstetrics and Gynecology, Am. Gynecol. Soc., Central Soc. for Clin. Research, Soc., Exptl. Medicine and Biology, State and local med. socs., Am. Soc. for Pharmacology and Exptl. Therapeutics, Assn. for Study Internal Secretions, Am., Central Assns. Obstetrics and Gynecology. Author: Toxema of Pregnancy. 2d. edit., 1956; also scientific publications; editor Am. Journal of Obstetrics and Gynecology. Home: 8120 S. Kingston Av., Chgo. 17. Office: 5841 Maryland Av., Chgo. 37. Died Aug. 15, 1957.

DIEDERICH, William Hunt (dēd'rĭk), sculptor; b. Hungary, 1884; s. Kurt and Eleanor (Hunt) D.; ed. boarding schools in Europe; m. Mary de Anders, 1911 (div.); children—Sybil D. Hansen, William Hunt; m. 2d, Countess Wanda v. Goetzen, May 1923 (dec. 1952); children—Diana Huberta, Harold Michael (USMC, killed in Korea 1952). Sculptor, 1909—, also engaged in other decorative arts; exhibited in Rome and Paris; one-man shows Rome 1912, in permanent collections, Metropoitan Museum, N.Y. City, Whitney Museum, Seattle. Recipient gold medal Archtl. League, 1922. Mem. Salon d'Automne, Paris, Nat. Inst. of Arts and Letters. Home: Tappan, N.Y. Died May 14, 1953.*

DIEHL, Edith, hand bookbinder; b. Brewster, N.Y., May 21, 1876; d. Philip and Josephine (Lee) Diehl; prepared for coll. at Montour Falls Acad.; student Wellesley Coll., Class of 1904; student Jena U., 1898-1900; studied craft of hand bookbinding in England, France and Belgium; unmarried. Teacher of hand bookbinding; lecturer on printing, binding, and evolution of the book. During World War organized Red Cross workrooms in New York; apptd. nat. dir. of training for Woman's Land Army. Clubs: Nat. Arts (New York), Lyceum (London). Author: The Kinds of Binding in The Dolphin (Vol. 2), 1935; Bookbinding. Its Background and Technique, 1946; article, "Bookbinding" (revised Chambers' Encyclopedia). Address: 455 E. 51st St., N.Y.C.; also Brewster, N.Y. Died May 12, 1953; buried Milltown Cemetery, Brewster, N.Y.

DIELS, Otto Paul Hermann, chemist; b. 1876; student U. Berlin; M.D. (hon.), U. Keil. Asst. chemistry instr. U. Berlin, 1899-1912, head dept., 1913, extraordinary prof., 1914; ordinary prof. U. Kiel, 1916, now prof. emeritus. Recipient Baeyer Meml. medal, 1931; Nobel prize for chemistry (with Kurt Alder), 1950. Mem. Acad. Halle, Acad. Gottingen, Acad. Munich, Royal Spanish Soc. Physics and Chemistry. Author books on chemistry. Home: Clausewitz St. 12, Kiel (24b), Germany. Died Mar. 7, 1954.

DIEMER, George Willis, (dēm'ĕr), coll. pres.; b. Arkansas City, Kan., Dec. 11, 1885; s. John Perdue and Amelia L. (Sylvius) D.; B.Pe., State Teachers Coll., Kirksville, Mo., 1911; studied U. of Mo., 1912-13; B.S., State Teachers Coll., Warrensburg, Mo., 1917; A.M., Teachers College, Columbia University, 1925; LL.D., Culver-Stockton College, 1953; married Myrtle S. Caselbolt, June 15, 1916; children—Dorothy Elizabeth, George Willis, John Irving, Emma Lou. Teacher, prin. and supt, rural and town schs. in Mo., 1905-21; prin. Henry C. Kumpf Sch., Kansas City, Mo., 1921-23; pres. Teachers Coll. of Kansas City, 1923-37; pres. Central Mo. State Coll., Warrensburg, Mo., 1937-56; pres. emeritus, 1956—; instr. U. Colo., summer sessions, 1928-36, U. of Kan., summer session, 1930. Served as 4-minute man and chmn. Clay County Chapter Am. Red Cross, World War I. Chmn. edn. com. Mo. State Council of Defense, 1942-45. Mem. U.S. Edn. Mission to Japan, 1946 and 1950; cons. Am. zone, for Dept. of State, summer 1951; mem. U.S. Nat. Commn., UNESCO, 1951-54; pres. Internat. Council on Edn. for Teaching, 1953; del. 16th Internat. Conf. on Pub. Edn., Geneva, Switzerland, 1953; mem. Nat. Commn. on Accreditation. Director Kansas City Council Boy Scouts. Mem. N.E.A., Mo. State Teachers Assn., Am. Assn. Teachers Colls. (chmn. com. on profl. ethics; mem. accrediting com., pres. 1947-48), Kappa Delta Pi, Phi Delta Kappa. Elder Disciples of Christ. Mason, K.T., Shriner, Eastern Star. Clubs: Schoolmasters' (Kansas City); Internat. Professional Men's, Rotary, Warrensburg Club (pres., dist. gov. 1948-49). Co.-author: Pupil Citizenship, 1931; A Platoon School in Kansas City, Missouri, 1925. Contbr. to nat. professional jours. Address: 7311 Manchester Rd., Kansas City, Mo. Died Aug. 13, 1956; buried Warrensburg, Mo.

DIERKS, DeVere, lumber mfg. exec.; b. Callaway, Neb., Jan. 18, 1893; s. Peter and LaDesha (Matthews) D.; student Mass. Inst. Tech., 1910, U. Neb., 1911; m. Pauline Atterbury, Sept. 24, 1914; children—Ruth (Mrs. Daniel Morgan), DeVere. Exec. v.p. Dierks Forests, Inc., Hot Springs, Ark., 1945—; dir. So. Pine Assn. Home: 5049 Wornal Rd. Office: Dierks Bldg., Kansas City 6, Mo. Died May 21, 1957.

DIETRICH, Herman Rudolph, consul-general; b. Utica, Mo., Jan. 6, 1862; ed. pub. sch. Farmer, 1884-8; became mcht., 1888; postmaster Utica, 1898-1903; owner and mng. editor Utica Herald, 1900; mem. Mo. legislature, 1902-3; consul-gen. to Ecuador, since Apr. 2, 1913-Dec. 12, 1912 (resigned). Home: Utica, Mo. Died Jan. 20, 1938.

DIETRICHSON, Gustav Johan Fredrik, bishop; b. Luther Valley, Wis., Apr. 8, 1855; s. Provost Gustav Fredrik and Pauline (Prens) D.; ed. U. of Christiania; m. Magdalen Odegaard, June 22, 1881. Removed to Norway with family when 5 yrs. old; ordained Luth. ministry, 1879; elected bishop of Tromso, Norway, Feb. 25, 1910. Dir. Norwegian Mission Soc. and Mission for Laplanders, Tromso. Suppliant Parliament of Norway, 1910-12. Knight Order St. Olaf, Norway. Address: Tromso, Norway. Died Mar. 1922.

DIETZ, Carl F. (dēts), corp. official; b. N.Y. City, Feb. 12, 1880; s. Frederick A. and Caroline (Behr) D.; M.E., Stevens Institute of Technology, 1901, Doctor of Engring. (honoris causa); P.G., Royal Tech. Coll., Berlin, 1902; m. Katherine Vane, Nov. 26, 1907; children—Katherine Caroline, Caroline Vane, Alan Vane. Metall. and cons. engr., 1903-11; successively plant engr., asst. sales mgr., gen. sales mgr. and v.p. Norton Co., Worcester, Mass., 1911-21; pres. and gen. mgr. Bridgeport Brass Co., 1921-27; industrial and banking consultant. 1928-29; exec. v.p. Commander Larabee Corp., Minneapolis, 1930-32; nat. code dir. wheat flour milling industry under NRA, 1933-35; now chmn. Lamson Corp., Del., pres. N.Y. Mail & Newspaper Transportation Co., Boston Pneumatic Transit Co.; director Adams Express Company, also director Financial Cons., Tucson, Ariz. Profl. engr. State of N.Y., and Conn., 1932, and all states with engring. registration burs. per Nat. Bur. of Engring. Registration; chmn. Lamson Mobilift Corp., Portland, Ore. Mem. Munitions Board Packaging and Materials Handling Industry Adv. Com. Industry Panel mem. War Labor Board, Region 2. Mem. New York State Com. on Displaced Persons; tripartite mem. for industry, N.L.R.B., New York State. Civic award, Humanitarian, Polish Legion Am. Vets. Mem. Council of Defense, Syracuse and Onondaga Co.; dir. War Fund and Community Chest of Onondaga County. Ex-chmn. Conn. Mfrs. Indsl. Relations Committee; national councilor U.S. C. of C., mem. advisory bd. dept. of mfr. Mem. finance bd. Bridgeport Community Chest. 1923-27; dir. Conn. and Bridgeport Mfrs. Assn., 1923-27; also dir. Boy's Club; formerly pres. Rotary and Engineers clubs of Bridgeport Fellow Am. Soc. M.E.; mem. Am. Inst. Mining and Metall. Engrs., Nat. Assn. Mfrs. (pres., mem. com. on labor negotiations), Mfrs. Assn. of Syracuse (chmn., mem. exec. com., chmn. govt. affairs com.), Conveyer Equipment Mfrs. Assn. (pres.), Technl. Club of Syracuse (bd. govs., chmn. civic affairs com.), Syracuse C. of C. (dir.), Am. Soc. Professional Engrs., Onondaga Health Assn. (dir.), Technology Club of Syracuse (hon.), Machinery and Allied Products Inst. (mem. Council for Technical Advancement), American Ordnance Association (dir. of Empire Post), Industrial College Armed Forces (mem. adv. com. materials handling), State Commn. Against Discrimination. Mem. Phi Sigma Kappa, Theta Nu Epsilon, Pi Tau Sigma (hon.). Republican. Episcopalian (vestryman). Mason (32°, Shriner). Clubs: Engineers (New York); Union League (Chgo.); Syracuse Technology (hon.), Century (Syracuse, N.Y.); Oswelewgois (Redfield, N.Y.). Contbr. engring and indsl. articles. Address: 515 Ponce de Leon Blvd., Belleair, Fla. Died Oct. 4, 1957; buried Mountain Grove Cemetery, Bridgeport, Conn.

DIFFENDORFER, Ralph Eugene (dĭf'fĕn-dôrf-ĕr); b. Hayesville, O., Aug. 15, 1879; s. Frank and Addie L. (Arnold) D.; A.B., Ohio Wesleyan U., 1902 (Phi Beta Kappa); B D., Drew Theol. Sem., 1907; studied Union Theological Sem., 1913-14; D.D., Ohio Wesleyan U., 1925, LL.D., 1942; LL.D., Ill. Wesleyan University, 1941; LL.D. Boston University, 1951; m. M. Edna Saylor, Nov. 4, 1903. Served as asst. sec. Epworth League, 1902-04; sec. Missionary Edn. Movement U.S. and Can., 1904-16; ednl. sec. Bd. Home Missions and Ch. Extension and Bd. of Foreign Missions, M.E. Ch., 1916-17; asso. sec. Centenary Commn., Br. of Home Missions and Ch. Extension, M.E. Ch., 1918; dir. of Home Missions Survey, Interchurch World Movement, 1919-20; sec. dept. of edn., com. on conservation and advance, M.E. Ch., Chicago, Ill., 1920-24; corr. sec. Bd. of Foreign Missions, M.E. Ch., 1924-40; exec. sec. Div. of Fgn. Missions of the Bd. of Missions and Ch. Extension, Meth. Ch., 1940-49. Del. 1st Internat. Conf. on Missionary Edn., Lunteren, Holland, 1911; del. to Gen. Conf. M.E. Ch., 1928, 32, 36, Newark Annual Conf.; del. to Internat. Missionary Council, Jerusalem, 1928; del. to Life and Work Council, Oxford, Eng., 1937; del. to Internat. Missionary Council, Madras, India, 1938; del. to Uniting Methodist Conf., Kansas City, Mo., 1939; member of Gen. Conf. Meth. Ch., 1940, 44, 48; mem. Exec. Com., Commn. on Internat. Justice and Goodwill of Fed. Council of Churches; mem. Foreign Mission Conference of N. America (chairman of com. of ref. and council, mem. Com. on Cooperation in Latin Am.; Chmn. advance program); mem., dir. Church World Service, Inc. (chmn. Christian literature Com.); pres. bd. founders Nanking Theol. Sem.; mem. Com of Council. Ad-interim Com. of International Missionary Council; dir. Conf. on Christian Bases of World Order, Del., O., Mar., 1945; conslt. for Fgn. Missions Conf. of N. Am. at First Assembly of World Council of Chs., Amsterdam, 1948. Pres., trustee Clifton Springs (N.Y.) Sanitarium; pres. of bd. trustees Santiago (Chile) Coll.; trustee Colegio Ward (Buenos Aires); pres. Japan Internat. Christian U. Found.; mem. Meth. deputation to Japan, 1941. Mem. Phi Beta Kappa, Pi Gamma Mu, Theta Phi. Award Order of the Jade, Chinese Govt., 1940. Author: Child Life in Mission Lands, 1904; Jr. Studies in the life of Christ, 1904; A Modern Disciple of Jesus Christ—David Livingstone, 1913; Thy Kingdom Come, 1914; Missionary Education in Home and School, 1917; The Church and the Community, 1920. Editor: The World Service of the Methodist Episcopal Church, 1923; China-Japan?, 1938; Church and Mission in Japan, 1941. Home: 48 Green Village Rd., Madison, N.J. Office: 44 E. 23d St., N.Y.C. 10. Died Jan. 31, 1951; buried Haysville, O.

DIGGES, Isaac Watlington (dĭgz), lawyer; b. West Point, Va., Apr. 15, 1897; s. Isaac and Elizabeth Robins (Watlington) D.; B.A., U. of Richmond (Va.), 1917; student law sch., George Washington U., Washington, D.C., 1922-25; grad. École Des Sciences Politiques, Paris, France, 1922; studied U. of Paris Law Sch., 1920-22; m. Louise Darrow; children—Sherrill Pierronet, Virginia Seward. Admitted to Va. bar, 1922, to New York bar, 1933; attorney for Federal Trade Commission, 1922-25; counsel for Bristol Myers Co., Bissell Carpet Sweper Co., Assn. Nat. Advertisers, Good Housekeeping Mag., DuPont Co., Printers' Ink, Motor and Equipment Mfrs. Assn., F. L. Smith & Co., O. M. Scott & Sons Co.; gen. counsel National Com. Democrats for Wilkie, 1940; asso. adminstr. War Savings Staff, U.S. Treasury, 1942-43; counsel War Shipping Administration, N.Y., 1943. Mem. Town Planning Bd., North Castle, N.Y.; Served as sergt. A.E.F., World War I. Mem. Am. Bar Assn., Am. Judicature Soc., U.S. Trade Mark Assn. (mem. lawyers adv. com.), Am. Arbitration Assn. (mem. trial panel), Phi Delta Phi, Kappa Sigma. Democrat. Clubs: Uptown. Decoration: Medal of Liberation (King Christian X). Author: The Modern Law of Advertising and Marketing, 1948. Contbr. articles on legal phases of business in Printers' Ink, etc. Home: Beford, N.Y. Office: 60 E. 42d St., N.Y.C. Died July 8, 1953.

DIGGLE, Roland (dĭg'l), organist, composer; b. London, Eng., Jan. 1, 1885; s. Charles Edmund and Helen (Fisher) D.; ed. pvt. tutors, Royal Coll. Music, London; m. Mary Webster, 1909; 1 dau., Dorothy May (Bertucci). Came to U.S., 1904, naturalized 1914. Organist, choirmaster, St. John's Episcopal Ch., Wichita, Kan., 1907-11, St. John's Cathedral, Quincy, Ill., 1911-14, St. John's Ch., Los Angeles, 1914—. Recitalist San Diego, San Francisco expn.; made several organ recital tours of U.S. Episcopalian. Mason. Composer organ and orchestral music; orchestral works performed by Los Angeles Symphony Orchestra; mem. Am. Soc. Composers, Authors and Publishers. Contbr. to The Diapason, Am. Organist, Musical Opinion, Etude, The Organ, etc. Home: 260 S. Citrus St. Studio: 514 W. Adams St., Los Angeles. Died Jan. 13, 1954.

DI GIORGIO, Joseph, fruit grower; b. Italy, June 10, 1874; s. Salvatore and Concetta (Scalco) Di G.; student pub. schs. of Italy; m. Beatrice Brackenridge, Sept. 8, 1910. Importer, 1893; was pres. Atlantic Fruit Co., now chmn. bd. dirs. Di Giorgio Fruit Corp., San Francisco. Decorated Commendatore Crown (Italy). Catholic. Elk. Club: Whitehall (N.Y.C.). Home: Di Giorgio Farms, Di Giorgio, Cal. Office: 433 California St., San Francisco. Died Feb. 25, 1951.

DIKE, Norman Staunton, ex-jurist; b. Bklyn., Oct. 22, 1862; s. Camden C. and Jeannie D (Scott) D. prep. edn. Bklyn. Poly. Inst.; Ph.B., Brown U., 1885, LL.D., 1933; LL.B., Columbia Law Sch., 1887; m. Evelyn Moore Bidle, June 30, 1917; 1 son, Norman Staunton. Admitted to N.Y. bar, 1887; elected mem. Bd. Suprs. Kings County, 1894 (pres. pro tem, 1896); apptd. sheriff of Kings County, 1902. county judge, 1906-19; justice Supreme Court of N.Y., 2d Dist., 1920-33; immediately upon retirement as justice Supreme Court was apptd. by Appellate Div., 2d Dept., as ofcl. referee Supreme Ct. N.Y. Lt. col. on staff of Gov. Morton, 1895-96. Served in O.T.C., Camp Plattsburg, N.Y., 1916. Mem. Am., N.Y. State, Bklyn. bar assns., Soc. Colonial Wars, S.R., Soc. War of 1812, Psi Upsilon. Republican. Conglist. Mason. Clubs: Union, University (N.Y.C.). Bar Harbor. Author of brochure: Narrative of Life of Anthony Dike, 1623, 1638. Home: 4 E. 65th St., N.Y.C. Died Apr. 15, 1953; buried Greenwood Cemetery, Bklyn.

DILLARD, James Edgar, clergyman; b. Danville, Va., June 3, 1879; s. Rev. Edward Banks (D.D.) and Annie Robertson) D.; A.B., William Jewell Coll., Liberty, Mo., 1900, D.D., 1913; A.M., Clarksburg (Mo.) Coll., 1901; student Washington U., 1912-14; studied Divinity School, University of Chicago, summers 1918, 28, 32, 35; LL.D., Howard College, 1927; married Lillian Madison, January 15, 1903; children—Reverend James Edgar, Lillian Lois (Mrs. Wheeler Tracy). Began preaching at 16; ordained ministry Missionary Bapt. Ch., 1896; pastor, Sturgeon, Mo., 1896-1900; pres. Clarksburg (Mo.) Coll., 1901-07; successively pastor Macon, Mo., Delmar Ch., St. Louis and First Ch., St. Joseph, Mo., until 1918; pastor Southside Church, Birmingham Ala., 1918-36; dir. of promotion Exec. Com. Southern Bapt. Conv., Nashville, Tenn., 1936-47, ret. Second v.p. So. Bapt. Conv., 1932-33; pres. Alabama Bapt. State Convention, 1933-34. Member Theta Phi Fraternity. Mason (32°, Shriner). Club: Cosmopolitan. Author: Anti-Rust Browning Book, 1908; Biblical Introduction (pamphlet), 1917; We Southern Baptists, 1937; What Next, 1940; Bible Stewardship, 1941; Romance of a Century, 1945; Building a Stewardship Church, 1947; Good Stewards, 1953; also tracts and articles on ednl. and religious subjects. Collaborator: Book of Daily Devotions, 1923; The Magnetic Master, 1937. Asso. editor, The Quarterly Review, 1938-47; compiler, Centennial Handbooks (19). Home: 3600 Sperry Av. Address: 127 9th Av. N., Nashville 3. Died July 9, 1953; buried Danville, Va.

DILLE, John Flint (dillē), newspaper exec.; b. Dixon, Ill., 1884; s. Jesse Brooks and Florence (Flint) D.; Ph.B., U. Chgo., 1909; m. Phoebe M. Crabtree, 1911; children—John Flint, Robert Crabtree. Began career in advt., 1910; founder Nat. Newspaper Syndicate, 1917, pres., 1917—; pres. Buck Rogers, Inc., John F. Dille Co.; creator Buck Rogers, 25th Century A.D. Awarded citation for pub. service U. Chgo., 1943. Mem. Phi Gamma Delta. Republican. Methodist. Clubs: Westmoreland Country (Wilmette, Ill.); Chicago Athletic Assn. Home: 2727 Lincoln St., Evanston, Ill. Office: 326 Madison St., Chgo. Died Sept. 10, 1957; buried Oakwood Cemetery, Dixon, Ill.

DILLEHUNT, Richard Benjamin (dĭl'lê-hŭnt), surgeon; b. Decatur, Ill., July 12, 1886; s. Benjamin Webster and Augusta (Buchert) D.; student U. of Ill., 1904-06; M.D., Rush Med. Coll. (U. of Chicago), 1910; unmarried. Began practice at Portland, Ore., 1914; with U. of Ore. Med. Sch. as prof. anatomy and asst. dean, 1912-17, dean, 1920-43, also clinical professor orthopedic surgery and head of dept.; surgeon in chief, Shriners' Hospital for Crippled Children, 1923-43; member surg. staff Emanuel Hosp., Multnomah County Hosp.; chief of orthopedic surg. staff, Doernbecher Memorial Hosp. for Children, 1926-43. Commd. 1st lt. Med. Corps U.S. Army, June 1917; capt. Jan. 1918; major, Jan. 1919; served as orthopedic surg. Base Hosp. No. 46, Am. Expeditionary Forces. Chmn. com. on Survey Oregon State Mental Hosps. since 1951. Member American Medical Assn. State Med. Soc., Multnomah County Med. Soc., N. Pacific Surg. Assn., Pacific Northwest Med. Assn., Pacific Coast Surg. Assn. (pres. 1939-40), Am. Acad. of Orthopedic Surgeons, Am. Orthopedic Assn., Western Orthopedic Association (honorary mem.), Oregon Mental Health Association (dir. 1950), North Pacific Orthopedic Society (president 1934), Phi Rho Sigma, Alpha Omega Alpha; fellow of A.C.S.; hon. mem. Seattle Surg. Assn. Republican. Mason (32°, Shriner). Clubs: University, Arlington. Home: 2607 N.W. Roanoke St., Portland 10, Ore. Died Oct. 31, 1953.

DILLER, Neal V. business exec.; b. Diller, Neb., 1899. Dir. Automatic Clothes Washer, Inc., George F. Brown and Sons, Inc.; pres., dir. Chase Candy Co. Home: 7551 Delmar Blvd., University City, Mo. Office: 4230 Gravois Av., St. Louis, 16. Died Dec. 7, 1959.

DILLON, John Thomas, industrialist; born Erie, Pa., Feb. 7, 1884; s. John Thomas and Catherine (Hanley) D.; student pub. schs. of Erie and Titusville, Pa.; tutored in metall., engring., Buffalo, N.Y., 1902-04; m. Kathryn Gibbs, Feb. 7, 1906; children—Katherine, Frances. Asst. foreman machine dept. Titusville Forge Co., gen. supt., later pres., 1907-17; gen. mgr. Titusville div. Bethlehem Steel Co., 1917-26; vice pres. of Struthers Wells-Titusville Corp. (now Struthers Wells Corp.), Warren, Pa., 1928-32, pres. 1932-56; chairman of the board, 1956—; president of the Titusville Iron Works Company, 1932—; dir. Titusville Trust Co. Mem. Pa. State Chamber of Commerce (treas. 1947-48), Newcomen Soc., Pa. Soc. Republican. Clubs: Engineers (N.Y. City); Wanango Country (Oil City, Pa.); Country (Titusville, Pa.). Home: 509 E. Main St. Office: 315 S. Franklin St., Titusville, Pa. Died May 12, 1958; buried Titusville.

DILLON, Robert E(mmet), pub. utilities exec.; b. North Attleboro, Mass., Dec. 29, 1883; s. Louis Willard and Emma Augusta (Horton) D.; S.B., Mass. Inst. Tech., 1910; m. Mona Audrey de Mare, Jan. 1934. Mech. engr. North Packing Co., 1910-11; with Boston Edison Co. since 1911, v.p. and asst. to pres. since 1948. Clubs: Boston City, Algonquin, Engineers. Home: 325 Winter St., Framingham, Mass. Office: 182 Tremont St., Boston 12. Died Nov. 2, 1952.

DIMITROV, Georgi, premier of Bulgaria; b. 1882. Politically active in Bulgaria, 1909—; mem. exec. com. Communist Internat., 1921-35, gen. sec., Moscow, 1935-42; prime minister People's Republic of Bulgaria. 1947. Awarded Order of Lenin, 1945. Author number publs. relating to worker and trade union movements, communism, related subjects. Address: Sofia, Bulgaria.* Died Feb. 7, 1949.

DIMOCK, Hedley S(eldon), educator; b. Nova Scotia, Can., Feb. 11, 1891; s. Charles T. and Catherine (Chase) D.; A.B., U. Saskatchewan, 1920; M.A., U. Chgo., 1925, B.D. and Ph.D., 1926; m. E. Marguerite Gardiner, Aug. 17, 1922; children—Dorothy Marguerite, Hedley Gardiner, Elizabeth Christine. Came to U.S., 1922, naturalized. 1937. Sec. Boys' Work Bd., Saskatchewan, 1920-22; instr. psychology and edn. Carleton Coll., Northfield. Minn., 1926-27; prof. religious edn. George Williams Coll., Chgo., 1927-34, dean and prof., 1934-52; coordinator of tng. YMCA, San Francisco, 1952-58. Coordinator of tng., dir. hdqrs. staff services U.S.O., Inc., 1943-46. Served with Princess Patricia Canadian Light Inf., Eng. and France, 1916-18. Mem. Am. Assn. Group Workers, Am. Acad. Social and Polit. Sci., Am. Assn. Adult Edn., Am. Camping Assn., Nat. Council on Relgion in Higher Edn., Nat. Conf. Social Work. Religious Edn. Assn., Assn. Secc. YMCA, Adult Edn. Council Chgo. (bd. dirs.). Baptist. Author: (with Charles E. Hendry) Camping and Character, 1929, Rediscovering the Adolescent, 1937; (with Taylor Statten) Talks to Counselors, 1939; (with Harleigh Trecker) Supervision of Group Work and Recreation, 1949; (with Roy Sorenson) Designing Education in Values, 1955. Editor: Character Education in the Summer Camp (monographs), 1930, 31, 35, 36, 39, 41, 42, 48; Administration of the Modern Camp, 1948. Home: 1449 Balboa Av., Burlingame, Cal. Office: 220 Golden Gate Av., San Francisco. Died Oct. 4, 1958.

DIMOCK, William Wallace, prof. vet. sci.; b. Tolland, Conn., Feb. 20, 1880; s. Henry Eugene and Ellen M. (Clark) D.; B.Agr., Conn. Agrl. Coll., 1901; D.V.M., N.Y. State Veterinary College (Cornell U.), 1905; D.V.M., University of Habana, Cuba, 1908, Professor Honoris Causa, 1945; married Ruth Attwill Mudge, Nov. 27, 1909; children—Phoebe, Betty Anne, Shubael Eugene, Gladys Eusebia, Ruth Mudge. Began practice as veterinarian in Conn., 1905; asst. chief animal husbandry, Cuban Expt. Sta., Santiago de los Vegus, Cuba, 1906-08; chief veterinarian, Nat. Bd. of Health, Cuba, 1908-09; prof. pathology and bacteriology, State Coll. of Ia., 1909-19; prof. vet. science, U. of Ky., since 1919, ex-head dept. animal pathology, Ky. Agrl. Expt. Sta. Mem. Am. Vet. Med. Assn. (pres. 1942-43), A.A.A.S., Ky. Vet. Med. Assn., Ia. Vet. Med. Assn., Ky. Acad. Science, U.S. Live Stock Sanitary Assn., Gamma Alpha, Phi Kappa Phi, Sigma Xi (pres. U. of Ky. Chapter 1930-31). Democrat. Presbyn. Author or joint author of 100 publs. on animal diseases. Home: Swigert Av., Lexington, Ky. Died Oct. 1953.

DIMOND, Anthony Joseph (dī'mŭnd), U.S. dist. judge; b. Palatine Bridge, N.Y., Nov. 30, 1881; s John P. and Emily (Sullivan) D.; student St. Mary's Catholic Inst., Amsterdam, N.Y., 1896-98; LL.D. (honorary) University of Alaska, 1950; married Dorothea Frances Miller, February 10, 1916; children—Marie Therese, John Henry, Anne Lillian. Taught sch., 1900-03; prospector and miner, 1904-12; in practice of law since 1913; U.S. commr., Chisana, Alaska, 1913; spl. asst. U.S. atty., Valdez, 1917; mem. Alaska Territorial Senate, 1923, 25, 29, 31; mayor of Valdez, 1920-22 and 1925-32; del. from Alaska, 73d to 78th Congresses (1933-45); U.S. dist. judge, 3d div., Anchorage, Alaska, since Jan. 1945. Mem. Am. Bar Assn. Catholic. Elk, Pioneer of Alaska. Home: Anchorage, Alaska. Died May 28, 1953.

DINES, Homer Duncan, lawyer; b. Shelbyville, Mo., Oct. 16, 1877; s. Henry B. and Mattie L. (Duncan) D.; student Chaddock Coll., Quincy, Ill., 1894-98, LL.B., 1900; m. May Dickson, Oct. 10, 1901; children—Ralph, Helen; m. 2d, Louise D. Seaton, June 2, 1934; stepson, Robert D. Seaton. Admitted to Ill. bar, 1900; private secretary to Judge Guy C. Scott, 1903-07; law practice, Quincy, Ill., 1900-09; sec. to Judge Geo. A. Cooke 1909-18; mem. Daily, Dines, Ross & O'Keefe, now Ross, McGowan & O'Keefe, Chgo., 1918—. Served with Ill. N.G., 3 yrs. Mason. Home: 3750 Lake Shore Dr., Chgo. 13. Office: 122 S. Michigan Av., Chgo. 3. Died July 22, 1959; buried Rosehill Mausoleum, Chgo.

DINGELL, John David (dĭng'ĕl), congressman; b. Detroit, Mich., Feb. 2, 1894; s. Joseph Adam and Mary (Knapp) D.; m. Grace Blossom Bigler, of Colorado Springs, Colo., Apr. 27, 1925; children—John David, Patricia Ann (dec.), James Victor, Julé Jane. Newspaperman, pipeline engineer, wholesale dealer in beef and pork products; mem. 73d-84th Congresses, from 15th Michigan District Organizer and ex-trustee Colo. Springs Labor College. Mem. Internat. Typog. Union, Knights of Columbus, Army and Navy Club. Democrat. Home: Detroit, Mich. Office: 1110 New House Office Bldg., Washington. Died Sept. 19, 1955; buried Holy Sepulchre Cemetery, Detroit.

DINKELSPIEL, Lloyd W., lawyer; b. San Francisco, Nov. 19, 1899; s. Samuel L. and Beatrice (Bachman) D.; A.B., Stanford, 1920; LL.B., Harvard, 1922; m. Florence Hellman, February 26, 1926 (dec. Jan. 1954); children—Frances (Mrs. William H. Green), Lloyd W.; m. 2d, Anna R. Ward, July 26, 1958. Admitted to Cal. bar, 1921, pvt. pactice San Francisco since 1922; partner Heller, Ehrman, White & McAuliffe 1927—. Pres. Jewish Welfare Fedns. of San Francisco, Marin Co. and Peninsula, Nat. Jewish Welfare Bd.; dir. Wells Fargo Bank, Stanford Research Inst., president Stanford, trustee 1953-58. Served as 2d lt. Inf., United States Army, 1918; maj. to lt. col., U.S.A.A.F., 1943-45. Decorated Legion of Merit. Mem. Am., San Francisco (pres. 1942-43) bar assns. Home: 2800 Broadway, San Francisco 15. Office: 14 Montgomery St., San Francisco 4. Died May 1959.

DINKMEYER, Henry William, educator; b. Carlinville, Ill., Feb. 17, 1892; s. John Henry and Augusta (Luessenhop) D.; student Elmhurst Coll., 1907-11, D.D. (hon.), 1942; student Eden Theol. Sem., Webster Groves, Mo., 1911-14; B.D., Yale, 1915; A.M., U. of Chicago, 1922; m. Lois Ely, Aug. 23, 1917; 1 son, Henry William. Ordained to ministry of the Evangelical and Reformed Ch., 1914, and served as minster St. John's Ch., Wright City, Mo., 1915-19, Bethany Evang. and Reformed Ch., Chicago, 1919-48; pres. Elmhurst (Ill.) Coll. since 1948. Club: Kiwanis (Elmhurst). Home: 170 Prospect St., Elmhurst, Ill. Died Feb. 16, 1957; buried St. Charles, Mo.

DINSMORE, Robert Scott, surgeon; b. Troy, Kan., Aug. 10, 1892; s. Robert Scott and Etha (Wilkinson) D.; A.B., U. Kan., 1914; M.D., Washington U., 1917; m. Alice J. Mattley, Apr. 13, 1940. Intern Lakeside Hosp., Cleve., 1917-18, resident surgery, 1919-23; mem. staff Cleve. Clinic Found., 1923—, chief surgery, 1949—. Trustee A.M. McGregory Home. Served with USMC, 1918-19. Crile European travelling fellow, 1923. Diplomate Am. Bd. Surgery. Mem. A.M.A. (chmn. sect. surgery 1937), Cleve. Acad. Medicine (pres. 1936-37), Am. (pres. 1953), So., Central surg. assns., Ohio Med. Assn., Eastern Surg. Soc., Am. Goiter Assn., Am. Assn. Ry. Surgeons, Delta Tau Delta, Nu Sigma Nu. Clubs: Pasteur, Medical Arts (Cleve.); Saddle and Sirloin (Chgo.); Catalia Trout Club (Castalia, Ohio). Home: Park Lana Villa, Park Lane and E. 105th St. Office: 2020 E. 93d St., Cleve. 6. Died Sept. 1957.

DIOR, Christian, fashion designer; b. Normandy, 1905; s. Maurice and Magdeleine (Martin) D.; student Nat. Sch. Polit. Science. Had picture gallery showing works of famous contemporary artists, including Dali, Berard, Cocteau, 1928-31; travelled in Russia, 1931, in Spain, 1934; fashion illustrator Figaro Illustrated, 1935; sold sketches of ideas for accessories and dresses, 1935-38; asst. to Piguet, 1938-39; designer for Lucien Lelong, 1942-45; has own house of fashion design 1946—; opened establishment, N.Y.C., 1948, and in Caracas, Venezuela, 1953. Served with French Army, World War II. Address: 30 Av. Montaligne, Paris 8e, France. Died Oct. 24, 1957 *

DISERENS, Paul, consulting engineer; b. Cincinnati, O., Jan. 9, 1882; s. Albert Day and Alice (Jefferies) D.; B.S., Purdue U., 1904, M.E., 1906; student U. of Ill., 1906-08; unmarried. Research asst. with Dr. W. F. M. Goss, 1904-08; in charge locomotive tests in study of superheated steam locomotive service, Carnegie Inst. of Washington, 1905-1906; research asst., studying Ill. coal, U. of Ill., 1907-09; engr. of test in charge research, Laidlaw Dunn Gordon Co., Cincinnati, O., 1909-19; asst. chief engr., Worthington Pump and Machine Corp., New York City, 1919-28, chief cons. engr., 1928—, dir. research, 1944-45, dir. research and development, Worthington Pump and Machine Corp. and subsidiaries, (Worthington-Gamon Meter Co., Ransome Machinery Co., Electric Machinery Co.), 1945-54; tech. advisor Compressed Air and Gas Inst. 1954—. Cons. Nat. Defense Research Com., 1941-44. Fellow Am. Soc. Mech. Engrs. (mem. power test codes com.) Mem. Am. Soc. Refrigerating Engineers, U.S. Nat. Com. Internat. Electrotech. Com. (director secretariat and also chairman of the technical committee on internal combustion engines). Republican. Clubs: Engineers (New York); Canoe Brook Country (Summit, N.J.); Baltusrol Golf (Springfield, N.J.); Cornell (N.Y.) Inventor of expander engines for refrigeration in gasoline industry; valves for compressors; hot oil pumps for oil refineries; holds U.S. and fgn. patents. Contbr. of articles to professional jours. Home: 1 Euclid Av., Summit, N.J. Died Oct. 6. 1958; buried Spring Grove Cemetery, Cin.

DISQUE, Brice P. (dĭsk), army officer, exec.; b. California, O., July 19, 1879; s. Henry Jacob and Ella (Pursell) D.; ed. pub. schs., Cincinnati, O., and Walnut Hill Sch.; distinguished grad. Inf. and Cav. Sch., 1906, Army Staff Coll., 1907; m. Mary Florence Coulter, Oct. 22, 1901; children—Brice Pursell, Gordon Coulter. Served from 2d lt. to brig. gen., U.S. Army, 1899-1919; brig. gen. U.S. Army Reserve Corps, 1919-49; served in Philippine Insurrection and World War; captured Aguinaldo's southern comdr., Emeterio Funes, and his troops, Feb. 21, 1901. Served as mgr. of Michigan State Prison (developed system providing gainful employment for all inmates and operated the prison at profit without financial aid from State), 1916-17; organizer and comdr. Spruce Division, U.S. Army, and pres. U.S. Spruce Corp., 1917-19; organizer, 1918, pres. 1918-19, Loyal Legion Loggers and Lumbermen for lumber industry in the Pacific Northwest (cont. after war period as coordinating agency, bringing industrial peace between employer and employes). Pres. G. Amsinck & Co., 1919-21, Johnson Cowdin & Co., 1921-27, United Industrial Bancstocks, 1930; v.p. The Aviation Corp., 1929; pres. U.S. Distributing Corp., Pattison and Bowns, Inc., 1933-36, Jansen Creek Orchards, Inc.; Pres. Anthracite Inst., 1931-33; dir. Murray Hill Trust Co., 1924-28, Peoples Nat. Bank & Trust Co., 1934-55; past pres. of the Coal Consumers Protective Assn., N.Y. City. Active duty War Department, 1941-42. Chmn. Area Advisory Com. on Local Distbn., Solid Fuels Adminstrn. for War, N.Y., 1943-46. Mem. S.R. Awarded D.S.M. (U.S.); Comdr. Order S.S. Maurice and Lazarus (Italy); commendation from govts. of Great Britain and France. Mem. Disciples of Christ Ch. Clubs: Metropolitan, Uptown (New York); Army and Navy (Wash.) Army and Navy (Manila). Home: Spuyten Duyvil, New York, N.Y.; (farm residence) Linlithgo, N.Y. Died March 1960.

DITTRICK, Howard, physician, editor; born St. Catharines, Ont., Can., Feb. 14, 1877; s. Duncan and Martha (Harper) D.; student, St. Catharines Collegiate Inst., 1890-95, Welland Model Sch., 1895-96; M.B., U. of Toronto, 1900, M.D., 1927; post-grad., Johns Hopkins, 1901; m. Gertrude B. Moore, Jan. 29, 1907; children—Douglas Harper, Harvey Hull (dec.), John Hull, Laurence Howard, Alan Everitt, Howard David, Paul Lindley. Came to U.S. 1900, naturalized 1911. Intern gynecology, Lakeside Hosp., Cleveland, 1900-01; resident in gynecology, 1902-05; demonstrator, dept. gynecology, Western Res. Univ., 1904-15, instr. 1915-25, sr. clin. instr. 1925-43; edit. dir., Cleveland Clinic, 1943-47; asso. prof. history of medicine, Frank E. Bunts Ednl. Inst., 1948; med. referee, Prudential Ins. Co., 1938-43; directing editor, Current Researches in Anesthesia and Analgesia, 1940—; mem. Cleveland Acad. Medicine (membership com., 1923, chmn. clin.-path. sect. 1927, chmn. programs 1928, dir. 1928, 29, 30, chmn. art exhibit 1933, editorial com. 1927-34, editor 1934-43, asso. editor 1943-45, adv. editor, 1945—), Med. Library Assn. (v.p. 1947; mem. various coms.); trustee Cleveland Med. Library 1927; dir. membership 1929-31, dir. programs 1932-34, curator museum 1929-35, dir. museum, 1935—, pres., 1945-46; pres. Cleveland Med. Examiners Club 1936-43; dir. Howard Dittrick Museum Hist. Medicine, Cleveland Med. Library; trustee Cleveland Health Museum, 1940—; chmn. med. adv. com. Greater Cleveland Hosp. Fund. 1945-46. Received Distinguished Service Award, Cleveland Acad. Medicine 1943. Served on med. adv. bd., World War I; charge first aid sta., Civilian Defense, World War II. Fellow American Medical Association; mem. Am. Assn. Museums, Internat. Assn. Hist. Medicine, Internat. Assn. Med. Museums, Am. Assn. Med. History, Ohio State, and Western Res. hist. socs., Canadian Univs. Assn. of Ohio (pres. 1947, 48), Cleveland Museum Art (life). Episcopalian. Clubs: Rowfant, Professional Men's (charter mem.), Pasteur (past pres. and charter mem.). Compiler: Medical Pioneers in Western Reserve, 1932; author: Some Old Hospitals in Spain, 1948; Some Important Contributions to Medicine by Clevelanders, 1948; also numerous articles on med. subjects, etc. Official del. of U.S. Govt. to Internat. Congress of History of Medicine, Spain 1935, Yugoslavia 1938. Home: 3320 Euclid Heights Blvd., Cleveland Heights 18, O. Died July 11, 1954; buried Lakeview Cemetery, Cleve.

DIXON, George Peleg, assn. exec., ret. army officer; b. Worcester, Mass., Jan. 29, 1889; s. Rufus S. and Cora I. (Bemis) D.; student Worcester Poly. Inst., 1912; m. Edna M. Spitzer, May 27, 1946; children—Patricia, Peter (by former marriage), Penelope Ann. Student engr. Pacific Tel. & Tel. Co., San Francisco, 1912-17; engr. Western Electric Co., N.Y.C., 1919-20; traffic supervisor, insp. N.Y. Telephone Co., 1920-25; gen. mgr. Worcester Spiral Ramp Garage Co., 1925-27; N.Y. Telephone Co., 1927-29; communications engr. Nat. City Bank, and asso. cos., N.Y.C., 1929-40; v.p. Internat. Tel. & Tel. Corp., 1945-50, regional v.p., Brazil, 1946-48; exec. v.p., editor Armed Forces Communications Assn., Washington, since 1950. Trustee Worcester Poly. Inst. Mem. Cal. N.G., 1916-17, served Mexican Border, 6 months; lt. to capt. Signal Corps, U.S. Army, 1917-19, overseas with 91st Div. and S.O.S., 1918-19; lt. col. Signal Corps, col. A.C., 1940-45; signal officer II Corps area, 1940-42; signal communications officer 8th Air Force Service Command, chief signal officer 8th Air Force, dir. communications, U.S.S.T.A.F., E.T.O., 1942-45; Signal Res., 1945-49. Decorated Silver Star (2), Legion of Merit, Bronze Star Medal (4), Commendation Medal, Victory Medal (World War I and II), Mexican Border Medal, World War I Occupation Medal, Am. Def. Medal, E.T.O. Medal, Am. Theatre Medal, World War II Occupation Medal; Officer Order Brit. Empire; Chevalier Legion of Honor, French Cross of War (2), Gen. Service Medal, Gold Palms Hon. Officer French Acad. Sci. (France); Belgium Cross of War. Mem. Am. Inst. Radio Engrs., Radio Engrs. Soc. (Gt. Britain), S.A.R., Armed Forces Communications Assn. (a founder), N.Y. Acad. Scis., Am. Legion, N.Y. State Soc. Mil. and Naval Officers, Mil. Order World Wars, Phi Gamma Delta. Episcopalian. Clubs: Army and Navy (Washington); Belle Haven Country (Alexandria, Va.); Governors Island Officers (N.Y. C.); Internacional (Rio de Janeiro). Home: 20 Belfield Rd., Belle Haven, Alexandria, Va. Office: 1624 Eye St., Washington 6. Died July 9, 1956; buried Arlington Nat. Cemetery.

DOBBIE, George Alexander, ins. and mfg. exec.; b. Lanark, Ont., Can., Apr. 21, 1880; s. Alexander and Edith (Lamont) D.; ed. pub. schs. of Brockville, Ont.; m. Jennie E. Scott, Apr. 8, 1908; children—Margaret E. (Mrs. J. G. Crean), Jean M. (Mrs. G. F. Pangman), George H. Chmn. bd., Dominion Life Assurance Co., Waterloo, Ont., since 1949; pres. Newlands & Co., Ltd., Galt, since 1915, C. Turnbull Co., Ltd., since 1946, Stauffer-Dobbie, Ltd., since 1915, Gypsum Lime & Alabastine Co., Ltd., Paris, Ont., since 1936; v.p., Cocksnutt Plow Co., Brantford, Ont., since 1937; dir. Minn. & Ontario Paper Co., British American Oil Co., Royal Bank of Canada, United Corp., Slimgsby Mfg., Ltd., Frost & Wood Co., Ltd. Mem. and past pres. Canadian Woolen and Knit Goods Mfrs. Assn.; mem. Canadian C. of C. Home: The Cedars. Office: Newlands & Co., Ltd., Galt, Ont., Can. Died May 24, 1951.

DOBBS, Hoyt McWhorter, bishop; b. Antioch, Cherokee County, Ala., Nov. 16, 1878; s. Samuel Lewis and Laura (Clayton) D.; student Verner Mil. Inst., Tuscaloosa, Ala., 1893-95; A.M., Southern U., Greensboro, Ala., 1899, D.D., 1914; B.D., Vanderbilt, 1904; D.D., Emory, 1913; LL.D., Birmingham-Southern Coll., 1922; Litt.D. conferred by Southern College, 1928; m. Lessie Rush Jackson, Nov. 14, 1906; children—Hoyt M., Mary Elizabeth (dec.), Margaret Jackson. Licensed to preach M.E. Ch. S., 1901; ordained deacon, Nov. 27, 1904, elder. Nov. 22, 1908; pastor Mt. Vernon Ch., 1904-06, Fountain Heights Ch., 1907, Highlands Ch., 1907-09 (all of Birmingham, Ala.), Central Ch., 1909-13, Troost Av. Ch., 1913-14 (both Kansas City, Mo.); First Ch., Ft. Worth, Tex., 1914-16; dean Sch. Theol. and prof. and lecturer on Christian Doctrine, Southern Meth. Univ., Dallas, Tex., 1916-20; pastor First Methodist Ch., Anniston, Ala., 1920-22; elected bishop May 16, 1922, and assigned to Brazil with official residence at Sao Paulo, 1922-26; assigned to 13th Episcopal Dist., embracing states of Ala. and Fla., with official residence at Birmingham, Ala., 1926-30; assigned to 12th Episcopal Dist., embracing states of La. and Ark., with official residence at Shreveport, La., 1930-34; assigned to 7th Episcopal Dist., embracing states of La. and Miss., official residence at Shreveport; retired June 24, 1944. Mem. Gen. Board Christian Edn. Del. to Gen. Conf. of Meth. Ch., 1918, 22. Mem. Phi Beta Kappa, Phi Delta Theta. Mason (33°, K.T., K.C.C.H., Red Cross of Constantine, Shriner). Club: Lions. Contbr. on religious and ednl. subjects. Address: 5900 Line Av., Shreveport, La. Died Dec. 9, 1954; buried Shrevport.

DOBRINER, Konrad (dō-brē'nẽr), research physician; b. Elberfeld, Germany, Oct. 14, 1902; s. Paul and Laura (Drey) D.; Gymnasium Cologne, Gymnasium Lennep, 1909-21, U. of Freiburg, 1921-25, U. of Munich, 1925-27; M.D., D.M.S., U. of Munich, 1927; m. Shirley FitzGerald, June 28, 1945; children—Madeleine Joan, Mark George. Came to U.S., 1934, naturalized, 1940. Intern II Medizinische Abteilung Krankenhaus Munich-Schwabing, 1927-28, assistenzarzt, 1928-33; specialist for internal med., Munich, 1932; research fellow U. of Rochester Med. Sch., 1934-36, Hosp of Rockefeller Inst., 1936-39; head dept. research chemistry Memorial Hosp., N.Y. City, 1939-47; mem. Sloan-Kettering Inst., N.Y. City, since 1947. Mem. Am. Soc. Biol. Chemists, Assn. Study Internal Secretions, Am. Assn. Cancer Research, Am. Soc. Clin. Investigation, Soc. Exptl. Biol. and Med., Harvey Soc., N.Y. Acad. Scis. Research in metabolism of steroid hormones; cancer research; prophyrin metabolism, metabolism of carcinogens, infra-red spectrometry. Home: 345 E. 68th St., N.Y. Ctiy 21. Office: 444 E. 68th St., N.Y.C. 21. Died Mar. 10. 1952; buried Simsbury, Conn.

DOBSON, Mason Henry, newspaper editor and publisher; b. Janesville, Wis., Oct. 18, 1891; s. Woodhouse Thomas and Annie Virginia (Covert) D.; ed. Beloit (Wis.) Coll. Acad.; m. Louise Ellen Garrigan, June 10, 1912; children—Mason, Donald, Betty. Began with Beloit Daily News, 1913, editor since 1924; now also publisher. Mem. Wis. Hist. Soc.; hon. mem. Sigma Delta Chi. Republican. Episcopalian. Mason (32°). Club: Beloit Country. With Am. Red Cross, July 1943-Feb. 1945, serving in N. Africa, Sicily and Italy as dep. dir. Civilian War Relief for Mediterranean Theater of Operations, and dir. CWR in Italy. Awarded Cross of Merit, First Degree, by the Order of Malta. Home: Littlebeck Farm, Shirland, Ill. (Durand, R.F.D. 1). Home: R. 1, Durand, Ill. Office: Daily News Pub. Co., Beloit, Wis. Died Dec. 9, 1952; buried Eastlawn Cemetery, Beloit, Wis.

DOCK, George, physician, educator; b. Hopewell, Pa., Apr. 1, 1860; s. Gilliard and Lavinia Lloyd (Bombaugh) D.; M.D., U. of Pa., 1884; hon. A.M., Harvard, 1895; Sc.D., U. of Pa., 1904; LL.D., University of Southern Calif., 1936; m. Laura McLemore, July 5, 1892; children—George, William; m. 2d, Miriam Gould, Oct. 17, 1925. Asst. clin. pathology, U. of Pa., 1887-88; prof. pathology, Tex. Med. Coll. and Hosp., 1888-91; prof. theory and practice of medicine and clin. medicine, U. of Mich., 1891-1908; prof. theory and practice of medicine, Tulane U., 1908-10; prof. medicine, Washington U. Med. School, 1910-22; hon. prof. medicine, University of Southern Calif. Member Assn. American Physicians (pres. 1916-17), A.M.A., etc.; fellow A.A.A.S. Club: University, Valley Hunt, Twilight (Pasadena); Athletic (Los Angeles). Author: Hookworm Disease (with C. C. Bass), 1940. Also numerous articles on med. subjects in jours. and text-books. Home: 397 E. Calaveras, Altadena, Calif. Died May 30, 1951.

DODD, Alvin Earl, assn. exec.; b. Hudson, N.Y., Mar. 11, 1883; s. Alvin Harvey and Edith (Merrill) D.; B.S., Armour Inst. Tech., 1905; LL.D., Temple U., 1948; m. Catherine Filene, Dec. 10, 1921 (div. 1930); 1 dau., Joan; m. 2d, Henrietta F. Coster, Aug. 31, 1941. Asst. prin. Fifth Ward Manual Tng. Sch. Allegheny, Pa., 1905-06; head manual arts dept. Mass. Normal Sch., North Adams, 1906-07; pres. Eastern Arts Assn., 1907-08; prin. North Bennett Indsl. Sch., Boston, 1908-12; dir. Nat. Soc. for Promotion of Indsl. Edn., 1912-16; mem. Com. on Classification of Personnel, Gen. Staff U.S. Army, 1917; head War Service Com., Retail Dry Goods Industry, 1918; dir. Retail Research Assn. and Asso. Merchandising Corp., 1917-21; mgr. distbn. dept. U.S. C. of C., 1921-27; mem. bd. dirs. Fgn. Policy Assn., 1927-28; dir. gen. Wholesale Dry Goods Inst., 1927-29; lectr. on trade and indsl. problems Northwestern U., U. Chgo., U. Wash., Stanford U., 1927-29; asst. to pres. Sears, Roebuck & Co., 1929-30; v.p. Kroger Grocery and Baking Co., 1930-33; exec. v.p. Am. Mgmt. Assn., 1934-35, pres., 1936-48, hon. pres., 1949-51. Cons. mem. staff William L. Batt, Chief of ECA mission to United Kingdom, 1950. Recipient Henry L. Gantt gold medal, 1947. Past mng. dir. U.S. council Internat. C. of C., exec. vice chmn., 1949. Mem. Am. Econ. Assn., Nat. Inst. Social Sciences, Am. Acad. Polit. and Social Sci., Fgn. Policy Assn., Am. Trade Assn., N.Y. Trade Assn. Execs. Clubs: Cosmos (Washington); Lake Shore Athletic (Chgo.); City, Lotos, Sales Executives (N.Y.C.). Home: 160 E. 48th St. Office: 330 W. 42d St., N.Y.C. Died June 2, 1951; buried Grand Detour, Ill.

DODD, Edwin Merrick, prof. of law; b. Providence, R.I., Oct. 31, 1888; s. Edwin Merrick and Ellen (Tiffany) Dodd; student Providence (R.I.) pub. and pvt. schs., 1893-1902, St. Mark's Sch., Southboro, Mass., 1902-06; A.B., Harvard Univ., 1910; LL.B., Harvard Univ. Law Sch., 1913; m. Winifred Hyde, June 20, 1928. Admitted to Mass. bar, 1913; engaged in gen. practice of law, Boston, 1913-16; prof. law, Washington and Lee Univ., Lexington, Va., 1916-17; again in practice of law at Boston, Mass., 1919-22; asst. prof., then prof. law, Univ. of Neb., 1922-27; prof. of law, Univ. of Chicago, 1927-28; prof. of law, Harvard Univ. Law Sch., 1928-46. Fessenden professor of law since 1946. Compliance Commr. War Production Board and Civilian Prodn. Adminstrn. since 1942. Mem. Am. Bar Assn., Mass. Hist. Soc., Phi Beta Kappa. Democrat. Episcopalian. Clubs: Harvard (Boston); Faculty (Cambridge). Contbr. articles on corpn. law and other legal subjects to legal publs. Home: 989 Memorial Drive, Cambridge, Mass. Died Nov. 3, 1951; buried Mt. Auburn Cemetery, Cambridge, Mass.

DODD, John Morris, surgeon; b. Waynesburg, Pa., Oct. 5, 1866; s. Samuel and Catharine (Morris) D.; ed. common schs.; M.D., Starling Med. Coll., Columbus, O., 1889; D.Sc., Northland Coll., 1925; m. Missouri Stoops, Dec. 23, 1889; children—Florence E., Edith M., Helen R., John M. Practiced, Ashland, Wis., since 1889; surgeon St. Joseph's and Ashland Gen. hosps.; pres. Ashland Gen. Hosp. Assn.; founder and pres. Ashland Clinic. Mayor of Ashland, 1911-13 and 1933-1939; sec. Wis. State Bd. of Med. Examiners, 1915-24. Pres. trustees Northland Coll.; trustee Interstate Post-Grad. Med. Assn. Maj. Med. Reserve Corps, U.S. Army. Fellow Am. Coll. Surgeons, A.M.A.; mem. Soo and C.&N.W. Ry. Surg. Assns. (ex-pres.), State Med. Soc. of Wis. (pres. 1911-12, councilor 1903-30). Mason (Past Grand Comdr., K.T. of Wis.), Elk, I.O.O.F., Rotarian. Author: The Autobiography of a Surgeon, 1928. Home: Ashland, Wis. Died Aug. 5, 1950; buried Ashland.

DODD, Monroe Elmon, clergyman; b. Brazil, Tenn., Sept. 8, 1878; s. William Henry and Lucy (Williams) D.; A.B., B.O., Union U., Jackson, Tenn., 1904, D.D., 1909, LL.D., 1930; corr. work U. Chgo., Crozer Theol. Sem.; D D., Baylor U., 1917; m. Emma Savage, Oct. 10, 1904. Ordained to Bapt. ministry, 1902; pastor Fulton, Ky., 1904-08, First Ch., Paducah, 1908-11, 22d and Walnut St. Ch., Louisville, 1911-12, First Ch., Shreveport, La., 1912-50, emeritus, 1950—; pastor Temple Bapt. Ch., Los Angeles, 1927. Sgt. 2d Tenn. Vols., Spanish-Am. War; YMCA service 12 mos., 6 mos. overseas, World War I. Mem. Bapt. $75,000,000 campaign commissions; mem. exec. com. Bapt. World Alliance, 1934—; pres. La. Bapt. Conv., 1926-27, So. Bapt. Conv., 1933-35. Democrat. Mason. Rotarian. Author: Jesus Is Coming to Earth Again, 1917; Baptist Principles, 1918; Jesus the Lily, Lamb, Lion, Lord, 1920; The Prayer Life of Jesus, 1923; The Democracy of the Saints, 1924; Concerning the Collection, 1929; Missions Our Mission, 1929; The Christ We Worship, 1930; Radio Revival Sermons, 1932; Communion Meditations, 1933; Girdling the Globe for God, 1935; The New Testament Three-Sixteens, 1936. Went around the world in 1934 on tour of mission fields. made all airplane missionary tour of S.A., 1938-June 1944, elected general director, Centennial Evangelistic Crusade, Southern Baptist, 1945. Made 25,000 mile airplane preaching tour of Australia and So. Pacific, 1946; toured Europe, Africa, South Am., 1947. Home: 601 Ockley Dr., Shreveport, La. Died Aug. 6, 1952.

DODDS, B(ernice) L(ee), coll. dean; b. St. Edward, Neb., Jan. 7, 1903; s. Oscar Leigh and Della Elizabeth (Karnes) D.; A.B., U. of Neb., 1926; A.M., U. of Wyo., 1936; Ed.D., Columbia, 1940; LL.D. (honorary), Purdue University, 1958; married

Doris Elsie Fonda, Oct. 3, 1928; children—Bernard Fonda, Barbara Bethyne. Teacher in pub. sch., Beaver Crossing, Neb., and Basin, Wyo., 1925-30; prin. high sch., Basin, Wyo., and Superior, Wyo., 1930-37; scholar, research asst., instr., Teachers Coll., Columbia, 1937-39; successively asst. prof., asso. prof., prof. edn., Purdue U., 1939-48, dir. div. of education and applied psychology 1948-53; dean, Coll. Edn., U. Ill., 1953-—. Mem. Phi Kappa Phi, ednl. bull., Sigma Xi, Kappa Delta Pi, Phi Delta Kappa, Pi Kappa Phi. Mason. Co-author: American High School Administration, 1951. Home: Edgewood, R.R. 3, Urbana, Ill. Died Mar. 23, 1959.

DODDS, Chauncey Y., govt. official; b. Mayfield, Ky., May 6, 1892; s. William De Castro and Lillie May (Yarbrough) D.; student, Ind. U., 1910-11; m. Charlotte Waterfield, July 12, 1925; children—Alan H., Chauncey Y. Officer First Nat. Bank, Mayfield, Ky., 1911-25; pvt. investment bus., 1926-33; chief examiner drainage, levee and irrigation div., R.F.C., Washington, D.C., 1933-38, chief small bus. div., 1946-47; dir. office of loans. Served as capt., 59th inf., A.E.F., U.S. Army, 1917-19. Democrat. Mason. Home: 4241 Garfield St. N.W. Office: 811 Vermont Av. N.W., Washington. Died Jan. 16, 1952; buried Arlington Nat. Cemetery.

DODGE, Martin, government official; born Auburn, Ohio, August 27, 1892; son Julius H. and Emma Gail (Bartholomew) D.; ed. Oberlin Acad.; A.B., Oberlin Coll., 1915; Ph.D., Columbia, 1918; m. D'Etta Brown, Nov. 10, 1917; children—Diana, Peter, Mgr. indsl. bur. Mchts. Assn. of N.Y., 1918-27; v.p. and sec. Am. Airports Corp., 1928; vice pres., sec. and dir. Aviation Securities Corp., 1928-32; staff exec. Young com., Fed. Res. System, 1932-33; partner Norman Bel Geddes & Co., 1933-35, Walter Dorwin Teague 1935-40; pub. relations counselor Martin Dodge & Carlton K. Matson, 1941-44, Martin Dodge & Co., 1944-46; pub. relations counselor Dodge & Mugridge, labor cons. 1946-53; dep. commr., Dept. of Commerce and Pub. Events, N.Y. C., 1955-—. Pub. D-M Digest gist of labor, leftwing and group press, 1944-50. Organized Council on Adult Edn. for the Fgn. Born, 1921. Pres. Oberlin Alumni Assn. of N.Y., 1926-28. Mem. Acad. Polit. Sci., Am. Viewpoint, Inc. (chmn.), Pub. Relations Society of Am. (past mem. bd. dirs. and exec. com.), Am. Management Assn. Mem. The Riverside Ch. Club: University. Author: The Administration of the City of Frankfort am-Main; Industrial Pensions; Newtown Creek Industrial District; Industrial Map of New York; Labor Public Relations; Labor-Management Melee; Labor-Management Revolution of 1947 Labor's Fourth Estate; Know Your Isms; Labor's Political PR; also numerous pamphlets and magazine articles on industrial, labor and pub. relations subjects. Home: 277 Park Av., N.Y.C. 17. Office: 500 Park Av., N.Y.C. 22. Died Nov. 25, 1957.

DODGE, Martin, real estate broker; b. Auburn, O., May 27, 1851; s. Joseph and Hannah C. D.; student Hiram Coll., 1871-75, A.M. (hon.), 1893; student Buchtel Coll., 1875; m. Anna Merchant, 1996. Admitted to Ohio bar, 1877, practiced in Cleve., 1881-1905, in Kan., 1879-81; real estate bus., Cleve., 1881-1905, Dodge Park, Md., 1905-—. Mem. Ohio Legislature, Ho. and Rep.s and Senate from 1891, reelected to Senate, 1899. Chmn. Good Rds. Commn. apptd. by Gov. McKinley, 1893; dir. Office of Road Inquiry, Dept. Agr., Washington, 1900-05. Republican. A leader in Good Roads movement. Address: Dodge Park, Md. Died Apr. 21, 1931; buried Ft. Lincoln Cemetery, D.C.

DODGE, Melvin Gilbert, librarian; b. East Rodman, N.Y., Feb. 17, 1868; s. William S. and Cynthia (Ballard) D.; A.B., Hamilton Coll., 1890, A.M., 1894; m. Dora M. Allen, July 17, 1901. Librarian Hamilton Coll., 1891-1901; asso. librarian Leland Stanford Jr. U., 1901-9; sec. Bd. of Edn., San Francisco, 1909-12; legislative reference librarian State Library, Sacramento, 1912-16; printer and book pub., Utica, N.Y., 1916-—. Mem. Phi Beta Kappa. Editor: Clark-Prize Book (with D. W. Burke), 1894; Alexander Hamilton, 1896; Fifty Years Ago (Half-Century Annalists' Letters to Hamilton Alumni), 1899. Compiler Class of 1890, Hamilton Coll., 1898; editor-in-chief Delta Upsilon Decennial Catalogue, 1903. Home: Utica, N.Y. Died Feb. 11, 1953.

DODGE, Nathan Phillips, real estate, banking; b. Council Bluffs, Ia., Mar. 24, 1872; s. Nathan Phillips (Sr. and Susannah Cane (Lockwood) D.; prep. edn. Williston Sem. (Easthampton, Mass.) and Phillips Exeter Acad.; B.A., Harvard, 1895, LL.B., 1897; m. Laura Collins Whitney, June 11, 1907; children—Nathan Phillips, Laura W., Henry Whitney. Admitted to Mass. bar, 1897, practiced at Boston, 1897-1900; moved to Omaha, Neb., 1900, and managed liquidation of Omaha Savings Bank 2 yrs.; in real estate business, 1902-—, buying and developing on a large scale; has platted and sold 163 subdivisions in 123 cities in 19 statse; pres. N. P. Dodge Corp. (Del.); chmn. bd. dirs. Council Bluffs Savings Bank, Rawley Land Co.; pres. Walnut Hill Cemetery Co., West Lawn Cemetery, Cedar Lawn Cemetery, Hillcrest Meml. Park, N. P. Dodge Co., Omaha Realty Co. Mem. Neb. Ho. of Rep., 2 terms, 1905-09, Senate 1911, 13; author Direct Primary Law and Election Commissioner Law; del. at large, Rep. Nat. Conv., 1916; pres. Hughes Alliance (Hughes Campaign). Republican. Unitarian. Mason (32°, Shriner). Home: R. 2 Omaha 12. Office: Keeline Bldg., Omaha, Neb. Died Sept. 19, 1950.

DODGE, Richard Elwood, educator; b. Wenham, Mass., Mar. 30, 1868; s. Robert Francis and Sarah Elizabeth (Wood) D.; A.B., Harvard, 1890, A.M., 1894; m. Stella Pomeroy Dalton, Aug. 19, 1896; children—Stanley Dalton, Margaret Belden, Philip Elwood. Asst. geology, 1891-94, and instr., 1894-95, Harvard; instr. geology and geography, 1895-96, asso. prof. natural science, 1896-97, prof. geography, 1897-1916, Teachers Coll. (Columbia); county agent leader, extension service, Connecticut, 1918-20; dean 2 yr. course, Conn. State College, 1920-30; prof. geog., 1926-38, prof. emeritus, U. of Conn., since 1938. Asst. U.S. Geol. Survey, Northeastern, Southern Appalachians, summers 1890-95. Received Distinguished waro, Nat. Council Geog. Teachers, 1946. Fellow N.Y. Acad. Scis., Geol. Soc. Am., A.A.A.S., Assn. Am. Geog. (pres. 1915), Sigma Xi; hon. corr. mem. Geog. Soc. of Australasia (Brisbane branch). Dist. gov. of 30th Dist. Rotary International, 1930-31. Author: Reader in Physical Geography for Beginners, 1900; Dodge's Geographies, 1903; Dodge's Geographical Note Books, 1912; Dodge-Lackey Geographies, 1927; also numerous articles on the teaching of geography; co-author Dodge and Kirchwey's Teaching of Geography in Elementary Schs.; Bowman and Dodge's English Edition of Brunhes' La Géographie Humaine; Foundations of Geography (with son Stanley Dalton Dodge), 1937; Economic Geography (with W. Harrison Carter, Jr.), 1939. Inaugurated Jour. Sch. Geography (Jour. Geography), 1897. Mason (32°). Home: Mansfield Center, Conn. Died Apr. 2, 1952; buried Wenham, Mass.

DODSON, Harry Lea, lawyer; b. Chgo.; s. William and Sarah (Ament) Dodson; prep. edn. U. Acad., Chgo.; LL.B., Northwestern U., 1907; m. Margaret Isabel Cormack, Apr. 3, 1895; children—Margaret Isabel, Sarah Ament. Admitted to practice in Patent Office, Washington, 1900, also admitted to U.S. and Ill. Supreme Court and U.S. Dist. Court; specializes in law of patents, trademarks and copyrights. Mem. Am., N.Y. patent law assns., Patent Law Assn. Chgo., N.Y. County Lawyers Assn., Am. Bar Assn. Clubs: Sound Beach (Conn.); University (Washington); Hamilton (Chgo.). Regarded as an authority in his spl. field; was the first to induce a court to recognize, in its decision, the tests of invention in a design (Bayley & Sons vs. Krich 264 Fed.). Home: Southfield Point, Stamford, Conn. Address: 41 Park Row, N.Y.C. Deceased.*

DOGGETT, Laurence Locke (dŏg-gĕt), educator; b. Manchester, Ia., Dec. 22, 1864; s. Simeon Locke and Mary Ann (White) D.; A.B., Oberlin Coll., 1886, A.M., 1890, B.D., 1890, D.D., 1911; student Union Theol. Sem., N.Y.C., 1889, U. Berlin, 1893-94; Ph.D., U. Leipzig, 1895; M.H., Internat. YMCA Coll., 1917; LL.D., Am. Internat. Coll., 1933, Amherst, 1936; Dr. Humanics, Springfield Coll., 1952; m. Caroline Gillespie Durgin, Oct. 8, 1894 (died 1932); children—Ruth Wedgwood Kennedy, Clinton Locke (dec.); m. 2d, Olive Dutcher, July 3, 1934. Asst. state sec. YMCA of Ohio, 1888, 90-93, state sec., 1895-96; sec. Oberlin YMCA, 1889-1890; pres. Internat. YMCA Coll., Springfield, Mass., 1896-1936, pres. emeritus, 1936-—; world tour visit 120 alumni of Springfield Coll. in 26 countries, 1936-37; special corr. Springfield Daily Republican, Pan-American Conf., Lima, Peru, 1938. Prin., Summer Training Inst., Silver Bay, Lake George, N.Y., 1903-11. Decorated Order of Orange Nassau, 1916; Second Order of Red Cross, Estonia, 1937; medal and diploma Czecho-Slovak Republic, 1939; recipient Silver Buffalo, Boy Scouts Am., 1936; Dir. Internat. YMCA Sch., Geneva, Switzerland. Mem. Mass. Soc. Descs. of Pilgrims, Assn. Employed Officers YMCA N.A. Conglist. Clubs: University (Boston); Rotary, Reality, Century, Foreign Policy, The Club (Springfield, Mass.). Author: History of the Young Men's Christian Association, Vol. I, 1896, Vol. II, 1922; History of Boston Young Men's Christian Association, 1901; Life of Robert R. McBurney, 1902; Man and a School, 1943. Home: Bradenton, Fla. Died Nov. 13, 1957.

DOHERTY, Robert Ernest (dō'ĕr-tĭ), coll. pres.; b. Clay City, Ill., Jan. 22, 1885; s. Anthony and Clara (Sauther) D.; B.S., U. of Ill., 1909; M S. Union Coll., Schenectady, N.Y., 1921; hon. M.A., Yale, 1931; hon. LL.D., Tufts Coll. and U. of Pittsburgh, 1936; honorary D.Sc. from Waynesburg College, 1948; married Pearl Edna Mills, June 20, 1911; children—Robert Ernest, Vera Maud, James Anthony. With Gen. Elec. Co., Schenectady, 1909-31, test engr., 1909-10, designing engr., 1910-18; asst. to Dr. C. P. Steinmetz, 1918-23, cons. engr., 1923-31; prof. elec. engring., Yale, 1931-33, dean of Sch. of Engring., Yale, 1933-36; pres. Carnegie Inst. Technology, Pittsburgh, 1936-50; chmn. Engrs. Council for Prof. Development, 1941-43; Production Planning Bd., O.P.M., 1941; mem. Nat. Advisory Com. for Aeronautics, 1940-41; mem. Advisory Com. for Engineering Science and Management War Training, 1940-46; chmn. Allegheny Conf. on Community Development, Pittsburgh, 1943-46; adv. committee, Army Specialized Training Division, 1943-46; Civil Adv. Council, Office Chief of Ordnance, 1942-45; mem. Bd. of Visitors to the United States Naval Acad., 1944. Dir. Forbes Nat. Bank, Montour Railroad; chmn. bd. Fed. Reserve Br., Pittsburgh, 1942-45. Mayor of Scotia, N.Y., 1922; mem. Bd. of Education, 1925-29. Awarded Lamme medals: for engring., Am. Inst. E E., 1937; for edn., Soc. for Promotion Engring Edn., 1945, 1st prize, oil painting, Asso. Artists of Pittsburgh, 1944. Mem. Am. Inst. Elec. Engrs., Social Science Research Council, Am. Soc. for Engring. Edn. (pres. 1943-44), Theta Tau, Sigma Xi, Tau Beta Pi, Eta Kappa Nu, Theta Delta Chi, Omicron Delta Kappa. Conglist. Clubs: Engineers, Duquesne, University. Author: Mathematics of Modern Engineering (with E. G. Keller), 1936; (paper) Edn. for Professional Responsibility, 1948. Contbr. tech. and ednl. articles. Home: 900 Park Av. N., Winter Park, Fla. Died Oct. 19, 1950; buried Clay City, Ill.

DOIDGE, Frederick Widdowson, government official New Zealand; born in Cootamundra, New South Wales, February 26, 1884; married to Lyle Clark; 1 son, Edwin. Served in New Zealand Div., in France, World War I. Entered newspaper work, London, Eng., 1918; became dir. London Daily Express, Sunday Express, Evening Standard; returned to New Zealand, 1935; minister of external affairs 1949-51; High Commr. for New Zealand in Gr. Britain since 1951. Address: 415, Strand, London, W.C. 2. Died May 26, 1954.

DOIG, Thomas W(illiam) (doig), credit union exec.; b. Minneapolis, Apr. 23, 1896; s. William and Isabelle (Frazier) D.; ed. pub. schs. of Minneapolis; LL.D. (honorary), St. Francis Xavier University; m. Beulah A. Hyers, Sept. 20, 1917; children —Mrs. Donald Stoneman, Mrs. Leo Mulrooney. Asst. station examiner, Post Office, Minneapolis, 1929-30; asst. exec. dir. Credit Union Nat. Extension Bur., 1930-35, asst. mng. dir. Credit Union Nat. Assn., 1935-45, mng. dir. since 1945; mng. dir. CUNA Mutual Ins. Soc., and CUNA Supply Cooperative since 1945. Federal Res. bd. advisor for consumer credit, 1941-51. Contbr. articles on credit unions in various publs. Speaker and lecturer on credit unions. Home: 2812 Oxford Road. Madison 5. Office: Credit Union Nat. Assn., Filene House, Madison 1, Wis. Died Dec. 19, 1955.

DOLAK, Michael Charles, life ins. exec.; b. Belle Plaine, Ia., Aug. 24, 1891; s. Michael J. and Anna (Holbrook) D.; B.S. in C.E., State U. Ia., 1912; m. Lillian Abbott, June 1923. Various positions civil engring., constrn., drafting and gen. engring., 1912-16; asst. engr. U.S. R.R. Adminstrn., 1919-23; sr. civil engr. Interstate Commerce Commn., 1916-1918; Financial dept. of N.Y. Trust Co., N.Y. City, 1933-1934; joined Conn. Mut. Life Ins. Co., Hartford, Conn., 1935, v.p. since 1947; com. mem. several r.r. re-orgns.; dir. Plume & Atwood Mfg. Co. Chmn. investment com., State of Conn. Contbr. articles newspapers and mags. Home: 22 Cornell Rd., West Hartford 7. Office: 140 Garden St., Hartford 15, Conn. Died July 6, 1955.

DOLAN, Elizabeth Honor, artist, mural painter; b. Fort Dodge, Ia., May 20, 1884; d. John and Mary (O'Donnell) Dolan; student U. Neb., 1903-04, Chgo. Art Inst., 1911-14, Art Students' League, N.Y.C., 1915-18. Beaux Arts, France, 1924-26, Fountainbleau, Rome, 1931-32; unmarried. Began as portrait painter, 1913; executed fresco in 13th Century Cathedral, Fourqueux, France; murals in Neb. State Capitol, Neb., State Mus., Natural History Mus., N.Y.C., All Soul's Ch., Lincoln, Neb., Lincoln YWCA, Mus. of Natural History (New York); Univ. of Neb.; 10 murals in New Masonic Temple, Lincoln, Neb., 1935; murals, U.S.O. Center, University Club, Students Union Bldg. and 4 portraits in Founders Room, Univ. Natural History Museum, Lincoln, Neb. Died May 26, 1948.

DOLE, James Drummond, chmn. bd. Hawaiian Pineapple Co., Ltd.; b. Jamaica Plain, Boston, Sept. 27, 1877; s. Charles Fletcher and Frances (Drummond) D.; prep. edn., Roxbury Latin Sch.; A.B., Harvard, 1899; m. Belle Dickey, Nov. 22, 1906; children—Richard Alexander, James Drummond, Elizabeth, Charles Herbert, Barbara. Took up homestead in Hawaiian Islands, 1900; started planting pineapples, 1901; organized Hawaiian Pineapple Co., Ltd., 1901, erected cannery, 1903, pack reaching 4,857,054 cases in 1931; guided the development of canning syrup, citric acid and pineapple bran from skins and ends of pineapple; of canned pineapple juice (1932); "liquid apple" type canned and bottled apple juice (1940); a corresponding natural type carrot juice (1937); originated and carried out first campaign of Associational Advt. for popularizing canned Hawaiian pineapple, 1908-09; helped establish research work in pineapple industry; pres., gen. mgr. Hawaiian Pineapple Co., Ltd., until 1932, chmn. bd. 1932-48; ret.; former chmn. James Dole Engring. Co., Chemical Process Co., now retired. Mem. of Territorial Bd. Agr. and Forestry, 1903-04; chmn. Territorial Food Commn., 1917-18; mem. Territorial Tax Commn.,

1884-88; became mcht., 1888; postmaster Utica, 1898-1928-32; pres. Hawaii Bur. Governmental Research, 1928-32. President Association Hawaiian Pineapple Canners for many yrs.; former trustee Palama Settlement and United Welfare Fund (Honolulu); Chief of Food Products Sect. of Div. of Process and Marketing of the A.A.A., Washington, 1933. Clubs: Pennask Lake (Brit. Columbia); Pacific (Honolulu); Pacific Union, Commonwealth (San Francisco); Harvard (N.Y.C.). Wrote: (pamphlet) Impressions of Five Months in Washington, 1934. Address: 2036 Alihilani Pl., Honolulu, Hawaii. Died May 14, 1958; buried Makawao Cemetery, Maui, Hawaii.

D'OLIER, Franklin (dōl'yā), insurance; b. Burlington, N.J., Apr. 28, 1877; s. William and Annie (Woolman) D.; B.A., Princeton, 1898; LL.D., University of Newark, 1940; married Helen Kitchen, November 11, 1903. President and treasurer, Franklin D'Olier & Co., Inc., founded by father, 1869, until 1926; pres. 1937-45; chmn. bd. Prudential Ins. Co., 1946, 1947; director Howard Savings Institution of Newark, National Biscuit Co., Pennsylvania R.R., General Refractories Company (Philadelphia), Morristown (N.J.) Trust Co. Trustee Princeton U. Commd. capt. U.S. Army, Apr. 1917; arrived in France, July 1917; organized salvage service of A.E.F.; hon. disch. as lt. col. Gen. Staff, Apr. 1919. Awarded D.S.M. (U.S.); Comdr. Legion of Honor (France). Elected first nat. comdr. Am. Legion, Nov. 12, 1919; mem. American Legion mission to England, 1941; N.J. State chmn. U.S.O., 1943-46; National War Fund and Treasury Bond Drives; chairman U.S. Strategic Bombing Survey in Germany and Japan, 1944-46. Received the Medal of Merit from the United States. Episcopalian. Clubs: Princeton (Phila.); University, Princeton (N.Y. City); Morristown, Essex. Mem. Soc. Colonial Wars. Home: R.D. 1, Basking Ridge, N.J. Office: 744 Broad St., Prudential Insurance Company, Newark 1, N.J. Died Dec. 10, 1953; buried St. Mary's Church Graveyard, Burlington, N.J.

DOLL, Alfred W., educator; b. Phila., June 5, 1903; s. Valentine and Katharine (Stift) D.; B.S., Central High Sch., Phila., 1920; B.S. in M.E., U. of Pa., 1924, M.E., 1931; M.A., Columbia, 1928; Ph.D., N Y. Univ., 1932; P.E., U. of State of New York, 1936; m. Helen A. Nicholson, June 4, 1932; children—Katharine Ruth, Susan Josephine. Mem. faculty Pratt Inst. Sch. of Engring., 1925—, beginning as instr. now prof. physics, head dept. physics, 1938-42, 1946-53. acting dean sch. engring., 1953-56, asst. dean, 1956—, head dept. mech. engring., 1942-46, curriculum chmn. mech. engring., 1940-46, supervisor of basic instrn., 1946—; Defense Training Inst. of Brooklyn as chmn., dept. of physics, 1940-43. Mem. Am. Assn. Physics Teachers, Am. Inst. Physics, Am. Soc. M.E., Am. Soc. E.E., Tau Beta Pi, Sigma Xi (hon. asso.). Presbyn. Author: Mechanics, Fluids and Heat Texts published by Pratt Inst. Home: 115 Dogwood Av., Malverne, L.I., N.Y. Office: 215 Ryerson St., Bklyn. 5. Died Dec. 23. 1957; buried Hillside Cemetery, Roslyn, Pa.

DOLLAR, R(obert) Stanley, shipping and exec.; b. Bracebridge, Ont. Can., July 6, 1880; s. Robert and Margaret (Proudfoot) D.; brought to the U.S. 1882, naturalized 1886; m. Esther Johnson, July 15, 1914; children—R(obert) Stanley, Diana (Mrs. Joseph C. Hickingbotham). Employed in father's steamship office, 1898; sec. M. S. Dollar Steamship Co., at time of incorporation, 1900, opened offices in various ports abroad, 1904-09; vice pres., gen. mgr., Dollar Steamship Lines, Inc., at time of consolidation in 1910, became pres., 1931; pres. Am. Mail Line in 1922; inaugurated Dollar Line 'Round-the-World Service, 1924; established Dollaradio, pvt. radio communications system, 1926, later a pub. system known as Globe Wireless, Ltd., pres., 1931—; purchased third interest in U.S. Lines, 1931, pres. 1932; pres., dir. The Robert Dollar Co., The Robert Dollar Co., Ltd. (Can.), Dollar Assocs., Inc., Globe Wireless Ltd.; chmn. bd. South Pacific Air Lines, Inc.; partner Dean Witter & Co., Ltd.; dir. Lucky Stores, Inc., First Western Bank & Trust Co., Pacific Nat. Fire Ins. Co., Pacific Ventures, Inc. (Reno). Regional v.p., dir. Nat. Fgn. Trade Council, Inc. (N.Y.). Dir. A.P. Giannini Scholarship Found.; trustee Webb Inst. Naval Architecture in N.Y., U.S. council Internat. C. of C., Inc. Mason (Shriner, K.T.). Clubs: Pacific Union, Bohemian (San Francisco); India House (N.Y.C.). Home: Walnut Creek, Cal. Office: Robert Dollar Bldg., 311 California St., San Francisco 4. Died Sept. 28, 1958.

DOLLENS, Burl Austin, engr.; b. Elnora, Ind., Dec. 10, 1901; s. James and Mary (Stalcup) D.; B.S., Purdue U., 1925, D.S. in Engr. (hon.), 1951; m. Neva E. Johnson, Dec. 20, 1924; daughters—Marilyn, Marjorie. With Gen. Motors Corp. since 1925, student tng. course, Delco Remy div., 1925-26, successively, industrial engineer, foreman prodn. dept., asst. supt., motor plant, plant engr. for entire div., asst. chief inspector of div., supt. Grey Iron Foundry, supt. motor plant, gen. supt. three aircraft aluminum foundries, mgr. foundries and world's largest automotive battery plants, Delco-Remy Div., Muncie, Ind., New Brunswick, N. J., 1923-45; gen. mgr. Saginaw (Mich.) Malleable Iron Div. (now Central Foundry Div.), 1945-46; asst. gen. mgr. Electro-Motive Div., La Grange, Ill., 1946-50; vice pres. General Motors Corp. and gen. mgr. Electro-Motive Div. since 1950. Mem. Ill. State C. of C. (dir.), Newcomen Society of England. Republican. Conglist. Clubs: Chicago, Executives, Indiana, Western Railway, Economic (Chicago). Home: 340 Cottage Hill Ave., Elmhurst, Ill. Office: Electro-Motive Div., General Motors Corp., La Grange, Ill. Died Feb. 9, 1952.

DOLMAN, John, Jr. (dŏl'măn), prof. English; b. Philadelphia, Pa., May 21, 1888; s John and Christine Harriet Melanie (Nickinson) D.; grad. Central Manual Training High Sch., Philadelphia, 1906; B S., U. of Pa., 1910, A.M., 1913; m. Ethel Louise Schatte, Sept. 2, 1912 (died Apr. 26, 1937); children—Barbara Caroline, John Phillips, Robert Effingham, Geofrey. Reader in English, U. of Pa., 1910-11, instr. in English, 1911-20, asst. prof. English, 1920-27, prof. since 1927, dir. summer sch., 1925-46. Editor Quarterly Jour. of Speech, 1923-26. Member Speech Assn. of America (pres. 1930), Eastern Public Speaking Conf. (pres. 1922), Nat. Assn. of Summer School Directors (pres. 1932), Nat. Theatre Conf., Am. Edn. Theatre Assn., Am. Iris Soc. Clubs: Players' (Swarthmore, pres. 1941-42); Art Alliance (Philadelphia). Author: A Handbook of Public Speaking, 1922 (revised), 1944; The Art of Play Production, 1928 (revised), 1946; Gogol's Inspector-General (adaptation, 1937): The Art of Acting, 1949; The Art of Reading Aloud, 1956; sundry articles on speech and drama. Home: 304 Vassar Av., Swarthmore, Pa. Died July 9, 1952; buried West Laurel Hill Cemetery, Phila.

DONAHUE, Joseph P., auxiliary bishop of New York. Address: 221 West 107th St., N.Y.C. Died Apr. 28, 1959.

DONALD, William Goodricke, physician and surgeon; b. San Francisco, Calif., Nov. 2, 1889; s. John Hugh and Elsie Francis (Wilson) D.; B.S., U. of Calif., 1911, M.D., 1923; m. Alice Minerva Osborn, Dec. 31, 1914 (dec.); children—William Goodricke, Edward Osborn, Alice (Edwards); m. 2d, Donna McDonald, Mar. 2, 1951; 1 dau., Moire Jean. Acting univ. physician U. Cal., 1923-24, asso., 1924-38, U Physician since 1938; pvt. practice gen. medicine and surgery since 1923; dir. State University Health Service. Lieutenant Sanitary Corps, U.S. Army, 1918-19; capt. Med. Corps, 159th Inf., 1923-25. Mem. A.M.A., World Medical Assn., Indsl. Med. Assn., A.A.A.S., Calif. Acad. Medicine, Alameda County Med. Assn. (past president), Alpha Omega Alpha, Delta Omega (pub. health soc.), Sigma Phi. Republican. Club: Bohemian (San Francisco). Home: 927 San Benito Road. Office: University of California, Berkeley, Cal. Died Dec. 30, 1957; buried Berkeley, Cal.

DONALDSON, John, political economist; b. Charlotte, N.C., Oct. 9, 1892; s. Charles and Mary (Hixson) D.; B.S., U. of M.D., 1910; univ. scholar, 1911-13, univ. fellow in polit. science, 1913-14, Johns Hopkins Ph.D., 1914; m. Frances G. (A.B. with distinction, George Washington U.), d. Henry and Katherine Flaacke, of N.Y. City, 1924; 1 son, John Charles Lockman. Successively instructor economics and sociology, Smith Coll., prof. political science and history, Mount Morris Coll., prof. economics and history, Roanoke Coll., till 1918; economist U.S. War Trade Bd., 1918-19. U.S. Shipping Bd., 1919-20, U.S. Dept. of State, 1920-22; lecturer Am. Univ. Grad. Sch. of Business Adminstrn., 1921-22; tech. adviser, Am. delegation Conf. on Limitation of Armament, Washington, D.C., 1921-22; sec. U.S. Interdepartmental Economic Liaison Com., 1921-22; prof. commerce, 1922-29, prof. polit. econ. 1929-47, ret. George Washington U., also exec. officer of dept. of economics to 1930. mem. Academic Council, 1924-46, acting dean Grad. Sch. Letters and Sciences, 1930, acting dean Columbian Coll., 1930-31. Editor for foreign countries, the Commerce Yearbook of 1923 (U.S. Dept. Commerce), 1924; mem. nat. com. Congress of Am. Industry, 1926; mem. for American of Internat. Com. on Research in Internat. Relations, Geneva, 1931-32; mem. Commn. on Internat. Phases of Justice, Industry and Finance, 1932; co-founder and chmn. bd. National Academy of Economics and Political Science (formerly The Acad. of World Economics) to 1948, hon. chmn. bd., 1948—; dir. of research Office of Special Adviser to the Pres. on Foreign Trade, 1934-35. Mem. Commn. on Cultural Relations, Inter. Am. Center of Fla. Fellow Royal Econ. Soc.; mem. Am. Acad. Polit. and Social Science, Am. Econ. Assn., Am. Acad. Political Science, Am. Assn. Univ. Profs., English-Speaking Union, Am. Assn. for Advancement of Science (member council, 1946-48), Pi Kappa Phi (past Archon, D.C. Alumni Chapter), Delta Phi Epsilon (national vice president, 1930-34, national pres., 1934-36), Pi Gamma Mu (governor D.C. Province, 1931-34 and hon. nat. vice pres., 1934—). Presbyn. Mason. Club: Cosmos. Author: State Administration in Maryland, 1916; The National Economy of Denmark and the European War; The Economic Situation in the Far East; The World Coal Trade; Trade and Shipping of Australasia; Tariff Discriminations; Commercial Treaty Policy; Currency Policy and Foreign Trade; Studies of Economic Relations Between U.S. and Various Foreign Countries; also other official works and archival brochures in field of international relations, 1918-22, and 1934-35; International Economic Relations—A Treatise on World Economy and World Politics, 1928, Spanish edit., 2 vols., 1931; The Dollar—A Study of the "New" National and International Monetary System, 1937; Contemporary World Politics—An Introduction to the Problems of International Relations (with others), 1939. Contbr. to Encyclopaedia of the Social Sciences, also to Am. and European jours. on economics and foreign affairs. Home: 601 N. Lake Av., Avon Park Fla. Died June 2, 1955; buried Rock Creek Cemetery, Washington.

DONALDSON, Kenneth Hume, educator; b. Greenwich, Conn., Sept. 15, 1888; s. Robert Montgomery and Ida Leonora (Schwacofer) D.; E.M., Columbia, 1912; m. Lillian Hughes, May 25, 1918 (dec. Jan. 1, 1951); 1 dau., Roberta Montgomery (Mrs. Howard Tidd Knox). Miner, sampler, investigator, testing engr., concentrator, supt., Ida., Mont., Colo., Ariz., 1912-21; with Case Inst. Tech., Cleveland since 1921, head dept. metall. engring. and metals research lab. since 1938; cons. iron ore benefication U.S.S.R., 1931-32; sci. investigator U.S. Fgn. Econ. Adminstrn., Eng., Germany, 1945. Mem. Am. Inst. Mining & Metall. Engrs., Am. Soc. Metals, Sigma Alpha Epsilon, Sigma Xi. Republican. Episcopalian. Clubs: University, Professional Men's (Cleveland). Contbr. Chem. Engrs. Handbook; report to State Dept., U. S.A. on Russian Trade. Home: 1596 Ansel Rd., Cleve. 6. Died Sept., 1953.

DONAT, Robert, actor; b. Withington, Manchester, Eng., Mar. 18, 1905; s. Ernst Emile and Rose Alice (Green) D.; m. Ella Annesley Voysey; m. 2d, Renee Asherson, 1952. First appearance in Julius Caesar, 1921; has since appeared in many stage successes in Eng. including Precious Bane, The Rivals, Sleeping Clergyman, The Devil's Disciple, Heartbreak House, Cure For Love, Much Ado About Nothing, and Murder In The Cathedral; also appeared in numerous motion pictures, notably in The Private Life of Henry VIII, The Count of Monte Cristo, The Thirty-nine Steps, The Ghost Goes West, Knight Without Armour, The Citadel, Goodbye, Mr. Chips, The Young Mr. Pitt, The Adventures of Tartu, Perfect Strangers, The Winslow Boy, The Cure for Love, The Magic Box, Lease of Life, Inn Of The Sixth Happiness. Recipient Academy Award, 1939. Address: care Christopher Mann Ltd., 140 Park Lane, London W. 1, Eng. Died June 9, 1958.

DONDLINGER, Peter Tracy, author, educator; b. Port Washington, Wis., Oct. 26, 1877; s. Nicholas and Katherine (Kyle) D.; A.B., Nat. Normal U., Lebanon, O., 1899; Ph.D., Yale, 1904; m. Mabel Bennett; children—Bennett, Alice. Prof. mathematics, Uraina Normal Coll., Glasgow, Ky., 1899-1900; tchr., pub. schs., Delaware County, Ind., 1900-01; prof. mathematics, Fairmount Coll., Wichita, Kan., 1904-06; with Fisk & Robinson, N.Y.C., 1906-07; pres. Stamford (Conn.) Mus., 1951-53. Mem. Nat. Geog. Soc., Am. Forestry Assn., A.A.A.S., Am. Breeders Assn., Am. Economic Assn. Author: Book of Wheat, 1907; What and Where in Up to Date G.I. Education. Address: New Haven, Conn. Died Oct. 4, 1954.

DONEGAN, Edmund Joseph, ins. exec.; b. Bklyn., Aug. 30, 1888; s. Edmund J. and Elizabeth A. (Riley) D.; student Coll. St. Francis Xavier, N Y. 1904, Bklyn. Law Sch., 1913; m. Lois Carlin, Apr. 13, 1914. Sec. Firemen's Ins. Co. of Newark, 1939—, also sec. affiliated firms; dir. Met. Casualty Ins. Co of N.Y. Dir. N.Y. Bd. Trade. Home: 302 W. 12th St., N.Y.C. 14. Office: 55 John St., N.Y.C. 38. Died 1959.

DONEGAN, Maurice Francis, judge; b. Welton, Ia., Sept. 2, 1875; s. Jeremiah and Mary (Lucey) D.; student St. Ambrose Acad., Davenport, Ia., 1889-90; A B., Creighton Coll., 1895; A.M., Georgetown U., 1898, Ph.D., 1900; LL.B., State U. Ia., 1901; LL D., St. Ambrose Coll., Davenport, Ia., 1941; m. Mary I. Martin, Nov. 29, 1905; children—Charles Maurice, Justin Martin, Mary Louise, Maurice Francis. Admitted to Ia. bar, 1901; practiced in Davenport, 1901-13, 21-33; city atty. Davenport, 1908-13; judge Dist. Court of Ia., 1913-21 (resigned); asso. justice Supreme Court of Ia., 1933-39, chief justice, 1936; U S. dist. atty. So. Dist. Ia., 1940—; resumed private practice of law as mem. Bollinger & Donegan, Jan. 1939. Chmn. Scott County Bd. Legal Examiners. World War. Mem. Am., Ia. Scott County (pres. 1904, 39) bar assns. Democrat. Roman Catholic. K.C. Home: 336 W. Columbia Av., Davenport, Ia. Died Mar. 24, 1950; buried Davenport.

DONEY, Carl Gregg (dô'nê), educator; b. Columbus, O., July 24, 1867; s. Abram Covert and Emily Victoria (Brock) D.; B.Sc., Ohio State U., 1891, LL.B., 1893, Ph.D., 1902; post-grad. in philosophy Harvard, 1891-92; A.M., Ohio Wesleyan, 1899; LL.D., Howard U., 1912; D.D., Willamette U., 1918; m. Jennie Anna Evans, Sept. 6, 1893; children—Paul Herbert, Hugh Abram. Entered M.E. ministry Oct. 1893; pastor, Bainbridge, O., 1893-95, Centenary Ch., Granville, O., 1895-98, St. Paul's Ch., Delaware, O., 1898-1900, King Av. Ch., Columbus, O., 1900-05, Hamline Ch., Washington, 1905-07; pres. W.Va. Wesleyan Coll., Buckhannon, 1907-15; pres. Willamette U., Salem, Ore., 1915-34, pres. emeritus,

1934—. Pres. D.C. Anti-Saloon League, 1906-07; formerly dir. W.Va. YMCA, and trustee W.Va. State Soc. of Hygiene. Study and travel in Europe, 1913-14. Mem. War Work Council, 1917; YMCA lectr. and liaison work in France, 1918; mem. exec. com. Ore. and Ida. YMCA, 1919—. Mem. Gen. Conf. M.E. Church, 1912, 28. Mem. Phi Beta Kappa, Beta Theta Pi, Phi Delta Phi. Mason (32°), Rotarian (hon.). Club: University. Author: The Throne Room of the Soul, 1906; An Efficient Church, 1907; God Answers Prayer, 1923; Half Way to Noon, 1929; Cheerful Yesterdays and Confident Tomorrows, 1942; The Broken Circle: A Life of Paul H. Doney, 1943; (brochure) Concerning Intelligence. Contbr. to mags. and periodicals. Home: 194 W. Royal Forest Blvd., Columbus 2, O. Died Nov. 5, 1955.

DONHAM, C(harles) R(umpel), veterinarian; b. Rockport, Ind., Aug. 1, 1898; s. Lewis Singleton and Amelia Rebecca (Rumple) D.; D.V.M., Ia. State Coll., 1921; M.S., Ore. State Coll. 1927; student, sch. of med., Washington U., summer part-time student U. Minn., 1929-35; m. Margaret Hyde Lysinger, June 18, 1921; children—Marion Margaret (Mrs. Joseph F. Jamison), James Charles. Pvt. practice in vet. medicine, 1921-22; instr., asst. prof. vet. medicine, Ore. State Agr. Coll., 1922-29; asst. prof., asso. prof. vet. medicine U. Minn., 1929-35; prof. vet. medicine Ohio State U., 1935-40; prof. vet. sci. Purdue U., 1940—. Mem. com. on brucellosis U.S. Live Stock Sanitary Assn.; adv. com. Bur. Animal Industry, U.S. Dept. of Agr.; mem. Nat. Com. on Brucellosis. Mem. Conf. of Ofcl. Research Workers in Animal Diseases in N. Am., Ind., Am. vet. med. assns., Sigma Xi, Phi Kappa Phi, Zeta Iota, Sigma Nu. Methodist. Mason. Rotarian. Home: 1519 Summit Dr., West Lafayette, Ind. Died Apr. 24, 1956; buried Ames (Ia.) Cemetery.

DONHAM, Wallace Brett (dŏn'ăm), educator; b. Rockland, Mass., Oct. 26, 1877; s. George E. and Sarah A. (Studley) D.; A.B., Harvard, 1898, LL.B., 1901, LL.D., 1939; LL.D., Juniata, 1942, N.Y.U., 1943, Trinity Coll., 1946; L.H.D., Colgate U., 1943; m. Mabel Higgins, Apri. 7, 1903. Admitted to bar, 1901, entered legal dept. Old Colony Trust Co., v.p., 1906-19; dean grad. sch. bus. adminstrn. Harvard, 1919-42, prof. adminstrn., 1942-48; vis. prof. human relations Colgate U., 1948-49; mng. dir. Harvard-Yenching Inst., 1950-54. Decorated Officer, Legion d'Honneur, 1930. Author: Business Adrift; Business Looks at the Unforeseen; Education for Responsible Living. Home: 987 Memorial Dr., Cambridge, Mass. Died Nov. 29, 1954.

DONN Edward Wilton, Jr., architect; b. Washington, D.C., Apr. 2, 1868; s. Edward W. and Laura (Gardner) D.; B.S., Mass. Inst. Tech., 1891; student Cornell U., 1892; traveled in Europe; unmarried. Chief designer in office of architect of the treasury, Washington, 1900-03; mem. Wood, Donn & Deming, Washington, 1903-12, Donn & Deming, 1912-24, Edward W. Donn, Jr., since 1924; dir. Northern Market Co. Architect for restoration and rehabilitation of "Wakefield," birthplace of George Washington, also architect for "Kenmore," home of Betty Washington, Fredericksburg, Va., also Woodlawn Mansion, Va., also Terminal Bldgs. at Mt. Vernon Gate, President Board Examiners and Registrars of Architects, D.C. Fellow A.I.A. (dir. also chmn. bd. of examiners); mem. Arch. Inst. America, Am. Fed. Arts, Washington Soc. Fine Arts, Zeta Psi. Episcopalian. Mason. Clubs: Metropolitan, Arts (dir.), Chevy Chase, Racquet (Washington) City (New York). Home: 10 E. Bradley Lane, Chevy Chase 15, Md. Office: 1920 K St., N.W., Washington 6. Died 1953.

DONNAN, Elizabeth (dŏn'ăn), educator; b. Morrow County, O.; d. John W. and Annie Grisell Donnan; A.B., Cornell U., 1907. Prof., dept. econs. Wellesley Coll., 1920-49, ret. Mem. Phi Beta Kappa. Editor: Papers of James A. Bayard, 1915; An Historian's World: Selections from correspondence of John Franklin Jameson (with Leo F. Stock). Author: Documents Illustrative of the Slave Trade to America, 4 vols., 1930-34; Economic Principles and Modern Practice (with H. R. Mussey), 1942, rev. 1947. Home: Spruce Ledge, Round Pond, Me. Died Mar. 15, 1955; buried Waterville, O.

DONNELL, Annie Hamilton, author; b. Kents Hill, Me., Sept. 11, 1862; d. Albert H. and Mary C. (Robinson) Hamilton; A.B., Woman's Coll., Kents Hill, 1881; m. Webb Donnell, July 8, 1886; children—Dorothy (Mr. H. G. Calhoun), Rachel, Lloyd Hamilton, Kenneth Woodbridge. Author: Camp Fidelity Girls, 1903; Rebecca Mary, 1905; The Very Small Person, 1906; Miss Theodosia's Heartstrings, 1916. Home: 529 Las Tunas Drive, Arcadia, Cal. Died 1943.

DONNELL, Ben Dobyns (dŏn'ŭl), newspaper editor; b. Greensburg, Ind., May 28, 1881; s. Luther and Elizabeth J. (Dobyns) D.; student, Ind. Univ., 1899-1900; m. Mathilde E. Christensen, Jan. 15, 1909; children—Mary E. (Mrs. Olin W. Harvey), Mathilde E. (Mrs. Arch A. Greenwood). William L., Ben Dobyns, Jennie June (Mrs. T. R. Boone), Ralph M. Teacher, rural sch., Indiana 1900-01; with Ye Old Book Shoppe, Chicago, Ill., 1902-03; reporter, Greensburg (Ind.) Daily News, 1904-05, Ft. Worth Telegram, San Angelo, Daily News, Ft. Worth Record, 1906-07; city editor, Wichita Falls (Tex.) Daily gram, San Angelo Daily News, Ft. Worth Record, News, since 1909; v.p., Times Publ. Co. (pub. of Times and Record News), since 1909. Chmn., housing authority, Wichita Falls, Tex. Mem. Tex. Mng. Editors Assn., Am. Soc. Newspaper Editors, Beta Theta Pi. Democrat. Presbyterian. Mason. Club: Rotary. Home: 1615 Tilden St. Office: Times Publishing Co., Wichita Falls, Tex. Died Mar. 28, 1952.

DONNELLEY, Thomas Elliott (dŏn'ĕl-lĭ), printer; b. Chicago, Ill., Aug. 18, 1867; s. Richard Robert and Naomi Ann (Shenstone) D.; B.A., Yale, 1889; m. Laura Leonora Gaylord, May 24, 1899 (died 1932); children—Clarissa, Elliott, Gaylord. Upon graduation, 1889, entered business established by his father, 1864; served as a workman in all depts., since death of father in 1899 and until 1934, as pres. R. R. Donnelley & Sons Co., chmn. bd., 1934-52; chmn., bd. Reuben H. Donnelley Corp. 1929-52, now hon. chmn. dir. Internat. Harvester Co., Protective Mutual Ins. Co., First Nat. Bank Lake Forest. Was director pulp and paper division of War Industries Board. Republican. Mem. First Bapt. Ch. Clubs: Commercial, Chicago, Union League, University, Quadrangle, Caxton, Onwentsia, Old Elm. Home: 902 N. Green Bay Rd., Lake Forest, Ill. Office: 350 E. 22d St., Chgo. 16. Died Feb. 6, 1955; buried Lake Forest, Ill.

DONNELLY, George J.; auxiliary archbishop Roman Catholic Church. Address: St. Pius Church, 3310 S. Grand Blvd., St. Louis. Died Dec. 13, 1950.*

DONNER, William Henry, mfr.; b. Columbus, Ind., May 21, 1864; s. Frederick and Mary Jane (Johnson) D.; Hanover Coll., 1882-83; m. Adella May Newson, 1890; children—Robert Newson, Joseph William; m. 2d, Dora Browning Rodgers, Mar. 27, 1909; children—William Henry, Elizabeth Browning, Dora Browning. Mgr. Donner Milling Co., Columbus, Ind., 1885-94; treas., mgr. Nat. Tin Plate Co., Anderson, Ind., 1894-99; a founder of Monessen, Pa., 1897, of Donora, Pa., 1899; pres. Union Steel Co., Donora, 1899-1903; one of receivers of Westinghouse Machine Co., Pitts., 1907; pres. Cambria Steel Co., 1912-16; chmn. Pa. Steel Co., 1914-16; pres. Donner Steel Co., Inc., 1916-29; chmn. bd. Otis Hidden Co., Louisville, Ky.; dir. Mellon Nat. Bank, Pitts., Fidelity-Phila. Trust Co. Pres. Internat. Cancer Research Found.; dir. Zool. Society of Phila.; mem. adv. bd. George S. Cox Med. Research Inst., U. of Pa. Mem. Am. Iron and Steel Inst. Republican. Presbyn. Clubs: Duquesne, Pittsburgh, Rittenhouse, Phila. Country, Union League (Phila.); Buffalo (Buffalo). Home: Camp Woods, Villa Nova, Pa. Office: 1616 Walnut St., Phila. Died Nov. 3, 1953.

DONOHOE, James A. (dŏn'ō-hō), judge; b. O'Neill, Neb., Aug. 9, 1877; s. John T. and Mary (Biggins) D.; B.S., Fremont (Neb.) Normal Coll., 1898; m. Florence M. Lowrie, Sept. 7, 1911. Began as teacher pub. schs.; later deputy county treas.; admitted to Neb. bar, 1905; in gen. practice law until 1933; mem. Neb. State Senate, 1908-09; mem. Constl. Conv. of Neb., 1918-19; judge U.S. Dist. Court since 1933. Democrat. Catholic. K.C. Club: Country. Home: 617 N. 90th St., Omaha, Neb. Died Feb. 26, 1956: buried Calvary Cemetery.

DONOVAN, William Joseph, lawyer, commr.; b. Buffalo, Jan. 1, 1883; s. Timothy P. and Anna (Lennon) D.; A.B., Columbia, 1905, LL.B., 1907; LL.D., Niagara U., 1919, U. of Notre Dame, 1929, Syracuse Univ., 1931; m. Ruth Rumsey, July 14, 1914; children—David Rumsey, Patricia (dec.). Began practice at Buffalo, 1907; counsel for N.Y. State Fuel Administration, 1924; Republican candidate for lieut. gov. of New York, 1922; U.S. dist. atty., Western District of N.Y., 1922-24; mem. U.S. delegation to customs regulations conf. between U.S. and Can., 1923; asst. atty. gen. of U.S., 1924-25; the asst. to the atty. gen., Mar. 1925-29; U.S. commr. and chmn. Rio Grande River Compact Commn., 1928-29; U.S. commr., chmn. Colo. River Commn. since 1929; mem. Donovan, Leisure, Newton and Irvine; counsel for Assn. Bar City New York and New York and Bronx County bar assns. in bankruptcy investigation, 1929; counsel to com. for revision New York state pub. service commn. laws, 1929. Ambassador of U.S to Thailand, 1953-54. Member Board Arbitration, under Nat. Mediation Bd., controversy between Am. Train Dispatchers Assn., and B. & M. R.R. Rep. candidate for gov. of N.Y., 1932. Served as capt. Troop I, 1st Cav., N. Y. Nat. Guard; asst. chief of staff, 27th Div., A.E.F., World War; maj., brigade, adj., 51st Brigade; maj., 165 Inf. (old 69th N.Y.) advancing to rank of col.; wounded three times; unofficial observer for sec. of navy, Great Britain, July-Aug. 1940, southeastern Europe, Dec. 1940-Mar. 1941; apptd. coordinator of information, July 1941; dir. Office of Strategic Services, June 1942; rank of maj. gen., U.S. Army. Decorated (World War I) Congressional Medal of Honor for conduct in action near Landres and St. Georges, France, Oct. 14-15, 1918; D.S.C. for conduct in crossing River Ourcq, July 28-31, 1918, D.S.M. for services in Bacarat sector, July 28-31, and Meuse-Argonne Offensive, Oct. 1918 (U.S.), Legion of Honor, Croix de Guerre with palm and silver star (France), Croci di Guerra (Italy); (World War II) Oak leaf cluster on D.S.M. for services as dir. of strategic services (U.S.), Order of Crown (Italy), Knight Comdr. Order of British Empire (Gt. Britain), Comdr. Legion of Honor (France), Grand officer Order of Leopold with palm (Belgium), Papal Lateran medal, Order St. Sylvester (Papal), Comdr.'s Cross with star of Polonia Restituta (Poland), 1st Class of Most Exalted Order of White Elephant, Santi Mala medal (Siam), Comdr. Cross with star Royal Order of St. Olav (Norway); Alexander Hamilton medal Assn. Alumni Columbia Coll. Mem. Assn. Bar City New York (exec. com. 1931), Phi Kappa Psi, Phi Delta Phi. Republican. Roman Catholic. Home: Chapel Hill Farm, Berryville, Va. Died Feb. 8, 1959.

D'OOGE, Benjamin Leonard, educator; b. Grand Rapids, Mich., 1860; s. Leonard and Johanna (Quintus) D.; A.B., U. Mich., 1881, A.M., 1884; Ph.D., U. Bonn, 1901; studied abroad, 1899-1901, 08-09, 27; m. Jennie E. Pease, June 25, 1885; children—Ida Joanna, Helen Irene, Leonard, Benjamin Stanton. Prin. high sch., Coldwater, Mich., 1881-83; instr. Latin, U. Mich., 1884-85; prof. Latin, Mich. State Normal Coll., 1886-1937. Mem. Am. Philol. Assn., Archaeol. Inst. Am., Classical Assn. Middle West and South, (pres. 1910-11), Phi Beta Kappa; Mich. Schoolmasters' Club (pres. 1893, 94, 1904). Editor: Colloquia Latina, 1888; Viri Romae, 1895; Easy Latin for Sight Reading, 1897; Caesar's Gallic War (with James B. Greenough and M. Grant Daniell), 1898; Second Year Latin (with same), 1899; Helps to the Study of Classical Mythology, 1899; Cicero, Select Orations, 1901; Latin Composition, 1901. Revised (with others) Allen & Greenough's Latin Grammar, 1903; Latin Composition for Secondary Schools, 1904; Latin for Beginners, 1910; Caesar in Gaul (with F. C. Eastman), 1917; Concise Latin Grammar, 1920; Elements of Latin, 1921; Junior Latin Lessons (with Dorothy M. Roehm), 1927. Contbr. to mags. Home: Ypsilanti, Mich. Died. 1940.

DOOLEY, Channing Rice (dōō'lē), industrialist; b. Rockville, Ind., Apr. 4, 1878; s. Rufus and Susan (Rice) D.; B.S., Purdue University, 1900, E.E., 1902, Dr. of Engring., 1944; m. Inez Jones, 1907; children—Phyllis A., David L. Began career as design engineer for the Westinghouse Elec. and Mfg. Co., East Pittsburgh, Pa., 1902-11, first head ednl. dept., 1911-19; pres. Westinghouse (formerly Casino) Tech. Night Sch., 1906-23; mgr. personnel and training, Standard Oil Co. (N.J.), N.Y. City, 1919-29; personnel mgr., Standard Oil Co. of N.Y., 1929-32; since merger of Standard Oil Co. of N.Y. with Vacuum Oil Co. in 1932, has been mgr. indsl. relations, Socony Vacuum Oil Co., Inc.; on leave since 1940, retired 1944. Organized and directed Training Within Industry, 1940, under Nat. Defense com.; continued as dir. T.W.I., under War Manpower Commn., Washington, D.C., 1942-Jan. 1. 1946; president T.W.I. Foundation since Jan., 1946. Spl. mission with I.L.O., Geneva, 1948, 49, 50, ECA, Paris, 1951, Mut. Security Adminstrn., 1952. Mem. bd. trustees Foremanship Foundation; mem. executive committee Jr. Achievement, Inc. Received with Walter Dietz, asso. dir. T.W.I., First Annual Award in field of human relations, by Soc. for Advancement of Management, 1944. Educational director vocational com. on education and special training. War Dept., World War I, 1918-19. Mem. Fed. Com. on Apprenticeship, 1934-46; served several terms as member board of trustees, Antioch College. Member American Inst. Elec. Engrs., American Society for Engring. Edn., Am. Assn. for Adult Edn., Am. Management Assn., Amateur Cinema League, American Soc. for the Advancement of Management, Indsl. Relations Research Assn., S.A.R., Silverbay Assn., Phi Kappa Psi, Tau Beta Pi. Rep. Presbyterian. Clubs: Purdue, Indiana, Downtown Athletic (N.Y. City). Author: articles on industrial relations topics. Home: 41 Oakland Pl. Office: Training Within Industry Foundation, 382 Springfield Av., Summit, N.J. Died June 25, 1956.

DOOLEY, Lucy, ex-coll. pres.; b. Atchison, Kan.; d. James and Catherine (Hurley) D.; LL.D., St. Benedict's Coll., 1926. Supr. Mt. St. Scholastica Convent, 1924-50; pres. Congregation of St. Scholastica, Mt. St. Scholastica Coll. 1926-50, ret. Home: Atchison, Kan. Died Apr. 19, 1951; buried Mount St. Scholastica Convent Cemetery.

DOOLEY, M(arion) S(ylester), physician, author; b. Cedar Grove, Mo., Dec. 23, 1879; s. Thomas Jefferson and Elizabeth Caroline (Howell) D.; A.B., U. Mo., 1907; med. student U. Mo., Harvard, 2 yrs.; M.D., Syracuse U., 1914; m. Mary Elizabeth Jadwin, Sept. 1, 1908; children—Elizabeth (Mrs. Frederick D. Becker), Alice Ann (Mrs. David Radford Serpell); m. 2d, Constance Howell, Mar. 1, 1943. Successively instr., asst. prof., asso. prof., prof. physiology and pharmacology Syracuse U. Coll. of Medicine, 1907-17, prof. pharmacology, 1917-45, emeritus prof., 1945—; drugs cons. University Hosp. staff, 1922-47, Bureau Hosp. Standards and Supplies, Inc., 1935—, W.P.B., 1943-45. Mem. U.S. Pharmacopoeia Revision Com., 1920-50. Fellow Internat. Coll. Anesthesia, A.M.A., Syracuse Acad. Medicine; mem. Internat. Anesthesia Research Soc. (hon. pres.), Am. Soc. Pharmacology and Therapeutics,

Soc. Exptl. Biol. and Medicine, Sigma Xi. Phi Kappa Phi, Alpha Omega Alpha. Unitarian. Author: Pharmacology and Therapeutics in Nursing, 1948; chmn. editorial com. Practitioners and Interns Handbook, 4 edits, 1928-49; co-chmn. editorial com. Drug Manual, 1949. Home: 417 Waverly Av., Syracuse 10, N.Y. Died Dec. 13, 1958; buried Fayetteville (N.Y.) Cemetery.

DOOLITTLE, Dudley; b. Cottonwood Falls, Kan., June 21, 1881; s. Joseph Harmon and May Coleman (Jones) D.; LL.B., U. Kan., 1903; m. Zula McQuillen, Dec. 1, 1915; children—Beverly, Dudley. Admitted to Kan. bar, 1903, began practice at Cottonwood Falls; pres. Strong City State Bank; dir. Exchange Nat. Bank; pros. atty. Chase County, Kan., 1908-12; mem. 63d to 65th Congresses, 4th Kan. Dist.; spl. rep. U.S. Treasury Dept. to Italy, 1919; mem. State Bd. of Regents, Kan., 1931-35; gen. agt., FCA, Wichita, Kan., 1934-38; pres. and trustee Coll. of Emporia, 1938-40. Mem. Sigma Chi. Presbyn. Mason (32°). Club: Kansas City (hon.). Home: Strong City, Kan. Died Nov. 14, 1957; buried Prairie Grove Cemetery, Cottonwood Falls, Kan.

DOOLITTLE, Frederick William, pub. utility exec.; b. Hopkinton, Ia., July 9, 1883; s. Fred William and Mary (Russell) D.; A.B., Princeton, 1905; B.S. in Civil Engring., U. Colo., 1907, M.S. and C.E., 1911; m. Madeleine Steele, Sept. 16, 1910; children—Frederick William, Russell Carter, Robert Winthrop (dec.). Pre-professional work with U.P. R.R.; with Boston Consol. Mining Co., Bingham, Utah, 1907, Consol. Coal & Coke Co., Dacono, Colo., 1908; instr. in mechanics and hydraulics U. Ill., 1908-09; designer of steel structures C.M.St.P. Ry., Chgo., 1909; in charge instrn. in structural engring. U. Colo., 1909-10; designer concrete structures C.M.&St.P. Ry., 1910; asst. prof. mechanics U. Wis., also expert on cost of r.r. operation, R.R. Commn., Wis., 1910-13; sec. Pub. Utilities Commn., Ill., 1913-14; dir. bureau fare research Am. Electric Ry. Assn., N.Y.C., 1914-16; cons. engr., 1916-23; v.p., mem. exec. com. The North American Co., 1923-36, dir. 1923-47, continues as consultant; dir. other pub. utility and coal mining cos. Treas. Transit Code Authority under NRA; chmn. com. on pub. utilities and law of Commerce and Industry Asso. of N.Y., 1937—. Mem. Bd. Edn., Garden City, 1940-1947; mem. Price Adjustment Bd., N.Y. Ordnance Dist. U.S. Army, 1943-44. Mem. Newcomen Soc., Am. Soc. C.E., Princeton Engring. Assn. (past pres.), Sigma Xi, Beta Theta Pi, Tau Beta Pi. Republican. Presbyn. Clubs: Recess (N.Y.C.); Engineers (St. Louis). Author: Cost of Urban Transportation Service, 1916. Contbr. to tech. jours. Home: 79 Brompton Rd., Garden City, N.Y. Office: 60 Broadway, N.Y.C. 4. Died Sept. 13, 1950.

DORAN, William Thomas, ret. clergyman, educator; b. Omaha, Neb., Feb. 6, 1870; s. Patrick and Mary (Hughes) D.; ed. St. Mary's Coll.; Creighton U.; A.M., St. Louis U., 1900. Joined Soc. of Jesus (Jesuits), 1890; ordained priest R.C. Ch., 1904; pres. U. Detroit, 1915-21; prin. Marquette High Sch., Milw., 1921-23; regent Schs. of Law, Commerce and Sociology, St. Xavier Coll., prin. St. Xavier Cin., 1923-24; pres. St. Louis U. High Sch., 1924-30; treas. St. Mary's Coll., 1930-46. Retired. Address: St. Mary's Coll., St. Marys, Kan. Died June 24, 1949.

DORCHESTER, Liverus Hull, clergyman; b. Charlestown, Mass., Aug. 27, 1864; s. Rev. Dr. Daniel and Mary Payson (Davis) D.; A.B., Boston U., 1886, S.T.B., 1889; D.D., Syracuse U., 1909; m. Nellie E. Hardy, June 10, 1889; children—Donald Hardy, Mrs. Ruth Allen. Ordained M.E. ministry, 1889; pastor St. Luke's Ch. (now Wesley Ch.), Springfield, Mass., 1889-94, First Ch., Westfield, Mass., 1894-99, People's Temple, Boston, 1899-1902, Newton Center, Mass., 1902, Lindell Av. Ch., St. Louis, 1903-07, Elm Park Ch., Scranton, Pa., 1907-12, Westville Ch., New Haven, Conn., 1912-14, Prospect M.E. Ch., Bristol, Conn., 1914-21, First Ch., Hartford, Conn., 1921-29, Simsburg Meth. Ch., 1930-36; ret. 1937; supply pastor, 1937-45. Pres. Conn. Federation Chs., 1923-26, exec. sec., 1929—. Home: Groton Long Point, Conn. Died Nov. 15, 1946.

DORRANCE, Gordon, publicist, writer; b. Camden, N.Y., June 14, 1890; s. Daniel James and Edith Lillian (Turner) D.; prep. edn. Manlius (N.Y.) Sch.; Forest Engineer, Biltmore (N.C.) Forest Sch., 1913, supplementary work at Technische Hochschule, Darmstadt, Germany; studied Grad. Sch., U. Pa., 1919-20; m. Emile Berthe de Vaulte, Sept. 12, 1922. With State Bd. Forestry, Md., 1913-17; pres., chmn. bd. Dorrance & Co., Inc., 1920-40. Served as lt. Engrs., U.S. Army, in France, 1918-19; capt. to maj. Reserves, 1925-30; maj. to lt. col. U.S. Army, 1942-45, with office of under sec. of war (internal security), later M.I., 1942; with gen. staff corps, 1943, U.S. Joint Chiefs of Staff and duty with War Dept. Gen. Staff, 1943-45; commn. M.I. Res. 1946; recalled to active duty, Feb., promoted to col. Sept. 1947. Decorated Comdr. Order of the Phoenix, 1930. Mem. Pa. Forest Commn., 1936. Mem. Soc. Mayflower Descs. Presbyn. Mason. Author: Broken Shackles, 1920; The Bonapartes in America, 1939 (co-author), Ten Commandments for Success (with others), 1947. Editor: The Pocket Chesterfield, 1920; Contemporary Poets, An Anthology of Fifty, 1927. Contbr. Sci. Am., Popular Sci. Monthly, London Times Imperial Trade Supplement, New York Times Annalist, Magazine of Wall St., etc. Address: 33 Roumfort Rd., Mt. Airy, Phila. 19. Died Mar. 22, 1957.

DORSEY, James Emmet, lawyer; b. Fergus Falls, Minn., Sept. 12, 1889; s. John George and Katherine (Pastoret) D.; A.B. with distinction, U. Minn., 1910; LL.B., Harvard, 1913; m. Loretta Mary Toomey, Jan. 18, 1916; children—Joan (Mrs. Roland Flinsch), John George, James Emmet, Peter, Rachel (Mrs. David G. Wyer, dec.). Admitted to Minn. bar, 1913, since practiced in Mpls.; partner Dorsey, Owen, Barker, Scott & Barber; dir. Cargill, Inc., Northrup, King & Co. Pres. The Cargill Found. Former pres. Legal Aid Soc. Mpls. Mem. Phi Beta Kappa. Clubs: Minneapolis, Minikahda (Mpls.). Home: 2204 West Lake of the Isles Blvd., Mpls. 5. Office: First National-Soo Line Bldg., Mpls. 2. Died Sept. 16, 1959.

DORSEY, LeRoy Howard, bus. exec., sportsman; b. Logansport, Ind., Jan. 19, 1887; s. Daniel Howard and Martha Elizabeth (Umbarger) D.; ed. pub. schs. of Ind.; unmarried. Salesman, 1904, later div. mgr., dir. Chicago Portrait Co., pres. since 1931; established Fine Arts Assn., 1923, pres. since 1931; pres. American Fine Arts Studios since 1932; dir. Empire Art Co., Pty., Ltd., Sydney, Australia, since 1931; pres. Corn Belt Farms, Inc., Kentland, Ind., since 1936; owner and operator Dorsey Farms, Kentland, Goodland and Chalmers, Ind., since 1933. Served in F.A. Officers Training Sch., World War I. Pres. Better Fishing, Inc., since 1946 (pioneering nat. fishing rodeos throughout U.S.A. children under license age); hon. president Internat. Fishing Rodeos in Mexico. Honorary rep. in U.S.A. Fed. Fishing Comm. Mexican Navy Dept.; honorary rep. Ministre Interior of Mexico. Decorated Mexican Aztec Eagle, 1949. Mem. Atlantic Tuna Club, New South Wales Game Fishing Assn.; Boca Del Rio; Club de Pesca, Acapulco; Ceylon Anglers, Colombo; Philippine Game Fishing Assn., Manila; Hawaii Big Game Fishing Club, Honolulu; Southern Calif. Tuna Club; Rod and Reel Club of Miami; Tuna Club, Avalon; Ocean Reef, Key Largo; West Palm Beach Fishing Club; Chicago Assn. Commerce, Mexican Chamber Commerce U.S., Chicago Press Club, Outdoor Writers Assn. of America, Am. Legion, Am. Museum Natural History, Am. Inst. of Park Execs.; Adventurers Club, Chicago; Executives Club, Chicago; Central Lions Club; Izaak Walton League; Ind. Soc. of Chicago. Methodist. Mason (32°, K.T., Shriner). Home: 5236 Lake Park Av., Chicago 15. Office: 509 S. Wabash Av., Chgo. 5. Deceased.

DORSEY, Thomas Francis (Tommy), orchestra leader; b. Mahoney Plains, Pa., Nov. 19, 1905; s. Thomas Francis and Theresa (Langton) D.; ed. public schools, Shenandoah, Pa.; m. Mildred Kraft; children—Patricia (Mrs. Lester Hooker), Thomas Francis, III; m. 2d, Pat Dane, Apr. 8, 1943; m. Jane New, Mar. 27, 1948; children—Susan, Stephen. Began career as trombonist with father's band and town band, 1919; later played with wellknown bands on road, in radio studios and theatres; with brother (Jimmy) organized band, 1934; made first appearance with own name band at French Casino, New York, N.Y.; leader of Tommy Dorsey orchestra; chmn. of the board of the Dorsey Brothers Music Company, Embassy Music Company, star own television series, Stage Show; on screen has appeared in pictures, Girl Crazy, Broadway Rhythm, Presenting Lily Mars, DuBarry Was a Lady, and Ship Ahoy, A Song Is Born; recorded for Victor, Decca and Bell. Author: The Modern Trombonist, 1944. Composed Trombonology. Home: Flagler Dr., Greenwich, Conn. Office: 1619 Broadway, N.Y.C. 19. Died Nov. 26, 1956; buried Kensico Cemetery, Valhalla, N.Y.

DOSDALL, Chester Arthur, bus. exec.; b. San Antonio, Dec. 3, 1882; s. Rev. Gottlieb and Elisha (Heins) D.; student Blinn Coll., Brenham, Tex., 1899-1901; m. Marie Culligan, May 22, 1926; children—Chester A., Thomas Edwrrd, Mary L. Clk. St. Paul & Marine Ins. Co., 1903, v.p., sec. 1943—, also dir.; dir., v.p., sec. Mercury Ins. Co.; sec. St. Paul-Mercury Indemnity Co.; dir. Western Adjustment & Inspection Co. (Chgo.), Ins. Fedn. of Minn., St. Paul Goodwill Industries, Gen. Adjustment Bur. N.Y. Mem. St. Paul Assn. Commerce (past dir.), Minn. Hist. Soc. (life). Republican. Methodist. Mason (Shriner). Clubs: St. Paul Athletic, White Bear Yacht, Minnesota. Home: 1141 Summit Av., St. Paul 5. Died Nov. 1949.

DOSS, (Henry) Clay (dŏs), business exec.; born Moulton, Ala.; s. James Mitchell and Sarah (Ponder) D.; A.B., Duke U., 1909, LL.B., 1912; m. Melanie Le Bosquet, Dec. 16, 1924; 1 son, Clay (dec.) Br. mgr. Ford Motor Co., successively in Oklahoma City, Kansas City, Mo., N.Y. City, Chicago, and Dearborn, Mich., 1919-39, gen. sales mgr., 1939-44; v.p. in charge sales Nash Motors, Detroit, 1944-54; exec. cons. Am. Motors Corp., 1954-55; v.p. Outdoor Advertising Inc., 1955—. Trustee Duke University. Served with USN, World War I. Mem. Alpha Tau Omega. Methodist. Clubs: Detroit Athletic, Detroit Golf and Country. Home: 20066 Stratford Rd. Office: General Motors Bldg., Detroit. Died May 10, 1958; buried White Chapel Cemetery, Bloomfield Hills, Mich.

DOTEN, Samuel Bradford (dō'tĕn), entomologist; born in Gold Hill, Storey County, Nevada, December 14, 1875; son of Alfred and Mary Calista (Stoddard) Doten; B.A., Univ. of Nevada, 1898, M.A., 1912; D.Sc., 1950; m. Laura Katherine Schweis, June 16, 1915. Instr. history and mathematics, 1898-1900, instr. mathematics and entomology, 1900-02, asst. prof., 1902-03, asst. prof. entomology, meteorology and mathematics, 1903-05, prof. entomology, since 1906, U. of Nev.; also entomologist and dir. Nev. Expt. Station, 1913-46. Fellow A.A.A.S.; member Phi Kappa Phi. Republican. Episcopalian. Rotarian. Author numerous bulls. and articles on entomol. subjects. Home: 129 Elm St., Reno, Nev. Died May 9, 1955; buried Masonic Cemetery, Reno.

DOUBLEDAY, George, ret. chmn. bd. Ingersoll-Rand Co.; b. Mar. 19, 1866; s. George A. and Mary (Brumley) D.; m. Mary May White; children—G. Chester, James Moffitt, Alice (Mrs. John Holbrook). With Ingersoll-Rand Co., mfrs. mining machinery, 1895—, serving as treas., 1st v.p., pres. (25 years), then chmn. bd., resigned 1955; dir. A. S. Cameron Steam Pump Co., Can. Ingersoll-Rand Co., Ltd., Corn Exchange Bank Trust Co., Lopatong Water Co., W. R. Grace & Co., West Easton Land Co. Mem. S.R. Episcopalian. Democrat. Clubs: India House, Engineers, Links, Down Town (N.Y.C.); Everglades, Bath and Tennis (Palm Beach). Home: Ridgefield, Conn. Office: 11 Broadway, N.Y.C. Died Dec. 6, 1955.

DOUGHERTY, Blanford Barnard (dô'hẽr-tĭ), ex-coll. pres.; b. Boone, N.C., Oct. 21, 1870; s. Daniel Boone and Ellen Caroline (Bartlette) D.; ed. Wake Forest Coll., 1892, Ed.D., 1936; Holly Spring Coll., 1893; B.S., Carson-Newman Col., 1896; Ph.B., U. N.C., 1899; D.Litt., Elon Coll., 1926. Co-founder, 1903, pres. Appalachian State Normal Sch. (now Appalachian State Teachers Coll.) until 1955. Baptist. Club: Commercial. Home: Boone, N.C. Died May 27, 1957; buried Boone, N.C.

DOUGHERTY, Denis J., cardinal; student St. Charles Sem., Overbrook, Pa.; became first Am. bishop of Nueva Segovia, P.I., 1903; bishop of Jaro, P.I., 1908, of Buffalo, 1915; archbishop See of Phila. and Province of Pa., July 1918; Cardinal, Mar. 1921. Address: 225 N. 18th St., Phila. Died May 31, 1951.*

DOUGHTON, Robert L. (dou-tŭn), ex-congressman; b. Laurel Springs, N.C., Nov. 7, 1863; s. J. H. and Rebecca (Jones) D.; ed. Laurel Springs High Sch.; LL.D., U. N.C.; J.D., Catawba Coll., Salisbury, N.C.; m. Lillie S. Hix, 1898. Mercantile business, farmer and stock raiser, Laurel Springs, 1894-1911; pres. Deposit and Savings Bank, North Wilkesboro, N.C., 1911-36. Member N.C. Senate, 1908-10; mem. 62d to 72d Congresses (1911-33), 8th N.C. Dist. and 73d to 82d Congresses (1933-53), 9th N.C. District; chmn. ways and means com. U.S. Ho. of Reps., 73d through 79th Congresses re-elected 81st. Nat. Dem. Committeeman for N.C. since 1952. Mem. State Bd. of Agr., 1903-09, State Prison Bd., 1909-11. Baptist. Home: Laurel Springs, N.C. Office: House Office Bldg., Washington. Died Oct. 1, 1954.

DOUGLAS, Arthur F., hotel exec., lawyer; b. San Luis Obispo, Cal., Oct. 14, 1902; s. William and Julia (Fiske) D.; A.B., Whitman Coll., 1924, LL.D., 1944; LL.B., Columbia, 1927; m. Florence N. Peebles, Jan. 5, 1927; children—Florence Noble, Nancy Archibald, Mary Alexander. Admitted to N.Y. bar, 1928; practiced law with Root, Clark, Buckner & Ballantine, corporate attys., N.Y.C., 1927-37; became sec.-treas. Hotels Statler Co., Inc., 1937, dir. 1938, exec. v.p. and treas., 1939, pres., 1945-54; pres., dir. N.Y. Hotel Statler, Statler Studios, Inc., Statler Management, Inc., Statler Cal. Corp.; sec.-treas., dir. Buffalo Jenny Co., Inc.; trustee Dollar Savs. Bank of N.Y.; dir. Sydney Blumenthal & Co. Mem. Beta Theta Pi, Phi Delta Phi. Clubs: Bronxville (N.Y.) Field (past pres.); University (N.Y.C.). Home: 44 Masterton Rd., Bronxville, N.Y. Office: Hotel Statler, N.Y.C. Died Mar. 9, 1956.

DOUGLAS, Charles Henry, editor, writer; b. Liberty, N.Y., June 10, 1861; s. Rev. Samuel J. and Annie Suthers (Jackson) D.; B.A., Colgate U., 1885, M.A., 1888, Litt.D., 1915; m. Talulah G. Abercrombie, Mar. 21, 1889 (died, 1926); 1 son, Kenneth A.; m. 2d, Winifred H. Barnes. Taught Delhi (N.Y.) Acad., 1885-86, Suffield (Conn.) Acad., 1886-88; prin. high sch., Keene, N.H., 1888-93, Hartford, Conn., 1893-95; editor in chief D. C. Heath & Co., 1895-1925. Mem. Phi Beta Kappa. Author: History and Government of Connecticut, 1896. Contbr. to pedagog. and lit. jours. Home: 92 Manet Rd., Chestnut Hill, Mass.; (summer) Pinecrest, Lake Spofford, N.H. Died Apr. 11, 1954; buried Newton, Mass.

DOUGLAS, David Dwight, banker; b. Detroit, Mich., Dec. 25, 1891; s. Samuel Townsend and Marion Lucretia (Dwight) D.; prep. edn., Detroit Univ. Sch. and Hotchkiss Sch., Lakeville, Conn.; B.S.,

Sheffield Scientific Sch. (Yale), 1914; m. Josephine Alger; children—Martha Dwight, David Dwight. Began with Detroit Trust Co., 1914; sec. 1st Nat. Co. of Detroit, 1919-21, v.p., 1921-24, pres., 1924-29, chmn. bd., 1929-30; v.p. First Nat. Bank in Detroit, 1922-26, acting pres., 1926, pres., 1927-31; v.p. Detroit Bankers Co., 1931-32; owner of the Industrial Coating Engineers of Detroit; exec. vice president and director Grosse Pointe Bank, Commonwealth Brass Corp.; dir. Michigan Consolidated Gas Co. Served as lt., capt., Air Service, U.S. Army, World War I; capt. U.S. Naval Res., Amphibious Forces, World War II. Trustee Grace Hosp.; dir. Detroit Community Fund. Member Book and Snake Soc. Republican. Episcopalian. Clubs: Detroit, Detroit Athletic, Yondotega, Grosse Pointe Country (Detroit), Bohemian (San Francisco), California (Los Angeles), River, Racquet, Yale, The Leash (N.Y. City). Home: 39 Dymar Lane, Grosse Pointe Farms, Mich. Office: National Bank Bldg., Detroit 26. Died July 23, 1951.

DOUGLAS, Frederic Huntington, curator, anthropologist; b. Evergreen, Colo., Oct. 29, 1897; s. Charles Winfred and Mary Josepha (Williams) D.; A.B., U. of Colo., 1921; post-grad. U. of Mich., 1921-22; student Pa. Acad. Fine Arts, 1922-26; Doctor Sci., University of Colorado, 1948; married Freda Bendix Gillespie, May 21, 1926; children—Ann Pauline and Eve (twins), David. Painter and wood-carver, 1926-29; pres. sch. bd. Evergreen, Colo., 1929-34; curator, dept. Indian Arts, Denver Art Museum, 1929-47, curator, dept. Native Arts, since 1947; dir. Denver Art. Mus., 1940-42; asst. prof. anthropology U. Denver, from 1934; lecturer in anthropology U. Colo., from 1946; research fellow in ethnology Harvard, 1952; director of edn. Fed. Indian Exhibit, San Francisco Fair, 1938-39; co-dir. North Am. Indian Art, Museum Modern Art, N.Y.C., 1940-41; member Anglo-Am. group inspecting Swedish and Finnish museums, 1946; commr. Fed. Indian Arts and Crafts Board, from 1946. Served as private, U.S. Inf., 1918; commd. capt. Med. Adm. Corps, Nov. 1942, major, 1944, lt. col., 1945; registrar 31st Gen. Hosp., 25 mos., on New Hebrides and Luzon; disch., Feb. 1946. Trustee Denver Art Museum, Museum of Northern Arizona, Museum of Man, San Diego; mem. of the editorial board F. W. Hodge Anniversary Fund. Sec. Clearinghouse for Southwestern Museums, 1938-51. Research in design, styles and techniques appearing in work of Indian tribes north of Mexico, in last 150 yrs., with special emphasis on history of each design, style and technique. Fellow A.A.A.S. (v.p. Southwest Div., 1942-47, pres., 1947-48), Royal Anthrop. Soc. of Gt. Britain; mem. Am. Anthrop. Assn., Soc. for Am. Archeology, Am. Folklore Soc., Societe des Americanistes de Paris; mem. Phi Gamma Delta, Sigma Delta Chi, Mu Alpha Nu. Republican. Episcopalian. Clubs: Denver Country, University, Mile-High, The Westerners (Denver, Colorado). Author and editor, Denver Art Mus. publs. in Indian art; Indian Leaflet Series, since 1930, Indian Design Series since 1938, etc.; author (with Rene d'Harnoncourt), Indian Art of the United States, 1941; The Inner Light (verses, 4 vols.), 1946-53. Contbr. articles to newspapers and jours. Home: 745 S. Jackson St. Office: 1300 Logan St., Denver. Died Apr. 23, 1956; buried Fairmount Cemetery, Denver.

DOUGLAS, Hamilton, lawyer; b. Atlanta, Ga., Nov. 11, 1887; s. Hamilton and Corinne (Williams) D.; B.S., Vanderbilt, 1908; LL.B., Atlanta Law Sch., 1910; hon. LL.D., Tulsa (Okla.) Law School, 1942; m. Sue Bradley Johnson, December 5, 1914 (divorced); children—Hamilton, Jr., Sue Bradley; m. 2d, Marian McTyeire. Admitted to Georgia bar, 1910, and began practice at Atlanta; asst. atty. gen., Ga., 1912 15; dean Atlanta Law School since 1922; pres. English Mica Co.; dir. Kings Mountain Mica Co., Atlanta Baggage & Cab Company, Yellow Cab Co. Mem. Am., Ga. State and Atlanta bar assns., Sigma Chi (grand trustee, 1929-33; grand consul 1933-35). Democrat. Unitarian-Universalist. Mason (32°, K. T.). Clubs: Lawyers, Burns, Civitan. Home: 512 Manor Ridge Dr. Office: Rhodes Haverty Bldg., Atlanta, Ga. Died July 10, 1958.

DOUGLAS, John Francis, corp. official; b. Goodwood, Ont., Can., Oct. 30, 1874; s. James Aaron and Annie (Scott) D.; came with parents to U.S., 1885; A.B., U. of N.D., 1896, LL.D., 1933; LL.B., Yale, 1898; m. Neva Bostwick, Dec. 28, 1898; children—John Scott, Neva Bostwick, James Bostwick. Admitted to North Dakota bar, 1898, and began practice at Grafton; removed to Seattle, Wash., 1900; partner Douglas, Lane & Douglas, 1900-07; an organizer, 1907, president Metropolitan Building Co., until 1933, now v.p., dir.; dir. Peoples Nat. Bank Seattle; dir. many Pacific Northwest cos.; chairman finance committee Carnation Co., 1942-51, now dir. Maj. Q.M. Corps, U.S. Army, 1918. Trustee Calif. Arboretum Found., Los Angeles; advisor Am. Mutual Fund, Inc., Los Angeles. Mem. King County Bar Assn., Book and Gavel (Yale), Phi Alpha Delta. Ind. Rep. Presbyterian. Mason (Shriner). Clubs: Rainier, Yale, China, Seattle Golf, Bankers (New York), Los Angeles Country. Author: Douglas on Washington Corporations, 1904. Home: 450 S. Lucerne Blvd., Los Angeles 5. Office: Statler Bldg., 900 Wilshire Blvd., Los Angeles 17. Died Nov. 29, 1952.

DOUGLAS, Lee, lawyer; b. Nashville, May 23, 1885; s. Byrd and Adelaide (Gaines) D.; A.B., Princeton, 1906; LL.B., Vanderbilt U., 1908; m. Mrs. Elizabeth Keith Caldwell, Jan. 30, 1929 (died Oct. 1932); m. 2d, Marguerite Redding, Apr. 6, 1946. Admitted to Tenn. bar, 1908, practicing in Nashville; apptd. U.S. atty. Middle Dist. of Tenn., by President Wilson, 1914; reapptd. 1919; resigned 1922; apptd. spl. asst. to atty. gen. of U.S. to prosecute spl. cases for the Govt.; also in gen. practice at Nashville; pres. Nashville and Decatur R.R. Mem. Am. Bar Assn., Phi Delta Theta, Phi Delta Phi. Sec. Woodrow Wilson Club of Tenn., 1912; del. Dem. Nat. Conv., 1924. Mem. Newcomen Soc., Nashville br. English-Speaking Union, Grad. Council, Princeton. Democrat. Presbyn. Mason (32°, Shriner). Clubs: Coffee House, Belle Meade Country, Cumberland. Home: W. Tyne Blvd., Bell Meade, Nashville. Office: Stahlman Bldg., Nashville 3. Died Aug. 17, 1959.

DOUGLAS, Lloyd C(assel), clergyman; b. Columbia City, Ind., Aug. 27, 1877; s. Rev. Alexander Jackson and Sarah Jane (Cassel) D.; A.B., Wittenberg Coll., Springfield, O., 1900, A.M., 1903; B.D., Hamma Div. Sch., Springfield, 1903; D.D., Fargo (N.D.) College, 1920, U. of Southern Calif., 1928, U. of Vt., 1931; LL.D., Gettysburg (Pa.) Coll., 1935; Litt.D., Northeastern U., 1936, Wittenberg Coll., 1945; m. Besse Io Porch, Apr. 7, 1904 (died Dec. 30, 1944); children—Besse Io, II (Mrs. J. Weldon Wilson), Virginia Vorys (Mrs. Howard L. Dawson). Ordained Luth. ministry, 1903; pastor Zion Ch., North Manchester, Ind., 1903-05, 1st Ch., Lancaster, O., 1905-08, Luth. Memorial Ch., Washington, 1908-11; dir. religious work U. of Ill., 1911-15; pastor First Congl. Ch., Ann Arbor, Mich., 1915-21, First Ch., Akron, 1921-26, First Ch., Los Angeles, 1926-29, St. James United Ch., Montreal, 1929-33; now engaged in writing and lecturing. Mem. Phi Gamma Delta. Mason. Clubs: St. Botolph (Boston); Authors, Jonathan. Author: Wanted—a Congregation, 1920; The Minister's Everyday Life, 1924; These Sayings of Mine, 1926; Those Disturbing Miracles, 1927; Magnificent Obsession, 1929; Forgive Us Our Trespasses, 1932; Precious Jeopardy, 1933; Green Light, 1935; White Banners, 1936; Home for Christmas, 1937; Disputed Passage, 1939; Doctor Hudson's Secret Journal, 1939; Invitation to Live, 1940; The Robe, 1942; The Big Fisherman, 1948. Home: 721 E. Charleston Blvd., Las Vegas, Nev. Died Feb. 13, 1951.

DOUGLAS, William Archer Sholte, newspaperman, historian; b. Dervock, Ireland, Apr. 6, 1886; s. Richard and Julia Lever (Bonorandi) D.; student Foyle Coll., Ireland and Bedford Sch., Eng.; m. Wilma Victoria Crane; 1 son, Edward Gerard; children by previous marriage—Richard Maginis (USAAF), William A. S. Came to U.S., 1908, naturalized, 1913. Began as reporter with Phila. North American, 1909; successively with N.Y. Jour., N.Y. Herald, Dallas News, Houston Post; editor Pathé News, 1913-14; ofcl. motion picture cameraman to Meixican govt., 1923-24; with Balt. Sun, 1925, Washington corr., 1927-28, London corr., 1928-29; Chgo. corr. Balt. Sun, N.Y. Herald Tribune, Boston Herald, 1931-33; Universal News corr. in Europe, 1935, Chgo. Herald-Examiner, 1936, Washington Times-Herald, 1937-40; corr. European war zone, 1939-40, 1944-45; editorial writer and columnist Chgo. Sun, 1941-46; injured in action. In British Army, advancing from bugler to captain, served as sgt.-maj. Engr. Corps, U.S. Army, later capt. Tank Corps, World War I; comdr. arty., rebel army, Port au Prince, Haiti, 1907. Mem. Am. Legion, British Legion, Am. War Corrs. Assn., Sigma Delta Chi. Clubs: National Press (Washington); Union League (Chgo.); Junior Army and Navy (London). Author: Long John Murray; Racketeers of Europe; The Midwesterner and Pioneer Railroad (with Robert J. Casey). Contbr. to Am. Mercury, Esquire, Coronet, Collier's, Am. Mag., etc. Home: Union League Club. Office: 20 E. Jackson Blvd., Chgo. Died July 1951.

DOUGLASS, Aubrey Augustus, educator; b. Eureka, Kansas, Feb. 26, 1887; s. Clifford Hannibal and Ella Erwin (Mains) D.; A.B., Kan. State Teachers Coll., 1912; M.A., Clark U., Worcester, Mass., 1915; Ph.D., 1917; m. Mary Evelyn Ftizsimmons, Apr. 20, 1918; children—James Brian, Malcolm Paul. High sch. teacher, 1910-12; prin. Wamego (Kan.) High Sch., 1912-14; asst. prof. edn., State Coll. of Wash., 1919-24; lecturer on edn., Harvard U. Grad. Sch. Edn., 1924-26; prof. and head dept. edn., Claremont (Calif.) Colls., 1926-35, dir. of graduate studies, 1937; chief of div. of secondary education, Calif. State Dept. of Education, 1935-37, asst. supt. of public instruction, 1938-43; superintendent, city schools, Modesto, 1943-47; asso. supt., Calif. State Dept. Edn., since 1947; vis. prof. summer sessions Pa. State Coll., Harvard, Stanford, U. of Chicago, U. of Washington, U. of Calif. Fellow, Oberlaender Trust in Germany studying schs., 1936. Mem. survey com. on needs of Calif. in higher edn., 1947-48. Served A.U.S., 1917-18. Mem. N.E.A. (department of superintendence), Calif. Soc. of Secondary Education, Phi Delta Kappa, Phi Kappa Phi, Kappa Delta Pi. Mason. Author: The Junior High School, 1917; Secondary Education, 1927; Modern Secondary Education, 1938; The American School System, 1934, rev. edit., 1940. Contbr. articles to ednl. jours. Home: 2225-22d Av., Sacramento, 18. Died May 8, 1952; buried Masonic Lawn, Sacramento.

DOUGLASS, Frederick Melvin, surgeon; b. Kalida, O., June 26, 1890; s. Curry Frederick (M.D.) and Kathrine Willoughby (Melvin) D.; M.D., U. Toledo, 1911; post-grad. study, Boston, London (Eng.), Mayo Clinic, and Chgo., 1914, 15; m. Ruth Jacobson, Nov. 2, 1913 (dec.); children—Kathryn Jane (Mrs. Nelson Montgomery Loud), Frederick Melvin (M.D.); m. 2d, Beatrice Ossege, Nov. 21, 1926. Intern St. Vincent's Hosp., Toledo, 1911-12; resident physician Lucas County Hosp., Toledo, 1912-13; practicing general surgeon with J. H. Jacobson, M.D., 1913-18; with C. W. McNamara and Richard Hotz, M.D., 1918—; dir. surgery St. Vincent's Hosp., 1926—. Trustee Endowment Fund of Toledo Med. Coll. Diplomate Am. Bd. Surgery (founders group). Fellow U.S. chpt. Internat. Coll. Surgeons (past chmn. bd. govs.), A.C.S. (life mem.), Am. Assn. Obstetricians, Gynecologists, and Abdominal Surgeons; mem. Acad. Medicine Toledo and Lucas County (pres. 1937-38, trustee 1938—), Northwestern Ohio Med. Soc. (pres. 1928-29), Am., Ohio med. assns. Presbyn. Mason (32°), Elk. Clubs: Inverness, Toledo. Contbr. sci. and med. articles. Home: 2029 Potomac Dr. Office: 421 Michigan St., Toledo. Died July 4, 1950.

DOUGLASS, George Shearer, banking exec.; b. Beattie, Kan., July 15, 1895; s. Phillip and Annie Wilson (Shearer) D.; B.S. in civil engring., Kan. State Agrl. Coll., 1916; m. Edythe Groh; 1 son, George Shearer. Railroad and municipal engr., 1916-20; continuously with bureau of valuation Interstate Commerce Commn. in railroad valuation work from 1920, became dir. bureau, July 1945; vice pres. chmn. bd. Old Dominion Bank, Arlington Va.; chairman bd. Bank of Anandale, Anandale, Va. Served with U.S. Army Air Force, World War I. Mem. Washington Soc. of Engrs. Protestant. Mason. Club: Federal (Washington). Home: 3706 17th St., N. Arlington, Va. Office: Interstate Commerce Commission Bldg., Washington 25. Died Jan. 5, 1953; buried Arlington Nat. Cemetery.

DOUGLASS, H(arlan) Paul, clergyman; b. Osage, Ia., Jan. 4, 1871; s. Truman Orville and Maria (Greene) D.; A.B., Ia. Coll., 1891, A.M., 1896; grad. Chicago and Andover Theol. sems., 1894; Williams fellowship, Harvard; courses U. of Chicago, Columbia and New York Sch. of Philanthropy; D.D., Drury Coll., 1905; m. Rena Sherman, June 25, 1895; 1 dau., Dorothea (Mrs. William A. Leech, Jr.). Ordained Congl. ministry, 1894; pastor, Manson, Ia., 1894-95, Ames, 1896-1900, Springfield, Mo., 1900-06; instr. in psychology, 1900-04, prof. philosophy, 1905-06, Drury Coll.; supt. of edn., Am. Missionary Assn., in charge of 75 schs. for Negroes and mountaineers in the South, 1906-10; corr. sec., Am. Missionary Assn., 1910-18; with A.E.F. in France as Y.M.C.A. sec. and mem. of Army Ednl. Corps, 1918-19; mgr. agrl. labor br. Interchurch World Movement, 1919-20. Research dir., Inst. of Social and Religious Research, 1921-33; dir. China Survey of Laymen's Foreign Missions Inquiry, 1930-34, Commn. of Appraisal of Am. Unitarian Assn., 1934-35; sec. Commn. to Study Christian Unity, Federal Council of Churches of Christ in America, 1937-42; chairman of research department, 1943; editor of Christendom, 1938-48, associate editor the Ecumenical Review, 1948-50; dir. Com. for Coöperative Field Research, 1945. Mem. Phi Beta Kappa fraternity. Author: Christian Reconstruction in the South, 1909; The New Home Missions, 1916; The Little Town, 1919; The St. Louis Church Survey, 1924; The Suburban Trend, 1925; How Shall Country Youth Be Served?, 1926; The Church in the Changing City, 1927; How to Study the City Church, 1928; Church Comity, 1929; City's Church, 1929; Protestant Coöperation in American Cities, 1930; Church Unity Movements in the United States, 1934; A Decade of Objective Progress in Church Unity; The Metropolitan Pittsburgh Church Study, 1948. Home: 129 Cooper Av., Upper Montclair, N.J. Office: 300 Fourth Av., N.Y.C. 10. Died Apr. 14, 1953; buried Phila.

DOUNCE, Harry Esty (douns), journalist; b. Syracuse, N.Y., Apr. 6, 1889; s. George A. and Cornelia (Esty) D.; B.S., Hamilton Coll., 1910; m. Margaret Lane, 1917; children—Roger Esty (dec.), Margaret (Mrs. R. P. Dale, Jr.). Reporter N.Y. Sun, 1910-12; spl. writer, dramatic editor Syracuse Herald, 1912-14; spl. writer N.Y. Sun (Sunday edition), 1916-19; editor Books, Book World, (N.Y. Sun) 1919-20; features editor N.Y. Evening Post, 1920-22; editorial asso. Collier's Weekly, 1923-25; book reviewer The New Yorker, 1925-26; editor The Literary Review (N.Y. Evening Post), 1926-28; mem. editorial staff Liberty mag., 1928-47. Contbr. fiction and articles to mags. Home: 211-26 34th Road, Bayside, N.Y. Died Mar. 26, 1957.

DOUTHIRT, Walstein F., former v.p., dir. Am. Natural Gas Co.; formerly American Light & Traction

Co.; b. Columbus, O., Sept. 25, 1867; s. Stephen T. and Mary (Brooks) D.; Ph.B., Kenyon Coll., Gambier, O., 1888; widower. Mem. Assn. Bar City N.Y. Retired. Died May 10, 1955.

DOUTHIT, Claude (douth'it), chmn. bd. Am. Hide & Leather Co.; b. Anderson County, S.C., Aug. 17, 1883; s. Joseph Benjamin and Mary (Watkins) D.; E.E., Clemson (S.C.) A. and M. Coll., 1902; married Martha D. Francis, June 10, 1913; 1 son, Claude; married 2d, Helen Manger, December 7, 1929. Cottonseed buyer and mill supt. Procter & Gamble Co., 1902-06, mill mgr., 1906-10; v.p., gen. mgr. Buckeye Cotton Oil Co., subsidiary of Procter & Gamble Co., 1910-23; chmn. bd. Am. Hide & Leather Co., 1928—. Home: R.D. 1, Westerly, R.I. Office: 17 East St., Boston. Died Feb. 14, 1957.

DOW, Allan Wade, chemical engr.; b. New York, N.Y., Aug. 24, 1866; s. Capt. John Melmoth and Elizabeth K. (Allan) D.; ed. pvt. sch.; Ph.B., Sch. of Mines, Columbia, 1888; m. Jessie Cecelia Frank, Nov. 10, 1892; children—F. Miriam, Allan W., John A. Asst. chemist, Barber Asphalt Paving Co., 1889-94; chemist to engring. dept. and insp. asphalt and cement for D.C., 1894-1906; mem. firm Dow & Smith, cons. engrs., specialists on road paving and paving materials, 1906-32; cons. engr. under name of A. W. Dow, Inc., same specialities, 1932—; v.p. and chief engr. Colprovia Roads, Inc., 1935-39. Past pres. Assn. Asphalt Paving Technologists; mem. Am. Chem. Soc., Internat. Soc. for Testing Materials, A.A.A.S., Am. Soc. for Testing Materials. Home: Old Gulph Rd., Bridgewater, Conn. Office: 801 2d Av., N.Y.C. 17. Died Dec. 8, 1955; buried Bridgewater.

DOWD, W(illiam) Carey, Jr., publishing exec.; b. Charlotte, N.C., Oct. 11, 1893; s. William Carey and Eloise Jordan (Butt) D., student Wake Forest (N.C.) Coll., 1910-13, student U. N.C., 1913-14; m. Ann Garvey Rogers, May 11, 1918; children—William Carey III, Marie Eloise (Mrs. Walter B. Latimer). With News Pub. Co., Charlotte, N.C., 1919-47, pres., pub. Charlotte News, 1927-47. Served as 1st lt. Q.M.C., U.S. Army, AEF, 1918-19. Mem. C. of C. (dir.), Am. Legion, N.C. Press Assn. (hon. life mem., past pres.), Sigma Chi. Democrat. Baptist (deacon). Clubs: Good Fellows (dir.), Charlotte Country, Charlotte City. Home: 1121 Queens Rd. W. Office: Dowd Press, Inc., Box 3155, Charlotte 3, N.C. Died Aug. 13, 1949.

DOWDELL, James Render, judge; b. nr. Lafayette, Ala., Apr. 2, 1847; s. James F. and Sarah H. (Render) D.; cadet in C.S.A., 1864-65; student U. Ala., 1864-5; A.B., Coll. at Auburn, Ala., 1867, A.M., 1869; m. Rosie Tuener, Sept. 6, 1871; 2d, Ella M. Ware, Dec. 12, 1878. Admitted to bar, 1870, engaged in practice at Lafayette; solicitor 9th Jud. Circuit, 1876-80; judge 5th Jud. Circuit, 1888-92; chancellor N. Eastern div., 1896-98; asso. justice Supreme Ct., Ala., 1898—, now chief justice. Methodist. Democrat. Home: Lafayette, Ala. Office: Montgomery, Ala. Died June 29, 1921.

DOWELL, Benjamin B(utterworth), govt. ofcl., lawyer; b. Silver Spring, Md., Oct. 18, 1895; s. Julian C. and Cynthia E. (Noyes) D.; LL.B., George Washington U., 1924; m. Edna C. Maedel, Nov. 16, 1927. Admitted to D.C. bar, 1923; mem. patent law firm Dowell & Dowell, Washington, 1923-40; dir. contract termination program, dep. Bur. Aero. Gen. Rep., Central dist., USN, Wright Field, O., 1944-47; indsl. adviser NPA, Def. Prodn. Adminstrn., 1950-53; spl. cons. Bus. and Def. Services Adminstrn., Dept. Commerce, 1955; chmn. Govt. Patents Bd., 1955—. Served as officer (pilot), USN, World War I, as Procurement and Contract adminstrn. officer, World War II; capt. Res. (ret.). Mem. Am., Fed., D.C. bar assns., Am. Patent Law Assn., Am. Judicature Soc., Early Naval Aviators, Naval Res. Officers Assn., Navy League U.S., Vets. Fgn. Wars, Sigma Alpha Epsilon. Republican. Club: Capitol Hill (Washington). Home: 2300 Connecticut Av, Washington 8. Office: Govt. Patents Bd., Dept. of Commerce Bldg., Washington 25. Died Oct. 29, 1958; buried Arlington Nat. Cemetery.

DOWNES, James R., ry. officer; b. Tyrone, Pa., Oct. 23, 1883; s. John and Catherine (Cushen) D.; ed. high school of Tyrone, Pa.; m. Caroline Poorman, Jan. 3, 1917; 1 dau., Elizabeth (Mrs. George W. Elkins, Jr.). Entered service with Pa. Railroad, 1901; supt. of freight transportation, Central Region, Pittsburgh, 1923-28, chief, Philadelphia, 1928-34, asst. v.p., Sept.-Oct. 1934; v.p. operations and maintenance, Assn. Am. Railroads, Washington, D.C. (on leave from Pa. R.R.), 1934-35; asst. to the pres. Pa. R.R., Phila., 1935-39, v.p.-asst. to pres. since Jan. 16, 1939. Club: Union League (Phila.). Home: Rittenhouse Claridge, Phila. 3. Died Feb. 15, 1955.

DOWNES, John, naval officer (ret.); b. Dorchester, Mass., Nov. 16, 1879; s. John and Emma Homer (Nazro) D.; B.S., U.S. Naval Acad., 1901; hon. LL.D., St. Ambrose Coll., 1943; m. Agnes Carlyle Bryant, Oct. 31, 1906; children—John, William Bryant, Sarah Fairfax Carlyle; m. 2d, Edith A. Steinbrecher, Aug. 12, 1952. Served as midshipman 3d class, Spanish Am. War, 1897; commd. ensign U.S. Navy, 1901, advanced through grades to rear adm., 1935; aide to supt. U.S. Naval Acad., 1916-18; comdr. heavy cruiser div., 1937-38; chief of staff to comdr. scouting forces, 1934-35; comdt. 9th Naval Dist., 1935-36, 40-42; ret. from active duty, 1944; with Chgo. chpt. A.R.C., 1944, Ford Motor Co., 1945; dir., Ill. Service Recognition Bd. (vets. bonus), 1947—. Decorated Spanish Am. War and spl. engagement medals, West Indian campaign medal, Victory medal with silver star (World War I), Legion of Merit (World War II). Republican. Clubs: Yacht (N.Y.C.); Army Navy (Washington); Chevy Chase (Md.); Chicago, Old Elm (Lake Forest, Ill.); University, Union League, Tavern (Chgo.). Home: 40 E. Shiller St., Chgo. 10. Office: 160 N. La Salle St., Chgo. Died Feb. 10, 1954; buried Annapolis, Md.

DOWNES, (Edwin) Olin, music critic; b. Evanston, Ill., Jan. 27, 1886; began study of music at age of 8, later studied piano, music history and analysis under Dr. Louis Kelterborn, piano under Carl Baermann, harmony under Homer Norris and Clifford C. Hielman, harmony and music appreciation John P. Marshall; Mus.D., Cin. Conservatory, 1939. Music critic Boston Post, 1906-24, N.Y. Times, 1924-55; lecturer on opera Boston U. under auspices of Mass. Extension and Lowell Inst.; asst. in music courses Boston U. and Harvard, summer 1911; lectr. on mus. theory, history and appreciation Chautauqua, N.Y.; lectr. Bklyn. Inst. Arts and Scis., 1932-34, Berkshire Mus. Center and Berkshire Music Festival with Boston Symphony Orchester under Dr. Serge Koussevitzky; chmn., lectr. 50th anniversary of Carnegie Hall; lectr. Phila. Forum, Curtis Inst., Met. Opera Assn., Met. Opera Guild, Jr. League of N.Y., N.Y. Town Hall, and music and ednl. instns. from coast to coast; dir. N.Y. music N.Y. World's Fair, 1938-39. Clubs: Century Assn., Coffee House. Author: The Lure of Music, 1918; Symphonic Broadcasts, 1932; Ten Operatic Masterpieces, from Mozart to Prokofieff, 1952. Editor: Songs of Russia. Contbr. to the Musical Quarterly, The Music Review, and others, also Cobett's Cyclopedia of Chamber Music; Oscar Thompson's Cyclopedia of Music and Musicians. Collaborator with Elie Siegmeister in Treasury of American Song. Home: 205 W. 57th St., N.Y.C. 19. Died Aug. 22, 1955.

DOWNEY, Hal, educator emeritus; b. State Coll., Pa., Oct. 4, 1877; s. John F. and Stella (Osborn) D.; B.A., U. Minn., 1903, M.A., 1904, Ph.D., 1909; studied U. Berlin, 1910, U. Strassburg, 1911; m. Iva Mitchell, June 7, 1905; children—Phyllis Mitchell, Richard Thomas, Jean Annis. Asst. in dept. of zoölogy U. Minn., 1903, successively instr., asst. prof., asso. prof., prof., 1917-29, prof. anatomy, Med. Sch. 1929-46; lectr. hematology Mayo Found. for Medical Research; research in hematology Dept. Anatomy, U. Minn., Mayo Found., 1947—. Pvt. Co. A, 13th Minn. Vol. Infantry, in P.I., 1898-99. Recipient Outstanding Achievement award, 1951; Distinguished Service award, 1957. Fellow Internat. Soc. Hematology (hon.), European Soc. Hematology (hon.). Mem. Assn. Am. Anatomists, Minn. Pathol. Soc., Sigma Xi. Contbr. papers on haematology to tech. jours. Editor, contbr. Handbook of Hematology (4 vols.), 1938; Am. editor, Folia Haematologia, 1928-41. Home: 2 Barton Av. S.E., Mpls. 14. Died Jan. 9, 1959; buried Ft. Snelling Nat. Cemetery.

DOWNEY, Mary Elizabeth, librarian; b. Sarahsville, O.; d. Hiram James (M.D.) and Martha (Ball) Downey; A.B., Shepardson (Ohio) Coll., 1895; A.B., Denison U., 1899, A.M., 1924; grad. U. Chgo. Library Sch., 1901. Asst. librarian Field Museum, Chgo., 1901-02; librarian Ottumwa (Ia.) Pub. Library, 1902-08; library organizer of Ohio, 1908-12; library sec. and organizer, Utah, 1914-21; dir. Ft. Douglass Library, 1917-19; librarian, dir. and sec. N.D. Library Commn., 1921-23; librarian Denison U. Library, 1923-29; library organizer of Ohio, 1929-31; dir. Chautauqua (N.Y.) Sch. for Librarians, 1906-35; dir. Utah summer library school, 1914, 20; librarian U.S. Sesquicentennial Commn., 1937-38, librarian Nat. Woman's Party, 1941—. Officer many library and lit. orgns.; mem. A.L.A. (chmn. religious books round table 1932-33), Ohio (pres. 1912-14; chmn. coll. and reference sect., 1925-27; chmn. College Librarians of the Middle West, 1926-27), Utah (pres. 1920-21), N.D. (pres. 1922-23), D.C. library assns. Chmn. Library Extension com. Ohio Fedn. Women's Clubs, 1929-32; sec. Trustees Chautauqua Bapt. Union, 1935-36; pres. W.C.T.U. Chautauqua, Frances Willard Union, 1935; dir. peace and internat. relations W.C.T.U. of D.C. 1938—; chmn. resolutions com. D.C. Fedn. Women's Clubs. Mem. U.S. Flag Assn., League Am. Pen Women (pres. Chevy Chase br. 1942-43; chmn. lecture com., South Atlantic sect.; pres. Md. state branch, 1946-48, adv. com. 1948—), Nat. and World Woman's Parties (mem. council chmn. D.C. branch, Nat. Women's Party, 1943-48), Am. Forestry Assn. Bapt. Clubs: Chautauqua Woman's, Bird and Tree; Political Study, Sunshine, Excelsior Literary, Ohio State Women (Washington). Contbr. profl. jours. Professional lecturer. Home: 203 Third St. N.E., Washington 2. Died May 25, 1949.

DOWNEY, William H(enry), economist; b. Antigo, Wis., Jan. 24, 1896; s. William and Margaret (Foster) D.; student Minn. Coll. Law, 1915-16, Marquette Coll. Law, 1917-18, Wis. State Tchrs. Coll., River Falls, 1919-20, U. Wis., summers 1920, 21; B.S., Valparaiso U., 1926; M.A., U. Notre Dame, 1928; grad. work U. Mich., summers 1929, 30; m. Norma Eulalia Carroll, June 24, 1925; children—Margaret Mary (Mrs. Donald Vetter), William H., John Carroll. With Downey-Campbell Constrn. Co., Milw., 1923-25; instr. U. Notre Dame, 1928-30, asst. prof., 1932-35, asso. prof., 1935-38, prof. econs., 1938—, head dept. econs., 1937-42; with dept. social science St. Mary's Coll., Notre Dame, Ind., 1934—. Sec. pub. affairs com. Milwaukee County Council of Defense, 1917-18. Mem. Gov. of Ind. Mediation Bd., 1939-40. Mem. Am. Econ. Assn., Cath. Econ. Assn. (co-organizer and 1st sec. 1940-43), A. A.A.S., Acad. Polit. Sci., Ind. Acad. Social Scis. (dir. 1937-39), Am. Assn. U. Profs. Roman Catholic. Home: 60 N. St. Joseph Av., Niles, Mich. Office: U. of Notre Dame, Notre Dame, Ind. Died Jan. 10, 1954; buried Niles, Mich.

DOWNING, Robert Everard, pres. Pike Coll., Mo., 1894—; b. Randolph Co., Mo., Feb. 6, 1864; grad. U. Mo., 1886; supt. schs. Huntsville, Mo., several yrs.; later prof. sci., higher mathematics, Stephens Coll., Columbia, Mo. Address: Bowling Green, Mo. Deceased.

DOWNS, Joseph, curator; b. Shutesbury, Mass., 1895; s. Daniel and Mary (MacDonald) D.; grad. Mus. Fine Arts Sch., 1921. Asst. Mus. Fine Arts, 1921-22; traveling scholarship, Europe, 1922-23; furniture designer, 1923-25; curator Pa. Mus. Art, Phila., 1925-32, Am. wing Met. Mus., 1932-49, H.F. duPont Winterthur Mus. since 1949. Mem. N.Y. Hist. Soc. (hon.), Am. Assn. Museums, Walpole Soc., Soc. for Preservation N.E. Antiquities (life). Club: Century Association. Author: American Furniture, 1952; also articles mus. bulls., profl. mags., jours. Home: Guilford, Conn. Office: care H.F. duPont Winterthur Museum, Winterthur, Del. Died Sept. 8, 1954.

DOWNS, William Smith, cons. engr., prof.; b. Martinsburg, W.Va., Mar. 15, 1883; s. Joseph Allen and Caroline Janet (Evans) D.; B.S. in Civil Engring., W.Va. U., 1906, C.E., 1915; m. Nellie Jane Albright, June 22, 1910; children—William Richard, James Albright, Jane. Topographer, Bolivian R.R. Commn., Bolivia, S.A., 1905-06; chief draftsman, M.&K. R.R., 1906-09; resident engr., Hydro Elec. Co. of W.Va., 1909-15; County Highway engr., Monongalia County, W.Va., 1915-19; div. engr., W.Va., State Rd. Commn., 1919-29; cons. engr., Morgantown, W.Va., 1929—; prof. Ry. and Highway Engring., W.Va. U.; consultant for Assn. Am. Railroads, W.Va. Pub. Service Commn., Pa. R.R., West Assn. R.R. Execs., Princeton U. State and Local Govt. Sect. Morgantown Municipal Planning Commission. Mem. Am. Soc. Civil Engring. (past pres. W. Va. sect.), W.Va. Soc. Prof. Engring. (past pres.), Am. Rd. Builders Assn. (dir. edn. div), Soc Promotion Engring. Edn., Beta Theta Pi, Tau Beta Pi, Chi Epsilon. Republican. Presbyterian. Club: Rotary (Morgantown, W.Va.). Contbr. to professional jours. Home: 204 Euclid Av., Morgantown, W.Va. Died July 12, 1954; buried East Oak Grove Cemetery, Morgantown.

DOYLE, Bernard Wendell, indsl. exec.; b. Leominster, Mass., Oct. 29, 1873; s. Bernard and Ann (Gurry) D.; grad. Eastman Coll., 1892; m. Elizabeth H.P. Haley, Feb. 22, 1909 (dec. Sept. 5, 1946); children—Louise L., Marjorie E. (Mrs. Richard C. Rockwell); m. 2d Rachael Butler Holbrook, Aug. 31, 1949. With Horn Supply Co., Leominster 1892, sec., gen. mgr., 1897 1917; treas. Paton Mfg. Co., Leominster, 1899-1912; established with A.S. Paton and Ludwig Stross the Viscoloid Co., 1901, sec. treas., 1901-12; sec. treas., gen. mgr. Sterling Comb Co., 1904-12; sec. treas. Harvard Novelty Co., 1906-12; pres. Viscoloid Co., 1918-25, sold to du Pont, v.p. du Pont Viscoloid Co., after 1925. Founder Merchant's Nat. Bank; v.p. Independent Lock and Lockwood Hardwood Co.; trustee Leominster Savs. Bank; dir. U.S. Rubber Co., Boston Edison Co., Mass. Mutual Life Ins. Co., Safety Fund Nat. Bank, Merchants Nat. Bank of Boston, Boston and Me. Rr. Trustee Cushing Acad., Northeastern U. Mayor city of Leominster Mass., 1926-30. Mem. Boston and Leominster C. of Cs., Asso. Industries of Mass., Nat. Assn. Mfrs., Isaak Walton League, Mass. Audubon Soc., Nat. Geog. Assn., Wildlife Management Inst., N.E. Council. Founded and donated site for Leominster Hosp. Republican (mem. Mass. Club; Worcester Co. League; del. Nat. Conv., 1926-30). Clubs: Algonquin, Fay and Home Market, Oak Hill Monoosnock, Worcester Country, Eastern, Corinthian, New Bedford Yacht, Navy League. The Links. Home: 245 Lindell Av., Leominster, Mass. Deceased Dec. 26, 1949.

DOYLE, Howard L., lawyer; b. Aug. 26, 1894; s. Frank and Catherine (Galvin) D.; LL.B., Georgetown U., 1917; m. Mary Finn, Sept. 1931; children—Patrick Finn, Katharine Ellen. Began practice law, 1921; became mem. law firm Le Forgee, Samuels & Miller; U.S. dist. atty., Southern Dist. of Ill., since Apr.

1935. Mem. Ill. Legislature, 1931-35. Pres. U.S. Attorneys Conf. Assn. since 1941. Mem. Decatur Bar Assn. Home: Decatur, Ill. Address: U.S. Court House, Springfield, Ill. Died Aug. 20, 1954.

DOYNE, John James, educator; b. Farmville, Va., Oct. 28, 1858; s. John and Agnes (Stratton) D.; prep. edn. high sch., Farmville; U. Va.; m. Ida Beard, Nov. 1, 1882. Tchr. pub. schs., Lonoke, Ark., 1879-88, Ft. Smith, 1888-90, Lonoke, 1890-9; county examiner, Lonoke Co., 14 yrs., Sebastian Co., 1 yr.; state supt. schs., Ark., 1898-02, 1906-8; pres. State Normal Sch., Conway, Ark., 1908—. Editor Arkansas Teacher. Mem. N.E.A., Southern Ednl. Assn. Democrat. Baptist. Mason. Home: Conway, Ark. Deceased.

DRAGER, Walter Louis (drā'gẽr), civil engr.; b. Hamilton, Ill., Feb. 23, 1886; s. Charles and Lesa P. (Winters) D.; student U. Cal., 1905-06, Cornell U., 1906-09; m. Alice E. Sickly, Feb. 29, 1908; children—Carl (dec.), Donald G., Susan Winters (Mrs. Kenneth K. Lawshe), Alice Anne (Mrs. Macon J. Fussell). Asst. city engr., Auburn, N.Y., 1909-10; asst. to cons. engr. Johnstown, Pa., 1910-11; asst. city engr., Schenectady, N.Y., 1912-13; asst. to constrn. engr. Grand Valley Dam, U.S. Reclamation Service, Grand Junction, Colo., 1914-15; asst. engr. Pub. Utilities Commn. on Denver water supply investigation, 1915-16; asst. engr. in charge investigations for Castle Peak Project, Utah Reconnaissance, U.S. Reclamation Service, 1917-20; office engr. U.S. Reclamation Service, Denver, 1920-22; engr. Bear River div. Salt Lake Basin Invesgitations, Utah, 1922-26; resident engr. J. G. White Co., Aguascalientes, Mexico, 1926-29; field engr. Stevens & Wood, Inc., 1929-31; asst. div. engr. N.J. State Water Policy Commn., Trenton, 1931-32; engr. and acting chief engr. RFC, 1932-37, chief engr. same and Def. Plant Corp., 1937-47, ret. 1947. Mem. Am. Soc. C.E., Theta Xi. Democrat. Mason. Home: 1919 Maine Av., Long Beach, Cal. Died Aug. 10, 1953; buried Forest Lawn Meml. Park.

DRAKE, Jeannette May, librarian; b. Argenta, Ill., Oct. 31, 1878; d. John Lewis and Aura Belle (Dickey) D.; B.L.S., U. Ill., 1903. Library organizer for Wis. Free Library Commn., 1903-05; librarian, Pub. Library, Jacksonville, Ill., 1905-08; instr., Wis. Library Sch. (U. Wis.), 1908-10; librarian, Pub. Library, Sioux City, Ia., Sept. 1910-Sept. 1917; prin. circulating dept. Los Angeles Pub. Library, 1917-19; librarian Pasadena (Calif.) Pub. Library, 1919—. Mem. Ia. Federation Women's Clubs (chmn. state art com., 1915-17), Ia. Library Assn. (pres. 1915-16), Cal. Library Assn. (pres. 1923-24), A.L.A.; Pasadena Civic League. Clubs: Pasadena College Woman's, Zonta. Given citation by Am. Legion, Pasadena, for promotion of intellectual freedom, 1934. Home: 3919 E. California St., Pasadena, Cal. Deceased.

DRAKE, Lauren J., tank car co. exec.; b. Keokuk, Iowa, Aug. 27, 1880; s. Lauren J. and Mary (Anthony) D.; grad. Shattuck Sch., Faribault, Minn., 1900; m. Edith Love, 1903; children—Mrs. Eliza Drake Lamberton, Mary Drake Freer, Julia Drake Holinger; m. 2d, Lorraine T. Ming, 1947. Pres. Galena-Signal Oil Co., 7 yrs.; pres. Union Tank Car Co., 1926-46, chmn. bd., 1946-52. Regional dir. Boy Scouts Am. Member of Bd. of Managers, Illinois Society, Sons of American Revolution. Clubs: Union League, Chicago Yacht, (Chicago). Home: 1550 N. State Pkwy., Chgo.; also Point Clear, Ala. Died Jan. 7, 1953.

DRANT, Patricia (Hart), dermatologist; b. Grenola, Kan., Jan. 27, 1895; d. James Lafayette and Nora Coombs (Demmitt) Hart; B.S., U. of Kan., 1918; M.D., Univ. of Pa., 1920; grad. student dermatology, U. of Pa. Graduate Hosp., Phila., 1921-22, St. Louis Hosp., Paris, 1924-25, Vienna, 1925, Budapest, 1925; m. Reginald Drant, Sept. 1, 1920 (divorced); m. 2d, William Warren Rhodes, exec. Du Pont Co., Aug. 18, 1934 (divorced 1949); married 3d James S. Collins, June 14, 1952. Dermatologist Abington Mem. Hosp., Pa., Methodist Hosp., Phila., Woman's Hosp., Phila. Diplomate of Am. Acad. Dermatology and Syphilology. Fellow A.A.A.S.; mem. Am. Acad. Dermatology and Syphilology, Am. Med. Assn., Phila. Dermatol. Soc., Phila. County Med. Soc., Alpha Omicron Pi. Club: Art Alliance. Home: "Rokeby," Westtown, Pa. Died Oct. 3, 1955; buried East Laurel Hill Cemetery, Phila.

DRAPER, Alfred Pearman, lawyer; b. Baldwinsville, N.Y., Dec. 29, 1891; s. Russell J. and Emily Ena (Pearman) D.; LL.B., Valparaiso (Ind.) U., 1922; m. Florence Leontine Porter, May 24, 1923; children—Donna Norene (Mrs. William J. Welter), Porter Russell. Admitted to Ind. bar, 1921 and since practiced in Gary; partner Draper & Eichhorn, 1943—; referee in bankruptcy, 1942-47. Mem. Am. Ind., Gary bar assns., Am. Judicature Soc., The Indiana Soc., Nat. Assn. Referees in Bankruptcy, Sigma Delta Kappa. Presbyn. Mason. Club: Gary Country. Home: 574 Monroe St. Office: 504 Broadway, Gary, Ind. Died July 28, 1955; buried Ridge Lawn Cemetery, Gary, Ind.

DRAPER, Ernest Gallaudet, mfr.; b. Washington, D.C., May 15, 1885; s. Amos Galusha and Luella Bell (Merrill) D.; B.A., Amherst 1906; M.A., 1936; LL.D., Gallaudet, 1951; m. Mary W. Childs, Feb. 7, 1911; children—William Hamlin Childs (dec.), Doris Bartlett, Mary; m. 2d, Theodora Trowbridge, Dec. 4, 1926. Began as clerk, New York, 1906; pres. Am. Creosoting Co., 1912-20; treas. and v.p. The Hills Bros. Co., packers Dromedary dates and other food products, 1920-35; asst. sec. of Commerce, 1935-38; mem. Bd. Govs., Fed. Reserve System since 1938; formerly v.p. The Dromedary Co. of Calif.; dir. Scoville Canning Co. Lt. sr. grade, U.S.N.R.F., 1918-19; asst. navigator U.S.S. Sierra, 1918. Mem. N.Y. State Commn. on Unemployment, 1930-35, mem. N.Y. City Art Commn., 1924-27; mem. N.Y. State Advisory Com. on Minimum Wage; apptd. mem. Nat. Labor Bd., 1934; apptd. mem. Business Advisory Council, Dept. of Commerce, 1935; mem. executive com. on Commercial Policy, 1936-38; mem. President's Com. on Crop Insurance, 1936; chmn. govt. unit, Am. Red Cross War Fund Drive, 1944. Mem. bd. dirs., Children's Hosp., Washington, D.C. Mem. bd. trustees Gallaudet Coll., Washington; dir. People's Inst., N.Y. City, 1920-35. Mem. Am. Assn. for Labor Legislation (pres. 1930-32), Mchts. Assn., New York (com. on industrial relations 1932-35), Am. Econ. Assn., Acad. Polit. Science, Alpha Delta Phi, Phi Beta Kappa. Presbyn. Clubs: University, Amherst; Metropolitan (Washington). Author: Navigating the Ship, 1920. Author with others Can Business Prevent Unemployment, 1925; and various publs. Home: 2408 California St. N.W., Washington. Retired 1951. Died Apr. 30, 1954; buried Woodlawn Cemetery, N.Y.

DRAPER, Ruth, actress (monologuist); b. in New York, N.Y., Dec. 2, 1884; d. Dr. William H. and Ruth (Dana) Draper, the fifth of six children—g.d. Charles A. Dana, early and famous editor of the New York Sun; ed. private tutors and one year at private school; hon. A.M., Hamilton Coll., 1926; Dr. Fine Arts, University of Me., 1941; L.H.D., Smith Coll., 1947; LL.D., U. Edinburgh, 1951, University Cambridge, Eng., 1954. First appearances, professionally, were at schools, colls., clubs, etc., 1911. In 1918 spent 7 months giving performances at A.E.F. camps in France; Aeolian Hall, London, 1920; West End Theater (alone) several weeks, 1924; toured the U.S.A., 1924-28; eighteen consecutive weeks in Comedy Theater, New York, 1928-29; toured South Africa, 1935; world tour, including Ceylon, India, Burma, Java, Australia and New Zealand, 1938; South America, 1940; Canada and the U.S.A., 1940-41, British Isles, Europe, United States, 1942—. Repertoire consists of 36 original monologues, including 57 characters. Translated from the Italian of Lauro de Bosis, poetic drama, Icaro (with preface by Gilbert Murray), 1933. Address: 66 E. 79th St., New York, N.Y., or Dark Harbor, Me. Died Dec. 30, 1956.

DREFS, Arthur George, business statesman; b. Buffalo, April 5, 1888; s. Charles Adam and Elizabeth (Farber) D.; B.S. in Econ., U. of Pa., 1909; m. Clara Artemisa Newman, Mar. 19, 1921. With Miller, Franklin, Stevenson & Co., N.Y. City, 1909-12; v.p. Miller, Franklin, Basset & Co., 1912-17; pres. Drefs, Cummings & Drefs, Detroit, 1919-20, dissolved 1921; v.p. and dir. McQuay-Norris Mfg. Co., St. Louis, 1921-23, sec.-treas. and dir., 1923-28, v.p., treas. and dir., 1929-44, pres. since April 1945, chmn. bd. since Apr. 1950. Sec.-treas. King Quality Products Co., 1928-44, pres. since 1945. Dir. Miss. Valley Trust Co., since 1940, Koken Cos., Inc., King Quality Products Co., St. Louis Pub. Service Co., Automotive & Aviation Parts Mfg. Inc., 1949. Representative Automotive and Aviation Parts Mfrs. on Automotive Safety Found., 1939-40, 1944-45; dir. Nat. Standard Parts Assn., 1938-40, Automotive Parts and Equipment Mfrs. Assn., 1938-40, 1944-45; dir. Nat. Mfrs. Assn. since 1943 (regional v.p. 1944, 47, 48; nat. v.p., 1949; mem. exec. com., 1944, 49); nat. councilor U.S. Chamber of Commerce; chmn. bd. St. Louis C. of C., 1944-45 (exec. com. 1944-47); mem., sr. adv. com. St. Louis Co. C. of C.; trustee Automotive Safety Found., 1949. Chief Administrative Br. Motor Vehicle Div., 1917-19; chmn. Metropolitan St. Louis Com. on Preparedness for Nat. Defense, 1940-42; mem. (1941-47), chief (1947-48) St. Louis Dist. Ordnance Adv. Bd.; Industry Mem. Mayor's (St. Louis) Labor Mgr. Com.; mem. exec. com. St. Louis-St. Louis County March of Dimes Campaign, 1947-48; mem. exec. com. St. Louis and St. Louis County chapter Nat. Found. for Infantile Paralysis, Inc.; mem. exec. com. Small Arms and Small Arms Ammunition Div., 1946-48, Army Ordnance. Trustee Southern Methodist Univ., St. Johns Meth. Ch., Nat. Soc. Indsl. Assoc., 1949; dir. Central Inst. for Deaf, Municipal Theatre Assn. of St. Louis, Corporate Bd. of Group Hosp. Service (1945-48), Adult Edn. Council of Greater St. Louis (1945-46), Barnes Hosp.; bd. govs. Automobile Club of Mo.; mem. president's council St. Louis U. since 1950. Mem. Pan-American Soc., Am. Ordnance Assn., Washington (mem.-at-large; dir. St. Louis Dist.). Methodist. Clubs: Noonday, Racquet, Bogey (St. Louis); Detroit. Home: 39 Glen Eagles Dr., St. Louis Country Club Grounds, Clayton 24, Mo. Office: 2320 Marconi Av., St. Louis 10. Died Nov. 1, 1950; buried Bellefontaine Cemetery, St. Louis.

DRESBACH, Melvin, physiologist; b. Hallsville, O., July 8, 1874; s. Harvey and Amanda (Orr) D.; B.Sc., Ohio State U., 1897, M.Sc., 1900; M.D., Ohio Med. U., 1903; spl. work, Woods Hole, Mass., summer 1903, Würzburg, Germany, 1904, Leyden, 1911; m. Sylvia Reedy, Dec. 28, 1899. Asst. in physiology Ohio State U., 1897-1902, instr., 1902-05; instr. physiology Cornell Med. Coll., 1908-09, asst. prof. pharmacology, 1909-10, asst. prof. physiology Albany Med. Coll. (Union U.), 1918-36; now engaged in research, U. Pa. Mem. Am. Physiol. Soc., Soc. Exptl. Biology and Medicine, A.A.A.S., Sigma Xi, Nu Sigma Nu. Democrat. Contbr. to med. publs. Home: 817 Madison Av., Albany, N.Y. Died Oct. 15, 1946; buried Chillocothee, O.

DRESCHER, Theodore Bausch, bus. exec.; b. Rochester, N.Y., Apr. 22, 1894; s. William Alexander Edward and Anna (Bausch) D.; student Rochester Inst. Tech., 1907-10, Worcester Acad., 1910-13, Cornell U., 1914-15; m. Rolena Utrich, Apr. 30, 1919; children—Ann Elizabeth, Marjorie. With Bausch & Lomb Optical Co. since 1917, asst. supt., 1917-18, supt., 1918-21, works mgr., 1921-22, vice pres. in charge of manufacture, 1932-50, vice pres. in charge of process development since 1950. Dir. Rochester Gen. Hosp. Mem. Phi Kappa Psi. Clubs: Country, Genesee, Valley, Cornell (Rochester). Home: 2615 East Av., Rochester 10. Office: 635 St. Paul St., Rochester, N.Y. Died Feb. 22, 1953.

DRESDEN, Arnold, mathematician; b. Amsterdam, Netherlands, Nov. 23, 1882; s. Mark and Anna (Meyerson) D.; student U. of Amsterdam, 1901-03; S M., U. of Chicago, 1906, Ph.D., 1909; m. Louise Schwendener, June 12, 1907; 1 son, Mark Kenyon. Came to U.S., 1903, naturalized citizen, 1912. Teacher of mathematics, University High Sch., Chicago, 1906-09; instr. mathematics, 1909-12, asst. prof., 1912-21, asso. prof., 1921-27, U. of Wis.; prof. mathematics, Swarthmore Coll., 1927—. Service with A.R.C. in France, Sept. 1918-June 1919. Fellow A.A.A.S.; mem. Math. Assn. America (pres. 1933-35), Am. Math. Soc., Académie of Macon, France, Société Mathématique de France. Author: Plane Trigonometry, 1921; Solid Analytical Geometry and Determinants, 1930; An Invitation to Mathematics, 1936; Introduction to the Calculus, 1940. Home: 606 Elm Av., Swarthmore, Pa. Died Apr. 10, 1954; buried Cumberland Cemetery, Media, Pa.

DRESSER, Horatio Willis, author; b. Yarmouth, Me., Jan. 15, 1866; s. Julius A. and Annetta G. D.; A.B., Harvard, 1895, A.M., 1904, Ph.D., 1907; m. Alice Mae Reed (A.B., Wellesley, 1893), Mar. 17, 1898; children—Dorothea, Malcolm. Telegraph operator and railroad agt. in Calif., 1879-1882; stenographer, reporter, proofreader, bookkeeper, Boston, 1885-88; editor and publisher Journal of Practical Metaphysics, 1896-98, and of The Higher Law, 1899-1902; asst. in philosophy, Harvard, 1903-11; prof. philosophy, Ursinus Coll., Collegeville, Pa., 1912-13; instructor church history, New Church Theological School, Cambridge, Mass., 1913-14. Lecturer on practical philosophy, 1893-1912. Consultant in psychology Associated Clinic, Brooklyn, New York, 1932—. Author: The Power of Silence, 1895; The Perfect Whole, 1896; The Heart of It, 1896; In Search of a Soul, 1897; Voices of Hope, 1898; Methods and Problems of Spiritual Healing, 1899; Voices of Freedom, 1900; Living by the Spirit, 1900; Education and the Philosophical Ideal, 1900; The Christ Ideal, 1901; A Book of Secrets, 1902; Man and the Divine Order, 1903; Health and the Inner Life, 1906; The Greatest Truth, 1907; The Philosophy of the Spirit, 1908; A Physician to the Soul, 1908; A Message to the Well, 1910; Human Efficiency, 1912; The Religion of the Spirit in Modern Life, 1914; Handbook of the New Thought, 1917; The Victorious Faith, 1917; On the Threshold of the Spiritual World, 1919; A History of the New Thought Movement, 1919; The Open Vision, 1920; Spiritual Health and Healing, 1922; Psychology in Theory and Application, 1924; Ethics in Theory and Application, 1925; History of Ancient and Medieval Philosophy, 1926; History of Modern Philosophy, 1928; Outlines of the Psychology of Religion, 1929; Knowing and Helping People, 1933. Editor: Spirit of the New Thought, 1917; The Quimby Manuscripts, 1921. Home: Flower Lane, Marshfield, Mass. Office: 50 Monroe Pl., Bklyn. Died Mar. 30, 1954.

DREW, Charles Richard, surgeon; b. Washington, June 3, 1904; s. Richard Thomas and Nora R. (Burrell) D.; grad. Amherst Coll., 1926; M.D., C.M., Faculty Med., McGill U., 1933; Med.D.Sc., Columbia Coll. Phys. and Surg., 1940; hon. D.Sc., Va. State, 1945, Amherst Coll., 1947; m. Minnie Lenore Robbins, Sept. 23, 1939; children—Bebe Roberta, Charlene Rosella, Rhea Sylvia, Charles Richard. Extern Royal Victoria Hosp., Montreal, Can., 1932-33; intern Gen. Hosp., Montreal, Can., 1933-34, resident in medicine, 1934-35; instr. in pathology Howard U., Washington, 1935-36, asst. in surgery, 1935-36, prof. surgery, head dept., 1941—; Rockefeller fellow in surgery Coll. Phys. and Surg. Columbia, also resident in surgery Presbyn. Hosp., N.Y.C., 1938-40; chief surgeon and chief of staff

Freedman's Hosp., Washington, med. dir. 1946-47; surg. cons. ETO (Army), 1949. Dir. first plasma div. Blood Transfusion Assn., supplying plasma to British, 1940-41; first dir. A.R.C. Blood Bank, supplying plasma to U.S. forces, 1941. Diplomate Am. Bd. Surgery, becaeme examiner, 1942. Recipient Springarn award, 1944, dir. D.C. chpt. Nat. Founds. Polyomyelitis, 1946, D.C. Soc. for Crippled Children. Mem. Am.-Soviet Science Com., 1944. Home: 328 College St. N.W. Office: Dept. of Surgery, Howard U., Washington. Died Apr. 1, 1950.

DREYFUS, Camille Edouard, corp. executive; b. Basel, Switzerland, Nov. 11, 1878; s. Abraham and Henrietta (Wahl) D.; grad. U. Basel, Switzerland, 1902, M.A., Ph.D.; Sorbonne, Paris, 1906, m. Jean Tennyson, 1931. Chmn. dir. Celanese Corp. Am.; pres., dir. of Canadian Celanese, Ltd., Montreal; mng. dir. British Celanese, Ltd., London. Trustee Pestalozzi Found. Decorated Officer of French Legion of Honor. Mem. Am. Chem. Soc., N.Y. State C. of C., Swiss Benevolent Soc. (adv. bd.). Mem. Congregation Emanu-El. Clubs: Manhattan, Chemists (N.Y.). Office: 180 Madison Av., N.Y.C. 16. Died Sept. 27, 1956; buried Salem Fields Cemetery.

DREYFUS, Carl, pub.; b. Boston, July 26, 1876; s. Jacob and Emilie (Weil) D.; student Boston Latin Sch., 1887-91, Harvard, 1891-94; m. Lilian Shuman, 1899 (died 1913); m. 2d, Sylvia Goulston, Aug. 19, 1914 (died 1942); children—Emile, Carl and Edward G. m. 3d, Edna Wetzler. Partner Jacob Dreyfus & Sons, shirt mfrs., 1900-23; pres. Dreyfus Properties, Inc.; mem. bd. trustees Boston Home Savings Bank; pub. Boston Record-American. Trustee Simmons Coll., Northeastern U., Boston City Hosp.; dir. Franklin Inst. Jewish religion. Mason. Clubs: Harvard, City, University (Boston); Harvard (N.Y.C.); Kernwood Country. Home: 312 Dartmouth St., Boston. Died Mar. 29, 1953.

DRINKER, Cecil Kent, physician; b. Philadelphia, Pa., Mar. 17, 1887; s. Henry Sturgis and Aimee Ernesta (Beaux) D.; B.S., Haverford College, 1908, D.Sc. (hon.), 1933; M.D., Univ. of Pa. Med. School, 1913; A.M. (hon.) Harvard, 1942; m. Katherine Livingston Rotan, Sept. 7, 1910; children—Anne, Cecil. Interneships and residence in hosps., 1913-17, became acting head dept. physiology, Harvard Univ. Med. Sch., 1917-18, asst. prof. physiology, 1918-19, asso. prof., 1919-23; sec. Com. on Indsl. Hygiene, 1918-22; mng. editor Jour. of Indsl. Hygiene, 1919-32; asst. to visiting physicians Boston City Hosp., 1922-24; prof. physiology, Harvard Univ. Sch. Pub. Health, 1923-48, asst. dean, 1924-35, dean, 1935-42; associate editor Jour. of Indsl. Hygiene and Toxicology, 1932-48; lecturer in physiology, Cornell Med. College, 1948-49; consulting physiologist U.S. Navy since 1951. Emeritus mem. American Soc. for Clin. Investigation; mem. Assn. of Am. Physicians, Am. Physiol. Soc., Royal Danish Acad. Sci. and Letters, Phi Beta Kappa, Alpha Omega Alpha, Sigma Xi. Republican. Home: Sippewissett Rd. Address: Box 502 Falmouth, Mass. Died Apr. 14, 1956; buried Phila.

DRISCOLL, Charles Benedict, editor, writer; b. Wichita, Kan., Oct. 19, 1885; s. Florence and Ellen (Brown) D.; A.B., Friends U., Wichita, Kan., 1912, Litt.D., 1937; spl. work U. Kan., U. Minn., New Sch. for Social Research, N.Y.C.; m. Genevieve Peterson, Oct. 8, 1918; children—Mary Ellen (Mrs. John Parker McKee), Patricia Virginia (Mrs. Daniel Schadle). Reporter for Wichita Eagle, 1912-13, Omaha Daily News, 1914-15; editorial writer and dept. editor St. Paul Daily News, 1916-17; mail service editor United Press Assn., N.Y.C., 1918-19; editor Wichita Eagle, 1919-23; asso. editor Cleve. Press, 1924; asso. editor, McNaught's Monthly, N.Y., 1925-27; exec. editor McNaught Syndicate, 1925-38. Mem. Will Rogers Meml. Commn. Mem. Authors' League Am., Pi Gamma Mu. Clubs: Players, Dutch Treat (N.Y.C.); Nat. Press (Washington). Author: Doubloons, the Story of Buried Treasure, 1930; Treasure Aboard, 1931; Driscoll's Book of Pirates, 1934; The Life of O. O. McIntyre, 1938; Pirates Ahoy!, 1941; Kansas Irish, 1943; Country Jake, 1946; also syndicated series of daily poems, 1916-18; Pirates Ahoy (a series of pirate tales), 1927-28; The World and All, daily editorial feature; daily column New York Day by Day, succeeding O. O. McIntyre in 1938; contbr. mags. Originator of school page, now a widely accepted feature of newspapers. Lecturer; radio broadcaster of pirate and treasure tales. Travels widely, following treasure clues; owns large library devoted to treasure and pirates; recognized as leading authority on these subjects; author Pieces of Eight, daily story strip syndicated to 100 newspapers, 1933-36. Home: 363 Glenbrook Av., Yonkers, N.Y. Office: Lincoln Bldg., N.Y.C. Died Jan. 15, 1951.

DRISCOLL, Denis J., ex-congressman; b. N. Lawrence, N.Y., Mar. 27, 1871; ed. Lawrenceville Acad., State Normal and Tng. Sch., Potsdam, N.Y., studied law privately; m. Elizabeth Biglan; 2 daughters. Prin. St. Mary's (Pa.) High Sch., 4 yrs.; admitted to Pa. bar, 1898, since practiced in St. Marys; sr. partner Driscoll, Gregory & Coppolo; U.S. atty. for Western Dist, Pa., 1920-21; mem. 74th Congress (1935-37), 20th Pa., Dist.; apptd. mem. (1937) Pa. Pub. Utility Commn. by Gov. Earle for 10 yrs. (chmn.), resigned 1940 to accept appointment by U.S. Ct., So. Dist. N.Y., as one of two trustees of bankrupt Asso. Gas & Electric Corp.; bankruptcy closed, trustees discharged 1946; elected a presdl. elector from Pa., 1944. Served as 2d lt. 16th Pa. Inf. in P.R., Spanish-Am. War; mem. Pa. N.G., 3 yrs. Pres. St. Marys Sch. Bd., 25 yrs. Del. Nat. Dem. Convs., 1916, 20, 24, 28, 52; chmn. Dem. State, 1905, mem. 1899-1922. Mem. Am., Pa., Elk County bar assns., United Spanish War Vets., Vets. Fgn. Wars. Address: 139 N. St. Michael St., St. Marys, Pa. Died Jan. 18, 1958.

DRISCOLL, Joseph, journalist; b. St. Louis, Mo., Jan. 5, 1902; s. Daniel Francis and Felicitas (Delaney) D.; ed. public and private schools; m. Eleanor McNamara, Dec. 27, 1930. Began on St. Louis Times and St. Louis Post-Dispatch; joined New York Herald Tribune 1930, covered Lindbergh Kidnaping case and trial of Hauptmann, chief corr. in charge London office, 1935-39, covered death of King George V, accession and abdication of King Edward VIII, coronation of King George VI, and the successive crises leading up to the Second World War; chief Washington corr., 1939-41, war corr. traveling through many lands, with Halsey and Nimitz in Pacific, and Patton across Europe, 1941-45; Post Dispatch nat. corr. since 1947. Chmn. Third Army War Correspondents. Mem. American War Correspondents Association (first president). Author: Dock Walloper, 1933; War Discovers Alaska, 1943; Pacific Victory, 1945. Contbr. to mags. Office: St. Louis. Died May 7, 1954.

DRISCOLL, Louise, writer; b. Poughkeepsie, N.Y., Jan. 15, 1875; d. John Leonard and Louise (Dezendorf) D.; ed. pub. schs., Catskill, N.Y., German and Italian under pvt. tutors. Began writing at 16; since writer novelettes, short stories, etc.; was awarded prize of $100 by Poetry, Chgo., for poem, The Metal Cheeks, published 1914. Presbyn. Mem. Poetry Soc. Am. Author: The Garden of the West (poems), 1922; Garden Grace (poems), 1924. Lectr.; librarian Catskill Pub. Library. Home: 120 Broad St., Catskill, N.Y. Died July 24, 1957; buried Jefferson Rural Cemetery, Catskill.

DRISCOLL, William H., v.p. staff Carrier Corp.; b. Jersey City, 1879. K.C. Home: 50 Glenwood Av., Jersey City, N.J. Office: Carrier Corp., 300 S. Geddes St., Syracuse 1, N.Y. Died Sept. 7, 1950.

DRIVER, Samuel Marion, judge; b. Wamic, Ore., May 22, 1892; s. Francis Marion and Adelia (Lucas) D.; LL.B., U. of Wash., 1916; LL.M., Georgetown U., 1926; m. Sue Glascock, Mar. 21, 1922; children—Garth Edward, Janeil. Admitted to Wash. bar, 1916; prosecuting attorney Douglas County, Washington, 1922-23; prosecuting attorney for Chelan County, Washington, 1935-37; U.S. atty. for Eastern Dist. of Wash., 1937-40; judge Wash. State Supreme Court 1940-46; judge U.S. Dist. Court, eastern dist. of Wash. since Apr. 1946. Mem. Wash. Judicial Council, 1935-37; mem. adv. com. of U.S. Supreme Ct. on Fed. Civil Procedure, 1947-56; member of the Supreme Court committee on administration of criminal law, 1956—. Served in 91st Division, U.S. Army, 1918-19; served with U.S. Army, Judge Advocate Generals Dept., Nov. 1942-Jan. 1946. Mem. Am. Bar Assn., Am. Judicature Soc., Am. Law Inst., Kappa Sigma, Phi Delta Phi. Democrat. Home: Route 1, Pasco. Wash Office: Federal Bldg., Spokane, Wash. Died Sept. 1958.

DROKE, George Wesley, mathematician; b. Morgan Co., Ind., Sept. 26, 1854; s. George and Diana (Etter) D.; A.B., U. Ark., 1880, A.M., 1884, LL.D., 1929; U. Mich., Johns Hopkins, U. Chgo., brief periods; LL.D., Hendrix Coll., 1919; m. Josephine Campbell, Sept. 24, 1879 (died 1886); children—George Prentice, Leila Ruth (dec.), Marvin Josephine; m. 2d, Inez James, Aug. 18, 1887 (died Apr. 1931); children—Albert Hill (dec.), Mary Inez, Louise Blanche, James Walling (adopted); m. 3d, Mrs. Belle Clayton Fenner, Feb. 20, 1932. Asst., 1st asst. tchr., prep. dept. U. Ark., 1880-85; head dept. of English, Coronal Inst., San Marcos, Tex., 1885-86; prin. high sch., Bentonville, Ark., 1886-87; with U. Ark., 1887-1929, prof. mathematics, astronomy, 1897-1929, emeritus prof., 1929—; dean Coll. Arts and Scis., 1915-25. Mem. Math. Assn. Am., Ark. State Tchrs'. Assn. (pres. 1910), Phi Beta Kappa (1932). Methodist. Home: Fayetteville, Ark. Died Sept. 4, 1936.

DROUGHT, Henry Patrick (Harry), lawyer; b. San Antonio, Tex., June 16, 1893; s. Henry Patrick and Ethel (Tunstall) D.; prep. student St. Mary's Coll., 1905, St. Anthony's Coll., San Antonio, 1909; LL.B., U. of Tex., 1915; LL.D. (hon.) St. Edward's Univ., Austin, Tex., 1938; m. Kathleen Lukin; children—Patrick, Mary (Mrs. Karl Streiber), James Lukin, Thomas. Engaged in active practice of law, since 1915; state dir. for Tex. Nat. Emergency Council, 1934-37, N.R.A., 1934, Fed. Housing Adminstrn., 1934; state adminstr. Work Projects Adminstrn., 1935-43; mng. partner H. P. Drought & Co. (investments, established 1883), 1917—; dir. Dallas Federal Reserve Bank. Chairman of the board of commissioners Housing Authority of the City of San Antonio. Mem. Regional Loyalty Board, U.S. Civil Service Commn., Region 14, 1948-53. Chmn. Dem. Congl. Exec. Com., 14th Tex. dist., 1930-32. Chmn. bd. trustees Our Lady of the Lake Coll. Mem. Am. Bar Assn., Am. Judicature Soc., State Bar of Texas, San Antonio Bar Assn., Texas Philos. Soc., Kappa Sigma, Phi Delta Phi. Hon. mem. La Asociacion Nacional De Abogados (Mexico). Order of the Alamo. Club: San Antonio Country. Author: Federal Tax Liens in Tex. (Texas Law Review), 1924. Home: 123 Charles Rd., San Antonio 9. Office: Alamo National Bldg., San Antonio. Died July, 1957; buried San Antonio.

DRUM, Hugh Aloysius, business exec.; b. Fort Brady, Mich., Sept. 19, 1879; s. Capt. John (U.S.A.) and Margaret (Desmond) D.; father killed at Battle of San Juan, Santiago, Cuba; honor grad. Army Sch. of the Line, 1911; grad. Army Staff Coll., 1912; A.B., Boston College, 1921; hon. Sc.D., Manhattan College, 1940; honorory LL.D., Boston Coll., 1923, St. Lawrence Univ., Fordham Univ., 1941, Loyola U., Columbia Univ., 1942, Rutgers Univ., New York Univ., 1943; hon. D.M.S., Pa. Military Coll., 1941, Georgetown Univ., 1943; University of Delaware, 1944; m. Mary Reaume, Oct. 14, 1903; 1 dau., Anna Carroll (Mrs. Thomas H. Johnson). Commd. 2d lt. 12th U.S. Inf., Sept. 9, 1898; promoted through grades to maj., May 1917; lt. col. (temp.), Aug. 5, 1917; col. (temp.), July 30, 1918; brig. gen. (temp.), Oct. 1, 1918; brig. gen. (temp.), Sept. 21, 1920-Mar. 4, 1921; brig. gen., U.S. Army, Dec. 6, 1922; maj. gen., U.S. Army, Dec. 1, 1931; lt. gen., Aug. 5, 1939. In Philippine Islands, 1898-1901, participating in Philippine Islands Insurrection; participated in campaign against Moros, also Lake Lanao Campaign; recommended for brevet as captain; aide de camp to General Baldwin; aide and adjutant general, Southwestern Division until 1906; again in Philippine Islands, 1908-10; instructor, director and assistant commandant Command and General Staff School, 1912-14; duty on the Mexican border, 1914; served as assistant chief of staff under Gen. Funston at Vera Cruz; asst. instr. in mil. art at army schs., later aide to Gen. Funston until latter's death, Feb. 19, 1917; asst. to chief of staff under Gen. Pershing, when latter succeeded Gen. Funston; detailed to Gen. Staff, June 4, 1917, and accompanied Gen. Pershing to France, as asst. chief of staff; chief of staff 1st Army, A.E.F., July 4, 1918-Apr. 1919; chief of staff Services of Supply, A.E.F., Apr.-July 1919; remanded to regular rank of maj. of inf.; dir. Army Sch. of the Line since 1919; comdt. General Service Schools, 1920-21; assigned to comd. coast and air defenses, 2d Corps Area, 1922; asst. chief of staff, in charge operations and training, Washington, 1923-26; comd. 1st Inf. Brigade, 1st Div., 1926-27; assigned to comd. 1st Div. Oct. 15, 1927; apptd. insp. gen., U.S. Army, rank of maj. gen., Jan. 29, 1930; comdr. 5th Corps Area and First Army, 1931-33; permanent rank of major general, Dec. 1, 1931; apptd. dep. chief of staff, Feb. 23, 1933; comdr. of Hawaiian Department, Honolulu, 1935-37; comd. Second Army and Sixth Corps Area, Chicago, Ill., 1937-38; comdg. First Army and Second Corps Area, Governors Island, New York, since 1938; appointed lt. gen., U.S. Army, Aug. 5, 1939; comdg. gen. Eastern Defense Command and First Army, Nov. 1940-Sept. 1943; apptd. lt. gen. N.Y. State Guard, 1943; apptd. chairman N.Y. State Veterans Commn., 1944; pres. Empire State, Inc. since 1944. Awarded silver star "for gallantry in action" at Battle of Bayan, Philippine Islands. Distinguished Service medal, with cluster; Commdr. Legion of Honor, and Croix de Guerre with 2 palms (French); Commander Order of Crown (Belgian); Commander Order of Crown (Italian), Comd. (with star) Royal Order of St. Olaf (Norway); Spanish War, Philippine Campaign, Mexican Service (Vera Cruz Expdn.), Mexican Border Service medals, Victory Medal with 4 battle clasps, Am. Defense and Am. Theatre ribbons; Medal of Merit, 1943. Roman Catholic. Mem. Am. Legion, Loyal Legion, Knights of Malta, Soc. of Friendly Sons of St. Patrick (N.Y.), Assn. Ex-members Squadron A (hon. 1942), Mil. Intelligence Res. Sec. (2d Service Command), Scabbard and Blade, Council on Foreign Relations, N.Y. Chamber of Commerce, N.Y. Soc., Mil. and Naval Officers of World Wars, 1944, St. Nicholas Soc. of the City of N.Y. Clubs: Union, University, India House, Overseas Press, Downtown Athletic, Lotos, Rotary, Officers of Army and Navy, Chevy Chase (Washington). Address: Empire State Bldg., N.Y.C. Died Oct. 3, 1951.

DRUMMOND, Alexander M., teacher; b. Auburn, N.Y., July 15, 1884; s. Robert Loudon and Anna E. (Burke) D.; A.B., Hamilton Coll., 1906, A.M., 1909; L.H.D. (hon.), 1938; M.A., Harvard, 1907; studied at Cornell U., 1908-10, 1912-15. Instr. in pub. speaking Cornell U., 1907-10, 12-15, asst. prof., 1915-18, prof., 1920—, head of dept., 1920-40; dir. Cornell U. Theatre, Cornell Summer Theatre; dir. Cascadilla Schs., 1918-21, trustee, 1921-25; dir. dramatics N.Y. State Fair, 1919-21. Corporate mem. ANTA. Mem. Nat. Inst. of Social Scis., Nat. Assn. Tchrs. of Speech (ex-pres.), Nat. Ednl. Theatre Assn., Nat. Theatre Conf. (hon. pres. 1948—). Delta Kappa Epsilon. Editor and author of various texts, regional plays, and contbr. to jours. in field of drama and speech. Home: 3 Reservoir Av., Ithaca, N.Y. Died Nov. 1956.

DRUMMOND, Huntly Redpath, banker; b. Montreal, Can.; s. Sir George and Helen (Redpath) D.; ed. Montreal High Sch., Rugby Sch. (Eng.); LL.D., McGill U.; D.C.L., Bishop's U.; m. Mary Reynolds, 1899 (dec.). Began as clerk, Bank of Montreal; later entered Can. Sugar Refining Co., Ltd., becoming pres., 1910; co. merged with Can. and Dominion Sugar Co., became v.p.; became dir. Bank of Montreal, 1912, v.p., 1927, pres., 1939, chmn. bd., 1942, now hon. pres.; dir., hon. pres. Royal Trust Co. Gov. Alexandra Hosp. Mem. council Montreal Art Gallery. Officer, Quebec div. Canadian Red Cross. Clubs: Mount Royal, Royal St. Lawrence Yacht, Montreal Ski, Montreal Amateur Athletic. Home: 3418 Drummond St., Montreal, Quebec, Can. Died Dec. 9, 1957.

DRUMMOND, James Herbert, timberman; b. Winslow, Me., Nov. 23, 1865; s. George Lincoln and Mary Partridge (Murphy) D.; ed. Oak Grove Sem., Vassalboro, Me.; corr. course in law; m. Grace Edith Day, Oct. 1, 1902. Began in lumber and timber bus., Iron River, Wis., 1892; pres., Flamish Timber Co., 1909—; pres. Bank of St. Andrews, St. Andrews Ice & Power Co.; mem. firm Ware Mercantile Co. Sergt. 4th Wis. Inf., Spanish-Am. War, 1898. Mayor of St. Andrews, 1908-11. Home: 1000 Arthur Av., Panama City - St. Andrews, Fla. Died Nov. 25, 1939; buried Greenwood Cemetery.

DRURY, Aubrey, writer; b. Sacramento, Cal., June 10, 1891; s. Wells and Ella Lorraine (Bishop) D.; A.B., U. Cal., 1914 (post grad. lang. and lit., 1914-15); unmarried. Writer, adv. bur., Southern Pacific R.R., 1914-17; lecturer Panama-Pacific Internat. Expn., San Francisco, 1915; editor extension div., U. Cal., 1919; asso. editor Jour. of Electricity, San Francisco, 1919-20; partner Drury Company, public relations San Francisco, since 1919. Served as pvt., Signal Corps., U.S. Army, 1917; 2d lt., U.S. Air Service, 1917-19; 1st lt., U.S.R., Air Service, 1919. Mem. Save-the-Redwoods League since 1920, adminstr. sec. since 1940. Publicized Apache Trail of Ariz., giving names to mountains and canyons; mem. Official Hist. Landmarks Com., State of Cal., 1929, chmn., 1952—; pres. Cal. Conservation Council, 1951-52. Fellow Inst. Am. Geneaology; mem. Nat. Audubon Soc. (dir. 1946-47, 55-57), Nat. Parks Assn. (trustee 1949), Am. Forestry Assn. (v.p. 1950), Cal. Statewide Com. on Higher Edn. (sec.), Cal. Hist. Society (director; president 1949-51), Sir Francis Drake Assoc. (pres. 1956, 57), Pan Am. Society, World Trade Club of San Francisco (sec. and manager 1919-22), Cal. Alumni Assn., Cal. Folklore Soc., Cal. Acad. Sciences, Am. Legion. Organized World Metric Standardization Conf., San Francisco, 1920; dir. All-Am. Standards Council since 1924; v.p. Metric Assn., 1941-62. Republican. Episcopalian. Clubs: Commonwealth of Cal. (San Francisco), Sierra, Contra Costa Hills. Author: California Tourist Guide and Handbook (with Wells Drury), 1913; World Metric Standardization, An Urgent Issue, 1922; California: An Intimate Guide, 1935, fifth edition, 1947; How to Retire to California, 1950; John A. Hooper and California's Robust Youth, 1952. Co-author: The Pacific Cosst Ranges (1946), other books. Editor, co-author: Point Lobos Reserve (Cal.), 1954. Contbr. to Motorland (Cal. State Automobile Assn.), other mags., newspapers, on Cal. and western travel. Home: 1540 Euclid Av., Berkeley 8, Calif. Address: 114 Sansome St., San Francisco 4, Died Oct. 23, 1959.

DRURY, Francis Keese Wynkoop, librarian, ret.; b. Ghent, N.Y., Feb. 9, 1878; s. John Benjamin (D.D.) and Henrietta Wynkoop (Keese) D.; A.B., Rutgers, 1898, A.M., 1905; B.L.S., U. Ill., 1905; m. Martha B. Walker, Aug. 28, 1907 (died Dec. 4, 1930); 1 son, John Benjamin II. Asst. librarian Gardner A. Sage Library, New Brunswick, N.J., 1899-1903; with U. Ill. Library, 1903, acting librarian, 1907-09, asst. librarian, 1909-19; asst. librarian Brown U. Library, 1919-28, asst. prof., 1920-28; exec. asst. for adult edn. A.L.A., Chgo., 1929-31; librarian Nashville Pub. Library, 1931-46, ret.; vis. prof. Peabody Library Sch., 1931—. In A.L.A. war service, 1918-19. Pres. Ill. Library Assn., 1914, R.I. Library Assn., 1923-25, Tenn. Library Assn., 1934-37; v.p. S.E. Library Assn., 1940-46. Mem. A.L.A., Zeta Psi, Phi Beta Kappa. Presbyn. Author: College Life and College Sport, 1924; Viewpoints in Modern Drama, 1925; Novels Too Good to Miss, 1926; Book Selection, 1930; Order Work for Libraries, 1930; The Broadcaster and the Librarian, 1931; What Books Shall I Read?, 1933; The Library in the Fraternity House, 1935; Specimens of Reading Lists, 1936; Drury's Guide to Best Plays, 1953. Compiler lists; contbr. library periodicals. Address: 4308 Esteswood Dr., Nashville. Died Sept. 6, 1954; buried Mt. Hope Cemetery, Franklin, Tenn.

DRYDEN, George Bascomb, ret. rubber exec.; b. Olmsted Falls, O., July 6, 1869; s. Cyrus Perry and Lucia (Stearns) D.; ed. pub. schs.; m. Ellen A. Andrus, June 20, 1901 (dec. 1950); children—George Eastman, Ellen Maria (Mrs. H. Curry Dearborn). Began in rubber bus., Chgo., 1901; dir. City Nat. Bank & Trust Co., Borg-Warner Corp. Trustee George Eastman House, Inc. Chief 4th procurement dist., Chmn. Warfare Service, AUS, World Wars I and II. Life trustee, Northwestern U.; trustee Chgo. Zoöl. Soc.; dir. Evanston Hosp. Assn. Republican. Clubs: Chicago, Chicago Athletic Assn., Glenview Golf, Northport Point Golf. Home: 1314 Ridge Av., Evanston, Ill. Office: 208 S. La Salle St., Chgo. Died Sept. 9, 1959; buried Meml. Park Cemetery.

DRYDEN, John Lester, director of Borg-Warner Corp.; president of Long Mfg. div. Borg-Warner Corp., Detroit. Home: P.O. Box 1727, University, Va. Office: Borg-Warner Corp., Long Mfg. Div., 12501 Dequindre St., Detroit 12. Deceased.

DRYDEN, John N., lawyer; b. Dane County, Wis., June 1, 1856; s. Nathaniel H. and Emily C. (Balch) D.; grad. Gibbon (Neb.) Acad., 1879; later took 3 yr. course, Neb. State U.; m. Helen M. Holmes, Jan. 31, 1884. Admitted to bar, 1886. Mem. Am. Bar Assn., Neb. State Bar Assn.; del. Universal Congress Lawyers and Jurists, St. Louis, 1904. Methodist. Republican. Address: Kearney, Neb. Died Dec. 10, 1931; buried Kearney.

DRYER, George William (drī'ĕr), lawyer; b. Placerville, Cal., Feb. 12, 1881; s. John Lewis and Mary Louella (Alexander) D.; A.B., Stanford, 1902; Stanford Law Sch., 1903-04; m. Louise Dickson, Sept. 18, 1915; children—Mary Louise (dec.), John Lewis. Admitted to Cal. bar, 1904, began practice at Los Angeles, mem. Dryer, Hails, Burris & Lagerlof. Pres. Los Angeles Orthopedic Found., Orthopedic Hosp., 1918-46. Chmn. bd., 1946—; dir. Community Welfare Federation, Los Angeles, 1924-54, mem. bd. govs. 1954—; dir. Los Angeles Area War Chest. Ex-pres. Los Angeles Stanford Club, Stanford Law Soc. So. Cal. Mem. Am., Cal., Los Angeles (past trustee) bar assns., Am. Judicature Soc., Stanford Assos. (bd. govs., 1941-44). Hist. Soc. of Southern Cal., Native Sons Golden West, Cal. Soc. S.R., Delta Chi. Methodist. Mason (32°, K.T., Shriner). Clubs: University (past pres.), Lincoln. Recipient Los Angeles Realty Bd. annual award for community service and citizenship for 1936. Contbr. hist. articles. Home: 133 S. Las Palmas Av. Office: Rowan Bldg., Los Angeles. Died Feb. 9, 1959.

DuBARRY, William H(agan), univ. administrator; b. Lewistown, Pa., June 25, 1894; s. Joseph N., Jr., and Rebecca (Hagan) DuB.; ed. Blight Sch., De Lancey Sch.; B.S., U. of Pa., 1916; LL.D., Dickinson Coll., 1944; unmarried. Asst. to provost and pres., U. of Pa., 1923-31, dir. scholarships and student finances, 1931-39, vice pres. asst. to pres., 1939-44, exec. v.p., 1944-54, v.p. for corp., 1954—; dir. Provident Mutual Life Ins. Co. of Phila. Served as 2d lt. U.S. Army, 1917-19. Pres. Wistar Inst. Anatomy and biology; trustee Moore Sch. Elec. Engring.; mem. bd. trustees Eastern Pa. Psychiartic Inst.; trustee House of Rest; mem. bd. mgrs. Univ. Museum. Phila. Grad. Hosp. Mem. Zool. Soc. Phila (dir.), Mil. Order Loyal Legion of the United States. The Society of the War of 1812. S.R. Republican. Sec. standing com. Protestant Episcopal Diocese of Pa., mem. vestry P.E. Ch. Holy Trinity. Clubs: Lenape, Rittenhouse. Home: The Barclay, Rittenhouse Square, Philadelphia 3. Office: College Hall, Univ. of Pennsylvania, Phila. 4. Died Feb. 6, 1958.

du BOIS, Coert (dû-bois'), diplomat; born at Hudson, N.Y., Nov. 10, 1881; s. John C. (M.D.) and Eva (Kimball) du B.; ed. Biltmore Forest Sch.; m. Margaret Mendell, August 1, 1910. With United States Forest Service, 1900-17, dist. forester, Calif. Dist, 1911-17; consul assigned Paris, 1919, Naples, 1920, Port Said, 1922, in charge Visa Office, State Dept., Washington, 1924-27; consul gen., Batavia, Java, 1927-30; fgn. service inspector, India, 1930; consul gen., Genoa, Italy, 1931, Naples, Italy, 1931-37, Havana, Cuba, 1937-41; in charge Caribbean Office, State Dept., Washington, D.C., Oct. 9, 1941; Jan. 1944; apptd. on President's Anglo-Am. Caribbean Commn., March 14, 1942; sec. in diplomatic service, Aug. 1935; now retired. Liaison officer, State Dept. and War Assets Adminstrn., Central and So. Am. and Caribbean, 1946-47; U.S. del., U.N. Security Council's Com. of Good Offices, Java, N.E. Indies, Jan.-July 1948, rank of minister. Commd. maj. engrs. U.S. Army, Aug. 1917; lt. col., Sept. 1918; served with 10th Engrs. in France, Sept. 1917-Sept. 1918; duty Office of Chief of Engrs., Sept.-Dec. 1918; hon. disch., Dec. 4, 1918. Sent to England, Ireland and the Continent of Europe, 1925, as rep. of U.S. Govt. to arrange for the examination of immigrants before leaving home countries. Club: Metropolitan (Washington). Episcopalian. Home: 13 Elm St., Stonington, Conn. Died March 6, 1960.

DuBOIS, Eugene Floyd, physiologist; b. West New Brighton, N.Y., June 4, 1882; s. Eugene and Anna Greenleaf (Brooks) DuB.; A.B., Harvard 1903; M.D., Coll. Phys. and Surg. (Columbia), 1906; Sc.D., U. Rochester (N.Y.), 1948; m. Rebeckah Rutter, June 4, 1910. Interne Presbyn. Hosp., N.Y., 1907-08, asst. pathologist, 1909; instr. applied pharmacology, Cornell U. Med. Coll., N.Y., 1910-17; asso. prof. medicine, 1919-30, prof. medicine, 1930-41, prof. physiology, 1941-50, emeritus prof., 1950—; med. dir. Russell Sage Inst. Pathology, 1913-50; dir., vis. physician Second Med. Div. of Bellevue Hosp., 1919-32; cons. physician, 1932—; physician-in-chief N.Y. Hosp., 1932-41. Chmn. com. on aviation medicine NRC, 1940-45. Lt., lt. comdr. Med. Corps, USNRF, 1917-18; capt. 1927; during war had charge of investigations dealing with aviation, gas warfare and submarine ventilation. Served as capt. M.C., USNR, 1942-45, Bur. Medicine and Surgery, USN. Decorated Navy Cross. Mem. Assn. Am. Physicians, Am. Assn. Clin. Investigation, Am. Physiol. Soc., Nat. Acad. Scis. Democrat. Episcopalian. Club: Century Assn. Author: Basal Metabolism in Health and Disease, 1924, 27, 36; The Mechanism of Heat Loss and Temperature Regulation. Compiler of Harvard University Songs, 1902. Research in metabolism. Home: 1215 Park Av., N.Y.C. 28. Died Feb. 1959.

DuBOIS, Gaston Frederic, consultant; b. Switzerland, Aug. 9, 1880; s. Louis Ferdinand and Lucy (Smith) DuB.; Chem.E., Fed. Poly. Inst., Zurich, Switzerland, 1903; spl. student electro-chemistry Technische Hoshschule, Dresden, Germany, 1904; m. Marguerite Gilli, Oct. 18, 1909; children—Rene Gaston, Louis Frederic, Jeanne Marguerite. Came to U.S., 1904, naturalized, 1920. With Monsanto Chem. Co., St. Louis, 1904-05, as mfg. chemist, 1904-13, prodn. mgr., 1913-20, v.p., tech. dir., 1920-30, v.p. charge research and development, 1930-39, v.p., mem. exec. com., 1939-45, dir. Monsanto and subsidiaries, 1906-49, ret. 1949. Recipient Perkin Medal, 1944. Mem. Am. Inst. Chem. Engrs., Am. Chem. Soc., Am. Soc. for Metals, Swiss Chem. Soc., Electrochem. Soc., Soc. Chem. Industry London, Ethical Soc. Clubs: Noonday, Missouri Athletic, University (St. Louis); Bellerive Country (Normandy, Mo); Chemists (N.Y.C.). Home: 8 Crestwood Dr., Clayton 5, Mo. Died Nov. 1, 1953; buried Oak Grove Cemetery, St. Louis.

duBOIS, Guy Pène (dü-bwä'), artist; b. Brooklyn, N.Y., Jan. 4, 1884; s. Henri Pène and Laura (Hague) duB.; student N.Y. Sch. of Art, 1899-1905, Colorossi's, Paris, 1905-06; m. Florence Sherman, Apr. 10, 1911; children—Yvonne Pène; (Mrs. Houghton Furlong), William Pène; step children—Virginia Duncan (Mrs. Edwin Earle Lucas), Donald Duncan, Robert Duncan. Reporter, music and art critic, N.Y. American, 1906-13; asst. art critic N.Y. Tribune, 1913-14; art critic N.Y. Evening Post, 1916-18; editor Arts and Decoration, 1913-16, 1917-22; lived and painted in France, 1924-30. Represented in Metropolitan Museum of Art, Whitney Museum of American Art, Museum of Modern Art, Galleries of Living Art (New York City), Newark Museum, Brooklyn, Institute of Arts and Scis., Phillips Mem. Gallery (Washington, D.C.); Museum of Fine Arts, Boston, Mass.; Wilwaukee (Wis.) Art Inst., Los Angeles Museum, Pittsburgh Athletic Club, Cleveland Museum of Art, Detroit Institute of Arts, Pennsylvania Academy of Fine Arts, Carnegie Institute Pittsburgh, and museums at San Diego, Andover, Baltimore, Toledo. Awarded purchase prize, Los Angeles Museum, 1928; Harris silver medal, Chicago Art Inst., 1930; 2d Altman prize, Nat. Acad. Design, 1936; 2d Corcoran prize, Washington, 1937; 1st Altman prize, N.A.D., 1945; 1st Salmagundi Club prize, 1946. Mem. Nat. Inst. Arts and Letters, Nat. Acad. Design, N.A. Mem. bd. editors Mag. of Art of Am. Fedn. of Art. Contbr. articles Mag. of Art, N.Y. Times Book Review Author: Artists Say the Silliest Things (autobiography), 1940. Address: 20 W. 10th St., N.Y.C. Died July 18, 1958.

DU BOIS, Julian Arthur, physician; b. Aztalan, Wis., Jan. 8, 1856; s. Darwin and Harriet (Leonard) D.; student U. Wis., 1873-77; M.D., Rush Med. Coll., Chgo., 1879; m. Laura R. Faville, Apr. 1, 1881; children—Benjamin Faville, Julian Faville, Faville (dec.). Began practice, Lake Mills, Wis., 1879; removed to Sauk Center, Minn., 1882; pres. 1st State Bank. Mayor of Sauk Center 2 terms; Dem. candidate for Congress, 6th Minn. Dist., 1902, 1914; mem. State Ednl. Commn. Mem. A.M.A., Minn. State Med. Soc., Crow River Med. Assn., Stearns, Benton and Sherburne County Med. Soc., State Hist. Soc. Minn. Club: Commercial. Physician, Home School for Girls. Surgeon for G.N. and N.P. rys. Home: Sauk Center, Minn. Died May 4, 1937.

DU BOIS, Mary Constance (dōō-bois), author; b. Phila., Mar. 28, 1879; d. Rev. Henry Ogden and Emily Stuart (Meier-Smith) Du Bois; attended Rye (N.Y.) Sem., 1891-97, Columbia, summer, 1903, Columbia ext. course, winter of 1903-04. Episcopalian. Author: Elinor Arden, Royalist, 1904; A Captive Choir, 1905; The Lass of the Silver Sword, 1909; The League of the Signet Ring, 1910; The Girls of Old Glory, 1918; Comrade Rosalie, 1919; White Fire, 1923; Captain Madeleine, 1928; Mother's Story Box, 1933; Patsy of The Pet Shop, 1937; Shadow Cove Mystery, 1940. Home: 390 West End Av., N.Y.C. Died June 19, 1959.

DU BOSE, Henry Wade, clergyman; b. Spring Hill, Tenn., May 18, 1884; s. William Thompson and Lucy (Wade) D.; prep. edn., Branham and Hughes Sch., Spring Hill; A.B., Vanderbilt U., 1904; B.D., Presbyn. Theol. Sem., Louisville, Ky., 1910; D.D., Southwestern Coll., Memphis, Tenn., 1918; m. Marie Webb, Apr. 14, 1915; children—Marie Lucile, James Webb, Henry Wade, William

Thompson. Teacher in prep schs. 3 years; ordained ministry Presbyn. Ch. of U.S., 1910; pastor successively Versailles, Ky., Government Street Ch., Mobile, Ala., First Ch., Danville, Va., until 1922. First Ch., Spartanburg, S.C., 1923-37, Highland Park Ch., Dallas, Tex., Dec. 1937-Dec. 1942, Trinity Presbyn. Ch., Montgomery, Ala., 1942-44; pres. Presbyterian Assembly's Training Sch., Richmond, Va., 1944-—. Vice pres. Am. Assn. Schs. of Religious Edn. Member Phi Beta Kappa, Delta Kappa Epsilon. Dem. Contbg. editor Christian Observer, Louisville. Home: 1204 Palmyra Av., Richmond 22, Va. Died Feb. 11, 1960.

DUDGEON, Matthew S. (dŭd'jŭn) ret.; b. Madison, Wis., June 18, 1871; s. Richard and Dilla (Ball) D.; A.B., Baker U., 1892, A.M., 1900; LL.B., U. Wis., 1895; m. Mabel Cunningham, July 11, 1900; children—Lucile, Edith. Pros. atty. Dane County, Wis., 1899-1903; mem. Wis. Ho. of Rep., 1903-04; sec. Wis. Free Library Commn. and dir. Library Sch., U. Wis., 1909-20; librarian Milw. Pub. Library, 1920-41, ret. Chmn. Milwaukee County Salvage Com., 1942-44. Served as pvt. Spanish-Am. War, 1st Regt., Wis., 1898. Mem. A.L.A. (treas. 1927-41; chmn. adult edn. bd. 1926-33; 2d v.p. 1941), Delta Tau Delta, Phi Delta Phi. Republican. Methodist. Club: Milwaukee City (pres. 1927-28). On leave of absence as mgr. camp libraries for soldiers and sailors, hdqrs. Washington, 1917, in U.S. and in France, 1918-19. Home: 2932 N. Hackett Av., Milw. Died July 26, 1949; buried Madison, Wis.

DUDLEY, Albert Henry, banker; b. Haleford, Va., Sept. 23, 1885; s. Albert McLeod and Ada Nye (Hancock) D.; student pub. schs. and Locust Dale (Va.) Acad.; m. Lillie Gaines Phillips, June 8, 1921; children—Maxwell Phillips, Albert Henry, Louis Roane. Began in employ of Farmers Bank (later First Nat. Bank), Martinsville, Va., 1904; bookkeeper and teller Nat. Exchange Bank, Roanoke, Va., 1906-13, asst. cashier, 1913-18; asst. federal reserve agt. Federal Reserve Bank of Richmond, 1918-22, mng. dir. Balt. br., 1922-31. Mem. bd. govs. Md. General Hospital. Virginians of Md. (Baltimore); mem. Nat. Council YMCA; dir. Balt. YMCA. Balt. So. Meth. (weekly newspaper). Democrat. Mem. M.E. Ch., South, and dist. lay leader Balt. Conf. Mason (K.T., Shriner), K.P., Elk. Clubs: Chesapeake, Press, Maryland, Baltimore Country (Baltimore); Commonwealth (Richmond). Home: 839 W. University Pkwy., Balt. Died Oct. 4, 1945; buried David Ridge Cemetery, Balt.

DUDLEY, Albertus True, author; b. Paris, N.Y., Jan. 19, 1866; s. Rev. Horace Franklin and Josephine (Lamson) D.; A.B., Harvard, 1887; studied in Germany; m. Frances Perry, July 2, 1890. Teacher Phillips Exeter Acad., 1887-95, Noble and Greenough's School, Boston, 1896-1917. Trustee U. N.H., 1928-1933. Author: Following the Ball, 1903; Making the Nine, 1904; In the Line, 1905; With Mask and Mitt, 1906; The Great Year, 1907; The Yale Cup, 1908; A Fullback Afloat, 1908; The School Four, 1909; At the Home Plate, 1910; The Pecks in Camp, 1911; The Half-Miler, 1913; The Unofficial Prefect, 1916; The King's Powder, 1923; A Spy of '76, 1933; also editorials and historical papers. Home: Exeter, N.H. Died Feb. 11, 1955.

DUDLEY, Frank Virgil, artist; b. Delavan, Wis., Nov. 14, 1868; s. James A. and Flora C. (Virgil) D.; ed. high sch.; studied Chgo. Art Inst.; m. Maida Lewis, May 21, 1913; 1 son, Paul B. Awarded Municipal Art League prize, Chgo., 1907; Municipal Art League purchase prize, 1914; Butler purchase prize, 1915; Martin B. Cahn prize, 1919; Logan medal and 1st prize, 1921; Arché Club prize, 1926; Studebaker Hoosier Salon prize, 1926; Beaumont Parks Salon prize, 1927; Butler Memorial Hoosier Salon prize, 1928, 30, 32. Mem. Municipal Commn. for Encouragement of Local Art. Mem. Painters and Sculptors Chgo., Chgo. Galleries Assn., Allied Arts Assn. Club: Cliff Dwellers. Home: 6356 Greenwood Av., Chgo. Died Mar. 5, 1957.

DUDLEY, Mrs. Guilford (Anne Dallas Dudley), suffragist; b. Nashville, Nov. 13, 1876; d. Trevanion Barlow and Ida (Bonner) Dallas; ed. Ward's Sem. and Price's Coll., Nashville; m. Guilford Dudley, 1902; children—Ida Dallas (dec.), Trevania Dallas (dec.), Guilford. Pres. first Nashville Equal Suffrage League, 1911-15; pres. Tenn. Equal Suffrage League, 1915-18; 3d v.p. Nat. Am. Woman Suffrage League, 1917-21; dir. suffrage forces. Tenn. ratification campaign, 1920. Apptd. by Sec. of Treasury, mem. Nat. Woman's Liberty Loan Com., 1917-19; state pres. Tenn. Woman's Liberty Loan Com., 1st, 2d and 3d Liberty Loan campaigns; 1st woman chmn. Asso. Dem. State Com., 1920; 1st woman del. at large to Dem. Nat. Conv., San Francisco, 1920. Chmn. bd. govs. Belle Meade Mansion. Mem. Colonial Dames, Assn. Preservation Tenn. Antiquities, D.A.R. Episcopalian. Clubs: Belle Meade Country, Centennial. Home: Hillsboro Rd., Nashville. Died Sept. 13, 1955; buried Mt. Olivet Cemetery, Nashville.

DUER, Caroline King, author; b. N.Y.C., Feb. 27, 1865; d. James G. K. and Elizabeth (Meads) Duer; ed. privately. Contbr. to mags. Former poet, editor Vogue mag. Author: Unconscious Comedians, 1901. Address: 60 E. 53d St., N.Y.C. Died Jan. 1956.

DUFF, Alexander Wilmer, educator; b. St. John, N.B., Can., May 23, 1864; s. Alexander and Lucy (McKenzie) D.; A.B., U. N.B., 1884, LL.D., 1920; A.B., London U., 1887; M.A., U. Edinburgh, 1888, D.Sc., 1901; m. Isabel Stuart McIntosh, June 21, 1894. Prof. physics, Madras, India, 1899-90, U. N.B., 1890-93, Purdue U. 1893-99, Worcester Poly. Inst., 1899-1936, prof. emeritus, 1936-—. Cons. and exptl. engr. U.S. Army, 1918-19. Fellow Am. Acad. Arts and Sciences, Am. Physiol. Soc. Presbyn. Author: Elementary Experiemntal Mechanics, 1905; Physical Measurements (with A. W. Ewell), 1910; College Physics, 1925; Elements of Physics (with H. T. Wood), 1928. Editor: A Text-book of Physics. Home: 52 Fruit St., Worcester, Mass. Died Feb. 24, 1951.

DUFF, G(eorge) Lyman, educator, pathologist; b. Hamilton, Ont., Can., Jan. 26, 1904; s. Charles and Elizabeth Anne (Ostler) D.; B.A., U. Toronto, 1926, M.A., 1927, M.D., 1929, fellow pathology, 1929-31, Ph.D., 1932; Nat. Research Council fellow medicine Johns Hopkins, 1931-32; m. Isobel Farrell Griffiths, Oct. 23, 1935; children—Sheila Louise, Graham Lyman, Ian Griffiths, Catharine Isobel. Asst. pathology Johns Hopkins, 1931-33, instr. pathology, 1933-35; asst. pathologist Johns Hopkins Hosp., 1933-35; lectr. pathology U. Toronto, 1935-37, asst. professor pathology, 1937-39; asst. pathologist Toronto General Hosp., 1935-39; asso. editor Am. Jour. Med. Sci. since 1938; prof. pathology, dir. path inst. McGill U. since 1939, hon. curator Royal Canadian Army Med. Corps Med. Mus., 1941-48, dean faculty medicine since 1949; cons. pathologist Montreal General Hosp., Childrens Meml. Hosp., Alexandra Hospital, Reddy Meml. Hosp., Jewish Hosp. of Hope, Montreal; asso. examiner pathology and bacteriology Med. Council Can., 1942-45; mem. asso. com. med. research Nat. Research Council Can., Ottawa, 1943-48, executive com., 1944-48; examiner pathology Royal Coll. Phys. and Surg. Can. since 1944; hon. cons. pathology Royal Victoria Hosp.; lectr. medicine Royal Coll. Physicians Can., 1947; editorial bd. Am. Heart Jour. since 1950, Lab. Investigation since 1953. Certified specialist in pathology Royal Coll. Phys. and Surg. Can. Recipient Flavelle Medal, Royal Soc., Can., 1956. Fellow Royal Society Can., Royal Coll. Physicians Can.; mem. Nat. Cancer Inst., Can. (dir., v.p. 1953-54, pres. 1954-55), Path. Soc. Gt. Brit. and Ireland, Am Assn. Pathologisst and Bacteriologists (mem. council 1950-53, v.p. 1953-54, pres. 1954-55), Canadian Cancer Soc. (nat. dir.), Internat. Assn. Med. Mus. (mem. council 1942-47, mem. editorial bd. Bull. 1947-52, v.p. 1949-50, pres. 1950-51), Montreal Medico-Chirurgical Soc., Que. Association Pathologists (pres. 1946-47), Am. Soc. Study Arteriosclerosis (bd. dirs. 1947-50, v p. 1950-51, pres. 1951-52), Soc. Exptl. Biology and Medicine, Canadian Med. Assn., Canadian Assn. Pathologists. Contbr. articles med. jours. Home: 730 Upper Roslyn Av., Westmount 6. Office: 3775 University St., Montreal 2, P.Q., Can. Died Nov. 1, 1956.

DUFF, Sir Lyman Poore, former chief justice Canada; b. Jan. 7, 1865; s. Rev. Chas. and Isabella (Johnson) D.; B.A., Toronto U., 1887, LL.B., 1889, LL.D., 1923; LL.D., Columbia, U. Pa., McGill U., Laval U., U. B.C., U. Montreal, U. Dalhousie; m. Elizabeth Eleanor Bird, 1898 (died 1926). Called to Ontario bar, 1893, B.C. bar, 1895; Queen's Counsel, 1899; counsel for B C. Legislature in Coal Lands Investigation, 1902; jr. counsel for Great Britain in Alaska Boundary Arbitration, 1903; judge of Supreme Court of B.C., 1904; judge, Supreme Court of Can., 1906-33, chief justice, 1933-44, retired. Mem. Judicial Com. of Imperial Privy Council. Royal commr. of Investigation of contracts of Shell Com., 1916; Central appeal judge under Mil. Service Acts, 1917-18; hon. bencher, Gray's Inn, 1924; gov. U. Toronto, 1926; adminstr. Govt. of Can., 1931, 43; chmn. of Transportation Commn. investigating railways in Can., 1932. Created Knight, 1934. Pres. Toronto U. Lit. and Scientific Soc., 1891. Clubs: Rideau, Country, Royal Ottawa Golf (Ottawa); Union (Victoria); Vancouver. Address: 488 Wilbrod St., Ottawa, Ont., Can. Died Apr. 26, 1955.

DUFF, William McGill, life ins. exec.; b. Pitts., Feb. 2, 1878; s. James Alexander and Charlotte (McGill) D.; grad. Allegheny High Sch., Pitts., 1895; m. Mary Prenter, July 19, 1919; children—Charlotte Duff McCrady, Letitia Duff Dyke. General agent for the Equitable Life Assurance Society. Trustee Westminster College, New Wilmington, Pa.; v.p. Am. College Life Underwriters (degree C.L.U.); mem. Pitts. Life Underwriters (ex.-pres., treas., dir.), Nat. Assn. Life Underwriters (ex-trustee). Dir. The Zoar House, Crippled Children's Assn. Mem. S.A.R. (pres.) Sigma Phi Epsilon. Republican. Presbyn. Mason. Clubs: Insurance, Duquesne; The Clan Chattan Assn. (Scotland); Shannopin Country, Longue Vue, Athletic Assn. (Pittsburgh), Republican (New York). Home: 707 Amberson Av., Pitts. Died Jan. 6, 1948.

DUFFY, Frank H., mem. Democratic Nat. Com. from Vt., 1916-—. Home: Rutland, Vt. Died May 21, 1950.*

DUFNER, Edward, painter; b. Buffalo, Oct. 5, 1871; s. Bernhard and Clara (Dold) D.; pupil Art Students' League, Buffalo, N.Y.C.; under James McNeil Whistler, Paris, and Acad. Julian under Laurens; m. Annie L. Collins, 1898; m. 2d, Ilka H. Renwick, 1933; m. 3d, Fern Bradley, 1943. Recipient Albright prize and scholarship Art Students' League, Buffalo, 1893; Wanamaker prize and honorable mention, Paris, France, 1899; bronze medal Buffalo Expn., 1901; hon. mention Paris Salon, 1902; fellowship prize Soc. of Artists, Buffalo, 1904; silver medal St. Louis Expn., 1904; William T. Evans prize Am. Water Color Soc., 1909; Julius Levy prize Peabody Inst., Balt., 1921; Walter Lippincott prize Pa. Acad. Fine Arts, 1924; gold medal Brown-Bigelow nat. art competition, N.Y.C., 1925; People prize Newport (R.I.) Art Assn., 1935; Lucille Dingley prize for figure composition Ogunquist Art Center, 1939; Founder's Special prize Sanity in Art Exhbn., Chgo., 1941. Instr. Art Students' League, Buffalo, 1903-07, N.Y.C., 1908-17, Carnegie Inst. Tech., 1921; now instr. painting and drawing of the class of profl. artists, Traphagen Sch., N.Y.C. Represented in the Buffalo Fine Arts Academy, Bklyn. Inst. Fine Arts, William M. Chase collection, N.A.D., Nat. Arts Club, Lotos Club (N.Y.C.), Milw. Art Soc., Fort Worth Art Museum, Montclair Art Museum, Randolph-Macon Women's College, Lafayette Art Assn., Parthenon Art Gallery (Nashville), Wesleyan College Collection (Macon, Ga.), Vanderpoel Art Assn., Chgo., Hanover (Ind.) College and many private collections and in Harvard Coll. library, Cambridge, Mass., A.N.A., 1910, N.A., 1929; mem. N.Y. Chgo., Water Color Club, Am. Water Color Soc., Am. Art Assn., Paris, Buffalo Fine Arts Acad., Allied Artists Am.; hon. mem. Buffalo Soc. Artists. Clubs: Salmagundi, Lotos, Nat. Arts. Patron Montclair Art Museum. Home and studio: 15 Wyndham Rd., Short Hills, N.J. Died Oct. 1, 1957; buried St. Helena Church Yard, Beaufort, S.C.

DUFY, Raoul, artist; b. Le Havre, France, June 3, 1877; studied at Ecole des Beaux-Arts (Le Havre); pupil of Leon Bonnat, Ecole Nationale des Beaux-Arts (Paris). One of the Modern French school of painters; also decorator, designer of fabrics, tapestries and ceramics, muralist, wood engraver, book illustrator. Work first exhibited in Paris at Salon des Artists Français, 1901; first one-man show Galerie Berthe Weill, 1906. Suffering from severe arthritis (uses left hand for painting), came to U.S. for treatment in Boston, 1950, and having greatly improved began to sketch and paint surrounding scenes; his Am. water colors were exhibited at Louis Carré Gallery, 1951, and later on nat. tour of U.S. Represented in European museums and prin. museums and galleries of U.S. Knight Legion of Honor. Address: care Louise Carré Gallery, 712 5th Av., N.Y. City 19. Died Mar. 23, 1953.

DUGGAN, B. O., state commr. of edn. Home: 303 High St., Chattanooga, Tenn. Office: State Dept. of Education, Nashville. Died Nov. 13, 1949; buried Murfreesboro, Tenn.

DUGGAN, John J., pres., gen. mgr. and dir. Chapman Valve Mfg. Co. Trustee Hampden Savings Bank, Springfield, Mass.; dir. Union Trust Co., Springfield, Mass., Perkins Machine & Gear Co.; dir. Mutual Fire Assurance Co., Milton Bradley Co., Springfield, Mass. Trustee, City Library Assn., Springfield. Home: 140 Oak St. Office: Chapman Valve Mfg. Co., 203 Hampshire St., Indian Orchard, Mass. Died Nov. 5, 1954.

DUGGAN, Stephen, coll. prof.; b. New York, Dec. 20, 1870; s. Hugh and Mary D. (Hayden) D.; B.S., Coll. City of New York, 1890, M.S., 1896; M.A., Columbia U., 1898, Ph.D., 1902; LL.D., Rollins Coll., Fla., 1927; Litt.D., San Marcos U., Peru, 1931; LL.D., U. of Mich., 1933; LL.D., Clark U., 1937, Oberlin Coll., 1937; L.H.D., Lafayette Coll., 1939; LL.D., U. of Maine, 1943; m. Sarah Alice Elsesser, Jan. 2, 1902; children—Mary Alice, Laurence (dec.), Stephen Pierce, Sally Ann. Instr., asso. prof. and prof. polit. sci., Coll. City of N.Y., 1896-1928; dir. Inst. Internat. Edn., 1919-46, now dir. emeritus; pres. N.Y. Acad. Pub. Edn., 1922-23; lecturer internat. relations, Columbia, 1924-25; sec. Am. Univ. Union in Europe since 1926. Mem. advisory bd. Div. of Cultural Relations, State Dept. Mem. Philippine Ednl. Survey Commn., 1925; mem. Am. Brazilian Commn. of Conciliation; mem. Am. Commn. on Intellectual Coöperation. Trustee Am. College for Girls at Istanbul, Asso. Boards for Christian Colleges in China, Am. Coll. at Athens, Greece, World Peace Found.; dir. Council on Fgn. Relations, League of Nations Assn., Carl Schurz Memorial Found., Netherlands-America Found. Mem. Am. Hist. Assn., Am. Polit. Science Assn., N.E.A., Phi Beta Kappa, Kappa Delta Pi. Commander Order of Crown of Italy; Officier Legion of Honor (France); Officer Order of White Lion (Czechoslovakia); Officer Order of Merit (Hungary); Comdr. Order of Star (Roumania); mem. Order of Merit (Chile); Order of Orange Nassau, 1949. Clubs: Century (New York); Cosmos

(Washington). Author: The Eastern Question—A Study in Diplomacy, 1902; A History of Education, 1916; The League of Nations, 1919; The Two Americas, An Interpretation, 1933; A Professor at Large, 1943; The Rescue of Science and Learning, 1948. Home: Old Long Ridge Rd., Stamford, Conn. Office: 2 W. 45th St., N.Y. City. Died Aug. 18, 1950.

DUGGAR, Benjamin Minge, univ. prof.; b. Gallion, Ala., Sept. 1, 1872; s. Dr. Reuben Henry and Margaret Louisa (Minge) D.; brother of John Frederick D.; student U. of Ala., 1887-89; B.S., Miss. A. and M. Coll. (1st honors), 1891; M.S., Ala. Poly. Inst., 1892; A.B., Harvard, 1894, A.M., 1895; Ph.D., Cornell, 1898; German universities and at Naples, Paris, and Montpelier, 1899-1900, 1905-06; LL.D., U. Mo., 1944; D.Sc., Washington U., 1953; m. Marie L. Robertson, Oct. 16, 1901 (died 1922); children—Marie Louise, Benjamin Minge, Anna St. Julian Guerard, George Strowan, Emily Westwood; m. 2d, Elsie Rist, June 6, 1927; 1 daughter, Gene Lorraine. Asst. dir. Uniontown (Ala.) Agrl. Expt. Sta., 1892-93; asst. botanist of Ill. State Lab. Natural History, 1895-96; cryptogamic botanist, Agrl. Expt. Sta. and instr. plant physiology, 1896-1900, asst. prof., 1900-01, Cornell; physiologist, Bur. Plant Industry, U.S. Dept. Agr., 1901-02; prof. botany, U. of Mo., 1902-07, prof. plant physiology, Cornell U., Feb. 1, 1907-12; research prof. plant physiology, Mo. Bot. Garden and Washington U., 1912-27; prof. physiology and economic botany, University of Wisconsin, 1927—, emeritus, June, 1943—; consultant, mycological research and production, Lederle Laboratories Div. American Cyanamid Co., Pearl River, N.Y., 1944. Acting prof. biology chemistry Washington U. Med. Sch., 1917-19. Awarded Medal of Honor of Public Education, Venezuela, 1951. Trustee emeritus Marine Biol. Lab., Woods Hole Oceanographic Instn. Fellow A.A.A.S. (v.p. section G, 1925); mem. Nat. Acad. Scis., Am. Philos. Soc., Phila. Acad. Science, Botanical Soc. of America (pres. 1923), Am. Soc. Plant Physiol. (pres. 1946-47), American Phytopathol. Soc., American Chem. Society, Soc. American Naturalists, American Pub. Health Assn., Torrey Botanical Club, Nat. Research Council (chmn. div. biology and agr., 1925-26), Sigma Xi, Phi Beta Kappa, Phi Sigma. Chairman Organizing Com. and general secretary Internat. Congress Plant Sciences, 1926. Speaker in sect. plant physiology, Internat. Congress of Arts and Sciences, St. Louis, 1904. Editor for physiology, Botanical Abstracts, 1917-26, Biological Abstracts, 1926-33, and Biological Abstracts of Radiation, 1936. Author: Fungous Diseases of Plants, 1909; Plant Physiology, 1911; Musroom Growing, 1915; A Textbook of General Botany with G. M. Smith, et al); also research articles. Home: 198 Braunsdorf Rd., Pearl River, N.Y. Died Sept. 10, 1956; buried Oak Hill Cemetery, Nyack, N.Y.

DUGGAR, Reuben Henry, physician; b. Petersburg, Va., June 16, 1837; s. Henry and Alice Goode (Vaughan) D.; removed to Ala., 1844; ed. at home and Madison Coll., Pa.; grad. med. dept. U. Pa., 1858; served asst. surgeon, C. S. A.; m. 1864, Margaret Louise Minge, 1864; children—David (dec.), John (dec.), Reuben Henry, Benjamin (dec.), Llewellyn. Was trustee Ala. Agr'l. and Mech. Coll. 6 yrs.; grand counselor State Med. Assn., and its 1st historian; 1st v.-p. Ala. State Hist. Soc. Democrat. Episcopalian. Address: Gallion, Ala. Died May 5, 1921; buried Faunsdale, Ala.

DUKE, Charles Wesley, writer; b. Tyrone, Pa., Apr. 17, 1885, s. George Washington and Mary Ann (Stratiff) D.; graduated Dickinson Jr. College, Williamsport, Pennsylvania, 1905; student Ohio Wesleyan; m. Edith May Butler, Oct. 21, 1910; children—Chas. W., Mary Louise, Suzanne Virginia (Mrs. Wayne Richardson Hess). City editor Daily Herald, Jersey Shore, Pa., 1905; reporter Sun, later Gazette & Bulletin, Williamsport, 1906, Philadelphia North American, 1907; with Phila. Evening Times, 1908-12; reporter, editor and feature writer Philadelphia Public Ledger, 1912-22; Sunday editor Phila. Public Ledger, 1922-34; with Watkins Syndicate, Phila., 1935; Sunday staff Phila. Inquirer, 1938-49; Phila. rep. Editor and Publisher, 1943-49; apptd. dir. med. information U. of Pa., 1949. Mem. Sigma Chi. Mason. Home: Aldan, Delaware County, Pa.; and Cape May, N.J. Office: 3457 Walnut St., Phila. Died Aug. 6, 1956; buried Arlington Cemetery, Drexel Hill, Pa.

DUKE, Samuel Page, coll. pres.; b. Ferrum, Va., Sept. 5, 1885; s. Thomas Page and Jennie Gray (Ward) D.; A.B., Randolph-Macon Coll., 1906; A.M., Columbia, 1913; LL.D., Hampden-Sydney College, 1931; LL.D., Bridgewater Coll., 1946; m. Lucile Campbell, Aug. 26, 1908; children—Samuel Page, Julia Lois, Robert Campbell, Marshall Ward. Instr. Willie Halsell Co., Vinita, Oka., 1906-08; prin. high sch., Chase City, Va., 1908-10; prin. city schs., Richmond, Va., 1910-14; dir. county teachers' insts., also dir. dept. of edn., State Teachers Coll. (Farmville, Va.) and state supr. secondary schs., Va., until 1919; pres. Madison Coll., 1919-49, pres. emeritus, 1949—. Past pres. Rockingham Meml. Hosp. Mem. N.E.A., Phi Delta Kappa, Kappa Alpha, Kappa Delta Pi, Phi Beta Kappa. Democrat. Methodist. Rotarian. Home: Harrisonburg, Va. Died Apr. 25, 1955; buried Harrisonburg.

DUKES, Richard Gustavus (dūks), educator; b. Findlay, O., Nov. 10, 1871; s. Eli and Mary Hannah (Delaney) D.; student De Pauw U., Mass. Inst. Tech.; M.E. in Elec. Engring., Cornell, 1896; m. Harriet Campbell, June 22, 1901 (died Dec. 1943); m. 2d, Mary Irene Hughes, Feb. 23, 1946; children—Elizabeth Mitchell (Mrs. C. D. Phillips), Martha Campbell (Mrs. F. H. Ryan). With Gen. Electric Co., Schenectady, 1898-1900; instr. in mech. engring. Worcester Poly. Inst., 1900-01; instr. dept. exptl. engring. Cornell U., 1901-03; prof. in charge applied mechanics Case Sch. Applied Science, 1903-09; prof. applied mechanics and head dept. Purdue U., 1909-42, prof. emeritus, 1942—, dean Grad. Sch., 1929-42, dean emeritus, 1942—. Mem. Soc. Promotion Engring. Edn., Am. Soc. for Testing Materials, Ind. Acad. Science, Scabbard and Blade, Sigma Xi, Delta Kappa Epsilon, Alpha Phi Omega, Tau Beta Pi. Presbyn. Club: Town and Gown. Home: 2 Stadium Rd., W. Lafayete, Ind. Died Aug. 12, 1950.

DULANY, George William Jr. (dû-lā'nē), lumberman, mfr.; b. Ft. Scott, Kan., July 11, 1877; s. George W. and Fanny (Williams) D.; grad. Phillips Andover Acad., 1895, Ph.B., Yale, 1898; m. Blanche E. Horst, Aug. 5, 1940; 1 son, George William III. Civil engr. Empire Lumber Co., Winona, Minn., 1898-1900; settled Mpls., 1900; organizer 1904, chmn. bd. Eclipse Lumber Co.; moved to Clinton, Ia., 1910; organizer, 1914, Climax Engring. Company; president Siuslaw Timber Co.; also president Fullerton Minerals Co., Gulf Lumber Co.; dir. La. Central Oil & Gas Co., Exchange Saw Mills Sales Co., La. Long Leaf Lumber Co., La. Central Lumber Co., R. J. Hurley Lumber Co., Grandin Coast Lumber Co., Fisher Flouring Mills Co., White-Dulany Co., Gallatin Valley Milling Co., Pettibone Timber Co., White Grandin Lumber Co., Ouchita & Northwestern Ry.; dir., treas. Timber Engring. Co. Seaman U.S.N., Span.-Am. War, 1898; lt. F.A., Minn. N.G., 1904-10; capt Iowa Nat. Guard, 1910-15; capt 126th F.A., 34th Div., U.S. Army, 1917. Mem. Nat. Lumber Mfr's. Assn. (hon. life dir.), Yale Engring. Assn., Miss. Valley Assn. (hon. life dir.), U.S. and Clinton C.'s of C., Clinton Junior C. of C., S.A.R., Spanish-Am. War Vets., Am. Legion, 40 and 8, Rotary, Chi Phi, Lumber Fraternity Hoo Hoo (past Snark of the Universe). Republican. Presbyn. Mason, Elk. Clubs: University, Commonwealth (Chgo.); Clinton Country (Ia.); Yale (N.Y.C.); Rancho Santa Fe Golf, La Jolla Beach and Tennis (La Jolla, Cal.); San Diego (San Diego, Cal.). Nat. councilor and Silver Beaver, Boy Scouts of America. Organizer 1916, and sec. soc. for Prevention of Calling Sleeping Car Porters "George" (40,000 mems.). Home: 7951 La Jota Way. Office: P.O. Box 858, La Jolla, Cal. Died May 15, 1959.

DULCAN, Charles B., dept. store exec.; b. Winnipeg, Can., Aug. 15, 1888; s. Harris and Sarah (Walkow) D.; came to U.S., 1894; naturalized 1918; m. Elizabeth R. Petrie, Apr. 30, 1918; children—Edward S., Alvin G., Charles B. With The Hecht Co., dept. store, Washington, D.C., since 1912, successively as salesman, asst. buyer, buyer, asst. mdse. mgr., gen. mdse. mgr., v.p., gen. mgr. 1936; exec. v.p., gen. mgr., 1950, v. chmn. bd. dirs., and mng. dir. Washington area, 1953, ret., 1953; director Nat. Bank of Washington. Dir., past v.p. Police Boys Club; dir. Met. area A.R.C., Fed. City Council; past trustee Am. Cancer Soc.; past mem. bd. Nat. Symphony Orchestra. Mem. comml. standards com. and adv. com. Dept. Commerce. Member exec. com. Greater Nat. Capitol committee Board Trade. Mem. President's Inaugural Committee, 1948, 52. Member American Institute of Management, Am. Retail Fed., Mutual Health Service, Nat. Retail Dry Goods Assn. (director; recipient gold medal, award, 1946). Selected Brand Name Retailer of Year, 1949, '51. Jewish Religion. Mason. Clubs: Advertising, National Press, Cosmopolitan (gold medal, 1951), Princeton, Variety (Washington); Woodmont Country (Rockville, Md.). Home: Westchester, Washington 16. Office: 1034 Woodward Bldg., Washington 5. Died Jan. 6, 1957.

DULLES, John Foster (dŭl'lĕs), Sec. of State; b. Washington, Feb. 25, 1888; s. Allen Macy and Edith (Foster) D.; B.A., Princeton U., 1908, LL.D., 1946; Sorbonne, Paris, 1908-09; LL.B., George Washington Univ., 1911; LL.D., Tufts, 1939, Wagner College, Northwestern U., 1947, Union Coll., 1948, U. of Pa., 1949, Lafayette, 1949, Amherst, Seoul Nat. U., 1950, U. Ariz., St. Josephs Coll., 1951, St. Lawrence U., Johns Hopkins U., Fordham U., Harvard, 1952, Columbia University, 1954, Georgetown U., 1954, U. S.C., 1955, Ind. U., 1955, Ia. State U., 1956; m. Janet Pomeroy Avery, June 26, 1912; children—John Watson Foster, Lillias Pomeroy (Mrs. Robert Hinshaw), Avery. Began practice, N.Y. City, 1911; mem. Sullivan & Cromwell, 1911-49; past trustee Bank N.Y. Chmn. Rockefeller Found., Carnegie Endowment for Internat. Peace, Gen. Edn. Bd. Past mem. N.Y. State Banking Bd. Past trustee Union Theol. Sem., N.Y. Pub. Library, Secretary of The Hague Peace Conference, 1907; member of the 2d Pan-Am. Scientific Congress, special agent Department of State, in Central America, 1917; captain and major U.S. Army, 1917-18; asst. to chairman War Trade Bd., 1918; counsel to Am. Commn. to Negotiate Peace, 1918-19; mem. Reparations Commn. and Supreme Econ. Council, 1919; legal adviser, Polish plan of financial stabilization, 1927. American rep. Berlin debt conferences, 1933. Mem. U.S. del. San Francisco Conf. on World Orgn., 1945, United Nations Gen. Assembly, 1946, 47, 50; acting chmn. U.S. delegation U.N. Gen. Assembly, Paris, 1948; adviser to Sec. of State at council of Fgn. Ministers, London, 1945, 1947, Moscow, 1947, Paris, 1949. Apptd. interim United States senator, 1949; consultant to Secretary of State, 1950; spl. rep. of President, with rank of ambassador, negotiated Japanese Peace Treaty, 1951, and Australian, New Zealand, Philippine and Japanese Security Treaties, 1950-51; apptd. Sec. of State, 1952. Member National Aeronautics and Space Administration; U.S. del. 13th UN general assembly. Member Association Bar City of New York, Phi Beta Kappa, Phi Delta Phi. Presbyterian. Clubs: University, Down Town Assn., Century (N.Y.); Metropolitan (Washington). Author: War, Peace and Change, 1939; War or Peace, 1950. Writer and speaker on internat. affairs. Home: 610 Park Av., N.Y.C.; also 2740 32d St., N.W., Washington. Office: Secretary of State, Washington. Died May 24, 1959; buried Arlington Nat. Cemetery.

DUMAINE, Frederic Christopher (dū-mān'); b. Hadley, Mass., Mar. 6, 1866; s. Christopher and Cordelia (Roberts) D.; ed. pub. schs. of Dedham; m. Louise Gould, Dec. 3, 1923. Pres. Commonwealth Corp.; v.p. and dir. Boston Railroad Holding Co.; pres. and trustee Amoskeag Co.; mem. exec. com. and dir. Boston Mfrs. Mutual Fire Insurance Co.; chmn. and pres. N.Y.,N.H.&H. R.R. Co.; chmn. John P. Maguire & Co., Inc.; dir. New Eng. Steamship Co., Paper Mill Mut. Ins. Co., Boston Garden Arena Corp., Baystate Corp.; mem. Boston Advisory bd. Guarantee Co. of N. America. Home: Groton, Mass. Office: 199 Washington St., Boston. Died May 27, 1951; buried Groton, Mass.

DUMAS, Gustave (dōō'mā), university administrator; born at Flushing, New York, June 11, 1898; son of Alexander and Margaret (Harkins) D.; A.B., Woodstock Coll., 1922, A.M., 1925; B.L. University of Montreal, 1924; Ph.D., University of Paris (Sorbonne), 1936; research U. of Montreal, Oxford, Lyons (France), Univ. of Amsterdam. Joined Soc. of Jesus (Jesuits), 1918; ordained priest of Roman Catholic Ch., 1930. Instr., St. Peter's Prep. Sch., Jersey City, N.J., 1925, Georgetown U., Washington, D.C., 1926-28; studies in Europe, 1928-36; asst. prof., Romance Langs., Fordham Grad. Sch., 1936, head of the department, 1937, dean 1938, administrator since 1951. Member of the general advisory bd. Anglo-Am.-Hellenic Bureau of Edn. Mem. Nat. Ednl. Assn., Nat. Cath. Ednl. Assn., Am. Assn. of Sch. Administrs., Am. Assn. for Advancement of Science, Cath. Hist. Assn. Author: Histoire du Journal de Trévoux, 1936. Contbr. to scholarly jours. Address: Fordham Univ., N.Y.C. 58. Died May 28, 1958; buried St. Andrews, Poughkeepsie, N.Y.

DUMAS, Walter A(lexander), army officer; born Sherman, Tex., Nov. 25, 1893; s. DeBerry Glenn and Bessie Holland (Leecraft) D.; B.S., Davidson (N.C.) Coll., 1915, M.A., 1916; Ga. Sch. Tech., summer, 1914; Med. Dept., Texas U., 1916-17; grad. Inf. Sch., 1923; Comd. and Gen. Staff Sch., 1933; Chem. Warfare Sch. and Army War Coll., 1936; m. Josephine Lawson, May 12, 1921; children—Joy Lawson (Mrs. John Bispham Stokes), Walter Arthur. Served with Siberian A.E.F., 1919-20, P.I., 1920-22; instr. Inf. Sch., Ft. Benning, Ga., 1923-27, 1940-41, Tactics Dept., U.S. Mil. Acad., 1927-31; gen. staff 9th Corps Area, Fourth Army and Western Defense Comd., 1936-40, 1941-42; comdr. 317th Inf.; comdr. Tank Destroyer Replacement Training Center, 1942-43; with gen. staff, overseas, 1943; promoted through the grades from 2d lt., 1917, to brigadier general, 1943; plans and operations officer (G-3) U.S.A.F., So. Pacific, 1943-44; 10th Army, 1944-45; G-3 sect. gen. staff Far East Comd. (Gen. MacArthur), 1945-47. Retired Oct. 1947 for phys. disability. World War II campaigns: No. Solomons, Ryukus (Okinawa) and others. Mem. S.A.R., Pi Kappa Alpha, Sigma Upsilon, Phi Chi. Mason (32°, K.T., Shriner. Nat. Sojourners). Decorations; Distinguished Service Medal, Legion of Merit (U.S. Army, U.S. Navy). Home: 3340 Santiago St., S.F. 16. Died Sept. 11, 1952; buried Arlington Nat. Cemetery.

DUMBAULD, Horatio Snyder, judge; b. Saltlick Twp., Fayette County, Pa., May 15, 1869; s. George Adams and Elizabeth (Snyder) D.; B.S., Mount Union Coll., 1895; m. Lissa Grace MacBurney, June 9, 1903; 1 son, Edward. Tchr. pub. schs. at various times, 1884-98; admitted to Pa. bar, 1899, began practice at Uniontown; mem. Pa. Ho. of Reps., 1899-1901; U.S. atty. Western dist., Pa., 1933-36; judge Ct. of Common Pleas, Fayette County, Pa., 1936—. Mem. Democratic Central Com., Fayette County several campaigns; del. Dem. Nat. convs., 1916, 1932. Mem. Pa., Fayette County bar assns., Sigma Nu. Democrat. Presbyn. Mason (Shriner), Elk. Club:

Triangle. Home: 44 S. Mt. Vernon Av., Uniontown, Pa. Office: Uniontown, Pa. Died Oct. 29, 1945; buried Dickerson Run Cemetery.

DUMLER, Martin George (dum'lẽr), composer; b. Cincinnati, O., Dec. 22, 1868; s. Martin and Magdalena (Diem) D.; prep. edn., St. Joseph Sch., Cincinnati, 1874-80, St. Xavier Coll., 1880-81; student Coll. of Music of Cincinnati, 1895-1901, Mus.M., from same, 1924, honorary Mus.D., 1934; LL.D., St. Xavier Coll., 1927; studied painting with Martin Rettig, Richard Busebaum and E. H. Potthast; m. Pearl Estelle Droste, Jan. 23, 1907; 1 son, Martin Henry. Began musical career as choir boy at St. Joseph's R.C. Ch., Cincinnati; visited mus. centers of Europe, 1889; has produced numerous sacred and secular compositions played in U.S. and Europe including Opus 40, a mus. setting of the "Stabat Mater" played by the Cincinnati Mus. Festival Assn., 1935. Received $500 Sachs Prize for outstanding achievement 1944, on composition Ballet Scenes, Opus 50, played by Cincinnati Symphony Orchestra under Eugene Goossens; Te Deum performed Cincinnati Musical Festival, 1946. With Chatfield & Woods Sack Co., pres. since 1929. Pres. Bruckner Soc. of America (hon. mem. Internat. Bruckner Soc. of Vienna); v.p. Coll. of Music of Cincinnati; dir. Cincinnati May Festival Assn.; life mem. Cincinnati Art Museum Assn.; mem. exec. com. Soc. of St. Gregory of America; mem. Nat. Assn. for Am. Composers and Conductors. Catholic. Clubs: Queen City, Cincinnati, McDowel, Musicians. Art (Cincinnati); Salmagundi (New York); Hyde Park Country. Home: 1607 Dexter Av., Cincinnati 6. Office: Arbor Place, Station O, Cin. 8. Died Oct. 19, 1958.

DUMOND, Frank Vincent, artist; b. Rochester, N.Y., 1865; s. A. M. and Elizabeth A. D.; pupil of Boulanger, Lefebvre and Benjamin-Constant, Paris; m. Helen Xavier, Mar. 9, 1896. Recipient 3d class medal, Paris Salon, 1890; gold medal, Boston, 1892, Atlanta Expn., 1895; 2 silver medals, Buffalo Expn., 1901; silver medal, St. Louis Expn., 1904. N.A., 1906; mem. Soc. Mural Painters, Archtl. League, Artists' Fund. Mem. Internat. Jury Awards, Panama Expn., 1915. Clubs: Century, National Arts, Lotos. Home: Lyme, Conn. Died Feb. 1951.

DUNBAR, (Helen) Flanders, psychiatrist; b. Chicago, Illinois; daughter Francis William and Edith (Flanders) Dunbar; grad. Brearley Sch., N.Y. City, 1919; B.A., Bryn Mawr Coll., 1923; M.A., Columbia, 1924, Ph.D., 1929, Med. Sc.D., 1935; B.S., Union Theol. Sem., 1927; M.D., Yale, 1930; m. George Henry Soule (retaining own name by law); 1 dau., Marcia Winslow Dunbar-Soule. Clinical research Worcester (Mass.) State Hosp., summer 1925, and various periods later; sub-internship New Haven Hosp., 1928; hospitant in Gen. and Psychiatric-Neurological Hosp. and Clinic of U. of Vienna, and asst. at Burghölzli, Zurich, 1929-30; asst. in medicine Columbia U. Coll. of Phys. and Surg. and Presbyn. Hosp., 1930-34; clin. asst. vis. physician Bellevue Hosp., 1935-37; instr. in psychiatry Columbia Univ. Coll. of Phys. and Surg. and asst. attending psychiatrist Presbyn. Hosp. and Vanderbilt Clinic, 1931-36. asso. in psychiatry, asst. physician and asso. attending psychiatrist, 1936-49; in charge psychosomatic research, 1932-49; asso. mem. staff Greenwich (Conn.) Hosp., 1944-49; practicing med. as specialist in psychiatry and psychosomatic problems; instructor N.Y. Psychoanalytic Institute. 1941-49. Diplomate Nat. Bd., Am. Bd. Psychiatry and Neurology. Qualified psychiatrist, N.Y. State, Conn. Mem. exec. com. N.Y. City Com. on Mental Hygiene; sec. Welfare Council and chmn. sub-com. on psychiat. problems in somatic disorders, 1936-48. Fellow N.Y. Acad. Medicine (neurology and psychiatry; sec., asso. treas., com. emotions and health 1932-38), Am. Psychiat. Assn. (sec.-treas. 1939-40, vice chmn. 1940-41. sect. psychoanalysis), Am. Geriatrics Soc., Internat. Assn. Gerontology, N.Y. Acad. Sci.; mem. A.M.A., A.A.A.S., Academy of Psychoanalysis, Association for Psychiatric Treatment of Offenders, New York Society of Clinical Psychiatry, Am. Psychoanalytic Assn. (treas. 1942-45), N.Y. Psychoanalytic Soc. (edn. com. 1942-44), Am. Psychopath. Assn. (v.p. 1942-45), Assn. for Research in Nervous and Mental Diseases, Internat. Psychoanalytic Assn., med. socs. County N.Y., State. N. Y., Nat. Com. on Alcoholism, Nat. Safety Council, N.Y. State Acad. Gen. Practice, World Med. Assn., UNICEF (U.S. Com., Inc.), American Orthopsychiat. Assn., Am. Psychomatic Soc. (council 1947; formerly Am. Soc. Research Psychosomatic Problems), American Com. for World Fedn. for Mental Health, Greenwich Med. Soc. Clubs: Colonial Dames, Bryn Mawr, Cosmopolitan. Author: Symbolism in Medieval Thought, 1929; Emotions and Bodily Changes, 1935, rev. 1954; Psychosomatic Diagnosis, 1943, rev. 1956; Mind and Body: Psychosomatic Medicine, 1947, rev. 1955; Synopsis of Psychosomatic Diagnosis and Treatment, 1948; Your Child's Mind and Body, 1949; Psychiatry in the Medical Specialties, 1959. Translator: Eugen Kahn's Psychopathic Personalities, 1931. Inaugurator Jour. Psychosomatic Medicine, exptl. and clin. studies, monograph supplements, editor in chief, 1938-47, now emeritus. Contbr. numerous sci. articles. Collaborating editor Psychoanalytic Quarterly, 1938-40, editor, 1939-40. Editor Acta Psychotherapeutica, Psychosomatica et Orthopaedagogica. Home: South Kent, Conn. Office: South Kent, Conn.; 1 E. 69th St., N.Y.C. 21. Died Aug. 1959.

DUNCA, Frederick S., gen. counsel. Am. Chain & Cable Co. Address: care American Chain & Cable Co., Inc., 929 Connecticut Av., Bridgeport, Conn. Died 1952.

DUNCAN, Carson Samuel, economist; b. Crawford County, Ill., Aug. 25, 1879; s. John Calvin and Sarah Jane (Martin) D.; A.B., Wabash Coll., 1901; A.M., Columbia, 1905; Ph.D., U. Chgo., 1913; m. Beatrice H. Sheets, Aug. 29, 1915; children—Hugh Scott, Roderick Martin. Prof. English, Ohio State U., 1906-14; asst. prof. marketing U. Chgo., 1915-18; statis. expert Am. Shipping Mission, London, Eng., 1918-19, U.S. Shipping Bd., 1918-19; at Peace Conf., Paris, 1919; chief investigator, Nat. Indsl. Conf. Bd., 1919-21; dir. Bur. of Research, Southern Wholesale Grocers' Assn., 1921-22; economist, Assn. Am. R.Rs., 1922. Mem. Am. Econ. Assn., Am. Statis. Assn, Phi Beta Kappa Club: Cosmos Presbyn Author: Argumentation (with other), 1910; Commercial Reearch, 1919; Marketing—Its Problems and Methods, 1920; A National Transportation Policy, 1936. Ret., 1949. Home: 23 Berenda Way, Ladera, Menlo Park, Cal. Died Oct. 1, 1958.

DUNCAN, Glenn A., educator; b. Huntington, Ind., Dec. 2, 1896; s. Allen Grant and Annie Ruth (Evans) D.; student Valporaiso U., 1915-16, Huntington Coll., 1916-17; A.B., U. Wis., 1930, grad. study, summers 1932, 34, 37, 40; m. Sybil Constance Robbins, July 10, 1925; 1 son, Glenn Allen. With Erie R.R., 1914-15, Simmons Co., Kenosha, Wis., 1919-21, Y.M.C.A., Madison, Wis., 1922-25, Karstens Clothing Store, 1925-26; head dept. English White Pine High Sch., Ely, Nev., 1930-50; state supt. pub. instrn. Nev., 1950——. Fire supr. Fred. Bur. Land Mgmt., summers, 1942-48. Served with A.E.F., 1917-19; disch. as sgt. Mem. Nev. Edn. Assn. (past pres., v.p since 1950), Nev. Class Room Tchrs. Assn. (past pres.), Am. Assn. Sch. Adminstrs., Western Adminstrn. Assn., State Sch. Officers Assn. (nat. chief), N.E.A., Nev. State Sch. Adminstrs. Assn., Am. Legion, 40 and 8. Club: Lions. Office: State Capitol, Carson City, Nev. Died June 27, 1956.

DUNCAN, Herschel Mills, coffee co. exec.; b. Fountain Run, Ky., Nov. 5, 1888; s. John G. and Amelia (Neal) D.; student U. Ky.; m. Linnie Dunn, June 5, 1912; children—Katherine (Mrs. Cummings), Amelia (Mrs. Lewis N. White), Herschel Mills, Harriet (Mrs. Paul E. Taft). Laborer Cheek Neal Coffee Co., Houston, 1907-18; founder, 1918, since pres., gen. mgr. Duncan Coffee Co., Houston. Dir. Houston Horse Show; past mem. bd. mgrs. Jefferson Davis Hosp. Ky. col. Mem. Nat. Coffee Assn. (dir.), Houston Fat Stock Show (life). Mason (Shriner). Clubs: River Oaks Country, Houston, Houston Country (Houston); Ramada; Tejas; Texas Corinthian Yacht. Home: 3320 Chevy Chase St., River Oaks, Houston 19. Office: 1200 Carr St., Houston. Died Feb. 15, 1957.

DUNCAN, Stuart, business exec. Chmn., dir. Marquette Cement Mfg. Co.; pres., dir. La Salle State Bank. Home: 801 7th St. Office: 654 First St., La Salle, Ill. Deceased.

DUNGAY, Neil Stanley (dŭn'gā), pub. health educator; b. near Faribault, Minn., Sept. 28, 1882; s. Moses L. and Ida M. (Herreman) D.; studied summers, Bklyn. Inst. Arts and Scis., Cold Spring Harbor, N.Y., Marine Biol. Lab., Woods Hole, Mass., U. Wis.; B.A., U. Minn., 1904, M.D., 1925; Ph.D., U Chgo, 1913; traveled and studied in England and Germany, 1929, Africa, Asia, 1937; m. Maude Belle Dodge, June 1907 (died 1927); m. 2d, Freda Esther Eyrich, Aug. 25, 1928. Instr. sci. high sch., Marshall, Minn., 1904-06; instr., acting prof., prof. biology Carleton Coll., 1907-25; physician with student health service U. Minn., 1924-25; dir. student health service, chmn. div. of health and physical edn. Carleton Coll., 1925-37, prof. hygiene and pub. health, 1925—. Mem. Woods Hole Corp. Served as pvt. and 2d lt. 2d Minn. Inf., N.G., 1909-11; with S.A.T.C., Ft. Sheridan, 1918. Fellow Am. Pub. Health Assn., A.A A.S., A.M.A.; mem. Minn. Med. Assn., Rice County Med. Soc., North Central Student Health Assn. (pres. 1936-37), Phi Beta Pi, Phi Beta Kappa, Sigma Xi, Alpha Omega Alpha. Ind. Republican. Conglist. Mason. Home: 611 E. Third St., Northfield, Minn. Died Sept. 19, 1958; buried Oaklawn Cemetery, Northfield, Minn.

DUNHAM, James Henry, clergyman, educator; b. Bedminster, N.J., July 31, 1870; s. Sering P. and Anna L. (Bergen) D.; A.B., Princeton, 1891, A.M., 1894; grad. Princeton Theol. Sem., 1895; studied U. Berlin, Germany, 1895-96; Ph.D., U. Pa., 1913; LL.D., Franklin and Marshall Coll., 1923, Temple U., 1945; m. Mary McMullin Barrows, June 10, 1904; 1 son, Barrows. Ordained to Presbyn. ministry, 1896; pastor 1st Ch., Mt. Holly, 1896-1912; tchr. Haverford (Pa.) Sch., 1914-15; prof. ethics Temple U., Phila., 1914-15, prof. philosophy, 1915-42, dean Coll. Liberal Arts and Sciences, 1915-42, dean emeritus, 1942—. Served as moderator of the Presbytery, 1902; commr. Gen. Assembly, 1905. Mem. Am. Philos. Assn., A.A.A.S., Am. Acad. Polit. and Social Science, Am. Assn. U. Profs., Pa. Acad. Fine Arts, Hist. Soc. Pa., S.R., Order Founders and Patriots (chaplain-general, 1938), Holland Soc. N.Y., Phi Beta Kappa. Club: University (Phila., Winter Park, Fla.). Author: Freedom and Purpose—The Psychology of Spinoza, 1916; John Fourteen, 1917; Principles of Ethics, 1929; The Religion of Philosophers, 1947. Home: Hamilton Ct., Phila. 4. Died Oct. 20, 1953.

DUNHAM, Robert James; b. Chgo., Mar. 12, 1876; s. James Sears and Mary E. (Brown) D.; student Harvard, 1895-97; m. Ethel L. Richardson, Dec. 6, 1899; children—Caryl, Robert J., Josephine A., Phelps; m. 2d, Edith Preston Drown, Apr. 19, 1923. Sec. Dunham Towing & Wrecking Co., 1897-1901; in vessel brokerage and marine ins. bus., 1901-03; pres. Shipowners' Dry Dock Co., 1903-06; treas. Western Cold Storage Co., 1907; entered employ Armour & Co., 1907, becoming asst. treas., 1909, later v.p., resigned 1920; v.p. Universal Oil Products Co. until 1931. Chmn. Ill. Emergency Relief Com., 1933-35; pres. Chgo. Park Dist., 1934——; adminstr. Ill. Works Progress Adminstrn., 1935-37. Clubs: Chicago, Saddle and Cycle, Casino. Home: 1500 Lake Shore Drive, Chgo. Died Feb. 1948.

DUNHAM, Russell H., explosives co. exec.; former pres., chmn. bd., chmn. finance com., dir. Hercules Powder Co.; dir. N.Y. Trust Co., Equitable Trust Co. Home: 1107 N. Broome St. Office: Delaware Trust Bldg., Wilmington 6, Del. Died Feb. 1, 1958.

DUNKLEY, Ferdinand Luis, musician; born London, Eng., July 16, 1869; s. Walter Samuel and Elizabeth (Walker) D.; student Trinity Coll. of Music, London, 1884-86; scholarship for composition Royal Coll. of Music, London, 1886-90; m. Maud Elizabeth Pitman, July 4, 1893 (died 1911); 1 dau., Eugenie Aleen (dec.); m. 2d, Margaret Mary Gwyther, June 3, 1912; 1 dau., Annabelle Margaret Elizabeth (Mrs. Peter W. Kecher). Came to U.S., 1893, naturalized, 1938. Master of music St. Agnes Sch., Albany, N.Y., 1893-99; mus. dir. Asheville (N.C.) Coll., 1899-1901; organist in churches of Vancouver, B.C., and Seattle, 1909-13; condr. Philharmonic Orchestra, New Orleans, 1913-14; organist and condr., Seattle and Tacoma, Wash., 1914-20, Birmingham, Ala., 1920-28; organist St. Charles Av. Presbyn. Ch., and Temple Sinai, New Orleans, 1929-44; prof. organ and composition, and teacher voice and piano, Loyola Coll. of Music, New Orleans, 1932——; organist, Unitarian Church, 1950——; past dir. Ursuline College Glee Club. Condr. music festival, Asheville, N.C., 1901; organizer New Orleans Choral-Symphony Soc., also music festivals in Old French Opera House, New Orleans; condr. "All Dunkley" program, New Orleans, 1948; gave world premier of From the Far West suite for orchestra, under Ole Windingstad, Albany, N.Y., 1947. At various times served as organist in chs. in Albany, N.Y., Asheville, N.C., and Birmingham, Ala.; now organist First Unitarian Ch., New Orleans. Fellow Am. Guild of Organists, Royal College of Organists London; mem. Am. Soc. Composers, Authors and Pubs., Nat. Assn. Teachers of Singing, Nat. Cath. Music Educators Assn. (past officer La. unit), New Orleans Music Teachers Assn. Episcopalian. Club: New Orleans Writers (president 1951; branch of National Writers Club). Compositions include: Rustic Suite for Orchestra; Cradle Song; Blessed Is the Man; Bring Flowers; (song) The Veil; Late September; The Wreck of the Hesperus; Sabbath Eve Service; Leif Erikson; The Blacksmith's Serenade; From the Far West. Author: The Buoyant Voice, Acquired by Pitch Control, 1942; Nature's Law of Voice, 1946. Home: 30 Moore Av., Waldwick, N.J. Died Jan. 5, 1956; buried Greenwood Cemetery, New Orleans.

DUNLEVY, Robert Baldwin, educator; b. Sparta, Wis., Dec. 14, 1870; s. Robert M. and Sarah Baldwin (Canfield) D.; B.L., U. Wis., 1893; post-grad. work U. Chgo., 3 quarters, 1894, 1906, 07; grad. student, asst. in chemistry, U. Wis., 1908-9, A.M., 1909; m. Edith May Andrus, June 22, 1897. Prof. chemistry and geology Southwestern Coll., Winfield, Kan., 1895—. Geologist, dir. Cowley Oil Co. Mem. City Council, Winfield, 1899-1907. Mem. A.A.A.S., Am. Chem. Soc., Kan. Acad. Sci., Delta Upsilon, Progressive Republican. Methodist. Club: Winfield Commerical. Home: Winfield, Kan. Died Dec. 31, 1948.

DUNN, Charles Wesley, lawyer; b. Annapolis, N. S., Can., July 26, 1885; s. Simeon Billingham and Emma (March) D.; brought to U.S. in childhood; student Monson (Mass.) Acad., 1899-1903; A.B., Princeton, 1907; A.M., Columbia, 1909; LL.B., N. Y.U., 1911; m. Alice Louise Hafner, Sept. 9, 1925; children—Anne Bemister, Charles Wesley. Admitted to N.Y. bar, 1911, and since practiced in N.Y.C.; gen. counsel for Grocery Mfrs. of Am., Inc., Am. Pharm. Mfrs. Assn., Premium Advertising Assn. of Am., World Med. Assn. (dir.; U.S. com. gen. counsel), and numerous mfrs. of food, pharm. and other products; pres. The Food Law Inst., Inc.; prof. law N.Y.U. in charge its pioneer nat. center grad. instrn. in food and drug law; mem. Atty Gen.'s Nat. Com. to study the anti-trust laws; corporator Norwalk (Conn.) Savs. Soc.; dir. Swiss Am. Corp., N.Y.

Mem. nat. citizens div. com. FAO; mem. nat. adv. com. to program in agr. and bus. Harvard Grad. Sch. Bus. Adminstrn. Trustee Nutrition Found. Mem. Am. Bar Asso. (chmn. com. on food, drug and cosmetic law, sect. corp., banking, bus. law; mem. FTC com. of sect. of anti-trust law), N.Y. State Bar Asso. (chmn. sect., food drug and cosmeitc law, chmn. sect. on anti-trust law; mem. spl. com. to study N.Y. State antitrust laws), Bar Assn. City of N.Y., Phi Gamma Delta. Republican. Presbyn. Clubs: N. Y.U. Faculty; University (N.Y.); Key and Seal (Princeton). Editor: Food, Drug and Cosmetic Law Journal. Author: Dunn's Food and Drug Laws, 1927; Dunn's Fed. Food, Drug, and Cosmetic Act, 1939; Dunn's Wheeler-Lea Act, 1939. Co-editor: Kleinfeld & Dunn's Federal Food, Drug and Cometic Act, 1938-49, also 1949-50, 1951-52; How to Comply With Antitrust Laws (book). Contributor to legl publs. Home: Wilson Point, S. Norwalk, Conn. Office: 608 5th Av., N.Y.C. 20. Died Nov. 2, 1959.

DUNN, Emmett Reid, coll. prof.; b. Alexandria, Va., Nov. 21, 1894; s. Emmett Clarke and Mary Cassandra (Reid) D.; A.B., Haverford Coll., 1915, M.A., 1916; Ph.D., Harvard, 1921; m. Alta Merle Taylor, Mar. 15, 1930. Teacher at Smith Coll., 1916-28; with Haverford (Pa.) Coll. since 1929, David Scull prof. biology since 1935; curator reptiles and amphibians, Phila. Acad. Natural Sciences since 1937. Served as ensign, U.S.N.R.F., 1918. Received John Simon Guggenheim Fellowship, 1928. Mem. Academia Colombiana de Ciencias, Am. Soc. Ichthyologists and Herpetologists (sec. and editor jour. 1924-29, pres. 1930 and 1931). Clubs: Harvard Travellers (Cambridge, Mass.); Explorers (New York). Home: 748 Rugby Rd., Bryn Mawr, Pa. Office: Haverford College, Haverford, Pa. Died Feb. 13, 1956; buried Alxanderia, Va.

DUNN, Gano, elec. engr.; b. New York, N.Y., Oct. 18, 1870; s. N. Gano and Amelia (Sillick) D.; B.S., Coll. City of New York, 1889; M.S., 1897; E.E., Columbia, 1891, hon. M.S., 1914; hon. D.Sc., Columbia, 1938, Rutgers, 1938, N.Y. University, 1941; Doctor of Engineering, Lehigh University, 1942; D.Sc. (honorary), City College, New York, 1947; LL.D. (honorary), Bowdoin College, 1947; married Julia Gardiner Gayley, Aug. 26, 1920 (died May 12, 1937). With the Western Union Telegraph Co., 1886-91, also Crocker-Wheeler Electric Mfg. Co., v.p. and chief engr., 1898-1911; v.p. in charge engring. and constrn., J. G. White & Co., Inc., New York, 1911-13; pres. The J. G. White Engring. Corp. since 1913; trustee Greenwich Savings Bank; dir. Guaranty Trust Co.; trustee and dir. Panhandle Eastern Pipe Line Co., 1936-43; dir. Radio Corp. of Am., Nat. Broadcasting Co., R.C.A. Communications, Inc.; dir. Regional Plan Assn., Inc. President New York Elec. Soc., 1900-02, Am. Inst. Elec. Engrs., 1911-12, United Engring. Soc., 1913-16; chmn. The Engring. Foundation, 1915-16; chairman Nat. Research Council, 1923-28; v.p. Internat. Elec. Congress, Turin, 1911; U.S. delegate and mem. exec. com., World Power Conf., 1936; chmn. Am. Com. World Powers Conf., 1946-52; mem. N.Y. State Committee on Tech. Industrial Development since 1944. Member War Dept. Nitrate Commn., 1916-18; chmn. Visiting Com. Bur. of Standards since 1928; chmn. State Dept. special com. on submarine cables, 1918. Hon. mem. Assn. Iron and Steel Engrs., Am. Institute E.E. (pres. 1911-12). Fellow Inst. Radio Engrs., Royal Micros. Soc., A.A. A.S., N.Y. Acad. Sciences, N.Y. Micros. Soc.; member Pan-American Society (honorary president), Am. Society Mech. Engrs. (hon. mem. 1944), Am. Soc. C.E., British Instn. E.E. (hon. sec. for U.S.), Franklin Inst., Illuminating Engring. Soc., New York Hist. Soc., N.Y. Zoöl. Soc., Pilgrims (chmn. exec. committee, Optical Society of America, Horological Institute of America, Nat. Acad. Sciences, Am. Acad. Arts and Sciences, Am. Philos. Soc. Mem. S.R., N.Y. Chamber Commerce. Mem. visiting com. Harvard Engineering School. Trustee Barnard College; chmn. trustees Cooper Union for Advancement Sci. and Art; mem. President's Com. on Civil Service Improvement, 1939; mem. Patent Office Adv. Com., 1939-41; member mayors Bus. Advisory Com., City of New York; consultant New York City Housing Authority, 1941; special consultant on power and steel, Office of Production Management; member board trustees Cathedral of St. John the Divine, Grant Monument Association, member Business Advisory Council for Department of Commerce; member Science Advisory Board, 1932-36; president Society of Older Graduates of Columbia, 1933-38; pres. Phi Beta Kappa Alumni in New York, 1940, Phi Beta Kappa Associates, 1944. War Dept. cons., 1947; mem. N.Y. State Univ. Commn., 1947. Awarded Townsend Harris medal, 1933, Edison medal, 1937; Hoover medal, 1939; Egleston medal, 1939; Modern Pioneer Award, National Association of Manufacturers, 1940; Pan-American Soc. Medal, 1947; Peter Cooper medal, 1950. Decorated Order Honor and Merit, Republic of Haiti, 1940. Clubs: Union, Univ., Knickerbocker, Fencers, Columbia Univ., Engineers', Recess, Century, Church, New York Yacht, Cruising Club of America, Tuxedo, Downtown (New York); Cosmos (Washington, D.C.). Contributor various papers on elec. and engring. subjects. Office: 80 Broad St., N.Y.C. 4. Died Apr. 10, 1953.

DUNN, Harvey, artist; b. Manchester, S.D., Mar. 8, 1884; s. Thomas and Bersha (Dow) D.; ed. Art Inst. Chicago, 1902-04; Howard Pyle Sch. Art, 1904-06; Doctor Fine Arts, South Dakota State College, 1952; m. Johanne Krebs, March 12, 1908; children—Robert Kruse, Louise (Mrs. John Randolph Rutherford). Magazine illustrator since 1906 for leading publications, murals, portraits; teacher Grand Central Sch., New York. Was official artist with A.E.F., capt. Mem. Nat. Acad. Design, Soc. Illustrators (pres. 1948-49). Mason. Clubs: Artists Guild, Salmagundi. Author: Evening in the Classroom, 1934; A permanent collection of more than 40 of his paintings acquired by S.D. State Coll., 1951. Home: 20 Forest Rd., Tenafly, N.J. Died Oct. 29, 1952.

DUNN, Ignatius J., lawyer; b. Sarpy County, Neb., Feb. 1, 1868; s. Michael and Mary (McBride) D.; ed. dist. sch.; m. M. Maud Wingrove, Apr. 16, 1900. Studied law while working as stereotyper; admitted to bar, 1890, since in practice at Omaha; dep. county atty. Douglas County, Neb., 1898-1901; dep. city atty., Omaha, 1906-11; Dem. nominee for Congress, 1896 (declined); del.-at-large Dem. Nat. Conv., Denver, 1908, Balt., 1912, Phila., 1936 (placed W. J. Bryan in nomination for presidency, 1908). Catholic. Home: 3323 Frances St. Office: First Nat. Bank Bldg., Omaha, Neb. Died Mar. 1958.

DUNN, Sir James Hamet, industrialist; b. Bathurst, N.B., Can., Oct. 29, 1875; s. Robert and Elizabeth (Joudrey) D.; LL.B., Dalhousie U., 1898, LL.D.; LL.D., U. N.B., U. Bishops Coll., Queen's U.; D.Sc., Laval U. Admitted to bars of N.S., Ont., P.Q., N.W. Territories; Kings Counsel of P.Q.; mem. Montreal Stock Exchange; sr. partner Dunn Fisher & Co., pvt. banking house, London, Eng.; pres., chmn. bd. dirs. Algoma Steel Corp. and subsidiaries, Sault Ste Marie, Ont.; dir., chmn. exec. com. Can. S.S. Lines. Created Baronet, 1921. Hon. col., 49th Heavy Anti Aircraft Regt., R.C.A., Canadian Army. Mem. Bar. of N.B. (hon.), Dalhousie U. Alumnia (pres., 1948). Home: Saint Andrews, New Brunswick. Office: Algoma Steel Corp., Sault Ste Marie, Ont., Can. Died Jan. 1, 1956.

DUNN, Joseph, educator; b. New Haven; s. Thomas K. and Abigail (Leary) D.; A.B., Yale, 1895, Ph.D., 1898; Officer d'Académie; grad. student Harvard, 1901-02, U. Frieburg, Baden, 1902-03, Faculté des lettres, Rennes, France, 1903-04. Instr. Latin, Cath. U. Am., 1898-1900, Romance langs., 1900-01, prof. Celtic langs. and lits., 1904—; lectr. Celtic, Linguistic Inst., Yale, 1928-29, Coll. City of N.Y., 1931. Fellow A.A.A.S.; mem. Phi Beta Kappa, Modern Lang. Assn. Am., Linguistic Soc. Am. (found. mem.), Irish Text Soc., Am. Irish Hist. Soc., Mediaeval Acad. Am., A.A.A.S., Folklore of Ireland Soc.; corr. mem. Instituto de Coimbra (Portugal). Catholic. Clubs: University (Washington); Graduate (New Haven). Author: A Grammar of the Modern Portuguese Language, 1927. Editor: Breton Mystery, Buez Sant Patrice, Paris, 1908; The Glories of Ireland (with P. J. Lennox), 1914. Translator: The Ancient Irish Epic Tale of Táin Bó Cúalnge, London, 1913. Contbr. to Am. and European revs., dictionaries and encys.; specialist-contbr. to Webster's New Internat. Dictionary. Address: 206 Park St., New Haven. Died Apr. 9, 1951; buried St. Laurence Cemetery, New Haven.

DUNN, Robert (Steed), explorer, writer; b. Newport, R.I., Aug. 16, 1877; s. Thomas and Kate (Hunter) D.; A.B. cum laude, Harvard, 1898. Newspaper corr. U.S. Dixie expdn. Mt. Pelee, Martinique, W.I., 1901; discovered and named Mt. Hunter (14,900 feet), McKinley Range, Alaska, 1903; Russian-Japanese War, 1904; first explored and climbed new volcano island, Perry, just risen in the Bering Sea, 1906; discovered on Umnak Id. (Aleutians) crater, of Mt. Okmok, largest caldera known western hemisphere, 1906; made world cruise, U.S. Fleet, 1907; seizure of Vera Cruz, 1914; with armies in Europe, 1914-15; expdn. of Gen. Pershing into Mexico, 1916. Attached to U.S.S. Conyngham, Queenstown, Ireland, 1917; commd. lt. (j.g.) USN, 1918; intelligence officer USN Hdqrs., London, Eng., 1918-19, with U.S. High Commn., Constantinople, Turkey, 1919-22; asst. naval attaché, Ankara, Turkey, 1942-44. Led first ascent of Mt. Wrangel, Alaska, 1908; explored Kamchatka River, Siberia, 1913. Clubs: Harvard (N.Y.C); American (London). Author: The Shameless Diary of an Explorer, 1907; The Youngest World (novel), 1914; Five Fronts, 1915; Horizon Fever (novel), 1932; And Least Love (poems), 1945; World Alive, 1956, English edit., 1958. Home: Uffculme, Katonah, N.Y. Died Dec. 24, 1955; buried Newport, R.I.

DUNN, Samuel O., editor; b. Bloomfield, Ia., Mar. 8, 1877; s. Samuel W. and Sarah J. (Hedrick) D.; Pratt (Kan.) High Sch., 1894; admitted to Ill. bar, 1911 (hon. A.M., Tufts Coll., Mass., 1921); m. Carrie E. Smith, Mar. 29, 1899; children—Fayette Smith, Elizabeth, Samuel O. Learned printer's trade, 1890-95; editor, Quitman (Mo.) Record, 1895-96; asso. editor, Maryville (Mo.) Tribune, 1896-1900; reporter Kansas City Journal, 1900-02; editorial writer, Kansas City Journal, 1902-04; railroad editor and editorial writer, Chicago Tribune, 1904-07; asso. editor, and mgn. editor, Railway Age, 1907-08; western editor and editor, Railway Age Gazette, and its successor, Railway Age, 1911-48; chmn. bd. Simmons-Boardman Pub. Corp., 1931-50, chmn. emeritus, 1950—. Mem. American Econ. Assn., Western Railway Club. Clubs: Union League, Chicago, Traffic. Author: American Transportation Question, 1912; Government Ownership of Railways, 1913; Railway Regulation or Ownership?, 1918. Home: 222 E. Chestnut St. Office: 79 W. Monroe St., Chgo. 3. Died Jan. 4, 1958; buried Maryville, Mo.

DUNNING, Charles A., milling exec.; b. July 31, 1885; m. Ada Rowlatt, 1913; children—Katherine, Avery. Chmn. Ogilvie Flour Mills Co., Ltd., Montreal; dir. Bank of Montreal, C.P. Ry. Served as minister of rys., Canadian Govt., 1917, minister of telephones, 1918, minister of agr., 1919; premier Province of Saskatchewan, 1922; rep. Regina, Saskatchewan, in Canadian Parliament, 1926-30; minister of rys. and canals, 1926; became mem. Privy Council, 1926; minister of finance, 1929-30, 1935-39. Address: 3940 Cote des Neiges Rd., Montreal, Can. Died Oct. 1958.

DUNNING, Henry Sage, oral surgeon; b. in 1881, D.D.S., New York Coll. Dentistry, 1904; M.D., Coll. Phys. and Surg. (Columbia), 1911; B.Sc., New York U., 1915. Practiced, N.Y. City, 1904—; prof. emeritus oral surgery Columbia U. Sch. Dental and Oral Surgery; cons. oral surg., Nat. Speech Disorders., Greenwich, Norwalk, N.Y., Foundling hosps.; cons. oral surgeon, Knickerbocker, St. Luke's, Roosevelt, St. Vincent's hospitals, Nassau, Minneola, Vassar Brothers' hosps.; attending oral surgeon; consulting oral surgeon Harlem Eve and Ear Hospital, Manhattan Eye, Ear, Nose and Throat Hosp.; consulting oral surgeon at Sloane, Babies', Mary Immaculate, Jamaica, North Hudson, Hackensack General, State Reconstruction (West Haverstraw) and United (Port Chester) hosps.; consulting oral surgeon to St. Joseph's Hosp., Stamford, Conn., Jersey City Med. Center, Jersey City. Fellow Am. Coll. Surgeons, mem. Am. and N.Y. State med. socs., Am. Bd. Plastic Surgery, Am. Laryngol., Rhinol. and Otol. Acad. of Medicine, Vets. Fgn. Wars. Home: 108 Weed St., New Canaan, Conn. Died Feb. 10, 1957.

DUNNING, James Edwin, clergyman; b. Three Springs, Pa., Jan. 23, 1886; s. Charles T. and Mary H. (Crever) D.; A.B., Dickinson Coll., 1905, A.M., 1912, D.D., 1930; m. Daisy Winande Fisher, June 20, 1906; children—James Fisher (dec.), Charles Wesley, Edwin Crever. Prof. mathematics, Union Coll., Barbourville, Ky., 1905-06; asst. prin., high sch. Bellefonte, Pa., 1906-07; ordained to ministry M.E. Ch., 1907; pastor, Center and Sandy Ridge, Pa., 1907-08, Lumber City, Pa., 1909-12, Howard, Pa., 1912-15, Louther Meml. Ch., Johnstown, Pa., 1915-17, Ford Meml. Ch., Ford City, Pa., 1917-21, Chesterfield Sq. Ch., Los Angeles, 1921-25, Euclid Heights Ch., Los Angeles, 1925-29, Pacific Palisades, 1929-33, Orange, Cal., 1933-35; dist. supt. San Diego-Phoenix Dist., 1935-39; exec. sec. Bd. Missions and Church Extension, So. Cal. Ariz. Conf., 1939-43; exec. sec. Los Angeles Missionary and Church Extension Soc., 1939-43; asso. minister First Meth. Ch., Los Angeles, 1943-50; field sec. Conf. Endowment Fund, 1950-55; asso. minister First Ch. Downey, Cal., 1955—. Del. to Gen. Conf. M.E. Ch., Columbus, O., 1936; reserve del. Uniting Conf. The Meth. Ch., Kansas City, mo., 1939; del. 1st Gen. Conf. Meth. Ch., Atlantic City, 1940, 1st Western Jurisdictional Conf. Meth. Ch., Sn Francisco, 1940. Mem. bd. mgrs. Bd. Foreign Mission M.E. Ch., 1939; trustee All Nations Foundation, Los Angeles Missionary and Ch. Extension Soc., mem. bd. Missions and Church Extension, So. Cal.-Ariz. Conf. chmn. Los Angeles Regional to Personnel Com., Methodist Bd. Missions; chmn. dept., Survey and Planning, So. Cal. Council Protestant Chs. Mem. Alpha Chi Rho, Phi Beta Kappa. Corr. The Christian Advocate. Home: 5560 Bradna Dr., Los Angeles 43. Office: 10801 S. Downey Av., Downey, Cal. Died Sept. 26, 1958; buried Inglewood Park Cemetery, Inglewood, Cal.

DUNNING, John Wirt, ex-coll. pres.; b. Corunna, Mich., Oct. 11, 1882; s. Homer Bailey and Mary Elizabeth (Burchard) D.; A.B., Alma (Mich.) Coll., 1904, D.D., 1917; student Princeton Sem., 1904-05; B.D., McCormick Theol. Sem., 1907; m. Anna Elizabeth Mahoney, Nov. 21, 1906; 1 dau., Catherine Estelle. Ordained to ministry Presbyn. Ch., 1907; pastor First Ch., Tecumseh, Mich., 1907-10, First Ch., Portsmouth, O., 1910-16, First Ch., Kalamazoo, Mich., 1916-38; pres. Alma Coll., 1938-42. Dir. Mich., Children's Aid Soc.; mem. Kalamazoo Charter Commn.; chmn. A.R.C. for Mich.; pres. Boy Scout Council, Kalamazoo. Republican. Mason (K.T.), Rotarian (hon. life mem. Kalamazoo). Author: The Eternal Riddle, 1911; The Fight for Character, 1938; The Presbyterian Church—Its History, Its Teaching, Its Call, 1940. Contbg. editor to Sermon Digest. Writes daily column for Booth Syndicate Newspapers. Home: Route 1, Hickory Corners, Gull Lake, Mich. Died Dec. 29, 1950; buried Kalamazoo, Mich.

DUNNING, Stewart N., lawyer; b. Peekskill, N.Y., Dec. 7, 1876; s. William B. and Emma Ada (Bancroft) D.; m. Hazel C. Case, Jan 25, 1905;

children—John Stewart, Harrison Freeman, Richard Bancroft, Dorothea (Mrs. Harold Faust), Hazel (Mrs. Adolph J. Rettig), Diana, Daphne (Mrs. Robert L. Kenderdine, Jr.). Admitted to Conn. Bar, 1903; gen. counsel, Fuller Brush Co.; dir. Park Street Trust Co., Fuller Brush Co. Republican. Christian Scientist. Club: Hartford. Home: 40 Cold Spring Dr., Bloomfield, Conn. Office: 3580 Main St., Hartford, Conn. Died Nov. 22, 1951; buried Bloomfield, Conn.

DUNSHEE, Jay Dee (dŭn'shē), health officer; b. at Milton, Ia., Dec. 30, 1884; s. James Allen and Ellen (Gates) D.; M.D., U. of Ia., 1908; m. Erol Reid Willey, July 25, 1908; 1 son, Wade Allen; m. 2d, Laura Christine Gahn, May 31, 1940. In pvt. practice, 1908-17; dir. Child Welfare, Los Angeles, Calif., 1921-26; health officer, Pasadena, Calif., 1929-34; dir. State Dept. of Health, Calif., Mar. 17, 1934-Sept. 17, 1935; became pub. health advisor to State Dept. of Public Welfare, Idaho, 1935; dir. State Dept. Health, medical director State Mental Instns.; 1936, dir. local health adminstrn., Ariz., 1937-44; prin. med. officer, Poston Gen. Hosp., Poston, Ariz., 1944-47, retired. Fellow Am. Pub. Health Assn. Served as captain, U.S. Medical Corps with British and A.E.F. in France, World War I. Formerly mem. American Assn. Social Workers, publishers Journal Mental Hygiene, Southern Calif. Member bd. dirs. Los Angeles and Pasadena Child Guidance Clinic. Pres. Southern Calif. Soc. for Mental Hygiene; mem. Council on Modern Parenthood, Phi Delta Theta, Alpha Kappa Kappa. Episcopalian. Mason. Address: 526 W. Monte Vista Rd., Phoenix, Ariz. Died Jan. 28, 1956; buried Lindsey, O.

DUNWODY, William Elliott (dŭn'wŏod-ĭ), mfr.; b. Savannah, Ga., Dec. 17, 1870; s. William Elliott and Aimee Taylor (LaRoche) D.; grad. 1st honor Boys' High Sch., Macon, Ga., at 13; won scholarship offered by City of Macon and entered Mercer Univ. at 13, but left in jr. yr. to enter business; m. Elizabeth Lowe Webster, Oct. 11, 1892; children—William Elliott, Kenneth Webster. Cashier, firm of Ballance & Sorrell, Boston, Mass., 1889-91; cashier Macon (Ga.) Hardware Co., 1891-94, Union Savings Bank and Trust Company, 1894-1900; chairman bd. Cherokee Brick and Tile Co.; pres. Standard Brick Co., 1904—; dir. Coleman-Meadows-Pate Drug Co., Citizens and So. Natl. Bank (Macon, Ga.), Louisville & Wadley R.R. Adviser to U.S. adminstrn. on Structural Clay Products Code, N.R.A.; active in war work and Liberty Loan drives during World War I. Mem. Alexander Sch. Bd., Macon, Ga. Past pres. Nat. Brick Mfrs.' Assn., Ga. Brick Mfrs.' Assn., Nat. Hollow Building Tile Assn., So. Clay Products Assn.; ex-pres. Ga. State Fair Assn. Mem. Macon C. of C. (past pres.), Alpha Tau Omega. Independent Democrat. Presbyn. Mason (K.T., Shriner). Clubs: Rotary, Idle Hour Country. Home: Dunwody Dr., Rivoli, Macon. Office: Cherokee Brick & Tile Co., Macon, Ga. Died Sept. 18, 1956; buried Riverside Cemetery, Macon, Ga.

DUNWOODY, Henry Harrison Chase, army officer; b. Highland County, O., Oct. 23, 1842; s. William and Sarah (Murphy) D.; grad. U.S. Mil. Acad., 1866; LL.B., Columbian (now George Washington) U., 1876, Commd. 2d lt. 4th Arty., 1866, advanced through grades to maj. Signal Corps, 1890; lt.-col., 1897; col. chief signal officer vols., 1898; col. U.S. Army, 1898; resigned from vol. service 1898; brig.-gen., 1904; ret. at own request after 40 yrs.' service, 1904. Recorder tactics bd., St. Louis, 1869-71; weather forecaster, signal officer, Washington, 1872-91; has been supervising forecast official. Address: War Dept., Washington. Died Jan. 1, 1933.

DUPLESSIS, Maurice L., premier, P.Q., Can.; b. Trois Rivieres, P.Q., Can., Apr. 20, 1890; s. Judge N. L. and Berthe (Genest) B.; B.A., LL.B., Laval U., hon. D., Laval, Bishop, McGill, Caen (France) univs. Mem. law firm Duplessis, Langlois & Lamothe, Trois Rivieres, P.Q.; first elected to Quebec legislature, 1927; became leader of Conservative Party, 1933; formed party, Union Ntionale, 1936; premier, pres. council, atty. gen. of Quebec, 1936-39, 44—. Home: 240 Bonaventure, Trois-Rivieres, P.Q., Can. Died Sept. 7, 1959.

DU PONT, Lammot; b. Wilmington, Del., Oct. 12, 1880; s. Lammot and Mary (Belin) du P.; B.S., Mass. Inst. Tech., 1901; m. 4th, Margaret A. Flett, Nov. 24, 1933. Dir., E. I. du Pont de Nemours & Co., pres., 1926-40, chmn. bd., 1940-48; dir. Wilmington Trust Co. Mem. Am. Chem. Soc., Mfg. Chem. Association (past president). Clubs: Metropolitan (New York); Union League (Philadelphia); Wilmington. Address: Du Pont Bldg., Wilmington 98, Del. Died July 24, 1952.

DU PONT, Pierre Samuel, mfr.; b. Wilmington, Del., Jan. 15, 1870; s. Lammot and Mary (Belin) du P.; prep. edn. Penn. Charter Sch., Phila., Pa., Mass. Inst. Tech., class of 1890; m. Alice Belin, Oct. 6, 1915. Pres. E. I. du Pont de Nemours & Co., 1915-19, chmn. bd., 1919-40, hon. chmn. 1940—; helped organize Gen. Mfrs. Corp., pres. 1920-23, chmn. bd. 1923-29. Apptd. liquor commr. of Del., 1933, for term 1933-38; tax commr., Del., 1925-37, and May 1944-Oct. 1949. Mem. State Bd. of Edn., Del., 1919-21. Mem. Corp. Mass. Inst. Tech., Am. Philos. Soc., Phi Kappa Sigma. Clubs: Wilmington, City (Wilmington); Metropolitan (New York). Home: Wilmington, Del. Died Apr. 5, 1954.

DURAND, William Frederick, mech. engr.; b. Bethany, Conn., Mar. 5, 1859; s. William L. and Ruth (Coe) D.; grad. U.S. Naval Acad., 1880; Ph.D., Lafayette Coll., 1888; LL.D., U. Cal., 1927; m. Charlotte Kneen, Nov. 23, 1883. Served in Engr. Corps, USN, 1880-87; prof. mech. engring. A. and M. Coll., Mich., 1887-91; prof. marine engring. Cornell U., 1891-1904; prof. mech engring. Leland Stanford Jr. U., 1904-24; now prof. emeritus. Sci. attaché Am. Embassy, Paris, and mem. Interallied Commn. on Inventions, 1918-19; mem. President's Aircraft Bd., 1925; adv. bd. engrs. Boulder Dam Project, 1929; chmn. Navy Depts. Spl. Com. in Airship Design and Constrn., 1935. Mem. NACA, 1915-33, 41-45, Nat. Research Council, 1915-45, War Service in Washington, 1941-45. Recipient Guggenheim medal award, 1935; John Fritz medal award, 1935; Franklin Inst. medal award, 1938; Presdl. Award of Merit, 1946; Wright Mem. Trophy, 1948. Fellow Am. Acad. Arts and Scis., A.A.A.S., Royal Aero. Soc., Inst. Aero Scis. (hon.); mem. Nat. Acad. Scis. (J. J. Carty medalist 1944), Am Philos. Soc., Soc. Naval Architects and Marine Engrs., Société Technique Maritime, Am. Soc. Naval Engrs. (life mem., gold medalist), A.S.M.E. (hon. mem., medalist 1945;. Assn. Italiana di Aerotecnica (hon.). Author Fundamental Principles of Mech., 1889; Resistance and Propulsion of Ships, 1898; Practical Marine Engineering, 1901; Motor Boats, 1907; Hydraulics of Pipe Lines, 1921; Biography of Robert Henry Thurston, 1929. Gen. editor Aerodynamic Theory (6 vols.), 1934. Contbr. to engring. jours. Home: 379 Washington Av., Bklyn. 38. Died Aug. 9, 1958.

DURANTY, Walter (dû-răn'tĭ), writer, fgn. corr., lectr.; b. Liverpool, Eng., May 25, 1884: student Harrow, Bedford; m. Mrs. Anna Enwright, Sept. 1957. Fgn. corr. N.Y. Times, 1913-39, with French Armies, 1917-18, in USSR (resident), 1921-34, roving, 1934-39; corr. N.A. Newspaper Alliance in Europe, USSR, Japan. 1939-41. Recipient O. Henry short story prize, 1929, Pulitzer prize, 1932. Club: Coffee House (N.Y.C.). Author: I Write As I Please 1935; One Life, One Kopeck, 1937; The Kremlin and the People, 1942; Search for a Key, 1943; USSR, 1944; Stalin and Co., 1949. Died Oct. 3, 1957.

DURET, Miguel Lanz, lawyer, pub.; b. Mexico, D.F., Jan. 12, 1909; s. Miguel Lanz Duret and Concepción Sierra; B.S., Colegio Frances Morelos, 1928; Law Degree, Nat. U. Mexico, 1934, Master Polit. Scis. (hon.); B.J. (hon.), Columbia; m. Francisca Dolores Valdés, Feb. 26, 1937; children—Miguel Lanz, Francisco, Carlos, Dolores. With El Universal, 1934—, successively mech. supt., advt. mgr., labor relations counsel bus. mgr., gen. mgr. dailies, pres., 1940—; pres. Banco de las Artes Gráficas. Mem. Mexico City Police Commn.; pres. Inter-Am. Tribunal for Freedom of Press. Served as brig. gen. Mexican Army, World War II; comdg. officer 15th Inf. Div. Decorated Medal of Mil. Merit (Mexico); recipient Medal Honor, U. Mo., 1943; Maria Moors Cabot medal, Columbia, 1946; medal Les Palmes de l'Academie (France). Mem. Bar Assn. Mexico, Am. Soc. Mil. Engrs., Inter-Am. Press Assn. (pres. 1953-54), Sigma Delta Chi. Clubs: Chapultepec Golf, Mexico City Country, Azteca Golf, Banqueros, Jockey (Mexico City). Home: Julio Verne 27, Mexico 5. Office: Avenida Juarez 88, Mexico 1, Distrito Fed. Died Mar. 24, 1959.

DURFEE, Edgar Noble, prof. of law; b. Detroit, May 19, 1882; s. Edgar Oren and Mary (Bassett) D.; A.B., Harvard, 1904; student law sch., U. of Mich., 1905-06; J.D., U. of Chicago, 1908; m. Amy Eleanor Savage, June 28, 1911; children—George Savage (deceased), Elizabeth (Mrs. Paul Oberst), Paul Savage (lt., j.g., U.S.N.R., killed in action, P.T.O., 1943). Admitted to Mich. bar, 1908, and practiced in Detroit, 1908-10; asst. prof. law U. of Ida., 1910-11; mem. faculty U. of Mich. Law School, 1911—, prof. of law, 1915—; adviser Am. Law Inst., Restatement of Contracts, Restitution and Specific Performance, 1930-31. Reporter Am. Law Inst. Injunction Against Tort, 1937-39 (with M. T. Van Hecke). Mem. Phi Delta Phi. Roman Catholic. Democrat. Author: Cases on Mortgages, 1915; Cases on Equity, 1928; Cases on Security, 1951; Cases on Remedies, Vol. 2 (with John P. Dawson), 1939. Contbr. articles in law revs. Home: 1926 Day St., Ann Arbor, Mich. Died July 5, 1958; buried St. Thomas Cemetery, Ann Arbor.

DURHAM, Donald B(lythe), univ. prof.; b. Reading, Pa., July 14, 1883; s. Albert R(iggs) and Sarah Ann (McCurdy) D.; A.B., Princeton, 1905, A.M., 1906, (fellow in classics, 1905-06, 1909-11), Ph.D., 1911; m. Mary Darland Banta, June 27, 1911; children—Albert Riggs, Marianne (Mrs. Emory Lakatos). Teacher Mt. Tamalpais Mil. Acad., San Rafael, Calif., 1906-07; Mr. Leal's Sch., Plainfield, N.J., 1907-09; instr. in classics, Princeton, 1911-15, asst. prof., 1915-18; asst. prof. Latin and Greek, Hamilton Coll., 1918-21, asso. prof., 1921-23, prof., 1923-36, Edward North prof. Greek since 1936. Mem. managing com., Am. Sch. of Classical Studies at Athens. Mem. Am. Philol. Assn., Classical Assn. of Atlantic States (pres. 1945-47), Am. Classical League, Am. Assn. Univ. Profs., Hellenic Soc. of London, Phi Beta Kappa. Presbyterian. Contbr. to classical periodicals. Home: 21 Marvin St., Clinton, N.Y. Died Sept. 28, 1951.

DURHAM, Edward Miall, Jr., ry. exec.; b. Memphis, Tenn., Oct. 23, 1875; s. Edward Miall and Emily Alberta (Perkins) D.; grad. Memphis Mil. Acad., 1891; C.E., Lehigh U., Bethlehem, Pa., 1896, D. Engring., 1939; m. Mary Grey Wilkins, Dec. 16, 1903; children—Edward Miall (dec.), Benjamin Wilkins. Began in hydrog. surveys, U.S. Dept. of War, 1896, later recorder deep waterways State of N.Y.; transitman C.&N.-W. Ry., 1899; asst. engr. Southern Ry., 1900; successively resident engr., prin. asst. engr., asst. chief engr., chief engr. and valuation engr., Atlanta, Birmingham & Coast Ry. and exec. gen. agt. Southern Ry., 1901-19; with U.S. R.R. Adminstrn., 1920-23, serving as mgr. dept. ways and structures and dir. div. of liquidation, 1923; asst. to pres. Mo.P. Ry., 1924; v.p., 1926, sr. v.p., 1927-35; chief exec. officer C.,R.I.&P. Ry., Dec. 1, 1935-July 15, 1942; retired. Mem. Am. Soc. C.E., Am. Ry. Engring. Assn., Delta Tau Delta. Clubs: Chevy Chase (Washington, D.C.); St. Louis Country; Chicago; Bogey. Home: 900 S. Price Rd., Clayton 24, Mo. Died June 6, 1954.

DURHAM, Fred Stranahan, business exec.; b. Williamport, Pa., July 2, 1884; s. Joseph Edward and Nellie Rebecca (Stranahan) D.; student Moravian Prep. Sch., Bethlehem, Pa., 1895-98; grad. Bordentown Mil. Inst., 1902; A.B., Princeton, 1906; m. Christine Witherspoon Bryden, Apr. 29, 1916; 1 son, Fred. S. Agent Penn Mutual Ins. Co., 1906; v.p.; treas., dir. Bonney Forge & Tool Works, and predecessor co., Bonney Vise & Tool Work of Phila., 1907-33, pres., dir., 1933—; v.p., dir. Nassau Products, Inc., Allentown, Pa., 1926—; pres., dir. Trexler Lumber Co., Allentown, 1944—; dir. Allentown Nat. Bank, Jordan Hills Realty Co., Pa. Power & Light Co. Councilman Borough Catasauqua, Pa., 1934-40; chmn. finance com. Catasauqua chpt. A.R.C. Mem. and past. dir. Nat. Standard Parts Assn., Automotive Equipment Assn., C. of C., Newcomen Soc. Eng. Republican. Presbyn. Mason. Clubs: Lehigh Country, Livingston (past pres.). Developed original idea for patented welding fittings now known as WeldOlet and ThreadOlet, 1932. Home: Third and Pine Sts., Catasauqua, Pa. Office: Bonney Forge & Tools Works, Allentown, Pa. Died May 28, 1949; buried Allentown.

DURKIN, Martin, labor union exec.; b. Chgo., Mar. 18, 1894; s. James J. and Mary Catherine (Higgins) D.; ed. grammar sch., 3 years evening sch.; m. Anna H. McNicholas, Aug. 29, 1921; children—Martin B., William J., John F. Began as steamfitters apprentice, Chgo.; later business mgr. local 597, Steamfitters, Chgo.; then dir. of labor. State of Ill.; gen. pres. United Association of Plumbers and Pipefitters of U.S. and Canada. Sec. of labor, Jan.-Sept. 1953 (resigned and returned to work with union). Mem. Nat. War Labor Bd. Served in 332d Field Arty. and 6th Cav., World War I. Home: 5614 Kirkswood Dr., Chevy Chase, Md. Office: 901 Mass. Av., N.W. Washington. Died Nov. 13, 1955.

DURLING, Edgar Vincent, newspaper columnist; b. N.Y.C., July 24, 1893; s. Charles and Lily (Robinson) D.; student Phillips Andover Acad.; B.S., Wesleyan U., 1913; m. Joan Marie Boissen, March 1920. Coll. corr. Springfield (Mass.) Republican, 1910-12; on editorial staff N.Y. Morning Telegraph, 1915-18, N.Y. Globe, 1923-24, N.Y. Herald, 1924; columnist Los Angeles Express, 1931, Los Angeles News, 1931-35, Los Angeles Times, 1935-39; with King Features Syndicate, 1939—, author column On the Side. Served with U.S. Coast Arty., World War I. Republican. Episcopalian. Office: King Features Syndicate, 235 E. 45th St., N.Y.C. Died Sept. 13, 1957.

DURYEA, Nina Larrey (Mrs. Chester B. Duryea), author; b. Cohasset, Mass., Aug. 11, 1874; d. Franklin Waldo and Laura (Bevan) Smith; student Miss Hubbard's Sch. (Boston), Madame Lang's (Brussels, Belgium); m. Chester B. Duryea, June 1, 1898; 1 son, Chester B. Founder and pres. Duryea War Relief, 1914-18. Hon. mem. Nat. Inst. Social Scis.; dir. World's Center for Women's Archives. Recipient Legion of Honor, Medaille d'Or, medal of Pas de Calais, medal Dames Française Croix Rouge (France); Queen Elizabeth Order (Belgium); Order of Valor (Italy); Order of St. Anne (Russia); Mil. medal (Montenegro). Republican. Episcopalian. Club: Garden (Lenox, Mass.). Author: The House of Seven Gabblers, 1908; A Sentimental Dragon, 1911; The Voice Unheard, 1913; Mallorca the Magnificent, 1927, 31; The Pride of Maura, 1932. Contbr. to mags. Home: The Mill, Stockbridge, Mass. Died Nov. 1, 1951.

DUSHMAN, Saul (dōōsh'măn), phys. chemist; b. Rostov, Russia, July 12, 1883; s. Samuel and Olga (Hurwitz) D.; came to America, 1891; B.A., U. of Toronto, Can., 1904, Ph.D., 1912; hon. D.Sc., Union Coll., Schenectady, N.Y., 1940; m. Amelia Gurofsky,

May 1, 1907 (died May 6, 1912); m. 2d, Anna Leff, June 28, 1914; 1 dau., Beulah. Demonstrator electrochemistry, U. of Toronto, 1904-09; lecturer, 1909-12; with Research Lab., Gen. Electric Co., Schenectady, N.Y., since 1912, asst. dir., 1928-48; dir. research div. Edison Lamp Works, Harrison, N.J., 1922-25; research consultant since 1950. Mem. Am. Phys. Soc., Am. Chem. Soc. Naturalized citizen of U.S., 1917. Jewish religion. Author: High Vacuum, 1923; Elements of Quantum Mechanics, 1938; Scientific Foundations of Vacuum Technique, 1949; Fundamentals of Atomic Physics, 1951; also numerous tech. articles. Office: Gen. Electric Research Lab., P.O. Box 1088, Schenectady, N.Y. Died July 7, 1954; buried Temple Gates of Heaven Cemetery, Schenectady, N.Y.

DUTCHER, George Matthew (dŭch'ẽr), educator; b. Pleasant Valley, N.Y., Sept. 16, 1874; s. Meritt Thomas and Mary Albertson (Stoutenburg) D.; A.B., Cornell U., 1897, Ph.D., 1903, Pres. White fellow history, Europe, 1900-01; LL.D., Allegheny Coll., 1939; m. Adrienne Van Winkle, June 17, 1909. Asst. in English history, Cornell, 1898-1900; asso. prof., 1901-05, prof., 1905-46, emeritus, 1946—; v.p. Wesleyan U., 1918-21; prof. hist., Cornell, summer 1912, Columbia, 1913, 24, U. Pa., 1917 U. Cal., 1918, 21, U. Mich. 1929, Northwestern U., 1936; lectr. history, Harvard, 1923-24; vis. prof. history, Yale, 1926-28. Trustee Conn. State Hosp., 1922—, chmn. 1931—. World tour, 1921-22, lecturing before univs., colls.; vis. prof. Carnegie Endowment for Internat. Peace to univs., Hawaii, P.I., China, Japan, 1930. Chmn. com. on hist. publs., mem. of Tercentenary Commn. of Conn., 1933-36; state historian of Conn., 1936-41. Mem. Am. Hist. Assn. (chmn. com. bibliography, 1915-28), New England History Tchrs. Assn. (pres. 1918-19), Conn. Hist. Soc. (v.p., 1945—), Middlesex County Hist. Soc. (v.p. 1916), Phi Beta Kappa. Clubs: Acorn (Conn.); University (Winter Park, Fla.;. Author: Political Awakening of the East, 1925. Contbr. New Internat. Ency., Dictionary Am. History, Am. Hist. Review, Jour. of Modern History, etc. Joint editor: A Guide to Historical Literature, 1931. Home: 77 Home Av., Middletown Conn. Died Feb. 22, 1959.

DuTREMBLAY, Pamphile-Real, senator, journalist; b. Ste. Anne de la Perade, P.Q., Can., Mar. 5, 1879; s. P.P.V. and Helene (Dufort) DuT.; student Trois-Rivieres Coll., P.Q. Normal Sch., Quebec, P.Q., student law, McGill, Laval U., Montreal; m. Angelina Berthiaume, Sept. 21, 1907. Admitted to the bar, 1901, created King's Council, 1917; practice of law; pres., gen. mgr. La Campaigne de Publication de la Presse Limitee, 1921; pres., gen. mgr. La Compagnie de Publication de la Patrio Limitee, actual; rep. Laurier-Outremont (Montreal) in House of Commons, Can., 1917-21; apptd. to Quebec Legislative Council for Div. of Sorel, Dec. 1924; apptd. senator to Canadian Senate, Nov. 19, 1942. Decorated Knight of the Legion d'Honneur (France), 1925; received title of hon. citizen of the City of Dieppe, France, 1930; recipient gold medal of the Academie Francaise awarded to newspaper La Presse, Montreal, 1931, medal of the Ligue Maritime at Coloniale, France, 1930, medal of the Jubilee of His Majesty the King, 1935, medal of the Coronation of His Majesty George VI, 1937; officer La Ligue d'Union Latine, France, 1938. Hon. vice pres. Quebec Provincial div., The Can. Red Cross Soc.; hon. mem. and gov. Hôpital Notre Dame, Montreal. Pres. la Federation des Oeuvres de Charite Canadiennes-Francaises, 1935-36, Liberal. Catholic. Clubs: Mount Royal, Reform, Royal Automobile of Can. (Montreal); Rideau, Ottawa. Home: The Chateau, 1321 Sherbrooke St., West, Montreal 25. Office: La Presse, 7 St. James St., West, Montreal 1, P.Q., Can. Died Oct. 6, 1955.

DUTTON, Edward A., lawyer; b. Savannah, Ga., Feb. 24, 1908; s. Sterling Monroe and Georgia Bell (Keller) D.; A.B. L.L.B., U. Ga. Admitted to Ga. bar, 1931, since practiced in Savannah. Mayor Savannah Beach, Tybee Island, Ga., 6 consecutive terms. Chmn. bd. dirs. Charity Hosp. and Tng. Sch. for Nurses; vice chmn. Family Service of Savannah, Inc. Mem. Am., Ga. (pres. 1953-54) bar assns., Ga. Municipal Assn. (pres.). Elk (grand exalted ruler, asst. to grand esquire, 1939—; v.p. Ga. 1949; grand lodge activities com. 1946, 50; grand treas. 1952), Mason (K.T., Shriner), Eagle. Clubs: Lions (past pres., (Port of Savannah). Home: Savannah Beach, Tybee Island, Ga. Office: Commercial Bldg., Savannah, Ga. Died May 23, 1954.

DUVAL, Laurel, produce exchange exec.; b. Wapakoneta, O., Mar. 31, 1887; s. August and Amanda Marie (Myers) D.; student Wooster Coll., 1903-05; m. Mary Elizabeth Fombelle, Dec. 26, 1908; 1 dau., Querida (Mrs. John Paul Dunn). Asso., A. M. Fombelle, grain bus., Wooster, O., 1906-07; aide, grain standardization, U.S. Dept. Agr., Baltimore, 1907-08, grain supervisor in charge Phila. dist., 1916-17, N.Y., charge Atlantic ports, 1918-21; charge Baltimore lab. U.S. Grain Standardization, 1909-12; chief, office of Estandardización de Granos, Argentina Ministerio de Agricultura, 1913-15; chief grain dept. N.Y. Produce Exchange, 1922-37, v.p., 1938-40, also chmn. finance and other coms., mng. dir. and mem. exec. com. since 1941, bd. mgrs. since 1938. Decorated Knight Order of Orange-Nassau, Queen Wilhelmina of the Netherlands, 1947. Mason. Clubs: Commodity (pres. 1943-48) (N.Y. City); Westchester Country (Rye, N.Y.). Author bulls., and article in Yearbook of Dept. Agr.; also articles in trade mags. Home: W. 72d St., N.Y. City 23. Office: 2 Broadway, N.Y. C. 4. Died Feb. 16, 1952.

DUXBURY, George H., ret. ins. exec.; b. Paterson, N.J., Aug. 12, 1893; s. John and Elizabeth (Cruikshank) D.; ed. pub. schs. of Paterson, N.J.; m. Esther E. Zabriskie, 1919. Spl. agent in eastern N.Y. state, North British and Mercantile Ins. Co., Ltd.; returned N.Y. office ofcl. capacity, promoted through various ranks; U.S. mgr., 1946-51; U.S. mgr. Ocean Marine Ins. Co., Ltd., 1946-51; pres., dir. The Mercantile Ins. Co., Am., The Commonwealth Ins. Co., N.Y., The Pa. Fire Ins. Co., The Homeland Ins. Co., Am. Dir. Gen. Adjustment Bur. Episcopalian. Clubs: Down Town (Phila.); Bankers, Wall Street, Union League (N.Y.C.); Bay Head (N. J.) Yacht. Home: 784 Park Av., N.Y.C. 21. Office: 150 William St., N.Y.C. 8. Died Apr. 27, 1956.

DWIGGINS, Clare Victor, illustrator, cartoonist; b. Wilmington, O., 1874; s. Charles B. and Mary (Shepherd) D.; ed. pub. schs. and acad.; m. Bess Lindsay 1899. Began in 1890, and has been cartoonist St. Louis Post Dispatch, New York Journal, Phila. Inquirer, N. American and Telegraph, and internat. syndicate; now art editor for M. Walter Dunne, publisher, New York. Illustrator: Crankisms, 1901, Brevities, 1903, Completed Proverbs, 1904, all by Lisle De Vaux Matthewman, C4; Whimlets, by Samuel I. Stinson, 1903 C4; Toasts, 1904. Author: Rubáiyát of an Egg, 1905; The Skull Toast Book, 1906. Residence: 74 Irving Pl. Office: 135 Fifth Av., New York. Died Oct. 1958.

DWIGGINS, William Addison, artist; b. Martinsville, O., June 19, 1880; s. Moses Frazer and Eva (Siegfried) D.; prep. edn., pub. schs., Richmond, Ind., and Cambridge, O.; student Sch. of Illustration, Chgo., 1899-1901; m. Mabel Hoyle, Sept. 8, 1904. Book designer and illustrator; cons. Mergenthaler Linotype Company, Alfred A. Knopf, Incorporated. Member of Society of Printers (honorary), (Boston), Double Crown Club (London), Am. Inst. Graphic Arts (N.Y.C.), Soc. Typographic Arts (Chgo.). Author. Paraphs (under pseudonym H. Püterschien), 1928; Layout in Advertising, 1928; Form Letters—Illustrator to Author, 1930; Towards a Reform of the Paper Currency, 1932; Marionette in Motion, 1939; WAD to RR, 1940; Millennium I, 1945; MSS by WAD, 1947; numerous articles in profl. jours. Designer Metro, Caledonia, Electra series and other series of type faces. Home: Leavitt St., Hingham, Mass. Died Dec. 25, 1956; buried Hingham Centre Cemetery.

DWIGHT, Harrison Griswold, writer; b. Constantinople, Aug. 6, 1875; s. Henry Otis and Adele M. (Griswold) D.; A.B., Amherst, 1898. U.S. Consulate, Venice, corr. Chgo. Record-Herald, 1898-1902; curator Authors Club, N.Y.C., 1903-06; mag. work in Europe and Near East, 1906-14; with Supreme War Council, Versailles, and Peace Commn., Paris, 1918-19; spl. asst. Dept. of State, 1920-25, returned to State Dept., 1930-33; asst. dir. Frick Collection, N.Y.C., 1936-46. Author: Constantinople, 1915, 26; Stamboul Nights, 1916; Persian Miniatures, 1917; The Emperor of Elam and Other Stories, 1920. Translator: The Empress Might-Have-Been (from the French, by Octave Aubry), 1927. Address: 31 E. 12th St., N.Y. C. Died Mar. 24, 1959.

DWIGHT, Minnie Ryan (Mrs. William G.), editor, pub.; b. Hadley, Mass., June 22, 1873; dau. Patrick and Catherine (Rielley) Ryan; grad. Hopkins Acad., Hadley, 1889; spl. work Mt. Holyoke Coll., 1895-96; L.H.D. (hon.), Am. Internat. Coll., Springfield, Mass., 1941, U. Mass., 1947; m. William G. Dwight, Nov. 5, 1896 (died 1930); children—Helen Mary (Mrs. Oscar E. Schoeffier), Laura Sluyter (Mrs. Richmond Lewis), William. Connected with Holyoke (Mass.) Daily Transcript, 1891—, editor-in-chief and pub., 1930—; pres., treas. Holyoke Transcript, Inc., Transcript-Telegram Pub. Co., 1930—; treas. Hampden-Hampshire Corp., 1940—, Radio Sta. WHYN, 1940—. Mem. Mass. Old Age Pension Commn., 1922-24, Hampden County Aid to Agrl. (mem. bd. trustees), Hampden County Extension Service (pres. home bur. 1917-49), Holyoke Parks and Recreation Commn., 1910-28, Holyoke Child Welfare Commn., 1913—, Holyoke Soldiers Meml. Commn., 1935—. Mem. Mass. Rep. State Com., 1920-34; del. to Progressive Conv., Chicago, 1916; del. to Rep. Nat. Conv., Kansas City, 1928. Pub. relations chmn., Office of Civilian Defense; dir. USO, Holyoke; Hampden County chmn. for Women for Liberty Loan and War Savings Campaigns, World War I; chmn. war com., Fruitland Park, Fla., World War II. Honored by French Govt. for War Relief Work, 1920; decorated by Vets. Fgn. Wars for civic service, 1947. Trustee Holyoke Hosp., Public Library, Am. Internat. Coll. Mem. bd. mgrs. Holyoke Home for Aged People, adv. council women's dept. Mass. State Coll. Dir. Holyoke Visiting Nurse Assn., Holyoke chpt. A.R.C., Holyoke Community Chest (a founder), Holyoke Tb Assn., Holyoke C. of C. (mem. exec. com., v.p.); dep. commr. Holyoke Girl Scouts, 1931-50. Mem. YWCA (past dir.), D.A.R. (hon.), Mass. Demonstration Council (past pres.), Am. Acad. Polit. Sci., Soc. Am. Editors, Am. Soc. Newspaper Editors, Women's Roosevelt Meml. Assn. (charter), Holyoke Council World Relations, France Forever (Boston). Episcopalian. Clubs: Press of Mass., Western Mass. Women's, Mass. Women's Rep. (charter); Hampden County Women's (a founder, pres.), Holyoke Women's (founder, 1st pres.), Business and Professional Women's (charter mem.), Quota (charter), Delphian (charter), Garden (Holyoke); Women's, Garden (Leesburg, Fla.). Home: 387 Appleton St., Holyoke; (winter) Pine Eden, Fruitland Park, Fla. Office: 180 High St., Holyoke, Mass. Died July 31, 1957; buried Bernardston, Mass.

DWIGHT, Richard Everett, lawyer; s. Melatiah Everett and Helen McClure (Kirby) D.; A.B., Princeton, 1897; LL.B., New York Law Sch., 1899; m. Gertrude Grace, Sept. 27, 1899 (died Oct. 1937); m. 2d, Emily H. Wright, Nov. 11, 1937. Practiced at N.Y. City since 1899; mem. Dwight, Royall, Harris, Koegel & Caskey; sec., dir. H. Boker & Co.; dir. Church & Dwight Co., Belding-Hemingway Co., Ft. Orange Paper Co., California Commercial Co., Inc., Thomas McMullen & Co., National Surety Co., Nat. Marine Ins. Co., Pilot Steel & Tool Co., Ltd., Schley Realty Co. Mem. Am. Bar Assn., N.Y. State Bar Assn., Assn. Bar City of New York. Republican. Conglist. Home: 375 Park Av. Office: 100 Broadway, N.Y. City. Died Sept. 28, 1951; buried Woodlawn Cemetery, New York.

DWYER, Edward Martin, educator, clergyman; b. Chestnut Hill, Pa., Mar. 6, 1906; s. James Marie and Katherine Agnes (Curry) D.; A.B., Villanova Coll., 1928; Ph.D., Julius Maximilian U., Wurzburg, Germany, 1933; S.T.L., Institute Angelicum, Rome, Italy, 1937; student U. Berlin, 1933. Entered Order Augustinian Fathers, 1924; ordained priest Roman Catholic Ch., 1931; master professed clerics, Augustinian Internat. Coll., Rome, Italy, 1933-37; prof. philosophy, chmn. dept. Villanova (Pa.) U., 1940—, dean, 1944-56; provincial definitor, 1956-57. Mem. Nat. Cath. Edn. Assn., Am. Cath. Philos. Assn. Address: Villanova University, Villanova, Pa. Died Sept. 10, 1957; buried Villanova.

DWYER, James A., business exec.; b. Phila., Oct. 17, 1896; s. Michael J. and Mary C. (Kennedy) D.; student The Roman Cath. High Sch., Phila., 1910-11, also various night sch. courses; m. Marie E. Cannon, April 18, 1917; 1 dau., Rose Marie (Mrs. Edward J. Walsh). Order clerk, Phila. branch, Crane Co. of Chicago, 1917-19, estimator-salesman, 1919-25, sales mgr., 1925-34, asst. mgr., 1934-35, mgr., 1935-36, dist. mgr.-Eastern dist., N.Y. City, 1937-43, mgr. branch houses, Chicago, since 1943, gen. mgr. sales and branches, 1944, vice pres. sales and branches, 1945-51, v.p. indsl. sales since 1951; dir. Crane Ltd. (Can.), Crane Export Corp., Crane of Minn. Served as 2d lt. San. Corps. overseas, 1918-19. Mem. Valve Mfrs. Assn. (pres. 1953—), Pipe Fitting Assn. (v.p. 1953—). Republican. Roman Catholic. Clubs: Chicago Athletic Assn., Lake Shore. Home: 1120 Lake Shore Dr., Chgo. 11. Office: 836 S. Michigan Av., Chgo. 5. Died May 15, 1956.

DWYER, James Francis, author; b. Camden, N.S.W., Australia, Apr. 22, 1874; s. Michael and Margaret (Mahoney) D.; pub. sch. edn.; m. Lena Cassandra Stewart, Nov. 7, 1894 (divorced); m. 2d, Catharine Galbraith Welch, Dec. 30, 1919. Traveled extensively as newspaper corr. in Australia and South Seas, 1898-1906; traveled through South Africa to Eng., 1906; came to America, 1907; traveled in India, Egypt, Australia, 1914; Spain, Algeria France, 1919-20; crossed the Desert of Sahara to Timbuktoo, 1935. Author: The White Waterfall, 1912; The Bust of Lincoln, 1912; The Spotted Panther, 1913; Breath of the Jungle, 1915; Evelyn, 1929; O Splendid Sorcery, 1930; Romantic Quest of Peter Lamonte, 1934; Cold Eyes, 1934; Hespamora, 1935; Lady with Feet of Gold, 1935; Leg-Irons on Wings, 1949. Contbr. to Collier's, Ladies' Home Journal, Woman's Home Companion, Delineator, etc. Founded in 1921 (with Galbraith Welch Dwyer) the Dwyer Travel letters. Address: 119bis Boulevard d'Alsace, Pau (Bassés-Pyrénées), France. Deceased.

DWYER, John B., educator; b. Dayton, Ohio, Jan. 8, 1910; s. James Francis and Frances Susanna (Staley) D.; A.B., U. Dayton, 1932; M.A., Xavier U., 1936; S.T.L., West Baden Coll., Loyola U., 1944; Ph.D., U. N.C., 1950. Entered Soc. of Jesus, 1932; instr. English John Carroll U., 1944, West Baden Coll., summer 1946, U. Detroit, 1938-40, asst. prof., 1950-53, asso. prof., 1953, dean coll. arts and scis., 1953-56; regional dir. edn. Jesuit Ednl. Assn., 1956—. Mem. Am. Assn. Colleges and Univs., Mediaeval Acad. Am., Modern Language Assn., Am. Dialect Soc., Nat. Coll. Assn. Tchrs. English, Mich. Acad. Arts, Scis. and Letters. Address: 509 N. Oak Park Av., Oak Park, Ill. Died Jan. 15, 1957; buried, Cemetery of Milford Novitiate, Milford, O.

DWYER, William Joseph, banker; b. Jersey City, N. J., Mar. 20, 1888; s. William J. and Katherine Loretta (Cogan) D.; ed. St. Paul's Acad., Jersey

City; m. Clara Virginia Daniels, Aug. 20, 1926; children—Nancy Elliott, William Daniels. Traveling salesman, 12 yrs.; field dir., A.R.C., 1920-23; founder, Bailey, Dwyer & Co., Jersey City, 1925, and served as v.p.; reorgn. Bergen Trust Co., 1940, pres. since Oct. 1940; dir. Westerleigh Hills Realty Corp. Served as state chmn. for N.J. Am. Bankers Assn. war bond com., 1944-45; v.p. N.J. div. Am. Cancer Soc.; state treas. Sister Kenny Found.; trustee men's adv. bd., Jersey City Y.W.C.A.; del. to S.N.J. Constl. Conv. rep. Hudson County, 1947; chmn. bd. trustees Stevens Hoboken (N.J.) Acad. Served as pvt. U.S. Army, 1917-19; with A.E.F.; disch. as capt. Mem. Am. Bankers Assn. (trustee), Am. Inst. Banking, Am. Legion, Community Chest. Republican. (electoral coll. nominee of N.J. 1939). Clubs: Lake Mohawk Country, Lake Mohawk Horse Show Assn. (chmn.); Theodore Roosevelt Assn. (Jersey City); Kiwanis, Jersey City Philharmonic (pres. 1945-46); Bond (N. J.); Lotos of N.Y. Home: Linden Ct., Jersey City, N.J.; (summer) Lake Mohawk, N.H. Office: 26 Journal Square, and 921 Bergen Av., Jersey City, N.J. Died 1948.

DYCHE, Howard Edward (dīk), prof. elec. engring.; b. Spring Valley, O., Jan. 19, 1884; s. Samuel Edward (M.D.) and Flora Alice (Carey) D.; grad. high sch., Spring Valley, 1901; M.E. in E.E., Ohio State U., 1906; m. Edith Mae Guy, Feb. 2, 1910; 1 son, Howard Edward. Engr., ry. dept. Westinghouse Electric & Mfg. Co., 1906-11; prof. elec. engring., Westinghouse Tech. School, Pittsburgh, 1909-11; instr. in mathematics and physics, U. of Pittsburgh, 1911, instr. in elec. engring., 1912-14, asst. prof. elec. engring., 1914-17, asso. prof., 1917-19, prof. and head of dept., 1919—; director of graduate work in industry, 1927-52, acting dean School of Engring. and Mining, 1950; cons. engr., registered profl. engr. Commonwealth of Pa., Asst. dir. war training, U. of Pittsburgh, 1918 and 1944. Member Am. Inst. E.E. (past chmn. Pittsburgh. sect.), Soc. Promotion Engring. Edn., Sigma Xi, Sigma Tau, Eta Kappa Nu. Lutheran. Mason (32°). Clubs: University, Faculty. Home: 317 South Av., Wilkinsburg, Pa., and Spring Valley, O. Address: University of Pittsburgh, Pitts. Died Apr. 11, 1954; buried Homewood Cemetery, Pitts.

DYE, Alexander Vincent; b. Flora, Ill., Feb. 11, 1876; s. Alexander Elbridge and Mary Caroline (Hudspeth) D.; A.B., William Jewell Coll., Liberty Mo., 1901, A.M., 1902; Ph.D., U. of Leipzig, Germany, 1904; m. Ida Miller, Apr. 15, 1903; children—Russell Vincent, Margaret Louise (Mrs. W. T. Whitman); married 2d, Alice McHardy Byrnes, Nov. 12, 1930; married 3d, Margaret Scott, July 15, 1948. Prof. modern langs., William Jewell Coll., 1904-09; Am. consul, Nogales, Mexico, 1909-13; asst. gen. mgr. Phelps Dodge Corp., Douglas, Ariz., 1916-17; spl. asst. to U.S. Dept. State and rep. of War Trade Bd., Norway, 1917-19; rep. Am. Internat. Corp., 1919-21; U.S. trade commr., London, 1921-23; commercial attaché, Mexico City, 1923-26, Buenos Aires, 1926-35; dir. Bur. of Foreign and Domestic Commerce, Washington, D.C., 1936-39; commercial attaché, London, 1939-41; retired from the foreign service, Mar. 1, 1941; economic consultant Nat. Foreign Trade Council, 1941-45; member com. on International Economic Policy; chmn. of Organizing Com. of Internat. Business Conference held at Rye, N.Y., 1944; member of advisory board Committee for Economic Development; member Council of Foreign Relations. United States delegate to International Commercial Conf., Rio de Janeiro, 1927; U.S. del. 6th Internat. Refrigeration Congress, Buenos Aires, 1932; adviser to Pan-Am. Commercial Conf., Buenos Aires, 1935; adviser to Am. delegations to 7th and 8th Confs. of Am. States at Montevideo, 1933, and Lima, 1938; federal commr. Pan-Am. Hernando de Soto Expn., Tampa, Fla., 1939. Decorated Order of St. Olav (Norway), 1919. Club: Cosmos (Washington). Contbr. to publs. Dept. Commerce. Address: Boxwood Terrace, Tryon, N.C. Died June 2, 1956; buried Calvary Episcopal Church Cemetery, Fletcher, N.C.

DYE, Eva Emery, author; b. Prophetstown, Ill., July 17, 1855; d. Cyrus and Caroline (Trafton) Emery; A.B., Oberlin Coll., 1882, A.M., 1889; m. Charles Henry Dye, July 1882; children—Emery Charles, Trafton Mickelwait, Everett Willoughby, Mrs. Charlotte Evangeline Hutchinson. Mem. Ore. Hist. Soc., Nat. Hist. Assn. Author: McLoughlin and Old Oregon, 1900; Stories of Oregon, 1900; The Conquest, 1902; McDonald of Oregon, 1906; numerous hist. sketches. Home: Oregon City, Ore. Deceased.

DYER, Clifton G(len), lawyer; b. Byron, Mich., Sept. 3, 1885; s. John and Rhoda (Davis) D.; A.B., U. of Mich., 1908, J.D., 1913; m. Bess B. Browne, Sept. 12, 1916. Prof. of pleading and practice, U. Detroit, 1916-23; admitted to Mich. bar, 1913; practiced as asso., firm of Angell, Bodman & Turner, Detroit, 1914-19; mem. firm of Angell, Turner & Dyer, 1920-28, Angell, Turner, Dyer & Meek, 1928-47; sr. mem. firm now Dyer, Meek, Ruegsegger & Batten 1947—; dir. United Light & Railways Co., 1942-49, Am. Natural Gas Co. (formerly Am. Light and Traction Co.), Mich.-Wis. Pipe Line Co., Am. La. Pipe Line Co. Mem. Am., Detroit (pres. 1929-31) bar assns., State Bar of Mich. Clubs: Detroit Athletic; Lawyers (Ann Arbor); Bankers of Am. Home: 19595 Argyle Crescent, Detroit 3. Office: Dime Bldg., Detroit 26. Died May 20, 1959.

DYER, John Napier; b. St. Louis, Jan. 14, 1877; s. John Napier and Corinne (Chouteau) D.; ed. Smith Acad. (Washington U.), Phillips Acad.; short courses, Ia. State Coll., Purdue U.; m. Marion Sims McKenney, Dec. 12, 1900; 1 son, Richard Napier. Pioneer builder of motor fire apparatus, pres., gen. mgr., Webb Motor Fire Apparatus Co., grower of peaches, apples, vegetables, Vincennes, Ind., 1907-10; prop., mgr., McKenney Farms, nr. Vincennes, Ind., 1908-38; pres. Dyer Realty Co., McKenney Farms Realty Co., 1920-35. Served as pvt., Battery A, Mo. Vols., Spanish-Am. War. Pres. Nat. Hort. Council, Knox County Hort. Soc., Ind. Hort. Soc.; mem. Am. Farm Bur. Fedn. (dir.), Ind. Farm Bur. (one of organizers), Ill. Hort. Soc., Ky. Hort. Soc., Tenn. Hort. Soc., Mo. Hort. Soc. Chmn. Am. Red Cross, Knox Co., 1918; dir. Pub. Realtions; Raw Materials Nat. Council. Progressive candidate for congress, 1912, U.S. senator, 1914; mem. Ind. State Legislature, 1933, 35, 36 (spl. session); vice chmn. State Adv. Bd., Fed. Emergency Adminstrn. Pub. Works, 1933-34. Trustee Ind. State Hosp. for Insane, Logansport, 1912-20. Progressive Democrat. Episcopalian. Rotarian. (dist. gov. 1918-19; 1st v.p. 1919-20, pres. Vincennes Rotary Club, 1918). Author: The Peril of Peasantry. Lectr., agrl. econ. analyst. Home: McKenney Farms, Vincennes, Ind. Died Jan. 4, 1954.

DYER, Leonard Huntress, inventor; b. Washington, D.C., May 13, 1873; s. George Washington and Kate (Huntress) D.; student Corcoran Scientific Sch., Columbian (now George Washington) U., 1893, Georgetown U. Law Sch., 1895. Nat. Law Sch., Washington, D.C., 1896; D.Sc., Rollins College, Winter Park, Fla., 1949; m. Josephine Duncan, July 10, 1905; children—Duncan (dec.), Katherine Huntress (Mrs. Elmer Puddington); m. 2d, Jessica Hofstetter, Oct. 14, 1927. Was admitted to D.C. bar, 1894; practiced patent law with brother, Frank L. Dyer, until 1897; practiced alone, 1897-1903, with others, in N.Y. City, until 1917. Commd. lt. U.S.N.R.F., Mar. 6, 1917, and apptd. comdr. 2d Sec., 3d Naval Dist., hdqrs. Bridgeport, Conn.; also assigned as comdr. Squadron 6, 3d Naval Dist. Invented an automobile with a direct drive, sliding transmission, selective gear shift and unit power plant; more than 100,000,000 automobiles have been made embodying this invention; also invented the flying boat, elec. steering gear, and improvements in steam turbines, etc. Also a landscape painter. Fellow Am. Geog. Soc. Mem. Soc. Colonial Wars, Spanish Inst. of Florida. Clubs: New York Yacht, University of Winter Park (Fla.); Anglers' Yacht. Author: The Evolution of the Motor Vehicle as Shown by Patents, 1955. Home: Winter Park, Fla. Died Nov. 16, 1955.

DYER, Leonidas Carstarphen, ex-congressman; b. Warren Co., Mo., June 11, 1871; s. James Coleman and Martha E. (Camp) D.; Central Wesleyan Coll., Warrenton, Mo., and Washington U., St. Louis; married. Admitted to Mo. bar, 1893, and since in practice at St. Louis. Asst. circuit atty., St. Louis, 1909-10; mem. 62d Congress (1911-13); received certificate of election to 63d Congress but was unseated after a partisan contest; mem. 64th to 72d Congresses (1915-33), 12th Mo. Dist. Republican. Served Spanish-Am. War, in Santiago campaign; on staff of Gov. Hadley, Mo., with rank of col.; comdr. in chief United Spanish War Vets., 1915-16. Mem. Christian Ch. Mason. Office: Chemical Bldg., St. Louis, Mo. Died Dec. 1957.

DYKEMA, Peter William (dī'kĕ-mȧ), prof. music; b. Grand Rapids, Mich., Nov. 25, 1873; s. Cornelius and Henrietta (Nutting) D.; B.L., U. Mich., 1895, M.L., 1896; studied voice with Franz Arens, N.Y.C., 1903, 04, theory, with Frank Shephard, 1904, 05; student Inst. Musical Art, N.Y.C., 1911-12; also studied in Berlin, Germany; m. Jessie Dunning, Dec. 24, 1903; children—Karl Washburn, Roger Dunning, Alice Mary Barnes, Helen Cargan Dengler, Peter Scot. Tchr. English and German, Aurora (Ill.) High School, 1896-98; prin. Jr. High Sch., Indpls., 1898-1901; in charge music Ethical Culture Sch., N.Y.C., 1901-13; prof. music U. Wis., 1913-24, also chmn. Dept. Pub. Sch. Music and dir. Madison Choral Union; leave of absence, 1918-19, while serving as song leader and supervisor of singing, S.A.T.C., in behalf of War and Navy Dept.; prof. music edn. Tchrs. Coll. (Columbia), 1924-40, prof. emeritus, 1940—; lectr., guest tchr. several univs. and colls. Mem. Music Educators Nat. Conf. (past pres.; chmn. com. past presidents, 1948), Nat. Research Council of Mus. (ex-chmn.), Music Tchrs. Nat. Assn., N.E.A., Phi Mu Alpha (supreme pres. 1922-28); mem. bd. of Control Nat. Bur. for Advancement of Music, 1932-43; mem. Com. on Music in Therapy, 1944—; pres. Hastings Taxpayers Assn., 1944—. Chmn. In and About N.Y. Mus. Edn. Club, 1934-39. Author: Music for School Administrators, 1931. Co-author: Festivals and Plays, 1913; New School Music Handbook Dykema and Cundiff, 1923 (rev. edit., 1939, rev. edit. School Music Handbook, New Edition, 1955; Modern Orchestra Series, Vol. 1, 1929, Vol. 2, 1931; Modern Band Series, Vol. I, Parts 1 and 2, 1939; Music Tests (with Kwalwasser), 1929 (rev. edit. 1949, Singing Youth, 1936; Music Series Singing School, 8 vols. (1939-48); The Teaching and Administration of High School Music, 1941; The Supervision and Administration of Music Edn., 1949; also four pamphlets on music and radio, 1937. Composer; Robin Hood and Allan a Dale, 1936; The Arrow and the Song, 1940, The Three Bears and Goldilocks, 1941; Text of Preludes to Eternity, 1946. Editor: Myths and Legends (drama), 1914; Sing! (with Stevens), 1938. Chmn. editorial bd. Twice 55 Community Songs, (7 vols.). Gen. editor The New Laurel Library (7 vols.). Editor Music Supervisors' Journal 7 years. Formerly spl. music adviser Nat. Recreation Assn. Home: Bovenop, 30 Floral Drive, Hastings-on-Hudson, N.Y. Died May 13, 1951.

DYKSTRA, Clarence Addison (dīk'strū), univ. pres.; b. Cleveland, O., Feb. 25, 1883; s. Lawrence and Margaret (Barr) D.; A.B., State U. of Ia., 1903; fellow in history and asst. in polit. science, U. of Chicago, 1903-04, 1906-08; L.H.D., Otterbein, 1935; Litt.D., U. of Cincinnati, 1937; L.H.D., Hobart Coll., 1938; LL.D., Ohio Wesleyan, 1934, Knox Coll., 1936, Hope Coll., 1937, Northwestern U., 1939, Johns Hopkins Univ., Harvard Univ., Rutgers Univ., 1941, University of California, Lake Forest College, and University of Denver, 1943, Occidental Coll., 1947; m. Ada M. Hartley, July 31, 1909 (died 1926); 1 dau., Elizabeth Sylvester; m. 2d, Lillian K. Rickaby, Dec. 25, 1927; 1 stepson, Franz Rickaby Dykstra. Teacher pvt. schs., Pensacola, Fla., 1904-06; instr. in history and govt., Ohio State U., 1907-09; prof. polit. science and head of dept., U. of Kan., 1909-18; exec. sec. Cleveland (O.) Civic League, 1918-20; sec. Chicago City Club, 1920-22, Los Angeles (Calif.) City Club, 1922-26, also commr. Dept. Water and Power, Los Angeles, 1923-26, dir. personnel and efficiency, same dept., 1926-30; prof. municipal adminstrn., U. of Calif., 1923-30; city mgr., Cincinnati, 1930-37; pres. Univ. of Wis., 1937-45; provost University of California, 1945—. Member technical advisory board, Nat. Emergency Pub. Works Adminstrn.; mem. Ohio State Advisory Com. of U.S. Employment Service. Pres. Internat. Assn. of City Mgrs., 1932-33; mem. President's Com. Fiscal Relations, Fed. Govt. and D.C.; chmn. Com. to Survey "The Role of the Urban Community in the Nat. Economy"—Nat. Resources Bd.; mem. exec. com. Tax Revision Council and chmn. sub-com. on allocation of functions between federal, state and local govts.; dir. Selective Service, 1940-Apr. 1941; mem. advisory com. on Education, Recreation and Welfare to Army and Navy; chmn. Nat. Defense Mediation Board until June, 1941. Mem. Nat. Municipal League (president 1937-40) National Conference on City Planning, American Political Science Assn. (president 1938), Am. Acad. Polit. and Social Science, Phi Beta Kappa, Phi Kappa Phi, Delta Upsilon. Mem. U.S. Nat. Com. of U.N.E.S.C.O., President's Medal for Merit 1946. Mem. Dutch Ref. Ch. Contbr. to Nat. Municipal Review, Annals Am. Acad. Polit. and Social Science, Am. City, Am. Polit. Science Review, Public Administration, etc. Home: University House, University of Calif. Office: Administration Bldg., University of California, Los Angeles. Died May 6, 1950; buried Inglewood (Cal.) Cemetery.

DYM, Aaron, rabbi; b. Sanok, Poland, Feb. 7, 1896; s. Moses and Sarah (Englard) D.; D.D., Yeshiva Coll., Sanok, Poland, 1913; student Univ. of Budapest, 1914-16; m. Miss Lustig, Sept. 1920; children—Helen, Fanny Gloria, Leah. Came to U.S., Dec. 25, 1925, naturalized, 1934. Asst. rabbi, Sanok, Poland, Apr. 1913-Aug. 1914; rabbi of Linsker Congregation, New York, N.Y., 1926-29; rabbi Nepolokowitz-Bukowina Congregation, New York, N.Y., 1930-40; rabbi Congregation Shaare Torah, New York, since 1941. Sec. Fedn. Orthodox Rabbis of Am., June 1926, exec. sec. since Jan. 1935. Home: 15A W. Polit. Action Com. for Palestine. Home: 15A W. 73d St., New York 23. Office: 252 East Broadway, N.Y.C. Died June 5, 1951.

E

EAGER, Helen (ā-gĕr), drama critic; born Marlborough, Mass.; d. Henry William and Jennie (Thompson) Eager; ed. Lasell Jr. Coll., Auburndale, Mass., and Pierce Sch., Boston, Mass.; unmarried. Feature writer, Boston Herald-Traveler, 1925-27; motion picture critic and editor, Boston Traveler, since 1927, drama critic and editor, since 1933. Home: 98 Charles St., Boston 14. Office: Boston Traveler, 80 Mason St., Boston 12. Died Oct. 23, 1952.

EAGER, John M. (ē'gĕr), army officer; b. Baltimore, Md., Aug. 20, 1889; s. John M. and Constance (Colclough) E.; student Georgetown Coll., 1908-09; A.B., Harvard Coll., 1912; grad. F. A. Sch., 1924, Command and Gen. Staff Sch., 1925, Chem. Warfare Sch., 1933; m. Kathryn Tydings, June 22, 1935; children—John Macaulay, IV, Mary Tydings. Commd. 2d lt., F.A., Mar. 1913, advanced through grades to brig. gen., Sept. 1942; asst. mil.

attaché and mil. attaché chief of Italy 1919-1923; gen. staff 1937-1943; chief of staff and comdg. gen., 5th Service command (Ohio, Ind., Ky. and W.Va.), 1940-43; organized and commanded Italian Service Units 1944-45 with hdqrs. at Ft. Wadsworth, N.Y. and units operating at all ports of embarkation, most Army depots, arsenals and numerous centers, posts, camps and stations in the U.S.; now Washington rep. of Heyden Chem. Corp. Editor U.S. Field Artillery Journal 1928-32; Clubs: Army and Navy, Army-Navy Country, Harvard (Washington, D.C.); Harvard (New York City). Home: 6301 Broad Branch Rd., Chevy Chase. Office: 917-15th St., N.W., Washington. Died Nov. 15, 1956; buried Arlington Nat. Cemetery.

EAGLETON, Clyde, prof. internat. law; b. Sherman, Tex., May 13, 1891; s. Davis Foute and Addie C. (Parker) E.; A.B., Austin Coll., Sherman, Tex., 1910, A.M., 1911, hon. LL.D., 1941; A.M., Princeton, 1914; A.B., Oxford, Eng. (Rhodes scholar), 1917; Ph.D., Columbia, 1928; m. Sara Virginia McKinney, Sept. 15, 1917; 1 son, Clyde. Teacher U. of Louisville (Ky.), 1918-19, Southern Meth. U., Dallas, Tex., 1919-23; with New York U., 1923——, prof. of internat. law until retirement in 1956; lectr. N.Y. University Sch. Law and Graduate School of Arts and Sciences, 1956-57, U. Wash., 1957; legal expert, Dept. of State, 1943-45. Member American Political Science Assn. (exec. council), Am. Soc. Internat. Law (exec. council), Assn. Am. Rhodes Scholars, League of Nations Assn. (nat. ednl. com.), Conf. Teachers of Internat. Law (exec. com.); vice chmn. Commn. to Study Orgn. of Peace; mem. Council Fgn. Relations (N.Y.); now prof. internat. law and dir. grad. programs in U.N. and World Affairs; consultant to Interim Com. of U.N., 1948, United Nations Internat. Law Commn., 1949; consultant to govts. in internat. law cases. Recipient 3 yr. grant for study internat. rivers Ford Found. Member New Commonwealth Soc. (editorial bd.), Internat. Law Assn. (exec. council; president), Phi Beta Kappa, Sigma Alpha Epsilon, Chin Tsai (Chinese hon. soc.). Democrat. Presbyterian. Technical expert, U. S. Delegation, Dumbarton Oaks Conf. (Washington, 1944); Com. of Jurists (Washington, 1945); United Nations Conf. on Internat. Orgn. (San Francisco, 1945). Club: Cosmos (Washington). Author: Responsibility of States in International Law, 1928; International Govt., 1932 (rev. edit., 1948); Analysis of the Problem of War, 1937; The Forces That Shape Our Future, 1945. Internat. law editor of N.Y.U. Law Quar. Review; mem. editorial bd. Am. Jour. of Internat. Law, and Am. Polit. Science Rev.; collaborator Revue de Droit International et de Legislation Comparée (Bruxelles). Editor of Annual Review of the United Nations. Home: 86 Brookdale Drive, Crestwood, Tuckahoe P.O. 7, N.Y. Address: New York University, Washington Square, N.Y.C. Died Jan. 30, 1958; buried Ferncliff, Hartsdale, N.Y.

EAMES, Alfred Warner (ēmz), packing co. exec.; b. Los Angeles, May 3, 1886; s. Alfred W. and Anna (Alward) E.; student Sanford; B.A., Cornell U., 1911; m. Carrie McLean, Oct. 7, 1913; children—Alfred Warner, Janet A., Alward F. Mgr. Hawaiian Islands Packing Co., 1912-14, became pres., 1914; mgr. Hawaiian interests Cal. Packing Corp., San Francisco, 1917-20, dir., 1920——, v.p., 1921-40, pres., 1940——; v.p. Cal. Processors & Growers, Inc.; chmn. bd., dir. Alaska Packers Assn.; dir. A., T. & S.F. Ry. Mem. Cal. C. of C. (dir.), Canners League Cal. (v.p.), Nat. Canners Assn. (v.p.), San Francisco Employers Council (dir.), N.A.M. (dir.). Republican. Clubs: Pacific-Union, San Francisco Golf (Ingleside); Menlo Country (Redwood City). Home: 600 El Camino Del Mar. Office: 101 California St., San Francisco. Died Oct. 28, 1948.

EAMES, Emma, operatic prima donna; b. of Am. parentage, Shanghai, China, Aug. 13, 1865; childhood spent in Boston; studied music; sang in ch. and concerts; studied in Paris; m. Julian Story (q.v.), 1891; 2d, Paris, Emilio de Gogorza, July 12, 1911. Début Paris Grand Opera, Mar. 13, 1889; in Juliette; Covent Garden, London, 1891; N.Y.C., 1891; since sung in regular opera seasons in London and U.S. Officier d'Académie (French); English Jubilee medal. Home: 30 Sutton Pl., N.Y.C. Died 1949; buried Bath, Me.

EAMES, Henry Purmort, pianist, lecturer; b. Chicago, Sept. 12, 1872; s. Melville C. and Olive Walworth (Purmort) E.; Cornell Coll., Ia., 1887-91; Mus.D., 1906; LL.B., Northwestern U., 1894; studied theory of music and piano under William Smith, Babcock Mathews and William Hall Sherwood, and in Europe under the late Madam Clara Wieck Schumann and Ignace J. Paderewski; m. Clara Boone Hansbrough, Sept. 11, 1895; children—Mrs. Jane Holdom, Mrs. Judith Balfour, Ruth Purmort). Toured America with Remenyi (Hungarian violinist), 1894-95; in Europe, 1895-97; toured America from coast to coast as solo pianist, 1897; dir. piano dept. and lecturer in theory and aesthetics music dept. U. of Neb., 1898-1908; concert tour in France, Great Britain and Ireland, and taught and lectured in Paris, 1908-10; concert tour in America, 1910-11; conducted travel parties through Europe; established and dir. Omaha Sch. of Music and Allied Arts, 1911-12; v.p. and dir. piano and orchestral depts. Cosmopolitan Sch. of Music, Chicago, 1912-20; dir. Ill. Wesleyan U. dept. of music and lecturer on aesthetics, at Bloomington, Ill., 1913-19; dir. of music, Brunswick Records, 1919-20; chmn. music div. Art Service League; on piano faculty and lecturer on history and aesthetics, Am. Conservatory, Chicago, 1923-28; prof. musical art and aesthetics, Scripps Coll., Claremont, Calif., 1928-41, prof. emeritus since Sept. 1941, prof. musical art and aesthetics, Claremont Graduate Coll., 1928-41; dir. musical art Olive Hill Foundation, Los Angeles, since 1946; visiting lecturer in musicology, U. of Calif., Los Angeles, 1946-47. Dir. music, lecturer on aesthetics, summer sch., U. of Calif. (adult education department); lecturer on musicology and piano recitalist in summer sessions, University of California, 1928, 29 and 30, University of N.M., 1933, Univ. of Hawaii, 1934, Claremont Grad. Colls., 1935; apptd. dir. for 1936 of Kokokahai Summer Sch. of Music, Hawaii; chmn. Southern Calif. Com. on Inter-American Cultural Relations; mus. consultant Padua Hills Inst. Pres. Am. Soc. Musicians, 1915-18, and 1925; pres. So. Calif. Soc. for Oriental Studies, 1943-46; member Am. Philos. Soc., Southwestern Archaeol. Federation, Native Composers of America, Am. Assn. Univ. Profs., American Soc. for Aesthetics, California Folk Lore Society, Beta Theta Pi. Republican. Mason. Club: Cliff Dwellers (Chicago). Premier of Second Orchestral Suite, at Pasadena, Mar. 29, 1941. Published over 30 songs, choruses and pageants. Made 14 annual lecture-recital tours of U.S. Home: 1034 Harvard Av., Claremont, Cal. Died Nov. 25, 1950; Oak Park Cemetery, Claremont, Cal.

EARHART, Harry Boyd, retired; b. Worthington, Pa., December 21, 1870; s. Joseph and Margaret (Boyd) E.; student public schools, Pennsylvania, 1876-87; hon. alumnus U. of Mich., 1932; m. Carrie L. Beal, Apr. 23, 1901 (died 1940); children—Margaret Beal (Mrs. Clement A. Smith), Louise (Mrs. Theophils Raphael), Richard, Elizabeth (Mrs. James A. Kennedy). Agt. and owner vessels, Great Lakes, 1888-1904; mfr. of machinery, 1904-10; pres. and chmn. bd. White Star Refining Co., 1910-32; dir. Vacuum Oil Co., 1920-34. Trustee Citizens Research Council of Mich.; founder Relm Found., trustee 1950-51; mem. Earhart Found.; asso. Cal. Inst. Tech.; dir. Am. Petroleum Inst., 1929-32; former dir. Nat. Safety Council. Republican. Methodist. Mason (32°). Clubs: University (Ann Arbor); Detroit. Home: 'The Meadows,'' Route 2, Ann Arbor. Office: First National Bldg., Ann Arbor, Mich. Died Oct. 21, 1954; buried Botsford Cemetery, Ann Arbor.

EARLE, Clarence Edwards, engr.; b. Bengies, Md., Aug. 27, 1893; s. William George and Annie Rebecca (Edwards) E.; student Baltimore Polytech. Inst., 1913; B.S. in Chem. Engring., George Washington U., 1923; m. Dorothy B. Stone, April 16, 1919; children—Leslie Marie (Mrs. Richard O. Thomas), Richard Stone. Teacher manual arts, science, mathematics, Del Norte, Colo., Richmond, Va., 1913-18; head aeronautical gas sect., Bur. Aeronautics, U.S. Navy, 1920-25; rep. U.S. helium plant, Ft. Worth, Tex., 1925-30; head chem. research and development sec., Bur. Aeronautics, U.S. Navy, 1930-42, chief chem. consultant, 1942-43; dir. Earle Research Lab., since 1939; research dir. Baltimore Engring. and Chem. Co.; president Breco Mfg. Company, director Medical Chemicals, Inc., Insl-X Company, Ossining, N.Y.; chief tech. consultant R.R. Engring. Co. (all Baltimore). Entered U.S. Naval Aviation, Jan. 8, 1918 as machinist mate 2d class, disch. as ensign U.S Naval Res., Apr. 1920. Mem. Am. Chem. Soc. Automotive Engrs., Washington Soc. Engrs. Protestant. Mason (Shriner). Clubs: University, Congressional Country (Washington, D.C.), Merchants' (Baltimore). Discovered and developed Lithium soap lubricating greases used in aircraft mfg., U.S. and fgn., World War II; originated, developed all-purpose hydraulic oil, chem. polar compounds for thin film preservation of metallic surfaces against corrosion, aircraft carbon monoxide detector, etc.; pioneered discovery and development of series of chem. compounds known as phenyl-amino salts used as mycotic drug in South Pacific. Home: 5025 Glenbrook Terrace, Washington 16. Office: Marsh Bldg., Washington 6. Died Nov. 25, 1953.

EARLE, Edward Mead, univ. prof.; b. N.Y. City, May 20, 1894; s. Stephen King and Helen Martha (Hart) E.; B.S., with highest honors, Columbia, 1917, Ph.D., 1923, LL.D., 1954; L.H.D., Union Coll., 1941, Colgate U., 1947; LL.D., Princeton U., 1947; m. Beatrice Lowndes, Feb. 11, 1919; 1 dau., Rosamond. Served as 2d and 1st lt., Field Arty., and A.S., U.S. Army, 1917-19, World War. With Nat. City Bank, New York, 1919-20; lecturer in history, Columbia, 1920-23, asst. prof., 1923-26, asso. prof. 1926-34; prof. Sch. of Hist. Studies, Inst. for Advanced Study, Princeton, since 1934; asso. mem. All Souls Coll., Oxford, 1950. Stafford Little lecturer, Princeton, 1941; Lamont lecturer, Yale, 1945; Chichele lectr. U. of Oxford, 1950. Fellow Mil. Sciences, Library of Congress since 1943. Mem. bd. analysts, Office Strategic Services, Washington, 1941-42; spl. consultant to the comdg. gen. Army Air Forces, 1942-45, on temporary duty with 8th and 9th Air Forces, U.S. Strategic Air Forces overseas, 1944-45; spl. asst. to Supreme Comdr. Allied Powers, Europe 1951. Rep. of Internat. Opium Commn., Turkey and Greece, 1924. Lect. Army War Coll., 1924-27, 1939-40, 50, Army Indsl. Coll., 1927, Army and Navy Staff Coll., 1944-46, Nat. War Coll., 1946-51, Joint Services Staff Coll. (Brit.), 1948-50, Imperial Defence Coll. (Brit.), 1948-51, Royal Naval War Coll. (Brit.), 1950; mem. bd. visitors Air U., U.S.A.F., 1952-55. Vice chairman Foreign Policy Association, 1924-27; ednl. dir. N.Y. chapter Am. Inst. Banking, 1921-27. Trustee Foundation for Social Sciences, U. of Denver; mem. bd. academic cons. Nat. War Coll., 1946-49. Awarded Presidential medal for Merit for war service; medal for Distinguished Public Service, Columbia University; Legion of Honor, Rank of Chevalier (French). Mem. Am. Hist. Assn., Am. Polit. Science Assn., Council on Foreign Relations, Phi Beta Kappa, Alpha Delta Phi. Specialist in military affairs and American foreign relations. Clubs: Century (New York); Army and Navy (Washington). Author: An Outline of Modern History, 1921; Turkey, The Great Powers, and Bagdad Railway (winner of George Louis Beer prize for best work of year on European diplomacy), 1923; Against This Torrent, 1941; American Views on Air Power (with Gen. Carl Spaatz), 1947. Editor and co-author: "Makers of Modern Strategy: Military Thought from Machiavelli to Hitler," 1943; Nationalism and Internationalism, 1950; Modern France: Problems of the Third and Fourth Republics, 1951. Contbr. articles in Pol. Sci. Quarterly, Yale Review, Fgn. Affairs, Am. Hist. Review, etc. Edited and wrote introduction to sesquicentennial edition of the Federalist, 1937. Home: 101 Battle Road. Address: Institute for Advanced Study, Princeton, N.J. Died June 24, 1954.

EARLE, Genevieve Beavers, ex-city ofcl.; b. N.Y.C., Apr. 25, 1883; d. George and Rose A. (Carruth) Beavers; B.A., Adelphi Coll., 1907, LL.D., (hon.), 1943; student N.Y. Sch. Social Work, 1908; m. William Pitman Earle, Jr., Oct. 25, 1913 (died 1940); children—William P. (died 1935), Mrs. Mary E. Stanton. Partner Earle Bros., N.Y.C., 1930-40; dir. Midwood Trust Co., 1930-31; adv. com. Mfrs. Trust Co., 1931-38. Staff, Bur. Municipal Research, N.Y.C., 1908-13; mem. City Bd. Child Welfare, 1917, City Indsl. Relations Bd., 1937; mem. City Council, 1937, 39, 41, 43, 45-49, minority leader, 1940-46, 46-49. Sec. N.Y. com. for outlawry of war, 1923, mem. Mayor Walker's com. on plan and survey, 1926, sec. Gov. Roosevelt's commn. on stblzn. of industry to prevent unemployment, 1930-31; chmn. women's div. Bklyn. Emergency Unemployment Commn., 1930-31; mem. N.Y.C. Charter Revision Commn., 1935-36, mem. Mayor's com. on city planning, 1937-38; chmn. or mem. various election coms., 1908-35. Mem. bd. trustees Bklyn. Pub. Library, 1934-38. Mem. City War Council, 1941. Recipient citation for distinguished pub. service Mayor LaGuardia, 1936; gold medallion Museum City N.Y.; gold medal Bklyn. Downtown Assn., 1937. Mem. United Neighborhood Guild (pres. 1924-31), League Women Voters (chmn. Bklyn. 1928-33). Bklyn. Jr. League, Kappa Alpha Theta. Independent Republican. Unitarian. Clubs: Women's City (exec. dir. 1933-36), Civitas. Address: 33 Bellport Lane, Bellport, L.I., N.Y. Died Mar. 6, 1956; buried Greenwood Cemetery, Bklyn.

EARLE, Walter Frank, banker; b. Belleville, N.J., Mar. 29, 1866; s. Reuben and Anna Eliza (Hewitt) E.; student Worcester Acad.; m. Elizabeth Hyde, Apr. 2, 1907; 1 son, Edward Hyde. With Harvard Trust Co. (formerly First Nat. Bank of Cambridge), 1889——, beginning as messenger and bookkeeper, successively cashier, clk. of bd., treas., pres., 1912-41, chmn., 1941-53, hon. chmn., 1953——; co-founder E. & R. Laundry Co., Cambridge, Mass., 1900; co-founder Phoenix Lace Mill (R.I.), 1908. Mem. bd., treas. Mt. Auburn Hosp., Cambridge, 1936-52. Home: 3 Concord Av., Cambridge. Office: Harvard Trust Co., Cambridge 38, Mass. Died Aug. 4, 1958; buried Mt. Auburn Cemetery, Cambridge.

EARLEY, John Joseph, archtl. sculptor; b. N.Y.C., Dec. 12, 1881; s. James Farrington and Mary (Kelley) E.; student St. John's Coll., 1894-99; m. Elizabeth Marie Viboud, Feb. 11, 1904; 1 dau., Frances Agnes (Mrs. John J. Kuhn). Began as apprentice in father's studio making archtl. ornaments, 1899; entered plastering contracting business, 1906, and developed archtl. concrete and plastic mosaic process which bears his name; collaborated with Lorado Taft in constrn. of Foundain of Time, 1921; built the Parthenon, Nashville, 1923; decorated interior of several notable churches, including Ch. of Sacred Heart, Washington; prepared and erected ornamentation of Baha'i Temple, Wilmette, Ill.; Mosaic ceilings U.S. Dept. of Justice, Washington, 1935; Thomas Alva Edison Meml. Tower, Menlo Park, 1937. Cons. on mosaic concrete for U.S. Naval Test Basin, Carderock, Md., 1938. Recipient Wason medal Am. Concrete Inst., H. C. Turner gold medal for development concrete as archtl. medium, 1934; Craftsmanship medal A.I.A., 1936. Mem. Am. Concrete Inst. (pres. 1938); asso. mem. A.I.A. Catholic. Club: Columbia Country. Contbr. tech. articles and periodicals. Home: 2700 Connecticut Av. N.W., Washington. Office: Rosslyn, Va. Died Nov. 25, 1945.*

EARLY, John Jacob, educator; b. South Bend, Ind., Jan. 15, 1878; s. Isaac and Mary Elizabeth (Irvin) E.; A.B., Indiana U., 1901; A.M., Columbia U., 1927; LL.D., hon., U. Wyo., 1951; m. Mary Whitmer, Aug. 20, 1902; 1 dau., Ruth Evelyn (Mrs. J. W. Sampson). Country school teacher, 1895-98; teacher physics and chemistry, Warsaw (Ind.) High Sch., 1901-03, prin. high sch., 1903-05, supt. schs., 1905-08; supt. schs. Sheridan, Wyo., 1908-1945, supt. emeritus, 1945-46; president Wyo. State Board of Education. Chmn. Sheridan County chpt. A.R.C., World War I. Recipient Wyo. Distinguished Service Award from Kiwanis Clubs of the state, 1947. Mem. State Bd. Ednl. Examiners, State Bd. Edn. (pres. from 1929), Y.M.C.A. Bd., Boy Scouts Council; trustee Perkins Foundation. Mem. N.E.A., Wyo. Edn. Assn. (past pres.), Phi Delta Kappa, Phi Gamma Delta. Republican. Presbyterian. Mason (Shriner). Clubs: Rotary (past pres.); Emeritus (Ind. U.). Home: 405 W. Works St., Sheridan, Wyo. Died Dec. 2, 1951; buried Mount Hope Cemetery, Sheridan.

EARLY, Maurice, newspaper political columnist; b. Cleveland, O., June 14, 1889; s. Henry and Emma F. (Niklaus) E.; student Marquette U., 1912-14; Wabash Coll., 1915; m. Josephine L. Zartman, Sept. 29, 1917; children—Elizabeth J. (Mrs. Arnold Goodman), Josephine L. (Mrs. Philip W. Rothrock), Charles. Political writer, Indianapolis (Ind.) Star since 1922, columnist since 1939. Recipient By-Line award, Marquette Univ. Sch. of Journalism, 1946, distinguished service award, Ind. Pub. Health Assn., 1951. Mem. Sigma Delta Chi. Club: Indianapolis (Ind.) Press (pres. 1934). Author of pamphlet, Constitutional Revision in Indiana (reprint of newspaper articles), 1929. Home: 4157 Central Av. Office: Indianapolis Star, Indpls. 5. Died Feb. 5, 1954; buried Holy Cross Cemetery, Indpls.

EARLY, Stephen, manufacturing exec.; b. Crozet, Va., Aug. 27, 1889; s. Thomas Joseph and Ida Virginia (Wood) E.; student pvt. schs. in Va., high schs., Washington, D.C.; m. Helen Wrenn, Sept. 17, 1921; children—Stephen T., Helen Virginia, Thomas Augustus. Mem. Washington staff, United Press, 1908-13, Associated Press, 1913-17 and 1920-27; advance rep. for Franklin D. Roosevelt, campaign of 1920; publicity dir. for bd. dirs. Chamber of Commerce of U.S., 1920-21; Washington rep. Paramount-Publix Corp. and Paramount News, 1927-33; asst. sec. to President Roosevelt, Mar. 4, 1933-July 1, 1937, sec., 1937-45; apptd. spl. asst. to President Truman; awarded D.S.M. by the President; vice pres. Pullman, Inc., 1945-48; v.p. Pullman Standard Car Mfg. Co., Jan. 1948-Apr. 1949; apptd. under sec. of defense, Apr. 1949, dep. sec. of defense Aug. 1949, resigned Sept. 1950; reelected v.p. Pullman, Inc., also Pullman-Standard Car Manufacturing Co., Sept. 1950. Served as capt. inf., U.S. Army, World War I. Awarded Silver Star citation. Democrat. Baptist. Clubs: The Chicago (Chicago), Metropolitan, National Press, Burning Tree. Home: 7704 Morningside Dr., Washington. Died Aug. 11, 1951; buried Arlington Nat. Cemetery.

EARNHEART, Harold, physician; b. Dongola, Ill., June 4, 1904; s. Ernest Griffith and Anna Mabel (Fink) E.; A.B., Oklahoma City U., 1924; student Washington U. Med. Sch., 1924-25; M.D., U. of Okla., 1929; m. Pauline Virginia Darling, Mar. 3, 1936; children—John Harold, Stephen Griffith. Intern Grad. Hosp. U. of Pa., 1929-30; resident training Broadstreet Hosp., N.Y. City, 1931, Women's Hosp., 1931-33, Michael Reese Hosp., Chicago, 1934, Chicago Lying-In Hosp., 1935; field rep., asst. dir. Am. Coll. Surgeons, Chicago, 1935-42; med. dir Swift & Co., Chicago since 1943. Fellow A.C.S., Am. Assn. Indsl. Phys. and Surgs., A.M.A.; mem. Phi Kappa Psi. Phi Beta Pi. Home: 518 Maple Av., Wilmette, Ill. Office: Swift & Co., Gen. Office, Chgo. 9. Died Feb. 7, 1953.

EARP, James William (ärp), writer; b. Clarence, Mo., June 15, 1888; s. William Samuel and Catherine (Cleary) E.; ed. pub. schs.; m. Marie Rita Rainville, Aug. 9, 1927; children—James Girouard, Rose Marie. Contbr. to high sch. paper at age of 15; condr. C.R.I. and P. Ry., in service, 1912-56, ret.; first success as mag. writer was series of articles entitled "Adventures of Railroad Students," Railroad Man's Mag., 1916; wrote series, "Tales by Jones the Boomer," Railroad Man's Mag., 1916-19, also "Southpaws and Others," "That Boxing Kangaroo," 1922, and "Mike Magee Stories," 1923, in Top-Notch Mag., "Corporal Brown Stories," War Stories, 1926-28, "Switch Shanty Tales," Railroad Man's Mag., 1929-31, "Railroad Fables," Railroad Stories, 1932-34, Slippery Buck series Railroad Stories, 1935-37, 1938-42, 1946-51, also stories appearing in Munsey publs., Smart Set, Action Stories, Am. Boy; 2-star story in O'Brien's Best Short Stories, 1929. Served as sergeant Co. C, 68th Engrs., later 56th Co. Transportation Corps, A.E.F.; sporting editor "The Camouflage," soldiers' paper, and mem. press special touring French battlefields and Germany, under auspices of the paper, "Stars and Stripes"; hon. disch., July 16, 1919. Mem. Order of Railway Condrs. K.C. Author: Boomer Jones, 1921. Address: 6334 Montgall, Kansas City 30, Mo. Died Nov. 18, 1958; buried Mount Olivet Cemetery, Kansas City.

EASTBURN, L(acey) A(rnold), coll. pres.; b. South English, Ia., May 19, 1889; s. James Wilson and Mary Cade (Arnold) E.; B.S. (edn.), S.W. Mo. State Teachers Coll., 1916; A.B., A.M., Drury Coll., Springfield, Mo., 1917; student (summer), U. Ariz., 1921-23, U. Cal., 1928-33; Ed.D., Stanford, 1936 (Cubberley teaching fellow, 1934-35); LL.D., Southwest Christian Seminary, 1950; married Viola B. Cox, Feb. 2, 1918; 1 dau., Viola Catherine (Mrs. John C. Jennings). Teacher, rural schs., Mo., 1908-13; teaching fellow Drury Coll., 1916-17; supt. schs., Golden City, Mo., 1917-18; instr. mathematics and physics, Northern Ariz. Normal Sch., 1919-21; dir. research and guidance, high schs., jr. coll., Phoenix, 1921-47; Cubberly teaching fellow Stanford, 1934-35; vis. prof. edn. U. Ariz., Ariz. State Colls., summers, 1936-43; pres. Ariz. State Coll., 1947—; dir. 1st Fed. Savs. & Loan Assn. (Phoenix). Mem. bd. dirs. YMCA, Community Chest. Served U.S. Army, Air Service, 1918-19. Mem. Nat. Soc. for Study Edn., Ariz. Council Edn. (pres., 1936-37), Ariz. Sch. Adminstrs. (pres. 1940-41), State Bd. Edn., N.E.A., Am. Assn. Sch. Adminstrs., Assn. Tchr. Edn. Instns., Nat. Commn. Accrediting, Phi Delta Kappa, Kappa Delta Pi. Mem. Christian Ch. Club: Kiwanis (mem. bd. dirs. past pres. Phoenix). Author: Relative Efficiency of Instruction in Large and Small Classes on Three Ability Levels, 1936; co-author: Planning Your Life, 1939. Contbr. articles to ednl. jours. Home: Arizona State College, Flagstaff, Ariz. Died Oct. 31, 1957; buried Memory Lawn Meml. Park, Phoenix.

EASTERBROOK, Arthur E., army officer; b. Amsterdam, N.Y., Nov. 4, 1893; s. Col. Arthur Edmund and Fannie (Luscombe) E.; student U. of Wash., 1915-17; grad. Army Field Officers Tactical Sch., Langley Field, Va., 1921; m. Gertrude L. Augustine, May 1, 1920; 1 son, Arthur Edward. Commd. 2d lt., inf., 1917, retired for disability in line of duty with rank of lt. col., 1939; returned to active duty, 1940; promoted brig. gen., 1944; comdg. officer Santa Ana Army Air Base, Santa Ana, Calif., since August, 1944. Decorated Distinguished Service Cross with oak leaf cluster, Purple Heart, Victory Medal with 4 stars (major campaigns in World War I), German Army of Occupation and Pre-Pearl Harbor ribbons, Legion of Merit; Croix de Guerre (France). Mem. Sigma Chi, Scabbard and Blade. Credited with shooting down 5 planes during World War I. Home: 2220 Greenleaf St., Santa Ana, Cal. Died July 24, 1952; buried Arlington Nat. Cemetery.

EASTMAN, Clarence Willis, coll. prof.; b. Concord, N.H., Jan. 3, 1873; s. Charles Leonard and Sarah (French) E.; B.S., Worcester Poly. Inst., 1894; studied U. of Göttingen, 1895-96, U. of Leipzig, 1896-98, Ph.D., 1898; hon. A.M., Amherst, 1912; m. Ann Hull Dey, Aug. 29, 1906; children—Anthony Dey, Philip Dey, Karl Dey. Asst. in modern langs., Worcester Poly. Inst., 1894-95; instr. German, 1898-1901, assistant professor, 1901-07, University of Iowa; asso. prof. German, 1907-09, prof. German lang. and literature, 1909-43, prof. emeritus, 1943, Amherst Coll. Mem. Modern Lang. Assn. of America, Modern Lang. Assn. New England (pres. 1920-21), Am. Assn. Univ. Profs. Member Plattsburg Training Camp, Aug. 1916; in charge mil. training, Amherst Coll., May-June 1917; tactical instr. R.O.T.C., Amherst, Apr.-May 1918; attended 4th O.T.C., Camps Devens and Lee; instr. mil. law, Amherst Unit of S.A.T.C.; translator P.O. Dept., 1918. Moderator town of Amherst, 1926-48; chmn. rationing bd., Amherst, July 1943-Feb. 1944. Episcopalian. Mason. Author: Die Syntax des Dativs bei Notker, 1899; An Account of Some of the Ancestors of Harry Thompson and Myra Hull, 1916. Editor of Goethe's Poems, 1941, and other texts. Address: 86 Northampton Rd., Amherst, Mass. Died Mar. 11, 1952; buried Wildwood Cemetery, Amherst, Mass.

EASTMAN, Hal Pond, industrialist; b. Oxford, Neb., 1885; s. Joseph Reed and Antoinette M. (Hill) E.; student U. of Mich., 1906-08; m. Edith M. Hall, 1913; 1 dau., Janet (Mrs. Carl West, Jr.); m. 2d, Maybelle Nordness, 1921; children—John, Paul, Robert Joseph, Hal Pond. Began with Crane Co., 1903; with J. H. Matthes Co., 1904, Idaho Placer Co., 1909-11, Crane Creek Land & Irrigation Co., 1911-13; chief engr. Am. Cyanamid Co., 1913-14, gen. supt., 1914-17, vice pres. and dir., 1947—, pres. North Am. Cyanamid, Ltd.; v.p., dir. Ariz. Chem. Co., Porocel Corp.; dir. So. Minerals, So. Pipeline, So. Petroleum corps., Berbice Co., Ltd. Republican. Episcopalian. Clubs: Rockefeller Center; Siwanoy Country. Home: 39 Edgewood Lane, Bronxville, N.Y. Office: American Cyanamid Co., 30 Rockefeller Plaza, N.Y.C. Died May 4, 1955; buried Monrovia, Cal.

EASTMAN, Helen, nature student; b. S. Newbury, Vt., Mar. 22, 1863; d. Charles Wesley and Elizabeth Chastina (Abbott) E.; ed. Wells River (Vt.) graded sch.; studied art and became tchr. painting, 1886-93, but health failing took up nature study. Mem. Evangelical Assn. Author: New England Ferns and Their Common Allies, 1904. Address: Wells River, Vt. Died Oct. 26, 1953; buried North Wilkesboro, N.C.

EASTMAN M(oses) Gale, univ. dean, dir. agrl. expt. station; b. Sanbernton, N.H., Sept. 13, 1886; s. George Prescott and Laurenia A. (Gale) E.; ed. New Hampton Literary Inst., 1904-08, Bates Coll., 1908-09; B.S., N.H. Coll., 1913; M.S., Cornell U., 1916, Ph.D., 1931; m. Josephine B. Currier, June 27, 1916; children—Laurenia Annie, David Gale. County agent, 1913-14; asst. commr. of agr., State of N.H., 1914-15; farm supt., New London, 1916-18; asst. prof. agronomy N.H. Coll. (now U. of N.H.), 1918-25, asso. prof., 1925-29, prof. agrl. economics, 1929-31, asso. dean College of Agriculture, 1931-33, dean 1933-48; asst. agronomist. Agrl. Expt. Station, 1918-25, asso. agronomist, 1925-29; asso. agrl. economist, 1929-31; dir, 1939-48. Member Durham Sch. Board, 1927-38, chmn. 1931-38. Mem. Alpha Zeta, Phi Kappa Phi. Alpha Tau Omega. Mason. ham, N.H. Died Jan. 2, 1953; buried Durham (N. H.) Cemetery.

EASTWOOD, Alice, botanist; b. Toronto, Can., Jan. 19, 1859; d. Colin Skinner and Eliza Jane (Gowdey) E.; grad. E. Denver High Sch., 1879. Tchr. E. Denver High Sch., 1879-89; curator herbarium Cal. Acad. Scis., 1892-49, ret. Fellow A.A.A.S., Cal. Acad. Scis. Author: Popular Flora of Denver, Colo., 1893; Popular Flora and Pacific Coast Edition, Bergen's Botany, 1897; Popular Flora and Rocky Mountain Edition, Bergen's Botany, 1900; Hand-Book of Trees of California, 1905; also many papers on systematic botany and articles for scientific mags. Address: 1221 Lombard St., San Francisco. Died Oct. 29, 1953; buried Toronto, Can.

EATON, Charles Aubrey, congressman; b. Nova Scotia, Can., Mar. 29, 1868; s. Stephen and Mary D. (Parker) E.; B.A., Acadia U., N.S., 1890, M.A., 1893; graduate Newton Theol. Instn., Mass., 1893; M.A., McMaster U., Toronto, Ont., 1896; (D.D., Baylor U., 1899, Acadia, 1907; LL.D., McMaster, 1916); m. M. Winifred Parlin, June 26, 1895; children—Marion Aubrey, Margaret Evelyn, Frances Winifred, Chas. Aubrey, Mary Rose, Catharine Starr. Ordained Bapt. ministry, 1893; pastor First Ch., Natick, Mass., 1893-95, Bloor St. Ch., Toronto, 1895-1901, Euclid Av. Ch., Cleveland, 1901-09, Madison Av Ch., New York, 1909-19; editor Leslie's Weekly, 1919-20. Expert in industrial relations. Sociol. editor Toronto Globe, 1896-1901; asso. editor Westminster, Toronto, 1899-1901; spl. Canadian corr. New York Tribune and Boston Transcript, 1897-1901; spl. corr. London Times. Head of nat. service sect. U.S. Shipping Bd. Emergency Fleet Corp., Nov. 1917-Jan. 1919; head industrial relations dept. Nat. Lamp Works, Gen. Electric Co. Editor of Light since 1923. Mem. 69th to 72d Congresses (1925-33), 4th N.J. Dist. and 73d to 82d Congress (1933-53), 5th N.J. Dist.; apptd. by Pres. Roosevelt as a U.S. del. to the United Nations Conf., San Francisco, Feb. 28, 1945, signed the Charter, June 26, 1945. Home: P.O. Box 126, Plainfield, N.J. Office: 1229 House Office Bldg., Washington. Died Jan. 23, 1953; buried Hillside Cemetery, Plainfield, N.J.

EATON, Emma Florence, editor; b. Wakefield, Mass., Feb. 26, 1874; d. Chester W. and Emma G. (Leach) Eaton; A.B., Smith Coll., 1896; post-grad., Oxford, 1899-1900 (receiving certificate from Assn. for Edn. Women of Oxford, 1900). Taught English in high schs. and N.H. Normal Sch.; editor Wakefield Citizen and Banner (now Wakefield Daily Item), 1905—. Author: Dramatic Studies from the Bible, 1906. Address: Wakefield, Mass. Died July 5, 1933; buried Wakefield.

EATON, Ernest Theophilus, educator, ex-lt. gov.; b. Atkinson, Me., Sept. 11, 1877; s. Thomas O. and Delia Ellen (Bolster) E.; B.S., Lenox (Ia.) Coll., 1897, M.S., 1899; Ph.B., U. Ia., 1899; LL.D., Intermountain Coll., 1931; m. Augusta M. Valiton, Sept. 6, 1911; children—Margaret Louise, Robert Thomas. Prin. pub. schs., Oak Park, Des Moines, Ia., 1900-02; supt. schs., Deer Lodge, Mont., 1902-08; also prin. Powell County (Mont.) High Sch., 1903-08; financial sec. Coll. of Mont., 1908; a founder, 1908, financial dir., bus. mgr. Billings Poly. Inst., 1908-31, pres., 1931-46. Mem. Mont. Ho. of Reps., 3 terms, 1917-18, 19-20, 25-26, chmn. com. on edn. 2 terms; State senator, terms 1927-39, chmn. com. on edn. 3 terms, pres. senate 1935; lt. gov. Mont., 1941-49. Mem. Am. Council State Govts., Nat. Econ. League, Acad. Polit. Science. Republican. Conglist. Mason. Clubs: Commercial, Kiwanis, Rod and Gun. Home: Polytechnic P.O., Billings, Mont. Died Aug. 1957.

EATON, George Franklin, lawyer; b. Brewer, Me., Mar. 15, 1892; s. Fred Gordon and Alice Louise (Gibson) E.; A.B., Bowdoin Coll., 1914; LL.B., U. Me., 1916; m. Elizabeth Gale Littlefield, Aug. 22, 1917; children—Franklin Wilmot, Richard Galen, Robert John, Dwight Littlefield. Admitted to Me. bar, 1917, law since practiced Bangor; mem. Eaton, Peabody, Bradford & Veague; pres. dir. European & N.A. Ry. Co.; pres., trustee Bangor Savs. Bank; dir. Community Broadcasting Service, Community Telecasting Service, Mchts. Nat. Bank; city solicitor, Bangor, 1921-25, councillor, 1932-33; co. atty., Penobscot Co., 1926-28. Mem. nat. com. Citizen's Com.

Reorgn. Exec. Br. of Govt. Mem. sch. bd. Bangor, 1926-31. Trustee Eastern Me. Gen. Hosp., Bangor Pub. Library. Served with A.S., U.S. Army, 1917-19; disch. as 1st lt. Mem. Am., Me. State (pres.), Penobscot bar assns., Fed. Tax Inst. N.E. (adv. com.), Alpha Delta Phi, Phi Alpha Delta, Phi Kappa Phi. Republican. Conglist. Mason (33°, K.T.). Clubs: Tarratine, Penobscot Valley Country, Rotary (Bangor); Bucks Harbor Yacht (Brooksville, Me.). Home: 85 Highland St. Office: 6 State St., Bangor, Me. Died Oct. 1, 1956.

EATON, Harvey Doane, lawyer; b. North Cornville, Me., Sept. 20, 1862; s. Augustus Barna and Harriet (Armstrong) E.; ed. dist. sch.; student Somerset Acad., 1874-81, Waterville (now Coburn) Classical Inst., 1881-83; A.B, Colby U. (now Colby Coll.), 1887; LL.B., Harvard Law Sch., 1891; m. Estelle Merrill Foster, Oct. 22, 1891 (died Feb. 28, 1908); children—Harvey Doane, Foster, Florence, Harriet (Mrs. Albert Raymond Rogers); m. 2d, Hazel Irene Fletcher, Oct. 29, 1914; children—Fletcher, John Colby, Arthur Tibbetts, Frances. Admitted to Me. bar, 1889; city solicitor Waterville, 1897-98; procured charter for Kennebec Water Dist., 1899 (first municipality of kind ever organied in Me.; plan now used throughout state); became connected with Central Me. Power Co., 1899, drew present charter, 1905, resigned as pres., 1924; now gen. practice law. Chmn. draft bd., 1917-19. Mem. bars of Me., U.S. Dist. Ct., U.S. Circuit Ct. Appeals of 1st Circuit, Supreme Ct. Mem. Me. Bar Assn., Delta Kappa Epsilon. Republican. Conglist. Home: 55 Silver St. Office: 50 Main St., Waterville, Me. Died Oct. 17, 1953.

EATON, James Murchie, vice-pres. Am. Overseas Airlines; b. Platka, Fla., Feb. 15, 1888; s. Charles Freedom and Alice Mabel (Murchie) E.; student Calais (Me.) Acad., 1902-06; B S. in Elec. Engring., U. of Me., 1910; unmarried. With Stone and Webster, engring., management and construction, 1910-20; charge of purchasing and distribution of materials for cantonment, Waco, Tex., and Am. Ordnance Depot, France, 1917; became interested in airplanes when he made his first flight with Ed Wiggins winter 1913; assisted in establishing service between Tampa and St. Petersburg, Fla. (21 miles), which is now credited with world's first scheduled airline, winter 1914; went to Europe to investigate possibility of using wartime aircraft for commercial operation, 1920; concluded such craft not adequate; engaged in mfg. and merchandising in Mass. and Ind. to 1928; associated with Pan-Am. Airways becoming gen. traffic mgr. (lines increased from 110 miles to 19,000 miles during period), 1928-31; pres. Ludington Airlines (New York to Washington every hour), 1931-33; aviation consultant, 1933-36; associated with Am. Export Steamship Lines, 1936; became vice-pres. Am. Export Airlines, Inc., 1936; now v.p. Am. Overseas Airlines Inc. Mem. advisory com. Daniel Guggenheim School of Aeronautics of the Coll. of Engring., N.Y. Univ. Mem. Phi Gamma Delta, University Club (Boston), Mason. Home: 125 E. 50th St. Office: 100 E. 42d St., N.Y.C. Died May 1, 1952.

EATON, James Shirley, ry. specialist; b. Nashville, Aug. 1, 1868; s. Brig.-Gen. John E. and Alice (Shirley) E.; A.B., Marietta Coll., 1889; A.M., Dartmouth, 1894; m. Ethel O. Mason, Sept. 24, 1908; children—Shirley Osgood (dec.), Phoebe Kimball, Osgood Shirley. Traveling auditor, So. Ry., 1894-97; expert in adaptation of electric tabulating machine to ry. accounting, 1898-99; statistician, Lehigh Valley R.R., 1899-1903; railroad edior Wall Street Jour., 1903-04; now statistician. Lectr. Tuck Sch., Dartmouth; lectr. ry. transportation, N.Y.U. Mem. Am. Econ. Assn. Club: Railroad. Author: Railroad Operations, 1900; Education for Efficiency in Railroad Service, 1910; Railroad Expense Handbook, 1911. Also monographs on ry. subjects. Examiner Fed. Trade Commn., 1917-20; statistician, economist Bur. Econs. and Engring. of Nat. Assn. Owners Ry. Securities, 1921-22; ry. expert work, N.Y.C., 1922-29. Wrote articles on N.E. Divs. Case and Potter plan. Home: 949 Ray Av., Ridgefield, N.J. Died Aug. 13, 1933; buried Sutton, N.H.

EATON, Joseph Oriel, mfr.; b. Yonkers, N.Y., July 28, 1873; s. Joseph Oriel and Emma (Goodman) E.; B.A., Williams, 1895; m. Edith Ide French, Apr. 26, 1910; children—Edith French (Mrs. Daniel Dewey), Caroline French, Winsor Brown French, Edward Savage French, Joseph Oriel, Margaret Adams (Mrs. Herbert M. Sichel), Martha (Mrs. Charles Hickok), Anne (Mrs. H. Whitney Dodge). Began with American Express Company, New York City, 1895; department mgr., George P. Ide & Company, shirt and collar mfrs., Troy, N.Y., 1897-1904; assistant general mgr. Empire Cream Separator Co., Bloomfield, N.J., 1904-06; organizer, 1906, treas. until 1910, Interstate Shirt & Collar Co., Troy; Founder, vice pres. and treas., Torbensen Gear & Axle Co., 1911; president The Torbensen Axle Co., 1916-19; organizer, 1919, president, 1919-23, The Eaton Axle Co.; pres. Eaton Mfg. Co., 1923-25, chmn. bd. since 1925; partner Otis & Co., investment brokers, 1921-31; chmn. bd. Eaton Mfg. Co., Cleveland; director and member executive com., Inland Investors, Inc., National Acme Company; dir. Berkshire Frozen Food Lockers, Inc. Served as private, 2d New York Vol. Inf., Spanish-American War. Mem. Gargoyle Alumnus, Delta Psi. Clubs: Union, Tavern, (Cleveland); St. Anthony, Williams (New York); Taconic Golf; Old Timers, Detroit; Faculty (Williamstown). Home: 2207 Devonshire Dr., Cleveland Heights; (summer) Williamstown, Mass. Office: 739 E. 140th St., Cleve. Died May, 1949.

EATON, L(ealdes) McKendree (Lee M.), physician; b. Owaneco, Ill., Feb. 3, 1905; s. Jordan Stewart, Sr., and Margaret (Barrett) E.; student James Millikan U., 1923-25; B.S., U. Chgo., 1927, M D., 1932; M.S., U. Minn., 1938; m. Mary Louise Long, Apr. 2, 1936; children—Elizabeth Barrett, Lynne St. Pierre, Emily Jordan, Charles McKendree, Thomas Lee. Intern Cook County Hosp., Chgo., 1931-33; fellow internal medicine Mayo Found., Rochester, 1933-34, fellow neurology, 1934-36, instr. neurology, 1938-41, asst. prof., 1941-46, asso. prof., 1946-50, prof., 1950-—; cons. neurology Mayo Clinic, 1936-47, head neurologic sect., 1947-54, chmn. neurology sections, 1954-—; research myasthenia gravis, polymyositis, other neuromuscular diseases. Med. adv. bd. Myasthenia Gravis Found., Inc., 1954-—. Diplomate Am. Bd. Psychiatry and Neurology. Mem. Central Neuropsychiat. Assn. (pres. 1953), Am. Neurological Assn., Am. Acad. Neurology, Assn. Research Nervous and Mental Disease (president 1958), American Medical Association (chairman section on nervous and mental disease 1956), Sigma Xi, Alpha Omega Alpha. Universalist. Author articles on neurologic subjects. Home: 909 Eighth St. S.W. Office: 200 First St. S.W., Rochester, Minn. Died Nov. 17, 1958.

EATON, Lucien, mining engr.; b. St. Louis, Mo., July 6, 1879; s. Lucien and Hannah Orr (Noyes) E.; A.B., magna cum laude, Harvard, 1900, M.S., 1902; S.B. in mining and metallurgy, Lawrence Scientific Sch., 1901; m. Eleanor Archibald Stevens, June 15, 1907 (dec. May, 1949); children—Elizabeth Stevens, Eleanor, Lucien; m. 2d, Charlotte Vose, July 8, 1952. On engring. staff Cleveland Cliffs Iron Co., Ishpeming and Ironwood, Mich., 1902-06; supt. Iron Belt & Shores Mines, same co., Iron Belt, Wis., 1906-09; supt. Ishpeming Dist. (with exception of few months), 1909-29; cons. mining engr. Roan Antelope Copper Company and Rhodesian Selection Trust, Ltd., 1929-33; consulting mining engineer gold mines of Australia, Western Mining Corp., Bendigo Mines, North Broken Hill, Broken Hill S., Zinc Corp., and other Australian mining cos., 1934-35; consulting engr. Copper Range Co. and Isle Royale Copper Co., 1937-38; general manager Isle Royale Copper Co., 1938-39; cons. mining engineer with H. A. Brassert & Co., New York, 1940-46; cons. engr. with Pierce Management, Scranton, Pa., for Turkish Govt. in Turkey, 1947; Cons. engr. Copper Range Co., since 1947; Big Sandy and other mining cos. and with H. A. Brassert & Co. (Mex.), 1946; pres. dir., Inca Mining & Development Co., Santo Domingo, Peru, 1925. Capt. engrs. U.S. Army, June-Dec. 1918. Mem. Am. Inst. Mining and Metall. Engrs., Mining and Metall. Soc. America, Lake Superior Mining Inst. (v.p. 1929), Am. Mining Congress (chairman standardization committee 1929) Republican. Mason. Unitarian. Member of Milton Hoosick Club. Made various improvements in mining practice and in design of rock drills and mech. equipment for handling ore. Author: Practical Mine Development and Equipment, 1934. Contbr. to tech. jours. Address: 79 Vose's Lane, Milton 87, Mass. Died Dec. 9, 1952; buried Milton Cemetery, Milton, Mass.

EATON, Marquis G(eorge), accountant; b. Hastings, Mich., Sept. 27, 1898; s. Walter Richie and Blanche (Troup) E.: student N.Y.U., 1919-26; m. Charlotte Goeppe, Aug. 15, 1922; 1 dau., Blanche (wife of Dr. Cluade L. Nabers). Sec., bookkeeper Middle States Oil Corp., N.Y.C., 1919-24; pub. accountant, N.Y.C., 1924-26; accountant Consol. Oil Co., Wichita Falls, Tex., 1926-27; staff accountant L. E. Cahill & Co., Tulsa, 1928-31; office mgr. Barrow, Wade, Guthrie & Co., Oklahoma City, 1932-36; C.P.A., San Antonio, 1936-—; partner Eaton & Huddle, 1943. C.P.A., Okla., Tex. Mem. Am. Inst. Accountants (pres., mem. council), Tex. Soc. C.P.A.'s (pres.). Contbr. articles trade mags. Home: 530 Grandview Pl. Office: Alamo National Bldg., San Antonio. Deceased.

EATON, Philip Bentley, coast guard officer; b. Elkins, N.H., Jan. 24, 1887; s. James Everett and Sophia Rebecca (Bentley) E.; ed. pub. sch. and high sch., Collinsville, Conn.; student Cooper Union, New York, N.Y., 1903-05, Webb Inst. of Naval Architecture, 1905-08, Coast Guard Acad., 1908; m. Anita Mera Anese McWynne, Feb. 9, 1917. Commd. ensign (engineering), U.S. Coast Guard, 1908, and advanced through the grades to rear adm., 1943; served 18 yrs. at sea, including 5 Arctic cruises on cutter Bear; apptd. naval aviator, 1917; patrol pilot and comdg. officer Naval Air Station, Chatham, Massachusetts, World War I; asst. engr.-in-chief, 1941-46, retired as rear admiral, September 1946. Chief inspector ships, Coast Guard, at Bath Iron Works (Bath, Maine), and Camden, N.J., 1931. Decorated Navy and Marine Corps Medal, Victory Medal with aviation clasp, Defense Medal, World War II Medal, Expert Rifleman. Mem. Am. Soc. Naval Engrs., Soc. Mil. Engrs. Newcomen Society of England. Clubs: Propeller, Army and Navy (Washington). Home: "Comynholm," Ocean View Highway, Westerly, R.I. Died May 18, 1958; buried Arlington Nat. Cemetery.

EATON, Walter Prichard, author, coll. prof.; b. Malden, Mass., Aug. 24, 1878; s. Warren Everett and Mary (Prichard) E.; A.B., Harvard, 1900; A.M., Yale, 1946; married Elise Morris Underhill, June 30, 1910. Reporter on Boston Journal, 1900; dramatic department New York Tribune, 1902-07; dramatic critic New York Sun, 1907-08; literature work since 1908; New York theatrical corr.; dramatic critic American Mag., 1909-18; prof. playwriting, Yale U., 1933-47. Visiting lecturer, U. of Tex., 1948, U. of N.C., 1948-49. Mem. Unitarian Com. of Appraisal, 1934-35. Mem. Nat. Inst. Arts and Letters. Clubs: Elizabethan (New Haven); Century, Coffee Ho. (N.Y.). Author: Am. Stage of Today, 1908; The Runaway Place (with Elise Underhill), 1909; At the New Theatre and Others, 1910; Boy Scouts of Berkshire, 1912; Boy Scouts in the Dismal Swamp, 1913; Barn Doors and Byways, 1913; The Man Who Found Christmas, 1913; Boy Scouts in the White Mountains, 1914; The Idyl of Twin Fires, 1915; New York, 1915; Boy Scouts of the Wild Cat Patrol, 1915; Plays and Players, 1916; The Bird House Man, 1916; Peanut, Cub Reporter, 1916; Green Trails and Upland Pastures, 1917; Newark, 1917; Boy Scouts in Glacier Park, 1918; Echoes and Realities (verse), 1918; In Berkshire Fields, 1919; On the Edge of the Wilderness, 1920; Boy Scouts at Crater Lake, 1922; Penguin Persons and Peppermints, 1922; Queen Victoria (a play with David Carb), 1923; Boy Scouts on Katahdin, 1924; Skyline Camps, 1924; The Actor's Heritage, 1924; A Bucolic Attitude, 1926; Hawkeye's Room Mate, 1927; Boy Scouts on the Green Mountain Trail, 1929; Ten Years of the Theatre Guild, 1929; New England Vista, 1930; The Drama in English, 1930; Everybody's Garden, 1932; Boy Scouts in the Grand Cañon, 1932; On Yankee Hilltops, 1933; Wild Gardens of New England, 1935; Boy Scouts in Death Valley, 1938. Lecturer on gardens and dramatic topics. Home: Sheffield, Mass. Died Feb. 27, 1957; buried Sheffield.

EATON, William Hanmer, paper mfr.; b. East Hartford, Conn., June 3, 1879; s. Arthur W. and Frances M. (Hanmer) E.; student Peekskill Military Acad., 1896; B.S., Trinity Coll., 1899; m. Isabel Westcott Nicholson, July 17, 1901; children—Hope (Mrs. Leonard A. Whipple), Isabel Wilmot (Mrs. Kimball Salisbury), Ethel Frances (Mrs. E. E. Colt), Cynthia Edith (Mrs. William Callan). With Eaton Paper Corp., 1899-—, dir., 1901-—, chairman co., 1935-53, ret., now bd. chmn. Mem. City Council, Pittsfield, 1904-05. Trustee Trinity Coll. Served as lt. col. U.S. Army, exec. asst. to Chief Ordnance Office A.E.F., World War I; col. F.A. Res., 1922-41; col. Intelligence Div., First Service Command, 1941-45. Club: St. Anthony (New York). Home: 76 Eleanor Road. Office: 75 Church Street, Pittsfield, Mass. Died Oct. 8, 1957.

EAVENSON, Howard Nicholas (ĕv'ĕn-sŭn), mining engr.; b. July 15, 1873; s. Alben Taylor and Susan (Bean) E.; student Public and Friends' Central School, Phila., Pa.; B.S., Swarthmore Coll., 1892, C.E., 1895; Dr. Engring., Univ. of Pittsburgh, 1928; m. Ada J. Daugherty, Sept. 20, 1898. Engring. work in Va., N.J. and with U.S. Lake Survey, 1892-97; with H. C. Frick Coke Co. and Allied cos. as div. engr., asst. chief engr., chief engr., Uniontown, Pa., 1897-1902; chief engr. U.S. Coal and Coke Co., Gary, W.Va., 1902-20; cons. engr., 1920-—, now head of Eavenson & Auchmuty; dir. Boone Co Coal Corp., Appalachian Coals, Inc.; pres. Bituminous Coal Research Inc., 1939-48. Trustee, Carnegie Inst. Mem. Am. Soc. C.E., Am. Inst. Mining and Metall. Engrs. (pres. 1934), Am. Soc. Testing Materials, Delta Upsilon, Tau Beta Pi. Republican. Mem. Society of Friends. Clubs: University, Duquesne, Rolling Rock. Author: Coal Through the Ages; The Pittsburgh Coal Bed—Its Early History and Development; First Century and a Quarter of American Coal Industry. Home: 4411 Bayard St. Office: Koppers Bldg., Pitts. 19. Died Feb. 16, 1953.

EBERHARTER, Herman Peter (ĕb'ĕr-här-tĕr), congressman; b. Pittsburgh, Apr. 29, 1892; s. Jacob and Louisa (Ramer) Eberharter; LL.B., Duquesne University, 1925; married Emma A. Naughton, January 13, 1934 (dec.); children—Herman Peter, James Jacob. Admitted to Pennsylvania bar, 1925, and practiced since in Pittsburgh Mem Pa. Ho. of Rep., 1935-36; mem. 75th-77th, 79th-82d U.S. Congresses, 32d Pa. Dist., 78th Congress, 31st District, 83d-85th Congresses, 28th District. Served as private 20th Inf., U.S.A. World War; maj. O.R.C. Mem. Allegheny County Bar Assn. Democrat. Catholic. Home: 5521 Wilkins Av. Office: New House Office Bldg., Washington. Died Sept. 9, 1958.

EBERSOLE, William Stahl, prof. emeritus; b. Mt. Pleasant, Pa., Nov. 13, 1862; s. Solomon Keister and Sarah Emily (Stahl) E.; A.B., Lebanon Valley Coll., Annville, Pa., 1885, A.M., 1888, Litt. D., 1904; post-grad., Yale, 1890-92; Am. Sch. Classical Studies, Athens, Greece, 1896-97; U. Munich, Bavaria, Germany, summer 1897; m. Florence

Adelaide Sheldon, Dec. 14, 1892. Prof. Greek and Latin, San Joaquin Valley Coll., Woodbridge, Cal., 1885, 87; prof. Greek, Lebanon Valley Coll., 1887-90, 1893-1910, prof. Greek and archaeology, 1910-34, registrar, 1919-34, 36-37, prof. emeritus, 1934-—; acting pres., 1922-23, and last half 1926-27, Cornell Coll., Ia. Mem. Bd. Edn. of Meth. Ch., 1924-32. Mem. Archaeol. Inst. Am., Am. Philol. Assn., Classical Assn. Middle West and South, Am. Classical League, Phi Beta Kappa. Author: The Metopes of the West End of the Parthenon; contbr. Am. Jour. of Archaeology, Classical Jour. (book reviews). Republican. Methodist. Home: Mt. Vernon, Ia. Died Mar. 5, 1952; buried Mt. Vernon (Ia.) Cemetery.

ECCLES, James A., financial cons.; b. Cambridge, Mass., June 17, 1887; s. David and Anne Hutchinson (Adams) E.; A.B. cum laude, Harvard, 1910; m. Mary McGibbon, June 17, 1920. With Harris Forbes & Co., New York and Boston, 1912-19, partner, 1921-33; pres. Harris Forbes & Co., Ltd., Montreal and Toronto, 1921-33; ret., 1933; financial consultant to Canadian corps.; v.p. and dir. Royal Trust Co., Montreal; mng. dir. Montreal London & Gen. Investors, Ltd.; dir. Bell Telephone Co. of Can., Brazilian Traction Light and Power, Bldg. Products, Can. Steamships, Canadian Internat. Paper Co., Shawinigan Water & Power Co., Governor McGill U., Royal Edward Laurentian Hosp., Montreal; pres. Royal Victoria Hosp. Received rank Comdr. Order of Agrl. Merit, P.Q. Mem. Montreal Bd. of Trade (past treas.), Investment Bankers Assn. of Can. (past pres.), Investment Bankers Assn. of Am. (past gov.). Clubs: Mount Royal (past chmn.), St. James (past chmn.). Home: 3940 Cote des Neiges Rd. Office: 465 St. John St., Montreal, P.Q., Can. Died March 3, 1960.

ECHOLS, Oliver P. (ĕk'ŏls), army officer (ret.); b. Charlottesville, Va., Mar. 4, 1892; s. William H. and Mary (Blakey) E.; student Va. Poly. Inst., 1908-10, U. of Va., 1910-13; grad. Army Industrial Coll., 1926, A.C., Engring. Sch., 1927, Command and Gen. Staff Sch., 1934, Army War Coll., 1939; m. Margaret Bailey, Dec. 28, 1920; 1 dau., Mary Beirne. Commd. 2d lt. U.S. Army, 1916, and advanced through grades to maj. gen., 1942; served A.C. Exptl. Engring. Sect., 1927-30; chief A.C. Procurement Sect., 1930-31; graduate of Air Corps Tactical School, 1932; chief engr. Material Div., 1934-38, asst. chief, 1939-40, chief, 1940-47. President Aircraft Industries Assn., 1947-49; chmn. bd., chief exec. officer Northrop Aircraft, Inc., Hawthorne, California since 1949. Served with U.S. Air Services, A.E.F., Aug. 1917-Apr. 1919; comd. 1st Observation Group, chief aviation, 1st Army Corps. Participated in battles of Champagne-Marne, Aisne Marne, St. Mihiel, Meues-Argonne. Chief Army A.F. Materiel Div., Oct. 1940-Apr. 1945; chief Internal Affairs and Communication Div., U.S. Control Council, Germany, May-July 1945; asst. dep. mil. gov., U.S. Mil. Govt. (Berlin) Germany, July 1945-Apr. 1946; chief civil affairs div., War Dept., Washington, D.C., Apr. 1946-47; retired. Decorations: D.S.M. with Oak Leaf Cluster, Legion of Merit, Purple Heart, Victory Medal with five battle clasps, Hon. Comdr. Order of British Empire. Home: 10425 Charing Cross Rd., Los Angeles 24. Office: Northrop Aircraft, Inc., Hawthorne, Cal. Died May 15, 1954.

ECHOLS, Robert, clergyman; b. Selma, Ala., Feb. 5, 1874; s. William Walter and Rebecca Louise (Harris) E.; A.B., Birmingham-Southern Coll., 1902; D.D., 1921; m. Edith Claire Howard, June 23, 1903; children—Roberts Wadsworth, Frank Howard, Edith Katherine (Mrs. J. M. Herren, Jr.), Rebecca Louise (Mrs. Albert E. Terry), Nelle Claire (Mrs. Paul L. Clem), Mary Julia, Eloise Christian. Ordained ministry M.E. Ch., South, 1902; pastor Blocton, Ala., 1903-04, Millport, 1905, Coleanor-Piper, 1906, Attalla, 1907-09; presiding elder, Haleyville Dist., 1910-13; pastor Walker Memorial Ch., Birmingham, Ala., 1914, Eleventh Av. Ch., Birmingham, 1915, Woodlawn Ch., Birmingham, 1916-18; presiding elder Birmingham Dist., 1919-22; pastor Woodlawn Ch., Birmingham, 1923-25, First Ch., Florence, 1926-27, First Ch., Tuscaloosa, 1928-29, First Ch., Huntsville, 1930-31, presiding elder Jasper Dist., 1932-35; pastor McCoy Memorial Ch., Birmingham, 1935-—. Mem. Conf. Bd. of Christian Edn. of N. Ala. Conf. Trustee Birmingham-Southern Coll., 1920-—, pres. bd., chmn. exec. com.; mem. bd. dirs. Ala. Meth. Orphanage. Mem. Kappa Alpha, Omicron Delta Kappa. Democrat. Mason, K.P. Home: 724 Eighth Av. W., Birmingham, Ala. Died May 26, 1949.

ED, Carl Frank Ludwig (ĕd), cartoonist; b. Moline, Ill., July 16, 1890; s. John and Eva (Bloom) E.; ed. high sch., Moline; Augustana Coll., Rock Island, Ill.; m. Ellen Margaret Schwack, June 9, 1911; 1 dau., Donna Jean (Mrs. Frederick Reynolds). With Rock Island Argus until 1917, resigning as city editor; cartoonist World Color Syndicate, St. Louis, 1912-18; sport cartoons for Chgo. Evening Am., 1918; with Chgo. Tribune, 1919-59: creator of Harold Teen. Home: 7914 Kolmar Av., Skokie, Ill. Died Oct. 10, 1959.

EDDY, Allen, newspaperman; b. Macedon, N.Y., Dec. 14, 1870; s. Marvin and Mary Jane (Howland) E.; ed. pub. schs.; m. Frances J. Clark, Apr. 14, 1897 (died 1911). Reporter, feature writer, editorial writer, political analyst Chgo. and N.Y.C. papers, 1890-—; spl. writer on politics Knickerbocker Press, Albany Evening News and other Gannett newspapers, 1924-33; editor the News and Knickerbocker Press, Albany, 1933-37; editor and pub. N.Y. State Journal, 1937-—. Home: De Witt Clinton Hotel. Office: 190 State St., Albany, N.Y. Died Feb. 23, 1957.

EDDY, Brayton, author, entomologist, lectr.; b. Providence, Jan. 13, 1901; s. Charles Zimri and Alace Edith (Kerr) E.; grad. Moses Brown Sch., Providence, 1917; Ph.B., Brown U., 1921; postgrad. Biol. Lab., Cold Spring Harbor, 1931, Cornell U. summers 1932-34; m. Emilia Robison, Feb. 13, 1928; 1 son, Charles Zimri II. Founder R.I. Insect Zoo, 1935, dir., 1936, 38; dir. Mich. Insect Zoo, 1937; extension lectr. Brown U., 1938; adminstr. R.I. Office of Entomology and Plant Industry, 1939-45; curator insects and reptiles N.Y. Zoöl. Soc., 1945-—. Fellow N.Y. Zoöl. Soc., 1946; mem. Am. Assn. Econ. Entomology, A.A.A.S., Entomol. Society Am., Bronx Beekeepers Assn., Am. Nature Study Soc., Am. Soc. Ichthyol. and Herpetol., Brown Alumni Assn., Delta Upsilon. Author: Strangeways (play), 1922; Rock Bottom (novel), 1923; Personality of Insects (with Royal Dixon), 1924; Personality of Water-Animals (with same), 1925; The Pick-up (skit), 1925; also plays Shallow Wells (with Michael Kallesser), 1926; The Way Out (with Michael Kallesser), 1926; Plenty Palavar; Night Caps (children's stories), 1928; A Couple of Brokers (skit), 1929. Contbr. short stories and articles to mags., newspapers. Address: care N.Y. Zoölogical Soc., Bronx Zoo, N.Y.C. 60. Died July 17, 1950; buried Palmer Cemetery, Somerset, Mass.

EDDY, Charles Brown, lawyer; b. New Britain, Conn., Nov. 29, 1872; s. James H. and Maria N. (Brown) E.; A.B., Yale, 1893; LL.B., N.Y. Law Sch., 1895; m. Ellen Coolidge Burke, June 7, 1902 (died 1941); children—James Henry, Charles Brown, John Burke. Began practice in N.Y. City, 1895; became associated with firm of Simpson, Thacher & Bartlett, 1901, partner, 1905-19; asst. gen. counsel U.S. R.R. Adminstrn., 1918, apptd. asso. dir. div. of finance, 1919; chmn. Greek Refugee Settlement Commn., under League of Nations, 1926-30. Mem. Am. Bar Assn., Assn. Bar City of N.Y., Bibliog. Soc. (London), Royal Soc. of Arts (London), Alpha Delta Phi, Phi Beta Kappa. Republican. Clubs: University, Grolier, Down Town Assn. (N.Y.C.); Metropolitan (Washington). Home: West Hartford, Conn. Died Jan. 9, 1951.

EDDY, Walter Hollis, physiol. chemist; b. Brattleboro, Vt., Aug. 26, 1877; B.S., Amherst, 1898; A.M., Columbia, 1908; Ph.D., 1909, Instr. sci., high sch., Amherst, 1898-1900, Passaic, N.J., 1900-03; head dept. biology, N.Y.C. High Sch. Commerce, 1903-17; asso. in biochemistry Coll. Phys. and Surg. (Columbia), 1908-13; research chemist N.Y. Hosp., 1913-—; with Tchrs. Coll. (Columbia), 1919-41, prof. physiol. chemistry, 1922-41, now emeritus; dir. Bur. Food, Sanitation and Health, Good Housekeeping Mag., 1927-41; cons. chemist and conductor, Food Forum program WOR, 1941-48; sci. dir. Am. Chlorophyll, Inc., Lake Worth, Fla., 1948-52, Am. Chlorophyll Div., Strong Cobb Co., 1952; research dir. Mangrove Products, Inc., West Palm Beach, Fla., cons. chem. engr., 1953-—; research cons. U.S. Vitamin and Pharm. Corp. Served from capt. to maj. Nutrition Div., U.S. Army, 1917-19; an organizer Div. Food and Nutrition, A.E.F., and made chief div. Author: Experimental Physiology and Anatomy, 1906; Vitamin Manual, 1921; Nutrition, 1928; The Avitaminoses, 1937, rev. edit., 1941, 1945. What Are the Vitamins?, 1941; We Need Vitamins, 1941; Vitaminology 1949, also many articles on foods and vitamins. Home: 1227 N. Lakeside Dr., Lake Worth, Fla. Died Oct. 1959.

EDENS, William Grant, banker, good roads promoter; b. Richmond, Ind., Nov. 27, 1863; s. Hervey D. Washington and Elsie Jane (Fought) E.; student pub. schs.; m. Lillian Maud Brunner, Dec. 9, 1896; 1 son, William McKinley. Began as messenger boy Western Union Telegraph Co., later mail carrier and in ry. service, advancing to freight and passenger conductor; vice-grandmaster Brotherhood of R.R. Trainmen, 1887-90, chief clk. and cashier nat. hdqrs., Galesburg, 1890-96; canvassed Ill. for William McKinley for President, 1895; state organizer Ill. Rep. League, later on staff Rep. Nat. Com., under director of Marcus A. Hanna, chmn., with supervision of orgn. of railroad voters, 1896; asst. gen. supt. free delivery system Postoffice dept., 1897-1904; resigned to serve in Rep. nat. campaign; with Central Trust Co. of Ill. (now Central Republic Bank and Trust Co.), 1905-31, v.p., 1919-31, retired. Organized Group Four, Ill. Bankers' Assn., 1907, and served as sec. and chmn.; sec. com. on agr. and vocational edn. Ill. Bankers' Assn., 1910, later chmn. good roads com.; mem. agrl. commn. Am. Bankers' Assn., 1919; mem. exec. council Am. and Ill. bankers' assns. Elected pres. Ill. Hwy. Improvement Assn., 1912, and conducted campaign culminating in adoption of $60,000,000 good roads bond issue in Ill., 1918; mem. Bd. Hwy. Advisers of Ill., 1917. Chmn. of Campaign Com. for William B. McKinley for U. S. senator in 1920. Represented organized railroad labor as chmn. legislative com., at 43d Gen. Assembly of Ill., brought about formation of labor conf. for entire state. Vice pres. (inactive) Chgo. Nat. Bank. Honorary recruiting officer, U.S. War Dept., World War I; mem. 17th Engrs. Regiment, AEF, 108th Engrs., Ill. N.G. Mem. Am. Inst. Banking, Am., Ill., Reserve City bankers assns., Dixie Highway Commn., Mississippi Valley Waterway Assn. (treas. Chgo. br.), St. Lawrence Deep Waterway Commn., Nat. Rivers and Harbors Congress for Ill. (v.p.), Am. Geol. Soc., Ill. Hist. Soc., Ohio, Ind. socs., Chicago Assn. Commerce, Nat. Assn. Letter Carriers (hon.), Old Time Printers' Assn. (hon.), Order of Bookfellow (charter mem.). Mem. Woodrow Wilson Found.; mem. bd. trustees Sarah Hackett Stevenson Meml. and Home for Aged and Disabled R.R. Employees; mem. Original Mount Harney Meml. Assn. (erecting monument on Rushmoore Mountain in Black Hills), Abraham Lincoln Assn. Washington rep. A Century of Progress Expn., Chgo., 1932; rep. Nat. Terra Cotta Mfrs. Assn., 1934; Edens Expressway named for him. Republican. Methodist. K. P. (grand chancellor Ill., 1903-04; mem. supreme lodge, 1905-—), Moose (life). Clubs: Hamilton (chmn. polit. action com.), Midday, Bankers, Traffic, Press, Ill. Auto (hon.), Bob O'Link Golf, Tam O'Shanter Golf. Received citation from WPB for directing national scrap metal salvage campaign for Brotherhood of Railroad Trainmen, 1942. Home: 1111 St. Johns Av., Highland Park, Ill. Office: 120 S. LaSalle St., Chgo. Died Nov. 14, 1957; buried Meml. Park, Skokie, Ill.

EDGAR, Graham, chemist; b. Fayetteville, Ark., Sept. 19, 1887; s. George Mathews and Rebecca (Fry) E.; B.S., U. Ky., 1907; Ph.D., Yale, 1909; m. Lucna N. Dunbar, Oct. 9, 1926; 1 dau., Nancy (Mrs. Warren Fales). Asst., later asso. prof. chemistry U. Va., 1909-17; prof. chemistry Cal. Inst. Tech., 1917-18; sec. researdh information service NRC, 1918-19; prof. chemistry U. Va., 1919-24; dir. research Ethyl Corp., 1924-52, v.p., 1932-52; v.p. Ethyl-Dow Chemical Co., 1933-52, retired; now cons. chem. engr. Cons. chemist Ordnance Dept., U.S. Army, 1918-19. Mem. Am. Chem. Soc., Am. Petroleum Inst., Soc. Automotive Engrs., Inst. Aero. Scis., Am. Soc. Testing Materials, Inst. Petroleum Technologists (London), Phi Beta Kappa, Sigma Xi, Tau Beta Pi. Democrat. Clubs: Chemists (N.Y.C.); Field (Bronxville). Contbr. Jour. Am. Chem. Soc., Am. Jour. Sci. Home: Riversville Rd., Greenwich, Conn. Died Sept. 8, 1955.

EDGE, Walter Evans, ex-gov., N.J., ex-senator, ex-ambassador; b. Phila., Nov. 20, 1873; s. William and Mary (Evans) E.; student pub. schs.; m. Lady Lee Phillips, June 10, 1907 (died 1915); m. 2d, Camilla Loyall Ashe Sewall, Dec. 9, 1922. Began as printer's devil Atlantic Review, Atlantic City; later established a nat. and internat. advt. agency; was propr. Atlantic City Daily Press, Atlantic City Evening Union, also identified with banking and other lines of business. Journal clk., N.J. Senate, 1897-99; sec. of senate, 1901-04; Rep. presdl. elector, 1908; del. at large Rep. Nat. convs., 1916-48; mem. N.J. Assembly, 1910, Rep. leader Senate, two terms 1911-16, Rep. leader 1912, pres. 1915, was chmn. economy and efficiency commn. and a leader in securing passage of workmen's compensation bill, state budget system bill and central purchasing bureau bill; gov. of N.J. for term 1917-20, resigned, 1919, to take seat in U.S. Senate, term 1919-25, re-elected for term, 1925-31, resigned; A.E. and P. from the U.S. to France, 1929-33; gov. of N.J., 1944-47. With Sec. of Treasury Mellon negotiated Franco-Am. Accord of July 6, 1931. Served as lt. Co. F, 4th N.J. Vol. Inf., Spanish-Am. War; later capt. Co. L, 3d Regt. N.J.N.G.; mem. staffs of Govs. Murphy and Stokes; was lt. col. and chief ordnance dept., staff of Maj. Gen. C. Edward Murray, N.J. Nat. Guard. Episcopalian. Clubs: Union League (Phila.); Book, Union League (N.Y. C.). Home: Princeton. Office: Press-Union Bldg., Atlantic City, N.J. Died Oct. 29, 1956.

EDGECOMBE, Samuel (Wheeler), horticulturist; b. Decatur, Ill., July 7, 1907; s. Robert and Luella (Wheeler) E.; B.S.A., U. Manitoba (awarded U. Gold Medal for Scholarship), 1930; M.Sc., Ia. State Coll. (fellow in pomology), 1931, Ph.D., 1936; m. Winnie Davis Slusser, June 10, 1932; children—Virginia Elaine (Mrs. Richard K. Johnson), Roberta-Gay (Mrs. Stephen Shadle). With Ia. Emergency Garden Relief Program, Ia. State Coll. Extension Service, 1933, forest pathologist, 1933; dir. subsistence gardens, Ia. Emergency Relief Adminstrn., 1934, dir. Ia. Service Bur. Transients, 1934-35; extension asst. prof. horticulture and chmn. hort. extension service, Ia. State Coll., 1935-42, extension asso. prof. and asso. research prof., 1941-42; asso. prof. plant sci., U. Manitoba, 1942-44; research dir., v.p., dir. of bd. W. Atlee Burpee Co., Phila., 1944-47, vegetable prodn. head, 1945-—; head, prof. horticulture, Winnipeg Victory Garden Program; chmn. Winnipeg Food Conservation Program Com., 1942-44; vegetable judge, All Am. Selections, 1946; 1st v.p. Am. Garden Found., 1947; pres. Winnipeg Hort. Soc. Assn., 1943-44; hon. pres. Ft. Garry Hort. Soc., 1943-44; dir. Manitoba Hort. Assn., 1942-44. Mem. Soc. Econ. Entomologists, Ia. Acad. Sci., Am. Soc. Hort Sci, (mem, com, edn., chmn. 1950-51), A.A.

A.S., Am. Polmol. Soc., Ia. State Hort. Soc. (dir. at large 1941-42), Utah, Wash., Colo. hort. socs., Western Canadian Soc. Hort. (1st pres., 1943-44), Agrl. Inst. Can., N.Y. Bot. Garden, Am. Acad. Polit. and Social Sci., Am. Hort. Soc., Pan Am. Assn. Phila., Am. Beekeepers Fedn. (chmn. honey and pollen plants com., 1948-52), Sigma Xi. Presbyn. Club: Utah Associate Garden. Contbr. articles hort. jours. Home: 493 W. 3d North, Logan, Utah. Died Feb. 5, 1959.

EDGELL, George Harold (ĕj'ĕl), historian of art; b. St. Louis, Mar. 4, 1887; s. George Stephen and Isabella Wallace (Corbin) E.; A.B., Harvard, 1909, Ph.D., 1913, Art D. (hon.) 1948; fellow Am. Acad. in Rome, 1910-12; m. Jean Walters Delano, June 13, 1914; children—George Harold, Delano (dec.), Henry Walters. Asst. in fine arts, 1909-10, instr., 1912-14, asst. prof., 1914-22, asso. prof., 1922-25, prof., 1925-35, dean faculty architecture, chmn. council Sch. of Architecture, 1922-35, Harvard; curator of paintings Mus. Fine Arts, Boston, 1934-38; dir. museum, 1935—. American commr. Interallied Commission for Propaganda, Italian General Staff, 1918; annual prof. Am. Acad. in Rome, 1919-20; exchange prof. to U. of Paris, 1929; overseer, Harvard U., 1936-42. Decorated Chevalier of Legion of Honor, 1937. Member Boston Art Commn., 1925-50; chmn. Mass. State Art Commn., 1941-51; trustee Boston Museum of Fine Arts, 1927—; pres. Am. Assn. of Mus., 1949-51. Mem. U.S. Commn. for UNESCO, 1947—. Fellow A.A.A.S; mem. Archaeol. Inst. Am., College Art Association of America, Phi Beta Kappa (president Harvard Chapter, 1940-42). Republican. Episcopalian. Clubs: Harvard, Tavern (Boston); Harvard, Century (New York), The Athenaeum (London). Author: (with Fiske Kimball) A History of Architecture, 1918; The American Architecture of Today, 1928; A History of Sienese Painting, 1932; The Bee Hunter, 1949. Contbr. to American Journal Arcraeology, l'Arte, Art in America, Gazette des Beaux Arts, etc. Home: Newport, N.H. Address: Museum of Fine Arts, Boston 15. Died June 29, 1954; buried North Newport, N.H.

EDINGTON, Arlo Channing (ĕd'ĭng-tŭn), author; b. Washington, Kan., Sept. 23, 1890; s. Talford Channing and Alice Rebecca (Baumbarger) E.; registered pharmacist, Kan., 1909; m. Carmencita Alicia Eunice Ursulla de Ballen, Oct. 2, 1920; children—Channing Crane, Nicida Ynez; m. 2d, Clelah Keltner Ross, Oct. 1935; m. 3d, Kathleen Paterson Sargent, April 17, 1947. Registered pharmacist, Kan., 1909-17; served as private, advancing to acting 1st sergt. in charge recruiting depot post, Ft. Douglas, Utah, later master engr., sr. grade, and batn. sergt. maj. 70th Engrs., U.S. Army, Nov. 1917-Jan. 1919; began in motion picture industry, 1919, as writer, editor, later dir.; sec., asst. gen. mgr. and dir. Edington-Witz Refining Co., Ltd.; dir. Edington-Witz Refining Co., Crude Oil Producing Co. Condidate for lt. gov. of Calif., 1934. Fellow Royal Soc. of Arts (London); life founder mem. Pacific Geog. Soc.; ex-pres. Calif. Gladiolus Soc.; mem. screen writers Guild; hon. mem. Eugene Field Soc. Republican. Co-Author (with wife): The Studio Murder Mystery, 1929; The House of the Vanishing Goblets, 1930; Tundra, 1930; The Monk's Hood Murders, 1931. Free lance writer for motion pictures. Home: 238 17th St., Santa Monica, Cal. Office: 941 Westwood Blvd., Los Angeles. Died Nov. 16, 1953.

EDISON, Mark Aaron, chain store exec.; b. Valdosta, Ga., Sept. 15, 1895; s. Abraham and Sarah (Halle) E.; student pub. schs.; m. Ida Edison, May 18, 1919 (dec.); children—Evelyn Francis (Mrs. Eric P. Newman), Julian Irving. Vice pres., treas. and dir. Edison Bros. Stores, Inc., St. Louis, 1922-51. Mem. Nat. Assn. Shoe Chain Stores (pres. 1948-51). Mason (32°). Club: Westwood Country. Home: Ladue. Mo. Office: 315 Washington Av., St. Louis 2. Died Mar. 2, 1951.

EDMAN, Irwin, prof. philosophy; b. N.Y. City, Nov. 28, 1896; s. Solomon and Ricka (Sklower) E.; B.A., Columbia, 1917, Ph.D., 1920; LL.D., Goucher, 1949; unmarried. Began as lectr. on philosophy, Columbia, 1918, instr., 1920-24, asst. prof., 1925-31, asso. prof., 1931-35, prof. philosophy since 1935, Johnsonian Prof. of Philosophy, 1950, exec. officer, dept. philosophy, 1945. Henry Ward Beecher lecturer, Amherst Coll., 1935; lecturer U. of Calif., summer 1939; visiting professor, Hamilton College, Clinton, N.Y., summer 1942; visiting lecturer Harvard, 1944; visiting prof. National Univ. of Brazil, Rio de Janeiro. 1945. Matchette lectr. Weslayan U. since 1947; Fulbright lectr., France, 1951-52. Recipient gold medal from N.Y. U. Soc. Libraries, 1949. Fellow Am. Acad. Arts and Scis.; mem. Am. Philos. Assn., N.Y. Philosophy Club, Am. Inst. of Arts and Letters, Phi Beta Kappa Fraternity. Clubs: Century, Coffee House (N.Y.C.), Columbia, Athenaeum (London). Author: Human Traits and Their Social Significance, 1920; Richard Kane Looks at Life, 1926; Poems, 1925; Adam, the Baby and the Man from Mars. 1929; The Contemporary and His Soul, 1932; The Mind of Paul, 1935; Four Ways of Philosophy, 1937; Philosopher's Holiday, 1938; Candle in the Dark, 1939; Arts and the Man, 1939; Fountainheads of Freedom, 1941; Philosopher's Quest, 1947. Co-author: Living Philosophies, 1931; Am. Philosophy Today and Tomorrow, 1935; Columbia Studies in the History of Ideas, 1935; On Going to College, 1937; I Believe, 1939; Landmarks in Philosophy, 1941; Under Whatever Sky, 1951. Editor of Works of Plato, 1927; The Philosophy of Santayana, 1936; Boethius' Consolation of Philosophy, 1943. Contributor to The Nation, New Republic, New York Times, Herald-Tribune, Harper's magazine, The Saturday Review, Atlantic Monthly, The New Yorker magazines. Member editorial bd. American Scholar. Home: 315 W. 106th St., N.Y.C. Died Sept. 4, 1954.

EDMUNDS, James Richard, Jr., architect; b. Baltimore, Md., Apr. 1, 1890; s. James Richard and Anna Smith (Keyser) E.; B.S., U. of Pa., 1912; studied abroad, 1911, 1919, 1923; m. Elizabeth Eddington Campbell, Nov. 26, 1913; children—James Richard III, Page II, Frances Campbell. Began as draftsman, Baltimore, Md., 1912; engaged as principal in practice of architecture, Baltimore, 1915, Canton, China, 1918-20; senior draftsman, office of Jos. Evans Sperry, Baltimore, Md., 1920-23, partner in firm, 1923-30; mem. firm Crisp & Edmunds, 1930-39; as James R. Edmunds, Jr., architect, since 1939; dir. Calvert Bank, Baltimore, since 1941. Chmn. Constrn. Advisory Council of U.S., 1948-49. Mem. and treas. Md. Bd. of Examiners and Registration of Architects, 1935-44. Chmn. Housing Authority of Baltimore, 1937-41; chmn. Lexington Market Authority, of Baltimore, since 1945. Past. pres. Baltimore Bldg. Congress. Trustee Children's Rehabilitation Inst., Inc., of Md. Fellow Am. Inst. Architects (treas. and dir., 1943-45, pres. 1945-47), Royal Inst. British Architects (hon. corr. mem. 1945), Md. Hist. Soc., Psi Upsilon, Sigma Xi. Clubs: Baltimore Country, Md., Merchants, Engineers (Baltimore, Md.); Gibson Island (Maryland). Home: 9 Blythewood Rd. Office: 130 W. Hamilton St., Balt. Died Feb. 4, 1953.

EDMUNDS-HEMINGWAY, Mme. (Clara), contralto, poet, artist composer, playwright, lectr., critic; b. Elmwood, Mich., Oct. 4, 1878; d. Dennis Bowen and Florence (Davis) Edmunds; student Mrs. J. N. Reed, Gertrude I. Smith, N.Y., N.Y., Althea Hillabrandt, Agnes Leist Beebe, Chgo.; pvt. course in poetry; m. Ray Rolfe Hemingway, June 28, 1900; 1 dau., Florence Clara (Mrs. Florence H. Pruitt). Review editor for poetry: Nat. League Am. Pen Women's Bull., 2 yrs.; Driftwind, Avon, Port O' Poets, Nebulae; conducted own column, Viewpoints, 5½ yrs.; has appeared on maj. radio stas., 1923—. TAPS broadcast overseas throughout World War II. Originator art-form Stories in Stone, or Rock Pictures, 1927. Awarded 1st and 3rd prizes, Little Theatre Contest, Gary, Ind.; 1st place for songpoem for bugle call, Taps, Chgo. Tribune Line dedicated to dead of 1st div. A.E.F. by Col. Robert R. McCormick, 1937 (used by many radio artists and read on U.S. Air Services Band's ½ hr., 1946 Chicagoland Music Festival); honorable mention; Nat. Pen Women's contest for 1 act plays. Hollywood Dramatic Reading Contest, Writers' Digest contest; 1st prize short story, Ill. Pen Women; 1st and 2d state prizes (articles) and 1st prize state poetry, Ill. Woman's Press; red and white ribbons, also hon. mention art, Chgo. Pen Women; Nat. Red Ribbon for ms. song, Allah, Nat. Soc. Arts and Letters; nat. 1st prize song-poem, Nat. League Am. Pen Women, 2d prize, bk. manuscript-poems, Chgo. Pen Women, 1954. Mem. Chgo. Artists Assn., Nat. Soc. Arts and Letters, Bookfellows, Nat. League Am. Pen Women, Nat. and Ill. Fedn. Music Clubs, Nat. and Ill. Woman's Press Assn., D.A.R., Rogers Park Woman's Club. Lakeview Mus. Soc., Municipal Arts. Author: Oak Roots (poems) and pub. song, Poetry and prose pub. in 134 mags. and newspapers; anthologies in Eng., Can., Alaska, U.S. Rep. Conglist. Home: 1082 Ogden Av., Benton Harbor, Mich. Died Dec. 31, 1958.

EDSON, Merritt Austin, maj. gen. USMC, ret; b. Rutland, Vt., April 25, 1897; s. Erwin A. and Lelia M. (Davis) E.; student U. Vt., 1915-17, LL.D. (hon.); m. Ethel W. Robbins, Aug. 16, 1920; children—Merritt A., Herbert R. Commd. 2d lt. USMC, advancing to maj. gen.; served with 11th Marine and 15th Separate Bn., France, 1918-19; firing mem. Marine Corps rifle team, 1921; qualified naval aviator, 1922, Marine Corps aviator, Guam, 1923-25, Caribbean and Nicaragua, 1927-29; instr. tactics basic schs., 1929-31; ordnance officer depot supplies, 1931-35; team capt. rifle and pistol teams nat. matches, 1935-36; service with 4th Marines, Shanghai, China, 1937-39; service hdqtrs., Washington, 1939-41; comdg. officer 1st raider bn., Feb.-Sept., 1942, 5th Marines, Sept. 1942-July 1943 (participated in Tulagi-Guadalcanal campaign, commanded troops which seized Tulagi); chief staff 2d Marine div., Aug. 1943-Jan. 1944 (participated in Gilberts (Tarawa) operations); asst. div. comdr. 2d Marine Div., Saipan-Tinian operations, Jan.-Aug. 1944; chief of staff Fleet Marine Force Pacific, Sept. 1944-July 1945; comdg. gen. Service Command, Fleet Marine Force Pacific, July-Dec. 1945; member staff Chief of Naval Operations Jan. 1946-Mar. 1947; retired Aug. 1947, Commissioner Public Safety, State of Vt., 1947-51; executive director Nat. Rifle Assn. of Am., 1951—. Decorated Congressional Medal of Honor, Navy Cross (2), Silver Star, Legion of Merit (2), Presidential Unit Citation (2) (U.S.), Medal of Merit (Nicaragua), D.S.O. (Great Britain). Mem. Am. Legion, Vets. Fgn. Wars, Patrons of Husbandry, Nat. Rifle Assn. Am. (past v.p., pres.), Disabled Am. Vets., Army and Navy Union. 1st Marine Div. Assn. (past pres.). Optimists, Nat. Skeet Shooting Assn., Alpha Tau Omega. Republican. Conglist. Mason. Clubs: Army-Navy, Columbia Country, Nat. Press, University. Died Aug. 14, 1955; buried Arlington Nat. Cemetery.

EDSON, Winfield, clergyman; b. Red Cloud, Neb., Dec. 5, 1907; s. Isaac William and Margaret Rosamond (Ricker) E.; B.S., Neb. State Tchrs. Coll., 1934; B.D., Berkeley Bapt. Div. Sch., 1937, D.D., 1944; m. Itha Anderson, Oct. 3, 1930; children—James William, Winfield Doyle. Ordained to ministry of Baptist Ch., 1937; asst. pastor First Ch., Oakland. Cal., 1935-37, Fremont, Neb., 1937-38; dir. pub. relations Berkeley Bapt. Div. Sch., 1938-39; pastor First Bapt. Ch., Long Beach, Cal., 1939—. Pres. Am. Bapt. Conv.; mem. bd. So. Cal. Bapt. Conv. Trustee U. Redlands, Berkeley Bapt. Div. Sch., Spanish-Am. Theol. Sem. Mason, Kiwanian. Home: 3939 Locust Av., Long Beach 7. Office: 1000 Pine Av., Long Beach 13, Cal. Died Apr. 19, 1956; buried Westminster (Cal.) Meml. Park.

EDWARDS, Charles William, educator; b. Arkadelphia, Ark., Dec. 13, 1873; s. Daniel William and Mary Jane (White) E.; A.B., Trinity Coll., Durham, N.C., 1894; M.A., Tulane, 1896; studied Columbia, 1896-97; M.S., N.Y.U., 1898; m. Marie Kramer, June 14, 1912; children—Charles William, Daniel Kramer, Mary Jane. Prof. physics, Trinity Coll., 1898, mgr. sci. depts., 1901-10. Mem. A.A.A.S., Am. Phys. Soc., N.C. Acad. Sci. (pres. 1900-01), Soc. Promotion Engring. Edn., N.C. Physics Tchrs.' Assn. (pres. 1921-22), Phi Beta Kappa, Sigma Xi; asso. mem. Am. Inst. E.E. Methodist. Author: Physical Measurement, 1915; Preliminary College Physics, 1925. Co-author: First Course in Physics for Colleges, 1928; A Manual of Experiments in Physics, 1930; also numerous articles sci. mags. Home: 406 Buchanan Boul., Durham, N.C. Died Nov. 17, 1955.

EDWARDS, Edward William, banker, mfr.; b. Cincinnati, O., May 1, 1874; s. Walter Raleigh and Ellen (Bryan) E.; ed. Woodward High Sch. and Nelson's Business Coll.; m. Eleanore Zimmerman, Nov. 14, 1901; daughter—Mrs. William Wood Prince. With Scott & Company, 1891-98, Reeves Iron Company, Dover, Ohio, 1898-1901; founder, 1901, The Edwards Manufacturing Company, mfrs. iron and steel; purchased Scott & Co., 1906, Canonsburg Steel and Iron Works, 1917, Kinnear Mfg. Co., 1919, now chmn. board; chmn. board The Edwards Manufacturing Company. President Cincinnati Rapid Transit Commn., 1914-Dec. 1928. Trustee Christ Hosp., Berea (Ky.) Coll., Cincinnati Inst. of Fine Arts, Cincinnati Music Hall Assn., Cincinnati Art Mus. Mem. Officers' Examining Bd., 1917-18. Chevalier of the Legion of Honor (France). Del Rep. Nat. Conv., 1924, delegate at large, 1932. Past vice president Southwestern District of Ohio Chamber of Commerce. Member Christian (Disciples) Ch. Clubs: Cincinnati (pres. 1913-14), Commercial (pres. 1921-22), Queen City, Cincinnati Country, Bald Peak Country, Cloud. Collector of pictures. Home: 2567 Observatory Rd. Office: Fifth & Butler Sts., Cin. Died July 23, 1956.

EDWARDS, Everett Eugene, historian; born at Waltham, Minn., Feb. 12, 1900; s. E. E. and Jennie A. (Hunt) E.; A.B., Carleton Coll., 1921; A.M., Harvard, 1924; m. Helen Evelyn Heckler, May 20, 1938; children—Thomas F., Terence E. Teacher in high sch. Grand Rapids, Minn., 1921-22; instr. hist. Northwestern U., 1923-25; visiting prof. history, Miami U., summer, 1926, Cath. U. of America, summer, 1936, U. of Mo., summer 1939, U. of Minn., summer, 1947; agrl. history work U.S. Dept. of Agr. since 1927, also teacher agrl. history Grad. School Dept. Agr. and American Univ. Sec. of Nat. Agricultural Jefferson Bicentenary Committee, 1943-44. Mem. Agrl. Hist. Soc. (life mem.; pres. 1939-40), Am. Assn. for State and Local Hist., Am. Hist. Assn., Miss. Valley Hist. Assn., Econ. Hist. Assn. (v.p., 1945-46; member editorial board) Minnesota Hist. Soc. (life mem.), Soc. Am. Archivists, Southern Hist. Assn. (life mem.), State Hist. Soc. of Wis. (life mem.). Club: Harvard (Washington, D.C.). Author of historiographical studies of F. J. Turner, Joseph Schafer, Ulrich B. Phillips; also bibliographies, govt. reports pub. by U.S. Dept. Agr. Editor of Agricultural History since 1931. Contbr. to hist. jours. Home: 8606 Jefferson St., Bethesda 14, Md. Office: U.S. Dept. of Agriculture, Washington 25. Died May 1, 1952; buried Rock Creek Cemetery.

EDWARDS, George William, economist; b. N.Y. City, Mar. 11, 1891; s. William and Pauline Elizabeth (Stein) E.; A.B., Coll. City of New York, 1911, fellow, 1911-14; A.M., Columbia, 1913, Ph.D., 1917; B.D., Union Theological Sem., 1944; m. Louise F. Stein, June 10, 1930; children—George Frank, Paul David. Teacher high schools, N.Y. City, 1914-17; research in foreign banking for Federal Reserve Board in United States and Europe, 1920-22; assistant prof. banking, Columbia, 1921-23; prof. banking, New York U., 1923-27; dean Sch. of Business and Civic Adm., Coll. City of N.Y., 1927-32, chmn. dept. economics 1927-47; ordained deacon, Episcopal Church, December 18, 1943, and priest, June 4, 1944. Vicar, St. Andrews, Hartsdale, New York, 1943-48. With Federal Reserve Board, 1920-22; director Institute of Internat. Finance, 1926-27. Spl. agt. U.S. Dept. Commerce, N.Y. City, 1923, in Europe, 1924; economist Bank of America, 1923-27; with Stone, Webster & Blodget, 1927-32; instr. on investments Grad. Sch. of Banking, Am. Bankers Assn., 1935-39. Member Am. Econ. Assn., Acad. Polit. Science, Phi Beta Kappa. Episcopalian. Club: Scarsdale Golf. Author: New York as an Eighteenth Century Municipality, 1917; (with H. P. Willis) Banking and Business, 1922; Foreign Commercial Credits, 1922; International Trade Finance, 1924; Problems and Questions in Banking, 1924; Investing in Foreign Securities, 1926; Principles of Bond Investments (with Lawrence Chamberlain), 1927; Principles of Banking and Finance, 1932; Investments, 1935; Evolution of Finance Capitalism, 1938. Co-author: Capital Expansion, Employment and Economic Stability, 1940; co-author: Regulations of the Security Markets, 1946. Home: Hawthorne Way, Hartsdale, N.Y. Died Mar. 4, 1954.

EDWARDS, Gordon L., steel corp. exec.; b. Bklyn., 1884; student pub. schs.; m. Mary E. Lawlor Edwards; children—Gordon Robert, Richard Albert Edwards. With U.S. Steel Corp. from incorporation 1901, until retirement, 1950, treas., 1927-46, v.p., treas., 1946-50; pres., dir. Seventy-One Broadway Corp.; asst. treas. Tenn. Coal, Iron & R.R. Co., many other indsl. corps. Dir., treas. U.S. Steel and Carnegie Pension Fund. Mem. Am. Iron and Steel Inst. Mason. Clubs: Montauk, Shelter Island Yacht. Home: 9 Prospect Park W., Bklyn. 15. Died June 14, 1956; buried Greenwood Cemetery, Bklyn.

EDWARDS, Granville Dennis, theologian; b. Hamilton, Mo., Dec. 2, 1868; s. Solomon and Zerilda Ann (Hale) E.; A.B., U. Mo., 1897 (Phi Beta Kappa); A.B., Harvard, 1898, A.M., 1899, also registered in Harvard Div. Sch., 1898-1900; studied univs. of Berlin and Marburg, Germany, 1910-11; study and research in Palestine and Egypt, 1922-23; D.D., Ind. Sch. Religion, 1929; m. Ida May Moore, Nov. 7, 1900 (died 1930); 1 son, Corwine D.; m. 2d, Mrs. Helen Gromer, Sept. 8, 1936. Oradined to ministry Disciples of Christ, 1893; pastor Salisbury and Mt. Carmel, Mo., 1894-97, Prairie View, 1895-97, Cowgill, Jan.-Oct., 1897, Nevada, Mo., 1900-05; First Christian Ch., Honolulu, Hawaii, 1905-07; field rep. Bible Coll. Mo., 1907-10; prof. O.T. lit. and interpretation, 1910-36, acting dean, 1912-14; dean, 1914-34; same coll.; leave of absence, 1936-39 to engage in writing and reseach; ret. 1939. Vice pres. Ariz. Council Chs., 1942-44; pres. religious conf. Ariz. State Tchrs. Coll. 1943, ret. 1944. Chmn. agitation com., Anti-Saloon League, Hawaiian Islands, 1906-07; pres. Ministerial Union, Honolulu, 1907; rec. sec. Bd. Edn. Disciples of Christ, 1915-35; mem. Commn. on Surveys of Internat. Conv. Disciples of Christ, 1926-32. Mem. Campbell Inst., Am. Oriental Soc., Soc. Biblical Lit. and Exegesis. Address: 121 Seminary Av., Cameron, Mo. Died June 2, 1952.

EDWARDS, Gurney, lawyer; b. Providence, May 25, 1897; s. Seeber and Sarah E. (Gurney) E.; A.B., Brown U., 1918; LL.B. cum laude, Harvard, 1921; m. Elizabeth Dealey, Sept. 15, 1927; children—Charles Gurney, James Seeber, George Dealey. Admitted to R.I. bar, 1921; asso. with Edwards and Angell, Providence, 1921-29; mem. firm, 1929—; instr. law Northeastern U., Providence Div. Law Sch., 1925-33. Served as cpl. U.S. Army, 1918. Mem. Children's Friend & Service (past pres.). Former mem. exec. com. Gen. Council Congl. Christian Chs.; alternate del. Rep. Nat. Conv., 1948. Mem. Am. Law Inst., Am., R.I. bar assns. Phi Beta Kappa, Delta Sigma Rho, Alpha Delta Phi. Author: Rhode Island Annotations to Restatement of Law of Contracts, 1933; Rhode Island Annotations to Restatement of Law of Agency, 1935. Home: 21 Arlington Av. Office: 15 Westminster St., Providence. Died Nov. 1, 1955.

EDWARDS, Leroy D(elos), univ. prof.; b. Lancaster, Wis., May 12, 1897; s. Charles Delos and Luella Jane (Bidwell) E.; B.S., U. of Wis., 1923; A.M., Western Reserve U., 1931, Ph.D., 1936; m. Hildegarde Anna Alt, Jan. 1, 1925; 1 dau., Edith Lou. Instr. pharmacognosy Indianapolis College of Pharmacy (now Butler U.), 1924-28; successively instr., teaching fellow, asst. prof., prof. pharmacognosy and pharmacology Western Reserve U., 1928-40; prof. pharmacognosy and pharmacology U. of Fla., 1940-45; prof. pharmacology Purdue U., 1945—. Served with U.S.N., in submarine service, WW I. Mem. A.A.A.S., Am. Pharm. Assn., Phi Beta Kappa, Sigma Xi, Phi Kappa Phi, Rho Chi, Theta Chi, Kappa Psi. Presbyterian. Clubs: Rotary, Elks. Research in action of soaps and drugs on skin, investigation on plant drugs, toxicology of drugs. Home: 608 Allen St., West Lafayette, Ind. Died Oct. 29, 1954.

EDWARDS, Paul Kenneth, educator; b. Oskaloosa, Ia., Oct. 26, 1898; s. David Morton and Della (Russell) E.; A.B., Earlham Coll., 1920; M.B.A., Harvard, 1922, D.C.S., 1936; m. Mary Louise Carroll, May 29, 1926; children—Patricia Ann, David Carroll. Prof. econs. Ursinus Coll., Collegeville, Pa., 1922-23; with Harvard Bur. Bus. Research, 1923-24; asst. prof. commerce U. Va., 1924; asst. to gen. sales mgr. Crosley Radio Corp., 1925; with Daniel Starch in marketing research, N.Y.C., 1926; sales research Simmons Co., N.Y.C., 1926-28; prof. econs. Fisk U., 1928-34; dir. sales promotion in Negro markets, Rumford Co., East Providence, R.I., 1932-38; prof. marketing, chmn. dept. U. Newark, 1937-42; prin. review and negotiations officer, U.S. Civil Service Commn., and acting chief clothing and textile br., Office of Relief and Rehabilitation Adminstrn., State Dept., 1942-43; asst. dir. research J. Walter Thompson Co., N.Y.C. 1943-46; prof., chmn. dept. marketing, sch. bus. adminstrn. Rutgers U. since 1946; cons. in marketing and marketing research. Mem. N.Y.C. Market Research Council. Mem. Am. Marketing Assn., Delta Sigma Pi, Beta Gamma Sigma. Mem. Soc. of Friends. Clubs: Harvard Bus. Sch., Harvard (N.Y.C.); Newark (N.J.) Athletic. Author: The Southern Urban Negro as a Consumer, 1932. Home: Three Winthrop Pl., Maplewood, N.J. Office: 18 Washington Pl., Newark 2. Died Dec. 1959.

EDWARDS, Richard Henry, clergyman, educator; b. Lisle, N.Y., Oct. 22, 1877; s. Hamilton and Martha Ann (Hanford) E.; grad. Phillips Acad., Andover, Mass., 1897; B.A., Yale, 1901, M.A., 1902; student Yale Div. Sch., 1902-04; grad. Union Theol. Sem., 1906; m. Anna R. Camp, Aug. 6, 1908; children—Elizabeth Ann (dec.), David Hamilton, Katharine Camp, Richard Pierrepont. Gen. sec. Yale U. Christian Assn., 1901-04; asst. pastor Old First Presbyn. Ch., N.Y. City, 1904-06; ordained Congl. ministry, 1906. Congl. univ. pastor U. of Wis., 1906-12; sec. for social study and service of Student Dept. Internat. Com. Y.M.C.A., 1912-17; sec. Nat. War Work Council Y.M.C.A. Bur. of Personnel, 1917-18, associate executive dept. of the East, 1918-19; exec. sec., Cornell United Religious Work, 1919-37. Exec. dir. Nat. Council on Religion in Higher Edn., 1924-31, counselor, 1931—; visiting prof. Grad. Divinity Sch. U. of Chicago, and Chicago Theol. Sem., summers, 1928-33; visiting prof. Colgate-Rochester Divinity Sch., 2d term, 1933; lecturer Psychol. Center, Paris, summer, 1934; visiting prof. Union Theol. Sem., New York, summer, 1935, Auburn Theol. Sem., summer, 1936, Southern Meth. U., winter, 1937, Scarritt College, winter, 1938, Southern Methodist Pastors Schools, summers, 1936-43, Howard U., fall quarter, 1943, Keuka College (spring Quarter), 1944, Spelman College, 1944-45, Bennett College, 1945-46; secretary to Arkansas Methodist Commission on Tenancy, 1938-39. Founder, with wife, Happy Valley Homes, Lisle, N.Y.; pres. Happy Valley, Inc., 1930-42; member Commn. on Survey of Auburn Theol. Sem., 1933; mem. bd. mgrs., Ithaca (N.Y.) Reconstruction Home for Infantile Paralysis, 1935-37; chmn. advisory com. Hazen Agency Grants, 1931-41; mem. commn. on Religion and Health, Fed. Council of Chs., 1941-46. Mem. Psi Upsilon, Skull and Bones. Republican. Author: Studies in American Social Conditions, 1910; Popular Amusements, Christianity and Amusements, 1915; Organizing Myself, 1932; The Place of Persons in the Educational Process, 1933; Coöperative Religion at Cornell University, 1939; A Person-Minded Ministry, 1940; What Can Make Higher Education Religious?, 1941. Co-author: A Life at Its Best, 1915; Christianizing Community Life, 1918; Student Counseling, 1927; Undergraduates, 1928; Happy Valley: An Adventure in Good Will, 1943; The Mastery of Fear, Anxiety and Hostility, 1943; The Edwards Family in the Chenango Country, 1947; Valiant for Truth, Life, Letters and Diaries of David Fay Edwards, 1952; (with sister) A Mother; 1953. With wife deeded Lisle, N.Y., properties to N.Y. Congl. Christian Conf., Inc., for permanent conf. center, 1942. Home: Lisle, N.Y.. Died Apr. 7, 1954; buried Lisle (N.Y.) Cemetery.

EDWARDS, Richard Stanislaus, naval officer; b. Phila., Feb. 18, 1885; s. Richard S. and Lucy Brooke (Neilson) E.; student Episcopal Acad., Phila., 1896-1903; B.S., U.S. Naval Acad., 1907; m. Hallie Ninan Snyder, Aug. 11, 1914. Commd. ensign, U.S. Navy, 1908; advanced through grades to rear adm., 1940, vice adm., 1942, admiral, 1945; dep. comdr. in chief, U.S. Fleet, vice chief Naval Operations, 1945-47, ret. 1947. Decorated Victory medal and Navy Cross. Clubs: Army and Navy, Chevy Chase (Wash.). Address: 25 Josepha Av., San Francisco 27. Died June 4, 1959.

EDWARDS, Thomas Allison, judge; b. Dover, Ark., Feb. 21, 1874; s. Thomas Samuel and Martha Isabel (Allison) E.; ed. U. of Ark.; m. Rose Catherine Leverett, Feb. 24, 1901; children—Thomas Leverett, Mary Merlin, Catherine, Donald Allison, John Charles. Admitted to Okla. bar, 1898, and began practice at Cloud Chief, Okla.; county atty., Washita Co., Okla., 1900-05; judge, Dis. Court, 17th Okla. Dist., 1915-25; judge, Criminal Court of Appeals, Okla., 1925—, presiding judge, 1929-37; retired from bench, 1937. Mem. Okla. State Hist. Soc. (dir.). Democrat. Methodist. Mason (Shriner). Author: Geronimo et al (poems), 1939. Home: Cordell, Okla. Died Jan. 5, 1955.

EDWARDS, William A., banker; b. N.Y. City, July 1, 1902; s. Edwin D. and Eulalie (Homier) E.; ed. in pub. schs., Kearney, N.J.; m. Rae Carpenter, Sept. 21, 1929; children—William C., S. McNeill. With Chemical Bank & Trust Co., N.Y. City, since 1916, vice pres. since 1948. Club: Montclair (N.J.) Golf. Home: 372 Highland Av., Montclair, N.J. Office: Chemical Bank & Trust Co., 165 Broadway, N.Y.C. Died 17, 1951.

EFFLER, Erwin R., lawyer; b. Toledo, Dec. 15, 1884; s. Jacob and Alice (Leibius) E.; A.B., St. John's High Sch. and Coll., 1905; M.A., Georgetown U., 1906, LL.B., 1908; m. Fanny Pilliod Effler, Apr. 30, 1913; children—James, Erwin R., Paul. Admitted to Ohio bar, 1908; asso. Smith & Baker, 1908; partner Effler, Eastman, Stichter & Smith, 1936—; dir. City Auto Stamping Co., City Machine & Tool Co. Mem. Am., Ohio State, Toledo bar assns. Home: 3532 Ridgewood Rd., Ottawa Hills, Toledo. Office: 240 Huron St., Toledo 4. Died Nov. 1, 1956; buried Mausoleum, Calvary Cemetery, Toledo.

EGAN, Louis Henry, elec. engr.; b. La Crosse, Wis., Nov. 21, 1881; s. John M. and Susanna (Gallagher) E.; Ph.B., Yale, 1904; m. Fanny James, Oct. 2, 1912. Asst. engr., div. mgr. Detroit Edison Co., 1905-09; gen. mgr. Kansas City Light & Power Co., 1910-16; with Union Electric Co. of Mo., 1916—, successively asst. gen. mgr., v.p., pres., 1920—; pres. Mississippi River Power Co. (Keokuk, Ia.), Ia. Union Electric Co., Union Electric Co. of Ill., Union Colliery Co., The St. Louis County Gas Co., Union Electric Land and Development Co., St. Louis & Belleville Electric Ry. Co.; dir. Mercantile-Commerce Bank & Trust Co., Mercantile-Commerce Nat. Bank. Trustee Edison Electric Inst. Mem. Am. Inst. Elec. Engrs. Home: 30 Brentmoor, Clayton, Mo. Office: 315 N. Twelfth Boul., St. Louis. Deceased.

EGAN, Thomas Aloysius, educator; b. Chicago, Ill., Nov. 13, 1884; s. John and Ellen (Bunyan) E.; student Loyola, Chicago, 1900 03; A.B., St. Louis U., 1908, A.M., 1910. Prof. sociology and regent colls. of Commerce and Law, Creighton U., Omaha, Neb., 1921-31; dean Coll. of Arts and Sch. of Social Work, Loyola U., 1931-37, dean University Coll., 1931-44, prof. religion, 1944—, trustee, 1931—. Mem. Am. Sociol. Soc., Am. Sociol. Assn., Am. Acad. Polit. and Social Science, Nat. Cath. Ednl. Assn., Alpha Kappa Delta. Catholic. Mem. Society of Jesus. Home: 6525 Sheridan Rd., Chicago 26. Office: 820 N. Michigan Av., Chgo. 11. Died Dec. 8, 1954; buried, All Saints Cemetery, Des Plaines, Ill.

EGELSON, Louis I., rabbi; b. Rochester, N.Y., Aug. 29, 1885; s. Samuel and Anna F. Egelson; A.B., Coll. City of N.Y., 1904; A.M., Columbia University, 1907; rabbi, Jewish Theol. Sem., New York N.Y., 1908; D.D. (hon), Hebrew Union Coll.-Jewish Inst. Religion, 1954; married Augusta Cronheim, January 27, 1920; 1 son, Louis I. Administrative sec. Union of Am. Hebrew Congregations since 1942; sec. Com. on Chaplain Procurement, 1942-47. Com. on Emergency Placement of Chaplains, 1943-47; mem. exec. bd. Central Conf. American Rabbis, 1946-49. Sec. Commn. on Information about Judaism, Commn. on Mil. Services. Editor, Liberal Judaism. Served as chaplain, 91st Div., A.E.F., World War I; participated St. Mihiel, Meuse-Argonne and Lys-Scheldt campaigns. Mem. Am. Legion, Mason. Author of pamphlets. Home: 240 Central Park South. Office: 838 Fifth Av., N.Y.C. 21. Died Apr. 10, 1957; buried Walnut Hills Cemetery, Cin.

EGGERS, George William (ĕg'ẽrz), prof. emeritus; b. Dunkirk, N.Y., Jan. 31, 1883; s. George A. H. and Josephine (Smith) E.; ed. at Pratt Inst., Brooklyn; European travel; m. Cornelia Bingham, Apr. 24, 1909; 1 dau., Dorothea C. (Mrs. Edwin V. Smith). Instructor Pratt Institute, 1905-06; head of art department, Chicago Normal Coll., 1906-16; acting director 1916-17, director 1917-21, Art Inst., Chicago; dir. Denver Art Museum, 1921-26; art editor Rocky Mountain News, 1923-26; dir. Worcester (Mass.) Art Mus., 1926-30; prof. of art and head dept., Coll. City of N.Y., 1930-48. Instr. and lecturer Chautauqua (N.Y.) Instn. several yrs. and at Teachers' Coll., Columbia, 1925-26, Honolulu Academy of Arts, 1932, Salem lecturer Colorado Coll., 1923; Cooke-Daniels lecturer, Denver Art Museum, 1926. Pres. art sect. N.E.A., 1907-08; mem. Denver Municipal Art Commn., 1922-26. Organizer and commr.-gen. Comprehensive Exhbn. of Am. Art, Royal Acad., Stockholm; Ny-Carlsberg Museum, Copenhagen; City Art Museum, Munich, 1930. Mem. board trustees, Am. Craftsmen's Educational Council, Coll. Art Assn., Hungarian-Am. Art Acad., N.E.A. (life mem.). Decorated Knight of North Star (Sweden), 1930, Logan prize Internat. Water Color Exhbn., 1932. Author: George Bellows. Collaborator with C. A. and O. L. McMurry in Teaching the Industrial Arts; art editor Webster's New Internat. Dictionary, 1927-34, contbr. to ednl. and art jours. Rep. in Art Institute of Chicago, Rhode Island School of Design Museum, Los Angeles Art Museum, New York Public Library, Okla. State Normal Univ., Honolulu Acad. of Arts; collections of R. Allerton, R. Garrison, A. C. Goodyear, Carl Milles, Booth Tarkington, Brenda Putnam, and others. Clubs: Arts (hon. mem.,

Chicago); Athenaeum (founder mem.), Town Hall (Ntw York City). Home: 720 Riverside Dr., N.Y.C. 31. Died Sept. 25, 1958; buried Chautauqua, N.Y.

EGGLESTON, Sir Frederic William, Australian diplomat; b. Melbourne, Australia, Oct. 17, 1875; s. John Waterhouse and Emily (Overend) E.; student Wesley Coll., Melbourne, Leys Sch., Cambridge, Eng., Melbourne U. Law Sch.; m. Louisa Augusta Henriques, May 10, 1904 (died Mar. 1, 1935); children—Egan Moulton, Hersilea Jean (Mrs. John Shannon), Frederic Felix Henriques. Admitted as barrister and solicitor, 1897; mem. Eggleston, Eggleston & Lee, Melbourne; mem. Victorian State Parliament, 1920-27; minister of railways, atty. gen., and chmn. state grants commn., 1933-41; minister to China, 1941-44; minister to U.S., 1944-46. Trustee Melbourne Nat. Gallery and Public Library. Recipient Bowen prize for English essay, U. Melbourne, 1894, Harbison Higginbotham Exhbn. for Hist. and Econ. Research, 1981. Mem. Royal Inst. Internat. Affairs (London), Inst. Pacific Relations, Australian Inst. Internat. Affairs. Author: Life of George Swinburne (Australian statesman); State Socialism in Victoria; Search for a Social Philosophy. Created Knight Bachelor, 1941. Home: 18 Royal Crescent, Chamberwell, Victoria, Australia. Office: 143 Queen St., Melbourne, Victoria, Australia. Died Nov. 12, 1954.

EGGLESTON, Joseph Dupuy, educator; b. Prince Edward County, Va., Nov. 13, 1867; s. Joseph Dupuy and Anne Carrington (Booker) E.; A.B., Hampden-Sydney Coll., 1886, A.M., 1897, LL.D., 1918; LL.D., Washington and Lee, 1917; m. Julia Johnson, Dec. 18, 1890. Taught in pub. schs., Va., Ga., and N.C., 1886-89; supt. schs., Asheville, N.C., 1891-1900, Prince Edward County, Va., 1903-05; state supt. pub. instrn. of Va., 1906-13; chief of field service in rural edn. U.S. Bur. Edn., 1913; pres. Va. Poly. Inst., 1913-19; pres. Hampden-Sydney College, Va., 1919-39, pres. emeritus, 1939—. Editor, sec. Bur. Information and Publicity. So. Edn. Bd., U. Tenn., 1902; has been editorial writer for leading papers in Va., N.C., and Tenn.; contbr. sch. mags. Mem. Phi Beta Kappa, Beta Theta Pi, Omicron Delta Kappa, Va. Hist. Soc., Soc. of Cincinnati, S.A.R., Soc. Preservation Va. Antiquities, Nat. Soc. Colonial Wars, Huguenot Soc., Founders of Manakin, Am. Classical Assn. (life). Author: (with R. W. Bruére) The Work of the Rural School, 1913. Home: Hampden-Sydney, Va. Died Mar. 13, 1953; buried Hampden-Sydney.

EGLOFF, Gustav, research in petroleum; b. N.Y. City; s. August and Mary E.; A.B., Cornell U., 1912; A.M., Columbia, 1913, Ph.D., 1915; D.Sc., Polytechnic Inst. Bklyn., 1938, Armour Inst. Tech., 1940, Philadelphia Coll. of Pharmacy and Science, 1944; married. Asst. in Chandler Mus., Barnard research fellow, 1914-15; chemist U.S. Bur. Mines, 1915-16, Aetna Chem. Co., Pittsburgh, 1916-17; dir. research Universal Oil Products Co., Chicago, 1917—. Holder of 250 patents on processing petroleum oil, coal, shale oil and chemical derivatives of hydrocarbons; delegate World Power Conference, London, 1928, 36, Berlin, 1930, Washington, 1936, London, 1950; delegate Congress for Automobile Transportation, Rome, 1928, World Engring. Congress, Tokyo, 1929, Internat. Bituminous Coal Conv., Pittsburgh, 1926, 28, 31, World Petroleum Congress, London, 1933, 37 (v.p. Congress); Internat. Congress of Chem., Rome, 1938; lectured before chem. symposium of Royal Inst. Chem., St. Andrews, Scotland, July 1947, Internat. Congress of Pure and Applied Chem., 1947, 1951; dir. sci. and tech. com., International Petroleum Expn. and Congress, Tulsa, Okla., 1948. Has lectured at Columbia, Princeton, Chicago, Northwestern, California, Southern Calif., Stanford, Mo., Mich., N.Y., Johns Hopkins; mem. com. on petroleum exhibits, Century of Progress, Chicago, 1933; chmn. sci. exhibit Internat. Oil Expn., Tulsa, 1938-42; apptd. by Am. Inst. Mining and Metall. Engrs. advisor to Mus. of Science and Industry, Chicago; mem. adv. bd. Chem. Warfare Service, Washington, D.C. Awarded gold medal of Am. Inst. Chemists, 1940; Octave Chanute medal (1939-40), by Western Soc. Engrs.; named "Modern Pioneer," by National Assn. of Manufacturers, 1940; Columbia Univ. Medal for Excellence, June 1943. Head of mission sponsored by Nat. Resources Commn. of China and Acting in an advisory capacity in establishment and development of modern petroleum refining industry in Republic of China; mem. Scandinavian research and industry tour sponsored by Royal Swedish Acad. of Engring. Research, 1946. Fellow Am. Inst. Chemists (pres. 1942-46), A.A.A.S., Royal Society of Arts of Great Britain; member American Chemical Society (councillor at large, dir. Chicago sect.; chmn. petroleum div. 1946-47), Am. Inst. Chem. Engrs. (dir.), Am. Inst. Mining and Metall. Engrs. (chmn. Chicago Section, 1934), Wash. Academy Sciences, Chmn. Inst. of Can., Ill. Soc. Engrs., Franklin Inst., Soc. Chem. Industry, Am. Petroleum Inst. (dir.), Nat. Petroleum Assn., Inst. Petroleum Technologists (London), Soc. Am. Mil. Engrs., Western Soc. of Engrs., (v.p., mem. development and library committees), Soc. Automotive Engrs., Am. Soc. for Testing Materials, Adult Edn. Soc. of Chicago (dir.), Ill. Acad. Science, Am. Geog. Society (fellow), Washington Award Commn., Sigma Xi, Phi Lambda Upsilon. Clubs: Chemists of Chicago (pres. 1934); Chemists of New York (v.p. 1939-41); Cosmos (Washington, D.C.). Author: Earth Oil, 1933; The Reactions of Pure Hydrocarbons, 1937; The Physical Constants of Hydrocarbons, Vol. 1, 1939, Vol. 2, 1940; Catalysis, 1940; Emulsions and Foams, 1941; Isomerization of Pure Hydrocarbons, 1942; Physical Constants of Hydrocarbons, Vol. III, 1946. Contbr. over 425 articles to tech. and trade journals on petroleum industry, particularly cracking and refining of oil. Elected by U. Edinburgh to give Romanes lecture in chemistry, 1951. Home: 2100 Lincoln Park West, Chicago 14. Office: 30 E. Algonquin Rd., Des Plaines, Ill. Died Apr. 29, 1955; buried Yonkers, N.Y.

EGLY, Henry Harris, investments; b. Brooklyn, N.Y., Jan. 28, 1893; s. Louis and Emma Bertha (Maturnas) E.; ed. business coll.; m. Matilda Anna Pasfield, Apr. 22, 1916; children—Jean E. (Mrs. Harold Cole), Patricia. Clerk Nat. Bank Commerce, 1908-09; with Wm. A. Read & Co., and successor Dillon, Read & Co. since 1909, v.p. and exec. Dillon Read & Co. since 1932; on leave to organize and head securities assn. unit of Securities and Exchange Commn., Washington, D.C., 1938-39; completed Washington assignment and returned as v.p. Dillon Read & Co., Inc., 1939; trustee Lincoln Savs. Bank, Bklyn. Dir. Beekman Downtown Hosp. Mem. bd. trustees Adelphi Coll. Republican. Protestant Episcopalian. Clubs: Recess, Bond, Southward Ho Country. Home: Bayberry Point Islip, N.Y. Office: 46 William St., N.Y.C. Died Sept. 3, 1958; buried Oakwood Cemetery, Bayshore, L.I., N.Y.

EGNER, Frank, publisher; b. N.Y. City, July 6, 1892; s. Frank Lewis and Caroline (Ritter) E.; Boy's High Sch., Brooklyn, 1907; student Wagner Coll., Rochester, N.Y., 1909-10; m. Lucy Margaret Rilling, Aug. 14, 1915; 1 dau., Mildred (Mrs. Ray Serenbetz). Sales corr. Am. Book Co., N.Y. City, 1907-18; advt. mgr. McGraw-Hill Book Co., N.Y. City, 1918-32, asst. v.p., 1932, v.p., 1933-46; pres. Falcon Press, N.Y. City, 1932-33; pres., dir. Funk & Wagnalls Co., 1946-51; v.p. Nelson Doubleday, Inc., 1951—; vice president Blakiston & Company, 1952-54; now vice president McGraw-Hill Book Company. Vice president bd. trustees Wagner Coll. Clubs: Advertising. Author: How to Make Sales Letters Make Money, 1938; Direct Mail Advertising and Selling (with L. R. Walter), 1940; Letters For Special Occasions, 1957. Home: 6 Health Pl., Garden City, N.Y. Office: 575 Madison Av., N.Y.C. Died Aug. 6, 1957; buried Greenfield Cemetery, Hempstead, L.I., N.Y.

EHRENFRIED, Albert (ā'rĕn-frēd), surgeon; b. Lewiston, Me., Feb. 9, 1880; s. George and Rachael (Blauspan) E.; grad. Boston Latin Sch., 1898; A.B., cum laude, Harvard, 1902; M.D., Harvard Medical School, 1905; surgical house officer, Boston City Hosp., 1905-07; m. Grace Waterman, July 3, 1912; children—George, Fredrika Jean, Constance. Practiced, Boston, 1907—; formerly senior visiting surgeon, Beth Israel Hospital consulting surgeon Jewis Memorial Hospital; assistant surgeon children's Hosp.; surgeon sanatorium div. Boston City Hosp.; asst. in atanomy Harvard Med. Sch.; asst. in surgery Harvard Grad. Sch. Mem. Brookline Town Meeting; member examining committee Boston Public Library. Trustee, Boston Medical Library. Fellow A. A.A.S., Am. Coll. Surgeons, A.M.A.; member Mass. Med. Soc. (councillor), Norfolk Med. Soc., (past pres.), Am. Genetics Assn., Am. Eugenics Assn., Eugenics Research Soc., Bostonian Society, Am. Jewish Com. (councillor Boston chapter), Phi Rho Sigma, Tau Epsilon Phi. Mem. Temple Sinai (hon. pres.). Club: Harvard. Author: Surgical After-Treatment (with L. R. G. Crandon), 1912. Editor and translator: Krause-Heyman Ehrenfried Textbook of Surgical Operations, 1915. Asst. editor of Norfold Med. News. Contbr. articles on surg. and related subjects. Home: 33 Centre St., Brookline, Mass. Office: 520 Beacon St., Boston. Died Sept. 25, 1951.

EHRLICH, Harry, surgeon; b. West Farms, N.Y., Mar. 22, 1909; s. Louis and Anna (Spummburgh) E.; U. Va., 1929; M.D., L.I. Coll. Medicine, 1933; m. Estelle Monaghan, July 13, 1935; children—Margery, John. Intern Kings Count Hosp., Brooklyn, 1933-35; asst. surgeon Nathan Littauer Hosp., Gloversville, N.Y., 1935-40; resident pathologist Beth Israel Hosp., 1940-42; asst. surg. resident, Rockefeller fellow and chief surg. resident Meml. Hosp., 1942-46; asso. Dr. Hayes Martin, 1946-47; asso. surgeon in charge head and neck surgery Mt. Sinai Hosp. since 1947, cons. head and neck surgeon, tumor clinic since 1947; specialist in treatment cancer of head and neck. Diplomate Am. Bd. Surgery. Fellow A.C.S.; mem. Am. Radium Soc., N.Y. Co. Med. Soc., A.M.A., N.Y. Acad Medicine, Am. Cancer Soc., James Ewing Soc., N.Y. Cancer Soc. Author articles med. jours. Asst. editor of Cancer, 1949-51. Home: 860 Fifth Av. Office: 715 Park Av., N.Y.C. 21. Died July 31, 1952; buried Ferncliff Cemetery, Hartsdale, N.Y.

EICHENAUER, Charles Frederick, editor; b. Warsaw, Ill., Oct. 9, 1882; s. Frederick and Elizabeth (Goebel) E.; A.B., Dartmouth, 1905; LL.B., Chgo.-Kent Coll. Law, 1909; hon. Litt.D., Culver-Stockton U., 1929. Tchr. history and civics, high sch., Quincy, Ill., 1905-07; admitted to Ill. bar, 1909; reporter, city editor Quincy Daily Herald, 1909-11, mng. editor, 1911-16, editor, 1916-26; editor Quincy Herald-Whig and Jour., 1926—. Conducted daily column, "The Editor's Telescope," in Quincy Herald, 1918-26, Quincy Herald-Whig and Jour., June 1, 1926—. Student Cost Arty. Sch., Fort Monroe, Va., 1917-18. Trustee MacMurray Coll. Women, Jacksonville, Ill., Cheerful Home Settlement (pres.), Quincy Y.M.C.A. (e-pres.; mem. nat. council 1939), Chaddock Boys' Sch., Quincy Home for Aged. Mem. Am. Soc. Newspaper Editors, Ill., Inland press assns., Ill. C. of C. (publicity com.), Quincy C. of C. (v.p.), Am. Legion, Sigma Delta Chi, Phi Beta Kappa. Methodist. Mason (33°; grand orator 1939). Elk. Clubs: Lions (Quincy); Dartmouth (Quincy and Chicago); Press (Chicago). Author of I Found a Story in Garbeheim and other essays, 1934; Contradictory Factors in Europe's Troubled Life, 1937. Mem. Am. Seminar to Europe, 1934, 37. Home: 1806 Grove Av. Office: Herald-Whig Sq., Quincy, Ill. Died Sept. 26, 1945; buried Quincy.

EICHER, Henry Martin, lawyer; b. Washington County, Ia, May 29, 1858; s. Benjamin and Lydia (Sommer) E.; ed. Eastern Ia. Normal Sch., 1875-6; studied law in office Judge Dewey, 1880-82, Washington, Ia.; m. Washington, Ia., June 26, 1888, Frances Celia McKee. Admitted to Ia. bar, 1883; asst. U.S. atty. So. dist., Ia., 1895-98. Mem. bd. dirs. Ia. State Children's Home, 1905; mem. Ia. State Bd. Edn., 1912—; appt. mem. Nat. Def. Council during World War I. Mem. Ia. State Bar Assn.; del. Universal Congress Lawyers and Jurists, St. Louis, 1904. Democrat. Address: Washington, Ia. Died July 28, 1919; buried Elm Grove Cemetery, Washington, Ia.

EICHHORN, William A., business exec.; b. Newark, Aug. 27, 1897; s. William H. and Louise (Ibenthaler) E.; ed. pub. schs. of N.Y. City; m. Frances Felter, Nov. 1, 1930; 1 son, William A. With American News Co., N.Y. City, 1911—, as mail boy, 1911-13, clerk 1913-30, asst. to v.p., 1930-33, asst. sec., 1933-40, sec., 1940-43, dir. 1941—, asst. treas., 1943-47, exec. v.p. and treas. 1947—; treas. The Union News Co. 1947—, dir. 1942—. Club: Wheatley Hills Golf. Home: Ten Cambridge Lane, Manhasset, L.I., N.Y. Office: 131 Varick St., N.Y.C. 13. Died Feb. 28, 1960.

EIKENBERRY, William Lewis (ī'kĕn-bĕr-ĭ), college prof.; b. Waterloo, Ia., July 12, 1871; s. William E. H. and Susan (Berkley) E.; student Mt. Morris (Ill.) Acad. and Coll., 1887-92; B.S., U. of Mich., 1894; studied U. of Chicago; m. Florence Shaw, June 30, 1903; 1 son. Robert S. Prof. sciences, Mt. Morris Coll., 1894-1901; instr. botany, Central High Sch., St. Louis, Mo., 1903-04; head dept. of botany, McKinley High Sch., St. Louis, 1904-09; instr. botany, University High Sch., U. of Chicago, 1909-16; asst. prof. edn., 1916-19, asso. prof., 1919-22, U. of Kan.; prof. and head dept. of science, State Teachers Coll., E. Stroudsburg, Pa., 1922-29; head of Science Dept., State Teachers Coll., Trenton, N.J., 1929-42; retired July 1, 1942; with training department, Eastern Aircraft, Trenton, N.J., 1942-43; with War Defense courses, Temple University, May-August, 1943; lecturer in physics Princeton, 1943-46. Lecturer and instr. in gen. science methods. Fellow A.A.A.S.; mem. American Botanical Soc., Nat. Assn. for Research in Science Teaching (pres. 1928-30), National Science Teachers Association (president 1939-40), Sigma Xi, Phi Delta Kappa. Republican. Member Church of the Brethren. Author: Problems in Botany, 1919; The Teaching of General Science, 1922. Co-Author: Elements of General Science, 1914 (with O. W. Caldwell), 3d edit., 1926; Laboratory Manual of General Science (with same), 1914; Laboratory Problems in General Science (with same), 1924; Educational Biology (with R. A. Waldron), 1929. Home: 709 S. Congress St., Polo, Ill. Died Dec. 20, 1957; buried Fairmount Cemetery, Polo.

EINSTEIN, Albert (in'stin), theoretical physicist; b. Ulm a. d. Donau, Germany, Mar. 14, 1879; s. Hermann and Pauline (Koch) E.; ed. Luitpold Gymnasium (Munich), Aarauer Kantonsschule (Aarau, Switzerland), Technische Hochschule, Zurich; Dr. honoris causa, Geneva, Oxford, Cambridge, Manchester, Princeton, Paris, Madrid, Rostock, Buenos Aires, Zurich, Yeshiva, Harvard, London, Brussels; m. Mileva Marec, 1901; children—Albert, Eduard; m. 2d, Elsa Einstein, 1917 (died 1936). Prof. at Universitat Zurich, Deutsche U. (Prague), Technische Hochschule (Zurich), Preuss, Akademie d. Wissenschaft (Berlin); came to U.S., 1933, became citizen, 1940; apptd. for life as mem. of Inst. for Advanced Study, Princeton, N.J., 1933; discoverer and exponent of the theory of relativity. Awarded Nobel prize, 1922; Franklin Inst. medal, 1935. Member Institut de France. Author: Meaning of Relativity, 1923; Sidelights on Relativity, 1923; Investigation on the Theory of the Brownian Movement, 1926; About Zionism, 1931; (with others) Living Philosophies, 1931; Builders of the Universe, 1932; On the Method of Theoretical Physics, 1933; (with Sigmund Freud) Why War?, 1933; The World as I See It, 1934; Evolution of Physics (with Leopold Infeld), 1938; also brochures and articles in mags. Home: 112 Mercer St., Princeton, N.J. Died Apr. 18, 1955.

EINSTEIN, Alfred, musicologist; b. Munich, Bavaria, Dec. 30, 1880; s. Ludwig and Johanna (Guttenstein) E.; Ph.D., U. Munich; Dr. H.C., Princeton, 1947; m. Hertha Heumann, Apr. 11, 1906; 1 dau., Eva Harriet. Came to U.S., 1939, naturalized, 1944. Editor Zeitschrift für Musikwissenschaft, Germany, 1918-33; music critic Berliner Tageblatt, Berlin, Germany, 1927-33; lived in London and in Mezzomonte nr. Florence, Italy, 1933-38; prof. music Smith Coll., Northampton, Mass., 1939-50. Mem. Am. Musicol. Soc., Music Library Assn., Royal Music Assn. (hon.). Writer on history of music, especially in connection with Italy in 16th century and Mozart. Author: History of Music, 1917; Gluck, 1936; Revision of "Kochel-Catalogue," 1937; Greatness in Music, 1941; Mozart, His Character, His Work, 1945; Music in the Romantic Era, 1947; The Italian Madrigal, 1949; Schubert, 1951. Editor: Musiklexikon (Riemann), 1919, 23, 29; Neues Musiklixikon, 1926. Home: 509 Village Dr., El Cerrito 8, Calif. Died Feb. 13, 1952; buried Berkeley, Cal.

EISENHOWER, Arthur B., banker; b. Hope, Kan., Nov. 11, 1886; s. David and Ida (Stover) E.; m. Louise Eisenhower; 1 dau., Katherine (Mrs. Berton Roueche). With Commerce Trust Co., Kansas City, Mo., 1905—, v.p., 1934, exec. v.p., dir. 1934-53, vice-chmn. bd. dirs., mem. exec. com., 1953-56, ret.; specialized in banking in grain trade and milling industries, also grain exports; pres. dir. Plaza Bank of Commerce, until 1956; dir. Interstate Securities Co., Central Surety & Ins. Corp., Coleman Co. (Wichita, Kan.), Gleaner Harvester Corp., Independence, Trans World Airlines, Inc., (Kansas City, Mo. and N.Y.C.). Hon. dir. Rockhurst Coll., Kansas City, Mo. Dir. Midwest Research Inst., Nat. Fund for Med. Edn. Dir., treas. Am. Cancer Soc., Am. Heart Assn., Kansas City, Mo., Arthritis Found.; dir. Brooking Inst. St. Louis (grain and milling research); life mem. Kansas City Art Inst., Nelson Gallery of Art. Trustee Mo. Pub. Expenditure Survey. Mem. Robert Morris Assos. (life mem., hon. mem.), Newcomen Soc., Wine and Food Soc. (past pres., hon. mem.). Republican. Mason (Shriner). Clubs: Seven-Eleven (past pres., hon. mem.), Forty Year Column, Kansas City (past pres., hon. mem.), C. of C. Mission Hills Country (Kansas City, Mo.), Links (N.Y.C.). Home: 6331 Ensley Lane. Office: 10th and Walnut Sts., Kansas City, Mo. Died Jan. 26, 1958.

EISENMAN, William Hunt (ī'sĕn-măn), b. Jamestown, O., July 7, 1886; s. Maurice and Margaret Hunt (Dempsey) E.; Ph.B., Kenyon Coll., Gambier, O., 1903; student Leland Stanford Jr. U. (now Stanford U.), 1903-06; A.M., Morningside Coll., Sioux City, Ia., 1907; student Ohio State U., 1910-11; m. Mildred Randle, Aug. 18, 1917; 1 son, William Hunt Eisenman, Jr. (lieut., Air Corps, killed 1943). Principal high sch., Olathe, Kan., 1907-10; head of chemistry dept., Racine Coll., 1911-14, supt. pub. schs., Elmhurst, Ill., 1914-17; founder, 1917, since nat. sec. Am. Soc. for Steel Treating (now Am. Soc. for Metals); president Association and Exposition Management, Inc.; gen. mgr. Metals Engring. Institute and Metall. Seminars; sec. of metals group National Research Council; mng. dir. Expn. of Am. Inventions, Nat. Metal Congress, Nat. Metal Expn., Western Metal Congress, Western Metal Expn.; dir. Am. Ceramic Expn., Am. Soc. of Inventors, Soc. of Collectors; sec. Am. Soc. Metals Found. Education and Research. Dir. Cleve. Conv. and Visitors Bureau Inc. Capt. Illinois National Guard, 1916-18. Engr. mem. Nat. Research Council; advisory com. Chicago "World's Fair," 1933. Mng. director "St. Louis on Parade," "Philadelphia on Parade," Kansas City (Mo.) "Jubilesta." Awarded gold medal First World Metall. Congress, gold medal, Am. Soc. Metals, 1956. Fellow Am. Inst. Chemists; mem. Am. Iron and Steel Inst., Soc. Automotive Engrs., Am. Soc. Testing Materials, Am. Foundrymen's Assn., Nat. Assn. Exhibit Mgrs. (pres.), Cleve. Engring. Soc.; hon. life mem. Iron and Steel Inst. Gt. Britain, Die Duetsche Gesellschaft fur Metallkunde, Germany, Société Française de Métallurgie, France, Assn. des Ingenieurs Sortis de l'Ecole de Liège, Belgium. Republican. Episcopalian. Mason. Clubs: Chemists' (N.Y.C.); Tennis, Racquet (Palm Springs, Cal.); Shadow Mountain (Palm Desert, Cal.); University, Rotary, Cleveland. Author: Chemistry for Girls, 1910; Chapter Know-How, 1948; How to Organize for Success. Home: 13300 Drexmore Rd. Office: 7301 Euclid Av., Cleve. Died June 1958.

EISNER, J. Lester, business exec.; born Red Bank, N.J., Mar. 18, 1889; s. Sigmund and Bertha (Weis) E.; student Phillips Exeter Acad., 1906-07; A.B., Harvard, 1911; m. Marguerite Davidson, Jan. 13, 1913 (died Feb. 28, 1924); children—Lester, Jacques (killed in action aboard U.S.S. San Francisco, battle of Savo Island, Nov. 12, 1942), Gerald; m. 2d, Virginia Scharf Steiner, Apr. 18, 1932; 1 step-son, Erwin B. Steiner. With Signumd Eisner Co., mfr. of uniforms, Red Bank, N.J., since 1911; pres., dir. Sego Trading Co. since 1922. Mem. Tri-State Treaty Compact (N.J., N.Y., Conn.), 1931-36; commr. and v. chmn. Interstate San. Commn., 1936-42 (chmn. N.J. Commn.). Organizer Nat. Recovery Adminstrn. for N.J., 1933, chmn., 1933-34; chmn. State Recovery Adminstrn. of N.J., 1933-34. Organizer Monmouth County (N.J.) Welfare Bd., 1928, vice chmn., 1928-39; mem. bd. overseers Graham-Eckes School, Palm Beach, Fla. Maj, Q.M.C., U.S. Army, 1917-18; lt. col., Q.M. Reserve Corps, 1919-35; lt. col., N.J. N.G., 1930-33; served as A.R.C. dir. of transportation for E.T.O., hdqrs. London and Paris, 1944-45. Mem. at large Nat. Council Boy Scouts of Am., Mem. bd. edn., Red Bank, 1917-20. Asso. mem. New Sch. for Social Research, N.Y. City. Mem. Am. Legion, Mil. Order World War, Mil. Order Fgn. Wars, League for Fair Play (dir.), Com. on Nat. Affairs (dir.), N.J. Taxpayers Assn. (dir.), Monmouth Hist. Soc. Republican. Elk, Mason, Nat. Sojourner. Clubs: Monmouth Boat; Shrewsbury River Ice and Yacht (Red Bank, N.J.); Army and Navy (Washington); Harvard, The Whist (N.Y.C.); Harvard (N.J.); Montauk (L.I.) Yacht; American (London). Home: 920 Fifth Av., N.Y.C. Office: 261 Fifth Av., N.Y.C. 16. Died May 27, 1955.

EISNER, Mark (īs'nẽr), lawyer; b. New York, N.Y., Dec. 15, 1886; s. David L. and Sophia (Silverthau) E.; A.B., Coll. of City of N.Y., 1905; LL.B., New York U., 1907; m. Helene Oettinger, June 7, 1922; children—Barbara, Mark. Admitted to N.Y. bar, 1907; lecturer on taxation N.Y. Univ. Sch. Finance, 1919-22; mem. Olvany, Eisner & Donnelly since 1924; dir. Bourjois, Inc., Skilmill, Inc. Prof. law of taxation, N.Y. Law Sch., 1935. Mem. N.Y. Legislature (Assembly), 1913-14; del. N.Y. State Constl. Conv., 1915; collector Internal Revenue, New York, 1915-19; counsel to NRA at New York, 1933. Trustee chmn. Bd. Higher Edn. City of N.Y., 1926-38; treas., dir. N.Y. Adult Edn. Council, Inc.; trustee Practicing Law Inst.; treas. College Arts Association; executive committee Tax Institute, pres., 1943-45; trustee Montefiore Hosp. Mem. Assn. Bar City of N.Y., County Lawyers Assn., Am. and N.Y. State bar assns., Delta Sigma Phi, Phi Beta Kappa, Phi Beta Kappa Assos. U.S. Regional Loyalty Bd., Am. Assn. Jewish Edn. (pres. 1939-47), pres. Alumni Assn. Coll. City of N.Y., 1943-45. Democrat. Jewish religion. Mason, Elk, K.P. Clubs: Salmagundi, Harmonie, City, Lawyers, National Democratic Club, National Art (N.Y.); Quaker Ridge Golf (Mamaroneck). Author: A Lay View of Higher Education. Editor: How Government Regulates Business. Contbr. series of lectures on taxation and govt. over radio. Home: 417 Park Av., New York 22. Office: 20 Exchange Pl., N.Y.C. Died Mar. 28, 1953.

EKELEY, John Bernard (ĕk'lē), chemist; b. Orebro, Sweden, Jan. 1, 1869; s. John and Ingeborg (Olson) E.; brought to U.S., 1872; A.B., Colgate U., Hamilton, N.Y., 1891, A.M., 1893 (Sc.D., 1911); Ph.D., U. of Freiburg, in Baden, Germany, 1902; studied Sorbonne, Paris, 1909-10, U. of Berlin, 1910; married Adelaide Evelyn Hobbs, July 18, 1894 (died August 5, 1943); married 2d, Viola Winifred Gaylord, Mar. 16, 1946. Assistant in chemistry at Colgate University, 1891-93; science master, St. Paul's School, Garden City, N.Y., 1893-1900; professor and head dept. of Chemistry, U. of Colo., 1902-37, emeritus, 1937, State chemist of Colo., 1911-33. Inventor, with W. B. Stoddard, of process for extraction of tungsten from tungsten ores; pres. Tungstic Acid Corp., 1922-28. Dir. Nat. State Bank, Boulder, Colo., mem. Colo. Coal Mine Commn., 1911. Fellow A.A.A.S.; mem. Am. Chem. Soc., Am. Electrochem. Soc., Am. Institute of Chemical Engineers, American Institute of Chemists, Colorado-Wyoming Academy of Science, Faraday Society, Royal Central Asian Society, Delta Kappa Epsilon, Phi Beta Kappa, Sigma Xi, Alpha Chi Sigma. Author: A Laboratory Manual of Inorganic Chemistry, 1912, revised, 1923, 28, 34; The Chief Laws and Theories of Chemistry Briefly Stated, 1924; also various research articles in Am. and European chem. journs. Home: 703 11th St., Boulder, Colo. Died Nov. 8, 1951.

EKERN, Herman Lewis, lawyer; b. Trempealeau County, Wis., Dec. 27, 1872; s. Even and Elizabeth (Grimsrud) E.; LL.B., U. Wis., 1894; hon. LL.D., 1944; LL.D., Capital, 1935, Thiel, 1939; m. Lily C. Anderson, Aug. 16, 1899; children—Elsie (Mrs. William G. Fisher), Lila (Mrs. Horace H. Ratcliff), John, George, Irene (Mrs. Winfield V. Alexander), Dorothy. Admitted to Wis. bar, 1894, and practiced at Whitehall until 1911, and at Madison and Chgo. after 1915; mem. firm Ekern & Meyers and Ekern, Meyers & Matthias, Ekern, Naujoks & Ekern, 1951—; dist. atty. Trempealeau Co., 1895-99; mem. Wis. Legislature (Assembly), 1903, 05, 07 (speaker of House, 1907); dep. commr. ins. of Wis. 1909-10, commr. of ins., 1911-15; atty. gen. of Wis., 1923-27; chmn. Wis. Unemployment Commn., 1931. Lt. gov. Wis., 1938. Chmn. Wis. Deep Waterway Commn. Regent U. Wis., 1939-43; dir. U. Wis. Found. Past pres. Luth. Brotherhood (legal res. life ins.), also Boy Scouts, Coll. Student and other benevolences. Dir. Fgn. Bondholders Protective Council, Nat. Multiple Sclerosis Soc. Mem. Am., Wis., Ill., Chgo. bar assns., A.A.A.S., Am.-Scandinavian Found., Acad. Polit. Sci., Newcomen Soc., also various fraternal, benevolent, ednl. and econ. assns. Del. Rep. nat. and state convs.; chmn. State Central Com. Wis., 1929-32. Republican. Luth. Author of the original soldiers' and sailors' War Risk Insurance Act; co-author Railroad Retirement Acts and Teachers Retirements Acts. Contbr. on ins. and econ. subjects. Home: 2809 Columbia Rd., Madison 5, Wis. Address: Suite 1755, 1 La Salle St. Bldg., Chgo. 2. Died Dec. 4, 1954; buried Madison, Wis.

EKLUND, Fred Nils, advt. exec., orgn. exec.; b. Forshaga, Sweden, July 8, 1904; s. Anders Fredrik and Charlotta (Gustavsson) E.; ed. pub. schs., Sweden; m. Astrid Nyquist, Feb. 15, 1930. Came to U.S., 1922, naturalized, 1943. Clerk, 1924-28; toolmaker, 1940-47; draftsman Globe Co., Chgo., 1947-49; asst. advt. mgr. Swedish Am. Tribune, Chgo., 1949-51, advt. mgr., 1951—. Mem. Internat. Order Good Templers, 1922—, sec. Central States Grand Lodge, 1933-38, pres., 1940-41, 45-47, Am. nat. pres., 1948-51. Mem. Chgo. Swedish Christian Male Chorus, Swedish Christian Assn. Chgo. Home: 7946 Rhodes Av., Chgo. 19. Office: 208 N. Wells St., Chgo. 6. Died Jan. 27, 1957.

EKWALL, William Alexander, judge U.S. Customs Court; b. Ludington, Michigan, June 14, 1887; s. Alexander and Emilie Ekwall; LL.B., Oregon Law School, Portland, Oregon, 1912; m. Lina Moser, June 19, 1915; children—Mrs. Joyce Atkinson, Jacqueline. Admitted to Oregon bar, 1912, and practiced in Portland as member firm of Senn, Ekwall & Recken until 1922; municipal judge, Portland, 1922-27; judge Circuit Court, 4th Dist., Dept. 8, Portland, 1927-35; mem. 74th Congress (1935-37), 3d Ore. Dist.; mem. law firm Morton & Ekwall, 1938-42; apptd. judge U.S. Customs Court, New York, by President Franklin D. Roosevelt, Feb. 13, 1942. Elected del. to Rep. Nat. Conv., Philadelphia, Pa., 1940, from Ore. 3d Dist. Served as pvt., inf., at Camp Pike, Ark., World-War. Mem. Am. Legion, 40 and 8, Delta Theta Phi. Mason (Shriner), mem. Elks (past exalted ruler), Woodmen of the World. Home: 9 Tanglewylde Av., Bronxville, N.Y. Office: 201 Varick St., N.Y.C. 14. Died. Oct. 16, 1956; buried Portland, Ore.

ELDER, Bowman, railway corp. exec.; b. Indianapolis, Ind., Mar. 4, 1888; s. William Line and Laura (Bowman) E.; grad. Chestnut Hill (Pa.) Acad., 1907; B.S., U. of Pa., 1911; m. Madeline Fortune, Sept. 30, 1914; children—Anne, William Line. Entered real estate bus. at Indianapolis, with father, as Wm. L. Elder & Bowman Elder, 1912-40; promoted Chamber of Commerce Office Bldg. and became sec.-treas. Chamber of Commerce Bldg., Corp.; receiver Ind. R.R. and as such lessee Pub. Service Company of Indiana and Indiana Service Corporation, 1933-41; vice president Circle Agencies, Inc., 1935-39; pres. and dir. of Southern Indiana Railway, Inc. Consular agent for France at Indianapolis, 1934-40. Commd. lt. C.A. Res. Corps, Nov. 27, 1917; capt., Apr. 5, 1918; served in France, July 30, 1918-Feb. 22, 1919; capt. Res., May 1, 1919; lt. col., July 5, 1923; col., July 16, 1926; mem. 5th Corps Area Advisory Bd., term 1931-39. Del. Dem. Nat. Conv., St. Louis, 1916, del. at large Dem. Nat. Conv., Chicago, 1932, del. Dem. Nat. Conv. Chicago, 1940; treas. Dem. State Com., Indiana, 1924-26. Mem. bd. dirs. American Red Cross; trustee Park School for Boys, 1934-40; trustee Crown Hill Cemetery Association (pres. and mem. bd. of mgrs.). Active in nat. affairs of Am. Legion, 1922—, nat. chmn. distinguished guests com., 1922, mem. nat. exec. com., 1923-27, nat. chmn. of France Conv. Com., in charge 2d A.E.F., 1927 (comprising 20,000 legionnaires, largest orgn. peace time movement in history), nat. treas. Am. Legion, 1928-33; also same, Legion Pub. Corp.; mem. Ind. Soc. Chicago, Indianapolis Chamber of Commerce, U. of Pa. Alumni Association, Indianapolis Real Estate Board, Reserve Officers Assns., Mil. Order Foreign Wars, Newcomen Society of England. Forty and Eight, Sons of Am. Revolution, Friars Sr. Soc. of Univ. of Pa., Zeta Psi. Officer Order Polonia Restituta (Poland); Order Legion of Honor (France). Presbyterian. Mason, Elk. Clubs: Army and Navy (Washington, D.C.); University, Dramatic, Indianapolis Athletic (dir. and treas.). Compiler: History of the 71st Artillery (C.A.C.) in the Great War, 1919. Home: New Augusta, Ind. Office: Chamber of Commerce Bldg., Indpls. 4. Died June 10, 1954; buried Crown Hill Cemetery.

ELDER, Orr Jay, ret. publisher; b. Farmington, Ill., Nov. 5, 1882; s. Manly P. and Isabel (Grinnell) E.; student Farmington High Sch. and Brown's Business Coll., Galesburg, Ill.; m. Elizabeth Stack, Feb. 6, 1919; 1 son, Orr Jay. Stenographer to Charles Austin Bates, 1901-02, Hampton Advt. Agy., 1902; with MacFadden Publications 1903-51, successivly asst. advt. mgr., advt. mgr., 1903-41, pres. and dir., 1941-51. Republican. Episcopalian. Home: 187 Old Short Hills Rd., Short Hills, N.J. Office: 205 E. 43d St., N.Y.C. Died May 2, 1957.

ELDRED, Byron E., mech. engr.; b. Jackson, Mich., Feb. 12, 1873; s. Zenas C. and Helen (Carter) E.; B.S., Dartmouth (class of 1896), hon. D.Sc., 1916; m. Mildred Carter, 1896 (div. 1911); m. 2d, Mary

Victoria Lawson, Apr. 22, 1911 (died 1930); m. 3d, Mrs. G. Norden Hawthorne, 1931. Engaged in research and engineering work; inventor of many comml. processs and products, among which is a substitute for platinum used extensively in mfr. of electric lamps and electrical contacts, temperature and volume of flame control, the optical light slit used generally in sound recording for theatre pictures, the Talking Book micro-photographic record of sound, and waste coal recovery process utilizing property of absorption of carbonaceous materials. Discoverer of effect of sinusoidal air wave for correcting defective audition and method for continuous casting of metals known as draw-casting. War work during World War I. Recipient John Scott legacy and medal City of Phila., Elliott Cresson gold medal by Franklin Inst. Pres. Nat. Assn. Engrs. Hoover for President, 1928; mem. exec. com. NRC, 1931-32. Del. U.S. Govt. to World Engring. Congress, Tokyo, 1929. Club: Engineers New York (pres. 1938-39). Home: Lime Rock, Conn. Died May 27, 1956.*

ELDRERGE, Elliott Minton (ĕl'drĕj), banker; b. Bklyn., Nov. 11, 1878; s. Orris King and Ella Virginia (Snyder) E.; Adelphi Acad., 1884-96, Ph.B., Wesleyan U., Middletown, Conn., 1900; m. Florence Goodliff Murphy, Nov. 19, 1903; children—Elliott Minton (dec.), Ashton Goodliff, Doris. Began with Wheelwright, Eldredge & Co., dry goods comm. merchants, N.Y.C., 1900-01; partner, Eldredge, Lewis & Co., 1901-10, West Baker & Co., 1910-16, Eldredge & Snyder, 1916-30; v.p., Williamsburgh Savs. Bank, 1939-42 became pres., 1942, chmn. bd., ret. 1956; dir. Savs. Bank Trust Co., Institutional Securities Corp. Dir. House of St. Giles the Cripple, Bklyn. Eye and Ear Hosp. Mem. Am. Inst. Banking, Bklyn. C. of C. (dir.), Alpha Delta Phi. Clubs: Bankers (Bklyn.); Huntington Country; Union League (N.Y.). Home: Halesite, N.Y. Died Oct. 13, 1959.

ELDRIDGE, Seba, sociologist; b. Johnston County, N.C., July 22, 1885; s. Josiah and Elizabeth (Phail) E.; prep. edn., Buies' Creek (N.C.) Acad. (now Campbell Coll.); B.E., N.C. State Coll., 1907; A.B., Columbia, 1911, Ph.D., 1925; m. Katherine Ruth Eldridge, Sept. 15, 1917; 1 son, Seba. Social and civic work, N.Y. City, 1908-16, including spl. agt. Charity Orgn. Soc., 1910-13; sec. Dept. of Social Betterment of Brooklyn Bur. Charities, 1913-15; organizer and dir. Com. on Federal Constn., 1914-16; asst. in philosophy, Columbia, 1917-18; asst. prof. sociology and economics, Smith Coll., 1918-19; prof. sociology and economics, Rockford (Ill.) Coll., 1919-21; asso. prof. sociology, U. of Kan., 1921-29, prof. since 1929. Mem. Am. Sociol. Soc., A.A.A.S., Am. Assn. University Profs. Author: Problems of Community Life, 1915; Social Legislation in Illinois, 1921; Political Action, 1924; The Organization of Life, 1925; An Introduction to Sociology (with others), 1927; Major Problems of Democracy (with Carroll D. Clark), 1928; The New Citizenship, 1929; Public Intelligence, 1935; New Social Horizons, 1941; Development of Collective Enterprise (with associates), 1943; Fundamentals of Sociology (with associates), 1950. Contbr. to various journals. Home: 1501 Crescent Rd., Lawrence, Kan. Died Feb. 16, 1953.

ELDRIDGE, William Angevine, banker; b. Great Neck, N.Y., Nov. 6, 1900; s. Lewis A. and Elizabeth M. (Huyck) E.; A.B., Harvard, 1921; m. Barbara F. Jones, Jan. 24, 1935; children—Janet, Robert H. With The Hanover Bank, N.Y.C., since 1921, v.p., 1930-50, v. chmn. since 1950, trustee since 1942; dir. F. C. Huyck and Sons, Homeland Insurance Co., Mercantile Ins. Co., United Nat. Indemnity Co., Commonwealth Ins. Co. of New York, N. British and Mercantile Ins. Co., Ltd. Served with United States Marine Corps, 1918. Mem. bd. mgrs. St. Luke's Hosp. Trustee of the Juilliard Musical Foundation. Member Phi Beta Kappa. Clubs: Harvard, Union (New York). Office: 70 Broadway, N.Y.C. Died Oct. 5, 1953.

ELIAS, Harold Lee, found. exec.; b. Charleston, S.C., Mar. 27, 1891; s. Louis and Rachael (Loeb) E.; LL.B., Georgetown U., 1914; unmarried. Admitted to D.C. bar, 1915. Field dir. Near East Relief campaign, hdqrs. N.Y. City, 1919, Wilfred T. Grenfell Labrador Mission campaigns, U.S. and Can., hdqrs. N.Y. City, 1920-22, German Child Feeding campaign, 1923-24, A.R.C., Salvation Army, Anne Morgan, Am. Assn. for Old Age Security, and other campaigns 1924-27; with Leonard Wood Memorial-Am. Leprosy Foundation, N.Y. City, since 1927, exec. sec. since 1940. Home: 198 W. Tenth St., N.Y. City 14. Office: 1 Madison Av., N.Y.C. Died July 19, 1956.

ELIOT, Amory, banker, trustee; b. Chicopee, Mass., May 26, 1856; s. William Prescott and Eleanor (Chapin) E.; grad. Phillips Exeter Acad., Exeter, N.H., 1873; A.B., Harvard, 1877, student Law Sch., 1877-79; m. Mary Clark, Dec. 7, 1881; children—Lydia (Mrs. Oliver Turner), Mary (Mrs. Richard Sears Loveing), Samuel, Rosamond (Mrs. Frederic Munroe Burnham). Admitted to Mass. bar, 1880, and began practice at Boston; pres. Webster and Atlas Nat. Bank, 1914-20, chmn. bd., 1920-—; with Samuel Eliot and R. E. Connor, trustees and agts., 1920-—; trustee Boston Chamber Commerce Realty Trust, Bus. Real Estate Trust, Suffolk Savs. Bank for Seamen and others. Clubs: Exchange, Essex County (ex-pres.), Harvard (Boston); Harvard (N.Y.C.). Home: Manchester-by-the-Sea, Mass. Office: 131 State St., Boston. Died Apr. 12, 1943.

ELIOT, Frederick May (ĕl'yăt), pres. Am. Unitarian Assn.; b. Boston, Mass., Sept. 15, 1889; s. Christopher Rhodes and Mary Jackson (May) E.; grad. Roxbury Latin Sch., 1907; A.B., Harvard U., 1911, A.M., 1912; S.T.B., Harvard Div. Sch., 1915; D.D., Carleton Coll., 1935, Meadville Theol. Sch., 1937; LL.D., University of Minnesota, 1937, Mount Holyoke College, 1948; married Elizabeth Berkeley Lee, June 25, 1915. Ordained Unitarian ministry, 1915; asso. minister First Parish Ch., Cambridge, 1915-17; minister Unity Ch., St. Paul, 1917-38; pres. Am. Unitarian Assn., 1937-—. Mem. bd. trustees Proctor Acad., Andover, Hackley Sch., Tarrytown, New York, Mount Holyoke College (president); president of American Unitarian Assn., 1937-—. Served as 1st lt., chaplain U.S. Army, World War I; with A.E.F., Aug. 1918-Mar. 1919, Base Hosp. No. 7, Tours, France. Fellow American Academy of Arts and Sciences; member Delta Upsilon. Author: The Unwrought Iron, 1920; Fundamentals of Unitarian Faith, 1926; Toward Belief in God, 1928; Samuel McChord Crothers, Interpreter of Life, 1930. Home: 89 Irving St., Cambridge, Mass. Address: 25 Beacon St., Boston 8. Died Feb. 17, 1958.

ELIOT, William Greenleaf, Jr., clergyman; b. St. Louis, Missouri, Oct. 13, 1866; s. Rev. Thomas L. (D.D., LL.D., Litt. D.) and Henrietta R. (Mack) E.; A.B., Washington U., 1888, LL.D., 1932; Harvard Divinity School, 1889-91; D.D., Meadville Theol. Sch., 1925; Litt.D., Reed College, 1944; m. Minna Sessinghaus, 1894 (died 1944); children—Clara Eliot (Mrs. R. B. Raup), William G. III, Mrs. Ruth Eliot Prentiss, Theodore S. Ordained to the ministry, 1894; was pastor successively Seattle, San Francisco, Milwaukee, Wis.; supt. Am. Unitarian Assn. in Pacific N.W., 1901-06; minister Ch. of Our Father, Portland, Ore., 1906-34, now emeritus. Dir. congresses and conferences Lewis and Clark Expn., 1905; regent Reed Coll., 1926-44, hon. trustee, 1944-—. Mem. Phi Beta Kappa. Club: City. Home: 1923 N.E. Schuyler St., Portland, Ore. Died June 8, 1956; buried Riverview Cemetery, Portland, Ore.

ELKIN, Daniel Collier, surgeon; b. Louisville, Ky., Mar. 26, 1893; s. Robert and Roberta (Collier) E.; A.B., Yale, 1916; M.D., Emory University, Atlanta, Ga., 1920; Sc.D., Northwestern University, 1952; D.Sc. (honorary), Centre Coll., 1956; married Helen McCarty, November 3, 1923; 1 son, Daniel C. Intern and resident surgeon, Peter Bent Brigham Hosp., Boston, Mass., 1920-24; asst. in surgery, Harvard, 1924; Whitehead prof. of surgery, Emory U., 1929-55, now emeritus. Mem. bd. trustees Univ. Kentucky. Served as colonel Medical Corps, Army of U.S., unit dir. 43d Gen. Hosp., 1941, chief of surg. service Ashford (W.Va.) Gen. Hosp., 1942-46. Apptd. brigadier gen., O.R.C., A.U.S., 1949. Awarded Matas medal for vascular surgery Tulane U., 1940; Legion of Merit, 1945, Fellow A.C.S. (pres.); mem. Soc. Vascular Surgery (president 1948), Soc. Medical Consultants (president 1949), Southern Surgical Assn. (president 1946), American Surgical Assn. (past pres.), American Assn. Thoracic Surgery, Soc. Clinical Surgery (pres. 1947). Presbyn. Clubs: Piedmont Driving, Capital City, (Atlanta); Pendennis (Louisville); Graduates (New Haven). Author: Medical Reports of John Y. Bassett, 1941. Contributor numerous papers relating to surgery of heart and blood vessels to sci. publs. Home: Lancaster, Ky. Office: Emory University, Ga. Died Nov. 3, 1958; buried Lancaster, Ky.

ELKINS, Davis, ex-senator; b. Wahington, Jan. 24, 1876; s. U.S. Senator Stephen B. and Hallie (Davis) E.; student Harvard; m. Mary Reagan; children—Hallie Katherine, Davis, Maureen. Left coll., 1898, to enlist as pvt. 1st W.Va. Vol. Inf., at beginning of Spanish-Am. War; commd. 1st. lt. and later served as capt. on staff of Brig. Gen. Theodore Schwan, in Cuba and P.R.; assumed charge of business interests of father, upon leaving army; apptd. by Gov. Glasscock of W.Va. to U.S. Senate to fill vacancy caused by death of father, serving Jan. 9-Jan. 31, 1911. Commd. maj. U.S. Army, Dec. 27, 1917, and served as adj. 13th Inf. Brigade, 7th Div., in Tex. and France; hon. disch., Dec. 27, 1918, after being elected in absence to U.S. Senate for term 1919-25. Republican. Clubs: The Links, Racquet and Tennis (N.Y.); Deepdale Golf. Home: 2029 Connecticut Av., N.W., Washington. Died Jan. 5, 1959.

ELLABARGER, Daniel Rudolph, coll. pres.; b. Dublin, Ind., Dec. 12, 1863; s. John Warfel and Mary (Herr) E.; Hartsville (Ind.) Coll. 3 yrs. until 1886; A.B., Ind. U., 1892; A.M., Huntington Coll., 1921; studied U. Chgo.; m. C. Luello Scudder, Mar. 25, 1885; 1 son, Lowell S. Supt. schs., Dublin, Ind., 1892-3, Knightstown, 1893-5; prin. high sch., Richmond, Ind., 1895-1908, Piqua, O., 1908-19; pres. Huntington Coll., 1919-25. Home: Hungtington, Ind. Died 1949.

ELLERHUSEN, Florence Cooney (ĕl'lĕr-hōō-zen), painter; b. Norwood, Ont., Can.; d. John Ward and Mary Ann (O'Callahan) Cooney; studied art at Art Inst. Chicago, Art Students' League (New York); pupil of William M. Chase, William H. Vanderpoel, George Elmer Brown and George Luks; m. Ulrich H. Ellerhusen, sculptor, Jan. 19, 1921. Exhibited at Art Inst. Chgo., N.A.D., Allied Artists Am., N.Y., Balt. Water Color Socs., Newport, Montclair art assns. Mem. Nat. Assn. Women Painters and Sculptors, Allied Artists Am., Morristown, Mountain Lake art assns. Pen and Brush Club, Art Council of N.J. (founder, dir. 1941-—, pres. 1948-—). Instr. in painting, Del. Arts Council of N.J., 1940-46. Received 1st prize for water color Morristown Art Assn., 1939, Art Centre of the Orange, 1940. Roman Catholic. Home and studio: Towaco, N.J. Died Apr. 20, 1950; buried Gate of Heaven Cemetery, Hanover, N.J.

ELLERHUSEN, Ulrich Henry, sculptor; b. Warren, Mecklenburg, Germany, Apr. 7, 1879; s. Henry Christopher and Mary (Quapp) E.; grad. high sch., Leipzig, 1892; studied Art Inst. Chgo, Art Students' League, and Cooper Union, New York, also with Karl Bitter; m. Florence Cooney (portrait and landscape painter), Jan. 19, 1921; (dec. 1950). Came to U.S., 1894, naturalized citizen, 1900. Exhibited N.A.D. Architects' League, Allied Artists Am. Union League Club (N.Y.C.), Pa. Acad. Fine Arts (Phila.), Carnegie Inst. (Pitts.), Corcoran Art Galleries (Washington), San Francisco Expn., Blackstone Galeries (Buffalo), St. Louis Art League (winner of design of St. Louis Art League, others. Prin. works: Meditation, and Maidens Bearing Garlands, also figures of Conception and Contemplation, Place of Fine Arts, San Francisco Expn.; Schwab meml. fountain Yale; Diana panel at Greystone, N.Y. estate of Samuel Untermeyer; rowing trophy for USN; war hero medals for Pa. R.R. Co.; Peace monument Elmwood Park, N.J.; communion rail, The Life of Christ, Ch. of St. Gregory, N.Y.C.; St. Michael, St. Mary's Coll., Notre Dame, Ind.; History of Religion, 21 statues, chapel U. Chgo.; statues and symbolical decorations main entrance, Ch. of the Heavenly Rest, N.Y.C.; exterior stone sculpture Oriental Inst., U. Chgo.; friezes La. State Capitol; colossal reliefs Electrical Bldg., Century of Progress, Chgo.; First Permanent Settlement of the Old Northwest monument, Herrodsburg, Ky.; frieze Post Office, Columbus, O.; Lewis and Clark and The Road to Oregon friezes, Kansas City (Mo.) City Hall: The Oregon Pioneer, figure for State Capitol, Salem, Ore.; Holy Trinity statues of St. Vincent de Paul and Joseph for Mary Immaculate Seminary, Northampton, Pa. Recipient the gold medal for sculpture, Archtl. League of N.Y., 1929, Allied Artists Am., 1934; named N.J. artist of the year, 1955. Hon. pres. Art Council N.J., N.A. Mem. Nat. Sculpture Soc. (v.p.), Archtl. League N.Y., Allied Artists Am. (pres.); hon. mem. Beaux Arts Inst. Design, Salmagundi Club; pres. Art Council of N.J.; instr. sculpture Beaux Arts Inst., 8 yrs.; also at Nat. Acad. Design school. Lutheran. Home and studios: Change Bridge Rd., Montville, N.J. Died Nov. 9. 1957; buried Gate of Heaven Cemetery, Hanover, N.J.

ELLETT, Thomas Harlan, architect; b. Red Oak, Ia., Sept. 2, 1880; s. Thomas Ely and Caroline Elizabeth (Bake) E.; certificate in Architecture, Armour Inst. Tech., 1903; B.S. in Architecture, U. Pa., 1906; awarded Arthur Spayd Brook medal and Cresson traveling fellowship; studied abroad and at Am. Acad. in Rome, 1907-09; m. Jane Poultney bigelow; Aug. 15, 1917; 1 dau., Jane Braxton (Mrs. William Hoffman Benjamin). Engaged in gen. practice of architecture, N.Y.C., 1915-—; designer Am. Mil. Chapel and development of cemetery at Thiaucourt, France; Cosmopolitan Club, N.Y.; country houses in vicinity of N.Y.; Bronx Post Office, N.Y.; cons. architect U.S. Dept. Treasury, 1934-36, 1939-40. Served as capt. 302d Engrs., A.E.F., World War. Decorated Silver Star medal (U.S.). Fellow of the Am. Inst. of Architects. Awarded silver medal for 1928 by Architectural League of N.Y. for design of residence for J. Seward Johnson, New Brunswick, N.J., and gold medal for 1933, for design of Cosmopolitan Club, N.Y., also gold medal, Montevideo, 1940; winner Covington, Ky., Post Office and Court House competition. Academician Nat. Acad. of Design. Mem. Nat. Inst. of Arts and Letters. Club: Century (N.Y.C.); Highland Country. Home: Garrison-on-Hudson, N.Y. Office: 101 Park Av., N.Y.C. Died 1951.

ELLICOTT, John Morris, naval officer; b. St. Inigoes, Md., Sept. 4, 1859; s. James Fox and Elvira Ann (Jones) E.; grad. U.S. Naval Acad., 1883; studied U.S. Naval War Coll. and Torpedo Sch.; m. Annie M. Williams, Dec. 29, 1887. Commd. ensign USN, 1885, ret. as capt., 1912, recalled artive duty, 1918-22; in flagship Tennessee, N. Atlantic sta., 1883-85; expdn. occupying Isthmus of Panama, 1885; in Ranger, N. Pacific sta., 1885-88; staff intelligence duty Navy Dept., 1888-91, Bennington, 1891-93; on flagship Chicago, European sta., 1894; instr. ordnance U.S. Naval Acad., 1894-96; Marion and flagship Baltimore, Pacific sta., 1896-98; flagship Baltimore, Asiaitc sta., 1898-99; staff Naval War Coll., 1900-01; participated in battle of Manila Bay, May 1; navigator Prairie, 1901-04; supt. of compasses Navy Dept., 1905-06; exec. officer Maryland, Asiatic sta.,

1906-07; comd. Solace, 1908; insp. 13th Light House Dist., Portland, Ore., 1909; comdg. U.S.S. Maryland, 1911-13; Navy Yard, Mare Island, Cal., 1914, capt., 1917-20. Recipient medal from Congress for services at Manila. Author: Justified (novel), 1891; Life of John Ancrum Winslow, 1900; Ellicott Valuation Contract Bridge, 1930; others. Address: Quarters 177, Mare Island Naval Shipyard, Cal. Died Sept. 16, 1955; buried Mare Island Naval Cemetery.

ELLIMAN, Lawrence Bogert, real estate broker; b. Flushing, N.Y., Sept. 11, 1876; s. William and Mary Lawrence (Bogert) Elliman; student Flushing Institute, 1890, Berkeley School, 1891-94; married Edyth Howard Coppell, November 18, 1902 (died August 13, 1941); children—Edyth (Mrs. Prentice Talmage), Lawrence Bogert, Jr.; m. 2d, Madelaine Chauncey Lynch, May 6, 1944. Entered real estate business with Pell & Graves, N.Y. City, 1897; formed as of Sept. 1897 firm of Pease & Elliman, Inc., 1901, now president; real estate business and management; v.p. McLean & McLean; dir. Commonwealth Ins. Co., Homeland Ins. Co.; pres. and dir. Hotel Barbizon; also pres. or dir. of numerous subsidiary or co-related bldg. corps. and civic assns. Served in N.Y. State Naval Militia, 1896-1901. Mem. Fifth Av. Assn. (dir.), Real Estate Bd. of N.Y. (hon. gov.), N.Y. Geneal. and Biol. Soc. (trustee, pres.), St. Nicholas Soc., Soc. of Colonial Wars, N.Y. Hist. Soc. Republican. Episcopalian. Clubs: Racquet and Tennis, Uptown (New York); Rockaway Hunting, Lawrence Beach. Home: 655 Park Av. Office: 660 Madison Av., N.Y.C. 21. Died July, 1954.

ELLINGSON, Carl Herman, banker; b. Willmar, Minn., Sept. 26, 1883; s. Elling and Sigrid (Christopherson) E.; graduate Willmar Seminary, 1903; m. Lady Marguerite F. Brereton. Admitted to the Washington State bar, 1916; comptroller and financial sec., War Prisoners' Aid Work, Berne, Switzerland, 1918-19; in chg. of commissary dept., Brit. Army of Occupation, Egypt and Palestine, 1919-20; pub. accountant, St. Paul, Minn., 1920-22; organizer, Minn. Bldg. and Loan Assn. (now Minn. Federal Savings & Loan Assn.), St. Paul, 1922, director, 1926-33; asst. general manager of savings and loan divison, Fed. Home Loan Bank Bd., Washington, 1933-37; organizer, mgr. pres., First Fed. Savs. & Loan Assn., Washington, 1937-51; organizer, 1955, since pres., dir. Nat. Security Savs., Bethesda, Md.; mem. Washington Bd. Trade. Republican. Author: Manual of Office Adminstrn., 1944; Federal Savs. and Loan Assns., Their Strength and Weakness, 1952. Contbr. articles on finance to mags. Home: 8517 Woodhaven Rd., Bethesda, Md. Office: 600 F St., Washington. Died Nov. 26, 1956; buried Fort Lincoln Cemetery.

ELLIOTT, Claude, coll. dean; b. Cross Plains, Tex., Sept. 21, 1896; s. Robert Mitchell and Martha Caroline (Smith) E.; student West Tex. State Tchrs. Coll., Abilene Christian Coll., Simmons Coll.; B.S., Southwest Tex. State Tchrs. Coll., 1923; A.M., U. Tex., 1928, Ph.D., 1934; m. Emma Edwin Moore, Sept. 6, 1927. Prin. Donna High Sch., 1922; supt. LaFeria Pub. Sch., 1923-27; mem. faculty Southwest Tex. State Tchrs. Coll. since 1929, prof. history, 1929-42, registrar, dir. personnel, 1942-49, coordinator, vets. affairs, 1943-45, dean grad. studies since 1949. Served with U.S. Navy, World War I. Recipient Rockefeller grant for Tex. history research, 1945, 47. Fellow and life mem. Tex. State Hist. Assn. (pres. 1953-55); mem. N.E.A., Am. Legion So. Hist. Assn., Tex. State Tchrs. Assn., Tex. Classroom Tchrs. Assn., Tex. Assn. Collegiate Registrars (pres. 1947), Hays County Tchrs. Assn., C. of C. Democrat. Mem. Ch. of Christ. Club: Kiwanis (lt. gov., Kiwanis Internat. 1946). Author: Leathercoat, Life of a Texas Patriot, 1938; Union Settlement in Texas, 1861-65 (monograph), 1948; Alabama and Texas Revolution (monograph), 1947; Freedman's Bureau in Texas, 1952; Theses on Texas History, 1955. Contbr. articles for Handbook of Texas; Collector of Texana (including Tex. postal cancellations relating to postal history of Republic of Tex.) as related to cultural background of Tex., especially as related to Anglo-Spanish cultural conflict still in progress in state. Home: 434 N. Comanche St., San Marcos, Tex. Died Oct. 1, 1958; buried San Marcos.

ELLIOTT, Edward Loomis, investment banker; b. Pitts., Dec. 6, 1899; s. James R. and Mary R. (Loomis) E.; Mining Engr., Stanford, 1921; m. Ellen Brailsford, Apr. 14, 1922; children—John B., Mary Elizabeth (Mrs. Wislar), David L. Mining engring., 1922-23; constrn. engr. Scofield Twaites Co., 1923-29; partner Van Alystyne, Noel & Co., 1939-52, Elliott & Co., N.Y.C., 1952—; dir. Chromalloy Corp., Dynamic Electronics-N.Y., Inc., Internat. Research and Exploation Corp., Metalsalts Corp. Mem. Am., N.Y. stock exchanges. Home: 30 West Rd., Short Hills, N.J. Office: 25 Broad St.,N.Y.C 4. Died Oct. 13, 1959.

ELLIOTT, Gertrude (Lady Forbes-Robertson), actress; b. (May Gertrude Dermot) Rockland, Me; d. Thomas and Mary Adelaide (Hall) Dermot; ed. pub. sch. and normal coll., New York; m. J. Forbes-Robertson, Dec. 22, 1900 (dec. 1937); children—Maxine, Jean, Dinah. Made profl. début, Sartoga, N.Y., Sept., 1894; starring alone under mgmt. of Liebler & Co., 1910-12; toured with husband in his farewell repertoire, 1912-14; starred in Eyes of Youth, St. James' Theatre, London, 1918-19. Home: London, Eng. Died Dec. 24, 1950.

ELLIOTT, Harrison Sacket, educator; born at St. Clairsville, Ohio, Dec. 13, 1882; s. Calvin Watson and Luella Augusta (Sacket) E.; student Antioch Coll., Yellow Springs, O., 1898-1900, Valparaiso (Ind.) U., 1900-01; A.B., Ohio Wesleyan U., 1905; B.D., Drew Theol. Seminary, 1911; A.M., Teachers College, Columbia, 1922; student at Oxford University, England, 1931; Ph.D., Yale, 1940; m. Grace Hunsberger Loucks, June 24, 1927; children—David Loucks, Donald Harrison, Margaret Jean. Secretary to James W. Bashford, bishop of M.E. Ch., China, 1905-08; corr. Asso. Press, Shanghai, China, 1906-08; assistant sec. Africa Diamond Jubilee, M.E. Church, 1909-10; sec. International Com., Y.M.C.A., 1910-22; sec. Nat. War Work. Council, Y.M.C.A., 1917-18; teacher Nat. Training Sch., Y.W.C.A., 1920-25; instr. of religious psychology, Drew Theol. Sem., 1911-23; mem. faculty Teachers Coll., Columbia, summers, 1923-29; asst. prof. religious edn. and psychology, Union Theol. Sem., N.Y., 1922-23, asso. prof., 1923-25, Skinner and McAlpin prof. of practical theology and head dept. religious edn. and psychology since 1925, dir. summer courses, 1937-43. Ordained to ministry of Meth. Ch., 1944. Chmn. bd. trustees, Exptl. Sch., N.Y., since 1948. Member Nat. Council Y.M.C.A.'s; chmn. nat. boys work com. Y.M.C.A.'s, 1927-46; chmn. bd. publs., since 1946. Mem. Religious Edn. Assn. (mem. bd. dirs.; vice pres. 1937-38; pres. 1939-42). Author: Student Standards of Action (with Ethel Cutler), 1914; How Jesus Met Life Questions, 1920; The Bearing of Psychology upon Religion, 1927; The Process of Group Thinking, 1928; Group Discussion in Religious Education, 1930; Solving Personal Problems (with Grace L. Elliott), 1936; Can Religious Education Be Christian?, 1940. Contbr. to religious and ednl. jours. Home: 404 W. 116th St., N.Y. City. Office: 3041 Broadway, N.Y. City 27. Died June 27, 1951.

ELLIOTT, Homer, lawyer; b. Martin County, Ind., Jan. 9, 1878; s. Jacob and Mary Elizabeth (Littell) E.; student Ind. State Normal Sch., Terre Haute, Ind.; 1897, Ind. U., 1898-99; m. Myrtle Leonard, Apr. 19, 1903; children—Martin Kelso, Virginia Evelyn. Admitted to Ind. bar, 1900, began practice at Spencer; U.S. atty. for Dist. of Ind., by appointment of Pres. Harding, Jan. 9, 1922; resigned Jan. 15, 1925, and apptd. spl. asst. to Atty. Gen. of U.S.; prosecuted the Gary Conspiracy and the Hawkins mail fraud cases, also the Gov. Warren T. McCray mail fraud case; judge Morgan Co. Circuit Ct., 1950-July 18, 1952. Mem. Am., Ind. State, Morgan Co., Indpls. bar assns. Republican. Methodist. Mason. Club: Columbia (Indpls.). Home: Martinsville, Ind. Died July 18, 1952; buried Martinsville.

ELLIOTT, Middleton Stuart, ret. naval officer; b. Beaufort, S.C., Oct. 16, 1872; s. Midleton Stuart and Ann (Rhett) E.; M.D., George Washington U., 1894; m. Alice Miller Sherwood, Sept. 14, 1898; children—Caryl Middleton (wife of Philip R. Osborne, USN), Alice Sherwood (wife of Joel Newsom, USN). Med. officer USN, 1896, advanced through grades to vice adm., 1942. Received Medal of Honor. Served in Spanish-Am. War, Philippine Insurrection, Vera Cruz, World War. Mem. Huguenot Soc. S C. Episcopalian. Club: New York Yacht. Home: Beaufort, S.C. Died Nov. 29, 1952.

ELLIOTT, Roy Gordon, greeting card exec.; b Cin., Apr. 18, 1899; s. Gordon and Anna (Meyer) E.; student pub. schs.; m. Gladys Irene Myers, Aug. 28, 1924; children—David Warren, Roy Gordon, Judith Annette. Pres., dir. Gibson Art Co., 1954—. Organized, incoporated and developed the Village of Amberley, 1939, first mayor, and served 3 terms. Mem. C. of C. Clubs: Rotary, Queen City, Cincinnati Country, Hyde Park Golf and Country (Cin.). Home: 7930 Ridge Rd., Cin. 37. Office: 233 W. Fourth St., Cin. 1. Deceased.

ELLIOTT, William Sanders, lawyer; b. Jacksonville, Ill., Feb. 20, 1880; s. Frank and Cornelia (Sanders) E.; A.B., Princeton, 1900; LL.B., Harvard, 1903; m. Ethel Buckingham, June 4, 1910. Practiced in Chgo, 1903—; mem. Holland & Elliott, 1907-12; with legal dept. Internat. Harvester Co., 1912-48, gen. counsel, 1924-46, v.p., 1934-46, sr. cons. 1946-48, ret. Mem. Phi Beta Kappa. Clubs: University, Commercial, Chicago, Princeton, Indian Hill. Home: 1361 Hackberry Lane, Winnetka, Ill. Died May 8, 1957.

ELLIS, Charles Calvert, clergyman, educator; b. Washington, July 21, 1874; s. Henry Jennings and Kate Calvert (Kane) E.; B.E., Juniata Coll., 1890, A.B., 1898, D.D., 1925; A.M., Ill. Wesleyan U., 1903, Ph.D., 1904; Ph.D., U. Pa., 1907; postgrad. Princeton. 1919-20, Harvard, summer 1922; B.D., Temple U., 1920; LL.D., Bridgewater, 1941; m. Emma Susan Nice, Dec. 25, 1902; chidren—Calvert Nice, John Dwight. Tchr. pub. schs., 1890-94; prof. English, Juniata Coll., 1898-99, 1900--01, head dept. edn., 1907-30, v.p., 1917-30, pres., 1930-43, pres. emeritus, 1943—; asso. pastor First Brethren Ch., Phila., 1899-1900, pastor, 1919-21; lyceum lecturer, 1908-13. Asso. Victoria Inst. (Gt. Britain). Mem. N.E.A., Pa. Ednl. Assn., Nat. Soc. for Study of Edn., Soc. Coll. Tchrs. Edn., Pa. Soc. Coll. Tchrs. Edn., English-Speaking Union; mem. Pa. Commn. for Study of Ednl. Problems, 1931-35; mem. exec. com. Pa. coop. Commn. for Study of Tchr. Edn., 1939-43; moderator Church of Brethren Nat. Conv., 1935, 1944; pres. Assn. Coll. Pres. Pa., 1936; pres. Gen. Edn. Board Ch. Brethren, 1931-42; dir. Bethany Bibl. Sem., 1930-47. Rotarian (past pres.). Author: Lancasterian Schools in Philadelphia (thesis), 1907; Studies in Doctrine and Devotion (Part III), 1919; The Religion of Religious Psychology, 1922, 28; The Christian Way of Life, 1924. Frequent speaker at religious and ednl. convs.; author of This Week's Teaching Principle in S. S. Times, 1919-30; His Days and Ours, 1946; Juniata College, History of Seventy Years, 1947. Contbr. to religious and ednl. publs. Home: 1830 Mifflin St., Huntingdon, Pa. Died June 27, 1950; buried Riverview Cemetery, Huntingdon, Pa.

ELLIS, Don Carlos, ednl. film producer; b. N.Y.C., Nov. 14, 1883; s. Benjamin H. and Ella P. (Platt) E.; A.B., Georgetown U., 1904, LL.B., 1908; A.M., Gonzaga, 1906; m. Helen G. Gordon, Oct. 10, 1913 (died Mar. 15, 1953); children—Joan (Mrs. Harry A. Tubbs), Mary Ellen (Mrs. James Orville Gibson), Charles Gordon. Instr. English and history Gonzaga Coll., Washington, 1906-07; in charge ednl. sect. U.S. Forest Service, 1909-17; sect. Nat. Adv. Bd., and v.p. Nat. Conservation Expn., Knoxville, Tenn., 1913; organizer and dir. motion picture sect. U.S. Dept. Agr., 1917-19; dir. ednl. production Universal Film Mfg. Co., 1920; sec. and dir. Nat. Non-Theatrical Motion Pictures, Inc., 1922-25; v.p. Harry Levey Service Corp., 1922-24; sec., treas. and dir. Gen. Vision Co., 1924-25; v.p. and gen. mgr. Bray Screen Products, 1925-27; editor Bray Screen Mag. 1926-27; dir. ednl. service Consolidated Film Industries, 1927-29; pres., gen. mgr. Films of Commerce Co., Inc., 1929-44; sec.-treas., dir. Visual Instrn. dep. N.E.A., 1938-39, treas., dir. N.Y. br., 1935-44; pres. Bd. Edn., Garden City, N.Y., 1932-44; motion picture dir. U.S. Dept. Agr., 1944-47, chief tng. aids div. Med. Illustration Service, Armed Forces Inst. Pathology, 1947—. Republican. Catholic. Author: (with Laura Thornborough) Motion Pictures in Education; writer, newspaper and mag. articles. Home: 1012 20th St. South, Arlington, Va. Office: Armed Forces Inst. Pathology, Washington 25. Died Mar. 15, 1953; buried Columbia Gardens Cemetery, Arlington, Va.

ELLIS, George Adams, lawyer; b. Castleton, Vt., July 25, 1881; s. Horace B. and Alice A. (Adams) E.; student Castleton (Vt.) Normal Sch., 1895-97; Horace Mann Sch., New York City, 1898-99; B.A., Columbia, 1904, LL.B., 1908; LL.D. (hon.) Univ. of Vermont, 1932, also Middlebury College, 1954; married to Margaret Richards; 1 daughter, Ann R. Admitted to New York bar, 1907; with law firm of Simpson, Thacher and Bartlett, New York, 1908-09; partner Booth & Ellis, New York, 1911-13; asst. gen. counsel Union Pacific R.R., New York, 1914-19; partner McKinstry, Taylor, Patterson & Ellis, New York, 1920; partner Clark, Carr & Ellis, New York, 1921—. Admitted to Vermont bar, 1945. Dir. and mem. exec. com. I.C. R.R., 1934-45; chmn. bd. and dir. 1st Nat. Bank of Bennington, Vermont, Vermont Copper Company, Incorporated; dir. New York Shipbuilding Corp.; dir. Moore Pub. Co., Jarka Corp., Avco Mfg. Co., ACF. Brill Corp., Ellis Trust (Vt.). Trustee Columbia Law Review, Bard Coll., Hist. Mus. and Art Gallery Cem. Assn., Bennington, Vermont. Member American Math. Soc. Am. Bar Assn., New York State Bar Assn., Bar Association City of New York, Vermont Bar Association. Republican. Unitarian. Clubs: Bennington, Bennington Country, Nat. Rep. (N.Y.), Tuxedo, Metropolitan (gov.), University, Whist, Wings, Rockefeller Center, (N.Y.C.); Bath and Tennis (gov.) (Palm Beach, Fla.). Home: Monument Av., Bennington, Vt. Office: Bennington, Vt.; also 120 Broadway, N.Y.C. 5. Died Oct. 4, 1955; buried Old Bennington (Vt.) Cemetery.

ELLIS, George Price, Sr., business exec.; b. Chgo., Feb. 10, 1888; s. William Humphrey and Mary (Hogan) E.; grad. sch. commerce, Northwestern, 1917; m. Thayer Carlisle, June 25, 1909; 1 son, George Price. Chief acct., gen. auditor Chgo. Bridge & Iron Co., 1906-16; sr. partner George P. Ellis & Co., C. P.A.'s, Chgo., 1916—; partner Wolf & Co., C.P. A.'s. dir. First Fed. Savs. & Loan Assn. Chgo. Comptroller, tax cons. Nat. Assn. Real Estate Bds.; cons. numerous trade assns.; mem. Nat. Com. Municipal Accounting; mem. bd. judges Louisville Nat. Municipal Finance Officers Award, 1940, 41, 42. Past pres. Agard Deaconess Rest Home, Lake Bluff, Ill.; former mem. bd. mgrs. Meth. Old People's Home, Chgo. Meth. Social Union (past pres.), Laymen's Assn. Rock River Conf. (past pres.); trustee Ill. Masonic Hosp. Mem. bd. dirs. Boys Clubs, 1921—, awarded Bronze Keystone, 1948. Mem. Am. Inst. Accountants (council mem., past pres.), Ill., Ohio, Wis., Tenn. socs. C.P.A.'s, Nat. Assn. Cost Accts., Internat. Accts. Soc. (faculty and exec. ednl. com.), Ill. C. of C. (past pres.), Northwestern U. Gen. Alumni Assn. (past treas.), Northwestern U. Found., Alpha Kappa Psi, Beta Alpha Psi. Methodist. Mason (32°, K.T., Shriner; chmn. finance com. Grand Lodge Ill.).

Clubs: Executives (past pres.), Kiwanis (past pres.), Union League (Chgo.). Author. lectr. profl. and bus. subjects. Home: 1710 Orrington Av., Evanston, Ill. Office: 7 S. Dearborn St., Chgo. Died May 1959.

ELLIS, J(ohn) Breckenridge, author; b. nr. Hannibal, Mo., Feb. 11, 1870; s. John William and Sallie (Breckenridge) E.; A.B., Plattsburg (Mo.) Coll., 1886, A.M., 1900; also good mus. edn.; Litt.D., Culver-Stockton Coll., 1927; unmarried. Prof. English lit., Plattsburg Coll., 1886-97, Central Christian Coll., Albany, Mo., 1900-02; engaged in lit. work, 1902—. Founded Advance Soc. and Ellisan Literary Soc. Edits. Jr. Life Club. Christian Standard, Cin. Pres. Mo. Writers' Guild 5 terms to 1926. Author: In the Days of Jehu, 1898; King Saul, 1898; Shem, Story of Captivity, 1899; The Dread and Fear of Kings, 1900; Garcilaso, 1901; The Holland Wolves, 1902; Adnah, Tale of the Time of Christ, 1902; The Red Box Clew, 1902; The Ellisan Literary Year Book, Nos. I and II, 1903, 1904; The Stork's Nest, 1905; The Keeneyes Series, 1906, 1907; Twin Starrs (dramatized), 1907; Arkinsaw Cousins (dramatized), 1908; Soul of a Serf, 1910; Fated to Win, 1910; Story of a Life, 1910; Something Else, 1911; Fran (dramatized), 1912; Little Fiddler of the Ozarks, 1913; The Third Diamond, 1913; Lahoma, 1913; The Woodneys, 1914; Agnes of the Bad Lands, 1916; His Dear Unintended, 1947; The Picture on the Wall, 1920; The Mysterious Dr. Oliver, 1929; When the Light Burned Low, 1930; Tied Up, 1931; My Window Toward Tibet, 1931; Old Steady, 1932; The Back Number, 1933; Adventure of Living, 1933; Lost and Found., 1934; Ripples from Stones, 1935; Two Masters, 1936; Once There Was a Bear, 1937; A Little Leaven, 1938; Beulah Looks In, 1939; How People Talk!, 1940; Other Things, 1940; Forever and Always, 1941; The Noland Way, 1943; Old Hippo Hunter, 1943. Founder Jr. Life Club and Boy Life Campfire. Address: Granite, Okla. Died Apr. 2, 1956; buried Plattsburg, Mo.

ELLIS, John Dayhuff, surgeon; b. Rensselaer, Ind., July 6, 1886; s. James Hervey Stewart and Jessie (Dayhuff) E.; grad. high sch., Rensselaer, 1905; S. B., U. of Chicago, 1909; M.D., Rush Med. Coll., 1911; Master in Anthropology, University Arizona, 1952; m. Gilberta Lutz, June 10. 1919; children—John Brockus, Liela Baldwin. Practiced medicine in Chicago, 1911—; now serving as senior surgeon St. Luke's Hospital; mem. Medical Corps, United States Army, 1918-19. Fellow Am. Coll. Surgeons (mem. fracture com.); mem. Inst. of Traumatic Surgery (dir.), Am. Assn. for the Surgery of Trauma, Chicago Surg. Soc., Am. Bd. of Surgery, Chicago Literary Soc. Renaissance Soc. U. of Chicago, Phi Delta Theta, Theta Nu Epsilon, Nu Sigma Nu, Sigma Xi, Red Cross of Constantine. Republican. Presbyn. Mason (32°, Shriner). Clubs: University, Caxton (Chgo.). Address: 7440 West 10th St., Denver. Died Mar. 9, 1956; buried Rensselaer, Ind.

ELLIS, Max Mapes, educator; b. Lawrence, Ind., Dec. 3, 1887; s. Horace and Grace (Mapes) E.; grad. Idaho State Normal Sch., 1904; A.B., Vincennes U., 1905, Sc.D., 1914; studied U. Ill., 1906; A.B., Ind. U., 1907, A.M., 1908, Ph.D., 1911; m. Marion Lee Durbin, Sept. 4, 1909; 1 dau., Cornelia Grace. Prof. natural sci. Vincennes U., 1909; fellow in zoölogy Ind. U., 1910-11; inst. biology U. Colo., 1911-14, asst. prof. biology, 1914-18; asst. prof. physiology U. Mo., 1919-23, asso. prof., 1923-27, prof., 1927-36, prof. physiology and pharmacology, 1936—. Dep. entomologist of Ind., summer 1909; in charge of Gimbel Scientific Expdn., British Guiana, 1910; U. Mich. Biol. Station, summers 1913-17; spl. invstigator Colo. State Fish Commn., 1915-18. Served as 1st lt. San Corps, U S. Army, as physiologist in Med. Research Lab. Air Service, 1918-19. Fellow A.A.A.S.; mem. Am. Physiol. Soc., Soc. Exptl. Biol. Medicine, Am. Assn. U. Profs., Sigma Xi, Phi Beta Kappa, Phi Rho Sigma, Kappa Sigma. Author numerous sci. papers on biol. and physiol. subjects. Physiol. research at Physiol. Inst., U. Glasgow, Scotland, and various other univs. in Europe, 1927-28. Home: 101 Willis Av., Columbia, Mo. Died 1953; buried Forest Lawn, Hollywood Hills, Los Angeles.

ELLIS, Ralph, ret. newspaperman; b. Iuka, Kansas, July 27, 1879; s. Wallace Augustus and Catherine Elizabeth (Axline) E.; A.B., U. Kan., 1900; m. Anna L. Orr; 1 dau., Mrs. Walter Bennett. Began as reporter Lawrence (Kan.) Gazette, 1900; later connected with Kansas City World, Kansas City Times and Chgo. Tribune; mng. editor and editor Kansas City Journal-Post, 1921-30; srved as editor Washington Times; now in adveritsing and publicity business, Chgo. Home: 6347 Winthrop Av. Office: 140 S. Dearborn St., Chgo. Deceased.

ELLIS, Thomas David, denominational sec.; b. Quitman County. Ga., Oct. 6, 1868; s. Thomas James and Rebecca (Gay) E.; A.B., Emory U., 1893, D.D., 1910; m. 2d, Vera Dorothy Sanders, Dec. 10, 1924; children of previous marriage—James Branch (dec.), Thomas David, Jr. Ordanined ministry M.E. Ch., S., 1897; pastor successively Blakely, Pelham, Centenary (Macon), Vineville (Macon), Ga.; presiding elder Savannah District; pastor Mulberry St. Ch. (Macon), Wesley Monumental Ch. (Savannah), Mulberry St. Ch. (Macon), all within South Ga. Conf. until 1922; secretary board of Church Extension, Methodist Church, South, 1922-42 (resigned, Dec. 1942). Trustee Wesleyan College, Methodist Orphanage (both Macon, Geo.gia). Mem. Gen. Conf. M.E. Church, S., 8 times, also 1 Spl. Gen. Conf.; mem. Commn. on Ch. Union of M.E. Ch., S., which submitted plan voted upon in 1925, and also mem. commn. which wrote plan for ch. union which has been adopted by M.E. Ch., Meth. Protestant Ch. and M.E. Ch., S.; mem. Uniting Conf., Kansas City, 1939, Gen. Conf. Meth. Ch., Atlantic City, 1940, Jurisdictional Conf., Asheville, 1940. Mem. Alpha Tau Omega. Democrat. Mason. Home: 4774 Rivoli Dr., Macon, Ga. Died July 7, 1952; buried Riverside Cemetery, Macon.

ELLIS, W(illiam R(obert), business exec.; b. Los Gatos, Calif., Sept. 6, 1886; s. John Edward and May (Carpenter) E.; grad. Stanford, 1909; m. Debra O'Keefe, July 2, 1910; children—William Charles, John R., Thomas Francis. In railroad engring. and constrn. work Ocean Shore R.R., San Francisco, part time, 1907-08; mining engring. Hellester Gold Mining Co. and Mariposa Creek Mining Co., California Mother Lode, part time, 1908-09, full time, 1910-13, Mascot Copper Co., Ariz., 1910-13; mem. procurement div. Panama Pacific Expn., 1914-15; explosives engr. Hercules Powder Co., 1915-30, asst. gen. mgr. explosives dept., 1930-34, gen. mgr., 1936-45, vice pres. since 1945, dir. since 1937. Mem. Am. Inst. Mining and Metall. Engrs., Am. Ordnance Assn., Zeta Psi. Republican. Episcopalian. Clubs: Wilmington, Wilmington Country; Family (San Francisco). Home: San Rafael, Cal. Died Jan. 30, 1955; buried Oaklawn Cemetery, San Jose, Cal.

ELLIS, William Thomas, writer; b. Allegheny, Pa., Oct. 25, 1873; s. Charles H. and Mary E. (Davis) E.; pub. sch. edn.; LL.D., Davidson Coll., 1913, Litt.D., Temple U., 1939; m. Margaret H. McKinnon, Oct. 3, 1899; children—Franklin Courtney, Mackinnon, Margaret Amelia. On staff Phila. dailies till 1894; editor the Internat. Christian Endeavor Organ, 1894-97; editor Forward, Presbyn. weekly, 1897-1902; on editorial staff Phila. dailies; toured the world investigating social religious and polit. conditions for syndicate of Am. newspapers, 1906-07, 10-11; toured Chinese famine field, winter of 1906-07, and by writings raised over million dollars for relief; at his suggestion in personal interview Pres. Theodore Roosevelt invited Chinese students to America and had govt. allocate part of Indemnity Fund for their support; interviewed Delai Lama, Kigng Ibn Saud of Arabia, last Sultan of Turkey, last Caliph of Islam; early writer about his friend, Lawrence of Arabia; travel in Russia, 1917, reporting revolution and advent of Bolshevism for Sat. Eve. Post; war corr. Russian, Persian, Caucasus, Rumanian and French fronts, 1917-18; the only corr. present at the first all-Am. action of the War, Battle of Apresmont; spl. corr. N.Y. Herald and asso. newspapers in Balkans, Turkey, Egypt, 1919; rep. Chgo. Daily News and asso. newspapers at Conf. on Limitation of Armament, Washington, 1921-22; in Near East for Sat. Eve. Post and other mags., 1923. Made complete tour of Bible lands, identifying real site of Kadeshbarnea in Mid-Sinai, 1925-26, revisited Sinai, Akaba and Petra, 1930; in Palestine and Near East for Herald-Tribune, 1938. Has lectured and addressed many conventions, especially of churchmen, in all parts of country; several seasons on Chautauqua circuits; writer of S.S. lessons in syndicate of newspapers, 1897—. Candidate for Congress, 1922. Sec. commn. on Christian publicity Men and Religion Movement, New York, 1912, and edited and largely wrote its vol. The Church and the Press. Author: Men and Missions; Billy Sunday—the Man and His Message; Advertising the Church; Bible Lands Today, 1927; Pilgrim Fare from Bible Lands, 1940; As the Shepherds Saw It, 1946. Contbr. mags.; newspaper columnist. Clubs: Cosmos, National Press, Overseas Writers (Washington). Author of Religion Day by Day and A Daily Prayer in War-Time, syndicated daily newspaper features. Originator of Nat. Recognition Day for Sunday Sch. Tchrs. Home: 28 N. Belmont St., York, Pa.; (summer) Lyndhurst, Ont. Died Aug. 14, 1950; buried Lyndhurst.

ELLISON, George Robb, judge; b. Canton, Mo., July 22, 1881; s. William Cowgill and Laura (Lucas) E.; A.B., Harvard, 1903; student in law, U. of Mo., 1903-04. Admitted to Mo. bar, in 1904; in practice, Maryville, 1904-07; mem. firm Shinabarger, Blagg & Ellison, 1907-27; commr. Supreme Ct. of Mo., 1927-30, jurge since 1931; city atty. Maryville, 1905-07; mem. Pub. Library Bd., 1908-12. Mem. Am. Law Inst., Am. and Mo. State bar assns. Democrat. Mason, Elk. Clubs: Country (Jefferson City and Maryville). Address: Supreme Court Bldg., Jefferson City, Mo. Died July 17, 1957; buried Jefferson City, Mo.

ELLISTON, Grace, actress; b. Memphis, Tenn., 1878; d. George R. and Sarah Virginia (Tarpley) Rutter; ed. St. Mary's Episcopal Sch. and pub. schs. Appeared in Wizard of the Nile, Casino Theatre, New York, 1895, in Two Escutcheons, Garden Theatre, 1896; played in Americans at Home, 1899, The Ambassador, 1900, The Shades of Night, 1901, Chattanooga, Grand Opera House, Chicago, 1901; in Arizona, on tour; appeared in The Importance of Being Earnest, at Columbia Theatre, San Francisco, with Henry Miller, 1902; played in The Only Way, same theatre, 1902; leading woman with Nat Goodwin, in The Usurper, 1904; played in A Blot in the Scutcheon, 1905, The Lion and the Mouse, Lyceum Theatre, 2 yrs., The Rector's Garden, 1908, Falling Leaves, 1908, The Devil, with George Arliss, 1908; starred in Jacquelin, 1909, Nest of Kin, 1910; played in Her Husband's Wife, with Henry Miller, 1910; appeared in Coming Home to Roost, 1912, Black Fear (moving picture), 1914; played in The Shadow, with Ethel Barrymore, at Empire Theatre, New York, 1915; appeared in The Country Cousin, Gayety Theatre, 1917, The Lucky One, Garrick Theatre, 1922. Contbr. articles about the theatre to the Springfield Republican. Home: Stockbridge, Mass.; and New York, N.Y. Died Dec. 1950.

ELLISTON, Herbert Berridge, editor; b. Wakefield, Yorkshire, Eng., Nov. 15, 1895; s. Frederick Thomas and Elizabeth (Berridge E.; came to U.S., 1921; m. Mildred Foster, 1923; 1 son, Stephen Foster; m. 2d. Joanne Shaw, August 9, 1941; 2 sons, Peter Berridge and Michael Shaw. Began as reporter on Midland Daily Telegraph (Coventry), Portsmouth Evening News, foreign correspondent Manchester Guardian and The New York Herald; editorial writer New York Herald. 1922-23; economic adviser, Chinese Govt., 1925-27; asst. director of research (economist), Council on Foreign Relations, New York, N. Y., 1927-30; joined Christian Science Monitor, 1930, financial editor and columnist, 1933-40; now editor Washington Post. Served as signaller in Royal Horse Arty., 1915-18, recommended on the field for commn., disch. as cadet. Awarded Pulitzer prize for editorial writing, 1949; decorated by Finnish, Belgian Governments, 1956. Mem. Am. Econ. Assn., Council on Foreign Relations, Royal Economic Society. Clubs: Century (New York); Royal Societies (London, Eng.); Cosmos, Metropolitan, National Press (all Washington, D.C.). Co-author and asso. editor, Am. Foreign Relations, 1927-30, yearly vol. pub. by Council on Fng. Relations, New York, N.Y. Author: Finland Fights. Contbr. to American and foreign press. Home: 2500 Massachusetts Av. N.W. Office: Washington Post, Washington. Died Jan. 22, 1957; buried Rock Creek Cemetery, Washington.

ELLMAKER, Lee, publisher and editor; b. Lancaster, Pa., Aug. 7, 1896; s. Alfred and Mary (Hess) E.; ed. West. Phila. High Sch., 1910-14; m. Myrtle Wolfe, Sept. 15, 1921; children—Lee, Jr., William. Employed as newspaper reporter, 1913-15; pvt. sec. to Hon. William S. Vare, 1915-18; v.p. Nat. City Bur., Washington, D.C., 1918-25, corr. for Internat. News Service, 1919-23; organized, 1926, and since pub. Phila. Daily News; pub. Liberty and other publs. for Macfadden Publications, 1927-31; pub. Pictorial Review, 1931-33; pub. Woman's World, 1932-40, Teck Publications, 1930-38; pres. Excello, Woman's World and Pictorial Review Pattern Cos., 1931-35; pres. Philadelphia Daily News, Inc. In radio service, U.S. Navy, 1918. Republican. Mason. Home: 37 Green Hill Lane, Phila. 31. Address: Daily News, 22nd and Arch Sts., Phila. 1. Died Mar. 27, 1951; buried West Laurel Hill Cemetery, Phila.

ELLSWORTH, Albert LeRoy, oil exec.; b. Welland, Ont., Can., July 2, 1876; s. George Alfred and Elizabeth (Foster) E.; student pub. schs. of Welland; m. Bessie B. Burgar, Aug. 31, 1907; 1 son, 3 daus. Established Brit. Am. Oil Co., Ltd., Toronto, 1906, pres. since 1927, now chmn. bd.; pres. Internat. Metal Industries, Ltd.; dir. Brit. Am. Oil Producing Co., Tulsa, Toronto Pipe Line Co., Tulsa (Del. corps.); chmn. bd. Toronto Iron Works, Ltd.; dir. other cos. Deceased.

ELLSWORTH, Franklin Fowler, lawyer, ex-congressman; b. St. James, Minn., July 10, 1879; s. Clinton and Louise (Manning) E.; student academic dept., U. Minn., 1897-99; LL.N., U. Minn., 1901; m. Lurline Mae Bader, July 27, 1902 (died Nov. 8, 1935); m. 2d, Florence R. Struthers, May 7, 1938. Admitted to Minn. bar, 1901; practiced St. James, Minn., 1901-10; became mem. Hughes & Ellsworth, Mankato, Minn., 1910. City atty., St. James, 1902-03, county atty., 1905-08; mem. 64th to 66th Congresses (1915-21), 2d Minn. Dist.; candidate at primaries for Rep. nom. for gov. of Minn., 1924. Mem. Ellsworth, Clinite & Drills. Pvt. Co. H, 12th Minn. Vols., Spanish-Am. War. Mem. Minn. State Bar Assn., Minn. Lawyers' Assn. (pres.), United Spanish War Vets., Mu Sigma, Phi Gamma Delta. Mason; mem. K. of P. (past Grand Chancellor for Minn.). Clubs: Commercial, North Minneapolis. Author: The Band Wagon, 3d edit., 1921. Home: 4858 Fremont Av., S. Office: McKnight Bldg., Mpls. 9. Died 1942; buried Lakewood Cemetery, Mpls.

ELLSWORTH, Fred Winthrop, banker; b. Battle Creek, Mich., June 27, 1872; s. Alfred Almeron and Mary Ellen (Iden) E.; ed. high sch., Battle Creek, Bryant & Stratton Bus. Coll., Chgo., and YMCA Sch., Chgo. grad. Am. Inst. Banking, N.Y.C., 1911; m. Emma Rosa Fairman, Aug. 12, 1897; children—Margaret L., Lois Winifred (dec.). Clk. First Nat. Bank, Chgo., 1892-1905, advt. mgr., 1905-09; same, Guaranty Trust Co., N.Y.C., 1910-16, sec., 1916-18; v.p. Hibernia Bank & Trust Co., New Orleans, 1918-33; v.p. Hibernia Nat. Bank, New Orleans, 1933-46;

ret. 1946. Mem. sch. bd., Westfield, N.J., 1916-18; dir. New Orleans Hosp. Service Assn., New Orleans Better Bus. Bur. (1930-46); mem. Nat. Citizens Com. for Welfare and Relief Mobilization, 1932; dir. New Orleans YMCA (pres. 1921-26); pres. Assn. Res. City Bankers, 1920, Chgo. chpt. Am. Inst. Banking, 1907; mem. Am. Bankers Assn., 1916-46 (chmn. bank mgmt. commn. 1930), Financial Pub. Relations Assn. (pres. 1919; sr. adv. council); chmn. finance com. New Orleans br. Brit. War Relief Co., 1941-46; mem. exec. com. New Orleans U.S.O.-Y.M.C.A., 1942-46, New Orleans United Community and War Chest, 1942-45; mem. New Orleans war price and rationing bd. OPA, 1943-46; W. O. New Orleans regt. Vol. Port Security Force of USCG, 1943-45. Mem. New Orleans Assn. Commerce, 1918—, treas., 1923-24, dir., 1923-24, 1933. Presbyn. Author of "Battle Creek High School," 1937; "B.C.H.S. '91—50th Anniversary," 1941; also booklets and pamphlets. Contbr. bus. and 15. Office: Hibernia Bank Bldg., New Orleans 12. financial publs. Home: 13 Richmond Pl., New Orleans Deceased.

ELLSWORTH, Lincoln, explorer, civil engr.; b. Chgo., May 12, 1880; s. James William and Eva (Butler) E.; prep. edn. Hill Sch., Pottstown, Pa.; student Columbia 2 years; M.S., Yale; LL.D., Kenyon Coll.; m. Mary Louise Ulmer, May 23, 1933. Axman on 1st survey Grand Pacific R.R. surveys of transcontinental route across Canada, 1902-07, then resident engr. Prince Rupert Terminal; later resident engr. on constrn. work west of Montreal, C.P. Ry.; prospector for gold, Peace River, 1909; became asst. engr. Kougarock Mining Co., Alaska, 1910; organizer Ellsworth Expdn., sponsored by Johns Hopkins, making geol. cross section of Andes Mountains from Pacific Ocean to headwarters of the Amazon, 1924; condr. and navigator N 24 on Amundsen-Ellsworth Polar Flying Expdn., reaching 88° N. Latitude; co-leader of Amundsen-Ellsworth-Nobile Transpolar flight from Kingsbay, Spitzbergen, to Teller, Alaska, May 11-13, 1926; dir. of scientific investigation Wilkins-Ellsworth Trans-Arctic Submarine Expdn., 1931; represented Am. Geog. Soc. on Graf Zeppelin Arctic flight, 1931; made airplane flight of 2,300 miles, crossing Antarctic, Nov. 1935; in recognition of this flight and for claiming 30,000 square miles of new land for U.S., awarded special gold medal by Congress; in 1939 made flight into interior of Antarctica on Indian Ocean side, south of Australia, claiming 81,000 square miles of ty. for U.S. Lt. comdr. USNR. Fellow Am. Museum Nat. History, Royal Geog. Soc.; asso. mem. Am. Soc. C.E.; hon. fellow and trustee Am. Mus., New York; trustee Western Reserve Acad., Hudson, O. Decorated Comdr. 1st Class Order St. Olav (Norway); awarded gold medal by Norwegian Parliament for saving 2 companions from drowning, 1925; awarded Great King Humbert medal of Italian Geog. Soc., 1920; Grand Cross Order of St. Olav, Norway, 1926; spl. gold medal, by President Hoover from Congress of U.S., 1931; David Livingston Centenary medal, Am. Geog. Soc.; Hubbard gold medal, Nat. Geog. Soc., also Explorer's gold medal; Elisha Kent Kane gold medal, Phila. Geog. Soc.; gold medal, Geog. Soc. of Chicago; Patron's gold medal, Royal Geog. Soc. Clubs: Union, Century Association, Explorers, Boone and Crockett (New York). Author: The Last Wild Buffalo Hunt, 1915; (with Capt. Roald Amundsen) Our Polar Flight, 1925; First Crossing of the Polar Sea, 1926; Search, 1932; Beyond Horizons, 1938. Address: care Morris & McVeigh, 60 Wall St., N.Y.C. Died May 26, 1951; buried Hudson, O.

ELMAN, Robert, surgeon; b. Boston, Mass., Nov. 9, 1897; s. Samuel and Bessie Marian (Schmidt) E.; B.S., Harvard, 1919; M.D., Johns Hopkins, 1922; m. Mima Kreykenbohn, June 15, 1928. Resident house officer Johns Hopkins, 1922-23; asst. in pathology Rockefeller Inst., 1923-25; mem. teaching staff Washington U. Med. Sch., St. Louis, since 1925, now prof. clin. surgery; asso. surgeon Barnes Hosp. and St. Louis Children's Hosp.; in pvt. practice surgery, St. Louis, since 1928. Dir. surg. service and chief of staff Homer Philips Hosp. Mem. committee on infected wounds and burns, committee on convalescence and rehabilitation, National Research Council, 1943-45. Member National Professional Advisory Council, Office of Vocational Rehabilitation, Federal Security Administration (chairman Missouri State Office of Vocatonal Rehabilitation Advisory Council). Diplomate American Bd. Surgery; fellow A.C.S., A.A. A.S., Internat. Soc. Surgery; mem. Harvey Society, Am. Surgical Assn., Am. Gastroenterological Assn. (president, 1955). Society Exptl. Biology and Med. (pres. Mo. sect. 1948), American Medical Association, Phi Beta Kappa, Alpha Omega Alpha, Sigma Xi. Author: (with Warren H. Cole) Textbook of General Surgery, 5 edits. since 1936; Parenteral Alimentation in Surgery, 1946 (awarded the quinquennial Samuel D. Gross award, Phila. Acad. of Surgery, 1945); numerous single chapters in surg. texts, many papers on surg. subjects including first report on use plasma transfusions in burns and on successful use of amino acid mixtures injected intravenously in the human for parenteral protein feeding; mem. editorial bd. of Gastroenterology, Archives of Surgery. Home: 4456 Maryland Av., St. Louis 8. Office: 600 S. Kingshighway, St. Louis 10. Died Dec. 23, 1956.

ELMEN, Gustaf Waldemar, elec. engr.; b. Stockholm, Sweden, Dec. 22, 1876; s. Claes Julius and Josephine (Ericson) E.; B.S., U. of Neb., 1902, M.A., 1904, D.Eng., 1932; m. Ruth M. Halvorsen, 1907; children—James Frederick, Richard Spencer, Paul Halvorsen; came to U.S., 1893, naturalized, 1918. Fellow in physics, U. of Neb., 1902-04; elec. engr. for Gen. Electric Co., 1904-06, for Western Electric Co., 1906-25, for Bell Telephone labs., 1925-41; magnetic consultant for Naval Ordnance Lab., Washington Navy Yard, 1941—. Mem. Sigma Xi. Awarded John Scott medal by City of Philadelphia, 1927, Elliott Cresson medal by Franklin Inst., Phila., 1928. Modern Pioneer Award Nat. Assn. Mfrs., 1940. Republican. Inventor magnetic materials used in elec. communications. Author of papers on magnetic properties of alloys. Home: 104 High St., Leonia, N.J. Address: Naval Ordnance Laboratory, Navy Yard, Washington. Died Dec. 10, 1957.

ELMER, William, railroading; b. Trenton, N.J., Sept. 29, 1870; s. William and Alice (Gray) E.; E.E., Princeton, 1894; m. Helen Gray, Sept. 12, 1906; children—William, Marie Louise (Mrs. Austin Woody). Apprentice, Meadows shops, Pa. R.R., 1896-1900; supt. electric ry. Atlantic City, N.J., 1900; asst. master mechanic, Altoona (Pa.) machine shops, 1900-02; asst. engr. motive power, Pa. R.R., Altoona, Pa., 1903-05, master mechanic, Pitts. div., 1905-11, supt. motive power No. div., Buffalo, 1911-16, supt. Schuylkill div., 1916-18, Phila. div., 1919-20, Middle div., 1920-26, asst. engr., chief engr.'s office, Phila., 1927-35, ret. from railroad work, 1935; tax assessor, Bay Head, N.J., 1940—. Decorated by King of the Belgians, 1919. Fellow Am. Soc. M.E.; mem. Am. Inst. E.E. Home: 32 North St., Bay Head, N.J.; also 222 South River Dr., Rockledge, Fla. Died May 6, 1947.

ELMER, William Price, lawyer, ex-congressman; b. Robertsville, Mo., Mar. 2, 1871; s. William John Horace and Sarah Elizabeth (Wagoner) E.; student Wingo Law Sch., 1890-92; m. Amie Adelmann, Dec. 9, 1896; children—William Doss (dec.), Victorene Dale (Mrs. W. C. Whitmire), McVeigh Adelmann, Billie Ruth (Mrs. R. W. Dent, dec.), Vivian Katrina (Mrs. F. G. Gatlin), Helen Willene (Mrs. J. E. Turner), Amelia Imogene (Mrs. Myron Hamilton), Lucille (dec.), Dorothy Elizabeth (Mrs. Charles Horn). Practiced Mo. courts, 1892—; pros. atty. Dent County, 1895-96, 1905-06, organized First Nat. Bank of Salem, Mo., 1906, Salem Light and Power Co., 1909; mem. 78th Congress, 8th Mo. Dist. Chmn. Dent County Rep. Com., 1906—; del. and alternate to Rep. Nat. Convs., 1904, 08, 12, 20; mem. Mo. Gen. Assembly, 1903, 21, 29, 31; party floor leader Mo. Ho. of Reps., 1931; originator of Old Age Pension law in Mo. Mem. 19th Jud. Bar Assn. Mo. (pres. 1938), Mo. Bar Assn., Lawyers Bar Assn., St. Louis, C. of C. Republican. Mason (32°). Home: Salem, Mo. Died May 11, 1956; buried Cedar Grove Cemetery, Salem.

ELMORE, George Sutherland, lawyer; b. Washington, Aug. 14, 1915; s. Alfred Robert and Edith Lee (Sutherland) E.; Diploma, Sidwell Friends Sch., 1933; A.B., Dartmouth Coll., 1937; student Cornell Law Sch., 1937-39; LL.B., Cath. U. Am., 1941; m. Mary Everett Marlow, June 29, 1938; children—George Sutherland, Edith Lee. Admitted to D.C. bar, 1941; asso. Covington, Burling, Rublee, Acheson & Shorb, Washington, 1941-42; sr. partner Elmore & Moore 1947—; v.p., dir. Wyo. Minerals Resources Corp.; sec., dir. Nuclear Magnetics, Inc. (Fla.); dir. Am. Mining & Development Co., Capital Res. Corp., Silver Sage Oil & Mineral Co. (Wyo.), Lt., USNR, 1944—, active duty, 1942-45; asst. counsel Bur. Ordnance, Office Gen. Counsel for Navy, 1946-47. Mem. Am., Fed., D C. bar assns., Sigma Nu, Phi Delta Phi. Episcopalian. Clubs: Capitol Hill, Sertoma, Metropolitan. Home: 5208 38th St., Washington 15. Office: 3900 Ingomar St., Washington 15; also Ring Bldg., Washington 6. Died Jan. 9, 1955; buried Arlington Nat. Cemetery.

ELMSLIE, George Grant, architect; b. Aberdeenshire, Scotland, Feb. 20, 1871; s. John and Jane (Wans) E.; ed. Duke of Gordon Schs., Huntly, Aberdeenshire, Scotland; came to U.S., 1885; m. Bonnie Marie Hunter (A.B., Wellesley Coll.), Oct. 12, 1910 (died 1912). Pupil in architecture with Adler & Sullivan, Chicago, 1890-95; asso. with Louis H. Sullivan in planning and designing, 1895-1910; in partnership with W. G. Purcell and George Feick, Jr., 1910-12, and with Purcell, 1912-20; practiced alone in Chicago since 1920. Fellow A.I.A. Democrat. Presbyterian. Author papers on architecture, etc. Home: 5723 Blackstone Av., Chgo. Died Apr. 23, 1952.

ELOFSON, Carl L., business exec.; b. Chicago, Dec. 23, 1893; s. Carl and Emma (Nero) E.; ed. public school and business coll.; m. Nellie Holmberg, Jan. 2, 1918; 1 son, Carl L. Began as mail boy, Internat. Harvester Co., later with advt. and sales depts.; became salesman New York branch Art Metal Construction Co., Jamestown, N.Y., 1918, branch mgr., Baltimore, Phila., and Chicago, later Western sales mgr., hdqrs., Chicago, then in charge all branches, Jamestown, 1934-36, vice pres. in charge sales, 1936-48, exec. vice pres., 1948—, also mem. bd. dirs. and mem. exec. com. Served with U.S. Air Force 1917-18. Home: 46 Westminster Dr. Office: Art Metal Constrn. Co., Jamestown, N.Y. Died Feb. 21, 1954; buried Lakeview Cemetery, Jamestown, N.Y.

ELROD, Ralph (Perry), bacteriologist; b. Oakland, Cal., Jan. 17, 1913; s. Ralph Leroy and Rose (Gyson) E.; A.B., Brown U., 1936, M.S., 1938; Ph.D., Ohio State U., 1941; m. Elizabeth Virginia Keefe, Oct. 30, 1942; children—Perry Keefe, Ralph George. Instr. Brown U., Providence, 1940-41; asso. Rockefeller Inst., Princeton, N.J., 1941-47; prof., chmn. dept. microbiology U. S.D., 1947—. Served as maj. San. Corps, U.S. Army, 1942-45, bacteriologist, serologist, and parasitologist. Mem. Am. Assn. Immunologists, Soc. Am. Bacteriol., Sigma Xi, Alpha Tau Omega. Author numerous articles in field of microbiology. Home: 920 E. Clark St. Office: U.S.D., Vermillion, S.D. Deceased.

ELSON, Henry William, historian, lecturer; b. Muskingum County, O., Mar. 29, 1857; s. Jacob and Clara (Swingle) E.; A.B., Thiel Coll., Pa., 1886, A.M., 1889; grad. Luth. Theol. Sem., Phila., 1889; spl. student U. Pa., 1895-96; Litt.D., Newberry Coll., 1906; m. Hannah E. Smith, 1889 (died 1895); children—Delma Viola, Harold Altair, Winfred Paul; m. 2d, Ida S. MacMullan, 1898. Pastor St. John's Evangelical Luth. Ch., Kittanning, Pa., 1889-93. St. Stephens, Phila., 1893-95; resigned the ministry and became writer and lecturer of Univ. Extension Soc. of Phila.; prof. history and econs. Ohio U., 1905-16; pres. Thiel Coll., Greenville, Pa., 1916-21; lectr. history N.Y.U., 1927-32. Mem. Ohio Constl. Conv., 1912; author proposal to enable three-fourths of a jury to render a verdict. Pres. Ohio Valley Hist. Assn., 1914-15. Del. Dem. Nat. Conv., St. Louis, 1916. Author: Side Lights on American History, 2 vols., 1899, 1900 (republished, 1928); Historical Biographies for Children—Andrew Jackson, U.S. Grant, Daniel Boone and Frances Willard, 1899; How to Teach History, 1901; Star-Gazer's Hand-Book, 1902; History of the United States, 1904, enlarged edit., 1926, rev., 1945, trans. revised, brought to date, 1945, into French, 1927, Spanish, 1932; History of the United States (5 vols.), 1906; A Guide to American History, 1909; Guide to English History, 1911; Modern Times, and the Living Past, 1921 (high school world history over one million sold); United States—Its Past and Present, 1925; Through the Years with Our Constitution, 1937. Wrote nearly 4 vols. of Review of Reviews' Photographic History of the Civil War, 1911. Home: 1314 Watchung Av., Plainfield, N.J. Died Jan. 29, 1954; buried Hillside Cemetery, Plainfield.

ELSTAD, Rudolph T., mining co. exec.; b. Independence, Wis., Aug. 23, 1895; s. James and Anne (Torgeson) E.; B.S., U. Minn., 1919; m. Elizabeth Dougher, Sept. 29, 1923; children—Elizabeth, Margaret. With Oliver Iron Mining Div., U.S. Steel Corp., Duluth, 1919—, successively mining engr., asst. gen. mining capt., asst. supt., asst. to v.p., asst. gen. mgr., gen. mgr., v.p. and gen. mgr., 1919-46, pres., 1946—. Dir. Duluth Community Chest, St. Luke's Hosp. Assn. Trustee Carleton College. Mem. Am. Iron Ore Assn. (dir.), Am. Mining Congress (dir.), Am. Inst. Mining and Metall. Engrs., Am. Iron and Steel Inst., C. of C. (dir.). Conglist. Clubs: Duquesne (Pitts.); Minneapolis, Mesabi Country, Kitchi Gammi, Northland Country, Rotary, Duluth Athletic. Home: 3018 E. 2d St. Office: Wolvin Bldg., Duluth, Minn. Died Dec. 1959.

ELTING, Howard, retired mfr.; b. N.Y.C., Feb. 15, 1869; s. Philip and Harriet (HasBrouck) E.; B.S. in Civil Engring., Rutgers, 1890; m. Florence West, Jan. 17, 1903; children—Carroll (Mrs. James M. Bovard), Howard. With local frt. office C., B.&Q.R.R., Chgo., 1891, later in claim dept. at St. Louis, and chief clk. to gen. frt. agt.; traveling frt. agt., gen. agt. and div. frt. agt. Hannibal & St. Joseph R.R. until 1900; local agt. and asst. supt. terminals of Burlington System, at St. Louis, until 1904; mem. of Adams & Elting Co., mfrs. paints, Chgo., 1904-19; pres. Health & Milligan Mfg. Co., paints, 1919-24; dir. Chgo. Commons. Trustee Rutgers Coll., 1910-15. Chmn. U.S.O., Santa Barbara. Mem. Chgo. Assn. Commerce (sr. council; gen. sec. 1910, v.p. 1912, pres. 1913), Nat. Paint, Oil and Varnish Assn. (pres. 1917) Field (life), Art Inst. (life), Delta Phi. Republican. Presbyterian. Clubs: Commercial (pres. 1920, Chicago); Valley Club of Santa Barbara. Home: 232 San Leandro Lane, Santa Barbara, Cal.; (summer) New Platz, N.Y. Died Mar. 21, 1954; buried New Platz.

ELTING, Victor, lawyer; b. Yonkers, N.Y., Oct. 13, 1871; s. Ezekiel Jan and Katherine Bevier (Hulbert) E.; A.B., Columbia, 1891; LL.B., U. of Mich., 1892; m. Mrs. Marie Winston Walker, Aug. 1, 1904 (died July 12, 1932); children—Victor, Winston, John. Admitted to Ill. bar in 1892; master in chancery of Superior Court, 1899-1906; trustee Civic Fedn. and Bureau of Public Efficiency. Pres. City Homes Assn., 1906-10; pres. Chicago Sch. of Civics and Philanthropy, 1908, until merged with U. of Chicago, 1920; dir. Nat. Housing Assn., 1911-13; pres. City Club of Chicago, 1906-08. Mem. New Trier Township High School Board, 1906-09, pres. 1909.

Trustee Knox Coll. Galesburg, Ill.; ex-pres. of English Speaking Union, Chicago. Mem. Am. Ill. State and Chicago bar assns., Law Club, Legal Club (ex-pres.), Am. Law Inst. (charter mem.), Chicago Council on Foreign Relations (ex-pres.), Council on Foreign Relations, New York, Columbia Alumni Assn. of Ill. (ex-pres.), League of Nations Association of New York. Vice-pres. United Nations Association (N. Y. and Washington). Dir. Greer Sch., Hope Farm, N.Y. National director American Protective League (auxiliary to Department of Justice), World War I. Decorated Médaille de la Réconnissance Française; awarded Columbia Univ. Medal of Excellence, 1936. Republican. Episcopalian. Clubs: University (Chicago); Century Assn., St. Andrews Golf (New York); Huron Mountain (Mich.); St. Maurice Fish and Game (Quebec). Author of Round the World—A Diary; Recollections of a Grandfather; various articles, travel narratives and revs. Home: University Club, 76 E. Monroe St., Chgo. Died Aug. 20, 1956; buried New Paltz, N.Y.

ELTON, J. O., metallurgist; b. Wash., 1879; s. J. W. and Mary J. (Davis) E.; student Wash. State Coll., 1899-1902; B.S. in Mining Engring., U. of Ida., 1909, hon. Metall. Engr., 1920; m. May McKenzie, May 9, 1904; children—James W., Richard M. Asst. testing engr., Anaconda Copper Mining Co., 1909-10; supt. Success Mine, Wallace, Ida., 1911-12; metallurgist, Anaconda Smelter Commn., 1913-15; supt. electrolytic zinc plants, Anaconda Copper Mining Co., 1916-18; asst. gen. supt., same, Great Falls, Mont., 1918-21; mgr. Internat. Smelting Co. and subsidiaries, 1921—; pres. North Lily Mining Co., Yankee Consol. Mining Co., Park Premier Mining Co., Pelleyere Mining Co., Mountain City Copper Co.; v.p. Walker Mining Co.; mgr. Tooele Valley R.R.; dir. Park Utah Consol. Mining Co.; v.p., gen. mgr. Nat. Tunnel & Mines Co.; v.p. Utah State Bldg. Commn. Pvt. U.S. Vols., in Philippines, 1898-99. Mem. Am. Inst. Mining and Metall. Engrs. (dir.; James Douglas medalist, 1932), Am. Chem. Soc., Am. Electro-Chem. Soc., Am. Zinc Inst. (v.p.). Republican. Clubs: Alta (Salt Lake City); Chemists (New York). Home: Highway 52, New Port Richey, Fla. Died Dec. 1, 1956; buried Pine Hill Cemetery.

ELWOOD, Robert Arthur, clergyman; lectr.; b. Newburgh, N.Y., Nov. 27, 1873; s. James and Mary Eggleson (Hoy) E.; student Cedarville (O.) Coll., 1894-95; Ref. Presbyn. Sem., Phila., 1895-96; Princeton Theol. Sem., 1896-97 (non-grad.); m. Eva Madden, Feb. 22, 1900; children—Russell M. and 4 not living. Began as office boy with F. Middleton & Co., Phila., later with John Wanamaker; entered evangelistic work, 1897; ordained Presbyn. ministry, 1899; pastor Absecon, N.J., until 1901, Olivet Ch., Wilmington, Del., 1901-05, 1st Ch., Leavenworth, Kan., 1905-08; founder, 1909, and pastor Boardwalk Ch., Atlantic City, N.J.; only ch. of kind in the world: "no members, no officers, no choir and no collection plates"; ret. 1940. Served two enlistments Pa. Nat. Guard; cpl. 6th Pa. Vols., Spanish-Am. War, 1898; YMCA worker early part World War; grad. Chaplains' Sch., Camp Taylor, Louisville, 1918; acting chaplain 157th F.A., 82d Div., Camp Gordon, Ga., 1918; chaplain O.R.C., U.S. Army. Mem. Presbytery of W. Jersey. Presbyn. Ch. U.S.A.; mem. Hotel Greeters Am.; nat. chaplain Nat. Restaurant Assn., 1928-30; chaplain N.J. Exempt Firemen's Assn., 1931—. Mem. United Spanish War Vets. (chaplain in chief 1911, 18), Lion, Kiwanian. Author: Meditations, 1900; Model Conditions of Life, 1904; He Is Coming, 1907; Travel Talks, 1915. Contbr. mags. Home: "Rest-Haven," Absecon, N.J. Died Sept. 18, 1949.

ELY, Hanson Edward (ē'lē), army officer; b. Independence, Ia., Nov. 23, 1867; s. Eugene Hanson and Julia (Lamb) E.; grad. U.S. Mil. Acad., 1891; distinguished grad. Inf. and Cav. Sch., 1905; grad. Army Staff Coll., 1906; m. Eleanor Boyle, July 6, 1910. Commd. 2d lt. 22d Inf., 1891, advanced through grades to col. (temp.), 1917; brig.-gen. to maj. gen. Nat. Army, 1918, brig. gen. to major gen. U.S. Army, 1923. Served in Mont., N.D. and Neb., 1891-97; prof. mil. sci. and tactics State U. Ia., 1897-98; with regt. at Camp Wikoff, N.Y., 1898; in Philippines, 1899-1901; comd. Gen. Funston's mounted scouts, later regtl. adj. and adj. gen. 3d Dist., Dept. So. Luzon; observer German maneuvers and studying European armies, 1906; in Philippines, 1907-12; arrived in France, 1917; apptd. col. 28th Inf., 1918; apptd. comdr. 3d Brigade Inf., 2d Div., 1st Army Corps, AEF, 1918, comdr. 5th Div. 3d Army Corps, 1918; comd. 28th Inf. when it captured Cantigny, and the 5th Div. when it forced Meuse crossing; ret. 1931. Decorated D.S.C., D.S.M. (U.S.); Comdr. Legion of Honor; also Officer Legion of Honor; 5 Croix de Guerre. Clubs: Army and Navy (Washington and Manila); Chevy Chase (Washington); Golf and Country (Des Moines, Ia.). Address: 2540 Massachusetts Av. N.W., Washington. Died Apr. 28, 1958; buried Arlington Nat. Cemetery.

ELY, Joseph Buell, lawyer, corp. exec.; b. Westfield, Mass., Feb. 22, 1881; s. Henry Wilson and Sarah N. (Buell) E.; A.B., Williams Coll., 1902, LL.D., 1931; LL.B., Harvard, 1905, also Wesleyan U., Holy Cross Coll.; m. Harriet Z. Dyson, May 1, 1906; 1 son, Richard. Began practice of law at Westfield, 1905; apptd. dist. atty. Berkshire and Hampden counties, 1915, elected, 1916; gov. of Mass., 1931-35; sr. partner Ely, Bradford, Bartlett, Thompson & Brown at Westfield, 1935—, also Ely, King, Kingsbury & Corcoran at Springfield; pres., dir. Am. Woolen Co.; dir. Hampden Nat. Bank & Trust Co. (Westfield), Internat. Hydro-Electric System, New England Power Assn., New England Electric System, The Torrington Co. (Conn.), Eastern Racing Assn. (Boston). Mem. Phi Delta Theta. Democrat. Conglist. Elk. Clubs: Tekoa Country (Westfield); Colony, Union, City (Boston). Home: 66 Broad St., Westfield, Mass. Office: 294 Washington St., Boston. Died June 13, 1956.

ELY, Sims; b. Overton County, Tenn., Jan. 7, 1862; s. Matthew Sims and Susan Jane (Carr) E.; ed. country schs., Tenn. and Kan., and Ill. Wesleyan U. Business Coll.; m. Elizabeth Northcutt, June 6, 1886 (died Jan. 7, 1940); children—Helen (Mrs. Harry Craig Richardson), Sims, Northcutt. Editor and owner Hutchinson (Kan.) Democrat, 1885-92; spl. commr. Supreme Court of Kansas (county seat litigation), 1892; sec. to U.S. Senator John Martin of Kan., 1893-94; sec.-treas. Hudson Reservoir Co. (Roosevelt Reservoir Project, Ariz.), 1897-1904; sec. and Spanish translator to Gov. Murphy of Ariz., 1898-1902; sec. to Gov. Joseph H. Kibbey, 1905-09; territorial auditor and bank comptroller, Ariz., 1908-09; chmn. Bd. of Equalization, Ariz., 1909, Board of Control, 1908-09, Arizona Ry. Commn., 1909; editor and mng. owner Arizona Republican, Phoenix, 1907-11; gen. mgr. Valley Bank Adj. Co., Phoenix, 1914-19; president Board of Edn., City of Phoenix, 1908-22; exec. sec. Ariz. Resources Bd., 1919-22, also spl. sec. to Gov. Thomas E. Campbell, and in these two positions cooperated with govs. of 7 states of Colorado river basin, 1919-21, in settling policies for storage of flood waters; at meeting of govs., Denver, Aug. 1920, apptd. with Judge Delph Carpenter to advise on definite policy, which led to adoption of Carpenter plan of interstate compact for allocation of flood waters among the 7 states; following adoption of their report by govs., was asso. with Carpenter in assuring passage of necessary legislation in basin states and congress, which was followed by "Santa Fe Compact" and constrn. Hoover Dam; chief clk., administrative asst., Dept. of Justice, 1922-23; dir. and treas. Federal Land Bank and Federal Intermediate Credit Bank, Berkeley, Calif., 1923-30; apptd., Oct. 1931, by Sec. Interior as city mgr. Boulder City, Nev., construction camp for Hoover dam; by operation of law was due to retire for age, 1939, but President U.S. by special order continued services for one year, and in 1940 repeated this order; retired as city mag., April 1, 1941, and joined son, Northcutt Ely, in law office, Washington, D.C. Clubs: Arizona (Phoenix); University (Washington). Author: The Lost Dutchman of Arizona. Home: Phoenix, Ariz. Address: Northcutt Ely Law Offices, Tower Bldg., Washington 5. Died Nov. 11, 1954; buried Greenwood Meml. Park, Phoenix.

ELY, Wayne, lawyer; b. Kennett, Mo., Apr. 30, 1891; s. Thomas Richard Rupe and Lulia (Page) E.; student Westminster Coll., 1906-08, Washington and Lee U., 1910-11; U. Mo., 1913; m. Amy Nelle Henderson, June 30, 1915; children—Betty Jean (Mrs. H. J. Hausner), Richard, Robert, Miriam (Mrs. William A. Zukoski). Admitted to Mo. bar, 1914; asst. U.S. atty., Eastern Mo., 1920-21; special asst. gen., Mo., 1926-27; practicing lawyer as partner Ely & Ely, St. Louis, specializing in trial of railroad and ins. cases, 1924—; div. counsel Mo. and Ill., G.,M.&O. R.R.; dist. atty. (Mo.) Wabash R.R.; local atty. Burlington Lines. Mem. Am., Mo. State, St. Louis bar assns., Am. Coll. Trial Lawyers, Internat. Assn. Ins. Counsel (v.p., 1930-33, mem. exec. com., 1947-50), Am. Judicature Soc., Newcomen Soc. Democrat. Presbyn. Mason. Clubs: Contemporary, Mo. Athletic, Noonday, Algonquin Golf. Home: 134 Gray Av., Webster Grove 19, Mo. Office: Ry. Exchange Bldg., St. Louis. Died Feb. 26, 1959; buried Oak Hill Cemetery, St. Louis.

ELY, Wilson C., architect; b. Trenton, N.J.; s. John H. and Lydia H. (Wilson) E.; m. Grace Chamberlain, June 2, 1897 (now deceased); children—Dorothy Grace (Mrs. R. B. Bigham), John Wilson m. 2d, Edith C. Johnson, June 25, 1936. Architect since 1896; dir. Nat. Newark and Essex Banking Co. Howard Savings Inst., N.J. Realty Co. Mem. advisory bd. of the Sch. of Architecture of Princeton Univ.; mem. bd. Eye and Ear Infirmary, Babies Hosp. Fellow Am. Inst. Architects; mem. Newark Museum Assn., N.J. Hist. Soc., N.J. Soc. Architects (past pres.). Mason. Clubs: Essex, Downtown (Newark, N.J.). Home: 375 Mt. Prospect Av. Office: 744 Broad St., Newark, N.J. Died Aug. 28, 1959.*

EMBLETON, Harry, educator; b. East Orange, N.J., Jan. 1, 1888; s. Robert and Eliza (King) E.; B.S., Cornell, 1912; m. Katherine Smith, Dec. 7, 1916 (died 1950); 1 son, Thomas William; married 2d, Marie J. Davidson, June 30, 1951. Asst. horticulturist, Citrus Exptl. Sta., Riverside, Calif.; with Purdue U., 1912-13; Sharples Separator Co., Chicago, 1914-15; Okla. A. and M. Coll., 1916-23; mem. faculty, U. of Ariz., since 1923, now prof. of poultry husbandry and chmn. dept. Hon. state farmer, Future Farmers of Am., 1941; mem. Poultry Sci. Assn., So. Ariz. Poultry Assn. (pres.), So. Ariz. Fair (mem. exec. com.), exec. com. of Boy Scouts of Pima County, Big Brothers (chmn.). Alpha Zeta, Alpha Gamma Rho. Mason (32°). Home: 2108 E. Silver St., Tucson. Died June 8, 1953; buried South Lawn Cemetery, Tucson.

EMERICK, Edson James, neurologist; b. Fayette, O., Oct. 28, 1863; s. James Porter and Mary Ann (Humphrey) E.; student U. Mich.; M.D., L.I. Med. Coll., 1887; m. Alice Cary Dill, Sept. 16, 1891. In gen. practice at Fayette, 1887-91, Columbus, 1891-1907; supt. Instrn. for Feebleminded, Columbus, 1907-24; one of founders, dir. Bur. Juvenile Research, 1924-30; practice limited to neurology, 1924—. Past pres. Nat. Assn. for Care and Study of Feebleminded. Columbus Acad. Medicine. Republican. Conglist. Mason (K.T., Shriner), K.P. Clubs: Columbus Athletic, Optimist, Crichton, Columbus Country. Home: 854 E. Broad St. Office: 33 E. Grant Av., Columbus, O. Deceased.*

EMERSON, Haven, physician; b. N.Y.C., Oct. 19, 1874; s. J. Haven and Susan (Tompkins) E.; A.B., Harvard, 1896; A.M., Columbia, 1899, D.Sc., 1954; M.D., Coll. Phys. and Surg. (Columbia), 1899; m. Grace Parrish, June 15, 1901; children—Ethel, Robert, J. Haven, Ruth, Ralph. Practiced in N.Y.C., 1899—; asso. in physiology and medicine Coll. Phys. and Surg., 1902-14; asst. vis. physician Bellevue Hosp., 1906-14; pres. Bd. Health, and commr. Dept. Health City N.Y., 1915-17; prof. preventive medicine Cornell U.; lectr. Tchrs. Coll. (Columbia), and N.Y. Sch. of Social Work; dir. Cleve. Hosp. and Health Survey, 1919-20; prof. of public health adminstrn. Columbia, 1922-40, emeritus, 1940—; professional lecturer U. Minn. 1943; vis. lectr. sch. pub. health U. Mich. Served from maj. to col. M.C., U.S. Army, AEF, 1918-19. Dir. health and hosp. surveys in many cities of U.S., also Athens, Greece, 1921-31; dir. New York Hosp. Survey, 1935-37. Mem. Board of Health, N.Y.C., 1937—; trustee Oberlaender Trust and W. K. Kellogg Found.; mem. Commn. Expert Statisticians of Health Sect. League of Nations, 1920-40; headed 7-man pub. health group sent to Germany by Unitarian Service Com. Teaching Mission, 1951. Mem. Am. Pub. Health Assn. (pres. 1933-34), Acad. of Athens (Greece). Decorated Médaille des Épidémies and Chevalier Legion d'Honneur (France); D.S.M. (U.S.); recipient Sedgwick medal Am. Pub. Health Assn., 1935, Lasker award, 1949; Gold Heart award Am. Heart Assn., 1953. Author: Alcohol, Its Effects on Man, 1934; reviser of Flint's Manual of Auscultation and Percussion, 1916. Editor: Alcohol and Man, 1932; The Baker Memorial, 1930-39, 1941, Administrative Medicine, 1942, Local Health Units for the Nation, 1945. Home: 156 E. 79th St. Office: 600 W. 168th St., N.Y.C. 32. Died May 21, 1957.

EMERSON, John, actor, playwright, producer; b. Sandusky, O., May 29, 1874; s. Henry Fry and Mary (Almond) E.; student Oberlin, Western Reserve, U. Chgo., Dramatic Sch. Chgo. Mus. Coll., Am. Acad. Dramatic Arts, N.Y.C.; m. Anita Loos, June 15, 1919. Acted and prod. plays for William Harris, Daniel Frohman, Shuberts, Clyde Fitch and others, 1904-10; gen. stage dir. for Charles Frohman 1910-14; wrote and played The Conspiracy, 1912, Step Lively, 1913; writer and producer motion pictures for Paramount, D. W. Griffith, Douglas Fairbanks, Mary Pickford, Constance Talmadge, etc., 1914-22; pres. Emerson-Loos Co., writers and producers motion pictures; writer and producer of plays for Metro-Goldwyn-Mayer, 1932-37; writer and producer of radio plays, 1937—. Mem. Actors' Equity Assn. (pres. 1920-28, hon. pres. 1928—), Am. Dramatists' Assn., Authors' League Am. Clubs: Players, Lambs, Coffee House, Lotos (N.Y.C.); Everglades, Seminole (Palm Beach). Author (with Anita Loos): How to Write Photoplays, 1920; Breaking Into the Movies, 1921; The Whole Town's Talking, 1923; The Fall of Eve, 1924; Gentlemen Prefer Blondes (stage version), 1925; Cherries Are Ripe, 1928; The Social Secretary, 1932. Home: 506 Ocean Front, Santa Monica, Cal. Died Mar. 8, 1956.

EMERSON, Robert, educator, researcher; b. N.Y.C., Nov. 4, 1903; s. Haven and Grace (Parrish) E.; A.B. cum laude, Harvard, 1925; Ph.D., Friedrich Wilhelm U., Berlin, Germany, 1927; m. Claire Garrison, Feb. 9, 1929; children—Kenneth, Stephen, David, Ruth. Nat. Research fellow, Harvard, 1927-29; asst. prof. biophysics Cal. Inst. Tech., 1929-46; on leave as research asso. Carnegie Inst. Washington, Stanford, 1937-40; research prof. botany U. Ill., 1946—; research on photosynthesis, especially investigation of maximum efficiency; Fulbright fellow, 1954. Mem. Nat. Acad. Scis., Am. Bot. Soc., Am. Soc. Plant Physiologists. Author sci. papers. Home: 806 W. Main St., Urbana, Ill. Died Feb. 4, 1959.

EMERSON, William, architect; b. N.Y.C., Oct. 16, 1873; s. Dr. John Haven (M.D.) and Susan Titus (Tomkins) E.; A.B., Harvard, 1895; hon. Dr. Arts, 1939; studied architecture Columbia, 1895-97; École des Beaux Arts, Paris, 1897-1901; m. Frances Hillard White, Jan. 14, 1913. Practiced at N.Y.C., 1901-18, specializing in model tenements and bank bldgs.; prof. architecture Mass. Inst. Tech., 1919-39, also chmn.

faculty and dean Sch. Architecture, prof. emeritus, 1939-—. Maj. and dir. Bur. Constrn., A.R.C. at Paris, 1917-19. Life mem. Corp. Mass. Inst. Tech.; mem. Corp. Simmons Coll.; chmn. Unitarian Service Com., 1940-—. Fellow A.I.A. (past pres. N.Y.), Am. Acad. Arts and Scis.; mem. Am. Assn. for UN (pres. 1944-54), Soc. Beaux Arts Architects (ex-v.p.), Boston Soc. Architects (pres. 1940-42), Delta Kappa Epsilon, Phi Beta (hon.) Pres. Assn. Collegiate Schools Architecture, 1921-23; v.p. The Byzantine Inst., 1935. Decorated Chevalier Legion of Honor (France). Unitarian. Clubs: Harvard, Union (Boston); Harvard, Century (N.Y.C.); Union Interalliée (Paris). Author: Old Bridges of France (with Georges Gromort), 1925; The Use of Brick in French Architecture (with Georges Gromort), 1935. Home: 159 Brattle St., Cambridge, Mass. Office: 107 Massachusetts Av., Boston 15. Died May 4, 1957; buried Concord, Mass.

EMERY, DeWitt McKinley, founder Nat. Small Business Men's Assn.; b. Grove City, Pa., Dec. 12, 1896; son of William S. and Mina Elizabeth (Alexander) E.; educated in high school, Youngstown, O.; m. Lillian Price, Nov. 27, 1917 (died Nov. 28, 1929); children—Marjorie Jane, Richard (dec.); m. 2d, Florence Price, July 7, 1931; 1 son, James DeWitt. Dir. of sales Monroe Letterhead Co., Huntsville, Ala., 1925-29, moved company to Akron, O., and incorporated as Monroe Letterhead Corp., 1929, pres. and treas. to 1950; partner DeWitt Emery and Associates, management counsel. Founded National Small Business Men's Assn., Akron, O., November 1937, pres., 1937-41 and since June 1942. Pres. Small Business Econ. Found. Columnist, small town weekly papers. Presbyn. Mason. Clubs: Chicago Executive (dir.), Sunset Ridge Country, Rotary. Home: 2235 Central Park. Office: 2834 Central St., Evanston, Ill. Died July 22, 1955; buried Meml. Park Cemetery, Ridge Rd., Evanston, Ill.

EMERY, James Augustan, lawyer; b. Detroit, Mar. 29, 1876; s. Augustan Havens and Mary (Harrington) E.; student St. Ignatius Coll., San Francisco; A.B., Santa Clara (Cal.) U., 1896; attended Hastings Coll. Law (U. Cal.), 1898; m. Emily Aloise Hartrick, Jan. 30, 1902; children—Mary Aloise, Letitia Alexia, Alice Suzanne. Admitted to Cal. bar, 1903, began practice at San Francisco; counsel Health Bd., San Francisco, 1903-04. Citizens' Indsl. Assn. Am., 1905-08; gen. counsel N.A.M., 1910-46 (resigned Dec. 1946), Nat. Founders Assn., 1920; assisted orgn. Nat. Indsl. Conf. Board, 1916; assisted in orgn. War Labor Board, 1917; adviser Employer Group of 1st Internat. Labor Conf., Washington, 1919, actively participated in presentation of indsl. questions in litigation and legislation; factor in transition of Am. industry from system of employers' liability to workmen's compensation. Roman Catholic. Clubs: Chevy Chase (Washington); and Bohemian (San Francisco). Author: Accident Prevention and Relief (with F. C. Schwedtman), 1911; Workmen's Compensation in the States (legal phase), 1917. Office: Investment Bldg. Washington. Died Sept. 28, 1955.

EMERY, Roe, motor transportation; b. Lake City, Minn., Oct. 31, 1874; s. Sloan Miller and Julia (Haas) E.; ed. Sch. of Agr., St. Paul, Minn., and Montana Agricultural Coll.; married Florence Garrard Brown, 1898 (died 1913); m. 2d, Jeannette Carpenter, June 30, 1917 (died 1943); children—Walter Carpenter, Rowena, Patricia Jeannette. In cattle business, Ten Sleep, Wyoming, 1898-1906; sheep raising, White Sulphur Springs, Mont., 1906-13; moved to St. Paul, Minnesota, 1913, moved to Denver, Colorado, 1915; president Rocky Mountain Parks Transportation Co., Denver Cab Co., Rocky Mountain Motor Co.—all consolidated into Rocky Mountain Motor Co., of which he is pres. Pres. National Western Stock Show, 1934-40. Episcopalian. Mason. Clubs: Denver, Denver Country. Motorized Glacier Nat. Park, 1914. Home: 648 Humboldt St. Office: 1730 Glenarm Pl., Denver. Died Feb. 4, 1953.

EMERY, William Orrin, chemist; b. Vernon, Vt., Mar. 29, 1863; s. Ira and Emmeline (Stearns) E.; B.S., Worcester Poly. Inst., in civ. engring., 1885, in chemistry, 1886; spl. work in chemistry, physics, geology, mineralogy, and bacteriology, Bonn and Berlin, 1886-93; pvt. asst. to Prof. Kekule and instr. chemistry, U. Bonn, 1887-92; Ph.D., U. Erlangen, 1888; m. Auguste Josephine Roetzel, Apr. 8, 1893; children—Alice, Gustav Harold. Pvt. docent in chemistry, U. Bonn, 1891-92, absent on leave, 1893-97; research chemist in Berlin and Chgo., 1893-94; prof. chemistry, Wabash Coll., 1895-1901; was research chemist, Crawfordsville, Bonn and Berlin, beginning 1902; organic chemist (1907; and chief Synthetic Products Lab., Bur. Chemistry, Dept. Agr., 1908-—; also charge spl. collaborative investigations of Food and Drug Adminstrn., 1929-—. Fellow A.A.A.S.; mem. Am. Chem. Soc., Washington Acad. Scis., Phi Beta Kappa, Sigma Xi. Club: Cosmos. Contbr. numerous papers Am. and fgn. periodicals. Home: 2232 Cathedral Av. N.W. Address: Bur. of Chemistry, Washington. Died May 3, 1946; buried Fort Lincoln Cemetery, Washington.

EMHARDT, William Chauncey, clergyman; b. Phila., Jan. 29, 1874; s. Charles Stokes and Anne Catharine (Burk) E.; grad. Episcopal Acad., Phila., 1890; B.A., U. Pa., 1894; post-grad. work, U. Pa., Columbia; student Phila. Div. Sch., 1895; S.T.D., 1931; grad. Gen. Theol. Sem., 1897; Ph.D., U. Kan., 1898; m. Anne Lindsey Haines, Oct. 25, 1900; children—Anne Catharine, Elisabeth Montgomery (dec.). Deacon, 1897, priest, 1898, P.E. Ch.; missionary Western Kan., Indian Ty. and Okla., 1897-98; curate St. Luke's Ch., Germantown, Pa., 1898-1902; rector Ch. of Ascension, Gloucester City, N.J., and St. Luke's Ch., Newton, Pa., until 1919; in charge Country Centre Mission, Bucks Co., Pa., 1911-19; sec. Commn. for Ch. work among Immigrants, Diocese of Pa., 1910-19, Providence of Washington, 1917-24; field dir. fgn. born work, Nat. Council P.E. Ch.; counselor on ecclesiastical relations, P.E. Ch.; vicar Pro-Cathedral of St. Mary, Phila., 1936-43, vicar emeritus 1943-—. Spl. chaplain of Archbishop of Canterbury, Lambeth Conf., London, 1930; trustee Near East Relief, etc., chmn. Commn. on Correlation of Chs. in Near East; chmn. Am. Com. of Russian Theol. Sem., Paris; chmn. Am. Com. on Greek Centenary (1830-1930); chmn. com. on Christian Approach to the Jew; mem. Federal Council Chs.; chmn. Hill Sch., Athens, Greece, 1927-37. Made hon. archpriest in Contantinople, 1922. Knight Comdr. Order of S. Saviour (Greece); Order of Holy Sepulchre; Distinguished Service Medal, Near East Relief, 1945. Mem. Am. Acad. Social and Polit. Science, Am. Schs. of Archaealogy, Am. Soc. Church History; Sons of the American Revolution, Colonial Soc. of Pa. Clubs: Clergy (N.Y.C.). Author: Oldest Christian People, 1926; Eastern Church in the Western World (with others), 1928; Religion in Sovietу Russia, 1929; (monograph) The Anglican Communion and Reunion, 1931. Home: 1482 Leeds Point Rd., Oceanville, N.J. Died Aug. 5, 1950.

EMIG, Arthur S(amuel) (ĕm'ig), univ. prof.; b. Farmington, Ia., Dec. 11, 1887; s. Dr. Charles Henry and Mary (Luedde) E.; A.B., U. of Mo., 1916; S.T.B., Boston U., 1921; Ph.D., Northwestern U., 1930; Frank D. Howard fellow, U. of Basel, Switzerland, Edinburgh U., Scotland, U. of Berlin; m. Constance Latshaw, Aug. 29, 1917. Asst. prof. philosophy Allegheny Coll., Meadville, Pa., 1923-27; asst. prof. sociology U. of Mo., 1927-30, prof. since 1931. Pres. bd. Columbia Social Service Soc., 1933-37. Fellow A.A.A.S.; mem. Am. Assn. Univ. Profs., Theta Chi, Phi Beta Kappa, Alpha Pi Zeta, Alpha Kappa Delta, Kappa Phi Kappa. Democrat. Methodist. Club: Columbia Rotary (pres. 1941). Home: 207 Edgewood Av., Columbia, Mo. Died Sept. 26, 1949; buried Mt. Washington Cemetery, Kansas City, Mo.

EMIG, Elmer Jacob, educator; b. Fowler, Ind., Mar. 27, 1898; s. Jacob Stafford and Carrie (Hanson) E.; B.A., Canterbury Coll., 1922; M.A., U. Wis., 1926, postgrad., summer 1927; m. Clara Louise Pennington, Feb. 19, 1921; children—Elmer Byron, Mary Jane. Instr. English, Elwood (Ind.) Sr. High Sch., 1922-25; copydesk Wis. State Jour., 1925-26; asst. prof. journalism U. Fla., 1927-28, prof., 1928-31, 49-—, head dept. journalism, 1928-49; instr. Stanford, 1931-32; editorial writer and editorial page columnist Fla. Times Union, 1945-47. Dir. goodwill tour of journalism students to Cuba under auspices Asso. Dailies of Fla., 1930. Served with U.S. Army, 1917-19, O.R.C., 1933-37; officer USN, 1942-45. Mem. Am. Legion (vice chmn. Fla. dept. Americanism Commn. 1934-35), Am. Assn. Tchrs. Journalism (Southeastern dir. 1938-39), S.A.R., Phi Delta Kappa. Sigma Delta Chi, Kappa Tau Alpha, Alpha Delta Sigma (so. v.p. 1951-53). Independent. Mason (K.T., Shriner). Author articles. Home: 2120 N.W. Third Pl., Gainesville, Fla. Died Oct. 16, 1957.

EMLAW, Harlan Stigand, mining engr.; b. Grand Haven, Mich., Aug. 8, 1873; s. Andrew Jackson and Louisa (Yates) E.; student Mich. State Coll., 1890-92; B.S. and M.E., Mich. Coll. of Mining and Tech., 1895, Dr. of Engring., 1942; m. Alice Lucy Bilz, June 26, 1901; 1 dau., Alice Louise (Mrs. Donald A. Lacoss). Engr. with Anaconda Copper Co., 1896-1903; acting and gen. superintendent of mines for Cerro de Pasco Mining Co., Peru, S.A., 1903-07; pvt. practice to 1919; gen. mgr., pres. and dir., Am. Potash and Chem. Corp., 1919-45; retired 1945. Mem. Am. Inst. Mining and Metall. Engrs., Mining and Metall. Soc. Am. Republican. Club: Mining (New York). Home: 724 Charlotte Av., Rock Hill, S.C. Died Feb. 5, 1953; buried Grand Haven, Mich.

EMMERSON, Henry Read, Canadian senator; born Dorchester, N.B., Can., Nov 7, 1883; s. Hon. Henry Robert and Emily C. (Record) E.; student Horton Collegiate Acad., 1897-99; A.B., Acadia U., 1904; m. Faulein B. Price, Dec. 28, 1905. Elected mem. House of Commons for the constituency of Westmorland, Province of N.B., 1935, re-elected 1940, 1945; called to Senate of Canada, 1949. Served in the Inf., Canadian Forces, 1914-18, in France, 1914-18, disch. as maj. Retired. Home: Dorchester, New Brunswick, Can. Died June 21, 1954; buried Amherst, Nova-Scotia, Can.

EMMET, Lydia Field, artist; b. New Rochelle, N.Y., Jan. 23, 1866; d. William Jenkins and Julia Colt (Pierson) Emmet; pupil of Bouguereau, and Fleury, Paris, and William Chase, Frederick MacMonnies, H. Siddons Mowbray, Kenyon Cox and Robert Reid, New York. Awarded medal Chgo. Expn., 1893; bronze medal Atlanta Expn., 1895; hon. mention Buffalo Expn., 1901; silver medal St. Louis Expn., 1904; Shaw prize, 1906; Proctor prize, 1907; Clarke prize, 1909; hon. mention Pitts. Internat. Exhbn., 1912; Phila. prize, Pa. Acad. Fine Arts, 1915; Corcoran popular prize, 1917; Maynard prize N.A.D., 1918; popular prize Newport (R.I.) Exhbn., 1921; Newport popular prize, 1923; Phila. Bok prize, 1925; A.N.A., 1909; N.A., 1911. Mem. Art Students League. Home: 214 E. 76th St., N.Y.C. Studio: 535 Park Av., N.Y. C.; also Stockbridge, Mass. Died Sept. 16, 1952.

EMMONS, Lloyd C., educator; b. Lawrenceville, Ill., May 4, 1887; s. Redmond W. and Dorinda E. (Shinn) E.; B.S., Central Normal Coll., 1907, A.B., Ind. U., 1909, A.M., Harvard, 1917; LL.D., Mich. State Coll., 1953; m. Pearle E. Conover, Jan. 31, 1909; children—Anna Dorinda (Mrs. Jack I. Green), Dorothy Elinor (Mrs. George Reid), Philip Richard. Rural sch. tchr., 1904; instr. math., Mich. State Coll., 1909-13, asst. prof., 1913-18, asso. prof., 1918-26, prof., 1926-—, research prof. Instnl. Adminstrn., 1929, dean of liberal arts 1934-44, dean Sci. and Arts, 1944-52, dean emeritus, 1952-—. Mem. Phi Kappa Phi, Pi Delta Kappa. Home: 1126 Sunset Lane, East Lansing, Mich. Died Dec. 8, 1957; buried Evergreen Cemetery, Lansing, Mich.

EMORY, Samuel T(homas), univ. prof.; b. Chase City, Va., Oct. 3, 1896; s. Eugene Samuel and Mary Carter (Bacon) E.; A.B., Randolph-Macon Coll., 1917, A.M., 1918; A.M., Columbia, 1921; Ph.D., U. of Chicago, 1939; m. Mary Dortch, June 14, 1923; children—Elizabeth Dortch, Samuel Thomas. Prin., Goldsboro (N.C.) High Sch., 1920-23; supt. Tarboro public schs., 1923-28; state rep. The MacMillan Co., Chapel Hill, N.C., 1928-32; asst. prof. U. of N.C., 1933-39, asso. prof., 1939-45, prof., 1945-—, acting chairman department geology and geography, 1949-51, chmn. dept., 1951-—; Fulbright lectr. Swedish and Finnish Comml. Univs., Helsinki, Finland. Chairman Chapel Hill Sch. Board. Served as candidate officer, inf., U.S. Army, 1918; 2d lt., U.S. Army Res., 1918-20. Mem. Assn. Am. Geographers, Nat. Council Geography Tchrs., Am. Geog. Soc., Sigma Xi, Kappa Sigma, Sigma Upsilon, Elisha Mitchel Soc. Democrat. Episcopalian. Contbr. articles to professional jours. Home: 722 E. Franklin St., Chapel Hill, N.C. Died Mar. 6, 1957; buried Chapel Hill Cemetery.

ENCKELL, Carl J(ohan) A(lexis), Finnish statesman; b. St. Petersburg, Russia, June 7, 1876; s. Carl and Helena (Bronikowsky) E.; grad. Finnish Cadet Corps Acad., Hamina, 1896; engring. diploma, Tech. U. Dresden, 1902; m. Lucy Ponsonby-Lyons, 1903 (dec. 1945); children—Marietta, Ralph, Estelle, Bernard. Employed in engring. field, 1903-17; asso. with various comml. enterprises from 1927. Minister to Soviet govt., 1917-18; minister fgn. affairs, 1918-19, 1922, 1942, also minister to France, 1919-27; minister fgn. affairs, 1944-50. Decorated Grand Cross Order White Rose (with diamonds), 1st Class Grand Star Order Cross of Liberty (Finland), Grand Cross Royal Order Vasa (Sweden), Grand Cross Order Danneborg (Denmark), Grand Cross Polonia Restituta, Grand Cross Order of Crown (Belgium), Grand Cross Anamite Dragon, Grand Cross Order of Falcon (Iceland), Grand Officer Legion of Honor (France). Address: Helsinki, Finland. Died Mar. 26, 1959.

ENDERS, John Ostrom, banker; b. Hartford, Conn., Dec. 3, 1869; s. Thomas Ostrom and Harriet Adelaide (Burnham) E.; ed. Stern's and Bowen's pvt. sch. and Phillips Exeter Acad.; m. Harriet Golden Whitmore, June 12, 1895; children—John F., Harriet B., Ostrom, Elvia. Began with U.S. Bank, Hartford, 1888, v.p., 1915-18, pres., 1918-23; pres. U.S. Security Trust Co. (cons. U.S. Bank Security Co. and Fidelity Trust Co.), 1923-25, chmn. bd., 1925-27; chmn. bd. Hartford Nat. Bank & Trust Co., 1927-35, chmn. exec. com., 1935-—; cons. Hartford-Aetna Nat. Bank, and U.S. Security Trust Co.; trustee Soc. Savs.; v.p. Dime Savs. Bank, dir. Aetna Casualty & Surety Co., Aetna Life Ins. Co., Automobile Ins. Co. of Hartford, Hartford Steam Boiler Inspection and Ins. Co., Hartford Nat. Bank & Trust Co. Mem. Conn. House Reps., 1899; chmn. bd. Hartford Hosp. Republican. Episcopalian. Mason (K.T.). Clubs: Hartford Club. Home: 17 N. Highland St., West Hartford. Office: Hartford Nat. Bank & Trust Co., Hartford, Conn. Died Apr. 2, 1958; buried West Hartford, Conn.

ENDICOTT, H(enry) Wendell; b. Dedham, Mass., Nov. 1, 1880; s. Henry Bradford and Caroline Williams (Russell) E.; Harvard, 1899-1901; m. Martha Waldron, d. C. W. Barron, Oct. 2, 1911; 1 dau., Martha Endicott; m. 2d, Priscilla Maxwell, Sept. 12, 1925; children—Bradford Maxwell, Priscilla. With Endicott-Johnson Corp., mfrs. leather and shoes, for many years from 1901, v.p., 1919; dir. Sears Roebuck & Co. (Chicago), Geo. E. Keith Co. (Campello, Mass.); trustee New England Conservatory of Music; president Boston Opera Association; director Metropolitan Opera Assn., Inc.; N.Y. City. Member Massachusetts Committee on Public Safety. Overseas commr. War Department in France and England, later chief research and specifications branch of Clothing and Equipage Division under Q.M. Gen., Washington, World War I, attaining to the rank of major; retired with rank of lt. col.; tech. cons. World War II, overseas; acting commr., Pacific Theater; dep. commr. Fgn. Liquidation Commn. Mem. Unitarian Ch. Clubs: Somerset, Harvard, Harvard Travelers (Boston); Dedham Polo and Country; Swan Island Shooting (N.C.); Moisie Salmon (Canada); Boone and Crockett (N.Y. City). Author: Adventures with Rod and Harpoon Along the Florida Keys, 1925; Adventures in Alaska and Along the Trail, 1928; Saga of the Tented Cities, 1952. Home: Dedham. Office: 831 Shawmut Bank Bldg., Boston. Died Apr. 20, 1954; buried Forest Hill Cemetery, Boston.

ENESCO, Georges, composer; b. Livehni, Rumania, Aug. 19, 1881; s. Constantin and Marie Enesco; student Vienna Conservatory, 1888-94 (Gesellschafts medal); Paris Conservatory, 1894 (1st prize for violin, 1899); m. Marie Rosetti-Tescano, Dec. 1936. Composer: Poeme Roumain for orchestra; 3 orchestra suites; 3-d, Villageoise; in rumanian folk-like character, composed for N.Y. Philharmonic Symphony Soc. 3 symphonies; 2 Rumanian rhapsodies; 1 symphonie concertante for cello and orchestra; 1 wind instrument distett; 1 string octett; 1 piano and string quintett; 2 piano and strings quartettes; 2 string Quartettes 3 violin and piano sonatas, 3-d, in rumanian folk-character; 2 cello and piano sonatas; 2 pianoforte sonatas; 3 pianoforte sonatas; 2 pianoforte suites; variations for 2 pianos; 10 published songs, Impressions d'Enfance, piano and violin; 1 opera, Oedipe; concert-overture on motives in Rumanian character, and other compositions. Guest condr. and violonist in Europe and America. Mem. Rumanian Acad., French Acad. Fine Arts, Commn. Legion d' Honneur. Founded National George Enesco Prize for works by young composers of Rumania, 1912; regarded as foundator of rumanian composing sch. Held courses of musical interpretation in Paris (Inst. Instrumental Astruc) Siena (Acad. Chigiana) Brithton, Romeo Draghici. Paganini Prize, SACEM-Paris. Mem. Christian Orthodox Church. George Enesco Mus. Bucharest-Rumania; triennal G. Enesco-Competition, 1958, the 1-st. Home: 26 rue de Clichy, Paris, France; also Hotel Atala, 10 rue Chateaubriand, Paris. Died May 4, 1955; buried Pere-Lach aise, Paris.

ENGEL, Albert Joseph (ĕng'ĕl), ex-congressman; b. New Washington, O., Jan. 1, 1888; prep. edn. Central Y.M.C.A., Chicago; LL.B., Northwestern U., 1910; m. Bertha M. Bielby; children—Margaret Ann, Albert Joseph, Helen Louise. Admitted to Mich. bar, 1910, and since practiced in Lake City; pros. atty. Missaukee County, 1917; mem. Mich. State Senate, 1921, 27, 29, 31; mem. 74th to 81st Congresses, 9th Mich. Dist. Served as 1st lt., later capt., Sheridan, Ill., War Dept., Washington, D.C., and in A.E.F. (23 mos.), 1917-19. Elected hon. alumnus Univ. of Mich., 1937. Republican. Home: Lake City, Michigan. Died Dec. 3, 1959.

ENGEL, Katharine Asher (Mrs. Irving M. Engel), orgn. exec.; b. New Haven, Oct. 27, 1898; d. Harry W. and Pauline (Housman) Asher; A.B., Smith Coll., 1920; postgrad. Oxford U., 1923-24; M.A. (hon.), Smith Coll., 1950; m. Irving M. Engel, Jan. 14, 1926; 1 dau., Susan Katharine (Mrs. Richard W. Levy). Nat. v.p., chmn. exec. com. Nat. Council Jewish Women, 1946-49, nat. pres., 1949-55, pres. N.Y. sect., 1955-57; chmn. bd. dirs. United Service for New Americans, 1946-48, hon. pres., 1951-54; mem. bd. U.-Inst.-Technion, 1950—; mem. Nat. Crusade council Crusade for Freedom, 1950; dir. Greater N.Y. United Jewish Appeal, 1946—, mem. adminstrv. and exec. coms. Nat. United Jewish Appeal, 1946-48, exec. com. Women's div., 1946-49; vice chmn. women's div. Bond Drive for Israel, 1951; mem. exec. com. Nat. Com. on Immigration Policy; mem. U.S. nat. commn. UNESCO, 1953; v.p. United Hias Service, 1954; asso. chmn. Am. Jewish Tercentary Com., 1953-54; mem. Women's Adv. Commn. on Def. Manpower, adv. com. for womens affairs Civil Def. Adminstrn. Gov. Hebrew U. in Jerusalem. Mem. Jewish Publs. Soc. (hon. v.p.), Phi Beta Kappa. Club: Smith College (N.Y.C.). Home: 575 Park Av., N.Y.C. 21. Office: 9 E. 69th St., N.Y.C. 21. Died Mar. 30, 1957.

ENGELHARDT, Nickolaus Louis, ednl. consultant; b. Naugatuck, Conn., Oct. 8, 1882; s. George J. and Helena (Deubel) E.; A.B., Yale, 1903; Ph.D., Columbia Univ., 1918; Butler medal, Columbia U., 1937; m. Bessie E. Gardner, June 14, 1905; children—Mrs. Helen Stonborough, Nickolaus, Hildagarde (Mrs. Dwight Crouse Baum). Teacher private schs., 1903-06; teacher and prin. secondary schools, 1907-12; supt. schools, Dunkirk, N.Y., 1912-16; asso. in education, Teachers Coll. (Columbia), 1916-18; asst. prof. education, 1918, asso. prof., 1919-21, prof., 1921-42, asso. dir., div. field studies, 1929-42, dir., 1942, chmn. exec. com., dept. of advanced professional edn., Teachers Coll., Columbia, 1939-42; on leave of absence, 1942-47, prof. 1948—; asso. supt. schools, in charge of Housing, Bus. Adminstrn., N.Y.C., 1942-47, planning N.Y.C.'s post war sch. bldg. program of 120 schs.; Manual Sch. Planning, Community Studies, Room Utilization Studies, Population Analyses, Furniture and Equipment Schedules, Check Lists, etc. bldg. advisor Resettlement Adminstrn., Wash., 1935-36. Dir. Aviation Edn. Research Project, Teachers Coll., resulting in Air-Age Series. mem. Engelhardt, Engelhardt, Leggett & Cornell, ednl. cons., N.Y. City, 1947—; school bldg. surveys, school finance, administrative studies, 1916—. Chairman Local Exemption Bd. No. 135, N.Y.C., 1918-19; spl. cons. Nat. Survey Sch. Finance. Member N.E.A., Am. Assn. Sch. Adminstrs. (pres. 1944-45, mem. yr. book commn.), Nat. Soc. Teachers Edn., mem. Health and Phys. Edn. Council N.Y. State (adv. com. N.Y. State bd. regents); mem. Sch. Bldgs. and Ground Council; mem. N.Y. State Council Sch. Supts.; co-chmn. Young Adult advisory com. N.Y. State Edn. Dept. Mem. Met. Mus. Art (ednl. com.); mem. Cleveland Conf.; advisor National Conf. on Facilities for Athletics, Recreation, Health and Phys. Edn.; Nat. Soc. Sci. Study Edn., N.Y. State Council Sch. Supts., Cleve. Conf., Am. Edn. Research Assn., Nat. Assn. Sch. Bldg. Officials, N.Y. Acad. Public Education. Kappa Delta Pi, Phi Delta Kappa. Presbyn. Mason. Author A School Building Program for Cities, 1918; School Building Programs in American Cities, 1928: Junior High School Standards, 1932; Elementary School Building Score Card and Survey Manual, 1936. Co-Author: Survey of the School System of St. Paul, 1917; The Classroom Teacher, 1919; The Elementary Principal's Record Book, 1919; Problems in Educational Administration, 1925; School Building Problems, 1927; Revised Standards for Elementary School Buildings (all with G. D. Strayer), 1933; (with Fred Engelhardt) Public School Business Administration, 1927; (with C. Alexander) School Finance and Business Management Problems, 1929; Planning School Building Programs (with Fred Engelhardt), 1930; Survey Manual for the Business Administration in Public Sch. Systems, 1936; (with N.L.E. Jr.), Planning the Community Sch., 1940; Engelhardt Elementary Classroom Portfolio, 1941; (with others) Manual of School Planning (New York Schs., 1943-47); Malden, Massachusetts, Survey; Standards for Church and Religious Education Plants, Engelhardt-Smith-Kline Arithmetic Series. Director or co-director and co-author school surveys of Atlanta, Baltimore, Phila., Chicago, Fort Worth and Beaumont, Tex., Springfield and Lynn, Mass., Tampa, Fla., Greensboro, N.C., Hartford, Conn., Evansville, Ind., Yonkers, Rye, Watertown, Newburgh, N.Y., St. Louis, Mo., Pittsburgh, Pa., Hartford, Conn., and many other cities, also sch. bldg. surveys of Del., Fla., Mo., Canal Zone and St. John's, Newfoundland. Planning High School Buildings, 1949; Planning Guide for San Francisco Schs., 1948; Planning Elementary School Buildings, 1952; The Junior High School, Its Furniture and Equipment, 1952; School Planning and Building Handbook, 1956. Cons. editor Am. Sch. and Univ. Yearbooks. Asso. editor Sch. Exec. Mag. Ednl. cons. on sch. bldgs. to bds. edn. and architects; pub. lectr. and contbr. to ednl. and archtl. mags. Home: 331 W. 250th St., N.Y.C. Office: 221 W. 57th St., N. Y.C. 19. Died Feb. 24, 1960.

ENGER, Melvin Lorenius (ĕng'ĕr), ret. coll. dean; b. Decorah, Ia., May 5, 1881; s. Lauritz Magnus and Bertha (Myran) E.; student U. Minn., 1900-02; B.S., U. Ill., 1906, C.E., 1911, M.S., 1916; m. Mary Adeline Crawford, Aug. 24, 1908; children—Bertha Marie, Walter Melvin. Instrumentman C., M.&St.P. Ry., 1906-07; instr. theoretical and applied mechanics U. Ill., 1907, 09, asso., 1909-11, asst. prof., 1911-17, asso. prof., 1917-19, prof. mechanics and hydraulics, 1919—, head dept. theoretical and applied mechanics, 1926-34, in charge research investigations in engring. materials, dean of engring. and dir. Engring. Expt. Sta., 1934-49, dean emeritus, 1949—. Mem. Am. Soc. C.E. (past dir.), Am. Soc. for Testing Materials, Am. Water Works Assn., Am. Soc. Engring. Edn., Ill., Western socs. engrs., Newcomen Soc., Ill. Acad. Science, A.A.A.S., Nat. Soc. Profl. Engrs., Sigma Xi, Tau Beta Pi, Phi Kappa Phi, Sigma Tau. Republican. Kiwanian. Home: 702 E. Fifth Av., Escondido, Cal. Died May 13, 1956; buried Escondido.

ENGLAR, D. Roger, lawyer; b. Medford, Md., Nov. 3, 1883; s. David and Martha E. (Shepherd) E.; A.B. summa cum laude, Western Maryland Coll., 1903, LL.D., 1942; LL.B. cum laude, Harvard Law Sch., 1906; m. Ethel Miller, June 5, 1909; 1 dau., Elizabeth Watts. Began as clerk in maritime law, N.Y.C., 1906; entered partnership with firm, Harrington, Bigham and Englar; now sr. partner, Bigham, Englar, Jones and Houston, specializing in admiralty and maritime law; dir. U.S. Guarantee Co. Trustee Western Maryland Coll. Mem. Maritime Law Assn. U.S. (former pres.), Am., N.Y. State bar assns., Bar Assn. City N.Y. Republican. Protestant. Clubs: University, Downtown Assn., India House, Harvard (N.Y.C.); Metropolitan (Washington). Home: 1095 Park Av., N.Y.C. Died Jan. 18, 1948.

ENGLE, Earl T., med. research, editor; b. Waterloo, Ia., Mar. 19, 1896; s. Levi H and Mary C. (Stephens) E.; A.B., Nebraska Wesleyan U., 1920; A.M., U. of Colorado, 1923; Ph.D., Stanford, 1925; m. Mirth Richardson, Jan. 1, 1917; children—Audrey Engle Hawthorn, Robert Gregg. Instr. zoölogy, U. of Colo., 1921-23, anatomy, Stanford, 1925-27; asst. prof., 1927-28; Coll. Physicians and Surgeons, Columbia, 1928-29; asso. prof., 1929-39, professor since 1939, assigned to obstetrics and gynecology, 1949; Sir William F. Shaw lecturer Royal College of Obstetrics and Gynecology, London, 1952. Director research, National Committee Maternal Health, 1937-47; chairman editorial com., Assn. Internal Secretions, 1942-48. Recipient award from Am. Urological Assn., 1946; award for research Am. Gynecol. Soc., 1950. Hon. mem. N.Y. Soc. Am. Urol. Assn., Western Urol. Association; mem. Am. Soc. Anat., Am. Soc. Physiol., Soc. Exp. Biol. Med., Soc. Gerontol. Assn., Study Internal Secretions, Nat. Research Council (mem. com. growth, 1945-50, committee human reprodn., 1947-50). Editor: (books) Diagnosis in Sterility, 1946; Problem of Fertility, 1946; Menstruation and Its Disorders, 1948; Studies on Ovary and Testis, 1952; Pregnancy Wastage, 1953; (with G. Pincus) Hormones and the Aging Process, 1956. Mem. Atomic Bomb Casualty Commn., Hiroshima, 1949. Address: La Orilla, Rancho Santa Fe, Cal. Died Dec. 17, 1957.

ENGLISH, Frank A., food mfr.; b. Wilkes-Barre, Pa., 1895. Pres., dir. Planters Nut & Chocolate Co., Wilkes-Barre, Pa.; dir. Miners Nat. Bank of Wilkes-Barre. Home: 555 Gibson Av., Kingston, Pa. Office: 632 S. Main St., Wilkes-Barre, Pa. Died Aug. 5, 1959.*

ENGLISH, Robert Byrns; b. Rushford, N.Y., Dec. 8, 1872; s. Charles and Frances (Byrns) E.; A.B., U. of Rochester, N.Y., 1896; A.M., 1898; U. of Chicago, summer, 1899; fellow in classics, U. of Mich., 1903-05, Ph.D., 1905; m. Grace May Hill, Aug. 9, 1900 (died Dec. 27, 1943); children—Byrns Hill, Helen Ruth, Charles Loyal; m. 2d, Mrs. Julia D. Baymiller, June 1, 1946. Prof., Latin, Greenville Coll., Ill., 1896-1903; prof., head dept. Latin, Washington and Jefferson Coll., 1905-23, dean, 1920-22, head dept. Romance langs., 1923-25, acting head of dept., 1925-27; prof. French, U. of Fla., summer 1927; prof. philosophy, U. of Miami, Fla., 1927-32; professor classic languages, Coburn Sch., Miami Beach, Fla., 1932-33; lecturer, instr. extension div. U. of Fla., 1933-37. War Work, A.E.F., France, 1918-19; mem. Army Ednl. Corps and dean of Am. students, U. of Grenoble, France, 1919. Former mem. mng. com. Am. Sch. of Classical Studies in Rome. Mem. Phi Beta Kappa, Phi Gamma Delta. Presbyterian. Contbr. to classical jours. Home: 541 San Lorenzo Av., Coral Gables, Fla. Died Nov. 27, 1952.

ENGMAN, Martin Feeney (eng-man), dermatologist; b. New Orleans, Aug. 20, 1868; s. Harry A. and Matilda (Feeney) E.; student U. Ky., U. Va.; M.D., N.Y.U., 1891; grad. study U. Heidelberg and in Paris, Berlin, Hamburg; m. Louise Charlott, 1897; children—Martin F., Walter C. Lecturer on dermatology and syphilis N.Y. Post Grad. Sch., 1894; began practice, St. Louis, 1897; lectr. on dermatology Marion-Sims Coll. of Medicine, St. Louis, 1898-99; clin. prof. dermatology Washington U., 1905—; pres., mem. bd. Bernard Free Skin and Cancer Hosp. One of the founders of the Nat. Leper Home and Bernard Free Skin and Cancer Hosp. Fellow A.M.A.; mem. Am. Dermatol. Assn. (ex-pres.), Mo. Social Hygiene Assn. (pres.); corr. mem. Danish Dermatol. Assn., French Dermatol. Assn. Episcopalian. Club: University. Discoverer of amoebic infection of the skin and five other hitherto unrecognized diseases of the skin. Home: 49 Fair Oakes, Clayton, Mo. Office: 3720 Washington Av., St. Louis. Died Oct. 12, 1953; buried Bellefontaine Cemetery, St. Louis.

ENGSTROM, Sigfrid Emanuel, clergyman, ch. exec.; b. Chicago, Ill., Feb. 15, 1907; s. Andrew Malcolm and Emily Christine (Chindblom) E.; A.B., Augustana Coll. Rock Island, Ill., 1930; B.D. Augustana Theol. Sem., 1932; Doctor Divinity, Capitol University, 1948; married Ida Christine Stenstrom, June 25, 1932; children—Nancy Emily, Robert Alan, John David. Shipping clerk, Bike-Web Mfg. Co., Chicago, Ill., 1921-23; trafic mgr., All-American Radio Corp., Chicago, 1923-26; ordained to ministry of Lutheran Ch., 1932; pastor, Gethsemane Ch., St. Louis, Mo., 1932-35; Faith Ch., Griswold, Ia., 1935-36, Bethany Ch., Des Moines, Ia., 1936-37. Field sec. and sec. of stewardship Iowa Luth. Conf., Augustana Church 1935-39; pres. Iowa Conf. Luther League, 1932-34; pres. Augustana Synod Nat. Luther League, 1934-36; pres. Luth. Home Mission Council of America, 1939-42; pres. Div. of American Missions of Nat. Luth. Council, 1942-46, sec., 1946-49; special commissioner to Finland, Lutheran World Fedn., 1948, delegate Hanover, Germany, 1952; executive dir. Board American Missions of Augustana Lutheran Church; director Luth. World Action for Augustana Lutheran Ch.; pres. Am. Lutheran Conf., 1953-54. Mem. Tau Kappa Alpha, Pi Kappa Delta. Editor Augustana Annual. Contbr. articles to church publs. Home: 4924 Maple Rd., Minneapolis 10. Office: 2445 Park Av., Mpls. 4. Died Apr. 28, 1955; buried Lakewood Cemetery, Mpls.

ENNIS, Joseph (Burroughs), director Am. Locomotive Co.; b. Wortendyke, N.J., May 29, 1879; s.

William C. and Kate E. (Burroughs) E.; grad. high sch., Paterson, N.J., 1895; D. Engring., Clarkson College of Technology, 1945; m. Lillian R. Jersey, Dec. 14, 1903; 1 dau., Ruth L. Draftsman, Rogers Locomotive Works, 1895-99; leading draftsman Schenectady (N.Y.) Locomotive Works, 1899-1900. Rogers Locomotive Works, 1900-01, Cooke Works of Am. Locomotive Co., 1901-02; in mech. engr.'s office of Am. Locomotive Co., N.Y. City, 1902-05, asst. to mech. engr., 1906-08, designing and estimating engr., 1908-12, chief mech. engr., 1912-17, v.p. engring., 1917-41, dir., 1924—, sr. v.p. engring. Am. Locomotive Co., 1941-47. Awarded Henderson medal by Franklin Inst., Apr., 1944. Fellow Am. Soc. M.E.; member Am. Soc. Metals, Newcomen Soc. of England (mem. of council, London). Methodist. Clubs: Engineers, Railroad, Metropolitan. Home: 9 Pope Rd., Paterson 4, N.J. Died Sept. 22, 1955.

ENNIS, Thomas Leland, lawyer; b. Rotterdam Junction, N.Y., May 8, 1891; s. Charles Alfred and Margaret Rose (Turnbull) E.; B.S., Union Coll., Schenectady, N.Y., 1914; LL.B., Columbia, 1917; m. Madeleine Smith, Aug. 30, 1919; 1 son, Thomas Allen. Admitted to N.Y. bar, 1917; asso. with Hughes, Schurman & Dwight, 1919-27; asst. to gen. counsel, Del. & Hudson Co., 1927-35, gen. counsel, 1935-41; vice pres. and gen. counsel since 1942; mem. bd. mgrs. since 1938 (v.p., gen. counsel and director of 10 companies controlled or affiliated with it, including the Delaware and Hudson Railroad Corporation. Enlisted as seaman in U.S.N.R.F., in World War 1, May, 1917; active duty successively as seaman, petty officer, chief boatswain's mate and ensign until discharged, June, 1919. Member Am. Bar Assn., N.Y. State Bar Assn., Assn. of Bar of City of New York, Association of Practitioners before the Interstate Commerce Commn., Alumni Assn. of Law Sch. of Columbia U., Alpha Delta Phi. Member bd. trustees, Boys' Club of New York. Republican. Episcopalian. Clubs: University (New York); Rockaway Hunting (Cedarhurst, N.Y.). Home: 850 Park Av. Office: 230 Park Av., N.Y.C. Died Sept. 30, 1952.

ENOS, George M(agee) (ē'nŭs), univ. prof., engr.; b. Dubuque, Ia., July 8, 1896; s. George Alfred and Evalyn (Magee) E.; B.S. in Metall. Engring., S.D. Sch. of Mines, 1921, Metall. E., 1922; M.Sc., Carnegie Inst. Tech., 1922; Ph.D., U. Cincinnati, 1925; m. Edna Jones, Feb. 21, 1924; children—Robert Jones, Ruth Evalyn. Teacher grade sch., S.D., 1914-15; asst., chem. labs., S.D. Sch. of Mines, 1916-21; jr. metallurgist U.S. Bureau of Mines, Pittsburgh, 1922-23; successively instr., asst. prof., asso. prof. metallurgy, U. Cincinnati, 1923-39; cons. metallurgist various Cincinnati firms, 1923-39; prof. metall. engring. Purdue U. since 1947, also chmn. of div.; cons. metallurgist. Served with U.S. Army, 1939-46; commd. capt. and advanced through grades to col.; comdg. officer, 5560th Organized Reserve Research and Dev. Group; dir. engring. Cincinnati ordnance dist. Ordnance Dept. Mem. Am. Inst. Mining and Metall. Engineers, Am. Soc. for Metals, Am. Ordnance Assn., Reserve Officers Association, Sigma Xi, Tau Beta Pi, Phi Lambda Upsilon, Acacia, Scabbard and Blade. Mason (32°). Author: Visual Examination of Steel, 1938; (with W. E. Fontaine) Elements of Heat Treatment (in press). Contbr. articles to professional jours. Home: 1215 Vine St., West Lafayette, Ind. Died Oct. 27, 1952.

ENRIGHT, Richard Edward, police ofcl.; b. Campbell, N.Y., Aug. 30, 1871; s. Michael H. and Jett (Bennett) E.; ed. high sch., Campbell, and Elmira Business Coll.; m. Jeane Paterson Smith, Nov. 27, 1918. Police commr., N.Y.C., 1918-25; now pres. Richard E. Enright, Inc.; v.p. Gainsborough Art Galleries. Decorated Comdr. Order of Vasa (Sweden); Order of Dannebrog (Denmark); Order of St. Olaf (Norway); Crown of Italy (Italy); Order of Isabella, the Catholic (Spain); Order of Leopold II (Belgium); Order of the Golden Cross (Austria), Order of St. Sava (Serbia); Officer Order of Ferdinand I (Rumania); Order of the Redeemer (Greece); Victorian Order (Gt. Britain); Order of the Sun (Peruvia); Chevalier Legion of Honor (France). Author: Vultures of the Dark, 1924; The Borrowed Shield, 1925. Home: 278 Garfield Pl., Bklyn.; (summer) Massapequa, L.I. Office: 222 W. 59th St., N.Y.C. Died Sept. 5, 1953.*

ENSLOW, Linn Harrison, cons. engr., editor; b. Richmond, Va., Feb. 26, 1891; s. Linn B. and Marie H. (Harrison) E.; B.S. in Engring. Chemistry, Va. Poly. Inst., 1912; grad. courses in chemistry Johns Hopkins, 1913-15; m. Mary Elva Glendy, Aug. 12, 1915; children—Harrison, Nancy Adair (Mrs. Lawton Spencer). Indsl. chemist Gen. Chem. Co., 1912-14; chemist Md. State Health Dept., 1914-17; chemist in charge water purification plants, Spartanburg, S.C., and Panama Canal, 1917-20; san. engr., chemist, Va. State Dept. Health, 1920-25; research and development engr. The Chlorine Inst. Am., 1925; apptd. editor Water Works and Sewerage (now Water and Sewage Works), Gillette Pub. Co., 1931, v.p. Gillette Pub. Co., 1934-53. Served with 1st Md. Cav. AUS, World War I; spl. cons. WPB, World War II. Fellow Am. Pub. Health Assn.; mem. Am. Soc. C.E. (past chmn. san engring. div.), Am. Water Works Assn. (Diven medal; Goodell prize; George W. Fuller Meml. award; chmn. publ. com.; dir.; mem. exec. com.; vice chmn. on awards; v.p.; pres. 1949; chmn. gen. policy com.; nat. water policy com.), New England Water Works Assn., Am. Inst. Chem. Engrs., Am. Fedn. Sewage Works Assn. (dir.; v.p.; chmn. publicity com.), N.Y. State (past pres.; chmn. program com.; exec. com.; v.p.), N.J. Sewage works assns., Pa. Water Works Operators Assn., Md.-Del. Water and Sewage Assn., (hon.) Inst. Sewage Purification (Brit.), Water and Sewage Works Mfrs. Assn. (dir.; past chmn. exec. com.), Kappa Alpha. Developer water and sewage treatment processes; inventor equipment for water and sewage purification control. Home: 3437 83d St., Jackson Heights, L.I.; also "sunnyside," Back Creek Valley, Pulaski County, Va. Office: Scranton Pub. Co., 1955 E. 44th St., N.Y.C. 17; also 185 N. Wabash Av., Chgo. 1. Died Nov. 3, 1957; buried New Dublin Presbyn. Ch. Cemetery, Dublin, Va.

ENSTROM, William N., banker; b. New York, N.Y., Sept. 9, 1888; s. Frederick and Anne Eugenie (Fisk) E.; LL.D., Hamilton Coll. Clk. N.Y. Nat. Exchange Bank, now Irving Trust Co., 1906, asst. cashier, 1917-19, v.p., 1919-40, dir., 1939, 1st v.p., 1940-42, pres., 1942-49, chmn. bd., 1949-57, chmn. exec. com., 1957—; director Canada Dry Ginger Ale, Inc., Warner-Lambert Pharmaceutical Company, Incorporated. Served as officer, USN, 1917-19. Clubs: Pilgrims, Racquet and Tennis, Recess, Union League, Brook (N.Y.C.); Augusta (Ga.) Nat. Golf; Nat. Golf Links (Southampton, N.Y.); Pine Valley (N.J.); Blind Brook (Port Chester, N.Y.). Office: 1 Wall St., N.Y.C. Died July 1, 1957.

EPPLEY, Eugene C. (ĕp'lē) hotel exec.; b. Akron, O., Apr. 8, 1884; s. Owen and Jessie C. (Phillips) E.; grad. Culver (Ind.) Mil. Acad., 1901; student Stanford, 1902-03; unmarried. Began with McKinley Hotel, Canton, O., 1903; pres. Eppley Hotels Co. 1915-56, operating 22 hotels; chairman of board Sheraton Cadillac Hotel, Detroit; hon. chmn. bd. Sheraton Corp. Am.; director Branliff Internat. Airways, Sheraton Corp. Am. Dir. Culver Ednl. Found.; president Eugene C. Eppley Foundation, Inc. Served as National Food Aministrator for Hotels, World War I; food consultant to Sec. of War, World War II. Dir. Mt. Rushmore Nat. Memorial Society of the Black Hills (South Dakota), Greater Omaha Assn., Omaha Chamber Commerce; mem. Hotel Men's Mut. Benefit Assn. of U.S. and Can (pres. 3 terms), Chi Psi (exec. council). Decorated Gold Cross of Social Welfare (French), 1926. Crowned King Ak-Sar-Ben XXXIX, legendary Nebraskan Empire of Quivera, Omaha, 1933. Mason (32°, Shriner), Elk. Clubs: Omaha, Omaha Athletic, Omaha Field, Omaha Country. Address: Hotel Fontenelle, Omaha, Neb. Died Oct. 14, 1958; buried Culver (Ind.) Masonic Cemetery.

EPSTEIN, Jacob, sculptor; b. of Russian-Polish parents, N.Y.C., 1880; student of art at Ecole des Beaux Arts and Julian Acad.; m. Margaret Gilmour Dunlop. Executed 18 figures for the bldg. of the British Med. Assn., 1908; designed tomb of Oscar Wilde, Pére Lachaise Cemetery, Paris, 1912; meml. to W. H. Hudson, Hyde Park, London, 1925; carved two groups, "Day" and "Night," 1928, for Underground New Bldg., Westminster, London S.W.; 5 works in Nat. Gallery of Modern British Art; portraits, Admiral Lord Fisher, Joseph Conrad, Duchess of Hamilton, Lady Gregory, Prof. John Dewey (Columbia U.), Winston Churchill; also "Adam," a 3-ton statue in pink alabaster, exhibtd. in N.Y.C., 1940, and "Genesis." Author: Let There Be Sculpture, 1940, autobiographical. Address: 18 Hyde Park Gate, London, Eng. Died Aug. 19, 1959.

EPSTEIN, Max, chairman Gen. Am. Transportation Corp.; b. Cincinnati, O., Feb. 6, 1875; s. Morris and Cecelia (Wertheimer) E.; ed. Coll. City of N.Y.; m. Leola S. Selig, 1907. Resident of Chicago, 1891—; chmn. exec. com. Gen. Am. Transportation Corp. and dir. in affiliated cos.; dir. Chicago Daily News; chairman advisory com. Federal Reserve Bank; chairman Draft Board during World War; lt. col., U.S. Army Reserves. Actively interested in philanthropy; donor Max Epstein Clinic of the Univ. of Chicago. Trustee U. of Chgo., Art Inst. of Chgo.; dir. Boy Scouts of Am., Am. Red Cross. Republican. Jewish religion. Home: 915 Sheridan Rd., Winnetka, Ill. Office: 135 S. La Salle St., Chgo. Died Aug. 22, 1954.

EPSTEIN, Ralph C(ecil), economist; b. Chgo., Sept. 25, 1899; s. Hugo and Ellinor (Schwerin) E.; A.B., Columbia, 1921; A.M., Harvard, 1925, Ph.D., 1926; m. Miriam Abrams, Oct. 14, 1922; children—Elizabeth Frances (Mrs. Edwin N. Barker), Joan Ellinor (Mrs. John D. Gill). Asst. economics, Northwestern U., 1921-22, instr., 1922-23; asst. in economics, Harvard, 1924-25, tutor in div. history, govt. and economics, 1925-26; asst. prof. economics and business orgn., U. Buffalo, 1926-29, prof. since 1929, dean Sch. of Bus. Adminstrn., 1935-47, head dept. econs., 1939—; chmn. bd. Smith, Keynes & Marshall, Inc., book pubs.; engaged in industrial engring. with Gerard, Graham & Co., 1919-20; econ. and editorial work A. W. Shaw Co., 1922-23; on staff of Com. on Govt. Statistics, Washington, D.C., 1934; cons. economist U.S. Dept. Commerce, 1930-32. Special economic adviser and consultant, War Production Board, Washington, D.C., 1942-43. Expert consultant to War Dept. (HQ, ASF), 1943-45; to Office Contract Settlement, Washington, D.C., 1944-45. Vice pres. Family Service Soc.; mem. nat. bd. govs. Atlantic Union Com. Pres. Buffalo chpt. Atlantic Union Com., representative to interview legislators and heads of state, in seventeen different countries, 1955; mem. of the advisory com. Graduate Faculty Polit. and Social Sci. of N.Y.; fellow Royal Econ. Soc.; mem. Am. Econ. Assn., Acad. Polit. Sci., Am. Statis. Assn. (v.p. 1937-38), Joint Com. on Income Tax Statistics, Auto. Industry Committee of Price Research Conference, Phi Beta Kappa. Clubs: Harvard, Buffalo. Author: The Automobile Industry—Its Economic and Commercial Development, 1928; Supplementary Readings in Economics, 1929; Trends in Buffalo Real Estate Assessments (with F. M. Clark), 1929; Source Book of the Study of Industrial Profits (with F. M. Clark), 1932; Industrial Profits in the U.S., 1934; History of General American Transportation Corp., 1948; Concentration and Price Trends in Rubber Manufacturing, 1949; Growth of the American Rubber Industry, 1953; How To Invest Your Money, 1957; Report on Asia, 1956; Report on Europe, 1956. Contbr. fgn. affairs publs., to econ. jours.; cons. indsl. corps. Address: 41 Irving Pl., Buffalo. Died Nov. 21, 1959.

ERB, Frank Otis, prof. religious edn.; b. St. John, N.B., Can., Aug. 14, 1878; s. George William and Eliza Ann (Riecker) E.; grad. Provincial Normal Sch., Fredericton, N.B., 1896; A.B., U. of N.B., 1900; student Colgate Theol. Sem., Hamilton, N.Y., 1901-03; grad. Rochester Theol. Sem., 1904; A.M., U. of Chicago, 1911, B.D., 1912, Ph.D., 1913; m. Emilie Hyatt, July 5, 1905; children—Karl Kierstead (dec.), Margaret Ballou (Mrs. Leston Fitch), Frances Elizabeth (Mrs. Fred Franz), Edgar Gillette. Came to U.S., 1901, naturalized citizen, 1917. Ordained ministry Bapt. Ch., 1903; pastor Glace Bay, N.S., 1904-09; asst. pastor Hyde Park Ch., Chicago, 1910-13, pastor Free Ch., Portland, Me., 1913-17; editor Young People's Publs., Am. Bapt. Pub. Soc., 1917-23; prof. religious edn., Colgate-Rochester Div. Sch., 1923-44, prof. emeritus since 1944; interim pastor, Calvary Bapt. Ch., Providence, R.I., 1944-45; interim pastor, Genesee Bapt. Ch., Rochester, N.Y., 1945-46, Lafayette Avenue Baptist Church, Buffalo, New York, 1946; visiting prof. School of Religious Edn., Auburn Theol. Sem., 1926-34; exten. lec. Univ. of Rochester, 1929-31. Rep. of Northern Baptist Conv. on Internat. S.S. Lesson Com., 1923-29; mem. edn. commission N.Y. State S.S. Assn.; chmn. N.Y. State Bapt. Commn. on Edn., 1927-31. Mem. Religious Edn. Assn., Nat. Soc. for Study of Edn., A.A.A.S., Theta Phi. Republican. Mason. Author: The Young People's Movement, 1916; Old Testament Leaders, 1921; New Testament Leaders, 1922; Life of Christ, 1923; Illustrated Bibles, 1937; Religious Education of Adults, 1938; also many articles in religious publs. Home: 251 Sherwood Av., Rochester 11, N.Y. Died Aug. 26, 1950; buried Evergreen Cemetery, Cazenovia, N.Y.

ERBEN, Henry Vander Bogert, elec. exec.; b. Schenectady, N.Y., Nov. 23, 1898; s. Hermann F. T. and Anna (Van der Bogert) E.; M.E., Yale, 1919; m. Frances Dey Carpenter, June 16, 1923; children—Alice Dey, Anna Louise. With General Electric Company, Schenectady, New York, 1920—, test course, 1920-22, lighting dept., comml. engring., 1922-23, apparatus div. central station dept., 1923-28, asst. mgr. apparatus div., 1928-29, mgr., apparatus div., 1929-33, mgr. switchgear div., 1933-39, asst. mgr. central station dept., 1939-41, mgr. 1941-44, commercial vice pres. and asst. gen. mgr. apparatus dept., 1944-48, v.p. and gen. mgr. apparatus dept., 1948-51, exec. v.p. apparatus group, 1951-54, exec. v.p. distbn. group, 1954—. Mem. Am. Inst. E.E., Newcomen Soc. Clubs: University, Engineers (N.Y.C.); Mohawk, Mohawk Golf (Schenectady). Home: Rosendale Rd., Schenectady, N.Y. Office: 570 Lexington Av., N.Y.C. 22. Died Dec. 26, 1956; buried Vale Cemetery, Schenectady.

ERDMAN, John Frederic, surgeon; b. Cin., Mar. 27, 1864; s. Zacharia and Maria Elizabeth (Lippert) E.; M.D., Bellevue Hosp. Med. Coll. (N.Y.U.), 1887, D.Sc., 1948; m. Georgiana Wright, June 20, 1894; children—Olivia Sturtevant, Sturtevant, Jane. Practiced at N.Y.C., 1887—; clin. prof. surgery, Univ. and Bellevue Hosp. Med. Coll. (N.Y.U.), 1893-1908; prof. practical anatomy, N.Y.U., 1895-1900; dir., prof. surgery, N.Y. Post-Grad. Med. Sch. and Hosp. Columbia, 1908-34; attending surgeon Post-Grad. Hosp., 1934-39; cons. surgeon since July, 1939; cons. surgeon, Gouverneur, Nassau, Mt. Vernon, Greenwich Gen. and Nyack, Rockland States, St. Luke's (Newburgh) hosps., State Hosp. at Central Islip, Home for Incurables, Hosp. Joint Diseases, Jersey City Med. Center, Union Hosp. (Bronx), Southampton Hosp. Capt., asst. surg., N.Y. Nat. Guard, 6 yrs. asst. surgeon U.S.R.C., 1912-15; lt. col. M.O.R.C. until 1929. Pres. Interstate Post. Grad. Med. Assn. N.A., 1936-37. Fellow A.C.S.; mem. A.M.A., Am. Assn. Obstetricians, Gynecologists and Abdominal Surgeons, N.Y. Surg. Soc., Am., N.Y. urol. socs., N.Y. Acad. Medicine, N.Y. County Med. Assn., Ohio Soc

N.Y., Bellevue Alumni. Episcopalian. Clubs: Union League, Devon Yacht, Maidstone (L.I.), L.I. Country, Hospital Graduates. Address: 122 E. 70th St., N.Y.C. Died Mar. 1954.

ERHARDT, John George (ĕr'härt), officer foreign service; b. Brooklyn, Nov. 4, 1889; s. John and Mary (Bader) E.; Ph.B., Hamilton Coll., Clinton, N.Y., 1915; student Fordham U. Law Sch., 1915-17, Am. Sch. for Classical Studies, Athens, Greece, 1921, U. of Bordeaux (France), 1933; m. Eleanor Davis, Feb. 21, 1920; children—Daniel Davis, Richard Hopkins. Admitted to N.Y. bar, 1919; in practice at N.Y. City, 1919-20; vice consul Athens, Greece, 1920, consul, 1920-24; consul Winnipeg, Can., 1924-26; assigned to commercial office, Dept. of State, 1926-30, chief, 1928-30; rep. Dept. of State at various foreign trade convs. and inter-departmental trade confs.; consul Bordeaux, France, 1930-33; consul gen. Hamburg, Germany, 1933-37; assigned to Dept. of State, 1937; inspector diplomatic missions and consular posts, 1937-39; consul gen. and first sec., London, 1939-41; chief, Div. of Fgn. Service Personnel, Dept. of State, since 1941; deputy dir. in charge of recruitment and training of personnel for service in liberated areas, 1943; dir., Office of the Foreign Service, 1944, political adviser to Commanding American General in Austria with personal rank of Minister, 1945; apptd. E.E. and M.P. to Austria, Aug. 2, 1946; del. to Council Fgn. Ministers, Moscow, Mar. 1947; last assignment E.E. and Ambassador E. to Union of South Africa. Served in U.S. Army, 1918-20. Mem. Am. Acad. Polit. and Social Science, Delta Upsilon, St. James Club, London. Presbyterian. Club: Cosmos (Washington). Address: Dept. of State, Washington. Died Feb. 18, 1951; buried Hamilton Coll. Cemetery, Clinton, N.Y.

ERICKSON, Cyrus, utilities exec.; b. Clinton, Minn., Mar. 8, 1898; s. John H. and Henrietta Rudolpha (Lee) E.; B.A., Carleton Coll., 1920; LL.B., Harvard, 1924; m. Dorothy Caswell, Mar. 22, 1929; 1 dau., Elizabeth. Editor Charletonian, 1919; asso. editor The Ortonville (Minn.) Independent, 1920-21; admitted to Minn. bar, 1924; practice of law, Mpls., 1924-26; with Northern States Power Co., Mpls., 1926—, gen. counsel, 1954—. Mem. Am. (mem. atomic power com.), Minn. (mem. com. atomic energy law), Hennepin County bar associations. Clubs: Minneapolis Athletic, Minneapolis Golf. Home: 2729 Drew Av. S., Mpls. 16. Office: 15 S. 5th St., Mpls. 2. Died Jan. 7, 1959.

ERICKSON, Frank Morton, educator; b. Kendallville, Ind., Sept. 21, 1870; s. Gunder and Mary Louise (Sharp) E.; A.B., Wabash Coll., 1892; M.A., U. Chgo., 1895; student archaeology, Athens, Greece, 1900; student Harvard, 1905-06, Stanford, 1915; Ed. D., Willamette U., 1934; m. Harriet Sophronia Shulze, June 14, 1893 (dec.); children—Frank Morton (dec.), Herbert Shulze, Mary Marilla. Tchr. Greek and Latin, Highland Coll., 1892-94; prof. Greek, Ripon Coll., 1895-14, dean, 1909-14; prof. edn., U. Ida., 1914-20; prof. edn., Willamette U., 1920-40, dean univ., 1931-40; ret. Sept. 1940. With Army Ednl. Corps, A.E.F. U. at Beaune, France, World War I. Mem. Soc. Coll. Tchrs. Edn., Am. Assn. U. Profs., Sigma Chi. Republican. Presbyn. Home: 3505 Foothill Road, Santa Barbara, Cal. Died Aug. 28, 1957; buried Kendallville, Ind.

ERICSSON, Frans August, coll. dean; b. Pjetteryd, Sweden, Aug. 15, 1883; s. Peter Erik and Ingrid Kajsa (Johannesson) Johansson; came to U.S., 1905, naturalized, 1911; A.B., Upsala Coll., East Orange, N.J., 1911, A.M., 1912; Ph.D., N.Y.U., 1932; LL. D. (hon.), Augustana Coll. and Theol. Sem., Rock Island, Ill., 1935; m. Gertie Helena Sandquist, Dec. 26, 1912 (died 1931); children—Vivie, Lennart, Margaret; m. 2d, Esther H. Fant, Nov. 25, 1932; stepdaus., Ruth, Barbara. Instr. German and Swedish, Upsala Coll., 1911-14, prof. German and Swedish, 1914-18, acting pres., 1918-20, 1936-38, dean since 1920, 1st Gustaf V. prof. Swedish lang. and lit. since 1945. Decorated Order of Vasa, 1st class, Sweden, 1943. Mem. bd. trustees Luth. Meml. Hosp., Newark. Mem. Assn. Coll. Deans, Swedish Cultural Society, Swedish-Am. Hist. Soc., Soc. Advancement Scandinavian Studies, Am. Assn. U. Profs., Phi Delta Kappa. Club: Rotary Internat. Home: 540 Springdale Av., East Orange, N.J. Died Mar. 30, 1952; buried Restland Meml. Park, Hanover, N.J.

ERIKSON, Carl Anthony, partner Schmidt, Garden & Erikson; b. Joliet, Ill., Aug. 15, 1888; s. August and Christine (Anderson) E.; B.S. in Architecture, U. of Pa., 1910; m. Ruth Howe, Nov. 20, 1913; 1 son, Carl Anthony. Draftsman various architects, 1905-13; with Schmidt, Garden & Martin, Chicago, Ill., 1913-25; partner Schmidt, Garden & Erikson, architects and engrs. specializing in hosp. work and industrial buildings since 1925. Trustee University of Pennsylvania. Fellow American Institute of Architects; mem. Am. Hosp. Assn., Phi Gamma Delta. Club: University (Chicago). Home: 200 E. Pearson St. Office: 104 S. Michigan Av., Chgo. Died Apr. 1958.

ERIKSON, Henry Anton, physicist; b. Mt. Morris, Wis., July 30, 1869; s. Hemming and Elizabeth (Tommeraas) E.; B.E.E., U. of Minn., 1896, Ph.D., 1908; student U. of Chicago, 1899, Cambridge U., Eng., 1908-09; m. Winifred Boynton, of New Lisbon, Wis., June 21, 1899; children—Hemming (dec.), Elizabeth W., Henry B. Instr. in science, high sch., Rochester, Minn., 1896-97; instr. physics, 1897-1906, asst. prof., 1906-14, asso. prof., 1914-15, prof. 1915-38, also chairman of dept., professor emeritus, 1938—, University of Minnesota. Fellow A.A.A.S.; mem. Am. Physical Soc., Sigma Xi, Tau Beta Pi, Theta Chi. Club: Cosmopolitan. Author: Elements of Mechanics; Manual of Physical Measurements, 1902. Contbr. on ionization in Physical Rev., Philos. Mag., others. Address: 1207 Genoa St., Coral Gables, Fla. Died June 22, 1957; buried Mount Morris, Wis.

ERK, Edmund Frederick, ex-congressman; b. Pitts., Apr. 17, 1872; s. Frederick J. and Johanna (Burke) E.; ed. pub. schs.; m. Martha H. Hervey, Nov. 18, 1914; 1 dau., Louise M. (Mrs. Lawson M. McKenzie). Clk. Com. on Foreign Affairs, Nat. Ho. of Rep., 1919-31; sec. Am. delegation to League of Nations Conf., Geneva, 1924-25; mem. 72d Congress (1931-33), 30th Pa. Dist. Republican. Mason. Club: Nat. Press (Washington). Author: A Merry Crusade to the Golden Gate, 1906; The First Born Documents of Popular Constitutional Liberty, 1925, 27; Peace the Birth-Song of Christianity, 1929. Compiler: Romance of the Mails, 1931. Home: 1208 Haslage Av., Pitts. Died Dec. 14, 1953.*

ERMINGER, Howell B., Jr., investment securities; b. Macon, Ga., July 8, 1882; s. Howell B. and Caroline (Woodson) E.; ed. Mercer U., Macon, Ga., 1899-1902; m. Lila Willingham, Apr. 27, 1910; children—Carolyn (Mrs. John de Laittre), Bertha (Mrs. Aldis J. Browne, Jr.). Began in the lumber business, 1903; pres. Builders Lumber & Supply Co., Macon, 1909-21; engaged in spl. financial work. Havana, Cuba, Boston, 1921-26; pres. Miami Corp., investment securities, since 1926; v.p. and dir. Nome Mines. Trustee Estate of Charles Deering; mem. bd. dirs. C.&O. Ry., Pere Marquette R.R.; dir. Greenbrier Hotel Corp. Mem. Phi Delta Theta. Presbyterian. Clubs: Chicago, Casino, Attic (Chicago); City Midday, The Links, Bankers (New York). Home: 219 Lake Shore Dr. Office: 410 N. Michigan Av., Chicago. Died Aug. 21, 1951; buried Chicago.

ERNST, August Frederic, coll. pres.; b. Hanover, Germany, June 25, 1841; s. Rev. Karl and Agnes (Brackebusch) E.; grad. Gymnasium, Celle, Hanover, Germany, 1859; studied U. Gottingen, 1859-62; m. Agnes Hartwig, Jan. 6, 1867. Came to U.S. 1863; served a Luth. congregation as pastor, 1863-68; pastor 1st Luth. Ch., Albany, N.Y., 1868-69; prof. Northwestern Coll., Watertown, Wis., 1869—, coll. pres., 1870—. Elected pres. joint Luth. synod Wis., Minn., and Mich., 1892, re-elected 1895, 97, 99. Active in politics only 1890, when State Wis. was carried by Democrats. Address: Watertown, Wis. Died Aug. 8, 1924.

ERNST, Fritz B., ret. exec.; b. Maidson, Ind., Oct. 23, 1877; s. Louis and Sophia (Bruner) E.; B.S. in C.E., Purdue U., 1900. With "Railway Age," 1900-01; tchr. car design, locomotive design, and ry. mech. engring. Purdue U., 1902-06; with Fitzhugh-Luther, six months 1906; with Am. Steel Foundries, 1906-47; ret. Jan. 1947. Dir. Chgo. Crime Commn., Chgo. City Opera Co.; mem. bd. Travelers Aid Soc., Boy Scouts Am. Clubs: Chicago, University, Tavern, Glen View; Bohemian (San Francisco). Author books including: Small Town Boy Goes Away to College. Home: Parkway Hotel, 2100 Lincoln Park W., Chgo. Died Feb. 1959.

ERSKINE, John, author; b. New York, N.Y., Oct. 5, 1879; s. James Morrison and Eliza Jane (Hollingsworth) E.; A.B., Columbia, 1900, A.M., 1901, Ph.D., 1903, LL.D., 1929; LL.D., Norwich U., 1919; Litt.D., Amherst, 1923; L.H.D., Hobart Coll., 1927; Litt.D., U. of Bordeaux, France, 1929; Mus.D., Rollins Coll., 1931; Pd.D., N.Y. State Normal Coll., 1934; Mus D., Cornell Coll., 1935; Mus.D., Ill. Wesleyan Univ., 1935; L.H.D., Boston University, 1935; married Pauline Ives, June 9, 1910 (divorced, 1945); children—Graham, Anna; m. 2d, Helen Worden, July 3, 1945. Instr. in English, 1903-06, asso. prof. 1906-09, Amherst College; adj. prof. English, 1909-16, prof. 1916-37, emeritus since 1937, Columbia U. Chmn. administrative com., Juilliard Sch. of Music, 1927-28, pres. 1928-37, dir. since 1927, chmn. bd. 1948; trustee Juilliard Musical Foundation since 1937, pres. 1948. Dir. Met. Opera Assn., 1935, chairman management com. Trustee French Inst., 1935-39. Vestryman, Corp. Trinity Parish, N.Y., 1916-41, warden 1939-41; trustee P.E. Pub. Schs., New York, 1916-41, chmn. school com. many years, pres. 1939-41. Director Winter Institute of Literature, University of Miami, 1945-46; Member Municipal Art Committee, 1935-37. Member Poetry Society America (president 1922). College English Assn.; N.Y. Bohemians, Delta Upsilon, Phi Beta Kappa, Phi Mu Alpha Sinfonia fraternities. Mem. exec. com. Am. Council Learned Soc., 1920-24, secretary, 1921-24; member National Institute Arts and Letters, American Acad. of Arts and Sciences, Soc. of American Historians. Awarded Butler medal, 1917; David Bispham Opera medal, 1933; chmn. Nat. Com. for Music Appreciation, 1940-41; chmn. Army Edn. Commn., A.E.F., 1918-19; ednl. dir. A.E.F. Univ. of Beaune, France, 1919. Decorated Chevalier Legion of Honor, France, 1919, officer, 1939; D.S.M., U.S., 1919. Hon. citizen of Beaune, France, 1919. Clubs: Columbia U., St. Andrews, Century. Author: The Elizabethan Lyric, 1903; Selections from Faerie Queene, 1905; Actaeon and Other Poems, 1906; Leading Am. Novelists, 1909; Written English (with Helen Erskine), 1910; The Golden Treasury (edited with W. P. Trent), 1912; Great American Writers (with W. P. Trent), 1912; Selections from the Idylls of the King, 1912; A Pageant in Honor of Roger Bacon, 1914; The Moral Obligation To Be Intelligent, 1915; The Shadowed Hour, 1917; Democracy and Ideals, 1920; The Kinds of Poetry, 1920; Collected Poems, 1922; The Literary Discipline, 1923; Sonata and Other Poems, 1925; The Private Life of Helen of Troy, 1925; The Enchanted Garden, 1925; Galahad, 1926; Prohibition and Christianity, 1927; Adam and Eve, 1927; The Delight of Great Books, 1928; Penelope's Man, 1928; Sincerity, 1929; Uncle Sam, 1930; Cinderella's Daughter, 1930; Unfinished Business, 1931; Jack and the Beanstalk, 1931; Tristan and Isolde, 1932; Bachelor of Arts, 1934; Helen Retires, 1934; Forget If You Can, 1935; Solomon, My Son! 1935; Influence of Women—And Its Cure, 1936; Young Love, 1936; (in collaboration) The President's Mystery Story, 1936; Brief Hour of Francois Villon, 1937; The Start of the Road, 1938; Give Me Liberty, 1940; Cassanova's Women, 1941; Song Without Words, 1941; Mrs. Doratt, 1941; The Complete Life, 1943; The Voyage of Captain Bart, 1943; The Philharmonic-Symphony Society of New York; Its First Hundred Years, 1943; What is Music?, 1944; Human Life of Jesus, 1945; The Memory of Certain Persons, 1947; My Life in Music, 1950; English titles for French films: Story of a Cheat, 1938; The Baker's Wife, 1939; My Life as A Teacher, 1948. Editor: books by Lafacadio Hearn; Interpretations of Literature, 1915; Appreciations of Poetry, 1916; Life and Literature, 1917; Talks to Writers, 1920; Books and Habits, 1921; Pre-Raphaelite and Other Poets, 1922; Musical Companion, 1935. Co-editor: Cambridge History of American Literature, 3 vols., 1917-19. Address: 540 Park Av., N.Y.C. Died June 2, 1951.

ERVIN, Morris Donaldson, newspaper corr.; b. Dayton, Ky., Feb. 1, 1894; s. John Newton and Elizabeth Templeton (Mollyneaux) E.; A.B., Wooster (O.) Coll., 1920; m. Louise Hauer, June 27, 1924; children—Donald, Suzanne (Mrs. John Felber). Reporter Commercial Tribune, Cincinnati, 1912-1915; reporter Cincinnati Times-Star, 1921-23, chief Columbus (O.) bureau, 1923-24, chief Washington bur., 1924-56, political and economic columnist, 1956—; asso. editor Sheridan Reveille (Army paper), Montgomery, Ala., 1917. Enlisted as pvt., Co. D, 146th Inf., U.S. Army, 1917; with A.E.F., 1918-19; hon. disch. as 2d lt., 1919. Newsweek Magazine Award, 1952, 54. Clubs: National Press (mem. bd. of govs., 1939-45), Girdiron (Washington). Contbr. to mags. Home: 7104 Leesville Blvd., Springfield, Virginia. Office: 1393 National Press Bldg., Washington. Died Nov. 2, 1956; buried Arlington Nat. Cemetery.

ERWIN, Clyde Atkinson, educator; b. Atlanta, Ga., Feb. 8, 1897; s. Sylvanus and Mamie (Putnam) E.; ed. U. of N.C.; Pd.D., Catawba Coll., Salisbury, N.C., 1935; Ed.D., North Carolina State College, Raleigh, 1950; m. Evelyn Miller, Apr. 28, 1920; children—Frances Elizabeth, Clyde Atkinson, Jr. Sch. teacher and prin., 1914-25; supt. Rutherford County Schs., N.C., 1925-34; state supt. of pub. instrn. for N.C. since 1934. Chmn. bd. of trustees, East Carolina Teachers Coll.; mem. bd. of trustees Greater Univ. of N.C., N.C. Coll., Agrl. and Tech. Coll., Elizabeth City State Teachers Coll.; mem. High Sch. Textbook Com., 1927-32; chmn. Elementary Textbook Commn., 1933-34; pres. Southern Council Chief State Sch. Officers, since 1944; mem. exec. com., chmn. legislative com. Nat. Council Chief State Sch. Ofcrs., 1945-47, v.p., 1948, pres. 1949; mem. Yearbook Com., Am. Assn. Sch. Adminstrs., 1945-46; consultant Nat. Safety Council; cons. Ednl. Policies Com. of Nat. Educational Assn.; consultant to Rural Editorial Service for State Education Assns.; mem. com. on Scouting in the Schs.; mem. nat. com. on Sch. Savings; mem. com. on ednl. bldgs. and equipment of Am. Council on Edn.; mem. N.C. chapter of Horace Mann League; mem. Nat. Commn. on Safety Edn.; consultant on regional Schs. at Southern Govs. Conf.; v.p. Regional Council for Edn.; mem. Army Adv. Com. in Raleigh; chmn. United States Delegation, 13th International Conference on Public Education, Geneva, 1950. Member N.E.A., N.C. Education Assn. (past pres), Sigma Chi, Phi Kappa Phi, Kappa Phi Kappa. Mason. Clubs: Kiwanis (Raleigh, N.C.), Rutherford County. Mem. bd. adv. editors of The School Executive. Home: 2609 Clark Av. Address: State Education Bldg., Raleigh, N.C. Died July 19, 1952.

ERWIN, George L., Jr., business exec.; b. Muskegon, Mich., June 14, 1895; s. George L. and Hattie (Brown) E.; M.E., Cornell, 1917; m. Helen Ruth Baldwin, May 10, 1930; 1 dau., Nancy Ann. Salesman Manning, Maxwell & Moore, St. Louis, 1921-22; advt. mgr. Kearney & Trecker Corp., Milw., 1923-25, gen. sales mgr., 1925-36; dept. mgr., dist. mgr., asst. to v.p. in charge sales Crane Co., Chgo., 1936-51, v.p. heating div., 1951—. Served as 1st lt. U.S. A.A.F., 1917; night bombing pilot 100th squadron, R.A.F., 1918. Trustee Village of Glencoe, 1946-50. Mem. St. Andrews Soc. Republican. Episcopalian. Mason (32°, K.T., Shriner). Clubs: University, Cornell (Chgo.); Chgo. Curling (Northbrook, Ill.); Skokie Country (Glencoe, Ill.); Rotary. Home: Cumnock Rd., Inverness Countryside, Palatine, Ill. Office: 836 S. Michigan Av., Chgo. 5. Died May 15, 1956; buried Memorial Park, Evanston, Ill.

ERWIN, Henry Parsons, investment banker; b. Newark, July 16, 1881; s. Orlando Richard and Mary Elizabeth (Parsons) E.; A.B., U. Mich., 1904; grad. Ill. Inst. Tech.; student U. Chicago, 1916-17; D.Sc. (hon.), George Washington University, 1952; married Helen Peck Blodgett, 1921; children—Eileen (Mrs. John Alvin Croghan), Hope (Mrs. Macdonald Goodwin), Henry Parsons. Engr., mfr., mem. Washington Stock Exchange; dir. Riggs Nat. Bank, Fed. Storage Co., Washington. Trustee, sec., chmn. finance com. bd. trustees George Washington U.; mem. Community Chest Fedn. Classification Com.; trustee United Community Services of Washington, trustee Boys Club of Washington, treas. Boys Club Found., treasurer of the National Capital Area Boy Scouts. Served as capt., comdr. Paterson (N.J.) Ordnance Depot, Feb.-Nov. 1918; served, Office Chief of Ordnance, Washington, 1918-20; lt. col., active duty, Ordnance Corps, U.S. Army, Washington, World War II; lt. col., U.S. Army Res. since 1943 to time of death, June 3, 1953. Member Am. Ordnance Assn. (founder, dir., treas.), A.S.M.E., Nat. Parks Assn. (sec.), S.A.R., Archaeol. Soc. of Washington (v.p.), Com. of One Hundred (Miami Beach, Fla.). Republican. Episcopalian. Clubs: Circumnavigators Around World; Athletic Assn., Quadrangle (Chicago); Metropolitan, Univ., Army and Navy, Army-Navy Country, Nat. Press (Washington); Chevy Chase (Md.); Surf (Miami Beach). Author: Ordnance Supply in Time of War and Peace, 1939; numerous elec. and hydraulic engring. articles. Home: Arbremont, Upton St. and Linnean Av. N.W., Washington; also (summer) Cragmere, Mackinac Island, Mich. Office: 723 15th St., Washington 5. Died June 3, 1953; buried Arlington Nat. Cemetery.

ERWIN, Marion Corbett, naval officer (ret.); b. Hartsville, Tenn., Mar. 15, 1893; s. William Jefferson and Jennie Belle (Filson) E.; student, Bus. Coll., Cincinnati, 1909-10, Navy Electric School, 1914-15; grad. Naval War Coll., 1934; m. Beatrice Helen Chacksfield, Jan. 7, 1919; 1 son, Marion Corbett. Enlisted U.S. Navy as apprentice seaman, 1910, commd. ensign, 1917, advanced through grades to rear adm., 1946; service in Turkey, 1911-12, with Armed Guard and Brit. Grand Fleet, 1917-18; with amphibious forces, Africa, Solomons, Guam, Iwo Jima, P.I., Japan landings, 1941-45; ret. from active duty, 1946; now associated with J. W. Malmberg Co., investments. Awarded 2 Bronze Stars, various campaign and area medals, ribbons and battle stars, letter of commdn. from comdr. in chief, Atlantic fleet. Mem. U.S. Naval Inst. Repub. Episcopalian. Mason. Club: San Diego (Calif.). Home: 3230 Trumbull St., San Diego 6, Cal. Died Oct. 6, 1954.

ESCHER, Franklin (ĕsh'ĕr), banker; b. New York, June 19, 1881; s. Henry and Louise (Fasnacht) E.; student Yale, 1902; m. Mildred B. Gleason, Oct. 19, 1909. Began editorial work in New York, 1900; editor Investment Magazine, 1910-13, finance editor of Harper's Weekly, 1908-13, spl. lecturer on finance, Am. Inst. Banking, Princeton, New York U., Dartmouth Coll., 1910-15; partner John Muir & Co., mem. N.Y. Stock Exchange, 1919-20; now mem. Dresser and Escher, bankers, New York. Author: Elements of Foreign Exchange, 1910; Practical Investing, 1913; Foreign Exchange Explained, 1917; Modern Foreign Exchange, 1933. Home: 71 Chestnut St., Englewood, N.J. Office: 111 Broadway, N.Y.C. Died May 29, 1952.

ESCOBAR, Adrian C. (ĕs-kō-bär), former Argentine ambassador to U.S.; b. Buenos Aires, 1881; s. Juan Miguel Escobar and María Juliana de Acevedo Ramos; student sch. Law and Social Scis., Nat. U. of Buenos Aires, 1902. Sec. to pres. of Argentina, 1906-08; nat. dep. for Province of Buenos Aires, 1908-24, 32-36; municipal commr. in Suipacha, 1930; dir. gen. mail and telegraphy works of the nation, 1938-43; Argentine del. Pan-Am. Conf. of Lima, 1938; ambassador to Spain, 1940; ambassador to U.S., 1943-44; v.p. Argentine delegation to UN conf., London, 1946; pres. Coll. of Law; mem. Nat. Commn. of Codification of Internat. Law, 1939. Decorated Knight of the Legion of Honor, Order of the Candor of the Andes, and Order of Bolivar. Author: Ideas of Government and Active Politics; Congress and the Confederacy of the Nations. Died Feb. 15, 1954.

ESHBACH, Ovid Wallace, educator; born Pennsburg, Pa., Apr. 13, 1893; s. Horace W. and Lena (Hill) E.; E.E., Lehigh U., 1915, M.S., 1920, E.D., 1948; D.Sc., Ursinus Coll., Collegeville, Pa., 1939; m. Clara E. Ortt, Oct. 4, 1919; children—John Robert, Frances Elinor. Asst. to chief engr. U.S. Naval Engr. Expt. Sta., Annapolis, Md., 1915-16; instr. Lehigh U., 1916-17, 1919-20, asst. prof. elec. engring. 1920-23; asst. engr. Bell Telephone Co. of Pa., Phila. 1923-25; spl. asst. Am. Tel. & Tel. Co., N.Y. City, 1925-39; dean Northwestern Tech. Inst., Evanston, Ill., 1939-53, Walter P. Murphy prof. engring. sci. and physics, 1953—; instr. night grad. sch., Brooklyn Poly. Inst., 1930, 32, 34, 36; nonresident instr. cooperative course in elec. engring. Mass. Inst. Tech., 1926-39. Served as pvt., U.S. Inf. and 3d O.T.C., 1917-18; 2d lt., Signal Corps, U.S. Army, 1918-19. Mem. bd. trustees Perkiomen Sch., Pennsburg, Pa. Awarded Octave Chanute medal, Western Soc. Engrs., 1945. Fellow Am. Inst. E.E., A.A.A.S.; mem. Am. Soc. Engineering Education, Western Society of Engineers (pres.), Sigma Xi, Eta Kappa Nu, Pi Tau Sigma, Tau Beta Pi, Triangle. Republican. Mem. Union Ch. Editor in chief; Handbook of Engineering Fundamentals, 1936. Home: 201 Kenilworth Av., Kenilworth, Ill. Office: Northwestern Technological Inst., Evanston, Ill. Died Mar. 4, 1958; buried Pennsburg, Pa.

ESKRIDGE, James Burnette (ĕsk'rĭj), educator; b. nr. Nashville; s. John Harper and Catherine Jamima (Castleman) E.; A.M., Burritt Coll., Spencer, Tenn., 1893; Ph.D. in Philosophy, Cumberland U., Lebanon, Tenn., 1897, LL.D., 1943; A.M. in Classical Langs., U. Chgo., 1903, Ph.D. in Classics, 1912; m. Nancy Ellen Hibbett, Dec. 2, 1892; children—Mrs. Leola Swann, James Burnette, Joseph Allen, Mrs. Mary Olive Alban. Instr. East Side Acad., Nashville, 1891-94; head Tng. Sch., Shelbyville, Tenn., 1894-96; prin. Springfield (Ten.) Collegiate Inst., 1896-97; instr. Latin and mathematics Boys' Tng. Sch., Montgomery, Ala., 1897-98; prof. classical langs. and lit. Tex. Christian U., Ft. Worth, 1898-1912; pres. Okla. (State) Coll. for Women, Chickasha, 1912-14; pres. Southwestern State Normal Sch., Weatherford, Okla., 1915-21; pres. Okla. Agrl. and Mech. Coll., 1921-23. Mem. N.E.A., Kappa Delta Pi. Democrat. Mem. Christian (Disciples) Church. Mason (32°), K.P. Author of The Influence of Cicero upon Augustine in the Development of His Oratorical Theory for the Training of the Ecclesiastical Orator, 1912. Home: 3113 E. Blackford, Evansville, Ind. Died Apr. 2, 1952; buried Mt. Olivet Cemetery, Nashville.

ESPENSHADE, Abraham Howry, educator; b. Lancaster, Pa., May 30, 1869; s. Benjamin and Esther Ann (Howry) E.; student Millersville and Westchester (Pa.) State normal schs., 1885-6, Lebanon Valley Coll., Annville, Pa., 1887; A.B., Wesleyan U., 1894; A.M., Columbian U., 1897; m. Fannie E. Wood, Dec. 19, 1901. Instr. English and history, Mercersburg (Pa.) Acad., 1894, Chauncy Hall Sch., Boston, 1895; univ. fellow English, Columbia U., 1896; instr. English, Barnard Sch., N.Y., 1897; asst. prof. English and rhetoric, Pa. State Coll., 1898—. Episcopalian Compiler of Forensic Declamations, 1901 S6. Author: Essentials of Composition and Rhetoric, 1904 H2. Address: State College, Pa. Deceased.

ESPINA, Concha, writer; b. Stantandez, Spain, Apr. 15, 1869; d. Victor Espina and Ascension Tagle; m. Ramon de la Senna, 1892; children—Ramon, Victor, Luis, Josefina. Mem. Hispanic Soc. Am. (v.p.), N.Y. Am. acads. arts and scis. Author numerous books published in Spanish. Home: 32 Alfonso XII, Madrid, Spain. Died May 19, 1955.

ESPINOSA, Aurelio Macedonio (ĕs-pē-nō-sä), educator; b. Carnero, Colo., Sept. 12, 1880; s. Celso and Rafaela (Martínez) E.; Ph.B., U. Colo., 1902, M.A., 1904; Ph.D., U. Chgo., 1909; hon. Litt.D., U. San Francisco, 1930; LL.D., U. N.M., 1934; m. Margarita Garcia, June 14, 1905; children—María Margarita, Aurelio Macedonio, José Manuel, María Josefita, Ramón Prof. modern langs., U. N.M., 1902-10; fellow and instr. Spanish, U. Chgo., 1908-09; asst. prof., asso. prof., prof. Romance languages, Stanford, 1910-47, head dept., 1932-47, emeritus. Editor Hispania, 1917-25, cons. editor, 1925—; asso. editor Jour. Am. Folk-Lore; hon. mem. N.M. Hist. Soc., Mexican Soc. Geography and Statistics, Chile Folk-Lore Soc.; corr. mem. Hispanic Soc. Am., Real Academia Española de la Lengua, Hispano-Americana de Ciencias y Artes de Cadiz. Spl. investigator in Spain under Am. Folk-Lore Soc. and the Junta para Ampliación de Estudios of Madrid, 1920; pres. Am. Folk-Lore Soc., 1923, 24, Am. Assn. Tchrs. Spanish, 1928, Pacific Coast Br. Am. Philol. Assn., 1929; Comendador con placa de la Real Orden de Isabel la Católica, 1922. Catholic. Author: Elementary Spanish Grammar; Beginning Spanish; Elementary Spanish Reader; First Spanish Reader; Elementary Spanish Composition and Conversation; Advanced Spanish Composition and Conversation; Easy Spanish Conversation; Cuentos y Romances; Primer of Spanish Pronunciation; Lecciones de Literatura Espanola; Studies in New Mexico Spanish; Cuentos Populares Españoles (3 vols.); El romancero español; Estudios sobre el español de Nuevo Mejico; Spanish Tradition in New Mexico; (brochure) Romancero Nuevomejicano; Romances tradicionales de Puerto Rico; Notes on the Origin of History of the Tar-Baby Story; España en Neuvo Méjico; España; Conchita Argüello; Historia de la literatura española; also many articles to jours. Editor of Martinez Sierra, Benavente, Echegaray, Ayala, Alvarez-Quintero, etc., for Am. schs. Translator into English various Spanish publs. and works from English into Spanish. Home: Stanford University, Cal. Died Sept. 4, 1958.

ESPINOSA DE LOS MONTEROS, Antonio, ambassador of Mexico to U.S.; b. Jan. 15, 1903; s. Antonio and Mari (Choza) E. de los M.; student Sacred Heart Coll., Denver; B.S., Gettysburg (Pa.) Coll., 1925; M.A., Harvard, 1927; m. Blanca Rico; children—Blanca, Antonieta. Economist, Ministry Finance, 1927-28, chief, econ. library and archives, 1929-30, chief, dept. alcohol, 1931-32, ofcl., bur. statistics, 1928-29, 1932-33; chief, dept. econ. studies, Ministry Nat. Economy, 1933-36; gen. mgr., later dir., Nacional Financiera, 1936—; ambassador to U.S., 1945—. Prof. econs. secondary sch. of Mexico City, 1927-31; prof. U. Nacional de México, 1929-34. Address: care Mexican Embassy, Washington. Died Sept. 19, 1959.*

ESSELEN, Gustavus John, research chemist; b. Roxbury, Mass., June 30, 1888; s. Gustavus John and Joanna (Blyleven) E.; A.B. magna cum laude, Harvard, 1909, A.M., 1911, Ph.D., 1912; m. Henrietta W. Locke, Sept. 18, 1912; children—Rosamond (Mrs. Bradford K. Bachrach), Josephine (Mrs. George Byron Hanson), Gustavus John, 3d. Mem. research lab. staff Gen. Electric Co., Lynn, 1912-14; asst. mgr., later mgr., Chem. Products Co., 1914-17; research staff Arthur D. Little, Inc., 1917-21; v.p. and dir. research Skinner, Sherman & Esselen, Inc., 1921-30; pres. and treas. Gustavus J. Esselen, Inc. (name changed to Esselen Research Corp. 1946), Boston, 1930-49; v.p. U.S. Testing Co., Inc., mgr. Esselen Research Div., 1950-52. President American Council of Commercial Laboratories, Incorporated, 1951-52. National Academy of Sciences delegate to Internat. Union of Chemistry, Liege, 1930, Lucerne, 1936. Chmn. bd. trustees Swampscott Pub. Library, 1928-38. Mem. Nat. Research Council, 1936-39 and 1940-43; mem. Mass. Bd. Registration Professional Engrs. and Land Surveyors, 1942-49, chmn. 1943, 48; mem. Referee Bd. Office Prodn. Research and Development, 1942-45 (chmn. joint Army-Navy-N.D.R.C. Committee on Tropical Deterioration, 1943-46). Served as a major and lt. colonel, Chemical Warfare Reserve, 1925-40. Received Pioneer Award of Nat. Assn. of Mfrs., 1940, Norris Award, 1948. Fellow A.A.A.S., Am. Inst. Chemists, Am. Acad. Arts and Scis. (council 1944-48); mem. Am. Chem. Soc. (dir. 1934-41; trustee permanent trust fund), Assn. Cons. Chemists and Chem. Engrs. (dir. 1936-39, 1946-49), Am. Inst. Chem. Engrs. (dir. 1931-33, 1934-36), Boston C. of C. (dir. 1943-46), Asso. Industries of Mass., Engineering Socs. N.E., N.E. Council, Tech. Assn. Pulp and Paper Industry, Soc. Chem. Industry of Great Britain (chmn. Am. sect. since 1949), Electrochem. Soc., Soc. Plastics Industry, Soc. Plastics Engrs., Alpha Chi Sigma, Sigma Xi. Conglist. Clubs: Harvard, Rotary, Union, Chemists (New York); Cosmos (Washington, D.C.). Author of numerous tech. papers and chapters on chem. products. Lecturer. Address: 99 Gale Rd., Swampscott, Mass. Died Oct. 22, 1952; buried Swampscott (Mass.) Cemetery.

ESSERY, Carl Vanstone, lawyer; b. nr. Croswell, Mich., Jan. 4, 1886; s. Evan and Victoria (Farewell) E.; A.B., U. Mich., 1910, J.D., 1912; m. Clara M. Mooney, Dec. 29, 1920. Admitted to Mich. bar, 1912, since practiced in Detroit; mem. Hill, Essery, Lewis & Andrews; chmn. bd., dir. Saturday Night Press, Inc., since 1948. Trustee Detroit Episcopal City Mission, Mariners' Ch., St. Peter's Home for Boys. Served as lt. (j.g.), U.S.N.R., World War I. Decorated Navy Cross. Mem. Maritime Law Assn. U.S. (exec. com. 1938-41; v.p. 1947-49), Am. (chmn. sect. bar orgn. activities 1937-38; mem. house dels. 1936-44; bd. govs. 1939-41; chmn. admiralty com. 1942-43, 46-49), Mich. State (pres. 1933-34), Pa. (hon.), Detroit bar assns., Am. Law Inst., Quarterdeck Soc. (hon. mem.), Detroit Bd. Commerce (v. chmn. port com. since 1946). Republican. Episcopalian. Mason. Clubs: Lawyers (U. Mich); Propeller U.S. (pres. Port Detroit 1937-38; nat. v.p. Lower Great Lakes 1945), Detroit, Detroit Boat, Thomas M. Cooley (Detroit). Home: Brookdale Rd., Birmingham, Mich. Office: Penobscot Bldg., Detroit 26. Died Sept. 18, 1953.

ESSEX, William Leopold, bishop; b. Piermont, N.Y., Feb. 8, 1886; s. William and Elizabeth (Looser) E; A.B, Columbia, 1906, S.T.D., 1937; B.D., Gen. Theol. Sem., N.Y. City, 1911, S.T.D., 1938; D.D., Nashotah (Wis.) House, 1936; m. Charlotte Josephine Nason, June 11, 1914; children—William Leopold, Charlotte Nason. Ordained ministry P.E. Ch., 1911; curate Trinity Ch., Newport, later of St. Peter's Ch., St. Louis; rector Trinity Ch., Rock Island, Illinois rector St. Paul's Church, Peoria; bishop Diocese of Quincy, 1936-58; ret. Mem. Delta Upsilon. Rotarian. Address: 1819 W. Moss Av., Peoria, Ill. Died Feb. 26, 1959; buried Christ Ch., Limestone.

ESTABROOK, Merrick Gay, Jr., army officer; b. Boston, July 12, 1886; s. Merrick Gay and Flora (Shaw) E.; student Pub. Latin Sch., Boston, 1900-05; A.B., Harvard, 1909; grad. Air Corps Engring. Sch., 1932, Army Indsl. Coll., 1936; m. Marion Ward Hartley, Sept. 5, 1912; 1 dau., Mary Ward (wife of Maj. William J. Headrick, Jr.). Commd. 1st lt., Aviation Sect., Signal Corps, U.S. Army, 1917, and advanced through the grades to brig. gen., Sept. 17, 1943; ret. Aug. 1944. Began as mine operator, 1909. With U.S. Army Air Corps, Patterson Field, 1943. Address: Patterson Field, Fairfield, O. Died Dec. 19, 1947.*

ESTILL, George Castleman, utilities exec.; b. Lexington, Ky., May 27, 1881; s. William Wallace and Harriet Hughes (Sheffer) E.; A.B., Ky. U., 1902; M.E., Cornell, 1907; m. Alice Dashiell Garth, Oct. 25, 1911; 1 dau., Alice Garth (Mrs. St. Julien Palmer Rosemond). Prin. asst. chief engr. Birmingham Ry. Light & Power Co., 1903-15; chief engr. Cumberland Power & Light Co., Portland, Me., 1915-19; mgr. for receiver Montgomery Light & Traction Co. (Ala.), 1919-21; supt. roadways New Orleans Pub. Service, 1921-24; gen. supt. Fla. Power & Light Co., Miami, 1924-32, dir., 1934-37, v.p., gen. mgr., 1932-34, pres., 1934-37; dir. Consumers Water Co., Miami Beach Ry. Co., Miami Water Co., 1925-37, v.p., gen. mgr., 1930-37. Dir. Community Chest, chmn. fund campaign, Miami; gen. chmn. Mercy Hosp. drive, Miami; vice chmn. bd. trustees U. Miami. Mem. C. of C. (dir.), Kappa Alpha. Clubs: Rotary (past pres., dir.), Biscayne Bay Yacht (Miami). Home: 2127 Brickell Av., Miami 36, Fla. Died June 15, 1957; buried Woodlawn Park Cemetery, Miami.

ESTY, William Cole, III, advertising; b. Urbana, Ill., Mar. 7, 1895; s. William and Julia (Coy) E.; student Amherst Coll., 1912-15; m. Gertrude Wilder, June 12, 1923; children—William Cole IV, Jane Chapin; m. 2d, Alice Stevens, June 8, 1936; children—Julia Cole, Edward Tuckerman, 2d. Western mgr., Motion Picture News, Chicago, 1915-17; advt. mgr., The Home Sector, N.Y., 1918-19, Butterick Pub. Co., N.Y., 1919-21; copy chief, J. H. Cross Co., Philadelphia, 1921-22; v.p. The Corman Co., N.Y., 1922-25. J. Walter Thompson Co., N.Y., 1925-32; pres., dir. William Esty & Co., 1932-47, chmn. 1948. Pvt. to 2d lt. machine gun cos., A.E.F., 1918-19. Mem. Psi Upsilon. Episcopalian. Clubs: Union League (New York, N.Y.); New Canaan Country (New Canaan, Conn.); Ox Ridge Hunt, Tokeneke (Darien, Connecticut); Marshepaug (gov.; Litchfield, Conn.). Home: New Canaan, Conn. Office: 100 E. 42d St., N.Y.C. 17. Died Jan. 21, 1954.

ETCHEVERRY, Bernard Alfred, irrigation engr.; b. San Diego, Calif., June 30, 1881; s. Bernard and Louise (Earle) E.; B.S. in C.E., Coll. Civ. Engring., U. of Calif., 1902; m. Helen Maude Hanson, of Berkeley, Calif., Aug. 6, 1903; children—Bernard Earle, Alfred Starr. Instr. in civ. engring., U. of Calif., 1902-03; asso. prof. civ. engring., U. of Nev., 1903-05; asso. prof. irrigation engring., 1905-17, prof. same, 1917—, U. of Calif. Consulting engr. for various projects and cos. in B.C., Wash. and Calif. Mem. Am. Soc. C.E., 1909; mem. Psi Upsilon, Phi Beta Kappa, Sigma Xi, Tau Beta Pi, Alpha Zeta, Chi Epsilon. Officer de l'ordre du Ouissam Alouite (Morocco), 1932. Dir. American Society Civil Engineers, 1934-36. Republican. Clubs: Commonwealth, University. Author: Irrigation Practice and Engineering, 3 vols.; Land Drainage and Flood Protection. Contbr. numerous articles on irrigation problems to tech. jours. Home: 2678 Buena Vista Way, Berkeley, Cal. Died Oct. 26, 1954; buried Sunet View Cemetery, Berkeley.

ETCHISON, Page McKendree, organization exec.; b. Jefferson, Md., Nov. 15, 1892; s. McKendree Reiley and Jeanette (Kessler) E.; student Milton Bus. Sch., Washington Coll. of Law, George Washington U.; B.S.L., Southeastern U., 1926; L.H.D., hon., Salem (W.Va.) Coll., 1942; m. Lucille Shannon, June 22, 1916; 1 son, Bruce. Religious work dir., Y.M.C.A., Washington, 1914-48; exec. sec. Washington City Bible Soc. since 1948; field sec. Am. Bible Soc. since 1948. Co-founder Organized Bible Class Assn., 1922, pres. since 1931; mem. N. Am. Administrative Com., World Council of Christian Edn.; mem. Washington Bd. of Trade, Chevy Chase Citizens Assn.; mem. official bd. Hamline Meth. Ch., Meth. Union. Hon. life mem. Am. Bible Soc.; life mem. Y.M.C.A.; mem. S.A.R., Masonic Vets. Assn. Republican. Methodist. Mason (32°), Odd Fellows, Loyal Knights of Round Table (past sec. and pres.). Author: Victory Through Faith. 1943; The Organized Bible Class Association—A Twenty-Five Year History, 1947. Weekly columnist News of the Bible Classes, Evening Star, Washington. Home: 3730 Appleton St., Washington 16. Office: Washington Bldg., Washington. Died June 2, 1952.

ETZ, Roger Frederick (ĕtz), clergyman; b. Akron, O., Apr. 30, 1886; s. George Emmet and Frances Adelaide (Rogers) E.; A.B., Tufts, 1909, S.T.D., 1929; S.T.B., Crane Theol. Sch. (Tufts), 1910; postgrad. Hartford Sch. Religious Pedagogy, 1917-18; D.D., Lombard Coll., Galesburg, Ill., 1927; m. Verta Atkinson Smith, June 11, 1913; children—Dorothy, John Rogers. Field sec. Young People's Christian Union, 1910-13, also editor Onward; ordained Universalist ministry, 1913; minister Concord, N.H., 1913-17; asst. pastor Hartford, Conn., 1917-18; sec. Universalist Gen. Conv. and Internat. Ch. Extension Bd., 1919-37; pastor Charlestown, Massachusetts, 1922-29; also general supt. Universalist Ch., 1929-38; pastor Newark, 1938-41; pastor First Universalist Ch., Medford, 1941-50. Sec. Joint Commn. Conglists. and Universalists on Comity and Ch. Unity; pres. Mass. Universalist Conv., 1948. Trustee Medford Pub. Library, 1948. With YMCA in France 1 yr., World War I; chaplain (capt.), 182d Inf., Mass. N.G., 1922-29. Republican. Mason. Home: 21 Rural Av., Medford, Mass. Died Dec. 19, 1950; buried Oak Grove Cemetery, Medford.

EUBANK, John Augustine, lawyer, educator; b. Balt., s. John and Mary (Richardson) E.; LL.B., St. Lawrence U.; LL.M., Bklyn. Law Sch. Admitted to N.Y. bar; practice of law, N.Y.C.; prof. aero. law Bklyn. Law Sch., 1932—. Del. to first Inter-Am. Bar Assn. Conf., Havana, Cuba, 1941. Conducted 3 nat. symposiums on aero. law, 1933, 38, 46. Recipient Aero. Progress award. Mem. Fed. Bar Assn. N.Y., N.J., and Conn. (chmn. com. on aero. law), N.Y. County Lawyers Assn., Aircraft Industries Assn., Am., N.Y. State bar assns., Nat. Aeros. Assn., Soaring Soc. Am., Nat. Geog. Soc., Inst. Aero. Scis., Am. Mus. Natural History, Speakers Club, Am. Horse Show Assn., Am. Soc. Internat. Law. Author: Aeronautical Jurisprudence (3 vols.). Contbr. numerous articles on aero. and air law to law revs., aviation jours. Office: 32 Broadway, N.Y.C. Deceased.

EUBANK, Victor (G.C.), newspaperman; b. Nodaway County, Mo., Aug. 14, 1883; s. Reuben B. and Mary Elizabeth (Campbell) E.; ed. pvt. and pub. schs. and Univ. Med. Coll., Mo.; unmarried. Began with Kansas City Star, 1903; with Chicago Inter-Ocean, 1904, later with Chicago Record-Herald, Chicago Evening Jour., Chicago Examiner and Chicago Tribune; joined Associated Press, 1913, as editor Chicago Bur.; lit. and supervisiong dir. Essanay Film Co., Chicago, 1914; in World War as lt. and capt. Signal Corps, U.S. Army, later capt. intelligence sect. O.R.C.; rejoined Associated Press, 1921, Far Eastern cable editor, San Francisco, 1922-24, cable editor, New York, 1924-25, chief Associated Press Bur., Tokyo, Japan, 1925-29; London Five-Power Naval Conf., 1930; chief Moscow Bur., 1930-31; Internat. Financial Conf., London, 1931; transferred to hdqrs. Associated Press, New York, 1931; writing leading Wall Street review daily for Associated Press 1931-48, now writing spl. features. Contbr. playlets, short stories and mag. articles. Home: 1 Bank St., N.Y. City 14. Office: Associated Press. 50 Rockefeller Plaza, N.Y.C. Died Dec. 11, 1955.

EULER, William Gilman Badger (ū'lẽr), utilities exec.; b. San Francisco, Sept. 24, 1883; s. Henry and Marie (Keeley) E.; B.S., U. Cal., 1905; m. Helen B. Shea, Sept. 8, 1916. Engr., Gen. Elec. Co., San Francisco, 1905-10; from div. supt. to gen. supt., Great Western Power Co. of Cal., 1910-30; with Pacific Gas & Elec. Co., San Francisco, 1930—, gen. supt., 1930-39, chief engr., 1939-44, v.p. charge of operations, 1944-47, v.p., gen. mgr., 1947-50, exec. v.p., 1950—, dir., 1948—. Mem. Edison Elec. Inst., Am. Inst. E.E., Am. Gas Assn., Pacific Gas Assn., Pacific Coast Elec. Assn., Alpha Tau Omega. Mason. Clubs: Engineers, Olympic, San Francisco Golf (San Francisco), Menlo Country (Redwood City, Cal.). Home: 119 Selby Lane, Atherton, Cal. Died Mar. 9, 1958.

EUSTACE, Bartholomew Joseph (ū'stās), bishop; b. New York, N.Y., Oct. 9, 1887; s. Bartholomew A. and Elizabeth (Nolan) E.; ed. St. Francis Xavier Coll., New York, 1902-10, St. Joseph's Sem., Yonkers, N.Y., 1910-11, North Am. Coll., Rome, Italy, 1911-15; LL.D., St. Bonaventure's College, 1948. Ordained priest of the Roman Catholic Church, in Rome, Nov. 1, 1914; asst. Ch. of Blessed Sacrament, New Rochelle, N.Y., 1915-16; prof. of philosophy, St. Joseph's Sem., Yonkers, 1916-37; rector Ch. of Blessed Sacrament, New Rochelle, Sept. 1937-Mar. 1938; named bishop of Camden, N.J., Dec. 16, 1937, installed, May 4, 1938. Home: 342 Kings Highway West, Haddonfield. Office: 721 Cooper St., Camden, N.J. Died Dec. 11, 1956.

EUSTIS, Arthur Galen, ednl. adminstr.; b. Strong, Me., May 31, 1901; s. Arthur G. and Marilla (Allen) E.; B.A., Colby Coll., 1923, L.H.D., 1956; M.B.A., Harvard Grad. Sch. Bus. Adminstrn., 1926; m. Lorinda B. Orne, June 29, 1929; children—Jon, Arthur G., Nancy O. Instr. Northeastern U., Colby Coll..; prof. Colby Coll., treas., bus. mgr., v.p., 1950-58, sr. v.p., 1958—; dir. C. F. Hathaway Co. Mem. bd. advs. St. Joseph Coll.; mem. econ. adv. bd. State Me. Trustee Goodwill Home Assn.; mem. bd. trustees, Thayer Hosp., Waterville Boys Club. Mem. Eastern Assn. Coll. Bus. Officers, Adv. Council Me. Unemployment Compensation Commn., State Legislature, 1925-27. Mem. Phi Beta Kappa. Mason. Republican. Conglist. Club: Rotary. Contbr. articles on hosp. adminstrn. and coll. financial policies. Home: Mayflower Hill Dr., Waterville, Me. Died Jan. 28, 1959.

EVANS, Alexander William, univ. prof.; b. Buffalo, N.Y., May 17, 1868; s. William A. and Maria Ives (Beers) E.; Ph.B., Yale, 1890, M.D., 1892, Ph.D., 1899, Doctor of Science (honorary), 1947; Universities of Munich and Berlin (Germany), 1894-95; m. Phoebe Whiting, Apr. 17, 1914; children—Margaret, Janet, Allison. Asst. prof. botany, 1901-06, prof. botany since 1906, Yale. Fellow A.A.A.S., Am. Acad. Arts and Scis.; mem. N.E. Bot. Club, Bot. Soc. of America, Conn. Acad. Arts and Sciences, Torrey Bot. Club; corr. mem. Acad. Sciences, Cherbourg. Club: Graduate. Home: 180 Livingston St., New Haven, Conn. Died Dec. 6, 1959.

EVANS, Alvin Eleazer, law educator; b. Valley, Neb., Sept. 16, 1878; s. Eleazer Davis and Elizabeth Lorinda (Peckenpaugh) E.; A.B., Cotner U., 1898; A.M., U. Neb., 1898; Ph.D., U. Mich., 1908, J.D., 1918; Harvard Law Sch., 1915-16; m. Georgina Palmer, July 24, 1909 (dec.); children—Palmer Evans, Patricia; m. 2d, M. Jean King, May 25, 1941. Asst. prof. Latin, U. Wash., 1908-09; prof. classics State Coll. Wash., 1909-15; dir. summer sessions, 1911-15; admitted to bar Mich., Neb., Ida., D.C., Ky.; mem. firm Cain & Evans, Falls City, Neb., 1916-17, Nisbett & Evans, Moscow, Ida., 1918-22; referee in bankruptcy for Dist. of Ida., 1919-22; prof. law U. Ida., 1917-22; prof. law George Washington, 1922-27; dean law sch. U. Ky., 1927-48; prof. law St. Louis Law Sch., 1949-50, dean, 1950-52, prof., 1952—; prof. law U. Tex., summer 1922, U. Cin., summer 1942, U. Mich., 1946, Western Reserve U., 1947. Ezra Ripley fellow Harvard Law Sch., 1935-36; recipient distinguished service award U. Neb., 1941. Mem. Am. Ky., Ida., Neb., D.C. bar assns., Am. Law Inst., Am. Assn. U. Profs., Fayette County chpt. Ky. Soc. for Crippled Children (pres. 1942-43), Delta Theta Phi, Order of the Coif. Democrat. Mem. Central Christian (Disciples) Ch. (former chmn. adminstrv. bd.). Mason. Rotarian. Reemployment committeeman for Selective Service, Ky.; adv. mem. Local Draft Bd., No. 42. Clubs: University, University of Kentucky Research (pres. 1939-40). Author: Roman Law Studies in Livy, 1910. Joint author of Volume IV of Michigan Studies, Humanistic Series, 1910. Contbr. some fifty articles in legal periodicals compiled set of cases on community property. Home: 744 Interdrive, University City, Mo. Office: 3642 Lindell Blvd., St. Louis. Died June 17, 1953.

EVANS, Donald, lawyer; b. Hampton, Ia., July 2, 1882; s. William D. and Julia Adelade (Stark) E.; Ph.B., Grinnell (Ia.) Coll., 1903; LL.B., Drake U. Law Dept., 1907; m. Edna Lydston Hooley, Oct. 24, 1907; children—Jean Lydston (dec.), Susan Lydston (Mrs. Hubert C. Jones). Admitted to Iowa bar, 1907; with Carr, Carr & Evans, 1909-18; gen. atty. M.&St.L. R.R., 1918-19, C.,St.P.,M.&O. Ry., 1919-20, Minneapolis & St. Louis R.R., 1920-22; member firm Evans, Riley, Duncan, Jones & Hughes (was Carr, Cox, Evans & Riley), Des Moines, Ia., since 1922. Trustee Grinnell College since 1944; dir. Central Life Assurance Soc. Mem. Ia. State and Am. bar assns. Republican. Conglist. Clubs: Des Moines, Wakonda Country (Des Moines). Home: 4104 Greenwood Drive. Office: 1215 Equitable Bldg., Des Moines, Ia. Died Jan. 7, 1954; buried Des Moines, Ia.

EVANS, Edgar Hanks, mfr.; b. Edmund Hanks, Saratoga Springs, N.Y., July 18, 1870; s. Jesse Turner and Mary (Olmsted) Hanks; adopted by George Thomas and Mary J. (Robertson) Evans, Indianapolis, Ind., 1874; student Rose Poly. Inst., 1887; A.B., Wabash Coll., 1892, hon. A.M., 1902; hon. LL.D., Hanover (Ind.) Coll., 1937; hon. Litt.D., Ind. Central Coll., 1938; m. Ella Laura Malott, April 18, 1899; children—Eleanor Macy (Mrs. Erwin Cory Stout), Mary Robertson (Mrs. Samuel Runnels Harrell), Caroline Malott (dec.). Partner Geo. T. Evans & Son, 1893-1909; treas. Acme-Evans Co., 1909, pres. 1909-33, chairman board of directors, 1932-45, hon. chairman, 1945—; dir. Union Trust Co., 1922-50, Citizens Gas Co., 1924-35, Ind. Nat. Bank, 1932—; past president Indianapolis Elevator Co.; v.p. Comet Electric Co., 1917-24, Am. Milling and Purifying Co., 1904, Alsop Process Co., 1905-08; treas. Winter Wheat Millers' League, 1896-1903; a founder, 1902, pres. and chmn. bd., 1931-32, hon. mem., 1940, Millers Nat. Fedn.; chmn. Ind. Wheat Improvement Com., 1905-30; mem. bd. govs. Indianapolis Bd. of Trade, 1898— (v.p. 1909-11; pres. 1911-12); mem. Indianapolis Chamber Commerce (mem., 1894—; awarded Staff of Honor 1940), Nat. Chamber of Commerce, Chicago Board of Trade; dir. 1893-98, pres. 1897, Boys Club Assn.; dir. Indianapolis Y.M.C.A., 1916-48 (pres. 1926-34, vice pres. 1934-43), Internat. Com. Y.M.C.A. 1917-26, Nat. Council Y.M.C.A., 1925; vice pres. Indianapolis Anti-Saloon League, 1934-41. Trustee Wabash College, 1918—, also national chairman million dollar campaign, 1924; trustee, 1923—, pres. bd. 1944-45, Long Junior Coll. for Women of Hanover Coll.; founded Citizens School Com., Indianapolis, 1921, chairman, 1921-25 and 1934-38; chairman Tabernacle Presbyn. Ch. $700,000 Bldg. Com., 1920-30 (citation 50 yrs. an elder, 1950); chmn. Indianapolis Near East Relief Campaign, 1921, Ind. Russian Relief Campaign, 1922; pres. Ind. Council Religion in Higher Education, 1935-48, honorary president, 1948—; member committee Presbyn. Gen. Assembly, 1936. Awarded Citation of Honor in Religion, 1940, by Ind. School of Religion; hon. chmn. Citizens Sch. Com., 1947; hon. mem. for 1946 Indianapolis Community Fund. Member Wabash College Alumni Association, Indiana Society Mayflower Descendant, Am. Hist. Society, Ind. Hist. Soc., Delta Tau Delta. Republican. Clubs: Columbia, Indianapolis Athletic, Woodstock, Dramatic, Contemporary, Century. Author: Let Us Develop Religion in College, 1940; Should All College Students Study the Bible, 1945. Home: 3445 N. Pennsylvania

St., Indianapolis, Ind. Died July 23, 1954; buried Crown Hill Cemetery, Indpls.

EVANS, Edward Andrew, editor; b. Pendleton, Ore., Apr. 15, 1892; s. A. Grant and Katharine (Robb) E.; student U. of Okla., 1908-11; m. Grace Millar, Sept. 11, 1916; 1 son, David Grant. Began as reporter Okla. City News, 1911; reporter Denver Express, 1912-15; successively reporter, city editor, night editor and mng. editor, Cleveland (O.) Press, 1915-23; editor Okla. City News, 1923-27; asso. editor San Francisco News, 1927-31; editor Columbus (O.) Citizen, 1931-35; editor news service of Wired Radio, Incorporated, 1935-36; editorial writer and member general editorial board Scripps-Howard Newspapers since 1936. Served as second lieut. U.S. Army, Central Officers Training Sch., Camp Zachary Taylor, Ky., 1918. Mem. Kappa Alpha, Sigma Delta Chi. Presbyterian. Club: National Press. Home: 1868 Columbia Road N.W. Office: 1013 13th St. N.W., Washington. Died July 25, 1951; buried Santa Barbara, Cal.

EVANS, Everett Idris, surgeon; b. Norfolk, Neb., Apr. 15, 1909; s. Rhys and Mary (Jones) E.; Ph.D., U. of Chicago, 1935, M.D., 1937; m. LaVerne Veatch, Sept. 14, 1936; children—Robert Rhys, Melissa Lee, Richard Idris. House surgeon, Pa. Hosp., Phila., 1937-39; asst. resident surgery, Med. Coll. of Va. Hosp., Richmond, 1939-40; Rockefeller Foundation Fellow in surgery, Mass. Gen. Hosp., Boston, 1940-41; resident in surg., Med. Coll. of Va. Hosp., 1941-42, asst. prof. surg., Med. Coll. of Va., 1942-43, asso. prof., 1943-48, prof. surg. and dir. surg. research lab. since 1948; responsible investigator, Office Sci. Research and Development, Med. Coll. of Va., 1940-46, prin. investigator Research and Development Bd., Office Surg. Gen., Dept. of Army since 1948; surg. cons., Atomic Bomb Casualties Commn., Far East Command (Japan) since 1948, Office of Surg. Gen., Dept. of Army since 1948; vis. prof. surgery pro tem, Ohio State Univ., 1950; MacArthur lecturer U. of Edinburgh, 1952-53. Member committee on surg., Nat. Research Council since 1946; mem. com. on blood and blood substitutes, Am. Red Cross since 1947, com. on atomic casualties, Nat. Research Council since 1947; mem. adv. bd. on Health Services, Am. Nat. Red Cross, since 1947. Mem. adv. com. on annual scientific award, Am. Pharm. Mfrs. Assn. since 1947. Awarded certificate of appreciation by Depts. of Army and Navy for work during World War II. Mem. Internat. Soc. Surgery, Soc. for Vascular Surg., Am. Surg. Assn., Southern Med. Assn., A.M.A., Am. Physiol. Soc., Am. Surg. Assn., Am. Coll. Surgs., Southern Surg. Assn., Richmond Acad. Med., Sigma Xi, Nu Sigma Nu, Alpha Omega Alpha. Democrat. Episcopalian. Club: Commonwealth. Mem. editorial bd. Annals of Surg. since 1947. Home: Llanfair, River Rd., Richmond. Office: 1200 E. Broad St., Richmond 19, Va. Died Jan. 14, 1954; buried St. Mary's Episcopal Church, Goochland County, Va.

EVANS, Frank, lawyer; b. Coalville, Utah, July 26, 1873; s. Henry Beck and Anna Catherine (Bruun) E.; student Brigham Young U., 1892-93, U. of Utah, 1896-98, U. of Chicago, 1899; m. Priscilla Livingston, Dec. 31, 1902. Worker in coal mine, later editor of country paper, 1892-94; teacher pub. sch., Coalville, 1894-96; supt. Summit County (Utah) schs., 1899-1900; teacher city schs., Ogden, Utah, 1901; admitted to Utah bar, 1902, and began practice at Coalville; city atty., Coalville and Park City, 1903-07; pros. atty., Summit County, 1905-07; atty. for Utah Farm Bureau, 1921-24; sec. and gen. marketing counsel Am. Farm Bureau, 1924-27; gen. counsel Am. Farm Bureau Fedn., 1927-29. Member Utah State Senate, 1915-17, Federal Farm Bd., 1931-33. Served with Am. Red Cross, overseas, World War. Regent U. of Utah, 1921-25. Pres. Salt Lake Exchange Club, 1929. Pres. Eastern States Mission Ch. of Jesus Christ of Latter Day Saints (Mormon), 1937-40; sec. for finance to first presidency Ch. of Jesus Christ of Latter Day Saints (Mormon), 1940-50. Trustee Clayton Investment Co.; dir. Zion's Savings Bank and Trust Co., Utah Savings and Trust Co., Zion's Securities Corp.; mem. The Newcomen Society of England. Pres. emeritus Club University of Utah. Author: Law of Agricultural Coöperative Marketing (with E. A. Stokdyk), 1937. Home: 105 E. South Temple St. Office: 47 E. South Temple St., Salt Lake City, Utah. Died Aug. 21, 1950; buried Coalville (Utah) City Cemetery.

EVANS, Frederic Dahl, army officer; b. Ill., June 29, 1866; grad. U.S. Mil. Acad., 1887, Army War Coll., 1906. Commd. add. 2d lt., 22d Inf., July 1, 1887; 2d lt. 18th Inf., Oct. 6, 1887; 1st lt. 24th Inf., Jan. 21, 1895; trans. to 18th Inf., May 16, 1895; capt., Mar. 2, 1899; maj. 17th Inf., Mar. 3, 1911; adj. gen., Mar. 2, 1912; assigned to 4th Inf., Jan. 31, 1915; col., 1917; brig. gen. N.A., Aug. 5, 1917. Comd. Seminole Negro Indian scouts until Apr. 1892; at Fort Bliss, Tex., 1893-8; ordered with regt. to Philippines, 1898; participated in battles of Manila, Aug. 13, 1898, of Jaro, Feb. 12, 1899, of Jaro River Mar. 16, 1899; adj. of Col. Carpenter's expdn. from Iloilo to Capiz, Panay Island, 1899; again in P.I., 1903-5; mem. Inf. Exam. Bd., Ft. Leavenworth, Kan., 1906-07; apptd. comdr. 152d Inf. Brigade, Camp Devens, Ayer, Mass., Sept. 1917; comdr. 156th Inf. Brig., 76th Div., A.E.F. in France, July 1918; hon. discharged as brig. gen., Nov. 27, 1918. Address: War Dept., Washington. Died May 1, 1953.

EVANS, George Watkin, mining engr.; b. Ystrad, Rhonnda Valley, Wales, Mar. 5, 1876; s. Watkin and Catherine (Hughes) E.; student Internat. Corr. Schs., Scranton, Pa., 1892-96; B.S. and E.M., State Coll. of Wash., Pullman, Wash.; m. Olivia Laird, Mar. 12, 1902; children—Watkin L., Blodwyn E., Lloyd George. Practical work in coal mines, 1888-96; later in the Klondyke and placer mines, Yukon; with Wash. Geol. Survey, 1899-1901; cyanide practice in gold mines, Colo., 1902; practiced as engr., 1903-08; geologist in charge coal surveys Wash. Geol. Survey, 1909-12; cons. mining engr. U.S. Bur. of Mines, 1911-—, also cons. Mining Engr. U.S. Navy; dist. mining engr. U.S. Bur. of Mines during World War I; cons. engr. for large fuel cos., also Canadian Nat. Rys.; now in practice as cons. mining engr. Mem. Am. Inst. Mining and Metall. Engrs., West Coast Engineers. Unitarian. Rotarian. Home: 3134 37th Pl., Seattle 44. Died Jan. 11, 1951.

EVANS, Harold Sulser, ins. exec.; b. Grinnell, Ia., June 7, 1895; s. John and Matilda (Sulser) E.; student Grinnell Coll., 1914-18; m. Lana Edna Eriksen, Apr. 9, 1922; children—John, Harold S. With Allied Mut. Casualty Co., Des Moines, 1930-—, successively claim adjuster, mgr. claim dept., v.p., sec. and mgr., 1930-38, pres., gen. mgr., 1938-—, chmn., 1949-—; dir. Town Mut. Dwelling Ins. Co. (Des Moines), Central Nat. Bank & Trust Co., Ia. Mut. Tornado Ins. Assn. Mem. Am. Legion, Ia. Assn. Mut. Ins. Assns. (past pres.). Mason (Shriner). Clubs: Wakonda, Des Moines Home: 3514 Fleur Dr. Office: Allied Mutual Casualty Co., 4th and Park Sts., Des Moines, Ia. Died Apr. 17, 1959; buried Masonic Cemetery, Des Moines, Ia.

EVANS, Henry Clay, clergyman, educator; b. nr. Maysville, Ky., Dec. 24, 1851; s. Milton and Naomi (Maple) E.; A.B., Westminster Coll., Mo., 1881, A.M., 1884, D.D., 1894; LL.D., Austin Coll., 1916; m. Elida Washington Scott, Aug. 8, 1883; children—Louise Scott (Mrs. Gaines B. Hall), Mary Maple (Mrs. E. M. Munroe), Henry Clay. Prof. mathematics, Synodical Female Coll., Fulton, 1881-87, pres. coll., 1888-93; ordained Presbyn. ministry, 1883; prof. Greek, Westminster Coll., Fulton, 1887-88; co-editor St. Louis Presbyn., 1893-94; pastor First Ch., Kirkwood, Mo., 1894-1902; pres. Tex. Presbyn. Coll., 1902-21; became sec. Monteagle (Tenn.) S.S. Assembly, 1908. Trustee Presbyn. Theol. Sem., Louisville, 1893-95. Democrat. Home: Monteagle, Tenn. Deceased.*

EVANS, Herbert P(ulse), mathematician; born Chattanooga, Tenn., Jan. 5, 1900; s. Oscar Ewel and Effie Gertrude (Pulse) E.; B.S., Univ. Wis., 1923, M.S., 1927, Ph.D., 1929; student Columbia, 1924-25; m. Rae Elbertine White, Dec. 27, 1929; children—Douglas Sherwood, Gail Kristine. Research engr. Bell Tel. Lab., N.Y. City, 1923-25; instr. elec. engring., Univ. Wis., 1925-28, research asst. in physics (and Columbia) 1928, mem. dept. of math. since 1928, instr., 1928-29, asst. prof., 1929-38, asso. prof., 1938-42, prof. since 1942, charge univ. extension math. dept. since 1945. Served in U.S.N.R.F. as elec. 3c, 2c, 1c, and chief p.o., 1917-19, in France, 1918-19. Fellow A.A.A.S. Mem. Am. Math. Soc., Math. Assn. of Am., Inst. Math. Statistics, Am. Statistical Assn., Am. Assn. Univ. Profs.; Sigma Xi, Pi Mu Epsilon. Club: Univ. Asso. ed. Am. Math. Monthly, 1944-49. Contbr. articles on electric circuit theory, boundary value problems, probability theory, and mathematical edn. in scientific jours. Home: 1101 Seminole Highway, Madison 5, Wis. Died June 2, 1959.

EVANS, Hugh Ivan, clergyman; b. Delaware, O., May 6, 1887; s. James and Mary Ella (Boyce) E.; grad. Wooster (O.) Acad., 1905; A.B., Woolster Coll., 1909, D.D., 1924; B.D., Princeton Theol. Sem., 1912; Dr. Sacred Theology (hon.), Carroll College, 1950; D.D. (hon.), Miami University, Oxford, O., 1957; m. Edith Bean, June 30, 1914; children—Hugh Bean, Edith Mabel (Mrs. Wallace Macgregor). Ordained Presbyn. ministry, 1912; pastor Gallipolis, O., 1912-16, Marysville, 1916-20, 2d. Ch., Portsmouth, O., 1920-23; Westminster Ch., Dayton, 1923-55. Moderator Presbyn. Snyod of Ohio, 1930-31; Moderator of Presbyterian Church, U.S.A., 1950, president bd. nat. missions, 1953-54; director The Found. of Presbyn. Ch. U.S.A., 1955-—. Member general council strategy com., chmn. 12 million dollar bldg. funds campaign, 1951, 52, 53; pres. Ohio Pastors' Conv., 1933-34; trustee Lane Theol. Sem. (president), Wooster College, Princeton Theological Seminary; gen. chairman Dayton War Chest Campaign, 1943; pres. Dayton Community War Chest, 1945-46; v.-chmn. War Fund Campaign for State of Ohio; mem. Am. Seminar in Europe, 1934; mem. Bd. of Presbyn. Nat. Missions (N.Y.); mem. Nat. Council of Chs. of Christ in U.S.A.; Newcomen Soc. N.A. Republican. Mason (32°, 33°, K.T.), Clubs: Rotary, Union League Ohio Soc. of N.Y. (chaplain). Ofcl. del. World Alliance Reformed Churches holding Presbyterian System, Geneva, Switzerland, 1948; represented Presbyterian Church, U.S.A. World Council of Chs., Amsterdam, Holland, 1948. Author: A Parson Travels, 1934; What the Years Have Taught Me, 1952. Home: One Lexington Av., N.Y.C. 10. Office: 156 Fifth Av., N.Y.C. 10. Died Apr. 23, 1958; buried Mound Hill Cemetery, Gallipolis, O.

EVANS, John Brooke, asst. treas. U.S.; b. Pottstown, Pa., Nov. 16, 1872; s. Jesse Worth and Ellie G. (Reifsnyder) E.; prep. edn. Hill Sch., Pottstown; LL.B., U. Pa., 1896; m. Mabel R. Senior, Oct. 28, 1903. Admitted to Pa. bar, 1896; and practiced in Pottstown; borough solicitor, Pottstown, 1899-07; asst. dist. atty., Montgomery County, Pa., 1908-11; asst. treas. of U.S., Phila., 1915; Democrat. Mem. Reformed Ch. (German). Home: Pottstown, Pa. Died Feb. 1956.

EVANS, John C., ret. ins. exec. Entered in bus. with Tex. Fire Protection Assn., 1908, later various field, managerial and ofcl. positions until 1934; with Great Am. Ins. Co., 1934, pres., 1947-55, ret., also dir.; pres., dir. Am. Nat. Fire Ins. Co., Detroit Fire & Marine Ins. Co., Mass. Fire & Marine Ins. Co. and Rochester Am. Ins. Co.; v.p., dir. Great Am. Indemnity Co.; v.p. One Liberty Street Realty & Securities Corp.; dir., mem. exec. com. Gen. Adjustment Bureau, Underwriters Salvage Co. of N.Y. Mem. Eastern Underwriters Assn. (exec. com.). Clubs: Drug and Chemical, Lawyers (N.Y.C.). Home: 240 Forest Av., Glen Ridge, N.J. Office: 1 Liberty St., N.Y.C. 5. Died Nov. 16, 1957.

EVANS, John Norris, ophthalmologist; senior surgeon Brooklyn Eye and Ear Hosp.; prof. emeritus ophthalmology Long Island Coll. of Medicine. Consultant L.I. Coll. Hosp. Fellow Am. Coll. Surgeons; mem. Am. Ophthalmol. Soc., Am. Acad. Ophthalmology and Otolaryngology, Society for Research of Ophthalmology. N.Y. Opthalmol. Soc., Brooklyn Opthalmol. Soc., N.Y. State Med. Soc., Kings County Med. Soc., Neon Soc., Med. Club of Brooklyn, Harvey Soc., Am. Academy of Compensation, Inc., Asso. Physicians of L.I. (hon.). Medalist, L.I. Coll. of Medicine, U. of Buffalo, Neon Med. Soc. Club: Tuscarora. Author: Clinical Scotometry. Asso. editor Quarterly Review in Opthalmology. Contbr. to med. jours. Office: 23 Schermerhorn St., Bklyn. 2. Died Apr. 8, 1953.

EVANS, Letitia Pate (Whitehead), philanthropist; b. Redford, Va., Feb. 21, 1872; d. Maj. Cornelius and Elizabeth (Stagg) Pate; student Miss Declik's Sch., Lynchburg, Va., Miss Leigh Breazel's French Sch., Bedford, Va.; m. Joseph Brown Whitehead, Oct. 8, 1894 (died 1906); children—Joseph Brown (dec.), Conkey Pate (dec.); m. 2d, Lt. Col. Arthur Kelley Evans, 1913 (died May 25, 1948). Pres. Whitehead Holding Co., Atlanta; dir. Coca Cola Co. Endowed Joseph B. Whitehead Chair of Surgery Emory U., chmn. bd. Joseph B. Whitehead Found; donated $3,000,000 to Emory U. Hosp., Atlanta, for Conkey Pate Whitehead Surg. Pavilion; donated Letitia Pate Evans dining hall to Agnes Scott Coll., Decatur, Ga., bequeathed $100,000 for maintenance; bequeathed $350,000 to build Episcopal Home for Old Ladies in Richmond, Va., $50,000 to Va. Episcopal Sch., Lynchburg, $500,000 to William and Mary Coll., Williamsburg; restored the Custom House, Yorktown, Va.; furnished ambulances for France, World War II; donated $32,000 gold reserve for Queen's Fund for air raid victims; equipped Canadian Hosp. at Taplaw on Astor estate. Trustee Am. Hosp., Paris, France, Emory U., Agnes Scott Coll., Museum of Fine Arts, Richmond, Va. Awarded Order of Purple Heart, Wings of Britain (Gt. Britain); spl. de lux vol. France's meml. publ. for N.Y. World's Fair (given 60 Americans). Mem. Va. Soc. Colonial Dames; life mem. Assn. for Preservation of Va. Antiquities, Va. Hist. Soc., Order First Families of Va., 1607-20 (mem. council), Daus. of Barons of Runnemede, Order of the Crown, Ams. of Royal Descent. Episcopalian. Home: Malvern Hall, Hot Springs, Va. Died Nov. 14, 1953; buried Hollywood Cemetery, Richmond, Va.

EVANS, Marcellus Hugh, lawyer, ex-congressman; b. Bklyn., Sept. 22, 1884; s. Timothy Joseph and Mary Agnes (Lynch) E.; student St. James Acad., Bklyn., 1895-1901; LL.B., Fordham U., 1910; m. Mary Agnes Sheehan, June 21, 1911; children—Marcellus Timothy (dec.), Mary Catherine, Joseph, Grace Mary, Virginia Mary, Margaret Mary. Admitted to N.Y. bar, 1910; mem. firm Evans & Evans, 1910-—; mem. Assembly, N.Y. State, 1922-26, Senate, 1927-34; mem. 74th to 76th Congresses, 5th N.Y. Dist. Catholic. Home: 305 E. 4th St., Bklyn. Office: 41 Park Row, N.Y.C. Died Nov. 1953.*

EVANS, Ray O., cartoonist; b. Columbus, O., Dec. 1, 1887; s. Oscar Benjamin and Mary (Barnett) E.; A.B., Ohio State University, 1910; married Helen H. Holter, October 11, 1911; children—Ray O., Dorothy Jane (deceased), Patricia Ann (Mrs. J. R. Kistler). Began as advertising artist, Columbus Dispatch, 1910; cartoonist, Dayton News, 1912-13, Baltimore American, 1913-20. Member Puck art staff, 1915-16; instr. in cartooning, Md. Inst., 1920; staff artist Baltimore News and American, 1920-22; Cartoonist Columbus Evening Dispatch since 1922. Creator of spl. features, "Maryland Movies," "Snapshots at Annapolis," "Pertinent Portraits," "Kindly Karicatures," "Uncle Funny Bunny" for school children, Am. Edn. Press.; illustrations for "The Diary of a Plain Dirt Gardener," for Better Homes and Gardens. Mem. advisory staff Federal Board of Cartooning. Presbyterian. Mem. Sigma Delta Chi, Sigma Pi. Mason (32°, Shriner). Clubs: University, Dispatch Country, Forty-One, Cartoonists Soc. Home: 2615 Wexford Rd. Address: The Columbus Dispatch, 34 S. 3d St., Columbus, O. Died Jan. 18, 1954.

EVANS, Rudolph Martin, mem. bd. govs. Fed. Res. System; b. Cedar Rapids, Ia., Nov. 4, 1890; s. Martin and Margaret (Ganshorn) E.; B.S., in Civil Engring., Ia. State Coll., 1913; m. Thurma Marguerite Allen, Apr. 15, 1919; children—Lenore Marguerite (Mrs. R. E. Dorsey), Nancy Lee (Mrs. J. W. Miller). With Allied Machinery Co. Am., 1916-21; farmer and livestock raiser, Laurens, Ia., 1921-33; with A.A.A. in Iowa, 1933-36; spl. asst. to Sec. of Agr., 1936-38; adminstr. A.A.A., 1938-42; now mem. bd. govs. Fed. Res. System. Candidate U.S. Senate, Ia., 1956. Served with 116th Engrs., U.S. Army, A.E.F., 1918-19. Mem. Kappa Sigma. Democrat. Episcopalian. Mason. Home: Arnolds Park, Ia. Office: Federal Reserve Bldg., Washington. Died Nov. 21, 1956; buried Laurens, Ia.

EVANS, Rudulph, sculptor; b. Washington, D.C., Feb. 1, 1878; s. Frank L. and Elizabeth Jeanette (Grimes) E.; ed. Corcoran Art Sch. (Washington, D.C.), Art Students' League (N.Y.C.), Julian Acad. and École des Beaux Arts (Paris, France); m. Jane Coleman Wood, Nov. 9, 1905. Exhibited in leading cities, including N.Y.C., Chgo., Washington, Paris, France, etc.; awarded bronze medal, Paris Salon, 1914, and French Cross of Legion of Honor, 1934; statue, "The Golden Hour," purchased by French Govt. for Luxembourg Mus., and replica of same, in marble, in Met. Mus., N.Y.C.; Watrous gold medal, Nat. Acad. Exhbn., N.Y.C., 1920; commd. for monuments or portrait busts, by Frank A. Vanderlip, John D. Rockefeller, Jr., Thomas F. Ryan, etc.; sculptor of McKinney memorial; J. Sterling Morton monument; Woolley Memorial at Detroit, Mich., Kiernan Memorial at Green Bay, Wis.; marble portrait of Gen. Bolivar, Gen. Miranda (Pan Am. Union, Wash., D.C.); bronze portraits of John Greenleaf Whittier, Owen D. Young, Bernard M. Baruch; bronze portrait of Longfellow and of George Bancroft, historian, for Hall of Fame, Grover Cleveland (Princeton U.), bronze statue of General Robert E. Lee in capitol at Richmond, Virginia, Jacob Loose at Kansas City, Mo., William Jennings Bryan and Sterling Morton, Washington, D.C.; heroic statue of Thomas Jefferson, Washington, dedicated on 200th anniversary of birth, Apr. 13, 1943; bronze bust of Bernard Baruch, bronze statue of William Jennings Bryan for State Capitol at Lincoln, Neb.; also executed sculptured portraits, busts, bronze statues of numerous notable Americans for the collections of various pub. instns. in U.S. Cavaliere Order of Crown of Italy. Hon. fellow Nat. Sculpture Soc.; mem. Met. Mus. Art, Nat. Inst. Arts and Letters, N.A. Studio: 1701 16th St. N.W., Washington 9. Died Jan. 16, 1960.

EVANS, Silas, educator; b. Scranton, Pa.; Feb. 12, 1876; s. Roland Hill and Sarah (Alban) E.; A.B., Ripon (Wis.) Coll., 1898; A.M., Princeton, 1900; B.D., Princeton Theol. Sem., 1901; (D.D., Carroll Coll., 1911, Middlebury Coll., Middlebury, Vt., 1913; LL.D., Lawrence Coll., Appleton, Wis., 1912); L.H.D., Ripon Coll., 1943; m. Nellie Bruce McAfee, Aug. 15, 1906; children—Bettye Bruce, Silas McAfee, Richard Harry. Ordained Presbyn. ministry, Sept. 15, 1901; asst. pastor, Hastings, Neb., prof. philosophy, Hastings Coll., 1901-03; prof. philosophy, pastor, Park Coll., Mo., 1903-09; prof. Hebrew and Hellenistic Greek, U. Wis., 1909-10; pres. Ripon Coll., Wis., 1910-17; pres. Occidental Coll., Los Angeles, 1917-21; pres. Ripon Coll., 1921-43; now minister Congl. Bapt. Ch., 1943-45; vis. prof. Bible and philos., Lindenwood Coll., Mo., 1945-46; asso. minister Westminster Presbyn. Ch., Milw., 1947-51; prof. Bible and philos. Carroll Coll., Waukesha, Wis. Author: Currency of the Invisible. Home: 3407 N. Frederick, Milw. Died Nov. 1, 1959; buried Ripon, Wis.

EVANS, Silliman, pres. Nashville Tennessean; b. Joshua, Texas, April 2, 1894; s. Columbus Asbury and Alice (Silliman) E.; studied Polytechnic Coll. (now Southern Methodist U.), Fort Worth, 1911-13; m. Lucille McCrea, Nov. 20, 1923; children—Silliman, Amon C. Began as newspaper reporter, 1913; reporter and desk exec., United Press, Internat. News Service, Dallas Morning News and reporter, member staff and Washington correspondent, Ft. Worth Star-Telegram, 1913-26; v.p. Tex. Air Transport until 1928, Southern Air Transport until 1929, Am. Airways, Inc., until 1932; 4th asst. postmaster gen., 1933-34; resigned to accept presidency Maryland Casualty Co., Baltimore, now dir.; president and publisher Nashville Tennessean; dir. Am. Airlines. Democrat. Clubs: Fort Worth; Nat. Press (Washington); Maryland (Baltimore); Belle Meade (Nashville); Cloud (New York); Tavern, Chicago, (Chicago). Home: Franklin Rd., Nashville 4. Address: 1100 Broadway, Nashville. Died June 26, 1955.

EVANS, Walter Chew, bus. exec.; b. Columbus, O., Aug. 27, 1898; s. Walter H. and Mary L. (Chew) E.; student U. of Ill., 1917-21, U. of Chicago, 1922; m. Georgina Burtis, Nov. 8, 1924; children—Barbara (Mrs. William K. Bixby II), Charles B.; married 2d Lee Huddleston, September 17, 1947. Vice pres. Westinghouse Electric Co.; pres., dir. Westinghouse Radio Stas., Inc.; v.p. and dir., Westinghouse X-Ray Co.; dir. Union Trust Co. of Md. Broadcast Music, Inc. Dir. Baltimore Assn. of Commerce, Radio Mfrs. Assn. Mem. Armed Forces Communications Assn., Inst. Naval Engrs., Inst. Radio Engrs., Chi Psi, Tau Beta Pi. Clubs: Maryland, Merchants (Baltimore), Penn. Athletic (Phila.), Annapolis Yacht. Home: 5 Eastern Av., Annapolis. Md. Office: Westinghouse Electric Corp., Balt. 3. Died May 28, 1952; buried Arlington Nat. Cemetery.

EVANS, Walter Howard, judge; b. New Middletown, Ind., Apr. 17, 1870; s. Isaac William and Mary Catherine (McRae) E.; B.S., Valparaiso U., 1899; LL.B., U. of Ore., 1905; m. May Ball, Aug. 11, 1898; children—Mary Catherine, Lillian Alice (Mrs. Floyd F. Bowles), Walter Howard. Teacher pub. schs., 1886-98; clk. Q.M. Dept., U.S. Army, 1898-1905; admitted to practice in Ore., 1905; asst. U.S. atty., Dist. of Ore., 1908-12; state dist. atty., 4h Jud. Dist., Ore., 1912-21; judge Circuit Court, 4th Jud. Dist., Ore., 1921-31; judge U.S. Customs Court, N.Y. City, since Feb. 1931. Hon. pres. bd. trustees Children's Farm Home, Corvallis, Ore. Hon. life mem. State Dist. Atty.'s Assn. of Ore.; mem. Am., Ore. State and Multnomah County bar assns. Republican. Presbyterian. Mason (K.T., Shriner). Mem. St. Andrews Soc. Home: 7806 27th Av., S.E., Portland, Ore.; and 425 Riverside Dr., New York. Address: 201 Varick St., New York, N.Y. Died July 13, 1959.*

EVANS, Ward Vinton, prof. chemistry; b. Rawlinsville, Lancaster County, Pa., June 8, 1880; s. Jacob and Elizabeth (Oldham) E.; prep. edn., Franklin and Marshall Acad.; Ph.B., Franklin and Marshall Coll., 1907; Ph.D., Columbia, 1916; m. Harriet Alice Mattson, June 30, 1922; children—Ward Vinton, James Trimble, Elizabeth Annetta. Asst. in chemistry, Columbia, 1915-16; instr. same, Northwestern Univ., 1916-17, asst. prof. phys. chemistry, 1918-19, asso. professor, 1919-28; professor, 1928-45; retired as head chemistry dept., 1945, to teach in Army universities in Europe; professor at Loyola University, 1945-—; con. gas explosions. Lieutenant, U.S. Army, 1917-18. Awarded Honor Scroll, Am. Inst. Chemists, 1946. Mem. Am. Chem. Soc. (chmn. phys. div., 1929-30, and of Chicago sect., 1929-30). Phi Lambda Upsilon. Alpha Chi Sigma, Sigma Xi. Clubs: University (Evanston); Chemists (Chicago). Contbr. on tech. subjects to Jour. Am. Chem. Soc. Home: 2711 Harrison St., Evanston, Ill. Died Aug. 2, 1957; buried Rawlinsville, Pa.

EVANS, William, theologian; b. Liverpool, Eng., Jan. 1, 1870; s. George and Margaret E.; prep. edn. pvt. sch. in Eng.; grad. Moody Bible Inst., 1892, Chgo. Luth. Theol. Sem., 1896, postgrad. course, B.D., 1900; Ph.D., Chgo. Theol. Sem.; Litt.D., John Brown U.; D.D., Wheaton Coll., 1906; m. Laura C. Torgerson, June 25, 1902; children—Dorothy L. (dec.), Louis H., Oren W., Paul H. Ordained, 1894; pastor, Goshen, Ind., 1895-97, later Wheaton and Chgo.; dir. of Bible course Moody Bible Inst., Chgo., 1901-15; asso. dean Bible Inst., Los Angeles, 1915-18; dir. Bible Confs., for U.S. and Can. 1918-—; exec. v.p. The John Brown Schools. 1943-44. Author: The Book of Books, 1902; How to Memorize, 1909; Outline Studies in Bible Books, 1909; Personal Soul-Winning, 1910; Studies in the Life of the Christian, 1911; The Great Doctrines of the Bible, 1912; How to Prepare Sermons, 1913; Outline Study of the Bible, 1913; Book Method of Bible Study, 1915; Epochs in the Life of Christ, 1916; The Pentateuch, 1916; Christian Science, 1916; The Gospels and Acts, 1917; Romans and Corinthians, 1918; The Shepherd Psalm, 1921; The Coming King, 1923; Christ's Last Message to the Church, 1926; What Happens After Death, 1926; Facing Calvary, 1928; Dr. Evan's Question Box. 1928; From the Upper Room to the Empty Tomb, 1934; Through the Bible —Series of Ten Volumes on Bible Exposition. Presbyn. Address: 1924 N. Gramercy Pl., Los Angeles 27. Died My 21, 1950; buried Forest Lawn Meml. Park, Glendale, Cal.

EVANS, William E., ex-congressman; b. Laurel County, Ky., ed. Sue Bennett Meml. Coll., London, Ky.; m. Cecil Corine Smith; 1 dau., Catherine Cecil. Admitted to Cal. bar and practiced law; sr. mem. firm Evans, Pearce & Campbell. Del. Rep. Nat. Conv., 1924; mem. 70th to 72d Congresses, 9th Cal. Dist. and 73d Congress, 11th Cal. Dist. Home: Hollywood, Cal. Office: 448 S. Hill St., Los Angeles. Died Nov. 1959.*

EVANS, William Lloyd, educator; b. Columbus, O., Dec. 22, 1870; s. William Henry and Anne (Lloyd) E.; B.Sc., Ohio State U., 1892, M.Sc., 1896, LL.D., 1948; Ph.D., U. Chgo., 1905; D.Sc. (hon.) Capital U., 1949; m. Cora Ruth Roberts, Mar. 9, 1911; children—Lloyd Roberts (M.D.), Jane Anne (Mrs. Alvin H. Nielsen), William Arthur (lt. j.g., U.S.N.R.; lost in action Mar. 27, 1944). Chemist with Am. Encaustic Tile Co., Zanesville, O., 1892-94; University fellow, Ohio State U., 1895-96; asst. dept. of ceramics, 1896-98; instr. chemistry Colorado Springs High Sch., 1898-1902; Univ. fellow and Lowenthal fellow in chemistry U. Chgo., 1903-05; lectr. chemistry, Starling-Ohio Med. Coll., 1911-15; asst. prof. chemistry Ohio State U., 1905-08, asso. prof., 1908-11, prof., 1911-41, chmn. dept. chemistry, 1928-41, prof. emeritus, 1941-—; cons. chemist The Lowe Bros. Co. (Dayton), Columbus Coated Fabrics Corp., Div. Carbohydrates Nat. Insts. Health. Mem. Nat. Research Council Com. on Carbohydrate Research, 1926-27, Nat. Research Council Div. of Chemistry and Chem. Tech., 1934-40. Commd. capt. O.R.C., U.S. Army, Oct. 11, 1917; maj. C.W.S., Offense Div., July 19, 1918; disch., Dec. 30, 1918; head of lab. insp. div. Edgewood Arsenal, World War I. Del. 10th Congress Internat. Union Chemistry, Liege, Belgium, 1930. Fellow A.A.A.S., Am. Acad. Arts and Sciences; mem. Am. Chem. Soc. (chmn. organic div. 1928; mem. exec. com. organic div. 1929; councilor at large 1934-40; pres.-elect 1940; pres., 1941), Ohio Acad. Sci. (pres. 1939-40; fellow; v.p. chemistry sect. 1933-34), Scabbard and Blade, Sigma Xi, Phi Eta Sigma, Phi Beta Kappa (hon.), Phi Lambda Upsilon, Alpha Chi Sigma, Gamma Alpha, Sigma Chi. Conglist. Mason (32°). Clubs: Ohio State University Faculty (pres. 1928), Torch (pres. 1933); Engineers (Dayton, O.). Author: Study and Quiz Outline in Chemistry, 1923. Co-Author: Laboratory Exercises in General Chemistry (with Wm. McPherson and W. E. Henderson), 1928; An Elementary Course in Qualitative Analysis (with J. E. Day and A. B. Garrett), 1938; Semimicro Qualitative Analysis (with A. B. Garrett and L. L. Quill), 1940, rev. edit. (with A. B. Garrett and H. H. Sisler), 1951. Mem. exec. bd., Ohio Jour. Science; mem. bd. editors Jour. of Higher Edn.; chmn. bd. editors, Songs of Ohio State U. (1st and 2d edits.). Contbr. Jour. Am. Chem. Soc. and Jour. Chem. Edn. Awarded William H. Nichols medal, 1929: gold medal Am. Inst. of Chemists, 1942. Home: 1975 Indianola Av., Columbus 1, O. Died Oct. 18, 1954; buried Columbus, O.

EVELYN, Sister Mary, educator; b. Kewanee, Ill.; d. John Terence and Mary Anne (McDonough) Murphy; prep. edn. Kewanee (Ill.) High Sch. and Saint Clara Acad., Sinsinawa, Wis.; A.B., St. Clara Coll., 1916; Ph.D., U. Fribourg, Switzerland, 1928. Prin. Sacred Heart Acad., Washington, 1916-18; dir. Institut de Hautes Etudes, Fribourg, 1918-24; dean Rosary Coll., River Forest, Ill., 1928-37, pres., 1937-43. Mem. Gen. Council of Congregation of the Most Holy Rosary, 1943-49, mother gen., 1949-55. Author: Life and Time of Blessed Clara Gambacarta, 1928. Address: Sinsinawa, Wis. Died Sept. 9, 1955; buried Sinsinawa.

EVENDEN, Edward Samuel (ē'vĕn-den), educator; b. Sheridan Ore. Oct. 29 1884; s. John and Sarah Anne E. (Cawston) E.; diploma State Normal Sch., Monmouth, Ore., 1903; A.B., Stanford, 1910, A.M., 1911; Ph.D., Tchrs. Coll. (Columbia) 1919; m. Louise Marcus 1912; 1 dau. Louise Anne. Critic tchr. and supt. State Normal Sch., Monmouth, Ore., 1903-07, head dept. edn., 1911-17; asst. and asso. in dept. ednl. adminstr. Tchrs. Coll. (Columbia), 1918-20, asst. prof. edn., 1920-22, asso. prof., 1922-23, prof., 1923-50, professor emeritus of edn., 1950-—, head of coll. relations div. Citizenship Edn. Project, chmn. com. on Ed.D. degree, Tchrs. Coll., 1944-47, exec. officer advanced sch. edn., 1947-50, com. on instrn., faculty of philosophy Columbia, mem. University Council, 1940-49. Asso. dir. Nat. Survey Edn. of Tchrs., 1930-33; vice chmn., later chmn., commn. on tchr. edn. Am. Council on Edn., 1938-44; chmn. Com. on Tchr. Edn. of Am. Council on Edn., 1944-46; cons. Com. of Trustees on Exptl. program No. 18, Washington, 1944; mem. exec. com. Ednl. Council of Nat. Council of YMCA, 1931-33; mem. Cleve. Conf., 1931-—; mem. advisory com. on sch. studies of Nat. Com. for Mental Hygiene; mem. com. on curriculum development in higher edn. of Soc. of Curriculum Specialists; consultant com. on accrediting Nat. League Nursing Edn., 1937-42; chmn. advisory com. on service to teachers colls., Nat. Soc. Prevention Blindness, 1935-39; mem. council on teacher edn. for N.Y. State Bd. of Regents; spl. cons. on tchr. edn. for N.Y. State Assn. Colls. and Univs., 1942-43. Fellow A.A.A.S. (v.p. and chmn. Sect. Q, edn., 1936, sect. committeeman 1939-47); life mem. N.E.A. (chmn. com. on techers' salaries, 1923; mem. com. on Tenure of N.E.A. 1933-36) Am. Assn. Sch. Adminstrs., Suprs. Student Teaching (nat. adv. com.). Nat. Soc. Study Edn., Coll. Tchrs. Edn. (exec. com. 1931-34, pres. 1934-35, com. on standards and surveys, research cons. to com. 1950, rep. Eastern States Assn. Profl. Schs., of A.A.T.C. to UN), Progressive Edn. Assn., Am. Assn. U. Profs., Phi Beta Kappa, Phi Delta Kappa, Kappa Delta Pi (Laureate counselor, 1946-48). Episcopalian. Mason. Author: Teachers Salaries and Salary Schedules in the U.S. (pub. by N.E.A.), 1918-19; (with Prof. N. L. Engelhardt) Score Card and Standards for City Church Plants, 1920; (with others) The Malden Survey, 1920; (with Prof. G. D. Strayer) A Syllabus of a Course in Principles of Education;

conducted the surveys of several cities, and building score cards for colleges, normal schs. and teachers colls.; standards for college bldgs. with G. D. Strayer and N. L. Engelhardt; study of normal school buildings in Massachusetts, 1923, Pennsylvania, 1924; dir. with Prof. R. J. Leonard, of survey of colleges of Un Luth. Ch. of America, 1926-28; made building surveys of univs. and colleges of Fla. and Me. and of normal schools and teachers colleges in Mass. and Pa.; survey of teacher preparation in Mo., 1929, of Chicago Normal Coll. and Crane Jr. Coll., Chicago, 1932; Volumes II and VI of the National Survey of the Education of Teachers (U.S. Office of Education), 1935; spl. studies of curriculum practices in normal schools and teachers colleges in the U.S. for Am. Assn. Teachers Colls.; Teacher Education in a Democracy at War, 1942; (with R. Freeman Butts) Columbia University Cooperative Program for the Preservice Education of Teachers, 1942: A Study of Recently Erected and Proposed Buildings of Teachers Colleges of the U.S., 1945; A Quarter Century of Standards; Control and Support of Teachers Colleges, 1948. Clubs: Cosmos (Washington); Coumbia U. Faculty (N.Y.C.). Home: 445 Riverside Dr., N.Y.C. Died Oct. 19, 1957.

EVEREST, David Clark (ĕv'ĕr-ĕst), chairman of the board Marathon Corporation; born Pine Grove, Mich., Oct. 13, 1883; s. John Henry and Gertrude (Clark) E.; student pub. schs., Gobles, Mich.; Dr. of Bus. Adminstrn., Northland Coll., 1946; LL.D., U. Wis., 1953, Lawrence Coll., 1954; m. Rita Gouin, September 20, 1905; children—Helen Gertrude (Mrs. Rowland Lilly), Ruth (Mrs. Norman E. Weaver), David Clark. Office boy and bookkeeper Bryant Paper Co., Kalamazoo, Mich., 1900-02; asst. mgr. Munising (Mich.) Paper Co., 1902-07; mgr. Williams Gray Co., Chicago, Ill., 1907-09; gen. mgr. Marathon Corporation, paper and food package mfr., Rothschild, Wis., 1909-50, pres., 1938-50 and 1951-52, chmn. bd., 1950—; chmn. bd. Marathon Paper Mills of Can., Ltd., 1946—; pres. Wausau Paper Mills C., Brokaw, Wis., 1948-50, chmn. bd., 1950—; pres. Wis. Valley Improvement Co. since 1950; v.p. D. J. Murray Mfg. Co. since 1951, First Am. State Bank, Wausau, Masonite Corp., Laurel, Miss., since 1926, Longview (Wash.) Fibre Co. since 1926, Employers Mut. Liability Ins. Co., Wausau, Wis. since 1920, also dir. these and many other cos. Chief cos. Chief cons. pulp and paper br. OPM, Washington, 1940-41; cons. pulp and paper br. NSRB, 1948-50, mem. adv. com. to Sec. of Agr. on forest pest control, 1952—; mem. forestry advisory committee State Conservation Commission, 1948—. Chmn. Marathon County chapter A.R.C., 1918—; vice chairman board, trustee Lawrence Coll., Appleton, Wis. Mem. Am. Paper and Pulp Assn. (pres. 1927-28, 1937-38; Gold Medal award 1944), Inst. Paper Chemistry (v.p. 1929—, trustee), Am. Forestry Assn. (pres. 1951—, dir. 1952-53; award 1949), Wis. State (pres. 1952—, mem. bd. curators; award of merit 1949), Marathon County (pres. 1952—), hist. socs. Republican. Episcopalian. Mason. Clubs: Athletic (Milwaukee); Wausau, Country (Wausau, Wis.). Home: 1206 Highland Park Blvd., Wausau, Wis. Office: Marathon Corporation, Rothschild, Wis. Died Oct. 28, 1955; buried Pine Grove Cemetery, Wausau, Wis.

EVERETT, Charles Horatio, edictor; b. Rock County, Wis., Mar. 22, 1855; s. Josiah Milton and Mary E. (Ross) E.; ed. high sch., Clinton, Wis.; m. Angerona B. Barningham, 1878 (died 1903); 1 son, Milton Wayne; m. 2d, Grace Lange, 1910. Engaged as dairy farmer in Wis. for 40 yrs.; editor The Wisconsin Agriculturist, Racine, 1901—. Conductor of Wis. farmers' insts. 14 yrs. and mem. State Bd. of Agr. during same period; pres. Wis. Live Stock Sanitary Bd., Wis. Dairymen's Assn.; Mem. Wis. Ho. of Rep., 1913, Senate 1915-17. Awarded testimonial by U. Wis., 1916, for eminent services in development of agricultural thought and practice. Republican. Conglist. Mason. Elk, Modern Woodman. Home: Racine, Wis. Died Mar., 1936.

EVERETT, George Abram, educator; b. Lawrence, N.Y., Apr. 18, 1875; s. Luther and Martha C. (Abram) E.; student Potsdam (N.Y.) State Normal Sch.; A.B., Cornell U., 1899, LL.B., 1901; m. Anna McEwen, Nov. 28, 1907; children—Martha Abram, Richard McEwen (dec.). Tchr. Flushing, L.I., 2 yrs., Lawrenceville Sch., 2 yrs.; asst. pub. speaking, Cornell U., 1899, later instr. and asst. prof. same, prof. extension teaching, 1912-43, prof. emeritus, 1943—. Admitted to N.Y. bar, 1901. Republican. Presbyn. Mason. Address: 4 Lawrence Av., Potsdam, N.Y. Died Sept. 15, 1958.

EVERETT, Harry Harding, surgeon; b. Troy Grove, Ill., Sept. 5, 1875; s. Milton Harkness and Delia (Harding) E.; B.Sc., U. Neb., 1897; M.D., Northwestern U., 1900; post grad. work N.Y. Post Grad. Sch., Johns Hopkins, U. Jena, U. Vienna; m. Blanche Hargreaves, Aug. 20, 1907; children—Jane, Betty, Harry Harding. Asst. surgeon Lincoln (Neb.) Sanitarium, 1901-16; instr. U. Neb., 1902; pres. and chief surgeon Lincoln Sanitarium, 1917-1928; attending surgeon Bryan Meml. Hosp. and St. Elizabeth Hosp.; chief of surg. staff Lincoln Gen. Hosp.; med. dir. Woodmen Central Life Ins. Co., and Woodmen Health & Accident Co.; surgeon C.B.&Q. R.R. at Lincom; county physician 4 yrs. Hon. V.P. Am. Hort. Soc. Fellow Internat. Coll. Surgeons, A.C.S.; mem. Am. Assn. Ry. Surgeons, A.M.A., Mo. Valley Assn., Am. Iris Soc. (dir.), British Iris Soc., Am. Ros Soc., Beta Theta Pi, Theta Nu Epsilon, Phi Rho Sigma. Republican. Mason (32°, Shriner). Clubs: Lincoln University, Lincoln Country, Round Table. Specialist in gardening. Home: 2433 Woodcrest Blvd. Office: 301 Woodmen Accident Bldg., Lincoln, Neb. Died Mar. 30, 1949.

EVERETT, William Wade, retail mcht.; b. Chelsea, Mass., Aug. 23, 1871; s. Shepard Silas and Emma Jane (Wade) E.; student pub. and pvt. schs.; m. Sarah Buckingham, June 9, 1897; children—Helen (Mrs. Dwight K. Terry), Edith (Mrs. Francis A. Murray), William Wade. Asst. cashier, Woodward & Lathrop, dept. store, 1888, successively buyer, gen. mgr., v.p., 1888-42, pres., 1942-49, retired, continues as trustee; dir. Am. Security & Trust Co., Chesapeake & Potomac Telephone Co. Dir. Washington Bd. Trade, Bliss Elec. Sch. Mem. S.A.R. Republican. Baptist (trustee). Mason, Rotarian (past pres.). Home: 3010 Woodland Drive, Washington 8. Office: care Woodward & Lahtrop, Washington 13. Died Mar. 15, 1949.*

EVERHART, Mahlon Thatcher, rancher; b. Martinsburg, Pa., Mar. 24, 1873; s. Marshal Henry and Mary Carolyn (Thatcher) E.; student Centennial High Sch., Pueblo, Colo., 1889-90, Kiskiminetas Springs Sch., Pa., 1890-91; m. Carolyn Fall, Dec. 1, 1909 (died Oct. 12, 1918); children—Clare (Mrs. William M. Zuendt), Mahlon Thatcher, Jack Fall. Bank employee, 1891-98; rancher, Ariz., 1898-1903; cattle raiser, operator of ranches in Mexico, N.M. and Colo., 1903—; pres. Hatchet Cattle Co.; dir. 1st Nat. Bank, Pueblo, 1st Nat. Bank, Florence, Colo. Home: 2331 Greenwood St. Office: 1st Nat. Bank, Pueblo, Colo. Died Apr. 13, 1955.

EVERSON, William Graham, clergyman; b. Wooster, Ohio; the son of Jacob Monroe and Annie Louise (Riddell) Everson; A.B., Franklin (Ind.) Coll., 1903; D.D., 1931; B.D., Newton Theol. Instn., 1908; spl. work, Baylor U. and Harvard; m. Mary Coon (A.B., Franklin), Aug. 31, 1904; children—John David, Mary Louise. Ordained Bapt. ministry, July 18, 1901; pastor Morgantown and Lewis Creek, Ind., 1901-03, First Ch., Columbus, Ind., 1903-05, Glendale Sq., Boston, 1905-08, College Av. Ch., Indianapolis, 1908-11, First Ch., Newport, Ky., 1911-13, Fourth Av. Ch., Louisville, Ky., 1913-15, Norwood Ch., Cincinnati, 1915-21, First Ch., Muncie, Ind., 1921-29, pastor emeritus, 1929-31; pastor First Bapt. Ch, Denver, 1931-32, First Ch., "The White Temple," Portland, Ore., 1932-39; pres. Linfield College, McMinnville, Ore., 1939-43; chmn. advisory com., Shriners Hospital for Crippled Children, Portland, Ore., 1944-47; exec. sec. Ore. Heart Assn., Inc., Portland. 1947—. In Spanish-American and World Wars, in France, Italy, Austria, Dalmatia, Serbia and Montenegro; commander only American sector in Italy and all U.S. troops east of Adriatic Sea; rep., United States in Fiume and supervised investigations and food distribution in Austria and Serbia after armistice; hon. disch. with rank of col., June 1919; promoted brig. gen. res., July 1922, and comd. 76th Inf. Brig.; maj. gen., U.S. Army, chief Nat. Guard Bur., 1929-31. Citations and decorations from Eng., France, Italy, Fiume, Serbia, U.S. and three battle clasps. Grad. Command and Gen. Staff School at Ft. Leavenworth, Kan. and Grad. Army War College, Washington, D.C.; retired January 19, 1945 with rank of major general. Chautauqua and Lyceum lecturer, 1919—; mem. Nat. Speakers' Bur. of Am. Legion; nat. chaplain Mil. Order Foreign Wars, 1923-26; past dept. chaplain United Spanish War Vets.; chaplain Am. Legion, 1923-24; past grand chaplain Ind. Masons; chairman Ore. Alien Enemy Hearing Bd. Life mem. Boston Ministerial Association. Member International Lyceum and Chautauqua Association, International Law Enforcement Officials, American Legion, United Spanish War Vets., Mil. Order of World Wars, Mil. Order of Fgn. Wars, Army-Navy Union, Scabbard and Blade, Purple Heart, Sigma Alpha Epsilon, Pi Gamma Mu, Phi Kappa Gamma, Pi Kappa Delta. Republican. Baptist. Mason. (32°, K.T., Shriner, Red Cross of Constantine). Rotarian. Author: Twenty Outline Studies of the New Testament, 1921; World War and Peace Potentialities, 1924. The Challenge of the Impossible, 1926; The Great Obstacle to World Peace, 1927; Forever As the Stars, 1932; Some Trails of Challenge, 1933. Contbr. on religious, health, peace and other subjects. Honorary life mem. Ind. State Police. Has traveled over 237,000 miles in 18 countries by airplane. Home: 3715 S.E. Tolman St., Portland 2, Ore. Died Sept. 3, 1954; buried Riverview Abbey, Portland.

EVERSULL, Harry Kelso, clergyman, educator; b. Cincinnati, O., Sept. 20, 1893; s. E. Elwood and Mattie May (Tallant) E.; A.B., Wabash Coll., 1919, LL.D., 1939; B D., Yale, 1922; grad. study Yale, 1922-24, U. of Cincinnati, 1926-28; D.D., Elon (N C) Coll., 1933; D.D., Rio Grande College (Ohio), 1948; married Anita Mueller, September 18, 1920; children—Gilbert Richard, Robert Elwood. Ordained to congl. ministry, Old Stone Ch., East Haven, Conn., 1922, pastor there 1920-24; pastor Walnut Hills Congl. Ch., Cincinnati, 1924-37; pres. Marietta Coll., 1937-42; executive secretary Cincinnati Council of Churches, 1942-46; became Presbyterian, 1946; pastor Walnut Hills Presbyterian Church since 1946. Moderator Miami Association, Congl. Churches, 1926, Cincinnati Congl. Union, 1931-32; mem. Mid West Regional Committee of Congregational Churches, 1934-38. Member Commission to Survey Cincinnati Public Schools. 1934-35; pres. Cincinnati Fed. Chs., 1934-36. Grand Chaplain Ohio Grand Council Royal and Select Masons since 1941; Grand Chaplain, Grand Lodge, F. and A. M. of Ohio, 1946-47; chaplain Masonic Meml. Chapel; dir. Spiritual Mobilization, Am. Econ. Found.; trustee Press Radio Bible Service. First lt. Inf., U.S. Army, 1918. Trustee Elon Coll. and Atlanta Found. Vanderbilt U. since 1932, O. Congl. Conf., 1928-31; dir. Cincinnati Red Cross, 1933-38, Internat. Order Knights of Round Table, 1929-31; mem. bd. mgrs. Y.M.C.A., 1936-38 and since 1942; member Commn. Interchurch Relations and Christian Unity, Gen. Council of Congl. Chs., 1940-46. Mem. Am. Assn. of School Administrators, Ohio College Association, Phi Gamma Delta, Sigma Alpha Chi (past national pres.), Sigma Mu Sigma (national pres.), Newcomen Soc. of Eng., Acacia. Republican. Presbyterian. Mason (33°, K.T., Shriner. Royal Order Jesters, Red Cross of Constantine). Clubs: Schoolmasters Yale, Clergy (Cincinnati); Univ. Ohio Soc. (N.Y.); Noontide (Detroit). Author: The Evolution of an Old New England Church, 1924; The Congregational Church, 1925; Howard Billman, 1935; Education and the Democratic Tradition, 1939; Sir Knight William McKinley, 1943; The Temples in Jerusalem, 1946. Home: 3442 Zumstein Av. Office: Gilbert Av. and William Howard Taft Boulevard, Cin. Died Sept. 13, 1953.

EWALD, Henry Theodore (ē'wäld), advertiser; b. Detroit, Mich., Apr. 20, 1885; s. Henry Charles and Theresa (Siefert) E.; ed. public schools, honorary degree, Detroit Central High School; honorary LL D. from Wayne University, 1941; married Oleta Alice Stiles, Jan. 26, 1911; children—Shirley Oleta (Mrs. Brewster Loud, Jr.), Henry T. With D. & C. Navigation Co., 1899-1908; with Studebaker Corp. of America, South Bend, Ind. and the E-M-F Automobile Co. of Detroit, 1908-11; sec. Campbell-Ewald Co., 1911-17, president since 1917; chmn. bd. Mack-Gratiot Co., Hanson Chevrolet Co.; dir. Nat. Outdoor Adv. Bur.; v.p. Wabeek State Bank, Traffic Audit Bureau, Inc., of N.Y. Was publicity dir. Liberty Loan drives for Detroit, and War Savings Stamp drive, also for $5,000,000 Y.M.C.A. Bldg. drive, $4,000,000 Woman's Bldg. drive, $3,000,000 Associated Buildings drive. Chairman of board Am. Assn. Adv. Agencies, 1932-33; dir. Boys Club of Detroit; dir. and trustee Grace Hosp., Salvation Army; chmn. exec. com. Detroit chapter, Am. Red Cross. Received, 1940, gold medal award in recognition of distinguished services to advertising; annual advertising award, sponsored by Advertising and Selling; medal for distinguished services, U. of Mo, May 14, 1942. Mem. Advertising Fedn. of Am., Soc. Automotive Engrs. Detroit Bd. of Commerce (ex-dir.). Rep. Protestant. Mason (K.T.). Clubs: Adcraft (founder and ex-pres.), Detroit Athletic (ex-dir.), Players, Detroit Boat, Bloomfield Hills Country (pres. and ex-dir), Rotary Country of Detroit, Recess, Theatre Arts, Grosse Pointe, Grosse Pointe Yacht; Advertising Club (New York); Bankers of Am., Detroit, Country. Home: 1453 Iroquois Av. Office: General Motors Bldg., Detroit. Died Jan. 9, 1953.

EWART, J(ohn) Kaye (ū'ĕrt), banker; b. Bellingham, Wash., Mar. 15, 1907; s. James Tully and Ellen Isabella (Kay) E.; ed. pub. schs. of Tacoma; grad. degree comml. banking, Am. Inst. Banking, 1932; student Pacific Coast Sch. Banking, U. Wash., 1940, grad. comml. div. 1957; m. Elsie Louise Hazelwood, May 31, 1936; 1 dau., Jane Kaye. Wholesale lumber bus., Tacoma, 1925-27; with Nat. Bank of Washington (formerly Nat. Bank of Tacoma), 1927—, messager, interior clerk, statement clerk and bookkeeper, 1927-34, mem. credit dept., 1934-37, dept. mgr., 1937-39, asst. cashier and charge orgn. and operation FHA Title I installment lending dept., 1939-41, personnel, new accounts dept., 1941-42, charge orgn. and dir. banks bus. development and public relations dept., 1942-45, asst. v.p., 1945-50, v.p. and comml. loan officer, 1950—. Bd. dirs. Tacoma Athletic Commn., Inc.; treas. and mem. exec. com. Tacoma Community Chest; mem. bd. regents, Grad. Sch. Banking, Rutgers U., 1949-50, mem. finance com., 1950. Mem. Am. Inst. of Banking (pres. local chpt. 1941-42; asso. council man for Western Wash. 1942-45; mem. nat. exec. council 1945-48, nat. v.p. 1949, pres. 1950; mem. exec. council 1949-50; mem. adminstrv. com. 1950; mem. exec. council 1949-50; mem. adminstrv. com. 1950), Wash. Bankers Assn., Tacoma Execs. Assn. Home: 805 North C, Tacoma. Died Aug. 2, 1957; buried Mt. View Cemetery, Tacoma.

EWEN, Edward C., naval officer; b. Portsmouth, N.H., May 26, 1897; s. George Swenson and Jessie (Coots) E.; student Tilton (N.H.) Acad., 1914-15; grad. U.S. Naval Acad., 1921, post-grad. 1929-32; m. Elizabeth R. Livingston, Sept. 5, 1923. Commd. ensign, USN, 1921, advanced through grades to rear adm., 1945; in naval aviation service 1924—; comd. U.S.S. Breton, 1943, U.S.S. Independence, 1944; became chief Naval Air Res. Tng., 1946; apptd. comdr. U.S. 1st Carrier Fleet in Pacific, 1950; ret. Decorated Navy Cross, Legion of Merit with gold star, Bronze Star Medal, Commendation Ribbon. Clubs: Chevy Chase, Army and Navy (Washington); Chicago, University (Chgo.); Glen View (Ill.); Onwentsia (Lake Forest, Ill.); Indian Hill (Winnetka, Ill.). Died Aug. 1959.

EWEN, W. C., business exec.; b. Carmel, N.Y. Dir. The Pacific Coast Co.; Pacific Coast Coal Co., Queensborough Bridge Ry. Co., N.Y.C., United Traction Co., Albany, N.Y. Pres. Putnam Co. C. of C. Clubs: Advt. (N.Y.C.); Bankers, Carmel Country. Home: Kent Cliffs Rd., Carmel, N.Y. Office: 618 Broadway, Hastings-on-Hudson 6, N.Y. Died Oct. 16, 1954.

EWING, Fayette Clay, otolaryngologist; b. Ariel Plantation, LaFourche Parish, La., May 28, 1862; s. Fayette Clay (M.D.) and Eliza Josephine (Kittredge) E.; ed. U. of the South and U. of Miss.; M.D., Jefferson Med. Coll., Phila., 1884; certificates of internship from several eye, ear, nose and throat hosps., London and N.Y. City; m. Martha Macdonald, 1885 (dec.); children—Fayette Clay (dec.), Ephraim Macdonald (dec.), Presley K., Donald Macdonald; m. 2d, Rowena Annette Clarke, 1924. Practiced gen. medicine, Washington, D.C., 1885-93; specialist in ear, nose and throat, St. Louis, 1896-1918; retired to enter U.S. Army, 1917; one of founders Am. Acad. Ophthalmology and Otolaryngology, 1896 (gen. sec., 1900); fellow A.C.S. (only living founder). Royal Soc. Medicine (Great Britain); mem. Am. Medical Association Command major, M.R.C., United States Army, January 7, 1918; served as chief of ophthalmology and otolaryngology dept., U.S. Rehabilitation Hosp. U.S.P.H.S., Camp Beauregard, 1919-27; now maj. inactive, M.R.C. Awarded Honor Scroll by Jefferson Med. Coll. Alumni, 1947; Golden medal from U. of the South, 1952. Del. of A.M.A. to Internat. Med. Congress, Rome, 1893; del. from Am. Acad. Ophthalmology and Otolaryngology to Internat. Ear Congress, London, 1899; selected by the Congress as sole speaker to rep. U.S. at internat. banquet, London, 1896. Mem. Sons of Revolution (through Gen. Robt. Ewing, Ky.); charter mem. U. Miss. chpt. Beta Theta Pi, only living founder; past pres. Beta Theta Pi Alumni Soc. of St. Louis; hon. mem. Rapides Parish Med. Soc. (past president); past pres. 8th Dist. Med. Soc. La.; former trustee U. of the South; joint-founder (1900) Scottish Terrier Club of Am. (hon. pres.); oldest Scottish Terrier breeder and promoter that ever lived; est. internationally known Nosegay Kennels, 1897; hon. pres. Scottish Terrier Club of Scotland (est. 1888), only American so honored; author of The Book of the Scottish Terrier (standard book of the breed in Britain and Am.); known as "the Father of Scottish Terriers in America," and "Dean of the Fancy"; hon. mem. various nat. canine clubs. Author: Hamlet, an Analytic and Psychologic Study, 1934; also author Shakespearean papers; lecturer on Shakespearean drama and Brit. and Am. poetry; world traveler. Formerly abstract editor of Laryngoscope and The Eye, Ear, Nose and Throat Monthly; contbr. to scientific jours. Democrat. Episcopalian. Home: "Nosegay," Pineville, La. Died Apr. 15, 1956.

EWING, Henry Ellsworth, entomologist; b. Arcola, Ill., Feb. 11, 1883; s. Joseph Henry and Ann Louisa (McDonald) E.; student Knox Coll., 1902-04; A.B., U. of Ill., 1906, A.M., 1908; Ph.D., Cornell U., 1911; m, Bertha May Wood Riley, Aug. 7, 1916; children—Paul McDonald, Lydia Frances. Science teacher Marshall (Ill.) High Sch., 1908-09; asst. in zoölogy, Ia. State Coll., 1909-10; Schuyler fellow Cornell U., 1910-11; asst. entomologist Ore. Agrl. Expt. Sta., 1911-14; asst. prof. of entomology, Ia. State Coll., 1914-16, asso. prof., 1916-19; specialist Bur. of Entomology, U.S. Department of Agriculture, 1919-23, associate entomologist, 1923-29, entomologist, 1929-45, collaborator since 1947. Fellow A.A.A.S., Iowa Academy of Science, Entomol. Soc. of America; mem. Am. Assn. Econ. Entomologists, Soc. of Mammalogists, Am. Soc. of Parasitologists (pres. 1944), Am. Soc. Ichthyologists and Herpetologists, Ecol. Soc. of Am., Ill. Acad. of Sci., Biol. Soc. Washington, Washington Acad. of Science, Helminthological Soc. of Washington (past pres.), Entomol. Society of Washington (pres. 1941), Phi Delta Theta, Sigma Xi. Author: A Manual of External Parasites, 1929, and scientific and tech. articles. Contbr. Encyclopaedia Britannica. Home: 7308 Willow Av., Takoma Park, Md. Office: U.S. National Museum, Washington. Died Jan. 5, 1951; buried Rock Creek Cemetery, Washington.

EWING, John Dunbrack, editor, publisher; b. New Orleans, La., Feb. 3, 1892; s. Robert and May (Dunbrack) E.; B.S., Va. Mil. Inst., 1913 (capt. basket ball team); m. Helen Hamilton Gray, Dec. 27, 1919; children—Helen May, John D. Circulation mgr. New Orleans States, 1913-15; asst. gen. mgr. Shreveport Times, 1915-17, asst. pub., 1919-31; pub. New Orleans States, 1931-33; pub. and editor Shreveport Times and News-Star-World, Monroe, La., since 1931; co-founder Monroe World, 1929; pres. radio stations KTBS and KWKH since 1934; trustee and pres. Ewing Estate since 1931. Capt. Inf. 32d Div., 1917-19. Awarded Croix de Guerre with Star, 1918, Purple Heart. Pres. Southern Newspaper Pub. Assn., 1938-39, chmn. bd. 1939; dir. K.C.S. and L.&A. Railroads; mem. American Legion (dept. comdr., 1921; chmn. bd. Am. Legion Monthly), Sigma Nu. Democrat. Episcopalian (vestryman). Mason (K.T., Shriner). Clubs: Boston (New Orleans); Shreveport Golf and Country: Augusta (Ga.) Masters; Deepdale (L.I.). Home: 910 Ockley Drive. Office: 408 Marshall St., Shreveport, La. Died May 17, 1952.

EWING, Lynn Moore, lawyer; b. Nevada, Mo., Oct. 3, 1903; s. Lee B. and Edith (Moore) E.; A.B., U. Mo., 1925, L.B., 1927; m. Margaret Ray Blair, Sept. 14, 1928; children—Lynn Moore, Blair Gordon. Admitted to Mo. bar, 1927; asst. atty. State Hwy. Commn., 1928-29; mem. Ewing, Ewing & Ewing at Nevada, Mo., 1929—. Mayor, Nevada, 1936-46, mem. Sch. Bd., 1937—, pres., 1948-50. Trustee Cottey Coll., 1943-50. Mem. Am. (state del. 1946-50), Mo. (pres. 1952-53, bd. govs. 1948-53), Vernon Co. bar assns., Am. Law Inst., Am. Judicature Soc., Phi Beta Kappa, Order of the Coif, Sigma Nu, Phi Delta Phi, Alpha Pi Zeta. Democrat. Presbyn. Elk. Clubs: University (Kansas City, Mo.); Rotary. Home: 700 North Washington St., Nevada. Office: Farm and Home Bldg., Nevada, Mo. Died July 5, 1958; buried Nevada, Mo.

EWING, William, clergyman; b. Melbourne, Quebec, Can., Dec. 9, 1853; s. John and Jeanette (Smith) E.; B.A., McGill U., 1878; grad. Congl. Coll. of Can. (affiliated with McGill U.), 1879; D.D., Olivet Coll., Mich., 1908; m. S. Henrietta Allworth, June 13, 1882; children—Anna Allworth, Marion Jeanette, Clara Muriel (Mrs. C. G. Smith), Gordon Banham. Ordained Congl. ministry, 1879; missionary in Canadian N.W.; established 1st Ch., Winnipeg, later pastor Plymouth Ch., Fargo, N.D.; supt. Congl. S.S. and Pub. Soc., N.D., 1887-91, Mich., 1891-1907; gen. sec. missionary and extension dept., Boston, 1907-17; apptd. field sec. N.Y.C., 1917. Traveled around the world, 1922-23; now connected with Pilgrim Place in Claremont, Cal. Mem. Afternoon Club. Trustee Fargo (N.D.) Coll., 1883-91, Olivet Coll., 1897-1907. Republican. Author: The Graded Sunday School, 1896; The Sunday School Century, 1918. Home: 487 W. 6th St., Claremont, Cal. Died Jan. 10, 1932.

EYRE, Laurence (âr), actor, playwright; b. Chester, Pa.; s. Caleb Churchman and Constance Isemberg (Stacey) E.; ed. pvt. schs.; m. Alice McFadden Brinton, June 25, 1925. Debut with Castle Square Stock Co., Boston, in Dion Boucicault's comedy, The Jilt, 1907; played with Julia Marlowe, Katherine Kidder and with Columbia Stock Co., Washington, Boston Theatre Stock Co., Master of the House Co., also played leading Shakespearean Characters with Ben Greet Co.; played Alexis in Anthony and Cleopatra, at dedicatory performance, New Theatre, N.Y., 1909. Author of Comedy, Mrs. Xmas Angel, prod. Harris Theatre, Oct. 19, 1912, and subsequently at Maxine Elliott Theatre and the Playhouse under title of The Things that Count, and ran for 250 nights. Author: The Things That Count, 1914; Sazus Matazus (first full length play dealing entirely with Negro life, all the characters being colored), prod. 1916; Driftwood, prod. 1917; Mis' Nelly o' N'Orleans, prod. 1919, London, 1921; Martinique, prod. 1920; The Merry Wives of Gotham, prod. 1923; The Steam Roller, 1925; One Trip of the Silver Star, prod. 1925; The Forcing Bed, 1929; Escapade, 1929; While Doctors Disagree, prod. 1932; Service for Two, prod. 1935. Address: Ridgefield, Conn. Died June 6, 1959.

EYRING, Carl Ferdinand (ī'rĭng), educator; b. Colonia Juarez, Chihuahua, Mexico, Aug. 30, 1889; of Am. parents; s. Henry and Deseret (Fawcett) E.; grad. Juarez Acad., at Colonia Juarez, 1908; A.B., Brigham Young U., 1912; A.M., U. Wis., 1915; Ph.D., Cal. Inst. Tech., 1924; grad. study Columbia, 1919, U. Chgo., 1920; m. Fern Chipman, Sept. 9, 1914; children—Robert Chipman, Elaine. Instr. mathematics and physics Juarez Acad., 1908-09; asst. in physics Brigham Young U., 1910-12, instr., 1912-14, asst. prof. physics, 1915-17, prof. physics and mathematics, 1917—, dean Coll. Arts and Scis., 1924—; asst. in physics U. Wis., 1914-15; asst. in physics Cal. Inst. Tech., 1922-23; acoustical engr. Bell Telephone Labs., 1929-31. Served as sgt. 1st class, Air Forces, U.S. Army, World War I, research div., air acoustics, Washington. Mem. Gen. Board Deseret Sunday School Union. Fellow Utah Acad. Science (pres. 1923); mem. Am. Physical Soc., A.A.A.S., Acoustical Soc. Am. (v.p. 1950-51). Democrat. Mormon; pres. New England Mission, Mormon Church, 1937-39. War research U. Cal., under-water acoustics USN Lab., San Diego, 1941-42, Rutgers U. jungle acoustics at Panama, 1944-45. Home: 827 N. University Av., Provo, Utah. Died Jan. 3, 1951; buried Provo City Cemetery.

EYSTER, George Senseny, army officer; b. Halltown, W.Va., Aug. 8, 1895; B.S., U.S. Mil. Acad., 1917; grad. Signal Sch., 1928, Inf. Sch., 1932, F.A. Sch. 1933, Chem. Warfare Sch., field officers course, 1937, Command and Gen. Staff Sch., 1938. Commd. 2d lt., inf., U.S. Army, 1917, and advanced through the grades to brig. gen., 1944; in charge def. housing sect., Fed. Works Adminstrn. Br., G-4, War Dept. Gen. Staff, Washington, 1940-42; chief, later exec. officer, unit tng. br., tng. div., Services of Supply, Washington, 1942-43; chief staff, 76th Inf. Div., Ft. George G. Meade, Md., Jan.-Aug. 1943; became chief, operations br., G-3 sect., Hdqrs. European Theater Operations, Aug. 1943. Home: 3900 Connecticut Av. N.W. Address: care The Adjutant General's Office, War Dept., Washington 25. Died Mar. 9, 1951.*

F

FACKLER, Edward Bathurst, actuary; b. N.Y. City, Oct. 13, 1879; s. David Parks and Elizabeth Leverett (Davenport) F.; A.B., Yale, 1900; LL.B., N.Y.U., 1905; m. Carrie Elizabeth Root, 1914; children—Elizabeth R., David E., Ruth T., Louis R. (dec.), John D. Became associated with father in actuarial bus. which later became Fackler & Co., cons. actuaries, 1900, mem. firm, 1907; v.p., actuary Western & Southern Life Ins. Co., Cincinnati, since 1950. Fellow Soc. Actuaries, Casualty Actuarial Soc.; mem. Internat. Congress Actuaries, Am. Math. Soc., Ins. Soc. of N.Y. Author: Notes of Life Insurance, 1907; co-author: Illinois Standard Tables (4 vols.), 1922; Complete Surrender Value Ready Reckoner, 1927; American Men Mortality Premium and Reserve Tables (3 vols.), 1927; also author articles, treatises. Editor: Principles and Practice of Life Insurance (9th edit.), 1939, (10th edit.), 1949. Home: Hotel Sheraton Alms, Cincinnati 6. Office: 400 Broadway, Cincinnati 1. Died Jan. 8, 1952.

FAGAN, William Long, farmer; b. Wetumpka, Ala., Nov. 20, 1838; s. Enoch F.; A.M., Howard Coll.; m. Annie E. Avery, Nov. 30, 1874. Capt., C.S.A., 1861-65; surrendered co of 65 (Co K, 8th Ala. inf.), probably the largest co. in Lee's army, at Appomattox C. H.; contbr. numerous articles to various jours. Compiler: Southern War Songs. Address: Havana, Ala. Died May 27, 1914; buried Havana, Ala.

FAGERBURG, Dewey Frank, lawyer; b. Champaign County, Ill., July 25, 1898; s. Edward H. and Charlotte (Anderson) F.; A.B., U. Mich., 1920, LL.B., 1922; m. Dorothy White, Dec. 22, 1922; children—Charlotte, Dewey Frank, Karin. Admitted to Ill. bar, 1922, since practiced in Chgo.; mem. Snyder, Chadwell & Fagerburg and predecessor firms since 1930. Served with U.S.N., World War I. Mem. Am., Ill. State, Chgo. bar assns., Phi Beta Kappa, Phi Delta Phi, Sigma Alpha Epsilon. Conglist. Mason. Clubs: Law, Legal, Univ., Swedish, Mid-Day, Econ., Execs. (Chgo), Hinsdale, Ill. Home: 4 E. Fifth St., Hinsdale, Ill. Office: 135 S. LaSalle St., Chgo. 3. Died June 13, 1958.

FAGLEY, Frederick Louis (făg'lē), clergyman; b. Bethel, O., May 8, 1879; s. Wallace Clark and Fannie (Brown) F.; student U. of Cincinnati, 1903-04; A.B., Evansville (Ind.) Coll., 1905, D.D., 1916; A.M., Oberlin Coll., 1910, D.D., 1948; B.D., Oberlin Theol. Sem., 1911; student Cambridge, summer, 1937; m. Hortense Martin, June 30, 1909; children—Richard Martin, Frances Joan (Mrs. Wm. A. Coury), Robert Earle. Prof. philosophy of edn., Moores Hill Coll., 1905-08; pastor Plymouth Congl. ch., Cincinnati, O., 1911-14; exec. sec. Cincinnati Federation of Chs., 1914-18; exec. sec. Commn. on Evangelism of the Congl. Chs., 1919-22; asso. sec. Nat. Council Congl. Chs., 1922-31; asso. sec. Gen. Council Congl.-Christian Chs., 1931-48, emeritus; exec. sec. Am. Com. Internat. Congl. Council, 1937; dir. German exchange projects, Nat. Council Chs. of Christ; mem. exec. com. Fed. Council of Chs. of Christ in Am. (chmn. advisory com., 1945-47), General Commission Army and Navy Chaplains (vice chmn., 1945-47), Commission for Camp and Defense Communities, Service Men's Christian League (vice chmn., 1945-47); chmn. Nat. Committee on Army and Navy Chaplains. Dudliean lectr. Harvard, 1951-52. Citation meritorious service, U.S. Army and USN, 1952. Sec. Congl. Christian Hist. Soc., 1951—. Mem. Am. Fern Society (past president). Clubs: New England Botanical, Quill (president 1950-51), National Arts (sec., 1948-51). Author: Parish Evangelism, 1923; The Congregational Churches, 1926; Your Church and You, 1928; Handbook on Teaching Religion, 1933; A Little Handbook on Adult Education, 1935; An Outline of Church History, 1935; The Religions of Mankind, 1936; A Guide to the Christian Year, 1937; History of American Congregationalism (with G. G. Atkins), 1942; History of Congregational Christian Chs., 1956. Home: 60 Gramercy Park, N.Y. C. 10; also Sunapee, N.H. Office: 289 Fourth Av., N.Y.C. 10. Died Aug. 25, 1958.

FAHEY, John H. (fā'hĭ), govt. ofcl.; b. Manchester, N.H., Feb. 19, 1873; s. Patrick and Maria F.; high sch. edn.; m. Margaret Quinn, Oct. 22, 1901; children—Margaret, Eleanor. Began newspaper work as reporter and news editor Manchester, N.H.; editor and later mgr. Eastern Associated Press, New Haven, until 1893; editor, day mgr. Associated Press, Boston, 1893-97, N.E. supt., 1897-1903, 2d v.p., 1909-10; editor, pub. Boston Traveler, 1903-10; pres. Boston Traveler Co., State Pub. Co.; pres., pub. Worcester

(Mass.) Post, 1914-37; pres. St. John's River Shipyard Co., Jacksonville, Fla., 1918-20; pres., pub. Manchester (N.H.) Mirror, 1922-25; pres. The Clarke Press, pub. New York Evening Post, 1923. Mem. U.S. section of Inter-Am. High Commn. Chmn. Fed. Home Loan Bank Bd., chmn. bd. dirs. HOLC, Washington, 1933-—; chmn. bd. trustees Federal Savings and Loan Ins. Corp., 1934-—; commr. Fed. Home Loan Bank Adminstrn., 1942-—. Former dir. and mem. exec. com. Boston C. of C., chmn. of delegation from chambers of commerce in U.S. vis. leading European cities, 1911; dir., chmn. exec. com. C. of C. U.S.A., 1912-13, pres., 1914-15, hon. vice pres., 1915-20, chairman com. on fgn. affairs; mem. sr. council C. of C. of U.S., 1921-23; chmn. organizing com. Internat. C. of C., 1919-20, Am. dir., 1921-26; hon. mem. Bolsa de Commercio de Buenos Aires; dir., chmn. exec. com. 20th Century Fund, Inc., 1929-39, pres., 1937; dir. Edward A. Filene Good Will Fund. Decorated Chevalier Legion of Honor, France, 1920; Comdr. Order of the Crown, Italy, 1920; Officer Order of the Golden Sheaf, China, 1916. Catholic. Clubs: Tedesco Country, Swampscott, Burning Tree (Washington). Home: Little's Point, Swampscott, Mass. Office: Federal Home Loan Administration, Washington. Died Nov. 19, 1950.

FAHNESTOCK, Zephine Huphrey (Mrs. Wallace Weir Fahnestock) (fä-nĕ-stŏk), author; b. Phila., Dec. 15, 1874; d. Zephaniah Moore and Harriette (Sykes) Humphrey; B. L., Smith Coll., 1896; m. Wallace Weir Fahnestock, Apr. 13, 1914. Episcopalian. Author: The Calling of the Apostle, 1900; Uncle Charley, 1902; Over Against Green Peak, 1908; Recollections of My Mother, 1912; The Edge of the Woods, 1913; Grail Fire, 1917; The Homestead, 1919; The Sword of the Spirit, 1920; Mountain Verities, 1923; The Story of Dorset, 1924; Winterwise, 1927; Chrysalis, 1929; The Beloved Community, 1930; Green Mountains to Sierras, 1936; Cactus Forest, 1938; 'Allo Good-by, 1940; A Book of New England, 1947. Co-author: The Friendly Mountains, 1943; God and Company, 1953. Home: Dorset, Vt. Died Nov. 14, 1956; buried Dorset (Vt.) Cemetery.

FAIG, John Theodore, (fāg), engineer, educator; b. Lexington, Ky., Feb. 5, 1875; s. John and Louisa (Hurst) F.; B.M.E., Univ. of Ky., 1894, M.E., 1897, D.Sc., University of Kentucky, 1948; married Frances Wiley, 1909. Draftsman Lane & Bodley Co., Cincinnati, 1894-96; instr. engring., U. of Mich., 1896-98; asst. prof. and prof. engring., U. of Ky., 1898-1906; prof. mech. engring. U. of Cincinnati, 1906-18, also head of dept.; pres. of depts., Ohio Mechanics Inst., Cincinnati, since 1918. In charge S.A.T.C., Ohio Mechanics Inst., 1918; supervised training of 1200 ex-service men, under Veterans' Bur., 1919-25; pres. United City Planning Com. of Cincinnati, 1927-28. Fellow A.A.A.S., Am. Soc. Mech. Engrs.; mem. Soc. for Promotion Engring. Edn., Am. Engring. Council, 1924-27, Newcomen Soc. (British), Tau Beta Pi. Mem. Internat. Jury Awards, San Francisco Expn., 1915. Presbyterian. Clubs: Cincinnati, Literary. Home: 3345 Whitfield Av., Cin. Died Apr. 8, 1951.

FAIRBANK, Janet Ayer (Mrs. Kellogg Fairbank); b. Chicago, Ill.; d. Benjamin F. and Janet (Hopkins) Ayer; ed. U. of Chicago; m. Kellogg Fairbank, May 29, 1900; children—Janet, Kellogg, Benjamin Ayer. Active in cause of woman suffrage and in politics; was chmn. western div. of woman's finance com. Prog. Party; mem. exec. com. Dem. Nat. Com., 1919; Ill. Dem. Nat. Committeewoman, 1924-28; many yrs. pres. bd. Chicago Lying-In Hosp.; was mem. Woman's Nat. Liberty Loan Com., World War I, and mem. Ill. Com., Woman's Division, Council National Defense. Clubs: Scribblers, Friday, Fortnightly (Chicago). Author: At Home, 1910; The Cortlandts of Washington Square (novel), 1923; The Smiths (novel), 1925; Idle Hands (short stories), 1927; The Lion's Den (novel), 1930; The Bright Land (novel), 1932; Rich Man—Poor Man (novel), 1936. Home: 1244 N. State St., Chgo. Died Dec. 28, 1951; buried Graceland Cemetery, Chgo.

FAIRCHILD, Arthur Wilson, lawyer; b. Marinette, Wis., Dec. 11, 1876; s. Hiram Orlando and Emma (Hough) F.; B.L., U. of Wis., 1897, LL.B., 1901; m. Edith Hansen, Apr. 19, 1911; 1 dau., Edith Fairchild (Mrs. Arthur J. Frank). Admitted to Wis. bar, 1901, and began practice at Milwaukee; became asso. with firm Miller, Noyes & Miller, 1901, becoming partner, 1905; partner Miller, Mack & Fairchild, 1906-51, Fairchild, Foley & Sammond since 1951; dir. Nat. Rivet & Mfg. Co., T. A. Chapman Co., Square D Co., Mid-State Mfg. Co., Shaler Co., Graham Transmissions, Inc., Riverside Realty Co., Centric Corporation, Milwaukee Sanitarium, Kurth Malting Co., Dartwell Co., Fox Point Corporation. Special attorney Federal Trade Commission, Washington, Aug. 1-Oct. 15, 1917. Commd. maj. Ordnance Dept., U.S. Res., 1917; lt. col. Ordnance Dept., U.S. Army, 1918. Mem. Am., Wisconsin and Milwaukee bar assns., Phi Beta Kappa, Phi Delta Phi, Phi Delta Theta. Republican. Clubs: Milwaukee, Milwaukee Country, University, Milwaukee Athletic (Milwaukee); University (Chicago). Home: 2242 N. Lake Drive. Office: 735 N. Water St., Milw. 2. Died Aug. 2, 1956.

FAIRCHILD, David, agrl. explorer; b. Lansing, Mich., Apr. 7, 1869; s. George Thompson and Charlotte Pearl (Halsted) F.; student Kan. State Agrl. Coll.; hon. degrees from Oberlin Coll., Fla. State Coll., Kan. State; m. Marian H. Bell, Apr. 25, 1905; children—Graham Bell, Barbara (Mrs. Leonard Muller), Nancy Bell (Mrs. Marston Bates). Expdns. in search of plants for introduction to U.S., with Barbour Lathrop, to Dutch E. Indies, 1895, to S. Sea Islands, Siam, Australia, New Zealand, 1896-97, to W. Indies, S.A., Egypt, Ceylon and Persian Gulf, 1901-02, Africa, 1903; organizer, in charge office plant introduction Dept. of Agr., 1904-28; Allison V. Armour expdns. to Morocco, Dutch E. Indies, W. Africa, Carribbean, 1925-27, 32-33; in charge sci. work of Fairchild Garden expdn. to Philippines, Celebes, Java, Bali and Moluccas, on Mrs. Anne Archbold's Chinese junk, Cheng Ho, 1939-40; collected plants in Colombia, Panama and Guatemala and Yucatan, 1944. Mem. bd. trustees Nat. Geog. Soc. Medallist Societe d'Acclimatacion France, Harvard Traveller's Club, Mass. Hort. Soc. (George Robt. White), Nat. Acad. Scis., Garden Club of Am., Men's Garden Clubs(Johnny Appleseed), Nat. Council State Garden Clubs (Gold seal), Fairchild Tropical Garden (Meyer medal, plant introduction); Fairchild Tropical Garden, Coconut Grove Fla. named in his honor. Fellow Linnean Soc. London; pres. Am. Genetic Assn.; hon. mem. Committee of One Hundred, Miami Beach. Author: Book of Monsters, 1914; Exploring for Plants, 1930; The World Was My Garden, 1938; Garden Islands of the Great East, 1945; The World Grows Round My Door, 1947. Home: 4013 Douglas Rd., Coconut Grove, Fla.; (summer) Beinn Bhreagh, Nova Scotia, Can. Died Aug. 2, 1954.

FAIRCHILD, Henry Pratt, social scientist; b. Dundee, Ill., Aug. 18, 1880; s. Arthur Babbitt and Isabel (Pratt) F.; A.B., Doane Coll., Crete, Neb., 1900, LL.D., 1930; Ph.D., Yale U., 1909; m. Mary Eleanor Townsend, June 2, 1909 (died Oct. 1, 1928); 1 dau., Eleanor Rogers. Instr. The Internat. Coll., Smyrna, Turkey, 1900-03; state sec. Doane Coll., 1903-06; prof. economics and sociology Bowdoin Coll., 1909-10; asst. prof. economics Yale, 1910-12, asst. prof. science of society, 1912-18, sec. Bur. of Appmts., 1917-18; asso. dir. personnel dept. War Camp Community Service, 1918-19; prof. social economy and dir. Bur. of Community Service and Research, N.Y.U., 1919-24, prof. sociology since 1924, chmn. dept. of sociology, Grad. Sch. Arts and Science, 1938-45, prof. emeritus 1945-—. Exec. sec. Conn. State Commn. on Child Welfare, 1919-21; ednl. dir. Univ. Settlement, N.Y., 1919-20. Lectr. U. Calif. Summer Sch., 1923; investigator Nat. Research Council and spl. immigration agent in Europe of U.S. Dept. Labor, 1923. Round Table leader Inst. of Politics, Williamston, 1924; lectr. U. So. Calif. summer sch., 1940; pres. Population Assn. of America, 1931-35, Eastern Sociol. Conf., 1931-32; pres. People's League for Econ. Security, 1934-38; chmn. Commonwealth Fed. of N.Y., 1934-37; pres. Film Audiences for Democracy, 1939-40; pres. Town Hall Club, 1934-40; v.p. Planned Parenthood Fedn., 1939-48; mem. exec. com. Am. Commonwealth Polit. special service engagement U.N., 1952. Fedn. Fellow Am. Geog. Society, A.A.A.S.; mem. Am. Sociol. Soc. (pres. 1936), Am. Eugenics Soc. (pres. 1929-31), Solvay Institute (Brussels, Belgium), Am. Assn. U. Profs. (member coun.). Trustee Tchrs. Ins. and Annuity Assn.; sec. Nat. Coun. Am.-Soviet Friendship. Club: Century (N. Y.). Author: Greek Immigration to the United States, 1911; Immigration, 1913; Outline of Applied Sociology, 1916; Elements of Social Science, 1924; The Melting-Pot Mistake, 1925; The Foundations of Social Life, 1927; Profits or Prosperity?, 1932; General Sociology, 1934; The Way Out, 1936; People: The Quantity and Quality of Population, 1939; Economics for the Millions, 1940; Main Street: The American Town, Past and Present, 1941; Race and Nationality: As Factors in American Life, 1947. Editor: Immigrant Backgrounds, 1927; The Obligation of Universities to the Social Order, 1933; Dictionary of Sociology, 1944; The Prodigal Century and Ours Versus: The Reflections of a Sociologist. Home: 230 E. 48th St. Address: New York Univ., Washington Square East, N.Y. C. 3. Died Oct. 2, 1956; buried Crete, Neb.

FAIRCHILD, Raymond Wilber, retired president of Illinois State Normal University; born Bismark Illinois, September 9, 1889; son Wilber Daniel and Serena Mattie (Johnson) F.; A.B., U. of Mich., 1914, A.M., 1919; Ph.D., Northwestern U., 1932; LL.D., Ill. Wesleyan U., 1935; m. Nellie M. Bronson, June 25, 1913; children—Ralph Bronson, Robert Eugene. Asst. prin. Vandalia (Ill.) High Sch., 1909-10; teacher and asst. prin. Moline High Sch., 1910-14; dean State Teachers Coll., Stevens Point, Wis., 1914-20; supt. of sch., Fond du Lac, 1920-23, Elgin, Ill., 1923-30; prof., sch. of edn., Northwestern U., 1930-33; pres. Ill. State Normal U. 1933-55, ret. Mem. N.E.A., Ill. Edn. Assn., Ill. Supts. Assn., Nat. Ninety-Six Club, Kappa Delta Pi, Phi Delta Kappa. Methodist. Contbr. to ednl. jours. Home: 307 W. Virginia Av., Normal, Ill. Died June 12, 1956.

FAIRHURST, William, mfg. exec.; b. Paterson, N.J., Nov. 10, 1891; s. Joseph and Ida (Thompson) F.; grad. Peddie Sch., 1911; Ph.B., Yale, 1914; m. Josephine Milson, Oct. 22, 1919; children—William Milson, Thomas Johnston. Apprentice Packard Motor Car Co., Detroit, 1914-17; mgr. Detroit and N.Y. City offices Taft-Peirce Mfg. Co., Woonsocket, R.I., 1919-25; sales mgr. Spicer Mfg. Corp., Toledo, 1925-35; v.p. Dana Corp. (hdqrs. Spicer mfg. div.) since 1935. Mem. bd. corporators Peddie Sch. Served as capt., comdg. machine gun co., inf. U.S. Army, France and Germany, 1917-19. Mem. Soc. Automotive Engrs., Army Ordnance Assn., Sigma Chi. Episcopalian (vestryman 1943-50, sr. warden, 1949). Mason (32°). Clubs: Yale (N.Y. City); Inverness, Toledo (Toledo); Athletic (Detroit). Home: 3759 Sulphur Spring Rd., Toledo 6. Office: 4100 Bennett Rd., Toledo 1. Died Oct. 2, 1953; buried Woodlawn Cemetery, Toledo.

FAIRMAN, F. E., Jr., business exec.; b. Pitts., Oct. 15, 1899; s. Francis Evarts and Dulce (Fiske) F.; grad. U.S. Naval Acad., 1921; m. Sarah Lawrence Cooper, Nov. 18, 1921; children—Francis E. III, Philip Benson, Sarah Lawrence (Mrs. Wilson F. Engel, Jr.). Engr. Gen. Electric Co., Schenectady, 1923-28, sales engr., 1928-33, sect. sales mgr., 1934-40, asst. div. mgr., 1941-45; v.p. Food Machinery Corp.; gen. mgr. Peerless Pump div., 1945-49; mgr. sales Transformer & Allied Products div. Gen. Electric Co., 1949-50, gen. sales mgr. Large Apparatus divs., 1950-51, gen. mgr. Transformer & Allied Products div., 1951-52, v.p., gen. mgr., 1953-54, cons. Transformer Div. 1954-—. Registered engr., Cal., Mass. Served as ensign USN, 1921-23. Fellow Am. Inst. E.E.; mem. Nat. Elec. Mfrs. Assn. Mason. Clubs: Court (Pittsfield); Mohawk (Schenectady); Engineers (N.Y.C.). Home: 1029 West St. Office: 100 Woodlawn Av., Pittsfield, Mass. Died Sept. 27, 1958.

FAIRWEATHER, Clement Wilson, architect; b. Newcastle-on-Tyne, Eng., May 8, 1882; educated in architecture as articled pupil fo John W. Dyson, architect, Newcastle-on-Tyne; m. Marion Isabel Gordon Harkness, June 10, 1911; children—Clement Wilson, Eleanor Alice (wife of Lt. Herbert Lovet Manchip, Royal Corps of Signals). Came to U.S., 1907, naturalized, 1917. Engaged in practice as architect, Metuchen, N.J., 1921-—. Designer of Parish House of St. James Episcopal Ch., Upper Montclair, N.J.; Theol. Sem. Chapel, New Brunswick, N.J.; Municipal Bldg., also War Memorial, Metuchen, N.J..; First Congregational Christian Ch., Irvington, N.J., Hay Harbor Golf and Yacht clubs (remodelled), Townley Presbyn. Ch., Union, N.J., Fishers Island. N.Y.; also residences in N.J., N.Y., Conn. and Mass.; engaged in rehabilitation of Hertzog Hall, New Brunswick, N.J.; Reformed Ch. of Levittown (N.Y.); Chapel of Southern Normal Sch., Brewton, Ala., Reformed Ch., Metuchen, N.J., Corpus Christi R.C. Church and Rectory, South River, N.J., St. John's R.C. Ch. and Rectory, Allentown, N.J., First Presbyn. Ch., Plainfeld, N.J., Employees Bldg., Camden (N.J.) Coke Plant. Mem. N.J. State Board of Architects, 1926-28. Fellow Am. Inst. Architects; (del. to Internat. Congress of Architects, Holland, 1927). Mem. gov.'s adv. council N.J. State Institutional Bldg. Program, 1950-52. Home: 39 Rector St., Metuchen, N.J. Died Apr. 15, 1957; buried St. Andrew's Cemetery, Newcastle-on-Tyne, Eng.

FAISAL II, King of Iraq (see Feisal II King of Iraq)

FAKE, Guy Leverne, judge; b. Cobleskill, N.Y., Nov. 15, 1879; LL.B., N.Y.U., 1904; m. Grace Elizabeth Mucklow; children—Leverne M., Elwood B. Admitted to N.J. bar, 1903, began practice at Rutherford; mem. N.J. Gen. Assembly, 1907-08; judge, Dist. Court, 2d Jud. Dist. of Bergen County, N.J., 1909-24; Supreme Court commr., 1926; judge, U.S. Dist. Ct., N J Dist., 1929-—, chief Federal judge, 1948-—, ret. 1951, ubut assigned to continue in service. Served in Spanish-American War, 1898. Mem. N.J. (hon.), Rensselaer County (N.Y.), Schoharie County (N.Y.) hist socs., Phi Gamma Delta, Theta Sigma Lambda. Presbyn. Mason. Home: Rutherford, N.J. Address: Postoffice Bldg., Newark 1. Died Sept. 23, 1957.

FALCK, Alexander Diven (fawlk), glass mfr.; b. Elmira, N.Y., Mar. 7, 1878; s. Col. William and Mary (McQuhae) F.; student Elmira (NY.) Free Coll., 1891-95; A.B., Williams Coll., 1899; studied Columbia Law School, 1899-1901; m. Elizabeth Arnot Rathbone, June 3, 1908; children—Alexander Diven, James Rathbone, Elizabeth Arnot. Admitted to N.Y. bar, 1901; practiced at Elmira, 1901-18; with Corning (N.Y.) Glass Works, 1918-—, hon. chmn. bd., dir.; pres., dir. The Rathbone Corp.; dir. Arnot Realty Corp., Corhart's Refractories-Co., Le Pyrex, Am.-LaFrance-Foamite Corp., Elmira Knitting Mills, Chemung Canal Trust Co. Pres. bd. Arnot Ogden Meml. Hosp., Elmira. Pres. Arnot Art Gallery. Mem. N.Y. State Bar Assn., Kappa Alpha, Phi Delta Phi. Republican. Episcopalian. Clubs: City, Country (Elmira); Adirondack League (Old Forge, N.Y.); University, Williams (N.Y.C.). Home: 722 W. Water St. Office: 415 E. Water St., Elmira, N.Y. Died Apr. 4th, 1950.

FALES, Frederick Sayward (fāls); b. Rockland, Me., Feb. 26, 1873; s. Albert Norris and Lucy Helen (Butler) F.; grad. Phillips Acad., Andover, Mass., 1892; A.B., Amherst Coll., 1896; m. Grace S. Hughes, May 9, 1900; 1 dau., Fredericka F. Monroe. Employee, Swift & Co., Chgo., 1896; purchasing agt. Libby, McNeil & Libby, Chgo., 1897-1903; with Standard Oil Co. of N.Y. (now Socony Mobil Oil Co., Inc.) from 1903, becoming dir. and mgr. marine dept. 1919; pres. Standard Oil Co. of N.Y., Inc.; v.p., dir. Socony-Vacuum Corp.; dir. Carrier Corp., Carrier Engring. Corp. Mem. War Labor Bd. 1941. Mem. bd. gov. New Rochelle Hosp. Trustee Amherst Coll. Republican. Conglist. Clubs: University, Amherst, Recess, Psi Upsilon, Tobique Salmon, Blind Brook; Highland Park (Fla.). Home: Premium Point, New Rochelle, N.Y. Died Sept. 24, 1955.

FALK, Harold Sands, mfg. exec.; b. Milwaukee, Dec. 24, 1883; s. Louis Wahl and Kitty (Sands) F.; B.S., U. of Wis., 1906, LL.D. (hon.), 1948; M.S. (hon.), Marquette U., 1930; m. Eugenia Bechtner, Apr. 21, 1908; children—Harold Frank, Louis Wahl, Richard Sands, Robert Paul, Mary Elizabeth (Mrs. B. A. Tompkins, Jr.). Asst. to supt., The Falk Corp., mfrs. indsl. machinery, Milwaukee, 1906, in various plant depts., 1906-20, v.p., works mgr. and dir., 1920-40, pres., dir., 1940—; v.p. Heil Co., 1933—; trustee, mem. exec. and finance coms. Northwestern Mut. Life Ins. Co., Milw.; dir. and mem. exec. com. Wis. Elec. Power Co.; dir. Employers Mut. Liability Ins. Co. of Wausau (Wis.), Protection Mut. Fire Ins. Co., Oilgear Co., Harnischfeger Corp., Wis. Telephone Co. Received Penton medal, Am. Foundrymen's Assn., 1939. Civilian Aide to Sec. of Army for State of Wis., 1931-52. Mem. Am. Soc. M.E., Am. Soc. Naval Architects and Marine Engrs., Am. Ordnance Assn., Am. Foundrymen's Assn., Am. Vocational Assn., Navy League of U.S., Newcomen Soc., Chi Psi. Clubs: University, Milwaukee, Wisconsin, Advertising, Press (Milwaukee); Chicago, Advertising (Chicago). Home: 1869 N. Cambridge Av., Milw. 2. Office: 3001 W. Canal St., Milw. 8. Died Oct. 7, 1957; buried Milw.

FALK, K. George, chemist; b. N.Y. City, Sept. 8, 1880; s. Arnold and Fannie (Wallach) F.; B.S., Columbia, 1901; Johns Hopkins, 1901-03; Ph.D., Strassburg U., 1905; Berlin U., 1905-06; m. Dora Lichten, May 31, 1909; m. 2d, Carolyn Rosenstein, Oct. 16, 1935. Asst. in phys. chemistry, Columbia, 1906-07, tutor in physics, 1907-09; research asso. in phys. chemistry, Mass. Inst. Tech., 1909-11; chemist Harriman Research Lab., Roosevelt Hosp., New York, 1911-28, Harriman Research Fund, New York U. Med. Coll., 1929-31; biol. chemist, Bureau of Labs., Health Dept., N.Y. City, 1931-39; prof. chemical bacteriology in preventive medicine, New York U. Med. Coll., 1933-36; dir. Lab. of Industrial Hygiene, Inc., since 1936; also consultant for various chem. companies. Capt. Sanitary Corps, U.S. Army, 1918-19. Pres. Hebrew Tech. Inst. Mem. Am. Chem. Soc., Am. Pub. Health Assn., Am. Soc. Biol. Chemists, A.A.A.S., Soc. Exptl. Biology and Medicine, Harvey Soc., N.Y. Acad. Sciences, London Chem. Soc., Am. Assn. for Cancer Research, Am. Inst., Am. Inst. of Chemists, Sigma Xi, Phi Lambda Upsilon. Clubs: Chemists, Columbia, Harmonie. Author: Chemical Reactions, Their Theory and Mechanism, 1920; Chemistry of Enzyme Action, 1921, 2d edit., 1924; Catalytic Action, 1922. Contbr. to scientific jours. Home: 40 E. 66th St., N.Y. City 21. Office: 254 W. 31st St., N.Y.C. 1. Died Nov. 22, 1953; buried Ferncliff Cemetery, Hartsdale, N.Y.

FALL, Frank Andrews, author; b. Flint, Mich., Aug. 24, 1878; s. Delos and Ida J. (Andrews) F.; A.B., Albion Coll., 1899, Litt.D., 1916; A.M., Columbia, 1902; m. Nelala B. Ramsdell, June 27, 1906; 1 son, Kingsley Ramsdell. Sec. to pres. of Bellevue and Allied Hosps., N.Y.C., 1902-05; bursar, N.Y. U., 1905-20; v.p., bus. mgr. Scudder Sch., 1921-22; asso. editor Mgmt. and Adminstrn., 1923-24; dir. edn. and research Nat. Assn. of Credit Men, 1925-31; mem. editorial staff Outlook and The Independent, 1930-32; asst. to pres. L.I. U., 1932-42. Mem. Co. L, 31st Mich. Vol. Inf., 1898. Mem. bd. mgmt., West Side YMCA; mem. Nat. Bd. of Review of Motion Pictures; mem. bd. govs. Eastern Rugby Union. Mem. Market Research Council, Conf. of Statisticians in Industry, Am. Econ. Assn., Fgn. Policy Assn., Am. Statis. Assn., Nat. Fire Waste Council, Alpha Tau Omega. Clubs: Quill, Union League, Writers Club. Author: Messages to Men, 1901; Steering Gear, 1902; Quill Points, 1903; Life-lines for Men, 1904; Blazed Trails, 1905; Developing a Positive, 1907; Working for the Boss, 1913; Little Stories of Progress, 1914; Effective Collection Methods (with E. H. Gardner), 1932; also mag. articles, short stories. Home: Alford, Mass. Died Sept. 6, 1959; buried Alford, Mass.

FALL, Gilbert Haven, educator; b. Somersworth, N.H., Mar. 27, 1883; s. John Albert and Susan (Lord) F.; grad. Somersworth High Sch., 1901; A.B., Dartmouth, 1905; hon. M.A., U. of Pa., 1931; m. Ethel May Bernier, June 1910 (died 1936); 1 son, Gilbert Haven; m. 2d, Florence Huff Candor, June 1938. Teacher of science, high school, Bellows Falls, Vt., 1905-06; with Chestnut Hill Acad., 1906—, as teacher of history, registrar, asst. to headmaster, and as headmaster, 1930-36, head department social studies, 1936—. Member Progressive Edn. Soc., Headmasters' Assn. of Phila. Dist., Headmasters' Assn. Country Day Schs., Chi Phi. Republican. Episcopalian. Mason. Home: 500 W. Willow Grove Av., Chestnut Hill, Pa. Died Sept. 11, 1956.

FALLIS, Iva Campbell Doyle (Mrs. Howard T. Fallis). Can. senator; b. Castleton, Ont., June 23, 1883; d. Michael John and Jessica (Stewart) Doyle; student Colbourne Collegiate, Toronto Normal Sch.; m. Howard T. Fallis, Dec. 8, 1909. Tchr. 5 yrs.; became speaker Conservative Party, 1923; later 1st v.p. Ont. Conservative Assn., 5 yrs.; 1st v.p. Nat. Exec., 3 yrs.; senator Can. Senate 1935—. Dir. Ont. Red Cross Soc., Ont. Girl Guides Assn. Mem. Peterborough Council Women, Beta Sigma Phi (internat. v.p., Can. sponsor). Clubs: Soroptimist (Peterborough, Ottawa); hon. v.p. Women's Canadian (Ottawa). Home: Peterborough, Ont. Office: The Senate, Ottawa, Can. Deceased.

FALLON, Bernard Joseph, corp. official; b. Rutland, Ill., Aug. 10, 1880; s. John and Catherine (Fitzgerald) F.; A.B. (scientific course), De La Salle Inst., Chicago, 1898; m. Frances Driscoll, Sept. 15, 1909; children—Mary Catherine, Frances Fay (dec.), Jack, David. With engring. dept. C.B.&Q. R.R., 1899-1907; engr. maintenance of way, Met. West Side Elevated Ry., 1907-09; asst. gen. mgr. same, 1909-11; engr. maintenance of way, Chicago Elevated Railroads, 1911-20; chief engr. Chicago, North Shore & Milwaukee R.R., 1916-25; asst. gen. mgr. Chicago Elevated Railroads, 1920-21, gen. mgr., 1921-25; v.p. Chicago Rapid Transit Co., 1925-34; v.p. Chicago, North Shore & Milwaukee R.R. Co., 1925-34; v.p. Chicago, Aurora & Elgin R.R. Co., 1925-34; trustee and exec. officer, Chicago Rapid Transit Co.; exec. officer for trustees, Chicago, North Shore & Milwaukee Ry. Co., pres., 1946—; v.p. and dir. Evanston Bus. Co. Cons. United Transit System, Chicago. Mem. Western Soc. Engrs. Chicago Assn. Commerce, Evanston Hist. Soc. Clubs: Chicago Athletic Assn., Chicago Engineers, Glen View. Address: 1500 Lake Shore Dr., Chgo. Died, Dec. 24, 1956.

FALLS, Raymond Leonard, dean Youngstown Coll. of Law Sch.; b. New Castle, Pa., July 12, 1899; s. Benjamin Francis and Katherine (Weir) F.; A.B., Thiel Coll., 1921, LL.B., Western Reserve Univ., 1926; m. Vernita B. Bowden, Sept. 10, 1927; children—Raymond Leonard, Jr., Phyllis Kay. Pvt. practice in Youngstown, O., since 1926; prof. of law, Youngstown Coll. Law Sch. since 1933, dean of Law Sch., since 1942; partner, Falls, Hazel & Kerr. Mem. bd. edn. Youngstown City Sch. Dist., 1944-48. Mem. nat. panel arbitrators Nat. Arbitration Assn. Mem. Mahoning County Bar Assn. (past pres.), Am. Bar Assn., Ohio Bar Assn. (publ. com.; com. on O. Judicial system; legal education committee, member of executive committee), Amrican Judicature Soc., Ohio League of Law Schools, Chamber Commerce (taxation and legislative coms.), Delta Sigma Phi, Phi Alpha Delta. Mason. Elk. Club: Optimist (past pres.). Home: 3521 Hopkins Rd. Office: Realty Bldg., Youngstown, O. Died Sept. 18, 1956; buried Forest Lawn Meml. Park Yongstown, O.

FALVEY, Wallace, business exec.; b. Norwich, Conn., May 1, 1894; s. Timothy J. and Mary Elizabeth (Cosgrove) F.; student Boston Latin Sch.; A.B., Harvard U., 1916; married. With investment firm of Jackson & Curtis, Boston, Mass., 1916; with Mass. Bonding and Ins. Co., N.Y. City, since 1917, now president; dir. Rockland-Atlas Bank of Boston. Mem. corp. Northeastern U.; bd. mgrs. Mass. Eye & Ear Infirmary. Served in World War I. Trustee Am. Mus. of Safety; dir. Nat. Safety Council. Clubs: Harvard, Boston Harvard, University, Racquet and Tennis (N.Y.C.); Metropolitan (Washington); Tedesco (Swampscott, Mass.); Apawamis (Rye, N.Y.); National Golf Links (Southampton). Office: 10 Post Office Square, Boston 9. Died Nov. 7, 1958.

FARIS, Ellsworth, sociologist; b. Salem, Franklin County, Tenn., Sept. 30, 1874; s. George Alexander and Sophie Jane (Yarbrough) F.; S.B., Tex. Christian Univ., Ft. Worth, 1894, A.M., 1906; Ph.D., Univ. of Chicago, 1914; m. Elizabeth Lee Homan, Oct. 3, 1901 (died July 31, 1937); children—Eugene Homan (dec.), Richard Alexander, Robert E. Lee, George, William Kercheval (dec.), Ellsworth; m. 2d, Ruth Greeley Wells, Jan. 1, 1941. Missionary to Congo, Africa, 1897-1904; asso. editor Christian Courier, Dallas, Tex., 1904-11; prof. philosophy and psychology, Tex. Christian U., 1906-11; scholar in psychology, U. of Chicago, 1911-12; fellow in philosophy, same, 1912-13; asst. prof. philosophy, State U. of Ia., 1913-14; instr. psychology, U. of Chicago, 1914-15, also Art Inst. Chicago; asso. prof. psychology, State U. of Ia., 1915-17, prof., 1917-18; dir. Ia. Child Welfare Research Sta., 1918-19; prof. sociology, U. of Chicago, 1919-39, chmn. dept. of sociology and anthropology, 1925-29, chmn. dept. of sociology, 1929-39, retired, 1939; visiting prof., U. of Wash., summer, 1930, Tulane, 1st semester, 1930-31, U. of Mich., summer, 1932, U. of Hawaii, 1938; Distinguished prof. sociology Tex. Christian U., 1949-50; prof. sociology U. of Utah, 1951; research in Belgian Congo and Anglo-Egyptian Sudan, 1932-33, Guatemala, Costa Rica, Mexico, 1947, Belgian Congo, Uganda, 1949. Editor Am. Jour. Sociology, 1925-36. Pres. Adult Edn., Council of Chicago, 1941-42. Mem. Sociological Research Association (charter mem.), Am. Sociol. Soc. (pres. 1937), Acacia, Sigma Xi. Awarded commemorative medal by King of the Belgians, 1930. Contbd. chpts. to Mathew's Contributions of Sci. to Religion, 1924, Burgess' Personality and the Social Group, 1929, Smith's Essays in Philosophy, 1929, Young's Social Attitudes, 1930; also articles on psychol., sociol. and anthropol. topics. Co-Editor: Intelligent Philanthropy, 1930; American Society in War Time, 1943. Author: The Nature of Human Nature, 1937. Clubs: Onwentsia, Quadrangle, University, Casino. Home: 1401 N. Green Bay Rd., Lake Forest, Ill. Died Dec. 19, 1953.

FARIS, James Edge, med. dir., U.S.P.H.S.; b. Red Hill, Va., Aug. 1, 1889; s. John Newton and Martha Anne (Edge) F.; student U. of Richmond, 1910-11; M.D., U. of Va., 1916; m. Elizabeth M. Sheldon, Oct. 22, 1921; children—James Edge, Elizabeth Anne, Mary Margaret. With U.S. Pub. Health Service since 1916; began as interne Ellis Island Hosp., 1916-17; commissioned assistant surgeon, 1917, passed assistant surgeon, 1921, surgeon, 1925, senior surgeon, 1937, medical director, 1943; quarantine officer Fort Monroe, 1917-21; anti-typhus work, Boston, March-July 1921; immigration examiner, Montreal, Can., August-November 1921; student officer, Hygienic Lab., Washington, D.C., 1922; exec. officer, Marine Hosp., Ellis Island, 1922-23; chief quarantine officer, Virgin Islands, 1923-25; medical clinic, U.S. Marine Hosp., N.Y. City, 1925-26; med. adviser to Am. Consul, Gothenburg, Sweden, 1926-28, to Am. Consul Gen., Genoa, Italy, 1928-31; hosp. adminstr., U.S. Indian Service, Washington, D.C., 1931-35; med. officer in charge Marine Hosp., Mobile, Ala., 1935-36; with Ala. State Health Dept., Montgomery, 1936-37, Neb. State Health Dept., 1937-38; med. officer in charge U.S. Quarantine Station, Fort Monroe, Va., since Sept. 1938. Home: 71 Fenwick Rd. Office: U.S. Quarantine Station, Fort Monroe, Va. Died Jan. 20, 1952.

FARLEY, Edward Philip, steamship company exec.; b. Madison, Wis., Oct. 18, 1886; student U. of Wis., 1905-07; m. Elise Inderrieden, Sept. 4, 1914. Chmn. bd., pres. Am.-Hawaiian Steamship Co.; dir., chmn. bd. Eastern Steamship Lines, Incorporated; director, chairman, member executive com. Am. Ship Building Co.; dir. Ore Transport Inc., Gen. Am. Investors Co., Inc. Chmn. U.S. Shipping Bd., June 1923-Feb. 1924; and pres. Emergency Fleet Corp. same period; dir. Glens Falls Ins. Co. Clubs: India House, Racquet and Tennis, Creek, The Brook (N.Y.); Chevy Chase, Metropolitan (Washington); Pacific-Union (San Francisco), Chicago. Home: 435 E. 52d St. Office: 90 Broad St., N.Y.C. Died Mar. 5, 1956.

FARLEY, Eliot, business exec.; b. Beverly Farms, Mass., 1885; s. James Phillips and Mary Eliot (Wells) F.; A.B., Harvard, 1907; m. Helen Grozier, May 16, 1916. Chmn. bd. Textron, Inc.; dir. Raymond Products Co., Berlin, Conn.; v.p. and dir. Pickering Coal Co., Salem, Mass. Clubs: Harvard, Tennis and Racquet, Somerset (Boston); Harvard, Racquet and Tennis (New York). Office: 27 State St., Boston. Died July 31, 1952.

FARLEY, J(ohn) W(ells), lawyer, corp. exec.; b. Brookline, Mass., June 15, 1878; s. James Phillips and Mary Eliot (Wells) F.; grad. Roxbury Latin Sch. 1894; A.B., Harvard, 1899, LL.B., 1903; m. Isabel Stewart McLennan, Sept. 15, 1911; children—Louise, Elizabeth, Isabel. Admitted to Mass. bar, 1903, since practiced in Boston; in law office of Alfred Hemenway, 1903-08; partner Hemenway, Barnes & Farley, 1908-13; sec. asst. counsel, Boston Finance Com., 1909; treas., pub. Boston Herald, 1911-13; partner Fish, Richardson, Herrick & Neave, 1913-16; partner Herrick, Smith, Donald & Farley 1916—; chmn. exec. com., dir. Merrimac Hat. Corp., Thompson Electric Welder Co.; pres., dir. Acme Fishing Tool Co., Indsl. Co.; dir. Am. Airlines, Inc., State St. Trust Co. Served as maj. 303d Infantry U.S. Army, 1917-19. Overseer, Harvard, 1941-47; pres. bd. trustees Children's Hosp. Boston 1944—; mem. corp. of Northeastern U., 1941—. Pres. Needham Taxpayers Assn., 1932-35; gen. chmn. Boston Emergency Relief Campaign, 1934; gen. chmn. Mass. Rep. Finance Com., 1936-37; gen. chmn. A.R.C. War Relief Campaign, 1940; exec. dir., Mass. Com. on Pub. Safety 1941-45, exec. com., dir. Boston Community Fund. Unitarian. Republican. Clubs: Tavern, Somerset, Dedham Country and Polo. (all Boston). Home: South St., Needham, Mass. Office: 294 Washington St., Boston. Died Mar. 12, 1959; buried Mt. Auburn Cemetery, Cambridge, Mass.

FARMER, August Neustadt (adopted name), educator; b. foothills of Carpathian Mts. near Kaschau, Austria-Hungary, May 26, 1872; s. Julius Neustadt came to U.S. at 10 yrs. of age and was adopted into family of George W. Farmer, of Spring Valley Minn., 1883; student U. Minn., 1896-98 and (law) 1900-02; B.L., Carleton Coll., Minn., 1899, LL.D.,

1952; married Nell Rafferty, December 27, 1899 (deceased February 19, 1954); children—Sterling Neustadt, Faith. Teacher, principal and superintendent schs., Minn., 1887-1912; educational research work, Bureau Municipal Research, New York City, 1912-15; reorganized ednl. dept. Nat. Cash Register Co., Dayton, O., 1915-16; supt. schs., Evanston, Ill., 1916-18; war camp community service, 1918-19; dist. rep. for War Camp Community Service and Community Service, Inc., New York, also exec. sec. Mich. Community Council Commn., 1919-21; mem. of staff of survey of N.Y. City schools, 1924-25; treas. Sand Products Corp. (Detroit). Mem. Delta Sigma Rho. Republican. Unitarian. Mason (32°, Shriner). Clubs: Midday; La Gorce Country, Com. of 100 (Miami Beach, Fla.). Author: Condition and Needs of Wisconsin's Rural Schools, 1913; (joint author) Survey University of Wisconsin, 1914; Conditions and Needs Wisconsin Normal Schools, 1914; Food Problems, 1918; Progress Report No. 1 (Mich. Community Council Commn.), 1920; Reorganization Michigan State Government (joint author), 1921; Report on Teacher Training in New York City Public Schools, 1925. Home: (summer) Lake Shore Hotel, Lakewood, O.; (winter) 1332 Biscaya Island Surfside, Miami Beach, Fla. Office: Perry Payne Bldg., Cleve. Died June 23, 1956.

FARMER, Clyde F., ry. official; b. Newark, O., s. M. L. and Ann (Duncan) F.; ed. pub. schs. and business coll.; married, Nov. 24, 1921; 1 son, Clyde F. Began as clerk, B.&O. R.R., Newark, O., 1909, later in traffic and operating depts., div. freight agent, Cleveland, later Akron and Youngstown, 1920-28, asst. gen. freight agent, Cleveland, 1928-29, gen. freight agent, Baltimore, 1929-31, asst. freight traffic mgr., St. Louis, 1931-37, freight traffic mgr., Pittsburgh, 1937-41; v.p. D.,L.&W. R.R. 1941—. Served with 36th Engrs., U.S. Army, in France, 14 mos., World War. Mason. Clubs: Duquesne (Pittsburgh); Cloud, Whitehall, Railroad (New York); Baltusrol Golf (Springfield, N.J.). Home: Summit, N.J. Office: 140 Cedar St., N.Y.C. Died Aug. 26, 1956; buried Cedar Hill Cemetery, Newark, O.

FARMER, Garland, Sr., editor, publisher; b. Durango, Tex., Aug. 8, 1897; s. Thomas Cinclar and Mary (Hargrave) F.; student Bedichek's Acad., 1910-11, Eddy Lit. and Sci. Inst., 1912-14; m. Agnes Langhorne, May 15, 1921; children—Garland, Tom, Jack and Gene (twins). With Postal Service, 1916-26; editor, pub. Henderson Times, 1927—; freelance writer, 1927—. Chmn. So. Council Research, 1939-49; dir. Nat. Library Newspapers. Pub. mem., vice chmn. 8th Regional War Labor Bd., Dallas, 1943-45. Author: The Realm of Rusk County, 1951; A Million Dollars Worth of Advice, as told Garland Farmer by prominent people, 1955. Home: 314 East St. Office: Times Bldg., Henderson, Tex. Died July 19, 1956; buried Lakewood Meml. Park, Henderson.

FARMER, S. J.; pres. Baptist Conv. of Ontario and Quebec. Address: 223 Church St., Toronto, Ontario, Can. Died Sept. 4, 1953.

FARNAM, Ruth Stanley (Baroness de Luze), author, lectr.; b. Patchogue, L.I., N.Y., Sept. 11, 1873; d. William Henry and Ida Jay (Overton) Stanley; ed. pub. schs.; m. Charles Henry Farnam, Jr., June 13, 1899 (died 1909); m. 2d, Baron Raymond de Luze, Feb. 25, 1928. Made hon. sgt. of Serbian Army; present at Battle of Bröd, Oct. 11, 1916; first woman to enter reconquered Serbian ty.; sent to Paris by Com. on Protection of Women, 1919; lectured throughout U.S. for Liberty Loan, raised large sums of money for Serbian relief. Decorated Serbian Order St. Sava, 3d Class and 5th Class; Order of Mercy, Order of Kossovo, Order Royal Serbian Red Cross, Grand Citation by the field marshal of Serbian Army, 1919; Order of the Redeemer (Greece). Mem. Nat. Soc. Colonial Daus. Clubs: Rotary, Kiwanis, Commercial of Duluth, Minnesota (all hon.); Rotary (Flint, Mich.); Sorosis, American Woman's (London, Eng.). Republican. Presbyn. Author: A Nation at Bay, 1918. Contbr. to mags. Home: 12 rue Alsace, Saumur, France. Died Dec. 7, 1956.

FARNHAM, Dwight Thompson, cons. engr.; b. Candor, N.Y., Oct. 15, 1881; s. LeRoy Dwight and Cora P. (Thompson) F.; A.B., Yale, 1904; m. Mateel Howe, June 16, 1910. With Clermont and Shawmut mfg. cos. of Pa., 1904-06; supt., gen. supt., mgr. Denny Renton Clay Coal Co., Seattle, 1906-14; studied conditions in Europe, 1914; supervising engr. Emerson Co., 1914-16; cons. practice, St. Louis, including spl. work for emergency Fleet Corp. and Ordnance Dept., during World War, 1916-20. Served as mem. faculty Sch. Bus. Adminstrn. St. Louis U.; studied indsl. conditions in France, Italy, Germany and Eng., 1920; in consulting indsl. and financial work, N.Y.C., 1920—; mgr. indsl. dept. Peat, Marwick, Mitchell & Co., 1924-33; became indsl. counsel Indsl. Relations Counselors, Inc., 1933. Mem. General Foods orgn., 1935. Lecturer univs. Former dir. Am. Mgmt. Assn., Soc. Indsl. Engrs. and Am. Ceramic Soc.; fellow Masaryk Acad. (Czechoslovakia); mem. Am. Soc. Mech. Engrs., Com. on Work Periods, Internat. Mgmt. Congress Com., Nat. Econ. League, Mayflower Soc., etc. Republican. Episcopalian. Club: Yale. Author: Scientific Administration and Scneitific Industrial Efficiency, 1916; Executive Control, 1918; America vs. Europe in Industry, 1921; Profitable Science in Industry (with others), 1924; The Vertical Trust, 1925; Types of Consolidations in America and Europe, 1929; The Effect of Currency Inflation, 1933; A Place in the Country, 1936; The Embattled Male or Why Women Are Queer, 1941; Be It Ever So Humble or Hellions on the Hearth, 1942; also some 50 articles in mags. and tech. jours. Home: Westport, Conn. Died Sept. 20, 1950.

FARNHAM, Mateel Howe (Mrs. Dwight Thompson Farnham), writer; b. Atchison, Kan.; d. Edgar Watson and Clara (Frank) Howe; grad. Mt. Vernon Sem., Washington; m. Dwight Thompson Farnham, June 16, 1910 (died 1950). Began writing for Atchison Globe, of which father was editor; winner of $500 prize offered by Portland Oregonian for essay on Portland; contbr. short stories to Delineator and Woman's Home Companion, and a novelette to Ladies' Home Jour.; won $10,000 Pictorial Rev.-Dodd, Mead & Co. prize with novel, Rebellion, 1927; also author of Marsh Fire, 1928; Wild Beauty, 1930; Battle Royal, 1931; Lost Laughter, 1933; Great Riches, 1934; Ex-Love, 1937; The Tollivers; contbr. to leading mags. Home: Westport, Conn. Died May 2, 1957.

FARNSWORTH, Charles Stewart, army officer; b. Lycoming County, Pa., Oct. 29, 1862; s. Isaac Francis and Sarah (Moore) F.; grad. U.S. Mil. Acad., 1887; distinguished grad. Army Sch. of the Line and Staff Coll., Ft. Leavenworth, Kan., 1909, 10; grad. Army War Coll., Washington, 1916; m. Laura J. Galey, July 20, 1887 (died May 20, 1890); 1 son, Robert James; m. 2d, Helen D. Bosard, Nov. 28, 1894 (died July 1951). Commd. 2d lt. 25th Inf., 1887, advanced through grades to maj. gen. Nat. Army, 1918; served in Dakota Ty., Mont. and N.D. until 1893; prof. mil. sci. and tactics U. N.D., 1893-97; with 7th Inf., Denver, 1897-98; at Chickamauga Park (Ga.), Tampa (Fla.), Santiago and Havana (Cuba) and Montauk Pt. (N.Y.) during Spanish-Am. War; in Alaska, 1899-1901; constructing cantonments at the Presidio, San Francisco, 1902-03; served in Philippines, Mont., Mich., and Kan., 1904-10; comdr. Ft. Gibbon, Alaska, 1910-11; instr., insp. Pa. N.G., 1911-13; served in Cal., Tex., and Washington, 1913-16; with Pershing's punitive expdn., in Mexico, 1916; comdg. base of communications Columbus, N.M., later asst. chief of staff, El Paso Dist., until 1917; comdt. Inf. Sch. of Arms, Fort Sill, Okla., 1917; comdg. 159th Inf. Brig., Camp Lee, Va., 1917-18, comdg. 37th Div., AEF, 1918-19, participating in occupation of the Baccarat (Vosges Mountains) and Panne (St. Mihiel) sectors and in the offensives in the Argonne-Meuse and Ypres and Lys; comdg. Camp Bowie, Tex., Inf. Sch. and Camp Benning, Ga., 1919-20; chief of Inf., 1920-25, ret. Decorated Silver Star, D.S.M. (U.S.); Croix de Guerre, comdr. Legion of Honor, Verdun Medal (France); comdr. Order of Leopold II (Belgium). Pres. Altadena Citizens' Assn., 1929. Altadena Beautification League, 1930-31; dir. LaViña Tubercular Sanitarium; dir., v.p. Los Angeles County Conservation Assn., 1934-38; dir. Foothill Health Sch. for Girls. Clubs: Twilight (Pasadena, Cal.); Los Fiesteros (Los Angeles), Army of Santiago de Cuba, Order of Midnight Sun. Home: 556 E. Las Flores Drive, Altadena, Cal. Died Dec. 19, 1955; buried Nat. Cemetery, Presidio of San Francisco.

FARQUHAR, Samuel Thaxter, book publisher; b. Newton, Mass., May 10, 1890; s. David Webber and Grace (Peloubet) F.; A.B., Harvard, 1912; m. Carley Frost, 1948; children, by previous marriage—Robert Leete, Francis Nelson, Jean Mather. Mgr. U. of Calif. Press, Berekeley, Calif., since 1943. Vice pres. Am. Inst. Graphic Arts. Clubs: Faculty, Rotary (Berkeley); University, Zamorano (Los Angeles); Roxbourghe (San Francisco); E. Clampus Vitus. Mason. Elk. Contbr. articles to profl. jours. Office: University of California Press, Berkeley 4, Cal.; and University of California Press, Royce Hall, University of California, L.A. 24. Died May 23, 1949; buried Sunset View Cemetery, Berkeley, Cal.

FARQUHARSON, James (fär'kwẽr-s'n), coll. prof.; b. Aberdeen, Scotland, Jan. 19, 1897; s. William and Annie (Fraser) F.; came to U.S., 1906, naturalized, 1931; D.V.M., Colorado State Coll., 1921; student Iowa State Coll., 1922, Mayo Foundation, Rochester, Minn., 1940; m. Margaret Mae McCabe, June 21, 1923; children—William Bruce, James Carey. Practicing veterinarian since 1921; asst. prof. anatomy, Colo. State Coll., Fort Collins, Colo., 1922-27, asso. prof., 1927-32, asso. prof. veterinary medicine, 1932-34, prof. vet. surgery and clinic and head of dept. since 1934. Served with Canadian Army, 1917-18. Mem. Colo. Vet. Med. Assn., Am. Vet. Med. Assn. (chmn. gen. practice, 1939; chmn. sect. surgery, 1942; asso. editor, 1938-43; mem. exec. bd., 1942; pres. elect, 1943; pres., 1944; mem. vet. research council since 1942), Research Workers of North America, Sigma Nu, Alpha Psi, Phi Kappa Phi, Am. Legion. Mason, Rotarian. Home: 1320 W. Oak St., Fort Collins, Colo. Died Mar. 11, 1954; buried Grandview Cemetery, Fort Collins, Colo.

FARRAND, Beatrix (Cadwalader) (făr'rănd), landscape gardner; b. N.Y., June 19, 1872; d. Frederick Rhinelander and Mary Cadwalader (Rawle) Jones; profl. edn. under Charles Sprague Sargent, dir. Arnold Arboretum of Harvard; M.A. (hon.), Yale, 1926; L.H.D. (hon.), Smith Coll., 1935; m. Max Farrand, Dec. 17, 1913. Designer of gardens or grounds for the late Clement B. Newbold of Jenkintown, Pa. (now destroyed), 1898; Grad. Coll., Princeton, 1912; G. H. Milliken, Northeast Harbor, Me., 1921; Meml. Quadrangle planting, Yale U., 1921; Robert Woods Bliss Washington, 1922; various bldgs., U. Chgo., 1930-31. Supervising landscape gardner Princeton, 1915-43; cons. landscape gardener Yale, 1922-45, U. Chgo., 1933-47, Dartington Hall and Estates, Totnes, Devonshire, Eng., 1933-44, Occidental Coll., Los Angeles, 1937-48; cons. landscape gardener Oberlin Coll., 1939-48, Dumbarton Oaks, Harvard, 1941-48, Arnold Arboretum, Jamaica Plain, Mass., 1949-54; cons. for landscape gardening, Santa Barbara Botanic Garden, 1944-50; founder, pres. Reef Point Gardens, Bar Harbor, Me., 1939. Recipient Garden Club of Am. Achievement Medal, 1947; Mass. Hort. Soc. Gold Medal, 1952; N.Y. Bot. Garden Distinguished Service Award, 1952. Fellow Am. Soc. Landscape Architects (charter mem.); hon. mem. A.I.A. Hon. trustee Santa Barbara Bot. Garden. Home: Garland Farm, R.F.D. 1, Bar Harbor, Me. Died Feb. 27, 1959.

FARRAND, George E., lawyer; b. Dogtown, Clarion County, Pa., Apr. 14, 1878; s. William and Jeanette (McKevett) F.; prep. edn., high sch., Ventura County, Calif.; student Hastings Law Sch., San Francisco, Calif., 1897-99; m. Alice Knox, Nov. 18, 1903; children—Knox, Stephen McKevett. Admitted to Calif. bar, 1899, and began practice in Ventura County; later moved to Los Angeles; gen. counsel Calif. Walnut Growers Assn. since 1910, Sunkist Growers, Incorporated, since 1913, Los Angeles Clearing House Assn.; orgn. gen. counsel Fed. Farm Bd., 1929. County clk. of Ventura Co., 1900-07, dep. dist. atty., 1907-09; mem. sch. bds., Santa Paula and San Buenaventura, 1900-16; mem. Calif. Constl. Commn., 1930. Trustee Cal. Institute of Technology since 1933. Member Am. Bar Assn., State Bar of Calif., Los Angeles Bar Assn., Calif. Inst. Associates, Order of Coif (hon.). Clubs: California, Los Angeles Athletic, Los Angeles Country; The Beach Club (Santa Monica). Home: 322 S. Windsor Blvd. Office: 215 W. 6th St., Los Angeles 14, Died May 31, 1954.

FARRAR, Gilbert Powderly (fărrow), cons. typographer, designer of newspapers and magazines; b. Lynchburg, Va., June 16, 1886; s. Jesse Madison and Christine (English) F.; ed. grammar sch.; m. Beatrice Breakspear, Aug. 24, 1913 (deceased); children—Mary L. (Mrs. Henry Bennett Burr), Frederic B., Beatrice Breakspear II; m. 2d, Carol A. Richards, June 6, 1953. Type compositor, 1900-08; designer of printing Internat. Corr. schs., Scranton, Pa., 1908-11; dir. of printing for advt. agencies, 1911-16; gen. cons. typographer, 1916—; lecturer on typography, New York U., 1918-28; designer of Los Angeles Times, Los Angeles Mirror, Hollywood Citizen-News, North Hollywood Cal. Valley Times, San Francisco Call Bulletin, N.Y. Tribune, Atlanta Journal, Houston Post, Houston Chronical, Dallas Times Herald, Dallas Morning News, Worcester (Mass.), Telegram, Worcester Gazette, Portland (Ore.) Journal, Brooklyn Eagle, Minneapolis Tribune, Minneapolis Star, Cleveland News, San Diego Union and Tribune, Deseret News, Fort Worth Star Telegram, Salt Lake (Utah) Tribune, Corpus Christi (Texas) Caller-Times, The Daily Press and Times-Herald (Newport News, Va.), Fort Wayne Journal Gazette, Vancouver (B C.) Sun, Montreal Standard, Edmonton Bulletin, Victoria Times, Anderson (S.D.) Independent and Daily Mail, The Reno Evening Gazette, Jersey Journal, Jamestown (N.Y.) Post-Journal, Charlotte (N.C.) Observer, Columbus (O.) Dispatch, Miami (Fla.) Daily News, Tex., Erie (Pa.) Morning News, 1957. Retail Daily, 1957. Quality group of 8 newspapers, Thomson Dailies (8), Ont., Can., Bridgeport Herald. Editor and Publisher etc.; typographic counselor and lecturer for printing machinery and type companies, 1927-37. Christian Scientist. Mason. Author: The Typography of Advertisements that Pay, 1917; How Advertisements Are Built, 1925; also articles in advertising and printing trade publications. Lecturer before advt. clubs, newspaper assns., etc. Home: Laguna Beach, Cal. Office: 121 Riverside Dr., N.Y.C. 24. Died Apr. 4, 1957.

FARRINGTON, Joseph Rider (făr'ĭng-tŭn), publisher; b. Washington, D.C., Oct. 15, 1897; s. Wallace Rider and Catherine McAlpine (Crane) F.; B.A., University of Wisconsin, 1919; married Mary Elizabeth Pruett, May 17, 1920; children—Beverly (Mrs. Hugh Richardson), and John. Began as reporter Philadelphia Public Ledger, 1919; Washington corr. Phila. Pub. Ledger and Honolulu Star-Bulletin, 1919-23; mng. editor Honolulu Star-Bulletin, 1924-33, v.p., 1929-34, pres. and gen. mgr. since 1934; pres. Hilo Tribune Herald, Honolulu Lithograph Co., Ltd. Sec. Hawaii Legislative Commn., 1932; mem. Territorial Senate, 1934-42; del. Congress from Hawaii, 1942; reelected, 1944, 46, 48, 50, 52. Enlisted U.S. Army, 1918; commd. 2d lt., Sept. 1918; hon. discharged, Dec. 1918. Director, secretary, treasurer and president Hawaiian Association Amateur Athletic Union of U.S.; member First Territorial Boxing Commn.,

1929. Mem. Am. Legion, Beta Theta Pi, Sigma Delta Chi. Clubs: Outrigger Canoe, Pacific Lions, Commercial (Honolulu). Author: American Samoan Commission's Visit to Samoa (with Reuel S. Moore), 1931. Home: 3180 Pacific Heights Rd. Office: 125 Merchant St., Honolulu, Hawaii. Died June 19, 1954; buried Nuuanu Cemetery, Honolulu, Hawaii.

FARRINGTON, Robert I., ry. ofcl.; b. Providence, Sept. 5, 1861; s. Preston M. and Caroline (Thayer) F.; ed. pub. schs., Providence; m. Caroline B. Burger, Dec. 1, 1885; children—Thayer B., Dorothy (Mrs. John P. Upham), John D. Clk. in auditor's office N.P. Ry., 1882-83, cashier freight office, Brainerd, Minn., 1883, chief clerk at Tacoma sta., 1883-84, clerk in office auditor frt. receipts, 1884-85; treas. receivers Cairo div., Wabash, St. Louis & Pacific Rd., 1885-88; with gen. auditor I.C. R.R., 1888; chief of disbursement div., accounting dept., St. Paul, Mpls. & Manitoba Ry., 1888-89; auditor disbursements, 1889-94, asst. comptroller, 1894, comptroller, 1894-1902, 2d v.p. 1902, v.p. G.N. Ry., 1909, ret., 1913, Chief of finance sect., accounts dept., purchase, storage and traffic div. of Gen. Staff U.S.A., Washington, 1918. Address: 2 E. 61st St., N.Y.C. Died Mar. 1948.

FARRIS, Frank Mitchell (făr'ĭs), banker; b. Nashville, Tenn., Nov. 23, 1890; s. Willis Manning and Tommie (Haynes) F.; grad. Bowen Prep. Sch., Nashville, 1909; student Vanderbilt U., 1909-10, U. of Mich., 1910-12; m. Mary Lellyett, Nov. 10, 1914; children—Frank Mitchell, Mary Ann (Mrs. M. Hugh Stuart), John Lellyett, Catharine Lee, Frances Elizabeth. Clerk State Bank & Trust Co., Nashville, 1912, asst. cashier, 1913, cashier, 1914-15; asst. cashier Cumberland Valley Nat. Bank, 1915-21; sec. Am. Trust Co., 1921-25 (also mgr. Cumberland Valley branch); cashier Am. Nat. Bank, 1925-27; organized Third Nat. Bank, 1927, exec. v.p., 1927-35, pres. since 1935; pres. Third Nat. Co.; dir. Farris Hardwood Lumber Co. Mem. bd. trustees George Peabody Coll. for Teachers and Joint U. Library. Mem. Newcomen Soc., Phi Kappa Sigma. Independent Democrat. Presbyn. Club: Belle Meade Country (Nashville). Home: Granny White Pike. Office: Third National Bank, Nashville. Died Apr. 19, 1950.

FARWELL, Arthur (făr'wĕl), composer; b. St. Paul, Minn., Apr. 23, 1872; s. George L. and Sara G. (Wyer) F.; ed. Baldwin Sem., St. Paul, to 1889; grad. Mass. Inst. Tech., 1893; spl. studies in elec. engring.; studied musical composition, 1893-99, under Homer Norris, Boston, Engelbert Humperdinck, in Germany, and Alexandre Guilmant, Paris; m. Gertrude Everts Brice, June 5, 1917; children—Brice, Arthur Bragdon, Beatrice, Sara Emerson, Emerson, Jonathan Kirkpatrick; m. 2d, Betty Richardson, Sept. 1939; 1 dau., Cynthia Torrance. Was lecturer on music at Cornell University, Ithaca, N.Y., 1899-1901; established Wa-Wan Press, Newton Centre, Massachusetts, for best American and Indian music; on staff Musical America, New York, since Jan. 1909; supervisor of municipal concerts, New York, 1910-13; dir. Music School Settlement, New York, 1915-18; acting head, dept. of music, U. of Calif., 1918-19. Holder of composer's fellowship of Pasadena Music and Art Assn., 1921-22-23. Founder and conductor Pasadena Community Music Meetings, 1922-23. Composer: American Indian melodies, 1901, and "Dawn" and "The Domain of Hurakan," 1901; Navajo War Dance; Symbolistic Studies, 1904-09; incidental music for "Joseph and His Brethren" and "The Gods of the Mountain"; music for pageant of Meriden, N.H., and pageant of Darien, Conn., 1913; music for community masque "Caliban," 1916, and "The Evergreen Tree," 1917; music for the "Pilgrimage Play," Hollywood, Calif., 1921; Symphonic Hymn on "March! March!" 1921; "The Hako," 1922 (string quartet); Prelude to a Spiritual Drama, 1928; Rudolph Gott Symphony (orchestra), 1932; "The Hound of Heaven" (for tenor), 1935; Piano Quintet in E minor, 1937; "Symbolistic Study, No. 6, Mountain Vision," two pianos and strings (Nat. Fed. of Music Club's prize, 1939); Polytonal Studies (piano); 40 Emily Dickinson Songs, 1941-43; "Indian Scene" and "Navajo War Dance, No. 2" (choruses), "Navajo War Dance, No. 2 (piano), 1946; "Cartoon" (opera), 1948. Lecturer Mich. State Coll.. 1927-39. Author: Intuition in the World-Making, 1938-45. Home: 684 Riverside Drive, N.Y.C. 31. Died Jan. 20, 1951.

FASSETT, Norman C(arter) (făs'sĕt), univ. prof.; b. Ware, Mass., Mar. 27, 1900; s. Joseph Lorenzo and Helen Stearns (Carter) F.; B.S., Harvard, 1922, A.M., 1923, Ph.D., 1925; m. Katherine Hill Knight, September 1, 1925 (div. 1950); children—Anne (Mrs. J. Sunshine), Marcia (Mrs. John Grimm); Charles. Instructor in botany, at University of Wis., 1925-30, asst. prof., 1930-37, asso. prof., 1937-45, prof. of botany since 1945; curator Herbarium since 1937; chmn. botany dept., 1948-49. Colombian Cinchona Mission, 1944. Mem. Am. Soc. Naturalists, A.A.A.S., Soc. Study of Evolution, Botanical Soc. of Am., Am. Soc. Taxonomists (sec. treasurer, 1936-44, president, 1953—), Wisconsin Academy Science, also member of Sigma Xi. Clubs: Torrey Botanical, New England Botanical. Protestant. Author: Manual of Aquatic Plants, 1940; Leguminous Plants of Wisconsin, 1939; Spring Flora of Wisconsin (1932) and subsequent editions). Contbr. articles on taxonomy, ecology and phytogeography, particularly of plants of the Middle West in 60 publs. Office: Dept. of Botany, Univ. of Wis., Madison 6, Wis. Died Sept. 14, 1954; buried Boothbay Harbor, Me.

FASTEN, Nathan, prof. zoölogy; b. Austria, Dec. 4, 1887; s. Schneier and Jane (Drillman) F.; brought to U.S., 1889, naturalized, 1896; B.S., Coll. City of New York, 1910; Ph.D., U. of Wis., 1914; m. Frieda Mayer, June 18, 1916; children—Janet Rebecca (Mrs. Leon Benson Levy), Marion (Mrs. Alexander Grinstein), Natalie (Mrs. Gilbert E. Rosenwald, Jr.), Head dept. of biology, Marshall College, Huntington, W.Va., 1910-11; asst. instr. zoölogy U. Wis., 1911-14; instr., asst. prof. zoölogy U. Wash., 1914-20; asso. prof. zoölogy and physiology Ore. State Coll., 1920-21, prof., head dept., 1921-45; chief biologist, chief tech. div. Wash. Pollution Control Commn., 1945-50, ret. chief biologist, cons. biologist, 1950—; summer work as asst. U.S. Bur. Fisheries, Woods Hole, Mass., 1911, investigator Wis. Fish Commn., 1912, 13, 14, Wash. Fish Commn., 1919, Ore. Fish and Game Commn., 1923, in charge invertebrate zoölogy Puget Sound Biol. Sta., 1915, 16, 20, charge animal biology B.C. Summer Session for Tchrs. 1922, 23; spl. investigator Oyster Culture and Pollution Problems, Pacific Spruce Corp., 1927-28; chmn. Ore. Basic Sci. Exam. Com., 1934-45. Fellow A.A.A.S.; mem. Am. Soc. Zoölogists, Am. Soc. Naturalists, Genetics Soc. Am., Western Soc. Naturalists (pres. 1924-25), Sigma Xi, Phi Kappa Phi, Gamma Sigma Delta, Phi Sigma. Jewish religion. Clubs: B'nai B'rith, Seattle Lodge, Mens, Temple de Hirsch. Author: Origin Through Evolution, 1929; Principles of Genetics and Eugenics, 1935; Principles of General Zoölogy, 1938; Introduction to General Zoölogy, 1941; General Zoölogy Laboratory Outlines, 1941; also articles profl. jours. Home: 2504 25th Av. N., Seattle 2. Died Sept. 19, 1953; buried Seattle.

FATH, Jacques F., couturier; b. Maisons-Laffitte, France, Sept. 6, 1912; s. Andre and Alphee (Storr) F.; student Hautes etudes Commerciales; m. Genevieve Bauchet de La Bruyere, Feb. 18, 1939; son, Philippe. Established dressmaking firm, Paris, 1937. Joined French Army as 2nd class gunner, World War II. Awarded Croix de Guerre (palmes d'argent). Home: 42 Cours Albert Ier, Paris 8. Office: 39 Av. Pierre Ier de Serbie, Paris, France. Died Nov. 13, 1954.

FAULK, C. E., airline exec.; b. Ouachita Parish, Pa., Aug. 19, 1878; s. Francis Lamy and Mary Elizabeth F.; m. Josephine McClendon, June 7, 1905; children—Clarence E., Eleanor Newcomb, Robert M. Pres. and dir. Delta Air Corp. since 1935; chmn. bd. Delta Air Lines, Inc., Municipal Airport, Atlanta; dir. Central Savs. Bank & Trust Co., Monroe, La. Mem. Monroe C. of C. K.P. Clubs: Lotus, Rotary (Monroe); Bayou DeSiard Country. Home: 207 McClendon Pl., West Monroe, La. Died Aug. 31, 1951.

FAULKES, James Nelson (fawlx), publisher; b. Cedar Rapids, Ia., Apr. 10, 1888; s. Fred Warren and Alice Mary (Miller) F.; student Coe Coll., 1909-11, State U. Ia., 1912. Circulation dept. Cedar Rapids (Ia.) Gazette, 1914-28, v.p., circulation mgr., 1928-43, pub. since 1943; pres., gen. mgr. Gazette Co. since 1943. Served with U.S. Army, World War I; disch. as sgt., 1918. Mem. Am. Legion. Elk, Mason (K.T., Shriner). Office: 500 Third Av. S.E., Cedar Rapids, Ia. Died Dec. 29, 1956.

FAULKNER, Charles James, lawyer; b. Martinsburg, W.Va., Aug. 23, 1877; s. Charles James and Sallie (Winn) F.; entered Washington and Lee U., 1893; B.L., 1898, LL.D., 1941; m. Elizabeth Durkee, Oct. 12, 1907. Admitted to bar Va., W.Va., 1898; settled in Chicago, 1899; with Peck, Miller & Starr, 1899-1903; gen. practice, 1903-05; became atty. for Armour & Co., 1905, asst. gen. counsel, 1914-17, gen. counsel 1917-46, ret., now dir., mem. exec. com. Mem. Am., Ill., Chgo. bar assns., S.C.V. (comdr.), S.A.R, Southern Soc Chgo, Phi Gamma Delta, Phi Beta Kappa Clubs: Chicago; Chevy Chase (Washington); Opequon Golf (Martinsburg, W. Va.); Virginia Seniors Golf Assn. Home: Martinsburg, W.Va. Died Sept. 3, 1953.

FAULKNER, Roy H., aviation, transportation exec.; b. Allegheny, Pa., Feb. 11, 1886; s. Samuel and Rachel (Hunter) F.; student Bryn Athyn (Pa.) Acad.; m. Agnes L. Stewart, Dec. 17, 1916; children—Cecil Stewart, Joan. Lumber salesman until 1916, then automobile retail salesman until 1916, then automobile retail salesman and later sales mgr. Oakland-Pittsburgh Co., and gen. mgr. Nash-Cincinnati Motor Co.; joined Auburn Automobile Co. as sales mgr., 1922, advancing to dir. of sales, v.p. in charge of sales and pres. 1931, resigned; became v.p. Studebaker Sales Corp., South Bend, Ind.; v.p. Pierce-Arrow Motor Co., Buffalo, 1933-34; returned to Auburn Co. as pres., 1934; later owner Roy H. Faulkner & Associates, Staman Building, Auburn, Ind.; Ind. rep. Mystic Adhesive Products Co., Chgo., at Fort Wayne, Ind. Mason, Swedenborgian. Address: Fort Wayne, Ind. Died Aug. 15, 1956.

FAUST, Albert Bernhardt (foust), univ. prof.; b. Baltimore, Apr. 20, 1870; s. John and Katherine (Kalbfleisch) F.; A.B., Johns Hopkins, 1889, Ph. D., 1892; matriculated in U. of Berlin, 1892; studied and traveled abroad, 1892-94; hon. Doctor. Univ. of Göttingen, 1937; m. Theodora Leisner, of Flensburg, Germany, July 20, 1921. Instr. in German, Johns Hopkins, 1894-96; asso. prof. German, Wesleyan U., Conn., 1896-1903; asst. prof. German, U. of Wis., 1903-04; asst. prof. German, 1904-10, prof., 1910-38, Cornell, prof. emeritus since 1938. Mem. Modern Lang. Assn. of America, Am. Hist. Assn., Goethe Gesellschaft, Phi Beta Kappa, Beta Theta Pi. Author: Charles Sealsfield (Carl Postl), Der Dichter beider Hemisphären, 1897; The German Element in the United States, 1909 (the first draft of this book was awarded Conrad Seipp Memorial Prize of $3,000, under the auspices of U. of Chicago; awarded Loubat prize by Royal Prussian Acad. Sciences, Berlin, 1911), revised edit., 1927; Das Deutschtum in den Vereingten Staaten, 2 vols., 1912; Guide to the Materials for American History in Swiss and Austrian Archives, 1916. Compiler: Lists of Swiss Emigrants to the American Colonies in the Eighteenth Century, 1920. Editor of series of college textbooks, and writer of historical and literary essays. Editor of John Quincy Adams's Translation of Wieland's Oberon, 1940. Author: The Bank War: An American Historical Drama, 1944. Visiting Carnegie prof. U. of Vienna, April-July 1933. Decorated golden cross of honor, Austria. Home: 125 Kelvin Place, Ithaca, N.Y. Died Feb. 8, 1951; buried Pleasant Grove Cemetery, Ithaca.

FAUST, Allen Klein, educator; b. Bernville, Pa., Aug. 20, 1869; s. Jacob L. and Lydia (Klein) F.; grad. Keystone State Normal Sch., Pa., 1893; A.B., Franklin and Marshall Coll., Lancaster, Pa., 1897, A.M., 1900; grad. Lancaster Theol. Sem., 1900; Ph.D., U. Pa., 1909; m. Mary E. Marden, Oct. 17, 1903; children—Lloyd Marden, Richard Allen. Tchr. pub. schs., Pa., 3 yrs.; sent to Japan by Bd. of Fgn. Missions, Ref. Ch. in U.S., 1900; tchr. history and sociology, North Japan Coll., 1900-13; pres. Miyagi Coll., Sendai, 1913-30; prof. social science, dean of men, Catawba Coll., 1930-44 Founder of Anti-Tuberculosis Assn. of Japan, 1910; engaged in famine relief, in recognition of which was presented with silver cup by the Japanese Imperial Govt.; decorated Order of Sacred Treasure, 4th Class (Japan). Author: Christianity as a Social Factor in Modern Japan, 1909; The Great Enemy of Society—Tuberculosis (in Japanese), 1910; Religious Pedagogy (in Japanese), 1912; The New Japanese Womanhood, 1926. Mem. Pi Gamma Mu. Address: Allenton, Pa. Died Sept. 13, 1953.

FAUST, John Bernard, ret. fgn. service ofcl.; b. Otranto Plantation, S.C., Sept. 18, 1898; s. John S. J. and Blanche (Walker); F.; B.Sc., Clemson Coll., 1918; student Georgetown U., 1925-26; M.A., U. Miami; m. Dorothy Shaw, July 12, 1928; children—Owen Hartley, Lucien Cornelius, Dorothy Claire. Engaged in chem. engring., 1918-25; appotd. fgn. service officer, 1926, served successively Buenos Aires, Asunción, Washington, Paris, Lisbon, Santiago de Chile, Tegucigalpa, and Beirut; Dept. of State, Washington, 1951-52; ret. 1952. Introduced China wood oil tree into S.C., Argentina, Paraguay. Home: Denmark, S.C.; also 1212 Cortez St., Coral Gables, Fla. Died July 3, 1957; buried Denmark, S.C.

FAUST, Paul E., advt. exec.; b. Ossian, Ia., 1878; married; 5 children. Formerly newspaperman in Ottumwa and Davenport, Ia.; entered advt. field, 1900; became pres. Mitchell-Faust Advt. Co.; became sec.-treas. Feature Radio Co., Inc. A founder Am. Assn. Advt. Agys. Address: Evanston, Ill. Died Sept. 24, 1952.*

FAUST, Walter Livingston, business exec.; b. Bryn Mawr, Pa., Aug. 4, 1895: s. Walter P. and Marion Adele (Byrnes) F.; grad. Mech. Engr., Stevens Inst. Tech., 1921; m. Gertrude Brigham, July 6, 1918; children—Mrs. Nancy Anderson, Mrs. Marion F. Walker. Chief engr. Whitlock Cordage Co., N.Y.C., 1922-29; with Socony Vacuum Oil Co., Inc., N.Y.C., 1929—, domestic marine sales mgr., 1929-32, gen. marine sales mgr., 1932-34, gen. mgr. marine and aviation sales, 1934-37, Eastern sales mgr., 1937-42, v.p., 1942—, dir., 1943—. Licensed profl. engr., N.Y., 1929-40. Dir. Downtown Beckman Hosp., Nat. Fgn. Trade Council. Mem. Authors League, Authors Guild, Playhouse Assn. Republican. Episcopalian. Clubs: New York Yacht, American Yacht, India House. Author: Mystery of Burnleigh Manor, Mystery of Villa Sineste; also plays (produced) Phantom Footsteps; This Rock; also articles and short stories. Home: 36 E. 36th St., N.Y.C.; also Daytona Beach, Fla. Office: 26 Broadway, N.Y.C. 4. Died July 20, 1956.

FAW, Walter Wagner, jurist; b. Johnson City, Tenn., July 3, 1867; s. Thomas Ambrose and Carrie Elizabeth (Wagner) F.; prep. edn., Science Hill Acad., Johnson City; Ky. Mil. Inst. (Farmdale); Va. Mil. Inst., Lexington: LL.B., Cumberland U. Law Sch., Lebanon, Tenn., 1889, LL.D., 1932; m. Martha Elizabeth Kernan, May 25, 1892 (dec.); children—Carrie Kernan (Mrs. Tom Watson Pointer), Margaret Wagner (Mrs. James Cannon III), Ruth (Mrs. Thomas Burns Carroll, dec.), Martha Elizabeth (Mrs. Clair D. Regen), Sarah (Mrs. Christopher V. Winfree). Admitted to Tenn. bar, 1889, and practiced at Johnson City, mem. Harr & Faw, 1889-91, Faw & Cox, 1891-95; moved to Franklin, Tenn., 1899; mem. Faw & Crockett, 1899-1905; 1st asst. atty. gen. and reporter, Tenn., 1905-13; spl. judge, Supreme Court, Tenn., 4 mos., 1914; judge Court of Civil Appeals (now Court of Appeals) from Sept. 1, 1918 (and presiding judge from 1923), to date of voluntary retirement from active service, effective Dec. 16, 1940. Alderman, Johnson City, 1891-93; city atty., Johnson City, 1893-94; mayor of Johnson City, 1896-98; mem. Tenn. Ho. of Rep., 1905. Recipient of the Award of Merit, D.A.R., 1954. Trustee Battle Ground Acad., Franklin. Mem. Am. Tenn. State and Williamson County bar assns., Alpha Tau Omega. Democrat. Methodist. Mason (K.T.), K.P. Home: 1003 W. Main St., Franklin, Tenn. Died May 18, 1956; buried Mount Hope Cemetery, Franklin, Tenn.

FAWCETT, William H., ret. banker; b. Pitts., March 4, 1883; s. James T. and Marion (Love) F.; ed. pub. schs. Pittsburgh; m. Laura Kelly, Oct. 31, 1904; children—James T. III, William H., Jr., John Kelly. Asst. cashier Peoples Nat. Bank, Pittsburgh, 1920-21; asst. cashier 1st Nat. Bank, Pittsburgh, 1921-33, v.p., 1933-46; became sr. v.p. Peoples 1st Nat. Bank & Trust Co. (mem. Fed. Res. Bank Dist. 4), 1946, now v. chmn., mem. bd. dirs., ret. Mem. Pitts. Athletic Assn. Republican. Methodist. Clubs: Duquesne, Field, (Pitts.). Home: 406 Gull Rd., Ocean City, N.J. Died Dec. 6, 1958.

FAY, Charles Robert, mfg. exec.; b. Springfield, O., Oct. 13, 1900; s. Charles Andrew and Frances Louise (Wade) F.; B.S., Purdue U., 1922; m. Vivian Melissa Kiser, Oct. 17, 1925; children—Elaine (Mrs. Richard Drisko), Louise (Mrs. Robert Grove), Miriam (Mrs. Wilbur K. Cox). Worked as a machinist and as production clk. Weidly Motor Co., 1922; shop foreman Thomas Skinner Steel Products Co., Indianapolis, 1923-25; with Westinghouse Elec. Corp., 1925-44, dir. employee accounts div., E. Pittsburgh, 1938-42, asst. to v.p. charge contract terminations, 1943-44; cons. controlled materials plan WPB, 1942-43; comptroller Pittsburgh Plate Glass Co., So. Minerals Corp., Corpus Christi, Tex., Columbia-So. Chem. Corp., Pitts., 1944-55; chmn., dir. Koppers Pitts. Co., 1947—; dir. Canadian Pittsburgh Industries, Ltd., 1949—; v.p., controller Pitts. Glass Co., 1955-56, v.p., dir., 1956—, dir. Mem. Controllers Inst. Am. Presbyn. Mason. Clubs: Duquesne, Oakmont Country, Longue Vue Country, University. Home: 16 Holland Rd., Pitts. 35. Office: 1 Gateway Center, Pitts. 22. Died July 19, 1959; buried Woodlawn Cemetery, Pitts.

FAY, George Morris, lawyer; b. Pittston, Pa., May 22, 1909; s. William Michael and Caroline (Runner) F.; A.B., Georgetown Univ., Washington, 1931, LL.B., 1935; m. Dorothy M. Donovan, Dec. 29, 1936; children—Dorothy Ann (wife of Richard S. Varney, U.S. Navy), Mary Lynn, Joan, William, Girard. Partner law firm, Fay & Anderson. Attorney, Bureau of War Risk Litigation, Department of Justice, 1935-40, criminal div., 1940-44, spl. asst. to atty. gen., tax div., 1946; U.S. atty., Dist. of Columbia (interim appointment), 1946-47, reapptd. and confirmed by U.S. Senate, 1947, 1951. Lieut., U.S. N.R., 1944-46. Mem. Am. Fed. and D.C. bar assns., Bar of Supreme Ct. of U.S. Democrat. Club: Metropolitan. Home: 6005 Cromwell Dr., Washington 16. Office: Fay and Anderson, Suite 911, Washington Bldg., Washington. Died Nov. 17, 1957; buried Gate of Heaven Cemetery.

FEATHERSTONE, William B., educator; b. Ia., Jan. 10, 1900; s. Robert L. and Mary B. (Webber) F.; A.B., U. Wyo., 1923; Ph.D., Columbia, 1932. Dir. secondary edn., Los Angeles, 1932-35; prof. edn., tchrs. coll., Columbia, since 1935. Mem. Nat. Soc. Study Edn., N.E.A., Internat. Council for Exceptional Children. Author: The Curriculum of the Special Class, 1932; Teaching the Slow Learners, rev. 1951; A Functional Curriculum for Youth, 1950. Home: 501 W. 120th St., N.Y. City 27. Died Apr. 13, 1951.

FEDERSPIEL, Matthew Nicholas (fĕd'ĕr-spēl), plastic and maxillo-facial surgeon; b. Lincoln, Kewaunee Co., Wis., Sept. 15, 1879; s. Peter and Kathryn (Forster) F.; D.D.S., Milwaukee Medical Sch., 1900; M.D., Marquette U., 1910, B.S., 1912; m. Bertha Agatha Knocke, June 24, 1903. Practiced at Milwaukee since 1910; prof. oral and maxillo-facial surgery, Dental Sch. Marquette U.; prof. plastic and maxillo-facial surgery, Med. Sch. Marquette U.; plastic and facial surgery, Milwaukee Hosp., St. Joseph's and St. Michael's Hosps. Fellow Am. Coll. Surgeons, Am. Coll. Dentists; mem. Am. Board Surgery, A.M.A., Am. Bd. Plastic Surgery, Am. Dental Assn., Wis. Acad. Dentists, Am. Soc. Orthodontists, Am. Assn. Ry. Surgeons, Wis. State and Milwaukee County med. societies, Wis. State Dental Soc., Milwaukee Acad. Medicine (life mem.). Republican. Roman Catholic. Elk. Author: Harelip and Cleft Palate, 1927; numerous articles in med. and dental publs. Address: 1403 N. Astor St., Milwaukee. Died Sept. 6, 1951; buried Holy Cross Cemetery, Racine, Wis.

FEE, Chester Anders, author, editor; b. Pendleton, Ore., July 26, 1893; s. Judge James Albert and Rose (Maney) Fee; A.B., U. of Ore., 1916; grad. student U. of Calif., 1919; m. Sara Campbell Robinson, July 8, 1922. Asst. phys. dir., Univ. High Sch., Oakland, Calif., 1920-22; dir. phys. edn., supervisor of attendance, field exec. Boy Scouts of America, Taft, Calif., 1922-27; feature writer Los Angeles Times, 1927; advt. mgr. Direct Mail Selling Assn., Los Angeles, 1927-28, Seaside Oil Co., Santa Barbara, 1928-30; wheat and pea farmer, 1930-38; instr. of English, U. of Ore., 1939-42; editorial asst. The Timberman and Western Building, 1943; asso. editor, The Lumberman and Pulp and Paper Industry mags. 1943-47; editor of Western Outdoors, 1948-49; in charge information and pub. relations Ore. Indsl. Accident Commn. since 1949; editor "Safer Oregon." Served as 1st lieutenant, 63d Infantry, with Intelligence Department, U.S. Army, 1917; 1st lt., Res Corps, 1920-32, capt. Nat. Guard Res., 1934-40. Mem. Am. Literary Assn., Brit. Poetry Soc., League of Western Writers (president Oregon 1939), Eugene Field Society, Oregon Society of Artists, American Legion, Beta Theta Pi, Sigma Upsilon and Sigma Iota Xi. Awarded 4th prize, Am. Voices, 1936; 2d prize, Yearbook of Contemporary Poetry, 1937; shared 1st prize, Poetry Studies (Brit.), 1938; 3d prize, Oregon Soc. of Artists Exhibit, 1945. Episcopalian. Author: Rimes o' Round Up, 1935; Chief Joseph; The Biography of a Great Indian, 1936; Wilderness Patriot; A Drama of Marcus Whitman, 1939; Major General Charles Lee: American Palladium, 1951. Contbr. verses, articles and fiction to mags. Home: 5032 S.E. 36th Pl., Portland 2. Office: Pub. Service Bldg., Salem; also 427 S.W. 11th St., Portland 5, Ore. Died May 24, 1951.

FEE, James Alger, judge; b. Pendleton, Ore., Sept. 24, 1888; s. James Albert and Rose (Maney) F.; A.B., Whitman Coll., 1910, LL.D., 1933; A.M., LL.B., Columbia, 1914; m. Frances Louise Waldo, Feb. 9, 1916 (died Sept. 20, 1935); children—Frances Louise (Mrs. George Conery Martin), Margery Waldo (Mrs. Ray Martin Steele), Lillian Adele (Mrs. Lauren Moore); m. 2d, Alice Emma Tomkins, Dec. 22, 1943. Began practice of law, 1914; mem. firm of Fee & Fee, 1915-16, 1920-27; city atty. Pendleton, 1916-17; mem. legal staff dir. sales, War Dept., 1919-20; judge Circuit Ct. Ore., 1927-31; judge U.S. Dist. Ct., Ore. dist., 1931-54, chief judge, 1937-54; U.S. Circuit judge, 9th Circuit, 1954—. Mem. Jud. Council State of Ore., 1928-31; U.S. Dist. Judges Ninth Circuit exec. sec., 1945-48, 1950-54, pres., 1948-50. Entered 2d O.T.C., Presidio, San Francisco, 1917; commd. 1st lt. Air Service, U.S. Army, 1917; instr., aerial gunnery, Reserve mil. aviator, 1918; 1st lt. Ore. N.G., 1926, advancing to lt. col. and asst. chief of staff, G-1, 41st Div., 1939. Mem. Bd. of Edn., Pendleton, 1922-31. Mem. bd. of overseers Whitman Coll., Chmn., Multomah County Law Library, until 1949, pres. 1941-49. Fellow Am. Bar Found.; mem. Am. (chmn. com. on cooperation with Fed. Judiciary, 1950-54), Ore. State bar assns., Am. Law Inst. (mem. council 1949—), N.G. Assn. of U.S. (life), Am. Judicature Soc., Selden Soc. of London (Am. mem.), Am. Legion, Mil. Order World War (Ore. State comdr. 1942-45), Am. Asso. Newcomen Soc., Beta Theta Pi, Phi Beta Kappa; founding mem. Phi Beta Kappa Assos. (bd. dirs. 1945-52). Republican. Episcopalian. Member of the board of editors Columbia Law Review, 1912-14, Oregon Law Review, 1924-31, Law lecturer. Contbr. to legal publs. Clubs: Pacific Union (San Francisco); University (Portland). Home: 901 California St. Office: U.S. Ct. of Appeals, Post Office Bldg., San Francisco. Died Aug. 25, 1959; buried Arlington Nat. Cemetery.

FEEMAN, Harlan Luther, educator; b. Champaign, Ill., Jan. 22, 1873; s. Henry Benjamin and Hannah Margaret (Ewing) F.; Ph.B., Adrian Coll., Mich., 1900, M.A., 1907; student Oberlin Coll., 1905; Drew Theol. Seminary, 1907-08; D.D., Adrian, 1909; LL.D., Western Maryland Coll.; m. Annie Cairns, Oct. 14, 1901; children—Hyrtl C., Margaret N. Teacher common schs., Ill., 1891-94; ordained M.P. ministry, 1903; pastor Pittsburgh, 1900-04; head of dept. of history and economics, 1904-07, dean Sch. of Theology, 1908-11, Adrian Coll.; head dept. of Bibl. and practical theology, Westminster (Md.) Theol. Sem., 1911-15; sec. Bd. of S.S. and Young People's Socs. of Meth. Protestant Ch., 1915-17; pres. Adrian Coll., 1917-40; pres. emeritus, 1940—. Mem. Sigma Alpha Epsilon, S.A.R. Club: Rotary. Author: The Kingdom and the Farm; Prayers for Strength, Comfort and Good Cheer; The Nurture of Vitality; The Story of a Noble Devotion. Home: Adrian, Mich.; (winter) Dayton Beach, Fla. Deceased.

FEGAN, Hugh J. (fā'gǎn), dean and prof. law; b. Washington, D.C., May 7, 1881; s. Hugh J. and Catherine (Wise) F.; A.B., Georgetown U., 1901, A.M., 1902, LL.B., 1907, Ph.D., 1916, LL.D., 1943; grad. work in history English law, Oxford and Cambridge univs., Eng., 1937-38; LL.D., St. Mary's Coll., 1934, Boston U., 1950; unmarried. Asst. solicitor U.S. Dept. Agriculture, 1907-11; prof. law and sec. law faculty Georgetown U., 1911-18, asst. dean, 1919-43, dean Sch. of Law since 1943. Served as capt., J.A.G. Dept., U.S. Army, 1918-19. Spl. atty. U.S. Treasury Dept., 1919. Mem. (life) Am. Law Inst., Am. Bar Assn., Bar Assn. of D.C., Oxford Soc. (Eng.). Club: Cosmos (Washington). Editor: Vance's Cases on Insurance (4th edit.), 1952. Contbr. articles to law periodicals. Home: 1801 16th St., Washington 9. Died Dec. 19, 1954; buried Rock Creek Cemetery, Washington.

FEILCHENFELD, Ernst H. (fīl'kĕn fĕld), educator, internat. lawyer; b. Berlin, Germany, Oct. 6, 1898; s. Dr. Hermann F. and Else (Orbach) F.; Dr. Juris Utriusque, Berlin U., 1922; spl. student London Sch. of Econs., 1923-24. Came to U.S., 1924, naturalized, 1936. Referendar, Berlin and Hamburg, 1921-26; assessor, Hamburg, 1926; research Bur. of Internat. Research, Harvard U. and Radcliffe Coll., 1924-30; asst. lecturer, asst. prof. law Harvard Law School, 1926-32; consultant in creation League of Nations' High Commn. for Refugees and League of Nation's research on internat. loan agreements, N.Y., 1933-36; supervisor advanced students preparing for Ph.D. in Law, Oxford U., 1937-39; with treasury dept., bd. of econ. warfare, Office of Foreign Relief and Rehabilitation, Washington, D.C., 1940-43; prof. internat. orgn. and internat. law, dir. of research, Inst. of World Polity, School of Foreign Service Georgetown U., since 1944. Asso. mem. Am. Bar Association; mem. Am. Soc. of Internat. Law, Pi Gamma Mu. Club: Cosmos. Author: Voelkerrechtspolitk als Wissenchaft, 1922; Public Debts and State Succession, 1931; Rights and Remedies of Foreign Bondholders 1934; The Next Step; A Plain Man's Guide to Internat. Principles, 1938; The Internat. Econ. Law of Belligerent Occupation (Carnegie Endowment for Internat. Peace, Washington, D. C.), 1942; Prisoners of War (Inst. of World Polity, Sch. of Foreign Service, Georgetown U., Washington, D.C.), 1948. Contbr. to profl. publs. and jours. Home: Cosmos Club, Washington 5. Address: School of Foreign Service, Georgetown U., Washington 7. Died Mar. 25, 1956; buried King David Meml. Gardens, Falls Church, Va.

FEININGER, Lyonel Charles Adrian (fīn'ĭng-ĕr), painter; b. New York City, July 17, 1871; s. Frederick William Carl and Elizabeth Cecilia (Lutz) F.; studied art at Sch. for Applied Arts, Hamburg, Germany, Acad. of Arts, Berlin; Colarossi, Paris; m. Julia Lilienfeld, Sept. 25, 1905; children—Andreas, Laurence, Theodore Lux. Caricaturist and illustrator for various weeklies in Germany and Paris, 1893-1908; Chicago Tribune (comic section), 1906; independent work as painter since 1907; instr. in painting and graphic arts, Bauhaus, Weimar, Germany (later moved to Dessau), 1919-32; teacher art, Mills Coll., Oakland, Calif., summers 1936, 37, Black Mountain College, N.C., 1945. Exhibited at Salon des Independants, Paris, 1911, 12, and later in many exhbns. and oneman shows in Europe. In U.S. exhibited with 19 Living Americans Exhbn., Museum of Modern Art, N.Y. City, 1930; Artists for Victory Exhbn., Metropolitan Museum, N.Y. City, 1942 (awarded 3d prize); represented in touring exhbn. Contemporary Am. Painting, shown in Latin America by Metropolitan Museum of Art. Executed murals for Marine Transportation Bldg., and courtyard of Masterpieces of Art, N.Y. World's Fair, 1939, 40. Represented in permanent collections of Metropolitan Museum, Whitney Museum of Am. Art, Museum of Modern Art, N.Y. City, Vassar Art Gallery, museums in Providence, R.I. Boston, Worcester, Mass., Springfield, Mass., Washington, D.C., Minneapolis, St. Louis, Detroit, San Diego, San Francisco, Wichita, Kan., Ft. Worth, Tulsa, Ft. Dodge, Okla. and many others. Home: 235 E. 22d St., N.Y. C. Died Jan. 13, 1956; buried Mount Hope Cemetery, Hastings-on-Hudson.

FEISAL II (fī'säl), King of Iraq; b. May 2, 1935; s. King Ghazi and Queen Aliyah; early edn. by pvt. tutors; student Sandroyd Prep. Sch., and Harrow (both Eng.). Succeeded to throne, following death of father, 1939; ascended throne, 1953. Decorated Order of Al Hashim, Order of Feisal I, Order of Al Rafidain, Order of Al Nahdha, Order of Al Istiqlal; Order of Hussein I (Jordan); Mil. Merit award (U.S.), Mil. Merit award (Spain); Order of Cedar (Lebanon); Order of Solomon (Ethiopia); Lion of Netherlands. Address: Qasr el-Zuhur, Baghdad, Iraq. Assassinated July 16, 1958.*

FEISS, Paul Louis (fīs), mfr.; b. Cleveland, O., June 3, 1875; s. Julius and Carry (Dryfoos) F.; ed. pub. schs. and University Sch., Cleveland; m. Edith Lehman, June 2, 1903; children—Julian William, Carl Lehman, Caroline Babette Farber, Gertrude Louise. Associated since 1892 with The Joseph & Feiss Co., manufacturer of men's clothing, Cleveland; vice-pres. of company at incorporation, 1920, gen. mgr., 1925, pres., 1927-38, chmn. bd. since 1938. Formerly v.p. Cleveland Community Fund; president National Information Bureau; member Cleveland Musical Arts Association (trustee), Cleveland Art Mus. (advisory bd.); ex-pres. Mount Sinai Hospital, Alta House. Mem. Cleveland Chamber Commerce (ex-pres.). Decorated Order of St. Sava, Yugo-Slavia. Clubs: Rowfant (past pres.), Mid-Day, City (Cleveland). Home:

12600 Cedar Rd., Cleveland Hgts. 6. Office: 2149 W. 53d St., Cleve. Died Jan. 20, 1952.

FELAND, Faris Robison, II, business exec.; b. Lawrenceburg, Ky., March 27, 1887; s. Faris Robison and Ella (King) F.; student State University of Kentucky; m. Ivy May Green, May 11, 1909; children—Faris Robison III, Mary (Mrs. Warren Wheaton), Jesse (Mrs. Wm. Bartel), William Gerdine, Quintus, Milner. Compositor and reporter on county weekly newspaper, Lawrenceburg, Ky., 1907-08; compositor, later advt. writer Elbert Hubbard, East Aurora, N.Y., 1908-09; with George Batten Co., since 1910, copywriter, 1910-15, head copy dept., 1915-28, vice pres., dir., 1917-28; v.p., dir. Batten, Barton, Durstine and Osborn, Inc., 1928-30, treas. since 1930, chmn. exec. com., since 1940. Club: The Players (New York). Home: 63 Enclosure, Nutley 10, N.J. Office: 383 Madison Av., N.Y.C. 17. Died Nov. 14, 1952.

FELDER, C. S., business exec.; b. Ushlfeld, Germany, Sept. 11, 1887; s. Sigmund and Sophie Felder; ed. in pub. schs. and high sch. Vice pres. in charge of stores V.P. Richman Bros. Co. Mem. Am. Legion. Mason, Elk. Home: 12700 Shaker Blvd. Office: 1600 E. 55th St., Cleve. Deceased.*

FELDMANN, Markus, ex-pres. of Switzerland; b. Thun, Switzerland, May 21, 1897; s. Markus F. and Maria (Zurlinder) F.; grad. U. Bern, 1921, LL D., 1924; m. Margrit Beck, June 30, 1922; 1 son. Admitted to bar, 1921; editorial staff Neue Berner Zeitung, 1922, editor in chief, 1928-45; sec. Burgerpartei, Bern, 1921; mem. Nat. Council, 1935-45, 47-51; pres. parliamentary press, 1938-45; chief dept. justice and police Fed. Council of Switzerland, 1951-57, v.p. Fed. Council, 1955, pres., 1956-57; pres. Bern Peasants, Artisans and Middle Class party, 1943-45; exec. council Bern canton, 1945-51, pres., 1947-48, dir. adminstrv. and health depts., 1945-46, edn. and church depts., 1946-51. Recipient 1st prize for treatise Swiss Soc. Jurists, 1931; 1st prize for book on corporations Econ. Soc. Bern, 1934. Mem. Bern Press Soc. (pres. 1929-31), Swiss Press Union (pres. 1933-35), Bern Glee Club. Author several books. Office: Palais Federal, Bern, Switzerland. Died Nov. 3, 1958.

FELDMANS, Jules, diplomat; b. Nigranda, Latvia, July 21, 1889; s. Frederick and Dorothy (Adamovic) F.; LL.M., U. of Moscow, 1915; m. Marianne Robin, Apr. 28, 1923. Legal adviser, chief of Russian div., Ministry Fgn. Affairs of Latvia, 1919-21; sec. Latvian legation, Paris, 1921; chief, League of Nations div., Ministry Fgn. Affairs, Riga, 1923; counselor Latvian legation, Paris, 1925, chargé d'affaires ad interim, 1925-27; chief, Eastern and Western divs., Riga, 1928-30; Latvian permanent del. League of Nations, Geneva, 1930, E.E. and M.P. to Switzerland, 1932; became Latvian envoy to King of Denmark, 1939; Minister Plenipotentiary, chargé d'affaires of Latvia, Washington, since 1949. Served with Latvian Army, World War I. Mem. Latvian Nat. Movement; chmn. Latvian Nat. Comm. Evangelical Lutheran. Home: Riga, Latvia. Office: Latvian Legation, 4325 17th St., Washington 11. Died Aug. 16, 1953.

FELIX, Anthony G., business exec.; b. Berks County, Pa., Jan. 25, 1885. Ret. sr. v.p. The Pa. Co. for Banking and Trusts; now chairman of executive committee of the Bankers Securities Corporation. Clubs: Philadelphia Country, Racquet, Union League (Phila.). Home: The Mermont, Bryn Mawr, Pa. Office: 1315 Walnut St. Died Jan. 20, 1958.

FELL, Harold Bertels, petroleum producer; b. Wilkes-Barre, Pa., Aug. 18, 1889; s. Daniel Ackley and Frances (Bertels) F.; prep. edn., Hillman Acad.; grad. Mercersburg (Pa.) Acad., 1907; C.E., Princeton, 1912; m. Georgie Simpson, Jan. 8, 1919 (div.); children—Frances Alice, Elizabeth Simpson, Engr. Lehigh Valley Coal Co., 1912-17; v.p., gen. mgr. Peerless Steel Co., Ardmore, Okla., 1919-21; v.p., gen. mgr., later pres. Simpson-Fell Oil Co., 1921-57; ret.; owner H. B. Fell Oil and Gas; pres., dir. Rickey Royalty Co. Mem. adv. council Geol. Engring. Dept., Princeton. Trustee Okla. Pub. Expenditures Council, So. Okla. Meml. Found. Served from 1st lt. to maj. F.A., U.S. Army, 1917-18; col. F.A. Res. Chmn. Okla. State Soldiers Relief Commn., 1921-22; pres. Okla. Am. Legion Endowment Fund Corp., 1925-28. Dir. Internat. Petroleum Expn., Tulsa. Mem. Am. Assn. Petroleum Geologists (asso.), So. Okla. Oil and Gas Assn. (ex-pres.), Am. Inst. Mining and Metall. Engrs., Am. Petroleum Inst., Princeton Engring. Assn., Mid-Continent Oil & Gas Assn. (dir.), Ind. Petroleum Assn. Am. (dir.), Okla. C. of C. (dir.), Ardmore C. of C. (pres. 1932-33), Am. Legion (dept. comdr. 1920-21), Reserve Officers Assn. of U.S. (pres. Okla. dept. 1927-28). Republican. Presbyn. Clubs: Dornick Hills Country (Ardmore); Tulsa; Beacon (Oklahoma City); Tiger Inn (Princeton). Address: P.O. Box 1146, Springfield, Ill. Died Jan. 12, 1959.

FELLER, Abraham Howard, U.N. counsel; b. New York City, Dec. 24, 1904; s. Julius and Jennie (Klein) F.; B.A., Columbia, 1925; LL.B., Harvard, 1928; student U. of Berlin, 1929-30; m. Alice Klein, Aug. 14, 1932; 1 dau., Caroline Josephine. Admitted to N.Y. bar, 1929, bar U.S. Supreme Court, 1934, District of Columbia bar, 1936. Asso. Inst. Fgn. Pub. Law and Internat. Law, Berlin, 1929-31; instr., Harvard Law Sch., 1931-32, Thayer teaching fellow, 1932-34; spl. asst. U.S. Atty. Gen., 1934-40; lecturer, Harvard Law Sch., 1937-38; T.N.E.C. counsel, 1938-39; asso. prof. law, Yale, 1940-44; spl. consultant, nat. defense mediation bd., 1941; consultant lend-lease adminstrn., 1941; dep. dir., Office Facts and Figures, 1941-42, O.W.I., 1942-43; gen. counsel, O.W.I., 1943-44; gen. counsel, U.N.R.R.A., 1944-45; U.N.R.R.A. rep., Internat. Labor Conf., 1944, Bretton Woods Monetary Conf., 1944, U.N. San Francisco Conf., 1945; U.S. alternate rep., U.N. Prep. Com., London, 1945; adviser to U.S. delegation, U.N. Gen. Assembly, London, 1946; gen. counsel and dir. legal dept., U.N., since 1946; legal advisor to numerous U.N. coms. and confs., 1946-51; vis. prof. of law, Stanford U., 1947; prof. internat. law, Ecole Libre des Hautes Etudes since 1949. First Am. lawyer to appear before Internat. Court of Justice, 1949. Member Am. Bar Assn., Am. Soc. of International Law (mem. exec. council), Association of the Bar, City of New York, Adv. Com. Research in Internat. Law, Phi Beta Kappa. Editor: Decisions of the German Supreme Court and digests of decisions of Permanent Court of Internat. Justice and of Permanent Court of Arbitration (all pub. Germany, 1931); Diplomatic and Consular Laws and Regulations (Carnegie Foundation, 1933). Author: The Mexican Claims Commn., 1935; United Nations and World Community. Home: 50 Central Park West. Office: United Nations, N.Y.C. Died Nov. 13, 1952.

FELLERS, Carl Raymond, educator; b. Hastings, N.Y., Oct. 4, 1893; s. Frank and Mary (Baratier) F.; ed. Mexico (N.Y.) Acad. High Sch.; A.B. in Chemistry, Cornell U., 1916; M.S., Rutgers U., 1916; Ph.D., 1918; m. Josephine Sanders, Mar. 28, 1921; children—Francis X., Mary J., Martha L., Anne M., John C., Paul J., David A., Stephen G. Bacteriologist (1st lt.) U.S. Pub. Health Service at Camps Greene, Bragg and Benning in lab. and field sanitation work, 1918-19; certificate of merit, from Surgeon Gen.; bacteriologist (food law enforcement) U.S. Bur. Chemistry and Soils, Washington, and San Francisco, 1920; research bacteriologist on seafoods and canned foods, Nat. Canners Assn., Seattle and State of Wash., 1921-23; asso. prof., food preservation (teacher and research in food tech., especially fish and marine products), U. of Wash., Seattle, 1924-25; research prof. food tech., Mass. State Coll. (now U. of Mass.) and Expt. Sta., Amherst, Mass., 1926, head of dept., 1941-57; food and nutrition consultant, 1957—. Food research, human and animal nutrition; dir. Blue Channel Corp., Beaufort, S.C. (packing marine products); abstractor for chem. abstracts, editor bd. Food Research and Quick Frozen Foods; food consultant. Served with U.S. Army, res. officer, Chem. Warfare Service, 1926-42; post chem. officer, Ft. Devens, Mass., 1942; army Command and Staff Sch., 1942; major and lt. col., Q.M.C., S.W. Pacific Theater, Australia and New Guinea, 1943-46 (army subsistence and liaison with Australian Govt.). Awarded Bronze Star; Babcock Award, American Institute of Nutrition 1950; Medal of Merit (Cuba). Fellow A.A.A.S., American Public Health Assn. (governing council 6 yrs. and chmn. food and nutrition sect., 1936); mem. Am. Chem. Soc. (councillor and sec.-treas. agr. and food sect., 1941-42, chmn. 1948), Soc. Am. Bacteriologists, Am. Soc. for Hort. Sci., Am. Fisheries Soc., N.Y. Acad. Sci., Inst. Food Tech. (pres. 1949, secretary 1947-48; founder and councillor), Sigma Xi, Phi Lambda Upsilon, Phi Kappa Phi, Theta Kappa Phi, Phi Tau Sigma (honorary pres.). Roman Catholic. K.C. Inventor of methods for pasturizing dried foods, canning Atlantic crabs, ascorbic acid antioxidants and use of chelating agents in foods. Author, many sci. and tech. articles on chemistry, bacteriology and tech. of foods; contbr. to several books, jours. and encys. Home: 52 Fearing St., Amherst, Mass. Died Feb. 22, 1960.

FELLHEIMER, Alfred, architect; b. Chgo.; B.S., U. Ill., 1895; m. Elizabeth Hull; children—Madelaine (Mrs. Carl Maas). Sr. partner Fellheimer & Wagner, N.Y.C., 1923—; prin. works include Union Sta., Cin., N.J. Turnpike Bldgs., Queens Coll. Sci. Bldg., Allied Chem. Co. Lab., Morristown, N.J. Registered architect N.H., N.Y. Fellow A.I.A.; mem. Am. Soc. C.E. Author: Forms and Functions of 20th Century Architecture, 1952. Address: 155 E. 42d St., N.Y.C. Deceased.

FELLOWS, Frank, ex-congressman; b. Bucksport, Me., Nov. 7, 1889; s. Oscar and Eva Maria (Fling) F.; student Bucksport (Me.) Sem., U. of Me.; LL.B., U. of Me. Law Sch.; m. Georgia Eleanor Maling, June 27, 1910; children—Elizabeth, Oscar, Joan Raymond, William. Admitted to Me. bar, 1911, and since in gen. practice at Bangor, Me.; clerk U.S. Dist. Court, Portland, Me., 1917-21; mem. firm Fellows & Fellows. Member 77th to 82d Congresses (1941-53), from 3d Maine District. Permanent chmn. Maine Republican State Convention, 1950. Member American, Maine State and Penobscot County bar assns., Phi Gamma Delta, Phi Delta Phi. Acted as spl. trial counsel for Pub. Utilities Commission of Maine in rate litigation, 1931-36. Republican. Unitarian. Clubs: Kiwanis, Tarratine (Bangor). Died Aug. 27, 1951; buried Silver Lake Cemetery, Bucksport, Me.

FELLOWS, Harold E(verett), assn. exec.; b. Amesbury, Mass., Mar. 22, 1899; s. Roscoe Conklin and Grace Adelaide (Hilliard) F.; student N.Y.U., 1916-17; m. Janet S. Edgerly, June 10, 1919; children—Barbara Louise (Mrs. Arthur S. Spangler), Jeanne Edgerly (Mrs. Keith C. Steele). Jr. exec. wholesale provision and cold storage bus.. Haverhill, Mass., 1919-27; radio dir. Greenleaf Co., Boston, 1928-30, gen. mgr., 1930-32; asst. mgr., comml. mgr. radio sta. WEEI, Boston, 1932-26, gen. mgr., 1936-44; mgr. N.E. operations C.B.S., Boston, 1944-51; pres. Nat. Assn. Broadcasters, Washington, 1951-54, pres., chmn. bd. 1954—. Mem. advt. com. Nat. Distribution Council, Dept. of Commerce; President's Citizens Adv. Com. Fitness Am. Youth. Dir. Advt. Council; bd. visitors sch. public relations and communications, Boston U.; mem. bd. dir. Nat. Conf. Christians and Jews. Chmn. Radio-TV com. U.S. com. UN; mem. Pres. Com. Employment of Physically Handicapped. Mem. United States C. of C., Theta Chi, Alpha Delta Sigma. Conglist. Clubs: Metropolitan, Broadcasters (chmn. bd. gov.) (Washington); Advertising (Boston). Home: Gilmanton Iron Works, N.H. Office: 1711 N. St., Washington 6. Died Mar. 8, 1960.

FELS, Mary (Mrs. Joseph Fels); b. Sembach, Germany, Mar. 10, 1863; d. Elias and Fannie (Rothschild) Fels; grad. Keokuk (Ia.) High Sch., student St. Mary's Acad., Notre Dame, Ind., U. Pa.; m. Joseph Fels, Nov. 16, 1881 (died Feb. 22, 1914). Organizer The Joseph Fels Found. (Inc.), for the enlightenment of Jews and Gentiles as to Israel's history and mission, the nonpolitical resettlement and reorganization of Palestine, the advancement of social justice and the promotion of the right relationship of man to the soil and to God and His law. Editor, The Public, New York, 1917-19. Author: Joseph Fels, His Life Work, 1916; Toward the Light, 1927. Home: 2 W. 86th St., N.Y.C. Deceased.

FELS, Samuel S., mfr.; b. Yanceyville, N.C., Feb. 16, 1860; s. Lazarus and Susannah F.; LL.D., U. Pa., 1937; D.Sc., Antioch Coll., 1947, Temple U., 1949; m. Jennie May, May 15, 1890. Partner Fels & Co., soap mfrs., 1881 until inc., 1914, since pres.; pres. Paschall Oxygen Co. Trustee Wistar Inst., Franklin Inst. (now v.p.); a founder, 1908, since trustee Phila. Bur. Municipal Research; established Crime Prevention Assn. Phila. 1932; Samuel S. Fels Fund, 1935 (pres.). Recipient Philadelphia (Bok) Award, 1948. Mem. Am. Philos. Soc., Sigma Xi. Author: This Changing World, 1933. Home: 39th and Walnut St. Office: 73d and Woodland Av., Phila. 42. Died June 23, 1950.

FELSING, William August, chemist; b. Denton, Tex., May 19, 1891; s. William and Anna Judith (Kurner) F.; A.B., U. of Texas, A.M., 1916; Ph.D., Mass. Inst. Tech., 1918; m. Stella Elizabeth Scorgie, Sept. 8, 1920; children—Barbara Ann, William August. Asst. prof. chemistry, U. of Texas, asso. prof., now prof., part-time research scientist, defense research lab.; with Underwater Sound Lab., Harvard, Mar.-Nov. 1943. Served as 1st lt., later capt., Chem. Warfare Service, U.S. Army, Mar.-Dec. 1918; engaged in making poison gas Edgewood Arsenal. Mem. Tex. Acad. Sciences, Am. Chem. Soc., Sigma Xi, Phi Lambda Upsilon, Phi Beta Kappa, Acacia. Mason. Author: Notes on Descriptive Chemistry, 1928; General Chemistry (with E. P. Schoch and G. W. Watt) 1938; (revised edit. 1946). Contbr. more than 50 research articles to sci. jours. Home: 3007 Washington Square, Austin 21, Tex. Died Oct. 5, 1952; buried Austin Meml. Park, Austin, Tex.

FELTES, Nicholas Rudolph, exec. v.p. Bastian-Morley Co., Inc., La Porte, Ind.; chmn. bd. dirs. Am. Trust Co., South Bend. Home: 627 W. Washington Av., South Bend, Ind. Office: Bastian-Morley Co., Inc., La Porte, Ind. Deceased.

FELTON, Lloyd Derr, physician; b. Pine Grove Mills, Pa., Nov. 18, 1885; s. Anthony K. and Amanda K. (Derr) Felton; A.B., Wooster Coll., 1910, D.Sc., 1925; M.D., Johns Hopkins, 1916; m. Margaret Crosser, June 28, 1916; children—Lloyd Crosser, Barbara Belle. Asso. in bacteriology and pathology, Johns Hopkins, 1916-20; asso. in pathology, Rockefeller Inst. of Med. Research, 1920-22; asst. prof. preventive med., hygiene, Harvard, 1922-35; asso. pathology, bacteriology Johns Hopkins, 1935-38; with USPHS, 1938-49, med. dir., 1944-49, ret. Served as contract surgeon U.S. Army, 1917-18. Trustee Wooster Coll., 1935-38. Fellow A.M.A., Am. Pub. Health Assn.; mem. Am. Chem. Soc., Soc. Am. Bacteriol., Am Assn Immunol. (pres. 1947), Washington Acad. Sci., N.Y. Acad. Sci., A.A.A.S., Am. Acad. Polit. and Social Scis., Mil. Surgeons, Sigma Xi, Phi Beta Kappa. Contbr. profl. jours. Home: 3701 Thornapple St., Chevy Chase 15, Md. Died Sept. 11, 1953; buried Arlington Nat. Cemetery.

FENETRY, Clare Gerald, judge, ex-congressman; b. Phila.; B.A., J.D., St. Joseph's Coll., Phila.; LL.B., U. Pa.; LL.D., Loyola Coll., Balt., Canisius Coll., Buffalo; Litt.D., St. John's U., Bklyn.; Dr.

Civil and Canon Law, Hahnemann Med. Coll.; L.H.D., St. Francis Coll., Loretto, Pa.; Ph.D., Phila. Coll. Law; certificate in internat. law Naval War Coll., Newport, R.I.; m. Miriam E. Loughran; 1 dau. Mem. law faculty Wharton Sch., U. Pa., 5 yrs.; mem. Phila. Bd. Law Examiners, 10 yrs.; asst. dist. atty., Phila., 1928-35; mem. 74th U.S. Congress, 3d Pa. Dist.; judge Common Pleas Court No. 5 of Phila., 1939—. Served with USN in France, 1917-18; re-entered Naval Res. as 1st (s.g.), 1930. Mem. Am. Legion, Vets. Fgn. Wars, Irish War Vets. U.S. (past nat. adv. gen.), Jewish War Vets. (hon. life), Friendly Sons of St. Patrick (past pres. Phila.), French Soc. Phila. (hon. chancellor), 315th Inf. Assn., Cath. War Vets. of Am. (past comdr.), Old Guard City Phila., Municipal War Vets. Moose, Elk, K.C. Contbr. prose and verse various mags. and periodicals. Died July 1, 1952; buried Holy Sepulchre Cemetery.

FENHAGEN, George Corner (fĕn-hā'gĕn), architect; b. Baltimore, Md., Dec. 7, 1884; s. Charles Denny and Jane (Corner) F.; student U. of Pa., 1903-05, Am. Acad. in Rome, Italy, 1906-07; m. Mildred Thurston Pierce, Sept. 10, 1911 (died 1919); children—George Corner, Jr., J. Pierce; m. 2d, Helen Weston, Oct. 14, 1921 (died 1926); 1 son, F. Weston; m. 3d, Mary Ford Pringle, June 30, 1929; 1 dau., Christina Wood. In employ Pell & Corbett, N.Y. City, 1905-06, 1907-10; asst. cons. architect, Philippine govt., 1911-14, const. architect, 1914-16; mem. firm Sill, Buckler & Fenhagen, architects, Baltimore, Md., 1916-21, Buckler & Fenhagen, 1921-46; firm name now Buckler, Fenghagen, Meyer & Ayers; asst. prof. design, U. of Pa., 1923. Fellow Royal Society of Arts, London; former member council Md. Hist. Soc. Fellow Am. Inst. Architects (past pres. Baltimore Chapter). Mem. Alumni Soc. Am. Acad. in Rome. Awarded Alumni traveling fellowship U. Pa., 1906. Democrat. Club: Philippine (N.Y.). Home: The Homewood Apts., Balt. 18. Office: Fed. Land Bank Bldg., Balt. Died Aug. 23, 1955; buried Greenmont Mausoleum, Greenmont Cemetery.

FENHAGEN, James Corner, banker; b. Baltimore, Aug. 10, 1875; s. Charles D. and Jane Dungan (Corner) F.; student Friends' Sch., Baltimore; m. Marion G. Stansbury, Sept. 12, 1899. Clerk and officer, Merchants Nat. Bank, Baltimore, 1892-1905; v.p. and cashier, Md. Nat. Bank, 1905-11; partner Robert Garrett & Sons, 1911-31; chmn. trust com., Baltimore Trust Co., 1932-33; chmn. exec. com., Baltimore Nat. Bank, 1933-41, vice chmn. bd., 1941-54; now chairman investment com. Fidelity-Baltimore National Bank & Trust Company; member executive and finance committees, director Commercial Credit Co.; mem. exec. com. and dir. Md. Casualty Co.; chmn. finance com. and dir. A. S. Abell Co. (pubs. Baltimore Sun); mem. exec. and finance coms. and dir. Am. Credit Indemnity Co. of N.Y.; dir. and mem. exec. com., Am. Health Ins. Corp.; dir. Md. Drydock Co.; dir. and mem. investment com., Provident Savings Bank. Mem. exec. com. Community Chest of Baltimore, Inc.; mem. bd. trustees Baltimore City Retirement System Com. Republican. Presbyn. Clubs: Maryland, Elkridge, Merchants (Baltimore). Home: Two Wyndhurst Av., Baltimore 10. Office: Baltimore Nat. Bank, Baltimore and Light Sts., Balt. 3. Died Mar. 2. 1955.

FENKELL, George Harrison, civil engr.; b. Chagrin Falls, O., Feb. 4, 1873; s. Delaville L. and Sarah Nancy (Foote) F.; B.S. in Civil Engring., U. Mich., 1926, as of 1895; m. Jeanie Harris, Feb. 22, 1897; children—Neal H., Margaret Susan (Mrs. Winston Mather). Civil engr. with Commrs. of Water Works, Erie, Pa., 1902-07, Pa. Dock Commn., 1908; civil engr. Dept. Water Works, Detroit, 1908-13; commr. pub. works, 1913-18, gen. mgr. Dept. of Water Supply, 1918-38, chief engr. New Water Supply Project, 1924-38. Mem. Recreation Commn., Detroit, 1914-18; mem. Engring. Bd. Review, San. Dist. Chgo., 1924-25. Pres. Mich. Engring. Soc., 1926. Detroit Engring. Soc., 1925-26. Recipient Norman medal Am. Soc. C.E., 1902. Hon. mem. Am. Soc. C.E. (dir. 1923-26), Am. Waterworks Assn. (pres. 1931), Mich. Engring. Soc. (pres. 1926-27); mem. Engring. Soc. Detroit, Tau Beta Pi. Mason. Address: Almont, Mich. Died Nov. 8, 1949.

FENNER, Clarence Norman, geologist; b. nr. Paterson, N.J., July 19, 1870; s. William Griff and Elmina Jane (Carpenter) F.; E.M., Sch. of Mines (Columbia), 1892, A.M., Columbia, 1909, Ph.D., 1910. Mining and econ. geol. work in U.S., Can., Mexico, Central and S. A., 1892-1907; petrologist Geophys. Lab., Carnegie Instn., Washington, 1910-37, research asso., 1937-38, engaged on researches in application of physics and chemistry to geology, ret., 1938; expdn. of N.Y. Acad. Sci. on geolog. reconnaissance of P.R., 1914; researches on optical glass for mil. purposes under War Industries Bd. (in charge one of prin. plants), 1917-1918; geologist Nat. Geog. expdn. to Valley of 10,000 Smokes, Alaska, 1919; leader of 2d expdn. sent by Geophys. Lab. to same locality, 1923; geol. investigations in Peru, 1939; rep. of Geol. Soc. Am. on Nat. Research Council, 1925-28 (mem. exec. com. div. geology and geography, 1926-28). Fellow Geol. Soc. Am., Am. Phys. Soc., A.A.A.S.; mem. Am. Inst. Mining and Metall. Engrs., Washington Acad. Scis., N.Y. Acad. Scis., Am. Geophysical Union (chmn. sect. of volcanology, 1933-35), Geol. Soc. of Washington (pres. 1933); fgn. corr. Geol. Soc. of London. Writer of many sci. papers, especially on geol. and volcanological subjects. Club: Cosmos. Home: 64 Broad St., Clifton, N.J. Died 1949.

FENOLLOSA, Mary McNeill (Sidney McCall), author; b. Mobile, Ala.; d. William Stoddard and Laura (Sibley) McNeill; grad. Irving Acad., Mobile, Ala.; m. Ernest F. Fenollosa, Dec. 28, 1895 (died Sept. 21, 1908); 2 children. Traveled in Europe and Japan; resided in Japan for about 8 yrs. Mem. Soc. Dramatists and Composers, Writers' Branch of Equal Suffrage, Pen and Ink Club. Author: Out of the Nest; A Flight of Verses, 1899; Children's Verses on Japanese Subjects; The Dragon Painter, 1906; (under nom de plum "Sidney McCall") Truth Dexter, 1906; The Breath of the Gods, 1906; Red Horse Hill, 1909; Blossoms from a Japanese Garden (illustrated from paintings by Japanese artists), 1915; Sunshine Beggars, 1918; The Stirrup Latch; Christopher Laird, 1919. Editor: Epochs of Chinese and Japanese Art, 2 vols. Contbr. to mags. Home: Cismont, Va. Died Jan. 11, 1954.

FENSTERWALD, Bernard, merchant; b. Nashville, Sept. 1, 1890; s. Joseph and Bertha (Moses) F.; B.S., Vanderbilt U., 1911; m. Blanche Lindauer, Nov. 9, 1916; children—Bernard, Ann (Mrs. Robert Eisenstein). Partner Burk & Co., Nashville, since 1911; dir. May Hosiery Mills. Trustee Vanderbilt U., Fisk U.; v.p. bd. hosp. mgrs., Vanderbilt U. since 1925. Mem. Phi Beta Kappa. Jewish religion. Clubs: Kiwanis, Woodmont Country, Shamus. Home: Clarendon Av., Bellemeade, Nashville 5. Office: 416 Church St., Nashville 3. Died 1952.

FENSTON, Earl J., lawyer; b. Mt. Jewett, Pa., Mar. 31, 1895; s. George Manford and Katherine Elizabeth (Brown) F.; B.A., U. Cal., 1915; A.B., Harvard, 1916; grad. study U. de Caen, France, 1919; m. Emma Margaruite Brix, April 11, 1920; children—Earl Brix, James Guthrie. Admitted to Cal. bar, 1917, pvt. practice 1920—; pub. Hanford Sentinel & Jour., Hanford, Cal., 1953—; owner Radio Station KNGS, 1953—; purchased Santa Maria Times, 1956. Regent U. Cal. 1948—. Republican (alternate del., 1952). Mason. Clubs: Sequoia Sunnyside, Rotary (Fresno); Bohemian, Press and Union League (San Francisco); Petroleum (Los Angeles). Home: 5424 E. Butler Av. Office: Helm Bldg., Fresno, Cal. Died Jan. 31, 1958; buried Fresno, Cal.

FENTON, Howard Withrow, banker; b. Indpls., Dec. 29, 1877; s. William Taylor and Mary Louise (Inskeep) F.; grad. high sch.; m. Ethel Beatrice Carpenter, May 22, 1901; children—Alice Beatrice (Mrs. Fenton Morrill); m. 2d, Lauretta Octigan White, Feb. 14, 1931. Began with N.W. Harris Co., 1895, continuing with its successor, the Haris Trust & Savs. Bank, of which was made treas., 1907, dir., mem. exec. com., 1909, v.p. 1911, pres. 1923, chmn. bd., 1943-47; ret. 1947. Mem. Ind. Soc. of Chgo. Republican. Clubs: Chicago, Union League. Old Elm. Home; Lake Forest. Office: 115 W. Monroe St., Chgo. 3. Died Aug. 30, 1958.

FENTRESS, Calvin, lumber and banking; b. Bolivar, Tenn., May 22, 1879; s. James and Mary Tate (Perkins) F.; A.B., Princeton, 1901; m. Paulina S. Lyon, Jan. 14, 1903; children—Dr. Thomas L., Mary (Mrs. Burwell Dodd), Calvin, Emily (Mrs. Fentress Ott), Paul Lyon, Harriet, James. Has been identified with lumber and banking interests, 1902—; treas., dir. Lyon, Gary & Co., until 1920, firm name was changed to Baker, Fentress & Co., now chmn. bd., dir.; mem. exec. com., dir. Chgo. Nat. Bank; chmn. bd., dir. Consol. Naval Stores Co., Flexonics Corp., Medford Corp., Clover Valley Lumber Co.; dir. Greenville & No. Ry. Co., Coos Bay Lumber Co., Caseades Plywood Corp. Mem. Northwestern U. Assos., U. Chgo. Citizens Bd. Hon. trustee Berkshire Sch. (Mass.); dir. Chgo. Crime Commn.; dir., former mem. exec. com. Chgo. chpt. A.R.C.; governing mem. Art Inst. Chgo. (life), Chgo. Zoöl. Soc.; life mem. Chgo. Hist. Soc., Field Mus ; mem. Newcomen Soc. of Eng. Former trustee North Shore Country Day Sch.; former mem. Winnetka Pub. Sch. Bd.; past pres. Princeton Club of Chgo., Class of 1901 Princeton, Western Assn. Princeton Clubs: former mem. Grad. Council, Princeton; asso. mgr. Central div. A.R.C., World War I. Clubs: Chicago, University (former dir.), Saddle and Cycle, The Attic, Commercial, Economic, Princeton (Chgo.); Indian Hill (Wilmette); Princeton (N.Y.C.); Nassau, Cap and Gown (Princeton). Home: 939 Green Bay Road, Hubbard Woods, Ill. Office: 208 S. La Salle St., Chgo. Died Feb. 6, 1957.

FENWICK, Charles Philip, physician; b. St. John's Newfoundland, July 10, 1891; s. Mark and Margaret (Hudson) F.; student Methodist Coll., St. John's; M.B., Toronto U., 1916; m. Jacqueline McCullough, June 8, 1921; children—Margaret (wife of Capt. Brian Hennessy), Jacqueline Anne. Capt. RCASCO Toronto Gen. Hosp., 1919-20; physician to Hydro Elec. Power Commn., hdqrs. Niagara Falls, 1920-21; pvt. practice, Niagara Falls, Ont., 1921-23, Toronto, 1923-39; asso. sec. Health League of Can., asso. coroner City of Toronto, physician to Royal York Hotel, 1928-39; chief med. services Canadian Pacific Ry. Co., Canadian Pacific Air Lines, Montreal, P.Q. 1946—. Served as capt. Canadian Army, 1916-19; overseas, France, Belgium; entered active duty as lt. col., Canadian Army, 1939, advanced through grades to maj. gen., 1945; dir. gen. med. service; A.D.M.S., 2d Can. Div., 1940-42, D.D.M.S. 2d Can. Corps, 1942-43, D.D. M.S., 1st Can. Army, 1943-44; dir. gen. Can., 1945-46; dir. gen. med. services, Royal Canadian Army M.C., Nat. Def. Hdqrs., Ottawa, 1945-46, ret. from Army, 1946. Decorated Comdr. of the Bath, 1945, Comdr. of the British Empire, 1943; Mil. Cross, 1917; Efficiency Decoration, 1939. Mem. Airlines Med. Dirs. Assn. (exec.), Assn. Am. R.R.'s, Aero Med. Assn. Clubs: Canadian Railway, Canadian. St. James, United Services, Grenadier Guards, (Montreal), Caduceus (Toronto). Home: 3445 Ridgewood Av. Office: Canadian Pacific Ry. Co., Windsor St., Montreal, P.Q., Can. Died Mar. 20, 1954.

FERGUSON, Fred Swearengin, newspaperman; b. Bargersville, Ind., Jan. 4, 1887; s. Alonzo and Elizabeth Jane (Swearengin) F.; ed. Indpls. pub. schs. and Manual Training High Sch.; m. Helen Charlotte McFlynn, Apr. 29, 1911; children—Betty Jane (Mrs. Robert Lee Henry), Fred Thayer. Began as reporter Indianapolis News, 1907; with United Press in various larger bureaus throughout country, 1908-16; war corr. with A.E.F. for United Press covering Cantigny, St. Mihiel, Battle of Marne, Soissons and Argonne, 1917-18; covered Armistice commn. and later Versailles Peace Conf.; v.p. and gen. news mgr. United Press, 1920-26; pres. NEA Service, Inc., 1926-59, ret. Mem. Society of The First Division. Clubs: Dutch Treat, Lambs (N.Y.C.); Huntington (L.I.) Country; Nat. Press (Washington). Home: 4 Wincoma Dr., Huntington, L.I., N.Y. Office: 461 8th Av., N.Y.C. Died Dec. 1959.

FERGUSON, Homer Lenoir, shipbuilder; b. Waynesville, Haywood Co., N.C., Mar. 6, 1873; s. William Burder and Laura Adelaide (Reeves) F.; grad. U.S. Naval Acad., 1892; graduate, Glasgow U., 1895; Dr. Commercial Science, Washington and Lee, 1930; LL.D., U. of Richmond, 1932; Dr. Engring., Worcester Polytech. Inst., 1933; D.Sc., Duke U., 1933; Dr. Engring., Rensselaer (N.Y.) 1937; D.Sc., William and Mary College, 1942; married Eliza Anderson Skinner, September 23, 1896. Assistant naval constructor, Columbian Iron Works, Baltimore, Maryland, 1895-96; adviser with Wolff & Zwicker, Portland (Ore.) Navy Yard, 1896-99, Navy Yard, Bremerton, Wash., 1899-1900; supt. constrn. Bath (Me.) Iron Works, 1900-02; asst. supt. constrn. Newport News (Va.) Shipbuilding & Dry Dock Co., 1902-04; with Bur. Constrn. and Repair, Washington, D.C., 1904-05; with Newport News Shipbuilding & Dry Dock Co. since 1905, pres. and gen. mgr., 1915-37, pres., 1937-40, pres. and chmn. bd., 1940-46, resigned as pres., 1946, chmn. bd., since Aug. 1946; pres., trustee Mariners Mus. of Newport News; dir. Chesapeake & Potomac Telephone Company of Virginia. President Chamber of Commerce of United States, 1919-20; member of the Nat. Indsl. Conference Bd. Mem. Acad. Political Sci., Soc. Naval Engrs., Soc. Naval Architects and Marine Engrs. (pres. 1928-29), Shipbuilders Council of America, National Association of Manufacturers, American Geographic Society (council), Phi Beta Kappa. hon. mem. Am. Soc. of Marine Engrs., Propeller Club of the United States. Awarded Diploma and Cross of Legion of Honor (France); Knight Comdr. Order Leopold II (Belgium). Episcopalian. Mason, Elk Clubs: Engineers (New York); Army and Navy, City (Washington, D.C.); James River Country (Newport News, Va.). Home: 20 Museum Dr., Warwick, Va. Office: Newport News Shipbldg. and Drydock Co., Newport News, Va. Died Mar. 14, 1953.

FERGUSON, John Lambuth, clergyman; b. Columbiana, Ala., May 12, 1892; s. John Lee and Claudia Jane (Cole) F.; grad. Birmingham So. Acad., 1910; student Vanderbilt U., 1910-13; A.B., Emory U., 1914, B.D., 1916; postgrad. U. Chgo., 1920-21, U. Edinburgh, 1919; D.D., Southwestern U., 1947; m. Olive Ann Watkins, 1921 (dec. 1924); 1 son, Oliver Watkins; m. 2d, Christine Franklin Beverly, Feb. 25, 1933; children—Franklin Cole, Alice Christine, John Lambuth. Prof. religious edn. Millsaps Coll., Jackson, Miss., 1919-23; ordained to ministry Meth. Ch., 1918; etension sec. Gen. Sunday Sch. Bd., hdqrs. Nashville, extension sec. Gen. Sunday Sch. Bd., hdqrs. Nashville, ville, 1928-30; v.p. Scarritt Coll., Nashville, 1930-33; dist. supt. Columbia dist. Tenn. Conf., Nashville, 1936-39; minister Belmont Ch., Nashville, 1939—. Served as chaplain U.S. Army, overseas service, 1918-19. Chmn. commn. on World Service and Finance, Tenn. Conf., 1943—; sec. commn. on budget, Southeastern Jurisdiction, 1944—; del. gen. conf. M.E. Ch. South, 1938, Uniting Conf., 1939, Jurisdictional Conf., 1940, 44; mem. bd. trustees of property of former M.E. Ch. South, Nashville, 1944—. Mem. Am. Legion (past dept. chaplain), Sigma Upsilon (hon.), Kappa Sigma. Democrat. Mason (garnd chaplain). Club: Pew-Pulpit. Contbr. to church sch. lit. and religious press, M.E. Ch. Home: 4005 Harding Pl., Nashville 5. Office: 2007 Acklen Av., Nashville 4. Died Mar. 30, 1950.

FERGUSON, Kenneth Reinhard, aviation consultant; born Milbank, South Dakota, June 21, 1904; s. William James and Matilda (Reinhard) F.; B.S. in Elec. Engring. (hon. scholarship award), U. Minn., 1926; student Mass. Inst. Tech., Extension Div., 1929; m. Dorothy Frances Geckler; children—Janice Carole, Kenneth Reinhard, Jr. Engring. sales rep. Westinghouse Electric, 1926-29; aeronautical ground sch. instr. Curtis-Wright, 1930; traffic rep. Northwest Airlines, Inc., gen. traffic mgr., 1931, asst. to v.p. in charge of operations, 1936-42, v.p. in charge of operations, 1942-45, v.p. in charge of engring. and planning, 1945-48, v.p. operations and engineering director, 1948-51; aviation consultant, 1951—. Mem. Am. Inst. Electrical Engineers, National Adv. Com. Aeronautics (former mem. operation com.), I.A.T.A., Chi Phi, Eta Kappa Nu. Clubs: Athletic (St. Paul); Minikahda (Minneapolis). Episcopalian. Home: 112 W. Minnehaha Parkway, Mpls. 19. Died June 13, 1954; buried Sunset Meml. Cemetery, Mpls.

FERGUSON, Milton James, librarian; b. Hubbardstown, W.Va., Apr. 11, 1879; s. of William Harvey and Nancy Ann (Strother) F.; A.B., U. of Okla., 1901, A.M., 1906; certificate N.Y. State Library Sch., 1902; H.L.D., New York U., 1933; m. Rose Margene Barnett, Sept. 5, 1903; 1 dau., Ruth B. Librarian U. of Okla., 1902-07; asst. librarian Calif State Library, 1908-17, librarian, 1917-30; chief librarian Brooklyn (N.Y.) Public Library 1930-49; consultant Chivers Bookbinding Co., 1949—; editor-in-chief of Dewey Decimal Classification. Member Am. Library Assn. (exec. bd., 1925-26, 1933-37, pres. 1938-39). Calif. Library Assn. (pres. 1918-19 and 1926-27); Nat. Assn. of State Libraries (pres. 1918-19), N.Y. Library Assn. (pres. 1932-33), N.Y. City Library Club (pres. 1932-33), Brooklyn Conf. Adult Edn (pres. 1932-33), Am. Assn. Adult Edn., N.Y. Adult Education, Am. Inst. of Graphic Arts, Print Makers Soc. of Calif. (hon.), Calif. Soc. of Etchers (hon.), Phi Beta Kappa, Calif. rep. of Library War Service during World War; mem. advisory war cabinet of State Council of Defense, Calif., 1918. Admitted to Calif. bar, 1912. Pres. League of Library Commns., 1923-27; pres. Sacramento council Boy Scouts of America, 1923; trustee Edn. Foundation of Lake Placid, 1937—; mem. Library Council of State of New York. Mem. New York Academy of Public Edn. Clubs: Rotary (pres. Sacramento 1921-22, Brooklyn 1939-40), Municipal (pres. 1944 45), Carteret Book, Rembrandt (Brooklyn); Old Field, Grolier, St. Andrew's Society of State of N.Y. Democrat. Mason (30°). Made library survey Union of South Africa, Rhodesia and Kenya Colony, for Carnegie Corp. of New York, 1928-29. Editor: American Library Laws, 1930. Home: 115 Willow St., Bklyn. 2. Office: Chivers Co., 33 Nassau St., Bklyn. Died Oct. 23, 1954; buried Green-Wood Cemetery, Bklyn.

FERGUSON, R(ussell) J(ennings), educator; b. Gowdy, Ind., Jan. 13, 1898; s. James Edward and Elizabeth Charlotte (Dwiggins) F.; A.B., Ind. U., 1921, A.M., 1924, Ph.D., 1928; m. Hannah May Broyles, May 29, 1922; children—Jeanne Anne, Robert Wayne, Elizabeth Ellen. Athletic dir. and instr. history Hanover Coll., 1921-23; acting instr. history and asst. coach Ind. U., 1923-25, instr. history, 1927-28; instr. history U. Pitts., 1925-27, asst. prof. history, 1928-32, asso. prof., 1932-45, prof., 1945—, acting head dept., 1954-55, head dept., 1955—; research asso. Western Pa. Hist. Survey, 1933-36. Served as fireman U.S.S. Kearsarge, USN, 1918; lt. comdr. and comdg. officer at Officer Tng. Unit, World War II. Mem. Am., Miss. Valley, Pa. hist. assns., Western Pa. Hist. Soc. Democrat. Christian (Disciple). Author: Early Western Pennsylvania Politics, 1938; Allegheny County-Sesqui-Centennial Review (Collaborated) Allegheny County Commrs., (1938); contbr. prof. jours. Home: 139 Edgewood Av., Pitts. 18. Died Aug. 20, 1955; buried Elwood, Ind.

FERGUSON, Smith Farley, clock mfg. co. exec.; b. Essex, N.Y., Sept. 8, 1872; s. Everard D. and Marion A. (Farley) F.; Ph.B., Yale, 1894; m. Margaret C. Florance, June 8, 1918. With Ludlow Valve Mfg. Co., Troy, N.Y., 1894-1903; pres. Mackenzie, Quarrier & Ferguson, Inc., engrs. and contractors, N.Y.C., 1903-14; mem. Hill & Ferguson, cons. engrs., N.Y.C., 1914-22; dir., active in mgmt. Seth Thomas Clock Co., 1925—; v.p. Gen. Time Instruments Corp., 1931-36, chmn. bd. dirs., 1936—. Dir. N.Y. Assn. for Blind. Mem. Clock Mfrs. Assn. Am. (pres. 1934-44), Delta Phi. Republican. Episcopalian (vestryman). Clubs: University, Yale, (N.Y.C.); Short Hills (Short Hills, N.Y.); Graduates (New Haven, Conn.). Home: Stewart Rd., Short Hills, N.J. Died July 21, 1950.

FERGUSON, William Scott, historian; b. Marshfield, P.E.I., Can., Nov. 11, 1875; s. Donald and Elizabeth (Scott) F.; A.B., McGill U., 1896, LL.D., 1921; A.M., Cornell U., 1897, Ph.D., 1899; Litt.D., U. Louvain, Belgium, 1927; LL.D., U. Toronto, 1934; studied at U. Berlin and Athens, Greece, 1899-1900; m. Mary Alena White, 1902; 1 dau., Elizabeth Frances. Instr. Greek and Roman history U. Cal., 1900-03, asst. prof., 1903-06, asso. prof., 1906-08; research asso. Carnegie Instn. of Washington, 1906-07; asst. prof. history Harvard, 1908-12, prof. ancient history, 1912-29, McLean prof. ancient and modern hist., 1929-45, emeritus, 1945—, dean faculty arts and sciences, 1939-42; prof. Am. Sch. Classical Studies, Athens, Greece, 1913-14. Fellow Am. Acad. Arts and Sciences; corr. fellow British Academy; mem. Am. Philol. Assn., Archeol. Inst. Am. (v.p. 1948), Am. Philos. Soc., Mass. Hist. Soc., Am. Hist. Assn. (pres. 1939), Soc. Hellenic Studies of London (hon.), Phi Beta Kappa. Clubs: Harvard (Boston); Faculty (Cambridge). Author: The Athenian Secretaries, 1898; The Athenian Archons, 1899; Hellenistic Athens, 1911; Greek Imperialism, 1913; The Treasurers of Athena, 1931; Athenian Tribal Cycles, 1932. Contbr. to Cambridge Ancient History and to hist., philol. and archeol. jours. in America, Eng., France and Germany. Address: 8 Scott St., Cambridge 38, Mass. Died Apr. 28, 1954.

FERLAINO, Frank Ralph, indsl. physician; born N.Y. City, Feb. 1, 1900; s. John and Angelina (Paola) F.; B.S., Princeton, 1922, M.S., 1923; M.D., Johns Hopkins, 1927; grad. study Columbia, 1934, 1938, 1941-43. Intern, resident physician Presbyn. Hosp. Med. Center, N.Y. City, 1927-30; med. asst. Med. Dept. Am. Telephone & Telegraph Co., N.Y. City, 1929-38; asst. physician L.I. Med. Coll. and Kings Co. Hosp., L.I., 1934-37; asst. physician, instr. N.Y. Post Grad. Med. Sch. and Hosp., N.Y. City, 1935-44, asst. attending physician since 1944, co-dir. Ann. Symposium Indsl. Medicine and Surgery, 1943-46; med. examiner N.Y. Life Ins. Co., N.Y. City, 1931-33; physician in charge Compensation Clinic, Gen. Accident Ins. Co., N.Y. City, 1932-34; med. examiner, cons. traumatic diseases and injuries Mass. Bonding Ins. Co., Employers Mutual Ins. Co. Wis., U.S. Fidelity and Guaranty Ins. Co., Home Indemnity Co., All-state Ins. Co. since 1932; med. cons. Stony Wold Sanatorium, Lake Kushaqua, N.Y. since 1938, mem. med. bd. since 1944; pvt. practice, specializing in heart and chest diseases, indsl. medicine and surgery, traumatic and indsl. med. cons., N.Y. City since 1930; asso. med. dir. Schenley Labs., N.Y. City, 1944-46; med. dir. Gen. Motors Corp., N.Y. City since 1946; staff physician Roosevelt Hosp., N.Y. City since 1945; asst. attending physician U. Hosp., N.Y. City since 1950; asst. clin. prof. indsl. medicine Inst. Indsl. Medicine, Bellevue Med. Center, N.Y.U. since 1949; chmn. med. adv. bd. N.Y. State Athletic Commn., 1948-50; lectr. Trudeau Sch. Tuberculosis since 1949. Served as seaman 1st class, U.S. Navy, World War I. Fellow Am. Coll. Chest Physicians; mem. A.M.A., Med. Soc. Co. Kings, Acad. Medicine Brooklyn, N.Y. State Med. Soc. (mem. subcom. on indsl. health and accident prevention), Indsl. Med. Assn. (dist. counsellor for N.Y. and No. N.J.), World Med. Assn., Am. Trudeau Soc. and National Tuberculosis Assn., A.A.A.S., Morgagni Med. Soc., Am. Pub. Health Assn., Am., N.Y. Heart assns., Am. Soc. Bacteriology, Am. Assn. Indsl. Physicians and Surgeons, Research and Edn. Found. for Study Common Cold, Johns Hopkins Med. and Surg. Assn., N.Y. State Soc. Indsl. Medicine, Soc. Med. Jurisprudence, N.Y. Acad. Scis., Soc. Alumni Presbyn. Hosp., Assn. Princeton Grad. Alumni, Phi Chi, Delta Tau Delta, Omega Alpha Pi. Republican. Clubs: Johns Hopkins (N.Y. City); Mt. Washington (Baltimore); Dial Lodge (Princeton); Lake Placid. Home: 519 Ocean Parkway, Brooklyn 17. Asso. editor Industrial Medicine and Surgery Medical Journal. Author articles on indsl. medicine. Office: 580 Park Av., N.Y. C. 21; 1775 Broadway, N.Y.C. 19. Died Sept. 1953.

FERMI, Enrico, physicist; b. Rome, Italy, Sept. 29, 1901; s. Alberto and Ida (de Gattis) F.; student U. Pisa, Italy, 1918-22; D.S. (hon.), Ruprecht Karls Universitat, Heidelberg, 1936, U. Utrecht, 1936, Columbia U., 1946, Washington U., 1946, Yale, 1946, Harvard, 1948, U. Rochester, 1952; LL.D., Rockford Coll., 1947; m. Laura Capon, July 19, 1928; children—Nella, Giulio. Came to U.S., Jan. 1939. Lectr. physics, U. Florence, Italy, 1924-26; prof. theoretical physics, U. Rome, 1927-38; prof. physics, Columbia, 1939-42; research atomic bomb, U. Chgo., 1942-45, prof. physics, 1946—. Recipient Premio Matteucci, 1926, Nobel Prize, 1938, Hughes Medal of Royal Soc., 1942, Congressional Medal for Merit, U.S.A., 1946, Transenster Medal, U. Lieges, Belgium, 1947, Franklin Medal, Franklin Inst., 1947, Medaglia Donegani per la Chimica, 1948, Barnard Medal, Columbia, 1950, Dr. Bimala Law Gold Medal, Indian Assn. Cultivation Sci., 1951; Rumford Medal, Am. Acad. Arts and Scis., 1953; Gold Medal, Italian-Am. Charitable Soc., 1954; Award of Merit, Pres. U.S.A., AEC, 1954; Lewis Prize, Am. Philos. Soc. Phila., 1946. Fellow Am. Acad. Arts, Scis., Royal Soc. Edinburgh, Scotland; mem. Reale Accademia d'Italia, Accademia Gioenia di Scienze Naturali, Societa Italiana delle Scienze o dei XL, Imperiale Accademia dei Naturalisti di Halle, Indian Acad. Scis., Wiener Akademie der Wissenschaften, Academia Rumena, Bucarest, Am. Philos. Soc. Phila., Nat. Acad. Scis., Franklin Inst. Phila., Order of Sons of Italy in Am., Fondazione Angelo della Riccia (hon. pres. 1946), Societa Italiana di Fisica, Royal Soc. London, Am. Phys. Soc. (v.p. 1952; pres. 1953), Swedish Engr. Soc. Chgo., Sigma Xi; corr. mem. Regia Accademia delle Scienze di Torino, Accademia delle Scienze di Leningrado, Academia Brasileira de Ciencias. Catholic. Author: Thermodynamics, 1937; Elementary Particles, 1951; also several books pub. in Italy. Contbr. to scientific jours. Research: atomic physics. Address: 5327 University Av., Chgo. 15. Died Nov. 28, 1954.

FERNALD, Henry Torsey, entomologist; b. Litchfield, Me., Apr. 17, 1866; s. Prof. Charles Henry and Maria Elizabeth (Smith) F.; B.S., U. Me., 1885, M.S., 1888; Ph.D., Johns Hopkins, 1890; m. Minna R. Simon, of Baltimore, June 9, 1890; children—Helen Elizabeth, Charles Henry, Ruth Louise (Mrs. C. B. Stone). Prof. zoology Pa. State Coll., 1890-99; prof. entomology Mass. Agrl. Coll., 1899-1930, also chmn. sch. sci., 1913-27, dir. grad. sch., 1927-30, retired 1930. State zoologist Pa., 1898-99; state nursery insp. Mass., 1902-18; entomologist Mass. Agrl. Expt. Sta., 1910-30. Fellow A.A.A.S.; mem. Assn. Econ. Entomologists (a founder, pres. 1914), Entomol. Soc. Am., Boston Soc. Natural History, Phi Beta Kappa, Phi Kappa Phi. Mem. Congl.-Christian Ch. Club: Men's University (Winter Park, Fla.). Author: Applied Entomology; also bulls., pamphlets, on zoology and entomology. Address: 1128 Oxford Rd., Winter Park, Fla. Died July 15, 1952; buried Palm Cemetery, Winter Park, Fla.

FERNALD, Merritt Lyndon, botanist; b. Orono, Me., Oct. 5, 1873; s. Merritt Caldwell and Mary Lovejoy (Heywood) F.; B.S., Harvard, 1897; hon. D.C.L., Acadia U., N.S., 1933; D.Sc., U. Montréal, 1938; m. Margaret Howard Grant, Apr. 15, 1907; children—Katharine, Mary (dec.), Henry Grant. Asst. in Gray Herbarium, Harvard, 1891-1902, curator, 1935-36, dir., 1937—, instr. botany, 1902-05, asst. prof., 1905-15, Fisher prof. natural history 1915-49, prof. emeritus, 1947—. Asso. editor of Rhodora (jour. of N.E. Bot. Club), 1899-1928, editor in chief, 1924—. Writer about 899 bot. papers and monographs. Editor: Gray's Manual of Botany, 7th edit. (with Benjamin L. Robinson). Hon. pres. Internat. Botanical Congress, Stockholm, 1950. Fellow Am. Acad. Arts and Scis. Bot. Soc. American (pres. 1942), A.A.A.S. (v.p. 1941); mem. Societas pro Fauna et Flora Fennica, Am. Soc. Plant Taxonomists (pres. 1938), Am. Philos Soc., Nat. Acad. Science, N.E. Bot. Club (pres. 1911-14), Acad. Natural Scis. Phila., Conn. Bot. Soc., Phila. Bot. Club, Bot. Soc. and Exchange Club of British Isles, Norske Videnskaps Akademi, Société Linnéane de Lyon, Societas Phytogeographica Suecana (hon.), Royal Soc. Scis. Uppasal (Sweden), Franklin Inst., Phila. (hon.). Pa. Hort. Soc. (hon.), Assn. Am. Geographers, Josselyn Bot. Soc. Me.; fgn. mem. Linnean Soc., London. Recipient Leidy gold medal Acad. Scis. Phila., 1940; gold medal Mass. Hort. Soc., 1944; Marie-Victorin medal la Fondation Marie-Victorin for outstanding services to botany in Can., 1950. Author: Edible Wild Plants of Eastern North America (with Alfred C. Kinsey); Gray's Manual of Botany, 8th and Centennial edit., 1950. Home: 14 Hawthorn St., Cambridge, Mass. Died Sept. 22, 1950; buried Mt. Auburn Cemetery, Cambridge.

FERNANDEZ, Antonio M., congressman, lawyer; b. Springer, N.M., Jan. 17, 1902; s. Jose Estevan and Maria Anita (Lopez) F.; student Highlands U., Las Vegas, N.M., 1921, Cumberland U., Tenn., 1931; m. Cleofas Chavez, June 12, 1924; children—Anita, Dolores, Antonio Manuel, Orlando Octaviano, Manuel Armando. Court reporter, 1924-30; admitted to N.M. bar, 1931, and since practiced in N M.; mem. Legislature, 1935; chief tax atty., 1935-36; asst. atty. gen., 1937-41; mem. Pub. Service Commn., 1941-42; mem. 78th to 84th Congresses, at large for N.M. Home: 501 Armenta St., Santa Fe, N.M. Address: 1023 H.O.B., Washington. Died Nov. 7, 1956; buried Rosario Cemetery, Santa Fe, N.M.

FERNBERGER, Samuel Weiller, prof. psychology; b. Phila., Pa., June 4, 1887; s. Henry and Julia (Weiller) F.; B.S., U. of Pa., 1908; A.M., 1909, Ph.D., 1912; m. Eve Wallerstein, July 12, 1922; children—Edward, John Marshall. Asst. in psychology, U. of Pa., 1908-10, instr., 1910-12; instr. psychology, Clark U., 1912-15, asst. prof., 1915-20; asst. prof. psychology, U. of Pa., 1920-27, prof. since 1927; lecturer, Curtis Inst. of Music, 1926-28. Chmn. com. for perceptual problems, Nat. Research Council, 1940-41. Mem. C6, Nat. Defense Research Com., 1941; tech. aide D7, Nat. Defense Research Committee, 1941-45. Served as 2d lt. then 1st lt. inf., U.S. Army, 1917-19. Decorated with the Croix de Guerre (France); President's Certificate of Merit, 1948. Fellow A.A.A.S.; mem. Am. Psychol. Assn. (past sec., treas.; pres. gen. sect. since 1952), Soc. Exptl. Psychologists (secretary 1928-48), Nat. Institute Psychology (president 1930-41). Eastern Psychol. Assn. (pres. 1936), Psychometric Soc., Sigma Xi. Democrat. Reformed Jewish religion. Mason. Clubs: Lenape, British Officers (Phila). Author: Elementary General Psychology, 1936. Contbr. monographs and articles to psychol. journs. Editor: The Psychological Bulletin, 1918-30, Journal of Experimental Psychology 1930-46. Co-operating editor, American Journal of Psychology since 1925. Home: 6314 Wissahickon Av., Phila. 44. Died May 3, 1956.

FERRARI, Louis, lawyer, banker; b. Bobbio, Italy, Feb. 10, 1879; s. Colombo and Anna (Zanardi) F.; came to U.S., 1879, naturalized by parents' naturalization; A.B., Stanford, 1901; m. Alice Elizabeth Crowe, Oct. 12, 1910; children—Louis, Anna Alice (Mrs. Cyril Doyle), Emilio, Bernardo (dec. World War II), Gerald. Admitted to Cal. bar, 1901; pvt. practice of law, San Francisco, 1901-18, 1944-50, sr. partner Ferrari & Ferrari, San Francisco, since 1950; dep. dist. atty., S.F., 1901-17; trust atty. Bank of Italy (now Bank of Am.), 1917-24, gen. counsel, Bank of Am., NT&SA, 1924-44, now dir. Pres. Italian Welfare Agy. Chmn. Am. Com. Italian Immigration. Democrat. Roman Catholic. K.C. Clubs: Olympic, Serra, Olympic-Lakeside Country, Menlo Country; Los Altos Country. Home: 151 Upper Terrace, San Francisco 17. Office: 300 Montgomery, San Francisco 4. Deceased.

FERRIS, Elmer Ellsworth, author, univ. prof.; b. Lamartine, Wis., Oct. 11, 1861; s. George Horace and Annette (Stowe) F.; grad. Wayland Acad., Beaver Dam, Wis., 1881; student U. of Chicago, 1886-87, 1899. 1900; m. Minnie F. Lum, July 6, 1889; children—Helen Josephine, Frederick Lum. Admitted to bar, 1888, and practiced at Hastings and Lincoln, Neb., until 1898; ordained Bapt. ministry, 1899; pastor Ashland, Neb., 1899-1900, 1st Ch. La Crosse, Wis., 1900-04, Tabernacle Ch., Milwaukee, 1904-07, 1st Ch., East Orange, N.J., 1907-09; retired from pulpit, on account of ill health; then traveling salesman, sales mgr., v.p. Calumet Tea & Coffee Co.; sales coach and salesman for Alexander Hamilton Inst., lecturer in sales training courses for Am. Gas. Assn., also for N.Y. Edison Co.; dir. sales training Internat. Merc. Marine Co.; lecturer on sales at Pace Inst.; gen. sales mgr. Phenix Cheese Co.; prof. N.Y. U. Sch. of Commerce, Accounts and Finance, 1920-30. Trustee Wayland Acad., 1904-06. Fellow Am. Geog. Soc.; mem. Inst. Polit. Science, Delta Kappa Epsilon, Beta Gamma Sigma. Republican. Author: Pete Crowther, Salesman, 1913; The Business Adventures of Billy Thomas, 1915; Developing Sales Personality, 1923; Salesmanship (with G. R. Collins), 1924; Text on Salesmanship Alexander Hamilton Inst., 1928; Who Says Old!, 1933; Making a Go of Marriage, 1937; Jerry of Seven Mile Creek, 1938; Jerry at the Academy, 1940; Jerry Foster, Salesman, 1942; also The Industrial Gas Salesman, and Selling Ocean Travel. Home: 114 Morningside Drive, N.Y. City 27. Died May 12, 1951.

FERRIS, Eugene B(everly) Jr., physician; b. McNeill, Miss., June 24, 1905; s. Eugene B. and Martha (Reynolds) F.; B.S., Miss. State Coll., 1925; M.D., U. of Va., 1930, M.S. (Dupont fellow, 1930-31), 1931; m. Charlotte Gordon Hopkins, June 6, 1936; children—Charlotte Beverly, Ann Gordon, Eugene Beverly. Interne, Boston City Hosp., 1931-33; resident U. of Mich. Hosp., 1933; asst. resident Thorndike Meml. Lab. and research fellow, Harvard Med. Sch., 1933-35; mem. faculty, U. of Cincinnati Coll. of Medicine, 1935-52, asso. prof. of medicine and asst. dir., dept. internal medicine, Cincinnati Gen. Hosp., dir. psychosomatic teaching program, 1947-51, prof. of medicine, 1951-52; prof. of medicine Emory U., chief of med. services Grady Hosp., 1952-—, Cons. in mental health and mem. com. on research of mental hygiene council, USPHS, 1946-51, cardiovascular study section, 1952-57; med. dir. Am. Heart Assn., 1957-—. Member of the medical teaching mission to Poland and Finland (sponsored by Unitarian Service Com. and World Health Orgn.), 1948. Dir. research project on aviation medicine for Office Scientific Research and Development, 1942-45; mem. sub. com. on decompression sickness, Nat. Research Council, 1942-46. Recipient Horsley prize for research from U. of Va., 1936; Certificates of appreciation from the War Dept., The Navy Dept., and Office of Scientific Research and Development for med. research (as civilian), World War II. Fellow A.A.A.S., A.C.P. (regent); mem. Am. Soc. for Clin. Investigation (mem. council, v.p., 1949, pres., 1950), Assn. Am. Physicians, Am. Psychosomatic Soc. (mem. council, sec., 1947, pres., 1950), A.M.A., Am. Heart Assn. (v.p., bd. govs. 1955-57), Council High Blood Pressure Research (chmn. 1955-56), Ohio Med. Assn., Cin. Acad. Medicine, Central Soc. Clin. Research, Phi Beta Kappa, Sigma Xi, Alpha Omega Alpha, Beta Theta Pi. Editor-in-chief, Cincinnati Journal of Medicine, 1945-47, Journal of Clinical Investigation, 1947-52, mem. editorial bd., 1952-—, Annals of Internal Medicine, Am. Jour. Medicine, Jour. Psychosomatic Medicine. Home: 1035 Park Av., N.Y.C. 28. Office: 44 E. 23d St., N.Y.C. Died Sept. 26, 1957; buried Holly Springs, Miss.

FERRIS, Ralph Hall, penologist, clergyman, author; born of American parents in Kolhapur, India, Dec. 10, 1880; s. Rev. George Henry and Lucy (Hall) F.; B.A., Coll. of Wooster, 1901; B.D., Union Theol. Sem., 1904; M.A., Columbia U., 1906; Ph.D., Detroit Inst. of Tech, 1936; m. Ethel June Essig, June 5, 1913; children—Ruth Amy (Mrs. Vernon T. Smith), Robert Wesley. Came to U.S., May 23, 1889. Lecturer N.Y. Bd. of Edn., 1903-07; fellow Union Theol. Sem., 1904-06; ordained Presbyn. minister, 1905, transferred to Congl. denom., 1909; pastor, first Congl. Ch., Closter, N.J., 1903-07; instr. new testament Union Theol. Sem., 1906-07; prof. Chicago Theol. Sem., 1907-11; pastor first Congl. Ch., East Orange, N.J., 1915-17; prof. philosophy and social work Detroit Inst. of Tech., 1927-37; pastor Blvd. Congl. Ch., Detroit, Mich., 1930-33; asso. pastor first Congl. Ch., Detroit, 1936-37; state dir. probation Lansing, Mich., 1937-47, state dir. pardons, paroles and probation, 1947-49; acting pastor St. Paul's Evang. and Reformed Ch., Lansing, Mich., 1949-50; pastor Memorial Presbyn. Ch., Bay City, Mich., 1950-51; pastor Community Congregational Church, Tombstone, Arizona, 1951-53. Served as major, inf., 1917-19. Dir. domestic relations div. Recorder's Ct., Detroit, Mich., 1922-35; mem. revision sec. Detroit Charter Commn., 1913-14. Mem. Michigan Probation and Parole Association (life), Am. Assn. of Social Workers, Am. Prison Assn., Nat. Probation Assn. Author: Bergson and Commonsense, 1912; Tempted in all Points, 1916; Handbook of Probation, 1938 (2d edit. 1947). Co-author: (with Sheldon Glueck et al.) Probation and Criminal Justice, 1933. Editor-in-chief: Social Services of the Circuit Court, I-Kent, 1944, II-Washtenaw, 1944, III-Muskegon, 1945, IV-Saginaw, 1946, V-Kalamazoo, 1947, VI-Barry-Eaton, 1947, VII-Ionia, 1948; County Juvenile Services, I-Kent, 1943, II-Bay, 1945, III-Waxford 1946, IV-Chippewa, 1947, V-Kalamazoo, 1947. Contbr. to mags. Home: 5555 E. Speedway, Tucson. Office: Community Congl. Church, Tombstone, Ariz. Deceased.

FERRIS, Walton C., foreign service officer; b. Philadelphia, Pa., Dec. 2, 1900; s. Walter and Hannah Brinton (Price) F.; grad. Riverside High School, Milwaukee, Wis., 1918; student Swarthmore (Pa.) Coll., 1918-21, U. of Wisconsin Law Sch., Madison, Wis., 1921-22, Marquette U. Evening Law Sch., Milwaukee, Wis., 1922-24; m. Sarah Gertrude Perrine, Apr. 23, 1927; 1 son, Wilson Perrine. Admitted to Wis. bar, 1924; law clerk, Lines, Spooner & Quarles, Milwaukee, Wis., 1922-24, lawyer, 1924-26; foreign service officer, 1926-31 and 1934-—, vice consul, Palermo, Italy, 1927-31, consul, 1931; resigned from fgn. service, 1931; with Div. Eastern European Affairs, U.S. Dept. of State, 1931-34; re-apptd. to fgn. service, 1934, consul, Sheffield, Eng., 1934-39, consul, London, Eng., 1939-41, 2d sec. of Embassy, London, 1941; Div. Fgn. Service Personnel, Dept. of State, 1942-45, asst. chief, 1945; fgn. service insp., 1945-46; attended Nat. War Coll., 1947-48; consul gen. at Quebec 1948-49; fgn. service insp., 1950-53; assigned Dept. of State, 1953-—. Address: 3120 38th St., Washington 16. Died May 9, 1955; buried Rock Creek Cemetery, Washington.

FERRY, David William, clergyman; b. Belfast, Ireland, Mar. 25, 1876; s. John and Sarah Ann (Reid) F.; came to U.S., 1905, naturalized, 1915; grad. Presbyn. Theol. Sem., Chgo., 1909; D.D., Whitworth Coll., 1918; m. Edith May Fenno, May 19, 1909; children—David Ernest, Frank W. Volunteer with British Forces, Boer War, S. Africa; chaplain of 158th Infantry, A.E.F., World War. Presbyn. clergyman 1909-—; pastor First Ch., Yakima, Wash., 1923-43. Medals with clasps for 3 yrs. service in Boer War; victory medal with clasps for service as chaplain in World War. Trustee Whitworth Coll.; moderator Synod of Wash. of Presbyn. Ch., U.S.A., 1936-37. Mason (32°). Author: Back to the Home, 1926. Home: 601 S. 7th Av., Yakima, Wash. Died Dec. 9, 1955; buried Terrace Hights Cemetery, Yakima, Wash.

FERRY, Dexter Mason, Jr., business man; b. Detroit, Nov. 22, 1872; s. Dexter Mason and Addie E. (Miller) F.; student U. Mich., 1892-95, M.A., 1933; A.B., Columbia U., 1898; m. Jeannette Hawkins, October 1, 1907; children—Dexter, Edith (Mrs. A. U. Hooper), Jean (Mrs. C. C. Davis), William Hawkins. Chmn. Ferry-Morse Seed Co.; chmn. Standard Accident Ins. Co. Mem. Mich. Ho. of Rep., 1901-04; pres. State Bd. Edn., 1908-12. Pres. Detroit Museum of Art, 1914-17; pres. Detroit Museum of Art Founders' Society 1920-1948. Republican. Presbyn. Member Delta Kappa Epsilon. Clubs: Detroit, Country U. (founder), Detroit Boat (ex-pres.). Commd. capt. Q.M.R.C., Feb. 1, 1917; active duty Ft. Sam Houston, Tex., May 10, 1917, adj., then comdg. officer Motor Truck Group; orgd., and officer in charge, Motor Convoy Service, Chgo. Dist., Feb. 1918; promoted maj., Aug. 1918; lt. col. Q.M.R.C. (M.T.C.), Sept. 1919; col., Dec. 1922; comdg. officer 5th Army Train, 1922-30. Home: Grosse Pointe, Mich. Office: Ferry-Morse Seed Co., Detroit. Died Dec. 1959.

FERRY, Ervin Sidney, physicist; b. Croydon, N.H., June 14, 1868; s. Harvey S. and Hattie W. (Eastman) F.; B.S., Cornell, 1889, grad. student, 1891-93, fellow in physics, 1902-03; grad. student, Upsala, Sweden, 1897-98; grad. student and fellow in physics Johns Hopkins, 1893-94; m. Ruth M. White, Aug. 21, 1900; 1 dau., Priscilla Grace. Prof. physics Purdue U., 1899-—. Mem. Am. Physical Soc., Am. Electro-chem. Soc., Astron. and Astrophys. Soc. Am., Société Française de Pshysique, Delta Kappa Epsilon, Sigma Xi. Author: Elementary Dynamics, 1906; Practical Physics (with A. T. Jones), 1907; Pyrometry (with others), 1917; General Physics and Its Application to Industry and Everyday Life, 1921; (with others), Physics Measurements (2 vols.), 1929; Applied Gyrodynamics, 1931. Home: Lafayette, Ind. Died Oct. 8, 1956.*

FERRY, George Francis, army officer, steel exec.; b. Ft. Adams, R.I., Oct. 14, 1894; s. George Francis and Sarah (Bowley) F.; grad. Staunton Mil. Acad., 1912; student Valparaiso U., 1912-14; m. Dorothy Helen Mustard, Feb. 12, 1915; children—Helen Beverly (Mrs. Clare Stengel), George Francis, John Robert, Thomas Spencer. Supt. standard structural mills Carnegie-Ill. Steel Co., South Chicago, 1916-—. Entered Ill. N.G. as pvt., 1920, pvt. to lt. col., active duty 131st Inf., trained at Camp Forest, Tenn., 1941; comdr. 2d Bn., 132d Inf., South Pacific Campaign, 1941-43; comdr. regt., Guadalcanal, 1942; returned to U.S., 1944; organized, comdr. regt. of inf., Camp Maxey, Tex., 1944; dir. tng. Camp Wheeler, Ga., 1945; separated from service, 1945; chief staff Ill. N.G., 1946; later organized, comdr. 132d Inf. Regt., W. Madison St., Chicago; apptd. brig. gen., assigned asst. comdg. gen. 33d Div., 1948; now maj. gen. Decorated: Presdl. Citation, Bronze Star Medal, Combat Infantryman Badge, 3 battle stars, Legion of Merit, Navy Citation. Mem. Am. Soc. Metals. Club: Lake Shore Country (Chicago). Home: 7746 Cregier Av., Chgo. 49. Office: care Carnegie-Illinois Steel Co., South Chgo., Ill.; also care Adjutant General, Department of the Army, Washington 25. Died Sept. 25, 1954; buried Ft. Sheridan, Ill.

FESSENDEN, Laura Dayton, author; b. New York; d. Abram Child and Maria Annis (Tomlinson) Dayton; m. Benjamin A. Fessenden. Corr. various papers; represented Harper's Bazar at World's Columbia Exposition. Member D. A. R. (state regent D. A. R., since 1905), Colonial Dames. Clubs: Woman's Fortnightly (Chicago); Highland Park Woman's. Author: Beth, 1878; Essie, 1878; A Puritan Lover, 1887; A Colonial Dame, 1897; Chronicle of a Branch of the Dayton Family, 1902; Moon Children, 1902; 2002. Child Life 100 Years from Now; Hatsu, A Story of Egypt, 1904; Dorothy Lee, A Story of the American Revolution, 1905. Contb'r. to mags., writer of songs, etc. Address: Highland Park, Ill. Deceased.

FETZER, Frank L., lawyer; b. Denver, Aug. 19, 1886; s. John L. and Lucretia (Elgin) F.; student Stanford, 1909; LL.B., Denver U., 1912; m. Alma Blood, on September 30, 1914; one son, James B. Admitted to Colo. bar, 1912; gen. civil practice, Denver, since 1912; judge supreme ct., Colo., 1942-43. Trustee of Herbert Hoover Foundation, Inc. Dir. Finnish Relief, 1940. Decorated Knight First Class, Order of White Rose of Finland, 1941; Congl. medal for Services as govt. appeal agt., World War II. Mem. Am., Colo. and Denver bar assns., C. of C., Colo. Interstate Chess Team, S.A.R., Kappa Sigma, Phi Delta Phi. Republican. Baptist. Mason. Clubs: Denver Law, Denver Athletic, City (past pres.), Lakewood Country, Arapahoe Gun. Home: 1582 Emerson St., Denver 18. Office: Midland Savs. Bldg., Denver 2. Died Dec. 28, 1955; buried Fairmont Cemetery, Denver.

FETZER, Wade, insurance executive; born in Ottumwa, Iowa, November 22, 1879; son of William Henry and Henrietta (Clark) F.; student pub. schs., Ottumwa; m. Margaret Spilman, June 11, 1901; children—John Clark, Wade, Margaret (Mrs. John H Sherman), Mary Jane (Mrs. Calvin S. Bryant). In insurance business, Chicago, Ill., since 1897; president W. A. Alexander & Company, insurance, since 1927, now chmn.; pres. The Fidelity & Casualty Co., New York, 1930, now dir.; dir. The Continental Insurance Co. of New York, La Salle Nat. Bank of Chicago, First Nat. Bank of Hinsdale, Ill. President Ins. Fed. America, 1920; 1st pres., 1913, now mem. exec. com. Nat. Assn. Casualty and Surety Agents. Trustee Beloit (Wis.) Coll., Union Ch. of Hinsdale, Ill., Northwestern Univ. Republican. Conglist. Mason. Clubs: Union League, Chicago, Chicago Athletic, Attic (Chicago); Hinsdale, Hinsdale Golf, Bankers (New York); Bath and Indian Creek Country (Miami Beach). Home: 737 S. Elm St., Hindale, Ill.; (winter) 6437 North Bay Rd., Miami Beach, Fla. Office: 135 S. La Salle St., Chgo. Died Sept. 22, 1956; buried Bronswood Cemetery, Hinsdale, Ill.

FEUCHTWANGER, Lion (foikt'väng-ĕr), author; b. Munich, Germany, July 7, 1884; ed. in Berlin; Ph.D., University of Munich, 1907; Doctor Juis Honoris Causa, Humboldt U., Berlin, 1954; Doctor Honoris Causa Litterature, Hebrew Union College, Cin. 1959 married to Martha Loffler, 1912. Recipient Lit. prize City of Munich, 1957, Nat. Art and Lit. prize, Berlin, 1953. Author: The Prisoners of War, 1918; The Ugly Duchess, 1928; Success, 1929; Josephus, 1932; Power, 1926; The Oppermanns, 1934; The Jew of Rome, 1936; The Pretender, 1937; Paris Gazette, 1940; The Devil in France, 1941; Josephus and the Emperor, 1942; Double, Double Toil and Trouble, 1943; Simone, 1944; Stories from Far and Near, 1945; Proud Destiny, 1947; The Devil in Boston (play), 1948; This Is the Hour, A Novel about Goya, 1951; 'Tis Folly To Be Wise, A Novel about Jean-Jacques Rousseau, 1953; Raquel, The Jewess of Toledo (novel), The Widow Carpet (play), 1956; Centum Opuscula (essays), 1956. Jephthah and

His Daughter, 1958. Home: 520 Paseo Miramar, Pacific Palisades, Cal. Died Dec. 21, 1958; buried Woodlawn Cemetery, Santa Monica, Cal.

FEUILLERAT, Albert Gabriel (fû-yē-rä), univ. prof.; b. Toulouse, France, July 16, 1874; s. Joseph F. and Jeanne Marie (Méda) F.; B.A., Lycée of Toulouse, 1891; M.A., U. of Toulouse, 1896; studied U. of Lyons, 1898-99; Docteur ès Lettres, U. of Paris; hon. Ph.D., U. of Louvain, 1908; D.Litt., U. of Manchester, Eng., 1914, Yale, 1920; m. Fanny Bourget, Oct. 14, 1901. Prof. English, Lycée and U. of Clermont-Ferrand, 1899-1901; prof. English lit., U. of Rennes, 1901-27; visiting prof., Harvard, 1923-24, Columbia, 1927-28, Yale, 1928-29; Sterling prof. emeritus, Yale, 1929-43, and asso. fellow Berkeley Coll. Mem. Modern Language Assn. America, Modern Humanities Research Assn., Andiron Club of N.Y. City, Société des Professeurs français en Amérique, Malone Soc., Phi Beta Kappa; nat. hon. mem. Phi Sigma Iota, Knight Legion of Honor (France); Officer Order of St. Sava (Jugoslavia). Clubs: Graduate, Elizabethan (New Haven). Author: John Lyly (Contribution à l'histoire de la Renaissance), 1910; Le Bureau des Menus Plaisirs à la Cour d'Elizabeth, 1910; French Life and Ideals, 1925; Comment Marcel Proust a composé son roman, 1934; Paul Bourget: Histoire d'un esprit sous la III République, 1937; Baudelaire et la Belle aux cheveux d'or, 1941; Baudelaire et sa mère (edit. Variétiés, Montreal), 1944. Shakespeare (Œuvres choisies with an introduction), 2 vols., 1922. Editor: A. Wilson, the Swisser (with an introduction), 1904; Documents relating to the Revels at Court in the time of Queen Elizabeth, 1908; Documents relating to the Revels at Court in the time of Edward VI and Mary, 1914; Sir Philip Sidney's Complete Works, 4 vols., 1912-26; Blackfriars Records (Malone Soc. Collections), 1914; Shakespeare, Poems, 1927. Has lectured extensively in U.S. Turnbull lecturer on poetry, Johns Hopkins, 1927. Home: 228 Park St., New Haven 11, Conn. Died Nov. 3, 1952.

FEWSMITH, Joseph, advt. exec.; b. Cleveland, May 18, 1889; s. Livingston and Anna Lee (Grant) F.; B.S.,Wooster (O.) Coll., 1911; m. Edith Phillips, May 8, 1915; children—Joseph, Phillips. Asst. to advt. mgr., advt. dept. Peerless Motor Car Co., Cleveland, 1911-14; copy writer Martin Kelley Advt. Agency, Toledo, 1914-17; copy writer and service N.W. Ayer & Sons, Phila., 1917-21; v.p., dir. Seeney James, Cleveland, 1921-30; orgn. bus. with late Barclay Meldrum under name Meldrum & Fewsmith, Cleveland, 1930, v.p., treas., art dir., 1930-45, pres. and treas., 1945-50, chmn. bd. since 1950. Mem. Cleveland C. of C., Alpha Tau Omega. Presbyn. Clubs: Union, Hermit, Country, Mid-Day, Advertising, (Cleveland); Athletic (Detroit); University (N.Y. City). Home: 2862 Manchester Rd., Shaker Heights 22, O. Office: 1220 Huron Rd., Carnegie Hall, Cleve. Died Mar. 12, 1953.

FIALA, Anthony (fē-a'lä), explorer; b. Jersey City Heights, N.J., Sept. 19, 1869; s. Anthony and Annie (Kohout) F.; student Cooper Union and N.A.D., N.Y.C.; m. Mary Clare Puryear, Dec. 6, 1905; children—Anthony, Reid Puryear, Mary Maury, Lenore Fontaine. Began business life as stone artist and designer of lithography; asst. in a physical and chem. lab., 5 yrs.; newspaper artist and cartoonist, 1890; cartoonist Grit, Williamsport, Pa., 1893-94; studied processes of photo-engraving and photogravure; installed photo-engraving plant for Bklyn Daily Eagle, 1894, also in charge art and engraving dept., 1894-99; now pres. Fiala Outfits, Inc. War corr. for Bklyn. Daily Eagle while trooper in Troop C, 1st N.Y. Vol. Cav., Spanish-Am. War, 1898; commd. 1st lt. 14th Regt. Nat. Guard, N.Y., 1900, and was instr. mil. engring. Photographer Baldwin-Ziegler Polar Expdn., 1901-02; comdg. officer Ziegler Polar Expdn., 1903-05, reaching 82° 4' north, discovered and mapped new islands, also surveyed and mapped accurately greater part of Franz Josef Archipelago, maps and records published by Nat. Geog. Soc., Washington, 1907. Commd. 2d lt., q.-m. Squadron C, N.G., N.Y., 1908, capt. 2d Cav., 1911. Fellow A.A.A.S., Royal Geog. Soc.; mem. Am. Geog. Soc.; hon. mem. Internat. Yukon Polar Inst. Cruising Club of Am. Episcopalian (vestryman). Mason. Clubs: Explorers, Arctic, Ends of the Earth, Camp Fire of America, Am. Canoe Assn., Squadron C Cavalry. Author: Troop "C" in Service, 1899; Fighting the Polar Ice, 1906. Accompanied Col. Theodore Roosevelt on his trip through the Brazilian wilderness, 1913-14; explored the Papagaio River and descended the Jurnena and Tapajos rivers of Brazil. Capt., Machine Gun Troop, Mexican border service, 1916-17; capt. 4th Co. 102d Ammunition Train, 1917; transferred to Ordnance R.C., Feb. 11, 1918; maj. N.A., July 31, 1918; officer in charge Small Arms Proving Ground, Springfield, Mass., July 1, 1918-June 4, 1919; hon. discharged, June 4, 1919; maj., Ordnance Sect. O.R.C., July 9, 1919. Home: 148 83d St., Bklyn. Office: 10 Warren St., N.Y.C. Died Apr. 8, 1950; buried Arlington Nat. Cemetery.

FICKEL, Jacob Earl, ret. army officer; b. Des Moines, Ia., Jan. 31, 1883; s. Joel and Margaret Maria (Jackson) F.; student Des Moines Coll., 1899-1902, Revenue Cutter Service, Cadet Sch., 1902-04, Air Corps Tactical Sch., 1924-25, Command and Gen. Staff Sch., 1925-26, Army War Coll., 1930-31; m. Marion Allison, Feb. 15, 1912; children—Arthur Allison, Stanton Livingston. Enlisted in U.S. Army as pvt. 1904; commd. 2d lt., 1907, advanced through the grades to maj. gen. U.S. Army, 1940; 1 aerial gunner 1910; trained as pilot 1918; comd. flying school, 1918, 35; staff AC, 1919-20, 22-23, 31-34; comptroller-treas. U.S. Spruce Production Corp., 1921; exec. Wright Field, 1926-30; staff 9th Corps Areas, 1936-39; dir. aircraft prodn., 1938; command First Wing G.H.Q., Air Force, 1939; asst. chief AC, 1940, comd. S.W. Air Dist., 1940, 4th Air Force, 1941, 3d Dist. Tech. Tng. Command, 1942, Eastern Tech. Tng. Command, 1943, Western Tech. Tng. Command, 1945, ret. 1946. Rated command pilot and combat observer. Methodist. Club: Army and Navy (Washington). Address: San Antonio. Died Aug. 7, 1956.

FICKEN, Henry Horlbeck, lawyer; b. Charleston, S.C., Aug. 17, 1872; s. John Frederick and Margaret Buckingham (Horlbeck) F.; B.A., Yale, 1893; m. Julia Ball, June 23, 1896. Admitted to S.C. bar, 1894, since practiced at Charleston. Chmn. bd. commrs., Charleston Orphan House. Mem. War Council, A.R.C., World War. Mem. Delta Kappa Epsilon. Democrat. Episcopalian. Clubs: University (N.Y.C.); Yeaman's Hall. Address: Charleston, S.C. Died Oct. 10, 1940.

FIEBACH, Albert H. (fē'bŏk), lawyer; b. Brownhelm, O., Aug. 28, 1876; s. Peter and Sarah (Leuszler) F.; student Oberlin Acad., 1892-95, Oberlin Coll., 1895-96, U. of Mich., 1896-98; A.B., Oberlin Coll., 1899; LL.B., Harvard University, 1902; m. June Bogart, November 30, 1905 (deceased December 2, 1950); 1 daughter, Mary Bogart (Mrs. Charles William Bliss). Admitted to the Ohio bar, Dec. 1902, and since practiced in Cleveland, sr. mem. Fiebach Hauser & DiLeone, specialist in corporation, finance, estate and labor law; director Ohio Forge & Machine Corp., other indsl. cos. Police prosecutor, traffic judge, clerk, auditor and solicitor of Bratenahl Village, 1914-34; dir. Pub. Health and Welfare City of Cleveland, 1935. Organizer, trustee Cleveland Federated Charities and Legal Aid Soc. Cleve. Mem. Am., Ohio State, Cleve. bar assns. Mason (33°, K.T., Shriner, Red Cross of Constantine, Royal Order Scotland, Jester), Imperial Potentate. Shrine, 1942-43; Most Illustrious Grand Sovereign Grand Imperial Council, R.C. of Constantine, 1948-49. Clubs: Rotary; Cleve. Singers'. Home: 10110 Lake Shore Blvd. Office: National City Bank Bldg., Cleve. Died July 16, 1955.

FIELD, Carter, newspaper man; b. Baltimore, Md., Dec. 19, 1885; s. Charles Carter, Jr., and Mary Virginia (Lane) F.; student Baltimore City Coll., 1905; studied Johns Hopkins; m. Kathryn R. Burns, Aug. 19, 1942. Reporter on Baltimore American, 1908-09, Baltimore Sun, 1909-10; telegraph editor Norfolk Landmark, 1910, also spl. writer Baltimore Sun; editor and mgr. Cumberland Press, 1912-13; U.S. Senate corr. United Press, 1913; Washington corr. N.Y. Tribune (now N.Y. Herald Tribune), Apr. 2, 1915-June 1, 1929; became Washington corr. Bell Syndicate, 1929; now spl. writer for McGraw Hill publications. Mem. Troop A, Md. N.G., 1906-07. Republican. Clubs: Nat. Press, Gridiron, Metropolitan, Overseas Writers, Chevy Chase. Author: Bernard Baruch-Park Bench Statesman, 1944. Home: Chevy Chase Club, Chevy Chase, Md. Died Oct. 13, 1957.

FIELD, Charles Neale, clergyman; b. Reading, Eng., July 10, 1849; s. Rev. John and Frances (Peers) F.; ed. Durham U.; B.A., Univ. Coll., 1870, Cuddesdon Theol. Coll., Oxford, Eng., 1872. Ordained deacon Ch. of Eng., 1872, priest, 1873; asst. priest Plympton St. Mary, 1873-6; entered Soc. St. John the Evangelist (Oxford Soc., commonly known as Cowley Fathers), 1876, professed 1879; asst. rector Ch. of St. Clements, Phila., 1880-91; resigned; asst. Ch. of St. John the Evangelist, Boston, priest in charge Mission Ch., St. Augustine; founder St. Martin's Ch. and other missions for colored people, 1891-1904; Provincial superior Soc. of St. John the Evangelist, Am., 1904-11. Vice pres. John Howard Indsl. Home for Discharged Prisoners; pres. Mass. Br. Soc. for Maintenance of Cath. Principles. Address: 33 Bowdoin St., Boston. Died Jan. 14, 1929; buried Foxboro, Mass.

FIELD, Fred Tarbell, judge; b. Springfield, Vt., Dec. 24, 1876; s. Frederic Griswold and Anna Melanie (Tarbell) Field; ed. Vt. Acad., Saxtons River; A.B., Brown U., 1900; LL.B., Harvard U., 1903; LL.D., Dartmouth, 1931, Amherst and Williams, 1939; U. Vt., 1940; D.C.L., Boston U., 1942; m. Gertrude Alice Montague, Oct. 11, 1922; 1 dau., Ann Montague. Admitted to Mass. bar, 1903, to U.S. Supreme Court, 1907; asst. atty. gen., Mass., 1905-12, mem. U.S. Advisory Tax Bd., 1919; mem. Goodwin, Proctor, Field & Hoar, 1919-23; justice Supreme Judicial Court Mass., 1929-38, chief justice, 1938-47, retired. Lectr. Boston U. Law Sch., 1913-17, Harvard Grad. Sch. of Business Adminstrn., 1921-23. Trustee Brown U., 1920-26. Pres. Am. Bapt. Fgn. Mission Soc., 1923-25; fellow of Brown U., 1926—; trustee Newton Theological Instn., 1917-45, pres. bd., 1928-35. Awarded Rosenberger medal Brown U., 1940. Fellow Am. Acad. Arts and Sciences; mem. Am. Law Inst., Am. Mass. bar assns., Bar Assn. City of Boston (v.p. 1927-29), Colonial Soc. of Mass. (v.p.), Mass. Hist. Soc., Am. Antiquarian Soc., Mass. Soc. of Cincinnati (hon.), Phi Beta Kappa (pres. Brown U. Chapter 1940-41). Clubs: Union, St. Botolph (hon.), Odd Volumes (Boston). Home: 36 Fairmont Av., Newton, Mass. Died July 23, 1950.

FIELD, Henry Alonzo, ins. exec.; b. Milford, Mass., Aug. 8, 1870; s. John A. and Mary A. (Phillips) F.; grad. Deerfield (Mass.) Acad., 1887; m. Margaret Owen, Oct. 23, 1901. With Phillips Mfg. Co., Springfield, Mass., 1890-98, Vacuum Oil Co., 1898-1908; mem. firm Oppenheimer & Field, gen. ins., Springfield, 1908-25; mem. firm Field, Eddy & Mulheron, 1925-34, Field, Eddy & Bulkley, 1934-—; chmn. bd. Springfield Nat. Bank, 1928—; v.p. Springfield Instn. for Savs.; dir. Springfield Mchts., Inc., New Eng. Ins. Co., Mich. Fire and Marine Ins. Co., Springfield Fire & Marine Ins. Co., Springfield St. Ry., Peerless Handcuff Co. (v.p.), Van Norman Co. Chmn. Hampden chpt. A.R.C., 1918-19; mem. City Planning Board, Springfield, 1921-25, Police Commn., 1925-30; pres. Springfield Hosp., 1923-48. Vice pres. City Library Assn.; trustee Springfield Coll., Deerfield Acad. Mem. George Washington chpt. S.A.R. (past pres.), Ins. Fedn. Mass. (pres. 1921), Union Relief Assn. (pres. 1921). Republican. Episcopalian. Mason (32°, K.T., Shriner). Clubs: Detroit, Colony Nayasset (past-pres.), Longmeadow Country; Metropolitan (N.Y.C.). Home: 57 Westminster St. Office: 1200 Main St., Springfield, Mass. Died Feb. 28, 1957; buried Center Cemetery, Ashfield, Mass.

FIELD, Herbert H., clergyman; b. Bklyn., Sept. 3, 1883; s. John H. and Alicia C. (Hicinbothem); student Bklyn. Poly Inst., Columbia, Union Theo. Seminary, N.Y.; D.D. Hastings Coll., 1928. Ordained to Presbyn. ministry, 1907; m. Catherine M. Williamson 1910; children, Herbert W., John W., Catherine V. Zupeck. Pastor Flushing (N.Y.) Presbyn., 1907-10, Flatbush Presbyn. Ch., Bklyn., 1910-43; exec. and stated clerk, Presbytery of Brooklyn-Nassau, 1943—. Home: 200 Congress St., Bklyn. Died May 28, 1955.

FIELD, Marshall, born Chicago, Ill., Sept. 28, 1893; s. Marshall, Jr., and Albertine (Huck) F.; reared and ed. in England; student Eton Coll. and Cambridge U.; m. 3d, Mrs. Ruth Pruyn Phipps, Jan. 15, 1936. Pres. The Field Found., Inc.; pres., dir. Field Enterprises Inc. (which publishes Chgo. Sun-Times, World Book Ency. and Child-craft; owner, operator Simon & Schuster, Pocket Books, Inc., Parade Publs., Inc., N.Y.C. Functional Music Inc., Chgo.; dir. American Houses, Inc. Trustee Chgo. Natural History Museum, Metropolitan Museum of Art, N.Y. Zoological Soc., New School Social Research, Sarah Lawrence College; hon. trustee U. of Chicago; gov. Menninger Foundation. Pvt. 1st Ill. Cavalry, 1917, afterwards 122d F.A., 33d Div.; promoted through grades to capt.; arrived in France, Mar. 1918; participated in St. Mihiel and Meuse-Argonne operations; honorably discharged, Feb. 20, 1919. Elected pres. Child Welfare League of Am., 1951. Democrat. Clubs: Chicago, University, Casino, (Chicago); Knickerbocker, Racquet and Tennis, Brook, Grolier, Meadow Brook, Turf and Field, N.Y. Yacht (N.Y. C.). Home: 740 Park Av., N.Y.C. 21; (country) Lloyds Neck, Huntington, L.I., N.Y. Offices: 250 Park Avenue, N.Y.C. 17; 211 W. Wacker Dr., Chgo. Died Nov. 8, 1956; buried Chgo.

FIELD, Oliver Peter, univ. prof.; b. Fergus Falls, Minn., Oct. 21, 1897; s. Peter Ole and Tonnetta Thorbia (Iverson) F.; A.B., St. Olaf Coll., 1919; A.M., U. of Minn., 1924; LL.B., Ind. U., 1927; S.J. D, Yale, 1928; m. Elsie Maurine Kimmell, Dec. 29, 1928; children—Janet Maurine, David O. Instructor political science, North Dakota Agricultural College, 1922-23; instructor political science, Indiana University, 1924-26, asst. professor, 1926-28; asso. prof. polit. science, U. of Minn., 1928-31, prof., 1931-39; prof. govt., Ind. U., 1939—; also head of department. Lecturer on government, Harvard, 1935-36. Mem. Am. Polit. Science Assn. (mem. exec. council 1937-40, v.p. 1950), Midwest Polit. Sci. Assn. (managerial com. 1942-46). Republican. Lutheran. Author: (with Frank G. Bates) State Government, 1928, 39; Cases on Constitutional Law, 1931, 36; Effect of an Unconstitutional statute, 1935; Civil Service Law, 1939; (with John E. Stoner) Public Health Service in an Indiana Defence Community; Unconstitutional Legislation in Ten Selected States. Contbr. to various law revs. Home: 1326 Maxwell Lane, Bloomington, Ind. Died Oct. 22, 1953; buried Bloomington, Ind.

FIELD, Richard Stockton, naval officer; b. Pocahontas, Miss., June 9, 1890; s. dr. Robert and Belle (Daniel) F.; grad. U.S. Naval Acad., 1911; grad. U.S. Naval War Coll., 1936; m. Mildred Fearn, Oct. 15, 1913; children—Richard Stockton, Fearn. Commd. ensign USN, 1912, advanced through grades to comdr., 1931, ret., 1937; dir. Bur. of Marine Inspection and Nav., U.S. Dept. of Commerce, Washington, 1937-—. With USCG, 1942— for duration of war; promoted capt., USN. 1942. Decorated Victory, Haitian, Mexican, Nicaragua campaign medals (U.S.); Commendatore of Order of Crown of Italy. Episcopalian. Club: Chevy Chase. Home: Chevy Chase Club, Chevy Chase, Md. Deceased.

FIELDER, James Fairman, ex-gov. N.J.; b. Jersey City, Feb. 26, 1867; s. George B. and Eleanor A. (Brinkerhoff) F.; LL.B., Columbia Law Sch., 1887; LL.D., Rutgers, 1914, Columbia, 1929; m. Mabel C. Miller, June 4, 1895. Practiced law. Mem. N.J. Ho. of Assembly, 1903, 04. State Senate, 1907-13 (pres. of Senate 1912-13); as pres. of Senate succeeded Woodrow Wilson to governorship of N.J., 1913-14, resigned as senator, 1913, thus creating vacancy in office of governor; in Nov. 1913, elected gov. for term, 1914-17; vice chancellor N.J. Court of Chancery, 1919-48, ret. Democrat. Conglist. Mem. Hudson County Bar Assn. Home: 210 Orange Rd., Montclair, N.J. Died Dec. 2, 1954; buried Bayview Cemetery, Jersey City.

FIELDS, Herbert, writer; b. N.Y.C., July 26, 1897; s. Lew and Rose (Harris) F.; student Columbia. Started writing career at Columbia writing varsity shows with Richard Rodgers and Lorenz Hart, 1920, 31; with them commd. to write 1st and 2d Garrick Gaieties; dissolved partnership, joined forces with Vincent Youmans in prodn. of Hit the Deck. Co-author: Dearest Enemy; The Girl Friend; Peggy Ann; Connecticut Yankee; Present Arms; (with B. G. De-Sylva) DuBarry Was a Lady, Panama Hattie, 1940-41; Something for the Boys, Mexican Hayride, Up in Central Park. Author: Fifty Million Frenchmen; The New Yorkers (produced by E. Gay Goetz and with music and lyrics by Cole Porter). Co-author of libretto of Let's Face It, 1942; Annie Get Your Gun, 1946. Home: The Warwick, N.Y.C. Died Mar. 1958.

FIELDS, Joseph E., business exec.; b. Fargo, N. D., 1878; student pub. schs. and business coll. Began with farm implement business; sales dept. Nat. Cash Register Co., Dayton, O., for 10 yrs.; distbr. Chalmers Motor Car Co., Fargo, N.D., and later with sales staff at factory, 2 yrs.; sales mgr. Hupp Motor Car Co., 4 yrs.; then sales mgr. Liberty Motor Car Co.; asso. with Walter P. Chrysler, 1922-25; became v.p. and dir. Chrysler Corp., Detroit, 1925, later pres. DeSoto div.; pres. Chrysler div., 1931-37; v.p. Chrysler Corp., 1937-43. Clubs: Athletic, Country, St. Clair River Country. Home: 2117 River Road, St. Clair, Mich. Died Mar. 12, 1951.

FIELDS, Louis Glenn, business exec.; b. Lovejoy, Ga., Dec. 23, 1900; s. James Wiley and Ida (Edwards) F.; B.S., U. Ga., 1921; m. Emily Holbrook, Sept. 12, 1926; children—Louis Glenn, James Holbrook. Br. mgr. Graybar Electric Co., Inc., Miami, Fla., 1928-40, peninsular dist. mgr., 1940-48, southeastern dist. mgr. since 1948, bd. dirs. since 1951. Fla. dist. chmn. Com. for Econ. Development, 1944. Mem. S.A.R. Phi Delta Kappa. Methodist (steward). Mason. Clubs: Optimist, Kiwanis (dir., Jacksonville). Home: 307 Clovelly Rd., Windsor Farms, Richmond. Office: 10 S. Sixth St., Richmond, Va. Died June 23, 1956; buried Hollywood Cemetery, Richmond, Va.

FIELDS, William Henry, clergyman; b. Washington County, Pa., July 30, 1869; s. Robert Matthew and Mary Elizabeth (Leonard) F.; student Cal. (Pa.) Normal Sch.; A.B., Bethany Coll., 1901; m. Ola Dove Scott, Mar. 11, 1902; children—Allen Scott, Zona Klief (Mrs. Edward J. Klee), Manton Baron, Clark William, Catharine Valpa. Ordained ministry Disciples of Christ Ch., 1901; pastor Beaver, Pa., 1901-05, Wheeling, W.Va., 1905-37; now sr. mem. Fields Funeral Home. Former pres. W.Va. Religious Edn. Assn. (former mem. bd., adult supt.). Trustee Bethany Coll.; dir. W.Va. Home for Aged and Friendless Women; pres. W.Va. Missionary Soc. (chmn. exec. com.; mem. bd. 1905—). Mem. Sigma Nu. Republican. Mason (32°), Eastern Star. Club: Civitan (hon. mem.). Address: 843 Main St., Wheeling, W.Va. Died June 21, 1945.

FIELDS, William Jason, ex-governor; b. Willard, Carter Co., Ky., Dec. 29, 1874; s. Christopher C. and Alice (Rucker) F.; ed. pub. schs., Carter Co., and Ky. U., Lexington; m. Dora McDavid, of Rosedale, Ky., Oct. 28, 1893; children—Forrest G., Robert Forde, Everett E., Frank C., William Earl, Elizabeth. Farmer, lawyer and real estate dealer, Olive Hill, Ky.; commercial traveler for wholesale grocers and dry goods, 1899-1910. Mem. 62d to 68th Congresses, 1911-25, but resigned from Congress Dec. 1923, having been elected gov. of Ky., for term, 1924-27, inclusive; now practicing law. Democrat. Mason. Home: Olive Hill, Ky. Died Oct. 21, 1954; buried Olive Hill Cemetery.

FIFE, Ray, educator; b. Van Wert, O., Dec. 1, 1883; s. James and Melissa (Hoaglin) F.; B.S., Ohio No. U., 1909; B.S. in Agr., Ohio State U., 1917; student Cornell U., summers 1921-23; Ph.D., Columbia, 1929; m. Flossie Hall, Oct. 30, 1917. Rural sch. teacher, 1901-05; rural supt. schs., Van Wert County, O., 1910-15; agrl. extension service Ohio State U., 1917-19, asst. to prof. agrl. edn., 1919-21; state supr. vocational agr. in Ohio, 1921-36; pres. N.M. State Coll., 1936-38; mem. research com. Am. Vocational Assn., 1940—. Mem. Am. Vocational Assn. (pres. 1933-35), Alpha Zeta, Phi Delta Kappa, Iota Lambda Sigma. Methodist. Mason. Author various bulletins and monographs. Contbr. to ednl. and agrl. mags. Home: 1944 Chatfield Rd., Columbus, O. Died May 16, 1950; buried Convoy, O.

FIFE, Robert Herndon, univ. prof.; b. Charlottesville, Va., Nov. 18, 1871; s. Robert Herndon and Sarah Anne (Strickler) F.; B.A., and M.A., U. of Va., 1895; studied Göttingen, 1898-99; Ph.D., Leipzig, 1902; L.H.D., Wesleyan U., 1920, Middlebury Coll., 1955; Litt.D., Columbia, 1929; U. Pa., 1946; Washington and Lee University, 1949; married Sarah Gildersleeve, March 7, 1913 (dec. 1949); m. 2d, Hildegarde E. Wichert, December 21, 1952. Instructor English and German, St. Alban's School, Radford, Virginia, 1895-98; instr. German, Western Reserve U., Cleveland, 1901-03; asso. prof. German, 1903-05, prof., 1905-20, Wesleyan U.; Gebhard prof. Germanic langs. and lit. and exec. officer of dept., Columbia, 1920-46; instr. German, summer schs., U. of Va., 1903-05, Columbia, 1907, 1917; lecturer Chautauqua Instn., 1917-18; Petri lecturer U. of Upsala (Sweden), 1927; Carnegie visiting prof., S. African Univs., 1931. Mem. Modern Lang. Assn. America, (pres. 1944), American Association Teachers of German (pres. 1933), Am. Scandinavian Found. (trustee since 1946), Phi Beta Kappa, Deutsche Philaligische Gesellschaft (hon.), Deutsche Akademie (hon. corresponding), Inst. Pacific Relations, Council on Foreign Relations. Trustee Conn. Hosp. for Insane, 1912-20; mem. Conn. State Bd. of Charities, 1915-20 (pres. 1919-20); chmn. Modern Foreign Lang. Study (nat. investigation modern lang. teaching), under Am. Council Edn., 1924-28, chmn. Com. on Modern Lang. 1931-49; dir. Germanistic Society of N.Y., Carl Schurz Memorial Foundation. Edited and translated The Vestry Book of King William Parish, Virginia, 1707-1750; Virginia Historical Magazine, Vols. XI-XIII. Editor: E. T. A. Hoffman's Meister Martin, 1907; Heine's Harzreise and Buch le Grand, 1911; Heine's Harzreise (sch. edit.), 1912; Publications of American Committee on Modern Languages (24 vols.), since 1927; also editor Germanic Studies, a research series. Co-editor Germanic Review since 1925. Co-editor: Letters of Ludwig Tieck, 1937. Author: Der Wortschatz des Englischen Maundeville, 1902; The German Empire Between Two Wars, 1916; Young Luther, 1928; Summary of Reports on Modern Foreign Languages, 1931; Tendencies in Education in East and South Africa, 1932; Teaching of English in Puerto Rico (with H. T. Emanul), 1952; The Revolt of Martin Luther, 1957; also author monographs on subjects connected with German literature, history, philology and with language study and teaching. Club: Century. Home: 2505 Bedford Av., Bklyn. 26. Office: 423 W. 117th St., N.Y.C. Died Aug. 1, 1958; buried Charlottesville, Va.

FIFIELD, Albert Frank, corp. official; b. Lowell, Mass., Feb. 8, 1876; s. Frank and Abigail Mary (Cummings); student Tilton (N.H.) Sem., 1892-96; m. Velma Faunce Linscott, May 25, 1904; children—Velma Louise (Mrs. John C. Daggett, dec.), Helen (Mrs. Robert Laurence Rice, Jr.); m. 2d, Mrs. Georgette Eveland, Oct. 7, 1930; step-children—Jule Eveland (Mrs. Frank H. Whaley, Jr.), Marilyn Eveland (Mrs. Robt. Sutcliffe). Operated machine repair shop in New Hampshire, 1897-1904; constrn. superintendent Jencks Machine Company, Quebec, Canada, 1904-07; in machinery and automobile business, 1907-14; engaged in munition manufacturing, 1914-18; identified with tool industry as mgr. T. F. Shurly Co., Ltd., St. Catharines, Ont., Can., 1919-33; chmn. bd. True Temper Corp. of Cleve., 1956—; v.p. Shurley-Dietrich-Atkins Co., Ltd.; dir. Welland Vale Mfg. Co., Ltd., Hayes Steel Products, Ltd., The Bishop & Babcock Mfg. Co., Cleve., Atlas Steels, Ltd., Port Weller Dry Docks, Ltd. Mem. bd. govs. Gen. Hosp., St. Catharines, Ontario. Clubs: Union (Cleve.); St. Catharines (Ont.); Castalia Trout (Castalia, O.); Niagara Falls Country, St. Catharines Golf, Seigniory (Montebello, Can.). Home: 157 Ontario St., St. Catharines, Ont., Can. Died May 21, 1958.

FIKE, Charles Laird (fīk), marine corps officer (ret.); b. Des Moines, Ia., Mar. 13, 1902; s. Clement Laird and Mary Jane (Campbell) F.; B.S., U.S. Naval Acad., 1924; M.S. in Engring., U. Mich., 1936; m. Helen Elizabeth Lytle, June 28, 1924; 1 son, Robert G. Commd. 2d lt. USMC, 1924, advanced through grades to brig. gen., 1946; Marine Corps aviation, 1926-46, ret., 1946; exec. engr. ry. car div., E. G. Budd Co., Phila. Distinguished Flying Cross, Bronze Star. Mem. Soc. of Automotive Engrs. Home: 1037 Edge Hill Rd., Roslyn, Pa. Died May 3, 1950.

FILBEY, Edward Joseph, educator, accountant; b. Oakfield, Wis., Jan. 18, 1879; s. Nathaniel and Emma (Neeb) F.; Ph.B., Lawrence Coll., Appleton, Wis., 1901; A.B., U. of Wis., 1903, Ph.D., 1908; student U. Ill., 1915, C.P.A., 1919; m. May Constance Vaughan, Aug. 15, 1906; children—Edward Vaughan (dec.), Dorothy May (Mrs. Frederick A. Ross), Constance Harriet (Mrs. Le Roy E. Allison), Nathan Vaughan. Instr. of mathematics, Madison (Wis.) High School, 1901-02; statistician Wis. Bureau of Labor, 1906-07; prof. classics, Peabody Coll., U. of Nashville, 1907-11; sec. to Pres. James, U. of Ill., 1912-17; accountant Albert T. Bacon & Co., Chgo., 1917-19; asst. prof. of accounting, U. of Ill., 1919-21, asso. prof., 1921-24, prof. 1924-47, emeritus; asst. dean Coll. Commerce, 1922-28; now pvt. practice C.P.A., sr. partner Filbey, Andrews & Filbey. Mem. Bd. of Edn., 1922-30; dir. Urbana Assn. Commerce, 1925-35. Mem. Ill. Soc. C.P.A.'s, Am. Inst. of Accountants, Am. Accounting Assn. (sec.-treas. 1920-25, pres. 1925-26), Phi Beta Kappa, Beta Gamma Sigma, Kappa Delta Rho, Beta Alpha Psi, Delta Sigma, Pi. Republican. Methodist. Club: Rotary. Author: Federal Income Tax Problems and Solutions, 1920-47 (new edit. annually); Sixteen Years at the University of Illinois (with Edmund J. James and others), 1920. Contbr. to mags. on accounting subjects, auditing and income taxation. Home and office: 706 W. Pennsylvania Av., Urbana, Ill. Died Mar 10, 1959; buried Woodlawn Cemetery, Urbana, Ill.

FILENE, Lincoln (fĭ-lēn') merchant; b. Boston, Apr. 5, 1865; s. William and Clara (Ballin) F.; student pub. schs., Lynn and Boston; hon. M.A., Dartmouth Coll., 1916; m. Therese Weil, May 1895. Pres., chmn. exec. com., dir. William Filene's Sons Co., Boston; chmn. bd. Federated Dept. Stores, N.Y.; hon. chmn. Retail Research Assn., Associated Merchandising Corp. Rep. Gov. Ely of Mass. in Seven Satate Commn. to study Unemployment Ins., 1931; mem. bus. adv. council for U.S. Dept. Commerce, 1933-38; mem. indsl. adv. bd. NRA. Trustee Beth Israel Hosp., Boston; mem. Overseers com. to visit Grad. School Bus. Adminstrn., Harvard; mem. Adv. Bd. Edn. (Mass.), 1909-35; dir. Am. Arbitration Assn. (New York); pres. Lincoln and Therese Filene Found. Elected hon. member Phi Beta Kappa, Coll. William and Mary, 1922, senator, 1940. Mem. N.E. A., Boston C. of C., C. of C. U.S. (dir. 1923-25; chmn. nat. trade relations com. 1925-26), Nat. Retail Dry Goods Assn. (dir. 1927-29; chmn. trade relations com. 1928), 250 Associates of Harvard U.; chmn. research com. N.E. Council, 1925-28; mem. Advisory Com. on Nation-wide Survey of Secondary Edn. conducted by Sec. of Interior, 1930. Knight Legion of Honor, 1927. Clubs: Harvard, Boston City (Boston); Harvard (N.Y.C.). Author: A Merchant's Horizon); Unfair Trade Practices—How to Remove Them; Toward Full Employment (with Dennison, Flanders and Leeds); a number of articles in mags. of social and economic matters. Office: 426 Washington St., Boston. Died Aug. 27, 1957.

FILES, Howard W., business exec.; b. Sioux Falls, S.D., Feb. 18, 1893; s. Frederick H. and Mary B. (Meserve) F.; ed. Coe Coll. and Minnesota Coll. of Law; m. Nora Bergseng, June 18, 1921; 1 dau., Marcia Mae. Employed by Pillsbury Flour Mills Co. (now Pillsbury Mills, Inc.), 1912—, became mgr. Durum wheat dept., 1919, mgr. bakery dept. 1922, asst. gen. sales mgr. 1925, mem. bd. dirs. 1928, gen. sales mgr. 1931, vice pres. 1933, v.p. in charge sales and advt., 1940, mem. Pillsbury mgmt. com., 1946, mem. exec. com., dir., 1951. Served as pvt. to 2d lt., Q.M. Corps, U.S. Army, World War 1. Mem. Millers' Nat. Fedn. (pres. 1950-52, mem. exec. com., dir.). Mason. Clubs: Minneapolis (Mpls.); Lafayette. Home: 510 Groveland Av., Mpls. Office: Pillsbury Bldg., Mpls. 2. Died Dec. 7, 1957.

FILLEY, Everett R(oswell), oil prodn. exec.; b. Filley, Neb., Sept. 5, 1894; s. O.E. and Katharine (Williams) F.; A.B., Baker U., 1915, LL.D., 1952; m. Velma Hopping, June 17, 1917; children—Velma (Mrs. J. S. Rowe), Everett Roswell, Alice (Mrs. R. A. Johns), Jane Ellen (Mrs. W. H. Bradfield). Active in production department of The Texas Company, 1915, land man, 1916-19, exec. secretary, 1919-28, asst. div. mgr., div. mgr., 1929-38, asst. mgr., 1938-47, manager at Houston, 1947-53, vice president, 1953-57, senior vice president, 1957—; pres., dir. Texas-Zinc Minerals Corp., Texaco Exploration Co. (Can.); dir. Seaboard Oil Co., Halliburton Oil Well Cementing Company, Methodist Publishing House. Trustee Baker U., Drew U. Mem. Mid-Continent Oil and Gas Assn. (pres. Okla.-Kan. div. 1932-35), Am. Petroleum Inst., Houston C. of C., Delta Tau Delta. Methodist. Mason. Clubs: Houston, Kiwanis (Houston); University, Cloud (N.Y.C.); Apawamis (Rye, N.Y.). Home: Beechcroft Rd., Greenwich, Conn. Office: 135 E. 42d St., N.Y.C. 17. Died Mar. 21, 1958; buried Memorial Park Cemetery, Tulsa.

FILLMORE, Charles, clergyman, educator; b. Indian Reservation, Minn., Aug. 22, 1854; s. Henry Gleason and Mary Georgina F.; self-educated; m. Myrtle Page, Mar. 1881 (died 1931); children—Lowell, W. Rickert, Royal (dec.); m. 2d, Cora G. Dedrick, Dec. 31, 1933. Co-founder, 1889, pres. United Sch. of Christianity, Kansas City, Mo. (sch. has 1700 brs., 2,000,000 students, pubs. 7 periodicals and many books). Author: Christian Healing, 1909; Talks on Truth, 1926; Twelve Powers of Man, 1930; Prosperity, 1936; Mysteries of Genesis, 1936, rev. and enlarged 1944; Jesus Christ Heals, 1939; Mysteries of John, 1946; Atom Smashing Power of Mind, 1949; Keep a True Lent, 1953; (with Cora Fillmore) Teach Us to Pray, 1941.

Address: Unity Village, Lee's Summit, Mo. Died July 5, 1948.

FINCH, Frederick L., physician; b. Youngstown, O., June 13, 1905; s. Frederick L. and Genevieve Elizabeth (Dobbins) F.; grad. N.Y. Prep Sch., 1925; student Coll. Wm. and Mary, 1925-28; M.D., Med. Coll. Va., 1932; m. Melba Mayhew Gravely, June 23, 1932; 1 dau., Carole Virginia. Intern St. Lukes Hosp., Richmond, Va., 1932-33; pvt. practice gen. med., Urbanna, Va., 1933-34; internal medicine, asso. indsl. physician Am. Tobacco Co., Richmond, 1934-42, physician-in-charge Va. div., practice internal medicine 1946—; asst. prof. pub. health Med. Coll. Va. 1946—. Entered M.C., USN, 1942; disch. to Res. as comdr., 1946. Fellow Indsl. Med. Assn.; mem. A.M.A., Tri-State Med. Soc., Med. Soc. Va., Richmond Acad. Med., Lambda Chi Alpha, Alpha Kappa Kappa, Theta Chi Delta, Chi Beta Phi. Home: 105 Seneca Rd., Richmond. Office: 1001 Franklin St., Richmond 20, Va. Died May 21, 1957.

FINCH, George Augustus; b. Washington, D.C., Sept. 22, 1884; s. James D. and Emma B. (Fitnam) F.; LL.B., Georgetown U., 1907; Doctor of Laws, University of Thessalonika, 1948; m. J. Mae Wright, 1905; children—Eleanor Harrison, Augusta Emma (Mrs. Gerald J. Davis), David Wright (dec.), Mary Roberta (Mrs. E. Orville Johnson), George Augustus, Beatrice Anne (Mrs. Ralph M. Richter). Clk. War Department, 1905; law clk., Department of State, 1906-11, secretary American Commn. to Liberia, 1909; expert on internat. questions, War Industries Bd., 1918; asst. tech. adviser Am. Commn. to Negotiate Peace, 1919; sec. board editors Am. Jour. Internat. Law, and asst. sec. Am. Soc. Internat. Law, 1909-24, mag. editor and sec., 1924-43, editor in chief and vice pres., 1943-53, honorary editor-in-chief, vice pres., 1953—; asst. sec. and asst. dir. Div. Internat. Law, Carnegie Endowment for Internat. Peace, 1911-40, sec., 1940-47, asso. dir., 1940-43, dir., 1943-47, counsellor, 1948-50, trustee, 1940-56, hon. trustee, 1956-57; del. of the Endowment to 2d Pan Am. Scientific Congress, Washington, 1915-16, to 3d, Lima, Peru, 1924-25; rep. of Endowment to the Orient, 1929; prof. of internat. law, Washington Coll. of Law, 1931-34; prof. internat. law, summer session, U. of Mich., 1932-38, McGill U., Montreal, 1939; University of Washington, summer sessions, 1948; lecturer internat. law, Academy Internat. Law, The Hague, 1935, Georgetown University sch. of Fgn. Service, 1945-54; mem. adv. com. research in internat. law, Harvard Law Sch., 1928-40. Asst. sec. gen. Am. Inst. of Internat. Law, 1927-42, mem. exec. council, 1942—; pres. Inter-Am. Acad. of Comparative and Internat. Law, 1945—. Knight Comdr., Order of Balboa (Panama), Order of Cespedes (Cuba). Mem. bar of D.C., Am. Bar Assn., Am. Soc. Internat. Law. Author: Sources of Modern Internat. Law; numerous articles and addresses. Club: Cosmos. Home: 4000 Virgilia St., Chevy Chase 15, Md. Office: 1346 Connecticut Av., Washington. Died July 17, 1957.

FINCH, Henry LeRoy, investment banker; b. Plainfield, N.J.; s. Edward L. and Annie Ridley (Crane) F.; educated Leal's School for Boys, Plainfield, and Phillips Andover; m. Mary Farquhar Baker, October 5, 1915; children—Henry LeRoy, Charles Baker, John Ridley, Stephen Baker. Organized with Wilbur S. Tarbell firm of Finch & Tarbell, members N.Y. Stock Exchange in 1916, succeeded by present firm of Finch, Wilson & Co., members N.Y. Stock Exchange, 1922; v.p., trustee Broadway Savings Bank, N.Y. Organized and conducted post exchange at Columbia U. for S.A.T.C., under Col. John P. Finley, comdg. officer during World War I. Hon. deputy chief N.Y. Fire dept. Trustee Corp. for relief of widows and children of clergymen of P.E. Church in State of N.Y.; trustee Buckley School Found.; v.p. and mem. bd. mgrs. Hosp. for Ruptured and Crippled, New York. Mem. St. Nicholas Society (president), S.R. Republican. Episcopalian. Jr. warden Saint James' P.E. Church, N.Y.C. Mason (32°, Shriner). Clubs: Union, Church (past v.p.), L.I. Country (past pres.), Bankers, Turf and Field, Seabright Lawn Tennis and Cricket. Home: 46 E. 74th St., N.Y.C. 21; also BreaBurn Farm, Middletown Township, N.J. Office: 120 Broadway, N.Y.C. 5. Died Feb. 1960.

FINCH, Morton Easley, pres. Am. Snuff Co.; b. Boydton, Va., Jan. 5, 1877; s. Langston Easley and Tabitha Walker (Boyd) F.; grad. N.Y. Law Sch., 1902; m. Katharine McIntyre Braden, June 18, 1902; children—Braden Langston, Virginia (Mrs. Ben Rush Waller). Admitted to New York bar, 1904, Tenn. bar, 1912; with law dept. Am. Tobacco Co., N.Y. City, 1899-1912; sec.-treas. and counsel Am. Snuff Co., Memphis, Tenn., 1912-35, v.p. and counsel, 1935-40, pres. and dir. since Mar. 6, 1940. Mem. industrial advisory committee Fed. Res. Bank, St. Louis. Mem. Am. and Memphis bar assns. Democrat. Methodist. Club: Country (Memphis). Home: 565 Goodwyn. Office: P.O. Box 217, Memphis 1. Died Oct. 18, 1949.

FINCH, Ruy Herbert, vocanologist; b. Sunbury, O., Aug. 31, 1890; s. Thacker Webb and Ida (Hubbard) F.; ed. George Washington U., U. Chgo.; independent studies in meteorology, seismology, volcanology with Dr. W. J. Humphreys and Dr. T. A. Jaggar, Jr.; m. Margaret Helena Harvey, Oct. 12, 1923; children—Robert H., Harvey E., Amy Jean. With U.S. Weather Bureau, 1910, meteorologist, 1919; asst. to Dr. Jagger, dir. Hawaiian Volcano Obs., 1919; asso. volcanologist U.S. Geol. Survey, 1924. Established obs. for study of Cascade Volcanoes at Lassen Peak, Cal., 1926, orchardist Watsonville, Cal., 1936-39; volcanologist Nat. Park Service, Hawaii, 1940-47, now U.S. Geol. Survey. Instr. meteorology USN, forecast at Naval Air Sta., Ireland, during World War I; del. 4th Pacific Sci. Congress, Java, 1929, 7th Congress, New Zealand, 1949. Fello A.A.A.S., Geophysical Union, Geol. Soc., Am.; mem. Seismol. Soc. Am. Presbyn. Contbr. on sci. topics to various publs. Address: Watsonville, Cal. Died Mar. 25, 1957; buried Golden Gate Nat. Cemetery, San Bruno, Cal.

FINCH, Vernor Clifford, geographer; b. Tecumseh, Mich., Oct. 18, 1883; s. Ornan B. and Delilah (Bryan) F.; B.S., Kalamazoo Coll., 1908, Sc.D., 1933; B.S., U. Chgo., 1908, postgrad., 1909-11; Ph.D., U. Wis., 1916; m. Louise Lassfolk, Aug. 28, 1912; children—John Vernor, Thomas Lassfolk. Tchr. sci., high sch., Mt. Pleasant, Ia., 1908; asst. instr. geography, U. Wis., 1911, instr., 1912, asst. prof., 1916, asso. prof., 1919, became prof. 1927, now prof. emeritus. Spl. expert U.S. Shipping Bd., 1918-19. Mem. Assn. Am. Geographers, Gamma Alpha, Sigma Xi. Baptist. Author: Geography of the World's Agriculture (with O. E. Baker), 1917; Economic Geography (with R. H. Whitbeck), 1924; Elements of Geography (with G. T. Trewartha), 1936. Home: 1226 Sweetbriar Rd., Madison, Wis. Died Oct. 23, 1959; buried Tecumseh, Mich.

FINCH, Volney Cecil, educator, cons. engr.; b. Smith River, Calif., Aug. 24, 1892; s. Daniel Wesley and Belle (Gray) F.; post grad., U.S. Naval Acad., 1925-26; S.M., Mass. Inst. Tech., 1927; m. Frances Bennett Meyer, July 3, 1922. Entered U.S. Navy, 1917, served as naval aviator, 1917-29 and 1941-46; chief engr. and v.p. Aerco, 1929-31; prof. aeronautical engring., Ala. Poly. Inst., 1930-33; asso. prof. and prof. mech. engring., Stanford, since 1933. Registered profl. engr., Calif. Mem. Inst. Aeronautical Scis., Internat. Assn. Hydraulic Structures Research, A.S.M.E., Am. Helicopter Soc., Sigma Xi, Tau Beta Pi, Theta Chi. Author: Airplane Designers Handbook, 1930; Preparing for Aviation, 1931; Aircraft Engines (with A.B. Domonoske, 1936; Non-Rigid Airships, 1942; Airship Rigging, 1943; Pump Handbook, 1948; Jet Propulsion (Turbojets), 1948; Jet Propulsion (Turboprops), 1950. Contbr. sci. and tech. jours. Home: 639 Mirada Av., Stanford, Cal. Died Nov. 9, 1953; buried Fort Rosecrans, San Diego County, Cal.

FINCKE, Clarence Mann, banker; b. Bklyn., Oct. 12, 1874; s. Charles Louis and Clara (Hutchinson) F.; B.A., Yale, 1897; m. Elisabeth Whitman, Oct. 18, 1900; children—Allen Whitman, Marion Meigs, McKenzie. With Franklin Trust Co., N.Y.C., 1917-20, Bank of Am., 1920-31; with Greenwich Savs. Bank, N.Y.C. 1932-56, formerly chmn. bd., pres.; dir. Home Life Ins. Co., Manhattan Fire and Marine Ins. Co., Seaboard Surety Co. Rep. Presbyn. Clubs: Union League; Knickerbocker Country (Tenafly, N.J.); Cruising Club of Am. Home: 164 Winthrop Pl., Englewood, N.J. Office: Broadway and 6th Av. at 36th St., N.Y.C. Died June 19, 1959.

FINDLAY, Hugh (fĭnd'lā), landscape architect; b. Ayr, Scotland, 1879; s. Francis and Christina (Morton) F.; brought to U.S. in infancy; student Clark U., 1 yr.; spl. course in horticulture Cornell U., 1908; B.S.A., Syracuse U., 1916; M.A., Columbia, 1922; M.L.A., Harvard, 1927; m. Mabel L. Chase, July 5, 1916. Prof. horticulture and agrl. botany N.Y. State Sch. of Agr., Morrisville, 1909-14; prof. horticulture Syracuse U. Coll. Agr., 1914-17; asst. in visual instrn. agrl., States Relations Service, Washington, 1917; dir. agrl. courses Nat. Service Sch., Washington, summer, 1918; organizer and insp. of camp farms, O.Q.M.G., 1918; lectr. in horticulture AEF, Beaune, France, 1919; lectr. horticulture Columbia U., 1925-27, asso. prof. landscape architecture, 1927-45, now emeritus; dir. Hamilton Arboretum and Gardens, Nevis, Irvington-on-Hudson, N.Y. Fellow Royal Hort. Soc. (Eng.), Am. Geog. Soc., Am. Soc. Landscape Architects, Sigma Xi. Presbyn. Author: House Plants, Their Care and Culture, 1916; Practical Gardening, 1917. Editor of Handbook for Practical Farmers, 1920; Garden Making and Keeping, 1926; Imperishable Earth (poems), 1934; Stone of Destiny (poems), 1940; Isle of Destiny (poems), 1941; Gardening for Health and Happiness, 1945. Home: 11 Madison St., Hamilton, N.Y. Died Aug. 23, 1950; buried Hatch Lake, R.F.D. Eaton, N.Y.

FINDLEY, Earl Nelson, editor, publisher; b. Xenia, O.; s. Robert Pressley and Carrie Belle (Nelson) F.; student pub. schs., Cin.; Litt.D., Parsons Coll., Fairfield, Ia., 1942; m. Gertrude Murray Train, Dec. 25, 1906 (dec.). Began in subscription dept. Ency. Brit., Cin., 1893-99; with Lockhart Iron & Steel Co., Pitts., 1900-02; asst. gen. sales mgr. Lake Superior Power Co., Saulte Ste. Marie, Can., 1903; with Parson Mfg. Co., N.Y.C., 1904-08; reporter and article writer, specializing in aviation N.Y. Tribune, 1908-15; aviation specialist N.Y. Times Sunday Mag., 1916-17; apptd. editor U.S. Air Service Mag. (oldest aeronautical monthly in U.S.), Dec. 7, 1918, while serving as capt. on staff of Dir. of Mil. Aeronautics, owner, pub. 1925—; pres., treas. Air Service Pub. Co., Inc. Clubs: Army and Navy (Washington). Home: 3051 Idaho Av. N.W. Office: Transportation Bldg., Washington 6. Died July 11, 1956; buried Arlington Nat. Cemetery.

FINESINGER, Jacob Ellis, physician; b. New Castle, Pa., Oct. 28, 1902; s. Hyman Joseph and Fannie M. (Kaplan) F.; A.B., Johns Hopkins, 1923, A.M., 1925, M.D., 1929; studied psychoanalysis in Vienna, 1933-34, conditioned reflex activity in Leningrad, under Professor Pavlov, 1934; married to Grace Lubin, June 24, 1932; children—Ruth Joan (Mrs. Sheppard Kellam), and Joe Lubin. Intern neurology Boston City Hosp., 1929, resident neurologist, 1930, jr. vis. neurologist, 1930-32; Commonwealth fellow Boston Psychopathic Hosp., 1932-35; asst. in neuropathology Harvard Med. Sch., 1930-32, research fellow in psychiatry, 1932-35, asso. in psychiatry, 1935-36, asst. prof. psychiatry, 1936-49; asst. psychiatrist Mass. Gen. Hosp., 1936-39, psychiatrist, 1939-49; prof. psychiatry and head dept. U. Md. Sch. Medicine since 1949, psychiatrist in chief U. Hosp. since 1949. Port exec., port of Boston, U.S. Shipping Bd., 1941-45; prin. investigator on studies on selection of air-craft pilots, U.S. Navy and Nat. Research Council, 1941-45; consultant to Surgeon Gens. Office, U.S. Army; mem. study health sect. for mental health, U.S.P.H.; mem. com. on psychiatry Nat. Research Council; mem. dean's subcom. for psychiatry U.S. V.A. and research council U.S. Army Chem. Center. Mem. A.M.A., Am. Psychiat. Assn., Am. Neurol. Assn., Am. Soc. for Clin. Investigation (editorial bd. Jour. Clin. Investigation, 1948-54, mem. adv. editorial bd. Human Relations), American Psychoanalytic Assn., Assn. for Research in Nervous and Mental Disease, Am. Acad. Neurology, Soc. Biol. Psychiatry, also local and state profl. socs. Tech. adviser series of sound films on therapeutic interviewing. Contbr. to monographs; author papers on neurol., psychiatric topics. Editor in chief Journal Nervous and Mental Disease, 1958—. Home: 4512 N. Charles St., Balt. 10. Office: Department of Psychiatry, U. Md. Sch. of Medicine, Balt. Died Jun 19, 1959.

FINGOLD, George, govt. ofcl.; b. Boston, Oct. 18, 1908; s. Hyman and Blanche (Handler) F.; LL.B., Suffolk Law Sch., 1931; m. Evelyn McLean, Feb. 15, 1942. Admitted to Mass. bar, 1931, since practiced Boston; formerly asst. dist. atty. Middlesex Co., Mass., and asst. atty. gen., Mass.; now atty. gen. Commonwealth of Mass. Mem. Boston Bar Assn., Nat. Assn. Attys. Gen. (v.p., chmn. Eastern sect., mem. exec. bd.). Home: 37 Lowell Rd., Concord, Mass. Office: State House, Boston. Died Aug. 31, 1958.

FINK, Colin Garfield, electrochemist; b. Hoboken, N.J., Dec. 31, 1881; s. Frederick William and Minnie (Spengeman) F.; B.A., Columbia, 1903; M.A., Ph.D., Leipzig, 1907; hon. Sc.D., Oberlin Coll., 1936; m. Charlotte K. Muller, June 6, 1910; children—Frederick William, Ernest Arthur (dec.), Harold Kenneth. Asst. in electrochemistry U. Leipzig, 1906-07; research engr. Gen. Electric Co., Schenectady, 1907-10, Edison Lamp Works, Harrison, N.J., 1910-17; head research lab. Chile Exploration Co., N.Y.C., 1917-21; head div. electrochemist, Columbia, 1922-50, also metall. and art research: cons. practice, 1922-50. Chmn. tungsten com. U.S. Munitions Board, 1939. Fellow A.A.A.S.; mem. Electrochem. Soc. (past pres., past sec.), Am. Chem. Soc., NRC, Am. Inst. Mining and Metall. Engrs., Met. Mus. Art. Sigma Xi, Phi Lambda Upsilon (asso.), Tau Beta Pi (hon.). Republican. Club: Faculty (N.Y.C.). Editor "Electrochemistry" of Chem. Abstracts, 1907—; contbg. editor Mineral Industry. Originator of the drawn tungsten filament; platinum substitute for tungsten lamps and radio tubes; insoluble anode for copper; process for tin smelting and refining; corrosion resistant metals; commercial chromium and tin plating; aluminum plate on steel, etc. War Work, Time Bomb, S.A.M. Labs.; govt. cons. on metals. Recipient of Edward Goodrich Acheson gold medal for outstanding accomplishments in electrochemistry; Perkin medal, 1934; Modern Pioneer Award, 1940. Home: 440 Riverside Dr., N.Y.C. 27. Died Sept. 16, 1953.

FINK, Denman, artist, archtl. designer; b. Springdale, Pa., Aug. 29, 1880; s. Rev. H. G. G. and Medie (Wagey) F.; student pub. schs. Pitts.; Pitts. Sch Design, Boston Museum Sch. Art, Art Students' League, N.Y.C.; m. Zillah Jenkins, Aug. 5, 1903; children—Rogert Kendall, Enna (Mrs. J. Allen Brown). Began as illustrator for magazines; did color illustrations for Colliers Weekly, Am. Mags., others; became art dir. of civil development and spl. adviser to Geo. E. Merrick, developer of Coral Gables; designed Venetian Pool, the four Portal Entrances to Coral Gables; collaborated with architects in designing Miami Biltmore Hotel, Coral Gables City Hall; executed murals for ceiling and stair well The Four Seasons; executed numerous murals for pvt. residences, also various portraits; dir. art dept. and prof.

drawing and painting U. Miami, 1930-52, ret. Exhibited N.A.D., Pa. Acad., Pitts. Internat., Chgo. Art Inst., City Mus. St. Louis, Pan Am. Exhbn., San Francisco. Selected as one of 21 nationally known artists to paint canvas for Fourth Liberty Loan and United War Work campaign, depicting activities of A.L.A. in World War I, latter receiving spl. showing in many cities, and Congl. Library, Corcoran Gallery, Washington. Recipient commns. for mural in Fed. Court Room, P.O. Bldg., Miami, Fla., also mural panel for Lake Wales, Fla., P.O. Eastern Airlines Ticket Office, Miami, Miami Sr. High Sch., St. Francis Hosp., Miami Beach. Mem. Nat. Soc. Mural Painters, Soc. Illustrators (N.Y.), Planning Bd. City Coral Gables. Club: Salmagundi. Home: 760 Anastasia Av., Coral Gables, Fla. Died June 6, 1956.

FINK, William Green, lawyer; b. Summers County, W.Va., s. Turpin Moses and Emily Caroline (Meador) F.; student Central Normal Coll., Great Bend, Kan., 1891-93; m. Georgia Mariner, Aug. 18, 1904; 1 dau., Christine M. (wife of Lt. Jack H. McDonald). Began as sch. tchr., 1895; admitted to Kan. bar, since engaged in practice in Fredonia; dir. First Nat. Bank, Home Bldg. & Loan Assn. Mem. Kan. Ho. of Reps., 1931-37; mem. Kan. Legislative Council, 1931-35; Dem. floor leaders, 2 sessions; chmn. Kan. Tax Com.; mem. State Bldg. and Loan Bd., 1931-34. Former mem. Dem. Nat. Com., Kan. Methodist. Mason. Address: Fredonia, Kan. Died Mar. 10, 1949; buried Fredonia City Cemetery.

FINKLE, Frederick Cecil, cons. engr.; b. Viroqua, Wis., May 3, 1865; s. Thurston and Sophia Amelia (Michelet) F.; student pvt. and high schs. and spl. course in engring. U. Wis.; m. Henrietta Catherine Billette, Oct. 10, 1924; children—Frederick Cecil, Yvette Catherine. Settled in Cal., 1887; chief engr. Jurupa Land & Water Co., and N. Riverside Land & Water Co., San Bernardino County, 1887-90; city engr. San Bernardino, 1890-92; chief engr. water supply Cal. State Instns., 1892-94; chief engr. E. Riverside Irrigation Dist. (later changed to Riverside Highland Water Co.) and Graepland Irrigation Dist., 1894-97; chief engr. Redlands Electric Light & Power Co., Cal. Power Co., 1897-1901; chief hydraulic engr. and geologist So. Cal. Edison Co., Los Angeles, 1901-07, cons. engr., 1907-13; cons. engr., gen. practice 1913-—. Mem. Rapid Transit Commn., Los Angeles, 1925-26. Has served as cons. engr. on many projects and for many domestic water supplies, among them Denver Union Water Co. and cities of San Bernardino, Long Beach, Ontario, Glendale, Burbank, Beverly Hills, Cal.; chief engr. of cons. engr. for eighteen important storage reservoir dams; had charge of flood protection works in Palo Verde Valley on Colorado River after overflow in 1922; has constructed many dams and hydro-electric power plants; designed Arrowhead Lake Dam, Boulder Creek Power Plant, others; now in practice as cons. engr. specializing in water supply for domestic and irrigation uses, and hydroelec. power development; large land owner, also owner Finkle Arms Apts., Finkle Manor Apts., and York Apts. (Los Angeles), Savoy Hotel (Burbank, Cal.). Mem. Am. Soc. M.E., Am. Assn. Engrs., Am. Inst. E.E., Am. Water Works Assn., Southside, Harbor Dist. (pres. 1941) C.'s of C., Wis. Alumni Assn. Republican. Roman Catholic. Elk. Club: California. Home: 805 N. Crescent Drive. Office: Lomitas Av. & Crescent Dr., Beverly Hills, Cal. Died Apr. 7, 1949; buried Calvary Cemetery, Los Angeles.

FINLAY, Walter Stevenson, Jr. (fin'lā), vice pres. J. G. White Engring. Corp; b. Hoboken, N.J., Aug. 18, 1882; s. Walter Stevenson and Amy Green (Ketcham) F.; M.E., Cornell U., 1904; m. Jean Falconer Perkins, Feb. 4, 1911; children—Walter Stevenson III, Henry Perkins, John Falconer, Elisabeth P. Began as asst. in motive power dept., Interborough Rapid Transit Co., N.Y.C., 1904; associated with Henry Gordon Stott until 1910 in research and construction work having to do with large power station engineering and operation; with father in importing and manufacturing business; 1910-15; in charge power engineering and constrn. work, Interborough Rapid Transit Company, 1915-17, also in charge entire power system, 1917-20; vice president and director engineering policy, American Water Works & Electric Co., 1920-27; pres. The West Penn Elecric Co., 1927-39; dir., vice pres. J. G. White Engring. Corp.; dir. Overseas Cons., Inc., Far East-Am. Council of Commerce and Industry, Inc. Fellow Am. Inst. E.E., Am. Soc. M.E. (ex-mgr.; ex-v.p.); former mem. Am. Engring. Council, United Engring. Soc., Engring. Foundation; mem. Delta Tau Delta, Quill and Dagger (Cornell U.). Republican. Presbyn. Clubs: Duquesne (Pittsburgh); Engineers, Cornell, University, India House, N.Y. Yacht (N.Y.). Address: 80 Broad St., N.Y.C. 4. Died June 17, 1953.

FINLAYSON, John Duncan, life ins. exec.; b. Thessalon, Ont., Can., May 16, 1886; s. Kenneth and Anna (Dickie) F.; student Alma (Mich.) Coll., 1907-08, LL.D., 1928; A.B., U. Mich., 1911; student Union Theol. Sem., and Columbia, 1911-12; B.D., Auburn Theol. Sem., 1914; studied Berlin and Göttingen; Th.D., Harvard, 1916; m. Virginia Joyce Crafts, Sept. 4, 1912; children—Joyce Louise, Judith Ann, Jeanne Tertia. Ordained to ministry Presbyn. Ch., 1914; pastor Ypsilanti, Mich., 1916-19; prof. psychology and philosophy Dubuque (Ia.) Coll., 1919-20; instr. psychology U. Mich., 1921-22; pres. Fairmount Coll., Wichita, Kan., 1922-26, lead successful movement for municipalization of Fairmount Coll., developing it into Municipal U. of Wichita, pres., 1926-27; chancellor U. Tulsa, 1927-34; pres. Beacon Life Ins. Co., 1934-35; dist. mgr. Mass. Mut. Life Ins. Co., 1935-—. YMCA regional ednl. dir. AEF, World War I; in charge work in central and so. France and for Army of Occupation in Germany, until Feb. 1919; ednl. dir. U.S. Army, at camps Dodge and Lewis, 1920-21. Mem. Assn. Coll. Pres.', N.E.A. (life), Okla. Acad. Sci., Pi Gamma Mu. Presbyn. Mason. Home: 2735 Bedford Rd. Office: First Nat. Bldg., Ann Arbor, Mich. Died June 4, 1950.

FINLEY, Charles William, biologist; b. Cooks Mills, Ill., Aug. 10, 1880; s. Thomas Putnam and Martha Elizabeth (Covert) F.; diploma State Normal Sch., Charleston, Ill., 1908; B.S., U. of Chicago, 1910, M.S., 1911; Ph.D., Columbia, 1926; m. Sylvia Fears Finley, Aug. 8, 1906; children—Charles Otis, Eleanor Eliza. Teacher rural schs., Ill., 1902-07; head of biol. dept., State Normal Sch., Macomb, Ill., 1912-17, Lincoln Sch. of Teachers Coll., Columbia, 1917-22, and prin. high sch. div. of same, 1922-27; dean of instrn. State Teachers Coll., Montclair, N.J., 1927-43. Fellow A.A.A.S.; mem. N.E.A., N.J. State Teachers Assn., Ill. Acad. Science, Am. Assn. Univ. Profs., N.J. Schoolmasters' Club, N.J. Council of Edn., N.Y. Farm Bur., Phi Delta Kappa, Sigma Xi, Kappa Delta Pi. Republican. Baptist. Mason, K.P., Granger. Author: Biology in the Public Press (with Otis W. Caldwell), 1923; Biology in the Secondary Schools and the Training of Biology Teachers, 1926. Contbr. to mags. Home: Keeseville, N.Y. Died Oct. 8, 1952; buried Cooks Mills, Ill.

FINLEY, Emmet, newspaper mgr.; b. Salem, O., May 22, 1881; s. Richard and Mary (Barr) F.; A.B., Adelbert Coll. (Western Reserve U.), 1903; m. Ruth Bissell Ebright, Aug. 24, 1910. Admitted to Ohio bar, 1907; reporter successively Canton (O.) Repository, Cleve. Plain Dealer, Cleve. Press, 1908-10; sec. Cleve. Street Ry. Commn., 1910-12; reporter and city editor Cleve. Press, 1913-16; asso. editor Newspaper Enterprise Assn., 1916-19; gen. mgr. Publishers Autocaster Service, 1919-38, sec., 1939-45; gen. mgr. Am. Press Assn., 1921-38, sec., 1939-45; gen. mgr. John H. Perry Newspapers (Jacksonville Journal, Reading Times, Pensacola Journal and News), 1926-32, gen. mgr. Star Adcraft Service, 1928-38; v.p. Midwestern Paper Co., 1938-45; v.p. Harry W. Brintnell Co., 1943-46; exec. v.p., treas. Western Newspaper Union, 1938-45, WNW Sales Corp., 1938-45. Mem. Phi Beta Kappa. Republican. Episcopalian. Home: 268 Palisade Av., Dobbs Ferry, N.Y. Died Dec. 13, 1950.

FINLEY, Joseph William (fin'ley), lawyer; b. Bird Island, Minn., Aug. 4. 1896; s. James J. and Jane (Reagan) F.; student St. Thomas Coll., 1914-15; LL.B., St. Paul Coll. Law, 1921; m. Susie L. Moore, Oct. 10, 1922; children—Joseph Moore, Paul Reagan, Ruth Ann. Admitted to Minn. bar 1921 and since practiced in St. Paul; mem. Bundlie, Kelley, Finley & Maun since 1936. Asst. U.S. dist. atty. Minn. State, 1930-34. Chmn. bd. trustees Memorial Day Assn., 1927-35. Served as Sgt., C.W.S., 5th Corps, A.E.F., World War I. Mem. Am. Legion (past state, dist. and post comdr.), Minn. State, Ramsey Co. (past pres.), Am. and St. Paul bar assns., Disabled Am. Vets., St. Mark's Holy Name Soc., St. Thomas Alumni Assn. (past mem. exec. council), Delta Theta Pi (past dean). Republican (chmn. city and co. coms. 1936-38). Roman Catholic. K.C. Clubs: Variety, Athletic, Lincoln (St. Paul). Home: 2107 Watson Av., St. Paul 5. Office: Hamm Bldg., St. Paul 2. Died Nov. 12, 1953; buried Resurrection Cemetery, Mendota, Minn.

FINLEY, Ruth Ebright (Mrs. Emmet Finley), author, editor; b. Akron, O., Sept. 25, 1884; d. Leonidas S. (M.D.) and Julia (Bissell) Ebright; student Oberlin Coll., 1902-03, Buchtel Coll. (now U. of Akron), 1904-05; m. Emmet Finley, Aug. 24, 1910. Editor of Woman's page, Cleveland (O.) Press, 1911; fiction editor Scripps-Howard Newspapers, 1912-18; mng. editor Washington (D.C.) Herald, 1919; woman's editor Newspaper Enterprise Assn., 1920-21; asso. editor McClure's Mag., 1926-28; editor Guide—The Woman's National Political Review, 1936-38. Trustee of Hempstead (N.Y.) Public Library, 1922-39. Chmn. nat. press com. Nat. Council Women of U.S., 1928-29; mem. Nat. Com. on Folk Arts of the U.S. Co-vice chmn. steering com. of Nat. Fedn. of Business and Professional Women's Clubs for Celebration of 100 Years of Woman's Progress in Business and the Professions, 1937; mem. Nat. Council of Women. Mem. D.A.R., Kappa Kappa Gamma. Republican. Episcopalian. Club: Women's Nat. Republican (N.Y.C.). Author: Old Patchwork Quilts, 1929; The Lady of Godey's—Sarah Josepha Hale, 1931. Contbr. to magazines. Home: 16 Dumbarton Drive, Huntington, L.I., N.Y. Died Sept. 24, 1955; buried Grandview Cemetery, Salem, O.

FINLEY, William Lovell, naturalist; b. Santa Clara, Cal., Aug. 9, 1876; s. John Pettis and Nancy Catherine (Rucker) F.; A.B., U. Cal., 1903; D.Sc., Ore. State Coll., 1931; m. Irene Barnhart, Feb. 21, 1906; children—Phoebe Katherine (Mrs. Arthur N. Pack), William Lovell. Writer Review of Reviews Co., 1904-05; lectr. Nat. Assn. Audubon Socs., N.Y.C., 1906-25; mem. Bd. of Fish and Game Commrs., Ore., 1911; state game warden, Ore., 1911-15; state biologist, 1915-19; mem. Ore. Game Commn., 1925-27. Mem. adv. bd. U.S. Dept. Agr., Migratory Bird Treaty Act; mem. Adv. Council on Outdoor Recreation. Republican. Methodist. Hon. pres. Ore. Audubon Soc.; mem. Am. Ornithologists' Union, Outdoor Writers Assn. Am. (dir.), Nat. Parks Assn. (adv. council), Wildlife Soc. (trustee), Sigma Xi; charter mem. Am. Soc. Mammalogists, Cooper Ornithol. Club, Pacific Northwest Bird and Mammal Soc. Author: American Birds, 1907; (with wife) Little Bird Blue, 1915, Wild Animal Pets, 1928; also many sci. papers on bird life and 2 bulls. on Ore. birds. Producer of Finley nature films (motion pictures). Asso. editor The Condor, 1906-09. Editorial staff Nature Mag., 1923-37; v.p. Izaak Walton League Am., Nat. Wildlife Fedn. Home: R.F.D. 10, Portland, Ore. Died June 29, 1953; buried Riverview Cemetery, Portland.

FINN, John F(rancis) X(avier), lawyer; b. N.Y. City, May 21, 1901; s. William A. and Charlotte C. (Tweedy) F.; A.B. summa cum laude, Coll. City of N.Y., 1920; LL.B. summa cum laude, Fordham U., 1923; m. Maria L. Marrin, June 27, 1928; children—John F. X., Maria T., Donald F. X., Paul J., Anna May, Anthony. Admitted New York bar, 1923, practiced since as member firm Lorenz, Finn & Lorenz, New York City. Member bar Supreme Court United States. Specialized appellate practice, corporate reorganizations, law of receivers and creditors' rights cases. Trustee reorgn. of $10,000,000 Childs Company, 1943-48; frequently served as referee Supreme Court New York State; expert law examiner Municipal Civil Service Commn. N.Y. City; professor law school Fordham U., 1924-—, dean Law Sch., 1954-56; member N.Y. State law revision commn. apptd. by Gov. Herbert H. Lehman, and reappointed by Gov. Thomas E. Dewey; counsel to com. on revision laws of U.S. House of Reps.; mem. com. to revise N.Y. Civil Practice Act, 1955-56. Served in U.S. Army, 1918; sr. res. lt., U.S. Navy, 1931-41. Dir. and vice pres. Hodgkin's Disease Research Foundation, Incorporated. Member following bar associations: American, New York (past chairman committee on state legislation, member committee on fed. constitutional amendments); N.Y. City (past chmn. com. on state legislation, mem. Admissions com., Nominating Com., N.Y. Co. Lawyers Assn. (dir. and chmn. com. on the city ct.); Am. Judicature Soc.; Civil Service Reform Assn.; Phi Beta Kappa (past pres., Gamma Chap.). Democrat. Roman Catholic. Clubs: Catholic, Manhattan, Ancient Order of Hibernians, K. of C. Author: Keener's Cases of Contracts (with I. Maurice Wormser), 1933; Carmody's Manual of New York Practice (with Edward Q. Carr, Leonard S. Saxe), 1946; Manual of New York Civil Practice (with Harold R. Medina, Edward Q. Carr), 1935; Ash's Greater New York Charter, 10 year Supplement (with Paul B. Carroll), 1937. Contbr. numerous articles to law jours. Home: 910 Fifth Av. Office: 165 Broadway, N.Y.C. 6. Died Sept. 8, 1956; buried St. Mary's Cemetery, Queens, N.Y.

FINNEGAN, James A(loysius), state ofcl.; b. Phila., Dec. 20, 1906; s. Owen and Mary (Egan) F.; student U. Pa., 1928-32. Sec. Nav. Commn. Del. River, State Pa., 1935-38; adminstrv. asst. Senator Francis J. Myers (Pa.), 1938-42; adminstrv. asst. to Michael J. Bradley, chmn. Dem. Party of Phila., 1947-48; chmn. Dem. Party, Phila., 1948-53; pres. City Council, Phila., 1953-55; sec. Commonwealth of Pennsylvania, 1955-—; campaign manager to Adlai E. Stevenson, 1956. Delegate to Democratic Nat. Conv., 1940, 48, 52. Served as lt. col., USAAF, 1942-46. Mem. Air Force Assn., Res. Officers Assn. K.C. Home: 5743 Springfield Av., Phila. 43. Office: Capitol Bldg., Harrisburg, Pa. Died Mar. 27, 1958.

FINNEGAN, Philip J., judge; b. Chicago, June 25, 1886; s. Richard and Ella (Biggs) F.; LL.D., Chicago Law Sch., 1913; m. Sue Moran, Sept. 22, 1923; children—Phyllis (Mrs. Thomas J. O'Brien, Jr.), Patricia (Mrs. Harry A. Hughes, Jr.). Admitted to Ill. bar, 1913; judge Municipal Court of Chicago, 1922-29; elected judge of Circuit Court, Cook County, 1929, reelected, 1933, 39, 45; apptd. judge of U.S. Court of Appeals, 7th Circuit, 1949. Mem. Chicago, Ill. and Am. bar assns., Phi Alpha Delta. Home: 247 East Chestnut St. Office: U.S. Court of Appeals, 1212 Lake Shore Dr., Chgo. 11. Died Jan. 1959.

FINNEGAN, Richard James, newspaperman; b. Chgo., Sept. 5, 1884; s. Richard J. and Ella (Biggs) F.; LL.B., Chgo. Law Sch., 1907; Dr. Journalism (Hon.), Northwestern U., 1947; m. Lucile Adams, July 6, 1907; children—Lucile (Mrs. Willard J. Loarie), Ruth Joan (Mrs. Charles R. Corcoran), Richard Adams. Reporter Chgo. Chronicle, 1901, Chgo. Inter Ocean, 1903-04; with Chgo. Daily Jour., 1904-29, city editor, 1914-15, mng. editor, 1916-25; co-editor, 1925-29; editor Chgo. Times, 1929-44, editor, pub., 1944-47; editor, exec. v.p. Chgo. Sun-Times, 1947-50, cons. editor, 1950-—; dir. Field Enterprises, Inc., Chgo. Co-founder Ill. Hwy. Improvement Assn., 1912, sec., 1912-18; Ill. v.p. Dixie Hwy. Assn., 1913-17; mem. nat. adv. heart council US PHS, 1950-52. Pres. City News Bur., 1939-51, La Rabida Jackson Park Sanitarium, Chgo., 1944-55; dir. Welfare Council Met. Chgo., Chgo. Heart Assn., Chgo. Council on Community Nursing, Chgo. Area Hosp. Fund, Fund for the Republic. Mem. pres.' com. U. Notre Dame; council on med. and biol. research U. Chgo.; citizens' adv. com. Loyola U.: mem. freedom of press com. Thomas Jefferson Meml. Found. Mem. Northwestern U. Assos., Am. Soc. Newspaper Editors, Chgo. Press Vets. Assn. (hon. chmn.). Phi Alpha Delta (nat. recorder 1907-08), Sigma Delta Chi. Clubs: Chicago, Tavern, Westmoreland, Press. Irish Fellowship (pres. 1940) (Chgo.). Home: 7462 Sheridan Rd., Chgo. 26. Office: 211 Wacker Dr., Chgo. 6. Died May 6, 1955.

FINTA, Alexander (fin'tȧ), sculptor, painter, author; b. Turkeve, Hungary, June 12, 1881; s. Alexander and Roza (Hajdu) F.; student Real Gymnasium, 1891-97; student European Art Schs. and academies, 1897-1912; student Columbia U., 1928; m. Eszter Finta, of Turkeve, Hungary, Apr. 25, 1914; 1 son, Alexander; m. 2d, Catherine Kantor, of Budapest, June 12, 1919. Came to U.S., 1923, naturalized, 1930. Sculptor, Twentiedth Century Fox Film Studio Company, Beverly Hills, California. Clubs: California Art, Painters and Sculptors (Los Angeles); South West Art Assn. Represented by statuary in Budapest, Hungary, Transylvania; monuments to war heroes in Jugoslavia, Czechoslovakia 16 piece group in Cathedral of Dom Pedro, Brazil 12 ft. granite monument "Strength," in Rio de Janeiro. Works shown in Nat. Museum and Fine Arts Museum, Hist. Museum, Budapest, Belles Arts Museum, Rio de Janeiro, Brooklyn Museum, Met. Museum of Art, Cleveland Pub. Library; represented by a collection of medals in The Numismatic Museum of N.Y.; portrait of Cardinals Hayes, Met. Museum of Art. Modeled the late Emperor Charles 4th of Austria; executed bronze memorial of Dr. Alfred E. Hess for Nat. Acad. of Medicine, Washington Irving, Walt Whitman and Robert Fulton memorials, bronze memorial Prof. William Hallock Park, Health Dept. New York; marble portrait of St. Stephen, King of Hungary for Cath. Ch. of St. Stephen, New York; bronze portrait relief of Michael de Kovats, drillmaster of Washington's cavalry, Historical Museum, New York; bust of Senator Robert F. Wagner; bronze portrait of Christae Myron, patriarch Greek Cath. Ch., bronze protrait Dr. Anna Williams; bronze portrait of Prof. Emory Holloway of Queens Coll. of N.Y.; bronze portrait of Countess Szechenyi née Gladys Vanderbilt; bronze portraits of George Kemeny and Arpad Tarnoczy Hungarian poets; bronze portraits of Ella Holloway and Catherine Finta; equestrian statue of General U.S. Grant for Federal Government; Civil War Memorial, Los Angeles; granite statue of Christ, Rio de Janeiro, Brazil; several commemorative medal; bronze medal, Fisk Jubilee Quintet; Prayer; bronze statue for His Royal Highness, Maharaja of Indore; bronze monument of Imre Madach; bronze portraits George Szechkay, Michael Kosztin: bronze meml. Louis Kossuth, Pitts., St. Louis; bronze monument Imre Madach, Cleve.; bronze portrait John Kiss, Hungarian poet, Doctor Louis Kossuth Birini; 25th Anniversary Commemorative Jubilee Medal for Painters and Sculptors Club of Los Angeles; bronze portraits: Dr., Mrs. Wm. G. Rethy, Cornelius Csongradi, Dr. C. H. Albaught, Lida and Stephen Izant; bronze monument Louis Kossuth, Los Angeles; bronze equestrian statue Michael de Kovats, Washington; bronze meml. tablet Agoston Haraszthy, Sonoma, Cal. Awards: Sculptors prize, silver medal and popular vote gold medal, Painters' and Sculptors' Exhibit, Los Angeles, 1941; first prize, gold medal for sculpture, Los Angeles Art Museum Exhibition, 1945; 1st prize for sculpture and Gold Medal, Painters and Sculptors Club, 1947; spl. Jubilee Medal, Ebel Club's Exhbn.; 1st prize for small sculpture, Greek Theater Exhbn., 1947; sculpture prize, 1947; sculpture prize Painters and Sculptors Club of Los Angeles, 1948, 49; sculpture prize, South West Art Assn., 1948, 49. Apptd. expert in art and archaeology by Hungarian Government, 1917. Honorary member Edgar Allan Poe Literary Society of America. Author: Herdboy of Hungary, 1932; Best Short Stories for Children, 1934; The Big Game Hunt (serial) 1936; My Brother and I; Kis Bojtar; Sanko, serially in Tarogato Mag., 1941-43; A Nagy-Majom Titka (published in Hungary), 1950. Epic poems; Ki Vagy?, the Wondervoiced Colt's Bell; two vols. of Lyric Poems; epic poem Attila. Contbr. mags. Lecturer. Home: 2823 S. Hobart Blvd., Los Angeles 18. Died Aug. 3, 1958; buried Inglewood (Cal.) Park Cemetery.

FIPPIN, Elmer Otterbein, agronomist; b. Columbus, O., Sept. 18, 1879; s. John and Sidney A. (Holt) F.; B.Sc. in Agr., Ohio State U., 1900; postgrad. Cornell U., 1904; m. Florence E. Postle, Nov. 21, 1901; children—Walter Russell, Robert Allen (dec.), William Howard, James Elmer (dec.), Julia Anne, Elizabeth Carol. Asst. in soil survey U.S. Bur. Soils, 1900-04; asst. prof., prof. soil technology Cornell U., 1905-19; dir. agrl. dept. Nat. Lime Assn., 1920, gen. mgr., 1921-22; cons. practice, Washington, 1923-24; dir. agrl. expt. stas., Republic of Haiti, 1924-26; exec. sec. and treas. State Conservation and Development Commn. of Va., 1926-30; N.E. rep. Fed. Farm Bd., 1931-32; economist A.A.A., 1933-34; agrl. adviser TVA, 1935-47, ret. Fellow A.A.A.S.; charter mem. Am. Soc. Agronomy; mem. Soil Science Soc. Am., Am. Farm Mgmt. Assn., Alpha Zeta. Author: Rural New York, 1921; First Principles of Cooperation in Buying and Selling in Agriculture, 1934; (with T. L. Lyon) Principles of Soil Management, 1909, Soils—Their Properties and Management, 1914; also five chapters on soils in Farmers' Handbooks of Knowledge, and various articles and repts. Home: 223 E. 6th Av., Fountain City, Tenn. Died Dec. 26, 1949.

FIRESTONE, Clark Barnaby, journalist, author; b. Lisbon, O., Sept. 10, 1869; s. Solomon Jefferson and Anna Elizabeth (Williams) F.;A.B., Oberlin Coll., 1891, honorary M.A., 1901; honorary LL.D., Oberlin College, 1951; married Beatrice Sturges, 1906; children—Laurence S., Robert B., Lorraine, Richard L. Reporter N.Y. Mail and Express, 1892-99, chief editorial writer, 1899-1901 and 1903-11, London corr., 1901-02; editorial writer N.Y. World, 1911-12; pres. Firestone Bank Lisbon, O., 1912-14, dir., 1912—; govt. World War historian, 1919-20; editorial writer Cincinnati Times-Star, 1921-30, asso. editor, 1930-54. Served as Liberty Loan chmn. Columbiana County, O., 1917-18. Pioneer in promoting building of Lincoln Highway. Recipient Sachs Award, Cin. Inst. Fine Arts, 1953. Republican. Clubs: Literary, Classical Round Table (Cincinnati). Author: Army Ordnance Districts—1918-19 (govt. publ.), 1920; The Coasts of Illusion, 1924; Enter Pauline (libretto), 1929; Sycamore Shores, 1936; The Winding Road (verse), 1937; Bubbling Waters, 1938; Journey to Japan, 1940; Flowing South, 1941; Tower Window, 1949; The Yesterdays (verse), 1953. Home: 3543 Zumstein Av., Cin. Died June 3, 1957; buried Spring Grove Cemetery, Cin.

FISCHER, Karl, R.R. ofcl.; b. Quincy, Ill., June 18, 1883; s. John and Nora (Eagen) F.; attended pub. schs. in Quincy and night school in St. Louis; m. Eva Pearl Robison, Feb. 7, 1915; 1 dau., Annabelle (Mrs. DeWitt Clifton Mullen). Began as timekeeper, C., B.&Q. R.R., 1909, successively tourists car conductor, depot passenger agt., city ticket agt., loading insp., gen. mgr. staff, asst. trainmaster, trainmaster, to 1921; transportation insp., supt. transportation staff, 1921-24; insp. transportation, gen. mgr. staff, 1924-25; asst. supt., 1925-29, supt., 1929-31; supt. relief and employment dept., chmn. pension bd., Chgo., 1934-35; land and tax commr., Chgo., 1935-42; on leave for spl. govt. service in Washington, 1940-42; asst. to pres. Burlington Lines, 1942-47, v.p. exec. dept. 1947—; dept. since 1947; dir. Mercantile Nat. Bank. Episcopalian. Clubs: Executives, Traffic (Chgo.). Home: 7649 N. Eastlake Terrace, Chgo. Died Nov. 23, 1950.

FISCHLER, Peter K. (fish-ler), naval officer; b. Wellsboro, Pa., Sept. 10, 1895; s. Peter and Lillie (Sticklin) F.; B.S., U.S. Naval Acad., 1917; m. Rachel Elizabeth Moore, Nov. 9, 1918; children—Louise Frances (Mrs. David Robert Dieffenbacher), Betty Jane (wife of 1st Lt. Walter Stanley Mattox), Patricia Ann. Commd. ensign USN, 1917, advanced through grades to rear adm., 1943; comdr. U.S.S. Meredith, Breckenridge, Bell, Robinson, Putnam, Preble, Farragut, Alaska; insp. Naval Reserve, Detroit, 1919-39; asst. chief of staff, Comdr. Service Force, Atlantic Fleet, 1941-42; operations officer, staff of comdr.-in-chief U.S. Fleet, 1942-44; comdr. battleship div., 1945; asst. chief of staff, staff of comdr.-in-chief Pacific Fleet, 1945-46; dep. comdr. 19th fleet, 1946-47; comdr. amphibious training command Pacific Fleet, 1947; comdr., amphibious group 1, Pacific Fleet, 1948—. Decorated Bronze Star, Legion of Merit, 2 commendation ribbons, Victory medals (World Wars I and II). 2d Nicaraguan campaign, Yangtze service medals, Navy Expeditionary medal, Am. Defense medal with fleet clasp, Asiatic-Pacific Theatre ribbon with stars, Philippine Liberation medal. Home: 145 E St., Coronado, Cal. Died July 14, 1950.

FISH, Alfred Lawrence, lawyer; b. Somerville, Mass., Nov. 20, 1877; s. Herbert F. and Lillian M. (Higgins) F.; A.B., Harvard, 1899, LL.B., 1906; student U. Chicago, 1899-1900; m. Helen Dennis Cole, June 30, 1903 (dec. Dec. 23, 1933); m. 2d, Grace Lillian Phillips, June 24, 1936. Admitted to Mass. bar, 1906; asst. economics Harvard, 1900-01; asso. Brandeis, Dunbar & Nutter, 1906-10, mem., 1910-16; mem. Dunbar, Nutter & McClennen, 1916-29, Nutter, McClennen & Fish, since 1929 (all Boston). Mem. Am., Mass. State, Middlesex Co., Boston bar assns. Clubs: Harvard, Union, Marshfield Country (Boston). Home: 68 Beacon St., Boston 8. Office: 75 Federal St., Boston 10. Died July 23, 1955; buried Marshfield Hills, Mass.

FISHBURN, Junius Blair, banker, publisher; b. Boone Mill, Va., Sept. 27, 1865; s. James Addison and Mary Louise (Boon) F.; ed. high schs. Danville, Ky., and Roanoke, Va.; Dr. Commercial Science, Washington and Lee U., 1941; m. Grace T. Parker, Sept. 5, 1893; children—Junius Parker, Mary Evelyn (Mrs. George Scott Shackelford, Jr.), Ernest Louise (Mrs. Louise F. Fowlkes). Cashier National Exchange Bank of Roanoke, Va., 1889-1806, president, 1906-19, chairman board, 1919-25; chairman board and executive committee First National Exchange Bank, Roanoke, 1925—; v.p. Times World Corp. Received Algernon Sydney Sullivan award from Coll. of William and Mary, 1937. Mem. English-Speaking Union, Am. Acad. Polit. and Social Science, Va. Mus. of Fine Arts; life mem. Va. Hist. Soc., Hist. Soc. of Pa., New England Hist. and Geneal. Soc., Wis. History Soc. National Geog. Soc. Democrat. Mem. M.E. Ch., South (trustee). Clubs: Shenandoah, Roanoke Country (Roanoke). Home: 714 13th St. S.W. Office: Times Bldg., Roanoke, Va. Died Apr. 1, 1955; buried Roanoke.

FISHBURN, Junius Parker, pub., editor; b. Roanoke, Va., Sept. 30, 1895; s. Junius Blair and Grace (Parker) F.; grad. Mercersburg (Pa.) Acad., 1914; Litt.D., Princeton, 1919; A.M., Columbia, 1923; D.C.S., Washington and Lee, 1936; m. Katherine Rodes Nelson, January 14, 1926; children—Sally Hart, Robert Nelson. Vice president Times-World Corp. (The Roanoke Times, The Roanoke World-News, Radio Station WDBJ), 1919-23, pres. since 1923; dir. First Nat. Exchange Bk. of Roanoke; dir. Fed. Reserve Bk. of Richmond, 1928-31; dir. Norfolk & Western Ry. Co., Old Dominion Fire Ins. Co., Chesapeake & Potomac Telephone Co. of Va.; chmn. board of governors Nation's Business, 1931-34. Chief petty officer, later ensign U.S.N.R., 1917, ensign U.S. Navy, 1918. Former mem. State Conservation and Development Commission, Virginia State Chamber Commerce (pres. 1926-29), Roanoke Chamber Commerce; dir. Chamber of Commerce of U.S., 1930, v.p., 1931-34. Mem. bd. of regents Mercersburg Acad.; trustee Hollins College. Mem. Am. Newspaper Pubs' Assn., Am. Soc. Newspaper Editors, Southern Newspaper Publishers' Assn., Am. Hist. Assn., Am. Econ. Assn., Am. Assn. Polit. Science, Phi Beta Kappa. Democrat. Presbyterian. Clubs: Rotary (pres., 1929-30), Shenandoah, Roanoke Country (Roanoke); Press (Washington); Princeton, University (New York). Home: 2731 S. Jefferson St. Office: Times Bldg., Roanoke, Va. Died Mar. 24, 1954.

FISHER, Alphonse Louis, clergyman, educator; b. Newport, Ky., Jan. 27, 1886; s. Edward and Josephine Mary (Pfirman) F.; A.B., St. Louis U., 1912, A.M., 1914; post grad. work, 1919-23; studied canon law, St. Stanislaus Sem., Cleveland,O., 1923-24. Joined Soc. of Jesus (Jesuits), 1907; instr. in English St. Mary's (Kan.) Coll., 1914-16, Xavier U., Cincinnati, 1916-18; ordained priest R.C. Ch., 1921; dir. Elet Hall, Xavier U., 1924-27; regent Sch. of Commerce and Coll. of Law, same univ., since 1927. Pub. speaker and lecturer on psychology and sociology. Mem. bd. trustees Xavier U. Home: 635 Sycamore St., Cin. Died Dec. 1, 1951.

FISHER, Anna, artist; b. Cold Brook, N.Y.; d. John H. and Rachel (Heifer) Fisher; ed. Fairfield (N.Y.) Sem.; grad. Pratt Inst., Brooklyn. Instr. art dept., Pratt Inst. Awarded Agar prize, Nat. Women Painters' and Sculptors Assn., 1918; Harriet Brooks Jones prize, Balt. Water Color Club, 1920, 1924; Hudnut prize, N.Y. Water Color Club, 1921; Joseph Isador prize (N.Y. Water Color Soc. and Am. Water Color Soc.), 1927; Harold Swift prize, Grand Central Art Galleries, 1930; Nat. Arts Club prize, 1932; "Reflections," purchased by people of Montclair for Montclair (N.J.) Mus.; "White Hollyhocks," Nat. Arts Club; "Venetian Glass and White Roses," Sci. and Arts Dept. of Pratt Inst., Bklyn.; "White Roses," Bklyn. Mus.; "Orchids," Womnen's Club of N.J., etc. Mem. bd. Louis Comfort Tiffany Found. A.N.A., 1920, N.A., 1932; mem. Am. Water Color Soc., Nat. Women Painters' and Sculptors' Assn., N.Y. Water Color Club, Allied Artists of N.Y. C., League of N.Y. Artists, N.Y. Soc. Painters Nat. Arts Club (life). Home: 939 8th Av., N.YC. Died 1942.*

FISHER, Ben S., lawyer; b. Anderson, Ind., June 13, 1890; s. Thomas C. and Elizabeth N. (Craig) F.; LL.B., U. Ill., 1914; m. Kate S. Chatburn, Dec. 25, 1920; children—Ben C., Nancy C. Admitted to Ore. bar, practiced in Coos Bay, 1914-30; dist. atty. Coos County, Ore., 1920-24; asst. gen. counsel Federal Radio Commn., Washington, 1930-35; atty. specializing in radio, 1935—. Served with 11th Co., Ore. N.G.; 1st lt., CAC, 1918; capt. Ore. N.G., 1920. Mem. Am. (chmn. communications com.), Dist. (dir.) bar assns., Communication Bar (pres. 1945), Am. Legion (state comdr. Ore., 1928, nat. committeeman 1929), Phi Delta Phi, Alpha Delta Sigma, Sigma Chi (v.p. Sigma Chi Found.; grand consul 1943-45; chmn. bd. trustees 1943). Republican. Presbyn. Elk (state pres. Ore. 1925). Mason (Shriner). Clubs: Coos Country (Coos Bay), Columbia Country; National Press, University (Washington). Home: 1837 Plymouth St. N.W. Office: Perpetual Bldg., Washington. Died Sept. 30, 1953; buried Washington.

FISHER, Bud (H. C. Fisher), cartoonist; b. Ill., Apr. 3, 1884; s. Albert A. and Nellie G. (Morse) F.; student Hyde Park High Sch., Chgo., U. Chgo.; m. Countess Adeita de Beaumont, 1924 (legal separation Feb. 8, 1927). Began as cartoonist in San Francisco, 1905; creator of the daily comic in newspapers; creator of Mutt and Jeff. The first cartoonist to syndicate his own work on a large scale; also appears in moving pictures, and in vaudeville personally. Author: Mutt and Jeff Cartoons, Book I, 1910, Book II, 1911, Book III, 1913, Book IV, 1915, Book V 1916. Commd. lt. F.A., Nat. Army. Aug. 27, 1917, resigned Feb. 1918. Died Sept. 7, 1954.*

FISHER, Charles Thomas, Jr., banker; b. Detroit, Mich., Feb. 14, 1907; s. Charles Thomas and Sarah Wilhelmina (Kramer) F.; B.S., Georgetown U., Washington, D.C., 1928, LL.D., 1939; m. Elizabeth J. Briggs, Feb. 2, 1929; children—Charles Thomas III, Mary Elizabeth, Jane Briggs, Frederick John II, Walter Briggs, Sarah Wilhelmina, John Allen. Pres. and dir. Nat. Bank of Detroit; dir. Detroit Edison Co., Briggs Mfg. Co., Am. Airlines, Inc., Cunningham Drug Stores, Inc., Mich. Bell Telephone Co., General Motors Corp., Am. Broadcasting Paramount Theatres, Inc., Federal Home Loan Bank of Indianapolis Nat. Steel Corp. Vice chmn. Mackinac Bridge Authority; mem. bus. adv. council Dept. of Commerce; civilian aide to sec. of army for Mich. Trustee Committee for Economic Development; asso. bd. lay trustees, finance com. U. Notre Dame. Republican. Catholic. Home: 5 Lake Ct., Grosse Pointe, Mich. Office: R.P.A. Box 116, Detroit 32. Died Apr. 14, 1958; buried Holy Sepulchre Cemetery.

FISHER, Dorothy Canfield (Dorothea Frances Canfield Fisher), author; b. Lawrence, Kan., Feb. 17, 1879; d. late James Hulme and Flavia (Camp) Canfield; Ph.B., Ohio State U., 1899; Ph.D., Columbia, 1904; D. Litt., Middlebury Coll., Vt., 1921, Dartmouth College 1922, U. of Vermont, 1922, Columbia, 1929 Ohio State University, 1935, Northwestern University, 1931, Williams College, 1935, University of Nebraska, 1937, Swarthmore College; married John Redwood Fisher, May 9, 1907; children—Sarah, James. Sec. Horace Mann Sch., 1902-05. Studied and traveled extensively in Europe; acquired several langs. in childhood. Three years in France doing war work. Mem. Nat. Inst. of Arts and Letters. Mem. State Bd. of Edn., Vt.; 1921-23. Author: Corneille and Racine in England, 1904; English Rhetoric and Composition (with G. R. Carpenter), 1906; What Shall we Do Now? (with others), 1906; Gunhild, 1907; The Squirrel-Cage, 1912; The Montessori Mother (also trans. into French, German and Danish), 1913; Mothers and Children (trans. into French and Dutch), 1914; Hillsboro People, 1915; The Bent Twig (appeared serially in France and Norway), 1915; The Real Motive, 1916; Fellow-Captains (with S. L. Cleghorn), 1916; Understood Betsy (trans. French, Norweigan, German), 1917; Home-Fires in France, 1918; The Day of Glory, 1919; The Brimming Cup (trans. into Swedish), 1921; Rough Hewn, 1922; Raw Material, 1923; The Home-Maker, 1924; Made-to-Order Stories (translated into German), 1925; Her Son's Wife, 1926 (translated into Italian, 1953); Why Stop Learning?, 1927; The Deepening Stream, 1930; Basque People, 1931; Bonfire, 1933 (translated into Norwegian); Fables for Parents, 1937; Seasoned Timber, 1939; Tell Me a Story, 1940; Nothing Ever Happens, 1940; Our Young Folks, 1943; American Portraits, 1946; Four Square, 1949; Something Old, Something New, 1949; Paul Revere and the Minute Men, 1950; Independence and the Constitution, 1950; A Fair World For All, 1952; Vermont Tradition: The Biography of an Outlook On Life, 1953; A Harvest of Stories, 1956; Memories of Arlington, Vermont, 1957. Translated Papini's "Christ" from the Italian, 1921, also translated Tilgher's "Work." 1930. Work in numerous anthologies. Contbr. short stories to mags. as Dorothy Canfield. Home: Arlington, Vt. Died Nov. 9, 1958; buried Churchyard of St. James Church, Arlington, Vt.

FISHER, Dorsey Gassaway, ex-fgn. service officer; b. Ft. Leavenworth, Kan., Feb. 12, 1907; s. Ronald E. and Ellen (Gassaway) F.; student U. Wash., 1923-25; A.B., Harvard, 1927, A.M., 1928. Apptd. fgn. service officer U.S. Dept. of State, 1929, vice consul, Calcutta, 1929-32, Havana, 1933-34, 3d sec. legation, San Salvador, 1935-37; assigned press office Dept. State, 1937-41, asst. chief div. current information, 1940-41; 2d and 1st sec. Embassy, London, 1941-46, asst. press officer UN Conf., San Francisco, 1945; mem. U.S. del. to 1st UN meetings, London, 1945-46; 1st sec. Embassy and pub. affairs officer, Mexico, 1947-50; 1st sec. Embassy, and pub. affairs officer, Madrid, 1951-52; resigned 1953. Mem. U.S. del. to 2d UNESCO Conf., Mexico, 1947. Mem. Soc. Cincinnati. Episcopalian. Club: Harvard of Mexico (pres. 1950) Died 1954.

FISHER, Franklin L., illustrations editor; b. Horseheads, N.Y., Aug. 24, 1885; s. Augustus H. and Emily Jane (Garlick) F.; ed. grammar sch. and high sch., Horseheads; m. Ami Dimond, Oct. 22, 1910. Engaged in supplying news and feature photographs to newspapers and mags., N.Y. City, 1907-10; founder, and mgr. 1910-15. Harris & Ewing News Photograph Service, Washington, D.C.; chief of illustrations div. National Geog. Mag. since 1915. Life trustee Nat. Geog. Soc. since May 1945. Served as lt. comdr. U.S. Navy. Mem. U.S. Naval Inst., Nat. Geog. Soc., Photographic Soc. America, White House

News Photographers Assn., Res. Officers Assn. of U.S. Clubs: Nat. Press, Overseas Writers, Cosmos, Chevy Chase; Elmira (N.Y.) Golf and Country, Elmira City. Home: 2101 Connecticut Av. N.W. Office: 1146 16th St. N.W., Washington. Died Aug. 12, 1953.

FISHER, Galen Merriam, social research; b. Oakland, Calif., Apr. 12, 1873; s. Galen Merriam and Susan (Talcott) F.; B. Litt., U. of Calif., 1896; M.A. Harvard, 1905; D.D., Pacific School of Religion, 1945; studied at Columbia U., 1913-14, and 1920-22; m. Ella L. Wilcox, June 5, 1900 (died July 21, 1947); children—Galen Merriam (dec.), Gerald Wilcox, Eleanor Talcott, Ralph Hart; m. 2d, Jessie Willis Brockman, Sept. 1, 1948. Student sec. Boston Y.M.C.A., 1896-97; sec., Japan, Internat. Com. Y.M.C.A., 1897-1919, sr. sec., 1900-19; asso. exec. sec. Rockefeller Inst. Social and Religious Research, 1921-22; exec. sec. of same, 1923-34; gen. dir. of research in India, China and Japan for Laymen's Foreign Missions Inquiry, 1930-31; director studies of Springfield Internat. Y.M.C.A. Coll. 1935, Pacific Sch. of Religion, 1938, So. Calif. Congl. Chs., 1941; cons. Office Strategic Services, Washington, D.C., lecturer Civil Affairs Training Sch., Stanford U., 1944; acting pres. Pacific School of Religion, 1945. Co-founder Com. on Am. Principles of Fair Play, 1941-45. Trustee Inst. of Pacific Relations; mem. nat. council and internat. bd. Y.M.C.A., Internat. War. Prisoners Aid Soc., 1940-46. Chmn. bd. trustees Pacific Sch. of Religion; trustee World Affairs Council No. Calif. Mem. Am. Sociol. Soc., Beta Theta Pi. Progressive Rep. Conglist. Author: Creative Forces in Japan, 1923; Public Affairs and Y.M.C.A.'s since 1844, 1948; articles on Japanese evacuation. Co-author: Undergraduates (with R. H. Edwards); 1928; Catholics, Jews and Protestants (with C. E. Silcox), 1934. Editor of Religion in American Colleges, 1928. Contbg. editor: Dictionary of Sociology, 1944. Translator; Philosophical Problems (by H. Höffding), 1905. Collaborator on Fact Finding Reports of Research Staff for Laymen's F.M. Inquiry, 4 volumes, 1933. Home: 850 Cragmont Av., Berkeley 8, Cal. Died Jan. 2, 1955; buried Mountain View Columbarium, Oakland, Cal.

FISHER, Gordon, mfr. welded tubular products; b. Swissvale, Pa., Nov. 2, 1874; s. Rev. Samuel J. (D.D.) and Annie (Shreve) F.; B.A., Princeton, 1895; LL.B., N.Y. Law Sch.. 1897; m. Matilda C. Milligan, July 6, 1901; children—Gordon, John M. Began practice with Dalzell, Scott and Gordon, Pitts. 1898, admitted to firm, 1906, under title of Dalzell, Fisher & Dalzell, and continued to practice until 1929; pres. Spang, Chalfant & Co., Inc., mfrs. seamless and welded tubular products, 1927-30, chmn. bd. 1930—; dir. First Nat. Bank (Etna, Pa.), Nat. Supply Co. (Pitts.). Formerly lectr. on med. law, U. Pitts. Pres. Allegheny Gen. Hosp., Pitts. Republican. Presbyn. Mason (32°, Shriner). Clubs: Duquesne, Pittsburgh Golf, Fox Chapel Golf. Home: 4 Colonial Place. Office: Grant Bldg., Pitts. Died Dec. 14. 1945.*

FISHER, Haldane S., chmn. bd., past pres. Emporium Capewell Co. Home: 1000 Mason St. Office: 835 Market St., San Francisco. Died Apr. 28, 1953.*

FISHER, Hammond Edward ("Ham"), cartoonist; b. Wilkes-Barre, Pa., Sept. 24, 1900; s. Edward John and Sadie (Breakstone) F.; grad. Wilkes-Barre High Sch.; self educated in art; 1 dau., Wendy. Became successively, cartoonist Wilkes-Barre Record, Wilkes-Barre Leader, cartoonist, columnist and contbr. to mags. pub. Wilkes-Barre Pictorial; advt. man with N.Y. Daily News, 1927-28; started cartoon, Joe Palooka, for McNaught Syndicate, 1930 now syndicated to 955 newspapers; v.p. Lancaster & Chester R.R.; dir. Am. Title & Mortgage Co., Miami, Fla. Mem. Writer's War Board. Member Society of Illustrators, Artists, Writers and Board of Cartoonists Soc. Am. Legion, Amvets, YMCA, Christian Athletes Fund. Clubs: Kiwanis, Cowboys Turtle Assn. Served as war corr. World War II; also in special work for Army, Navy and Office of War Information; broadcaster to overseas troops; contbr. to Stars and Stripes and camp papers. Awarded citations by Navy, Air, War Dept. and State of Pa. Mt. Joe Palooka, Pa.; statue to Joe Palooka, Bedford, Ind. Author: Boxing; Joe Palooka of War; (monthly comic books) Joe Palooka, Humphrey Pennyworth; (radio program) Joe Palooka (Columbia network); 1943; Hill-Billy Comics and books; Little Max and Humphrey Pennyworth. Joe Palooka pictures featured by United Artists, also shorts by Warner Brothers, 1935-37; TV Joe Palooka Story National Syndicated; writer motion pictures for Monogram Pictures Corp. Lecturer. Awarded hon. doctor degree Hamilton Coll. Home: 20 E. 74 St., N.Y.C. Died Dec. 27, 1955.

FISHER, James Blaine, mfg. exec.; born Johnstown, O., Jan. 28, 1884; s. Melancthon and Jenny (Leonard) F.; student pub. schs., Alliance, O.; m. Emily Anderson, June 2, 1914; children—Virginia (Mrs. Edward Doherty), Clark, Gordon. Clerk, Am. Steel foundries, Alliance, 1901-04; shop apprentice Alliance Machine Co.. 1904-08; draftsman Federal Steel Co., Waukesha, Wis., 1909-14; chief engr. Waukesha Motor Co., internal combustion engines, 1914-49, vice president, 1935-49, director since 1935,

cons. engineer since 1949. Served on war adv. com. Ordnance Dept., World War II. Mem. Soc. Automotive Engrs., Am. Soc. for Testing Materials, Am. Petroleum Inst., Am. Soc. Agrl. Engrs., Soc. Am. Mil. Engrs. Republican. Methodist. Club: City (Milwaukee). Home: Route 6, Waukesha, Wis. Died Apr. 8, 1953.

FISHER, John Wesley, agrl. dir., b. Evergreen, La., Aug. 1, 1907; s. Willie Lester and Mary (Simpson) F.; B.S. in agr., Southern U., Baton Rouge, Ia., 1932; M.S. in vocational agr., Ia. State Coll., 1938; grad. student, U. of Ill.; m. Deborah Eva Shackelford, June 4. Instr. horticulture, Southern U., 1932-38, asst. dir. agr., 1938-39, dir. agr., 1939—, prof. agr. Assisted in organizing La. Interscholastic Athletic and Literary Assn., to promote better conditions in public schools for Negroes, 1938; chmn. exec. com. Troup 43, Boy Scouts of Am.; chmn. Univ. Red Cross, March of Dimes drives; consultant, state farmers' orgns. Hon. Modern Farmer Degree, New Farmers of Am. Democrat. Baptist. Mem. Am. Hort. Soc., Nat., La. edn. assns., Rural Sociological Society, Phi Beta Sigma, Beta Kappa Chi, Alpha Phi Omega, Alpha Tau Alpha (charter member). Mason. Author: Year Around Vegetable Gardening in Louisiana, 1938. Address: Southern University, Southern Branch P.O., Baton Rouge 5. Died Apr. 8, 1956.

FISHER, Russell Todd, assn. exec.; b. Gloucester, Mass., July 3, 1892; s. William F. and Anne (Todd) F.; student Worcester Poly. Inst., 1910-11; B.T.E., Lowell Textile Inst., 1925; m. Patricia Webb, Mar. 17, 1920; children—Anne Wilmouth. Patricia Webb, Willa Todd. In employ Marshall Field & Co., N.Y.C., 1914-17; asst. chief textile sect. Bur. Standards, Washington, 1917-22; tech. sec. Nat. Assn. Cotton Mfrs., 1922-25, sec., 1926-36, pres., 1936——. Mem. Nat. Safety Council, Am. Soc. Testing Materials, Q.M. Assn., Boston Trade Assn. Execs. Served as capt. U.S. Army. Republican. Conglist. Club: University (Washington). Home: 121 Summit Av., Wollaston, Mass. Office: 80 Federal St., Boston. Died Apr. 24, 1951.

FISK, Louisa Holman Richardson (Mrs. Everett O. Fisk); b. Prince Edward Island, Can., Mar. 1, 1861; d. James and Martha (West) Holman; adopted in childhood by uncle and aunt, Mr. and Mrs. George W. Richardson, of Winchester, Mass.; A.B., Boston University, 1883, A.M., 1887, Ph.D., 1891, L.H.D. (honorary), 1941; student Newnham College, Cambridge, England, 1890-91; holder of first European fellowship Association Collegiate Alumnae; traveled in Europe, 1895, 1900; married Everett Olin Fisk, June 6, 1915. Teacher Greek and Latin, Lasell; Auburndale, Massachusetts, 1883-85; Professor Latin, Carleton Coll., Northfield, Minn., 1885-1902; asso. dean of women and prof. history of art, Ohio Wesleyan U., Delaware, 1902-04; gen. and exec. sec. Brit.-Am. Y.W.C.A., and Student Union, Paris, France, 1904-14; mem. Nat. Com. Y.W.C.A. of France, 1907-14; dean of women and prof. Latin, Olivet (Mich.) Coll., 1914-15; now v.p. and treas. Fisk Teachers' Agencies, Boston. Hon. pres. Boston Univ. Women's Council, 1925—; president Mass. Society for University Education of Women, 1930-33, vice-pres., 1924——; was member board managers Deaconess Assn., Boston Y. W.C.A.; mem. Waldernsian Aid Society of Boston (dir.), Florence Crittenden League of Compassion (executive committee), Phi Beta Kappa. Mem. Ecumenical Conf. of Methodism, Atlanta, 1931. Pres. Boston Br. of Am. Assn. of University Women, 1919-23; president Woman's Graduates' Club of Boston University, 1922-23; member Academy of Political Sciences; trustee Boston U., 1922——. Methodist. Clubs: College, Professional Women's, Women's Republican. Women's City (Boston); Twentieth Century. Speaker on missionary and ednl. topics. Made tour around world studying missions, 1936-37, six months in India. Home: 135 Winthrop Rd., Brookline, Mass.; (summer) Barter's Island, Trevett, Me. Address: 120 Boylston St., Boston, Mass. Died Mar. 18, 1955; buried Dell Park Cemetery, Natick, Mass.

FISKE, Adam Hastings, pharm. mfr.; b. Wrightsville, Pa., Sept. 27, 1894; s. Paul E. and Edith (Nace) F.; Pharm.D., Phila. Coll. Pharmacy and Sci., 1916. D.Sc. (hon.), 1956; m. Ethel Durno, Mar. 1, 1921. Instr. Phila. Coll. Pharmacy and Sci., 1916-17; with Eli Lilly & Co., 1919——, v.p., 1945—, dir., 1947——. Trustee Phila. Coll. Pharmacy and Sci., Health, News Inst. 2d lt., A.S., U.S. Army, 1917-19. Mem. World Med. Assn. (bd.), Am. Pharm. Assn., N.Y. Acad. Sci., A.I.M., C. of C., Am. Legion. Mason. Home: 6360 Around the Hills Rd., Indpls. Office: 740 S. Alabama St., Indpls. 6. Died Aug. 25, 1959.

FITCH, Florence Mary, educator; b. Stratford, Conn., Feb. 17, 1875; d. Rev. Frank S. and Anna Eliza (Haskell) F.; A.B., Oberlin Coll., 1897; U. Munich, 1901; A.M., Ph.D., U. Berlin, 1903; Litt. D., Oberlin Coll. 1947. Tchr. Masten Park High Sch., Buffalo, 1897-1900; sec. to pres., instr. philosophy Oberlin Coll., 1903-04, dean of coll. women, 1904-20, prof. philosophy, 1904-11, prof. Bibl. lit. 1911-40, prof. emeritus, 1940——. Conglist. Author: The Daughter of Abd Salam; One God: The Way We Worship Him; Their Search for God: Ways of Worship in the

Orient; Allah, The God of Islam; A Book About God; The Child Jesus; The Boyhood of Jesus (pub. posthumously). Home: 97 Elm St., Oberlin, O. Died June 2, 1959; buried Buffalo.

FITCH, John Andrews; b. Cumberland, Wis., Apr. 20, 1881; s. Edwin P. and Elizabeth (Powers) F.; B.A., Yankton Coll., 1904, LL.D., 1929; grad. study U. Wis., 1906-07, fellow in econs., 1908-09; m. Florence Lee, Sept. 1, 1909; children—Faith Lee (Mrs. Benjamin J. Hill), Jean Andrews (Mrs. John L. Rockwell). Instr. Weeping Water (Neb.) Acad., 1904-06; mem. staff Pitts. Survey, 1907-08; expert N.Y. State Dept. Labor, 1909-10; editor industry dept. The Survey, N.Y.C., 1911-19; mem. faculty N.Y. Sch. Social Work, Columbia, 1917-46, prof., 1940-46, now emeritus; lectr. econs. Columbia, 1924-26, 36-39, lectr. sch. bus., 1947-48, 53-54; lectr. New Sch. for Social Research, 1950-51; extension div. N.Y. State Sch. Indsl. and Labor Relations, Cornell; dir. study of trade unions under auspices Nat. Council Chs. Christ in U.S., 1947-55. Mem. Nat. Ry. Labor Panel, 1942-47; mem. pub. panel Nat. War Labor Bd., Region 2, N.Y., 1943-45. Mem. Am. Econ. Assn., Acad. Polit. Sci., Nat. Conf. Social Work, Am. Acad. Arbitrators, Indsl. Relations Research Assn. Author: The Steel Workers, 1911; The Causes of Industrial Unrest, 1924; Capital and Labor, 1929; Vocational Guidance in Action, 1935; The Social Responsibilities of Labor Organizations, 1957. Home: 39 Claremont Av., N.Y.C. 27. Died June 1959.

FITCH, Rachel Louise, research; b. Galva, Ill., Sept. 27, 1878; d. Elmer Eli and Rachel (Helgesen) Fitch; A.B., Knox Coll., 1902, A.M., 1911, Litt.D. (hon.), 1932; grad. work U. Cal., 1914-15, U. Ore., 1921. Tchr. Ill., 1895-96, 1902-03, N.D., 1898-99; editor, mgr. Galva (Ill.) Weekly News, 1906-08; editor, mgr. Trident of Delta Delta Delta, 1905-15; librarian Cambridge (Ill.) Pub. Library, 1911-14; speaker Chautauqua Circuit, 1918-19; editor Jour. Am. Assn. Univ. Women, 1922-23; dean women, Whitman Coll., 1924-26; dean women, Cornell U., Ithaca, N.Y., 1926-41; sponsored by Reader's Digest to make study of and lecture on Old Age, 1945-47; research and lectr. on Gerontology, 1947—. Spl. reporter for Y.W.C.A. in France, 1918. Mem. Hoover's Com. on Food for Small Democracies. Fellow Allied Scientists of World; mem. Am. Guild Organists, Gerontol. Soc., Mountaineers, Zonta, League Am. Penwomen (nat. v.p. for Ore. 1924-26), Women's Overseas Service League (nat. recording sec. 1933-35), Am. Forestry Assn., Nat. Council Family Relations, Acad. Polit. Scis., Conf. on Aging, Bus. and Profl. Women, Assn. Social Workers, Am. Sociol. Soc., Oldsters Club, Inc., English Speaking Union, D.A.R., Grandmother's Club (hon.), Mortar Bd., Delta Delta Delta (nat. v.p. 1904-05; nat. editor 1905-15; nat. pres. 1915-19; nat. Panhellenic officer 1925-31), Phi Kappa Phi, Pi Lambda Theta, Delta Kappa Gamma, Phi Beta. Republican. Author: Madame France, 1918. Publisher of A Detailed Record of Delta Delta Delta, 1907. Contbr. articles on Coeducation and Sororities to Ency. Brit. As first vis. officer for coll. sorority visited 130 Colls.; now condr. research, and lect. old age; speaker before clubs, etc. Address: 511 N. C St., Tacoma. Deceased.

FITE, Emerson David, educator; b. Marion, O., Mar. 3, 1874; s. Lemuel and Louisa (Smiley) F.; student Hillsdale (Mich.) Coll., 1892-94; A.B., Yale, 1897; Ph.D., Harvard, 1905; m. Alice Louise Nye, Sept. 1, 1904; children—Katherine Boardman, Marcia. Tchr. Latin and history Mt. Hermon (Mass.) Sch., 1897-1901; Austin teaching fellow Harvard, 1904-06; instr. history Yale, 1906-09, asst. prof., 1909-13; prof. polit. sci., Vassar Coll., 1913-44, prof. emeritus, 1944—. Mem. N.Y. State Assembly, 1934-43. Mem. Phi Beta Kappa. Republican. Episcopalian. Author: Social and Industrial Conditions in the North During the Civil War, 1910; The Presidential Campaign of 1860, 1911; History of the United States, 1916; The United States, 1923, (with Archibald Freeman) A Book of Old Maps, 1926; Government by Cooperation, 1932. Home: 112 Market St., Poughkeepsie, N.Y. Died May 10, 1953; buried Poughkeepsie Rural Cemetery.

FITE, Warner, college prof.; b. Philadelphia, Mar. 5, 1867; s. George and Sallie Gibbs (Liddle) F.; A.B., Haverford (Pa.) Coll., 1889; Phila. Div. Sch., 1889-90; post-grad student, univs. of Pa., 1890-91, Berlin, 1891-92, Munich, 1892-93, Pa., 1893-94, Ph. D., 1894; LL.D. (honorary), Haverford College, 1939; married Esther Wallace Sturges, Oak Park, Ill., June 29, 1901 (died Oct. 2, 1916); children—Charles S., George L., Mary D., Franklin K.; m. 2d, Florence Odell, of Chicago, Oct. 10, 1930. Instr. philosophy, 1894-96, and dean of faculty, 1895-97, Williams Coll.; docent, asst., and instr. psychology, U. of Chicago, 1897-1903; instr. philosophy, U. of Tex., 1903-06; jr. prof. philosophy, 1906-08, prof., 1908-15, Ind. U., Bloomington; Stuart prof. ethics, 1915-35, professor emeritus, 1935—, Princeton University. Lecturer in philosophy, Harvard Univ., 1911-12; acting prof. philosophy, Leland Stanford Jr. U., fall semester, 1913. Mem. Am. Philos. Assn., Phi Beta Kappa. Author: Introductory Study of Ethics, 1903; Individualism, 1911; Moral Philosophy—the Critical View of Life, 1925; The Living Mind, 1930; The Platonic Legend, 1934; Jesus, the Man—A Critical Essay, 1943. Translator: Mist ("Niebla"), by Miguel de Unamuno, 1928. Contbr. to mags. Home: Hopewell, N.J. Died June 23, 1955.

FITE, William Benjamin, educator; b. Marion, O., Aug. 23, 1869; s. Lemuel and Louisa (Smiley) F.; Hillsdale (Mich.) Coll., 1888-91; Ph.B., Cornell, 1892, Ph.D., 1901; married 1903. Tchr. mathematics Mich. Mil. Acad., Orchard Lake, 1892-98; instr. mathematics Cornell, 1901-05, asst. prof., 1905-10; became prof. mathematics Columbia, 1910, exec. officer dept., 1928-42, Davies prof. mathematics, 1936-42, Davies prof. emeritus of mathematics, 1942—; vis. prof. mathematics Rollins Coll., 1943-44; Stevens Inst. Tech., spring session 1946. Mem. Am. Math. Soc., Math. Assn. Am., Delta Tau Delta, Sigma Xi. Author: College Algebra and First and Second Courses in Algebra; New First Course in Algebra (with F. J. McMackin), 1928; Advanced Calculus, 1938. Home: 44 Morningside Dr., N.Y.C. 25. Died 1952.

FITTS, William Cochran, lawyer; b. Tuscaloosa, Ala., Jan. 29, 1866; s. Philip A. (D.D.) and Sophia (Cochran) F.; grad. spl. course Southwestern Presbyn. U., Clarksville, Tenn., 1884; B.L., U. Ala., 1886; studied U. Va. Law Dept., summer 1886; LL.D., Southwestern U., Memphis, 1927; m. Eleanor Hewitt, Apr. 23, 1890; children—Mrs. Harriet F. Ryan, Mrs. Holland F. Garner, Eleanor, William C. Practiced at Tuscaloosa, Ala., 1886-1901, Mobile, as mem. Fitts & Leigh, 1901-11, Birmingham, 1911-14, as Harsh & Fitts; spl. asst. to atty. gen. of U.S., 1914-17, asst. atty. gen. of U.S., 1917-19; mem. Mooney, Fitts & Rowe, N.Y.C., 1919—; spl. counsel RFC, 1933—. Atty. gen. of Ala. 2 terms, 1894-98; commr. of endowment U. Ala., 1898-1901; mem. Constl. Conv. of Ala., 1901 Del. Dem. Nat. Conv., 1932. Mem. Alpha Tau Omega. Democrat. Episcopalian. Club: University (Washington). Home: 2320 Ashmead Pl. N.W., Washington. Died Feb. 26, 1954; buried Birmingham, Ala.

FITZ, Reginald, physician; b. Boston, Mass., Feb. 28, 1885; s. Reginald Heber and Elizabeth Loring (Clarke) F.; A.B., Harvard, 1906, M.D., 1909; hon. D.Sc., Western Reserve University, 1943; LL.D. (hon.), Hahnemann Medical Coll., 1947; m. Phoebe Marion Wright, June 29, 1918; children—Phoebe Marion, Reginald Heber, Elizabeth Jean, William Richard Wright, Edith. House officer Mass. General Hosp., 1909-11; vol. asst. Johns Hopkins Med. Clinic, 1911-13; asst. resident physician Peter Bent Brigham Hosp., 1913-15, Rockefeller Inst. Hospital, N.Y.C., 1915-17; staff Mayo Clinic, 1920-22; associate professor medicine Harvard Med. Sch., 1922-36, lecturer in history of medicine since 1936, also assistant dean since 1947; Wade professor of medicine, Boston U., 1936-40; dir. Evans Memorial, 1936-40; clin. asso. Thorndike Memorial Lab., Boston, since 1940; mem. bd. hon. consultants to Army Med. Library (Washington), 1943-52; mem. Nat. Bd. Med. Examiners, 1932-45 and since 1947; chmn. med. adv. bd. No. 13, Selective Service, Boston, 1940-47; med. advisor Boston met. chapter Am. Red Cross. Served as capt. and maj. Med. Corps, U.S. Army, 1917-19. Trustee Perkins Inst. for Blind, 1943-46, pres. since 1946; trustee Brookline Pub. Library, Wellesley Coll., Boston Medical Library; university marshal, Harvard. Mem. Am. Bd. Internal Medicine, 1936-46, chmn., 1944-46. Mem. bd. regents Am. Coll. Physicians, 1939-47, since 1950, 1st v.p., 1947-48, pres., 1949-50; pres. Boston Tuberculosis Assn., 1946-49. Mem. A.M.A. (mem. council med. edn. and hosps. 1929-49), Mass. Heart Association, Mass. Med. Soc. (chmn. com. on med. edn. and diplomas, 1930-40; pres., 1945-46); Suffolk Dist. Med. Soc. (pres. 1938-40), Am. Assn. Hist. Med., Med. Library Assn., Spl. Library Assn., Am. Acad. Arts and Scis., Colonial Soc. Mass. Clubs: Harvard, Tavern (Boston); Century Assn. (New York); Brookline Country. Mem. editorial bd. Archives of Internal Medicine. Home: 56 Walnut Pl., Brookline, Mass. Office: 319 Longwood Av., Boston. Died May 27, 1953.

FITZGERALD, E. Roy, business exec.; b. Staplehurst, Neb., May 29, 1893; s. James Corbett and Catherine Agnes (Ryan) F.; student Mankato (Minn.) Tchrs. Coll., 1907-09; m. Susanne E. Youngblood, July 9, 1941; children—Michael Roy, Barbara Geraldine. Conducted own business, Eveleth, Minn., 1920-25; with Royal Rapid Transit Co., Madison, Wis., 1925-27; pres. Rex Finance Corp., Chgo., Southern Ltd., Inc., Chgo., 1928-36; pres. Nat. City Lines, Inc., Chgo., 1936—, also dir.; pres. Nat. Hotel Enterprises, Inc., Chgo.; chmn. bd St. Louis Pub. Service Co., Los Angeles Transit Lines, Ry. Equipment & Realty Co., Oakland, Cal.; dir. Key System Transit Lines. Clubs: Athletic, Edgewater Golf (Chgo.); Missouri Athletic (St. Louis). Home: Blackstone Hotel, Chgo. Office: Prudential Plaza, Chgo. Died June 15, 1957.

FITZGERALD, John Francis, ex-congressman, exmayor; b. Boston, Feb. 11, 1863; s. Thomas and Rosanna F.; ed. in Eliot Grammar and Boston Latin schs., and short course in Harvard; LL.D., U. Notre Dame, 1915; m. Josephine Mary Hannon, Sept. 18, 1889. Mem. Boston Common Council, 1892; Mass. Senate, 1893-94; mem. 54th to 56th Congresses; mayor of Boston, 1906-07, 10-14; mem. Boston Port Authority, 1934. Dem. candidate for U.S. Senate, 1916, for gov., 1922; pres. Mass. Electoral Coll., 1933; press. Electoral College, 1944. Home: Hotel Bellevue, Boston. Died Oct. 2, 1950.*

FITZGERALD, John Joseph, lawyer, judge; born Brooklyn, Mar. 10, 1872; s. Patrick P. and Catharine T. (McMahon) F.; A.B., Manhattan Coll., 1891, A.M., 1893; studied New York Law Sch.; LL.B. cum laude, regents U. State of N.Y., 1893; LL.D., Manhattan Coll. and St. John's Coll.; m. Kathleen L. Ferris, 1901; children—Justin S., John J., Kathleen L., Paul J., Edmund J., Muriel M., Gerard. Admitted to bar, 1893, and since in practice at New York. Mem. 56th and 57th Congresses (1899-1908), 2d N.Y. Dist., and 58th to 64th Congresses (1903-17), 7th Dist.; resigned from Congress, Dec. 31, 1917, to resume practice at N.Y. City; sr. mem. firm Fitzgerald, Stapleton & Mahon; became counsel to Bd. of Transportation, N.Y. City, Jan. 1, 1930; apptd. judge, Kings County, Feb. 16, 1932, for term ending 1936, elected. Nov. 1932. for 14 yr. term; retired and resumed pvt. practice of law, Jan. 1, 1943. Del. Dem. Nat. Conv., 8 times since 1900. Trustee Manhattan Coll. Home: 881 Ocean Av. Address: 32 Court St., Bklyn. Died May 13, 1952.

FITZGERALD, John Morton, ret. ry. exec.; b. Phila., Apr. 26, 1877; s. Samuel William and Laura Neff (Morton) F.; ed. pub. schs., Phila., LL.D., U. of Pittsburgh, 1931; m. Eleanor Milson, Feb. 5, 1902; 1 son, Colonel Herbert Morton. Rodman with Phila., Harrisburg & Pittsburgh Ry., 1891; engring. dept. Columbus, Sandusky & Hocking R.R., 1893; successively engring. construction, maintenance and operating dept., Choctaw, Okla. & Gulf R.R., asst. gen. mgr. Va. and Southwestern Ry., v.p. Pitts. Terminal R.R. & Coal Co., pres. Davis Coal & Coke Co., v.p., pres. Western Md. Ry. Co., vice chmn. Eastern R.R., ret. Pres. Conf. Com. on Pub. Relations. Chmn. bd. Asso. Traffic Clubs of Am.; dir. Greater N.Y. Safety Council; trustee, Am. Museum of Safety. Member Engineers Soc. Western Pa., American Society of Political and Social Science, The Economic Club of New York, American Institute Mining and Metall. Engineers, Academy Polit. Science, Newcomen Soc. of England, Tau Kappa Epsilon, Omicron Delta Kappa, Sigma Tau, Beta Gamma Sigma, Delta Mu Delta, Alpha Kappa Psi, hon. mem. Transportation Society U. of Pa., Finance Forum New York U., Alpha Lambda Sigma, U., United Assns. of Railroad Vets. Rep. Episcopalian. Mason. Clubs: Union League, Bankers (N.Y. City), The Chicago Club (Chicago), University, Duquesne (Pittsburgh); Traffic Clubs of N.Y. City, St. Louis, Chicago, Reading, Lehigh Valley. Home: 125 E. 50th St., N.Y.C. 22. Died Feb. 25, 1960.

FITZGERALD, Leo David, lawyer, ins. exec.; b. Livingston Manor, N.Y., June 2, 1896; s. David Henry and Wilhelmina Teresa (Smith) F.; LL.B. cum laude, Fordham U., 1924; m. Frances E. Doyle, Oct. 9, 1930; children—Frances E., Mary Agnes, Leo David. With Equitable Life Assurance Soc. of U.S., N.Y.C., 1917—, successively chief legal reference div. dept. policy claims, asst. supt. dept. policy claims, asso. counsel, counsel, 1936-55, v.p., counsel, 1955—; sec., dir. Life Ins. Guaranty Corp. Gov. New Rochelle (N.Y.) Hosp. Served with Inf., U.S. Army, A.E.F., World War I. Mem. Am., N.Y. State bar assns., N.Y. Law Inst., Assn. Life Ins. Counsel, Am. Legion, Lyncroft-Broadview Assn. (pres., dir. 1953). K.C. (4°). Wykagyl Country (New Rochelle). Home: 88 Paine Av., New Rochelle N.Y. Office: 393 7th Av., N.Y.C. 1. Died Jan. 1960.

FITZGERALD, Maurice A., govt. official; b. Brooklyn, Jan. 9, 1897; s. William R. (nom de plume—Corrig O'Sheen) and Mary A. (Cherry) Fitz G.; student Excelsior Bus. Sch., 1914-16; m. Catherine Walsh, Apr. 19, 1930; children—Kathleen, Maurice L., Thomas. Elected mem. N.Y. State Assembly, 9 terms, 1929-37 (chmn. com. on public service); sheriff, Queens Co., N.Y., 1938-41; commr. borough works, Queens Co., 1942-49; pres. Borough of Queens since Jan. 1950, chmn. local bd. public improvement since 1950. Mem. bd. estimate, N.Y. City, since 1950. Borough chmn. Catholic Charities, 1947-48. Mem. Queens Coll. Assn., Queens Soc. Arts and Crafts, Bowne House Hist. Soc., Queens Music Council, County Council Boy Scouts. Democrat (mem. state com. since 1940, presidential elector, Dem. candidate, N.Y., 1948). K.C. Elk. Club: Lions. Home: 129-16 134th St., S. Ozone Park, N.Y. and Four Highview Dr., Huntington Bay Hills, L. I. Office: Borough Hall, Kew Gardens, N.Y. Died Aug. 25, 1951.

FITZGERALD, Thomas, ret. street ry. exec.; b. Balt., May 30, 1878; s. Thomas and Fanny (Kettlewell) F.; A.B., Johns Hopkins, 1898; m. Laura Unger, Dec. 5, 1899; children—Elizabeth K. (Mrs. Francis P. Browning, dec.), Thomas, Frances K. (Mrs. Lynford A. Keating). Gen. supt. Norfolk, Portsmouth & Newport News Co., 1902-03; gen. mgr. Lexington Ry. Co., 1903-05; purchasing agt., asst. to v.p. Cin. Traction Co., 1905-07; asst. gen. mgr. same and Ohio Traction Co., 1907-13, gen. mgr. both cos., 1913-17; cons. electric ry. engr., Pitts., 1920-24; gen. mgr. Pitts., Rys. Co., 1924-25, v.p., Pitts. Rys. Co. and Pitts., Motor Coach Co., also dir. 37 subsidiaries, 1925-38; trustee and gen. mgr. Rys. Co. and Pitts., Motor Coach Co., 1938-51, ret.; trustee dir. Transit Research Corp., 1937. Pres., dir. Pitts. Conv. Bureau. Maj. inf., U.S. Res., 1917; maj. inf. U.S. Army, 1918, lt. col., 1918-19. Mem. Am. Transit Assn., Soc. Am. Mil. Engrs., Engring. Soc. Western Pa., C. of C. (dir. 1945—), Vets. Fgn. Wars, Am. Legion, Kappa Alpha. Mason (K.T., Shriner). Clubs: Duquesne, University, Traffic, Railway, Fellows, Rotary. Home: 5820 Elwood St., Pitts. 32. Office: 435 Sixth Av., Pitts. 19. Died Nov. 26, 1956.

FITZGERALD, William Joseph, lawyer; b. Brooklyn, N.Y., Nov. 19, 1877; s. Daniel H. and Margaret J. (Kelly) F.; student St. Thomas' Coll. (now U. of Scranton), 1892-94, Holy Cross Coll., 1894-96; A.B., Georgetown U., 1898; m. Clare P. McGrath, Nov. 9, 1916. Prin. pub. sch., Scranton, Pa., 1898-1902; admitted to Lackawanna County (Pa.) bar, 1902; and since in practice at Scranton; partner Fitzgerald, Kennedy, Eckersley & O'Brien. Mem. Am. Bar Assn., Pa. Bar Assn. (pres., 1932-33), Lackawanna Bar Assn. (pres., 1928-32). Cath. Club: Scranton Country (Clarks Summit, Pa.). Author articles on legal subjects. Home: 1617 Madison Av., Dunmore, Pa. Office: Scranton Life Bldg., Scranton 3, Pa. Died Oct. 17, 1955.

FITZGIBBON, John Harold, physician; b. Portland, Ore., Jan. 26, 1894; s. Edward H. and Terese (Rodgers) F.; A.B., U. of Oregon, 1917, M.D., Rush Med. Coll., 1920; m. Elizabeth Smith, June 17, 1921; children—John Harold, Mary Elizabeth (Mrs. John B. Dimick), Edward Leslie, Elizabeth Jean (Mrs. Charles G. Dimon, Jr.). Intern Presbyn. Hosp., Chgo., 1920-21; pvt. practice of medicine, 1922—; clinical prof. medicine, Univ. of Oregon Medical School (chief, division gastro-enterology); member staff, St. Vincent's Hosp., and Multnomah County Hosp. (both Portland), 1922—; cons. gastro-enterologist U.S. Vets. Adminstrn. Bd. of Trustees, Nat. Physicians Co. (1942-47); pres. Clackamas Broadcasters, Inc., (KGON), 1947—. Diplomate American Board Internal Medicine. Fellow Am. Coll. Phys. Member Am. Med. Assn. (chmn. council med. service and pub. relations, 1944-45, mem. bd. trustees, 1945-50), Am. Gastro-enterol. Assn., International Soc. Gastro-enterol., N. Pacific Soc. Internal Medicine (past pres.), Pacific Interurban Clin. Club, Ore. State and Multnomah County med. socs., Portland Acad. Medicine, Am. Gastroscopic Soc. (pres. 1946-47), Am. Radio Relay League, (hon.) Japan Med. Assn., Beta Theta Pi, Nu Sigma Nu, Sigma Xi. Roman Catholic. Club: University, Waverley. Home: 9900 S.E. Cambridge Lane, Milwaukie 22, Ore. Office: 812 S.W. Washington St., Portland, Ore. Died Sept. 4, 1957.

FITZHUGH, Percy Keese (pseudonym Hugh Lloyd), author; b. Bklyn., Sept. 7, 1876; s. William Wyvill and Mary (Keese) F.; student pub. schs., Pratt Inst., Bklyn.; m. Harriet Lloyd LePorte, July 13, 1900; children—Lawrence Stetson, Millicent Alden (dec.). Author: The Golden Rod Story-Book, 1906; The Colonial Series (6 vols.), 1907; The Story of a Fight, 1907; The Galleon Treasure, 1908; King Time, 1908; Along the Mohawk Trail, 1912; For Uncle Sam, Boss, 1913; In the Path of La Salle, 1914; Tom Slade, Boy Scout of the Moving Pictures, 1915; Uncle Sam's Outdoor Magic, 1916; Tom Slade at Temple Camp, 1916; Tom Slade on the River, 1917; The Boys' Book of Scouts, 1917; The History of the United States from Appomattox to Germany, 1918; Tom Slade with the Colors, 1918; Tom Slade with the Boys Over There, 1918; Tom Slade on a Transport, 1918; Tom Slade, Motorcycle Dispatch Bearer, 1918; Tom Slade with the Flying Corps, 1919; Roy Blakeley, Scout, series (5 vols.), 1918; The Winning of the Golden Cross, 1920; Bobby Cullen on the Mississippi, 1920; Tom Slade Back Home, 1920; Tom Slade, Scout Master, 1920; Tom Slade, Scout Hero; Tom Slade on Mystery Trail; Roy Blakeley's Motor Caravan; Roy Blakeley—Lost, Strayed or Stolen; Tom Slade at Black Lake, 1921; Roy Blakeley at the Haunted Camp; Roy Blakeley's Bee Line Hike; Roy Blakeley's Funny Bone Hike; Pee-wee Harris, 1922; Pee-wee Harris on the Trail, 1922; Pee-wee Harris in Camp, 1922; Pee-wee Harris in Luck, 1922; Pee-wee Harris Adrift, 1922; Tom Slade's Double Dare, 1923; Pee-wee Harris, F.O.B. Bridgeboro, 1923; Tom Slade on Overlook Mountain, 1924; Pee-wee Harris, Clean-up Worker, 1924; Roy Blakeley on the Tangled Trail, 1924; Westy Martin, 1924; Westy Martin in the Yellowstone, 1924; Tom Slade at Bear Mountain, 1924; Pee-wee Harris As Good As His Word, 1925; Roy Blakeley On the Mohawk Trail, 1925; Westy Martin in the Rockies, 1925; Tom Slade Forest Ranger, 1926; Roy Blakeley's Elastic Hike, 1926; Pee-wee Harris Mayor for a Day, 1926; Tom Slade in the North Woods, 1927; Roy Blakeley's Roundabout Hike, 1927; Pee-wee Harris and the Sunken Treasure, 1927; Hervey Willetts, 1927; Tom Slade at Shadow Isle, 1928; Pee-wee Harris on the Briny Deep, 1928; Roy Blakeley's Happy-go-lucky Hike, 1928; Westy Martin in the Purple Sage, 1928; Skinny McCord, 1928; Tom Slade in Haunted Cavern, 1929; Roy Blakeley's Go As You Please Hike, 1929; Pee-wee Harris in Darkest Africa, 1929; Westy Martin on Old Indian Trail, 1929; Wigwag Weigand, 1929; Spiffy Henshaw, 1929; Westy Martin in the Sierras, The Parachute Jumper, Pee-wee Turns Detective, Roy Blakeley up in the Air, Mark Gilmore—all 1930; The Hermit of Gordon's Creek, Kidnaped in the Jungle, The Copperhead Trail Mystery, The Mysterious Arab, The Smuggler's Secret—all 1931; Our West with Westy Martin, 1933; Adventures of Holman Barcley, 1934; Skippy Dare Stories, 3 vols., 1935; The Concise Biographical Dictionary, 1935. Editor Every Girl's Library (10 vols.), 1909. Co-editor Lossing's History of the United States. Contbr. to mags. Home: 283 Maple Av., Oradell, N.J. Address: care Grosset & Dunlap, Publishers, N.Y.C. Died July 5, 1950.

FITZMAURICE, John E., bishop; b. Ireland, Jan. 9, 1840; s. James and Katherine F.; ed. Ireland and U.S.; grad. St. Charles Sem., Phila.; D.D., Georgetown U., 1889. Ordained priest, 1862; was consecrated bishop of Amisus and coadjutor bishop of Erie with right of succession, Feb. 1898; succeeded, Sept. 1899. Address: Erie, Pa. Died June 18, 1920.

FITZPATRICK, Morgan C., ex-congressman; s. J. M. and Elizabeth F.; ed. U. of Ohio; LL.B., Cumberland U.; m. Maggie May De Bow, 1894. Admitted to bar, 1890; engaged in practice at Gallatin, Tenn.; editor Hartsville Vidette, 1895-6; mem. Tenn. Ho. of Rep., 1894-8 (speaker, 1897-8); chmn. State Dem. Com., 1898-1902; state supt. schs., 1899-1903; mem. 58th Congress, 4th Tenn. Dist. Address: Gallatin, Tenn. Died June 29, 1908.

FITZ-RANDOLPH, Corliss, educator; b. New Milton, W.Va., July 24, 1863; s. Franklin and Mary Elizabeth (Fox) Fitz R.; A.B., A.M., Alfred (N.Y.) U., 1888, hon. L.H.D., 1903; grad. student in classical philology, Columbia, 1896-99; Ph.D., Salem Coll., W.Va., 1904 (LL.D. 1913); m. Marion Melissa Howard, Mar. 18, 1890 (she died Feb. 21, 1921); 1 dau., Mildred; m. 2d, Mrs. Grace Dawson Bell, July 7, 1926. Teacher in public schs., New Milton, W.Va., 1879-84, Montclair (N.J.) High School, 1889-91; prin. pub. sch., Ashaway, R.I., 1888-89, Staten Island, N.Y., 1892-96, and Newark, N.J., 1899-1933. Editor Alfred U. Quarterly, 1896-98; lecturer classical philology, Alfred University, 1899-1901; editor School Exchange, Newark, 1907-11. Trustee Alfred Univ., 1896-1938, honorary trustee since 1938. Mem. Nat. Inst. Social Scis., 1915-48, Sons Am. Rev. Editor and contbr. to Seventh Day Baptists in Europe and America, 1910. Author: History of Seventh Day Baptists in West Virginia, 1905; Report on European Schools, 1909; History of German Seventh Day Baptists, 1910; Rogerines, 1910; Education, and not Instruction, 1913; Anniversary Addresses, 1922; The Sabbath and Seventh Day Baptists, 5th revision, 1945; A Century's Progress: A History of the First Seventh Day Bapt. Church of New York City, 1948. Joint Author: A Manual of Seventh Day Baptist Procedure, 1923, 2d edit. 1926. Editor: Autobiog. of Rev. Samuel D. Davis, 1942; Seventh Day Baptist Year Book, 1914-28. President American Sabbath Tract Soc., 1914-41, trustee, 1890-1941, pres. emeritus, 1941—; pres. and librarian Seventh Day Baptist Hist. Soc., 1916—; pres. Seventh Day Baptist General Conference, 1931-32 (sec. Sabbath School Board, 1901-11); dir. Seventh Day Baptist Missionary Soc., 1920-42; visitor to European schs., 1909. Mem. N.J. Hist. Soc., Nat. Inst. Social Sciences. Am. Soc. of Ch. History, Am. Hist. Soc., Société Académie et Historique Internationale (Paris), Congregational Hist. Soc. (England). Club: Author's (London). Home: 83 Jefferson Av., Maplewood, N.J. Died Nov. 6, 1954; buried Hillside Cemetery, Plainfield, N.J.

FITZSIMON, Laurence Julius (fits'sim'un), bishop; b. San Antonio, Tex., Jan. 31, 1895; s. John Thomas and Theodora (Okelmann) FitzSimon; student St. Anthony's Coll., San Antonio, 1907-11; Ph.D., North Am. Coll., Rome, Italy, 1914, S.T.B., 1916; student St. Meinrad Sem., St. Meinrad, Ind., 1920-21. Ordained priest, R.C. Church, May 17, 1921; prof. St. John's Seminary, San Antonio, 1921-25; pastor churches at Runge, Karnes City and Kenedy, 1925-32, St. James Ch., Seguin (all of Tex.), 1932-41; apptd. chancellor of Archdiocese of San Antonio, 1941; consecrated bishop of Amarillo, Oct. 22, 1941. Served in U.S. Navy, 1917-19. Mem. Am. Legion, Vets. Fgn. Wars, North Sea Mine Force Assn. Address: 1800 N. Spring St., P.O. Box 2009, Amarillo, Tex. Died July 2, 1958; buried Amarillo.

FITZWATER, Perry B., clergyman; b. Hardy County, W.Va., Sept. 8, 1871; s. Cyprianus and Clerenda (Delawder) F.; grad. teachers' course, Bridgewater (Va.) Coll., 1894; spl. study, same coll., 13 mos.; student, Moody Bible Inst., Chicago, 1898-99; grad. Xenia Theol. Sem., 1905; postgrad. work, Princeton Theol. Sem., and Princeton Univ., 1911-12; D.D., Muskingum Coll., 1909; m. Addie Frances Kaylor, July 1898; children—Joseph Kaylor, James Perry, Timothy Titus. Formerly teacher and prin. pub. schs.; ordained ministry, 1909; mem. Presbyn. Ch.; dean Bible dept. Manchester (Ind.) Coll., 1905-11; dean Bible dept., La Verne Coll. (Calif.), 1912-13; mem. faculty Moody Bible Inst., 1913—, dean Evening Sch. of the Inst., 1923-26, and dean Day and Evening Schools, 1926-29, director pastor's course, 1934—; acting dean, Moody Bible Institute, 1941-42. Was for about 20 yrs. writer of Sunday Sch. lessons for Moody Bible Institute Monthly, also newspaper syndicated lessons pub. in about 2,600 papers in America. Republican. Author: The Church and Modern Problems, 1914; God's Code of Morals, 1926; Why God Became Man, 1934; The Doctrines of the Christian Faith (for Corr. Sch.); Christian Theology, 1948; Woman: Her Mission, Position and Ministry, 1950; Preaching the Bible, 1953; Preaching and Teaching the New Testament, 1957. Cons. editor Internat. S.S. League; contbg. editor Standard Reference Bible. Home: 1006 Brummel St., Evanston, Ill. Address: 820 N. La Salle, Chgo. Died Dec. 29, 1957; buried Memorial Park Cemetery, Skokie, Ill.

FLACK, Joseph, diplomat; b. Grenoble, Pa., Dec. 5, 1894; s. Roland and Sallie Russell (Walter) F.; B.S. in Econ., U. of Pa., 1916, post grad. student, 1919-20; m. Aloisia Schmid, Aug. 25, 1932. Began as consular officer, 1916; vice-consul, Liverpool, Eng., 1917-19; apptd. sec. of Embassy, 1920; 3d sec. Embassy, Paris, 1920; at La Paz, Bolivia, 1922; at Santo Domingo, Dominican Republic, 1924; 2d sec. Legation, Vienna, 1925; 2d sec. Embassy at Santiago, Chile, 1929; 1st sec. Embassy, Warsaw, Poland, 1931, at Madrid, 1932, Berlin, 1933; European Div., Dept. of State, 1936; became consul gen., 1937; counselor of Embassy, Madrid, 1940; counselor of Embassy, Caracas, Venezuela, 1941-45; State Dept., 1945-46; ambassador to Bolivia, 1946-49; A.E. and P. to Costa Rica, 1949-50, to Poland since 1950. Spl. rep. Pres. of U.S.A. with rank of spl. ambassador, to inauguration of Pres. Hertzog of Bolivia, 1947 and to inauguration of Pres. Ulate of Costa Rica, 1949. Presbyn. Club: Metropolitan (Washington). Home: 110 East Ashland St., Doylestown, Pa. Address: Dept. of State, Washington. Died May 8, 1955; buried Neshaminy Cemetery, Warwick, Pa.

FLACK, Marjorie, author, illustrator; b. Greenport, L.I., N.Y., Oct. 23, 1897; d. George Nelson and Charlotte Augusta (Brooks) Flack; student Art Students League, N.Y. City, 1918-20; m. Karl Larsson, Dec. 25, 1919 (divorced 1940); 1 daughter, Hilma (Mrs. Jay Hyde Barnum); m. 2d, William Rose Benét, June 21, 1941 (deceased May 4, 1950). Author and illustrator, 1927—; lectr. Writers' Conf. U. Utah, 1950, U. Conn., 1951, Ind. U., 1951. Fellow MacDowell Colony, Peterboro, N.H. Club: Womens City (N.Y.C.). Author: Taktuk, An Arctic Boy, 1928; All Around the Town, 1929; Angus and the Ducks, 1930; Angus and the Cat, 1931; Angus Lost, 1932; Ask Mr. Bear, 1932; Wag-Tail-Bess, 1933; The Story About Ping, 1933 (selected by Mus. Modern Art of Manhattan, award of merit Columbus O. Film Festival, included Internat. Venice Film Festival, frequently used on TV 1956), Humphrey, 1934; Tim Tadpole and the Great Bullfrog, 1934; Topsy, 1935; Christopher, 1935; Up in the Air, 1935; Wait for William (illustrated with Richard Holberg), 1935; What to Do About Molly, 1936; Willy Nilly, 1936; Walter, The Lazy Mouse, 1937; Lucky Little Lena, 1937; The Restless Robin, 1937; William and His Kitten, 1938. Illustrator: Scamper, 1934; Scamper's Christmas at the White House, 1934; The Country Bunny and the Little Gold Shoes (text by Du Bose Heyward), 1939; Pedro (with Karl Larsson), 1940; Adolphus, the Adopted Dolphin (text by William Rose Benét), 1941; The New Pet, 1943; I See a Kitty, 1943; Away Goes Jonathan Wheeler, 1944; The Boats on the River, Neighbors on the Hill (textbook), 1946; The Happy Birthday Letter, 1947. Address: Pigeon Cove, Cape Ann, Mass. Died Aug. 29, 1958.

FLAHERTY, Robert Joseph, explorer, producer; b. Feb. 16, 1884; s. Robert Henry and Susan (Kloeckner) F.; student Upper Canada Coll., Toronto; hon. Dr. Fine Arts, U. Mich., 1950; m. Frances J. Hubbard, 1914; 3 daughters. Led. 4 expdns. into subarctic eastern Canada; explored and mapped island archipelago known as Belcher Islands, Hudson Bay; explored and mapped barren lands of Northern Ungava, 1910-16; produced motion picture, Nanook of the North, 1920-22, Moana, 1923-25, Man of Aran, 1932-34; co-producer motion picture, Tabu, 1929-31; Elephant Boy, 1935-36; The Land (for Department of Ariculture), 1939-41; film sequences for War Dept., 1942; documentary film for Museum of Art, Providence, 1944; produced documentary film for Botanical Garden, New York, 1946; series of documentation films for Sugar Research Found., New York; recently produced and directed film, Louisiana Story, in La. (judged best documentary film of 1949). Chevalier Legion of Honor. Clubs: Coffee House, Explorers, The Players, Century (New York). Author: The Captain's Chair; My Eskimo Friends; White Master; also monographs and articles. Home: Black Mountain Farm, R.F.D. 1, Brattleboro, Vt. Died July 23, 1951.

FLANAGAN, James Wainwright, mining engr.; b. Henderson, Tex., Oct. 26, 1872; s. Robert Buck and Anna Bell (Cornelius) F.; ed. pub. schs. and pvt. study; m. Panchita G. Love, Jan. 1902; 1 son, James W. (dec.); m. 2d, Hazel B. Brown, Dec. 10, 1913; 1 dau., Diva B. Railroad work and mining, 1888-

1912, in Cuba, Mexico and U.S.; foreign financial assn., 1913-19, with Sir Herbert Holt, pres. Royal Bank of Can.; organized, 1919, Andian Nat. Corp., of Toronto, Can., to build 615 miles petroleum pipe line from Cartagena to Barranca Bermeja in Colombia, S.A., and to purchase wharf and terminals at Cartagena; obtained concession from Colombian Govt. and completed construction; was 1st v.p. and gen. manager Andian National Corp., Ltd., pres., 1925-42; spl. asst. to exec. officer of petroleum for war, serving Puerto Rico, Cuba and West Indies, Nov. 1942-44. dir. International Petroleum Corp.; dir. Macassa Mines, Ltd., Toronto, Ont., 1930. Served as lieut. col. Cuban Army, 1896-97; awarded Medal of Mil. Merit; spl. assignment on staff of Brig. Gen. W. W. Gordon, U.S. Army, 1898; commd. hon. lt. col., 2d Bn., Irish Regt. of Canada, Dec. 1940, and of 1st Bn., Irish Regt. of Canada, July 1941. Hon. mem. Cuban Expn. at St. Louis, Mo., 1904. Democrat. Roman Catholic. Decorated by Pope Pius XI, as Comdr. Order of St. Gregory, 1926; decorated Cross of Boyacá, in the official and military class, Colombia, 1933. Clubs: Bankers, New York Athletic, India House, Canadian Club, Army and Navy, Catholic (New York); Denver Country; Jockey (Lima, Peru); Jockey, Anglo-American (Bogota, Colombia); Cartagena (Cartagena). Address: Waldorf Astoria Hotel, New York, N.Y.; also Shamrock Hotel, Houston, Tex. Died July, 1950.

FLANAGAN, John, sculptor; b. Newark; pupil of Augustus St. Gaudens, New York, and of Henry Chapu and Alexandre Falguière, École des Beaux Arts, Paris (recipient various medals and prizes). Executed Monumental Clock, Library of Congress, Washington; large bronze relief Antique Education, Free Pub. Library, Newark; large tinted marble relief Aphrodite; bronze meml. portrait Samuel Pierpont Langley, Smithsonian Instn.; Bulkeley meml., bronze and marble, Aetna Life Ins. Co., Hartford, Conn.; statue of Joseph Henry, Albany, N.Y.; Dept. of Agr. war meml. large relief in marble, Washington; and other large works in the round, and in relief; various portrait busts and heads in the round, portrait plaquettes, and commemorative medals, including the medal commemorating the visit of Prince of Wales, Verdun Medal, presented by President Harding in the name of Congress and the People of U.S. to City of Verdun for its heroic defense in the World War, and Am. Acad. Arts and Letters medal for good diction on radio; designed George Washington 25 cents piece now minted by U.S. Treasury. Represented in medal collection of the Musée du Jeu de Paume, Paris; Museum of Ghent, Belgium; Met. Museum, and Am. Numismatic Soc., New York; Art Inst. Chgo.; Carnegie Inst., Pittsburgh; Art Museum, Newark, N.J.; St. Louis and Brooklyn museums. Recipient silver medal Paris Expn., 1900, Buffalo Expn., 1901, St. Louis Expn., 1904; medal of honor, sect. of medals, San Francisco Expn., 1915; Saltus Medal of Am. Numismatic Soc., for signal achievement in the art of the medal, 1921; medal Paris Salon, 1931; Watrous medal, N.A.D., 1932; decorated Chevalier Legion of Honor, 1927, officer, 1934 (France). N.A., 1928; mem. Nat. Inst. Arts and Letters, Am. Numis. Soc., Nat. Sculpture Soc. (hon.). Studio: 1947 Broadway. Home: N.Y.C. Died Mar. 28, 1952.

FLANDERS, Fred C., newspaper editor; b. Ottumva, Ia., July 16, 1883; s. Edward and Ella (Smith) F.; student Northwestern U. Law Sch., m. Mabel Marian O'Neill, May 29, 1911; children—Neil Fred, John Elbridge, Mary Jane, Dale Chester, Marian Ruth. Reporter Aurora Beacon, Aurora News, 1906; city editor Beacon-News, 1908, mng. editor 1912-55, ret. Mem. Am. Legion. Elk, Moose. Home: 20 S. Russell Av. Office: 1 E. Main St., Aurora, Ill. Died Sept. 1959.

FLANNAGAN, John William, Jr., ex-congressman; b. Trevilians, Va., Feb. 20, 1885; s. John William and Bessie Haskins (Wills) F.; LL.B., Washington and Lee U., 1907; m. Frances Deel Pruner, Sept. 25, 1910; children—John William III, Mrs. J. Rosser Murray, Jr., Francis Wills, Haskins (dec.). Began practice at Appalachia, Wise County, Va., 1907, settled in Bristol, Va.; mem. Morrison, Rouse & Flannagan; pres. Dickenson County Bank, Clintwood, Va., 1917-30. Mem. 72d to 80th Congresses (1931-49), 9th Va. Dist.; chmn. House Com. on Agriculture. Mem. Va., Bristol and Dickenson County bar assns. Democrat. Presbyterian. Mason (Shriner), Odd Fellow, Modern Woodman, Moose. Club: Westmoreland (Richmond). Home: Bristol, Va. Died Apr. 27, 1955; buried Mountain View Cemetery, Bristol.

FLANNERY, John Spalding, lawyer; b. Baltimore, Md., May 16, 1870; s. John A. and Margaret E. (Reilly) F.; LL.B., Georgetown U., 1894, LL.M., 1895; m. Isabel Gautier Gregory, June 23, 1909 (dec.); children—Virginia M. Early, Fontaine F. de Geofroy, Anne Dudley Pini. Admitted to D.C. bar, 1895, and practiced since at Washington; mem. firm of Flannery, Craighill & Aiello; gen. counsel F. A. Delano, federal receiver of Red River Valley in boundary suit of Oklahoma vs. Texas, 1920-26; counsel Pennsylvania R.R. System, American Security and Trust Company; special master in Texas versus Florida, 1938. Member American Bar Association, Society Internat. Law. Ind. Democrat. Roman Catholic. Clubs: Metropolitan, Chevy Chase, Lawyers. Home: Hotel Claridge, 820 Connecticut Av. Office: 725 15th St., Washington, 5. Died Feb. 17, 1954; buried Rock Creek Cemetery, Washington.

FLANNERY, Vaughn, painter; b. 1898; s. James Benjamin and Nancy Kent (Maddox) F.; student Art Inst. Chgo., pvt. study; m. Elizabeth Anderson Ettinger; children—Kent Vaughn, Liza Maddox. Permanently represented in Carnegie Museum, Pitts., Balt. Mus., Phillips Memorial, Washington; Whitney Gallery and Kraushaar Galleries, N.Y.C., Toledo Museum, and pvt. collections. Club: Maryland Jockey (dir.). Home: Cockade Farms, Harford County, Md. Address: care Kraushaar Art Galleries, 32 E. 57 St., N.Y.C. 22. Died Dec. 25, 1955.

FLEEK, John Sherwood, investment banker; b. Newark, O., Aug. 29, 1893; s. Henry Sherwood and Fanny (Moore) F.; grad. Phillips Exeter Acad., 1911; A.B., Harvard, 1915, M.B.A. cum laude, 1921; m. Hester Noyes, July 7, 1921; children—Henry Sherwood, John Sherwood, Hester. Asso. Hayden, Miller & Co., investment bankers, Cleve., 1921—, partner 1926—, spl. partner, 1950—; pres. Midwest Vessel Corp., 1936-43; pres. Fleek & Son Co. of Newark, O., wholesale grocers; dir. Alliance Ware, Inc. Exec. mgr. Victory Fund Com. for Fourth Fed. Res. Dist., Cleve., directed 1st and 2d war loan campaigns 1942, 43; trustee Cleve. Crime Commn., 1927-47, Cleve. chpt. A.R.C., 1943-47. Trustee Cleve. Inst. Music, 1925-30; trustee, treas. John Huntington Benevolent Fund. Served as capt. F.A., World War I. Decorated Croix de guerre. Mem. Investment Bankers Assn. Am. (pres. 1941-42), Asso. Harvard Clubs (pres. 1946-47), Harvard Alumni Assn. (dir. 1945-47, v.p. 1953-54). Clubs: Union, Tavern, Harvard (Cleve.). Home: 17500 S. Woodland Rd., Shaker Heights, O. Office: Union Commerce Bldg., Cleve. 14. Died Mar. 27, 1957.

FLEESON, Howard Tebbe, lawyer; b. Sterling, Kan., Aug. 7, 1895; s. William and Helen (Tebbe) F.; A.B., U. Kan., 1920; LL.B., Yale, 1922; m. Katherine Murdock, Nov. 21, 1927; 1 son, Allen. Admitted to Kan. bar, 1922, since practiced in Wichita; mem. Fleeson, Gooing, Coulson & Kitch, and predecessors, since 1923, sr. partner since 1935; dir. First Nat. Bank, Kan. State Bank, Wichita Eagle, Inc., radio sta. KFH Co., KFH Bldg., Inc., Union Nat. Bank Bldg. Operating Co. Served as 1st lt., 12th aero squadron A.S., U.S. Army, France and Germany, 1917-19. Decorated D.S.C. and Oak leaf. Mem. Am., Kan. State bar assns , Delta Upsilon. Republican. Episcopalian. Club: Wichita Country. Home: 346 N. Belmont Av., Wichita. Office: First Nat. Bank Bldg., Wichita 2. Died May 7, 1957; buried Wichita Park Cemetery, Wichita, Kan.

FLEISCHMANN, Max C. (flĭsh'män), mfr.; b. Riverside, O., Feb. 26, 1887; s. Charles and Henriette (Robertson) F.; educated public schools and Ohio Military Institute; LL.D. (hon.), Univ. of Nevada; m. Sarah Hamilton Sherlock, Dec. 20, 1905. Entered mfg. dept. of the Fleischmann Co., Cincinnati, at 18, became chmn. bd.; on acquisition of co. by Standard Brands, Inc , became dir. of latter; dir. Security Nat. Bank. Dir. gen. Nev. State Museum; v.p., trustee Santa Barbara Museum of Natural History; trustee Save-the-Redwoods League. Served in O. Nat. Guard 6 yrs. (2d lt.); 1st lt. Ohio Vol. Cav. Spanish-Am. War; maj. comdg. Balloon Corps, A. E.F., 1917-18. Fellow Royal Geog. Soc. Republican. Mason (32°). Clubs: New York Yacht, Explorers (life); Santa Barbara, Valley Club of Montecito. Author: After Big Game in Arctic and Tropic (pvt. circulation), 1909. Home: Glenbrook, Douglas Co., Nev. Office: 595 Madison Av., New York, N.Y.; and 1st Nat. Bank Bldg., Reno. Died Oct. 16, 1951; buried Mountain View Cemetery, Reno.

FLEISHER, Walter Louis, engr.; b. Phila., Pa., July 18, 1880; s. Simon and Rosa Wolf F.; B.S., Univ. of Pa., 1900, M.S. 1901, M.E. (hon.) 1931; m. Marcia Garrick 1938 (died 1947); children—Walter L., Anna (Mrs. Jerome Shore), Jeffrey. Engr.-in-chief firm of Francis Bros. and Jellett, N.Y. City, 1903-11; formed W. L. Fleisher & Co., Inc., 1911 and served as pres., treas. and chief engr. until merger with 2 other cos. under name of The Cooling and Air Conditioning Corp. and served as vice pres. and chief engr. to 1930; established consulting office Walter L. Fleisher, N.Y.C., 1930, since served as pres. and treas.; pres. Air & Refrigeration Corp. since 1934. Life mem. Am. Soc. Heating and Air Conditioning Engrs., Inc. (2d v.p., 1939, pres., 1941; chmn. com. on air conditioning in industry). Recipient F. Paul Anderson award, 1953; citation U. Pa., 1955. Fellow Am. Soc. Heating and Air Conditioning. Am. Soc. Refrigerating Engrs.; mem. Am. Soc. Bakery Engrs., A.S.M.E. (life), Heating, Piping and Air Conditioning Contractors Nat. Assn. (hon. mem., chmn. standards com.); mem. Princeton U. Adv. Council Dept. of M.E., since 1940. Club: Princeton. Editor-in-chief ASHVE Guide, 1932-33; mem. bd. cons. and cont. editors of Heating, Piping and Air Conditioning since 1929. Contbr. chpts. to tech. publs. Mem. ASHVE Speakers Bur. Holder 100 Am. and fgn. patents. Home: Saw Mill Farm, New City, N.Y. Address: 439 Madison Av., N.Y.C. 22. Died Apr. 18, 1959.

FLEISHHACKER, Herbert, banker; b. San Francisco, Nov. 2, 1872; s. Aaron and Delia (Stern) F.; ed. pub. schs. and business coll.; m. May Belle Greenbaum, Aug. 9, 1905. Began as bookkeeper, father's paper business, 1887, later salesman for the house and established paper mills in Ore. and electric power plants in Cal.; became mgr. London, Paris and Am. Bank, San Francisco, 1907, later pres. Anglo and London Paris Nat. Bank, 1911-32; bank consolidated with Anglo Cal. Trust Co., 1932, as the Anglo Cal. Nat. Bank became pres.; officer or dir. various other corps. Office: 1 Sansome St., San Francisco. Died Apr. 2, 1957.

FLEMING, Sir Alexander, univ. rector; b. Lochfield, Darvel; son Hugh Fleming; ed. Kilmarnock Acad., St. Mary's Hosp. Med. Sch.; M.B., B.S., London; Dr. honoris causa many univs. in Europe and Am.; married Sarah Marion McElroy (dec. 1949); 1 son; married 2d, Amalia Coutsouri, 1953. Rector U. Edinburgh; prof. emeritus bacteriology U. London; capt. Royal Army M.C.; pvt., London Scottish for 14 yrs. Recipient Nobel prize; Humanitarian award, Variety Clubs of Am.; many medals from learned socs. Decorated Comdr. Legion of Honour. Fellow Royal Soc., Royal Coll. Surgeons, Royal Coll. Physicians; mem. Pontifical Academy Scis., Soc. Gen. Microbiology (past pres.), London Ayrshire Society (hon. pres.); hon. mem. many acads. and science socs. throughout world. Clubs: Athenaeum, Chelsea Arts, Savage, Caledonian. Published numerous articles on bacteriology, immunology and chemotherapy including the original descriptions of penicillin and lysozyme. Address: The Wright-Fleming Institute of Microbiology, St. Mary's Hosp. Med Sch., London W2, Eng. Died Mar. 11, 1955; buried Crypt of St. Paul's Cathedral.

FLEMING, Dewey Lee, newspaperman; b. Whitmer, W.Va., July 19, 1898; s. Sidney Albert and Hattie Alice (Bowers) F.; B.A., Davis and Elkins College, West Virginia, 1918, LL.D., 1944; student Columbia University, 1922; married Elizabeth Walker, January 4, 1932 (died April 21, 1938). Reporter Elkins West Virginia, Inter-Mountain, 1917-19, Baltimore, Md., American, 1922-23; city reportorial staff Baltimore Sun, 1923-26, Washington bur., 1926-27, New York corr., 1927-28, Chicago corr., 1928-29, London correspondent, 1929-31, Washington bureau since 1931, chief of Washington bureau since 1941. Awarded Pulitzer Prize for reporting of national affairs during the year 1943. Students Army Training Corps, 1918. Trustee, Davis and Elkins Coll., Elkins, W.Va. Democrat. Presbyterian. Mason. Clubs: Gridiron, Overseas Writers, National Press (Washington, D.C.). Home: 4201 Mass. Av. N.W. Address: 1214 National Press Bldg., Washington. Died May 18, 1955; buried Buckhannon, W.Va.

FLEMING, Frederic Sydney, clergyman; b. Calais, Me., Mar. 7, 1886; s. John and Isabel Maude (Crawley) F.; student Lewis Inst., Chgo., 1906-08; S.T. B., Western Theol. Sem., Chgo., 1911, D.D., 1933; D.D., Nashotah House, 1926, Trinity Coll., 1948; LL.D., Hobart Coll., 1933; S.T.D., Gen. Theol. Sem., 1935; D.C.L., U. of South, 1938; m. Margaret Frederick Moore, Nov. 4, 1916; children— Mary Louise (Mrs. Fortunato Jerace), Thomas Crawley. With Nat. Biscuit Co., junior exec. and asst. to pres., 1900-06; deacon and priest, P.E. Ch., 1911; curate St. Bartholomew's Ch., Chgo., 1911; priest St. Paul's Ch., La Salle, Ill., 1912-15; rector Ch. of the Atonement, Chgo., 1915-27, St. Stephen's Ch., Providence, 1927-30; vicar Chapel of the Intercession, Trinity Parish, N.Y.C., 1930-32; rector Trinity Parish, 1932-51. Elected bishop of Northern Ind., also Olympia, 1924, declined. Dep. General Convention P.E. Ch., 1922, 25, 34, 37, 40, 43, 46; pres., trustee Trinity Sch.; trustee Columbia, Sailors' Snug Harbor, Gen. Theol. Sem., Seamen's Ch. Inst. of N.Y., Cathedral of St. John the Divine, N.Y.C., Am. Ch. Bldg. Fund. Mem. fo Bd. Youth Consultation Service, Leake and Watts Children's Home, Soc. for Promoting Religion and Learning; chaplain, New England Society; member and chaplain St. George's Society; member The Pilgrims, English-Speaking Union, N.Y. Marine Soc. Republican. Clubs: Century, Down Town Assn. Home: Central Valley, N.Y. Office: 74 Trinity Pl., N.Y.C. 6. Died June 19, 1956; buried Trinity Parish Cemetery, N.Y.C.

FLEMING, John Adam, magnetician, geophysicist; b. Cincinnati, O., Jan. 28, 1877; s. Americus V. and Catherine B. (Ritzmann) F.; B.S., U. of Cincinnati, 1899, D.Sc., 1933; D.Sc., Dartmouth Coll., 1934; m. Henrietta C. B. Ratjen, June 17, 1903 (died Mar. 26, 1912); 1 dau., Margaret Catherine; m. 2d, Carolyn Ratjen, Oct. 30, 1913. Aid, U.S. Coast and Geod. Survey, 1899-1903, asst., 1903, magnetic observer, 1904-10; chief magnetician of the dept. of terrestrial magnetism, Carnegie Institution, Washington, 1904-46, chief observatory div., 1915-18, chief magnetic survey div., 1919-21, assistant director, 1922-29, acting director 1929-34, director 1935-46, retired in 1946; adviser of Carnegie Institution, Washington, in international scientific relations, 1946-54. Trustee of Woods Hole Oceanographic Institute, 1930-50, Washington Biophysical Institute, 1940-46; president Temporary Commission on Liquidation of International Polar Year, 1932-33, 1948-50. President Assn. Terrestial Magnetism and Elec. International Union of Geodesy and Geophysics, 1930-48; mem. Internat. Commn. Terrestrial Magnetism and Atmospheric Electricity, 1930-46; mem. International Commission for Polar Year, 1931-47; member of executive council Internat. Council of Scientific Unions, since 1937 (president 1946-49); member National Research Council, del. to assemblies of Internat. Union Geodesy and Geophysics; acting chairman, American section Aeroartic, 1929-33. del. from Nat. Research Council to Stockholm Assembly, 1930, Lisbon Assembly, 1933, Edinburgh Assembly, 1936, Washington Assembly, 1939, of Internat. Union Geodesy and Geophysics. Fellow A.A.A.S., Washington Academy Sciences, American Physical Society, American Geog. Soc.; mem. Nat. Acad. Sciences (chairman section on geophysics, 1951-54), American Institute of Mining and Metallurgic Engineers, American Geophysical Union (gen. sec., 1925-47, hon. president since 1947), Seismol. Soc. of America, Md. Acad. Science, Philos. Soc. Washington (sec. 1913-16, pres. 1925), Nat. Inst. of Social Sciences, Sigma Xi; hon. mem. State Russian Geog. Soc., Royal Soc. of New Zealand, corr. mem. Michelsen Inst. Science and Intellectual Freedom of Norway, Geophysical Society of Finland; mem. Norwegian Acad. Sciences and Letters, Geological Soc. of Peru, Geographical Soc. of Lima. Awarded William Bowie medal of Am. Geophysical Union, 1941; Charles Chree medal and prize of The Physical Soc. (London) 1945; certified effective service O.S.R.D., 1945; certificate exceptional service, Bureau of Ordnance, United States Navy, 1945; Commander of the Order of St. Olav of Norway, 1948. Republican. Presbyterian. Club: Cosmos. Editor and co-author: Scientific Results of the Ziegler Polar Expedition of 1903-05, 08. Co-author of vols. II to VII, Researches of Department of Terrestrial Magnetism, Carnegie Institution, Washington, 1915, 17, 21, 25, 27, 46; Scientific Results of Cruise VII of the Carnegie during, 1928-29, 1943-46. Editor of Journl Terrestrial Magnetism and Atmospheric Electricity, 1927-49. Contributor numerous articles and reviews on geophysics. Address: The Cosmas Club, Washington. Died July 29, 1956; buried Woodlawn Cemetery, Nashville.

FLEMING, Philip Bracken, engr., ex-ambassador; b. Burlington, Ia., Oct. 15, 1887; s. John Joseph and Mary (Bracken) F.; student U. of Wis., 1905-07; B.S., U.S. Mil. Acad., 1911; student Army Eng. School, 1912-13; LL.D., St. Francis Coll.; J.C.D., George Washington U.; m. Dorothy Carson, Dec. 5, 1914; children—Carson, Jocelyn. Commd. 2d lt. C.E., U.S. Army, 1911, and advanced through grades to maj. gen., 1942 (temp. col. during World War); grad. mgr. of athletics West Point, 1926-33; exec. officer and dep. adminstr. Pub. Works Adminstrn., 1933-35; in charge Passamaquoddy Project, 1935-36; co-ordinator Resettlement Adminstrn., 1936-37; dist. engr. St. Paul, 1937-39; adminstr. Wage and Hour Div., Dept. of Labor, 1939-41, Fed. works adminstr., 1941-49; chmn. U.S. Maritime Commn., 1949-50; under sec. of commerce for transportation, 1950-51; ambassador to Costa Rica, 1951-53, ret. Chmn. Pres.' Hwy. Safety Conf., 1946-49, Pres.' Conf. on Fire Prevention, 1947-49. Mem. Ia., N.H., Minn. hist. socs., Am. Soc. C.E., Soc. Am. Mil. Engrs., Permanent Internat. Assn. Nav. Congresses (chmn. Am. sect., mem. permanent council), Delta Upsilon, Roman Catholic. Clubs: Minnesota, University, Somerset (St. Paul); Army and Navy, Army and Navy Country (Washington); Chevy Chase; Engineers (N.Y.C.). Home: 1554 34th St. N.W. Office: Am. Embassy, San Jose, Costa Rica. Died Oct. 6, 1955; buried Arlington Nat. Cemetery.

FLEMING, Wallace B., educator; b. Cambridge, O., Nov. 22, 1872; s. William A. and Mary A. (Glenn) F.; A.B., Muskingum Coll., 1894, A.M., 1897, D.D., 1912; B.D., Drew Theol. Sem., 1897; Ph.D., Columbia, 1914; LL.D., West Virginia. Wesleyan Coll., 1922, Baker U., 1936; L.H.D., Muskingum Coll., 1944; m. Bertha G. Baldwin, Apr. 3, 1897 (died Oct. 10, 1931); children—Paul, Bertha Jane; m. 2d, Helen Wilson, Dec. 16, 1932. Ordained M.E. ministry, 1897; pastor N. Paterson, N.J., 1897-99, Bayonne; 1899-1904, Maplewood, 1904-11; prof. Hebrew and Greek, Drew Theol. Sem., Madison, N.J., 1911-15; pres. W.Va. Wesleyan Coll., Buckhannon, W.Va., 1915-22; pres. Baker U., 1922-36, pres. emeritus 1936—; v.p. W.Va. Wesleyan Coll., 1937-44; ret. Mason. Rotarian. Author: History of the City Tyre, 1915; Guide Posts to Life Work, 1923; Genealogy of a Fleming Family, 1947. Home: Buckhannon, W.Va. Died June 30, 1952; buried Heavner Cemetery, Buckhannon, W.Va.

FLETCHER, Frank Morley, artist; b. Whiston, Lancashire, Eng., Apr. 25, 1866; s. Alfred Evans and Sarah Elizabeth (Morley) F.; ed. University Coll., Liverpool, University Coll., London; art edn. St. John's Wood Art Sch., studio of Hubert Voss, London, and Atelier Cormon, Paris, to 1891; m. Maude Evelyn Brown, Mar. 28, 1895. Became naturalized citizen of U.S., 1929. Mem. faculty of London County Council Central Sch. of Arts, 1896-98; dir. Dept. of Fine Art, University Coll., Reading, 1898-1906; H.M. insp. sch. of art, Bd. of Edn., London, 1906-07; 1st dir. Edinburgh Coll. of Art, 1907-23; invited to Santa Barbara, Cal., by Community Arts Assn., 1923; dir. Santa Barbara Sch. of Arts until 1930; mem. Central Com. of Selection for Scholarships and Fellowships of Carnegie Corp., N.Y. Exhibited paintings and prints, Paris Salon, Royal Acad., London, Berlin, Dresden, Milan, N.Y. etc. Awarded medal Chgo. Expn., 1893, Internat. Expn., Milan, 1906; Fellowship Edward MacDowell Assn., 1938. Prints in British Mus., U.S. Nat. Mus. etc. Officer and instr. in field engring., 1917-18, World War. Fellow British Inst. Indsl. Art; mem. Art Workers' Guild, London. Protestant. Author: Woodblock Printing, 1916; Colour Control, 1936. Home: Ojai, Cal. Deceased.

FLETCHER, Henry, lawyer; b. Bklyn., Sept. 29, 1877; s. George H. and Ida (Sharp) F.; student gymnasium, Hanover, Germany; grad. Adelphi Acad., Bklyn., 1894; A.B., Yale, 1898, A.M., 1901; LL.B. cum laude, Harvard, 1901; m. Mary Sinclair Sloane, June 7, 1909 (died Nov. 1910); m. 2d, Ethel Thompson, June 3, 1913. Mem. firm Fletcher, Sillcocks & Leahy, 1902-20, now Fletcher & Brown; dir., mem. trust com. Irving Trust Co.; dir., mem. exec. com. Directory of Directors Co.; dir.; pres. Fletcher Bros.; chmn. bd. Swan & Finch Co. (Standard Oil subsidiary), 1915-22; dir. Arex Indemnity Co. Mem. reception com. to French and British War Commn., May 1917; mem. Oil Trade Com. of All Liberty Loan Drives; mem. citizens com. N.Y. Public Library; mem. City Com. Citizens Union (formerly v. chmn.); pres., trustee McAuley Water Street Mission; dir. Fedn. Protestant Welfare Agencies, Inc.; mem. bd. mgrs. Am. Tract Society; mem. exec. bd., bd. dirs. Protestant Council of N.Y.C.; v.p., past pres. Nat. Inst. Social Sciences; v.p., dir., chmn. finance com., mem. exec. com. Putnam Trust Co.; mem. adv. com. Individual Underwriters. Mem. Bd. of Estimate and Taxation, Greenwich; mem. Greenwich Library (formerly pres.); trustee Yale Library Associates, Yale-In-China, Textile Museum of Washington; hon. dir., past pres. Greenwich Hosp. Mem. banking and currency com., past dir. Commerce and Industry Assn. Mem. Am., N.Y. State N.Y. County bar assns., Assn. Bar City N.Y., Am. br. Internat. Law Assn., Nat. Council Nat. Econ. League, N.Y. Geneal. and Bibliog. Soc., Am. Museum Natural History, Am. Geog. Soc., Archeol. Inst. Am., Am. Econ. Assn., Bibliog. Soc. London, Am. Acad. Polit. and Social Science, Soc. for Preservation of N.E. Antiquities, English-Speaking Union, Legal Aid Soc., New Eng. Soc. (past dir.), Civil Service Reform Assn., Am. Econ. Assn., Acad. Polit. Science, Nat. Municipal League, U.S., N.Y. and Greenwich (Conn.) C.'s of C., Harvard Econ. Soc., Bibliophile Soc. (Boston), St. Nicholas Soc., Council Fgn. Relations, Vermont Soc., N.Y. Zoöl. Soc. Gov. Thomas Dudley Family Assn., Descs. Colonial Governors, Order Founders and Patriots of America, S.R., Phi Delta Phi, Pi Gamma Mu, Selden Soc. (Gt. Britain), Royal Econ. Soc. (London), Greenwich Soc. Artists (asso.), Phi Beta Kappa. Clubs: Down Town, Century, University, Grolier, Harvard, Yale (life), City, Uptown, Ft. George (Fla.); Yeamans Hall (S. C.); Graduates (New Haven); Greenwich Country, Greenwich Field, Round Hill, Beach (Greenwich); Manursing Island (Rye, N.Y.); Book Club of Calif. Contbr. on financial topics. Home: Field Point Park, Greenwich, Conn. Office: 21 E. 40th St., N. Y.C. 16. Died June 5, 1953.

FLETCHER, Henry Prather, diplomat; b. Green Castle, Pa., Apr. 10, 1873; s. Lewis Henry Clay and Martha Ellen (Rowe) F.; ed. Chambersburg (Pa.) Acad.; LL.D., U. Chile, Juniata Coll., Dickinson Coll., Lafayette Coll.; m. Beatrice Bend, July 25, 1917 (died Sept. 9, 1941). Admitted to bar, 1894; official reporter 39th Judicial Dist., Pa., 1891-98. Private Troop K, 1st U.S. Cavalry Vol. (Rough Riders), 1898; 1st lt., batn. adj. 40th U.S. Vol. Inf., serving in P.I., 1899-1901; 2d sec. Am. Legation, Cuba, 1902-03, China, 1903-05; sec. Am. Legation to Portugal, 1905-07; 1st sec. Am. Legation, China, 1907-09; charge d'affaires, 1907-08, 1909-10; apptd. E.E. and M.P., Chile, 1909; apptd. A.E. and P., Chile, 1914, Mexico, 1916, resigned, 1920; under sec. of state, 1921-22; A.E. and P. Belgium, 1922-24; A.E. and P. Italy, 1924-29, when resigned. Chmn. of U.S. delegation to 5th Pan-Am. Conf., Santiago, Chile, 1923; del. 6th Pan-Am. Conf.. Habana, 1928; chmn. U.S. delegation to Internat. Conf. for Protection of Literary and Artistic Property, Rome, 1928; mem. Spl. Commn. to Investigate and Report upon Conditions in Haiti, 1929; chmn. U.S. Tariff Commn., 1930-31; chmn. Rep. Nat. Com., 1934-36; del. to Rep. Nat. Conv. 1936, 1940; gen. counsel Rep. Nat. Com., mem. exec. com., 1936-44; spl. adviser Sec. of State, 1944-45. Mem. Am. Soc. Internat. Law, Council, of Fgn. Relations, S.A.R., Scotch-Irish Soc. of Pa., Kittochtinny Hist. Soc. Clubs: Metropolitan (Washington); The Brook, The Links, Regency (N.Y. C.); Fountain Head (Md.); Reading Room, Country, Clambake (Newport). Home: Newport, R.I. Office: 563 Park Av., N.Y.C. 21. Died July 10, 1959; buried Arlington Nat. Cemetery.

FLETCHER, John Gould, author, poet; b. Little Rock, Ark., Jan. 3, 1886; s. John Gould and Adolphine (Krause) F.; student Phillips Andover Acad., Harvard Coll.; LL.D., U. Ark., 1933; m. Florence Emily Arbuthnot, July 5, 1916; m. 2d, Charlie May Hogue, Jan. 18, 1936. Author: Fire and Wine, 1913; Irradiations—Sand and Spray, 1915; Goblins and Pagodas, 1916; Japanese Prints, 1918; The Tree of Life, 1918; Breakers and Granite, 1921; Paul Gauguin, His Life and Art, 1921; Preludes and Symphonies, 1922; Parables, 1925; Branches of Adam, 1926; John Smith—also Pocahontas, 1928; The Black Rock, 1928; The Two Frontiers, 1930; XXIV Elegies, 1935; The Epic of Arkansas, 1936; Life Is My Song (augobiography), 1937; Selected Poems, 1938; South Star, 1941; The Burning Mountain, 1946; Arkansas (prose history), 1947. Translator: The Dance Over Fire and Water (by Elie Faure), 1926; The Reveries of a Solitary (by J. J. Rousseau), 1927. Recipient Pulitzer Prize for poetry, 1939. Mem. Nat. Inst. Arts and Letters. Home: Johnswood, R.D. 5, Box 435, Little Rock, Ark. Died May 20, 1950; buried Little Rock.

FLETCHER, Robert Stillman, librarian; b. Hartford, Conn., Sept. 12, 1874; s. William Isaac and Annie LeBarron (Richard) F.; A.B., Amherst, 1897; m. Charlotte I. Stephenson, Nov. 19, 1907; 1 dau., Suzanne Stephenson (Mrs. Henry G. Dravneck). Successively with Buffalo Pub. Library, 1898-1900, Carnegie Library, Bradford, Pa., 1900-03, Bklyn. Pub. Library, 1903, Carnegie Library, Pitts., 1904-08; became connected with Amherst Coll. Library, 1908; librarian, 1911-35, retired on leave of absence because of ill health, librarian emeritus 1939—. Mem. A.L.A. Republican. Conglist. Mem. Chi Psi. Home: Amherst, Mass. Died Jan. 23, 1953.

FLETCHER, Samuel Johnson, fgn. service officer; b. Portsmouth, N.H., Sept. 17, 1891; s. John Joseph and Ellen Idellia (Johnson) F.; student Plymouth Bus. Sch., 1909-10, Columbia, 1916-17; m. Elizabeth Wentworth Huelin, Feb. 10, 1921. Clk. Boston & Maine Ry., 1910; clk. in various offices Portsmouth Navy Yard, 1911-16; vice consul, Barranquilla, Colombia, 1917, Cartagena, Colombia, 1917-21, LaGuaira, Venezuela, 1921-23, LeHavre, France, 1923-28; consul, Bluefields, Nicaragua, 1928-30, Montreal, Can., 1930-35 Canton China, 1935-39, Foochow, China, 1939, Tientsin, China, 1939-41; detained by Japanese 1941; returned to U.S., 1942, on exchange vessel Gripsholm; first sec. of Embassy and consul, Havana Cuba, 1942-43; apptd. consul Calcutta, India, 1943; apptd. consul general, Calcutta, India, 1945, Goteborg, Sweden, 1947; Melbourne Australia, 1947. Home: Kittery Point, Me. Address: care Dept. of State, Washington. Died Nov. 3, 1958; buried Kittery Point, Me.

FLETCHER, William Bartlett, naval officer; b. St. Albans, Vt., Jan. 7, 1862; s. John Bartlett and Louisa Ballard (Williams) F.; grad. U.S. Naval Acad., 1882, Naval War Coll., 1915; m. Malene R. Asserson, Apr. 4, 1888. Commd. ensign USN, 1884, advanced through grades to rear adm.; served in the battleship Massachusetts, Spanish-Am. War, 1898; at Naval War Coll., Newport, R.I., 1902-04, 1907-09, 11-12, comdr. Birmingham, 1909-11, Montana, 1912-13, Kansas, 1913-14, mem. Gen. Bd. Navy Dept., 1916-17; comdr. Squadron Three, Patrol Force, Atlantic Fleet, 1917. 7th Naval Dist., 1918-19; comdr. 14th Naval Dist., 1919, Naval Sta., Hawaii, 1919. Decorated Medals for West India and Santiago Campaign, Philippine Campaign, Spanish-Am. War. Conglist. Club: Army and Navy (Washington). Home: Orrs Island, Me. Office: care Navy Dept., Washington. Died June 29, 1957; buried U.S. Naval Acad., Annapolis, Md.

FLEXNER, Abraham, educator; b. Louisville, Nov. 13, 1866; s. Morris and Esther (Abraham) F.; A.B., Johns Hopkins, 1886; A.M., Harvard, 1906, U. Berlin, 1906-07; LL.D., Western Reserve U., 1914, Swarthmore Coll., 1934; M.D. honoris causa, U. Berlin, 1929, U. Brussels, 1930; LL.D., N.Y. U., 1936, Princeton, 1940, Johns Hopkins, 1949, Washington U., 1950; Litt.D., U. Ia., 1936; m. Anne Laziere Crawford, June 23, 1898; children—Jean Atherton (Mrs. Paul Lewinson), Eleanor. Began teaching, Louisville High Sch., 1886; staff mem., Carnegie Found. for Advancement of Teaching, N.Y., 1908-12; asst. sec., 1913-17, sec., 1917-25, dir. div. of studies, med. edn., 1925-28, Gen. Edn. Bd.; dir. Inst. for Advanced Study, 1930-39; dir. emeritus 1940—. Comdr. Legion of Honor (France), 1926. Rhodes memorial lectureship, Oxford, Eng., 1927-28, also the Taylorian lectureship, Oxford, 1928; lectr. Fondation Universitaire, Belgium, 1929. Author: The American College, 1908; Medical Education in the United States and Canada, 1910; Medical Education in Europe, 1912; Prostitution in Europe, 1913; A Modern School, 1916; A Modern College, 1923; Medical Education, A Comparative Study, 1925; Do Americans Really Value Education?, 1927; Universities—American, English, German, 1930; I Remember: An Autobiography, 1940; Henry S. Pritchett, A Biography 1943; Daniel Coit Gilman: Founder of the American Type of University, 1946; ednl. papers. Home: Falls Church, Va. Died Sept. 21, 1959.

FLEXNER, Anne Crawford (Mrs. Abraham Flexner), playwright; b. Georgetown, Ky.; d. Louis G.

and Susan (Farnum) Crawford; A.B., Vassar Coll., 1895; m. Abraham Flexner, June 23, 1898; children —Jean Atherton (Mrs. Paul Lewinson), Eleanor. Mem. Soc. Am. Dramatists. Club: Cosmopolitan. Author: (plays) Miranda of the Balcony, 1901; Mrs. Wiggs of the Cabbage Patch, 1903; A Lucky Star, 1909; The Marriage Game, 1913; The Blue Pearl, 1918; All Souls Eve, 1919; Aged 26, 1936; also (book) The Marriage Game, 1916; Aged 26 (book), 1937. Home: Stanhope Hotel, Fifth Av. and 81st St., N.Y.C. Died Jan. 12, 1955.

FLICK, Walter A(braham), educator; b. Dayton, Va., June 19, 1895; s. Abraham Berkeley and Ida Sarah (Fletcher) F.; A.B., Bridgewater Coll., 1922; A.M., Washington and Lee U., 1924; Ph.D., Ohio State U. (hon. fellow), 1928; m. Ileita Frances Lee, Oct. 23, 1921; 1 son, Walter Berkeley (dec.). Prin. The Broadway High Sch., Broadway, Va., 1919-21; prof. of math., Shenandoah Coll., Dayton, Va., 1921-23; prof. of edn. and psychology, Washington and Lee U., 1924—, chmn. dept. of edn. and psychology 1930—; indsl., pub. relations cons.; vis. lectr. U. Alaska, 1954. Trustee Shenandoah Coll. Served as 2d lt. inf. AEF, 1917-18; civilian lectr., World War II. Mem. N.E.A., Kappa Phi Kappa, Phi Delta Kappa. Methodist. Club: Ruritan. Home: Walieta Farm, Fairfield, Va. Office: Washington and Lee U., Lexington, Va. Died Nov. 27, 1958; buried Fairfield (Va.) Cemetery.

FLINNER, Ira Arthur, educator; b. New Brighton, Pa., Jan. 31, 1884; s. Adam and Mary (Schaffer) F.; grad. Slippery Rock (Pa.) State Normal Sch., 1902; Ph.B., Grove City (Pa.) Coll., 1906, LL.D., 1927; A.B., Harvard, 1911, A.M., 1919, Ed.M., 1925, Ed. D., 1926; m. Bertha B. Welsh, Aug. 22, 1906. Prin. North Washington (Pa.) Inst., 1906-09; instr. in mathematics, Grove City Coll., summer, 1911; headmaster Huntington Sch., 1911-25; edn. dir. Lake Placid Club Edn. Foundation 1925-51, trustee, 1925— headmaster Northwood Sch. 1925-51, Blair Acad., 1951—. Member Headmaster's Assn., N.E. Assn. Colls. and Secondary Schs., N.E.A., Nat. Secondary Sch. Assn., Phi Delta Kappa. Republican. Conglist. Mason. Home: Blairstown, N.J. Died Apr. 30, 1954; buried Blairstown.

FLINT, Austin, physician; b. Ballston, N.Y., July 30, 1868; s. Austin and Elizabeth (McMaster) F.; grad. Phillips Andover Acad.; M.D., Bellevue Hosp. Med. Coll., N.Y.U., 1889; hon. A.M., Princeton, 1894; m. Marion Wing, 1895; 1 dau., Adelaide (Mrs. Reginald L. Whitman). Practiced in N.Y.C., 1889-1929; now retired; prof. obstetrics U. and Bellevue Hosp. Med. Coll., 1895-32, prof. emeritus, 1932—; cons. obstetrician Bellevue Hosp.; cons. surgeon Woman's Hosp., N.Y.C., Hosp. for Ruptured and Crippled, Newport Hosp., ret. active practice 1938. Fellow A.C.S.; mem. Am., N.Y. State and N.Y. County med. assns., N.Y. Acad. Medicine, N.Y. Obstet. Society, Alumni Bellevue and Woman's hospitals. Republican. Episcopalian. Specializes in diseases of women and obstetrics. Home: Venice, Fla. Died July 20, 1955; buried Woodlawn Cemetery, N.Y.C.*

FLINT, Leon Nelson, educator; b. Thayer, Kan., Oct. 8, 1875; s. Horatio Nelson and Mary Sophia (Miller) F.; A.B., U. Kan., 1897; m. Elizabeth Browning, Sept. 6, 1904; children—Maurice Browning, Robert Leon, George Miller. Prin. Olathe (Kan.) High Sch., 1900-01; pub. Manhattan (Kan.) Nationalist, 1901-05; sec. Alumni Assn. U. Kan., editor Grad. Mag., 1905-16; lectr. journalism U. Kan., 1906-09, asst. prof. journalism, 1909-13, asso. prof., 1913-16, prof., chmn. dept., 1916-41, prof. journalism, 1941-46, now ret. Editor The Kansas Editor, 1917-41. Mem. Am. Assn. Tchrs. of Journalism, Am. Assn. Schs. and Depts. of Journalism (pres., 1927) Kan. Editorial Assn., Phi Beta Kappa. Author: Newspaper Writing in High Schools, 1918; The Editorial, 1920; Ten Tests of a Town, 1921; The Conscience of the Newspaper, 1925. Contbr. to mags. and newspapers. Home: Lawrence, Kan. Died Sept. 30, 1955.

FLOM, George Tobias (flŭm), philologist; b. Utica, Wis., Apr. 12, 1871; s. Ole O. Torjussen and Martha Jonsson (Borlaug) F.; B.L., U. Wis., 1893; A.M., Vanderbilt U., 1894; studied U. Wis., 1896-97, Columbia, 1897-98 (fellow in Germanic philology), univs. of Copenhagen and Leipzig, 1898-99; Ph.D., Columbia, 1900; m. Loretta Regina Muldoon Dec. 26, 1900; children—George Reginald (dec.), Elizabeth Edda (Mrs. Arthur T. Gorman), Mary Antoinette (Mrs. John R. Thim). Asst. in French and German, Vanderbilt U., 1899-1900; instr., later prof. Scandinavian langs. and actg. prof. English philology, Ia. State U., 1900-09; prof. Scandinavian langs., U. Ill., 1909-27, Scandinavian langs. and English Philology since 1927. Editor Scandinavian Studies and Notes, 1911-20; asso. editor Ill. U. Studies in Lang. and Lit., 1915-40; coop. editor, later asso. editor, Journal of English and Germanic philology, 1902-26, mng. editor 1926-40. Decorated Knight Order of St. Olaf, 1st class (Norway), 1939. Fellow Det Norske Videnskaps-Akademie i Oslo in the div. of foreign members. Mem. Modern Lang. Assn. (past v.p.), Norwegian-Am. Hist. Soc., Soc. Advancement of Scandinavian Study (past pres.), Forening for Norske Maal og Minne (Oslo), Soc. for Northern Research (London), Normandsforbundet (Oslo), Linguistic Soc. of America (past pres.), Am. Assn. University Professors (charter member), Phi Beta Kappa. Author: Scandinavian Influence on Lowland Scotch, 1900; Chapters on Scandinavian Immigration to Iowa, 1906; History of Scandinavian Study in American Universities, 1907; History of Norwegian Immigration to the United States, 1909; Fragment R.A. 58 C of the Konungs Skuggsjá, 1911; The Phonology of the Dialect of Aurland, 1915; Studies in Scandinavian Paleography, 1915-17; South Scandinavian Rock-Tracings, 1921; Language of the Konungs Skuggsjá—A.M. 243, B.a., part I, 1921, part II, 1923; Old English Grammar and Reader, 1930. Editor: Björnson's Synnöve Solbakken, 1905, 1918; Tegner's Frithiofs Saga, 1909; American Facsimile Edition of Konungs Skuggsjá; Arnamagnean Manuscript 243, B.a., Folio in Phototypic Reproduction with Diplomatic Text, Introduction and Notes, 1916; The Borgathing Law of the Codex Tunsbergensis, 1925; A.M. 315 E. Folio, Fragment of an Old Norwegian Legal Codex of ca. 1225, Facsimile with Introduction on the Script and the Language, 1928; A.M. 619, 4to, An Old Norwegian Homiletic Codex of ca. 1200, Diplomatic Text with Eight Facsimile Pages and Introduction, 1929; The Old Norwegian General Law of the Gulathing. According to Codex Gl. k.S. 1153, Folio. Diplomatic Edition with Linguistic-Paleographic Introduction and Four Facsimile Pages, 1937. Morphology of the Dialect of Aurland in Sogn. Norway, 1944. Contbr. to Am. and European philol. and linguistic jours. Home: 2127 Osceola Drive, Ft. Myers, Fla. Died Jan. 1960.

FLOOD, Francis Arthur, fgn. service officer; b. Oakland, Ia., Nov. 13, 1896; s. James Francis and Jennie (Meeks) F.; A.B., U. Neb., 1920; m. Helen Janet Maitland, June 27, 1925; children—Barbara Joan, Francis A., Maitland Kirk. Homestead, Wyo., 1920-22; instr. U. of Neb., 1922-23, Ia. State Coll., 1923-24; asso. editor Nebraska Farmer, Lincoln 1924-27, Farmer-Stockman, Okla. City, 1937-42; fgn. writer for agrl. mags., 1927-33; asst. to adminstr. A.A.A., U.S. Dept. Agr., 1933-37, asso. dir., fgn. agrl. relations, 1943-47; apptd. fgn. service officer U.S. Dept. of State. 1957, agrl. attaché and 1st sec. U.S. Embassy, Ottawa, Can., 1947-53, counselor of Embassy, Rome, Italy, 1953-55; consul-gen. Glasgow, Scotland, 1955—. Served seaman 2d class USN, World War I; asst. to War Food adminstr., World War II. Mem. Agrl. Inst. Can., Kappa Lambda Alpha, Alpha Gamma Rho. Clubs: Rotary (Ottawa); Explorers (N.Y. C.). Home: 3715 Chevy Chase Lake Dr., Chevy Chase 15, Md. Office: care U.S. Fgn. Service, Dept. of State, Washington 25. Died Aug. 21, 1956; buried Arlington Nat. Cemetery.

FLOOD, Walter Vincent, mfg. exec.; b. N.Y. City, Aug. 9, 1897; s. Thomas and Marguerite Flood; graduate St. Francis College; married Mary M. Flood; children—Walter, John, Thomas, Janet, Mary, James. Secretary and treasurer, Moto-Meter Gauge & Equipment Corp.; v.p. and comptroller Auto-Lite Battery Corp., Niagara Falls; v.p. and comptroller Electric Auto-Lite Co., Toledo, O., Prest-O-Lite Battery Corp., Indianapolis, Auto-Lite Battery Corp. of Calif., Oakland. Republican. Catholic. Home: 3765 Brookside Rd. Office: 1200 Champlain St., Toledo, O. Deceased.

FLORANCE, Howard, editor; b. Yonkers, N.Y., Nov. 6, 1885; s. Charles and Cora (Smith) F.; ed. pub. schs. of N.Y.C.; m. Jessie Lyng, Oct. 29, 1909 (dec.); children—Maida (Mrs. Albert M. Cusick), Elizabeth (Mrs. Gordon V. Reid). Began as office boy, 1898; photographers' asst., 1899, pub. stenographer, 1901; with editorial staff Review of Reviews (mag.) in various capacities, including financial editor, mng. editor, 1905-37; mng. editor, sec.-treas. Literary Digest, 1937-38; became asso. editor The Readers Digest, 1938, later sr. editor, now ret. Republican. Presbyn. Home: 103-16 Springfield Blvd., Queens Village 9, N.Y. Died Jan. 1959.

FLORER, Warren Washburn, author; b. Loda, Ill., May 17, 1869; s. William Jefferson and Mary Ann Louise (Washburn) F.; A.B., DePauw, 1890, A.M., 1894; studied Cornell, 1891-93, U. of Leipzig, 1893-96; fellow in German, Cornell U., 1896-97, Ph.D., 1897; m. Jeannette Smith, June 22, 1898; children —Frances Mary, Herbert Washburn. Instr. German, 1897-1906, asst. prof., 1906-18, U. of Mich.; now mgr. Mut. Benefit Life Ins. Co. Faculty comdr. R.O.T.C., 1917-18. Mem. Modern Lang. Assn. America, Delta Tau Delta, S.A.R. (state historian, 1917-19), Imperial Institute of the University of Leipzig, Academic Modern Philological Society of Germany. Author: Substantivflexion bei Martinus Luther, 1899; Biblische Geschichten und Kapitel aus Weizsäckers und Lutuher's Bibelübersetzungen, 1900-02; Luther's Use of the Pre-Lutheran Versions of the Bible; Heyse's l'Arrabbiata (edit. for direct method), 1902; selections from Luther's Bible Translation (text edit.), 1903; Schiller's Jungfrau von Orleans, 1907; Baumbach's Der Schwiegersohn, 1909; Wildenbruch's Novellen; Frenssen's Jörn Uhl; Hillern's Höher als die Kirche, 1917; Liberty Writings of Dr. Hermann Kiefer, 1917; German Liberty Authors, 1917; The Revolution of 1848, 1918; also articles on Luther's lang. German lit., Revolution of 1848, pedagogy, and guides for the study in German of Goethe's Herman and Dorothea Egmont, Schiller's Wilhelm Tell and various short stories. Address: Ann Arbor, Mich. Died Apr. 1958.

FLORSHEIM, Irving S., chmn. bd. Florsheim Shoe Co.; b. Chgo., Oct. 27, 1893; s. Milton S. and Gertrude (Stern) F.; B.A., Cornell U., 1914; children —Mary Elizabeth (Mrs. Allan Jones), Nancy Jane (Mrs. Bertrand Goldberg); married Helen Titus Ford, Aug. 6, 1951. Became asso. with the Florsheim Shoe Co., Chgo., pres., 1926-46, chmn. bd., 1946—. Served as lt. (j.g.) USNR, 1917-18. Clubs: Standard, Lake Shore Country, Mid-Day, Tavern. Home: S. Milwaukee Av., Libertyville, Ill. Office: 130 S. Canal St., Chgo. 6. Died Oct. 18, 1959.

FLORY, Ira S(amuel) flō'rē), law educator; b. Bridgewater, Va., Aug. 24, 1883; s. Joel Soloman and Sarah Margaret (Miller) F.; B.A., Mount Morris (Ill.) Coll., 1907; LL.B., U. Va., 1909; summer student Columbia U. Law Sch., 1917; m. Ella Eugenia Early, Sept. 20, 1905; children—Harold Michael, Frances Willard, Ira Samuel. Instr. mathematics Mount Morris Coll., 1905-07; admitted to Va. bar, 1909; instr. law, U. Va., 1909-12; prof. law La. State U., 1912-17, 1919—, acting dean, 1933-35, 39-41; law clk. Carter, Ledyard & Milburn, N.Y.C., 1917-18. Served in F.A. officers' tng. sch., Camp Taylor, Ky., 1918. Mem. Phi Delta Phi, Phi Kappa Phi, Omicron Delta Kappa, Order of the Coif. Democrat. Methodist. Mason. Home: 3353 Byron St., Baton Rouge 5. Office: La. State U. Law School, Baton Rouge 3. Died Sept. 3, 1950; buried Roselawn Meml. Park, Baton Rouge.

FLOTA, George W., judge; b. Pitts., 1893; s. Adam and Anna F.; m. Ruth Coles, 1928; children—Claire, Richard; son by previous marriage, George W. (USN). Sec. to govs.' Strong and Bone of Alaska; admitted to bar, 1927; apptd. asst., dist. atty. 1st Jud. div. Alaska, 1927, counsellor-at-large Interior Dept. for Alaska, 1940, U.S. dist. judge, 1st Div. Alaska, 1947. Mason, Elk (life). Died June 4, 1955; buried Juneau, Alaska.

FLOURNOY, Harry L(ightfoot) (flur-noi), newspaper editor, writer; b. Romney, W.Va., Mar. 5, 1878; s. Samuel Lightfoot and Frances Anne (White) F.; student U. W.Va., 1896-1900. Law clk. Flournoy, Price & Smith, 1900-08; auditor, City of Charleston, W.Va., 1908-12; real estate bus., 1912-14; dep. officer Kanawha Co., W.Va., Bur. Internal Revenue, 1914-18; joined Charleston (W.Va.) Gazette, 1918, asso. mng. editor, chief editorial writer since 1942; writer 200 local feature fiction stories, Adventures of Old Man Heck, 1925-30. Mem. Charleston Planning Commn.; chief clk. Draft Bd., Charleston, World War I. Mem. Allied Artists. Presbyn. Elk. Clubs: Old Man Heck (pres. 1949-50), Press (Charleston, W.Va.). Author: Chips and Whetstones, 1950. Office: care The Gazette, Charleston, W.Va. Died Dec. 31, 1954.

FLOWERS, James Nathaniel, lawyer, retired r.r. exec.; b. Carroll Co., Miss., July 17, 1870; LL.B., U. of Miss., 1896; widower. Admitted to Miss. State Bar, 1896; asst. atty. gen. of Miss., 1903-06; atty. for Gulf, Mobile and Ohio R.R. Co., 1906-47; gen. counsel and dir. of that co. and New Orleans Gt. Northern, 1928-47, and v.p. both cos., 1940-47; mem. law firm at Jackson, Miss., since 1906, present style of which is Flowers, Brown & Burns. Mem. Miss Bar Assn. (pres., 1925). Home: 1505 North State St. Office: First National Bank Bldg., Jackson, Miss. Died May 5, 1952.

FLOWERS, Robert Lee, univ. pres.; b. York Collegiate Inst., North Carolina, Nov. 6, 1870; s. George Washington and Sarah (Haynes) F.; grad. U.S. Naval Acad., 1891; hon. A.M., Trinity College (now Duke Univ., Durham, N.C., 1900; LL.D., Davidson College, 1927; LL.D., University of North Carolina, 1942; m. Lily Virginia Parrish, June 22, 1905 (died May 22, 1948); children—Virginia, Sybil Parrish. Prof. mathematics, Duke U., 1891-1934; v.p. in charge of business div., 1925-41, pres. 1941-48, trustee of the univ., sec. since 1910, treas., 1928-48, chancellor since 1948. Mem. bd. trustees of the Duke Endowment since 1926. Dir. Durham & Southern Ry. Co., Fidelity Bank. Mem. bd. visitors, U.S. Naval Acad., 1946. Trustee Greensboro Coll., Methodist Orphanage, Oxford Orphanage, N.C. Coll. for Negroes, Lincoln Hosp. for Negroes. Mem. Bd. Edn. of N.C. Conf. M.E. Ch., S., since 1916. Mem. N.C. Acad. Science, Alpha Tau Omega, Omicron Delta Kappa, Phi Beta Kappa. Mason. Rotarian. Home: Durham, N.C. Died Aug. 24, 1951; buried Maplewood Cemetery, Durham.

FLOYD, Ivy Knox, clergyman; b. Whitesville, Ky., Sept. 15, 1885; s. Harden Lawrence and Sallie (Douthitt) F.; student Bethel Coll., McKenzie, Tenn., 1911-13; B.S.L., Oskaloosa (Ia.) Coll., 1914; m. Clyde Godbold, May 3, 1908; children—Vernon Lamar, Walter Ray, Floyd Godbold, Melba Laurence. Tchr. pub. schs. 7 yrs.; ordained ministry Cumberland Presbyn. Ch., 1909; pastor Trenton, Tenn., 1912-14, First Ch., Austin, Tex., 1916-17, First Ch., Dallas, 1923—. Moderator Gen. Assembly Cumberland Presbyn. Ch., 1926. Served as chaplain 7th Tex. Inf.,

131st M.G. Batt., Development Batt., World War; now chaplain 132d F.A., Tex. N.G. Ch. reporter on Dallas Dispatch, 1926-29; now reporter, religious editorial writer Dallas Jour., in addition to pastoral work. Home: 810 S. Beacon St., Dallas. Deceased.

FLOYD, Richard C(lark), b. Brookline, Mass., Oct. 28, 1886; s. Eugene Benton and Mary Cleaveland (Taylor) F.; A.B., Harvard, 1911, grad. study, grad. sch. bus. adminstrn., 1910-11; m. Nancy Ogden, Dec. 7, 1929; children—Mary Cleaveland, Nancy Ogden, Richard Clark. Formerly v.p., dir. Bird & Son, Inc.; later asso. dir. Mass. div. Am. Cancer Soc.; dir., mem. exec. com. Norfolk Co. Trust Co.; mem. corp. Brookline Savs. Bank; dir. Coolidge Coop. Bank. Has served Town of Brookline, as park commr., chmn. playground commn., mem. Limited Town Meeting Assembly, mem. sch. com., mem. finance com., chmn. gymnasium and baths commn., dir. citizens com. Dir. Boys Club Camp Wing; mem. boys work com. Boston Y.M.C.A.; trustee Dexter Sch., Longwood, Park Sch., Brookline. Served as capt. C.W.S., U.S. Army, World War I. Mem. bd. dirs. Inter-Collegiate Assn. Amateur Athletes of Am.; rep. Intercollegiate Assn. to convs. of Amateur Athletic Union and of Am. Olympic Assn.; twice elected mgr. Am. Olympic Team; chmn. com. on rules of athletic competition of Intercollegiate Athletic Assn., mem. games com., Harvard rep. Mem., v. chmn. overseers' com. on athletic sports Harvard; v.p., dir. Harvard Alumni Assn., mem. permanent class com., chmn. class 25th reunion; Harvard commencement marshal, dir. Harvard Alumni Bull.; mem. standing com. Harvard Ch. Mem. Boston C. of C., S.R., Delta Kappa Epsilon. Republican. (mem. state com. and exec. com. of Mass.; del., v.p. Mass. state conv.). Episcopalian. Clubs: Harvard (N.Y.C.); Harvard (bd. govs.); Madison Square Garden, University (Boston); Phoenix S-K, Hasty Pudding and Institute of 1770 (Harvard); Country and Polo (Dedham); Longwood Cricket (Chestnut Hill); The Country (sec., mem. bd. govs.), Commercial (Brookline); Lipton League; Middlesex; Republican of Mass., Norfolk County Republican. Address: 207 Fisher Av., Brookline, Mass. Died Sept. 15, 1953.

FLYNN, Edmund W., jurist; b. Providence, Jan. 9, 1890; s. James A. and Elizabeth J. (Kelly) F.; grad. magna cum laude, Holy Cross, 1910; grad. Georgetown Law Sch., 1915. Admitted to R.I. bar, 1917; mem. R.I. Ho. of Reps., 1931-35; chief justice Supreme Ct. of R.I. since 1935. Served with U.S. Army, World War I. Mem. Am. Bar Assn. Home: 252 Rhodes St., Providence. Died Apr. 1957.

FLYNN, Edward, ry. ofcl.; b. Bement, Ill.; s. John and Martha (Yost) F.; student pub. schs.; m. Lucy Alice Fletcher, July 8, 1916. With C., B.&Q. R.R. Co., 1897-47, successively brakeman, condr. train master, asst. supt., div. supt., gen. supt., gen. mgr., v.p. operation, 1897-1935, exec. v.p., 1935-47, ret.; dir. C., B.&Q. R.R. Co. and C.&S. lines, Chgo. Union Station Co., Terminal R.R. Assn. of St. Louis, Mercantile Trust & Savings Bank, (Chgo.), U.S. Nat. Bank (Omaha). Club: Chicago (Chgo.). Home: 181 Lake Shore Dr., Chgo. Died June 5, 1954; buried Denver.

FLYNN, Edward Joseph, lawyer; b. N.Y. City, Sept. 22, 1891; s. Henry T. and Sarah (Mallon) F.; LL.B., Sch. of Law, Fordham U., 1912; LL.D., 1925; m. Helen Margaret Jones, June 15, 1927; children—Edward Patrick, Richard Michael, Sheila. Admitted to N.Y. bar, 1913; assemblyman Bronx County, N.Y., 1918-21, sheriff, 1922-25; mem. firm Goldwater & Flynn since 1924; chamberlain City of N.Y., 1926-28; sec. State of N.Y., 1929-39; commr. gen. U.S. Worlds Fair Commn., 1939 to closing. Chmn. exec. com. Democratic County (Bronx) Com. since 1922; nat. committeeman from State of N.Y. since 1930; chmn. Democratic National Com., 1940-42. Roman Catholic. Knight of Malta. Author: You're the Boss, 1947. Home: 2728 Henry Hudson Parkway, Bronx, N.Y. City. Office: 60 E. 42d St., N.Y. City 17. Died Aug. 18, 1953.

FLYNN, Errol Leslie, actor, author; b. Hobart, Tasmania, June 20, 1909; s. Theodore Thomson and Marelle (Young) F.; student St. Paul's Sch., South Western London Coll. (both of London), North Shore Grammar Sch. (Sydney) and King's Sch. (Ireland); m. Lilliane Marie Madeleine Carré (Lili Damita), May 5, 1935 (div. Mar. 31, 1942); 1 son, Sean Leslie; m. 2d, Nora Eddington (div.); 2 daus. Came to U.S., 1936, naturalized, 1942. Actor, Northampton Repertory Co., Eng. Malvern Festival, 1934; with Warner Bros. Pictures Corp., 1935—; starred in Captain Blood, Robin Hood, Gentleman Jim, Objective Burma, San Antonio, Silver River, Adventures of Captain Fabian, Mara Maru, Crossed Swords, Lilacs in the Spring, The Warrior; pres. Thomson Productions, Inc., Adventures of Don Juan, Kim, That Forsythe Woman, Against All Flags, Master of Ballantrae. Served as patrol officer New Guinea Govt. Service, 1929; mem. Hong Kong Volunteers, 1932. Mem. Royal Geographic Soc. Club: California Yacht. Author: Beam Ends, 1937; Showdown, 1946; My Wicked, Wicked Ways. Address: 7740 Mulholland Dr., Los Angeles 46. Died Oct. 14, 1959.

FLYNN, Vincent Joseph, clergyman; b. Avoca, Minn., Sept. 11, 1901; s. John Edward and Estella (Farrell) F.; A.B., Coll. of St. Thomas, St. Paul, Minn., 1923; student St. Paul Sem., 1921-27; S.T.B., Catholic U. of America, 1927; A.M., U. of Minn. 1929; Ph.D., U. of Chgo., 1939; LL.D., St. Ambrose Coll., 1950, U. of Notre Dame, 1951. Ordained priest Roman Catholic Ch., 1927; asst. pastor Ch. of Incarnation, Minneapolis, summer 1927; instr. in Latin and English, St. Thomas Mil. Acad., St. Paul, Minn., 1927-30; assistant professor of English, College of St. Thomas, 1935-39, professor of English and chairman of department, 1940-44, pres. of the college since Jan. 1944; visiting lecturer Cath. U. of America, summers 1939-41. Awarded Guggenheim fellowship, 1942-43. Sec.-treas. of corporation Coll. of St. Thomas. Catholic co-chmn. North Central region Nat. Conf. Christians and Jews. Mem. bd. of dir. J. J. Hill Reference Library, St. Paul Inst.; consultant Board of Edn., Nat. Catholic Welfare Conf.; member of the National Commission on Accrediting; Minnesota State bd. of directors UN Association; Citizens Com. Hoover Report. Mem. bd. govs. Menninger Found., Topeka, Kan., 1954—. Recipient outstanding achievement award, University of Minnesota, 1953. Member Modern Language Association, Medieval Academy, American Catholic Historical Assn., Bibliog. Soc. America, Lambda Alpha Psi, Delta Epsilon Sigma. K.C. Clubs: Cosmos (Washington), Skylight, Minneapolis (Mpls.), Town and Country (St. Paul), Chicago Athletic. Editor: Prose Readings—An Anthology for Cath. Colls., 1942; A Shorte Introduction of Grammar (by William Lily, 1567), 1945. Traveled and worked in libraries in Eng., France, Italy, Germany and Belgium, 1934-35; discovered manuscript relating to history of Anglo-Italian relations and general cultural history in last half of 15th Century, Venerable English Coll., Rome. Address: College of St. Thomas, St. Paul 1. Died July 6, 1956; buried Mendota Heights, Minn.

FLYTHE, William P., newspaper corr.; b. Conway, N.C., Mar. 19, 1893; s. James H. and Jimmie (Walton) F.; student Acad. Richmond Co., Augusta, Ga., 1903-07; m. Marion Nichols, Dec. 24, 1939; children—(by previous marriage to Julia Hatcher), Wm. P., Mrs. Jack Morris. Reporter Pitts. Gazette Times, 1909-10; city editor Augusta Herald, 1911-12, Atlanta Georgian, 1912-15; city editor Savannah Press, 1915-16; corr. Internat. News, White House, 1917-37; publicity, indsl. relations J. A. Jones Constrn. Co., 1940-45; editor, bur. mgr., corr. polit. analysis, Hearst Bur., Washington, 1945—. Mem. White House, State Dept. corr. assns. Club: National Press (Washington). Home: 1301 15th St., Washington. Office: Times-Herald Bldg.; also Pennsylvania, Bldg., Washington. Died Jan. 22, 1956; buried Augusta, Ga.

FOGHT, Harold Waldstein (fōt), educator; b. Fredrickshald, Norway, Dec. 7, 1869; s. Capt. John E. and Laura (Arneberg) F.; student Fredrikshald Latin Sch., 1875-81; grad. Ord (Neb.) High Sch., 1890; student U. Neb., 1893-95; A.B., Ia. Coll., 1897; A.M., Augustana Coll., Rock Island, Ill., 1900; grad. study, Royal Frederick U., Copenhagen, 1900-01; Ph.D., Am. U., 1918; m. Alice Mabel Robbins, Dec. 28, 1897. Tchr. rural and village schs., 1890-93; prof. history and sociology, Elk Horn Coll., 1895-97, headmaster, 1897-99; prof. history and edn., Blair (now Dana) Coll., Blair, Neb., 1899-1900; pres. Ansgar Coll., Hutchinson, Minn., 1901-03; prin. acad., Midland Coll., Atchison, Kan., 1903-06; prof. history and edn., Midland Coll., 1906-08; prof. rural edn., Mo. State Tchrs. Coll., Kirksville, 1908-12; specialist in rural edn., U.S. Bur. Edn., 1912-14; specialist in rural sch. practice, 1914-17, chief rural school div., U.S. Bur. Edn., 1917-19; pres. No. State Tchrs. Coll., Aberdeen, S.D., 1919-27; pres. Municipal U. of Wichita, 1927-33; became supt. and spl. disbursing agt. for Cherokee Indians, U.S. Office Indian Affairs, 1933. Chmn. ednl. com. Nat. Survey Assn.; mem. country ch. and country life com., Fed. Council Chs.; mem. N.E.A. (mem. Ednl. Council, 1916; chmn. Com. of 100 on Rural Edn., 1923; v.p., 1925). Dir. provincial ednl. survey of Saskatchewan, 1917; dir. state ednl. surveys S.D., Ala., etc. Mason (32°). Author: Trail of the Loup, 1906; The True Significance of the Norse Discovery of America, 1900; The American Rural School, 1910; Rural Denmark and Its Schools, 1915; The Rural Teacher and His Work, 1915; Unfathomed Japan, 1928. Collaborator on "Educational Resources of Rural and Village Communities," and Comparative Educational Systems, 1917, and many bulletins of U.S. Govt.; lectr. nat. and state ednl. assns., univs. and coll. summers schs.; spl. lectr. on rural edn. in Japan (on invitation of Japanese govt.), 1924. Home: Mound, Lake Minnetonka, Minn. Deceased.

FOGLESONG, John E(dward), (fō'gĭl-sông); chemist; b. Lucerne, Ind., July 20, 1885; s. Peter John and Mary Adaline (Long) F.; A.B., Wabash Coll., 1910; A.M., Ohio State U., 1912; Ph.D., Cornell U., 1919; m. Florence Eugenia Young, June 2, 1915 (dec.); 1 son, William Peter. Chemist DuPont Co., Wilmington, Del., 1912-13, Union Carbide Co., Niagara Falls, N.Y., 1913-16, The Barrett Co., Phila., 1919-21; instr. Cornell U., 1917-19; asst. prof. chemitsry U. of the South, 1921-23; asst. prof. Trinity (Conn.) Coll., 1923-28; asst. prof. U. Miss., 1928-30, asso. prof., 1930-45, prof. analytical chemistry, 1945—. Mem. Am. Chem. Soc., Gamma Alpha, Alpha Chi Sigma, Phi Delta Chi, Sigma Xi. Methodist. Mason (grand high priest Miss. 1949). Author: Exercises in Quantitative Analysis, 1943. Contbr. articles to chem. jours. Home: 20 N. 14th St., Oxford, Miss. Office: University, Miss. Died Dec. 19, 1956.

FOGO, James Gordon, Can. senator, steel exec.; b. Halifax, N.S., July 9, 1896; s. Adam G. and Alice (Hanway) F.; LL.B., Dalhousie U., 1924; m. Helen Fisher, Oct. 11, 1927; children—James, Annette Elizabeth. Admitted to N.S. bar, 1924, and practiced with Burchell, Smith, Parker & Fogo, Halifax, 1926-46; v.p. Algoma Steel Corp., Ltd., Ottawa, since 1946. Apptd. mem. Senate of Can., 1949. Created Kings Counsel, 1938. Served as asso. co-ordinator of controls, Dept. Munitions and Supply of Can., Ottawa, 1942-44, mem. war contracts depreciation bd., 1943-44, dir. Wartime Shipbldg., Ltd., 1943-44. Pres. Nat. Liberal Fedn. of Can. since 1946. Clubs: Rideau; York; Halifax. Home: 260 Metcalfe St. Office: 140 Wellington St., Ottawa, Ont., Can. Died July 6, 1952.

FOLEY, Frederick Clement, ex-coll. pres.; b. Lowell, Mass., Mar. 9, 1904; s. Michael and Margaret (Heeland) F.; A.B., Providence Coll., 1927; A.M., Cath. U. Am., 1932, grad. work in philosophy and theology, 1932-34. Prof. religion Providence Coll., 1934-44, asst. dean, 1936-44, pres., 1944-47, superior of Dominican Fathers of the faculty, 1944-47; now mem. faculty Aquinas Coll. High Sch., Columbus, O. Vice pres. and treas. Providence Coll. Corp.; chaplain, mem. bd. govs. Providence Coll. Alumni Assn. Mem. Order of Preachers (Dominican). Mem. Thomistic Inst., Delta Epsilon Sigma. Home: 557 Mt. Vernon Av., Columbus, O. Died Aug. 17, 1955.*

FOLLANSBEE, John, retired exec.; b. Pitts., May 11, 1868; s. Gilbert and Marie Jackson (Haynes) F.; student pub. schs. Pittsburgh, Pa.; m. Alice P. Kerr, June 1, 1899 (dec. 1934); children—John Haynes, Robert Kerr, Rebecca R. (Mrs. Mifflin W. Blackstone). Chmn. Follansbee Steel Corp., Pitts., 1940-47, retired; pres. Lustro Coated Sheets Co., 1912—. Republican. Presbyn. Clubs: Duquesne, Field (Pitts.). Home: Bent Oak, Fox Chapel Rd., Sharpsburg, Pa. Died Oct. 9, 1957.

FOLLETT, Charles Walcott, bookseller, pub.; b. Indianapolis, Dec. 28, 1882; s. Nathaniel and Martha (Duncan) F.; ed. pub. schs., Indianapolis; children—Dwight, Garth, Robert, Nathaniel. Bookselling, pub. bus. since 1902, pres., treas. J.W. Wilcox & Follett Co., established 1873, The Follett Book Co., established 1929, The Follett Pub. Co., established 1922; dir. chmn. exec. com., Central Nat. Bank, Chicago. Served as pvt. 158th Ind. Regt., Spanish-Am. War. Vice pres. John Howard Assn. A founder Ill. Booksellers' Assn. (ex-pres., sec.). Republican. Unitarian. Club: City (Chicago). Home: 190 E Chestnut St. Office: 1255 S. Wabash Av., Chgo. Died Dec. 9, 1952; buried Oakridge Mausoleum.

FOLTZ, Frederick Steinman, army officer; born Lancaster, Pa., Dec. 15, 1857; s. Surgeon Gen. Jonathan M. (U.S.N.) and Rebecca (Steinman) F.; grad. U.S. Mil. Acad., 1879; m. Mary F., d. Maj. T. B. Keefer, U.S.A., July 11, 1883. Commd. 2d lt. 1st Cav., June 13, 1879; 1st lt., Mar. 26, 1888; capt. 2d Cav., June 23, 1898; maj. 15th Cav., Sept. 13, 1906; lt. col. cav., Feb. 29, 1912; col. of cav., Sept. 27, 1914; assigned to comd. of 1st Cav., Dec. 14, 1914; brig. gen. N.A., Aug. 5, 1917. Duty with Maj. Gen. Miles in Cuba and P.R., July-Aug. 1898; collector of customs, Batavano, Cuba, 1898-99; served successively as supervisor of police, Havana, chief of secret service of Cuba, provost marshal and capt. of Port of Havana; in P.I., 1906; gov. Province of Havana, 1908. Apptd. comdr. 182d Inf. Brigade, A.E.F., Sept. 1917, 91st Div., July 1918; hon. discharged as brig. gen. N.A., Nov. 11, 1918. Mem. Soc. Santiago, Loyal Legion, Aztec Club. Club: Army and Navy. Address: 2022 Columbia Rd., N.W., Washington. Died Aug. 28, 1952; buried Arlington Nat. Cemetery.

FOLTZ, James A(rthur), Jr., newspaper exec.; b. Ft. Smith, Ark., Aug. 31, 1903; s. James Arthur and Jane (Price) F.; student Culver Mil. Acad., 1920-22, U. Mo., 1922-27; m. Josephine Henry, June 16, 1928; children—James Arthur, Clinton Henry. Advt. salesman Ft. Worth Press, 1927-35, advt. dir., 1940, bus. mgr., 1940-45; bus. mgr. Comml. Appeal and Memphis Press Scimitar, 1945-47; asst. gen. mgr. and bus. mgr. Cleve. Press, 1947-53; bus. mgr. Memphis Publishing Co. since 1953. Mem. bd. Shelby Co. Red Cross, Community Council; budget com. Memphis Community Chest. Mem. C. of C. (indsl. council), Am., So. newspaper pubs. assns., Sigma Delta Chi, Phi Delta Theta. Republican. Mem. Christian Ch. Clubs: Memphis Country, Tennessee. Office: 33 W. Galloway Dr., Memphis. Died Apr. 28, 1956; buried Forest Park, Ft. Smith, Ark.

FOLZ, Stanley, lawyer; b. Phila., Sept. 22, 1878; s. Leon H. and Alice (Rhine) F.; A.B., U. Pa., 1900, LL.B., 1903; m. Blanche Marks, Dec. 11, 1916. Admitted to Pennsylvania bar, 1903, since practiced in Philadelphia, partner Folz, Bard, Kamsler, Goodis & Greenfield since 1916; director City Stores Co., Bankers Securities Corporation. Member American, Pa. State, Phila. bar assns. Republican. Jewish religion. Club: Locust. Home: Chateau Crillon, Rittenhouse Sq., Phila. 3. Office: 1315 Walnut St., Phila. 7. Died Nov. 2, 1954.

FONTAINE, Lamar, civil engineer; b. Laberde Prairie, Austin's Colony, Tex., Oct. 10, 1829; s. Edward F.; captured by Comanche Indians; prisoner over 4 yrs.; later escaped from camp, head of Zuñi River, and returned 750 miles, alone and afoot, to Austin, Tex.; later 6 yrs.; in U.S.N. under instruction of Lt. Matthew Fontaine Maury (his kinsman) and Lt. Louis Herndon; afterward traveled over Europe, Africa, Asia (from Kamtchatka to Chinese Wall and south to Ceylon), South and Central America; was with Russian army at siege of Sebastapol, winning iron cross of Peter the Great for marksmanship; was civ. eng'r. in Central America, 1860; at Pensacola, Fla., Jan., 1861, in capture of navy yard, redoubt, Fts. Barrancas and McRee; pvt. 10th Miss. inf., March, 1861; transferred to his father's co., "K," 18th Miss., June 1861; wounded at 1st Manassas; transferred to Troop I, 2d Va. cav.; scout for Gen. T. J. ("Stonewall") Jackson, Nov., 1861, to May, 1853; then courier between Gens. Joseph E. Johnston and Pemberton. During siege of Vicksburg, though suffering from 3 severe wounds and a partially paralyzed right arm, made way through Federal lines on crutches into Vicksburg with 40,000 gun caps and dispatches for Gen. Pemberton, and, 10 days later, with dispatches to Johnston and many solidiers' letters to Jackson, Miss.; famous as marksman; 5 times captured by Federals, but each time made successful daring escape. Was in 27 battles, 57 skirmishes and 100 individual skirmishes and was wounded 67 times. Wrote war songs: All Quiet Along the Potomac; Oenone; Only a Soldier; Good Old Rebel; Dying Prisoner at Camp Chase; etc. m. June 20, 1866, Lemuella S. Brickell. Address: Lyon, Miss. Died Oct. 1, 1921.

FONVILLE, Richard Henry, pharmacist; b. Center. Tex., Apr. 30, 1882; s. Washington Jefferson and Mary (Garett) F.; student Nacogdoches (Tex.) High Sch., 1896-97, Barnes Med. Coll., St. Louis, 1898-1900; m. Lillian Racke, Jan. 23, 1907 (died 1916); children—Beverly (Mrs. William Keesee Van Zandt), Irma (Mrs. J. B. Garrett), Dorothy) m. 2d, Clara McCormick, Apr. 20, 1925; 1 dau., Clarita Ann. In retail drug bus., Houston, 1903—; mayor City of Houston, 1937-38 (refused renomination), chmn. Houston Bd. Health; chmn. Houston Bd. Edn. (pres. 1924-28; instituted $11,000,000 bldg. program and complete reorganization for pub. schs.); organized 1st br. Am. Social Hygiene Assn. in Tex., 1932. Democrat. Mem. Anglican Ch. Mason (Shriner). Address: 2219 Yorktown Dr., Houston. Died Dec. 13, 1954; buried Hollywood Cemetery, Houston.

FOOT, Edwin Hawley, business exec.; b. Red Wing, Minn., Jan. 6, 1876; s. Silas Buck and Lorena (Park) F.; student Trinity Coll., Hartford, Conn., 1895-96; m. Evalyn Lawther, Nov. 8, 1898. Pres., gen. mgr. S.B. Foot Tanning Co., Red Wing, 1908-45, chmn. since 1945; dir. Goodhue Co. Nat. Bank, Trout Brook Realty Co., Superior Real Estate Co. Member Christ Ch. Mason. Clubs: Rochester (Minn.) Country; Commercial, Golf (Red Wing); Minnesota (St. Paul). Home: 1015 Fourth St. Office: Tannery Rd., Red Wing, Minn. Died July 4, 1957.

FOOT, Nathan Chandler, pathologist; b. N.Y. City, July 27, 1881; s. James Dwight and Ellen Bellows (Chandler) F.; A.B., Harvard, 1903; M.D., Columbia, 1907; m. Emma May Cobb, Jan. 11, 1910; children—Louise K. Foot Besson, Dr. Ellen B. Foot Neumann. Surg. intern, N.Y. Hospital, 1908-10; assistant instructor and instr. pathology, Harvard Medical Sch., 1912-19; instructor comparative pathology, 1919-22; assistant professor, associate professor, and prof., pathology, Coll. of Medicine, U. of Cincinnati, 1922-32; prof. surg. pathology, Cornell Med. Coll. and surg. pathologist, N.Y. Hosp. 1932-48; prof. emeritus surg. pathol.; cons. surg. pathol., N.Y Hosp., since July 1948; consulting path., Armed Forces Inst., Washington. Research in cancer detection, dept. pathology, med. coll. Cornell U. Diplomate Am. Bd. Pathology (pres.). Fellow Coll. Am. Pathologists; mem. Intersociety Cytologic Com., Am., N.Y. Co. med. socs., Pathol. Society of Argentina (corr.), N.Y. Acad. Medicine, Am. Assn. Pathologists and Bacteriologists, Am. Soc. Exptl. Pathology, N.Y. Pathol. Soc., Harvey Soc., A.A.A.S., Phi Rho Sigma, Sigma Xi, Alpha Omega Alpha. Unitarian. Clubs: Century Assn., New York Practitioners' Soc. Editor: Studies on Tsutsugamushi Disease (by Dr. Rinya Kawamura). Author papers on pathology, experimental pathology and morphology; Pathology in Surgery, 1945; Identification of Tumors, 1948. Home: 106 Tanglewylde Av., Bronxville, N.Y. Address: 1300 York Av., N.Y.C. 21. Died Sept. 4, 1958.

FOOTE, Mark, newspaper writer; b. Battle Creek, Mich., July 21, 1882; s. Dr. Lewis Adelbert and Adella (Inman) F.; student St. John's Coll., Annapolis, Md.; A.B., U. of Mich., 1903, hon. M.A., 1941; married Mildred E. Gove, Aug. 4, 1918; children—Grace (Mrs. David Brownlie), Barbara (Mrs. Joseph K. Layos), Jeanne (Mrs. William J. Dalton). Mem. of editorial staff System Magazine, Chicago, 1903-04; with Grand Rapids (Michigan) Press, 1905-13; Washington correspondent Booth Newspaper Syndicate, 1913—; one of 20 American newspaper men who went to Manila in 1935 as guests of Philippine government to witness setting up of new Philippine Commonwealth and inauguration of Manual L. Quezon as president; traveled in Japan and China, writing series of newspaper articles on conditions in Far East. Graduate J. Russell Young School of Expression. Dir. National Press Building Corporation, Newsweek Mag. Award, Master of Prophecy, 1946, 52. Member Michigamua, Michigan State Society, Sigma Delta Chi. Unitarian. Mason. Clubs: Gridirion (ex-pres.), Nat. Press (ex-pres.), Overseas Writers, Univ. of Michigan (pres. 1932). Home: 4816 Quebec St. N.W. Office: Colorado Bldg., Washington. Died July 26, 1957; buried National Meml. Park, Falls Church, Va.

FOOTE, William Wirt, librarian; b. Cleve.; s. William Wirt and Emaline (Brooks) F.; student spl. courses, Oberlin College & Sons. of Music, 1895-1900; bibliography and library sci., Oberlin Coll., 1900-02; pvt. instrn. Cleve., 1898-1900; m. Ethel L. Healey (died Oct. 13, 1958), July 20, 1898; 1 dau., Audrey Brooks (Mrs. A. Bruce Brown). Tchr. and profl. singer, 1898-1901; asst. librarian, Oberlin Coll., 1902-10, Miss. A. & M. Coll., 1911-13; librarian Oklahoma A. & Coll., 1914-15; librarian State Coll. of Washington, 1915-46; librarian emeritus, 1946—. Served as Washington state dir. library publicity, U.S. Food Adminstrn., World War. Mem. Am., Pacific N.W. library assns., Wash. State Tchrs. Assn., N.E.A., Phi Mu Alpha. Presbyn. Club: Wranglers. Author or editor and compiler of State College of Wash. Library Bulletin: U.S. Food Adminstrn. Weekly News Letter; spl. bibliographies, articles, etc. Address: 44 Roycroft Av., Long Beach, Cal. Died Oct. 20, 1953; buried Sunnyside Meml. Park, Long Beach.

FORBES, Allan, banker; b. Boston, Mass., Nov. 20, 1874; s. J. Murray and Alice B. (Bowditch) F.; A.B., Harvard, 1897; m. Josephine M. A. Crosby, June 4, 1913; children—Phyllis Forbes Leland, R. Bennet (dec.), Allan, Jr., James, Henry. Pres. State St. Trust Co., 1911-50, chmn. bd., 1950-55, co-chmn. adv. com. 2d Bank, 1955. Pres. Boston & Albany R.R. Co.; dir. Boston Ins. Co., N.E. Mut. Life Insurance Company, Boston Consolidated Gas Company; trustee of the Franklin Savings Bank. Mem. Mass. Hist. Soc. (treas. and mem. finance com.). Repub. Unitarian. Clubs: Somerset, Down Town (Bos.); Dedham Country and Polo. Home: Westwood, Mass. Office: Second Bank-State St. Trust Co., Boston 1. Died July 9, 1955; buried Westwood, Mass.

FORBES, B(ertie) C(harles), writer, pub.; b. New Deer, Aberdeenshire, Scotland, May 14, 1880; s. Robert and Agnes (Moir) F.; ed. University Coll., Dundee, Scotland, night schools; Litt.D., U. of Southern Calif., 1935; m. Adelaide Stevenson, Apr. 20, 1915; children—Bruce Charles, Malcolm Stevenson, Gordon Buchan, Wallace Federate. Learned shorthand at 13; printer's devil at 14; reporter on Dundee Courier at 17; sub-editor and editorial writer at 19; went to S. Africa, 1901; assisted in founding Rand Daily Mail, Johannesburg; came to New York, 1904, and started as reporter Jour. of Commerce, later financial editor same and editorial writer Financial and Commercial Chronicle; business and financial editor New York American, 1912; resigned to found Forbes Mag. (semi-monthly), of which is editor and publisher; writer of syndicated column; chmn., Heritage Mag., Inc., 1948-49. Naturalized citizen of United States, 1917. Member Academy Polit. Science, Met. Museum Art, St. Andrews Soc., Burns Soc., Inst. of Journalists (London). Mem. Bd. of Edn., Englewood, 1939-41. Pres. Investors Fairplay League 1942-50. Presbyterian. Clubs: Knickerbocker Country, Palm Beach Golf League. Author: Finance, Business and the Business of Life, 1915; Men Who Are Making America, 1917; Keys to Success, 1919; Forbes Epigrams, 1922; Men Who Are Making the West, 1923; Automotive Giants of America, 1925; How to Get the Most Out of Business, 1927; The Salesman's Diary, 1937, 46; Little Bits About Big Men, 1940; 499 Scottish Stories—For the Price of 500, 1945; Among Books: Editor, America's 50 Foremost Business Leaders, 1948; 101 Unusual Experiences Gleaned from the Careers of Business Leaders, 1952. Freedom Found., Honor Medal, 1952. Office: 70 5th Av., N.Y.C. Died May 6, 1954.

FORBES, Harriette Merrifield, author; b. Worcester, Mass., Oct. 22, 1856; d. William Trowbridge Merrifield; grad. Oread Collegiate Inst., Mass., 1873; m. William Trowbridge Forbes, Feb. 5, 1884; children—William T. M., Allan W., Cornelia B., Katharine M., Esther L., Malcolm S. (dec.). Mem. Worcester Hist. Soc., Colonel Tim Bigelow Chpt. D.A.R., N.E. Historic-Geneal Soc. Author: The Hundredth Town, 1889; The Diary of Rev. Ebenezer Parkman, 1899; Gravestones of Early New England, 1927. Compiler: New England Dairies (1602-1800), 1924. Home: 23 Trowbridge Rd., Worcester, Mass. Died Oct. 12, 1951.

FORBES, Russell, researcher, cons.; b. West Middlesex, Pa., Feb. 29, 1896; s. Thomas Leroy and Frances Josephine (Sweesy) F.; A.B., Westminster Coll., New Wilmington, Pa., 1918; A.M., Colo. Coll., 1919; M.A. in Pub. Adminstrn., N.Y. Tng. Sch. for Pub. Service, 1924; Ph.D., Columbia, 1929; LL.D., Westminster Coll., New Wilmington, Pa., 1942; m. Mary Grace Springer, Aug. 29, 1925; children—James Russell, Malcolm Kingsbury. Instr. English, U. Me., 1919-20; sec. C. of C., Mercer, Pa., 1920-22; research sec. Nat. Assn. Purchasing Agts., N.Y.C., 1923-26; lectr. on municipal govt. N.Y.U., 1926-29, asst. prof. govt., 1929-30, asso. prof., 1930-33, prof. and dir. Div. Research in Pub. Adminstrn., 1933; dir. Municipal Adminstrn. Service, 1927-33; sec.-treas. Governmental Research Assn., 1927-32; sec. Nat. Municipal League, 1928-33; cons. govtl. purchasing to Nat. Assn. Purchasing Agts.; commr. of purchase N.Y.C., 1934-41; v.p., gen. mgr. Air Cargo, Inc., 1941-44; cons. bus. econ. Bur. Fed. Supply, U.S. Treasury Dept., 1946-47; leader Fed. Supply Project, Commn. on Orgn. Exec. Br. of Govt., 1948; cons. Boston Finance Commn., 1949; chmn. com. on Army Supply Methods, 1949; dep. adminstr. Gen. Services Adminstrn., 1949-53; acting adminstr. Def. Materials Procurement Agy., 1953; chief cons. 2d Hoover Commn., 1953-55; research and cons. Louis J. Kroeger & Assos., San Francisco, 1955—. Served as pvt. inf. U.S. Army, 1918. Recipient Shipman medal Nat. Assn. Purchasing Agents, 1934; Hughes Memorial medal, N.Y.U., 1937; 4th ann. award of City Club of New York for outstanding public service to the City, 1940. Mem. Govtl. Research Assn., Nat. Municipal League (hon. v.p. 1933—), Tau Kappa Alpha. Independent Democrat. Presbyterian. Author: Governmental Purchasing, 1929; Centralized Purchasing, 1931 (revised 1941); Purchasing Laws for State, County and Municipal Governments, 1931 (revised 1941); Organization and Administration of a Purchasing Office, 1932 (revised, 1941); Purchasing for Small Cities, 1932 (2d edit. 1939). Contbr. to The Purchasing Agent, The Nat. Municipal Review, The American City, Public Management, Ency. of the Social Sciences. Home: 601 Forest Av., Tampa 3, Fla. Office: 64 Pine St., San Francisco. Died June 18, 1957; buried West Middlesex, Pa.

FORBES, W(illiam) Cameron, b. Milton, Mass., 1870; s. William Hathaway and Edith (Emerson) F.; g.s. Ralph Waldo Emerson; A.B., Harvard U., 1892, LL.D., 1912; also LL.D., Trinity Coll., 1924; LL.D., Bates College, Lewiston, Me., 1932; unmarried. Was clerk with Jackson & Curtis, bankers & brokers, Boston, 1894-95; chief financial dept. Stone & Webster, elec. engrs., 1897-1902; partner J. M. Forbes & Co., mchts., Boston, 1899—; past v.p. Mass. Hosp. Life Ins. Co.; mem. corp. Provident Institution for Savings. Mem. Philippine Commn., and sec. commerce and police in government of Philippine Islands, 1904-08; vice governor of P.I., July 1, 1908-Nov. 10, 1909, gov. gen., Nov. 11, 1909-Sept. 1, 1913, when resigned. Receiver Brazil Ry. Co., 1914-19. Mem. Wood-Forbes Mission sent by Pres. Harding to investigate conditions in P.I., 1921; chmn. President's commn. for study of conditions in Haiti, 1930; ambassador to Japan, June 1930-Apr. 1932; chmn. Am. Economic Mission to the Far East, 1935. Overseer Harvard U., 1914-20. Life mem. emeritus Mass. Institute of Technology Corp. Honorary Pres. China Soc. Am.; mem. Mass. Hist. Soc., Coll. Electors Hall of Fame (N.Y.U.) Fellow Am. Acad. Arts and Sciences. Clubs: Union, Tavern, Harvard (Boston); Harvard, India House, N.Y. Yacht (New York); Manila Polo (Manila); Harvard Travellers. Home: Hotel Vendome. Office: 199 Washington St., Boston. Died Dec. 1959.

FORCE, Raymond Charles, corp. official; born Croton, Mich., July 28, 1880; s. George Henry and Laura Evelyn (Allen) F.; pres. Caterpillar Tractor Co. (Calif.), 1925-30; chmn. exec. com., 1930-40; now dir. and mem. exec. com.; dir. Soundview Pulp Co., Bank of Calif., N.A., San Francisco. Home: Diablo, Calif. Office: 800 Davis St., San Leandro, Calif. Died Nov. 15, 1951.

FORD, Amelia Clewley, educator, b. Searsport, Me., Sept. 9, 1875; d. Alfred Blanchard and Charlotte L. (Butman) Ford; student Bridgewater (Mass.) Normal Sch., 1892-95; A.B., Radcliffe, 1905; A.M., U. Wis., 1906, Ph.D., 1908. Tchr. elementary schs., 1895-1900; tchr. history and English, high sch., Melrose, Mass., 1903-05; instr. history, Milw.-Downer Coll., 1908-14; prof., 1914—. Mem. Am. Hist. Assn., Am. Assn. U. Woman (Milw. br.), Radcliffe Alumnae Assn. Wilson Democrat. Unitarian. Author: (thesis) Colonial Precedents for Our Lady System as It Existed in 1800, 1910. Lectr. before women's clubs. Address: Milwaukee-Downer College, Milw. Deceased.

FORD, David McKechnie, ry. exec.; b. Glasgow, Scotland, July 26, 1883; s. Robert and Jane (McKechnie) F.; m. E. C. Hilda Owen, July 12, 1911. Moved to Can., 1905. Mem. staff Canadian No. Ry., Toronto, 1905; chief clerk, operating and accounting depts., Halifax and Southwestern Ry., N.S., 1905-10, accountant and cashier for company's Quebec lines, 1916; accountant, eastern lands dept. Canadian Nat. Ry., 1916; became chief clerk, pres.'s office

Canadian Nat. Rys. and Canadian Govt. Merchant Marine, 1918, office asst. to pres., 1922; asst. to v.p. of purchases and stores, Canadian Nat. Rys., 1923-41, v.p., 1941—. Home: 1321 Sherbrooke St. W. Office: 355 McGill St., Montreal, Que., Can. Died Mar. 1953.

FORD, Frazer L., bank pres.; b. Forest City, Mo., Dec. 20, 1883; s. Jacob Marion and Nannie (Litsey) F.; student Hotchkiss Sch., Conn., 1901-02; A.B., Yale, 1906; m. Marjorie George, Mar. 4, 1914; children—Jacob Marion, Margot, Frazer Lee. In wholesale dry goods business, 1906-10, investment banking, 1910-14; pres. First Nat. Bank, St. Joseph, Mo., 1920—; pres. First Trust Co., First St. Joseph Stock Yards Bank; dir. St. Joseph Union Dept. Co. Trustee Endowment Fund of Meml. Home of St. Joseph, Mo. Mem. Zeta Psi. Democrat. Methodist. Clubs: Benton, St. Joseph Country. Home: 2820 Lovers Lane. Office: First Nat. Bank, St. Joseph, Mo. Died Apr. 10, 1947; buried Mount Mora Cemetery, St. Joseph, Mo.

FORD, Harriet French (Mrs. Fordé Morgan), playwright; b. Seymour, Conn.; d. Samuel and Isabel Stoddard Ford; student pub. schs., New Haven and Boston; took course at Am. Acad. Dramatic Arts and studied with David Belasco; m. Fordé Morgan, M.D., Jan. 29, 1930. Mem. Authors' League Am., Dramatists' Guild. Episcopalian. Plays: The Greatest Thing in the World (with Beatrice de Mille), 1900; A Gentleman of France, 1902; Audrey, 1903; The Fourth Estate and The Little Brother of the Rich (with Joseph M. Patterson), 1910; (following 1912-21) The Agryle Case, The Dummy, Polygamy, The Dickey Bird, Mr. Lazarus, On the Hiring Line, When a Feller Needs a Friend, Old P.Q., Orphan Aggie, Main Street (with Harvey O'Higgins); The Land of the Free (with Fannie Hurst), 1919; In the Next Room (with Mrs. August Belmont), 1924, and Christopher Rand, 1929; etc. Home: 1328 University Av., N.Y.C. Died Oct. 12, 1949.

FORD, Jeremiah Denis Matthias, educator; b. Cambridge, Mass., July 2, 1873; s. J.D. and Mary Agnes (Collins) F.; A.B., Harvard, 1894, A.M., 1895, Ph.D., 1897, studying in Coll. Law Sch. and Grad. Sch.; élèv École des Hautes Études, U. Paris 1897-98, student Sorbonne, École des Chartes and Collége de France; hon. Docteur-ès-lettres, U. Toulouse, 1922; D.Litt., Nat. U. Ireland, 1932, Trinity Coll., Dublin, 1934, Bowdoin Coll., Brunswick, Me., 1935; L.H.D., Fordham U., 1940; Litt.D., Harvard, 1942; m. Anna Winifred Fearns, Jan. 1, 1902; children—Anita Winifred (Mrs. Hubert S. Packard), Robert, Elizabeth Frances (Mrs. Rawson Lyman Wood), Richard. Instr. French, Harvard, 1895, later Harris fellow same in residence U. Paris; again instr. French, 1898-1900; instr. Romance langs., 1900-02, asst. prof., 1902-07, Smith prof. French and Spanish langs., 1907-43, Harvard and Radcliffe Coll.; chmn. dept. Romance langs. Harvard, 1911-43, Smith prof. emeritus, 1943—. Chief examiner for Spanish under Coll. Entrance Examining Bd., 1908-21. Lectr. Spanish lit., Lowell Inst., 1918; exchange prof. Harvard, to U. Paris and to Spanish univs., 1921-22; dir. Am. U. Union for Continent of Europe, hdqrs. Paris, 1925-26; vis. prof. to French and Spanish univs., 1925-26; dir. Harvard Council on Hispano-Am. Studies; editor in chief Speculum, 1927-36. Fellow Am. Acad. Arts and Scis. (pres. 1931-33), Medieval Acad. Am. (pres. 1939-41), A.A.A.S.; mem. Modern Lang. Assn. Am. (v.p. 1910-11, 1927-28), Am. Assn. U. Profs., Am. Dialect Soc. Dante Soc. (pres., 1932-40), Am. Cath. Hist. Assn. (pres. 1935), Humanities Research Assn. of Eng. (pres. 1937-38), Italian Hist. Soc. Mass. (pres., 1930-40), Am. Council Learned Socs., American Folk-Lore Society, Am., History Sci. Soc., Société de Linguistique (Paris), Comité France-Amérique (Paris), Hispanic Soc. Am. (v. p.); corr. mem. Académie des Inscriptions et Belles-Lettres (Paris); Spanish Acad. (Madrid), Spanich Acad. Belles Lettres (Barcelona), Institute de France. Comdr. Order of Isabella the Cath. (Spain); Officer Legion of Honor (France); Officer Order of Crown (Italy); Knight Royal Order of Cultural Merit (Rumania); Officer Order of Pub. Instrn. (Portugal); awarded Laetare medal by U. Notre Dame, 1937; 3 medals Hispanic Soc. Am.; Cervantes Medal, Fla. Clubs: Cambridge Club (pres. 1933), Faculty (Cambridge, Mass.); Harvard, Club of Odd Volumes (Boston); Club de la Renaissance (Paris, France), Roman Cath. Author: The Old Spanish Sibilants (Vol. VII of Harvard Studies and Notes), 1900; Exercises in Spanish Composition, 1901; Spanish Grammar, 1904; First Spanish Course, 1917 and 1941; Main Currents of Spanish Lit., 1919; Portuguese Grammar, 1925; Spanish Grammar for Colls., 1928. Editor: Chivalrous Romanes in Italian Verse, 1904; Goldoni's Curioso Accidente, 1899; Moratin's Sí de las niñas, 1899; Alarcon's capitan Veneno, 1900; A Spanish Anthology, 1901; Old Spanish Reading, 1906; Selections from Don Quixote, 1908; Spanish Fables in Verse, 1918; Letters of John III of Portugal, 1931; Bibliography of Cerantes, 1931; Bibliography of Brazilian Belles-Lettres, 1931; Bibliography of Cuban Belles-Lettres, 1932; Letters of the Court of John III of Portugal, 1933; Crónica de João de Castro of Leonardo Nunes, 1935; Suñe's Bibliografia del Quijote, 1939; The Lusiad—now newly put into English by Richard Fanshaw (reprint edit., London, 1955), 1940. Annotated ed. Os Lusiadas of Camoes, 1946, Italian and Spanish editor of New Internl. Encyclopedia, 1901-04; contbr. Spanish and Italian articles to Johnson's Ency., Cath. Ency., and Ency. America. Contbr. to philol. publs.; gen. editor of Henry Holt & Co.'s. Spanish series. Home: 9 Riedesel Av., Cambridge, Mass.; also Peterborough, N.H. Died Nov. 13, 1958.

FORD, Joseph C., mfg. exec.; b. Scottdale, Pa., May 21, 1889; s. Albert and Jane V. (Garwood) F.; M.E., Cornell, 1911; m. Vera Veerhusen, June 29, 1916. With Gen. Electric Co., Cleveland, N.Y. City, Chicago, 1911-14; asst. mgr. and sec. Ray-O-Vac Co., Madison, Wis., 1914-25; pres. The Celon Co. since 1926; dir. Wis. (Bell) Telephone Co. since 1947; First Nat. Bank, Madison, Ray-O-Vac Co. Founder, chmn. Madison Com. Trust Fund; trustee, pres. Village of Maple Bluff; dir. Madison Meml. Found., Madison and Wis. Found. Mem. Wis. Mfrs. Assn. (dir.). Republican. Clubs: Madison, University, Maple Bluff Golf (Madison); Cornell (N.Y. City). Home: 500 Farwell Dr., Maple Bluff, Madison 4, Wis.; also Delray Beach, Fla. Office: 2030 Pennsylvania Av., Madison 4, Wis. Died Oct. 19, 1956.

FORD, Mason (French), business exec.; b. N.Y. City, Feb. 16, 1899; s. Ives Mason and Sophie Magdalene (Patterson) F.; B.S., Georgetown U., 1924; m. Dorothy Henley Burns, June 18, 1921. Served with Am. del., Tacna-Arica Plebescitary Commn., Northern Chile, 1926; asst. trade commr. Am. Embassy, Buenos Aires, 1927-28; regional dir. Latin Am. for St. Regis Paper Co., Buenos Aires, Argentina, since 1928, dir. internat. div. since Jan. 1949; vice pres. and dir. St. Regis Paper Co., N.Y. City, since 1943; dir. Bulkley Dunton Paper Co., S.A., Cia T. Janer, Cia Colombiana de Empaques Bates. Episcopalian. Mason. Clubs: Bankers, Metropolitan, Union League (N.Y. City); Jockey (Buenos Aires); Jockey Bragileiro (Rio De Janeiro); Club De La Union (Santiago, Chile). Home: Praça Da Republica 77, São Paulo, Brazil. Office: 230 Park Av., N.Y. City 17. Died July 30, 1951; buried São Paulo.

FORD, Richard Clyde, educator; b. Clarence Twp., Calhoun County, Mich., May 17, 1870; s. Charles Albert and Meranda Elizabeth (Floyd) F.: Ph.B., Albion (Mich.) Coll., 1894, Ph.M., 1897, Litt.D., 1934; studied U. Freiburg, Germany, 1894, also Geneva and Paris; Ph.D., U. Munich, 1900; m. Grace Augusta Cogshall, June 25, 1895; children—Dorothy (dec.), Richard, Anne Elizabeth. Tchr. country sch. and supt. village sch. tchr. Anglo-Chinese Sch., Singapore, Malaysia, 1891-92; asst. prof. French and German, Albion Coll., 1894-99; prof. modern langs. No. State Normal Sch., Marquette, Mich., 1901-03, Mich. State Normal Coll. (now Eastern Mich. Coll.), Ypsilanti, 1903-40. Mem. State Hist. Commn. Mem. Assn. Mod. Lang. Tchrs. Central W. and S. Mich. State Tchrs. Assn., Mich. Schoolmasters' Club, Delta Tau Delta. Republican. Clubs: Twenty, Rotary. Author: Elementary German for Sight Translation, 1902; (with Charles O. Hoyt) John D. Pierce (biography), 1905; The White Captive (novel), 1915; Sandy MacDonald's Man (novel), 1928; Heroes and Hero Tales of Michigan, 1930; Red Man or White (novel), 1931. Editor: Sudermann's Teja (drama), 1906; De Tocqueville's En Amérique, 1909; Wildenbruch's Die Rabensteinerin, 1912. Translator; Jour. of the Pontiac, Conspiracy, 1913. Home: Ypsilanti, Mich. Died May 8, 1951; buried Highland Cemetery, Ypsilanti.

FORD, Thomas Francis, ex-congressman, editor; b. St. Louis; s. Thomas and Ellen (Ferris) F.; ed. pub. and pvt. schs., St. Louis and Toledo, O.; m. Lillian Cope Cummings, June 21, 1911. With newspapers in Wash., Ida., Washington, and Cal., 1913—; lit. editor The Times, Los Angeles, 1919-29; editor The Times Illus. Mag., 1919-23; publicity dir. Los Angeles Dept. Water and Power, 1929-31. Mem. City Council, Los Angeles, 1931-33; mem. 73d to 78th Congresses, 14th Cal. Dist. Spl. lectr. on internat. trade, U. So. Cal., 1920-21. Democrat. Unitarian. Clubs: University, X Club: Cosmos (Washington). Author (with Lillian C. Ford) The Foreign Trade of the United States, 1920. Travel and economic research in Europe, 1927. Spl. articles on European conditions for various publs. Home: 1244 Summit Dr., Encinitas, Cal. Died Dec. 1958.

FORD, Willard Stanley, educator; b. Monticello, Wis., April 20, 1890; s. James and Ellen (Turner) F.; A.B., Lawrence Coll., Appleton, Wis., 1915; studied U. of Wis., summer 1916, Stout Inst., summer 1919; A.M., Teachers Coll. (Columbia), 1925, Ph.D., 1927; m. Etta Anna Hammond, Aug. 9, 1916; children—Jack Hammond, Carolellen, Richard Stanley. Teacher rural sch., Wis., 1908; teacher grammar grades, Elmwood, Wis., 1909; teacher science and mathematics, Ft. Atkinson, Wis., 1913-16; supt. schs., New London, Wis., 1916-19; dir. vocational edn., Appleton, Wis., 1919-24; lecturer U. of Mo., summer, 1926; prof. edn. U. of Southern Calif., 1926-34, also asst. dean Sch. of Edn.; chief deputy supt. Los Angeles City Schs., 1934-38; supt. Glendale City Schools, 1938-47; now prof. edn., Chico (Calif.) State Coll. Co-dir. with O. R. Hull, of an educational survey of Los Angeles City Schs., 1933-34. Mem. bd. trustees Glendale Y.M.C.A. Mem. Am. Assn. Univ. Profs., Nat. Soc. Coll. Teachers of Edn., Supervisors of Student Teaching, Nat. Soc. for Study on Edn., N.E.A., Am. Assn. of Sch. Adminstrs., Public Sch. Business Officials Assn. of Southern Calif., Sigma Phi Epsilon, Phi Beta Kappa, Phi Kappa Phi, Phi Delta Kappa, Tau Kappa Alpha. Methodist. Mason; mem. Order Eastern Star. Club: Rotary. Author and co-author of numerous school surveys. Address: 939 Arbutus St., Chico, Calif. Died Mar. 11, 1951.

FORDHAM, Herbert (fôrd'âm), lawyer, publicist; b. Greenport, N.Y., Nov. 23, 1869; s. Thomas Dering and Lydia M. (Latham) F.; Ph.B., Cornell U., 1894 (Phi Beta Kappa), LL.B., 1895; m. Inez Robbins, June 21, 1900. Admitted to N.Y. bar, 1895, and since practiced in N.Y. City; head of title business of Reeve & Bartlett from 1902, and for many yrs. sole owner until sale in 1925 of plant at Riverhead to Title Guarantee & Trust Co. Apptd., Jan. 1926, by Appellate Div., 2d Dept., Supreme Court of N.Y., mem. Com. on Character and Fitness of Applicants for Admission to the Bar; resigned Nov. 1926, for reasons stated to the court and given wide publicity; this and later action considered of weight in securing from Court of Appeals increased requirements for admission to the Bar of N.Y. Mem. Am. and N.Y. State bar assns., N.Y. Law Inst., Assn. Bar City of New York, Archaeol. Inst. America, Am. Econ. Assn., Acad. Polit. Sci., N.Y. State Hist. Assn., Suffolk Co. Hist. Soc., L.I. Hist. Soc., N.Y. Bot. Garden, Phi Beta Kappa Alumni Assn.; fellow Am. Geog. Soc. Author: A Voice from the Past (Old Southold Town's Tercentenary), 1940. Home: (country) Oak Farm, near Greenport, L.I., N.Y. Died Sept. 10, 1953; buried Stirling Cemetery, Greenport, L.I., N.Y.

FORDYCE, Claude Powell (fôr'dĭs). eye, ear, nose and throat specialist, author; b. McLean, Ill., Mar. 6, 1883; s. Charles and Marie (Gray) F.; A.B., Neb. Wesleyan U., 1905, B.Sc., 1907; student U. of Neb., 1907-09; M.D., Washington U., 1910; m. Dora Maude Maddox, June 22, 1910; 1 dau., Marileen Ann. Scholar in zoölogy, U. of Neb., 1907-08; began practice Falls City, Neb., 1915; surgeon Neb. Soldiers' Hosp., Grand Island, 1911-13; spl. representative of gov. of Neb. at Nat. Parks Conf., Des Moines, Ia., 1921; health editor Adventure Mag., camping editor of Outdoor Life and Recreation Magazine, 1922-29; asso. editor publs. Am. Med. Assn., 1929-31; formerly med. dir. Merck & Co., Rahway, N.J., specializing in indsl. medicine and surgery; now doing research and special scientific writing; specialist in eye, ear, nose and throat. Member advisory com. Nat. Safety Council. Mem. Am. Med. Assn., Neb. State Med. Assn. (v.p.; councillor 1927), Mo. State Med. Assn., Authors' League Am., Soc. Midland Authors' (Chgo.), Neb. Acad. Sci., Neb. Outboard Motorboat Assn. (pres.), Mo. Valley Boat Racing Assn. (vice commodore), Sea Scouts Am. (exec. com. 6th area), Neb. Writers Guild (pres. 1928), Nat. Conf. in State Parks (dir.), Am. Assn. Industrial Physicians and Surgeons, N.Y. Acad. Medicine (asso.), The Writers, Sigma Chi, Nu Sigma Nu. Democrat. Methodist. Clubs: Rocky Mountain (Denver); Sierra (San Francisco); Mazama (Portland, Ore.); Mountainers' (Seattle). Author: Touring Afoot, 1916; (booklet) Taking the Place of the Doctor, 1920; Trial Craft, 1922; (monograph) Auto Camps and Tours, 1924. Camping editor Outdoorsman (Chgo.). Contbr. articles to mags. Home: 2522 Mulberry St., St. Joseph 49. Office: 412 Kirkpatrick Bldg., St. Joseph, Mo. Died Aug. 18, 1953.

FOREHAND, Brooks, univ. prof.; b. Fort Deposit, Ala., Aug. 18, 1899; s. William Glenn and Mary Read (Williamson) F.; A.B., Univ. of Ala., 1921, A.M., 1924; A.M., Harvard, 1931; student Univ. of Wis., summer 1929, Princeton, 1930-31; m. Margaret Beery, Dec. 22, 1934; children—Margaret Lee, Mary Read, Elizabeth Evans. Instr. in English, Ga. Sch. of Tech., 1921-22, Univ. of Ala., 1922-23, asst. prof. of English, 1924-30, asso. prof., 1931-44, prof. of English since 1944, acting head dept. English, 1945-46, head dept.of English since 1946. Mem. Modern Lang. Assn., Mediaeval Acad., Modern Humanities Research Assn., S. Atlantic Modern Lang. Assn., Ala. Assn. Coll. Teachers of English, Am. Assn. Univ. Profs., Phi Beta Kappa, Phi Kappa Phi, Omicron Delta Kappa, Sigma Upsilon, Lambda Chi Alpha, Jasons. Democrat. Methodist. Clubs: Phoenix. Home: 1200-13th St., Tuscaloosa, Ala. Died Dec. 20, 1957.

FOREMAN, Albert Watson, army officer; b. Wilmington, Del., Aug. 11, 1874; s. Thomas Nicholson and Mary Louise (Watson) F.; grad. Army Sch. of the Line, 1915, Army War Coll., 1921; m. Rebecca Marchand Conner Milligan, Sept. 17, 1901 (died 1930); 1 daughter, Estelle Josephine. Commander 2d lt., Delaware Volunteer infantry, 1898; appointed 1st lt. Regular Army, February 1901, advancing through the grades to col., 1927; retired from active duty, 1938; recalled to active duty, 1942, again retired from active service, December 1946; dir. internal security, Hdqrs. 2d Service Command, Governor's Island, N.Y., Sept. 1942; retired from active duty, Oct. 1943; apptd. acting state dir. Selective Service System, Del., Nov. 1943, state dir. since Apr. 1944.

Participated in Spanish-Am. War, Philippine Insurrection, Pulajan Campaign (Samar, P.I.), Mex. Border Service and in Mexico, World War I (A.E.F.), World War II (Atlantic Sector). Prof. mil. science and tactics, Miss. Agrl. and Mech. Coll., Starkville, Miss., Nov. 1, 1916-July 1, 1917. Organized and comd. 3d Civilian Conservation Corps Dist., 1st Corps Area, 1933-34. Decorated Distinguished Service Medal, Legion of Merit with oak leaf cluster (U.S.), Cross of Order l'Etoile Noir (France); awarded gov.'s med. by governor of Delaware, 1946, apptd. a.d.c. to gov., 1947; recipient citation for Army Service ribbon from sec. of war. Mem. Order Founders and Patriots Am., Huguenot Soc. N.E., S.A.R., Mayflower Descendants, Mil. Order of Carabao, 80th Div. Vets. Assn., Mil. Order World War, Inf. Assn. (Washington), Soc. Am. Wars, Commandery Commonwealth of Mass., Soc. Colonial Wars, S.R., Magna Charta Soc. (papers finally completed and accepted just prior to death), Ancient and Hon. Arty. Co. of Mass., Soc. War 1812, Am. Legion. A "freeman" of Gov. and Co. of Mass. Bay in N.E. Mason (Lafayette Lodge No. 14, A.F. and A.M. of Wilmington, Del.), Sojourner, Heroes of '76. Clubs: Army Athletic Assn. (West Point); Army and Navy (Washington); Algonquin (Boston); Bedford, Kiwanis, Wilmington Country, Wilmington, Social Service (Wilmington). Home: 803 N. Franklin St., Wilmington 6, Del. Died Aug. 12, 1950; buried Arlington Nat. Cemetery.

FOREMAN, Alvan Herbert, lawyer; b. Great Bridge, Va., Mar. 1, 1878; s. Esmond Olando and Anna Luke (Tatem) F.; A.B., Coll. of William and Mary, 1899; LL.B., U. of Va., 1907; m. Alma J. Large, Nov. 12, 1912 (died Apr. 1937); 1 dau., Mrs. Margarette Aurelia Hargroves; married 2d, Grace Branch Carrington, Dec. 27, 1940. Prin. pub. sch., Norfolk, Va., 1901-05; supt. pub. schs., Norfolk County, 1909-17; admitted to Va. bar, 1907; since practicing in Norfolk; dir. Tidewater Perpetual Bldg. & Loan Association. Chmn. Norfolk George Washington Bicentennial Commn., chmn. Norfolk Schl. Bd., 1930-43; board of visitors College of William and Mary, 1923-52, rector, 1946-49, vice rector, 1949-52; chairman bd. trustees Norfolk Poly. Coll., 1944; member adv. commission Norfolk Division, Va. State Coll.; dir. Norfolk Pub. Library, 1930-43, Norfolk Chapter Am. Red Cross, 1933-52; sec., treas., dir. Patriotic Education, Inc.; mem. jury of awards of Freedoms Found., 1951. Mem. S.A.R. (pres. Va. 1943-44; mem. nat. exec. com. 1943-47, 48—, member of national board of trustees, 1943—, chmn. nat. com. on orgn. 1943-44; v.p. gen. S. Atlantic dist. 1942-43; nat. pres. gen. 1947-48; twice awarded Florence Kendall medal), Va. State and Norfolk-Portsmouth bar assns., Phi Beta Kappa, Phi Sigma Kappa, Pi Gamma Nu, Phi Kappa Phi. Recipient Algeron Sydney Sullivan award, William and Mary College, 1929; medallion, by General Alumni Association of William and Mary, 1934, for service and loyalty to mother college; new stadium at Norfolk Div. of Coll. (seating capacity 25,000) named Foreman Field, 1936; selected as first citizen of Norfolk, 1935, and recipient of distinguished service medal; Minute Man award by the National Society S.A.R. Member Va. Club. Democrat. Methodist. Mason (Shriner). Clubs: Lions, Sports, Cosmopolitan (hon.), Yacht and Country (Norfolk); Ruritan of Great Bridge (hon.). Home: 927 Larchmont Crescent. Office: Western Union Bldg., Norfolk, Va. Died Mar. 23, 1958.

FOREMAN, Grant, author; b. Detroit, Ill., June 3, 1869; s. Abner W. (M.D.) and Elizabeth R. (Hayden) F.; LL.B., Law Dept., U. of Mich., 1891; m. Carolyn Thomas, July 26, 1905. Admitted to Ill. bar, 1891, U.S. Supreme Ct., 1910; with the Commn. to Five Civilized Tribes, 1899-1903; formerly practicing lawyer in Oklahoma. Mem. Okla. State Historical Society (dir.); member Society of American Historians; Phi Beta Kappa. Republican. Student of Indian and western history and contributor to numerous mag. articles on these subjects. Author: Pioneer Days in The Early Southwest, 1926; Indians and Pioneers, 1930; Indian Removal, the Emigration of the Five Civilized Tribes, 1932; Advancing the Frontier, 1933; The Five Civilized Tribes, 1934; Fort Gibson—A Brief History, 1936; Down the Texas Road, 1936; The Adventures of James Collier, 1937; Adventure on Red River, 1937; Sequoyah, 1938; Marcy and the Gold Seekers, 1939; A Pathfinder in the Southwest, 1941; A History of Oklahoma, 1942; Muskogee—The Biography of an Oklahoma Town, 1943, The Last Trek of the Indians. Editor: A Traveler in Indian Territory, The Journal of Ethan Allen Hitchcock, 1930; Indian Justice, an account of a Cherokee murder trial as reported by John Howard Payne, 1934. Address: 1419 W. Okmulgee Av., Muskogee, Okla. Died Apr. 21, 1953; buried Greenhill Cemetery, Muskogee, Okla.

FOREMAN, Harold Edwin, banker; b. Chicago, Ill., Aug. 30, 1888; s. Edwin G. and Rose (Kohn) F.; A.B., Dartmouth, 1909; m. Florence Born, June 5, 1912; children—Harold E., John B. Began as messenger Corn Exchange Nat. Bank, Chicago, 1909; with Foreman Bros. Banking Co., 1910, v.p., 1914-21, pres. 1921-29; chmn. bd. Foreman-State Nat. Bank, 1929-31; also chmn. bd. Foreman-State Trust & Savings Bank until 1931. Home: 955 Sheridan Rd., Glencoe, Ill. Died July 1958.

FORESMAN, Hugh Austin, publisher; b. Easton, Pa.; s. Robert and Elizabeth (Reiley) F.; A.B., Lafayette Coll., Easton, Pa., 1887; m. Lila Patterson, Oct. 21, 1896; children—Emily (Mrs. R. W. Kenyon), Dorothy (Mrs. Warren McCracken), Patty (Mrs. Theron Chapman). Taught in Union High Sch., Coleraine, Pa., 1888-91; with Silver, Burdett & Co., Chgo., 1891-95; joined in organizing Scott, Foresman & Co., pubs. of sch. books, 1895; pres., 1929-43, chmn. bd., 1943-55, hon. chmn. bd., 1955—. Mem. bd. trustees Lafayette Coll. Clubs: University, Quadrangle, Indian Hill, Barrington Country. Home: Fox Lane, Winnetka, Ill. Office: 433 E. Erie St., Chgo. Died Jan. 1960.*

FORKER, John Norman, consultant; born Mercer, Pa., Nov. 25, 1885; s. George Campbell and Caroline Belle (Moon) F.; B.S. in M.E., Pa. State Coll., 1907, Graduate Degree of Fuels Engineer 1948; m. Mary Katharine Fencil, Oct. 9, 1915; children—Robert Fencil, Helen Louise. Engr. with steel corps., 1907-15; engr. with Koppers Co., Pittsburgh, Pa., 1915-25; pres. Am. Tar Products Co., 1925-31; pres. Koppers Products Company, 1931-36; v.p. Koppers Co., Inc.; retired. Exec. dir. Gen. State Authority and The State Hwy. and Bridge Authority, Commonwealth of Pa. Trustee Pa. State U. Mem. A.S. M.E., Am. Iron and Steel Inst., Am. Gas Assn., Phi Kappa Phi, Pi Tau Sigma. Republican. Episcopalian. Clubs: Duquesne (Pitts.); Union League (N.Y.C.); Fox Chapel Golf. Home: 7 Pawcatuck Av., Watch Hill, R.I. Office: 1700-14 Wall St., N.Y.C. Died Sept. 19, 1956.

FORREST, Aubrey Leland, chancellor; b. Eastland, Tex., Aug. 17, 1912; s. James Alonzo and Saphronia Elizabeth (Young) F.; A.B. magna cum laude, Abilene Christian Coll., 1933; M.A., Mich. State Coll., 1940; student U. of Chicago, summer 1944, Pacific Sch. of Religion, summer 1945; Ph.D., U. of So. Calif., 1948; m. Frances June Seth, Nov. 30, 1933; children—Aubrey Lester, James Franklin, Mary Frances. Instr. in Spanish, Warner Coll. Acad., Eastland, Tex., 1932, instr. in English Bible, Anderson (Ind.) Coll., 1945; counselor-chaplian, Juvenile div., Los Angeles County Penal Instns., 1945 46; instr. in English and history Culter Acad., Los Angeles, 1945-46; prof. of religious edn. and dir. student personnel Taylor U., Upland, Ind., 1946-47, dean 1948-51; dean Nebraska Wesleyan U., 1951-54, univ. chancellor, 1954-57. Former mem. Church Commn. on World Service, Ch. com. on Relief and Rehabilitation, Anderson, Ind., active in Ind. Conf. of Ch.-related and Independent Colls. Mem. N.E.A., Am. Assn. U. Profs., Neb. Assn. Colls. and Univs. (pres. 1955), Schoolmasters Club, Nat. Assn. Bibl. Instrs., Am. Acad. Polit. and Social Sci., Scholarship Soc. South, Urban League. Rotarian. Author: The Youth Fellowship in Your Church, 1943; also articles various ednl. periodicals. Researcher in social history and influence of protest groups in religious life. Address: Neb. Wesleyan U., Lincoln, Neb. Died. May 7, 1957; buried Lincoln Meml. Park.

FORRESTAL, Frank Vincent, banker; m. Kathleen Murphy Forrestal; children—Frank, Mrs. Annie Quigg, Mrs. Kathleen Carley. Vice pres. fgn. dept. Bankers Trust Co. of N.Y. until 1959, ret. 1959. Served with AEF, World War I. Home: 1040 Park Av. Office: 16 Wall St., N.Y.C. Died Aug. 1959.

FORRESTER, D(avid) Bruce (fŏr'rĕs-tẽr), director of General Box Co.; b. Chanute, Kansas, Nov. 4, 1881; s. William S. and Charlotte Bruce (Millar) F.; student Mo. State U., 1901-03; m. Maude Kimball Swentzel, Jan. 14, 1908; children—Barbara (Mrs. Philip F. Rahm), David Bruce, twins. Box mfg. bus. since 1903 with father and succeeding him, in Forrester-Nace Box Co., merged with General Box Co., 1922; became vice pres. General Box Co., 1922, later became chmn. of the bd., now director; chmn. Industrial Loan Com. of Fed. Reserve Bank of Kansas City, Mo., 10th Dist. One of founders and first dirs., Asso. Industries of Mo. Member board directors American Red Cross of Kansas City, Community Fund of Kansas City. Past president Club Presidents Round Table. Dir Southern States Indsl. Council, Citizens Regional Planning Council, Central Indsl. Dist. Assn.; pres. Employers Assn., Kansas City Chamber of Commerce; mem. bd. election commrs., Kansas City, Mo. Trustee Kansas City Art Institute. Mem. Sigma Alpha Epsilon. Republican. Presbyterian. Clubs: Kansas City Athletic (pres.), Kansas City, University, Mission Hills Country, Saddle and Sirloin, Hoof and Horn (Kansas City, Mo.). Home: The Walnuts, 5049 Wornall Rd. Office: 1600 W. 8th St., Kansas City, Mo. Deceased.*

FORREY, George C., Jr. (fô-rē), investment banker; b. Anderson, Ind., Jan. 31, 1882; s. George C. and Mary (Baxter) F.; grad. Culver (Ind.) Mil. Acad., 1899; A.B., Williams, 1903; m. Lucia Hurst, 1913; children—Elheurah F. (Mrs. N. C. Stilwell), George C. III. Salesman E. M. Campbell & Co., brokers, Indianapolis, Ind., 1903-05; with Breed & Harrison, 1905-12, Breed, Elliott & Harrison, 1912-20; first v.p. and dir. Fletcher Am. Nat. Bank, 1923-32; receiver Indianapolis Street Ry., 1930-32; v.p., dir. and mem. exec. com. Indianapolis Rys., Inc., since orgn., 1932; chmn. bd. Indianapolis Bond & Share Corp., 1949—; dir., mem. exec. com. Gary Rys., Inc.; dir. Hook Drugs, Inc.; dir., mem. exec. com. Union Title Co., Indianapolis, 1924—; also dir. various realty companies. Mem. Ind. state exec. com. for all Liberty Loan campaigns, World War; asst. chief ednl. sec. Ordnance Dept. Ind., 1918. Mem. Sons of Am. Revolution. Theta Delta Chi. Republican. Presbyterian. Mason (32°). Clubs: Country, Players, Contemporary, Rotary (Indianapolis); Ft. Lauderdale (Fla.) Country; Tippecanoe Lake (Ind.) Country. Home: 3261 N. Pennsylvania. Address: Indpls. Bond and Share Corp., Indpls. Died Sept. 21, 1954; buried Anderson, Ind.

FORSTMANN, Curt Erwin, business exec.; b. Passaic, N.J., Feb. 19, 1907; s. Julius and Adolfine (Lynen) F.; student Riverdale Sch., Lawrenceville Sch. and Coppet, Switzerland; m. Elizabeth F. Allen, Oct. 26, 1931; children—Peter Allen, Anna Louise, Richard Lynen. Volunteer various European textile mills; became exec. asst. to father, founder Forstmann Woolen Co., until 1939, pres., dir. since 1939; chmn. bd., dir. Julius Forstmann & Co., Inc. Pres. Carl Forstmann Meml. Found. Worked with Army and Navy procurement officers in development of new mil. fabrics during World War II. Home: 196 Upper Mountain Av., Montclair, N.J. Office: 2 Barbour Av., Passaic, N.J. Died Jan. 19, 1950.

FORSYTHE, W(illia)m B(oore), ret. business exec.; b. Balt., June 3, 1897; s. William Sayers and Sarah (Boore) F.; ed. Ont. Normal Model Sch., Ont. Normal Sch., Internat. Corr. Sch.; m. Nena Florence Rice, Sept. 11, 1926; 1 dau., Betty Lou. Spent 1914-15 learning father's bus., Forsythe Loundry Ltd., Toronto, Can.; timekeeper, foreman and constrn. supt., Atlas Constrn. Co., Montreal, and Joseph E. Nelson Co., Chgo., 1919-22, salesman, 1922-24; salesman, br. mgr., Eastern regional mgr., Coca-Cola Co. of Can., 1924-28, spl. rep. and asst. to European gen. mgr., Coca-Cola Co. of Europe, 1928-31; gen. mgr., v.p. subsidiaries Consol. Beverages of Can., 1931-39; mng. dir. Pepsi-Cola Co. Ltd., Eng., 1939—; apptd. mgr. Pepsi-Cola Co. (Del. Corp.) Export Div., 1941, became v.p., 1942, dir., 1949—, now 1st v.p., dir.; chmn. bd., pres. Pepsi-Cola Internat., 1954-57, ret.; dir. Pepsi-Cola Co. of Can. Served Canadian Army, 1915-19. Mem. Nat. Fgn. Trade Council. Mem. Ch. of Eng. Clubs: Royal Canadian Yacht, Stamford Yacht, Export Mgrs. Home: Byways, Cedar Heights Rd., Stamford, Conn. Office: Pepsi-Cola Co., N.Y.C. 19. Died Mar. 8, 1959.

FORT, Gerrit, ret. rialroad exec.; b. Cedar Rapids, Ia., Nov. 12, 1865; s. Hiram Pratt and Caroline (Van Dyck) F.; student pub. schs. Cedar Rapids; m. Eleanor Cleary, Sept. 5, 1892; children—Garritt, Henrietta, Louise. With pass dept. N.Y.C.&H.R. R.R., 1889-96; sec. Central Pass. Assn., Chgo., 1897-1900; asst. gen. passenger agt. U.P. R.R., 1900-07; asst. to v.p. and gen. passenger agt. N.Y.C.&H.R. R.R., 1907-10; passenger traffic mgr U.P. System, comprising the U.P. R.R., Ore. Short Line and Ore.-Wash. R.R. & Navigation Co., 1910-18; asst. dir. U.S.R.R. Adminstrn., 1918-19; v.p. B.&M. R.R., 1920-27, later exec. asst.; pres. Raymond & Whitcomb Co., 1927-31; chmn. Boston Tidewater Terminal, Inc., 1931-40; pres. Mystic Terminal Co., 1933-40; retired. Home: 4190 Palmetto Way, San Diego, Cal. Deceased.*

FORT, Jardine Carter, lawyer; b. Lumpkin, Ga., Mar. 16, 1889; s. George Hudson and Martha (Carter) F.; student U. of Mich., 1907-08; LL.B., Georgetown U., Washington, D.C., 1911; m. Helen Sellman Nicholson, June 25, 1914 (dec.); children—Jardine Carter, Harriet Morton (Mrs. George Wood Wilson, Jr.), Anne Ducachet (Mrs. Guy Bowman Mercer); m. 2d, Eloise Orme Robinson, Sept. 12, 1952. Admitted to D.C. bar, 1911, and practiced law in Washington, D.C., 1911-14; atty., then asst. chief counsel, Interstate Commerce Commn., 1914-24; commerce atty., Ill. Central Sys., Chgo., 1924-28, asst. gen. counsel, 1928-32, gen. atty., 1932-34; gen. solicitor, Assn. of Am. Railroads, Washington, D.C., 1934-41, gen. counsel, 1941-44, vice president and gen. counsel since 1944. Mem. Am. and D.C. bar assns., Delta Chi. Episcopalian. Clubs: Chevy Chase (Washington, D.C.); The Chicago (Chicago). Home: 3009 32d St. N.W. Address: 815 17th St. N.W., Washington. Died May 10, 1956; buried Rock Creek Cemetery, Washington.

FORT, Joel B., Jr., banker; b. Springfield, Tenn., Aug. 8, 1888; s. Joel B. and Sallie (McKay) F.; ed. Wallace Prep. Sch., Nashville, Tenn.; m. Emma Vaughn, Oct. 1921. Began with Am. Nat. Bank, Nashville, 1909; with Cumberland Valley Nat. Bank, 1911-18; utility clk., Nashville Br. Federal Res. Bank of Atlanta, Ga., 1920, cashier, 1921-25, became mng. dir., 1925; vice pres. Fed. Res. Bank of Atlanta (Ga.), also mgr. Nashville (Tenn.) Branch, since 1947. Served in Aviation Corps, United States Army, World War. Member Nashville Chamber Commerce (pres. 1949). Democrat. Baptist. Mason (Shriner). Home: Vaughn Rd. Office: Federal Reserve Bank, Nashville. Died Oct. 17, 1951.

FORTENBAUGH, Robert, educator; b. Harrisburg, Pa., July 17, 1892; s. James Penrose and Mary Jeannette (Zimmerman) F.; A.B., Gettysburg Coll., 1913; grad. Luth. Theol. Sem., Gettysburg, Pa., 1916; A.M., Syracuse U., 1920; Ph.D., U. Pa., 1926; m. Lena Schweinberger, Aug. 16, 1921; children—Robert B., Ruth E. (Mrs. N. Neiman Craley Jr.), Ann E. (Mrs. Paul S. Eicholtz). Ordained to ministry Luth. Ch., 1916; pastor Ch. of the Atonement, Syracuse, N.Y., 1916-23; instr., then asst. prof. sociology Syracuse U., 1918-23; acting, then Adeline Sager prof. history Gettysburg Coll., 1923—, vice chmn. adminstrv. com., 1955-56; summer term faculty Pa. State U., U. Pa., Bucknell U., U. Chattanooga. Clerical mem. Central Pa. Synod, United Luth. Ch. Am. Recipient medal, Freedoms Found., Inc., 1950. Mem. Am., Pa. (pres. 1945-48) hist. assns., Am. Assn. U. Profs., Phi Beta Kappa, Phi Kappa Phi, Phi Alpha Theta, Kappa Phi Kappa, Alpha Tau Omega (nat. v.p. 1954-56). Republican. Author: The Synodical Polity of the Lutheran Church in America, 1926; (with H. J. Tarman) Pennsylvania: The Story of a Commonwealth, 1940; The Nine Capitals of the United States, 1948; Lincoln and Gettysburg, 1949; (with H. J. Tarman) The Pennsylvania Story, 1950. Contbr. hist. and religious periodicals. Home: 150 W. Broadway, Gettysburg, Pa. Died Mar. 15, 1959; buried Evergreen Cemetery, Gettysburg.

FORTESCUE, Granville (Roland), (fôr′tĕs-kū), writer; b. New York, N.Y., Oct. 12, 1875; s. Robert Francis and Marion Theresa (O'Shea) F.; U. of Pa. (left coll. at outbreak of Spanish-Am. War); m. Grace Hubbard Bell, June 4, 1910; children—Thalia, Marion, Helene. Pvt. and corp. 1st U.S. Cav. (Rough Riders), 1898, wounded at San Juan Hill; 1st lt. 26th U.S. Vol. Inf., campaign P.I., 1899-1901; apptd. 2d. lt. 4th U.S. Cav., 1902; grad. staff coll., 1904; 1st lieut., 10th U.S. Cavalry, comdg. Troop A.; military attaché with Japanese Army before Port Arthur. Served as mil. aide to President Roosevelt at White House; resigned from U.S. Army, 1906; capt. and spl. agent Cuban rural guard, 1906. Spl. corr. London Standard with Spanish army in Riff War, 1909; exploration interior of Venezuela, headwaters of Orinoco River to mouth; corr. London Daily Telegraph, with Belgian, French, English, Russian and Turkish armies in the field. Commd. maj., O.R.C., N.A., 1917, and in active service with 314th F.A., A.E.F. in France, 1917-18; wounded at Montfaucon; ret. maj. F.A., 1928. Republican. Awarded certificate of merit and Distinguished Service Cross, Victory Medal, 3 bars; Spanish War medal; Philippine Insurrection War medal; Order of Purple Heart (United States). Order of the Rising Sun (Japan), Japanese War Medal. Clubs: Army and Navy (Washington, D.C.); Metropolitan, Turf and Field (New York). Author: At the Front with Three Armies, 1914; Russia, the Balkans and the Dardanelles, 1915; What of the Dardanelles?, 1915; Fore-Armed, 1916; France Bears the Burden, 1917; (plays) Dolores, 1915; Love and Live, 1921; The Unbeliever, 1925; Front Line and Dead Line, 1937. Fiction editor of Liberty Mag., 1930. Home: Bayport, N.Y. Office: Lantana, Fla. Died Apr. 21, 1952; buried Arlington Cemetery.

FORTIER, Michel J., bus. exec.; b. Jeanerette, La., Dec. 6, 1903; s. Edmund L. and Stella (de la Croix) F.; ed. pub. schs.; m. Thelma Self, Jan. 11, 1921; children—Michel J., Robert H. Trade sales rep., Sherwin-Williams Co., New Orleans, La., 1931-35, div. mgr., 1935-40, mgr. Miss. Valley Dist. St. Louis, 1940-42, mgr. North Central District, Cleveland, 1942-43; vice pres. and gen. mgr. Acme White Lead & Color Works, Detroit, 1943-44; vice pres., dir. and exec. asst. to pres. Sherwin-Williams Co., Cleveland, Dec. 1944-45, vice pres., dir. and gen. mgr. since Dec., 1945; vice pres. and dir. Acme White Lead and Color Works, Detroit, John Lucas & Co., Philadelphia, Rogers Paint Products, Inc., Detroit, Martin-Senour Co., Chicago, Hemingway & Co., New York, Texarkana Paint Co., Texarkana, Texas, dir. The Lowe Bros. Co., Dayton, all affiliates of Sherwin-Williams Co., since 1945. Republican. Mason. Clubs: Canterbury Golf Union, Pepper Pike Country (Cleveland). Home: South Park Manor, 13800 Fairhill Rd., Shaker Heights 20, O. Office: Midland Bldg., Cleve. 15. Died May 31, 1952.

FORTUNE, Alonzo Willard, clergyman; b. Holmes County, O., June 29, 1873; s. William S. and Emily A. (Middaugh) F.; A.B., Hiram (O.) Coll., 1898, A.M., 1900; student Rochester Theol. Sem., 1903-04; B.D., U. Chgo., 1905, Ph.D., 1915; LL.D., Transylvania Coll., Ky., 1930; m. Bessie Hale, June 29, 1898; children—Carl Hale, Emily Elizabeth. Ordained ministry Christian (Disciples) Ch.; pastor Chagrin Falls, O., 1899-1901, First Ch., Rochester, N.Y., 1901-04, Walnut Hills Ch., Cin., 1907-12; prof. doctrine Coll. of Bible, Lexington, Ky., 1912-22, dean of coll., 1917-22; pastor Central Ch., Lexington, 1922-44, ret.; tchr. practical theology Coll. of the Bible. Recipient Algernon Sydney, Sullivan award U. Ky., 1944; Lexington Optimist Cup, 1945; Hiram Coll. Alumni awrd, 1946. Mem. Pi Kappa Alpha, Theta Phi. Democrat. Rotarian. Author: The Conception of Authority in the Pauline Writings, 1918; Origin and Development of the Disciples, 1924; The Church of the Future, 1930; The Disciples in Kentucky, 1932; brochure for Am. Bible Soc., 1937; Thinking Things Through With E. E. Snoddy, 1940; Adventuring with Disciple Pioneers, 1942. Pres. Internat. Conv. of Disciples of Christ, 1936-37. Home: 624 Elsmere Park, Lexington, Ky. Died Dec. 26, 1950; buried Lexington Cemetery.

FOSBROKE, Hughell Edgar Woodall, theologian; b. Netherton, Worcestershire, Eng., Apr. 5, 1875; s. Charles Baldwin and Charlotte (Elton) F.; came to U.S., 1890; prep. edn. Shattuck Sch., Faribault, Minn., 1890-93; student Harvard, 1893-95; B.D., Nashotah House, Wis., 1901, D.D., 1909, LL.D., 1927; D.D., Episcopal Theol. Sch., 1916, Columbia, 1923; S.T.D., General Theol. Sem., 1934; D.D., Boston Univ., 1939; m. Blanche Esther Peter, June 12, 1901; children—Hughell Edgar Woodall (dec.), Esther. Deacon and priest P.E. Ch., 1900; instr., prep. dept. Nashotah House, 1900-01; instr. Hebrew, 1901-02, prof. O.T., 1902-09, prof. history and religion of Israel, 1909-16, Episcopal Theol. Sch.; dean, Gen. Theol. Sem., N.Y. City, 1917-46; retired since Aug. 1, 1947. Dep. Gen. Conv. P.E. Ch., 1907. Mem. Soc. Bibl. Lit. and Exegesis, Am. Oriental Soc. Home: Winchester Center, Conn. Died Oct. 19, 1957; buried Winchester Center.

FOSHAG, William Frederick (fō′shăg), museum curator; b. Sag Harbor, N.Y., Mar. 17, 1894; s. William Frederick and Joanna Eva (Riegler) F.; A.B., U. of Calif., 1919, Ph.D., 1923; m. Merle Crisler, Sept. 5, 1923; 1 son, William Frederick. Chemist Riverside Portland Cement Co., Riverside, Calif., 1917-18; asst. curator U.S. Nat. Museum, 1919-29, curator, 1929-48, head curator, department of geology, 1948—. Fellow Mineral Society America (pres. 1940, Roebling medalist 1953), Geol. Soc. Am. (v.p. 1941), Geophys. Union (v.p. 1947-48, pres. volcanology sect. 1953-55), Soc. Econ. Geol. Soc. for Research on Meteorites (v.p. 1933-34), Washington Acad. of Science, Geol. Soc. of Mexico (hon.), Alpha Chi Sigma, Theta Tau, Sigma Xi; corr. mem. Sociédad Cientifica Antonio Alzate de Mexico. Author: (with George P. Merrill) Minerals from Earth and Sky, 1929; Birth and Development of Paricutin Volcano, 1956. Pre-Columbian Art (with others), 1957. Home: 5202 Westwood Dr., Washington 16. Address: U.S. National Museum, Washington. Died May 21, 1956.

FOSS, George Ernest, commercial sec.; b. Pittsfield, N.H., Mar. 10, 1873; s. Horace Melvin and Abigail Hannah (Green) F.; A.B., Dartmouth, 1897; m. Martha Longfellow Brown, June 28, 1899 (died July 19, 1936); 1 son, Bradbury Poor; m. 2d, Olive Anderson Sipe, May 25, 1938 (died Oct. 21, 1941). Began as principal of grammar and high schools, New Hampshire, 1897-1901, junior high schools, Springfield, Mass., 1901-14; gen. sec. Springfield Chamber of Commerce, 1914-19, Pa. State Chamber of Commerce, 1919 to retirement; retained in advisory position. Dollar-a-year man in Ordnance Dept., Western Mass. Dist., Jan. 11, 1918-Mar. 24, 1919. Mem. Charter Revision Commn., Springfield, 1912-13. Mem. Harrisburg Chamber of Commerce, Nat. Assn. State Chamber of Commerce Officials, Nat. Assn. Commercial Organization Secretaries (ex-pres.), Sons of American Revolution, Dartmouth Alumni Assn., Phi Kappa Psi. Republican. Presbyterian. Clubs: Dartmouth of Central Pa. (ex-pres.), Rotary of Harrisburg (ex-pres.). Home: 1915 N. Front St., Harrisburg, Pa. Died June 28, 1950; buried Pittsfield, N.H.

FOSS, Wilson (Perkins), Jr., chmn. bd. New York Trap Rock Corp.; b. Haverstraw, N.Y., Dec. 17, 1890; s. Wilson P. and Anna (De Baun) F.; student Hill Sch., Pottstown, Pa., 1906-10; Ph.B., Sheffield Scientific Sch. (Yale), 1913; m. Mary Burns, Dec. 7, 1923; children—Wilson III, Hugh H., Mrs. Mary Foss Howard. With New York Trap Rock Co., 1914-16, 30—, salesman, 1916-17, now chmn. bd.; pres. Haverstraw Crushed Stone Co., 1916-17; with Tex. Oil Co. in Spain, 1919-20; v.p. Parish-Watson & Co. (works of art), 1920-43. Served as capt. inf., overseas 17 months on special duty with M.I. Div., U.S. Army, World War I. Republican. Presbyn. Mason (32°). Clubs: Union, Yale, Rockland Country; Creek Country; Triton Fish and Game Club (Quebec, Can.). Home: 155 E. 72d St., N.Y.C. Office: 230 Park Av., N.Y.C. 17. Died Nov. 17, 1957.

FOSTER, Charles Henry Wheelwright; b. Brookline, Mass., Nov. 30, 1859; s. Charles Orin and Caroline Blanchard (Candler) Foster; A.B., cum laude, Harvard University, 1881; married Mabel Chase Hill, 1885; children—Charles O. (deceased), Catherine H. (Mrs. R. M. Tappan), Reginald C. (deceased), Hilda C., Edith H. (Mrs. Albert D. Farwell), Ruth M. (deceased) Caroline W. (Mrs. Theodore Sizer), Barbara (Mrs. J. Linzee Weld) (dec.), John W. (dec.); m. 2d, Mrs. E. B. Van Winkle, 1927 (dec.). Organized Brookline Nat. Bank, 1886, later became pres., sold it to a syndicate, 1904; became treas. of Chickering & Sons, 1891; dir. Northern R.R. of N.H., Foster's Wharf Co. Trustee Harvard Mutual Foundation and several large estates. Unitarian. Clubs: Union, Eastern Yacht, Country; Dedham Country and Polo. Home: Ship's Cabin, Marblehead, Mass. Office: 791 Tremont St., Boston. Died Sept. 22, 1955.

FOSTER, Finley M(elville) K(endall), prof. English; b. N.Y.C. Jan. 27, 1892; s. Finley Milligan and Sallie Cecil (Neer) F.; A.B., N.Y.U., 1913, A.M., 1914; Ph.D., Columbia U., 1918; m. Janet Elizabeth Muchmore, June 2, 1915. Asst. in English, New York U., 1913-14, instr., 1914-16; instr. English, U. of Del., 1917-18, dir. extension div., 1919-20, asst. prof. 1918-21, asso. prof., 1921-25; asso. prof. English, U. of Wis., 1925-28; visiting prof. English, U. of Wash., summer 1927; Oviatt prof English lit., Western Res. U., since 1928, editor The Broadside since 1941, chmn. div. English since 1944. Lecturer on lit. and art, U. of Del., U. of Toronto, 1942. Member advisory council, Cleveland Museum of Art. Member Modern Language Association, American Society for Aesthetics, Am. Assn. Univ. Profs., Phi Beta Kappa, Phi Kappa Phi, Theta Chi. Episcopalian. Clubs: Rowfant, Philosophical (Cleveland); Andiron (N.Y. City). Editor: English Translations from the Greek, 1918; W.S. Landor Poems to Ianthe, 1922; Victorian Prose (with Helen C. White), 1930; One Hundred Books Which An Intelligent American Should Have Read, 1937; Voices of Liberty (with Homer A. Watt), 1941. Contbr. Dictionary of the Arts, 1945. Advisory editor in literature Ency. Americana, 1947. Chmn. bd. trustees Cleveland Hearing and Speech Center. Home: 2164 Briarwood Rd., Cleveland Heights 18. Office: Western Reserve University, Cleve. 6. Died Oct. 30, 1953; buried Knollwood Mausoleum, Cleve.

FOSTER, George Burgess, Jr., ret. army officer, physician; b. Salem, Mass., July 27, 1884; s. George Burgess and Maria Christine (Hanson) F.; M.D., Jefferson Med. Coll., Phila., 1907; hon. grad., Army Med. Sch., Washington, 1910; Dr. Ph., Harvard Med. Sch., Boston, 1917; grad. Med. Field Service Sch. (Army), Carlisle, Pa., 1921, advanced course, 1929; m. Sara Ellis Thomas, Sept. 4, 1912; children—Ellis Anne (Mrs. William R. Lonsdale), George Burgess III, Katherine Christine (Mrs. Charles Stuart O'Malley, Jr.). Intern Phila. Gen. Hosp., 1907-09; commd. 1st lt., Med. Corps, U.S. Army, 1909, advancing through the grades to brig. gen., 1944; served overseas in Philippine Islands, Hawaii and France. Comdg. officer, O'Reilly Gen. Hosp., 1941-44; comdg. gen. O'Reilly Gen. Hosp., 1944-46; retired with rank of brig. gen., 1946; med. dir. Cambridge (Mass.) City Hosp. 1946—. Decorated Legion of Merit (U.S.), Legion of Honor (France); Philippine Campaign, Victory (World War I), Army of Occupation in Germany, Mexican Border, American Defense, Am. Theatre and Victory (World War II) medals. Fellow Am. Coll. Physicians, Am. Med. Assn.; mem. Mil. Surgeons U.S., Am. Pub. Health Assn., Am., Mass. hosp. assns., Pathol. Soc. Phila., Mass. Med. Soc., New England Hosp. Assembly. Club: Harvard (Boston). Contbr. to med. literature. Address: Oxford Courts, 5 Arlington St., Cambridge 40, Mass. Died Dec. 31, 1949.

FOSTER, George Nimmons, lawyer; b. Sterling, Neb., Dec. 29, 1885; s. Frank B. and Mary E. (Nimmons) F.; LL.B., U. Neb., 1911; Ph.B., U. Chgo., 1912, J.D., 1914; m. Esther Mosher Burritt, Sept. 2, 1914; children—Georgette, Frank Burritt. Prof. law, U. Neb., 1912-23, also gen. practice, 1915-22; counsel for Union Auto Ins. Co. and Union Fire Ins. Co., Lincoln, Neb., 1923; moved to Los Angeles, 1925; consul, 1925, v.p., 1926-29, Union Auto Ins. Co., Los Angeles; now gen. practice law at Los Angeles. Served on staff Adj. Gen's Dept., World War; maj. Judge Adv. Gen.'s Dept., Am. Legion. Mem. Order of Coif, Acacia, Phi Delta Phi. Republican. Methodist. Mason (33°). Club: Nebraska. Writer on legal and Masonic subjects. Home: 814 Glenmont Av., Los Angeles. Died Nov. 7, 1952; buried Sterling, Neb.

FOSTER, Henry Bacon, judge; b. May 9, 1863; s. Joshua Hill and Frances Cornelia (Bacon) F.; A.B., U. Ala., 1882, A.M., LL.B., 1884; m. Jennie Hester. Tchr. Gadsden, Ala., 1882-83; admitted to Ala. bar, 1884, and began practice at Tuscaloosa; mayor of Tuscaloosa, 1890-94; mem. Ala. Ho. of Rep., 1898-1902; served as judge Ct. Appeals, Ala. Served as maj. 2d. Regt., Ala. Vols., Spanish-Am. War, 1898. Democrat. Home: Tuscaloosa, Ala. Deceased.

FOSTER, Israel Moore, ex-commr. ct. claism; b. Athens, O.; s. Franklin E. and Mary (Rice) F.; Ph.B., Ohio U., 1895 (LL.D.); studied law, Harvard, 1895-96; LL.B., Ohio State U. Law Sch., Columbus, O., 1898; m. Frances Bayard Witman, Oct. 26, 1898. Began practice at Athens, 1898; mem. Foster & Wells; dir. Security Savings Bank. Sec. Rep. State Central Com., 1912; pros. atty., Athens County, O., 3 terms, 1902-10; mem. 66th to 68th Congresses (1919-25), 10th Ohio Dist.; commr. Court of Claims, Washington, 1925-42; retired. Trustee, secretary Ohio U.; local chmn. Mil. Tng. Camps Assn. Sec. A.R.C. Mem. Am. Bar Assn., Phi Delta Theta, Phi Delta Phi. Presbyn. Mason (Shriner). Clubs: Nat. Press, Cosmos, University (Washington). Home: Athens, O. Died June 10, 1950.*

FOSTER, John Merrell, packer; b. Ottumwa, Ia., Nov. 25, 1894; s. Thomas Dove and Eliza Jane (McClelland) F.; student Shattuck Sch., Faribault, Minn., 1908-09, Lawrenceville (N.J.) Sch., 1909-13, Ia. State Coll., Ames, 1914-16, U.S. Naval Acad., 1918;

m. Mrs. Iva Gilbertson Scripps, Oct. 20, 1920 (divorced); 1 son, James Whitney; m. 2d, Wilma Charlotte Koenig, May 2, 1936; 1 dau., Linda. With John Morrell and Co., since 1916, beginning as laborer, asst. to supt., 1917, sales dept., 1919-26; sec., dir. and asst. mgr. Sioux Falls, S.D., plant, 1926-38, manager 1939-44, 1st v. pres. in charge of operations 1944-52, pres., 1952-54, v.p., dir. sales, 1954-56, vice pres. merchandising and procurement, 1956—; dir. Northwest Bancorporation. Chmn. American Meat Inst.; trustee American Meat Institute Foundation. Served as dist. chmn. Com. for Econ. Development. Served in U.S. Navy, 1917-19; ensign A.E.F., 1918-19. Mem. exec. com. Ia. Mfrs. Assn.; mem. Quiet Birdmen, Phi Kappa Psi. Republican. Presbyn. Clubs: University (Chgo.); Ottumwa Country; Minneapolis. Home: B & B Ranch, West Golf Rd., Ottumwa, Ia. Died Aug. 24, 1958; buried Ottumwa.

FOSTER, Major Bronson, economist; b. Robertsville, Tenn., Jan. 6, 1892; s. Joshua Burnsides and Sarah Ann (Du Pee) F.; grad. Chilhowee Inst., Seymour, Tenn., 1907; A.B., Carson-Newman Coll., Jefferson City, Tenn., 1910, A.M., 1911; studied, Cornell U., 1911-13; m. Helen Margaret Vertner, Oct. 12, 1918; 1 dau., Marjorie Helen. Teacher pub. schs., Tenn., 1907; instr. physics Carson-Newman Coll., 1909-10; prin. Watauga Acad., Butler, Tenn., 1910-11; fellow polit. economy Cornell U., 1912-13; asst. to dean, instr. econs. N.Y.U. Sch. Commerce, Accounts and Finance, 1913-15; asst. prof. econs., sec. Sch. Commerce, Accounts and Finance, 1915-18; asst. to chmn. bd. dirs. Fed. Res. Bank of N.Y., 1918-19; automobile distbr., 1919-20; adminstrv. Officer Alexander Hamilton Inst., 1920-29, now pres.; also pres. Alexander Hamilton Inst., Ltd. (Canada); prof. banking and finance N.Y.U., 1923—, chmn. dept., 1923-55. Dir., mem. exec. com. Cheltenham Art Center. Mem. Am. Econ. Assn., Am. Academy Polit. and Social Science, Royal Econ. Society (London), Delta Sigma Pi, Phi Alpha Kappa, Lambda Chi Alpha, Theta Nu Epsilon. Republican. Baptist. Mason (32°, Shriner). Clubs: Lawyers, Lotos (N.Y. City). Author: Banking, 1917. Co-author: Money and Banking, 1936. Editor-in-chief: Modern Business Series, Business Conditions Service. Home: Hedgehurst, Rowland Av. and Croyden Rd., Cheltenham, Pa. Office: 71 West 23d St., N.Y.C. 10. Died July 4, 1958.

FOSTER, Theodosia Toll (Faye Huntington), author; b. Verona, N.Y., 1838; d. Daniel and Ruth Hollister (Hills) Toll; grad. Oneida Sem., 1861; m. James H. Foster, 1869 (died 1872). Many yrs. prin. Home Sch., Verona, N.Y.; pres. W.C.T.U. of Oneida County, N.Y. Author: In Earnest; Through Patience; Kitty Farnham; Allan Phillips; Fred Roberts; Mr. McKenzie's Answer, 1876; Ripley Parsonage, 1877; From Different Standpoints (with Mrs. Alden), 1878; Echoing and Re-echoing, 1879; Mrs. Deane's Way, 1880; Millerton People, 1884; What Fide Remembers, 1885; Competitive Workmen; St. Paul's Problem, 1887; The Boynton Neighborhood, 1895; A Modern Exodus; His First Charge, 1897; Lewis Elmore—Crusader, 1898; A Break in Schedule Time, 1901; Opportunity Circle, 1901. Address: Verona, N.Y. Deceased.

FOSTER, Thomas Henry, meat packer; b. Chicago, Ill., Jan. 31, 1875; s. Thomas Dove and Elizabeth (Thompson) F.; grad. Parsons Acad., Fairfield, Ia., 1893; student Parsons Coll., 1893-94, B.S. in Bus. Adminstrn., 1929, Litt.D. (hon.), 1945; LL.D. (hon.). Westminster Coll., Salt Lake City, 1947; m. Mary Frances Bulger, July 25, 1898; children—Katherine Margaret (Mrs. Ralph Benedict Vernon), Gertrude Elizabeth (Mrs. Harold Edward Purdy), Robert Thompson. With John Morrell & Co., meat packers, Ottumwa, Ia., since 1894, mgr. of one of plants, 1909-15, v.p., gen. mgr., 1915-21, pres., 1921 to June 20, 1944; chmn. since June 20, 1944; dir. John Morrell & Co., Ltd. (Liverpool and London, Eng.), Victoria Cold Stores, Ltd. (Liverpool): trustee Morrell Refrigerator Car Co.; dir. Chicago, Burlington & Quincy R. R., Colo. and So. Ry. Chmn. War Relief drives, Ottumwa, four minute man, World War I. Mem. bd. dirs. Nat. Assn. of Mfrs., 1936; dir. Inst. Am. Meat Packers (chmn. bd. 1938-39, 1943-44), Chicago Bd. of Trade, C. of C. of U.S. (dir. 1923), Ottumwa Chamber Commerce (dir. 1914-26), Ia. State Historical Soc., Beta Gamma Sigma (hon.). Dem. Presbyn. Clubs: Embassy (Des Moines); Tavern, Univ. (Chicago); Grolier (New York). Author: (with Malcolm G. Wyer) Bookplates in Iowa, 1914; A Letter from the Fire, 1923; A Little Journey to the Valley of the Loire, 1945; Shakespeare—Man of Mystery, 1946; America's Most Famous Book, 1947; Beadles, Bibles and Bibliophiles, 1948; The Unbought Grace of Life and Other Essays, 1950. Collector of rare books, manuscripts, prints, etc. Home: 1560 N. Elm St., Ottumwa, Iowa. Died Nov. 14, 1951.

FOSTER, William Frederick, artist; b. Cin., Aug. 13, 1882; s. William Bolliver and Emma (Koch) F.; art. edn., Cin. Art Acad., 1898-1900, Art Students' League, N.Y., 1901-03, Chase's Sch., N.Y.C., 1903-05; Julian Acad., Paris, 1912-14; m. Mary Bramhall, 1909; 1 dau., Lonna Averill; m. 2d, Audrey Marye, 1920. Illustrator for Life, 1905-10; later illustrator for Saturday Evening Post, Harper's, Cosmopolitan, Scribner's, Liberty, Pierre La Fitte Publs. (Paris, Washington and London), etc.; now portrait painter. Instr. Art Inst. of Chgo., 1919-20. Served as ambulance driver, France, 1916-18. Awarded Clarke prize, Nat. Acad. Design, 1926, auction prize, 1927; A.N.A., 1926; mem. Soc. Ind. Allied Artists, Salmagundi Club. Republican. Address: 54 W. 74th St., N.Y.C. Died 1953.

FOSTER, William Henry, chmn. bd. General Fireproofing Co.; b. Kingston, Pa., 1866; s. David and Jane (Clark) F.; m. Josephine Orr, 1893. Chicago sales mgr. The Salem Wire Nail Co., 1892-94; v.p. and sales mgr. Falcon Iron and Nail Co., Niles, O., 1894-1901; sec. and sales mgr. The Youngstown Sheet and Tube Co., 1901-03; sec. General Fireproofing Co., 1903-06, v.p., 1906-12, pres., 1912-27; chmn., board since 1927; dir. Ohio Leather Co., Gen. Fireproofing Corp. of Ill., Crab Creek Land Co., Ohio Edison Co. Home: Orchard Hill Farm, Hubbard, O. Office: General Fireproofing Co., Youngstown, O. Died Oct. 18, 1951.

FOSTER, William James, retired elec. engr.; b. Argyle, N.Y., Sept. 17, 1860; s. James and Martha (Dobbin) F.; A.B., Williams Coll., Williamstown, Mass., 1884, A.M., 1885, D.Sc., 1923; M.S., Cornell, 1891; m. Caroline McEachron, Sept. 16, 1896; 1 son, William James. Instr. mathematics, William Coll., 1885; asst. prin. Burr & Burton Sem., Manchester, Vt., 1885-86; tchr. sci. and mathematics, Hill Sch., Pottstown, Pa., 1886-90; engr. Thomson-Houston Co., Lynn, Mass., 1891-94; asst. engr. Gen. Electric Co., Schenectady, N.Y., 1894-1925, cons. engr., 1925-29 (now retired). Fellow Am. Inst. E.E., A.A.A.S.; mem. Acad. Polit. Sci., Phi Beta Soc. Hudson Valley Soc. Recipient medals for machine design by St. Louis, San Francisco, and other expns., Lamme medal of Am. Inst. E.E., 1931. Republican. Mem. Ref. Church of Am. Clubs: Mohawk Golf; Williams (New York); Taconic Golf (Williamstown, Mass.). Contbr. articles to tech. publs.; also wrote Descendants of John Dobbin of Connagher. Home: 2 Douglas Rd., Schenectady. Died July 2, 1943; buried Argyle (N.Y.) Cemetery.

FOSTER, William Trufant, economist; b. Boston, Jan. 18, 1879; s. William Henry and Sarah Jennie (Trufant) F.; A.B., Harvard, 1901, A.M., 1904; Ph.D., Columbia, 1911; LL.D., Colo. Coll., 1913, Western Res. U., 1916, U. Me., 1936; L.H.D., Rollins Coll., 1947; Litt.D., Reed Coll., 1948; m. Bessie Lucile Russell, Dec. 25, 1905; children—Russell Trufant, Le Baron Russell, Faith, Trufant. Instr. English, Bates Coll., 1901-03; prof. Eng. and argumentation Bowdoin Coll., 1905-10; pres. Reed Coll., Portland, Ore., 1910-20; dir. Pollak Found. for Econ. Research, 1920—; lectr. principles of edn. Harvard, summers 1909, 19, Columbia, 1911; fellow in edn. Columbia, lectr. in edn1. adminstrn., 1909-10. Inspr. in European service for A.R.C., 1917. Mem. Public Affairs Com. of New York; mem. Consumers adv. bd. NRA, 1933-35; mem. State Planning Bd. Mass.; econ. adviser Internat. Labor Conf., Geneva, 1938. Trustee, Rollins Coll., 1947—. Fellow A.A.A.S.; mem. Phi Delta Kappa. Author: Argumentation and Debating, 1908; Administration of the College Curriculum, 1910; Essentials of Exposition and Argument, 1911; Should Students Study?, 1917; Money (with Waddill Catchings), 1923; Profits (with same), 1925; Business Without a Buyer (with same), 1927; The Road to Plenty (with some), 1927; Progress and Plenty (with same), 1930; Basic Principles of Speech (with Lew Sarett), 1936; Speech, 1942. Editor and Part Author: Social Hygiene and Morals, 1913. Editor: (with Warren M. Persons) The Problem of Business Forecasting, 1924. Editor: Modern Speeches on Basic Issues, 1939. Contbr. to newspapers and mags. Address: 1399 Aloma Av., Winter Park, Fla. Died Oct. 8, 1950.

FOSTER, William Wallace, chmn. Union Trust Co. of Rochester; b. Syracuse, N.Y., Jan. 1, 1873; s. William Augustus and Celia (Raynor) F. Became pres. Trust Company of Rochester, 1930, now chairman of the board; director of various corporations. Clubs: Genesee Valley, Rochester County (Rochester). Home: 34 S. Goodman St. Office: 19 Main St., W., Rochester. Died Sept. 5, 1956.*

FOTHERGILL, John Vincent, ins. exec.; b. Birkenhead, Eng., June 2, 1871; s. John and Gertrude Mary (Herd) F.; student Birkenhead and other pvt. schs. of Eng.; m. Gertrude Damon, Dec. 15, 1909; children—John Damon, Margery (Mrs. Stockman). Vice pres. London & Lancashire Indemnity Co. of Am. since 1926; asst. sec. London & Lancashire Ins. Co., Law, Union & Rock Ins. Co., Ltd.; asst. sec., dir. Orient Ins. Co., Safeguard Ins. Co. of N.Y. Republican. Club: Hartford Golf. Home: 12 Staples Pl., West Hartford 7. Office: 20 Trinity St., Hartford, Conn. Died Jan. 20, 1953.

FOTITCH, A(lexander) Constantin (fō'tĭch), diplomat; b. Sabac (Schabatz), Jugoslavia, Feb. 4, 1891; s. Alexander and Pola F.; grad. U. Law, Bordeaux, France, 1912; m. Tatiana Zurunich, Oct. 23, 1922; 1 dau., Pola. Began as soldier, 1912; began diplomatic service, 1915, as attaché Ministry Fgn. Affairs; with legation in Berne, 1917, Paris, 1918; sec. legation, Stockholm, 1919, Vienna, 1920; with dels. to Peace Conf., Paris; sec. legation, London, 1921-24; gen. consul, Vienna, 1924, Constantinople, 1924-26; counsellor legation, Rome, 1926; del. to 3d session Polit. Econ. Commn. for Conf. for Disarmament, Geneva, 1926; expert to 7th Congress of League of Nations, Geneva, 1926; del. League of Nations each yr., 1927-31, also v.p. 5th commn., 1928, pres. advisory opium commn., 1929 and del. to council, to assembly and to spl. session at Madrid, 1930; counsellor legation, Prague, 1927; del. Plenary Commn. for Disarmament, Geneva, 1927, 10th and 11th Internat. Labor Confs., Geneva, 1927-28; pres. delegation to Internat. Conf. for Econ. Statistics, Geneva, 1928; dir. polit. div. Ministry Fgn. Affairs, 1929; E.E. and M.P. to Moscow, 1929; del. 2d Hague Conf., 1930; del. Conf. for Regulation Hungarian War Reparations, Paris, 1930; mem. royal delegation to Conf. Fgn. Ministers of Little Entente, 1930; under sec. Ministry Fgn. Affairs, 1930; E.E. and M.P. to U.S. from Jugoslavia, 1935-42; A.E. and P. Oct. 5, 1942-July 14, 1944; resigned. Served as capt. in Balkan War, 1912-13, in army of Jugoslavia throughout World War I. Decorated White Eagle; gold and silver medals for bravery; medal of Serbian-Turkish War, 1912, Serbian-Bulgarian War, 1913, World War, 1918; Order of St. Sava, 1st class; Grand Officer Legion of Honor (France), etc. Author: The War We Lost, 1948. Home: 4112 Jenifer St. N.W., Washington. Died Feb. 14, 1959; buried Serbian Orthodox Monastery, Libertyville, Ill.

FOULDS, Henry W(illiam), mfg. exec.; b. Edinburgh, Scotland, Jan. 10, 1891 (parents U.S. citizens); s. Henry T. and Marie Anne Elizabeth (Pillans) F.; Chem.E., U. Pa., 1914; m. Rose Huntington, 1922; children—Henry William, Ralph H., Robert S., Mrs. John D. Plant, Jr. With Electric Storage Battery Co., Phila., 1914-16, Fairbanks-Morse, Buenos Aires, 1919-25. Servel, Inc., 1926-30, Goulds Pumps, Seneca Falls, N.Y., 1930-34; with Permutit Co., N.Y.C., 1935—, pres., dir., 1944—, chmn., 1957—; pres., dir. Permutit Co. of Can., Ltd., Montreal, 1936—; pres., dir. Simplex Valve & Meter Co., Phila., 1946-57, chmn. bd., 1957—. Officer, World War I. Mem. Pan-Am. Soc. U.S., Am. Soc. M.E., Am. Water Works Assn., The Camp Fire Club of Am. Clubs: Union League. Died Apr. 4, 1959.‡

FOULK, Charles William (fŭlk), chemist; b. Warren, O., Apr. 26, 1869; s. Elias James and Louisa (Paltzgrove) F.; A.B., Ohio State U., 1894; grad. study Mass. Inst. Tech., summer, 1897, Physico-Chem. Inst., Leipzig, Germany, 1899-1901; D.Sc., Mt. Union Col., Alliance, O., 1934; m. Elma Brooks Perry, Sept. 12, 1905. Asst. to chemist O. State Bd. Agr., 1894-96; prof. analytical chemistry, Ohio State U., 1908—, emeritus prof., 1939; cons. chem., Geol. Survey of O., 1914-16. Past chmn. tech. com. no. 3, joint research on boiler feed water studies (Am. Boiler Mfrs. Assn., Am. Ry. Engring. Assn., Am. Water Works Assn., Nat. Electric Light Assn., Am. Soc. Testing Materials, Am. Soc. M.E.). Fellow A.A.A.S.; mem. Am. Chem. Soc., Sigma Xi, Phi Beta Kappa, Phi Lambda Upsilon. Clubs: University Faculty, Torch. Author: Introductory Notes on Quantitative Chemical Analysis, 2d edit., 1910; General principles and Manipulation of Quantitative Chemical Analysis, 1913; Industrial Water Supplies of Ohio, 1925. Contbr. jours. of Am. Chem. Soc., Jour. Am. Water Works Assn. Inventor of density measuring apparatus. Home: 275 East Lane Av., Columbus, O. Died Dec. 15, 1958; buried Piqua, O.

FOUNTAIN, Percy Coleman, lawyer; b. Monroeville, Ala., Jan. 10, 1907; s. Murdoch McCorvey and Evelyn Margaret (Nettles) F.; A.B., U. Ala., 1927, LL.B., 1929; m. Rebecca Buck, Dec. 18, 1943; children—Percy Coleman, John Ernst. Admitted to Ala. bar, 1929, practiced in Monroeville, 1929-31, Mobile, 1931-39, asso. Smith & Johnston; first asst. U.S. atty. So. Dist. Ala., 1939-42, 45-48, U.S. atty. 1948—. Served as lt. U.S.N.R., 1942-45. Mem. Ala., Mobile Co. bar assns., Phi Kappa Sigma, Phi Alpha Delta. Democrat. Baptist. Kiwanian. Home: 209A Desales Av. Office: Federal Bldg., Mobile, Ala. Died Feb. 1, 1956; buried Pine Crest Cemetery, Mobile.

FOUNTAIN, William Alfred, Sr., bishop; b. Elberton, Ga., Oct. 29, 1870; s. Richard and Virginia F.; normal course, Allen U., Columbia, S.C., 1892; A.B., Morris Brown U., Atlanta, 1901; B.D., Turner Theol. Sem., Atlanta, 1902; M.A., Northwestern U., 1919; D.D., Wilberforce (Ohio) U., 1920, LL.D., 1927; studied U. of Chicago and Garrett Biblical Inst.; m. Jessie Williams June 29, 1894 (died Sept., 1898); m. Julia Allen, Oct. 24, 1899. Ordained ministry A.M.E. Ch., 1894; pastorates in Ga. and Wilmington, N.C.; presiding elder Athens (Ga.) Dist.; pres. Morris Brown U. since 1911; elected bishop, 1920, and assigned to 18th and part of 13th dists. from Cal. to West Indies and S. Am., presided over 6th Episcopal District including Ga., 12th District including Ark. and Okla., now 9th Dist. including Ala. Chmn. Edn1. Bd. and Religious Edn. Dept. of A.M.E. Ch., Nat. Council Chs. of Christ in U.S.A. Mem. exec. bd. Boy Scouts; mem. Interracial Com. of Ga. Pres. bd. trustees Morris Brown Coll.; trustee Atlanta U., Wilberforce U., Morehouse Coll., Daniel Payne Coll. (chmn.). Mem. Sigma Pi Phi. Sr. bishop emeritus A.M.E. Ch. Home: 242 Boulevard N.E., Atlanta. Died Apr. 23, 1955.

FOUSE, Winfred Eugene, business exec.; born Akron, O., Dec. 24, 1877; s. Reuben E. and Salina (Royer) F.; grad. Hartville High Sch. and Eastman Business Coll., Poughkeepsie, N.Y.; m. Elva Corl, Mar. 30, 1902; children—Harlan C., Eugene Kenneth, Betty Frances, Elva Marie. Teacher, school near Hartville, O.; in engring. dept. Wheeling & Lake Erie R.R., 1900-02; with B. F. Goodrich and Diamond Rubber Co., Akron, O., 1902-05; credit mgr. Firestone Tire & Rubber Co., Akron, 1905-09; with W. O'Neil, organized Western Rubber & Supply Co., Kansas City, Mo., 1909, and The Gen. Tire & Rubber Co., Akron, 1914; dir. The Gen. Tire & Rubber Co., 1914— (past v.p., treas.). Past pres., hon. life trustee Akron Y.M.C.A. Republican. Conglist. Mason (33°, K.T., Shriner). Clubs: Portage Country, Masonic, Akron City, Congress Lake Country, Rotary. Home: 1215 W. Market St., Akron. Office: The General Tire & Rubber Co., Akron, O. Died July 22, 1958; buried Rose Hill Cemetery, Akron, O.

FOWLER, (Harry) Alfred, editor, pub.; b. Paola, Kan., Dec. 1, 1889; s. Harry Turton and Anna (St. Louis) F.; ed pub. schs. and privately; m. Eleanor Morrison, Nov. 12, 1918; 1 dau., Gloria Eleanor; m. 2d, Wilma Hall, Nov. 14, 1940. Owner Alfred Fowler, Publisher; formerly editor Print Survey, The Quarterly Notebook, The Golden Galleon, The Bookplate Ann., The Romance of Fine Prints, The Print Collectors' Chronicle, The Print Collectors' Quarterly. Served from lt. to capt. Signal Corps, U.S. Army, World War I; capt. to lt. col. USAAF, 1942-45. Mem. Soc. Print Collectors (dir.), Bibliog. Soc., Am. Inst. Graphic Arts, Am. Soc. Aesthetics. Episcopalian. Clubs: Grolier (New York); Print Collector (London). Author of books on bookplates, radio and fine prints. Address: 311 N. Thomas St., Alexandria 3, Va. Deceased.

FOWLER, Charles Rollin, lawyer; b. Jordan, Minn., Sept. 17, 1869; s. R. D. and Jane (Varner) F.; LL.B., U. Minn., 1892; m. Caroline Blair Jones, Nov. 5, 1895 (died Dec. 17, 1941). Admitted to Minn. bar, 1892, N.D. bar, 1893; mem. Fowler, Youngquist, Furber, Taney & Johnson; specializes in ins. corp. and utility law; apptd. co-receiver Minn. & Ontario Paper Co., 1931; former dir. Minn. Loan & Trust Co. Mem. Minn. Ho. of Rep., 1911-12, Minn. Senate, 1919-22. Mem. Co. B, 1st Regt. Minn. State Militia, 1886-91; chmn. Legal Advisory Bd., Div. 3, Mpls., under SSS, 1917-18. Mem. Am. (gen. council 1932-34), Minn., Hennepin County bar assns., Am. Liberty League (nat. lawyers com.), U. Minn. Law Alumni Assn. (pres. 1908), Mpls. Soc. Fine Arts, Orchestral Assn. Mpls., Delta Chi. Mason (32°), Elk. Clubs: Minikahda (gov. 1910-41; pres. 1916, 30, 40), Minneapolis (gov. 1939-42); Minneapolis Athletic (pres. 1916); Minnesota (St. Paul); Bankers (N.Y. C.). Author: (pamphlets) Encroachment by Government on the Domain of Private Business; Nationalization by Coercion; Message from an American Who Has Lived Three-Quarters of a Century. Home: 1921 Humboldt Av. S. Office: Northwestern Bank Bldg., Mpls. Died May 26, 1950; buried Lakewood Cemetery, Mpls.

FOWLER, Harold North, educator; b. Westfield, Mass., Feb. 25, 1859; s. Samuel and Maria (Jones) F.; A.B., Harvard, 1880; studied Am. Sch. Classical Studies, Athens, 1882-83, university Bonn and Berlin, 1883-85; Ph.D., Bonn, 1885; Litt.D., Western Reserve U., 1939; m. Helen, d. Ex-Governor Charles H. Bell, of N.H., Dec. 23, 1890 (died Aug. 18, 1909); m. 2d, Mary Zay, d. Frank Price Blackford, of Ohio, June 30, 1925. Instructor, Harvard, 1885-88; prof., Phillips Exeter Acad., 1888-92; prof. Greek, U. of Tex., 1892-93, Coll. for Women, Western Reserve U., 1893-1929, prof. emeritus since 1929; consultant in classical lit., Library of Congress, 1929-32, now hon. consultant. Professor Greek lang. and lit. Am. School Classical Studies, Athens, 1903-04, 1924-25, research prof., 1929; editor-in-chief Am. Journal of Archaeology, 1906-16. Mem. Am. Philol. Assn. (president 1913), Archaeol. Inst. America (v.p. 1916-36), Soc. for Promotion Hellenic Studies, Am. Fed. of Arts, English-Speaking Union; corresponding member Deutsches Archäol. Institut. Editor: Thucydides, Book V, 1888; Plautus, Menaechmi, 1889; Quintus Curtius, Books III and IV, 1890. Allen and Greenough's Ovid, 1891; also Corinth, Volumes I, III, IV, VI, VIII and IX. Joint Author: Tuell and Fowler's First Book in Latin, 1893; Tuell and Fowler's Beginners's Book in Latin, 1900; Fowler and Wheeler's Handbook of Greek Archaeology, 1909; The Picture Book of Sculpture (with Mary B. Fowler), 1929; Corinth, Vol. I (with Richard Stillwell), 1932. Author: History of Ancient Greek Literature, 1902; History of Roman Literature, 1903; A History of Sculpture, 1916. Translator: Plato, Vol. I, in the Loeb Classical Library, 1914, Vol. 11, 1921, Vol. III, 1925, Vol. VI, 1926; Plutarch's Moralia, Vol. X, 1936. Contbr. on classical subjects to revs. and mags. Home: 936 S. Main St., Findlay, O. Died Sept. 29, 1955; buried Westfield, Mass.

FOWLER, James Alexander, lawyer; born Knox County, Tennessee, Feb. 22, 1863; s. Joseph W. and Mary (Connor) F.; grad. E. Tenn. Wesleyan U. (now U. of Chattanooga), 1884, LL.D., 1910; m. Lucy Ellen Hornsby, May 28, 1885; children—Harriet Vivian (Mrs. Rowntree), Harley Grey, Hornsby Joseph, James Alexander, Edward Cornelius, Samuel Francis. Tutor, E. Tenn. Wesleyan U., 1884-85; prin. Clinton High Sch., 1885-86; admitted to bar, 1886, and since in practice at Clinton and Knoxville, Tenn. Presdl. elector, 1896; Rep. nominee for gov. Tenn., 1898, asst. atty. gen. U.S., 1908-11; asst. to atty. gen., U.S., May 15, 1911-July 31, 1913; spl. asst. to atty. genl. Aug. 1913-June 1914, and Mar. 9, 1921-Sept. 30, 1926; mayor of Knoxville, 1927-29; Rep. nominee for U.S. Senate, 1928; del. Rep. Nat. Conv., 1932; mem. Rep. Program Com., 1938. Del. M.E. Gen. Conf., 1896; trustee U. of Tenn., Tenn. Wesleyan Coll., 1928-48 (pres. bd.). Home: 3311 Broadway N.E. Office: Hamilton Bank Bldg., Knoxville, Tenn. Died Nov. 18, 1955; buried Greenwood Cemetery.

FOWLER, Robert Lambert, mfg. exec.; b. Danville, Ill., Oct. 4, 1876; s. Robert E. and Ellen (Dillon) F.; B.S., U. of Ill., 1899; married Georgiana Savage, June 26, 1907; children—Georgiana, Mary Elizabeth. In private engineering, 1899-1903, Salt Lake City, Utah, engineer of mines Utah Fuel Company, 1903-06; chief engineer Dawson Fuel Company, 1906-08; superintendent Manhattan Trap Rock Company, 1908-10; manager Barber Asphalt Paving Company, 1910-18; in charge of prodn., Pierce Oil Corp., 1918-21; v.p. marketing Pierce Petroleum Corp., 1921-27; mgr. factories Sears Roebuck & Co., 1927-31; pres. Florence Stove Co., 1931-45, chmn. bd., pres., 1945—; dir. Florence Stove Co., Am. Rock Wool Corp., Fry Roofing Co. Pres., dir. Am. Asphalt Association. Mem. Delta Tau Delta, Tau Beta Pi. Clubs: Exmoor Country, Bob O'Link Golf (Highland Park, Ill.); Oak Hill Country (Fitchburg, Mass.). Home: 16 Warwick Rd., Winnetka, Ill. Office: Merchandise Mart, Chicago 54. Died Mar. 6, 1958; buried Christ Church Cemetery.

FOWLER, Russell Story, surgeon; b. Brooklyn, N.Y., May 1, 1874; s. George Ryerson and Louise Rachel (Wells) F.; grad. Brooklyn Polytechnic Inst., 1891; M.D., Coll. Physicians and Surgeons (Columbia) 1895; grad. study, Allegemeine Krankenhaus, Vienna, 1900-01; m. Rose Blanche Beauchesne, Aug. 11, 1933; children—Rachel Story, George Ryerson, and (by former marriage) Russell Story. Held various minor hosp. and dispensary positions, 1895-96; adjunct surgeon Brooklyn Hosp., 1896-1906; acting attending surgeon 2d Div., Meth. Episcopal Hosp., 1898-99, asst. surgeon, 1898-1906, attending surgeon, 1906-27, cons. surgeon, 1927-29, sr. surgeon, 1929-34, cons. surgeon, 1934—; asst. surgeon German Hosp. of Brooklyn, 1899-1906; chief surgeon German Hosp. (Wyckoff Heights Hospital of Brooklyn), 1906-48, chief consultant surgeon, 1948—, now hon. dir. emeritus surgery; lecturer New York Polyclinic, 1896-97; former consultant surgeon Huntington Hospital and Hebrew Orphan Asylum Brooklyn; former cons. surgeon Beth Moses Hosp. and Bay Ridge hospitals, Brooklyn. Member N.Y. State Com. Council Nat. Defense, 1917, 18; chmn. Auxiliary Med. Defense Com. of Kings County, 1917, 18; organizer of Kings County and Long Island Med. Advisory Bd.; mem. Med. Advisory Bd. No. 17, Censor Med. Soc. County of Kings, 1909, v.p., 1914, pres., 1915, trustee, 1916-20 and 1927-33, chmn. Centenary Celebration Com., 1921-22; mem. Joint Com. on Graduate Edn. of Med. Soc. County of Kings and L.I. Med. Coll., 1925-29. Licentiate (founders group) Am. Bd. Surgery. Fellow Am. Coll. Surgeons (one of founders; gov. several times), N.Y. Acad. Medicine, Societe Internationale de Chirurgie; sr. fellow Brooklyn Surg. Soc. (past pres.), A.M.A., Am. Med. Editors' and Authors' Assn., Med. Soc. of State of N.Y., N.Y. Physicians Mutual Aid Assn., Am. Geog. Soc., Nat. Geog. Soc. N.Y. Zoöl. Soc. Brooklyn Inst. Arts and Sciences, Brooklyn Museum, Am. Mus. Natural History, etc.; founder and past pres. Clin. Soc. of Wyckoff Heights Hosp.; hon. mem., one of founders and former concillor Trail Riders Assn. of Canadian Rockies. Republican. Episcopalian (trustee Ch. of the Messiah 1922-26). Clubs: Montauk (Brooklyn); Nassau Country, Alpine of Canada, Campfire of America, Brooklyn Hosp. No. 1. Author: Surgery of the Spleen, and Operations Upon the Small Intestine, Mesentery and Omentum (Johnson's Operative Therapeusis); The Operating Room and the Patient, 3 edit.; Minor Surgery in Bryant & Buck System, 1906. Collaboraor in G. R. Fowler's Surgery, 1906. Contbr. to surgery mags. Home: 155 Stratford Rd., Bklyn. 18. Died Jan. 5, 1959; buried Greenwood Cemetery.

FOWLER, Walter William, ret. transportation exec.; b. Allison Prairie, Ill., Mar. 3, 1888; s. William H. and Elizabeth Jane (Calvert) F.; student Charleston (Ill.) Normal Sch., 1904; m. Pearl Marie Hasecoster, Oct. 5, 1910; children—Jane, Betty (Mrs. Ashton Laidlaw), Susan (Mrs. Robert G. Beisel). Began with Big 4 R.R., 1904; in various positions successively with S. J. Fowler Coal Co., East St. Louis, Sterling Coal Co., Chgo., Star Coal Co., Kansas City, Pitts. & Ohio Coal Co., Chgo. and Northwest Trading Co., Chgo. until 1919; with Gen. Am. Car Co., Chgo., 1919-41; with Gen. Am. Transportation Corp., Chgo., 1944-52, v.p., dir., 1946-52. Head of Mission Bd. of Econ. Warfare, Fgn. Econ. Adminstrn., China, 1943-44. Mem. Far East com. Nat. Fgn. Trade Council. Republican. Clubs: Union League, South Shore Country (Chgo.); Metropolitan, India House (N.Y. C.). Home: 65 W. Jackson Blvd. Office: 135 S. La Salle St., Chgo.

FOX, Andrew Fuller, congressman; b. Pickens Co., Ala., April 26, 1849; studied law in Grenada, Miss.; admitted to Miss. bar, 1877; has practiced in Miss. since; delegate to Dem. Nat. Conv., 1888; State senator, 1891-93; U.S. att'y for Northern dist. of Miss., 1893-6; mem. Congress 1897-1903, 4th Miss. dist.; Democrat. Home: West Point, Miss. Deceased.

FOX, Carl, lawyer; b. nr. Slate Springs, Webster County, Miss., Apr. 27, 1876; s. Hally and Angeline (Cooke) F.; B.S., Miss. State Coll., 1897; student Columbian Law School, Washington, 1897-98; m. Mary Evelyn Cottrell, Nov. 29, 1905; children—Carl, Albert Cottrell, Sophia Wilsford (Mrs. Bruce Kenamore), Mary Evelyn (Mrs. Harry R. Maxon, Jr.). Admitted to Miss. bar, 1899, and began practice at West Point; practiced at Vicksburg, 1900-10; asst. atty. gen. of Miss., 1910-12; entered law dept. of Mobile & Ohio R.R. Co., Mobile, Ala., 1912, gen. solicitor law, under federal control, 1918-20, gen. counsel for receivers, St. Louis, 1932-40; gen. solicitor G., M. & O. R.R., 1940—. Served as pvt. and corpl. Co. A, 2d Miss. Regt., Spanish-Am. War, 1898. Democrat. Home: 1006 Government St., Mobile 20. Office: 104 St. Francis St., Mobile 13, Ala. Died Dec. 18, 1958.

FOX, Fred Lee, judge; b. Braxton County, W.Va., Oct. 24, 1876; s. Camden and Caroline (McMorrow) F.; LL.B., W.Va. Univ., 1899; m. Annie Lee Frame, June 27, 1900; children—Gordon Byrne, John Holt, George McMorrow, Agnes Jane, Rebecca Ellen (Mrs. Charles A. Duffield, Jr.), Anna Jean (Mrs. J. Fleet Greene). Admitted to W.Va. bar, 1899, and practiced in Sutton until 1933; mem. State Senate, 1912-20; state tax commr., 1933-36; judge Supreme Court of Appeals since 1937. Mem. Am. and State bar assns. Democrat. Presbyterian. Mason. Home: 206 Ruffner Av. Address: State Capitol, Charleston, W.Va. Died Aug. 8, 1952.

FOX, Genevieve (Mrs. Raymond G. Fuller), writer; b. Southampton, Mass.; d. Samuel Barker and Louisa Caroline (Gray) Fox; B.A., Smith Coll., Northampton, Mass., 1911; m. Raymond G. Fuller, Nov. 5, 1932. Editorial asst. Ginn & Co. and Silver, Burdette & Co., 1911-18; publicity writer Nat. Playground Assn., 1920-22, Met. Life Ins. Co., 1925-33; tutor Bryn Mawr Summer Sch. for Indsl. Workers, 1922. Served as research worker and writer for War Work Council, YWCA, 1918-20. Mem. Phi. Beta Kappa. Club: Pen and Brush (New York). Author: Mountain Girl, 1932; Mountain Girl Comes Home, 1934; Lona of Hollybush Creek, 1935; Susan of the Green Mountains, 1937; Border Girl, 1939; Green Treasure, 1941; Sir Wilfred Grenfell, 1942; Army Surgeon, 1944; Cynthia of Bee Tree Hollow, 1948. Contbr. fiction and articles to mags. Died Oct. 6, 1959.

FOX, Howard, dermatologist; b. London, Eng., July 4, 1873; s. George Henry and Harriet Lovisa (Gibbs) F.; brought to America in infancy; A.B., Yale, 1894; M.D., Coll. Physicians and Surgeons, Columbia, 1898; post-grad. work univs. of Berlin and Vienna; Sc.D., Rollins Coll., Winter Park, Fla., 1931; unmarried. Practiced, New York, since 1903; prof. dermatology, Dartmouth Med. Coll., Jan. 1913; dermatol. asst., Vanderbilt Clinic, 1903-13; attending dermatologist U.S.P.H.S., Dist. 2; prof. dermatology, N.Y. Polyclinic Med. Sch., 1923-24; emeritus prof. dermatology and syphilology, New York U.; Hon. cons. dermatologist and syphilologist, Bellevue Hosp.; cons. dermatologist various hosps. Lt. Col., M.C. U.S. Army, comdg. officer Base Hosp. No. 136, Vannes, France, 1918-19; active service in war, 1917-19; consultant to Sec. of War in tropical medicine during World War II; now col. Med. R.C. Pres. Am. Bd. of Dermatology and Syphilology, 1932-45; pres. Med. Soc. County of New York, 1938; 1st pres. Am. Acad. Dermatology and Syphilology, 1938; pres. N.Y. Soc. of Tropical Medicine, 1939; 1st pres. Assn. of Dermato-Syphilologists of Greater New York. Mem. Am. Dermatol. Assn. (hon.), (pres. 1924-25), N.Y. Acad. Medicine, Am. Med. Assn., N.Y. State Med. Soc., Psi Upsilon; corr. mem. Swedish Dermatol. Soc., Brit. Assn. of Dermatology and Syphilology, Danish Dermatol. Soc., Med. and Surg. Soc. of Sao Paulo (Brazil); hon. mem. Society of Investigative Dermatology, New York Dermatol. Society, Manhattan Dermatol. Society, N.E. Dermatol. Society, Pittsburgh Dermatol. Soc., Royal Society of Medicine (Sect. of Dermatology), Cuban Dermatol. Soc., Société Française de Prophylaxie Sanitaire et Morale, Société Française de Dermatologie et de Syphiligraphia, Hungarian Dermatol. Soc., Spanish Acad. of Dermatol. and Syphilology. Austrian Dermatol. Soc., Polish Assn. of Dermatology and Syphilology, Sociedad de dermatol. y syphilografia of Argentina, Italian Soc. Dermatology and Syphilology (hon.), N.H. State Med. Soc., Plainfield Med. Soc.; Med. Assn. of Peru; v.p. 8th Internat. Congress Dermatology, Copenhagen, 1930; hon. pres. 9th Internat. Cong. of Dermatology, Budapest, 1935.

Clubs: Omega, Phi Alpha Sigma, Psi Upsilon. Contbr. Personal Hygiene (Pyle), 1909; Mod. Treatment (Hare), 1910; Skin Diseases in Infancy and Childhood, 1929; "Eliot's Quiz." 1938; Clinical Tropical Medicine (Z. T. Bercovitz), 1944. Editor-in-chief Archives of Dermatology and Syphilology, 1937-47. Address: 145 E. 54th St., N.Y.C. 22. Died Oct. 1954.

FOX, Victor Samuel, corp. exec.; b. Nottingham, Eng., Apr. 13, 1893; s. Joseph and Betsy (Duschac) F.; brought to U.S., 1898, naturalized, 1904; student pub. schs. Fall River, Mass.; m. Carolyne Bellvage, Aug. 8, 1943; 1 dau., Victoria Ann. Pres., chmn. bd. Consol. Maritime Lines, Inc., shipbuilders and operators, 1919-22; indsl. engr., adv. on re-orgns. to large corps., 1922-35; pres. Fox Feature Syndicate, Inc., N.Y.C., and pubs. and printers, N.Y.C. and Wilkes-Barre, Pa., 1935-45; indsl. engr., adviser on corporate financing; pres. Key Industries, Inc., and Renard Investments, Ltd., 1945—. Home: Palmer Hill Rd., Old Greenwich, Conn. Office: 142 E. 49th St., N.Y.C. 17. Died July 3, 1957.

FOX, William, film producer; b. Tulchva, Hungary, Jan. 1, 1879; s. Michael and Anna (Freid) F.; brought to U.S. in infancy; ed. pub. schs., N.Y.C.; m. Eva Leo, Jan. 1, 1900. Began as theatrical mgr., Bklyn., 1904; later pres. Fox Circuit of Theatres, Fox Film Corp.; prod. Victor Hugo's Les Miserables, Dickens' Tale of Two Cities, Romeo and Juliet, A Daughter of the Gods, Salome, Cleopatra, Evangeline, Over the Hill, Queen of Sheba, etc. Chmn. theatrical team A.R.C. drive, 1917; chmn. theatrical and motion picture com. United War Work Campaign Fund drive, 1918. Mason, K. of P. Home: Woodmere, L.I., N.Y. Died May 8, 1952.*

FOX, William Henry, museum dir.; b. Phila., Nov. 10, 1858; s. Daniel Miller and Elizabeth Caroline (Korn) Fox; A.B., U. Pa., 1881, LL.B., 1883, Litt. M., 1920; Litt.D., St. John's Coll., Bklyn., 1922; m. Catherine Thomas Dobbins, Feb. 25, 1904 (died 1950). Sec. dept. art and sec. Internat. Art Jury Awards, and mem. representing Russia, St. Louis Expn., 1904; dir. Herron Art Inst., Indpls., 1905-10; sec. gen. U.S. Sect., and mem. and sec. of Internat. Jury of Awards, Internat. Expn. of Art and History, Rome, Italy, 1911; became curator in chief Museums of Bklyn. Inst. Art and Science, 1913, dir., 1914, dir. emeritus, 1934. Was founder Bklyn. Mus. Quar. Mag. Mem. adv. com. for fine arts, Panama P.I. Expn. and mem. Internat. Art Jury Awards representing Sweden. Trustee Rollins Coll., 1935-47, trustee dir. art dept., 1936-40. Mem. Ind. chpt. A.I.A., Am. Museums Assn., Am. Fedn. Arts, Am. Art Directors' Assns., S.R., N.Y. Soc. S.R. Decorated Knight Officer of the Crown of Italy; Knight of the Polar Star of Sweden; Chevalier Legion of Honor (France); Comdr. Order of Donnebrog (Denmark); Order of Crown of Belgium; Grand Silver Cross of Merit (Austria). Quaker. Clubs: National Arts, Century (N.Y.C.). Authors' (London). Contbr. of articles to various newspapers and periodicals. Trustee Rollins Coll. Address: 500 W. Chelton Av., Germantown, Phila. 44. Died Jan. 18, 1952; buried West Laurel Hills, Phila.

FOX, William H(iram), educator; b. Bicknell, Ind., Jan. 17, 1906; s. Harmon Britain and Nellie (Antibus) F.; scholarship Juilliard Sch. Music, 1925-27; Mus.B., Ind. U., 1927, M.A., 1930, Ph.D., 1946; m. Martha Mae McEwen, June 9, 1930; children—Wilhelmina Sue (Mrs. Frederick Murray Robinson), Roberta Lou. Instr. Ind. Central Coll., 1930-33; asso. prof. Murray State Coll., 1933-42; prof. edn., asst. dir. research and field service Ind. U., 1946—; cons. evaluation and research Prasarn Mil. Coll., Bangkok, Thailand. Mem. Am. Assn. U. Profs., Am. Ednl. Research Assn., Am. Psychol. Assn., Ind. State Tchrs. Assn., Ind. U. Alumni Assn., Inst. Math. Statistics, Nat. Council Measurement, N.E.A., Nat. Soc. Study Edn., Assn. Sch. Coll. and U. Examiners, Phi Delta Kappa, Phi Mu Alpha, Ind. Schoolmen's Club, Phi Gamma Delta. Contbr. profl. publs. Home: 816 S. Fess Av., Bloomington, Ind. Died June 14, 1958; buried Rose Hill Masoleum, Bloomington, Ind.

FRAILEY, Carson Peter, pharmacist, assn. exec.; b. Emmitsburg, Md., Aug. 12, 1887; s. Oscar D. and Clara M. (Hoke) F.; Pharm.D., Univ. of Md., 1908, D.Sch., (hon.), 1946; LL.D. (hon.) Southeastern Univ., Washington 1949; m. Rebecca Gray Houck, 1912; 1 son, Carson Gray. With retail drug stores Blue Ridge Summit, Pa., Baltimore, Md., Washington, D.C., 1908-12; Armour & Co. (now The Armour Labs.), Chicago, 1912-14; H. K. Mulford Co., mfg. chemists, Phila., 1914-23; exec. vice pres. and sec. Am. Drug Mfrs. Assn., Washington, D.C. since 1923; professorial lecturer on indsl. pharmacy, George Washington Univ. Commd. major, R.C., U.S. Army; Asst., in studies of med. supply program against a nat. emergency; served as chmn. drugs resources adv. com., Army and Navy Munitions Bd. 1940-44, chmn. com. attached to Office The Surgeon Gen. of the Army since 1944. Mem. Com. on Revision of Constn. and By-Laws of U.S. Pharmacopoeial Conv.; mem. Nominating Com. and bd. trustees U.S. Pharm. Convention, 1950-60. Mem. bd. trustees Southeastern Univ. Mem. Am. Pharm. Assn. (awarded 1 yr. mem. by Md. Bd. of Pharmacy for highest gen. average, 1908, mem. lab. com.), Am. Foundation for Pharm. Edn. (hon. mem.), Nat. Drug Trade Conf. (pres., since 1930), Kappa Psi, Y.M.C.A. (pres. since 1944, chmn. executive com.), S.A.R. Gold Key Award for Service to Youth, Y.M.C.A. Registered pharmacist Md., D.C. Mem. Rho Chi. Mem. Luther Pl. Meml. Ch. (past pres. ch. council). Home: 3704 Livingston St. N.W., Washington 15; and Emmitsburg, Maryland. Office: Albee Bldg., Washington 5. Died Mar. 13, 1954; buried Emmitsburg, Md.

FRAKER, George W., banker (ret.); b. Oshkosh, Wis., Oct. 10, 1874; s. E. L. and Helen (Porter) F.; ed. in pub. schs.; m. Agnes F. Warren, Nov. 14, 1899; children—Margaret, Helen, George W., Harrison Shedd. Formerly vice pres. Nat. City Bank of N.Y.; dir. Cannon Mills Co., Am. Enka Corp., Pocahontas Fuel Co., Inc., Moore Corp. Clubs: Union League, Down Town Assn. (New York); Plainfield (N.J.) Country. Home: 909 Park Av., Plainfield, N.J. Office: 20 Exchange Pl., N.Y.C. Died May 30, 1951.

FRAME, James Everett, theologian; b. Boston, Mar. 24, 1868; s. James and Martha (Clark) F.; A.B., Harvard, 1891, A.M., 1892, S.T.D., 1913; grad. Union Theol. Sem., 1895; studied univs. of Berlin and Göttingen, Germany, 1895-97; m. Jean Herring Loomis, May 22, 1906; children—Sutherland, Dorothy, Donald. Fellow Union Theol. Sem., 1895-97; instr. N.T., 1897-1901, asst. prof., 1901-03, asso. prof., 1903-05, Edward Robinson prof. of Bibl. theology, 1905-19, Baldwin prof. Sacred Literature, 1919-38, prof. emeritus, 1938—, Union Theol. Sem. Presbyterian. Fellow Am. Acad. Arts and Sciences; mem. Am. Oriental Soc., Soc. Bibl. Lit. and Exegesis. Author: Commentary on the Epistles of St. Paul to the Thessalonians (Internat. Critical Commentary), 1912. Home: 7 Edgehill St., Princeton, N.J. Died Dec. 30, 1956.

FRANCE, Charles E., lawyer; b. nr. Cleo Springs, Okla. Terr., Nov. 8, 1900; s. Morris Elmer and Ada (Ginder) F.; student U. Mo., 1919-21; LL.B., U. Okla., 1923; m. Gudrun Engell of Copenhagen, Denmark, July 26, 1945; 1 son, Charles Engell. Admitted to Okla. bar, 1923, since practiced Oklahoma City; mem. firm Burford, Miley, Hoffman & Burford since 1923, now sr. partner successor firm; sec., dir. Suburban Water Company; vice president, general counsel Standard Food Markets, Humpty Dumpty Super Markets, Folding Carrier Corp. and affiliated cos. Volunteered for mil. service in Feb. 1942 as legal officer in Air Force; transferred to Judge Advocate General's Dept. staff Judge Advocate for XII Air Force Service Command and Army Air Force Service Command, Mediterranean Theater Operations; disch. as lt. col. Mem. Okla. City Library Bd. Trustees; sec. and a founder Okla. Art Center; mem. A.R.C. (past county dir., past chmn.). Mem. Am., Okla. (pres. 1945) and Okla. Co. (past dir. and pres.) bar assns., Phi Alpha Delta, Beta Theta Pi. Club: Beacon. An author of law providing public support for Crippled Children's Hosp. and Soc. of Okla. Interested in art and modest collector Am. art and etchings. Home: 321 N.W. 14th St. Office: 16 S. Pennsylvania Av., Oklahoma City. Died Nov. 10, 1952.

FRANCE, Melville Jefferson, lawyer; b. Brooklyn, N.Y., Oct. 29, 1878; s. Thomas Jefferson and Addie (Clark) F.; A.B., Columbia, 1900; Teachers Coll. (Columbia U.), 1900; LL.B., New York Law Sch., 1902; m. Annie Franklin Wilson, Oct. 29, 1904; m. 2d, Adele Dyott Hart, December 22, 1953. Admitted to N.Y. bar, 1902, and began practice in Brooklyn; asst. corp. counsel City of New York, 1914-15; U.S. atty. Eastern Dist. of N.Y., 1915-19; mem. Wood, Molloy France & Tully, since 1919; trustee Kings Highway Savings Bank, Brooklyn. Member Bar Assn. City of New York, Am., N.Y. and Brooklyn bar assns. Democrat. Presbyterian. Clubs: Columbia, University. Home: 135 E. 54th St., N.Y.C. 22. Office: 25 Broad St., N.Y.C. Died July 22, 1955; buried Walton, N.Y.

FRANCHOT, Charles Pascal (frăn'shō), lawyer; b. Olean, N.Y., Oct. 8, 1886; s. Nicholas Van Vranken and Annie Conyne (Wood) F.; student Olean (N.Y.) High Sch., 1901-04, Phillips Acad., Andover, Mass., 1905-06; A.B., Yale, 1910; LL.B., Harvard, 1914; m. Lillian Winston, Apr. 8, 1920; 1 dau., Fendall Winston (Mrs. Arthur Burtis Lawrence, Jr.). Admitted to N.Y. bar 1914, and since in practice at Buffalo and New York; admitted to District of Columbia bar, 1946; member Kenefick, Cooke, Mitchell & Bass, 1920-26; mem. Franchot & Warren, 1928-37, Franchot & Schachtel, 1937-42; practiced alone, Jan. 1943-May 1944, mem. Franchot & Dessner, 1944-46; Franchot, Corwin & Dessner, May 1946-53; with offices in N.Y. and Washington, D.C.; v.p. and gen. counsel Rand Kardex Bureau, Inc., 1926-27; director and general counsel Remington Rand Inc., 1927-45; pres. and gen. counsel Buffalo Electric Furnace Corp.; chmn. bd. dirs. and gen. counsel Sonotone Corp.; Royal Crown Beverage Co., DeLisser Machine & Tool Corporation; pres. and dir. Cheekmaster Systems, Incorporated; spl. legal adviser to dir. Naval Petroleum Reserves, 1946-50, James Petroleum Corp. Served as 1st lt., later capt. and maj. cav. A.E.F., World War I; lt. col., cav. O.R.C. Capt. U.S.N.R.; served as spl. asst. to judge advocate gen. of U.S. Navy, May 1944-May 1946. Received citation by Gen. Pershing, with award of Purple Heart, "for meritorious service" on staff, A.E.F. Awarded Commendation Ribbon by secretary of Navy. Mem. Am., District of Columbia and N.Y. State bar associations, Assn. Bar City of New York, Phi Beta Kappa, Psi Upsilon, Skull and Bones (Yale), Am. Soc. of French Legion of Honor. Republican. Episcopalian. Clubs: Yale, Midday (New York), Metropolitan (Washington). Home: 1067 Fifth Av. Office: 1636 Lincoln Bldg., N.Y.C. 17; also 1741 K St. N.W., Washington 6. Died Sept. 8, 1953; buried Olean, N.Y.

FRANCIS, James Draper, corp. exec.; b. Pikeville, Ky., Feb. 25, 1884; s. David Livingston and Kate (Dean) F.; grad. Pikeville Coll. (Ky.); student Center Coll.; LL.B., U. Va., 1908; LL.D., Marshall Coll., 1939, W.Va. U., 1949, David and Elkins Coll., 1954; H.H.D., Pikeville (Kentucky) College, 1956; married Permele Crawford Elliott, June 14, 1910; children—John Elliott (dec.), James Draper (dec.), David Livingston, Ellie M. (dec.), Permele Francis Meacham. Admitted to bars of Va., W.Va. and Ky., 1908; mem. law firm Auxier, Harman & Francis, 1908-18; atty. Island Creek Coal Co., 1911-18; v.p. and gen. counsel Island Creek Coal Co., Pond Creek Pocahontas Co. and Mallory Coal Co., 1918-34; pres. Appalachian Coals, Inc., 1932-34; pres. Island Creek Coal Co., Pond Creek Pocahontas Co., 1934-49, chmn. boards of both companies and their subsidiaries 1949-52; chmn. bd. Powellton Coal Co. and Mallory Stores, Inc.; chmn. bd. Princess Elkhorn Coal Co., Princess Coal Sales Co.; director Appalachian Coals, Incorporated. Mem. bd. trustees Pikeville (Ky.) Coll.; v.-chmn. Regional exec. com., Region 4, Boy Scouts of Am. Past dir. Huntington (W.Va.) C. of C., U.S. C. of C., Nat. Assn. of Mfrs., W.Va. Coal Assn., Am. Mining Congress, So. States Indsl. Council; dir. Nat. Coal Assn., 1926—; member business advisory council U.S. Department of Commerce; dir. Nat. Indsl. Conf. Recipient James F. Rand medal Am. Inst. Mining and Metall. Engrs. Ky. bar assns., Delta Chi, Raven Soc. U. Va. Presbyn. Mason (32°). Clubs: Guyan Country (Huntington); University (Washington); Queen City (Cin.); Rockefeller Center Luncheon, Recess (N.Y.C.). Home: The Hemlocks, 250 Ridgewood Road, Park Hills, Huntington. Office: West Virginia Bldg., Huntington, W.Va. Died Jan. 8, 1958.

FRANCIS, John, Jr., writer; b. Iola, Kan., May 6, 1875; s. John and Lodeska F.; grad. St. Johns Mil. Sch., Manlius, N.Y., 1893; student U. of Kan., 1897-98; LL.B., Columbian (now George Washington) U., Washington, D.C., 1903; hon. M.A., Dickinson Coll., Carlisle, Pa., 1918; married Louise Frances Bartlett, Apr. 22, 1907 (died December 18, 1949). Admitted to District of Columbia bar, 1903; chief of Land Div., Indian Office, Washington, D.C., 1909-12, chief of Edn. Dept., 1912-17; supt. U.S. Indian School, Carlisle, Pa., 1917-18. Served as 1st lt. and adj. U.S.G., Fort Niagara, N.Y., and Phila., Pa., 1918-19; asst. field director Am. Red Cross, U.S. Naval Hosp., Chelsea, Mass., 1919. Mem. Phi Kappa Psi. Republican. Episcopalian. Mason. Author: The Triumph of Virginia Dale, 1921; The Successful Mr. Bagley, 1926. Contbr. Dictionary of Am. Biography and Dictionary of Am. History. Home: The Ontario, Washington. Retired. Died Jan. 2, 1954.

FRANCIS, Parker B(rowne), mfr.; b. Hartford, Conn., June 18, 1886; s. Parker Browne and Elinor Camille (Van Amringe) F.; A.B., Harvard, 1908; m. Mary Bainbridge Love, May 17, 1916; children—John Byers, Parker Browne III, Richard Love. Chem. engr. Parke-Davis Co., 1909-11; with J. F. Hartz Co., 1911-13; became sec. and part owner, Puritan Compressed Gas Corp., Kansas City, Mo., 1913, v.p., 1923, pres. and owner, 1932, chmn. bd., 1957—; pioneered use of compressed gas in World War I, asso. WPB, Washington, World War II. Mem. Compressed Gas Assn. (past mem. exec. bd.), Better Business Bur. (director), Civic Research Institute, Am. Royal Live Stock Assn. Trustee Kansas City Museum, Art Inst., Philharmonic Orchestra; trustee, Midwest Research Institute, Kansas City Assn. Harvard Chemists. Mem. American Royal Association (board of governors), American Chem. Soc., Am. Electro Chem. Soc., Starlight Theatre Assn. of Kansas City. Unitarian. Clubs: University, Kansas City Country; Harvard (New York); Harvard Varsity. Home: 2015 Drury Lane, Kansas City 15, Mo.; (summer) Ludington, Mich. Office: 2012 Grand Av., Kansas City 8, Mo. Died Sept. 13, 1957; buried Mount Washington Cemetery, Kansas City.

FRANCIS, W(illiam) A(lvah), educator; b. Bigbee Fork, Miss., Aug. 30, 1875; s. William Byrd and Nancy Jane (Tankersley) F.; Diploma, Peabody Normal Coll., 1901; A.B., U. Nashville, 1902; A.M., U. Tex., 1922; Litt.D., Austin Coll., 1939; m. George Offutt, Aug. 28, 1912; children—William Alvah, Harold Offutt, George Claggett. Prin. Beeville (Tex.) High Sch., 1902-05, 1908-12, Harlingen 1905-07; prof. English, Sam Houston State Coll., 1912-20, 1922-25; instr. English, U. Tex., 1920-22; prof. English, dir. dept., Tex. Coll. Arts and Industries, 1925-46, prof. English, 1946-49, ret. 1949. Mem. A.A.A.S., Nat. Council Tchrs. English, Modern Lang. Assn. Am., Shakespeare Assn. Democrat. Presbyn. Mason (K.T., past comdr.; Shriner). Contbr. Early Modern English Dictionary, in process of pub., Oxford U., Eng. Splties: Lexicography, English grammar and usage; also Shakespeare. Home: 529 W. Richard Av., Kingsville, Tex. Died Sept. 3, 1957; buried Beeville, Tex.

FRANCIS, William Howard Jr., lawyer, govt. ofcl.; b. Ft. Worth, Nov. 11, 1914; s. William Howard and Frances (Lysaght) F.; A.B., Rice Inst., 1935; LL.B., Tex. U., 1938; m. Caroline Keith Wiess, May 25, 1946. Admitted to Tex. bar, 1938; with Vinson, Elkins, Weems & Francis, 1938-41, 1945-49; pvt. practice of law, Houston, 1949—; oil operator, 1949—; pres. Texas Fund, Inc., Houston, 1955-57; apptd. asst. sec. defense, 1957—. Served as capt. M.I., AUS, 1941-45. Mem. Am., Tex., Harris County bar assns. Episcopalian. Clubs: Houston Country, River Oaks County, Ramada, Tejas, Bayou, Allegro. Home: 2923 Inwood Dr., Houston. Office: San Jacinto Bldg., Houston 2. Died May 24, 1958.

FRANCIS, William Mursell, stained glass artist; b. London, Eng., Jan. 6, 1870; s. John and Jane (Edwards) F.; prep. edn. pvt. schs., student Kings Coll., London, 1887-91; m. Margaretta A. Stimpson, July 27, 1895; 1 dau., Elsie Marguerita (Mrs. Charles R. MacDonald). Came to U.S. 1913. Artist and craftsman in stained glass and mfg. of stained glass windows, 1920—; mem. firm Reynolds, Francis & Rhonstock. Represented by windows in Riverside Ch. (N.Y. City), Princeton U. Chapel. Mercersburg Acad. Chapel, Glens Falls (N.Y.) Presbyn. Ch., Wellesley Coll. Chapel, Cathedral of St. John the Divine. East Liberty (Pa.) Presbyn. Ch., Shore Mem. Chapel, Colo. Coll., Am. Memorial Chapel (Belleau Wood, France), Washington (D.C.) Cathedral, St. Paul's Ch. (Winston-Salem, N.C.), Cenacle Convent Chapel (Newport, R.I.). Awarded gold medal Tercentenary Fine Arts Exhbn., Boston, 1930. Mem. Boston Soc. of Arts and Crafts. Episcopalian. Home: 51 Worthen Av., Weymouth, Mass. Office: 1 Washington St., Boston, Mass. Died July 7, 1954; buried Blue Hill Cemetery, Braintree, Mass.

FRANK, Eli, lawyer; b. Baltimore, Md., Feb. 8, 1874; s. Moses and Isabella (Cohen) F.; A.B., Johns Hopkins, 1894; LL.B., U. of Md., 1896; m. Rena Ambach, Dec. 8, 1897; children—Margaret R. (Mrs. Bertram M. Friedman), Eli, Jr., Isabel (Mrs. Sydney M. Cone, Jr.). Admitted to Maryland bar, 1896, and began practice at Baltimore; prof. law, U. of Md., 1900-44, professor emeritus, 1944—; judge, Supreme Bench, Baltimore, Maryland, 1922-44. Chmn. commission to revise laws affecting crimes and punishment, Maryland. Former president Asso. Jewish Charities of Baltimore, Hebrew Hosp. of Baltimore City; former v.p. Enoch Pratt Free Library; former mem. Board of School Commrs., Baltimore; mem. exec. com. Am. Jewish Com. Trustee Johns Hopkins U. Member Board of Municipal Music of Baltimore City. Mem. Am. Bar Assn., Am. Law Inst., Md. State Bar Assn. (pres. 1943-44), Bar Assn. Baltimore City (former pres.), Order of the Coif, Phi Beta Kappa. Democrat. Jewish religion. Clubs: Suburban, University. Author: Title to Real and Leasehold Estates, 1912. Home: 2007 Sulgrave Av., Baltimore 9. Office: First National Bank Bldg., Balt. 2. Died July 25, 1959.

FRANK, Jerome N., judge; b. N.Y.C., Sept. 10, 1889; s. Herman and Clara (New) F.; Ph.B., U. Chgo., 1909, J.D., 1912, LL.D., 1953; m. Florence Kiper, July 18, 1914; 1 dau., Barbara. Admitted to Ill. bar, 1912; practiced in Chicago, 1912-29, in New York, 1930-33 and 1936-37; research asso. Yale Law Sch., 1932; gen. counsel Agrl. Adjustment Administration, Washington, D.C., May 1933-Feb. 1935; gen. counsel Federal Surplus Relief Corp., Washington, 1933-35; spl. counsel to R.F.C., in railway reorganization matters, Washington, 1935; commr. Securities and Exchange Commn., 1937-41, chairman May 1939-April 1941; judge U.S. Court of Appeals for 2d Circuit, May 1941—; visiting lecturer in law, Yale Univ., 1946—. New School, 1946-47, Brandeis U., 1954-55. Mem. Assn. Bar City of New York, Phi Beta Kappa, Order of the Coif. Author: Law and The Modern Mind, 1930; Save America First, 1938; If Men Were Angels, 1942; Fate and Freedom, 1945; Courts on Trial, 1949; Not Guilty (with Barbara Frank), 1957. Contributor to legal and other periodicals. Address: U.S. P.O. Bldg. & Courthouse, New Haven. Died Jan. 13, 1957.

FRANK, Joseph Otto, prof. chemistry and science edn.; b. Lebanon, Ind., Feb. 14, 1885; s. John Henry and Margaret Alice (Garner) F.; A.B., Indiana U., 1909, A.M., 1912; grad. study, U. of Wis., summer, 1921, U. of Chicago, summer, 1925, Columbia, summer, 1926, State U. of Ia., summer, 1929, U. of Mich., summer, 1938; m. Lora Jane Spence, Nov. 6, 1906; children—John Otto, Joseph Henry, Loren Spence, Lora Jane. Prof. chemistry and biology, Winona Coll., Warsaw, Ind., 1909-11; prof. chemistry and biology, State Teachers Coll., Oshkosh, Wis., 1912-16, head of coll. dept., 1916-25, prof. chemistry and science edn. since 1925; asst. in dept. natural science, Columbia, summer, 1926; gave courses in teaching of chemistry and teaching of gen. science, U. of Colo., summer, 1924, Harvard, summer, 1927; U. of Ala., summer, 1931. Studied violin under Franz Stahr, Cologne, Germany, 1905; organizer and dir. First Am. Legion Band of Wis., 1921-22. Mem. American Chemical Society, N.E.A., Central Association Science and Mathematics Teachers, Alpha Chi Sigma, Phi Delta Kappa, Kappa Delta Pi; fellow Am. Assn. Advancement Science. Conglist. Mason. Author: Elements of Quantitative Chemical Analysis, 1914; Brief Outline of Qualitative Analysis, 1917; Teaching First Year Chemistry, 1921; How to Teach General Science, 1924; High School Science Terminology (with H. K. White), 1930; Mystery Experiments and Problems (with Guy J. Barlow), 1933; Chemicals in the Home, 1937. Contbr. to leading ednl. jours. Contbg. editor Journal of Science Edn. Home: 650 Elmwood Av., Oshkosh, Wis. Died Aug. 9, 1949; buried Lake View Meml. Park, Oshkosh.

FRANK, Theodore, pres. Seneca Nation; b. Salamanca, N.Y., Mar. 14, 1894; s. George Henry and anna (Jimerson) F.; grad. Carlisle U., 1917; m. Flora B. Barney, Nov. 21, 1929; children—Betty Lou, Larry Eugene. Farmer, 1919-24; partner Putnam's Garage, 1924—, operating garage and service station, Onoville, N.Y., also Corydon, Pa. (mgr. of Corydon branch). Elected to Council of Seneca Nations of Indians, 1938, clerk of the Nation, 1942-44, pres., July 1944— (to fill vacancy), elected treas. Nov. 1944, for 2 yr. term. Enlisted in 16th Engrs., U.S. Army, 1917, served with AEF, 1917-19. Republican county committeeman Cattaraugus County, N.Y., 1925-34. Mem. Vets. Fgn. Wars. Home: Onoville, N.Y. Died Mar. 18, 1952; buried Steamburg, N.Y.

FRANKE, Gustav Henry, army officer; b. Manning, Ia., Sept. 7, 1888; s. Gustav Henry and Dorathea (Pevestorf) F.; B.S., U.S. Mil. Acad., 1911; student Field Arty. Class, Ft. Sill, Okla., 1924-25; distinguished grad. Command and Gen. Staff Sch., 1926, Army War Coll., 1937; m. Mildred Dixon McKee, Mar. 12, 1912; children—Mildred McKee (Mrs. Edwin H. Kerrison, Jr.), Helen Dorathea (Mrs. Christian Hanburger), Gustav Henry. Commd. 2d lt., Coast Arty. Corps, June 13, 1911; transferred to Field Arty., Jan. 13, 1917; promoted through grades to col., March 1, 1940; apptd. maj. gen., U.S. Army, Apr. 17, 1942; served in P.I., 1912-15; instr. in mathematics, U.S. Mil. Acad., 1915-17; with 1st Div. and at Gen. Hdqrs., France, July-Dec. 1918; prof. mil. science and tactics, Colo. Agrl. and Mech. Coll., 1922-24; gen. staff and acting corps area engr., 4th Corps Area, Atlanta, Ga., 1927-31; prof. mil. science and tactics, Ala. Poly. Inst., 1931-36; comdr. 2d Field Arty., Panama, 1937-40; post exec., Ft. Bragg, Jan.-May 1941; comdr. Field Artillery Replacement Center, Ft. Bragg, N.C., May-Aug. 1941, arty., 6th Div., Aug. 1941-Apr. 1942, 81st Div., Apr.-Aug. 1942; mem. War Dept. Dependency Bd., Mar. 1943; retired for physical disability, January 1, 1944. Awarded Victory medal with 4 bars, Croix de Guerre with silver star, Mexican Border Service Ribbon, Army Commendation Ribbon. Mem. Scabbard and Blade, Omicron Delta Kappa. Clubs: Army and Navy (Washington). Address: Myrtle Beach, S.C. Died Mar. 19, 1953; buried West Point, N.Y.

FRANKFORT, Henri, archeologist; b. Amsterdam, The Netherlands, Feb. 24, 1897; s. Benjamin Philippe and Mathilde (Israëls) F.; student U. of Amsterdam, 1917-20; M.A., U. of London, 1924; Ph.D., U. of Leiden, 1927; student British Sch. of Archeology at Athens, 1925; m. Henriette Antonia Groenewegen, Dec. 31, 1923 (divorced); 1 son, Johannes Benjamin; m. 2d, Enrigueta Harris, June 27, 1952. Came to U.S., 1938, naturalized, 1944. Dir. of Excavations for Egypt Exploration Soc., London, at Abydos, Tell El Amarna and Erment, 1925-29; field dir. of Iraq Expedition (Tell Asmar and Khorsabad) of Oriental Inst. of U. of Chicago, 1929-37; extraordinary prof. of the history and the archeology of Ancient Near East, University of Amsterdam, 1932-38; research professor oriental archeology, Oriental Institute, University of Chicago, 1932-49; now director Warburg Institute and professor history of pre-classical antiquity U. London, 1949—. Served in Netherlands Army, 1915-17. Fellow Royal Anthropology Inst. Gt. Britain and Ireland; mem. Am. Philos. Soc., Egypt Exploration Soc. Author: Studies in Early Pottery of the Near East, I, 1924, II, 1927; (with others) The Mural Painting of El-Amarneh, 1929; Archeology and the Sumerian Problem, 1932; (with others) The Cenotaph of Seti I at Abydos, 1933; Cylinder Seals, a Documentary Essay on the Art and Religion of the Ancient Near East, 1939; Sculpture of the Third Millennium B.C. from Tell Asmar and Khafajah, 1939; More Sculpture from the Diyala Region, 1943; The Intellectual Adventure of Ancient Man, 1947; Kingship and the Gods, An Essay on Ancient Near Eastern Religion as the Integration of Society and Nature, 1947; Ancient Egyptian Religion, 1948; The Birth of Civilization in the Ancient Near East, 1951; the Art and Architecture of the Ancient Orient, 1954; Stratified Cylinder Seals from the Diyala Region, 1955. Contbr. articles profl. jours. Address: Warburg Institute, Univ. of London, Imperial Inst. Bldg., London, S.W. 7, Eng. Died July 16, 1954; buried London, Eng.

FRANKFORTER, George Bell, chemist; b. Potter, O., Apr. 22, 1859; s. Andrew and Elizabeth (Clunk) F.; A.B., U. Neb., 1886, A.M., 1888; chem. course Bergakademie, Berlin; Ph.D., U. Berlin, 1893; m. Mary Spalding Carter, 1898; children—Alice Sylvia, Mary Elizabeth (Mrs. Charles Christian Hewitt), Eleanor Evans (dec.), George William Carter. Instr. chemistry U. Neb., 1885-87, prof. chemistry, 1893-94; high sch., Lincoln, Neb., 1887-88; dean Sch. Chemistry and dir. Chem. Lab., U. Minn., 1894-1917, prof. organic and indsl. chemistry, 1920-25, prof. emeritus, 1927—. Prof. chemistry, Stanford, 1925-26. Mem. State Council Def. Maj., Ordnance Dept. U.S.A., 1918; chief chem. supervisory br. of inspection div.; dir. Ordnance Technol. and Officer's Tng. Sch., at DuPont Powder Plant, Carney's Point, N.J.; dir. supervisory and control lab., Phila.; examiner, explosives, chemicals and loading, Ordnance Claims Bd.; tech. adv. War Claims Bd., 1919-20. U.S. Mint commr., 1900. Fellow A.A.A.S.; mem. Am. Chem. Soc., Am. Electrochem. Soc., Soc. Chem. Industry, Ordnance Assn., Mil. Order World War, Asso. Tech. Adv. Corpn., Phi Beta Kappa, Sigma Xi, Gamma Alpha, Phi Lambda Upsilon. Republican. Conglist. Clubs: Chemists', Skylight. Author numerous papers on chem. subjects; also series of bulls. on explosives. Home: 525 East River Rd., Mpls. Died Sept., 1947.

FRANKL, Paul Theodore, designer; b. Vienna, Austria, Oct. 14, 1886; s. Julius and Emma (Friedman) F.; student U. of Vienna, 1904-06, U. of Berlin, 1907-11, art schs., Paris and Munich, 1911-13; m. Isabelle Dorn, 1920; 1 son, Peter Paul; m. 2d, Mary Irwin, Feb. 8, 1936; 1 dau., Paulette. Came to U.S., 1914, naturalized, 1925. Began as architect in Vienna and Berlin; became president Frankl Galleries, 1914; now head Paul T. Frankl Associates; held position as lecturer with Metropolitan Museum, New York City; prof. New York U.; asso. prof. U. of Southern Calif., Los Angeles; designer for Johnson Furniture Co., Hart Mirror Co., Grand Rapids. Author: New Dimensions, 1928; Form and Reform, 1930; Machine Made Leisure, 1932; Space for Living, 1938; American Textiles, 1953; also articles. Home: 633 Via Horquilla, Palos Verdes Estates, Cal. Died Mar. 21, 1958.

FRANKLIN, Chester Arthur, newspaper editor; b. Denison, Tex., June 7, 1880; s. George Francis and Clara Belle (Williams) F.; grad. Omaha (Neb.) High Sch., 1896, student U. of Neb., 1896-98; LL.D. (hon.) Samuel Houston College, Austin, Tex., 1947; m. Ada Crogman, July 25, 1925. Began as printer's apprentice, 1891; family moved to Denver, Colo., and father purchased newspaper, Denver Statesman, 1899; upon father's death took over management of the paper, changed its name to Denver Star and continued its operation, 1901-13; moved to Kansas City, Mo., 1913; founded Kansas City Call, 1919, has continued as editor, pres. of co. and prin. owner. Has been active in civic work. Home: 1717 E. 18th St. Office: 1715 E. 18th St., Kansas City, Mo. Died May 7, 1955; buried Highland Cemetery, Kansas City, Mo.

FRANKLIN, Lewis Battelle, banking; b. Flushing, N.Y., Nov. 24, 1878; s. Lindley Murray and Martha L. (Mann) F.; ed. pub. sch., Flushing; D.C.L., U. of the South; m. Martha Dandridge, June 8, 1918; children—Isabelle Lawrence (Mrs. M. E. Devendorf), Martha Littlefield (Mrs. Christy W. Bell), Ann Dandridge. Began bus. career in N.Y., 1895-1917; v.p. Guaranty Trust Co. of N.Y., 1909-18; dir. war loan orgn., Treasury Dept., Washington, 1918-19; treas. Missionary Soc. of P.E. Ch., 1919-48. Pres. Investment Bankers' Assn. Am., 1917-18. Clubs: Wee Burn Golf, U.S. Seniors Golf, Noroton Yacht, Century Assn. Home: Noroton, Conn. Died Mar. 21, 1959.

FRANKLIN, Lynn Winterdale, foreign service officer; b. Ocean Grove, N.J., June 11, 1888; s. Charles and Jenny (Jones) Winterbothm; after death of father and re-marriage of mother, adopted by step-father, George L. Franklin; educated Western High School, private tutors, read law, and studied comml. sch., Washington, D.C., 1906-11; m. Butler-Brayne Thornton Robinson, June 11, 1925; children—Butler-Brayne Thornton, Jenny-Lynn, Bessie Forbes, Lynn Winterdale, Jr. Entered foreign service at legation, Tegucigalpa, Honduras, 1912; vice and deputy consul general at legation and consulate gen., San Salvador; vice consul at Callao-Lima, 1916-18, Guayaquil, 1918-19; delegate to Pan-Am. Commercial Conf., 1919; vice-consul and attaché to legation at San Salvador, 1919-24; consul at San Salvador, Hongkong, Saltillo, Hankow, Chefoo, Amoy, Barcelona, Stockholm (served as secretary of the embassy, 1938), Fort Erie and Niagara Falls (Canada); consul gen., Curacao, N.W.I., 1945. Episcopalian. Club: Hongkong Golf. Compatriot, S.A.R. Home: "Fall Hill," Fredericksburg, Va. Died July 8, 1952; buried City Cemetery, Fredericksburg, Va.

FRANKLIN, Samuel Petty, univ. prof.; b. Glensboro, Ky., June 23, 1895; s. Benjamin and Kate Franklin; A.B., Union Coll., 1919; A.M., Northwestern U., 1921; S.T.B., Boston Univ. Sch. of Theology,

1924; Ph.D., U. of Iowa, 1925; m. Laura Maria Wilcox, May 29, 1919; children—Harriet Maria, Helen Louise. Prof. psychology and religion, Union Coll., 1921-23; ordained Methodist ministry, 1918; professor religious edn., Baldwin-Wallace Coll., Berea, O., 1925-31; head of dept. religion and religious edn., U. of Pittsburgh, 1931-46; taught summer sch. at Ia. State Teachers Coll., Extension Sch., 1924, Northwestern University, 1928, 29, 36; chmn. administrative com. Sch. of Edn., University of Pittsburgh, 1943. Dean, School of Education, Univ. of Pittsburgh, 1944-55, ret. chmn. Western Pa. Edn. Conf., 1944. Mem. bd. directors of Shadyside Academy, since 1948. Pres. Religious Education Association, since 1948. Member Religious Edn. Assn. (dir.), Internat. Council Religious Edn., Am. Assn. Univ. Profs., N.E.A., Phi Delta Kappa. Contbg. author Creative Personalities, Vol. I and II, 1940. Contbr. to ednl. and relig. publs. Address: 5539 Guilford Av., Indpls. Died Oct. 13, 1956; buried Elm Ridge Cemetery, Muncie, Ind.

FRANKLIN, Walter Alexander, educator; b. Alvarado, Tex., Apr. 18, 1891; s. Willis Burton and Sarah Rebecca (Coats) F.; A.B., U. Tex., 1924, A.M., 1926, Ed.D., 1949; m. Ida Mae Jones, July 4, 1911; children—Evelyn (Mrs. G. D. Bowie, Jr.), Elta Rose (Mrs. R. E. Wentling), Walter Alexander, Janice (Mrs. L. A. Edwards, Jr.), Dan Roger. Tchr., prin., supt., pub. schs. of Tex., 1916-45; tchr., head social sci. dept. Midwestern U., 1947—, now prof. edn. and dir. extension div. Dem. delegate Texas State Democrat Convention, 1948, 1950. Served as capt. Tex. State Guard, 1941-45. Mem. N.E.A., State Tchrs. Assn., Phi Delta Kappa, Phi Gamma Mu. Mem. Christian Ch. (elder). Mason. Club: Kiwanis International. Author: San Antonio Road (hist. novel), 1951. Contbr. to daily press and periodicals. Home: 1813 Garfield, Wichita Falls, Tex. Died Jan. 6, 1955; buried Rosemont Cemetery, Wichita Falls.

FRANTZ, Frank Flavius, educator; b. Daleville, Va., Aug. 23, 1874; s. Thornton Petit and Sarah Jane (Petit) F.; B.A., Central Coll., Mo., 1900; M.A., Vanderbilt U., 1902, Ph.D., 1910; m. Mary Evalin Brown, Sept. 12, 1912; children—Laurent Brown, John Marshall, Marie Therese (dec.), Mary Evalin, Frank Callum. Teaching fellow in French, Vanderbilt U., 1901-05; prof. French, Peabody Coll. for Tchrs., 1905-11; prof. modern langs., Central Coll., 1911-15; acting prof. Romance langs., Vanderbilt U., 1915-16; prof. Romance langs. U. Tenn., 1916-49. Mem. Phi Beta Kappa, Phi Kappa Phi, Sigma Nu. Democrat. Methodist. Mason. Author: Oreste dans la Tragèdie Française, 1910. Editor: Noiraud of Halèvy (with Mme. Pauline G. Delpuech), 1922. Home: 3906 Woodhill, Knoxville, Tenn. Died Apr. 9, 1957.

FRANZHEIM, Kenneth, architect; b. Wheeling, W. Va., Oct. 28, 1890; s. Charles William and Lida Riddle (Merts) F.; B.S., Mass. Inst. Tech., 1913; m. Bessie Simms, May 12, 1919; children—Lillie Weir (Mrs. Myrlin McCullar), Elizabeth F. (Mrs. R. S. Reese), Kenneth, II. Began as architect for theatre and office bldgs., Chgo., Washington, Bklyn., 1920-24, office bldgs., nurses homes, hosps., and coml. bldgs., Houston, Galveston, Baytown, Tex., 1933-—, bank bldgs., Houston, 1954-—. Mem. bd. Soc. for Prevention Cruelty to Animals. President The Frederick R. Lummis Med. Found. Recipient A.I.A. Award of Merit in comml. architects, Foley's Dept. Store, Houston, 1950. Fellow A.I.A. (past pres., Houston chpt.), Allied Arts Assn. (past chmn. bd.), Sociedad de Arquitectos Mexicanos (hon.), National Sculpture Society (hon.), Phi Gamma Delta. Presbyterian. Clubs: Coronado, Ramada, Bayou. Home: 900 S. Wayside, Houston, also Alta Vista 40, Villa Obregon, Mex. Office: 802 Lovett Blvd., Houston 6. Deceased.

FRAPRIE, Frank Roy (fră'prē), editor; b. Fall River, Mass., July 14, 1874; s. Stephen Thomas and Caroline Mary (Goodrum) F.; B.S., Lawrence Scientific Sch. (Harvard), 1898, S.M., 1902; student U. of Munich, 1902-03; m. Mary Otis Sampson, Sept. 19, 1911; m. 2d, Marjorie Russell Purchase, Jan. 21, 1928. Instr. Chelsea High Sch., 1898-99, U. of Ill., 1899-1900; prin. Steep Brook Sch., Fall River, 1900-01; asso. editor Photo Era, Boston, 1900-05; editor Am. Photography, 1905-49, Electrician and Mechanic, 1905-13, Popular Photography, 1912-16, Practical Photography since 1915, and Am. Annual of Photography, 1927-49. Treas. Am. Photographic Publishing Co., C. P. Goerz Am. Optical Co. Am. commr. Internat. Photographic Expositions, Dresden, 1909, Budapest, 1910. Awarded gold medal of Vienna Photographic Soc. for preëminent achievement, 1933. Hon. Fellow and medalist Royal Photographic Soc. of Gt. Britain; hon. fellow, Photographic Soc. of Am.; mem. of Boston Camera Club, Boston Y.M.C.U. Camera Club, Am. Cryptogram Assn., Boston Mineral Club, Am. Soc. of Bookplate Collectors and Designers, Société Française de la Photographie. Republican. Unitarian. Author: A Manual of Photography, 1906; Among Bavarian Inns, 1906; Castles and Keeps of Scotland, 1907; The Art of the Munich Galleries (with Florence Jean Ansell), 1910; The Raphael Book, 1912; Practical Photography series, 13 vols., 1915-39; Cash from Your Camera, 1921; The Spell of the Rhine, 1921; Boston Cross Word Puzzle Book, 1925; Portrait Lighting, 1935; Photographic Amusements, 1937; also papers on chem. and mineral. subjects. Translator: Optics for Photographers (from German of Dr. Hans Harting), 1918; The Spell of Alsace (from French of André Hallays), 1919; The Spell of the Heart of France (Hallays), 1920; The Spell of Provence (Hallays), 1923; Bromoil Printing and Bromoil Transfer (from German of Dr. Emil Mayer), 1923; Portrait Photography (from German of Franz Fiedler), 1936. Travel in Europe, Asia, Africa and America. Home: 40 Cummings Rd., Brookline 46, Mass. Died June 20, 1951.

FRASER, Alexander David, educator; b. Scotsburn, N.S., May 25, 1886; s. Rev. James William and Isabella (Mackay) F.; student Pictou (N.S.) Acad., 1905; A.B., Dalhousie U., 1910; A.M., Johns Hopkins, 1919; Ph.D., Harvard, 1924; m. Norah Winifred Binns, June 20, 1927; children—Douglas Ferrar, Penelope. Came to U.S., 1924. Tutor in classics, Dalhousie U., 1915-18; prof. classics, Jamestown (N.D.) Coll., 1922-23; prof. classical langs., Alfred U., 1925-30; asso. prof. archaeology, U. Va., 1930-45, prof. classical archaeology and history, 1945—; asst. dir. Am. Sch. Classical Studies at Athens, summer 1935. Mem. mng. com. Am. Sch. Classical Studies, 1939—. Served as gunner, 10th siege battery, Canadian Army, 1918. Life mem. Assn. Guillaume Budè (France), Classical Assn. (Eng.); mem. Am. Philol. Assn., Archaeol. Inst. Am., Am. Classical League, Classical Assn. Middle West and S., Classical Assn. Va. (pres. 1940-42), Albemarle Co. Hist. Soc. Ind. Episcopalian. Club: Keswick Country. Author: An Ancient Monument of Pictou, N.S., 1921; The Potamic System of the Trojan Plain, 1937. Contbr. articles and revs. in sci. jours. Home: 2300 Stadium Rd., Charlottesville, Va. Died Aug. 1, 1955; buried Scottsburn, lottesville, Va. Died Aug. 1, 1955; buried Scottesburn, N.S.

FRASER, Chelsea Curtis, author and violin maker; b. New Sarum, Ont., Can., Aug. 28, 1876; s. Oliver Leroy and Emma Maletta (Atherton) Fraser; ed. public schs. of Saginaw, Mich.; summer courses, Mich. State Coll.; unmarried. Began as messenger Western Union Telegraph Co., 1892; mandolin, guitar and banjo inlayer, 1893-99; corr. Montgomery Ward & Co., Chicago, 1900-02; mandolin and guitar maker, Kalamazoo, Mich., 1904-05; adv. mgr. Saginaw Milling Co., 1906-07; furniture insp. War Dept., 1909-11; instr. industrial arts, Sigsbee Sch., Grand Rapids, 1913-31. Mem. of the Mich. Authors' Assn. Author: Good Old Chums, 1911; Every Boy's Book of Handicraft, Sports and Amusements, 1913; The Boy Hikers, 1918; The Boy Hikers Homeward Bound, 1919; Boys' Book of Battles, 1919; Boys' Book of Sea Fights, 1920; Young Citizen's Own Book, 1920; Secrets of the Earth, 1921; Work-a-Day Heroes, 1921; Story of John Paul Jones, 1922; Around the World in Ten Days, 1922; Herooes of the Wilds, 1923; Heroes of the Sea, 1924; Practical Book of Home Repairs, 1925; Heroes of the Air, 1926; Boy's Busy Book, 1927; The Story of American Engineering, 1928; Heroes of the Farthest North and Farthest South, 1930; Model Aircraft Builder, 1931; Story of Aircraft, 1933, rev. edit., 1939, 1944; Famous American Flyers, 1941, enlarged edit., 1942; The Messiah, 1945; Boyhood of Abraham Lincoln, 1948; Silver Strings, 1952. Since age of 16 contbr. juvenile and tech. articles to mags., etc. Home: 2025 Stark St., Saginaw, Mich. Died Nov. 7, 1954: buried Oakwood Cemetery, Saginaw.

FRASER, Duncan William, chmn. Am. Locomotive Co.; b. Churchville, Nova Scotia, June 2, 1875; s. Simon and Harriet Fraser (Cameron) F.; ed. high sch.; m. Edna Hubley, Sept. 3, 1932; vice-pres. Am. Locomotive Co., 1920-40, pres., 1940-45, chmn. since 1945; chairman and director Montreal Locomotive Works. Limited; director Canada Iron Foundries, Ltd.; dir. Gen. Steel Castings Corp., Otis Elevator Co. Mason. Clubs: Railroad, Railroad-Machinery, St. James, Canadian, The Recess, Westchester Country, Mount Royal, Metropolitan, Bankers. Home: 330 Park Av., N.Y.C. 22. Office: 30 Church St., N.Y.C. Died Dec. 21, 1954.

FRASER, Forrest L(ovat), sales exec.; b. Corning, N.Y., Sept. 18, 1909; s. Forrest Lovat and Grace James (Heinen) F.; student Dartmouth Coll.; m. Eleanor Kitchen, July 21, 1931; 1 son, Forrest Lovat. Buyer, mdse. mgr. George B. Peck, Inc., Kansas City, Mo., 1940-44; sales and mdse. mgr. Sole Works, Inc., Loveland, O., 1944-45; dir. grocery mdse. The Kroger Co., Cin., 1945-51; exec. v.p. Pabst Brewing Co., 1951-56; exec. v.p. Am. Optical Co., 1956. Clubs: Sunset Ridge Country (Winnetka, Ill.); Chicago Athletic Assn. (Chgo.). Home: 1930 E. Ridgewood Lane, Glenview, Ill. Office: 221 N. LaSalle St., Chgo. Died July 12, 1956.

FRASER, Harry Wilson (frā'zẽr), pres. Order of Ry. Conductors of Am.; b. Topeka, Kan., June 7, 1884; s. Lewis Peter and Lavara Virginia (Weltner) F.; m. Lillian Elisabeth Spane, Sept. 8, 1905. Ry. clerk, 1900-07, brakeman, 1907-09, conductor, 1909-23; sec. to pres. Order Ry. Conductors, 1929-32, chief clerk, 1932-34, deputy pres., 1934-38, v.p., 1938-40, senior v.p., 1940, pres., 1941-—. Active Boy Scout work, 1933-—, pres. Waubeek Area council, 1940-41, mem. nat. council, 1943. R.R. Labor mem. Nat. Mgmt.-Labor Policy Com., War Manpower Comn., 1943-44-45. Sec., trustee Nat. Planning Assn., 1945-46-47; vice chmn. Ry. Labor Exec. Assn., chmn., 1947-—; chmn. bd. dirs. Labor, nat. weekly newspaper. Del. Inland Transport Com. ILO, Geneva, Switzerland, 1947; study labor conditions, transport industry, Germany (by apptmt. OMGUS), 1947; workers' del. adviser, 30th session ILO, Geneva, 1947, workers' del. adviser 31st session, San Francisco, 1948. Mason (K.T., 32° Shriner), Elk. Clubs: High Twelve (Cedar Rapids). Home: 1412 E. Pikes Peak Av., Colorado Springs, Colo. Office: Order of Railway Conductors Bldg., Cedar Rapids, Ia. Died May 13, 1950.

FRASER, Hugh John, company exec.; b. Brockville, Ont., Can., Oct. 15, 1897; s. Oliver K. and Margaret A. (Braniff) F.; B.S., Queen's U., 1923; m. Muriel Dunne, Sept. 1, 1927; children—Margaret Joan, Dorcas Eleanore. Joined Internat. Nickel Co., 1923, various tech. and operating capacities to asst. mgr. prodn., N.Y.C., 1935, asst. v.p. Internat. Nickel Co. of Can., 1943, Internat. Nickel Co., Inc., 1943-47, v.p., 1947, v.p. in charge all co. plant operations in U.S. since 1947. Mem. Am. Inst. Mining and Metall. Engrs., Am. Soc. Metals, Mining and Metall. Soc. Am., Canadian Inst. Mining and Metallurgy. Clubs: Mining, City Midday (N.Y.C.); Larchmont (N.Y.) Yacht. Home: 45 Woodbine Av., Larchmont. Office: 67 Wall St., N.Y.C. 5. Died Aug. 22, 1952.

FRASER, James Earle, sculptor; b. Winona, Minn., Nov. 4, 1876; s. Thomas Alexander and Cora E. (West) F.; student pub. schs., Mpls., Art Inst. Chgo., Ecole des Beaux Arts and Colorossi and Academie Julian, Paris; m. Laura Gardin, Nov. 27, 1913. Instr. Art Students' League N.Y., 1906—, also dir.; former asst. to Augustus St. Gaudens. Prin. works include bust of Theodore Roosevelt, Senate Chamber, 4 pediments Commerce Bldg., pediment Constitution Av. side and 2 heroic figures for front Archives Bldg., 2 heroic figures before Supreme Ct. Bldg., Flaming Sword, 2d Div. Meml., Albert Gallatin statue, north portico Treasury Bldg., two heroic equestrian groups for bridgehead Lincoln Meml. Circle, Alexander Hamilton, Treasury Bldg., John Ericsson Monument, Journey Through Life, Rock Creek Cemetery (all in Washington); Buffalo nickel; monuments to Bishop Potter, Cathedral St. John the Divine, N.Y., to John Hay, Cleve., Thomas Edison, Edison Inst., Dearborn, Mich., Mayo Bros., Rochester, Minn., Harvey Firestone, Akron, O., Franklin, Springfield, Ill.; equestrian relief portrait of children of Harry Payne Whitney; fountain group for E. H. Harriman, Arden, N.Y.; portrait relief of Morris K. Jesup, Am. Mus. Natural History; statues: End of the Trail, Panama P.I. Expn., Canadian Officer, Winnipeg, Victory, Bank of Montreal, Can., Primitive Inventor of Water Power, figure in fron of City Hall, Niagara Falls; Thomas Jefferson and Lewis and Clark, Mo. State Capital; 2 groups Discoverers and Pioneers, on Meml. Bridge, Chgo.; portrait bust, Elihu Root; portrait relief, Dr. Wm. M. Polk; portrait bust Augustus Saint Gaudens, Lincoln Statue, Jersey City; for N.Y. State, Theodore Roosevelt Meml., figures of Boone, Audubon, Lewis and Clark, and equestrian group of Theodore Roosevelt connected with Natural History Mus., N.Y.C.; figure of Franklin for Franklin Inst., Phila. Recipient 1st prize, best work of sculpture, Am. Art Assn., Paris, 1898; 1st prize, competitive medal for design, and many medals for nudes; Edison medal, 1906; gold medals Panama P.I. Expn., 1915; gold medal of honor Archtl. League, 1925; Saltur medal for Art of the Medal; decorated Knight Order of Vasa (Sweden); gold medal Nat. Inst. Arts and Letters, 1950; Century Assn. medal and Nat. Sculpture Soc. Medal of Honor. N.A., 1917; mem. Am. Acad. Arts and Letters, Nat. Sculpture Soc. (pres. 1925-26; hon. pres.), Nat. Inst. Arts and Letters (v.p.). Clubs: Century Association, Architectural League, Nat. Arts. Home: North Av., Westport, Conn. Died Oct. 11, 1953; buried Willowbrook Cemetery, Westport, Conn.

FRASER, Malcolm, illustrator; b. Montreal, Can., Apr. 19, 1869; s. W. Lewis F.; student pub. schs. N.Y.; studied art under Wyatt Eaton; at Art Students' League under Carroll Beckwith and Kenyon Cox, Gotham Art Students under Walter Shirlaw, in Paris at Académie Julian, under Boulanger, Lefèbvre and Benjamin Constant and in the Beaux Arts with Léon Jerome; m. Katharine Church, June 10, 1897 (died Jan. 6, 1930); 1 dau., Phyllis; m. 2d, Mary Austin Aldrich (sculptress), Feb. 14, 1933. Black and white work in Century, St. Nicholas, Ladies' Home Jour., etc. Illustrator of Richard Carvel, Caleb West, Bret Harte stories, etc. Producer of mural decorations, symbolic paintings and portraits; alter piece, Madonna and child; portrait of the Rt. Rev. John D. Wing, Bishop of S. Fla. (both St. Luke's Cathedral, Orlando, Fla.). Painter of 56 symbolic paintings for which the citizens of Ormond, Fla., erected a permanent war meml. Art Gallery. Capt. A.R.C. with AEF, World War I. Recipient 8 decorations for allied govts.; U.S. Life-Saving Medal by special act of Congress; Congressional Medal of Honor. Member of the Veterans of Foreign Wars U.S., Orlando Art Assn. Club: Salmagundi. Lecturer on art topics. Home: (summer) Brookhaven, L.I., N.Y.; (winter) Orlando, Fla. Died June 12, 1949; buried Brookhaven, L.I., N.Y.

FRASER, Peter, prime minister of New Zealand; b. Fearn, Ross-shire, Scotland, Aug. 28th, 1884; student primary schs., night schs., pub. and reference libraries; LL.D., Aberdeen U., 1941, Cambridge, 1944; m. Jeanet Kemp, 1918 (died 1945). Resident New Zealand, 1910—; 1st nat. sec. Social Dem. Party, hdqrs. Wellington, 1913-16; mem. nat. exec. New Zealand Labour Party, 1916, then v.p., pres., sec. to Parliamentary Labour Party, Wellington, 1919-33, dep. leader, 1933-40, minister of edn. health and marine, 1935-40; prime minister of New Zealand, 1940—. Mem. N.Z. del. to Empire Parliamentary Assn., London, 1935-48; cons. with British Govt. on N.Z. war effort, 1939; as mem. Brit. War Cabinet participated in discussions in G.B., 1941; visited U.S. and addressed Fgn. Affairs com. Ho. of Rep., 1942; signed Canberra Pact, 1943; attended British Commonwealth P.M. conf., London, 1944-48, 49; ILO conf. at Phila., 1945; visited Italy con., U.S.A., and United Kingdom, 1944; leader N.Z. delegation UN Conf. on Internat. Orgn., San Francisco, 1945; chmn. UN Com. dealing with Internat. Trusteeship, San Francisco, 1945; addressed session Fgn. Affairs Com. of U.S. Senate, also ILO Conf., Phila., 1945; chmn. Social, Cultural and Humanitarian Com., UN first Gen. Assembly, London, 1946; leader N.Z. delegation, 3d session UN Gen. Assembly, 1948. Attended British Empire Prime Ministers' Conf., London, 1944, 1948; del. Empire Parliamentary Conf., 1935, 1948. Decorated Privy Councillor, 1940, Companion of Honour, 1946. Recipient Freedom of the City, Aberdeen, Glasgow, Inverness, Edinburg, London, Swansea, Derby, Tain, Dingwall. Mem. N.Z. Labor Party. Author: In Time of War (collection of speeches made during World War II). Home: 86 Mortimer Terrace, Wellington. Office: Parliament Bldg., Wellington, New Zealand. Died Dec. 12, 1950.

FRASER, Samuel, fruitgrower, nurseryman; born, Cheadle, Cheshire, Eng., Feb. 2, 1876; s. John and Frances C. (Widdison) F.; student, Cheshire Agrl. Coll., Holmes Chapel, Eng., 1896-98; M.S. in agr., Cornell U., Coll. of Agrl., 1905; m. Nicolas M. Shaw, Aug. 26, 1903 (dec.); children—Douglas S. (dec.), Rachel S. (Freeman); m. 2d, Mrs. Dorothy Yates Coates, Sept. 29, 1951. Came to U.S., 1900, naturalized, 1913. Farm laborer, 1890-95; asst. Cheshire Agrl. College, Holmes Chapel, Cheshire, Eng., 1896-98; mgr. butter factory, 1899; agriculturist, Sch. of Agrl. and Horticulture, Briarcliff Manor, N.Y., 1900-03; asst. agronomist, Cornell Univ., College of Agr., 1903-05; agent W. A. Wadsworth Estate, Geneseo, N.Y., 1906-14; fruitgrower, nurseryman, since 1906; economist, Internat. Apple Assn., 1919-41, sec. 1941-51, exec. v.p. 1951-55, cons. 1955—. National Diploma in Dairying, Great Britain. Diploma, fellow First Place, Highland and Agricultural Society (Scotland); fellow Royal Soc. of Arts (London, Eng.); fellow A.A.A.S., diploma, medallist, life mem. Royal Agr. Soc. (London, Eng.); mem. Sigma Xi; charter mem. organizing aid, Cosmopilation Clubs 1904; life mem. various hort. socs. Republican. Author: The Potato, 1905; Distribution of Fruits and Vegetables (with R. G. Phillips), 1922; American Fruits, 1924, rev. edit. 1927; The Strawberry, 1927; also numerous bulls., articles, reports. Home: 22 Main St., Geneseo, N.Y. Retired. Died May 17, 1959; buried Genesco, N.Y.

FRASIER, George Willard (frā'zhĕr), educator, b. Marlette, Mich., Sept. 21, 1890; s. James Oliver and Susan Margaret (Emerick) F.; A.B., Mich. State Normal Coll., Ypsilanti, 1916, M.Ed., 1930; A.M., Stanford, 1918; Ph.D., Columbia, 1922; LL.D., Colo. Coll., 1924; LL.D., U. Colo., 1927; Sc.D., Colo. State Coll. Edn., 1951; m. Rhea Dorothy Thompson, Feb. 20, 1914; 1 dau., Jane (Mrs. Richard A. Smith). Tchr. high school, Harbor Beach, Mich., 1911-12; supt. schs., Coleman and Mayville, Mich., 1912-15; prof. edn., dir. research, Eastern Wash. Coll. Edn., Cheney, Wash., 1916-20; asso. in ednl. adminstrn. Tchrs. Coll. (Columbia), 1920-21; dir. dept. classification and statistics, pub. schs. Denver, 1921-23; dean grad. sch. Colo. State Coll. Edn., Greeley, 1923-24, pres., 1924-48, pres. emeritus, 1948—; vis. prof. Stanford, winters 1949-51, lectr. in edn., 1951—, expert cons. on tchr. tng., Office Edn., Dept. Interior, 1930-33; ednl. cons. Civil Aeros. Adminstrn., 1942-48. Del. White House Conf. on Child Health and Protection, 1930. Ednl. adv. Gen. Fedn. Women's Clubs, 1936—. Mem. cons. editorial bd. Nat. Com. for Mental Hygiene, 1937—. Pres. Am. Assn. Tchrs. Colls., 1930-31; chmn. Tchrs. Coll. Personnel Assn., 1931-39; mem. adv. com. Coop. Test. Service, Am. Council on Edn., 1931-37. Mem. com. on the tchr., Am. Hist. Assn., 1930-35. Mem. Nat. Council Boy Scouts Am., 1935-48, mem. regional exec. com., 1942-48; mem. nat. bd. dirs. 1942-48; member Camp Fire, 1924-29. Life mem. N.E.A. (pres. normal schs. and tchrs. coll. sect., 1924-25; com. higher edn., 1936-37); N. Central Assn. Colls. and Secondary Schs. (2d v.p. 1931), Nat. Kindergarten Assn. (v.p. 1930), Phi Delta Kappa, Kappa Delta Pi, Pi Kappa Delta. Conglist. Mason. Rotarian. Author: Control of City Sch. Finance, 1922; Introduction to Edn. (with W. D. Armentrout), 1924; Experiments in Teachers College Administration (with others), 1929. Teachers College Finance (with F. L. Whitney), 1930; An Introduction to the Literature of Education (with W. D. Armentrout), 1931; Principles of Teaching (with George Drayton Strayer and W. D. Armentrout), 1936. What You Can Make High Schools Do (social studies with Wm. McAndrew), 1935, Scientific Living Series, 1937-52; Learning to Spell, 1939; An Introduction to the Study of Education, 1951. Home: 360 Forest Av., Palo Alto, Cal. Died Apr. 28, 1958.

FRAWLEY, John Edward, hotel mgr.; b. Glens Falls, N.Y., Sept. 5, 1894; s. John and Ellen (Noonan) F.; student Ogden Sch., Chgo., and bus. coll.; m. Ina Curtis, July 28, 1915; 1 dau., Patricia Ann. Began as bellman, 1908; clerk, Blackstone Hotel, Chgo., 1910-16; asst. mgr. Muehlebach Hotel, Kansas City, Mo., 1917-21; owner El Dorado (Kan.) Hotel, 1921-23; mgr. Hollenden Hotel, Cleve., 1923-26, Hotel Fort Shelby, Detroit, 1927-31; exec. v.p. Nat. Hotel Mgmt. Co., N.Y.C., 1931-39; gen. mgr. Hotel Fort Shelby, Detroit, 1939-50; pres. Frawley Hotel Co. until 1950, retained McLure Hotel, Wheeling, W. Va. Pres. Am. Hotel Assn.; v.p. Detroit Conv. and Tourist Bureau; pres. Detroit Meml. Hall Commn. Civilian cons. to sec. War Food Service Program. Clubs: The Old (Sainte Claire Flats, Mich.); Players (Detroit). Home: 525 W. Lafayette St. Office: Hotel Fort Shelby, Detroit 26. Died Aug. 17, 1956.*

FRAZAR, Everett Welles, import-export exec., ret.; b. Shanghai, China, Aug. 17, 1867; s. Everett and Annie (Lindsley) F.; student Columbia; M.E. Stevens Inst. Tech., Hoboken, N.J., 1890; m. Maud Wolcott, Oct. 7, 1896; children—Anna Halstead (Mrs. A. Frazar Hawkins), Everett (dec.). Began with Edison Phonograph works, West Orange, N.J., 1890 later transferred to lab. of Thomas A. Edison; two years later went to Europe to demonstrate electrically propelled and operated torpedo invented by Mr. Edison and a Mr. Scott; on returning to U.S., assisted in development pneumatic dynamite gun invented by Mr. Dana Dudley; joined firm of father, Frazar & Co., Japan, 1896, in charge of engring. dept., also rep. Henry Ford, Baldwin Locomotive Works, Victor Talking Machine Co., and many other Am. mfrs., erected factories for production of steel tubes, wire nails, etc. On declaration of war on Japan, 1941, all interest in Jana, Manchuokuo, and China frozen; sr. partner Frazar & Co., N.Y.C. established 1872; partner in Frazar & Hansen, 301 Clay St., San Francisco, established 1920, now retired. Served 2 yrs as asst. commr. A.R.C. of Siberia hdqrs. Vladivostock, during World War I. Decorated Order of Rising Sun, 3d° (Japan). Mason (33°). Episcopalian. Republican. Clubs: India House, Columbia University, Rotary, Lawyers (N.Y. C.). Home: 520 Ocean Dunes Rd., Daytona Beach, Fla. Died Oct. 14, 1951; buried Forest Hills Cemetery, Boston.

FRAZER, William Henry, clergyman, educator; b. LaFayette, Ala., Sept. 16, 1873; s. John Alexander and Nancy Emiline (Abernethy) F.; A.B., Southwestern Presbyn. U., 1897, LL.D., 1937; B.D., Union Theol. Sem. in Va., 1899; D.D., Presbyn. Coll. of S.C., 1909; Litt.D., Davidson (N.C.) Coll., 1926; m. Sarah Winnie Jones, Oct. 25, 1899; children—Winnie Love, William Henry (dec.), Emily Jones. Ordained Presbyn. ministry, 1899; pastor Georgia Av. Ch., Atlanta, Ga., 1899-1901, Tatnall Sq. Ch., Macon, 1901-06, 1st Ch., Anderson, S.C., 1906-17; pres. Bellhaven Coll., Jackson, Miss., 1917-21, Queen's Coll., Charlotte, N.C., June 1921-39; pastor Pineville (N. C.) Ch., 1939-47; ret. 1947; stated supply Government St. Ch., Mobile, Ala., First Church, Tampa, Fla., Shenandoah Ch., Miami, Fla., Lakeland Ch., Lakeland, Fla., Second Church, Charleston, S.C., Oakland Church, Oakland, Florida. Democrat. Mason (32°, K.T., Shriner), Kiwanian. Author: Bible Notes for Bible Students, 1924; The Possumist; Challenging Mantles; Fireside Musings of Uncle Rastus and Aunt Randy. Lecturer, after-dinner speaker. Home: Nations Ford Rd., Charlotte, N.C. Died June 19, 1953; buried LaFayette, Ala.

FRAZIER, Clarence Mackay, manufacturing; born Great Falls, Mont., Nov. 27, 1903; s. Walter Alvin and Margaret (Engle) F.; B.A., Stanford U., 1926; m. Dorothy Evelyn Williams, June 16, 1926; children—Diane, Daniel Roderick. Gen. mgr., Hale Brothers Dept. Store, San Jose, Calif., 1934-41; asst. to pres., Food Machinery & Chemical Corp., San Jose, 1941-42, vice-pres., 1943-44 and since 1949; mem. bd. dirs. and exec. com., Food Machinery & Chem. Corp. since 1949; vice-pres. and mgr., Peerless Pump div., 1944-45, vice pres. in charge operations, 1945-49; director California Manufacturers Corp.; past pres. Merchants Assn., San Jose; past dir. San Jose C. of C. Past dir. Nucleus Bldg. and Loan, San Jose. Dir. San Jose Community Chest. Mem. Phi Kappa Psi. Clubs: Rotary, St. Claire. Home: 1621 University Way. Office: 333 West Julian St., San Jose 5, Cal. Died Nov. 10, 1952.

FRAZIER, Raymond Robert, banker; b. Viroqua, Wis., Mar. 21, 1873; s. William and Pluma (Powell) F.; student U. Wis., 1896-97; m. Augusta Wood, Feb. 22, 1898. Personal sec. to gov. of Wis., 1890-93, exec. clerk, 1893-96; Am. consul at Cpoenhagen Denmark, 1902-05; banking business, Seattle, 1906—; v.p., gen. mgr. Wash. Mutual Savings Bank, 1906-15, pres., 1915-34, chmn. bd., 1934-41, adviser to bd., 1941—; dir. Pacific Nat. Bank, 1929-34; trustee Seattle Times Co., 1930-32; v.p. Rainier Nat. Park Co., 1925-27, dir., 1920-40. Activee promotor savings bank legislation; pres. savs. bank div. Am. Bankers Assn., 1921, state v.p., 1931-34, 38-39, chmn. spl. com. in negotiations with sec. of treasury in connection with refunding maturing war debts; pres. Wash. Savings Banks Assn. 1926; mem. Com. on Federal Legislation and Com. on Extension of Savings Assn., 1926; mem. Com. on Federal Legislation and Com. on Extension of Savings Bank System, Nat. Assn. Mut. Savings Banks, also mem. council of adminstrn., 1920-36. Mem. Psi Upsilon. Unitarian. Elk. Clubs: College (pres. 1915-16); Italian; Seattle Golf (trustee 1935-38); Union (Victoria, B.C.). Home: 1000 8th Av., Seattle 4. Office: 1101 2d Av., Seattle 1. Died Oct. 4, 1955.

FREDENTHAL, David, artist; b. Detroit, Apr. 28, 1914; s. Robert and Faigle (Demsky) F.; student Cranbrook Acad. Art., Bloomfield Hills, Mich., 1935-38, Colorado Springs Fine Art Center, summer, 1936. Instr. Cranbrook Acad., 1937-38, classes for children and adults, Bissel Hanover, N.H., 1942-43; studio classes in drawing and watercolor, 1948; instr. Columbia summer 1950; guest instr. John Herron Art Inst., Indpls., 1951, Norton Art Gallery, West Palm Beach, Fla., winter 1955; one-man shows: Downtown Gallery, N.Y.C., Asso. Am. Artist's Gallery; exhibited Flint Art Inst., Golden Gate Expn., Whitney Mus., Met. Mus., Carnegie Inst., Nat. Acad., and others; represented in collections: Milw. Art Inst., Mus. Modern Art, Ency. Brit. Collection, Met. Mus. Art, IBM, Am. Acad. Arts and Letters, Art Mus. New Britain Inst., Abbott Labs., and several others, both public and pvt.; illustrator numerous books and other publns.; served as war corr. Life Mag., 1944-46; mem. editorial bd. Mag. of the Year, 1947-48. Recipient 1st prize, Mich. Artists Ann. Exhbn., 1936; Guggenheim Found. Fellow, 1938-40; 1st prize Ann. Water Color Exhbn., Jackson, Miss., 1942; 1st award Cal. Watercolor Soc., 1943; Kohnstamm prize, Chgo. Art. Inst., 1946. Author books and articles, represented in several published collections. Home: 637 Madison Av., N.Y.C. 22. Office: care Downtown Gallery, 32 E. 51 St., N.Y.C. Died Nov. 13, 1958.

FREDERICKSON, Charles Richard, corp. exec.; b. Lawrence, Kan., Oct. 3, 1875; s. Anthony and Anna Louise (Larson) F.; grad. Lawrence Bus. U., 1892; m. Elizabeth Brent, Apr. 18, 1899; children—Mary Flemings (Mrs. Arthur Oudry Davis), Phebe Brent (Mrs. John Alfred Wright), Charles Richard (dec.), Elizabeth Brent (Mrs. Stuart Holness Lane); m. 2d, Mrs. Phoebe Nixon Williams, Dec. 1, 1936. Began as printer's apprentice Sports Afield, Denver 1892; organized Frederickson Co., Chgo., 1908; Am. Art Works, Inc., pres., 1911—, treas., 1914—; chmn. bd. Am. Colortype Co., Clifton, N.J., 1944—, chmn. exec. com., 1931—. Recipient Silver Beaver and Silver Antelope awards Boy Scouts Am. Del. Rep. Nat. Conv., 1928-40. Pres. Ohio Mfrs. Assn., 1924-25; v.p. Ohio C. of C., 1929-32. Clubs: Coshocton Town and Country; The Regency (New York). Home: Cambridge Rd. Office: 400 Pine St., Coshocton, O. Died June 26, 1955.

FREE, Arthur Monroe, ex-congressman, lawyer; b. San Jose, Calif., Jan. 15, 1879; s. George A. and Ellen Elizabeth (Littlefield) F.; student at College of the Pacific, Stockton, Calif., 1896-97; A.B., Stanford, 1901, LL.B., 1903; m. Mabel Carolyn Boscow, Nov. 11, 1905. Began practice at San Jose, 1903; city atty. Mountain View, Calif.; dist. atty. Santa Clara County, 3 terms, 1907-19; mem. 67th to 72d Congresses (1921-33), 8th Calif. Dist.; now mem. Rea, Free, Jacka & Frasse. Republican. Mason (32°, K.T., Shriner), Elk, I.O.O.F., Kiwanian. Home: 66 S. 14th St., San Jose, Cal. Died Apr. 1, 1953; buried Oak Hill Meml. Park, San Jose.

FREE, Lincoln Forrest, coll. dean; b. San Francisco, Calif., Apr. 8, 1903; s. Charles Lincoln and Gertrude (Laubach) F.; A.B., Lafayette Coll., Easton, Pa., 1925; A.M., 1932; Ph.D., New York U., 1939; grad. student Lehigh U., 1930-32, Columbia, 1931-33; m. Edith Louise Smith, Sept. 7, 1927; children—Elaine Louise, Jeannette Gertrude. Instr. in education, West Chester (Pa.) State Teachers Coll., 1925-29; instr. mathematics, Lafayette Coll., 1929-35; instr. mathematics and dir. of guidance, Hofstra Coll., New York U., 1935-37; dean of men and professor mathematics and astronomy, Western Maryland Coll., Westminster, Md., 1937-52; dean of instrn. State Tchrs. Coll., West Chester, Pa., since 1952. Mem. N.E.A., Eastern Assn. of Coll. Deans and Advisers of Men (pres. 1945). Club: Rotary. Home: 402 W. Union St., West Chester, Pa. Died Apr. 29, 1959.

FREEBOURN, Harrison (Harry) J., judge; born Erie, Pa., Feb. 17, 1890; s. John and Agnes (Brown) F.; ed. pub. schs., Pa., Ia. and Mont.; studied law with I. G. Denny, Butte, Mont., 1915-17; m. Anne Donnelly, Jan. 18, 1911 (died 1932); children—James D., William B., Harriet (Mrs. Robert T. Hansen),

Patricia (Mrs. George Thomas), Geraldine (Mrs. G. Joe DeVine); m. 2d, Mary Elizabeth Moran, Nov. 30, 1936; children—Michael, Pamela, Sean. Employe East Butte Copper Mining Co., 1911-18; admitted to Mont. bar, 1918, practiced in Butte, 1918-49; county atty. Silver Bow County, 1929-36; atty. gen. of Mont., 1937-40; asso. justice Mont. Supreme Ct. since Jan., 1949. Boxing commr. Silver Bow County, 1922. Mem. Mont. Bar Assn., Vets. Fgn. Wars (post counsel, 1940-48). Eagle. Home: 416 S. Crystal St., Butte, Mont. Office: Supreme Court, Helena, Mont. Deceased.

FREEBURG, Victor Oscar, writer, painter; b. Stanton, Ia., Mar. 22, 1882; s. Andrew Victor and Margaret Charlotte (Erickson) E.; A.B., Yale, 1905, A. M., 1908; Ph.D., Columbia, 1915; studied art at Art Students League of N.Y. and under Birger Sandzén and Wayman Adams; m. Dorothy Dumble, Mar. 25, 1943. Instr. English, U.S. Naval Acad., 1906-07; instr. pub. speaking, Coll. of City N.Y., 1908-13; instr. English, Haverford Coll., 1913-15; instr. English, Columbia, 1915-16, instr. photoplay writing, 1915-17; editor Swedish-Am. Trade Jour., 1919-22; asst. dir. Am. Swedish News Exchange, 1922-25; mem. publicity staff, Tamblyn and Brown, 1925-29; spl. writer on staff Milbank Meml. Fund, 1931-36; editor The Am. Swedish Monthly, 1936-46. Served as ensign U.S. Navy during World War I. Mem. SSS, Local Bd. 3, N.Y., 1942-43. Author: Disguise Plots in Elizabethan Drama, 1915; The Art of Photoplay Making, 1918; Pictorial Beauty on the Screen, 1923. Trans. six stories of Prince William of Sweden, 1927; editor, William Henry Welch at Eighty, 1930. Contbr. to mags. Painter of portraits and landscapes. Mem. Rockport Art Assn., Am. Vets. Soc. Artists. Home: 8 High St., Rockport, Mass. Died Jan. 11, 1953; buried Lindsborg, Kan.

FREED, Emerich Burt, judge; b. Hungary, Nov. 22, 1897; s. Nicholas and Sarah (Benfield) F.; came to United States, 1910; A.B. cum laude, Western Reserve University, 1918, LL.B., 1920; m. Gertrude Davies, May 8, 1930; children—Robert Emerich, Margot Lee. Admitted to Ohio bar, 1919; in private practice of law, 1918-29; first assistant criminal div., prosecuting attorney's office, Cuyahoga County, O., 1929-32; pros. atty., same county, 1932-33; 1st asst. county prosecutor, Jan.-Aug. 1933; apptd. U.S. atty., Northern Dist. Ohio, Aug. 15, 1933; apptd. U.S. dist. judge, Northern Dist. of Ohio, Oct. 15, 1941. Mem. Cleveland Bar Assn., Am. Judicature Soc., Am. Bar Assn. Mason. Club: Cleveland Athletic. Home: 2707 Colchester Rd. Address: Federal Bldg., Cleve. Died Dec. 1955.

FREEMAN, Alfred Bird, business exec.; b. Dalton, Ga., Jan. 13, 1881; s. Charles Benjamin and Rosa Norissa (Bird) F.; ed. pub. elementary sch.; m. Ella Moore West, Oct. 23, 1902 (dec., Apr. 17, 1941); children—Mary Ella (Mrs. William B. Wisdom), Rosa (Mrs. Charles Keller, Jr.), Richard West; m. 2d, Domenica Massina Mallard, June 29, 1945. Sec.-treas. La. Coca-Cola Bottling Co., New Orleans, 1906-43, pres., 1943-47, chmn. of bd., since Mar. 25, 1947; dir. Wesson Oil and Snowdrift Co., New Orleans, New Orleans Pub. Service, Inc., The Coca Cola Company. Democrat. Presbyterian. Mason. Clubs: Boston, Country (New Orleans). Home 560 Audubon St. Office: P.O. Box 1140, New Orleans. Died Nov. 3, 1957; buried New Orleans.

FREEMAN, Allen Weir, sanitarian; b. Lynchburg, Va., Jan. 7, 1881; s. Walker Burford and Bettie Allen (Hamner) F.; student Richmond (Va.) Coll., 1895-1900, B.S., 1899; M.D., Johns Hopkins, 1905, LL.D., 1952; Sc.D., U. Richmond (Va.), 1950; married Julia Griffin Brown, June 30, 1906; children—Bettie Charter (Mrs. Cuthbert Rogerson), Margaret Brown (Mrs. L. A. Poole, Jr.). Interne Newark (N.J.) City Hosp., 1905-06; demonstrator in physiology, Med. Coll. of Va., 1906-07; med. insp. Richmond Health Dept., 1907-08; asst. commr. of health, Va., 1908-15; state dir. Rockefeller Hookworm Commission for Va., 1910-14; epidemiologist U.S. P.H.S., 1915-17; state commr. of health, Ohio, 1917-21; with Johns Hopkins U. since 1921, as res. lecturer pub. health adminstrn., School of Hygiene and Pub. Health, 1921-23, prof., 1923-46, dean, 1934-37, prof. emeritus since 1946; cons. Md. State Health Dept. Commd. major Med. Corps, U.S. Army, 1918; was epidemiologist to bd. for investigation of pneumonia in Army camps, Camp Funston, Kan., and Camp Pike, Ark.; special member Rockefeller Foundation, 1926; lecturer, University of Rio de Janeiro, Brazil, 1926. Fellow American Public Health Assn. (pres. 1942). Mem. A.M.A., Medical Soc. of Va., Phi Gamma Delta, Sigma Xi, Phi Beta Kappa, Delta Omega (nat. pres. 1932). Democrat. Episcopalian. Club: Johns Hopkins (Baltimore). Author: Five Million Patients. Contbr. numerous articles pertaining to epidemiology and public health adminstrn. Home: Wyman Park Apts., Baltimore 11. Office: 2411 N. Charles St., Balt. 18. Died July 3, 1954; buried Hollywood Cemetery, Richmond, Va.

FREEMAN, Douglas Southall, writer; b. Lynchburg, Va., May 16, 1886; s. Walker Burford and Bettie Allen (Hamner) F.; A.B., Richmond Coll., 1904; fellow, 1906-07, Ph.D., 1908, Johns Hopkins; LL.D., Washington and Lee, 1919, William and Mary Coll., 1920, U. of Richmond, 1923; Wake Forest, 1933, Coll. of Charleston, 1938; U. of Pa., 1942; Dickinson College, 1944, Univ. Calif., 1947; Johns Hopkins, 1948; Litt.D., Dartmouth, 1935, U. of Wis., 1936, Wesleyan, 1936, Lafayette, 1940, Marshall, 1937, Rochester U., 1943, Northwestern, 1943, Columbia, 1945, N.Y.U., 1945, Harvard, 1949; Bucknell, 1946, Yale, 1946, Princeton, 1947; L.H.D., Pittsburgh U., 1936; D.C.L., Univ. of the South, 1948; D.Sc., Hamden Sidney, 1951; m. Inez Virginia Goddin, Feb. 5, 1914; children—Mary Tyler (Mrs. Leslie Cheek, Jr.), Anne Ballard (Mrs. J. O. Adler, Jr.), James Douglas. Editor Richmond (Va.) News Leader, 1915-49; vis. prof. journalism, Columbia, 1934-35, prof. (not in residence), 1936-41; rector and pres. board trustees Univ. of Richmond 1934-49; lecturer Army War College since 1936. Member Advisory Council, Hist. Div., War Dept.; mem. President's Commn. Higher Edn.; mem. Planning Com., Library Congress. Chmn. adv. com. Princeton edit. writings of Thomas Jefferson; mem. adv. bd. Dictionary of Am. Hist., Atlas of Am. History; historian-in-chief, S.C.V.; mem. adv. com. Am. Inst. France; ret. trustee Rockefeller Found., Gen. Edn. Board, Woodrow Wilson Found.; trustee Carnegie Endowment Internat. Peace, dir. Equitable Life Assn. Soc., So. Ry. Member Nat. Council Boy Scouts of Am., Nat. Adv. Council Girl Scouts, Nat. Citizens Com. Community Chests of Am.; mem. council and hon. lay canon Washington Cathedral. Member Nat. Acad. Arts and Letters, American Philsophical Soc. (Franklin medalist, 1947), Southern Historical Society (president), Soc. Am. Historians (1st pres.), Am. Antiquarian Soc., Mass. Hist. Soc. (corr.), N.E. Hist. Genealogical Soc., Va. Hist. Soc. (hon. and exec. com.), Am. Academy Arts and Science, Newcomen Soc.; mem. adv. council Mt. Vernon Ladies Assn., adv. council Robert E. Lee Mem. Foundation, Patrick Henry Mem. Foundation (trustee). Mem. Soc. of the Cincinnati, Sons of Revolution, S.C.V., American Society of Newspaper Editors, also Phi Gamma Delta, Phi Beta Kappa, Omicron Delta Kappa, Sigma Delta Chi (hon. president 1948-49), Pi Delta Epsilon. Medalist S.C.V., 1939 and Virginians of Md., 1941; Va. Press Assn. distinguished service award, 1946; medallion U.S. Command and Staff College, 1949. Baptist. Clubs: Commonwealth, New York, Southern, Country Club of Virginia. Author: Reports on Virginia Taxation, 1912; Virginia—A Gentle Dominian (In These United States), 1924; The Last Parade, 1932; R. E. Lee (4 vols.), 1934 (pulitzer Prize, 1934); The South to Posterity, 1939. Lee's Lieutenants (3 vols., 1942-44); John Stewart Bryan, 1947; George Washington, Vols. I, II, 1948, Vols. III, IV, 1951, Vol. V, 1952, Vol. VI, 1954; Lee of Virginia, 1958; also other studies in Virginia, and Confederate Military History. Editor: Calendar of Confederate Papers, 1908; Lee's Dispatches, 1915. Home: Westbourne, Hampton Gardens. Address: P.O. Box 8748, Richmond, Va. Died June 13, 1953.

FREEMAN, Ernest Harrison, elec. engr., educator; b. Topeka, Kan., Sept. 26, 1876; s. Harrison and Marinda D. (Hunter) F.; B.S., Kan. State Coll., 1895; D.Eng., 1935; grad. Kan. State Tchrs. Coll., 1897, Eng. D. (hon.), 1935; B.S., Armour Inst. Tech., 1902, E.E., 1906; married. Taught sch. in Kan., 1897-99; tchr. Armour Inst. Tech. (now Ill. Inst. Tech.), 1902-—, prof. and head dept. elec. engring., 1909-41, prof. elec. engring., 1941-—, prof. emeritus elec. engring., 1944-—; inventor, cons. elec. engr. Mem. Am. Inst. E.E., Eta Kappa Nu, Tau Beta Pi, Phi Kappa Phi. Home: 601 Laurel Av., Wilmette, Ill. Address: 3300 Federal St., Chgo. Deceased.

FREEMAN, Hadley Fairfield, engineer and patent lawyer; b. Sandusky, O., June 27, 1893; s. Thomas Edward and Mary Ann (Talbot) F.; B.S., Case Sch. Applied Science, Cleveland, 1914; LL.B., George Washington U., Washington, D.C., 1918; m. Gertrude Veronica Browne, Aug. 10, 1918; children—Thomas Hadley, James Janvrin. Examiner U.S. Patent Office, 1915-18. Air Service, U.S. Army, 1918; patent and trademark lawyer and engineer, New York, 1919-20, Milwaukee, 1920-23, 1931-34, Cleveland, 1923-46, Chicago, 1929-43, Pittsburgh since 1946. Dir. Research, Edwin L. Wiegand Co. Mem. Am. and Allegheny Co. bar assns., Am. and Pittsburgh patent law assns., Internat. Assn. for Protection of Industrial Property, Am. Inst. E.E., Engring. Soc. of W. Pa., Am. Soc. for Metals, Patent Inst. of Canada, Eta Kappa Nu. Clubs: Cosmos (Washington, D.C.), University Club of Pittsburgh. Home: 4735 Bayard St. Office: 7500 Thomas Blvd., Pitts. Died May 28, 1951; buried Lakewood, O.

FREEMAN, Miller, publisher; b. Ogden, Utah, July 20, 1875; s. Legh Richmond and Ada Virginia (Miller) F.; ed. pub. sch. Ahtanum, Wash.; hon. A.M., Whitman Coll., Walla Walla, Wash.; m. Bessie Lea Bogle, Oct. 15, 1906; children—William Bogle, Frederick Kemper, Miller. Founder and became pub. The Ranch, 1897 (merged with Wash. Farmer), Idaho Farmer, Oregon Farmer (operated as N.W. Farm Trio) 1912-15, Pacific Fisherman, 1903, Pacific Motor Boat, 1908, Motorship, 1916, Canning Age, 1919, Pulp & Paper, 1926, Mining World, San Francisco, 1939, The Lumberman; pres. Miller Freeman Publs. (Seattle). Western Trade Jours. (San Francisco); dir. Pacific Nat. Bank. Founder Naval Militia, Wash., 1910, rank of comdr., 1910-19; capt. naval res., 1919-37; comdt. U.S. Naval Training Camp, Seattle, 1917-19. Chairman Pacific Fisheries Conf. Cons. N. Pacific Fisheries Treaty. Mem. Rep. National Committee, 1937-40. Mem. Wash. Ho. of Rep., 1913, Wash. State Veterans Commn., 1919-22, International Fisheries Commn., 1925-33, Wash. State Planning Council, 1934-41. Republican. Clubs: Rainier, Seattle Yacht; Overlake Golf and Country (Bellevue). Home: Bellevue, Wash. Office: 71 Columbia St., Seattle. Died Sept. 18, 1955.

FREEMAN, Talbot Otis, pub. relations cons.; b. Boston, Sept. 11, 1890; s. Daniel Allen and Lucy Talbot (Swanton) F.; S.B., Harvard, 1914; m. Ellen Roy Goldsborough, July 27, 1934; children—Talbot Otis, Elizabeth Carroll. Mgr. Hartford (Conn.) Home Co., ins., 1921-23; dir. Community Bond & Mortgage Co., Waterbury, Conn., 1925-26; treas., dir., mem. exec. com. Colonial Air Transport, Hartford and N.Y.C., 1926-29; v.p., dir., mem. exec. com. Fairchild Aviation Corp., N.Y.C., 1928-30; dir. Aero Supply Mfg. Co., College Point, N.Y., 1928-30; asst. to pres. Aviation Corp., N.Y.C., 1929-30; mem. exec. com. Waco Aircraft Corp., Troy, O., 1929-30; v.p., dir., mem. exec. com. Air Investors, Inc., N.Y.C., 1929-34; v.p., sec., dir., mem. exec. com. Fed. Broadcasting Corp., N.Y.C., 1933-34; regional group supr. Travelers Ins. Co., Hartford, 1934-39; v.p. Pepsi-Cola Co., L.I. City, N.Y., 1940-50; v.p., dir. Compagnia Ingenos Azuoarreros Matanzas, Cuba, 1944-50. Dir., sec., chmn. pub. relations adv. com. Grocery Mfrs. Am., 1946-50; trustee Nutrition Found., Inc., 1947-50; dir., exec. com. Food Industry War Com., and successor Food Industry Council, 1944-47. Mem. soft drink industry adv. com. W.P.B. Mem. gov.'s staff Conn., 1925-31, first aviation insp., 1923-25; pilot inaugural flight, air mail, New York-Boston, July 2, 1926. Served as 1st lt. 140th Air Squadron, overseas, 1917-18; maj., comdg. 43d Div. A.S., Conn. N.G., 1923-25. Mem. Nat. Aero. Assn. (chmn. legislative com. 1926-32), Pub. Relations Soc. Am., Mass. Soc. Mayflower Descs., Am. Arbitration Assn. Republican. Episcopalian. Club: Harvard (N.Y.C.). Co-Author: World Situation on Sugar, 1946. Contbr. to mags. Home: 103 E. 86th St., N.Y.C. Died Dec. 6, 1955.

FREEMAN, William Perry, editor; b. Miller County, Mo., June 15, 1858; s. Andrew Jackson and Editha Abagail (Tinsley) F.; d. pub. schs.; m. Alice Harris, Sept. 19, 1881 (died Nov. 16, 1917); 1 dau., Elsie (Mrs. Lewis A. Ellis); m. 2d, Gladys Eckman, May 29, 1932; 1 dau., Lucy Mae. Admitted to Okla. bar, 1898; clerk U.S. Ct. of Appeals, Ind. Ty., 1898-1907; practiced at McAlester, 1907-12; dir., later pres., now v.p. First Nat. Bank of McAlester; editor Okla. Mason, 1919-—, sec. McAlester Scottish Rite bodies 1927-31, sec. emeritus, 1931-—. Mem. Exemption Bd., McAlester, World War. Republican. Mem. Christian (Disciples) Ch. Mason (past grand master grand lodge Okla. 1914). Elk. Home: 537 E. Adams Av. Office: Masonic Temple, McAlester, Okla. Died July 9, 1944; buried Masonic Sect., Oak Hill Cemetery, McAlester.

FREER, Romeo Hoyt, ex-congressman; b. Bazetta, O., Nov. 9, 1845; s. Josiah D. and Caroline P. (Brown) F.; ed. Grand River Inst., Austinburg, O.; m. Mary Iams, July 8, 1884. Served in Union Army, 1862-5; subsequently capt., maj., col. 1st regt., W. Va. N.G.; admitted to bar, 1868; asst. pros. atty. Kanawha County, W.Va., 1868-70, pros. atty., 1870-73; U.S. consul Nicaragua, 1873-7; mem. legislature, 1891; pros. atty. Ritchie Co., 1892-97; judge 4th Jud. Dist., 1896-99; mem. 56th Congress; atty.-gen., W.Va., several yrs. from 1901; postmaster of Harrisville, W.Va., 1907-—. Republican. Grand Master, I.O.O.F.; dept. comdr. G.A.R Address: Harrisville, W.Va. Deceased.

FREIBERG, Leonard Henry (fri'berg), lawyer; b. Cincinnati, Dec. 23, 1885; s. Bernhard and Nettie Jeanette (Moss) F.; A.B., Yale, 1908; LL.B., U. Cincinnati, 1911; m. Henrietta Weihl, June 12, 1913; children—Carlotta Graeham, Leonard Henry. Admitted to Ohio bar, 1911 and since practiced in Cincinnati; asst. city solicitor, asst. co. prosecutor Hamilton Co., 1931-32; candidate for city council, pros. atty., co. commr. various times. Mem. Cin. City Charter Com. Pres. Home for Jewish Aged, 1936; mem. bd. Cin. Social Hygiene Soc. Pres. Internat. Assn. Torch Clubs, 1951-52. B'nai B'rith (pres. dist. grand lodge 2, 1930-31. Home: 849 Clifton Hills Terrace, Cin. 20. Office: 1st National Bank Bldg., Cin. 2. Died Feb. 4, 1954; buried Cin.

FREIN, Pierre Joseph, educator; b. Alford, Mass., June 22, 1869; s. Joseph and Marie (Marchant) F.; A.B., Williams Coll., 1892; Ph.D., Johns Hopkins, 1899; grad. study Johns Hopkins and in Europe, 1895-99; m. Emma Blanche Macleod, Aug. 26, 1899; 1 dau., Alice Virginia Crawford (Mrs. Jesse Charles Johnson). Tchr. German and French, Holbrook Mil. Acad., 1892-93; prof. French and Greek, Oahu Coll., 1893-95; instr. Stanford, 1899-1900, asst. prof. Romance langs., 1900-03; prof. French and Italian, U. Wash., 1903-18, prof. Romance langs., 1918-47, ret.; prof. summer sessions Stanford, 1920, U. So. Cal.,

1927, U. Mich., 1931. In charge French classes S.A.T.C., U. Wash., World War I. Decorated Officer de l'Instruction Publique, 1931, Chevalier de la Legion d & d'Honneur, 1935 (France). Mem. Modern Lang. Assn. An., Nat. Fedn. Modern Lang. Tchrs., Am. Assn. U. Profs., Alliance Francaise Seattle (founder), Art Inst. Seattle (charter mem.). Unitarian. Club: Faculty Men's. Home: 4317 15th Av. N.E., Seattle. Died Aug. 1954.

FREITAG, Walter, trade union ofcl.; b. Remscheid, Germany, Aug. 14, 1889; student pub. schs.; married. Apprentice tool maker; head dist. council Metal Workers Union, Hagen, 1920-33; chmn. Social-democratic Party, Dist. Hagen-Schwelm, 1931, mem. Prussian Provincial Diet, 1932; concentration camp, later under Nazi police supervision, 1933-45; cooperation in re-establishment Metal Workers Union, and Social-democratic Party, 1945; chmn. Metal Workers Union, 1946; mem. Northrhine-Westphalian Diet, 1947; mem. Bundestag, 1949-53; pres. German Fedn. Trade Unions, 1952—. Adv. com. European Coal and Steel Community, 1952—; exec. bd. ICFTU, 1952—, v.p., 1953—. Address: Vorsitzender, Düsseldorf, Hans-Böckler-Haus, Stromstrasse 8, Germany. Died July 6, 1958.

FREMMING, Morris A., govt. ofcl.; b. Ft. Dodge, Ia., July 27, 1902; s. Andrew A. and Mathilda (Soder) F.; student Tobin College, 1922-23; married to Patricia Dorothy Morgan, on June 9, 1928; children—Richard Arthur, Michael Douglas, Patrick David. Agent Bureau Internal Revenue, Dallas, 1935-41, group chief field and office group, 1945-51, asst. internal revenue agt. in charge, 1951-52, dist. commr., Birmingham, Ala., 1952-53, regional commr., San Francisco, since 1953. Served as lt. comdr., U.S. Navy, PTO, 1943-45. Decorated: Am. Def., Am. Area, Pacific Area with 3 battle stars, World War II medals (Navy). Lutheran. Address: 7011 Shook Rd., Dallas. Died Nov. 17, 1953; buried Field of Honor, Restland Meml. Park, Dallas.

FREMSTAD, Olive, soprano; b. Stockholm, Sweden; d. Olaf and Anna (Runquist) Fremstad; appeared as concert pianist at age of 5; brought to Am. at age of 10, and lived in Miami; unmarried. Taught music in Mpls., Duluth, Chgo., N.Y.C.; went to Germany, 1892, studied under Lilli Lehmann. Made début in Cologne Opera House, as Azucena, in Trovatore, 1898; subsequently engaged at Royal Opera House, Munich; sang two seasons at Covent Garden, London; engaged for Metropolitan Opera Co., N.Y.C., 1903. Sings in all prin. Wagnerian rôles, also many in French and Italian. Best known rôles: Isolde, in Tristan and Isolde; Brünnhilde. in The Ring; Kundry, in Parsifal; Venus, Tosca, Armide, and Salome. Address: Irving-on-Hudson, N.Y. Died Apr. 21, 1951.

FRENCH, Burton Lee, ex-congressman; b. Delphi, Ind., Aug. 1, 1875; s. Charles A. and Mina P. (Fisher) F.; A.B., U. Ida., 1901, LL.D., 1921; fellow polit. sci. U. Chgo., 1901-03, Ph.M., 1903; LL.D., Miami U., 1948; m. Winifred Hartley, June 28, 1904 (died Jan. 31, 1934). Lawyer, lecturer and writer on law and polit. sci. Mem. Ida. Ho. of Reps., 1898-1902, Rep. floor leader, 1900-02; mem. 55th to 72d Congresses, except two Congresses, 1st Ida. Dist., mem. com. on appropriations, chmn. Naval sub-com. on appropriations eight yrs.; del. U.S. Congress to Interparliamentary Union Conv. London, 1930, Bucharest, 1931; now prof. emeritus govt. Miami U., Oxford, O. Apptd. mem. Fed. Loyalty Review Board, 1947. Am., Ida. bar assns., Am. Polit. Science Assn., Acad. Polit. and Social Science, Am. Soc. Internat. Law, Phi Delta Theta, Delta Sigma Rho, Omicron Delta Kappa, Phi Beta Kappa. Republican. Presbyterian. Mason. Home: Oxford, O. Died Sept. 1954.

FRENCH, Edward Vinton, fire ins. co. exec.; b. Lynn, Mass., Mar. 11, 1868; s. Benjamin Vinton and Elisa (Tufts) F.; B.S., Mass. Inst. Tech., 1889; m. Mary O. Wentworth, Oct. 26, 1892; children—Helen Wentworth (Mrs. Jerome C. Greene), Margaret Vinton (Mrs. Sandford G. Gorton). Hydraulic testing, elec. engring. and spl. inspections, Asso. Factory Mut. Fire Ins. Cos., 1892-1906; v.p., engr. Arkwright Mut. Fire Ins. Co., 1906-20, pres., 1920-43, chmn. bd., 1943-46; dir. Ark. Mut. Fire Ins. Co., Brockton Edison Co.; trustee Eastern Utilities Assos. Served as maj. U.S. Army in charge fire protection work, France, World War I. Mem. Am. Soc. M.E., Am. Soc. E.E., Am. Water Works Assn., N.E. Water Works Assn., Nat. Fire Protection Assn. Episcopalian. Clubs: Engineers, Down Town, Episcopalian, North Andover Country. Home: 20 School St., Andover, Mass. Died Dec. 19, 1957.

FRENCH, Frank Chauncey, engr., educator; b. Humboldt, Ia., Feb. 20, 1876; s. David Baker and Mary Rachel (McConnell) F.; B.C.E., Ia. State Coll., 1896, C.E., 1905; m. Theo. C. Plambeck, Jan. 1, 1907; children—Frank C., Dorothy Josephine, Tom Ellis, Montana Wanda, David Jerry. Served as location and constrn. engr. rys. and as asso. prof. civ. engring., Ia. State Coll., until 1906, sr. constrn. engr., with U.S. Govt., P.I., 1906-07; asso. prof. civil engring., U. Utah, 1907-09; cons. engr., Salt Lake City, 1910-11; designing engr. Butte Superior Copper Co., 1912-14; supt. constrn. Kennecott Copper Corp., Latouche, Alaska, 1915-17; supt. and chief engr. Colo. Consol. Mines & Power Co., Lake City, Colo., 1919-23; became dean Marquette U., Milw., 1924; cons. civil and mining engr. and county judge of Hinsdale County, Colo.; cons. engr. U.S. Treasury Dept., 1931-42. Commd. capt. engrs., U.S. Army, 1917, maj., 1918, lt. col. O.R.C., 1924, col. 1935. With War Dept., U.S. Army Engrs., 1942-46, ret., 1946—. Formerly mem. Am. Soc. C.E., Ia. Engrs. Soc., Milw. Engrs. Soc. Am. Assn. Cooperative Schs. (dir.). Democrat. Mason (Shriner). Home: Box D, Lake City, Colo. Died Dec. 23, 1956.

FRENCH, Mary Montagu Billings (Mrs. John French); b. Woodstock, Vt., Mar. 5, 1869; d. Frederick and Julia (Parmly) Billings; ed. Miss Brackett's Sch., N.Y. City, 1881-86, Miss Porter's Sch., Farmington, Conn., 1886-88; hon. A.M., Middlebury Coll., 1939; m. John French, June 1, 1907; children—John, Mary (Mrs. Laurance Spelman Rockefeller), Elizabeth (Mrs. Ethan Allen Hitchcock). Member Y.W.C.A. (pres. 1938-40). Mem. Nat. Soc. Colonial Dames. Mem. Worlds Y.W.C.A., Nat. Inst. of Social Services. Presbyterian. Clubs: Cosmopolitan, Woodstock Country. Home: Woodstock, Vt. Died June 14, 1951; buried Woodstock.

FRENCH, Robert Dudley, prof. English; b. New Haven, Conn., Nov. 4, 1888; s. Joseph Richardson and Mary Amanda (Bradstreet) F.; A.B., Yale U., 1910, A.M., 1914, Ph.D., 1920; m. Margaret Stewart Means, Oct. 1, 1914. Tutor Hotchkiss Sch., 1910-12; instr. in English, Yale U., 1914-19, asst. prof. English, 1919-26, asso. prof., 1926-30, prof. English and master of Jonathan Edwards Coll., 1930-53. Trustee The Westminster Sch., Simsbury, Conn.; mem. bd. dirs. The Family Soc. of New Haven. Mem. Modern Language Assn. America, Modern Humanities Research Assn. Episcopalian. Clubs: Century (N.Y. City); Elizabethan (New Haven). Home: King's Hwy., North Haven, Conn. Died Aug. 22, 1954.

FRENCH, Seward Haight, Jr., business exec.; born Binghamton, N.Y., Nov. 5, 1907; s. Seward Haight and Mary Rust (Halley) F.; B.S., U. Pa., 1930, LL.B., 1935; m. Jean Crouse, Apr. 3, 1948; children—Seward Haight, Calvin K., Elizabeth S. With Merck & Co., Inc., Rahway, N.J., 1930-32; admitted to Pa. bar; legal dept. Penn Mut. Life Ins. Co., Phila., 1935-37; mem. firm Reed, Smith, Shaw & McClay, Pitts., 1937-47; asst. to pres. charge indsl., pub. relations Crucible Steel Co. of Am., Pitts., 1947-53, v.p. charge indsl., pub. relations, 1953—. Dir. Psychol. Service of Pitts. Mem. Pitts. C. of C. (labor-management council), Pa. State C. of C. (mem. indsl. relations com.), U.S. C. of C. (Internat. Labor Orgn. employer rep. group), Am. Arbitration Assn. (nat. panel arbitrators), Am. Iron and Steel Inst. (indsl. relations com.), Pitts. Personnel Assn. (dir.), Allegheny Roundtable (adv. com.), Soc. Advancement Management, Am., Pa. State, Allegheny Co. bar assns. Republican. Protestant Episcopal. Clubs: Duquesne, Athletic Assn., Harvard-Yale-Princeton (Pitts.); St. Anthony (N.Y.C.). Home: 5615 Aylesboro Av., Pitts. 17. Office: P.O. Box 88, Pitts. 30. Died Sept. 20, 1954.

FRENCH, Willard S., advt. exec.; b. Three Rivers, Mich., 1887. Vice chmn. Brooke, Smith, French & Dorrance Co.; dir. French Paper Co., Niles, Mich. Home: 2239 Burns Av. Office: E Jefferson Av. at Burns, Detroit 14. Died Dec. 1959.

FRERICHS, William Reinhard (frā'rěks), clergyman, educator; b. Wilhelmshaven, Germany, Aug. 26, 1877; s. Johann Friedrich and Gesche Maria (Hillers) F.; B.A., Carthage (Ill.) Coll. 1906; diploma Colgate-Rochester Div. Sch., 1909; studied univs. of Wash. and Ore., M.A., U. Ore., 1929; Ph.D., U. Greifswald, Germany, 1931; LL.D. (honoris causa) Linfield Coll., 1948; m. Carrie Frances Thompson, Aug. 20, 1908; children—Carl William, Robert Thompson, Ruth Elinor (Mrs. James P. Senter), Margaret Louise. Came to U.S., 1895, naturalized, 1904. Ordained Bapt. ministry, 1909; pastor Hillsboro, Ore., 1909-11, Ducor, Cal., 1911-12; prof. German (and Greek), Linfield Coll., McMinnville, Ore., 1912—, librarian, 1914-24, editor coll. publs., 1919—, acting pres., 1931-32, dean 1938-43; ret. Mem. Am. Assn. Tchrs. German, Pi Gamma Mu, Delta Phi Alpha. Author: Georg Ruseler; ein beitrag zur niederdeutschen literaturgeschichte. Republican. Editor: Pacific Baptist, 1918-19. Home: Box 144, McMinnville, Ore. Deceased.

FREUCHEN, Peter, author, explorer; b. Nykobing Falster, Denmark, Feb. 20, 1886; s. Lorenz Benzon and Frederikke (Rasmussen) F.; student Cathedral Sch., Nykoping Falster, 1895-1904, U. Copenhagen, Denmark, 1904-06; m. Navarana (eskimo of Thule, North Greenland), 1911 (dec. 1921); children—Mequsaq Avataq Igimaqsusuktoranguapaluk, Pipaluk Jette Tukuminguaq Kasaluk Palika Häger m. 2d, Dagmar Muller, June 23, 1945. Became sailor after leaving high sch.; mem. Arctic expdn., Danmark Expeditionen, 1906-08; in London, 1910, Thule, North Greenland, 1910-26, engaged in exploration, trading; second-in-command Fifth Thule Expdn., 1921-25; bought Island Enehoje, Denmark, 1926; in Greenland, 1927, 30, Russia and Spitzbergen, 1928; staff motion picture, Eskimo, Hollywood, Cal., also Alaska, 1932-34; in Hudson Bay, Can., 1934, S.A., 1936, Siberia, 1938, Lapland, 1939; lectr. U.S., 1935-37; lived underground in Denmark, 1940-43, captured by Germans, 1943, escaped to Sweden, 1944; brought to U.S. by Am. mil. plane, 1944, since lectured U.S.; member of the Danish Arctic Institute Council. Awarded Order of Merit with two bars (Denmark), Hans Egede Medal, Walker Medal, Danish Liberation Medal. Fellow Am. Geog. Soc.; mem. Danish Royal Geog. Soc. (mem. council), Danish Authors League, Maitre éf Jeux Florimontains de l'Academie, Chambery, Internat. Mark Twain Soc. Club: Explorers of Am. (N.Y. C.). Author: Eskimo, 1930; Sea Tyrant, 1931; Ivalu, 1934; Arctic Adventure, 1936; It Is All Adventure, 1937; White Man, 1946; Larion, 1948, Sibivian Adventure, 1949; Vagrant Viking, 1953; Ice Floes, 1954; Book of the Seven Seas, (with David Loth); Arctic Year (with F. Salomonsen). Contbr. articles mags. Home: 444 E. 57th St., N.Y.C. 22. Office: United Nations, N.Y.C. Died Sept. 2, 1957.

FREULER, John Rudolph, motion picture exec.; b. Monroe, Wis., Nov. 17, 1872; s. John R. and Rosina (Miller) F.; ed. pub. schs. and comml. coll., Milw.; m. A. Jessie Golz, Mar. 2, 1897 (dec.); children—Mrs. Gertrude Hammelman, Mrs. Loraine Walker. Employed by brokerage firm, Milw., 1890; entered storage warehouse bus., 1893, land bus., 1902; opened Theater, Comique (motion pictures), Milw., 1905; organized Am. Film Co., Inc., 1910, Mut. Film Corp. 1912 (now RKO Corp.), N. Am. Film Corp., 1914; pres. Mut. Film Corp., 1915-18. Pioneered wave of high salaries by paying Charles Chaplin $670,000 for appearing in 12 comedies in 1916; chmn. 1st motion picture bd. trade, 1915; now pres. White Front Theater Corp., Century Theatre Co. One of founders Milw. Downers Coll. Mem. Soc. Motion Picture and TV Engrs. Home: 241 Fairview Rd., Glencoe, Ill. Died Dec. 19, 1958; buried Forest Home Cemetery, Milw.

FREUND, Erwin O., business exec.; b. Chgo., Jan. 5, 1888; s. Gustav and Mina (Oppenheimer) F.; student Armour Inst. Tech., 1902-06, U. Chgo., 1906-07; m. Rosalind Heims, Sept. 28, 1912; children—Gustav, II, Katharine, Ruth. Began as office clk. S. Oppenheimer & Co , 1907; with S. Oppenheimer & Co., Ltd., London, 1910-12, S. Oppenheimer & Co., Chgo., 1912-19; pres. Shanghai (China) Bye Products Co., 1919-22; v.p. Ind. Casing Co., Chgo., 1923-26; pres. Visking Corp., mfrs. cellulose sausage casings and plastics, Chgo., 1926—. Home: R.F.D. 1, Hinsdale, Ill.; 3738 Pine Tree Drive, Miami Beach, Fla.; and 5009 Ellis Av., Chgo. Office: 6733 W. 65th St., Chgo.; also 135 S. La Salle St., Chgo. Died Nov. 12, 1947.*

FREUND, Hugo Abraham, physician; b. 1881; s. Adolph and Henrietta (Newman) F.; A.B., U. of Mich., 1903, M.D., 1905. Practiced in Detroit since 1907; married Hortense Goldsmith, Nov. 9, 1909 (died September 1936); children—Lisette F. Malbin, Richard A., Margaret F. Alexander; married 2d, Ruth H. Taylor. July 1950. President of $10,000,000 corporation, entitled Children's Fund of Michigan, donated by United States Senator James Couzens, principal and income to be disbursed in 25 years from 1929; senior consulting physician Department of Internal Medicine, Harper Hospital; cons. physician Mich Children's and Detroit Receiving hosps., St. Joseph's Hosp. (Pontiac, Mich.). Vice pres. Am. Ednl. Foundation. Certificate of Merit, A. M.A. Exhibit on Rheumatoid Arthritis, 1947. Fellow A.M.A.; mem. Am. Coll. Physicians, Am. Assn. Pathologists and Bacteriologists, Mich. Med Soc., Central Soc. for Clinical Research, Am. Rheumatism Assn. A.A.A.S. Clubs: Recess, Bloomfield Hills Country, Franklin Hills Country. Author numerous scientific papers. Home: 2651 Lone Pine Rd., R.F.D. No. 3, Pontiac, Mich. Office: 62 Kirby Av., Detroit. Died Dec. 24, 1952.

FREUND, Sanford H. E. (froind), lawyer; b. N.Y. City, June 26, 1880; s. Albert and Sophia (Eisner) F.; A.B., Harvard, 1901, LL.B., 1903, Began practice of law at Boston, 1903; eastern attorney C.,R.I.&P. Ry., 1910-12; gen. attorney and asst. gen. counsel Gt. Northern Ry., 1912-18; dir. div. of operations, U.S. Employment Service, 1918-19; asst. gen. counsel U.S. Railroad Adminstrn., in charge of financial work, 1919-20; gen. counsel U.S. Shipping Bd., 1922-23, also of U.S. Shipping Bd. Emergency Fleet Corp.; mem. Shearman & Sterling & Wright, New York, since 1923. Has lectured at Harvard on criminal law, Boston Univ. on conflict of laws, and corps., and U. Chgo. on conflict of laws and criminal law. Mem. Internat., Am. bar assns., Bar Assn. City of Boston, Assn. Bar City of New York, N.Y. County Lawyers Assn., N.Y. State Bar Assn., Conn. State Bar Assn., Internat. Law Soc., Am. Br. Internat. Law Assn., Maritime Law Assn. of U.S., Phi Beta Kappa, Phi Delta Phi. Clubs: Metropolitan (Washington, D.C.); Harvard, City Mid-day, Bankers (New York); Harvard (Boston); University (Chicago). Home: "Ashtoncroft," Ridgefield, Conn. Office: 20 Exchange Pl., New York 5, N.Y. Died Nov. 29, 1954.

FREUTEL, Guy Scott, banker; b. Chgo., Dec. 6, 1921; s. Edward C. and Kathryn (Scott) F.; A.B., U. Cal. at Los Angeles, 1947, A.M. in Econs., 1948; Ph.D. in Econs., Harvard, 1957; m. Dorothy Locke, Mar. 6, 1943; children—Guy Scott, Eric L. Mem. faculty econs. Washington U., 1951-55; research cons. Fed. Res. Bank St. Louis, 1951-55, asst. v.p., 1955-57, 1st v.p., 1957—; teaching fellow Harvard, 1950. Dir. St. Louis Met. Planning Assn. Served as lt. (j.g.) USNR, 1942-46. Mem. Econometric Soc., St. Louis C. of C., Beta Gamma Sigma, Pi Gamma Mu, Beta Theta Pi. Home: 1313 Forest Av., Kirkwood 22, Mo. Office: P.O. Box 442, St. Louis 66. Died Aug. 29, 1959.

FREY, Charles Daniel, advertising exec.; b. Denver, Oct. 9, 1886; s. Daniel and Augusta Eleanora (Stone) F.; ed. pub. schs.; m. Mary Ross Burch, Oct. 17, 1908 (died June 2, 1945); children, Mary Elizabeth (Mrs. Gail Borden), Charles Jr., Barbara Ross (Mrs. Eugene F. Graves, Jr.); m. 2d Charlotte Goodlett Caldwell, Feb. 18, 1950. In editorial and art dept. Chgo. Examiner, 1905-06, Chgo. Evening Post, 1906-09; organized Charles Daniel Frey Co., advt. illustrations copy, Chgo., N.Y., 1910; reorganized into advt. agency, Chgo., 1921; liquidated, 1948; dir. Chgo. Times, Inc., 1939-47. Chmn. finance com. Municipal Voters League, 1920-26. Vice chmn. bd. Am. Assn. Advt. Agencies, 1934, mem. exec. bd., 1932-35. Mem. reorgn. com. and trustee Chgo. Latin Sch., 1926-32, Girls Latin Sch. of Chgo., 1928-34. Organizer Chgo. br., 1917, and nat. dir. Am. Protective League, Dir. Chgo., Press Veterans Association; mem. Chgo. board Salvation Army; dir. Civic Music Assn., Chgo., Lyric Opera of Chgo. Trustee Chgo. Musical Coll.; mem. citizens bd., U. Chgo.; mem. bd. Chgo. U.S.O. Served as capt., Mil. Intelligence Div. Gen. Staff, Washington. World War I. Decorated Medaille de la Reconnaissance Française. Republican. Episcopalian. Mason. Clubs: Chicago, Commonwealth, Economic, Caxton, Casino, Farmers Tavern (Chgo.); Bohemian (San Francisco). Home: 232 E. Walton Pl., Chgo. 11. Office: 230 N. Michigan Av., Chgo. 1. Died Nov. 1959.

FREY, John Philip, ret. trade unionist; b. Mankato, Minn., Feb. 24, 1871; s. Leopold and Julia Philomen (Beaudry) F.; student pub. schs.; m. Nellie Josephine Higgins, June 10, 1891; children—Leslie L., Arwin P., Hattie E. Editor Molders' Jour., 1903-27; sec-treas. metal trades dept. AFL, 1927-34, pres. metal trades dept., 1934-50, pres. emeritus, 1950—; spl. lectr. econ. and trade-union topics U. Chgo., 1907; labor mem. of Federal Commn. investigating sci. mgmt.; chmn. bd. Nat. Bur. Econ. Research, Inc., 1922-28; mem. exec. bd. Workers Edn. Bur., 1923-28; mem. permanent com. on edn. AFL; pres. Ohio State Fedn. Labor, 1924-28; labor expert Am. delegation to Internat. Econ. Conf., Geneva, Switzerland, 1927; mem. Labor Advisory Bd. under NRA; mem. Fed. Com. on Apprentice Tng. Labor mem. shipbuilding stblzn. com. WPB. Lt. col. Specialist Res., U.S. Army. Pres. Bd. Edn., Norwood, O., 1917-21. Mason. Clubs: Cosmos (Washington); Literary (Cin.). Author: An American Molder in Europe, 1911; The Labor Injunction, 1922; Craft Unions of Ancient and Modern Times, 1944; also numerous pamphlets, including Scientific Management and Labor, 1916; Calamity of Prosperity, 1931; Bankers Domination, 1933; Calamity of Recovery, 1935. Address: 3031 Sedgwick St., Washington 8. Died Nov. 29, 1957; buried Arlington Nat. Cemetery.

FREY, John Walter, internal med.; b. Pittsburgh, Jan. 7, 1892; s. John and Hedwig (Feibelman) F.; B.S., U. of Pittsburgh, 1913, M.D., 1916; grad. study, Johns Hopkins, 1921; m. Annette Hirsch, Dec. 18, 1919; children—John Walter, William Arthur, Margaret Ann. Interne Allegheny Gen. Hosp., 1916-17; resident Children's Hosp., 1917; instr. in U. of Pittsburgh, 1919-22; asst. in clin. diagnosis, St. Francis Hosp., 1922-23; research work Mellon Institute, Pittsburgh, Pa., 1928, 1930, 1932; specializes in internal medicine; medical staff, Presbyterian Hospital; instructor physical diagnosis, University of Pittsburgh Medical School, 1943. Served as captain Medical Reserve Corps, World War, 1917-19, Base Hospital 114, Beau Desert, France, 1918-19. Fellow Am. Medical Assn.; member Allegheny County Med. Soc., Diabetes Assn. Pittsburgh, Phi Rho Sigma. Republican. Mason (Shriner, Past Commander Legion of Honor Syria Temple). Clubs: University, Oakland Lions (pres. 1937). Contbr. to mags. Home: 5700 Centre Av. Office: Schenley Apartments, Pitts. Died Mar. 16, 1955.

FRICK, John Henry, educator; b. nr. Liberty, Mo., Mar. 13, 1845; s. William Frick; A.B., Central Wesleyan Coll., 1870; m. Kathryn Hartel, July 14, 1872. Tchr. pub. schs., 2 yrs.; taught prep. dept., Central Wesleyan Coll., 1870-71, prof. mathematics and natural scis., 1871-1920. Police judge, 1927. Has served on State, county and congl. coms. Served with Union army, Aug. 1864-65. Mem. A.A.A.S., Internat. Geol. Soc., Acad. Scis., St. Louis; mem. G.A.R. Republican. Author: Textbook in German for Epworth League, Die Himmel erzdhlen die Ehre Gottes. Address: Warrenton, Mo. Died Dec. 28, 1927; buried Warrenton.

FRIDGE, Benjamin Franklin; b. Baton Rouge, La., Feb. 24, 1856; s. John D. and Adaline Christine (Wolff) F.; ed. Peabody Free Sch., Baton Rouge; m. Alice P. Steadman, Mar. 24, 1886. In gen. mercantile business, 1878-02; pres. Tallahala Lumber Co., Ellisville Home Improvement Co., Hotel & Lodge Co., Fridge-Sinnon Realty Co.; v.p. Lavery Lumber Co. Mem. for Miss. of Prog. Nat. Com. Presbyn. Address: Ellisville, Miss. Deceased.

FRIEDEL, Francis Joseph, educator, clergyman; b. Cleve., Aug. 9, 1897; s. Jacob and Rosina (Willkomm) F.; A.B., U. Dayton, 1917; M.A., Cath. U. Am., 1935; Ph.D., U. Pitts., 1950; S.T.B., U. Fribourg, Switzerland, 1925, S.T.L., S.T.D., 1926. Professed in the Soc. of Mary, 1914; ordained priest, Roman Catholic Ch., 1927; instr. U. Dayton, 1927-34, prof. sociology, head dept., dean coll. of arts and scis., dir. eve. classes, 1935-43, dean, arts and scis., 1950-53, temp. ret.; pres. Trinity Coll., Sioux City, Ia., 1943-49. Asso. with Council of Social Agencies in Dayton, pres. bd dirs. Guidance Center, 1938-42. Mem. Am. Sociol. Soc., Am. Cath. Sociol. Soc. (pres. 1941), A.A.A.S. (fellow), Mariological Soc. Am., Provincial Chpt. Soc. Mary, Delta Epsilon Sigma (a founder), Alpha Sigma Tau (organizer). K.C. (4°). Author: Mariology of Cardinal Newman, 1928; Our Social World, 1939; Social Problems, 1940; also religious booklets. Address: U. Dayton, Dayton, O. Deceased.

FRIEDEN, Alexander, chemist; b. Lithuania, Oct. 5, 1895; s. Abraham and Sarah (Rubin) F.; B.S., U. Va., 1919, M.S., 1919; M.A., Columbia, 1920, Ph.D., 1923; m. Evelyn Gutman, Nov. 13, 1920; children—Dr. Julian, Dr. Carl. Came to U.S., 1912, naturalized, 1919. Tchr. Charlottesville (Va.) High Sch., 1917-18, Columbia, 1920-23; with cons. labs. of Dr. Raymond F. Bacon, 1923-33; ind. cons., 1933-36; lectr. food and nutrition coll. New Rochelle (N.Y.), 1935-36; tech. dir. food products dept. Stein, Hall & Co., Inc., N.Y.C., 1936-39, tech. dir., 1939-41, v.p., 1941-46; dir. research Pabst Brewing Co., Milw., 1946-53, v.p. research, 1953—. Mem. food engrng. council Ill. Inst. Tech., 1949—; bd. visitors Agrl. Research Inst., N.R.C. Served with C.W.S., U.S. Army, 1918. Mem. Cerevisiae Yeast Inst. (dir.), Am. Chem. Soc., A.A.A.S., Am. Soc. Cereal Chemists, Am. Soc. Brewing Chemists, Inst. Food Technologists, Textile Research Inst., Tech. Assn. Pulp and Paper Industry, Am. Soc. Textile Chemists and Colorists, N.Y. Acad. Sci., Chemists Club N.Y., Sigma Xi. Mem. Ethical Culture Soc. Contbr. sci. and tech. publs., chpts. sci. books. Patentee in field. Home: 746 E. Beaumont Av., Milw. 17. Office: 1037 W. McKinley Av., Milw. 3. Died Apr. 21, 1956.

FRIEDEN, Pierre, diplomat of Luxembourg; b. Oct. 28, 1892; m. Madeleine Kinnen, 1946. Dir. Nat. Library, 1929-42; minister of edn., Luxembourg, 1944-45, councilor of state, 1946-48, minister edn., 1948—, minister interior affairs, 1951—, now prime minister. Address: Office of Prime Minister, Luxembourg, Luxembourg. Died Feb. 23, 1959.*

FRIEDENWALD, Harry, ophthalmologist; b. Balt., Sept. 21, 1864; s. Dr. Aaron and Bertha (Bamberger) F.; Baltimore City Coll., 1879; A.B., Johns Hopkins, 1884; M.D., Coll. Phys. and Surgs., Balt., 1886; D.H.L., Jewish Inst. Religion, N.Y.C., 1932; D.Sc., U. Md., 1932; post-grad. work univ. of Berlin and Vienna; m. Bertha Stein, June 28, 1892. Resident physician City Hosp. of Balt., 1886-87; asst. at Prof. Hirschberg's Augenheilanstalt, Berlin, 1887-89; asso. prof. ophthalmology and otology Coll. Phys. and Surg., Balt. (now U. Md., 1894-1902, prof., 1902-29, now emeritus; ophthalmic surgeon Balt. Eye, Ear and Throat Charity Hosp. and Mercy, Sinai, Union Meml. and Woman's hosps. Dir. Jewish Theol. Sem. Am.; gov. Dropsie Coll., Phila. Fellow A.A.A.S., A.C.S.; mem. A.M.A., Am. Ophthal. Soc. (pres. 1936-37), Am. Otol. Soc., Ophthal. Congress Oxford, Ophthal. Soc. United Kingdom, Med. and Chirurg. Faculty of Md., Phi Beta Kappa. Club: University (Balt.) Author: Life, Letters and Addresses of Aaron Friedenwald, 1906; The Jews and Medicine, 1944; Jewish Luminaries in Medical History and a Catalogue of Works bearing on the subject of Jews and Medicine from his library, 1946. Home: 2412 Rogers Av. Office: 1212 Eutaw Pl., Balt. Died Apr. 8, 1950.

FRIEDENWALD, Jonas Stein, ophthalmologist; b. Baltimore, Md., June 1, 1897; s. Harry and Bertha (Stein) F.; A.B., Johns Hopkins, 1916, M.D., 1920; A.M., Harvard, 1922; m. Marie Louise Sherwin, Apr. 19, 1925. Instr. ophthalmic pathology, Johns Hopkins, 1923-29, asso. in clin. ophthalmology, 1929-31, asso. prof. since 1931; asst. visiting ophthalmologist, Johns Hopkins Hosp., 1929-31, visiting ophthalmologist since 1931; ophthalmic surgeon, Baltimore Eye and Ear, Union Memorial, Women's Sinai and Provident hosps. Fellow Am. Coll. Surgeons; mem. A.M.A., Am. Ophthal. Soc., Am. Optical Soc., Am. Acad. Ophthalmology and Otolaryngology, Am., Assn. Clin. Investigation, Ophthal. Soc. United Kingdom, Awarded medal research ophthalmology A.M.A., 1935, Lucien Howe medal, Am. Ophthal. Soc., 1951; Howe prize in ophthalmology U. Buffalo, 1948; Proctor award medal, 1949; Donders award medal, Dutch Ophthal. Soc., 1952. Jewish religion. Club: University. Author: Pathology of the Eye, 1929. Contbr. to profl. jours. Address: 1212 Eutaw Pl., Balt. 17. Died Nov. 5, 1955.

FRIEDLANDER, Theodore, mfr.; b. San Francisco, Calif., Mar. 6, 1886; s. Louis and Jennie (Magnes) F.; student high sch., 1901-02; m. Louise Silberman, Dec. 27, 1915; children—Theodore, Gardner, Richard. With Phoenix Hosiery Co., Milwaukee, since 1909, as Pacific Coast rep., 1909-12, v.p. and gen. mgr., now pres.; dir. Marine Nat. Bank, Milwaukee. Mem. advisory bd. Wisconsin State Industrial Commission; mem. exec. bd., mem. at large, Milwaukee County Council Boy Scouts of America; mem. exec. bd., Milwaukee chapter Red Cross. Trustee, Layton Art Gallery. Republican. Mason. Jewish religion. Clubs: Milwaukee Athletic, University, Lake, Country (Oconomowoc). Home: 3439 N. Summit Av. Office: 320 E. Buffalo St., Milw. Died Dec. 3, 1952.

FRIEDMAN, Elisha Michael (frēd'măn), cons. economist; b. N.Y.C., May 25, 1889; s. Louis and Miriam Deborah (Friedman) F.; B.S. cum laude, Coll. City N.Y., 1908; B.C.S., N.Y.U., 1913. Engaged in bus. adminstrn. and sci. mgmt., 1910-16; with Eugene Meyer, Jr. & Co., 1916-17; statistician to Adv. Commn., Council Nat. Def., and War Industries Bd., 1917-18, War Finance Corp., 1918-20; mem. Econ. Liaison Com. (interdepartmental group of U.S. Govt. economists), 1919-20; mem. Group Com. of U.S. Sect., Inter-Am. High Commn., 1920-28; asst. to pres. Overseas Securities Corp., 1921, v.p. 1922-23, spent most of 1922 in fourteen European countries in connection with interests of corporation; engaged in investment banking, 1923-29; mgr. investment fund, 1929-39; mem. com. organizing Amalgamated (Labor) Bank of New York, 1928; cons. economist, 1939—; lectr. on finance, sch. commerce N.Y.U., 1920-29, New Sch. for Social Research, 1927-30. Before congl. coms. initiated efforts to revise taxes on capital gains, 1938, and to eliminate double tax on income of corps., 1942; to maintain full employment through flexible wages, 1944, and by profit-sharing to stabilize employment and prodn., 1939, to finance small bus. by holding cos., without govt. aid, 1943; to establish, under Bretton Woods legislation, an Internat. Bankruptcy Ct. for defaulting fgn. loans, to eliminate by treaty, double inheritance taxes on estates of Americans with property abroad, 1945; advocated integrating utility holdings cos. into regional systems, 1943; consol. r.r.'s into few systems, 1939; stopping wasteful labor practices on railroads, 1938; participation by stockholders in reorganizing bankrupt railroads, 1945. Chmn. econ. adv. group of European and Canadian bankers and economists conferring with U.S. govt. officials on war problems, 1941-45. Fellow, A.A.A.S., Mem. Council on Fgn. Relations, Am. Acad. Polit. and Social Sci., Am. Econ. Assn., Royal Econ. Soc. (life), Am. Statis, Assn. Am. Sociol. Soc., Acad. Polit. Science, Am. Soc. Pub. Adminstrn., Nat. Child Labor Com., Am. Jewish Hist. Soc., Judaeans, Nat. Consumers League, Phi Beta Kappa. Clubs: Bankers, New York University Faculty (N.Y.C.); Century Country (White Plains); Cosmos (Washington); Authors (London). Author: Labor and Reconstruction in Europe, 1919; International Commerce and Reconstruction, 1919; International Finance and its Reorganization, 1922; Survival or Extinction, Aspects of Jewish Question, 1924; Russia in Transition, 1932. Editor: American Problems of Reconstruction, 1918; America and the New Era, 1920; writer on economic questions. Home: 25 E. 67th St., N.Y.C. 21. Office: 20 Broad St., N.Y.C. 5. Died Mar. 25, 1951.

FRIEDMAN, Emanuel David, neuropsychiatrist; b. at New York City, Aug. 25, 1884; s. Louis and Miriam Deborah F.; B.S., College of City of New York, 1903; M.D., New York Univ. Coll. of Medicine, 1907; studied U. of Vienna, 1908-09, U. of Berlin, 1913; m. Rose Borgenicht, June 30, 1908; children—Nathan Baruch, Harold Herman, Renee Vivian. Instr. medicine, New York Univ. College of Medicine, 1913-18, instructor neuropathology, 1919-22, lecturer, neuropathology, 1922-24, clin. prof. neurology, 1924-27, prof. neurology and head of department, 1927-47; prof. emeritus, 1947—; assistant attending physician Central Neurol. Hospital, 1912-21; C.A. Herter fellow, in research medicine, 1914-15; contract surgeon, U.S. Army, 1918, adjunct attending physician Bellevue Hosp., 1917-19, adjunct neurologist, 1919-22, associate, 1922-31, visiting neuropsychiatrist, 1931-49, consulting neuropsychiatrist, 1949—; adjunct neurologist Mt. Sinai Hospital, 1920-25, associate, 1925-32; associate neurologist Montefiore Hosp., for Chronic Diseases, 1921-23; attending neurologist Israel-Zion Hosp., Brooklyn, 1922-25, chief neurological service, 1925-43; consulting neurologist, 1943—; senior attending neurologist Beth Israel Hospital, 1930-49, cons. neuropsychiatrist, 1949—; neuropsyhchiatrist in charge New York University division, Goldwater Memorial Hospital, N.Y., 1943-47; consulting neuropsychiatrist, since 1947; consultant neuropsychiatry, Vet. Adminstrn., 1946; consulting neurologist Jersey City, University, Manhattan General and Beth David hospital, chairman committee on neurology of Workmen's Compensation Board, 1935-38. Neuropsychiatrist Medical Advisory Board under Selective Service Act, 1940-43. Lecturer, N.Y. Univ. School of Military Neuropsychiatry, 1944-45. President Association Alumni New York University College of Medicine, 1937-38. Member sub-committee on technical and scientific research, Noise Abatement Commission of N.Y. City. Diplomate American Board Neurology and Psychiatry. Mem. A.M.A., Med. Soc. State of N.Y., N.Y. County Med. Society, N.Y. Acad. Medicine (sec. sect. of neurology and psychiatry, 1925; chmn. of sect. 1926. Mem. Com. on admission, 1933-37) American Neurol. Assn., N.Y. Neurol. Soc. (v.p. 1938-39; pres. 1939-40), Assn. for Research in Nervous and Mental Diseases, Harvey Soc., Am. Psychiatric Assn., Phi Beta Kappa, Phi Delta Epsilon, Alpha Omega Alpha, N.Y. Univ. Chapter, Sigma Xi, Authors Club of London. Jewish religion. Contbr. to symposium, America and the New Era, 1920. Contbr. on internal medicine and neurology. Home: 1200 5th Av. Office: 1192 Park Av., N.Y.C. Deceased.

FRIEDMAN, Herbert Jacob, lawyer; b. Chicago, Mar. 2, 1876; s. Jacob and Henrietta (Kahn) F.; A.B., Harvard, 1897, LL.B., 1900; m. Elsie Sidenberg, Oct. 1, 1907. Lecturer, John Marshall Sch. of Law, 1902-06; instr. and lecturer, Northwestern U. Law Sch., 1904-08. A counsel for Civil Service Commn. of Chicago, 1911, and active in vice and police investigation at that time. Del. Internat. Prison Conf., 1910; an organizer of 1st Nat. Conf. for Reformation of Criminal Law and Criminal Procedure; consolidated all forces in Chicago interested in the housing problem, 1914, and now sec. Chicago Housing Assn.; one of organizers Am. Symphony Orchestra of Chicago; pres. Chicago Forum Council, 1927-29; dir. Young Men's Associated Jewish Charities (1st pres.), Chicago-Winfield Tuberculosis Sanitarium, Legal Aid Soc. Writer on spl. subjects in Cyclopedia of Law and Procedure, Harvard Law Review, Yale Law Review, etc. Democrat. Clubs: City, Harvard, Book and Play (pres. 1928-30), Chicago Law, Northmoor Country, Standard, Attic; Penguins (Washington, D.C.). Govt. appeal agt., 1917-18; gov. "Four Minute Men" of Chicago. Dir. of speakers 7th Federal Dist. for 4th Liberty Loan. Mem. Federal Industrial Commn., 1918; mgr. with Senator Walsh of nat. senatorial campaign, 1920; pres. Political Amnesty Com., 1923. Former sec. Municipal Voters' League, Pres., 1932—. Home: 1086 Old Elm Lane, Glencoe, Ill. Office: 120 S. LaSalle St., Chgo. Died. Oct. 21, 1956.

FRIEDMAN, Lee Max, lawyer; b. Memphis, Dec. 29, 1871; s. Max and Tillie (Marks) F.; A.B. magna cum laude, Harvard, 1893, LL.B., 1895; D.H.L. (honorary), Hebrew Union Coll., 1943; D. Jurisp. (hon.), Suffolk University, 1952. Admitted to Mass. bar, 1895; associate Ropes, Gray & Loring, 1895-97; with Morse, Hill & Hodges, 1897-98, Morse & Friedman, 1898-1912, Friedman & Atherton, 1912-14, Swift, Friedman & Atherton, 1914-19, Friedman & Atherton, 1919-23, now Friedman, Atherton, Sisson & Kozol, specializing in corp., equity and probate matters. Organizer Juvenile Ct., Boston, 1905; past mem. Boston Municipal Research Bur.; Mass. Spl. Com. on discrimination. Former trustee Children's Instn. Dept., Beth Israel Hosp., Asso. Jewish Philanthropies. Trustee, past pres. Pub. Library; trustee Gen. Theol. Library; dir. Nat. Jewish Welfare Bd. U.S. govt. appeal agt., local bd., Boston, World War I. Mem. vis. com. Print Dept. Boston Mus. Fine Arts, Harvard Library, Harvard Coll. Semitic and Egyptian Civilization. Member American Massachusetts State and also the Boston bar assns., Am. Jewish Hist. Soc. (honorary president), American Antiquarian Society, Jewish Publication. Soc. Am. (hon. v.p.), Mass. Hist. Soc. (Council), Anglo-Jewish Hist. Soc. London (corr. mem.). Mem. Temple Israel of Boston (hon. life pres. 1954, hon. life trustee 1943); hon. mem. exec. com. Union American Hebrew Congregations; mem. governing body World Union Progressive Judaism. Author: Early American Jews, 1934; Robert Grosseteste and the Jews, 1934; Zola and the Drefus Case, 1937; Rabbi Haim Isaac Carigal, 1940; Jewish Pioneers and Patriots, 1943; Pilgrims In A New Land, 1948; also mag. articles. Collector Hebraica and Judaica, one of the largest pvt. collections of books dealing with post-bibl. Jewish history. Home: 206 Bay State Rd., Boston 15. Office: 30 State St., Boston 9. Died Aug. 7, 1957; Forest Hills Cemetery, Boston.

FRIEDMAN, Sol H., steel exec.; b. Russia, Apr. 14, 1895; (Am. citizenship through father); s. Harry and Roza (Fleshin) F.; m. Cele B. Akers, May 30, 1920; children—Daniel A., Stanford J. Sec.-treas. Friedman Bros. & Co., Inc., 1924-37; pres., treas. Reliance Steel Corp., 1937-44, solar Steel Corp., Cleve., 1944—. Trustee Euclid Av. Temple, Mt. Sinai Hosp. (both Cleve.). Clubs: Oakwood Country (Cleve.); Franklin Hills Country (Detroit). Home: 2952 Glengary Rd., Shaker Heights, O. Office: Union Commerce Bldg., Cleve. 14. Died Mar. 14, 1957.

FRIEDMANN, Max E., dept. store pres.; b. Milwaukee, Wis., Mar. 2, 1890; ed. pub. schs. and Univ. of Wis.; m. Helene Freda Jaehrling, 1924 (div. 1935); children—Freda Katerina, Maxine Alberta; married 2d, Elinore Weinhold, 1947. Pres., Ed. Schuster & Co., Incorporated, dept. store, Milwaukee; dir. Cavendish Trading Corp., N.Y. Trustee Citizens' Governmental Research Bureau of Milwaukee; trustee Metropolitan Milwaukee War Memorial; dir. Milwaukee Assn. of Commerce; vice pres. and dir. Credit Bureau of Milwaukee; trustee Milwaukee Art Inst. Home: 8560 North 76th St. Office: N. 3d St. and West Garfield Av., Milw. Died Mar. 31, 1954.

FRIEL, Arthur Olney, author; b. Detroit, May 31, 1885; s. George William and Lucy Locke (Thompson) F.; A.B., Yale, 1909; m. Elizabeth Genevieve Knowlton, Dec. 31, 1911. Editor Asso. Press, N.Y., 1911-18, 19-20; began freelance writing, as contbr. adventure tales to mags., 1919. War editor Concord (N.H.) Monitor-Patriot, 1942-44; editorial writer and columnist Manchester (N.H.) Union Leader, 1944-46; asst. editor N.H. Sunday News, 1946-48. Explored, Rio Ventuari, affluent of Orinoco, solving mystery of traditional White Indians, 1922. Formerly fellow Royal Geog. Soc., Am. Geog. Soc.; mem. Authors League Am., Am. Newspaper Guild. Author: King, of Kearsarge, 1921; The Pathless Trail, 1922; Tiger River, 1923; Cat-o'-Mountain, 1923; The King of No Man's Land, 1924; The River of Seven Stars, 1924; Mountains of Mystery, 1925; Hard Wood, 1925; Renegade, 1926; Forgotten Island, 1931; also many mag. stories and articles. Address: care Authors League, 6 E. 39th St., N.Y.C. Died Jan. 27, 1959.

FRIEND, Albert Mathias, Jr., archaeologist, educator; b. Ogontz, Pa., Feb. 27, 1894; s. Albert Matthias and Clara Belle (Tappen) F.; student U. Pa., 1910-11; Litt. B., Princeton, 1915, A.M., 1917. Instr. art and archaeology Princeton, 1921-24, asst. prof., 1924-27, asso. prof., 1927-36, prof., 1936-46, Marquand prof. art and archaeology since 1946; dir. studies Dumbarton Oaks, Harvard since 1944. Trustee Am. Acad. Rome, Procter Found. Served as corpl. 29th Engr. Corps, France, 1918-19. Fellow Mediaeval Acad. Am. (1st v.p.), Pierpont Morgan Library; mem. Am. Philos. Soc., Societe Nationale des Antiquaires de France, Am. Numismatic Soc. (council). Club: Nassau (Princeton, N.J.). Author articles in profl. publs. and coll. bulls. Editor: The Illustrations in the Manuscripts of the Septuagint since 1941; Studies in Manuscript Illumination since 1947. Home: 10 Mercer St., Princeton, N.J. Died Mar. 1956.

FRIERSON, Horace (fri-ersun), lawyer; b. Columbia, Tenn., Feb. 5, 1881; s. Horace and Jeannie (Phillips) F.; grad. Wallace U. Sch., Nashville, 1898; LL.B., Vanderbilt U., 1902; m. Julia Warfield, Oct. 20, 1909; children—Horace Jr., Chloe. Practiced at Lawrenceburg, Tenn., 1902-09; dist. atty. 11th Circuit, Tenn., 1910-17; practiced at Columbia, Tenn., 1919-34; U.S. atty. Middle Dist. of Tenn. Jan. 1934-Aug. 1947; sec., treas. Maury Drilling Co., 1930—. Trustee of the Columbia Military Academy. Served in Spanish-Am. War and Philippine Insurrection, July 1898-Nov. 1899; maj. 114th F.A. World War, June 1917-Apr. 1919; in France, May 1918-Mar. 1919. Chmn. Dem. State Exec. Com. of Tenn., mng. state campaign of Franklin D. Roosevelt, Sept. 1, 1932-Aug. 31, 1934. Mem. Tennessee (past president), Maury County (past president) bar associations, American (past commander), Kappa Alpha. Presbyn. Club: Graymere Country. Home: R.F. D. 1. Address: 810 S. Garden, Columbia, Tenn. Died Aug. 30, 1956; buried Columbia.

FRIERSON, John Woods, newspaperman; b. Shelbyville, Tenn., Mar. 10, 1897; s. Albert and Kate (Fogelman) F.; student Webb Sch., Bell Buckle, Tenn., 1913-14, Branham and Hughes Sch., Springhill, Tenn., 1914-15; m. Waldo Meyer, Jan. 8, 1934; children—John Woods, Albert Meyer, Waldo Lynn. Classified advt. salesman Memphis Press, 1922-24; advt. salesman 1924-28; advt. mgr. El Paso (Tex.) Post, 1928-29; bus. mgr. El Paso Herald-Post, 1929-35; Birmingham (Ala.) Post, 1935—; pres., dir. Birmingham Post Co. and asst. gen. mgr. Birmingham News 1950—. Served as cpl. 11th Aero Squadron, 1st Day Bombardment Group, 1st Army, AEF, 1917-19. Democrat. Presbyn. Clubs: Birmingham Country, Downtown, The Club. Home: 4241 Cliff Rd. Office: Birmingham Post, Birmingham, Ala. Died Aug. 1959; buried Elmwood Cemetery, Birmingham.

FRIERSON, William Little, lawyer; b. Shelbyville, Tenn., Sept. 3, 1868; s. Robert Payne and Mary (Little) F.; A.B., Southwest Presbyn. U., Clarksville, Tenn., 1887; LL.D., Southwestern at Memphis, 1929; m. Margaret Daniel, Apr. 20, 1892; children—Mrs. Margaret Williamson, Robert Payne, Mrs. Sue Lawwill. Began practice at Shelbyville, Tenn., 1889; settled in Chattanooga, 1890; mem. Anderson & Frierson, 1891-93; Shepherd & Frierson, 1893-1906, Coleman & Frierson, 1906-17; city atty., 1912-15; spl. judge Supreme Court of Tenn., 1916; asst. atty. gen. of U.S., 1917-20; solicitor gen. of U.S., 1920-21; mem. Williams & Frierson, Chattanooga, 1921—. Mayor of Chattanooga, 1905-07. Mem. Am., Tenn. State (pres. 1922-23) bar assns. Home: Hotel Patten. Office: Chattanooga Bank Bldg., Chattanooga, Tenn. Died May 25, 1953.

FRIES, Elmer Plumas (frēz), editor; b. Carson City, Nev., July 10, 1884; s. Albert N. and Margaret (Fraser) F.; ed. Woodward High Sch., Cincinnati; m. Estelle A. Wild, Oct. 5, 1907. Formerly on editorial staffs of Cincinnati Commercial Tribune, Chicago Journal, Phila. North American and New York Press; editor Cincinnati American, 1913-14, Cincinnati Post, 1921-29; initiated newspaper crusade which was followed by adoption of city manager government in Cincinnati; dir. of Democratic State News Service, Columbus, Ohio, 1929-34; now editorial writer and polit. columnist, Columbus Evening Dispatch. Presbyterian. Elk. Clubs: University (Columbus); National Press (Washington). Home: 1188 E. Broad St., Columbus, O. Died May 18, 1949; buried Walnut Hills Cemetery, Cincinnati.

FRIESEN, Abraham Penner (frē'zĕn), educator, physicist; b. Manitoba, Can., June 2, 1887; s. Johann Isaac and Helena (Penner) F.; student Mennonite Collegiate Inst., Gretna, Manitoba, 1902-03, 1904-06, 1915-16; student Provincial Normal Sch., Winnipeg, fall terms, 1906, 13, summers 1921, 22; student N.D. U., summer 1917; B.A., Bethel Coll., N. Newton, Kan., 1924; M.A., U. Colo., 1928; Ph.D., U. Kan., 1935; m. Agatha Hamm, July 25, 1907; children—Wilhelmina (wife of Lt. G. A. Ediger), Elfriede (Mrs. P. G. Pankratz), Louise (wife of Dr. P. D. Hooge), Wilfred John. Flour mill apprentice Steinbach, Man., 1900-02; night miller, 1903-04, 10-11; rural sch. tchr., Manitoba, 1906-09; tchr. mathematics, phys. sci. Mennonite Collegiate Inst., Gretna, Man., 1909-10, 16-19; prin., tchr. math., phys. sci. Steinbach, 1911-15, 19-23; grad. asst. physics U. Colo., 1924-25; asst. to librarian summers 1926, 27, 28; instr. physics, asst. chemistry Bethel Coll., 1925-28, asst. prof. physics, asst. instr. chemistry, 1928-31, prof. physics, chmn. natural sci. div., 1932-43; asso. prof., acting head dept., physics Southwestern U., Georgetown, Tex., 1943-49; prof., head dept. physics, 1940—. Fellow A.A.A.S.; mem. Am. Assn. Physics Tchrs. (charter mem.), Am. Phys. Soc., Optical Soc. Am., Am. Council Math. Tchrs., Kan. Acad. Sci., Texas Acad. Sci., Sigma Xi. Methodist (mem. bd. Stewards, St. John's Methodist Ch., also mem. Ch. Brotherhood). Contbr. articles to popular, religious, scientific publs. Home: 401 Walnut St., Georgetown, Tex. Died 1953.

FRIESNER, Ray Clarence (frēz'nĕr), coll. dean; b. Bremen, O., Feb. 8, 1894; s. Emanuel Stephen and Sarah Elizabeth (Myers) F.; A.B., Ohio Wesleyan U., 1916, D.Sc., 1950; Ph.D., U. Mich., 1919; m. Bessie Ball, 1916 (dec.); m. 2d, Gladys Miller, 1922. Grad. asst. in botany U. Mich., 1916-17, research fellow, 1917-9, instr. summers, 1918-19; asst. prof. botany Butler U., 1919-22, asso. prof., 1922-25, prof., 1925-—, dir. div. grad. instrn., 1944-47, dean Coll. Liberal Arts and Scis., 1947-—. Mem. Ind. Acad. Scis. (sec. 1926-35, pres. 1936), Bot. Soc. America, Ohio, Mich., Ill., Wis. acads. of science, Eugenics Research Assn., Am. Eugenics Soc., Am. Genetic Assn., Biol. Soc. Washington, Am. Soc. Plant Taxonomy, A.A.A. S., Sigma Xi, Phi Beta Kappa, Phi Kappa Phi, Phi Sigma. Democrat. Mem. Disciples of Christ Ch. Contbr. papers to bot. jours.; editor Butler U. Bot. Studies. Home: Brendonwood, Indpls. 44. Died Dec. 1, 1952; buried Bremen, O.

FRILEY, Charles Edwin (fri'lĭ), coll. pres.; b. Ruston, La., Aug. 27, 1887; s. William Christopher and Ellen (Douglas) F.; grad. Sam Houston Teachers Coll., 1905; student Baylor U., 1905-07; B.S., A. and M. Coll. of Tex., 1919; A.M., Columbia, 1923; grad. study summers, U. of Chicago, 1926-31; LL.D., Hardin-Simmons U., 1929; LL.D., Agrl. and Mech. College of Texas, 1940; Sc.D., Cornell College, 1942; married Nina Lynn Wood, June 21, 1913 (died October 28, 1918); children—Charles Edwin, William Alva; married second, Vera Foreman, June 22, 1921 (deceased, May 26, 1947); one daughter, Frances Foreman; married 3, Magdalen Ranney, April 16, 1951. Teacher public schools Texas and Louisiana, 1907-10; registrar A. and M. Coll. of Tex., 1912-24, dean of Sch. of Arts and Sciences, 1924-32; visiting prof. of edn., U. of Chicago, summers, 1930, 31; dean of Div. Science, Ia. State Coll., 1932-36, v.p., 1935-36, pres., Mar. 17, 1936—. Mem. Tex. Commn. on Accredited Schs., 1917-32; sec. Southwest Athletic Conf., 1925-32; sec. Assn. Tex. Colls., 1925-27, pres., 1928; chmn. Com. on Selection of Rhodes Scholars Tex., 1931, Ia., 1937-52, mem. of exec. com. Assn. Land Grant Colleges and Univs., 1933-43; member problems and plans com. American Council on Edn.; chmn. board of review North Central Assn. of Colleges and Secondary Schools (president 1942-43); chairman board of trustees Ia. State Coll. Agrl. Foundation. Member Survey Commission, U. of Illinois, 1942; College of City of New York, 1943. Vice president National Council Presbyn. Men, 1946-50. Fellow Iowa Acad. of Science; member American Association Coll. Registrars (pres. 1929; hon. life mem. 1933), Nat. Collegiate Athletic Assn. (mem. exec. council, 1928-32), Sigma Alpha Epsilon, Phi Kappa Phi, Phi Mu Alpha. Mem. ex officio Ia. State Fair Board and Ia. Geol. Survey. Democrat. Episcopalian. Mason (33°). Contbr.

articles on coll. adminstrn. Home: Brookhill, R.F.D. 3, Ames, Ia. Died July 11, 1958; buried Iowa State College Cemetery, Ames.

FRISCH, Martin, engring. exec.; b. Csebze, Hungary, Nov. 22, 1899; came to U.S., 1909, naturalized, 1917; student Washington U., 1917-19; B.S., U. Ill., 1921; m. Anita Laurence Barnard, Apr. 3, 1937. With Combustion Engring. Corp., N.Y. City, successively as field research engr., assit. mgr. service and erection dept. and mgr. field engring. dept., 1923-29; with Foster Wheeler Corp., N.Y. City, since 1929, successively chief engr. pulverizer div. chief engr. steam div., dir. engring. and dev., 1940-47, v.p. and chief engr., 1947-52, v.p., general mgr. equipment div. since 1953, dir. since 1948, member executive com. since 1944. Instr. mechanics and strength of materials U. Wis., 1922. Served as 2d lt. F.A., O.R.C., U.S. Army, World War I. Fellow Am. Soc. M.E. (boiler code com.); mem. Am. Soc. Naval Engrs., Am. Soc. Testing Materials, Pi Tau Sigma, Tau Beta Pi, Sigma Xi (asso.). Republican. Unitarian. Mason. Clubs: Lawyers, Engineers (N.Y. City). Numerous patents in pulverization, steam generation, combustion. Author articles and papers in tech. jours. Home: 65 Central Park W., N.Y. City 23. Office: 666 Fifth Av., N.Y.C. 19. Died June 16, 1959.

FRITSCH, Homer Charles, business exec.; b. Piqua, O., July 23, 1894; s. Charles and Mary Adeline (McMaken) F.; B.S., Ohio State, 1916; m. Myrl Ruth Beckwith, Oct. 4, 1924; children—Homer C., Thomas D. Chemist, Parke, Davis & Co., Detroit, Mich., 1916-17, vice pres. and gen. mgr. Parke, Davis & Co., 1942-51, exec. v.p. 1951—, dir. 1946—; dir. Takamine Lab. Inc., Pffeifer Bremey Co., Trenton Chemical Co. Commr., pres. pro tem, Village Grosse Pointe Park (Mich.) Commn., 1939—; became pres. Village Grosse Pointe Park, 1948; mayor City of Grosse Pointe Park, Dec. 1950—. Mem. bd. of visitors, Ohio State Univ. 1940-44. Served as mem. penicillin, streptomycin, pharm and biol. adv. coms. to War Prodn. Bd., mem. drug and chemical adv. com. Army and Navy Munitions Bd., World War II. Mem. Am. Pharmaceutical Assn., Am. Chem. Soc., Mich. Acad. of Sci., Detroit Engring. Soc., Phi Delta Chi. Republican. Presbyn. Mason. Clubs: Detroit, Detroit Boat, Univ., Det. Athletic (Det.); Chemists (N.Y. City). Home: 1009 Harvard Rd., Grosse Pointe 30, Mich. Office: care Parke, Davis & Co., Detroit 32. Died Apr. 8, 1957; buried Woodlawn Cemetery, Detroit.

FRITZ, John Henry Charles, clergyman; b. Martin's Ferry, O., July 30, 1874; s. John and Catherine (Kirchner) F.; student Concordia Coll., Fort Wayne, Ind., 1894; grad. Concordia Sem., St. Louis, Mo., 1897; D.D., Concordia Coll., Adelaide, Australia, 1930; m. Emilie Koerber, Dec. 29, 1898; children—Martha Esther (Mrs. Walter A. Baepler), Ruth Emilie (Mrs. Adolph R. Meyer), Henry Arthur Paul. Ordained Lutheran ministry, 1897; pastor at Bismarck and Pilot Knob, Mo., 1897-1901, Brooklyn, New York, 1901-14, Bethlehem Ch., St. Louis, 1914-20; dean Concordia Theol. Sem., 1920-40, now instr. homiletics. Pres. Western Dist. Evang. Luth Synod of Mo., Ohio and other states, 1919-20. Author: The Practical Missionary, 1919; Church Finances, 1922; Pastoral Theology, 1932; The Preachers Manual, 1941; Essentials of Preaching, 1948. Home: 6525 San Bonita, St. Louis. Died Apr. 12, 1953; buried New Bethlehem Lutheran Cemetery, St. Louis.

FRITZ, Oscar Marion, justice; b. Milw., Mar. 3, 1878; s. Theodore Herman and Dorathea (Glatz) F.; student Milw. Law Sch. (now Marquette U.), 1898-99; LL.B., U. Wis., 1901, LL.D., 1953; m. Ena B. Lorch, Aug. 30, 1902 (died Sept. 8, 1945); children—Marion Theodore, Norma Louise; m. 2d, Anna M. Millman, June 21, 1947. Admitted to Wis. bar, 1901, began practice at Milw.; mem. firm Kronshage, McGovern, Goff, Fritz & Hannan to 1912; judge Circuit Court, Milw., 1912-29; justice Supreme Court Wis., 1929—, chief justice, 1950—. Mem. Am., Wis., Chief Justice since January 1, 1950. Member American Milwaukee County bar assns. Home: 3404 N. Summit Av., Milw. Address: State Capitol, Madison, Wis. Died Oct. 5, 1957; buried Forest Home, Milw.

FROEDTERT, Kurtis R., grain and malt exec.; b. Milwaukee, June 3, 1887; s. William and Laura (Wagner) F.; ed. Mich. Mil. Acad.; m. Mary Helf, Jan. 3, 1926. Chmn. bd., pres. Froedtert Grain & Malting Co., Inc., since 1915; pres. Froedtert Enterprises, Inc.; dir. Wis. Meml. Park Co. Mem. City of Milwaukee Land Commn. Mem. Master Brewers Assn. Am. Mason (Shriner), Elk. Clubs: Wisconsin. Milwaukee Athletic. Home: 5200 N. Lake Dr., Whitefish Bay, Wis. Office: 3830 W. Grant St., Mil. Died Dec. 6, 1951; buried Wis. Meml. Park Company, Milw.

FROEHLINGER, Richard Anthony, corp. ofcl.; b. Balt., June 20, 1887; s. Joseph G. and Josepha M. (Hochhaus) F.; student parochial schs.; m. Elizabeth J. Waldhauser, Nov. 9, 1910; children—Barbara Elizabeth, Ruth Mary, Margaret Amelia, Marie Teresa, Richard Anthony, Mary Agnes. Clk. advancing to bookkeeper J. A. Manger Co., grain mchts., Balt., 1901-11; bookkeeper Furst-Clark Constrn. Co., Balt., 1911; successively bookkeeper, asst. treas., treas. Md. Dredging & Contracting Co., 1911-19; asst. treas. Arundel Corp. (formed by merger), Balt., 1919-22, treas., 1922-37, sec.-treas., 1937-40, exec. v.p., treas., 1940-41, pres., 1951—; v.p., treas. Md. Slag Co., 1941—; pres., treas. Arundel-Brooks Concrete Corp., 1941—. Democrat. Roman Catholic. Home: 117 St. Albans Way, Balt. 12. Office: Pier 2, Pratt St., Balt. 2. Died Sept. 8, 1955; buried Holy Redeemer Cemetery.

FROHRING, William Otto, dir. and spl. tech. consultant; b. Cleveland, July 1, 1893; s. William E. and Martha L. (Bliss) F.; Ohio State U., 1915; m. Gertrude Arvilla Lewis, 1916; children—Roger, Lloyd, Elaine, Glenn. Dir. labs. Telling-Belle Vernon Co., Cleveland, 1916-25; v.p. and gen. mgr. S.M.A. Corp., Cleveland, 1925-38, pres. and dir. research, 1938-42, chmn. bd., 1942-43; now dir. and spl. tech. consultant Am. Home Products Corp., N.Y. City; v.p. and dir. R. L. Frohring Machine Co.; chmn. bd. Lewis Machine Co. (merged with Curtis Mfg. Co.), 1954-55; dir. Curtis Mfg. Co.; pres. Bio-Medical Instrument Co.; chmn. Newbury Industries; research asso. in pediatrics Western Res. Sch. Med., 1946-50. Mem. A.A.A.S., Am. Chem. Soc., Soc. Am. Bacteriologists, Soc. Chemistry Industry, Dairy Science Assn., Biochemical Soc. of Gt. Britain. Home: Munn Rd., Newbury. Office: Route 87, Newbury, O. Died Sept. 11, 1959.

FROST, Frances, writer; b. St. Albans, Vt., Aug. 3, 1905; d. Amos and Susan (Keefe) Frost; student Middlebury Coll., 1923-26; Ph.B., U. of Vt., 1931; m. W. Gordon Blackburn, Apr. 4, 1926 (divorced 1931); children—Paul, Jean; m. 2d, Samuel Stoney, September 1933 (divorced). Began as reporter, 1927; instructor in creative poetry, U. of Vt., 1929-31. Author: (verse) Hemlock Wall, 1929; Blue Harvest, 1931; These Acres, 1932; Pool in the Meadow, 1933; Woman of This Earth, 1934; Innocent Summer (novel), 1936; Road to America (poems), 1937; Yoke of Stars (novel) 1939; Uncle Snowball (novel), 1940; Kate Trimingham (novel), 1940; Village of Glass (novel), 1942; Christmas in the Woods (poetry), 1942; Legend of the United Nations 1943; American Caravan, 1944; Mid-Century (poems), 1946; Windy Foot at the County Fair (juvenile), 1947; Christmas is Shaped Like Stars (poetry), 1948; The Little Whistler (children's poems), 1949; Maple Sugar for Windy Foot (juvenile), 1950; Then Came Timothy (juvenile), 1950; The Cat That Went to College (juvenile), 1951; Little Fox (juvenile), 1952; Rocket Away (juvenile), 1953; Star of Wonder, 1953; This Rowdy Heart (poems), 1954; Fireworks for Windy Foot (juvenile), 1956. Contbr. verse and fiction to New Yorker, Am. Mercury, Sat. Eve. Post, etc. Home: 79 Horatio St., N.Y.C. 14. Died Feb. 11, 1959.

FROST, Henry Atherton, univ. prof.; b. Newton, Mass., Feb. 8, 1883; s. William Atherton and Myra Ames (Tilton) F.; A.B., Harvard, 1905, M.Arch., 1918; m. Anna Partenheimer Lochman, June 28, 1911; children—William Atherton, Henry Atherton. Prof. architecture, Grad. School of Design, Harvard; chmn. dept. archtl. science, Harvard, now prof. emeritus; vis. prof. architecture Ohio U., 1950-51. Episcopalian. Club: Harvard Faculty. Home: Congress Apts., Athens, O. Died May 26, 1952; buried Mt. Auburn Cemetery, Cambridge, Mass.

FROST, Henry Weston, clergyman, author; b. Detroit, Jan. 7, 1858; s. Mahlon S. and Frances (Foster) F.; ed. Princeton; D.D., Westminster Coll., New Wilmington, Pa., 1922; m. Abbie Gridley Ellinwood, Sept. 12, 1883; children—Ellinwood Alden, Inglis Folger, Elisabeth Stirling, Hilda (Mrs. Charles Custer Rockafellow), Freda (Mrs. George H. Carey), Reginald Radcliffe, Folger Weston. In bus., Attica, N.Y., 1880-88; ordained ministry Presbyn. Ch., 1904: sec. China Inland Mission, 1889-93, home dir., 1893-19 Republican. Club: Ivy (Princeton). Author: Heart Songs, 1917; Men Who Prayed, 1914; Matthew 24 and the Revelation, 1924; Outline Bible Studies, 1925; Effective Praying, 1926; Little Sermons from the Pentateuch, 1928; Miraculous Healing. Home: 24 Hibben Rd., Princeton, N.J. Office: 237 School Lane, Germantown, Phila. 44. Died Jan. 8, 1945.

FROST, Joseph H., banker; b. San Antonio, Tex., Aug. 20, 1881; s. Thomas C. and Josephine (Houston) F.; grad. San Antonio Acad., 1898; B.S., Princeton, 1902; m. Eda Kampmann, Nov. 23, 1912 (died Dec. 1, 1918); children—Joseph Hardin, John II; m. 2d, Julia King Gleaves, Sept. 13, 1930. With Frost Nat. Bank, San Antonio, June 1902—, chmn. bd. 1949—; dir. Southwestern Life Ins. Co., San Antonio Belt & Terminal Railroad Company. Former mem. Federal Advisory Council, 11th Federal Reserve Dist. Bd. trustees, Trinity U. Elk. Club: San Antonio Country. Address: Frost National Bank, San Antonio, Texas. Died July 31, 1956.

FROST, William Dodge, bacteriologist; b. Lake City, Minn., Sept. 13, 1867; s. Benjamin Cutler and Lucy Jane (Dodge) F.; B.S., U. of Minn., 1893, M.S., 1894; Ph.D., U. of Wis., 1903; Dr. P.H., Harvard, 1913; m. Jessie H. C. Elwell, of Minneapolis, Jan. 1, 1895; children—Herbert Cutler (dec.), Russell Elwell, Theodore Dodge. Biologist in lab., Minn. State Bd. Health, 1894-95; asst. in bacteriology, 1895-98; instr., 1898-1902, asst. prof., 1902-07, asso. prof., 1907-15, prof. agrl. bacteriology, 1916-38, U. of Wis. Trustee Congl. Sum. Assembly, Frankfort, Mich. Fellow A.A.A.S., Am. Pub. Health Assn.; associate fellow A.M.A.; member American Association Medical Milk Commissions (pres.), Society American Bacteriologists, Nat. Soc. Study and Prevention Tuberculosis, Wis. Anti-Tuberculosis Assn. (dir.), Madison Anti-Tuberculosis Assn. (dir.), Wis. Acad. Sciences, Royal Inst. Pub. Health (London), Sigma Xi, Alpha Zeta, Farm House; life mem. Am. Missionary Assn. Pres. The Morningside Sanatorium. Author: Laboratory Guide in General Bacteriology, 1901; General Bacteriology (with E. G. McCampbell), 1911; The streptococci (with Mildred A. Englebrecht), 1940; also collaborator, Marshall's Microbiology. Originator of "cellular test" for pasteurized milk and "little plate" method of counting bacteria in milk. Contbr. tech. jours. on bacteriology, especially the hemolytic streptococci of milk. Address: 1010 Grant St., Madison, Wis. Died Jan. 25, 1957; buried Forest Hill Cemetery, Madison.

FROTHINGHAM, Channing, physician; b. Bklyn., May 10, 1881; s. Channing and Elizabeth (Gerrish) F.; prep. edn., Poly. Prep. Sch., Bklyn.; A.B., Harvard, 1902, M.D., 1906; m. Clara Morgan Rotch, 1907; children—Channing, Mary Eliot, Joseph Rotch, Timothy Gerrish (dec.), William Rotch, Virginia, Thomas Eliot. Began practice at Boston, 1907; mem. faculty of Harvard Med. Sch. in different capacities, 1908-33; physician to Peter Bent Brigham Hosp., 1912-33, cons. physician since 1933; physician in chief Faulkner Hosp., 1933-46, cons. physician 1946—. 1st lt.-lt. col., Med. R. C., 1917-18. Trustee Boston Psychopathic Hosp.; overseer Harvard Coll., term, 1936-42. Chmn. Com. of Physicians for Improvement of Med. Care, Inc., 1941-47; chmn. Com. for the Nation's Health. Mem. Assn. Am. Physicians, Mass. Med. Soc. (pres. 1937, 38). Clubs: Tavern, Tennis and Racquet (Boston); Country (Brookline, Mass.). Home: 186 Reservoir Rd., Brookline, Mass. Office: 275 Charles St., Boston. Died Aug. 11, 1959.

FROTHINGHAM, Theodore Longfellow, lawyer; b. Bklyn., Sept. 10, 1863; s. James Harding and Wilhelmine Edith (Vietor) F.; A B., Harvard, 1884, LL.B., 1887; m. Elizabeth F. Mason, Dec. 2, 1901 (died Jan. 22, 1937); children—Theodore, Elizabeth. Admitted to N.Y. bar, 1887; clk. law office Evarts, Choate & Beaman, 1886-92, Seward Guthrie & Morawetz, 1892-93; practiced alone, 1893-98, 08-35; mem. firm Steele, DeFriese & Frothingham, 1899-1907; now retired, 1935. Former trustee Bklyn. Hosp., Polytechnic Inst. Bklyn., Bklyn. Pub. Library, others. Mem. Assn. Bar City of N.Y., N.E. Soc., L.I. Hist. Soc., N.E. Historic Geneal. Soc., Phi Beta Kappa. Unitarian. Club: Century. Home: (summer) Bass River, Cape Cod, Mass. Died Feb. 8, 1951; buried South Yarmouth, Mass.

FROTHINGHAM, Thomas Goddard, author; b. Boston, July 9, 1865; s. Thomas Goddard and Frances Adeline (Cook) F.; grad. Boston Latin Sch., 1883; hon. A.M., 1930; m. Eleanor Felton Whiting, Dec. 30, 1903; 1 dau., Eleanor. Trustee estates. Capt. U.S.A., World War, now capt. U.S.R. Pres. Bunker Hill Monument Assn. Mem. Copley Soc. (pres.), Bostonian Soc. (librarian), Soc. Preservation N.E. Antiquities, Mil. Hist. Soc. Mass., Mass. Hist. Soc., U.S. Naval Inst., Zeta Psi. Clubs: St. Botolph, Boston Athletic, Eastern Yacht, Myopia Hunt. Author: A Guide to the Military History of the World War, 1914-18, 1920; A True Account of the Battle of Jutland, 1920; The Crisis of the Civil War—Antietam (monograph), 1922; The Naval History of the World War—Offensive Operations, 1914-1915, 1924; The Naval History of the World War—The Stress of Sea Power, 1915-1916, 1925; The Naval History of the World War—The United States in the War, 1917-1918, 1926; The American Reinforcement in the World War, 1927; George Washington, The American Commander in Chief, 1930. Home: 74 Chestnut St. Office: 18 Tremont St., Boston. Died Mar. 17, 1945; buried Mt. Auburn Cemetery, Cambridge, Mass.

FRUEAUFF, Harry Day, petroleum exec.; b. Columbia, Pa., Aug. 15, 1875; s. John F. and Annie Day (Taggart) F.; ed. pub. schs.; m. Lena Russell, July 20, 1914. Started in book and stationery bus., 1894; with Pueblo Gas & Fuel Co., 1907-12; salesman, sec., then v.p., gen. mgr. with City Light & Traction Co., Sedalia, Mo., 1912-16; Montgomery (Ala.) Light & Water Power Co.; Oil Marketing and Refining Div., N.Y.C., 1917-51, ret. Pres. Charles A. Frueauff Found. Mem. Doherty Men's Frat. Club: Advertising (N.Y.). Home: 12 E. 86th St., N.Y.C. Office: 70 Pine St., N.Y.C. 5. Died Mar. 1959.

FRY, Clements Collard, physician; b. Jersey City, Nov. 15, 1892; s. Edward and Susan (Norman) F.; B.S., Mich. State Coll., 1917; M.D., Northwestern, 1923. Intern Lsvl. City Hosp., 1923-24; intern, asst. med. officer, resident Boston Psychopathic Hosp., 1924-26; asst. psychiatry, med. sch. Harvard, 1925-26; clin. instr. mental hygiene and psychiatry Yale, 1926-29, instr., 1929-30, asst. prof., 1930-34, asso. prof., 1934-40, lectr. psychiatry and mental hygiene since 1940, psychiatrist div. student mental hygiene, dept. univ. health since 1926; asso. psychiatrist New Haven Hosp., New Haven Dispensary. Med. cons. to Lend-Lease Adminstrn., 1942-43; prin. investigator union OSRD contract Nat. Research Council, 1943-47, prin. investigator under Med. Research and Development Bd., Dept. of Army, 1947. Mem. A.M.A., Conn. State, New Haven Co. med. socs., Am. Psychiat. Assn., Am. Orthopsychiat. Assn., Am. Psychosomatic Soc., Am. Group Psychotherapy Assn., Inc., A.A.A.S., Nu Sigma Nu, Psi Upsilon. Clubs: Beaumont Med., Yale (N.Y.C.); Book and Snake, Graduate (New Haven). Author: The Anatomy of Personality (with Howard W. Haggard), 1936; Mental Health in College (with Edna G. Rostow), 1942. Home: 1253 Trumbull Coll., New Haven. Died Nov. 24, 1955.

FRY, Harry Shipley, prof. chemistry; b. Cincinnati, Oct. 24, 1878; s. Harry Oliver and Emma Elizabeth (Richards) F.; B.A., U. of Cincinnati, 1901, M.A., 1902, Ph.D., 1905; m. Corinne Angele Lacroix, June 16, 1904; 1 son, Harry Lacroix (M.D.). With faculty Univ. of Cincinnati since 1901, professor and head department of chemistry since 1918. Professor emeritus 1945. Former mem. Nat. Research Council (div. chemistry and chemical technology), Nederlandsche Chemische Vereeniging, Nat. Inst. of Social Sciences. Fellow A.A.A.S.; mem. Am. Chem. Soc., Sigma Xi, Phi Lambda Upsilon. Protestant. Author: The Electronic Conception of Valence and the Constitution of Benzene, 1921. Contbr. many articles in Am. and foreign tech. publs. First to propose and apply the term "electromer" and "electronic tautomerism" as fundamental concepts in the development of the electronic conception of valence and explanation of chem. reactions of compounds of carbon. Home: 6371 Grand Vista Av., Cincinnati. Died May 18, 1949; buried Spring Grove Cemetery, Cincinnati.

FRY, William Wallace, lawyer; b. Mexico, Mo., Aug. 22, 1886; s. William Wallace and Annette (Bourne) F.; grad. Mo. Mil. Acad., 1903; LL.B., U. of Mo., 1909; m. Velma Johnson, Oct. 19, 1912. Admitted to Mo. bar, 1909, and since practiced in Mexico, Mo.; mem. firm Fry, Edwards & Wright; mem. bd. dirs. Mexico Savings Bank. Mem. State Bd. Law Examiners, 1930-46. Served as 1st lt. Army Service Corps, United States Army, 1918. Trustee Law School Foundation, University of Missouri. Member board curators, Lincoln (Mo.) University, 1939-42. Member Am. Bar Assn. (mem. house of dels., 1938-42), Mo. Bar Assn. (pres. 1937-38; mem. bd. govs., 1944-46), Am. Counsel Assn. (pres. 1953-54), Am. Judicature Soc., Am. Law Inst., 1940-46, Am. Legion, Forty and Eight, S.A.R., Order of the Coif, Phi Delta Phi, Sigma Nu. Democrat. Methodist. Clubs: Rotary, Mexico, Country (Mexico, Mo.); University (St. Louis, Mo.). Home: 3 Elm Tree Dr. Office: 123 E. Jackson St., Mexico, Mo. Died Nov. 23, 1953; buried East Lawn Meml. Park, Mexico, Mo.

FRYE, Jack, business exec.; m. Nevada Smith, July 21, 1950; 1 dau., Lili Nevajac. Partner Burdett Flying Sch., 1923-24; pres. Aero Corp. of Cal., 1926-30; pres. Standard Air Lines, 1928-29; v.p. charge of operations Western Air Express Corp., 1930; v.p. operations Transcontinental & Western Air, Inc., Kansas City, Mo., 1930-34, pres., 1934-47; pres. Gen. Aniline & Film Corp., 1947-55; pres., chmn. bd. The Frye Corp., 1955—; mem. bd. dirs. Maryland Casualty Co. Decorated Medal for Merit; Grand Officer Crown of Italy. Fellow Inst. Aero Sciences. Clubs: Family (San Francisco); California (Los Angeles); Cloud, Wings, Sleepy Hollow Country (New York); Army and Navy (Washington); Conquistadores del Cielo. Home: 306 N. Alvernon St., Tucson. Office: 617 Texas St., Ft. Worth. Died Feb. 1959.

FRYE, Newton Phillips, corp. exec.; b. Chicago, June 24, 1894; s. Charles S. and Sadie Ellen (Brown) F.; student pub. schs. of Chicago; m. Esther Frances Ennis, Nov. 10, 1917; children—Newton Phillips, Marilyn Frye Barrett. Former mgr. financial dept. Chicago Daily News; vice pres. P. W. Chapman & Co., Chicago, Minton, Lampert & Co., Fed. Securities Corp. and Central-Ill. Co.; now chmn., dir. Central Republic Co., Chgo.; pres., dir. Midwest United Investors, Inc.; dir. Insurance Exchange Building Corp., Dodge Mfg. Co., Seabrooke Farms Corp., Booth Fisheries Corp. Clubs: Tyron (N.C.) Country; Chicago, Bond (Chgo.); Exmoor Country (Highland Park, Ill.); Recess (N.Y.C.). Home: 430 Oakdale Av., Glencoe, Ill. Office: 209 S. La Salle St., Chgo. Died May, 1957.

FRYE, William Clinton, industrialist; b. Milwaukee, Wis., Aug. 21, 1877; s. Oscar Bell and Emma (Sivyer) F.; married Elsie Dyer, April 22, 1908; children—Stephen, Mary (Mrs. J. S. Owen). Clerk Chain Belt Co., Milwaukee, 1895-1923, pres. 1916-23, resigned, 1923, now dir. and mem. exec. com. Dir. various cos. Chmn. bd. Boy Scouts, Milwaukee Found.; dir. Rogers Memorial Found., Milw. Children's Hosp.; trustee Milw. Downer Coll. Adv. bd. Milw. Art Inst.; mem. sr. council Wis. Anti-Tuberculosis Assn.; mem. adv. com. Milw. Children's Hosp. Republican. Episcopalian. Clubs: Milwaukee, University (Milw.); Chicago (Chgo.); Oconomowoc Golf (Oconomowoc, Wis.). Home: 2655 N. Lake Dr., Milwaukee 11, Wis. Died Nov. 15, 1954; buried Forest Home Cemetery, Milw.

FUERST, P. Placidus, clergyman; b. Bremen, Germany, June 8, 1868; s. Phil. F.; grad. Mt. Angel Coll., Ore., 1890. Mem. Order of Benedictine Fathers, Order Maryknoll Missioners; ordained 1891; elected abbot of Mt. Angel Abbey, and pres. Mt. Angel Coll., 1910, resigned, 1921, did parish work, 1921-38; composer of popular sacred music; rector Mt. Angel Coll., prof. music, physics and chemistry. Address: Mt. Angel Abbey, St. Benedict, Ore. Died Aug. 16, 1940; buried Cemetery of Mount Angel Abbey, St. Benedict, Ore.

FULCHER, Paul Milton, educator; b. Eureka, Ill., Nov. 10, 1895; s. George Alfred and Joan Antoinette (Palmer) F.; A.B., W.Va. U., 1916; A.M., Harvard, 1917; studied Oxford U., Eng., 1 term, 1919, U. of Mo., 1920; Ph.D., U. of Wis., 1925; married Louise Dwyer, February 9, 1929 (deceased January 18, 1949). Instructor in English, University of Missouri, 1919-20; instr. in English, U. of Wis., 1920-25, asst. professor, 1925-30, associate professor, 1930-43; professor since 1943. Ambulance driver with American Field Service, in France, 1917-19. Awarded Croix de Guerre (France). Member Modern Language Association America, Phi Beta Kappa (honor society). Presbyterian. Author: Guests of Summer (novel), 1930. Compiler: Foundations of English Style, 1927; Descriptive Passages, 1928; Short Narratives, 1928. Editor: Wuthering Heights (by Emily Brontë), 1929; Literary Masters of England (with Bushnell and Taylor), 1936, rev. edition, 1950. Contbr. to mags. Home: 6008 Winnequah Rd., Madison 4, Wis. Died Jan. 1958.

FULLAM, James Edson, ret. communications exec.; b. Brookfield, Vt., May 9, 1890; s. Frank Nelson and Frances Emma (Blakebrough) F.; B.S., U. Vt., 1911, M.E., 1922; M.B.A., N.Y.U., 1921; m. Ruth Chester Tyler, June 5, 1923; 1 dau., Margaret Louise. Engr. N.Y. Telephone Co., 1911-16, 19-21; sales mgr. Bell Telephone Securities Co., 1922; v.p. Internat. Tel. & Tel. Securities Corp., 1923-30; treas. Internat. Tel. & Tel. Corp., 1930-33, v.p., 1934-48, retired; v.p. Internat. Standard Electric Corp., 1931—; chmn. bd. Shanghai (China) Telephone Co.; vice chmn. bd. China Electric Co. Served with U.S. Army; pvt. 1916-17, capt. to maj. ordnance, 1917-19; lt. col. Ordnance Res., 1928-33. Mem. exec. com. China Am. Council of Commerce and Industry; dir. China Soc.; mem. China com. Nat. Fgn. Trade Council. Mem. Am. Asiatic Assn. (exec. com.), Phi Delta Theta, Phi Beta Kappa. Club: Broad Street (N.Y.C.). Home: Newtown, Conn. Office: 67 Broad St., N.Y.C. 4. Died Feb. 21, 1951.

FULLER, Alfred Howard, business exec.; b. Hartford, Conn., Mar. 27, 1913; s. Alfred Carl and Evelyn W. (Ells) F.; student Kingswood Sch., Duke, Harvard, m. Dora Baker, June 24, 1936; children—Alfred Carl, II, Cynthia, Daphne. Began as dealer; with The Fuller Brush Co., 1936—, elected v.p., dir., 1937; pres., 1943—. Mem. Sigma Mu. Republican. Clubs: Hartford, Yacht (N.Y.C.); Hartford, Wampanoag Country; Larchmont (N.Y.) Yacht; Essex (Conn.) Yacht; Seawanhaka-Corinthian Yacht; Cat Cay (Bahamas). Home: Hunter Dr., West Hartford, Conn. Office: 3580 Main St., Hartford, Conn. Died May 9, 1959; buried Fairview Cemetery, West Hartford.

FULLER, Alvin Tufts, ex-gov. Mass.; b. Boston, Feb. 27, 1878; s. Alvan Bond and Flora A. (Tufts) F.; student pub. schs.; L.L.D., Boston U., Tufts Coll., Holy Cross Coll., Bates Coll., Boston Coll.; m. Viola Davenport, July 12, 1910: children—Lydia (Mrs. George T. Bottomley), Mary (Mrs. Robert L. Henderson), Alvan Tufts, Peter Davenport. Owner Cadillac-Oldsmobile Co., Boston. Mem. Mass. Ho. of Reps., 1915; del. Rep. Nat. Conv., Chgo., 1916; mem. 65th and 66th Congresses, 9th Mass. Dist., resigned; lt. gov., Mass., 1921-25, gov. 2 terms, 1925-29. Trustee Boston Mus. Fine Arts, Boston U., Newton Theol. Instn., N.E. Conservatory Music, Boston Symphony Orchestra. Baptist. Odd Fellow, Mason (33°), Elk, K. of P. Clubs: Algonquin, Union Boat, Essex County, Brookline Country. Home: 150 Beacon St. Address: 808 Commonwealth Av., Boston. Died Apr. 30, 1958.

FULLER, Ellis Adams, clergyman, sem. pres.; b. Cross Hill, S.C., April 1, 1891; s. John Rhett and Ida Lee (Adams) F.; A.B. Presbyn. Coll. S.C., Clinton, 1912, D.D. 1924; Th.M., So. Bapt. Theol. Sem., 1921, post-grad work, 1 yr.; m. Elizabeth West Bates, Dec. 17, 1925; children—Ellis Adams, Sara Elizabeth (Mrs. James M. Miller), Ida Lee (Mrs. Terry G. Waddle). Ordained to Bapt. ministry; pastor Greenwood, S.C., 1922-24, Greenville, S.C., 1924-25; gen. supt. evangelistic work (17 states and D.C.), So. Bapt. Conv., 1925-28; pastor First Ch., Atlanta, Ga., 1928-42; pres. Southern Bapt. Theol. Sem., Louisville, 1942—. Pres. Bapt. Home Mission Bd. of Southern Bapt. Conv., 1928-42; chmn. Ga. Bapt. Hosp. Commn., 1938-42; pres. Ga. Bapt. Conv., 1939-42; chmn. exec. com., 1940-42. Mem. exec. com. Bapt. World Alliance. Democrat. Mason, Rotarian. Home: 1042 Alta Vista Rd. Office: Southern Baptist Theological Seminary, 2825 Lexington Rd., Louisville. Died Oct. 28, 1950; buried Cave Hill Cemetery, Louisville.

FULLER, Frank Lanneau, lawyer; b. Fayetteville, N.C., Jan. 14, 1868; s. Thomas C. and Caroline Douglas (Whitehead) F.; student Horner Mil. Acad., Oxford, N.C.; Davidson (N.C.) Coll., 1885-1887; studied law in Law Sch. of Col. Geo. N. Falk, Cilley, N.C.; m. Lillian Arnold Day, N.C., Nov. 23, 1892. Practiced in Durham, N.C., 1889-1911; was mem. Fuller & Fuller, later Winston & Fuller, then Fuller & Fuller, again; counsel Liggett & Myers Tobacco Co., 1911-41, ret. Mem. N.C. Ho. of Rep., 1893. Mem. Assn. Bar City N.Y., So. Soc., N.C. Soc., Kappa Alpha. Democrat. Presbyn. Clubs: Metropolitan, Hudson River Country. Home: 290 Park Av., N.Y.C. Died Sept. 1952.

FULLER, Frank Manly, physician; b. Keokuk, Ia., Sept. 29, 1868; s. Euclid Erastus and Cecilia (Gerard) F.; A.B., Parsons Coll., Fairfield, Ia., 1888, A.M., 1891; M.D., Keokuk Med. Coll., 1897; grad. study Met. Schs. Medicine, London, Eng., 1898; Allgemeine Krankenhaus und Policlinic, Vienna, Austria, 1901; m. Anna M. Ballinger, Sept. 2, 1897 (died 1908); children—Frank Lapsley, Madison Ballinger, John Davis; m. 2d, Caroline T. Davis, Nov. 15, 1911. Began practice at Keokuk, 1897; prof. clin. diseases of children, Keokuk Med. Coll., 1897-1908; chief staff, St. Joseph's Hosp., Keokuk, 1914-27; sec. Ia. State Bd. Med. Examiners, 1924-38, pres., 1938-41; ret. Served as 1st lt., Ia. Nat. Guard, 1889-97; capt., M.C., U.S. Army, in France, 1917-19. Mem. city council, Keokuk, 2 terms. Pres., physician Bd. Keokuk. Pres. Fedn. Med. State Examining Bds. U.S., 1943—, v.p., 1939-40, mem. bd. dirs., 1940-42. Fellow A.C.P.; mem. A.M.A., Ia. State (pres. 1925), S. Eastern Ia. (ex-pres.), Lee County (ex-pres.) med. socs., Ia. Clin. Med. Soc. (pres. 1923), Interstate Post Grad. Assembly (ex-v.p.). Republican. Presbyn. Mason. Elk. Clubs: Keokuk, Keokuk Country. Home: 217 High St., Keokuk, Ia. Died 1946.

FULLER, Harold deWolf, found. exec.; b. S.I., N.Y., Oct. 11, 1874; s. of Ralzamon Jesse and Belle (deWolf) F.; A.B., Harvard, 1898, A.M., 1900, Ph.D., 1902; traveling fellow, 1902-04, Germany, France, England, and Holland; m. Carla Graham, on October 18, 1911 (died March 1955). Instructor in English and comparative literature at Harvard, 1904-10; asst. editor The Nation, 1911-13, and editor, 1914-17. Joint-editor (with Fabian Franklin) of The Review (polit. weekly), from May 1919, which after acquisition, Oct. 1921, of The Independent, was known as The Independent and The Weekly Review, sole editor, 1922-24 (retired); editor "New York" (weekly), 1927-1930; professor journalism, New York University, 1926-33; executive director Netherland-Am. Found. since 1935, v.p. since 1944; regular contbr., on staff Think mag. since 1938. Officer Order of Orange-Nassau. Clubs: Century, Authors. Author: The Sources of Titus Andronicus, 1901; Romeo and Juliette, 1905; Beatrice (a metrical transl. of a Dutch legend), 1909; Lyric Poetry, 1926; Opportunities for College Editors, 1927; Loose Ends of Truth, 1930. Contbr. article on Oliver Wendell Holmes in Am. Writers on Am. Lit., 1931. Home: 3 East 63d St., N.Y.C. 21. Office: 590 Madison Av., N.Y.C. 22. Died May 2, 1957.

FULLER, Henry Jones, manufacturer; b. St. Johnsbury, Vt., Dec. 12, 1873; s. Homer Taylor and Etta (Jones) F.; prep. education Worcester Academy; B.S. in M.E., Worcester Poly. Inst., 1895; m. Nancy Archibald, Feb. 19, 1902; children—John Archibald, Elinor Constance, Mary Leslie, Engineer E. & T. Fairbanks & Co., St. Johnsbury, 1895-97; mgr. The Fairbanks Co., Montreal, 1897-1905; pres. Canadian Fairbanks, Morse Co., Ltd., 1905; v.p. Fairbanks, Morse & Co., 1913; pres. E. & T. Fairbanks & Co., 1917; chmn. bd. Gorham Co., Gorham Mfg. Co. Alvin Corp.; director Iowa Public Service Company, Remington Rand, Ltd., Canada Cement Co., Ltd., Canadian-Ingersoll Rand Co., Black, Starr & Gorham, Inc., Page Hersey Tubes, Limited, Remington Rand, Inc., Savage Arms Corp., Pittston Co., Clinchfield Coal Co., Davis Coal & Coke Co., Cuno Engring. Corp.; mem. adv. bd. Chase Nat. Bank, N.Y.C. Mem. bd. trustees Worcester Poly. Inst., St. Johnsbury Acad., Grand Central Art Galleries. Member Phi Gamma Delta. Republican. Presbyterian. Clubs: University, Piping Rock, Blind Brook, Richmond County Country, Fishers Island Club; Hope (Providence, R. I.); Uptown Club (New York); Mont Royal (Montreal, Can.). Home: 1035 5th Av., New York; (country) Fishers Island, N.Y. Office: 60 E. 42d St., N.Y. C. 17. Died Apr. 21, 1956; buried Mount Royal Cemetery, Montreal, Can.

FULLER, Margaret, author; b. Brooklyn, N.Y., d. Capt. James Ebenezer and Rebecca Phillis (Hope) F. Author: A New England Childhood, 1916; One World at a Time, 1922-23; Alma, 1927; Her Son, 1929; The Golden Roof, 1930; The Complete History of the Deluge, 1936; It is All So Simple, 1947; This Awakening, 1948; Sonnets and Songs, published in 1955. Contributor Poet Lore, also others. Republican Episcopalian. Home: 1 Canterbury Rd., Norwich Town,

Conn. Died Feb. 1, 1954; buried Yantic Cemetery, Norwich, Conn.

FULLER, Warner, lawyer, railroad exec.; b. Clinton, Ia., Aug. 12, 1901; s. George Raymond and Florence Mary (Warner) F.; B.S., U. Ore., 1924; LL.B., Yale, 1927; m. Florence Buck, Sept. 1, 1928. Research asst. Yale Law Sch., 1927-28; admitted to Cal. bar, 1929; asso. law firm McCutcheon, Olney, Mannon & Greene, San Francisco, 1928-32; asst. prof. law Duke, 1932-36; prof. law Washington U., St. Louis, 1936-45, acting dean law sch., 1942-44, dean, 1944-45; v.p., gen. counsel Terminal R.R. Assn. of St. Louis, 1945—. Spl. cons. Fed. Coordinator of Transportation, 1934-36; compliance commr. St. Louis area, WPB, 1942-45; pub. rep. St. Louis area, War Labor Bd., 1943-45; dir. U.S.O. Council of St. Louis, 1951—; commr. Bryan Mullanphy Emigrant and Travelers Relief Fund 1946-52; mem. bd. mgrs. St. Louis R.R. YMCA, 1947—. Mem. Am., Ore., Cal., Mo., St. Louis (chmn. com. legal edn. 1949-52) bar assns., Family Service Soc. of St. Louis County (pres. 1946-48, dir. 1943-48), Social Planning Council of St. Louis and St. Louis County (chmn. exec. com., family and children div., also dir. 1949-51), Order of Coif, Delta Tau Delta, Delta Theta Phi, Omicron Delta Kappa. Clubs: Contemporary, Noonday (St. Louis). Editor: Symposium on Three Years of the Securities Act, Jan. and Apr. 1937 issues Law and Contemporary Problems. Co-draftsman Amended Railroad Bankruptcy Statute of 1935 (sect. 77). Contbr. profl. jours. Home: Conway Rd., east of Woods Mill Rd., Box 138, Route 1, Creve Coeur, Mo. Office: Union Station, St. Louis 3. Died June 11, 1957.

FULLER, Wiley Madison, govt. ofcl.; b. Hillsboro, Tex., Feb. 13, 1890; s. Wiley Madison and Eva Montgomery (Carter) F.; student U. Tex., 1910-11; 1912-13; LL.B., George Washington U., 1920; m. Willie O'Neal Brown, Dec. 3, 1917; 1 dau., Elizabeth Carter. Stenographer Civil Service System, Washington, 1916; various clerical adminstrv. positions Treasury Dept., 1919-27, legal staff div. loans and currency, 1927-34, atty. in charge staff, 1934-42, atty. in charge legal staff Chgo. br. Bur. Public Debt, 1942-52, chief counsel, Washington, 1952—; admitted to D.C. bar, 1920, mem. Campana, Fuller & Turner, 1924-25. Charter mem. Arlington Hosp. Assn., treas., 1938-39. Served as 1st lt. 130th F.A., 35th div., U.S. Army, 1917-19. Mem. Am. Legion, Fed. Bar Assn. Home: 626 S. Adams St., Arlington 4, Va. Office: Treasury Dept., Washington 25. Died Sept. 29, 1954; buried Arlington Nat. Cemetery.

FULLERTON, Charles Alexander, music tchr.; b. Manchester, N.H., Oct. 11, 1861; s. Neil and Mary (Kerr) F.; B.S., Ia. State Normal Sch., 1890; M. Mus., Chgo. Mus. Coll., 1931; m. Alma Estelle Gray, June 23, 1897; children—Roderick Craig, Ruth Jeanette (dec.), Margaret Gray, Craig Kerr. With Ia. State Tchrs. College, 1897—, emeritus prof. music, doing part time service in Extension Div. 1934—, formerly head dept. music; made spl. study of democracy in music edn. for over 40 yrs.; developed system known as the "Choir Plan," which brings music as an art directly to children daily by phonograph as means of standardizing the singing of each individual. Founding mem. Music Educators Nat. Conf., pres., 1912. Conglist. Compiler: Choice Songs, 1900; Glee Club Songs, 1906; New Song Book and Music Reader, 1910; A One Book Course in Elementary Music and Selected Songs for Schools, 1925; New Elementary Music, 1936; Together We Sing, 1950. Home: Cedar Falls, Ia. Died Dec. 14, 1945; buried Cedar Falls.

FULMER, Ellis Ingham, professor physical chemistry; b. Gibbon, Neb., Apr. 12, 1891; s. Clark Adelbert and Evalena Anna (Ingham) F.; A.B., Neb. Wesleyan U., 1912; A.M., U. of Neb., 1913; grad. study, U. of Pa., 1913-14; Ph.D., University of Toronto, 1919; D.Sc., Nebraska Wesleyan University, 1944; m. Ruth Emma Files, June 15, 1915 children—Norman Clark, Robert Ellery. Chemist Agr. Expt. Sta., U. of Neb., summers 1913-14; in charge chemistry dept., Leander Clark Coll., Toledo, Ia., 1914-15; same, Friend's U., Wichita, Kan., 1915-16; chemist, Aetna Explosives Co., 1917; chemist, expt. farms, Ottawa, Can., 1918; asst. prof. biophysical chemistry, Ia. State Coll. Agr. and Mechanic Arts, 1919-20, asso. prof., 1920-23, prof., 1923—, asst. to dir. Inst. Atomic Research, 1947—. Fellow A.A.A.S., mem. Am. Chem. Soc., Sigma Xi, Phi Kappa Phi, Gamma Sigma Delta, Phi Lambda Upsilon, Alpha Chi Sigma, Theta Chi. Conglist. Home: 2060 Cessna St., Ames, Ia. Died Feb. 10, 1953.

FULTON, Chester Alan, mining engr.; b. Brooklyn, December 18, 1883; s. Charles Alexander and Anne (McGinness) F.; Engr. of Mines, Columbia U., 1906; m. Ethel Belle Pagan, Jan. 20, 1909; children—John Charles, Ethel Bette (Mrs. Arthur Morris Nelson). Assayer, Standard Smelting Co., Rapid City, S.D., 1906; shift boss, Cyanide plant, Peregrina M. & M. Co., Guanajuato, Mex., 1907; mine supt., Guanajuato M. & M. Co., Guanajuato, Mex., 1908-12; professional work in Mexico. Central Am., U.S., 1912-14; supt. Lo Increible Mine, Venezuela, 1914-16; professional work in Cuba, 1916-18; mgr. Davison Sulphur Co., Cienfuegos, Cuba, 1918-21; cons. engr., Davison Chemical Co., Baltimore, Md., 1921-28; v.p. Southern Phosphate Corp., Baltimore, Md., 1928-32, president 1932-45, director and president (1944). Am. Inst. Mining and Metallurgical Engrs., Theta Delta Chi. Clubs: Baltimore Country (Baltimore); Columbia University, Engineers, Mining (New York). Mason. Home: 302 Somerset Rd., Baltimore 10. Office: 10 E. 40th St., N.Y.C. 16. Died Aug. 16, 1951; buried Yonkers, N.Y.

FULTON, James A., ins. exec.; b. Dover, Del., Aug. 18, 1889; s. Cecil C., and Anna (Meredith) F.; LL.B., U. Md.; m. Helen Siessen, Aug. 18, 1944; 1 dau., Meredith Anne. Admitted to bar, Del., Md. Formerly v.p. Continental Am. Life Ins. Co., Wilmington, Del.; supt. Agencies Home Life Ins. Co., N.Y.C., 1927, agy. v.p., 1928, pres., dir., 1929—; dir. Seaman's Bank for Savings, Corn Exchange Bank Trust Co. Clubs: Union, Metropolitan, Merchants, Down Town Assn. Home: One Fifth Av. Office: 253 Broadway, N.Y.C. Died Sept. 21, 1950.

FULTON, Kerwin Holmes, advt. exec.; b. Truro, N.S., Can., Mar. 17, 1885; s. Suther Brown and Mary Elizabeth (Vance) F.; ed. pub. schs., Nova Scotia; m. Harriet E. Van Hoff, Jan. 26, 1910. Began with Van Beuren Billposting Co., 1902, v.p. and gen. mgr., 1913-17; pres. Van Beuren & N.Y. Billposting Co., 1917-26; pres. Poster Advertising Co., 1917-26; pres. O. J. Gude Co., 1919-31; pres. Gen. Outdoor Advt. Co., 1925-31 (now dir.); pres. and dir. Outdoor Advertising Incorporated, 1931-55, chairman and chief executive officer, 1955—; trustee Kings County Trust Co.; mem. adv. bd. Fifth Av. Br., Chem. Bank & Trust Co.; former sec.-treas., dir. Traffic Audit Bur., Inc., N.Y.; dir. The Advt. Council, Inc., N.Y. Former dir. Outdoor Advt. Assn. Am., and U.S. C. of C. Presbyn. Clubs: Uptown, Advertising, Deepdale (Great Neck, L.I.); Camp Fire of America, Canadian of N.Y.; Recess (Detroit). Home: 1 W. 81st St. N.Y.C. 24. Office: 60 E. 42d St., N.Y.C. 17. Died Dec. 10, 1955.

FULTON, Samuel Alexander, business exec.; b. Clay County, Ill., Nov. 13, 1877; s. James Mackey and Jane Walker (Patton) F.; student Gem City Business College, Quincy, Illinois, 1901-02; LL.D., (hon.) Monmouth College, 1948; m. Luella McChesney, Sept. 19, 1906 (deceased Mar. 1952); m. 2d, Gladys Western Swartz, Dec. 2, 1952; 1 step-dau., Donna Swartz Burke. Traveling salesman, Iowa Soap Co., 1903-10; retail dept. store business, 1910-13; established The Fulton Co., Marshalltown, Ia., 1913. Chmn. Building Fund for Gideons headquarters bldg., 1927; mem. Gideons (pres., v.p., trustee, chaplain, treas.; served on cabinet 29 yrs.). Mem. West Allis Vocational and Adult Edn. School Bd., also mem. senate, Monmouth Coll., Ill. Republican. Mem. United Presbyn. Ch. N. Am. Moderator, Gen. Assembly United Presbyn. Ch. of North America. Address: 7325 Maple Terrace, Wauwatosa, Wis. Died Jan 2, 1954; buried Highland Meml. Cemetery.

FULTON, Walter Scott, ret. army officer; b. Lyndoch, Ont., Can., Mar. 23, 1879; s. James and Jennie (Grey) F.; brought to U.S., 1880; B.S., U.S. Mil. Acad., 1904; grad. Command and Gen. Staff Sch., 1925, Army War Coll., 1929; m. Helen Rose Bennet, Feb. 27, 1911; children—Helen Bennet (Mrs. Stephen W. Ackerman), Walter Scott. Commd. 2d lt. Inf., June 15, 1904, and advanced through the grades to brig. gen., 1942; retired, 1944. Home: 1815 Starke Av., Columbus, Ga. Died June 24, 1950.

FUNCHESS, Marion Jacob (fŭn'chĕs), adminstr.; b. Orangeburg, S.C., Apr. 9, 1884; s. Jacob Sebastion and Ella Mariah (Andrews) F.; B.S., Clemson (S.C.) Agrl. Coll., 1908; M.S., U. of Wis., 1911; m. Agnes Eloise McCants, June 21, 1911; children—Jean Eloise, Helen, Kenneth McCants, Mary Ella. Asst. prof. agronomy, Ala. Poly. Inst., 1909-12, asso. prof., 1912-15, prof., 1915-20, head of Agronomy Dept., 1920-24, dean of Coll. of Agr. and dir. Agrl. Expt. Sta., 1924-51, dean emeritus, 1951. Past pres. Assn. So. Agrl. Workers. Fellow Am. Soc. Agronomy (ex-pres.); mem. A.A.A.S., Alpha Gamma Rho, Phi Kappa Phi, Gamma Sigma Delta, Alpha Zeta. Democrat. Methodist. Mason. Club: Auburn Outing. Home: 343 S. College St., Auburn, Ala. Died Feb. 19, 1953; buried Pine Hill, Auburn, Ala.

FUNK, Charles Earle, editor, lexicographer; b. Springfield, O., Apr. 4, 1881; s. Benjamin F. and Cynthia (Layton) F.; student New York U., 1899-1902; B.S., U. of Colo., 1904; Litt.D., Wittenberg College, 1937; m. Beulah Messinger Johnson, Oct. 23, 1912; children—Charles Earle, John Capron, Marion Elizabeth (Mrs. Gene Valente), Donald Messinger, Priscilla Ann (Mrs. Arthur T. Martin), William Benjamin. Engr., Colo., Wyo., Idaho and Ore., 1904-11, asso. editor The Engineering Mag., 1911-15, mng. editor, 1915-17; editor and sec. Industrial Extension Inst., 1916-22; asso. editor New Standard Dictionary and abridgments, 1921-27, 1931-38, editor, 1939-47; asso. editor Lexicographer's Easy Chair, 1931-37; asst. editor New Standard Ency., 1931, New Internat. Year Books, 1932-38, editor, 1939-47; cons. editor, Funk & Wagnalls Co., 1947—; radio quiz program Say It with Words, Mut. network, 1938; syndicated column, Power with Words, 1951-53; interim speech consultant C.B.S., 1950-51. Compiler: (with L. A. Leslie) 25,000 Words Spelled, Divided, and Accented, 1935. Author: What's the Name, Please?, 1936; A Hog on Ice, and Other Sayings, 1948; Thereby Hangs a Tale, 1950; Heavens to Betsy, and Other Savings, 1955; Horsefeathers, 1958. Editor: (with Dr. Frank H. Vizetelly) New Comprehensive Standard Dictionary, 1937; editor Standard Junior Dictionary, 1939; New Practical Standard Dictionary, 1946; New College Standard Dictionary, 1947. Mem. Zeta Psi. Republican. Conglist. Mason. Clubs: Rotary, Mt. Dora Bowling. Home: Mt. Plymouth, Sorrento, Fla. Died Apr. 16, 1957; buried Morvian Cemetery, S.I., N.Y.

FUNK, John Clarence, author, lawyer; b. Harrisburg, Pa., Jan. 29, 1884; s. David Sieber (M.D.) and Matilda (Motzer) F.; A.B., Princeton, 1905; student law dept. U. Pa., 1906; LL.B., Dickinson Coll., 1909, A.M., 1909; D.Sc., Susquehanna U., 1926; m. Ada Cynthia Pruden, May 15, 1926. Vice agt. U.S. Dept. Justice, 1912-13; dep. clerk U.S. Dist. Ct., Middle Dist. Pa., 1914; U.S. Navy law enforcement rep. Commn. on Tng. Camp Activities, portion of 1917; mem. U.S.N.R.F., 1917; supervising inspector Office Naval Intelligence, 1919; supervising field agt. U.S. Interdepartmental Social Hygiene Bd., 1920; dir. Bur. Protective Social Measures, Pa. State Dept. Health, 1921; sci. asst. USPHS, 1922, regional dir., 1936, spl. atty., 1922, later chief bur. of pub. health edn., Pa. State Dept. Health; dir. health edn., Va. State Dept. Health, 1936-46; former exec. sec. Pa. Pub. Health Assn. Lt. comdr. USNR, ret. Mem. bar Supreme Ct. Pa., Phi Delta Theta, Nat. Reciprocity Club (hon.). Presbyn. Mason. Author: Vice and Health (text book on social sanitation), 1921; So This Is America! (an Am. travel book), 1923; How to Live Longer, 1927; Stay Young and Live!, 1943. Formerly health feature writer for Western Newspaper Union and contbr. mags. Home: R.D. 1, Box 103, Fayetteville, Pa. Deceased.

FURAY, James Henry (fū'rā), ret. newspaper man; b. Omaha, Dec. 4, 1879; s. John Baptist and Catharine (McShane) F.; A.B., Creighton U., Omaha, 1898, LL.D., 1938; m. Mabel Elizabeth Beeman, Feb. 15, 1908; children—James Henry (dec.), Eleanor Catherine (Mrs. Charles E. Pierson), Henry Beeman. In newspaper work as reporter and desk editor Omaha Daily News, Chicago American, St. Paul News, Chicago Inter-Ocean and Indianapolis Star, 1899-1905; with Cleveland Press, 1905-08; with United Press, 1908-1947, mgr., Chicago div., 1908-10, Mountain div., 1910-15, Pacific Coast div., 1915-18, foreign editor, N.Y. Office, 1918-24, v.p., 1924-47, dir. 1926-47. Mem. Sigma Delta Chi. Rom. Cath. Clubs: Ekwanok Country (Manchester, Vt.) Received Rochester U. award for distinguished service to Pan-Am. unity, 1943. Home: Manchester, Vt. Died July 20, 1955; buried Manchester, Vt.

FURBER, Fred Nason, lawyer; b. Detroit Lakes, Minn., Dec. 17, 1882; s. James Cate and Elizabeth T. (Nason) F.; LL.B., U. Minn., 1904, LL.M., 1905; m. Dorothy Morse, May 14, 1920 (died Dec. 16, 1938); 1 dau., Elizabeth Nason; m. 2d Alta B. Morse, July 11, 1942 (died Mar. 17, 1948). Admitted to Minn. bar, 1904, since practiced in Mpls.; mem. Youngquist, Furber, Comaford Danforth & Clarkson; spl. atty. Dept. Justice, 1920. Served as pvt. to 1st lt. U.S. Army, 1917-19, with A.E.F., 1918-19, adj. Army, Occupation, Sinzig, Germany, 4th A.A.C. Mem. Am., Minn. and Hennepin Co. bar assns., Mil. Order World Wars, Am. Legion, Minn. Civic and Commerce Assn. Rep. Episcopalian (a founder, vestryman and sr. warden emeritus St. George Ch., St. Louis Park, Minn.). Mason (32°, Shriner). Clubs: Professional Mens, Auto, Athletic, The Minneapolis, Minikanda. Home: 5421 Minnetonka Blvd., St. Louis Park, Mpls. 16. Office: Northwestern Bank Bldg., Mpls. 2. Died May 14, 1958.

FURBER, Henry Jewett, retired lawyer; b. Green Bay, Wis., 1865; s. Henry Jewett and Elvira (Irwin) F.; B.S., U. of Chicago, 1886; studied univs. of Berlin, 1886-87, Vienna, 1887-88, Leipzig, 1888-89, Halle, Germany, 1889-90; A.M., Ph.D., magna cum laude, Halle, 1891; studied law Northwestern U. Law Sch.; hon. A.M., Bowdoin, 1889; unmarried. Prof. economics, Northwestern U., 1892-94; in France and Italy, 1894-96; was instrumental in opening univs. of France to foreigners on virtually same basis as those of Germany; 1st v.p. Nat. Life Ins. Co., Washington, 1897-1900; general counsel Chicago Bd. of Underwriters, 1904-12. Elected, 1901, pres. Internat. Olympic Games Assn. of 1904. Comdr. Legion of Honor, France; mem. Chicago Athletic Assn., Japan Society (N.Y.); honorary life member Chicago Academy Sciences; mem. National Institute of Social Sciences. Colonel Infantry, Minnesota National Guard. Wrote: Geschichte der Oekonomischen Theorien in Amerika (doctor's thesis) 1891. Contbr. Providence Jour., World War I. Awarded a 2d prize in internat. literary contest commemorative of XXVI centennial of Japan, in 1941 at Tokyo. Inventor of method of mathematically locating masked batteries and detecting submarines and aircrafts by sound waves (phonotelemetry), and automatic sales system, and calculating apparatus. Address: care Bankers Trust

Co., Fifth Av. and 44th St., N.Y.C. Died June 6, 1956.

FURBRINGER, Max Henry, (fŭr'bring-ĕr), architect; b. St. Louis, Mo., July 26, 1879; s. Henry and Dora (Ockel) F.; student Washington U., 1896-98, Beaux Arts Soc., New York, 1898-1900; m. Marzie Harris, 1901; children—Louis, Victor; m. 2d, Sophye Buchanan, 1921. Archtl. draftsman, Eames & Young, St. Louis, Mo., 1900-02; partner, Jones & Furbringer, Memphis, Tenn., 1902-35, Furbringer & Ehrman, since 1935. Chmn. City Planning Comn. Trustee Memphis Acad. of Arts. Fellow A.I.A. Mason (32°, Scottish Rite). Club: Lions (Memphis, Tenn.) Author: Domestic Architecture, 1916. Home: 1437 Goodbar Ave. Address: 1004 Union Planters Bldg., Memphis. Died Jan. 17, 1957.

FURMAN, Lucy, author; b. Henderson, Ky.; d. William Barnard (M.D.) and Jessie (Collins) F.; ed. pvt. schs., Henderson, Sayre Inst., Lexington, Ky., and spl. courses U. of Cincinnati. Worker for many years at Hindman (Ky.) Settlement Sch. Methodist. Author: Stories of a Sanctified Town, 1897; Mothering on Perilous, 1913; Sight to the Blind, 1915; The Quare Women, 1923; The Glass Window, 1925; The Lonesome Road, 1927; also many articles on conservation of wild life. National vice pres. Anti-Steel-Trap League. Home: 722 W. Main St., Lexington, Ky. Died Aug. 1958.

FURNESS, Clifton Joseph, tchr., author; b. Sheridan, Ind., Apr. 30, 1898; s. T. Chalmers and Clara E. (Spray) F.; A.B., Northwestern U., 1921; A.M., Harvard, 1928; unmarried. Began as tchr. piano, 1914; tchr. music, Northwestern U., 1919-21, of English and music, Horace Mann Sch. Boys, N.Y.C., 1922-27, of English, Northeastern U., 1928-29, Bradford (Mass.) Coll., 1929-31, Harvard Grad. Sch., 1929-34, of biography and music, Katharine Gibbs Schs., 1929-40; supr. academic studies, N.E. Conservatory Music 1930—. Mem. S.A.T.C., Northwestern U., 1918. Received grants-in-aid to complete biography of Walt Whitman from Carnegie Corp. through Am. Council Learned Socs., 1938-40. Mem. Modern Lang. Assn. Am., Kappa Gamma Psi, Pi Kappa Lambda. Mem. Soc. Friends. Author: Walt Whitman's Workshop, 1928; The Genteel Female, 1931; Lotos Petals—A Story of the Life and Work of Rudolf Steiner, 1935; also author of chpt. on Schumann Heink in Famous Americans (2d series), 1944. Editor: Facsimile Reprint of 1855 Edition of Walt Whitman's Leaves of Grass, 1939. Collaborated with Dr. Clara Barrus, Whitman and Burroughs, Comrades, 1931. Contbr. to mags. Home: Hudson, N.Y. Address: New England Conservatory of Music, Boston. Deceased.

FURROW, Clarence Lee, educator; b. Grand Junction, Ia., Mar. 22, 1896; s. A. M. and Blanche (Van Horn) F.; student Okla. Bapt. U., 1916-17; A.B., U. Okla., 1921, M.A., 1922; grad. study Princeton, 1922-23, U. Ill., 1923-24; Ph.D., State U. Ia., 1933; m. Esther Yakish, Aug. 12, 1918; children—Clarence Lee, Jr., Marjorie Helen. Instr. zool. U. Kan. 1924-26; spl. vis. instr. Neb. State Tchrs. Coll., 1925; asst. prof. biology Knox Coll., 1926-33, prof., 1933-40, Clara A. Abbott prof. biology, 1940—, also chairman of the dept. of biology; visiting prof. U. Minn. summers, 1945—, U. Chgo. summers, 1945—. Dir. study, com. on liberal arts edn. N. Cenrtal Assn., 1948—; mem. Nat. Com. on Gen. Edn., 1950—. Fellow A.A.A.S., Am. Microscopic Soc., Ill. State Acad. Sci. (past pres.); mem. Am. Association of University Professors, American Assn. Biology Tchrs., Am. Soc. Zoologists, Sigma Xi, Tri Beta (v.p.). Methodist. Contbr.: General Education in Transition; also to sci. jours. Editor North Central News Bull. Home: 819 Bateman St., Galesburg, Ill. Died Mar. 9, 1955; buried Meml. Park, Galesburg.

FURTWANGLER, Wilhelm (fōōrt'vĕng-lĕr), conductor; b. Berlin, Germany, Jan. 25, 1886; s. Adolf and Adelheid (Wendt) F.; musical edn. in theory and composition, Munich; Dr. (hon.), U. Heidelberg; m. Zita Lund, 1923. Began as chorus dir. and condr. in operas at Breslaus, Zurich, Munich and Strassburg; condr. of symphony and philharmonic choruses in Lübeck, 1911-15; 1st condr. the Mannheim Opera, 1915-20; condr. State Opera Concerts, Berlin, Museum Concerts, Frankfurt, Tonkunstler Orchestra, Vienna, 1920-22; dir. Berlin Philharmonic Konzerte, 1922-34, 35—; dir. Gwendhauskonzerte, Leipzig, 1922-28; dir. N.Y. Philharmonic Orchestra, 1925-27, Vienna Philharmonic Konzerte, 1927-30; dir. Berlin State Opera, 1933-34, guest condr., 1936—; guest condr. Bayreuth Festival, 1935-38; dir. Vienna Philharmonic Konzerte since 1938; guest dir. of operas in London, Paris, Zürich, elsewhere. Named hon. senator U. Jena; senator German Acad., Munich; hon. citizen of Mannheim; mem. German and Swedish acads. of arts, Royal Acad. St. Cecelia, Rome, Soc. of Friends of Music, Vienna, Carl Schurz Soc., Vienna and Berlin philharmonic orchestras, German Soc. of Musical Learning. Decorated Officer's Cross of the Crown of Italy, Goethe medal, Brahms medal, 1937. Home: Potsdam, Germany. Died Dec. 1, 1954.*

FUSON, Samuel Dillard, advt., public relations; b. Seymour, Mo., June 26, 1890; s. James Wayne and Sarah Temperance (McMahan) F.; student Drury Coll., 1908-09; Columbia U., 1922; m. Dagmar Nelson, Aug. 20, 1921; 1 dau., Patricia. Newspaper reporter, editor, various papers in St. Louis, Springfield, Joplin, Mo., Little Rock, Memphis, 1912-20; staff writer, editor, Asso. Press in St. Louis, Columbus, Trenton, Boston, N.Y. City, 1920-24; New York corr., Chicago Tribune, 1924-27; mng. editor, Christian Herald Mag., 1927-30; dir. publicity, Erwin Wasey & Co., 1930-35; v.p. in charge public relations, Arthur Kudner, Inc., 1935-45; v.p., dir. Kudner Agency since 1945. Pres. Nat. Assn. Public Relations Counsel, Inc., 1945; vice chmn. New York Red Cross Public Relations Com., 1942-44; chmn. public relations com., New York War Finance Com., 1941-43; chmn. Pub. Relations Soc., Am. Mason (Shriner). Clubs: Advertising, Military-Naval, St. Nicholas, Circus Saints and Sinners, Wings (N.Y. City); National Press (Washington); Recess (Detroit). Home: Headquarters Farms, R.F.D., Stockton, N.J. Office: 575 Madison Av., N.Y.C. 22. Died Nov. 4, 1954.

FUSTING, Frederick Erwin, mfg. exec.; b. Baltimore, Apr. 19, 1882; s. Charles Francis and Lily (Albert) F.; student Mt. St. Joseph's Coll., Baltimore; m. Marie Hammond, Apr. 15, 1914. With Crown Cork & Seal Co., Inc., Baltimore, and predecessor co., since 1903, v.p., 1927—. Home: 3 Overhill Rd., Balt. 10. Office: Crown Cork and Seal Co., Inc., Balt. 3. Died Feb. 24, 1953.

FUTRELL, Junius Marion, ex-gov. Ark.; b. Greene Co., Ark., Aug. 14, 1872; s. Jeptha and Arminia F.; student, U. Ark., 1892-93; m. Tera Ann Smith, Sept. 14, 1893; children—Bill Nye (Mrs. H. G. McCall), Selma Prentiss (Mrs. J. H. Farrell), Junius Byron, Ernie Exah (wife of Dr. A. H. Maddox), Olive Janice (Mrs. Clem Moore), Daniel Wood. Began as sch. tchr., 1892; tchr., farmer, later circuit clk.; admitted to Ark. bar, 1913; mem. Ark. Ho. of Res., 1897-99 and 1901-03; state senator, 1913-17; pres. of senate, 1913-15; acting gov. Ark., 5 mo. from Mar. 13, 1913; circuit judge, 1922; state chancellor, 1923-33; gov. of Ark., 1933-37; now in spl. legal work for Dyess Colony, Inc. Home: 4121 Woodlawn Av., Little Rock, Ark. Deceased.

G

GABBERT, Mont Robertson (găb'bĕrt), prof. philosophy; b. Casey Creek, Ky., Aug. 29, 1889; s. Zachary Taylor and Agatha (Robertson) G.; prep. edn., Lindsay Wilson Training Sch., Columbia, Ky.; A.B., Transylvania Coll., 1915, A.M., 1916, LL.D., 1947; Ph.D., U. of Chicago, 1921; m. Myra Anna Love, Sept. 7, 1921; 1 dau., Eleanor Frances (dec.). Ordained ministry Disciples of Christ Ch., 1911; pastor Junction City (Ky.) Christian Ch., 1913-16; served with Y.M.C.A., Chicago, July 1917-Sept. 1918; prof. psychology and edn., Hiram (O.) Coll., 1918-20; asst. prof. philosophy, U. of Pittsburgh, 1921-24, prof., 1924-54, head dep. 1926-54, ret. Mem. Am. Philos. Assn., Southern Assn., Philosophy and Psychology, British Institute of Philosophy, A.A.A.S., American Association University Professors, Sigma Xi. Mason. Clubs: Faculty of the University of Pittsburgh (president, 1933-35), Quiz, Philosophy, Longue Vue. Contbr. chapter to Religion and the Modern Mind, 1929. Home: 520 S. Murtland Av., Pitts. 8. Died Apr. 3, 1955; buried Philo, Ill.

GABLEMAN, Edwin Wilson, publicist; b. Waverly, O., Dec. 21, 1885; s. Philip and Margaret (Breinig) G.; student Purdue, 1906-08; married Ellen Ann Rogers, April 22, 1922; 1 daughter, Barbara (Mrs. Gordon F. Bell). Began newspaper work with Portsmouth (Ohio) Times, 1903; city editor Lima Times-Democrat, 1909-13; reporter, Cincinnati Enquirer, 1916-19, corr. at Columbus, O., 1919, head of Washington bur. of Enquirer, 1920-43, Sun Oil Co., Washington, D.C., since 1943. Democrat. Episcopalian. Mason (K.T.). Clubs: Nat. Press, Gridiron (pres. 1936), Alfalfa, Columbia Country, Chevy Chase. Political commentator Nat. Broadcasting Co., 1936-37. Home: 3133 Connecticut Av. N.W. Office: American Security and Trust Bldg., Washington. Died June 10, 1954.

GABRIEL, Charles L(ester), business exec.; b. N.Y.C., Sept. 28, 1891; s. Lewis and Charlotte (Bibo) G.; S.B., Mass. Inst. Tech., 1912, M.S., 1913; m. Ruth V. Katz, June 5, 1923; children—Charlotte J. (Mrs. David Leaness), Dorothy J. Plant supt. Baryta Mfg. Co., New Market, N.J., 1914-16, Port Morris Chem. Co., Nicholasville, Ky., 1916-18; sales mgr. Comml. Solvents Corp., Terre Haute, Ind., and N.Y.C., 1920-23, v.p., 1924-38; pres., dir. Resinox Corp., N.Y.C., 1934-38; v.p., dir. Publicker Industries, Inc., Phila., 1942—. Mem. adv. com. Temple U. Research Inst. Served as 1st lt., C.W.S., U.S. Army, 1918-19. Recipient Letter of Commendation for unusual service, 1919. Mem. Am. Chem. Soc., Am. Inst. Chemists, Am. Inst. Chem. Engrs., Franklin Inst., Mil. Order World Wars, Soc. Am. Wars, C.W.S. Vets. Assn. Clubs: Chemists (N.Y.C.); M.I.T. (Phila.). Contbr. articles to chem. jours., and Ency. of Chem. Technology. Patentee prodn. of methanol, prodn. of normal butyl lactate, lacquer composition, coated paper, synthetic resin varnishes. Home: 1927 Wynnefield Terrace, Phila. Phila. 31. Office: 1429 Walnut St., Phila. 2. Died Sept. 24, 1949; buried Roosevelt Cemetery.

GABRIEL, Gilbert Wolf (gā'brĭ-ĕl), critic, author; b. Brooklyn, N.Y., Jan. 18, 1890; s. Samuel and Anna (Lavine) G.; prep. edn., Peekskill Mil. Acad. and Polytechnic Prep. School, Brooklyn; B.A., Williams College, 1912, hon. M.A., 1937; m. Ada Vorhaus, June 3, 1918. Reporter New York Evening Sun, 1912-15, lit. editor, 1915-17, music critic, 1917-24; dramatic critic New York Telegram-Mail, 1924-25, New York Sun, 1925-29, N.Y. American, 1929-37, Cue mag. since 1949; lectr. drama, criticism N.Y.U. Served as 2d lt. inf., U.S. Army, at Plattsburg T.C., Camp Upton and Camp Lee, World War. Chief of Alaska Mission, Overseas Branch, Office of War Information, Anchorage, Alaska, 1942-43; public relations and propaganda officer, G-2, Alaska Defense Command, 1943; deputy chief publs., Psychological Warfare Division, Supreme Headquarters, London, 1944. Mem. Authors League of Am. (officer, mem. council). Clubs: Dutch Treat, Williams Coll., N.Y. Critics' Circle; Critics' Circle of London (hon.). Author: The Seven Branched Candlestick, 1916; Jiminy, 1922; Brownstone Front, 1924; Famous Pianists and Composers, 1928; I, James Lewis, 1931; Great Fortune, 1933; I Got a Country, 1943; Love from London, 1946; I Thee Wed, 1948; also stories, articles and motion pictures. Home: Brewster, N.Y. Died Sept. 3, 1952.

GADE, John Allyne (gä'dê), b. Cambridge, Mass. Feb. 10, 1875; s. Gerhard and Helen Rebecca (Allyne) G.; B.S., Harvard University, 1896; M.A., Columbia 1948, Ph.D., 1950; m. Ruth Sibley, November 18, 1907; children—Fredrick Herman, Margaret Durbin, Ruth Allyne. Practiced architecture in N.Y. City. Mem. Commn. of Relief for Belgium, 1916-17; naval attaché U.S. Legation, Copenhagen, Denmark, 1917-19; mem. Baltic mission; entered diplomatic service, 1919; served as rep. of State Dept. in the Baltic provinces; mem. White, Weld & Co., bankers; returned to Naval Service; capt. U.S.N.R. 1938; naval attaché U.S. Embassy, Brussels and United States Legation, Lisbon; ret. naval service, 1940. Awarded Navy Cross (U.S.), Faithful Service Medal (Navy); var. fgn. decorations. Clubs: Knickerbocker, Harvard. Author: Book Plates, Old and New, 1898; Cathedrals of Spain, 1911; Charles XII, King of Sweden, 1917; Christian IV, 1928; Life of Cardinal Mercier, 1934; All My Born Days, 1942; Life and Times of Tycho Brahe, 1947. Address: 920 Fifth Av., New York, N.Y. and St. James, L.I., N.Y. Died Aug. 16, 1955.

GAEHR, Paul Frederick, educator; b. Thoune, Switzerland, May 15, 1880; s. Gottlieb and Jakobea (Zurbruegg) G.; brought to U.S. 1889; A.B., Cornell U., 1902, A.M., 1905, Ph.D., 1918; m. Pauline Collin, June 11, 1908; children—Dorothy, Robert Edward. Asst. in physics Cornell U., 1901-03, instr., 1903-08; head math. dept. Robert Coll., Constantinople, Turkey, 1908-11; prof. physics, Wells Coll., 1911-45, retired; engr. Western Electric Co., summer 1918; acting prof. physics S.A.T.C., Cornell U., 1918. Fellow A.A.A.S.; mem. Am. Phys. Soc., Opt. Soc. Am., Sigma Xi Republican. Presbyn. Mason. Home: Aurora, N.Y. Died Nov. 12, 1955; buried Cleve.

GAERTNER, Carl Frederick (gârt'nĕr), artist; b. Cleveland, O., Apr. 18, 1898; s. Henry Fred and Nellie (Metzler) G.; student Western Reserve U., 1918; studied Cleveland Sch. of Art, 1920-23; m. Adelle Potter, September 7, 1938; children—Frederic Lucian, Carl Potter. Instructor in drawing, South Side High School, Cleveland, Ohio, 1918-20, John Carroll University, 1920-24; instr. in painting, Cleveland Sch. of Art since 1925; instr. John Huntington Poly. Inst., 1929-30, Western Reserve U. Sch. of Architecture since 1925; free lance designer and painter since 1921. Represented in Cleveland Museum of Art, Kenyon Coll., Cleveland pub. libraries, Cleveland Municipal Art Gallery, Metropolitan Mus., Am. Acad. of Arts and Letters, Whitney Mus. of Am. Art, Ill. State Mus. of Art, Chicago Art Inst., New Britain Art Institute, Pepsi Cola Collection, Toledo Museum of Art, Swope Art Gallery (Terre Haute), Ball State Teachers College (Indiana), Awarded: Cleveland Mus. of Art 1st prize, oil painting, 1923-28; 2d prize, oil painting, 1922, 31; 1st prize landscape painting, 1941; hon. mem. indsl. painting, 1941; special award, landscape painting, 1942, 44; Cleveland Mus. of Art, 1943; 1st prize, landscape, hon. mention water color painting and still life painting; Art Inst. of Chicago, hon. mention, landscape painting, 1942; Altman Prize, Nat. Acad. of Design, 1944; 1st prize Cleveland Museum, 1945; Portrait of Am. Exhbn., $500 prize, 1945; Watson F. Blair, $600 prize, Chicago Art Inst., 1946; Salmagundi prize, 1947; 50; Herbert L. Pratt Purchase award, 1952; Carnegie Prize, Nat. Academy of Design, 1950. One-man show, Macbeth Gallery, New York, 1945, 47, 50, 52; Ruth Coulter Galleries, Cleve., 1934; Cleve. Inst. Art, 1941; Colby Jr. Coll., Canton (O.) Art Inst., Dayton (O.) Art Inst., 1946; Phila. Art Alliance, 1947, 48; Ten Thirty Gallery, Cleve., 1948. President Cleveland Society of Artists, 1935-38. Member Alpha Beta Delta, Epsilon Delta Rho. Mason. Clubs:

Salmagundi, Audubon Artists, Water Color of Phila. Home: Hemlock Hill Farm, River Rd., R. 4, Willoughby O. Address: Cleveland Inst. of Art, Cleve- Died Nov. 4, 1952; buried Lakeview Cemetery.

GAERTNER, Herman Julius, educator; b. Klausthal, Germany, July 11, 1866; s. Christian and Adolphine (Becker) G.; came to Am., 1880; B.S., Ohio No. U., 1888, Ped.D. (hon.), 1912; A.B., Ind. U., 1892; A.M., Ohio Wesleyan, 1896; m. Nellie J. Hornbeck, Aug. 16, 1894; children—Harold H., Marion A., Herman J., Paul C., Nellie Jane. Supt. schs., Deshler, O., 1887-92; prof. mathematics, Wilmington (O.) Coll., 1894-96; supt. schs., Perrysburg, 1896, Fairburn, Newnan and Waynesboro, Ga., to 1907; co-founder, head, Ga. Mil. Acad., 1901-02; prof. history, Ga. Normal, Indsl. Coll., 1908-13; dean, Sch. of Edn., Oglethorpe U., 1920-47; head Grad. Sch. and extension work, 1926-47, prof. emeritus, 1947—. Trustee Oglethorpe U. Mem. Sigma Nu, Phi Gamma Mu. Democrat. Presbyn. Mason (K.T.). Writer, lectr. on edn. Home: 39 Huntington Rd., Atlanta. Died Mar. 1, 1958; buried Clarkston, Ga.

GAFFNEY, Dale V., army officer; b. Mass., Feb. 18, 1894; grad. AC Tactical Sch., 1936, Command and Gen. Staff Sch., 1937; rated command pilot, combat and tech. observer. Pvt. advancing to sgt., 5th Inf., Mass. N.G., 1916-17; pvt. aviation sect. Signa Corps, 1917; commd. 2d lt., 1918, advanced through the grades to brig. gen. AC, 1943; dep. comdr. Air Force Proving Ground, Eglin AFB, Fla. Address: care War Dept., Washington 25. Died Mar. 28, 1950.*

GAGGIN, Edwin Hall, architect; b. Erie, Pa., Nov. 12, 1866; s. Richard Francis and Gertrude Phoebe (Hall) G.; B.Arch., Syracuse U., 1892; studied École des Beaux Arts, Paris, 1895-97; m. Eva Roe, Jan. 11, 1911; 1 son, John Bridge (dec.). Began practice in Syracuse, 1902; prof. architecture U. Syracuse, 1892-1902. Methodist. Mem. Delta Kappa Epsilon. Mason (32°). Home: 846 Ostrom Av., Syracuse, N.Y. Died Apr. 19, 1959; buried Oakwood Cemetery Syracuse.

GAIL, William Wallace, editor, speaker; b. East Aurora, N.Y., June 29, 1880; s. William Henry and Julia (Wallace) G.; A.B., Cornell U., 1905; m. Virginia Irene Gunderman, Mar. 25, 1905; children—Wallace Henry (dec.), William Morrison, Robert Woodard. Reporter and mng. editor Cripple Creek (Colo.) Times, 1905-08; editorial writer and news editor Colorado Springs Gazette and Evening Herald, 1908-13; mng. editor Billings (Mont.) Gazette, 1913-16; owner Gail-Billings Advt. Co.; exec. v.p. Associated Industries of Billings and mem. exec. com. Asso. Industries of Mont.; trustee Nat. Small Business Men's Assn. since 1941. Mem. Phi Beta Kappa. Protestant. Clubs: Commercial, Rotary. Author: Yellowstone County, Montana, in the World War, 1919. Known as speaker before industrial relations and civic groups, convs. and as humorous dinner speaker and toastmaster. Home: R.F.D. No. 3, Billings. Office: Stapleton Bldg., Billings, Mont. Died Feb. 20, 1951.

GAILOR, Frank Hoyt, judge; b. Sewanee, Tenn., May 9, 1892; s. Thomas Frank and Ellen Douglas (Cunningham) G.; student Racine (Wis.) Coll., 1906-08; A.B., Univ. of the South, Sewanee, Tenn., 1912, D.C.L., 1928; student Columbia U., 1912-13; M.A. (Rhodes Scholar), New College, Oxford U., Eng., 1916; m. Mary Louise Pennel, Aug. 9, 1922; children—Mary Ann, Ellen Douglas, Nancy Pennel. Admitted to bar, Tenn., 1919; mem. Tenn. Legislature, house of representatives, 1921, senate, 1923; county trustee Shelby County, 1924-36, county atty., 1936-41; circuit judge, 1941-42; associate justice Supreme Court of Tenn., 1942—. Served as 2d lt., Royal Garrison Arty., B.E.F., 1916-18; 1st lt., F.A., U.S. Reserve, 1918-19. Mem. Alpha Tau Omega, Am. Legion. Club: University (Memphis, Tenn.). Home: 1343 Goodbar Place, Memphis 4, Tenn. Office: Supreme Court Bldg., Nashville 3. Died Apr. 8, 1954; buried Elmwood Cemetery, Memphis.

GAINES, L. Ebersole, bus. exec.; b. Fayetteville, W.Va., Mar. 9, 1893; s. Ludwell Graham and Martha (Ebersole) G.; ed. Lawrenceville Sch.; Litt.B., Princeton, 1916; m. Betty Chilton, Jan. 31, 1925; children—Martha, L. Ebersole, George C., Ludwell Graham, Stanley. Lawyer since 1925; admitted to practice West Virginia Supreme Court, Federal District Courts and U.S. Treasury Dept., 1928, U.S. Supreme Ct., 1935; became vice pres. Amherst Coal Co. and Logan County Coal Corp., 1935; pres. New River Co., Mount Hope, W.Va., 1939—, director; vice pres. and dir. Amherst Coal Co., Amherst Fuel Co., Logan County Coal Corp., Buffalo Creek Coal and Coke Co., Merchants and Miners Nat. Bank (Oak Hill, W.Va.), Campbells Creek R.R. Co., Fayette Nat. Bank, Chesapeake & Potomac Telephone Co. of W.Va. Served as seaman 2d class, C.Q.M., 1917, ensign, U.S. Naval Flying Corps, 1918-19. Mem. at large, grad. council, Princeton U.; mem. bd. trustees The Lawrenceville School. Mem. West. Va. (pres.) and Nat. (past pres.) coal assns., Am. and W.Va. bar assns. Clubs: Links, Princeton (New York); University Cottage (Princeton); Metropolitan (Washington). White Oak, Edgewood, Hawks Nest Country; Rotary International (hon.). Home: Fayetteville, W.Va. Office: 409 Main St., Mount Hope, W. Va. Died Apr. 16, 1954; buried Huse Meml. Cemetery, Fayetteville, W.Va.

GAITHER, Frances (Mrs. Rice Gaither), (gă'thẽr), novelist; b. Somerville, Tennessee, May 21, 1889; daughter of Paul Tudor and Annie Matilda (Smith) Jones; B.A., Miss. State Coll. for Women, 1909; m. Rice Gaither, Apr. 25, 1912. Contbr. stories to popular magazines, 1919-28. Wrote centennial pageant, The Shadow of the Builder, prod. U. of Va., 1921; pageant, The Clock and the Fountain, prod. Miss. State Coll. for Women, 1935. Author: The Painted Arrow, 1931; The Fatal River—Life and Death of La Salle, 1931; The Scarlet Coat, 1934; Little Miss Cappo, 1937; Follow the Drinking Gourd, 1940; The Red Cock Crows, 1944; Double Muscadine, 1949 (Book of the Month Club selection). Home: 460 W. 24th St., N.Y.C. Died Oct. 28, 1955; buried Corinth, Miss.

GALE, Hoyt Stoddard, geologist; b. Cleveland, O., Dec. 9, 1876; s. George Rodney and Helen Maria (Richardson) G.; A.B., Harvard, 1900, S.B., 1902; m. Almira Miller, June 18, 1902; 1 son, Hoyt Rodney. Asst. geologist, U.S. Geol. Survey, 1902-10, geologist since 1910; in charge section of non-metalliferous deposits, 1912-20; chief geologist of the various foreign subsidiaries of Gulf Oil Corp., 1921-23; in charge Gulf Co.'s operations in Calif. and on Pacific Coast, 1923-29; survey oil possibilities S. Africa, 1938-39; now geologist in cons. practice. Fellow Geol. Society America (mem. of council 1937-39), Soc. Economic Geologists, A.A.A.S. Unitarian. Author of U.S. Geol. Survey bulletins on coal fields, of northwestern Colorado, borax, potash and nitrate deposits in the U.S., and miscellaneous contbrns. on geologic subjects, including Geology of Southern California, guidebook for 16th Internat. Geological Congress, 1933, Geology of the Kramer borate deposits, Calif., 1945, etc. Home: 1775 Hill Drive, Eagle Rock, Los Angeles 41, Cal. Died July 6, 1952.

GALER, Roger Sherman, lawyer; b. Hillsboro, Ia., June 27, 1863; s. Washington M. and Lucinda (Terrill) G.; Ph.B., State U. of Ia., 1885, A.M., 1888; studied law, same univ.; LL.D., Lombard (Ill.) Coll., 1925; m. Lola Goan, Mar. 23, 1887 (died 1909); 1 son, Paul B.; m. 2d, July 1, 1912, Laura Bowman (grad. Radcliffe Coll., Ia. State Teachers Coll. and Lombard Div. Sch.). Pres. Southern Ia. Normal Sch., 1887-92; prin. Iowa City Acad., 1892-93; practiced law at Mt. Pleasant, Ia., since 1893; sr. mem. Galer & Galer; referee in bankruptcy, 1898-1904. Pres. trustees Lombard Coll., 1920-30, Mt. Pleasant Public Library, 1925-28. Pres. Universalist Gen. Conv., 1919-23, trustee, 1919-27, and 1931-33; pres. Ia. State Universalist Conv., 1919-24; mem. Nat. Council Fed. of Religious Liberals (pres. 1927-31); editor with wife of Universalist Sunday School Helper, 1924-28. Trustee Meadville Theol. Sch., Chicago, 1934-42, Lombard Coll. since 1937. Mem. American Bar Assn., Internat. Law Assn., Ia. State Bar Assn. Odd Fellow. Club: Authors' (London). Author: A Layman's Religion, 1921; Old Testament Law, 1922. Home: 403 E. Washington, Mt. Pleasant, Ia. Died Dec. 27, 1950; buried Mt. Pleasant.

GALES, George M., chmn. exec. com. Liggett Drug Co.; b. Raleigh, N.C., Aug. 6, 1876; s. Seaton and Mary (Cameron) G.; ed. pub. schs.; m. Helene Seymour Houghton, Nov. 16, 1910; children—Helene, Seaton. Chmn. exec. com. Liggett Drug Co.; dir. Rexall Drug Co., Boots Pure Drug Co., England. Episcopalian. Clubs: Union League, Creek, Piping Rock. Home: Locust Valley, Long Island, N.Y. Office: 71 W. 23d St., N.Y.C. Died Aug. 15, 1954.

GALL, John Christian, lawyer; b. Lenoir, N.C., Feb. 1, 1901; s. John Jacob and Bertha Babcock (Smyer) G.; student The Citadel, 1917-18; LL.B., George Washington U., 1923; m. Elsie Grafton Rosenberger, Oct. 9, 1924; children—John Christian, Joseph Grafton, Howard Smyer. Bookkeeper, cotton mfrs., 1919-20; employee U.S. Treasury Dept., 1920-21; legal dept. N.A.M., 1921-41; now in pvt. practice; admitted to D.C. bar, 1923, Va. bar, 1927. Mem. Am., D.C. bar assns., Am. Trade Assn. Execs., Am. Aberdeen-Angus Assn. (v.p.), Phi Delta Phi, Sigma Phi Epsilon. Democrat. Episcopalian. Clubs: University, Metropolitan (Washington). Author booklets in legal field; contbr. mags. in mfg. field. Home: Amandale Farm, Upperville, Va. Office: Commonwealth Bldg., Washington 6. Died Dec. 13, 1957.

GALLAGHER, Charles Eugene, ret. pub. utilities exec.; b. Salamanca, N.Y., May 15, 1876; s. Charles Edward and Catherine (Lanning) G.; student schs. of Salamanca; m. Alice V. Forker, June 22, 1899; children—Doclie, Eugenia. Accountant and telegraph operator Mountain State Gas Co., Parkersburg, W. Va., 1893-94, United Gas Co., Bradford, Pa., 1894-95, Oil City Fuel Supply Co. (Pa.), 1895-99; with East Ohio Gas Co., Cleve., 1899-1941, pres., 1933-41; now retired; dir. Nat. City Bank of Cleve., Hercules Motor Corp. (Canton, O.). Dir. Greater Cleve. council Boy Scouts Am. Clubs: Cleveland Athletic. Home: 19901 S. Woodland Rd., Shaker Heights, 22, O. Died Mar. 7, 1951.

GALLAGHER, Daniel J., lawyer; b. Newton, Mass., Aug. 31, 1873; s. Owen and Ann G.; A.B., Boston Coll., 1892, A.M., 1894, LL.D., 1917; LL.B., Boston U., 1895; m. Mary A. Cronin, Nov. 26, 1898 (dec.); children—Edwin D., Louis M. Neville, Owen A., Alice C. Dooley, Florence M. Adams. Practice, Boston, 1895; del. Mass. Constl. Conv., 1917-18; U.S. atty. for Dist. of Mass., by apptmt. of Pres. Wilson, June 8, 1920-Mar. 4, 1921, then reapptd. ad interim by Judge James M. Morton of U.S. Dist. Court. Democrat. Mem. K.C., Catholic Order of Foresters. Home: 17 Ocean St. Office: 209 Washington St., Boston. Died Mar. 23, 1953.

GALLAGHER, Francis Edward, mfr.; b. Salamanca, N.Y., Nov. 21, 1884; s. Charles Edward and Catharine (Lanning) G.; A.B., Cornell U., 1906; m. Frances L. Coons, July 13, 1907; children—Catharine (Mrs. M. F. Witherell), Ralph, Barrett, Eileen (Mrs. A. Warren). Physicist, Bureau of Soils, U.S. Dept. Agr., 1906-07; research chemist Arthur D. Little, Inc., Boston, 1907-13; chemist, engr. John A. Manning Paper Co., Troy, N.Y., 1913-23; chemist, engr. Behr Manning Corp., sand paper mfrs., Troy, 1913-23, pres. 1938-50, chmn. bd., 1950—; v.p. John A. Manning Paper Co.; dir. Norton Co., Mfrs. Nat. Bank. Trustee Rensselaer Poly. Inst.; trustee Samaritan Hosp., Troy. Mem. Am. Chem. Soc., Newcomen Soc. Eng. (Am. br.), Sigma Xi. Republican. Clubs: Troy, Troy Country (Troy, N.Y.); Chemists (N.Y.C.); Mountain Lake (Fla.). Home: 21 Westover Rd. Office: Behr Manning Corp., Troy, N.Y. Died Mar. 23, 1950; buried Troy, N.Y.

GALLAGHER, Michael, pub. utilities; b. Latrobe, Pa., Sept. 3, 1870; s. William and Mary (Welsh) G.; student pub. sch.; m. Sarah Luella Humphreyville, May 10, 1891; children—Pauline (Mrs. Baird R. Tewksbury), William, Mary (Mrs. H. Church Bacon), Helen (Mrs. William E. Woods), Sarah. Began as coal operator, 1893; now asst. to pres. and dir. N.Y.C.&St.L. R.R. Co.; pres. Peoples Nat. Bank, Mount Pleasant, O.; chmn. bd. The Midland S.S. Lines, Inc., Cleve.; dir. Haile Mines, Inc. Mem. Ohio Soc. N.Y. Clubs: Cloud, National Republican (N.Y.C.); Union, Pepper Pike (Cleve.); Fort Henry (Wheeling, W.Va.). Home: 3001 Fairmount Blvd., Cleveland Heights. Office: Terminal Tower Bldg., Cleve. Died Aug. 1957.*

GALLAGHER, Ralph W., former chairman Standard Oil (N.J.); b Salamanca, N.Y., May 27, 1881; formal schooling ended at age of 16; private study engring.; widower; 2 daughters, 1 son. Began in Olean (N.Y.) pumping station of N.Y. Transit Co., pipe line owners, 1897; became tank gauger, fireman, relief telegrapher, constn. foreman for Nat. Transit Co. and United Pipe Lines Co.; became paymaster and asst. supt., East Ohio Gas Co., 1900, in charge trunk line work and supt. distributing plants, 1906, supervisor all company properties, 1908, dir., gen. mgr. and v.p., 1923, pres., 1926; became supervisor natural gas production, Standard Oil (N.J.), 1933, dir., 1933, v.p. 1937, pres., Jan., 1943, chmn. bd., June 12, 1944-Jan. 1, 1946; retired. Dir. J. P. Morgan & Co., Inc. Home: 1040 Park Av., N.Y.C. Died July 31, 1952; buried Gate of Heaven, Hawthorne, N.Y.

GALLAGHER, Sears, artist; b. Boston, Mass., April 30, 1869; s. William and Mary M. (Sears) G.; pupil Tomaso Juglaris, Boston, Jean Paul Laurens, and Benjamin-Constant, Paris; m. Charlotte K. Dodge, 1895; children—Bradford Dodge, Katherine Sears. Exhibited in the Salon, Paris, the most important exhbns. in America, and the Paris Expn., 1900. Logan medal Chicago Soc. of Etchers, 1922; silver medal, Print Makers Soc., Cal., 1929; City of Boston tercentenary medal for etching, 1930; Richard Mitton medal for water color painting, 1937. Mem. Boston Society Water Color Paniters, Guild of Boston Artists, The Soc. of Am. Etchers. Club: Charles River Country. Home and studio: 307 LaGrange St., West Roxbury, Mass. Died June 9, 1955; buried Walnut Hills Cemetery, Brookline, Mass.

GALLATIN, Albert Eugene (găl'ă tĭn), painter, author; b. Villa Nova, Pa., July 23, 1881; s. Albert H. and Louisa B. (Ewing) G.; g.g.s. Albert G., sec. U.S. Treasury, 1801-1813, and minister to France and Eng. Has exhibited paintings: Durand-Ruel Gallery, New York; Galerie Pierre, Paris; Mayor Gallery, London; Arts Club of Chicago; San Francisco Mus. of Art; Inst. of Modern Art, Boston; Honolulu Art Mus., and elsewhere. Represented in permanent collections: Phila. Mus. of Art; Berkshire Mus., Pittsfield, Mass.; Phillips Memorial Gallery, Washington; Mus. of Modern Art, New York. Mem. council New York U.; founder, 1927, New York U. Mus. of Living Art (own collection of 20th century paintings); this collection was transferred to Phila. Mus. of Art, 1943. Trustee Phila. Mus. Art, Jesup Memorial Library (Bar Harbor, Me.). Visitor, Libraries of Harvard U. Mem. Fed. Grand Jury Assn. of N.Y., The Pilgrims, Ends of the Earth, Am. Abstract Artists, Bibliog. Soc. America, Motor Car Touring Soc. (pres.), Soc. of the Cincinnati (French branch); life mem. Holland Lodge (N.Y.), Soc. Colonial Wars, St. Nicholas Soc., French Inst. in U.S., N.Y. Hist. Soc.; fellow Royal Soc. of Arts (London),

Metropolitan Mus. of Art (New York). Clubs: Grolier, Union (New York); Lenox (Mass.); Philadelphia (Pa.); Travellers (Paris); Pot and Kettle, Bar Harbor (Bar Harbor, Me.); Harvard Faculty (Cambridge, Mass.). Author: Whistler's Art Dicta, 1940; Whistler—Notes and Footnotes, 1907; Modern Art at Venice, 1910; Whistler's Pastels and Other Modern Profiles, 1912; Certain Contemporaries, 1916; Vermeer of Delft, 1917; Portraits of Whistler, 1918; Walter Gay—Paintings of French Interiors, 1920; Modern Fine Printing in America, 1921; American Water-colorists, 1922; Gaston Lachaise, 1924; Charles Demuth, 1927; Jacques Mauny, 1928; Gallatin Iconography, 1934; Georges Braque, 1943; Max Beerbohm; Bibliographical Notes, 1944; Of Art: Plato to Picasso, 1944; Aubrey Beardsley—Catalogue of Drawings and Bibliography, 1945. Home: 655 Park Av., N.Y.C. Died June 15, 1952.

GALLICO, Paolo, pianist; b. Italy, 1868; s. Guglielmo and Adele Gallico; married; 1 son. Studied in Trieste and made 1st public appearance there at age of 15 yrs. Next went to Vienna for further study and traveled in Europe in concert tours, 1888-92; in 1892 settled in N.Y.C., where he has since remained teaching and playing in concerts. Major compositions: Euphorion, Rhapsodie Mondiale, Rhapsodie Montereyan; a symphony; Harlequin (a lyric opera); The Apocalypse (a dramatic oratorio). Home: Hotel Ansonia, N.Y.C. Died July 6, 1955.

GALLIE, William Edward, surgeon; b. Barrie, Ont., Can., Jan. 29, 1882; s. William and Annie M. (Gray) G.; M.D., U. Toronto, 1903; Sc.D. honoris causa, McGill U., 1948; m. Janet Louise Hart, Mar. 3, 1914; children—Alan Edward, Marion Louise, Hugh Richmond. Intern Hosp. for Sick Children, Toronto, 1903-04, resident surgeon, 1906-07, jr. surgeon, 1907-12; asso. surgeon, 1912-19, surgeon-in-chief, 1919-29, cons. surgeon since 1929; intern Toronto Gen. Hosp., 1904-05, jr. surgeon, 1909-12, surgeon-in-chief, 1929-47, intern Hosp. for Ruptured and Crippled, N.Y. City, 1905-06, hon. surgeon-in-chief, 1937; with Faculty of Medicine, U. Toronto, as jr. demonstrator, 1906, demonstrator of anatomy, 1906-09, demonstrator of pathology, 1909-12, asst. prof. of surgery, 1919-29, prof. of surgery and head of dept., 1929-47, emeritus prof. of surgery since 1947, dean of Faculty of Medicine, 1936-46; Hunterian prof., Royal Coll. of Surgeons, England, 1924. Charles Mickle Fellowship, U. Toronto, 1929. Served as capt., Canadian Army Med. Corps, 1917, maj. (acting), 1919. Fellow Royal College of surgeons of Eng. (hon. gold medal 1947), Royal Coll. of Surgeons of Can., A.C.S. (past pres.); hon. fellow Royal Soc. Medicine, Western Surg. Assn., Acad. Orthopaedic Surgeons, Assn. of Surgeons of Great Britain and Ireland; mem. Am. Orthopedic Assn. (pres.), Am. Surg. Assn. (pres. 1948), Central Surg. Assn., Am. Interurban Surg. Soc., Am. Interurban Orthopaedic Soc., Can. Physiol. Soc., Can. Med. Assn., Canadian Soc. of Clin Surgs., British Orthopaedic Soc. (hon.), Internat. Orthopaedic Soc., Internat. Soc. of Surgeons, Presbyterian. Clubs: York, Rosedale Golf (Toronto). Author papers and lectures on med. and surg. subjects. Home: 181 Teddington Park Av. Office: Medical Arts Bldg., 170 St. George St., Toronto 5, Ont., Can. Died Sept. 1959.

GALLOWAY, Charles Anderson, clergyman; b. Norris City, Ill., Dec. 20, 1876; s. William Marshall and Louisa Angeline (Morris) G.; ed. pub. schs., summer normal schs., securing 1st grade tchr's. certificate; m. Cora McMurtry, Oct. 27, 1901; children—Frieda (Mrs. A. E. Neas), Cleta (Mrs. Robert W. Wilcox, Jr.), Kathryn Louise, Charles Everette. Tchr. pub. schs. 9 yrs.; ordained ministry Cumberland Presbyn. Ch., 1910; pastor successively Fairfield, Lincoln, Ill., Bowling Green, Ky., Jackson, Richard City, Tenn., until 1925, Lebanon, Tenn., 1926-27; Presbyterial missionary, Madison Presbytery, Jackson, Tenn., 1927-29; pastor of Jefferson Av. Cumberland Presbyn. Ch., Evansville, Ind., 1929-35, Waynesboro Ch., 1935—. Apptd. postmaster, Waynesboro, Tenn., 1939. Served as pvt. Co. C, 4th Ill. Vol. Inf., Spanish-Am. War, 1898-99. Pres. Bd. of Edn., Cumberland Presbyn. Ch., 1921-25; pres. Bd. of Missions Ind. Presbytery, 1929-35; mem. Bd. of Tithing and Budget, Cumberland Presbyn. Ch., 1930-35; writer, editor of Advanced Tchrs'. Quar., Cumberland Presbyn. Bd. of Publ. Democrat. Mason, Odd Fellow, Maccabee. Home: Waynesboro, Tenn. Died May 2, 1954; buried Greenwood Cemetery, Waynesboro.

GALLOWAY, David Henry, physician, surgeon; b. Bellevue, Ia., Jan. 24, 1859; s. John and Elizabeth (Hall) G.; Cornell Coll., 1879-80; Ph.G., Chgo. Coll. of Pharmacy, 1885; studied chemistry Harvard 3 yrs.; M.D., Coll. Phys. and Surg., Chgo., 1893; m. Mrs. Myra G. Schwartz, Aug. 6, 1921. Prof. analytical chemistry Chgo. Coll. of Pharmacy, 1888-90; lectr. in chemistry, Coll. Phys. and Surg., Chgo., 1892-93; settled at Roswell, 1904. Mem. A.A.A.S., Am. Genetic Assn., Am. Econ. League, Am. Secular Union, Mus. Natural History, N.M. Archaeol. Soc. Republican. Agnostic. Home: Roswell, N.M. Deceased.

GALLOWAY, Floyd Emerson, army officer; b. Falmouth, Ky., Sept. 11, 1890; s. Grant and Alice (Moreland) G.; student U. of Ky., 1911-14; grad., Air Service Pilots Sch., 1921, Air Service Observation Sch., 1922, Air Corps Tactical Sch., 1933, Command and Gen. Staff Sch., 1938, Army War Coll., 1941; 1 dau., Mary Ann; m. 2d, Martha Gardener, June 8, 1929; children—Mary Ann (by 1st marriage), Patton, Floyd Emerson. Fibre specialist with Philippine govt., 1914-17; commd. 2d lt., U.S. Army, June 16, 1917, and advanced through the grades to brig. gen., Nov. 4, 1942; served in World War I with A.E.F. in Siberia; has comd. Bolling Field, Washington, D.C., Maxwell Field, Montgomery, Ala., Crissy Field, San Francisco, Calif., and Albrook Field, Canal Zone; organized and comd. Air Force Service Command in the Caribbean Area. Mason, Elk. Club: Army and Navy (Washington, D.C.). Home: Glen Iris Farm, Paris, Ky. Died Sept. 19, 1955; buried Paris, Ky.

GALLOZZI, Tommaso, vocal tchr.; b. Rome, Italy, Jan. 25, 1873; s. Michael Angelo and Marie Civita (Volpini) G.; grad. Municipal High Sch., Rome; studied in Budapest, Hungary, under Q. Merli, 5 yrs., Milan, Italy, with Signoretti 2 yrs.; m. Helen Travaglini, Feb. 7, 1892. Sang leading tenor rôles at Budapest 19 yrs.; appeared in theatres throughout Europe; came to U.S., 1912, naturalized citizen, 1917; operatic coach; developed 32 pupils for grand opera and the concert stage. Composer Gallozzi's 50 New Vocalizes, 1916. Republican. Catholic. Home: 234 S. Huntington Av., Jamaica Plain, Boston. Died Mar. 8, 1938; buried St. Michael's Cemetery, Boston.

GALLUP, Anna Billings, curator; b. Ledyard, Conn., Nov. 9, 1872; d. Christopher Milton and Hannah Eliza (Lamb) Gallup; grad. State Normal Sch., New Britain, Conn., 1893; S.B. in Biology, Mass. Inst. Tech., 1901. Tchr. Hampton (Va.) Normal and Agrl. Inst., 1893-96; tchr. biology R.I. State Normal Sch., 1901-02; with Children's Mus., Bklyn., 1902-37, became curator 1904, now curator-in-chief emeritus. Studied and collected specimens at Marine Biol. Lab., Bermuda, and traveled in Europe studying museums. Recipient Hudson Fulton bronze medal, 1909; gold medal Nat. Inst. Social Sciences, 1930; William Hornaday Meml. award for service and leadership in jr. mus. field, 1955. Mem. Nat. Inst. Social Sciences, Am. Assn. Audubon Socs., Nat. Council Adminstrv. Women in Edn., Bklyn. Botanic Garden, The Auxiliary Bklyn. Children's Museum, L.I. Fedn. Women's Clubs, Bklyn. Nature Club, Am. Assn. Museums, Am. Nature Study Soc., Alumni Assn. and Women's Assn. Mass. Inst. Tech. Republican. Christian Scientist. Home: North Stonington, Conn. Died Oct. 1956.

GALLUP, Frank Amner, educator; b. Cassville, N.Y., Sept. 13, 1863; s. David Budlong and Elizabeth Ann (Amner) G.; grad. Colgate Acad., Hamilton, N.Y., 1883; A.B., Colgate U., 1890, U. Chgo., 1895-96, Am. Sch. Classical Studies at Rome, 1901; m. Effie Deklyn Lloyd, 1890 (died 1899); m. 2d, Elizabeth Chard Smith, June 24, 1902. Prof. Latin, Colgate Acad., 1890-1902; dir., classical dept. Packer Collegiate Inst., Bklyn., 1902-4; editor Watertown (N.Y.) Standard, 1904-7; mgr. Yonkers (N.Y.) Daily News, 1908; prin. Egberts High Sch., Cohoes, N.Y., 1908-9; asso. prin. Albany (N.Y.) High Sch., 1909-11, prin., 1911-16; pres. St. Lawrence U., Canton, N.Y., 1916-18; lit. work, 1919; dir. lang. dept. Ensley High Sch., Birmingham, Ala., 1920-22; prin. High Sch., Clinton, N.Y., 1923—. Mem. Beta Theta Pi, Phi Beta Kappa. Republican. Presbyn. Mason. Compiler: Select Orations and Letters of Cicero, 1897; A Latin Reader, 1913. Home: Cassville, N.Y. Died Feb. 1951.

GALVIN, Joseph A., drug co. exec.; b. Hyde Park, Mass., Apr. 16, 1883. Treas., Rexall Drug, Inc., 1920-24, v.p. and treas., 1925-39, exec. v.p., 1940-41, pres., 1941-43, chmn. bd. since 1943; dir. Rexall Drug Inc., Rexall Drug, Ltd., Toronto, Seamless Rubber Co., New Haven, Conn. Liberty Mutual Fire Ins. Co., Boston. Clubs: Los Angeles Country; University (Boston). Home: 341 S. Bristol Av., Los Angeles 24. Office: 8480 Beverly Blvd., Los Angeles Died May 10, 1954.

GALVIN, Leroy Spahr, editor, pub.; b. Jamestown, O., June 2, 1875; s. William Spahr and Huldah Anne (Fichthorne) G.; A.B., Miami U., Oxford, O., 1898; m. Nella E. Richie, Nov. 25, 1901; 1 dau., Catharine Richie. Began in newspaper business with father, Jamestown, O., 1889; founder, 1897, since editor and pub. Lima Evening and Sunday News; pres. Galvin-bros. Corp., Lima News Pub. Co.; dir. The Metropolitan Bank, Lima, also News Journal, Wilmington, O. Times-Bulletin, Van Wert, O., Record-Herald, Washington Court House, O. Trustee Miami U. Aide de camp to governor of Kentucky, rank of col. Mem. Ohio Soc. of New York, Beta Theta Pi. Republican. Episcopalian. Clubs: Rotary, Lima, Shawnee Country. Home: 637 W. Market St. Office: 121 E. High St., Lima, O. Died Mar. 1, 1952; buried Woodlawn Cemetery, Lima.

GALVIN, Paul Vincent, mfg. exec.; b. Harvard, Ill., June 29, 1895; s. John and Alice (Brickley) G.; student U. Ill., 1914-17; LL.D., Loyola U., Chgo., 1951; m. Lillian Guinan, Apr. 1920 (died 1942); 1 son, Robert W.; m. 2d Virginia Critchfield, Nov. 21, 1945. Founder in 1928 and since pres. Galvin Mfg. Co. (name changed to Motorola, Inc. 1946), chmn. bd. Motorola, Inc., Chgo., 1956—. Mem. pres.' council Loyola U. Served as 2d lt. to 1st lt. F.A., U.S. Army, 1917-19, with 131st F.A. regt., 36th Div. in France, 1918. Mem. Radio Television Mfrs. Assn. Am. (pres. 1943-45), Phi Kappa. Knight of Malta. Clubs: Chicago Athletic Association (Chgo.); Westmoreland Country (Wilmette, Ill.); LaGorce Country (Miami Beach, Fla.). Home: 3038 Normandy Pl., Evanston, Ill. Office: 4545 Augusta Blvd., Chgo. 51. Died Nov. 5, 1959; buried All Saints Cemetery, Des Plaines, Ill.

GAMAGE, Frederick Luther (găm'āj), educator; b. Hopkinton, Mass., June 19, 1860; s. Henry Richard and Abbie (Lackey) G.; A.B., Brown U. 1882, A. M., 1885; D.C.L., Hobart, 1898; m. Isabella Horner, Sept. 23, 1886; children—Margaret Edgerton, Frederick Luther. Instr. Greek, Delaware Acad., Delhi, N.Y., 1882-85; prin. Oxford (N.Y.) Acad., 1885-93; head master St. Paul's Sch., Garden City, L.I., 1893-1907; founded, now headmaster emeritus and chaplain Pawling (N.Y.) Sch. Mem. S.R. Club: University (N.Y.C.). Home: Pawling, N.Y. Deceased.

GAMBER, Branson Van Leer, architect; b. Phila., Aug. 19, 1893; s. Branson Van Leer and Margaret (O'Brien) G.; student Brown Coll. Prep Sch. and Drexel Inst. Art and Sci., Phila.; hon. M.S. in Engring., Detroit Inst. Tech., 1941; m. Gula B. McElwee, July 20, 1915 (div. 1936); children—Gula Margaret (Mrs. Francis J. Zaher), Branson Van Leer III (dec.). Draftsman, designer and chief craftsman, 1907-23; registered architect, and engaged in pvt. practice in Mich., 1923—; tchr. archtl. design and history, evening sch. Detroit Inst. Tech., 1 yr. Served with U.S. Army, Inf. O.T.C., 1918. Mem. Detroit Plan Commn., 1½ yrs.; v.p. Detroit Housing Commn., 1 yr. Fellow A.I.A. (mem. bd. dirs.; pres. Detroit 3 terms); mem. Mich. Soc. Architects (pres. 1 term), Engring. Soc. Detroit, Detroit Hist. Soc., Am. Legion. Club: Detroit Athletic. Home: 1516 Vinewood Av., Detroit 16. Died Oct. 12, 1949.

GAMBLE, Cecil Huggins, philanthropist; b. Cin., Apr. 25, 1884; s. David Berry and Mary Augusta (Huggins) G.; student Franklin Sch., 1895-1900, Lawrenceville Sch., 1900-01; A.B., Princeton, 1905; student Cin. Law Sch., 1905-06; LL.D., Centre Coll., 1933, Tusculum Coll., 1934; m. Marguerite Louise Gibbs, Nov. 5, 1908; children—Mrs. Hugh McD. Ritchey, Mrs. Joseph D. Messler, David Gibbs, Edwin Cecil, Mrs. Harlan J. Swift, James Neare. With Procter & Gamble Co., 1906-17, became sec., 1915, now dir.; dir. Equitable Fire Ins. Co.; dir. Little Miami R.R. Co. Chmn. Cin. Civil Service Commn., 1926-41; pres. YMCA of Cin. and Hamilton County, O., 1925-49, pres. emeritus 1949—; v.p. Little Traverse Hosp. Petoskey Mich. Hon. trustee Cin. Children's Home Christ Hosp., Spring Grove Cemetery Assn. Republican. Presbyn. Clubs: Commercial, Commonwealth, Queen City, University, Cincinnati Country. Home: 4 Westmoreland Pl., Pasadena 3, Cal. Office: Union Central Life Bldg., Cin. Died June 19, 1956.

GAMBLE, James Lawder, pediatrician; b. Millersburg, Ky., July 18, 1883; s. Edwin and Elizabeth (Lawder) G.; A.B., Stanford U., 1906; M.D., Harvard U. Med. Sch., 1910; M.S. (hon.), Yale, 1930; M.D. (hon.), U. Zurich, 1950; Sc.D., U. Chgo., 1952; m. Elizabeth Chafee, Apr. 26, 1916; children—Jane, Sheila, James Lawder, Edwin Francis, John. Instr. pediatrics, Johns Hopkins U. Med. Sch., 1915-22; asst. prof. pediatrics, Harvard U. Med. Sch., 1922-29, prof., 1929-50, emeritus since 1950. Served as physician A.R.C. France, 1917-19. Borden Award, Am. Acad. Pediatrics, 1946, Chapin Award, R.I. Med. Soc., 1950, Kober Award, Assn. Am. Physicians, 1951; Moxon Award Royal Coll. Physicians, 1954; Howland award, American Pediatric Society, 1955. Member American Pediatric Soc., Assn. Am. Physicians, Am. Soc. Biol. Chemists, Am. Academy of Arts and Sciences, Nat. Acad. Sciences, Société de Pediatrie de Paris. Clubs: Century Association (New York); Harvard, Tavern (Boston). Contbr. papers reporting researches in body fluid physiology. Editor: Am. Jour. Clinical Investigation, 1941-47. Home: 33 Edge Hill Rd., Brookline, Mass. Office: Children's Hosp., Boston. Died May 28, 1959.

GAMBLE, Ralph Abernethy, ex-congressman; b. Yankton, S.D.; s. Robert J. (ex-senator of S.D.) and Carrie O. G.; Litt.B., Princeton, 1909; law student George Washington U., 1909-11; LL.B., Columbia, 1912; m. Virginia Nesbitt, Apr. 19, 1911 (died Mar. 1937); m. 2d, Mrs. Ruth G. Daniels, June 19, 1958. Admitted to N.Y. bar, 1913; mem. McInnes & Gamble; counsel, Town of Mamaroneck, 1918-34, Larchmont, 1926-28. Mem. N.Y. State Assembly, 2d Dist., Westchester County, 1931-37; elected to 75th Congress, 25th N.Y. Dist., 1937, to fill vacancy; re-elected 76th to 78th Congresses, 79th to 82d, 28th Dist., 83d-84th Congresses, 26th Dist. Apptd. mem. Joint House-Senate Com. on Housing, 1947. Mem. N.Y. State Commn. for Chgo. World's Fair, 1933-34.

Republican. Home: St. Michaels, Md. Office: 551 Fifth Av., N.Y.C. Died Mar. 4, 1959.

GAMBLE, Robert Howard, chmn. Federal Reserve Branch Bank of Jacksonville; b. Tallahassee, Florida, Dec. 18, 1888; s. Robert and Mary Margaret (Summer) G.; student Law Sch., Yale, 1911; m. Mildred Franklin, Feb. 23, 1929; children—Catharine Bruce, Robert Howard. Began as runner Redmon & Co., N.Y. City; jr. partner Prince & Whitely, N.Y. City, later sr. partner, 1919-24; member National Code Authority, 1933-35; chmn. Regional Face Brick Code Authority No. 4, Washington, D.C., Regional Structural Clay Tile Code Authority No. 5, and Regional Common Brick Code Authority No. 19, 1933-35; co-founder Structural Clay Products Inst., Washington, D.C., dir. since 1934; labor advisor for Structural Clay Products Industry, Dept. of Labor, Walsh Healey div., Washington, since 1939; dir. Federal Reserve Branch Bank of Atlanta, Ga., Dist. No. 6, Jacksonville, Fla., since 1938; chmn. Duval County-Jacksonville Defense Council; mem. Industry Committee for Clay Products Industry, Labor Department; chmn. of Board of Directors Ga. Ice Co., Savannah; pres. Gamble Holding Corp., Jacksonville, Fla., Fla. Ice & Coal Co., Fla.-Ga. Brick & Tile Co., Fla. Brick & Tile Corp., Magaba Corp. Enlisted in Am. Field Service for service with French Army; returned to U.S., Sept. 1917 and transferred to U.S. Naval Aviation; placed on inactive duty, Jan. 1919 with rank of lieutenant-commander; resumed active duty, U.S. Navy, June 13, 1942, with rank of Commander; spl. asst. to Adm. A. B. Cook, Chief Air Operational Training Command, U.S. Naval Air Sta., Jacksonville, Fla.; transferred overseas as asst. and aide to Vice Adm. Cook, 1943; asst. and aide to Vice Adm. W. R. Munroe, Comdr. Gulf Sea Frontier, 1944; now asst. and aide to W. S. Anderson, Commandant 7th Naval Dist. and Comdr. Gulf Sea Frontier. Mem. Southern Clay Products Assn. (pres.), Fla. Brick Makers Assn. (pres.). Democrat. Episcopalian. Home: New Cut Plantation, Wadmalaw Island, S.C. Died Feb. 10, 1953; buried Oak Lawn, Jacksonville, Fla.

GAMBRILL, James Henry, Jr., mfr.; b. Baltimore, Md., Mar. 9, 1866; s. James Henry and Antionette Francis (Staley) G.; ed. Frederick (Md.) Acad., 1878-82; m. Susan May Winebrener, Oct. 31, 1890; (dec.); children—James Henry, 3d, Susan May (Mrs. C. S. Lane, 3d). Milling and grain business, 1882-88; mercantile business, Ala., 1888-93; flour, feed, grain, farm products, 1893-1909; mfr. crackers, biscuits, bread, animal feeds, Frederick, Md., since 1909; pres. Dietrich & Gambrill, Inc., G. L. Baking Company, Glade Valley, Maryland Milling Supply Company; director Citizens National Bank of Frederick. Pres. bd. of trustees Frederick Home for Aged, Stronghold, Inc. (Dickerson, Md.); mem. bd. trustees Dietrich Found., Philadelphia, Pa.; dir. of Hood Coll.; pres. Confederation of Western Md. Communities, Inc. Served as chmn. Frederick County Enrollment Bd. for Mil. Census, mem. Dist. Bd. Selective Service, insp. local draft bd. during World War. Mem. Izaak Walton League America, Am. Forestry Assn., Nat. Parks Assn., New York Zoological Soc. Democrat. Episcopalian. Mason. Club: Rotary (Frederick); Woodmont Rod and Gun (Hancock). Home: 112 Court St. Office: Carroll St., Frederick, Md. Died Oct. 17, 1951; buried Mount Olive Cemetery Frederick, Md.

GAMBRILL, J(ohn) Montgomery, educator; b. Baltimore County, Md., May 9, 1880; s. Dr. William Bartlett and Mary Elizabeth (Nichols) G.; grad. Balt. Poly. Inst., 1897; grad. student Columbia, 1907, 12-15, A.M., 1913, Masters Diploma in Teaching. Tchrs. Coll., 1913; m. Maude R. Mayfield, July 28, 1903; children—Winifred, Helen Mayfield (Mrs. Louis Dorsey Clark), Larner Montgomery; m. 2d, Olive Moore, May 31, 1935. Instr. high sch. Ellicott City, Md., 1898-99, supervising prin. publ. schs., 1899-1901; instr. dept. of English and history Balt. Poly. Inst., 1902-04, head dept. history and civics, 1906-13; instr., asst. prof., asso. prof. and prof. history, Tchrs. Coll. Columbia, 1913—, vice chmn. div. instrn., 1934-36, prof. emeritus of history, Columbia, 1943—, mem. faculty of polit. science Columbia, 1934—, asst. to dir. extension teaching, in charge extramural centres, 1914-16; vis. prof. of Am. history Johns Hopkins, 1942-46, lectr., 1948-53; vis. prof. history Smith Coll., 1947-48. Asst. state supt. pub. instrn. Md., 1904-06; treas. Md. State Bd. Edn., 1904-06; editor Atlantic Ednl. Jour., 1906-11; editor dept. secondary schs., History Teachers' Mag., 1912-14, editor book review dept. Hist. Outlook, 1921-25. Pres. Alumni Assn. Balt. Poly. Inst., 1905-08; mem. Am. Hist. Assn., Fgn. Policy Assn., Nat. Council for Social Studies (pres. 1927-28), Assn. History Tchrs. of Middle States and Md. (pres. 1922-23), The Hist. Assn. (London), Econ. History Assn. Clubs: Columbia University and Faculty of Columbia University (N.Y.C.); Johns Hopkins (Balt.). Author: Leading Events of Maryland History, 1903 (rev. and enlarged 1910, 17); 1 Bibliography of History for Schs. and Librarians (with Charles M. Andrews and Lida Lee Tall), 1910; Exptl. Curriculum-Making in the Social Studies (report of an investigation for the Commonwealth Fund) 1924; Hist. Tests for Elementary Grades (with Olive Moore and I. Jewell Simpson), 1928. Editor: Selections from Poe, 1907 (rev. and enlarged 1936); Socializing the Child (by Sarah Dynes), 1916; Our Ancestors in Europe (by Jennie Hall), 1916; How the Old World Found the New (by Eunice Fuller Barnard and Lida Lee Tall), 1929; My Maryland (by Beta Kaessman, Harold R. Manakee and Joseph L. Wheeler), 1934; The Westward Movement: A Book of Readings on Our Changing Frontiers (with Ina F. Woestemeyer), 1939. Home: 2942 Wyman Pkwy., Balt. 11. Died Jan. 13, 1953; buried Cemetery of the Chapel of the Good Shepherd, Howard County, Md.

GAMEWELL, Francis Dunlap, ret. missionary; b. Camden, S.C., Aug. 31, 1857; s. John N. and Sarah (Thornton) G.; student civil engring. Rensselaer Poly. and Cornell U.; A.B., Dickinson Coll., 1881, A.M., 1884, Ph.D., 1901; hon. M.S., Columbia, 1901; LL.D., Syracuse U., 1908; D.D. Northwestern U., 1926; m. Mary Porter, June 29, 1882 (died Nov. 27, 1906); m. 2d, Mary, d. Bishop William X. Ninde, May 12, 1909 (died Aug. 26, 1947). Engaged in ednl. work, Peiping, China, 1881-84; supt. West China Mission, 1884-87; prof. chemistry and physics Peking U., 1889-1900; chief-of-staff, fortifications, British Legation, Siege of Peking, June 20-Aug. 14, 1900; field sec. and exec. sec. Bd. Fgn. Missions of M.E. Ch., N.Y.C., 1901-08; sec. of edn. for China, M.E. Ch., 1909-25; gen. sec. Ednl. Assn. of China (now China Christian Ednl. Assn.), 1912-25; asso. sec. Eastern Asia, China, Japan and Korea, Bd. Foreign Missions M.E. Ch., N.Y.C., 1924-29; coöperating sec. China Christian Ednl. Assn.; mem. China Ednl. Commn. Retired 1930. Trustee Yenching U. Peking, China. Corr. mem. N.E.A. Mem. Phi Beta Kappa. Address: Clifton Springs Sanitorium, Clifton Springs, N.Y. Died Aug. 7, 1950; buried Hackensack (N.J.) Cemetery.

GAMMAGE, Grady (găm-māj), coll. pres.; b. Prescott, Ark., Aug. 5, 1892; s. Thomas Mancion and Elizabeth (Greer) G.; A.B., U. Ariz., 1916, A.M., 1922, LL.D., 1926; Ed.D., N.Y.U., 1940; Litt.D., Southwest Christian Seminary, 1952; m. Dixie Dees, Aug. 21, 1913 (died Sept. 11, 1948); m. 2d Kathryn R. Klink, Nov. 19, 1949; 1 son, Grady. Tchr. pub. schs., Ark., 1909-12; prin. high sch., Winslow, Ariz., 1920-23, supt. schs., 1923-25; dir. training Northern Ariz. State Tchrs. Coll., Flagstaff, 1925-26, pres., 1926-33; pres. Ariz. State U., June 20, 1933—; spl. lecturer on edn., N.Y. U., summer 1945. Member Ariz. State Bd. Edn., Ariz. Bd. of Vocational Edn., Ariz. United War Fund, Inc. Chairman of board of directors and director of War Drives. Mem. bd. directors Phoenix Symphony Assn., Marshall Foundation, Nat. Conf. Christians and Jews, Nat. War Fund. On spl. mission to Germany, 1947, to study teacher edn. Recipient Legion of Merit Medal (Denmark), Certificate of Merit. (China). Mem. Am. Institute Fgn. Trade (dir.), Assn. Applied Solar Energy (dir.), Navy League, Phoenix C. of C. (dir.), Am. Assn. Coll. Tchrs. English, Order of Distinguished Americans, Western College Assn., N.E.A., Newcomen Society N.A., Horace Mann League, Am. Assn. Tchrs. Colls. (pres. 1945-46), S.A.R., Ariz. Edn. Assn., Phi Kappa Phi, Phi Delta Kappa, Kappa Delta Pi, Phi Eta Sigma, Epsilon Pi Tau, Iota Sigma Alpha, Tau Kappa Epsilon. Democrat. Methodist. Mason. Clubs: Rotary, Paradise Valley Country, Executives, Hiram, Arizona Newcomen Soc. Author: Rural Education in Arizona; A Survey of Ariz. State Teachers College; contbr. articles to mags. Speaker on civic and ednl. topics. Address: Ariz. State U., Tempe, Ariz. Died Dec. 1959.

GANNETT, Anne Macomber (Mrs. Guy Patterson Gannett), orgn. exec.; b. Augusta, Me.; d. George E. and Sarah (Johnson) Macomber; grad. Bradford (Mass.) Jr. Coll., 1903; A.M., Bates Coll., 1946; m. Guy Patterson Gannett, June 6, 1905; children—Madeleine (Mrs. Creighton Gatchell, dec.), John, Jean (Mrs. Roger Chilton Williams). Vice pres., treas. Guy P. Gannett newspapers, Portland, Me. Active in philanthropy and music; mem. Nat. Fedn. Music Clubs (pres. 1941-47; Me. Fedn. pres. 1932-36; mem. nat. bd., 1924—, nat. pub. chmn. 1935-39, legislative chmn. and eastern regional v.p. 1939-41, initiated music in hosp. service program, established regional conf. scholarships Nat. Music Camp, Interlochen, 1944, dir. internat. music relations program 1947—, trustee Found. for Advancement of Music). Dir Met. Opera Guild. Trustee New Eng. Conservatory Music; mem. bd. Koussevitzky Music Found.; v.p. Nat. Music Council; mem. sub-com. on music. Nat. Bd. YWCA; mem. Nat. and Inter-Am. Music Week Com. A founder and head women's com. Portland (Me.) Symphony Orch. Mem. Sigma Alpha Iota. Republican. Christian Scientist. Club: Mountain Lake, Lake Wales, Fla. (mem. bd. trustees). Home: Grey Rocks, 882 Shore Rd., Cape Elizabeth, Me. Office: Press Herald Bldg., Portland, Me. Died May 22, 1951.

GANNETT, Farley, cons. engring.; b. Washington, May 6, 1880; s. Henry and Mary Ellen (Chase) G.; B.S., Mass. Inst. Tech., 1902; m. Janet Rand Sanders, June 14, 1905; children—Juriel, Jane, Alice. Engr. on Harrisburg (Pa.) Filter Plant; chief engr. Pa. Water Supply Commn.; pres., dir. Gannett, Fleming, Corddry & Carpenter, Inc., 1915-57, chairman of the board, 1957—; vice president, director Engineers Water Works Corp.; dir. Cayuga Rock Salt Co. Mem. Am. Soc. C.E. Club: Beaufort Hunt. Home: 2841 N. 2d S.t Office: 600 N. 2d St., Harrisburg, Pa. Died Jan. 20, 1958.

GANNETT, Frank Ernest (găn-nĕt′), editor, pub.; b. Bristol, N.Y., Sept. 15, 1876; s. Joseph Charles and Maria (Brooks) G.; A.B., Cornell, 1898; hon. A.M., Wesleyan U., 1929; LL.D., Alfred U., 1935, Hobart Coll., 1937; Ph.D., Oglethorpe Univ., 1939; Litt.D., Keuka College, 1939; LL.D., Hartwick College, 1941, St. Bonaventure College, 1947, University N.B., 1951, Syracuse University, 1953; Doctor Journalism (hon.), Bradley University, 1955; married Caroline Werner March 25, 1920; children—Sarah Maria (Mrs. Charles V. McAdam, Jr.), Dixon. Editor of Cornell Alumni News, 1900; mng. editor and mgr., Ithaca (N.Y.) Daily News, 1900-05; editor Pittsburgh (Pa.) Index, 1905-06; editor and part owner Elmira (N.Y.) Gazette, 1906, Elmira Star-Gazette since 1906; sole or controlling owner Rochester Times-Union, Rochester Democrat and Chronicle, Albany Knickerbocker-News, Utica Observer-Dispatch, Utica Press, Elmira Star-Gazette, Elmira Advertiser, Elmira Telegram, Newburgh News, Ithaca Journal, Ogdensburg Journal, Beacon News, and Malone Evening Telegram, Saratoga Springs Saratogian, Olean Times-Herald, Massena Observer, Binghamton Press, Niagara Falls Gazette (all N.Y.), Hartford (Conn.) Times, Plainfield (N.J.) Courier-News, Danville (Ill.) Commercial-News; promoter Teletypesetter; director Teletypesetter Corp.; pres. emeritus Gannett Co., Inc. Sec. to late Jacob G. Schurman, pres. first Commn. to Philippines, 1899. Mem. exec. com. Cornellian Coun. (pres. 1925-26). Awarded medal and citation Cath. War Vets, 1948; gold citizenship award Vets Fgn. Wars, 1949; Fairbanks Citation, 1951; George Washington Carver Meml. Inst. award of merit and hon. fellowship, 1952; Civic medal Rochester Mus. Arts, Scis., 1955; decorated Chevalier Legion of Honor. Mem. bd. dirs. Rochester Inst. Tech. (founders award, 1952); trustee emeritus Cornell; trustee Keuka Coll. Candidate for Rep. nomination for pres., 1940; v. chmn. Nat. Com., 1942. Mem. Soc. the Cincinnati, N.Y. State Publishers' Asso. (pres. 1921-27), N.Y. Press Assn. (ex-pres.). N.Y. Associated Dailies (ex-pres.), S.A.R. (medal citizen award, 1951), Phi Beta Kappa (hon. 1937), Soc. of the Genesee (ex-pres.). Unitarian. Mason (K.T., Shriner), Elk. Founded Frank E. Gannett Newspaper Found., Inc., to perpetuate for service Gannett Newspapers. Clubs: Rochester City, Rochester Country, Oak Hill Country, Genesee Valley, Rochester Yacht, Rochester Ad, Cornell (Rochester); Advertising, University (New York); Bath, Indian Creek (ex-pres.), Committee of 100 (mem. bd. govs.) (Miami Beach, Fla.). Rotary Club. Author: Britain Sees It Through 1944; The Fuse Sputters in Europe, 1946; Winging Round The World, 1947. Translator: Friars and Filipinos (from the Spanish), 1900. Developer revolutionary engraving process. Home: 195 Sandringham Rd. Rochester, N.Y.; also (winter) 5641 Collins Av., Miami Beach, Fla. Office: Times Sq., 55 Exchange St., Rochester, N.Y. Died Dec. 3, 1957.

GANNETT, Guy Patterson, publisher; b. Augusta, Me., Nov. 27, 1881; s. William H. and Sarah N. (Hill) G.; ed. Andover Acad. and Yale University, LL.D., Portland University, 1951; married Anne J. Macomber, June 1905; children—Alice Madeliene (dec.), John Howard, Jean. Pres. Guy Gannett Pub. Co., pubs. Portland Press-Herald, Evening Express, Portland Sunday Telegram, Waterville Sentinel and Kennebec Journal; president of Guy Gannett Broadcasting Services (stas. WGAN, WGUY, WGUY-FM), Bangor; dir. Union Mut. Life Inst. Co. Col., spl. adv. Nat. Comdr. Civil Air Patrol. Former member Rep. Nat. Com., Me. Legislature and Senate. Served as div. rep. Am. Red Cross, in France, 6 mos., 1918. Trustee Bates Coll. Home: 882 Shore Rd., Cape Elizabeth, Me. Office: 390 Congress St., Portland, Me. Died Apr. 24, 1954.

GANO, Seth Thomas (gā-nō′), corp. treas.; b. Westville, N.Y., July 2, 1879; s. Thomas P. and Clymena (Saxton) G.; A.B., summa cum laude, Harvard, 1907; m. Adelaide E. Beunke, Dec. 3, 1907; children—Barbara A. (Mrs. William A. B. Hamilton), Priscilla (Mrs. Gano Bowen), and Cynthia (Mrs. George M. Walker). Treasurer and director of Gauley Coal Land Company since 1911; president, dir. Reliance Co-operative Bank; trustee, Ontario Mining Lands Trust; v.p., trustee Belmont Savings Bank; trustee Belmont Hill Co.; dir. Sharon Sanatorium, Rockland Atlas Nat. Bank. Decorations: Russian Red Cross (ancien régime), with diploma, 1926; Palme académique (France) 1930, Cruz Vermille de Dedi cacao (Portugal), 1942; Legion of Honor (France), 1951. Fellow of Royal Society of Arts, 1939. Former moderator Town of Belmont; trustee Belmont Public Library; member Harvard Alumni Commencement Committee; member Unitarian Service Com. Mem. Archaeol. Inst. America (treas.), The Byzantine Inst. (asst. treas. and sec.), Mediaeval Academy America (member exec. com.), Phi Beta Kappa (treas. Harvard chapter, 1924-39; v.p. 1940-42, pres. 1942-44). Republican. Unitarian. Clubs: Harvard, Union (Boston); Faculty (Cambridge); Harvard (New York). Home: 70 Clark St., Belmont 78, Mass. Office: 199 Washington St., Boston 8. Died Feb. 2, 1955; buried Belmont, Mass.

GANUS, Clifton L. (găn ûs) restaurant chain exec.; b. Hillsboro, Tex., Oct. 25, 1903; s. William E. and Mary (Jackson) G.; student pub. schs. of Hillsboro; LL.D., Harding Coll.; m. Jewell Bearden, Feb. 21, 1921; children—Clifton L., Arvis Dale, James W., Joy Carleen. Wholesale grocery salesman, Dallas, 1921-24; purchasing agt. Pig Stands Co., Dallas, 1924-29; opened first of 12 A & G restaurants, New Orleans, 1932, chmn. bd. Finest Foods, Inc. (operators A and G restaurants in New Orleans, also Mrs. Drake's Sandwiches in New Orleans and Memphis, 1932—; exec. v.p. Progressive Bank & Trust Co.; mem. bd. Industries Sales Corp. Mem. Mayors Adv. Com., Housing Authority Bd. R.R. Terminal Bd., Sewerage and Water Bd., New Orleans. Chmn. bd. trustees Lake Terrace Sch.; trustee Harding Coll.; mem. bd. YMCA, Goodwill Industries Mem. C. of C. (bd.). La. Restaurant Assn. (pres. 1944-47). Rotarian. Home: 517 Amethyst St., New Orleans 19. Office: 2627 Canal St., New Orleans. Died Sept. 20, 1955; buried Garden of Memories.

GARBER, Daniel, painter; b. N. Manchester, Ind., April 11, 1880; s. Daniel and Elisabeth (Blickenstaff) G.; student Cincinnati Art Acad. and Pa. Acad. Fine Arts; m. Mary Franklin, June 21, 1901; children—Tanis, John Franklin. Mem. faculty, Pa. Acad. Fine Arts since 1909. 1st Hallgarten prize, Nat. Acad. Design, 1909; hon. mention, Carnegie Inst., 1910; 4th Clark prize and hon. mention, Corcoran Gallery Art, Washington, 1910; hon. mention Art Club of Phila., 1910, bronze medal, Internat. Expn., Buenos Aires, 1910; Walter Lippincott prize, Pa. Acad., 1911; Potter Palmer gold medal and 1st prize $1,000, Art Inst. Chicago, 1911; awarded $1,500 and Corcoran silver medal for painting "Wilderness," 1912; gold medal, San Francisco Exposition, 1915; 2d Altman prize, N.A.D., 1915; Shaw prize, Salmagundi Club, 1916; H. S. Morris prize, Newport (R.I.) Art Assn.; 1st Altman prize for figure painting, N.A.D., 1917; Edward Stotesbury prize, Pa. Acad. Fine Arts, 1918; Temple medal, Pa. Acad., 1919; $2,000 and 1st Clark prize, Corcoran Gallery of Art, Washington, 1921; 1st Altman prize for landscape, N.A.D., 1922; gold medal, Art Club of Phila., 1923; Carnegie prize, N.A.D., 1923; 3d prize Internat. Exhibit Carnegie Inst., 1924; gold medal, Sesquicentennial Expn., Phila., 1926; 1st Altman prize for landscape painting, awarded 2d time, 1927; gold medal of honor, Pa. Acad. Fine Arts, 1928; Sesnau medal in landscape, Pa. Acad. Fine Arts, 1937; gold medal, Phila. Water Color Club, 1942; Gribbel Memorial Prize, Print Club of Phila., 1942. Fellowship Prize, Penna. Acad. Fine Arts, 1947. Represented in permanent collections of City Art Museum, St. Louis; Corcoran Gallery of Art, Washington, D.C.; U. of Mo., Columbia; Mary Ann Brown Memorial, Providence, R.I.; Art Inst. Chicago; Carnegie Inst., Pittsburgh; Nat. Arts Club, New York, Museum of Arts and Science, Los Angeles; Pa. Acad. of Fine Arts; Nat. Gallery of Art, Washington, D.C.; Duncan Philips Memorial Collection, Washington, D. C.; Wilstach Collection, Memorial Hall, Phila.; Mt. Holyoke College; Albright Gallery, Buffalo; University Club, Phila.; John Herron Art Inst., Indianapolis; Met. Museum of Art, New York; Reading (Pa.) Mus.; Hackley Museum, Muskegon, Mich., N.A., Phila. Museum of Art, Woodmere Gallery, Phila. Mem. Nat. Inst. Arts and Letters, Nat. Acad. Design, Soc. Am. Etchers, Gravers and Woodcutters, Inc. Clubs: Art (Phila.); Nat. Arts, Salmagundi (New York). Address: Lumberville, Bucks County, Pa. Died July 5, 1958.

GARBER, Frederick William, architect; b. Cincinnati, O., s. Frederick William Christopher and Elise (Rabbe) G.; student Mass. Inst. of Tech., 1900-03; m. Alice Noble Woodward, May 14, 1907; children —Stanley Thomas, Frederick William, Woodward, Charles Stedman. Architect, firm of Garber & Woodward, 1904-32; in practice under own name, 1932—. Fellow A.I.A. (past dir.); mem. McDowell Soc. Mason. 28 Oak Av., Glendale, O. Office: Union Central Bldg., Cin. Died Aug. 7, 1950.

GARCIA, Fabian (gär-sē'à), horticulturist; b. Chihuahua, Mex., Jan. 20, 1871; s. Ricardo and Refugio (Rivera) G.; brought to U.S. in 1873, naturalized 1889; B.S., N.M. Agrl. Coll., 1894, M.S.A., 1906, D.Agr., 1927; spl. work, Cornell U., 1899-1900; m. Julieta J. Amador, Aug. 14, 1907 (died Dec. 5, 1920). Asst. in agr. N.M. Agrl. Coll., 1894-1906, prof. horticulture, 1906—, horticulturist Expt. Sta., 1906-13, dir., 1913—, extension lectr. in horticulture, gen. agr., rural edn., English, Spanish, 1918—. Pres. Dona Ana County Fair, 1912; dir. Dona Ana County Fair Assn. Mem. Am. Pomol. Soc., Am. Hist. Assn., A.A.A.S., Alpha Zeta, Epsilon Sigma Phi. Catholic. Rotarian. Contbr. numerous articles and bulls. on agrl. and other sci. topics. Home: Las Cruces, N.M. Address: State College, N.M. Died Aug. 6, 1948; buried Las Cruces, N.M.

GARDINER, James L., clergyman; b. Mount Forest, Ont., Can., Apr. 2, 1872; s. Thomas and Amy (Wright) G.; grad. Model Tchrs.' Tng. Sch., 1890; B.D., Garrett Bibl. Inst., 1901; D.D., De Pauw U., 1914; m. Mary A. Stansfield, June 18, 1901. Came to U.S., 1895, naturalized citizen, 1902. Ordained ministry M.E. Ch., 1901; pastor St. Clair, Mich., 1901-04, Tabernacle Ch., Detroit, 1904-08, First Ch., Trenton, N.J., 1908-13, St. Paul's Ch., South Bend, Ind., 1913-22, Austin M.E. Ch., Chgo., 1922-29, St. James' Ch., Chgo., 1929-34, State Street Ch., Trenton, N.J., 1934—. Served as spl. preacher under Nat. War Work Council, YMCA in Eng. and France, 1918-19. Republican. Mason (32°). Clubs: Union League (Chgo.); Flossmoor (Ill.) Country; Rotary of South Bend (former chaplain). Home: State St. Church, Trenton, N.J. Deceased.

GARDINER, William Howard, publicist; b. Boston, Mass., Mar. 24, 1875; s. William Howard and Helena Lawrence (Baird) G.; ed. Jesuit boarding sch. in France, 1882-88; Boston Latin Sch., 1889; Hopkinson's and Hale's pvt. schs., Boston, 1889-92; special student Mass. Institute Technology, 1892-96; Naval War College, Newport, 1922-23; m. Mary Ruth McBurney, May 16, 1918 (died September 26, 1947). Chemist, electrical and traction engineer, 1900-07; consultant engineer gas cos. in Boston; became asso. partner with Henry L. Doherty, New York, 1907, in engring. management and financing pub. utilities; retired from business, Aug. 1914, for war work, and since has given his time to foreign affairs and naval policy of the U.S.; in 1931, persuaded Canadian government to veto Lord Curzon's proposal for renewal of the Anglo-Japanese Alliance. Author of view that "North America, particularly the United States, has ceased being virtually self-sufficient and is taking on the character and outlook of a great island centrally placed in the oceanic world." Has written many articles on this and kindred subjects in Yale Rev., Atlantic Monthly, North Am. Rev., etc. V.p. Navy League of U.S., 1928-33 (resigned 1935). Worked on global policy with White House and Dept. State, during World War II. Now Gardiner prof. Oceanic Hist. and Affairs, Harvard. Former pres. Fed. Grand Jury Assn. So. Dist. of N.Y.; mem. Grand Jury Assn. of N.Y. County; mem. U.S. Naval Inst., Naval History Found., Inst. of Am. Genealogy, Hist. Soc. of Pa., New England Historic Geneal. Soc.; v.p. gen. Gen. Soc. of the War of 1812 (pres. New York div. 1937-46); former dep. gov., N.Y. Soc. Order of the Founders and Patriots of America; mem. St. Nicholas Soc. of New York, Sons of the Revolution, Soc. of Colonial Wars, Mil. Order Loyal Legion of U.S.; Colonial Order of the Acorn. Worked on global policy with White House and State Dept. during World War II. Episcopalian. Home: 333 E. 57th St., N.Y.C. Died June 21, 1952.

GARDINER, William Tudor, ex-governor; b. Newton, Mass., June 12, 1892; s. Robert Hallowell and Alice (Bangs) G.; graduate of Groton School, 1910; A.B., Harvard, 1914; LL.D., Bates, 1929; Univ. of Maine, 1932, Bowdoin College, 1945; student Harvard Law School, 2 years; m. Margaret Thomas, Sept. 16, 1916; children—Tudor, Thomas, Margaret, Sylvester (died 1947). Admitted to Mass. bar, 1917, to Maine bar, 1919; began practice of law at Augusta; formerly mem. firm Andrews, Nelson & Gardiner; chmn. Inc. Investors, Nat. Dock & Storage Warehouse Co.; v. chmn. Pacific Coast Co.; dir. Rayonier, Inc. Enlisted as pvt., 1st Me. Heavy F.A., reorganized as 56th Pioneer Inf.; advanced through grades to 1st lt.; served in Meuse-Argonne offensive, World War I; commd. maj. U.S. Air Force, Mar. 1942, advanced to colonel; placed on inactive list, July 1945, World War II. Mem. Me. Ho. of Rep., 1921-25 (speaker of house 1925); elected governor of Me. two terms, 1929-33; vice-pres. and dir. Incorporated Investors; director U.S. Smelting, Refining & Mining Co., Northwest Airlines, Inc., Nat. Dock & Storage Warehouse Co. Mem. Am. Legion. Republican. Episcopalian. Mason (33°). Elk, Grange. Clubs: Brookline Country, Somerset, Harvard, Tavern Union Boat (Boston); Harvard (New York). Home: Gardiner, Maine. Office: 200 Berkeley St., Boston. Died Aug. 2, 1953.

GARDNER, Charles M., writer, lecturer; b. Huntington, Mass., July 19, 1872; s. William F. and Maria (Spring) G.; ed. pub. schs. of Westfield, Mass.; m. Elizabeth L. Hayward, Sept. 26, 1906; 1 son, Bryant Hayward. Treas. Home Newspaper Pub. Co., Westfield, Mass., 1894-1905; asso. editor Comml. Bull., Boston, 1905-09; mgr., editor, treas., Nat. Grange Monthly, Springfield, Mass., 1911-46; dir. Grange Publicity Bur., 1923-49. Mem. Mass. State Legislature, Ho. of Rep., 1909-10; head Mass. State Dairy Dept., 1909-13; mem. Mass. State Bd. Agr., 1909-14. Dir Farmers & Trades, Life Ins. Co., Syracuse, N.Y. 1932—, Nat. Grange Fire Ins. Co., Keene, N.H., 1934—. Mem. Nat. Grange (Patrons of Husbandry, State Master, 1909-13, High Priest of Demeter, Nat. Grange 1913—). Republican. Conglist. K.P., Red Man (Metocomet Tribe). Author: The Grange-Friend of the Farmer. Author pubs. to agrl. and rural edn. Contbr. spl. articles on farm matters, grange to Christian Science Monitor. Home: 41 Ridgewood Pl. Office: Myrick Bldg., Springfield, Mass. Died Jan. 21, 1954.

GARDNER, Edward Joseph, economist; b. Hamilton, O., Aug. 7, 1898; s. Edward and Mary (Long) G.; B.C.S., Night Coll. Commerce and Finance, St. Xavier U., Cincinnati, 1921; night student Wharton Sch. of Bus., U. Pa., and U. Cincinnati; m. Esther Pring, Oct. 12, 1926; children—Edward Austin, Patricia Marie. Vice-mayor of Hamilton, O., 1926-28; Ohio state rep., 1937-38 and 1941-42; sec. Ohio State House Taxation Com., 1937-38; chmn. joint com., Ohio State House and Senate for studies of causes delinquent taxes, 1938; mem. 79th Congress (1945-47), 3d Ohio Dist. Awarded Phillip C. Swing Scholarship at U. Cincinnati, 1941. Served with U.S. Army, World War I. Exec. chmn. Butler County Dem. Orgn. Mem. Pub. Accountants Soc. of Ohio (pres. 1943), Am. Econ. Assn., Am. Menagerie Club, Am. Legion (adj.; chef de gare 40 and 8), K.C. (4°, past grand knight), Elk, Moose. Home: 822 Minor Av., Hamilton, O. Office: First National Bank Bldg., Hamilton, O. Died Dec. 7, 1950; buried St. Mary Cemetery, Hamilton.

GARDNER, Edward Tytus, business exec.; b. Middletown, O., Sept. 16, 1879; s. Colin and Elizabeth (Tytus) G.; ed. pub. schs., Middletown; grad. Franklin High Sch., Cincinnati; m. Janet Earnshaw, Apr. 15, 1909; children—Edward T., William Earnshaw. Treas. The Colin Gardner Paper Co., Middletown, 1900-17, pres., 1917-23; an organizer The Gardner-Harvey Paper Co., Middletown 1908, v.p. and treas., 1908-23; pres. The Gardner-Harvey Paper Co., The Gardner Paper Bd. Co. and The Colin Gardner Paper Co., 1917-23; these cos. consolidated, 1923, pres. and exec. head successor firm Gardner & Harvey Co., 1923-32, this firm purchased board Mills, Folding Box plant and other properties of The Richardson Co. of Lockland, O., 1932, and operated as the Gardner-Richardson Co., pres. and gen. mgr., firm name changed to The Gardner Board & Carton Co., 1949, later pres., chmn. bd. till 1957 when co. merged with Diamond Match Co. and name became Diamond Gardner Corp., now dir., mem. exec. com.; dir. Wrenn Paper Co., Middleton. Rep. Baptist. Clubs: Racquet and Tennis (N.Y.C.); Moraine Country (Dayton). Home: 255 Park Rd., Dayton 19, Ohio. Office: 407 Charles St., Middletown, Ohio. Died Feb. 22, 1960.

GARDNER, Eugene Elmore, educator; b. Orangeburg, S.C., June 7, 1890; s. Milton Elmore and Annie Eliza (Able) G.; A.B., Furman U., Greenville, S.C., 1914; M.A., U. Chgo., 1923; Ph.D., Duke, 1937; postgrad. study, U. Mexico, 1948; m. Blanche King, July 19, 1927. Instr. English and German, Cumberland Coll., Williamsburg, Ky., 1914-18; instr. English and French, Okla. Bapt. U., Shawnee, 1920-21; with Furman U., 1921—, successively asst. and asso. prof., prof. and head dept., 1939—, chmn. faculty, 1954. Served in U.S. Army, 1918. Mem. South Atlantic Modern Lang. Assn., Assn. U. Profs., Kappa Alpha. Democrat. Baptist. Club: Thirty-Nine. Home: 4 Jones Av., Greenville, S.C. Died Dec. 17, 1955; buried Springwood Cemetery.

GARDNER, Herbert Spencer, advertising; b. Warsaw, Mo., Dec. 22, 1872; s. Nicholas Spencer and Susan Frances (Holmes) G.; ed. pub. schs.; m. Mary Read, Apr. 8, 1896; children—Edward Read, Herbert Spencer, Charles Holmes: m. 2d, Louise Gay Reeves, Jan. 9, 1939. Clerk Frisco R.R., 1888-94; chief rate clk. and adv. agt. Cotton Belt R.R., 1894-1902; v.p. H. E. Leason Adv. Agency, 1902-08; pres. Gardner Adv. Co., 1908-35; chmn. bd. since 1935; pres. Twinplex Sales Co., 1911-35, Wizard Co. (now Trimfoot Co.), 1913-41, chmn. bd. 1941-48; dir. Nat. Outdoor Adv. Bur. Dir. publicity 8th Federal Res. Dist., 3d, 4th and Victory liberty loans, World War I. Received Wilkinson award for outstanding service during liberty loan campaigns. Pres. Am. Assn. Adv. Agencies, 1924-25. Republican. Conglist. Club: Biltmore Forest Country (Asheville, N.C.). Home: 880 Fifth Av. Office: 9 Rockefeller Plaza, N.Y.C. Died May 4, 1955; buried Bellefontaine Cemetery, St. Louis.

GARDNER, Horace John, writer and radio commentator; b. Grenloch, N.J.; s. John Walker and Anna Anderson (Myers) G.; grad. Woodbury High Sch., N.J., 1913; student Univ. Pa., 1915; m. Mildred Rainier, Mar. 22, 1919. Suburban newspaper editor, Grenloch, N.J., 1914-15; writing for newspapers and mags. since 1919; conducted "The Literary Parade" on radio, 1935-37; former v.p. charge sales, dir. A. S. Barnes & Co., N.Y. City. Presbyn. Club: Fifth Estate (New York). Author: Games and Stunts for All Occasions, 1935; The Year 'Round Party Book, 1936; Courtesy Book, 1937; Both Sides of the Microphone, 1938; The Book of Original Plays and How to Give Them, 1938; Happy Birthday to You!, 1939; Let's Celebrate Christmas!, 1940; Let's Celebrate Patriotic Days, 1943; Let's Celebrate Thanksgiving, 1947; several radio features. Address: 250 E. 35th St., N.Y.C. 16. Died Dec. 24, 1950; buried Bethel Cemetery, Hurffville, N.J.

GARDNER, Kirtland C., mfg. exec.; b. Cleveland, O., Aug. 5, 1876; s. George William and Rosalie Lucretia (Oviatt) G.; student Univ. Sch., Case

Sch. Applied Science; m. Myrta E. Neubauer, Sept. 10, 1901; children—Mary, Isabel, Kirtland, Louise, Frank. Sales engr. Lloyd Booth Co., Youngstown, O., 1899-1901; with United Engring. and Foundry Co., Pittsburgh, Pa. since 1901, pres. and gen. mgr., 1943-52, chmn. bd. and chief exec. officer since 1952; chmn. bd. Adamson-United Co. (Akron, O.); dir. Tristate Indsl. Assn., Davy-United Engineering Co., Ltd. (Sheffield, Eng.), Woodings-Verona Tool Works (Verona, Pa.), Stedman Foundry & Machinery Co. (Aurora, Ill.), Labdell-United Co. (Wilmington). Member of the advisory board of the Pittsburgh Ordnance; dir. Pittsburgh Testing Lab. Mem. Am. Iron and Steel Inst., Am. Soc. M.E., Army Ordnance Assn., Pittsburgh C. of C., Greater Pittsburgh Parks Assn. (dir.), Nat. Assn. Mfrs., Newcomen Soc. of Eng. Clubs: Duquesne, Edgeworth (Pittsburgh); Youngstown Country, The Youngstown (Pa.); Allegheny Country. Home: Coraopolis Hghts., Caraopolis Pa Office: 948 Fort Duquesne Blvd., Pitts. 22. Died Apr. 15, 1955.

GARDNER, Lester Durand, aero. exec.; b. N.Y.C., Aug. 7, 1876; s. Harry and Frances (Scott) G.; S.B., Mass. Inst. Tech., 1898; postgrad. Columbia, 1899; LL.D., Polytech. Inst. Bklyn., 1943; m. Margaret Kettle, Sept. 2, 1913. Staff N.Y. Mail, Sun, Times, and with Everbody's and Collier's mags.; pres., 1916-27, The Gardner Pub. Co., pubs. Aviation and Aero. Engring., Who's Who in American Aeronautics; pres. The Overbrook Press, Highland, N.Y.; pres. Aero. Industries, 1928; pres. Aero. C. of C. Am., 1928; exec. Inst. Aero. Scis., 1932-36; pres. Aero. Archives, 1932-36. Private 1st Plattsburg Regiment, 1915; commd. 1st lieutenant Signal Officers R.C., Aug. 1917; capt. Aviation Sect., Signal Corps, U.S. Army, Sept. 1917; maj. Air Service, Sept. 17, 1918; comdg. officer Aviation Camp, Waco, Tex., and mem. Bd. of Control, Dept. Mil. Aeronautics; on flying status when hon. discharged Dec. 13, 1918. Flew 26,000 miles over European airways, 1926. Del. U.S. Dept. of Commerce to 4th Internat. Civil Aviation Congress, Rome, 1927; apptd. by President Coolidge del. on the part of U.S. to Internat. Conf. on Civil Aeronautics, Washington, 1928; aero. mem. com. of N.Y. Statewide Econ. Congress, 1928; mem. Nat. Panel of Arbitrators, Am. Arbitration Assn., 1928; Am. del. German Aero Expn. and Conf., Berlin, 1928; as pres. Aero C. of C. Am., presented in 1928, cooperatively with Motion Picture Producers and Distbrs. Am., hist. film of Col. Charles A. Lindbergh's flying career, to U.S. State Dept., for U.S. Govt. archives; also to M. Laurent Eynac, French minister for air, at Aero Club de France, Paris, for French Govt. archives; to M. Lippens, Belgian minister of railroads and aeronautics, at Brussels for Belgian Govt. archives; to Sir Samuel Hoare, sec. of state for air of Great Britain, at Air Ministry, London, for British Govt. archives; Am. del., British Aircraft Expn., London, 1929; guest speaker, Internat. Advt. Conv., Berlin, 1929. Flew New York-Moscow-Rome-London via Hindenburg and European airlines. Del. to Lilienthal Soc., Berlin, 1936. Recipient Diploma of Honor, Ligue Internat. des Aviateurs, 1934; Daniel Guggenheim Medal for contbns. to aviation. Del. 1st World Congress Aero Press, Rome, 1939. Mem. aviation com. N.Y. World's Fair; mem. S.A. Reed, Octavo Chanute, Lawrence Sperry, Collier Trophy bds. of award. Hon. fellow Royal Aero. Soc.; mem. Soc. Automotive Engrs., Aero Med. Assn. U.S. (hon.), Am. Soc. M.E., N.Y. Mil. and Naval Officers of World War, Mass. Inst. Tech. Alumni Assn., S.A.R., Mil. Order World War, Am. Legion, Soc. Colonial Wars, Mil. Order Fgn. Wars, Soc. War 1812, Gamma Alpha Rho. Republican. Clubs: University, Wings Club (N.Y.C.); Army and Navy (Washington); Aviation Country (L.I., N.Y.). Home: 875 West End Av., N.Y.C. 25. Died Nov. 23, 1956; buried Arlington Nat. Cemetery.

GARDNER, Percy W., lawyer; b. Wakefield, R.I., July 17, 1881; s. Thomas A. and Sarah A. (Brett) G.; lineal desc. John Alden and Priscilla Mullins, of the Mayflower; Ph.B., Brown U., 1903; student New York Law Sch., 1903-05; m. Mary F. Pearse, Apr. 16, 1906; children—Thomas R., Mary E. Admitted to R.I. bar, 1905, U.S. Supreme Court bar, 1911; also mem. Mass. bar; specializes in corp. law; former investment counsel, chmn. finance com. and dir. Am. Unitarian Assn.; former trustee Meadville Theol. Sem., Chicago; former trustee and chmn. finance com. Hackley School, Tarrytown, N.Y.; chmn. of investment com. S. Co. Hosp. Mem. bd. mgrs., counsel Wakefield Trust Br. of Industrial National Bank; pres., dir., chmn. finance com. Providence Mutual Fire Ins. Company; director Providence Steel & Iron Company. Member American Bar Association, International Law Association, American Judicature Soc., R.I. Bar Assn., R.I. Soc. Mayflower Descendants (ex-gov.), R.I. Soc. for Prevention of Cruelty to Animals (ex-pres.); mem. Soc. of Colonial Wars State of R.I., Phi Delta Theta. Former col., 1st Light Infantry Regt., R.I. Militia. Republican. Formerly pres. Unitarian Layman's League. Clubs: Turks Head, Players; Union (Boston), Mason (32°). Author: Lawyer's Philosophy of Life, 1935. Home: 273 President Av., Providence. Office: Turks Head bldg., Providence. Died Sept. 28, 1955.

GARDNER, Robert Abbe, investment securities, brokerage; b. Hinsdale, Ill., Apr. 9, 1890; s. Henry Alansin and Deborah Chandler (Fessenden) G.; prep. edn., Phillips Acad., Andover, Mass.; B.A., Yale, 1912; m. Katherine Keep, May 6, 1916; children—Mary Blair, Robert A., Jr., Henry Keep. In employ of the Consumers Co., Chicago, 1912-15; with the Peabody Coal Co., 1915-19; mem. firm Mitchell-Hutchins & Co., investment securities, 1919—. Served as 1st lt., Field Arty., U.S. Army, with A.E.F., World War I. Col. A.U.S., July 1942-Nov. 1944, World War II. Pres. Community of Chicago, 1941-42 and 1945-47. Pres. United Charities of Chicago, 1934-36; chairman of Community Fund Campaign, 1932; trustee Northwestern U.; trustee Phillips Acad., Andover, Mass. Clubs: Chicago, University, Attic. Home: Lake Forest, Ill. Office: 231 S. La Salle St., Chgo. Died June 20, 1956; buried Lake Forest (Ill.) Cemetery.

GARDNER, Wallace John, bishop; b. Buffalo, N.Y., July 25, 1883; s. Frederick A. and Sarah Jane (McConnell) G.; A.B., St. Stephen's Coll., Annandale, N.Y., 1906, A.M., 1906, hon. D.D.; student Gen. Theol. Sem., N.Y. City, 1908-11, S.T.D., 1937; unmarried. Taught private schs., 1906-08; ordained deacon P.E. Ch., 1911, priest, 1912; chaplain schs. Garden City, 1911-19; rector St. Paul's Ch., Flatbush, Brooklyn, N.Y., 1919-33; vicar Chapel of Intercession, N.Y. City, 1933-36; bishop coadjutor Diocese of N.J., 1936-37; bishop of N.J. since Nov. 1, 1937. Trustee Gen. Theol. Sem. Mem. Sigma Alpha Epsilon. Club: Canadian (N.Y. City). Home: 323 Wood St., Burlington, New Jersey. Office: 808 W. State Street, Trenton, N.J. Died Oct. 22, 1954; buried St. Mary's Church Yard, Burlington, N.J.

GAREY, Enoch Barton, educator; b. Tuckahoe Neck, Md., Aug. 7, 1883; s. Robert J. and Vashti (Saulsbury) G.; A.B., St. John's Coll., Annapolis, Md., 1903, LL.D., 1933; grad. U.S. Mil. Acad., 1908; LL.D., Washington (Md.) Coll., 1923; m. Alice Brewer Ross, Dec. 31, 1914; children—Enoch Barton, Albert Ross, Arthur Ellis, Wilson Saulsbury, Alice Ross, Stewart Towers, Barbara Lyden. Commd. 2d lt. inf., Feb. 1908, advanced through grades to maj., regular army, 1920; Jan.-Sept. 1917, with AEF, 1918. comdr. 18th Machine Gun Batt. in France; resigned July 1923 to become pres. St. John's Coll., Annapolis; pres. The Garyey Sch., Aberdeen, Md., 1933-37. Supt. Md. State Police, 2 terms. Decorated Citation and D.S.C. (U.S.); Croix de Guerre (France). Mem. Omicron Delta Kappa, Phi Sigma Kappa. Republican. Presbyn. Clubs: Johns Hopkins, University (Balt.). Co-Author: Plattsburg Manual, 1917; Junior Plattsburg Manual, 1918; Guide Book to Frnce and its Battlefields, 1920; R.O. T.C. Manuals and numerous other military textbooks. Address: 590 Moreno Av., Brentwood Heights, Los Angeles.

GAREY, Eugene Lester, lawyer; b. Chicago, Ill., Aug. 28, 1891; s. Eugene Francis and Ellen Frances (O'Boyle) G.; LL.B., Chicago-Kent Coll. of Law, 1913; LL.D., Villanova College, 1948; married Margaret Kashner, May 12, 1923. Admitted to Ill. bar, 1913, N.Y. bar, 1925; United States Supreme Ct. bar, 1918; various U.S. Cts. and fed. agencies; senior partner, firm Garey & Garey; counsel, New York State Joint Legislature Committee to investigate administration and enforcement of the law, 1937-39; gen. counsel Select Com. Ho. Reps. to Investigate Fed. Communications Commn. (78th Congress, 1943-44); dir. Butte Copper and Zinc Co. Delegate to Constitutional Convention, 13th Senate Dist. of N.Y., 1938. Received honorary membership in Honor Legion of N.Y. City Police Dept., 1933. Decorated Knight (Papal) Sovereign Military Order of Malta. Mem. Pres. Com., U. of Notre Dame, 1950-51; mem. advisory council, Villanova Coll. Roman Catholic. Mem. Am. (mem. spl. com. on adminstrn. law, 1938-39; standing committee on communications, 1939-52) and N.Y. State bar assns., N.Y. Co. Lawyers Assn., N.Y. Co. Criminal Cts. Bar Assn. Life mem. Friendly Sons of St. Patrick. Life mem. Chicago Art Institute. Democrat. Clubs: Metropolitan, Recess, Catholic (New York); Metropolitan (Washington); Blind Brook. Contbr. articles to professional jours. Home: Mt. Kisco, N.Y.; 111 E. 56th St., N.Y.C. Office: 63 Wall St., N.Y.C. 5. Died May 20, 1953.

GARFIELD, Abram, architect; b. Washington, D.C., Nov. 21, 1872; s. James Abram (20th pres. U.S.) and Lucretia (Rudolph) G.; A.B., Williams, 1893; B.S., Mass. Inst. Tech., 1896; m. Sarah Granger Williams, Oct. 14, 1897 (died Feb. 3, 1945); children—Edward W., Mary Louise; m. 2d, Helen Grannis Matthews, Apr. 12, 1947. Practiced in Cleveland since 1898, with F. B. Meade. 1898-1905, alone, 1905-35, became mem. Garfield, Harris, Robinson & Schafer, now Garfield, Harris, Schafer, Flynn & Williams, 1935, ret. Chmn. City Plan Commn., 1929-42. Apptd. mem. Commn. Fine Arts (national), 1925. Fellow Am. Inst. Architects (dir. 1919-22, v.p. 1923-25); mem. Nat. Acad. Design N.Y., Alpha Delta Phi. Republican. Clubs: Union, Tavern (Cleve.); Williams Coll., Century Assn. (N.Y.C.). Home: 298 Corning Dr., Cleve. 8. Office: 1740 E. 12th St., Cleve. 14. Died Oct. 16, 1958; buried Lakeview Cemetery, Cleve.

GARFIELD, Irvin McDowell, lawyer; b. Hiram, O., Aug. 3, 1870; s. James Abram (20th President of U.S.) and Lucretia (Rudolph) G.; prep. edn., St. Paul's Sch., Concord, N.H.; A.B., Williams Coll., 1893; LL.B., Harvard, 1896; m. Susan Emmons, Oct. 16, 1906; children—Eleanor, Jane, Irvin McDowell. Admitted to Mass. bar, 1896, and began practice at Boston; mem. Warren, Garfield, Whiteside & Lamson; chmn. bd. Lawrence Gas & Electric Co. Mem. corp. and trustee Warren Institution for Savings (Boston); trustee Peter Bent Brigham Hosp. Mem. Am. and Boston bar assns., Alpha Delta Phi. Republican. Unitarian. Clubs: Somerset (Boston); Woods Hole Golf (Falmouth, Mass.); Williams (New York). Home: Woods Hold, Falmouth, Mass. Office: 30 State St., Boston. Died July 19, 1951.

GARIS, Charles Frederick Fleming (gär'is), mathematician; b. Easton, Pa., Feb. 1, 1881; s. Cornelius Weygant and Minnie (Fleming) G.; Ph.B., Lafayette Coll., 1903, A.M., 1906, Sc.D., 1923; studied U. Chgo., 1908; m. Rose Lansing, 1908; 1 dau., Drusilla Lansing. Instr. mathematics Union Coll., Schenectady, 1903-06, asst. prof., 1906-08, prof., 1908—, also dean of students, 1919—, and dean of Coll., 1933—. Mem. Am. Math. Soc., Am. Assn. U. Profs., Sigma Nu, Phi Beta Kappa, Sigma Xi. Republican. Presbyterian. Home: 910 Union St., Schenectady. Died Jan. 2, 1957; buried Vale Cemetery, Schenectady.

GARIS, Lilian C. (Mrs. Howard R. Garis), author; b. Cleveland, O.; d. Edward J. and Winifred (Noon) McNamara; studied in private schools and academies and Columbia U.; m. Howard Roger Garis, Apr. 26. 1900; children—Roger Carroll, Cleo Fausta (Mrs. John J. Clancy). Began writing verse for newspapers, 1890; in charge Woman's Work, Newark (N.J.) Evening News, 1895-1900. Originator movement for playgrounds, Newark; active in pub. affairs, woman suffrage, war work, etc.; councillor Girl Scouts of America. Catholic. Author: Two Little Girls, 1901; followed by many girls' books in series, under various pen names; also (under own name) Girl Scout Series (5 vols.); Gloria Books (2 vols.); Joan Books (2 vols); Jane Allen Books (4 vols.); Nancy Brandon (2 vols.); Mystery series; Melody Lane series, etc. Home: 97 Spring St., Amherst, Mass. Died Apr. 19, 1954; buried Amherst Catholic Cemetery.

GARLAND, Robert, author, newspaperman; born Baltimore, Apr. 29, 1895; s. Walter and Rebecca Stewart (Smith) G.; ed. pub. and private schs., Baltimore and abroad; m. Queenie Smith, May 17, 1931 (divorced 1937). Feature writer, Baltimore News, 1920-22; dramatic editor and critic Baltimore American, 1922-24; dramatic editor, critic and columnist Baltimore 22 Daily Post, 1924-26; columnist N.Y. Telegram, 1927, dramatic critic N.Y. World-Telegram, 1928-37; motion picture critic N.Y. American, 1937; pub. relations counsel N.Y. Fed. Theatre, 1937-38; asso. editor Musical Record, New York, 1941, Doubleday-Doran, Inc., 1942; drama critic and spl. writer N.Y. Jour. Am., and Internat. News Service. Served as 1st lt., U.S. Army, Siberia, World War I. Mem. N.Y. Drama Critics Circle. Democrat. Episcopalian. Clubs: University, Baltimore Country (Baltimore). Author: (plays and scenarios) The Double Miracle, 1915; Importance of Being a Roughneck, 1919; At Night All Cats Area Grey, 1933; Calling All Men (with Leonard Sillman), 1937; You've Got Something There (with Harold Sherman), 1937; Between Parades(with B. M. Kaye), 1938; No More Perfect Paradise (with Cynthia White), 1941; also many 1-act plays, short stories and articles in Sat. Eve. Post, Pictorial Rev., Forum, Theatre Arts, Theatre Time, Cosmopolitan, Esquire, and other publs. Appeared in role of Harold Sigrift, in revival of Brief Moment (S. N. Behrman), summer circuit 1947; role of Judge Heath in Night of January 16th (Ann Rand), 1949; title role, Clutterbuck (Ben Levy), 1950. Received award from Theatre Time for valuable contbn. to Am. theatre. Home: 34 W. 75th St., N.Y.C. 23. Died Dec. 27, 1955.

GARNETT, Porter, writer, retired; b. San Francisco, Mar. 12, 1871; s. Louis Anacharsis and Maria Champe (Garnett) G.; student pvt. schs. and tutors; m. Edna Foote, June 1, 1907. Contbr. to the Lark, 1895-97; dramatic and musical critic various San Francisco papers, 1892-1901; asso. editor Argonaut, 1905-06; asst. curator Bancroft Library, U. Cal., 1907-12; lit. editor San Francisco Call, 1912-13. Producer of Bohemian Club midsummer grove plays: The Hamadryads (by Will Irwin), 1904; The Triumph of Bohemia (by George Sterling), 1907; The Green Knight, 1911; asso. prof. graphic arts Carnegie Inst. Tech., 1922-35; established Lab. Press. Carnegie Inst. Tech. Decorated Chevalier Legion of Honor (France): recipient gold medal Am. Inst. Graphic Arts, 1932. Hon. life mem. Am. Inst. Graphic Arts. Clubs: Zamorano of Los Angeles, (hon.); Bohemian (San Francisco). Editor: The Grove Plays of the Bohemian Club, 1918; The Fine Book, a Symposium, 1934; A Laboratory Press Anthology, 1935. Author: The Bohemian Jinks, 1908; The Green Knight, 1911; San

Francisco One Hundred Years Ago (translation), 1913; A Pageant of May, 1914; The Inscriptions at the Panama-Pacific Internat. Expn., 1915; Stately Homes of California, 1915; A Documentary Account of the Beginnnigs of the Laboratory Press, 1927, etc. Home: R.F.D. 1, Calistoga, Cal. Died Mar. 20, 1951.

GARRABRANT, Arthur Anderson, business exec.; b. New Gretna, N.J., Dec. 13, 1889; s. Dr. Clarence and Mary Miller (Mathis) G.; student Princeton; m. Marguerite Craven, Oct. 26, 1921; children—Emilie Elaine (Mrs. Edwin H. Stulb, 3d), Arthur Anderson, Marguerite (Mrs. Harpur A. Tobin, Jr.), Alyce Pabst. Asst. dispatcher Atlantic City & Shore R.R., Atlantic City, N.J., 1912-15; stenographer Atlantic Refining Co., Phil., Pa., 1916-19, export corr., 1919-21, became asst. gen. manager of export sales, 1921, vice-president since 1937, director since 1941; manager of foreign sales since August 1943. Mem. Am. Petroleum Inst., S.A.R. Republican. Presbyterian. Clubs: Racquet, Cricket (Phila.). Home: 645 Westview St., Germantown, Phila. 19. Office: Atlantic Bldg., Phila. Died July 1, 1951.

GARRETT, Erwin Clarkson, author; b. Germantown, Phila., Mar. 28, 1879; s. George L. and Sophia Cooper (Gray) G.; B.S., U. Pa., 1906. Served as pvt., cos. L and G, 23d U.S. Inf., Troop I, 5th U.S. Cav., in Philippine Insurrection, 1899-1902. Made trip around world, including Central Borneo, home of the head hunting Dyaks, crossed the Emperor's closed, "sacred," red bridge at Nikko, Japan, 1908; went to France, Aug. 1917, as civilian, at own expense, so as to insure "front line" service in the World War, enlisted in Paris, Sept. 1, 1917, became pvt., Co. G, 16th U.S. Inf., 1st Div., AEF, serving until 1919 (wounded at Soissons, in 2d Battle of the Marne, 1918). Decorated Order of Purple Heart, Silver Star (U.S.), regiment and division awarded the fourragère from French Govt. Mem. Rittenhouse Astronomical Soc., Hist. Soc. of Pa., Colonial Soc. of Pa., Soc. of Colonial Wars (Pa.), S.A.R., Mil. Order Loyal Legion of U.S. (Pa.), Soc. of First Div. AEF (2d v.p., mem. bd. dirs. nat. soc.), Soc. of Descs. Continental Congress (v.p.), Plantagenet Soc. (recorder), Barons of Magna Charta (herald), Colonial Order of the Crown (justiciar). Author: Army Ballads and Other Verses, 1916; Trench Ballads and Other Verses, 1919; Jenghiz Khan and Other Verses, 1924; Io Triumphe and Other Verses, 1928. Contbr. army verse 1904—. Lectr. on astronomy. Address: 431 W. Stafford St., Germantown. Address: 1528 Walnut St., Phila. Died Oct. 1954.

GARRETT, Finis James, judge; b. on farm in Weakley County, Tenn., Aug. 26, 1875; s. Noah and Virginia (Baughman) G.; A.B., Bethel Coll., McKenzie, Tenn., 1897; m. Elizabeth Harris Burns, Nov. 27, 1901 (dec.); children—Burns, Mrs. Virginia G. Koehler. At 18 became editor of Weakely County Democrat, Dresden, Tenn. (a weekly); later edited McKenzie Herald, 2 yrs.; prin. Como (Tenn.) High Sch., and prin. high sch. dept., Milan, Tenn., 1897-99; admitted to bar, 1899; master in chancery, 1900-05; mem. 59th to 70th Congresses, 9th Tenn. Dist., minority floor leader of 68th Congress; became asso. judge U.S. Court of Customs and Patent Appeals, 1929, and presiding judge, 1937; now commr. Am. Battle Monuments Commn. Democrat. Home: 3550 Springland Lane, Washington 8. Office: Internal Revenue Bldg., Washington 25. Died May 26, 1956; buried Dresden, Tenn.

GARRETT, Garet (christened Edward Peter Garrett), writer; b. at Pana, Ill., Feb. 19, 1878; s. Charles J. and Alice Loretta (Conrad) G.; ed. pub. schs.; married Dorothy Williams Goulet, Aug. 15, 1947. Financial writer New York Sun, 1903-05, New York Times, 1906-07, Wall Street Journal, 1907-08, Evening Post, 1909-12; editor New York Times Annalist, 1912-14; asst. editor New York Tribune, 1916-19. Clubs: Salmagundi (N.Y.); The Family (San Francisco). Author: Where the Money Grows, 1911; The Blue Wound, 1920; The Driver, 1921; The Cinder Buggy, 1922; Satan's Bushel, 1923; Ouroboros, 1925; Harangue, 1927; The American Omen, 1929; The Bubble that Broke the World, 1932; On The Wings of Debt, 1943; A Time Is Born, 1944; The Revolution Was, 1944; Laissez Faire, 1949; Ex America, 1951; Rise of Empire, 1951; The Wild Wheel (published), 1952; The People's Pottage (pub), 1952; The American Story, 1955; also econ. and polit. essays. Editorial writer in chief Saturday Evening Post, 1940-42; editor American Affairs, 1944-50. Home: Tuckahoe, N.J. Died No. 6, 1954; buried Head of River Cemetery, Tuckahoe, N.J.

GARRETT, Paul Loos, educator; b. Waddy, Ky., Nov. 2, 1893; s. Craven and Florence (Gray) G.; A.B., Georgetown (Ky.) Coll., 1914, A.M., 1915, LL.D., 1938; grad. student U. of Chicago, and U. of Ky.; m. Virginia Ryland Ellis, June 1, 1921; children—Paul Ellis, Harvey Thornton, Ryland Gray. Prin. Crittenden (Ky.) High Sch., 1915-17, Campbellsburg (Ky.) High Sch., 1917-18, New Castle (Ky.) High Sch., 1919-24; supt. Versailles (Ky.) City Schools, 1924-37; dir. personnel div. State of Ky., Feb.-Sept. 1937; pres. Western Ky. State College since 1937. Served in 325th Field Arty. U.S. Army, with A.E.F., 1918-19. Pres. Ky. Assn. Colls. and Secondary Schs., 1937-38. Mem. N.E.A., Ky. Edn. Assn., Am. Legion, Phi Delta Kappa. Democrat. Baptist. Clubs: Rotary, Filson (Country (Bowling Green). Address: College Heights, Bowling Green, Ky. Died Feb. 28, 1955; buried Bowling Green, Ky.

GARREY, George Henry (găr'rē), cons. mining geologist, engr.; b. Reedsville, Wis., June 29, 1875; s. John Eugene and Harriet (Anderson) G.; B.S. U. Chgo., 1900, M.S., in Geology, 1902; E.M., Mich. Coll. Mines, 1904; m. Anna Reynolds Morse, Dec. 10, 1938. Served as econ. geologist with U.S. Geol. Survey, 1904-06; asst. chief geologist Am. Smelting & Refining Co., Am. Smelters Securities Co. and allied Guggenheim interests, 1906-08; mem. Spurr & Cox, Inc., 1908-11; partner J. E. Spurr in gen. cons. bus., 1911; again with Am. Smelting & Refining Co., etc., as chief geologist, 1911-14; cons. practice, 1914-15; in charge exploration dept. Tonopah Belmont Development Co., 1915-23; cons. mining geologist and engr., 1923—. Mem. Mining and Metall. Soc. Am., Soc. Econ. Geologists, Am. Inst. Mining and Metall. Engrs., Geol. Soc. Washington, Phi Delta Theta, Sigma Rho, Alpha Nu. Republican. Mason. Clubs: Engineers (Phila.); Denver Mile High, Denver Country, Cactus (Denver). Author or co-author various profl. papers, many repts. and bulls. of U.S. Geol. Survey, etc. Home and office: 1300 E. 7th Av., Denver 3. Died July 23, 1957; buried Fairmont Cemetery, Denver.

GARREY, Walter Eugene (găr'ĕ), physiologist, educator; b. Reedsville, Wis., Apr. 7, 1874; s. John Eugene and Harriet (Anderson) G.; B.S., Lawrence U., 1894; studied U. Berlin, 1898; Ph.D., U. Chgo., 1900; M.D., Rush Med. Coll., 1909; m. Charlotte Eaton, Dec. 31, 1901; 1 son, Walter Eaton. Extension instr. in zoölogy U. Chgo., 1894-98, fellow in physiology, 1898-1900; prof. physiology Cooper Med. Coll., San Francisco, 1900-10; asso. prof. physiology Washington U., 1910-16; prof. physiology Tulane U., 1916-25; prof. physiology Vanderbilt U. Med. Sch., 1925-44, prof. emeritus, 1944. Lectr. on gen. physiology Marine Biol. Labs., Woods Hole, Mass., also mem. research staff. Mem. bd. trustees Marine Biol. Lab., Nat. Bd. Med. Examiners. Mem. A.M.A., A.A.A.S., Am. Physiol. Soc. (pres. 1937, 1938), Am. Soc. Biol. Chemists, NRC, San Francisco Acad. Medicine (hon.), Phi Beta Kappa, Alpha Omega Alpha, Sigma Xi. Contbr. many articles, original research, chiefly on the heart. Address: Vanderbilt Hospital, Nashville 4. Died June 15, 1951; buried Woods Hole, Mass.

GARRISON, John Boggs, physician and surgeon; b. Blawenburg, N.J., Jan. 8, 1849; s. Peter Sutphen and Hannah Deweese (Boggs) G.; pvt. sem., Hopewell, N.J.; M.D., N.Y. Homoe. Med. Coll. and Hosp., 1882; m. Emma Hill, Apr. 18, 1883 (dec. Jan. 28, 1920); m. 2d, Francis Hill Riley, Nov. 9, 1921. Practiced in N.Y., 1882—; clinician to Dispensary N.Y. Homoe. Coll.; laryngologist, N.Y. Ophthalmic Hosp., Hahnemann Hosp., Laura Franklin Free Hosp. for Children; cons. laryngologist, N.Y. State Dept. of Health. Ex-editor, founder Homoe. Eye, Ear and Throat Jour. Democrat. Old School Baptist. Sr. mem. Am. Inst. Homoeopathy (censor); mem. N.Y. State Homoe. Med. Soc. N.Y. County Homoe. Med. Soc. (ex-pres.), Am. Homoe. Ophthal., Otol. and Laryngol. Soc., S.R. of N.J., etc.; charter mem. Unanimous Club, N.Y. Mem. Vol. Med. R.C. Home: Hopewell, N.J. Office: 19 E. 111th St., N.Y.C. Deceased.

GARTLAND, Joseph Francis, govt. ofcl.; b. Antrim, Pa., Oct. 4, 1880; s. Joseph Sweeney and Ellen (Nash) G.; student pub. schs., Wellsboro, Pa.; m. Jane O'Connor, June 20, 1906; children—Robert Joseph, Charlotte Ellen. With U.S. Post Office service, 1898—, successively clk., insp., 1913, post office insp. in charge AEF, France and Germany, 1918-20, asst. dir. Postal Savings system, 1920, post office insp., 1921, chief insp. Dept. of Interior, 1924-29, post office insp., condr. and organizer of schools for instrn. of post office inspectors, 1930-31, asst. supt., post office service, 1931-32, asst. chief post office insp., 1933-42, chmn. operations bd., 1942-46, and dir. of budget, Adminstrn. and Mgmt. Planning, Post Office Dept., 1942—. Made studies of postal service in England, Scotland and Ireland, 1938, also in all states and territories of U.S. at various times. Mem. Soc. for Advancement Mgmt., U.S. Budget Officers Conf., Newcomen Soc. of England. Home: 1634 19th St., Washington 9. Office: Post Office Dept., 12th and Pennsylvania Av., Washington 25. Died Apr. 11, 1949; buried Wellsboro, Pa.

GARVER, Frank Harmon, educator; b. Albion, Ia., Mar. 9, 1875; s. Andrew A. and Diana (Ballard) G.; student Albion (Ia.) Sem.; grad. Epworth (Ia.) Sem., 1895; A.B., Upper Ia. U., 1898; A.M., State U. Ia., 1908, Ph.D., 1912; m. Edna Sniffen, Aug. 14, 1900; children—Raymond J. (dec.), Jeannette. Prof. history and politics, Morningside Coll., Ia., 1898-1911; fellow in history, State U. Ia., 1901-02; prof. history, Mont. State Normal Coll., U. Mont., 1911-26, acting v.p., 1925-26; lectr. in polit. sci. U. Wash., summer 1924; prof. history, U. Southern Cal., 1926-48, chmn. hist. dept., 1929-32, lectr. in history, U. Mont., summer 1935. Trustee Sioux City Pub. Library, 1908-10. Mem. Am. Hist. Assn., Am. Polit. Sci. Assn., Miss. Valley Hist. Assn., State Hist. Soc. of Ia., Pi Gamma Mu, Alpha Pi Zeta, Phi Kappa Phi, Phi Alpha Theta (Xi Chapt.). Democrat. Methodist. Author: What Made the United States Great; also monograph: Attendance at the First Continental Congress. Contbr. to Am. Polit. Sci. Rev., Social Studies, Social Edn., Pacific Hist. Rev., Proc. Miss. Valley Hist. Assn., Ia. Jour. of History and Politics, Fgn. Affairs Interpreter, etc. Home: 4126 4th Av., Los Angeles. Died Sept. 24, 1952; buried Inglewood Park Cemetery.

GARVER, John Newton, Jr., banker; b. Peoria, Ill., Apr. 15, 1897; s. John Newton and Anna (Geiger) G.; A.B., Ohio Wesleyan U., 1919; m. Dorothy Millar Lamy, June 28, 1927; children—John Newton, Theodore Meyer Edward Bruce. Asst. mgr. Better Bus. Bur., Toledo, 1920-21, mgr. Akron, O., 1921-22, asst. mgr. Boston, 1922-23, mgr., Buffalo, 1923-25, pres. Buffalo Better Bus. Bur., 1926-50; pres. Nat. Assn. Better Bus. Burs., Fla., 1925-26; chmn. bd. govs. Assn. Better Bus. Burs., N.Y. City, 1946-52, now director; director Buffalo Better Bus. Burs. Assistant secretary Mfrs. & Traders Trust Co., Buffalo, 1926-33, v.p., 1933—, dir., 1943—. Trustee Buffalo Community Chest; dir. Buffalo Municipal Bur.; pres. and dir. Buffalo Conv. and Tourist Bur.; director Buffalo Area council Boy Scouts of America (president 1951-52). Member Phi Kappa Psi. Republican. Methodist. Clubs: The Mid Day, Greater Buffalo Advertising, The Buffalo (Buffalo). Home: 60 Hodge Av., Buffalo 22. Office: 284 Main St., Buffalo 5. Died Oct. 30, 1957.

GARVEY, Mary Patricia, Sister, coll. pres.; b. Ludington, Mich., Apr. 20, 1888; d. Patrick and Sarah (Shannon) Garvey; student Mich. State Normal Coll., Notre Dame U.; Ph.D., Marquette U., 1938. Prin. high sch., Ludington, Bay City, Mich., 1923-35; prof. Our Lady of Cincinnati Coll., Cin., 1937-40; pres. Mercy Coll., 1941—. Mem. N.E.A., Am. Cath. Philos. Assn., Nat. Cath. Ednl. Assn. Roman Catholic. Author: St. Augustine: Christian or Neo-Platonist, 1939; St. Augustine: Against the Academicians, 1942; article philos. jour. Home: Mercy College, 8200 W. Outer Dr., Detroit 19. Died Aug. 1952.

GARVIN, Jay Earle, textile mfr.; b. Pendleton, S.C., Oct. 28, 1898; s. James E. and Emma (Ellison) G.; B.S., Clemson (S.C.) A. and M. Coll., 1920; m. Abbie Gaillard; children—Eoline (Mrs. Richard Few), Jay Earle, Emma, Elizabeth. Designer, overseer Brogan Mills, Anderson, S.C., 1920-24; overseer, asst. supt. Judson Mills, Greenville, S.C., 1924-30; supt. Gossett Mills, Anderson, S.C., 1931-33; gen. supt. Dilling Mills, Kings Mountain, N.C., 1933-36; plants mgr. Burlington Mills, Altavista, Va., 1937-46, filament div. mgr., Greensboro, 1946-48, v. p. charge mfg., 1948-50, v.p. charge filament div., 1950-56. Rotarian. Home: 805 Sunset Dr. Office: 301 N. Eugene St., Greensboro, N.C. Died Dec. 21, 1957; buried Forest Lawn Cemetery, Greenboro, N.C.

GARWOOD, Irving, educator; b. Ada, O., Nov. 28, 1883; s. Isaac and Minverva (Longenecker) G.; Ph.B., Ohio Northern U., 1912; M.A., Harvard, 1917; Ph.D., U. of Chicago, 1922; m. Eileen Youngberg, July 15, 1918; 1 daughter, Ruth Elizabeth (Mrs. Eugene Arnold). Teacher public schools, Ohio, S. Dakota, Pa. and Nebraska, 1902-16; associate professor English, U. of N.Dak., 1918-19; spl. lecturer in English, Northwestern U., 1919-21; head of English dept., Westminster Coll., New Wilmington, Pa., 1921-23; prof. English, U. of Richmond, 1923-24; head of English dept., Western Ill. State Teachers College, 1924-46, emeritus professor of English, 1950—. President Community Artists Association, 1942-48. Mem. Am. Assn. Univ. Profs., Pierian Sodality (Harvard), Soc. of Midland Authors, Institut Littéraire et Atistique de France, Tau Gamma Delta, Sigma Tau Delta. Mason (32°). Member Christian Church. Clubs: Philosophy (president 1954), Kiwanis. Author: Questions and Problems in American Literature, 1927; Heath Manual of Literature of England, 1930; The American Periodicals from 1850 to 1860, 1931; New Studies in American Literature, 1937; The College Assembly, 1947; also lecturer: A Pilgrimage to the Literary Shrines of America, America's Home Songs in Picture and Story, The World of William Shakespeare, The Bible as Literature, and With the Literary Vagabond in the Old World, The Mysterious Box of Pandora; Spoon River; Realistic Portraits of Small Town Lives in the Midwest, The Words We Use and How. Educational Collaborator for Coronet Instructional Films and for Encyclopedia Britannica Films. His Home is noted for Shakespeare garden, "The Forest of Arden," where Shakespearean plays are presented on stage covered with earth brought from Stratford-upon-Avon. Home: 216 N. Normal St., Macomb, Ill. Died June 8, 1957.

GARY, Hampson, lawyer, diplomat; b. Tyler, Tex., Apr. 23, 1873; s. Franklin Newman and Martha Isabella (Boren) G.; ed. Bingham Sch., Bingham, N.C., and U. Va.; children—Mrs. Bernard A. Moran, Franklin. Admitted to Texas bar, 1894, practice of law at Tyler, Tex., until removal to Washington, 1914; was referee in bankruptcy, 4 yrs.; standing master in chancery U.S. Court, 2 yrs.; apptd. spl. counsel Dept. of State, Dec. 9, 1914, to assist in the consideration of matters arising out of war situation in Europe; advanced to regular service and made a solicitor, same, June 8, 1915; diplomatic agt. and consul gen. to Egypt, rank of minister resident, Oct. 2, 1917-Apr. 7, 1920. While serving in Cairo was in charge of Am. interests in Palestine, Syria and Arabia; at the front beyond Jerusalem with Field Marshal Allenby for a while in 1918; called to Paris, 1919, for work with Am. Commn. to Negotiate Peace; E.E. and M.P. to Switzerland, Apr. 7, 1920-June 1, 1921; in gen. law practice, Washington, 1921-32, N.Y.C., 1931-34. Mem. Fed. Communications Commn. (first chmn. radio-broadcast div.), 1934-35; gen. counsel, 1935-38; solicitor U.S. Export-Import Bank, 1938-46; retired. Capt. U.S. Vols. Spanish-Am. War, 1898; col. 3d Tex. Inf. Mem. Tex. Ho. of Reps., 1901-02; regent U. of Tex., 1909-11. Mem. Am. Bar Assn., Am. Soc. Internat. Law, U. of Va. chpt. Phi Beta Kappa, Alpha Tau Omega, Soc. Colonial Wars, S.R. Episcopalian. Clubs: Metropolitan, Chevy Chase (Washington). Home: Metropolitan Club, Washington. Died Apr. 18, 1952; buried Arlington Cemetery, Washington.

GARY, Theodore, business executive; s. George and Catherine (Pettit) G.; educated district schools in Missouri, 18 weeks; honorary LL.D., University of Mo., 1928; m. Helen Fairbanks Larrabee, Nov. 1, 1882; children—Hunter Larrabee, Mary (Mrs. Wesley H. Loomis, Jr.); m. 2d, Annie Laurie Larrabee, Oct. 8, 1938. Formerly in real estate and loan business; acquired telephone plant at Macon, Mo., 1897; with others effected consolidation of the Kansas City Home and the Bell Telephone cos. of Kansas City, Mo., regarded as the largest physical consolidation of telephone properties up to 1922; organizer, dir. Theodore Gary & Co., investments, Kansas City; pres. and dir. Gary-Loomis Co.; mem. Theodore Gary & Partners (New York). A founder, first president and now president Macon Public Library. President Independent Telephone Assn. of U.S., 1907-08; chmn. Mo. State Highway Com., 1921-26; chmn. Mo. State Survey Commn., 1929; trustee and v.p. Mo. Hist. Soc. Republican. Home: "Oakhill," Macon, Mo. Died Nov. 4, 1952.

GASKILL, Alfred, forester; b. Phila., Nov. 6, 1861; s. Joshua W. and Caroline E. C. (Lippincott) G.; ed. Friends' schs., Phila.; spl. studies Harvard, forestry Balt., N.C., U. Munich, Germany; m. Marion E. Nickerson, May 19, 1906; 1 dau., Margaret Nickerson. Supt. of large glass mfg. bus., Millville, N.J., Phila., 1881-98; gave up mfg. to study and practice forestry when the field was new; with U.S. Forest Service, 1901-06; state forester of N.J., 1907-22; dir. State Dept. of Conservation and Development, 1915-22; now ret. Democrat. Quaker. Mem. Soc. Am. Foresters, Am. Forestry Assn., Washington Acad. Scis. Home: R.D. 2, Brandon, Vt. Died Sept. 6, 1950.

GASSER, Lorenzo Dow, army officer; b. Lykins, O., May 3, 1876; s. Frederick and Lycinda (Rhoad) G.; ed. pub. schs., Tiffin, O.; grad. U.S. Gen. Staff Coll., Langres, France, 1918; grad. Army War Coll., Washington, 1921; m. Molly Gregory Sugrue, September 5, 1904. Captain 2d Ohio Inf., 1898-99; apptd. lt. 43d U.S. Inf., 1899; commd. 2d lt. Regular Army, 1901, advanced through grades to maj. gen., 1942; dep. crief of staff, U.S. Army, retired, 1940; returned to active duty, 1941; pres. War Dept. Manpower Bd., ret. 1945. Decorated D.S.M. with two oak leaf clusters, Legion of Merit (U.S.); French Legion of Honor. Clubs: Army and Navy, Chevy Chase. Home: 36011 Connecticut Av., N.W., Washington. Died Oct. 29, 1955.

GASTON, Arthur Lee, judge; b. Chester, S.C., Aug. 14, 1876; s. Thomas Chalmers and Adelaide (Lee) G.; A.B., Davidson (N.C.) Coll., 1896; student U. Va., 1896-97; m. Virginia Aiken, Dec. 3, 1902 (died 1907); 1 son, David Aiken; m. 2d, Edith Byrd Smith, Apr. 20, 1910; 1 dau., Sarah Elizabeth. Admitted to S.C. bar, 1897, and practiced at Chester; became mem. Gaston, Hamilton & Gaston; judge 6th Judicial Circuit of S.C., 1934-48; pvt. law practice, 1948—. Mem. S.C. Ho. of Reps., 1900-06, 30-34, chmn. judiciary com., 1932. Dem. Nat. Conv., 1920. Served as 1st lt. 1st S.C. Vol. Inf., Spanish-Am. War; lt. col., staff of Gov. R. I. Manning during World War I. Recipient citation for distinction in law Davidson Coll., 1948. Commr. to Gen. Assembly Presbyn. Ch. in U.S., 1951. Chmn. bd. regents S.C. State Hosp. 1928. Mem. Chester Bar Assn. (pres.), C. of C. (pres. 1926-27), Kappa Alpha. Democrat. Presbyn. Rotarian (past pres.). Author: Remarks and Reminiscences. Home: Chester, S.C. Died Aug. 13, 1951.

GATCH, Thomas Leigh, lawyer; born at Salem, Ore., Aug. 9, 1891; s. Claud and Helen (Plummer) G.; student Ore. State Coll., 1906-08; grad. U.S. Naval Acad., 1912; LL.B., George Washington U., 1922; LL.D., Willamette U., Salem, Ore., 1944; m. Nancy Dashiell, June 13, 1917; children—Nancy, Eleanor, Thomas. Entered U.S. Navy, 1908, and advanced through the grades to vice adm., 1945; judge adv. gen., 1943-45; comd. U.S.S. South Dakota in battles of Santa Cruz and Guadalcanal, 1942, wounded in action; retired from navy, 1947; member law firm of Boyd and Erwin, 1947—. Decorated Navy Cross with gold star, Purple Heart. Address: 90 Gloucester St., Annapolis, Md. Died Dec. 16, 1954; buried Ft. Rosecrans, San Diego, Cal.

GATES, Caleb Frank, chancellor; b. Constantinople (now Istanbul), Turkey, Dec. 24, 1903; s. Caleb Frank and Mary Ellen (Moore) G.; student The Hill Sch., 1919-22; B.A., Princeton U., 1926; B.A., Oxford U. (Rhodes scholar), 1929; M.A., 1931; post-grad. student, Princeton, 1932-33; m. Elizabeth Whipple Farnum, June 28, 1928; children—Caleb Frank, Betsy Ann, Mary Ellen, Gwynne; m. 2d, Mabel Ridge, Apr. 15, 1955; 1 dau., Donna Stanton. Tchr. and administrv. work, Robert Coll., Istanbul, 1929-32; instr. history, Princeton, 1933-36, asst. dean Coll., asst. to dir. of Admissions, 1936-41; chancellor U. Denver, 1941-47, prof. history, 1947—. Served in U.S. Army, 1943-46. Mem. Assn. Am. Rhodes Scholars, Am. Hist. Soc., Acad. Polit. Sci., Am. Acad. Polit. and Social Sci. Clubs: Alpine (London); American Alpine, University (N.Y.C.); Denver Country. Home: 737 Emerson St., Denver 18. Died Dec. 21, 1955; buried Golden Gate Nat. Mil. Cemetery, San Bruno, Cal.

GATES, Eleanor (Mrs. Frederick Ferdinand Moore), author; b. Shakopee, Minn., Sept. 26, 1875; d. William Cummings and Margaret (Archer) G.; student Stanford U., 1894-95, U. Cal., 1899-1901; m. Richard Walton Tully, Jan. 26, 1901 (div. 1914); m. 2d, Frederick Ferdinand Moore. Was on the staffs of Examiner, Call and Chronicle (San Francisco) and Enquirer (Oakland, Cal.) while pursuing studies; held one of the eight scholarships for women founded by Mrs. Phoebe A. Hearst. Mem. Prytanean Soc. (U. Cal.), Pacific Coast Woman's Press Assn. Author: The Biography of a Prairie Girl, 1902; The Plow-Woman, 1906; Good Night, 1907; Cupid, the Cow-Punch, 1907; The Justice of Gideon, 1910; The Poor Little Rich Girl (play and novel), 1913; We Are Seven (play, 1913; Apron-Strongs (play and novel), 1917; Phoebe, 1918; Piggie, 1919; The Rich Little Poor Boy, 1921; Darling of the World (play), 1922; Out of the West (play), 1924; Pa Hardy, 1926; Fire (play), 1927; Fish-Bait (play), 1928. Address: Los Angeles. Died Mar. 7, 1951.

GATES, Paul Hayden, engr., state ofcl.; b. Franklin, Vt., June 17, 1895; s. Charles Winslow and Mary Elizabeth (Hayden) G.; Ph.B., U. Vt., 1915; m. Vera Hugh Horne, Sept. 5, 1919 (dec.). Mgr. rural utilities 1916—; commr. highways State Vt. 1951—; asst. prof. mil. sci. and tactics Ga. Sch. Tech., 1942-44. Served with U.S. Army, 1917-19, 34-38, 40-45. Home: Franklin. Office: Montpelier, Vt. Died June 15, 1956; buried Franklin, Vt.

GATES, William Benjamin, educator; b. Rose Hill Nelson County, Va., Aug. 23, 1877; s. Rev. James Edward and Pattie Pryor (Goodwin) G.; grad. Randolph-Macon Acad., 1896; A.B., Randolph-Macon Coll., 1900, A.M., 1902; grad. study Univ. of Va., 1902; m. Fanny Robbins Ladew, June 17, 1903; children—Mrs. Fanny Goodwin Carr, William Benjamin, Mrs. Anna Magruder Nash, Mrs. Marjorie Nelson Robertson, Robbins Ladew. Teacher, Millersburg (Ky.) Mil. Inst., 1902-03; prin. high sch., Suffolk, Va., 1904-07, Martinsville, Va., 1907-15; div. supt. schs., Henry County, Va., 1915-24; v.p. Blackstone (Va.) Coll., 1924-26, pres. 1926-36; pres. and owner Fairfax Hall (girls junior coll.) since 1936; pres. Park View Land Co. Chmn. Am. Red Cross and Pub. Safety Com., Henry County, World War. Mem. bd. dirs. Citizens-Waynesboro Bank and Trust Co., Early Dawn Dairy. Chmn. bd. trustees Fishburne-Hudgins Ednl. Found. Member Pi Gamma Mu, Phi Kappa Sigma. Methodist. Democrat. Mason, K.P. Club: Rotary. Address: Fairfax Hall, Waynesboro, Va. Died July 6, 1959; buried Waynesboro, Va.

GATES, William Frederick, pres. Prairie Pipe Line Co.; b. Hillsdale, Mich., Aug. 15, 1867; s. William Wells and Viola Elizabeth (Farnsworth) G.; ed. pub. schs.; m. Cora Minnie Ora Coursey, Dec. 21, 1901. Began as laborer with W.Va. Transportation Co., Volcano, W.Va., 1884; with Buckeye Pipe Line Co., Lima, O., 1887-90; gauger and foreman, same co., The Indiana Pipe Line Co., 1890-1902; gen. supt., v.p. The Prairie Oil & Gas Co., Neodesha and Independence, Kan., 1903-15; pres., gen. mgr., Prairie Pipe Line Co., Independence, Kan., 1915—. Republican. Mason (32°, K.T., Shriner). Clubs: Rotary, Elks, Country. Home: Independence, Kan. Died Nov. 24, 1938; buried Independence.

GATHERCOAL, Edmund Norris, educator; b. Sycamore, Ill., Dec. 23, 1874; s. John and Jane Gertrude (Sweet) G.; Ph.G., Chgo. Coll. Pharmacy, 1895; Pharm. M., Phila. Coll. Pharmacy and Sci., 1934; m. Cordelia Marion Poole, Sept. 24, 1899; children—Marion G. (Mrs. George R. Lund), Norris M., Jean C. (Mrs. A. T. Christensen). Instr. and prof. pharmacognosy, U. Ill., 1910—; now emeritus. Awarded Ebert prize medal, 1913; mem. U.S. Pharmacopoeial Rev. Com., 1920, 30; chmn. Nat. Formulary Rev. Com., 1930. Mem. Am. Pharm. Assn. (pres. 1938), Sigma Xi, Rho Chi, Kappa Psi. Republican. Baptist. Co-author: Pharmacognosy Text Book, 1947; National Formulary, 6th edit., 1936. Home: P.O. Box 72, Pentwater, Mich. Office: 808 S. Wood St., Chgo. Died Dec. 27, 1954; buried Pentwater Cemetery.

GAUGLER, Ray(mond) C(hristopher) (gŏg'lẽr), business exec.; b. Pittsburgh, Aug. 3, 1892; s. Emil and Barbara (Woelful) G.; m. Eva Lord, Nov. 26, 1914; children—Gladys (Mrs. Frank A. Stevens), Mercedes (Mrs. Richard V. Arnold), Blanche (Mrs. Lewis O. Wardell, Jr.), Jeanne (Mrs. Joseph V. Hogue, Jr.). Pres. and dir. Am. Cyanamid Co., N.Y. City; dir. Jefferson Chem. Co., Guaranty Trust Co. of N.Y., So. Minerals Corp., So. Pipe Line Corp. Republican. Roman Catholic. Clubs: Winged Foot Golf (Mamaroneck, N.Y.); Larchmont (N.Y.) Shore. Home: 14 N. Chatsworth Av., Larchmont, N.Y. Office: 30 Rockefeller Plaza, N.Y.C. Died Jan. 11, 1952; buried Gate of Heaven Cemetery, Pleasantville, N.Y.

GAULEY, Robert David, artist; b. Carnaveigh County Monaghan, Ireland, Mar. 12, 1875; s. James and Ellen (Perry) G.; came to Am. with parents, 1885; studied with Denman W. Ross, Cambridge, Mass., Edmund Tarbell and Frank Benson, Mus. of Fine Arts, Boston, Bouguereau and Ferrier, Acad. Julian, Paris; m. Hélène Marie White, Oct. 11, 1920. Awarded bronze medal Paris Expn., 1900; hon. mention Buffalo Expn., 1901; hors concours, Charleston (S.C.) Expn., 1902; bronze medal, St. Louis Expn., 1904; Isidor portrait prize, Salmagundi Club, 1907, 1912; Thomas B. Clark prize, Nat. Acad. of Design, 1908; 3d best figure exhibit, Appalachian Expdn., Knoxville, Tenn., 1910; silver medal, Panama P.I. Expn., San Francisco, 1915. A.N.A., 1908. Mem. Am. Water Color Soc., New York Water Color Club. Home-Studio: 517 Shepherd Av., Winter Park, Fla. Died 1943.*

GAULT, James Sherman, elec. engr.; b. Detroit, June 23, 1899; s. James Robert and Etta May (Eby) G.; student Detroit City Coll. (now Wayne U.), 1917-19; B.S., U. of Mich., 1921, M.S., 1924; m. Wilma Hazel Smith, June 14, 1924; children—Margaret, Marian, Madelaine. Test dept. Gen. Elec. Co., Schenectady, N.Y., 1921-22, turbine engring. dept., Lynn, Mass., May-Sept. 1922; mem. faculty U. of Mich. since 1922, prof. elec. engring. since 1946, in charge of A-C machinery and indsl. control courses since 1944; elec. engr. Holland, Ackerman & Holland, Chicago, and Ann Arbor, Mich., 1926-48. Fellow Am. Inst. E.E. (chmn. com. on indsl. power systems). Alumni Assn. U. of Mich. (past dir.), Sigma Xi, Iota Alpha, Eta Kappa Nu (asso.). Club: Exchange (Ann Arbor). Author: Alternating-Current Machinery (with Benj. F. Bailey), 1951. Died Nov. 16, 1951.

GAUNT, Alfred Calvin, mfr., b. Worcester, Mass., Apr. 30, 1882; s. Henry and Mary Lyle (Weir) G.; grad. Lawrence Commercial School, 1899, Lowell Technol. Institute, 1903; married Bertha Fisher, Sept. 12, 1906; children—Henry T. (dec.), E. Abbot, Persis Lovejoy (Mrs. James B. Woodman, Jr.), Nancy Lyle (Mrs. Wilber B. Bradford). Began as apprentice in Methuen, Mass., 1895, designer, 1900-02, supt., 1903-06; pres. Merrimac Mills, Methuen, since 1913; dir. Methuen Co-operative Bank, Methuen Nat. Bank. Chmn. Nat. Adv. Council Independent Smaller Business, 1939; pres. New England Smaller Business Assn., 1938-39. Founder Methuen Public Forum and chairman, 1925-38. Dir. Essex County Rep. Club. Formerly dir. Nevins Home for Aged, Am. Business Congress. Trustee Mass. Congregational Conference. Member Massachusetts Governor's Executive Council, 1947-48. Former chmn. of the Fifth Victory Loan, Tax Payers Association, Methuen Red Cross. Founder Chi Beta Kappa (church fraternity), 1910. Republican. Conglist. Mason (Shriner) and Odd Fellow. Author: Smaller Business Lifts Its Eyes, 1938: Smaller Business and Democracy, 1939. Home: 56 Pleasant St., Methuen, Mass. Died Jan. 21, 1959; buried Walnut Grove Cemetery, Methuen.

GAUSS, Christian (gous), univ. prof.; b. Ann Arbor, Mich., Feb. 2, 1878; s. Christian and Katherine (Bischoff) G.; A.B., U. of Mich., 1898, LL.D., 1933; Litt.D., Washington, 1914; L.H.D., Lehigh, 1928, Washington and Jefferson Coll., 1946; Litt.D., New York U., 1947; LL.D., Kenyon Coll., 1947; m. Alice Hussey, June 15, 1902; children—Katherine, Dante Christian, Natalie, Hildegarde. Instr. Romance langs., U. of Mich., 1899-1901; Lehigh U., 1901-03; asst. prof. Modern languages, Lehigh U., 1903-05; asst. prof. Romance langs., 1905-07, prof. Modern langs. since 1907, chmn. dept., 1913-36, and since 1943, dean of the College, 1925-45, Princeton; dean emeritus, dean of alumni, since 1946. Pres. Am. Com. Baltic Univ. in Exile, 1948; pres. New Jersey World Federalists, 1947. Non-resident lectr. on Ropes Found. for Comparative Literature, U. of Cincinnati, 1913; grad. lectr., New York U., 1915-16; lectr., Columbia U. Inst. Arts and Sciences. Lit. editor Princeton Alumni Weekly, 1914-20, asso. editor Jour. of Education, mem. editorial bd. The Am. Scholar.

Trustee and v.p. Princeton U. Press, Teachers Ins. and Annuity Assn., 1928-40. Mem. exec. com. Nat. com. for Democracy and Intellectual Freedom, 1939-40; chmn. Am. Assn. for a Democratic Germany, 1944; mem. Nat. Com. Am. Civil Liberties Union, Modern Language Assn. (mem. exec. council). Decorated Knight of Legion of Honor of French Republic, 1935. Mem. Balzac Soc. America (v.p.), Kappa Sigma, Phi Beta Kappa (senator; pres. United Chapters, 1946), pres. Dante League America, 1918-20. Clubs: Princeton (N.Y.), Century, Nassau. Translator: Ferrero's The Women of the Caesars; (with Alice Gauss) Bainville's History of France, 1925. Editor: Selections from J. J. Rousseau, 1914; Democracy Today, An American Interpretation, 1917; Flaubert's Madame Bovary, 1930. Author: The German Emperor, 1915; Through College on Nothing a Year, 1915; Why We Went to War, 1918; Life in College, 1930; A Primer for Tomorrow, 1934. Co-author: America Now, 1938; The City of Man, 1940; American Thought, 1947; Modern Princeton, 1947. Home: 24 Bayard Lane, Princeton, N.J. Died Nov. 1, 1951; buried Greensboro, Vt.

GAUTHIER, Eva (gō-tē-ā'), mezzo-soprano; d. Ottawa, Can., Sept. 20, 1885; d. Louis and Parmelia (Laporte) Gauthier; ed. St. Joseph's Sch., Rideau St. Convent, Collegiate Inst., Ottawa; studied voice at Conservatoire, Paris, under Jacques Bouhy and Mme. Schoen-René (Berlin), London, Milan, Italy; m. F. M. Knoote, June 30, 1911 (div.). Toured as contralto with Emma Albani, Eng., Can.; operatic début in Carmen, at Royal Opera, Pavia, 1909; sang in opera in Eng.; made tour of the world, studied Oriental Music; toured Europe, made coast to-coast tours of U.S.; gives recitals of modern music and unknown classics, folk songs, especially Oriental; first to introduce Am. jazz on concert program of modern music; toured Australia, New Zealand with Mischa Elman; appeared with Berlin, London Philharmonic, Boston Symphony, Phila., Cin., San Francisco orchestras; now engaged in teaching, N.Y. Represented Canadian artists at Diamond Jubilee of Confederation of Can. Gov. Am. Guild of Musical Artists. Recipient silver medal Dominion Can.; decorated by Queen of Denmark. Catholic. Home: 33 W. 51st St., N.Y.C. Died Dec. 1958.

GAUVREAU, Emile Henry (gōv-rō'), editor, author; b. Centerville, Conn., Feb. 4, 1891; s. Alphonse and Malvina (Perron) G.; ed. Provencher Acad., Montreal, Can., and pub. schs. and high sch., New Haven, Conn.; m. Sarah Welles Joyner, Aug. 1, 1915 (divorced 1936); children—Alphonse Perron, Henry Welles; m. 2d, Winifred C. Rollins, Dec. 5, 1936. Began as newspaper reporter, 1909, later cartoonist; became night editor New Haven Journal-Courier, 1915, and legislative reporter, later mng. editor, Hartford Courant, 1924; editor and publisher, New York Evening Graphic, 1924-29; mng. editor New York Daily Mirror and Sunday Mirror, 1929-35; also daily columnist as news commentator; launched nat. editorial campaign which established Mark Twain's home as lit. shrine in Hartford, Conn.; dir. in chief, pooling of patents investigation conducted by Com. of Patents, House of Reps.; special observer with Congl Mission to Soviet Russia on recognition study; assigned as spl. agt. of Congress to study Good Neighbor policy in Cuba; editor Rotogravure mag. of Phila. Sunday Inquirer and editor of Click, picture monthly, 1937-40. Club: Authors. Author: Hot News, 1931; Scandal for Sale, Heroes All (motion pictures) 1932; The Scandal Monger, 1932; What So Proudly We Hailed (an analysis of Russia), 1935; My Last Million Readers (autobiography), 1941; Billy Mitchell, Prophet Without Honor, 1942; Saboteurs of the Air, 1943; The Wild Blue Yonder (analysis of U.S. air power), 1944; Cabin Fever, 1947; Biography of Warden Lewis E. Lawes of Sing Sing Prison, 1949; Dumbbells and Carrot Strips—the Life and Times of Bernarr Macfadden (book published), 1953; literary works published in England, France, Holland, Finland, and Russia; compiler biography General William Mitchell for Encyclopedia Britannica, 1945. Contbr. articles and fiction to mags., serial to Saturday Evening Post., etc. Director Com. of Public Information, Bucks County, Pa., Defense Council, World War II. Am. advisor to official delegation of Korean Provisional Govt., United Nations Conf., Calif., 1945. Active in restoring posthumous mil. honors to Gen. William Mitchell. Home: Tinicum Pines, Point Pleasant, Pa. Died Oct. 15, 1956.

GAVER, Harry Hamilton, educator; b. Berryville, Va., Dec. 21, 1886; s. James Watts and Elizabeth (Hardesty) G.; A.B., Randolph-Macon Coll., 1907; M.A., U. Va., 1912; student Johns Hopkins, 1921-22; m. Helen Gerard, June 15, 1915; 1 son, Harry Hamilton. Instr. mathematics, sci. Norfolk (Va.) Acad., 1907-10; instr. mathematics University Va., 1911-13; instr. mathematics, sci. Woodberry Forest Sch., Va., 1913-16; instr. mathematics U.S. Naval Acad., 1916-23; headmaster Urban Acad., Los Angeles, 1925-29, Black Foxe Mil. Inst., 1929—. Mem. Cal. Assn. Ind. Schs. (pres. 1948-50), Raven Soc., Kappa Sigma. Home: 637 N. Wilcox Av., Los Angeles 4. Died Mar. 7, 1954; buried Berryville, Va.

GAVIT, Bernard Campbell (gă'vĭt), educator; b. Saginaw, Mich., Oct. 12, 1893; s. John Albert and Emma (Campbell) G.; A.B., Wabash College, Crawfordsville, Ind., 1915, LL.D., 1936; J.D., U. of Chicago, 1920; m. Nettie Sue Bledsoe, Aug. 1, 1922; children—Susanna Campbell, Albert McQueen, George Bernard. Admitted to Ind. bar, 1920; mem. Ibach, Gavit, Stinson and Gavit, Hammond, Ind., 1920-28; asst. prof. law, U. of Ore., 1928-29; prof. law, Ind. U., 1929—, dean of Sch. of Law, 1933—; dir. and sec. The Principia Press, Inc. Mem. Indiana State Board of Law Examiners, 1931-39; sec. Ind. Jud. Council, 1935—; chmn. Ind. State Com. Governmental Economy, 1934-35, Ind. Commn. Uniform Laws, 1933-37; sec.-treas. Assn. Am. Law Schs., 1941-42, 1946, president, 1948; gen. counsel War Manpower Commn., 1942-43. Served with A.E.F., World War I. Member Phi Delta Phi, Phi Delta Theta, Order of Coif, Phi Beta Kappa. Democrat. Author: The Commerce Clause of the U.S. Constitution, 1932; Indiana Law Future Interests, Wills and Descent, 1934; Indiana Cases and Materials on Trial and Appellate Procedure, 1935; Cases and Materials on an Introduction to Law and the Judicial Process, 1936; Cases on Procedure (2 vols.), 1940, 41; Revision of Browne's Blackstone, 1941; Indiana Procedure (2 vols.), 1941-43; Revision of Thompson's Indiana Forms, 3 vols., 1947. Contbr. articles to law publs. Home: 1320 South Downs Dr., Bloomington, Ind. Died Jan. 16, 1954; buried Rosehill Mausoleum, Bloomington Cemetery.

GAVIT, John Palmer (gă-vĭt'), editor, writer; b. Albany, N.Y., July 1, 1868; s. Joseph and Fanny Breese (Palmer) G.; spl. studies Hartford and Chgo. Theol. sems.; L.H.D., Dartmouth, 1935; m. Lucy Lamont, May 8, 1890; children—Joseph Lamont (dec.), Lamont (dec.). Newspaper work in Albany and Hartford, Conn., 1884-93; social welfare and settlement work, Hartford, Chgo. Commons and Pitts. region, 1893-1902; with Associated Press as Albany corr., 1902-09, chief of Washington bur., 1909-11, supt. central div. at Chgo., 1911-12; with N.Y. Evening Post as Washington corr., 1912-13, mng. editor, 1913-18, v.p. and dir., 1920-22; dir. and mem. lit. conf. Harper Bros., 1918-20; traveled much abroad; writer on edn. and internat. affairs; v.p. Survey Associates, and asso. editor The Survey, 1927—. Trustee Common Council for American Unity. Mem. N.Y. Microscopic Society, Authors' League Am. Clubs: Gridiron, National Press (Washington); Century (N.Y.C.); Winter Park (Florida) University. Author: Reporter's Manual, 1903; Some Information for Mother, 1912; Americans by Choice, 1922; College, 1924; Americans from Abroad (booklet), 1926; Opium, 1927. Home: Alabama Hotel, Winter Park, Fla. Address: P.O. Box 447, Winter Park, Fla. Died Oct. 27, 1954; buried Brookside Cemetery, Englewood, N.J.

GAW, Allison, prof. English; b. Phila., Pa., May 23, 1877; s. Horace Denton and Mary (Tudor) G.; A.B., Central High Sch., Phila., 1896; B.S., U. of Pa., 1900; A.M., 1906, Ph.D., 1907; m. Ethelean Tyson, June 30, 1909. Harrison grad. scholar, 1900-01, Harrison fellow, 1906-07, 1907-08, U. of Pa.; prof. English, Temple U., Phila., 1901-06; asst. prof. English, State Coll. of Wash., Pullman, Wash., 1908-11; prof. English 1911-14, head of dept., 1914-24, chmn. div. of English lang. and lit., speech, journalism and comparative lit., 1921-38, U. of Southern Calif., also mem. exec. council, Sch. of Research, 1933—. Spl. examiner in English, Calif. State Bd. Edn., 1914-17; mem. bd. publs. Calif. State Council of Defense, 1917-18. Mem. Nat. Council Teachers of English, Modern Lang. Assn. America, Pacific Coast Br. Am. Philol. Assn., Modern Humanities Research Assn., Shakespeare Assn. America, Am. Assn. Univ. Profs., Browning Soc., Phi Beta Kappa of Southwest (vice pres., 1924-25), Phi Kappa Phi (pres. Southern Calif. Chapter, 1926-27), Sigma Tau Delta, Alpha Phi Epsilon, National Collegiate Players; pres. Epsilon of Calif. chapter, Phi Beta Kappa, 1933-34. Methodist. Clubs: University, Schubert (hon.), American College Quill Club (nat. vice chancellor 1932-33). Author: Sir Samuel Tuke's Adventures of Five Hours, 1917; Studying the Play, 1921, 3 rev. edits.; Centres of Interest in Drama and Types of Dramatic Conflict (contbd. to Schelling Anniversary Papers), 1923; The Origin and Development of Henry VI in Relation to Shakespeare, Marlowe, Peele, and Greene (constituting U. of Southern Calif. Studies, Vol. I), 1926, 27; The Evolution of the Comedy of Errors, 1926; Development of Graduate Work at the University of Southern California, 1910-35; (with Ethelean Tyson Gaw) Pharaoh's Daughter (play), produced 1925, published 1928; (articles) Time in Shakespeare, 1946. Editor: Studies in English Drama (first series), 1917; Shakespeare's Much Ado About Nothing, 1946. Editor (with E. T. Gaw) of The Lyric West (mag. of Am. verse) 1925, 26, 27; also contbr. to periodicals; author of series of articles "The Artistry of the Stanza"; collaborator in Bull. 2, 1917, U.S. Bureau Edn., on Reorganization of English in Secondary Schools; co-editor (with Louis Wann and R. T. Thompson) of Univ. of Southern Calif. Poems (one of the University's semi-centennial publications), 1930; collaborator (with Wm. G. Campbell) on A Form Book for Thesis Writers, 1933. Now prof. emeritus. Home: 1924 N. Las Palmas Av., Los Angeles 28. Died May 17, 1954; buried Forest Lawn, Glendale, Cal.

GAW, Cooper, newspaper editor; b. Easton, Pa., July 7, 1877; s. Alexander Moore and Mary Brandon (Wright) G.; grad. Easton Acad. and St. Austin's Sch., S.I., N.Y.; A.B., Harvard, 1898; m. Eva Ellsworth Schwall, Oct. 3, 1905. Began as reporter Worcester (Mass.) Evening Gazette, 1898; with New Bedford Evening Standard, 1899—, Sunday editor, 1907-14, editorial writer, 1914—. Mem. New Bedford Bd. Health, 1906, 15-24. Trustee New Bedford Free Pub. Library, 1929-38. Mem. New Bedford Port Soc., Old Dartmouth Hist. Soc., Sigma Alpha Epsilon. Republican. Club: Harvard. Home: Drift Road, South Westport, Mass. Address: The Standard-Times, New Bedford, Mass. Died Oct. 30, 1956.

GAY, Frederick Parker, pathologist, bacteriologist; b. Boston, July 22, 1874; s. George Frederick and Louisa Maria (Parker) G.; A.B., Harvard, 1897; M.D., Johns Hopkins, 1901; Sc.D. George Washington U., 1932; m. Catherine Mills Jones, Oct. 18, 1904; children—Louisa Parker, Lucia Chapman, Frederick P. (dec.), William. Asst. on Johns Hopkins Med. Commn. to Philippines, 1899; asst. demonstrator pathology U. Pa., 1901-03; fellow Rockefeller Inst. for Med. Research, 1901-03; research student Pasteur Institute, Brussels, 1903-06; bacteriologist Danvers Insane Hosp., 1906-07; asst. and instr. in pathology Harvard Med. Sch., 1907-10; prof. pathology, U. Cal., 1910-21, prof. bacteriology, 1921-23; prof. bacteriology, Columbia, 1923—. Maj., M.C., U.S.A., 1918-19; mem. med. sct. NRC, 1917-24, chmn., 1922-23, chmn. Med. Fellowship Bd., 1922-26; C.R.B. exchange prof. to Belgian univs., 1926-27. Fellow A.M.A., A.A.A.S.; mem. Nat. Acad. Science, Assn. Am. Physicians, Am. Assn. Pathologists and Bacteriologists, Soc. Experimental Biology and Medicine Assn. Am. Bacteriologists, American Assn. Immunologists. Comdr. Order of Crown of Belgium. Republican. Clubs: Faculty (Columbia and U. Cal.); Century (N.Y.C.). Author: Studies in Immunity, 1909; Typhoid Fever, 1918; Agents of Disease and Host Resistance (with others) 1935; The Open Mind—a Life of Elmer Ernest Southard; also contbr. scientific jours. on bacteriology, immunology and pathology. Home: New Hartford, Conn. Office: 630 W. 168th St., N.Y.C. Died July 14, 1939; buried Old Town Hill Cemetery, New Hartford, Conn.

GAY, Maude Clark, author; b. Waldoboro, Me., Sept. 28, 1876; d. Webster C. Mayo and Annie (Atherton) Clark; grad. Lincoln Acad., Damariscotta, Me., 1895; m. John T. Gay, Jr., Feb. 10, 1896. Mem. Ho. of Rep., State Me., 1932-34; State Senator, 1934-36. Mem. Me. Fedn. Womans Clubs (pres. 1935-37). Contbr. from girlhood to newspapers, mags., etc., poems and short stories. Author: The Knitting of the Souls, 1904; Paths Crossing, 1908. Address: Waldoboro, Me. Died Sept. 11, 1952.

GAYER, Arthur David (gā'ĕr), prof. econ.; b. of English parentage, Poona, Brit. India, Mar. 19, 1903; s. Jack Arthur and Marie (Milionchick) G.; student St. Paul's Sch., London, Eng., 1916-21; B.A., Oxford U., 1925, M.A., 1927, Ph.D., 1930; grad. student Columbia, 1927-29. Came to U.S., 1927; m. Muriel Stirling Coeyman, Sept. 25, 1943 (divorced); 1 son, Paul Arthur. Research fellow in econs., Oxford U., 1925-27, Rockefeller Foundation, N.Y., 1927-30; research asso. Nat. Bur. Econ. Research, New York, 1930-31; lecturer and asst. prof. economics, Columbia, 1931-40; asso. prof. and prof. econ., Queens Coll., N.Y., since 1940, chmn. econ. dept. since 1942; visiting prof. Columbia Business School, summer 1945, Columbia Coll., 1946, New York University since 1946. Research sec., Economic and Financial Group, Council on Foreign Relations, 1943-45; econ. cons. to the United Nations since 1946; was executive secretary Columbia Commission on Economic Reconstruction, 1932-34; research economist Federal Public Works Administration and consultant Nat. Planning Bd., Washington, D.C., 1933-34; chmn. Commn. on Puerto Rico sugar industry, 1936-37; sr. economist bd. of govs. Federal Reserve System, Wash., 1936-37; consultant Nat. Resources Planning Board, 1939. Mem. Economists' Nat. Com. Monetary Policy since 1935; gov. Soc. for Stability in Money and Banking since 1936. Mem. Royal Econ. Soc., Am. Statis. Assn., Am. Econ. Assn. Clubs: Oxford Union (Oxford, England), Columbia Faculty, New York. Wrote: Fluctuations of Industry and Employment in England, 1815-50, 1930; Economic Reconstruction, Report of the Columbia Commission (in part), 1934; Public Work and Economic Planning, 1934; Monetary Policy and Economic Stabilization, 1935, 2d edit., 1937; Public Works in Prosperity and Depression, 1935; Unemployment Relief and Public Works in the United States, 1936; The Sugar Economy of Puerto Rico, 1938; American Economic Foreign Policy (with C. T. Schmidt), 1939; How Money Works, 1940; Obras Públicas, 1942; The Problem of Lend-Lease, 1944; The Control of International Cartels, 1944; Basic Economics (with Harris, Spencer), 1951; Readings in the History of Economic Thought (with Ph. Newman), 1952; The Growth and Fluctuation of the British Economy, 1790-1850, (with W. W. Rostow and A. J. Schwartz), 2 vols., 1953. Editor: The Lessons of Monetary Experience, 1937. Contbr. articles to N.Y. Times, also econ. and statis. jours. Home: 456 Riverside Dr., N.Y.C. 27. Died Nov. 17, 1951; buried London, Eng.

GAYLE, R(obert) Finley, Jr., physician; b. nr. Norfolk, Va., Dec. 18, 1891; s. Robert Finley and May Jeanette (Young) G.; M.D., Med. Coll. Va., 1915; post grad. Columbia, 1921; m. Elizabeth Marshall Cole, Aug. 16, 1919 (dec. Aug. 14, 1944); children—Elizabeth Marshall (Mrs. Parke S. Rouse, Jr.), Robert Finley, III, John Cole; m. 2d, Sarah Geer Dale, Nov. 3, 1945. Intern Tucker Hosp. Richmond, Va., 1915-16, asso. chief staff, 1919-29; residency Phila. Orthopedic Hosp. and Infirmary for Nervous Disease, 1916, Neurol. Inst., N.Y. City, 1916-17; pvt. practice neurology and psychiatry since 1919; professor and chairman of the department neurology and psychiatry Medical College of Virginia since 1937, chief neurologist and psychiatrist, hosp. div., since 1937; vis. psychiatrist Crippled Children's Hosp., Home for Incurables, Johnston-Willis Hosp., Retreat for the Sick, St. Lukes Hosp., Sheltering Arms Hosp., Stuart Circle Hosp., St. Elizabeth Hosp.; psychiatric cons. V.A. Mem. Governor's Adv. Bd. on Mental Hygiene; bd. mem. Va. Dept. Mental Hygiene and Hosps. Served as capt., 3rd div., U.S. Army, A.E.F., Army of Occupation, World War I; cons. Selective Service, World War II. Diplomate Am. Bd. Neurology and Psychiatry. Fellow A.C.P., A.M.A., Am. Neurol. Assn., Am. Psychiatric Assn. (past president), Medical Society of Virginia, American Academy Neurology, So. Psychiatric Association (past pres.); mem. A.A.A.S., So. Med. Assn. (excouncilor), Neuropsychiatric Soc. Va. (past pres.), Richmond Acad. Medicine (past pres.). Virginia Democrat. Episcopalian. Mason. Clubs: Commonwealth, Country Club of Va., Farmington Country, Deep Run Hunt. Contbr. articles profl. jours. Home: 311 Charmian Rd., Richmond 26. Office: 414 W. Franklin St., Richmond 20, Va. Died Nov. 4, 1957; buried Richmond.

GAYLORD, Clifford Willard, bus. exec.; b. Lockport, Ill., Oct. 10, 1883; s. Albin Pascal and Virginia (Snow) G.; ed. pub. sch., academy, and U. of Chicago; m. Catherine Pirrung, June 9, 1923; stepchildren—Jane Pirrung Flynn, Gilbert R. Pirrung, Henriette Pirrung Snyder. Entered business, Chicago, 1902; with Gaylord Container Corp., St. Louis, Mo., since 1920, pres. since 1921, also dir.; dir. First Nat. Bank St. Louis, Ill. Central R.R. (Chicago, Ill.). Served as lt. col., asst. chief of staff, 77th Div., A.E.F., 1917-19; brig. gen. comdg. Mo. Nat. Guard, 1941-45; adj. gen. State of Missouri, 1941-45. Certificate of Merit, Naval Air Reserve. Past chairman bd. dirs. St. Louis C. of C.; dir. Washington Univ. (St. Louis), chmn. exec. com. City Airport Commn., St. Louis; v.p., mem. exec. Com., Jefferson Nat. Expansion Assn.; mem. bd. dirs. Boys Clubs Am.; mem. exec. com., bd. dirs . Miss. Valley Assn.; mem. bd. trustees, Govt. Research Inst. Baptist. Mem. Am. Legion, Legion of Honor, De Molay. Mason (32°). Clubs: Chicago; St. Louis Country. Home: 29 Westmoreland Pl. Office 111 N. 4th St., St. Louis. Died Jan. 7, 1952.

GEAR, Harry Barnes, ret. elec. engr.; b. Marietta, O., Mar. 6, 1872; s. George Rufus and Julia (Barnes) G.; A.B., Marietta Coll., 1892; M.E., Cornell, 1895; m. Bertha Riley, Jan. 4, 1897; children—Margaret (Mrs. Roland H. Lawrence), Robert Barnes. Insp., Commonwealth Edion Co., Chgo., 1895-1900, chief insp., 1900-11, engr. distbn., 1911-21, asst. to v.p., 1921-35, v.p. operating and engring., 1936-44, ret., 1944. Fellow Am. Inst. E.E.; mem. Western Soc. Engrs. Republican. Baptist. Home: 10018 Bell Av., Chgo. 43. Died Mar. 27, 1959; buried Marietta, O.

GEARHART, Bertrand Wesley, lawyer; born Fresno, Calif., May 31, 1890; s. John Wesley and Mary Elizabeth (Johnson) G.; LL.B., U. of Southern Calif., 1914; unmarried. Admitted to Calif. bar, 1913; also admitted to bar of U.S. Supreme Court; in practice, Fresno, California, 1914-17 and since 1919; dist. atty., Fresno Co., 1917-23; mem. 74th to 80th Congresses (1935-49), 9th Calif. Dist. (Ways and Means Com.); exec. dir. Orgn. to Repeal Fed. Income Taxes, Inc. Second lieutenant, Air Service, U.S. Army, World War I. Member State Athletic Commn., 1931; dir. Calif. Veterans' Home, 1932; mem. Calif. Constl. Conv. of 1933. Mem. Am. Legion (past comdr. Calif.; former nat. committeeman), Soc. Am. Legion Founders, Native Sons Golden West (past pres.), S.A.R., Zeta Psi, Phi Delta Phi. Republican (mem. state and county coms.). Elk (dist. dep. G.E.R.). Clubs: Sequoia Towne, Sunnyside Country (Fresno); University, National Press (Washington); Commonwealth, Sierra (San Francisco). Home: 941 Yale Av. Office: T. W. Patterson Bldg., Fresno, Cal. Died Oct. 11, 1955; buried Mountain View Cemetery, Fresno, Cal.

GEBHARDT, Raymond L., railroad exec.; b. Easton, Pa., Sept. 9, 1882; s. Christopher and Sarah M. (Ricker) G.; student Lerche's Prep. Sch.; C.E., Lafayette Coll., 1908; m. Ida Miller, Jan. 14, 1909; children—Richard V., John L., Katherine E. (Mrs. Samuel Miller), Jean E. (Mrs. Norman A. Hill). With engring. group Lehigh Valley Ry. Co., successively div. engr., trainmaster, supt. various divs.; exec. asst. N.Y., O. & W. Ry., 1941-42, v.p., 1944, trustee since 1944. Mem. Newcomen Soc. of N.Y., Tau Beta Beta Pi. Clubs: Traffic, Railroad, Canadian, Downtown Athletic (N.Y. City). Home: 325 E. 41st St., N.Y.C. 17. Died Jan. 28, 1953.

GEDDES, Sir Auckland Campbell, diplomat; s. Auckland Campbell G.; ed. Edinburgh U., London Hosp. and U. of Freiburg, Germany; m. Isabella Ross, 1906; 4 sons, 1 dau. Served as demonstrator and asst. prof. anatomy, Edinburgh U., and prof. anatomy, McGill U., Montreal, Can.; mem. British Cabinet, 1917-20; A.E. and P. from Great Britain to U.S., 1920-24. Created Knight Comdr. of the Bath, 1917, Companion of the Bath, 1917. Address: British Embassy, Washington. Died Jan. 8, 1954.

GEDDES, Norman Bel (gĕd'ĕs), designer, author, theatrical producer; b. Adrian, Mich., Apr. 27, 1893; s. Clifton Terry and Lulu (Yingling) G.; student Cleve. Sch. of Art, Art Inst. Chgo.; M.A., U. Mich., 1937; LL.D., Adrian College, 1936; B.F.A., Syracuse U., 1940; m. Helen Belle Sneider, Mar. 9, 1916 (dec.); children—Joan, Barbara; m. 2d, Frances Resor Waite, Mar. 3, 1933 (dec.); m. 3d, Ann Howe, 1944 (div.); m. 4th, Edith Luytens, 1953. Pioneer in Am. stage design, 1914, in present day methods of stage lighting, 1916; designer, dir., coauthor or producer of more than 200 plays, musicals, operas, motion pictures, and for the circus; planner or designer numerous theatres in U.S. and Europe, including Theatre Guild, Roxy Theatre (N. Y.C.), Ukrainian State Opera House (Karov, USSR), Copa City (Miami, Fla.); designer Gen. Motors Corp. bldg. and exhibit, Futurama, N.Y. World's Fair, 1938, master plan for City of Toledo, 1944, NBC studios, 1955; asso., archtl. commn., Century of Progress Expn., Chgo., 1938; indsl. designer, 1927—; pioneer designer indsl. products, including streamlined automobiles, 1928, railways trains, 1931, ocean liner, 1932, airplane interiors, 1933, electric typewriter, 1946; originator methods and techniques for use by U.S. Army, USN, USAF, OSS, as techniques for ship identification, aircraft recognition, "natural" camouflag (Corps Engrs.,) model constrn. and photograph (USN), Mark IV submarine trainer, stop motion tng. films, rubber mat processes, psychol. warfare weapons (OSS), method, equipment and bldg. Air Force Strategic Command trainer; ofcl. record Battle of Midway (sec. of def.); mem. Inventors Council; adviser QMG, U.S. Army, also OWI. Exhibitor in museums in U.S., Europe, Africa, Asia, 1912—; represented in collections of museums in U.S., Europe, Asia. Mem. NRC, Authors League Am., United Scenic Artists Union, Illuminating Engring. Soc., Archtl. League of N.Y., U.S. Naval Inst., Mediaeval Acad. Am., Royal Soc. Arts (London), (hon.) Arquitectura de Mexico. Clubs: Players, Coffee House, North American Yacht Racing Union. Author: Theatrical Presentation of the Divine Comedy of Dante, 1923; Horizon, 1932; Magic Motorways, 1940. Contbr. encys. and mags. Address: 350 Park Av., N.Y.C. 22. Died May 8, 1958.

GEDDY, Vernon Meredith, lawyer; b. Williamsburg, Va., Nov. 11, 1897; s. Thomas Henley and Martha Virginia (Piggott) G.; A.B., Coll. of William and Mary, 1917; grad. study U. Chicago, 1917; law student, U. Va., 1919-20; m. Carrie Cole Lane, Oct. 24, 1923; children—Vernon Meredith, Caroline Cole (Mrs. Fred L. Frechette). Admitted to Va. bar, 1920; judge Juvenile and Domestic Relations Ct., Williamsburg and James City Co., Va., 1922-24; commonwealth atty., Williamsburg and James City Co., 1924-28; incorporator Colonial Williamsburg, Inc., trustee since 1948, and Williamsburg Holding Corp. (latter now Williamsburg Restoration, Inc.), 1928, successively sec., asst. to pres., v.p., 1st v.p., exec. v.p., 1930-48, dir. since 1948; asso. Murray, Aldrich & Webb, 1930-31, Milbank, Tweed, Hope & Webb, 1931-34 (both N.Y. City); dir. Peninsula Bank & Trust Co. Trustee Endowment Assn. of Coll. of William and Mary; mem. bd. Va. State Hosp. Served as 2d lt., C.A.C., U.S. Army, 1918. Recipient Coll. of William and Mary Alumni Medallion for service rendered to coll. Mem. Am., Va. State bar assns., Va. State C. of C., Soc. Alumni Coll. of William and Mary, Phi Beta Kappa, Phi Kappa Phi, Omicron Delta Kappa, Kappa Sigma. Episcopalian (trustee, vestryman). Clubs: Rotary (Williamsburg); Princess Anne Country (Virginia Beach, Va.). Home: Williamsburg, Va. Died Oct. 18, 1952.

GEE, Edward (Artley), educator; born Wayne, Michigan, Sept. 28, 1893; s. Edward Francis and Mabel (Melvina) G.; student Mich. State Normal Coll., 1912-14; A.B., U. of Mich., 1923, A.M., 1926; student Harvard, 1937-38; married Inez Bayes, August 1, 1917; married 2d, Edna Mae Oatley, February 9, 1924. Supt. of schs., Bellaire, Mich., 1916-18, Mancelona, Mich., 1918-21; instr. in accounting U. of Mich., 1922; asst. prof. Mich. State Coll., 1923, asso. prof. economics, 1929, prof. and head dept.of business adminstrn. since 1944, head of department of accounting since 1950; director East Lansing Building & Loan Assn. Mem. management panel, legislative com., Reorganization State Govt. Sec. Ingham Co. Tb. Soc. Served as chmn. Antrim Co. War Preparedness Bd.; chmn. war Bond Drives; sec. Y.M. C.A.,World War I; mem. fiscal branch Detroit Ordnance Dist., War Dept., 2½ yrs. World War II. Member American Accounting Association, National Assn. Cost Accountants, Mich. Govtl. Accountants Assn., Inter-City Wranglers, Delta Sigma Pi, Theta Chi, Beta Gamma Sigma (hon.), Beta Alpha Psi (hon.). Meth. Clubs: Economic, Kiwanis (Lansing); State Coll. (E. Lansing); Economic (Detroit). Author: Accounting for Engineers, 1931. Mem. bd. cons. editors Accountants Handbook. Contbr. tech. articles. Home: 219 Oxford Rd., East Lansing, Mich. Died Mar. 22, 1957; buried Evergreen Cemetery, Lansing, Mich.

GEER, Everett Kinne, physician; b. St. Paul, Jan. 14, 1893; s. Ethelbert F. and Helen (Hazen) G.; ed. Central high sch. (St. Paul); B.S., U. Minn., 1915; M.D., 1917; post grad. Trudeau Sch. Tb (Saranac Lake, N.Y.), June-July 1921; m. Olive Barnett Lewis, May 15, 1918; children—Patricia (Mrs. John W. Donahower), Everett Kinne (lt. USAAF, killed in action, May 1944), Thomas Brownell. Engaged in practice of medicine, specializing in diseases of chest; chief tb div. Ancker Hosp.; med. dir. Children's Preventorium, Ramsey County; asst. prof. medicine Minn. U. cons. tb. br. Area 8 VA. Served as lt. M.C. USN, 1917-19. Fellow A.C.P.; mem. A.M.A., Am. Heart Assn., Am. Trudeau Soc. (mem. council 1941-43), Central Soc. for Clin. Research. Internat. Union against Tb, Minn. Acad. Med. Minn. Soc. Internal Med., Minn. Pathol. Soc., Minn. Med. Assn., Minn. Trudeau Soc., Nat. Tb Assn., Ramsey County Med. Soc., Minn. Pub. Health Assn. (mem. exec. com.) Phi Gamma Delta, Nu Sigma Nu. Independent Republican. Unitarian. Author of many med. papers. Home: 1050 Lombard Av., St. Paul 5. Office: Lowry Medical Arts Bldg., St. Paul 2. Died May 3, 1950.

GEER, E(zra) Harold, organist, prof. music; b. Tabor, Ia., Mar. 5, 1886; s. Ezra Benoni and Lucy Jane (Spees) G.; diploma in music, Amity Coll., 1903; A.B., Doane Coll., 1906, M.A. (in absentia), 1910, Mus.D. (hon.), 1949; Mus.B., Oberlin (O.) Conservatory of Music, 1907, grad. student in organ and composition, 1907-09; music study in Paris with Charles M. Widor and André Gedalge, 1911-13; studied organ with T. Tertius Noble, N.Y., 1915-16; conducting and composition with André Bloch, Fontainebleau, 1923; m. Ednah Wynne Phelps, July 5, 1918; children—Francis Harold (dec.), Ednah Harriette, Hardison Joyner, Lucien Miner. Instr. in organ and history of music Lake Erie Coll., Painesville, O., 1907-09; instr. in organ and theory of music, Albion (Mich.) Coll., 1909-11; organist and choirmaster First Congl. Ch., Fall River, Mass., 1913-16; with Vassar Coll., 1916-52, as asst. prof. of music, 1916-19, asso. prof., 1919-22, prof. of music, 1922-52, dir. of Vassar Coll. Choir, 1920-52, chmn. dept. music, 1944-50; organ recitals in Europe, 1924, various parts of U.S.; over 650 organ recitals at Vassar; cons. music Pa. Coll. for Women, 1952-54; prof. music, acting head dept., Hood Coll. 1954-56. Chmn. ednl. com., Hymnal for Colls., and Sch., 1956. Fellow Am. Guild of Organists, 1916; mem. Am. Assn. Univ. Profs., Pi Kappa Lambda. Republican. Conglist. Editor and arranger: Vassar Choral Music, 1926—; Sacred Choruses and Choral Arrangements for Women's Voices, 1932—; numerous other titles of choral music. Composer and arranger of organ music; contbr. to musical jours. Author: Scales and Arpeggios for the Organ, 1945; Organ Registration in Theory and Practice, 1957. Address: Center Sandwich, N.H. Died Dec. 23, 1957.

GEHL, Edward J(ohn), judge; b. Hartford, Wis., Jan. 26, 1890; s. Peter L. and Margaret (Wegmann) G.; LL.B., U. Wis., 1913; m. Jessie Colburn, Nov. 26, 1923; 1 dau., Mary Lou. Admitted to Wis. bar, 1913, and practiced in West Bend, 1913-17, Hartford, 1919-40; U.S. atty., Milwaukee, 1932-33; judge, 13th Jud. Circuit of Wis., West Bend, 1940-50; asso. justice Supreme Ct. of Wis., Madison, since 1950. Served as capt., U.S. Army, World War I. Mem. Am. Legion, Vets. Fgn. Wars, Order of Purple Heart. Home: 745 E. Gorham St. Office: State Capitol, Madison, Wis. Died Aug. 28, 1956; buried West Bend, Wis.

GEHRMANN, Bernard John, ex-congressman; b. East Prussia, Germany, February 13, 1880; s John Gehrmann and Rose (Bader) G.; brought to United States, 1893, naturalized, 1901; ed. common schs., Germany, and night sch., Chicago; m. Mary Miller, Jan. 12, 1904; children—Arthur, Joseph, Leona (Mrs. Vern Henderson), Rose (Mrs. Prosper Heinzen), Victor, John, Loraine (Mrs. Elmer Anderson), Mary (Mrs. Irving Justice), Dorothy, Bernard, Edward. Began as farmer, Neillsville, Wis., 1896; removed to Mellen, Wis., 1915; clerk sch. bd., 1916-34; town assessor, 1916-22; chmn. town bd., 1922-30; conducted farmers institutes throughout state, for Coll. of Agr., U. of Wis., 1920-33; mem. State Legislature, 1927-33; state senator, 1933-34; mem.

74th to 77th Congresses (1935-43), 10th Wis. Dist.; dir. various farmers' coöp. socs. Mem. Am. Soc. of Equity (past state pres.). Progressive. Catholic. Mem. K.C., Eagles. Home: Mellen, Wis. Died July 12, 1958; buried Mellen Union Cemetery.

GEHRMANN, George Howard, physician; b. Norwalk, Conn., Oct. 11, 1890; s. Charles Henry and Ida (Cummings) G.; M.D., Long Island Coll. Hosp., 1913; m. Henrietta Walters, Nov. 20, 1940. Interne, Long Island Coll. Hosp., 1913-15; plant physician, du Pont Co., Wilmington, Del., 1915-18, 1919-26, became med. dir. 1926, ret.; asst. prof. preventive med., Va. Med. Coll., Richmond, 1937—. Served as 1st lt., M.C., U.S. Army, 1918-19. Fellow A. M.A., Am. Coll. Phys., Am. Pub. Health Assn., Am. Acad. Occupational Med. Home: Chadds Ford, Pa. Office: Nemours Bldg., Wilmington, Del. Died Sept. 1959.

GEHRON, William, architect; b. Williamsport, Pa., July 9, 1887; s. Jacob and Marguerite (Dechert) G.; A.B. in Arch., Carnegie Institute of Technology, 1912; A.F.D. (honorary), Denison University; m. Grace Patricia McDermott, Nov. 10, 1917; children—Grace Patricia (Mrs. John Edward Heilmann), William Jules. Asso. with Arnold W. Brunner, New York, 1912-25; Gehron & Ross, New York, 1925-32; ind. practice, New York and Williamsport, Pa., 1932-53; with Gehron & Seltzer, 1953—; buildings designed, 1925— include, The Pennsylvania State Capitol group, Harrisburg, Pa. (North Office Bldg., Education Bldg., Finance Bldg., Soldiers and Sailors Memorial Bridge, People's Court, New Center Wing of Capitol, general plan Capitol group extension), United States Military Acad., West Point, New York (Washington and Grant Halls), Veterans Memorial Bridge, Rochester, N.Y., Jewish Theol. Sem., New York, N.Y., Young Men's Hebrew Assn. Bldg., Lexington Av., N.Y.C., Union Temple, Brooklyn, gen. plan for Denison Univ., Granville, O. (chapel, library, science bldg., Curtiss Hall, Shaw Hall, dormitory bldgs., sorority and frat. houses, Physical Edn. and Community Center, Music and Art Bldg.), Harlem Hosp. Out Patient Depts., N.Y., N.Y., State Hosps., Criminal Court & Prison, Queens; McDonald Obs., Tex.; Queens Borough Hall, Queens, N.Y.; Halloran Gen. Hosp. and Staten Island for U.S. Army, new standard mobilization hosp. designs for Army Engrs. pub. sch. 192, Manhattan, N.Y., nurses residence and sch., Queens Gen. Hosp., New York, N.Y., med. and surg. bldg., Utica (N.Y.) State Hosp., Pennsylvania; Hinley and Royle schs., Darien, Conn., also pvt. homes. Served as archtl. consultant for Housing div. Fed. Dept. of Pub. Works, 1934-36. Awarded Silver medal Architectural League for works of major importance, 1932. Fellow Am. Inst. of Architects, Denison Univ., Granville, O. Mem. Century Assn., Architectural League of N.Y., Nat. Acad. of Design, Nat. Inst. for Archtl. Edn., N.A.D. Lutheran. Home: 66 Highbrook Av., Pelham 65, N.Y. Office: 101 Park Av., N.Y.C. 17. Died Nov. 1958.

GEIER, Philip Otto (gī'ẽr), mfr.; b. Cin., Sept. 18, 1876; s. Philip and Sophia Louise (Otten) G.; student pub. and tech. schs.; m. Gladys Jones, Nov. 15, 1913; children—Philip Otto, Eugene Walter. Chmn. bd., and treas. Cin. Milling Machine Co.; dir. Cin. Grinders, Inc.; pres., dir. Bacon Realty Co.; trustee Cin. So. Ry.; treas., dir. Factory Power Co., Factory Colony Co.; dir. First Nat. Bank of Cin. Mem. C. of C., Ohio Mfrs. Assn. (trustee, v.p.). Republican. Presbyn. Mason (32°, K.T., Shriner). Clubs: Queen City, Camargo, Cincinnati Country (Cin.). Home: Route 1, Box 54R, Madisonville, Cin. O. Office: 4701 Marburg Av., Oakley, Cin. Died Apr. 21, 1954.*

GEIFFERT, Alfred Jr. (gī'fẽrt), landscape architect; b. Cincinnati, O., Dec. 22, 1890; s. Alfred Frederick and Emma Paulina (Boehme) G.; educated public schools, Jersey City, N.J., and extension courses Columbia University; m. Anna Zeydel, July 14, 1912; children—Hugo Herman, Alfred 3d, Martha, Ruth, Franklyn; m. 2d, Lu Duble, June 9, 1944. Began as asst. to Ferruccio Vitale, 1908; partner Vitale, Brinckerhoff & Geiffert, 1917-23, Vitale & Geiffert, 1923-34, Vitale & Geiffert-Gilmore D. Clarke, gen. practice landscape architecture, 1934-39, Alfred Geiffert, Jr., 1939—; dir. Architects Offices, Inc.; cons. landscape architect to U. Ill., Rutgers U., Bd. of Architect Consultants of U.S. Treasury N.J. Coll. for Women, Rockefeller Center, Princeton U., Bell Labs., Murray Hill, N.J., etc.; mem. bd. design Chgo. Century of Progress, 1933; collaborator Bd. Design N.Y. World's Fair, 1939; made town plans of Scarsdale, N.Y., Pleasantville, N.Y., etc.; architect for many parks, subdivisions and private estates; consultant in defense housing for Public Bldgs. Adminstrn. Recipient gold medal Archtl. League, 1920, 34, President's medal, 1945; Gold Medal of Honor, Nat. Sculpture Soc., 1951. Trustee Am. Fine Arts Society, Beaux-Arts Inst. Design, Nat. Sculpture (v.p., mem. council), Civil Service Reform Assn., Nat. Acad. Assn. Fellow Am. Soc. Landscape Architects (trustee, mem. exec. com. and past pres. N.Y. chpt.); mem. Municipal Art Soc. (past pres.; mem. bd. dirs.), Archtl. League of N.Y. (v.p.), Fine Arts Fedn. N.Y.C. (del.), Artists for Victory (v.p.), N.A.D. Republican. Club: Century Assn. Contbr. on landscape architecture to Ency. Brit., Bailey's Cyclopedia of Horticulture. Home: Dover Plains, N.Y.; also 27 W. 10th St., N.Y.C. Office: 101 Park Av., N.Y.C. Died Aug. 26, 1957.

GEIGER, Alfred B., printing exec. with Chicago Rotoprint Co., Chicago, Ill., since 1922, beginning as gen. supt. of plant, became vice pres., 1926, pres. since 1928; also pres. W. F. Hall Printing Co., Chicago, (of which Chicago Rotoprint Co. is a subsidiary) since 1936. Jewish religion. Clubs: Standard, Bryn Mawr Country. Home: Edgewater Beach Hotel. Office: 4600 Diversey Parkway, Chgo. Died Dec. 1958.

GEISER, Karl Frederick (gī'zẽr), educator; b. Fairbank, Ia., June 18, 1869; s. John and Agatha (Haist) G.; A.B., Upper Iowa U., 1893; Ph.D., Yale, 1900; post-grad. U. Berlin, 1905-06, Harvard, 1918-19; m. Addie M. Finch, Sept. 19, 1899 (died Jan. 20, 1909); m. 2d, Florence Mary Chaney, Sept. 10, 1912; 1 dau., Gretchen Eleanor (Mrs. T. S. Sappington). Began as tchr., 1893; asst. in Am. history Yale, 1899-1900; professor political science Iowa State Normal School, Cedar Falls, Iowa, 1900-07, Oberlin College, 1908—; teacher summer sessions, successively, University Ill., Columbia, U. Cal. U. Minn. and Ohio State U., 1906-26; lectr. Inst. Politics, U. Va., 1934, also in Hochschule für Politik, Berlin, U. Berlin, U. Marburg, U. Göttingen, U. Münster, Hochschule of Danzig and U. Königsberg, 1936-37. Fellow in Germany of Oberlaender Trust, 1936-37. Mem. Am. Hist. Assn., Am. Polit. Sci. Assn., Am. Soc. Internat. Law. Author: Redemptioners and Indentured Servants in the Colony and Commonwealth of Pennsylvania, 1901; The Government of Iowa (with Jessie Macy), 1905; Democracy versus Autocracy, 1918; Political Philosophy from Plato to Bentham (with Engelmann and Jászi), 1927; American Political Ideals (in German), 1934. Translated and edited Sombart's Deutscher Sozialismus under title, A New Social Philosophy, 1937; translated and edited Sombart's Der Moderne Kapitalismus. Contributed articles to Cyclopedia of Am. Govt. and New Dictionary of Am. Biography; also mag. articles to Am. periodicals. Home: Oberlin, O. Died Apr. 1, 1951.

GEIST, Walter (gīst), corp. official; b. Milwaukee, Wis., Dec. 1, 1894; s. Christian and Annette (Haagenson) G.; studied evenings, extension and correspondence courses; LL.D. (hon.) Lawrence Coll., Marquette U.; D. Engring. (hon.), Mich. Coll. Mining and Technology; m. Florence E. Kopperud, July 21, 1917; children—Kenneth Robert, Janet Lucille Bugni. With Allis-Chalmers Mfg. Co. since 1909, blue print and errand boy, held positions of tracer, draftsman, designer and engr. in charge, 1909-19, asst. mgr. milling machinery dept., 1919-33, gen. sales mgr., 1933-36, v.p., 1936-42, pres. since 1942, now also dir. and mem. executive committee; dir. York Corp.; dir. and mem. exec. com. First Wis. Nat. Bank, 1st Wis. Trust Co.; director Wis. Bankshares Corp., Chicago & Northwestern Railway. Director Wisconsin Mfg. Association, Nat. Assn. of Mfg., Milwaukee Post Army Ordnance Assn., Milwaukee Council of Navy League of U.S. Mem. exec. com. of Wis. Citizens Pub. Expenditure Survey; assoc. Northwestern Univ.; trustee St. Olaf Coll., Northfield, Minn.; mem. board of govs., Marquette Univ.; trustee, Nat. Council for Community Improvement, Milwaukee Hosp. Dir. De Mille Found. for Polit. Freedom. Recipient Modern Pioneer award, 1940; Knight's Cross of St. Olav (Norway); Industrialist of the Year 1950 (Marquette U. chpt. Inst. Indsl. Engrs. and Execs.; cited by U.S. Navy Bur. of Ships for contbn. to Navy in World War II. Mem. Am. Soc. M.E., Engrs. Soc. of Milwaukee Nat. Security Indsl. Assn. (vice chmn. bd.), Transportation Assn. Am. (dir.), Elec. Mfrs. Club (bd. govs.). Republican. Lutheran. Mason (33°). Clubs: Milwaukee Athletic (dir.), Milwaukee, Chicago, Wisconsin Newcomen (chmn. for Wis.), Wisconsin. Home: 2630 E. Shorewood Blvd., Milwaukee 11. Office: Allis-Chalmers Mfg. Co., Milwaukee 1. Died Jan. 29, 1951.

GEMMILL, William Headrick, educator; b. White Lake, Ont., Can., Mar. 4, 1871; s. John and Sarah (Headrick) G.; brought to U.S. in infancy; B.S., Ia. State Coll. Agr. and Mechanic Arts, 1894; student Highland Park Coll., Des Moines Coll., Drake U.; M.A., Highland Park, 1911; m. Birdie D. Richards, Aug. 13, 1895; children—Agnes (Mrs. W. H. Brown), John Du Mont, Helen, Iva May (Mrs. Robert Morris). County supt. schs., Keokuk County, Ia., 1898-1902; supt. schs., Dallas Center, Ia., 1901-11, Carroll, Ia., 1911-13; sec. Ia. State Bd. Edn., 1913-37; supt. of documents, Ia. State Coll. 1937—. Mem. N.E.A., Ia. State Tchr's. Assn., Ia. Acad. Sci., Nat. Geog. Soc., Am. Mus. Nat. History Republican. Methodist. Mason, Odd Fellow. Address: Supt. of Documents, Iowa State Coll., Ames, Ia. Died May 22, 1945.

GENTH, Lillian, painter; born Philadelphia, Pa.; d. Samuel Adams and Matilda Caroline (Rebsher) Genth; ed. pvt. and pub. schs., Phila., grad. Sch. of Design, Phila., 1900 (fellowship to Paris); studied under James MacNeill Whistler and at Colorossi Atelier; unmarried. Won Mary Smith Prize, Pa. Acad. of Fine Arts, 1904; Shaw Prize, Nat. Academy of Design, 1907; gold medal, Am. Art Soc., Phila., 1907; bronze medal, Exposicion Internacional de Arte, Buenos Aiers, 1910; 1st Hallgarten prize, Nat. Acad. Design, 1911; bronze medal, Nat. Arts Club, New York, 1913. Represented at Carnegie Inst. (Pittsburgh); Art Club of Phila.; Engineers' Club (New York); Cremer Collection, Germany; Detroit (Mich.) Club; Met. Mus., New York; Grand Rapids (Mich.) Art Assn.; Nat. Arts Club, New York; Brooklyn Inst.; Nat. Gallery, Washington; Rochester (N.Y.) Art Museum; Muncie (Ind.) Art Assn.; Dallas (Tex.) Art Assn.; Des Moines (Ia.) Art Assn.; Mus. of History and Science, Los Angeles. Fellow Pa. Academy Fine Arts; A.N.A., 1908. Mem. Union Internationale Beaux-Arts et des Lettres (Paris), Royal Soc. Arts (London), Nashville Art Assn., Nat. Arts Club (New York). Home: 225 W. 86th St., N.Y.C. Died Mar. 28, 1953.

GENTILE, Felix Michael, social worker; b. Bronx, N.Y.C., Feb. 16, 1910; s. Michael and Carmelina (Rizzone) G.; B.S., Manhattan Coll., 1932; diploma social work Fordham U., 1934; m. Elizabeth Steele Schumacher, Jan. 20, 1940; children—Elizabeth Steele, Philip Steele. Social worker N.Y. State Dept. Social Welfare, 1933-35, sr. social worker, 1935-36; social research analyst Works Project Adminstrn., 1936-37; asso. tech. advisor Social Security Adminstrn., 1937-41, pub. assistance analyst, 1941-42; exec. sec. La. Soc. Mental Health, 1942-44; sec. La. Child Care Com., chmn. mental health com. Office Civilian Def., 1943-44; sec. Governor's Commn. on Mental Health Laws, 1944-45; lectr. sch. social work Tulane U., La. State U.; dep. dir. welfare Italy Mission, U.N.R.R.A., 1944-45; dep. dir. Adminstrn. Services charge overseas service, 1945-46; research asso. Russell Sage Found., 1946-47; exec. dir., bd. community relations City of Toledo, 1947-52; lectr. community orgn. U. Toledo, 1950-51; exec. dir. Big Bros. Am., Inc. since 1952. Mem. Am. Assn. Social Workers, Nat. Conf. Social Work, Civil Rights Com. (bd. mem., chmn. 1949-51). Club: Phila. Torch. Contbr. articles profl. publs. Home: 1319 Warner Rd., Meadowbrook, Pa. Office: Suburban Station Bldg., Phila. 3. Died May 12, 1957.

GENTLE, Alice True (Mrs. Jacob R. Proebstel), dramatic soprano; b. Chatsworth, Ill., June 30, 1888; d. John Glidden and Emma Catharine (Shroyer) True; ed. pub. schs.; m. Jacob Robinson Proebstel, Apr. 28, 1921. First operatic and stage experience received in chorus of Oscar Hammerstein's Manhattan Grand Opera Co.; went to Italy and was engaged as leading soprano at La Scala Theatre, Milan; with Met. Opera Co., 1918—; has been identified with Scotti Grand Opera Cos. Ravinia Park, Chicago, Chicago Civic Opera Co., etc.; prin. rôles: Carmen, Santuzza, in Cavalleria Rusticana; Anita, in Massenet's La Navarraise; Floria, in La Tosca; Fédora; Zaza; La Forza del Destino. Home: 275 N. Banciforte Av., Santa Cruz, Calif. Died Feb. 28, 1958.

GENTRY, Charles Burt (jĕn'trĭ), educator; b. Drexel, Mo., Oct. 3, 1884; s. John Henry and Sarah Elizabeth (Beaty) G.; Pd.B., Pd.M., Warrensburg (Mo.) Normal Sch., 1908, A.B., 1911; student U. Mo., summers, 1909, 10; B.S. in Edn., U. Chgo., 1912; M.S. in Agr., Cornell, 1919; studied Tchrs. Coll., Columbia, 1919-20, 1927-28, Harvard Grad. School of Edn., 1936; m. Kathleen Moore, Aug. 8, 1912; children—John Louis, Robert Wilton, Charles Edwin, Jean Frances. Tchr. rural schs., Drexel, 1904-05; prin. high sch., Booneville, Mo., 1908-11; tchr. agr. State Normal Sch., Conway, Ark., 1912-14; prof. agr. Tchrs'. State Coll., Springfield, Mo., 1914-18; asso. prof. agrl. edn. Rutgers Coll., New Brunswick, N.J., 1919-20, also asst. state supr. agrl. edn.; dean div. of tchr. tng. U. Conn., 1920-38, dir. div. resident instrn., 1931-1940; dean univ., 1940-50, dean univ., prof. emeritus, 1950—, acting pres., 1928-29, 35; state supr. agrl. edn. Conn. State Bd. of Edn., 1921-31; tchr. summer sch., U. Ariz., 1922, U. Tenn., 1923, Utah Coll. Agr., U. Cal., 1924, Colo. Agrl. Coll., 1926, Cornell U., 1928, 30, Ohio State U., 1931, 41, U. N.H., 1932. Fellow A.A.A.S.; mem. Am. Acad. Polit. and Social Sci., Nat. Edn. Assn., Am. Vocational Assn., Am. Assn. for Advancement of Agrl. Teaching, N.E. Assn. Colls. and Secondary Schs., Nat. Soc. Coll. Tchrs. Edn., N.E. Assn. Coll. Tchrs. of Edn., Conn. Assn. Sch. Supts., Phi Delta Kappa, Sigma Chi. Conglist. Mason. Home: Storrs, Conn. Died Nov. 16, 1955.

GENTRY, Martin Butler, mining engr., corp. exec.; b. Kansas City, Oct. 13, 1886; s. Richard and Susan (Butler) G.; B.S. Sheffield Sci. Sch., Yale, 1906, E.M., Columbia Sch. Mines, 1909; m. Margaret Tomlinson, May 24, 1922; children—Margaret G. Yingling, Martin B. Churn drill foreman Chile Exploration Co., Chuquicamata, Chile, 1912-13; scout engr. Bolen Darnell Coal Co., 1914, William Braden & Andes Exploration Co., Chile, 1915, engr., mine supt., 1916-18; mine mgr. Santiago Mining Co.; rep. Anaconda Copper Mining Co., Santiago, 1919-25; r.r. supt. Andes Copper Mining Co., 1925-27, Allied Chem. and Dye Corp., 1927-30; asst. to pres. Solvay Process Co.,

N.Y.C., 1927-30; Beryllium Co. of Am., 1930-32, Union Sulphur Co., 1932-34, Beryllium Products Co., 1934-35; asst. to pres. Freeport Sulphur Co., 1935-41, v.p., 1941-49, ret.; v.p., dir. Sulphur Export Corp., N.Y.C., ret. Dec. 31, 1949. Former v.p., treas. Am. Arbitration Assn Mem. Amer. Inst. Mining and Metall. Engrs., Mining and Metallurgical Soc. of Am. (past pres.), Am. Soc. for Metals. Republican. Presbyn. Clubs: Cloud, Mining, University, Explorers, Yale. Home: Southern Pines, N.C. Died July 31, 1956.

GEOFFROY, W(ilfrid) J(oseph), govt. official; b. Worcester, Mass., Sept. 10, 1895; s. Joseph and Elsina Barton (Reed) G.; m. Helen Leonard, Sept. 8, 1922; 1 dau., Marion (Mrs. Donald McKeown). With Gen. Motors Acceptance Corp., 1920, mgr. various branches in west and middle west; leave of absence, 1943, resigned, 1947; with Reconstrn. Finance Corp. since 1943, chief adminstrv. officer since 1948, chmn. review com. since 1948; mem. War Contracts Price Adjustment Bd. since 1948. Served as sergt., 11th Photog. Sect., Air Service, World War I. Home: 4018 Veazey St. N.W., Washington 16. Office: 811 Vermont Av., Washington. Died Apr. 7, 1952.

GEOGHAN, William F. X. (gē'găn), lawyer; b. Philadelphia, Pa.; s. John and Ellen F. (Laragy) G.; A.B., St. Joseph's Coll., Phila., 1903, A.M., 1905; LL.B., Georgetown U., 1906; m. Gertrude M. Conway; children—Margaret M., Helen G., William F. X. Admitted to N.Y. bar, 1907, and began practice at N.Y. City; asst. dist. atty. Kings Co., N.Y., 1923-29, chief asst. dist. atty., 1930, dist. atty., 1931-40. Mem. Emerald Assn., St. Patrick's Soc. of Brooklyn, Friendly Sons of St. Patrick of Brooklyn. Brooklyn Bar Assn., N.Y. State Bar Assn. Knight of Columbus, Elk. Democrat. Club: Bathing and Tennis (Spring Lake, N.J.). Home: 1842 Bedford Av. Office: 26 Court St., Brooklyn, N.Y. Died Nov. 24, 1959. Buried St. Charles Cemetery, Farmingdale, L.I., N.Y.

GEORGE, VI (Albert Frederick Arthur George), King of Great Britain, Ireland and the British Dominions Beyond the Seas; born Sandringham, Dec. 14, 1895; s. King George V and Queen Mary (dau. of Duke of Teck); m. Lady Elizabeth Angela Marguerite Bowes-Lyon, Apr. 26, 1923; children—Queen Elizabeth Alexandra Mary, (m. H.R.H., Prince Philip, Duke of Edinburgh, 1947), H.R. H., Princess Margaret Rose. Became midshipman in Royal Navy, 1913. Adm. of the Fleet, Field Marshal, Marshal of the Royal Air Force, 1936. Created Duke of York, Earl of Inverness and Baron Kilarney in peerage of the United Kingdom, 1920; became Duke of Rothesay, Earl of Carrick and Baron of Renfrew in the peerage of Scotland upon accession to the throne; succeeded his elder brother, Edward VIII, 1937; crowned at Westminster Abbey, May 12, 1937. Died Feb. 6, 1952; buried St. George's Chapel, Windsor.

GEORGE, Charles Albert, librarian; b. New York, Oct. 11, 1867; s. Charles Timmons and Mary Louisa (Huff) G.; grad. Peddlie Inst., Highstown, N.J., 1893; A.B., Princeton, 1897, A.M., 1899; m. Mary Leslie Guion, Aug. 9, 1900; 1 dau., Julia Guion. Asst. to librarian and chief of catalogue dept., Princeton U. Library, 1898-1909; librarian, Pub. Library, Elizabeth, N.J., 1909-50; mem. A.L.A., N.J. Library Assn. (pres. 1908-09), N.J. Hist. Soc., Historic Commn, City of Elizabeth. N.J. Trustee Union County Hist. Soc., Alpha Phi. Address: Public Library, Elizabeth, N.J. Died Aug. 2, 1950; buried Moravian Cemetery, New Dorp, S.I., N.Y.

GEORGE, Walter Franklin, senator; b. Preston, Ga., Jan. 29, 1878; s. Robert Theodric and Sarah (Stapleton) G.; B.S., Mercer, 1900, B.L., 1901, LL.D., 1920; married Lucy Heard, July 9, 1903; children—Heard Joseph, Joseph Marcus (killed in action 1944). Began practice at Vienna, Georgia, 1901; solicitor general Cordele Judiciary Circuit, Ga., 1907-12; judge Superior Court, same circuit, 1912-17; judge Court of Appeals of Ga., Jan. 1, 1917-Oct. 1, 1917, resigned; asso. justice Supreme Court of Ga., 1917, resigned, 1922; U.S. senator, 5 terms, 1922-51, re-elected for term ending 1957; spl. asst. to Pres. U.S. as ambaddador to NATO, 1957—. Home: Vienna, Ga. Died Aug. 4, 1957; buried Vienna, Ga.

GEORGE, W(illiam) Perry, fgn. service ofcr., ret.; b. Gadsden, Ala., Nov. 25, 1895; s. Robert Conklin and Alice (Hollingsworth) G.; student Dubose Acad., Univ. of Grenoble, Am. Sch. of Classical Studies, U.S. Naval Acad.; m. Eileen Dolores Patricia Hayes, May 18, 1921; children—William Patrick Michael, Peter; married 2d, Elizabeth Hardy-Wrigley, May 10, 1947. Vice-Consul Grenoble, France, 1916-17, Athens, 1918-22; consul Canary Islands, 1923-24, Buenos Aires, 1925, Riviere-du-Loup, 1926-28, Belgrade Yugoslavia, 1928; sec. of legation, Belgrade, 1929-31; consul Izmir, Turkey, and for Italian Islands of Aegean, 1932-33; charge d'affaires ad interim, Addis Ababa, 1934-35; consul at Malta, 1935; special mission to Yugoslavia, 1936; consul at Bordeaux, 1936-39, Barcelona, 1939-41, Valencia, 1941. Assitant chief, Division of Western European Affairs, Dept. of State, 1941-45; counselor of Embassy, London, 1945-46; mem. Am. del. Tangier Conf., Paris, 1945; spl. mission to Yugoslavia, 1946; retired, Mar. 1947; pvt. bus. in Spain, 1947—. Clubs: Pilgrims, Girondins. Author of civil and commercial codes for The Special Court (mixed justice) in Ethiopia. Home: Gadsden, Ala. Address: Barcelona, Spain. Died July 22, 1955.

GERAN, Elmer Hendrickson, ex-congressman; b. Matawan, N.J., Oct. 24, 1875; s. Charles A. and Lydia H. Geran; grad. Peddie Inst., Hightstown, N.J., 1895; A.B., Princeton, 1899; LL.B., N.Y. Law Sch., 1901; m. Lysbeth Frick Ward, July 19, 1924. Admitted to N.J. bar, 1901, and began practice at Jersey City. Mem. Ho. of Assembly, 1911-12; mem. N.J. State Water Supply Commn., 1912-15, asst. prosecutor Monmouth County, N.J., 1915-17; mem. and minority leader N.J. Ho. of Assembly, 1916-17; sheriff of Monmouth County, 1917-1920; apptd. U.S. dist. atty. for N.J., 1920, by President Woodrow Wilson, resigned, 1921, and resumed practice at Asbury Park; mem. 68th Congress, 3d N.J. Dist. Democrat. Baptist. Home: Wooleytown Rd., Matawan, N.J. Died Jan. 12, 1954.

GERARD, James Watson (jĕ-rärd'), diplomat, lawyer; b. Geneseo, N.Y., 1867; s. James and Jenny (Angel) G.; A.B., Columbia, 1890, A.M., 1891, LL.D., 1930; m. Mary, d. late Marcus Daly, mine owner, of Montana. Admitted to bar, 1892, and began practice at New York City. Elected asso. justice Supreme Court of N.Y. for term 1908-21; resigned, July 1913, upon appmt. as A.E. and M.P. to Germany; recalled upon breaking off of diplomatic relations, Feb. 3, 1917. Dem. nominee for U.S. senate (while at Berlin), 1914; treas. Dem. Nat. Com. to 1932, chmn. finance committee, 1934; appointed mem. advisory board Point Four Program. Author: My Four Years in Germany, 1917; Face to Face with Kaiserism, 1918. Represented President as spl. ambassador to coronation of King George VI. Home: 1014 5th Av. Office: 41 E. 57th St., N.Y.C. Died Sept. 6, 1951.

GERBER, Frank, business exec.; b. Douglas, Mich., Jan. 12, 1873; s. Joseph and Agnes (Moyer) G.; student Normal Sch., Valparaiso, Ind., 1888; m. Pauline Platt, April 29, 1897; one son, Daniel F. Clerk, D. Gerber's Sons, Tanners, Fremont Can- 1889-1893, partner, 1894-1905; mgr. Fremont Canning Co., Fremont, Mich., 1904-16, pres., 1917-41; pres. Gerber Products Co., successor to Fremont Canning Co., 1941-44, chmn. bd. since 1944. Pres. Nat. Canners Assn., Washington, D.C., 1919. Christian Scientist. Republican. Home: 120 E. Dayton St. Office: Gerber Products Co., Fremont, Mich. Died Oct. 7, 1952.

GERDES, John (gĕr'dĕs), lawyer; b. N.Y.C., Sept. 26, 1886; s. Herman and Sophia (Garland) G.; B.Litt., Berea Coll., 1907; A.M., N.Y.U., 1918, LL.B., 1910, LL.M., 1911, J.D., 1912; m. Theodora M. McCaren, Feb. 17, 1916; children—Janet, Margery. Admitted to New York bar, 1909; senior mem. Gerdes, Montgomery & Miller, N.Y.C.; former prof. law of corporate finance and corporate reorgn., N.Y.U.; former gen. counsel, v.p., chmn. exec. com. and dir. C.R.I.&P. R.R.; treas. and dir. Law med. Foundation, Howes Leather Co., Inc., C. F. Mueller Co., Knapp Bros., Shoe Mfg. Corp., Zion Industries, Inc. counsel N.Y.U. Mem. Nat. Bankruptcy Conf. (chmn. com. on reorganizations); adviser Restatement of the Law of Bus. Assns. of Am. Law Inst.; mem. rules com. Federal Court in N.Y.; rep. to 2d Internat. Congress of Comparative Law, League of Nations, The Hague; sec. N.Y. State Com. of Nat. Progressive Party, 1913-16; N.Y. presdl. elector (Republican), 1916; mem. Am. Judicature Society, American Law Institute, Am. Bar Association (chmn. com. on reorgn.; section on corporation banking and mercantile law), New York State Bar Assn., Assn. Bar City of New York, Nat. Acad. Social Sci., Phi Gamma Delta, Phi Delta Phi. Clubs: Piping Rock, Pilgrims, Union, Church, Downtown Association, Cold Spring Harbor Beach. Episcopalian. Author: Gerdes on Corporate Reorganization (3 vols.). Contbr. articles to law revs. and other legal publs. Home: 570 Park Av., N.Y.C.; and Pepperidge Point Mill Neck, Oyster Bay, Long Island, N.Y. Office: 1 Wall St., N.Y.C. 5. Died Dec. 1959.

GERE, George Grant, physician; b. Greene, N.Y., Dec. 27, 1848; at age of 16 joined 1st Neb. Vet. Cav.; served until war closed; M.D., Eclectic Med. Inst., Cin., 1871; m. Sarah J. Wood, 1890. Practiced in Western states 10 yrs.; prof. anatomy Cal. Med. Coll., 1881-86, prof. surgery, 1886-1906. Formerly pres. of State, v.p. of Nat. Eclectic Med. socs., sec. Bd. of Med. Examiners, Cal. Author: Lectures on Callopractic Surgery; also various med. monographs. Home: 1762 Waller St. Office: Pacific Bldg., San Francisco. Died Dec. 29, 1918.

GERHAUSER, William Henry (gĕr'hou-zĕr), shipbuilder; b. Detroit, Mich., Jan. 7, 1889; s. Wm. and Mary Catherine (Klippel) G.; grad. Detroit Univ. Sch., 1906; B.Ch.E., U. of Mich., 1911; m. Amy Jean Farr, June 13, 1914; children—William Farr, Merton Farr, Henry Farr, Frederick Farr. Asst. sec. Detroit Bd. of Commerce, 1911-14; supt. Williams Bros. Co., Detroit, 1915-17; asst. to pres. Am. Shipbuilding Co., 1917-18, v.p., 1918-28, pres. since 1928; dir. American Shipbuilding Company, Union Bank of Commerce (Cleveland), Ohio Bell Tel. Co., Harshaw Chemical Co., Ferry Cap & Set Screw Co.; director, Cleveland Cliffs Iron Co. (Cleveland). Trustee Webb Institute Naval Architecture (N.Y.), Western Reserve Acad. (Hudson, O.). Mem. Soc. Naval Architects and Marine Engrs., Chi Psi. Republican. Presbyterian. Clubs: Union, Kirtland, Tavern (Cleveland); India House (New York); Toledo (Toledo, O.). Home: 2301 Coventry Road. Address: Am. Shipbuilding Co., Cleve. Died Nov. 23, 1952.

GERIG, John Lawrence (gĕr'ĭg), educator; b. Columbia, Mo., Nov. 30, 1878; s. Francis Joseph and Caroline (Degan) G.; A.B., U. Mo., 1898, A.M., 1899, LL.D., 1941; Ph.D., U. Neb., 1902; Élève Titulaire de l'École des Hautes-Études, U. Paris, 1903-05; Columbia U.; Litt.D. ad honorem, U. of Rome, 1927; m. Vianthia Savannah Crim, Dec. 21, 1911 (died July 15, 1947). Teaching fellow in Romance langs. U. Mo., 1898-99, U. Neb., 1899-1901, also instr. in Romance langs., Sanskrit and comparative philology, 1901-03; mem. faculty summer sessions univs. Mo., 1899, and Neb., 1901; instr. Romance langs. Williams Coll., 1905-06; lecturer Columbia, 1906, tutor, 1908, instr., 1909, asst. prof. Romance langs., 1910, asst. prof. Celtic, 1911, asso. prof., 1911, prof., 1924-44, prof. emeritus of Celtic, 1944—, exec. officer dept. Romance langs. 1919-29; hon. dir. dept. of Spanish Studies, U. of P.R., 1926—; taught Celtic, Linguistic Inst. Am., summer 1930, and Lang. Inst., summer 1932. Pres. and founder Istituto di Coltura Italiana negli Stati Uniti, 1923-29, and Inst. of Rumanian Culture, 1926—; v.p. Instituto Italo-Americano di Cultura Presso L'Universita di Roma, 1950—; pres. Italian Digest and News Service, 1926—; pres. Italian Hist. Soc. Am., 1927-32; founder and mem. exec. council Institut des Études Françaises aux États-Unis, Instituto de las Españas en los Estados Unidos, 1921-29; pres. Italian House Fund; trustee Am. Iona Soc., Inc., 1930—, pres. 1945—; chmn. com. on French lit. Facsimile Texts Soc. Am., 1930—; pres. India Acad. of America, 1930-33; founder Society of Friends of Universities of Ireland, 1930; v.p. India Soc. of Am., 1930—, Soc. of Friends of U. Rome, 1930—, Italian Institute of Culture, 1934—, Fedn. Irish Socs. of N.Y. 1936—; trustee Irish Palace Found., 1945—; founder, v.p. Permanent Italian Book Exhbn., 1928-31; hon. v.p. Gaelic Musical Soc. 1938—. Hon. mem. Accademia Ital. di Scienze e Lettere, Am. Irish Hist. Soc. (also mem. exec. council 1939—), Am. Inst. Rumania, Am. Celtic Inst.; corr. mem. Hispanic Soc. Amer.; Am. mem. Internat. Com. of Experts in Ling. Bibl., Internat. Com. of Lit. Hist.; gov. Bd. of Internat. Cultural Assn., 1946; mem. Société des Anciens Textes Français, Poetry Soc. Am., Linguistic Soc. Am. Philol. Assn.; charter mem. Amer.-Armenian Cultural Assn., 1946; mem. Societe des Anciens Textes Francais, Poetry Soc. Am., Linguistic Soc. Am., Am. Assn. Univ. Profs., Met. Mus. Art, Am. Mus. Natural History, Phi Beta Kappa, and many other socs. Decorated Cavaliere della Corona d'Italia, for distinguished services to Italian culture in America, 1925; Chevalier Legion of Honor (France), 1927; Comdr. of Crown of Rumania, 1931. Awarded Gold Medal by Am. Irish Hist. Soc. in tribute to his eminence in Celtic scholarship, Nov. 17, 1944; honorary scroll of Celtic Soc. Coll. Univs. Assistant editor Edgren's Italian Dictionary, 1902; asso. editor, 1910; editor-in-chief, 1925-27, and advisory editor, 1937-46. Romanic Review; associate editor Bulletins of Inst. of Rumanian Culture, Inst. di Colt. Ital., etc.; asso. founder Revista de Estudios Hispánicos; founder and advisory editor, 1938—, Celtic Digest. Clubs: Authors' (London); Men's Faculty of Columbia University. Author: Antoine Arlier and the Renaissance at Nimes, 1929. Editorial reviser Celtic literature, modern philology and Oriental literature in New Internat. Ency. (2d edit.), Ex-Libris, Romanic Review, Les Annales du Midi, Revue de la Renaissance, Am. Journal of Philology, Mélanges Émile Picot (Paris, 1913), La Vie Universitaire, New Armenia, Americana Annual, etc. Address: 39 Claremont Av., N.Y.C. 27. Died Sept. 20, 1957; buried New Salem Cemetery of Ashland, Mo.

GERLACH, George W., storage and warehouse exec.; b. Ossining, N.Y., June 2, 1879; s. Henry and Elizabeth (Dee) G.; student Mt. Pleasant Mil. Acad.; m. Mary Fowler, June 19, 1901; 1 dau., Elizabeth Van Wagenen. Pres. and dir. Manhattan Storage and Warehouse Co., N.Y.C., 1936—; dir. Manhattan Storage Safe Deposit Co. Chmn. Zoning Appeals Bd., Westchester County; pres. Bd. Edn., Ossining, N.Y. Treas., Lulu Thorley Lyons Home for Crippled and Delicate Children; treas. Walter Scott Free Sch. for Crippled Children. Mem. N.Y. State C. of C., N.Y. Real Estate Bd., 42d St. Assn., 6th Av. Assn. (dir.). Home: Ossining, N.Y. Office: Manhattan Storage and Warehouse Co., 7th Av. and 52d St., N.Y.C. Died Aug. 24, 1954.

GERLAUGH, Paul (gĕr'lâ), animal science research; b. near Osborne, O., April 21, 1891; s. Charles Lewellen and Julia Alnetta (Hower) G., S.B., O. State U., 1913; S.M., Pa. State Coll., 1917; m. Anna Rebecca Brosey, Feb. 7, 1914; children—Julia Ann (Mrs. Richard B. Bogner), Donald Brosey. Instr., Pa. State Coll., 1913-17; county agrl. agent, Wood County, O., 1917-21; livestock extension specialist, O. State U., 1921-28; chief, dept. of animal industry, O. Agrl. Exptl. Sta., 1928-47; asso. in animal science since 1948. Mem. Am. Soc. of Animal Prodn. (pres. 1948), Alpha Zeta, Gamma Alpha Delta, Sigma Xi. Presbyterian. Home: 1019 Forest Dr. Office: Ohio Agriculture Experimental Station, Wooster, O. Died Aug. 10, 1951; buried Wooster Cemetery.

GERLING, Henry Joseph, supt. schs.; b. Normandy, Mo., Feb. 20, 1870; s. Frank A. and Pauline (Weiskittel) G.; A.B., Pe.B., LL.B., U. Mo., 1894, L.M., 1896; grad. study, dept. social and polit. scis., Cornell U., 1896-99, pres. White fellow, 1896-97; LL.D., Muskingum Coll., 1931, Washington U., 1932, U. Mo., 1933; m. Vinnie Adams, Aug. 24, 1896; children—John H., Pauline (Mrs. P. J. Hickey). Teaching fellow, U. Mo., 1893; prin. high sch., Columbia, Mo., 1894-95; asst. to librarian, Cornell U., 1897-99; prin. elementary schs., St. Louis, 1899-1908; prof. social sci., Harris Tchrs. Coll., St. Louis, 1908-10; prin. Observation Sch., St. Louis, 1911-15; asst. supt. schs., St. Louis, 1915-29, supt., 1929-40; ret. 1940. Mem. N.E.A., Mo. State Tchrs. Assn. (pres. 1929-30), Cornell U. Alumni Assn., St. Louis C. of C., Phi Beta Kappa, Sigma Alpha Epsilon. Baptist. Mason (32°), Odd Fellow. Clubs: University (U. of Mo.), Town and Gown, Missouri Athletic. Home: 945 Beverly Av., Glendale, Mo. Office: 911 Locust St., St. Louis. Died Aug. 2, 1948; buried Oak Grove Mausoleum, St. Louis.

GERMANOS, archibishop of Thyateira, b. Delliones, Silivria, Eastern Thrace, Sept. 15, 1868; s. Pandelis and Helen (Kyropoulos) Stenopoulos; Th.M., Theol. Sch. of Halki, Constantinople, 1897; Ph.D., U. Leipzig, 1903; Th.D., Oxford U., Athens U., Gen. Theol. Sem., N.Y.C. Teacher and preacher, Rodosto, 1897-1900, prof., 1904-07, prin., 1907-22; elected Exarch, Western and Central Europe with See in London, 1922; accomplished missions for Oecumenical patriarchate in Russia, Finland, Sweden, Latvia, Switzerland, U.S., and elsewhere; rep. Oecumenical patriarch to Archbishop of Canterbury, to the Swedish Ch., to the Old Catholics in Switzerland; one of 6 presidents World's Council of Chs. Decorated Grand Cordon (Russia, Yugoslavia, Sweden, Latvia), Knight Comdr. of Victoria Order (Great Britain), Knight Comdr. of Greek Order, Phoenix, Saviours, 3d Class. Hon. v.p. Anglo-Hellenic League (London). Club: Athenaeum (London). Contbr. articles to religious publs. Greek Orthodox Ch. Home: 8 Dawson Pl., London W. 2, Eng. Died Jan. 23, 1951; buried Orthodox Greek Cemetery, London.

GERNON, Frank E., investment banker; m. Mrs. Helen J. Gernon; children—Mrs. Richard Valentine, Mrs. Miles Hirson, James D., Frank E. Joined Hayden, Stone & Co., as mgr. investment dept., 1923, became partner, 1929, retired, 1942; partner Carl M. Loeb, Rhoades & Co., 1943—. Former gov. Investment Bankers Assn., chmn. N.Y. group. Clubs: Westchester Country, Bankers, Bond (N.Y.C.). Home: Harrison, N.Y. Office: 42 Wall St., N.Y.C. 5. Died Dec. 2, 1956.

GEROULD, Gordon Hall (jĕr'ăld), educator; b. Goffstown, N.H., Oct. 4, 1877; s. Rev. Samuel Lankton and Laura Etta (Thayer) G.; B.A., Dartmouth, 1899; B.Litt., Oxford U., 1901; m. Katharine Fullerton, June 9, 1910 (died July 27, 1944); children—Christopher, Sylvia. Reader in English, 1901-02, Bryn Mawr Coll., asso. English philology, 1902-05; asst. prof. English, Princeton, 1905-16, prof. English, 1916-38, Holmes prof. belles lettres, 1938, chmn. dept. Eng., 1942, emeritus 1946—. Fellow Mediaeval Acad. Am. Author: The North English Homily Collection, 1902; Sir Guy of Warwick, 1905; The Grateful Dead, the History of a Folk-Story, 1908; Saints' Legends, 1916; Peter Sanders, Retired (novel), 1917; Youth in Harley (novel), 1920; Filibuster, 1924; A Midsummer Mystery (novel), 1925; The Ballad of Tradition, 1932; How to Read Fiction, 1937; The Patterns of English and American Fiction, 1942. Editor: Selected Essays of Fielding, 1905; (with Charles Bayly, Jr.), Contemporary Short Stories, 1927; Poems of James Thomson, 1927; Mediaeval Literature, Sixteenth Century (2 vols. in Nelson's English Readings), 1929. Translator: Beowulf and Sir Gawain, 1933. Contbr. to philol. publs. and mags. Capt., U.S. Army, 1918. Home: 4 Mercer St., Princeton, N.J. Deceased.

GEROULD, James Thayer, librarian; b. Goffstown, N.H., Oct. 3, 1872; s. Samuel Lankton and Laura Etta (Thayer) G.; A.B., Dartmouth, 1895, Litt.D., 1932; m. Mary Aims Chamberlain, Sept. 18, 1900 (died 1939); 1 son, Albert Chamberlain; m. 2d. Winifred Gregory, Dec. 6, 1940. Asst. librarian Gen. Theol. Sem., 1896-97; chief of dept. Columbia U. Library, 1897-1900; librarian U. Mo., 1900-06, U. Minn., 1906-20; librarian Princeton, 1920-38, emeritus, 1938—. Literary editor The Bellman, 1916-18; history asso. Current History Mag., 1926-33. Asst. mgr. no. div. A.R.C., 1917-19. Mem. A.L.A., Bibliog. Soc. Am., Phi Beta Kappa, Delta Kappa Epsilon. Author: Sources of English History of the Seventeenth Century, 1603-1689, 1921; College Library Building: its planning and equipment, 1932. Compiler: selected articles on interallied debts, and revision of the debt settlement, 1928; selected articles on the pact of Paris, officially the general pact for the renunciation of war, 1929; (with Mrs. Gerould). A Guide to Trollope, 1948. Democrat. Episcopalian. Home: 601 Pollard Park Dr., Williamsburg, Va. Died June 8, 1951.

GEROULD, Winifred Gregory (jĕr'ăld), bibliographer; b. Independence, Ia., Oct. 14, 1885; d. Alonzo Goodrich and Almira (Webster) Gregory; educated univs. of Iowa and Minn., also U. of Wis. Library School, 1909-10; m. James Thayer Gerould, Dec. 6, 1940. Librarian Sch. of Mines, U. of Minn., 1911-16; hosp. librarian, Asheville, N.C., 1918; librarian, technol. div. St. Paul Pub. Library, 1917-19; asst. in technol. div. Carnegie Library, Pittsburgh, 1920-23; editorial work for Am. Library Assn. and Bibliog. Soc. of America since 1924; research in nat. and univ. libraries in Europe, 1929-30 and 1937. Rep. Am. Library Assn. at Internat. Congress on Bibliography, Rome, 1930. Mem. Am. Library Assn., Bibliog. Soc. America, D.C. Library Assn. Author: Bibliography of Minn. Mining and Geology, 1915; (with J. T. Gerould), A Guide to Trollope, 1948. Editor; Union List of Serials in Libraries of U.S. and Canada, 1927; List of Serial Publications of Foreign Governments, 1932; Union List of Newspaper Files in Libraries of U.S. and Canada, 1936; International Congresses and Conferences, 1840-1937, 1938; Union List of Serials, 2d ed., 1943. Home: 601 Pollard Park Drive, Williamsburg, Va. Died Dec. 10, 1955.

GERRER, Gregory, clergyman; b. Alsace Lorraine, France, July 23, 1867; s. F. X. and Caroline (Gross) Gerrer; was brought to U.S., 1872; entered Sacred Heart Monastery, Okla., 1891; hon. LL.D., U. of Notre Dame, 1918. Ordained priest R.C. Ch., in Buckfast Abbey, Devonshire, Eng., 1900; studied art at Paris and Rome, remaining abroad, 1900-04; painted official portrait of Pope Pius X, exhibited at St. Louis Expn., 1904, replica painted for the Vatican. Painter of portraits, murals and scenery. Admitted to Okla. Hall of Fame, 1931. Address: Shawnee, Okla. Died Aug. 24, 1946.

GERRISH, Thornton, ret. banker; b. Bklyn., July 17, 1879; s. William Lawrence and Florence (Churchill) G.; A.B., Harvard, 1901; m. Madeleine Broun, Jan. 17, 1912; 1 son, Thornton. Clerk Farmers Loan and Trust Co., N.Y.C., 1901-06, trust officer, 1906-17; v.p. Franklin Trust Co., 1917-20; v.p. Bank of America, 1920-31; v.p. Bklyn. Savings Bank, 1931-39, pres., 1939-44, chmn. bd., 1944, ret. Trustee Poly. Prep. Country Day Sch., Bklyn. Home: 25 Seneca St., Rye, N.Y. Died July 4, 1955.

GERRY Peter Goelet, ex-senator; b. N.Y.C., Sept. 18, 1879; s. Elbridge Thomas and Louisa Matilda (Livingston) G.; S.B., Harvard, 1901; m. Edith Stuyvesant Vanderbilt. Admitted to R.I. bar, 1906; mem. Representative Council, Newport, R.I., 1912; del. Dem. Nat. Conv., from R.I., 1912, 1916, 1932; mem. 63d Congress, 2d R.I. Dist.; U.S. senator, 1917-23, 23-29, 35-41, 41-47; mem. Dem. Nat. Com., 1932-36. V.p. Am. Humane Assn. Episcopalian. Clubs: Hope, Squantum, University (Providence). Home: 62 Prospect St., Providence 6. Office: 68 S. Main St., Providence 3. Died Oct. 31, 1957.

GERSTENBERGER, Henry John, pediatrist; born Cleveland, O., Jan. 9, 1881; s. John H. and Clara E. (Schake) G.; student Corcordia Coll., Ft. Wayne, Inc., 1899; M.D., Western Reserve U., 1903; m. Else B. Schweitzer, March 28, 1913; children—Paula Ruth, Else Louise (Mrs. Emil Brinker) (deceased), Gretel, Katherine. Practiced at Cleveland 1906—; professor of pediatrics, Western Reserve University Med. Sch. until 1945, prof. emeritus since 1945; dir. of pediatrics, Babies and Childrens, U., and Cleveland City hosps. Mem. A.M.A., Ohio State Med. Assn., Am. Acad. Pediatrics, Am. Pediatric Soc., Am. Inst. Nutrition, Am. Pub. Health Assn., Nat. Tuberculosis Assn., A.A.A.S., Internat. Pediatric Cong., Union Internat. de Secours aux Enfants, Alpha Omega Alpha, Sigma Xi; hon. mem. Deutsche Gesellschaft für Kinderheilkunde, Sociedad Mexicana de Pediatria; hon. sci. benefactor El Hospital del Nino, Mexico, 1945. Chmn. U.S. delegation, 4th Internat. Pediatric Cong., and 2d Internat. Cong. for Protection of Childhood, Rome, Sept. 1937. Clubs: University, Ohio Society of New York. Home: 1500 Crest Rd., Cleveland Heights 21. Address: Babies and Childrens Hospital, Room 624, 2103 Adelbert Rd., Cleve. 6. Died June 24, 1954.

GERWIG, George William, b. Paris, O., Jan. 18, 1867; s. Charles W. and Henrietta (Taylor) G.; B.A., U. Neb., 1889, M.A., 1891; Ph.D., Western U. Pa. (now U. Pitts.), 1904; D.H.L., U. Tampa, 1941; m. Margaret McGrew, June 4, 1896 (died 1901); children—Percy McGrew, Margaret Darsie. Began, 1892, as sec. Bd. of Edn., Allegheny, Pa. (now North Side, Pitts.), continued as sec. Bd. of Edn., Pitts. until 1929; pres. Percy Pub. Co.; in charge U.S. Census, Pitts. Dist., 1910; trustee H. C. Frick Ednl. Commn., (sec. and treas. 1926—); trustee Chautauqua Institution; dir. State Child Welfare Assn., Inc.; guest lectr. U. Tampa. Mem. Phi Delta Theta. Republican. Mem. Christian (Disciples) Ch. Author: Art of the Short Story, 1909; Schools With a Perfect Score, 1918; Washington, the Young Leader, 1923; Chautauqua, An Appreciation, 1924; The Declaration of Independence for Young Americans, 1926; Templed Hills, 1929; Shakespeare's Ideals of Womanhood, 1929; Character, 1930; Emotion, 1931; Guideposts to Character, 1932; Jesus: A Sisters Memories, 1934; Everychild—An American Ideal, 1942. Home: 1121 Davis Av., N.S. Office: Union Trust Bldg., Pitts. Died 1950.

GESELL, Robert, neurophysiologist; b. Alma, Wis., June 23, 1886; s. Gerhard and Christina (Geisen) G.; A.B., U. Wis., 1910; M.D., Washington U., 1914; m. Cora Lees, 1912; 1 dau., Christine (Mrs. Roger Stevens). Asst. zoology U. Wis., 1909-10; asst. physiology Washington U., 1910-12, instr., asso. and asso. prof. physiology, 1912-19; prof. physiology U. Cal., 1919-22, U. Mich. since 1923. Mem. Am. Physiol. Soc., Am. Soc. Exptl. Biology. Contbr. med. articles profl. publs. Home: 3 Ridgeway, Ann Arbor, Mich. Died Apr. 19, 1954.

GETTELL, Raymond Garfield (gĕt'tĕl), educator; b. Shippensburg, Pa., Mar. 4, 1881; s. John Jacob and Zora Lindlay (Hollar) G.; grad. State Normal Sch., Shippensburg, 1898; A.B. summa cum laude, Ursinus Coll., Pa., 1903; A.M., U. Pa., 1906; Litt.D., Trinity Coll., 1941; m. Nelene, Groff Knapp, Apr. 18, 1906; children—Dorothy Bates, Richard Glenn. Asst. prin. high sch., Duncannon, Pa., 1898-99; instr. State Normal Sch., Shippensburg, 1899-1900, Ursinus Coll., 1902-04; prof. history and econs. Bates Coll., Lewiston, Me., 1906-07; Northam prof. history and polit. sci. Trinity Coll., Hartford, Conn., 1907-14; prof. polit. sci. Amherst, 1914-23; prof. polit. sci. U. Cal., 1923—, dean summer session, 1934-42; prof. polit. sci. summers, U. Me., 1910, U. Ill., 1913, U. Tex., 1915, Columbia, 1916, U. Mich., 1917, Cornell U., 1919-20, U. Hawaii, 1934; vis. prof. U. Cal., 1920-21. Recorder U.S. Shipping Bd., 1917-28. Mem. Am. Hist. Assn., Am. Polit. Science Assn., Phi Beta Kappa. Republican. Clubs: University, Chit Chat, Bohemian. Author: Introduction to Political Science, 1910; Problems in Political Evolution, 1914; History of Political Thought, 1924; The Constitution of the United States, 1924; History of American Political Thought, 1928; Political Science, 1933, rev. edit. 1949; also numerous articles in various periodicals. Compiler: Readings in Political Science, 1911. Home: 2825 Piedmont Av., Berkeley, Cal. Died Oct. 9, 1949.

GEYER, Ellen M(ary), univ. prof.; b. Cedar Rapids, Ia., Aug. 22, 1879; d. Henry William and Barbara (Kiefer) Geyer; Ph.B., U. of Ia., 1902; A.M., 1910; student U. of Chicago, 1916-17, Columbia, 1929-30. High sch. teacher, Tipton, Ia., 1902-04; instr. in English, Ia. Coll. of Engring. and Mech. Arts, 1906, State U. of Ia., 1907-17; teaching fellow and asst. prof. English, U. of Chicago, 1918; instr. and dir. of English, U. of Ia. High Sch., 1918-19; prof. English, U. of Mont., 1919-24; prof. English and edn. U. of Pittsburgh, 1924-51; instr. English and edn., charge practice tchrs. Seton Hill Coll., 1951—. Mem. Nat. Council Teachers of English, Am. Assn. Univ. Profs., English Assn. Western Pa., Cath. Bus. and Professional Women, Delta Kappa Gamma, Theta Phi Alpha, Mortar Board. Republican. Roman Catholic. Author: (with Wolfe) Enjoying English, 1939; (with Carver) Communicating English, 1940. Home: 4733 Maripoe St., Pitts. 13. Died, Feb. 2, 1953; buried Linnwood Cemetery, Cedar Rapids, Ia.

GHORMLEY, Ralph K. (gôrm'lê), cons. surgeon orthopedic surgery, Mayo Clinic; b. Portland, Ore., Feb. 10, 1893; s. David O. and Alice M. (Irwin) G.; B.S., Whitworth Coll., Tacoma, Wash. (now in Spokane), 1914; M.D., Johns Hopkins U., 1918; m. Jean McDougall, June 25, 1924; children—Ralph M., Alice E., now (Mrs. Charles D. Baker). Served at Letterman General Hospital, United States Army Hospital, in San Francisco, California, 1919; interne Johns Hopkins Hospital and Children's Hospital, Baltimore, Maryland, 1919-20, New York Hosp., 1920-21; asst. resident surgeon, Johns Hopkins Hosp., 1921-22; assistant in orthopedic surgery, Harvard Univ., 1922-23, instr., 1923-29; practiced orthopedic surgery, Boston, Mass., 1922-29; with Mayo Foundation, Rochester, Minn., 1929-58, instr. in orthopedic surgery, 1929-32, asso. prof., 1932-37, prof., 1937-58, prof. emeritus 1958—; asso. in orthopedic surgery, Mayo Clinic, 1929-38, head of section, 1938-58, senior consultant in orthopedic surgery, 1955-58; cons. U.S. Naval Hospital, Oakland, California; also honorary consultant Peninsula Community Hospital, Carmel, California. Consultant Orthopedic Surg., Vets. Adminstrn., Washington, D.C. Certified specialist orthopedic surg. by Bd. Orthopedic Surgery. Served as pvt., lieut., capt., Med. Corps, A.E.F., 1917-19. Fellow Am. Coll. Surgeons; mem. Am. Orthopedic Assn. (sec. 1933-40, pres. 1948-49), Clin. Orthopedic Soc. (pres. 1941), Am. Acad. Orthopedic Surgeons, Am. Surg. Assn., A.M.A., Am. Bd. Orthopedic Surgery (pres. 1951-52), Western Surg. Soc., Am. Assn. for Surgery of Trauma, Robert Jones Orthopedic, Society, International Surgery Society, International Society Orthopedic Surgery and Traumology, Alpha Omega Alpha, Sigma Xi; corr. mem. Scandanavian, Belgian orthopedic socs. Club: Harvard (Boston). Author: Diagnosis in Joint Disease (with Nathaniel Allison), 1931. Home: P.O. Box 4223, Carmel, Cal. Died June 6, 1959.

GHORMLEY, Robert Lee (gôrm'lē), naval officer; b. Portland, Ore., Oct. 15, 1883; s. David Owen and Alice Minerva (Irwin) G.; A.B., U. Ida., 1902, LL.D., 1946; B.S., U.S. Naval Acad., 1906; m. Lucile Elizabeth Lyon, Oct. 20, 1911; children—Daniel Dyer, Alice Elizabeth (Mrs. W. C. F. Robards), Robert Lee. Commd. ensign USN, advanced through grades to vice adm., 1941; asst. chief staff, U.S. Fleet, 1931-32; comd. U.S.S. Nevada, 1935-36; Fleet operations officer, 1936-37; dir. war plans div., Office Chief of Naval Operations, Navy Dept., 1938-39, asst. to chief of Naval operations, 1939-40; spl. naval observer, London, Eng., 1940-42; comdr. U.S. Naval Forces European Waters, 1942; comdr. South Pacific Force and South Pacific Area, 1942; comd. allied forces during seizure of Guadalcanal-Tulagi, 1942; comdr. Hawaiian Sea Frontier, comdt. 14th Naval Dist., 1943-44; comdr. U.S. Naval Forces, Germany, 1944; retired from active duty, 1946. Decorated: D.S.M. (Army and Navy), Nicaraguan Campaign badge, Mexican Campaign badge, Legion of Merit; Pacific and Atlantic Campaign badges, Victory medals, World Wars I and II. Mem. Phi Beta Kappa, Phi Delta Theta. Presbyterian. Club: Army-Navy (Washington). Home: 3305 Macomb St. N.W., Washington 8. Died June 21, 1958; buried Arlington Nat. Cemetery.

GHULAM Mohammed, ex-government official; born in Lahore, West Pakistan, on August 29, 1895; M.A. and LL.B., M.A.O. College, Aligarh, India, LL.D., Punjab, 1949. With Indian Audit Dept., 1920-32; commr. development, Bhopal State, 1932-34; dep. dir. finance, posts and telegraphs, also financial adviser, communications, Govt. of India, 1934-39, controller-gen. purchases, 1940, additional sec. Dept. Supply, 1941; mem. exec. council, mem. court Muslim U., Aligarh, 1940; mem. court Aligarh and Delhi U., 1940; finance minister Nizam's govt., Hyderabad-Deccan, 1942-45; dir. Tatas, Ltd., 1945-47; minister finance, econ. affairs, Pakistan, 1947-51, gov. for Pakistan, Internat. Bank Reconstrn. and Development, also Internat. Monetary Fund, 1950; gov. gen. Pakistan, 1951-55. Comdr. Indian Empire, renounced Knighthood, 1947. Pres. Internat Islamic Econ. Orgn. Died Aug. 29, 1956; buried Karachi, West Pakistan.

GIANELLONI, Vivian Joseph, sugar corp. exec.; b. East Baton Rouge Parish, La., Oct. 28, 1892; s. Sabin and Julia (Lefebvre) G.; B.S. in sugar engring., Audubon Sugar Sch., La. Univ.; m. Marcelle Tarilton, Feb. 26, 1918; children—Vivian Joseph Jr., Giles Sabin, Arthur Louis, Ignatius Loyola; m. 2d, Marjorie Daniell, Nov. 26, 1940. With the Rio Cauto Sugar Co., 1913, Compañia Azucarera, Fla., 1916, Punta Alegre Sugar Corp. v.p., 1938-52, pres., 1952—. Served as 1st lt. and adjutant, 62d Arty., C.A.C., A.E.F., 1917-19. Mem. Am. Soc. M.E., Am. Chem. Soc., Cuban Soc. of Engrs., Assn. Cuban Sugar Technologists. Clubs: American, Havana Biltmore Yacht and Country, International Yacht. Address: Apartado 1938, Habana, Cuba. Office: Royal Bank Bldg., Aguiar 367, Habana, Cuba. Died Nov. 13, 1957; buried Roselawn Cemetery, Baton Rouge.

GIANNINI, Lawrence Mario; b. San Francisco, Calif., Nov. 25, 1894; s. Amadeo Peter and Clorinda Agnes (Cuneo) G.; LL.B., Hastings Coll. of the Law (Univ. of Calif.), 1920; married Anna Mercedes Collins, April 17, 1929; children—Anne, Virginia. Began with Bank of Italy (later Bank of America National Trust & Savings Association), San Francisco, 1918, became senior vice-president; now pres., chmn. exec. com., Bank of Am. Nat. Trust & Savings Assn.; chmn. bd. Occidental Life Ins. Co.; pres. and dir. Bank of America (Internat.); dir. Transamerica Corp., Pacific Nat. Fire Ins. Co., Fireman's Fund Insurance Co., Inter-Am. Corp., Nat. City Bank of N.Y., City Bank Farmers Trust Co. Member President's Com. for Financing Fgn. Trade. Mem. Com. on Internat. Econ. Policy; mem. Calif., San Francisco bar assns., Native Sons of the Golden West. Democrat. K.C., Elk. Clubs: Bohemian, Olympic, Commonwealth, Commercial (San Francisco); Jonathan, Los Angeles Athletic (Los Angeles). Home: Atherton, Cal., also 945 Green St., S.F. Office: 300 Montgomery St., S.F. Died Aug. 19, 1952.

GIBB, Arthur Norman (gib), architect; b. Quebec, P.Q., Can., May 23, 1868; s. John Lawson and Elizabeth Murison (McCallum) G.; student Ecole Nippel, Neuchatel, Switzerland, 1882-83, Trinity Coll. Sch., Port Hope, Ont., Can., 1883-84, Upper Can. Coll., Toronto, 1884-86; B.Arch., Cornell U., 1890; m. Henrietta Merriam Collins, June 1, 1897; children—John Collins, Mary Murison (Mrs. Leslie Irving Nichols). Came to U.S., 1886, naturalized, 1897. Practiced architecture in Ithaca, N.Y., 1890—; draftsman, W. H. Miller, 1890-92; jr. partner Vivian & Gibb, 1892-1904; under own name, 1904-16; sr. mem. Gibb & Waltz, 1916-28; under own name, 1928-38; sr. mem., Arthur N. Gibb, Architects, 1938-48; mem. Hilt & Gibbs asso. architects, 1948—. Alderman, chmn. finance com. City of Ithaca, 1914-16, 40-43, 44-47; mayor, 1947; mem. San. Sewer Commn., Ithaca, 1906. Fellow A.I.A. (mem. central N.Y. chpt.); mem. Social Service League of Ithaca (ex. com. and treas.), N.Y. Assn. Architects, Am. Mus. Natural History, Chi Phi. Mason. Clubs: Rotary, Yacht, Cornell (Ithaca). Home: 1022 Stewart Av., 119 S. Seneca St., Ithaca, N.Y. Died Dec. 25, 1949.

GIBBON, John Heysham, surgeon; b. Charlotte, N.C., Mar. 16, 1871; s. Robert (M.D.) and Mary Amelia (Rogers) G.; prep. edn. Macon Sch., Charlotte; M.D., Jefferson Med. Coll., 1891; m. Marjorie G. Young, Sept. 2, 1901; children—Marjorie Young, John H., Samuel Young, Robert. Prof. surgery and clin. surgery Jefferson Med. Coll., 1907-31 (emeritus); cons. surgeon Pa., Jefferson Med. and Bryn Mawr hosps. Surgeon U.S. Vol. Engrs., Spanish-Am. War, 1898; col. M.C.U.S. Army and cons. in surgery to AEF, World War I. Fellow, ex-pres. Am. Surg. Assn., Coll. Physicians of Phila., Phila. Acad. Surgery; mem. A.M.A., Med. Soc. State of Pa., Phila. Pediatric Soc., Nat. Soc. Study and Prevention Tb, etc. Contbr. to Reference Hand-Book of Medical Sciences, Keen's System of Surgery, many articles to surg. jours. Address: Lynfield Fram, Media, Pa. Died Mar. 13, 1956; buried Old St. David's Ch., Radnor, Pa.

GIBBONS, (Austin) Cedric, motion picture art dir.; b. N.Y.C.; s. Austin Patrick and Veronica Florence (Fitzpatrick) G.; ed. pvt. tutor; art edn. Art students League, N.Y., 4 yrs.; m. Dolores Del. Rio, Aug. 16, 1930 (div. 1941); m. 2d, Hazel Brooks, Oct. 1944. Draftsman in father's archtl. office, 1911-13; art. dir. Thomas A. Edison Studios, Bedford Park, N.Y., 1915-17, Goldwyn Studios, 1918-24, Metro-Goldwyn-Mayer Studios, 1924—. Served in U.S. Navy, 1918. Catholic. Won Acad. awards for art direction on Bridge of San Luis Rey, 1929, Merry Widow, 1933, Pride and Prejudice, 1940, Blossoms in the Dust, 1941, Gaslight, 1944; The Yearling, 1948, Little Women, 1949, An American in Paris, 1951, The Bad and the Beautiful, 1952; Julius Caesar, 1953; Soc. of Soc. Motion Picture Art Dirs. award for consistent creative excellence, 1950. Office: Metro-Goldwyn-Mayer Studios, Culver City, Cal. Deceased.

GIBBONS, George Rison, aluminum mfr.; b. Bartow County, Ga., July 18, 1879; s. John Rison and Annie America (Felton) G.; prep. edn. Piedmont Inst., Rockmart, Ga., 1894-97; A.B., Emory Coll. (now Univ.), 1900; m. Helen L. Maxfield, July 12, 1919; children—George Rison, Maxfield Scott, Felton Lewis. With Aluminum Co. of Am., 1901—, v.p., 1911—, sr. v.p., 1931—, also dir.; pres., v.p. or dir. associated and subsidiary cos.; dir. Fidelity Trust Co., Union Barge Line Corp. Trustee Emory U. Mem. Delta Tau Delta. Republican. Presbyn. Clubs: Duquesne, University, Fox Chapel Country, Pittsburgh Golf (Pitts.); Rolling Rock (Ligonier, Pa.); University (N.Y.C.). Home: 5455 Dunmoyle Street. Office: Gulf Bldg., Pitts. Died Sept. 3, 1950; buried Homewood Cemetery, Pitts.

GIBBONS, James Edmund, investment banker; b. Boston, Aug. 4, 1890; s. Patrick J. and Helena J. (Daly) G.; A.B., Boston Coll., 1912; m. Ruth Cummings, Oct. 29, 1919; children—Robert E., Nancy M., Ruth (Mrs. Robert F. Costello). With Am. Tel. & Tel. Co., 1912-24; partner Cotter Advt. Agy., 1924-29; exec. v.p. Inc. Investors, Boston, 1929—. Office: 200 Berkeley St., Boston 16. Died Apr. 30, 1959.

GIBBONS, Stephen B., ex-asst. sec. of U.S. Treasury; m. Mary Elizabeth Clayton, June 30, 1919; 1 dau. Anne Barbara (Mrs. William F. Ross). In bus. until 1912; then private sec. to William Gibbs McAdoo; became private sec. to Judge Samuel Seabury, 1916; then income tax examiner Feb. Bur. of Internal Revenue, N.Y., until 1926; asst. sec. of U.S. Treasury, 1933-39; v.p. Hudson Trust Co., Union City, N.J., 1939—. Home: 12 E. 97th St., N.Y.C. 29. Died May 1958.

GIBBS, John Sears, Jr., mfr.; b. St. Louis, June 28, 1876; son John Sears and Helen (Macqueen) G.; student pvt. sch., Balt.; m. Ethel Fairbanks Dixon, Dec. 15, 1903 (dec.); children—William T. Dixon, Sarah Macqueen (Mrs. J. McKenny Willis), Mary Bartlett (Mrs. Lawrason Riggs). Chmn. bd. Gibbs & Co., Inc.; dir., 1st Nat. Bank, Eutaw Savings Bank (Balt.). Past pres., mem. bd. trustees, Johns Hopkins Hosp.; mem. bd. trustees Johns Hopkins U. Clubs: Maryland, Elkridge, Merchants (Balt.); Chesapeake Yacht (Easton, Md.); Porcupine (Nassau, Bahamas). Home: Tyreonnell, Woodbrook 12, Baltimore County. Office: 2235 Boston St., Balt. 31. Died Oct. 29, 1953; buried Easton, Md.

GIBBS, Robert Adams, educator; b. Fort Ann, N.Y., Oct. 6, 1871; s. Theron Z. (M.D.) and Mary J. (Thomas) G.; student Stanford U., 1893-96, U. Cal., summer 1906; A.B., U. So. Cal., 1908; m. Della M. Page, Apr. 7, 1909 (died Feb. 10, 1937); 1 dau., Edith Caroline (Mrs. Earle Russell Vaughan); m. 2d, Mrs. Lilian (Clark) Schouten, May 13, 1941. Founder, 1908, head master, Page Mil. Acad., Los Angeles. Recommended by Redfield Proctor, Sec. of War, as lt., U.S. Army, 1892. Maj. Cal. N.G. Republican. Baptist. Fellow Am. Geog. Soc.; mem. Soc. Colonial Wars, S.R., N.E. Hist. and Geneal. Soc., Inst. Am. Genealogy, Assn. Ind. Schs. Los Angeles County (pres. 1939-40), Pi Gamma Mu; founder, life mem. Pacific Geog. Soc. Mason (32°), Elk. Rotarian. Author: Western Tales, 1925; Sea Stories, 1926. Address: Page Military Academy, 1201 S. Cochran Av., Los Angeles 35. Died July 23, 1952.

GIBBS, Wolcott, writer, critic; b. New York, N.Y., Mar. 15, 1902; s. Lucius Tuckerman and Angelica Singleton (Duer) G.; student Hill Sch., Pottstown, Pa., 1917-20; m. Elinor Mead Sherwin, Oct. 14, 1933; children—Wolcott, Janet. Reporter various newspapers, 1922-27; copyreader The New Yorker, 1927-28, asso. editor, 1928-37, editorial writer, 1937-42, drama critic, 1940—, motion picture critic, 1944-45. Co-founder, editor The Fire Islander, 1954. Member Soc. of The Cincinnati. Club: Century Association (New York City, 1956). Author: Bed of Neuroses, 1937; Season in the Sun, 1946; Season in the Sun (play), 1950; More in Sorrow, 1958. Contbr. weekly criticism, occasional fiction and articles to The New Yorker. Home: Ocean Beach, Fire Island, N.Y. Office: 25 W. 43d St., N.Y.C. Died Aug. 16, 1958.

GIBSON, Charles Hammond, author; b. Boston, Nov. 21, 1874; s. Charles Hammond and Rosamond (Warren) G.; student pvt. sch., Boston and St. Paul's Sch., 1889-92; student architecture Mass. Inst. Tech., 1893-94; studied in Brit. Museum, architecture and landscape architecture in Eng. and France, 1894. Real estate and investments, Boston, 1894-1915. Went to Eng., 1894, as sec. to Alfred Harmsworth (Lord Northcliffe) as asst. in organizing Jackson-Harmsworth Polar Expdn., 1894-95; visited France and made researches in French history; organized lectures in U.S., 1896-97, to revive interest in the history and architecture of Touraine. Delivered courses of lectures on politics, lit. and travel, 1904-14; park and recreation commr, City of Boston, 1914-16; sec. Mass. Prison Reform League, 1913-16. Mem. Nat. Allied Relief Com., 1915, Bunker Hill Monument Assn., Japan Society, Boston, Mass. Hort. Soc., Mass. Audubon Soc., Fgn. Policy Assn., Italy Am. Soc., Navy League U.S., Am. Poetry Assn. (pres. 1925-26), Poetry Soc. Great Britain (v.p.), Acad. Polit. Sci. Student 1st OTC., Plattsburg, N.Y., 1915. Clubs: Boston Authors, Trinity, Episcopalian, Nahant Garden Club. Author: Two Gentlemen in Touraine (pen-name Richard Sudbury), 1900; Among French Inns, 1905; The Spirit of Love and Other Poems, 1906; The Wounded Eros (sonnets), 1908; The Prisoner's Hymn, 1914; At Lincoln's Memorial, 1924; England, A Pindaric Ode, 1930. Composer. Editor Reminiscences of Annie Crowninshield Warren, 1910; Year Book of Poems of Boston Chapter Am. Lit. Assn., 1925, and Am. Poetry Assn., 1926. Contbr. Our Unknown Dead and other odes to Am. and European mags. Home: 137 Beacon St., Boston; (summer) Nahant, Mass. Died Nov. 17, 1954.

GIBSON, Edwin T., univ. ofcl.; grad. Cornell U. Law Sch., 1907; m. Wilmoth Cosby, 1916; children—Edwin C., Wilmoth C. Uellendahl. Gen. law practice New York, 3 yrs.; trial counsel Legal Aid Soc., New York; legal dept. Nat. Biscuit Co., 1912-15; asst. to pres., sec. Am. Sugar Refining Co., 1915-26; pres. Brooklyn Cooperage Co., 1926-30; exec. vice pres. Empire Bond & Mortgage Corp., 1930-32; exec. v.p. Gen. Foods Corp., dir., 1946, member exec. com., 1950, ret., 1951; research dir. Kraft Paper Industry, 1955-59; chmn. bd. Market Research Corp. of Am., 1958—; dir., mem. exec. com. Mchts. Refrigerating Co., First Fed. Savs. and Loan Assn. Administrator D.P.A., 1951; member board governors Refrigeration Research Foundation. President Eisenhower Exchange Fellowships, Inc. Am. mem., chmn. Internat. Materials Conf., Washington, 1951; vice chmn. Mut. Security Adminstrn. Evaluation Group, 1953—. Trustee, mem. exec. com. Cornell U. Served in A.U.S., maj., ordnance A.E.F., World War I. Decorated Order of World Wars; named Man of the Year, Nat. Assn. of Mfrs., 1953. Mem. Nat. Planning Assn., Phi Kappa Psi, Phi Delta Phi. Mem. Am. Legion. Clubs: American Yacht; Cornell University (N.Y.); Army and Navy (Washington). North Fork Country (Cutchogue, L.I.); Cavalry (Bklyn.). Home: Rt. 3, Box 341, Montgomery Rd., Savannah, Ga. Office: 149 E. 78th St., N.Y.C. Died Feb. 23, 1959; buried Kensico Cemetery, Valhalla, N.Y.

GIBSON, Harvey Dow, banker; b. North Conway, N.H., Mar. 12, 1882; s. James L. and Addie (Dow) G.; A.B., Bowdoin Coll., 1902, LL.D., 1919; LL.D., U. N.H., 1933, Northeastern, 1945; m. Carrie Hastings Curtis, June 10, 1903; m. 2d, Helen Whitney Bourne, Mar. 12, 1926. Entered employ Am. Express Co., at Boston, 1902, and became asst. mgr. financial dept. at N.Y.C.; asso. with others and purchased control Raymond & Whitcomb Co., of which was v.p.; apptd. asst. to pres. Liberty Nat. Bank, 1912, v.p.,

1913-17, pres., 1917-21, when Liberty Nat. Bank was merged with N.Y. Trust Co., elected pres. of latter co.; pres. Mfrs. Trust Co. of N.Y., 1931—, chmn. bd., 1931-47; chmn. bd. Nat. Bondholders Corp., Textile Banking Co.; dir. Shuron Optical Co., Huron Holding Corp., Chesapeake Ohio Ry., N.Y.,N.J.&H. R.R. (exec. com.), Am. Home Products Corp., U.S. Lines Co. (exec. com.), Internat. Mercantile Marine Co., Western Electric Co. (exec. com.), Brooklyn-Manhattan Transit Corp., Distillers Corp., Seagrams, Ltd., Paramount Pictures, Inc. (exec. com.), New England Pub. Service Co., Home Ins. Co. (exec. and finance com.), Hershey Creamery Co. Chmn. N. Y. County chpt. A.R.C., 1917; apptd. gen. mgr. A.R.C., 1917, also mem. War Council and War Finance Com., commr. for France, 1918, and for Europe, 1919; A.R.C. commr. to Great Britain, 1942-45, commr. to Gt. Britain and Western Europe, 1944-45; nat. chmn. 1946-47 Fund Campaign, gov., mem. exec. com., 1947. Mem. N.Y. World's Fair Finance Com., Inc., chmn. 1936-41, mem. exec. com., 1936-41; chmn. bd., 1939-41; incorporator, Nat. Orgn., 1919, dir. N.Y. chpt. A.R.C.; chmn. Emergency Unemployment Relief Com., N.Y.C., 1931-33; chmn. American Com. of Short-term Creditors of Germany. Served as lt. col. to col., U.S. Army, 1919. Decorated citation by Pres. Truman; Medal of Merit, 1945; Asso. Comdr. Order of St. John (Brit.); Officer of Legion of Honor (France); Comdr. Order of the Crown (Belgium); Knight Order of Vasa (Sweden); Order of the Crown (Rumania); recipient Gold Medal award; Assn. of N.Y., 1934; Curtis Bowdoin prize, 1938; certificate by Pres. F. D. Roosevelt, for service overseas, 1942; ann. award by U. N.H. of Pette Medal, 1948. Trustee and chmn. finance com. of Bowdoin Coll.; pres. bd. trustees Fryburg Academy; trustee Northeastern Univ., Florence Nightingale Internat. Foundation, Am. Foundation for Blind, Helen Keller Endowment Fund; treas. Jane A. Delano Meml. Fund; treas., dir. Beekman-Downtown Hospital; trustee, mem. exec. com. Community Service Soc. N.Y.; dir. Am. Horse Shows Assn., Am. Arbitration Assn. Mem. Piping Rock Horse Show Assn. (pres.), English Speaking Union (dir.), Greater N.Y. Fund (dir.), Newcomen Soc. of Eng., Am. br., N.Y. State C. of C. (v.p., 1947), Bond of N.Y. (mem. adv. council), Buck's (London), National Golf Links of America, Recess Travellers (Paris), Union Interalliee, Maine Society, Theta Delta Chi. Republican. Presbyn. Clubs: Bankers of America, Links, Links Golf, Nat. Golf Links, Racquet and Tennis, Turf and Field, Recess Union League, University, Piping Rock, River, Wall Street, Meadown Brook, Madison Sq. Garden (pres. and gov.), The Creek (pres.), N.Y. Yacht (gov.), Meadow Brook Hounds (past master of foxhounds). Home: 52 E. 69th St., New York; (country) Locust Valley, N.Y. Office: 55 Broad St., N.Y.C. Died Sept. 11, 1950; buried North Conway (N.H.) Cemetery.

GIBSON, Hugh; b. in Los Angeles, Calif., Aug. 16, 1883; s. Frank A. and Mary G.; grad. École Libre des Sciences Politiques, Paris, 1907; LL.D., M.A., Pomona; Dr. Dip. and Polit. Sci., Louvain; LL.D., University of Brussels and Yale; married at Brussels, Ynés Reyntiens, February 27, 1922 (deceased, March 1950); 1 son. Apptd. sec. of legation, Tegucigalpa, Honduras, 1908, 2d secretary Am. Embassy, London, 1909-10; pvt. sec. to legation at Tegucigalpa, Honduras, July 31, 1908; 2d sec. Am. Embassy, London, 1909-10; pvt. sec. to asst. sec. of state, Washington, D.C., 1901-11; sec. of legation, Havana, Cuba, 1911-13; mem. spl. mission to observe elections in Santo Domingo, Dec. 1913; sec. of Legation, Brussels, 1914-16; assigned to Embassy, London, May 16, 1916, to Dept. of State, Feb. 28, 1917; attached to British sec. of state for foreign affairs during visit to U.S., Apr.-June 1917; attached to Belgian War Mission during visit of the Mission to U.S., June-Aug. 1917; apptd. 1st sec. Embassy, Paris, Mar. 1918; duty with Mr. Hoover, dir. gen. of relief, Nov. 1918-Apr. 1919; mem. Inter-Allied Mission to countries of former Austro-Hungarian Empire, Dec. 1918-Jan. 1919; apptd. first E.E. and M.P. to Poland, Apr. 16, 1919; apptd. E.E. and M.P. to Switzerland, 1924-27; vice-chmn. Am. delegation to Internat. Conf. for Control of the Traffic in Arms, Geneva, 1925; chmn. Am. delegation to Preparatory Commn. for Disarmament Conference, 1926-27; ambassador to Belgium and E.E. and M.P. to Luxemburg, 1927-33, and 1937-38; ambassador to Brazil, 1933-37. Del. to Conf. on Pvt. Manufacture of Arms, 1927; chmn. Am. Delegation to Conf. for Limitation of Naval Armament and chmn. on the conf., 1927; del. to London Naval Conf.; acting chmn. U.S. Delegation at Disarmament Conf., Geneva, 1932, U.S. rep. on Mediatory Group to end Chaco War, Buenos Aires, 1935; director general for Europe of Commn. for Polish Relief and Commn. for Relief in Belgium, 1940-41; delegate to Chaco Peace Conf., Buenos Aires, 1935; director Commn. for Relief in Belgium and Belgian-American Educational Found.; dir. Provisional Intergovernmental com. on Movement of Migrants from Europe, 1952—. Trustee of French Institute in America. Clubs: University, Links, Dutch Treat (New York); Metropolitan (Washington, D.C.); University, Sunset, Friday Morning (Los Angeles, Calif.); Royal Golf (Brussels). Author: A Journal from Our Legation in Belgium, 1917; Rio, 1937; Belgium, 1939; The Problems of Lasting Peace (with Herbert Hoover), 1942; The Road to Foreign Policy, 1944; The Basis of Lasting Peace (with Herbert Hoover), 1945. Address: 63 rue des Pâquis, Geneva, Switzerland. Died Dec. 12, 1954.

GIBSON, James Edgar, author, builder; b. Williamsport, Pa., May 1, 1875; s. William and Mary Alice (Otto) G; ed. private and pub. schs. and grad. Wharton Sch. of Finance and Economy, U. of Pa., 1896; m. Eleanor Landell Fox, Oct. 10, 1906. Salesman of bldg. supplies, 1897-99; supt. of constrn. Keystone Fireproofing Co., Phila., 1899-1901, v.p., 1901-03, pres., 1903-17; pres. Metropolitan Fireproofing Co., New York, 1908-17; treas. and gen. mgr. Victoria Gypsum Mining & Mfg. Co., Can., 1908-17; gen. mgr. Keystone Plaster Co., Chester, Pa., 1908-17; sec. and treas. Price Engine Co., Phila., Pa., 1917-24; concrete specialist, engaged in polychrome concrete work, concrete roof constrn., since 1924; an asst. to chief of ordnance, U.S. Army, Middle Div., 1917-18; sec. Claims Bd. U.S. Army Ordnance Dept., Middle Div., 1918-22. Member Philadelphia County Board of Public Assistance of Commonwealth of Pa. since 1943. Republican. Episcopalian. Author: Dr. Bodo Otto and the Medical Background of the American Revolution, 1937. Contbr. to hist. jours.; also "Bodo Otto, Senior Hospital Physician and Surgeon of Valley Forge," in Historical Review of Berks County, 1936; chapter "Captured Medical Men and Hospitals of the American Revolution" to the Annals of Medical History, 1938; The Historical Background of German Emigration, pub. by The Hist. Soc. of Berks County, Pa., 1940; The German Academy or Seminary in Philadelphia, 1773-1777, pub. by The Luth. Ch. Quarterly, 1941; Blood Transfusion in Reverse, to gen. mags. and Hist. Chronicle, 1944; John Bullus Reading, Physician and Navy Surgeon, 1945; Some Ancestors of the Rapalje Family; Benjamin Rush Terminates Postwar Mutiny; Dr. Benjamin Rush's Apprenticed Medical Students; The Role of Disease in the 70,000 Casualties of the American Revolutionary Army; Bodo Otto, Junior; Smallpox in the Am. Revolutionary Army; Third Party, 1829; Pennsylvania Provincial Conference of 1776; Modern Trend in Care and Recreation of the Aged; Biography of Major Gen. John Borrows; Biography of Dr. John Augustuus Otto. Home: 500 W. Chelton Av., Phila. Died Feb. 9, 1953.

GIBSON, Stanley, physician; b. Jacksonville, Ill., Apr. 9, 1883; s. George C. and Lavina (Carlisle) G.; A.B., De Pauw U., Greencastle, Ind., 1907; A.M., Northwestern U., 1912, M.D., 1913; m. Virginia Woltersdorf, Sept. 30, 1922. Practiced in Chgo., 1913—; prof. emeritus of pediatrics Northwestern U. Med. Sch.; cons. pediatrician St. Luke's Hosp., cons. in cardiology Children's Meml. Hosp. Capt. M.C., U.S. Army in World War, serving 18 mos. overseas at Base Hosp., No. 12, Camiers, France. Mem. Phi Beta Kappa, Alpha Omega Alpha, Sigma Psi, Delta Upsilon, Nu Sigma Nu. Club: University. Contbr. to med. journals. Home: 1710 Wesley Av., Evanston, Ill. 707 W. Fullerton, Chgo. Died Oct. 1956.

GIDE, André Paul Guillaume (zhēd), French author; b. Paris, France, Nov. 22, 1869; s. Paul and Juliette (Rondeaux) G.; student Lycee Louis Le Grand, Paris; m. Madeleine Rondeaux, 1895. Author of Les cahiers d'Andre Walter, 1891; Le voyage d'Urien, 1893; Paludes, 1895; Les Nourritures terrestres, 1897; Lettres a Angele, 1900; L'Immoraliste, 1902; La Porte étroite, 1909; Isabelle, 1911; Souvenirs de la Cour d'Assises, 1913; Les Caves du Vatican, 1914; Symphonie pastorals, 1919; Corydon, 1924; Si le grain ne meurt, 1926; Incidences, Les faux monnayeurs, 1926; Voyage au Congo, 1927; l'Ecole des femmes, 1929; Oedipe, 1931; Persephone, 1933; Retour de l'U.R.S.S., 1936; Retouches a mon Retour de l'U.R.S.S., 1937; Journal, 1939, 46, 50; wrote critical studies of Dostoevski and Oscar Wilde; translations of English classics as Shakespeare, Whitman, Blake, etc.; now considered one of the foremost contemporary novelists and writers of France. Recipient Nobel Prize for Literature, 1947. Fellow: Royal Soc. of London. Address: Paris VII, Ibis rue Vaneau, France; also care Justin O'Brien, Columbia U., N.Y.C. 27. Died Feb. 19, 1951; buried Cuverville-en-Caux, Normandy, France.

GIDEON, Valentine, lawyer; b. Iron County, Mo., Jan. 11, 1859; s. Calvin and Artemesia (Matkin) G.; B.S., Carleton Coll., Farmington, Mo., 1886; student St. Louis Law Sch., 1888-89; m. Elizabeth L. Lang, July 24, 1889; 1 son, Reinhart L. Began practice at Ogden, Utah, 1890; commr. Supreme Court of Utah Ty., 1892-96; mem. Bd. of Edn., Ogden, 1897-1900; city atty., Ogden, 1912-15; apptd. asso. justice Supreme Court of Utah, Mar. 1917, and elected to same position, Nov. 1918, for term ending Jan. 4, 1927, chief justice, 1925-26; reapptd. to Supreme Court by governor Feb. 1927, to fill out term expiring Jan. 1, 1929; in practice of law, Ogden, Utah, since 1929. Retired 1945. Democrat. Conglist. Mem. Am. and Utah State bar assns. Mason (K.T., Shriner), K. of P. Address: 69 Foxcroft Rd., W. Hartford, Conn. Died Feb. 11, 1951; buried Fairview Cemetery, West Hartford.

GIES, William John (gīz), biological chemist; b. Reisterstown, Md., Feb. 21, 1872; s. John Jr., and Ophelia Letitia (Ensminger) G.; B.S., Gettysburg, 1893, M.S., 1896, Sc.D., 1914, LL.D., 1924; Ph.B., Yale, 1894, Ph.D., 1897; LL.D., Baylor Univ., 1924; Sc.D., Temple Univ., 1938; Sc.D., U. of Maryland, 1940; studied U. of Berne, 1899; Marine Biol. Lab., Woods Hole, Mass., 1901, 1902; m. Mabel Loyetta Lark, May 24, 1899; children—John, James Tressler, Robert Henry, Mary. Asst. in physiol. chemistry, 1894-98, in zoölogy, 1895, tutor in physiology, 1896-98, Yale; instr. physiol. chemistry, 1898-1902, adj. prof., 1902-05, prof., 1905-07, prof. biol. chemistry, 1907-55, Columbia. Sec. of faculty of Coll. Phys. and Surg. (Columbia), 1905-21; prof. physiol. chemistry, New York Coll. of Pharmacy, 1904-22, Teachers Coll. (Columbia), 1909-28; cons. chemist New York Bot. Garden, 1902-21, and mem. board of scientific directors, 1911-28; consulting pathol. chemist, Bellevue Hosp., 1910-22. Pres. Ann. Conf. of Biol. Chemists, 1917-18; dir. Lutheran Hosp., 1917-19; chmn. exec. com. N.Y. Sch. of Dental Hygiene, 1916-17; sec. administrative bd. Sch. of Dentistry, Columbia U., 1917-21; chmn. Dental Adv. Board N.Y. Dept. of Health, 1926-35; mem. com. New York State Department of Health on fluoridation of Water Supplies since 1944. In charge study of dental education for Carnegie Foundation, 1921-31. Fellow A.A.A.S. (organizer, sec. sect. K, 1905-09), Am. Coll. Dentists (asst. sec. 1933-43; chmn. N.Y. sect. 1939-40, hist., 1947), Am. Acad. Periodontol., N.Y. Acad. Dentistry (v.p. 1938-40, pres. 1940-41, first hon. fellow, 1945); asso. fellow N.Y. Acad. Med., mem. Am. Philos. Soc., Soc. Exptl. Biol. and Med. (sec. 1903-09, v.p. 1909-10, 1914-15, pres. 1917-19), Am. Soc. Biol. Chemists (sec. 1906-10), Internat. Assn. Dental Research (hon. pres. 1922-28; sec. 1928-38; pres. elect 1938-39; pres. 1939-40), Am. Assn. Dental Editors (pres. 1935-36), Pan-Am. Odontol Assn. (pres. 1943-44); N.Y. State Dental Society (hon.), Allied Dental Council (hon.), American Physiological Society, Soc. Pharmacology and Exptl. Therapeutics, Phi Beta Kappa, Phi Sigma Kappa, Sigma Xi, Nu Sigma Nu, Omicron Kappa Upsilon, Theta Kappa Psi; hon. member Austrian and Danish dental societies. Choice of alumni for pres. of Gettysburg Coll., 1904, alumni trustee, 1908-20; trustee Irving Coll., 1900-10. Author: Biochemical Researches (8 vols.), 1903-27; Text-Book of General Chemistry, 1904; Text-Book of Organic Chemistry, 1905, 09; Laboratory Work in Biological Chemistry, 1906; Bull. on Dental Edn., for Carnegie Foundation, 1926. Editor Am. Dental Assn. vol. on Dental Caries, 1939, 2d edit., 1941, Wells Memorial vol., 1948. Editor Am. Coll. of Dentists volume on Dental Care Under Clinical Conditions, 1943; editor vol. for N.Y. Inst. Clin. Oral Path., on Fluorine in Dental Public Health, 1945. Founder, editor Proc. Soc. Exptl. Biology and Medicine, 1904-10, Proc. Am. Soc. Biol. Chemists, 1907-10, Bio-chem. Bull., 1911-16; Jour. Dental Research, 1919-36, editor emeritus since 1936; Jour. Am. Coll. of Dentists, 1934-38; asst. editor, 1938-40; editor dept. of biol. chemistry in Chem. Abstracts, 1911-21; asso. editor New York Jour. of Dentistry, 1935-36; contbg. editor Annals of Dentistry, 1936-42, mem. editorial bd., 1947-52; editor History of First Three Decades of N.Y. Acad. of Dentistry 1953. Past director research under auspices National Dental Research Commn., N.Y. State Dental Soc., First Dist. Dental Soc. State of N.Y. and N.Y. Sabbath Com.; chmn. Research Council of N.Y. Acad. Dentistry, 1927-41. Collaborator for various chemical, medical, and biological journals since 1895. Award of merit Rhode Island State Dental Soc., 1927; Callahan medal of Ohio State Dental Soc., 1928; permanent ann. fellowship in biol. chemistry, Columbia, founded in his honor, 1928, by pupils and colleagues; permanent dental research awards and fellowships founded in his honor, 1937, by Am. Coll. Dentists. Recipient of distinguished service award, Gettysburg Coll., 1938, Alpha Omega Frat., 1940, Sigma Epsilon Delta, 1948. Gies Found. for Advancement of Dentistry established by dentists, 1951; Spenadel and Burkhart awards by N.Y.C. and State dental socs., 1951, 52; Pa. ambassador (Manheim), 1951; inscribed bas-relief portrait-plaque erected 1952, as founder Columbia U. Dental Sch. Address: 502 W. Orange St., Lancaster, Pa. Died May 20, 1956.

GIESE, Oscar W. (gēs'e), lawyer; b. Baltimore, Nov. 25, 1905; s. Frederick A. and Gertrude (Stolzenbach) G.; student Baltimore Poly. Inst., 1923; John Hopkins, 1925; U. of Fla., 1926; LL.B., George Washington U., 1930; m. Virginia Buell, Oct. 4, 1929; children—Ann Mather, Carr William, Robert Buell. Engr. Fla. Power and Light Co., 1926-27; law practice, Washington, D.C., 1930; private law practice Minneapolis, 1930-42; v.p. McGraw Electric Co., 1946-48; private law practice, Washington, D.C., since 1948. Served as major, chief patent officer, Q.M. Corps, U.S. Army, 1942-45. Mem. Am. Bar Assn., Am. Patent Law Assn. Nat. Assn. Mfrs. (com. on patents and research). Clubs: Minneapolis (Minn.); Army and Navy, National Press (Washington). Home: 3045 Foxhall Rd. N.W. Office: National Press Bldg., Washington. Died Dec. 12, 1956; buried Arlington Nat. Cemetery.

GIESEKING, Walter Wilhelm, concert pianist; b. Nov. 5, 1895; s. Wilhelm and Martha (Bethke) G.; m. Anne Haake, 1925; 2 daus. First appeared in concerts, 1913; toured in concerts throughout Europe, 1920—, North America, 1926—, England, 1928, also elsewhere abroad. Prof. State Conservatory of Music, Sarrebruck. Composer musical works including: Sonatina for Flute and Piano, 1937; Serenade for String Quartet, 1939; also other chamber music. In mil. service, 1916-18. Address: Saarbrücken Saar, Kohlweg 18. Died Oct. 26, 1956.

GIFFORD, George, banker; b. Schenectady, N.Y., Dec. 15, 1881; s. William and Adelaide Grigsby (Richardson) G.; A.B., Union Coll., Schenectady, 1908. Banking business at Schenectady since 1898; pres. Mohawk Nat. Bank since 1924. Mem. Psi Upsilon. Presbyn. Clubs: Mohawk, Mohawk Golf. Home: 9 N. Church St. Office: 216 State St., Schenectady, Died July 19, 1951; buried Vale Cemetery, Schenectady.

GIFFORD, Glen J., govt. ofcl.; b. Tipton, Ind., Sept. 17, 1877; s. George H. and Anna R. (Smiley) G.; A.B., Ind. U., 1899; m. Edith C. Holland, Jan. 1, 1901; 1 dau., Georgeann (Mrs. Russell G. Bishop). Admitted to Ind. bar, 1898; atty. Tipton County, Ind., 1901-28; judge 36th Judicial Circuit, Ind., 1929-34; solicitor agr., U.S. Dept. of Agr., 1934-46, hearing examiner, 1946-52, chief hearing examiner, 1952-56. Served with U.S. Army, World War I. Mem. Phi Delta Theta. Presbyn. Mason. Clubs: University (Washington). Home: 3150 16th St. N.W., Washington 10. Office: 417 West Adminstrn. Bldg., Washington 25. Retired. Died Apr. 18, 1958; buried Arlington Nat. Cemetery.

GIFFORD, Ralph Clayton, banker; b. North East, Md., Jan. 19, 1889; s. David LeGrande and Sallie Rebecca (Read) G.; B.S., U. of Pa., 1913; m. Lalla Robinson Swearingen, Apr. 21, 1914; 1 son, killed in action. Salesman Lamson Co., Boston, Mass., 1913-14; real estate business Louisville, Ky., 1914-16; with First National Bank and Kentucky Trust Co., Louisville, 1916-18; vice pres. both banks, 1918-27, exec. vice pres., 1927-31, pres. 1931-44, chmn. bd. since 1944; dir. Louisville Ry., 1927-30, Chesapeake & Ohio Ry. Co., 1939-42, N.Y. & Chicago R.R. Co., 1939-42; dir. Louisville br. Fed. Reserve Bank of St. Louis, 1938-43. Member Fed. Adv. Council, representing Eighth Fed. Res. Dist. Trustee Speed Memorial Museum. Treas. Community Chest, 1926-35. Mem. Newcomen Soc. Eng., Delta Upsilon. Republican. Presbyn. Club: Pendennis (Louisville). Home: The Mayflower, Virginia Beach, Va. Office: First Nat. Bank, 216 S. 5th St., Louisville. Died Feb. 25, 1959.

GIFFORD, Roy Wellington, chmn. Borg-Warner International Corp.; b. South Lyon, Mich., Oct. 25, 1883; s. Myron Wentworth and Elizabeth Rebina (Echlin) G.; B.S., U. of Mich., 1906; m. Lena Antoinette Fairweather, Sept. 2, 1910; children—Theron Fairweather, Margaret Antoinette. Grad. apprenticeship Seager Engine Works, 1906-08, asst. sec.-treas. and export mgr., 1908-10; supt. Deyo-Macey Engine Co., Binghamton, N.Y., 1910-13. gen. mgr. and treas., 1913-15; supt. munitions Massey-Harris Co., Toronto, Can., 1916-17, factory mgr., 1918-23, dir. in charge all mfg., Can. and plants in 4 countries, 1923-31; asst. to pres. Borg-Warner Corp., Chicago, Ill., 1931-34, pres. Borg-Warner Internat. Corp., 1934-36, became chmn. bd., 1946, Norge machine products div., 1940-48; chmn. bd. Robotyper Corp., Hendersonville, N.C.; retired, 1949. Extensive European travel from 1909, and building factories, France and Germany, 1926-28. Active in E.C.A. problems. Testified on reciprocal trade treaties before ways and means com. U.S. Ho. of Reps., 1940. Mem. Detroit Bd. of Commerce (chmn. fgn. trade com.), C. of C. (mem. joint Canadian and U.S. com. Nat. Chambers of Commerce), Nat. Elec. Mfg. Assn. (mem. tariff and export com.), Tau Beta Pi. Republican. Presbyn. Clubs: Detroit Athletic, Lochmoor Golf, Rotary. Home: 3130 Washington Rd., West Palm Beach, Fla. Died Nov. 1, 1951; buried Imlay City, Mich.

GIFFORD, Walter John, coll. dean; b. Pittsfield, O., July 15, 1884; s. Frank Augustus and Harriet Evelyn (Avery) G.; A.B., Oberlin Coll., 1907; M.A. Columbia, 1911, Ph.D., 1918; m. Litta Phelon McMeeken, Mar. 21, 1912; children—Daisy May (Mrs. Roland E. Jones), Robert Walter. Tchr. elementary sch., Pittsfield, 1901-03, Windom Inst., Montevideo, Minn., 1907-09; prof. Wooster (O.) Coll., 1911-14; asst. edn. Columbia, 1914-16; prof. edn. Goucher Coll., Balt., 1916-18; ednl. dir. Army Y.M.C.A., Newport News, Va., 1918-19; dean, prof. edn. Madison Coll., Harrisonburg, Va., 1919—, chmn. exec. com. adminstrn., 1948-49. Mem. N.E.A., Va. Edn. Assn., Phi Beta Kappa, Phi Delta Kappa, Kappa Delta Pi. Methodist. Rotarian. Author: Historical Development of the New York State High School System, 1918; Introduction to Psychology, 1922; Introduction to the Learning Process, 1923; Syllabus in the History of Education, 1928; Problems in Educational Psychology (with Clyde P. Shorts), 1931. Home: 700 Ott St., Harrisonburg, Va. Died Apr. 26, 1957.

GIGLI, Benjimino (jēl'yē), tenor; b. Recanati, Italy, Mar. 20, 1890; s. Dominico and Ester (Magnaterra) G.; studied at Liceo St. Cecilia, Rome, under Enrico Rosati; m. Costanza Cerroni, Apr. 1915; children—Ester, Enzo. Début as Enzo, in "La Gioconda," at Rovigo, Italy, Oct. 15, 1915; sang throughout Italy, Europe, S. and Central America; joined Met. Opera Co., New York, 1920; prin. rôles in "Andrea Chénier"; "Cavalleria Rusticana"; "Fedora"; "Lucia"; "Traviata"; "Tosca"; "Bohème"; "Iris"; "Mefistofele"; "Amore Tre Re"; "Lucrezia Borgia"; "Francesca da Rimini"; "Romeo e Giulietta" (in French); "Lohengrin"; "Butterfly"; "Rigoletto"; "Africana"; "Gianni Schicchi"; "Martha"; "I Compagnacci"; "Manon Lescaut"; "Pagliacci"; "La Favorita"; "Mignon"; "Manon", in French and Italian; "Ballo in Maschera"; "L'Elisir d'Amore"; "Adrienne Lecouvreur"; "Roi d'Ys"; "Rigoletto"; "Cena delle Beffe"; "Amico Fritz"; "Don Giovanni"; "Falstaff"; "Sonnambula", etc. Served in Italian Army, 1909-11, and 1915. Grand Ufficale Crown of Italy; Commendatore of Gregorio Magno, by the Pope; Comendador Royal Order of Isabel la Catolico; Commendatore S.S. Maurizio and Lazzaro; Chevalier de la Legion d'Honneur. Catholic. Address: Via Serchio 2, Rome, Italy. Died Nov. 30, 1957; buried family tomb, Recanati, Italy.

GILBERT, Albert Clark, paper mfr.; b. Neenah, Wis., Nov. 20, 1887; s. William Markley and Priscilla Arabelle (Hartsock) G.; grad. Mohegan Lake (N.Y.) Sch., 1907; m. Frances Mabel Kimberly, May 25, 1916; children—Frances Kimberly (dec.), Priscilla, Katharine, Gloria, Alice Markley, Nicholas T. Associated with Gilbert Paper Co., Menasha, Wis., since 1907, as treas. and dir., 1907-18, v.p., 1918-26, pres. since 1926; v.p. and dir. Nat. Mfg. Bank of Neenah, Neenah, Wis. Mem. Phi Delta Theta. Presbyterian. Mason (32°). Clubs: North Shore Golf (Neenah, Wis.); Riverview Country (Appleton, Wis.); Tavern (Chicago). Home: 620 E. Wisconsin Av., Neenah, Wis. Office: 330 Ahnaip St., Menasha, Wis. Died Mar. 14, 1952; buried Neenah, Wis.

GILBERT, Charles Calvin, Sr., assn. exec. b. nr. Bethel, Tenn., Mar. 12, 1877; s. Capt. J. Calvin and Tranquilla Gracey G.; ed. pub. schs. of Lawrenceburg, Tenn., business coll., Nashville; m. Alma Bradford, June 20, 1900; children—Mary Louise (Mrs. J. L. Templeton), Charles Calvin, Elizabeth (Mrs. James H. Armistead). Stenographer and bookkeeper So. Soda Works, Nashville, 1893-1906; sec.-treas. So. Baking Powder Co., 1906-08; bookkeeper and office mgr. So. Automobile Co., 1909-11; asso. sec. Nashville C. of C., 1911-12; sec.-treas. Tenn. Mfrs. Assn., 1912—. Mem. Nashville City Council, 1909-13, Tenn. Legislature, 1913-15; mem. Nashville C. of C., pres. Memphis-to-Bristol Highway Commn.; sec. Southern States Indsl. Council; exec. dir. Nat. Fifty Years in Bus. Club, pub. Fifty Years in Bus. Mag. Mem. staff Gov. H. H. Horton, with rank of gen., 1928-32, staff Gov. Gordon Browning, with rank of col., 1937-39; comdr. Tenn. Colonels. Pres. Presbyn. Officers Union; elder Nashville Presbytery (deacon, Trinity Presbyn. Ch.). Clubs: Kiwanis of Nashville (sec. 1923-28, pres. 1944; dist. gov., Tenn., Ky., 1924-25), Nashville Execs. (sec., treas.), Belle Meade Golf and Country (Nashville); Mountain City (Chattanooga); Missouri Athletic (St. Louis). Owns and operates farm near McMinnville, Tenn. Home: 1805 Ashwood Av. Office: Stahlman Bldg., Nashville. Died June 2, 1954.

GILBERT, Charles Kendall, ret. bishop; b. Bainbridge, N.Y., Aug. 6, 1878; s. Don A. and Amelia H. (Bixby) G.; A.B., Hamilton Coll., 1902, A.M., 1905, D.D., from same, 1926; graduate General Theological Seminary, 1905, S.T.D., 1931; Litt. D., Hobart College, 1947; D.D., Trinity Coll., 1949; S.T.D., Columbia U., 1950; m. Anna Louise Brownell, June 21, 1906 (dec.); 1 son, Frederic D. H. Deacon, 1905, priest, 1906, P.E. Ch.; rector Trinity Ch., New Dorp, S.I., N.Y., 1905-06, Grace Ch., Millbrook, N.Y., 1906-12; sec. social service commn., Diocese of N.Y., 1912-13; editor of The Churchman, 1913-18; rector Church of St. James, Scarsdale, N.Y., 1918-20; executive secretary Social Service Commn. Diocese of N.Y., 1920-30; suffragan bishop, Diocese of New York, 1930-46; bishop of N.Y. Diocese, 1947-50. ret. 1950. Sec. Convention Diocese of N.Y., 1916-30. Dir. Youth Cons. Service. Officer French Legion of Honor, 1951. Mem. Chi Psi. Democrat. Clubs: Century Association, University. Author: Foreigners or Friends (with Thomas Burgess and C. T. Bridgeman), 1921; The Social Opportunity of the Churchman, 1921. Address: Charlemont, Mass. Died Nov. 18, 1958; buried Cathedral Ch. of St. John the Divine, N.Y.C.

GILBERT, Charles Pierrepont H., ret. architect; b. N.Y.C., Aug. 29, 1863; s. Loring and Carolyn C. (Etchebery) G.; prepared for coll.; took spl. courses in civil engring. and architecture; also studied painting, sculpture and fine arts, abroad; m. Florence Cecil Moss, Sept. 14, 1896 (died 1946); 1 son, Dudley Pierrepont. In active practice of architecture, 1889-1933; now cons. architect. Fellow A.I.A.; mem. Archtl. League, Soc. Colonial Wars, S.R., N.E. Soc., Soc. War of 1812, C. f C. Charter mem. Squadron A, N.G.N.Y. Clubs: Metropolitan, Racquet and Tennis. Home: 216 Townsend Av., Pelham Manor N.Y. Died Oct. 25, 1955.

GILBERT, Donald Wood, educator; b. Rochester, N.Y., Jan. 29, 1900; s. Avery Sanford and Emily Charlotte (Wood) G.; A.B., U. Rochester, 1921, M.A., 1923; M.A., Harvard, 1925, Ph.D., 1932; m. Eleanor Ruth Garbutt, Aug. 19, 1922; children—Emily Eleanor, Virginia Mary. Asst. in econs. U. Rochester, 1922-23, instr. econs., 1925-28, asst. prof., 1928-32, jr. prof., 1932-39, prof., 1939—, dean grad. sch., 1940-48, chmn. dept. econ., 1946-48, provost, 1948-51, v.p. charge university development, 1951-53, dir. Canadian studies program, 1953-54; asst. in econs. Harvard, 1924-25. Trustee Rochester Savings Bank, 1948—; bd. dirs. Rochester Bureau Municipal Research, 1948—. Mem. S.A.T.C., 1918. Pub. Triparite Panel chmn. 2d Regional War Labor Bd., 1943-45; chmn. resrch. com., Council on Postwar Problems, Rochester and Monroe County, 1943-45. Trustee, Rochester C. of C., 1944—; mem. bd. dirs. Rochester Council Society Agencies, 1946-51, Rochester Assn. UN, 1946-48; econ. cons. N.Y. State Joint Legis. Com. on Interstate Co-op., 1945-49; commr. Nat. Commn. on Accrediting, 1950-51. Mem. Am. Econ. Assn., Phi Beta Kappa, Psi Upsilon. Presbyn. Clubs: Pundit, University (Rochester). Author articles on taxation, business cycles and municipal finance to econ. jours. Home: 1 Chelmsford Lane, Rochester 18. Office: 15 Prince St., Rochester, N.Y. Died Aug. 26, 1957; buried White Haven Meml. Park, Rochester.

GILBERT, George Burton, ret. physician; b. Thomaston, Conn., Sept. 28, 1881; s. George Colton and Elizabeth W. (Judd) G.; A.B., Yale, 1903; M.D., Johns Hopkins, 1908; m. Elinor Drane Lillard, Apr. 6. 1915 (dec.); 1 son, George Robert; m. 2d, Catherine B. White, May 23, 1921 (div. 1933); 1 son, William Burton; m. 3d, Margaret C. Thomas, June 14, 1935. Intern Hartford (Conn.) Hosp., 1908; res. physician Cragmor Sanatorium, 1909-10; physician specializing in tb and internal medicine, Colorado Springs, Colo., 1911—; cons. physician Glockner and St. Francis Hosp. and Sanatoria, Meml. Hosp.; now retired. Mem. A.C.P., A.M.A., Am. Clinical and Climatol. Assn., Nat. Tb. Assn., Trudeau Soc., Am. Coll. Chest Physicians, Colo. Foundation for Research in Tb in Denver (asso. research dir.). Republican. Methodist. Home: 214 E. San Rafael St., Colorado Springs, Colo. Died Apr. 6, 1951; buried Evergreen Cemetery, Colorado Springs.

GILBERT, Harvey Wilbarger, oil, lumber, land; b. Beaumont, Tex., Feb. 18, 1884; s. John Nathan and Annie Webster (Wilbarger) G.; grad. Bingham Military Acad., Asheville, N.C., 1902; grad. student U. of Va., 1902-03; grad. Soulé Business Coll., New Orleans, 1904; married Hortense Gibbons, February 18, 1914; children—John Nathan, II, Eleanor Hortense (Mrs. Marshall Muse, Jr.). Began in oil and lumber business, Tex., 1903; pres. Harvey W. Gilbert Petroleum Co., Gilbert Lumber Co., Gilbert Tidewater Industrial Sites, Gilbert Tidewater Industries, Nona Oil Co., Nona Lumber Mills, Cheltenham Import & Export Co. Promoter Beaumont-Port Arthur Ship Channel; chmn. Beaumont-Port Arthur Indsl. Commn., since 1925; builder of Kansas City Southern Industrial R.R. Belt Line, Jefferson County Court House, Beaumont-Port Arthur Fresh Water Canal, Beaumont-Port Arthur Blvd. (12 mile blvd. 200 feet wide, paralleling ship channel), Beaumont-Port Arthur Metropolitan Airport; promoter and one of builders, Rockland Dam System on Neches River; Inter-city Indsl. Canal, Inter-city Indsl. Belt Railroad, Beaumont-Port Arthur-Houston Short-Line Highway. Mem. Sons of Am. Revolution (state dir.), East Tex., Pan-American Seaway, Inter-City Belt Indsl. R.R. Hist. Soc., Tex. State Hist. Soc., Old Spanish Trail Assn., Sons of Republic of Texas, Phi Kappa Sigma, Delta Theta. Ind. Democrat. Mem. Ch. of Christ, Scientist. Mason (32°). Clubs: Beaumont Country, Port Arthur Country. Contbr. industrial articles newspapers and jours. Home: 870 Calder Av. Office: Gilbert Bldg., Beaumont 1, Tex. Died Mar. 1955.

GILBERT, Katharine, teacher; b. Newport, R.I., July 29, 1886; dau. Thomas Jefferson and Sue (Morrison) Everett; A.B., Brown Univ., 1908, A.M., 1910, Litt.D., 1945; Ph.D., Cornell, 1912; m. Allan H. Gilbert, Aug. 1, 1913; children—Everett Eddy, Creighton Eddy. Teacher ungraded sch., Mount Hope, Conn., 1903-04; asst. to editor Philosophical Review, Cornell, 1915-19; Kenan Research fellow in philosophy, Univ. of N.C., 1922-28, acting prof. of philosophy, 1928-29; prof. of philosophy, Duke Univ., 1930-41, head dept. of aesthetics, art and music since 1942. Rep. U.S. Dept. of State Mission to students of philosophy in Italy, 1947. Organized portion on edn. of women for Duke Univ. Centennial Celebration, 1938. Mem. Am. Philos. Assn. (pres. Eastern div., 1946), Am. Soc. for Aesthetics (pres. 1947-48), Am. Assn. Univ. Women (mem. nat. com. on standards, 1942-46). Author: Maurice Blondel's Philosophy of Action, 1924; Studies in Recent Aesthetic, 1927; A History of Esthetics (with Helmut Kuhn), 1939; Aesthetic Studies: Architecture and Poetry, 1952. Contbr. articles in philos. and aesthetic subjects in scholarly jours. Home: 503 Compton Pl. Office: College Sta., Durham, N.C. Died Apr. 28, 1952.

GILBERT, Newell Clark, physician; b. Clinton, Ill., Dec. 5, 1880; s. Newell Darrow and Elizabeth (Clark) G.; B.S., U. of Wis., 1903; student U. of Mich., 1904; M.D. and M.S., Northwestern U., 1907; m. Charlotte Louise Pettibone, Sept. 22, 1914; children—Robert Pettibone, Mary Elizabeth. Interne St. Luke's Hosp., 1907-09, attending physician since 1916; prof. emeritus, past chmn. dept. of internal medicine, Northwestern U. Med. School. During World War served as capt., and later maj., Med. Corps, later lt. col. Med. O.R.C. Fellow A.A.A.S.; mem. Central Soc. for Clin. Research, Illinois State and Chicago med. socs., Chicago Soc. of Internal Medicine, Inst. of Medicine of Chicago, Am. Soc. for Clin. Investigation, Assn. of Am. Physicians, Am. Med. Assn., (past chmn. sect. pharmacol. and exptl. therapeutics; past chmn. sect. on med.), S.R., Sigma Alpha Epsilon, Phi Rho Sigma, Sigma Xi, Pi Kappa Epsilon. Republican. Baptist. Club: University. Contbr. to various med. jours. editor. Home: 5740 S. Kenwood. Office: 104 S. Michigan Av., Chgo. Died Aug. 1953.

GILBERT, S(tirling) Price, ret. justice; b. Stewart County, Ga., Jan. 31, 1862; s. Jasper Newton and Sarah Louise (Redding) G.; B.S., Vanderbilt U., 1883; LL.B., Yale, 1885; LL.D., Oglethorpe U., 1939; m. Mary Howard, Dec. 12, 1895; children—Price, Francis Howard (dec.). Began practice in Atlanta, 1885, firm of Gilbert & Brandon (Morris Brandon); removed to Columbus, 1886; mem. Ga. Ho. of Reps., 1888-93; solicitor gen., Ga., 1893-1908; judge Superior Court, Ga., 1908-16; justice Supreme Court, Ga., 1916-37, retired; chmn. Commn. to Revise Code of Ga., 1929, by apptmt. of Supreme Court, reappointed by legislative resolution, 1933, code adopted as statute law, effective Jan. 1, 1935. Mem. bd. regents U. System of Ga., 1943-50. Capt. Ga. N.G. 1887-93; mem. State Mil. Adv. Bd., 1890-93 (resigned). Commn. adv. bd., Tallulah Falls Sch. Mem. Ga. Bar Assn. (hon.), Phi Delta Theta (nat. treas. 1886-89), Phi Delta Phi; curator Ga. Hist. Soc. Democrat. Methodist. Mason. Clubs: Capital City (hon. life), Atlanta Athletic (hon.), Druid Hills Golf (hon.); Rotary (Brunswick, Ga.). Author: A Georgia Lawyer, 1946; Chief Justice Bleckley of Georgia; The Lamars of Georgia (Am. Bar Assn. Jour.). Author (brochure); James Clark McReynolds, late Justice Supreme Court, U.S. Home: Sea Island, Ga. Address: (summer) 675 W. Wesley Rd. N.W., Atlanta. Died Aug. 28, 1951; buried West View Cemetery.

GILBOY, Glennon, cons. engr.; b. Duryea, Pa., Sept. 11, 1902; s. James Bernard and Agnes Veronica (Glennon) G.; student Wyo. Sem., Kingston, Pa., 1921; B.S., Mass. Inst. Tech., 1925, M.S., 1927, D.Sc., 1928; m. Elizabeth Lane Waterman, Apr. 19, 1930 (div. Nov. 1953). Architect's asst., 1917-21; mem. staff Mass. Inst. Tech., 1925-29, asst. prof., 1929-32, asso. prof., 1932-37; pvt. cons. practice, 1937-55; with C. J. D'Amato & Assos., 1955—. Spl. engring. adviser to adminstr. OPA, 1942-43; U.S. del. World Power Conf., Stockholm, 1933, Washington, 1936. Recipient Desmond Fitzgerald medal Boston Soc. C.E., 1935. Mem. Am. Soc. M.E., Boston Soc. C.E., Am. Acad. Arts and Scis., A.A.A.S., Sigma Xi, Tau Beta Pi, Chi Epsilon. Home: 521 Beacon St. Office: 50 Beacon St., Boston. Died Aug. 18, 1958.

GILCHRIST, Beth Bradford, author; b. Peacham, Vt., Apr. 14, 1879; d. Oscar James and Martha Elizabeth Earl (Bradford) G.; A.B., Mt. Holyoke Coll., 1902. Conglist. Author: The Life of Mary Lyon, 1910; Helen Over the Wall, 1912; Helen and the Uninvited Guests, 1913; Helen and the Find Out Club, 1914; Helen and the Fifth Cousins, 1915; The Camerons of Highboro, 1919; Cinderella's Granddaughter, 1918; Kit, Pat and a Few Boys, 1921; Trail's End, 1925; also under pseudonym John Prescott Earl wrote series of boys prep-school stories including: The School Camp; On the School Team. Home: 79 Center St., Rutland, Vt. Died Apr. 23, 1957; buried Evergreen Cemetery, Rutland.

GILCHRIST, Fred C(ramer) (gil'krist), ex-congressman; b. California, Pa., June 2, 1868; s. James Cleland and Hannah (Cramer) G.; B.D., State Teachers Coll., Cedar Falls, Ia., 1886; LL.B., State U. Ia., 1893; m. Ellen Hurley, May 16, 1896; children—Frances (Mrs. Ledyard B. Hakes), Fred Cleland, Mavis (Mrs. B. Wilmot Allen). Tchr. and supt. schs. until 1890; county supt. schs. Pocahontas County, Ia., 1890-92; began law practice at Laurens, Ia., 1893; mem. Ia. Ho. of Rep., 1902-04; mem. law firm Gilchrist & Gilchrist, 1922—; mem. Ia. State Senate, 1923-31; mem. 72d Congress, 10th Ia. Dist., 73d to 77th Congresses, 8th Ia. Dist., 78th Congress, 6th Ia. Dist. Pres. Bd. Edn., Laurens, 1905-28. Republican. Mason. Home: Laurens, Ia. Died Mar. 10. 1950; buried Laurens Cemetery.

GILDER, Rodman, publisher; b. N.Y.C., Jan. 8, 1877; s. Richard Watson and Helena (de Kay) G.; A.B., Harvard, 1899; m. Comfort Tiffany, Apr. 20, 1911; children—Rodman, Mrs. A. E. Treat, Mrs. A. A. Miller. Identified with monthly, daily and weekly journalism in New York. Capt., later maj., U.S. Army Air Service, 1917-19. Trustee the Art Guild. Clubs: Century Association, Harvard (N.Y.C.); Cold Spring Harbor Beach. Author: Joan, the Maiden, 1933; The Battery, New York—a History, 1935. Address: 108 E. 82d St., N.Y.C. 28. Died Sept. 30, 1953.

GILE, John Fowler, surgeon; b. Tewksbury, Mass., July 5, 1893; s. John M. and Vesta F. (Fowler) G.; A.B., Dartmouth Coll., 1916, hon. A.M., 1937; M.D. Harvard, 1920; m. Nettie E. Edmunds, June 22, 1922; children—John F., Jane, Amos W., Nancy. Intern Worcester (Mass.) City Hosp., 1920-22; mem. surg. staff, Mary Hitchcock Meml. Hosp., Hanover, N.H., since 1922; instr. anat., Dartmouth Medical Sch., 1922-25; instr. physical diagnosis, 1925-34, instr. anat., 1930-39, prof. clinical surgery, since 1939. Pvt., M.C., U.S. Army, 1917-18. Life trustee Dartmouth Coll. Mem. Adv. Bd. "B," N.H., World War II. Fellow Am. Coll. Surgeons; mem. A.M.A., Am. Bd. Surgery (mem. founders group), Am. Assn. Surgery Trauma, New England Obstet. and Gynecol. Soc., New Eng. and Surg. Soc. (sec. 1937-46), New England Cancer Soc., N.H. Med. Soc. (v.p. 1944-45), Grafton County Med. Soc. (past pres.), Kappa Kappa Kappa, Sphinx. Clubs: Rotary, Eastern Surgical, N.H. Surgical. Contbr. articles to med. soc. meetings. Home: 17 Choate Rd. Office: Hitchcock Clinic, Hanover, N.H. Died Jan. 29, 1955; buried Hanover, N.H.

GILES, Howard Everett, painter; b. Bklyn., Feb. 10, 1876; s. Frank W. and Mary Ella (Bennett) G.; grad. high sch., Newark, N.J.; studied Art Students' League, N.Y.; spl. studies with Jay Hambidge, 1916-19; and with Dr. Denman W. Ross, 1922-26; m. Evelyn Carter, Mar. 18, 1933. Represented in permanent collections of Bklyn. Inst. of Art, Denver Mus. of Art, Boston Mus. of Art, Decatur (Ill.), Mus. Fine Arts, Art Inst. Chgo., Pa. Acad. Fine Arts, Fogg Art Mus. (Harvard), Gallery Fine Arts (San Diego, Cal.), John H. Vanderpoel Meml. Gallery (Chgo.), Mus. Fine Arts (Boston, Houston, Texas, Brooklyn, Montpelier, Vermont), Bennington Hist. Mus. (Vt.); pvt. collections of Mrs. J. D. Rockefeller, Jr., and Mr. John Spalding of Boston, etc. Awarded Shaw purchase prize ($500); Shaw water color prize; Inness gold medal, N.A.D., 1918; Beck prize, Pa. Acad., 1917; silver medal, $1000 prize, Carnegie Inst., 1921; Kramer prize, Art Inst. Chgo. (internat. Water Color Exhbn.), 1921; hon. mention Art Institute Chicago, 1918; first hon. mention Grand Central Galleries, 1931; Dana Gold medal, Pa. Acad., 1932; hon. mention Ogonquit Nat. Exhbn., 1935; medal (first class), Montclair Mus. of Art. 1934, Dean emeritus fine arts dept. Master Inst. of Roerich Mus., N.Y. Instr. drawing and composition. Lectr. on elements of design, N.A. Mem. Am. Water Color Soc., Phila. Water Color Club, Balt. Water Color Club. Clubs: Nat. Arts (life), Century (N.Y.C.). Home: South Woodstock, Vt. Died 1955.

GILES, Malcolm R., fraternal exec.; b. Somerset County, Md., May 3, 1894; s. John Rigby and Emma A. (Carew) G.; student Bryant and Stratton Bus. Coll., Baltimore, Md., 1912-13; Dr. of Social Science, Univ. of Maryland, 1951; married Marie Iris Treman, June 24, 1920 (dec.); 1 son, Malcolm R.; m. 2d, Kathleen M. Howard, Jan. 6, 1936; children—Richard Howard, Barbara Kay. Farmer, 1908-11; accountant and with U.S. Postal Service, 1913-15; chief clerk, Loyal Order Moose, 1915-17; dist. supervisor N.C. and S.C., Loyal Order of Moose, 1919-24; supreme sec., 1925-49; comptroller, 1931-39, organizer membership enrollment dept., 1934; exec. dir., 1945-49, dir. gen. since 1949. Sergt., Army Service Corps, U.S. Army, 1918-19; with A.E.F. 14 months. Dir. Aurora (Ill.) Nat. Bank. Mason (Shriner), Moose, Odd Fellow, K.P., Elk. Club: Country (Aurora, Ill.). Home: 71 Gladstone Av., Aurora, Ill. Office: Mooseheart, Ill. Died Sept. 29, 1953; buried Lincoln Meml. Park, Aurora, Ill.

GILHAMS, Clarence C., ex-congressman; b. Brighton, Ind., Apr. 11, 1860; s. Aaron and Mary Jane G.; ed. State Normal Sch., Terre Haute, Ind. Taught sch., LaGrange Co., Ind.; ex-auditor LaGrange Co.; elected to 59th Congress, No. 6, 1906, for unexpired term 1906-07), of N. W. Gilbert, resigned; reëlected to 60th Congress 1907-09); Republican. Address: LaGrange, Ind. Died June 5, 1912.

GILKEY, Geraldine Gunsaulus Brown, ex-pres. YWCA in the U.S.A.; b. Chesterville, O., June 24, 1889; d. Clarence Talmage and Lillian (Gunsaulus) Brown; Ph.B., U. Chgo., 1912; m. Charles Whitney Gilkey, July 26, 1915; children—Mary Jane, Langdon Brown. Gen. sec. YWCA of U. Chgo., 1913-14; chmn. student dept. Central Field, YWCA, 1915-18; chmn. adv. bd. YWCA of U. Chgo., 1926-29; v.p. YWCA, U.S.A., 1926-30, pres., 1930-32. Mem. nat. bd. YWCA, convener Central Region, 1933-37, mem. nat. YWCA pub. affairs com., 1934—, Chgo. met. bd. (chmn. pub. affairs com., 1934-37; v.p. 1937—); mem. mid-west com. Fed. Council Chs.; mem. auxiliary com. Univ. Clinics. Mem. Am. Assn. Univ. Women, Mortar Bd. Baptist. Clubs: Contemporary, Woman's City, Fortnightly, Chicago Alumnae, University Settlement League. Home: South Yarmouth, Mass. Died Nov. 11, 1955; buried Beechwood, Centerville, Mass.

GILKISON, Frank E., judge; b. Martin County, Ind., Nov. 3, 1877; s. John and Matilda (Inman) G.; LL.B., Indiana U., 1901; m. Eva Edwards, June 15, 1925; 1 son, Frank Edward. Admitted to Ind. bar; deputy prosecuting atty., 1907-09; judge, 49th Judicial Circuit of Ind., 1935-45; judge, Supreme Court of Ind. since Jan. 1945. Republican county chmn. Martin County, Ind., 1928-34. Mem. Ind. State Bar Assn. Mason (32°, K.T.). Home: 906 E. Walnut St., Washington, Ind. Office: State House, Indpls. Died Feb. 25, 1955; buried Bethany Cemetery, Daviess County, Ind.

GILL, Everett, church official; b. Huntsville, Mo., Nov. 4, 1869; s. Adam Fisher and Mary Ann (Fairchild) G.; A.B., William Jewell Coll., Liberty, Mo., 1890; Th.M., Southern Bapt. Theol. Sem., Louisville, Ky., 1894, Th.D., 1895; D.D., Georgetown (Ky.) College, 1910; D.D., Wake Forest (North Carolina), 1944; m. Emma Geraldine Wililiams, Oct. 10, 1895; children—Harrison Williams, Charles Fairchild, Everett, Geraldine (dec.), Mary Elizabeth. Ordained ministry Southern Bapt. Church, 1891; pastor Fifth Street Ch., Hannibal, Mo., 1896-1903, East Ch., Louisville, 1903-05; supt. North Italian Mission, Rome, Italy, 1905-19; pastor Westport Ch., Kansas City, Mo., 1919-21; European rep. Foreign Mission Bd., Southern Bapt. Conv., 1921-39, retired; engaged in literary work and lecturing. Member staff American Relief Administration in Russia, and among the first to provide for distribution of food and clothing during the great famine, 1921-22. Capt Am. Red Cross, Italian front, 1918. Decorated Royal Italian Medal for relief work among survivors of earthquake, 1915, and Service medal (Italian), World War. Mem. bd. dirs. Bapt. theol. sems., Budapest (Hungary) and Bucharest (Rumania). Mem. S.R., Vets. Foreign Wars, Phi Gamma Delta. Mason (K.T.). Clubs: Knife and Fork (Kansas City); Anaconda (Danville, Ky.). Author: The School of the Church (in Italian); New Testament Churches; Europe and the Gospel; Bible Doctrines; Bible Geography; Europe: Christ or Chaos; A. T. Robertson—A Biography. Home: Wake Forest, N.C. Died Feb. 5, 1958; buried Hollywood Cemetery, Richmond, Va.

GILL, Richard C(ochran), research-explorer, author; b. Washington, Nov. 22, 1901; s. Dr. William Tignor Gill and Flora May (Allen) G.; B.A., Cornell U., 1924; grad. student Columbia, N.Y.U., 1926-27; m. Ruth Lenfest, Apr. 19, 1926. Instr. English, Lafayette Coll., Easton, Pa., 1925-28; field mgr. in Ecuador, Peru, Bolivia, S.A., B. F. Goodrich Rubber Corp., 1928-30; pres. Gill, Miller Co., ranching, Ecuador, 1930—; pres. Gill, Dundas and Co., Palo Alto, Cal., leader Gill-Merrill expdn., other S.A. (upper-Amazonian) expdns. in ethno-botany, tropical Am. pharmacognosy, etc.; ethnographic exploring chiefly in ethnobotany of drug curare, and clin. application to spastic paralysis, and its accepted clin. application in shock-therapy method of treating mental diseases, more recently its use as an adjuvant in anesthesia and an anti-convulsant in other fields; pvt. research in evolution and clin. application of new therapeutic curare variant of higher alkaloidal potency; evolution of economical prodn. technique for chem. pure d-tubocurarine, its clin. uses in acute anterior poliomyelitis, obstet. anaesthesia, allied gynecologic employments, recent easier co-adminstrn. with intravenous anaesthetics; writer, lectr., 1930—; acting adviser on tropical Am. def. commodities and drugs, def. facilities and terrain; pres. Gill-Merrill Participants; bot. collections N.Y. Bot. Garden, Arnold Arboretum (Harvard), Kew Gardens (London), referable elsewhere; pres., founder S.A. mfg. base, Transandino Co., curare and other tropical drugs; founded tech. library, over 5000 items on history, botany, pharmacognosy, pharmacology and clin. reprints and curare, curare synthetics, anti-curare agts. Recipient 2 citations from Republic of Ecuador. Fellow Am. Geog. Soc., Am. Polar Soc.; mem. Hakluyt Soc. (Great Britain), Explorers Club, A.A.A.S., Am. Acad. Polit. and Social Sci.; Cal. Acad. Scis., Am. Pharm. Assn., Torrey Bot. Club, Sigma Phi Sigma. Baptist. Author: Manga, 1937; Volcano of Gold, 1938; Kalu, 1939; White Water and Black Magic (a history of curare), 1940; Paco Goes to the Fair (a Jr. Lit. Guild book), 1940; The Other America, 1941; The Flying Death (Curare): A Manga Book, 1942; Francisco de Oreliana, a Biography (in prep.); Scientific Bibliography of Curare (1595-1945) (in prep.); Clinical Employments and History of Modern Curarization (in prep.); Physico-Chemical Determination of d-Tubocurarine in Therapeutic Formulations in prep.); South American juvenile books, Contbr. articles to Ency. Britannica; Saturday Evening Post, Yale Rev., Nat. Geographic, Technology Rev., Natural History sci., med. publs. Home: Presque Isle, Me.; also P.O. Box 281, Palo Alto, Cal. Died July 7, 1958; buried Rock Creek Cemetery, Washington.

GILLEAUDEAU, Raymond, publisher; b. N.Y.C., Feb. 8, 1887; s. Joseph R. and Emma (Kane) G.; m. Aimee Larkin, 1921. Lawyer, 1912-17, 1919-20; printer and pub. This Week Mag., 1920-42; now pub.; became pres. United Newspaper Mag. Corp., 1934;

now ret. Served in U.S. Army, 1917-18. Roman Catholic. Home: 55 Park Av. Office: 420 Lexington Av., N.Y.C. Died Oct. 1958.*

GILLEN, Charles P., city official; b. Roscommon, Ireland, Aug. 6, 1876; s. Thomas and Mary A. (Conry) G.; brought to U.S. at age of 10; ed. Seton Hall Coll., South Orange, N.J.; m. Margaret Carey, Feb. 1923; children—Charles P., Colleen. Real estate business, 1894—; pres. Charles P. Gillen Co. Mem. Bd. of Works, Newark, 2 terms, 1912-18; mayor of Newark, 1917-21; became city dir., 1921-33. Mem. Am.-Irish Hist. Soc. Democrat. K.C., Elk, Eagle. Home: 113 Prospect Av., North Arlington, N.J. Died June 30, 1956.

GILLEN, Courtland C., ex-congressman; b. Roachdale, Ind., July 3, 1880; s. Columbus and Rachel E. (Edwards) G.; student De Pauw U. 4 terms; LL.B., U. Indpls., 1905; m. Nelle F. Williams, May 31, 1922; children—Wayne G., Mary Elizabeth, Rachel Mae. Began practice at Greencastle, Ind., 1905; pros. atty. 64th Jud. Circuit, Ind., 1917-18; mem. Bd. of Edn., Greencastle, 1913-17; asso. in practice with Benjamin F. Corwin, 1918-30, with Glenn H. Lyon, 1930-33; mem. 72d Congress, 5th Ind. Dist. Democrat; judge Putnam Circuit Ct., 1934-40; returned to pvt. practice. Methodist. Mason, Elk, Eagle, Rotarian. Home: Greencastle, Ind. Died Sept. 1, 1954.

GILLES, Verner Arthur (gĭl'ĕs), geologist; b. Kirwin, Kan., Jan. 3, 1886; s. Arthur William and Sarah (Weaver) G.; B.S., U. of Ore., 1911; m. Eva Kathleen Norris, Sept. 20, 1920. Began as mining engr., June 1911; const. engr. N.P. Ry. Co., 1911-16; intermittently with several mining companies, 1916-21; cons. engr. Lewisohn Bros., 1921; geologist N.P. Ry. Co., 1921-26, asst. chief geologist, 1926-40, chief geologist 1940-54. Mem. Am. Inst. Mining and Metall. Engrs., Am. Assn. Petroleum Geologists, Delta Tau Delta, Acacia. Clubs: Hilands Golf (Billings, Mont.). Mason (K.T., Shriner). Home: Western Apts., 33rd and Division Sts. Office: 201 Yale Bldg., Billings, Mont. Died Nov. 9, 1954.

GILLESPIE, Alexander Garfield (gĭl-lĕs'pē), army officer; b. Gaines, Mich., Aug. 19, 1881; s. Alexander and Sarah (Gillespie) G.; B.S., U.S. Mil. Acad., 1906; diploma Coast Arty. Sch., 1911, Command and Gen. Staff Sch., 1924, Army War Coll., 1929; m. Mildred Hathaway Green, July 23, 1908; children—Marguerite Alice (wife of Colonel William G. Bartlett), Alexander Garfield (dec.). Served with various units of the Army in U.S., Philippines and France, 1906-19; asst. mil. attaché, Tokyo, Japan, 1920-22; corps area ordnance officer, Chicago, 1924-28; prof. of ordnance and science of gunnery, U.S. Mil. Acad., 1929-33; in command of Rock Island (Ill.) Arsenal, 1934-37; in Washington, 1937-40; in command of Watervliet (N.Y.) Arsenal, 1940-45; chief of indsl. service, Ordnance Dept., Washington, D.C., 1945-46; retired since 1947. Awarded Purple Heart, Distinguished Service Medal, Legion of Merit. Member Army Ordnance Assn. Methodist. Mason. Club: Army and Navy (Washington). Address: 3415 34th Pl. N.W., Washington 16. Died Jan. 7, 1956.

GILLESPIE, George Benjamin, lawyer; b. Vienna, Ill., June 3, 1863; s. James Bryson and Mary Levice (Enloe) G.; ed. pub. schs.; LL.B., Ill. Wesleyan U., 1887; m. Mary Juette Oliver, Nov. 19, 1890; children—James Alfred (dec.), George Marion (dec.), Loui Frank. Apptd. dep. clerk Johnson County, Ill., 1883, clk., 1884; law partner Judge A. K. Vickers, 1885-86; admitted to Ill. bar, 1887, practiced in Vienna until 1906, Springfield 1906—; partner H. J. Hamlin, 1906-08, Hamlin, Gillespie & Fitzgerald, 1908-09, Gillespie & Fitzgerald, 1909-16, Gillespie & Gillespie, 1919-27, Gillespie, Burke & Gillespie, 1927—; consul for ry., insurance companies of America. Member of America, Illinois State, Sangamon, County bar assns., Phi Delta Phi. Republican. Methodist. Mason (32°, K.T., Shriner). Club: Sangamo. Contbr. to law jours., etc. Home: 1421 Lowell Av. Office: Reisch Bldg., Springfield, Ill. Died Aug. 4, 1944.

GILLESPIE, James Frank, ex-congressman; b. White Sulphur Springs, W. Va., Apr. 18, 1869; s. James and Henrietta G.; student Concord (W.Va.) Normal Sch., 2 yrs., Central Coll., Danville, Ind., 1 yr. Taught in pub. schs. of W.Va.; prin. White Sulphur Springs High Sch., 1891; admitted to W.Va. bar, 1892, Ind. bar, 1894; since in practice of law; served in Ill. Legislature, 2 yrs.; mem. 73d Congress 17th Ill. Dist. Democrat. Home: Bloomington, Ill. Died Nov. 26, 1954.

GILLESPIE, William Lane, banker; b. Albany, N.Y., 1881; s. Matthew and Margaret (Goodrich) G.; m. Florence L. Hummell, 1904. Chmn. bd. and dir. National Commercial Bank & Trust Company of Albany; trustee Home Savings Bank; director Delaware & Hudson Co., Delaware & Hudson R.R. Corp., Consol. Car Heating Co., United Traction Co., Albany, N.Y.; chmn. finance com. N.Y. State Teachers Retirement Board; ex-pres. N.Y. State Bankers Assn. Mason (Shriner). Clubs: University, Albany Country, Fort Orange (Albany, N.Y.); Bankers of America (New York). Home: 399 State St. Office: 60 State St., Albany, N.Y. Died Aug. 18, 1949.

GILLET, Joseph Eugene (jĭl-let'), educator; b. Hasselt, Belgium, Aug. 14, 1888; s. Léopold and Hélenè (Uytterschout) G.; ed. Royal Athenaeum, Hasselt; Ph.D., U. Liège, 1910; studied univs. Paris, Leyden, Munich, Berlin; m. Myrtle Margaret Mann, 1915. Came to U.S., 1913, naturalized, 1918. Asst. lectr. French, U. Edinburgh, 1910-11; instr. German, U. Wis., 1913-15; asso. in comparative lit. and Romance langs., U. Ill., 1915-18; asst. prof. Romance langs., U. Minn., 1921-24; asso. prof. Spanish, Bryn Mawr Coll., 1924-29, prof., 1929, head dept. 1924; prof. Spanish, U. Pa. 1949—; vis. prof. Spanish, U. Chgo., summers 1923, 29, Princeton, 1st semester, 1928-29, 1929-30, Univ. of Pennsylvania, 1st semester, 1940-41; U. Cal., Berkeley, spring term, 1948-49. Served in U.S. Army, 1918-19. Mem. Am. Assn. Univ. Profs., Modern Lang. Assn. Am. (monograph com., com. on research activities), Hispanic Soc. Am., Academia de Bellas Artes, Valladolid. Author: Molière en Angleterre (1660-70), Paris, 1910; Micael de Carvajal, Tragedia Josephina, Princeton and Paris, 1932; Bartolomé de Torres Naharro, Propalladia and other works, Vol. I, 1943, Vol. II, 1946, Vol. III, 1951; other edit. 16th Cent. Spanish plays. Translator; Dr. C. Snouck Hurgronje, The Holy War "Made in Germany," N.Y., London, 1915. Contbr. articles and reviews in European, Am. periodicals on Spanish and Spanish Am. lit., linguistics. Editor: The Hispanic Rev. (U. of Pa.); asso. editor Romance Philology (U. Cal.). Address: 302 Berkeley Rd., Merion Sta., Pa. Died June 4, 1958; buried West Laurel Hills Cemetery, West Philadelphia, Pa.

GILLETT, Leonard Godfrey, banker; b. Gananoque, Ont., Can., April 16, 1893; s. Richard Clay and Helen Elizabeth (Bird) G.; student Wykeham Ho. Sch., Montreal, Quebec; m. Joan Wallace Miller, Dec. 29, 1913; children—Richard Charles, Adrienne Margaret G. Goodfellow, Joan Alison (Mrs. Marshall P. Lee), Helen Frances (Mrs. J. Fred Dixon). Began with The Bank of Toronto, Montreal, Canada, 1909, Western Canada, 1912-26, chief inspecting officer, Toronto, 1928, asst. mgr., Montreal, 1929, mgr., Montreal, 1938, asst. gen. mgr., Toronto, 1943, gen. mgr., 1948, now vice president, director; also dir. Dominion of Can. Gen. Ins. Co., Can Permanent Trust Co., Casualty Co. of Can. Pres. Canadian Bankers' Assn.; mem. Toronto Bd. Trade. Anglican. Clubs: National, Granite, Toronto Golf, Toronto Skating, Toronto Hunt, St. James's, Toronto (Montreal), Montreal Badminton and Squash, York; Canadian of New York. Home: 10 Benevenuto Pl., Toronto 7. Office: 55 King St. W., Toronto 1, Ont., Can. Died Mar. 9, 1956.

GILLETTE, Albert Cooley, lawyer; b. Wiscoy, N.Y., Mar. 12, 1876; s. Frank Bangs and Evaline (Cooley) G.; student Geneseo (N.Y.) Normal Sch., 1896-98; M.A., Columbia, 1904, LL.B., 1905; m. Annie White, June 5, 1911; children—Dale (wife of Dr. Frank Tipton Rogers), Maud (Mrs. Donald C. MacDonald), Alberta (wife of Robert E. Whitcomb, USNR). Admitted to N.Y., Minn. bars, 1905; asso. lawyer Washburn, Bailey & Mitchell, Duluth, Minn., 1905-11, mem. firm, 1911-29; mem. Mitchell, Gillette & Carmichael, Duluth, 1929-37; sr. mem. Gillette, Nye, Harries & Montague, Duluth, 1937—; pres., dir. Minn. & Manitoba R.R. Co., Can. & Atlantic Transit Co., Duluth & Va. Realty Co.; chief counsel Minn. Power & Light Co.; dir., mem. exec. com. No. Nat. Bank of Duluth; dir. several other corps. Trustee Forest Hill Cemetery Assn. Mem. Am., Minn., 11th Judicial Dist. bar assns. Republican. Presbyn. Clubs: Kitchi Gammi, Northland Country (Duluth); Bath, Indian Creek Golf (Miami Beach, Fla.). Home: 711 Irving Pl. Office: Alworth Bldg., Duluth, Minn. Died Feb. 7, 1950.

GILLETTE, Halbert Powers, editor, engr.; b. Waverly, Ia., Aug. 5, 1869; s. Theodore Weld and Laetitia S. (Powers) G.; grad. Hammond Hall Acad., Salt Lake City, 1886; E.M., Sch. of Mines, Columbia Univ., 1892. Asst. N.Y. state engr., 1896-98; contractor, 1898-1902; asso. editor, 1903-05, Engineering News; president Gillette Pub. Co. Chief engineer of Washington R.R. Commn., 1906-07. Member American Society C.E. Author: Economics of Road Construction, 1901; Earthwork and Its Cost, 1903; Rock Excavation—Methods and Cost, 1904; Handbook of Cost Data, 1905; Concrete Construction—Methods and Cost (with Charles S. Hill), 1908; Cost Keeping and Management Engineering (with Richard T. Dana), 1909; Clearing and Grubbing, 1917; Handbook of Electrical and Mechanical Cost Data (with Richard T. Dana), 1918; Handbook of Construction Cost, 1922; Road and Street Construction (with J. C. Black), 1940; also many articles on weather, climatic and geol. cycles, 1928-48. Editor Roads and Streets. Home: 1125 Oak Grove Av., San Marino 9, Cal. Office: 22 W. Maple St., Chgo. 10. Died June 18, 1958.

GILLETTE, John Morris, sociologist; b. nr. Maryville, Mo., Aug. 9, 1866; s. William W. and Jane (Radford) G.; A.B., Park Coll., Parkville, Mo., 1892, LL.D., 1928; grad. Princeton Theol. Sem., 1895; A.M., Princeton U., 1895; Ph.D., Chicago Theol. Sem., 1898; Ph.D., U. of Chicago, 1901; m. Margaret Carolyn Morgan, Sept. 4, 1901. Ordained Presbyterian ministry, 1895; pastor, Dodge City, Kan., 1895-96; lecturer and librarian Bible Normal Coll., Springfield, Mass., 1898-99; prin. Chadron (Neb.) Acad., 1899-1900; pres. Acad. for Young Women, Jacksonville, Ill., 1901-03; prof. history and sociology, State Normal Sch., Valley City, N.D., 1903-07; prof. and head of dept. sociology, U. of N.D., since Sept., 1907; chmn. N.D. State Child Labor Co., 1913-20; state supervisor rural research, Federal Emergency Relief Adminstrn. Chmn. advisory com. on personnel, N.D. Workmen's Compensation and Unemployment Ins. Div., 1937-40. Member advisory board Nat. Child Labor Com., 1918-22; dir. N.D. State Hist. Society; mem. Am. Sociol. Soc. (1st v.p. 1926, pres. 1928), Nat. Conf. Social Work, American Assn. for Labor Legislation, American Country Life Association, State Educational Assn. of N.D., etc.; asso. mem. Internat. Inst. of Sociology; advisory mem. Nat. Acad. Agriculture of Czechoslovakia. Mem. Phi Beta Kappa. Clubs: Grand Forks, Fortnightly, Franklin. Author: Culture Agencies of a Typical Manufacturing Group—South Chicago, 1901; Vocational Education, 1910; Constructive Rural Sociology, 1913; The Family, 1913; Rural Communities, 1915; Sociology, 1916; Rural Sociology, 1922, revised, 1936; (with J. M. Reinhardt) Current Social Problems, 1933, revised 1937; Problems of a Changing Social Order (with J. M. Reinhardt), 1942; Social-Economics of North Dakota, 1942; Mounds and Mound Builders of the U.S., 1944; North Dakota Weather and Rural Economy, 1945. Home: Grand Forks, N.D. Died Sept. 24, 1949.

GILLETTE, Wilson D. (jĭl-lĕt'), congressman; b. Sheshequin, Bradford County, Pa.; ed. Ulster High Sch., Susquehanna Collegiate Inst.; married. Began as clerk in gen. store; dealer of automobiles since 1913. Mem. Pa. House of Reps., 1930-40; elected to 77th Congress, Nov. 1941, to fill unexpired term of Albert G. Rutherford; mem. 78th to 82nd Congresses (1943-53), 14th Pa. Dist. Republican. Methodist. Mason. Rotarian. Home: 102 York Av., Towanda, Pa. Office: House Office Bldg., Washington 25. Died Aug. 7, 1951; buried Oak Hill Cemetery, Towanda, Pa.

GILLICK, James T. (gĭl'lĭk), ret. ry. ofcl.; b. Glencoe, Minn., June 1, 1870; student pub. schs. Entered services of C.,M.&St.P. Ry. (now C.,M., St. P.&P. Ry.) 1886; continued successively as telegraph operator, train dispatcher and chief dispatcher, 1890-1903, trainmaster, 1903-07, supt. div., 1907-13, asst. gen. mgr., 1913-17, gen. mgr., 1917-25, became chief operating officer, 1925, v.p. in charge of operation, 1945, cons. v.p., 1945-48, also officer in various subsidiaries; retired June 1, 1948, dir. Mercantile Nat. Bank of Chgo. Home: 3500 N. Lake Shore Drive. Office: Union Station, Chgo. Died Dec. 1956.

GILLIES, Donald B., steel corp. exec.; b. Bruce Mines, Ont., Can., Nov. 4, 1872; Mining Engr., Mich. Coll. Mining and Tech., 1893, D.Eng., 1931; LL.D., Mont. Sch. Mines, 1939; m. Mary Lou Yancey; 3 children. Joined Mont. Ore Purchasing Co. as slag pot pusher, 1893, later in drafting room and smelter field; was asst. assayer Parrott Silver & Copper Co., then mining engr. for W. A. Clark properties in Butte, later chief engr., gen. supt., finally mgr. all Clark properties; with Corrigan, McKinney & Co. of Cleve., 1910-35, mgr. Mexican properties, 1910-18, v.p. charge mining operations in U.S. and Mexico, 1918-32, pres., 1932-35, co. merged with Republic Steel Corp., of which was v.p., 1935-47, mining cons., 1947—. Active Cleve. Community Fund, 1932—, bd. trustees; treas. local chpt. A.R.C., 1952, 53. Mem. C. of C. (chmn. river and harbor com.), Am. Inst. Mining Metall. and Petroleum Engrs. (pres. 1939), Mining and Metall. Soc. Am., Mont. Soc. Engrs., Cleve. Engring. Soc. (trustee), Lake Superior Iron Ore Assn. (pres. 1947-51, chmn. bd. dir., 1951-56). Clubs: Union, Kirtland, Chagrin Valley Hunt, Pepper Pike, Mid-Day Tavern (Cleve.); Miscowaubik (Calumet, Mich.). Home: 2460 Edgehill Rd., Cleveland Heights, O. Died Sept. 29, 1956; buried Myrtle Hill Cemetery, Rome, Ga.

GILLILAN, Strickland (gĭl'ĭ-ăn), journalist; b. Jackson, O.; s. Lewis and Mary Alice (Clare) G.; attended Ohio U. to junior yr.; m. Alice Hendricks, Mar. 27, 1894 (died 1901); 1 dau., Marjorie Hendricks Ellensen; m. 2d, Harriet Nettleton, June 9, 1903; children—Harriet Nettleton Buchheister, Burdette Strickland. Began newspaper work on Jackson Herald, 1887; on Athens (O.) Herald, 1888-92; city editor Daily Telegram, Richmond, Ind., 1892-95; city editor Richmond Daily Palladium, 1895-1901; reporter and editor Marion (Ind.) Daily Tribune, 1901; on staff of Los Angeles Herald, 1901-02, Baltimore American, 1902-05; free-lance writer, 1906—, also lyceum lecturer and after dinner speaker, 1899—; broadcaster. Well known writer of humorous stories and verse. Past pres. Am. Press Humorists. Author: Including Finnigin, 1910 (including the popular line, "Off agin on agin, gone agin, Finnigin"); Including You and Me, 1917; Sunshine and Awkwardness, 1918; A Sample Case of Humor, 1919; Laugh It Off, 1924; Danny and Fanny, 1928; Gillilan, Finnigin & Co., 1940. Address: care B. S. Gillilan, Arlington, Va. Died Apr. 25, 1954.

GILLILAND, John W., oil producer; b. Tioga, Tex., May 6, 1881; s. Mathias Wesley and Mattie (Masters) G.; student pub. schs. Nashville; married; children—Chapman (dec.), Ruth (Mrs. W. L. Histler, Jr.). In real estate business, Artesia, N.M., 1901-03; mgr. Tioga (Tex.) Milling Co., 1903-04; asst. cashier First Nat. Bank, Tioga, 1904-05; clk. Exchange Nat. Bank, Dallas, Tex., 1905-06; real estate business, Holdenville, Okla., 1906-09; v.p. Okla. State Bank, Holdenville, 1909-12; organized, 1912, and since pres. Southwestern Oil Co.; moved office to Tulsa, 1916; pres. Gilliland Oil Co., First Nat. Bank (Holdenville, Okla.); v.p. Guaranty State Bank (Muskogee); dir. First Nat. Bank (Tulsa), State Nat. Bank (Oklahoma City), Drumright (Okla.) State Bank. Republican. Methodist. Mem. YMCA. Mason (32°, Shriner), Elk. Clubs: Country (Tulsa); Kansas City (Kansas City); Toledo (Toledo, O.). Home: 1616 S. Denver St. Office: First Nat. Bank Bldg., Tulsa. Died Mar. 29, 1957.

GILLIN, John Lewis (gĭl'ĭn), educator; b. Hudson, Ia., Oct. 12, 1871; s. Samuel Brallier and Anna Louisa (Straley) G.; B.Litt., Upper Ia. U., 1894; A.B., Ia. (now Grinnell) Coll., 1895, LL.D., 1930; A.M., Columbia, 1903, Ph.D., 1906; B.D., Union Theol. Sem., 1904; m. Etta Shaffner, May 18, 1897 (died Nov. 1944); 1 son, John Philip; m. 2d, Mary W. McCutcheon, Jan. 3, 1946. Prof. social sci. Ashland (O.) Coll., 1905-06, pres., 1906-07; asst. prof. polit. economy and sociology State U. Ia., 1907-11, prof., 1911-12; asso. prof. sociology U. Wis., 1912-15, prof., 1915-42, prof. emeritus, 1942, chmn. dept. sociology and anthropology, 1937-41. Sec. dept. gen. information and welfare of extension div., U. of Wis., 1912-18. Pub. mem. Nat. War Labor Bd., 6th region, 1943. Recipient Alumni award of Grinnell Coll., 1950. Ex-pres. Wis. State Conf. Charities and Correction; dir. dept. of civilian relief, Central Div. A.R.C., 1917-19; nat. dir. ednl. service, A.R.C., 1921-22. Democrat. Ex-pres. Am. Sociol. Soc.; mem. Nat. Conf. Social Work. Mem. P.B.K., Alpha Kappa Delta, Alpha Kappa Lambda. Author: A History of Legislation for the Relief of the Poor in Iowa, 1914; (with F. W. Blackmar), Outlines of Sociology, 1915, 30; Wholesale Citizens and Spare Time, 1918; Poverty and Dependency, 1920-26, 32; Criminology and Penology, 1925, 35, 56; (with others) Social Problems, 1928, 32, 43; Taming the Criminal, 1931; Social Pathology, 1933, 39, 46; (with others) The Madison Community, 1934; Introduction to Sociology (with John P. Gillin), 1942; The Wisconsin Prisoner, 1946; Cultural Sociology (with John P. Gillin), 1948; Predicting Criminal Behavior, 1952. Life mem. Social Sci. Research Council. Home: 2211 Chamberlain Av., Madison 5, Wis. Died Dec. 8, 1958; buried Madison.

GILLIS, James Martin (gĭl'ĭs), clergyman, editor; b. Boston, Mass., Nov. 12, 1876; s. James and Catharine (Roche) G.; grad. Boston Latin Sch., 1895; A.B., St. Charles Coll., 1896; grad. St. Paul's Coll., Washington, D.C., 1900; S.T.L., Cath. U. of America, 1903; hon. Litt.D., Coll. of Mount St. Vincent, 1934, Fordham U., 1935, St. Francis Coll., 1935; St. Benedict's Coll., Atchison, Kan., 1940, Boston Coll., 1941; LL.D., U. of Detroit, 1940; S.T.D., College Angelicum, 1951. Joined Paulist Fathers, 1900; ordained priest R.C. Ch., 1901; mem. bd. editors Cath. Book Club, 1928-48. Mem. Cath. Press Assn., Cath. Interracial Council; academy mem. Gallery of Living Catholic Authors. Speaker on Catholic Hour, National Broadcasting Co., 1930-41. Author: False Prophets, 1925; The Catholic Church and the Home, 1928; (syndicated article) Sursum Corda: What's Right with the World, 1928—; The Ten Commandments, 1931; Christianity and Civilization, 1932; The Paulists, 1932; This Our Day, 1933, vol. II, 1949; So Near is God, 1953; On Almost Everything, 1955; This Mysterious Human Nature, 1956; My Last Book, 1957. Editor Catholic World, 1922-48; contbg. editor since 1948. Lecturer. Home: 415 W. 59th St. Office: 411 W. 59th St., N.Y.C. Died Mar. 14, 1957; buried Crypt Church of St. Paul the Apostle, N.Y.C.

GILLMOR, Reginald E., corp. exec.; b. Menomonie, Wisconsin, July 13, 1887; s. Daniel Webster and Jane (Shipman) G.; graduate U.S. Naval Academy, 1907; children—William Sims, David Spear. With Sperry Gyroscope Co., Brooklyn, 1912-13; Sperry Gyroscope Co., Ltd., London, 1913-17; Sperry Gyroscope Co., Brooklyn, 1918-19 and 1924-45, pres., 1932-45; v.p. Sperry Corp. 1945—; loaned to State Dept. as industry dir., Am. Mission to Greece, Aug. 1947-June 1948, vice chmn. Nat. Security Resources Bd., Sept. 1948-Feb. 1949. Served with U.S. Navy, 1907-12, 1917-18. Trustee Barnard Coll., Hampton Inst., Webb Inst. Naval Architecture. Mem. Army Ordnance Assn. (dir.), Sci. Apparatus Makers of Am. Home: 2801 Quebec St. N.W., Washington. Office: 30 Rockefeller Plaza, N.Y. City. Died Feb. 7, 1960.

GILLMORE, Quincy Adams, army officer; b. West Point, N.Y., Jan. 12, 1881; s. Quincy O'Mahr and Margaret (Van Kleeck) G.; pre. edn., Mohegan Lake (N.Y.) Sch. and Preston Sch., Washington, D.C.; student Colo. Sch. Mines, 1898-1900; grad. U.S. Mil. Acad., 1904; m. Frances West Hemsley, Nov. 16, 1904; children—Quincy A., Frances West, Frederick Hemsley. Commd. 2d lt., Arty., U.S. Army, 1904, resigned, 1907; col., F.A., N.J. Nat. Guard, 1917, brig. gen., 1922, maj. gen., 1924; comdg. gen., N.J. Nat. Guard, and 44th Div. (N.Y. and N.J. troops), 1924-32, resigned. Comd. 112th F.A., A.E.F., 1917-19. Mem. Huguenot Soc., Soc. Colonial Wars, Loyal Legion. Awarded Distinguished Service Medal, State of N.J. Republican. Episcopalian. Clubs: Rittenhouse, Racquet (Philadelphia, Pa.); Union, Racquet and Tennis, Turf and Field. Home: 840 Park Av., N.Y.C. 21. Died Jan. 5, 1956; buried West Point Cemetery, West Point, N.Y.

GILMAN, Albert Franklin, chemist; b. Hallowell, Me., Sept. 9, 1871; s. William Franklin and Julia Ann (Gordon) G.; grad. Kent's Hill (Me.) Acad., 1892; student, Wesleyan U., Conn., 1893-94; S.B., Amherst Coll., 1897, A.M., 1901; postgrad. U. Tenn., 1902, Harvard 1903, U. Chgo., 1905, 1906; Ph.D., U. Denver, 1913; m. Agnes Geneva McGlynn, Sept. 28, 1899 (dec.); children—Albert Franklin, Gertrude Marcelle. Tchr. sci., Farmington, Me., 1897-98; prof. science Dow Acad. Franconia, N.H., 1898-99; prof. chemistry and physics Maryville (Tenn) Coll., 1900-06; prof. chemistry Ripon (Wis.) Coll., 1906-17, Huron (S.D.) Coll., 1917-18, Ill. Wesleyan U., 1918-20, Carroll (Wis.) Coll., 1920-21, Central YMCA Coll. of Arts and Scis., Chgo., 1921-42. Toured Europe during 1910 to study methods used in chemical labs. Fellow A.A.A.S., Royal Soc. Arts, Am. Inst. Chemists, Inst. Am. Genealogy; mem. Am. Chem. Soc., Wis., S.D., Ill. acads. sci., Delta Tau Delta, Phi Lambda Upsilon. Republican, Mason. Author: A Laboratory Outline Quantitative Analysis, 1908; Laboratory Outline Qualitative Analysis, 1908; (brochure), Origin of the Republican Party, 1915; Organic Reactions (with son), 1931. Collector of statistics and sociol. data for Dietary Studies in Rural Regions of Eastern Tenn., U.S. Bull. No. 221. Writer various chem. papers. Home: 948 Chicago Av., Oak Park, Ill. Died May 18, 1951; buried Forest Home Cemetery, Forest Park, Ill.

GILMAN, John R., bus. cons.; b. Everett, Mass., Apr. 19, 1895; s. Dennis J. and Martha L. (Riley) G.; A.B., Harvard, 1917; m. Philomene F. Gradie, June 5, 1923; children—John R., Jr., Barbara A., Philomeme F., Martha Ann. With Lever Bros. Co., Boston, 1917-48, v.p. and dir., 1945-48; v.p., Colgate, Palmolive Peet Co., Jersey City, 1949-52; v.p. Roy S. Durstine, Inc., N.Y.C., 1952-54; bus. cons. 1954, ret. Trustee Newton Coll. Club: Harvard. Contbr. articles on advt. Home: Punkateest Neck Rd., Tiverton, R.I. Died Apr. 30, 1958; buried St. Joseph's Cemetery, West Roxbury, Mass.

GILMAN, Margaret, coll. prof.; b. Meadville, Pa., Aug. 14, 1896; d. Nicholas P. and Mary S. (Stubbs) Gilman; A.B., Bryn Mawr Coll., 1919, A.M., 1920, Ph.D., 1924. Instr French Bryn Mawr (Pa.) Coll., 1923-26, asso., 1926-30, asso. prof., 1930-47, prof. since 1947, chmn. dept. French since 1948; vis. prof. French Columbia, 1946-47; vis. lectr. French lit. Harvard, 1950-51. Fellow Guggenheim Foundation, 1954-55. Member Modern Language Association (executive council, 1955-58), Internat. Federation Modern Languages and Literature (v.p., 1954-57), Am. Assn. Teachers of French, American Society for Aesthetics, American Association University Profs., Assn. Internat. des Etudes Francaises, Phi Beta Kappa. Author: Othello in French, 1925; Baudelaire the Critic, 1943; The Idea of Poetry in France, 1958. Contbr. lit. and lang. jours. Office: Bryn Mawr Coll., Bryn Mawr, Pa. Died May 27, 1958.

GILMER, Albert Hatton, prof. speech and drama; b. Loraine, Ill., Dec. 31, 1878; s. Park Hatton and Elizabeth (Riggs) G.; B.S., Knox Coll., 1900, A.M., 1911; studied U. Chicago, summer 1905; grad. student, U. Munich, Germany, 1908-09, Harvard, 1912-14, Oxford, Eng., summer 1925, U. London, 1934; (hon.) Litt.D., Knox Coll., 1936; m. Mabel Bishop, June 25, 1910. Teacher pub. schs., Kewanee, Ill., and Detroit U. Sch., 1900-08; instr. English, Bates Coll., Lewiston, Me., 1909-10; instr. then prof. English and later of dramatic literature, Tufts Coll., Medford, Mass., 1910-28; prof. speech and dramatic art, Lafayette Coll., Easton, Pa., 1928-47, prof. emeritus since 1947. Mem. Am. Assn. Univ. Profs., Nat. Assn. Teachers of Speech, Phi Beta Kappa, Beta Theta Pi. Hon. Officer French Acad. of Edn.; awarded "Plams" as speaker rep. of Lafayette Coll. and Am. Friends of Lafayette at 100th anniversary memorial celebration of death Gen. Lafayette in Paris, 1934. Republican. Author: (plays) The Edge of the World, 1912; Old John Brown, 1913; A Wake or a Wedding, 1936; (play) A Voice for Freedom (prod. by Phoenix Little Theatre), 1950. Writer and dir. of pageants Lafayette Centennial, 1932; City of Easton Golden Jubilee Celebration, 1937; Washington Meets Lafayette, World's Fair, 1939. Home: 4733 N. 14 St., Phoenix, Ariz.; (summer) Isle of Birches, Lovell, Me. Died June 5, 1950; buried Woodmere Cemetery, Detroit.

GILMER, Elizabeth Meriwether ("Dorothy Dix"), journalist; b. Montgomery County, Tenn., Nov. 18, 1861; m. George O. Gilmer, Nov. 21, 1884. Editor woman's dept. New Orleans Picayune, 1896-1901; contributed to that paper series of papers called Dorothy Dix Talks; joined New York Journal staff as writer on spl. topics, April 8, 1901; joined Wheeler Syndicate staff, Jan. 1917; joined staff of Ledger Syndicate, Jan. 15, 1923; joined Bell Syndicate staff, Jan. 1933. Author: Mirandy; Mirandy Exhorts; Fables in Slang; Hearts a la Mode; A Joy Ride Around the World; Dorothy Dix, Her Book; How to Win and Hold a Husband. Home: 6334 Prytania St., New Orleans. Died Dec. 16, 1951; buried Metairie Cemetery, New Orleans.

GILMORE, Eugene Allen, educator; b. at Brownville, Nebraska, July 4, 1871; s. Andrew Hall and Sarah Jane (Allen) G.; A.B., De Pauw, 1893, LL.D., 1922; LL.B., Harvard, 1899; LL.D., University of Iowa, 1941; D.C.L., University of Pittsburgh, 1942; m. Blanche Basye, Dec. 27, 1899; children—Eugene Allen, Elizabeth Basye, John Andrew. Mem. of bar in Mass., Wis., Iowa and Indiana. Practiced Boston, 1899-1902; asst. prof., 1902-03, prof. law, 1903-22, acting dean, 1912-13, U. of Wis. Law Sch.; vice-gov. and sec. pub. instrn., Philippine Islands, 1922-30; acting gov. gen. Philippine Islands, 1927-29; dean State U. of Ia. Coll. of Law, 1930-34, pres. State Univ. of Iowa, 1934-40; dean Univ. of Pittsburgh Law School, 1940-42; prof. law, University of Iowa, since 1942. Visiting professor law, University of Calif., U. of Chicago, Columbia U.; nonresident lecturer on law, U. of Philippines. Ex-commr. Nat. Conf. Commrs. on Uniform State Laws from Wis. and Ia. (ex.-sec.). Fellow Am. Inst. of Criminal Law and Criminology (ex-sec.); ex-pres. Assn. Am. Law Schs., 1919-20; chmn. Com. on Indonesian Customary Law of Am. Council Learned Socs. since 1934; mem. Advisory Council of Philippine Research Bur. since 1935; mem. bd. trustees Carnegie Foundation for the Advancement of Teaching since 1938. Conglist. Mem. Am. Law Inst., Am. Bar Assn., Ia. State Bar Assn., Phi Beta Kappa, Delta Kappa Epsilon, Phi Alpha Delta. Clubs: Triangle, Univ. of Iowa. Author treatise on Partnership; also monographs on franchises, interstate commerce, assignments, reparian rights, legal education, etc. Editor: Cases on Partnership; Modern American Law, 15 vols. Joint Editor: Documentary History of American Industrial Society. Home: 109 E. Market St. Office: Law School, University of Iowa, Iowa City, Ia. Died Nov. 4, 1953.

GILMORE, Maurice E. (gĭl'mōr), ex-commr. Public Works Adminstrn.; b. Somerset, Ky., Sept. 14, 1878; s. Cyrus Beattie and Elizabeth (MacQuarrie) G.; student Haskell Inst., 1892-94; B.S., Henry Kendall Coll. (Tulsa Univ), 1899, Mo. Univ., 1898; grad. Army War Coll., 1918; m. Mary Wells Barnes, Feb. 3, 1937; children—Maurice Eugene, George Barnes, Mary Elizabeth. Engring. asst., 1899; engr. on allotment of Indian Reservations in Okla., Interior Dept., Indian Affairs, 1899-1906; constrn. engr. Panama Canal and Panama R.R. (levelman to supt. public works), 1906-13; constrn. and operation of Elec. Power Plant and St. R.R. and Municipal Development in Panama, 1913-15; with Elec. Bond & Share Co., 1915-17; R. W. Hebard & Co., Inc., in South and Central America, 1919-33; state engr. insp. N. Y., Public Works Adminstrn., 1933-37, regional director, region No. 1, 1937-40, commissioner 1940-44; director Department of Transportation and Economic Development; coordinator of Inter-American Affairs, 1944-47. Retired February 1947. Served in Spanish American War with Rough Riders, 1898; Mexican Campaign, 1914; commissioned capt. and advanced through grades to colonel, World War I, 1917-19. Democrat. Roman Catholic. Mem. Am. Soc. C.E., Soc. Am. Military Engrs., Am. Soc. for Testing Materials, Am. Geog. Soc. Clubs: Army-Navy (Washington, D.C.); Club Union, Country (Panama); Club International, Club Union, Country (San Salvador). Home: 5111 Moorland Lane, Bethesda, Md. Died Nov. 19, 1957; buried Arlington Nat. Cemetery.

GILMORE, Thomas Francis, pub.; b. Chgo., Aug. 15, 1904; s. Alson B. and Anna (Moster) G.; student Campion Coll., 1922-24, Cath. U., 1924-25; LL.B., U. Ill., 1927; m. Alice Horan, July 27, 1933; 1 son, Thomas F. Admitted to Ill. bar, 1927, practiced in Chgo., 1927-37; with Commerce Clearing House, Inc., 1937—, successively asso., editorial mgr. fed. tax publs., v.p., West Coast mgr., gen. sales mgr., exec. v.p., 1937-56, dir., 1955—, pres., 1956—; pres., dir. Commerce Clearing House Products Co., 1956—; v.p. Commerce Clearing House Canadian, Ltd. Mem. Am. Bar Assn., Ill. C. of C. Chgo. Assn. Commerce and Industry, Kappa Sigma. Club: North Shore Country. Home: 1006 Seneca Rd., Wilmette, Ill. Office: 4025 W. Peterson Av., Chgo. 30. Died May 1959.

GILMOUR, Abram David Pollock (gĭl-mour'), clergyman; b. Helensborough, Scotland, Oct. 5, 1876; s. Matthew and Susan Roberta (Pollock) G.; brought to U.S. in infancy; A.B., Hampden-Sydney (Va.) Coll., 1896, A.M., 1897; studied Princeton and Princeton Theol. Sem.; D.D., Washington and Lee U., 1909; m. Elizabeth Monroe Taylor, June 4, 1907 (died 1932); children—Monroe Taylor, Matthew Pollock, Elizabeth Roberta; m. 2d, Nancy Lee Janney, Jan. 22, 1935. Ordained to Presbyn. ministry, 1901; pastor Windsor Av. Ch., Bristol, Tenn., 1901-05; financial agent, asst. prof. Hebrew Union Sem., Richmond, Va., 1905-08, asso. prof., 1908-11; pastor Purity Ch., Chester, later First Ch., Spartanburg, S.C., until 1922, First Ch., Wilmington, N.C., 1922-41, ret. 1941. Chmn. War Camp Community Service for Camp Wadsworth, S.C., World War. Moderator Synod of N.C., 1931, chmn. work com., 1928—; chmn. ad interim com. on revision of Directory of Worship and Optional Forms, Gen. Assembly; chmn. Gen. Assembly Stewardship Com; trustee Presbyn. Coll. of S.C., Flora McDonald Coll. (N.C.), Peace Inst. (N.C.). Mem. Soc. of Lees of Va., Beta Theta Pi, Friars (Princeton). Author: The Denominational College, a Denominational Necessity, 1909. Home: Leeton House, Leesburg, Va. Died May 14, 1948; buried Hollywood Cemetery, Richmond, Va.

GILPATRIC, Guy, author; b. N.Y.C., Jan. 21, 1896; s. John Guy and May (Smith) G.; student Columbia Grammar Sch., N.Y.C.; m. Louise Lesser, Mar. 27, 1920. Began as aviator, 1912; instr., exhibition and test pilot for various firms in U.S. and Can., 1912-17; established altitude record for U.S. (one passenger) at Dominguez, Cal. (4665 ft.), 1912; advt. and story writing, 1918-30, writing books, 1930—. Served from 1st lt. to capt. U.S. Air Service, AEF, 1917-18. Author: Scotch and Water, 1931; Half Seas Over, 1932; French Summer, 1933; Brownstone Front, 1934; Mr. Glecannon, 1935; Three Sheets in the Wind, 1936; The Glencannon Omnibus, 1937; The Gentleman with the Walrus Mustache, 1938; The Compleat Goggler, 1939; Glencannon Afloat, 1941; Second Glencannon Omnibus, 1942; Action in the North Atlantic, 1943; Mr. Glencannon Ignores the War, 1944; Guy Gilpatric's Flying Stories, 1945; The Canny Mr. Glencannon, 1947. Contbr. fiction to mags. Home: 1806 El Encanto Rd., Santa Barbara, Cal. Died July 6, 1950; buried Evergreen Cemetery, Elizabeth, N.J.

GILRUTH, Irwin Thoburn, lawyer; b. Argmere, India, May 14, 1889 (parents U.S. citizens); s. Archibald and Agnes Jane (Mulligan) G.; A.B., Ohio Wesleyan U., 1910, LL.D., 1947; J.D., U. Chgo., 1917; m. Anna May Hardman, Nov. 30, 1917; children—Jane Gilruth McCarthy, Roger Oldham. Admitted to Ill. bar, 1917, since practiced in Chgo.; mem. firm Gregory, Gilruth & Hunter, 1944—. Mem. Am., Ill., Chgo. bar Assns., Art Inst. (life), Phi Delta Theta. Republican. Methodist. Clubs: Law, University, Cliff Dwellers, Chicago Literary (Chgo.). Home: 7206 Euclid Av., Chgo. 49. Office: 105 La-Salle St., Chgo. 3. Died Aug. 11, 1957.

GILTNER, Leigh Gordon, author; b. Eminence, Ky.; d. William Spencer and Sara Elizabeth (Raines) Giltner; ed. U. Chgo.; A.M., Eminence (Ky.) Coll.; ed. in music Chgo. Mus. Coll. and under several noted pvt. tchrs.; in expression, Morgan Sch., Chgo., Hart Conway, Chgo. Clubs: Filson (Louisville), Woman's of Central Ky. Author: (poems) The Path of Dreams; also contbr. short stories, sketches and verse to mags. Home: 171 Ashland Av., Lexington, Ky. Deceased.

GILTNER, Ward, dean of veterinary medicine; b. Ithaca, N.Y., Apr. 5, 1882; s. Richard Dana and Frances Victoria (Knickerbocker) G.; D.V.M., Cornell U., 1906; M.S., Ala. Poly. Inst., 1908, Dr. P.H., U. Mich., 1933; m. Mabel A. Decker, Dec. 20, 1902; children—Dorothy (Mrs. Charles Parrish), Alice (Mrs. Richard Teel), Elizabeth (dec.), William Ward, David. Asst. in vet. sci. Ala. Polytech. Inst., 1906-08; research asst. in bacteriology Mich. State Coll., 1908-12, prof., 1912-23, dean vet. medicine, 1923—, also dir. biol. scis.; dir. East Lansing State Bank, East Lansing Bldg. & Loan Assn. Fellow A.A.A.S., Am. Pub. Health Assn.; mem. Soc. Am. Bacteriologists, Am. Assn. Pathologists and Bacteriologists, Am. Chem. Soc., Mich. Acad. Sci., Am., Mich. vet. medicine assns., Sigma Xi, Phi Sigma, Delta Omega. Clubs: Wranglers (Lansing), Mich. State Coll. Faculty. Home: 652 Hillcrest Av., East Lansing, Mich. Died July 14, 1950; buried Evergreen Cemetery, Lansing, Mich.

GINGRICH, Curvin Henry (ging'rik), astronomer; b. York, Pa., Nov. 20, 1880; s. William Henry and Ellen (Kindig) G.; B.A., Dickinson Coll., Pa., 1903, M.A., 1905; U. of Chicago, summers, 1909-12, Ph D., 1912; Yerkes Observatory (Univ. of Chicago), 1911-12; Sc.D., from Dickinson College, 1941; m. Mary Ann Gross, Aug. 10, 1915; 1 daughter, Gertrude. Teacher of mathematics, Maryville Sem., Mo., 1903-05, Northwest Mo. Coll., Albany, 1905-07, Baker Univ., Baldwin, Kan., 1907-09; instr. mathematics, 1909-12, prof. mathematics and astronomy since 1912, acting dean, 1914-15, dean, 1915-17; asst. to the pres., and registrar, 1917-19, Carleton Coll.; at Mt. Wilson Obs., 1921-22; in charge courses in astronomy, Columbia, summers, 1929, 30; lecturer Adler Planetarium, summers, 1931, 32, 33; research asst. at McCormick Obs., summer 1935. Asso. editor Popular Astronomy, 1912-26, editor since 1926. Astron. work at Goodsell Obs., Carleton Coll., principally micrometric measures of comet positions and double stars, also celestial photography and photographic determinations of positions of asteroids; stellar photometry. Mem. Am. Astron. Soc., Math. Assn. America, Phi Beta Kappa, Sigma Xi, Kappa Sigma. Mason. Methodist. Home: Northfield, Minn. Died June 17, 1951; buried Oak Lawn Cemetery, Northfield, Minn.

GINSBURGH, A(braham) Robert, ret. A.F. officer; b. Warsaw (then Russian Poland), May 30, 1895; s. David and Anne (Ellion) G.; came to U.S., 1901, naturalized, 1901; A.B., Harvard, 1917, LL.B., 1936; A.M., U. of Louisville, 1922; A.M., U. of Mo., 1931; grad. Field Arty. Sch., 1921, Army Indsl. Coll., 1939, Army-Navy Staff Coll., 1943; m. Elsie Bullitt Pinney, Dec. 29, 1922; children—Robert Neville, Anne and Martha, twins. Commd. 2d lt., U.S. Army, 1917, and advanced to brig. gen., 1948, ret., 1953; served as capt., F.A., in Philippines, 1919-20, France, 1933; col. Gen. Staff Corps, Southwest Pacific Theater, 1943-45, Japan, 1945-46; mem. staff F.A. Sch., 1921-25; recruiting publicity bureau, 1925-28; battery comdr. and mem. Pack Arty. Bd., 1928-30; mem. staff Sec. of War Hurley, 1931-33, asst. Sec. of War Johnson, 1937-40, Asst. and Undersec. of War Patterson, and chief indsl. services div., 1940-43, Sec. of War Patterson, 1946-47, Sec. of Army Royall, 1947-48; dep. dir. public relations U.S. Air Force, 1948-49; mem. staff Sec. of Defense Johnson, 1949-50, mem. staff Secretary of Defense Marshall, 1950-51, Secretary of Defense Lovett, 1951-52, Sec. of Defense Wilson, 1952-53, ret. 1953; asso. editor U. S. News and World Report, 1953—. Reporter for the New York World, 1925-27; admitted to D. C. bar, 1937. Decorated D.S.M., Legion of Merit, Air medal, Bronze Star medal, Distinguished Service Star (Philippines). Mem. Caribou Society, Aviation Writers Association. Phi Beta Kappa. Delta Sigma Rho. Unitarian. Clubs: National Press, Army-Navy. Home: 2572 Military Rd., Arlington, Va. Office: 24th N St. N.W., Washington. Died June 27, 1958; buried Arlington Nat. Cemetery.

GINTHER, Mrs. Pemberton, artist and author; b. Phila.; d. David and Mary Esther (Shapley) Ginther; studied Sch. of Design (Phila.), Pa. Acad. Fine Arts; m. Willis A. Heyler, Sept. 25, 1915. Painter Landscapes and figures; has exhibited at Pa. Acad. Fine Arts, Art Club (Phila.), Rochester, N.Y. and Rotary Shows in N.Y., Ohio and the South. etc.; also private exhibitions of oil, water color and charcoal; designed stained glass windows: "Peter and John at the Tomb," St. John's P.E. Church, Suffolk, Virginia; "John on Patmos," Church of the Restoration, Phila., and others. Awarded gold medal, 1940, by the Plastic Club. Episcopalian. Author: Miss Pat Series (10 vols.), 1915; Beth Anne Series (4 vols.), 1915; Betsy Hale Series (4 vols.); Hilda of Grey Cot Series (4 vols.), 1922-25; The Secret Stair, 1928; The Jade Necklace, 1929; The Thirteenth Spoon, 1930; Through the Wilderness. Illustrates own books. Awarded Federation prize for verse, In Bucks County. Awarded Federation 1st prize for 1 act play, "One of Those Things;" portrait prize Miss. Art Assn. Mem. Fellowship Pa. Acad. Fine Arts. Clubs: Plastic, Odds and Ends (pres.), Colonial (pres.), Delaware Valley Music. Woodmere Gallery. Home: Street Rd., Lahaska, Pa. Died Aug. 7, 1959.

GINZBERG, Louis, college prof.; b. Kowno, Russia, Nov. 28, 1873; s. Isaac and Cecelia (Jaffe) G.; educated universities of Berlin, Strassburg and Heidelberg; D.H.L., honoris causa Jewish Institute of Religion, 1932, Dropsie College, 1941, Hebrew Union College, 1943; Ph.D., University of Heidelberg, 1898; D.D., honoris causa, Harvard University, 1936; married Adele Katzenstein, May 23, 1909; children—Eli, Sophie. Came to America, 1899; professor Talmud and Rabbinics, Jewish Theological Seminary, N.Y., since 1902. Author: Die Haggada bei den Kirchenvätern, 1899; Die Haggada bei den Kirchenvätern und in der Apokryphischen Litteratur, 1900; The Legends of the Jews, 7 vols., 1909-28; The Geonim, and their Halakic Wrightings, 1909; Genziah Studies, 1909; (brochure) Der Anteil R. Simons an der ihm zugeschriebenen Mekilta, 1911; (brochure) Studies into the Origin of the Mishnah, I, 1920; Eine unbekannte jüdische Sekte, I, 1922; (brochure) Some Observations on the Attitude of the Synagogue Towards the Apocalyptic-Eschatological Writings, 1922; (brochure) Notes on Philosophical Terms in the Moore Nebukim, 1924; Genizah Studies, Vol I, 1928, Vol II, 1929; Students, Scholars and Saints, 1928; A Commentary on the Palestinean Talmud, 3 vols., 1941; On Jewish Law and Lore, 1954; The Legends of the Bible, 1956; also many pamphlets. Editor: Yerushalmi Fragments, 1909. Home: 514 W. 114th St., New York 25. Office: 3080 Broadway, N.Y.C. 27. Died Nov. 11, 1953.

GIORDANO, Alfred S., physician; b. Avellino, Italy, Feb. 3, 1893; s. Antonio and Maria (Urciuoli) G., S.B., Syracuse (N.Y.) U., 1918, M.D., 1920; S.M., U. of Minn., Fellowship, Mayo Clinic, 1923; m. Alice Gracy, M.D., Aug. 28, 1923; children—Carol, Robert P., Nancy R., David A. Director, South Bend Med. Lab., later South Bend Med. Foundn., 1923—. Mem. A.M.A., Ind. State and St. Joseph County med. socs., Am. Soc. Clin. Pathologists (sec.-treas. 1930-48; Gold Merit medal 1950, Ward Burdick Gold medal 1952), Am. Assn. Pathologists and Bacteriologists, Coll. of Am. Pathologists, Ind. Assn. of Clin. Pathologists. Contbr. to sci. publs. Home: 1518 E. Colfax Av. Office: 531 N. Main St., South Bend, Ind. Died Feb. 15, 1958; buried South Bend.

GIPPRICH, John L., clergyman, physicist; b. Balt., Jan. 5, 1880; s. Anton and Mary (Hopf) G.; A.B., Loyola Coll., 1900; studied Johns Hopkins, 1908-09. Joined Soc. of Jesus (Jesuits), 1900; ordained priest R.C. Ch., 1913; prof. physics, Holy Cross Coll., 1903-05, Boston Coll., 1906-07; prof. mathematics, Fordham, 1907-08; prof. physics, Georgetown U., 1914-29; became regent Med. and Dental schs., same univ., 1929; prof. physics St. Joseph's Coll., Phila., 1935-36; pastor Southern Md. Chs., 1936-44; mem. faculty Georgetown U., 1944—. Mem. Washington Acad. Sci., Royal Astron. Soc., London. Author: Laboratory Manual of Mechanics, Heat and Sound, 1927. Address: Georgetown U., Washington. Died Mar. 7, 1950; buried Georgetown U.

GIST, Arthur Stanley (gĭst), coll. exec.; b. Marion, Ia., Jan. 19, 1883; s. William Wesley and Lillian (Hurlburt) G.; B.Di., Ia. State Teachers Coll., Cedar Falls, 1904; A.M., U. of Washington, 1918; m. Ruth Palmer, June 2, 1928; children—Ruth Lillian (Mrs. John C. Baldwin), Mary. Began as a rural teacher; president of the Humboldt State Coll., Arcata, Calif., 1930-50, ret.; now dir. of instruction Golden Gate Coll. Mem. Phi Delta Kappa. Conglist. Rotarian. Mason. Author: Elementary School Supervision, 1926; The Administration of an Elementary School, 1928; Clarifying the Teacher's Problems, 1932. Co-Author: The Teaching and Supervision of Reading (with W. A. King), 1927; New Stories from Eskimo Land (with A. H. Eide and R. P. Gist), 1930 Administration of Supervision, 1934. Editor of five year-books, Dept. of Elementary School Principals, N.E.A. Contbr. on ednl. topics. Home: 10 Blair Av., Piedmont, Cal. Died Oct. 25, 1952; buried Mountain View Cemetery, Oakland, Cal.

GITTINGER, Roy (gĭt'tĭng-ẽr) univ. prof.; b. Melrose, Ia., Jan. 12, 1878; s. James F. and Nancy (Applegate) G.; Simpson Coll., Indianola, Ia., 1897-98, 1899-1900; B.A., U. of Okla., 1902; A.M., U. of Chicago, 1906; Ph.D., U. of Calif., 1916; m. Frances Price, Mar. 10, 1900; children—James Price, Dorothy, John William. Mem. faculty, U. of Okla., 1902—; dean of undergraduates, 1915-22, prof. English history, 1905—, registrar, 1919-25, acting dean Graduate School, 1925-26, dean of administration, 1926-41, dean admission, 1941-46, regents' prof. history, 1946-50, professor emeritus, 1950—. Chmn. Cleveland County (Okla.) Council of Defense, 1917-19. Mem. Oklahoma Ednl. Assn. (life mem.), Phi Beta Kappa. Presbyterian. Democrat. Mason. Author: Formation of State of Oklahoma, 1917, 2d edit., 1939; The University of Oklahoma, a History of Fifty Years, 1942. Contbr. to Ency. Britannica, 12th, 13th, 14th, and later edits. Home: 225 W. Duffy, Norman, Okla. Died Oct. 13, 1957; buried I.O.O.F. Cemetery, Norman.

GITTINGS, J(ohn) Claxton, pediatrist; b. Pa., May 23, 1874; s. J. B. Howard and Katherine Scott (Claxton) G.; M.D., U. Pa., 1895; m. Katherine Colhoun, Sept. 23, 1903. Lectr. pediatrics, Johns Hopkins Sch. Medicine. Mem. Am. Pediatric Soc. (emeritus); fellow Coll. of Physicians, Phila. Episcopalian. Clubs: St. Elmo, University Barge (Phila.); South River Club (Md.). Address: Harwood, Md. Died Mar. 8, 1950.

GIVEN, John LaPorte, newspaper man; b. Bellefonte, Pa., Oct. 3, 1871; s. John LaPorte and Isabel (Macbride) G.; Litt.B., Cornell, 1896; m. Irene Heinz, Oct. 24, 1899 (dec.); children—Sarah Given Larson, John LaPorte. Reporter and city editor Altoona (Pa.) Times, 1890-92; on staff New York Evening Sun, 1896-1902; spl. writer, 1902—; dir. H. J. Heinz Co. Clubs: University, Cornell University, Garden City Golf (N.Y.C.); Ekwanok Country (Manchester, Vt.); Pinehurst (N.C.) Country; St. Bernard Fish and Game (Can.). Author: Making a Newspaper, 1907. Home: Manchester, Vt. Died May 20, 1957; buried Dellwood Cemetery, Manchester.

GIVLER, J(ohn) P(aul), educator; b. Paola. Kan., Aug. 4, 1882; s. Henry Vine and Elizabeth Ann (Good) G.; Ph.B., Hamlin U., 1906, A.M., 1912; grad. study Johns Hopkins, 1906-07, 1909-10; Columbia, 1916-17; Yale (Army course), 1918; m. Mary Charlotte Shepherd, Aug. 29, 1907; 1 dau., Genevieve Shepherd (Mrs. Jas. E. Hines). Prof. biology, Southwestern Coll., Kan., 1907-09, 1911-16; instr. Haverford Coll., 1910-11, City Coll. of N.Y., 1916-17; instr. Johns Hopkins, summers 1912, 13, 14; instr. zoology U. Tenn., 1917-18; prof., head dept. biology Woman's Coll., U. N.C., 1920-49, chmn. faculty math. and the scis., 1923-34. Served as 1st lt., Sanitary Corps, U.S. Army, 1918-20; bacteriologist in Am. hosps. Fellow A.A.A.S. Mem. Kan., N.C., N.Y. Acads. Sci. (past mem), Soc. of Sigma Xi. Presbyn. Author: A Practical Textbook in General Biology, 1933; Laboratory Directions for General Biology (with E. Inez Coldwell), 1946. N.C. sci. editor and contbr. Every Week mag., 1917-18. Contbr. to scientific pubs. chiefly on meaning of sci.

edn. in relation to life. Home: 213 Westover Terrace, Greensboro, N.C. Died June 10, 1957.

GLADDING, Ernest Knight, chemist; b. Newport, R.I., Aug. 16, 1888; s. Henry and Mary Elizabeth (Dennis) G.; B.S., Worcester Poly. Inst., 1910; m. Elizabeth Boss Congdon, Oct. 10, 1914; children—Prescilla C. (Mrs. Victor J. D. Moore), Elizabeth K. (Mrs. Weston J. Donehower), Anne (Mrs. Oscar N. Stern), Thomas C., Marcia (Mrs. John C. Guthrie). Chemist eastern lab. DuPont Powder Co., 1910, Kenvil lab., 1910, DuPont, Wash., 1910-15, E. I. du-Pont de Nemours & Co., Inc., Parlin, N.J., 1915, acid supt., later asst. plant supt., Hopewell, Va., 1915-18, plant supt., Old Hickory, Tenn., 1918-19, chem. dir. dye works, 1919-20; supt. royal plant Du-Pont Fibresilk Co., Buffalo, 1920-24, asst. prodn. mgr., 1924-25; prodn. mgr. DuPont Rayon Co., Buffalo, 1925-28, gen. mgr. tech. dept., N.Y.C., 1928-30, Buffalo, 1930-32, asst gen. mgr., 1932-36; asst. mgr. tech. div. rayon dept. E. I. duPont de Nemours & Co., Inc., Buffalo, 1936-38, mgr. nylon div. rayon dept., Wilmington, Del., 1938-44, dir. development dept., 1944-51, ret. 1951. Dir. Chem. Fund. Mem. A.A.A.S., Army Ordnance Assn., Am. Chem. Soc., Am. Geog. Soc. Home: 913 Stuart Rd., Wilmington 67, Del. Died July 16, 1958.

GLADSTONE, Robert William, Can. senator; b. Kent Co., Ont., Sept. 13, 1879; s. David and Sarah (Abray) G.; student Ridgetown Collegiate Inst., 1893-96, Chatham Model Sch., 1897; m. Elizabeth Lyons, Jan. 10, 1912; 1 son, John Kenneth. Tchr. pub. schs., Kent Co., Ont., Can., 1899-01; pres. Armco Drainage Products Co., Ltd., Guelph, Ont., 1908-32. Mem. Dominion Parliament, 1935-49; apptd. to Can. Senate, 1949. Mem. United Ch. Can. Mason. Club: Rotary (Guelph). Home: 21 Oxford St., Guelph City, Ont. Office: The Senate, Ottawa, Can. Died May 31, 1951.

GLAMAN, Eugenie Fish (Mrs. August Frederick Glaman) (glă'măn), artist; b. St. Joseph, Mo., Jan. 25, 1872; d. Henry and Catherine Shepherd Fish; grad. Art Institute of Chicago, 1897; studied Kansas City Art Institute and with Emmanuel Fremiet, Lucien Simon and Charles Cottet, Paris, also at Calderon's School of Animal Painting, London, and with Briton Rivière; m. August Frederick Glaman, Feb. 16, 1895 (died 1926); children—Frederick (died in infancy, 1906), Johanna. Specializes in landscapes and animal subjects. Exhibited, Art Inst. of Chicago; Acad. of Design, New York; St. Louis Expn., 1904; Carnegie Exhibition, Pittsburgh; Pennsylvania Academy Fine Arts; New York World's Fair, 1939; Metropolitan Museum of Art, Museum of Modern Art. Royal Soc. Painters, Etchers and Engravers of London, 1954, Ill. State Fair Art Exhbn., 1956. Bronze medal, St. Louis Expn.; E. B. Butler prize, Art Inst., Chicago, 1913; prize for etching, Ind. Soc. Print Makers, 1945; Kate W. Arms Memorial Prize, Soc. Am. Etchers, 1946; first award for etching Phila. Sketch Club, 1955. Chief works: The Old Sheepfold, purchased by Chicago Commn., 1914; Two Friends, Union League Club, Chicago; represented Ill. State Museum, State Library (Springfield), Nat. Collection Smithsonian Inst. and Nat. Museum (Washington); arms collection of Contemporary Am. Prints, Met. Mus., Warren Mack Meml. Collection Pa. State Coll.; in collection of The Saddle and Sirloin Club, also collections of E. B. Butler, Curtis Camp, R.F. Goodman, Charles H. Swift, Edmund D. Hulbert, William O. Goodman, Arthur G. Leonard, Mrs. Frank G. Logan, Thomas E. Wilson, Chicago; F. L. Gilbert, Duluth, Minn.; Capt. James Hoatson, Calumet, Mich.; G. L. Berg, Seattle, Wash. Mem. Assn. Chicago Painters and Sculptors, Chicago Soc. Etchers, Chgo. Soc. Artists, Alumni Art Inst. Chicago, Woman's Salon, Chicago; Soc. Am. Graphic Artists. Conn. Acad. Fine Arts, Hartford, Conn., Artists Equity Assn., Artists League of the Midwest, Chicago. Address: Tree Studio Bldg., 4 E. Ohio St., Chgo. II. Died Oct. 19, 1956; buried Mount Auburn Cemetery, Berwyn, Ill.

GLANCY, Alfred Robinson, mfr.; b. Miamiville, O., July 17, 1881; s. Augustus C. and Louise (Robinson) G.; M.E., Lehigh U., 1903, Dr. Engring., 1943; m. Lenora Courts, Nov. 14, 1906; children—Alfred Robinson, Lenora Courts (Mrs. Richard L. Hull), Louise Courts (Mrs. Inman Brandon). In mining engring., 1903-10; pres. Glancy Malleable Corp., 1922-30; chmn. bd. A. R. Glancy, Inc.; pres. Oakland Motor Car Co., 1924-30; v.p. General Motors Corp., 1926-30, ret. 1931. Chief of Ordnance, OPM, 1941. Brig. gen., U.S. Army, Dept. Chief of Ordnance. Chief, Tank-Automotive Center, Aug. 1942. Chmn. Mich. State Planning Commn.; chmn. Mich. Pub. Trust Commn. Trustee Lehigh U. Awarded Legion of Merit, U.S. Army, 1943. Mem. Theta Delta Chi. Clubs: Detroit, Detroit Country, Bloomfield Hills Country; Royal Bermuda Yacht; Capital City, Piedmont Driving (Atlanta, Ga.). Home: 3206 Arden Road, Atlanta, Ga.; (winter) Somerset Bridge, Bermuda. Died Aug. 4, 1959.

GLASER, Lulu, actress; b. Allegheny City, Pa., June 2, 1876; d. Louis A. and Caroline (Auerbacher) G.; m. Thos. D. Richard, July 10, 1916. Studied music and joined Francis Wilson Opera Co. as understudy for Marie Jansen; subsequently took various rôles as leading comedienne with co. and has, 1900—, successfully starred at the head of her own organization in Sweet Anne Page; starred in Dolly Varden, 1901-04; in The Madcap Princess, and Miss Dolly Dollars, 1904-06; Aero Club, 1906-07; Lola from Berlin, 1907-08; Mlle. Mischief, 1908-09; One of the Boys, 1909-10; The Girl and The Kaiser, 1910-11; Miss Dudlesack, 1911-12. Mem. Audubon Soc., Toledo Mus. Art, etc.; life mem. Asso. Actresses Am. Home: Mt. Vernon, N.Y. Died Sept. 1958.

GLASER, Otto (Charles) (glā'sĕr), biologist; b. Wiesbaden, Bermany, Oct. 13, 1880; s. Charles and Eleanore (Blum) G.; brought to U.S. in infancy; A.B., Johns Hopkins, 1900, Ph.D., 1904; studied U. Budapest, 1911-12; m. Dorothy Gibbs Merrylees, Sept. 1, 1909; children—Comstock, Victoria; m. 2d, Anita Gibson Glaenzer, 1934 (died 1940); m. 3d, Dorothy Wrinch, Aug. 20, 1941. Demonstrator in comparative anatomy, embryology and biology Coll. Phys. and Surg. (now University Maryland), Baltimore, 1901-03; fellow Johns Hopkins, 1903-05; investigator oyster culture North Carolina Geological Survey and U.S. Bureau Fisheries, 1901-02; in charge oyster culture Gulf Biol. Station, La., 1903-04; instr. zoölogy and embryology Marine Biol. Lab., Woods Hole, Mass., 1905-07; with U. Mich., 1905-08, advancing to asso. prof. biology; prof. biology Amherst (Mass.) Coll., 1918—, Harkness prof., 1939—; lectr. on biology New Sch. for Social Research, N.Y.C. Trustee clk. of corp. Marine Biol. Lab., Woods Hole. Fellow A.A.A.S.; mem. Am. Soc. Naturalists, Am. Soc. Zoölogists, Am. Physiol. Soc., Soc. Exptl. Biology and Medicine, N.Y. Acad. Science, Soc. Growth and Development, Phi Beta Kappa, Sigma Xi. Contbr. to sci. jours. on developmental physiology and growth. Home: 33 Kendrick Pl., Amherst, Mass. Died Feb. 7, 1951.

GLASGOW, Arthur Graham (glăs'gō); b. Buchanan Va., May 30, 1865; s. Francis Thomas and Anne Jane (Gholson) G.; M.E., Stevens Inst. Tech., 1885; E.D., 1928; D.Sc., Washington and Lee University, 1930; LL.D., Wabash College, 1950; married Margaret Elizabeth Branch, 1901. Joined United Gas Improvement Company, 1885; secreatry and mgr. Lewiston (Me.) Gas Light Co., 1886; engr. Kansas City (Mo.) Gas Light & Coke Co., 1888; gen. inspector The United Gas Improvement Co., 1890; gen. mgr. and chief engr. Standard Gas Light Co. of City of N.Y., 1891; est. firm of Humphreys & Glasgow, London, Eng., 1892, now chmn. bd.; installations of Humphreys-Glasgow plant and processes aggregate daily capacity over 2,500 millions cubic ft., chmn. and pres. Bldg. Supplies Corp. Norfolk, Va., Chmn. U.S. Del. World's Gas Congress, Paris, 1900; chmn. Com. on Electrolysis of Am. Gas Light Assn., 1903-06; rep. Am. Gas at Paris Conf. for Standardizing Threads, 1908. Vice chmn. Red Cross Mission to Rumania, 1917; with U.S. War Dept., Washington, France and England, 1918; fixed-nitrogen adminstr., U.S. War Dept. (est. U.S. Fixed-Nitrogen Lab., now administered by Dept. of Agr.), 1919. Pres. Alumni Assn. of Stevens Inst. Tech., 1906, alumni trustee, 1907-10, now special life trustee, recipient Alumni Award 1951. Awarded Rhoads Medal, Va. Museum Fine Arts (with wife), 1952. Life member of Institute Civil Engineers, Inst. Mechanical Engineers, American Society M.E., American Society Civil Engineers; honorary member Inst. Gas Engrs. (Gt. Britain). Gold medalist Am. Gas Assn., 1910, Franklin Inst., 1928. Clubs: Metropolitan (Washington, D.C.); Commonwealth (Richmond, Va.); Everglades, Bath and Tennis (Palm Beach, Fla.); University, Down Town (New York); Am., Carlton, R.A.C., Wentworth (London). Many patents and other contbns. to Gas Technology, also numerous articles opposing isolation, etc. Series Letters Concerning Better Government, republished in pamphlet form, following the brochure "Making Democracy and the World Mutually Safe." (some 200,000 issued). Address: (winter) 80 Middle Rd., Palm Beach, Fla. Died Oct. 28, 1955; buried Hollywood Cemetery, Richmond, Va.

GLASS, Carter, Jr., publisher, editor; b. Lynchburg, Va., Mar. 29, 1893; s. Carter and Aurelia (Caldwell) G.; A.B., Washington and Lee U., 1913; m. Ria Binford Thomas, Apr. 24. 1918; children—Carter, III, Ria Delos, Thomas Reakirt. Began as linotype operator, 1913; reporter The Daily Advance, Lynchburg, 1915, Washington corr., 1915-16, telegraph editor, 1919-25, editor, 1925-43; co-publisher with sister and nephew, of The News (morn.), The Daily Advance (afternoon). Served on Mexican border, 1916-17; 1st lieutenant of Infantry, U.S. Army, 1917-19. Commissioned major in U.S. Army, Jan. 1943; discharged as lt. col., Sept. 1945. President Lynchburg Chamber of Commerce, 1936-41; mem. Lynchburg Sch. Bd.; pres. Am. Philatelic Soc., 1937-39. Member Va. State Senate, 1940-44. Mem. Kappa Sigma. Democrat. Methodist. Elk. Club: Oakwood Country (Lynchburg). Author: History of Virginia Democracy (with Robert C. Glass), 1937. Home: 3620 Manton Dr. Office: The News-Daily Advance. Lynchburg, Va. Died Dec. 1, 1955; buried Springhill Cemetery, Lynchburg, Va.

GLASS, Robert Camillus, journalist; b. Lynchburg, Va., June 13, 1885; s. Edward Christian and Susie Gathright (Carter) G.; A.B., Washington and Lee U.; m. Susie Gray Wright, June 5, 1926 (dec.). Tchr. pub. sch., 1907; mng. editor Richmond, Va., 1912-14; editorial writer Richmond Times-Dispatch, 1914; editor The News and Daily Advance, Lynchburg. Mem. Am. Soc. Newspaper Editors, Am. Acad. Polit. Sci., Sigma Delta Chi. Methodist. Democrat. Clubs: Boonsboro, Sphex (Lynchburg), Commonwealth (Richmond). Author: History of the Democratic Party in Virginia (with Carter Glass, Jr.), 1938. Home: Sheringham Place. Office: The News, Lynchburg, Va. Died July 6, 1958.

GLASSFORD, William Alexander, II, ret. naval officer, corp. ofcl.; b. San Francisco, June 6, 1886; s. William Alexander and Allie (Davis) G.; student N.M. State Normal U., 1901-02; B.S., U.S. Naval Acad., 1906; U.S. Naval War Coll., 1929-32; m. Eleanor Phelps, June 1, 1909; children—Eleanor Phelps (Mrs. Ernest von Helmburg), Thomas Phelps, Margaret Phelps; m. 3d, Henrietta Sherwood, Oct. 1946. Commd. ensign U.S. Navy, 1908, and advanced through the grades to vice adm., 1942; comdr. U.S. Naval Forces, Southwest Pacific, 1941-42; personal rep. of President, with rank of Minister, French W. Africa, 1943; deputy comdr. U.S. Naval Forces in Europe, 1944; comdr. U.S. Naval Forces, Mediterranean, 1945; comdr. U.S. Naval Forces, Germany, 1945-46; ret., 1947; now European mgr. RCA; partner Glassford Farms, Phoenix, now ret. Decorated Navy D.S. M.; awarded gold star in lieu of 2d D.S.M.; Order Orange and Nassau; Order Star of Africa; Order Crown of Italy; Order of the Bath. Episcopalian. Clubs: Army and Navy (Washington); Chevy Chase (Md.); New York Yacht, Ends of the Earth (N.Y.C.). Address: Santa Barbara, Cal. Died July 30, 1958.

GLAZEBROOK, Otis Allan, Jr., investment banker; b. Elizabeth, N.J., July 6, 1887; s. Otis A. and Virginia Calvert Key (Smith) G.; grad. Pingry Sch., Elizabeth, 1904; student Princeton, 1904-05; m. Lucy King, June 10, 1916; children—Lucy Glazebrook Bradley, Otis A., Virginia Anne. With Fifth Av. Bank of N.Y., 1906-07, Lawrence & Co., 1907-08; asst. Cashier Union Exchange Nat. Bank of N.Y., 1908-14. Met. Bank of N.Y., 1915; with Grayson M.-P. Murphy & Co., 1915-42, partner, 1926-42, mng. partner, 1937-42, also dir. Finance and Trading Corp., owned and controlled by firm, 1916-26. pres., 1921-26, when merged with controlling co.; partner Hornblower & Weeks since 1942; pres. and dir. Kreutoll Realization Co.; exec. com. Am. Hide and Leather Co., Bridgeport Brass Co., Can. Dry Ginger Ale, Inc., Chromium Corp. Am., White Motor Co., Bridgeport Brass Co. (chmn.), N.Y. City Omnibus Corp., the Omnibus Corp.; dir., chmn. exec. com. Nat. Aviation Corp.; dir., mem. exec. com., finance com., voting trustee S.A.L. Ry. Co.; dir. Drilling & Exploration Co., Inc. Ecuadorian Corp., Ltd., Eureka Williams Corp., Holland American Merchants Corporation, Internat. Products Corp., National Aviation Research Corporation, The White Motor Co. Formerly: pres. and dir. Victor Box Mfg. Co., Tindel Morris Co., Stanley Insulating Co., Am. Thermos Bottle Co., Nizer Mfg., Graymur Corp.; v.p, and dir. New Process Cork Co.; v.p., treas. and dir. Kelvinator Corp ; dir., chmn. exec. com. Nat. Aviation Corporation; member board directors Thomas & Betts Co., Glenn L. Martin Co., Am. Ice Co., Amalgamated Leather Cos., Inc., Wm. Jameson & Co., Inc., Interborough Rapid Transit Co.; mem. adv. com. Staten Island branch Bank of the Manhattan Co. Served as chmn. 1st and consol. 6 per cent bond holders com. Seaboard Air Line Ry. Co., 1938-46, one of 3 reorgn. mgrs., 1944-46. Trustee Staten Island Hosp., New Brighton, 1921-36. Treas. Staten Island Defense Recreation Com., Inc., 1944-48. Republican. Episcopalian. Clubs: Union League, Links, Knickerbocker, Richmond County Country, Lake Placid, Downtown Assn. (New York); Metropolitan (Washington). Home: Benedict Rd., Dongan Hills, Staten Island 4, N.Y. Office: 40 Wall St., N.Y.C. 5. Died May 23, 1954; buried Moravian Cemetery, S.I., N.Y.

GLAZIER, Robert Cromer, ret. chmn. Soc. for Savings; b. Hartford, Conn., May 17, 1870; s. Isaac and Mary Safford (Mather) G.; student pub. schs.; m. Mary Skinner Chapin, Apr. 22, 1912. Began as clk. Charter Oak Nat. Bank, 1888, asst. cashier, 1900-07; treas. Riverside Trust Co., 1907-22; v.p. Hartford Aetna Nat. Bank, 1922-27; pres. Soc. for Savings, 1927-48, chmn., 1948-50; dir. Hartford Nat. Bank & Trust Co., Torrington Co., Enfield Construction Co. Club: The Hartford. Home: 165 Steele Rd., West Hartford, Conn. Died Dec. 9, 1954.

GLEASON, Gay, lawyer, ins. exec.; b. Somerville, Mass., Nov. 4, 1888; s. Joseph H. and Mary L. (Gay) G.; A.B., Dartmouth, 1910; LL.B., Harvard, 1913; m. Winifred Nowell Gaskin, June 5, 1923; children—Noel Gay (Mrs. Edward C. Edwards, Jr.), Persis Elizabeth, Edward Stone. Admitted to Mass. bar, 1913; mem. Sawyer, Hardy, Stone & Morrison, Boston, 1919-48; gen. counsel, dep. mgr. Employers Liability Assurance Corp., Ltd., 1942—; v.p., gen. counsel Am. Employers Ins. Co., Employers Fire Ins.

Co.; 1st v.p., trustee Employers Group Assos. Mem. Ins. Library Assn. Boston (trustee), Ins. Fedn. Mass. (exec. com.), Am., Mass., Boston bar assns., Newcomen Soc. Mason. Clubs: Algonquin, Down Town, Harvard (Boston); Brae Burn Country (Newton, Mass.). Home: 55 Farlow Rd., Newton 58, Mass. Office: 110 Milk St., Boston 7. Died June 25, 1955; buried Newton (Mass.) Cemetery.

GLEASON, James, actor, writer, director; b. N.Y. C., May 23, 1886; s. William and Mina (Crolius) G.; ed. pub. schs. N.Y. and San Francisco; m. Lucille Webster, Aug. 22, 1906; 1 son, Russell. At age of 2 mo. was carried on stage in play, Clouds; played with numerous stock companies; appeared at the Casino, N.Y., 1914, Park, 1919, Lyric, 1919, Bijou, 1920; played Hap Hurley in Is Zat So, also playing same part in first appearance, Apollo Theatre, London, 1926; became producing mgr. with Messrs. Booth and Ernest Truex, producing Pomeroy's Past and Sure Fire, 1926; played Mickey Shannon in Shannons of Broadway; commenced film career in 1928; appeared in Count of Ten, and many others including My Gal Sal, Manhattan Tales, Strictly Dynamite, Manila Calling, Crash Dive, A Guy Named Joe, My Client Curley. Wrote the films: The Fall Guy, Dumbells in Ermine, Women of all Nations, Rain or Shine, Is Zat So, Sure Fire, etc. Wrote the plays: Shannons of Broadway, Is Zat So, The Fall Guy, Rain or Shine. Served 12 yrs., U.. Army in Cav., F.A. Tank Corps. Mil. Intel. Service. Mem. So. Cal. Dem. Com., Nat. Found. Infantile Paralysis, Inc. Clubs: The Players, Lambs (N.Y.C.); Riviera Country, Uplifter's Polo (Santa Monica); The Masquers (Hollywood). Address: 3381 Mandeville Canyon Rd., Los Angeles. Died 1959.

GLEIS, Paul G(erhard), educator; b. Rheine, Westphalia, Germany, Jan. 5, 1887; s. Henry and Anna (Ruediger) G.; grad. Gymnasium, Rheine, 1907; grad. student U. Munich, Berlin, Leipzig, Münster, 1907-11; m. Anna Louise Roleder, Sept. 1, 1921; children—Paul F., Eric H. Came to U.S., 1911, naturalized, 1935. Mem. faculty Catholic U. Am. since 1911, prof. German lang. and lit. since 1925, head, dept. of German and comparative philology since 1911, summer faculty U. Notre Dame, 1929-31. Mem. Modern Lang. Assn. Am., Am. Assn. Tchrs. German, Cath. Commn. on Internat. and Cultural Affairs, Soc. for History of Germans of Md., Goethe Soc. Am. Author: History of the Prospect Hill Cemetery Society of Washington, D.C., 1858-1950, 1950. Editor: Catholic University Studies in German, 24 vols. 1954, Washington Journal, weekly, 1914—. Contbr. to tech. jours. Home: 4711 Oliver St., Riverdale, Md. Office: Mullen Library, Catholic University of America, Washington. Died July 11, 1955; buried Prospect Hill Cemetery, Washington.

GLEN, James Allison, ex-govt. ofcl.; b. Renton, Dumbartonshire, Scotland, Dec. 18, 1877; s. David and Mary (Bain) G.; came to Can., 1911; ed. Renton and Alexandria pub. schs., student U. Glasgow, 1903-04; m. Mary Helen Law, Dec. 14, 1905; 1 son, David Paul. Admitted to bar, 1912; gen. practice of law, Russell, Manitoba, 1914—: first elected to House of Commons, 1926, re-elected 1935-40, speaker of House, 1940-45; minister of Mines and Resources 1945-48. Pres. Manitoba Sch. Trustees Assn., 1920-24; pres. Manitoba Econ. Conf., 1924-26. Liberal-Progressive. Mem. United Ch. of Can. Club: Royal Ottawa Golf. Address: Russell, Manitoba, and Ottawa, Ontario, Can. Died June 27, 1950.

GLENN, Edgar Eugene, army officer; b. Kansas City, Kan., Oct. 27, 1896; s. Stephen Edgar and Rose (Scanlon) G.; student, U. Ill., 1917-18; grad. Advanced Pursuit Sch., 1922, AC Tactical Sch., 1935, Command and Gen. Staff Sch., 1936; m. Ethel Foster, Oct. 13, 1921. Began as private Aero Squadron, 1917; commd. 2d lt. Aviation Sect., 1918, advanced through the grades to brig. gen., 1942; flying instr., 1918-19; pursuit tng., 1922; observation, 1923; bombardment, 1923; Panama Canal Zone, 1923-25; on faculty Ga. Sch. Tech., 1926-27; in charge Organized Res., Colo.-Okla., 1928-29; sec. and operations officer Advanced Flying Sch., Kelly Field, Tex., 1930-33; staff, 2d Wing, 1937-40; became chief of staff First Air Force, Mitchel Field, N.Y., 1942; spl. observer, Eng. and Ireland, 1941-42; chief of staff for Maj. Gen. Claire Chennault of 14th Air Force, 1943-45; wounded in action, Apr. 28, 1943; chief of staff 1st Air Force, 1945—; rep. USAF at Korean truce negotiations, 1953. Decorated D.S.M., Legion of Merit with oak leaf cluster, Air Medal, Purple Heart (U.S.); Chinese Hero medal, Chinese Cloud Banner (China). Mem. Phi Gamma Delta. Club: Meadowbrook Hunt (Army). Home: 67 Hilton Av., Garden City, L.I., N.Y. Died Mar. 9, 1955.

GLENN, Gustavus Richard, coll. pres.; b. Jackson County, Ga., Dec. 5, 1848; s. James Russell G.; A.B., University of Georgia, 1871, A.M., 1872; LL.D., Peabody Normal (Nashville), 1899; married Nellie Verstille, July 22, 1875. Pres. Columbus Female Coll., 1875-84 (coll. destroyed by fire); prof. natural sci., Wesleyan Coll., Macon, 1884-94; state sch. commr., Ga., 1895-1903; pres. N. Ga. Agrl. and Mech. Coll., 1904—. Mem. N.E.A. (pres. dept. superintendence, 1901-02), So. Ednl. Assn. (pres. 1900-01). Address: 1080 Reeder Circle, Atlanta. Died Jan. 23, 1939; buried Decatur, Ga.

GLENN, James Dryden, steel exec.; b. Pitts., May 27, 1905; s. David and Emma J. (Biven) G.; student pub. schs., Wooster, O.; m. Treva Hartman, Dec. 4, 1927; children—James Dryden 2d and Trevor D. (twins) Sales dept. Central Alloy Steel Corp., 1927-30, Asso. Alloy Steel Co., 1930-32; asst. mgr. stainless and alloy div. Sharon Steel Corp., 1932-37, mgr., 1937-44, asst. gen. mgr. sales, 1944; v.p. sales Eastern Stainless Steel Corp., 1945-47; gen. mgr. stainless steel sales Crucible Steel Co. Am., 1948-54, gen. mgr. sales, 1954-55, v.p., gen. mgr. sales, 1955-56, v.p. sales, 1956—. Chief stainless steel sect., iron and steel div. NPA, 1952. Mem. Am. Iron and Steel Inst., Am. Soc. Metals, Am. Ordnance Assn., Nat. Indsl. Conf. Bd., Am. Steel Warehouse Assn., Farm Equipment Inst., Newcomen Soc. N.A., Pitts. C. of C., Pitts. Civic-Business Council. Clubs: Duquesne, Chartiers Country, Pittsburgh Athletic (Pitts.). Home: 90 Lambeth Dr., Bridgeville, Pa. Office: Oliver Bldg., Pitts. 22. Died May 8, 1958; buried Mt. Lebanon Cemetery.

GLENN, John Mark, ret. found. exec.; b. Balt., Oct. 28, 1858; s. William Wilkins and Ellen Mark (Smith) G.; M.A., Washington and Lee U., 1879, LL.D., 1907; student Johns Hopkins, 1879-80; LL.B., U. Md., 1882; hon. M.A., Johns Hopkins, 1902; m. Mary Willcox Brown, May 21, 1902. Admitted to bar, 1882; mem. supervisors of city charities, Balt., 1898-1907, pres. 1904-07; gen. dir. Russell Sage Foundation ($15,000,000 for the betterment of social and living conditions), 1907-31. Pres. Nat. Conf. Charities and Correction, 1901; mem. exec. com. and social service dept. Federal Council Chs. Ex-trustee Russell Sage Foundation, Regional Plan Assn. of New York. Fellow A.A.A.S.; mem. Phi Beta Kappa. Clubs: Century, National Arts (N.Y.C.); University (Balt.). Democrat. Episcopalian. Home: 45 Park Av., N.Y.C. 16.

GLENN, Leonidas Chalmers, geologist; b. Crowder's Creek, N.C., Sept. 9, 1871; s. William Davis and Sarah P. (Torrence) G.; A.B., U. of S.C., 1891; Ph.D., Johns Hopkins, 1899; m. Nellie Louise McCullough, Sept. 12, 1900; children—William David, Hugh Wilson. Taught in secondary schs., 1891-94; supt. town schs., Darlington, 1894-96; student Harvard Coll., summer, 1895; Johns Hopkins, 1896-99; adj. prof. biology and geology, S.C. Coll., Columbia, 1899-1900; adj. prof. geology, Vanderbilt University, 1900-03, professor, 1903-42, head of division of science, 1928-42, professor emeritus since 1942. Recently engaged in work for North Carolina, Kentucky, Tennessee, and U.S. geol. surveys and U.S. Forest Service; mem. faculty George Peabody Coll. for Teachers, 1914-15; oil geologist, Sinclair Oil Co., 1916-17 and 1918; actg. state geologist of Tenn., 1918; spl. agt. U.S. Internal Revenue Dept., oil and gas valuation works 1918-19; investigated changes in Red River, Tex. Okla. boundary, for U.S. Dept. Justice, 1919-21; studied mining for oil and oil shale industry in Europe, 1923. Mapping W. Ky. coal field for Ky. Geol. Survey since 1924; cons. geologist Tenn. Valley Authority and U.S. Army Engrs. Fellow A.A.A.S.; Geol. Soc. Washington, Am. Inst. Mining and Metall. Engrs., Geol. Soc. America, Seis. Soc. Am., Tenn., Ky. Acads. Science, Phi Beta Kappa, Sigma Xi, Kappa Sigma. Contbr. to scientific periodicals. Presbyterian. Democrat. Address: 2111 Garland Av., Nashville 5. Died Jan. 11, 1951.

GLENN, Otis Ferguson, ex-senator; b. Mattoon, Ill., Aug. 27, 1879; s. Joseph C. and Mary (Ferguson) G.; LL.B., U. Ill., 1900; m. Anna Martin, Oct. 28, 1911; children—Mary Elizabeth, Martha. Admitted to Ill. bar, 1902, and began practice at Murphysboro, Ill.; mem. Glenn, Real & Browning, Chgo. State's Atty., Jackson County, Ill., 1906-08, 16-20; mem. Ill. State Senate 1920-24; spl. asst. atty. gen. Ill. for Herrin massacre trials, 1922; U.S. senator, 1928-32; apptd. spl. counsel to trustees C.,R.I.&P. Ry., 1935. Republican. Mason. K.P. Clubs: Union Leaague, Lake Shore Athletic (Chgo.); Annapolis (Md.) Roads. Home: Portage Point, Manistee, Mich. Office: 134 S. La Salle St., Chgo. Died Mar. 11, 1959.*

GLORE, Charles Foster, investment banker; b. Eureka Springs, Ark., Nov. 16, 1887; s. Charles B. and Laura (MacAdams) G.; student Lewis Inst., Chgo., 1905-08, U. Chgo., 1910; Ellen Josephine Hixon, Sept. 11, 1915; children—Frances Hixon (Mrs. Kellogg C. Beach), Charles Foster, Robert Hixon. Identified with banking business in Chgo., 1910—; partner Glore, Forgan & Co., offices Chgo. and N.Y.C.; chmn. exec. com. and dir. The Chicago Corp., Anderson Prichard Oil Corp.; mem. exec. com., dir. Continental Assurance Co., Continental Casualty Co., Libby, McNeil & Libby, Stewart-Warner Corp.; dir. The Englander Co., Inc., Studebaker Corp., Spiegel, Inc. Served as major Inf., attached to Gen. Staff, 1st Army AEF, World War I. Trustee Art Inst. Chgo., St. Luke's Hosp. Mem. Delta Kappa Epsilon. Republican. Episcopalian. Clubs: Attic, Chicago, Commercial, Old Elm, Onwentsia, Shoreacres; The Links (N.Y.C.). Home: 301 N. Sheridan Rd., Lake Forest, Ill. Office: 135 S. La Salle St., Chgo. Died Oct. 6, 1950; buried Lake Forest, Ill.

GLOVER, David D., ex-congressman; b. Prattsville, Ark., Jan. 18, 1868. Tchr. pub. schs. 10 yrs.; admitted to Ark. bar and practiced in state and federal courts; mem. Ark. Ho. of Rep., 1909, 11; served as pros. atty., 7th Jud. Dist. of Ark.; mem. 71st to 73d Congresses, 6th Ark. Dist. Democrat. Home: Malvern, Ark. Died Apr. 5, 1952; buried Shawow Lawn Cemetery, Malvern.

GLOVER, Frederic Samuel, business exec.; b. Delaware, O., Mar. 18, 1879; s. Samuel and Margaret (Means) G.; student U. Minn., class of 1901; m. Eva Haldeman, Nov. 26, 1903; children—Frederic Samuel, John Haldeman. Gen. mgr. Gas Traction Co., Mpls., 1907-12; v.p. Emerson-Brantingham Co., Rockford, Ill., 1912-17; v.p. then pres. Timken-Detroit Axle Co., Detroit, 1919-33; pres. Reo Motor Car Co. (then Reo Motors, Inc.), Lansing Mich., 1938-40; chief, optics, fire control and radio communications sect. OPM, 1941; chmn. joint optics com., chmn. joint jewel bearing com., dir. automotive div. W.P.B., 1942-45; dir. bur. industry operations Civilian Prodn. Adminstrn., 1945; now dir. automotive div. NPA. Served as col. U.S. Army as chief motor transport service, 1917-19. Mem. Chi Psi. Republican. Address: 26029 E. River Rd., Grosse Ile, Mich. Died Jan. 13, 1954.

GLOVER, Roy Henry, lawyer; b. Goldendale, Wash., July 15, 1890; s. Waldo Edwin and Mary Margaret (Mahan) G.; LL.B., U. Ore., 1915; m. Helen A. Henderson, Oct. 5, 1910. Admitted to Ore. bar, 1915, practiced in Portland since 1916; admitted to Mont. bar, 1918; clk., later asst. atty. Mont. State Counsel for G.N. Ry., Gt. Falls, 1919-36; mem. Cooper, Stephenson & Glover, 1936-43; legal staff Anaconda Co. (was Anaconda Copper Mining Co.), Butte, Mont., 1943-45, western gen. counsel, 1945-51, v.p., gen. counsel, dir. 1951-55, chmn., 1955—. Chmn. Chile Copper Co., Chile Exploration Co., Andes Copper Mining Co.; pres. Mines Investment Co., Heisey Co.; dir. Am. Brass Co., Anaconda Aluminum Co., Anaconda-Am. Brass Co., Ltd., Anaconda Export Co., Anaconda Sales Co., Anaconda Wire & Cable Co., Andes Exptl. Co., Me., Butte, Anaconda & Pacific Ry. Co., Butte Water Co., Chile Steamship Co., Greene Cananca Copper Co., Internat. Smelting & Refinery Co., Potrerillos Ry Co., Santiago Mining Co., 1st Nat. Bank, Gt. Falls, 1st Bank Stock Corp., 1st Nat. City Bank, N.Y. Decorated Knight Comdr. Order of Merit Bernardo O'Higgins (Republic of Chile); named Man of the Year, Montana, 1955. Served as sgt., Overseas Courier, World War I. Mem. Am., Mont. State, Fed. Power bar assns., Butte C. of C., Gt. Falls YMCA, Am. Judicature Soc., Am. Inst. Mining and Metall. Engrs., Acad. Polit. Sci., Am. Mining Congress, Am. Inst. Mining Engrs., Newcomen Soc. N.A., Confrerie des Chevaliers du Tastevin (France), Inst. Polit. and Adminstrv. Scis. U. Chile (asso. mem.), Nat. Mining Soc. Chile (hon.). Clubs: Lawyers, Country, Rotary, Town, Trap & Skeet (Butte); City Midday, Sleepy Hollow. Home: 280 Park Av., N.Y.C. Office: 25 Broadway, N.Y.C. 4; also Hennessy Bldg., Butte, Mont. Died Mar. 31, 1958.

GOBEILLE, Harrold Le Fevre (gō-bĕl), business exec.; b. Cleve., Nov. 2, 1894; s. William Mitchell and Nettie (Le Fevre) G.; student pub. schs.; m. Luise R. Beck, Apr. 19, 1917; children—Dorothy (Mrs. William F. Rappich), Harrold Le Fevre. With Cleveland-Cliffs Iron Co., Cleve., 1916—, mgr. marine dept., 1944—, v.p., 1952—; with Cleveland-Cliffs S.S. Co., Cleve., 1916—, v.p., 1944—, also dir.; sec., treas., dir. Great Lakes Protective Assn.; dir. Lake Carriers' Assn., Cleve. Mem. Am. Bur. Shipping, Assn. Naval Architects and Marine Engrs. Clubs: Union, Cleveland Athletic, Westwood Country, Propeller. Home: 14915 Lake Av., Lakewood 7, O. Office: Union Commerce Bldg.. Cleve. 14. Died Mar. 31, 1958.

GODBOLD, Edgar, college president; b. Auburn, Franklin County, Miss., Dec. 2, 1879; s. Thomas Rowan and Mary S. (Terry) G.; B.S., Miss. Coll., 1905, M.A., 1910, LL.D., 1931; student U. of Chicago, 1906, 07; LL.D., Howard Payne Coll., 1923; m. Irene Coleman, June 16, 1909; m. 2d, Lucie T. Yates, April 12, 1940. Principal Lawrence County High School, Silver Creek, Miss., 1905-06; professor biology, Miss. College, 1906-12, La. Coll., 1913-18; sec. La. Bapt. Edn. Commn., 1912-18, La. Bapt. State Bd., 1919-23; pres. Howard Payne Coll., 1923-29; gen. supt. Mo. Baptist Gen. Assn., 1929-42; pres. Louisiana Coll. since 1942. Mem. regional loyalty bd. Fed. Civil Service Commn. Overseas Y.M.C.A. work, World War, 1918-19. Chmn. La. Moral and Civic Foundation since 1942; mem. La. Edn. Foundation since 1945. Mem. N.E.A. Club: Rotary. Home: Military Highway. Address: Louisiana College, Pineville, La. Died Nov. 21, 1952; buried Forest Lawn Cemetery, Pineville, La.

GODBOUT, Joseph Adelard, Canadian senator; b. St. Eloi, Temiscouata, Sept. 24, 1892; s. Eugene and Marie-Louise (Duret) G.; B.A., Ste-Anne Agrl. Coll., 1919; B.S.A., Mass. Agrl. Coll., 1922; D.Sc. A. (hon.), Laval U., 1931, D.M.V. (hon.), Montreal U., 1932; D.C.L. (hon.), McGill U., 1931, Bishop U., 1943, Mass. State U., 1943; m. Marie Dorilda

Fortin, Oct. 9, 1923; children—Jean, Pierre, Marthe (Mme. Georges Bussieres), Rachel, Therese. Prof. animal husbandry Ste-Anne Agrl. Coll. and agronomist L'Islet Co., 1922-29; hon. prof. Laval U., 1940—; elected to Quebec Legislature, 1929; minister of agr., 1930-36, premier of Quebec, 1936, 39-44, also pres. exec. council, minister agr. and minister colonization, 1939-44; senator of Montarville, 1949—; farmer, breeder purebred Shorthorn and Azrshires cattle, and apple grower, 1931—. Leader Liberal party, 1938, leader Liberal opposition, 1944-48. Mem. Canadian Agrl. Inst., La Corporation des Agronomes de Quebec, Le Cercle Universitaire de Montreal, K.C. Clubs: The Reform of Quebec and Montreal. Home: Frelighsburg, P.Q. Office: The Senate, Ottawa, Can. Died Sept. 1956.

GODCHAUX, Charles (gŏdshō), sugar mfg. exec.; b. New Orleans, La., Jan. 8, 1869; s. Leon and Justine (Lamm) G.; student Phillips Exeter Acad.; m. Bonita Hiller, May 24, 1899. Pres. Godchaux Sugars, Inc., 1919-53, chmn. bd. 1953—; dir. Leon Godchaux Clothing Co., Ltd., Whitney Nat. Bank. Home: 8 Garden Lane. Office: Carondelet Bldg., New Orleans. Died Oct. 23, 1954.

GODCHAUX, Jules, sugar mfr.; b. New Orleans, July 11, 1872; s. Leon and Justine (Lamm) G.; student Phillips Exeter Acad., Class of 1889; student mech. engring., Mass. Inst. Tech. Class of 1893; m. Cora Dorothy Tanner. Vice pres. in charge of operations Godchaux Sugars, Inc., producers of sugar cane, raw sugar and refined sugar Raceland (La.) Factory, and Reserve (La.) Refinery; chmn. bd. Raceland Bank Trust Co.; pres. Luling-Hahnville Bank, Luling, La. Hon. life mem. La. Engring. Soc., Am. Sugar Cane League of U.S.A.; mem. Iota Mu chapter Phi Gamma Delta; mem. Rep. La. Third Dist. Com. Home: 1319 Eleonore St. Office: Godchaux Sugars, Inc., Carondelet Bldg., New Orleans. Died July 5, 1951.*

GODDARD, Calvin Hooker, army officer, military historian, criminologist; born Baltimore, October 30, 1891; s. Capt. Henry P. and Eliza W. (Acheson) G.; A.B., cum laude, Johns Hopkins, 1911, M.D., 1915; honor grad. Army Med. Sch., Washington, 1917; m. Eliza Cunningham Harrison, Aug. 3, 1915; children —Eliza Cunningham (Mrs. Harry Bacas), Mary Woodbridge (Mrs. Henry Zon). Commissioned first lieutenant, Medical Corps, United States Army, Feb. 18, 1917; promoted through grades to maj., Mar. 28, 1918; served in U.S., France, Germany and Poland; resigned June 2, 1920; assistant director (business adminstrn.) Johns Hopkins Hospital, 1921-24; administrative dir. Cornell Clinic, New York, 1924-25; developed the science of identifying fired bullets and empty cartridge cases, now known as forensic ballistics, N.Y., 1925-29; managing director Scientific Crime Detection Lab. Northwestern Univ., 1929-33; dir. research, 1933-34, prof. police science, law faculty, 1930-34. Awarded fellowship by Guggenheim Foundation, 1935, to write book on arms identification; fellowship from Oberlaender Trust (Phila.), 1936, to permit studies in Europe. Mem. bd. dirs. Soc. American Military Engrs., 1940-42; collaborator (ordnance), National Park Service, U.S. Dept. Interior, since 1940; member board editors and advisors Encyclopedia Britannica since 1940. Recalled to active service as lt. col., U.S. Army, and assigned to hist. section Army War Coll., 1941-42; chief, hist. sect. Ordnance Dept., 1942-45; mem. hist. div., War Dept. Spl. Staff, 1945-47; mem. hist. sect. G/2 Gen. Hdqrs., Far East Command, Tokyo, Japan, to 1948, Chief of Criminal Investigation Lab., Far East Command, Tokyo, 1948-51; chief Hist. Unit, Army Med. Service, since 1951; cons. on mil. history to surgeon gen., U.S. Army; promoted to col., 1950. Awarded Legion of Merit, 1951; Order of the Crown of Italy, 1946. Mem. Soc. Am. Mil. Engrs., Assn. Mil. Surgs., Army Ord. Assn., Am. Military Inst., Am. Acad. Forensic Scis., Internat. Soc. for Detection of Deception, Internat. Assn. for Indentification, Am. Hist. Assn., Soc. War 1812 (N.Y.), Veteran Corps of Arty. (N.Y.), Order Indian Wars, French Soc. for Advancement of Science, Phi Kappa Psi, and Pi Gamma Mu. Episcopalian. Club: Cosmos (Washington). Contbr. articles on ordnance and munitions, Ency. Brit., Ency. Brit. Year Book, Junior Ency., etc. Home: 3533 Quebec St. N.W., Washington 16. Died Feb. 22, 1955; buried St. Peters Episcopal Church, New Kent County, Va.

GODDARD, Charles William, playwright; born Portland, Me., Nov. 26, 1879; s. Judge Charles William and Rowena Caroline (Morrill) G.; A.B., Dartmouth, 1902; unmarried. Reporter, Boston Post, 1903; editorial staff, New York Sunday American, 1904-18. Mem. Delta Kappa Epsilon Fraternity, also Casque and Gauntlet. Republican. Author: (motion picture serials) The Perils of Pauline; The Exploits of Elaine; The Goddess; The Mysteries of Myra; The Seven Pearls; The Hope Diamond Mystery. Co-author: (plays) The Ghost Breaker; The Misleading Lady; Miss Information; The Last Laugh; The Broken Wing; Silver Wings; also short stories. On staff of American Weekly, since 1923. Address: 149 N.E. 93d St., Miami Shores 38, Fla. Died Jan. 11, 1951; buried Portland, Me.

GODDARD, Henry Warren, ret. judge; b. N.Y.C., 1876; s. Frederick Bartlett and Lydia Jane (Mason) G.; student N.Y. Law Sch., 1901; m. Mabel Gordon Moorman, May 1912. Formerly mem. Gay & Goddard; judge U.S. Dist. Ct., So. Dist. of N.Y., by apptmt. President Harding, 1923-54, ret. Mem. Squadron A, N.Y. Nat. Guard, 12 yrs.; mem. Draft Bd. 13 mos., then entered O.T.C., Camp Taylor, Louisville; hon. disch. 1918; past pres. N.Y. Hosp. Mus. Assn.; v.p., chmn. bd. N.Y. Assn. for the Blind. Mem. Assn. Bar City N.Y. Republican. Presbyn. Clubs: Union, Racquet and Tennis, Lawyers', Nat. Republican (dir. 1912-14), Downtown Assn., Century. Home: 215 E. 72d St. Office: U.S. Court House, Foley Sq., N.Y.C. Died Aug. 26, 1955.

GODDARD, Karl B(lake), lawyer; b. Harvard, Ill., Sept. 15, 1886; s. Charles W. and Caroline (Blake) G.; LL.B., U. Mich., 1910; m. Ethel Green, Sept. 25, 1915. Admitted to Mich. bar, 1910; partner Goddard, McClintock, Fulton & Donovan, Detroit, since 1913; v.p., dir. Universal Products Co., Inc. Mem. Phi Delta Phi. Home: 403 Notre Dame, Crosse Pointe 30. Mich. Office: Ford Bldg., Detroit 26. Died Dec. 1953.

GODDARD, Oscar Elmo, clergyman; b. Hartford, Ark., Sept. 1, 1867; s. Columbus Evans and Narcissa Theresa (Smedley) G.; A.B., Hendrix Coll., Conway, Ark., 1893, D.D., 1910; m. Mary Leila Robins, June 22, 1893; children—Lily Ruth (Mrs. W. W. Jackson), Leila Lois (Mrs. D. N. Morrison), Oscar Paul (dec.), Margaret Elizabeth (Mrs. Rufus F. Walker), Virginia Theresa (Mrs. Embree Du Bose); m. 2d, Mrs. J. C. Holcombe, Sept. 21, 1929. Ordained to ministry M.E. Ch., S., 1894; missionary to China and v.p. Anglo-Chinese Coll., 1894-95; pastor Magnolia, Monticello and Ft. Smith, Ark., until 1901; presiding elder Harrison dist., 1901-02; pastor Morrillton, Ark., 1902-05; First Ch., Muskogee, Okla., 1905-09; presiding elder Muskogee Dist., 1909-10; pastor of St. Paul's Ch., Muskogee, 1911-13, First Ch., Galveston, Tex., 1913-17, First Ch., Beaumont, Tex., 1917-18; home mission sec. M.E. Ch., S., 1918-21; pastor McKendree Ch., Nashville, 3 mos., 1922, First Ch., Conway Ark., 1922-26; became fgn. sec. Bd. Missions, M.E. Ch., S., 1926; pastor Fort Smith, Ark., 1937-40, ret. 1950. In charge evangelistic campaign of M.E. Ch., S., in Czechoslavia, 1921. Mem. Interdominational Tour of The Holy Land, 1924; Mission Tour of Belgian Congo, Africa, 1928. Trustee Okla. Meth. Coll. Author: Some Facts About China; Making America Safe; The Bible and Finance; Handbook on Revivals; Modern Evangelism on Fundamental Lines; The Methodist Evangel. Address: 1321 Davis St., Conway, Ark. Died Apr. 29, 1950; buried Fort Smith, Ark.

GODEHN, Paul M., lawyer; b. Moline, Ill., Oct. 29, 1891; s. Charles H. and Ida (Anderson) G.; LL.B., U. Mich., 1915; m. Myrtle Penniman, Sept. 26, 1927. Admitted to Ill. bar, since practiced Chgo.; mem. Mayer, Meyer, Austrian & Platt; mem. bd. dirs. United Air Lines, Inc. Mem. Am., Ill. State, Chgo. (bd. mgrs.) bar assns. Republican. Presbyn. Clubs: Tavern, Attic, Chicago, Saddle and Sirloin (Chgo.); Barrington (Ill.) Hills Country. Home: Barrington. Office: 231 S. LaSalle St., Chgo. Died Jan. 31, 1952.

GODLOVE, Isaac Hahn, color physicist; b. St. Louis, June 13, 1892; s. Lewis and Lillie G.; B.S., M.A., Washington U., 1915; Ph.D., U. Ill., 1926; m. Esther Alice Hurlbut, Dec. 22, 1923; 1 son, Terry Francis; m. 2d, Margaret Noss, Aug. 6, 1949. Prof. chemistry Mo. State Normal Sch., 1915-16; asso. prof. U. Okla., 1921-26; research dir. Munsell Color Co., 1926-30; dir., exhbn. color N.Y. Mus. Sci. and Industry, 1930-31; color editor Webster's New Internat. Dictionary, 1931-32; propr. Color Service Labs., 1932-35; chemist and physicist DuPont Co., 1935-43, Gen. Aniline & Film Corp., 1943—. Trustee Munsell Color Found. Mem. Optical Soc. Am. (com. colorimetry), Am. Assn. Textile Chemists and Colorists (chmn. color com.), Inter-Soc. Color Council (chmn. 1948-49, editor), Wash. Oratorio Soc. (v.p.), Sigma Xi, Alpha Chi Sigma. Author articles on color physics and psychology. Joint author: The Science of Color, 1953. Co-author: The Smithsonian Tables of Physical Constants, 1954. Home: 127 Spring Garden St. Office: General Aniline & Film Corp., Easton, Pa. Died Aug. 14, 1954; buried Greenwood Cemetery, Lancaster, Pa.

GODSHALL, Wilson Leon, prof. polit. science (internat. relations); b. Landsdale, Pa., April 26, 1895; s. Wilson Hackman and Blanche (Rosenberger) G.; B.S., U. of Pa., 1919, A.M., 1920, Ph.D., 1923; m. Annetta Howard Metcalf, Sept. 8, 1920. Head polit. science dept., Union Coll., 1923-34, Penfield Traveling Scholarships, 1924-25, 1931-32; head history and polit. science dept., Dickinson Jr. Coll., 1934-39; vis. prof., Pa. State Coll., 1935-39; prof. diplomatic history and internat. relations, Lehigh Univ. since 1939, head, dept. of internat. relations since 1946, on leave as cultural affairs officer Am. Embassy, Tokyo, 1952-54; exec. sec. Fulbright Commn., Japan; vis. prof., U. Wash., U. Pa., St. John's Univ. (Shanghai), Lingnan Univ. (Canton), University of the Philippines, U. of Maine, Miami U., U. of Conn. Chief quartermaster, U.S.N.R.F., 1917-18; col. (ret.) M.I., A.U.S. Res. Mem. Am. Polit. Sci. Assn., Am. Acad. Polit. and Social Sci., Am Soc. Internat. Law, Internat. Platform Assn. (pres. 1954—), Chinese Soc. and Polit. Sci. Assn., Philippine Acad. Social Sci., Am. Assn. U. Profs., S.A.R., Fgn. Policy Assn., Pi Gamma Mu (nat. pres.), Lambda Chi Alpha, Tau Kappa Alpha. Mason. Club: Rotary. Author: Tsingtau Under Three Flags, 1929; Am. Fgn. Policy, 1937; Map Studies in European History and Internat. Relations, 1940; also sect. in encys., 1954. Co-author: Introduction to Politics, 1941; Contemporary Europe, 1941, 1947; Major Problems of Internat. Politics, 1948; Origin and Consequences of World War II, 1948. Editor and co-author: Principles and Functions of Govt. in U.S., 1948. Home: 1892 Homestead Av. Office: Lehigh Univ., Bethlehem, Pa. Died June 1, 1956.

GODWIN, Earl, b. Washington, D.C.; s. Harry Post and Annie Falconer (Stoppard) G.; ed. public schools, Washington, D.C., and Passaic, N.J. and Emerson Inst., Washngton, D.C.; m. Elizabeth Cromelin, Aug. 1938. Polit. writer and spl. corr. Washington Star, Milwaukee Sentinel and Montreal Star, 1908-17; asso. editor Washington Times, 1917-19; asst. to pres. of Chesapeake and Potomac Telephone Co., 1920-23; accompanied President Harding to Alaska as spl. rep. of Bell Telephone System, July and August 1923; chmn. of publicity coms., both inaugurals of President Wilson and for President Roosevelt's third inaugural; publicity for Am. Econ. Inst., 1924-25; publicity dir. of various polit. orgns. supporting prohibition, 1925-33; polit. expert and White House corr. Washington Times-Herald, 1933-40; spl. Washington corr. Western Newspaper Union, 1933-37; radio news analyst for Washington Times, 1934; special broadcaster Nat. Broadcasting Co. on Southern chain, 1938-39; Washington observer for N. B.C., network commentator and television reporter, 1950; news broadcaster on Blue Network "Watch the World Go By," 1942. 1st lt. C.W.S. U.S. Army, 1918-19. Award for news analysis United Bus. Men's Assn. Phila., 1946; decoration for news analysis from King of Norway, 1947; certificate of appreciation from S.S.S., 1952; citation, Am. Legion, 1934; Freedoms Found. award, 1953. Chmn. publicity for President's Com. for Boy Scouts' Jamboree, Washington, 1937, mem. nat. publicity council Boy Scouts Am. 1945—. Sec. D.C. Bd. Appeals for Selective Service. Mem. White House Corrs. Assn. (pres. 1938-40), Radio Corrs. Assn. (pres. 1939-45). Episcopalian. Club: National Press (ex-pres.). Home: R.F.D. 2, Alexandria, Va. Office: Sheraton Park Hotel, Washington 8. Died Sept. 24, 1956.

GOESSMANN, Helena Theresa, educator, lectr.; b. Charles Anthony and M. A. (Kinney) G.; grad. Sacred Heart Acad., Providence, 1885; studied in Europe 2 yrs.; M.Ph., Ohio U., 1897. Mem. English faculty Mass. Agrl. Coll., 1910—; known as lectr. on ednl. and cultural subjects; chmn. adv. bd. Woman's Auxiliary of Catholic Summer Sch., Cliff Haven, N.Y., 1898—. Organizer, 1900, and 1st pres. Elmhurst (Sacred Heart) Alumnae Assn.; mem. Amherst Hist. Soc., U.S. Cath. Hist. Soc., Delta Phi Gamma (hon.), etc. Clubs: Amherst Woman's Hampden County Woman's, Tuesday. Wrote: (pageant plays) The Vision of Mary Chester; By the River of Holy Memories; (French folk play) The Little Sister of Lisieux; etc. Home: Amherst, Mass. Died Aug. 19, 1926.

GOETZ, Philip Becker (gĕts); b. Buffalo, N.Y., July 20, 1870; s. George and Catherine (Hausauer) G.; A.B., Harvard, 1893; m. Linda Alvord Graves, July 7, 1897; children—Theodore Becker, Esther Becker. Mem. faculty Central High Sch., 1893-1903, Lafayette High Sch., 1903-10, Nichols Sch., 1910-13 —all of Buffalo; chmn. of faculty of dept. of arts and sciences, U. of Buffalo, 1913-22, sec. Council since 1920, emeritus prof. Latin and Greek since 1926. Mem. N.Y. Classical Assn., Phi Beta Kappa, Delta Upsilon. Republican. Unitarian. Club: Buffalo. Author: (poem) Kallirrhoe, 1896; Poems, 1898; Interludes, 1904; (play) The Summons of the King, 1911; (brochure) Reflections on the Great War, 1917; Lyrics and Meditations, 1925; also songs, articles in mags., etc. Contbr. weekly column of "Comment" to Buffalo Evening News. Home: 715 Delaware Av., Buffalo 9. Died Dec. 1, 1950; buried Forest Lawn, Buffalo.

GOETZE, Arthur Burton, telephone exec.; b. Chgo., June 8, 1901; s. Richard and Sophia (Hoffmeister) G.; student Armour Inst., 1917-18, 1919-21; m. Evelyn Gunderson, Nov. 15, 1924; children—Shirley June (Mrs. D. R. Russell, Jr.), Alan Burton. With the engineering department Western Electric Co., 1917-42, personnel dir., 1942-48, works mgr., 1948-49, v.p. mfg., 1952-54, v.p. finance, 1954-56, vice pres. manufacturing, 1956, president, 1956—, bd. dirs., exec. com., 1953—; v.p. charge personnel Chesapeake & Potomac Telephone Co., 1949-50; v.p. charge operations Ohio Bell Telephone Co., 1950-52, bd. dirs., executive committee, 1950-52; bd. dirs., exec. com. Teletype Corp., Chgo.; mem. adv. com. Chem. Corn Exchange Bank; dir. Mfrs. Junction R.R., Bell Telephone Labs, Sandia Corp., Nassan Smelting and Refining Co., Weco Corp., Westrex Corp., Northern electric Co. Ltd. (Montreal, Can.). Mem. Nat. Elec. Mfrs. Assn., N.A.M., Am. Mgmt. Assn., U.S. C. of C., Am. Ordnance Assn., Newcomen Soc. Eng., Armed Forces Communication Assn. Clubs: Railroad Machinery (N.Y.C.); Canoe Brook Country (Summit, N.J.). Home: 286 Hartshorn Dr., Short Hills, N.J. Office: 195 Broadway, N.Y.C. 7. Died Mar. 9, 1959; buried St. Stephens Cemetery, Short Hills, N.J.

GOETZE, Frederick Arthur (gĕt'zē), univ. treas.; b. Jersey City, Apr. 17, 1870; s. Frederick A. and Sarah C. (Gee) G.; student Stevens Prep. Sch., 1882-85, Columbia Sch. Mines, 1893-95, M.Sc., Columbia, 1905, D.Sc., 1929; m. May L. Martin, Feb. 11, 1896; children—Robert Addison (dec.), Marjorie, Dorothy, Richard Baron. Asst. supt. and supt. of bldgs. and grounds Columbia U., 1895-1907; dean schs. mines, engring. and chemistry Columbia, and cons. engr., 1907-16, comptroller, 1913-25, treas., 1916—; dir., v.p. University Patents, Inc.; dir. Merchants Fire Assurance Corp. of N.Y., Washington Assurance Corp. of N.Y., Mchts. Indemnity Corp. of N.Y. Mem. sub-com. War Industries Bd., Washington, World War I. Dir. Research Corp.; trustee Tchrs. Ins. and Annuity Assn. Am. (exec. com.), N.Y. Mus. Sci. and Industry (trustee, mem. exec. and finance coms.). Mem. Am. Soc. M.E., Acad. Polit. Science, Real Estate Bd. N.Y., Tau Beta Pi. Clubs: Columbia University, Down Town Association, Union, Men's Faculty, Phi Delta Theta. Address: 75 Maiden Lane, N.Y.C. 7. Died Mar. 7, 1950.

GOETZMANN, Jule Lawrence (gĕts'măn), govt. ofcl.; b. St. Paul, Dec. 12, 1912; s. George L. and Myrtle (Rinehart) G.; A.B., St. Ambrose Coll., Davenport, Ia., 1934; student, grad. sch., Northwestern U., 1948-49; m. Charlotte Ehler, July 16, 1937. Apptd. fgn. service officer U.S. Dept. State, 1937; vice consul, Habana, Cuba, 1937-39, Yokahama, 1939-41, Bilbao, Spain, 1942-46; 2d sec. of Embassy and consul, San Jose, Costa Rica, 1947-48; economist, (internat. and fiscal), Monetary Affairs staff, U.S. Dept. State, 1949—. Mem. Am. Econ. Assn. Home: 1825 Columbia Rd. N.W., Washington. Office: U.S. Dept. State, Washington 25. Died July 23, 1956.

GOGARTY, Oliver St. John (gō'găr-ty), author; b. Dublin, Ireland, Aug. 17, 1878; s. Dr. Henry J. K. and Margaret (Oliver) G.; student Trinity Coll., Dublin, 1897, Worcester Coll. Oxford, 1904; M.D., Royal Coll. Surgeons (fellow 1906), 1907; m. Martha Duane, Aug. 1906; children—Oliver Duane, Dermot St. John, Brenda Beatrice. Gov., Richmond, Hardwick and Whitworth hosps., Dublin, 1915—; vis. surgeon Meath Hosp., Dublin, 1910. Mem. Irish Senate, 1922-34. Author: (plays) Blight, A Serious Thing; The Enchanted Trousers (produced Abbey Theatre, Dubln), 1920; (poetry) Wild Apples, 1919; An Offering Of Swans, 1924, Elbow Room, 1940, Perennial (a selection), 1948), Selected Poems, 1933, Collected Poems, 1951; As I Was Going Down Sackville Street, 1937; I Follow St. Patrick, 1938; Tumbling In The Hay, 1938; Going Native, 1940; Mad Grandeur, 1947; Intimations, 1950; Rolling Down The Lea, 1950; also articles in lit. mags. Address: 45 E. 61st St., N.Y.C. 21. Died Sept. 22, 1957; buried Ballinakill, Country Galway, Ireland.

GOHDES, Conrad Bruno, educator; b. Wangerin, Pomerania, Germany, Mar. 19, 1866; s. Otto annd Ulrica (Gross) G.; student Royal Gymnasium, Dramburg, Germany, 1877-83; Capital U., Columbus, O., 1884-88, A.B., A.M.; Litt.D., Susquehanna U., 1917; m. Clara Heiser, June 5, 1893; children—Gladys Maud (wife of Rev. L. Redelfs), Mabel Elizabeth (wife of Rev. H. Trump), Otto Conrad, Clarence Louis Frank, Francis Nicholas, Dorothy Eleanor (Mrs. John Rupprecht). Was ordained to ministry Luth. Ch., 1888, and established congregations at Peru, W.Va.; Grace English Luth. Ch., New Orleans, Grace English Luth. Ch., San Antonio, Beitel Meml. Ch. and Bull Verde chs., Bexar County, Tex.; prof. history, Capital U., 1912—. Naturalized citizen of U.S., 1890. Author: Christian Frederic Schwartz, the Apostle to India, 1923; Fuel for the Fire, 1927. Editor: Reu's Catchetics (in English), 1918; Does the Modern Papacy Require a New Evaluation? (book), 1940. Translator parts of Luther's German and Latin Works for Am. Lenker edit. Editor Lutheran Youth. Contbr. to several anthologies of verse, writer for young people. Advocate of the English lang. in the religious lit. and ednl. work of Luth. Ch. Am. Home: 1392 E. Mound St., Columbus, O. Deceased.

GOIN, Sanford Williams, architect; b. Frankfort, Ky., June 17, 1908; s. Newbold Loescher and Mariam (Jett) G.; student U. Fla., 1930; m. Elisabeth Henderson Johnson, July 18, 1935; children—Sanford W., Newbold Crittenden, Mary Elisabeth, David Neville. Draftsman, Gainesville, Fla., 1927-35, practice of architecture, 1935—; mem. Goin & Moore, Architects; dir. Gainesville Mutual Building and Loan Assn. Member Alachua County Zoning Commn., 1947-49, 52—. City Planning Bd., Gainesville, 1946-48, Bd. City Commrs., 1948-51. Trustee Alachua County Hosp., 1938-42. Served with 25th Sea Bees, USNR, 1942-45. Fellow A.I.A. (dir. S. Atlantic region, 1957— nat. dir. 1957—) mem. Fla. Assn. Architects (pres. 1950-52), Am. Legion, 40 and 8, Newcomen Soc. Presbyn. Mason. Clubs: Kiwanis, Golf and Country (Gainesville). Home: 518 N.E. 4th Av., Gainesville, Fla. Died Sept. 12, 1958.

GOLD, Howard R., clergyman; b. Nazareth, Pa., Nov. 2, 1878; s. Stephen Henry and Mary Ann (Remaly) G.; B.A., Lafayette Coll., 1903; grad. Luth. Theol. Sem., Mt. Airy, 1907; studied Columbia Univ., Univ. of Wis.; D.D., Gettysburg (Pa.) College, 1932; m. Margaret Hoffman Coover, June 28, 1923 (died Apr. 8, 1959). Ordained to ministry, Luth. Ch., 1907; pastor Luther Meml. Ch., Madison, Wis., 1907-16; one of organizers of student pastor movement, 1907; exec. sec. Gen. Luth. Com. to celebrate 400th anniversary of beginning of the Reformation, 1916-17, inaugurating proceedings that led by amalgamation to orgn. of United Luth. Ch.; corr. sec. Bd. of Edn., United Luth. Ch., also chmn. Publicity Com. same; field sec. Nat. Luth. Commn. for Soldiers and Sailors' Welfare during World War. Dir. Lutheran Bur. of Nat. Luth. Council, New York, until 1923; pastor Trinity Ch., New Rochelle, N.Y., 1923-39; former pastor St. Paul's Luth. Ch., Williamsport, Pa.; now exec. sec. of Council of Chs. of Williamsport. Chairman commn. for survey of higher edn., United Luth. Ch. in America; formerly pres. bd. edn. United Luth. Ch. in America. Author: Bible Stories Told Again, 1929 religious features for pub. press. Address: 1566 Reservoir Av., Roslyn, Pa. Died Feb. 17, 1959.

GOLDEN, John, playwright, producer of plays; b. N.Y. City, June 27, 1874; s. Joel and Amelia (Tyreler) G.; family moved to Wauseon, O., 1875; ed. pub. and night schs., and New York Univ. Law Sch.; Dr. of Pub. Service, Oglethorpe Univ. Super at Harrigan Theatre, and actor in stock, repertoire and Shakespeare; comic journalist and rhymester, then studied music under Damrosch; wrote many songs (Poor Butterfly, etc.), also many short plays and lyrics; comp. the music for over a dozen mus. com. Major O.R.C., U.S. Army; maj. N.Y. Police Reserves. Mem. Am. Soc. Composers, Authors and Publishers. Moose. Clubs: New York, Lambs (shepherd), Lotos, Flushing Country, Belleclaire Golf, Lakeville Golf, Bayside Yacht Club, Atlantic Yacht; Green Room (London); Coldstream Golf, Sands Point Country, Artists and Writers Club. Author or producer (plays): Turn to the Right; Lightnin' (1,291 consecutive performances, New York); Three Wise Fools; Thunder; Dear Me; The First Year; The Wheel; Spite Corner; The Seventh Heaven; Chicken Feed; The Serpent's Tooth; The Streak; The Wisdom Tooth; 2 Girls Wanted; Four Walls; Eva the 5th; Night Hostess; Let Us Be Gay; Salt Water; When in Rome—; That's Gratitude; As Husbands Go; Riddle Me This; When Ladies Meet; The Bishop Misbehaves; A Touch of Brimstone; Susan and God; Skylark; Claudia; Theatre; Counselor at Law, Three's a Family; A Place of Our Own; Made in Heaven; short plays: River of Souls; The Clock Shop. Musical comedies: The Little Colonel; Miss Print; The Hoyden; Forward March; Over the River; The Candy Shop. Shows at the Hippodrome: Hip Hip Hooray, 1915-16; The Big Show, 1916-17; Cheer Up, 1917-18; Everything, 1918-19. Produced Revival of They Knew What They Wanted, 1949; The Male Animal, 1952. Member of the bd. dirs. Am. Theatre Wing War Service and N.Y.C. Center of Music and Drama; chmn. entertainment div. N.Y. Defense Recreation Com.; dir. U.S.O. camp shows: trustee United Seaman's Service; dir. Percy Williams Home, Actor's Fund, Queensboro Soc. Prevention Cruelty to Children; sponsored playwriting contest for U.S. soldiers, sailors and airmen and prize play contest for Navy; originated plan for free entertainment of soldiers; twice produced Red Cross at War, for Red Cross War Fund. Received citation from War and Navy Depts., United China Relief, Finnish Relief; Army Dept. highest civilian decoration for distinguished service. N.Y.C. chmn. for observance of UN Day, 1950—. Home: Bayside, L.I. Office: St. James Theatre Bldg., 246 W. 44th St., N.Y.C. Died June 17, 1955.

GOLDEN, S. M., railroad exec. Vice pres. Chicago Great Western Railway Co. Address: 309 West Jackson Blvd., Chicago, Ill. Died Dec. 28, 1950.*

GOLDENWEISER, Emanuel Alexander (gōl'dĕn-vī-sēr), economist; b. Kiev, Russia, July 31, 1883; s. Alexander S. and Sofia (Munstein) G.; grad. First Kiev Gymnasium, 1902; A.B., Columbia, 1903; A.M., Cornell U., 1905; Ph.D., 1907; m. Ann Allen, Dec. 1916; children—Margaret Ellen, John Alexander. Came to U.S., 1902, naturalized citizen, 1907. Spl. investigator U.S. Immigration Commn., 1907-10; spl. agt. U.S. Census, 1910-14; statistician, Office of Farm Management, Dept. of Agr., 1914-19; asst. statistician Federal Reserve Bd., 1919-24; asst. dir. Div. of Research and Statistics. 1925, dir., 1926-45; mem. Inst. for Advanced Study, Princeton, N.J., 1946-51; economist Federal Open Market Committee, 1936-45; tech. advisor U.S. Bituminous Coal Comm., 1920. Fellow Am. Statis. Assn. (pres. 1943); mem. Am. Econ. Assn. (pres. 1946). Club: Cosmos (Washington). Author: Immigrants in Cities, (Vols. 26 and 27 of Reports of Immigration Commn.), 1909; (with L. E. Truesdell) Farm Tenancy in the United States (U.S. Census), 1924; Federal Reserve System in Operation, 1925; Jobs, 1946; Monetary Management in the U.S., 1949; American Monetary Policy, 1951; also articles in econ. jours. Home: 30 N. Stanworth Dr., Princeton, N.J. Retired. Died Mar. 31, 1953.

GOLDING, Louis, author and world traveller; b. Manchester, England, Nov. 19, 1895; s. Philip and Yetta (Trotsky) G.; ed. Manchester Grammar Sch.; M.A., Queen's Coll., Oxford, 1921; married. Author: Forward from Babylon, 1932; Magnolia Street, 1932; Five Silver Daughters, 1934; Mr. Emmanuel, 1939; In the Steps of Moses the Conqueror, 1939; The World I Knew, 1940; Who's There Within?, 1942; No News from Helen, 1943; Pale Blue Nightgown, 1944; The Glory of Elsie Silver, 1944; Three Jolly Gentlemen, 1947; Honey for the Ghost, 1949; The Dangerous Places, 1952; The Loving Brothers, 1952; To the Quayside, 1953; Goodbye to Ithaca, 1955; Mr. Hurricane, 1957; (films) Mr. Emmanuel, 1945; Rome, 1946; worked on Arnhem (Netherlands) film, Theirs Is the Glory, 1945. Fellow Royal Soc. Lit. Contbr. Eng. and Am. journals. Lectr. in U.S. Home: 16 Hamilton Terrace, London, N.W. 8, England. Address: care Curtis Brown, Covent Garden, London W.C. 2. Died Aug. 1958.

GOLDMAN, Edwin Franko, condr., composer; b. Louisville, Ky., Jan. 1, 1878; s. David and Selma (Franko) G.; ed. pub. schs., N.Y. City; student Nat. Conservatory of Music, N.Y. City; studied cornet under Jules Levy and Carl Sohst; Mus.D. (hon.), Phillips University, 1934, Boston University, 1936, DePauw University, 1953; married Adelaide Maibrunn, Oct. 8, 1908; children—Richard Franko, Louise Elizabeth. Cornetist, Met. Opera House orchestra, 1895-1905; teacher, band instruments, 1905-18; was mem. faculty, Columbia, 1919-26; organizer, 1911, since condr. Goldman Band; mgr. and condr. Goldman Band Free Summer Concerts (Columbia campus, later in Central Park, also on campus New York U.) since 1918; concerts in Prospect Park, Brooklyn, since 1934; Decorated Officier de l'Instruction Publique, for services in cause of French music, 1929; Cavaliere of Order of Crown of Italy, 1933; Order of White Lion (Czechoslovakia), 1936; gold medal from City of N.Y., 1923; 1st official gold medal, American Bandmasters Assn., 1932; medal Eastern States Exposition, 1933; Citizenship Medal from the Vets. of Fgn. Wars, 1949; Outstanding Musician medal, National Association of American Conductors and Composers, 1950; Lincoln Award for outstanding citizen of country, 1951; Ky. Col.; also awards and testimonials from cities and organizations throughout the U.S. Organizer and 1st pres. Am. Bandmasters' Assn., elected hon. life pres., 1933. Member American Society of Composers, Authors and Publishers; honorary mem. Kappa Kappa Psi, Alpha Mu Pi, Phi Alpha Mu, Toronto (Can.) Mus. Protective Assn., Newark (N.J.) Musician's Union, New Haven (Conn.) Musicians' Union, Pa. Bandmasters' Assn., Assn. of Mus. Instrument Dealers of New York; hon. mus. counsellor 4H Clubs of U.S., Boy Scouts of America. Made chief of Pawnee Indians, title Chief Bugle, 1935; hon. mem. Ottawa and London, Ont. Musicians Unions. Club: The Bohemians. Composer over 110 marches and numerous other compositions for band, also a large number of solos for various wind instruments, etc. Visited Philippines and Japan for USO, Oct. 1945; made report on Am. Army bands to Pres. Truman, General Eisenhower, and Secretary of War Patterson. Author of The Band Guide and Aid to Leaders, 1916; Band Betterment, 1934; The Goldman Band System for Developing Tone, Intonation and Phrasing, 1935. A pioneer in presentation of symphony music by all-wind band. Apptd. maj., city Patrol Corps, N.Y. City, 1942. Home: 1 University Pl., N.Y.C. Died Feb. 21, 1956.

GOLDMAN, Solomon, rabbi; b. Kozin, Volhynia, Russia, Aug. 18, 1893; s. Abraham Abba and Jeannette (Grossman) G.; prep. edn., Rabbi Isaac Elchanan Seminary; A.B., New York U., 1917; rabbi, Jewish Theol. Sem., 1918, D.H.L., 1936, D.Litt., 1946; D.D., Jewish Inst. Religion, 1947; grad. study Columbia and U. of Chicago; m. Alice Lipkowitz, June 23, 1918; children—Geulah (Mrs. Joseph Epstein), Naomi (Mrs. Albert Zemel). Rabbi B'nai Israel Congregation, Brooklyn, 1917-18; B'nai Jeshurun Congregation, Cleveland, Ohio, 1919-22, Jewish Center, Cleveland, 1922-29, Ansche Emet Synagogue, Chgo., Ill., since 1929. Formerly mem. Com. of 100 and New Charter Commn. of Cleveland; v.p. Am. Zionist Orgn.; hon. pres. Nat. Hebrew Assn.; del. World's Zionist Congress, 1937, vice pres., same, 1939; conducted Jewish National Fund campaign in South Africa, 1937; mem. Hillel Foundation Commn.; made goodwill tour of South America, 1941. Mem. United Palestine Appeal (hon. vice-chmn.); co-chmn. United Jewish Appeal; trustee Jewish Publication Soc. of America. Member Rabbinical Assembly, American Acad. Polit. and Social Science, Am. Oriental Soc., Linguistic Soc. America, Societas Spinoza; pres. Zionist Organization of America, 1938-40. Recipient Phi Beta Delta Award, 1938; Ginzberg Citation, 1943. Joint editor Brooklyn Jewish Forum, 1909-10; asso. editor Journal of Religious Education. Author: A Rabbi Takes Stock, 1931; The Jew and the Universe, 1936; The Golden Chain, 1937; Crisis and Decision, 1938; Prayers and Readings, 1938; Undefeated. 1940; also the author of The Words of Justice Brandeis, 1953; The Ten

Commandments, 1956. Co-author: Hashebil and Songs and Readings, 1938; The Book of Books, 1948; In the Beginning, 1948. Editor: Schecter Memorial Volume; Frischman's Stories; Feierberg's L'On; Letters and Essays of Ahad Ha-am; Peretz Stories, 1938; Bialik's Stories, 1940; Brandeis on Zionism. Author of script "The Romance of a People." Contributor to Reflex, Menorah Journal, New Palestine, Journal of Religious Education, Seven Arts Syndicate, Hadaor, Gilynot (Palestine) Hetakuphah. Clubs: Covenant, Standard, Bryn Mawr (Chicago); Woodmont Country (Washington, D.C.). Home: Elm Rd., Vernon Twp., R. 1, Mundelein, Ill. Died May 14, 1953; buried Meml. Park, Evanston, Ill.

GOLDSBOROUGH, Laird S(hields) (gōldz'bûr-ō), editor; b. La Fayette, Ind., Mar. 6, 1902; s. Winder Elwell and Charlotte Poole (Wallace) G.; A.B., Yale, 1924; fellow Royal Univ. of Norway; m. Forence Maconaughy in Goldsborough, Eng., June 17, 1929. Asso. editor Fortune mag., 1929-34; foreign affairs editor of Time mag., 1925-40; became spl. asst. to chmn. bd. Time, Inc., 1941. Became co-ordinating officer in New York for Counter Espionage, U.S. Army Office of Strategic Services, 1943. Clubs: Union Interalliée (Paris); Yale (New York); Elizabethan (New Haven). Home: 1200 Fifth Av. Office: 9 Rockefeller Plaza, N.Y.C. Died Feb. 14, 1950; buried Evergreen Cemetery, Gettysburg, Pa.

GOLDSBOROUGH, T(homas) Alan, judge; b. at Greensboro, Md., Sept. 16, 1877; s. Washington E. and Martha P. (Laird) G.; A.B., Washington College, 1899, LL.D., 1935; LL.B., University of Maryland, 1901; m. Laura Hall, June 16, 1909; children—Martha Winder, Thomas Alan, Eliza Hall, George Hall. Began practice at Denton, Md., 1901; state's atty., Caroline County, Md., 1904-08; mem. 67th to 76th Congresses (1921-41), 1st Md. Dist.; resigned to accept apptmt. as U.S. Dist. Judge for D.C., 1939. Democrat. Episcopalian. Home: Denton, Md. Address: U.S. District Court, Washington 1. Died June 16, 1951.

GOLDSBOROUGH, W(inder) Elwell, engr. and economist; b. Balt., Oct. 10, 1871; s. Washington Elwell and Martha Pierce (Laird) G.; M.E., Cornell U., 1892; m. Charlotte Poole Wallace, Dec. 20, 1899; children—Winder Elwell (dec.), Laird Shields. Engr. Colliery Engring Co., Scranton, Pa., 1892-93; prof. elec. engring., Ark. U., 1893-94; cons. engr., Edison Elec. Illuminating Co., Balt., 1894-96; prof. elec. engring., Purdue, 1894-1905, also dir. Sch. Elec. Engring., 1896-1905; asst. to pres., 1905-06, bus. mgr. engring. dept., 1906-07, J. G. White & Co., N.Y.C.; dir., v.p. and gen. mgr. Denver (Colo.) Reservoir Irrigation Co., 1907-10; pres. Platte Valley Land Co., 1908—; pres. the Goldsborough Co., engrs., 1910-23; gen. mgr. Laramie (Wyo.) Water Co., 1910-13; gen. and financial mgr. New Home Sewing Machine Co., 1918-20; cons. engr., N.Y. City, 1914-23; with Henry L. Doherty & Co., N.Y., 1923-32; mgr. and dir. research Power Div. Labs., Combustion Utilities Corp., New York, 1924-32; cons. engr. and economist, 1932—. Major, Cornell Univ. Cadet Corps, 1892; maj. Ark. State Guards, 1893-94; comdt. cadets Ark. U., 1893-94. Mem. or del. to Internat. Elec. congresses, Chicago, 1893, Paris, 1900, St. Louis (v.p.), 1904; chief of dept. electricity, St. Louis Expn., 1902-05; mem. jury of awards, Buffalo Expn., 1901; mem. superior jury Internat. Jury of Awards, St. Louis Expn., 1904; mem. com. com. of Nat. Electric Light Assn. on Arc Light Photometry, 1900-03; chmn. exec. com. Electric Ry. Test Commn., 1903-07. Commerative Medal Univ. Expn., 1904. Decorated Order of Crown (Italy), 1904. Fellow A.A.A.S., Am. Inst. E.E. (v.p. 1901-05); asso. fellow American Electro-Therapeutic Assn.; mem. or past mem. Am. Soc. M.E., Inst. Elec. Engrs. of England, Franklin Inst., Internat. Assn. Testing Materials, Soc. Promotion Engring. Edn., Nat. Inst. Social Sciences, Ind. Acad. Science, Am. Electro-Chem. Soc., New York Southern Soc., Beta Theta Pi. Clubs: (mem. or past mem.): Denver, University, Country, Transportation (Denver); St. Louis, Mercantile (St. Louis); Lawyers, Engineers, Nat. Arts, Cornell, Purdue (New York); Country (South Norwalk). Inventor and patentee of numerous machines and devices. Author of ednl., literary, scientific, econ. and engring. books, monographs, papers and reports. Home: Bonniebrook Rd. and Richards Av., Norwalk, Conn. Died Jan. 12, 1957.

GOLDSCHMIDT, Jakob, banker; b. Eldagsen, Germany, Dec. 31, 1882; s. Marcus and Lina (Bacharach) G.; ed. in German schools; Dr. of Social Science (hon.), U. of Heidelberg, 1927; m. Sophie Joseph, Apr. 8, 1913 (died 1922); 1 son, Alfred Erwin. Bank clk., 1908; formed firm Schwartz, Goldschmidt & Co., 1910; managing dir. Nat. Bank Fuer Deutschland, 1918, which merged with Deutsche Nat. Bank Bremen, Darmstaedter Bank to form Darmstadter Und Nat. Bank of which pres., 1922; founder Internat. Bank of Amsterdam, vice chmn., 1924; formerly mem. bds. dirs. German, Austria and Policy Indstl. Cos.; chmn. bd. dirs. and exec. com. Pierce Governor Co., Inc., Anderson, Ind.; mem. bd. dirs. and exec. com. Tenn. Corp., Tenn. Copper Co., Birdsboro Steel Foundry & Machine Co., Birdsboro Armorcast. Mem. N.Y. State C. of C., Fgn. Policy Assn., Acad. Polit. Science, Museum of Modern Art, Metropolitan Museum. Clubs: Wall St., Economic (N.Y.). Home: 32 E. 64th St., N.Y. City 21. Office: 30 Broad St., N.Y.C. 4. Died 1955.

GOLDSCHMIDT, Richard Benedict, zoologist; b. Frankfurt on Main, Germany, Apr. 12, 1878; s. Solomon and Emma (Flürscheim) G.; Ph.D., U. Heidelberg, 1902; also student U. Munich; M.D. (hon.), U. Kiel, 1929; D.Sc. (hon.), U. Madrid, 1934; Dr. (hon.), Berlin, 1953; m. Elsa Kühnlein, Mar. 15, 1906; children—Ruth Emma (Mrs. H. Williams), Hans. Came to U.S., 1936. Asst. U. Heidelberg, 1900; lectr., asst. and asso. prof. U. Munich, 1903-14; mem. and dir. Kaiser Wilhelm Inst. for Biol. Research, Berlin, 1914-36; prof. zoölogy Imperial U., Tokyo, 1924-26; prof. zoölogy U. Cal., 1936-48, emeritus; Silliman lectr. Yale, 1939-40. Mem., hon. mem., fgn. mem. numerous academies, learned socs. in 12 different countries. Author: The Mechanism and Physiology of Sex Determination, 1923; Physiological Genetics, 1938; Ascaris: The Biologist's Story of Life, 1937; The Material Basis of Evolution, 1940; Understanding Heredity, 1952; Theoretical Genetics, 1955; Portraits from Memory, 1956; 12 books in German on genetics, sex, travel, popular sci., pub. Germany, many trans. other langs. Contbr. articles on biology to tech. jours. U.S. and Europe. Home: 590 Arlington, Berkeley, Cal. Died Apr. 24, 1958.

GOLDSMITH, Milton, author; b. Phila., May 22, 1861; s. Abraham and Cecilia (Adler) G.; A.B., Central High Sch., Phila., 1877; course in literature, langs. and music at U. of Zurich, 1877-80; m. Sophia Hyman, of New York, Feb. 14, 1899; children—Rosalind, Madeleine. In wholesale clothing business, 1882, 1904; pres. Goldsmith-Leving Co., embossing of works of art, calendars, pictures, etc. Contbr. of many short stories in mags., local papers and Jewish papers, several hundred poems in Puck, Judge, Life, Cosmopolitan, etc.; also several mus. compositions and songs; also several dramatic works in prose and verse, of which a comedy, "A Romance of Kief," and a mus. comedy, "Jay Caesar, Esq.," have been performed; "The Little Brother" (drama, performed London and New York), 1918. Spent yrs. 1910 and 1911 in Berlin and Paris, translating a number of German and French plays into English for Am. stage. Clubs: Mercantile, Pharisees, American Dramatists. Author: Rabbi and Priest, 1882; A victim of Conscience, 1903; Max Geller, Student (psychol. novel); Adventures of Prince Charming, 1912; I Wonder Why, 1919; Practical Things, 1920; I Wonder How, 1922; Old Mother Earth and Her Family, 1930; In Search of a Soul, 1931. Address: 22 Shadow Lane, Larchmont, N.Y. Died Sept. 21, 1957.

GOLDSMITH, Philip H., sports good mfr.; born Cin., May 23, 1897; s. Oscar and Minnie (Hess) G.; m. Cecile Crager, Sept. 18, 1922; 1 dau., Minette. Chmn. MacGregor Sport Products, Inc., dir.; dir. The MacGregor Co., MacGregor Golf Co. Mason. Home: 160 South Island, Golden Beach, Fla., also 3555 Glen Edge Lane, Cin. Office: Spring Grove Av., Cin. 32. Died Sept. 18, 1958.

GOLDSTEIN, Sidney Emanuel, rabbi; b. Marshall, Tex., Mar. 7, 1879; s. Jacob and Golda (Mesritz) G.; B.A., U. of Cincinnati, 1904; Bachelor of Hebrew Literature and Rabbi, Hebrew Union College, Cincinnati, 1905; grad. work in social sciences, Univ. Cin., U. Chgo., Columbia U.; D.D. honorus causa, Jewish Institute of Religion, N.Y., 1945; m. Susan Sugarman, July 23, 1906; children—Eleanore Mattye (Mrs. Hugo Nichthauser), Beatrice Sidbeth (Mrs. Harvey Konheim). Assistant superintendent at Mt. Sinai Hospital, New York, 1905-07; associate rabbi Free Synagogue, New York, since 1907; prof. social service, Jewish Inst. of Religion, New York, since 1922. Mem. exec. com. Social Justice and Peace, Central Conf. Am. Rabbis; chmn. Jewish Inst. on Marriage and The Family since 1937; chmn. N.Y. State Conf. on Marriage and the Family, 1936-46; pres. National Conf. on Family Relations, 1944-46; mem. tech. adv. com. of Nat. Conf. on Family Life; mem. planning com. of White House Conf. on Children in a Democracy, 1939-40; mem. exec. com. Planned Parenthood Fedn. of Am.; chmn. exec. com. War Resistors League of Am., 1930-41; mem. N.Y. State Com. on Discrimination in Employment, 1941-44; mem. exec. com. Nat. Council for a Permanent Fair Employment Practice Com.; chmn. exec. com., Joint Com. on Unemployment, 1930-34; mem. exec. com. City Affairs Com. of N.Y., 1930-41. Home: 500 West End Av. Office: 30 W. 68th St., N.Y.C. 23. Died Mar. 19, 1955.

GOLDSTINE, Harry, business exec.; b. Chgo., June 5, 1892; s. Soloman and Rosa (Swartz) G.; student U. Ill. Coll. Pharmacy, 1914; m. Ruth South, Nov. 12, 1921. Store mgr. Walgreen Co., Chgo., 1914-20, dist. mgr. 1920-29, store operations and merchandising, 1929—, v.p., dir., 1930—. Mem. bd. dirs. Ill. Protestant Children's Home. Mem. Am. Legion (past comdr.; mem. past comdrs. club). Mem. Christian Science Ch. Mason (32°, Shriner). Clubs: Dorchester, Kiwanis, Executives. Home: 7136 Bennett Av. Office: 744 Bowen Av., Chgo. Died Aug. 1959.

GOLDTHWAIT, Nathan Edward, capitalist; b. Mendon, Mass., Dec. 29, 1872; s. Stephen and Polly L. (Wheelock) G.; ed. Worcester and Uxbridge acads., Mass.; A.B., Brown U., 1952, A.M.; m. Mary A. Thayer, Aug. 25, 1852. Tchr. Worcester Acad., 1852-53; prin. Uxbridge Acad., 1853-55; lumber mcht., La Crosse, Wis., 1855-59; pres. Wis. Female Coll., 1859-63; prof. mathematics, Des Moines (Ia.) Coll., 1873-86 (trustee, 1872-1902). Extensively engaged in real estate bus., 1868—; editor, propr. Boone County Republican, 1886-99, Boone News and Republican, ret. Lincoln Republican. Baptist. Mem. Ia. Acad. Scis., Delta Kappa Epsilon. Address: Boone, Ia. Died Feb. 1918.

GOLDTHWAITE, du Val R., corp. official; b. Montgomery, Ala., Aug. 23, 1893; s. Robert and Annie Paul (Nesbitt) G.; ed. Harvard, 1917; m. Mary Stringfellow, May 30, 1930. Began with Vacuum Oil Co., 1918-20; with Congoleum Co., 1920-25; with Dillon, Read & Co., 1925-31, partner, 1930-31; dir. Internat. Printing Ink Corp. (now Inter-Chem. Corp.), 1928—, exec. v.p., 1931-32, pres., 1932—; chmn. bd. Interchemical Corp., N.Y.C. Home: Englewood, N.J. Office: 67 W. 44th St., N.Y.C. 36. Died Apr. 26, 1954.

GOLLOMB, Joseph, (gŏl lŭm), author; b. St. Petersburg, Russia, Nov. 15, 1881; s. Julius and Rachel G.; came to U.S., 1891; B.A., Coll. City of New York, 1902; M.A., Columbia, 1908; m. Zoe Beckley, Nov. 14, 1914. Tchr., lectr. pub. schs. of N.Y., 1902-12; reporter Evening World. Evening Mail, Evening Post, 1912-14; dramatic critic Evening Mail, New York Call, The Nation, 1914-17; served on the staffs of scenario departments Vitagraph Company, Universal Film Company, 1914-16, Paramount Productions, Metro-Goldwyn-Mayer, Fox Films and others, 1933-34. Special writer for Evening Post, and went to Europe for paper, 1919. Mem. N.Y. Acad. Sci., Am. Soc. for Research in Psychosomatic Problems. Author: Songs for Courage (with Zoe Beckley), 1917; That Year at Lincoln High, 1918; Working Through at Lincoln High, 1921; The Girl in the Fog, 1923; Tuning in at Lincoln High, 1925. Translator Brunet's German Constitution, 1923; Master Man Hunters, 1926; The Portrait Invisible, 1927; The Subtle Trail, 1929; The Curtain of Storm, 1932; Unquiet, 1935; Armies of Spies, 1939; What's Democracy To You, 1940; Young Heroes of the War, 1943; Up at City High, 1945; Tiger at City High, 1946; Window on the World, 1947. Home: 214 E. 17th St., N.Y.C. 3. Died May 23, 1950.

GOLUB, Jacob Joshua (gō'lūb), physician, hospital administrator; born July 25, 1891; son of Joshua and Rebecca (Langer) G.; M.D., Boston University School of Medicine, 1915; married Helene Dankner, Mar. 8, 1925; children—Grace, Elsa, James Robert. Interne Mass. Memorial Hosp., 1915-16; physician in U.S. Pub. Health Service, 1918-20; med. and health commr. for Volhynia, Ukraine, of the Am. Joint Distbn. Com., 1921-23; head of med. service for Poland, 1923-24, now chmn. of its Health Committee for overseas health of war stricken areas. Assistant director Mount Sinai Hospital, New York, 1926-27; med. dir. Beth Moses Hosp., Brooklyn, 1924-25, 1928-29; med. dir., exec. v.p., Hosp. for Joint Diseases, N.Y., 1929-52; cons. in planning of the Rothschild-Hadassah Hosp. and Hebrew U. Med. Sch., Jerusalem, Palestine, and in the planning of many hospitals in U.S. Member Saratoga Springs Authority and Commn. of N.Y.; v.p., dir. Hosp. Council of N.Y.; mem. council on hosp. planning of Am. Hosp. Assn.; mem. N.Y. State Com. of Nat. Assn. for Practical Nurse Edn. Mem. N.Y. Acad. Medicine, N.Y. Med. Soc., A.M.A., Am. Hosp. Assn. (mem. council on hosp. planning), Am. Pub. Health Assn., N.Y. Hosp. Assn., Am. Assn. Hosp. Consultants (charter mem.). Contbr. to med. jours. Home: 1160 Park Av., New York 28. Office: 1919 Madison Av., N.Y.C. 35. Died Sept. 22, 1953.

GONCE, John Eugene, Jr. (gŏns), pediatrician; b. Elkton, Md., Oct. 17, 1893; s. John Eugene and Eliza (Bratton) G.; A.B., U. of Del., 1913; M.D., U. of Pa., 1918; m. Louise Allyn, Sept. 3, 1927; children—John Eugene III, Allyn. Interne U. Hosp., Phila., Pa., 1918-19; instr. clinical medicine, U. of Wis., 1919-25; interne Children's Hosp., Phila., Pa., 1922-23; asso. in pediatrics, U. of Wis., 1925-26, asst. prof. pediatrics, 1926-30, asso. prof. pediatrics, 1930-32, prof. pediatrics, since 1932; pediatrician to Wis. Gen. Hosp., since 1925. Fellow Am. Coll. Physicians; mem. Dane County Med. Soc. (pres., 1945-46), Wis. Med. Assn., A.M.A., Am. Acad. Pediatrics, Sigma Xi, Sigma Sigma, Kappa Alpha. Club: Blackhawk Country. Contbr. to med. jours. and Grulee and Eley's textbook of pediatrics. Home: 2221 Chamberlain Av., Madison 5. Office: 1300 University Av., Madison 6, Wis. Died Mar. 25, 1956.

GONZALEZ, Bienvenido M. (gŏn'thä'lĕs), biologist; b. Apalit, Pampanga, P.I., Mar. 22, 1893; s. Joaquin and Florencia (Sioco) G.; B.Agr., U. Philippines, 1913; M.S., U. Wis., 1916; D.Sc. in hygiene, Johns Hopkins, 1922; m. Concepcion Rafols, Jan. 1, 1917; children—Manuel Amado, Gonzalo Wilfrido, Eva Beatriz, Lilia Cristina, Bienvenida Maria.

Grad. asst. in animal husbandry, U. Philippines, 1914-16, instr., 1916-17, asst. prof., 1917-18, asso. prof., 1919-20, prof., 1920—, head dept., 1923-39, dean Coll. Agr., 1927-39; pres. U. Philippines, 1939-51, ret., regent, 1919-21, 39—; v.p., dir. Pambul, Inc.; dir, Pampanga Sugar Development Co. pres., 1951-53; chmn. bd. Review for Moving Pictures for the Philippines. Trustee Maquiling Sch. (founder 1924, pres. 1924-40). Fellow A.A.A.S.; mem. Nat. Research Council of Philippines (chmn.), Nat. Council Edn., Philippine Soc. Tech. Agriculturists, Los Baños Biol. Club, Philippines Soc. Advancement Research, U. Philippines Alumni Assn. (exec. bd.), Phi Kappa Phi. Editor: The Philippine Agriculturist, 1929-39. Home: 3667 Taft Av., Pasay, Rizal, P.I. Died Dec. 30, 1953; buried South Cemetery, Makati, Rizal, P.I.

GOOCH, Tom Carbry, editor; b. Bonham, Tex., Jan. 25, 1880; s. Harold and Mattie Revel (Taylor) Gooch; great grandson of Mrs. Mabel Gilbert, first white woman to come to Dallas; educated public schools and Art Inst., Chicago, 1 year; m. Lula Flateau, November 25, 1908; Began as reporter, Ft. Wayne (Ind.) News, 1900; with Dallas (Tex.) Times Herald since 1901, editor in chief since 1910; president The Times Herald Printing Co., Dallas. Chmn. bd. radio sta. KRLD, Inc. Dir. State Fair of Tex. Member Dallas Art Assn., Southwestern Medical Foundation, Texas Press Association, Texas Publishers Association, Amer. Newspaper Publishers Assn., Sons of Republic of Texas, Dallas Symphony Soc. Episcopalian. Mason (32°, K.C.C.H.). Clubs: Dallas Country, Brook Hollow Country, Little Sandy Hunting. Home: 3724 Armstrong Av., Dallas, Tex.; and Sandy Bottoms Farm, Hawkins (P.O.), Tex. Office: Herald Square, Dallas. Died June 13, 1952.

GOOD, Alice Campbell (Mrs. William H. Good), Dem. nat. committeewoman, N.Y.; b. Brooklyn; d. Felix and Mary (Martin) Campbell; ed. Brooklyn Heights Sem.; LL.D., St. John's U., Brooklyn, N.Y., 1937; m. William Howard Good, Nov. 20, 1901 (died Oct. 13, 1933); children—Alice Campbell (wife of Capt. Gerald Smith), Felix Campbell. Became member New York State Reconstruction Commn. (chmn. demobilization comm.), 1919, N.Y. State Roosevelt Memorial Com., 1926, Bd. of Higher Edn. of New York, 1928-37. Del. at large from N.Y. to Dem. nat. convs., 1924, 28, 32, 36, 40 and 44; mem. electoral college of N.Y. State, 1933—, temporary chmn. 1941 and 1945; Dem. nat. committeewoman for N.Y., 1936—. Awarded gold medal as outstanding citizen by Downtown Brooklyn Assn., 1945; recipient Papal decoration Pro Ecclesia et Pontifice, 1953. Mem. bd. dirs. Brooklyn chapter Am. Red Cross. Mem. Brooklyn Inst. Arts and Sciences (trustee). Club: Cosmopolitan. Home: 3 Pierrepont Place, Bklyn. Died Jan. 13, 1956.

GOOD, Charles Winfred, educator, research exec.; b. Saginaw, Mich., May 17, 1893; s. Charles Henry and Mary Winnifred (Farrar) G.; B.S., U. of Mich., 1918; m. Vera L. Tibbetts, Apr. 8, 1923; children—Martha Ann (Mrs. F. C. Vibrans), Phoebe J. (Mrs. D. L. Trezise), Charles Hansen. Instr., auto mechanics, U. of Mich., 1918, in mech. engring., 1918-25. asst. prof., 1925-33, asso. prof., 1933-43, prof. of mech. engring. since 1943, on leave as engring. cons. Am. Car & Foundry Co. in its Albuquerque, N.M. operations for AEC until 1953; asst. to dir., dept. of engring. research (changed to Engring. Research Inst., 1948), 1923-36, asst. dir., 1936-51; cons. mech. engr. since 1925; cons., indsl. research and development div., Office of Tech. Service, 1946-47. Mem. A.S.M.E. (life mem.; chmn. profl. divs. com.), Society Automotive Engineers, American Society Engineering Education, Engineering Society of Detroit, Gamma Alpha, Delta Alpha Epsilon, Tau Beta Pi. Clubs: University, Michigan Union (Ann Arbor). Author: Internal Combustion Engines (with Lay and Vincent), 1931. Contbr. articles to tech. publs. Home: 2307 Hill St., Ann Arbor, Mich. Died Sept. 6, 1956.

GOODALE, Stephen Lincoln, univ. prof.; b. Saco, Me., Aug. 31, 1875; s. Benjamin Nourse and Ella Adelaide Augusta (Scammon) G.; Ph.B., Colo. Coll., Colorado Springs, 1899, A.M., 1909, D.Sc., 1921; E.M., Colo. Sch. of Mines, Golden, 1904; studied Harvard Summer Sch., 1910; m. Nelle Priscilla Sater, May 22, 1906; children—Priscilla Harriet, Prudence Nourse, Stephen Lincoln. Spent summers, 1901-04, working in mines of Colo.; asst. in chemistry, Colorado Coll., 1901-02; at Camp Bird Mine, Ouray, Colo., 1904-06; assayer Annie Laurie Mine, Utah, summer, 1906; independent profl. work, Lander County, Nev., 1906-08; asst. supt. Bristol Consol. Mining & Smelting Co., nr. Pioche, Nev., 1908-09; head department of metallurgy, Sch. Mines, U. Pitts., 1909-39, prof. of metallurgy, 1939—, retired from active teaching 1945; profl. engr. in mining and metallurgy. Presbyterian. Served inf., U.S. Army, World War I. Mem. A.A.A.S., Am. Inst. Mining Engrs., Am. Electrochem. Soc., Engrs.' Soc. Western Pa., Am. Soc. for metals, Sigma Gamma Epsilon, Sigma Tau. Author: Chronology of Iron and Steel. Contbr. to scientific mags. Home: 1156 Murrayhill Av., Pitts. 17. Died Jan. 14, 1957.

GOODBAR, Joseph Ernest, educator, lawyer, economist; b. St. Louis, Mo., Jan. 31, 1890; s. Joseph Lee and Kate (De Pass) G.; A.B., U. of Ark., 1910; LL.B., magna cum laude, Boston U., 1930; LL.M., Harvard, 1931, S.J.D., 1933; married Octavia Walton. Clerk with Alfred Peats Co., Boston, Mass., 1910-12 and 1914-17; in mercantile business, Portland, Me., 1912-14; pres. Wall-Goodbar Co., Boston, 1917-26; admitted to Mass. bar, 1930, Ill., 1932, N.Y., 1937, Me., 1948; practiced law in Chgo., 1931-32; legal practice and research in money, banking and economics, Boston and N.Y. City, 1933-46; lecturer at Boston U. Sch. of Law; head dept. of bus. adminstrn. U. of Tampa since 1949; lectured in Berlin, Munich and Budapest, 1938, on money and banking; testified before House and Senate Coms. on banking measures, 1937, 1938, before Ways and Means Com. on taxation, 1942; spl. consultant, U.S. Dept. Commerce, 1942. Advisor Endicott College; counsel Made in America Foundation; director and vice president Phi Beta Kappa Associates, 1940-44. Director, Cavalcade of Maine Youth, 1946. Member American and Boston bar associations, Assn. of the Bar of the City of N.Y., Acad. of Political Science, A.A.A.S., American Economic Association, Phi Beta Kappa, Delta Theta Phi. Mason (32°, K.T., Shriner). Methodist. Clubs: Harvard (N.Y. and Boston); Torch (Tampa); Cosmos (Washington); Royal Automobile (London). Author: Managing the People's Money, 1935; A Creative Capitalism (with Lorenzo Bergeron) 1948. Contributor of articles to Boston U. Law Rev., Current History Mag., law revs. and other nat. publs. Address: 1501 Bayshore Blvd., Tampa, Fla.; also 146 Dartmouth St., P.O. Box 840, Portland, Me. Died July 21, 1953; Pine Grove Cemetery, Falmouth Foreside, Me.

GOODELL, Raymond Batchelder, lawyer; b. Salem, Massachusetts, July 30, 1886; s. George Zina and Esther Frances (Chase) G.; A.B. cum laude, Harvard, 1908, LL.B., 1911, student Sch. Bus. Adminstrn., 1911-12; m. Grace Alma Price, Sept. 12, 1918 (divorced); children—Jeanne Amory, Barbara Patricia (Mrs. Norman Flynn); m. 2d, Dorothy Marie McDonald, Jan. 17, 1932; children—Melisande Roberta, James McDonald. Admitted to Mass. bar, 191‸ N.Y., 1928; staff bur. commn. research, legal dept. Am. Tel.& Tel. Co., 1912-14; staff Price Waterhouse & Co., C.P.A.'s, N.Y.C., 1915-29, Sullivan & Cromwell, N.Y.C., 1929-34; practice law N.Y.C., 1934—; tax counsel Scandrett, Tuttle & Chalaire, N.Y.C., 1935-47, Coudert Bros., N.Y.C., 1939—; dir. C.P.A., N.Y., 1927. Mem. Am. Bar Assn., Am. Soc. Internat. Law, Bar Assn., N.Y.C., Am. Inst. Accountants, N.Y. Soc. C.P.A.'s, Essex Inst. Mass. Clubs: Harvard, Advt., City Midday (N.Y.C.); University (Washington). Home: Hevelyn Rd., Elmsford, N.Y. Office: 488 Madison Av., N.Y.C. 22. Died Oct. 2, 1958.

GOODENOUGH, Luman W(ebster) (good'ē-now), lawyer; b. Ludington, Mich., Jan. 1 1873; s. Daniel W. and Lodema (Olney) G.; student Albion (Mich.) Coll., 1892; B.L., U. Mich., 1896, LL.B., 1898; m. Eliza Wing Noble, Mar. 22, 1904; children—Elizabeth L. (Mrs. George A. Schemm), Eleanor (Mrs. Wm. John Spicer), Daniel W. Admitted to Mich. bar and began practice at Detroit, 1898, ret. 1940. Formerly dir. numerous indsl., comml., banking and real estate corps. and trust cos.; formerly trustee several ednl., civic and charitable instns.; one of original mems. Detroit Bd. of Commerce, Detroit Athletic Club, Detroit Community Fund, Boys' Club Detroit; former pres. bd. trustees Mich. Sch. Religion. First pres. Rotary Club, Detroit. Served as chmn. Mich. War Savings, dir. YMCA, chmn. YMCA war work campaign, mem. Liberty Loan Com. and local draft bd., counsel Am. Protective League; four minute man. Mem. Am., Mich. State, Detroit, N.Y.C. bar assns., Phi Delta Phi, Delta Tau Delta. Ind. Episcopalian. Home: Longacres, Farmington, Mich.; (winter) Winter Park, Fla. Address: care Daniel W. Goodenough, Penobscot Bldg., Detroit. Died Jan. 4, 1947.

GOODERHAM, Melvill Ross, ins. executive; born Toronto, Ont., Can., Jan. 10, 1877; s. George and Harriet (Dean) G.; student Model Sch., Toronto; Ridley Coll., St. Catherines, Ont., Warren Hill, Eng., Osgoode Hall, Toronto; m. Charlotte Wheeler Taylor, 1898. Read law with T. G. Blackstock; called to the bar of Ontario, 1900; created K.C., 1928; mem. firm of Gooderham Martin & Co., Toronto; formerly v.p., Mfrs. Life Ins. Co., pres., 1935—. Pvt. Queen's Own Rifles (Toronto), 1893-95; lt. 48th Highlanders. 1915; seconded to 74th bn., C.E.F., 1917, as major, trans. to arty., Eng., 1916; served in France with 40th Battery, 1917 to end of war. Mem. bd. govs., Ridley Coll., St. Catharines, Ont. Mem. St. George's Soc. Clubs: York, Albany, Toronto Hunt, Toronto Golf, Royal Canadian Yacht. Home: 8 Elm Av., Toronto. Office: 200 Bloor St., Toronto 5, Ont., Can. Died Nov. 24, 1951.

GOODKIND, Gilbert E(lliott), trade assn. exec.; b. New York, N.Y., Dec. 14, 1913; s. Samuel and Sarah (Sussman) G.; student Coll of City of N.Y., 1930-33; LL.B., N.Y. Univ., 1938; m. Mildred Wicksman, Apr. 16, 1939; 1 son, Robert W. Admitted to the New York bar, 1941; with Dept. of Investigation of City of New York, 1934-37; asst. to pres. of Borough of Manhattan, 1938-45; budget officer United Nations Relief and Rehabilitation Adminstrn. 1945-46; exec. sec. Am. Booksellers Assn., since 1946; U.S. rep. to U.N.E.S.C.O. Book Conf., Paris, 1949. Served with U.S. Army, 1943-45. Mem. Nat. Retail Adv. Com., U.S. Dept. of Commerce. Mem. Trade Assn. Execs. Home: 142 Harrow Lane, Manhasset, N.Y. Office: 31 Madison Av., N.Y.C. 10. Died Jan. 29, 1951; buried Ferncliffe, N.Y.

GOODMAN, Daniel Carson, author; b. Chgo., Aug. 24, 1883; s. Louis C. and Anna (Goodman) G.; M.D., Washington U., 1905; grad. work, Heidelberg U., Germany; diploma, U. Vienna, 1908; m. Winifred Spear, Oct. 19, 1935. Practiced at St. Louis, 1905-16; original research on cell division, 1914; v.p., exec. officer Internat. Films Corp. and Cosmopolitan Film Corp., 1922-24; produced Enemies of Women, Janice Meredith, Zander the Great, Never the Twain Shall Meet, etc. Mem. A.M.A., Authors' League of Am. Author: (novels) Unclothed, 1912; Hagar Revelly, 1913; Travail (serial), 1915; The Taker, 1918; Sad, Sad Lovers, 1928; Battle of the Sexes (photoplay), 1928; Kaleidoscope (novel, 2 vols.), 1935; Fan Dance at Cockcrow (psychol. novel), 1941; The Dead Come to Life (collection short stories), 1943; They Came to See Dr. Arkady (novel), 1943. Wrote and produced (movie plays) Has the World Gone Mad? What's Wrong?, The Daring Years, Week-End Husbands, 1921-22; Narrow Their Heaven, 1939. Co-Author: A Compend on Materia Medica, 1904; A Man Among Women (play), 1926; On to Washington (play), 1927. Also author of play, Roof Overhead, 1931; (play) Courtyard in the Reich, 1943; (play) According to Plan, 1948. Home: Flemington, N.J. Office: 10 Park Av., N.Y. C. Died May 16, 1957.

GOODMAN, Frank Bartlett, newspaper editor; b. Denver, Colo., Mar. 13, 1878; s. John Bartlett and Mary Anita (Gollaher) G.; grad. Hyde Park High Sch., Chicago, Ill., 1895; student U. of Notre Dame, 1895-96, U. of Denver, 1896-97; m. Irene Miller, Mar. 1897; children—Frank B. Jr. (dec.), Mary Anita (dec.), John Bartlett, III; m. 2d, Charlotte McNamara, Nov. 16, 1929. Market editor Denver Times, 1897-98, Denver Times and News, 1898-99; sports editor Rocky Mountain News, 1899-1901, night city editor, 1901-02; reporter San Diego Union, 1902-03, telegraph editor, 1903-05; with Evening Tribune (now San Diego Tribune-Sun), San Diego, Calif., 1905—, as telegraph editor, city editor, and editor, 1930—. Former chmn. Calif.-Nevada Associated Press. Served in 1st Colorado Infantry 2 years. Republican. Elk. Clubs: Cuyamaca (San Diego); life mem. Fellowship (Los Angeles); Automobile of Southern Calif.; former dir. Chamber of Commerce. Home: 4327 N. Talmadge Dr. Office: Tribune-Sun, San Diego, Cal. Retired 1948. Died Mar. 7, 1954; buried Glen Abbey Meml. Park, San Diego.

GOODMAN, Frank Croly, radio exec.; b. Bklyn., June 22, 1878; s. Thomas and Elizabeth (Mildenhall) G.; m. Cora H. Irwin, Nov. 1907, children—Wesley B., Frank Croly. Asst. sec. Wm. A. Sunday Evangelistic Assn. N.Y., 1917-20; exec. sec. Religious Work Dept. Greater N.Y. Fedn. Chs., 1920-23; exec. sec. religious programs under auspices Greater N.Y. Fedn. Chs. Sta. WEAF, 1923-25; producer religious programs Sta. WJZ, 1925; exec. sec. network religious programs under auspices City, County and State Councils Chs. in U.S., NBC, 1926—; exec. sec. religious programs under auspices Fed. Council Chs. Christ Am., 1929—; established Dept. Nat. Religious Radio, exclusively for network broadcasting under joint co-operation of constituent bodies of Fed. Council Chs., and in co-op. with Nat., Am., Mut. Broadcasting cos.; dir. local sta. religious programs for interdenominational ch. bodies, 1937; mem. bd. mgrs. Am. Bible Soc., 1944—; mem. 20 Year Club Radio Pioneers. Rep. Meth. Home: 1312 E. 35th St., Bklyn. 10. Office: 297 Fourth Av., N.Y.C. 10. Died July 11, 1958.*

GOODMAN, Jack Arthur, editor, author; b. Montreal, Can., Dec. 13, 1908; s. Arthur and Gladys (Levy) G.; student N.Y.U., 1926-27, Coll. City of N.Y., 1927-29; brought to U.S., 1910, naturalized, 1939; m. Agnes Creighton Rumsey, Apr. 22, 1937; children—John Arthur, Jill Rumsey. Advt. copywriter Green-Brodie, Inc., N.Y.C., 1929-31; account rep. Schwab & Beatty, Inc., 1931-35; advt. mgr. Simon & Schuster, Inc., N.Y.C., 1935-40, exec. editor 1940—, v.p., dir. 1946—. Mem. Zeta Beta Tau. Author: I Wish I'd Said That! (with Albert Rice), 1935; A Discussion of the Art of Repartee by Two Good Listeners, 1935; How To Do Practivally Anything, 1942; While You Were Gone, 1946. Editor: The Fireside Book of Dog Stories, 1943. Contbr. articles, fiction, mags. Home: 22 Bank St., N.Y.C. Office: 630 Fifth Av., N.Y.C. 20. Died July 22, 1957.

GOODMAN, Nathan Gerson, historian, journalist; b. Phila., Pa., Jan. 9, 1899; s. Louis Jacob and Bertha (Bamberger) G.; A.B., U. of Pa., 1920, A.M., 1922, Ph.D., 1924; research and travel in Europe, 1923, 25, 28; m. Julia Nusbaum, Dec. 25, 1924; 1 dau., Susan. Instr. in English history, U. of Pa., 1920-22, modern European history, 1922-23,

English constl. history, 1924; University scholar in history, 1923-24; research work in British archives, 1923; European travel, 1925, 1928. Contbr. hist. and lit. articles to newspapers and mags. since 1924, including sketches of noted Americans who flourished before 1900; formerly lit. editor Atlantic City Press; regular contbr. to newspapers; publishers' reader and editor; book reviewer for Philadelphia Enquirer. Mem. American Historical Soc., Hist. Soc. of Pa., Germantown History Soc., Authors League of America, Franklin Inst., Am. Civil Liberties Union, Am. Education Fellowship, Internat. Mark Twain Soc., Soc. Am. Historians. Author: Diplomatic Relations Between England and Spain (1597-1603), 1925; Benjamin Rush, Physician and Citizen (1746-1813), a Biography, 1934; Benjamin Franklin's Own Story, 1937; Famous Explorers, 1942; Famous Authors, 1943; Famous Generals and Admirals, 1944; Famous Pioneers, 1945 (all Young People); A Benjamin Franklin Reader, 1945. Compiler: One Hundred Books Chosen by Prominent Americans, 1931, and 1938, and various other reading lists. Editor: The Ingenious Dr. Franklin, 1931; The Autobiography of Benjamin Franklin and Selections from His Other Writings, 1932. Editor: Profile of Genius: Poor Richard Pamphlets (Franklin Inst.), 1938. Home: 301 W. School House Lane, Germantown, Phila. 44. Died Aug. 22, 1953.

GOODMAN, William M., army officer (ret.); b. Norfolk, Va., Sept. 5, 1892; s. Hayman and Fannie (Kaminsky) G.; B.S., Va. Mil. Inst., 1912.; grad. Command and Gen. Staff Sch., 1931, Army War Coll., 1936, Navy War Coll., 1937; m. Marjorie Whitaker, Sept. 8, 1923; 1 dau., Marjorie Frances. Commd. 2d lt. CAC, U.S. Army, 1916, and advanced through the grades to maj. gen., Feb. 21, 1944; served with AEF, France, 1918-19, with 40th Artillery Brigade (ry.) and at headquarters S.O.S.; served War Dept. Gen. Staff (supply div.) July 1937-Feb. 1942; comd. Antiaircraft Def., Los Angeles, Feb. 1942-July 1942; charge of Oversea Supply Div., N.Y. Port Embarkation, 1942-45, San Francisco Port Embarkation 1945-1946. Awarded D.S.M. Club, Army and Navy (Washington). Mason. Address: 1458 Hampton Rd., San Marino 9, Cal. Died Dec. 13, 1958; buried San Francisco Nat. Cemetery.

GOODRICH, Annie Warburton, nursing edn.; b. New Brunswick, N.J., Feb. 6, 1866; d. Samuel Griswold and Annie Williams (Butler) G.; ed. under governesses and in pvt. schs., U.S., Eng. and France; registered nurse, N.Y. Hosp., 1892; hon. Sc.D., Mount Holyoke Coll., S. Hadley, Mass., 1921; hon. A.M., Yale, 1923; hon. LL.D., Russell Sage Coll., Troy, N.Y., 1936. Supt. nursing N.Y. Post-Grad. Hosp, 1893-1900, St Luke's Hosp. 1900-02 N.Y. Hosp., 1902-07; gen. supt. Tng. Sch. for Nurses, Bellevue and Allied Hosps., 1907-10; insp. nurses tng. schs., N.Y. State Edn. Dept., 1910-14; asst. prof. nursing and health, Columbia, 1914-23; dir. nurses, Henry St. Visiting Nurse Service, 1917-23; dean of Yale U. Sch. of Nursing, prof. nursing edn., 1923-34, dean emeritus, 1934—. Pres. Assn. Collegiate Schs. of Nursing, 1934-36, hon. mem. 1937—. Dean of Army Sch. of Nursing, 1918-19. V.p. Florence Nightingale Internat. Found. Mem. Nat. League Nursing Edn., Am. Nurses Assn. (pres. 1916-18), Internat. Council of Nurses (hon. v.p.), Am. Assn. Univ. Women; pres. Am. Fed. Nurses, 1909. Awarded medal, Inst. Social Sciences, 1921; D.S.M. (U.S.), 1923; Medaille d'Honneur de l'Hygiene Publique (France), 1928. Protestant. Club: Town Hall. Contbr. to Am. Jour. Nursing, etc. Home: Colchester, Conn. Died Dec. 31, 1954.

GOODRICH, Chauncey William; b. Cleve., Nov. 17, 1864; s. William Henry and Mary (Prichard) G.; prep. edn., Hopkins Grammar Sch., New Haven, Conn.; B.A., Yale, 1886; postgrad. study, Yale and in Europe; grad. Union Theol. Sem., 1891; D.D., Bowdoin, 1915; m. Annie Blair Stephens, Nov. 27, 1894; children—Mary Prichard, Eleanor Bruce. Ordained ministry Presbyn. Ch., 1893; asst. minister Madison Sq. Presbyn. Ch., N.Y.C., 1891-94; successively pastor St. Cloud Ch., Orange, N.J., Bolton Av. Ch., Cleve., Am. Ch., Paris, France, Fifth Av. Ch., N.Y.C., First Parish, Congl. Ch., connected with Bowdoin Coll., until 1917, Am. Ch., Paris, 1917-23, ret. 1926. Am. rep. Central Bur. for Relief of Evang. Chs. in Europe, also sec. Commn. on Relation with Religious Bodies in Europe of the Federal Council of Chs., N.Y.C., 1923-26. Mem. Psi Upsilon, Phi Beta Kappa. Chevalier Legion of Honor (France). Republican. Conglist. Home: Brunswick, Me. Died Oct. 6, 1956; buried Pine Grove Cemetery, Brunswick, Me.

GOODRICH, David Marvin, chmn. bd. B. F. Goodrich Co.; b. Akron, O., June 22, 1876; s. Benjamin Franklin and Mary (Marvin) G.; prep. edn., Germany and France, 1886-88, St. Paul's Sch., Concord, N.H., 1888-94; A.B., Harvard, 1898; m. Ruth Pruyn, June 2, 1903; 1 dau., Anne Marvin; m. 2d, Beatrice Morgan Pruyn, Nov. 13, 1936. Chmn. bd. B. F. Goodrich Co., 1927-50; dir. Commercial Solvents Corp., Freeport Sulphur Co., Sulphur Export Corp. Served as lt., Roosevelt's Rough Riders, Spanish-Am. War; lt. col. U.S. Army, World War. Home: Mt. Kisco, N.Y. Office: 230 Park Av., N.Y. C. 17. Died May 17, 1950; buried Lakeview Cemetery, Jamestown, N.Y.

GOODRICH, Ernest Payson, cons. engr.; b. Decatur, Mich., May 7, 1874; s. Edward Payson and Mary Isabelle (Hall) G.; B.Pd., Michigan Normal College, 1898; B.S., in C.E., U. of Mich., 1898, C.E., 1901, hon. D.Eng., 1935; hon. M.Ed., Michigan Normal Coll., 1936; D.Eng., Polytechnic Institute, 1955; married to Mildred Louise Weed, May 18, 1899; 1 son, Ernest Weed (dec.). Commd. civ. engr. (lt. jr. grade), U.S. Navy, 1899; resigned, 1903; chief engr. Bush Terminal Co. and affiliated cos., New York, 1903-07; pvt. practice since 1907, designing harbors in many parts of world, surveying zoning and planning cities and regions, including new capital of Nanking Whampoa, port of Canton, China, Bogota, Colombia, S.A., Los Angeles, Portland, Ore., Newark, N.J., etc.; cons. eng. N.Y. City Govt., 1910-16; managing director N.Y. Bureau Municipal Research; N.Y. City dir. Mil. census and inventory, 1917-18; cons. Regional Plan of N.Y. and Environs, also Cincinnati, Norfolk, Newark, Springfield, and New Haven; deputy commissioner and chief engr. Dept. of Sanitation, N.Y. City, later commr., 1933-34; port engr. and subsequently consultant, Albany Port Commn., 1924-1933; prof. engring. economics, N.Y. Univ., 1934-35; mem. tech. adv. com. War Claims Bd. after World War I; mem. Price Adjustment Bd., U.S. Navy, 1943. Past pres. Inst. Traffic Engrs.; trustee Brooklyn Poly. Inst., Packer Collegiate Inst. Lecturer and writer on tech. subjects, Inventor of the progressive sysvem of electric light signal street traffic control; discoverer of laws of population distribution; made extended studies of the application of sunlight to building orientation and city planning. Fellow A.A.A.S.; mem. (life) Am. Soc. Civil Engrs. (past dir.; Collingswood prize, 1905), Am. Inst. Cons. Engrs. (pres. 1951), Soc. Terminal Engrs. (past dir.), Am. Inst. of Planning (past dir.), Phi Gamma Delta and Tau Beta Pi fraternities. Conglist. Clubs: Engineers, Univ. of Michigan Club, Rembrandt. Translator; Der Eisenbetonbau (Concrete Steel Construction), by Prof. Emil Mörsch, 1909. Home: 161 Henry St., Brooklyn 2, N.Y. Office: 115 Broadway, N.Y.C. 6. Died Oct. 7, 1955; buried Forest Hill Cemetery, Ann Arbor, Mich.

GOODRICH, James Clarence, educator; b. nr. Fayetteville, Tenn., Jan. 11, 1879; s. William Cary and Elizabeth (Dollins) G.; grad. Morgan Sch., Howell, Tenn., 1899; B.S., in Ed., U. Ala., 1930; m. Omagh Knight, Dec. 27, 1911. Prin. Lynchburg (Tenn.) Tng. Sch., 1900-04; tchr. Morgan Sch., Fayetteville, 1904-08, Butler Sch., Huntsville, Ala., 1908-13; prin. Goodrich Sch., Huntsville, 1913—; supt. City Schs., Shelbyville, Tenn., 1921-29. Sec. Columbia, S.C. YMCA, 1918-21; mem. State Exec. Com. YMCA; dir. Army YMCA, 1917-18. Democrat. Methodist. K.P. Address: Fayetteville, Tenn. Died Feb. 27, 1931.

GOODRICH, James Edward, lawyer, banker; b. Cameron, Mo., Sept. 20, 1871; s. Nathan Sheward and Annie Fleming (Frame) G.; A.B. cum laude, U. of Missouri, 1891, LL.B., 1893; m. Harper Riggins. Began practice of law at Cameron, 1893; cashier First Nat. Bank of Cameron, 1893-95; judge Circuit Court, Jackson County, Mo., 1907-13; gen. counsel Federal Reserve Bank of Kansas City, 1918-24, Commerce Trust Co. 1917-47; gen. counsel for receivers Kansas City Rys. Co., 1920-26. Mem. bd. curators U. of Mo., 1919-32, pres. bd., 1921-32. Mem. Am. Bankers Assn. (exec. com. trust div. 1931-34), S.A. R., Phi Beta Kappa, Phi Delta Phi, Sigma Nu. Republican. Episcopalian (vestryman St. Paul's Episcopal Ch., Kansas City). Mason, Odd Fellow. Clubs: University, Kansas City, Kansas City Country. Home: 5215 Sunset Drive. Office: Commerce Bldg., Kansas City, Mo. Died Oct. 22, 1952; buried Evergreen Cemetery, Cameron, Mo.

GOODRICH, Nathaniel Lewis, librarian; b. Concord, N.H., Feb. 9, 1880; s. Arthur Lewis and Mary Eastman (Bachelder) G.; A.B., Amherst, 1901; B.L. S., N.Y. State Library Sch., Albany, 1904; M.A., Dartmouth Coll., 1920; Litt.D., Amherst Coll., 1941; m. Alice Lyman, July 30, 1908. Reporter Utica Press, 1901-02; in charge of order section, New York State Library, 1904-07; librarian, W.Va. U., 1907-09, U. of Tex., 1909-11, Dartmouth Coll., 1912-50. Capt. Mil. Intelligence Div., Gen. Staff, July-Dec. 1918. Mem. A.L.A., Beta Theta Pi. Conglist. Clubs: Appalachian Mountain, Canadian Alpine, American Alpine; Ski Club of Gt. Britain. Retired. Home: Hanover, N.H. Died Apr. 30, 1957.

GOODRICH, (John) Wallace, musician; b. Newton, Mass., May 27, 1871; s. John B. and Anna L. (Woodward) G.; ed. Newton High Sch., 1888; attended Royal Acad. of Music, Munich, 1894-95; student in Paris and Leipzig, 1895-97; Mus. Doc., Northwestern U., 1931; m. Madeleine Boardman, Apr. 20, 1904; children—John Wallace, Madeleine B. (deceased). Member faculty since 1897, dean, 1907-30, director, 1931-42, director emeritus since 1942, New England Conservatory of Music; organist, Trinity Church, Boston, 1902-09; founded, 1901, conducted, 1901-07, Choral Art Society of Boston; choral conductor Worcester County Musical Assn., 1902-07; organist at concerts of Boston Symphony Orchestra, 1897-1909; condr. Cecilia Soc. of Boston, 1907-10; condr. Boston Opera Co., 1909-12. Sec. Joint Commn. on Ch. Music, P.E. Ch., 1919-48; trustee Paderewski, Frank Huntington Beebe funds. Fellow American Acad. Arts and Sciences, Chevalier Légion d'Honneur (France). Clubs: Somerset, Tavern, Essex County. Home: Manchester, Mass. Address: N.E. Conservatory of Music, Boston. Died June 6, 1952; buried Manchester, Mass.

GOODRIDGE, Malcolm, physician; b. Flushing, N.Y., Feb. 28, 1873; s. Edwin Alonzo and Anna Margaret (Field) G.; A.B., Princeton, 1894; M.D., Coll. Physicians and Surgeons (Columbia), 1898; m. 2d, Elizabeth C. Stone, Aug. 11, 1930; children of 1st marriage—Malcolm, Edwin Tyson. Practiced at N.Y.C. since 1899; former prof. clin. medicine, Cornell U., Med. Coll.; cons. physician New York Hosp. (hon. mem. bd. govs.), Bellevue Hospital, Neurological Institute (New York); Mercy Hosp. (Hempstead). Trustee Home for Old Men and Aged Couples, New York. Fellow A.M.A., N.Y. Acad. Med. (hon.; p. pres.; chairman committee on med. and the changing order); member Nu Sigma Nu. Republican. Clubs: University, Century, Grolier. Contributor chapter on The Treatment of Arteriosclerosis in George Blumer edition of Billings-Forchheimer's Therapeusis of Internal Diseases; chapter on Diseases of the Arteries, in a Textbook of Medicine by Russell L. Cecil, M.D.; contbr. chapter "General Principles Involved in Treatment of Infectious Diseases," in Therapeutics of Internal Diseases by George Blumer. Home: 333 E. 57th St., N.Y.C. 22; also The Ugly Duckling, Woodstock, Vt. Died July 16, 1956; buried Woodstock, Vt.

GOODWILLIE, David Herrick, v.p. Libbey-Owens-Ford Glass Co.; b. Oak Park, Ill., Jan. 15, 1887; s. David Lincoln and Rose (Herrick) G.; M.E., Cornell U., 1908; m. Elsie Harriet Byrant, Jan. 23, 1912; children—David Bryant, John Herrick, Robert Bryant. Engr. Am. Steel & Wire Co., 1908-09; supt. filtration plant, Toledo, O., 1910-11; supt. water works, Toledo, 1912-13; cons. engr., Toledo, 1914-15; dir. of pub. service, Toledo, 1916-20; engr. and mgr. Ford Plate Glass Co., Toledo, 1920-30; exec. v.p. Libbey-Owens-Ford Glass Co., Toledo, since 1931; v.p. Canadian Libbey-Owens-Ford Glass Co.; pres. Am. Bicheroux Co. President Toledo Board of Education, 1930-33; mem. City Council of Toledo, 1937-38. Mem. Delta Phi. Clubs: Toledo, Toledo Country; Duquesne (Pittsburgh); Grosse Pointe Yacht, Recess (Detroit). Home: 2428 Scottwood Av. Office: Libbey-Owens-Ford Glass Co., Toledo. Died Oct. 17, 1952.

GOODWIN, Charles Archibald, lawyer; b. Hartford, Conn., Nov. 18, 1876; s. Francis and Mary Alsop (Jackson) G.; A.B., Yale University, 1898; LL.B., Harvard University, 1901; LL.D., Trinity College, 1948; married Ruth Cheney, June 29, 1912; children—Charles, Dorothy Cheney, Jonathan, Nancy, Benjamin Cheney. In practice of law at Hartford, 1902—; mem. Bennett & Goodwin, 1902-19, Shipman & Goodwin, 1919—; pres. State Savings Bank; dir. Phoenix State Bank & Trust Co. (now Conn. Bank & Trust Company); director, and member of finance com. Aetna Ins. Co., Conn. Gen. Life Ins. Co., Holyoke Water Power Co. (v.p.); dir. Church Life Ins. Co. Served as chmn. Com. on Military Census, Conn., 1917; mem. State Council of Defense, Conn., 1917-18; mgr. supply div. Emergency Fleet Corp., 1918-19. Chmn. Metropolitan Dist. Commn. of Hartford Co., 1929-48. Pres. Wadsworth Athenaeum; dir. Conn. Humane Soc. Chmn. distribution com. Hartford Foundation for Public Giving. Republican. Episcopalian; trustee Ch. Pension Fund; chancellor Christ Ch. Cathedral. Clubs: Hartford, Dauntless, Yale. Home: 84 Scarborough St. Office: 15 Lewis St., Hartford, Conn. Died Oct. 7, 1954.

GOODWIN, Clarence Norton, judge, lawyer; b. Penn Yan, N.Y.; s. R. La Barre and Belle (Norton) G.; A.B., Syracuse, LL.D., 1928; LL.B., Harvard; m. Augusta MacDonald, Nov. 11, 1912; children—MacDonald, Norton. Admitted to Ill. bar, 1897. Asst. corp. counsel, Chicago, 1899-1903; spl. counsel Chicago Bd. Edn., 1906-11; traction counsel to mayor of Chicago, 1907; judge Superior Ct., Cook Co., Ill., 1911-15; justice Ill. Appellate Ct., 1915-17; resumed law practice, Dec. 1917; spl. asst. to atty. gen. of U.S., 1918-21, in litigation, U.S. Circuit and Supreme courts which established navigability of Des Plaines River and permitted completion of Lakes to Gulf waterway; special assistant atty. gen. assigned to Bridges deportation proceedings, 1941-42; mem. firm Goodwin, Rosenbaum, Meacham & White. Chairman Nat. Conference on Legal Edn., Washington, February 22-24, 1922; chairman Conference of Bar Assn. Dels., 1921-22; del. to Democratic Nat. Conv., 1932; presidential elector, 1933. Mem. Am. and Chicago bar assns., Am. Law Inst. (charter mem.), Am. Jud. Soc. (chmn. bd. 1929-37), Harvard Law Soc. of Chicago (pres. 1928-30), Harvard Law Sch. Assn., Assn. Bar City of N.Y., Phi Beta Kappa, Delta Upsilon, Psi Eta (Harvard), Phi Alpha Delta, S.R. Democrat. Presbyn. Mason. Clubs: University, Law (Chicago); Harvard (N.Y.). Home: Sherra-moor, Damascus, Md. Office: 824 Connecticut Av. N.W., Washington. Died Sept. 21, 1956.

GOODWIN, Frank Judson, clergyman; b. Rye, N. Y., Mar. 19, 1862; s. Charles Trafton and Emily Gertrude (Wyckoff) G.; grad. Poly. Inst., Bklyn., 1879; B.A., Am. Inst., 1884; grad., Union Theol. Sem., 1888; D.D., Amherst, 1913; m. Grace Hayward Duffield, Nov. 11, 1891. Ordained Congl. ministry, 1888; pastor Glen Ridge, N.J., 1888-99, 1st Ch., Pawtucket, R.I., 1899-1910, Mt. Pleasant Ch., Washington, 1910-12. Moderator N.J. Conf. Congl. Chs., 1911—; dir. Congl. Bd. Ministerial Relief. Mem. Am. Bd. Congl. Fgn. Missions, Alpha Delta Phi (Amherst). Club: Cosmos (Washington). Author: A Harmony of the Life of St. Paul, 1895. Address: Westfield, N.J. Died Apr. 3, 1953.

GOODWIN, Harry Manley, physicist, educator; b. Boston, Apr. 18, 1870; s. Richard D. and Sarah (Clisby) G.; S.B., Mass. Inst. Tech., 1890; student Harvard Grad. Sch., 1890, 1891; Ph.D., U. Leipzig, 1893; U. Berlin, 1894; m. Mary B. Linder, Apr. 16, 1906; 1 son, Richard Hale. Asst. in physics, Mass. Inst. Tech., 1890-92, instr., 1892-97, asst. prof., 1897-1903, asso. prof. physics, 1903-06, prof. physics and electrochemistry in charge dept. of electrochemistry, 1906-34, dean of Graduate School 1932-40, prof. emeritus, 1940—. Fellow Am. Acad. Arts and Sciences, Washington Acad. Sciences, A.A.A.S., Am. Physical Soc.; mem. Am. Astron. Soc., Sigma Xi. Clubs: Harvard Club of Boston, Harvard Travellers, The Country Club. Author: Physical Laboratory Manuals; The Precision of Measurements and Graphical Methods. Contbr. of papers on physics and electrochemistry to scientific jours. Home: 424 Walnut St., Brookline, Mass. Died June 26, 1949.

GOODWIN, Philip Lippincott, architect; b. New York, N.Y., Mar. 14, 1885; s. James Junius and Josephine Sarah (Lippincott) G.; grad. Groton (Mass.) Sch., 1903; B.A., Yale, 1907; studied architecture Columbia, 1909-12, Paris, France, 1912-14; unmarried. Draftsman for Delano & Aldrich, architects, N.Y. City, 1914-16; partner Goodwin, Bullard & Woolsey, 1916-21; practiced alone, 1921-54, ret.; trustee J. J. Goodwin Estate; designed houses for N. B. Judah, Lake Forest, Ill.; H. Phipps, Fla.; Ralph Pulitzer, Jr., Long Island; R. D. Cutler, also Essex Bldg., Hartford, Conn.; 400 E. 57th St., N.Y. City, Christ Church Parish House, Hartford, Conn., Museum of Modern Art, N.Y. City, Yale U. Art Gallery, 1947. Served as 1st Lieut., Inf. A.E.F., World War I; member International section, Am. Com. to Negotiate Peace, Budapest, Hungary, 1919. Trustee of the Museum Modern Art, Fellow Am. Inst. Architects; mem. Archtl. League. Hon. corr. mem. Brazilian and Mexican Insts. Clubs: Knickerbocker, University, Yale, Century (N.Y.C.). Author: (books) French Provincial Architecture (with H. O. Milliken), 1925; Rooftrees, 1933; Brazil Builds, 1943. Home: 2 E. 70th St., N.Y.C. 21. Office: 445 Park Av., N.Y. C. 22. Died Feb. 12, 1958.

GOODWIN, Richard Vanderburgh, insurance exec.; b. New York, N.Y., Nov. 20, 1895; s. Eben W. and Mary E. (Vanderburgh) G.; student Albany (N.Y.) Mil. Acad., 1905-08; student Univ. of Washington, 1912, Columbia, 1914; m. Martha E. Chapman, June 22, 1929; children—Elizabeth Goodwin (Mrs. Lewis T. Bennett), Richard V. Began career as underwriter, Norwich Union Fire Ins. Co., New York, 1913-14; vice pres., Fireman's Fund Indemnity Co., New York, since 1934, vice pres. Western National Indemnity Co., New York since 1943; vice pres. and dir. New York Bd. of Trade since 1944. Served Mexican border, 1916; served with U.S. Army as capt. inf., World War I. Dir. Greater New York Safety Council, Ins. Fed. of New York, Ins. Soc. of New York, (pres., dir.), Assn. Casualty and Surety Cos. (past pres.), Insurance Inst. of N.Y. (vice pres. and director), New England Soc. Mem. Insurance Inst. of Am. (v.p., dir.), State Ins. Comm., State of New York, Grand Jury Assn. (dir.), Am. Female Guardian Soc. (mem. bd. councillors), U.S. Chamber of Commerce (nat. councillor), Am. Legion, S.A.R. (past pres. Empire state soc., past vice pres. gen., nat. soc.). Presbyn. (elder). Mason (P. M.). Clubs: Union League, Nat. Rep., Bankers, Drug and Chem., Casualty and Surety (past pres.), Shinnecock Hills Golf. Author and lecturer throughout country on patriotic, religious and ins. subjects since 1924. Home: 136 E. 64th St. N.Y. City. Office: 116 John St., N.Y.C. 7. Died Apr. 1, 1952.

GOODWIN, Wilder, lawyer, author; b. N.Y.C., Jan. 14, 1887; s. Almon and Maud (Wilder) G.; A.B., cum laude, Harvard, 1907; U. of Berlin; Columbia U. Law Sch.; m. Elizabeth Griffin, 1919; 1 dau., Jacqueline. Admitted to N.Y. bar, and since practiced in N.Y.C.; mem. Reynolds, Goodwin & Flack. Beck prize, in Real Property Law, Columbia 1909. On Mexican border duty, Squadron A, New York Cav., June-Dec. 1916; commd. capt. Cav. U.S.R., Oct., 1916; with 78th Div. in Flanders and in St. Mihiel and Argonne-Meuse offensives; severly wounded and twice cited for bravery in action at Grand Pré, France, 1918. Awarded decorations of Silver Star and the Purple Heart. Mem. Assn. Bar City of New York. Republican. Clubs: Harvard, Century. Author: The Up Grade (novel), 1926. Wrote Daring the Danger Zone (serial in Argosy Mag., 1916-17, under pen name Norcross Forbes); also various mag. articles. Home: 135½ E. 62 St. Office: 36 W. 44th St., N.Y.C. Died Nov. 1955.

GOODWIN, Willard T(erry), transportation exec.; b. Newburyport, Mass., Mar. 2, 1893; s. Ralph Cowles and Mary Louise (Jenkins) G.; Ph.B., U. Chgo., 1915; m. Lulu Bridgeman, Apr. 25, 1920; 1 dau., Martha Louise (Mrs. Allan Putnam). Joined Am. Pres. Lines, 1915, v.p. Far Eastern div., 1948—. Mng. dir. India, Ceylon, Burma, War Shipping Adminstrn., 1942-45. Elk. Home: 540 State St., Oswego, Ore. Office: American Pres. Lines, Manila, P.I. Died Aug. 7, 1953; buried Riverview Cemetery, Portland, Ore.

GOODYKOONTZ, Colin Brummitt, educator; born Atlanta, Ind., Dec. 14, 1885; s. Marion Putnam and Jeannie (Brummitt) G.; A.B., U. of Colo., 1912; Litt.M., U. of Calif., 1914; Ph.D., Harvard, 1921; m. Susan Blakey, Dec. 29, 1921; children—Mary Lois (dec.), Anna (Mrs. William A. Edmonds). Tutor history, government and economics, Harvard, 1916, Austin teaching fellow in history, 1917-18; instr. Bowdoin Coll., 1918-19, Yale, 1919-20; asst. prof. of history, U. of Colo., 1921-22, asso. prof., 1922-24, prof., 1924-54, professor emeritus, 1954—, acting dean college of arts and sciences, 1928-29; member editorial board Mississippi Valley Hist. Review, 1950-53. Recipient Stearns award, University of Colorado, 1953. Mem. Am. (pres. Pacific Coast br. 1953), Miss. Valley hist. assns., Agricultural History Society, Colorado-Wyoming Social Science Association (pres. 1938), Phi Beta Kappa, Delta Sigma Rho and Phi Alpha Theta. Congregationalist. Author: Home Missions on the American Frontier, 1939; First Congregational Church of Boulder, all Historical Sketch, 1939. Editor: (with James F. Willard) Experiments in Colorado Colonization, 1926, The Trans-Mississippi West, 1930; Papers of Edward P. Costigan relating to the Progressive Movement in Colorado, 1941. Home: 1064 10th St., Boulder, Colo. Died Jan. 6, 1958; buried Green Mountain Cemetery.

GORDON, Armistead Churchill, Jr., educator; b. Staunton, Va., July 9, 1897; s. Armistead Churchill and Maria Breckinridge (Catlett) G.; A.B., Coll. of William and Mary, 1916; A.M., U. of Va., 1918, Ph.D., 1921; m. Cornelia Daniel Waddell, Aug. 29, 1922; 1 dau., Ann Waddell (Mrs. Richard Henry Webster). High sch. teacher, Staunton, 1916-17; instr. English, U. of Va., 1919-22, asst. prof., 1922-28, asso. prof., 1928-40, prof. English, 1940—. Served as pvt., Chem. Warfare Service, U.S. Army, 1918-19; lt. U.S.N.R., 1942-44; lt. comdr., U.S.N.R., 1944-46; cons. Research and Development Bd., Nat. Mil. Establishment, Dec. 1950-Feb. 1951. Mem. Pi Kappa Alpha, Phi Beta Kappa. Jeffersonian Democrat. Episcopalian. Author: Virginian Writers of Fugitive Verse, 1924. Asst. editor Southern Life and Literature, Vols. 1-3, 1941-42. Contbr. to Nat. Cyclopedia of American Biography, Dictionary of American Biography, and various jours. and revs. Home: 1844 Westview Rd., Charlottesville, Va. Died May 12, 1953; buried U. Va.

GORDON, Frederic Sutterle, business exec.; born Brooklyn, July 2, 1887; s. George Gaynor and Mary Louise (Palmer) G.; student pub. schs. N.Y. City; m. Winifred Clara Martin, Oct. 9, 1915; children—Norma Palmer, Frederic Sutterle, George Stennet. Started as errand boy Colgate Hoyt Co., members N.Y. Stock Exchange, N.Y. City, 1901, partner since 1919; v.p. and dir. Internat. Delavaud Mfg. Co., Centrifugal Pipe Corp., Jersey City, N.J., since 1923; 1st v.p., dir. and mem. exec. com. U.S. Pipe & Foundry Co.; dir. Sloss Sheffield Steel & Iron Co. Vice-pres., trustee N.Y. Museum Science and Industry. Republican. Episcopalian. Clubs: Racquet (Phila.); Lawyers (N.Y. City); Riverton (N.J.) Country. Home: Edgewater Park, N.J. Office: 14 Wall St., N.Y. City. Died Aug. 9, 1951; buried Evergreen Cemetery, Elizabeth, N.J.

GORDON, George Anderson, diplomatic service; b. Huntsville, Ala., Nov. 19, 1885; s. Percy and Nancy Reed (French) G.; A.B., Harvard, 1906; LL.B., Columbia, 1912; m. Alice Vandergrift, July 7, 1930; 1 dau., Audrey. Practice of law with Murray, Prentice & Howland, N.Y.C., 1912-16. Served on Mexican Border, 1916; overseas with AEF, 1st lt. cav., later capt. arty., 1917-19; with Am. Commn. to Negotiate Peace, Paris, 1919; sec. Am. Embassy, Paris, 1920-23; assigned to Dept. State, 1923-25; 1st sec. Am. Legation, Budapest, 1925-27; tech. asst. to Am. del. to Prep. Commn. for Disarmament Conf., Geneva, 1st sec. Am. Embassy, Paris, adv. to Am. del. to Conf. for Limitation of Naval Armament, Geneva (all 1927); tech. expert Internat. Conf. Treatment of Foreigners, Paris, 1929; adv. London Naval Conf., 1930; counselor of embassy, Paris, 1930; counselor of embassy, Berlin, 1930; adv. Conf. of Ministers for Moratorium on Intergovernmental Debts, London, 1931; charge Am. Embassy at Rio de Janeiro, 1934-35; E.E. and M.P. to Haiti, 1935; The Netherlands, 1937; assigned State Dept. for emergency duty, 1940; ret., 1945. Mem. S.R. Clubs: Union, Brook (N.Y.C.); Travellers (Paris). Home: Oceanic Cottage, Palm Beach, Fla.; also 52 E. 69th St., N.Y.C. Died May 11, 1959.

GORDON, Gurdon Wright, lawyer; b. Sheffield, Mass., Nov. 26, 1871; s. Nelson Eliada and Caroline Augusta (Wright) G.; A.B., Williams Coll., 1897; student George Washington U., 1898; LL.B., Boston U., 1900; m. Ellen Beekman Walsh, Nov. 3, 1903 (died Feb. 1937); children—Gurdon Wright, Clyde Beekman; m. 2d Ethel Sugden Edwards, Mar. 24, 1938. Admitted to Mass. bar, 1900; tchr., Southington, Conn., 1891-92, Ashley Falls, Mass., 1892-1903, Sedgwick Inst., 1897-98; tchr. mathematics Wayland Coll., 1898-99; with U.S. Census, 1900-02; tchr. constl. law and legal ethics Springfield br. law sch. Northeastern U., 1922-35; dir. Monarch Life Ins. Co. (formerly Masonic Mut. Accident Co.), 1915—, now v.p., gen. counsel and dir.; mem. Gordon, Doherty, Buckley & Godfrey; dir. Springfield Fire & Marine Insurance Company, New England Insurance Company. Chairman of the Springfield Board Health, 1905-12; mem. Mass. Ho. of Reps. 1912, Mass. Senate, 1913-16; presidential elector for Mass. Rep. party, 1916; mem. spl. commn. investigating problems of st. rys. of Commonwealth, 1917; apptd. U.S. commr., Springfield, 1923; alternate del.-at-large Rep. Nat. Conv., 1920, dist. del., 1928; apptd. spl. judge of probate and insolvency Hampden Co., 1929. Mem. Am., Mass. State, Hampden County bar assns., Gargoyle, Phi Gamma Delta, Phi Delta Phi. Conglist. Mason. Home: 763 North St., Suffield, Conn. Office: 365 State St.; also 31 Elm St., Springfield, Mass. Died Feb. 9, 1959; buried Oak Grove Cemetery, Springfield.

GORDON, Irwin Leslie, journalist, author, publicity manager; b. Lowell, Massachusetts, October 24, 1888; s. Reverend John (D.D.) and Caroline A. (Irwin) G.; special course Temple University. Joined editorial staff Philadelphia Public Ledger, 1909; an editor Evening Public Ledger from its foundation, 1914 to 1921; was head Department of Journalism, Temple University; publicity manager of Reading R.R., editor Reading Railroad magazine. Enlisted as chief petty officer U.S.N.R.F., Dec. 13, 1917; commd. ensign, Apr. 20, 1918. Mem. Exec. Advisory Pub. Relations Com. Assn. of Am. Railroads, Washington, D.C. Mem. exec. com. Associated Railroads of Pa. Fellow Royal Geographical Soc. (London). Republican. Author: The Log of the Ark (with A. J. Frueh), 1915; What Allah Wills, 1917. Home: Bywood, Pa. Office: Reading Terminal, Phila. Died July 21, 1954.

GORDON, James Marcus, educator; b. Sheridan, Ark., June 27, 1875; s. James Armenius and Florence Elizabeth (Wallace) G.; student Baylor U., Waco, Tex., 1899, U. of Tex., 1901, U. of Chicago, 1902; A.B., Trinity Univ., Tex., 1903, LL.D., 1919; A.M., U. Chgo., 1908; grad. student Coll. Adminstrn., Columbia, 1924-25, also summers 1924, 25; m. Alice Land, Dec. 20, 1896; children—James Maurice, Wilson Harold, Gerald Grayson, Lynn Gray, Betty Alice. Teacher rural schs., Tex., 5 yrs.; connected with Trinity U., 1903-16, dean, 1908-16; pres. East Central State Normal Sch., Ada, Okla., 1916-20; pres. U. Tulsa, 1920-24; dean div. of Arts and Sciences, Texas Tech. Coll. also dir. summer sessions, 1925-45, dean emeritus, 1945—, also dean of men to 1937. Mem. Standards Com., Assn. of Tex. Colls., 15 years, pres. 1935-36. Mem. N.E.A. (life), Tex. State Teachers' Assn., Phi Delta Kappa. Active in Presbyn. Church; rep. at Presbyteries, Synods, and General Assemblies; moderator of El Paso Presbytery; Moderator, Synod of Texas, U.S., 1940. Rotarian. Democrat. Mason (32°, K.T.). Home: 2023 17th St., Lubbock, Tex. Died May 14, 1951.*

GORDON, John, clergyman; b. Gray County, Can., Feb. 5, 1878; s. Robert and Margaret (Davidson) G.; brought to U.S., 1889; prep. edn., high sch. and normal sch., Angola, Ind.; student Butler Coll., Indianapolis, 1899; B.D., Chicago Theol. Sem., 1905, D.D., 1919; D.D., Rockford Coll., 1937; m. Leona B. Brown, Aug. 5, 1907; children— Lea B., Elizabeth M. Ordained Congl. ministry, 1903; pastor Grand Rapids, Mich., 1903-07, Ravenswood, Chicago, 1907-12, 2d Ch., Rockford, Ill., since 1912 (over 1500 members); elected pastor for life, 2d Ch., Rockford, 1933. With Y.M.C.A., on transport between U.S. and France, World War; sent to England by Carnegie Commn. in interest of internat. friendship, 1919; chaplain on trip around the world, 1923, and 2 trips to North Cape in same capacity; second cruise around world, investigating missionary work of Congl. Ch., 1931. Lecturer on pastoral theology, Chicago Theol. Sem., 1926. Spent summer of 1934 in Russia and Germany, studying conditions and later giving lectures on that subject; spent spring of 1938 in Palestine, studying situation of the Jew and Arab. Republican. Mason, K.P., Elk. Rotarian. Home: Faust Hotel, Rockford, Ill. Died Jan. 26, 1956; buried Willwood Cemetery, Rockford, Ill.

GORDON, Robert, clergyman; b. Scotland, May 21, 1875; s. James and Jane (Hargie) G.; A.B., Kalamazoo (Michigan) College, 1907; studied University of Chicago, 1908, Divinity School, same university, 1909; winner of state-wide prohibition oratorical contest, 1900, and of inter-collegiate oratorical contest, 1905; m. Edith May Thoms, October 24, 1907; children—James Deane, Margaret May, Frank Craig, Robert Grenfell, Edith Belle, Mary Louise, Charles Thoms,

George Gregg, Helen Jane, Ruth Jeanette. Ordained Baptist ministry, 1906; pastor First Church, Milwaukee, 1907-12, First Ch., Topeka, Kan., 1912-19; Wis. state dir. city surveys for Interch. World Movement, 1919-20; pastor First Ch., Fond du Lac, Wis., 192?-30; editor The Baptist, 1930-33; pastor First Church, Stevens Point, Wis., 1933-36, First Church, Kenosha, Wisconsin, 1936-48, retired as pastor emeritus. Young Mens Christian Assn. speaker at mil. camps, 1918; with A.E.F. part of 1919. Mem. bd. mgrs. Wis. Bapt. State Conv.; trustee Wayland Acad. Mason (32°). Club: Lions. Lecturer before clubs and for World Alliance for International Friendship Through the Churches. Home: Washington Island, Wis. Died June 24, 1951; buried Washington Island, Wis.

GORDON, Thomas Sylvy, congressman; b. Chicago, Ill., Dec. 17, 1893; ed. parochial schools, Chicago; grad. St. Stanislaus Coll., Chicago, 1912; m. Celia Balcer; children—Phil, Thomas, Romona, Natalie. Began in banking business; became clerk in Polish Pub. Co. (Polish Daily News) and advanced to cashier and office mgr.; apptd. commr. Chicago West Side Parks, 1933, commr. Public Vehicle Licenses, 1936; treas. City of Chgo., 1939-42. Mem. 78th-84th Congresses, 8th Ill. Dist. Democrat. Del. to Dem. Nat. Conv., Phila., 1936. Mem. Polish Roman Cath. Union, Polish Nat. Alliance, Polish Alma Mater, K.C. Home: Chgo. Died Jan. 22, 1959.

GORE, Claude, mfr. cotton goods; b. Wilmington, N.C., July 19, 1878; s. Daniel Lenox and Elizabeth Rosalie (Lennon) G.; B.A., Wake Forest (N. C.) Coll., 1899; m. Anne Bruce Brewer, July 2, 1902; children—Claude (dec.), John William, Elizabeth Rosalie (Mrs. W. L. Parsons, Jr.), Mrs. Minor T. Hinson, Bruce Brewer (Mrs. E. R. Tull), Daniel Lenox. Vice pres., sec., treas., Great Falls Mfg. Co., 1902, pres., treas., 1924; treas. Marlboro Cotton Mills (McColl, S.C.), Raeford (N.C.) Cotton Mills Co.; pres. Bank of Rockingham, 1910-16; v.p. D. L. Gore Co., Wilmington, N.C. Mem. Country Bankers Assn. (pres. 1912). Pres. bd. trustees Wake Forest Coll., 1933-37. Baptist. Home: Rockingham, N.C. Died July 30, 1944; buried Eastside Cemetery, Rockingham.

GORMAN, Herbert Sherman, author; b. Springfield, Mass., Jan. 1, 1893; s. Thomas Jerome and Mary (Longway) G.; ed. Tech. High Sch., Springfield; m. Jean Wright, 1921; m. 2d, Claire O. Crawford, 1932. Began as reporter Springfield Republican, 1915; with Springfield Union, 1916-18, New York (N.Y.) Sun, 1918-21, New York Evening Post, 1921-23, New York Times, 1923-27, New York Herald-Tribune, 1927-28; extension lecturer, New York University, 1926-29. Author: The Fool of Love, 1920; (verse) The Barcarole of James Smith, 1922; The Procession of Masks, 1923; (with Jean Wright Gorman) The Peterborough Anthology, 1923; James Joyce—His First Forty Years, 1924; Gold by Gold, 1925; The Two Virginities, 1926; A Victorian American—Henry Wadsworth Longfellow, 1926; Notations for a Chimaera, 1926; Hawthorne—A Study in Solitude, 1927; The Place Called Dagon, 1927; The Incredible Marquis, 1929; Scottish Queen, 1932; Jonathan Bishop, 1933; Suzy, 1934; The Mountain and the Plain, 1936; James Joyce: A Biography, 1940; Brave General, 1942; The World's Great Novels, 1944; The Wine of San Lorenzo, 1945; The Cry of Dolores, 1948; The Breast of the Dove, 1949. Contbr. to mags. Special script writer N.B.C. University of the Air. Address: care Rinehart and Co., Inc., 232 Madison Av., N.Y.C. Died Oct. 28, 1954; buried Woodlawn Cemetery.

GORMAN, Lawrence Clifton, clergyman, educator; b. New York, N.Y., Sept. 28, 1898; s. Lawrence P. and Anna Theresa (Nagle) G.; A.B., Fordham U., 1920; A.M., Boston Coll., 1926; Ph.D., Gregorian U., Rome, Italy, 1938; LL.D., Loyola Coll., Baltimore, Md., 1943. Entered Soc. of Jesus, 1920; ordained R.C. priest, Woodstock Coll., Md., 1932; asst. prof. chemistry, Georgetown U., 1926-29, also dir. dept., 1933-35, acting dean, Coll. of Arts and Sciences, 1934; v.p. and dean of studies, Loyola Coll., Baltimore, 1936-42; pres. Georgetown University, 1942-49; v.p., also dean Graduate and Undergraduate Schools, University of Scranton (Pennsylvania) since 1950. Mem. Am. Council on Edn., A.A.A.S., American Assn. Colleges, Eastern Assn. College Deans and Advisers of Men, Catholic Ednl. Assn., Jesuit Ednl. Assn. Address: U. of Scranton, Scranton 3, Pa. Died Dec. 27, 1952; buried Jesuit Community Cemetery, Georgetown U., Washington.

GORMAN, Michael Arthur, editor; b. Cleveland, O., Sept. 18, 1892; s. John Vincent and Mary Stella G.; A.B. (honorary), U. Michigan; unmarried. Reporter Saginaw Courier-Herald, 1910-13; successively editor for telegraph news, sports, city editor, mng. editor, Saginaw Daily News, 1913-28; editor Flint (Mich.) Jour. since 1928. Dir. Mich. Health and Welfare Fund; mem. Flint Naval Adv. Com., Army Community Relations Com.; Asso. Press Managing Editors Association and Flint Children's Center; member board of governors Rackham Research Endowment Fund, Michigan State College; member adv. bd. U. Mich. Social Sci. Research Project, St. Joseph Hosp.; dir., chmn. exec. com., Flint College, Cultural Development; dir. U. Mich. Development Council, State Development Council; trustee Flint Inst. Arts, Clara Elizabeth (Knudsen) Maternal Health Fund, Cranbrook Acad. of Art (Bloomfield Hills, Mich.), Gabriel Richard Found., U. Mich.; Sci. Service; bd. govs. U. Mich. Inst. Indsl. Health; internat. trustee Kiwanis, 1925-29; regional adv. bd. Boy Scouts America (Silver Beaver, Silver Antelope). Member American Society Newspaper Editors (dir.), U. Mich. Press Club (ex-pres.), Sovereign Military Order of Malta in U.S., Knight of the Holy Sepulchre, Sigma Delta Chi. Hon. alumnus, University of Michigan, 1936. Catholic. Clubs: Town, Country, Flint City, U. of Mich. of Flint and of Detroit; Saginaw; Detroit, Detroit Adcraft, Detroit Economic, Detroit Athletic; Owosso City; Barton Hills Country; University, University of Mich., Union, (Ann Arbor); National Press (Washington, D.C.). Home: 2008 Calumet St., Flint, Mich. Died Oct. 11, 1958; buried Mt. Olivet Cemetery, Saginaw, Mich.

GOSE, Mack F., judge; b. Sullivan County, Mo., July 8, 1859; s. John M. and Hannah J. G.; ed. Whitman Sem., Walla Walla, Wash.; m. Lelah B. Seeley, Oct. 30, 1886. Began law practice at Pomeroy, Wash.; asso. justice Supreme Ct. Wash., 1909-15, when ret.; now farming. Chmn. bd. overseers, Whitman Coll. Mayor Pomeroy, 1898-99. Pres. Wash. State Bar Assn., 1915-16. Republican. Episcopalian. Mason, K.P. Address: Olympia, Wash.; (summer) Pomeroy, Wash. Deceased.

GOSHORN, Clarence Baker (gŏs'hôrn), advt. exec.; b. Saugatuck, Mich., May 12, 1893; s. William S. and Ida (Baker) G.; A.B., U. of Michigan, 1917; m. Gladys Musselwhite, July 30, 1917; children—Robert Musselwhite, William Webster. Instr., U. Mich., 1915; with Curtis Publishing Co. Phila., 1919-30; advertising exec., Erwin, Wasey & Co., Inc., N.Y.C., 1930-34, Arthur Kudner, Inc., N.Y.C., 1934-37; vice pres., Benton & Bowles, Inc., N.Y.C. 1937-42, pres. 1942—. Served as 2d lt., U.S. Army 1917-18. Chmn. bd. A.A.A.A., 1949-50. Mem. Phi Beta Kappa. Home: Malvern, Pa. Office: 666 Fifth Av., N.Y.C. Died Dec. 10, 1949; buried St. Peters, Malvern, Pa.

GOSHORN, Lenore Rhyno (gos'horn), publisher; b. Winterset, Ia., Mar. 13, 1893; d. Walter Preston and Eva (Abrams) Rhyno; A.B., U. Ia., 1914; m Robert C. Goshorn, Dec. 11, 1920; 1 dau., Betty (Mrs. Weldon). Asst. to pub. News Tribune, Capital News, Jefferson Ctiy, 1927-53, pub., 1953—; pres. News Tribune Co., 1953—, Capital Broadcasting Co. 1953—. Mem. Eastern Star, D.A.R., P.E.O. Am Assn. U. Women, Phi Beta Kappa, Delta Delta Delta. Home: 1720 Hayselton Dr. Office: 210 Monroe St., Jefferson City, Mo. Died July 8, 1959. buried Riverview Cemetery, Jefferson City, Mo

GOSHORN, R. C., (gŏs'horn), newspaper publisher; b. Winterset, Ia., May 8, 1890; s. Arthur and Kate (Shriver) G.; student Ia. State U., 1909-11; m. Lenore Rhyno, Dec. 11, 1920; 1 dau., Betty (Mrs. W. H. Weldon). Pub. weekly newspaper in Winterset, Ia., 1912-17, Eagle Grove, Ia., 1920-26; pub. two daily newspapers in Jefferson City, Mo., since 1926. Served in armed forces in World War I. Pres. Tribune Printing Co., News Tribune Co., Capital Broadcasting Co. Past pres. Mo. Press Assn., C. of C.; mem. Sigma Delta Chi. Mason (Shriner); Elk. Club: Rotary (Jefferson City, Mo.). Home: 1720 Hayselton Dr. Office: 210 Monroe, Jefferson City, Mo. Died Apr. 14, 1953; buried Mausoleum, Jefferson City, Mo.

GOSS, Albert S. (gaws), master Nat. Grange; b. at Rochester, N.Y., October 14, 1882; s. John W. and Flora M. (Alling) B.; ed. high sch. and business coll., Portland, Ore.; m. Minnie E. Hand, Dec. 21, 1907; children—Ruth Dorothy Hanssen, Warren Hand, Betty Jane Guill. Began as bookkeeper, 1901, later connected with cereal and flour milling, general store, telephone business, and farming; actively identified with Grange affairs, 1920-33; master Washington State Grange, 1922-33; land bank commr., Farm Credit Administration, 1933-40. Chmn. exec. com. National Grange, 1924-33, now master National Grange. Mem. exec. com. Internat. Fed. Agrl. Producers; mem. advisory bd. Federation for Railway Progress. Mem. Public Adv. Bd. Presbyterian. Mem. Woodmen of World. Home: 2800 McKinley Pl. N.W. Office: 744 Jackson Pl. N.W., Washington. Died Oct. 25, 1950; buried Forest Lawn Meml. Park, Glendale, Calif.

GOSS, Harvey Theo, exec. engr.; b. El Campo, Tex., Oct. 6, 1900; s. John Harvey and Mary Elizabeth (Thomas) G.; B.S., Tex. A. and M. Coll., 1922; m. Helen Rowe, July 24, 1927; children—Emily Caroline, Robert Warren, Jr. Engr. Empire Cos., Bartlesville, Okla., 1922-23, engr., 1923-24; natural gas engr. Cities Service Gas Co., 1924-29; engr. Ark. Natural Cos., Shreveport, La., 1929-32, chief engr., 1932-45, v.p., chief engr., 1945—; v.p. Ark. Natural Gas Corp., Ark. Fuel Oil Co., Ark. La. Gas Co. Ark. Pipeline Corp.; sec., adv. chief engr. Cities Service Def. Corp., 1941—. Councilman Eagle Dist. Boy Scouts. Mem. Am. Gas Assn., So. Gas Assn., So. Gas Assn., Am. Petroleum Inst. (councilor), Mid-Continent Oil and Gas Assn. (exec. com. La.-Ark. div.), Army Ordnance Assn., Shreveport C. of C. Mason. Clubs: Pipeliners, Shreveport Country, Shreveport Riding, Shreveport. Home: 251 Patton Av. Office: P.O. Box 1734, Shreveport, La. Died Feb. 10, 1959.

GOSSARD, Harry Clinton (gŏs'sẽrd), educator; b. Helena, O., Mar. 13, 1884; s. William Howe Kiler and Helen Matilda (Canfield) G.; B.S., Ohio Northern Univ., 1907, Ed.D., 1937; Ph.D., Johns Hopkins Univ., 1912; m. Zella May Zahniser, June 23, 1909; children—Gene Michel, Betty Lee, Mona Eloise. Teacher of rural schs. in Sandusky and Wood Counties, O., 1900-01; teacher high sch., Bellefontaine, O., 1904-06, Montclair, N.J., 1909-10; prof. mathematics, U. Okla., 1912-16, U.S. Naval Acad., 1916-18, again at U. Okla., 1918-19, U. Wyo., 1921-25, Neb. Wesleyan U., 1926-31; pres. N. Mexican Highlands Univ., 1931-39; dean Eastern N. Mex. Coll. Portales N.M., 1939-50; with Office of Mil. Govt., Stuttgart, Germany 1950-54. Methodist. Home: 322 S. E. Montana, Portales, N.M. Died Dec. 7, 1954.

GOSSETT, Benjamin Brown, cotton textile exec.; b. Williamston, S.C., Aug. 18, 1884; s. James Pleasant and Sallie A. (Brown) G.; Clemson (S.C.) Coll., 1899-1901; U.S. Naval Academy, Annapolis (Maryland), 1903-05; D.Sc., N.C. State Coll., Raleigh, N. C., 1939; LL.D., Presbyterian Coll. of South Carolina, 1943; m. Katharine Coleman Clayton, Dec. 19, 1906; children—James Pleasant II, Katharine Clayton (Mrs. F. Jones), Philip Clayton. Lt. U.S. Marines, 1905-07 (resigned); in cotton mfg. since 1907; v.p., asst. treas. Williamson (S.C.) Mills, 1908-28; v.p., asst. treas. Brogon Mills., 1909-22; pres., treas. Riverside Mfg. Co., 1913-28, Toxaway Mills, 1913-28; pres. Panola Cotton Mills, 1920-21, Cohannet Mills, 1919-23; pres. and treas. Chadwick-Hoskins Co., 1921-46; pres. Martinsville (Va.) Cotton Mill. Co., 1921-45; v.p., treas. Gossett Mills, 1928-36, pres., treas., 1936-46; pres., treas. Calhoun Mills, 1936-46; pres. Hoskins Corp., N.Y., 1928-40; dir. Textron, Inc., 1945-46; chmn. bd. Textron Southern, Inc., 1946; pres. Bank of Calhoun Falls, S.C., 1912-18; v.p. Citizens Nat. Bank (Anderson, S.C., 1916-21; v.p. American Trust Co., 1924-30, dir., 1919-33; dir. Republic Cotton Mills, 1926-33, Judson Mills, 1915-25, Southern Worsted Co., 1922-26, Dan River Mills, Inc., The Liberia Co., Stettinius Assos.-Liberia, Inc., Pharis Tire & Rubber Co., Carlisle Tire and Rubber Co., P. & N. Ry. Co., M.D. & S. R.R. Co., Turner, Halsey Co., Liberty Mutual Ins. Co., Fed. Fuel Administr. for S.C., 1917-18; chmn. commerce and industry div. of State Bd. Conservation and Development of N.C., 1927-30; mem. code authority cotton textile industry under N.R.A.; mem. N.C. Tax Classification Amendment Commn., 1937-38; mem. bd. visitors Clemson Coll.; trustee N.C. State Coll. Commd. capt., U.S. Army, 1918. Mem. Cotton Textile Inst. (dir., mem. exec. com.), Navy League of U.S. (v.p. and dir. for N.C.), N.Y. Southern Soc., Am. Cotton Mfrs. Assn., Am. Legion, S.A.R., Soc. of Sons of Confederate Vets., Newcomen Soc. of Eng., United Confederate Vets. (hon. maj. gen.), Mil. Order World Wars. Dem. Mason (K.T. Shriner), Clubs: Carlotte Country, Charlotte City, Poinsett, Biltmore Forest Country, Army and Navy, Merchants (N.Y.), Execs., Ponte Vedra, Circus Saints and Sinners. Home: 923 Granville Rd. Office: 1119 Johnston Bldg., S. Tryon St., Charlotte, N.C. Died Nov. 13, 1951; buried Forest Lawn Cemetery, Charlotte, N.C.

GOTTESMAN, D. Samuel, banker; pres. Gottesman & Co., Inc., Allied Internat. Corp., Central Nat. Corp., Gottesman & Co., Inc., N.Y., Gottesman & Co. A/B, Stockholm, Wooddike Realty Corp.; dir. Rayonier, Inc., Eastern Corp. Clubs: Bankers. Dartmouth, Harmonie, Inwood Country. Home: 730 Park Av., N.Y.C. 21. Office: 100 Park Av., N.Y.C. 17. Died Apr. 1956.

GOTTWALD, Klement, Czechoslovakian premier; b. 1896. Engaged in carpenter trade, one of founders of Czechoslovak Communist Party and editor of Communist paper after World War I; elected to Party Chair, 1936; went to Russia, 1938 and became leader of Soviet branch of Czechoslovak liberation movement; vice premier of Czechoslovakia, April 1945, prime minister, 1946-48, pres., 1948—. Address: Prague, Czechoslovakia. Died Mar. 13, 1953.*

GOTWALS, John C., civil engr.; b. Norristown, Pa., Nov. 4, 1884; s. Abraham G. and Mary (Logan) G.; grad. Pa. State Coll., 1906, C.E., 1907; m. Muriel C. Clemens, Nov. 10, 1927; children—Katharine, Mary Muriel. Engring. work with Pa. R.R. and Catskill Aqueduct, N.Y., until 1913; commd. 2d lt. engrs., U.S.A., Mar. 8, 1913; capt., July 1, 1916; maj. (temp.), Aug. 5, 1917; lt. col. (temp.), 1918-20; maj. engrs., U.S.A., July 1, 1920. Organized and comd. 56th Engrs. in France; in charge searchlight operations, A.E.F., Aug. 1917, to close of war; apptd. chief engr. Alaska Rd. Commn., July 1, 1920; v. chmn. Alaska R.R., Apr. 1-Sept. 30, 1923, chief engr. since Oct. 1, 1923-Mar. 15, 1924; U.S. dist. engr., St. Louis, Mo., 1924-30; engr. commr. Dist. of Columbia, 1930-34; ret. as lt. col., 1934. Mem. Am. Soc. Mil. Engrs., Delta Upsilon; asso. mem. Am. Soc. C.E. Presbyn. Address: 11321 Conway Rd., St. Louis 31. Died Jan. 15, 1946; buried Calvary Cemetery.

GOULD, Edwin Miner Lawrence (gōōld), psychologist; b. Montreal, Can., May 4, 1886; s. Edwin and Elizabeth (Whittemore) G.; B A., McGill U., 1907; The New Church Theol. School, Cambridge, Mass., 1908-10; graduate studies New York School of Social Work and Fordham Univ., 1931-33; m. Caroline Louise Wunsch, June 14, 1910 (divorced 1932); children—Nancy Lawrence (Mrs. Robert Wood), Carol (Mrs. Robert Gilmartin); married second, Harriet Hebbard, July 14, 1932. Came to United States, 1907, naturalized citizen, 1918. Instructor classics, Urbana (Ohio) University, 1907-08; ordained ministry Church of the New Jerusalem (Swedenborgian), 1910; assistant and associate pastor, Newtonville, Massachusetts, 1910-22; pastor, Brooklyn, N.Y., 1922-32; sec. Council of Ministers of General Conv. of New Jerusalem, 1916-20; editor New Church Messenger, 1920-32; dir. New Church Press, Swedenborg Publishing Assn., 1922-36, School of Human Relations (New York), 1933-34. Chief Yeoman U.S.N.R.F., 1917-18; 1st lt. chaplain U.S. Army, 1918-19; chaplain 1st Coast Defense Command Massachusetts National Guard, 1920-22. Member of Phi Kappa Pi. Club: Leewood Golf. Democrat. Author: Problems of the New Christianity, 1922; Fundamentals of the New Christianity, 1924; A Modern Pilgrimage, 1925; The Business of Living, 1926; If We Were Christians, 1931, The Way to Be Happy, 1948; Your Most Intimate Problems, 1948; Mirror of Your Mind, 1949; The Commonsense of Psychoanalysis, 1950. Now cons. psychologist, writer and author syndicated newspaper column, Mirror of Your Mind. Address: 140 E. 46th St., N.Y.C. 17. Died Dec. 26, 1952; buried Mt. Royal Cemetery, Montreal, Can.

GOULD, Frank Jay, capitalist; b. N.Y.C., Dec. 4, 1877; s. Jay and Helen Day (Miller) G.; ed. Berkeley Sch. and New York U.; m. Margaret Kelly, 1901; m. 2d, Edith Kelly, 1909; m. 3d, Florence La Caze, 1923. Entered ry. service, 1897; also officer or dir. of other cos. Office: 149 Broadway, N.Y.C. Died Mar. 31, 1956.

GOULD, William Edward, b. Cairo, Ill., Dec. 6, 1867; s. George and Anna Letitia (Clitherow) G.; student Oberlin Coll.; m. Harriet Bates, 1902; children—Harriet Barodel (Mrs. Ellis J. Waller), Eleanor Bates (Mrs. W. H. Grant, Jr.). In banking bus., Kewanee, Ill., 1900-27; now mortgage loan and gen. financing bus.; dir. Grain Marketing Co., Chgo.; author Nornbeck-Nelson bill in Congress, 1923, also Gould plan for purchase by U.S. Govt. of 50,000,000 bushels of wheat to be shipped to Europe. Local chmn. Liberty Loan dr., War Savs. Stamp dr., World War. Conglist. Mason (32°, Shriner). Home: 7729 N. Ashland Av. Office: 39 S. LaSalle St., Chgo. Died Dec. 21, 1958.

GOULDING, Edmund, motion picture dir., writer; b. London, Eng., Mar. 20, 1891. Actor, London state, 1909-14; with Army in France, 1915-19; writer, dir., U.S., 1919—; prod. Dancing Mother (with Edgar Selwyn), N.Y.C.; sound dir. motor pictures, including Grand Hotel, Dawn Patrol, Dark Victory, Claudia, Razor's Edge, Mister 880, others. Office: 10201 W. Pico Blvd., Los Angeles. Died Dec. 1959.

GOURLEY, Louis Hill, fgn. service; b. Springfield, Ill., Oct. 17, 1889; s. Albert Francis and Jeannette (Craig) G.; B.A., U. Ill., 1912; M.A., George Washington U., 1916; internat. law and polit. sci., Columbia, 1915; studied law, LaSalle Extension U.; studied Alliance Française, Paris, France, 1909, N.Y. U., 1940; unmarried. Prof., San Luis Potosi, Mexico, 1912-13; vice consul, Vera Cruz, Mexico, 1916-19, Warsaw, Poland, 1919-21; consul on detail at Warsaw, 1922-25; consul at Lourenço Marques, Portuguese E. Africa, 1925, at Port Elizabeth, Union S. Africa, 1926-27; detailed to Dept. State, Oct. 5, 1927; consul on detail Sao Paulo, Brazil, 1928-31; consul Medan, Sumatra, 1931-33, Hong Kong, 1933-36, Shanghai, 1936-Feb. 1938, Tsingtao, China, Mar.-June, 1938; consul Kobe, Japan, July 1938-July 1940, Darien, Manchuria, Aug. 1940, Harbin, Manchuria, 1940-42; Dept. State, June-Aug. 1942; returned Apr. 30, 1943. Mem. Phi Beta Kappa, Kappa Delta Pi, Lambda Chi Alpha. Address: Southwestern Presbyterian Sanatorium, Albuquerque, N.M. Died Mar. 28, 1950; buried Acacia Park Cemetery, Birmingham, Mich.

GOVE, George, architect; b. Rochester, Minn., Aug. 28, 1870; s. Royal H. and Nancy A. (Farnham) G.; student schs., Atelier, Paris, 1905-06. Practice of architecture, 1907—; with Heath, Gove & Bell, Tacoma, 1911-52; pvt. practice as George Gove, architect, 1952—; architect McNeil Fed. Penitentiary, 1928-41; designer hosps., sch. bldgs., churches. Fellow A.I.A. Mason. Home: 311 North L St. Office: Puget Sound Bank Bldg., Tacoma. Died Aug. 31, 1956; buried Mountain View Cemetery, Tacoma.

GOWDY, Robert Clyde, physics; b. Springfield, O., Mar. 10, 1886; s. William Fishell and Rhoda Elizabeth (Vose) G.; B.A., U. of Cincinnati, 1906, M.A., 1907, Ph.D., 1909; studied Trinity Coll. (U. of Cambridge), Eng., 1909-10, College de France, Paris, 1910-11; D.Sc. (honorary), University of Cincinnati, 1947; m. Mabel Greely, Dec. 19, 1914; 1 son, William Robert. Instr. physics, Lehigh U., 1911-12; instr. physics, U. of Cincinnati, 1912-16; asst. prof., 1916-19, asso. prof., 1919-20, prof. since 1920, also acting dean Grad. Sch., 1924, asst. dean Coll. Engring. and Commerce, 1925-28 and since Sept. 1932, acting dean, 1928-32, and 1939-40, dean, Jan. 1940, to Sept., 1946, dir. Sch. Applied Arts, 1940-46, dean emeritus, Coll. of Engineering since Sept. 1946. Commd. 1st lt. Ordnance Dept., U.S. Army, Jan. 1918; capt. Chem. Warfare Service, July 1918. Mem. A.A.A.S., Am. Physical Soc., Societe Physique. Phi Beta Kappa, Sigma Xi, Tau Beta Pi, Omicron Delta Kappa, Delta Tau Delta. Republican. Presbyterian. Club: Literary. Home: 2111 Auburn Av., Cincinnati 19. Died Mar. 27, 1950.

GOWEN, James Bartholomew, army officer; b. N.Y.C., Sept. 25, 1872; s. Michael Duggan and Elizabeth (O'Connell) G.; grad. U.S. Mil. Acad. 1898; honor grad. Army Sch. of Line, 1912; grad. Army Staff Coll., 1916, Army War Coll., 1923; m. Helene Lily Burlinson; children—Dorothy Aline (wife of Haydon L. Boatner, U.S. Army), Helene Burlinson, Mildred Muriel (wife of W. Spencer Rockwell, U.S. Army), Elizabeth Lucille (wife of Richard G. Prather, U.S. Army), Mary Marjorie (wife of Robert H. Sanders, U.S. Army), Kathleen Constance (wife of James M. Worthington, U.S. Army). Asst. cashier Parke, Davis & Co., 1889-94; commd. 2d lt., inf., U.S. Army, 1898; advanced through grades to brig. gen., 1929. Served in Cuban and Philippine campaign against San Ildefonso, P.I., Dec. 1899; acting mil. gov. Nueva Viscaya, P.I., 1900; chief staff, 38th Div., AEF, 1917-18; duty with Gen. Staff, G.H.Q., France, 1918-19; exec. officer Army War Coll., 1919-22, chief staff, 5th Corps Area, 1927-29; comdg. 1st F.A. Brigade, Ft. Hoyle, Md., 1929-32, 11th F.A. Brig., Schofield Barracks, H.T., 1932-34; 21st Brig., Schofield Barracks, H.T., 1934-36; ret., 1936. Campaign badges for Spanish-Am. War, Philippine Insurrection, Cuban Pacification, World War. Decorated Purple Heart. Catholic. Address: care Maj. R. G. Prather, West Point, N.Y. Died Aug. 9, 1958.

GRACE, Joseph Peter, bus. exec.; b. Great Neck, N.Y., June 29, 1872; s. W. R. and Lillius Gilchrest) G.; A.B., Columbia, 1894; LL.B., N.Y. Law Sch., 1895; m. Janet Macdonald, Aug. 1, 1908. Dir. W. R. Grace & Co.; also officer or dir. many other corps. Mem. Alpha Delta Phi. Clubs: Columbia University, Catholic University, Meadow Brook. Home: Manhasset, L.I. Office: 7 Hanover Sq., N.Y.C. Died July 15, 1950.*

GRACE, William Joseph, clergyman, educator; b. St. Louis, Feb. 23, 1882; s. Thomas Clancy and Elizabeth J. (Patterson) G.; B.A., St. Louis U., 1900, M.A., 1908, post-grad., 1914-18; student St. Stanislaus Sem. and Normal Tng. Sch., Florissant, Mo., 1902-06. Joined Soc. of Jesus (Jesuits), 1902; tchr. classical langs. John Carroll U., 1909-10, Xavier U., 1910-14, 18-19; ordained priest R.C. Ch., 1917; dean Coll. Arts and Scis., Creighton U., 1920-25, pres. 1925-28; dean Coll. Liberal Arts and dir. Summer Session, Marquette U., 1928-38; dean faculties, 1938-40; prof. Religion and Faculty Moderator of athletics, St. Louis U., 1940-41; asst. pastor St. Aloysius Ch., Kansas City, Mo., 1941-42; asst. pastor Gesu Ch., Milw., 1942—. Address: 1131 W. Wisconsin Av., Milw. 3. Died Apr. 16, 1959.

GRADLE, Harry Searls, oculist; b. Chgo., Dec. 31, 1883; s. Henry and Fanny (Searls) G.; grad. Univ. Sch. of Chgo., 1902, A.B., U. Mich., 1906; M.D., Rush Med. Coll., 1908; m. Alice Perry, November 29, 1906 (died 1944); m. 2d, Audrey M. Hayden, April 28, 1945. Prof., ophthalmology, U. Ill., attending ophthalmologist Michael Reese Hosp., chief staff Illinois Eye and Ear Infirmary. President Pan-American Congress of Ophthalmology, 1940. Mem. A.M.A., Ill., Chgo., Chicago medical socs., Am. Academy Ophthalmology and Oto-Laryngology (pres. 1938), Am. and Chgo. Ophthal. socs., Delta Upsilon, Phi Rho Sigma. Clubs: Tavern (Chicago); Army and Navy (Washington, D.C.). Contbr. tech. articles on med. topics. Home: 14060 Valley Vista Blvd., Sherman Oaks, Calif. Office: 58 E. Washington St., Chicago. Died May 25, 1950; buried Forest Lawn Cemetery, Los Angeles.

GRADY, Daniel Henry, lawyer; b. Columbus, Wis., Aug. 13, 1872; s. Daniel and Honora (Lavery) G.; LL.B., U. of Mich., 1894; m. Julia Ruth O'Brien, June 25, 1912. Admitted to Wis. bar, 1894; in gen. practice at Portage; spl. counsel for State of Wis. in prosecution of state anti-trust violations, investigation of receivership C.,M.&St.P. Ry. Co., investigation of Indian Affairs, litigation involving validity of ins. and ry. laws. Regent U. of Wis., 1924-30, 1932-38 and for term ending 1951, pres. of board, 1927-30. Mem. American and Wis. bar assns. Democrat. Catholic. K.C., Elk. Clubs: University (Milwaukee); Madison (Wis.). Home: Portage, Wis. Died May 11, 1954.

GRADY, Henry Francis, American ambassador; b. San Francisco, Feb. 12, 1882, s. John Henry and Ellen G. (Rourke) G.; A.B., St. Mary's University, Balt., 1907; Catholic U., Washington, 1906-07, U. Cal., 1915-16, Columbia. 1916-17; Ph.D., 1927; LL.D., U. San Francisco, 1943; m. Lucretia del Valle, Oct. 18, 1917; children—Reginald del Valle, Patricia Louise, Henry Francis, John Weston. Lecturer, evening session College City of N.Y., 1916-17, Columbia summer, 1917 and term 1917-18; spl. expert, Bur. of Planning and Statistics, U.S. Shipping Bd., 1918-19; U.S. trade commr. to London and continental Europe to report on postwar financial conditions, 1919-20; acting commercial attaché, London, Aug. 1919-Feb. 1920, Holland, Apr.-July 1920; acting chief of div. research, Bur. Foreign and Domestic Commerce, 1921; lectr., Foreign Service Sch., Gerogetown U., spring 1921, U. Cal., 1921-28; prof. internat. trade and dean of Coll. of Commerce, U. Cal., 1928-37; vice chmn. U.S. Tariff Commn., 1937-39; asst. sec. state, Aug. 1939-Jan. 1941; pres. Am. President Lines, Ltd., 1941-47; Am. ambassador to India, 1947-48; American ambassador to Greece 1948-50, United States ambassador to Iran, 1950. Trade adviser San Francisco C. of C., 1922-34; chmn. Foreign Commerce Association of San Francisco, 1922-34; vis. prof. Institute of Pacific and Oriental Affairs, Honolulu, summer 1932. Impartial chairman Regional Labor Board for San Francisco, 1933-34; chief of Trade Agreements Division, Dept. of State, Washington, D.C., 1934-36. Pres. Pan-Am. Soc. (San Francisco), 1933-34; dir. Inst. of World Affairs, Riverside, Cal., 1930. 33. Mem. of Economics Com. (chmn., 1940—), and Raw Materials Com., League of Nations, 1937; mem. Com. on Internat. Polit. and Social Problems, C. of C. U.S.; mem. business adv. council for Dept. Commerce; head Am. Tech. Mission to Indian, Mar. 1942; served as v.p., in charge economic sect., Allied Control Commn., in Italy, carrying the rank of United States Minister, Dec. 1943-July 1944; chmn. United States Delegation, Internat. Business Conf., Rye, N.Y., 1944-47; chmn. bd. dirs. and Federal Reserve agent of the Federal Reserve Bank of San Francisco, 1944-47. Pres. San Francisco C. of C., 1945; chmn. San Francisco Citizen's Com., UN Conf. on Internat. Orgn., 1945; head U.S. Section, Allied Mission for Observing the Greek Elections, 1945-46, with rank of U.S. Ambassador; chmn. Bd. Alternates, Cabinet Com. on Palestine and Related Problems, rank of Ambassador. Decorated Officer Legion of Honor. Mem. Acad. Polit. Sci., Fgn. Policy Assn., Am. Econ. Assn., Beta Gamma Sigma, Pan Xenia, Delta Sigma Pi, Lambda Chi Alpha, Phi Gamma Mu. Democrat. Clubs: Commercial, Commonwealth, The Family, Pacific Union (San Francisco); Metropolitan. Author: British War Finance, 1914-19, 1927; The Port of San Francisco (with Robert M. Carr), 1933. Contbr. to Currencies After the War, 1919; also to San Francisco business and various economic and trade jours., etc. Home: 137 Jordan, San Francisco. Died Sept. 1957.*

GRAEBNER, August Lawrence, educator; b. Frankentrost, Mich., July 10, 1849; s. Rev. John H. P. and Jacobina G.; acad. edn. St. Louis; collegiate edn. Concordia Coll., Ft. Wayne, Ind.; student in theology Concordia Sem., St. Louis; m. Anna Schaller, Aug. 14, 1873. Ordained to Luth. ministry, 1878; prof. in high sch., St. Louis, 1872-75; prof. Northwestern U., Watertown, Wis., 1875-78; prof. theology Luth. Theol. Sem., Milw., 1878-87; prof. church history, hermeneutics, liturgics, theology Concordia Sem., St. Louis, 1887—. Mem. Bd. Fgn. Missions of Synod Mo., Ohio and other states. Author: First Course in Composition and Grammar, 1878; Life of Luther, 1883; History of the Lutheran Church in America (in German), 1892; Half a Century of Sound Lutheranism in America, 1893; Outlines of Doctrinal Theology, 1898; Sunday School Texts, 1900; also numerous books in German on theol. subjects. Editor: Theological Quarterly. Contbr. encys. and mags. Address: Concordia Seminary, 801 De Mun Av., St. Louis 5. Died Dec. 7, 1904; buried Concordia Cemetery, St. Louis.

GRAEBNER, Martin Adolph Henry (grāb'nĕr), educator; b. Milw., Sept. 22, 1879; s. Augustus Lawrence and Anna (Schaller) G.; grad. Holy Cross Sch., St. Louis, Mo., 1893, Concordia Coll., Fort Wayne, Ind., 1898, Concordia Sem., St. Louis, 1901, D.D., 1942; m. Anna Albers, May 31, 1906; children—Paul William, Robert Carl, Martin Luther, Ruth Elizabeth, Lawrence Arthur, Herbert John. Ordained Luth. Ch., 1901; pastor Cushing, Okla., 1901-02, Oklahoma City, 1902-10; prof. Greek, St. John's Coll., Winfield, Kan., 1910-22; prof. classics, Concordia College, Milw., 1922-27; pres. Concordia College, St. Paul, Minn., 1927-46; now professor of classics; European dir. Lutheran Relief and Rehabilitation, 1947, headquarters Frankfurt, Germany. Admitted to bar, 1914; legal adviser. Missouri Synod Church Extension Board, 1918-27; member Missouri Synod College Curriculum Com.; member Minn. Univ. Com. on Educational Research. Mem. Kansas State Council of Defense, World War. Chmn. Minn. State Com. on Tolerance, Unity and Loyalty, St. Paul School Investigation Com., 1944. Mem. State Speakers Bur.; Honor Soc. Lutheran Acad. for Scholarship. Author: The Lord's Prayer and the Christian Life; Meditations on Psalm 119. Co-author: Vesper Sermons. Address: 1270 St. Anthony Ave., St. Paul, Minn. Died Nov. 12, 1950.

GRAEBNER, Theodore, prof. theology, author; b. Watertown, Wis., Nov. 23, 1876; s. Augustus L.

(D.D.) and Anna (Schaller) G.; grad. Luther Coll., New Ulm, Minn., 1893; A.B., Concordia Coll., Ft. Wayne, Ind., 1894; grad. Concordia Sem., St. Louis, Mo., 1897; D.D., Lutheran Seminary, Adelaide, Australia; m. Selma Brohm, Aug. 20, 1900; children—Gunhild (Mrs. G. Mahler), Eugene, Oliver, Alexander, Margaret. Prof. history, Walther Coll., St. Louis, 1897-1900; teacher of English, Luth. Ladies' Sem., Red Wing, Minn., 1900-06; pastor Jehovah Ch., Chicago, 1907-13; prof. theology, Concordia Theol. Sem., St. Louis, since 1913. Editor Luth. Herald, 1909-13, Der Lutheraner, 1913-17; dept. editor Lehre and Wehre, and Homiletic Mag., 1913-18; editor Lutheran Witness, 1914-49, Bible Student (quarterly) since 1921; lecturer Bad Boll, Germany, 1948, 49. Mem. National Committee for Civic Recovery, Concordia Historical Institute (director), Civic Union (director), Council on Education in Government, Philos. Society of Great Britain, Missouri Acad. of Science. Author: Lessons for Sunday School, 1905; The Dark Ages, 1917; Prophecy and the War, 1917; The Expository Preacher, 1919; Spiritism, 1920; Evolution, 1920; The Pastor as Student and Literary Worker, 1921; Bible Dictionary, 1922; Essays on Evolution, 1925; The Secret Empire, 1927; Touring with God, 1927; A Handbook for Congregational Officers, The Story of the Catechism, 1928; The Story of the Augsburg Confession, A Short History of the Augsburg Confession, The Pope and Temporal Power, 1929; Pastor and People, God and the Cosmos, 1932; Borderland of Right and Wrong, Problem of Lutheran Union, 1935. Translator of Luther's Commentary on Galatians, 1939; War in the Light of Prophecy, 1941, The Business Man and the Church, 1941; co-author, Toward Lutheran Union, 1943; Annotated Pocket New Testament, Church Bells in the Forest, 1944; Prayer-Fellowship, 1945; Is Masonry a Religion?, 1946; Handbook of Organizations, 1948. Co-editor, What Lutherans Are Thinking, 1947. Home: 7542 Byron Pl. Office: 801 De Mun St., St. Louis 5. Died Nov. 14, 1950; buried Concordia Cemetery, St. Louis.

GRAFF, Fritz William, educator, coll. dean; b. Marshall, Tex., Nov. 4, 1887; s. George Frederick and Frederica (Wind) G.; A.B., (Levi scholar 1908-11) University Texas, 1911; M.B.A., 1920; LL.D., (honorary), John Carroll University, 1956; married Agnes M. Frazer, May 21, 1928. Businessman, 1911-13; admitted to Texas bar, 1913; secretary to president University Texas, 1913-17, sec. to pres., editor univ. publs., 1917-20; mem. bd. control U. War Schs., 1917-18, asst. to pres., 1920-23, asso. prof. bus. adminstrn., 1920-24; prof. bus. adminstrn. U. Tex., 1924-25; vis. prof. bus. adminstrn. U. Wash., summer, 1924; asso. prof. bus. adminstrn. Cleveland Col., Western Res. U., 1925-28, prof. bus. adminstrn., head dept. accounting, acting head dept. trade and industry, 1928-34; prof. bus. adminstrn. John Carroll U., 1934—, dir. dept., 1934-45, dean sch. bus. econs. and govt., 1945-56, emeritus 1956, asso. treas., 1946—. C.P.A., O. Mem. Am. Bar Assn., Am. Inst. Accountants, Ohio Soc. C.P.A.'s, Am. Accounting Assn., Am. Statis. Assn., Econometric Soc., Am. Assn. U. Profs., Phi Beta Kappa, Beta Gamma Sigma, Beta Alpha Psi, Delta Kappa Epsilon, Alpha Kappa Psi. Episcopalian. Author: Elements of Accounting Analysis, 1932. Home: 2555 Eaton Rd., Cleve. 18. Died Apr. 21, 1957; buried Schulenburg City (Tex.) Cemetery.

GRAFFLIN, Douglas Gordon, educator; b. Washington, Mar. 10, 1911; s. Samuel Walter and Alma Snow (Parsons) G.; student Stevens Inst. Tech., 1927-28; B.A., Ohio University, 1931; M.A., New York U., 1933; m. Alice Wardell, June 22, 1935; children—Douglas Gordon, Alice, Wendelin, Susan, Mary. Teacher, McBurney Sch., N.Y. City, 1931-33, asst. head, 1933-35; teacher Battle Hill Sch., White Plains, N.Y., 1935-37; headmaster Brooklyn Friends Sch., 1937-42; dist. prin. The Pub. Schs., Chappaqua, N.Y., since 1942. Recipient Brooklyn Young Men's C. of C. award, 1941. Mem. N.E.A., N.Y. State Teacher's Assn., Phi Delta Kappa. Member Society of Friends. Home: 162 N. Bedford Rd. Office: The Public Schools, Chappaqua, N.Y. Died Aug. 23, 1959.

GRAHAM, Albert D.; chmn. bd. First Nat. Bank of Baltimore; dir. Eutaw Savings Bank, Fairfield Western Maryland Dairy Corp. Pres. Children's Hosp. Sch. Home: Lutherville, Md. Office: Light and Redwood Sts., Balt. Died May 16, 1957.

GRAHAM, Christopher, physician; b. Cortland County, N.Y., Apr. 1856; s. Joseph and Jane T. Graham; B.S., U. Minn., 1887; V.M.D., U. Pa., 1892, M.D., 1894; m. Elizabeth Blanche Brackenridge, 1899; children—Elizabeth Blanche, Malcolm Brackenridge. Asso. with Mayo bros. in practice at Rochester, 1894-1919; chmn. Union Nat. Bank of Rochester. Episcopalian. Home: 813 3d Av. S.E., Rochester, Minn. Died June 20, 1952; buried Oakwood Cemetery, Rochester, Minn.

GRAHAM, Dale, banker; b. Litchfield, Ill., Aug. 2, 1900; s. George H. and Alice (McPeak) G.; student Washington U., 1921-23; LL.B., Benton Coll. Law, St. Louis, 1926; m. Dorothy A. Gahre, Dec. 6, 1929; children—Marilyn Louise, Irene Ivel. Asst. v.p. Miss. Valley Trust Co., St. Louis, 1925-28, Nat. Park Bank, N.Y.C., 1928-29; 2d v.p. Chase Nat. Bank, 1929-31; cashier Canal Bank & Trust Co., New Orleans, 1931-33; v.p., cashier Nat. Bank of Commerce, 1933-46, sr. v.p., 1946-50, pres. since 1950, also chairman of the board and director; director Wesson Oil & Snowdrift Co., Inc., New Orleans. also So. Cotton Oil Co., Inc. Mem. Newcomen Soc. La. Clubs: Boston, New Orleans Country, Louisiana, Lake Shore, Stratford, Petroleum. Home: 1 Farnham Pl. Office: 210 Baronne St., New Orleans. Died June 3, 1958.

GRAHAM, Dorothy (Mrs. Graham Bennet), author; b. New Rochelle, N.Y., Dec. 13, 1893; d. Leo and Emma (Welton) Graham; educated in Lausanne, Switzerland, Florence, Italy; m. James W. Bennett, July 23, 1924 (div. 1942). Fellow Am. Geog. Soc.; mem. Internat. Soc. Women Geographers, P.E.N. (rep. congress Venice 1949), MacDowell Assn. (corporate mem.). Author: Through the Moon Door, 1926; Lotus of the Dusk, 1927; Brush Strokes on the Fan of a Courtesan, 1927; The French Wife, 1928; The China Veture, 1929; Candles in the Sun, 1930; Chinese Gardens, 1938; Flight Into Day, 1940; Wind Across the World, 1947; Far Horizons, 1954. Contbr. articles, essays, short stories to mags. in U.S. and Eng. Lectured on Oriental Subjects. Home: 1036 Park Av., N.Y.C. Died June 22, 1959; buried Kensico, Valahalla, N.Y.

GRAHAM, Edwin Charles; b. Warren County, Ill., June 21, 1871; s. Benjamin F. and Lucy (Brooks) G.; ed. public schs.; m. Annie L. Barron, 1894; (dec.); children—Lorraine (Mrs. Morgan B. Callahan, dec.), Edwin M., Anne (Mrs. Homer O. Eimers, dec.). Began in elec. supply business, Washington 1890; became pres. Nat. Electrical Supply Co., 1898; pres. Hamilton National Bank, 1933-46, later chmn. bd., now dir. (retired since 1946); v.p., dir. Washington Hotel Co.; dir. Chesapeake & Potomac Telephone Co., Acacia Mut. Life Ins. Co. Past pres. Bd. of Edn., Washington. Mason, Elk. Clubs: Nat. Press, University, Rotary, Columbia Country (Washington); Engineers' (N.Y.). Address: 2921 44th Pl., N.W., Washington. Died May 4, 1953; buried Rock Creek Cemetery, Washington.

GRAHAM, Edwin Eldon, pediatrist; b. Phila., Feb. 28, 1864; s. Archibald Hunter (M.D.) and Eliza J. (Sampson) G.; Harvard, 1882-84; M.D., Jefferson Med. Coll., 1887; intern Phila. Hosp., 1887-88; studied, Göttingen, Berlin and Munich, 1888-89; m. Lorraine Goodrich, Jan. 2, 1893. Prof. diseases of children, Jefferson Med. Coll., 1899—; pediatrist Phila. Hosp., 1903-18. Mem. A.M.A., Med. Soc. State Pa., Am. Pediatric Soc., Phila. Pediatric Soc. Presbyn. Clubs: Rittenhouse, Merion Cricket, Mill Dam. Address: 1713 Spruce St., Phila. Deceased.

GRAHAM, Evarts Ambrose, surgeon; b. Chicago, Ill., Mar. 19, 1883; s. David Wilson and Ida Anspach (Barned) G.; A.B., Princeton, 1904; M.D., Rush Med. Coll., 1907; Sc.D., Cincinnati, 1927; LL.D., Central Coll., 1927; hon. M.S., Yale, 1928; Sc.D., Princeton Univ, 1929; Sc.D., Western Reserve University, 1931; Sc.D., U. of Pa., 1940; Sc. D., U. of Chicago, 1941; Sc.D., McGill, U., 1944, Emory University, 1954, New York University, 1955; LL.D. University of Glasgow, 1951, Johns Hopkins U., 1952. Washington U., 1952, U. Leeds (England), 1954; special student chemistry, University Chgo., 1913, 14; m. Helen Tredway, January 29, 1916; children—David Tredway, Evarts Ambrose. Interne Presbyn. Hosp. Chgo., 1907-08; asst., also instructor surgery, Rush Medical College, 1909-15; asst. attending surgeon, Presbyterian Hosp., Chgo., 1912-15; mem. staff Otho. S. A. Sprague Meml. Inst., Rush, Chgo., 1912-15; chief surgeon Park Hosp., Mason City, Ia., 1915-17; professor surgery Washington U. Sch. of Medicine, 1919-51, prof. emeritus since 1951; emeritus surgeon in chief Barnes Hosp. and St. Louis Children's Hosp.; mem. Presidents Commn. on Health Needs of Nation, 1952; apptd. by Rockefeller Foundation to investigate teaching of surgery in British medical school, 1922; Harvey Soc. lecturer, 1924 and 1934; Mütter lecturer, 1924; McArthur lecturer, 1926; Shattuck lecturer, 1928; Alvarez lecturer, 1930; Joyce lecturer, 1931; Bevan lecturer, 1932; Caldwell lecturer, 1933; Balfour lecturer, 1934; Judd lecturer, 1937; Lister orator, London, 1947; Fraser lectr., Edinburgh, 1954; surgeon in chief Peter Bent Brigham Hosp., 1925; temp. prof. surgery St. Bartholomew's Hosp., London, 1939. Mem. Nat. Research Council (med. fellowship bd.), 1925-39; chmn. com. on surgery, 1940-46. Captain Medical Corps, U.S. Army, Jan. 1918; maj. May 1918; served with Sch. of Neurol. Surgery, Chicago, later as mem. Empyema Commn., Camp Lee, Va.; spl. lab. research on empyema, at Baltimore, Md.; comdg. officer Evacuation Hosp. No. 34, in France, Sept. 1918-May 1919; hon. discharged, 1919. Mem. com. apptd. by sec. of war to study activities of Medical Department of U.S. Army, 1942. Pres. bd. trustees John Burroughs School, St. Louis, 1930-37; mem. Nat. Bd. Med. Examiners, 1924-33. Chairman Am. Board of Surgery (1937-41); fellow Am. Coll. Surgeons (pres. 1940-41); Am. Med. Assn. (chmn. sect. gen. and abdominal surgery, 1925); mem. Am. Surg. Assn. (pres. 1937), Soc. Clin. Surgery, Am. Assn. Thoracic Surgery (pres. 1928), St. Louis Assn. Surgeons (pres. 1925), Soc. for Clin. Research. Société Internationale de Chirugie; Kaiserlich Deutsche Akad, d. Naturforscher (1932); National Academy Sciences (1941), Am. Philos. Soc. (1941); hon. fellow Assn. of Surgeons of Great Britain and Ireland, Royal College of Surgeons (London, Eng.); honorary mem. Society of Thoracic Surgeons of Great Britain and Ireland, Sociedad Argentina de Cirujanos Royal Society of Sciences, Uppsala, Sweden, others; mem. Nu Sigma Nu, Alpha Omega Alpha fraternities. Author: Empyema Thoracis, 1925; Diseases of the Gall-Bladder and Bile Ducts, 1928. Editor: Surgical Diagnosis, 1930. Wrote sect., "Treatment of the Acute Empyema," for Medical and Surgical History of World War (published by Surgeon General's Office), 1924. Editor, Year Book of Surgery. Awarded Gross prize in surgery, 1920; Leonard prize by American Roentgen-Ray Society, 1925; gold medal by the American Radiol. Soc., 1925, for the development of cholecystography; gold medal and certicate of merit from St. Louis Medical Society, 1927, for development of cholecystography; gold medal by Southern Medical Association, 1934, for scientific research; John Scott medal by City of Philadelphia, 1937; received St. Louis Award, 1942; Lister Medal of Royal Coll. Surgeons, Eng., 1942; Roswell Park medal, 1949; American College Chest Physician medal, 1949; Miss. Valley Med. Soc. medal, 1949; distinguished service medal of A.M.A., 1950; Bigelow Medal of Boston Surgical Soc., 1951, Charles Mickle Fellowship, Univ., Toronto, 1943. Gave expositions of disturbed mechanics of respiration and circulation when normal intrathoracic pressures are altered; developed method for cholecystography, or the X-ray visualization of the gall-bladder; new treatment for chronic abscess of the lung; contbns. to pathology and treatment of carcinoma of bronchus, explanation of particular toxicity of choloroform and similar anaesthetic agents; etc. Co-editor Archives of Surgery, 1920-45 and of Annals of Surgery, 1935-45; editor Journal of Thoracic Surgery since 1931; editor Year Book of Surgery, 1926-27. Home: Old Jamestown Rd., R.R. 2, Box 256, Florissant, Mo. Office: Barnes Hospital, 600 S. Kingshighway, St. Louis 10. Died Mar. 4, 1957.

GRAHAM, Henry Tucker, clergyman; b. Winchester, Va., Aug. 21, 1865; s. James Robert and Fanny Bland Tucker (Magill) G.; A.B., Hampden-Sydney Coll., 1886; B.D., Union Theol. Sem., Richmond, Va., 1891; D.D., Washington and Lee U., 1910, U. Pitts., 1912; LL.D., Hampden-Sydney Coll., 1934; m. Lilian Gordon Baskerville, Aug. 12, 1891; 1 dau., Alice Sturdivant (wife of Rev. Henry Graybill Bedinger). Ordained Presbyn. ministry, 1891; missionary in Japan, 1891-96; pastor, Fayetteville, N.C., 1897-1904, Farmville, Va., 1904-08; pres. Hampden-Sydney (Va.) Coll., 1908-17; pastor 1st Presbyn. Ch., Florence, S.C., 1917-40, retired. Moderator Presbyn. Synod of S.C., 1924; mem. Gen. Assembly's com. on closer relations with other Presbyn. chs.; mem. of Pan-Presbyn. Alliance at Montreal, Can., 1937; del. to Western Section Presbyn. Alliance, 1939-40; spl. del. from Synod of S.C. to the Sesquicentennial of the Synod of the Carolinas at Mt. Mourne, N.C. Mem. Phi Kappa Psi, K. of P. Club: Kiwanis. Author: Men of Might; An Old Manse and Other Sermons; The Praying Christ; Christ the Supreme Teacher; The Greatest Book in the World; Mother, a Kiwanis Address; The Minister—The Man and His Task; Objections to Reunion; Some Things for Which the South Did Not Fight in the War Between the States; Richard McIlwaine—a Sketch. Address: Pineville, N.C. Died Jan. 8, 1951; buried Florence, S.C.

GRAHAM, Horace Reynolds, mining exec.; b. N.Y. C., June 11, 1886; s. William Horace and Theresa L. (Reynolds) G.; M.E., Columbia, 1908; m. Leah Chambers, Apr. 22, 1913; children—Leah T., Horace R., Marguerite C. Laborer mines, Cripple Creek, Colo., 1907; laborer, engr. Nevada Consol. Copper Co. 1908-10; engr. Braden Copper Co., Rancagua, Chile, 1910-19; joined Guggenheim mining interests, Bolivia, 1919-29; nitrate industry, Chile, 1929—; pres., dir. Anglo-Lautaro Nitrate Corp., 1951-54, cons., 1954—; also partner Guggenheim Brothers, N.Y.C.; dir. Chilean Nitrate & Iodine Sales Corp., (Chile), Chilean Nitrate Sales Corp. (U.S.A.), Minerec Corp., Pacific Tin Consol. Corp. Representative Metals Res., Exim Bank, Defense Supply, Internat. Tng.; also chmn. Coordinators Com., Chile, World War II. Mem. Council Inter-Am. Cooperation (v. chmn.), Pan Am. Union (Chile), Am. Assn. Soc. of Chile, Pan Am. Soc. (v.p.), Chile Am. Assn., U.S. Inter-Am. Council (chmn.). Roman Catholic. Clubs: Prince of Wales Golf, The Phoenix, Polo, Union (Santiago, Chile); University, Columbia, Mining, Bankers, Anglers, Metropolitan, Winged Foot Golf, Blind Brook (N.Y.C.); Bohemian (San Francisco). Home: 1 Beekman Pl., N.Y.C. 22. Office: 120 Broadway, N.Y.C. 5. Died Nov. 8, 1954; buried Gate of Heaven Cemetery, Westchester County, N.Y.

GRAHAM, Hugh, educator; b. County Down, Ireland, Nov. 18, 1878; s. James and Ellen (Burns) G.; Teachers Diploma, De La Salle Coll., Waterford, Ireland, 1898; A.B., Royal U., Ireland, 1907; Higher Diploma in Edn., Queen's U., Belfast, 1914; A.M., U. Minn., 1919, Ph.D., U. of Minn., 1929; m. Susan McKay, Aug. 17, 1909 (died Nov. 16, 1919); children—James Gerard, Mary Teresa (Maureen) (Mrs. Charles Leo Beatty); m. 2d, Margaret T. Meagher, Sept. 18, 1922. Came to U.S., 1917, naturalized, 1924. Prin. elem. schs., County Down, 1899-1917; supt. pub. schs., Minn., 1918-20; head dept. edn., Coll. St. Teresa, Winona, Minn., 1920-27; prof. edn., St. Louis U. and supervisor teacher tng., 1927-30; dir. dept. edn., John Carroll U., Ursuline Coll. and Notre Dame Coll., Cleveland, since 1930; dir. grad. studies, John Carroll U. 1946-49. Mem. A.A.A.S., Am. Assn. U. Profs., N.E.A., Nat. Soc. Study Edn., Medieval Acad. Am. Cath. Hist. Assn., Minn. Hist. Soc., Ohio Coll. Assn. (mem. legislative com. 1935-1950), Ohio Coll. Teachers Edn. (pres. 1933-34), Phi Delta Kappa. Author: Ulster Folk Tales, 1906; Gaelic League; Early Irish Monastic Schools, 1923. Contbr. articles and book revs. in histl., lit., and ednl. periodicals. Address: 16307 Lotus Dr., Cleve. 28. Died May 2, 1952; buried Calvary Cemetery, Cleve.

GRAHAM, John Howard (grā'âm), chemist; born Phila., Pa., Dec. 29, 1880; s. Jonathan Wesley and Anna Elizabeth (Mifflin) G.; A.B., Central High Sch., 1898; B.S., U. of Pa., 1902, A.M., 1927; m. Lillian Mae Cogswell, June 19, 1906; children—Marguerite Rae (Mrs. Robert G. Wetmore), Dorothy Cogswell (Mrs. David C. Miller), Ruth Eleanor (Mrs. Herbert S. Simons), Lois Adele (Mrs. Roy G. Anderson), Janet Mae. Began as chief chemist, Spanish-American Iron Company, Daiquiri, Cuba, 1902; teacher chemistry, Central High School, Philadelphia, also Drexel, Central, Frankford, Mastbaum, and Germantown evening schools and Central High Summer Sch., 1903-30; chemist, Smith, Kline, French Co., Henry K. Wampole Co., Rohm and Haas Co.; consultant Central Railway Signal Co. Professor and head dept. organic chem., Temple U. Pharmacy Sch. since 1930; business manager, the Catalyst. Dir. Westminster Cemetery. Mem. A.A.A.S., Am. Assn. Univ. Profs., Pa. Acad. Science, Am. Chem. Soc., Pa. Bee Assn., Sigma Xi. Republican. Presbyterian (elder). Mason (32°, Shriner). Home: 113 Cliveden Av., Glenside, Montgomery County, Pa. Office: 3223 N. Broad St., Phila. 40. Died Oct. 5, 1951.

GRAHAM, Robert X(avier), univ. prof.; b. Moosic, Pa., Mar. 26, 1902; s. James and Catherine (Drexel) G.; A.B., Colgate Univ., 1925; A.M., Univ. of Wis., 1933; student, Univ. of Pittsburgh, 1935-37; m. Eleanor Kathryn Warner, Nov. 21, 1931. Instr. and asst. prof. English and journalism, Westminster Coll., 1925-35, dir. of pub. relations, 1927-35, coach of track and cross country, and asst. athletic dir., 1928-35; instr. English and journalism, Pa. Coll. for Women, 1935-36, dir. of publicity, 1935-36; dir. of pub. relations, Univ. of Pittsburgh, 1935-42, asso. prof. and head, Div. of Journalism, since 1945. Served in U.S. Naval Res., advancing from lt. to lt. comdr., 1942-45. Mem. Am. Coll. Pub. Relations Assn. (nat. editor, 1934-38; nat. pres., 1938-39), Am. Assn. Teachers of Journalism, Baker St. Irregulars, Pi Delta Epsilon, Omicron Delta Kappa, Kappa Delta Rho. Republican. Presbyterian. Author: A Bibliography in the History and Backgrounds of Journalism (privately pub.), 1940, Mechanics of Newspaper Editing, 1947; Ethics in Publicity in College Publicity Handbook, 1948; The College Newspaper (Pi Delta Epsilon), 1949. Editor of various club and assn. publs., 1935-39. Contbr. articles to trade, professional, fraternal and gen. mags. Home: 2333 McNary Boulevard, Pitts. 35. Died Feb. 4, 1953; buried Oak Park Cemetery, New Castle, Pa.

GRAHAM, Samuel Jordan, judge; b. Lexington, Rockbridge County, Va., July 27, 1859; s. Edward Lacy and Mary Lucy (Jordan) G.; student Washington and Lee U., 1881; m. Sue Finney Neal, Oct. 31, 1890 (died 1919); 1 dau., Mary Carter (Mrs. Stuart C. Gillmore); m. 2d, Leila H. B. Smith, July 2, 1924; m. 3d, E. Norma Purcell, Oct. 18, 1938. Practiced law at Lexington, 1881-90; moved to Pitts., 1890; pres. bd. examiners for admission to bar, Pitts., 3 yrs. Del. from Va. to Dem. Nat. Conv., Chgo. 1884, rep. to delegation on Com. on Credentials; del. Dem. Nat. Conv., Baltimore, 1912, mem. com. from Pa. to notify Woodrow Wilson of nomination; asst. atty. gen. of U.S., 1913-19; judge U.S. Court of Claims, 1919-30; retired. Mem. Am. Soc. Internat. Law, Am. Bar Assn., Sigma Alpha Epsilon, Phi Beta Kappa. Presbyn. Clubs: Metropolitan, Chevy Chase (Washington). Author: Some Reflections on the League of Nations; The Economic Organizaion of Peace. Address: Hotel Roanoke, Roanoke, Va. Died Jan. 20, 1951; buried Stonewall Jackson Meml. Cemetery, Lexington, Va.

GRAHAM, William Alexander, retired army officer, author; b. Chgo., Jan. 23, 1875; s. William Robinson (maj. U.S.A.) and Martha Smith (Hawkins) G.; student Beloit Coll. Acad., 1891-93, Beloit Coll., 1893-94, Stanford U., 1894-96, LL.B., U. Ia., 1897; m. Ada Jane Houck, June 25, 1902 (dec.); 1 son, Alexander (col. U.S.A.); m. 2d, Helen Jeanette Bury, Nov. 28, 1935; 1 son, William Alexander, Jr. (midshipman U.S. Naval Acad.). Admitted to Ia. bar, 1897, in gen. practice, Cedar Falls, 1897-1902, Des Moines, 1902-16; capt. of inf., Ia. Nat. Guard, 1912-17, Mexican Border, 1916-17; major, judge advocate, 88th Div., 1917-19; with A.E.F., 1918-19; commd. lt. col., Judge Advocate General's Dept., U.S. Army, 1920, col., 1931; retired, 1939. Decorated Mexican Border service medal, Victory medal with Meuse-Argonne and Defensive Sector bars. Mem. Alpha Tau Omega, Phi Delta Phi. Clubs: University, Lake Shore Ahtletic, Illinois Athletic (Chicago). Author: The Story of the Little Big Horn, 1926; The Custer Myth, 1953; Abstract of the Reno Court of Inquiry, 1954. Home: 555 Radcliffe Av., Pacific Palisades, Cal. Died Oct. 8, 1954; buried Arlington Nat. Cemetery.

GRANAHAN, William Thomas, congressman; born Phila., July 26, 1895; grad. LaSalle Extension U.; m. Kathryn O'Hay McNally, Nov. 20, 1943. Engaged in bldg. business, Phila. Mem. Democratic State Com., 4 yrs.; Democratic leader, 52d Ward, Phila.; former supr. inheritance tax and chief disbursing officer State Treasury, Commonwealth of Pa.; elected rep. 2d Pa. Dist., 79th Congress, 1944; re-elected to 81st-84th Congresses. Served with Army of Occupation, Germany, World War I. Member Am. Legion, Irish War Vets., Catholic War Vets, 20 and 8, Vets. Fgn. Wars. Democrat. Home: 2491 N. 50th St., Phila. Office: House Office Bldg., Washington 25. Died May 25, 1956; buried Easton, Pa.

GRANBERY, John Cowper, educator, editor born in Richmond, Virginia, June 15, 1874; son of Bishop John Cowper (D.D.) and Ella Fayette (Winston) G.; A.B., Randolph-Macon College, 1896; B.D., Vanderbilt, University, 1899; A.M., University of Chicago, 1908, Ph.D., 1909; D.D., Kentucky Wesleyan, 1913; married Mary Anne Catt, Jan. 22, 1903. Ordained ministry M.E. Ch., S., 1897; pastor Berlin Circuit, Williamsburg, Charlotte Circuit, Rocky Mount, Boydton, and Asbury Ch., Manchester, to 1909, Philippi and Barboursville, W.Va., and Paintsville, Ky., to 1913; prin. Sandy Valley Sem., Paintsville, Jan.-Sept. 1913; acting head dept. of edn. and asst. prof. sociology and economics, 1913-14, prof. sociology, economics and polit. science, 1914-25, Southwestern U.; head Dept. of History (including philosophy, sociology, and anthropology), Tex. Tech. College, 1925-32; engaged in travel, study, writing, and speaking, in Brazil, 1932-34; acting prof. philosophy and polit. science, Southwestern U., 1934-35, head of department of philosophy, 1935-38; founder (with May C. Granbery), publisher and editor of The Emancipator, 1938; visiting prof. history and economics, U. of San Antonio, summer, 1939-42. Visiting professor of Government, Our Lady of the Lake College, 1944; Government and History, Trinity Univ., 1944-45; prof. Greek, 1944-45, classical languages, 1945-46. President Methodist Council of Social Agencies of San Antonio District since 1947. War Work under Y.M. C.A. with American, French and Greek armies, 1917-1920. Decorated twice by Greek Government, golden cross of Order of Saviour, and Mil. Merit. Author: Outline of New Testament Christology, 1909; Students' Prolegomena to Philosophy, 1931. Contbr. articles and book revs. Made survey of Northern Africa, Balkans, and Eastern Europe for World League Against Alcoholism, summer, 1923. Contbg. editor Social Science. Address: 3305 W. Ashby, San Antonio 1. Died May 5, 1953.

GRANFIELD, William Joseph, judge; b. Springfield, Mass., Dec. 18, 1889; s. John and Ellen (O'Connor) G.; grad. Williston Sem., Easthampton, Mass., 1910; LL.B., U. Notre Dame, 1913; m. Jane Campbell, Aug. 30, 1919 (died Aug. 28, 1929); children—Eleanor Jane, William Joseph, John Campbell; m. 2d, Elsie I. Bemis, July 26, 1938; m. 3d, Ruth R. Belding, July 28, 1950. Began practice at Springfield, 1917. Mem. Common Council, Springfield, 1915-16; mem. Mass. Ho. of Reps., 1917-19; mem. Constl. Conv., Mass., 1917-18; del. Dem. Nat. Conv., 1924-28, del. at large, 1932, 36, asst. parliamentarian, 1940, elected mem. 71st Congress, 2d Mass. Dist., at spl. election, Feb. 1930, to fill vacancy caused by decease of William K. Kaynor; mem. 72d to 74th Congresses (1931-37); apptd. presiding justice, Dist. Ct. of Springfield (life term), July 22, 1936; ret. 1949. Mem. Spl. Commn. to Investigate Conn. River Navigation, 1946. Catholic. Address: 340 Arcadia Blvd., Springfield, Mass. Died May 28, 1959; buried St. Michael's Cemetery, Springfield.

GRANT, George Camron, coll. dean; b. Parkersburg, W.Va., Apr. 1, 1893; s. Jerry William and Minnie Belle (Brock) G.; student, Howard U., 1912-15; A.B., Morgan Coll., 1923, A.M., Columbia U., 1927, grad. work, 1932-33; D.Litt. (hon.). W. Va. State Coll., 1954; m. Marguerite Vandelia Westcott, July 15, 1915; children—George Camron, Earl Westcott, Ethel Minerva (Mrs. Clifton Scott Murray), Bernard Chivers. High sch. prin., 1923-25; supervisor of Kent County, Md., schs., 1925-27; prin. Morgan Acad., 1927-29; head dept. of edn., Morgan Coll., Balt., 1929-36, acting dean, 1936-37, dean since 1937. Dir. Community Fund of Baltimore, Inc., Metropolitan Board, Y.M.C.A., Balt. Council of Social Agencies (v.p.), Nat. Assn. of Collegiate Deans and Registrars in Negro Sch. (pres.), Md. Ednl. Assn. (pres. 1943), Mental Hygiene Soc. of Md., Balt. Urban League, Balt. Area Council, Boy Scouts of Am. Mem. Commn. on Med.-Legal Psychiatry, Md. Examiners Commn.; mem. com. Medical Care of State Planning Commn. Mem. Middle States Assn. Colls. and Secondary Schs., Am. Teachers Assn. Eastern Assn. of Coll. Deans and Advisers of Men. Southern Assn. Coll. and Secondary Schs., Kappa Delta Pi, Pi Lambda Psi, Gamma Boule, Sigma Pi Phi, Omega Psi Phi. Clubs: Monumental Golf, 25 Club, The Club (pres.) (Balt.). Contbr. to ednl. jours. Home: Morgan State Coll., Balt. Died Dec. 12, 1959.

GRANT, George Ernest, editor; b. Flushing, L.I., N.Y., Dec. 19, 1903; s. William Walter and Laura Louise (Perpall) G.; A.B., Colgate U., 1924; m. Marjorie Perez, May 24, 1935; children—Jenifer, Geoffrey Taylor, Philip Frisbie. With advt. dept. Certain-teed Products Corp., N.Y. City, 1925-30, Sloane-Blabon Corp., 1930-33; joined Reader's Digest Assn., Pleasantville, N.Y., 1933, sr. editor, 1945—. Trustee North Castle Free Library 1945-53, pres., 1953-55; trustee Urban League, v.p., 1953-55; trustee Community Coll. (both Westchester Co. N.Y.). Member Westchester County Historical Society, Westchester Co. Assn. Club: Whippoorwill (Armonk, N.Y.). Author: (booklet) A Project to Establish a Westchester County Museum. Home: Quartermile Rd., Armonk. Office: Reader's Digest Assn., Pleasantville, N.Y. Died June 19, 1955.

GRANT, James Richard, educator; b. Dover, Ark., Mar. 16, 1880; s. Daniel Richard and Mary Elizabeth (Aikins) G.; B.A., U. of Ark., 1908; Ph.B., DeKalb (Ill.) State Normal Sch., 1911; M.A., U. of Chicago, 1914; diploma, Teachers' Coll. (Columbia), 1918; Ph.D., Peabody Coll. for Teachers, 1925; LL.D. (hon.), Ouachita Coll., 1949; m. Gracey Sowers, Aug. 24, 1910; children—Bertie Elizabeth, James Richard, George Shell (killed in France on D-day, June 6, 1944), Grace Harriet, Daniel Ross. Teacher, principal and supt. pub. schs. in Ark. and Mo., 1909-12, prof. edn. and dir. teacher-training, U. of Ark., 1912-20; state supervisor rural schs. of Ark., 1920-26; pres. Ark. Polytechnic Coll., Russellville, 1926-31; mem. gen. extension faculty, Ark. State Teachers Coll., Conway, 1931-32; vice pres. and prof. edn. Ouachita Coll., 1932-33, pres. 1933-49, emeritus since 1949. Citation for Distinguished Alumnus, U. Ark., June 1949. Mem. N.E.A., Ark. Ednl. Assn. (pres. 1925-26), Phi Delta Kappa, Tau Kappa Alpha. Democrat. Baptist. Author: Acquiring Skill in Teaching, 1922; Pupil's Work Book in Arkansas Geography, 1922; A State's Teacher Training Problem, 1925; Life of Thomas C. McRae, 1930. Coauthor: History of Arkansas, 1935. Home: 1512 S. Pierce, Little Rock. Died Nov. 4, 1951; buried Rose Lawn Meml. Park, Little Rock.

GRANT, Richard Frank, coal and iron mcht.; b. Owatonna, Minn., Dec. 1, 1879; s. Frank Freeman and Mary (DeGolyer) G.; Ph.B., Yale, 1899; LL.B., N.Y. Law Sch., 1901; m. Elise Benton Hanchett, Feb. 10, 1910; children—Benton Hanchett, Richard De Golyer. Admitted to Minn. bar, 1902; mem. Sullivan & Grant, Duluth, 1903-09; mem. Ho. of Rep., 1908-09; apptd. gen. counsel M. A. Hanna & Co., Cleve., 1909, partner, 1917; v.p. The M. A. Hanna Co., 1923-28; also pres. Susquehanna Collieries Co. and Lytle Coal Co., 1923-28; pres. Lehigh Valley Coal Corp., 1928-33. Mem. Nat. War Finance Com., Am. Red Cross, World War I, also campaign mgr. Red Cross for Ohio, Ind. and Ky. Mem. Am. Bar Assn., Am. Iron and Steel Inst., Cleveland C. of C., (pres. 1923-24). U.S. C. of C. (pres. 1924-25). Book and Snake Soc. (Yale). Republican. Episcopalian. Home: R. 1, Vanderbilt, Mich. Died May 26, 1957; buried Minwendam Hills, Vanderbilt, Mich.

GRANT, Richard Ralph Hallam, corporation executive; b. Ipswich, Mass., Nov. 26, 1878; s. George Franklin and Anne (Hallam) G.; A.B., Harvard, 1901; m. Laura Elinor Williams, Sept. 1, 1906; children—Richard Hallam, Thirza Elinor (Mrs. A. R. Holladay). Gen. sales mgr. Nat. Cash Register Co., 1913-15; gen. mgr. Delco Light Co., 1915-20, pres. 1920-24; also pres. Frigidaire Co.; v.p. Chevrolet Motor Co., 1924-29; v.p. Gen. Motors Corp., 1929-44. mem. bd. dirs., 1932-53; mem. adminstrn. com. until retirement, Jan. 1944; now chmn. bd. The Reynolds & Reynolds Co., Dayton, O. Episcopalian. Clubs: Ye Buz Fuz, Miami Valley Hunt and Polo, Moraine Park Country (Dayton); Gulf Stream Bath and Tennis, Gulf Stream Golf (Delray Beach, Fla.); Union Harvard (N.Y.C.). Address: 740 Park Av., N.Y.C. Died Sept. 24, 1957; buried Centerville, O.

GRANT, Thomas McMillan, clergyman; b. Wilmington, N.C., July 28, 1886; s. Reuben and Elizabeth (McMillan) G.; A.B., Trinity Coll. (now Duke U.), 1909; D.D., High Point (N.C.) Coll., 1943; m. Malene Harrell, Dec. 28, 1910; children—Isa Costen (M.D.), Malene Elizabeth, M.D., (wife of C. Fred Irons, M.D.); m. 2d, Marie Hooker, June 12, 1919; one daughter, Ruby (Mrs. W. D. Bennett). Ordained to ministry of M.E. Church, South; deacon, 1911, elder, 1913; pastor (junior preacher),

Duke Memorial, Durham, North Carolina, 1909-10, Leasburg, N.C., 1910, Mangum St. Church, Durham, 1910-11, North Gates, N.C., 1911-15, Hillsboro, N.C., 1915-17, Hookerton, N.C., 1917-19, Hertford, N.C., 1919-23, Lumberton, N.C., 1923-27, Wilson, N.C., 1927-32; presiding elder, New Bern Dist., N.C., 1932-36, Jarvis Memorial, Greenville, N.C., 1936-41; dist. supt. Elizabeth City Dist., 1941-42, Rocky Mount. District, 1942-47; First Church, Rocky Mount, N.C., since 1947; mem. General Bd. Pensions, Methodist Ch., 1948-52. Trustee N.C. Conf. Methodist Ch.; sec. N.C. Conf. Meth. Episcopal Ch., South, 1925-38; sec. N.C. Conf. Meth. Ch. since 1938 (dir. superannuate endowment, 1929-39; pres. conf. Epworth League, 1923-31; mem. bd. missions and ch. extension). Mem. Gen. Conf., 1930, 34, 38, 40, 44, Uniting Conf., 1939. Trustee Duke U. Editor, N.C. Conf. Jour., Meth. Episcopal Ch., South, 1925-38, N.C. Conf. Jour., Meth. Ch., S.E. Jurisdiction, since 1939. Address: 1652 La Fayette Av., Rocky Mount, N.C. Died Dec. 31, 1952; buried Pineview Cemetery, Rocky Mount, N.C.

GRANT, William Thomas, insurance exec.; b. Middleport, O., Nov. 30, 1878; s. William H. and Ella J. (Logan) G.; ed. high sch., Ellinwood, Kan., Kan. U. Law Sch.; m. Frances Downing, 1908; children—Lucy Jane (Mrs. Clarence E. Cather), Frances Elizabeth, Esther Jane (Mrs. F. Douglas Williams), William Downing. Spl. representative Nat. Life Ins. Co. of U.S.A., Denver, 1902-03, state mgr. at Butte, Mont., 1903-04, agency mgr. at Kansas City, Mo., 1904, at Pittsburgh, Pa., 1905, again at Kansas City, 1906-09; organized Business Men's Assurance Co., Kansas City, 1909, sec., 1909-20, vice president, 1920-22, pres., 1922-44, chmn. bd. since 1945; dir. Emery Bird Thayer Dry Goods' Co., Peoples Securities Corp., Kansas City Fire and Marine Ins. Co., Metropolitan Savings & Loan Assn., Kansas City Airways. Chmn. bd. Kansas City Conservatory of Music; trustee Kansas City Philharmonic Orchestra Assn., Kansas City Y.W.C.A., U. of Kansas City; dir. Life Ins. Assn. Am.; member of board of Chevy Chase School, Washington, D.C.; mem. exec. com. Kansas City War Fund Chest; mem. Kansas City Chamber Commerce (es-pres.); mem. bd. govs. Am. Royal Livestock and Horse Show; former gen. chmn. Kansas City United Charity Campaign; former pres. Am. Life Conv., Health and Accident Underwriters Conf., International Claim Assn. Episcopalian. Clubs: Kansas City, Cooperative (ex-pres.), Mission Hills Country (ex-pres.). Home: 1241 W. 58th St. Office: Business Men's Assurance Bldg., Kansas City, Mo. Died Dec. 29, 1954.

GRANT, William West, lawyer; b. Davenport, Ia., June 27, 1881; s. William West and Adeline (Moseley) G.; A.B., Dartmouth Coll., 1903, also hon. A.M.; LL.B., U. Va., 1906; LL.D., Denver U., 1953; m. Gertrude Hendrie, Nov. 3, 1906; children—Edwin Hendrie, William West III, Melanie Mortimer. Admitted to Colo. bar, 1899, began practice at Denver; mem. Morris & Grant, 1910-16, Macbeth & Grant, 1923-27, Grant, Ellis, Shafroth & Toll., 1927-37, Grant, Shafroth & Toll., 1937—. Pres. Colo. Civil Service Commn., 1913, Denver Civil Service Commn., 1929; mem. Denver Zoning Commn., 1924, Denver Bd. Adjustment, 1925-35. Mem. Denver Bd. Edn., 1944-52, pres. 1947-49. Served as pvt. F.A., Replacement, U.S. Army, 1918; capt. O.R.C., 1918-28. Mem. bd. trustees Dartmouth, 1931—; mem. Nat. Council Episcopal Ch., 1940-46; chancellor P.E. Diocese Colo. Decorated Order Brit. Empire, 1949. Mem. Am., Colo. (pres. 1925), Denver (v.p. 1925) bar assns., Nat. Civil Service Reform League (mem. council), Am. Law Inst., Am. Judicature Soc., Psi Upsilon, Phi Delta Phi, Casque and Gauntlet. Episcopalian. Clubs: Arpahoe Hunt, Denver, Mile High, Denver Country. Home: 101 S. Humboldt St. Office: Equitable Bldg., Denver 3. Died June 30, 1957.

GRANVILLE, 4th Earl (William Spencer Leveson-Gower) (lōō'sŭn-gōr'), b. London, July 11, 1880; s. Granville George, 2d Earl Granville and Castalia Rosalind (Campbell) Leveson-Gower; LL.D. (hon.), Queen's U., 1950; m. Lady Rose Constance Bowes-Lyon, 1916; children—Mary Cecelia, James (Lord Leveson). Served with Grand Fleet Flotilla, European War, 1914-19; chief staff, maintenance capt. The Nore, 1924-27; naval a.d.c. to His Majesty, 1929; rear adm., comdg. Coast of Scotland, 1931-33; apptd. lt. gov. Isle of Man, 1937; hon. col., 15th (Isle of Man) Light Anti-Aircraft Regt., R.A., 1939; gov. No. Ireland, 1945-52. Decorated Knight of St. John; Companion Distinguished Service Order, Companion of the Bath, Knight Comdr. Victorian Order. Club: United Service (Pall Mall, London). Home: Pearsie, Kirriemuir, Angus, Scotland. Died June 25, 1953.

GRASON, C. Gus, judge; b. Towson, Md., Nov. 8, 1881; s. John and Ida (Brown) G.; student U. Md. Law Sch.; m. Muriel Skipwith Powers, 1910; children—Lelia Skipwith, W. H. Powers, Richard. Clerk, stenographer and rate clerk; then private law practice, Towson, 1908-26; asso. judge of Third Circuit Court of Appeals of Md., 1926-41, chief judge, 1942—. Home: Towson, Md. Deceased.

GRASSE, Edwin, violin virtuoso; b. N.Y.C., Aug. 13, 1884; s. Louis and Marie Ida (Sieghortner) G.; lost eyesight in infancy; studied violin under Carl Hauser, N.Y.C., until 1898; then under César Thomson, Brussels, Belgium; pupil Royal Conservatory, Brussels, winning 1st prize, with distinction, 1900, and Prix de Capacité, 1901; unmarried. Made debut in Berlin, Feb. 22, 1902, his first concert bringing him immediate success; has played in prin. cities of Europe and America; organist Bklyn. Inst. Arts and Scis., 1928; ret. 1940. Composer of suite for full orchestra, symphony, violin concertos, string quartette, 2 trios for piano, violin and cello, 4 sonatas for piano and violin, 20 songs without words for violin and piano; Am. Fantasie for violin and orchestra; also concert organist, composer for organ. Home and Studio: 220 W. 107th St., N.Y.C. Died. Apr. 1954.*

GRASSHOFF, Frank O., publisher; b. West Alexandria, O., Jan. 29, 1894; s. Henry and Mary (Zimmerman) G.; B.S., Wittenberg Coll., 1928, M.A., 1934; m. Norma Ludy, June 3, 1917. Supt. schs., 1919-20; dean Miami Jacobs Coll., 1929-42; sec., controller Jour. Herald Pub. Co., 1945-46, sec.-treas., 1946-48, exec. v.p., treas. since 1948, dir. since 1945; dir. Gen. Transportation & Storage Co. Served as 2d lt., U.S. Army, 1917-18; lt. col., A.C., 1942-45. Mem. Am. Newspaper Pubs. Assn., Controllers Inst. Am., Research Inst. Am., Y.M.C.A., Dayton Art Inst., Dayton C. of C., Am. Legion, Phi Delta Kappa. Methodist. Mason (Shriner), Lion. Clubs: Engineers, Miami Valley Golf, Executives. Home: 447 Cherry Dr., Dayton 2, O. Died May 8, 1952.

GRATZ, W. Edward J., clergyman; b. Hull, Can., Dec. 2, 1873; s. William Ernst and Kathrine (Steller) G.; came to U.S., 1881; student U. Minn., 1896-99; D.D., Hamline U., 1912; m. Emma Amelia, d. of Rev. J. G. Bauer, May 31, 1899; children—Dorothy Faith (dec.), Doris Hope (Mrs. Edward Tamm), Wesley Wilford, Gretchen Lois (Mrs. F. C. Potter), Darrel Bauer (dec.). Entered M.E. ministry, 1899, ordained, 1902; pastor successively, Melrose, Detroit, Princeton, Two Harbors (all Minn.), Joyce Memorial Ch., Mpls., Central Park Ch., St. Paul, St. Paul Ch., Lincoln, Neb.; sec. Dept. Institutes and Life Work of Epworth League, 1920-24; editor The Epworth Herald and Epworth League Publications of the M.E. Ch., 1924-40; pastor Our Saviors Meth. Ch., Evanston, 1941-43; pastor Emmanuel Meth. Ch., Evanston, 1943-46, acting gen. sec. Epworth League, 1924-25. Recording sec. Bd. of Edn., M.E. Ch., 1924-32; trustee Neb. Wesleyan U., 1917-20, Dakota Wesleyan U., 1924-40. Mason (K.T., 32°). Asso. editor: National Temperance Digest. Home: 820 B. Judson Av., Evanston, Ill. Died 1954.

GRAUER, Natalie Eynon, artist, teacher; b. Phila., Aug. 10, 1895; d. Wm. and Ann (Stewart) Eynon; student Nat. Acad. Design, 1915-18, Art Students League, 1915-20, Sch. Fine and Applied Arts, N.Y. City, 1915, Chicago Art Inst., 1923-24; m. Wm. C. Grauer, June 10, 1924; children—Blanche Eynon, Gretchen De Sanze, Portrait painter since 1925; owner, dir. Summer Sch. of Painting, East Claridon, O. Work exhibited Pa. Acad. Fine Arts, Nat. Acad. Design, Whitney Mus. Modern Art, Art Inst. Chicago, High Mus. of Atlanta, Acad. Fine Arts of Richmond, Cleveland Mus. Art. Rep. in permanent exhibitions, Laird Memorial Collection, Montgomery, W.Va., Washington and Lee U., Cleveland Coll., St. Johns Hospital, Cleveland, and pvt. collections. Organizer art dept., Cleveland Coll., Western Reserve U., 1935, and since named co-dir.; Old White Art Sch. and Colony, White Sulphur Springs, W.Va., 1932-42. Founded Old White Art Gallery at The Greenbriar, White Sulphur Springs. Awarded Larkin prize, Nat. Assn. Women Artists. N.Y. City, 1941; Awarded second prize Cleveland Mus. of Art, 1938, Four Honorable mentions, Cleveland Mus. of Art, 1940-45. Address: Grassmere, East Claridon, O. Died Oct. 28, 1955.

GRAVES, Charles Marshall, newspaper editor; born Charles City County, Va.; s. Richard Marcellus and Charles Anna (Otey) G.; direct desc. Capt. Thomas Graves who arrived in Jamestown Island, Va., 1608; mem. Yeardley Assembly, Jamestown, Virginia, 1619; g g s. Colonel Richard Croshaw Graves, comdg. troops New Kent and Charles City Counties, Va., during Revolutionary War; B.A., Univ. of Richmond (Va.), 1896; post-grad. study 1 yr. in classics, same univ.; m. Mary Blair Harvie, Apr. 30. 1903; children—Mary Michaux (Mrs. Francis Slade Danzoll), Va. Bernard (Mrs. Miles Cary). Was city editor of Richmond Times-Dispatch, 1903-07; on editorial staff since Sept. 30. 1907, news editor since 1912, editor of Sunday Rotogravure Picture Section, 1914-38 (first rotogravure editor in America), New York Times; gen. mgr. New York Times Wide World Photos (orgn. by him), 1919-41; under Arthur Hays Sulzberger, pub. New York Times, directed successful development first practical means in America for transmission photographs by ordinary telephone wires, Austin G. Cooley system. Democrat. Mem. Jamestowne Soc., Phi Chapter Phi Kappa Sigma, Phi Beta Kappa; founder and dir. Poe Memorial Society. Editor: Poems and Tales by Poe, 1906. An authority on Poe's life and writings. Contbr. to mags. Clubs: Englewood, Knickerbocker Country (Englewood, N.J.); Commonwealth, Country Club of Va. (Richmond). Home: Hotel Lucerne. Address: The Times, 229 W. 43d St., N.Y. City. Died Dec. 26, 1952; buried Hollywood Cemetery, Richmond, Va.

GRAVES, Eugene Silas, manufacturer; b. Chicago, Nov. 20, 1876; s. Eugene Luther and Fannie Mould (Brainard) G.; grad. Case Sch. Applied Science, 1899; grad. study Columbia, 1900-01, Farberei und Appreturschule, Crefeld, Germany, 1901-02; m. Delia Newton, June 4, 1902; children—Albro Newton, Eugene Brainard, Hubert Newton, Jean Graves Lynch, Hope, Franklin. Prof. chemistry New Bedford (Mass.) Textile Sch., 1901-08; treas. and gen. manager New Bedford and Agawam Bleachery, 1909-10; became v.p. and gen. mgr. Franklin Process Co., 1913, pres., 1922-45, chmn. bd., 1945-48, also of subsidiary cos., Southern Franklin Process Co., Central Franklin Process Co., Franklin Process Spinning Mill, Inc. Mem. Zeta Psi. Republican. Conglist. Home: 195 George St., Providence 6. Died Jan. 4, 1951.

GRAVES, Frank Pierrepont, educator, lawyer; b. Brooklyn, N.Y., July 23, 1869; s. Horace and Annie (Hall) G.; Brooklyn Poly. Prep. Sch., 1886; A.B., Columbia, 1890, A.M., 1891, Ph.D. (psychology and edn.), 1912, Doctors diploma in edn., 1912; Ph.D. (Greek and philosophy), Boston U., 1892; Litt. D., Heidelberg Coll. (Ohio), 1897, U. of Rochester, 1923, Canisius Coll., 1935; L.H.D., Tufts Coll., 1921, Colgate, 1922, Yeshiva, 1940; D.C.L., Ursinus Coll., 1937, University of the South, 1939; J.U.D., U. of Pa., 1940; LL.D., Alfred, Bethany, Boston, Bucknell, Columbia, Fordham, George Washington, Hamilton, Hanover, Hobart, Houghton, Juniata, Manhattan, Miami, Missouri, Niagara, Oberlin, Ohio, Pennsylvania, St. Bonaventure, St. John's (N.Y.), Syracuse, Union, Univ. State of N.Y., Washington (Md.), Western Reserve, William and Mary, Wyoming; LL.B., Albany Law Sch., 1943; m. Helen Hope Wadsworth, Dec. 18, 1895 (died Feb. 22, 1943); children—Katharine Bradford (Mrs. Edward B. Greene), Alden Wadsworth, Eleanor Hall (Mrs. W. Lewis Lyon), Richard Wadsworth; married 2d Mrs. Jessie Chase Malcolm, May 22, 1944 (dec. April 7, 1952), Assistant professor Greek, 1891-93; professor classical philology, Tufts Coll., 1893-96; president University of Wyoming, 1896-98; U. of Wash., 1898-1903; prof. history and principles of edn., and acting dean Teachers' Coll., U. of Mo., 1904-07; prof. history and philosophy of edn. and dean summer session, Ohio State U., 1907-13; prof. history of edn., summer 1907, U. of Wis., summers of 1912, 13, U. of Chicago, summer 1917, Columbia U. and summer 1925, U. of Calif.; prof. history of edn., and dean Sch. of Edn., U. of Pa., 1913-21; pres. U. of State of N.Y., and commr. of edn., 1921-40, retired; attorney for N.Y. State Teachers Assn. 1947—, visiting Carnegie prof., U. of Louvain, Belgium, 1928; editor Ednl. Review, 1920-24. Admitted to N.Y. State bar, 1943. Trustee City and County Savings Bank of Albany; voting trustee Williams Press, Inc., Albany. Alumni trustee Teachers' Coll. (Columbia), 1920-22; ex-officio trustee Cornell U. (mem. exec. com. and agrl. council), State Coll. Forestry, N.Y. State Teachers' Coll., and state agrl. schs., Russell Sage Coll., Albany Law School, Dudley Research Obs. (pres.). Mem. bd. govs. Union Univ., 1946—; v.p. Trans-Miss. and Internat. Expn., 1898. Mem. bd. visitors, U.S. Naval Acad., 1925. Decorated Knight of Crown of Belgium, 1925; Officer Legion of Honor, Fr., 1937. Awarded Butler medal for ednl. adminstrn., 1927; medal of Acad. of Pub. Edn., 1936; gold medal of Holland Soc., 1937; Am. Ednl. Award (Asso. Exhibitors), 1941. Mem. Nat. Advisory Com. on Edn., 1929-31. Fellow A.A.A.S.; mem. N.E.A., Am. Assn. of Sch. Adminstrs. (hon. life mem. 1941), Coll Teachers of Edn. (pres. 1920), Am. Assn. U. Profs, N.Y. State Historial Assn., English-Speaking Union, Am. Philos. Soc. (councillor 1933-36), Soc. of the Old Grads. of Columbia U., Foreign Policy Assn. (chmn. Albany br., 1940-41), Phi Beta Kappa (pres. Upper Hudson Chapter, 1925-26; senator of United chapters, 1928-52; nat. pres. 1937-40), Phi Delta Kappa, Phi Kappa Phi, Kappa Phi Kappa, Omicron Delta Kappa, Laureate Chapter of Kappa Delta Pi, Cum Laude, Pi Gamma Mu. Republican. Presbyterian (elder First Church). Clubs: University (Albany), City, Columbia Univ. (New York). Author: Burial Customs of the Ancient Greeks, 1891; The Philoctetes of Sophocles, 1893; A First Book in Greek (with Dr. E. S. Hawes), 1895; The State University Ideal, 1897; A History of Education Before the Middle Ages, 1909; A History of Education During the Middle Ages and the Transition to Modern Times, 1910; Great Educators of Three Centuries, 1911; Peter Ramus and the Educational Reformation of the Sixteenth Century, 1912; A History of Education in Modern Times, 1913; A Student's History of Education, 1915 and 1937; What Did Jesus Teach?, 1919; Administration of American Education, 1932; Addresses and Papers, 1921-26, 1926-31, 1931-36, 1936-40. Contbr. numerous articles on history of edn. and ednl. problems. Home: 303 Woodlawn Av. Address: 152 Washington Av., Albany, N.Y. Died Sept. 13, 1956; buried Albany, N.Y.

GRAVES, Henry Solon, forester; b. Marietta, O., May 3, 1871; s. William Blair and Luranah (Hodges) G.; A.B., Yale, 1892. A.M., 1900; spl. studies in forestry, Harvard and Univ. Munich; hon. A.M., Harvard, 1911; LL.D., Syracuse U., 1923, Yale, 1940; m. Ella Marian Welch, Dec. 19, 1903. Prof. forestry and dir. Forest Sch., Yale, 1900-10; chief of U.S. Forest Service, 1910-20; dean Sch. of Forestry, Yale, 1922-39; provost of Yale U., 1923-27, prof. emeritus, 1939—. Mem. Miss. Valley Com. (P.W.A.); pres. New Haven Park Commn. Served as lt. col. Corps Engrs., U.S. Army, 1917; A.E.F. Hon. mem. Am. Acad. of Arborists, Royal British Arboricultural Soc., Royal Scottish Arboricultural Soc.; fellow Soc. of Am. Foresters, Am. Geog. Soc.; mem. Am. Forestry Assn., A.A.A.S., Sigma Xi, Société Forestière de Franche-Comté de Belfort, and numerous assns. for the advancement of forestry and conservation. Author: Forest Mensuration, 1906; Principles of Handling Woodlands, 1911; also various bulls. Joint Author: The White Pine, 1896; Forest Education, 1932. Home: 339 Prospect St., New Haven, Conn. Died Mar. 7, 1951.

GRAVES, James Wesley, clergyman; b. Brookston, Ind., Jan. 25, 1868; s. Elza B. and Emily Jane G.; A.B., Franklin Coll., Ind., 1896; grad. Rochester (N.Y.) Theol. Sem., 1899; D.D., Des Moines Coll., 1912; m. Flora Emma Pierce, July 24, 1892; children—Mrs. Ruth Vivian Dooley, Mrs. Esther Bernice Preston, Mrs. Thelma Blanche Rogers, Winifred Virginia (Mrs. John R. D. Ransom). Ordained Baptist ministry, 1899; pastor, Mendon, N.Y., 1896-97, Gibbon, Neb., 1899-1902, Waverly, Ia., 1902-04, Dubuque, Ia., 1904-07, Calvary Ch., Des Moines, Ia., 1907-12; gen. sec. of Inter-Church Council, Des Moines, 1912-14; pastor First Church, Muscatine, Ia., 1914-18; orgn. sec. temperance work for Bapt. denomination, Phila., 1918; asso. sec. Temperance Commn. and Nat. Temperance Council of Federal Council Chs. of Christ in America, 1918; rep. Nat. Com. Northern Bapt. Laymen, 1919; pastor First Church, Clarksburg, W.Va., 1919-25, Binghamton, N.Y., 1925-1932; First Ch., Des Moines, Mar.-May 1933; exec. sec. All Ia. Prohibition Emergency Com., Apr.-July 1933. Pres. of Pub. Welfare Commn., Des Moines, 1911-14; sec. social service commission of Bapt. World Alliance, 1911; alt. mem. exec. com. Federal Council Chs. of Christ in America, 1911; trustee of Des Moines Coll., 1908; mem. bd. Iowa Bapt. Conv., 1908-18; mem. exec. bd. W.Va. Bapt. State Conv., 1920-25; mem. bd. mngrs. Am. Bapt. Publ. Soc. (vice chmn. bd., 1924-25; 1st v.p., 1924-25); mem. bd. trustees Anti-Saloon League of N.Y.; v.p. Colgate-Rochester Div. Sch. Alumni Assn., 1932-33. Mem. Phi Delta Theta. Mason. Home: 4134 Sixth St. S., St. Petersburg 5, Fla. Died Aug. 22, 1950; buried Meml. Park Cemetery, St. Petersburg.

GRAVES, John (Lafayette), govt. official; b. Butler, Mo., Sept. 25, 1901; s. Waller Washington and Alice Medora (Ludwick) G.; A.B., William Jewell Coll., Liberty, Mo., 1923; student, U. of Mo. Law Sch., 1923-25; m. Alice Barnett, June 20, 1934; 1 dau., Alice Medora. Admitted to Mo. bar, 1925; asso. atty., law firm Jourdan & English, St. Louis, 1925-31; asso., law firm Dearmont & Russell, Cape Girardeau, Mo., 1931-33; bond atty. State of Mo., 1933-43; sr. atty. legal div., bur. of pub. dept. U.S. Treasury, 1943-45, chmn. com. on practice, 1946—. Mem. Mo. Bar Assn., S.A.R., Boy Scouts of Am., Kappa Alpha. Democrat. Methodist. Club: Kiwanis Internat. Home: 3355 S. Stafford St., Arlington, Va. Office: U.S. Treasury Dept., Washington. Died Jan. 8, 1953; buried Oakhill Cemetery, Butler, Mo.

GRAVES, Robert John, surgeon; b. Boscawen, N.H., June 22, 1878; s. Eli Edwin and Martha Annette (Williams) G.; B.S., Harvard, 1900, M.D. from same, 1903; m. Helen McGregor Ayres, Oct. 10, 1905; children—Katharine (Mrs. Russell R. Larmon), Jane Phillips (Mrs. Woodbury Howard), John Kimball, Robin McGregor (wife of Dr. Henry J. Koch, Jr.). Began practice at Concord, 1904; medical director United Life and Accident Ins. Co. since 1917; chief surgeon B.&M. R.R. since 1921; dir. Mechanicks Nat. Bank; trustee Loan & Trust Savings Bank. Maj. Med. Corps, U.S. Army, chief of orthopedic service, Ft. McHenry, nr. Baltimore, Md., World War. Conglist. Mason (32°). Clubs: Snow Shoe (Concord); Harvard (Boston). Home: Beech Hill, Hopkinton, N.H. Office: 5 S. State St., Concord, N.H. Died Sept. 1950.

GRAVES, William Washington, neuropsychiatrist; b. La Grange, Ky., Nov. 13, 1865; s. David William and Julia Ann (Crockett) G.; M.D., St. Louis Coll. Phys and Surg., 1888; post graduate work London, Heidelberg, Berlin and Vienna, 1901-04; m. Helena J. Sessinghaus, June 9, 1891; 1 dau., Helen (dec.). With St. Louis U. Med. Sch., 1905—, prof. nervous and mental diseases, 1914—, dir. of dept., 1923—. Mem. A.M.A., A.C.P., St. Louis Med. Soc., Am. Neurol. Assn., Am. Psychiatric Assn., Alpha Kappa Kappa, Alpha Omega Alpha. Awarded Certificate of Merit and gold medal for scientific accomplishment based on his classification of scapulae and his discovery of the age-incidence principle of investigation, St. Louis Med. Soc., 1939. Democrat. Baptist. Mason (32°), Elk. Home: 5136 Enright Av. Office: 1402 S. Grand Blvd., St. Louis, Mo. Died Apr. 18, 1949.

GRAY, Carl Raymond, Jr., ret. VA ofcl.; b. Wichita, Kan., Apr. 14, 1889; s. Carl Raymond and Harriette (Flora) G.; student Western Mil. Acad., Alton, Ill.; A.B., U. of Ill., 1911; m. Gladys Beach, Oct. 16, 1911 (dec.); children—Gladys (Mrs. Maxwell Dieffenbach), and Carl Raymond III. Began with St. L.&S.F. R.R., 1911; asst. engineer Ore. Electric Ry. and S.P.&S. Ry., 1911-12; trainmaster and supt., 1912-13; asst. to gen. mgr. C.,B.&Q. R.R., 1913-14; asst. to gen. supt. St.L.&S.F. R.R., 1914-15; asst. engr. Consolidated Coal Co., Baltimore, Md., 1916; pres. Peach Bottom Slate Corp., 1916-17; gen. supt. Montgomery Ward & Co., 1919-20, gen. mgr. Chicago house, 1920-21; gen. mgr. City Ice Co., Kansas City, Mo., 1922-23, v.p. and gen. mgr., 1923-25; v.p. Central Mfg. District Bank, Chicago, 1926; mgr. industrial dept. C.&N.W. Ry. and C.,St.P.,M.&O. Ry., 1928-29; gen. mgr., C.,St.P.,M.&O. Ry. at St. Paul, 1929, v.p. and gen. mgr. of operation and maintenance, 1930-37, exec. vice pres., 1937-46; v.p. Chicago & Northwestern System, 1946-48; dir. Investors Mutual, Inc., subsidiary Investors Syndicate; administrator Veterans Affairs, VA, 1947-53. Served as capt., maj. and lt. col., U.S. Army, World War I; later, col., U.S. Engr. Res.; apptd. brig. gen. in charge railway transportation Allied European Theater War, 1942; promoted maj. gen., 1945. Decorated D.S.M., Legion of Merit with oak leaf cluster, Bronze Star Medal, Army Commendation Medal (U.S.); Italian War Cross for Merit, Order Crown of Italy; Knight Comdr. Brit. Empire (Gt. Brit.); Officer Legion of Honor, Croix de Guerre with 2 palms (France); Order Crown of Belgium. Mem. Soc. American Railway Engrs., Am. Mil. Engrs., Soc. Mayflower Descendants, S.A.R., Sons Confederate Vets., Order Founders and Patriots of America, Am. Legion. Military Ry. Service Veterans, Mil. Order World War, Reserve Officers Association, Sigma Alpha Epsilon. Republican. Baptist Clubs: St. Paul Athletic, Minnesota, Midway, Transportation (St. Paul); Interfraternity, Economic, Traffic (Chicago). Home: 1021 Third St., Hudson, Wis. Died Dec. 2, 1955; buried Willow River Cemetery, Hudson, Wis.

GRAY, Charles Harold, educator; b. Guthrie, Okla., Feb. 13, 1892; s. George Edwin and Marion Alice (Paddock) G.; A.B., U. of Wash., 1913; student Lincoln Coll., Oxford U., 1914-17; M.A., Columbia U., 1924, Ph.D., 1931; m. Helen Lenore McGregor, Dec. 22, 1919; children—McGregor, Carlyle. Instr. English, Reed Coll., Portland, Ore., 1917-20, asst. prof., 1920-21; research asst., Columbia U., 1922-23; asst. prof. English, Adelphi Coll., Brooklyn, 1923-24; prof. English, St. John's Coll., 1924-25; asst. prof. English, Bowdoin Coll., 1925-28, asso. prof., 1928-30, prof. and Pierce prof. English, 1930-33; mem. faculty, Bennington Coll., 1933-40; dean Bard College, Columbia Univ., 1940-44; pres. Bard College, 1944-46; head of English dept., Rensselaer Polytechnic Inst., Troy, N.Y., 1947-53; Fulbright vis. prof. U. Philippines, 1951-52; dir. div. academic studies Juilliard Sch. Music, N.Y.C. since 1953. Awarded Rhodes scholarship, 1914-17; U. fel. Columbia, 1921-22. Democrat. Episn. Author: Theatrical Criticism in London to 1795, 1931. Editor: Hazlitt Essays, 1928. Home: 50 Morningside Dr., N.Y.C. 25. Died May 14, 1959.

GRAY, Finly H., ex-congressman; b. on farm, Fayette County, Ind., July 24, 1864; s. John G. and Mercie B. (Demeree) G.; pub. schs., Fayette County; m. Alice Green, 1901. Admitted to Ind. bar, 1892, began practice at Connersville; mayor of Connersville, 1904-09. Mem. 62d to 64th and 73d to 75th Congresses, 6th, later 10th Ind. Dist. Democrat. Modern Woodman. Home: Connersville, Ind. Died May 8, 1947; buried Dale Cemetery, Connersville.

GRAY, Henry G., lawyer; b. N.Y. City, Oct. 4, 1875; s. John Clinton and Henrietta P. (Gunther) G.; student Pensionnat Haccius, 1890-92; A.B. magna cum laude, Harvard, 1897, A.M., 1898, LL.B. cum laude, 1900; m. Edith Deacon, Nov. 9, 1916. Admitted to N.Y. bar, 1900; dep. asst. dist. atty., N.Y. Co., 1902-05; partner Sage, Gray, Todd & Sims, and predecessors, N.Y. City, since 1907. Trustee Lawrenceville Sch., 1922-43, trustee emeritus since 1943; v.p., mem. exec. com. Prison Assn. of N.Y.; chmn. local draft bd. 91, N.Y. City, World War I. Home: 340 E. 72d St., N.Y. City 21. Office: 37 Wall St., N.Y.C. 5. Died July 5, 1954.

GRAY, Howard Adams, corp. exec.; b. Alton, Ill., Nov. 16, 1878; s. Howard Pinkney and Imogen (Skinner) G.; ed. Evanston (Ill.) Twp. High Sch., 1893-94, St. Paul's Sch., Concord, N.H., 1895-97; m. Gertrude Marie Lacey, Aug. 18, 1919; children—Mary Imogen, Howard Adams, Gertrude Lacey. Clerk Hanover Fire Ins. Co., 1897-1901; with Joseph T. Ryerson & Son, steel mfrs., Chgo., 1901-24, Ulster Iron Works, 1924-27; exec. v.p. Yates Am. Machine Co., Beloit, Wis., 1927-31; became dir. inspection div. Fed. Emergency Adminstrn. Pub. Works, Washington, 1933, dir. housing div., July 1936; asst. adminstr. Pub. Works Adminstrn., 1937-39; dir. Bituminous Coal Div., Dept. Interior, 1939-41; dep. solid fuels adminstrn. for war, Dept. Interior, 1941-43; now ret. Democrat. Episcopalian. Home: Ashburn Farm, Ashburn, Va. Died June 2, 1958.

GRAY, Howard Kramer, surgeon; b. St. Louis, Mo., Aug. 28, 1901; s. Carl Raymond and Harriette (Flora) G.; B.S., Princeton U., 1923; student U. of Neb., Coll. of Med., 1923-25, D.Sc. (honorary); M.D., Harvard, 1927; M.S., in surgery, Univ. of Minn., Mayo Foundation, 1932; D.Sc. (hon.), Lafayette College; married Lila DeWeenta Conrad, September 2, 1925; children—Howard Kramer, DeWeenta Russell (Mrs. Walter I. Bones, Jr.). Fellow in surgery, Mayo Foundation, 1928-32; jr. surgeon, Mayo Clinic, 1932-35, surgeon and head of a sect. in surgery since 1935; professor, Mayo Foundation, Graduate Sch., U. of Minn., since 1935. Captain U.S. Naval, Med. Corps Res. Fellow A.C.S., So. Surg. Assn. A. M.A.; mem. Am. Surg. Assn., Am. Assn. Thoracic Surgery, Western Surgical Assn., Soc. of Clinical Surgery, Surgeons' Club, Minn. State Med. Assn., Minn. Surg. Assn., Southern Minn. Med. Assn., Nu Sigma Nu. Independent. Baptist. Clubs: Ivy (Princeton, N.J.); Rochester Country, Rochester Tennis. Contbr. to med. jours. Home: 612 10th Av., S.W. Office: Mayo Clinic, Rochester, Minn. Died Sept. 6, 1955; buried Rochester, Minn.

GRAY, James Alexander, chairman of board of directors R. J. Reynolds Tobacco Company; born at Winston-Salem, North Carolina, August 21, 1889; s. James Alexander and Aurelia (Bowman) G.; A.B., University of North Carolina, 1908, LL.D., 1941; LL.D., Duke University, 1952; married Pauline L. Bahnson, Apr. 18, 1918; children—James A., Bahnson, Howard, Christine, Pauline, Aurelia. Began as clerk Wachovia Nat. Bank, Winston-Salem, 1908; asst. treas. Wachovia Bank & Trust Co., 1911-15, treas., 1915-18, v.p., 1918-19; mem. bd. dirs. since 1918; v.p. R. J. Reynolds Tobacco Co., 1920-34, pres, 1934-46, chmn. exec. com., 1946-49, mem. bd. dirs. since 1919, chmn. since 1949. Mem. City Hosp. Com., 1914. Chmn. Co. Highway Bd., Forsyth Co., N.C., 1915-16; mem. No. Carolina Senate, 1917-20. Pres. N. C. Bankers Assn., 1918-19; mem. exec. council Am. Bankers Assn., 1920-21. Trustee University of N.C., Methodist Children's Home. Democrat. Methodist. Clubs: Rotary, Twin City, Old Town, Forsyth Country. Address: R. J. Reynolds Tobacco Co., Winston-Salem 1, N.C. Died Oct. 29, 1952; buried Salem Cemetery, Winston-Salem, N.C.

GRAY, Joseph M. M., clergyman; b. Montgomery, Pa., Aug. 31, 1877; s. Joseph and Mary Ann (Miller) G.; A.B., Dickinson Sem., 1896; B.D., Drew Theol. Sem., 1901; D.D., Baker U., Baldwin, Kan., 1914; Litt.D., Syracuse Univ., 1923; S.T.D., Dickinson Coll., Carlisle, Pa., 1931; H.H.D., Ohio Wesleyan Univ., 1949; m. Elizabeth McCurdy, Oct. 14, 1903; children—Charles M., Joseph C., Elisabeth. Ordained M.E. ministry, 1901; pastor Rogers Meml. Ch., Balt., 1901-04, Wesley Chapel, Balt., 1904-06, Havre De Grace, Md., 1906-08, East Baltimore Station, 1908-11, Hamline Ch., Washington, 1911-13, Grand Av. Ch., Kansas City, Mo., 1913-20, Elm Park Ch., Scranton, Pa., 1920-28, Central Ch., Detroit, 1928-34; chancellor American University, Washington, 1934-40; pastor Bexley Meth. Ch., Columbus, O., 1941—. Lectured on hist. and religious subjects in army camps, England and France, 1918. Mem. Gen. Conf. M.E. Ch., 5 times, Uniting Conf., Meth. Ch., 1939. Republican. Mason (33°). Author: Old Faith in the New Day, 1915; The Contemporary Christ, 1921; An Adventure in Orthodoxy, 1923; Sufficient Ministers, 1925; Concerning The Faith, 1928; Prophets of the Soul, 1936; The Post-War Strategy of Religion, 1944. Exchange preacher in Eng., summer 1923. Retired 1950. Home: 4 Ridgefield Rd., Winchester, Mass. Died Jan. 9, 1957.

GRAY, Louis Herbert, comparative philologist, Orientalist; b. Newark, N.J., Apr. 10, 1875; s. Thomas Jefferson and Anna Elizabeth (Earl) G.; A.B., Princeton, 1896; fellow in classics, 1896-97; A.M., Columbia U., 1898, Ph.D., 1900; fellow Indo-Iranian, Columbia, 1897-1900; m. Florence Lillian Ridley, June 8, 1905 (died June 8, 1942). Chief cataloguer and instructor in Indo-Iranian, Princeton University, 1900-02; editor departments of etymology and the modern history of India, New International Encyclopedia, 1902-03; reviser translations for The Jewish Encyclopedia, 1904-05; asst. editor of and contbr. to Hastings' Encyclopaedia of Religion and Ethics (Edinburgh), 1905-15; editor of Mythology of All Races, 1915-18. With Am. Commn. to Negotiate Peace, 1918-19; attached to U.S. embassy, Paris, 1920; asso. prof. philosophy, U. of Neb., 1921-23, prof. comparative philology and Oriental langs., 1923-26; prof. Oriental langs., Columbia, 1926-35, prof. comparative linguistics, 1935-44; prof. emeritus, 1944—. Mem. American Oriental Soc., Linguistic Soc. of Am., Philol. Soc. (London), Société de Linguistique de Paris, corresponding mem. Societe d'histoire et d'archéologie de Senlis. Ratanbai Katrak lecturer on Zoroastrainism, Oxford U., 1925. Fellow Am. Acad. Arts and Scis. Episcopalian. Author: Indo-Iranian Phonology, 1902; The Hundred Love-Songs of Kamal ad-Din of Isfahan (with Ethel Watts Mumford), 1904; translation and edition of Vasavadatta, a Sanskirt Romance by Subandhu, 1913; Spitzhergen and Bear Island, 1919; Foundations of the Iranian Religions, 1929; Introduction of Semitic Comparative Linguistics, 1935; Foundations of Language, 1939; History of the Parish of St. Ignatius, New York City, 1946; also numerous articles on languages, literatures and religions of India, Armenia and Persia and on comparative linguistics, in various tech. journals. Editor: George Louis Beer's posthumous African Questions at Paris Peace Conference, 1923; Wisdom of the East (Vol. I of Columbia U. Course in Literature), 1928. Address: 450 Riverside Drive, N.Y.C. 27. Died Aug. 18, 1955.

GREATOREX, Kathleen Honora, artist; b. Hoboken, N.J., Sept. 10, 1851; d. Henry Wellington and Eliza (Pratt) G.; studied art in N.Y., Rome and Munich; unmarried. Besides decorative work and book illustration, has done much work in painting flower pieces, etc., which she has exhibited in the Paris Salon and elsewhere; hon. mention, Paris Salon; gold medals, Phila., Chgo. and Atlanta expns. Address: Moret, Seine et Marne, France. Deceased.

GREAVES, Joseph Eames, biochemist; b. Logan City, Utah, Nov. 2, 1880; s. Joseph C. and Catherine (Eames) G.; B.S., Utah Agrl. Coll., 1904; M.S., U. of Ill., 1907; Ph.D., U. of Calif., 1911; m. Pernecy Dudley, June 10, 1907 (died May 9, 1918); children—Joseph D., Florence D., Pernecy D., Vera D., Mary Oretta; m. 2d, Ethelyn Oliver, May 5, 1920; children—Marguerite Oliver, Thelma Mae, Oliver. Began as instructor in chemistry, Utah Agrl. Coll., 1907, asst. prof., 1908-10, asso. prof. physiol. chemistry, 1911-13, professor bacteriology and physiological chemistry, 1913-27, professor bacteriology and public health, 1927-29, professor bacteriology and biochemistry since 1929; also bacteriologist Utah Experimental Sta. Member Logan City Bd. of Health. Mem. Am. Chem. Soc., Am. Bacteriol. Soc., A.A. A.S., Am. Public Health Assn., Am. Soc. Biochemists, Utah Acad. Science Arts and Letters (pres. 1947). Latter Day Saint. Author: Agricultural Bacteriology, 1922; Bacteria in Relation to Soil Fertility (with E. O. Greaves), 1925; Elementary Bacteriology (with same), 5th edit., 1945; also over 100 articles in professional jours. Cons. editor Soil Science; contributing editor Americana Annual. Home: 445 North 3 E., Logan City, Utah. Died June 6, 1954; buried Logan City, Utah.

GREELEY, William B., forester; b. Oswebo, N.Y., Sept. 6, 1879, s. Frank Norton and Anna Cheney (Buckhout) G.; LL.B., Univ. of Calif., 1901, LL.D. (hon.), 1925; M.F., Yale, 1904, M.S., 1924; m. Gertrude Maxwell Jewett, Dec. 30, 1907; children—Molly (Mrs. J. A. Harvey, Jr.), Arthur W., Henry J., David C. With U.S. Forest Service, Cal., Hot Springs, Missoula, Mont., Washington, D.C., 1904-17, 1919-28, chief forester, 1920-28; sec.-mgr. West Coast Lumbermen's Assn., Seattle, 1928-45; bd. chmn. Am. Forest Products Industries, Inc., Seattle, 1946—. Mem. Wash. Forest Products Inst. Commn. Served as major and lt. col., U.S. Corps Engrs., 1917-19; organized 10th engrs. (forestry), head forestry sect. A.E.F. on timber operations in France, 1918-19. Decorated Chevalier Legion of Honor (France), 1918; Distinguished Service Order (England), 1919; Distinguished Service medal (U.S.), 1919; Sir William Schlich Forest medal, 1946. Fellow Soc. Am. Foresters (council mem.), West Coast Lumbermen's Assn. (vice pres.), Am. Forestry Assn. (vice pres.), Keep Wash. Green Assn. (pres.), Delta Upsilon, Phi Beta Kappa. Republican. Clubs: Cosmos (Washington, D.C.); Wash. Athletic (Seattle). Author: Forests and Men; Forest Policy. Home: Star Route, Suquamish, Wash. Office: Stuart Bldg., Seattle 1. Died Nov. 30, 1955.

GREEN, Allen Percival, fire brick mfr.; b. Jefferson City, Missouri; son of Joseph H. and Eliza (McHenry) G.; student Sch. of Mines and Metallurgy (U. of Mo.), D.Eng., 1935; LL.D., Westminster College, Missouri, 1933; D.Sc., Alfred (N.Y.) U., 1943; m. Josephine Brown, June 17, 1903; children—Elizabeth C. (Mrs. Arthur D. Bond), Martha McHenry (Mrs. Walter Goodwin Staley), Josephine (Mrs. Neal Shackleford Wood), Allen Percival, Robert Stafford. Formerly civil and mining engr., gen. practice; dir., gen. mgr. sales, Harbison-Walker Refractories Co., Pitts.; v.p. Evens & Howard Fire Brick Co., St. Louis; pres. A. P. Green Fire Brick Company, Mexico, Missouri, 1910-46, chmn. board 1946—; pres. A. P. Green Fire Brick Co., Ltd. (Toronto), Cia. Mexicana Refractories A. P. Green (Mexico City); pres. Bigelow Liptak Corp. (Detroit); partner, Cia. Mexicana de Refractarios A. P. Green, S.A.; dir., mem. exec. com. Wabash Ry.; dir. Ann Arbor R.R., New Jersey, Ind. & Ill. R.R., Liptak Furnace Arches, Ltd., London, Mercantile Trust Co., St. Louis. Mem. Com. of R.R. Dirs., Commr. Plan R.Rs. West of Miss. River. Mem. adv. com. Senate Capehart Com. of Fair Trade Practice. Mem. Refractories Inst., Am. Chem. Soc., Am. Ceramic Soc., A.S.M.E., State Hist. Soc. Mo. (v.p.). Democrat. Presbyn. Clubs: Missouri Athletic Assn., Racquet (St. Louis); Bath, Surf. Home: 16 S. Jefferson Rd. Office: care A. P. Green Fire Brick Co., Mexico, Mo. Died June 9, 1956; buried Mexico, Mo.

GREEN, Charles Henry, expn. dir.; b. Albion, Mich., Apr. 17, 1867; s. Henry S. and Mary E. (Ketcham) G.; ed. Homer Acad., Mich.; registered chemist in Mich.; m. Ada May Kerhaghan, July 16, 1890 (died Oct. 16, 1917); children—Lloyd Francis, Harold Clement; m. 2d, Adele Wright Drummond, Nov. 26, 1920; 1 dau., Marilynn Adele. Advt. and sales mgr. Shredded Wheat Co., Niagara Falls, N.Y., 1900-02; in expn. work as mng. dir. or pres. of over 50 trade expns., 1903-13; chief Dept. of Mfrs. and Varied Industries, Panama-Pacific Internat. Expn., San Francisco, 1913-15; U.S. commr. to Japan and China in interest of same; mem. Superior Jury Internat. Jury of Award, Panama P.I. Expn., 1915. Mng. dir. Nat. Music Show, Internat. Silk Expn., Internat. Fur Expn., Archtl. and Allied Arts Expn., Internat. Fabric Expn.; del. representing Archtl. League N.Y. to Paris Decorative and Indsl. Arts Expn., 1925. Tech. adv. N.J. Commn. N.Y. World's Fair, 1939. Veteran Co. A, 4th Regt. Mich. N.G. Received Chia Ho decoration from Pres. of China, 1916; Gold Medal of Honor, Archtl. League N.Y., 1925. Republican. Episcopalian. Home: Ridgewood, N.J. Office: 127 W. 43d St., N.Y.C. Deceased.

GREEN, Conant Lewis, lawyer; b. Attica, Ind., May 16, 1884; s. Alonzo Philip and Esther (Thompson) G.; student liberal arts, U. Mich., 1902-04, LL.B., 1907; m. Edna Glenn Simison, June 24, 1909; children—Esther Glenn (Mrs. Don Menke), Enid Gwendolyn (dec.), Adda Miriam (Mrs. J. E. Ross), Doris Elizabeth (Mrs. Thoburn Wiant). Edward Simison, Lt. Richard Lewis (lost at sea, Apr. 14, 1944), Constance Anne (Mrs. Joseph Wick), Alice Amber (dec.), Keith Alonzo (dec.). Admitted to Ind. bar, 1906, Ill. bar, 1912; in practice at Attica, 1907-11, 13-31, Danville, Ill., 1911-13, Indpls., 1931—, Noblesville, Ind., 1947—; atty. for Wabash R.R. and C.&E.I. R.R. Pres. Sch. Bd., Attica, 9 yrs. Mem. Sigma Nu, Barristers Sinfonia. Republican. Methodist. Clubs: Kiwanis (pres.), Harrison Hills Country (Attica); Columbia (Indianapolis); Lions (Carmel, Ind.). Home: Trails End Road. R.R. 5. Office: Hamilton Bldg., Noblesville, Ind. Deceased.

GREEN, Darrell Bennet, prof. elec. engring.; b. Martinsville, Ill., Feb. 11, 1893; s. Henry Alvarado and Catherine Anne (Bennett) G.; student, Central Normal Coll., 1912-19; A.B., A.M., Ph.D., Ind. Univ., 1921-37; student U. of Wis., 1925, Ohio State, 1931, Ia. Univ., 1929; m. Minnie Jean Lotich, 1917; children—Ursula Kathryn, Nona Jean. Became public sch. teacher, 1912, high sch. teacher, 1916; coll. prof. since 1925. Director of engring. Ohio Univ., 1943-47, chairman electrical engring., 1937-57. Mem. Internat. Illuminating Commn., Zurick, 1955. Licensed professional engineer, Ohio, 1946. Mem. Inst. of Radio Engrs., Am. Inst. E.E. Illuminating Engrs, Soc., Phi Delta Kappa. Sigma Xi. Home: 5 Arden Place, Athens, O. Died Feb. 20, 1959; buried West Union St. Cemetery, Athens.

GREEN, Dwight H., ex-governor; b. Ligonier, Ind., Jan. 9, 1897; s. Harry and Minnie (Gerber) G.; student Wabash College, 1915-17; Stanford University, 1919; Ph.B., University of Chicago, 1920, J.D., 1922; LL.D., MacMurray College, Blackburn College, 1941, Northwestern Univ., Illinois Wesleyan U., 1942; Knox College, 1945; Monmouth College, Lake Forest Coll., 1947; m. Mabel Victoria Kingston, June 29. 1926; children—Nancy Kingston (Mrs. J. B. Gilbert), Gloria K. (Mrs. W. McPherson). Admitted Ill. bar, 1922, and practiced at Chgo. until 1926; spl. atty. Bur. of Internal Revenue, Washington, D.C., 1926; apptd. spl. rep. gen. counsel, same bur., Chicago, 1927; served as spl. asst. to U.S. atty. for Northern Dist. of Ill., in charge income tax matters; conducted prosecutions for United States against Al Capone and other notorious gangsters also against public office holders charged with acceptance of bribes and graft; United States district attorney No. Dist. Ill., 1932-35; gov. Ill., 1941-49. Keynoter, Rep. Nat. Conv., 1948. Mem. bd. dirs. Research Found.; bd. trustees Wabash Coll. Served as 2d lt. Air Service, U.S. Army, 1917-19; army pilot and flying instr., Mather Field, Sacramento, Calif., 1918-19. Member American, Ill. State and Chicago bar assns., Ind. Soc. of Chgo. (pres. 1950-51, 54-55), Mil. Order of World Wars, Legal Club of Chgo., Fed. Bar Assn., United Cerebral Palsy Association of Chicago (pres., 1956—, chmn. bd. 1957), Kappa Sigma, Phi Alpha Delta (supreme justice 1936-38), Am. Legion, 40 and 8. Republican. Episcopalian. Mason (33°, Shriner). Clubs: Law, Tavern, Executives, Mid-Day, Chicago Athletic Assn., Saddle and Cycle (Chgo.). Address: 231 S. La Salle St., Chgo. 4. Died Feb. 20, 1958.

GREEN, Edward Brodhead, architect; b. Utica, N.Y., May 10, 1855; s. William Harry and Cornelia (Blackmar) G.; B.Arch., Cornell, 1878; m. Harriet B. Edson, June 16, 1887; children—Edward Brodhead, Mrs. Cornelia Coe, Paul Edson. Mem. Green & Wicks, Auburn, N.Y., 1880-83, Buffalo, 1883-1917; Edward B. Green & Sons, 1917-33; Green & James, 1933-45, Green James & Meadows, 1945—. Architect for Albright Art Gallery, Toledo Art Gallery, Marine Trust Co. (Buffalo), 3 bldgs. for Agrl. Coll. of Cornell U., Scranton Library, Buffalo Savings Bank, Art Inst. of Dayton (O.), Toledo Music Hall, Genesee Bldg., Erie County Jail, Buffalo Meml. Auditorium, 5 Fed. housing projects for Buffalo Municipal Housing Authority and one State housing project for Tonawanda Housing Authority; also Lockwood Meml. Library, Norton Hall, Crosby Hall and Gymnasium for U. Buffalo. Pres. State Bd. for Registration and Examination of Architects. Recipient U. Buffalo chancellor's medal, 1938. Fellow A.I.A.; dir. Buffalo Fine Arts Acad. (pres. 1915); mem. Kappa Alpha. Clubs: Saturn, Canoe, Buffalo, Buffalo Athletic. Home: 19 Mayfair Lane, Buffalo 1. Office: 250 Delaware Av., Buffalo 2, N.Y. Died Feb. 11, 1950.

GREEN, Edwin Luther, educator; b. Milton, Fla., Dec. 13, 1870; s. Alexander Hamilton and Lauretta Virginia (Fisher) G.; A.B., Washington and Lee U., 1892, Litt.D., 1942; Ph.D., Johns Hopkins, 1897; m. Gertrude Priest Cravens, Dec. 22, 1909; children—Edwin Luther, Estill Cravens (dec.), Christopher Ayer. Prof. Greek and German, Central U., Richmond, Ky., 1898-99; adj. and asso. prof. ancient langs., U. S.C., 1900-10, prof., 1910—. Mem. Am. Philol. Assn., Classical Assn. Middle West and South (sec.-treas. So. sect. 1921-25, pres. 1929-30), Phi Beta Kappa. Presbyterian. Author: School History of Florida, 1898; Indians of South Carolina, 1904; History of the University of South Carolina, 1916; History of Richland County (S.C.), 1932; George McDuffie, 1936. Unpublished manuscript, Life of William C. Preston, in Library of Congress. Home: 328 Sims Av., Columbia, S.C. Died Aug. 8, 1948; buried Elmwood Cemetery, Columbia.

GREEN, Francis Harvey, educator; b. Booth's Corner, Delaware County, Pa., May 19, 1861; s. Sharpless and Mary (Booth) G.; ed. West Chester (Pa.) State Normal Sch., Amherst Coll., Harvard; A.M., Dickinson Coll., 1893; Litt.D., Temple U., 1909; LL.D., Juniata Coll., 1931; m. Gertrude (Langdon) Heritage, Sept. 12, 1911. Prof. English, Juniata Coll., Huntingdon, Pa., 1884-88; head Dept. English, West Chester (Pa.) Normal Sch., 1888-1920; headmaster Pennington Sch., 1921—. Pres. Y.M.C.A. Mem. Transatlantic Soc. (Phila.), Dickens' Fellowship (Chester, Pa.), Chester County Hist. Soc. (pres.), Am. Asiatic Assn., Pa. State Teachers' Assn., N.E.A. Clubs: Harvard (Phila.); Pittsburgh Traffic; British Empire (Providence, R.I.); Ancient and Hon. Mech. Assn. of Baltimore. Republican. Methodist. Mason. Author: Notes on Rhetoric, 1909; Desirable Degrees, 1922; also verse and prose in mags. Compiler: Quotations from Great Authors, 1912; What They Say Day by Day, 1916; What Others Say Each Passing Day, 1920. Home: Lowellden, Pennington N.J. Died Jan. 23, 1958.

GREEN, Frank Russell, painter; b. Chgo., Apr. 16. 1856; s. Russell and Caroline G.; acad. and coll. edn.; studied art at Académie Julian, under Boulanger and Lefebvre, Colorossi Acad. under Collin and Courtois, Paris, France, criticism of Benjamin Constant; married. Hon. mention Paris Salon, 1900; awarded Shaw prize, Morgan prize, Lotos prize Nat. Acad. Design; medals for oil and water color paintings. A.N.A.; mem. Am. Water Color Soc., N.Y. Water Color Club (life mem. of both). Clubs: Salmagundi, Lotos. Address: Salmagundi Club, 47 Fifth Av., N.Y.C. Died 1940.*

GREEN, Frederick, educator; b. Cambridge, Mass., Feb. 28, 1868; s. Nicholas St. John and Cornelia (Henshaw) G.; A.B., Harvard, 1889, A.M., 1893, LL.B., 1893; m. Lois Shepherd, Sept. 7, 1920; children—Cornelia, Frederick Shepherd. Practiced in N. Y.C., 1893-1900; prof. law, U. Ill., Sept. 1904—. Mem. Ill. State Bar Assn., Am. Law Inst. (mem. com. which drafted the re-statement of agy.), Psi Upsilon, Phi Delta Phi, Phi Beta Kappa. Author: Cases on Carriers, 1910, 2d edit., 1927. Contbr. to law reviews. Home: 805 W. Green St., Urbana, Ill. Died July 27, 1956; buried Mt. Auburn Cemetery, Cambridge, Mass.

GREEN, Harold L., chmn. bd. and dir. H. L. Green Co., Inc. Home: Newtown, Conn. Office: care H. L. Green Co., 902 Broadway, N.Y.C. Died Apr. 13, 1951.*

GREEN, Henry Irvin, lawyer; b. Danville, Ind., Sept. 5, 1875; s. Francis M. and Kansas Ann (Clark) G.; ed. high sch., business coll., law offices and as official court reporter; m. Eva Clevenger, March 13, 1898 (deceased); 1 son, Francis Clevenger; m. 2d Elsie Mansfield, June 8, 1949. Admitted to Illinois bar, 1897, U.S. Supreme Court, 1915. General practice in State and Federal courts since 1900; sr. mem. Henry I. Green law offices, Urbana and Champaign; also firm Green & Hoagland, Alton, Ill. Corp. counsel, City of Urbana many yrs.; gen. solicitor Ill. Traction Co., Ill. Power & Light Corp.; vice pres. and gen. solicitor, Ill. Terminal R.R. System. Mem. Ill. Constl. Conv., 1920-22. Associated with U.S. Senator W. B. McKinley. Mem. Am. and Ill. state bar assns., Phi Delta Phi, Acacia, Rotary. Republican. Methodist. Clubs: Union League (Chicago), Flossmoor, and other clubs and professional orgns. Home: 503 W. Green St. Office: 136 W. Main St., Urbana, Ill.; and 113 N. Neil St., Champaign, Ill. Died

Nov. 10, 1954; buried Woodlawn Cemetery, Urbana, Ill.

GREEN, Howard Whipple, statistician; b. Woonsocket, R.I., Apr. 25, 1893; s. George Walter and Alice Judson (Paine) G.; A.B., Clark U., Worcester, Mass., 1914; B.S., San. Engring., Mass. Inst. Tech., 1916, Harvard, 1916; m. Leona Mildred Thacher, Nov. 30, 1919; children—Patricia Anne (Mrs. William H. Robinson, Jr.), Howard Thacher, Rod-man, instrument-man, cost engr., H. Koppers Co., constrn. of by-product coke plant, Lorain, O., 1916-17; san. engr. and bacteriologist, Miraflores water purification plant, and engr. of tests, municipal engring. div., Panama Canal, 1917-19; san. engr. malaria control work Internat. Health Bd., Rockefeller Found., Eudora, Ark., Mound, La., 1919-20, Aguirre, P.R., 1920-23; dir. bur. statistics and research, Cuyahoga County Pub. Health Assn., 1923-25; sec. and dir. statistics and research, Cleve. Health Council, 1925—; asso. in pub. health adminstrn., Sch. of Med., Western Reserve U., 1928—; supr. 6th O. Dist., 15th decennial census, Bur. of Census, 1930, spl. census of unemployment, Cleve., Bur. of Census, 1931; dir. Real Property Inventory, Met. Cleve. 1932—; tech. cons. real property inventory unit, Bur. Fgn. and Domestic Commerce, 1933-34; supr. real property inventory, Cleve. met. dist., Bur. Fgn. and Domestic Commerce, 1934; consultant div. housing, Federal Emer. Adminstrn. of Pub. Works, 1933-34, County Record Bur. Cuyahoga County, 1939-42; mem. health edn. com., Cleveland Health Council 1925—; adv. bd., Cleve. Div. of Health, 1934—; research com. Welfare Fed., Cleve., 1934—; sec. survey com., dept. health, O. Govt. Survey, 1935; incorporator, trustee, sec. Cleve. Health Mus. 1937—; chmn. Main Av. bridge dedication com., 1939; nutrition com., Welfare Fed.; research, records adv. com., Work Projects Adminstrn., Dist. 4, 1940-42; chmn. subcom. on health, Mayor's adv. com. to study health and hosps., 1940-46. Mem. Cleve. C. of C. (chmn. com. pub. health and welfare); chmn. Cain Park Theatre Citizens Com. 1940-43; mem. com. Indsl. Health of Mayor's War Production Com., 1942-45, med. adv. com. to Bd. Trustees on Tuberculosis, Cuyahoga Co., 1942—, Cuyahoga Co. Council for Civilian Def. War Service Bd., 1942-45, Soc. Welfare and Health Com., 1941-45, Social Protection Com., 1942—, War Housing Service, 1941-45, chmn. Health Com., 1941-45, Survey Com. on Housing Needs, 1941-45; mem. exec. com. First Victory Loan Drive, 1942; chmn. survey com. to adv. bd., Cleve. Div. Health, 1944-49; panel mem. Am. Arbitration Assn., 1944—; v.p. Cleve. Real Estate Bd., 1946-47; chmn. Citizens' Com. for the 3 Levies, Cuyahoga County, 1946-47; mem. Cleveland Rent Adv. Bd. since 1947; chmn. Cleveland Citizens. Com. for the 17 Bond issues and the Charter Levy, 1948; trustee Cleve. Bur. Govtl. Research since 1948; ex officio mem. adv. com. to Bur. Census 1951—. Fellow Am. Geo. Soc., Am. Pub. Health Assn. Trustee Regional Assn. Cleve., Real Property Inventory of Met. Cleve.; mem. Econometric Soc., Am. Assn. Social Workers, Am. Statistical Assn. (chmn. com. on census enumeration areas), Am. Marketing Assn. (treas. 1940-43; pres. 1944), Am. Sociol. Soc., Am. Soc. Civil Engrs., Am. Soc. Planning Officials, Urban Land Institute Population Assn. Am. Am. Econ. Assn., Nat. Conf. Social Work, Gryphon, Soc. of Mayflower Descs., S.A.R., Sigma Xi, Kappa Phi. Republican. Presbyn. Mason. Club: Mid-day (Cleve.). Contbr. numerous demographical studies and many articles presenting community data by census tacts. Home: 2231 Delamere Drive, Cleveland Heights 6, O. Office: 1001 Huron Rd., Cleve. 15. Died July 8, 1959; buried Lakeview Cemetery, Cleve.

GREEN, John Webb, lawyer; b. Oxford, Miss., June 9, 1859; s. Francis Marion and Susan Edmondson (Webb) G.; ed. Webb Sch., Bellbuckle, Tenn., 1874-76, Southwestern Presbyn. U., Clarksville, Tenn., 1876-79; LLD. (hon.), 1948; m. Ellen Marshall McClung, Jan. 26, 1897. Admitted to Tenn. bar, 1881; mem. Green & Shields, 1894-1903, Green, Webb & Tate, 1910-18, Green, Webb & Cowan, 1910-23, Green, Webb & Bass, 1925-36, Green, Webb, Bass & McCampbell since 1936; appointed special judge Supreme Court, Tenn., for 3d time, 1936; special judge Court of Civil Appeals, 1916; appointed, 1941, by United States District Judge for East Tennessee mem. Rules Committee for this district. Apptd. 1936, by Gov. McAllister mem., representing state of Tenn., on Com. for Arranging Celebration of 150th Anniversary of Constitution of U.S.; chmn. Standing Committee on Admission to Bar of U.S. Court at Knoxville. Fuel adminstr. for Knox County, during World War; former mem. Knoxville Bd. Edn.; former trustee Eastern Hospital for Insane. Trustee Lawson McGhee Library. Mem. Tenn. Hist. Commn. since 1943. Mem. American, Tennessee and Knoxville bar assns., Tenn. Soc. S.R., Phi Beta Kappa, Kappa Sigma. Democrat. Methodist. Author: Travels of a Lawyer, 1927; Other Travels of a Lawyer, 1930; Bench and Bar of Knox County Tennessee, 1947; Lives of the Judges of the Supreme Court of Tennessee, 1947, Law and Lawyers, 1950. Contbr. Tenn. Law Review. Home: Ridgeview, Fountain City, Knoxville. Office: Burwell Bldg., Knoxville, Tenn. Died May 26, 1957.

GREEN, Nathan Williams, surgeon; b. Ceylon, 1871; A.B., Yale, 1894; M.D., M.A., Columbia U. Coll. of Physicians and Surgeons, 1898; m. Anna L. Harrigton; children—Thomas D., John H. Asso. attending surgeon, St. Luke's Hosp.; asso. surgeon Memorial Hosp.; cons. St. Bartholomew's Hosp.; cons. surgeon, New York City Hosp., North Eastern Dispensary, Rockingham Hosp. (Bellows Falls, Vt.). Fellow A.C.S.; mem. A.M.A., Am. Assn. for Thoracic Surgery (past pres.). Address: Box 926, New Canaan, Conn. Died Apr. 21, 1955; buried Lakeview Cemetery, New Canaan.

GREEN, Norvin Hewitt, business exec.; b. N.Y. City, Oct. 20, 1893; s. Dr. James O. and Amy (Hewitt) G.; A.B., Columbia, 1917; m. Irene Pierce, Nov. 20, 1922 (div.); children—Amy (Mrs. Tracy W. Brown), Nancy (Mrs. Floris Ferwerda). Chmn. bd. dirs., The Gauley Mountain Coal Co., Ansted, W.Va., 1941—, Ringwood Co., Ringwood, N.J., 1944—, Electric Ferries, Inc., N.Y. City, 1949—, Green & Hewitt, Inc., N.Y. City, 1948—; dir., mem. exec. and finance com., Internat. Bus. Machines Corp., 1939—; dir. and mem. exec. com., The Okonite Co., 1935—, Intertype Corp., 1938—; trustee Bklyn. Savs. Bank. Reorgn. mgr. N.Y., Susquehanna & Western R.R., 1952. Treas. Borough of Ringwood (N.J.), 1919-24, mayor, 1924-30. Mem. bd. visitors Letchworth Village, 1942-51. Trustee, treas. Burke Relief Foundation; trustee Polytechnic Institute of Brooklyn, Brooklyn Institute of Arts and Sciences. Served as 1st lieutenant New York State Guard, 1917-18; 209th Field Signal Battalion, 9th Division, 1918-19. Member Danish American Greenland Commission, 1940-41. Awarded King Christian X medal of Danish Liberation, 1946. Trustee and treas. Winifred Masterson Relief Found., 1938—, Sheltering Arms Children's Service, 1923-38, Tuxedo Park Country Day Sch. (and pres.), 1942-43. Mem. N.Y. Hist. Soc. (past trustee), N.Y. State C. of C., Hugenot Soc., Soc. War 1812, Century Assn., S.R., Ry. and Locomotive Hist. Soc. Democrat. Episcopalian. Clubs: Lotos; The Cloud, St. Anthony, The Collectors, Grolier, Union League, Union, Century Assn. (N.Y.C.); Arcola Country; Phoenix Country, The Kiva (Phoenix). Home: 781 Fifth Av., N.Y.C. 19. Office: 500 Fifth Av., N.Y.C. 18. Died Apr. 11, 1955; buried Greenwood Cemetery, Bklyn.

GREEN, Percy Warren, judge; b. Booth's Corner, Delaware County, Pa., Aug. 18, 1889; s. Charles and Elizabeth Ellen (Talley) G.; B.S., in Economics, Wharton Sch. of Finance (U. of Pa.), 1911; A.M., U. of Pa., 1912; read law with William S. Hilles, of Wilmington, Delaware, 1913-16; m. Edith M. George; children—Pennvia Ellen (Mrs. William G. Whitaker), Warren. Assistant in finance, Wharton School of Finance (University of Pennsylvania), 1911; assistant professor in finance and transportation, Washington State Coll., Pullman, Wash., 1912-13; dep. atty. gen. State of Del., 1917-19; chief deputy, 1919-21; atty. for Levy Court, Newcastle County, Del., 1921-22; asst. city solicitor Wilmington Del., 1921-23; chief dept. atty. gen. of Del., 1933; apptd. atty. gen. of Del., July 6, 1933, and elected Nov. 1934, for term of 4 yrs. from Jan. 1, 1935; chief atty. Legislature of Del., 1939; deputy judge Municipal Court, Wilmington, Del., 1941-43; apptd. judge Court of Common Pleas, for term 12 yrs., New Castle County, 1943, 1955. Mem. Am. Bar Association (mem. bd. govs.), Del. State bar assn. Served as govt. appeal agt., World War I. Chmn. war work com. for Del. bar assns., World War II. Mem. Swedish Colonial Soc. of Del. (past pres.), Lincoln Club of Del. (past pres.), Kiwanis, S.A.R. (pres. Del. Soc.). Republican. Methodist. Mason. Home: 1202 Lovering Av. 12. Office: Public Bldg., Wilmington, Del. Died May 21, 1958.

GREEN, Perry Luther, former farm bur. exec., ins. exec.; b. North Royalton, O., June 5, 1879; s. Worthy Streator and Wealthy (Edgerton) G.; student Hiram Coll., 3 yrs.; m. Mabel Mary Alden, Sept. 7, 1904; children—Naoma Diantha, Alden E., Caspar D., Edward W. Farmer nr. Mantua, O.; dir. agr. Ohio, 1929-30; pres. Ohio Farm Bur., 1933-48; chmn. bd. Nation Wide Life Ins. Co.; mem. exec. com., investment com. all Nation Wide Ins. Cos.; dir., mem. investment com. Nat. Casualty Ins. Co., Detroit; Nation Wide Corporation & Approved Finance; dir. Tectum Corporation, Peoples Development Company, Peoples Broadcasting Co. (owner WGAR Cleve.); mem. bd. Coop. League of U.S.A.; promoted nat. coop. finance assn. in U.S., and agrl. credit corp. in Ohio. Mem. Ohio Legislature, 1921-29, mem. and chmn. state controlling bd. and finance com., 1925-26; mem. Pres. Hoovers Drought Relief Com., 1929-30. Trustee Hiram (O.) Coll., 1927-39; mem. bd. American Farm Bureau Federation, 1939-45. Author: A History of the Ohio Farm Bureau Federation and Its Subsidiaries. Home: R.D. 2, Mantua, O. Died July 28, 1957; buried Mantua Center, O.

GREEN, Robert McCay, lawyer; b. Phila., Oct. 14, 1903; s. Frank Delaplaine and Frieda (Goldsmith) G.; B.S. in Econs., Wharton Sch., U. Pa., 1925; LL.B., U. Pa., 1929; m. Eleanore Frances Reiley, July 5, 1930. Admitted to Pa. bar, 1930; practice in Phila., 1930-35, mem. firm Murdoch, Paxson, Kalish & Green, 1935-44; asst. gen. mgr. The Phila. Inquirer, 1944-46; mem. Dilworth, Paxson, Kalish & Green, 1946—; city solicitor, Phila., 1943-44; sec., dir. Sellers Injector Corp., Comprehensive De- & Dickerson, Inc., Dickson Fuel Corp., Phila. Meml. Park. Chmn. Phila. Water Commn., 1946-47. Trustee Junto, Inc., The Rittenhouse Found. Mem. Phi Sigma Kappa, Phi Delta Phi. Clubs: Union League, University, Midday, Phila. Country (Phila.); Maine Country, Yacht (Portland). Home: 250 S. 18th St. Office: Fidelity-Phila. Trust Bldg., Phila. 9. Died Oct. 22, 1956.

GREEN, Thomas Dunbar, hotel owner, trade assn. exec.; b. Columbia, S.C., July 6, 1870; s. John and Mary (Green) G.; m. Julia Dismukes, Nov. 1, 1899; children—John Dismukes, Julia (Mrs. Julia Green Sturges). Began business with father, cotton mfr., Lexington, S.C.; began hotel bus. Asheville, S.C., 1895; owner and operator Hotel Woodward, N.Y.C., 1908-36; pres. and treas. Am. Hotel Assn. Directory Corp. Pres. Hotel Assn. of N.Y.C., 1914-22; pres. and exec. dir. Am. Hotel Assn., 1925-41, now chmn. finance com. Active in work of Liberty Loan, Red Cross, Salvation Army, etc., during World War I; in charge hotels, restaurants, steamships and dining cars in N.Y., N.J., Pa. and Del. under Food Conservation Adminstrn. Decorated Comdr. Order of Crown (Belgium and Italy), Chevalier Legion of Honor (France). Mem. Mayflower Descendants, Society Colonial Wars. Clubs: Metropolitan, Tavern; Dering Harbor Golf and Yacht (Shelter Island). Home: 171 W. 57th St. Office: 221 W. 57th St., N.Y.C. Died May, 1954.

GREEN, Walton Atwater, lawyer, editor; b. N.Y. City, Nov. 4, 1881; s. George Walton and Harriet Brodhead (Atwater) G.; grad. Phillips Exeter Acad., 1900; A.B., Harvard, 1904, LL.B., 1909; m. Eleanor Munroe, June 22, 1904; 1 dau., Gloria. Editor and pub. Boston Journal, 1913-17; mem. New York Stock Exchange firm, 1919-25; chief prohibition investigator, Washington, D.C., 1925—. Sec. Mass. Spl. Commn. on Mil. Edn. and Reserve, 1915; chmn. Mass. Commn. on State Constabulary, 1916-17; mem. exec. com. Mass. Com. on Pub. Safety, 1917—. Commd. maj. inf., 1917; served in France at Gen. Staff Coll. and as batln. comdr. 108th Inf. Republican. Clubs: Union Boat, St. Botolph (Boston); Harvard (Boston and New York); Union, Rockaway Hunt (N.Y.). Home: Cedarhurst, N.Y. Died Dec. 2, 1954.

GREEN, William, labor leader; b. Coshocton, O., Mar. 3, 1870; s. Hugh and Jane (Oram) G.; ed. pub. schs.; hon. Dr. Industrial Sci., Oglethorpe University, 1936; Doctor of Law (hon.), Kenyon Coll., 1948; married Jennie Mobley, Apr. 1892; children—Flora, Esther, Nellie, Clara, Ruth, Harry. Sub-dist. pres. United Mine Workers of America, 1900-06; pres. Ohio Dist. Mine Workers' Union, 1906-10; mem. Ohio Senate, 2 terms; internat. sec.-treas. United Mine Workers of America, 1912-24; apptd. mem. exec. council Am. Fedn. of Labor, 1913, became pres. Dec. 19, 1924. Alternate at large from Ohio to Dem. Nat. Conv., San Francisco, 1920, del. at large, Baltimore, 1912, and New York, 1924. Apptd. mem. Advisory Council to Com. on Economic Security, 1934; mem. original Nat. Labor Bd.; mem. Ohio Building Commn. which erected new $6,000,000 State Office Bldg., Columbus, Ohio; served on governing bd. Internat. Labor Orgn., 1935-37; also served as mem. Advisory Council of NRA. Mem. Am. Acad. Polit. and Social Science. Baptist. Odd Fellow, Elk. Author of Ohio Workmen's Compensation Law. Awarded gold medal of honor, by Roosevelt Memorial Assn., for distinguished service in promotion of industrial peace, 1930. Editor of Am. Federationist. Author of "Labor and Democracy.' Home: 409 S. 4th St., Coshocton, O. Address: American Federation of Labor 901 Mass. Av. N.W., Washington 1. Died Nov. 21, 1952.

GREEN, William Charles, lawyer; b. Stephen, Minn., Oct. 8, 1886; s. Frank Adelbert and Bertha (Anderson) G.; ed. pub. schools, business school; private study of law; m. Erna Daisy Krueger, June 30, 1909; children—William A., Katharine (Mrs. Robert J. Greene), Robert A. Admitted to N.D. bar, 1913, Minn. bar, 1928; asst. states atty., Cass County, N.D., 1914-18, states atty., 1918-22; asst. U.S. atty., N.D., 1923-28; spl. counsel Com. Interstate Commerce U.S. Senate, 1928-31; spl. asst. atty. gen. Minn., 1929-42, and 1947—; asst. atty. gen., 1942-47; mem. Silver, Green & Goff, St. Paul, 1947—. Mem. Am., Minn. State bar assns., Kiwanis Internat. (past internat. trustee, v.p.). Republican. Presbyn. Mason (Shriner, 32°). Author articles legal jours. Home: 1847 Fairmount Av. Office: Minnesota Bldg., St. Paul 1. Died Sept. 14, 1952.

GREENAWALD, Paul Benjamin, bus. exec.; born Windsor Castle, Pa., Jan. 12, 1894; s. Milton A. and Sarah C. (Smith) G.; grad. Keystone State Normal Sch. (now Kuztown State Teachers Coll.), 1911; B.S., Pa. State Coll., 1920; m. Helen M. Adam, May 31, 1921; children—Emily S. (Mrs. John Shalter), Ralph A., Henry A., Kenneth A. Rural sch.

teacher near Reading, Pa., 1911-14; asst. metallurgist, Am. Steel & Wire Co., Worcester, Mass., 1920-24; asst. in metall. dept., The Carpenter Steel Co., Reading, Pa., 1924-35, metall. engr., 1935-44, gen. supt. of plant, 1944-45, vice pres. and plant mgr. since June 1945, dir. since 1945. Served as 2nd lt., Ordnance, U.S. Army, 1917-18. Mem. Am. Iron and Steel Inst., Mfrs. Assn. of Berks County (treas.). Republican. Mason. Address: 4238 7th Av., Temple, Berks Co., Pa. Died Sept. 4, 1952; buried Fleetwood Cemetery, Fleetwood, Berks Co.

GREENE, Edward Belden, industrialist; b. Cleveland, O., July 26, 1878; s. John Eliot and Mary Elizabeth (Seymour) G.; A.B., Yale, 1900, A.M., 1925; m. Helen Wade, Nov. 18, 1909; 1 dau., Helen Wade (Mrs. A. Dean Perry). With Cleveland Trust Co., 1900-33; with Cleveland-Cliffs Iron Co., 1933, now hon. chmn. bd.; pres. dir. Lake Superior & Ishpeming R.R. Co.; vice pres. and dir. Cliffs Dow Chemical Co., Wade Realty Co.; dir. Goodyear Tire & Rubber Co., Medusa Portland Cement Co., N.Y.C. R.R., Eaton Mfg. Co., Harshaw Chemical Co., Montreal Mining Co., Jones & Laughlin Steel Corp., Lake Superior Iron Ore Assn., Lake Carriers Assn. Dir. mil. relief, Lake div., Am. Red Cross, and mem. exec. com. Mil. Training Camps Assn., World War. Trustee Cleveland Museum Art, Cleveland Community Fund, Univ. Hospitals, Cleveland Sch. of Art; trustee Yale, 1925-47; trustee John Huntington Art and Polytech. Inst., Peabody Museum Natural History. Mem. Cleveland C. of C. (pres. 1924), Alpha Delta Phi, Wolfs Head Soc. Clubs: Tavern, Pepper Pike, Union, Kirtland, Chagrin Valley Hunt (Cleveland); University, Yale, Links (New York). Home: 10831 Magnolia Drive. Office: Union Commerce Bldg., Cleve. Died Oct. 20, 1957.

GREENE, Edward Martin, educator; b. Nashua, N.H., Nov. 4, 1875; s. Martin Van Buren and Isabel (Colton) G.; A.B. cum laude, Harvard, 1903 (hon. mention in French); A.M., U. Wis., 1910; student Universités de Rennes et de Paris, 1913-14; m. Helen Carter, Nov. 23, 1910; children—Robert Treat, Edward Carter, John Colton. Head dept. French, Hotchkiss Sch., Conn., 1907-09; teaching fellow, French, U. Wis., 1909-10; head dept. French, Butler U., Indpls., 1910-19; head dept. French, Univ. S.D., 1919—; chmn. state M.F.L. Round Table; prof. French, summer session, U. Ind., 1918. Served as official translator and corr. to War Orphans Com. World War I. Award by French Ednl. Commn. 1918-19. Mem. Modern Fgn. Lang. Assn., S.D. Ednl. Assn. (hon. life), Am. Assn. Teachers French. Conglist. Republican. Editor and part author bulletin 13 pub. by state of S.D. Curricula for Teaching Modern Fgn. Langs. in High Sch. of S. Dakota. Home: 323 Lewis St. Office: University of S.D., Vermillion, S.D. Died Jan. 26, 1952.

GREENE, Edwin Farnham, mfr.; b. Hills Grove, R.I., Feb. 9, 1879; s. Stephen G. and Natalia L. (Schubarth) G.; A.B., Brown U., 1901; m. Mrs. Helen B. Howell, Nov. 26, 1930. Pres. Lockwood Greene Co., 1901-26, chmn., 1926-30; treas. (chief exec.), Pacific Mills, 1907-28; pres. Edwin Farnham Greene, Inc.; former dir. Am. Tel. & Tel. Co., B.&M. R.R. and other corporations. Pres. Nat. Assn. Cotton Mfrs., 1912-13; mem. Pres. Wilson's First Industrial Commn., 1919; pres. bd. trustees, Wellesley Coll., 1916-26; trustee Museum of Fine Arts (Boston), 1918-28; treas. and trustee, N.E. Conservatory of Music, 1918-27; trustee Brown U. since 1910. Republican. Episcopalian. Clubs: University (Boston); University, Merchants, Manhattan (New York); Country (Fairfield, Conn.). Address: Hotel Langdon, 2 E. 56th, N.Y.C. Died Dec. 6, 1953.

GREENE, Floyd L., corp. exec.; b. McConnellstown, Pa., Nov. 30, 1888; s. Wilson E. and Florence (Yocum) G.; student Juanita Coll., Pa. State Coll., bus. coll.; m. Ella M. Huyette, July 3, 1911 (dec.); children—Anna Florence (Mrs. Henry Stultz), Herbert F., Richard S., Harold H., Robert E.; m. 2d, Betty Jane Korb, July 23, 1949. Served in various capacities with Gen. Refractories Co. and acquired cos., 1913—, pres. 1937-52, chmn. bd., 1952—, also pres., dir. several subsidiaries; chmn. bd. First Nat. Bank, Claysburg, Pa.; dir. First Nat. Bank, Alexandria, Pa. Clubs: Union League, Duquesne, Oakmont Country, South Shore Country of Chicago. Home: Barree, Pa. Office: 1520 Locust St., Phila. 2. Died Apr. 13, 1954.

GREENE, Henry Copley, author; b. Vienna, Austria, Nov. 21, 1871; s. J. S. Copley and Mary A. (Mayer) G.; A.B., Harvard U., 1894, A.M., 1924; m. Rosalind Huidekoper, May 14, 1907; children—Francesca Copley, Joy, Katrine Rosalind, Ernesta Copley (dec.). Clerk to Art Commn., Boston, 1907-17 and since 1921; research fellow, Boston sch. for Social Workers, Oct. 1908-June 1909; agt. for conservation of eyesight, Massachusetts Commn. for the Blind, 1909-17. Instr. division of philosophy, Harvard Univ., 1926-28; sec. of History Reference Council, 1926-40. Vice pres. France Forever in Boston, 1941-44; mem. staff Unitarian Service Com., Paris, Jan.-Aug. 1945. Club: Tavern. Author: The Children's Crusade (translated from the French of Marcel Schwob, with an introduction), 1898 (revised edition with essay on Marcel Schwob), 1905; Theophile, a Miracle Play, 1898; Plains and Uplands of Old France, a Book of Prose and Verse, 1898. Plays in verse: Pontius Pilate, 1903; Saint Ronan of Britanny, 1903; Theophile, 1903; The Childhood of Christ (translated from the Latin, with an introduction by Alice Meynell), 1904; The Father (a drama), 1904; Ophthalmia Neonatorum in Ten Massachusetts Cities, 1911; (with Katherine Tayor) The Shady Hill Play Book, 1928; also articles, Century, Atlantic Monthly, Speculum, Isis. Editor: Wisdom of Shakespeare, 1909; Listen In—Radio Health Talks, 1923. Translator: Medical Experimentation (by Claude Bernard), 1927. Delegate French War Emergency Fund, visiting army hosps., May 1916-Sept. 1917, lt. in charge reconstruction and relief, Am. Nat. Red Cross, Noyon, France, Sept. 1917; dist. mgr. Laon-Aisne, 1909-20; maj., Am. Red Cross; hon. discharged July 1920. Exec. sec. health service Boston Metropolitan Red Cross, 1920-24; with French Red Cross in France, 1940. Awarded Croix de Guerre and silver medal Reconnaissance, Francaise, 1918 Medaille du devouement, French Red Cross, 1940; Medaille de Vermeil, Reconaissance Francaise, 1948; Legion d' Honneur, Chevalier, 1948. Home: 10 Longfellow Park, Cambridge 38, Mass. Office: Faneuil Hall, Boston. Died Dec. 29, 1951.

GREENE, Henry Vincent, banker; b. Lawrence, Mass., Apr. 5, 1888; s. Robert Francis and Elizabeth Aloysia (Santry) G.; ed. pub. schs.; m. Josephine Virginia Hayes, June 17, 1919. Founder, H. V. Greene Co., investment bankers, 1916, established 115 br. offices in U.S. and Can.; founder 1st People's Trust, capital thirty million dollars; organized Mut. Finance Corp., Comml. Finance Corp., both comml. bankers; pres. Pulp & Paper Corp. Am.; dir. Cal. Carbon Co. Treas. Coll. of the Spoken Word, Inc. Clubs: Boston City, Boston Press, Woodland Golf. Home: Glen Rd., Weston, Mass. Office: 25 Huntington Av., Boston. Died Nov. 15, 1954.

GREENE, Howard, investment banking (ret.); b. Milwaukee, May 17, 1864; s. Thomas Arnold and Elizabeth Lynes (Cadle) G.; student Milwaukee Acad., 1877-82; Litt.B., U. of Wis., 1886; m. Louise McMynn, Oct. 27, 1890 (died 1932); children—Howard (dec.), Charles (dec.), John, Elizabeth M. (Mrs. Austin Ross), dec.; m. 2d, Carolyn Anderson, Feb. 1, 1936; children—Andrew Anderson, Abigail Carolyn, Martha Marie. With Greene and Button, wholesale druggists, 1886-94; president Fidelity Trust Company, 1902-12; became secretary Wisconsin Securities Company, 1912, now chaiman board; trustee Northwestern Mutual Life Insurance Co.; director Northwestern Nat. Ins. Co., Pusey Jones Corp. (Wilmington, Del.). Served as capt. and adjutant, 4th Wis. Vol. Inf., 1898-99; maj. engr. corps, 107th Engrs., U.S. Army, 1917-19; lt. col. O.R.C. Mem. Wis. State Hist. Soc., Chi Psi. Republican. Episcopalian. Mason (32°), K.T. Clubs: Milwaukee, University Wilmington Country, Wilmington. Home: Christiana, Del. Died July 10, 1956; buried Milw.

GREENE, James Sonnett, physician; b. N.Y.C., Dec. 25, 1880; s. Jacob J. and Doris (Harrow) G.; M.D., Cornell U., 1902; post grad. studies at Univ. Berlin, Allerheilegen Hosp. (Breslau), Univ. Jena, 1906-12; m. Emilie Josephine Wells, Aug. 27, 1919. Began practice at N.Y.C., 1902; founded Nat. Hosp. for Speech Disorders (devoted solely to diagnosis and treatment of voice and speech disorders), N.Y.C., 1916, and since med. dir.; prof. of speech, Coll. of Dental and Oral Surgery, N.Y.C., 1916-18; lectr. on voice and speech disorders, Grad. Sch. Med., U. Pa. Cons. on speech disorders, N.Y. Eye and Ear Infirm., Meml. Hosp., N.Y.C. Awarded spl. gold medal by Am. Laryngol., Rhinol. and Otol. Soc., 1940. Fellow N.Y. Acad. Medicine; mem. Med. Soc. Co. of N.Y., A.M.A, Am. Acad. Ophthalmology and Otolaryngology, Am. Laryngol., Rhinol. and Otol. Soc., Am. Group Therapy Assn., A.A.A.S.; sustaining mem. Nat. Assn. Teachers Speech; mem. Am. Soc. for Research in Psychosomatic problems. Clubs: Cornell Lotos (N.Y.). Author: The Cause and Cure of Speech Disorders (with E. J. Wells), 1927; I Was a Stutterer, 1932; Straight Talk (essays) 1948, also many monographs on speech and voice disorders. Editor of Talk (published by National Hospital for Speech Disorders); asso. editor of Better English in Speech and Writing. Contbg. editor to Year Book of the Eye, Ear, Nose and Throat, 1938. Contbr. to med. jours. Address: 61 Irving Place, N.Y.C. Died Sept. 17, 1950.

GREENE, Jerome Davis, ednl. adminstr.; b. Yokohama, Oct. 12, 1874; s. Daniel Crosby and Mary Jane (Forbes) G.; A.B., Harvard, 1896; U. of Geneva, Switzerland, 1896-97; Harvard Law Sch., 1897-99; hon. A.M., Harvard, 1914, Rutgers, 1915; LL.D., Harvard, 1937, Norwich Univ., 1937; m. May Tevis, April 28, 1900; 1 son, Jerome Crosby; m. 2d, Dorothea Dusser de Barenne, August 20, 1942; 1 son, David. Asst. to gen. mgr. Univ. Press, Cambridge, Mass., 1899-1901; sec. to pres. Harvard, 1901-05, to Corp. of Harvard U., 1905-10, 1934-43; mem. bd. overseers Harvard, 1911-13, 1917-23, 1944-50, sec. bd., 1938-43; gen. mgr. Rockefeller Inst. Med. Research, N.Y., 1910-12, trustee, 1912-32; asso. with John D. Rockefeller in mgmt. his various interests, 1912-14; trustee, sec. Rockefeller Found., 1913-17, trustee, 1928-39; trustee Gen. Edn. Bd., 1912-39; with Lee Higginson & Co., N.Y.C., 1917, mem. firm, 1918-32. Exec. sec. Am. sect. Allied Maritime Transport Council, London, 1918; sec. Reparation Commn., Peace Conf., Paris, 1919. Mem. Internat. Health Commn. Rockefeller Found., 1913-17; trustee Inst. for Govt. Research, Washington, 1917-28, Brookings Instn., Washington, 1928-45, Am. Hist. Assn., 1937-39, Boston Symphony Orchestra, 1938-48 (pres. 1942-45); treas. Am. Social Hygiene Assn., 1920-32, Am. Council Inst. Pacific Relations, 1926-29 (chmn. 1929-32, internat. chmn., 1929-33) pres. Am. Asiatic Assn., 1929-33; trustee Cambridge Hosp., 1935—. Resident of Toynbee Hall, London, 1918; prof. internat. politics U. Wales, 1932-34; director Harvard Tercentenary Celebration, 1934-37. Life mem. of Am. Acad. in Rome. Chmn. distbn. com. Cambridge Found., 1949—. Trustee Dowse Inst., Cambridge, 1937—, N.E. Conservatory of Music, 1937—, Mt. Auburn Hosp. 1935—; trustee, treas. Isabella Stewart Gardner Mus., 1937—. Pres. E. Asiatic Soc. of Boston, 1950—. Decorated Legion of Honor (France), Grand Officer Order of St. Sava (Yugoslavia), Officer Order Orange Nassau (Netherlands). Fellow A.A.A.S.; mem. N.Y. Hist. Soc., Medieval Acad. Am., Colonial Soc. of Mass. Clubs: Harvard (N.Y. and Boston); Century (N.Y.C.); Tavern (Boston); American (Tokyo); Rotary (Cambridge). Home: 54-A Garden St., Cambridge, Mass. Office: 294 Washington St., Boston. Died Mar. 29, 1959; buried Pine Grove Cemetery, Westborough, Mass.

GREENE, Joseph Ingham, army officer, mil. editor; b. Watertown, N.Y., Dec. 11, 1897; s. Will Camp and Mabel (Sanford) G.; B.S., U.S. Mil. Acad., 1923; grad. Inf. Sch., Ft. Benning, Ga., 1937; Command and Gen. Staff Sch., Ft. Leavenworth, 1938; m. Marjorie Kennard Hutchins, May 29, 1930. Reporter Daytona (Fla.) Daily News, 1915-18; served as private and corpl., 48th, 89th and 46th Inf., U.S. Army, 1918-19; cadet, U.S. Military Acad., West Point, 1919-23; commd. 2d lt., U.S. Army, 1923, and advanced through grades to col., 1943; service in Panama, Philippines, China and United States; assistant editor Panama American, 1926; corr. Manila Daily Bulletin, 1931; editor Tientsin Sentinel, China, 1932; asst. editor Inf. Sch. Mailing List, 1935-36; asso. editor Infantry Jour., 1938-40, editor, 1940-50, editor, gen. mgr., 1946-50; editor U.S. Army Combat Forces Journal, 1950; retired from Army, 1945, recalled to active duty, 1945; relieved, 1946. Member panel, Council on Books in Wartime for selection of useful books, 1943. Staff mem. Bread Loaf (Vt.) Writer's Conf., 1944-46). Sec.-treas. U.S. Inf. Assn. Sec. Assn. U.S. Army, 1950. Awarded Legion of Merit, 1946. Mem. Assn. Grads. U.S. Mil. Acad., Nat. Rifle Assn., Am. Military Institute (president, 1948), Military Order World Wars, Retired Officers Assn. Clubs: Army-Navy, Cosmos, National Press, Army War Coll. Mess, (Washington, Dist. of Columbia). Author: What You Should Know About Ground Forces, 1943, Asso. editor: Living Thoughts of Clausewitz; editor, The Infantry Journal Reader, 1943. Editor of mil. books, Spl. edit. Am. College Dictionary, 1947; editor (with Elizabeth Abell) anthology, First Love, 1948. Contributor articles to Infantry Journal and other mags. Home: 3601 Connecticut Av., Washington 8. Office: 1529 18th St. N.W. Washington. Died June 25, 1953; buried Arlington Nat. Cemetery.

GREENE, Raleigh W., banker; b. Opelika, Ala., July 2, 1893; s. James and Julia (Casey) G.; student pub. schs., Opelika; m. Anne M. Kenny, Sept. 28, 1921; 1 son, Raleigh W.; m. 2d, Evelyn S. Shabbot, May 3, 1939. With Weil Bros., Montgomery, Ala., 1913-17; founder First Fed. Savs. & Loan Assn., St. Petersburg, 1933, chief exec., dir. since 1933. Mem. War Price and Rationing Bd., 1941-46, chmn., 1943-46. Served as lt. col. G-1, 9th corps U.S. Army, 1917-20. Mem. Nat. (pres.), Fla. (past pres.) savs. and loan leagues, St. Petersburg C. of C. (past mem. bd. govs.). Clubs: Lions (past pres.), Ambassador, Rotary, Yacht, Bahama Shores Yacht Assn. Home: 1858 Brightwaters Blvd., Snell Isle, St. Petersburg. Office: First Federal Bldg., St. Petersburg 1, Fla. Died Apr. 28, 1954.

GREENE, Richard Thurston, lawyer; b. Port Henry, N.Y., June 29, 1867; s. James Gardner and Mary Helen (Rice) G.; B.S., Rutgers U., 1889; LL.B., Albany (N.Y.) Law Sch., 1891; m. Charlotte Louise Berry, Jan. 21, 1896; children—Charlotte Louise, Helen (Mrs. James C. Heminway), Marion (Mrs. Ferdinand K. Thun), Karolyn (Mrs. John O. Cole), Turston. Admitted to New York and Federal bars; pvt. practice, 1891—; dir. Lawyers Trust Co., Cutler Mail Chute Co. Former pres. Montclair (N.J.) Board of Edn. Life trustee Rutgers U.; trustee, treas. Montclair Y.M.C.A. Mem. Am., N.Y. State bar assns., N.Y. County Lawyers Assn., Bar Assn. City of New York, N.Y. Geneal. and Biog. Soc., S.A.R., New England Soc., Soc. of the Genesee (ex-pres.), Delta Kappa Epsilon (ex-pres.). Republican. Conglist. (former pres. and trustee). Mason. Clubs: University, India House (New York). Home: 239 S. Mountain Av., Montclair, N.J. Office: 61 Broadway, N.Y.C. 6. Died Oct. 30, 1949; buried Beechwood Cemetery, Centerville, Mass.

GREENE, Theodore Ainsworth, clergyman; born Andover, Mass., Jan. 12, 1890; s. Rev. Frederick William and Eliza Farrar (Walter) G.; A.B., Amherst Coll., 1913; A.M., 1916; B.D., Union Theol. Sem., 1918; A.M., Columbia, 1922; D.D., Piedmont Coll., 1936; m. Dorothy Goldthwait Thayer, May 23, 1918; children—Theodore Phinney, Thayer Ainsworth. Grad. sec. Amherst Christian Assn., 1913-14; dir. religious work, Amherst Coll., 1914-15; student asst. Broadway Tabernacle, New York, 1915-16; dir. religious edn. First Presbyn. Ch., Brooklyn, 1916-18; ordained to ministry of Congl. Ch., 1918; asst. pastor Brick Presbyn. Ch., New York, 1918-25; pastor First Ch. of Christ (Center Congl.), New Britain, Conn., since 1925. Dir. Grenfell Assn. America since 1917, sec., 1922-25; dir. Internat. Grenfell Assn. since 1920, vice chmn. since 1930; asso. sec. Am. Sect. Universal Christian Council on Life and Work, Stockholm, Sweden, 1923-25, chmn. exec. com., 1936; pres. Conn. Council Religious Edn., 1928-31; chmn. com. on internat. relations, Gen. Council Congl. and Christian Chs. in U.S., 1931-34; chmn. Conn. Conf. Congl. Chs., 1938-39; trustee Piedmont Coll. since 1933, Hartford Seminary since 1940, Madura College, India, since 1943; delegate World Conference on Church, Community and State, Oxford U., 1937. Mem. Alpha Delta Phi, Am. Soc. Ch. History, exec. coms. Gen. Council Congl. Chs. and World Alliance for International Friendship through Churches since 1939; mem. Prudential Com., Am. Board Commrs. for Foreign Missions since 1941, vice chmn., 1942-44, chmn. since 1944; mem. Am. Joint Com., World Council of Chs. since 1941; chmn. Dept. of Field Adminstrn., Fed. Council of Churches of Christ in America, 1942-44; delegate of Gen'l Council Cong'l Churches to Latin America, 1944; chmn. Commn. on World Council Services, 1944-46; v.p. Church World Service, Inc., since 1946. Alternate del. Congl. Chs., U.S., World Council Chs., Amsterdam Assembly, 1948; chmn. alternate com., Reconstrn. and Inter-Ch. Aid, Amsterdam. Clubs: University (New York); Shuttle Meadow, New Britain (New Britain); Dublin Lake (Dublin, N.H.); Thorndike (Jaffrey, N.H.); Get-Together (Hartford, Conn.). Author of "Ecclesiastical Organization of Geneva in Time of Calvin" and "What Can Christians Do for Peace," 1934; "Worship Services for Peace and Brotherhood," 1940. Contbr. to religious jours. Home: 33 Lexington St., New Britain, Conn. Died June 9, 1951; buried Jaffrey, N.H.

GREENE, Ward, writer; b. Asheville, N.C., Dec. 23, 1892; s. Allison Lawson and Susan Caryl (Rosenbury) G.; student University of the South, 1912-13; m. Edith Pfeil, May 8, 1942; 1 son, Charles Thomas. Newspaper reporter Atlanta Journal, 1913-17, New York Tribune, 1917; corr. in France and Germany, Atlanta Journal, 1918-19; writer, exec. editor, editor and gen. mgr. King Features Syndicate, 1921—; bd. dirs. Hearst corp.; trustee Hearst Found. Mem. Sigma Alpha Epsilon. Author: Cora Potts, 1929; Ride the Nightmare, 1930; Weep No More, 1932; Death in the Deep South, 1936; (play) Honey, 1937; King Cobra (under pseudonym of Frank Dudley), 1940; Route 28, 1940; What They Don't Know, 1944; (play) Blue Bonnets, 1945; Forgetful Elephant (under pseudonym of Jean Greene), 1945; Lady and the Tramp, 1954. Editor: Star Reporters and 34 of Their Stories, 1948. Contbr. of fiction to various periodicals. Home: Rockleigh, N.J. Office: 235 E. 45th St., N.Y.C. Died Jan. 22, 1956.

GREENLEAF, Carl Dimond, mfr.; b. Wauseon, O., July 27, 1876; s. Charles Carroll and Mary Susan (Dimond) S.; student Northwestern Normal Sch., Wauseon, 1894, Morgan Park (Ill.) Acad., 1895; B.S., U. Chgo., 1899; m. Deacon Jennings, Oct. 4, 1900; children—Dorothy Carroll (Mrs. Charles T. Boynton), Leland Burleigh, Harvey Dimond, Charles Willard. Began in bus. with father in firm Lyon & Greenleaf, flour millers, 1899, in charge, 1910-15, v.p. to 1950; pres. C. G. Conn, Ltd., band instrument mfrs., 1915-49, chmn. bd., 1949—; pres. Truth Pub. Co., Elkhart Hotel Co. to 1948; v.p. Foster Machine Co., 1922-41; dir. Buescher Band Instrument Co. Mem. Nat. Assn. Band Instrument Mfrs. (pres. 1916-27), U.S. C. of C. (dir. mus. industries, 1918-27), Elkhart C. of C. (1st pres.), Delta Tau Delta. Rep. Unitarian. Clubs: Christina Country (Elkhart); University (Chicago). Home: 1415 Greenleaf Blvd. Office: care C. G. Conn., Ltd., Elkhart, Ind. Died July 10, 1959.

GREENMAN, Jesse More, botanist; b. North East, Pa., Dec. 27, 1867; s. James William and Clarissa (More) G.; B.S., U. Pa., 1893; M.S., Harvard, 1899; Ph.D., U. Berlin, 1901; m. Anne Louise Turner, Sept. 20, 1902; children—Jesse More, Milton Turner. Asst. in botany, 1890-92, instr., 1893-94, U. of Pa., asst. Gray Herbarium, Harvard, 1894-99; Kirkland fellow from Harvard at U. Berlin, 1899-1901; asst. Gray Herbarium; instr. Harvard, 1902-05; asst. curator botany, Field Museum, Chgo., 1905-13; asst. prof. bot., U. Chgo., 1908-13; asso. prof. bot., 1913-16, prof., 1917-45, prof. emeritus 1945—; in charge grad. Henry Shaw Sch. Botany, 1927, Washington U.; emeritus curator herbarium, Mo. Bot. Garden, 1948—. Editor taxonomy vascular plants, Bot. Abstracts, 1917-27. Hon. chmn. U. of Pa. Bicentennial Com. St. Louis Dist. Fellow A.A.A.S. (chmn. sect. G 1936-37); mem. Bot. Soc. Am., Ecol. Soc. America, Am. Soc. Naturalists, N.E. Bot. Club, Germanistic Soc. St. Louis, Am. Assn. University Professors, New York Academy of Science, St. Louis Acad. Sci., Ill. Acad. Science, Sigma Xi, Phi Beta Kappa (pres. Washington U. chapter 1936-37), Phi Sigma, Sigma Alpha Epsilon; corr. mem. Phila. Acad. Natural Sciences. Democrat. Presbyn. Clubs: University, Harvard (St. Louis); Faculty (Washington U.). Contbr. numerous articles on flora of N. America and Mexico, also monograph on Genus Senecio. Home: 4129 Magnolia Av. Address: Missouri Botanical Garden, St. Louis, Mo. Died Jan. 20, 1951; buried West Laurel Hill Cemetery, Bala-Cynwyd, Pa.

GREENSFELDER, Albert Preston, constrn. engr.; b. St. Louis, Mo., July 6, 1879; s. M. B. and Carrie G.; B.S. in C.E., Washington U., St. Louis, 1901; m. Blanche Younker, Jan. 24, 1909. Engr. on constrn. Kan. Interurban Ry., 1901-02; asst. engr. with Terminal R.R. Assn., St. Louis, 1902-05; constrn. supt., 1906, sec. Fruin Colnon Contracting Co., 1908-27, pres., 1927-40, chmn., 1940-50, cons. constructor, 1950; dir. Mercantile Trust Co., Mo. Portland Cement Co. Past chmn. Univ. City Planning Commn.; past mem. Nat. Capital Planning Commn.; pilot Miss. River Parkway Planning Commn. former vice chairman Mo. Conservation Commn. and dir. City of St. Louis and U.S. chambers of commerce. Hon. chmn. Cons. Constructors Council of A.; dir. Asso. Gen. Contractors of America (ex-pres.); mem. Business Advisory Council of Dept. of Commerce; hon. mem. A.S. Civil Engrs., Engrs. Club at St. Louis. Mason. Clubs: University, Engineers (ex-pres.), Circle, Mo. Athletic (St. Louis); Engineers (N.Y.C.); Cosmos (Washington); Westwood Country. Home: 7041 Lindell Av., St. Louis, 5. Office: 1706 Olive St., St. Louis 3. Died Apr. 11, 1955.

GREENSLET, Ferris, publisher, author; b. Glens Falls, N.Y., June 30, 1875; s. George Bernard and Josephine (Ferris) G.; A.B., Wesleyan U., Conn., 1897, A.M., 1898; Ph.D., Columbia, 1900; Litt.D., Dartmouth, 1924; m. Ella S. Hulst, Apr. 25, 1903; children—Magdalena, George. Asso. editor Atlantic Monthly, 1902-07; lit. adviser to Houghton Mifflin Company, 1907, dir. 1910—, gen. mgr. trade dept., later v.p., gen. mgr., editor in chief, to 1942, lit. advisor 1942-47. Mem. Phi Beta Kappa, Nat. Inst. Arts and Letters, Mass. Hist. Soc., Am. Antiquarian Soc. Clubs: Century (New York), Saint Botolph (Boston). Author: Joseph Glanvill—A Study in English Thought and Letters of the Seventeenth Century, 1900; The Quest of the Holy Grail, 1902; Walter Pater, 1903; Life of Lowell, 1905; Life of Thomas Bailey Aldrich, 1908; Under the Bridge, 1943; The Practical Cogitator (with C. P. Curtis), 1945; The Lowells and Their Seven Worlds, 1946. Address: 2 Park St., Boston. Died Nov. 19, 1959.

GREENSTEIN, Jesse P(hilip), biochem. research; b. N.Y.C., June 20, 1902; s. Louis and Lena (Birnbaum) G.; B.S., Polytech. Inst. Bklyn., 1926; Ph.D., Brown U., 1930; m. Lucy Louise Mitchell, May 19, 1933; children—Louise (Mrs. Warren Brill), Michael Efrem. NRC fellow Harvard, 1930-31, instr., 1933-39; NRC fellow Kaiser Wilhelm Inst., Dresden, Germany, 1931-32; instr. U. Cal., 1932-33, vis. prof., 1948; chief biochemist National Cancer Inst., Nat. Insts. of Health, Bethesda, Md., 1939—, chief biochemistry lab., 1945—. Mem. com. sci. advisors Inst. Microbiology, Rutgers U., 1958-59; mem. Am. delegation Cancer Colloquium, Rome, 1949. Recipient Neuberg medal in biochemistry, 1950; Distinguished Service award U.S. Dept. Health, Edn. and Welfare, 1954; Hillebrand prize from Wash. chpt. Am. Chem. Soc., 1957. Hon. mem. Japanese Found. for Cancer Research, Japanese Biochemical Society; member American Chem. Society (chmn. div. biol. chemistry), Am. Soc. Biol. Chemistry, Am. Assn. Cancer Research, Nat. Research Council (mem. com. biochemistry, 1957-59, chmn. sub-com. on amino acids). Author: Biochemistry of Cancer, 2d edit. 1954. Editor Cancer Research Advances in Cancer Research, Archives of Biochemistry; co-author: Chemistry of the Amino Acids, 1960. Home: 1606 Highland Dr., Silver Spring, Md. Office: Nat. Cancer Inst., Bethesda, Md. Died Feb. 12, 1959; buried King David Meml. Garden, Falls Church, Va.

GREENSTONE, Julius Hillel, author; b. Russia, Apr. 27, 1873; s. Pesach David and Leah (Puskelinsky) G.; A.B., Coll. City of New York, 1900; rabbi Jewish Theol. Sem., 1900; A.B., U. of Pa., 1902, Ph.D., 1905, L.H.D., honoris causa, 1925; m. Carrie E. Amram, 1902 (dec.); m. 2d, Mrs. Ray Abeles, Sept. 5, 1916; children—Leah G. Farber, Gella G. Kraus, Deborah Greenstone. Teacher, Gratz Coll., Phila., 1905-33, prin., 1933-45, emeritus, 1945—. Mem. bd. dirs. United Synagogue of Am. Editor: S. Morais' Italian Hebrew Literature, 1926. Author: The Religion of Israel, 1902; The Messiah Idea in Jewish History, 1906; Methods of Teaching the Jewish Religion in Junior and Senior Grades, 1915, revised edit. The Jewish Religion, 1920; Numbers with Commentary, 1939; Jewish Feasts and Fasts, 1944. Contbr. to Rabbinic dept. Jewish Ency.; also to Jewish Quarterly Rev., Am. Jewish Year Book, etc. Home: 6429 N. 16th St., Phila. 26. Died Mar. 7, 1955.

GREENWALD, Herbert S., builder, developer; b. St. Louis, Aug. 16, 1915; s. Jacob W. and Clara (DeBirn) G.; student U. Chgo., 1940; m. Lillian Feldman, Apr. 14, 1940; children—Bennet B., Michael P. Pres. Metropolitan Corp. of Am., Herbert Realty & Constrn. Cos., Chgo., 1946—; works include skyscraper apts. on Chgo. lake front, redevelopment Lafayette Park in Detroit, Willoughby Walk, Bklyn., Battery Park, N.Y.C., Pavilion and Colonnade Apts., Newark. Dir. Winfield Hosp.; trustee Francis W. Parker Sch. Mem. Modern Poetry Soc. (dir.). Clubs: Standard, Arts (Chgo.). Home: 330 W. Diversey Pky., Chgo. Office: 135 S. LaSalle St., Chgo. 3. Died Feb. 3, 1959.

GREENWAY, Isabella Selmes (Mrs. Harry Orland King), ex-congresswoman; b. Bonne County, Ky., Mar. 22, 1886; d. Tilden R. and Martha Macomb (Flandrau) Selmes; ed. pub. schs., St. Paul, Minn., Chapins Sch., N.Y. City; m. Robert H. Munro Ferguson, July 15, 1905 (died 1922); children—Martha Munro (Mrs. Charles H. Breasted), Robert Munro; m. 2d, John C. Greenway, Nov. 4, 1923 (died 1926); 1 son, John S.; m. 3d, Harry Orland King, Apr. 22, 1939. Owner and operator, Ariz. Inn, Tucson, Ariz., 1929—; owner Gilpin Air Lines, Los Angeles, 1929-34; owner XX Cattle Ranch, Williams, Ariz., 1926—; mem. 73d Congress (1933-35) to fill unexpired term of L. H. Douglas; elected to 74th Congress (1935-37), Ariz. at large. Mem. Dem. Nat. Com., 1928-34. Chmn. Woman's Land Army of N.M., 1918. Home: 1634 N. Olsen Av., Tucson. Died Dec. 18, 1953; buried Boone County, Ky.

GREENWOOD, Ernest, ex-congressman of New York; born in Yorkshire, England, on November 25, 1884; the son of William and Mary (Cookson) G.; ed. pub. schs. Halifax Eng., Evening Tech. Inst. and Coll.; courses Columbia and Coll. City N.Y.; m. Sarah Emma Mosley, Aug. 7, 1909; 1 dau., Dorothy (Mrs. Charles Oliver Banks). Came to U.S., 1910, naturalized, 1916. With engring. firms, Hadfields and Sir John Brown, Sheffield, Eng., 1905-06; Campbells Gas Engine Co., Halifax, 1907-10; Gen. Elec. Co., Schenectady, N.Y., 1910-14; pub. sch. teacher, Schenectady, 1914-16; head vocational dept. Islip High Sch., 1916-20; supervisor Fed. Bd. Vocational Edn., 1920-22; asso. head master Dwight Sch. for Boys, and N.Y. Prep. Evening Sch. for Adults, 1922-27, headmaster, 1927-46, chmn. bd. trustees, 1946—; dir. First Nat. Bank of Islip, N.Y. Mem. 82d Congress (1951-53), 1st Dist. of N.Y. Mem. Islip Town Rationing Bd., 1942-45; chmn. planning com. Bd. Edn., Bay Shore, N.Y., 1947-48, treas., 1947-50. Mem. com. Census and Inventory of Mil. Resources, World War I; Civil Defense Council, World War II. Mem. bd. dirs. Girl Scouts. Mem. N.Y. Prep. Evening Sch. Assn. (pres., 1927-50), Nat. Com. for Citizens Com. for Reorganization of Exec. Br. of Govt., Pvt. Summer High Schs. Assn. of N.Y. and Vicinity (pres., 1927—). Liberal-Democrat. Episcopalian (vestryman). Mason. Club: Rotary (pres. 1948-49). Home: 53 Ocean Av., Bay Shore, N.Y. Office: Old House Office Building, Washington 25. Died June 15, 1955; buried Oakwood Cemetery, Bay Shore, N.Y.

GREER, Hilton Ross, writer; b. Hawkins, Tex., Dec. 10, 1879; s. Samuel Jeffries and Isabella Jane (Boren) G.; studied at U. of Texas; Litt.D., Austin Coll., 1924; m. Imogene Puryear Agard, June 20, 1914; children—Isabella Jane (Mrs. Homer Ezell), and Hilda Imogene (Mrs. R. E. Janes, Jr.). Newspaper reporter and editor Sherman, Denison and Austin, Tex., and Shreveport, La., until 1910; mng. editor Daily News, Amarillo, 1910-14; editorial writer Dallas Journal, 1914-33, columnist, 1933-35, lit. editor, 1935-38; lit. columnist Dallas Morning News, 1938-42; editorial writer since 1942. An organizer Poetry Soc. of Tex. (pres. 1921-41, hon. pres. since 1941), mem. Poetry Soc. America, Texas Geographical Soc., Texas Inst. of Letters (pres. 1942-44), Sigma Delta Chi. Democrat. Presbyterian. Author: Sungleams and Gossamers, 1903; The Spiders, and Other Poems, 1906; A Prairie Prayer, and Other Poems, 1912; Ten and Twenty Aprils, 1935. Editor: Voices of the Southwest, 1923; Best Short Stories from the Southwest, 1928; Best Short Stories from the Southwest (2d series), 1931; New Voices of the Southwest (with Florence E. Barns), 1934; An Introduction to Texas Literature, 1941. Lecturer on lit. subjects. Home: 3450 Asbury Av. Office: News Bldg., Dallas. Died Nov. 26, 1949; buried Hillcrest Meml. Park, Dallas.

GREER, Margaret R., librarian; b. Minneapolis, Minn., Feb. 13, 1891; d. John Nathan and Elizabeth (Russell) Greer; student Vassar Coll., 1909-10; A.B., U. of Minn., 1913; B.S., Simmons Coll., 1917; unmarried. Librarian Central High Sch. Library, Minneapolis, Minn., 1913-32; dir. sch. libraries and librarian, Bd. Edn. Library 1931-53; instr. div. library instruction, U. of Minn., 1933-45, and summers 1926, 1928, 1938. Visiting instr., Syracuse U., summers 1927, 1929-36, 1940-42, Columbia, 1937, U. of Denver, 1939. Mem. Am. Library Assn. (chmn. sub-com. or sr. high com. on edn., 1928-30, chmn. com. on coop. with N.E.A., 1936-37, chmn. joint com. on N.E.A. and A.L.A., 1937-38, chmn. com. on textbook inclusion in booklist, 1939-40, mem. bd. on library service to children and young people in pub. libraries and schs., 1939-41; chmn. work with teachers and sch. administrs. round table, since 1942, 2d vice pres., 1944). Co-author (with Elizabeth Scripture) Find It Yourself, 1927. Contbr. to ednl. and library jours. Home: 1812 Dupont Av. South, Mpls. 5. Died Nov. 1957.

GREGG, Alan, physician; b. Colorado Springs, Colo., July 11, 1890; s. James Bartlett and Mary (Needham) G.; prep. edn., Cutler Acad., Colorado Springs; A.B., Harvard, 1911; M.D., Harvard Med. Sch., 1916; m. Eleanor Agnes Barrows, July 2, 1923; children—Peter Alan, Nancy Barrows, Richard Alexander, Michael Barrows. Interne, Mass. Gen. Hosp., Boston, 1916-17; served with Royal Army Med. Corps, B.E.F., 1917-19; field staff mem. internat. health bd. Rockefeller Foundation, 1919-22, asso. dir. div. med. edn., 1922-28, asso. dir. med. sciences, 1929-30, dir. med. sciences, 1930-51, vice pres., 1951-56. Decorated Chevalier Legion d'Honneur, 1951; recipient Lasker award Am. Pub. Health Assn., 1957. Fellow A.A.A.S., Am. Acad. Arts and Scis., N.Y. Acad. Medicine, American Coll. Surgeons; hon. member Alpha Omega Alpha, American Association Physicians; mem. Am. Philosophical Society, Phi Beta Kappa (1936). Club: Century (N.Y.C.); Cosmos (Washington). Home: Big Sur, Cal. Died June 9, 1957; buried Westwood Cemetery, Oberlin, O.

GREGG, Alexander White, Jr., lawyer; b. Palestine, Tex., Aug. 17, 1899; s. Alexander White and Mary (Brooks) G.; grad. high sch., Palestine, 1916; A.B., George Washington U., 1921, A.M., 1925, LL.B., 1923; m. Dorothy Mondell, July 26, 1927 (divorced 1934); m. 2d, Eleanor Pocock, Aug. 2, 1940. With Bur. Internal Revenue, Feb. 1920—; legal and econ. work until 1923; spl. asst. to Sec. of Treasury, handling legislative matters, especially tax legislation, 1923-25; solicitor of internal revenue, 1925-26; gen. counsel Treasury Dept. until Oct. 10, 1927; mem. Gregg & Charest; now ranching in Sheridan, Wyo. Served as 2d lt. inf., U.S. Army, June 1918-Jan. 1919. Mem. Sigma Chi. Presbyn. Address: Sheridan, Wyo. Died June 23, 1958; buried Palestine, Tex.

GREGG, John Andrew, clergyman; b. Eureka, Kan., Feb. 18, 1877; s. Alexander and Eliza Frances (Allen) G.; A.B., U. Kan., 1902; M.A., Morris Brown U., 1915; D.D., Wilberforce, 1916; m. Celia A. Nelson, Aug. 20, 1900; m. 2d, Melberta McFarland, 1946. Pres. Bethel Inst., Cape Town, S. Africa, 1903-06; pastor A.M.E. Ch., Leavenworth, Kan., 1906-08, St. Joseph, Mo., 1908-13, elected bishop, Kansas City, Kan., 1924; pres. Edward Waters Coll., Jacksonville, Fla., 1913-20, Wilberforce U., 1920-24. Apptd. rep. Fraternal Council Negro Chs., vis. war fronts, 1943-44. Served six mos. in Cuba as q.m. sgt. 23d Kan. Vols., Spanish-Am. War. Recipient Award of Merit from Sec. of Army, 1947. Mem. Nat. Assn. Tchrs. Colored Schs. (pres. 1922-23), N.E.A. Republican. Mason. Club: Greene Country (O.), Rifle (pres.). Author: Christian Brotherhood, 1930; Superlative Righteousness, 1944; Of Men and of Arms, 1945. Address: 1150 Washington Blvd., Kansas City, Kan. Died 1953; buried Kansas City, Kan.

GREGG, Paul L., clergyman; b. Wichita, Kan., Dec. 10, 1901; s. James Lawrence and Alice (Maher) G.; student St. Mary's (Kan.) Coll., 1922-24 and 1935-39; A.B., St. Louis (Mo.) U., A.M., 1934; LL.B., Georgetown U., Washington, D.C., 1928, LL.M., 1941. Entered Society of Jesus, 1929; ordained priest Roman Catholic Ch., 1938; prof. of law, Creighton U. Sch. of Law since 1941, regent since 1944. Mem. Phi Alpha Delta. Address: Regis College, Denver. Died Sept. 23, 1955; buried Mt. Olivet Cemetery, Denver.

GREGG, J. A., bishop; b. Eureka, Kan., Feb. 18, 1877; s. Alexander and Eliza Frances (Allen) G.; A.B., U. of Kansas, 1902; m. Celia Ann Nelson, Aug. 20. 1900 (died 1941); m. 2d, Mrs. Mlberta McFarland, Dec. 1945. School teacher, Oskaloosa, Kan., 1902-03; ordained to ministry of African Meth. Episcopal Ch.; pastor, Emporia, Kansas, 1903; missionary teacher, Cape Town, South Africa, 1903-06; pastor, Leavenworth, Kan., 1906-08, St. Joseph, Mo., 1908-13; pres. Edwards Coll., Jacksonville, Fla., 1913-20, Wilberforce U., 1920-24; elected bishop, 1924; assigned 17th Episcopal Dist., South Africa, 1924-28, 5th Episcopal Dist., 1928-36, 4th Episcopal Dist., 1936-48, 11th Episcopal District since 1948; president Bishops Council African M.E. Church since 1948. Served as sergeant, later second lieutenant, 23d Kansas Volunteers, during Spanish-American War. Pres. trustee bd. Payne Theol. Sem. (Wilberforce U.); elected pres. Howard U., 1926, but declined position. Recipient Award for Merit by sec. of Army Kenneth C. Royall, 1947; Citation by Univ. of Kan., 1948. Pres. Fla. State Teachers Assn., 1916, Nat. Assn. Preachers in Colored Schs., 1922, African Meth. Episcopal Coll. Presidents Assn., 1922-24. Mem. Alpha Phi Alpha, Sigma Pi Phi. Mason, Knight of Pythias, Elk. Author: (pamphlets) Christian Brotherhood, 1930; Superlative Righteousness, 1944; Of Men and Of Arms, 1945. Delivered keynote address 8th Worlds Christian Endeavor, Berlin, Germany, 1930, invocation Nat. Rep. Conv., Philadelphia, 1940. By invitation of the president visited all war fronts, except Alaska, representing Fraternal Council of Negro Churches, 1943-44. Home: 1150 Washington Blvd., Kansas City 2, Kan. Office: Edward Waters College, Jacksonville, Fla. Died Feb. 1953.

GREGG, John B., physician; b. Gladbrook, Ia., Sept. 28, 1888; s. Daniel and Lillie A. (Sharp) G.; A.B., State U. of Ia., 1915, M.D., 1915, M.S., 1916; m. A. Elida Bailey, Aug. 10, 1921; children—John Bailey, Charles Dan, Mary Elida, Elizabeth Ann, Margaret Jane. Sr. clinical assistant oto-laryngology; State University of Ia., 1915-17; maj. Medical Reserve Corps, U.S. Army, assigned to British Royal Army Medical Corps, 1917-19; asso. prof. oto-laryngology, State U. of Ia., 1919-20; private practice, specializing in oto-laryngology, Sioux Falls, S.D., since 1920. Fellow Am. Coll. Surgeons; mem. A.M.A., S.D. State Med. Soc., Am. Acad. Ophthalmology and Otolaryngology, Am. Laryngol., Rhinol. and Otol. Soc., Newcomen Soc. of England, Alpha Omega Alpha, Sigma Xi, Phi Rho Sigma. Decorated British Mil. Cross, 1918. Republican. Episcopalian. Mason (Shriner). Club: Minnehaha Country. Home: 309 N. Duluth Av. Office: Security Nat. Bank Bldg., Sioux Falls, S.D. Died Mar. 3, 1954; buried Woodlawn Cemetery, Sioux Falls, S.D.

GREGG, John Price, govt. official; b. Portland, Ore., Sept. 8, 1891; s. John Thomas and Eva (Price) G.; A.B., Stanford, 1913, grad. studies, law and economics, 1913-14; student Univ. of Paris (Sorbonne), 1919; m. Elizabeth Emily Dyer, Apr. 2, 1929; 1 son, Lawrence Alexander. Admitted to bar of Ore., 1915, Mont., 1917, New York, 1925, Dist. of Columbia, 1935. Regional dir. Am. Relief Administrn. southern and eastern European relief and famine operations, London, England, 1920-23; asst. to Sec. of Commerce, Washington, D.C., 1926-27; mgr. Am. sect. and sec. Am. Com. Internat. Chamber of Commerce, Washington, D.C., 1927-35; sec. com. for reciprocity information, State Dept., 1937-41; asst. dep. and dep. chief, Priorities, War Prodn. Bd., 1941-42; U.S. sec. combined prodn. and resources bd., Washington, D.C., 1942-43; chief staff operations, War Prodn. Bd., Washington, D.C., 1943-44; exec. dir. U.S. Assos. Internat. Chambers of Commerce, New York, 1945-46; mem. U.S. Tariff Commn. since Sept. 1946. Commd. 2d lt., U.S. Army, Nov. 1917; served overseas Mar. 1918 to hon. disch. as capt., Mar. 1920. Mem. Alpha Delta Phi. Republican. Presbyterian. Clubs: Army and Navy Country, Cosmos (Washington, D.C.); University (New York, N.Y.); Devon Yacht (Amagansett, N.Y.). Home: 4313 Yuma St., Washington 16. Office: U.S. Tariff Commission, Washington 25. Died Oct. 29, 1952.

GREGOR, Elmer Russell, author; b. N.Y.C., Dec. 23, 1878; s. Charles Russell and Hester Ann (Gregory) Mc Gregor; grad. Bernard Mil. Acad., N.Y.C., 1897; m. Ida M. Frame, June 6, 1906. Traveled much in the mountains, east and west; contributed series of old-time Indian stories to juvenile publs. and many articles and stories to outdoor mags. Mem. S.R., Soc. Colonial Wars. Clubs: Camp-Fire of America, Forest Lake. Author: Camping in the Winter Woods, 1912; Camping on Western Trails, 1913; The Red Arrow, 1915; Indian Adventure Stories, 1916; White Otter, 1917; Running Fox, 1918; Warpath and Hunting Trail, 1919; The White Wolf, 1920; The War Trail, 1920; Spotted Deer, 1922; Three Sioux Scouts, 1922; Jim Mason—Backwoodsman, 1923; Jim Mason—Scout, 1923; Captain Jim Mason, 1924; The Medicine Buffalo, 1925; The War Eagle, 1926; Mason and His Rangers, 1926; The War Chief, 1927; The Mystery Trail, 1927; The Oswego Trail, 1928; The Spotted Pony, 1928; Three Wilderness Scouts, 1928. Founder with others Buckskin Men of Am., forerunner of Boy Scouts. Home: Southport, Conn. Died Apr. 4, 1954.

GREGORY, Chester Arthur, educator; b. Shelbyville, Ind., Jan. 24, 1880; s. Samuel H. and Elizabeth G.; B.S., Marion (Ind.) Normal Sch., 1903; B.A., Ind. U., 1908, M.A., 1914; Ph.D., State U. Ia., 1920; m. Sadie Elizabeth Smith, 1902; 1 dau., Helen Virginia; m. 2d, Corinne M. Taylor, 1942. Supt. public schools in Ind., Ill., and Minn., 10 yrs.; prof. edn., Parsons Coll., Fairfield, Ia., 1914-16; prof. sch. adminstration, U. Ore., 1917-24, also dir. bur. ednl. research; prof. school adminstrn., U. Cin., 1924-37, also director bur. administrative research; pres. C. A. Gregory Co., 1931—. Mem. Ednl. Research Assn., N.E.A., Phi Delta Kappa. Republican. Presbyterian. Author: The Proficiency of Oregon Children in the Tool Subjects, 1921; The Gregory American History Tests, 1922; The Fundamentals of Educational Measurements with the Elements of Statistical Method, 1923; Muddling Along, 1940. Part Author: The Gregory-Spencer Geography Tests, 1921; Statistical Method in Education and Psychology, 1929; Writer's Manual, 1935; Gregory Diagnostic Tests in Language, 1935. Home: 2907 Clifton Av. Office: 345 Calhoun St., Cin. Died Dec. 4, 1956; buried Spring Grove Cemetery, Cin.

GREGORY, David Thomas, bishop; b. Martinsburg, W.Va., July 16, 1889; s. Joseph T. and Sarah H. (Fulk) G.; student Shenandoah Collegiate Inst., 1910-15; A.B., Lebanon Valley Coll., Annville, Pa., 1917, D.D., 1924, B.D., Bonebrake Theological Sem. 1920; LL.D. Albright Coll., 1954; LL.D. Otterbein Coll., 1954; m. Margaret L. Broy; 1 dau., Thelma Davileah. Pastor Jones Springs, W.Va., 1914, Shenandoah, Va., 1915, Lebanon, Pa., 1916-17; asso. editor Religious Telescope, 1920-21; pres. Shenandoah Coll., 1922-26; pastor Euclid Av. U.B. Ch., Dayton, O., 1926-36; supt. Miami Conf., 1932-37; exec. sec. Council of Adminstrn. of Evang. United Brethren Church, 1937-50, bishop, 1950—. Trustee Bonebrake Theol. Sem., Otterbein Home and Orphanage; pres. Flat Rock Childrens Home Bd. and Ministerial Pension Bd. Mem. Nat. Council Chs. of Christ. Mason (32°). Kiwanian. Author: The Minister and Local Church Finance; Stewardship the Key to Christian Service. Home: 900 East End Av., Pitts. 21. Died Dec. 27, 1956; buried Martinsburg, W.Va.

GREGORY, Herbert Bailey, judge; b. Westmoreland County, Va., Apr. 10, 1884; s. Werter Hancock and Sallie James (Payne) G.; prep. edn., Randolph Macon Acad., Bedford, Va.; LL.B., Washington and Lee U., 1911; m. Margaret Kossen, Oct. 26, 1916; children—James Blair, Herberta Payne, Kossen. In practice of law at Roanoke, Va., 1911-23; judge Circuit Court, 20th Va. Jud. Circuit, 1923-26; judge Law and Chancery Court, City of Roanoke, 1926-30; justice Supreme Court of Appeals, Va., since 1930. Mem. American Va. State and Roanoke bar assns., Kappa Sigma, Phi Delta Phi, Omicron Delta Kappa (hon.), Phi Beta Kappa. Democrat. Methodist. Mason. Home: 530 Cassel Lane, Roanoke, Va. Died Mar. 1951.

GREGORY, Herbert E(rnest), geologist, educator; b. Middleville, Mich., Oct. 15, 1869; s. George Albert and Anne (Bross) G.; A.B., Yale, 1896, Ph.D., 1899; D.Sc. hon., Doane Coll., 1934; m. Edna Earle Hope, June 30, 1908; 1 dau., Anne Cutts (Mrs. John L. Scarlett). Asst. in botany Yale, 1896-98, instr. phys. geography, 1899-01, asst. prof. physiography, 1901-04, Silliman prof. geology, 1904-36, emeritus since 1936; asst. geologist U.S. Geol. Survey, 1900-09, geologist, 1909-48; supt. Conn. Geol. and Natural History Survey, 1916-20; acting dir. Bernice P. Bishop Museum, Honolulu, T.H., 1919-20, dir., 1920-36, emeritus dir. since 1936; chmn. bd. regents U. Hawaii, 1937-42; organized 1st Pacific Sci. Congress, 1920; del. European sci. congresses, 1948, 1950. Mem. bd. water supply, Honolulu, 1928-36. Trustee Palama Settlement, Honolulu, 1934-42. Served as maj., supervisor sci., com. edn. and special training War Dept., 1918. Fellow Geol. Soc. Am., Assn. Am. Geographers, Am. Acad. Arts and Scis., Washington Acad. Sci., Am. Philos. Soc.; mem. Nat. Research Council. Author geol. articles profl. jours. Asso. editor Am. Jour. Sci., 1904-28. Home: 3066 Wailani Rd. Office: Bishop Museum, Honolulu 17, Hawaii. Died Jan. 23, 1952; buried Honolulu, Hawaii.

GREGORY, John, sculptor; b. London, Eng., May 17, 1879; s. John and Amelia Elizabeth (Read) G.; student Art Students' League, N.Y.C., 1900-03, Ecole des Beaux Arts, Paris, 1904-06, Am. Acad. in Rome, 1912-15; pupil of George Grey Barnard and Anton Mercie; m. Katharine Van Rensselaer Crosby, June 7, 1922; 1 son, John Delafield. Assoc. in modeling Columbia, until 1925. Served as asst. insp., naval constrn. camouflage Navy Dept., 1918. Principal works include: Panels on Folger Shakespeare Library, Washington; Huntington Mausoleum, San Marino, Cal.; Albert J. Beveridge Meml., Indpls.; equestrian Gen. Anthony Wayne, Phila. Exhibited Nat. Sculpture Soc., Archtl. League, N.Y.C., Phila. Acad. Fine Arts, Art Inst., Chgo. Recipient Medal of Honor, Architectural League, 1921; Concord Art Association, 1926; National Sculpture Society, 1956; George D. Widener Meml., Pa. Acad. Fine Arts, 1933. Mem. Nat. Sculpture Soc. (pres. 1934-39, hon. pres. 1953—), Nat. Acad. Design, Nat. Inst. Arts and Letters; hon. mem. Beaux Arts Inst. Design (N.Y.C.), A.I.A. Mem. Art Commn. of N.Y.C., 1957—. Home: 222 E. 71st St., N.Y.C. 21. Died Feb. 21, 1958.

GREGORY, John Goadby, writer; b. Milw., July 11, 1856; s. John and Elizabeth (Goadby) G.; ed. pub. schs.; m. Caroline Paul, 1883 (dec. May, 1891); children—Marian Elizabeth, Caroline Strong (Mrs. William Wallace Rinehart), Paul Goadby, William Oliver (dec.); m. 2d, Victoria Winburn Smalley, 1892; (died Feb. 1946), 1 dau., Elizabeth Winburn (dec.). Type-setter Evening Wis., 1868-70; Compositor Milwaukee Sentinel, 1870-75; compositor Evening Wis., 1875-77, reporter, 1877-85, Commercial editor, 1882-85, City editor, 1885-89, editor 1889-1905, editor in chief, 1905-18; editor Northwestern Trade Bulletin, 1880-83; Special writer Sentinel, 1881-82; editor Milwaukee Miner and Mfr., 1887-89; ret.; professor journalism, Marquette U., 1919; sec. Wis. War History Commn., 1919-23; chief war history dept., Wis. State Hist. Soc., 1923-25. Member board of regents Marquette University. Mem. Wis. State Hist. Soc., Wis. Acad. Scis., Arts and Letters, Wis. Archeol. Soc., Milw. Co. Hist. Soc. Clubs: City, Milwaukee Press, Parkman, Old Settlers of Milwaukee County. Author: Beauty of Thebes (verse); History of Milwaukee, 1931; History of Southeastern Wisconsin, 1932; History of Southwestern Wisconsin, 1932; History of

West Central Wisconsin, 1933; also monographs on Northwestern history, biography, etc. Home: 1431 N. Jefferson St., Milw. Died Apr. 12, 1947; buried Forest Home Cemetery, Milw.

GREGORY, Leslie Roscoe, educator; b. Seneca, Kan., Sept. 16, 1888; s. Marion Wallace and Nettie Helen (Linn) A.; prep. edn., York (Neb.) Coll. Acad., 1905-09; A.B., York Coll., 1917; M.A., Tchrs. Coll., Columbia, 1924, grad. study, 1924-26; grad. study U. Neb., U. Chgo.; Pd.D., Albany State Tchrs. Coll., 1933; Ed.D., Columbia, 1943; m. Margaret C. Anderson, June 27, 1923; children—Sheila Jeanne, Jane Carolyn. Supervising prin. schs., Cowles, Neb., 1909-13; supt. schs., Exeter, Neb., 1917-19, Tecumseh, Neb., 1920-23; prin. high schs., Bronxville, N.Y., 1923-24; exec. sec. Inst. Child Welfare, Tchrs. Coll., Columbia, 1925-26; also research asso.; dir. research, pub. schs., Louisville, 1926-29; supt. schs., Louisville, 1929-31; pres. State Tchrs. Coll., Fredonia, N.Y., 1932—. Mem. State Com. Tchr. Edn.; mem. nat. com. Tchr. Exams.; mem. accrediting com., Am. Assn. Tchrs. Coll., 1941-46, chmn., 1946. Served as 2d lt. F.A., U.S. Army, June 1918-Jan. 1919. Pres. Ky. Edn. Assn., 1930-31; mem. N. E.A., N.Y. State Tchrs. Assn. (pres. Western Zone 1936), N.Y. State Assn. Colls. and Univs. (mem. exec. com.), Phi Delta Kappa, Kappa Delta Pi. Republican. Presbyn. Clubs: Rotary (past pres.), Shorewood (dir.). Home: Fredonia, N.Y. Died July 24, 1954; buried Fredonia.

GREGORY, Louis Hoyt, prof. zoölogy; b. Princeton Mass., July 21, 1880; d. Josiah David and Emily Du Puy (Skinner) Gregory; prep. edn., Dana Hall, Wellesley, Mass., 1897-99; A.B., Vassar Coll., 1903; A.M., Columbia, 1907; Ph.D., 1909; unmarried. With Barnard Coll., N.Y.C., as asst. in zoölogy, 1908-09, tutor, 1909-12, instr., 1912-17, asst. prof., 1917-23, asso. prof., 1923-36, prof., 1936—, asso. dean, 1932-49, prof. emeritus, 1949—. Fellow A.A. A.S.; mem. Am. Soc. Zoölogists, Soc. for Exptl. Biology and Medicine, Harvey Soc., Sigma Xi. Conglist. Clubs: Vassar, Cosmopolitan (New York). Home: 1160 5th Av., N.Y.C. Died Nov. 2, 1954.

GREGORY, Raymond William, educator; born Mooresville, Ind., Sept. 6, 1893; s. Corden Everett and Arminta Sarah (Marley) G.; B.S.A., Purdue U., LaFayette, Ind., 1918; M.S., Cornell U., 1924; Ph.D., 1937; married Bertha Jane Morgan, May 1, 1919 (died June 15, 1948); children—Sarah Jane (dec.), Richard Morgan, Robert Sandborn; married Bertha Vaughan Akin on June 21, 1950. Teacher of vocational agriculture and science, Mooresville, (Indiana) High School., 1919-23; assistant in rural education, Cornell U., 1923-24; asso. prof. agrl. edn., Purdue U., 1924-36, asst. state supervisor agrl. edn., State of Ind., 1928-36; specialist agrl. edn. U.S. Office of Edn., Washington, D.C., 1936-41; asst. dir. Rural War Production Training; special lecturer and teacher, university summer sessions, 1941-45; dep. dir. Surplus Property Utilization, 1945-46; asst. U.S. Commissioner for Vocational Education, 1946-52; spl. asst. to Commissioner of Education since 1952; commercial orchardist and farmer, since 1919. Served in U.S. Army, July-Nov. 1918. Mem. War-Navy Com., U.S. Armed Forces Institute; member board visitors Marine Corps Inst. since 1951; chmn. United States delegation Inter-American Seminar on Vocational Education, 1952. Member American Vocational Association (chmn. publs. com. 6 yrs.; mem. national advisory com. on agrl. education 3 yrs.), N.E.A., American Legion, Sigma Pi, Sigma Delta Chi, Alpha Zeta, Kappa Delta Pi, Phi Delta Kappa, Iota Lambda Sigma. Quaker. Mason. Agricultural editor for F. A. Davis Pub. Co., Phila., 1933-35, J. B. Lippincott Pub. Co., Phila., since 1936. Editor of Am. Vocational Assn. Jour., 1928-32; mem. editing managing board Agrl. Edn. Mag., 1929-42 (one of organizers 1929), editor of professional sect. (with A. K. Getman), same, 1936-42; special editor Little Livestock Lessons, Breeders Gazette, 2 yrs. Home: 4531 Van Ness St., N.W. Office: U.S. Office of Education, Washington. Died June 2, 1954; buried Mooresville, Ind.

GREGORY, Thomas B., oil and gas producer; b. Phila., Oct. 15, 1860; s. William Sheed and Amanda Walton (Miller) G.; ed. Brooks Mil. Acad., Cleve.; m. Adda S. Whitling, June 21, 1888; children—Ruth Whitling (Mrs. Richard G. Soper), Katherine Elizabeth (Mrs. Charles McGill Thomas). Began in oil business at Foxburg, Pa., 1885; mem. firm Crawford & Gregory; dir. Lone Star Gas Co., Dallas, Tex., Mountain Fuel Supply Co., Salt Lake City, Utah; Quaker State Oil Refining Corp., Oil City, Pa., Union Heat & Light Co., Grove City, Pa. Asst. to dir. oil production, U.S. Fuel Adminstration, later dir. Bur. Natural Gas, World War I. Mem. Am. Petroleum Inst., Am. Gas Assn. Episcopalian. Home: 5833 Aylesboro Av. Office: 894 Union Trust Bldg., Pitts. 19. Died July 1951.

GREGORY, William Edward, educator; b. Blanchester, O., July 3, 1901; s. William Charles and Birdie Grace (Parker) G.; B.S., Miami U., Oxford, O., 1924; grad. Field Arty. Sch., U.S. Army, 1931; M.A., U. of Mich., 1934; Ed.M. (Austin scholar), Harvard, 1935; Litt.D., Colgate U., 1940; m. Iris Beryl Hinton, of Middlesex, England, June 25, 1945. Began as educator, 1922; prin. Hanover High Sch., Hamilton, O., 1923; instr. mathematics, Culver Mil. Acad., Culver, Ind., 1924-27, tactical officer, F.A., 1927-30, asst. headmaster, 1930-33, dean, 1935-39, acting supt., 1939-40, supt. since 1940. Mem. bd. dirs. Culver Ednl. Foundation. Past. president Private Schools Association. With 12th U.S. Army Group, May 1942-July 1945; colonel Headquarters, October 1943 July 1945. Awarded Legion of Merit, Bronze Star Medal with Oak Leaf Cluster (United States); Legion of Honor, Croix de Guerre with Palm (France); Croix de Guerre with Palm (Belgium); Couronne de Chene (Luxembourg). Mem. N.E.A., Am. Acad. Polit. and Social Science, Pvt. Schs. Assn. of Central States, Association of Military Colleges and Schools, Delta Kappa Epsilon, Phi Delta Kappa, Cum Laude Soc., Kappa Delta Pi, Phi Beta Kappa. Presbyterian. Clubs: University, Harvard (Chicago); Army and Navy (Washington). Address: Culver Military Academy, Culver, Ind. Died Mar. 14, 1956; buried Culver Masonic Cemetery, Culver, Ind.

GREGORY, William Logan, banker; b. English, Ind., Sept. 21, 1898; s. William Lewis and Dovie (Benham) G.; ed. Colo. Sch. Mines; m. Catherine Keelan, Nov. 3, 1923; 1 dau., June. Served successively as asst. auditor, accountant and mgr. Marine Ins. Div., Am. Express Co., Buenos Aires, 1920-22; successively clerk and mgr. War Savings Dept., asst. mgr. Transit Dept., rep. Bank Relations Dept., asst. examiner Fed. Res. Agent's Dept., clerk for spl. study, audit dept., asst. statistician and chief clerk, Fed. Res. Agent's Dept., acting asst. Fed. Res. Agent, Fed. Res. Bank of St. Louis, 1922-30; v.p., cashier, dir. The Plaza Bank of St. Louis, and its predecessors, Guaranty-Plaza Trust Co., and Guaranty Bank & Trust Co., 1930—; now pres., dir. Easton-Taylor Trust Co., St. Louis. Lectr. Grad. Sch. Banking, Rutgers U., New Brunswick, N.J., bd. regents, 1951-53. Mem. exec. council Am. (state bank div.), Ind. (past pres.) bankers assns., Kappa Sigma. Clubs: Racquet, University. Home: R.D. 1, St. Louis Rock Rd., Villa Ridge, Mo. Office: 4915 Delmar Av., St. Louis 8. Died Apr. 28, 1959; buried English, Ind.

GREHAN, Bernard H(enry), civil engr.; b. New Orleans, Sept. 4, 1893; s. Bernard and Caroline (Simon) G.; B.C.E., Tulane Univ., 1915, C.E., 1923; m. Marie Louise LeMore, Aug. 25, 1917; children—Gloria Marie (Mrs. William C. Ellis), Bernard Albert, Patricia Ann (Mrs. J. W. Pou), Marie Le More (Mrs. Luther E. Hall III). With U.S. Engrs., in charge of hydrog. and topographic surveys, 1915-16; asso. with J. F. Coleman, cons. engrs., 1916-17; in gen. contracting bus., constrn. of bldgs. and foundations with George J. Glover Co., Inc., 1919—, v.p. and dir., 1925-47; asso. with Boh Bros. Construction Co., 1949—. Mem. La. State Bd. of Engring. Examiners, mem. bd. of adminstrs., Louise S. McGehee Sch. for Girls, 1941-49, Tulane U., 1949—, v.p. 1951. Served as 1st lt. U.S. Engrs. Corps, 1917-19; A.E.F., 1918-19. Mem. Am. Soc. Civil Engrs. (pres., La. sect., 1928), La. Engring. Soc. (pres. 1938), Asso. Gen. Contractors of Am. (pres., New Orleans chapter, 1946-47), Tau Beta Pi, Phi Kappa Sigma. Roman Catholic. Clubs: Louisiana, Recess, Boston (New Orleans). Home: 1670 Soniat St., New Orleans 15. Office: 2400 Cypress St., New Orleans 19. Died Dec. 15, 1952.

GRESHAM, James Wilmer (grĕsh'ăm), clergyman; b. Ocean Springs, Miss., July 13, 1871; s. James McAllister and Emily Alice (Seymour) G.; B.D., U. of South, 1896, D.D., 1915; m. Emily Williamson Cooke, Sept. 28, 1898. Deacon, 1895, priest, 1896, P.E. Ch.; curate Trinity Ch., New Orleans, La., 1896; rector St. James Ch., Baton Rouge, La., 1897-1900, Grace Ch., Charleston, S.C., 1900-04, Trinity Ch., San Jose, Cal., 1904-10; dean Grace Cathedral, San Francisco, 1910-39, dean emeritus, 1939—. Elected bishop of Philippines, 1918, but declined. Mem. Phi Beta Kappa. Mason (K.T.), Elk. Clubs: Commonwealth, University. Author: The Beatitudes of Jesus, 1908; The Young Man, 1909; The Wings of Healing, 1926; Upon the Harp, 1931. Home: "Eventide," 363 14th Av. Address: Cathedral House, 1051 Taylor St., San Francisco. Died Mar. 21, 1958.

GRESHAM, LeRoy (grĕs'săm), clergyman; b. Madison, Ga., Sept. 21, 1871; s. Thomas B. and Lula (Billups) G.; grad. Lawrenceville Sch., 1888, A.B., Princeton, 1892, A.M., 1893; studied Johns Hopkins; LL.B., U. Md., 1896; B.D., Union Theol. Sem. Va., 1906; D.D., King Coll., Bristol, Tenn., 1914, Washington and Lee U., 1924; m. Jessie Rhett (dec.), Jan. 7, 1903; children—Thomas B. (dec.), Francis R. (dec.). Practiced law in Balt., 1896-1903; ordained ministry Presbyn. Ch. U.S., 1906; pastor Chapel Hill, N.C., 1906-09, Salem, Va., 1909-46; ret. Mem. Phi Beta Kappa, Alpha Delta Phi. Democrat. Author mag. articles and reviews. Home: 535 Market St., Salem, Va. Died Feb. 16, 1955; buried Sherwood Park, Salem.

GREW, Henry S., mfr.; b. Boston, Mass., Nov. 1, 1875; s. Edward Sturgis and Annie Crawford (Clark) G.; A.B., Harvard U., Cambridge, Mass., 1896; m. Ethel G. Hooper, Nov. 17, 1897; children—Henry S., James H., Agnes H. (Mrs. Alexander Wheeler), Ethel H. (Mrs. Frederick Robinson). Chmn. exec. com. West Point Mfg. Co., Boston, since 1933, State St. Trust Co., Boston; dir. Wellington, Sears Co. Trustee N.E. Conservatory of Music. Home: 254 Marlborough St. Office: 111 Devonshire St., Boston. Died July 20, 1953.

GRIER, Albert Oliver Herman (grēr), editor; b. Milford, Del., Mar. 4, 1867; s. William George and Elma (Collins) G.; grad. Wilmington High Sch., 1885; m. Sarah Elizabeth Baylis, Dec. 24, 1895; children—George Martindale, Warren William, Albert Oliver Herman. Began as printer's apprentice on Wilmington (Del.) Every Evening, 1885, reporter, 1895-96, city editor, 1896-1927, editor, 1927-33 asso. editor Journal-Every Evening, 1933-34; editor Journal-Every Evening since 1934. Member of the American Society of Newspaper Editors, Delmarva Press Association, Wilmington Society Fine Arts Sons of Del., Wilmington Y.M.C.A. (life member 1948). Democrat. Episcopalian. Odd Fellow. Clubs: Torch of Delaware, Church of Delaware; Poor Richard Club (Philadelphia); Nat. Press (Washington). Author: This Was Wilmington, 1945. Contbr. articles to mags. Home: 115 W. 24 St., Wilmington 2. Office: News-Journal Bldg., Wilmington 99, Del. Died Jan. 23, 1953; buried Riverview Cemetery, Wilmington, Del.

GRIER, Francis Ebenezer, textile exec.; b. Due West, S.C., Nov. 17, 1899; s. Paul Livingston and Effie (Pressly) G.; A.B., Erskine Coll., Due West, 1920; m. Malvina Kennedy, Nov. 29, 1923; 1 son, Francis Calvin. With Nat. Union Bank, Rock Hill, S.C., 1920-21; treas., bus. mgr. Erskine Coll., 1921-24, treas., 1924—; pres. 1st Trust & Savs. Bank, Due West, 1924-27; v.p. Central Union Bank, Rock Hill, 1927-30, Greenwood (S.C.) br., 1930-33; pres. Bank of Greenwood, 1933-42; pres., dir. Abney Mills (merged with Brandon Corp. and Belton Mills, 1949). Dir. Greenwood C. of C. Democrat. Presbyn. Clubs: Biltmore Forest Country (Asheville, N.C.); Piedmont (Spartanburg, S.C.); Greenwood Golf. Home: 211 Jennings Av. Office: Abney Mills, Greenwood, S.C. Died Oct. 13, 1959.

GRIER, Norman MacDowell, biologist, educator; b. Pittsburgh, Pa., June 12, 1890; s. James B. and Marian (Gibson) G.; B.S., U. of Pittsburg, 1911, M. A., 1912, Ph.D., 1919; studied Cold Spring Harbor Biol. Lab., 1911, Yale, 1912-14, Harris Teachers' Coll., 1914-18, U. of Paris, 1919, Columbia, 1928-31; m. Margaretta Gibson, Aug. 30, 1915; 1 dau., Elizabeth Frances; m. 2d, Christine Ruth, Feb. 21, 1925; children—John James, Benjamin. Instr. physiology, Central High Sch., St. Louis, Mo., 1914-18; prof. zoology, Hollins Coll., 1919-20, Washington and Jefferson Coll., 1920-23; asst. prof. evolution Dartmouth Col., 1923-26; prof. and head of dept. biology, Des Moines U., 1926-27; head dept. science, and prof. biology, Westchester (Pa.) State Teachers Coll., 1927-28; prof. biology, Elizabethtown (Pa.) Coll., 1928-30, also head science dept.; prof zoology, Evansville (Ind.) Coll., 1930; prof. biology, Wagner Coll., S.I., N.Y., 1930-33; research in higher edn. and Inst. of Edn., New York U., 1933-34; dir. Industrial Survey Lebanon County, 1934; area dir. for Pa., Nat. Youth Adminstrn., 1935-36; founder and chmn. Lebanon County Mental Health Clinic, Lebanon. Pa., 1936—; personnel expert, Pa. Social Security Adminstrn., 1937; mem. Pa. State advisory board, Fed. Writers' Project, 1938-39; mem. Nat. Committee for Planned Parenthood since 1939; with Veterans Adminstrn., Washington, D.C., 1944; exec. officer, Veterans Adminstrn. Guidance Center, U. of Pa., 1945. Asso. Am. Psychol. Assn., 1945. Lecturer at Hahnemann Med. Coll., 1945-46; prof. histol. and embryol. Pennsylvania State Coll. Optometry, Phila., 1946-49; lecturer Philadelphia Junto since 1949. Member Committee on Religion and Health, Fed. Council, Churches of Christ in Am. since 1943. Instr. Biol. Lab., Cold Spring Harbor, N.Y., summers 1921, 22, in charge field systematic botany, 1923-26; lecturer Wagner Free Inst. of Science, Phila., 1928, Coll. of New Rochelle, 1932-33; Columbiona fellowship, 1929. In charge of mussel survey of Upper Miss. River, U.S. Bur. of Fisheries, 1920, 25; Commd. 2d lt. inf., Pa. N.G., 1911; 1st lt. C.W.S., U.S. Army, Aug. 1918; asst. gas. officer 5th A.C., A.E.F., 1918-19. Fellow A.A.A.S. (com. on place of science in edn. 1925-32), Ia. Acad. Science, 1927; mem. St. Louis Acad. Science (sec. 1916-18), Paleontol. Soc. America, Am. Eugenics Soc. (Pa., com. 1929), Am. Soc. Zoologists, Ecol. Soc. America, Bot. Soc. America (sec. syst. sect. 1932), Am. Assn. Univ. Profs., Pa. State Edn. Assn., State Conservation Assn., Pa. State Acad. Science, L.I. Biol. Assn., Am. Acad. Polit. and Social Science, Geographic Players (advisory bd.), Phi Delta Theta, Phi Sigma, Pi Delta Epsilon, Pi Gamma Mu, Phi Delta Kappa, Am. Legion, Vets. Fgn. Wars. Chmn. Lancaster County (Pa.) Wild Flower Preservation Soc. America, 1929; local chmn. United Welfare Fund of Lebanon County; member executive com. Lebanon County Boy Scouts. Mem. Disciples of Christ Ch.; mem. bd. ednl. survey Colls. of Ch. of the Brethren, 1932. Author of various tech. papers and book reviews in biol. subjects and higher edn. Asso. editor Am. Midland Naturalist, 1923-35;

editorial staff Biological Abstracts since 1950. Lecturer. Home: 207 Hathaway Park, Lebanon, Pa. Died Dec. 26, 1951; buried Mt. Lebanon Cemetery, Lebanon.

GRIES, John Matthew (grēs), economist; b. nr. Urbana, Champaign County, O., June 22, 1877; s. Alexander and Mary Ellen (Scarborough) G.; student Ohio Northern U., Ada., O.; A.B., Miami U., Oxford, O., 1905, A.M., 1906, LL.D., 1923; grad. student in economics, U. of Wisconsin, 1906-07, Columbia, 1907-08; m. Ethel Martha Goff, Dec. 22, 1909; children—John Paul, Robert Goff, George A. Financial sec. University Settlement, New York, 1907-08; spl. agt. U.S. Bur. Corp., Washington, 1908-14; lecturer, later asst. prof., Harvard, 1914-21; dir. Harvard Bur. Business Research, 1918; examiner U.S. Federal Trade Commn., 1917; expert U.S. Shipping Bd., 1918; chief Div. of Building and Housing, Bur. of Standards, U.S. Dept. Commerce, 1921-28, chief Div. of Public Construction, 1929-30; exec. sec. President's Conf. on Home Bldg. and Home Ownership, 1930-32; mem. Federal Home Loan Bank Board, 1932-33. Mem. of President Harding's Conf. on Unemployment, 1921; mem. Com. on Seasonal Operation in Constrn., same, 1923-24; apptd. by Sec. of Commerce Hoover a mem. Nat. Conf. on Street and Highway Safety, 1924; rep. U.S. Dept. Commerce at Internat. Housing and Town Planning Congress, Vienna, 1926; chmn. Am. delegation to Congress of Internat. Fed. Bldg. and Pub. Work, London, 1930. Mem. Am. Planning and Civic Assn. (dir.), Am. City Planning Inst. (hon.), Delta Upsilon, Phi Beta Kappa, Acacia. Mem. Christian Church. Mason; mem. O.E.S. Joint Author: How to Own Your Home, 1923; Seasonal Operation in the Construction Industries, 1924; also articles on housing. Editor (with J. Ford) of 11 vols. on housing. Home: Rosewood, O. Died Sept. 23, 1953; buried Rosedale Cemetery, Careysville, O.

GRIFFIN, Cardinal Bernard, archbishop of Westminster; b. Birmingham, Eng., Feb. 21, 1899; s. William and Helen (Swadkins) G.; student Cotton Coll., Staffs, Eng., Oscott Coll., Birmingham, Eng. Venerable English College, Pontifical Beda Coll., Rome; D.D. (Rome) 1925, D.C.L. (Rome), 1927; LL.D. (hon.) Fordham U., 1946, Birmingham U., 1946; D.D. (hon.) Louvain, 1948; LL.D. (hon.), Nat. Univ. of Ireland, 1955. Ordained priest Roman Cath. Ch., Nov. 1, 1924; pvt. s.c. to the archbishop of Birmingham, 1927-37; chancellor archdiocese of Birmingham, 1929-38; adminstr. Fr. Hudson's Homes, Coleshill, 1937-43; aux. bishop of Birmingham, 1938-43; archbishop of Westminster, December 18, 1943; created cardinal priest, Feb. 18, 1946; papal legate to Hierarchy Centenary Congress, 1950. Club: Athenaeum. Home: Archbishop's House, Westminster, London, S.W. 1, Eng. Died Aug. 20, 1956; buried Westminster Cathedral Crypt.

GRIFFIN, Carroll Wardlaw, educator; b. Lockhart, S.C., Oct. 14, 1900; s. Robert Lee and Madge (Wardlaw) G.; B.S., Clemson Coll., 1921; M.S., U. Va., 1923, Ph.D., 1927; m. Virginia Henshaw Cowherd, Nov. 26, 1925. Teaching fellow chemistry U. Va., 1921-23, 25-27; prof. chemistry high sch., Anderson, S.C., 1923-24; asso. prof. chemistry, physics Brenau Coll., 1924-25; prof. chemistry Miss. Woman's Coll., 1927-31; N.J. Gas Assn. fellow Rutgers U., 1931-32; asst. prof. chemistry Vassar Coll., 1932-39, asso. prof., 1939-45, prof., 1945-53, chmn. dept., 1955—; staff Mathew Vassar Found., 1953—. Member American Chemical Society, Southern Society of N.Y.C., Sigma Xi, Phi Lambda Upsilon, Alpha Chi Sigma. Republican. Baptist. Club: University (Poughkeepsie). Author: Inorganic Semimicro Qualitative Analysis (with Mary Alys Plunkett), 1951; Inorganic Quantitative Analysis (rev. edit.), 1954; Solutions to Problems in Inorganic Quantitative Analysis, 1955. Contbr. articles to scientific jours. Home: Wing Farm, Vassar College, Poughkeepsie, N.Y. Died May 4, 1959; buried Poughkeepsie Rural Cemetery.

GRIFFIN, James Arthur, banker; b. Fowltown, Ga., May 4, 1874; s. Andrew Richard and Louise Georgia (Hagood) G.; ed. pub. schs.; m. Nannie Marshal Johnson, Nov. 12, 1902; children—George Richard, James Arthur, Mary Louise (dec.), Albert, Nannie Marshal Christian, Thomas (dec.), Jack. Began as clk. and bookkeeper, First Nat. Bank of Ocala, Fla., 1891; with Exchange Nat. Bank, Tampa, since 1895, cashier, 1903-20, v.p., 1920-22, president, 1922-52, chairman of the board since 1952; pres. Tampa Investment & Securities Co.; chairman bd. Exchante National Bank, Winter Haven, Florida; Florida State Fair and Gasparilla Assn., Children's Home; member executive com. Community Chest of Tampa; an incorporator U. of Tampa (trustee). Mem. American Bankers Association, Florida Bankers Assn. (past pres.), Florida Historical Society, Florida Hort. Society, Newcomen Society, Florida Forest and Park Assn. Democrat. Episcopalian. Mason (32°, K.T., Shriner), Elk. Clubs: Rotary (charter mem.), Italian, Palma Ceia, Centro Asturiano, Centro Español, Ye Mystic Krewe of Gasparilla, Jesters. Home: 801 S. Delaware Av. Office: Exchange Nat. Bank, Tampa 1, Fla. Died Oct. 25, 1958.

GRIFFIN, James H., engr.; b. Ft. Edward, N.Y., Sept. 3, 1889; s. James J. and Sarah (Stevens) G.; B.E., Union Coll., 1912; m. Dorothy Van Valkenburgh, May 25, 1918; 1 dau., Janet (Mrs. Robert J. O'Connell). Surveyor and field engr., barge canal dept. State of N.Y., Waterford, 1912-13; with Pub. Service Commn., 1st dist., State N.Y., and successor bodies, Transit Commn. and Bd. Transportation, City of N.Y., 1913—, jr. engr., 1913-17, asst. engr., 1917-39, div. engr., 1939-45, dep. chief engr., 1945. chief engr., 1945—. Served as capt. 5th U.S. Engrs., 1917-18; maj. Engrs. Res. Corps, 1924-40. Mem. Am. Assn. Engrs. (nat. pres., 1931-32), Am. Soc. C.E., Soc. Am. Mil. Engrs. (pres., N.Y. City post), Am. Legion (post comdr.), Phi Gamma Delta. Clubs: The Engineers, N.Y. Railroad. Home: Hillcrest Av., Darien, Conn. Office: 370 Jay St., Bklyn. 1. Died Sept. 17, 1955.

GRIFFIN, John Howard, editor, columnist; b. Holyoke, Mass., June 7. 1898; son Jeremiah C. and Katherine Frances (Howard) G.; A.B., Cath. Univ. of Am., 1921; student Harvard, 1921-22; m. Alice L. Barry, Aug. 3, 1927; children—Richard, John, Maureen, Kevin, Carol, Gerald. Reporter, Springfield (Mass.) Union, 1923-26, Boston Herald, 1926-30; reporter Boston Post, 1930—, columnist, 1932—, Sunday editor 1940-52, editor-in-chief, 1952—, established The Boston Post Magazine. Roman Catholic. Contbr. to Am. mags. Home: 96 Russell Av., Watertown, Mass. Office: 259 Washington St., Boston. Died Jan. 31, 1954.

GRIFFIN, William Vincent, corp. exec.; b. Middletown, Conn., Jan. 1, 1886; s. John H. and Katherine (Stack) G.; LL.B., Yale, 1908, B.A., 1912; m. Isabel Shumard Carden, June 25, 1914 (dec. 1954); son William V. (dec.). Vice pres. chmn. Time, Inc., chmn. Brady Security & Realty Corp., Purolator Products. Inc., pres., dir. Tiblemont Island Mining Co., Smith-Tiblemont Mines, Ltd., Dobie Mines, Ltd.; dir. Chase Manhattan Bank, Nat. Shares Corp., Dresser Industries, Inc., Servel, Inc., Manati Sugar Co., Somerset Hills Development Corp., Cia. Ganadera Becerra, Wharton & No. R.R., Wenner-Glen Found.; trustee Estate, James C. Brady, N.Y., Emigrant Industrial Savings Bank. Assistant administrator Lend-Lease Administration, 1942-44; assistant to adminstr., dir. Brit. Empire Br., Fgn. Econ. Adminstrn., 1944-45. Dir. Trudeau Sanatorium; trustee United Hosp. Fund, N.Y., Yale Pub. Assn. Created Knight Comdr. Order of St. Gregory, 1926; Knight Official of the Crown of Italy, 1928; Papal Chamberlain — Cape and Sword, 1929; Knight of Malta, 1940; Knight Order of the Holy Sepulchre, 1956; Knight of the Order of Saint John of Jerusalem; Knight Commander British Empire, 1952. Presidential Certificate of Merit, 1947. Member English Speaking Union (past pres.), Delta Kappa Epsilon, Phi Delta Phi, Scroll and Key. Catholic. Clubs: Recess, Grolier, Racquet and Tennis, Essex Fox Hounds, Union, Somerset Hills Country, Yale; Metropolitan (Washington, D.C.). Home: Peapack, N.J. Office: 20 Exchange Place, N.Y.C. 5. Died Jan. 1958.

GRIFFITH, Chauncey H., corp. exec.; b. Sherrits, O., 1879. With Mergenthaler Linotype Co., 1906—, asst. to the pres., 1916, v.p. in charge typographic development, 1936-50, ret. 1950. Mem. Engrs. Club. Am. Inst. Graphic Arts, Grolier Club. Developed several type faces both English and in several Oriental langs. Home: 330 E. 43d St. N.Y. City. Office: 29 Ryerson St., Bklyn. Died Oct. 6, 1956.

GRIFFITH, Clark, baseball club exec.; b. Vernon Co., Mo., Nov. 20, 1869; s. Isaiah and Sarah Ann (Wright) G.; ed. public schs. Normal, Ill., Ill. Wesleyan, 1888-89; night law school, 1895; m. Ann Robertson, Dec. 2, 1900. Began as ball player, pitcher, 1887-1907; mgr. and pitcher, Am. League, 1903-09; mgr. Cincinnati Club, 1909-11; mgr. Washington, D.C., 1912-20; pres. Washington Baseball club, 1919—. Elected to Hall of Fame, Cooperstown, N.Y., 1946. Mason. Home: 4720 16th St. N.W. Office: Seventh and Florida Av. N.W., Washington. Died Oct. 27, 1955.

GRIFFITH, Franklin Thomas, lawyer; b. Mpls., Feb. 6, 1870; s. William A. and Hannah (Keefe) G.; educated high school and academy; m. Etta Pope, July 15, 1896; children—Harriet (Mrs. Zina A. Wise), Janet (Mrs. Raymond Sprague). Admitted to Ore. bar, 1894, practiced in Portland; mem. Griffith, Peck, Phillips & Coughlin; from orgn. with Portland Ry., Light & Power Co. (now Portland Gen. Electric Co.); gen. attorney pres., 1913-40, chmn. bd. 1940-47; chmn. Portland Traction Co.; pres. Title & Trust Co., Firtex Insulating Bd. Co., Griffith Rubber Mills Co. Republican. Mem. Am. Bar Assn., Ore. State Bar Assn. Mason (32°). Clubs: Arlington, Multnomah Athletic. Home: 1909 S.W. Laurel St. Office: Electric Bldg., Portland, Ore. Died. Nov. 7, 1952.

GRIFFITH, Hall McAllister, editor, writer, clergyman; b. San Francisco, Calif., Jan. 16, 1900; s. Harry Howard and Elizabeth Regina (Geraldson) G.; A.B., U. of Calif., 1922; student Princeton Theol. Sem., 1923-25, Grad. Sch. of Princeton U., 1924-25; D.D., Wheaton (Ill.) College, 1936; m. Clatherine Hughena Macneil, Jan. 11, 1926; children—Catherine Elizabeth, John Gresham Machen. Served with U.S. Army, 1918. Asst. editor Sunday School Times, 1922-23; ordained to the Presbyterian ministry, 1925; pastor, Marion Bridge, N.S., 1925-26, Scotsburn, N.S., 1926-30; mng. editor Christianity Today, 1930-35; pastor Hollond Memorial Presbyn. Ch., Phila., 1931-33; editor The Presbyterian Guardian, and gen. sec. the Presbyn. Constitutional Covenant Union, 1935-36; mgr. Independent Board for Presbyterian Foreign Missions, 1937-38, exec. sec., 1938-40; lecturer in church history, Faith Theol. Seminary, 1937-40; lecturer and associate, Business Counselors, Inc., 1940-41; gen. sec. Am. Council of Christian Chs., 1941-45; dir. pub. relations, Laymen's Nat. Com., 1946; asso. in pub. relations, Nat. Econ. Council, 1947-50; member sec. Independent Board for Presbyn. Fgn. Missions, 1933-36, 40. Elected commr. to Presbyn. Gen. Assembly, 1932, 34 and 35; unseated at 1935 assembly because of refusal to resign from The Independent Bd., as ordered by the Assembly of 1934; withdrew from denomination, 1936. Presiding officer at orgn. of First Gen. Assembly of Presbyterian Ch. of America (now Orthodox Presbyn. Ch.), 1936; ecclesiastical counsel Presbyn. Church of America, 1936; co-founder Bible Presbyterian Synod, 1937; clerk of General Synod, The Bible Presbyn. Church, 1938, 39; withdrew from that denomination, Apr. 1946. Author: The Case for Compromise, 1938; Termites in the Cross, 1947; Is There a Jewish Problem?, 1947. Contbr. to religious, econ. and gen. publs. Died Aug. 1957.

GRIFFITH, Reginald Harvey, college prof.; b. Charlotte, N.C., Feb. 3, 1873; s. Richard Henry and Mary Ann (Coleman) G.; student Greenville (S.C.) Mil. Inst., 1885-87; M.A., Furman U., Greenville, 1892, Litt.D., 1925; Johns Hopkins U., 1894-96, scholar, 1895-96; sr. fellow in English, U. of Chicago, 1901-02, Ph.D., 1905; student, Library of Congress, 1900-01, British Museum, summer of 1904, libraries University of Wis., summer, 1906, Harvard, summers 1903, 10, British Museum, 1912-13, 35, 52; Bodleian libraries, 1952; married Alice Mary Matlock, Aug. 3, 1906; children—Richard Henry, Mary Nell, Regina Helvetia. Teacher public schools, North Carolina and S.C., 1892-94, 1896-98, 1899-1900; prof. English, Furman U., 1898-99; instr. English, 1902-08, adjunct prof., 1908-14, asso. prof., 1914-19, prof., 1919—, prof. in graduate faculty, 1925—, research prof., 1935-36, curator, Wrenn Library, 1918—, U. of Tex., elected professor emeritus, 1952; professor English University Chicago, summer 1922, 31, 45, U. of Colo., 1926, Columbia, 1930, Duke, 1937. Appointed member board of visitors to U.S. Naval Academy, 1910. Mem. Modern Lang. Assn. America, Am. Assn. Univ. Profs., Phi Beta Kappa, Chi Psi. Democrat. Baptist. Clubs: University, Fortnightly. Author: Sir Percival of Galles—A Study of the Sources of the Legend, 1911; Alexander Pope—A Bibliography, Vol. I, Part I, 1923, Part II, 1927. Editor: A Descriptive Catalogue of an Exhibition of Manuscripts and First Editions of Lord Byron (with H. M. Jones), 1924. Contbr. to the Cambridge Bibliography of English Literature, 1940; (U. of Texas) Studies in English; also to philol. and other jours. Address: University Station, Austin 12, Tex. Died Dec. 10, 1957; buried Oakwood Cemetery, Austin.

GRIFFITH, W. M., oil exec.; b. Butler, Md., Nov. 11, 1897; s. William T. and Rosa (Bond) G.; grad. high sch.; m. Mary Hobbs, June 3, 1926; 1 son, Charles Hobbs. With Plymouth Oil Co., 1924—, v.p., dir.; dir. Melben Oil Co., Gen. Oil Sales Corp., Peoples Lumber Co., San Pat Lumber Co. Mason (32°, Shriner). Home: Box 387. Office: Box 968, Sinton, Tex. Dec. Nov. 20, 1954.

GRIFFITHS, Farnham Pond, lawyer; b. Alturas, Cal., Nov. 25, 1884; s. Rev. Griffiths and Hester (Horder) G.; B.L., U. Cal., 1906, LL.D., 1952; B.A. (Rhodes scholar), Oxford U., Eng., 1910, M.A., 1925; LL.D., Kenyon Coll., 1941; m. Marjorie Blanchard Morse, May 21, 1913; children—Gordon, Penry, Quentin. Admitted to Cal. bar, 1913; sec. to pres. U. Cal., 1906-07, 10-13, lectr. law, 1910-20; asso. McCutchen, Thomas, Matthew, Griffiths & Green (and predecessor firms), San Francisco, 1913—, partner, 1919—. Trustee Mills Coll., 1930-34, San Francisco Hosp. for Children and Tng. Sch. for Nurses, San Francisco Law Library; regent U. Cal., 1948-51. Asst. to chmn. com. sci. personnel OSRD, Washington, 1942, acting chmn., 1943. Recipient St. Thomas More award U. San Francisco, 1948. Mem. Assn. Marine Underwriters, Assn. IC C Practitioners, Am. Bar Assn., Internat. Law Assn. (pres. 1938-39), Am. Law Inst., Maritime Law Assn. U.S. (v.p. 1938-40), Bar Assn. San Francisco (pres. 1944), Marine Exchange of San Francisco (pres. 1940-41), Assn. Am. Rhodes Scholars (dir.), Balliol. Soc., Oxford U. Union, Mus. Assn. San Francisco (dir.), Am. Mcht. Marine Library Assn., San Francisco Com. Fgn. Relations, World Affairs Council, Army Ordnance Assn., English Speaking Union U.S., U. Cal. Law Sch. Assn., Delta Sigma Rho, Phi Beta Kappa, Phi Sigma Kappa, Phi Delta Phi. Clubs: Century Assn., The Players, Cercle de l'Union, Pacific Union Propeller of U.S., Bohemian (pres. 1938-40) (San Francisco); Cosmos (Washington); Old Capital (Monterey, Cal.).

Home: 1590 La Vereda, Berkeley 8, Cal. Office: Balfour Bldg., 351 California St., San Francisco 4. Died June 30, 1958.

GRIGGS, David Cullen, mfg. exec.; b. Waterbury, Conn., June 30, 1871; s. Henry C. and Mary Bassett (Foote) G.; Ph.B., Sheffield Sci. Sch., Yale, 1892; m. Helen Trowbridge Williams, June 6, 1904; children—Henry C., Eleanor Rice (Mrs. E. B. Powell, Jr.). Mech. engr., sec., pres. Waterbury Ferrel Foundery & Machine Co., 1893-97, dir., 1899—, chmn. bd., 1947—; dir. Waterbury Buckle Co., Waterbury Savs. Bank, Colonial Trust Co., Waterbury. Club: Waterbury. Home: 175 Pine St. Office: 453 Bank St., Waterbury, Conn. Died Oct. 9, 1958; buried Riverside Cemetery, Waterbury.

GRIGGS, Edward Howard, lecturer, author; b. Owatonna, Minn.; s. Joseph Emerson and Mary Ellen (Little) G.; A.B., Ind. Univ., 1889, A.M., 1890; spl. studies, U. of Berlin; L.H.D., U. of Me., 1905; LL.D., Colby Coll., Waterville, Me., 1922; Litt.D. from Ohio U., 1926; m. Jennie Taylor Fry, July 5, 1889 (died 1896); m. 2d, Mary Pratt Little, June 2, 1898 (died 1906); m. 3d, Margaret Keating Higgins, Apr. 25, 1940. Instr. English lit., Ind. U., 1889-91; asst. prof. ethics, Stanford U., 1891-92; prof. lit., Ind. U., 1892-93; prof. ethics, 1893-97, head of combined depts. of ethics and edn., 1897-98, Stanford U.; pub. lecturer since Jan. 1899. Author: The New Humanism, 1900; A Book of Meditations, 1902; Moral Education, 1904; The Use of the Margin, 1907; Human Equipment, 1909; The Philosophy of Art, 1913; Self-Culture Through the Vocation, 1914; Friendship, Love and Marriage, 1915; The Soul of Democracy, 1918; For What Do We Live?, 1921; Blossomed Hours, 1922; American Statesmen, 1927 (adopted for Ill. State Teachers' Reading Circle 1929); Socrates—Teacher and Martyr, 1932; The Story of an Itinerant Teacher, 1934; Earl Barnes, 1935; Beauty in Nature and Art, 1938; Great Leaders in Human Progress, 1939; Moral Leaders, 1940; also 16 handbooks to courses of lectures. Pres. dept. of philosophy and chmn. of the council, Brooklyn Inst. of Arts and Sciences. Has given two lectures annually at the Inst., for the past 50 yrs. Mem. Am. Acad. Polit. and Social Sci. Gave 32 broadcasts on "Lives of Great Men" over nat. hookup, 1938-39; 13 on "Torch of Progress," 1939-40. Club: Town Hall (N.Y.). Home: 515 N. Washington, Alexandria, Va. Died June 6, 1951.

GRIGGS, Frederick; b. St. Charles, Mich., Mar. 23, 1867; s. Ezra Samuel and Diantha (Mansfield) G.; ed. Battle Creek (Mich.) Coll., Chicago Normal Sch., U. of Buffalo; m. Blanche W. Eggeston, Aug. 17, 1892; children—Bruce, Donald, m. 2d Mabel S. Murrin, Aug. 6, 1940. Prin. prep. dept., Battle Creek Coll., 1891-1900, S. Lancaster (Mass.) Acad., 1900-07; sec. dept. edn., Seventh Day Adventist Denomination, 1907-10; pres. Union Coll., College View, Neb., 1910-13; ednl. sec. Seventh Day Adventist Denomination for N. America, and sec. dept. of edn. of Gen. Conf., Washington, 1914-18; pres. Emmanuel Missionary Coll., Berrien Springs, Mich., 1918-25; field sec. Far Eastern Div. of Gen. Conf. of Seventh Day Adventists, 1925-30; pres. Far Eastern Div. of Gen. Conf., 1930-36; pres. China Div. of Gen. Conf., 1936-38; gen. field sec. Gen. Conf. of Seventh Day Adventists 1938-50; retired 1950. Chmn. bd. Coll. of Med. Evangelists, Los Angeles, Pacific Press Assn. Author: Talks to My Students, 1905. Editor: The Million Dollar Moment, 1951. Home: 3868 Dwiggins St., L.A. 33. Died Aug. 10, 1952; buried Forest Lawn Cemetery, Glendale, Cal.

GRIGSBY, Bertram James, bus. exec.; b. Cuba, Ill., Jan. 15, 1884; s. George Nathaniel and Flora Annette (Snively) G.; student U. Ill., 1904-06; m. Elsie Ida Whiting, June 14, 1911; children—Raymond, James, Peggy Ethel. Mng. dir. Benjamin Electric, Ltd., 1908-16; v.p. Anderson Electric & Equipment Co., 1916-21; became pres. Grigsby-Grunow Co., 1921, chmn. bd., 1929-33; investments, 1933—; dir. Grigsby-Allison Co., Inc. Asso. mem. Am. Inst. E.E., Inst. Electric Engrs. (London). Republican. Mason. Clubs: Chicago Athletic Assn.; Barrington Hills Country; Park Ridge Country. Home: Barrington, Ill. Died 1954.

GRIGSBY, William Fred, jurist; b. nr. Maud, Ky., Nov. 21, 1876; s. William and Margaret (Weathers) G.; grad. Central Normal Coll., Waddy, Ky., 1899; m. Lulie Cokendolpher, Sept. 10, 1902; children—Henry Marshall, Margaret Eva. Admitted to Ky. bar, 1901, and began practice at Springfield; city atty., Springfield, 1906-28; v.p. Peoples Deposit Bank; former atty. Union Water Works Co., Cumberland Pub. Service Co., etc.; judge Ct. Appeals, Ky., 1929-31; now practice of law. Active A.R.C. and Liberty Loan drives, World War. Republican. Mem. M.E. Ch., S. Mason; mem. Maccabees, Woodmen of the World. Home: Springfield, Ky. Died Nov. 20, 1940; buried Springfield, Ky.

GRIM Paul Ridgeway, educator; b. Highland Co., O., Aug. 24, 1910; s. Omer Frank and Austa Gertrude (Ridgeway) G.; B.S., Ohio State U., 1932, M.A., 1935, Ph.D., 1938; m. Vivian Ione McMillen, Aug. 24, 1935; children—Douglas Paul, Corinne Vivian. High sch. tchr., Ripley, O., 1932-35; research asst., bur. ednl. research Ohio State U., 1935-37; supervisor Western Wash. Coll. Edn., Bellingham, 1937-42, dir. campus sch., student teaching, 1942-45; asst. prof. edn. Washington U., St. Louis, 1945-46; asst. prof. edn. U. Minn., 1946-47, dir. lab. experiences, chmn. dept. theory and practice of teaching since 1946, asso. prof. edn., 1947-51, prof. edn. since 1951; summer sch. faculty U. Ore., U. California, Syracuse University. Mem. Minn. Soc. Study Edn., Nat., Minn. edn. assns., Mpls. Citizens Com. for Pub. Edn., Civic League Greater Mpls., P.T.A. (past pres.), Am. Ednl. Research Assn., Assn. Student Teaching (national president 1953-54), Association for Supervision and Curriculum Development, National Society Coll. Teachers Education, National Society Study Edn., John Dewey Soc., Assn. for Higher Edn., Phi Delta Kappa. Methodist. Author: Principles and Practices of Secondary Education (with Vernon E. Anderson, William T. Gruhn), 1951: The Student Teacher in the Elementary School (with John U. Michaelis). 1953; The Student Teacher in the Secondary School (with John U. Michaelis), 1953. Editor: The Evaluation of Student Teaching, 1949. Home: 728 S.E. Sixth St., Mpls. 14. Died Sept. 18, 1956; buried Greenfield, O.

GRIMBALL, Elizabeth Berkeley, producer of plays; b. Union, S.C.; d. Harry Morris and Helen Emily (Trenholm) Grimball; grad. Charleston Female Sem.; grad. Boston Sch. Expression, 1900, post-grad. course, 1905; spl. summer course, Oxford U., Eng., 1900; studied stage design and prodn. with Norman Geddes, N.Y.C., 1922-24. Producer of Shoot, revival of March Hares, by Harry Wagstaff Gribble, and of Tyrants, by Thaddeus Rittner—all in N.Y.C., with profl. casts; stage dir. The Manhatters, musical comedy, 1927; founder, 1922, dir. Inter-Theatre Arts Sch. Acting and Prodn., now dir. Elizabeth B. Grimball Studio of Acting and Dramatic Tng.; dramatic instr. on staff Opera Comique Sch.; dir. Am. Theatrical Seminar in Salzburg, Austria; pioneer Am. woman to head Dept. at Mozartum Acad., Salzburg; dir. Jr. Footlight Players; founder, dir. N.Y. Sch. of Theatre; co-dir. The Playhouse, Brattleboro, Vt.; dir. Dramatic Tng. Studio, Charleston, S.C. Entertainer with A.E.F. in Fance. 1918-19. Chmn. recreation facilities com., Citizens Service Corps, Office Civilian Def., Charleston. Named to Carnegie Hall Gallery Famous People in N.Y.C., 1951. Mem. Art Aliance Am., N.Y. Soc. Craftsmen, Colonial Dames Am., Soc. Order Colonial Lords Manor Am. Democrat. Episcopalian. Author: The Snow Queen, 1920; The Waif, 1924; Costuming a Play (with Rhea Wells), 1925. Address: 56C Hasell St., Charleston, S.C. Died Aug. 30, 1953; buried Magnolia Cemetery, Charleston.

GRIMES, Charles Pennebaker, lawyer; b. Tacoma, May 31, 1904; s. Rt. Rev. Charles Ysla and Rose (Pennebaker) G.; grad. Taft Sch., 1924; A.B., Yale, 1927, LL.B., 1930; m. Louise Ireland, Mar. 18, 1933; children—Charles Livingston, Arline Ireland, Lucy Lee Custis. Admitted to N.Y. State bar, 1933, since practiced N.Y.C.; partner firm of Cole, Grimes, Friedman and Deitz; senior review counsel, Public Works Administration, 1933-34; senior counsel National Recovery Administration, 1934-35; deputy assistant district atty., N.Y. County, on staff of Thomas E. Dewey, spl. rackets prosecutor, 1935-37; asst. dist. atty., N.Y. County, on staff of Thomas E. Dewey, 1938-42; chmn. bd. dirs. DeLanoy & Kipp, Inc., 1944-47; chief counsel International Security Subcommittee, United States Senate, 1954. Member American, New York State, New York City bar assns., Non-Partisan Civic Assn., Inc. (dir.), Phi Delta Phi. Clubs: N.Y. City Church, Racquet and Tennis, Yale, Union League (N.Y. City); Piping Rock (Locust Valley, N.Y.), Creek (Locust Valley); Beaver Dam Winter Sports (Mill Neck, N.Y.). Home: "Green Arbors," Locust Valley, L.I., N.Y. Office: 30 Broad St., N.Y.C. Died Oct. 30, 1957.

GRIMES, William Middleton, army officer; b. Ft. Barrancas, Fla., Mar. 4, 1889; s. George S. and Margaret (McArthur) G.; student Manlius (N.Y.) Sch., 1908-11, Phillips Exeter Acad., N.H., 1906-08; grad. Cavalry Sch., 1922, Command and Gen. Staff Sch., 1925, Army War Coll., 1933; m. Mabel Lowe, Dec. 17, 1913; children—Peggy Lowe (wife of Capt. Sherbourne Whipple, Jr.), William Middleton. Commd. 2d lt., U.S. Army, Sept. 29, 1911; promoted through grades to brig. gen., 1941, maj. gen., May 1942; has been instr. The Cavalry Sch., Inf. Sch., Command and Gen. Staff Sch.; mem. War Dept, Gen. Staff, 1938-40. Awarded Silver Star citation. Episcopalian. Clubs: Army and Navy, Army-Navy Country (Washington); Potomac Hunt (Potomac, Md.). Address: Ft. Riley, Kan. Died Apr. 2, 1951.

GRIMM, John Hugo, lawyer; b. St. Louis, Mo., Jan. 17, 1864; s. Valentine I. and Magdalen (Jaeckel) G.; LL.B., summa cum laude, Washington U., St. Louis, 1886; Ph.D., St. Louis Univ., 1888, LL.D., 1912; m. Sophie E. Gruen, Nov. 18, 1891; children—Elmer H., Roland J. V., Thomas C., Horace F., Herbert Hadley. Admitted to Mo. bar, 1886, and began practice at St. Louis; judge Circuit Ct., St. Louis, 1908-25; prof. law, St. Louis U., 1908-26; lecturer on trademarks and unfair competition, Kansas City Sch. Law, 1926; mem. Mo. Bd. Law Examiners, 1926-31. Field dir. Am. Red Cross, Jefferson Barracks, Mo., 1917. Pres. State Conf. Mo. Judges, 1924-25; formerly dir. Mo. Conf. Social Welfare and chmn. Court of Honor Boy Scouts of America, St. Louis; mem. Civic Union. Del. from Mo. Bar Assn. to Am. Law Institute, 1928. Mem. Missouri State and St. Louis bar assns., Mo. Hist. Soc. (dir.), Soc. of St. Louis Authors, St. Louis Chamber of Commerce; one of organizers Mo. Assn. for Criminal Justice. Republican. Unitarian. Mason (K.T., Shriner). Club: Missouri Athletic Assn. Home: 575 Purdue Av., University City, St. Louis. Office: Central Nat. Bank Bldg., St. Louis. Died Oct. 1, 1954; buried Oak Grove, St. Louis.

GRINDAL, Herbert W(eld), ret. investment banker; b. Bklyn., Feb. 12, 1889; s. Herbert White and Sarah (Ten Broeck) G.; ed. pub. schs. of Bklyn.; m. Marion Merrill, Oct. 1911 (died 1948); children—Ernestine (Mrs. Charles M. Clarke, Jr.), Jean (Mrs. Carl Stobbe); m. 2d, Elsie Brewer Colby, Nov. 5, 1949; 1 step dau., Alice Colby. Banking and financial bus., Boston, 1906-21; with Guaranty Trust Co., N.Y.C., 1921-22, financial sec. Am. Fore group ins. cos., 1922-25, Lehman Bros., 1925-30; partner F. A. Willard & Co., 1930-34, Reynolds & Co., 1934-57, ret.; dir. Emery Air Freight Corp., Blue Ridge Mut. Fund, Inc., Baily Selburn Oil & Gas, Ltd. Clubs: Bankers, Camp Fire of America, Economic, Union League (N.Y.C.); Blind Brook (Port Chester, N.Y.); Augusta (Ga.) National Golf; Gatineau Fish and Game (Ottawa, Can.). Home: San Antonio. Died May 29, 1959.

GRINDON, Joseph, Sr., dermatologist; b. St. Louis, Mo., Aug. 20, 1858; s. Arthur St. Leger and Kelis (Chérot-Dupavillon) G.; educated St. Louis public schools, 1868-74; M.D., St. Louis Medical Coll., 1879; Ph.B., St. Louis U., 1884; Sc.D., St. Louis U., 1943; m. Lina Boislinière, Sept. 30, 1903 (deceased); children—Pauline C., Joseph B. (deceased), Dorothy M. (Mrs. A. B. Murphy, Jr.), Joseph B. (M.D.). Began practice, 1879; lecturer on diseases of the skin, 1886-95, prof. physiology, 1894-95, prof. dermatology, 1895-1900, St. Louis Med. Coll.; prof. clin. dermatology and syphilology, Washington U., 1900-12; prof. dermatology, St. Louis U., 1912-44; prof. emeritus since 1944; physician to St. Louis Smallpox Hosp., 1881-83; formerly dermatologist to O'Fallon Dispensary; dermatologist to St. John's, St. Mary's, Desloge and St. Louis City hospitals. Diplomate Am. Bd. Dermatology and Syphilus. President Medical Soc. of City Hosp. Alumni, 1897, St. Louis Med. Soc., 1899, St. Louis Dermatol. Soc., 1914-24; fellow A.M.A.; mem. Am. Dermatol. Assn. (pres. 1928), Mo. State Medical Assn. (v.p. 1931-32), Chicago Dermatol. Society, Dermatol. Conf. Mississippi Valley, Am. Acad. of Dermatology, Soc. for Investigative Dermatol., Archaeol. Inst. Am., St. Louis Acad. Scis., Mo. State Acad. Sci.; corr. mem. Société Francaise de Dermatologie et de Syphiligraphie. Author: Diseases of the Skin, 1902; also several chapters in American Text-Book of Genito-Urinary Diseases, Syphilis and Diseases of the Skin, 1898; Handbook of Cutaneous Therapeutics (with Dr. W. A. Hardaway), 1907. Contbr. to med. jours. Home: 7029 Westmoreland Av., St. Louis 5. Died Apr. 1, 1950; buried Calvary Cemetery, St. Louis.

GRINNELL, George Morton (grĭn-nĕl'), investment banker; b. N.Y.C., Feb. 22, 1902; s. William Morton and Elizabeth Lee (Ernst) G.; student Harvard, 1921-25; m. Elizabeth Cole, Nov. 6, 1926; children—Jeanne (Mrs. Stig Host), George James. With Roosevelt & Son, 1926-33; with Dick & Merle-Smith since 1933, partner, 1935-47, sr. partner since 1947, specializing in r.r. securities, finance; dir. Fundamental Investors, Investors Management Fund. Author articles on investment securities. Home: 57 E. 80th St., N.Y.C. 21. Office: 30 Pine St., N.Y.C. 5. Died Jan. 19, 1953.

GRISCOM, Ludlow (grĭs'kum), ornithologist; b. N.Y.C., June 17, 1890; s. Clement Acton and Genevieve Sprigg (Ludlow) G.; A.B., Columbia, 1912; A.M., Cornell U., 1915; m. Edith Sumner Sloan, Sept. 14, 1926; children—Edith Rapallo (Mrs. P. O. Daley), Andrew, Joan Ludlow. Instr. elementary biology, Cornell U., 1915-16; asst. in Am. Mus. Natural History, 1917-20, asst. curator ornithology, 1921-27; research curator zoölogy, Mus. Comparative Zoölogy, Harvard, 1927-48, and research ornithologist, 1948—. Mem. zool. exploration parties in Panama, 1924, 27, Yucatan, 1926, Nicaragua, 1917, Guatemala, 1930; vol. asst. with Gray Herbarium Expdn. to Arctic Newfoundland, 1925, and Gaspé Peninsula, 1923. Served as 2d lt. U.S. Army, 1917-19; U.S. del. 2d Interallied Propaganda Conf., London, 1918. Del. 8th Internat. Ornithol. Congress, Oxford, Eng., 1934. Recipient Conservation medal, 1956. Fellow A.A. A.S., Am. Ornithologists Union (pres. 1956), N.Y. Acad. Scis., Linnaean Soc. N.Y. (pres. 1927); mem. Ecol. Soc. Am. British Ornithologists Union, Nat. Audubon Soc. (chmn. bd. dirs.), Boston Soc. Natural History (trustee, pres. 1948, hon. curator birds), Children's Mus. of Boston (trustee), Mass. Fish and Game Assn. Am. Mus. Natural History, Mass. Audubon Soc. (dir.), Colonial Soc. Mass., Sigma Xi. Protestant. Clubs: Union, Harvard (Boston); Faculty (Cambridge); Union, Century (N.Y.C.); Cosmos

(Washington). Author: Birds of the N.Y. City Region, 1923; Distribution of Bird Life in Guatemala, 1932; Ornithology of the Republic of Panama, 1935; A Monographic Study of the Red Crossbill, 1937; Modern Bird Study, 1945; Birds of Nantucket, 1948; Birds of the Concord Region, a Study in Population Trends, 1949. Origin and Distribution Birds of Mexico, 1940; Distributional Check-List Birds of Mexico, Part I, 1940. Birds of Massachusetts, 1955, Annotated and Revised Checklist, with Dorothy E. Snyder, 1955. Contbr. articles to ornithol. and bot. jours.; spl. field of research birds of C.A., field identification of N. Am. birds, conservation. Contbg. editor Nat. Audubon Mag.; asso. editor, Audubon Field Notes. Home: 21 Fayerweather St., Cambridge 38, Mass. Died May 28, 1959; buried Mt. Auburn Cemetery, Cambridge.

GRISCOM, Rodman Ellison, banker; b. Phila., Oct. 21 1870; s. Clement Acton and Frances Canby (Biddle) G.; Ph.B., U. Pa., 1889; m. Anne Starr, Feb. 17, 1897 (died June 14, 1919), dir. Phila. Nat. Bank, Pennroad Corp., Am. Scantic S.S. Co.; mgr. Western Savs. Fund. Mem. Zeta Psi. Clubs: University, City, Midday, Nat. Golf Links (N.Y.C.); Philadelphia (Phila.). Home: Haverford, Pa. Office: Land Title Bldg., Phila. Died Mar. 4, 1944.

GRISER, John Millen, shipbldg. exec.; b. Charleston, S.C., Apr. 29, 1896; s. John Joseph and Marion (Brunson) G.; student pub. schs., Charleston; m. Florence Louise Slater, Feb. 8, 1919; 1 dau., Marion (Mrs. George Schmohl). Apprentice, mechanic Charleston Navy Yard, 1911-17; with Found. Co., New Orleans, 1919; supt. Chickasaw (Ala.) Shipbldg. & Car Co., 1919-20; mechanic, supt. Ala. Dry Dock & Shipbldg. Co., Mobile, 1917-19, supt., 1921-25, gen. supt., 1925-36, v.p. charge operations, 1936-44, pres., 1944—, dir. 1926—; v.p., dir. Pinto Island Metals Co., Mobile; pres., dir. Warrior-Tombigbee Development Assn., Birmingham, Ala.; dir. First Nat. Bank of Mobile, Am. Waterways Operators, Inc., Miss. Valley Assn. Mem. Ala. State C. of C. (v.p., dir.), Shipbuilders Council Am. (dir.), Am. Bur. Shipping (mem. bd. mgrs.), Lloyd's Register Shipping. Home: Route 4. Box 48. Office: P.O. Box 190, Mobile 2, Ala. Died Oct. 15, 1957.

GRISMORE, Grover Cleveland (griz' mōr), educator; b. Pandora, O., Oct. 27, 1888; s. Henry and Frances (Guinther) G.; student Oberlin Coll., 1907-09; A.B., U. of Mich., 1912, J.D., 1914; S.J.D., Harvard, 1921; m. May Aileen White, Sept. 1, 1917; 1 son, Roger. Mem. faculty, law sch., U. of Mich., since 1914, prof. law since 1920; Ezra Ripley Thayer teaching fellow, Harvard, 1920-21; acting prof. of law, Stanford, summer 1928, Cornell, summer 1929, U. of So. Calif., summer 1940. Served with U.S. Army, 1917-19; disch. rank of bn. sergt. major. Mem. Ann Arbor City Bd. of Pub. Works, 1940-45. Mem. Am. Bar Assn., Order of the Coif, Phi Alpha Delta. Republican. Club: Lawyers. Author: Principles of the Law of Contracts, 1947; Compiled Cases on the Law of Contracts, 1931. Home: 1914 Day St., Ann Arbor, Mich. Died Mar. 10, 1951.

GRISWOLD, Dwight Palmer, U.S. Senator; b. Harrison, Neb., Nov. 27, 1893; s. Dwight H. and Clarissa (Palmer) G.; student Neb. Wesleyan U., 1910-12; A.B., University of Nebraska, 1914; m. Erma Elliott, Sept. 25, 1919; children—Dorothy Helen (Mrs. John H. Gayer), Dwight (dec.). Connected with First Nat. Bank, Gordon, Neb., 1914-22, successivley as bank clk, asst. cashier, cashier, dir. since 1919; editor and pub. Gordon Jour., 1922-40; pres. Gering (Neb.) Natl. Bank since 1951. With mil. govt. in Germany, Jan.-June 1947; named chief Am. Mission for Aid to Greece, June 1947, resigned Sept. 1948. Mem. Neb. Ho. of Reps., 1921, Neb. St. senate, 1925, 27, 29; elected gov. of Neb. 1940, 42, 1944; elected United States senator from Neb., 1952. Served as sergt., 4th Neb. Infantry on Mexican Border Service, 1916; 1st lieut. and capt., 127th F.A., 1917-18. Mem. Neb. Press Assn. (state pres. 1931), Am. Legion (state comdr. 1930), Alpha Tau Omega. Republican. Presbyterian. Mason (Shriner). Home: Scottsbluff, Neb. Died Apr. 12, 1954; buried Scottsbluff, Neb.

GRISWOLD, Glenn, pub. relations exec.; b. Benton Harbor, Mich., June 19, 1886; s. Elbert Guy and Lura (Abbe) G.; ed. pub. and high sch.; m. Inez Haney, Sept. 12, 1910; 1 dau., Rita Mae; m. 2d, Denny Prager, 1938. Publisher of country newspaper at 17; joined staff of Chicago Inter-Ocean, 1908, Chicago Examiner, 1910; financial editor of Examiner, 1914-16, Chicago Tribune, 1916-18; western business mgr. Wall Street Journal, 1918-20; with Chicago Journal of Commerce, 1920-31, editor and pub., 1922-31; elected v.p. Fox Film Corp., 1931; publishing dir. and editor Business Week, New York, 1933-38; head of Glenn Griswold Associates, 1938-41; public relations director Conf. of Alcoholic Beverage Industries, Inc. Mem. Am. Economic Assn., Nat. Economic League (council), Izaak Walton League America (dir.). Episcopalian. Mason (K.T.). Clubs: Campfire, Advertising, Sales Executive (New York). Publisher, Public Relations News. Home: 815 Park Av. Office: 52 Vanderbilt Av., N.Y.C Died May 15, 1950.

GRISWOLD, Hervey DeWitt, ret. missionary; b. Dryden, N.Y., May 24, 1860; s. Benjamin and Laura Eliza (Hurd) G.; B.A., Union Coll., Schenectady, N.Y., 1885, M.A., 1900, D.D., 1910; grad. Union Theol. Sem., 1888; studied univs. of Oxford and Berlin, 1888-90; Ph.D., Cornell U., 1900; m. Frances Sheldon, June 25,- 1890; children—Laura Katharine (Mrs. Donald Mackenzie), Arthur Sheldon, Elizabeth (dec.), Frances Louise (Mrs. George A. Ballentine). Ordained Presbyn. ministry, 1890; missionary in India, 1890-1926; dist. missionary, 1890-94; prof. philosophy, Forman Christian Coll., Lahore, (now Pakistan), 1894-1914; sec. Council Am. Presbyn. Missions in India, 1914-19, 23-26; vis. lectr. religions of India, Columbia U., 1928-29. Mem. Am. Oriental Soc., Phi Beta Kappa, Phi Delta Theta. Author: Brahman (a Study of Indian Philosophy), 1900; Religion of the Rigveda, 1923; Insights into Modern Hinduism, 1934; also pamphlets on religious sects of modern India. Joint editor Religious Quest of India series. Contbr. articles encys. Address: 4611 Main St., Stratford, Conn. Died May 15, 1945; buried Dryden, N.Y.

GRISWOLD, James F., corp. exec.; b. Chicago, Ill., 1883; m. Lucy Griswold; children—James, Mrs. Ruth Lapp, Mrs. Marion Grey. Chmn. and dir. Chicago Mill & Lumber Co., Chicago; vice pres. and dir., Chestnut St. Corp., Helena Southwestern R.R.; dir. Liquid Carbonic Corp., Chicago. Home: 2164 Hyde St., San Francisco. Office: 33 S. Clark St., Chgo. Died Apr. 2, 1957. Buried San Francisco.

GRISWOLD, Morley, lawyer, ex-gov.; b. Elko, Nev., Oct. 10, 1890; s. Chauncey Warner and Mary Ellen (Dakin) G.; A.B., U. of Mich., 1913, LL.B., 1915; m. Marianne Williamson, Aug. 4, 1920; children—Mary Louise, Morley Williamson. Admitted to Nev. bar, 1915; in practice at Reno, splty. corp. mining, water, ins. law; elected lt. gov., 1926; gov. after death of Gov. Balzar, Mar. 1934-Jan. 1935. First lt. A.E.F., World War. Mem. Am., Nev. State and Washoe County bar assns., Am. Legion. Republican. Episcopalian. Mason. Home: 1010 La Rue St. Office: Reno National Bank Bldg., Reno. Died Oct. 3, 1951.

GRISWOLD, Oscar Woolverton, army officer; b. Ruby Valley, Nev., Oct. 22, 1886; s. Willard Smith and Margaret (Woolverton) G.; student U. of Nev., 1905-06; B.S., U.S. Military Acad., 1910; grad. Command and General Staff School, 1925, Army War College, 1929; LL.D., University of Nevada, 1946; married Elizabeth Katherine Matile, July 1, 1911; children—Matile (wife of Lt. Col. William Lyons Porte, U.S. Army), Katherine (dec.), George Matile. Commd. 2nd lt., Inf., U.S. Army, 1910, advanced through grades to lt. gen., 1945; fgn. service in China, 1914-17; served as maj. and lt. col., A.E.F., 1918-19; on War Dept. Gen. Staff, 1929-31; in Air Corps, July to Sept., 1931; comd. XIV Corps, during recapture of Luzon, P.I., 1945, in operations from Guadalcanal to Luzon. Legion of Merit, Distinguished Service Medal with Oak Leaf Cluster, Army, Navy Distinguished Service Medals, Silver Star with Oak Leaf Cluster, Bronze Star Medal, Air Medal, Purple Heart. Episcopalian. Mason (32°), Shriner, Retired. Home: The Broadmoor, Colorado Springs, Colo.

GROAT, Carl D., editor; b. Troy, N.Y., Dec. 7, 1887; s. Lester and Phoebe (Williams) G.; B.S., Dartmouth Coll., 1911; m. Ethel Robb Swindells; children—Barbara Helen, Mavis Irene. Reporter on Pittsfield (Mass.) Eagle, Springfield (Mass.) Union, Washington (D.C.) Times, 1911-12; corr. for United Press, 1912-18, Berlin (Germany) corr., 1918-25; Washington mgr. United Press, 1926-28, news dir., 1928-33; editor of Cincinnati Post since 1933. Clubs: Queen City, Cincinnati, Literary, Optimists, Torch (Cincinnati); National Press (Washington). Home: 3427 Whitfield. Office: Cincinnati Post, Cin. Died July 26, 1953.

GROAT, George Gorham, economist; born Green Island, N.Y., Dec. 15, 1871; s. William Henry and Fidelia Anna (Gorham) G.; A.B., Syracuse U., 1895; Pd.M., N.Y. State College for Teachers, 1897; A.M., Cornell Univ., 1901; Ph.D., Columbia U., 1905; m. Elizabeth Westeen Schiffer, June 18, 1902; 1 dau., Ruth Elizabeth. Teacher, Round Lake Acad., N.Y., 1895-96, N.Y. State Coll. for Teachers, 1897-1903, Morris High Sch., New York, 1904-06; lecturer New York U. Sch. of Commerce, Accounts and Finance, 1905-07; prof. economics and sociology, and sec. of faculty, Ohio Wesleyan U., 1907-13; prof. and head of department economics, University of Vermont, since 1913; professor emeritus of economics since June, 1944. V.p. Vt. State Conf. Social Work, 1919-22. Mem. Am. Econ. Assn., Am. Assn. for Labor Legislation, Delta Upsilon, Phi Beta Kappa. Independent. Congregationalist. Author: Trade Unions and the Law in New York, 1905; Attitude of American Courts in Labor Cases, 1911; An Introduction to the Study of Organized Labor in America, 1916, revised edit., 1926. Contbr. to econ. periodicals. Home: Burlington, Vt. Died Sept. 10, 1951.

GROEDEL, Franz Maximilian (grō'dĕl), physician; b. Bad Nauheim, Germany, May 23, 1881; s. Maximilian J. and Rosa (Klopfer) G.; ed. Univs. of Munich, Giessen and Leipzig, 1899-1904 (M.D., U. of Leipzig, 1904); unmarried. Came to U.S. 1934, naturalized, 1939. Chief X-ray dept., Holy Ghost Hosp., Frankfurt am Main, Germany, 1910-34; instr. U. of Frankfurt, 1919-34, prof. on med. faculty, since 1929; director Kerckhoff Heart Research Institute, Bad Nauheim, since 1929; cardiologist Heart Sanitarium, Bad Nauheim, 1904-34; licensed to practice medicine in New York State, 1934; now practicing in New York City; cons. cardiologist Lenox Hill Hosp.; attending cardiologist Beth David Hosp.; cardiol. St. Anthony's Hosp.; research fellow Biological Inst., Fordham Univ. Formerly pres. Deutsche Röntgengesellschaft and Frankfurter Röntgengesellschaft; formerly bd. dirs. German Heart Assn., Deutsch Balneologische Gesellschaft, etc. Founder Am. Coll. Cardiology; mem. Am. Physiol. Soc., Am. Heart Assn., New York Heart Assn., N.Y. Cardiol. Soc., A.M.A., N.Y. County Medical Soc., N.Y. State Med. Society, Am. Assn. History of Medicine, New York Phys. Therapy Soc., N.Y. Med. Union, Internat. Soc. Med. Hydrology; honorary member X-ray Society of Chicago, Ill., Detroit Roentgen Ray Society, American College Radiology, Med. Soc. Bologne, Italy, Hessian Roentgen Soc., Deutsche Kreislanfforsching Ges. Served as mil. surg. during World War. Author of many books, also brochures and articles on X-ray and diseases of the heart. Address: 829 Park Av., N.Y.C. Died Oct. 12, 1951.

GROESBECK, Alexander J. (grōs'bĕk), ex-gov.; b. Warren, Twp., Macomb County, Mich., Nov. 7, 1873; s. Louis and Julia (Coquillard) G.; ed. public schs., Mt. Clemens, Mich.; LL.B., U. of Mich., 1893. Admitted Mich. bar, 1893; atty. gen. of Mich., 1916-20; gov. of Mich., 3 terms, 1921-27. Republican. Home: 2990 E. Grand Blvd. Office: 2380 Penobscot Bldg., Detroit. Died Mar. 10, 1953.

GROESBECK, Herman V. S., lawyer; b. Chittenango, N.Y., July 8, 1849; s. Peter Walter and Hannah (Van Valkenburgh) G.; ed. Yates Poly. Inst., Chittenango. County supt. schs., Jefferson County, Ark., while prin. White High Sch., Pine Bluff, Ark., 1874-75, prin. high sch., supt. schs., Cadillac, Mich., 1877-78; began practice of law, Laramie, Wyo., 1881; police justice, Laramie, 1883-85; mem. Ho. of Reps., Wyo. Legislature, 1884, mem. territorial auditing bd.; county and pros. atty. Albany County, Wyo., 1883-85, 1889-90; city atty. Laramie, at various times; chief justice Supreme Ct. Wyo., 1890-96; atty. in office of asst. atty. gen. of Dept. Interior, 1897-1900; was asso. in practice with Col. S. W. Downey, del. in Congress for Wyo., and later with Charles E. Carpenter; now mem. Groesbeck & Elby. Formerly Republican, now Socialist. Universalist. Address: Laramie, Wyo. Deceased.

GROFF, George Weidman (grōf), agrl. missionary; b. Annville, Pa., Mar. 29, 1884; s. Abram Lafever and Lizzie (Weidman G.; B.S. in Agr., Pa. State Coll., 1907, M.S., 1918; grad. study, U. of Calif., 1926-27; m. Eva Brinser, Dec. 19, 1911. Agrl. missionary in China as rep. Pa. State Coll. as prof. horticulture, Lingnan, U., Canton, China, dean, dir. Coll. Agr., Lingnan U., 1921-34; dir. Plant Exchange, 1936-47, base in Florida, 1941-54; made various agricultural explorations in South China, Indo China, Siam and Malaya, 1911-40; began introducing new economic plants in China, 1912; field asst. U.S. Dept. Agr. in citrus canker eradication, southern U.S., 1917; field asst. Office of Crop Physiology and Breeding, U.S. Dept. Agr., in China, part time, 1918-20; adviser on plant introdn. Bur. Agr., Kwangtung, 1924-34; directed Nat. Geog.-Lingnan U. expdn. into northern Kwangsi to study bot. and ethnol. of area, 1937; agrl. rehabilitation officer with UNRRA in China, 1946-47. Horticulturist, directing plant exchange through missions, Christian Service Training Center, Babson Park, Fla., 1949. Lecturer in world agr., Pa. State College, 1944-47. Fellow A.A.A.S., Peking Natural History Soc.; mem. Soc. for the Advancement of Edn., Royal Asiatic Soc., China Soc., Science and Arts, The Christians Rural Fellowship, Alpha Zeta, Delta Upsilon, Delta Sigma Rho, Phi Kappa Phi, Phi Sigma, Sigma Xi, Phi Tau Phi (China). Presbyterian. Club: Rotary International (Sarasota, Fla.). Author: The Lychee and Lungan. Contbr. numerous articles to bulletins and jours. Home: Laurel, Fla. Address: American Foundation, Lingnan University, 475 Riverside Dr., N.Y.C. Died Dec. 4, 1954.

GROLL, Albert Lorey (grōl), artist, etcher; b. New York, Dec. 8, 1866; s. Carl and Caroline (Lorey) G.; ed. Royal Acad., Munich, 1899; m. Mary Champney Lowell, 1913; m. 2d, Henrietta L. Beinhorn, 1932. Engaged as landscape artist since 1895; Morgan prize, Salmagundi Club, 1903, Shaw prize, same, 1904; silver medal, St. Louis Expn., 1904; gold medal, Pa. Acad. of Fine Arts, 1907; medal, Buenos Aires and Santiago expns., 1910; Inness gold medal, Nat. Acad. Design, 1911; silver medal, San Francisco Expn., 1915; medal Nat. Arts Club, 1938. Represented in Corcoran Gallery, Washington; Carnegie Inst., Pittsburgh; Brooklyn Museum Arts and Sciences; Richmond (Ind.) Museum; Nat. Gallery, Washington; Minneapolis Museum; Met. Museum, New York; Newark (N.J.) Museum; Providence (R.I.) Museum; St. Louis, Ft. Worth (Tex.),

Santa Barbara (Calif.), Toledo (O.), Camden (Tenn.), Milwaukee (Wis.), Boston (Mass.) and Munich (Germany) museums; Pub. Library, New York; Philips Memorial (Washington, D.C.). Nat. Academician, 1910; mem. Nat. Inst. of Arts and Letters, Artists' Fund Soc., New York Water Color Club, Am. Water Color Soc. Clubs: Lotos (life), Salmagundi, Nat. Arts (life). Address: 222 W. 59th St., N.Y.C. Died Oct. 2, 1952.

GROOVER, Paul, textile mfr.; b. Quitman, Ga., Aug. 26, 1898; s. Fuller and Minnie (Thomas) G.; A.B., Va. Mil. Inst., 1920; advanced management program, Harvard Grad. Sch. Bus. Adminstrn., 1951; m. Madeleine Everett, Dec. 23, 1933. With Pepperell Mfg. Co., 1925-42; joined Pacific Mills, 1942, v.p., 1948-52, exec. v.p., July 1952—. Clubs: Biltmore (N.C.) Forest Country; Piedmont (Spartanburg, S.C.). Home: 29A Chestnut St., Boston 8. Office: 140 Federal St., Boston 10. Died July 8, 1954; buried Richmond, Va.

GROSE, George Richmond, clergyman; b. Nicholas County, W.Va., July 14, 1869; s. Andrew Dixon and Mary Estaline (Harrah) G.; A.B., Ohio Wesleyan U., 1894, A.M., 1896, D.D., 1908, LL.D., 1916; S.T.B., Boston U. Sch. of Theology, 1896; m. Lucy Dickerson, of Cadiz, O., June 28, 1894; children—Mrs. Mary Frances Witman, Wilbur Dickerson, Helen (Mrs. Helen Fallon), Virginia (Mrs. Virginia LaFever), William Edwin. Ordained M.E. ministry, 1896; pastor Cherry Valley Ch., Leicester, Mass., 1894-97, 1st Ch., Jamaica Plain, Boston, 1897-1900, 1st Ch., Newton, Mass., 1900-05, 1st Ch., Lynn, Mass., 1905-08, Grace Ch., Baltimore, 1908-12; pres. De Pauw U., Oct. 1912-24; bishop M.E. Church, assigned to Peking, China, 1924-32 (resigned as bishop). Mem. Ind. State Bd. Edn., 1913-24. Mem. Gen. Conf. M.E. Ch., 1916, 20, 24; pres. Ednl. Assn. M.E. Ch., 1917; mem. Univ. Senate; formerly mem. N. Indiana Conf. Mem. Sigma Alpha Epsilon. Clubs: Twentieth Century (Boston); Eclectic, City (Baltimore); Columbia (Indianapolis); University (Pasadena). Author: The Outlook for Religion, 1913; Religion and the Mind, 1915; Life of James W. Bashford, 1922; The New Soul in China, 1927; Edward Rector—A Story of the Middle West, 1928; The Man From Missouri — Mr. J. E. MacMurray, 1943. Contbr. to various periodicals. Religion editor Pasadena Star-News. Home: 1420 Morada Pl., Altadena, Cal. Died May 6, 1953; buried Greencastle, Ind.

GROSS, Charles Welles, lawyer; b. Hartford, Conn., Oct. 13, 1876; s. Charles E. and Ellen Clarissa (Spencer) G.; A.B., Yale, 1898; LL.B., cum laude. Harvard University, 1901; LL.D., Trinity College, 1939; m. Hilda Frances Welch, Nov. 2, 1905; children—Spencer, Mason W., Cornelia. Practiced Hartford, 1902—; mem. Gross, Hyde & Williams; dir. Hartford Nat. Bank & Trust Co., Aetna Ins. Company, and affiliated companies, Phoenix Mutual Life Ins. Co., Arrow-Hart & Hegeman Electric Co., Case, Lockwood & Brainard Co.; trustee Society for Savings. Mem. of State Board of Finance and Control, 1933-37; mem. State Advisory Council on Banking, 1937—, State Investment Com., 1937-39. Mem. Bd. St. Commrs., Hartford, 1907-09, Bd. Park Commrs., 1913-23, Draft Exemption Bd., 1917-19. Democrat. Conglist. Former moderator Conn. Conf. of Congl. Churches. Pres. trustees Hartford Sem. Foundation, 1915-45; trustee Horace Bushnell Memorial Hall Corp., Cedar Hill Cemetery; corporate mem. A.B.C. F.M. Mem. Am. Bar Assn., State Bar Assn. of Conn., Assn. Bar City of N.Y., Hartford Co. Bar Assn. (ex-pres.), Soc. Mayflower Descendants, Soc. Colonial Wars, Soc. of the Cincinnati, S.A.R., Phi Beta Kappa. Clubs: University, Hartford (Hartford); Graduate (New Haven). Home: 229 Kenyon St. Office: 49 Pearl St., Hartford, Conn. Died Mar. 30, 1957.

GROSS, Milt, cartoonist, author; b. N.Y.C., Mar. 4, 1895; s. Samuel and Rose (Spivak) G.; student high sch., Kearney, N.J., 1½ years; m. Anna Abramson, Dec. 14, 1920; children—Herbert, Jerrold, Stephen. Office boy New York American, 1912-13; comic artist Am. Press Assn., 1913-15, New York Evening Journal, 1915-17; with New York Tribune, Mar.-Aug. 1919; producer of "Animated Cartoons," 1919-22; with New York World, 1922—; drew daily news cartoon, then Banana Oil, 1925; creator of Gross Exaggerations, and Nize Baby, Dunt Esk. Served as pvt. 328th and 64th inf., U.S. Army, World War I. Jewish religion. Mason. Author: Nize Baby (book), 1926; Hiawatta with no Odder Poems, 1926; Dunt Esk (book), 1927; De Night in De Front From Chreesmas (book), 1927; Famous Fimales from Heestory, 1928. Died Nov. 29, 1953.*

GROSS, Walter W(oolf), lawyer; b. Troy, N.Y., Oct. 31, 1895; s. Marks and Estella (Kritzman) G.; A.B., Harvard, 1916, LL.B., 1920; m. Harriet R. Shoben, July 12, 1932; children—Woolf Paul, Martin Louis, Annette Marian. Admitted to N.Y. bar, 1920; practice of law, N.Y.C., 1920-53; gen. counsel, v.p., dir. Am. Broadcasting-Paramount Theatres, Inc., 1949—. Home: 14 E. 90th St., N.Y.C. 28. Office: 1501 Broadway, N.Y.C. 36. Died Feb. 16, 1956.

GROSSCUP, Walter T., corp. exec.; b. Camden, N.J., Sept. 14, 1883; s. Edward E. and Sally (Finlaw) G.; ed. South Jersey Inst.; m. Gertrude Gould; 1 son—Charles G. Bank examiner State of N.J., 1912-18; asst. Federal Reserve Agent, Federal Reserve Bank, Philadelphia, 1918-24; v.p. and treas. Colonial Trust Co., 1924-28; pres. and dir. Bankers Security Corp., 1929—, Land Title Bldg. Corp., South Penn Square Corp., Fourteen Twenty Walnut Corp., Ritz-Carlton, Sylvania and Adelphia Hotels (all Phila.); v.p. and dir. Bankers Bond & Mortgage Guaranty Co. of Am., Touraine Apts., Inc., Phila. Credit Bureau, Inc., Factors Corp.; treas. and dir. Nat. Consumer-Retailer Council, Inc. (N.Y. City); chmn. Liquor Control Bd., Pa., 1935-37; dir. Albert M. Greenfield & Co., Bankers Bond and Mortgage Co. of Phila., City Stores Co. (N.Y. City), Bonwit Teller (Phila.), Girard Life Ins. Co., Loveman, Joseph & Loeb (Birmingham, Ala.), Southwestern Market Co., 17th and Chestnut Sts. Holding Corp., Oppenheim Collins & Co., Inc. (N.Y. City); John Bartram Hotel, Phila. Dir. Bd. Trade, Phila. Mem. adv. com. Phila. region, War Assets Adminstrn.; mem. adv. com., R.F.C.; former chmn. bd., Smaller War Plants Corp., Region 3. Chmn. Phila. Highway Traffic Bd. Mem. Edward Powell Fund Award Com. Mem. Phila. Merchants Assn., Pa. Retailers Assn., C. of C. Mason (Shriner). Clubs: Racquet, Manufacturers, Country (Phila.); Bankers (New York). Home: 6635 McCallum St., Germantown. Office: 8th and Market Sts., Phila. 5. Died Sept. 24, 1950.

GROSZ, George, artist; b. Berlin, Germany, July 26, 1893; s. Karl and Marie (Schultze) G.; student Royal Acad., Dresden, Kunstgewerbeschule, Berlin, Acad. Calarossi, Paris; m. Eva Peter, May 26, 1920; children—Peter Michael, Martin Oliver. Guggenheim Fellow, 1937-38. Exhibited Amsterdam, Grenoble, London, Paris, Art Inst. Chicago, Whitney Mus., Detroit Inst. Arts, Los Angeles Mus., Minneapolis Inst. Art, Springfield (Mass.) Mus., Germanic Mus., Harvard U., Met. Mus., N.Y., Mus. Modern Art, N.Y., Cleveland Inst. Art. Awarded Gold medal Dusseldorf, 1927; medal Exhbn. Art Olympic Games, 1930; Blair pripe Internat. Watercolor Exhbn., Chicago, 1931; Block medal by Pa. Acad. Fine Arts, 1940; Purchase prize Chicago Art Inst., 1940; 2nd prize by Carnegie show, 1945; Gold medal National Acad. Arts and Letters, 1959. Mem. Nat. Acad. of Design. Author: A Little Yes, a Big No, 1946; published 52 Drawings, 1944; 30 Drawings and Watercolors, 1944. Home: The Cottage, Hilaire Farm, Huntington, L.I. Died July 6, 1959.

GROTE, August D. (grō'tē), business exec.; b. Hanover, Germany, Feb. 2, 1888; s. Dietrich and Dorothea (Eschenhorst) G.; came to U.S., 1891, naturalized, 1896; student evening classes Northwestern U., 1909-19; m. Esther N. Dahlman, May 1, 1908. Communications business since 1909; supervisory and management positions Ill. Bell Telephone Co., 1912-30, chief accountant, 1930-36, comptroller, 1936-44, vice pres. and comptroller, 1944-49, now v.p. in charge of finance; pres. and dir. Central Union Telephone Co. Mem. Telephone Pioneers of Am. (pres. Theodore N. Vail chapter 1, 1938), Controllers Inst. Am. (dir. 1943, pres. Chicago Control 1944-45), Chicago Assn. Commerce and Industry. Republican. Augustana Lutheran. Clubs: Executives', Union League (Chicago). Address: 4420 Palmarito St., Carol Gables, Fla. Died Aug. 23, 1951; buried Oak idge Cemetery, Ill.

GROUT, Frank F(itch), educator; b. Rockford, Ill., Jan. 24, 1880; s. Carlos Leroy and Carrie Louise (Fitch) G.; student Throop Poly. Inst., Pasadena, Cal., 1899; B.S. in Chemistry, U. Minn., 1904, M.S., 1908; Ph.D., Yale, 1917; m. May W. Browne, July 11, 1906. Chemist state geol. surveys, 1904-06; instr. geology U. Okla., 1907; mem. faculty U. Minn., 1907-48, emeritus, now prof. geol. and mineral., Geologist various state geol. surveys, and geologist U.S. Geol. Survey, 1918-24; spl. expert U.S. Shipping Bd., 1918. Dir. Minn. Geol. Survey, 1944-46. Del. U. Minn. and Minn. Geol. Survey to 18th Internat. Geol. Congress, London, 1948. Mem. Am. Chem. Soc., A.A.A.S., Am. Inst. Mining Engrs., Geol. Soc. Am., Soc. Econ. Geologists, Sigma Xi, Alpha Chi Sigma, Gamma Alpha, Sigma Gamma Epsilon, Acacia. Universalist. Mason. Author: The Clays and Shales of Minnesota (University of Minn.), 1914; (with others) The Clay and Shales of Minnesota (U.S. Geol. Survey, 1919; The Duluth Gabbro, 1918; The Magnetite Deposits of the Eastern Mesabi Range of Minnesota (with T. M. Broderick), 1919; (bull.) Geology and Magnetite Deposits of Northern St. Louis County, Minn., 1925; Petrography and Petrology, 1932; Problems of the Batholiths, 1933; The Rove formation, 1933; Geology of the Anorthosites of Minn. coast of Lake Superior (with G. M. Schwartz), 1939; Cuyuna manganese resources, 1942; vein carbonates, 1946. Revisor: Kemp's Handbook of Rocks, 1940. Home: 911 7th St. S.E., Mpls. Died Aug. 1, 1958.

GROVE, Charles Gerden, railroad engr.; b. Muddy Creek Forks, Pa., Dec. 20, 1890; s. Alexander Martin and Barbara Elizabeth (Uffelman) G.; B.S. in Civil Engring., Pa. State Coll., 1912; graduate York Collegiate Inst., 1908; m. Martha Caroline Srodes, Oct. 21, 1921. Successively track supervisor, div. engr., supt., supt. passenger transportation, engr. maintenance of way, chief engr. maintenance of way Western region, chief engr. Western region Pennsylvania R.R., 1912-55, area engineer, 1955—. Served as lieutenant 104 Engineers, 29 Division, France, World War I. Mem. Am. Ry. Engring. Assn. (pres. 1954). Rep. Presbyn. Mason. Club: Western Ry. (Chgo.). Home: 605 Wayland Av., Kenilworth, Ill. Office: Union Station, Chgo. 6. Died Nov. 18, 1957.

GROVER, Delo Corydon, clergyman, educator; b. Hartsgrove, O., May 29, 1869; s. Corydon Timothy and Eunice A. (McElroy) G.; Ph.B., Oberlin Coll., 1891; LL.B., U. Mich., 1893; S.T.B., Boston U., 1898, M.A., 1912; Ph.D., Grove City (Pa.) Coll., 1912; m. Anna Diedler, July 19, 1893; children—Marguerite (dec.), Dorothy, Kathryn. Prin. Orwell (O.) High Sch., 1889-90; practiced law, Cleve., 1893-94; ordained M.E. ministry, 1898; pastor successively Cleve., Woodsfield, Garrettsville, Cleveland heights and Youngstown until 1908; acing prof. philosophy and econs., Baldwin U. (now Baldwin-Wallace Coll.), Berea, O., 1908; dean, prof. psychology, Bible and econs. Scio Coll., 1909-11; prof. philosophy and psychology Mt. Union Coll., 1911-16; v.p., prof. philosophy Baldwin-Wallace Coll., 1916-21, v.p., prof. psychology, 1921-22, v.p., prof. philosophy and psychology, 1922—, now acting pres., 1933-34, v.p., prof. philosophy and psychology, 1934-39, emeritus, 1939—. Mem. Theta Kappa Nu. Mason. Author: Volitional Element in Knowledge and Belief, 1911. Address: 318 Front St., Berea, O. Died Jan. 25, 1955; buried Windsor, O.

GROVER, Nathan Clifford, civil engr.; b. Bethel, Me., Jan. 31, 1868; s. Daniel Barker and Martha Matilda (Eames) G.; B.C.E., U. Me., 1890, C.E., 1897, D.Eng., 1930; B.S., Mass. Inst. Tech., 1896; m. Anna Allen, June 14, 1900; children—Dorothy Allen, Mary Hamilton (Mrs. John Douglass Fitch). Instr. civil engring. U. Me., 1891-94, asst. prof., 1894-95, asso. prof., 1895-97, prof., 1897-1903; engr. U.S. Geol. Survey, 1903-07; hydraulic, constrn. and irrigation engr. with J. G. White & Co., N.Y.C., 1907-11; chief engr. Land Classification Bd., 1911-13, chief hydraulic engr. charge water resources br. U.S. Geol. Survey, 1913-39; ret. 1939. Conglist. Mem. Am. Soc. C.E., Washington Soc. Engrs., Washington Acad. Scis., Phi Kappa Phi, Tau Beta Pi, Beta Theta Pi. Club: Cosmos (Washington). Author: River Discharge (with J. C. Hoyt), 1907; Notes on Framed Structures (with H. S. Boardman), 1902. Home: 4505 Dexter Road, Washington. Died Nov. 29, 1957; buried Rock Creek Cemetery, Washington.

GROWER, Roy William; ret. army officer; b. Richland, N.Y., Jan. 27, 1890; s. William Seth and Elizabeth Ellen (Thomas) G.; E.E., Syracuse U., 1913; grad. co. Officers Course Engr. Sch. U.S. Army, 1922; 1 son, William L. Grower. Apptd. assistant supt. Bur. Gas & Elec., City of Syracuse, 1914. Served as 1st lt. O.R. with 56th Engrs. 2d Army, France, World War I; later detailed in A.C. with All-Am. Pathfinders; 1st lt. C.E. U.S. Army, 1920, advanced through grades to Brig. Gen., 1944; trooop duty with 2d and 6th Engrs., R.O.T.C. and staff details; asst. C. A. engr. 1st C. A. (Boston); assistant adminstr. engineer W.P.A., New York City, 1935-36; asst. dept. engr. Panama Canal Dept., 1937-39; dist. engr., St. Louis Engr. Dist., 1939-42; base sec. engr. Eastern Base Sec. (Eng.), 1943; base sec. comdr. Eastern Base Sec. (Eng.), 1st Base Sec., Brittany Base Sec. (France), 1944; retired 1946. Decorated Legion of Honor, Grand Officer Chevalier de Tastevin (France); Croix de Guerre (Luxembourg); Legion of Merit (U.S.). Mem. Tau Beta Pi, Scabbard and Blade. Mason. Address: 40 Devon Dr., Clearwater Beach, Fla. Died Jan. 31, 1957.

GROZA, Petre, pres. of Rumania; b. 1884; ed. univs. of Budapest, Berlin, and Leipzig. Former lawyer and landowner in Deva, Transylvania; minister of public works, 1926; vice premier in Sanatescu govt., 1944; leader in Ploughman's Front (peasant party); now Pres. of Rumania; leader Nat. Democratic Front since 1945. Dir. various companies. Address: Bucharest, Rumania. Died Jan. 7, 1958.

GRUBB, George Albert, dean emeritus of dental school; b. Pawnee County, Neb., Feb. 18, 1880; s. William Henry and Mary Jane (Clark) G.; D.D.S., U. of Neb., 1912, A.B., 1923; m. Amy Shively, Jan. 7, 1913. Practiced as dentist, Lincoln, Neb., 1912-1923; part time mem. faculty, Coll. of Dentistry, U. of Neb., 1913-23, prof. of dental lit. and science, prof. of operative dentistry and dean, 1923-39, dean emeritus since 1939, also prof. of dental history, ethics, lit., 1939-40. Mem. Med. Appeal Bd., Lancaster County, Neb., during World War I. Mem. Am. Dental Assn. (mem. since 1913), Neb. State Dental Assn. (sec. 1922, treas. 1923-24, v.p. 1925, pres. 1926; Neb. del. to Am. Dental Assn. many times), Am. Assn. Dental Schs. (mem. exec. com. 1936-39, v.p. 1939-40), Am. Assn. of History of Medicine, A.A.A.S., Xi Psi Phi (bd. dirs. Supreme Chapter 1919-31; pres. 1929-31), Omicron Kappa Upsilon, Lincoln Dist. Dental Soc. (past pres.), Fellow Internat. Coll. Dentists. Republican. Mason. Mem. Lincoln Grace Meth. Ch. (dir. ushers, mem. bd. trustees). Club: Kiwanis. Contbr. to dental jours.; editor Jour. Neb. State Dental Assn., 1917-18, 1940-53. Home: 2919 Garfield St., Lincoln, Neb. Died Nov. 1, 1953; buried Wyuka Cemetery, Lincoln, Neb.

GRUBER, John Lewis, musical educator; b. Shelbyville, Ky., Sept. 28, 1888; s. Henry Calvin and Mittie B. (Davis) G.; student U. Ky., 1909-10, U. Louisville, 1928-31; m. Caroline Manes, Oct. 3, 1910; children—Mittie Mathilda, Dorothe Carolyn. Began as pub. stenographer, Louisville, 1907; ct. stenographer, 1909-11; ofcl. police ct. stenographer, 1911-21; corr. sec. Louisville Conservatory Music, 1921-22, sec., 1922-24, v.p., treas., 1924-25, pres., treas., 1925—; v.p. Louisville Coll. Music, 1925-26, pres., 1926—, now also treas. Mem. Ky. Soc. S.A.R., Pi Gamma Mu. Democrat. Kiwanian. Home: 1508 Edgewood Pl., Louisville. Died Sept. 8, 1944; buried Cave Hill Cemetery, Louisville.

GRUEN, George John (grōō'ĕn), mfr.; b. Columbus, O., Aug. 11, 1877; s. Dietrich and Pauline (Wittlinger) G.; ed. public schools and bus. coll.; m. Emilie Thauwald, Nov. 17, 1904; children—George Thauwald, Robert Dietrich, Emily Pauline (Mrs. Arthur Jones Seaman). Began with Gruen Watch Makers Guild, 1895; treas., 1900-35, 1st v.p. and treas., 1916-35; v. chmn. bd., 1935-40, chmn. bd. since 1940; dir. Gruen Nat. Watch Caase Co. Mem. Cincinnati Chamber of Commerce. Trustee of Deaconess Hosp., Coll. of Music. Mem. Cincinnati Wholesale Jewelers and Mfrs. Assn. (pres. 1910), Cincinnati Assn. of Credit Mem (pres. 1920), Nat. Assn. of Credit Men, N.Y. (pres. 1927-28). Lutheran. Clubs: Cincinnati (pres. 1924); Rotary, Queen City (Cincinnati). Home: 2356 Park Av., Cincinnati 6. Office: Time Hill, Cin. Died June 3, 1952; buried Spring Grove Cemetery, Cin.

GRUENSTEIN, Siegfried Emanuel (grōōn'stīn), publisher, organist; b. Charlestown, Ind., Mar. 26, 1877; s. Rev. Elias E. and Louise (Schorer) G.; student Lake Forest Coll., 1895-96; hon. M.A., 1926; m. Miriam McNitt, Aug. 14, 1901. On staff Chicago Evening Post, 1895-1909; telegraph editor Chicago Daily News, 1909-17; founder, 1909, since editor and pub. The Diapason, a monthly mag. for organists, choirmasters and builders of organs—the official paper of the Am. Guild of Organists and of Canadian Coll. of Organists, also official paper of Hymn. Soc. of America; organist First Presbyterian Ch. of Lake Forest, Ill., 1891-1939. Mem. Am. Guild of Organists (dean Ill. Chapter, 1922-24); made hon. mem. Nat. Assn. Organists for services to the profession. Republican. Presbyterian. Has given organ recitals and played at organ dedications in various parts of the country. Home: 611 Ash St., Winnetka, Ill. Office: 25 E. Jackson Blvd., Chicago. Died Dec. 6, 1957.

GRUWELL, Hugh Clifton, banker; b. West Branch, Ia., Oct. 28, 1891; s. Elmer Thomas and Anna Belle (Jackson) G.; grad. Cornell Coll. Acad., 1909; student Cornell Coll., 1909-11; A.B., Harvard, 1916; m. Gertrude LaVon Kint, Feb. 6, 1917 (dec. Feb., 1954); m. 2d., Mrs. J. G. Kennedy, Jan. 1955; stepchildren—Mrs. George Stollwerck, Jesse Kennedy, John Kennedy, James Kennedy. Assistant cashier Farmers State Bank, Wilsall, Mont., 1912-20; mgr. credit dept. U.S. Nat. Bank, Portland, Ore., 1920-27; v.p. Peoples Nat. Bank of Wash., Seattle, 1927-36, Bank of Am., Los Angeles, 1936-45; exec. v.p. First Nat. Bank of Ariz., Phoenix, 1945-47, pres. 1947-55, chairman of the board, 1955—; president of the Nat. Ins. Agy., Phoenix since 1947. Ariz. chmn. U.S. Def. Bonds; chmn. Army adv. com. Ariz.; mem. world com., Nat. Bd. and Nat. Council of Y.M.C.A., pres. Phoenix Y.M.C.A. Director Good Samaritan Hosp., Am. Inst. Fgn. Trade. Mem. Am. (mem. pub. relations council) and Arizona bankers assns., Newcomen Soc. Eng., Sigma Alpha Epsilon. Methodist. Clubs: Country, Arizona, Saddle and Sirloin, Kiva, Press, Executives (Phoenix). Home: 1205 E. Thomas Rd. Office: First National Bank of Arizona, Phoenix. Died Aug. 23, 1946; buried Greenwood Meml. Park.

GUDGER, Eugene Willis (gŭd'jẽr), ichthyologist; b. Waynesville, N.C., Aug. 10, 1866; s. James Cassius Lowry and Mary Goodwin (Willis) G.; student Emory & Henry Coll., Va., 1883-87; B.S., U. of Nasvhille, 1892, M.S., 1893; Ph.D., Johns Hopkins, 1905; unmarried. Instr. science high sch., Asheville, N.C., 1893-94, Asheville Coll., 1894-59, Peabody High Sch., Little Rock, Ark., 1895-1901; lab. asst. Gen. Biol. Lab., Johns Hopkins, 1902-04; prof. biology, N.C. Coll. for Women, Greensboro, N.C., 1905-19; investigator U.S. Bur. Fisheries, Beaufort, N.C., 1902-11; research asso., Tortugas Lab., Carnegie Inst., 1912-15; editor Vol. III, Bibliography of Fishes (Am. Museum), 1919-23; asso. in ichthyology, Am. Museum, 1921, bibliographer in ichthyology, 1923-38, associate curator, 1935-38; now hon. associate in ichthyology, Am. Museum and librarian Dean Memorial Library. Fellow A.A.A.S., New York Zoöl. Society; mem. Am. Museum of Natural History (life), Am. Soc. Zoölogists, Am. Soc. Naturalists, History of Science Soc., N.C. Acad. Science (sec. 1907-18; pres. 1918; life mem.); hon. corr. mem. Salmon-Trout Association of Gt. Britain; corr. mem. Zoöl. Soc. of London, 1939. Mason. Author: (brochures) Breeding Habits of Segmentation of Egg of Pipe Fish, 1908; Habits and Life History Toadfish, 1910; History of the Spotted Eagle Ray, 1914; Natural History of the Whale Shark, 1915; Structure and Habits of Barracuda, 1918; Use of the Sucking Fish for Catching Fish, 1919; Myth of Ship-holder, 1919; Rains of Fishes, 1921; Smallest Shark-suckers, 1926; Live Fishes in Throat of Man, 1926; Nesting Habits of Gunnell, 1927; A Three-eyed Haddock, 1928; Nicolas Pike's Fishes of Mauritius, 1929; The Candiru, the Only Vertebrate Parasite of Man, 1930; Fishes with Two Mouths, Some Spider Fishermen, Fourth Florida Whale Shark and Model in American Museum, The Opah on the California Coast, 1931; Cannibalism among Sharks, Dolphin on Coast of North Carolina, 1932; Abnormal Dentition in Rays, 1933; Ambicoloration in Flatfishes, 1934; Geographical Distribution of the Whale Shark; Breathing Valves in Sharkes and Telcosts, 1935; Reversal in Flatfishes, 1935; Beginnings of Fish Teratology (1555-1642), 1936; Natural History and Geographical Distribution of the Pointed-tailed Ocean Sunfish, Abnormal Dentition in Sharks, 1937; Two-headed Trout, 8 inches long—the Record Size, 1938; A School of Whale Sharks in the Bahama Islands, 1938; Whale Sharkes in Gulf of Mexico, 1938; Whale Sharks Rammed by Steamers, Pugnacity of Swordfish Shown in Attacks on Vessels, Swordfishing in the Strait of Messina, Breeding Habits and Embryology of Frilled Shark (all 1940); Feeding Organs and Food of Whale Shark, Behavior of Whale Shark, Quest of Smallest Fish (all 1941): Giant Fresh Water Fishes of North America, Swordfishing with Harpoon in New England Waters, 1942; Fish-Eating Bats of India and Burma, 1943; The Stingray's Sting Poisonous to Man; The Earliest Winged Fish-catchers; Fishes That Play Leapfrog, Fishes That Swim Tandem-fashion, 1944; Fish-eating Bats of the Caribbean Region, The Frogfish (Antennarius) and the Anglerfish Use Their Lures in Fishing, 1945; Oral Breahting Valves in Fishes (1685-1935), 1946; Pomacentrid Fishes Symbiotic with Giant Sca Anemones, Utricularia, the only known Fish-Catching Plant, 1947; The Tiger Shark on the N.C. Coast and its Food there, 1948. Editor of Bashford Dean Memorial Volume; editor for ichthyological terms in 2d edit. Webster's New Internat. Dictionary, 1935. Home: Waynesville, N.C. Address: American Museum of Natural History, N.Y.C. 24. Died Feb. 19, 1956.

GUENTHER, Louis (gŭn'thẽr), publisher; b. London, Eng., Aug. 4, 1874; s. Otto and Rose G.; ed. pub. schs. and home study; m. Hedda Dawn Engel, Feb. 14, 1934. In advertising business, 1886-99; with father established a monthly trade paper, The Mail Order Journal, 1892, pub. until 1907; pub. (with father until 1905) The Financial World since 1902, publisher and editor since 1905. Mason. Clubs: Downtown Athletic, Masonic, N.Y. Athletic (member board of governors 1942-44). Author: Investment and Speculation, 1912; Intelligent Investment Planning, 1936. Home: 32 Washington Sq. W. Office: 86 Trinity Pl., N.Y.C. Died Mar. 11, 1953; buried Woodlawn Cemetery, N.Y.C.

GUERARD, Albert Leon, author; b. Paris, France, Nov. 3, 1880; s. Marcel Theophile and Marie (Collot) G.; B.A., Paris, 1899; post-grad. studies, London and Sorbonne, Paris; Agrégé, 1906; Litt.D., Geneva Coll., Beaver Falls, Pa., 1936, Brandeis U., Waltham, Mass., 1957; m. Wilhelmina Macartney, 1907; children—Sydney (dec.), Therina, Albert Joseph. Traveling scholarship in Eng., 1901-03; jr. prof. lit. and examiner in history Paris Normal Sch., 1904-06; instr. Williams Coll., 1906-07; asst. and asso. prof. French, Stanford U., 1907-13, prof. gen. lit., 1925-46, emeritus, 1946—; prof. French, Rice Inst., Houston, 1913-24, U. Cal., So. br., 1924-25; prof. French, U. Chgo., summer 1916, 20, U. Cal., 1921, 22, 26, U. Wis., 1923, U. Hawaii, 1930, U. Ore., 1931; prof. English, Harvard, summer 1949, U. Hawaii, 1950; prof. comparative lit. Brandeis U., 1950-53; lectr. French civilization New Sch. for Social Research, 1951, Radcliffe Coll., 1951-52; asso. in Humanities, Stanford, 1957—. Served with U.S. Army, intelligence and liaison services during World War I; with OWI, 1942-45. Mem. Phi Beta Kappa, Pi Delta Phi, Pi Sigma Alpha. Episcopalian. Decorated Chevalier of Legion of Honor (France); Crown of Rumania. Author: French Prophets of Yesterday, 1913; French Civilization in the XIX Century, 1914; Five Masters of French Romance, 1916; French Civilization from Its Origins to the Close of the Middle Ages, 1920; International Languages, 1921; The Napoleonic Legend, 1923; Honoré de Balzac (pamphlet), 1924; Beyond Hatred, 1925; Life and Death of an Ideal, 1928; L'Avenir de Paris, 1929; Literature and Society, 1935; Art for Art's Sake, 1936; Preface to World Literature, 1940; The France of Tomorrow (de luxe edit.), 1941, (complete), 1942; Napoleon III, 1943; Europe Free and United, 1945; France: A Short History, 1946; What the Teacher Learned (4 vols.), 1948—; Napoleon III, 1955; Napoleon I, 1956; Fossils and Presences, 1957; Joan of Arcc, 1957; France: A Modern History, 1959. Address: 635 Gerona Rd., Stanford, Cal. Died Nov. 13, 1959.

GUERRERO, Jose Custavo, internat. jurist; born San Salvador, El Salvador, June 26, 1876; s. Francisco and Louise (Lara) G.; ed. U. San Salvador; LL.D., Law Sch. of Guatemala; m. Adrienne Premi, Oct. 3, 1911. Entered diplomatic career in 1902; has served successively as consul at Bordeaux; consul gen. at Genoa, Italy; sec. of Legation at Washington; charge d'affaires, Rome, Italy; minister in Spain, Italy, and at the Holy See; minister fgn. affairs, El Salvador, minister of Justice, of Pub. Instrn., now permanent del. at League of Nations; head of Salvadorian delegation to Assembly of League of Nations, 1920-30; mem. Council of League of Nations; pres. 10th Assembly of League of Nations, 1929; head of Salvadorian delegation Pan.-Am. Conf. at Havana; v.p. Internat. Conf. on the commerce and traffic in arms; head of del. Conf. on Codification of Internat. Law at The Hague, 1930; head of delegation Internat. Conf. in Paris concerning the Treatment of Foreigners, etc. Elected member Permanent Court of Internat. Justice, 1930, v.p., 1931-36, pres., 1937-45. Elected mem. Internat. Court of Justice of United Nations, 1946, pres. of Court, 1946-49, vice pres. 1949. Decorated Grand Officer de la Legion d'Honneur, Grand Officer de la Couronne d'Italie, Grand Croix d'Isabelle la Catholique, Grand Croix de L'Ordre Carlos Manuel de Cespedes de Cuba, Grand plaque d'or de l'Order Jose Matias Delgada du Salvador, and others. Mem. Union juridique internationale de Paris, Academie diplomatique de Paris (pres.), Netherlands Acad. of Scis., etc. Author: La responsabilidad internacional de L'Estado; La Codification de droit internations; L'Order international Hier-Aujourd'hui-Deman; Les Cours de jurisdiction internationals; Tratado de derecho internacional, Catholic. Address: Vila La Chispa, Liserb-Superieur, Nice, France; Peace Palace, The Hague, Holland. Died Oct. 26, 1958.

GUEST, Edgar Albert, writer; b. Birmingham, Eng., Aug. 20, 1881; s. Edwin and Julia (Wayne) G.; brought to U.S., 1891; ed. grammar and high schs., Detroit; m. Nellie Crossman, June 28, 1906; children—Edgar A., Janet. Connected with Detroit Free Press since 1895; conducts column of verse and humorous sketches. Mem. Am. Press Humorists (ex-pres.). Mason (33°). Author: (verse) A Heap o' Livin', 1916; Just Folks, 1917; Over Here, 1918; Path to Home, 1918; When Day Is Done, 1921; All That Matters, 1922; The Passing Throng, 1923; Rhymes of Childhood, 1924; The Light of Faith, 1926; Harbor Lights of Home, 1928; The Friendly Way, 1931; Life's Highway, 1933; Collected Verse, 1934; All in a Lifetime, 1938; Today and Tomorrow, 1942; Living the Years, 1949. Home: 17471 Hamilton Drive, Detroit 3. Office: The Detroit Free Press, Detroit 31. Died Aug. 5, 1959; buried Woodlawn Cemetery, Detroit.

GUEST, Harold Walter, educator; b. nr. Otsego, Mich., Mar. 22, 1895; s. Henry Alden and Nellie May (Wood) G.; A.B., Albion Coll., 1921; A.M., U. Ill., 1922; Ph.D., Stanford, 1926; m. Marian Bernice Horner, Sept. 7, 1923; children—Margaret Ann (Mrs. J. R. Walter), Robert Horner. Asst. in econs., U. Ill., 1921-22; instr. econs., Lafayette Coll., Easton, Pa., 1922-24; acting asst. prof. econs., Stanford, 1924-25, lectr., 1925-26; prof. econs. and bus. adminstrn. Baker U., 1926—, also head div. social scis.; prof. econs. (on leave) Army U., Biarritz, France, 1945-46. Mem. Baldwin Sch. Bd., 1935-44, 48-53, chmn., 1949-52. Asso. adminstr. Kan. War Savs. Staff, 1942-43; economist U.S. Bur. Labor Statistics, 1943-44. Mem. commn. world peace Kan. Conf. Methodist Ch. Served as pvt., Field Hosp. No. 15, 2d Div., U.S. Army in France, 1917-18, Germany, 1918-19. Mem. Am., Midwest econ. assns., Am. Assn. U. Profs., Am. Finance Assn. Indsl. Relations Research Assn. Methodist (mem. S. Central jurisdiction bd. of Christian social relations. Rotarian. Author: Public Expenditure, 1927; also articles and pamphlets in field. Home: Baldwin, Kan. Died July 8, 1957; buried Oakwood Cemetery, Baldwin.

GUFFEY, Joseph F., ex-senator; b. Westmoreland County, Pa., Dec. 29, 1870; s. John and Barbaretta (Hough) G.; prep. edn., Princeton (N.J.) Prep. Sch.; student Princeton, 1890-92. In U.S. postal service, Pitts., 1894-99; sec. Phila. Co., pub. utilities, Pitts., and affiliated corps., 1899-1901, gen. mgr., 1901-18; ex-pres. Guffey-Gillespie Oil Co., Atlantic Gulf Co., Columbia Syndicate. Mem. War Industries Bd., Petroleum Service Div., and dir. bur. of sales, alien property custodian's office, World War I. Mem. Dem. Nat. Com. from Pa., 1920—. U.S. senator from Pa. for term 1935-47. Author: Seventy Years on the Red Fire Wagon, 1952. Address: Dresden Apt., 2126 Connecticut Av. N.W., Washington. Died Mar. 6, 1959; buried West Newton, Pa.

GUGGENHEIM, M. Robert, diplomat; b. N.Y.C., May 17, 1885; s. Daniel and Florence (Schloss) G.; student Drisler Sch., N.Y.C., also Sch. Mines, Columbia, 1907; grad. Army War Coll., 1925; m. Rebecca Pollard, 1938; 1 son by previous marriage, M. Robert. Dir., mem. exec. com. Am. Smelting & Refining Co.; sec., v.p. U.S. Zinc Co.; dir. Daniel and Florence Aviation Safety Center, Cornell, 1952—; apptd. U.S. ambassador to Portugal, 1953-54. Dir. Nat. Symphony Orchestra Bd., Washington, Daniel Florence Guggenheim Found. 1924— (sponsor ann. summer band concerts, N.Y.C.) Served as maj. U.S. Army, World War I; staff War Dept., 1932-33; now col. Decorated Purple Heart, Silver Star; hon. col. Ecuadorean Army. Clubs: Army Navy, Army Navy Country (Washington). Home: 4400 Board Branch Rd. Office: 2800 Albermarle St., Washington. Died Nov. 16, 1959.*

GUGGENHEIMER, Charles S., lawyer; b. N.Y.C., Sept. 11, 1877; s. Randolph and Eliza (Katzenberg) G.; A.B., Johns Hopkins, 1897; LL.B., N.Y. Law Sch., 1899; m. Minnie Schafer, Apr. 22, 1903; children—Randolph, Sophie G. Untermeyer. Admitted to N.Y. bar 1899, D.C. bar; partner Guggenheimer & Untermyer, N.Y.C., 1907—, Guggenheimer, Untermyer, Goodrich & Amram, Washington, since 1936; dir. Miami Copper Co., Gen. Development Co., Kerr Lake Mines, Ltd., Kerr Lake Mining Co., Rimu Gold Dredging Co., Ltd., Tenn. Corp., Warner Bros. Pictures, Inc., Tenn. Copper Co., Stanley Co. of Am., S.A. Gold & Platinum Co., K.L. Corp., Castle Dome Copper Co., Inc., Copper Cities Mining Co. Trustee Freedman Home. Democrat. Hebrew. Clubs: National Democratic, Bankers, Southern Society. Home: 270 Park Av. Office: 30 Pine St., N.Y.C.; also Ring Bldg., Washington. Died Nov. 7, 1953.

GUGLIELMI, Louis O. (gōō-yĕl'mē), artist, painter; b. Cairo, Egypt, Apr. 9, 1906; s. Talmiro and Domitilla (Secchi) G.; brought to U.S., 1914, naturalized, 1927; ed. pub. schs. and high sch., N.Y. City; student Nat. Acad. of Design, 1920-25; m. Ann de Maggio, May 22, 1939; 1 son, Stephen Austin. Has exhibited in major museums and galleries, including those of S.A. and Paris. Held one-man shows: Downtown Gallery, Magic Realists Exhbn., Mus. of Modern Art, Art Inst. of Chicago. Represented in pvt. and pub. collections, including those of Metropolitan Museum of Art, Museum of Modern Art, Whitney Museum of Am. Art, Newark. Hon. mention Carnegie Inst., 1945; Temple gold medal, Pa. Acad., 1952. Prof. of art La. State U., summer 1950, asso. prof., 1953; instructor of art New Sch. of Soc. Research, N.Y. City, 1950-51. Served with U.S. Army Air Corps, World War II; disch. 1945. Home: 1430 Second Av., N.Y.C. 21. Died Sept. 3, 1956; buried East Hampton, N.Y.

GUILL, John Hudson, govt. ofcl.; b. Chico, Cal., Dec. 28, 1879; s. John Hudson and Mary Jane (Bryan) G.; State Normal Sch., Chico, Calif., 1899; B.S. Agr., U. Cal., 1903; m. Ethel Gardner, May 12, 1908 (died 1941); children—Mary Jane, Samuel Gardner, Ethel May, John Hudson, Ida Virginia, Charles Lee; m. 2d, Margaret F. Demaree, Jan. 7, 1944. Farmer; mem. Cal. Assembly, 1911-12, 1913-14; chmn. bd. Freeholders for drafting charter for County of Butte, Calif., 1916; v.p. Fed. Land Bank of Berkeley, Cal., 1917-22; mem. Farm Loan Bd., Washington, D.C., 1922-33; dep. land bank commr., 1933-36; vice-pres. Federal Farm Mortgage Corp., 1936-47. Trustee State Normal School, Chico, 1916-20. Democrat. Methodist. Home: 2408 Cameron Mills Rd., Alexandria, Va. Died Oct. 9, 1959; buried Fort Lincoln Cemetery, Washington.

GUILLEBEAU, Joseph Edwin (gĭl'lĕ-bō), educator; b. Lincolnton, Ga., Sept. 8, 1894; s. Robert Franklin and Nora (Elam) G.; A.B., Mercer U., Macon, Ga., 1917; m. Ruby Ward, Dec. 28, 1920; children—Alice Sentilia, Joseph Edwin. Sci. tchr. Locust Grove Inst., 1917-18; instr. sci. Gordon Mil. Coll., 1918-20, 23-29, pres., 1929—; prin. high sch., Lincolnton, Ga., 1920-23. Baptist. Clubs: Civitan, Rotary. Address: Lincolnton, Ga. Died Sept. 15, 1956.

GUINEE, William Fenton, vegetable oil processing exec.; b. Memphis, Jan. 30, 1893; s. T. C. and Josephine (Reilly) G.; A.B., Christian Bros. Coll., 1912; m. Laura Mai Andrews, Aug. 4, 1926; children—William Fenton, Donald Griffin. V.p., dir. Refuge Cotton Oil Co., 1935—, Southern Cotton Oil Co., 1940—, Wesson Oil & Snowdrift Co., 1944—; pres. Meridian Fertilizer Co., Hattiesburg, Miss. Mem. Internat. House, New Orleans. Democrat. Roman Catholic. Clubs: Boston, New Orleans Athletic. Home: 25 Versailles Blvd. Office: Canal Bldg., New Orleans. Died Aug. 12, 1956; buried Metairie Cemetery, New Orleans.

GUINTHER, Robert (gin'ther), lawyer; b. Utica, O., Mar. 11, 1890; s. I. C. and Mary (Rexroth) G.; Ph.B., Coll. of Wooster, 1911; J.D., U. Chicago, 1915; m. Winifred Winn, Sept. 12, 1917; children—Annie Lee (Mrs. A. J. Peterson), Mary Catharine (Mrs. Ralph S. Brown). Admitted to Ohio bar, 1915, since practiced law Akron; mem. Slabaugh, Guinther & Pflueger, 1920—; dir. Seiberling Rubber Co., Robinson Clay Product Co., First Nat. Bank of Akron, Akron Standard Mold Co., Akron Realty Co. Pres. Akron bd. edn., 1928. Trustee Kent State U., Akron City Hosp. Served as lt. C.A.C., World War I. Mem. Ohio Judicial Council, Ohio State (pres., 1933), Am., Akron bar assns. (pres., 1924), Akron C. of C. (pres., 1932), Order of Coif, Am. Legion, Phi Beta Kappa, Delta Sigma Rho, Alpha Tau Omega. Presbyn. (trustee). Mason (Shriner, 33°). Clubs: Rotary, Portage Country, City, University. Home: 137 Fairlawn Blvd. Office: Second National Bldg., Akron. Died 1955.

GUINZBURG, Ralph K., bus. exec.; b. N.Y. City, Feb. 11, 1891; s. Victor and Henrietta (Kleinert) G.; m. Edna Stern, May 12, 1915; children—Jeanette, Margorie. Labor specialist, N.Y. Evening Mail, 1912; editor and pub., Westchester (N.Y.) County Budget, 1913-14; advt. mgr., I. B. Kleinert Rubber Co., N.Y. City, 1915-17, asst. treas., 1917, v.p., 1918-28, pres. and dir. since 1928. Trustee, Fedn. Jewish Philanthropies; pres., Jewish Family Service, 1944-49; asst. sec., Nat. Jewish Welfare Bd.; dir. Fed. Employment Service; past chmn., Com. for Coordinating Jewish Community Service for Vets. Mem. Nat. Notion Assn. (past pres.). Club: Harmonie (N.Y. City). Address: 485 Fifth Av., N.Y. C. 17. Died Jan. 15, 1957.

GULICK, Charles P. (gū'lĭk), hon. chmn. bd. Nat. Oil Products Co.; b. Newark, N.J., May 21, 1885; s. Jacob W. and Florence (Nicoll) G.; student coll. extension courses in law and chemistry; m. Ruth B. Nye, June 15, 1910 (divorced 1947); children—Richard, John, George; m. 2d, Florence Schwinn, 1948. Clerk Nat. Oil & Supply Co., Newark, N.J., 1904-05, sec. and treas., 1905; treas. Nat. Red Oil & Soap Co., 1907-12; treas. Nat. Oil Products Co., Harrison, N.J., 1912, Metasap Chem. Co., 1917; pres. Nat. Oil Products Co. (named NOPCO Chemical Co. since 1947), 1932-38, chmn. bd., 1938-40, pres. and chmn. bd., 1940-49, chairman of board, 1949-54, honorary chairman of the board, 1954—. Ex-pres. and founder Sulphonated Oil Mfrs. Assn. Mem. trustee advisory com., N.J. Coll. of Pharmacy, Rutgers U.; mem. bd. Y.M.C.A., Newark. Mason (K.T., Shriner). Clubs: Newark Athletic; Rotary of Newark (pres. 1943); W. Hudson Manufacturers (Harrison). Home: Forest Way, Essex Falls, N.J. Office: Essex and 1st Sts., Harrison, N.J. Died Sept. 4, 1955.

GUMPERT, Martin (gōōm'pĕrt), physician; b. Berlin, Germany, Nov. 13, 1897; s. Ely and Elise (Abraham) G.; studied medicine Univ. of Heidelberg; M.D., U. of Berlin, 1923; m. Charlotte Blaschko, Jan. 27, 1923 (died 1933); 1 dau., Nina. Came to U.S., 1936, naturalized, 1942. Resident asst. Rudolf Virchow Hosp., Berlin, 1923-27; dir. city clinic for skin and venereal diseases, Berlin-Wedding, 1927-33; engaged in practice as physician, also writer, New York, New York, 1936—; staff member Goldwater Memorial Hosp. research service; chief of Geriatric Clinic, Jewish Memorial Hospital; medcial adviser Time Magazine, 1943-45. Fellow American Geriatric Soc., A.M.A.; mem. Gerontological Soc.; New York Medical Society, American Public Health Association, Am. Authors League. Author: Verkettung, 1916; Heimkehr des Herzens, 1921; Venereal Diseases in Childhood, 1926; Handbook of Deformity Diseases, 1931; Hahnemann Biography, 1934; Life for the Idea, 1935; Trailblazers of Science, 1936; Dunant, Story of the Red Cross, 1938; Hell in Paradise: Autobiography, 1939; Heil Hunger! Health under Hitler, 1940; First Papers, 1941; You Are Younger Than You Think, 1944; Birthday (novel), 1949; Reports from Abroad, 1949, The Prejudice Against Old Age, 1951, Anatomy of Happiness, 1951. Contbr. articles to mags., including Readers Digest, Red Book, Coronet, Nation, Survey Graphic. Home: 315 E. 68th St. N.Y.C. Died Apr. 18, 1955.

GUNN, Walter Thomas, former judge; b. La Salle County, Ill., June 4, 1879; s. Luther V. and Alice E. (Rogers) G.; A.B., Greer Coll., Hoopeston, Ill., 1898; student Ill. Wesleyan U., 1899-1900; studied law, Ill. Wesleyan U.; m. Vina D. Dayton, June 29, 1904; children—Horace E., Margery. Admitted Ill. bar, 1902, and began practice in 1902; asst. states atty., Vermilion County, Ill., 1903-08; master in chancery U.S. Circuit Court, 1906-12; corp. counsel City of Danville, Ill., 1915-19; justice Supreme Court of State of Ill., 1938-51; now mem. firm Bookwalter, Carter, Gunn & Hickman; dir. Second Nat. Bank. Mem. Am. Bar Assn., Ill. State Bar Assn., Phi Delta Phi. Republican. Presbyterian. Mason, Elk, K.P. Home: 1205 W. Voorhees St. Office: First National Bank Bldg., Danville, Ill. Died Oct. 13, 1956; buried Springhill Cemetery, Danville.

GUNTER, Clarence (gŭn'tĕr), surgeon; b. Montgomery, Ala., Jan. 16, 1879; s. William Adams and Ellen Florence (Poellnitz) G.; prep. edn., Univ. Sch., Montgomery; M.D., Coll. Phys. and Surgeons, Columbia, 1901; m. Laurette O'Connell, June 30, 1909 (died in 1932); children—Manning, Randolph, Lovell; m. 2d, Evelyn Camilla Nolstad, Dec. 1936. Began the practice of medicine at Cananea, Sonora, Mexico, 1902; surgeon and asst. chief surgeon, S.P. R.R. of Mexico, 1900-16; div. surgeon, Ariz. Eastern R.R., 1916-24; dist. surgeon, S.P. R.R., 1924—. Served as surgeon, 18th Inf., United States Army Mexican border, 1916; capt., Med. R.C., 1917. Del. to Dem. Nat. Conv., 1924; mem. Dem. Nat. Com., 1928-32. Apptd. by Ariz. legislature mem. com. of 5 to assist in Arizona's fight on Boulder Dam in Congress, 1927. Pres. Board of Trusteees Globe Schs. Fellow A.C.S.; mem. Ariz. Med. Assn. (past pres.), Gila County Med. Soc. (past pres.). Presbyterian. Clubs: Cobre Valle Country; Arizona Club (Phoenix). Address: Globe, Ariz. Died Mar. 1955.

GUNTHER, Charles Otto, prof. mathematics and ordnance engring.; b. N.Y.C., May 21, 1879; s. Otto and Anna (Eybel) G.; M.E., Stevens Inst. Tech., 1900, D.Sc., 1950; m. Beatrice Disbrow, Feb. 19, 1901; children—Beatrix (Mrs. Fred B. Llewellyn), Jack Disbrow. With Stevens Inst. of Tech. 1900—, as instr. in mathematics, 1900-02, asst. prof., 1902-03, asst. prof. mathematics and mech. drawing, 1903-04, mathematics and mechanics, 1904-08, prof. and head of dept., 1908-36, prof. mathematics and ordnance engring., 1936-50, emeritus prof. mathematics and engring., 1950—, dean of student activities, 1920-25, dean of sophomores, 1927-28. Served with Ordnance Dept., U.S. Army, 1918-19; now lt. col. Ordnance Dept. Army U.S., inactive duty. Recipient of Stevens Honor Award, 1947; Stevens Alumni award, 1957. Fellow A.A.A.S.; mem. Army Ordnance Assn., Assn. Mathematics Teachers of New Jersey (past president, member council), Am. Soc. Civil Engrs. (life member), Am. Society Mech. Engrs., Soc. Am. Mil. Engrs., Societe Astronomique de France, Tau Beta Pi, Sigma Nu. Club: Officers of Army and Navy (New York). Author: Integration by Trigonometric and Imaginary Substitution, 1907; The Identification of Firearms from Ammunition Fired Therein, 1935. Contbr. to jours. Home: Grand View-on-Hudson, Nyack 9, N.Y. Office: Stevens Institute of Technology, Hoboken, N.J. Died June 8, 1958.

GUPTILL, Arthur Leighton, author, pub.; b. Gorham, Me., Mar. 19, 1891; s. Edward William and Nellie Ann (Stewart) G.; grad. in architecture Pratt Inst., Bklyn., 1912; student Mass. Inst. Tech., 1914-16; m. Ethel Marguerite Weir, Aug. 4, 1914; 1 son, Arthur Leighton. Registered architect, 1916—; partner Bearse & Guptill, archtl. designers and illustrators, N.Y.C., 1919-25; also free-lance specialist in design, free-lance advt. artist, cons. to advt. agencies, tchr. profl. art schs., 1916-37; part-time art dir. Reinhold Pub. Corp., 1930-37; condr. Guptill's Corner in archtl. mag. Pencil Points, 1934-37; exec. v.p. Watson-Guptill Publications, Inc., N.Y.C., 1937-51, pres., 1951—; editor, pub. (with Ernest W. Watson and Ralph W. Reinhold) mag. Am. Artist. Fellow Royal Soc. Arts London; mem. A.I.A., Amateur Artists Assn. Am., Inc. (founder pres.). Republican. Conglist. Club: Art Directors, (N.Y.C.). Editor, designer and pub.: Type Specimens (Longyear) 1940; Lumiprinting (d: Gemma), 1942; Studio Secrets (Taubes), 1943; Oil Painting for the Beginner (Taubes), 1944; Masks (Benda), 1945; Animal Drawing and Painting (Wilwerding), 1946; Pastel Painting (Sears), 1947; Painter's Question and Answer Book (Taubes), published in 1948; Scratchboard Drawing (Cutler), published in the year 1949; How to Draw the Dog (Thorne), 1950; Type and Lettering (Longyear), 1950; Watercolor Painting for the Beginner (Smith), 1951; Figure Indication (Schoor), 1952; Art and Hand-Lettering (Wotzkow), 1952; How to Make a Living as a Painter (Harris), 1954. Editor and pub.: Is That Me? (Levy), 1947; Painting with Jerry Farnsworth (Farnsworth), 1948; Applied Lettering and Design (Holub), 1948; Pen, Brush and Ink (Pitz), 1949; Scripts (Holub), 1950; Casein Painting (Gasser), 1950. Author: Sketching and Rendering in Pencil, 1922; Drawing with Pen and Ink, 1928; Freehand Drawing Self-Taught, 1933; Color in Sketching and Rendering, 1935; Sketching as a Hobby, 1936, Pen Drawing, 1937; Norman Rockwell, Illustrator, 1946; Pencil Drawing Step-by-Step, 1949; Oil Painting Step-by-Step, 1953; Watercolor Painting Step-by-Step, 1955; Home Study Course in Drawing and Painting (Annual), 1954, 1955; also various portfolios. Contbr. to art and archtl. periodicals. Home: 65 Prospect St., Stamford, Conn. Died Feb. 29, 1956; buried Gorham, Me.

GURIAN, Waldemar, prof. of polit. science; b. St. Petersburg, Russia, Feb. 13, 1902; s. Naoum and Clara (Lurje) G.; student Univs. of Munich, Breslau, Bonn; Ph.D., Univ. of Cologne, 1923; m. Edith Schwarzer, Jan. 7, 1924; 1 dau., Joan. Came to U.S., 1937, naturalized, 1943. Editor Koelnische Volkszeitung, 1923-24; lecturer, teacher Acad. of Politics, 1931-32; asso. prof. of politics, U. of Notre Dame, Ind., 1937—, prof. of political science, 1944—. Roman Catholic. Author: Bolshevism, 1932; Future of Bolshevism, 1936; Hitler and the Christians, 1937; Rise and Decline of Marxism, 1938; Die Politischen und Socialen Ideen des Franz, Katholismus, 1929; Der Integrale, Nationalismus in Frankreich, 1931; Um des Reiches Zukunft, 1933; Bolschevism an introduction to Soviet Communism, 1952. Editor for Review of Politics, Notre Dame, Ind. Contbr. to Foreign Affairs, Dublin Review, Commonweal, America, American Political Science Review, etc.; articles on totalitarianism. Russia, Germany, Comparative Government, International Relations. Home: 119 Hawthorne, South Bend, Ind. Address: University of Notre Dame, Notre Dame, Ind. Died May 26, 1954.

GUSHEE, Edward T. (gōō shā), public utilities exec.; b. Los Angeles, Jan. 10, 1895; s. Rev. Richard H. and Dagmar (Tisdale) G.; student Kent Sch., Pomona Coll.; m. Norine Bordley, June 28, 1924;

children—Richard B., Edward T., John W. H., Stephen H. Mgr. Castle Hot Springs (Ariz.) Hotel, 1915-20; dir. Aircraft Development Co., 1929-30; exec. v.p., dir. Electromaster, Inc., 1929-33; joined Detroit Edison Co., 1920, v.p., 1935-39, dir., 1936-39, asst. to chmn., 1945-48, v.p., 1948—; exec. v.p., dir. Union Electric Co. Mo., and subsidiaries, 1939-42. Gen. chmn. Community Chest of Met. Detroit, 1948, dir., 1948—; pres. Sts. and Traffic Commn., 1952-53. Dir. United Found.; pres. bd. trustees Kent (Conn.) Sch., 1949—; mem. adv. com. sch. bus. adminstrn. Wayne U., Detroit, 1947—. Served as capt. 64th Inf., 7th Div., A.E.F., 1917-18. Chief purchase policy br. Army Ordnance 1942; chmn. prodn. urgency com. W.P.B., 1943-45; dist. chief Detroit Ordnance Dist., 1947-53. Awarded Shipman Gold Medal, 1937. Mem. Am. Standards Assn. (v.p. 1952-53), Am. Legion, Newcomen Soc., Am. Ordnance Assn. Republican. Episcopalian (vestryman; del. Gen. Conv. 1949, 1952). Author: Scientific Purchasing (with Boffey), 1928; The Church Teaches, 1946. Home: 1783 Iroquois Av., Det. 14. Office: 2000 Second Av., Det. 26. Died Dec. 15, 1954; buried St. Johns Cemetery, Balt.

GUSS, Uriah Cloyd, banker; b. Juniata County, Pa., Apr. 16, 1860; s. Uriah and Catharine (Sieber) G.; ed. acads. and bus. coll.; m. Rebecca J. Snyder, Dec. 1, 1881. In lumber bus., Ulysses, Neb., 1884-90; bank cashier Ulysses, 1890-92; removed to Guthrie, Okla., 1892; in banking bus. Guthrie, 1892-1912; now dir. 1st Nat. Bank, Guthrie, Bank of Crescent. Okla. Rep. Christian Scientist. Mason. Home: 617 E. Cleveland Av. Office: 202 W. Oklahoma Av., Guthrie, Okla. Died Apr. 19, 1938.

GUST, John Lewis, lawyer; b. Ettrick, Wis., Dec. 13, 1878; s. William Frederick and Johanna (Ackerman) G.; B.Ph., Dakota Wesleyan U., 1906; M.A., LL.B., Northwestern U., 1909; m. Ada Lee Rebstock, June 8, 1914; children—Ada Lee (Mrs. John George Griffiths), John Devens. Admitted to Ill. and Ariz. bars, 1909; began practice of law in Phoenix, Ariz., 1909; mem. Gust, Rosenfeld, Divelbess, Robinette & Linton; legal adviser to Salt River Valley Water Users Assn., 1918-32; counsel in important Ariz. water litigation and numerous municipal bond issues. Dir. Valley Nat. Bank of Phoenix, Phoenix Title and Trust Co. Dir. Good Samaritan Hosp. Sec. Ariz. bd. of bar examiners, 1925-34; sec. com. on examinations and admissions, Ariz. State bar, 1934—. Mem. Am. and Ariz. State bar assns. Republican. Methodist. Office: 323 Security Bldg., Phoenix, Ariz. Died Oct. 20, 1949.

GUSTAFSON, Gilbert Eugene, radio mfg. exec.; b. Rock Island, Ill., Nov. 15, 1905; s. Gustaf A. and Hannah C. (Swanson) G.; student Augustana Coll., Rock Island, 1925; E.E. (honorary), Stevens Institute Technology; m. Norma M. Militzer, October 10, 1929; children—Warren N., David F., Gail L., Steven. Began in engring. dept. Zenith Radio Corp., 1925-27; chief engr. WJAZ Broadcast Station; engr. dept. Zenith Radio Corp., 1932-34, chief engr., 1934-43, v.p. in charge engring. since 1943. Fellow, Inst. of Radio Engrs.; mem. Am. Radio Relay League. Lutheran. Club: Radio Engineers (Chicago). Home: 1423 Lathrop St., River Forest, Ill. Office: 6001 W. Dickens Av., Chgo. Died Apr. 24, 1958.

GUSTAVUS V (gŭs-tä'vŭs), King of Sweden; b. Drottningholm, Sweden, June 16, 1858; s. King Oscar and Queen Sophia Wilhelmina; ed. in private schools in Stockholm, Sweden, and in Norway; m. Victoria (d. Frederick William Louis, Grand Duke of Baden), 1881 (died 1930); children—Eric (dec.), Oscar Fredrik Wilhelm Olaf Gustaf Adolf (Crown Prince), William. Served as lt. gen., Swedish Army; acted as regent during parts of father's reign; ascended throne, 1907. Address: Royal Palace, Stockholm, Sweden. Died Oct. 29, 1950; buried Riddarholm Ch., Stockholm.*

GUSTE, William Joseph, Sr. (gust), lawyer; b. New Orleans, Sept. 29, 1893; s. Edward F. and Delia (Murray) G.; A.B., Tulane, 1913, LL.B., 1915; m. Marie Louise Alciatore, July 6, 1921; children—William Joseph, Roy Francis, Rev. Robert Ignatius, Jules Anthony. Admitted to La. bar, 1915; practice of law, New Orleans, 1915—; sr. partner Guste, Barnett & Little 1918—; instructor department law, Loyola U., 1922-28; atty. Housing Authority, New Orleans. Dir. community chest, New Orleans; chmn. Parish, New Orleans Depts. Pub. Welfare; pres. Nat. Housing Conf., 1947-48, mem. nat. bd., 1944—. Mem. Nat. Assn. Housing Ofcls. (regional pres.), Assn. Commerce (chmn. members' council), New Orleans, Am., La. bar assns., Phi Beta Kappa. Elks. K.C. (supreme bd. dirs.). Club: Young Men's Business (past pres.). Home: 2200 Napoleon Av. Office: National Bank of Commerce Bldg., New Orleans. Died Aug. 4, 1957.

GUTENBERG, Beno (gōō'tĕn-bĕrg), prof. geophysics; b. Darmstadt, Germany, June 4, 1889; s. Hermann and Pauline (Hachenburger) G.; student Technische Hochschule, Darmstadt, 1907-08; Ph.D., U. of Göttingen, 1911; Ph.D. (honorary), U. Uppsala, Sweden, 1955; m. Hertha Dernburg, Aug. 17, 1919; children—Arthur, Stephanie. Came to U.S., 1930, naturalized, 1936. Began as asst. in central office Internat. Seismol. Assn., Strasbourg, 1913; prof. geophysics, U. Frankfurt am Main, 1926-30; professor geophysics, Cal. Inst. Tech., Pasadena, since 1930. Pres. Internat. Assn. for Seismology and Physics of Interior of Earth, 1951-54. Awarded Prix de Physique du Globe, Acad. Royal de Belgique. Served in German Army, World War, 1914-18. Recipient William Bowie Medal, 1953; Wiechert Medal 1956. Fellow Royal Astronomical Society; foregin member Geological Society, London; member Seismol. Soc. Am. (pres. 1945), Geol. Soc. Am., Am. Geophys Union, A.A.A.S., Soc. Exploration Geophysicists, Nat. Acad. Sci.; hon. mem. Royal Soc. New Zealand; corr. mem. Finnish Geog. Soc.; foreign mem. Academy Lincei, Rome; Swedish Acad. Sci.; Finnish Acad. Letters and Science. Author: Seismicity of the Earth (with C. F. Richter), 1949. Author, co-author or editor several books pub. in Germany; also more than 150 scientific papers. Editor: Internal Constitution of the Earth. Made first exact determination of radius of earth's core; regarded as authority on earthquakes. Home: 526 S. Sierra Vista Av., Pasadena 10. Office: Seismological Laboratory, 220 N. San Rafael Av., Pasadena 2, Cal. Died Jan. 1960.

GUTERMAN, Carl Edward Frederick (gōōt'ẽr-măn), plant pathologist; b. West Springfield, Mass., Oct. 27, 1903; s. Hans Wilhelm and Edith Arbella (Williams) G.; B.Sc., Mass. State Coll., 1925; Ph.D., Cornell, 1930; m. Hilda La Verne Kelly, July 7, 1926; children—Phyllis May, Donald Carl; m. 2d Mary M. Wetzsteon, July 21, 1949; step-children—Ross D. Wetzsteon, R. Scott Wetzsteon. Asst. plant pathology, Cornell, 1925-27, lily disease investigation fellow, 1927-30, asst. prof., 1930-36, prof., 1936—, asst. dir. Agr. Expt. Sta., 1936-42, dir. 1942—; dir. research, N.Y. State Coll. Agr. and N.Y. State Coll. Home Econs. (Cornell), 1942—. Mem. food protection com. Nat. Research Council 1950-53, N.Y. State Council, U.S. Dept. Agr., 1948—, N.Y. State Agr. Mobilization Commn., 1951-54. Dir. Cornell Research Found. Fellow A.A.A.S.; mem. Am. Inst. Biol. Scis., Am. Phytopath. Soc. (plant disease prevention com. 1944-48), Forest City Grange, N.Y. State Agr. Soc., Land Grant College Assn. (chmn. expt. sta. sect. 1952-53, sec. div. agr. 1952-53), Kappa Sigma, Gamma Alpha, Phi Kappa Phi, Sigma Xi. Unitarian. Clubs: Cornell of Ithaca, Statler. Contbr. articles on plant diseases and adminstrn. of agrl. research. Home: "The Byway," Forest Home, Ithaca, N.Y. Died Mar. 27, 1957; buried East Lawn Cemetery, Ithaca.

GUTHEIL, Emilian Arthur (goot-hile), physician; b. Czerlany, Poland, Jan. 21, 1899; s. Jacob and Regina (Baar) G.; M.D., U. of Vienna, 1930; m. Lilly Heitlinger, Mar. 15, 1935; children—Thomas Gordon, John Gordon. Came to U.S., 1937, naturalized, 1942. Neuro-psychiatric U. Clinic, Vienna, 1932-34; personal asst. to psychoanalyst, Dr. Wm. Stekel, 1921-36; co-founder active-analytic clinic, Vienna, 1932. Mt. Sinai Hosp., N.Y. City, psychiatric clinic, 1937-42; dir. publs. and instr. Postgrad. Center for Psychotherapy, N.Y. City since 1949. Diplomate Am. Bd. Psychiatry and Neurology. Mem. Assn. for Advancement Psychotherapy (founder; sec., treas., 1940-50; pres.), A.M.A., Am. Psychiat. Assn., N.Y. Soc. Clin. Psychiatry, Soc. Psychopath. & Psychother., N.Y. Co. Soc. Author books: The Handbook of Dream Analysis, 1951. Editor Am. Jour. Psychotherapy since 1947. Author articles. Address: 16 W. 77th St., N.Y.C. 24. Died July 7, 1959.

GUTHNER, William Ernest, govt. official; b. Dec. 18, 1884; s. Kaspar and Louise (Deininger) G.; grad. Sch. of Automatic Arms, 1917; Command and Gen. Staff Sch., 1929, Gen. Officers Course, 1941; m. Hannah Barrett, 1907; 1 dau., Dorothy R. (wife of Col. Howard M. Williams); m. 2d, Alyce Maus, 1930; children—Barbara Louise (wife of 1st Lt. Richard W. Hazen, A.C.), William E., Jr. Entered U.S. Army from Colo., served as pvt., corpl. and sergt., 6th U.S. Cavalry, 1901-04; capt., 157th Inf., A.E.F., 1917-19; successively maj., lt. col. and brig. gen., U.S. N.G., 1921-40, comdg. gen., 89th inf. brigade, 45th div., 1934-42, brig. gen., U.S. Army, 1941-46, with duty as brigade comdr., provost marshal, dir. security and intelligence, VI Corps Area and Sixth Service Comd., Chicago, 1942-46. Dir. pub. safety, Denver, 1934-40, exec. sec. Ill. Highway Traffic Safety Com., 1946-49. Awarded Legion of Merit with bronze cluster, 1944. Mem. Am. Legion, U.S. War Vets., Vets. Fgn. Wars (nat. chief of staff, 1936, nat. council adminstrn., 1929-35, v.p. Nat. Home bd., 1937-39). Mason. Club: Civitan. Home: 7924 Keystone Av., Skokie, Ill. Died Jan. 24, 1951; buried Fairmount Mausoleum, Denver.

GUTHRIE, Stanley Walter, lawyer; b. Titusville, Pa., June 24, 1889; s. Edward Marshall and Ella (Porter) G.; A.B., Stanford, 1913; m. Alice E. Cline, Sept. 17, 1913; 1 dau., Phyllis (Mrs. William S. Shinner); m. 2d Gladys McMurray, Feb. 17, 1949. Admitted to Calif. bar, 1914, U.S. Supreme Ct., 1929; practicing lawyer, Los Angeles, since 1913; sr. partner Guthrie, Darling & Shattuck since 1930; dir. Vernon Tool Co., Ltd., Schalk Chem. Co.; mem. adv. bd. Bank of Am. Mem. Calif. State (bd. govs. since 1949, v.p., 1951-52) and Los Angeles bar assns., Phi Alpha Delta, Delta Upsilon. Home: Bradbury Estates, Duarte, Calif. Office: 523 W. Sixth St., Los Angeles 14. Died Dec. 10, 1952; buried Forest Lawn, Glendale, Cal.

GUTHUNZ, Henry, ins. exec.; b. St. Paul, Oct. 11, 1893; s. Henry and Julia (McMahon) G.; student Minn. U.; m. Helen Hinrichs, Sept. 10, 1921; 1 dau., Dorothy Jane (Mrs. W. J. Lauer). Mgr., Wight-Phinney Co., 1920-24; pres. Ins. Service Agency, 1924-27; chmn. bd. Anchor Casualty Co., St. Paul; pres. Queen City Ins. Co., Sioux Falls, S.D.; dir. Empire Nat. Bank St. Paul. Mason. Clubs: Minnesota (St. Paul), Town and Country. Home: 1383 W. Maynard Dr. Office: 2700 University Av., St. Paul. Died June 26, 1957; Oakland Cemetery, St. Paul.

GUTSTADT, Richard E., orgn. exec.; b. San Francisco, Calif., May 13, 1888; s. Herman and Sarah Woolf) G.; m. Neva Jane Platt, Aug. 6, 1911; children—Miriam (Mrs. David Apter), Sylvia Jane (Mrs. Irwin Olcott), Richard H., Dr. Joseph Platt. Nat. dir. Anti-Defamation League of B'nai B'rith, 1931-48, exec. vice chmn. since 1948. President Temple Sinai. Chicago; hon. vice pres. Leo N. Levi Hosp., Hot Springs, Ark. Club: Covenant (Chgo.). Home: 7136 S. Oglesby Av., Chgo. Office: 327 S. La Salle St., Chgo.; also 212 Fifth Av., N.Y.C. 10. Died May 22, 1954; buried Cypress Lawn, San Francisco.

GUTTERSON, Henry H(igby), architect; b. Owatonna, Minn., Sept. 8, 1884; s. Arthur Lincoln and Mary (Higby) G.; student Univ. of Calif., 1903-05; L'Ecole des Beaux Arts, Paris, France (Victor Laloux patron), 1906-09; m. Helen Arnett, July 5, 1911. Office training, Grosvenor Atterbury, New York, 1910-16, John Galen Howard, San Francisco; design staff Panama-Pacific Exposition and city architect's staff, Oakland, Calif.; pvt. practice San Francisco since 1916; sup. architect St. Francis Wood and other residential developments; buildings include many churches, Christian Science Sanatorium for Pacific Coast, key bldgs. for Principia Coll., Ill., Berkeley (Calif.) High Sch. (in asso. with Will G. Corlett); teacher sch. of architecture Univ. of Calif., 1910-11, 1920-21. During World War I served church as camp welfare worker; bldg. counselor and regional exec., U.S.O., World War II; co-founder and dir. San Francisco Fed. Savings & Loan; mem. State Bd. Archtl. Examiners, 1924-27; mem. Berkeley City Planning Commn., 1942-45; mem. archtl. adv. com., San Francisco Civic Center during expansion studies. Fellow Am. Inst. of Architects (Sierra Nevada dir. 1942-45, Northern Calif. chapter pres. 2 terms); mem. soc. of Beaux Arts Architects, State Assn. Calif. Architects (founding mem., dir.), Delta Kappa Epsilon, Sigma Tau Delta (hon.). Republican. Christian Scientist. Home: 1644 Monterey Blvd., San Francisco. Office: 421 Powell St., San Francisco 2. Died Aug. 20, 1954.

GUY, J(ames) Sam(uel), prof. chemistry; b. Chester, S.C., Apr. 1, 1884; s. John Samuel and Margaret (Hardee) G.; B.S. Davidson Coll., 1905, M.A., 1906, hon. D.Sc., 1945; Ph.D., Johns Hopkins, Allie Candler, June 12, 1917; children—Florrie (Mrs. James Funk). John Slaughter Candler, James Samuel. Prof. mathematics, Fredericksburg (Va.) Coll., 1906-08; asst. in chemistry, Johns Hopkins, 1911-13; prof. chem., Agnes Scott Coll., Decatur, Ga., 1913-15, U. of Ark., 1915-18; prof. chem. Emory U., 1918-52, ret. 1952. Vice pres., treas., DeKalb Fed. Bldg. & Loan Assn., Decatur. Awarded Leon P. Smith medal by Crucible Club of Wesleyan Coll., Macon, Ga. (annual award to teachers of chemistry or biology in Southeast), 1939; Herty medal by Ga. sect. of Am. Chem. Soc., Herty Day, May 1940, at Ga. State Coll. for Women, Milledgeville, for notable contribution to the field of chemistry in the South. Mem. Am. Chem. Soc., Am. Assn. Univ. Profs. (v.p. 1930-32), Phi Beta Kappa, Gamma Alpha, Kappa Alpha, Rotary Club of Decatur, Ga. (pres.). Democrat. Presbyterian. Mason (32°). Author: A Course in Quantitative Analysis, 1931; also various monographs, also articles pertaining to physical chemistry, in leading chem. jours. Home: 1669 N. Cecatur Rd. N.E., Atlanta, Ga. Died Aug. 16, 1953.

GWALTNEY, Leslie Lee (gwält'nē), editor, clergyman; b. Elberon, Va., Mar. 5, 1876; s. John Avington Merritt and Sarah Rebecca (Deering) G.; student U. Richmond, 1899-1904, Union Theol. Sem., Richmond, 1904-05; Th.M., So. Bapt. Theol. Sem., Louisville, 1908; S.T.D., Ptomac U., 1909; Litt.D., Howard Coll., Birmingham, Ala., 1927; m. Richie Thornton Peters, Sept. 23, 1902; children—Rachel (dec.), Leslie Lee, Raecile (Mrs. Fred Alvis Davis), Virginia (dec.), Richard Merritt. Ordained ministry So. Bapt. Ch., 1902; pastor successively Prattville, Greenville, 1st Ch., Florence (all in Ala.), until 1919; editor Ala. Bapt., 1919-50. Past pres. Ala. Bapt. State Conv., 1935-37. Past pres. Ala. Temperance Alliance; trustee So. Bapt. Theol. Sem.; organizer Bapt. Found.; mem. Bapt. Conf. Com. on Pub. Relations, Washington. Democrat. Mason. Author: Man's Fairest Hope, 1924; A Rosary of Facts, 1936; Christ and Our Liberties, 1937; Herald of Freedom, 1939; Forty of the Twentieth, or The First Forty Years of the Twentieth Century, 1940; A Message for Today, 1941, etc. Home: 1326 N. 24th St., Birmingham, Ala. Died Nov. 10, 1955; buried Forest Hill Cemetery, Birmingham.

GWATHMEY, Edward Moseley (gwäth'mê), college pres.; b. Richmond, Va., Oct. 13, 1891; s. Robert Ryland and Hattie Payne (Winston) G.; student Richmond Acad., 1906-07; A.B., Richmond Coll., 1912; A.M., U. of Va., 1917, Ph.D., 1925; LL.D., University of South Carolina, 1943, U. of Richmond, 1949; m. Mildred Bates, June 25, 1927 (died Apr., 1956); children—Mary Winston, Anne Bates, Edward Moseley, Jr. Teacher high sch., Louisa, Virginia, 1913-16; with George H. McFadden and Bro., New York, 1919-20, J. P. Taylor Tobacco Co., Richmond, Virginia, 1920-21; instructor English, College of William and Mary, 1921-22, associate professor, 1922-24, prof., 1925-33; prof. of English summers, U. of Toulouse, France, U. of Utah, 1927, U. of Va., 1930-31; dir. Norfolk div. Coll. of William and Mary, 1932; pres. Converse Coll., Spartanburg, S.C., 1933-55, emeritus, 1955—. Served as seaman, later ensign and lt. (j.g.) U.S.N.R.F. World War. Sec.-treasurer Southern University Conference. Mem. Phi Beta Kappa, Phi Kappa Phi, Omicron Delta Kappa, Kappa Alpha. Democrat. Episcopalian. Clubs: Rotary, Country (Spartanburg). Author: Life and Works of John Pendleton Kennedy, 1931. Home: 176 N. Fairview Av., Spartanburg, S.C. Died June 7, 1956.

H

HAAG, Joseph, Jr., shipbuilding exec.; b. N.Y. City, Sept. 14, 1895; s. Joseph and Nellie (Grandon) H.; graduate Stevens Institute of Technology, Hoboken, New Jersey, 1918, M.E. (honorary), 1944; m. Camilla Marie Ashurst, Oct. 24, 1935. Began as apprentice Quintard Iron Works (subsidiary of Todd Shipyards Corp.), N.Y. City, 1917, later, estimator Clinton Dry Docks (Todd Shipyards Corp. subsidiary), Brooklyn, and since filled various positions with Todd Shipyards Corp. and its subsidiaries and affiliates, dir. Todd Shipyard Corp., N.Y.C., 1939—, pres., 1953—; vice pres. and dir. Todd Atlantic Shipyards Corp.; dir. Thermo Projects, Inc. Member of the classification committee of theAmerican Bureau Shipping. Served as lt., United States Navy, 1917-19. Mem. A.S.M.E., Shipbuilders Council Am. (dir.), Soc. Naval Architects and Marine Engrs., N.E. Coast Instn. Engrs. and Shipbuilders, Am. Welding Soc., Maritime Assn. Port of N.Y. Roman Catholic. Clubs: University, N.Y. Yacht, Whitehall, N.Y. Athletic, Downtown Athletic; Stevens Metropolitan, India House, Propeller (N.Y.C.). Home: 66 Sheldrake Rd., Scarsdale, N.Y. Office: 1 Broadway, N.Y.C. Died Mar. 10, 1958.

HAAKON VII (hä kŭn), King of Norway; b. Aug. 3, 1872; s. King Frederik VIII of Denmark and Queen Louise; baptismal name, Christian Frederik Carl Georg Valdemar Axel; trained as officer with Royal Danish Navy; m. Princes Maud, d. King Edward VII of Great Britain, 1896 (died 1938); 1 son, King Olav V. After separation of Norway and Sweden, was elected king of Norway, Nov. 1905; crowned king, Trondheim, 1906; following German invasion of Norway, 1940, maintained Norwegian govt. in exile, London, this govt. continuing war against Germany until end of World War II, 1945; returned to Norway, June 1945. Address: Oslo, Norway. Died Sept. 21, 1957; buried Palace of Akershus, Oslo, Norway.

HAAS, Francis Joseph, bishop, R.C. Diocese of Grand Rapids; b. Racine, Wis., March 18, 1889; s. Peter F. and Mary L. (O'Day) H.; St. Francis Sem., Milw., Wis., 1904-13; Ph.D., Cath. U. Am., 1922; LL.D., U. Wis., 1936, Ordained priest R.C. Ch., 1913; domestic prelate with title of Right Rev. Monsignor, 1937; prof. English, St. Francis Sem., 1915-19; prof. sociology St. Francis Sem., Marquette U. dean of Coll. Dept., St. Francis Sem., 1922-31; pres., Nat. Cath. Sch. Social Service, Washington, 1931-35, rector St. Francis (Wis.) Sem., 1935-37; dean Sch. of Social Sci. Cath. U. Am., 1937-43; bishop Diocese of Grand Rapids, 1943—. Editor The Salesianum (quarterly), 1922-31. Impartial chmn. Milw. Newspaper Industry, 1929; mem. exam. bd. Milwaukee County Civil Service Commn., 1929; gen. sec. Milwaukee County Assn. for Promotion Old Age Pensions, 1925-31; mem. Nat. Labor Bd., 1933-34; mem. Com. on Cultural Relations with Latin Am., 1929—; pres. Cath. Assn. for Internat. Peace, 1929-30; mem. Labor Adv. Bd., NRA, 1933-34; mem. Labor Policies Bd., Works Progress Adminstrn., 1935-39; special commr. of conciliation, U.S. Dept. of Labor, 1935-43; mem. Wis. Labor Relations Bd., 1937-39; mem. Com. on Long Range Work Relief Policies, Nat. Resources Planning Bd., 1940-43; chmn. Shoe Industry, Leather, Puerto Rico Wage Coms., 1939—, Wage and Hour Division, U.S. Dept. of Labor; chmn. Pres. Com. on Fair Employment Practice, 1943. Mem. Am. Econ. Assn., Cath. Conf. on Indsl. Problems (a founder), co-chairman, Council Against Intolerance in America; vice pres. American Assn. for UN, League of Nations Assn. (adv. council), Carnegie Ch. Peace Union (dir.). Author: Shop Collective Bargaining, 1922; Man and Society, 1930, rev. edit. 1951; An Introduction to Sociology, 1930; Security, Work and Relief Policies (as mem. com. on long range work relief of Nat. Resources Planning Bd.); also various sociol. pamphlets, and several publs. of NRA and Works Progress Adminstrn. Contbr. to Am. Ecclesiastical Rev., etc. Home: 2006 Lake Drive S.E. Office: 265 Sheldon Av., Grand Rapids, Mich. Died Aug. 29, 1953.

HAAS, Otto, chem. mfg. exec. Chmn. bd., pres. Rohm & Haas, mfrs. Plexiglas and various other chem. products for industry. Office: 222 W. Washington Sq., Phila. 5. Deceased.

HACKER, Fred A., business exec.; b. Quincy, Ill., Jan. 24, 1891; s. Fred Gottlieb and Adelaide (Bernhard) H.; student Art Inst. of Chicago, 1909-11, Ph.B., State Teachers Coll., Warrenburg, Mo., 1914; student evening classes Chicago U., 1915-17, Columbia U., 1919-23, N.Y. Trade Sch., 1920-22, N.Y. Employing Printers, 1923-26, La Salle Extension U., 1930-34; m. Alma Beck, Sept. 8, 1928. Apprentice pressman Dayton Printing Co., Quincy, Ill., 1907-09; pressman Poole Bros., Printers, Chicago, 1909-11; instr. indsl. arts Bd. of Edn., Kansas City, Mo., 1915-16, Chicago, 1916-17; advt. prodn. mgr. Barron G. Collier, Inc., N.Y., 1919-23; gen. mgr. Tabard Press, N.Y., 1923-31; cons. printing processes and equipment Wallace and Tiernan Products, Inc., Belleville, N.J., 1928-32; partner Reehl and Hacker, N.Y., 1932-35; vice pres. product research and development Am. Type Founders, Inc., Elizabeth, N.J., since 1934. Served as ensign, U.S.N.R., World War I. Member Young Lithographers Assn., N.Y. Lithographers Nat. Assn., Tech. Photographic Soc. of Am. Clubs: Printing House Craftsmen, Litho of New York. Patented portable plate-making machine, 1948, vibrating jogger, 1947. Home: 8 Riverside Dr., Cranford, N.J. Died May 30, 1958.

HACKER, Newton, lawyer; b. in Greene Co., Tenn., Mar. 3, 1936; s. Jacob and Sarah (Lloyd) H.; ed. public schs., Greene Co., Tenn., Tusculum Coll., Tenn., A.B., 1860; m. Antoinette Bradley, Oct. 3, 1867. Served in Union Army as pvt., 1st lt. and capt., Jan. 26, 1863-Aug., 1865; mustered out at Nashville, Tenn. Admitted to bar, 1866; mem. Tenn. legislature from Washington Co., Tenn., 1867; atty.-gen. for 1st Jud. Circuit, Tenn., 1870-78; circuit judge, same circuit, 8 yrs.; since then in practice of law at Jonesboro, Tenn. Was pres. 1st Nat. Bank, Greenville, Tenn., several yrs. Presbyn. Republican. Address: Jonesboro, Tenn. Died Aug. 22, 1922.

HACKETT, Charles Wilson, educator; b. Chilton, Tex., June 19, 1888; s. James Franklin and Mittie Matilda (Greer) H.; B.A., U. Tex., 1909; Stanford, 1910-11; M.A., U. Cal., 1914, Ph D., 1917; m. Jean Nette Hunter, June 30, 1915; children—Frances Blackburn (Mrs. Whitmell T. Rison), Charles Wilson. Asst. in history Stanford, 1910-11, vis. prof. history, 1929-30; fellow in history U. Cal., 1914-15, teaching asst. in history, 1915-17, research fellow Native Sons of Golden West, 1917-18; adj. prof. history, U. Tex., 1918-20, adj. prof. Latin-Am. history, 1920-23, asso. prof., 1923-25, prof., 1925—, dir. Inst. Latin-Am. Studies, 1940-51; exchange prof. Nat. U. of Mexico, summer 1922, also 3 summers research work in Nat. Archives of Mexico; vis. lectr. on Latin-Am. history and economics Harvard, 1925-26. Leader of Round Table, Inst. of Politics, Williamstown, Mass., 1928; lecturer, Seminar in Mexico, 1931-33; leader Round Table, Inst. Pub. Affairs, U. Va., 1935; prof. extraordinario, Nat. U. of Mexico, summers 1943-46. U.S. del. to Pan-American Congress, City of Panama, 1926, to 3d Gen. Assembly, Pan-Am. Inst. Geog. and Hist., Lima, Peru, 1941; mem. exec. com. Nat. Com. on Latin-Am. Research, 1933. Fellow Tex. State Hist. Assn.; mem. Am. Hist. Assn., Texas Philosophical Soc. (v.p.), Phi Kappa Sigma, Phi Beta Kappa; corr. mem. Hispanic Soc. of Am.; mem. council Quivira Soc.; hon. mem. N.M. Hist. Soc. Diploma de Honor, Academia Mexicana de la Lengua; Académico Crrespondiente, Academia Nacional de Ciencias, Antonio Alzate (Mexico), 1943; corr. mem. Sociedad Mexicana de Geografia y Estadistica, 1944. Democrat. Methodist. Club: Town and Gown (Austin). Editor (for Carnegie Inst.) of Historical Documents Relating to New Mexico, Nueva Vizcaya and Approaches Thereto, to 1773 (collected by Adolph F. A. Bandelier and Fanny R. Bandelier; Spanish texts and English translations), vols. I-III, 1923-37; editor joint translator of Pichardo's Treatise on the Limits of Louisiana and Texas, vols. I-IV, 1931-46; Revolt of the Pueblo Indians of New Mexico and Otermin's Attempted Reconquest, 1680-1682, Vols. I, II, 1942. Author: The Mexican Revolution and the United States (1910-1926), 1926; also article on Mexico in 14th edit. Ency. Britannica. Mem. editorial bds. various hist. revs. and mags.; mng. editor Southwestern Hist. Quarterly, 1937-39. Traveled extensively in Central America, Mexico, West Indies and S. America. Contbr. numerous hist. articles to mags. Home: 102 W. 33d St., Austin, Tex. Died Feb. 26, 1951; buried Austin Meml. Park, Austin, Tex.

HACKETT, E(dmond) Byrne, publisher; b. Kilkenny, Ireland, June 8, 1879; s. John Byrne (M.D.) and Bridget (Doheny) H.; ed. Kilkenny and Clongowes Wood colls., Ireland, St. Frances Coll., Crawley, Sussex, Eng.; hon. M.A., Yale, 1914; m. Margaret Carson, Dec. 11, 1903; children—Florence Mary D., Frances Byrne; m. 2d, Helen E. Plechner, Jan. 1923; 1 daughter, Helen Byrne (Mrs. Giles Merritt Kelly); m. 3d, Isabel La Monte, Feb. 12, 1927. Came to America in 1899. Connected with Doubleday, Page & Co., pubs., New York, 1901-07; head pub. dept., The Banker & Taylor Co., New York, 1907-09; 1st dir. Yale Univ. Press, New Haven, Conn., 1909—. Founder and pres. Brick Row Book Shop, New York. Past chmn. State of N.J. Advisory Council of History and Archives. Clubs: Elizabethan (Yale); Quadrangle (Princeton); Old Book Table. Home: Piedmont Farm, Bound Brook, N.J. Office: 140 Cedar St., N.Y.C. Died Nov. 10, 1953.

HACKETT, Frank D., army officer; b. Minn., Aug. 11, 1889; grad. Air Corps Tech. Sch., armament course, 1929, Engr. Sch., 1932, Tactical Sch., 1937. Served as 1st lt., aviation sect. Signal Officers Res. Corps, 1917-20; commd. pilot 1st lt. A.S., U.S. Army, 1920, advanced through the grades to brig. gen., 1945; ret. from USAF, 1948. Address: Hdqrs., USAF, Washington 25. Deceased.

HACKETT, Frank S., educator; b. Albany, N.Y.; s. Barthelmew John and Elizabeth (Clark) H.; graduate Trinity Sch., N.Y.C., 1895; B.A., Columbia, 1899; Litt.D., 1946; M.A. (hon.), Williams Coll., 1927; m. Frances Dean Allen, Dec. 17, 1904 (dec.); children—R. Allen, Robert S., Daniel C., Frederick K., Caroline E., Stephen H. Tchr. dept. English, Columbia, 1900; asst. headmaster Berkeley Sch., N.Y.C., 1905-07; founder, 1907, and headmaster Riverdale Country Sch. ret. 1949; established Camp Riverdale, summer camp for boys, 1912; founder Riverdale Sch. of Music, 1918, Riverdale Sch. for Girls, 1935. Student Mil. Tng. Camp, Plattsburg, 1916; organized information Bur. for Dept. Pub. Information, Washington, 1918; speaker for Nat. Security League. Trustee Hartley House (social settlement), N.Y.C. Mem. Schoolmasters' Assn. N.Y. and Vicinity (pres. 1919-20), Country Day Sch. Assn. (pres. 1924-25, Headmasters' Assn., Pub. Edn. Assn., Camp Dirs.' Assn. Am., Phi Delta Theta. Episcopalian. Clubs: University, Columbia University, Adirondack Mountain. Contbr. to mags. Awarded univ. medal, Columbia Univ., 1931. Home: 5635 Netherland Av., N.Y.C. Deceased.*

HACKETT, Richard Nathaniel, ex-congressman; b. Wilkesboro, N.C., Dec. 4, 1866; A.B., U. N.C., 1887; admitted to bar, 1888; m. Lois Long, Jan. 31, 1907. Was chmn. Wilkes County Dem. Exec. Com.; mem. Dem. State Exec. Com., 15 yrs., now mem. central adv. com.; mayor Wilkesboro 2 terms. Dem. nominee for N.C. Ho. of Rep., 1896; asst. to sec. of state of N.C., 1901-06; mem. 60th Congress, 8th N.C. Dist. Mason. Address: Wilkesboro, N.C. Deceased.

HACKMAN, Abe, retail exec.; b. N.Y.C., Apr. 6, 1910; s. Harry and Sarah (Schwartz) H.; B.A., Trinity Coll., 1930; M.S., Rensselaer Poly. Inst., 1931, Ph.D., 1933; m. Rose Strowiss, May 12, 1934; children—Michael, Jonathan. Statistician N.Y. State Temporary Emergency Relief Adminstrn., 1934-36; with R. H. Macy & Co., Inc., N.Y.C., 1936-43, 45—, v.p., controller, 1947—. Staff UNRRA, Washington and Rome, 1943-45. Mem. Met. Controllers Assn. (former pres.), Nat. Retail Dry Goods Assn. (dir. controllers cong.), Am. Marketing Association, Am. Statistical Association, Phi Beta Kappa, Sigma Xi. Club: Town (Scarsdale). Home: 52 Lincoln Rd., Scarsdale, N.Y. Office: 151 W. 34th St., N.Y.C. 1. Died Mar. 1960.

HACKNEY, Ed(ward) T., lawyer; b. Mt. Pulaski, Ill., Nov. 1, 1870; s. Oscar J. and Lena (Clark) H.; Southwestern Coll., Winfield, Kan., 1889-93; A. B., U. Kan., 1895; m. Mabel Rogers, Nov. 14, 1900. Practiced, Wellington, Kan., 1897—; mem. firm of Hackney & Shinn; v.p. Aetna Mill & Elevator Co. Mem. Kan. Ho. of Rep. (chmn. jud. com.), 1897-99; mem. Kan. Senate, 1930-36; pres. bd. administration various state ednl. instns. of Kan. Methodist. Pres. Wellington Library Assn., Lecture Club. Mem. Sigma Nu. Clubs: Commercial, Parliamentary, Rotary. Address: Wellington, Kan. Died Apr. 16, 1953; buried Wellington, Kan.

HADDEN, Charles (Wesley), business exec.; b. Peterboro, N.Y., Aug. 26, 1883; s. Albert C. and Gertrude (Blakeman) H.; A.B., Colgate U., Hamilton, N.Y., 1906; A.M., Dickinson Coll., Carlisle, Pa., 1908; grad. work U. of Grenoble, France, 1911; m. Polly Johnson, June 29, 1927. Taught and coached athletic teams in boys schs., Carlisle, Swarthmore, Pa., and Minneapolis, 1906-16; with Minneapolis Moline Co., 1916-22, export mgr. N.Y. office, 1919-22; asst. to pres. Maxwell Motors, 1922-25; sales mgr. Velie Motors, Moline, Illinois, 1925-26; sales exec. Copeland Products, Detroit, 1926-33; with Kelvinator of Can., Ltd., London, Ont., since 1934, gen. mgr. 1935-43, pres. and dir. since 1943; pres. and dir. Refrigerator Supplies Co.; dir. Geo. White & Sons, Ltd. Mem. London C. of C. Western Fair Bd., Canadian Mfrs. Assn., Canadian Elec. Mfrs. Assn.,

Canadian Elec. Assn., Phi Beta Kappa. Mem. Anglican Ch. Clubs: London, London Hunt (Ont.). Address: 1802 N. 7th Av., Phoenix. Died Apr. 14, 1953; buried Greenwood Meml. Park Mausoleum, Phoenix.

HADEN, Russell Landram, med. educator; b. Palmyra, Va., May 22, 1888; s. Clifton James and Nicie Delima (Landram) H.; A.B., U. of Va., 1910, A.M., 1911; M.D., Johns Hopkins, 1915; m. Isabel McLeod Smith, Oct. 6, 1917; children—Russell Landram, James Coke. Resident house officer, Johns Hopkins Hosp., 1915-16; asst. resident physician, Henry Ford Hosp., Detroit, Mich., 1916-17; dir. of labs., same hosp., 1917-18, 1919-21; asso. prof. medicine, U. of Kan., 1921-23, prof. exptl. medicine, 1923-30; head of dept. medicine, Cleveland (O.) Clinic, 1930-49, ret. 1949, now consultant in medicine and research. First lt. Med. Corps, U.S. Army, asst. chief med. service, base hosp., Camp Lee, Va., 1918-19. Fellow Am. Coll. of Physicians; mem. A.M.A., Am. Assn. of Pathologists and Bacteriologists, Am. Soc. for Clin. Investigation, Am. Clin. and Climatol. Assn., Assn. Am. Physicians, Central Soc. for Clin. Research, Society for Experimental Medicine and Biology, American Society of Clinical Pathologists, Phi Beta Kappa, Sigma Xi, Theta Delta Chi, Nu Sigma Nu, Alpha Omega Alpha, Pithotomy, Rowfant and Pasteur clubs. Democrat. Methodist. Author: Clinical Laboratory Methods, 1923; Dental Infection and Systemic Disease, 1928; Principles of Hematology, 1939. Awarded gold medal by Radiol. Soc. America for contributions to dental roentgenology, 1929. Contbr. on diseases of the blood, focal infection and intestinal obstruction. Home: Brightberry Farm, Crozet, Va. Died Apr. 26, 1952; buried Monticello Meml. Park, Charlottesville, Va.

HADLEY, Chalmers, librarian; b. Indpls., Sept. 3, 1872; s. Evan and Ella (Quin) H.; B.L., Earlham Coll., 1896; N.Y. State Library Sch., Albany, 1905-06; Litt.D., U. Denver, 1914; m. Edna Florence Hendrie, 1917. Engaged in newspaper work at Phila. and Indpls., 1898-1905; sec. and state organizer Ind. Library Commn., 1906-09; dir. Ind. Summer Library Sch., 1906-09; sec., exec. officer A.L.A., 1909-11; librarian Denver Pub. Library, 1911-24; librarian Pub. Library of Cin. and Hamilton County, 1924-26, ret. 1946. Pres. League Library Commns., 1907-08, Colo. Library Commn., 1913-18, Colo. Library Assn., 1914, A.L.A., 1919; pres. Ohio Library Assn., 1925; pres. Ohio Hist. and Philos. Soc. of Ohio, 1945—; gov. Soc. of Colonial Wars in Ohio, 1932-33; mem. Am. Library Inst. Mem. State Council Defense, 1918, Colo. Bd. War Camp Community Service, 1917-18; library dir. for Colo. of U.S. Food Administration, 1917-18, U.S. Boys Working Reserve, 1918; vol. library war service, 1918-19. Contbr. to library publs. Home: Birdwhistle, Box 48A, R.R. 5, Wyoming, Ohio. Address: P.O. Box 716, Cin. 1. Died May 12, 1958.

HADLEY, Charles William, lawyer; b. West Chicago, Ill., Oct. 17, 1875; s. Philip L. and Mary E. (Roundy) H.; A.B., Wheaton Coll., 1899; LL.B., Northwestern U. Law Sch., 1902; m. Harriet R. Guild, Feb. 4, 1904. Admitted to Ill. bar, 1902, and practiced at Wheaton and Chicago, until 1906, at Wheaton since 1906; state's atty. Du Page County, Ill., 1906-20; apptd. spl. atty. gen. by Edward J. Brundage, atty. gen. of Ill., Nov. 1922, and assigned to "clean up" work in City of Rock Island, later assigned to prosecution of interest suit against Gov. Small; re-apptd. spl. atty. gen. by Oscar E. Carlstrom, atty. gen. of Ill., Jan. 1925, and assigned to the same interest suit; also apptd. spl. state's atty. McHenry County, 1928; city atty. of City of Wheaton. Member Hadley & Leren; president and dir. Warrenville State Bank. Chmn. Ill. Commerce Commn., 1929-32. Mem. Ill. State, Am. and Du Page County bar assns. Phi Alpha Delta. Republican. Methodist. Mason (K.T.). Home: 215 E. Wesley St. Office: Century Bldg., Wheaton, Ill. Died 1951.

HADLEY, Edwin Marshall; b. Peoria, Ill., Oct. 14, 1872; s. of James Marshall and Margaret (Widenham) H.; eighth in lineal descent from Edward Fitz Randolph, from Nottinghamshire to New England, 1630; ed. Ill. Wesleyan and Northwestern univs.; m. Jessie Seymour McCarthy, June 21, 1904; children—James M., Edwin M., Jr., Raymond W. An organizer, 1898, of H. W. Dudley Coffee Co. and Ceylon Planters Tea Co., of which was sec., treas. and dir. until 1906; served as chmn. bd. Chicago-Cleveland Car Roofing Co., 1906-25, and as v.p. Pioneer Cast Steel Truck Co., Sullivan Metallic Packing Co., Reliable Ry. Equipment Co. Lt. col. Ill. Nat. Guard; maj. Mil. Intelligence Res., U.S. Army; completed mil. intelligence course, Army War Coll., 1928; Ill. chmn. Civilian Aides Com., for enlistments, Army Air Forces, World War II. National president. The Paul Reveres, Inc.; member S.R., S.A.R., Order of Runnymede, Ill. Chamber Commerce, Chicago Assn. Commerce, American Coalition, American Alliance, Am. Legion, Beta Theta Pi (past pres. Chicago Alumni). Republican. Reformed Episcopalian. Mason (K.T., 32°, Shriner). Sojourners. Grange. Clubs: Adventurers, Forty, Chicago Athletic, Union League, Executives, So. Shore Country (Chicago); Army and Navy (Washington, D.C.); Green Lake Yacht; Authors' (London). Received Northwestern U. Alumni Merit Award "in recognition of worthy achievement," 1945; Distinguished Service Citation, American Legion (Boone County), 1940. Author: Credenda, 1924; The Thoughtful Hour, 1925; Sinister Shadows, 1929; T.N.T., 1931; The Rape of the Republic, 1935. Editor Revere sect. of Chicago Leader. Pub. speaker. Farmer. Home: 690 Longwood Av., Glencoe, Ill. Office: 11 S. LaSalle St., Chgo. Died Feb. 16, 1953; buried Rosehill Cemetery, Chgo.

HADLEY, Ernest Elvin, psychiatrist; b. Alton, Kan., Aug. 2, 1894; s. John McCracken and Luella (Marshall) Hadley; S.B. in Medicine, U. Kan., 1918, M.D., 1920; m. Agnes Marie Hackerott, Aug. 5, 1919; children—Alice Marie (Mrs. Watson W. Eldridge, III), Virginia Lee (Mrs. Joseph D. Jeffrey), Arianne (Mrs. C. Stanley Lowell). Rotating interne Walter Reed U.S. Gen. Hosp., 1920-21; mem. psychiatric staff St. Elizabeth's Hosp., Wash., 1921-29; pvt. practice of psychiatry, 1929—. Director Washington-Baltimore Psychoanalytic Inst., 1949-52, Washington Psychoanalytic Institute, 1952—. Trustee and sec. William Alanson White Psychiat. Found., 1933-45; chmn. publs. com. and co-editor, Psychiatry, 1938-45; sec. Washington Sch. of Psychiatry, 1936-45, dir., 1936-43, dir. emeritus, 1943, fellow, 1943-45. Served as private, Enlisted Reserve Corps, U.S. Army, 1918; chmn. central examining board for neurology and psychiatry, Selective Service System, 1941; chmn. psychiatry panel, Army Induction Board, Fort Myer, Va., 1942-44. Mem. pub. health com. Washington Bd. of Trade. Fellow Am. Coll. Physicians, Am. Psychiat. Assn., George M. Kober Med. Soc. (pres. 1932-33), A.M.A.; mem. Am. Psychoanalytic Assn. (sec. 1930-36), Washington Soc. for Mental and Nervous Diseases (pres. 1930). Washington Psychopath. Soc. (pres. 1930), Washington Psychopath. Soc. (pres. 1928), Washington Psychoanalytic Soc. (pres. 1933, 41, 53, 54—). Am. Sociol. Assn., Southern Psychiatric Assn., Am. Genetic Assn., N.Y. Acad. of Science, History of Science Soc., Phi Beta Pi. Contbr. to scientific publs. Home: 4304 Forest Lane, N.W., Washington 7. Office: 1835 Eye St. N.W., Washington 6. Died Aug. 10, 1954.

HADZSITS, George Depue, college prof.; b. Detroit, Mich., Jan. 30, 1873; s. George and Clemmy Louise (Depue) H.; A.B., U. of Mich., 1895, A.M., 1896, Ph.D., 1902; studied Am. Sch. Classical Studies at Rome, 1900-01; m. Gertrude Cronbach, Sept. 8, 1910; 1 dau., Marcia Louise. Acting asst. prof. Latin, U. of Cincinnati, 1903-05, U. of Wis., 1905-06; research fellow in classics, 1906-09; instr. Latin, 1909-11, assistant professor, 1911-23, prof., 1923-43, emeritus professor, University of Pennsylvania; visiting professor of Latin, Indiana U., 1943-44, Johns Hopkins U., 1944-46, Swarthmore Coll., 1947-48; prof. pharmaceutical Latin, Temple U., 1947-50; prof. Latin, summers, U. of Colorado, 1926, 27, 31, 32, U. of Chicago, 1928, Leland Stanford U., 1933, Indiana U., 1943; visiting prof. Am. Acad., Rome, 1929-30. Mem. Am. Philol. Assn. (president, 1945), Archaeol. Institute America, Phila. Oriental Soc., Phila. Classical Club (pres. 1916-17). Classical Assn. Atlantic States (pres. 1937-38), Phila. Soc. Promotion Liberal Studies (pres. 1919-20, 1921-23, 1925-27), Am. Assn. Univ. Profs., Vergilion Soc. (past pres.), Phi Beta Kappa, Alpha Omega, Lambda Chi Alpha, Eta Sigma Phi (hon.), Baltimore Classical Club (hon.). Sons American Revolution. Republican. Episcopalian. Mason. Author: Prolegomena to a Study of the Ethical Ideal of Plutarch, 1906; also chapter on "Roman Religion," in Religions Past and Present, 1917; Handbook of the University of Pennsylvania Chapter of Phi Beta Kappa, 1919, Lucretius and His Influence, 1935. Editor-in-chief of the "Our Debt to Greece and Rome Library" of 45 volumes, 1922—; editor of "Classical Studies in Honor of John C. Rolfe," 1931; co-editor of "The Living Language," 2 vols. (with W. L. Carr), 1933-34. Editor of Publ. Am. Philol. Assn., 1939-41. Contbr. numerous monographs and articles in classical jours. Address: 1 Snowden Rd., Bala-cynwyd, Pa. Died June 9, 1954.

HAFEY, William Joseph (hā'fē), bishop; b. Springfield, Massachusetts, March 19, 1888; s. James J. and Catherine (Mulcahy) H.; prep. edn., high school, Chicopee, Mass.; B.A., Holy Cross Coll., Worcester, Mass., 1909; student Georgetown Law Sch., 1909-10; M.A., Mt. St. Mary's Sem., Emmitsburg, Md., 1914. Ordained priest R.C. Ch., 1914; asst. pastor St. Joseph's Ch., Baltimore, Md., 1914-20; chancellor archdiocese of Baltimore, 1920-25; consecrated bishop Diocese of Raleigh, July 1, 1925; later coadjutor bishop and since Mar. 25, 1938, bishop of Scranton, Pa. Home: 315 Wyoming Av., Scranton, Pa. Died May 12, 1954.

HAFFENREFFER, Rudolf Frederick, brewing co. exec.; b. Boston, June 22, 1874; s. Rudolf Frederick and Katherine (Burkhardt) H.; student Chauncey Hall Sch., Boston; grad. Mass. Inst. Tech., 1895; student Rauscher Inst. Polytechnicum, Stuttgart, Germany, 19— to 19—; D.B.A., (hon.), Providence Coll., 1948; m. L. Maude Munroe, Jan. 29, 1902; children—Rudolf Frederick, Carl W. Chmn. bd. Narragansett Brewing Co.; treas., gen. mgr. Old Colony Brewing Co., Old Colony Products Co., Fall River, Mass.; pres. Automatic Telephone Co., Utah-Apex Mining Co., Montezuma-Apex Mining Co., Herreshoff Mfg. Co., Mt. Hope Bridge Corp.; asst. treas. Mt. Hope Farms. Founder King Philip Mus., Bristol. Dir. R.I. chpt., vice chmn. Providence Co. chpt. Nat. Found. Infantile Paralysis; dir. R.I. Heart Assn.; trustee Mus. of the Am. Indian (Heye Found.). Chmn. R.I. Water Resources Commn., Bristol Co. Water Commn., Watuppa Water Bd., Fall River, Mass., Watuppa Reservoir Commn.; mem. R.I. Port and Indsl. Commn. Trustee R.F. Haffenreffer Family Found., Narragansett Brewing Co. Found. Mem. Fall River Hist. Soc. (dir.), Bristol City Nursing Assn. (dir.), Squantum Assn., R.I., Bristol hist. socs. Elk. Clubs: Mass. Inst. Tech. (Fall River, also R.I.), Turks Head, Bristol Yacht. Home: Bristol, R.I. Office: Elmwood Station, Providence 7. Died Oct. 9, 1954; buried Lawn Point Cemetery, Providence.

HAFNER, John A., business exec.; b. Chicago, July 24, 1892; s. John A. and Caroline (Kegebein) H.; student Northwestern U.; m. Irma E. Alexander, Nov. 26, 1919; children—Jeanne, Marilyn H. Kehl. John A. With Wilson and Co., Inc., Chicago, since 1914; vice pres. since 1946. Clubs: Edgewater Golf, Lake Shore. Home: 2048 Farwell Av. Office: 4200 S. Ashland, Chgo. Died Jan. 11, 1955.

HAGAN, Edward James, clergyman; b. Belfast, No. Ireland, Apr. 6, 1879; s. Samuel and Isabella (Cameron) H.; student Royal Belfast Academical Instn., 1893-98; B.A., New Coll. Queens U., Belfast, 1901; D.D., U. Edinburgh, 1939; m. Agnes Pairman Cormack, June 2, 1908. Ordained to ministry, Ch. of Scotland, 1907; pastor Cockenzie, 1907-11, Elgin, 1911-20, Hillhead Ch., Glasgow, 1920-26, Warrender Ch., Edinburgh, 1926-51; moderator Gen. Assembly Ch. of Scotland, 1944-45. Served as chaplain, Brit. Forces, France, 1915-18. Decorated Officer Order of Brit. Empire, 1918. Mem. World Presbyn. Alliance (pres. 1948-54), Brit. Council Chs. (v.p. 1946-48). Home: 12 Bruntsfield Gardens, Edinburgh, Scotland. Died Jan. 11, 1956.

HAGAN, John Campbell, Jr., investment banker; b. Richmond, Va., July 21, 1899; s. John Campbell and Alice (Nipe) H.; grad. McGuire's U. Sch., Richmond, Va., 1916; A.B., Va. Mil. Inst., 1921; m. Eliza Tabb Mason, Oct. 25, 1924; childeren—John Campbell, III, Anthony Mason. Tchr., asst. comdt. Castle Heights Mil. Acad., Lebanon, Tenn., 1921-22; security salesman Frederick E. Nolting, Inc., Richmond, 1922-24; v.p., mgr. investment dept. Grace Securities Corp., Richmond, 1926-29; pres., dir. Mason-Hagan, Inc., Richmond, 1929—; chmn. Eastern Life & Casualty Co., Richmond; dir. Va. Tel. & Tel. Co., Charlottesville, Va., P.C. Gwaltney, Jr. & Co., Inc., Smithfield, Va., S. H. Heironimus Co., Inc., Roanoke. Dir. Richmond Boys Club. Pres. George C. Marshall Research Found., Inc., Lexington, Va.; pres. Va. Mil. Inst. Found., 1943-46, dir., 1936—; bd. visitors Va. Mil. Inst., 1946-54, pres., 1952-54; trustee Sisters of Charity of St. Joseph Acad. and Orphan Asylum, v.p., 1942—. Served with USMC, 1918; as lt. col. USAAF, World War II. Decorated Bronze Star Medal. Mem. Investment Bankers Assn. Am. (v.p., exec. com. 1954-56), Nat. Assn. Securities Dealers (dist. chmn. 1950), Richmond C. of C. (dir. 1935—, pres. 1938), Richmond German Soc., Soc. Va. Creepers, Kappa Alpha. Clubs: Commonwealth (bd. govs.), Country of Va., Downtown (Richmond); Farmington Country (Charlottesville); City Mid-Day (N.Y.C.). Home: Weyanoke Farm, Charles City, Va. Office: 1110 E. Main St., Richmond 10, Va. Died Nov. 1959.

HAGEN, Harold C. (hä'gĕn), ex-congressman; b. Crookston, Minn., Nov. 10, 1901; s. Gudbrand T. and Anna (Brovold) H.; A.B., St. Olaf Coll., Northfield, Minn., 1927; m. Audrey Melton, Nov. 22, 1928; children—Harold Melton, Andora Audrey. Newspaper reporter, 1920-23; pub. dir., 1923-28; pub. weekly newspaper, 1928-32; salesman, 1932-34. Congl. sec., 1934-42; mem. 78th to 83d Congresses, 9th Minn. Dist. (elected to 78th Congress as mem. Farmer-Labor party, 79th-83d Congresses mem. Rep. party); pub. relation work, Washington, 1955—. Awarded plaque by Congl. Secs. Club of the U.S. Congress as the outstanding Congl. sec. in 1941. Mem. Little Congress, United Comml. Travelers, Sons of Norway, Norwegian Soc. of Washington. Lutheran. Mason (Shriner), Elk, Eagle, Rotarian. Author: Congressional Handbook or Manual of Information (with W. H. Hackett), 1941. Home: 317 Lincoln Av., Crookston, Minn. Address: 1405 New House Office Bldg., Washington. Died Mar. 19, 1957; buried Oakdale Cemetery, Crookston, Minn.

HAGEN, Oskar Frank Leonard, university professor; b. Wiesbaden, Germany, Oct. 14, 1888; s. Nestor William and Ellen Marion (Owen-Snow) H.; father a citizen of U.S. and mother an English woman; student univs. of Berlin, München; Ph.D., U. of Halle, 1914; m. Thyra A. Leisner, Aug. 23, 1914 (died Oct. 1938); children—Holger Edward, Uta Thyra; m.

2d, Beatrice Bentz, April 16, 1940. Privat docent, later professor extraordinarius history of art, U. of Göttingen. 1918-25; Carl Schurz memorial prof. art history, U. of Wis., 1 semester, 1924, prof. history and criticism of art, 1925-—, also head dept., of which was organizer; curator of university art collection. Served as organizer, 1921, and chief dir. Göttingen Händel-Festivals. Has lectured widely in U.S. Mem. com. on medieval and renaissance studies, Archeol. Inst. of America; hon. fellow University of Göttingen; fellow Royal Society of Arts; member Am. Hist. Assn., Medieval Acad. of America, Wis. State Hist. Soc., Am. Assn. Univ. Profs., College Art Association of America, Phi Beta Kappa, Sigma Delta Pi Episcopalian. Clubs: University, hon. mem. Göttingen Handel Soc. Author: Correggio Apokryphen, 1915: Matthias Grünewald, 1919, 3d edit., 1923; Deutsches Sehen, 1920, 24, 33; Vincent van Gogh, 1920; Deutsche Zeichner, 1921; Art Epochs and their leaders, New York, 1927; Hans Baldung, 1927; Patterns and Principles of Spanish Art, 1934, 2d edit., 1943; The Birth of the American Tradition in Art, New York, 1940. Editor and reviser various Handel operas. Composer: Chorol Rhapsody, 1944, concerto grosso, 1945; violin sonata, 1945; string quartet, Wisconsin Summer, 1946; Carducciana for choir a capella, 1948. Home: 1620 Adams St., Madison 5, Wis. Died Oct. 4, 1957.

HAGEN, Sam (hä'gĕn), economist; b. Northwood, N.D., Sept. 2, 1891; s. Ole H. and Ingeborg (Amundson) H.; A.B., St. Olaf Coll., 1916; A.M., U. of N.D., 1925, Ph.D., 1934; post doctoral study, U. of Ia., summer 1935, U. of Wash., summer 1940; m. Beatrice M. V. Page, Oct. 19, 1917; children—Lorraine Page (Mrs. H. E. Westerberg), Beverly Jane. Grade sch. prin., Edinburg, N.D., 1916-19; supt. schs, Crystal, N.D., 1919-24, Starbuck, Minn., 1924-27, Hawley, Minn., 1927-32; grad. asst. in economics U. of N.D., 1932-34, instr., 1934-35, asst. prof. economics. 1935-38, asso. prof., 1938-40, prof. economics since 1940, acting dean of School of Commerce, 1948-50, head of department of economics since 1950. Mem. N.D. Teachers Assn., Alpha Pi Zeta, Beta Gamma Sigma. Methodist. Home: 2508 Fifth Av. N., Grand Forks, N.D. Died Apr. 21, 1952; buried Meml. Park of Grand Forks.

HAGER, George Caldwell, lawyer and ret. corp. exec.; b. Bristol, Tenn., Jan. 1, 1893; s. John Jackson II, and Maude Livingstone (Caldwell) H.; A.B., King Coll., Bristol, 1911, LL.D., 1939; LL.B., U. Tenn., 1916; m. Grace Leslie Wilson, Sept. 15, 1923. Prin. high sch., Wyndale, Va., 1911-12; head dept. Latin, High schs., Knoxville, Tenn., 1912-14; admitted to Tenn. bar, 1915, and began practice at Knoxville with Jourolman & Welcker; with Maynard & Lee, 1916-17, Ayres, Broughton & Hager 1919-20; sec., dir. Cook County Supply Co. and subsidiaries, Chgo., 1920-21; gen. atty. Consumers Co. (consolidated with Cook County Supply Co.), 1921-25, v.p., 1925-39, also sec. 1929-39; dir. Chicago Federal Savings & Loan Assn., 1933-—, pres. 1934-39. Organizer Jr. Achievement, Chgo., 1940; v.p. Latin America, Eversharp, Inc., 1940-41, v.p. of adminstrn. and export, 1941-44; also v.p. War Products Div. Enlisted as pvt. U.S. Army, advancing to sgt., 2d lt., radio and gas officer, F.A., Meuse-Argonne offensive, with Army of Occupation until May 1919; attended O.T.S., Camp Gordon, Ga., La Courtine and Saumur Arty. Schs., France; served as judge advocate with Army of Occupation; maj. F.A., later Judge Adv. Gen. Reserve until 1942. Dir. and mem. exec. com. Rotary Internat., 1933-34, 38-40, also served as chmn. or mem. numerous other coms., 1932-53; pres. Rotary Internat., 1938-39 (made ofcl. tour in 43 countries during year); pres. Constl. Protective League of Ill., 1936-38. Decorated Order of St. Sava, first class (Jugoslavia) 1938; Grand Officer, Order of the Condor de los Andes (Bolivia), 1939; Comdr. Order of El Sol del Peru, 1939; Comdr. Order of Merit (Chile), 1939; Comdr. Order of Vasco Nunez de Balboa (Panama), 1939; Officer Order of the Southern Cross (Brazil), 1941; Honor Guest of Nation Nicaragua, 1939. Mem. Heroes of 1776, Am. Legion, Sigma Alpha Epsilon. Republican. Presbyn. Mason (32°, K.T.). Clubs: Lake Shore, Rotary (pres. 1932-33) (Chgo.); Sojourners. Contbr. to mags. and trade publs. Home: 1130 Lake Shore Dr., Chgo. Died Dec. 1958; buried Bristol, Tenn.

HAGGARD, Howard Wilcox, educator, author; b. La Porte, Ind., July 19, 1891; s. William Henry and Elsie (Wilcox) H.; prep. edn., Phillips Exeter Acad.; Ph.B., Yale, 1914, M.D., 1917; m. Josephine Foley, Sept. 9, 1916; children—Howard Wilcox (dec.), William Henry, Marjorie Marie (Mrs. William F. Bigoney, Jr.). Physiologist United States Bureau Mines, 1917; capt. Chem. Warfare Service, U.S. Army, 1917-18; cons. physiologist U.S. Bur. Mines, 1919-22; instr. physiology, Med. Sch., Yale, 1919-23, asst. prof., 1923-26, asso. prof. applied physiology, Sheffield Scientific Sch., Yale, 1926-38; prof. and dir. Lab. of Applied Physiology, Yale, since 1938, director of the office of U. Development, 1948-51. Physiologist N.Y. and N.J. Tunnel Commn.; mem. 3d Resuscitation Commn. Mem. Am. Soc. of Biol. Chemists, Am. Physiol. Soc., Internat. Anæsthesia Soc., Am. Soc. Hygiene Association, Connecticut Medical Society, Connecticut Academy of Arts and Sci., Nu Sigma Nu, Phi Sigma Kappa, Sigma Psi, Aurelian Soc. (Yale). Clubs: Elizabethan, Beaumont, New Haven Yacht, Essex Yacht. Author: Are You Intelligent?, 1926; Noxious Gases and the Principles of Respiration Influencing Their Action (with Yandell Henderson), 1927; The Science of Health and Disease, 1927; What You Should Know About Health and Disease, 1928; Devils, Drugs and Doctors, 1929; Schädliche Gase, 1931; The Lame, the Halt and the Blind, 1932; Mystery, Magic and Medicine, 1933; The Doctor in History, 1934; Diet and Physical Efficiency, 1935; The Anatomy of Personality, 1935; Staying Young Beyond Your Years, 1937; Man and His Body, 1938; Alcohol Explored (with E. M. Jellinek), 1942. Editor, Quarterly Journal of Studies on Alcohol; mem. editorial bd. Personnel Journal. Contbr. numerous papers on physiological subjects. Pres. Nat. Com. for Edn. on Alcoholism. Research work on noxious gases, alcohol, physiology of industrial fatigue and effiency. Home: Plantation Key, Fla. Died Apr. 22, 1959.

HAGGE, Hans Jergen, ins. exec.; b. Andover, Ia., Oct. 20, 1886; s. Henry and Anna C. (Sieck) H.; ed. pub. schs. of Ia.; m. Helen Single, Oct. 15, 1913; children—Robert Single, Daniel Lamoreaux. With Employers Mutual Liability Ins. Co., Wausau, Wis., since 1911, president since 1931, chairman of board since 1952; president and director Insurance Finance Company since 1935; v.p. and dir. Marathon Electric Mfg. Co., Wausau since 1925; dir. First Am. State Bank, Mont.-Dakota Utilities Co., Gen. Telephone Co. of Wis. Mem. C. of C. Presbyn. Mason. Clubs: Wausau, Wausau Country; Milwaukee, Athletic (Milw.). Home: 507 McIndoe St. Office: 407 Grant St., Wausau, Wis. Died Jan. 6, 1959; buried Pine Grove Cemetery, Wausau.

HAGGERSON, Fred H., corporation exec.; born Spalding, Mich., 1884; chmn. bd. Union Carbide and Carbon Corp., Electric Furnace Products; trustee, Central Hanover Bank & Trust Co. Address: 30 E. 42d St., N.Y.C. 17. Died Oct. 14, 1952; buried Nassau Knolls Cemetery, Port Washington, L.I.

HAGGIN, (James) Ben Ali, artist; b. N.Y.C., Apr. 20, 1882; ed. Pomfret (Conn.) Sch., Thatcher Sch., Ojai, Cal., Art Students League, N.Y.C., Acad. Munich, Germany. Noted for paintings of thoroughbred horses including Twenty Grand; Porter and Bonus; designer theatrical sets Ziegfield Follies; produced setting and entertainments for balls Metropolitan Opera, 1933, 34, 35, Beaux Arts pageant, 1927-32; former instr. Munich (Germany) Acad. Home: N.Y.C. Died Sept. 1951.*

HAGSTROM, G(ustavus) Arvid, clergyman; b. Sundsvall, Sweden, Sept. 8, 1867; s. Anders Gustav and Marie Elizabeth (Hernlund) H.; student bus. sch. of Mpls. and extension courses, Des Moines (Ia.) U.; grad. Div. Sch., U. Chgo. (formerly Bapt. Union Theol. Sem.); D.D., Wake Forest (N.C.) Coll., 1914; m. Caroline Wilhelmina Anderson, June 1, 1892 (dec. Feb. 1933); 1 dau., Marion (Mrs. L. J. Melrose); m. 2d, Ebba Brundin, July 26, 1934. Licensed to preach in Mpls., 1889; pastor, Kenyon, Minn., 1890-91, Newark, Ill., 1891-93; ordained to ministry Bapt. Ch., 1892; Sunday Sch. missionary for Am. Baptist Pub. Soc. and Ill. Swedish Bapt. Sunday Sch. Union, 1893-96; pastor First Swedish Bapt. Ch., Chgo., 1896-1907 (largest ch. in Swedish branch of Bapt. denomination in U.S.); missionary sec., corr. and financial sec. Swedish Bapt. Gen. Conf. of America, and supt. missionary work in U.S. and Can., 1907-09; pastor First Swedish Ch., St. Paul, 1909-13; pres. Bethel Inst. and prof. Bethel Theol. Sem. and Jr. Coll., St. Paul, 1914-41, pres. emeritus and mem. faculty, 1941-43; pastor Emerald Av. Bapt. Ch., Chgo.; gen. and promotional sec. Swedish Bapt. Gen. Conf. of America, 1930-33, chmn. Future Policy Com.; pres. of Minn. Bapt. Conv. Editor Young People's Paper for Swedish Baptists, 1895-96, The Church and Home (Forsamlingen och Hemmet), 1896-1907, Veckobulletinen, 1909-14; dept. editor Swedish mag. Hemmets Vän, Chgo. Life mem. and pres. Am. Baptist Foreign Mission Soc.; trustee, sec., treas. North Western Bapt. Hosp.; trustee Twin City Bapt. Union, Swedish Bapt. Gen. Conf. of America; mem. Minn. Hist. Soc. (life), Scandinavian Am. Found., Soc. Advancement of Scandinavian Lang. and Lit., Swedish Hist. Soc., America, Pi Gamma Mu. Co-editor Swedish hymn books, Valda Hymner, Triumfs Sånger, Fridsröster. Author of histories 1st Swedish Bapt. Ch., Chgo., 1906, St. Paul, 1913, 47, Mpls., 1921, 46, Bethel, Mpls., 1946. 60th anniversary history of Emerald Av. Bapt. Ch.; also biography of Dr. Frank Peterson. Co-editor: Biography Dr. E. Sandell. Home: 1281 Folsom St., St. Paul 3. Died Sept. 16, 1953; buried Lakewood Cemetery, Mpls.

HAGUE, Frank (hāg), ex-mayor; b. Jersey City, Jan. 17, 1876; s. John D. and Margaret (Fagen) H.; ed. pub. schools and pvt. tutors; m. Jennie W. Warner, Apr. 15, 1903; children—Frank, Peggy Ann. Began in sheriff's office, Hudson County, N.J., later mem. Street and Water Bd. of Jersey City; elected to first Bd. of Commrs., 1913, when the city govt. was changed to commn. form; mayor of Jersey City 1917-47; now retired; mem. Dem. Nat. Com. since 1922. Home: Boulevard and Duncan Av. Address: City Hall, Jersey City, N.J. Died Jan. 1, 1956.

HAGY, Henry B., banker; b. Reading, Pa., Aug. 2, 1864; s. William and Sarah A. (Bitler) H.; grad. high sch., Reading, 1883; m. Mary E. Eby, Oct. 11, 1899. Began with Kendall Bros., 1883; with H. T. & J. V. Kendall, bankers, 1884-86; with Pa. Trust Co., 1886, treas. and trust officer, 1904-12. 2d v.p., 1912-16, v.p., 1916-21, became pres., 1921, now retired; was mem. loan com. Nat. Credit Corp. No. 2 of 3d Federal Reserve Dist. Chmn. first two Liberty Loan drives of Berks County, World War. Trustee and pres. bd. YMCA, Reading. Republican. Episcopalian (vestryman Christ Ch.). Clubs: Wyomissing, Berkshire Country, Washington Library. Home: Reading, Pa. Died June 23, 1955.

HAHN, Herman F., banker; b. Chgo., Sept. 10, 1902; s. Harry W. and Daisy (Kohn) H.; student pub. schs. Kenilworth, Ill.; m. Louise Getz, Aug. 21, 1928; children—Mary, Ann, John, Peter. Employed Home Savs. Bank, later became Cal. Bank, Los Angeles, 1920-27; securities bus., Los Angeles and Chgo., 1928-30; v.p., dir. Union Bank & Trust Co. of Los Angeles, 1930-49, exec. v.p., 1949-50. pres., 1950-—. Treas., mem. bd. trustees Cedars of Lebanon Hosp. (Los Angeles); treas., dir. Welfare Fedn. of Los Angeles; dir. United Cerebral Palsy Assn., Inc., Hollywood (Cal.) Bowl Assn. Mem. Los Angeles C. of C. (dir.), Assn. Res. City Bankers, Am. Bankers Assn., Cal. Bankers Assn., Independent Bankers Assn. of So. Cal. (past pres.), Nat. Assn. Mfrs. Home: 1021 N. Beverly Dr., Beverly Hills. Office: 760 S. Hill St., Los Angeles 54. Died 1954.

HAHN, Lew, dept. stores; b. Jersey City, N.J., June 21, 1882; s. Lewis B. and Carrie Amelia (Van Tine) H.; ed. pub. schs.; m. Ethel Winifred Hesketh, May 28, 1910; children—Douglas Hesketh, Dane Francis. Newspaper work, N.Y. and Nev.; gold and silver mining, Nev., 1906-10; retail editor Fairchild Publs., N.Y., 1911-18; mng. dir. Nat. Retail Dry Goods Assn., 1918-28; pres. and gen. mgr. Hahn Dept. Stores (merger of 27 dept. stores throughout the country), 1929-31, chmn. bd., July 1931-Sept. 1933; pres. Hahn Dept. Stores Purchasing Corpn.; formerly mem. advisory bd. N.Y. Trust Co., North Am. Inter-Insurers. Formerly treas., gen. mgr. Nat. Retail Dry Goods Assn., former pres., now pres. emeritus; mem. adv. com. Affiliated Underwriters; mem. bd. dirs. Prince Sch. of Edn. for Store Service, Boston; ex-pres., mem. Council, Borough of Glen Rock, N.J. Chmn. Nat. Retail Code Authority until Jan. 1934; mem. indsl. adv. bd. NRA, 1934-35; mem. bus. adv. and planning council U.S. Dept. of Commerce. Hon. mem. Eta Mu Pi (New York U.). Republican. Clubs: Union League (N.Y.); Ridgewood Country, Bay-Head Yacht. Writer, lectr., tchr. on getting goods from production to consumption. Author: (with Percival A. White) Merchants' Manual, 1926; Stores, Merchants and Customers, 1952. Home: 441 Hawthorne Pl. Ridgewood, N.J. Died July 26 1956; buried Paramus, N.J.

HAHNE, Ernest Herman, univ. pres.; b. Walker Kan., Oct. 20, 1890; s. Herman and Virginia (Kitchen) H.; A.B., U. of Neb., 1911, LL.B., 1913; A.M., Harvard University, 1914; Ph.D., University of Chicago, 1930; LL.D., Ripon College, 1950; m. Helen Madeleine Jess, July 2, 1917; children—Dorothy Joan, Ruth Elizabeth. Asst. in economics, U. of Neb., 1910-13; admitted to Neb. bar, 1913; asst. in sociology, U. of Chicago, 1915-16; chmn. Dept. of Economics and Sociology, Dak. Wesleyan U., Mitchell, S.D., 1916-18; instr. in economics, Northwestern U., 1919-22, asst. prof., 1924-29, asso. prof. 1929-35, prof. 1935-46; also asst. dean College Liberal Arts, 1925-30, dir. summer session 1930-39; engaged in research in spl. assessments, U. of Chicago, 1922-24; now pres. Miami Univ., Oxford, Ohio; dir. Cincinnati br., Cleveland Fed. Reserve Bank, 1948. Administration member of national code authority under N.R.A. for cotton cloth glove, academic costume, and household ice refrigerator industries, special assessment and federal tax consultant; mem. research staff, Rep. National Committee, 1944. Member Headquarters Company, 354th Regiment, 89th Division, and personnel officer 7th (Dev.) Batt., Camp Dix, N.J., for alien enemies, World War I. Pres. Assn. of Summer Sessions Dirs., 1934. Mem. Am. Econ. Assn., Farm Econ. Assn., Am. Assn. of Univ. Profs., Nat. Tax Assn., Am. Legion, Phi Delta Phi, Beta Gamma Sigma, Delta Sigma Rho, Phi Beta Kappa, Acacia. Methodist. Mason. Clubs: University (Cincinnati); Kiwanis. Contbr. to encyclopedias and author of articles on finance. Home: Lewis Pl. Office: Miami Univ., Oxford, O. Died Nov. 25, 1952.

HAIG, Robert Murray (hāg), prof. emeritus polit. economy; b. Columbus, O., Oct. 3, 1887; s. James and Mary Caroline (Murray) H.; A.B., Ohio Wesleyan Univ., 1908, LL.D., 1925; A.M., University of Illinois, 1909; Ph.D., Columbia, 1914; LL.D., Rollins College, 1944; m. Gertrude M. Hopping, June 20, 1912; children—James, Robert Murray. With Columbia University, 1912-—, prof. bus. adminstrn., 1916-31, became McVickar prof. polit. economy 1931, now prof. emeritus, chmn. dept. of economics, 1940-43. Investigator for Com. on Taxation, N.Y.C., 1914-15, for Survey Com. of State Affairs, State of Colo., 1916; spl. service Fed. Treasury, 1917; spl. adviser to minister of municipalities, Province of Saskatchewan, Can., 1918; adviser to provincial treas., Alberta, 1918, to Taxation Bd., B.C., 1918-19; as mem. Com. on War Finance of Am. Economic Assn. sent to Eng. to study spl. British War taxes, 1919-20; counsel to N.M. Spl. Revenue Commn., 1920-21; sec. and chief of staff Spl. Joint Com. on Taxation and Retrenchment of Legislature State of N.Y., 1921-22; mem. Ednl. Finance Inquiry Commn., 1922-25; financial adviser to Govt. of Puerto Rico, 1924-26, 1945-46; dir. econ. survey, Regl. Plan of New York, 1923-27; adviser, Gov.'s Commn. on Sch. Finance, N.Y., 1926; sent to France by Columbia U. to study post-war finances, 1926-27; adviser to Mayor's Com. Plan and Survey, 1927-28; adviser and dir. research, Cal. Tax Commn., 1928-29; principal taxation economist, Forestry Service, U.S. Dept. Agr., 1929-30; chmn. St. Lawrence Power Development Commn. of N.Y. State, 1930-31; exec. sec. and dir. research, N.Y. State Commn. for Revision of Tax Laws, 1930-32; mem. Mayor's Com. on Taxation, 1930-32; pres. Nat. Tax Assn., 1931-32; sent to Hungary by Carnegie Endowment for Internat. Peace to study economic conditions, 1931; mem. bd. of consultants, Nat. Survey of Sch. Finance, U.S. Office of Edn., 1931; consultant on taxation, U.S. Treasury, 1933, 1934; cons. Nat. Resources Com., 1935; dir. research, N.Y. State Commn. on State Aid, 1935-36; sent to Australia by Columbia U. to study tax adminstrn., 1937; adviser N.Y. State Budget, 1934-43; mem. Joint Legislative Economy Commn., N.Y. State, 1942-43. Mem. Am. Econ. Assn., Am. Assn. Univ. Profs., Acad. Polit. Sci. Nat. Tax Assn., L'Institut Internat. de Finances Publiques (Paris), Internat. Assn. Pub. Finance and Fiscal Law (The Hague), Delta Tau Delta, Phi Beta Kappa, Beta Gamma Sigma; fellow Am. Acad. Arts and Scis.; trustee Acad. Polit. Science, 1940—. Methodist. Clubs: Century, Faculty. Author: A History of the General Property Tax in Illinois, 1914; The Exemption of Improvements from Taxation in Canada and the U.S., 1915; Some Probable Effects of the Exemption of Improvements from Taxation in the City of N.Y., 1915; The Taxation of Excess Profits in Great Britain (with others), 1920; The Federal Income Tax (with others), 1921; The Financing of Public Education in the State of New York (with G. D. Strayer), 1923; Economic Factors in Metropolitan Growth and Arrangement (with R. C. McCrea), 1927; The Finances and Financial Adminstration of New York City (with H. L. McBain and L. Rogers), 1928; The Public Finances of Post-War France (with others), 1929; The Sales Tax in the American States (with Carl Shoup), 1934; also numerous reports, articles, etc. Home: 400 W. 119th St., N.Y.C. 27. Died June 9, 1953.

HAIGHT, George Ives, lawyer; b. Christiana Twp., Dane County, Wis., Mar. 26, 1878; s. Stephen and Ettie (Ives) H.; ed. dist. sch.; high schs., Cambridge and Ft. Atkinson, Wis.; B.L., U. Wis., 1899; LL.B., Northwestern U., 1902; M.A., U. of Wis., 1928; LL.D., 1947; Northwestern U., 1940; m. Edith N. Adcock, June 6, 1906 (died 1941); children—Valerie Elizabeth (Mrs. Edward A. Haight), Daniel; m. 2d, Kathleen M. McKitrick in 1942. Admitted to Illinois bar, 1902, since practiced in Chgo.; pres. Wis. Alumni Research Found., 1925—. Spl. master in Cal.-Ariz. dispute over water rights on Colo. River, U.S. Supreme Ct., 1954—. Mem. Delta Chi. Republican. Episcopalian. Mason (chpt. K.T., Scottish Rite, Shrine). Clubs: Union League, Chicago, Arts, Chicago Yacht, Law, Executives, U.W., Wisconsin Society, Indiana Society (Chgo.). Home: 1000 Lake Shore Blvd., Evanston, Ill. Office: 209 S. La Salle St., Chgo. 4. Died Sept. 30, 1955.

HAINES, Frank David, jurist; b. Colchester, Conn., Jan. 16, 1866; s. David and Amanda (Taylor) H., prep. edn., Bacon Acad., Colchester; LL.B., Yale, 1893; M.A. (hon.), Wesleyan U., Conn., 1914, LL.D., 1927; m. Nellie E. Burke, 1887; children—Elmer B., Warren (dec.). With Jackson & Co., bankers, Middletown, 1883-90; admitted to Conn. bar, 1893; served as pros. agt. Middlesex County; exec. sec. Gov. Coffin, 1895-96; corp. counsel City of Middletown, asso. judge City Court, and pres. Bd. of Edn.; state's atty. Middlesex County, 1904-18; mem. bd. to revise Conn. Statutes, 1915-17; judge Superior Court of Conn., 1918-25; justice Conn. Supreme Court of Errors, 1925-36; retired by age limiation, Jan. 16, 1936, now state referee for life. Mem. Am., Conn. bar assns., Yale Alumni Assn., Middlesex County Hist. Soc. Republican. Episcopalian. Mason. Clubs: Graduate (New Haven); University (Hartford). Home: 337 Main St., Portland, Conn. Office: Middletown, Conn. Died Jan. 20, 1959; buried Trinity Cemetery, Portland.

HAINES, Thomas Harvey, psychologist, psychiatrist; b. Moorestown, N.J., Nov. 4, 1871; s. Zebedee and Anna Philips (Harvey) Haines; A.B., Haverford (Pa.) Coll., 1896; Ph.D., Harvard, 1901; M.D., Ohio State U., 1912; spl. studies in neurology and psychiatry, Munich, Zurich and London, 1912-13; m. Helen Manley Hague, Aug. 15, 1912. Asst. prof. philosophy, prof. psychology Ohio State U., 1901-15. First asst. phys., Boston Psychopathic Hosp., 1913-14, also prof. psychology Smith Coll. (part time); clin. dir. Ohio Bur. Juvenile Research, 1914-17; prof. medicine (nervous and mental diseases) Ohio State U., 1915-20. Fied cons. and dir. mental health surveys for Nat. Com. for Mental Hygiene in Ky., Ala., Miss., La., Mo., Md., Ariz., N.D., 1917-22; dir. div. on mental deficiency Nat. Com. for Mental Hygiene, 1922-25. Psycho. examiner Camp Dix and Camp Stuart, 1917-18; mem. com. on psychol. exam. of recruits, Nat. Research Council, 1917; psychiatrist at N.Y. Hosp. Out-Patient Dept., 1932-42. Fellow A.A.A.S., Am. Psychiatric Assn. (life mem.); mem. Med. Soc., State N.Y., Med. Soc. County N.Y., Phi Rho Sigma, Sigma Xi, Phi Beta Kappa. Mem. Religious Soc. of Friends. Author: Mental Measurement of the Blind, 1915; reports of mental hygiene studies in many states and bills offered to legislatures to improve administration in mental health fields; some fifty other titles in psychol. and med. jours. Home: 58 Tuxedo Rd., Montclair, N.J. Died Mar. 2, 1951; buried West Grove, Pa.

HAIRE, Andrew J., publisher; b. Brooklyn, N.Y., Sept. 20, 1881; s. Andrew J. and Maria G. (Owen) H.; M.E. in Elec. Engring., Cornell U., 1905; m. Alice O'Sullivan, Nov. 18, 1909; children—Andrew J., Jr., Thomas Brett, Mary Eileen McCann, Margaret Alice Mitchell, John (dec.). Chmn. board Haire Pub. Co. since 1909; past pres. Associated Business Publs., Nations Notion Assn.; dir. Mag. Pubs. Assn.; trustee Emigrant Industrial Savings Bank; publisher 12 specialized business papers: Home Furnishings, Toys and Novelties, Linens and Domestics, Luggage and Leather Goods, Crockery and Glass Journal, Corset and Underwear Rev.; Notion and Novelty Rev., Infants' and Children's Rev. Giftwares, Housewares Review, Handbags and Accessories. Republican. Roman Catholic. Clubs: Advertising (pres.), University, Catholic, Rotary (N.Y. City, past pres.); Westchester (N.Y.) Country. Friendly Sons of St. Patrick, Knights of Malta, Indian Creek (Fla.); Surf (Fla.). Home: 1120 Fifth Av., N.Y.C. 28. Office: 111 Fourth Av., N.Y.C. 3. Died Sept. 24, 1956.

HAKANSSON, Erik Gösta (hä'kän-s'n), naval officer; b. Sweden, Sept. 4, 1886; came to U.S., 1909, naturalized, 1915; M.D., U. of Ill., 1915; grad. Naval Med. Sch., Washington, 1917, Gorgas Memorial Laboratory, 1937; m. Dorothy Elizabeth Dorset, June 20, 1942. Interne Cook County (Ill.) Hosp., 1915-17; commd. lt. Med. Corps, U.S. Navy, 1917, advanced through the grades to capt., 1941; comdg. Naval Med. Research Inst., Bethesda, Md., 1943-48; ret. Mem. A.M.A., A.A.A.S., Am. Assn. Tropical Medicine, Acad. Tropical Medicine, Phi Chi, Alpha Omega Alpha. Club: Army-Navy Country (Washington). Home: R. 10, Richmond, Va. Office: Naval Medical Research Institute, Bethesda, Md. Died June 19, 1950; buried Arlington Nat. Cemetery.

HAKE, Harry, architect; b. Cincinnati, O., July 8, 1871; s. Charles Frederick and Caroline (Lukens) H.; student Ohio Mechanics Inst., Cincinnati, 1889-92, Cincinnati Art Acad., 1890-92; Sc.D., Lincoln Memorial U., 1928; m. Minnie Spreen, Dec. 2, 1899; children—Dorothea Caroline, Harry. Began as draftsman with L. F. Plimpton, Cincinnati, 1889; in practice as architect since 1897; mem. firm Harry Hake & Harry Hake, Jr., since 1946. Prin. bldgs.: Masonic Temple; Telephone bldgs.; group of bldgs., U. of Cincinnati; Queen City Club Bldg.; Central Vocational High Sch.; bldgs. for The Western & Southern Life Insurance Company (all in Cincinnati); Ohio State Office Bldg., Columbus, O. Fellow American Inst. Architects. Awarded 4 prizes for bldgs. in Cincinnati, Cincinnati Chapter Am. Inst. Architects. Received L'atelier Award for Excellency in Design, archtl. dept., U. of Cincinnati. Home: 2552 Madison Rd. Office: 2400 Gilbert Av., Cin. Died Sept. 13, 1955.

HALDEMAN-JULIUS, E(manuel), editor, author, pub.; b. Phila., Pa., July 30, 1889; s. David and Elizabeth (Zamost) Julius; prefixed Haldeman to surname after marriage to Marcet Haldeman, writer, actress, June 1, 1916 (died Feb. 13, 1941); children—Alice, Henry. Pres. Haldeman-Julius Pub. Co., pubs. Little Blue Books, Big Blue Books, The Key to Culture, The American Freeman, Agnostic. Author: The Color of Life, 1920; Dust (novel; with wife), 1921; The Art of Reading, 1922; Miscellaneous Essays, 1922; Literary Essays, 1923; Studies in Rationalism, 1924; Culture and Its Modern Aspects, 1925; Iconoclastic Literary Reactions, 1925; Today's Persons and Personalities, 1926; An Agnostic Looks at Life, 1926; Free Speech and Free Thought in America, 1926; Myths and Myth-Makers, 1927; Snapshots of Modern Life, 1927; Sane and Sensible Views of Life, 1927; The First Hundred Million, 1928; The Outline of Bunk, 1929; The Big American Parade, 1929; Violence (novel, with wife). Editor, with an introduction, The Story of Religious Controversy, 1929; Is Hitler a Maniac?, 1939; A Book of Problems, Puzzles and Brainteasers, 1939; Questions and Answers (26 vols.), 1942 (treating of internat. affairs, science, philosophy, religion, literature, politics and govt.); "How To" series (with H. G. Wells and Bertrand Russell), 1943, "The Self-Educator" (with Joseph McCabe), 1943; 2 vols. of short stories, with wife; biographies of Hitler, Stalin, Churchill, Chiang Kai-Shek, Roosevelt, 1945; Anthology, Notable Short Stories; The World's Great Isms, 1945; How to Become a Writer, 1946; What Can a Freeman Believe, 1945; My First 25 Years (autobiography), 1949; My Second 25 Years (autobiography), 1950; novels: Everybody, 1950; The Hawk and the Sparrow, 1950. Editor: 27 vols. of Americana, 1946. Editor The Critic and Guide, 1948. Home: Girard, Kan. Died July 31, 1951; buried Cedarville, Ill.

HALDEN, Alfred A(ugustus), mfg. exec.; b. N.Y. City, Jan. 31, 1895; s. Isidor and Rose (Miller) H.; B.S., Columbia, 1915, Chem.E., 1917; m. Dorothy Cohn, May 6, 1920; 1 dau., Babara Jean. Engr., The Barrett Co., 1917; with Nat. Starch Products, Inc., N.Y. City, since 1919, dir. and sec., 1930, exec. v.p. since 1942; dir. and sec. Nat. Adhesives (Can.), Ltd., since 1947. Served as staff sgt., U.S. Army, 1917-19. Mem. Am. Chem. Soc. Clubs: Chemists (N.Y. City); Beach Point (Mamaroneck, N.Y.). Home: 784 Park Av., N.Y.C. 21; also 15 Colonial Rd., Scarsdale, N.Y. Office: 750 3d Av., N.Y.C. 17. Died Mar. 19, 1956.

HALDEN, Leon Gilbert (häl'dĕn), professor of govt.; b. Austin, Tex., Dec. 1, 1893; s. Harry and Katherine (Seekatz) H.; A.B., U. of Tex., 1923, A.M., 1924, grad. work, 1928-30; grad. work, U. of Calif., 1925-26; Carnegie fellow, U. of Mich., 1937; m. Sallie Fellman, June 11, 1922; 1 son, Leon Gilbert. Prin., Tex. State Sch. for the Blind, 1915-16; county supt. of pub. instrn., Travis County, Tex., 1916-25; instr., U. of Calif., 1925-26; dean, Daniel Baker Coll., Brownwood, Tex., 1926-28; instr., U. of Tex., 1928-30; asso. prof., Sam Houston State Coll., 1930-34; became asso. prof., U. of Houston (Tex.), 1934, now prof. Served as capt., Specialist Reserve, Allied Control Commn.; with allied military government, North Africa and Italy. Awarded Mediterranean Theatre medal with two battle stars. Lecturer, War Dept., Bur. of Pub. Relations, Fed. Forum Project, Bur. of Edn. (Washington, D.C.), City Charter Commn. (Austin, Tex.). Awarded Rockefeller scholarship. Mem. Carnegie Commn. for Study of Post War Problems; member Texas Efficiency and Economy Commission. Fellow Acad. of Internat. Law; mem. Nat. Acad. Polit. and Social Sci., Nat. Municipal League, Nat. Polit. Science Assn., Nat. Com., Defense of America, Pi Gamma Mu, Pi Sigma Alpha, Phi Delta Kappa. Mason, Shrine, Acacia. Club: Kiwanis (Houston, Tex.). Author: Current Problems in Government, 1935; Ethiopian Crisis, 1936; Japan—Colossus of the Far East, 1937; Currency Problem, 1938; Red Fascism, 1947; Behind the Scenes in American-British Relations, 1951. Contbr. McCalls Mag., Polit. Sci. Quarterly, Dallas News, Houston Post. Home: 1801 Rosedale St., Houston. Died July 26, 1954.

HALE, Chandler, ex-3d asst. sec. of state; b. Washington, Mar. 2, 1873; s. Eugene and Mary Douglas (Chandler) H.; m. Rachel Cameron, Sept. 28, 1897. Asst. sec. Am. delegation to Internat. Bimetallic Conf., Brussels, 1892; sec. Am. Embassy at Rome, 1897; sec. Am. Legation and Embassy at Vienna, 1901-5; sec. Am. delegation to 2d Peace Conf., The Hague, 1907; 3d asst. sec. of state, U.S., 1909-13; Republican. Home: Ellsworth, Me. Died May 1951.

HALE, Florence, educator; b. Athol, Mass.; d. Henry and Anna (Perry) Hale; grad. State Normal Sch., Fitchburg, Mass., 1903; post-grad. work State Normal Sch., Hyannis, Mass., Columbia, Harvard univs.; L.H.D., Colby Coll., 1932. Tchr. high sch., Leominster, Mass., 1903-04; dir. training, Aroostook State Normal Sch., Presque Isle, Me., 1905-16; Me. state dir. rural edn., 1916-32. Mem. bd. trustees Westbrook Junior Coll., Portland, Me. Life mem. N.E.A. (pres. 1931-32; mem. bd. trustees); mem. Me. State Teachers' Assn.; Nat. Council Administrative Women in Edn. (dir.), Good Teeth Council for Children (dir.); charter mem. National Motion Picture Council Am. Republican. Unitarian. Lectr. gen. edn. for N.E.A. also radio broadcaster for same. Editor in chief The Grade Teacher. Home: Hale Rd., Darien, Conn. Died Dec. 2, 1959; buried Highland Cemetery, Athol, Mass.

HALE, Hugh Ellmaker, cons. engr.; b. Minomen, Minn.; s. William Wilberforce and Ann Graham (Patterson) H.; prep. edn. Selwyn Hall, Reading, Pa., Bethlehem (Pa.) Prep. Sch.; C.E., Lehigh U., 1897; m. Marianna Buckner Clark, June 27, 1904. Asst. engr. Pa. R.R., Phila., 1896-98, Altoona, Pa., 1898-99, asst. supr. signals, Jersey City, 1899-1901, supr. signals, Camden, N.J., 1901; div. engr. B.&O. R.R., Phila., 1902, supt., Butler, Pa., 1903-05, engr. maintenance of way, Balt., 1905-08; engr. of design, Mo.Pac. R.R., St. Louis, 1908-10, prin. asst. engr., 1910, engr. maintenance of way, Little Rock, Ark., 1911-14; engr. Eastern group, Pres.' Conf. Com., Fed. Valuation of R.R.'s in U.S., 1914-26, vice chmn. 1926-31; sr. mem. H. E. Hale & Co., cons. engrs., 1931-36; investment dept. Equitable Life Assurance Soc. of U.S., 1936-45; cons. engr.,

1945—. Mem. Am. Soc. C.E., Am. Ry. Engring. Assn., Soc. Am. Mil. Engrs., Sigma Phi. Republican. Episcopalian. Mason. Contbr. to tech. papers, etc. Home: 1165 5th Av. Office: 1165 Fifth Av., N.Y.C. 29. Deceased.

HALE, Lincoln Bell, govt. ofcl.; b. Ansonia, Conn., Aug. 23, 1899; s. Bernard Orlando and Elizabeth (Gale) H.; B.D., Yale U., 1927, M.A., 1933, Ph.D., 1936; Doctor of Laws, Vincennes University, 1950; married Sallie Elizabeth Watton, June 23, 1928. Draughtsman and machinist Farrel Foundry & Machine Co., Ansonia, 1916-21; asst. secretary Ansonia Y.M.C.A., 1921-23; ednl. sec. New Haven (Conn.) Y.M.C.A., 1923-27; asst. dir. Thessalonica Agrl. and Industrial Inst., Salonica, Greece, 1927-30; ordained ministry Congl. Ch., 1927; pastor Oxford (Conn.) Congl. Ch., 1930-34; field rep. for Conn. Survey Com. on the transition from sch. to coll. planned and directed study, Yale U., 1933-36; dir. personnel and placement services, Carleton Coll., 1936-39; dean and registrar, Evansville Coll., 1939-40, acting president, May 1940-June 1941, pres., 1941-54; director U.S. Operations Mission to Israel, 1954—. Served as private, 420th Telegraph Batt., A.E.F., July 1918-April 1919. Dir. Evansville Philharmonic Orchestra; pres. Evansville War Chest, 1943-44; pres. Indiana Association of Church Related and Independent Colleges, 1944-45. Mem. American Coll. Personnel Assn., Am. Legion, Veterans of Foreign Wars, Pi Gamma Mu. Conglist. Club: Rotary (Evansville, hon. mem. Tel Aviv, Israel). Author: Transition from High School to College, 1933; Encouraging Vital Religion in Our Schools, 1935; From School to College (with Hugh Hartshorne), 1939. Home: 42 Fifth St., Ansonia, Conn. Office: care Am. Embassy, Tel Aviv, Israel. Died Jan. 1958.

HALE, Oscar, judge; b. Wapello, Ia., Feb. 27, 1867; s. John and Clara (Rhodes) H.; student Valparaiso (Ind.), 1883-86 (B.S.), Law Sch. of State U. of Ia., 1893-94; m. Caroline Sillick, Feb. 20, 1899; 1 son, John. Tchr., 1887-93; admitted to bar, 1893, practiced in Wapello, Ia., 1894-1913; judge Dist. Ct., Ia., 1913-39; justice Supreme Ct., Ia., 1939—. Mem. Am. and Ia. bar assns. Republican. Mason (K.T.), Elk. Address: Wapello, Ia. Died Dec. 9, 1950.

HALE, Ralph Tracy, publisher; b. Newburyport, Mass., Dec. 29, 1880; s. Edward Augustine and Elizabeth Pike (Akerman) H.; A.B., Harvard, 1902; m. Margaret Stone Greenleaf, May 23, 1905; 1 son, Albert Greenleaf. Asst. in English, Harvard, 1902-03; editorial staff Ladies' Home Journal, 1903-04; editor Bobbs-Merrill Co., Indpls., 1904-07, Small-Maynard Co., Boston, 1907-20; treas. and mng. dir. The Medici Soc. of America, pubs., 1920-29 (combined with Hale, Cushman & Flint, Inc.; pres. Hale, Cushman & Flint, Inc., Publishers, 1927-42; withdrew from Hale, Cushman & Flint, Inc., buying its book publishing business which continued as Ralph T. Hale & Co., 1942-47; sold, 1947, to Charles T. Branford Co., Boston, to engage in special research and literary work; dir. The Talisman Press, pubs., 1947. Mem. Hist. Soc. of Old Newbury, Winchester Hist. Soc. Unitarian. Clubs: Boston Authors', Lincoln Group (Boston); Winchester Coffee, Monday (Winchester); Dalton (Newburyport). Author: (with Captain Robert A. Bartlett) The Last Voyage of the Karluk, 1916; (with Frederick W. Colburn) revision and completion of Philip L. Hale's "Vermeer", 1937. Address: 44 Lloyd St., Winchester, Mass. Died Sept. 1951.

HALE, Reuben Brooks, merchant; b. Elmira, N.Y., June 11, 1869; s. Marshal and Prudence (Dyckman) H.; B.S., U. of the Pacific, San José, Cal., 1890; m. Leonetia May Johnston, Jan. 1, 1895. Pres., dir. Hale Bros. Realty Co., Panama Realty Co., San Francisco; dir. Hale Bros. Stores, Inc., with stores at San Francisco, Oakland, San José and Sacramento, Cal.; v.p., dir. F. A. B. Mfg. Co., Oakland, Cal.; dir. Fullerton Oil Co., Broadway Dept. Store, Inc. (Los Angeles). Trustee San Francisco Pub. Library, 1906-41. Mem. Relief Com. of 50 and Reconstruction Com. of 40 after disaster at San Francisco, 1906; originator, one of organizers, and v.p. Panama-Pacific Internat. Expn., 1915; an organizer and ex-pres. Cal. State C. of C. pres. commn. extraordinary to Europe apptd. by Pres. Taft to visit foreign countries in behalf of Panama-Pacific Internat. Expn. Chmn. exec. com. Region 12, Boy Scouts of Am. for 4 years, mem. Nat. Exec. Bd., Boy Scouts of Am. Dir. San Francisco Chpt. Am. Nat. Red Cross, 1925-43. Republican. Mason (K.T., Shriner). Clubs: Pacific Union, Bohemian, Commercial, Commonwealth, Athens Ahtletic (Oakland); California (Los Angeles). Home: La Mirada, Hill Av., Saratoga, Cal. Office: 867 Market St., San Francisco 3. Died Nov. 3, 1950.

HALE, William Green, prof. law.; b. Hillsboro, Ore., Oct. 30, 1881; s. Greenville Nathaniel and Emma Nettie (Vite) H.; B.S., Pacific U., Forest Grove, Ore., 1903; LL.B., Harvard, 1906; m. Jessie McConnell, Nov. 2, 1907; 1 daughter, Genevieve; married second Ethel McConnell Hicks, 1949. Admitted to Ore. bar, 1906; practiced in office of Gammans & Malarkey 1 yr., as mem. Hale & McConnell, 2 yrs.; instr. law, U. of Ill., 1909-11; reëntered law practice at Portland, 1911; prof. law, U. of Ill., 1912-20; dean of Law Sch. and prof. law, U. of Ore., 1920-27; dean of Law Sch. and prof. of law, Washington Univ. Sch. of Law, 1927-30; dean and prof. law U. of Sou. Calif. Law Sch., 1930-47, prof. since 1947; prof. of law Hastings College of Law since 1949; prof. law Stanford, summer 1921, U. of Calif., summer 1923, U. of Mich., summer 1929, U. of Chicago, summer 1934, Stanford, summer 1937. Appointed commr. on Uniform State Laws for State of Mo., 1928. Asso. editor Ore. Law Rev., 1920-27. Mem. and vice chmn. Code Commn. State of Calif., 1931-41 and since 1947. Adviser Am. Law Inst. on Evidence Code since 1939. Mem. compliance commn., div. priorities, War Production Bd. since 1942. Member Oregon and California bar associations Theta Chi, Order of the Coif; president of Ill. br. Am. Inst. Criminal Law and Criminology, 1917-18. Republican. Author: Law of the Press, 1923, 3d ed., 1948. Editor in chief Ill. Law Bull., 1917-20. Home: 2431 Bryant, Palo Alto, Cal. Died June 26, 1952.

HALE, William J., chemist; b. Ada, O., January 5, 1876; s. James Thomas and Emma Elizabeth (Ogle) H.; A.B., A.M., Miami U., 1897, LL.D., 1937; A.B., Harvard Univ., 1898, A.M., 1899, Ph.D., 1902; traveling fellow in chemistry, Technische Hochschule, Berlin, and U. of Göttingen, 1902-03; m. Helen, d. Herbert H. Dow, Midland, Mich., Feb. 7, 1917 (died Oct. 16, 1918); 1 dau., Ruth Elizabeth (Mrs. Wiley T. Buchanan, Jr.). Research assistant, University of Chicago, 1 term, 1903; instructor, chemistry, 1904-08, asst. prof., 1908-15; asso. prof., 1915-19, U. of Mich.; dir. organic chem. research, Dow Chem. Co., Midland, Mich., 1919-1934, research consultant since 1934; president Verdurin Co., Detroit and Midland, Mich., since 1951. Chairman division of chemistry and chemical technology, Nat. Research Council, Washington, D.C., 1925-27; vis. prof. chemurgy, Conn. Coll., 1936-39. Fellow A.A.A.S., London Chem. Soc.; mem. American Chem. Soc., Société Suisse de Chimie, Société Chimique de France, Deutsche Chemische Gesellschaft, Phi Beta Kappa, Sigma Xi, Phi Lambda Upsilon, Alpha Chi Sigma. Author: A Laboratory Outline of General Chemistry (with Alexander Smith), 1907; The Calculations of General Chemistry, 1909; A Laboratory Manual of General Chemistry, 1917, 2d edit. with Wm. G. Smeaton, 1930; Chemistry Triumphant, 1932; The Farm Chemurgic, 1934; Prosperity Beckons, 1936; Farmward March, 1939; Farmer Victorious, 1949; Chemivision, 1952; papers organic chem., addresses chemurgic development for industrialization agr. Patentee of new process for mfr. of phenol, aniline, acetic acid, butadiene and their derivatives. Clubs; Detroit Club; Chemists (New York); Cosmos (Washington). Home: Midland, Mich. Office: The Dow Chemical Co., Midland, Mich. Died Aug. 8, 1955.

HALEY, William J., petroleum exec.; b. Phila., Aug. 27, 1891; s. William J. and Sally B. (Duffy) H.; M.E., U. Pa., 1914; post grad. work U.S. Naval Acad., 1918; m. Lucy Mansur Stirling, June 14, 1921; children—Katharine (Mrs. Frank M. Donahue), Louis Stirling, Ann Stirling. With Standard Oil Co. (N.J.), N.Y.C., or its affiliates both here and abroad, 1914—, pres. Esso Export Corp. until 1954, ret., dir.; pres., dir. United Petroleum Secs. Corp., Mediterranean Standard Oil Co.; cons. Commonwealth Oil Co., Puerto Rico, Moeller Steamship Co., Copenhagen, Denmark. Chmn. Caribbean Area Petroleum Com., World War II. Served with U.S. Navy, World War I. Mem. Alpha Chi Rho, Tau Beta Pi. Address: Kirby Lane, Rye, N.Y. Died Sept. 25, 1957.

HALIFAX, Earl of (Edward Frederick Lindley Wood), diplomat; b. England, Apr. 16, 1881; s. Charles Lindley (2d Viscount) and Lady Agnes Elizabeth (Courtenay) H.; student Eton Coll., M.A., Christ Ch., Oxford U.; fellow All Souls Coll., Oxford U., 1903; hon. LL.D., Leeds, 1923, Cambridge, St. Andrews, Sheffield, 1931; Toronto, 1932, Dublin, Liverpool, London, 1934; hon. D.C.L., Oxford, 1931, U. South, Sewanee, Tenn., 1942, Durham, 1935; hon. LL.D., Columbia, Yale, Harvard, 1941, Nashotah House, Syracuse, Princeton, 1942, Laval, State Coll. of Idaho, Coll. of Puget Sound, 1943; hon. Dr. Canon Law, Divinity Sch., Phila., 1942; hon. Dr. Humanities, Ohio Wesleyan U., 1942; m. Lady Dorothy Onslow, 1909; children—Charles Ingram Courtenay, Francis Hugh Peter Courtenay (killed in action, 1942), Richard Frederick, Anne Dorothy (Countess of Feversham). Asst. sec. Ministry of Nat. Service, 1917-19; British del. League of Nations Assembly, 1923; under sec. of state for colonies, 1921; pres. Bd. Edn., 1922-24; minister of agr., 1924-25; viceroy and gov. gen. of India, 1926-31; pres. Bd. of Edn., 1932-35; sec. of state for war, 1935; Lord Privy Seal, 1935-37; leader of House of Lords, 1935-38; Lord Pres. of Council, 1937-38; sec. of state for foreign affairs, 1938-40; ambassador to U.S., 1940-46. Served as lt. col. Yorkshire Dragoons, 1915-17; hon. col. since 1935. Chancellor U. Oxford, U. Sheffield, Order of Garter. Decorated Knight of Garter, Knight Grand Comdr. of Star of India, Knight Grand Cross St. Michael and St. George (grand master), Knight Grand Comdr. Indian Empire, Territorial Decoration. Mem. Ch. of England (Episcopalian). Home: Garrowby, York, Eng. Died Dec. 23, 1959; buried Kirby Underdale, York, Eng.

HALL, A(lbert) Neely, author; b. Chicago, Ill., May 31, 1883; s. Olin H. and Sarah (Neely) H.; grad. Lewis Inst., Chicago, 1901; Chicago Sch. of Architecture, 1902; m. Bertha E. Cassidy; 1 dau., Ruth Marion (Mrs. Robert J. Smith). Mem. nat. council Boy Scouts of America, also counselor in handicraft. Republican. Member Reformed Episcopalian Church. Author: The Boy Craftsman, 1905; Handicraft for Handy Boys, 1911, revised edition, 1933; The Handy Boy, 1913, revised edition, 1935; Wonder Hill, 1914; Homemade Toys for Girls and Boys, 1915; Handicraft for Handy Girls (with Dorothy Perkins), 1916; Carpentry and Mechanics for Boys, 1918; Homemade Games and Game Equipment, 1922, revised edit., 1935; Church and Sunday School Handicraft for Boys, 1922; Home Handicraft for Boys, 1922, revised edit., 1935; Outdoor Boy Craftsmen, 1925; Making Things With Tools, 1928; Big Book of Boys' Hobbies, 1929; Craft Work-and-Play Things, 1936; Outdoor Handicraft for Boys, 1938; Home Handicraft for Girls (with dau. Ruth Hall), 1941; 12 Craft Pattern Packets, 1950. Producer of Craft Patterns, a syndicate pattern feature supplied to leading newspapers of U.S., known as A. Neely Hall Productions. Home: 177 E. St. Charles Rd. Studio: N.E. corner North Av. and Route 83, Elmhurst, Ill. Died Feb. 20, 1959; buried Mount Emblem Cemetery, Elmhurst.

HALL, Alton Parker, business exec.; b. Kingston, N.Y., Mar. 9, 1900; s. Rev. Charles Mercer and Bertha (Parker) H.; student Kent Sch., 1912-18; A.B., Princeton, 1922; m. Emmeline Grace, June 19, 1926; children—Penelope, Alton Parker; m. 2d, Carol Sue Leguore, Mar. 1, 1941. With mfg. div. Bethlehem Steel Co., 1922-25, sales dept., 1925-42, asst. sales mgr., 1935-42; gen. sales mgr. Am. Chain & Cable Co., N.Y., 1944-48, v.p. and gen. mgr. sales since 1948. Served with S.A.T.C. and R.O.T.C., Princeton, 1918-22; 2d lt., F.A.O.R.C., 1922-26. Mem. Am. Iron and Steel Inst., Navy League of U.S., N.E. Iron and Hardware Assn., Eastern Car Foreman's Assn., Automobile Old Timers, St. Andrew's Soc. of N.Y. State. Clubs: Mohawk (Schenectady); New York Railroad, Sales Executives, Eastern Hardware Golf Assn., University, Princeton (New York); Bridgeport, Brooklawn Country, University (Bridgeport); Rockland Country (Sparkhill, N.Y.). Home: 22 E. 36th St., N.Y. City 16. Office: 230 Park Av., N.Y.C. 17. Died Aug. 31, 1951.

HALL, Charles Philip, ret. army officer; b. Sardis, Miss., Dec. 12, 1886; s. James Gatlin and Isabel Thornton H.; student Jefferson Mil. Coll., Natchez, 1900-04, U. of Miss., 1905-07; B.S., U.S. Mil. Acad., 1911; grad. Advanced Course, Inf. Sch., 1924; distinguished grad. Command and Gen. Staff Sch., 1925; grad. Army War Coll., 1930; m. Isabel Durand Mayor, Oct. 20, 1920; 1 dau., Gail Thornton. Commnd. 2d lt., U.S. Army, 1911; advanced through the grades to lt. gen., 1945. Served in U.S. Army in U.S. and Philippines; with 2d Div. in France and Germany in World War I; with 3d Div., Fort Lewis, Wash., 1941; comdg., gen. 93d Inf. Div., 1942; comdg. XI corps, S.W. Pacific, 1942 until ret.; service in New Guinea and Luzon. Decorated D.S.M. with oak leaf cluster, 1945; D.S.C., silver star with three oak leaves, Bronze Star Medal, Purple Heart, Legion of Honor, Croix de Guerre, Victory medal with 5 clasps. Mem. Phi Delta Theta. Club: Army and Navy (Washington). Died Jan. 26, 1953; buried Fort Sam Houston Nat. Cemetery, San Antonio.‡

HALL, Damon Everett, lawyer; b. West Dennis, Mass., Dec. 6, 1875; s. Almon E. (clergyman) and Caroline (Beard) H.; A.B., Williams Coll., 1897; LL.B. cum laude, Boston U. Law Sch., 1899; hon. LL.D., Williams Coll., 1940, Boston U., 1940; m. Isabel Leighton, Oct. 1, 1902; children—Isabel Kingsbury (Mrs. Arthur C. Bliss), Barbara Brightman (Mrs. George W. Stedman, Jr.), Ruth Leighton (Mrs. Stephen H. Sampson). Admitted to Mass. bar, 1899; asso. Hurlburt, Jones & Cabot, 1899, later becoming trail counsel for various st. ry. cos.; sr. mem. Hurlburt, Jones, Hall & Bickford, ret. 1949; counsel for B.&M. R.R., N.E. Power Co., Boston Mutual Life Co. and various individuals and corps. Served asst. atty. gen., Commonwealth of Mass., in legislative investigation Boston Police Dept., 1930; spl. counsel for Commonwealth water supply project for City of Boston, 1933-35. Mem. Salvation Army Adv. Bd., 1935—. Vice pres., dir. Boston Mutual Life Ins. Co. Trustee Williams Coll., 1931-56, Cushing Acad., Ashburnham, Mass., 1949—. Moderator Town of Belmont, 1940-41. Chmn. Tyng Scholarship Com. Williams College. Mem. Am., Mass. State, Essex County, Middlesex County, Boston bar assns. (pres. Bar Assn. City of Boston 1937-39). Independent Republican. Conglist. Mason. Clubs: Algonquin (Boston); Williams (N.Y.C.). Home: 204 Prospect St., Belmont, Mass. Office: Exchange Bldg., Boston. Died Dec. 18, 1953; buried Mt. Auburn Cemetery, Cambridge, Mass.

HALL, David McKee, Jr., congressman; b. Sylva, N.C., May 16, 1918; s. David M. and Edith (Moore)

H.; certificate of law, U. N.C., 1947, LL.B., 1948; m. Sarah McCollum, July 14, 1944; children—Sarah Anne, Edith Allison, Hannah McKee. Self-employed, gasoline, automobile, retail bus.; admitted to N.C. bar, 1947; with Hall & Thornburg, Sylvia, 1948—; atty. Town of Dillsboro, 1948—, Jackson County, 1952—; mem. 86th Congress, 12th Dist. N.C., mem. sci. and astronautics com., mem. Nat. Rivers and Harbors Congress. Sec.-treas. Jackson County Savs. and Loan Assn., 1953—; pres. Jackson County Industries, Inc., 1953—. Vice chmn. Jackson County Democratic Exec. Com., 1948-54; treas. Jackson County Indsl. Com., 1951—; mem. N.C. Senate, 1955; mem. N.C. bd. water commrs., 1956—; sr. Dem. liaison officer N.C. Young Dem. Clubs, 1956—. Regional fund chmn. A.R.C., 1956-58; dir. Carolinas Community Services, Jackson County United Fund, Inc., mem. Morehead scholarship com. U. N.C. Mem. Am., N.C. bar assns., Phi Delta Phi. Methodist (trustee). Elk, Rotarian. Home: Sylva, N.C. Office: Old House Office Bldg., Washington 25. Died Jan. 29, 1960.

HALL, Edwin S., petroleum exec.; b. Esso Standard Oil Co. and its parent co. Standard Oil Co. (N.J.), 1920-50, became gen. counsel Esso Standard Oil Co., 1927, head law dept., 1933, dir., 1934, v.p., 1940-49, pres., 1948-50, ret.; pres. Esso Standard Oil Co. (Pa.) until it became part of Esso Co. Home: Lake Mohawk, N.J. Office: 26 Broadway, N.Y.C. Died Aug. 13, 1953.*

HALL, Elmer Edwards, marine corps officer (ret.); b. Rocky Bar, Ida., Apr. 20, 1890; s. Joseph N. and Louise (Lovell) H.; E.M., U. of Ore.; student Ore. State Coll., 1 yr.; m. Emma B. Wootton, Feb. 14, 1918; 1 dau., Nancy Louise (wife of Comdr. E. J. Pawka). Began as miner in Eastern Ore.; commd. 2d lt., USMC, 1917, and advanced through grades to brig. gen., 1942; ret., 1946. Mem. Sigma Nu. Home: 6203 Waverly Av., La Jolla, Cal. Died Sept. 1958.*

HALL, Ford Poulton, prof. of govt. science; b. St. Paul, Minn., Nov. 21, 1898; s. Edward Collingwood and Jennie (Howard) H.; A.B., Carleton Coll., 1921; B.A., Oxford U., Eng., 1924, M.A., 1930, B.C.L., 1925; LL.M., U. of Minn., 1927; m. Frances Nimerfro, 1929. Instr. U. of Minn., 1925-27; asso. prof. of polit. science, Ind. U., 1927-36, prof. and head department of government since 1936, dean of the faculties, 1943-44, dean of Div. of Adult Edn., Pub. Services since 1946. Spl. representative U.S. Employment Service, 1934-38; mem. state advisory council, Ind. State Employment Service, 1935-39; chmn. joint com. on personnel adminstrn. for Ind. Dept. Pub. Welfare and Unemployment Compensation Div., 1936; chmn. county dept. Pub. Welfare, 1935-43. Mem. Indiana Merit System Council, 1940-41; acting dir. of Ind. Bureau of Personnel, 1941; tech. advisor to Ind. Merit System Assn., 1940-50; chairman division on social adminstrn., Ind. State Conf. on Social Work, 1944; chairman division on government changes, Ind. War History Com., 1943-44. Served in U.S. Army, 1918. Rhodes scholar to Oxford, 1922-25. Mem. Am. Polit. Science Assn., Am. Assn. Univ. Profs., Am. Soc. for Pub. Adminstrn. Phi Beta Kappa. Democrat. Author: Government and Business, 1934. rev., 1950; Concept of a Business Affected with a Public Interest, 1940; State Control of Business Through Certificates of Convenience and Necessity, 1947; Nat. Govt.: Law and Practice (with others). Contbr. articles to law jours. Home: 804 S. Woodlawn, Bloomington, Ind. Died Sept. 21, 1951.

HALL, Frank Hillman, lawyer; b. Washington, D.C., July 13, 1870; s. Hillman Allyn and Jennie (Carpenter) H.; A.B., Princeton, 1892; student George Washington U. Law Sch., 1892-93, N.Y. Law Sch., 1893-95; m. Alice Scudder, Apr. 22, 1897; children—Alice May (Mrs. Donald W. Sinclair), Frank Hillman; m. 2d, Frances B. Venino, of New York, Feb. 19, 1921. Admitted to N.J. bar, 1895, and began practice at Jersey City; mem. Dickinson, Thompson & McMaster, 1895-98, Thompson & Hall, 1898-1906; admitted to N.Y. bar, 1907; mem. Steele, Otis & Hall, 1906-10; practiced alone, N.Y. City, 1910—; vice-pres. Corn Products Refining Company; dir. Geo. W. Rogers Construction Corp. Republican. Clubs: Princeton, Whitehall (N.Y.C.); Englewood, Knickerbocker Country (Englewood). Home: 256 Lydecker St., Englewood, N.J. Office: 17 Battery Pl., N.Y.C. Died Nov. 2, 1957.

HALL, Gene W., engr.; b. Bklyn., Nov. 25, 1898; s. George Fowler and Lucy (Holmes) H.; m. Marguerite Mars, June 27, 1923; 1 dau., Jean Lois. With Parsons, Brinckerhoff, Hall & MacDonald, N.Y.C., 1919—, mem. firm, 1932—, pres. subsidiary, Parklap Nat. Builders, 1936—; pres. Housing Co. of Dundalk, Linden Housing Corp., Liberty Park Housing Corp.; pres. Cornwall Manor, Inc., 142 Maiden Lane Corp. Commd. brig. gen., U.S. Army, 1945. Elk. Home: 168 West Blvd., Bay Park, N.Y. Office: 51 Broadway, N.Y.C. 6. Died Nov. 30, 1951.

HALL, James Glenn, banker; b. Weston, Mo., Mar. 6, 1902; s. Charles Decatur and Laura Brown (Williams) H.; B.S., U. Mo., 1923; m. Helen Frances Day, Oct. 27, 1931; children—Glenice Kathryn, Helen Frances, Clara Virginia. Bookkeeper, Bank of Weston (Mo.), 1918-19, cashier, 1923-26; asst. nat. bank examiner 10th Federal Reserve Dist., 1926-28; clerk Central Nat. Bank and Trust Co., Tulsa, 1928-29; credit mgr. Exchange Nat. Bank, Tulsa, 1929-32; pres. Security Nat. Bank, Arkansas City, Kan., 1932-37; v.p. Home Nat. Bank, Arkansas City, Kan., 1937-38; exec. v.p. Nat. Bank of Topeka (Kan.), 1938-42; exec. v.p. First Nat. Bank, Birmingham, Ala., 1942-53, pres., 1953—. Mem. Phi Gamma Delta. Club: Mountain Brook Country (Birmingham). Home: 1401 Wellington Road. Office: First National Bank, Birmingham, Ala. Died June 13, 1953.

HALL, James Norman, author; b. Colfax, Ia., Apr. 22, 1887; s. Arthur Wright and Ella Annette (Young) H.; Ph.B., Grinnell (Ia.) Coll., 1910; married Sarah Winchester; children—Conrad L., Nancy E. (Mrs. N. G. Rutgers, Jr.). Author: Kitchener's Mob, 1916; High Adventure, 1918; Fairy Lands of the South Seas (with C. Nordhoff), 1921; On the Stream of Travel, 1926; Mid-Pacific, 1928; Falcons of France (with C. Nordhoff), 1929; Flying with Chaucer, 1930; Mother Goose Land, 1930; Mutiny on the Bounty (with C. Nordhoff), 1933; Men Against the Sea (with same), 1934; Pitcairn's Island (with same), 1934; The Tale of a Shipwreck, 1935; The Hurricane (with C. Nordhoff), 1936; The Dark River (with C. Nordhoff), 1938; The Friends, 1939; Out of Gas (with C. Nordhoff), 1939; Oh, Millerville! (under pseudonym Fern Gravel), 1940; Doctor Dogbody's Leg, 1940; Botany Bay (with C. Nordhoff), 1941; Men Without Country (with C. Nordhoff), 1942; Under a Thatched Roof, 1942; Lost Island, 1944; The High Barbaree (with C. Nordhoff), 1945; A Word for his Sponsor, 1949; The Far Lands, 1950; The Forgotten One and Other South Sea Narratives, 1951; Memoirs, 1952. Home: Papeete, Tahiti, Society Islands. Died July 6, 1951; buried Arue, Tahiti.

HALL, Leland, author; b. Malden, Mass., July 20, 1883; s. Osborn Boylston and Lydia Abbott (Lord) H.; A.B., Harvard, 1905; A.M., U. Wis., 1912. Tchr. music, history, U. Wis., 1910-12; lectr. Columbia, 1913-17. Harvard and Radfliffe 1920-22; prof. music, Smith Coll., 1930-52, prof. emeritus, 1952—; editor Art of Music, 1914-17. With A.R.C. in France, 1918. Author: Sinister House, 1919; Timbuctoo, 1927; Salah and His American, 1934; They Seldom Speak, 1936; Listener's Music, 1937. Contbr. to various publs. Home: Northampton, Mass. Died Feb. 8, 1957; buried Forest Dale Cemetery, Malden, Mass.

HALL, Louis Harrison, lawyer; b. Naugatuck, Conn., June 5, 1875; s. Billeous Cook and Adelaide (Smith) H.; grad. Wilbraham Acad., 1893; B.S., Amherst Coll., 1897; LL.B., Columbia, 1900; m. Georgiana Coyle, Sept. 7, 1905; children—Virginia (Mrs. Paul Webb), Louis Harrison, Jr., Adelaide (Mrs. David C. McIntosh, Jr.). Admitted to N.Y. bar, 1899, Conn. bar, 1907; with firm Putney, Twombly, Hall & Skidmore, N.Y.C., predecessor firms, 1900—, mem. firm, 1908—; asso. judge Town Ct., New Canaan, Conn., 1939; v.p., dir. Internat. Salt Co., Scranton, Pa.; dir., gen. counsel Botany Mills, Inc., Passaic, N.J., Bishop, McCormick & Bishop, N.Y.C., J. F. Douglas and Co., N.Y.C. Mem. Am., N.Y. State bar assns., Assn. of Bar City of N.Y., Psi Upsilon. Republican. Conglist. Clubs: Amherst, Lawyers, Union League (N.Y.); Norwalk (Conn.); Yacht. Home: S. Main St. and Woodland Rd., New Canaan, Conn. Office: 165 Broadway, N.Y.C. 6. Died Nov. 17, 1949; buried Lakeview Cemetery, New Canaan, Conn.

HALL, Percival, coll. pres. emeritus; b. Georgetown, D.C., Sept. 16, 1872; s. Asaph and Chloe A. (Stickney) H.; A.B., Harvard, 1892; M.A., Gallaudet College, 1893, Columbian (now George Washington) Univ., 1898; Litt.D., George Washington Univ., 1914; L.H.D., Gallaudet College, 1935; m. Carolyn Clarke, June 12, 1895; m. 2d, Ethel Zoe Taylor, June 20, 1900; children (by second marriage)—Percival, Marion Ethel, Jonathan. Instr. School for the Deaf, Washington Heights, New York, 1893-95; instr. and prof. mathematics, 1895-1910, pres., 1910-45, pres. emeritus, 1945—, Gallaudet College. Unitarian. Mem. Delta Upsilon. Clubs: Harvard, Cosmos, Rotary, Palaver. Home: 9 Kendall Green N.E., Washington 2. Died Nov. 7, 1953; buried Cedar Hill Cemetery, Washington.

HALL, Philo, ex-congressman; b. at Wilton, Minn., Dec. 31, 1865; s. Philo and Mary E. (Green) H.; ed. in pub. and pvt. schs., Waseca, Minn., Bapt. Coll., Sioux Falls, S.D.; studied law under Judge J. O. Andrews, Brookings, S.D., and admitted to bar, 1887; m. Mary A. Cooke, Apr. 30, 1890. Pros. atty. Brookings Co., 1893-97; mayor Brookings, 1895; mem. S.D. Senate, 1901-03; atty. gen. S.D., 1903-07; mem. 60th Congress (1907-09), S.D.-at-large; sr. mem. Hall, Roddle & Purdy, Aug. 1, 1908—. Mem. State Bar Assn. of S.D. Republican. Address: Brookings, S.D. Died Oct. 9, 1938.

HALL, Ray Ovid, economist-statistician; b. Stephentown, N.Y., Aug. 9, 1891; s. Wyatt Emerson and Jennie (Shaw) Hall; ed. comml. coll., Northampton, Mass., U. of Lausanne, Switzerland; A.M., Columbia, 1914, Ph.D., 1922; m. Dorothy Murphy Whalen, Feb. 8, 1939; step-children—Dorothy Geraldine, Sally Ann; 1 son, Stephen Goodspeed (dec.). Instr. comml. subjects Robert Coll., Constantinople, Turkey, 1909-12; lectr. on econ., indsl. history Cooper Union Inst., N.Y.C., 1912-14; dir. Peking (China) Sch. Commerce and Finance, 1914-17; instr. accounting Alexander Hamilton Inst. N.Y., 1917-19; regional economist on Near East, Dept. of State, Washington, 1919-21; sec. Econ. Liaison Com., prof. of foreign trade, Am. U., 1919-21; asst. chief Eastern European div., Bur. of Foreign and Domestic Commerce, Washington, 1921-22; comml. attaché, Athens and Constantinople, 1922-26; sr. econ. analyst, U.S. Dept. of Commerce, Washington, 1926-31; free-lance writer, lectr. 1931-33; chief statistician Indian br. Civilian Conservation Corps, later chief economist Indian Land Unit, Nat. Resource Bd., Washington, 1933-34; chief div. of internat. accounts, Nat. Indsl. Conf. Bd., N.Y. 1934-36; dist. auditor of Civilian Conservation Corps, Indian reservations, Mont., 1936-38; statistical asst., Office of Indian Affairs, Washington, 1938-40; economist, monetary research div., U.S. Treasury Dept.; sr. economist Office of Price Adminstrn., 1942-46; SCAP, Tokyo, 1946; chmn. regional rev. bd., 1946-47; adv. staff Office Internat. Trade, 1948—. Mem. Acad. Polit. and Social Sci. Author: Chapters and Documents on Chinese Nat. Banking, 1920; International Transactions of the United States, 1936; Tabular Presentation, 1943; Science of International Payments, 1945; also many reports and surveys. Contbr. many articles to financial publs., etc. Address: 1763 Columbia Rd., Washington. Died Nov. 19, 1952.

HALL, Sharlot Mabridth, author; b. Prosser Creek, Kan., Oct. 27, 1870; d. James Knox Polk and Adeline Susannah (Boblett) H.; high sch., Prescott, Ariz., Cumnock Sch. of Expression, Los Angeles; B.A. (hon.), U. of Ariz., 1921. Has traveled extensively over unsettled regions of desert and mountains in Southwest, studying Indians in their home environment; practical experience in mining, stock-raising, farming, etc.; student of Southwestern history and collector relics for hist. and archaeol. purposes. Asso. editor Out West (magazine), 1906-07. Arizona historian (appointive office created by act of legislature), 1909-12. Republican presdl. elector, 1924. Curator Pioneers' Mus., Prescott. Author: Cactus and Pine (verse), 1910. Home: 112 Capitol St., Prescott, Ariz. Died Apr. 9, 1943.

HALL, Sidney Bartlett, state supt. schs.; b. Great Bridge, Va., Feb. 5, 1895; s. Martin Wesley and Laura Virginia (Curling) H.; B.A., Coll. of William and Mary, 1918; M.A., U. Va., 1924; Ed.D., Harvard, 1926; m. Stella Reynolds, July 26, 1917; children—Stella Louise, Sidney Bartlett. Tchr. rural sch., Norfolk County, Va., 1913-16; asst. prin. high sch., Wise County, Va., 1916-18; prin. Western Br. High Sch., Norfolk County, 1918-19; supervising prin. elementary schs., Portsmouth, Va., 1919-21; prin. high sch., Danville, Va., 1921-24; supr. high schs. Va. Dept. Edn., 1924-25, 26-28; prof. secondary edn. George Peabody Coll. for Teachers, 1928-31; supt. pub. instrn., Va., 1931—. Mem. bd. visitors U. Va., Coll. William and Mary, Va. Poly. Inst., Va. Mil. Inst. Mem. N.E.A., also Dept. Superintendence, Dept. Adult Edn. and Dept. Secondary Prins. of same, Va. Edn. Assn., Phi Beta Kappa, Pi Kappa Alpha, Kappa Delta Pi, Pi Gamma Mu, Phi Delta Kappa. Democrat. Mem. Disciples of Christ Ch. Contbr. to Va. Jour. of Edn., The School Review, Jour. Ednl. Research, etc. Home: 4536 W. Seminary Av. Office: State Bd. of Edn., Richmond, Va. Died Aug. 1946.

HALL, Thomas, retired secretary of state for North Dakota; born at Cliff Mine, Michigan, June 6, 1869; son of Richard and Ellen (Peters) H.; student Concordia Coll.; m. Anna M. Grafenstein, Sept. 1, 1897; children—Richard G., Lucille (Mrs. James K. Blunt), Ellen (Mrs. Henry A. Hornthal), Edna (Mrs. Adolph Rumreich). Began as newspaper reporter, later shorthand reporter; sec. Bd. R.R. Commrs., Bismarck, N.D., 1909-13; sec. of state for N.D., 1913-24, 43-55, ret.; mem. U.S. Congress, 2d N.D. Dist., 1924-33; rancher. Served as mem. Co. B, N.D.N.G. Mason (Shriner), Elk. Republican. Methodist. Home: 600 W. Broadway, Bismarck, N.D. Died Dec. 4, 1958; buried Fairview Cemetery, Bismarck, N.D.

HALL, Walter Perley, lawyer; b. Manchester, N.H., May 9, 1867; s. James Perley and Catherine (Willey) H.; grad. Worcester High Sch., 1885; student Brown U., 1885-88, LL.D., 1928; Harvard Law Sch., 1888-90; m. Anna Bigelow Davis, Dec. 4, 1893. Admitted to Mass. bar, 1891; town solicitor, Clinton; city solicitor, Fitchburg; asst. dist. atty., Middle Dist., Mass., 1905; 1st asst. atty.-gen., Mass., 1906-07; chmn. Mass. R.R. Commn., 1907-11; justice Superior Ct. of Mass., 1911-22, became chief justice, 1922. Formerly capt. Mass. Vol. Militia. Mem. Rep. State Com., 1898; presdl. elector, 1904. Unitarian. Club: St. Botolph (Boston). Home: Fitchburg, Mass. Died 1942.*

HALL, Willard Merrill, labor relations cons.; b. Whipple Barracks, Ariz., May 16, 1896; s. William Richardson and Mary Hepburn (Hough) H.; grad. U.S. Mil. Acad., 1917; m. Mildred E. Sidwell, Apr. 12, 1927; children—Ruth Carroll, William Richardson, Richard Merrill. Vice chmn. management com., dir. Creole Petroleum Corp., N.Y. City, 1946-50; now cons. Internat. Labor Relations. Served as capt., U.S. Army, 1918, maj., 1943-44. Mem. Am. Inst. Mining and Metall. Engrs. Home: 581 Sylvan Dr., Winter Park, Fla. Died Apr. 9, 1953.

HALL, Wilmer Lee, librarian; b. Ruther Glen, Va., July 20, 1885; s. Judson Bunyan and Sarah Jane (Jennings) H.; A.B., Randolph-Macon Coll., Ashland, Va., 1906, LL.D., 1942; A.M., U. Chgo., 1911, postgrad., 1915-16; m. Eugenia Eleanor Close, Oct. 30, 1920. Head cataloger Va. State Library, 1912-13, acting head dept. of archives and history, 1914, and of reference div., 1915; sub-librarian N.Y. State Library, Albany, 1916-20; asst. state librarian Va. State Library, 1920-34, state librarian, 1934-46, head publs. div., 1947-56, 1956, ret. Mem. A.L.A. (chmn. catalog sect. 1926-27), Va. Library Assn. (pres. 1936-37), Nat. Assn. State Libraries (pres. 1936-37), Bibliog. Soc. America, Va. Hist. Soc., Sons of Confederate Vets., Phi Beta Kappa. Democrat. Episcopalian. Author of various bulls., among them: Handbook of Virginia State Library, 1921; Bibliography of Taxation in Virginia since 1910, 1925; Check-List of Virginia State Publications (5 vols.), 1927-34; A Bibliography of Virginia, Part IV, 1932. Editor: Notes on Southside Virginia (by Walter A. Watson), 1928; Executive Journals of the Council of Colonial Virginia, Vol. 5, 1945; Vestry Book of the Upper Parish, Nansemond County, Va., 1743-93; Journal of the Senate of Va., Oct. Session, 1792. Journal of the Senate of Virginia, November Session, 1794, 1951; journals of the Council of the State of Virginia, Vol. 3, 1952. Contbr. to mags. Home: 206 S. Mulberry St., Richmond, Va. Died Jan. 25, 1957.

HALLE, Samuel H., merchant; b. Cleveland, Ohio, 1868. Chmn. of bd. and dir. Halle Bros. Co., Cleveland. Home: 2163 Harcourt Drive, Cleveland Heights. Office: 1228 Euclid Av., Cleve. 15. Died Aug. 11, 1954.

HALLETT, Herbert K., banker; b. Oakland, Me., Sept. 18, 1867; s. Julius F. and Mehitable (Kimball) H.; student pub. schs.; m. Grace E. Farr, Dec. 20, 1892; children—Dorothy, Barbara. Began in banking business at Oakland, 1886; was cashier Littleton (N.H.) Nat. Bank; pres. Atlantic Nat. Bank, Boston, 1904-12; became pres. Fourth-Atlantic Nat. Bank, 1912; now chmn. bd. Atlantic Nat. Bank; chmn. dirs. Atlantic Corp. of Boston; dir. local bd. Am. Surety Co. of New York; dir. Clinton Market Co., Parker-Young Co., Security Safe Deposit Co., Warren Steam Pump Co., Waldorf System, Inc. Mem. Fed. Adv. Council, 1930, 31. Mem. Boston Clearing House Assn. (clearing house com.), Mass., Boston C.'s of C., Am. Bankers Assn. Home: 156 Highland St., West Newton, Mass. Office: 10 Post Office Sq., Boston. Died 1950.

HALLETT, Robert Leroy, engr.; b. Estes Park, Colo., July 13, 1881; s. William Leroy and Elvena Ada (Sessions) H.; E.M., Colo. Sch. of Mines, 1905; m. Phebe Louise James, June 10, 1911 (died 1933); 1 dau., Frances (Mrs. Arthur A. Denton, Jr.); m. 2d, Ann Elizabeth Beyer, Oct. 24, 1942. Chemist, Selby Smelting & Lead Co., Selby, Calif., 1905-08; mill supt., Midas Gold Mining Co., Knob, Calif., 1908-09; chemist and engr., Consolidated Arizona Smelting Co., Humboldt, Ariz., 1909-11; chemist and engr., Nat. Lead Co., New York, 1911-48, chief chemist, 1938-48; cons. mining and indsl. engr., New York, since 1949. Chmn. sub-com. on tin, Army and Navy Munitions Bd., 1939; adviser on tin, Council of Nat. Defense, Washington, D.C., 1940-41. Member Mining and Metall. Soc. of Am. (pres. 1947), Am. Inst. of Mining and Metall. Engrs., Am. Chem. Soc., Am. Soc. Testing Materials. Republican. Protestant Episcopalian. Club: Mining of New York (pres. 1949-50). Author: chapter on Paint Industry, Warshow's Representative Industries in the United States, 1928; section on Lead, Ency. Britannica, 1929 and 1947; sect. on Tin Industry, Metals Handbook, 1939; chapter on Tin, Liddell's Handbook of Nonferrous Metallurgy, 1945. Examined and investigated mining properties particularly those containing lead, tin, titanium and antimony for Nat. Lead Co. Made many mine examinations in the United States from 1911-46, in Brazil, 1924, Spain, 1926 and 1929, Norway, 1927, Germany, 1926, 1928 and 1929, Canada, 1927. Home: 49 E. 19th St., Brooklyn 26, N.Y. Office: 132 Nassau St., N.Y.C. 7. Died May 17, 1952.

HALLEY, Rudolph, lawyer; b. Harrison, N.Y., June 19, 1913; s. Henry and Pauline (Shipman) H.; A.B., Columbia University, 1932, LL.B., 1934; married Grace Ralston (divorced); children—Marian, Henry; m. 2d, Janice Brosh, 1951. Admitted to New York State bar, 1935, practiced as law secretary United States District Judge William Bondy, 1934-37; asst. U.S. atty. Southern Dist. of N.Y., N.Y. City, 1937-42; asst. counsel U.S. Senate War Investigating Com. (Truman com.), 1942-44, Com. on Oil and Fuel Shortages, 1943-44; chief counsel U.S. Senate War Investigating Com., 1944-45, Spl. Com. Investigating Organized Crime in Interstate Commerce, 1950, Crime Investigating Com. (Kefauver Com.), 1950-51; mem. law firm Fulton, Walter & Halley, N.Y. City and Washington, 1950—. Mem. D.C. bar, 1945—, U.S. Supreme Ct. bar, 1944—. Elected pres. N.Y.C. Council on Liberal ticket, 1951. Mem. N.Y. Bd. of Estimate, Health Ins. Bd.; bd. trustees N.Y. City Employees Retirement System, Mus. City of N.Y., N.Y. Pub. Library, Queens Boro Pub. Library. Mem. Am., N.Y. City bar assns. Kent Scholar, Columbia Law School, 1932, scholarship, Columbia, 1933-34. Editor Columbia Law Review, 1932-34. Address: 30 Rockefeller Plaza, N.Y.C. 20. Died Nov. 19, 1956.

HALLGREN, Mauritz Alfred, editor; b. Chicago, Ill., June 18, 1899; s. Alfred Aaron and Maria Katherine (Carlson) H.; ed. pub. schs., Chicago, and U. of Chicago; married to Elisabeth Steele, on Octover 12, 1921; children—Katherine (Mrs. Frank Sheridan), Elisabeth Lynn. Began as reporter Chicago Daily News, 1920; telegraph editor South Bend (Ind.) Tribune, 1920-22; asst. news editor Cincinnati Times-Star, 1922; editor for Associated Press, at Chicago, 1922-25; state dept. corr., Washington, D.C., for Internat. News Service and United Press, 1926-28; European corr., Berlin, for United Press, 1928-30; asso. editor The Nation, New York, 1930-34; asso. editor Baltimore Sun, 1934-38. Served in U.S. Marine Corps, in France, June 1918-Sept. 1919. Author: Seeds of Revolt, 1933; The Gay Reformer, 1935; The Tragic Fallacy, 1937; All About Stamps, 1940; Landscape of Freedom, 1941. Contbr. to mags. Home: Taylor's Island, Md. Died. Nov. 10, 1956; buried, Cemetery of Old Trinity Church, Church Creek, Md.

HALLIBURTON, Erle Palmer, business exec.; b. Ripley, Tenn., Sept. 22, 1892; s. Edwin Graves and Lou (Cothran) H.; student pub. schs. of Tenn.; m. Vida C. Taber, Sept. 11, 1915 (dec.); children—Erle Palmer, Zola Catherine (Mrs. John Rex), Vida Jessie (Mrs. Arthur Wayne), Ruth Lou (Mrs. William M. Hall), David John. Oil field worker, Cal., 1915-19; cons. engr., 1919-20; pres., gen. mgr. Halliburton Oil Well Cementing Co., Duncan, Okla., 1920-47, chmn. bd., 1947—; pres. Erle P. Halliburton, Incorporated, Los Angeles, 1933-48; partner Erle P. Halliburton Company, 1948—; also president and director of the Halliburton Portland Cement Co., Corpus Christi, Tex., Security Nat. Bank, Duncan, Okla. Received Modern Pioneer award, 1940; named 1st Citizen, Duncan, 1953. Mem. Am. Petroleum Inst., Am. Inst. Mining and Metall. Engrs., Tau Beta Pi, Beta Gamma Sigma. Republican. Presbyn. Clubs: Engineers, Bel-Air Bay, California, Los Angeles Country. Home: Los Angeles; also Duncan, Okla. Office: 1709 W. 8th St., Los Angeles 14; also Duncan, Okla.; and 1200 Navigation Blvd., Corpus Christi, Tex. Died Oct. 13, 1957.

HALLIGAN, Howard Ansel; b. Shelburne Falls, Mass., June 13, 1874; s. James and Flora Augusta (Strong) H.; B.A., Amherst, 1896; m. Mary Griswold Ballard, Nov. 22, 1898. With Western Electric Co., 1896—, v.p., 1908—. Conglist. Clubs: University, India House, Montclair Golf. Home: 52 Lloyd Rd., Montclair, N.J. Office: 195 Broadway, New York, N.Y. Died June 18, 1950.

HALLOCK, Henry Galloway Comingo, missionary; b. Holliday's Cove, Hancock County, W.Va., Mar. 31, 1870; s. Herman Benjamin and Adelia (Farnsworth) H.; bro. of Gerard B. F. H.; A.B., Princeton, 1893; grad. Princeton Theol. Sem., 1896; Ph.D., Richmond, O., Coll., 1896; unmarried. Ordained by Presbytery of Steubenville, O., Apr. 21, 1896, and apptd. missionary to China; became a self-supporting missionary, 1905. Prof. homiletics and dean of Theol. Sch. of U. of China; at Chenju, near Shanghai, 1925-27. Asst'd. Chinese Tract Soc., Shanghai, with half time, 1906; actg. Nat. Christian Endeavor gen. sec. for China, 1907-08; hon. sec. Internat. Bible Reading Assn. for Empire of China, 1906-14; founder, now sec., treas., Nat. Tract. Soc. for China; founder and sec. Anti-Cigarette Soc. of China; sec. Met. Mission. Engaged in S.S. work for Chinese in Shanghai; pastor Endeavorers' Church, Shanghai. Was intered in Shanghai, China, by the Japanese. Author: The Chinese Almanac (40th year 1942); The Concordance of the Whole Bible (Chinese); Bible Dictionary (Chinese); Topical Text Book (Chinese); Pocket Concordance of Chinese Bible Revised Version; also many tracts, articles in religious and secular jours., and several hymns in Chinese, and many sermon booklets in English; the Endeavourers' Daily Manna, The Endeavourers' Daily Portion, The Endeavourers' Daily Devotions, Moments of Blessing for Endeavourers, Daily Strength for Daily Duties for Endeavourers. Home: 480 Chapoo Rd., Shanghai, China. Died Jan. 24, 1951.

HALLOCK, Mary Elizabeth (Mrs. Frank L. Greenewalt), pianist; b. in Beirut, Syria; d. of Samuel and Sara (Tabet) Hallock; ed. under German Deaconess Sisters, Beyrouth; came to Am., 1882; grad. Chelten Hills Sch., Phila., 1888; studied piano with Theodore Leschetizky, Vienna; grad. Phila. Musical Acad., 1893; m. Frank Lindsay Greenewalt, M.D., July 14, 1898; 1 son, Crawford Hallock. Piano soloist with Pitts., Phila. symphony orchestras in tours; concertized in piano recital throughout country; lectured on rhythm at U. of Kan., Ia., Grinnell, Earlham, Holyoke, Vassar colls.; concertizing throughout Am., 1909-10, 1912-13. Hon. mem. Browning Soc.; mem. Illuminating Engrs'. Soc., Soc. of Arts and Letters; life mem. Women Suffrage Soc. of county of Phila. Del. to 45th Annual Conv. the Nat. Am. Woman Suffrage Assn. Editor authorized textbook of the Leschetizky method by Marie Prentner. First to use a color lighting accompaniment shifting in sympathetic feeling with the phases of a musical composition during its performance. Inventor basic patents dealing with method for use of light as means of expression and with rhythmic sound; mfr. light and color players. Hon. mem. Thursday Musical Club, Mpls.; chmn. 4th Congressional Dist. Nat. Woman's Party. Gold medallist, Phila. Conservatory; award gold medal Sesquicentennial Expn., Phila., 1926, for developing illumination as means of expression; adjudged inventor of light-color play as a means of human expression in combination with rhythmic sound, by Federal Dist. Ct. of Del., Fed. Circuit Ct. 3d Dist. Coined Words "nouarathar" and "sarabet" to designate the art of light-color play and the instrument used. The Hist. Soc. of Pa. is repository of her light-color play documents. Author: Light-Fine Art the Sixth, 1916; Nouarathar: A Compendium of the Fine Art of Light-Color Playing, 1946. Wrote first text book on fine art of light-color playing, also mag. articles representing original research. Home: Hotel du Pont, Willmington, Del. Died Nov. 27, 1950.

HALPIN, George H., business exec.; b. Rock Island, Ill., Nov. 2, 1889; s. Thomas and Elizabeth (Cavanaugh) H.; student St. Louis U., 1908-11; m. Margaret Moyer, Mar. 8, 1946. Shipping clerk Am. Glue Co., St. Louis, 1911, salesman, 1912-17, sales mgr., Chgo., 1919-21; v.p., sales mgr. and dir. Baeder Adamson & Co., Phila., 1921-30; became exec. v.p. and dir. Minn. Mining and Mfg. Co., 1949, now vice chmn. exec. com.; dir. Mid-States Gummed Paper Co., Chgo. Served from 1st lt. to capt. AS, U.S. Army, 1917-19. Mem. Am. Supply and Machinery Mfrs. Assn. (pres. 1938), Am. Hardware Mfrs. Assn. (pres. 1950). Republican. Clubs: Minnesota, St. Paul Athletic, Somerset Country (St. Paul); Minneapolis, Woodhill Country (Mpls.). Home: Route 5, Orono, Wayzata, Minn. Office: 900 Fauquier St., St. Paul 6. Died Oct. 1959.

HALSEY, Benjamin Schuyler, business exec.; b. Newburgh, N.Y., Jan. 4, 1873; s. Lewis Benjamin and Sarah Frances (Sheffield) H.; A.B., Princeton, 1896; m. Katharine Walsh, Nov. 28, 1913; children—Benjamin Schuyler, Frances (Mrs. Justin T. Callahan), Anne (Mrs. Charles S. Roberts), Sheffield J., Robert A. Treas., gen. mgr. Sheffield Farms, 1896-1902; became dir. Sheffield Farms-Slawson-Decker Co., 1902, later became sec.; became dir., v.p. Sheffield Farms Co., Inc., 1917, exec. v.p. until 1953, ret. 1953; dir. Nat. Dairy Products Corp. Dir. Greater N.Y.-N.J. Milk Inst., Milk Research Council. Republican. Presbyn. Clubs: Princeton, Athletic (N.Y.C.); Sleepy Hollow Country. Home: Grey Towers, Harriman Rd., Irvington, N.Y. Office: 524 W. 57th St., N.Y. C. 19. Died Dec. 11, 1956.

HALSEY, Jesse (hôl'tsē), clergyman; b. Southhampton, L.I., N.Y. May 3, 1882; s. Charles Henry and Melvina Dunreath (Terry) H.; ed. Princeton Theol. Sem. 1906-08, Princeton Grad. Sch. 1907-09; B.D., Union Theol. Sem., 1910; D.D., Wooster (O.) Coll., 1927; m. Helen Isham, Mar. 26, 1910; children—Charles Henry, Frederick Isham (dec.), Helen Augusta, Wilmun Haynes (dec.), Abigail Fithian. Ordained Presbyn. ministry, 1910; with Sir Wilfred T. Grenfell's Labrador Med. Mission, 1910-13; pastor Seventh Presbyn. Ch., Cin., 1913-42; prof. practical theology, McCormick Theol. Sem., Chgo. 1941-52, ret. 1952. Lectr. Columbia Summer Sch., 1937. With Y.M.C.A. in Russia, 1917; Am. agt. and chaplain British Navy, Mourmansk, N. Russia, 1918. Trustee Western Coll., Oxford, O., Lane Theol. Sem., Cin.; mem. Bd. of Pensions of Presbyn. Ch.; mem. Presbyn. Camp and Church Com., 1941-45; visitor to VI Service Command for Gen. Commn. on Army and Navy Chaplains, 1944-45; dir. Bethesda Hosp., Cin., Presbyn. Homes, O. Synod; pres. Cin. Council of Chs., 1938-39; vice-moderator 121st Gen. Assembly, Presbyn Ch., U.S.A.; moderator Synod of O., 1940-41. Mem. Consumers League, Americanization Com., Asso. Charities Bd., Cincinnatus Assn. (charter mem.). Clubs: Clerical, Lake Shore. Contbr. articles to religious and secular publs.; compiler of A Living Hope, 1932; Think on These Things, 1942. Home: 846 Chalmers Pl., Chgo. Died Jan. 12, 1954.*

HALSEY, William Frederick, naval officer; b. Elizabeth, N.J., Oct. 30, 1882; s. William Frederick and Anne Masters (Brewster) H.; student U. of Va., 1899-1900; **B.S., United States Naval Academy, 1904; LL.D., Columbia University, 1947, Lehigh U., Washington University, American International College, Lafayette College, 1954; married Fanny Cooke Grandy, Dec. 1, 1909; children—Margaret Bradford Halsey Spruance, and William Frederick, III. Commissioned ensign U.S. Navy, 1906, and advanced through the grades to rear adm., 1938; rank**

of vice adm., June 13, 1940; rank of adm., Nov. 18, 1942, and Dec. 11, 1945 took oath as fleet adm. comdg. U.S. Third Fleet in Pacific; retired, Apr. 1, 1947. Member board of dir. Bullock's Found. Decorated Navy Cross, Distinguished Service medal with 3 gold stars, Army D.S.M., Victory Medal with Destroyer clasp, Am. Area Campaign medal, Am. Defense Service medal, Philippine Liberation Campaign ribbon with 2 stars, Gold Cross of Chevalier, Order of the Redeemer (Greece), Insignia Al Merito (1st class), Diploma (Chile), Hon. Knight Comdr. British Empire. On good will tour to S.A. in summer of 1946; awarded Order of Naval Merit (Cuba), Order of the Liberator (Venezuela), Order of Ayacucho (Peru), Grand Cross of Legion of Merit (Chile), Abdon Calderon of Balboa (Panama), Supreme Chief in the Order of the Inotzal (Guatemala), Nat. Order of the Southern Cross (Grand Cross), Brazil. Mem. Delta Psi. Episcopalian. Clubs: Army and Navy, Chevy Chase (Washington, D.C.), Military Order of the Carabao; Metropolitan, Racquet and Tennis University, The Brook (New York). Home: 530 Park Av. Office: 90 Church St., N.Y.C. 7. Died Aug. 16, 1959.

HALSTEAD, Laurence, army officer; b. Cin., Oct. 21, 1875; s. Col. Benton and Rowena (Smith) H.; grad. U.S. Mil. Acad., 1899; honor grad. Army Sch. of the Line, 1910; grad. Army Staff Coll., 1911, Army War Coll., 1925; m. Ann Louise Maus, Feb. 10, 1903; children—Laurence, Mervin. Commd. 2d lt. inf., U.S. Army, 1899; promoted through grades to brig. gen., 1935; with the 11th Inf., P.R., 1899-1900, 13th Inf., Philippine Islands and San Francisco, 1901-04, 6th Inf., 1905-13; chief of staff 84th Div., Camp Taylor, Ky., 1917; asst. chief of staff 1st Army, France 1918-19; instr. Army Center of Arty. Studies, Trier, Germany, 1919; with War Dept. Gen. Staff, 1922-24; comdr. 27th Inf., 1926-28; chief of staff 7th Corps Area, Omaha, Neb., 1929-31; exec., office of chief of inf., Dept. of War, Washington, 1931-34; comdr. 12th Inf., Ft. Howard, Md., 1934-35; comdr. Pacific Sector, Panama Canal, 1935-38; ret. May 31, 1938. Decorated D.S.M. (U.S.). Club: Corinthian Yacht, Army and Navy. Home: 3311 Macomb St. N.W., Washington. Died June 1, 1954.

HALSTED, Thomas Henry, otologist; b. Listowel, Ontario, Canada, July 8, 1865; s. James Addison and Jane (Hacking) H.; Toronto U., 1883; M.D., Toronto Med. Sch., Toronto U., 1887; mem. Coll. Physicians and Surgeons, Ont., 1887; studied New York, Vienna, Heidelberg, Berlin, Budapest and London; m. Lola B. Bridgford, 1889 (died 1895); m. 2d, Charlotte C. Palmer, Oct. 7, 1897 (died 1932); m. 3d, Maida Lawrence Smyth, Sept. 30, 1933. In practice at Syracuse, 1889-1937; laryngologist and otologist, Syracuse Meml., St. Joseph's hosps.; became prof. laryngology and otology, Syracuse U., 1899, now emeritus. Unitarian. Fellow A.C.S., Am. Laryngol. Assn. (ex-pres.), Am. Otol. Soc., Am. Laryngol. Rhinol. and Otol. Soc., Am. Bronchoscopic Soc.; mem. A.M.A., N.Y. State Med. Soc. (ex-pres.), Onondaga County Med. Soc., Syracuse Acad. Medicine, Nu Sigma Nu, Alpha Omega Alpha. Mason. Home: Engelwood, N.J. Office: 475 Fifth Av., N.Y. C. Died Nov. 20, 1956.*

HAM, Arthur Harold, v.p. Provident Loan Soc., N.Y.; b. Livermore Falls, Maine, July 2, 1882; s. Joseph Gardiner and Mary Emma (Chandler) H.; ed. pub. schs.; A.B., Bowdoin Coll., 1908; fellow Bur. Social Research, N.Y. Sch. of Philanthropy, Columbia, 1908-09; m. Gertrude Christopher, May 31, 1910. Dir. Div. of Remedial Loans, Russell Sage Found., N.Y., 1909-18; v.p. Provident Loan Soc. of N.Y., 1918—. Trustee, treas. Russell Sage Found. Dir. Bush Terminal Bldg. Co. During the World War, dir. War Sav. Socs., N.Y., served in War Savs. Div. of Treas. Dept. at Washington. Overseer Bowdoin Coll. Mem. Phi Beta Kappa. Clubs: Union League (N.Y.C.); Scarsdale Golf, Blind Brook, Cruising of America. Author: Chattel Loan Business, 1909; Credit Union Primer, 1914; also miscellaneous pamphlets and articles on remedial loan movement. Home: 46 Fenimore Rd., Scarsdale, N.Y. Office: 346 4th Av., N.Y. C. Died Apr. 14, 1951.*

HAM, Marion Franklin, clergyman; b. Harveysburg, O., Feb. 18, 1867; s. George Wilson and Marcia Emily (Haynes) H.; ed. pub. schs.; D.D., Meadville Theol. Sch., Chicago, 1942; m. Mary Louise Jenkins, Jan. 27, 1902; children—Robert E., Marcia L. Rightmire. Newspaper reporter, Chattanooga, Tenn., 1891-92; clk. in Chattanooga banks, 1892-97; ordained Unitarian ministry, 1898; minister All Souls Ch., Chattanooga, 1898-1904; First Unitarian Ch., Dallas, Tex., 1904-09; Unitarian Ch., Reading, Mass., 1909-34 (now emeritus), Waverly Unitarian Ch., Belmont, Massachusetts, 1934-42; now emeritus; Unitarian Church, Gardner, Massachusetts, 1943-45, emeritus since 1945. Citation of Honor, The Religious Arts Guild, 1947; citation of honor, Chattanooga Audubon Soc., 1949. Honorary chaplain Reading Masonic Lodge and the Belmont Masonic Lodge. Member Hymn Society of America, Unitarian Ministerial Union, Cambridge Assn. of Ministers. Author: The Golden Shuttle (verse), 1910; The Kinchin Stories (negro dialect for pub. readings), 1914; hymns for Unitarian Hymnal, 1914 and 1937; I Hear Thy Voice (song for ch. choirs), 1915; Songs of the Spirit (religious verse), 1932; Songs of Faith and Hope (collected hymns), 1940; The King of Love (song for ch. choirs), 1941; Christmas Bells (song for ch. choirs), 1941; O Mother-heart (song for Mother's Day), 1941; America: Keeper of the Flame, 1945; Freedom, 1950; Songs at Sunset (collection of 13 hymns), 1951; Songs of a Lifetime, 1953; In a Rose Garden, 1954. Hymns used in many Am. and Brit. Hymnals, 1 translated into Japanese. Home: 10 Whitcomb St., Belmont 79, Mass. Died July 23, 1956.

HAM, Roscoe James, coll. prof.; b. Peabody, Mass., Apr. 3, 1875; s. James Nelson and Florence Angella (Billings) H.; A.B., Harvard, 1896; Harvard and University of Berlin, 1897-99; A.M., Bowdoin, 1907, L.H.D., 1944; m. Mary Cowell, Sept. 5, 1901 (died Dec. 1953); 1 son, Edward. Instr., Cascadilla Sch. Ithaca, New York, 1899-1901; instructor modern langs., 1901-03, assistant prof., 1903-06, prof., 1906-07, Bowdoin; prof. Romance langs., Trinity Coll., Conn., 1907-09; prof. German, Bowdoin, July 1, 1909-June 1945; prof. emeritus since June 1945. Author: Brief German Grammar (with A. N. Leonard), 1909; Quiz Questions on German Grammar, 1911; Einleitung in die Deutsche Sprache, 1915. Spl. asst. to Am. ambassador at Petrograd, engaged in war relief work, June 1916-Jan. 1917. Address: 3 Bath St., Brunswick, Me. Died Dec. 26, 1953; buried Pine Grove Cemetery, Brunswick, Me.

HAMAKER, John Irvin, biologist; b. Elizabethtown, Pa., Nov. 29, 1869; s. Jacob and Martha (Gish) H.; A.B., U. Kan., 1893; A.B., Harvard, 1894, A.M., 1895, Ph.D., 1897; studied U. Berlin, 1910-11; m. Ray Parker, Aug. 12, 1914; children—Madeline, Marjorie Love, Templin (dec.), Richard Franklin. Prof. biology Trinity Coll., Durham, N.C., 1897-1904; prof. biology Randolph-Macon Woman's Coll., 1904-45, emeritus, 1945—. Fellow A.A.A.S.; mem. Am. Soc. Zoölogists, Pa. German Soc. Methodist. Author: A Compend of the Principles of Biology, 1905; The Principles of Biology, 1913; The Elements of Biology, 1929; Matthias Gish of White Oak—The History of an American Family, 1940. Home: 223 S. Princeton St., Lynchburg, Va. Died July 24, 1956.

HAMERSLAG, Victor, newspaperman; b. Elizabeth, N.J., Mar. 7, 1904; s. Morris and Pauline (Herbst) H.; student high sch.; m. Nell Broudy, Jan. 19, 1936. Began newspaper career as space-rate reporter, Newark, 1923, and since engaged in work as reporter and writer, including radio bradcasting of news program for papers; handling local and state politics in N.J. and covering Republican and Democratic Nat. convs., 1936, 40; ran Coast Guard blockade aboard rum-runner during prohibition; covered death of six men in electric chair; interviewed Dutch Schultz in tavern two days before he was killed; movie press agent Warner Brothers, 1929; city editor, Newark Star-Ledger, 1943-48; pub. relations dept. Port of N.Y. Authority, 1948. Mem. Newsweek Mag. presdl. forecast panel, 1944. Mem. Am. Newspaper Guild. Jewish religion. Home: 209 Prospect St., East Grange, N.J. Died May 12, 1953.

HAMILL, Alfred Ernest, banker (ret.); b. Chicago, Sept. 16, 1883; s. Ernest Alfred and Eliza (Corwith) H.; student The Hill Sch., 1899-1901; A.B., Yale, 1905; D.L.C. (hon.), Lake Forest (Illinois) Coll., 1939; m. Clarice Griffin Walther, Oct. 1, 1908; children—Ernest Alfred, Corwith, Clarice (Mrs. Nelson L. Barnes, Jr.). Clerk Northern Trust Co., Chicago, 1906-09; with Hathaway, Smith, Folds & Co., 1909-15, partner, 1915-27; sr. partner Hathway & Co., 1927-32; partner Goldman, Sachs & Co., N.Y. City and Chicago, 1932-48; dir. Yates-Am. Machine Co., Phoenix Hosiery Co. Trustee Lake Forest Pub. Library (pres. since 1932), Art Inst. of Chicago (v.p.), Newberry Library (pres. since 1930), Chicago Child Care Society. Mem. council Am. Acad. in Rome. Alderman 2d ward Lake Forest, 1914-15. Republican. Clubs: The Attic, Casino, Caxton Commercial (Chgo.); Grolier (N.Y. City). Author: The Sonneteering of Petrarchino, 1926; Serenade, 1931; This Last Devotion, 1940. Home: 1115 E. Ill. Rd., Lake Forest, Ill. Office: 208 S. LaSalle St., Chgo. 4. Died July 12, 1953.

HAMILTON, Bertis Frank, metal furniture mfr.; b. Jackson County, Ind., Oct. 9, 1884; s. Grover and Anna (Sanders) H.; m. Nell Pruit, Apr. 1906. Supt. J. E. Farber Co., Flint, Mich., 1920-23; prodn. and efficiency engr. Arvin Industries, Inc., 1923-46; pres. Hamilton Mfg. Co., Columbus, Ind., 1945-54, chmn. bd., 1954—; dir. Irwin Union Trust Co., Columbus. Dir. Asso. Colls. of Ind. Mason, Kiwanian. Home: 1950 Franklin St. Office: 1503 Cottage Av., Columbus, Ind. Deceased.

HAMILTON, Charles Robert, clergyman; b. Lebanon, Ind., June 18, 1872; s. Samuel Luther and Elizabeth Sophia (Wheeler) H.; student Emporia Coll., 1889-91; A.B., Hanover Coll., 1893, A.M., 1895, D.D., 1913; B.D., McCormick Theol. Sem., 1896; M.Th., Princeton, 1922; m. Edith Alice Crooks, Aug. 3, 1907; children—Kingsley Wheeler, Miriam Nellie (Mrs. M. C. Freudenberg), Ralph Crooks. Ordained to ministry of Presbyterian Church, 1896; pastor, First Presbyn. Ch., Manchester, Ia., 1896-99, Kenmore Presbyn. Ch., Buffalo, N.Y., 1899-1907; apptd. to Philippines by Presbyn. Bd. Fgn. Missions, 1907; missionary, Laguna province, Pagsanjan, 1907-13, Santa Cruz, 1915-17, Los Banos, 1917-29; acting pres. Silliman U., P.I. 1930-32; pres. Union Sem., P.I., 1932-41. Editor Philippine Presbyn., 1915-29, lecturer Princeton Theological Seminary, 1921-22; trustee Silliman U., 1923-40. Union High Sch., Manila, P.I., 1937-41; pastor Ellinwood Church, Manila, P.I., 1937-38, Chinese United Evang. Ch., Manila, P.I., 1937-39, Leper Ch., San Lazaro Hosp., Manila, P.I., 1937-39. Head Financial Dept. and field rep. Anti-Saloon League, Ohio, 1942-45; head English and Latin Depts. of High Sch., Fredericksburg, O., 1945-46. Mem. exec. com. Philippine Presbyn. Mission, 1919-21, 1924-27, 1937-40, and sec. exec. com. 1920, 1937-40. Acting sec. Presbyn. Bd. Fgn. Missions, New York, 1935, chmn. Church Union Com. effecting union Presbyn., United Brethren and Congl. Chs. as United Evangelical Church of Philippines, 1929 (sec. 1937-39); Commr. to Gen. Assembly of Presbyn. Ch. in U.S. from Dubuque Presbytery, 1899, from Buffalo, 1905, Manila, 1914; del. to Gen. Assembly from Philippine Mission, 1921-35, 41, and from Presbyn. Bd. Fgn. Missions, 1942; chmn. com. on Comity and Ch. Relations, Nat. Christian Council, Philippines, 1930-37; chmn. com. on Cooperation and Union, Fedn. Evang. Chs., Philippines, 1937-41; moderator Philippine Synod, 1919-20. Prohibition nomine for gov. of Ohio, 1948. Mem. Phi Gamma Delta, Lions. Republican. Author: Church Union Opposed, 1927; History of the Presbytery of Wooster, 1952; co-author: The Christian Use of Money; Sectarian Religious Teaching in the Public Schools, 1938. Home: 433 Bloomington Av., Wooster, O. Died Apr. 4, 1954; buried Riverside Cemetery, Cleve.

HAMILTON, Frederic Rutherford, educator; b. Richland Center, Wis., July 31, 1881; s. Andrew and Jane (Hessen) H.; grad. State Normal Sch., Oshkosh, 1901; Ph.B., U. of Wis., 1906, Ph.M., 1917; Ph.D., Columbia, 1925; m. Marion Ethel Warren, June 26, 1906; children—Hope Mayhew (Mrs. Merrill Heiser), Ernestine Hamilton (dec.). Supt. city schs., Milton, Wis., 1901-04, Jefferson, 1906-08, Hudson, 1908-12; with U. of Wis. extension div., 1912-14; dir. extension div., U. of Kan., 1914-19; with U.S. Army Sanitary Corps, Hosp. Service, Waynesville, S.C., Boston, 1918-19; pres. Marshall Coll., Huntington, W.Va., 1919-23; asso. in edn. Teachers Coll., Columbia, 1923-24; pres. Bradley Poly. Inst., Peoria, Ill., 1925-46, pres. emeritus, 1946-52; exec. dean, U. Ill., Galesburg div., 1946-47; asst. Div. Higher Edn., U.S. Office of Edn., 1942-43; lecturer summers, U. Wis., 1939, 40; pres. Fedn. Ill. Colls.; exploratory-photographic expdn. to C. and S. Am., 1947-49, Australia, New Zealand, 1950, South Africa, 1951-52. Mem. N.E.A., Phi Delta Kappa. Presbyn. Clubs: University, Rotary, Booklovers', Galesburg. Author: Fiscal Support of State Teachers' Colleges, 1924. Lectr. Home: 136 Golfview Av., Iowa City, Ia. Died Feb. 19, 1952; buried Hinsdale, Ill.

HAMILTON, Isaac Miller, chmn. Federal Life Ins. Co.; b. Ash Grove, Ill., Sept. 6, 1864; s. Ephraim S. and Celia B. (Miller) H.; ed. Grand Prairie Sem., Onarga, Ill., and by pvt. tutors; m. Amanda S. Ernst, June 11, 1907; 1 dau., Mrs. Miriam Celia Keare. Admitted to Ill. bar, 1899, and engaged in gen. practice also in banking; mem. Ill. Senate, 1896-1900; pres. Federal Life Ins. Co. since its orgn., 1900-46, chmn. since 1946; chairman The Illinois Canning Company; chairman board directors Lake Shore National Bank. President Illinois Republican League, 1898-1900, Nat. Rep. League, 1900-02. Mem. Ill. State Bar Assn. Mason (32°, K.T.), K.P. Clubs: Union League, Hamilton, Chicago Athletic, Chicago Yacht, South Shore Country, Bob O'Link Golf, Chicago, Exmoor Country, Ill. Athletic; Bankers (N.Y.), Bath (Miami Beach, Fla.). Home: 3117 N.E. 7th Av., Miami 37, Fla. Office: Federal Life Bldg., 168 N. Michigan Av., Chgo. 1. Died Aug. 11, 1952; buried Roschill Cemetery.

HAMILTON, James E., chmn. and dir. Merchants Nat. Bank; m. Maude Helené Hazeltine; children—John T. II, Mrs. Richard E. Killian. Treas. and dir. Intern-Ocean Reinsurance Co., Cedar Rapids, Ia.; chmn. bd. and dir. Merchants Nat. Bank (est.1881), Cedar Rapids, now chmn. exec. com. Home: 2345 Linden Dr. Office: Merchants Nat. Bank, Cedar Rapids, Ia. Died Feb. 27, 1959.

HAMILTON, John Carroll, utilities exec.; b. Palestine, Tex., Dec. 11, 1891; s. Jesse Bradley and Ida (Foster) H.; student Austin Coll., 1908-10; m. Leila Broyles, June 30, 1917; children—John Carroll, Jean (Mrs. Robert C. Buckner). Pres. Arkansas Louisiana Gas Co., Shreveport, La., 1955—, also dir. Pres. Community Chest of Caddo and Bossier Parishes, La., 1947-48, dir. 1946-52, 56—; pres. YMCA, Shreveport, 1942-44, dir. 1930—. Chmn. bd. Shreve Meml. Library, Shreveport, 1942—; trustee, mem. exec. com. Centenary Coll. of La., 1952—. Mem. Am., So. gas assns. Clubs: Lions (past pres.), Shreveport Country, Shreveport. Home: 1108 Ontario

St. Office: Box 1734, Shreveport, La. Died Dec. 19, 1957; buried Forest Park Cemetery, Shreveport.

HAMILTON, John Leonard, architect; b. Bloomington, Ill., Mar. 7, 1878; s. John Marshall and Helen Maria (Williams) H.; ed. Chgo. Manual Training Sch.; m. Rose Marie Boomer, Sept. 2, 1901; children—Helen Pauline, John Leonard, Katherine, Philip Alexander. Began practice Chgo., 1905; atchitect for commrs. of Lincoln Park, 1907-11; mem. firm Perkins, Fellows & Hamilton, 1905-27, Hamilton, Fellows & Nedved, 1927-34; practiced under own name, 1934—. Architect Evanston Twp. High Sch., Mid City Trust & Savs. Bank, Wyandotte High Sch., Kansas City, Kan., Ia. City High Sch.; architect for Richmond, Ind., pub. schs., 1920-42, also for many pub. schs., coll. bldgs. in various states. Commr. Winnetka Park Dist., 1910-15, pres., 1914-15; mem. Zoning Bd. of Appeals, War Price and Rationing Bd., Winnetka. Received, 1912, from Ill. chpt. A.I.A. gold medal for design of the Lion House, Lincoln Park. Mem. 1st Ill. Inf., Spanish-Am. War, 1898. Fellow A.I.A.; mem. Ill. Soc. Architects. Conglist. Home: 789 Cherry St., Winnetka, Ill. Deceased.

HAMILTON, J(ohn) Taylor, bishop; b. Antigua, W.I., Apr. 30, 1859; s. Rev. Alan and Jane (Taylor) H.; pre. edn. Moravian boarding sch., Fulneck, Eng.; grad. Moravian Coll., Pa., 1875, Moravian Theol. Sem., 1877; D.D., Lafayette Coll., 1901; L.H D., Moravian Coll., 1928; m. Cecilia Elizabeth Beck, June 7, 1886 (died, 1944); children—Mrs. Constance Beck, Martin, Arthur Beck, Kenneth Gardiner. Tchr. Nazareth Hall, 1877-81; pastor Second Moravian Ch., Phila., 1881-86; resident prof. Moravian Coll. and Theol. Sem., 1886-1903, pres., 1918-28, pres. emeritus, 1928—; mem. Moravian Mission Bd., Herrnhutt, Germany, 1903; bishop Moravian Church, 1905—; pres. gen. exec. bd., 1914-32, now dean of bishops Moravian Ch., U.S. Asso. editor The Moravian, 1883-93, sole editor, 1893-94, 97, 99; mem. adminstrv. bd. Moravian Ch. N., 1898-1903; sec. Soc. for Propagating the Gospel, 1886-98, 1902, 03. Author: History of the Moravian Church in the United States (Am. Church History series), 1895; A History of the Moravian Church During the Eighteenth and Nineteenth Centuries, 1900; A History of Moravian Missions, 1901; Twenty Years of Pioneer Missions in Nyassaland, 1912; The Recognition of the Episcopate of the Maravian Ch. by Act of Parliament, in 1749, 1925; The Contacts of the Moravian Church with the Iroquois League, 1931. Home: 1444 Main St., Bethlehem, Pa. Deceased.

HAMILTON, Maxwell M(cGaughey), foreign service; b. Tahlequah, Okla., Dec. 20, 1896; s. Wallace Maxwell and May Calvin (Dobson) H.; student Washington and Jefferson Coll., 1914-15; Litt.B., Princeton, 1918; D.Litt., Calif. Coll. in China (Peiping), 1940; m. Julia Fisher, Dec. 20, 1924; 1 dau., Julia Frances. Entered foreign service as student interpreter at Am. Legation, Peking (now Peiping), China, May 20, 1920; promoted consul, 1924; vice consul and consul, Canton, 1922-25; consul, Shanghai, 1925-27; jr. and sr. assessor Mixed Court, Shanghai, 1925-27; assigned for duty in Div. of Far Eastern Affairs, Dept. of State, 1927, asst. chief, 1931-37, chief, 1937—; apptd. minister counselor Am. Embassy, Moscow, U.S.S.R., June 1943; assigned Dept. of State and appointed special asst. to Sec. of State, Sept. 1944; designated by President as U.S. rep. in Finland with personal rank of ministtr, Dec. 1944; minister to Finland, 1945-47, resigned to work with State Dept. on Japanese peace treaty; assigned t State Dept., 1948—; apptd. U.S. rep. on Far Eastern Commn. with rank of Ambassador, 1949—, elected chairman 1949, tchr. course U.S. diplomatic history Mills Coll., 1956-57. Served in U.S. Army, 1918. Instr. Tome Sch., 1919-20. Mem. Phi Beta Kappa, Phi Delta Theta. Clubs: Peking (China); Nat. Press, Metropolitan (Washington). Address: 1256 Martin Av., Palo Alto, Cal. Died Nov. 12, 1957; buried Golden Gate Nat. Cemetery, San Bruno, Cal.

HAMILTON, Roy William, coll. pres.; b. Detroit, Mich., Mar. 25, 1883; s. William Robertson and Jessie Dean (Mitchell) H.; A.B., U. of Michigan, 1906, A.M., 1914; student Union Theol. Sem., New York, N.Y., 1907-09, U. of Marburg, Gernay, 1909; diploma, Auburn Theol. Sem., Auburn, N.Y., 1910; LL.D., Alma (Mich.) Coll., 1943; m. Frances Jean Smith, September 7, 1910; children—Carolyn E. (Paukratz), Constance S. (Lehuer), McDonald K. Ordained to minstry of Presbyn. Ch., 1910; pastor, Immanuel Presbyn. Ch., Harrisburg, Pa., 1910-12, First Presbyn. Ch., Ypsilanti, Mich., 1912-14; university pastor, U. of Mich., 1914-17 U. of Colo. 1917-19; prof. Eng. lit. and v.p., Alma Coll., 1919-43, acting pres., 1942-43, pres., 1923-47, ret. 1947, prof. Eng. lang. and lit. since 1947; dir. Am. Annuity Savings Assn., Lansing, Mich. Served as soldier counselor, representing bd. of Christian edn. Presbyn. Ch. U.S.A., Camp Grant, Ill., 1917-18; chaplain, training battalion, U. of Colo., 1918-19. Sec.-treas. Gratiot County Council of Defense, Alma, Mich. Mem. Presidents Assn. Mich. Church-Related Colls. (vice pres.), Mich. Edn. Assn., Mich. Schoolmasters Club, Rotary Internat. Mason. Club: Pine River Country (Alma). Home: 619 West Center St., Alma, Mich. Died Mar. 29, 1952; buried Alma.

HAMILTON, Samuel L., professor of education; b. Nov. 1, 1885; s. William and Sarah (Wightman) H.; A.B., Princeton U., 1910; B.D., Drew Theol. Sem., 1913; grad. study, Columbia U., New York U.; m. Jeanette Eckert, June 12, 1912; children—Janet, Stuart, Muriel. Pastor, Stony Brook Methodist Ch.; gen. sec. N.J. Council of Religious Edn., 1924-29; chmn. dept. religious edn., School of Edn., New York U., since 1929; mem. Internat. Council of Religious Edn., chmn. com. on research; chmn. com. on parent edn. and home religion, Greater New York Fedn. of Churches; mem. ednl. com., The Protestant Council of City of N.Y.; mem. gen. com. Fed. Council of Churches of Christ in Am. Pres. bd. trustees, Newark Free Public Library, Newark, N.J.; mem. bd. trustees, Am. Seamen's Friend Soc., Newark Museum; pres. Trustees Assn., N.J. Library Assn.; mem. Citizens' Adv. Com., Central Planning Bd., Newark, N.J.; mem. N.Y. East Conf. Meth. Ch.; dir. Intercollegiate Br., N.Y. City Y.M.C.A.; asso. bd. fgn. missions of Meth. Ch.; mem. adv. com. on publs. of Haxen Found.; mem. National Christian Teaching Mission. Served as 1st lt. inf., U.S. Army, 1917-18. Awarded St. Mihiel and Meuse-Argonne combat stars. Member John Dewey Soc., Am. Assn. Univ. Profs., Kappa Delta Pi, Beta Pi. Clubs: Cartaret, Princeton Terrace, New York University Faculty, Monday. Author numerous articles in cultural mags. Home: 240 Montclair Av., Newark, N.J. Office: School of Edn., New York U., Washington Sq. East, N.Y.C. 3. Died Feb. 9, 1953.

HAMILTON, Walton Hale, lawyer, educator; b. Hiwassee College, Tenn., Oct. 30, 1881; s. Rev. Hale Snow and Bettie Dixon (Hudgings) H.; prep. edn., Webb Sch., Bellbuckle, Tenn., 1898-1901; student Vanderbilt U., 1901-03; B.A., U. Tex., 1907; Ph.D., U. Mich., 1913; M.A. (hon.), Yale, 1928; m. Lucile Elizabeth Rhodes, 1909; children—Richard Hale, Edward Rhodes, Jean; m. 2d, Irene Till, July 20, 1937; children—Robert, Douglas, Leslie. Instr. in prep. schs. until 1909; instr. medieval history U. Tex., 1909-10; instr. in econs. U. Mich., 1910-13, asst. prof. polit. economy, 1913-14; asst. prof. polit. economy U. Chgo., 1914-15; prof. econs. Amherst Coll., 1915-23, Robert Brookings Graduate Sch., 1923-28; prof. law Sch. of Law, Yale, 1928-48; with law firm Arnold, Fastar & Porter, 1945—. Mem. Nat. Recovery Adminstrn. Bd., 1934-35; del. of U.S. Govt. to ILO Conf., Geneva, 1935; spl. asst. to atty. gen., 1938-45; mem. Ga. bar. Served on presdl. fact-finding bd. arbitrating Pullman wage dispute. Author: Current Economic Problems, 1915, 25; The Control of Wages (with S. May), 1923; The Case of Bituminous Coal (with W. H. Wright), 1925; A Way of Order for Bituminous Coal (with same), 1928; The Power to Govern (with D. Adair), 1937; Price and Price Policies, 1938; The Pattern of Competition, 1940; Antitrust in Action (with I. Till), 1940; Patents and Free Enterprise, 1941; The Politics of Industry, 1951. Contributor to legal and economic periodicals. Home: 4630 32 Rd. N., Arlington, Va. Office: 1200 19th St. N.W., Washington. Died Oct. 27, 1958.

HAMILTON, Williard I., ret. life ins. exec.; b. Cleve., Aug. 2, 1867; s. Edward L. and Sarah C. (Lum) H.; grad. Newark (N.J.) Acad., 1885; m. Lettie Thompson, Apr. 9, 1896 (died 1923); children—Ethel Hamilton, Raymond L., Stuart W.; m. 2d, Cornelia F. Foster, Mar. 16, 1927. With Prudential Life Ins. Co., 1885-1937, sec. 1912-37, v.p., 1918-37; now pres. Haskell Improvement Co., Inc. Chmn. N.J. Water Policy Commn., 1925-1934; mem. N.J. Bd. Agr., 1928-29; mem. nat. adv. com. N.Y. World Fair, 1939. Mem. N.J. C. of C. (pres. 12 terms), Nat. Assn. of State C.'s of C. (past pres.), Foreign Policy Assn., Acad. of Polit. Sci. Republican. Presbyn. Clubs: Lake Valhalla Country (N.J.); Bald Peak Country (N.H.). Home: 71 Durand Rd., Maplewood, N.J. Died Nov. 28, 1955.

HAMILTON, William Pierson, banker; b. N.Y.C., Feb. 5, 1869; s. William Gaston and Helen M. (Pierson) H.; student St. Paul's Sch., Concord, N.H.; Ph.B., Yale, 1891; m. Juliet Pierpont, 1894; m. 2d, Theodosia G. S. Carlin, Jan. 2, 1924. After leaving college, 1891, entered office of Manhattan Trust Co., becoming treas. and dir.; entered office of J. P. Morgan & Co., 1897, and was made mem. of firm in 1900, also mem. firms of J. P. Morgan & Co. (N.Y.C.), Drexel & Co. (Phila.), Morgan, Harjes & Co. (Paris), Morgan, Grenfell & Co. (London), retired 1921. Mem. St. Nicholas Soc., S.R., Delta Psi. Clubs: Union, Racquet and Tennis, New York Yacht Club (N.Y.C.); Montecito Country, Valley (Montecito); Santa Barbara Club; Bar Harbor Club, Kebo Valley (Bar Harbor, Me.). Home: Thirlstane House, Bar Harbor, Me., and The Grange, Lingate Lane, Santa Barbara, Cal. Died May 1950.

HAMILTON, Wilson H., judge; b. Delta, Ia., May 1, 1877; s. James Alexander and Matilda (Vert) H.; LL.B., Drake U. Law Sch., 1900; m. Ethel L. Jacobs, May 9, 1901; children—Edgar Clifton, Wilson John, Martha Elizabeth (Mrs. Roy J. Hansen). Admitted to Ia. bar, 1900; county atty. Keokuk County, 1902-04; mayor of Sigourney, 1906-08; gen. practice of law in Sigourney, Ia., 1904-34; asso. justice of the Ia. Supreme Court, 1935-Jan. 1, 1941; chief justice, July 1, 1937-Jan. 1, 1938; again practicing in Sigourney, mem. firm Hamilton & Updegraff. Candidate for congress from 6th Dist. Ia., 1914. Mem. Ia. State Bar Assn. Democrat. Methodist. Mason, Odd Fellow, Woodman, Club: Lions. Home: Sigourney, Ia. Died Dec. 9, 1949.

HAMLEN, Joseph Rochemont, advt. exec.; b. Portland, Me., Mar. 15, 1881; s. James Clarence and Caroline Cushing (White) H.; student Milton Acad.; grad. Harvard, 1904, A.M. (hon.), 1933; m. Martha Thorndike, May 4, 1918; children—Joseph Rochemont, Paul (dec.), William, John. Operating head J. H. Hamlen & Son, Little Rock, Ark., 1905-25; exec. Harvard U. alumni orgns., 1925-29, pres., pub. Harvard Alumni Bull. since 1928; v.p. Albert Frank-Guenther Law, Inc. since 1929. Chmn. local chpt. A.R.C.; mem. Mass. Pub. Safety Com., Greater Boston Vets. Service Com., World War II. Trustee Pan Am. Soc. N.E. Decorated Brazilian and Chilean Red Cross. Clubs: Tavern, Harvard, Somerset (Boston). Home: 417 Beacon St. Office: 10 Post Office Sq., Boston. Died Jan. 3, 1957.

HAMLET, Harry Gabriel, U.S. Coast Guard officer; b. Eastport, Me., Aug. 27, 1874; s. Oscar Charles and Annie (Holland) H.; student Mass. Inst. Tech., 1892-93; grad. U.S. Coast Guard Acad., 1896; m. Francel Allen Hastings, Apr. 26, 1905; 1 dau., Jean Hastings. Ensign, Apr. 27, 1896; promoted through grades to vice-adm., comdt., June 14, 1932; retired. Awarded Gold Life Saving Medal (U.S.); Silver Star (U.S.N.); Victory Medal; Comdr. Crown of Italy. Mem. Mil. Order World War, Am. Legion, Vets. Fgn. Wars, Mil. Order of Carabao, Sigma Alpha Epsilon, Pi Gamma Mu. Episcopalian. Mason (32°), Elk. Clubs: Army and Navy (Washington); Army and Navy (Chicago); Army and Navy (San Francisco); Jibboom (New London, Connecticut). Home: 7110 Beechwood Dr., Chevy Chase 15, Md. Died Jan. 24, 1954.

HAMLIN, Fred(eric) (Albert), writer; b. Hannibal, Mo., May 13, 1905; s. Roy Miller and Alice Ruth (Clarke) H.; A.B., U. Pitts., 1927; m. Margaret Meriwether Bartlett, 1934; children—Frederic Albert, David Meriwether. Reporter, Sharon (Pa.) Telegraph, 1919-22, Pittsburgh Gazette-Times, 1923; mem: staff, World's Work Mag., 1927-28, Plain Talk Mag., 1928; mng. editor Christian Herald Mag., 1929-30, assigned to feature writing trip around world, 1930; staff writer New Yorker Mag., 1931; public relations work, N.Y.C., 1932-41; dir. information and statistics CAA, 1941-43; mem. editorial staff Ziff-Davis Pub. Co., 1943-48; staff writer for Hoover Commn., 1948; pub. Aircraft Year Book, Aero Digest; pres., treas. Lincoln Press, Inc., Aero. Digest Pub. Corp., 1949-56; publishers consultant, 1957—. Mem. Omicron Delta Kappa, Sigma Delta Chi. Clubs: Overseas Press, Nat. Press. Author: S. Parkes Cadman (a biography); Treasures in the Earth; Land of Liberty. Address: 5704 Huntington Pkwy., Bethesda, Md. Address: Nat. Press Bldg., Washington 4. Died Feb. 7, 1959; buried Hannibal, Mo.

HAMLIN, John, author; b. Verdi, Nev., Jan. 16, 1880; s. Sylvester Augustus and Mary Ellen (Meacham) H.; student Reno High Sch., 1893-95, U. of Nev., 1895-99; m. Rebie Kelley, 1913; 1 dau., Evelyn. Boyhood years lived in lumber camps in Nev. and Calif.; moved to Reno, Nev., in 1890; reporter Nev. State Jour., 1900-02, Reno Evening Gazette, 1902-03; opened Reno Free Library, 1904; chief librarian till 1913; with Paul Elder Co., San Francisco, 1914-19; author since 1900. Mem. League of Western Writers, Author's League of America. Republican. Protestant. Clubs: California Writer's (pres. Oakland branch, 1930-31); Commonwealth (San Francisco). Author: Beloved Acres, 1925; Fighting Wades, 1926; Range Rivals, 1927; Loot of Lava Beds, 1928; Desert Dancer, 1931; Whirlpool of Reno, 1932; Tales of an Old Lumber Camp, 1936; Death Rider, 1939; Phantom Rider, 1940; By Paddle Wheel and Pack Train, 1941; Flying Horses, 1942. Contributor to Western Story Mag., Triple-X, Rangeland Love Stories. Youth's Companion and other magazines; author of western stories and serials for radio and motion pictures. While reporting on Nevada State Jour. and Reno Gazette, wrote many feature stories for San Francisco dailies; also had a number of short stories pub. in San Francisco Argonaut and contributed to the D.C. Cook County juvenile papers, Youth's Companion and other periodicals. Address: Los Gatos, Cal. Died June 13, 1951.

HAMLIN, Talbot Faulkner, architect; b. New York, N.Y., June 16, 1889; s. Alfred Dwight Foster and Minnie Florence (Marston) H.; A.B., Amherst, 1910; B.Arch., Columbia U. Sch. of Architecture, 1914; D.Sc. (honorary) Dickinson College, 1952; married Hilda B. Edwards, Sept. 11, 1916 (divorced); children—Wilfrid Gardner, Talbot Fancher, Norman Anderson; m. 2d, Sarah H. J. Simpson, Nov. 17, 1926 (died 1930); m. 3d, Jessica V. Walters, June 10, 1931. Began as draftsman with Murphy & Dana, N.Y. City, 1914, partner, 1920; partner Murphy, McGill & Hamlin,

1920-23, McGill & Hamlin, 1925-30; in practice alone, 1930-34; among bldgs. erected, Ginling Coll., Nanking, China, Dormitory and Science buildings, College of New Rochelle; instructor and lecturer on history and theory of architecture, Columbia U. Sch. Architecture, 1916-47, prof., 1947-54, emeritus, 1954—; librarian Avery Library, 1934-45, Fine Arts Library, Columbia, 1935-45; editor, Columbia School Architecture, of Forms and Functions of Twentieth-Century Architecture, 1945—. Fellow A.I.A.; mem. Phi Beta Kappa. Socialist. Author: The Enjoyment of Architecture, 1920; The American Spirit in Architecture, 1926; Some European Architectural Libraries, 1939; Architecture Through the Ages, 1940; Greek Revival Architecture in America, 1944; Architecture; An Art for All Men, 1947; We Took to Cruising (with Jessica Hamlin), 1951. Editor, author: Forms and Functions of 20th Century Architecture (4 vols.), 1952; Benjamin Henry Latrobe (Pulitzer Prize biography), 1955. Editor for architecture, New National Encyclopedia, 1932-33. Contbr. to encys. and archtl. jours. Address: School of Architecture, Columbia U., N.Y.C. Died Oct. 7, 1956.

HAMM, Beth Creevey (Mrs.), painter; b. Bklyn., Apr. 5, 1885; d. John Kennedy and Caroline Alathea (Stickney) Creevey; grad. Packer Inst., Bklyn., 1903; A.B., Smith Coll., 1905; student New York Sch. of Art (winner 1st prize scholarship award), 1905-10, Kirkland Sch. of Art, Denver, 1938-39; m. Capt. Arthur Ellis Hamm, Aug. 18, 1917 (killed in action World War I). Solo exhbns. by invitation Denver Art Mus., 1943, Staten Island Art Mus., 1945, Kenneth Taylor Galleries, Nantucket, 1945, etc.; exhibited with Allied Artists Assn., Am. Watercolor Soc., Nat. Assn. Women Artists, Pen and Brush Members' Shows (hon. mention); 2 solo shows at Argent Galleries, New York; has participated in many group shows in New York and elsewhere; represented in permanent collections Denver Art Mus., Smith Coll. Club of New York; exhibited in Europe at Stedelyjk Museum in Amsterdam, also Brussels, Antwerp, Liege, Ghent, Ostend. Vice pres. and vice commr. in France of Am. Com. for Devastated France, 1918-24; 1st vice pres. Am. Friends of France (acting pres. May-Nov. 1946), 1946. Decorated Merite Agricole for work of orgn. Agrl. Syndicates in France, by Fr. govt. 1923; recipient 1st prize in water color Nat. Assn. Women Artists, 1949, Medal of Honor, 1957. Mem. bd. Frontier Nursing Assn.; dir. League Women Voters 15th Assembly Dist., 1942-44. Founded Arthur Ellis Hamm scholarship prize, Smith Coll., 1918. Mem. Smith Coll. Alumnae Assn. (1st v.p. 1939-42), Art Students League (life mem.), Nat. Assn. Women Artists (pres. 1944-46; hon. life mem. bd. dirs. 1955—), Phi Beta Kappa. Republican. Presbyn. Clubs: Smith Coll. (dir. 1939-44), Cosmopolitan, Pen and Brush (hon. life mem.) (N.Y.C.). Author: In White Armor, 1920; Fragments, 1920. Contbr. articles to nat. mags. Home; and studio: 164 E. 72d St., N.Y.C. 21. Died Nov. 21, 1958.

HAMMEL, William Charles Adam, teacher; b. Balt., May 31, 1869; s. John and Mary (Dell) H.; A.B., Baltimore City Coll., 1884; grad. Md. State Normal Sch., 1887; spl. studies in sci. Johns Hopkins; work in Sloyd, Nass, Sweden; m. Bertha Balls, June, 1895 (dec.). Dir. physics and manual arts, State Normal Sch., Balt., 1888-1903; organizer, state dir. Manual Tng. Sch. of Md., 1899-1903; dir. physics and manual arts State Normal Coll., Greensboro, N.C., 1903—; lectr. on sci. and indsl. subjects. Organizer, pres. Md. Audubon Soc., 1899-1903; mem. com. on Internat. Art Congress, Dresen, 1912. Mem. Nat. Civic League, Am. Health Assn., Nat. Soc. for Promotion Indsl. Edn., N.E.A., Md. Acad. Sci., A.A.A.S., Eastern Manual Teachers' and Art Assn., Am. Fedn. of Arts, N.C. Sci. Assn., etc. Writer on physics and manual training. Expert radiographer. Was first to discover that a magnet can affect a sensitive photo plate. Address: Greensboro, N.C. Died Jan. 29, 1946.

HAMMER, Edwin Wesley, cons. engr.; b. Newark, N.J., Dec. 16, 1867; s. William Alexander and Anna Maria Nichols (Lawton) H.; descendant on maternal side of Michael Hillegas, of Phila., first treas. of United States, and the Pilgrim, John Howland, on paternal side of George Frederick Hammer of Pa.; ed. pub. schs.; m. Emily Augusta Thompson, May 28, 1890; 1 son, Wesley Thompson. With Thomas A. Edison and Edison Cos., 1884-87; mgr. Edison Elec. Illuminating Co., Fall River, Mass., 1887-88; asst. engr. New York Edison Co., 1888-89; with Thomas A. Edison at Paris Expn., 1889-90, Northwestern Expn., 1890-91; engr. for legal dept. Edison Electric Light Co. and Gen. Electric Co., 1891-96; engr. Bd. of Patent Control, Gen. Electric Co., and Westinghouse Electric & Mfg. Co., 1896-1911; cons. practice, 1911—; professional engr., State of N.Y. Served as commr. water supply East Orange, N.J.; consultant to U.S. Navy, 1917-18. Fellow Am. Inst. Elec. Engrs.; mem. Am. Soc. Mech. Engrs., N.Y. Elec. Soc., Franklin Inst., Am. Water Works Assn.; asso. Am. Electro-Therapeutic Assn. (founder mem.), Edison Pioneers (pres. 1941-42). Mem. Society Colonial Wars, S.R., New Eng. Soc. of Oranges. Republican. Presbyterian. Club: Bankers. Co-Author: The X-Ray, or Photography of the Invisible, 1896; Cataphoresis, 1898. An inventor and patentee and has had much to do with patents and inventions as technician and patent expert. Home: 10 Crestmont Rd., Montclair, N.J. Died Oct. 11, 1951; buried Fall River, Mass.

HAMMOND, Charles Parker, radio exec.; b. N.Y.C., Apr. 13, 1909; s. Franklin P. and Grace Irene (Creegan) H.; A.B., Cornell U., 1931; m. Rosemary Sistrom, Sept. 16, 1938; children—Mary Louise, Deborah. With Cornell Daily Sun 1928-30; editorial staffs N.Y. World, N.Y. Post, Lit. Digest, 1930-36; promotion mgr., bur. of advt., Am. Newspaper Pubs. Assn. 1936-42; dir. advt. and promotions, N.B.C., 1944, v.p. 1947—, asst. to pres., 1948—, charge of advt., promotion, research, guest relations, information. Mem. Zeta Psi. Zeta Psi Alumni Assn. Conglist. Clubs: Players, Advt., Radio Executives, Rockefeller Center Luncheon (N.Y.C.). Home: Old Farm Rd., Chappaqua, N.Y. Office: National Broadcasting Co., 30 Rockefeller Plaza, N.Y.C. 20. Died June 29, 1950.

HAMMOND, Harry Parker, coll. dean; b. Asbury Park, N.J., Dec. 21, 1884; s. George A. and Sarah J. (Snyder) H.; grad. Wilmington (Del.) High Sch., 1902; B.S. in civil engring., U. fo Pa., 1909, C.E., 1915; hon. D.Eng., Case Sch. of Applied Science, 1931; LL.D., U. Vt., 1943; D.Eng., U.N.C., 1951; m. Margaret Raymond, Sept. 8, 1913. Instr. in civil engring., U. of Pa., 1909-11, Lehigh U., 1911-12; asst. prof. of civil engring., Poly. Inst. of Brooklyn, 1913-18, prof. of sanitary-hydraulic engring., 1918-27, prof. of civil engring., head of dept., 1927-37; dean Sch. of Engring., Pa. State Coll., 1937—. Chairman, Com. on Technical Institutes, Engineers' Council for Professional Development. Mem. Am. Soc. for Engineering Education (asso. dir. investigation, 1924-29; dir. summer schs., 1929-34; vice president, 1934-35; pres. 1936-37; Lamme medalist, 1945). Recipient J. H. McGraw Award in Tech. Inst. Edn., 1950. Mem. Am. Soc. Civil Engrs., m. Soc. Mech. Engrs., The Newcomen Soc. of England, Army Ordnance Assn., Am. Soc. Photogrammetry, Am. Soc. for Testing Materials, Triangle, Tau Beta Pi, Delta Kappa Pi, Pi Kappa Phi, Cong. Author: Lectures on the Engineering Profession. Contbr. on engring. edn. to Jour. of Engring. Edn. and publs. of Am. Soc. of Civil Engrs. Home: 432 W. Fairmount Av., State College, Pa. Died Oct, 21, 1953; buried Kensico Cemetery, Valhalla, N.Y.

HAMMOND, James (Thomas) Jr.; b. Tolu, Ky., Aug. 1, 1892; s. James Thomas and Susan (Partain) H.; ed. Henderson Coll., Arkadelphia, Ark., 1909-11; m. Beatrice R. Ralph, May 5, 1915; children—James Thomas III, Betty Sue. Cashier Chicot Bank & Trust Co., Lake Village, Ark., 1912-17; cashier Army Nat. Bank, Camp Pike, Ark., 1918; successively asst. cashier, cashier and v.p. W. B. Worthem Co., bankers, Little Rock, 1919-22; treas. Lord & Taylor, N.Y. City, 1922-26; also sec. Asso. Dry Goods Corp.; pres. Gimbel Bros., dept. store, Pittsburgh, 1927-32; pres. and pub. Detroit Times, 1932-33, Commercial Appeal (Memphis), 1933-36; chmn. board Cleveland (O.) Automatic Machine Co. Democrat. Episcopalian. Mason (K.T., 32°, Shriner). Clubs: Memphis Country, Hunt and Polo (Memphis); Havana Country (Cuba); Metropolitan (N.Y. City); Union, Country (Cleveland); Everglades (Palm Beach, Fla.); Pine Valley (Clementon, N.J.); Denver (Colo.). Home: "Mimosa," Germantown, Tenn.; and Palm Beach, Fla. Office: Sterick Bldg., Memphis, Tenn. Died Aug. 1951.

HAMMOND, Lyman Pierce, public utilities; b. Bridgeport, Conn., Oct. 30, 1880; s. Myron Burdett and Zelda (Pierce) H.; student high sch., Bridgeport, 1894-97; married Margaret Rusling, January 19, 1904 (died July 16, 1945); 1 dau., Mrs. Edward Hawley Roper; married second, Louise B. Warren, May 25, 1946. Accountant. 1897; machinery salesman until 1910; sales mgr. Colo. Power Co., 1910, subsequently gen. mgr., pres. until 1924; v.p. Bonbright & Co., 1917-20; from 1924 with Electric Bond and Share interests in various exec. positions and in charge operations of Mexican subsidiaries of American and Fgn. Power Co., Inc. and pres. Mexican Electric Enterprises, Inc. and several other subsidiaries from 1928 to retirement in 1947. Made econ. survey of Philippines for Gov. Gen. Henry Stimson, 1927. Now writes on econs. and pub. affairs. Clubs: Union League (N.Y. City); Fairfield Beach (Conn.). Home: Green's Farms, Conn. Died Nov. 14, 1952.

HAMMOND, Ogden Haggerty, ex-ambassador; b. Louisville, Oct. 13, 1869; s. John Henry and Sophia Vernon (Wolf) H.; Ph.B., Yale, 1893; m. Mary P. Stevens, 1907 (died 1915); children—Mary Stevens, Millicent Vernon, Ogden Haggerty; m. 2d, Marguerite McClure Howland, Dec. 18, 1917; stepson, McClure Meredith Howland. Began in real estate bus., 1907; pres. Broadway Improvement Co.; pres., dir. Hoboken Land & Improvement Co., Hoboken Development Co.; dir. 1st Nat. Bank of Jersey City, Hoboken R.R. Warehouse and Steamship Connecting Co. Mem. N.J. Ho. of Reps. 2 terms, 1914-17; chmn. State Bd. Charities and Corrections of N.J., 1918-20; mem. Rep. State Com., N.J.; del. Rep. Nat. Conv., 1916-24; mem. Com. for Reorganization of the Fgn. Service, 1919; chmn. State Bd. of Control (N.J.), 1918-21; A.E. and P. to Spain, 1925-29. Founder, trustee Mary Stevens Hammond Meml. Home for Destitute Children. Recipient Gold Cross of Isabella, Spain. Mem. Hoboken C. of C. (past pres.). Presbyn. Clubs: Knickerbocker. Recess, Somerset Hills Country, Essex, Newport Country. Home: 18 E. 82d St., N.Y.C. Office: 1 Exchange Pl., Jersey City. Died Oct. 29, 1956.

HAMMOND, Stevens Hill, mfg. exec.; b. Chicago, Ill., Aug. 30, 1910; s. Thomas Stevens and Barbara (Whiting) H.; attended Chicago Latin Sch., Culver (Ind.) Mil. Acad.; m. Mary Lou Pike, Dec. 28, 1950; children—Michael, Suzanne, Thomas. Office boy Whiting Corp., Harvey, Ill., summers 1923-26, apprentice, 1926-31, mgr. personnel dept., 1931-32, asst. to pres. 1933-34, v.p. and mgr. combustion div., 1934-35, v.p. and dir. underfeed stoker div., 1935-41, v.p. and dir., field force, 1941-42, v.p., mem. exec. com. and supervisor of all sales activities, 1942-43, exec. v.p., 1943-45, pres. 1945-51, chmn. bd. since 1951; dir. Ingalls Meml. Hosp., Harvey, Ill., B.&O. C.T. R.R. Republican. Episcopalian. Clubs: Chicago, South Shore Country (Chgo.); LaGorce Country (Miami Beach, Fla.); Flossmoor (Ill.) Country. Home: Greenacres Stud Farm, R.F.D. 2, Box 225, Chino, Cal. Office: Whiting Corp., Harvey, Ill. Died Apr. 28, 1958.

HAMMOND, Thomas Stevens, mfr.; b. Crown Point, N.Y., Oct. 29, 1883; s. Charles Lyman and Mary E. (Stevens) H.; student U. Mich.; m. Barbara Whiting, June 2, 1907; children—Stevens Hill, Thomas Lyman. Began with Whiting Foundry Equipment Co. (now Whiting Corp.), 1907, successively purchasing agt., asst. sec., v.p. and sec., treas., pres. and gen. mgr., resigned 1942; prodn. adviser Chgo. Ordnance Dist., 1942; became chief of prodn., later dist. chief to 1944, dep. dist. chief, 1946; returned to Whiting Corp. as pres., gen. mgr., 1944, became chmn. bd., 1945. Formerly v.p. Swenson Evaporator Co.; dir. Ill. Bell Telephone Co., Lumbermen's Mutual Casualty Company, Whiting Corp., Am. Airlines, Inc. Director Harvey Meml. YMCA, Ingalls Meml. Hosp.; past president Electric Overhead Crane Institute; trustee Illinois Institute of Technology. Member Nat. Defense Commn., bus. adv. council Dept. of Commerce. Served as 1st lt. F.A., Ill. N.G., 1916; from capt. to lt. col. F.A., U.S. Army, 1917-19; col. F.A., Ill. NG, 1921-31, brig. gen., 1931-40; brig. gen. U.S.R. 1932-40, retired as major gen, 1940. Decorated Officer Legion of Honor (France). Mem. U.S. C. of C., Nat. Founders' Assn. (past pres.), Am. Foundrymans' Assn. (past pres.), Nat. Metal Trades Assn. (past pres.), Chgo. Assn. Commerce (past pres.), Army Ordnance Assn. (past pres. Chgo. Post), Midwest Mfrs. Assn. (dir.), Ill. chpt. Rainbow Div. Vets. Republican. Episcopalian. Clubs: Chicago, Chicago Farmers, Chicago Golf. Racquet, Golf, Saddle and Cycle (Chicago); "M" Club (Ann Arbor, Mich.). Home: R.F.D. 3, Box 611, Aurora, Ill. Office: Whiting Corp., 33 S. Clark St., Chgo. Died June 15, 1950.

HAMPDEN, Walter (Walter Hampden Dougherty), actor; b. Brooklyn, N.Y., June 30, 1879; S. John Hampden and Alice (Hill) Dougherty; student Harvard, 1896-97; B.A., Poly. Inst., Brooklyn, 1900; m. Mabel Moore, 1905. First appearance on stage with F. R. Benson's Co., in classical repertoire, in Eng., 1901; leading man at Adelphi Theatre, London, 3 seasons; acted Hamlet, 1905, succeeding the younger Irving in the part; returned to U.S., 1907, and was engaged as support to Mme. Nazimova, at Bijou Theatre, New York; appeared as Manson in "The Servant in the House," 1908, later in "The Yellow Jacket," "Salome," "The Tempest," "Macbeth," "Othello," "Romeo and Juliet," "Taming of the Shrew," "The Wayfarer," etc.; season, 1923-24 revived "Cyrano de Bergerac" at National Theatre, New York, leased for year; in 1925 leased Colonial Theatre, renamed it Hampden's; appeared there, 1925-26, co-starring with Ethel Barrymore in "Hamlet" and "Merchant of Venice"; played at Hampden's in "Caponsacchi," 1926-27; in Ibsen's "An Enemy of the People," 1927-28; in "The Light of Asia," 1928-29, "The Bonds of Interest," 1929-30; "Richlieu," 1930; "Admirable Crichton" at New Amsterdam Theater, 1931; tourned "Cyrano," 1932, and in repertoire 1933-35; layed "Richard III," 44th St. Theater, New York, spring of 1935, and in "Achilles Had a Heel," same theatre, fall of 1935; toured in "Cyrano," spring of 1936; returned to stage as Sir Anthony Absolute in "The Rivals" (Theatre Guild), 1941-42; "Arsenic and Old Lace" (tour), 1942-43; Thomas Jefferson in "The Patriots" (The Playwrights), 1943-44; on various occasions played the leading roles in "A Successful Calamity," "Our Town," "Ethan Frome," "The Third Floor Book," "Trilby," (as Svengali); "Henry VIII," (Cardinal Wolsey); appeared in various motion pictures, on the radio, starring in "The Adventures of Leonidas Witherall." Appeared on Broadway in The Crucible, 1953. Pres. The Players Home: Ridgefield, Conn. Died June 11, 1955.

HAMPTON, Aubrey Otis, physician; b. Copeville, Tex., Sept. 10, 1900; s. Calvin Wade and Mary Catherine (Hornbuckle) H.; student Ride Inst., 1918-19, Baylor U., 1919-21; M.D., Baylor Coll. Medicine, 1925; m. Marian Greene, May 30, 1928, remarried

Apr. 23, 1955; 1 son, Aubrey Otis; m. 2d, Mrs. Astrid Young, Sept. 16, 1946; 1 dau., Julie Astrid. Intern St. Pauls Sanitarium, Parkland Hosp., Dallas, 1925; city physician, Ft. Worth, 1926; asst. resident radiology Mass. Gen. Hosp., Boston, 1927-28, radiologist, 1928-40, radiologist-in-chief, 1941-46; also asst. prof. radiology med. sch. Harvard; sr. partner Groover, Christie and Merritt, radiologists, Washington, 1946—; chief dept. radiology Garfield Meml. Hosp., Washington, 1946—; chief cons. radiology VA.; con radiology Dept. Army, Walter Reed Gen. Hosp., Armed Forces Inst. Pathology. Rep. Am. Roentgen Ray Soc. and V.A. to Nat. Research Council. Served as col., chief, sect. radiology, Walter Reed Gen. Hosp., Med. Corps, U.S. Army, 1942-45. Decorated Commendation Ribbon, Am. Campaign Medal, Victory Medal. Awarded Gold medal sci. exhibit by Am. Roentgen Ray Soc., 1936. Fellow Am. Coll. Radiology; mem. A.M.A., Am. Roentgen Ray Soc., Radiol. Soc. North Am., Med. Soc. D.C., S.E. Surg. Congress, Clinico-Path. Soc., Hippocrates-Galen Soc., Phi Beta Pi, Theta Nu Epsilon. Clubs: Army-Navy, Congressional Country, Rotary, (Washington); Aesculapian (Harvard). Editor of Am. lectr. series roentgenology. Contbr. med. jours. Home: South Weare, Mass. Died July 17, 1955; buried South Weare Cemetery.

HAMPTON, Edgar Lloyd, editor, author; b. Pilot Grove, Ia., June 25, 1872; s. Milton Jacob and Mary (Griffin) H.; grad. Pacific Acad., Newberg, Ore., 1892; student Pacific Coll., Newberg, 1893-94, and business coll., Seattle, Wash.; m. Genevieve Scott, Oct. 26, 1895; 1 dau., Ruth Haisley. Began as reporter, Seattle, 1898; founder, 1899, and editor Seattle Mail and Herald, 1899-1905; founder, 1905, and editor Westerner Magazine, Seattle, 1905-14; pres. and gen. mgr. Animated Ednl. Film Co., Seattle, 1914-16; has devoted attention since 1916 to magazine writing; mem. bd. of governors Colorado Life Co. Mem. Authors' League of America, Pacific Geog. Soc. (regent), Los Angeles Chamber Commerce, Los Angeles Pageant Association. Clubs: La Jolla Beach and Yacht. Contributor of serials, fiction, articles on conservation, reclamation and American ethnology, etc., to Saturday Evening Post, Metropolitan, Century, American, The Golden Book, etc. Author: The Wind in the South (novel), 1921; Everybody's Business; (brochures) Shifting America's Industrial Centre, 1934; The Open Shop Movement in the United States, 1934; Los Angeles County (history), 1938; Pacific Mercado (promotion of Pan-Americanism), 1938; One Hundred Landmarks (with Mrs. A. S. C. Forbes; Southern Calif. landmarks since 1769), 1939; Belated Interviews (brochure), 1948; Listed in Boston Transcript's fiction honor roll 1915. 21. Home: 2174 Beachwood Terrace, Los Angeles 28. Deceased.

HAMRIN, Shirley Austin, univ. prof.; b. St. Paul, Minn., Aug. 26, 1900; s. Rev. Christopher N. and Sarah (Hays) H.; B.A., summa cum laude, Hamline U., 1921; M.A., U. of Chicago, 1926, Ph. D., Northwestern University, 1931, Ed.D. (hon.) Hamline University, 1944; m. Margaret Hanson, Aug. 15, 1924 (dec.); children—Donald Clayton, Phyllis Margaret; m. 2d, Hazel Sundell, Feb. 21, 1934; 1 son, Robert Sundell. Began as high sch. teacher, Long Prairie, Minn., 1922; dean Junior Coll., Winnebago, Minn., 1923-24; prin. Moorhead (Minn.) High Sch., 1924-25; dept. of edn., Moorhead State Teachers Coll., 1925-29; instr. edn., Northwestern U., 1929-31, asst. prof., 1931-33, asso. prof., 1933-39, prof., 1939—, also dir. summer session, 1939-42, and dir. Univ. Coll., 1940-43, Veteran of World War. Mem. Senate of Methodist Ch., numerous ednl. orgns. and Phi Delta Kappa. Republican. Methodist. Mason. Author: Organization and Administrative Control in High Schools, 1932; Co-Curricular Activities in Elementary Schools (with H. J. Otto), 1937; Guidance in the Secondary School (with C. E. Erickson), 1939; Making Good in High School (with L. McColloch), 1939; Guidance Manual for Teachers (with C. E. Erickson), 1939; Guidance Practices in Public High Schools (with C. E. Erickson and M. O'Brien), 1940; Teachers Manual for Use of Occupational Materials, 1945; 4 Square Planning for Your Career, 1946; Improving Guidance and Personnel Services Through Research (edited with F. S. Endicott), 1946; Guidance Talks to Teachers, 1947; Counseling Adolescents (with Blanche Paulson), 1949; Chats with Teachers About Counseling, 1950; Initiating and Administering Guidance Services, 1953; Guidance Talks to Students (with Hubert W. Houghton), 1960. Also numerous professional book reviews and articles. Home: 2762 Woodbine Av., Evanston, Ill. Died Mar. 15, 1958.

HAMSUN, Knut (häm'sŭn), author; b. Norway, Aug. 4, 1859; s. Peder Pedersen and Tora (Olsdatter) H.; m. Marie Andersen; 5 children. Began as apprentice to cobbler, later clerk in store, post office; farmer; country sch. tchr.; longshoreman, coal-trimmer; came to U.S., was farm hand; lectr. and street-car conductor, Chgo.; returned to Norway, then to U.S. where lectr.; later fisherman at Newfoundland; writing, 1899—; now also farming. Awarded Nobel Prize for Lit., 1921. Author: Shallow Soil, 1914; Growth of the Soil, 1920; Pan, 1920; Hunger, 1921; Mysteries, 1927; Women at the Pump, 1928; Chapter the Last, 1929; Vagabonds, 1930; August, 1932; Benoni and Rosa, 1932; The Road Leads On, 1935; The Ring Is Closed, 1937; Look Back on Happiness, 1940. Address: Grimstad, Norway. Died Feb. 19, 1952.*

HANAU, Kenneth John, banker, business exec.; b. Bklyn. Nov. 6, 1895; s. Nathaniel and Emma (French) H.; student U. of Va., 1916; m. Elizabeth Oliver, Feb. 12, 1920; children—Dorothy, Helen, Kenneth, Douglas. Began as Bond salesman Spencer Trask & Co., N.Y.C.; sales mgr. Redmond & Co., investment bankers, 1921-25; partner J. & W. Seligman, private bankers, 1925-32; exec. v.p., treas., gen. mgr., mem. exec. com., dir. Wagner Baking Corp., Newark, 1934-54, ret., now dir., mem. exec. com.; chmn. exec. com. Nat. State Bank of Newark, 1954—, dir., 1940—; chmn. bd., mem. exec. com. United Cigar-Whelan Stores Corp., 1948-51; dir. and mem. exec. com. 1st Nat. Bank & Trust Co., Montclair, 1946-51, Can. Dry Ginger Ale, Inc., Krueger Brewing Co., Union Bag & Paper Corporation; dir., mem. exec. com. and finance com. M-K-T R.R., 1936—, Pub. Service Gas & Electric Co.; dir., mem. finance com. Merchants and Mfrs. Fire Ins. Co., Am. Equitable Assurance Co. of N.Y., 1936—; dir., mem. auditing com. Broad Street Investing Corp., 1935-51; Capital Adminstrn. Co., Ltd., 1935—; dir., mem. investment com. Colonial Life Ins. Co.; dir. Tri Continental Corp. Served in U.S. Army, 1917-19. Mem. Nat. War Labor Bd., 1942-45. Vice chmn. Montclair U.S.O., 1942-44. Pres. bd. trustees Montclair Acad., 1936-46. Trustee Montclair Community Chest, 1943-48. Chmn. War Fund Drive, 1945. Trustee Montclair Red Cross. Mem. Delta Kappa Epsilon. Clubs: Golf (pres. and mem. bd. trustees, 1943, 44, 45), (Montclair); Down Town (Newark); City Midday, D.K.E., Manhattan (N.Y.C.); The Chicago, (Chgo.); Country, Beach, (Madison, Conn.). Home: 333 Crestmont Rd., Upper Montclair, N.J. Office: Nat. State Bank, Newark 5. Died Apr. 27, 1957.

HANCHETT, Lafayette, mining man; b. Fulton, N.Y., Aug. 12, 1868; s. Silas and Mary (Chaffee) H.; student Denver U., 1888; m. Nellie Fonda, Mar. 22, 1893; 1 dau., Helen Francis (Mrs. Russell V. Williams). Manager Lamartine Mine, Idaho Springs, 1894-1904; mgr. Newhouse Tunnel, Idaho Springs, 1900-04; mgr. Boston Consol. Mining Co., Salt Lake City, Utah, 1904-10; v.p., United Hydro-Electric Co., Georgetown, Colo., 1900-15; v.p. and mgr. Thousand Springs Power Co., Ida., 1912-15; pres. Intermountain Electric Co., 1910—; pres. Utah Power & Light Co., 1920-29, chmn. bd., 1929—; dir. Nat. Copper Bank-Bankers Trust Co., 1910-28; dir. Federal Reserve Bank of Salt Lake City, 1919-35; sec., dir. Dixie Power Co. First to use steam shovel mining methods in Utah copper mines, 1905. Mem. Bd. of Appeals, U.S., Salt Lake City, 1917; chmn. Bd. of County Commrs., Salt Lake County, 1917; chmn. Civil Service Commn., Salt Lake City, 1923-24. Mem. Am. Inst. Mining and Metall. Engrs. Democrat. Clubs: Alta, Commercial, Bonneville. Home: 983 Third Av., Salt Lake City, Utah. Deceased.

HANCOCK, Glover Dunn, economist; b. Los Angeles, Jan. 10, 1878; s. Thomas D. and Laura (Dunn) H.; A.B., William Jewell Coll., Liberty, Mo., 1898, A.M., 1899; Ph.D., in economics, U. of Wis., 1908; m. Mabel Kimzey, June 29, 1911. Taught as prin. of high schs., coll. prep. sch., 1900-05; spl. agent Wis. State Tax Commn., parts of 1905, 06, 07; asst. prof. econs. Amherst Coll., 1908-10; prof. econs. and commerce, dir. Sch. of Commerce, Washington and Lee U., Lexington, Va., 1910-19; dean of Sch. of Commerce and Adminstrn., 1919-49; spl. lectr. in econs. Johns Hopkins, 1912; prof. econs., U. Va., summer 1922. Mem. Va. State Com. on State Personnel Adminstrn., 1938-40, 40-41. Mem. State Commn. on State Fund for Workmen's Compensation Ins., 1930-31; pres. Va. Social Sci. Assn., 1937-38. Mem. Am. Econ. Assn., Am. Polit. Sci. Assn., Am. Acad. Polit. and Social Sci., Sigma Nu. Episcopalian. Home: Lexington, Va. Died Oct. 27, 1955; buried Stonewall Jackson Cemetery, Lexington, Va.

HANCOCK, John M., industrial banker; b. Emerado, N.D., Feb. 2, 1883; s. Henry and Isabella (Irvine) H.; A.B., University of North Dakota, 1903, LL.D., 1932, Hamilton College, 1950; D.S.C. (honorary), New York University, 1950; m. Ida M. Buckingham, June 23, 1904; children—Ruth Laura, Ralph Henry (dec.). Partner Lehman Bros.; v.p. Jewel Tea Co., 1919-22, pres. 1922-24, chmn. bd., 1924-42, 1948-54, hon. chmn., 1948—, chmn. exec. com., 1942-48; chmn. bd. Lever Brothers, 1950-55; chmn. exec. com., Flintkote Co., Inc.; dir. Underwood Corp., Nat. Surety Corp.; International Silver Co.; Sears, Roebuck & Co., American Stores Co., A. Stein & Co., National Surety Marine Insurance Corp., Van Raalte Co., W. T. Grant Co., The Lehman Corp., John Hancock Mutual Life Ins. Co. Mem. War Resources Board, 1939; associate with B. M. Baruch in rubber survey, 1942; adv. unit, Office War Mobilization for War and Post-war Adjustment Policies, 1943-Sept. 1944. Chmn. Bd. Am. Management Assn. since 1946; alternate to B. M. Baruch as U.S. Rep. on United Nations Atomic Energy Commn., 1946; trustee Inst. for Advanced Study, Princeton, N.J. since 1948, Hamilton College, Clinton, M.I.T. Corp.; dir. at large Empire State Found. since 1952. In charge Navy purchasing comdr. Supply Corps, U.S.N., 1914-19; awarded Navy Cross; Medal for Merit, 1948 Republican. Baptist. Clubs: Union League (N.Y.C.); Blind Brook (Port Chester, N.Y.); Clove Valley Rod and Gun (N.Y.). Home: Scarsdale, N.Y. Office: 1 William St., N.Y.C. Died Sept. 25, 1956; buried Kensico Cemetery.

HAND, Augustus Noble, judge; b. Elizabethtown, N.Y., July 26, 1869; s. Richard Lockhart and Mary Elizabeth (Noble) H.; student Phillips Exeter Acad., 1886; A.B., magna cum laude, Harvard U., 1890, A.M., LL.B., cum laude, 1894; LL.D., Middlebury Coll., 1918, Williams Coll., 1928, U. of Pa., 1938, Yale, 1939, Harvard, 1944 Columbia, 1944, Princeton, 1952; m. Susan Train, Aug. 5, 1899; 1 dau., Serena (Mrs. William Lyttleton Savage, dec.). Began practice at N.Y.C., 1895; mem. Curtis, Mallet-Prevost & Colt, 1897-1901, Hand, Bonney & Jones, 1901-14; judge U.S. Dist. Ct., So. Dist. N.Y., by apptmt. of Pres. Wilson, 1914-27; judge U.S. Circuit Ct., by apptmt. Pres. Coolidge 1927-53. Pres. Havens Relief Fund, 1910-49. Overseer Harvard U., 1936-42. Mem. Am. Law Inst. (mem. council, exec. com., 1936—), Am., N.Y. State bar assns., N.Y. County Lawyers Assn., Assn. Bar City N.Y., Harvard Alumni Assn. (pres. 1944), Harvard Law Sch. Assn., N.Y. (pres. 1919-20), N.Y. Phillips Exeter Alumni Assn. (pres. 1921). Trustee Episcopal Theol. School, Cambridge, Mass., 1919-49; warden, Grace Ch., N.Y. City. Democrat. Clubs: Century, Harvard (v.p. 1943). Home: 11 E. 68th St. Address: U.S. Court House, N.Y.C. Died Oct. 28, 1954; buried Elizabethtown, N.Y.

HAND, Thomas Millet, congressman; b. Cape May, N.J., July 7, 1902; s. Albert Reeves and Sara (Millet) H.; LL.B., Dickinson Sch. Law (editor in chief law rev.), 1922; m. Mary Mercer Worth, Mar. 1, 1930, (dec.); 1 son, T. Millet; m. 2d Elizabeth Frost Spang, Dec. 31, 1950. Admitted to New Jersey bar, 1924, and engaged in practice of law, Cape May City, N.J.; also became newspaper publisher; served as clerk, Bd. Chosen Freeholders of Cape May County, 1924-28; prosecutor of the pleas, Cape May County, 1928-33; mayor, City of Cape May, 1937-44; mem. 79th, 80th, 82d, 83d, 84th Congresses, 2d N.J. Dist. Mem., vice chmn. Rep. State com., 1941-44. Mem. bar Supreme Court of N.J., Supreme Court of U.S. Mem. Cape May County (past pres.) and N.J. State bar assns., Phi Kappa Psi. Mason. Clubs: Union League (Phila.); University, National Press Capitol Hill, (Washington). ‡ Died Dec. 26, 1956; buried Cold Springs, N.J.

HANDLIN, Frank Augustine, banker; b. Allegheny City, Pa., Nov. 23, 1860; s. John and Rose H.; student high sch. and St. Joseph's Coll.; m. Helen M. McCarthy, Dec. 20, 1888; children—Claire V., Rosemary, Francis. Formerly with post office, Ft. Smith; began as bookkeeper with First Nat. Bank, Ft. Smith, promoted through various positions, pres. 1914—; dir. Ft. Smith Compress Co., Reynolds-Davis Grocery Co.; trustee Estate of George T. Sparks, 1907—. Republican. K.C., Elk. Clubs: Business Men's Country. Home: 423 N. 15th St. Office: First Nat. Bank, Ft. Smith, Ark. Died Oct. 28, 1925.

HANDWORK, Bentley S., business exec.; b. Birdsboro, Pa., 1885; children—Mrs. Frank R. Elliott Jr., Ben T. Pres. and dir. Joslyn Mfg. and Supply Co., N.Y.C., until 1953, chmn. bd. 1953-54. Ret. Ore. Crossarm Co., Portland, v.p., dir. Fed Tool Co., Chgo.; dir. South East-Joslyn Co., Cin., Southern Joslyn Co., New Orleans, Jobbers Supply Co., St. Paul. Home: 3000 Sheridan Rd. Office: 20 N. Wacker Dr., Chgo. Died Oct. 1956; buried Meml. Park Cemetery.*

HANDY, Burton, coll. pres.; b. Oct. 26, 1884; s. Hiram Cole and Ellen Margaret (Gowthrop) H.; A. B., Tri State Coll., Angola, Ind., 1907, A.M., 1926; postgrad. U. Chgo., 1916-17; m. Jeanette Maud Watson, Nov. 27, 1907; children—Russell Franklin, Burton, Lucy Ellen; m. 2d, Blanche Bruner, Dec. 30, 1948. Tchr. in pub. schs., 1901-09, in bus. schs., 1909-13; prin. comml. dept. Tri State Coll., 1913-20, prof. mathematics, 1920-28, sec., treas., 1928-34, pres. 1935-46, pres. emeritus, 1946—. Mem. Angola City Council, 1929-38. Republican. Mem. Mirror Lake Christian Ch. Mason. Rotarian. Address: 529 12th St. N., St. Petersburg, Fla. Died July 12, 1955; buried Circle Hill Cemetery, Angola, Ind.

HANDY, William Christopher, composer; b. Florence, Ala., Nov. 16, 1873; s. Charles Bernard and Elizabeth Brewer; ed. pub. schs., Florence, 1880-92; m. Elizabeth V. Price (dec.), July 19, 1898; children—Lucille (Mrs. Allan Springer) (dec.), Katherine Eugenia (Mrs. Homer Lewis), William Christopher, Florence Beatrice (dec.), Elizabeth Virginia White (dec.), Wyer Owens; m. 2d, Irma Louise Logan, January 1, 1954. School teacher, 1892-93; teacher and band master 1893-96; band master Maharas Minstrels 1896-1900, 1933; tchr. music dept., A. and M. Coll., Normal, Ala., 1900-02; band and orchestra leader Memphis, 1905-18; composer, pub., 1912—; pres.-treas. Handy Bros. Music Co., Inc., N.Y.C. Mem. Am. Fedn. Musicians; Am. Soc. Composers,

Authors and Pubs., Music Pubs. Protective Assn., Song Writers Protective Assn. Treas. Negro Actors' Guild, Inc., N.Y. City. Nat. Assn. Negro Musicians, Nat. Assn. Adv. of Colored People. Republican. Methodist. Mason (33°), Elk (life). Author: Negro Authors and Composers of the United States, 1935; W. C. Handy's Collection of Negro Spirituals, 1938; Father of the Blues (autobiography), 1941; Unsung Americans Sung, 1944; A Treasury of the Blues, 1949. Editor of: Blues (an anthology), 1926. Composer: St. Louis Blues, Memphis Blues, Beale Street Blues; (march) Hail to the Spirit of Freedom, The Big Stick Blues March; Go Down Moses March; anthem, They That Sow in Tears; Aframerican Hymn: Blue Destiny Symphony, and other compositions. Memorials include: W. C. Handy Sch. (Florence, Ala.), W. C. Handy Theatre, (Memphis), Handy Park and Square (Memphis), W. C. Handy Found. for the Blind, Inc., W.C. Handy Swimming Pool, Henderson, Ky. Home: 19 Chester Dr., Yonkers, N.Y. Office: 1650 Broadway, N.Y.C. 19. Died Mar. 28, 1958; buried Woodlawn Cemetery, N.Y.

HANES, Robert March, banker; b. Winston-Salem, N.C., Sept. 22, 1890; s. John Wesley and Anna (Hodgin) H.; student Woodberry Forest Sch., Orange, Va., 1907; A.B., University of North Carolina, 1912, LL.D., 1945; student Harvard University School of Business Adminstrn., 1912-13; m. Mildred Borden, July 3, 1917; children—Frank Borden, Sara Anne. Sec., treas. Crystal Ice Co., Winston-Salem, 1913-17; v.p. Wachovia Bank & Trust Co., Winston-Salem, 1920-31, pres., 1931-56, hon. chmn., 1956—; dir. So. Ry. Co., P. H. Hanes Knitting Co., Hanes Dye & Finishing Co., Security Life & Trust Co., R. J. Reynolds Tobacco Co., Borden Mfg. Co., Chatham Mfg. Co., Piedmont Nat. Gas Co., Piedmont Pub. Co., Carolina Power & Light Co. Chief E.C.A. Mission to Belgium and Luxembourg, 1949; dir. Economic Affairs for Western Germany, 1949-50; mem. bus. adv. council for sec. of commerce; civilian aide to sec. of army; chmn. commerce and industry div. N.C. Dept. Conservation and Development; pres. Gov.'s Research Triangle Com. of N.C. Mem. N.C. Gen. Assembly, 1919, 1931, Senate, 1933. Trustee Morehead Found., U. N.C. Served from 1st lt. to maj., arty., U.S. Army, 1917-18, AEF. Selected as Man of Year in N.C. by Newcomen. Mem. Am. (pres.), N.C. (pres.) bankers assns., C. of C. (pres.), Assn. Reserve City Bankers (pres.), Sigma Alpha Epsilon. Democrat. Methodist. Clubs: Twin City, Forsyth Country, Old Town, Dunes, Rotary (pres.), Lint Head Shoot, Rainbow Springs, Coral Bay. Home: 140 Stratford Rd., Winston-Salem, N.C. Died Mar. 10, 1959; buried Winston-Salem.

HANKS, Lucien Mason, banker; b. Madison, Wis., June 27, 1868; s. Lucien Stanley and Sybil (Perkins) H.; B.L., U. Wis., 1889; studied U. Berlin, Germany, 1 yr.; m. Mary Esther Vilas, Oct. 10, 1898; children—William Vilas (dec.), Sybil Anna, Lucien Mason. With State Bank, Madison, 1891-1906; sec. Central Wis. Trust Co., 1906-08; pres. 1908-27; chmn. bd., 1927-34, pres., 1934-40; was pres. First Nat. Bank; which was merged with Central Wis. Trust Co., 1922; dir. Nekoosa Edward Paper Co.; trustee Estate of William F. Vilas. Trustee Zoöl. Soc., Madison; sec.-treas. Wis. Alumni Research Found.; treas. State Hist. Soc. of Wis.; chmn. local chpt. A.R.C., 1942-46; treas. Dane County Chpt., Nat. Found. for Infantile Paralysis, Inc.; sec. treas. Wis. Alumni Research Found., 1927-47; mem. Chi Psi. Republican. Clubs: Madison, University. Home: 525 Wisconsin Av. Office: First Nat. Bank Bldg., Madison, Wis. Died Apr. 29, 1950; buried Forest Hill Cemetery, Madison, Wis.

HANLEY, John Chaney, ret.; b. East Liverpool, O.; s. Charles Hanley and Elizabeth Susan (Curby) H.; A.B., Westminster Coll., New Wilmington, Pa., 1897, D.D., 1927; grad. Pitts. Theol. Sem., 1900; m. Diana Pomeroy, Dec. 14, 1904. Ordained ministry United Presbyn. Ch. of N. Am. 1900; pres. Sayre Coll., Lexington, Ky., June 1, 1925-June 1, 1942. Address: care Sayre Coll., Lexington, Ky. Died Nov. 28, 1949.

HANLEY, L. E., mining exec.; b. Deadwood, S.D., Sept. 14, 1880; s. Thomas F. and Hatiea (Higgins) H.; student Wallace (Ida.) High School, Idaho, 1900; m. Persis Bailey, Nov. 9, 1911; children—Frances, Jean, Thomas. Began as asst. assayer Standard Mining Co.; assayer Helena Frisco Mining Co.; became assayer, head office, gen. supt. Hecla Mining Co., pres. and mgr. Hecla Mining Co. until 1951, now chmn. bd.; pres. Sullivan Mining Co.; pres. Polaris Mining Co.; v.p. Resurrection Mining Co.; dir. Coeur d'Alene Hardware & Foundry Co. Mem. Am. Inst. Mining & Metall. Engrs. Republican Clubs: Shosbone (Ida) Country; City, University (Spokane) Address: Wallace, Ida. Died Nov. 16, 1952.*

HANLEY, Miles L(awrence), univ. prof.; b. Xenia, Ohio, Nov. 14, 1893; s. William Alonzo and Mary Sophronia (Lloyd) H.; A.B., Wittenberg Coll., Springfield, O., 1914; A.M., Ohio State U., 1916; Charles Dexter Traveling Fellow, Harvard, 1926, A. M., Harvard, 1927; m. B. Louise Wardell, June 22, 1915. Instr. in English, U. of Kan., 1916-17, Northwestern U., 1917-18, U. of Tex., 1919-23; asst. and tutor Harvard U. and Radcliffe Coll., 1923-27; asst. prof. English, U. of Wis., 1927-31, asso. prof., 1931-39, prof. since 1939; asso. dir. Linguistic Atlas of New England, 1931-34 (mem. exec. com. 1930); lecturer in English, Yale, 1931-32; lecturer on English, Harvard, 1932-34; cons. linguistic matters to various advt. and bus. orgns. Served as 2d lt., 20th Inf., U.S. Army, 1918-19. Del. for U. of Wis., 2d Internat. Congress of Phonetic Scis., London, 1935. Harvard Tercentenary, 1936. Mem. Internat. Phonetic Assn. (certif. in phonetics 1/c. 1926). Am. Dialect Soc. (life mem.; sec.-treas. 1928-40), Modern Lang. Assn. (life mem.; sec. and chmn. coms. since 1924; mem. editorial adv. com.; chmn. com. on courses in phonetics, 1938; various times sec. or chmn. practical. phonetics, exptl. phonetics and present day English groups), Linguistic Soc. of Am. (exec. com. 1936; chmn. com. on courses in phonetics 1938), Am. Council Learned Socs. (mem. com. on non-English dialects 1940), Mediaeval Acad., Modern Humanities Research Assn., A.A.A.S., Am. Assn. Univ. Profs., Essex Inst. of Salem (Mass.), English Speaking Union, Wis. Hist. Soc., Phi Gamma Delta. Clubs: University (Madison); Longwood Cricket (Chestnut Hills, Brookline, Mass.); Harvard, Phi Gamma Delta (New York). Author: Materials and Methods of Reproducing Research Materials (with R. Binkley), 1936; Linguistic Atlas of New England, 3 vols., Am. Council Learned Socs. (as asso. dir.), 1939-43; Synonyms and Antonyms, Am. Coll. Dictionary (phonetic adviser), 1948. Phonographic recorder of about 1500 field records of New England pronunciation (now preserved in Rackham Hall of Grad. Studies, Univ. of Mich.), 1933-34; contbr. to Talking Books for the Blind; Good American Pronunciation (record), 1941. Compiler: Word Index to James Joyce's Ulysses, 1937, rev. edit., 1951. In charge of synonyms and antonyms American College Dictionary, 1947. Cons. in pronunciation Webster's New International Dictionary, 2d edit., 1934; chmn. com. on pronunciation Thorndike-Century Dictionaries, 1936-41. Contbr. articles in philolo. publs. Assembling collection of evidence on Am. and Modern English pronunciation (now preserved in English Lang. Sem., U. of Wis.) since 1931. Radio broadcaster on The Language We Speak, since 1927. Specialisms: phonetics, history of the English lang., history of modern English pronunciation, the English lang. in Am., Chaucer, Old and Middle English. Home: 803 State St., Madison 5, Wis. Died Feb. 4, 1954; buried Xenia, O.

HANLEY, Sarah Bond, former state rep.; b. Leon, Ia., Jan. 21, 1865; s. Jesse Walton and Ann Caroline (Harrah) Bond; student Monmouth (Ill.) Coll., 1882-85; m. John Hamilton Hanley, Sept. 5, 1889 (dec. July 15, 1936); 1 dau., Helen Hanley Brown. Charter mem. Woman's Dem. Club, Monmouth, 1888, the first polit. club for women; mem. Dem. State Central Com. of Women, 1925-36; del. Dem. Nat. Conv., 1924; Ill. mem. of com. to notify Gov. Charles W. Bryan of his nomination for v.p. of U.S.; elected to Gen. Assembly, Ill., 1926, reelected, 1928; del. at large Dem. Nat. Conv., 1928, 32; permanent chmn. Dem. State Conv., 1930. Mem. State Commn. on Washington Bi-Centennial, 1932; mem. Ill. State Commn., Century of Prograss Expn. Charter mem. Puritan Cavalier Chapter D.A.R., 1896, now hon. regent; unanimously elected 7 times as state officer, D.A.R., v.p. Gen. Nat. Soc., 1925-28, and dir. Nat. Officers' Club of D.A.R., 1927-30; was treas. 15th Dist. Fedn. Woman's Club, 1898. Mem. State Hist. Soc. of Ill., Nat. League of Am. Penwomen. Episcopalian. Writer on early Ill. hist. subjects. Home: Springfield, Ill. Died Apr. 1959.

HANLIN, Merton L., vice-pres., Clark Equipment Co.; b. Grinnell, Ia., Nov. 19, 1876; s. James and Margaret Ann (Leibee) H.; student pub. schs. of Chicago; m. Leonore Stults, Sept. 19, 1899 (died 1935); m. 2d, Florence E. Caine, January 8, 1938; children—Helen, Donald, Harold, Philip. Clerk Belt Ry. of Chicago, 1893-1902; chief clerk Ill. Steel Co., South Chicago, Ill., 1902-05; gen. mgr. Celfor Tool Co., Buchanan, Mich., 1905-17; v.p. Clark Equipment Co., mfrs. drills, reamers, etc., Buchanan, 1917-45; ret., 1945. Mason (32° Shriner). Home: 113 Clark St. Buchanan, Mich. Died Dec. 9, 1955; buried Oak Ridge Cemetery, Buchanan, Mich.

HANLON, Edward K(elly), lawyer; b. Taftville, Conn., Jan. 21, 1891; s. Edward and Ellen Jane (Kelly) H.; A.B., Loyola Coll., Balt., 1909; LL.B., Harvard, 1912; m. Rachel Ridder, Apr. 9, 1917 (dec. Dec. 1932); m. 2d, Regina Keenan Kniffen, Apr. 24, 1937. Admitted to N.Y. bar, 1913; mem. Beekman & Bogue, N.Y.C., 1917—, partner, 1926—. Mem. Am. Law Inst., Am., N.Y., Nassau Co. bar assns., Bar Assn. City N.Y. Clubs: Rockville Country (Rockville Centre); Broad Street (N.Y.). Home: 142 Morris Av., Rockville Centre, L.I., N.Y. Office: 15 Broad St., N.Y.C. 5. Died May 2, 1956; buried Cemetery of the Holy Rood, Westbury, L.I., N.Y.

HANN, Charles, lawyer; b. Montgomery, Ala. Feb. 7, 1888; s. Charles and Annie (Sykes) H.; A.B., Harvard, 1911, Carnegie Found. fellow in internat. law, 1912-13; A.M., LL.B., Columbia, 1915. Admitted to N.Y. bar, 1915, and later to bar U.S. Supreme Ct.; admitted to Cal. bar, 1932; began practice in N.Y.C.; dep. atty. gen. of N.Y., 1920; sr. mem. Hann and Hann; dir. Anderson Die Casting & Engring. Corp.; v.p. treas. Canadian U.S. Knitting Co. of St. Hyacinthe, Que. Served in USN, 1917-19, advancing to lt. comdr.; put U.S.S. Edorea in commn.; organized and directed Officers' Material Sch. (deck) and in charge sea tng. 4,250 naval officers for troop and cargo transports operated by U.S. Navy (4 mos. tng. for commns. instead of customary 2 yrs. for licenses). Named by Gov. Miller to represent state of N.Y. at ceremonies incident to burial of Unknown Soldier, at Arlington, Va., 1920. Del. to Internat. Congress of Interallied Veteran's Fedn., Warsaw, 1926, London, 1927, Bucharest, 1928, Belgrade, 1929, Lisbon, 1932 (chmn.), Casablanca, 1933 (chmn.). Trustee Am. Seamen's Friend Soc.; nat. v.p. Bundles for Am. and Bundles for Bluejackets. Mem. Am., N.Y. State bar assns., N.Y. County Lawyers' Assn., Harvard, Columbia law sch. assns., Maritime Law Assn. U.S., Rep. County Com., Am. Legion (comdr. N.Y. County, 1936, 1st dist. 1922), Navy League U.S. (v.p.), Mil. Order World Wars (past comdr.-in-chief), Naval Order U.S. (comdg. gen.), Soc. Mil. and Naval Officers World Wars (perpetual). Mil. Order Fgn. Wars (registrar), Soc. Am. Wars (past commander-general), Army and Navy Union U.S.A. (past comdr.), F I D A C (v.p. 1932-33), 40 and 8 (avocat), Rep. Service League (treas.), Am. Soc. French Legion of Honor (dir.), Bolivarian Soc. (dir.), 1937 N.Y. Nat. Conv., Am. Legion Corp., (ex-com.), Am. Nautical Cadets (pres.), Am. Emergency Vol. Ambulance Corps (treas.). Decorated Officer Legion of Honor (French); Order of Crown (It.); Polonia Restituta (Polish); Gen. Haller Swords; Macedonian (Greek); Bolivarian; Columbia Conspicious Service; Victory; N.Y. State, c.-in-c.'s Medal, M.O.W.W.; Medal of Army, Navy, Air Force Veterans in Can. Episcopalian. Clubs: Bankers of Am., Harvard, Delta Kappa Epsilon, Economic, Ends of Earth, N.Y. Yacht, University, Embassy, Nat. Republican, Propeller, Harvard Varsity, Columbia C, The Pilgrims, Church, English Speaking Union; Phi Sigma Omega (hon.), Sigma Phi Upsilon, Pershing Hall (Paris). Presented with loving cup by Harvard football players, 1912, by undergrads. of Columbia, 1914. Homes: 536 Hardee Rd., Coral Gables 46, Florida; and S. Sea Av., West Yarmouth, Cape Cod, Mass. Office: 12 E. 41st St., N.Y.C. 17. Died June 5, 1957.

HANNA, Charles Augustus, banker; b. Cadiz, O., Dec. 28, 1863; s. Neri A. and Eliza Jane (Phillips) H.; M.A., 1902, L.H.D., 1925, Marietta (O.) Coll.; m. Elizabeth Fleming Harrison, Oct. 19, 1905 (died Feb. 2, 1945); children—Mrs. Elizabeth Harrison Howell, Mrs. Mary Eleanor Adams, Virginia Lee, Phillips Hanna (dec.). Began banking career at Lincoln, Neb., 1885; v.p. First Nat. Bank, Lincoln, Neb., 1891-97; treas. Neb. Stock Yards Co.; nat. bank examiner for N.Y., 1899-1911; examiner for N.Y. Clearing House, 1911-1939. Mem. N.Y., N.J., Ohio, Va. hist. socs., N.J., N.Y., New Eng. geneal. socs., Soc. Colonial Wars, S.A.R. Republican. Presbyn. Club: Montclair Golf. Author: Historical Collections of Harrison County, O., 1900; Ohio Valley Genealogies, 1900; The Scotch-Irish, 1902; The Wilderness Trail, 1911. Home: 15 Rockledge Rd., Montclair, N.J. Died May 19, 1950.

HANNA, Mrs. John M. (Sallie L.), nat. bd. Y.W.C.A.'s of U.S.; b. Marquette, Mich., Nov. 24. 1869; d. Rev. Henry S. and Anna Hazzard (McCarer) Little; ed. Ferry Hall, Lake Forest, Ill., and Lindenwood Coll., St. Charles, Mo.; LL.D., Lindenwood Coll., 1956; m. John M. Hanna, Oct. 18, 1888 (died 1926). Chmn. Southwestern Field Com. Y.W.C.A., 1914-19; 1st v.p. Y.W.C.A.'s of U.S.A., 1922-24, pres., 1926-30, mem. nat. bd., 1914—. Chmn. Y.W.C.A. War Work, southwestern field, World War I. Mem.-at-large Tex. Council of Church Women; chmn. spl. gifts, Women's Div., Community Chest, Dallas Co., 1942-48; member Texas Interracial Commn., Southern Regional Council, Inc.; dir. Dallas Y.W.C.A.; mem. Am. Fedn. of Internat. Insts., Federal Council of Chs. (mem. Women's Cooperating Commn.), Dallas County League of Women Voters, Dallas Women's Chamber of Commerce, D.A.R. Delta Kappa Gamma (hon.), Beta Sigma Phi (hon.). Presbyterian. Club: Pilot (hon.). Received Zonta Annual Award, 1935, for spl. community contbn., Beta Sigma Phi award, 1945. Home: 3307 Drexel Dr., Dallas 5. Died Nov. 8, 1957; buried Denison, Tex.

HANNA, Leonard Colton, Jr., business exec.; b. Cleve., Nov. 5, 1889; s. Leonard Colton and Coralie (Walker) H.; student Univ. Sch., Cleve., 1900-04, Hill Sch., Pottstown, Pa., 1904-09, Yale, 1913. With The M. A. Hanna Co., Cleve., 1913—, partner, 1917-23, v.p., 1923-26, dir., mem. exec. com., 1923—. Served as 1st lt. Signal Corps, U.S. Army, World War I; with A.R.C. in England, World War II. Trustee The Play House. Karamu House, Cleve.; first v.p. The Cleve. Mus. Art. President Leonard C. Hanna, Jr. Fund. Member of Delta Kappa Epsilon. Clubs: Union, Tavern (Cleve.); Kirtland Country (Willoughby, O.); Yale (N.Y.C.). Home: Hilo Farm. Mentor. O. Office: Leader Bldg., Cleve. 14. Died Oct. 5, 1957.

HANNA, Margaret M., ret. fgn. service officer; b. Ann Arbor, Mich.; d. Edwin Phillips and Lucretia (Hynes) H.; ed. high school, Washington, fgn. lang. schs. and under pvt. tutors. Apptd. pvt. sec. Dept. of State, 1895, and advanced through grades to chief of Office of Coordination and Review, 1924; detailed to asst. Am. delegation to Pious Fund Arbitration, The Hague, 1902, Venezuelan Claims Commn., Caracas, 1903, 2d Peace Conf., The Hague, 1907, 4th, 5th and 6th Internat. Conf. of Am. States, 1910, 23, 28; consul at Geneva, Switzerland, 1937-39, ret. Mem. Kan. State Soc. Presbyn. Club: Women's University. Home: 1529 Varnum St. N.W., Washington. Died Mar. 30, 1950; buried Rock Creke Cemetery, Washington.

HANNA, Philip Sidney, ret. editor; b. Aurora, Ill., Mar. 9, 1887; s. James Carswell and Idella Medora (Hawley) H.; A.B., U. Ill., 1922; m. Marian A. Barlett, Nov. 22, 1913; children—Elizabeth (Mrs. F. R. Miller), Barbara (Mrs. E. S. Englebert), Nancy (Mrs. C. S. Robinson), Philip S. Stenographer The Economist, Chgo., 1912; financial asst. Chicago Tribune, 1913; cashier Bank of Sanborn, N.D., 1914-15, Coleman (Mich.) State Bank, 1916-17; state bank examiner of Mich., 1918-19, chief examiner, 1920; financial editor Mich. Manufacturer, 1921; mgr. Detroit News bur. of Wall St. Jour., 1922-27, 30-31; editor Chicago Jour. of Commerce, 1931-41; bus. editor Chicago Sun, 1942-43; bus. columnist Chicago Daily News, 1944-55, ret. Sec. Jr. Achievement of Chicago. Mem. Phi Kappa Psi. Democrat (Jeffersonian). Episcopalian. Home: 215 N. Garfield St., Hinsdale, Ill. Died Jan. 5, 1958.

HANNAGAN, Stephen (Steve) Jerome, publicity; b. Lafayette, Ind., Apr. 4, 1899; s. William John and Johanna Gertrude (Enright) Hannagan; student Purdue Univ., 1917-19; married Ruth Ellery, October 29, 1931 (div.); m. 2d, Suzanne Brewster, November 1939 (div. 1943). Began as reporter, Lafayette Morning Journal while attending high sch., became sports editor and city editor; with Indianapolis Star, 1918-19; with Russel M. Seeds Co., advt. agency, Indianapolis, 1919; became dir. of publicity Indianapolis Motor Speedway, 1919; with United Press, New York, 1920, later feature writer and New York columnist for Newspaper Enterprise Assn. and United Feature Syndicate; became head of own publicity organization, 1924, and conducted public relations for Internat. 500-mile motor race at Indianapolis, City of Miami Beach, Fla., Gene Tunney, Jack Dempsey, Gar Wood; v.p. Lord & Thomas, advt. agency, N.Y. Chicago, 1933-35; publicity office under own name, N.Y. City, since Aug. 1935, conducting publicity for Sun Valley, Ida., Coca-Cola Co., Union Pacific R.R. Company, Owens-Illinois Glass Co.; Olin Industries, Electric Auto-Lite Co., Admiral Corp., Thor Corp. Member Sigma Delta Chi. Roman Catholic. Contbr. to Cosmopolitan, Colliers, Liberty, etc. Flew around the continent with Capt E. V. Rickenbacker, 1921. Home: 280 Park Av. Office: 247 Park Av., N.Y.C. Died Feb. 3, 1953; buried St. Ann's Cemetery, Lafayette, Ind.

HANRAHAN, Edward Mitchell, surgeon; b. Binghamton, N.Y., Oct. 16, 1892; s. Edward M. and Julia (Stack) H.; A.B., Cornell, 1915; M.D., Johns Hopkins, 1919; m. Evelyn Barton Randall, Feb. 3, 1923; children—Julia Stack, Edward Mitchell. Intern, asst. resident Johns Hopkins Hosp., 1919-21; asst. resident Union Meml. Hosp., Balt., 1921-22; grad. study surgery, Vienna, Austria, 1922; instr. surgery and anatomy med. sch., Johns Hopkins, 1923-26, asso. surgery, 1936-45, asst. prof., 1945-49, asso. prof. plastic surgery since 1949; vis. surgeon plastic surgery Johns Hopkins Hosp., 1926-49, plastic surgeon in charge since 1949; vis. plastic surgeon Union Meml. Hosp., Balt. City Hosp., U.S. Marine Hosp., Balt.; cons. plastic surgery Hanover (Pa.) Gen. Hosp. Served with S.A.T.C., Med. Officers Res. Corps. Diplomate Am. Bd. Surgery (fdr.), Am. Bd. Plastic Surgery. Fellow A.C.S.; mem. A.M.A., So. Surg. Assn., Brit. Assn. Plastic Surgeons, So. Med. Assn., Am. Soc. Plastic and Reconstrn. Surgery, Alpha Delta Phi. Democrat. Episcopalian. Club: Halsted. Contbr. to med. books and encys., also articles to jours. Home: Cambridge Arms Apt., Balt. 18. Office: 1201 N. Calvert St., Balt. Died 1952.

HANSCOM, Elizabeth Deering, educator; b. Saco, Me., Aug. 15, 1865, d. George Albert and Lizzie (Deering) H.; A.B., Boston U., 1887, A.M., 1893; Ph.D., Yale, 1894. In lit. work, Boston, 1887-92; teacher of English, Smith Coll., since 1894, now prof. Mem. Phi Beta Kappa, Kappa Kappa Gamma. Author: Lamb's Essays—A Biographical Study, 1891; The Friendly Craft, 1908; Sophia Smith and the Beginnings of Smith College (with Helen F. Greene), 1925. Edited 2d part Henry IV, Tudor edition, Shakespeare, 1912; The Heart of the Puritan, 1917. Home: Northampton, Mass. Died Feb. 2, 1960.

HANSEL, John Washington, ret. business exec.; b. Kansas City, Mo., Jan. 1, 1889; s. John Washington and Christina (Mowat) H.; student U. Ill., 1908-10; m. Clare Pearl Livingston, Nov. 25, 1915; children—John W., David D., Christina M. Rep. Nat. Advt. Agency, Chgo., 1912-13; Western advt. mgr. The American Boy, 1913-14, Good Housekeeping, 1915-17; mgr. Chicago office N. W. Ayer & Son, Inc., 1918-22, resident partner, Chgo., 1922-28, v.p. charge Chgo. office, 1928-40, exec. v.p. and dir., Phila., 1940-54, ret. Clubs: Racquet, Merion Golf (Phila.); University (Chgo.); Detroit, Detroit Athletic (Detroit). Home: Rt. 2, Box 879, Tucson. Died Dec. 1957.

HANSEN, Alice G., business exec.; b. N.Y. City, June 6, 1913; d. Anthony Arthur and Senta (Ittlinger) Hansen; B.S., Columbia, 1932; post grad. student New York U. Founder, 1941 and since pres. Pittsburgh Mill Steel Co.; pres. Service Steel Corp. since 1942, acquired plants at Crum Lynne and at Baltimore, 1949. Assisted in developing prodn. low phosphorous pig iron in East Tex. ore fields, 1945. Mem. Am. Soc. Refrigeration Engrs., N.Y. Bd. of Trade, U.S. C. of C. Dem. Roman Catholic. Clubs: Womens Traffic, Advertising Womens (New York); Montauk Yacht. Designer new refrigerator. Home: 221 Griffin Av., Scarsdale, N.Y. Office: 336 Madison Av., N.Y.C. Died Oct. 18, 1953; buried Gate of Heaven Cemetery.

HANSEN, Armin Carl, artist; b. San Francisco, Oct. 23, 1886; s. Hermann Wendelborg and Olga (Josué) H.; ed. Mark Hopkins Inst. of Art, San Francisco, 1903-06; Royal Acad., Stuttgart, Germany, under Carlos Grethe, 1906-08; studied in Paris, Antwerp, Nieuwpoort; m. Frances Rives, June 16, 1922; 1 son, Wendelborg. Marine and figure painter. Exhibited at Art Inst., Chgo.; Acad. Fine Arts, Phila.; Nat. Acad. Design, N.Y.C., Cleve. Mus. Art; Palace Fine Arts, San Francisco; Library of Congress, Washington; Cleve. Mus.; Norfolk Mus.; Oakland Mus.; Los Angeles Mus. of History Sci. and Art; also various European salons. Recipient cash award Internat. Expn. Brussels, 1910; silver medal, San Francisco Expn., 1915; silver medal for painting, also for drawing, San Francisco Art Assn., 1916, gold medal for painting, drawing, 1918; first Hallgarten prize, N.A.D., 1920, gold medal, 1922, Huntington prize, 1923. Internat. Etching Expn., Los Angeles; Ranger fund purchase, N.A.D., 1925; gold medal Painters of the West—1925; Chas. M. Lea prize, Print Club of Phila., 1927; Internat. Gold Medal for etching, Paris, 1938; 1st Chgo. Soc. of Etchers award, 1947. Mem. San Francisco Art Assn., Cal. Soc. Etchers, Printmakers of Cal., Société Royal des Beaux Arts, Brussels, Bklyn. Soc. Etchers. A.N.A., 1926. Home: 254 Eldorado St., Monterey, Cal. Died Apr. 23, 1957.

HANSEN, Hans Christian Svane, Prime Minister of Denmark; b. Aarhus, Denmark, Nov. 8, 1906; student Heimvolkschochschule, Schloss Tinz Thuringen, 1928; m. Gerda Nielsen, 1930; children—Inge, Kirsten, Annelise. Chmn. Social Democratic Youth Orgn. of Denmark, 1933-37, Internat. Socialist Youth Orgn., 1935-39; mem. Parliament, 1936—; sec. Social Democratic Party, 1939-41, 45, chmn. 1955; minister finance, 1945, 1947-50, minister trade, 1950, minister fgn affairs, 1953-55; prime minister and minister for fgn. affairs, 1955—. Author: New Generation—New Strength, 1932; Hans Hedtoft, His Life and Work, 1955. Co-author: Th. Stauning, Son of the People, Prime Minister of Denmark, 1942. Home: Osterbrogade 95, Copenhagen, Denmark. Died Feb. 19, 1960.

HANSEN, Niels Ebbesen, horticulturist; b. nr. Ribe, Denmark, Jan. 4, 1866; s. Andrew and Bodil (Midtgaard) H.; came to U.S. with parents, 1873; B.S., Ia. Agrl. Coll., 1887; M.S., 1895; Sc.D., U. of S.D., 1917; m. Emma Elise Pammel, Nov. 16, 1898 (died Dec. 16, 1904); children—Eva Pammel (Mrs. David L. Gilkerson), Carl Andreas; m. 2d, Dora Sophie Pammel, Aug. 27, 1907. In practical horticulture, commercial Iowa nurseries, 1888-91; asst. prof. horticulture, Ia. Agrl. Coll., 1891-95; prof. horticulture, S.D. Agrl. College and Expt. Station, 1895-1937, prof. emeritus of horticulture since 1937. Spent 4 months, 1894, in hort. study in 8 countries of Europe, including Russia; made 10 months' exploration trip, 1897-98, for U.S. Dept. Agr., collecting new economic seeds and plants in Russia, Turkestan, Western China, Siberia, Transcaucasia; made 6 months' exploration, 1906, for U.S. Dept. Agr. around the world through Lapland, Finland, Russia, Siberia, Manchuria and Japan; made 9 months' exploration, 1908-09, for U.S. Dept. Agr. to Siberia, Mongolia, Manchuria, Turkestan, Transcaucasia and N. Africa; went to North China (Manchuria) for State of S.D., 1924; del. Internat. Congress Horticulture, London, 1930; originator new fruits, especially the Hansen hybrid plums, now extensively grown in the West; introduced the Turkestan, Siberian and many other alfalfas; also introduced and named the Cossack alfalfa, now widely grown in the prairie Northwest, developing from a spoonful of seed in 1906 to over one thousand bushels of seed in 1916; originated a method of field hybridization of hardy alfalfas by transplanting; made 5 months' exploration for alfalfa for S.D. in Siberia, 1913; also imported the Siberian fat-rumped sheep from which Director James W. Wilson developed a tailless breed of sheep; made exploration tour of 4 mos., 1934, at invitation of the Soviet govt., to East Siberia, with son, Carl A., as tech. asst.; a program of experiments in horticulture and agriculture, covering 100 points, was completed Mar. 1935, and published in 4000 copies by the U.S.S.R., 1937. Awarded George Robert White gold medal of honor "for eminent service in horticulture," by Mass. Hort. Soc., 1917; Marshall P. Wilder silver medal, Am. Pomol. Soc. (for new fruits), 1929; Cosmopolitan gold medal "for public service," Sioux Falls, 1933; awarded A. P. Stevenson gold medal by the Manitoba Hort. Soc. (for new fruits), 1935; Alumni Merit Award, Chicago Alumni Assn., 1942; Medal of Honor, Iowa, Iowa State Horticultural Soc., 1944; Medal of Honor, S.D. Hort. Soc., 1946. Sec. S.D. State Hort. Soc., 1895-1929, pres., 1929-32, pres. emeritus, 1936. Life mem. (hon.) Saskatchewan Hort. Soc., 1946. Mason. Author: Handbook of Fruit-culture and Tree-Planting (in Danish-Norwegian), 1890; Systematic Pomology (with J. L. Budd), 1903. Writer on horticulture. Home: Brookings, S.D. Died Oct. 5, 1950; buried Brookings.

HANSEN, William W(ebster), physicist; b. Fresno, Calif., May 27, 1909; s. William George and Laura Louise (Gillogly) H.; m. Betsy Ross, Oct. 18, 1938; A.B., Stanford, 1929, Ph.D., 1932. Instr. in physics, Stanford, 1930-34; Nat. Research fellow, 1932-34; asst. prof. of physics, Stanford U., 1935-37; asso. prof., 1937-42; prof., 1942—; research engr., Sperry Gyroscope Co., Garden City, N.Y. cons. to Nat. Def. Research Com., 1941-45. Recipient Liebmann prize of Inst. Radio Engrs. for work in electromagnetic theory, 1945. Fellow Am. Phys. Soc., Inst. Radio Engrs., A.A.A.S.; mem. Am. Assn. Physics Tchrs., Phi Beta Kappa, Sigma Xi. Contbr. articles to sci. jours. Specialist in physics, microwaves, nuclear induction. Home: 515 Gerona, Stanford University, Cal. Died May 23, 1949.

HANSMANN, William H., fidelity and surety exec.; b. Chicago, May 20, 1888; m. Cecelia Adams, 1927; children—Jeanne Adams, Dale. In fidelity and surety bus. since 1902; with Chicago br. Fidelity and Deposit Co. of Md. since 1920, v.p. and dir.; v.p. Am. Bonding Co. of Baltimore. Mem. Ins. Fedn. Ill., Assn. Casualty and Surety Mgrs. Chicago, Surety Underwriters Assn. Chicago. Clubs: Union League (Chicago); Sunset Ridge Country (Winnetka, Ill.). Home: 1220 Maple Av., Wilmette, Ill. Office: 166 W. Van Buren St., Chgo. 4. Died Dec. 5, 1952.

HANSON, Felix Valentine, clergyman; b. Veddige, Halland, Sweden, Nov. 26, 1877; s. Adolph and Elida (Peterson) H.; brought to U.S., 1880; A.B. Augustana Coll., Rock Island, Ill., 1900, A.M., 1907; B.D., Augustana Theol. Sem., 1903; Ph.D., Central U., Indpls., 1912; D.D., Upsala Coll., East Orange, N.J., 1949; m. Josephine Lindquist, June 24, 1903. Ordained to ministry of Luth. Ch., 1903; pastor Bethlehem Ch., Red Oak, Ia., 1903-10, Immanuel Ch., Jamestown, N.Y., 1910-54. Pres. N.Y. Conf., Augustana Luth. Ch., also sec. Synodical Council. Formerly Chmn. Bd. Pub. Welfare, Jamestown, N.Y., also mem. Jamestown Gen. Hosp. Commn., Jamestown Bd. Health, Emergency Relief Bur., Community Chest Bd., Red Cross Bd. Dir. Upsala Coll.; pres. bd. Gustavus Adolphus Children's Home, Jamestown. Decorated Knight Royal of Vasa, 1st class; delivered principal address at 85th birthday observance of King of Sweden at Washington, D.C. Author: Chivalry, 1907; Studies in Genesis, 1911. Contbr. to synod publs. Home: 556 E. 2d St., Jamestown, N.Y. Died May 24, 1956; buried Hill Cemetery, Jamestown.

HANSON, Richard Locke, drug co. exec.; b. Guatemala, C.A., Apr. 22, 1899; s. Henry Hall and Carmen (deMatheu) H.; B.A., Columbia, 1922; m. Frances Leich, June 21, 1923. Various exec. capacities, including sales mgr. Charles Leich & Co., wholesale druggists, Evansville, Inc., 1922-40; div. mgr. McKesson & Robbins, Inc., Providence, 1940-42, v.p. exports, N.Y.C., 1944-48, asst. to regional v.p., N.Y.C., 1948-53, dist. v.p. Rego Park, N.Y., 1953—. Mem. exec. com. bd. trustees Evansville Coll., 1938-40; mem. bd. Evansville Art Mus., Evansville Philharmonic. Served as seaman, USN, 1917-19; capt., U.S. Army, 1942-43. Mem. Nat. Wholesale Druggists Assn. (chmn. bd. control, exec. com.; pres. 1958), Soc. Colonial Wars, Phi Delta Theta (pres.), Phi Beta Kappa. Clubs: Columbia University; Providence (R.I.) Art; Varsity C. Grolier. Home: 110 East End Av., N.Y.C. 28. Office: 90-30 Metropolitan Av., Rego Park 74, N.Y. Died July 1, 1958.

HANZLIK, Paul John, prof. pharmacology; born Shueyville, Ia., July 24, 1885; s. Martin and Mary (Kreysa) H.; Ph.G., State U. of Ia., 1902, Ph.C., 1908; A.B., U. of Ill., 1908, A.M., 1911; M.D., Western Reserve U., 1912; m. Bertha Shimek, Aug. 1909; children—Harold, Dorothy. Demonstrator in pharmacology, Western Reserve U., 1912-13, instr., 1913-15, asso., 1915-17, asst. prof., 1917-20, asso. prof., 1920-21; prof. pharmacology Stanford Univ., 1921-50, prof. emeritus since 1950; cons. pharmacologist San Francisco Dept. Health, since 1934. U.S. Dept. Agriculture, 1936-44. With Pharmacological Inst. and Physico-Chemical-Biological Inst., U. of

Vienna, 1913-14. Served as capt. Med. Corps, U.S. Army, attached to Chemical Warfare Service, 1918. Mem. Am. Med. Assn., Am. Physiol. Soc., Soc. Pharmacology and Exptl. Therapeutics, Soc. Exptl. Biology and Medicine, A.A.A.S., Calif. Acad. Medicine, Calif. Med. Assn., Com. on Research on Syphilis, Inc., Internat. Assn. Dental Research, Sigma Xi, Phi Rho Sigma, Alpha Omega Alpha; fellow Am. Coll. Physicians, Am. Coll. Dentists (hon.), Am. Social Hygiene Assn., Inc. Republican. Author: Actions and Uses of the Salicylates and Cinchophen in Medicine, 1927; (with Prof. T. Sollman), Fundamentals of Experimental Pharmacology, 1928, 2d ed., 1939; Handbook of Accepted Remedies, Symptoms and Treatment of Poisoning, Diagnostic Procedures and Miscellaneous Information, 1940, 3d edit. Contbr. to med. and scientific periodicals. Home: 303 Franklin St., San Mateo, Calif. Office: 2398 Sacramento St., S.F. 15. Died Feb. 1, 1951; buried Columbarium, Cypress Lawn.

HANZSCHE, William Thomson (hăn'shē), clergyman, editor; b. Baltimore, Md., July 28, 1891; s. William Thomson and Mary McLean (Hunt) H.; prep. edn., Baltimore Poly. Inst.; student Johns Hopkins, 1910-11; A.B., Washington and Lee U., 1913, D.D., 1928; student Union Theol. Sem., Richmond, Va., 1913-15; A.M., Princeton, 1916; B.D., Princeton Theol. Sem., 1916, M. S.Th., 1917; grad. study U. of Chicago, 1917-18; m. Miriam Elizabeth Woolf, Oct. 3, 1917; 1 dau., Elizabeth. Ordained Presbyn. ministry, 1917; served as chaplain Western Mil. Acad. and pastor Upper Alton Ch., Alton, Ill.; pastor Union Tabernacle, Phila., Pa., 1919-22, Prospect Street Ch., Trenton, New Jersey, since 1922; editor The Presbyterian Magazine, New York City, 1929-33; mem. operating com., Presbyn. Ch., 1927-32. Trustee Presbyn. Gen. Assembly since 1936, Presbyn. Hist. Soc. Editor Pageant, 1936; chmn. Publ. Bd. Presbyn. Life, since 1945. Exchange preacher in Eng., summer 1934, Germany, France, 1937. Mem. Delta Upsilon, Delta Sigma Rho, Pi Gamma Mu, Phi Beta Kappa. Ind. Rep. Past pres. Trenton Kiwanis. Author: The Great Themes of Jesus, 1926; The Oracles of God, 1929; Our Presbyterian Church, 1933; The Presbyterians—A Stanch and Sturdy People, 1934; And They Went Forth, the story of 100 years, 1937; Jesus and the Pursuit of Happiness, 1939; Section on History of the Denominations in Myers 4 vol. History of New Jersey, 1943; Moulders of American Church and State, 1945; Forgotten Founding Fathers of American Church and State; also The Christian Way of Life, Immortality, This is Protestant Christianity, and other booklets. Contbr. articles to mags. Radio speaker as "The Trailfinder," over Radio National Broadcasting Co. Blue, Red, Mutual Networks, for Federal Council of Churches; Faith in Our Time, over Mutual Network; "Morning Chapel," Dumont Television Network. Home: Edgewood Rd., Yardley, Bucks Co., Pa. Address: Prospect St. Church, Trenton, N.J.; (summer) "Appidon," Eagle Mere, Pa. Died June 21, 1954.

HAPGOOD, Neith Boyce (Mrs. Hutchins Hapgood), author; b. Franklin, Ind., Mar. 21, 1872; d. Henry H. and Mary E. (Smith) Boyce; m. Hutchins Hapgood, June 1899; children—Boyce (dec.), Charles Hutchins, Miriam, Beatrix. Author (under name Neith Boyce): The Forerunner, 1903; The Folly of Others, 1904; Eternal Spring, 1906; The Bond, 1908; Enemies (with Hutchins Hapgood), 1916; Two Sons, 1917; Proud Lady, 1923; Harry, 1923; Winter's Night, 1927. Home: Richmond, N.H. Died Dec. 2, 1951; buried Petersham, Mass.

HARBISON, Ralph Warner, mfr.; b. Alleghney, Pa., Feb. 20, 1876; s. late Samuel Pollock and Emma Jane (Boyd) H.; A.B., Princeton, 1898; LL.D., Washington and Jefferson Coll., 1937; m. Helen Harris, 1905; children—Marjorie Stabler, E. Harris, Samuel P., Frederick H. Dir. Harbison-Walker Refractories Co., Pittsburgh (founded by father). Was mem. exec. com. War Work Council of Y.M.C.A. during World War I; dir. Pittsburgh Y.M.C.A., Presbyn. Hosp. (Pitts.); trustee Hosp. Service Assn. West Pa.; v.p. bd. trustees Pa. Coll. for Women; trustee Am. U. Cairo (Egypt); trustee Western Theological Sem.; mem. trustees Lake Placid Ednl. Foundation; member Nat. Bd. Y.M.C.A.; mem. Internat. Board Y.M.C.A.; pres. Nat. Council of Y.M.C.A., 1939-41. Clubs: Harvard-Yale-Princeton, Edgeworth, Allegheny Country, Lake Placid. Home: Pine and Woodland Rd., Sewickley, Pa. Office: Farmers Bank Bldg., Pitts. Died Dec. 1959.

HARBISON, William Albert; b. Allegheny, Pa., Nov. 14, 1874; s. Samuel Pollock and Emma Jane (Boyd) H.; student U. of Western Pa., 1894-96; Princeton, 1896-98; m. Harriet Virginia Euwer, Nov. 2, 1911 (died Dec. 11, 1945); 1 dau., Cynthia Courtney (Mrs. Carl W. Heye). Pvt. sec. to father, pres. Harbison-Walker Fire Brick Co., 1898-1905; mng. executor Estate of Samuel P. Harbison, 1905-25; pres. Agusan Coconut Co. (Manila, P.I.). Trustee of Bukidnon Assos. (treas.), Grove City (Pa.) Coll. (mem. finance com.), Harbison Agrl. Inst., Irmo, S.C., mem. finance com. Poly. Inst., Puerto Rico; mem. bd. govs. Stony Brook (N.Y.) Assembly, of Stony Brook Sch. for Boys. Mem. Am. Bible Soc. (dir.); mem. fgn. agencies com.), Am. Tract Soc. (v.p.; exec. com.; chmn. Internat. Bunyan Tercentenary Com.), Fed. Council Chs. of Christ Am. (Evangelistic Commn.), Internat. Reform Fed. of Washington (dir.), Lord's Day Alliance of U.S. (dir.), Met. Assn. Daily Vacation Bible Schs. (bus. men's com.), World Sunday Sch. Assn. (bd. mgrs.), World Alliance for Internat. Friendship Through the Chs. (adv. bd.), Greater N.Y. Fed. of Chs. (mem. Bus. Men's Com. of week day Bible sch. work), Am. Mission to Lepers (mem. finance com.), Internat. Assn. Daily Vacation Bible Schools (dir.), World's Assn. of Daily Vacation Bible Schs. (director), World's Foundation Daily Vacation Bible Schs. (pres.), N.Y. State Civic League (pres.). Republican. Presbyn. Clubs: Clergy, Union League, Westchester Hills Golf, Westchester Sr. Golf Assn., National Republican (mem. nat. affairs com., N.Y.); Pa. Soc. of N.Y. Home: Sunnylea, 567 North St., White Plains, N.Y. Died Sept. 9, 1950.

HARCOURT, Alfred, publisher; b. New Paltz, Ulster County, N.Y., Jan. 31, 1881; s. Charles M. and Gertrude M. (Elting) H.; ed. New Palz State Normal Sch.; A.B., Columbia, 1904; m. Susan Harreus, April 21, 1906 (died Aug. 14, 1923); 1 son, Hastings; m. 2d, Ellen Knowles Eayrs, Jan 19, 1924. Began with Henry Holt & Co., pubs., New York, 1904, and became dir. and sec.; resigned June 1919, and founded Harcourt, Brace Co. of which was pres. until voluntary retirement, 1942; special consultant, George S. Armstrong & Co., indsl. and management engrs., since 1942; founded Blue Ribbon Books, Inc. Democrat. Clubs: Greenwich (Conn.) Country, Valley, Santa Barbara, Calif. Compiler (with Crosby Gaige) Books and Readings, 1908. Office: 383 Madison Av., N.Y.C. Died June 20, 1954; buried New Paltz, N.Y.

HARCUM, Edith Hatcher (Mrs. Octavius Marvin Harcum), educator; b. Richmond, Va.; d. William Eldridge and Virginia Oranie (Snead) Hatcher; B.L., Woman's Coll., Richmond, Va.; studied piano with Safonoff, New York, Phillip, Paris, Leschetizky, Vienna; m. Octavius Marvin Harcum, Feb. 17, 1913; children—Edith Virginia, William Marvin. Concert pianist; soloist with symphony orchestras; established music dept. Fork Union Mil. Acad.; former head of piano dept. Shipley Sch., Bryn Mawr, Pa.; founder and pres. Harcum Junior Coll., Bryn Mawr, Pa. Clubs: Art Alliance, Plays and Players, Print, Main Line Music. Home: Bryn Mawr, Pa. Died Dec. 1958.*

HARDEE, Cary Augustus, ex-gov.; b. Taylor County, Fla., Nov. 13, 1876; s. James Blacksher and Amanda Catherine (Johnson) H.; student pub. schs.; m. Maud Randell, Feb. 7, 1900. Tchr. pub. schs., Fla., until 1900; admitted to bar, 1900, practiced at Live Oak, Fla.; state's atty. 3d Jud. Circuit, Fla., 1905-13; mem. and speaker Fla. Ho. of Reps., 1915-17; gov. of Fla., 1921-25. Democrat. Baptist. Mason, K.P., Elk, Woodman. Home: Live Oak, Fla. Died Nov. 21, 1957; buried Oakridge Cemetery, Madison, Fla.

HARDEN, Orville, v.p. Standard Oil Co. (N.J); b. Chicago, Ill., Apr. 4, 1894; s. Charles F. and Flora Kimball (Tice) H.; ed. pub. sch. vice pres., dir., vice chmn. exec. com. Standard Oil Co. (N.J.); dir. Arabian Am. Oil Co. Recipient Order of Comdr., French Legion of Honor. Clubs: Links, Knickerbocker. Home: 400 Park Av., N.Y.C. 22. Office: 30 Rockefeller Plaza, N.Y.C. 29. Died Aug. 17, 1957.

HARDESTY, Frederick A(rchibald), naval officer (ret.), tchr.; b. Astoria, Ore., Jan. 16, 1893; s. Millard Fillmore and Nettie Blanche (Harriman) H.; A.B., U. Ore., 1915; student Harvard, 1917, Ensign's Sch., 1918, Submarine Sch., 1922, Naval War Coll., 1926-27, USN, Postgrad. Sch., 1931-33; m. Hannah Florence Kelly, Oct. 4, 1923 (dec. Feb. 14, 1930); 1 son, John Frederick; m. 2d, Elizabeth Fuller Collingwood, June 17, 1931; 1 son, William Harriman. Tchr. high sch., Ore., 1915-17; entered USNR, 1917; commd. ensign USN, 1918, advanced through grades to capt., 1943; ret. as rear adm., 1947. Served in U.S.S. Ohio, World War I; exec. officer, U.S.S. Heywood, 1940-42, comdg. officer U.S.S. Schuylkill, 1943-44, U.S.. Rocky Mount, 1944-45. Decorated with World Wars I and II medals, Bronze Star, Philippine Liberation medal, various campaign and battle ribbons and stars. Mason. Club: Players' (Swarthmore, Pa.). Home: Moylan, Pa. Died June 6, 1956; buried Arlington Nat. Cemetery.

HARDESTY, Shortridge, civil engr.; b. Weston, Mo., Sept. 13, 1884; s. John H. and Bertie Malin (Railey) H.; A.B., Drake University, Des Moines, Ia., 1905, LL.D., from same, 1928; C.E., Rensselaer Poly. Inst., 1908, D.E., 1951; D.E., Union College, 1949; married Adelia V. Ferrell, August 20, 1910; children—Julia H. Davidson, Egbert Railey. Draftsman and designer, Waddell & Harrington, Kansas City, Mo., 1908-15; designing engr., Waddell & Son, 1916-17; mem. Waddell & Son, Inc., 1918-19; asso. engr. with J. A. L. Waddell, N.Y. City, 1920-26; partner Waddell & Hardesty, New York City, 1927-38; in practice as Waddell & Hardesty, 1938 to 1945; partner Hardesty & Hanover, 1945—; in charge work 1920—, including Washington Bridge over Housatonic River, Missouri River Bridge at Lexington, Mo., Goethals Bridge and Outerbridge Crossing for Port of New York Authority, North End Bridge, Springfield, Mass., four vertical lift spans in Jersey Central Bridge over Newark Bay, Kennebec bridge at Bath, Maine, Mississippi River bridge at Cairo, Ill., Standard Highway bridge plans for the Cuban Government, Cooper River Bridge at Charleston, S.C., lift span in Suisin Bay Bridge of Southern Pacific Ry., Anthony Wayne River Bridge at Toledo, O., Hudson River bridges at Albany and Troy, N.Y., Grand Island bridges over Niagara River, Pa. R.R. bridges over Passaic and Hackensack rivers, Marine Parkway Bridge over Rockaway Inlet, Allegheny County Bridges, Pittsburgh, Flushing River Bridge of Bronx-Whitestone Bridge Project, Perisphere and Trylon for New York World's Fair, 1939, bridges on Cross Bay Parkway and Circumferential Parkway in New York City, Rainbow Arch Bridge at Niagara Falls, Res. Basin bridge, Phila. Navy Cross Bronx Expressway and Van Wyck Expressway, in New York City, bridges for Virginia Highway Dept.; Captree State Parkway, Atlantic Beach Bridge, Niagara Thruway in Buffalo, Ohio Turnpike, Garden State Parkway in New Jersey, Cuyahoga River Bridges in Cleveland for W.&L.E. Ry., Nickel Plate Ry., and B.&O. Ry.; Jamaica Bay Bridges in N.Y.C.; Bd. Transportation. Chmn. Column Research Council; mem. Am. Soc. Civil Engrs., Am. Inst. Consulting Engineers, Society Am. Military Engrs., Am. Ry. Enging. Assn., Am. Soc. for Testing Materials, Am. Concrete Inst., Am. Toll Bridge Assn., Internat. Assn. for Bridge and Structural Engring., Rensselaer Soc. Engrs., Rensselaer Tech. Soc., Phi Beta Kappa, Sigma Xi, Tau Beta Pi. Democrat. Mem. Christian (Disciples) Ch. Club: Winged Foot Golf, Engineers. Home: 12 Cambridge Court, Larchmont, N.Y. Office: 101 Park Av., N.Y.C. 17. Died Oct. 16, 1956; buried Kensico Cemetery, Valhalla, N.Y.

HARDIN, Charles Roe, lawyer; b. Newark, N.J., Dec. 29, 1894; s. John Ralph and Jennie Josephine (Roe) H.; A.B., Princeton U., 1915; LL.B., Harvard University, 1919; married Emma Downer March 6, 1920 (died April 22, 1941); children—Charles Roe, Jr., Dorothy Downer (Mrs. Sidney Gordon Dillon), William Downer, Robert Downer; married 2d, Grace Valentine Wiss, February 6, 1946. Admitted to New Jersey bar as atty., 1920, as counsellor, 1923; engaged in gen. practice of law at Newark, N.J., as mem. firm Pitney, Hardin and Ward since 1923; dir. Nat. Newark & Essex Banking Co., Am. Ins. Co. Served as 1st lt. inf. U.S. Army, 1917-19. Unsuccessful candidate N.J. State Senate, 1926. N.J. mem. Nat. Conf. of Commrs. on Uniform State Laws. Mem. Essex Co. Park Commn. Trustee Babies' Hosp. Mem. Newark C. of C., Am., N.J. State bar assns., Essex Co. Bar Assn. (pres. 1935). Dem. Episcopalian. Mason. Clubs: Essex, Down Town (Newark, N.J.); Somerset Hills Country (Bernardsville, N.J.); Princeton (N.Y.). Home: 520 Parker St. Office: 744 Broad St., Newark, N.J. Died June 21, 1951.

HARDING, Albert Austin, band dir.; b. Georgetown, Ill., Feb. 10, 1880; s. Conway Augustus and Jennie (Stewart) H.; engring. student U. Ill., 1902-06, B.Mus., 1916; Mus. Doc., Phillips U., Enid, Okla., 1936, Davidson (N.C.) Coll., 1936; m. Margaret Rogers, June 11, 1913; 1 dau., Jane Austin (Mrs. Robert C. Moss). Dir. of bands, orchestras, etc., Paris, Ill., Terre Haute, Ind., Champaign and Urbana, Ill., 1898-1905; dir. bands dept. U. Ill., 1905-48, prof. music, 1918-48; dir. Univ. Symphony Orchestra, 1918-31; dir. of bands Nat. Music Camp, 1930-33; founder, conductor Nat. Band Clinics, U. of Ill.; guest condr. Chicagoland, Tri-State and various other music festivals, music camps, etc.; adjudicator Nat. Sch. Band Contests, Chicago World's Fair Bandmaster Contest, Am. Legion Nat. Band Contest, also many state band contests; spl. adviser to british music pubs., 1936. Chmn. band com. Music Educators Nat. Conf.; mem. adv. council Nat. Music Camp; mem. bd. dirs. Ill. State Municipal Band Assn. Served with Ill. N.G., 1899-1902; commd. col. Ill. State Militia, Oct. 1941. Mem. Am. Bandmasters Assn. (past v.p. and treas., past pres.), Nat. Sch. Band Assn. (mem. adv. com.), College Band Directors Assn. (hon. life pres.) Sinfonia, Phi Kappa Psi, Pi Kappa Lambda (past treas.-gen.); hon. pres. Ill. School Band Assn. Methodist. Rotarian. Editor: Manual of School Band Music, 1931; also numerous transcriptions for symphonic band; adv. editor various Am. band publs. Home: 710 S. Elm St., Champaign, Ill. Died Dec. 1958.

HARDING, Charles L(aban), business exec.; born Payson, Utah, June 9, 1906; s. Laban and Mary (Page) H.; S.B., Utah Agrl. Coll., 1928; LL.B., U. of Calif., 1933; m. Aleen Bird, Aug. 21, 1929; children—Marianna, Charles, Catharine Bee. With Shell Oil Co. and affiliated cos., San Francisco and New York, 1933-42, asso. Socony-Vacuum Oil Co., Inc., since 1944; dir. Socony-Vacuum Oil Co., Inc., Trans-Arabian Pipe Line Co., Arabian Am. Oil Co., Socony Vacuum Overseas Supply Co., Counsel Dist. 1, Petroleum Adminstrn. for War, 1942, dir., 1942-43; petroleum industry and fgn. operations coms., 1943-44; dir. in charge Dist. 1, Petroleum Adminstrn. for War, 1945. Mem. New York and Calif. bar assns., Council

Fgn. Relations, Inc., Am. Acad. Polit. and Social Sci. Clubs: Adirondack League (Old Forge, N.Y.); University, Downtown Assn. (New York). Home: 316 Manhasset Woods Rd., Manhasset, N.Y. Office: 26 Broadway, N.Y.C. Died Sept. 23, 1953; buried Nassau Knolls Cemetery, Port Washington, N.Y.

HARDING, George M., artist; b. Phila., October 2, 1882; s. Joseph and Charlotte Elizabeth (Matthews) H.; brother Charlotte Harding Brown; ed. Pa. Acad. Fine Arts, and with Howard Pyle, 1902-03; studied architecture; m. Anita Cotheal Nisbett, 1916 (dec.); children—Anita N. (Mrs. John Kistler), George M. Sent to northern ice fields, West Indies by Harper's, 1908, 10, 11; spl. artist, Harper's Mag., on journey around the world, working in Australia, New Guinea, Arabia, Dutch East Indies, Malay States, China, 1912-13. Mem. faculty Pa. Acad. of Fine Arts, dept. mural decoration. Mural decorations in First Nat. Bank, Corn Exchange Nat. Bank (Phila.), Germantown Trust Co.; war decoration State of Pa. Winner competition for mural decorations in U.S. Custom House., Phila., 1935, 2 panels in Post Office Bldg., Washington, D.C., 1936, murals in Phila. Post Office, 1937, mural in Legislative Hall, U.S. Government Building, New York World's Fair, 1339; murals in main hall of new Municipal Court, Phila., 1940; Murals in Common Pleas Court No. 7, City Hall, Philadelphia; five murals Montgomery Country Court House; mural designer for interior of Audubon Shrine Mus. 1st home of John James Audubon, Montgomery Co., Pa. Pictures in permanent collections of Pa. Academy Fine Arts and Chrysler collection and many private collections. Member board directors Pennsylvania Academy Fine Arts, 1958-59. Awarded E. T. Statesbury prize Pa. Acad. Fine Arts, 1938, Gold Medal of Honor, 1953, Fine Arts award, A.I.A., 1953, gold medal for mural painting, Architectural League New York, 1953. Drawings shown in United States, England and Australia. Commanding captain engineers, U.S. Army, 1918, and apptd. one of official artists of A.E.F.; made sketches and covered Château Thierry defense, Marne offensive, St. Mihiel offensive, Argonne-Meuse offensive, besides all American sectors from Amiens to Baccarat; accompanied Army of Occupation through Lorraine, Luxemburg and Germany; disch. May 1919; U.S. Marine Corps, June 1942, served as major in New Georgia Vella la Vella, Bougainville Emerau and Guam invasions. Dir. Abbey Scholarship Found. Mem. Acad. Natural Scis., U.S. Naval Inst., Soc. Am. Mil. Engrs., Pa. Art Commn., Nat. Soc. Mural Painters, Pa. Hist. Society; fellow Royal Geog. Soc.; National Academy; hon. mem. Tau Sigma Delta. Clubs: Century (N.Y.); Racquet. Home and Studio: Wynnewood, Pa. Died Mar. 26, 1959; buried St. David's Churchyard, Radnor, Pa.

HARDING, Louis A.; cons. engr.; b. Factoryville, Pa., Oct. 16, 1876; s. Henry L. and Luzette I. (Maynard) H.; student Keystone Acad., 1890-91; Centenary Collegiate Inst., 1893-95; B.S. in M.E., Pennsylvania State Coll., 1899; m. Charlotte Hanes Phelps, Oct. 6, 1923. Engr., Dickson Mfg. Co., Scranton, Pa., 1899, Lackawanna Steel Co., 1900; instr. machine design Cornell U., 1900-01; supt. coal washeries Lackawanna Coal & Coke Co., 1901-02; mgr. Pa. Engrg. Co., 1902-03; br. mgr. Armstrong Cork Co., 1903-05, chief engr., 1906-09; partner Cumming's-Harding, Inc., 1909-10; head dept. mech. engring., Pa. State Coll., 1910-13; cons. engr. N.Y., 1913; prof. expert mech. engr. U. Ill.; 1913-15; chief engr. John W. Cowper Co., 1915-21; pres.-treas. Harding & Crea, Inc., 1921-23; treas. Leach Steel Corp., fabricators, 1923—; pres. L.A. Harding Constrn. Corp., contractors, 1924-34; treas. Wilkeson Harding Corp., 1923—, also director; pres. Harding-Carlton Corp., 1934-36; commr. pub. works City of Buffalo, 1936-40; treas. and dir. N.Y., Leach Steel Corp., Rochester, N.Y. Fellow Am. Soc. M.E., 1943; mem. Am. Soc. C.E., Am. Soc. Heating and Ventilating Engrs. (pres. 1930), Sigma Psi, Phi Kappa Sigma, Pi Tau Sigma. Mason. Clubs: Buffalo, Niagara Falls City. Contbr. to Kent's Mechanical Engineers' Pocket Book, 1916-45; written on Mechanical Equipment of Buildings, 1916; Heating, Ventilating and Air Conditioning, 1932; Steam Power Plant Engineers, 1932; Heating and Air Conditioning Manual, 1935; A Brief History of the Art of Navigation, 1952. Address: 85 Cleveland Av., Buffalo 22. Deceased.

HARDING, Robert Ellison, banker; b. Paris, Tenn., Mar. 7, 1883; s. Noah and Celia (Matthewson) H.; prep. edn., Fort Worth (Tex.) U.; student U. of Tex., 1900-03; m. Merle Reynolds, Jan. 4, 1911; children—Robert E. Jr., Sue. With Ft. Worth Nat. Bank, summers 1897-1903, clk., 1903-1906, became asst. cashier, 1908, vice pres., 1914, president, 1930-51, chairman of board, 1951—; member Federal Advisory Council of Federal Reserve System, 1937-41; dir. Riverside State Bank, Fort Worth; vice pres., director Acme Brick Company; dir. State Reserve Life Ins. Co., Tex. Electric Service Co., Tex. Pacific Coal & Oil Co., T. & P. Ry., Internat.-Gt. Northern Railroad Co., M.P. R.R. Co., N.O., Tex. & Mexico R.R. Co., Ellison Furniture and Carpet Co. of Fort Worth, Fort Worth Lloyds, Fort Worth Belt Ry., West Side State Bank, Ft. Worth, Agrl.-Livestock Finance Corp., Citizens Hotel Co., Fed. Royalties Co.; dir. Fed. Reserve Bank of Dallas Tex., 1930-36. Trustee Texas Christian Univ., Fort Worth; v.p. Tex. Christian Univ. Stadium Assn. Mem. Assn. Reserve City Bankers (pres. 1933 and dir.), Fort Worth Chamber of Commerce (pres. 1928-29), Beta Theta Pi. Presbyn. Mason (32°, Shriner). Clubs: Fort Worth (v.p.), River Crest Country (v.p.), Rotary (hon.), Colonial. Home: 69 Westover Terrace, Ft. Worth 7. Address: care Fort Worth National Bank, Box 2050, Fort Worth. Died Feb. 20, 1952.

HARDISON, Osborne Bennett, ret. naval officer; b. Wadesboro, N.C., Dec. 22, 1892; s. William Cameron and Harriett Eleanor (Bennett) H.; A.B., U. of N.C., 1911; grad. U.S. Naval Acad., 1916; m. Ruth Morgan, Nov. 28, 1926; children—Osborne Bennett, William Gerry Morgan. Commd. ensign, USN, 1916, advancing through the grades to rear adm., 1942; served on U.S.S. Texas, 1916-20, operating in association and cooperation with British Grand Fleet during World War I; exec. officer U.S.S. Wickes, 1920-21, later serving on destroyers Claxton and Parrott; assigned to presdl. yacht U.S.S. Mayflower, 1922; became naval aviator, 1923, joining aircraft squadron, Scouting Fleet, 1923; observer, army air station, Selfredge Field, Mt. Clemens, Mich., 1925; instr. in dept. engring. and aeros., U.S. Naval Acad., 1925-27; comdg. officer, fighting squadrons based on U.S.S. Lexington, 1927-29; on duty, Navy Dept. Washington, 1929-32; operations officer on staff Rear Adm. John Halligan, Jr., U.S.S. Lexington; comdr. aircraft, Battle Force, U.S.S. Saratoga, 1932-34; navigator, U.S. Langley, 1934-35; with Bur. Aeros. and Bur. of Navigation, 1935-36; aviation officer Office of Chief of Naval Operations, 1936-38; exec. officer U.S. Ranger, 1938-39; aviation officer on staff Adm. James O. Richardson, comdr. in chief U.S. Fleet, 1939-40; comdg. officer naval air station, Anacostia, D.C., also on duty Bur. Aeros., 1940; aide to asst. sec. of navy for air, 1941-42; comdg. officer U.S.S. Enterprise, 1942-43, engaging in battles of Santa Cruz and Solomon Islands and other operations in vicinity of Solomons; comdr. Fleet Air in South Pacific, 1943-44; became chief of naval air primary tng., 1944 (with hdqrs. Kansas City, Kan., removed to Glenview, Ill., July 1944); dir. Pan-Am. Affairs, Office, Chief of Naval appropriations, now ret. Decorated Navy Cross, Legion of Merit, with star. Presidential Unit Citation. Mem. Phi Delta Theta. Clubs: Chevy Chase (Washington); Glen View (Glenview, Ill.). Home: 3315 Rowland Pl. N.W. Office: Navy Dept., Washington. Died Mar. 1959.*

HARDT, John William, banker; b. Frederick, Md., Apr. 3, 1884; s. William McCulley and Mary Ida (Keller) H.; B.S.E., U. Pa., 1906; m. Apr. 14, 1909. Asst. nat. bank examiner, 1906-07; various positions Franklin Nat. Bank, Phila., 1908-10. asst. cashier, 1910-16, cashier, 1916-21. v.p., 1921-28 (merged with Phila. Nat. Bank, 1928); v.p. Phila. Nat. Bank, 1928-47, exec. v.p., chmn. bd., 1947-49, now dir., mem. exec. com.; dir. Am. Stores Co., Interstate R.R. Co. Mem. Phi Delta Theta. Republican. Presbyn. Clubs: Union League, Rittenhouse, Midday (Phila.). Home: 6398 Church Rd., Overbrook, Phila. Office: Phila. Nat. Bank Bldg., Phila. Died Mar. 1960.

HARDY, Charles J., lawyer; b. N.Y. City; s. Michael and Elizabeth (Farrell) H.; student Coll. City of New York; LL.B., Columbia; LL.D. (De Paul University, Chicago); m. Virginia T. Taylor; 1 son, Charles J. Mem. Hardy, Stancliffe & Hardy. Trustee N.Y. Mil. Academy. Mem. Am. Bar Assn., N.Y. State Bar Assn., N.Y. County Lawyers Assn., Internat. Law Assn., Am. Judicature Soc., Phi Gamma Delta. Democrat; presdl. elector, 1932; N.Y. State rep. National Econ. Council, 1934. Catholic. Clubs: Metropolitan. Nat. Golf Links of America, Winged Foot Golf. Catholic, New York Athletic, Phi Gamma Delta, Manhattan, Long Island Country. Home: Hampton Bays, Long Island, N.Y. Office: 30 Church St., N.Y.C. Died Jan. 17, 1956.

HARDY, David Phillip, business mgr.; b. Petaluma, Calif., May 24, 1890; s. Henry and Louise (Daum) H.; B.S. in M.E., U. of Cal., 1912; m. Roena Vina Hinkle, Santa Cruz, Mar. 3, 1918; children—Charles Edward, James Herbert. Tchr. San Rafael Military Acad., Cal., 1912-16; high sch. tchr., prin., San Francisco Pub. Schs., 1916-24; dep. supt. schs., 1924-45 (leave for army service); asst. supt. of schs., San Francisco, 1945-48. With Cal. N.G., 1914—, beginning as private; served on Mexican border, 1916; capt. C.A., U.S. Army, 1917-19; col. 250th C.A., U.S. Army, 1940; brig. gen., 1941; now brig. gen. Cal. Def. and Security Corps. Mem. Am. Legion, Pi Kappa Phi. Republican. Club: Commonwealth of California. Address: 500 Rivera St., San Francisco. Died Sept. 17, 1957; buried San Francisco Nat. Cemetery.

HARDY, Edwin Noah, clergyman; b. Nelson, N.H., Mar. 1, 1861; s. Noah W. and Maria Rollins (Stone) H.; A.B., Amherst, 1887, A.M., 1904; B.D., Hartford Theol. Sem., 1890; Ph.D., Boston U., 1906; m. Nellie M. Severy, Oct. 22, 1890; children—Noah Phillips, Freeman Severy (dec.), Miriam, Christine Nellie. Ordained to ministry Congl. Ch., 1890; asso. pastor Phillips Ch., South Boston, 1890-1893; pastor Bethany Ch., Quincy, Mas., 1895-1911, 1st Ch., La Grange, Ill., 1911-16; field sec. Am. Tract Soc., 1918-22, exec., and rec. sec., 1922-41, now sec. emeritus; former chmn. Gen. Com. Immigrant Aid. Ellis Island and New York. Ex-pres. Brotherhood Andrew and Philip; 1st pres. Hardy Family Assn., 1930-37; pres. Ill. Home Missionary Soc., 1914-16. Fellow Inst. Am. Genealogy. Republican. Clubs: Congregational, Amherst, New Hampshire. Author: The Churches and Educated Men, 1904; A Manual of American Citizenship, 1919 (rev. 1925); also (booklets) The Story of the English Bible; A Century of Temperance Effort; Christ in the Life of Today; Speeding the World O'er Land and Sea; The Challenge of the New Era; Handbook for Christian Literature. Co-editor and reviser of Uncle John Vassar, Apostle of Personal Evangelism, by T. E. Vassar, 1931. Compiler and editor (with Dr. H. Claude Hardy) The Hardy Family History and Genealogy, 1935; George Whitefield—The Matchless Soul-Winner, 1938. History of the American Tract Society 1825-1944 (1945). Home: Greenwich, Conn. Died Aug. 1950.

HARDY, James Graham, college prof.; b. Easton, Pa., Mar. 13, 1874; s. Joseph Johnston and Mary Lewis (Montague) H.; A.B., Lafayette Coll., Pa.. 1894, A.M., 1898; Ph.D., Johns Hopkins, 1898; m. Nona Burnett Mills, Dec. 22, 1905. Began as instr. mathematics, Williams Coll., 1898, successively asst. prof., asso. prof., and prof., July 1, 1913—. Progressive. Presbyn. Mem. Am. Math. Soc., Phi Beta Kappa, Phi Gamma Delta. Author: Applications of the Theory of Limits to Elementary Geometry, 1907. Address: Williamstown, Mass. Died Sept. 5, 1953.

HARDY, Lamar, lawyer; b. Meridian, Miss., May 29, 1879; s. William Harris and Hattie (Lott) H.; Ph.B., U. of Miss., 1898; LL.B., Vanderbilt U., 1900; LL.D., U. of Miss., 1931; m. Micheline Michel, Oct. 1, 1914; 1 dau., Micheline Hardy (Mrs. William B. Clagett). Admitted to N.Y. bar, 1904; mem. of Davies, Hardy, Schenck & Sons; spl. asst. to atty. gen. of U.S. to serve as hearing officer under Selective Service Act of 1948; corp. counsel of City of N.Y., 1915-17; U.S. atty. for Southern Dist. of New York, 1935-38. Independent Democrat. Mem. Am. and N.Y. State bar assns., N.Y. So. Soc., Phi Delta Theta. Clubs: Recess, Blind Brook. Home: 840 Park Av., N.Y.C. Office: 1 Wall St., N.Y.C. Died Aug. 18, 1950.

HARDY, Le Grand Haven, ophthalmologist; b. Provo City, Utah, June 13, 1894; s. Milton Henry and Elizabeth (Smoot) H.; A.B., Brigham Young U., 1916; grad. study, U. of Chicago, 1917; B.S., Columbia, 1919, M.D., 1921; m. Susanna Edwards Schuyler Haigh, July 9, 1923. Began practice as ophthalmologist at N.Y. City, 1922; asst. surgeon N.Y. Eye and Ear Infirmary, 1924-30; ophthalmologist Northern Dispensary, 1924-29, consultant since 1929; ophthalmic surgeon Midtown Hosp., 1925-29; dir. ophthalmology Fifth Avenue Hosp., 1929-36; prof. of clin. Ophthalmology Coll. P and S. Columbia U., attending ophthalmologist Presbyterian Hospital and Vanderbilt Clinic; staff member Inst. of Ophthalmology; dir. Functional Testing and Physiologic Optics Labs., Inst. of Ophthalmology. Fellow A.C.S., A.M.A., N.Y. Acad. Medicine, Am. Ophthalmol. Soc., N.Y. Ophth. Soc., Am. Acad. Ophthalmology and Otolaryngology, A.A.A.S., Association Research Ophthalmologists, American Orthoptic Council (pres. since 1938), Inter-Society Color Council. Auhthor: History and Technic of Scotometry, published by American Ophthal. Society, 1931; also articles on illumination as it affects the eye, orthoptics, the bases of color vision, measurements of sight, etc. Co-author: The Geometry of Binocular Space Perception, 1953. Co-inventor: Hardy-Rand-Ritter Pseudoisochromatic Plates. Home: 21 E. 79th St., New York 21. Office: 23 E. 79th St. N.Y.C. Died Apr. 14, 1954.

HARDY, Oscar J., business exec.; b. Oshkosh, Wis., July 4, 1874; s. Louis and Augusta (Nemitz) H.; ed. in pub. schs.; m. Gertrude Weidner, Mar. 23, 1914; children—Susan (Mrs. Samuel W. Heaney), Doris (Mrs. A. Thomas Schwalm). Pres., pub. Oshkosh (Wis.) Daily Northwestern, 1917—; chmn. bd. Oshkosh Nat. Bank, 1934—; pres., dir. Oshkosh Motor Truck, Inc., 1936-44; dir. Wis. Nat. Life Ins. Co., 1928-49. Mem. Wis. Daily Newspaper League, Oshkosh Found., Am. Newspaper Pubs. Assn., Inland Press. Republican. Conglist. Elk, Mason. Apptd. col., governor's staff, 1939. Home: 541 Algoma Blvd. Office: Oshkosh Daily Northwestern, Oshkosh, Wis. Died Aug. 6, 1950; buried Riverside Cemetery.

HARDY, Ralph W(illiams), broadcasting exec.; b. Salt Lake City, May 6, 1916; s. John Kay and Clare (Williams) H.; student U. Utah, 1933-34-45; m. Maren Eccles, Mar. 10, 1939; children—Ralph Williams, Clare, Alison, Maren, David Eccles. Various positions sales and programming, radio sta. KSL, Salt Lake City, 1937-41, coordinator war activities, 1941-43, program dir., 1943-45, exec. asst. in charge pub. affairs, 1945-48, asst. gen. mgr., 1948-49; dir. govt. relations Nat. Assn. Radio and TV Broadcasters, Washington, 1949-53, v.p., 1953-55; v.p.

CBS, Inc., 1955—; dir. Advt. Council, Inc., 1949-53. Mem. advt. adv. com. Sec. Commerce, 1949-50; sec. Broadcast Adv. Council, 1950-52; bd. govs. Assn. Better Bus. Burs., 1951-54; mem. U.S. Nat. Commn. UNESCO, 1953—, vice chmn., 1955—, mem. U.S. delegation 8th World Conf. UNESCO, Montevideo, Uruguay, 1954, 9th World Conf., New Delhi, India, 1956; adv. council World Affairs Center U.S., 1956—. Mem. nat. council Boy Scouts, 1955—. Mem. U.S. C. of C., S.A.R. (past pres. Utah). Mem. Ch. of Jesus Christ of Latter-Day Saints (bishop 1941-49; 2d asst. gen. supt. YMMIA 1948-49, gen. bd. 1949—; high council Washington Stake 1949—, chmn. gen chaplain's com. 1952—). Clubs: Nat. Press, University, Columbia Country (Washington). Home: 3330 Stuyvesant Pl., Washington 15. Office: 1735 De Sales St., Washington 6: Died Aug. 5, 1957; buried Ogden, Utah.

HARDY, Summers, lawyer; b. Scotland, Van Buren County, Ark., May 23, 1875; s. Henry and Martha Adelaide (Underwood) H.; student Quitman (Ark.) Coll. to 1892; m. Laura V. Scrivner, July 29, 1900; children—Calla Mae, Milton Welch. Admitted to bar, Ardmore, I.T., 1897; practiced at Ardmore and Madill; pres. bd. Madill City pub. schs., 1907-08; chmn. Marshall County Dem. Conv., 1908; mem. Dem. State Central Com., Okla., 1910; judge 6th Jud. Dist., Okla., 1911-13, 26th Jud. Dist., 1913-14; asso. justice Supreme Ct. of Okla., 1915-21 (chief justice, 1919); resigned 1919; became counsel Sinclair Cos., Tulsa; retired from legal dept. Sinclair Cos., engaged in gen. law practice at Tulsa, 1942—; dean Law Sch., U. Tulsa. Mem. Am., Okla., Tulsa County bar assns., S.A.R. Brig. gen. United Sons Confed. Vets., 1900; pres. High-Twelve Internat., 1930-31. Methodist. Mason. Home: 1702 S. Madison. Office: Ritz Bldg., Tulsa. Died Oct. 18, 1950.

HARE, Marmaduke, clergyman; b. Knottingley, Eng., Apr. 6, 1856; s. Robert Henry and Margaret (Leighton) H.; Bath Coll.; Hull Med. Sch., 1875; King's Coll., London, 1878; Dorchester Coll., Oxford, Eng., 1878; M.D., Ghent, 1888; D.D., Seabury Div. Sch., 1921; m. Anna Frances Lyster, June 28, 1910; 1 dau., Alice. Ordained to ministry P.E. Ch., deacon, 1879, priest, 1881; chaplain British Army, S. Africa, 1880-84; asst. Battersea, London, 1884-85; vicar of Clay Hill, London, 1885-89, Christ Ch., Watney St., London, 1889-92; rector Bow and Surrogate, London, 1892-98; acting rector St. Paul's Ch., Albany, N.Y., 1899; asst. rector St. George's Ch., Toronto, Can., 1900-04; rector All Saints' Ch., New Milford, Conn., 1904-07; dean Trinity Cathedral, Davenport, Ia., 1907-28; emeritus. Del. Gen. Conv., 1910, 13, 20, 29. Dir. YMCA, Davenport, People's Union Mission. Clubs: Commercial, Contemporary. Address: care St. John's Cathedral, N.Y.C. Died Dec. 12, 1942.

HARGADON, I. Leo, dir. University Libraries, Fordham U.; b. Balt., Dec. 20, 1880; A.B., Loyola Coll., 1899; studied Jesuit House Classical Studies, Frederick, Md., Poughkeepsie, N. Y., 1900—04; Woodstock Coll., 1904-07, 1912-16. Ordained priest Roman Cath. Ch. 1916; tchr. mathematics Fordham U., 1907-12, 1919-24; librarian Fordham U., 1924-50, dir. libraries, 1950—. Mem. Soc. of Jesus. Address: care Fordham University, E. Fordham Rd., N.Y.C. 58. Died July 16, 1952; buried St. Andrew-on-Hudson, Poughkeepsie, N.Y.

HARGER, Charles Moreau, editor; b. Phelps, N.Y., Jan. 23, 1863; s. Henry and Martha (Densmore) H.; grad. Phelps Classical Sch., 1881; L.H.D., Bethany Coll., 1901; Litt.D., Baker U., 1909; m. Blanche Bradshaw, of Hope, Kan., Oct. 3, 1889; children—Lois Blanche (Mrs. Ross I. Parker), Ruth Moreau (Mrs. Giles S. Maxwell), Dorothy Jean (Mrs. H. Donald Harris). Principal of schools at Hope, Kan., 1886-88; editor Abilene Daily Reflector, 1888—; pres. Reflector Pub. Co.; dir. Abilene Nat. Bank. Dir. and lecturer, dept. of journalism, U. of Kan., 1905-10; chmn. Nat. Journalism, Teachers' Assn., 1909-10. Pres. Nat. Citizens' League for Kan. Asst. sec. Rep. Nat. Conv., 7 sessions, 1908-36; postmaster, Abilene, 1912-13; pres. State Bd. Corrections, 1915-16. Mem. State Bd. of Regents, 1925-38, chmn., 1929-38; president State Hist. Soc., 1930-31; mem. Kansas World's Fair Commn., 1937-39. Mason. Rotarian. Editor and compiler Poetry in Song. Contbr. to Century, Harper's, Scribner's, and other mags. Home: Abilene, Kan. Died Apr. 3, 1955; buried Abilene.

HARGREAVES, John Morris, air force officer; b. La Moille, Ill., Feb. 26, 1901; s. John Robert and Bessie (Kay) H.; A.B., Macalester Coll., 1920; B. S., U. Minn., 1921, M.G., 1924, M.D., 1925; m. Hartie Noel Mickel, Mar. 31, 1929; children—John Joaquin, Hardy Mickel. Intern Letterman Gen. Hosp., San Francisco, 1925-26; commd. 1st lt. M.C., U.S. Army. 1925, and advanced through grades to major gen., 1949; assigned to various Air Force and Ground Force hosps., Philippine Islands, 1927-30; dir. eye, ear, nose and throat, Sch. of Aviation Med., Randolph Air Force, Tex., 1935-40; asst. air surgeon Office of the Air Surgeon, Washington, 1940-42; command surgeon Air Material Command. 1942-45; surgeon 8th Air Force, Okinawa, Aug. Dec. 1945; command surgeon hdqrs. Pacusa, Jan.-Oct. 1946; dep. air. surgeon Air Surgeons Office, USAF, Washington, 1946-49; became air surgeon Continental Air Command, 1949. Decorated Am. Defense Service, World War II Victory, Legion of Merit and Bronze Star medals. Fellow A.C.S.; mem. A.M.A., Aero Med. Assn., Assn. Mil. Surgeons. Clubs: Army-Navy, Manila University, Manila Polo, Belle Haven Country. Author treatises: Protection Against Night Blindness, 1938; Testing of Hearing with Audiometer, 1939; Aviation Deafness, 1940; Ophthalmological Factors Selections of Military Aviators, 1940; Transportation of Patients by Airplane, 1942. Address: USAF. Died June 1959.

HARGROVE, Reginald Henry, corp. exec.; b. Marshall, Tex., Oct. 6, 1897; s. Oswald Lenoir and Nettie (Leonard) H.; student Rice Inst., 1914-15; m. Hallie Ward, Aug. 25, 1917; children—Robert Clyde, James Ward, Joseph Leonard. Clk. Comml. Nat. Bank, Shreveport, La., 1915-17; gen. mgr. Caddo Abstract Co., 1919-28; head land dept. Palmer Corp. of La., 1928-29; v.p. La. Gas & Fuel Co. and subsidiaries (including Palmer Corp. of La.), 1929-30; v.p., dir. all active domestic subsidiaries United Gas Corp., 1930-37; v.p., gen. mgr., dir. United Gas Pipe Line Co., Union Producing Co., United Oil Pipe Line Co., 1937-44, also v.p.; dir. Duval Tex. Sulphur Co. (all subsidiaries United Gas Corp.); v.p. United Gas Corp., 1944-47; pres. Tex. Eastern Transmission Corp., Shreveport, 1946—. Served with O.T.C., 1917; commd. 2d lt., C.A.C., 1917; with AEF, France; disch., 1919. Mem. Am. Gas Assn. (pres. 1946-47). Home: 525 Southfield Rd. Office: Texas Eastern Bldg., Shreveport 94, La. Died Jan. 10, 1954; buried Forest Park Cemetery, Shreveport.

HARING, Clarence Melvin, prof. veterinary science; b. Freeville, N.Y., June 1, 1878; s. Purley Work and Ellen Augusta (Ainsworth) H.; student Colgate Acad., 1897-98; D.V.M., N.Y. State Vet. Coll., Cornell U., 1904; m. Grace E. Moody, Aug. 22, 1908. Asst. in vet. anatomy, Cornell U., 1903-04; instr. vet. science, 1904-06, asst. prof., 1906-10, veterinarian and bacteriologist at Agrl. Expt. Sta. U. of Calif., 1910-13, dir. same, 1920-24; prof. veterinary science, U. of Calif., since 1913. Dir. Calif. anti-hog cholera serum lab., 1911-18. Consultant Calif. State Dept. Pub. Health since 1928;consultant War Manpower Commission, 1942-45. Second lieut. Vet. R.C., Feb.-Apr. 1918; 1st lt., Vet. Corps N.A., Apr.-June 1918; capt., Vet. Corps U.S. Army, July 1918-Jan. 1919. Baptist. Fellow A.A.A.S. Mem. Am. Vet. Med. Assn. (sec. 1915-16), Soc Am. Bacteriologists, Sigma Xi, Alpha Zeta, Delta Omega, Phi Zeta. Mason. Club: Faculty. Contbr. to agrl. and vet. publs.; investigator of animal diseases. Home: 2405 Hillside Av., Berkeley 4, Cal. Died July 9, 1951; buried Riverside, Cal.

HARKINS, William Draper, educator, cons. chemist; b. Titusville, Pa., Dec. 28, 1873; s. Nelson Goodrich and Sarah Eliza (Draper) H.; A.B., Stanford, 1900, Ph.D., 1907; post-grad. U. Chgo., 1901, 04, Stanford, 1905-06, Institut für Physikalische Chemie, Karlsruhe, Germany, 1909; research asso. Research Lab. Phys. Chemistry, Mass. Inst. Tech., 1909-10, 11; m. Anna Louise Hatheway, June 9, 1905; children—Henry Nelson, Alice Marion. Asst. and instr. chemistry Stanford, 1898-1900; prof., head dept. U. Mont., 1900-12; chemist in charge of smelter smoke investigation Anaconda Farmers's Assn., 1902-10, Mountain Copper Co. of Cal., 1904, U.S. Dept. of Justice, 1910-12; research work for Carnegie Instn., Washington, 1911; asst. prof. gen. chemistry U. Chgo., 1912-14, asso. prof., 1914-17, prof. physical chemistry 1917—, Andrew MacLeish Distinguished Service prof., 1935—, dir. rubber research, 1942—; professorial lectr. Mellon Inst. Indsl. Research, 1916-17; lectr. U. Ill., 1918-19; cons. chemist U.S. Bur. Mines, 1920-22; cons. engr. U.S. Air Service, 1924-27; cons. C.W.S., 1927—; cons. chemist Libbey-Owens-Ford Glass Co., 1929—, Universal Oil Products Co., 1930—, U.S. Rubber Co., 1939—, Nat. Def. Research Com., 1941—; George Fisher Baker lectr. Cornell Univ., 1936-37. Mem. Internat. Com. on Atoms, 1932—; Chgo. Commn. on Ventilation, 1916-28. Editor, sect. gen. and phys. chemistry Chem. Abstracts, 1912-16. Pres. Missoula (Mont.) City Bd. of Health, 1906-12. Fellow A.A.A.S. (v.p.); mem. Am. Chem. Soc. (chmn. Chgo. sect. 1915-16, chmn. div. phys. and inorganic chemistry 1919-20), Nat. Acad. Sciences, Am. Philos. Soc., hon. mem. Alpha Omega Alpha. Episcopalian. Awarded Willard Gibbs medal by Am. Chem. Soc., 1928. Author of over 200 papers on heat of sun and stars, stability of atomic nuclei and physics and chemistry of surfaces. Home: 5437 Ellis Av., Chgo. 15. Died Mar. 7, 1951; buried Chgo.

HARKNESS, William Hale, investments; b Cleveland, July 13, 1900; s. William Lamon and Edith (Hale) H.; student Browning Sch., New York, 1910-13; student St. Paul's Sch., Concord, N.H., 1913-18; B.A., Yale, 1922; LL.B., Harvard, 1925; m. Elisabeth Grant, June 13, 1932 (divorced Dec. 1945); 1 dau., Anne; m. 2d, Rebekah West Pierce, Oct. 1, 1947; 1 dau., Edith Hale. Admitted to New York bar, 1927, asso. in practice of law Murray, Aldrich & Webb, 1926-30; kept own office for management of investments, 1930—. Dir. Hoving Corp., Va. Hot Springs, Inc., Republic Foil & Metal Mills Inc., The New York Trust Co. Served in Yale unit S.A.T.C., 1918, 2d lt., O.R.C., 1918-20. Served as lt. col., U.S. Army Air Force in Washington, D.C., Mar.-July 1942, hdqrs. 8th Fighter Command, Watford, Eng., and Charleroi, Belgium, July 1942-July 1945. Decorated Bronze Star medal, Croix de Guerre avec Etoile de Vermeil, Europeon, African, Middle Eastern Ribbon with 5 battle stars (Germany, Air Offensive Europe, Normandy, Northern France, Central Europe). Mem. Am. Geog. Soc. (v.p.), Am. Mus. Natural Hist. (trustee), Boys' Club of N.Y. (v.p.), Presbyn. Hosp. in the City of New York (v.p.), Episcopalian. Clubs: Downtown Assn., The Links Madison Square Garden, New York Yacht, Racquet and Tennis, River, University, Yale (New York City); Yeamans Hall (Charleston, S.C.). Home: 778 Park Av. Office: 654 Madison Av., N.Y.C. 21. Died Aug. 12, 1954; buried Woodlawn Cemetery, N.Y.C.

HARL, Maple Talbot, business exec.; b. Marshall, Mo., Feb. 4, 1893; s. Baldwin Evans and Maxcy Jane (Campbell) H.; A.B., William Jewell Coll., Liberty, Mo., 1914 LL.D., 1952; U. of Chgo. Law Sch., 1916-17; m. Maybelle Mayfield, July 12, 1920; 1 dau., Suzanne. Former pres. Denver Safe Deposit Co.; v.p. Englewood Colo. State Bank, 1923-25; state bank commr. Colo., 1939-45; dir. F.D.I.C. (chmn. bd. dir. 1945-53); bd. dirs. United Am. Life Ins. Co., D.&R.G.W. R.R. National Commander Disabled American Veterans of the World War, 1937. Former director Denver Chamber of Commerce, Salvation Army, Denver chapter American Red Cross. Enlisted as private U.S. Army, 1917; commd. 2d lt. and advanced through grades to maj., 1918, with A.E.F., 1918-19; hon. disch., 1919. Trustee, Colo. Women's Coll. Former vice pres. Nat. Assn. State Bank Supervisors. Mem. Am. Legion, Vets. of Fgn. Wars, D.A.V., Forty and Eight Soc., Phi Gamma Delta, Phi Delta Phi, Beta Gamma Sigma. Baptist. Mason (32°, K.T., Shriner). Clubs: Kiwanis of Denver (past pres., gov. Rocky Mt. Dist.). Metropolitan, National Press, Army and Navy (Washington); Denver, Denver Country (Denver). Home: 800 Ogden St., Denver 18; also The Westchester, Washington. Office: National Press Bldg., Washington. Died Apr. 17, 1957; buried Fairmont Mausoleum, Denver.

HARLING, W(illiam) Franke, composer; b. London, Eng., Jan. 18, 1887; s. Joseph Edmund and Emily (Patterson) H.; brought to U.S., 1888; student pub. schs., Boston, and Grace Ch. Choir Sch., New York; student London Acad. Music; pupil of Théophile Ysaye, Brussels, 4 yrs.; m. Carry Van Lellyveld, Sept. 1914; one son, Joseph Edmund; m. 2d, LuGarda Salome Mayer, March 18, 1920; m. 3d, Elma Jascha, June 19, 1937. Organist and choir dir. Ch. of the Resurrection, Brussels, 1907-08, U.S. Mil. Acad., West Point, N.Y., 1909-10. Mem. A.S. C.A.P. Episcopalian. Composer: The Corps (West Point Mil. Acad. hymn); West Point Forever (official march); A Light from St. Agnes (grand opera in one act), performed by Chicago Civic Opera Co., Dec. 26, 1925, and in Paris, June 1929 (1st Am. opera ever sung in Fr.; awarded David Bispham medal); (symphonic works), The XXIII Psalm of David (symphonic poem with narrator, women's chorus, organ, 2 pianois); Exordium and Psalms with narrator, women's chorus, orchestra and 2 pianos; A Bible Trilogy (based on O.T. for full symphony orchestra, 2 pianos, choruses, soloists and narrator); Three Elegiac Poems for cello and orchestra, 1946; Monte Cassino, In Memoriam—1944 (orchestral tone poem with narrator), 1944; Chanson Popularies (tone poem performed Los Angeles Philharmonic orchestra directed by Artur Rodzinski); Before the Dawn (Persian idyl for symphony orchestra, solos for tenor, cello and harp, and male chorus, the Hollywood Bowl, 1933, with Richard Crooks, soloist); Oh, Captain, My Captain (symphonic ballad for baritone, male chorus and orchestra); At the Tomb of the Unknown Soldier (tone poem); The Miracle of Time (prize composition for soloists, double chorus, and orchestra, performed at the Tri-City Festival, Newark, May 1918); Mirra (miracle play); musical score, Heritage; Ave Maria (for voice, harp, cello, orchestra); (stage prodns. in N.Y.C.) Deep River, Paris Bound, Machinal, Salvation (produced by Arthur Hopkins); Outward Bound, In Love with Love, The Outsider (produced by Wm. Harris Jr.); Miss Nellie of N' Orleans, Wake Up, Jonathan (produced by Sam Harris); stage presentations for Roxy Theatre, New York, include The Trial of Joan of Arc, A Venetian Fantasy, Jazz Concerto. Also 100 published works, including operas, songs, cantatas; musical scores for motion pictures, including Tabu, Monte Carlo, Cradle Song, Trouble in Paradise, Broken Lullaby, Man's Castle, Bitter Tea of General Yen, By Candle Light, Madam Butterfly, Scarlet Empress, So Red the Rose, Souls at Sea, Men With Wings, Stagecoach (Award of Merit, 1939), Adam Had Four Sons, Penny Serenade, Adventure in Washington, The Lady Is Willing, I Escaped from the Gestapo, Soldiers of the Soil, Three Russian Girls, When the Lights Go On Again; Red Wagon (documentary film on life of Gustavus Swift). Home: 4053 Stone Canyon, Sherman Oaks, Cal. Address: American Society of Composers, Authors and Publishers, 30 Rockefeller Plaza, N.Y.C. Died Nov. 22, 1958.

HARLOW, Ralph Volney, author, educator; b. Claremont, N.H., May 4, 1884; s. Alvin Braley and Hattie (Grout) H.; grad. Mt. Hermon (Mass.) Sch., 1905; A.B., Yale, 1909, A.M., 1911, Ph.D., 1913; m. Judith Elizabeth Moss, June 21, 1921; children—Judith Mary, Janet Mabel, Elizabeth. Instr. in history, Simmons Coll., Boston, 1913-19, asst. prof., 1918-20; asst. prof. hist., Boston U., 1920-26; asso. prof. history, Yale, 1926-29; prof. history, Syracuse U., 1929-48; retired June 1948. Mem. Am. Hist. Assn., Phi Beta Kappa. Protestant. Author: A History of Legislative Methods, 1917; Samuel Adams, 1923; Growth of the United States, 1925 (revised edit., 2 vols., 1943); A History of the United States, 1934; Story of America, 1937; Gerrit Smith, Philantropist and Reformer, 1939, The United States from Wilderness to World Power, 1949, English edit., 1955. Home: Old Clinton Rd., Westbrook, Conn. Died Oct. 3, 1956; buried Cypress Cemetery, Westbrook.

HARLOW, Victor Emmanuel, coll. pres.; b. Chantilly, Mo., Nov. 23, 1876; s. James and Mary Adeline (Davis) H.; A.B., La Grange (Mo.) Coll., 1896; A.M., Shurtleff Coll., Alton, Ill., 1899, U. Okla., 1931; studied U. Mo.; m. May Van Hooser, June 1900 (deceased May 1903); children—Victor E., William V.; m. 2d, Gertrude Grindling, June 17, 1911; children—James G., John Hampden, Dorothea, Bryce N. Tchr. pub. schs., 1891-96; prof. nat. science Webb City (Mo.) Coll., 1897; prof. Latin and Greek, La Grange Coll., 1898; pres. Webb City Coll., 1899-1901; editor Enid Democrat, 1906, 07, Shawnee Herald, 1909-11, New State Tribune, 1911; founder Harlow's Weekly and editor, 1912—; pres. Harlow Pub. Corp.; pres. Kingfisher (Okla.) Coll., 1948—. First sec. and organizer State Bd. Pub. Affairs, Okla., 1909. Pres. bd. Okla. City Carnegie Library, 1941-46. Mem. Soc. Bibl. Lit. and Exegesis, U.S., Oklahoma City (dir.) C.'s of C. Democrat. Conglist. Club: Oklahoma University. Author: The Nations (verse), 1895; Jesus the Man, 1924; A Bibliography and Genetic Study of American Realism, 1931; Oklahoma, a History, 1934; Jesus' Jerusalem Expedition, 1936; The Destroyer of Jesus, The Life of Herod Antipas, 1953. Home: 4908 N.W. 23d St. Office: 532 N.W. 2d St., Oklahoma City. Died Oct. 6, 1958.

HARLOW, William Elam, evangelist; b. Salem, Ill., Feb. 22, 1860; s. Robert Allen and Margaret (Williams) H.; grad. Dr. Parkyn's Sch. Psychology, Chgo., also St. Louis Sch. Suggestive Therapeutics; m. Mary Kennedy, Aug. 18, 1883. Began as evangelist, 1890. Mem. Christian (Disciples) Ch. Prohibitionist. Author: Mental and Moral Therapeutics, 1890, rev. 1910. Address: 1359 Washington Av., Springfield, Mo. Died Dec. 23, 1922.

HARMELING, Stephen John, horticulturist; b. Sheboygan Falls, Wis., Mar. 8, 1951; s. Gerritt John and Everdinah (Hyink) H.; A.B. and A.M., Hope Coll., Holland, Mich.; B.D., Rutgers Theol. Sem.; m. Alida Maria Binnekant, Apr. 12, 1876; children—Stephen J., Gertrude Henrietta (Mrs. George Ensing), Emma Johannah (Mrs. S. W. Libbey), Henry, Geral Ridboeck, Kate (Mrs. Guy Bernisse), Philip, Margaret (Mrs. W. E. Gorsuch), Elmer, Edward Benjamin. Missionary Dutch Ref. Ch. in the states west of Mississippi River, 1882-1902, retiring on account of ill health; has devoted much time to horticulture and botany; propr. Island Nurseries, Vashon, Wash. Under commn. of Gov. Lister of Wash., organized and drilled 105 men for the war, 1918. Republican. Mason; Past Eminent Comdr. Vashon Island Commandery, K.T., also Past High Priest Chapter 48, Wash. Widely known as lecturer on hort. and landscape gardening subjects. Home: Vashon, Wash. Died Nov. 1940.

HARMON, Andrew Davidson, clergyman, educator; b. Auburn, Neb., Dec. 13, 1870; s. Henry and Margaret (Handley) H.; A.B., Cotner U., Bethany, Neb., 1893, A.M., 1894, LL.D., 1921; LL.D., Transylvania Coll., 1922, Texas Christian U., 1923; m. Alice Gadd, July 11, 1893; children—Margueritte, Harriet, Henry, Aldrew. Ordained Christian (Disciples) ministry, 1893; head dept. of Latin and v.p. Cotner U., 1896-97; pastor 1st Ch., St. Paul, 1897-1911 (built up from mission ch. of 33 members to a leading ch. of the city); spl. lecturer in colleges, 1912-13; pastor 1st Ch., Omaha, Neb. 1914; head dept. of sociology and pres. Cotner U., 1916-22; pres. Transylvania Coll. and Coll. of the Bible, Lexington, Ky., 1922-28; pres. Nat. Bd. of Edn. of the Disciples of Christ, 1921; pres. Internat. Conv. Disciples of Christ Chs., 1925-26; pres. Ministers Life and Casualty Union Ins. Co., Mpls., 1930-41; pastor Cable Community Congl. Church, 1941—. Democrat. Mason. Address: Lock Box 15, Cable, Wis. Deceased.

HARMON, Arthur Loomis, architect; b. Chgo., June 13, 1878; s. Henry Warren and Elizabeth (Pickering) H.; B.S., Columbia U. Sch. of Architecture, 1901; m. Anne Hallock, Nov. 2, 1907; children—David, Hallock. With McKim, Mead & White, N.Y.C., 1902-11; practiced individually, 1913-28; partner Shreve, Lamb & Harmon, N.Y.C., now asso.; consultant in design to Q.M., U.S. Army, 1926-27. Prin. individual work; Hotel Shelton, New York; YMCA Bldg., Jerusalem, Palestine; Juilliard Sch. of Music, New York; monuments for Am. Battle Monument Commn. for various locations in France. Partnership work; alteration of Bankers Trust Bldg., New York; Empire State Bldg., New York; Acacia Ins. Co. Bldg., Washington; buildings for Conn. Coll. for Women, New London Vladek Houses, Hunter College, N.Y.C. Group Plan, Engineering School and Chem. Engring. Bldg., Cornell U.; brs. for Chase Nat. Bank, N.Y. Times Bldg. addition, bldgs. at Kent (Conn.) School; cons. design for Parkchester and Stuyvesant Town Housing. Recipient gold medals A.I.A., Archtl. League, also awards by Fifth Av. Assn. Fellow A.I.A. (past pres. N.Y. chpt.), N.A.D.; mem. Archtl. League of N.Y. (past pres.), Beaux Arts Inst. of Design. Clubs: Century Assn., Columbia University. Home: 383 Grasslands Rd., White Plains, N.Y. Office: 11 E. 44th St., N.Y.C. Died Oct. 17, 1958; buried Ferncliff.

HARMON, Austin Morris, educator; b. Brockport, N.Y., Sept. 28, 1878; A.B., Williams Coll., 1902, L.H.D., 1927; A.M., Yale, 1903, Ph.D., 1908; student Göttingen and Am. Sch. Rome. Instr. Princeton U., 1907-16; prof. of Greek, Yale, 1916-45, emeritus, 1945—; Lampson prof. of Greek and associate fellow Jonathan Edwards Coll. Vice pres. Am. Philol. Assn., 1937-39, pres. 1939. Fellow Am. Acad. Arts and Sciences. Home: Chebeague Island, Me. Died June 29, 1950; buried Chebeague, Me.

HARMON, Claude Moore, realtor; b. Stoney Creek, Mich., Feb. 17, 1868; s. George W. and Alvena (Moore) H.; student pub. schs., Detroit; m. Margaret Cain, Jan. 28, 1895; children—Austin, John M. Engaged in real estate bus., Detroit, Mich., since 1899; established, co-partner, C. M. Harmon Co., Detroit, since 1928; dir. Detroit Bank, Detroit Fire & Marine Ins. Co. Trustee Kalamazoo Coll. Mem. Mil. Order Loyal Legion. Republican. Baptist. Clubs: Detroit, Detroit Golf. Home: 15 E. Kirby St., Detroit 2. Office: Penobscot Bldg., Det. 26. Died Dec. 7, 1951; buried Woodlawn Cemetery, Det.

HARMON, Hubert Reilly, air force officer; b. Chester, Pa., Apr. 3, 1892; s. Millard Fillmore and Madelin (Kendig) H.; B.S., U.S. Mil. Acad., 1915; grad. Army Flying Sch., 1917; m. Rosa-Maye Kendrick, Feb. 19, 1927; children—Eula Wulfjen, Kendrick. Served in Air Arm of Army or in USAF, 1917—; apptd. lt. gen. USAF, 1945; comd. 6th Air Force, 13th Air Force, also dep. comdr. aircraft, S. Pacific Theater, World War II; USAF Rep. UN Mil. Staff Com., also U.S. del. Inter-Am. Def. Bd., and spl. asst. to Chief of Staff USAF, for Air Force Acad. matters, 1947-53, ret. June 1953, recalled to active duty 1953; supt. USAF Acad., 1954-56, ret. Decorated D.S.M. (with Oak-Leaf Cluster), 2d, D.S.M. (with two Oak-Leaf Clusters), 1956, Legion of Merit, Distinguished Flying Cross (U.S.); also fgn. decorations. Rated command pilot, combat observer and aircraft observer. Clubs: Army and Navy (Washington); Chevy Chase (Md.); San Antonio (Tex.) Country; Cherry Hills, Denver Country (Denver). Home: 312 Westover Rd., San Antonio. Died Feb. 22, 1957; buried Cemetery at USAF Academy, Colorado Springs, Colo.

HARMON, John Francis, church efficiency worker; b. Olney, Ill., May 1, 1858; s. John and Charity (Bullard) H.; student State Normal Sch., Carbondale, Ill., Central State Normal, Danville, Ind.; grad. Garrett Bibl. Inst., Evanston, Ill., 1888; D. D., McKendree Coll., Lebanon, Ill.; m. Mary C, Murvin, Sept. 26, 1882; children—Stennie, Raymond (dec.), Mrs. Grace McGary, John F. (dec.), Mrs. Lillian Cook, Mrs. Marian Plater. Ordained to ministry M.E. Ch., 1886; pastor, Hawthorne, Ill., 1888-90, Metropolis, Ill., 1890-93, Mt. Carmel, 1893-97, Mt. Vernon, 1897-1902, East St. Louis, Ill., 1902-08; pres. McKendree Coll., 1908-15, Kan. Wesleyan U., Salina, 1915-18; ch. efficiency work from 1918; now retired. Mem. 5 Gen. Confs. M.E. Ch. and for 12 yrs. chmn. So. Ill. Conf. dels.; mem. Meth. Book Com., 1904-12. Prohibitionist. Home: Louisville, Ill. Died June 27, 1943; buried Shouse Chapel Cemetery, Clay County, Ill.

HARN, Orlando Clinton, gen. counsel Audit Bur. Circulations; b. Dayton, O., Mar. 25, 1871; s. Ira Baker and Renzilla Neocia (Fitch) H.; student Ohio Wesleyan U., Ph.B., Cornell U., 1894; m. Merry Christmas Williams, June 25, 1902. Began with Cleveland Leader, 1894, later successively telegraph editor Cleveland Press, news editor Scripps-McRae Assn., editor Architect and Builder and Inland Grocer (all of Cleveland); adv. mgr. H. J. Heinz Co., Pittsburgh, Pa., 1904-05; adv. mgr. Nat. Lead Co., 1905-27; one of founders Audit Bureau of Circulations (including more than 3,000 pubs. of U.S. and Canada), pres. 1920-27, mng. dir. 1927-39. Member United States Govt's. Div. of Advertising of Com. on Pub. Information, World War I. Pres. Tech. Publicity Assn., 1910-11; pres. Assn. Nat. Advertisers, 1911; chmn. of Advertising Council (Chicago), 1931; mem. board of govs. Advt. Fedn. Am., 1928-38, Chicago Fedn. Advt. Clubs. Mem. Phi Gamma Delta. Awarded Bok gold medal, 1926, by Harvard Sch. of Business Adminstrn., "for distinguished service to commerce and industry." Republican. Protestant. Clubs: Advertising (Chicago); Retired Profl. and Bus. Men's (Santa Barbara). Author: Marketing a Nationally Advertised Product (monography), 1915; Lead, the Precious Metal, 1924. Home: 1915 Santa Barbara St., Santa Barbara, Cal. Died Oct. 10, 1955; buried Santa Barbara Cemetery.

HARNER, Nevin Cowger, religious educator; b. nr. Berlin, Pa., Feb. 5, 1901; s. James Philip and Myrtie Dare (Cowger) H.; A.B., Franklin and Marshall Coll., 1921; B.D., Theol. Sem. Ref. Ch. in the U.S., 1924; S.T.M., Union Theol. Sem., N.Y. City, 1925; Ph.D., Columbia, 1931; D.D., Franklin and Marshall Coll., 1940, LL.D., Franklin and Marshall College, 1946; married Flora Balch Morton, Aug. 2, 1926; children—Nevin Louis, Philip Balch. Part-time instr. in French, Franklin and Marshall Coll., 1922-23; ordained ministry Ref. Ch. in the U.S., 1924; dir. religious edn., Zion Ref. Ch., Lehighton, Pa., 1925-28; instr. in religious edn., Theol. Sem. of Evang. and Reformed Ch., 1929-31, prof. Christian edn., 1931-45, dean, 1943-45; pres., Heidelberg College, 1945-47; prof. Christian edn., Theological Seminary of Evangelical and Reformed Church since 1947. Lecturer on religious education and psychology, Union Theol. Sem., 1944-45. Mem. bd. Internat. Missions, Evaneglical and Reformed Church; vice-chmn. Internat. Council of Religious Education; delegate and speaker at Quadrennial Council of Alliance of Reformed Chs. throughout the World Holding the Presbyn. System, Belfast, Ireland, 1933. Del. to confs. on Life and Work at Oxford, and Faith and Orders in Edinburgh, 1937. Mem. Federal Council, Chs. of Christ in America. Mem. Religious Edn. Assn., Phi Beta Kappa, Sigma Pi. Author: Factors Related to Sunday Sch. Growth and Decline in the Eastern Synod of the Reformed Ch. in the U.S., 1931; The Educational Work of the Church, 1939; Youth Work in the Church, 1942; (with David D. Baker) Missionary Education in Your Church, 1942; Religion's Place in General Education, 1949. Address: 523 W. James St., Lancaster, Pa. Died July 24, 1951.

HARPER, Cornelius Allen, physician; b. Hazel Green, Wis., Feb. 20, 1864; s. Moses Allen and Hester (Lewis) H.; B.S., U. Wis., 1889, LL.D., 1945; M.D., Columbian (now George Washington) U., 1893; D.Sc., Lawrence Coll., 1941; m. Elisabeth L. Bowman, Apr. 23, 1901; children—Cornelius Allen (dec.), Samuel Bowman. Practiced, Madison, Wis., 1894—; sec. exec. officer Wis. State Bd. of Health. 1904-43, specialist advisor of State Bd. Health and asst. health officer, 1943—. Pres. State and Provincial Health Officers N.A., 1908-09; mem. Wis. Tb com. to select site and erect first Tb sanitarium in Wis., 1903; mem. Assembly Wis. legislature, 1911; mem. State Soldiers' Rehabilitation Bd., 1923; mem. State Com. on National Council of Defense. Fellow Am. Pub. Health Assn.; mem. A.M.A., Wis. Med. Soc. (pres. 1930-31), Wis. Anti-Tb Assn. (dir.), Wis. Conf. of Social Work (exec. com.), Phi Kappa Psi, Madison Club. Author of bulls. on health, hygiene, etc. Home: 520 N. Pinckney St., Madison 3, Wis.

HARPER, Donald, lawyer; b. Rome, Ga., Sept. 20, 1868; s. Col. Charles Mallary and Georgia Houstoun (McDonald) H.; B.A., Mercer U., 1887; LL.B., U. Ga., 1889 (pres. class); m. Jeanne Bernard, May 5, 1896; children—Raymond, Helene (Countess Alexandre de Saint Phalle), Donald, Jacqueline (Mrs. André de Saint Phalle), Francis A. Admitted to Ga. bar, 1889, N.Y. bar, 1898. Apptd. commr. to Paris Expn. by Gov. Chandler of Ga., 1900. Engaged many yrs. in internat. law, Paris; was mem. law firm O'Brien, Boardman, Harper & Fox, N.Y.C., later mem. Harper, Szlapka & Harper, Paris; gen. counsel, dir. N.Y. Herald Co., Paris. Decorated Officier Légion d'Honneur (France). Mem. Am. Bar Assn., N.Y. County Lawyers Assn., N.Y. Southern Soc., Am. Soc. Internat. Law, Phi Delta Theta. Past pres. Am. Club, Paris. Club: The Nassau. Address: 108 Mercer St., Princeton, N.J.; also 32 Avenue de l'Opera, Paris, France. Died Apr. 24, 1954.

HARPER, George Washington Finley, banker; b. Lenoir, N.C., July 7, 1834; s. James and Caroline Ellen (Finley) H.; ed. Classical Schs., Lenoir, 1847-53; Davidson Coll., N.C., 1885-6; m. Ella A. Rankin June 14, 1859 (dec. 1909); children—George F., Ellen (Mrs. Bernhardt). In mercantile business at Lenoir, 1853-61 and 1865-94; built sect. of Chester & Lenoir R.R. from Lenoir to Hickory, 1873-9, and later pres. same; pres., gen. mgr. Carolina & Northwestern Ry. Co., 1893-1900; pres. Bank of Lenoir since its orgn., 1893; pres. Green Park (N.C.) Improvement Co.; v.p. Lenoir Cotton Mill; partner Benhardt-Seagle Hardware Co.; etc. Served in C.S.A. under Gens. Bragg, Johnston and Hood; was wounded and disabled at Battle of Resaca, Ga., May 15, 1864; advanced to maj. 58th N.C. Regt., which comd. at Battle of Bentonville, N.C., Mar. 19 and 20, 1865; surrendered at Greensboro, N.C., May, 1865. Co. register and justice of peace Caldwell Co., N.C., 1856-62; mem. N.C. Ho. of Rep.,

1880-1; del. Dem. Nat. Conv., St. Louis, 1888. Trustee Davidson Coll., 1900-12, Western N.C. State Hosp. for Insane, 1893-01. Democrat. Presbyn. Comdr. Confederate Vets. Camp Lenoir. Author: Caldwell County, N.C., in the Great War of 1860-65, 1910. Home: Lenoir, N.C. Died Mar. 16, 1921.

HARPER, Harvey W., mfg. exec.; b. Kidderminster, Eng., Aug. 13, 1878; s. John and Sarah Ann (Wilson) H.; married; children—Donald A., Helen (Mrs. Neville Brown). Naturalized citizen. Founder Tung-Sol Electric, Inc., Newark, now chmn. Home: 475 Park Av., Belleair Estate, Clearwater, Fla. Office: 95 8th Av., Newark 4. Died Nov. 23, 1958.

HARPER, Samuel Williams, banker; b. Wheeling, W.Va., Apr. 7, 1874; s. Henry Martin and Marion L. (Williams) H.; ed. Linsly Inst., Wheeling; m. Lillie E. Vance, Oct. 17, 1901; children—Louise E. (Mrs. D. T. Rownd), Nelson Vance, Virginia. Mgr. Harper & Bros., jobbers, Wheeling, 1891-1908; v.p. Consol. Telephone Co., 1908-15; pres. Southeastern Ohio R.R. Co., 1916-24; became pres. Wheeling Bank & Trust Co., 1919; now pres. Wheeling Dollar Savings & Trust Co. Chmn. personnel bur., Am. Red Cross, Washington, D.C., 1917-18. Trustee Linsly Inst., Children's Home. Republican. Presbyterian. Mason. Clubs: Fort Henry, Wheeling Country, New York Athletic (New York). Home: Echo Point, W.Va. Office: Wheeling Dollar Savings & Trust Co., Wheeling, W.Va. Died Dec. 10, 1950; buried Greenwood Cemetery, Wheeling.

HARR, Luther, economic consultant; b. Phila., Pa., April 10, 1896; s. Milton K. and Annie W. (Baum) Harr; grad. William Penn Charter Sch., Phila., Pa., 1914; B.S. Wharton Sch. of Finance and Commerce, U. of Pa., 1918; A.M., U. of Pa., 1920, Ph.D., in econ., 1924; m. Kathryn Cressman, Aug. 21, 1919; children—Luther, Virginia Anne. Instr. in economics U. of Pa., 1919-21, in finance, 1921-25, asst. prof., 1925-31, prof. of finance, 1931-40; econ. adviser and treas. Philadelphia Record, Courier Post Co. (Camden, N.J.), 1934-41; sec. of banking Commonwealth, Pa., 1935-37; treas. City of Philadelphia, 1938-42; counsel U.S. Bituminous Coal Consumers, June 1941-Aug. 1943; pres. and dir. Research and Planning, Inc., Phila., dir. China Forest Products Industries, Inc. Studied operation of English banking system in England, 1926-27; chmn. Pa. Bldg. and Loan Bd., 1937; chmn. Pa. Banking Bd., 1935-37. Mem. Pennsylvania State advisory committee National Youth Adminstrn.; chmn. exec. com. Nat. Assn. of Supervisors of State Banks, 1936-37; chmn. Gov. Earle's Financial Survey Com., 1934; chmn. Pa. Committee on Public Education, 1939. Served in R.O.T.C., 1917; statis. expert Ordnance Dept., U.S. Army, 1917-18. Dir. Phila. Forum, Lutheran Brotherhood. Mem. Am. Arbitration Assn., Delta Kappa Epsilon. Democrat. Lutheran. Mason, Moose. Clubs: Racquet, Philadelphia Country (Philadelphia). Author: Branch Banking in England, 1929; Banking Theory and Practice (with W. Carlton Harris), 1928, revised, 1936. Contbr. articles to jours.; co-editor Webster's Internat. Dictionary. Home: 3101 W. Penn St., Philadelphia 29. Office: 1616 Widener St., Phila. 3. Died Aug. 30, 1950.

HARR, William R., lawyer; b. Washington, July 5, 1872; s. Peter and Adelaide L. (Schleigh) H.; student pub. schs., D.C., LL.M., Georgetown U., 1896; m. Martha Beach Harvey, Aug. 1, 1900 (died June 28, 1948); children—Elizabeth (Mrs. T. H. Breeze, dec.), Richard Whitmore, (dec.). Admitted to D.C. bar, 1897; sec. to Justice John M. Harlan, 1896-1901; atty. Dept. Justice, 1902-09; asst. atty. gen. of U.S., 1909-13; in private practice, 1913-30; commr. U.S. District Court, D.C., 1930-48. Mem. Washington Nat. Monument Soc. Unitarian. Club: Cosmos. Home: 36 Primrose St., Chevy Chase, Md. Died June 17, 1950.

HARRAH, William Ferguson (hâr'rä), manufacturer; b. Brookfield, Mo., Nov. 12, 1871; s. Rev. Charles Clark and Sarah (Ferguson) H.; prep. edn. Browns Business College, Peoria; student Grinnell Coll., Ia., 1890-91; m. Marie E. Even, Feb. 19, 1894; 1 son, Charles Clayton. Export mgr. Rouse Hazard & Co., bicycle mfrs., Peoria, 1892-97; vice pres. and mgr. Harrah & Stewart Mfg. Co., mfrs. bicycles and woodenware, Des Moines, Ia., 1897-1905; sec. Nat. Wire Cloth Co., Niles, Mich., 1905-11; treas. Nat. Cable & Mfg. Co., Niles, 1907-13; v.p. and mgr. Niles div. Am. Wire Fabrics Co., 1911-22; co-founder and pres. Nat.-Standard Co. (Niles), 1913-34, hon. chmn. bd. 1934-52; dir. Nat. Standard Co., Can., Nat. Standard Co. of England. Member City Council, Niles, 6 yrs. Mem. Mich. State War Bd., World War. Formerly dir. Nat. Assn. Mfrs., and nat. councillor U.S. Chamber of Commerce. Republican. Presbyterian. Mason (32°, Shriner), Elk. Clubs: Rotary, Orchard Hills Country (Niles); Union League (Chicago); Home: Berrien Crest Farm, Niles, Mich. Office: National Standard Co., Niles, Mich. Died Apr. 16, 1959; buried Silverbrook Mausoleum, Niles.

HARRELSON, John William, chancellor; b. Cleveland County, N.C., June 28, 1885; s. John Hart and Ellen (Williams) H.; B. Engring., N.C. Coll. Agr. and Mechanic Arts (now N.C. State Coll. of Agr. and Engring.), 1909, M.E., 1915; LL.D., Wake Forest College, 1941; D.Ed., N.C. State Coll. Agr. and Engring., 1953; m. Elizabeth Connor, Dec. 14, 1935. Instr. mathematics, N.C. State Coll. of Agr. and Engring., 1909-15, asst. prof., 1915-17, asso. prof., 1920-21, professor, 1921-33, dean of administration, 1934-45; chancellor, 1945-53; emeritus, 1953—; dir. N.C. Dept. Conservation and Development, 1929-33. Grad. mgr. athletics N.C. State Coll., 1911-17, 1921-23; pub. dir. N.C. Cotton Growers Coop. Assn., Merit System Council of N.C., 1941-43 (chmn. 1941). Served in N.C. Nat. Guard, 1908-11; commd. 1st lt. coast arty., 1915, capt., 1916; mustered into U.S. Army, 1917, commd. major coast arty., 1918, hon. disch., 1919; col. field arty., O.R.C., since 1927; dep. chief Army specialized training div. Hdqrs. Fourth Command, Atlanta, Ga., 1943-44; col. A.U.S. (ret.) since 1948. Awarded Legion of Merit. Trustee Saint Mary's School and Junior College, Saint Augustine's College. Member Delta Sigma Phi, Tau Beta Pi, Phi Kappa Phi, Theta Tau, Omicron Delta Kappa, Blue Key, Pine Burr Society (North Caroline State College). Democrat. Episcopalian. Mason (32°). Clubs: Kiwanis, Carolina Country (Raleigh). Home: 1016 Harvey St., Raleigh, N.C. Died Mar. 12, 1955; buried Raleigh, N.C.

HARRIMAN, Henry Ingraham, public utilities; b. Bklyn., Dec. 26, 1871; s. Daniel Gould and Sally (Ingraham) H.; Ph.B., Wesleyn U., 1895; Ph.D., 1930; LL.B., N.Y. Law Sch., 1897; m. Edith Graves, July 7, 1898; children—Eunice A., Barbara (dec.), Gordon. Began with Am. Loom Co., 1899; later mgr. The Stafford Co., mfrs. cotton weaving machinery, Hyde Park, Mass.; organized and was pres. New England Power Co. and its associates; now vice chmn. bd. New England Power Association; dir. Federal Reserve Bank, Boston. Dir. Met. Planning Bd. of Mass.; past pres. C. of C. of U.S.; now U.S. employers' rep. to ILO; mem. bus. adv. council Dept. of Commerce; mem. sr. council U.S. C. of C.; vice chmn. Am. Youth Commn., State Planning Board (Mass.). Trustee Northeastern U., Wesleyan U. Clubs: University, Algonquin, Twentieth Century, Brae Burn Country. Home: 825 Centre St., Newton, Mass. Office: 441 Stuart St., Boston. Died July 4, 1950.

HARRINGTON, Frank Annibal, lawyer; b. Bowling Green, O., July 8, 1895; s. Newton Ross and Laura Belle (Case) H.; A.B., Miami U., 1920; student Dartmouth, 1915-17; Ohio State U., 1920-21; J.D., U. Chicago, 1922; m. Lillian R. Lindow, Jan. 13, 1956; 1 dau. (adopted), Barbara Ann (Mrs. James Walerius). Admitted to Ohio bar, 1921; asso. atty. Tracy, Chapman & Welles, Toledo, 1921-26; mem. law firm of Fuller, Harrington, Seney & Henry; v.p., dir. Short Way Lines, Inc.; pres., dir. Stollberg Hardware Co.; dir., chmn. exec. com. Gt. Lakes Terminal Warehouse Co.; sec., dir. Theatre Leasehold Corp.; sec., dir. Shurhit Products, Inc., Maumee Valley Transportation Company; director of Cameron Machine Company. Director Goodwill Industries, Inc. Served as sgt., U.S.M.C., 1917-19. Mem. Am., Ohio State bar assns., Toledo C. of C., Delta Kappa Epsilon, Phi Alpha Delta, Tau Kappa Alpha. Presbyn. Clubs: Lions, Toledo. Home: 325 N. Prospect St., Bowling Green, O. Office: Ohio Bldg., Toledo 4. Died May 28, 1959.

HARRINGTON, John Walker, author; b. Plattsburg, Mo., July 8, 1868; s. Frank and Margaret (Walker) H.; grad. U. Wooster, 1890; Ph.M., 1893; m. May Edwards Lewis, June 8, 1898; 1 dau., Ruth. Has been in newspaper work, 1890—; was on staff Cleve. Leader and the N.Y. Tribune; on N.Y. Herald, 1892 1915, N.Y. Times, 1917; spl. work London Times, 1898; feature writer N.Y. Herald-Tribune, N.Y. Times, other newspapers and syndicates, ret. 1942. Episcopalian. Contbg. author A Popular History of American Invention, 1924; editor of Derricks of Destiny (autobiography of Samuel G. Bayne), 1925. Also author of several juvenile books and various pamphlets. Contbr. to med., chem. and sci. jours., also popularized articles on sci. subjects to mags. and newspapers. Home: Hillside Rd., Greenwich, Conn. Died June 27, 1952.

HARRINGTON, Louis Clare, mining engr., educator; b. Ludington, Mich., Oct. 28, 1880; s. Jackson Davis and Emma Ada (Ink) H.; student Mich. Coll. of Mines, Houghton, 1901-03, B.S. in civil engring., U. of Mich., 1908; E.M., Mich. Coll. of Mines, 1909; m. Alberta Harriet Amstein, June 13, 1912. Miner in Mich., 1902; mining engr., Bisbee, Ariz., 1903-06; prof. geology and engring., Western Md. Coll., 1909-12; with Univ. of N.D. since 1912, as instr. mining and metallurgy, 1912, asst. prof., 1913-20, asso. prof., 1920-21, prof. since 1921, dir. of civ. of mines and mining experiments since 1931, dean of Coll. of Engring. since 1932; summer work in mine examination in Nevada City, Calif., 1913, Jackson, Ky., 1915, Ketchikan, Alaska, 1916, survey of lignite mines for State of N.D., 1919, 20, 26, 28, 30, Hyder, Alaska, 1922, 24. Mem. Am. Inst. Mining and Metall. Engrs., Mining and Metallurgical Society of America, Am. Soc. Testing Materials, Am. Chem. Soc., Soc. for Promotion Engring. Edn., N.D. Acad. Science, Am. Assn. Univ. Profs., Sigma Xi, Sigma Tau, Lambda Chi Alpha. Republican. Presbyn. Mason. Club: Grand Forks Country. Author of reports on investigations of lignite. Home: 319 S. 6th St., Grand Forks, N.D. Died Feb. 3, 1951; buried Toledo.

HARRINGTON, Thomas F., corp. exec.; b. Boston, July 12, 1902; s. John J. and Margaret J. (Campbell) H.; student Burdette Bus. Coll., Boston U.; m. Rose Elizabeth Williams, July 12, 1930; children—Donald Thomas, Richard Loring. Began with Batten, Barton, Durstine & Osborn, advt. agy., Boston, 1919, with contact staff, N.Y.C., 1924-31, dir. daytime radio programs, radio prodn. staff, 1931-34; radio dir. Young & Rubicam, advt. agy., 1934-36, mgr. Los Angeles office, dir. Jack Benny program, supr. all radio prodn., 1936-38, v.p. stockholder, 1940, mem. permanent plans bd., 1943-44; joined Ted Bates & Co., 1944, as v.p., mem. firm and account supr., currently mng. partner, group supr. Brown & Williamson Tobacco Corp., also partner charge radio, TV and publicity; chmn. board Ted Bates & Company, 1955—. K.C. Clubs: Candlewood Yacht, Candlewood Isle Assn. (Conn.); Ridgewood Country. Home: 1035 Park Av., N.Y.C. 28. Office: Ted Bates & Co., 630 Fifth Av., N.Y.C. Died July 10, 1955.

HARRIS, Agnes Ellen, home economist; b. Cedartown, Polk County, Ga., July 17, 1883; d. James Coffee and Ellen (Simmons) Harris; grad. Ga. Woman's Coll., 1902; B.S. in Edn., Columbia, 1910, M.A., same, 1925; hon. LL.D., University of Alabama, 1941. Teacher of home economics, high sch., Macon, Ga., 1903-07; State Agrl. Sch., Douglas, Ga., 1907-08; dir. dept. home econs. Fla. State Coll. for Women, 1908-19; mem. summer sch. faculty Johns Hopkins, 1911-14; state supr. home econs., Tex., 1919, 20; field agt. home econs. U.S. Dept. Agr., Washington, 1920-22; dean of women and state home demonstrations agt. Ala. Poly. Inst., Auburn, 1922-27; dean of women and dean sch. of home econs. U. Ala., 1927-45, dean sch. home econs., 1945—. Mem. Pres.'s Conf. on Home Building and Home Ownership; dir. 4th Dist. Ala. Fedn. Women's Clubs; rec. sec. Ala. Fedn. Women's Clubs: formerly ednl. chmn.); state pres. Ala. Home: Econs. Assn., 1943. Mem. Am. Home Econs. Assn., Nat. Assn. Deans of Women (past pres.), Ala. Edn. Assn., State Assn. Advisers to Girls, State Parent Teachers Assn. (chmn. summer Inst., Am. Assn. U. Women (ex-pres. Ala. br.; past religion v.p. South East Central Sect.), Nat. Congress Parents and Tchrs. (life mem.), Delta Kappa Gamma (past pres. state). Hon. v.p. Ala. Congress of Parents and Teachers. Presbyn. Home: University, Ala. Died Dec. 18, 1952: buried Myrtle Hill Cemetery, Rome, Ga.

HARRIS, Arthur Emerson, clergyman, educator; b. Montreal, Can., May 3, 1870; s. Edward and Sarah Maria (Gatland) H.; prep. edn. under tutors; grad. Crozer Theol. Sem., Chester, Pa., 1898; D.D., Bucknell University, Lewisburg, Pa., 1917; m. Anna Loomis Meredith, Oct. 29, 1902 (died Dec. 5, 1936); m. 2d, Ruth Naomi Chase, December 16, 1939. Telegrapher, 1888-92; in banking business, 1892-95; ordained Bapt. ministry, 1898; pastor successively at Newark, N.J., Meriden, Conn., and Phila., Pa., until 1926; asso. pastor with Russell H. Conwell, at Bapt. Temple, Phila., 7 yrs.; registrar and prof. psychology, sec. of faculty and dir. extension div., Eastern Bapt. Theol. Sem., Phila., 1925-38, prof. Biblical introduction and homiletics, 1938-51, prof. emeritus since 1951, sec. faculty, 1925-47; pastor Overbrook Bapt. Ch., 1942-49, pastor emeritus since 1950. Republican. Club: Union League (Phila.). Author: Perfected Character, 1894; Poems, 1895; Bible Books Outlined (O.T.), 1917; Bible Books Outlined (N.T.), 1918, 3d edit., 1933; The Psalms Outlined, 1925, 2d edit., 1948; The Household of Faith, 1938; The Book of Job Outlined, 1949; Personal Glimpses of Russel H. Conwell, 1949. Home: 6405 Overbrook Av., Phila. 31. Died Mar. 8, 1954.

HARRIS, Credo Fitch, author; b. nr. Louisville; s. Theodore Harding and Mary Jane (Schooley) H.; LL.D., Asbury College, Wilmore, Ky., 1934; m. Maud May Blanc. Served with U.S. Army in France, 1917-18. Mem. Soc. of Colonial Wars (Ky. gov. 1929-30), S.A.R., Ky. Hist. Soc., N.Y. Southern Soc. Vice-pres. Little Theatre Co., 1939-40. Organized, 1922, WHAS, the first licensed radio station in Ky. and directed it for 20 years. Author: Toby, A Novel of Kentucky, 1912; Motor Rambles in Italy, 1913; Sunlight Patch, 1915; Where the Souls of Men Are Calling, 1918; Wings of the Wind, 1920; Microphone Memoirs, 1937. Clubs: Arts (pres. 1923, 1932-33), Pendennis, Louisville Country, Filson. Episcopalian. Home: 2225 Village Dr. Address: The Courier Journal, Louisville. Died Apr. 4, 1956.

HARRIS, Dawson Bailey, banker; b. Murray Co., Ga., Dec. 6, 1891; s. Thomas Jefferson and Katherine (Keith) H.; student pub. schs.; m. Grace Evelyn Davies, Sept. 2, 1916; 1 son, Dawson Bailey. Messenger Hamilton Nat. Bank, Chattanooga, 1908-10, became asst. cashier, 1921, asst. v.p., 1926, v.p., 1928, exec. v.p., 1946, pres. since 1948, also dir.; v. chmn., dir. Ross-Meehan Foundries, Inc.; director Hamilton Nat. Bank, Knoxville, Tenn., Hamilton Nat. Asso., Inc., Interstate Life & Accident Co., Title

Guaranty & Trust Co. Tenn. Natural Gas Lines, Inc., East Tenn. Natural Gas Lines, Inc. Mem. Tenn. Bankers Assn. (pres. 1949-50), Chattanooga Mfrs. Assn., C. of C. Baptist. K.P. Club: Mountain City. Home: 488 S. Crest Rd., Chattanooga. Office: 7th and Market sts., Chattanooga 1, Tenn. Died Sept. 1953.

HARRIS, Everett Earl, author; b. nr. Jackson, O., July 6, 1887; s. George W. and Harriet (Case) H.; prep. edn., Martin Boehm Acad., Westerville, O.; A.B., Otterbein Coll., 1921, D.D., 1929; B.D., Bonebrake Theol. Sem., 1924; m. Nettie M. Welch, Oct. 28, 1909. Licensed to preach, 1907; ordained ministry U.B. Ch., 1914; pastor Browntown circuit, O., 1908-12, Crooksville, O., 1912-15; student pastor, 1915-19; field sec. Christian Endeavor, S.E. Ohio Conf., U.B. Ch., 1919-24; dir. religious edn. S.E. Ohio Conf., U.B. Ch., 1924-26; editor The Watchword, 1926-46; asso. editor The Telescope Messenger (weekly Evang. United Brethren Ch.), 1947-50. Trustee Internat. Soc. Christian Endeavor. Home: 723 W. Fairview Av., Dayton, O. Deceased.

HARRIS, George Stiles, educator, lawyer; b. Stowe, Vt., Feb. 26, 1887; s. Whitman Ferrin and Ellen (Stiles) H.; Ph.B., U. Vt., 1909; LL.B., N.J. Law Sch. (now by merger, Rutgers Law Sch.), 1922; m. Anne Smith, June 29, 1921; children—George S., John Smith, James Thomas. High sch. instr., Barre, Vt., 1909-10, Morristown N.J., 1910-14, Montclair, 1914-22; head English dept. Montclair High Sch., 1919-22; admitted to N.J. bar, 1922, as counsellor, 1925; practiced in Montclair, 1922-46; mem. faculty N.J. Law Sch., 1922-28, dean, 1928-36; prof. law U. Newark Law Sch., 1936-40, dean, 1940-46; dean Rutgers Law Sch., 1946-52, dean emeritus, 1952—; municipal counsel, Montclair, 1924-46; counsel, Bd. of Edn., 1924-47, Joint Meetings, Glen Ridge, Bloomfield, Montclair, and Newark, 1928-46; pub. panel rep. Nat. War Labor Bd., 2d region, 1942-44. Counsel N.J. State Tchrs. Assn., 1934, 35, 36. Mem. Am. Arbitration Assn. (arbitrator), Am. Law Inst., Am. Bar Assn. (mem. com. on zoning, chmn. com. on adminstrv. law, municipal sect.), Phi Beta Kappa, Phi Delta Theta, Delta Theta Phi. Clubs: Rotary (past pres.), Commonwealth (past pres.) (Montclair). Author: Legal Primer for Freshmen, 1925; Pleading and Practice in New Jersey, 1926, rev., 1939. Editor: Case books on: Criminal Law, 1923, rev., 1930; Statutes, 1927; Municipal Corps., 1928, rev. 1934; Domestic Relations, 1932. Contbr. articles in legal jours. Home: Walpole, N.H. Died Oct. 27, 1957.

HARRIS, George Waldo, coal and potash mining; b. Oskaloosa, Ia., May 8, 1876; s. Alexander Byron and Amanda (Harding) H.; ed. pub. schs. and bus. coll., Oskaloosa; m. Ella McCarty Masden, June 1, 1904; children—Charles Masden, George Robert, Mrs. Elouise Helen Tettemer, John Lloyd. Pres. Harris Bros & Yenney, 1900; pres. Harris Bros. Co., 1901; pres. Union Supply Co., Fraker, Ia., 1903; pres. Excelsior Coal Mining Co., Oskaloosa, 1904; pres. and founder, Colo. and Utah Coal Co., 1914-28, Colony Coal Co., 1917-28, Harris Coal Co., 1921-28. Harris Mines Co., 1924-38, Grassy Creek Coal Co., 1925, Hayden Coal Co., 1930 (chmn. bd., 1947—), Potash Co. of America, 1931-36 (now dir.), Chem. Securities Co., 1931. Mem. Denver C. of C., U.S. C. of C. Republican. Mason (K.T., 32°, Shriner). Clubs: Denver, Cherry Hills Country. Home: 3901 S. University Blvd., Englewood, Colo. Office: First National Bank Bldg., Denver 2. Died Apr. 16, 1950; buried Fairmount Mausoleum, Denver.

HARRIS, Gilbert Dennison, geologist; b. Jamestown, N.Y., Oct. 2, 1864; s. Francis E. and Lydia Helen (Crandall) H.; Ph.B., Cornell U., 1886; m. Clara Stoneman, Dec. 30, 1890; 1 dau., Rebecca Stoneman. On U.S., Tex. and Ark. geol. surveys, 1887-93; investigated tertiary deposits of Southern Eng. and Northern France, 1894; asst. prof. paleontology and strategraphic geology, 1894-1909, prof., 1909-35, now emeritus, Cornell; founder Paleontol. Research Instn., 1932. State geologist of La., 1899-1909. Editor and propr. Bulls. of Am. Paleontology, 1895—, and of Paleontographica Americana. Consulting geologist, Trinidad Petroleum Development Co., Trinidad, B.W.I., 1919-23; paleontologist to Standard Oil Co. of Venezuela, 1923-25; visiting grad. lecturer in Geology, Tex. State U., 1927; paleontologist to the Oldenbergische Erdölgesellschaft, Germany, 1929. Fellow Geol. Soc. Am. (v.p. 1937); Paleontological (pres. 1936); mem. Société Geologique de France, Palaeontologische Gesellschaft v. Deutschland, Société géologique de Suisse, Acad. Nat. Sci., Phi Beta Kappa, Sigma Xi. Home: 126 Kelvin Pl. Office: Paleontological Research Inst., 109 Dearborn Pl., Ithaca, N.Y. Died Dec. 4, 1952.

HARRIS, Henry Hiter, banker; b. Louisa County, Va., July 31, 1893; s. Henry Francis and Lecky H.; ed. public schs. of Louisa County, Am. Inst. of Banking; m. Mary Murdoch, Oct. 16, 1919; 1 son, Henry Hiter. Clerk Merchants Nat. Bank, Richmond, Va., 1912-18, auditor, 1919-20, asst. cashier, 1920-23, cashier, 1923-26; Merchants Nat. consolidated with First Nat. to form First and Merchants Nat. Bank of Richmond, 1926, asst. cashier, 1926-29, asst. v.p., 1929-34, v.p., 1934-38, exec. v.p., 1938-39, pres. since 1939, dir. since 1935; pres. and dir. First Nat. Bank Bldg. Corp.; dir. and mem. investment com. Lawyers Title Ins. Corp., Life Ins. Co. of Va.; chmn. adv. com. R.F.C. Richmond Loan Agy.; dir. Richmond Fredericksburg & Potmoac R.R. Co., Sulphur Mining and R.R. Co., Gen. Baking Corp., Tredegar Co., Va. Fire & Marine Ins Co.; dir. and mem. exec. com. Va.-Carolina Chem. Corp. Dir. and mem. exec. com. Richmond Area Community Chest; dir. Abingdon Barter Theatre. Mem. endowment fund, investment com., and treas. of Va., for Robert E. Lee Meml. Found.; v.p., dir. and mem. exec. com. Richmond Community Meml. Hosp.; mem. adv. council U. of Va. Dev. Fund; trustee, mem. exec. and financial coms. U. of Richmond; trustee and chmn. exec. com. Fork Union Mil. Acad., Crippled Children's Hosp.; trustee Banking research fund Assn. of Reserve City Bankers. Mem. Newcomen Soc. of Eng. (treas. Va. com.), Am. Bankers Assn. (mem. com. pub. relations; mem. commerce and marine commn.), U.S. C. of C. (com. on policy), Richmond C. of C. (nat. councilor), Clearing House Assn. of Richmond (chmn. clearing house com.). Served with U.S.N.R., 1918-19; commd. ensign, Supply Corps, June 1918. Baptist. Mason (K.T., Shriner). Clubs: Country of Va., Deep Run Hunt, Commonwealth (Richmond). Home: 23 Maxwell Rd., Richmond 21. Office: First & Merchants National Bank, Richmond 17, Va. Died Jan. 13, 1952; buried Hollywood Cemetery, Richmond.

HARRIS, John Augustus, adjutant gen. of Mo.; b. Centralia, Mo., Mar. 4, 1890; s. Edwin Ruthven and Mary (Gillaspy) H.; student Univ. of Mo., 1911-12; m. Susan Luella Chambers, May 31, 1913; children—John Robert, Ann Elizabeth. Sec. State Supt. of Pub. Schs., Jefferson City, Mo., 1915-19; chief advisor for 4-state area, Mo., Kan., Ia., Neb., rehabilitation div., Fed. Bd. Vocational Edn. (forerunner of Vets. Adminstrn.), 1919-20; industrial journalist and publisher since 1920; member board dirs. of National Guardsman Pub. Co. Enlisted F.A., 1918; attended O.T.S., F.A., Camp Taylor, Ky.; organized Hdqrs. Co., 4th Mo. Inf., M.S.G., Columbia, Nov. 1940, capt. and advanced through the grades to maj. gen., April 1945; adj. gen. of Mo. since Apr. 18, 1945; comdg. gen. Mo. N.G. and all state's mil. forces, Mar. 1946; apptd. dir. Selective Service for Mo., 1948; apptd. mem. Army's Com. on Civilian Components, 1949. Member National Guard Assn. of U.S. (mem. exec. com.), Am. Legion. Democrat. Baptist. Mason (Shriner). Clubs: Scabbard and Blade, Rotary, Jefferson City Country. Member of the 9th generation of family founded, Jamestown, Va., in 1630's by Robert Harris, son-in-low of Sir William Claiborne, 1st sec. Colony of Va. Home: Jefferson City, Mo. Office: Adj. Gen. Office: Jefferson City, Mo. Died Oct. 20, 1951.

HARRIS, John Burke, lawyer; b. Macon, Ga., June 10, 1887; s. Nathaniel E. and Fannie (Burke) H.; A.B., U. Ga., 1908; LL.B., Mercer U., 1909; m. Louise Erminger, Nov. 5, 1912; 1 son, John Burke. Admitted to Ga. bar, 1909, since practiced in Macon; mem. Harris, Russell, Weaver & Watkins since 1912. Mem. Am., Macon, Ga. (sec. 1932-42, pres. 1942-43) bar assns., Soc. Colonial Wars, Phi Beta Kappa, Chi Phi. Methodist. Mason, Elk. Club: Civitan (past pres., Macon, Ga.). Editor of Georgia Bar Journal since 1938. Contbr. legal jours. Home: Dempsey Hotel. Office: Persons Bldg., Macon, Ga. Died Nov. 10, 1957.

HARRIS, John Warton, obstetrician, gynecologist; b. Reidsville, N.C., Jan. 12, 1891; s. Robert and Ella Kerr (Lea) H.; Reidsville Sem., 1898-1907; A.B., U. of N.C., 1911, A.M., 1912; M.D., Johns Hopkins U., 1916; m. Margaret Price Ivey, Sept. 14, 1921; children—John W., Jr., Thomas Ivey. Resident in obstetrics, Johns Hopkins Hosp., 1916-19, asst. obstetrician, 1920-25, asso. obstetrician, 1925-28, asst., 1916-18, instr., 1918-21, asso., 1921-25, asso. prof., 1925-28; prof. obstetrics and gynecology, U. of Wis., obstetrician and gynecologist in chief, State of Wis. Gen. Hosp., since 1928. Mem. A.M.A., Am. Gynecol. Soc., Wis. Soc. Obstetricians and Gynecologists, Central Assn. Obstetricians and Gynecologists (founder), Wis. Med. Soc., Dane County Med. Soc., A.A.A.S. (fellow), Sigma Chi, Sigma Xi. Club: University. Baptist. Home: 1713 Summit Av., Madison 5, Wis. Died Jan. 14, 1955; buried Reidsville, N.C.

HARRIS, Louis Marshall, naval officer; b. Mineola, Tex., Dec. 24, 1900; s. William Milton and Mary Lucy (Jenkins) H.; B.S., U. of Texas, 1926; M.D., U. of Ark.; M.Sc. in Med., U. of Pa., 1939, D.Sc., 1949; m. Fannie Muriel Coltharp, Apr. 9, 1926; children—Frances, Barbara (Mrs. R. S. Stallings). U.S. Navy, 1931, advanced through the grades to capt., Med. Corps, 1945; regimental surg. 9th Marines and comdg. officer 1st Corps Medical Bn., Fleet Marine Force, Southwest Pacific, 1942-44; medical officer in charge appointments and reserve personnel, V-12 medical tng. program. Bureau of Medicine and Surgery, Navy Dept., Washington, 1944-45; now chief department obstetrics and gynecology National Naval Medical Center, Bethesda, Maryland with additional duty BuMed and Navy Dispensary. Associated obstetrics and gynecology Northwestern U. Sch. Medicine since 1946. Served with 3d Marine Div., Bougainville and Solomon Islands campaigns. Decorated Purple Heart, Bronze Star Medal with combat citation, Commendation (Bougainville campaign), Commendation Ribbon (from sec. of navy). Certified by Am. Bd. Obstetrics and Gynecology, 1945. Fellow A.C.S., Am. Assn. Obstetricians Gynecologists and Abdominal Surgeons, A.M.A., American Academy Obstetrics and Gynecology; mem. Assn. Mil. Surgeons, Phi Chi. Mason. Presbyn. Author articles in profl. jours. Address: 1805 Melody Lane, Garland, Tex. Died Nov. 11, 1955; buried Arlington Nat. Cemetery.

HARRIS, M(artha) Anstice, educator; b. Madison, Wis.; d. Samuel and Martha (Anstice) H.; Ph.D., Yale, 1896; unmarried; adopted daus., Gertrude Louis Spratte, Doris Marjorie Hopkins. Began teaching, 1886; dean Elmira (N.Y.) Coll. for Women, 1901-30, dean emeritus, 1930-56. Pres. trustees Pub. Library, Martinsburg, N.Y. Mem. Modern Lang. Assn. America, Coll. English Conf. Assn. Episcopalian. Club: Golf (pres.). Author: A Glossary of the West Saxon Gospel (Yale Studies in English), 1894; The House of Happiness, 1911, 29; also brochures on ednl. subjects. Home: 910 W. Church St., Elmira, N.Y. Died Jan. 14 1956.

HARRIS, Mary Belle, federal instn. supt.; b. LaPlume, Pa.; d. John Howard and Mary (Mace) Harris; A.B., Bucknell U., 1894, A.M., 1895; Ph.D., U. of Chicago, 1900; hon. LL.D., Bucknell U., 1927; Morris Harvey Coll., 1940. Engaged in teaching Latin, 1900-12; studied in Europe, 1912-14; supt. women, workhouse, Blackwell's Island, N.Y., 1914-17; supt. Reformatory for Women, Clinton, N.J., 1918-19; supt. State Home for Girls, Trenton, N.J., 1919-25; supt. Federal Industrial Instn. for Women, Alderson, W.Va., 1925-41; retired. Awarded Scroll of Honor for work in penal field, from Gen. Fed. of Women's Clubs, 1941; Woman of Week, Hour of Charm, 1940. Trustee Bucknell U. Pres. Civ. Club, 1946-50; vice president Union Co. Cancer Society, 1950-53. Awarded medal as Distinguished Daughter of Pa., 1954. Mem. Am. Assn. U. Women, Pi Beta Phi. Baptist. Author: I Knew Them in Prison, 1936; Kalidasa; Poet of Nature, 1936. Contbr. to mags. Mem. Pa. Bd. of Parole Apr. 1942-May 1943. Subject of book published in Denmark; Tro Paa Mennesker, by Gerda Mundt. Home: 9 Market St., Lewisburg, Pa. Died Feb. 22, 1957; buried Lewisburg.

HARRIS, Montefiore M., newspaper editor; b. Roxbury (Boston), Mass., Nov. 5, 1884; s. George and Fannie (Reinstein) H.; LL.B., Boston U., 1906, LL.M., 1907; m. Josephine Josey, Aug. 24, 1913; children—Josephine (Mrs. Louis Halperin), Janet Frances (Mrs. Ben Polin). Reporter San Antonio Express, 1909, staff corr. Austin, 1911-13, chief editorial writer, 1914-18; editor San Antonio Express and San Antonio Evening News, 1918-46; editor San Antonio Express, 1946-56, editor emeritus, 1956—. Trustee and secretary board Texas State Juvenile Training Sch., 1912-18; trustee San Antonio Pub. Library, 1921-23, 1929-54 (pres. bd. 1933-39 and 1941-54); mem. adv. bd. St. John's Coll.; mem. adv. com. Tex. State Library Planning Orgn.; mem. exec. com. trustees' sect. and mem. publicity com., Am. Library Assn., 1936-39, mem. trustees' jury of award 1941-44; mem. nat. plans com. 1947; director trustees div. 1948; awarded national citation for trustee 1945); recipient Key Stone award Boys Clubs Am., also golden medallion. Life mem. Tex. Library Assn. (2d v.p. 1937-40), co-chmn. People's Library Movement for Tex., 1938-39, pres. 1941; dir. Tex. Safety Assn., San Antonio Safety Council; pres. League of Texas Library Trustees 1936-38; San Antonio Boys Clubs; mem. Nat. Municipal League. Lecturer Nat. Acad., 1946. Pub. speaker and writer on library orgn. and service. Home: 151 Morningside Drive, San Antonio 9. Office: Express Publishing Co., San Antonio 6. Died Aug. 20, 1956.

HARRIS, Peter Charles, army officer; b. Kingston, Ga., Nov. 10, 1865; s. Charles Hooks and Margaret (Monk) H.; grad. U.S. Mil. Acad., 1888; honor grad. Inf. and Cav. Sch., 1895; Army War Coll., 1908; m. Mary Gughrie, Sept. 30, 1894 (dec.). Commd. 2d lt., 13th Inf., 1888, promoted through the grades to col., adj. gen., 1917; brig. gen. N.A., 1917; adj. gen. of Army, rank of maj. gen., 1918; retired 1922. In Battel of San Juan Hill and siege of Santiago de Cuba, 1898; in active operations against Philippine insurgents, 1899-1900; rep. of War Dept. at Buffalo Expn., 1901; again in Philippines, 1905-07, 12-15; duty Gen. Staff, 1907-11; duty in office of Adj. Gen., Washington, 1916-22. Nominated by Pres., bvt., capt., for gallantry in battle at Santiago de Cuba, 1898. Decorated D.S.M. (U.S.); Comdr. Legion of Honor (France); Comdr. Order of the Crown (Italy). Democrat. Presbyn. Clubs: Army and Navy (Washington and Manila). Home: The Highlands, Washington. Died Mar. 18, 1951.

HARRIS, Philip H(oward), elec. utility exec.; b. Portland, Me., Mar. 11, 1881; s. Newton W. and Lizzie (Huston) H.; B.S. in E.E., U. Me., 1903; m. Ida Wright, June 7, 1911; 1 dau., Tillie C. Test course, Gen. Electric Co., 1903-05; with Carolina Electric Power Corp., 1905-06; in service dept. Westinghouse Elec. & Mfg. Co., 1906-15, except 1 yr. when engr. Pocahontas Fuel Co.; with Pa. Electric Co. and its predecessor cos., 1915-46, successively supt. distbn., dist. supt., gen. supt., supt. power houses, supt. power houses and engrin. dept., gen. mgr. Pa. Elec. Co., Johnstown Fuel Supply Co. and other subsidiaries in western Pa., from 1928, later pres.; also chmn. bd. Pa. Edison Co., Altoona, Pa.; retired from business 1946. Dir. Cambria County chpt. A.R.C.; pres. Johnstown Community Chest; dir. Community Nursing Service, 1946-48. Mason (Shriner). Home: 208 Luzerne St., Johnstown, Pa. Died Apr. 4, 1956; buried Bristol, Va.

HARRIS, Mrs. Ralph A., Rep. nat. committeewoman; ed. Convent of Sacred Heart, St. Louis; owner and publisher (with 2 sons) Hutchinson (Kan.) News-Herald, Chanute (Kan.) Tribune, Ottawa (Kan.) Herald, Burlington (Ia.) Hawk Eye Gazette. Active in Rep. Party, state and nat., for many years; Rep. committeewoman for Kan. since 1936. Home: 424 Elm St., Ottawa, Kan.* Died Mar. 13, 1952.

HARRIS, Reese Harvey, lawyer; b. Factoryville, Pa., July 3, 1883; s. John Howard and Lucy A. (Bailey) H.; A.B., M.A., Bucknell U., 1903; LL.B., Harvard, 1908; m. Christine Richards, June 1, 1910; children—Reese Harvey, Elizabeth (Mrs. Philip W. Scheide), Isabella (Mrs. William L. Acker). Admitted to Pa. bar, 1909; mem. O'Malley, Harris, Harris & Warren, Scranton, Pa., 1913—; spl. dep. atty. gen., Pa., 1932-35; pres. U.S. Lumber Co.; chmn. bd. Miss. Central R.R. Co.; dir. First Nat. Bank, Scranton Lackawanna Trust Co., Pa. Coal Co. Presdl. elector, 1928; mem. Pa. State Bd. Governance, 1936-48. Trustee Keystone Jr. Coll., LaPlume, Pa., 1926—, Bucknell U., Lewisburg, Pa., 1930-35. Mem. Am., Pa. State bar assns. Home: LaPlume, Lackawanna Co. Office: Scranton Electric Bldg., Scranton, Pa. Deceased.

HARRIS, Seale, physician; born Cedartown, Ga., Mar. 13, 1870; s. Charles Hooks and Margaret Ann (Monk) H.; U. Ga.; M.D., U. Va., 1894; grad. study N.Y. Polyclinic, 1898; U. Chgo., 1904, Johns Hopkins, 1906, U. Vienna and other European clinics, 1906; hon. LL.D., U. Ala.; m. Stella Rainer, on April 28, 1897 (dec. 1940); children—Seale (deceased 1943), Josephine Anne (Mrs. John J. Keegan). General private practice medicine, Union Springs, Ala., 1894-1906; physician-in-chief Mobile (Ala.) City Hosp., 1906-13; prof. medicine U. Ala., 1906-13, now prof. emeritus med. coll.; founder, dir. Seale Harris Clinic, 1922-56, ret. Served as maj., M.C. Res., U.S. Army, 1917; staff Surgeon Gen. Gorgas Hosp., 1918-19; sec. research com. A.R.C., France, 1918-19; investigated food conditions and nutritional diseases in Italy, Austria and Germany, Jan.-Feb. 1919; cons. physician Pres. Wilson's Party, Italy, Jan. 1919; col. (ret.), M.C. Res. Recipient Distinguished Service Medal, A.M.A., Research Medal, So. Med. Assn. for discovery (1923) of hyperinsulinism, 1949; citation by Gen. Pershing for conspicuous and meritorious service in France. Fellow A.C.P., Am. Geriatrics Soc.; mem. Jefferson Co. Med. Soc., Ala. Med. Assn., So. Med. Assn. (past pres. and sec.), A.M.A., Am., Ala diabetes assns., Jefferson Co. Diabetes Soc., Am. Therapeutic Soc., Am. Gastroenterological Assn., Am. Medical Editors Assn. (past pres.), Sigma Alpha Epsilon, Phi Chi. Independent Presbyn. Club: Mountain Brook. Author: Clinical Pellegra, 1940; Banting's Miracle, 1946; Woman's Surgeon, 1950. Editor-owner Southern Medical Journal, 1910-22; editor War Medicine, Paris, France, during World War I. Home: 3822 Jackson Blvd., Birmingham 13. Office: 2219 Highland Av., Birmingham, Ala. Died Mar. 16, 1957; buried Elmwood Cemetery, Birmingham.

HARRIS, Walter Alexander, lawyer; b. Macon, Ga., Nov. 17, 1875; s. Nathaniel Edwin and Fannie (Burke) H.; A.B., U. of Georgia, 1895, LL.B., 1896, also LL.D., 1928; m. Emily Williamson, Jan. 9, 1901 (died June 5, 1936). Admitted to Ga. bar, 1896, and practiced in Macon; mem. Harris, Russell, Weaver & Watkins. Mem. Bibb County Bd. of Edn., 1905-12. Pvt., 1st lt. and capt., 3d Ga. Vols., May 1, 1898-Apr. 22, 1899; served in Cuba with Army of Occupation; comd. Ga. Brig. U.S. Nat. Guard. on Mexican border, 1916-17; comdg. 61st Inf. Brig., 31st Div., 1917-18; comdg. 31st Div., A.E.F., Sept. 28-Nov. 14, 1918; returned in command 174th Inf. Brig., 87th Div., Jan. 10, 1919; hon. disch., Jan. 21, 1919. Maj. Gen. Ga. N.G. (ret.). Mem. Am., Ga. bar assns., Macon Bar Assn., Macon Hist. Soc. (pres.), Soc. for Ga. Archaeology (mem. exec. com.). Trustee emeritus Wesleyan Coll. Mem. Chi Phi, Phi Beta Kappa. Comdr. Ga. Dept. Am. Legion, 1919. Democrat. Episcopalian. Club: Kiwanis. Author: Emperor Brim, 1937. Home: 644 College St. Office: Persons Bldg., Macon, Ga. Died Mar. 15, 1958.

HARRIS, Walter William, lawyer; b. Lewisburg, Pa., Mar. 11, 1894; s. John Howard and Lucy Adelaide (Bailey) H.; A.B., A.M., Bucknell U., Lewisburg, 1914; LL.B., U. Mich., 1918; m. Dorothy Vaughn Payne, Dec. 24, 1925; children—Walter William, Stephen Vaughn. Admitted to Pa. bar, 1918 and practiced in Scranton; local counsel for nat. corps. and pub. utilities; dir. East Scranton State Bank. Mem. Internat. Assn. Ins. Counsel, Am., Pa. and Lackawanna Co. (past dir.) bar assns., Phi Delta Gamma. Mason (32°). Home: 422 Glenburn Rd., Clarks Green, Pa. Office: Scranton Electric Bldg., Scranton 3, Pa. Died Feb. 7, 1952; buried Abington Hills Cemetery, Clarks Summit, Pa.

HARRIS, W(illiam) John, surgeon; b. Shrewsbury, Eng., June 17, 1852; s. Thomas and Martha (Gould) H.; ed. in London; came to U.S. 1871; M.D., Homeopathy Med. Coll. of Mo. (valedictorian), 1875; m. Jessie Fremont Gibbs, Sept. 26, 1878; children—Martha Gould (Mrs. Charles A. Soch), William J. Was prof. anatomy, later clin. medicine and sanitary science, Homoeopathic Med. Coll. of Mo., mem. Hosp. Bd., St. Louis, 1909-13. Fellow Internat. Homeopathy League; mem. Am. Inst. Homoeopathy, Am. Pub. Health Assn., Mo. Inst. Homoeopathy (ex-pres.), Homeopathy Hosp. Assn. Mo. Home: Norrington, R.F.D. 2, Valley Park, Mo. Died Dec. 25, 1946.

HARRISON, B(enjamin) George, insurance exec.; b. St. Francis, Kan., Apr. 27, 1889; s. L. E. and Cora L. (Tippen) H.; grad. Kan. Wesleyan U.; m. Vera Cover, Sept. 10, 1911; children—Harriet (Mrs. Robert T. Rushmore), Hubert L., Corinne (wife of Dr. John K. Griffith). With Franklin Life Ins. Co., Springfield, 1940—, sec.-treas., 1940-45, v.p., treas., 1945—. Mem. C. of C. Rotarian. Home: 1905 Wiggins St. Office: 812 S. Sixth St., Springfield, Ill. Deceased.

HARRISON, Carter Henry, ex-mayor; b. Chicago, Ill., Apr. 23, 1860; s. Carter Henry H. (five times mayor of Chicago—killed by assassin, Oct. 28, 1893); A.B., St. Ignatius Coll. (Loyola U.), Chicago, 1881, LL.D., 1900; LL.B., Yale Univ., 1883; Litt.D. (honorary), Loyola University, 1949; married Edith Ogden, Dec. 14, 1887; children—Carter Henry, Edith Harrison Manierre. Practiced law Chicago, 1883-89; in real estate business, 1889-91; publisher and editor Chicago Times, 1891-94; mayor of Chicago, 5 terms, 1897-1905 and 1911-15; collector of internal revenue, 1st Ill. Dist., 1933-45. Chmn. Ill. Advisory Bd. of Fed. Emergency Adminstrn. of Pub. Works, 1933. Dem. Mem. S.R., S.A.R., Soc. of the Cincinnati, Gov. Ill. Chapter Soc. of Colonial Wars, Soc. of War of 1812, Mil. Order of Fgn. Wars, Vets. of Fgn. Wars, Am. Legion. Officer Legion of Honor (France). Clubs: University, Cliff Dwellers, Huron Mountain, Camp Fire. Mason (K.T.). Pres. Commn. for Encouragement of Local Art, Chicago, 1918-45. In charge Am. Red Cross activities in 12 hosps., nr. Toul, France, Oct. 1, 1918-Apr. 1, 1919. Author: Stormy Years (autobiography), 1935; Growing up with Chicago (Sequel to Stormy Years), 1944; With the American Red Cross in France, 1918-1919, 1947. Home: 2100 Lincoln Park West, Chgo. 14. Died Dec. 25; 1953; buried Graceland Cemetery, Chgo.

HARRISON, Charles A(llison), utility exec.; b. Colorado Springs, Colo., Aug. 28, 1893; s. Richard Knight and Anna (Graham) H.; A.B., Colo. Coll., 1916; U.S. Naval Acad., 1919; m. Gertrude Ashley, June 19, 1924; children—Charles Allison, Walter Ashley. Engr. Denver Gas & Electric Co., 1917. Cheyenne (Wyo.) Light Fuel & Power Co., 1919-20, Salina (Kan.) Light, Power & Gas Co., 1920-22, Pub. Service Co. of Colo., Denver, 1922-25, 1925-27; staff engr. Cities Service Co., N.Y.C., 1927-35; asst. gen. mgr., dir. Toledo Edison Co., 1935-43, v.p., sales mgr., dir., 1943—. Commnd. ensign, U.S. Navy, 1919. Mem. Am. Gas Assn., Toledo C. of C. (past pres.), Illuminating Engrs. Soc., Phi Beta Kappa, Phi Gamma Delta. Mason (Shriner). Clubs: Toledo, Sylvania. Home: 2819 Inwood Dr., Tol. 6. Office: Toledo Edison Co., Tol. 4. Died June 15, 1955.

HARRISON, Charles Yale, author; b. Phila, Pa., June 16, 1898; s. Lewis and Sophie (Frumer) H.; ed. pub. schs., New York and Montreal; m. Emily Courtier, Apr. 20, 1920 (died Sept. 2, 1931); 1 son, Yale Peter; m. 2d, Edna Margolin, Feb. 14, 1932 (divorced); m. 3d, Eva Shapiro, May 4, 1940. Newspaperman with Canadian and Am. publs., 1919-29; novelist since 1930. Enlisted 244th Batt., C.E.F., 1916; served in France and Belgium, 1916-18; wounded with 14th Royal Montreal Regt., Amiens, France, Aug. 8, 1918. Author: Generals Die in Bed, 1930; A Child Is Born, 1931; Clarence Darrow, 1931; There Are Victories, 1933; Public Housing, 1937; Meet Me on the Barricades, 1938; Nobody's Fool, 1948; Thank God for My Heart Attack, 1949. Contbr. to leading magazines and newspapers. Home: 235 E. 22d St., N.Y.C. 10. Died Mar. 17, 1954.

HARRISON, Earl Grant, lawyer; b. Phila., Apr. 27, 1899; s. Joseph Layland and Anna (MacMullen) H.; A.B., U. of Pa., 1920, LL.B., 1923; LL.D., Lafayette Coll., 1947; L.H.D., Yeshiva U., 1947; m. Carol R. Sensenig, Apr. 2, 1923; children—Carol Hope (dec.), Paul, Joseph Barton, Earl Grant Jr. Admitted to Pa. bar, 1923; associate in Saul, Ewing, Remick & Saul, Phila., 1923-32; partner Saul, Ewing, Remick & Harrison, 1932-45; instr. U. of Pa. Law Sch., 1932-33, 1936-37, prof. and dean, 1945-48, former vice pres. the univ. Partner firm of Schnader, Harrison, Segal & Lewis, 1948—; dir. Home Insurance Company, Penn Mutual Life Insurance Co., Industrial Trust Company, Samuel S. Fels Fund. Carnegie Endowment for Internat. Peace. Director alien registration U.S. Department of Justice, 1940-41; special asst. to U.S. atty. gen., 1941-42; U.S. commr. of immigration and naturalization, 1942-44; U.S. rep. on Intergovt. Com. on Refugees, 1945-46. Served as 2d lieutenant, inf., U.S. Army, July-Dec. 1918. Pres. Pub. Charities Assn. of Pa. ,1936-43; vice chmn. Phila. Award Trustees, 1939—. Trustee University of Pennsylvania, 1939-49. Pres., Law Alumni Soc. U. of Pa., 1943-45. Mem. Am. Bar Assn., Pa. Bar Assn. (regional dir. 1940-41, 1942-43), Phila. Bar Assn. (bd. govs. 1934-36), Lawyers' Club of Phila. (pres. 1945), Phi Beta Kappa (v.p. Phila. Assoc.), Alpha Chi Rho, Delta Sigma Rho, Phi Delta Phi, 1946 general campaign chairman, Phila. United War Chest, chmn. Nat. Comm. on Post War Immigration Policy. Clubs: Midday, University, Franklin Inn (Phila.). Home: Rose Valley Road, Moylan, Rose Valley, Pa. Office: Packard Bldg., Phila. 2. Died July 28, 1955; buried cemetery of the Providence Meeting of the Religious Society of Friends, Media, Pa.

HARRISON, Edith Ogden, author; b. New Orleans; d. Judge Robert Nash and Sarah (Beatty) Ogden; ed. Convent of Sisters of Mercy, and afterward grad. Peabody High Sch., New Orleans; m. Carter Henry Harrison, Dec. 14, 1887. Decorated by French Govt. with Le Palmier, as patron of fine arts and for work done for French people in Chicago. Mem. Colonial Dames of Am. Roman Catholic. Clubs: Fortnightly, Friday, Twentieth Century. Author: Prince Silverwings, 1902; Star Fairies, 1903; Moon Princess, 1905; The Flaming Sword, 1908; Ladder of Moonlight, 1909; Mocking-Bird, 1909; Polar Star, 1909; Princess Sayrane, 1910; Lady of the Shows, 1912; Enchanted House and Other Fairy Stories, 1913; Clemenica's Crisis, 1915; Below the Euator, 1918; All the Way 'Round, 1922; Lands of the Sun, 1925; Gray Moss, 1929; The Scarlet Riders, 1930; Strange to Say - Early Recollections of Chicago, 1949. Home: 2100 Lincoln Park W., Chgo. 14. Died May 22, 1955; buried Graceland Cemetery, Chgo.

HARRISON, Francis Burton, ex-gov.-gen. P.I.; b. New York, Dec. 18, 1873; s. Burton and Constance (Cary) H.; A.B., Yale, 1895; LL.B., New York Sch. of Law, 1897; m. Mary Crocker, June 7, 1900 (died 1905); m. 2d, Magel Judson, 1907; m. 3d, Elizabeth Wrentmore, May 15, 1919 (divorced, 1927); m. 4th, Margaret Wrentmore, Apr. 8, 1927. Instructor in New York night law school, 1897-99; admitted to bar, 1898; private Troop A, N.Y. Vol. Cav., and capt. and adj.-gen. U.S. Vols., Spanish-Am. War, June 20, 1898-Jan. 31, 1899; mem. 58th Congress (1903-05), 13th N.Y. Dist., 60th, 61st, 62d Congresses (1907-13), 16th Dist., and 63d Congress (1913-15), 20th Dist.; resigned from 63d Congress, 1913; gov.-gen. P.I., 1913-21. Dem. candidate for lt.-gov. of N.Y., 1904. Home: Teaninich, Alness, Scotland. Died Nov. 21, 1957.*

HARRISON, George L.; banker; b. San Francisco, California, Jan. 26, 1887; s. George Francis Edward and Mary Ross (Ray) H.; A.B., Yale, 1910, M.A. (hon.), 1929; LL.B., Harvard, 1913; LL.D. (hon.), Colgate, 1933, Wesleyan, 1934; m. Gertrude Gordon Grayson, Mar. 2, 1940. Admitted to D.C. bar, 1914, N.Y. bar, 1937; legal sec. to Justice Oliver W. Holmes, of U.S. Supreme Ct., 1913-14; asst. gen. counsel Federal Res. Bd., Washington, 1914-18, gen. counsel, 1919-20; dep. gov. Fed. Res. Bank of N.Y., 1920-28, gov., 1928-36, pres., 1936-41; dir. N.Y. Life Ins. Co., 1941—, pres., 1941-48, chmn. bd. 1948-54; dir. RCA, N.B.C., Inc., RCA Communications, Inc., Harper & Bros. Spl. consultant to Sec. of War, 1943-46; alternate chmn., Interim Policy Com. on Atomic Energy; chmn. adv. com. fiscal and monetary problems E.C.A. Trustee Columbia U. Fgn. Service Ednl. Found. Trustee Com. Econ. Development. Capt. A.R.C., overseas 1918, bd. incorporators, 1936, central com., 1937, bd. dirs. N.Y. chpt., 1937, v. chmn. 1945. Decorated U.S. Medal for Merit; Order of Polonia Resituta, Comdrs. Cross with stars. Mem. Pilgrims of United States, Newcomen Soc. of England. Clubs: Century, Yale, (New York); Links, Turf and Field (L.I.); Alfalfa, Metropolitan (Washington); Chevy Chase (Md.). Home: 200 E. 66th St., N.Y.C. 21. Office: 51 Madison Av., N.Y. C. 10. Died Mar. 5, 1958; buried Rock Creek Cemetery, Washington.

HARRISON, Joseph Le Roy, librarian; b. North Adams, Mass., Oct. 12, 1862; s. John Le Roy and Ellen Maria (Hawkes) H.; student Drury Acad., Casadilla Sch., and Cornell U., U. Heidelberg, Germany, 1890, N.Y. State Library Sch., Albany, N.Y., 1901-03, B.L.S., conferred by regents U. State of N.Y., 1893, M.L.S., 1912. Mem. editorial staff N.Y. Comml. Advertisers, 1885-88, asst. Washington corr., 1888-89; sub-librarian, legislation, N.Y. State Library, Albany, 1893-94; librarian Providence Athenaeum, 1894-1911, Forbes Library, Northampton, 1912—. Mem. A.L.A., Mass. Library Club, Western Mass. Library Club, N.Y. State Library Assn., N.Y. State Library Sch. Assn., Soc. Colonial Wars, S.A.R., Northampton Hist. Soc. (clk., dir.), S.A.R. (sec., treas. Seth Pomeroy chpt. 1924—), Inst. Am. Genealogy, Pocumtuck Valley Meml. Assn. Club: Lake Placid. Editor: Cap and Gown—Some College Verse, 1893; With Pipe and Book—A Collection of College Verse, 1898; In College Days—Recent 'Varsity Verse, 1901; (with Williams Haynes) Camp-fire Verse, 1917; Fisherman's Verse, 1918; Winter-sports Verse, 1919. Author: The Great Bore, Souvenir of Hoosac Tunnel, 1891; Guide to the Study of James Abbott McNeill Whistler (with W. G. Forsyth), 1895; Forbes Library: The Half-Century, 1894-1944. Home: Northampton, Mass. Died May 19, 1950.

HARRISON, Leland, diplomat; b. N.Y. City, Apr. 25, 1893; s. W. Henry and Helen (Skidmore) H.; B.A., Harvard, 1907; m. Anne C. Coleman, June 27, 1925. Pvt. sec. to ambassador to Japan, 1907-08; apptd. 3d sec. Embassy, Tokyo, 1908; 2d sec. Legation, Peking, 1909; 2d sec. Embassy, London, 1910; sec. Legation Bogotá, Colombia, 1912; assigned duty Dept. State, 1915; diplomatic sec. Am. Commr. to Negotiate Peace, rank of councilor, Nov. 30, 1918; councilor Am. Embassy, Paris, May 1920; spl. duty Dept. State, 1921; expert asst. to Am. commrs. Conf. on Limitation of Armament, 1921-22; became asst. sec. of state, Mar. 31, 1922; apptd. E.E. and M.P. to Sweden, 1927; chmn. Am. delegation Internat. Telegraph Conf., Brussels, 1928; E.E. and M.P. to Uruguay, 1929-30; chief internat. relations div. U.S. Tariff Commn., Nov. 1930-Nov. 1931; Am. mem. Internat. Concilliation Commn. under Treaty with Estonia, 1934-35; E.E. and M.P. to Rumania, 1935-37, Switzerland, 1937-47. Chmn. Am. delegation, also diplomatic rep. to Internat. Red Cross Conf., Geneva, 1949. Clubs: Union (N.Y. City); Philadelphia; Metropolitan, Chevy Chase, Alibi (Washington); Somerset (Boston). Home: 3041 White Haven St., Washington. Died June 6, 1951; buried St. James the Less, Phila.

HARRISON, Luther, writer, lecturer; b. Blue Mountain, Miss., Nov. 21, 1877; s. Thomas Caldwell and Kittie (Stewart) H.; student Hendrix Coll., Conway, Ark., 1900-01, Erskine Coll., Due West, S.C., 1902-04; D.Litt., Erskine Coll., 1939; m. Leona Sharp, Dec. 24, 1910; 1 dau., Margaret. Began as reporter Russellville (Ark.) Courier-Democrat, 1904; editor and pub. Higgins (Tex.) Pilot, 1907-08, Wetumka (Okla.) Gazette, 1910-11, Wewoka (Okla.) Democrat, 1912-18, Holdenville (Okla.) Democrat, 1921-23; editorial writer Ada (Okla.) Evening News, 1919-21; chief editorial writer Daily Oklahoman, Oklahoma City, 1923—. Mayor of Wetumka, 1911; mem. Okla. Ho. of Reps., 1915-16, State Senate, 1919-23. Presdl. elector at large Dem. nat. ticket, 1928. Orator at unveiling of Will Rogers monument, Statuary Hall, Washington, 1939. Mason. Democrat. Home: 1143 W. 38th St. Office: Oklahoman Bldg., Oklahoma City. Died Jan. 16, 1959.

HARRISON, Maurice Edward, lawyer; b. San Francisco, Calif., Aug. 1, 1888; s. Edward Charles and Mary Gertrude (Bodkin) H.; A.B., U. of Calif., 1908, J.D., 1910; LL.D., St. Mary's Coll., 1937; m. Agnes Ballard Welsh, Jan. 8, 1913 (died Oct. 13, 1917); children—Ruth (dec.), Maurice Edward; m. 2d, Margaret Perkins Hayne, June 16, 1919; children—Sally Hayne, Margaret Anne, Lucy Duncan. Practiced at San Francisco in partnership with father, 1910-23; lecturer in law, University of California, 1911-19; prof. law and dean Hastings Coll. of Law, U. of Calif., 1919-25; mem. Brobeck, Phleger & Harrison since 1925. Mem. Calif. Code Commn., 1929-32; director Hastings Coll. of Law since 1935, Roman Catholic Sem., of San Francisco, since 1939; chmn. Dem. State Central Com., Calif., 1932-34; mem. U.S. Constitution Sesquicentennial Commission, 1935-39; mem. Alien Enemy Hearing Bd., 1942-43. Regent U. of Calif. since 1944. Decorated Officier Legion of Honor. Mem. Bar Assn. of San Francisco (pres. 1929-30). Roman Catholic. Clubs: Pacific Union, Bohemian. Home: 901 California St. Office: 111 Sutter St., San Francisco. Died Feb. 10, 1951.

HARRISON, Perry G(albraith), mining engr.; b. Mpls., Mar. 6, 1885; s. Hugh and Teresa V. (Scott) H.; student Columbia, 1909-10; E.M., Mich. Coll. Mines, 1909; m. Alice L. Smith, 1917 (dec.); 1 son, Hugh Howard; m. 2d, Virginia Climo, 1955. Mining engineer Meriden Iron Company, 1911-14; supt. Nat. Mines Co., 1911-17; cons. engr., geologist with H. V. Winchell, 1917-20; gen. supt. Campania Minera del Misrasol, Mexico, 1921; gen. mgr. Portland Gold Mining Co., 1922; mine supt. Smuggler Union, 1923; gen. mgr. Cusi Mining Co., 1924-27, North Range Mining Co., 1927-37; gen. mgr. Evergreen Mines Co., 1927-46, pres., 1937-46; v.p., dir. Hanna Coal & Ore Corp. since 1946 (also subsidiaries); ore sales manager M. A. Hanna Company, Cleve., 1946-57, now iron ore consultant; dir. Wheeling Steel Corp. Mem. Am. Iron and Steel Inst., Am. Mining Congress, Am. Inst. Mining and Metall. Engrs. Clubs: Kitchi Gammi (Duluth); Country, Union (Cleve.); Fort Henry (Wheeling, W.Va.). Home: 18000 S. Woodland Rd., Shaker Heights 22, O. Office: Leader Bldg., Cleve. 14. Died Nov. 11, 1959.

HARRISON, Ray, banker; b. Fort Adams, R.I., Sept. 13, 1895; s. George F. E. and Mary (Ray) H.; B.S., U. S. Mil. Acad., 1917; m. Elizabeth Love, Nov. 25, 1920; children—Ray, Jr., William D. Commd. 2d lt., U.S. Army, 1917, and advanced through grades to capt., F.A.; resigned Oct. 1, 1922; with Nat. Bank of Commerce, N.Y.C., 1922-29, Mellon Nat. Bank & Trust Co., Pitts., 1929—, now v.p.; dir. Montour R.R. Co., Aetna-Standard Engring. Co., Youngstown & So. R.R. Co. Clubs: Pittsburgh Golf, Duquesne, Fox Chapel Golf, Rolling Rock. Home: 1405 Squirrel Hill Av. Office: Mellon Square, Pitts. 30. Died July 13, 1957; buried Homewood Cemetery, Pitts.

HARRISON, Ross Granville, biologist; b. Germantown (Phila.), Pa., Jan. 13, 1870; s. Samuel and Katherine (Diggs) H.; A.B., Johns Hopkins, 1889, Ph.D., 1894, LL.D., 1942; M.D., U. Bonn, 1899; A.M. (hon.), Yale, 1907; D.Sc., U. Cin., 1920, U. Mich., 1929, U. of Dublin, 1932, Harvard, 1936, Yale, 1939, Columbia, 1940, U. Chgo., 1949; Ph.D. (hon.), U. of Freiburg, 1929; M.D. (hon.), U. of Budapest, 1935; Dr. Rev. Nat., University of Tübingen, 1953; m. Ida Lange, Jan. 9, 1896; children—Dorothea Katharine, Elizabeth Ross, Richard Edes, Eleanor Barrington (Mrs. Rufus Putney, Jr.), Ross Granviille. Lectr. on morphology Bryn Mawr Coll., 1894-95; instr. and asso. in anatomy Johns Hopkins, 1896-99, asso. prof. anatomy, 1899-1907; prof. comparative anatomy Yale, 1907-27, Sterling prof. of biology, 1927-38, prof. emeritus, 1938—. Chmn. NRC, Washington, 1938-46; pres. 6th Pacific Sci. Congress, 1939; Dunham lectr. Harvard, 1926; Croonian lectr. Royal Society, London, 1933; Linacre lectr. St. John's College, Cambridge, 1939; Silliman lectr. Yale, 1949. Mem. science com. Nat. Resources Planning Bd., 1938-43; mem. U.S. Nat. Com. for UNESCO, 1946-51. Conf. bd., Assoc. Research Councils (chmn., 1944—). Mng. editor Jour. Exptl. Zoology, 1903-46; trustee Marine Biol. Lab., Woods Hole, Mass., 1908-40, trustee emeritus, 1940—; bd. dirs. L.I. Biol. Sta.; trustee Bermuda Biol. Sta. (treas. 1930-46), Woods Hole Oceanographic Inst., Science Service. Mem. adv. bd. Wistar Inst.; bd. sci. dirs. Rockefeller Inst. Med. Research (v.p., 1939-—); bd. sci. advisers, Jane Coffin Childs Fund for Med. Research. Fellow Am. Acad. Arts and Scis., A.A.A.S. (v.p. 1936); mem. Nat. Acad. Sciences (council 1932-46), Conn. Acad., Am. Philos. Soc. (council 1941-44, v.p. 1947-50), Am. Soc. Zoologists (pres. 1924), Soc. Study Development and Growth (pres. 1946-47), Beaumont Med. Club (pres. 1933), Am. Assn. Anatomists (pres. 1912-13), Anatomische Gesellschaft (pres. 1934-35), Royal Physiog Soc. (Lund), Royal Soc. Science (Uppsala), Am. Soc. Naturalists (sec. 1902-04, pres. 1913), Am. Neurol. Assn., Soc. Exptl. Biology and Medicine; corr. member Göttingen Akad der Wissenshaften, Deutsche Acad. Sciences, Bavarian Acad. Science, Acad. Nat. Sci. Phila., Acad. des Sciences de l'Institut de France, Soc. de Biol., Paris; hon. mem. Conn. Med. Soc., Harvey Society, Royal Acad. Medicine, Turin, Royal Acad. Medicine, Belgium, N.Y. Acad. Science; fgn. asso. Acad. de Medecine, Paris; fgn. mem. Royal Netherlands, Norwegian, Royal Swedish acads. sci., Acad. Nazionale Lincei, Rome, Stockholm, Zool Soc., London, Royal Society, London. Fgn. corr., Acad. Science of Institute of Bologna, Italy. Awarded (1914) The Archduke Rainer medal of Imperial Royal Zoölogical Botanical Soc. of Vienna, 1925; John Scott medal and premium, of the City of Philadelphia, "for the invention of devices for tissue grafting and for tissue culture." John J. Carty Medal, Nat. Acad. Sciences, 1947; Antonio Feltrinelli International prize Accademia Nazionale de'l Lincei, Italy, 1956. Author numerous scientific papers on development of fishes, nervous system, embryonic transplantation and cultivation of animal tissues outside the organism. In 1907 first adapted the hanging drop culture method to the study of embryonic tissues and demonstrated directly the outgrowth of the developming nerve-fiber. Home: 142 Huntington St., New Haven. Died Sept. 30, 1959.

HARRISON, William Henry, judge, Supreme Ct., N.B.; b. St John, N.B., Sept. 25, 1880; s. Legh Richmond and Susan Louise (Thorne) H.; student Rothesay Collegiate Sch.; B.A. U. N.B., 1900, LL.D., 1938; LL.B., Harvard Law Sch., 1903; m. Constance Roy, Sept. 15, 1909; children—Patricia Louise (Mrs. Maj. Paul Maurice Blanchet), Janice Dorothea (Mrs. George F. Teed), Constance Mary. Called to N.B. bar, 1903; King's counsel, 1923; partnership Powell and Harrison, barristers, Saint John, 1906-19; edited New Brunswick Law Reports, 1908-19; entered firm of Barnhill, Sanford and Harrison (later Sanford and Harrison), 1919; elected to Provincial Legislature for City of St. John, Aug. 10, 1925, re-elected, June 1930, apptd. pres. Exec. Council, May 1931; apptd. atty. gen. of Province of N.B., 1933; called to Bench, Aug. 1935; judge, Chancery and Appeal Div., Supreme Ct. of N.B. Chmn. Bd. of Referees Excess Profits Tax Act, 1940-44. Served as major and lt. col. comdg. Divisional Ammunition Column, 2d Can. Div., 1914-18; comd. 3d N.B. Medium Brigade Royal Canadian Arty., 1919-22. Awarded D.S.O., 1917; three times mentioned in dispatches. Med. Bd. of the Provincial Mus. of N.B.; mem. Senate U. N.B.; trustees Lord Beaverbrook Scholarships; pres. Canadian Legion for N.B., 1928-29; pres. St. George's Soc., 1929, 30. Clubs: Union, Riverside Golf and Country, Canadian (past pres.), Mount Royal (Montreal). Mason. Mem. Angelican Ch. Home: 142 Mount Pleasant Av. Address. Supreme Court, Saint John, N.B., Can. Died July 18, 1955; buried Saint John.

HARRISON, William Henry, communications engr.; b. Bklyn., June 11, 1892; s. John and Ann (Terahin) H.; student Pratt Inst., 1913-15; D. Engring. (hon.), Polytech. Inst. Bklyn., 1938; LL.D. (hon.), Notre Dame U., 1939, Hofstra Coll., 1951; D. England (honorary) Renssalaer Poly. Inst., 1946, Manhattan College, 1950; Master of Procurement (hon.), Signal Supply Sch., Ft. Horabird, Md., 1952; married Mabel Gilchrist Ouchterloney, Apr. 14, 1915, children—William Henry, John Grant. Repairman and wireman, N.Y. Telephone Co., 1909-14; in engring. dept., Western Electric Co., New York, N.Y., 1914-18; engineer equipment and bldg. engr., and plant engr., Am. Telephone and Telegraph Co., N.Y. City, 1918-33; v.p. and dir. The Bell Telephone Co. of Pa. and The Diamond State Telephone Co., 1933-37; asst. v.p., Am. Telephone and Telegraph Co., N.Y.C., 1937-38; v.p. and chief engr., 1938-45, v.p. department operational engineering, 1945-48, pres., dir., 1948—; chmn. divs. of Internat. Tel. & Tel. Corp., subsidiaries; dir. subsidiary cos. Chief Shipbuilding, Construction and Supplies Branch, Office of Prodn. Management, 1941-42; dir. of Production, W.P.B., 1942. Apptd. brig. gen., U.S. Army, 1942, maj. gen., 1943; director construction division National Defense council, 1940; dir. of procurement and distribution service, Office of Chief Signal Officer, 1943-45; adminstr. N.P.A., 1950-51, D.P.A., 1951. Awarded D.S.M., 1945; Hon. Comdr. Order British Empire, 1946; Hoover Medal, 1946; Cross French Legion of Honor (Officer) 1947. Dir. Nassau Hosp.; mem. bd. gov. N.Y. Hospital; trustee Pratt Institute, Manhattan Coll. Mem. Am. Inst. Electric Engrs. (expresident), Newcomen Society, Eta Kappa Nu, Tau Beta Pi. Clubs: University, Downtown Athletic (New York); North Fork Country (Cutchogue, N.Y.); Garden City Golf, Cherry Valley (Garden City); Chevy Chase (Wash.); India House; Chgo. Home: 120 Kensington Rd., Garden City, N.Y. Office: 67 Broad St., N.Y.C. 4. Died Apr. 21, 1956.

HARROFF, Fred F(remont) (hare'uff), company exec.; b. Canfield, O., July 2, 1896; s. John W. and Elva (Collar) H.; A.B., Western Res. U., 1920; m. Grace Acker, June 30, 1923 (dec. July 21, 1950); children—Don F., Robert A.; m. 2d, Grace Withington, Aug. 27, 1952. Joined lamp div. Gen. Electric Co., Cleve., 1920, various positions mfg., marketing, adminstrn., 1920-38, asst. to v.p. in charge of lamp div., 1938-43, asst. gen. mgr. lamp div., 1943-48, gen. mgr., 1948-53, v.p. co., 1950-53, cons. lamp div. since 1953. Mem. Phi Beta Kappa, Delta Sigma Rho, Phi Alpha Delta, Lambda Chi Alpha. Home: 535 North Griffing Blvd., Asherville, N.C. Died Mar. 27, 1955.

HARSHA, William Thomas, surgeon; b. Decatur, Ill., May 14, 1884; s. William M. and Delia (Hutchinson) H.; student U. Chgo., 1902-04; M.D., Northwestern U., 1908; m. Pauline Palmer, Dec. 22, 1906. Intern Chicago Hosp., 1908-09; surgeon in charge I.C. R.R. Co., ret. 1949. Fellow A.C.S.; mem. A.M. A., Ill., Chgo. med. socs., Chgo. Surg. Soc. Home: 5718 S.W. 49th, Miami, Fla. Died Dec. 15, 1950; buried Oak Woods Cemetery.

HART, Charles A., clergyman; b. Ottawa, Ill., Sept. 6, 1893; s. John Joseph and Mary Etta (Donovan) H.; A.B., St. Viator Coll., 1917, A.M., 1919, LL.D., 1936; student St. Paul (Minn.) sem., 1917-19; J.C.B., Catholic U. of America, 1920, S.T.B., 1920, Ph.D., 1930; student Columbia, 1920, U. of Munich, 1924. Ordained Catholic priest, 1919; instr. philosophy, Cath. U. Am., 1921-31, asst. prof., 1931-36, asso. prof., 1936-52, prof. since 1952; prof. philosophy, Coll. of Notre Dame, Baltimore, Md., 1934; made domestic prelate by Pope Pius II, 1957. Founder and dir. Catholic Evidence Guild, Washington, D.C., 1931—. Awarded Papal medal Bene Merenti, 1939. Mem. Federation Internationale des Philosophie, British Institute Philosophy, Internat. Congress of Philosophy, Am. Philos. Assn., Am. Cath. Philos. Assn. (nat. sec. since 1930; editor of Proceedings since 1930), Medieval Acad., Cath. Ednl. Assn., Pi Gamma Mu, Phi Eta Sigma, Phi Kappa. Asso. editor New Scholasticism 1933—. Author: Thomistic Concert of Mental Faculties, 1930; Thomistic Metaphysics, 1959. Editor and contbr.: Aspects of New Scholastic Philosophy, 1931; Philosophy of Society, 1933; Philosophy of State, 1940. Contbr. to symposia: Twentieth century Religion, 1947; Builders of American Culture, 1947; Integration of the Catholic College Curriculum, 1950. Address: Catholic University of America, Washington 17. Deceased.

HART, Charles Arthur, entomologist; b. Quincy, Ill., Oct. 12, 1859; s. William Henry and Janet Elizabeth (Hoffman) H.; student State Normal U., 1881-82. Entomologist of Ill. Biol. Sta., 1894—; specialist in aquatic insect life; asst. Ill. State Lab., 1884-1900; asst. entomologist State Ill., 1900—. Mem. Soc. Am. Zoologists, Assn. Econ. Entomologists, A.A.A.S. Author: Entomology of the Illinois River (bull. State Lab. of Natural History), and various other entomol. articles. Address: Urbana, Ill. Died Feb. 18, 1918; buried Quincy, Ill.

HART, Edwin Bret, biochemist; b. Sandusky, O., Dec. 25, 1874; s. William and Mary (Hess) H.; student U. of Mich., 1892-97; U. of Marburg, Germany; U. of Heidelberg, Germany, 1900-01; m. Ann Virginia De Mille, Nov. 18, 1903; 1 dau., Margaret Virginia. Asst. chemist, N.Y. Agrl. Exptl. Station 1897-1902, asso. chem., 1902-06; prof. agrl. chemistry, U. of Wis.; chemist, Wis. Exptl. Station since 1906. Fellow A.A.A.S.; mem. Nat. Acad. Science, Am. Chem. Soc., Soc. Biol. Chemists, Soc. Animal Production, Soc. Dairy Science. Home: 302 Lathrop. Office: Biochemistry Bldg., U. of Wis., Madison 6, Wis. Died Mar. 12, 1953; buried Forest Hill Cemetery, Madison.

HART, George H(art), veterinarian; b. Phila., Pa., Oct. 10, 1883; s. John Robbins and Jane (Sheard) H.; V.M.D., Univ. of Pa., 1903; M.D., George Washington University, 1908; LL.D., University of California, 1958; married Eva M. Cadman, Nov. 13, 1912 (dec. Nov. 1949); m. 2d, Theresa A. Dennis, Jan. 6, 1954. Asst. bacteriology, pathology, pathol. div., bur. animal husbandry U.S. Dept. Agr., Washington, D.C., 1903-08, field worker, 1908-10; city veterinarian Health Dept., Los Angeles, Calif., 1910-17; asso. prof. vet. sci., Coll. of Agr., Univ. of Calif., 1917-24, prof., 1924-26, prof. and head div. of animal husbandry, 1926-48, dean Sch. Vet. Med. U. Cal., prof. vet. sci., 1948-54, dean emeritus, 1954—; Fulbright lectr. U. Sydney, Australia, 1955. U.S. Govt. del. to 13th Internat. Vet. Congress, Zurich, Switzerland, 1938, World Veterinary Congress, Stockholm, 1953. Del. National Research Council to 7th Pacific Science Congress, Auckland and Christ church, New Zealand, February 1949. Chairman com. on animal health, Nat. Research Council, 1943-44, 45; mem. coms. on animal nutrition, vet. services for farm animals and training of research workers in agr., Nat. Research Council, 1944-47. Recipient Internat. Vet. Congress prize, 1938; Borden award Am. Vet. Med. Assn., 1953. Member of the A.A.A.S., Am. Assn. Univ. Profs., Am. Vet. Med. Assn. (mem. research council 1941-50), Am. Soc. Animal Prodn. (pres. 1940, 1947 honor guest), U.S. Livestock Sanitary Assn., Wilderness Soc., Soc. Exptl. Biol. and Med., Sigma Xi, Delta Tau Delta. Republican. Episcopalian. Home: 114 E St., Davis, Cal. Died Aug. 2, 1959.

HART, Irving Harlow, educator; b. Grinnell, Ia., Sept. 3, 1877; s. Alexis Crane and Elizabeth Edith (Biggar) H.; A.B., Grinell (Ia.) Coll., 1898; post-grad. work in history and law State U. of Ia., 1900-01; m. Ida Fay Pew, Dec. 22, 1902 (dec. May 20, 1932); children—Elizabeth Fay, Mary Leota, Irving Harlow, Evan Alexis; m. 2d, Winfred Martha Tuttle, May 26, 1933. Instr. and comdt. various mil. acads. in West and Southwest until 1906; headmaster Lakeside Classical Inst., San Antonio, 1906-07; prin. Bradford Sch., San Antonio, 1907-08; supt. schs., Allison, Ia., 1908-12; county supt. schs., Butler County, Ia., 1912-14; prof. rural edn. Ia. State Teachers' Coll., 1914-15, dir. extension, 1915-48, archivist and historian, 1948—, sponsored Radio Service, and supervised service until 1948; participant weekly TV series Landmarks in Iowa History, 1952. Chmn. Sartori Hosp. Bd., 1937-48. Served from pvt. to cpl. K Co., 50th Ia. Inf., Spanish-Am. War, Apr.-Dec. 1898; ednl. sec. Army YMCA, Camp Dodge, Ia., Apr.-Nov. 1918, Camp Eustis, Va., Nov. 1918-Jan. 1919; ednl. dir. at Port of Debarkation, Newport News, Va., Jan.-Apr. 1919. Mem. N.E.A., Minn. (life), Ia. hist. socs., Minn. Archeol. Soc., Spanish War Vets., C. of C. (pres. 1936, 37), Soc. Mayflower Descendants, Ia. State Teachers Assn. (pres. 1932-33), Phi Beta Kappa, Phi Delta Kappa. Republican. Mason. Author: The First Seventy-Five Years, a history of Iowa State Teachers College, 1876-1951, 1951; numerous other hist. articles. Home: 2516 Walnut St., Cedar Falls, Ia. Died July 12, 1958.

HART, James A., hotel exec.; b. Ottumwa, Ia., June 12, 1900; s. William Archibald and Elizabeth Jane Hart; ed. Drake U., 1918; student Ia. Success Bus. Tng. Sch., 1919; m. Elizabeth Augusta Doeckel, Jan. 28, 1919. Gen. hotel tng. Harper Hotel, Rock Island, Ill., 1919-20; successively with Jefferson Hotel, Peoria, Ill., Quincy (Ill.) Hotel and Newcomp Hotel; exec. asst. mgr., Hotel Sherman, Chgo., 1920-26, later became pres. now v. chmn. bd.; mgr. dir., St. Clair and Eastgate Hotels, 1926-32; mgr. dir. Croyden Hotel, 1932; exec. asst. mgr. Palmer House, 1933; resident mgr. Ambassador Hotels, East and West, 1934-45; gen. mgr., 1945-49, later pres., now chmn. bd.; gen. mgr. The Pump Room; pres. The Buttery; v.p. Mexican Hotels, Ltd., 1945-52; partner The Freehart Corp., 1945-52; pres. Sherman Products Co., 1951-59. Mem. bd. lay trustees DePaul U.; dir. St. Josephs Hosp. Decorated Knight Equestrian Order of Holy Sepulchre of Jerusalem. Mem. Chgo. Conv. Bur. (dir.), Greater Chgo. Hotel Assn. (dir.) Phi Gamma Lambda. Clubs: Executives, Forty, Tavern, Beau Nash, Edgewater Golf. Home: Ambassador East Hotel, State and Goethe Sts. Office: Sherman Hotel, Clark and Randolph, Chgo. Died Feb. 1960.

HART, Michael James, ex-congressman; b. Waterloo, Quebec, Can., July 16, 1877; s. Timothy and Catherine Theresa (McGuirk) H.; brought by parents to U.S., 1880; ed. pub. schs.; m. Zola Hudson, July 9, 1904; children—Irving McGregor, Harry Howard, Richard James, Doris Ann and Virginia Jean (twins), Frances Joan; m. 2d, Wilma Ruth Slinkard, Feb. 11, 1924. Teacher pub. schs., Saginaw County, Mich., 1896-98; partner and gen. mgr. Hart Bros., farmers and shippers of produce, 1902—; mem. 72d and 73d Congresses, 8th Mich. Dist. Democrat. K.C. Club: Saginaw. Home: Saginaw, Mich. Deceased.

HART, Oliver Philip, city mgr.; b. Mooresville, N.C., Dec. 18, 1898; s. Spruce Maroney and Jane Elizabeth (West) H.; A.B., Davidson (N.C.) Coll., 1919, A.M., 1920; student U. of Chicago, summer 1927; Ph.D., U. of N.C., 1930; m. Lorraine Elizabeth Page, Sep. 14, 1927; 1 son, Oliver Philip. Asst. prof. of physics, Miss. State Coll., 1921-24, Clemson Coll., 1924-25; head physics U. of Miami (Fla.), 1926-32; supt. of public works projects, dir. of research, City of Miami, 1932-46, asst. city mgr., 1946-48, city mgr., 1948-50. Mem. Army Advisory Com. (3rd Army) and Naval Aviation Associate. Mem. Internat. City Mgrs. Assn., Sigma Upsilon. Presbyn. (treas.). Club: Rotary Internat. (Miami). Home: 1847 Crystal Terr., Miami 45. Office: Dade County Courthouse, Miami 45, Fla. Died Nov. 9, 1951; buried Woodlawn Cemetery, Miami.

HART, Theodore Stuart, physician; b. Groving, Ill., Feb. 25, 1869; s. Charles Langdon and Sarah (Franks) H.; A.B., Yale, 1891, A.M., 1893; M.D., Columbia U. Coll. Phys. and Surg., 1895; m. Mary Robbins, June 12, 1901. Intern Presbyn. Hosp., N.Y. C., 1895-97; vis. physician Seton Hosp., 1901-11; instr. Coll. Phys. and Surg., 1903-13, asst. prof. clin. medicine, 1913-22; vis. physician Presbyn. Hosp., 1914-22, cons. physician, 1922—; cons. physician Manhattan Eye, Ear and Throat Hosp., 1922—, Neurological Inst., 1936—. Mem. Conn. N.G., 1891-92; cardio-vascular cons. to U.S. Army, 1917, N.Y. Draft Board, 1918. Mem. U.S. Citizens Defense Corps, Emergency Medical Reserve Pool, 1941—. Diplomate Am. Bd. Internal Medicine. Mem. Assn. Am. Physicians, Am. Soc. Clin. Investigation, A.M. A., N.Y. Acad. Medicine, N.Y. Heart Assn. (pres. 1920-24), Am. Heart Assn. (chmn. exec. com., 1924-31), N.Y. Tb and Health Assn. (director 1924-31), Harvey Soc., Zeta Psi, Chi Delta Theta, Elihu Club. Republican. Presbyn. Author: The Diagnosis and Treatment of Abnormalities of Myocardial Function, 1917; Taking Care of Your Heart, 2d edit., 1937. Contbr. many papers on metabolic disorders and diseases of the circulation to med. jours. Clubs: University (N.Y.C.); West Side Tennis (L.I.). Home: 410 Park Av., N.Y.C. Died Jan. 1, 1951.

HART, William Lee, medical officer U.S. Army; b. Yorkville (now York), S.C., Jan. 27, 1881; s. George Washington Seabrook and Ellen Almene (Hackett) H.; M.D., Univ. of Md., 1906; LL.D., Baylor Univ., May 28, 1945; L.H.D., Southwestern Med. Foundation, June 10, 1946; grad. Army Medical School, 1908, Command and General Staff Sch., 1926, Army Industrial Coll., 1927, Army War Coll., 1931; m. Mariana Catherine Franklin, June 30, 1920; children—William Lee II, Mariana Catherine II. Pvt. practice, 1906-07; with Med. Corps U.S. Army, 1908—. Served as pvt. to capt. S.C. Militia and N.G., 1898-1908; 1st lt., advancing to col., U.S. Army, 1908-34; promoted to brigadier general, March 16, 1945; now brigadier general, United States Army, retired. Served as chief Overseas Div., Office of Surgeon General; with A.E.F. and with Army in France and Germany; various stations in the United States and P.I.; commanded 12th Med. Reg. in Philippines; pres. 7th C.A. Medical Research Board. Dean, Southwestern Medical College, 1946-49; dean S.W. Med. Sch. U. of Tex., 1949-50, dean emeritus, 1950—; professor pub. health, Southwestern Med. Coll., 1948-49, S.W. Med. School U. of Texas, 1949-50. Made researches in Philippines, in cholera; helminthology, and effects of tropical light on white people, also researches in typhoid fever, smallpox, etc., in U.S. Decorations from Bolivia, Ecuador, Serbia, Poland, France, Montenegro, Panama, etc. Awarded Founders' Medal by Assn. Mil. Surgeons of U.S., 1942. Ho Din, Southwestern Med. Foundation, 1944. Co-founder Celsus Soc. of San Antonio. Fellow A.M.A., Am. Coll. Phys., Am. Coll. Surg., A.A.A.S., Am. Pub. Health Assn., Scientific Soc. of San Antonio (pres. 1940-41); hon. mem. York County (S.C.) Med. Soc.; mem. Texas Acad. Science, Soc. of the Cincinnati, Geog. Soc. of Mexico, Pi Delta Upsilon, Nu Sigma Nu, Theta Nu Epsilon, Pi Gamma Mu, Upsilon Pi, Alpha Omega Alpha, Sigma Xi. Dem. Episcopalian. Clubs: Cosmos, Army and Navy (Wash.); Lambs (N. Y.). Compiler: History of Base Hospital No. 53. Contbr. on med. and scientific subjects. Address: 133 E. Mulberry Av., San Antonio 12. Died Dec. 22, 1957; buried York, S.C.

HARTER, Isaac, mech. engr.; b. Mansfield, O., Jan. 2, 1880; s. Michael Daniel and Mary Lucinda (Brown) H.; grad. Episcopal Acad., Phila., Pa., 1896, St. Paul's Sch., Concord, N.H., 1897; B.S., U. of Pa., 1901; m. Elizabeth Farrington, Mar. 15, 1904; 1 son, Isaac; married 2d, Alice Crane Howland, June 6, 1956. With Aultman & Taylor Machinery Co., Mansfield, O., 1901-05, The Stirling Co., Barberton, O., 1905-07; with The Babcock & Wilcox Co. as supt. Barberton Works, 1907-10, Bayonne (N.J.) Works, 1910-20, asst. to pres., 1920-25, v.p. and dir. 1924-47; exec. v.p. and dir. The Babcock & Wilcox Tube Co., 1924-47, chmn. bd., dir., 1947—. Mem. Am. Soc. M.E., Inst. of Metals (London), Ohio Society of New York, Am. Welding Soc., Sigma Xi, Phi Kappa Sigma. Republican. Episcopalian. Clubs: University, Engineers (New York); Piping Rock (Locust Valley, N.Y.); Seawanhaka-Corinthian Yacht (Oyster Bay, N.Y.). Address: 36 E. 72d St., N.Y.C. Died Aug. 22, 1957; buried Mansfield, O.

HARTFORD, George L.; chmn. bd. of dirs. Great Atlantic & Pacific Tea Co. Home: Montclair, N.J. Office: 420 Lexington Av., N.Y.C. Died Sept. 1957.*

HARTFORD, John A., chmn. bd. Great Atlantic & Pacific Tea Co.; b. Orange, N.J., 1872; s. George Huntington Hartford; mem. Pauline Corwin (divorced 1920; remarried, 1925); m. 2d, Frances Belger, 1920 (divorced 1920). At age 16 began in father's store (founded as tea store, Jersey City, N.J., 1859); proposed present policy of cash-and-carry, 1912, and followed with rapid expansion by branches; began policy of super-markets, 1930; now operating 4,700 stores with 120,000 employees and $3,000,000,000 annual sales; became chmn. of bd., 1949; also dir. Guaranty Trust Co., Long Island R.R., N.Y., N.H. & H. R.R., Prudential Ins. Co., Chrysler Corp. Home: Valhalla, N.Y. Office: 420 Lexington Av., N.Y. City. Died Sept. 20, 1951.*

HARTLEY, Roland H., ex-gov. Wash.; b. Shogomoc, York County, N.B., Can., June 26, 1864; s. Rev. Edward Williams and Rebecca Barker (Whitehead) H.; student pub. schs. and Mpls. Acad.; m. Nina M. Clough, Aug. 22, 1888; children—Edward Williams, David Marston, Mary. Settled at Brainerd, Minn., 1878; served as pvt. sec. to Gov. Clough, 1897, 98; moved to Everett, Wash., 1903, and engaged in lumber business; mayor of Everett, 1910, 11; mem. Wash. Ho. of Reps., 1915, 16; gov. of Wash., 1925-33. Served with Gen. Staff Minn. N.G., 8 yrs.; capt. O.R.C., U.S. Army. Republican. Mason (Shriner), Elk. Home: 2320 Rucker Av., Everett, Wash. Died Sept. 21, 1952; buried Everett.

HARTMAN, Gertrude, editor, author; b. Phila., Pa.; grad. Phila. Normal Sch. for Girls; A.B., Bryn Mawr, 1905; grad. student Teachers Coll. (Columbia), 1917-19. Teacher of English, Ballwin Sch., Bryn Mawr, 1905-07; head of English dept., Veltin Sch., New York, 1907-11; asst. to prin., Winsor Sch., Boston, 1911-14; examiner in English for Experiment Bd. of Head Mistresses Assn., 1912-16; dir. Merion Country Day Sch., Merion, Pa., 1915-17; research worker Bureau Ednl. Expts., New York, 1917-21; editor Progressive Education, 1924-30. Author: The Child and His School, 1921; Home and Community Life, 1923; The World We Live In, 1931; Creative Expression, 1931; These United States, 1932; Medieval Days and Ways, 1937; Finding Wisdom, 1938; Machines, 1939; The Making of a Democracy, 1940; Builders of the Old World, 1946; America—Land of Freedom, 1946; In Bible Days, 1948. Address: 140 E. 63d St., N.Y.C. Died May 12, 1955.

HARTMAN, Howard Russell, physician; b. Toledo, Dec. 11, 1887; s. George D. and Emma Elizabeth (Fauster) H.; A.B., U. Mich., 1911, M.D., 1914; m. Ila Fern Alexander, January 27, 1915; 1 daughter, Ruth Forrest (Mrs. James S. Ross). Fellowship Mayo Clinic, 1914-19, member of the permanent staff, 1915—, asso. prof. medicine, Mayo Found., 1940-53, head of section in medicine, 1938-53, mem. emeritus staff, 1953—. Developed Latin Am. Clientele at Mayo Clinic. Decorated El Sol del Peru (Peru), La Orden de Bayaca (Colombia). Fellow A.C.P.; mem. Am., So. Minn. med. assns., Am. Gastro-Enterol. Assn., Nu Sigma Nu, Alpha Omega Alpha, Sigma Xi. Republican. Baptist. Home: 800 12th Av. S.W. Office: Mayo Clinic. Rochester, Minn. Died Oct. 6, 1959.

HARTMAN, Lewis Oliver, ret. bishop; b. La Grange, Ind., May 3, 1876; s. Samuel Brenton and Mary Elizabeth (Mason) H.; A.B., Ohio Wesleyan U., 1899, A.M., 1902, D.D., 1922, Litt.D., 1935; S.T. B., Boston U., 1902, Ph.D., 1909, L.H.D., 1941; m. Helen Marion Nutter, Dec. 21, 1922; children—Mason Nutter, Richard Otis. Ordained M.E. ministry, 1903; pastor Bond Hill and Pleasant Ridge, O., 1903-04, Christie Chapel, Cin., 1904-09, Union Ch., Cin., 1910; Ohio State supt. Bd. Sunday Schs. of M.E. Ch., 1910-12, supt. inst. dept., 1912-14, foreign dept., 1914-20; editor Zions Herald, 1920-44; elected bishop Meth. Ch., 1944; resident bishop Boston area, 1944-48, retired. Del. Ecumenical Meth. Confs., London, 1921, Atlanta, 1931; del. Gen. Confs. M.E. Ch., 1924, 28, 32, 36, 40, 44, mem. Uniting Conf. Meth. Ch., 1939; del. Northeastern Jurisdictional Conf., 1940, 44; mem. gen. exec. com. Bd. Missions and Ch. Extention Meth. Ch.

and chmn. Joint Com. on Missionary Personnel; chmn. Interboard Com. on Missionary Edn. Pres. Meth. Fedn. for Social Service. Pres. Mass. Council Chs.; mem. Fed. Council of Churches of Christ in Am.; mem. corp. New England Deaconess Assn. Mem. Boston br. N.A.A.C.P. Trustee Boston U., New England Deaconess Hospital. Mem. Beta Theta Pi, Theta Phi, Pi Gamma Mu. Clubs: Puddingstone, Religious Press, Lincoln Group of Boston. Author: Popular Aspects of Oriental Religions, 1917. Home: 226 Bay State Rd., Boston. Died June 30, 1955.

HARTMAN, Siegfried Frisch, lawyer; b. Baltimore, Md., Mar. 19, 1888; s. Jacob and Regina (Frisch) H.; B.S., Coll. City New York, 1908; LL.B., Columbia, 1911; married Vera J. Cassel. Law practice in New York City, 1911; associated with firm of Stanchfield & Levy, 1911-16, mem. firm, 1916-21; practiced alone 1921-36; thereafter mem. Hartman & Craven, later Hartman, Craven & Fuld, now Hartman & Craven; referee N.Y. Supreme Ct. Mem. bd. visitors Manhattan State Hosp.; trustee, mem. exec. com., chmn. law com. Fedn. Jewish Philanthropies, N.Y.; dir. N.Y. Adult Edn. Council, 1943 48; adv. bd. Welfare Council N.Y. City; mem. N.Y. Co. Lawyers Assn. (dir.), Assn. Bar of City of N.Y., Phi Beta Kappa, Phi Epsilon Pi. Clubs: Hopewell Valley Golf, Lawyers, City Athletic, New York Musicians. Home: One E. 66th St., N.Y.C.; and Farm, Lambertville, N.J. Office: 39 Broadway, N.Y.C. Died Sept. 1, 1953.

HARTMANN, George W(ilfred), univ. prof., psychologist; b. Union Hill, N.J., Mar. 29, 1904; s. Herman C. and Veronica (Ruff) H.; A.B., Columbia, 1924, A.M., 1925, Ph.D., 1928; m. Esther Leah Norton, Aug. 27, 1927; children—Gretchen Beatrice, Eleanor Margaret. Instr. psychology, Dartmouth Coll., 1925-27; prof. psychology, Pa. State Coll., 1928-35; prof. edn., Teachers Coll., Columbia, 1936-49; chmn. dept. of psychology Roosevelt Univ., 1949—; dir. research, Cambridge-Somerville Youth Study, Ella Lyman Cabot Foundation; visiting lecturer psychol., Harvard, 1942-44; vis. prof., Ala. Poly. Inst., 1945; visiting professor, University of Puerto Rico, 1948; guidance cons. Newark Coll. Engring., 1946-49; editor Social Frontier, 1937-39; founder Jane Addams Peace School; chairman War Resisters League; chmn. Peace Now Movement, 1943-44; chairman, New York Fellowship of Reconciliation; Socialist candidate lt. gov. N.Y., 1938, for mayor N.Y. City, 1941. Awarded fellowship by Social Sci. Research Council for study in Berlin, 1930, Leipzig, 1931. Fellow A.A.A.S., Soc. for Psychol. Study Social Issues (pres. 1939); mem. Am. Ednl. Research Assn., Eastern Psychol. Assn. (dir. 1938-42). Author: Gestalt Psychology, 1935; Industrial Conflict, 1940; Educational Psychology, 1941; Democratic Socialism, 1948. Contbr. numerous articles to ednl. and other jours. Mem. adv. editorial bd. Jours. Social Issues. Home: 815 Travers Lane, Flossmoor, Ill. Office: Roosevelt Univ., Chgo. 5. Died June 11, 1955.

HARTREE, Douglas Rayner, educator; b. Cambridge, Eng., Mar. 27, 1897; s. William and Eva (Rayner) H.; B.A., M.A., Ph.D., St. John's Coll., Cambridge; M.Sc., U. Manchester; m. Elaine Charlton, Aug. 21, 1923; children—Nesta Margaret (Mrs. Edward L. Booth), Oliver Penn, John Richard. Research fellow St. John's Coll., Cambridge, 1924-27, Christ's Coll., Cambridge, 1928-29; prof. applied mathematics U. Manchester, 1929-37, prof. theoretical physics, 1937-45; prof. math. physics Cambridge U., 1946—, acting chief, Inst. Numerical Analysis, U.S. Bur. Standards, U. Cal., 1948; vis. prof. Princeton, 1955. Served with anti-aircraft exptl. sect. Munitions Inventions Dept., Ministry Munitions, 1916-19; with sci. research sect. Ministery of Supply, 1940-45. Recipient Rockefeller fellowship for study Inst. Theoretical Physics, Copenhagen, 1928. Mem. Royal Soc., Inst. Physics, Inst. Elec. Engrs., Cambridge Philos. Soc Author: Calculating Instruments and Machines, 1949; Numerical Analysis, 1952. Home: 21 Bentley Rd. Office: Cavendish Laboratory, Cambridge, Eng. Died Feb. 12, 1958.

HARTT, George Montgomery, newspaper editor; b. N.Y.C., Dec. 10, 1877; s. George le Baron and Margaret Florence Montgomery (Hartt) H.; grad. Passaic High Sch., 1895; hon. D.C.L., Acadia U., Wolfville, N.C.; m. Marie Russell, Aug. 29, 1913 (died Oct. 6, 1928); m. 2d, Dorothy Barbara Goldsmith, June 10, 1930. Reporter, Passaic Daily Journal, 1895; with the Central Monthly, N.Y.C., 1896; with Passaic Daily News, 1896-1900, city editor, 1898-1900; with Paterson (N.J.) Morning Call, 1900; editor in chief Passaic Daily News, 1901-32, Passaic Herald-News (a consolidation), 1932-45, now editor emeritus; dir. N. J. Mortgage and Title Ins. Co. (Passaic). Mem. Passaic Bd. Edn. Gov. Passaic Gen. Hosp. Republican. Episcopalian. Clubs: Rotary, Kenilworth (Passaic); Pica (Paterson); Upper Montclair Country (Montclair, N.J.). Home: 88 Boulevard, Passaic, N.J. Died Oct. 28, 1954; buried Cedarlawn, East Paterson, N.J.

HARTUNG, Albert Michael, lawyer; b. Lancaster, N.Y.; s. Martin and Julia (Rine) H.; student Canisius Coll., Buffalo; LL.B., U. Buffalo, 1908; m. Marian Kelly, Nov. 25, 1908 (died Jan. 12, 1929); children—Albert H., Mary Furman, Jane Gregory; m. 2d, Nora Purcell Ticknor, Oct. 1, 1932. Admitted to N.Y. bar, 1908, and began practice in Buffalo; in claim dept. Erie R.R. Co., 1909-12, law dept., 1912-17; in law dept. Wells Fargo & Co., 1917-18; asst. to gen. counsel Am. Ry. Express Co., 1918-19, gen. atty., 1919-23, gen. solicitor, 1923-29; gen. solicitor Ry. Express Agency, Inc., 1929-38, v.p. personnel and chmn. com. on personnel and labor relations, 1938-49, v.p. personnel and pub. relations, 1949—; mem. exec. and finance coms., bd. dirs. Expressmen's Mut. Life Ins. Co., Self-Insurers Assn. of N.Y. (mem. exec. com.); appeared before numerous bds., apptd. by Pres. of U.S., under provision of Railway Labor Act, to consider wage disputes in express industry; served on cons. staff of House Appropriations Com. to analyze the 1954 Federal budget. Admitted to practice in Supreme Ct. of U.S., several U.S. circuit courts of appeal and district courts. Mem Am. Bar Assn., Assn. of Practitioners before ICC. Phi Delta Phi. Roman Catholic. Club: Baltusrol Golf Club. Home: 445 Harding Dr., South Orange, N.J. Office: 230 Park Av., N.Y.C. Died May 10, 1958.

HARTWELL, Henry Walker, architect; b. Boston, Sept. 4, 1833; s. Alonzo and Sarah Lunt (Walker) H.; student Lawrence Acad., Groton, Mass.; studied architecture in offices of Joseph E. & Hammatt Billings, Boston; m. Sarah E. Miller, June 9, 1857. Began practice of architecture at Boston, 1855. Served in Union Army, 1862-63. His firm designed Fall River Acad. of Music; Central Ch., Fall River; Youth's Companion Bldg., Boston; High Sch., Springfield, and many other public buildings. Address: 147 Summer St., Waltham, Mass. Died Dec. 30, 1919; buried Mt. Feake Cemetery, Waltham.

HARTWELL, Shattuck Osgood, former supt. schs.; b. Littleton, Mass., Mar. 20, 1865; s. Shattuck and Catherine Stone (Mussey) H.; grad. Boston Latin Sch., 1883; A.B., Amherst, 1888; m. Kate W. Hitchcock, July 5, 1894; children—Edward W., Katharine. Shattuck W. Instr. Bklyn. Coll. and Poly. inst., 1888-89; prin. Kalamazoo High Sch., 1889-1901; supt. schs., Kalamazoo, Mich., 1901-15, Muskegon, Mich., 1915-18; supt. schs., St. Paul, 1918-36, supr. profl. tng., 1936-38. retired. Conglist. Wrote: Overcrowded Schools and the Platoon Plan (in Cleve. Sch. Survey), pub. by Russell Sage Found., 1915. Home: 1446 Fairmount Av., St. Paul. Died Nov. 4, 1946; buried Kalamazoo, Mich.

HARVEY, Basil Coleman Hyatt, educator; b. Watford, Ont., Can., Jan. 16, 1875; s. Dr. Leander H. and Anne (Wilson) H.; A.B., U. Toronto, 1894, M.B., 1898; M.D., 1928; grad. Normal College of N.S., 1895; member College of Physicians and Surgeons, Ontario, 1898; student U. Basel, Switzerland, 1903; m. Janet Hinsdill Holt, Sept. 1, 1904. Demonstrator of anatomy U. Toronto, 1895-97; practiced medicine, Watford, Ont., 1898-1901; asst. in anatomy U. Chgo., 1901-02, asso., 1902-04, instr., 1904-08, asst. prof., 1908-11, asso. prof., 1911-17, prof., 1917-40, emeritus, 1940—, dean med. students, 1923-40, dean students of biol. science div., 1931-40; recalled as acting dean of med. students and students in biol. sciences, 1943-44. Served as maj. Med. Dept., U.S. Army, AEF, during World War. Treas. Assn. Am. Med. Colls., 1933-35. Vice pres. Inst. Medicine (Chicago), 1933; mem. Assn. Am. Anatomists, A.A.A.S., Sigma Xi, Alpha Kappa Kappa. Clubs: Quadrangle, University, Olympia Fields Country. Translator: The Inheritance of Acquired Characters, Rignano. Author: The Nature of Vital Processes According to Rignano; Simple Lessons in Human Anatomy. Asso. editor Anat. Record, 1928-40; Papers on Anatomy; article on anatomy, Ency. Britannica. Home: 1326 E. 58th St., Chgo. 37. Died Feb. 15, 1958.

HARVEY, Byron Schermerhorn; b. Leavenworth, Kan., Aug. 31, 1876; s. Frederick Henry and Barbara (Mattas) H.; grad. Phillips Acad., Andover, Mass., 1895; Ph.B., Sheffield Scientific Sch. (Yale), 1898; married Helen Daggett, April 16, 1902 (died June 28, 1948); children—Byron S., John Stewart, Charles Daggett. Began, 1899, in catering business, established by father, at Kansas City, Missouri; removed to Chicago, 1903, as manager Chicago office; vice-president Fred Harvey, Inc., 1919-28; president Fred Harvey, 1928-46, chairman and chief executive officer since 1946. Mem. Chicago Assn. Commerce, U.S. Chamber Commerce, Art Inst., Chicago, Chicago Hist. Soc. Episcopalian. Clubs: Chicago, Commercial, Shoreacres, Casino, Tavern, Racquet, University: Yale (N.Y.); The Onwentsia. Home: 1100 Lake Shore Dr. Office: 80 E. Jackson Blvd., Chgo. 4. Died Dec. 19, 1954; buried Chgo.

HARVEY, Charles Milton, banker; b. Trezevant, Tenn., July 21, 1869; s. Giles Josephus and Eliza Ann (Christy) H.; ed. high sch., Booneville Ark.; m. Bessie Parker, Sept. 30, 1896; (dec.); children—Paul, Charles Milton, Rufus Marion (dec.); m. 2d, Maude Irene Phillips, Jan. 18, 1924; 1 son, Eldon Phillips. Began as owner and pub. country newspaper, Paris, Ark., 1891, owner and pub. Dardanelle (Ark.) Dispatch, 1893-95; grocer, Miami, India Ty., 1895-98; engaged in mining, 1898-1939; v.p., Commerce Mining & Royalty Co., Miami, Okla., 1913-19; pres. Security Bank & Trust Co., El Paso, Tex., 1915-22, Border National Bank, El Paso, 1922-23; president Harvey Investment Company, Harvey Sheep & Cattle Company, Harvey Farms Co.; an organizer and pres. El Paso Nat. Bank, 1925-44; chmn. bd. dirs. since 1944; v.p. N.E. Okla. Ry. Co. (Miami, Okla., 1928-39), Hotel Paso Del Norte (El Paso, Tex.), Member El Paso Chamber of Commerce; president El Paso Y.M.C.A., 1916. Methodist. Mason (33°, K.T., Shriner). Mem. El Paso City Civil Service Commn., 1933-37. Clubs: El Paso Automobile (pres.), El Paso Country, Knife and Fork Club (dir.). Home: 1407 Elm St. Office: El Paso Nat. Bank, El Paso, Tex. Died Feb. 15, 1952; buried Evergreen Cemetery, El Paso.

HARVEY, Edmund Newton, physiologist; b. Phila., Nov. 25, 1887; s. William and Althea Ann (Newton) H.; grad. Germantown (Pa.) Acad., 1905; B. Sc., U. Pa., 1909; Ph.D., Columbia, 1911; m. Ethel Nicholson Browne, Mar. 12, 1916; children—Edmund Newton, Richard Bennet. Instr. physiology Princeton, 1911-15, asst. prof., 1915-19, prof. 1919-33, H. F. Osborn prof., 1933—; vis. lectr. in biilogy Mass. Inst. Tech., 1940-41. Trustee Bermuda Biol. Sta.; v.p., trustee Marine Biol. Lab., Woods Hole, Mass. Vis. lectr. Inst. de Biofisica, Rio de Janeiro, 1946. Recipient John Price Wetherill medal Franklin Inst. Pa., 1934, Rumford medal Am. Acad. Arts and Scis., 1947; Certificate of Merit, U.S. Armed Forces; decorated Officer Nat. Order do Cruzerio do Sul (Brazil). Mem. A.A.A.S., Am. Soc. Naturalists, Am. Soc. Biol. Chemists, Am. Physiol. Soc., Soc. Exptl. Biology and Medicine, Am. Soc. Zoölogists, Growth Soc., Nat. Geog. Soc., Am. Assn. U. Profs., N.Y. Acad. Scis., Soc. Am. Bacteriologists, Bot. Soc. Am., Harvey Soc., Am. Philos Soc., Nat. Acad. of Sciences, Am. Acad. Arts and Sciences Boston, Internat. Soc. of Cell Biology (v.p. 1947-50), Nat. Research Council, Sigma Xi. Author: The Nature of Animal Light, 1920; Laboratory Directions in General Physiology, 1933; Living Light, 1940. Has made special studies in bioluminescence, cell permeability, nerve conduction, regulation in plants, ultrasonic radiation, cell surface tension, brain potentials, decompression sickness, mechanism of wounding, etc. Editor Survey of Biological Progress. Asso. editor Biol. Bull., Biol. Abstracts; Jour. of Cellular and Comparative Physiology. Home: 48 Cleveland Lane, Princeton, N.J. Died July 21, 1959.

HARVEY, Eli, artist, sculptor; b. Ogden, O., Sept. 23, 1860; s. William P. and Nancy M. H.; pupil Acad. of Fine Arts, Cin., under Profs. Leutz, Noble and Rebisso; Académie Julian, Paris, under Lefébvre, Benjamin Constant and Doucet; at the Académie Délécluse. under Delance and Callot, and with Frémiet, at the Jardin des Plantes, for animal sculpture; m. Mary Anna Baker, June 1893 (dec. Sept. 1919); m. 2d, Grace G. Harvey, June 8, 1921 (dec. Jan. 1924); m. 3d, Edith James, Apr. 11, 1925. Exhibited at the Paris salons in painting and sculpture, 1894-28, and Expn., 1900. Awarded gold medal 1st class, "Paris et Province" Exhbn., 1900; John Wanamaker prize for sculpture, Am. Art Assn., Paris, 1900; 3d medal for sculpture, Buffalo Expn., 1901; received commn. from N.Y. Zoöl. Soc., 1901, to do all sculpture for Lion House, New York Zoöl. Park; medal, St. Louis Expn., 1904; medal, Panama-Pacific Expn., 1915. Represented by sculpture in Met. Mus. of Art (N.Y.), Mus. of Fine Arts (St. Louis), Cin. Mus. of Arts, Library Art Assn. of Newark, London, Liverpool, and Brookgreen Gardens, S.C. Presented 16 bronzes to Expn. Park Mus., Los Angeles, 1943. Modeled portrait of gorilla for N.Y. Zoo Soc., 1916; eagles for Victory Arch, N.Y., 1919; medal for Am. Numis, Soc. to commemorate U.S. entrance into World War, 1917; meml. tablet for Met. Mus. of Art, 1919, for Am. Mus. Natural History, 1919; executied a pair of large lions for Eaton mausoleum, Toronto; large elk for Order of Elks; Brown Bear Mascot from Brown U., 1923; Am. Bald Eagle with Fasces (bronze), Ohioana Library Assn., Columbus, O., 1947; African Elepphant Scenting Danger (bronze), nat. collection Fine Arts Museum, Washington, 1948. Mem. Archtl. League (emeritus), N.Y. Zoöl. Soc. (life), Am. Art Assn. of Paris (charter); asso. mem. Société Nationale les Beaux Arts, Paris, 1928. Home: 130 Champion Pl., Alhambra, Cal. Died Feb. 10, 1957; buried Springfield Friends Ch. Cemetery, Wilmington, O.

HARVEY, Horace, Chief Justice of Alberta, Can.; b. Elgin County, Ont., Can., Oct. 1, 1863; s. William and Sophronia (Mack) H.; student St. Thomas Coll. Institute, Ontario, 1881-82; B.A., Univ. of Toronto, 1886, LL.B., 1888, LL.D., 1936; LL.D., Univ. of Alberta, 1917; married Nora Louise Palmer, July 21, 1893 (died May 13, 1948); 1 son, Alan Burnside. Barrister, 1899; practiced in Toronto, 1889-93, Calgary, Alberta, 1893-96; registrar of land titles, South Alberta, 1896-1900; dep. atty. gen., N.W. Ter., 1900-04; judge Supreme Court of N.W. Ter., 1904-07, Alberta, 1907-10; chief justice of Alberta, 1910. Chmn. board of govs., U. of Alberta, 1917-40; chmn. Mobilization Bd. for Alberta from 1940 till end of war. Life mem. Can. Bar Assn.; hon. mem. Am. Bar Assn. Mem. Anglican Ch. Home: 10226 Connaught Drive. Office: Supreme Court of Alberta, Edmonton, Alberta, Can. Died Sept. 9, 1949.

HARVEY, Ralph Hicks, jurist; b. Atlanta, Tex., July 20, 1893; s. John and Dora (Wright) H.; LL. B., U. Tex., 1921, post grad., 1921; unmarried. Teacher history and Latin, Linden High Sch., 1914, prin. Hughes Spring High Sch., 1912-13; supt. Linden Pub. Schs., 1914; county supt. pub. instrn. Cass County, 1915-18; admitted to Tex. bar, 1921, and practiced in Atlanta, 1921-27; county judge Cass County. 1927-28; practiced, Linden, 1929-31; dist. judge. 5th Jud. Dist., 1932-44; asso. justice Sixth Ct. Civil Appeals, Texarkana, 1944-49; asso. justice Supreme Ct. Tex. since 1949. Pres. Linden Bldg. & Loan Assn. since 1940; chmn. bd. dirs. 1st Nat. Bank of Linden. Served on the substantive law, real estate and probate law coms. State Bar of Tex.; former pres. Cass County Bd. Edn., Atlanta Ind. Sch. Dist. Bd.; dir. Boy Scouts. Mem. A.R.C. (county chmn.), Cass County Bar Assn., Linden C. of C. (past pres.), Delta Theta Phi. Methodist. Mason. Home: Atlanta, Tex. Office: 108 W. 15th St., Normandie Arms; also Capitol Sta., Austin, Tex. Died Sept. 8, 1950; buried Pine Crest Cemetery, Atlanta, Tex.

HARVEY, Samuel Clark, surgeon; b. Washington, Conn., Feb. 12, 1886; s. Calvin Ferry and Ellen Sophia (Clark) H.; Ph.B., Yale, 1907, M.D., 1911; Sc.D., Western Res. U., 1931; m. Katharine Kingsley Farnam, June 29, 1921; children—Elizabeth Kingsley, Louise Farnam, Samuel Clark. Instr. surgery Yale, 1919-21, asso. prof., 1921-24, William H. Carmalt prof. surgery, 1924-47, prof. surgery (oncology), 1947-52, ret. and continued research in field. Served as lt. to maj. Med. O.R.C., U.S. Army, 1917-18; active service in France. Fellow A.C.S.; mem. N.E. Surg. Soc., Soc. Clin. Surgery, Soc. Neurol. Surgery, A.A.A.S., A.M.A., Am. Surg. Assn., Am. Assn. for Thoracic Surgery, Sigma Xi. Clubs: Graduate (New Haven); Century, Yale (N.Y.C.). Home: 211 Highland St., New Haven 11; (summer) Race Hill Rd., Madison, Conn. Died Aug. 23, 1953; buried Grove St. Cemetery, New Haven.

HARVEY, William Riggs, lawyer; b. Newport, R.I., Aug. 31, 1877; s. Charles E. and Nettie P. H.; A.B., Brown U., 1901; LL.B., Harvard, 1904; m. Sarah Ward, June 24, 1908; children—Annette Ward and Bernice Sherman (twins), William Ward, Hope. Began practice at Newport, 1905; chmn. bd. Edward A. Sherman Pub. Co.. 1934-49, now dir.; president Aquidneck Nat. Bank, 1934-50; treas., dir. Aquidneck Realty Co.; chmn. local bd. of Management R.I. Hosp. Trust Co.; dir. Newport Coop. Assn. for Savs. & Bldg. Dir., trustee Newport Hosp. (pres. 1930-32); dir. Eppley Found. for Research. Mem. Rep. Council of Newport, 1906-14 (chmn. 1913-14); mem. Newport Bd. of Health, 1910-19; mem. Pub. Sch. Com., 1914-27, chmn., 1927-31; dir. Y.M.C.A.; mem. Judicial Council, State of R.I., 1939-45; mem. Tercentenary Com. Active as four-minute man and on war bds. Mem. Am., R.I., Newport bar assns. Newport Assn. Am. War Dads (pres. 1941), Newport Hist. Soc. (v.p.), Newport C. of C. (dir. 1920-21). Phi Delta Theta. Republican. Unitarian. Mason. Rotarian. Home: 45 Everett St., Office: 223 Thames St., Newport, R.I. Died May 27, 1953

HARWOOD, Charles, ex-gov. Virgin Islands; b. Bklyn.; s. Israel and Johanna H.; A.B., Hamilton Coll., 1902, A.M., 1905, LL.D., 1941; LL.B., N.Y. Law School, 1904; m. Alma H. Hendricks, Dec. 27, 1915; 1 son. Charles; stepchildren—Henry H., Mrs. Dorothy Herbert. Admitted to N.Y. bar, 1904, practiced in N.Y.C., 1904-35; spl. asst. to U.S. atty. gen., 1936-37; judge U.S. Dist. Ct., Dist. of Canal Zone, 1937-38 (resigned); became gov. Virgin Islands, 1941. Mem. N.Y. State Assembly, 1910. Maj. judge advocate gen. U.S. Reserve. Mem. Am., N.Y. State, Westchester bar assns., Assn. Bar City N.Y., N.Y. County Lawyers Assn., Am. Legion, Phi Beta Kappa, Delta Kappa Epsilon. Democrat. Mason (32°, Shriner). Clubs: Bankers, Manhattan, National Democratic; Westchester Country (Rye, N.Y.); University (Washington); Dartmouth College. Home: Stratford Road, Harrison, N.Y. Address: Charlotte Amalie, Virgin Islands; and 77 Cortlandt St., N.Y.C. 7. Died Oct. 23, 1950.

HARZA, Leroy Francis, engr.; b. Brookings County, S.D., Feb. 6, 1882; s. William Frederick and Clara Samantha (Jolley) H.; B.S. in M.E., S.D. State Coll., 1901, D.Eng., 1950; B.S. in C.E., U. of Wis., 1906, C.E., 1908; m. Zelma (Davidson) Hoffman, May 27, 1922; 1 son, Richard Davidson, and stepson, Arthur Charles Hoffman. Instr. mathematics, Mich. Agrl. Coll., 1902-04; hydraulic engring., U. of Wis., 1905-06. Cons. engineer investigation, design and construction of dams, hydraulic works, hydroelectric projects, bridges in U.S., Can., Uruguay, Argentina, El Salvador, India, Philippines, France, Iraq. Pres. Harza Engring. Co., Chgo. Awarded Citation, U. Wis., 1949; John Croes Medal, Am. Soc. C.E., 1950. Mem. Am. Soc. C.E., A.S.M.E., Am. Inst. Elec. Engrs., Western Soc. Engrs., Engr-

ing. Inst. Can., Tau Beta Pi. Presbyn. Mason. Club: Engineers. Author articles in tech. periodicals. Home: 215 Pierce Rd., Highland Park, Ill. Office: 400 W. Madison St., Chgo. 6. Died Nov. 22, 1953; buried Brookings, S.D.

HASCHE, Rudolph Leonard, cons., mfr.; b. Doon, Ia., June 20, 1896; s. Carl Harmann and Clara Belle (Lemon) H.; B.S., Tarkio (Mo.) Coll., LL.D., 1953; M.S., Washington and Jefferson Colege, 1919, Ph.D., Johns Hopkins, 1924; fellow U. Cal., 1924-25, univs. Berlin and Vienna, 1925-26; m. Blanche Knox, Aug. 25, 1920; 1 dau., Blanche Geraldine (Mrs. Richard P. Clarke). Research chemist for Am. Smelting & Refining Co., 1926-30, supt. research, 1930-31; dir. chem. research A. O. Smith Corp., 1931-34; supt. research and development div. Tenn. Eastman Corp., 1934-43, sci. counsel, 1943-52; pres., chmn. bd. Carbonic Development Corp., 1931——; pres. Hasche Engring. Co., 1950——, Hasche Process Co., 1958——; also pvt. cons. Cons. WPB, 1943, F. E.A., 1945, investigator chem. plants in Germany, 1945. Technical Deferment Com., WPB, 1943. Served in poison gas research dept., C.W.S., U.S. Army, World War. Nat. Research fellow of Rockefeller Found., 1924-25; Internat. Edn. Bd. fellow, 1925-26. Recipient certificate of appreciation Dept. of Army, 1951. Fellow A.A.A.S.; mem. Am. Gas Assn., Am. Inst. C.E., Am. Chem. Soc., Soc. Chem. Industry (London), Am. Petroleum Inst., Am. Soc. Refrigerating Engrs., Phi Beta Kappa, Sigma Xi, Gamma Alpha. Republican. Episcopalian. Clubs: University, Chemists. Author: Plastics, Theory and Practice, 1947. Contbr. to chem. jours. Holder of patents on Hasche process for mfg. dry ice, gas reforming and other chem. and liquefaction process. Home: 1107 Southwest Av. Office: P.O. Box 384, Johnson City, Tenn. Died Jan. 8, 1959.

HASKELL, Clinton Howard, pres. Beatrice Foods Co.; born Lynxville, Wis., July 7, 1888; s. John Franklin and Helen Lorraine (Peck) H.; ed. pub. schools; m. Ethel Miller, Dec. 3, 1908; children—Lorraine (Mrs. Wm. H. East, Jr.), Virginia (Mrs. Daniel J. Ball). President, Beatrice Foods Co., since 1928; director Chicago Cold Storage Warehouse Co., Lackawanna Cold Storage Co., Scranton, Pa., Terminal Refrigeration Co., Los Angeles. Mem. Chicago Mercantile Exchange, N.Y. Mercantile Exchange, Bd. of Trade; dir. U.S. Chamber Commerce, Washington, 1936-38; mem. agrl. com. Nat. Assn. of Mfrs.; past pres. Am. Butter Inst.; mem. War Food Adminstrn. Milk Conservation Com., 1944-45. Mem. Internat. Dairy Expn., Inc. (dir. Indianapolis), Nat. Dairy Council (dir.), Ill. State C. of C. Independent. Presbyterian. Clubs: Tavern, Caxton, Mid-Day, Agricultural (Chicago). Westmoreland Country (Wilmette, Ill.). Home: 1426 Chicago Av., Evanston, Ill. Office: 120 S. La Salle St., Chgo. 3. Died Mar. 21, 1952.

HASKELL, Harold Clifford, corp. exec.; b. Rockland, Me., Jan. 21, 1885; s. Charles Alton and Jessie (Hatch) H.; A.B., Tufts Coll., Medford, Mass., 1906, A.M., 1944; LL.B., Harvard, 1909; m. Ruth A. Sibley, Nov. 15, 1910. Mem. law firm, Perkins, Haskell and Perkins, Boston, Mass., 1909-24; dir. legal dept., Hood Rubber Co., Watertown, Mass., 1924-30; asst. dir. legal dept E. I. du Pont De Nemours & Co., Wilmington, Del., 1930-40, dir. of dept., 1940-50, dir. of company, 1941-50, gen. counsel, 1943-50; retired, 1950; dir. Security Trust Co. Dir. Knox County Gen. Hosp. Served as 1st lt., F.A., U.S. Army, World War I. Served successively as probation officer, clerk and spl. justice Brookline (Mass.) Municipal Ct., 1924-30. Member Am. and Del. bar assns., Harvard Law Sch. Assn., Am. Legion. Clubs: Wilmington, Harvard of Delaware (Wilmington); Rotary (Rockland, Me.); Camden Yacht; Megunticook Golf. Home: Diamond Hill, Rockport, Me. Died June 30, 1957; buried Achorn Cemetery, Rockland, Me.

HASKELL, Harry Garner, industrialist; b. N.Y.C., Sept. 30, 1870; s. Samuel and Mary Frances (Amory) H.; student pvt. schs.; E.M., Columbia, 1893; m. Elizabeth Scott Denham, 1914; children—Elizabeth, Harry Garner. Dir. E. I. du Pont de Nemours & Co., Noranda Mines, Ltd., Toronto, Can., Internat. Mining, N.Y. Home: Mount Salem Lane. Office: du Pont Bldg., Wilmington, Del. Died Jan. 4, 1951; buried Wilmington.

HASKELL, Henry Joseph, newspaper man; b. Huntington, O., Mar. 8, 1874; s. Henry Charles and Margaret (Bell) H.; B.A., from Oberlin Coll., 1896, Litt.D., 1917; LL.D., Missouri Valley Coll., 1930, U. of Mo., 1935, Marietta Coll., 1937; m. Isabel Cummings, 1901 (died 1923); 1 son, Henry Cummings; m. 2d Katharine Wright, 1926 (died 1929); married third, Agnes Lee Hadley (widow of former Governor Herbert S. Hadley), 1931 (died 1946). On staff Kansas City Star since 1898, editor since 1928; dir. Kansas City Star Co. Awarded Pulitzer prize for excellence of editorial page under his direction, 1933; for distinguished editorial writing, 1944; citation from Am. Classical League, 1943. Trustee Kansas City Art Institute. Mem. Phi Beta Kappa. Clubs: Kansas City, University, Kansas City Country, Cosmos, Nat. Press (Washington, D.C.). Author: The New Deal in Old Rome, 1939; This Was Cicero, 1942.

Especially interested in foreign affairs since boyhood spent in missionary family in Bulgaria. Home: 1035 W. Meyer Blvd., Kansas City 5, Mo. Office: The Star, Kansas City 17, Mo. Died Aug. 20, 1952.

HASKELL, William Edwin, Jr., newspaper exec.; b. Mpls., Mar. 28, 1889; s. William Edwin and Olga (von W.) H.; prep. edn. Shattuck Mil. Acad. (Faribault, Minn.), Haverford (Pa.) Sch., Worcester (Mass.) Acad.; student Dartmouth Coll., 1906-08; m. Elizabeth Lewis Osgood, Dec. 19, 1934. With Boston Herald, 1908-10; sales, adv. and promotion mgr. N.Y. dept. stores, 1911-14; advt. mgr. N.Y. Herald and Telegram, 1914-16; mem. advt., promotion and circulation staffs N.Y. Tribune (now N.Y. Herald Tribune), 1919——, asst. to pres., 1931——; pres. Philosopher Tobacco Co. Trustee Northern Dispensary, N.Y.C. Lecturer and writer on journalism. Awarded Gold Key by Columbia Scholastic Press Assn. in recognition of service, 1939. Served as capt. inf., World War I, AEF, 2 yrs. Decorated Croix de Guerre. Mem. Sigma Delta Chi. Republican. Unitarian. Mason (32°). Home: Putman Valley, N.Y. Address: New York Herald Tribune, 230 W. 41st St., N.Y.C. Died Aug. 28, 1953.

HASKELL, William Nafew, army officer; b. Albany, N.Y., Aug. 13, 1878; s. William and Sarah (Churchill) H.; grad. U.S. Mil. Acad., 1901; distinguished grad. Inf. and Cav. Sch., 1904; grad. Army and Staff Coll., 1905; grad. Staff College, Langres, France, 1918; LL.D., Georgetown, 1925; m. Winifred Farrell, July 3, 1901; children—John H. F., William N. (dec.), Joseph F., Mary. Commd. 2d lt., Feb. 18, 1901; promoted through grades to lt. col., Sept. 17, 1920; retired with rank of lieutenant general, 1942. Served in the Philippine Islands, 1901-02, 1906-07, 1912-14; commanded regt. on Mexican border, 1916-17; arrived in France, Feb. 1918; asst. chief of staff, 77th Div., and with 4th A.C.; participated as chief of operations, St. Mihiel offensive, also assisted in operations south of Metz; deputy chief staff and chief of operations 2d Am. Army; detailed as head of Am. Relief Mission to Rumania, under U.S. Food Administration, and later apptd. allied high commr. to Armenia, representing Great Britain, France, Italy and U.S., and dir. gen. all relief in the Caucasus; apptd. by Herbert C. Hoover as chief of Am. Relief Mission to Russia, leaving U.S. with staff, Sept. 3, 1921, and returning 1923; also Red Cross Commr. in Greece, in charge relief work incident to the Smyrna disaster, 1922-23. Apptd. maj. gen. N.Y. Nat. Guard, 1926. On active duty as maj. gen. comdg. the 27th Div. U.S. Army, stationed at Fort McClellan, Ala., 1940-41. Organized Army Emergency Relief, hdqrs. in Washington, D.C., Feb.-May 1942; dir. Civilian Protection, State of N.Y., May-Dec. 1942; apptd. mem. staff in charge of field operations by Dir. of Office of Fgn. Relief and Rehabilitation Operations, State Dept., Washington, D.C., Jan. 1, 1943. Apptd. National Dir. Office Civilian Defense, February 28, 1944. Executive director Cooperative for American Remittances to Europe, Inc., Europe, Inc., Jan. 1946-Apr. 1947, cons. to Oct. 1947; v.p. Save the Children Fedn., since March 1947. Awarded D.S.M. (United States); Officer Legion of Honor (France); Comdr. of Crown (Rumania); Comdr. Polonia Restituta (Poland); Comdr. Cross of the Redeemer (Greece); Order of Regina Maria, 1st class and Grand Officer of the Crown (Rumania); Order of White Lion (Czechoslovakia); U.S. Certificate of Merit. Conspicuous Service medal, State of N.Y. Catholic. Clubs: Union (New York). Century, Army and Navy (Washington). Home: 20 Church St., Greenwich, Conn. Died Aug. 13, 1952; buried U.S.A. Cemetery, Westpoint, N.Y.

HASKINS, Samuel Moody, lawyer; b. Salt Lake City, Jan. 20, 1872; s. Thomas Wilson and Frances Emily (Austin) H.; B.A., U. Cal., 1893; studied law pvtly.; m. Elisa Bonsall, Apr. 15, 1902; children—Samuel Moody, Barbara Haskins Niven, Janet Haskins Farr. Admitted to Cal. bar, 1895, since practiced in Los Angeles; partner Gibson, Dunn & Crutcher, 1908-—, sr. partner, 1931——; pres. Los Angeles Ry. Corp., 1932-36; dir. Security-First Nat. Bank of Los Angeles, Los Angeles Transit Lines, Pacific Mutual Life Ins. Co., Consolidated Steel Corp., Union Oil Co. of Cal. Mem. Am., Los Angeles bar assns., State Bar Cal., Delta Kappa Epsilon. Democrat. Club: California (Los Angeles). Home: 354 S. Kingsley Drive. Office: 634 S. Spring St., Los Angeles 14. Died Oct. 26, 1948.

HASLUP, Lemuel A(llen), prof. law; b. near Laurel, Md., July 23, 1896; s. James P. and Annie (Gaither) H.; student Charlotte Hall (Md.) Mil. Acad., 1911-14; B.S., Univ. of Md., 1917; LL.B., George Washington Univ., 1934; m. Mildred Motts, June 5, 1923; children—Allen Lee. Commd. 2d lt., in the United States Marine Corps, 1917, and advanced through grades to capt.; served in Haiti, Dominican Republic, Nicaragua, Guam, China and at sea; legal aide to comdt. Norfolk Navy Yard, 1934-38; retired for phys. disability, 1938, recalled to active duty, June 1941; lt. col., ret. list, Marine Corps, since 1946; on active duty, court martial rev. sect. Office of Judge Adv. Gen., Navy Dept., Washington, 1941-46. Admitted to D.C. bar, 1934, Supreme Ct. of U.S., 1938; lecturer in law, John B. Stetson U., 1938, dean and prof. of law Coll. of Law since 1946; asst. prof. Law Sch., U. of Miami, 1939-41; professorial lecturer, Law Sch., George Washington U., 1946. Mem. Am., Fla. State bar assns., Maritime Law Assn. of U.S., Am. Acad. Polit. and Social Sci., Am. Law Inst. (hon.), Am. Legion, Delta Sigma Phi. Episcopalian. Mason. Club: Rotary. Home: Box 116, DeLand, Fla. Died Aug. 9, 1953; buried Arlington Nat. Cemetery.

HASSE, Adelaide (häs'ē), bibliographer; b. Milw.; d. Dr. Herman E. and Adelaide (Trentlage) Hasse; student pub. schs. and pvt. tutors. Asst. librarian Los Angeles Pub. Library, 1889-95; librarian office supt. of documents, Washington, 1895-97; librarian document dept. N.Y. Pub. Library, 1897-1918; research work for War Labor Policies Bd., 1918-19; organized War Industries Bd. war records, 1919-21; office Asst. Sec. of War, statis. br., 1921; bibliographer to Brookings Instn., Washington, 1923-32; chief of index div. U.S. Daily, 1929-39; research cons. Works Progress Adminstrn., 1934-39; served as editorial analyst Temporary Nat. Econ. Com., 1939-41, SEC, 1941; lectr. Geroge Washington U., 1933-37, Cath. U. Am., 1940-41. Editor: Bradford's Journal 1693 (the first book printed in New York); New York House Journal 1695; Index to Economic Material in U.S. State Documents, 14 vols.; also of Special Libraries (monthly mag.). Compiler of Bibliography of Explorations, 1899; Bibliography of Official Publications of Colonial New York, 1903; Index to U.S. Daily, vols. 1, 1926, 32. Home: Silver Spring, Md. Died July 28, 1953.

HASSELMANS, Louis, conductor; b. Paris, France, July 25, 1878; s. Alph and Anna (de Boudagoff) H.; ed. Conservatoire de Musique, Paris (1st prize, cello, 1893); pupil of J. Delsart, A. Lavignac, and Benj. Godard; m. H. Copillet, Oct. 1902; children Henri Colette, Simone; m. 2d, Minnie Egener, Aug. 1921, 1 dau., Geraldine; m. 3d, Frances Stephens, Aug. 1933. Cellist (soloist and mem. Capet Quartette), 1893-1909; making frequent tours in Europe; 1st condr. Opéra Comique. Paris, 1909-11; dir. Montreal Opera Co., 1911-13; dir. Concerts Classiques, Marseilles, 1913-14; 1st condr. Chgo. Opera Co., 1918-20; again with Opéra Comique, 1920; became French condr. Met. Opera Co. and Ravinia Park, Ill., 1921; condr. N.Y. Met. Opera orchestra, 1924-26; resigned from Met. Opera Co., 1936. Died Dec. 1957.*

HASTINGS, Edgar Morton, civil engr.; b. Lutherville, Md., May 5, 1882; s. Robert John and Ada (Heilig) H.; student Baltimore City Coll., 1899-1900, Balt. Poly. Inst., 1901-02; hon. alumnus Va. Mil. Inst.; m. Carmen Robertson, Feb. 27, 1908; children—Edgar M., David C. Rod and instrument man, B.&O. R.R., Western Pa. and W.Va., 1901-03; R.F.&P. R.R. Co., Va., 1903-06, resident engr., 1906-20, prin. asst. engr., 1920-22, chief engr. in charge of all engring., design, constrn. signals, communications, 1922—. Dir. Richmond Land Corp. Cons. China Aid Program, Survey Mission to China, 1948. Past chmn. Richmond planning com. and bd. of zoning appeals. Mem. Nat. Tech. Adv. Com., 1940—. Dir. and pres. Richmond Home for Ladies, 1935—. Mem. Am. Soc. C.E. (pres. 1947), Am. Ry. Engr. Assn. (pres. 1939-40), Am. Soc. Testing Materials, Nat. Soc. Profl. Engrs., Engrs. Joint Council (1947-48). Democrat. Methodist. Mason. Clubs: Engineers, Hampton Roads, Central Va. (past pres.), Va. Peninsula, Lions. Home: 515 N. Boulevard, Richmond 20. Office: Broad St. Sta., Richmond 20, Va. Deceased.

HASTINGS, George Aubrey, author, public relations counselor; b. Constable, Franklin County, N.Y., Mar. 26, 1885; s. Albern E. and Anna (Hastings) Aubrey (adopted maternal surname); grad. Franklin Acad., Malone, N.Y.; student Syracuse U., 1904-06; spl. student New York Sch. of Social Work, 1912; m. 2d, Rosina Brice West, Nov. 11, 1927; children—Aubrey C. (by previous marriage), Anne Aubrey. Was reporter on Syracuse Post-Standard and Yonkers Statesman and correspondent New York newspapers, 1906-15; asst. sec. N.Y. State Charities Aid Assn., 1915-31; publicity writer and adviser to social service and pub. health orgns.; lecturer N.Y. City Bd. of Edn., 1921-28; instr. in orgn. of pub. opinion, extension dept., Columbia U., 1928-31; administrative asst. to President Hoover, June 1, 1931-Feb. 15, 1932. Extension dir. White House Conf. on Child Health and Protection, 1932-33; dir. public relations, Tamblyn & Tamblyn, New York; established independent pub. relations orgn., 1936. Spl. instr. Sch. Journalism, New York U., 1933-41; member advisory committee on medicine and public health of N.Y. World's Fair. Republican candidate for 77th Congress, 14th N.Y. Dist., 1941. Mem. Nat. Inst. Social Sciences, S.A.R., Delta Upsilon. Republican. Methodist. Author: Happy Journeys to Yesterday, 1933. Contbr. articles and editorials to newspapers and mags. Address: 227 Woodside Av., Ridgewood, N.J. Died Mar. 30, 1956; buried Constable, N.Y.

HATCH, Emily Nichols, artist; b. Newport, R.I.; d. Alfrederic Smith and Theodosia (Ruggles) Hatch; ed. Miss Bulkley's Sem. for Girls, Tarrytown, N.Y.; Artist Artisan Inst., under John Ward Stimson; painting under William M. Chase and Charles Hawthorne and Eugene Paul Ullman in Paris, France. Teacher of drawing, New York Collegiate Institute, 7 yrs. Exhibited Nat. Acad. Design; Carnegie Inst., Pittsburgh; Art Inst. Chgo.; Corcoran Art Gallery; Nat. Assn. Women Painters and Sculptors; Brooklyn, Detroit, St. Louis and Buffalo, museums; best known painting, "Rosamond Enters," exhibited throughout country and in Rio de Janeiro and Buenos Aires. Represented in National Museum in Washington, D.C., by "Washington's Birthday, 1918." and museum of the Richmond (Indiana) Art Assn. Awarded Emerson McMillan portrait prize, for portrait of Arthur Shattuck, by Woman's Art Club, N.Y.C., 1st prize, spring exhibition of Pen and Brush Club, 1931 for "Repose," hon. mention by same, 1934; Cooper portrait prize, Nat. Assn. Women Painters and Sculptors, 1935 for "Alice"; Edith C. Moore prize for figure painting, Hudson Valley Art Assn., 1941 for "Daca and His Guitar"; hon. mention by Pen & Brush for "Alice," 1934; Hudson Valley Art Association, 1946; annual Mr. and Mrs. Franklin Q. Brown Prize for print, The Abyss Poems publ. with music: Life's Ecstasy, A Little Child Came He, Holy Dawn, The Soul of the Garden; Rossini's Tarantelle (transl.); On the River; Father Abraham (1865); Oasis, Madonna, Snowflakes, Shadows, Gayety, Mystery, Festival. Mem. Nat. Assn. Women Painters and Sculptors (pres. 4 terms), Pen and Brush Club (dir. 3 yrs.), MacDowell Club of N.Y. C. (chmn. painting com., 5 yrs.), Hudson Valley Art Assn. (pres.; bd. dirs. 3 yrs.), New York Soc. of Painters, Westchester Guild of Arts and Crafts, Yonkers Art Assn. of N.Y.C.; hon. mem. Soroptimist Club, Republican Committee of 100; founder and dir. Tarrytown (N.Y.) Art Center. Presbyterian. Lecturer. Singer and writer of verse and lyrics for songs, among latter the Health Crusaders' Song, sung by 50,000 children in Washington, D.C., before President Wilson. Studio: 28 Le Grande Av., Tarrytown, N.Y. Address: care Pen and Brush Club, 16 E. 10th St., N.Y.C. Died Dec. 1959.

HATCH, L. Boyd, business exec.; b. Logan, Utah, Jan. 9, 1897; s. H. E. and Georgia (Thatcher) H.; student Utah State Agrl. Coll., 1 yr.; m. Anne McQuarrie, June 3, 1918. Asso. with ins. agency, Logan, Utah, from end of World War I until 1924; dir., chmn. bd. Ambassador Hotel of N.Y., Inc.; pres., dir. Knickerbocker Investing Corp.; dir. Mercast Corp., Bermuda Development Co., Ltd., Atlas Corp., City Investing Co., Ambassador Internat. Corp., French & Co., Howe Sound Co., Sperry & Hutchison Co., Utah Sand & Gravel Products Corp., George A. Fuller Co., Utah Lime & Stone Co. with U.S. Army, World War I. Address: Ambassador Hotel, Park Av. at 51st St., N.Y.C. 22. Died Aug. 31, 1957; buried Logan, Utah.

HATCH, Leonard Williams, former mem. N.Y. State Indsl. Bd.; b. Traverse City, Mich., June 30, 1869; s. Reuben and Marion Julia (Pierce) H.; A.B., Oberlin Coll., 1892; A.M., U. Wis., 1893; student U. Berlin, 1893-94; Ph.D., Columbia, 1895; m. Jennie M. Higinbotham. Lectr., Columbia, 1895-96; instr. Bowdoin Coll., 1896-97; statistician N.Y. State Dept. of Labor, 1897-1908, chief statistician, 1907-20; mgr. N.Y. State Ins. Fund, 1920-24; dir. bur. statistics and information N.Y. State Dept. of Labor, 1924-27; mem. N.Y. State Indsl. Bd., 1927-35; cons. Conn. Dept. Labor and Industry, 1935. Fellow Casual actuarial soc.; mem. Am. Econ. Assn., Am. Statis. Assn., Am. Assn. Labor Legislation. Author: Government Industrial Arbitration, 1905. Contbr. civic and sci. articles. Home: 425 Pelham Manor Rd., Pelham Manor, N.Y. Died Nov. 23, 1958; buried Westwood Cemetery, Oberlin, O.

HATCH, Pascal Enos, banker; b. Springfield, Ill., May 8, 1867; s. Ozias Mather and Julia (Enos) H.; grad. high sch., Springfield, 1884; A.B., Washington U., 1888; LL.B., Harvard, 1892; m. Ellen Dean Smith (Wellesley, '98), Jan. 10, 1911; 1 dau., Julia Enos (Mrs. Samuel P. Goddard, Jr.). Admitted to Illinois bar, 1891, and practiced at Springfield until 1905; member Hatch & Hatch; secretary Springfield Homestead Association, 1895-1905; sec. First Trust & Savings Bank, 1905-19; v.p. Sangamon Loan & Trust Co., 1919; v.p. 1st Nat. Bank, 1919-27, pres., 1927-48, chmn. bd. 1948—. Pres. Civil Service Commn., Springfield, 2 terms. Trustee Ill. Coll., Ill. Children's Home and Aid Soc. Rep. Episcopalian, jr. warden, Christ Ch. Parish, Springfield. Odd Fellow, K.P. Clubs: Sangamo, Illini Country. Home: 1005 N. 7th St. Office: First Nat. Bank, Springfield, Ill. Died Aug. 17, 1952; buried Oak Ridge Cemetery, Springfield.

HATCH, Vermont, lawyer; b. Heber City, Utah, May 14, 1893; s. Abram and Ruth (Woooley) H.; A.B. cum laude, Harvard, 1913; LL.B., Columbia, 1916; m. Nita Cowlishaw. Admitted to N.Y. bar, 1916, Utah bar, 1927; staff White & Case, 1916, partner, 1925—, in charge Paris office, 1930-31. Dir. Alpha Portland Cement Co., Unity Fire and General Ins. Co. Dir. Cornwall (N.Y.) Hosp., 1941-48, also v.p.; chmn. com. Columbia Law Sch. Sustaining Fund, 1951-53; trustee Columbia U., 1952—. Awarded Alumni Fedn. medal, Columbia, 1951. Mem. Am. Bar Assn. (com. peace and law through UN, 1950—; com. on facilities Law Library of Congress 1948-50), Assn. Bar City of N.Y. (chmn. com. on fed. legislation 1935-37), Alumni Assn. Law Sch. Columbia (pres. 1948-51, dir. 1951-53, bd. advisers 1953—), N.Y. State (com. on Am. citizenship 1948-52, 1955—), Utah, Orange County bar assns., N.Y. County Lawyers Assn., Am. Judicature Soc., Am. Law Inst. Clubs: Downtown Assn., Manhattan, Harvard (N.Y.C.), Columbia U., Storm King Golf. Home: R.D. 4, Box 222, Newburgh, N.Y.; also 40 Fifth Av., N.Y.C. 11. Office: 14 Wall St., N.Y.C. 5. Died Apr. 4, 1959.

HATCHER, James Fulton, lawyer; b. Stonewall, Okla., Jan. 17, 1890; s. Thomas Benjamin and Mary Ellen (Falter) H.; grad. Central State Normal Sch., Edmond, Okla., 1911; A.B., U. of Okla., 1913; B.S., U. of Fla., 1915; legal edn., U. of Okla.; m. Rebecca King Armstrong, May 24, 1922; 1 dau., Mary Lee. Began as pub. sch. teacher, 1910; prin. Madill (Okla.) High Sch., 1913-14, Walton County High Sch., De Funiak Springs, Fla., 1915-17, Chickasha Jr. High Sch., 1919-21, Sr. High Sch., 1921-26; admitted to Okla. bar, 1919, and practiced at Chickasha since 1926; sr. partner Hatcher & Bond; mem. State Bd. of Edn., 1929-35, State Pardon and Parole Board, 1935-39, chairman, 1943-47; former mem. and chmn. executive council Supreme Court of Oklahoma; member Chickasha Chamber of Commerce (director; past president). Served in United States Navy Reserve Force, World War, 1917-19; grad. Emergency Naval Acad., Hampton Roads, Va., 1918; hon. disch. as ensign. Past post comdr. Am. Legion, past dept. comdr. State of Okla., heading campaign which raised $200,000 for orphans of veterans. Mem. Am., Okla. State and Grady County bar assns., Phi Beta Kappa. Democrat. Methodist. Mason (32°, K.T., Shriner), Lion (past pres.), Modern Woodman. Club: Schoolmasters. Author: (with T. T. Montgomery), Elementary History of Oklahoma, 1925. Home: 1028 Chickasha Av. Office: Petroleum Bldg., Chickasha, Okla. Died Dec. 26, 1955.

HATCHER, Samuel Claiborne, clergyman, former coll. exec.; b. Springfield, Va., May 24, 1869; s. John Henry and Lucy Claiborne (Gregory) H.; student McGuire U., Richmond, Va., 1889-91; student Randolph-Macon Coll., 1891-94, D.D., 1909; m. Mary Louise Kern, Dec. 5, 1895 (dec. Mar. 1927); children—Gertrude Claiborne (Mrs. Arthur St. Clair Sloan), Samuel Paul, Mary Kern (Mrs. Lloyd Hanson), Anne Rebecca (Mrs. E. C. Smith, Jr.), Jane Gregory (dec.); m. 2d, Lululee Inez Johnson, Dec. 17, 1945. Ordained to ministry Meth. Ch., 1897; pastor Richmond, Va., 1893-98, Norfolk, Va., 1898-1902, Petersburg, Va., 1901-05, Farmville, Va., 1905-09, Richmond, Va., 1909-11; v.p., sec.-treas. Randolph-Macon Coll., 1911-47; retired. Acting pres., 1938-39, now sec.-treas., bd. trustees, dir. Hanover Nat. Bank; treas. College Park, Inc. Chmn. Hanover Sch. Bd. Mem. Phi Kappa Sigma, Omicron Delta Kappa. Democrat. Mason (K.T.). Home: Ashland, Va. Died Apr. 14, 1952; buried Blandford Cemetery, Petersburg, Va.

HATFIELD, Charles James, physician; b. Phila., Jan. 23, 1867; s. Daniel Keyser and Margaret Alexander H.; A.B., Princeton, 1888, A.M., 1891, Sc.D., 1938; M.D., U. Pa., 1900; student U. Göttingen, 1901, U. Vienna, 1902; m. Louise Müller Spear, Sept. 14, 1901 (died Aug. 22, 1909). Practiced in Phila., 1903—; asso. dir. and chmn. bd. Henry Phipps Inst. for Study and Prevention of Tb., 23 yrs. Ex-chmn. S.E. Pa. chpt. A.R.C.; pres. Potts Meml. Inst., Keene Valley Neighborhood Hosp., Phila. Tb and Health Assn. Fellow Coll. Physicians of Phila.; mem. A.M.A., Nat. Tb Assn. (sec.), Sigma Xi. Trustee U. Pa. Republican. Presbyn. Home: 8614 Montgomery Av., Chestnut Hill, Phila. Office: Henry Phipps Institute, 7th and Lombard Sts., Phila. Died Aug. 25, 1951.

HATFIELD, George (Bennett), clergyman, educator; b. Withamsville, O., Dec. 2, 1875; s. John Crossley and Mary (Bennett) H.; A.B., Oberlin Coll., 1908, B.D., 1908; S.T.M., Harvard, 1915; student U. of Berlin, Duquesne U.; m. Mary Louise Tatman, June 11, 1902. Began as teacher high schs.; ordained to ministry Congl. Ch., 1903; Congl. minister, 1902-12; non-resident minister, 1912-16; pres. Kingfisher Coll., 1916-17; prof. history Grove City Coll., 1918-21, prof. Medieval European and Semitic history and history of religions, U. Pitts., 1921-46; retired, 1946. Mem. Medieval Acad., Am. Hist. Assn., Am. Assn. U. Profs., Archaeol. Soc. Am., Philol. Soc., Phi Alpha Theta, Sigma Alpha Epsilon. Democrat. Translator: F. Rittlegneyer's Jesus (Behind The Man); Karl Heim's Das Gewissheitsproblem in Systematischen Theologie. Home: Batavia, O. Died Mar. 23, 1957.

HATFIELD, George Juan, farmer and lawyer; b. of Am. parents traveling abroad, at Waterloo, Ont., Can., Oct. 29, 1887; s. William Melancthon and Harriet Juanita (Bingham) H.; B.A., Stanford, 1911, M.A. in Polit. Science, 1912, J.D., 1913; m. Judith Barlow Hogan, Dec. 12, 1917; children—Lady Jane, Mary Elizabeth, Georgette Judith. Admitted to Calif.

bar, 1912; with Morris, Dunne & Brobeck, San Francisco, 1913-17; practiced alone, 1917-18, then McWilliams & Hatfield until 1922, Sapiro, Levy, Hatfield & Hayes, 1923-24, Hatfield, Wood & Kilkenny, 1927-33; U.S. dist. atty., Northern Calif. Dist., 1925-33; lt. gov. of Calif., 1935-38; state senator from Merced and Madera County since 1943; mgr., dir. James J. Stevinson (corp.). Pvt. F.A. Replacement Troops, 1918; lt. comdr. U.S. Naval Reserve since 1929. Asst. in dept. polit. economy, Stanford, 1910-11, and asst. in Law Sch., 1911-13; instr. Golden Gate Coll., 1913-17. Mem. Calif. State and San Francisco County bar assns., Calif. Acad. Science, Order of Coif, S.A.R., Am. Legion, Reserve Officers' Assn., Phi Beta Kappa. Republican. Episcopalian. Mason (32°, K.T., Shriner), Sciots, Elks, Eagles, Moose. Club: Bohemian (San Francisco). Author: Comparative Study of Code Pleadings in California and England, 1913. Author of vets.' welfare legislation, State of Calif., under which 1,500 vets. were educated and $90,000,000 invested in homes and farms for 14,000 vets. Home: P.O. Box 818, Newman, Calif. Office: Flying H. Ranch, Merced Country, Cal. Died Nov. 15, 1953.

HATFIELD, Joseph Clayton, ins. exec.; b. Milford, O., Oct. 3, 1877; s. John C. and Mary (Benett) H.; grad. Lebanon Normal Sch., 1900; m. Edna Hatfield Gaskins, Oct. 1904; children—Lucile (Mrs. Frank), Dr. Ralph Eugene, Mary Jane (Mrs. Folz). Tchr. Clermont County, public schools, 1900-04; personnel dir. Union Central Life Ins. Co., Cincinnati, 1922-23, asst. auditor, 1924-33, auditor, 1934, asst. v.p., 1933-34, v.p. since 1935. Methodist. Mason (32°), Eagle. Home: 3743 Reading Rd., Cincinnati 29. Office: Union Life Insurance Co., Cin. Died Oct. 6, 1952.

HATFIELD, (Livius) Lansing, singer; b. Franklin, Va.; s. Livius Lafayette and Lydia Anne (Parrish) H.; A.B., Lenoir-Rhyne Coll., 1930; certificate Peabody Conservatoory of Music Balt. 1936; m. Jeanne body Conservatory of Music Balt. 1936; m. Jeanne Elliott McGee Sept. 5, 1937. Singer at local concerts and radio; soloist St. Thomas' Ch., Balt., 1934-35; first New York appearance in mus. show, Virginia; created role Daniel Webster in Devil and Daniel Webster; baritone lead in Susanna Don't You Cry; joined Met. Opera Assn., 1941; soloist with N.Y. Philharmonic Symphony, and N.Y. Oratorio Soc.; starred in summer prodns. at St. Louis Municipal Opera, Los Angeles Light Opera Assn., San Francisco Light Opera Assn., Dallas State Fair Opera, Detroit Civic Light Opera Assn., sang the part of Rev. Davidson in the Rouben Mamoulian production of Sadie Thompson, spent six months in S.W. Pacific Theater singing to troops; was guest soloist at President Roosevelt's 4th Inaugural Dinner; starred in Carnegie Hall annual March of Dimes benefit concert; gave $200,000 7th War Loan concert in Pottsville, Pa.; made series of V-Discs for armed forces; recorded devotional songs for use of U.S. chaplains; recorded series of prayers for muzak radio religious programs throughout country; soloist with Phila. Orchestra and Mpls. Symphony, 1945-46, guest artist on many radio shows; averaging over 50 engagements a concert season, 1938—; with local radio stas., later music dir. Grove Park Inn, Asheville, N.C., 1951—. Home: Asheville, N.C. Died Aug. 22, 1954.

HATHAWAY, Charles Montgomery, Jr., fgn. service officer; b. Deposit, N.Y., Mar. 31, 1874; s. Charles Montgomery and Eliza (Grant) H.; B.A., Yale, 1899, M.A., 1901, Ph.D., 1902; m. Frances Elizabeth, Sept. 1, 1904; 1 son, Elbridge W. Asst. prof. English, Adelphi Coll., Bklyn., 1903-03; tutor in English, Columbia, 1903-05; instr. English and law U.S. Naval Acad., 1905-11; Am. consul. Puerto Plata, Dominican Republic, 1911-13, Hull, Eng., 1914-17, Queenstown, Ireland, 1917-19, Bombay, India, 1921-22, Dublin, Ireland, 1922-24; consul gen., Dublin, Ireland, 1924-27, Munich, Germany, 1927-39. On detail with Am. commr. in Hungary, at Budapest, 1920. Retired 1939. Mem. Phi Beta Kappa. Home: 1723 Grand Av., Santa Barbara, Cal. Died July 20, 1954.

HATHAWAY, Robert Joseph, surgeon; b. Ovid, Mich., Jan. 21, 1874; s. Joseph Obed and Martha (House) H.; student med. dept. U. of Mich., 3 yrs.; M.D., College of Medicine, University of Illinois, 1902; post-grad. work, University of Paris, University of Vienna; married Myrta A. Bement, 1897 (died 1901); 1 son, Robert J. Began practice at Glendive, Mont., as health officer Dawson County, 1902; chief surgeon Grace Hosp., 1905-17; capt., maj. and lt. col. Med. Corps, U.S. Army, World War; in France with A.E.F.; resumed practice at Glendive, 1919; supt. State Hosp., Warm Springs, Mont., 1921-25; settled at Evanston, Ill., 1926. Del. World Peace Conf., London, 1918. Fellow Am. Coll. Surgeons, A. M.A.; mem. Chicago Med. Soc., Chicago Soc. Industrial Medicine and Surgery. Mason (32°, K.T., Shriner), Sovereign Master Red Cross of Constantine; Grand Master of Masons of Mont., 1920. Office: Glendive, Mont. Died July 15, 1955; buried Middleburry Cemetery, Ovid, Mich.

HATHAWAY, Warren, pastor Cong'l Ch., Blooming Grove, N.Y., 1866—; b. Saratoga Springs, N.Y., Nov. 10, 1828; studied, Lockport, N.Y., and Oberlin, O., 1848-53 (D.D., Merom Coll., Ind); m. Cornelia Day; children—Alice, Rhoda, Jennie, Elizabeth, Warren Stanley; m. 2d E. M. Miller, Mar. 1877. Non resident prof. homiletics in Christian Biblical Inst. Author: A Faithful Pastor (biography Rev. John Ross); Lectures on Living Questions, F2; Studies in Nature and Grace; a vol. of sermons and more than 30 dedication discourses. Address: Blooming Grove, Orange Co., N.Y. Died Apr. 4, 1909.

HATHWAY, Marion (Mrs. Theodore R. Parker), educator, social worker; b. North Tonawanda, N.Y., July 31, 1895; d. William W. and Alice R. (Shelley) Hathway; A.B., Radcliffe Coll., 1916; A.M., U. Chgo., 1927, Ph.D., 1933; m. Theodore R. Parker, June 6, 1936. Began teaching, 1916; with Y.W.C.A. Central Com., Denver, 1920-21; asst. dir., bur. attendance Denver Pub. Schs., 1921-26; faculty mem. U. Wash., 1927-31; mem. faculty, asst. dir., div. social work, U. Pitts., 1932-38, mem. faculty sch. social work, 1941-51; exec. sec. Am. Assn. Schs. Social Work, 1938-41; prof. social economy, dir. grad. dept. Bryn Mawr (Pa.) Coll. since 1951. Mem. Nat. Conf. Social Work (sec. 1949-50), Am. Assn. Social Workers, Am. Assn. U. Profs. Author: The Young Cripple and His Job (social service monograph), 1928; Public Relief in Washington, 1853-1933 (with John Rademaker), 1934; The Migratory Worker and Family Life, 1937. Editor, co-author: Education for the Public Social Services, 1941; editor Social Service Series, Houghton-Mifflin Co. Office: Bryn Mawr College, Bryn Mawr, Pa. Died Nov. 18, 1955.

HATOYAMA, Ichiro, former prime minister of Japan; b. Tokyo, Japan, Jan. 1, 1883; s. Kazuo and Haruko (Taga) H.; Hogakushi, Tokyo Imperial U., 1907; m. Kaoru Terada, Sept. 18, 1908; children—Yuriko (Mrs. Junichi Furusawa), Reiko (Mrs. Michio Hatoyama), Setsuko (dec.), Iichiro, Keiko (Mrs. Shigeru Yamanaka), Nobuko (Mrs. Akeo Watanabe). Lawyer, Tokyo, 1907-15; mem. Japanese House of Reps., Tokyo, 1915—; chief sec. of cabinet, 1927-29, minister of edn., 1931-34; prime minister, 1954-56. Pres. Liberal Democratic Party. Home: 7-10. Otowacho, Bunkyoku, Tokyo, Japan. Died Mar. 1959.

HATT, Paul Kitchener, sociologist; b. Vancouver, B.C., Can., Oct. 30, 1914; s. Harold Oscar and Margaret (Millard) H.; came to U.S., 1937, naturalized, 1941; A.B., Linfield Coll., McMinnville, Ore., 1936; A.M., U. of Wash., 1940, Ph.D., 1945; m. Hertha Klein, 1937; 1 son, Peter McLeod; m. 2d, Genevieve Southard Gibbard, April 12, 1947; 1 step-dau., Patricia Jane Gibbard. Instr., U. of Ida., 1941-42; asst. field dir. and field dir., Am. Nat. Red Cross, 12th Naval Dist., 1942-44; instr., Miami (O.) U., 1944-45; asst. prof., Ohio State U., 1945-46; asso. dir. Am. Council on Edn. Coll. Study in intergroup relations, Wayne U., 1946-47; vis. prof. U. of Minn., Duluth br., summer 1947; asst. prof., Princeton, 1947-49; vis. lecturer, U. of Puerto Rico, 1947; continuing cons. Columbia U. Bur. of Applied Social Research, 1948-49; prof. of sociology, Northwestern, since 1949; vis. prof., U. of Wash., 1950. Mem. Am. and Rural sociol. socs., Sociol. Research Assn., Population Assn. of Am., Midwest Sociol. Soc., Sigma Xi, Alpha Kappa Delta. Contbr. articles in profl jours. Home: 1725 Orrington Av., Evanston, Ill. Died Jan. 6, 1953.

HAUBERG, John Henry, lumber exec.; b. Hillsdale, Ill., Nov. 22, 1869; s. Mark Detlef and Anna Margaret (Frels) H.; A.B., Valparaiso U., 1897; LL.B., U. Mich., 1900; LL.D., Augustana Coll. and Theol. Sem., 1930; m. Susanne Christine Denkmann, June 29, 1911; children—Catherine Denkmann (Mrs. Edward C. Sweeney), John Hauberg. Admitted to Ill. bar, 1901, practiced law, Moline, 1901-11, Rock Island, 1911-14; in lumber and timber bus. since 1914; pres. Denkmann Lumber Co., Rock Island Millwork Co. Founder Camp Hauberg for boys; originator Indian pow-wow council and founder Black Hawk Museum; pres. Black Hawk Hiking Club; chmn. Co. Forest Preserve Assn.; pres. Chippianock Cemetery Assn.; donor (with son and dau.) meml. Y.W.C.A., Rock Island; in memory of Mrs. John H. Hauberg, dec.; v.p. Rock Island Y.M.C.A.; dir. Tri-City Symphony Orchestra; past pres. State Luther League, State Sunday Sch. Assn., State Anti-Saloon League, County Old Settlers, Rock Island Hist. Soc. Mem. Rock Island C. of C. (past pres.), Ill. State, Rock Island Co. bar assns., Ill. State Archaeol. Soc. (dir.), Ill. State (dir., past pres.), Ia., Wis., Minn., Miss. Valley, Chgo. hist. socs. Club: Rotary (past pres.). Republican. Lutheran. Author hist. papers. Home: 24th St. and 13th Av., Rock Island, Ill. Deceased.

HAUGHT, Thomas William, educator; b. nr. Sistersville, W.Va., Nov. 25, 1871; s. Benjamin and Catherine (Shuman) H.; A.B., W.Va. U., 1896; student Harvard, 1½ yrs.; M.A., W.Va. Wesleyn Coll., 1916, D.Sc., 1929; spl. work, Johns Hopkins; m. Helen Grace Wetmore, July 7, 1903; children—Thomas Wetmore, John William, Fred Benjamin, Florence Anna. Formerly tchr. sci. W.Va. Wesleyan Coll., dean, 1909-29, acting pres. during four different periods, prof. geology, 1929-41, prof. emeritus, 1941—; instr. 49th Army Air Corps, organized on campus, 1942-44. Mem. Sigma Chi, Phi Beta Kappa. Republican. Methodist. Rotarian. Home: 66 College Av., Buckhannon, W.Va. Died Aug. 28, 1957.

HAUSER, Ernst A(lfred), educator, consultant; b. Vienna, Austria, July 20, 1896; s. Alfred C. (dec.) and Alice (Sobotka) H.; ed. K.K. Akademisches Gymnasium (Vienna); Ph.D., U. of Vienna, 1921; Sc.D. (hon.), Worcester Polytech. Inst., 1952; m. Vera M. Fischer, Apr. 8, 1922; children—Ernst F., Wolf Dieter, George W. Came to U.S., 1935, naturalized, 1940. Asst., U. Goettingen, 1921-22, res. chemist, 1922-25; chief chemist, Colloid Labs., Metallges, A.G., Frankfurt am Main, Germany, 1925-32, Semperit, Vienna, 1932-35; non-res. asso. prof. chem. engring. Mass. Inst. Tech., 1928-29, res. asso. prof. chem. engring., 1935-48, prof. chem. engring. 1948-56, dir. Div. Cooloid Chemistry, Dept. Chem. Engring.; vis. prof. colloid chemistry Worcester Poly. Inst. 1948-52. Served as capt., Austrian Army, 1914-18; recipient citations and honors. Fellow Am. Inst. Chemists, A.A.A.S., Royal Inst. Rubber Industry (London, Eng.); mem. Am. Chem. Soc. (past chmn. Div. Colloid Chemistry), Nat. Research Council. Am. Inst. Chem. Engrs., Soc. Chem. Industry, Sigma Xi, Alpha Chi Sigma. Episcopalian. Club: Chemists (N.Y.C.), Author: Latex, 1927; The Colloid Chemistry of the Rubber Industry, 1928; Handbook of Rubber Technology, 1925; Colloidal Phenomena, 1939; Experiments in Colloid Chemistry, 1940; Silicic Science, 1955; also many sci. publs. in fields of rubber, clays, theoretical and applied colloid science. Home: 15 Robinson St., Cambridge 38, Mass. Died Feb. 10, 1956; buried Cathedral of the Pines, N.H.

HAVEMEYER, Horace, corp. exec.; s. Henry Osborne and Louisine Waldron (Elder) H.; m. Doris A. Dick. Pres. Havemeyers' & Elder, Inc.; v.p. Bklyn. Elevator & Milling Co., Scranton & Lehigh Coal Co., Bklyn. Eastern Dist. Terminal; dir. Bankers Trust Co., South Porto Rico Sugar Co., Remington Arms Co., Great Western Sugar Co., Savannah Sugar Refining Co. Trustee Met. Mus. Art, Frick Mus. Home: 720 Park Av., N.Y.C. Office: 99 Wall St., N.Y.C. Died Oct. 25, 1956.

HAVENHILL, L. D. (hā'vĕn-hĭll), educator; b. Newark, Ill., Apr. 5, 1870; s. Asher D. and Ermina (Crum) H.; Ph.C., U. Mich., 1893, Ph.M., 1894, M.S. (hon.), 1940; B.S., U. Kan., 1903; m. Myra Buck, June 8, 1897; children—Marshall Asher, Robert Samuel. Pharm. chemist, Honolulu, Hawaii, 1894-95; chemist Chgo. & Aurora Smelting & Refining Co., 1896-99; asst. prof. pharmacy U. Kan., 1899-1906, asso. prof., 1906-07, prof. pharmacy, 1908-25, 40-45, also acting dean, 1925-26, dean, prof. pharmcy and materia medica, 1926-40, prof. emeritus, 1945—; fed. food and drug inspection chemist N.Y.C., 1907-08; chief drug lab. Kan. Bd. Health, 1909-25, dir., 1925-40. Mem. 10th and 11th revision coms. U.S. Pharmacopoeia, auxiliary mem. 12th rev. com. Pres. Am. Assn. Colls. of Pharmacy, 1933-34. Mem. Am. Chem. Soc. (pres. Kansas City sect. 1914), Am. (v.p. 1914), Kan. (hon.) pharm. assns., Kan. Acad. Sci. (pres. 1918), Phi Delta Chi, Sigma Xi. Republican. Conglist. Author: Essentials of Pharmacy (Sayre and Havenhill), 1918; Pharmaceutical Arithmetic, 1912; State Boards of Pharmaceutical Questions, 1917. Home: 1539 Vermont St., Lawrence, Kan. Died Apr. 29, 1950.

HAVENS, Donald, lawyer; b. Bklyn., Sept. 15, 1892; s. Edwin Taylor and Lillie Edith (Murphy) H.; Litt.B., Rutgers U., 1913; m. Mary Louise Pott, Oct. 1, 1924; children—Nancy (Mrs. Jay R. Rodgers), Philip Valentine, Donald Jr. Admitted to New York bar, 1919, U.S. Supreme Ct., 1925; practiced in N.Y.C. since 1919, partner Haight, Smith, Griffin & Deming, 1930—, Haight, Gardner, Poor & Havens, 1955—; sec., dir. U.S. Aviation Underwriters, Inc.; dir. Aircraft Radio Corp., Angostura-Wupperman Corp. Mem. Maritime Assn. Port of N.Y., Ins. Soc. N.Y., Am. Bar Assn., Bar Assn. City N.Y., Delta Upsilon. Clubs: Propeller, India House, University; Yacht, Golf (Sakonnet); Beach (Warren's Point). Home: Little Compton, R.I. Office: 80 Broad St., N.Y.C. Died Mar. 25, 1959.

HAVENS, Raymond Dexter, educator; b. Rochester, N.Y., July 25, 1880; s. Charles Wesley and Persis Elizabeth (Mack) H.; A.B., U. Rochester, 1902, Litt.D., 1926; Ph.D., Harvard, 1908. Instr. mathematics Pratt Inst. High Sch., 1902-04; mem. faculty U. of Rochester, 1908-25, prof. English, 1921-25; prof. English, Johns Hopkins, 1925-47, emeritus, 1947—. YMCA war work, 1917-19. Fellow A.A.A.S.; mem. Psi Upsilon, Phi Beta Kappa. Democrat. Baptist. Author: The Influence of Milton on English Poetry, 1922; The Mind of a Poet (Wordsworth), 1941. Home: 3700 N. Charles St., Balt. 18. Died 1958.

HAVERSTICK, Edward Everett, dentist; b. DeSoto, Mo., Dec. 6, 1873; s. William Jennings and Elizabeth (Vinyard) H.; student State Normal Sch., Cape Girardeau, Mo., University Acad., Columbia, Mo., U. Mo.; D.M.D., Mo. Dental Coll. (now Washington U. Sch. Dentistry), 1901; m. Laura Krenning, Oct. 23, 1905; children—Edward Everett, William Krenning. Devoted much time to study and compilation of dental history lit.; founder St. Louis Dental

Soc. Library (named after him), librarian, 1925-41; chmn. bd. Radio St. Louis, Inc., operating sta. KSTL; v.p., dir. White Hall Sewer Pipe and Stoneware Co. Fellow Am. Coll. Dentists; mem. Fedn. Dentaire Internationale, St. Louis Soc. Dental Sci. (pres. 1903-04), St. Louis Dental Soc. (pres. 1924), Mo. Dental Soc. (chmn. com. charge publ. History of Dentistry in Mo. 1932-41, pres. 1950-51), Am. Dental Assn., Omicron Kappa Epsilon, Delta Sigma Delta (chmn. history com. 1945-50). Co-author: History of Dentistry in Missiouri, 1938; History of Delta Sigma Fraternity. 1950. Home: 7346 Westmoreland Dr. Office: 346 N. Boyle Av., St. Louis. Died Nov. 26, 1955.

HAVILAND, James Thomas, ins. exec.; b. Aurora, Ill., June 20, 1889; s. William Crane and Florence (Hollister) H.; B.S., U. Chgo., 1912; LL.B., Northwestern U., 1914; m. Marjorie S. Benton, Mar. 25, 1916; children—Marjorie (Mrs. L. W. Arny), Nancy (Mrs. F. C. McCown). Admitted to Ill. bar, 1914, practiced in Chgo., 1914-19; atty. Lumbermens Mut. Casualty Co., Chgo., 1917-19, asst. sec., mgr. eastern dept., Phila., 1919-24, v.p., eastern mgr., 1924-54, sr. v.p. 1954—; sr. v.p., dir. Am. Motorists Ins. Co.; v.p. Am. Mfrs. Mutual Ins. Co., Fed. Mutual Fire Ins. Co.; vice chmn., dir. James S. Kemper & Co. Mem. Mayor's Bd. Traffic and Transportation, Phila. Hwy. Safety Adv. Council. Mem. Ins. Fedn. Pa. (dir.), Am. Automobile Assn. (dir.), Delaware Valley Council (director), Philadelphia Safety Council (gov.), Phila. C. of C. (chmn. urban traffic com.), Pa. Motor Fedn. (chmn. safety com., exec. com.), Phi Kappa Psi. Mason. Clubs: Automobile (pres., dir.), Northwestern University (chmn. bd.), Racquet (Phila.); St. Davids (Pa.) Golf; Edgemere (Dingsmans, Pa., pres.); Seaview Golf (Absecon, N.J). Home: 504 N. Wayne Av., Wayne, Pa. Office: 12 S. 12th St., Phila. 7. Died Apr. 28, 1957; buried Valley Forge Gardens, Inc., King of Prussia, Pa.

HAVNER, Horace Moore, lawyer; b. Wayne County, Ia., Nov. 22, 1871; s. John David and Rachel (Moore) H.; student Simpson Coll., 1892-96; LL.B., U. Ia., 1899; m. Ada La. Forest Dean, Jan. 3, 1900; children—Ada (Mrs. Kenneth F. Jones), Rachel (Mrs. L. Maynard Kyner). Admitted to Ia. bar, 1899, practicing in Marengo, 1899-1917; atty. gen. Ia., 1917-21; pvt. practice, Des Moines, 1921—; mem. Havner, Flick & Powers, 1924—; pres. Dallas Fuel Co., 1928—. Del. from 9th Gen. Conf. Dist. to gen. confs. M.E. Ch., 1908, 12, 16, 20, mem. book com. 1912-32. Trustee Simpson Coll., 1919-40. Served in Spanish-Am. War; 50th Ia. Inf., 1898-99. Mem. Ia. Hist. Soc., Spanish War Vets. (judge adv. gen. 1941-42; mem. nat. legislative com. United Spanish War Vets., 1942-45, sr. vice comdr. in chief 1946—), Sons of Union Vets., Nat. Econ. League, Phi Delta Phi. Methodist. Mason (32°, K.T.), K.P. Clubs: Conopus-Exchange (Des Moines); Union League (Chicago). Home: 1721 Pleasant St. Office: Insurance Exchange Bldg., Des Moines, Ia. Died July 30, 1949; buried Resthaven Meml. Park, Des Moines.

HAWKES, Clarence, lecturer, author; b. Goshen, Mass., Dec. 16, 1869; s. Enos S. and Edlah (Gurney) H.; grad. Perkins Inst., S. Boston, 1890; spl. studies in oratory and music; A.M., Hobart Coll., 1917; M.Litt., Syracuse, 1917; A.M., Amherst, 1919; L.H.D., Am. Internat. College, 1938; m. Bessie W. Bell, Oct. 30, 1899. In 1879 had leg amputated; in 1883, accidentally shot in eyes, causing total blindness. Began public lecturing 1891, and writing 1893. Mem. Am. Bison Soc., S.A.R., Sons of Veterans; v.p. English-Speaking Union, 1919. K.P. Clubs: Boston Authors, Northampton, Lions. Chmn. parade com. for 250th anniversary of the settlement of Hadley, Mass., 1909. Author: Pebbles and Shells, 1895; Three Little Folks, 1896; Idyls of Old New England, 1897; Songs for Columbia's Heroes, 1898; Hope of the World, 1900; Master Frisky, 1902; Little Foresters, 1903; Stories of the Good Green Wood, 1904; Shaggy Coat, 1906; The Trail to the Woods, 1906; Tenants of the Trees, 1907; Little Water Folks, 1907; Black Bruin, 1908; Shovelhorns, 1909; The Wilderness Dog, 1910; King of the Thundering Herd, 1911; Master Frisky's Heroism, 1911; Nature's Children, 1911; Piebald, King of Bronchos, 1912; The Boy Woodcrafter, 1913; Field and Forest Friends, 1913; Hitting the Dark Trail, 1915; King of the Flying Sledge, 1915; Woods and Water Friends, 1917; Trail to Woods and Waters, 1921; Pep, 1922; Wanted, a Mother, 1922; Dapples of the Circus, 1923; The Way of the Wild, 1923; The White Czar, 1923; A Gentleman from France, 1924; Silversheene, 1924; Pal o' Mine, 1925; Jungle Joe, 1926; Redcoat, 1927; Patches (Wizard of the Cattle Trail), 1928; Bing (story of a small dog's love), 1929; Big Brother, 1930; Peter, 1931; Dr. Thinkright, 1934; The Light That Did Not Fail, 1935; Roany (the Horse That Smelled Smoke), 1935; The Master of Mills Haven, 1936; Igloo Stories, 1937; Notes of a Naturalist, 1938; Christmas All the Year, 1938; Uncle Billy—The Curios Cobbler, 1939; Holiday Hopes, 1939; My Country (The America I Knew), 1940; The Strange Adventures of Mr. Turtle, 1944; The Service Man's Friend, 1944. Contributor stories, articles and verse. Lecturer upon nature subjects. Home: Hadley, Mass. Died Jan. 19, 1954; buried Old Hadley Cemetery, Hadley, Mass.

HAWKES, William F., editor; b. Bloomington, Ill., Oct. 20, 1898; s. William and Addie (Garland) H.; student Northwestern U.; m. Muriel Thomas, May 7, 1942; 1 son by previous marriage, William E. City editor Springfield (Ill.) News-Record, 1917-18, St. Louis Star, 1920-29; mng. editor, Phila. Record, 1930-44; writer war articles, 1945; mng. editor San Diego Journal, 1945, retired 1946; traveling Central America. With AEF, 1918. Club: Pen and Pencil (Phila.) Author: What Time Is It?, Two Days More. Address: care Atty. Joseph Sharfsin, Lincoln-Liberty Bldg. Died 1950.

HAWKINS, Arthur Hanson, surgeon; b. La Plata, Md., Dec. 27, 1868; s. Samuel and Jane (Robertson) H.; M.D., U. of Md. Coll. Physicians and Surgeons, 1895; m. Louise Brokenborough Price, 1901; children—Arthur Hanson, Helen Brokenborough; m. 2d, Lou Finzel, 1921. Began practice at Cumberland, 1901; chief of staff Memorial Hosp., Cumberland; consulting surgeon, Miner's Hosp., Frostburg, Md. Chmn. and surgeon, med. advisory bd., World War; now chmn. and surgeon med. advisory bd. and chmn. Army examining bd. Memorial Hosp., Cumberland. Past pres. Allegany-Garrett County Med. Soc.; past pres. Med. and Chirurg. Faculty of Md. Fellow Am. Coll. Surgeons, A.M.A.; mem. Sigma Alpha Epsilon. Mason (32°, K.T., Shriner), Elk. Clubs: Cumberland Rotary (past pres.); University (Baltimore); Cumberland Country, AliGhan Shrine Country. Home: Hill Crest Drive. Office: Memorial Hospital, Cumberland, Md. Died June 9, 1952.

HAWKINS, Hamilton Smith, ret. army officer; b. Dakota, Ty., Sept. 25, 1872; s. Brig. Gen. Hamilton Smith (U.S. Army) and Annie (Gray) H.; grad. U.S. Mil. Acad., 1894; distinguished grad. Army Sch. of Line, 1911; grad. Army Staff Coll., 1912. Commd. add. 2d lt. 4th Cav., 1894; promoted through grades to brig. gen., 1928. Detailed as mem. Gen. Staff Corps, 1918; chief of staff 35th Div., Argonne-Meuse offensive, 1918-19; asst. comdt. Cav. and Mounted Service Schs., Ft. Riley, Kan., 1919-23; comdg. Ft. Myer, Va., 1923-26; chief of staff Philippine Div., 1926-28; comdg. 14th Inf. Brigade, Ft. Omaha, Neb., 1928-29; comdg. 1st Cav. Brigade, Ft. Clark, Tex., 1929-34, 1st Cav. Div., Ft. Bliss, Tex., 1934-36; retired, 1936. Contbd. articles to cav. jour. Address: 3508 Lowell St., Washington. Died Oct. 19, 1950; buried Cemetery West Point, N.Y.

HAWKINS, Laurence Ashley, elec. engr.; b. Pittsfield, Mass., Mar. 22, 1877; s. William J. and Harriet E. (Foxcroft) H.; B.A., Williams Coll., Williamstown, Mass., 1897, Sc.D., 1944; B.S., Mass. Inst. Tech., 1899; m. Florence Kellogg, June 12, 1902; children—Laurence K., Elizabeth (Mrs. Raymond E. Booth); m. 2d, Ruth Kellogg, Aug. 10, 1910; m. 3d, Ann D. Krebs, Dec. 16, 1931. Elec. engr. Stanley Elec. Mfg. Co., Pittsfield, Mass., 1899-1903; asst. patent atty., patent dept. Gen. Electric Co., Schenectady, 1903-08, engr. ry. signal dept., 1908-11, exec. engr. research lab., 1912-45, cons., 1945-48, retired; pres. Mahwak Development Service, Inc. Mem., past pres. Boy Scouts Council. Mem. Am. Inst. E.E. (life), Illuminating Engring. Soc., Theta Delta Chi, Phi Beta Kappa, Sigma Xi. Clubs: Mohawk, Mohawk Golf, Rotary (Schenectady). Awarded Order of Ky. Colonels. Contbr. articles and lectures on indsl. research. Home: 1130 Wendell Av., Schenectady. Died May 15, 1958; buried Pittsfield, Mass.

HAWKINS, William Waller, newspaper mgr.; b. Springfield, Missouri, April 19, 1883; son of Xenophon and Fannie Butler (Menzies) H.; graduate Springfield High School, 1901; married Margaret Forster Wright, June 16, 1909; children—George Wright, William Waller, Jr., Ewing Butler; married 2d, Margaret Culbertson Scripps, October 21, 1943. Began newspaper work with Springfield (Missouri) Republican, 1901, becoming city editor, 1902; staff of Times, 1903, Herald, 1904, Courier-Journal, 1905-06, Louisville, Ky.; N.Y. staff of Publishers' Press Assn., 1906-07; with United Press Ass. since its orgn., 1907; mgr. at Albany, N.Y., San Francisco and Washington, D.C., 2d v.p. and gen. news mgr., Jan. 1, 1912, 1st v.p. and gen. mgr., 1915-20, pres., 1920-23, dir. and mem. exec. com., 1920-53; gen. exec. mgr. Scripps-Howard Newspapers, 1923-27, vice chmn. bd., 1927, chmn. bd., 1937-52; chmn. adv. council, Jan. to Feb. 1953. Address: Glenbrook, Nev. Died Feb. 19, 1953.

HAWKS, Charles, Jr., congressman; b. Horicon, Wis., July 7, 1899; s. Charles and Linda (Yankey) H.; grad. Horicon High Sch., 1917; student U. Wis., Sch. of Commerce, 1919-22; m. Lucile Alma McGinnis, of Waukesha, Wis., Sept. 1, 1928; children—Ann, Charles, III. Salesman Union Carbide & Carbon Co., 1922-25; insurance, own business, Horicon, 1925-28; with Edgar Ricker & Co., investment banking, Milwaukee, 1928-31; insurance, investments, own business, Horicon, since 1931; mem. 76th Congress (1939-41), 2d Wis. Dist.; mem. Bd. of Supervisors, Dodge County, Wis., 1935-39. Served in U.S. Navy, 1917-19. Mem. Am. Legion, Vets. of Foreign Wars. Clubs: Army and Navy (Washington, D.C.). Home: Horicon, Wis. Died Jan. 6, 1960.

HAWLEY, Frederick William, coll. pres.; b. Carthage, Ill., July 16, 1866; s. Joseph William and Sarah Frances (Symonds) H.; A.B., Carthage Coll., 1888, A.M., 1893, D.D., 1911; grad. McCormick Theol. Sem., 1892; D.D., Center Coll., Ky., 1911; LL.D., Knox College, Galesburg, Illinois, 1916; L.H.D., University Tulsa, 1945; m. Pauline Aston, June 30, 1895; children—Herrick Kent, Frederick William. Ordained to ministry Presbyn. Ch., 1892; pastor Oklahoma City, 1892-97; supt. missions Okla. Ty. and Ind. Ty., 1897-1906; pastor Bloomington, Ill., 1906-11; pres. Henry Kendall Coll., Tulsa, 1911-15; pres. Park Coll., 1915-37, acting pres. 1944-45, hon. pres. 1945—. Home: Parkville, Mo. Died July 29, 1953.

HAWTHORNE, Hildegarde, author; b. New York; d. Julian and Mary Albertina (Amelung) Hawthorne; ed. abroad and pvtly.; m. John Milton Oskison, July 16, 1920. Engaged in war work in France for Y.M.C.A. and Am. Red Cross, 1918; traveling abroad and in America, 1923-28. Member of the Authors' League of America; hon. mem. of MacDowell Club since its foundation; mem. Calif. Writers Club, Pen and Brush Club. Author: A Country Interlude, 1904; Poems, 1904; Essays, 1907; The Lure of the Garden, 1911; A Peep at New York, 1911; Old Seaport Towns of New England, 1916; Rambles Through College Towns, 1917; Girls in Bookland, 1917; Makeshift Farm, 1925; Corsica, 1926; Maybe True Stories, 1926; Island Farm, 1926; Deedah's Wonderful Year, 1927; Mystery at Star-C Ranch, 1929; Secret of Rancho del Sol, 1931; Wheels Toward the West, 1931; Mystery of Navajo Canyon, 1931; Romantic Rebel, The Life of Hawthorne, 1932; Riders of the Royal Road, 1932; Open Range, 1932; Lone Rider, 1933; Tabitha of Lonely House, 1934; Youth's Captain, Life of Ralph Waldo Emerson, 1935; Enos Mills of the Rockies (with E. B. Mills), 1935; Poet of Craigie House, the Life of Longfellow, 1936; On the Golden Trail, 1936; Phantom King, the Life of Napoleon's Son, 1937; Rising Thunder, the Life of Jack Jouett, 1937; The Miniature's Secret, 1938; The Happy Autocrat, a Life of Oliver Wendell Holmes, 1938; Romantic Cities of California, 1939; No Road Too Long, 1940; Concord's Happy Rebel (the Life of H. D. Thoreau), 1940; Williamsburg, Old and New, 1941; The Long Adventure (Churchill's Life), 1942; Ox-Team Miracle, The Life of Alexander Majors, 1942; California's Missions, 1942; No Road Too Long, 1942; Matthew Fontaine Maury, Trail Maker of the Seas, 1943; Give Me Liberty, The Story of Patrick Henry, 1945; Westward the Course: The Story of The Lewis and Clark Expedition, 1946; Born to Adventure: Story of John Charles Fremont, 1947; His Country Was the World, a Life of Thomas Paine, 1949. Reviewer with New York Times, 1917-25. Contributor poems, short stories and articles to mags. Home: East Ridge, Ridgefield, Conn. Died 1952.

HAY, Arthur Douglas, judge; b. Scotland, Oct. 24, 1884; s. Alexander and Jessie (Bruce) H.; came to U.S., 1906, naturalized 1918; student Heriot-Watt Coll., Edinburgh, 1901-05; LL.B., U. of Ore., 1911; m. Edith Mary Lawson, Nov. 3, 1914; children—Margaret (Mrs. Bob H. Napier), John Ralph, Douglas Lawson. Admitted to Ore. bar, 1911, and practiced in Portland, 1911, Klamath Falls, 1912-15, Lakeview, 1915-33; dist. atty., Lake County, 1925-26; circuit judge, 14th Jud. Dist., 1933-42; asso. justice, Supreme Court of Ore., since Nov. 28, 1942. Mem. Queen's Edinburgh Vol. Brig., The Royal Scots, 1903-05. Mem. Am. and Ore. bar assns., Am. Judicature Soc., Phi Delta Phi., Alpha Tau Omega. Republican. Episcopalian. Mason (grand master, Ore. 1941-42). Clubs: Rotary (Salem, Ore.). Home: 1415 S. Liberty St. Address: Supreme Court Bldg., Salem, Ore. Died Dec. 19, 1952.

HAY, Earl Downing, prof. engring.; b. New Goshen, Ind., Sept. 19, 1886; s. Walter Bruce and Valora Adela (Downing) H.; student Ind. U., 1905-06; B.S., Rose Poly. Inst., Terre Haute, Ind., 1910, M.S., 1915, M.E., 1921; grad. student U. of Wis., 1911-12; m. Bessie Louise Whipp, Aug. 14, 1913; children—Flavia Valora (Mrs. Charles Hazen), Charrie Anne (Mrs. Thurman Kepner), Helen Louise (Mrs. Jack Richardson), David Earl. Designer Nat. Malleable Castings Co., Indianapolis, 1910-11; design instructor, Univ. of Wis., Coll. of Engring., 1911-13; head dept. of design, Oshkosh (Wis.) State Teachers Coll., 1913-18; asso. in design, U. of Ill. Coll. of Engring., 1918-20; dean, Coll. of Engring., Des Moines (Ia.) U., 1920-24; dean, Coll. of Engring. Univ. of Wyo., 1924-28; head depts. of mechanics and industrial engineering, University of Kansas, 1928-46; head design dept. of mechanical engring., Iowa State Coll. since 1946. State representative to World Power Conf., Washington, D.C., 1936; mem. Airport Bd., Lawrence, Kan. Sec., mem., State Registration Board for Professional Engrs. Licensed professional engr., Kan. and Iowa. Mem. Am. Soc. Mech. Engrs. (chairman Kansas City Sect., 1939-40), secretary-treasurer, Central Iowa Section, 1946-47, chairman, Central Iowa section, 1948-49), Soc. for Engineering Education (pres. Kan.-Neb. section, 1935, 1941), Engrs. Council Professional Development (mem. accrediting com.), Kan. Engring. Society, Tau

Beta Pi, Phi Kappa Phi, Pi Tau Sigma, Tau Omega, Theta Tau. Republican. Methodist. Co-author: Trade Foundations, 1918; Education Through Woodworking, 1923. Contbr. articles and fiction to popular science publs., also tech. jours. Home: 523 Beech Av., Ames, Ia. Died Jan. 1, 1953.

HAY, John W., banker; b. nr. Fairfield, Ill., Sept. 11, 1864; s. L. P. and Jane (Borah) H.; educated public schools; LL.D., University of Wyoming; married Mary Blair, November 16, 1892; children—Archibald L. (dec.), Beulah (Mrs. William A. Radford), Lucy (Mrs. C. Hopkin Johnson), Mary (Mrs. George W. Hegewald), Hannah (Mrs. George H. Force), Jane, John W., Leonard W. Formerly ry. telegraph operator, advancing to asst. supt. U.P. Ry. in Wyo.; cattle and sheep raiser since 1900; pres. Rock Springs Nat. Bank, Am. Nat. Bank. Mason (33°). Republican. Home: Rock Springs, Wyo. Died Oct. 5, 1951.

HAYCOX, Ernest, author; b. Portland, Ore., Oct. 1, 1899; s. William James and Bertha (Burghardt) H.; student Reed Coll., Portland, 1919-20; B.A., U. Ore., 1923; Litt.D., Lewis and Clark Coll., 1946; m. Jill Marie Chord, Mar. 4, 1925; children—Mary Ann, Ernest James. Entered mil. service, 1915; on Mexican border with 3d Ore. N.G., 1916; in France, 1917-19. Chmn. Selective Service Board No. 1, Multnomah County, Ore. Mem. Ore. State Library Bd. Pres. U. Ore. Alumni Assn., 1946-47, Dad's Club, U. Ore., 1948-49. Mem. Am. Legion, Delta Tau Delta. Republican. Methodist. Rotarian. Author: Free Grass, 1929; Chaffee of Roaring Horse, 1930; Whispering Range, 1930; Starlight Rider, 1933; Riders West, 1934; Rough Air, 1934; The Silver Desert, 1935; Trail Smoke, 1936; Trouble Shooter, 1936; Deep West, 1937; Sundown Jim, 1938; Man in the Saddle, 1938; The Border Trumpet, 1939; Saddle and Ride, 1939; Rim of the Desert, 1940; Trail Town, 1941; Alder Gulch, 1942; Action by Night, 1943; The Wild Bunch, 1943; Bugles in the Afternoon, 1944; Canyon Passage, 1945; Long Storm, 1946. Contbr. to Collier's Magazine, Saturday Evening Post. Screen Stories: Union Pacific, Stagecoach, Apache Trail, Abilene Town, Canyon Passage. Home: 4700 S.W. Humphrey Blvd., Portland 1. Office: Failing Bldg., Portland 4, Ore. Died Oct. 13, 1950.

HAYDEN, Josiah Willard, foundation pres.; b. Boston, May 2, 1874; s. Josiah Willard and Emma A. (Tirrell) H.; grad. Pa. Mil. Acad., 1890; hon. LL.D., Manhattan Coll., 1946, Boston U., 1944; hon. L.H.D., Fordham, 1947; m. Nellie Blanche Littlefield, Oct. 9, 1904. Pres. Charles Hayden Found., Boston, since 1937; dir. Eastern Steamship Lines, Inc.; exec. position Y.M.C.A., 1942. Life mem. bd. trustees Mass. Inst. Tech. Recipient Order of Distinguished Auxiliary Service, Salvation Army. Clubs: Univ. (N.Y. City and Boston); Yacht, El Country (Habana, Cuba). Home: Lexington, Mass. Office: 10 Post Office Sq., Boston. Died June 15, 1955.

HAYES, David J(ohn), A(rthur), lawyer; b. Chgo., June 16, 1900; s. Jeremiah G. and Anna Louise (Quigley) H.; student Crane Jr. Coll., Chgo., U. Chgo.; LL.B., Chicago Kent Coll. Law, 1922; m. Lucille Margaret Johnson, Oct. 1, 1927; children—David J. A., Richard Johnson. Admitted to Ill. bar, 1922 and since in gen. practice, specializing in law applicable to wills, trusts and estates; admitted to practice before Supreme Ct. U.S., 1927; atty. for pres. Bd. Local Improvements of Chicago, 1925-27; atty. Pub. Guardian Cook County, Ill., 1923-35; prof. med. jurisprudence Chicago Med. Sch., 1925-26; commr. Supreme Ct. Ill., 1937-39. Mem. Chicago Black Horse Troop, 1930-36; govt. appeal agt. Selective Service Cook County Bd. 6, 1940-46, local bd., 1948—. Mem. bd. edn. Oak Park and River Forest High Sch., 1949-55. Mem. Chgo. (bd. mgrs. 1943-45), Ill. (bd. govs. 1946-56, v.p. 1956-59), Am. (chmn. com. on law lists 1951-59) bar assns., Internat. Acad. Trial Lawyers, The Fellow of Am. Bar Assn., Selden Soc., Chgo. Law Inst., Am. Judicature Soc., Amateur Cinema League, Inc., Chgo. Council Fgn. Relations, English-Speaking Union, Pan Am. Council, Am. Legion (judge adv. Oak Park post 15, 1936-43), Art Inst. Chicago (life), Phi Alpha Delta. Clubs: Chicago Athletic Assn., Economic, Executives, Campfire, Chicago Black Horse Troop (1st pres.) (Chgo.); Oak Park (Ill.) Country. Contbr. to law revs. and legal publs. Home: 1311 Park Av., River Forest, Ill. Office: One N. LaSalle St., Chgo. 2. Died June 17, 1959; buried Queen of Heaven Cemetery, Hillside, Ill.

HAYES, Edward Arthur, lawyer; b. Morrisonville, Ill., Jan. 5, 1893; s. Michael Patrick and Mary Ellen (Bray) H.; grad. St. Theresa's Parochial Sch., 1910; LL.B., St. Louis U., 1915; m. Margaret M. Muleady, Sept. 10, 1918. Admitted to Ill. bar, 1915, and practiced in Decatur, Ill., mem. firm Hayes & Downing, 1915-40; mem. firm Damon, Hayes White & Hoban, Chicago, since 1945; one of the gen. counsel, Bowser, Inc., since 1945; pres. Defense Identification Service, Inc., since 1951. Served as apprentice seaman, U.S. Navy, 1917, ensign U.S.N.R., aide to Adm. Moffett, 1918-19; comd. lt. comdr., U.S. N.R., 1933. Mem. Am. Legion (dep. comdr., Ill. dept., 1929-30; nat. comdr., 1933-34 mem. nat. exec. com., since 1931), Am., Ill. and Chicago bar assns. Republican. Mem. Americans for America (nat. chmn.), K.C. (4°). Clubs: Chicago Athletic Association. Home: 2130 Lincoln Park West, Chicago 14. Office: 33 LaSalle St., Chgo. 2. Died Apr. 1, 1955.

HAYES, George Miller, publishing exec.; b. Owensboro, Ky., Aug. 19, 1897; s. William Foster and Susan Ambie (Miller) H.; student James Millikin U., 1916-18; U. Chgo. Grad. Sch., 1920-26; m. Jessie A. Thistle, June 1919; 1 son, James A.; m. 2d, Adeline Zuley, Apr. 1937; 1 son, John Miller. High sch. tchr., 1919-27; with Field Enterprises, Inc., Chgo., and predecessor firms, 1927—, successively salesman, sales mgr., 1927-51, v.p., gen. mgr. ednl. div. 1951—, also dir.; pres., dir. World Book-Childraft, Ltd., Toronto, Can., 1956—; president of Field Enterprises Educational Corp. Mem. Am. Textbook Pubs. Inst. Clubs: Chicago Athletic Assn., Merchants and Manufacturers (gov.) (Chgo.). Home: 203 Sheridan Rd., Winnetka, Ill. Office: Merchandise Mart Plaza, Chgo. 54. Died Oct. 10, 1957.

HAYES, Henry Reed, financial consultant; b. Boston, Mass., Mar. 26, 1879; s. John J. and Caroline L. (Raymond) H.; grad. Roxbury (Mass.) Latin Sch., 1897; A.B., Harvard, 1901; m. Yvonne Stoddard, Oct. 24, 1917; children—Henry Reed, Howland, David, Philip. With Stone & Webster, Boston, 1901-10, later New York, in investment banking div., 1912-27; v.p. Stone & Webster, Inc., 1925-30; v.p. and dir. Stone & Webster and Blodget, N.Y.C., 1927-33. Served as major, later lt. col., U.S. Army, World War. Chmn. Rep. Town Com., Dedham, Mass., 1909-12; mem. exec. com. Mass. Rep. State Com., 1912. Pres. Investment Bankers Assn. of America, 1927. Dir. Better Business Bureau of N.Y.C., New York Sch. for the Deaf; trustee, mem. exec. com. Teachers Ins. and Annuity Assn. of America; dir. The Columbia Gas System, Inc., General Public Utilities Corp. Episcopalian. Clubs: Harvard, The Players (New York). Home: Dan's Highway, New Canaan, Conn. Office: 74 Trinity Pl., N.Y.C. 6. Died June 29, 1955.

HAYES, John Russell, librarian; b. at West Chester, Pa., June 25, 1866; s. William Mordecai and Rachel Hutton (Russell) H.; A.B., Swarthmore, 1888; A.B., Harvard, 1889; LL.B., U. Pa., 1892; univs. of Oxford and Strassburg, 1892-93; m. Emma Gawthrop, June 30, 1892; children—Esther Rachel, Katharine Russell, Eleanor Gawthrop. Instr. English, 1893-95, asst. prof., 1895-1906, college librarian, 1906-27; librarian Friends Hist. Library, 1927-36, Swarthmore College, retired, 1936. Mem. Phi Beta Kappa, Delta Upsilon. Mem. Soc. of Friends. Author: The Old-Fashioned Garden and Other Verses, 1895; The Brandywine, 1898; Swarthmore Idylls, 1899; Scholar's Ideal (Phi Beta Kappa ode), 1904; Old Quaker Meeting-Houses, 1909; Brandywine Days, 1910; In Memory of Whittier, 1910; Molly Pryce, 1913; Roger Morland, a Quaker Idyll, 1915; Collected Poems, 1916. Home: Embreeville, Pa. Died Dec. 29, 1945; buried Romansville Friends Meeting, Pa.

HAYES, Myron J., business exec.; b. Bristol, Ontario, N.Y., Feb. 18, 1891; s. Arza and Dora (Fox) H.; grad. high sch.; night sch. student Rochester Bus. Inst., 6 yrs.; also pvt. instrn. in spl. courses in law, comml. law, bus. adminstrn., psychology and econs.; m. Claribel Hilborn, June 25, 1914: children—Theda (Mrs. Robert E. Consler), Wilda (Mrs. Thomas A. McDowell). Accountant, Eastman Kodak Co., 1912-29, mgr. camera works, 1929-38, gen. mgr. camera works, hawkeye works and Navy ordnance div., 1938—, vice pres., 1943—; dir. Central Trust Co., Rochester, N.Y. Mem. Rochester Citizen's Com., Firemen's Benefit Fund, Police Benevolent Assn. Mem. Rochester C. of C., Nat. Assn. Accountants. Republican. Baptist. Clubs: Genesee Valley, Monroe Golf, Lake Placid, Spot, Rotary. Home: 15 Briar Patch Rd., Rochester 18. Office: 333 State St., Rochester 4, N.Y. Died Nov. 22, 1956; buried Honeoye, N.Y.

HAYES, Samuel Perkins, psychologist; b. Baldwinsville, N.Y., Dec. 17, 1874; s. M. D. L. and Mary Ellen (Perkins) H.; B.A., Amherst, 1896; B.D., Union Theol. Sem., 1902; M.A., Columbia, 1902; fellow Clark U., 1902-03; studied U. Berlin and Sorbonne, Paris, 1903-04; Ph.D., Cornell, 1906; studied Cambridge U., Eng., 1912; m. Agnes Hayes Stone, July 23, 1903; children—Lyman Stone, Mary Ellen, Samuel Perkins, Janet Card, Betsy Wanton. Prof. psychology Mt. Holyoke Coll., 1906-40; head dept. personnel Perkins Instn. and Mass. Sch. for Blind, 1940-55; cons. Am. Found. for Blind, 1932-54. Mem. Am. Psychol. Assn., Phi Beta Kappa, Sigma Xi, Chi Phi. Unitarian. Address: 29 Dempsey Av., Princeton, N.J. Died May 7, 1958.

HAYES, Thomas Sumner, educator; b. Bath, Me., June 10, 1902; s John P. and Jenna (Footer) H.; Ph.B., Georgetown U., 1924; m. Juana J. Janer, Nov. 23, 1928; children—Helen, Joan, Marjorie, Mary Jo. Tchr. high schs., Ponce, P.R., also San Juan, 1924-27; high sch. prin., Humacao, Arecibo, also Cayey, P.R., 1927-32; instr. English U. P.R., 1931-41, asst prof. English, 1941-42, prof. English lit., univ. librarian since 1942; sec. to Gov. P.R., 1942-43; columnist El Mundo of San Juan, 1949-51, 1954—. Member Am. Assn. Profs. Contbr. articles Ency. Americana, also P.R. newspapers, periodicals. Home: Avenida Universidad 50, Río Piedras, P.R. Died May 18, 1959; buried Porta Coeli Cath. Cemetery, Bayamon, P.R.

HAYES, Wade Hampton, banker; b. Norfolk, Va., May 12, 1879; s. William Arnold and Emma (Mathews) H.; Norfolk Academy; special course in political science, Columbia, 1899-1900; m. Julia Florence Yard, Dec. 14, 1905; 1 daughter, Sally. Sunday editor New York Tribune, Feb. 1908-14; member Hayes & Lord, investment bankers, and vice-president Chase Securities Corporation, investment bankers; now chairman Edmundsons Electricity Corp., Ltd.; dir. English Electric Co., Ltd., Utilities Corp. (Poland), Ltd., Marconi's Wireless Telegraph Co., Ltd., Marconi Instruments, Ltd., D. Napier & Son, Ltd., Edmundsons Electricity Corp., Ltd., and various other electric cos. in Eng. Enlisted 4th Regt. Va. Nat. Guard, 1896, and with same regt. in Spanish-Am. War as chief of couriers, staff of Maj. Gen. Fitzhugh Lee, Fla., Ga. and Matanzas, Cuba; mustered out, Nov. 1899; served as col. 107th Regt., N.Y. Nat. Guard, until 1931; was lt. col. 107th U.S. Inf., service in France, 1917-19; on staff of Gen. Pershing in operations section Gen. Staff, Gen. Hdqrs., A.E.F., June 1918-Feb. 1919; now brig. gen. retired; comdg. 1st American Squadron (Home Guard, Great Britain). Past comdr. Am. Legion, Dept. N.Y. Comdr. Legion d'Honneur (France); Comdr. Order British Empire. Mem. Southern Soc., Va. Soc., S.C. Soc., S.C.V., 7th Regt. Vet. Assn. Democrat. Clubs: Salmagundi, Down Town (New York); Carlton, City Athenaeum, American, Turf (London). Home: 48 Ennismore Gardens, London, S.W. 7. Office: 30 Gillingham St., S.W. 1, London, Eng. Died Sept. 4, 1956.

HAYES, Webb Cook II, naval officer; b. Toledo, O., Sept. 25, 1890; s. Birchard Austin and Mary (Sherman) H.; B.S., U.S. Naval Acad., 1911; LL.D. (hon.), Bowling Green State U.; m. Martha Baker, Apr. 29, 1919; children—Webb Cook III, Arthur Baker, Scott Birchard. Commd. ensign, U.S. Navy, 1911, and advanced through the grades to rear adm., 1954; served on destroyer, U.S.S. Trippe, World War I; transferred to U.S.N.R., 1928; recalled to active duty, 1941; dir. recruiting and induction, Navy Dept., 1941-44; comd. U.S.S. West Point (Am.), 1944-45. Pres., dir. Pemiscot Land & Cooperage Co., 1930—; dir. and chmn. exec. com. Baker Brothers Machine Tool Co., 1933-51. Trustee Ohio Hist. Soc., Meml. Hosp. of Sandusky County, O., Birchard Library, Fremont, O.; pres., trustee Rutherford B. Hayes Found. Awarded B.S.M. by Pres. U.S.; Commendation with ribbon by Sec. of Navy (U.S.); Order of Avis (Portugal). Clubs: Army and Navy, Chevy Chase (Washington); New York Yacht; Toledo Country, Toledo (O.); Everglades (Fla.). Address: Spiegel Grove, Fremont, O. Died July 10, 1957.

HAYHOW, Edgar Charles, hosp. dir.; b. N.Y.C., July 21, 1894; s. Henry Herbert and Lina Caroline (Buehlmaier) H.; B.S., Fordham U.; B.C.S., M.A., Ph.D., N.Y.U.; also postgrad Columbia. Successively asst. supt. Presbyn., St. Luke's and Lenox Hill hosps., N.Y.C., 1916-24; supt. New Rochelle (N.Y.) Hosp., 1924-27; hosp. cons., 1927-30; supt. Paterson (N.J.) Gen. Hosp., 1930-46; dir. East Orange (N.J.) Gen. Hosp., 1946—; lectr. on instnl. mgmt. N.Y.U., 1924-28. Mem. lay council Tchrs. Coll. Columbia; expert examiner Municipal Civil Service Commn., N.Y.; mem. Hosp. Survey of New York, 1937 (member gen. com.); mem. bd. trustees Am. Hosp. Assn., 1940-43 (1st v.p. 1939; chmn., mem. several councils); mem. Joint Com. of Edn. of Am. Hosp. Assn. and Am. Coll. Hosp. Adminstrs. Mem. Nat. Com. Mental Hygiene; chmn. com. on hosps. and instns. Midcentury White House Conf. Children and Youth. Served with Hosp. Service, BEF, later AEF, 1916-17; capt. Med. Adminstrv. Res. Corps, U.S. Army. Fellow Am. Coll. Hosp. Adminstrs. (regent 1938-52, pres. 1947-48); asso. fellow N.Y. Acad. Medicine; mem. adm., Internat., Inter-Am., N.Y., N.J. (pres. 1937) hosp. assns., Am. Acad. Polit. and Social Science, Lambda Sigma Phi, Phi Delta Kappa. Republican. Methodist. Clubs: Army and Navy, Railroad and Machinery (N.Y.C.). Contbr. to hosp. and social service mags. Home: 283 S. Center St., Orange, N.J. Address: East Orange General Hospital, East Orange, N.J. Died Aug. 23, 1957.

HAYKIN, David Judson, librarian; b. Russia, Jan. 18, 1896; s. Joseph L. and Grace R. (Rosenstein) H.; A.B., U. Neb., 1921; B.L.S., U. State N.Y., 1925; m. Irene Atwood Wilson, May 18, 1918; children—Joan Irene (Mrs. Marvin S. Weinstein), David Judson. Came to U.S., 1909, derivative citizen. Various profl. capacities U. Neb. Library, 1917, 18-24; head cataloger N.Y. State Library, 1925-27; head cataloging dept., instr. library sch. Queens Borough Pub. Library, N.Y.C., 1927-30; in charge office decimal classification A.L.A., Washington, 1930-31; chief div. documents Library Congress, Washington, 1932-34, chief coop. cataloging service, 1934-40, chief subject cataloging div., 1940-52, cons. classification and subject cataloging, 1952—; editor Dewey Decimal Classification, 1954-56. Mem. U.S. Bd. Geog. Names. Mem. American Documentation Institute, A.A.A.S., A.L.A. (pres. div. cataloging and classification 1952-53), Bibliog. Soc. Am., Am. Name Soc., Spl. Library Assn., Music Library Assn., D.C. Library Assn. (pres. 1945-47). Author: Subject Headings, a practical guide, 1951. Contbr. articles profl. jours. Home: 4958 Brandywine St., Washington 16. Office: Library of Congress, Washington. Died May 4, 1958.

HAYNES, Carlyle Boynton, clergyman, author; b. Bristol, Conn., May 24, 1882; s. Samson Miles Scribner and Lauretta (Bazzell) H.; prep. edn., South Lancaster (Mass.) Acad.; student Washington Missionary Coll., 1904-05; m. Alfreda Weber, Apr. 21, 1906; 1 son, Donald Frederick; married 2d, Elsie M. Argent, January 21, 1952. Active in city evangelistic campaigns, 1908-19; head of War Service Commn., Gen. Conf. Seventh-Day Adventists, 1918; pastor City Temple, New York, 1919-23; became pres. Greater New York Conf. Seventh-Day Adventists, 1923, Mich. Conf. of Seventh-Day Adventists, Jan. 1934; also pres. Gr. New York Corp. Seventh-Day Adventists, Gr. New York Book and Bible House. Apptd. Pres. of S. Am. Div. of Gen. Conf. of Seventh-Day Adventists (supervising all denom. work in S.A.), 1926; pres. Mich. Conf., 1934; World Evangelist of denomination, 1930; sec. War Service Commn., 1941; exec. sec. Council on Indsl. Relations, 1945; sec., Commn. on Rural Living, 1946; chmn. Com. on Calendar Revision, 1947. Republican. Author: The Other Side of Death, 1916; The Christian Sabbath, 1916; Our Lord's Return, 1918; Russellism; or the Coming of a False Christ, 1919; Spiritualism versus Christianity, 1918; Bible Prophecies Unfolding, 1919; What Is Coming?, 1920; Satan—His Origin, Work and Destiny, 1920; On the Eve of Armageddon, 1924; Christianity at the Crossroads, 1924; Twelve Great Signs of the Return of Jesus, 1925; The Return of Jesus, 1926; The Hour of God's Judgment, 1926; The Bible—Is it a True Book?, 1927; From Sabbath to Sunday, 1927; Our Times and Their Meaning, 1929; The Gift of Prophecy, 1931; Spiritism and the Bible, 1931; The Promised Land, 1933; When Christ Comes Again, 1934; God's Book, 1935; Earth's Last Hour, 1937; Living Evangelism, 1937; The Quest for the True Church, 1938; The Divine Art of Preaching, 1939; Seventh-Day Adventists; Their Teaching and Work, 1940; The Blackout of Civilization and Beyond, 1941; One World, One Government, One Sovereign, 1943; One World in Prophecy, 1944; Calendar Change Threatens Religion, 1944; World Calendar versus World Religion, 1944; Medical Soldiers in Training and Action, 1944; When God Splits the Atom, 1946; America and Its Prophetic Destiny, 1946; When a Man Dies, 1948; Palestine, Israel, and Bible Prophecy, 1949; The Book of All Nations, 1950; On the Throne of the World, 1952; Life, Death and Immortality, 1952; The Legion of the Tenth, 1957. Address: 6902 Sycamore Av., Washington 12. Died Mar. 11, 1958; buried George Washington Cemetery, Takoma Park, Md.

HAYNES, Daniel H(agood), business exec.; born Selma, Ala., Feb. 9, 1882; s. Arthur and Jessie (Lafayette) H.; B.S., Ala. Poly. Inst., 1901; m. Courtenay Collins, 1913; children—Hagood, Douglas. With Am. Tobacco Co., New York, 1907-10, Durham Duplex Razor Co., 1910-14; treas., Am. Machine & Foundry Co., 1914-23, 2d vice pres., 1919-22, vice pres., 1922-51, treas., 1949-51, vice chmn., chmn. exec. com. since 1951, director since 1915; treasurer International Cigar Machinery Company, New York, 1914-23, 2d vice pres., 1919-22, vice pres., 1922, v.p. and treas., 1922-23, v.p., 1923-41, president, 1941—. Member adv. board Chem. Corn exchange Bank. Republican. Clubs: Links (New York); Nat. Golf Links (Southampton, L.I); Southside Sportsmen's of Long Island. Home: 28 E. 73 St., N.Y.C. 21. Office: 261 Madison Av., N.Y.C. 16. Died Feb. 28, 1959.

HAYNES, Eli Stuart, astronomer; b. Trenton, Mo., July 12, 1880; s. Aaron and Philena (Biggs) H.; A.B., U. of Mo., 1905, A.M., 1907; Ph.D., U. of Calif., 1913; m. Mamie Ruth Mode, May 20, 1908 (died Feb. 1934); children—Charles Mode, Willis Stuart, Mary Ruth (dec.); m. 2d, Nola Lee Anderson, July 9, 1938. Asst. in mathematics, Univ. of Mo., 1905-06; research asst. Laws Obs., same univ., 1906-08; instr. in astronomy, U. of Mo., 1908-11, in charge dept., 1909-11; fellow in astronomy, 1911-12, instr., 1912-13, U. of Calif.; Martin Kellogg fellow, Lick Obb., 1913-14; asso. prof. astronomy, 1914-15, prof. 1915-23, Beloit Coll., also dir. Smith Obs.; prof. astronomy and dir. Laws Obs., U. of Mo., 1923-50, professor emeritus of astronomy, 1950—. Member board of trustees Christian College, Columbia, Mo., 1937-54. Fellow A.A.A.S. (mem. council 1935-38); mem. Am. Astron. Soc., Phi Beta Kappa, Sigma Xi, Delta Tau Delta. Mem. Christian (Disciples) Church. Mason (grand treas. Grand Chap. R.A.M., Mo., 1945—). Contbr. on variable star photometry, orbits of comets and asteroids and orbits of spectroscopic binaries. Home: 1408 Rosemary Lane, Columbia, Mo. Died Sept. 13, 1956; buried Memorial Park Cemetery, Columbia.

HAYNES, Elizabeth A. Ross (Mrs. George Edmund Haynes), polit., social worker; b. Lowndes County, Ala.; d. Henry and Mary Ross (both formerly slaves); diploma, State Normal Sch., Montgomery, Ala., 1898; A.B., Fisk U., Nashville, 1903; studied U. Chgo., summers 1905-07; M.A., Columbia, 1923; m. George Edmund Haynes, sociologist, Dec. 14, 1910; 1 son, George Edmund. Tchr. of Latin, Sumner High Sch., St. Louis, 1903-04; head tchr. tng. dept. State Normal Sch., Montgomery, Ala., 1905-08; first sec. of colored work, Nat. Bd. YWCA, 1908-10; vol. worker Nat. Bd. YWCA, 1910—; elected first colored rep. Nat. Bd. YWCA, 1924, serving until 1934; mem. Mayor La Guardia's City Planning Commn. Mem. exec. com. Interracial Com. of Federal Council of Churches. Dollar a year worker Women's Bur., U.S. Dept. Labor, 1918-20; sec. Domestic Service Sect. U.S. Employment Service, D.C., 1920-22. Sec. bd. mgmt. A. Clayton Powell Home for the Aged, N.Y.C.; mem. Brownell Commn. to Study Conditions of Negroes in N.Y.C.; mem. exec. com. of sect. on care of aged, Welfare Council of N.Y.C.; mem. Adv. Com. on Women's Participation in New York World's Fair, 1939. Mem. Nat. Assn. Colored Women, A.K.A. Sorority. Author: Unsung Heroes (biog. sketches), 1921; The Negro in Domestic Service in the United States, 1923; Black Boy of Atlanta, 1952. Home: 411 Convent Av., N.Y.C. Died Oct. 26, 1953.

HAYNES, Evan, lawyer; b. St. Louis, Missouri, July 23, 1895; s. Edgar Allan Poe and Cora Idella (Schwinn) H.; A.B., U. of Calif., 1922, J.D., 1924; m. Irene Whitford, July 23, 1928; children—Diana, Duncan. Admitted to Calif. bar, 1924, practiced law in San Francisco with Garret W. McEnerney, 1924-27; teacher Sch. of Jurisprudence, U. of Calif., 1927-29, 1930-35, 1936-42, acting dean, 1941-42; teacher, Columbia Law Sch., 1929-30; practiced law with Brobeck, Phleger & Harrison, 1935-36; head of Compliance Sect., Office of Price Adminstrn., Washington, D.C., 1942; regional rent exec., Pacific Coast Region, 1942-43; various posts in Foreign Economic Administration, Washington, D.C., 1943-44; partner Brobeck, Phleger & Harrison, San Francisco, since 1945. Served as private, lt., and capt., 58th Inf., 4th Div., 1917-19. Mem. State Bar of Calif., Am. Bar Assn., Sigma Pi, Phi Alpha Delta. Author: Selection and Tenure of Judges (Nat. Conf. Judicial Councils 1944), articles in legal periodicals. Home: Rt. 1, Box 30, Calistoga, Cal. Office: 111 Sutter St., San Francisco 4. Died Mar. 18, 1955; buried Mountain View Cemetery, Oakland, Cal.

HAYNES, George Edmund, sociologist; b. Pine Bluff, Ark., May 11, 1880; A.B., Fisk U., 1903; A.M., Yale, 1904; postgrad. U. Chgo., summers 1906, 07; grad. N.Y. Sch. Social Work, 1910; Ph.D., Columbia, 1912; m. Elizabeth A. Ross, Dec. 14, 1910 (dec. 1953); 1 son, George Edmund; m. 2d, Olyve Jeter, Apr. 12, 1955. Sec. colored men's dept. Internat. Com. Y.M.C.A., 1905-08; organizer, prof. social sci. Fisk U., Nashville, 1910-20; spl. asst. on Negro economics to sec. U.S. Dept. Labor, 1918-21; co-founder former exec. dir. Nat. Urban League; spl. adviser on Negro work, Interch. World Movement of N. Am., 1920-22; mem. Pres.'s Unemployment Conf., 1920-21; cons. on work among natives in South Africa, Internat. Survey of YMCA, 1930; sec. dept. race relations Fed. Council Churches Christ in Am., 1922-46; cons. for Africa, World's Com. of YMCA's, 1947; lectr. Coll. City N.Y., 1950-59. Mem. N.Y. Temporary Commn. for Study of Need for State Univ., 1947-48; mem. N.Y. State U. Bd. trustees, 1948-54, originator of Race Relations Sunday and Inter-racial Clinic; founder, first sec. Assn. Negro Colls. and Secondary Schs.; treas. Am. Com. on Africa; formerly vice moderator and 1st v.p. Home Bd. Congl. Christian Churches. Mem. Am. Social Workers Assn., Nat. Conf. Social Work, Church Conf. Social Work, Am. Sociol. Soc., A.A.A.S. Author: The Negro at Work in New York City, 1912; The Negro Newcomer in Detroit, Mich., 1917; The Trend of the Races, 1922; Along the Interracial Front, 1945; The Clinical Approach to Race Relations, 1946. Co-author: Studies in Cotton-Gowing Communities, No. 1, Alabama, 1933, No. 2, Arkansas, 1935; Africa-Continent of the Future, 1950. Contbr. articles to various publs. including Ency. Brit. Home: 303 Tecumseh Av., Mount Veronn, N.Y. Office: World's Com., YMCA, 347 Madison Av., N.Y.C. Died Jan. 8, 1960; buried Woodlawn Cemetery, N.Y.C.

HAYNES, Ira Allen, ret. army officer; b. in Ky., Sept. 10, 1859; grad. U.S. Mil. Acad., 1883; grad. Arty Sch., 1888. Commd. 2d lt. 3d Arty., 1883; promoted through grades to col. C.A.C., 1912; brig. gen. N.A., 1917; brig. gen., regular army, 1923. Duty with Va. State Militia at Richmond, Va., 1893; at Washington Barracks, D.C., 1893-95; at Honolulu, Hawaii, 1899; comdt. Coast Arty. Sch., 1913-16; apptd. comdr. 64th F.A. Brigade, Camp Beauregard, Alexandria, La., 1917; served in France, 1918-19; later comdr. 9th Coast Arty. Dist., San Francisco, retired, 1923. Home: 47 Hamilton Court, Palo Alto, Cal. Died Feb. 25, 1955.*

HAYNES, Robert Blair, mfg. exec.; b. St. Louis, Mar. 18, 1898; s. Matt Mortimer and Pearl (Wheeler) H.; student pub. schs. of Anderson, Ind.; m. Ruth N. Hall, Mar. 22, 1919 (died May 1950); children—Norma Y., Dorothy (Mrs. Irwin Carr), Joyce M. (Mrs. Albert E. Chiles); m. 2d Florence B. Pimblett, Jan. 26, 1951. Plant mgr. Electric Auto-Lite Co., Toledo, 1923-31; v.p. Dana Corp. 1935—, now mfg. cons. Mem. Soc. Automotive Engrs., Am. Soc. Tool Engrs. Mason (32°, Shriner). Clubs: Detroit Athletic. Toledo. Deceased.

HAYNES, Thornwell, consular service; b. Grindell Shoals, S.C., May 20, 1870; s. Hilliard and Sara (Lee) H.; A.B. and A.M., Wofford Coll., S.C., 1893; A.M., Vanderbilt U., Tenn., 1894; m. Minnie Lee Bowers, 1899. Teacher, 1894-1900; Am. consul at Rouen, France, 1900-05; at Nanking, China, 1905-07; consul-gen. at Singapore, 1907-09; supt. graded schs., Central S.C., 1909-11; supt. city schools, High Point, N.C., 1911-15; pres. Birmingham (Ala.) Coll., 1915-17; Am. consul at Helsingfors, Finland, 1917-19; diplomatic commr. to Finland with rank of minister plenipotentiary, 1919-20; consul at Berne, Switzerland, Aug. 1920—. Methodist. Extensive traveler. Mem. Chi Phi, Nat. Geog. Soc., N.E.A., U.S. Embassy Assn., etc. Author and contbr. to mags. Address: Columbia, S.C. Died Oct. 2, 1953.

HAYS, Arthur Alexander, theologian; b. Washington, Pa., June 23, 1875; s. Dr. George Price and Eleanor (Wherry) H.; A.B., Washington and Jefferson Coll., 1895, A.M., 1898, D.D., 1914; instr. high sch. and prin. schs., Washington, Pa., 1895-1900; McCormick Theol. Sem., 1900-03, and awarded at graduation, 1903, Bernadine Orme Smith Fellowship and 1st T. B. Blackstone Fellowship in N.T. Greek; post-grad. work, U. of Jena, Germany, 1903-05; B.D., McCormick Theol. Sem., 1909; m. Mary Johnston, June 14, 1910. Prof. Greek lang. and lit. Washington and Jefferson Coll., 1905-09; instr. history and N.T. Greek, McCormick Theol. Sem., 1909-14, prof. ecclesiastical history, 1914-45, prof. emeritus, 1945—. Trustee Washington and Jefferson Coll. Mem. Soc. for Bibl. Research, Am. Soc. Church History, Chicago Church History Club, Phi Delta Theta, Phi Beta Kappa. Presbyn. Author: (brochures) How a Medieval Monk Became Martin Luther, 1915; Pilgrim, Puritan, Protestant, 1920; Tyndale's Ploughboy Opens His Bible Collaborator: The Handbook to the Hymnal; From the Pyramids to Paul; The Study of the Bible, Today and Tomorrow. Home: 154 S. Wade Av., Washington, Pa. Died June 12, 1959; buried Washington Cemetery.

HAYS, Arthur Garfield, lawyer; b. Rochester, N.Y., Dec. 12, 1881; s. Isaac M. and Laura (Garson) H.; B.A., Columbia, 1902, M.A., 1905, LL.B., 1905; m. Blanche Marks, 1908; 1 dau., Lora Frances; m. 2d, Aline Davis Fleisher, June 12, 1924; 1 dau., Jane Darline. Admitted to N.Y. bar, 1905, and began practice at N.Y. City; mem. Hays, St. John, Abramson & Schulman, N.Y. City. Practiced internat. law in London, World War, 1914-15; active in many cases involving civil liberties; in opening up closed towns during coal strike in Pa., 1922; Scopes case in Tenn., 1925; Sweet case, Detroit, involving Negro segregation, 1925; case of Senator Wheeler, Washington, 1925; American Mercury case, Boston, 1926; Countess Cathcart immigration case; Sacco-Vanzetti case, 1927; appeared for defendants in Berlin and Leipzig, Germany, charged with burning of Reichstag, 1933; conducted investigation (1937) of civil liberties in Puerto Rico. Chmn. Progressive Party state campaign, N.Y, 1924; nat. dir. Am. Civil Liberties Union. Mem. New York State and New York County bar assns., Assn. of Bar of City of N.Y. Jewish religion. Author: Enemy Property in America, 1923; Let Freedom Ring, 1928 (rev. edit., 1937); Don't Tread on Me (with others), 1928; Trial by Prejudice, 1933; Democracy Works, 1939; City Lawyer, 1942. Contbr. to Nation and other mags. Home: 24 East 10th St., New York; and Sands Point, L.I. Office: 120 Broadway, N.Y.C. Died Dec. 14, 1954.

HAYS, Frank Lazmer, justice of supreme court; b. Council Bluffs, Ia., Feb. 12, 1889; s. Adam M. and Mary Elizabeth (Kirkendall) H.; student Drake U., Des Moines, Ia., 1909, 1915-17; LL.B., Creighton U., Omaha, Neb., 1918; m. Frances Eleanor Lundborg, Mar. 9, 1921; children—Frank Lazmer, Jr., Stanley Robert, Beverly Jean. Admitted to Colo. bar. 1920 and since practiced in Denver; asst. city atty., 1924-36; first asst. city atty., 1936-46, city and co. of Denver; justice Colo. Supreme Court, Denver, since 1946. Mem. Colo. and Denver bar assns. Mason. Central Christian Ch. Club: Denver Athletic. Home: 4139 Batavia Pl. Office: 355 State Capitol, Dener. Died May 29, 1951.

HAYS, Will H., lawyer; born in Sullivan, Indiana, November 5, 1879; son of John T. and Mary (Cain) Hays; A.B., Wabash College, Indiana, 1900, A.M., 1904; LL.D., Lincoln Memorial Univ., 1919; LL.D., Mt. Union Coll., 1926; LL.D., Wabash College, 1940; m. Helen Louise Thomas, Nov. 18, 1902; 1 son, Will H.; m. 2d, Jessie Herron Stutsman, Nov. 27, 1930. Admitted to Ind. bar, 1900; city atty., Sullivan, 1910-13; mem. Hays & Hays. Elected Rep. precinct committeeman before age of 21; chmn. Rep. County Com., Sullivan County, and mem. Rep. State Advisory Com., Ind., 1904-08; chmn. speakers' bur. Rep. State Com., 1906-08; dist. chmn. Rep. State Com., 2d

Dist., Ind., 1910-14; chmn. Rep. State Central Com., Ind., 1914-18; chmn. Ind. State Council of Defense, 1917-18; chmn. Rep. Nat. Com., Feb. 1918-June 7, 1921; postmaster gen. of U.S. by appt. of Pres. Harding, Mar. 5, 1921-Mar. 4, 1922; pres. Motion Picture Producers and Distributors of America, Inc., 1922-45, advisor, 1945-50; dir. Continental Banking Company, Chicago & Eastern Ill. R.R. Co.; vice president Roosevelt Memorial Assn.; trustee Institute for Crippled and Disabled Men; mem. Nat. Council Boy Scouts of America, Citizens Com. of Salvation Army, Am. and Ind. State bar assns., Nat. Inst. Social Science, Acad. Polit. Science, Phi Delta Theta (pres. for Ind. 6 yrs., nat pres., 1920-22); chmn. coördinating com. Am. Red Cross and Near East Relief, by appmt. of President Harding, Oct. 1922. Mem. Nat. Bd. of Incorporators, Am. Red Cross. Col. O.R.C. Elder Presbyn. Ch.; apptd. chmn. laymen com. Presbyn. Bd. Ministerial Relief and Sustentation, May 17, 1923; trustee Wabash Coll. Mason (33°, K.T., Shriner); K.P., Elk, Loyal Order of Moose. Clubs: Columbia, Indianapolis Athletic, Sullivan Rotary (hon.), Indianapolis Country (Ind.); Terre Haute (Ind.) Country; Ill. Athletic, Chicago Club, Indiana Soc. (Chicago); Metropolitan, Nat. Press, University (Washington, D.C.); Chevy Chase (Md.); Union League, Nat. Republican, Bankers, Chamber of Commerce Club, Friars, Advertising, Nat. Geographic, Economic, Hudson River Country, The Cloud, Sleepy Hollow Country, Rockefeller Center Luncheon, The Coffee House (New York); Lincoln, Hollywood Athletic, California Club, Bohemian (Calif.). Home: Sullivan, Ind. Office: 630 Fifth Av., N.Y.C. Died Mar. 7, 1954.

HAYWARD, Ralph A., mfr.; b. St. Clair, Mich., Apr. 16, 1895; s. George W. and Susan W. (Lowe) H.; B.S. in C.E., Univ. of Mich.; m. Marion MacGregor, Oct. 6, 1917. Began with Peninsular Paper Co. in 1916, and in 1917 joined the Spanish River Pulp & Paper Co.; assoc. with R. B. Wolf Co., as cons. engr., 1919-23; prof. chem. engineering U. of Mich.; vice pres., dir. Kalamazoo Vegetable Parchment Co., 1924-36, pres., dir. since 1936; pres. The KVP Co., Ltd., Espanola, Ont., KVP Co. of Texas, Houston, Tex.; chmn. bd., Appleford Paper Products, Hamilton, Ont., Harvey Paper Products, Sturgis, Mich. Served in Ordnance Dept., U.S. Army, World War I. Dir. Mich. Bell Telephone Co., Sutherland Paper Co., First Nat. Bank & Trust Co. (both Kalamazoo). Trustee, Kalamazoo Coll., Kalamazoo, Mich.; mem. bd. of Regents, U. of Mich. Clubs: Gull Lake Yacht, Kiwanis Detroit; Chemists (New York); Lake Shore (Chicago). Home: 315 Park Av. Office: Parchment (Kalamazoo Co.), Mich. Died Jan. 11, 1951; buried Riverside Cemetery, Kalamazoo, Mich.

HAYWARD, William Leete, clergyman; b. Morley, N.Y., Mar. 15, 1870; s. William Stone and Martha Jane (Avery) H.; grad. Nashotah Theol. Sem., Wis., 1893, B.D., 1894; unmarried. Ordered deacon, 1903, ordained priest, Episcopal Ch., 1894; asst., 1894-1906, vicar, Oct., 1906—, St. Elizabeth's Ch., Phila. Mem. Congregation of the Companions of the Holy Savior. Author: Obsequiale, or Rites or Burial of Dead, 1907 L4. Address: 1606 Mifflin St., Philadelphia. Deceased.

HAYWOOD, Allen S., labor orgn. exec. Vice pres. and dir. Congress Industrial Organizations. Address: 918 W. Rich St., Taylorville, Ill. Died Feb. 21, 1953; buried Oak Hill Cemetery, Taylorville.

HAYWOOD, Harry LeRoy, editor, author; b. Clermont County, O., Nov. 1, 1886; s. Newton Hutchinson and Alice Lauretta (Hughes) H.; rep. edn. Steele High Sch., Dayton, O.; student Bonebrake Theol. Sem., Dayton, 1906-07, Lawrence Coll., Appleton, Wis., 1908-09; m. Edith Agnes Shipley, Feb. 19, 1908; children—Ruth Ellen, Helen Naomi, Donald Newton. Pastor churches in Wis., Ind. and Ia., 1917-19; lectr. on lit. Grinnell (Ia.) Coll., 1919-20; editor The Builder, official jour. Nat. Masonic Research Soc., St. Louis, 1920-25; editor N.Y. Masonic Outlook, 1925-30; later writing for Grand Lodge N.Y. F. and A.M.; with Masonic History Co., Chgo., until 1944; now historian Cedar Rapids Masonic Library. Republican. Mason. Mem. Outer Circle Quatour Coronati Lodge, London. Author: Christian Mysticism, 1917; The Visitant (brochure), 1922; Symbolical Masonry, 1923; Great Teachings of Masonry, 1923; Am. Introduction to Masonry, 1926. Co-author: A History of Masonry (with J. E. Craig), 1927. Home: Cedar Rapids, Ia. Died 1955.

HAZARD, Daniel Lyman, magnetician; b. Narragansett Pier, R.I., Aug. 26, 1865; s. Thomas George and Mary King (Brooks) H.; student Brown U., 1880-81; A.B., Harvard, 1885. Bookkeeper and land surveyor until 1889; computer Mass. Topog. Survey Commn. on triangulation of Mass., 1889-92; apptd. computer U.S. Coast and Geod. Survey, 1892, later chief magnetician Div. Terrestrial Magnetism and Seismology until retirement, 1936. Fellow A.A.A.S.; mem. Am. Geophys. Union, Washington Acad. Sciences, Washington Soc. Engrs., Philos. Soc. Washington (pres. 1924). Unitarian. Club: Cosmos. Author: Directions for Magnetic Measurements, 1911, 31; The Earth's Magnetism, 1925; U.S. Magnetic Tables and Magnetic Charts for 1925, 1929. Contbr. to Jour. Terrestrial Magnetism, also article for Am. Year Book, 1915-19, 25-31. Editor of most of the publs. connected with magnetic work of the bur., 1908-35. Home: Narragansett, R.I. Died Sept. 21, 1951.

HAZARD, Henry Bernard, ret. asst. commr. Immigration and Naturalization Service; b. Washington, July 24, 1880; s. Hamilton Harvey and Lillie Eudora (Warder) H.; LL.B., U. Ore., 1916; LL.M., American U., 1923, D.C.L., 1925; m. Ettie Louise Thompson, December 14, 1904; married 2d, Sally MacLeod Dallas, June 2, 1953. Admitted to Ore. bar, 1916, U.S. Supreme Court, 1920; at Seattle in U.S. Dept. of Justice, 1908-09, Dept. of Commerce and Labor, 1909-13; naturalization examiner in charge Dept. of Labor, Portland, Ore., 1913-18, later chief naturalization examiner Phila.; chief examiner in charge of citizenship tng. Bur. of Naturalization, 1918-25, atty., 1925-28, chief counsel 1928-33, chief atty. and asst. to commr. of immigration and naturalization, 1933-39; dir. research, information and edn. Immigration and Naturalization Service, 1939-43, dir. research and ednl. services, 1943-47; asst. commr. for research and edn., 1947-49, ret.; rep. for adminstrv. naturalization overseas of members U.S. Army and Navy, 1943-45 (assimilated rank of col.). Decorated by Sec. of War, Medal of Freedom, 1946; recipient European-African-Middle East, Asiatic-Pacific civilian theater emblems. Mem. adv. bd. Nat. Citizenship Edn. Program, 1940-41. Adviser on nationality Harvard Law Sch., 1928-29; U.S. rep. com. on assistance to indigent foreigners, 1936-38, and adv. com. on social questions, 1937, League of Nations, Geneva; lectr. on internat. law, 1928-33; adj. prof. internat. law, 1933-34; adj. prof. polit. sci. Am. U. Grad. Sch., 1934-43. Mem. exec. bd. Nat. Council on Naturalization and Citizenship, Am. Fedn. Internat. Insts. Mem. Mass. Assn. Tchrs. Adults, Am. Soc. Internat. Law (mem. exec. council 1930-33, 38-41), Am. Assn. for Adult Edn., Pi Gamma Mu. Mason. Author: Operation Citizenship. Home: 81 Bearse Rd. Office: P.O. Box 448, Hyannis, Mass. Died Nov. 27, 1954; buried Beechwood Cemetery, Centerville, Mass.

HAZARD, Spencer Peabody, business exec.; b. London, Eng., Feb. 28, 1872 (parents U.S. citizens); s. Samuel and Blanche Crissy (Peabody) H.; student Germantown Acad., Phila., 1889; m. Serena Bluxome Hawley, June 1, 1918; children—Georgiana, Samuel. Clk. Pa. R.R., 1888; with R. D. Wood & Co., 1899-1934; pres., dir. R. D. Wood Co., 1934-47, now chmn.; chmn. Florence Pipe Foundry & Machine Co., 1947—. Trustee Germantown Acad. Mem. Mil. Order Loyal Legion. Republican. Episcopalian. Clubs: Union League, Philadelphia Cricket, Germantown Cricket. Home: 3009 Queen Lane, Phila. 29. Office: Public Ledger Bldg., Phila. 5. Died Oct. 22, 1957.

HAZARD, Willis Hatfield, clergyman, editor; b. West Chester, Pa., July 26, 1866; s. Willis Pope and Susan Robinson (Gilpin) H.; A.B., Haverford Coll., Pa., 1887; grad. Gen. Theol. Sem., 1891; grad. student U. of Pa., 1888, Columbia, 1891; A.M., Harvard (honors), 1892, Ph.D., 1894; m. Mary Dunbar Creigh, Nov. 14, 1898; children—Vincent Hatfield and Colton Dunbar (twins), Willis Gilpin. Deacon, 1891, priest, 1896, P.E. Ch.; rector Concord, Pa., 1895-98, Worcester, Mass., 1898; editorial writer on The Churchman, New York, 1899; editorial dept. D. Appleton & Co., 1900; dist. mgr. New England Mut. Life Ins. Co., 1904-15; editor New England Pilot and head of dept. of publs., N.E. Mut. Life Ins. Co.; retired as editor emeritus, Mar. 1, 1941. Asso. Victoria Inst. of Great Britain; mem. Am. Oriental Soc., Society Bibl. Lit. and Exegesis, Oriental Soc., A.A.A.S., Am. Acad. Polit. and Social Science, Business Hist. Society (Harvard), Foreign Policy Assn. (mem. council Boston br.); mem. bd. mgrs. Am. S.S. Union, Phila. Clubs: University, Harvard (Phila.); Harvard, Union, 20th Century, Appalachian Mountain, Classical Club of Greater Boston. Author of introduction to The Reasons for the Higher Criticism of the Hexateuch (by Rev. Isaac Gibson), 1897; The Fathers of Level Premium Mutual Life Insurance (historicocritical study). Contbr. to various revs. Outside lecturer on insurance, Grad. Sch. of Business Administration, Harvard. Home: 35 Greenough Av., Jamaica Plain 30. Office: 501 Boylston, Boston. Died Mar. 22, 1950; buried Oaklands Cemetery, West Chester, Pa.

HAZELTON, John H., lawyer; b. Boscobel, Wis., s. George Cochrane (M.C. from Wis.) and Ellen (Van Antwerp) H.; bro. of George Cochrane, Jr.; A.B., Johns Hopkins, 1893; LL.B., Columbian now George Washington) U., 1895; LL.M., 1896; m. Elizabeth Margaret Scholz, July 30, 1908; children—Hampden Thacher, Robert Cochrane (capt. in Mcht. Marine). Practiced in Washington, 1896-98, in New York, 1899—; asso. in practice with late Col. Robert G. Ingersoll. Author: The Declaration of Independence—Its History, 1906. Now writing a 4-vol. work on the Constitution of the U.S. Home: 688 Front St., Hempstead, L.I., N.Y. Died Dec. 20, 1957; buried Pinelawn (N.Y.) Cemetery.

HAZEN, Henry Honeyman, dermatologist; b. Oldwick, New Jersey, July 21, 1879; s. David Henry and Emma Louise (Honeyman) H.; A.B., Johns Hopkins, 1902, M.D., 1906; A.M., Georgetown University, 1925; Dr. Science, Howard University, 1944; m. (Miss) Laura Mae Ross, June 1, 1908 (dec.); m. 2d, Anita Burt, July 20, 1922; 1 son, Henry H. Began practice at Washington, 1908; prof. dermatology, Howard U., 1911-44; same, Georgetown U., 1913-34; cons. dermatologist, U.S. Pub. Health Service, since 1926 (com. for evaluation of serodiagnostic tests for syphilis), spl. cons., U.S.P.H.S., since 1918; dir. post-grad. course in venereal disease control, Howard U., 1937-42; attending physician, D.C. Health Dept., 1942-46; cons. syphilol., D.C. Health Dept.; chmn. Nat. Prophylactic Com.; pres. Social Hygiene Soc. of Dist. of Columbia; chmn. advisory com. on public edn. for the prevention of venereal diseases, U.S.P.H.S., since 1943. Certified by Am. Bd. Dermatol. and Syphilol., 1939. Fellow A.M.A.; member Am. Dermatol. Assn., Am. Roentgen Ray Soc., Social Hygiene Soc. of D.C. (pres., 1937-45), Am. Social Hygiene Assn. (hon. life). Club: Cosmos. Author: Diseases of the Skin, 1915, 3d ed., 1927; Skin Cancer, 1916; Syphilis, 1919, 2d ed., 1928; Cutaneous X-ray and Radium Therapy, 1931; Syphilis in the Negro, 1942. Contbr. to Jour. A.M.A., Archive of Dermatology and Syphilology, Am. Jour. of Syphilis, Am. Jour. Roentgenology. Home: 3708 Ingomar St., Washington 15. Died May 1, 1951.

HAZLETT, Samuel M., lawyer; b. Harrison Twp., Allegheny Co., Pa., Aug. 24, 1879; s. John M. and Ella (Kelly) H.; A.B., Waynesburg Coll., 1901; Litt.D. (hon.), 1939; m. Mary E. Baxter, Aug. 12, 1902; children—Helen (Mrs. Norman Jacobs), Howard J., Samuel M. Began career as sch. teacher, Tarentum, Pa., 1901; admitted to bar, 1907, and since in practice of law, Pittsburgh, Pa.; pres. Chautauqua (N.Y.) Reorganization Corp., to re-finance Chautauqua Instn., 1933-36, trustee and chmn. exec. bd., Chautauqua Institution, 1937-45, exec. v.p., 1941-45, pres. since 1945. Dir. Tarentum (Pa.) Sch. District, Tarentum Y.M.C.A., active in fund campaigns for Y.M.C.A. and Allegheny Valley Hosp. Presbyterian. Republican. Mason. Home: 321 E. 10th Av., Tarentum, Pa. Office: 708 Park Bldg., Pitts. 22. Died July 23, 1956; buried Prospect Cemetery, Brackenridge, Pa.

HAZLEWOOD, Craig Beebe, banker; b. East Aurora, N.Y., May 7, 1883; s. Clarence Stephen and Ora (Beebe) H.; grad. Lewis Inst., Chicago, 1902; student Univ. of Chicago 1 yr.; m. Estelle Neighbors, Dec. 18, 1912 (died 1935); children—Dorothy A. (Mrs. John Bainbridge), Ora Jean (Mrs. Richard Widmark) Craig B.; m. 2d, Ruth S. Copeland, July 18, 1943. Began with Union Trust Co., Chicago, 1904, v.p., 1917-29; v.p. First National Bank, 1929-37. Member American Bankers Association (1st v.p. 1927-28; pres. 1928-29), Reserve City Bankers Assn. (pres. 1923-24), Bankers Club of Chicago (pres. 1923-24). Trustee Lewis Inst. (now Ill. Inst. Tech.), Chgo. Republican. Home: 222 E. Chestnut St., Chgo. 11. Office: 38 S. Dearborn St., Chgo. Died June 25, 1953; buried Meml. Park Cemetery, Evanston, Ill.

HEAD, Walter William, life insurance exec.; b. on farm near Adrian, Ill., Dec. 18, 1877; s. Alfred Walter and Margaret Jane (Lambert) H.; educated normal school and business college; LL.D., Hastings Coll., 1927, Park Coll., 1950; m. Della Thompson, Mar. 7, 1900; 1 dau., Audrey Vernelle (Mrs. Raymond A. Baur). Prin. pub. schs., De Kalb, Mo., 1901-02 and 1903; cashier De Kalb State Bank, 1903-06; nat. and state bank examiner, 1906-08; cashier Am. Nat. Bank, St. Joseph, Mo., 1908-17; v.p. Omaha Nat. Bank, 1917-20, pres. 1920-29; pres. State Bank of Chicago, 1929, Foreman-State Nat. Bank, 1929-31; pres. Morris Plan Corp. of America, 1931-33; pres. Gen. Am. Life Ins. Co., St. Louis, 1933-51, chmn. board directors since 1951. Member board corporators. Presbyterian Ministers Fund for Life Insurance, Phila.; member Nebraska State Capitol Commission (having charge constrn. of $10,000,000 bldg.). Pres. National Council Boy Scouts of America, 1926-46 (hon. life v.p.); state chairman Missouri War Finance Com., 1942-46; chmn. Citizens Com. for Postwar Improvements and Employment in St. Louis, 1944-49; pres. St. Louis U.S.O. Council, and state chmn., U.S.O., for Mo., 1941-47; served as chmn. St. Louis Civilian Aides Com., appointment and procurement div., Army Air Forces, 1942; chmn. Anti-Slum Commn. of St. Louis, 1946-49; trustee Pub. Sch. Retirement System, St. Louis; dir. Nat. Comn. for Boys and Girls Club Work, St. Louis Crime Commn.; mem. met. bd. Y.M.C.A.; mem. nat. bd. dirs. Nat. Conf. Christians and Jews; trustee Lindenwood Female Coll. St. Charles, Mo., Am. Heritage Found., Governmental Research Inst., Westminster Coll., Fulton, Mo. Mem. American Geographical Soc., Am. Civic Assn., Am. Peace Soc., Pan-Am. Soc., Acad. Polit. Science; pres. Am. Bankers Assn., 1923-24. Mason (32°, Shriner). Clubs: Racquet, Noonday, Bogey Golf (St. Louis); St. Joseph (Mo.) Country. Home: 4931 Lindell Blvd. Office: 1501 Locust St., St. Louis. Died May 3, 1954.

HEADLEY, Cleon, lawyer; b. Fairmont, Minn., Nov. 14, 1887; s. Charles Wesley and Sara (Sherman) H.; B.S., Beloit (Wis.) Coll., 1909; LL.B., Harvard, 1914; m. Gertrude Knight, Dec. 10, 1917; children—David K., Richard K., Beth. Admitted to N.Y. bar, 1915; asso. Elkus, Gleason & Proskauer, N.Y. City, 1914-16; admitted to Minn. bar, 1917 and since practiced in St. Paul; mem. Morgan, Headley, Raudenbush & Morgan and predecessor firms since 1923. Pres. St. Paul Community Chest, 1943-44; mem. bd. Minn. div. Am. Cancer Soc. Served as capt., U.S. Army Inf., World War I. Mem. Am., Minn. State and Ramsey Co. (pres. 1937-38) bar assns. Clubs: Minnesota, Athletic (St. Paul). Home: 1173 Davern St., St. Paul 5. Office: First Nat. Bank Bldg, St. Paul 1. Died Jan. 1, 1954.

HEADLEY, John William, coll. pres.; b. Filley, Neb., May 5, 1901; s. Fidelis F. and Nancy Elizabeth (Daugherty) H.; B.A., Gen. Beadle State Tchrs. Coll., 1931; M.A., Colo. State Coll. Edn., Greeley, 1934, Ed.D., 1941; m. Leona Lorraine Erickson, Nov. 20, 1926; 1 son, John William. Tchr., athletic coach Jr. High Sch., Garden City, Hayti, Bryant, S.D., 1921-29; biology lab. asst. Gen. Beadle State Tchrs. Coll., 1929-31, dir. spl. services div., 1938-45; supt. of schs., Colman, S.D., 1931-35, Winner, S.D., 1935-38; pres. State Tchrs. Coll., Mayville, N.D., 1945-47; pres. State Tchrs. Coll., St. Cloud, Minn., 1947-51, S.D. State Coll. Agr. and Mech. Arts, 1952—; dir. curriculum revision and research com. State Dept. Pub. Instrn., Pierre, S.D., 1940-42. With USN, attached to recruiting service, 1942-45. Member S.D. Secondary Sch. Principals (pres. 1937), S.D. Sch. Adminstrs. (pres. 1938), S.D. Deans of Edn. (pres. 1941), S.D. Congress Parents and Tchrs. (state legislation chmn. 1940-42), S.D. Ednl. Assn. (mem. research com.), N.D. Congress Parents and Tchrs. (state chmn. cooperation with colls. 1946), Nat. Congress Parents and Tchrs. (treas.), Nat. Commn. on Safety Edn., Am. Legion, Phi Delta Kappa, Pi Kappa Delta, Delta Psi Omega. Mason. Club: Kiwanis. Editor course of study for elementary grades of S.D., 1940-42; contbr. articles on ednl. methods and finance to profl. jours. Home: 929 Tenth St., Brookings. Office: S.D. State Coll., College Station, S.D. Died Nov., 1957.

HEADLEY, Roy, forester; b. Sangamon County, Ill., Dec. 21, 1878; s. Edwin Ray and Minnie (Ridgeway) H.; ed. pub. schs.; prep. dept. U. Ida.; m. Rose St. Clair, Jan. 1, 1907; 1 son, Robert St. Clair. Farmer, logger, teamster, Ida., 1897-1901; timber cruiser, 1901-07; forest ranger, forest supr., Ida., Mont., 1907-09; asst. regional forester, Cal. region, 1909-17, in charge region, 1917-19; asst. forester, in charge bus. mgmt. personnel, fire control Forest Service, U.S. Dept. Agr., 1919-35, chief Div. Forest Fire Control, 1935-42; now ret. Mem. Soc. Am. Foresters. Home: 2934 Chesapeake St., Washington 8. Died Jan. 31, 1951; buried Moscow (Ida.) Cemetery.

HEAL, Gilbert B(urmester), editor; b. Eureka, Utah, Apr. 28, 1887; s. Edwin Lewis and Mollie (Finch) H.; ed. pub. schs.; m. Frankie Leyshon, Oct. 5, 1913; children—Edwin Lewis, James Patrick. Began as reporter Salt Lake Herald-Republican, 1910; city editor Ogden Standard Examiner, 1911-12, Salt Lake Telegram, 1912-14; mng. editor, later editor Salt Lake Herald-Republican, 1914-20; mng. editor Salt Lake Tribune, 1927-29, editor 1930—. Mem. Salt Lake City C. of C. Home: 803 4th Av. Address: Salt Lake Tribune, Salt Lake City. Died Feb. 8, 1951.

HEALD, Frederick De Forest, botanist; b. Midland City, Mich., July 23, 1872; s. Henry Francis and Hettie (Charles) H.; grad. prep. dept. U. S.D., 1891, B.S., U. Wis., 1894, fellow in botany, 1894-96, M.S., 1896; Ph.D., U. Leipzig, 1897; m. Nellie Townley, Dec. 27, 1899 (died 1939); children—Doris Adelaide, Henry Townley, Marian Rosey; m. 2d, Mrs. Charlotte Chamberlin, Nov. 5, 1942. Prof. biology Parsons Coll., Fairfield, Ia., 1897-1903; adj. prof. plant physiology U. Neb., 1903-06; asso. prof. botany, botanist, Neb. Expt. Sta., 1905-06; prof. agrl. botany, botanist, Neb. Expt. Sta., 1906-08; head botany U. Tex., 1908-12; pathologist Pa. Chestnut Tree Blight Commn. U. Pa., agent in forest pathology U.S. Dept. Agr., 1912-14; prof. plant pathology, Wash. State Coll., and plant pathologist Wash. State Expt. Sta., 1915-17; head dept. plant pathology, Wash. State Coll., Pullman, Wash., 1917-41, prof. emeritus, 1941—. Collaborator, 1905-08, 15, expert, 1909-10, Bur. Plant Industry, Washington; state botanist, Neb., and asso. chief Neb. State Insect Pest and Plant Disease Bur., 1907-08. Spl. research work in plant physiol. and pathol.; asso. editor Phytopathology, 1911-16, 19-21, 31-33. Fellow A.A.A.S.; mem. Bot. Soc. Am., Am. Phytopathol. Soc., Am. Forestry Assn., Am. Micros. Soc. (pres. 1912), Wash. Hort. Assn., N.W. Sci. Assn. (sec. 1923-26), Sigma Xi, Phi Beta Kappa, Phi Kappa Phi, Alpha Zeta, Phi Sigma; sec. Neb. Acad. Sciences, 1904-06. Conglist. Republican. Author: Revision of Analytic Keys to Genera and Species of North American Mosses, by C. R. Barnes, 1897; Laboratory Manual in Elementary Biology, 1902; Symptoms of Disease in Plants, 1909; Experiments in Plant Physiology (with I. M. Lewis), 1910; Manual of Plant Disease, 1926, 2d edit., 1932; Introduction to Plant Pathology, 1937, 2d edit., 1943; Bunt or Stinking Smut of Wheat, a World Problem (with C. S. Holton), 1941; also Neb., Tex. and Wash. agrl. expt. sta. bulls. and reports. Editor Plant Pathology and Mycology, Webster's New Internat. Dictionary, 2d edit., 1935. Contbr. to bot. mags. 1894—, cyclopedias. Address: 312 Howard St., Pullman, Wash. Died Apr. 24, 1954; buried Riverside Park Mausoleum, Spokane, Wash.

HEANEY, John William (hē'nē), lawyer; b. San Francisco, Calif., Jan. 14, 1891; s. William Peter and Mary L. (Hayes) H.; LL.B., University of Calif., 1913; m. Matilde A. Coffield, December 17, 1917 (div.); children—Sally, John William; m. 2d Viola C. Glaister, Jan. 17, 1949. Admitted to California bar, 1913 and practiced in San Francisco, 1913-15, in Santa Barbara since 1915; founder Richards, Carrier & Heaney, now Heaney, Price, Postel & Parma; director First Nat. Trust & Savings Bank. Served in Batt. C, 144th F.A., Sept. 1917; 1st lt. May 1918; capt., Sept. 1918; hon. disch. Dec. 1918. Rep. U.S. Army on Lumber Commodity Com., War Prodn. Bd. Chmn. com. to restore St. Francis Hosp., destroyed in 1925; chmn. advisory com. on restoration Santa Barbara Mission destroyed in 1925. Attended joint meeting British-Canadian-Am. Bar, London, 1924. Mem. Am., Nev. State and Santa Barbara County bar assns., State Bar of Calif., bar of U.S. Supreme Court. Mem. Am. Legion, Phi Alpha Delta. Republican. Clubs: Valley (charter mem.), Santa Barbara, (hon. mem.). Home: 2441 Garden St., Santa Barbara, Cal. Died Aug. 12, 1953; buried Santa Barbara Cemetery.

HEANEY, Noble Sproat, (hā'nē), physician; b. Mendon, Ill., May 8, 1880; s. Samuel William and Ettie May (Sproat) H.; A.B., U. of Chicago, 1903; M.D., Rush Med. Coll., 1904; assistant in University Frauenklinik, Heidelberg, 1907, Vienna, 1908; m. Floyd Chamberlin, Oct. 1, 1908 (divorced 1947); children—Susan Eleanor, Ruth Alice, Noble Sproat, Samuel Willis; m. 2d, Ruth Ainsworth, June 26, 1948. Emeritus Rush prof. obstetrics and gynecol., U. of Ill. Med. Coll.; cons. gynecol. to Hollywood Presbyterian Hospital, Cedars of Lebanaon Hospital, Los Angeles, Calif. Fellow Am. College Surgeons; mem. A.M.A., American Gynecol. Soc., Chicago Gynecol. Soc., Chicago Inst. Med. Pacific Slope Obstet. and Gynecol. Soc. Club: University (Chicago). Home: 435 S. Curson Av. W., Los Angeles 6. Office: 9730 Wilshire Blvd., Beverly Hills, Cal. Died Sept. 26, 1955.

HEARST, John Randolph, publisher; b. N.Y.C., Sept. 26, 1909; s. William Randolph and Millicent (Willson) H.; student Oglethorpe U., 1927-28; 1 son by former marriage John Randolph, m. Fanne Wade, Nov. 5, 1938; children—Joanne (Mrs. John Herndon), William Randolph, II. Deborah. Asst. to pub. Atlanta Georgian, 1927; asso. editor Cosmopolitan Mag. and Photoplay, 1928; pres. Harpers Bazaar-Cosmopolitan Book Corp., 1929-31; gen. mgr. Hearst Radio, 1931-34; v.p., asst. gen. mgr. Internat. Mag. Corp., 1931-32; pub. N.Y. Daily Mirror, 1932-34; pres. N.Y. Eve. Jour., 1936-37; asst. gen. mgr. Hearst Newspapers since 1941. Clubs: Montauk Yacht (vice commodore 1936-37), Metropolitan; Southampton Yacht, Shinnecock Hills Golf Club. Home: 61 East 80th St., N.Y.C. 21. Office: 959 Eighth Av., N.Y.C. 19. Died Nov. 13, 1958.

HEARST, William Randolph, newspaper pub. and editor; b. San Francisco, Apr. 29, 1863; s. George (U.S. senator) and Phoebe (Apperson) H.; student Harvard, 1882-85; LL.D., Oglethorpe, 1927; m. Millicent Willson, Apr. 28, 1903. Editor and propr. of San Francisco Examiner, Los Angeles Examiner, Los Angeles Herald and Express, Chicago Herald-American, Boston American, Boston Sunday Advertiser, Boston Record, New York Journal-American, New York Mirror, Albany Times Union, Baltimore Sunday American, Baltimore News-Post, Pittsburgh Sun-Telegraph, Detroit Times, Seattle Post-Intelligencer, San Francisco Call-Bulletin, Oakland Post-Enquirer, San Antonio Light, Milwaukee Sentinel; Hearst's Cosmopolitan, Good Housekeeping, Harper's and Junior Bazaars, Motor, Motor Boating Mag., Am. Druggist, Town and Country, House Beautiful; editor, propr. Good Housekeeping (London); Connoisseur inc. with Internat. Studio, Harper's Bazaar inc. with Vanity Fair. Elected to 58th and 59th Congresses (1903-07) 11th N.Y. Dist. Democrat. Candidate for mayor New York, on municipal ownership ticket, 1905, on Independent League ticket, 1909, for gov. N.Y., 1906, on Independent League and Dem. tickets. Home: Beverly Hills, Died Aug. 14, 1951; buried Cypress Lawn Cemetery, Colma, Cal.

HEATH, Edwin Joseph, clergyman, educator; b. St. Jan, Danish West Indies, Dec. 27, 1880; s. George Octavius and Charlotte Elizabeth (Reinke) H.; prep. edn., Fulneck Sch., Leeds, Eng.; A.B., Moravian Coll., Bethlehem, Pa., 1904, A.M., 1916, LL.D., 1942; B.D., Moravian Theol. Sem., 1907; D.D., Ursinus Coll., 1930; m. Mabel Mary Graham, Oct. 17, 1908; children—Barbara Mary (Mrs. J. J. H. Drury), Edwin Clifford, Marian Graham. Came to U.S., 1901, naturalized, 1924. Ordained ministry Moravian Ch., 1904; supt. Moravian mission, Trinidad, B.W.I., 1907-11; pastor St. John's Ch., Antigua, B.W.I., 1911-14; also warden Antigua mission, and dir. Tchrs. Tng. Coll., Antigua, 1911-14; exec. sec. Salem Acad. and Coll., Winston-Salem, N.C., 1914-26; pastor Immanuel Ch., Winston-Salem, 1915-20; head of history dept. Salem Coll., 1914-26; pres. Moravian Sem. and College for Women, Bethlehem, 1926-49, pres. emeritus, 1949—. Mem. Am. Hist. Soc., Moravian Hist. Soc., Am. Acad. Polit. and Social Science, Newcomen Soc., Nat.. Assn. Bibl. Instrs., Pa. Assn. Colls. and Univs. Democrat. Rotarian. Home: 310 Trenton Blvd., Sea Girt, N.J. Died Oct. 24, 1953; buried Nisky Hill Cemetery, Bethlehem, Pa.

HEATH, Fred H(arvey), chemist; b. Warner, N.H., Feb. 25, 1883; s. Benjamin Franklin and Julia Augusta (Wadleigh) H.; B.S., U. of N.H., 1905; Ph.D., Yale, 1909; grad. student U. of Marburg, Germany, 1909; m. Winnifred A. Grant, Apr. 20, 1911 (died 1918); 1 son, Frank Harvey; m. 2d, Mrs. Ida M. Erickson, Sept. 7, 1921 (died 1928); m. 3d, Mrs. Errah Shannon Schindler, June 8, 1932. In chem. analysis of waters and water problem research N.D. State Biol. Station, 1914-16; investigation on platinum ores of Washington, 1921-22; invented seleniam mustard gas, 1918. Instr. phys. chemistry Mass. Inst. Tech., 1909-10; instr. gen. chemistry Case Sch. of Applied Sci., 1910-11; instr. Wesleyan U. Conn., 1911-12; instr. and asst. prof. U. of N.D., 1912-17; asst. prof. U. of Washington, 1917-23; prof. U. of Fla. since 1923. Gas consultant to Fla. Defense Council, World War II, reserve officer Chem. Corps since 1924. Mem. several years of com. on examinations, div. of chem. edn., Am. Chem. Soc. Mem. Am. Chem. Soc. (pres. Puget Sound sect., 1919; sec. Florida sect. 1924-26, pres. 1943), Fla. Acad. Sci., Alpha Chi Sigma, Phi Lambda Upsilon, Gamma Sigma Epsilon. Democrat. Baptist. Mason. Club: Rotary (Gainesville). Author: Laboratory Manual of Quantitative Analysis, 1910, 1921-22, Laboratory Manual of General Chemistry (with W. H. Beisler), 1926, 1934, General Chemistry Text Book (with others), 1926, 2d edit., 1927. Contbr. chem. research articles to professional jours. Special work in photography. Home: 561 N.E. 7th Av., Gainesville, Fla. Died Jan. 26, 1952.

HEATH, Harold, zoölogist; b. Vevay, Ind., June 5, 1868; s. Charles Wesley and Sarah Ann (Cowgill) H.; A.B., Ohio Wesleyan U., 1893, Sc.D., 1919; Ph.D., U. Pa., 1898; m. Elsie Hjerleid Shelley, May 13, 1897; children—Ronald Wayland, Phyllis Thoburn, Sivert H. (dec.), James Procter. Asst. in biology Ohio Wesleyan, 1891-93; prof. biology U. of Pacific, 1893-94; instr. zoölogy Stanford, 1894-98, asst. prof., 1898-1904, asso. prof., 1904-09, prof., 1909-33, now emeritus. Mem. Ohio Wesleyan U. expdn. to Fla., 1890; naturalist, U.S. Fish Commn. Str. Albatross, 1904, exploration Cal. coast, summer, 1905, Japanese expdn., summer, 1906; naturalist on Pribilof Islands, summers 1910, 17; zoölogist, Stanford expdn. to Brazil, summer 1911; naturalist on Forrester Island, Alaska, summer 1913. Fellow Cal. Acad. Sci.; mem. Am. Soc. Zoölogists, A.A.A.S., Western Soc. Naturalists, Phi Beta Kappa, Sigma Xi. Home: care Hopkins Marine Station, Pacific Grove, Cal. Died Apr. 22, 1951.

HEATON, Arthur B., architect; b. Washington, D.C., Nov. 12, 1875; s. Francis M. and Mabel (Berthrong) H.; ed. pub. schs., Washington, D.C.; m. Mabel Williams, Oct. 1, 1902; children—Doris (Mrs. Charles M. Nash), James. Engaged in practice as architect, Washington, D.C., since 1900; supervising architect, Washington Cathedral, during first 13 yrs. of its construction. Served in construction div., U.S. Army during World War I. Fellow Am. Inst. Architects. Mem. bd. Equitable Co-operative Bldg. Assn., Washington Bldg. Congress. Clubs: Cosmos, Columbia Country (Washington). Home: 3041 Sedgwick St. N.W., Washington, D.C. Office: 1211-A Connecticut Av. N.W., Washington 6. Died Dec. 6, 1951; buried Rock Creek Cemetery, Washington.

HEATON, Harry Clifton, educator; b. Waterbury, Conn., Mar. 21, 1885; s. Thomas and Grace Higby (Benham) H.; B.A., Yale, 1907; studied U. Paris, 1907-10; Ph.D., Columbia, 1916; m. Andrée Thomas, Aug. 3, 1920; m. 2d, Fritsa Hansen Miller, June 24, 1939. With N.Y.U., 1910—, instr. in French until 1916, asst. prof. Romance langs., 1916-22, asso. prof. Spanish, 1922-26, asso. prof. Romance langs., 1926-27, prof., 1927—, head of dept., 1926—. Served with Am. YMCA in France, 1918-19; with Army Ednl. Corps as asst. to Am. dean at U. of Paris, 1919. Mem. Modern Lang. Assn. Am., Am. Assn. Tchrs. of Spanish, Phi Beta Kappa; corr. mem. Hispanic Soc. Am., Real Academia Espanola (Madrid). Officer d'Académie Instruction Publique (France). Conglist. Club: Faculty (N.Y.U.). Editor The Gloria d'amor of Fra Rocaberti, 1916; El Ingrato agradecido by Juan de Matos Fragoso, 1926. Editor and co-translator of The Discovery of the Amazon, by José Toribio Medina, 1934; contbr. to philol. jours. Home: 288 Pennsylvania Av., Crestwood, Yonkers, via Tuckahoe 7, N.Y. Died Dec. 28, 1950; buried Valley View Cemetery, Dover Plains, N.Y.

HEATON, Lucia Elizabeth, physician; b. Canton, N.Y., June 18, 1856; d. Ira Wilmarth and Lucinda (Langdon) Heaton; B.S., St. Lawrence U., 1879, M.S., 1882; M.D., Woman's Med. Coll., N.Y. Infirmary, 1892; post-grad. courses, N.Y. Polyclinic and N.Y. Post-Grad. Med. Sch. Gen. practice 1892-1920. Trustee St. Lawrence U. Mem. N.Y. State Med. Assn., Woman's Med. Assn. N.Y. State, also of N.Y. City, St. Lawrence County Med. Assn., Phi Beta Kappa, Kappa Kappa Gamma. Patrons of Husbandry. Universalist. Extension lectr. Coll. of Agr., Cornell U. Home: Canton, N.Y. Deceased.

HÉBRARD, Jean (ā-brär'), educator; b. Paris, France, Dec. 31, 1878; s. Jean and Caroline (Jacki) H.; student Ecole des Beaux-Arts, Paris, 1897-1904; Architecté diplomé, govt. of France, 1903; m. Karoline Syren, June 15, 1931. Prof. arthitecture Cornell U., 1907-11; practicing architect, Paris, 1911-26; prof. architecture U. Pa., 1926-31, U. Mich., 1931-39, emeritus, 1939—. Served as lt., inf. French Army, World War I. Decorated Croix de Guerre; awarded Gold Medal, Salon des Artistes Francais, 1903. Fellow A.I.A.; mem. Am. Soc. Planning Ofcls., Société des Architectes Diplomés par le gouvernement, France, Tau Sigma Delta, Alpha Rho Chi. Author: A World Center of Communication (with Henrick C. Anderson and Ernest Hébrard), 1913. Address: 596 Kuehnle Av., Ann Arbor, Mich. Died Feb. 20, 1959.

HECHT, David Stanford, lawyer; b. N.Y.C., Feb. 6, 1908; s. Samuel and Mary (Kaplan) H.; B.S., Coll. City of N.Y., 1927; LL.B., Columbia, 1930; m. Alyce L. McDonough, Dec. 12, 1949; children—David Stanford, Anthony McDonough. Admitted to N.Y. bar, 1931; asso. Chadbourne, Stanchfield & Levy, 1930-36; partner Hecht, Hadfield, Farbach & McAlpin (predecessor firms), 1937—; asst. gen. counsel Lend-Lease Adminstrn., 1943; v.p., dir., gen. counsel Hotel Pierre, N.Y.C.; dir., v.p., gen. counsel Mission Development Corp., Wilmington, Del.; dir. Parke-Bernet Galleries, Inc., N.Y.C., Thiokol Corp., Trenton, N.J.; v.p., dir., Pacwest Realty Corp., N.Y.C.; dir. Tide Water Oil Co., San Francisco, Pacific Western (Iran), Ltd. Trustee The Paul Getty Mus. Mem. Judge Adv. Generals Assn., Am. Bar Assn., Bar Assn. City of N.Y. Clubs: Southampton; Lawyers (N.Y.C.). Home: 2 E. 61st St., N.Y.C. 21. Office: 11 Broadway, N.Y.C. 4. Died July 1959.

HECHT, Julius Lawrence, pub. service official; b. Chicago, Ill., May 6, 1881; B.S., Mass. Inst. Tech., 1904; m. Irene M. C. King, Feb. 28, 1905; children—Lawrence Charles, Kenneth George, Rene Mary King. Began with North Shore Electric Co. (a predecessor of Pub. Service Co. of Northern Ill.), 1905; v.p in charge operations Pub. Service Co. of Northern Ill., 1923-53; retired, 1953. Member Am. Inst. E.E., Western Soc. Engrs. (pres. 1922-23), Nat. Dist. Heating Assn. (pres. 1920-21). Episcopalian. Mason. Home: Wilmette, Ill. Office: 72 W. Adams St., Chgo. Died June 9, 1955; buried Memorial Park Cemetery, Skokie, Ill.

HECHT, Moses S., business exec. Chairman and dir. Hecht Co. Home: 7310 Park Heights Av., Baltimore 13. Office: Baltimore and Pine Sts., Baltimore 1. Died Jan. 6, 1954.

HECHT, Rudolf S., banker; b. Ansbach, Germany, June 3, 1885; ed. in Germany; m. Lynne, d. late Judge Linn Boyd Watkins, 1911. Came to U.S., 1903; with Nat. Bank of the Republic, Chgo., 1903-05, Comml. Nat. Bank, 1905-06; asst. fgn. exchange mgr. Hibernia Bank & Trust Co. (now Hibernia Nat. Bank), New Orleans, 1906, promoted through various offices to pres., 1918, chmn. bd. 1933-45, now retired; mng. partner R. S. Hecht & Co., investment bankers; chmn. Miss. Shipping Co.; dir. Wesson Oil & Snowdrift Co., So. Cotton Oil Co., Hemisphere Internat. Corp. Pres., life mem. Bd. Liquidation City Debt (New Orleans); pres. Bd. Port Commrs., 1921-28. Pres. Am. Bankers Assn., 1934-35; chmn. bd. Internat. House (New Orleans); chmn. Thos. F. Cunningham Library; chmn. exec. com. Internat. Trade Mart, Cordell Hull Found. Internat. Edn.; vice chmn. Inter-Am. Council Commerce and Prodn.; dir. Nat. Fgn. Trade Council; trustee Internat. C. of C. Recipient Times-Picayune loving cup, 1922, Thomas F. Cunningham cup, 1948. Clubs: Pickwick, Country. Home: 16 Audubon Pl., New Orleans. Died Jan. 18, 1956; buried Trinity Episcopal Church Cemetery, Pass Christian, Miss.

HECK, Nicholas Hunter, hydrog. and geodetic engr.; b. Heckton Mills, Pa., Sept. 1, 1882; s. John Lewis and Mary Frances (Hays) H.; B.A., Lehigh, 1903, C.E., 1904. D.Sc., 1929; D.Sc., Fordham University, New York, N.Y., 1941. With U.S. Coast Survey, 1904-45; in charge wire drag parties, Atlantic Coast, 1906-16, comdr. schooner Mathlcess, 1917; lt. and lt. comdr. USNRF, New London, Conn., London, Eng., 1917-19, in charge location of submerged forest in Lake Washington, nr. Seattle, 1919-20; comdr. steamer Explorer, 1920-21; chief div. geomagnetism and seismology Coast and Geodetic Survey, 1921-42, asst. to dir., 1942 45, ret. 1945. Recipient William Bowie medal, Am. Geophys. Union, 1942. Fellow A.A.A.S., Am. Geog. Soc., Philos. Soc. Washington (pres. 1938), Washington Soc. Engrs., Wash. Acad. Sci., Am. Geophys. Union (chmn. 1935-38), Geol. Soc. Am.; mem. Am. Soc. C.E., Geol. Soc. Washington, Seismol. Soc. Am. (pres. 1936-39), Soc. Am. Mil. Engrs., Internat. Seismol. Assn. (pres. 1936-45), Tau Beta Pi, Phi Beta Kappa, Sigma Xi. Presbyn. Club: Cosmos. Author: Earthquakes; also govt. publs. concerning wire drag and sweep work of Coast and Geodetic Survey; compensation of the magnetic compass; velocity of sound in sea water; radio acoustic method of determining position in hydrography; earthquake history of U.S. and articles relating to magnetism and seismology. Home: 3421 Northampton St., Washington 15. Died Dec. 21, 1953; buried Arlington Nat. Cemetery.

HECK, Robert Culbertson Hays, mechanical engr.; b. Heckton Mills, Pa., Oct. 30, 1870; s. John Lewis and Mary Frances (Hays) H.; M.E., Lehigh U., 1893, hon. D.Eng., 1927; m Anna Wilson, Sept. 10, 1902; children—Margaret Wilson, Robert C. H., Mary Hays. Instr. mech. engring., 1893-1903, asst. prof., 1903-07, prof. exptl. engring., 1907-08, Lehigh U.; prof. mech. engring., Rutgers Coll., 1908-35, research prof. of mechanical engring., 1935-41, now emeritus, but teaching Army spl. training students, 1943. Republican. Presbyn. Fellow A.A.A.S.; mem. Am. Soc. Mech. Engrs., 1906, Soc. Promotion Engring. Edn., Nat. Research Council (1932-37), Tau Beta Pi, Phi Beta Kappa, Sigma Xi. Author: Notes to Supplement Holmes' Steam Engine, 1902; Manual for Course in Engineering Laboratory, Lehigh Univ., 1903; The Steam Engine and other Steam Motors, Vol. I, 1905, Vol. II, 1907; Notes on Elementary Kinematics, 1910; Notes on the Graphics of Machine Forces, 1910; The Steam Engine and Turbine, 1911; Steam Formulas, 1920; Mechanics of Machinery—Mechanism, Kinematics and Dynamics, 1925; Ideal Combustion-Engine Cycles, 1926; New Specific Heats, 1940. Home: 51 Adelaide Av., New Brunswick, N.J. Died Sept. 22, 1951; buried Riverview Cemetery, Heckton, Pa.

HECKERT, John Walter, educator; b. Germany, Jan. 21, 1872; s. August and Emilie H.; came to U.S., 1887; Ph.B., Hamline U., 1900; A.M., Columbia, 1905, Ph.D., 1917; m. Winifred Esther Yahn, June 13, 1901; children—Winfield Walter, Donald Henry, Dorothy Winifred, Richard Edwin. Supt. schs., Excelsior, Minn., 1900-01, Renville, 1901-04; tchr. edn. and prin. Model Sch., La. State Normal Sch., Natchitoches, La., 1906-09; prof. edn. and dir. div. elementary edn. Miami U., Oxford, O., 1909-42; retired. Fellow A.A.A.S.; mem. Nat. Soc. Study of Edn., Coll. Teachers of Edn., N.E.A. Mason. Author: The Organization of Instruction Materials, 1917; also articles The Cleveland Survey Tests in Arithmetic in the Miami Valley, Curricula for the Training of Teachers of the Elementary Grades, The Effect of Supervised Study Upon Children's Ability to Write Compositions. Home: 18 Tallawanda Rd., Oxford, O. Died June 6, 1952.

HECKMAN, Samuel B., ednl. dir.; b. Union, O., May 27, 1870; s. David and Hannah (Brumbaugh) H.; Ph.B., Earlham Coll., 1893; A.B., Harvard, 1894; A.M., U. of Pa., 1905, Ph.D., 1906; m. Winifrede Adelaide Ward, Sept. 4, 1918. Prof. English lit. and modern langs., Juniata Coll., Pa., 1895-97; instr. modern langs., Cheltenham (Pa.) Mil. Acad., 1898-1900; asst. commr. edn., Porto Rico, 1900-02; prof. psychology, Temple U., 1904-06; successively instr., asst. prof., asso. prof., prof. and head dept. of edn., and prof. ednl. psychology, and acting dean School of Education, Coll. of City of New York, 1908—; organized, 1913, and developed Ednl. Clinic in connection with dept. of edn., to render service to children in the solution of ednl., vocational and social problems; prof. emeritus edn., Coll. of the City of New York, 1939—. Fellow A.A.A.S.; mem. Am. Psychol. Assn., Am. Assn. Clin. Psychologists, Am. Assn. Univ. Profs., N.E.A., New York Acad. Public Edn., New York Soc. for Exptl. Study of Edn., Ohio Soc. Clubs: Harvard, New York City. Author: The Religious Poetry of Alexander Mack, Jr. Home: Wayne, Me. Died July 26, 1957; buried Bethel Cemetery, Union, O.

HEDBACK, Axel Emanuel, surgeon; born near Karlstad, Sweden, April 21, 1874; son Robert Wilhelm and Christine (Arn) H.; brought to U.S., 1882; graduate high school, New Richmond, Wis., 1893; M.D., cum laude, U. of Minn. Med. Sch., 1897; grad. work, Harvard, New York Polyclinic, Johns Hopkins, U. of Vienna; m. Gladys Margaret Webb, July 2, 1914; children—John William, Elizabeth Ann (Mrs. Don O. Lampland), Margaret (Mrs. David Paul Keefe), Susan (Mrs. Dwaine Lindberg). Prison physician, Stillwater, Minnesota, 1897; practiced medicine in Barron, Wisconsin, 1898-1903, Minneapolis since 1905; phys. Swedish Hosp., chief of staff, 1918; phys. in charge Home of Shelter; mem. staff Franklin and Parkview Hosps., Minneapolis. First phys. and organizer Welfare Dept. Federal Reserve Bank, Minneapolis. Mem. Com. of Management and chmn. of Physical Depts. Com. of Minneapolis Central Y.M.C.A. for many years; capt. of team in raising 1½ million dollars for new Y.M.C.A. Building; mem. bd. dirs. Minneapolis Council Social Agencies; mem. Minneapolis Municipal Charter Com., Minneapolis Traffic Safety Council; mem. Lay Advisory Council 3d Dist. Minn. Nurses Assn., Minneapolis Municipal Auditorium Organ Com. First lt. Med. R.C., U.S. Army, 1914-17. Chmn. Med. Adv. Bd., Minneapolis, 1917-19; mem. Minn. State Bd. of Health, 1919-23. Fellow A.M.A., Am. Geriatrics Soc.; mem. Minn. State Med. Assn. (v.p. 1932) Hennepin Co. Med. Soc. (pres. 1928), Am. Inst. Swedish Arts, Lit. and Science. Mason (32°). Conglist. Republican. Editor of Modern Medicine; editor Geriatrics, Jour. Am. Geriatric Soc. Mem. editorial bd. The Journal-Lancet. Home: 2108 Oliver Av. S. Office: Donaldson Bldg., Mpls. Died Dec. 31, 1951.

HEDGES, Joseph Harold, mining engr., govt. ofcl.; b. Lansing, Mich., June 9, 1882; s. Hiram C. and Louise (Gibson) H.; B.S., Mich. State Coll., 1903; E.M., Mich. Coll. Mines, 1905; m. Ethel Adams, Sept. 5, 1916; children—Dorothy, Florence (Mrs. P. L. Norton), Charles. Engr. Copper Range Cons. Mines Co., 1905; engr., mine supt. Mex. Cons. Mining and Smelting Co., 1906-11, Guanajuato Development Co., 1912; chief engr. Moctezuma Copper Co., 1913-16; asst. mgr. Utah Minerals Concentrating Co., 1917; mine foreman United Verde Extension Mining Co., 1918; gen. supt. Prince Cons. Mining and Smelting Co., 1918-22; field engr. Mining Corp. Can., Ltd., 1923-25; asst. to dir. U.S. Bur. Mines, 1926-40; sr. mining engr. U.S. Bur. Mines, College Park, Md., 1940-42; chief Tucson div., 1942-49, chief minerals division, Washington, 1949-50, special assistant to the director since 1951. Minerals advisor Military Govt., Germany, 1945. Mem. Am. Inst. Mining and Metall. Engrs., Tau Beta Pi. Club: Cosmos. Home: 4809 De Russey Parkway, Chevey Chase 15, Md. Office: U.S. Bureau Mines, Washington 25. Died Jan. 12, 1956.

HEDGES, Marion Hawthorne, research dir.; b. Winamac, Ind., Sept. 14, 1888; s. Thomas Benton and Charlotte Anne (Mullin) H..; A.B., Depauw U., 1910; M.A., Harvard, 1912; m. Agnes Elisabeth Becker, June 30, 1913; 1 dau., Elisabeth Suzanne. Prof. of English, Beloit Coll., 1913-20; reporter on Minneapolis Star, 1920-24; engaged in research for Internat. Brotherhood of Elec. Workers, 1924—. Sec. Council on Industrial Relations for Elec. Constrn. Industry. Spl. consultant on labor relations to TVA; tech. adviser and dep. del. of first U.S. labor delegation, Internat. Labor Conf.; tech. adviser World Textile Conf., Washington, 1937, Am. delegation, Internat. Labor Conf., 1935-38; cons. Fed. Social Security Bd.; chmn. Fed. Com. on Apprenticeship for Constrn. Industry; vice chmn. Nat. Econ. and Social Planning Assn. (founder); mem. planning com. WPB; sec. Nat. Joint Com. on Apprenticeship Standards for Elec. Constrn. Indsutry; mem. bd. Occupational Analysis, U.S. Employment Service; adminstrv. officer, ECA. Recipient gold medal award Nat. Planning Assn. Mem. Am. Acad. Polit. and Social Sci., Am. Econ. Assn., Phi Beta Kappa, Phi Gamma Delta, Sigma Delta Chi (nat. founder). Author: Iron City, 1919; Dan Minturn, 1928; A Strikeless Industry, 1932. Co-author: Educating for Industry through Apprenticeship. Editor: A Short, Simple Course in Speaking, 1924. Contbr. to Ency. Social Sciences, etc. Home: 5606 Warwick Pl., Chevy Chase 15, Md. Died Jan. 6, 1959.

HEDLEY, Frank, ry. exec.; b. Maidstone, Kent, Eng., Jan. 9, 1864; s. James and Emily (Miskin) H.; g.g. nephew of William Hedley, who designed and built the first locomotive traction engine (1813), from which Stevenson obtained his ideas for the locomotive (1825); common sch. edn.; m. Emmeline Minnie Mason, Dec. 24, 1885 (died 1944); children—Nellie, Mrs. Walter J. Hadley, Mrs. H. Henemier, Frank C., Mrs. E. Roy Moffat. Came to U.S., 1822; learned trade of machinist and employed on Erie and N.Y.C. rys.; with Interborough Rapid Transit Co., N.Y., 1903—, successively gen. supt., gen. mgr., v.p., gen. mgr., 1908-19, pres., gen. mgr., 1919-32 succeeding Theodore P. Shonts gen. mgr. receivers, 1932-34, gen. adviser for receiver, 1934-40 (system including all elevated and subway lines in boroughs Manhattan, Bronx, and 3 tunnels extending into Bklyn., Queens, excepting B.-M.-T. Lines and the Independent Subway operated by City N.Y.); elected v.p., gen. mgr. N.Y. Rys. Co., 1912, apptd. gen. mgr. by the receiver, 1919; now ret. Has instituted many improvements in transportation, among them the speed control system, ten-car trains, side doors to center of cars, fans in subways, multiple unit door control system, automatic turnstiles, numerous devices, now widely adopted, adding to comfort, safety of passengers. Republican. Episcopalian. Clubs: Railroad (bd. govs.), New York Railroad (ex-pres.), Engineers'. Home: 29 Fanshaw Av., Yonkers, N.Y. Died July 9, 1955.

HEDRICK, Charles Embury, educator; b. Hurricane, W.Va., Apr. 13, 1881; s. John Andrew and Nancy Lucinda (Boothe) H.; student Marshall Coll., 1899-1904; A.B., Lebanon U., 1908; A.M., U. Chgo., 1915; Ph.D., Peabody, 1927; m. Emma Barnhart, Aug. 30, 1911; children—Charles Barnhart, Dorothy Isabel. Began as prin. of grade and high schsools; prof. of history and v.p. Glenville State Teachers Coll., 1911-18; war work, 1918-19; prof. of history Marshall Coll., Huntington, W.Va., 1919-41, chmn. of Grad. Council and prof. of history, 1941—. Mem. Am., W.Va. hist. assns., N.E.A., Kappa Delta Pi, Phi Delta Kappa. Republican. Baptist. Kiwanian. Home: 1671 5th Av., Huntington, W.Va. Deceased.

HEDRICK, E.H., ex-congressman; b. Mercer Co., W.Va., Aug. 9, 1894; s. Clowney Spotts and Sallie (Thompson) H.; M.D., U. of Marvland, 1917; m. Myrtle Adelle Wade, June 23, 1943. In general practice of medicine, Beckley, W.Va., 1919-45; also in real estate business. Served several terms as health officer Raleigh County, West Virginia; superintendent Pinecrest Tubercular Sanitarium, Beckley, West Virginia, 1942-45; co-owner Guyan Utilities Co., Corinne Coal Land Co. (both Corinne, W.Va.), Beckley (W. Va.) Theater Corp.; vice pres. and dir. The Raleigh County Bank, Beckley, W.Va. Mem. 79th, 80th to 82d Congresses (1945-53), 6th Dist., W.Va. Served as 1st lt., Med. Corps, U.S. Army, during World War I. Mem. A.M.A., Raleigh County Med. Soc., Am. Legion. Democrat (candidate for gov. primary 1952). Moose. Address: 713 Woodlawn Av. Beckley, W.Va. Died Sept. 20, 1954; buried Sunset Meml. Park, Beckley, W. Va.

HEDRICK, Ulysses Prentiss, author, horticulturist; b. Independence, Ia., Jan. 15, 1870; s. Benjamin Franklin and Mary Catherine (Myers) H.; B.S., Mich. Agrl. Coll., 1893, M.S., 1895; D.Sc., Hobart Coll., 1913; LL.D., Utah Agrl. Coll., 1938; m. Amy Willis Plummer, June 23, 1898; children—Catherine Layton, Penelope (dec.), Ulysses Prentiss (dec.). Asst. horticulturist, Mich. Agrl. Coll., 1893-95; prof. botany and horticulture Ore. Agrl. Coll., 1895-97, Utah Agrl. Coll., 1897-99; prof. horticulture Mich. Agrl. Coll., 1899-1905; horticulturist N.Y. Agrl. Expt. Sta., 1905-30, dir. 1928-37, emeritus. Fellow A.A.A.S., N.Y. Hist. Assn.; mem. Am. Soc. for Hort. Sci., Am. Pomol. Soc., Sigma Xi, Kappa Alpha, Alpha Zeta. Democrat. Episcopalian. Author: Grapes of New York, 1908; Plums of New York, 1910; Cherries of New York, 1915; Peaches of New York, 1917; Manual of American Grape Growing, 1919; Sturtevant's Notes on Edible Plants, 1919; Cyclopedia of Hardy Fruits, 1921; The Pears of New York, 1922; Systematic Pomology, 1925; Small Fruits of New York, 1925; The Vegetables of New York, 1929; A History of Agriculture in the State of New York, 1933. Fruits for the Home Garden, 1944; Grapes and Wines from Home Vineyards, 1945; Land of the Crooked Tree, 1948; History of Horticulture in America to 1860, 1950. Home: 600 S. Main St., Geneva, N.Y. Died Nov. 14, 1951; buried Geneva, N.Y.

HEDTOFT, Hans, prime minister of Denmark; b. Aarhus, Denmark, Apr. 21, 1903; s. Hans Peter Hansen and Marie (Nielsen) H.; student pub. schs. in Denmark and abroad; m. Ella Holleuter, May 12, 1927, children—Bjarne, Annemarie, Karin. Began as lithograph's apprentice, Aarhus; sec., later mgr. Socialdemokratisk Ungdom (orgn. for social democratic youth of Denmark), 1922; asst. to Social Demokratisk Forbund, 1929; sec. to social dem. group of Parliament, 1929-35; sec. Social Dem. Party, 1935, leader of party, 1939; by German demand forced from leadership and other tasks in labor movement and trade union, 1941; mem. dirs. Star Brewery, 1941-45; minister of labour and social affairs, 1945, also returned as chmn. for Social Dem. Party; prime minister of Denmark, 1947-50, 1953—; mem. Parliament, 1935—, mem. com. foreign affairs, 1939—; mem. exec. com. for fund of Danish-Norwegian co-operation, 1945—; mem. Danish-Iceland Bd.; mem. bd. Danish-Iceland Fed. Alliance. Democrat. Home: Fuglsangalle 63. Office: Social demokratisk Forbund, Rosenornsalle 14, Copenhagen, Denmark. Died Jan. 29, 1955.

HEED, Thomas D., past chmn. Edward Hines Lumber Co.; b. St. Louis, Mo., Mar. 19, 1875; s. Thomas D. and Mary (Barnett) H.; ed. Coll. of Emporia, Kan., 1890-92; m. Augusta Miller Charlier, Nov. 19, 1907 (died July 19, 1922); m. 2d, Ruth Martha Byers, May 6, 1925. Entered ry service, Jan. 1896, in general auditor's office M.K.&T. Ry., St. Louis, Mo.; then field paymaster for constrn. dept. Standard Oil Co.; cashier Southwestern Passenger Bur.; chief clerk treasury dept., St.L.&S.F. Ry., and asst. sec. and asst. treas. same road, Apr. 1903-13; also asst. sec. and asst. treas. C.&E.I. Ry.; asst. to receiver same road, 1913-15, receiver and pres., 1918-20, financial asst. to receiver, 1920-22, dir., 1921-31; dir. St.L.&S.F. Ry., 1920-21; pres. and dir. Chicago Transfer & Clearing Co., 1922-25, also pres. Nev. Land Co., Nev. Mining Co., Judson Land Co., Judson Mining Co.; also mgr. Estate H. H. Porter; sr. partner Colvin & Co., investment bankers and brokers, 1925-31; became chmn. bd. Edward Hines Lumber Co., 1931; chmn. board and director The Laporte Corp., LaPorte, Ind.; chmn. exec. com. and dir. Clearing Indsl. Dist., Inc.; dir. Edward Hines Lumber Co., Ore. & Northwestern R.R.; now retired. Chmn. U.S. Navy Price Adjustment Bd. Chicago div., 1942-45; founded Heed Ophthalmic Found. for advanced study ophthalmology, 1946. Clubs: Midday, Tavern (Chicago); City Mid-day (New York). Address: 2435 Sycamore Canyon Rd. Montecito, Santa Barbara, Cal. Died Jan. 29, 1957; buried Santa Barbara.

HEELY, Allan Vanderhoef, headmaster; b. Brooklyn, N.Y., Feb. 2, 1897; s. Augustus Vanderhoef and Jessie (Ross) H.; grad. Phillips Acad., Andover, Mass., 1915; A.B., Yale, 1919; student Oxford U., Eng., 1929-30; A.M., Columbia, 1934; LL.D., Lafayette Coll., 1937; Litt.D., Princeton, 1938; L.H.D., Rollins College, Winter Park, Fla., 1942; m. Frances Torrey Thompson, June 25, 1927. With Wendell P. Colton Co., N.Y. City, advertising, 1919-21; asst. sec. Claflins, Inc., N.Y. City, wholesale drygoods, 1921-24; instr. English, Phillips Acad., 1924-34, asst. dean, 1933-34; headmaster The Lawrenceville (N.J.) Sch., 1934—. Dir. Interscholastic Found. Served as 2d lt. field arty., AUS, 1918. Trustee Lawrenceville Sch., Darrow Sch., St. Mary's Hall, Harvey Sch.; mem. com. Ednl. Research Fund of Tuition Plan, New York City. Mem. Headmasters Club of Philadelphia, Headmasters Association (president 1951-52), Alpha Delta Phi. Republican. Presbyterian. Clubs: Elizabethan (New Haven); University, Century Association, Coffee House (New York City); Ausable (St. Hubert's, New York); Yeamans Hall (Charleston, S.C.). Author: Why The Private School?, 1951. Address: Foundation House, Lawrenceville, N.J. Died July 7, 1959.

HEENEHAN, James T., lawyer; b. Palmer, Mass., Oct. 17, 1891; s. James and Elizabeth (O'Keefe) H.; A.B., Dartmouth Coll., 1914; LL.B. cum laude, Boston U., 1916; m. Marian C. O'Brien, Oct. 13, 1920; children—James T., Janet Rose (Mrs. Harry A. Kearney, Jr.), David Gerald, Dorothy Helen. Admitted to Mass. bar, 1916, and practiced in Springfield, 1916-23; admitted to N.Y. bar, 1923, practiced N.Y. City, 1923-30; counsel N.Y. State Banking Dept., 1930-34; partner firm Sullivan, Donovan and Heenehan (now Sullivan, Donovan, Heenehan & Hanrahan), 1934—. Mem. bd. gov. New Rochelle Hosp. Assn. Served as 1st lt., inf., U.S. Army, 1917-19, A.E.F., 1918-19. Trustee Iona Coll., New Rochelle, N.Y. Mem. Am., N.Y. State and N.Y. City bar assns., New York Co. Lawyers Assn., Phi Delta Phi. Roman Catholic. Clubs: Dartmouth College, Bankers (N.Y. City); Wykagyl (New Rochelle, N. Y.). Home: 1273 North Av., New Rochelle, N.Y. Office: 14 Wall St., N.Y.C. 5. Died Jan. 18, 1958; buried Gate of Heaven Cemetery, N.Y.

HEFELBOWER, Samuel Gring, coll. prof., author; b. Newville, Pa., Nov. 11, 1871; s. Samuel and Anna Elizabeth (Gring) H.; B.A., Gettysburg Coll., 1891, M.A., 1894, LL.D., 1925; grad. Luth. Theol. Sem., Gettysburg, 1894; studied univs. of Leipzig, 1895-96, 1901-02, Halle, 1902, Princeton, 1910-11, Harvard, 1911-14; M.A., Ph.D. Harvard, 1914; D.D., Dickinson, 1905; m. Edna M. Loomis, 1897 (died 1899); 1 dau., Edna Elizabeth; m. 2d, Anna E. Hitchins, 1902 (died 1922); m. 3d, Lillian Gantt, 1926. Ordained Luth. ministry, 1894; pastor Manheim, Pa., 1896-99, Frostburg, Md., 1899-1901; prof. German, 1902-04, pres., 1904-10, Gettysburg Coll.; prof. philosophy, Washburn Coll., Topeka Kan., 1914-20; prof. philosophy, Carthage (Ill.) Coll., 1920-36, Wagner Coll., S.I., N.Y., 1936-47, prof. emeritus, 1947—. Mem. Am. Philos. Assn., Phi Beta Kappa. Author: The Relation of John Locke to English Deism, 1918; The Place of Scholarship in Ministerial Training (bulletin), 1922; The History of Gettysburg College, 1932. Home: Chautauqua, N.Y. Died Sept. 12, 1950; buried Gettysburg, Pa.

HEFFELFINGER, Frank Totton, grain merchant; b. Mpls., Sept. 20, 1869; s. Christopher B. and Mary Ellen (Totton) H.; student high sch. and Phillips-Exeter Acad.; m. Lucia Louise Peavey, Oct. 31, 1895; children—Frank Peavey, Totton Peavey, George Wright Peavey, Mary Peavey (Mrs. H. Terry Morrison). In grain business, 1897—; pres. F. H. Peavey & Co., 1907-45, now chairman of the board. Manager of the northern division A.R.C., 1917-19; gen. chmn. Community Fund, Mpls., 1928-30. Presbyn. Clubs: Minneapolis, Minikahda (Mpls.); Woodhill Country (Wayzta, Minn.); Chicago, Old Elm (Ill.); Cypress Point (Pebble Beach, Cal.). Home: Maplewood, Wayzata, Minn. Office: Grain Exchange Bldg., Mpls. Died July 11, 1959; buried Lakewood Cemetery, Mpls.

HEFLIN, J(ames) Thomas, ex-senator; b. Louina, Ala., Apr. 9, 1869; s. Dr. W. L. and Lavicie Catherine (Phillips) H.; student So. U., A. and M. Coll., Auburn, Ala.; m. Minnie Kate Schuessler, Dec. 18, 1895 (dec.); 1 son, J. Thomas. Admitted to Ala. bar, 1893; register in chancery, 1894-96; sec. of state, 1902-04; mem. 58th to 66th Congresses, 5th Ala. Dist., resigned 1920; U.S. senator, 1920-31. Mayor of Lafayette, 2 terms; mem. Ala. Ho. of Reps., 1896-1900. Mem. Dem. State Exec. Com., 1896-1902; del. Constnl. Conv., 1901. Home: Lafayette, Ala. Died Apr. 21, 1951.*

HEIL, Charles Emile, artist; b. Boston, Feb. 28, 1870; s. Charles Theodore and Louisa (Poole) H.; ed. pub. schs., Boston; art edn., Cowles Art Sch., Boston, under De Camp and Major, 1891-95, Colorossi Acad. and Delacluse Acad., Paris, France, under Courtois and Blanc, 1895-96; m. Christina J. Sanders, July 16, 1902. Tchr. drawing, Boston Art Club, 1896-1901, Boston Free Evening Drawing Schs., 1903-10; has specialized on painting and etching of birds. Represneted in permanet collections of Nat. Mus., Washington, Bibliothéque Nationale, Paris, Print Div., State Galleries, Munich, Germany, Art Inst. Chgo., Cleve. Mus. Art, Cin. Mus., Worcester (Mass.) Art Mus., Milw. Art Inst., Los Angeles Mus. Art. Cal. State Library, N.Y. Pub. Library, Municipal Collection, Phoenix, Malden (Mass.) Pub. Library, Concord (Mass.) Art Assn., Framingham (Mass.) Pub. Library, Library of Congress, Washington, Yale Gallery of Art, Honolulu Acad. Art, Lawrence Coll., Appleton, Wis., U. Neb., Fogg Mus., Harvard, Museum of Fine Arts, Boston. Recipient gold medal Panama-Padific Expn., 1915; Richard Mitton gold medal for water color, Boston, 1938; Dawson Meml. medal, Pa. Acad. of the Fine Arts, 1940; first prize for Book-plate, Soc. Mayflower Descendants, Mass. Mem. Soc. Am. Etchers, Chgo. Soc. Etchers, Print Makers Soc. Cal., Boston Soc. Water Color Painters, Phila. Water Color Club, Guild Boston Artists, N. Shore Arts Assn. Represented in permanet collection of Children's Mus., Boston, Mass. Home: 35 Roseway St., Jamaica Plain, Mass. Died Apr. 28, 1950; buried Forest Hill Cemetery, Boston.

HEILAND, Carl August, geophysicist; b. Hamburg, Germany, July 16, 1899; s. Carl Heinrich and Emilie (Gruetter) H.; grad. Wilhelm Gymnasium, Hamburg, 1917; Dr. rer. nat., U. of Hamburg, 1923; student U. of Hamburg, 1918-22, U. of Heidelberg, 1922-23. Came to United States, 1925, naturalized, 1935. Married Peggy Johnston, May 24, 1947; one daughter, Ann, one son John Thomas. Geophysical field work State of Hamburg, 1921-22, A. Raky Drilling Company, 1922-23; in charge geophys. dept. Askania Werke, Berlin, 1924-25, Am. rep., 1925-26; prof. of geophysics and head dept., Colo. Sch. of Mines, 1926-48; pres. Heiland Research Corp., Denver, pres. div. of Minneapolis-Honeywell Regulator Co. Collaborator in seismology, U.S. Coast & Geodetic Survey. Fellow Geol. Society of America; Mem. Am. Geophys. Union, Soc. Exploration Geophysicists, Am. Inst. Mining and Metall. Engrs., Seismol. Soc. Am., Am. Assn. Petroleum Geologists. Republican. Lutheran. Clubs: Teknik, Denver (Denver). Author: Geophysical Exploration, 1940. Contbr. many geophys. and geol. articles to tech. jours. Home: 935 Field St., Lakewood, Colo. Office: 130 E. Fifth Av., Denver. Died Feb. 23, 1956.

HEILBRUNN, Lewis Victor, biologist; b. Bklyn., Jan. 24, 1892; s. Victor and Matilda (Biedermann) H.; A.B., Cornell U., 1911; Ph.D., U. Chgo., 1914; m. Marion Applebee Kerr, Jan. 13, 1923 (dec.); 1 dau., Constance; m. 2d, Ellen Donovan, June 3, 1932. Asso. in zoölogy, U. Chgo., 1914-16; instr., U. of Ill., Med. Sch., 1916-17; instr. of zoölogy, U. of Mich., 1919-21, asst. prof., 1921-29; Guggenheim Meml. Found. fellow, 1927-28; asso. prof. zoölogy, U. Pa., 192943, prof. 1943—. Mem. Nat. Research Council (Div. of Biology and Agriculture), 1935-38; trustee Marine Biol. Lab., Woods Hole, Mass., 1931—. Served as 1st lt. Air Service, U.S. Army, 1917-19; later capt., Air Corps Res., 1919-29. Awarded Silver Star with 2 oak leaf clusters. Fellow A.A.A.S.; mem. Am. Soc. Zoölogists (v.p. 1932), Am. Soc. Naturalists, Amer. Physiol. Soc., Soc. for Exptl. Biology and Medicine, Soc. Gen. Physiologists (pres., 1946). Author: The Colloid Chemistry of Protoplasm, 1928; An Outline of General Physiology, 1937; 2d ed., 1943. Former mng. editor Protoplasm monographs; mem. editorial bd. Physiol. Zoölogy. Address: Zoöl. Laboratory, Univ. of Pa., Phila. 4. Died Oct. 1959.

HEIMANN, Henry Herman, exec. mgr. Nat. Assn. of Credit Men; b. Aviston, Ill., Sept. 26, 1891; s. Bernard Henry and Mary Ann (Peek) H.; student St. Mary's (Kan.) Acad., 1905-08; LL.B., St. Louis U., 1914; m. Florentine Catherine Giller, July 25, 1915; children—Olivia Martha, Henry Herman (dec.). Began as an accountant, 1915; auditor Kawneer Co., 1917-19, asst. treas. and credit mgr., 1919-21, treas., 1921-27, v.p. same, and 4 affiliated cos., 1927-31; exec. mgr. Nat. Assn. of Credit Men since 1931, also ex-pres.; exec. vice pres., Credit Research Foundation. Chmn. safety bd., Niles, Mich.; chmn. Dem. State Com. of Mich., 1928-30; del. Dem. Nat. Conv., Houston, Tex., 1928, Chicago, Ill., 1932; mem. exec. com. of Business Advisory and Planning Council for U.S. Dept. of Commerce; vice-chmn. industrial com. NRA; dir. U.S. Shipping Bd., Jan. 1-June 1, 1934. Capt. U.S.N.R. Chmn. Com. of Causes and Remedies Accident Prevention Conf., Natural Business Year Council; pres. The Service Corp. of Nat. Assn. of Credit Men. Chmn. bd. Citizens Com. for Army, Navy and Air Force, Inc. Democrat. Catholic. Clubs: Rotary, Union League (New York); Wykagyl Country (New Rochelle); Orchard Hills Country; Piping Rock Locust Valley, L.I.); Bohemian (San Francisco). Author: America's Balance Sheet; numerous mag. articles. Home: 1219 Cedar St., Niles, Mich. Office: 229 4th Av., N.Y.C. Died Sept. 12, 1958; buried Silver Brook Cemetery, Niles.

HEIMBACH, Arthur E(rdman), mfg. exec.; b. Allentown, Pa., Dec. 23, 1902; s. Harry R. and Ella M. (Erdman) H.; B.S., Pa. State Coll., 1924; m. Nina Elizabeth Nagle, Oct. 4, 1924; 1 son, Karl N. Engr. Union Switch & Signal Co., 1924-27; train control supervisor to prin. asst. engr. P.&L.E. R.R., Pitts., 1927-41; sales engr. Gen. Ry. Signal Co., 1941-45; resident mgr., Chgo., 1945-48, western mgr., Chgo., 1948-50, v.p., Rochester, 1950-53, exec. v.p., 1953-55, pres., 1955—, also director; member board directors Genesee Valley Union Trust Co. Dir. Rochester Travelers Aid. Home: 2 Southern Pkwy., Rochester, 18. Office: 801 West Av., Rochester 2, N.Y. Died Oct. 17, 1958; buried Grandview, Allentown, Pa.

HEINBERG, John Gilbert, univ. prof.; b. Jackson, Mo., July 22, 1901; s. John George and Annie (Wessell) H.; A.B., Washington U., 1923, A.M., 1924; Ph.D., Brookings Grad. Sch. of Economics and Govt., 1927; Social Sci. Research Council fellow for study on French govt., 1929-30; m. Pauline Dorsey, Aug. 1, 1931; children—John Dorsey, Nancy. Mem. dept. of polit. sci., U. of Mo. since 1926, prof. polit. sci. since 1939, now chairman of department of political science. Panel chairman War Labor Bd.; performed govt. services for nat. and state merit systems; speaker in Mo. cities for adoption of United Nations. City Management form of govt. Mem. Am. Polit. Sci. Assn., Am. Assn. Univ. Profs. Episcopalian. Author: Comparative Major European Governments, 1937; (with A. C. Breckenridge) Law Enforcement in Missouri, 1942. Compiler: Manual on Federal-State Relations for the Missouri Constitutional Convention of 1943. Contbr. to symposia published as papers delivered at annual meetings of Am. Polit. Sci. Assn. Home: 29 W. Parkway Dr., Columbia, Mo. Died July 5, 1953; buried Meml. Cemetery, Columbia, Mo.

HEINL, Robert D. (hī'n'l), newspaper corr.; b. Terre Haute, Ind., Apr. 4, 1880; s. John G. and Mary Marguerite (Debs) H.; ed. pub. schs., and Rose Poly. Inst., Terre Haute; m. Helen M. Corbin; 1 son, Robert D., Jr. (U.S. Marine Corps). With New York City News Assn., 1905-06; New York Sun, 1906-10; Washington correspondent Leslie's Weekly, 1910-13; asso. editor The Nation's Business, official mag. Chamber of Commerce U.S.A., 1915-17; head of publications sect. U.S. Emergency Fleet Corp., during World War I; with Nat. Geographic Magazine, 1918-20; organized, edited Heinl News Service, 1924—; editorial staff Washington Post, 1926-34. Mem. White House Correspondents' Assn., Senate Press Gallery. Clubs: National Press; Overseas Writers, Friendship Fire Assn. Home: 2400 California St., Washington. Died Nov. 29, 1950; buried Oak Hill Cemetery, Washington.

HEINO, Albert Frederic, architect; b. Chgo., Jan. 28, 1905; s. John Fred and Anna Mabel (Knowles) H.; B.S., Armour Inst. Tech., 1926; A.M., U. Ill., 1928; m. Doris Pauline Monson, Apr. 26, 1930; children—Margaret Jean, Richard Lee (adopted). Instr. design U. Ill., 1926-28; pvt. practice architecture, Chgo., since 1932, specialized instnl. bldgs., chiefly ecclesiastical architecture; became co. architect United Air Lines, engaged in design airports and bldg. facilities, in charge research development covering future airport requirements, 1942, dir. design bldgs. and airports, 1947; prin. Albert F. Heino & Assos. since July 1948. Bldgs. include Peace Meml. Ch., Chgo., Luth. Student Center, U. Ill., Champaign, Concordia Coll. Campus, Springfield; cons. services Phila., Seattle, Denver; architect many churches and church schools. Pres. bd. edn. District 148, Ill., 1949-52. Mem. A.I.A. (1st v.p., dir. Chgo. chpt.). Architects Assn. Ill (del., mem. legislative com., Chicago Association of Commerce and Industry; awarded medal of excellence; chmn. nat. com. honor awards), Am. Scandinavian Found., Ch. Archtl. Guild Am. (N.Y.C.), Theta Xi, Scarab. Clubs: Beverly Lions (past pres.), University, Builders Tee (Chgo.). Author articles profl. publs. Contbr.: Forms and Functions of 20th Century Architecture (Columbia U.). Originator Unit Terminal Plan for air terminals. Home: Palos Park, Ill. Office: 10041 S. Western Av., Chgo. 43. Died Feb. 12, 1955; buried Mount Hope Cemetery.

HEINRICH, Edward Oscar (hīn'rĭch), chemical-legal expert; b. Clintonville, Wis., Apr. 20, 1881; s. August Frederick and Albertina Otilla (Zempel) H.; licentiate in pharmacy, Wash., 1899; B.S., U. of Calif., 1908; m. Marion Allen, Sept. 28, 1908; children—Theodore Allen, Mortimer Allen. Began as pharm. chemist, at Tacoma, Wash., 1899; chem. and sanitary engring. practice, Tacoma, 1908-17; also served as city chemist, engr. of tests and as expert in criminal investigations; chief of police, Alameda, Calif., 1917; city mgr., Boulder, Colo., 1918-19; practice, San Francisco, since July 1919. Lecturer on criminal investigation, University of California, 1917-25, 1938-39; research asso. in police science, 1930-31, lecturer in polit. science, 1943, lecturer in industrial plant protection, Engineering, Science, and Management War Training, 1943. Expert on questioned documents and other scientific evidence in Hindu-Ghadr revolution plot trials, San Francisco, 1917, also in cases of United States vs. William (Jack) Dempsey, United States vs. Levin (income tax frauds), People vs. Roscoe Arbuckle, People vs. William Hightower, the d'Autremont train bandits, Ore., St. Francis Dam failure, Los Angeles, 1928, U.S. vs. Germany (Black Tom cases, 1930-34), U.S. in re Harry Bridges, 1939, and other celebrated cases. Participant XVth International Criminal Police Commission Conference, Berlin, 1939. Captain Engineer Res., U.S. Army, 1917-32. Mem. Am. Inst. Criminal Law and Criminology, Am. Chem. Soc., Soc. Am. Mil. Engrs., Soc. of Pub. Analysts (Eng.), L'Académie Internationale de Criminalistique, Acacia, Phi Lambda Upsilon; hon. fellow Internat. Medico-Legal Assn. Democrat. Protestant. Mason (K.T.). Clubs: Hillside (Berkeley); Faculty (University of California); Engineers (San Francisco). Author: Introduction to Signature Inspection and Authentication, 1947; Flow Sheet for Criminal Investigation, 1952; articles and reports on subjects pertaining to detection of forgery, criminal investigation, city management, etc. Home: 1001 Oxford St., Berkeley 7, Calif. Office: Marvin Bldg., 24 California St., San Francisco 11. Died Sept. 28, 1953; inurned Chapel of the Chimes, Columbarium, Oakland, Cal.

HEISERMAN, Clarence Benjamin, lawyer; b. Urbana, O., Sept. 18, 1862; s. Aaron and Maria Louisa (Stuart) H.; A.B., Ohio Wesleyan U., 1884; m. Lillian Brown, Oct. 28, 1890; 1 son, Robert Brown. Admitted to Ohio bar, 1887, and began practice at Urbana; pros. atty., Champaign County, O., 1889-94; judge Court of Common Pleas, 2d Dist. of Ohio, 1894-1901, resigned; solicitor P., C.,C.&St.L. Ry. Co., at Urbana; gen. solicitor Pa. Lines, Pitts., 1910-14, gen. counsel, 1914-21; gen. counsel Pa. system, Phila., 1921-23, v.p. and gen. counsel, 1923-32, now spl. counsel. Mem. Am. and Various state bar assns., Pa. Scotch-Irish Soc., Pa. Soc. of N.Y., Chi Phi. Republican. Presbyn. Mason (32°). Clubs: Duquesne (Pitts.); Rittenhouse (Phila.). Home: Haverford, Pa. Office: Broad St. Sta. Bldg., Phila. Died 1950.

HEITMAN, Charles Easton; b. McLean County, Ky., Nov. 12, 1874; s. John and Isabel (Moore) H.; ed. pub. schs.; studies law; C.S.B., Mass. Metaphysical Coll., Boston, 1923; m. Mary Elizabeth Sproul, Dec. 1, 1906. Hudson-Fulton commr., 1909; financial editor Cassiers Mag., New York, 1910-13; mem. N.Y. City Real Estate Bd., 1911-23; first reader, 2d Ch. of Christ, Scientiest, N.Y. City, 1918-21; mem. Christian Science Com. on Publication, State of N.Y., 1922-26; pres. The Mother Ch., Boston, 1923-24; asso. editor Christian Science Monitor, 1926-27; former mem. editorial bd., Christian Science Monitor, and mgr. Christian Science Publishing Soc., now dir. The Mother Church, 1st Ch. of Christ, Scientist, Boston. Trustee Gifts and Endowments Fund of the Mother Ch., 1926-27. Served as corporal 1st Vol. Cav., U.S. Army (Roosevelt's Rough Riders), Spanish-American War. Mem. Am. Arbitration Soc. (trustee), Columbia Univ. Acad. Polit. Science. Republican. Mason (32°, K.T.). Clubs: University (Boston); Bankers (New York); National Press (Washington). Home: 8 W. Cedar St. Office: 107 Falmouth St., Boston, Mass. Died Oct. 1, 1948.

HEKMAN, John business exec.; b Winschoten, The Netherlands, Oct. 21, 1886; s. Edsko and Hendrikje (Ymker) H.; came to U.S., 1893, naturalized, 1900; ed. pub. schs., Grand Rapids, Mich.; m. Frederika Haan, July 20, 1912 (died May 20, 1916); children—Edward J., Frederika (Mrs. Samuel W. Tamminga); married second, Cornelia Haan, April 18, 1917 (died December 1958). Began as baker with Hekman Biscuit Company, 1900-17, partner, 1917-28, president since 1928; gen. mgr., vice pres. and dir. United Biscuit Co. of Am. since 1928; v.p. and dir. Peoples Nat. Bank of Grand Rapids since 1934; dir. Hekman Furniture Co., Hekman Rusk Co. Trustee Grand Rapids Christian High Sch., Calvin Coll., Butterworth Hosp. Served as pres., Community Chest and War Chest. Dir. Rehabilitation League. Mem. Christian Psychopathic Hosp. Assn. (pres. since 1940), C. of C. (past pres.), West Mich. Tourist and Resort Assn. (past pres.). Republican. Mem. Christian Reformed Ch. Clubs: Rotary (past pres.), Blythefield Country, Peninsular. Home: 757 Plymouth Rd. S.E., Grand Rapids 6. Office: 310 28th St. S.E., Grand Rapids 8, Mich. Died Nov. 23, 1951.

HEKTOEN, Ludvig (hĕk'tōn), pathologist; b. Westby, Wis., July 2, 1863; s. Peter P. and Olave Hektoen; A.B., Luther Coll., Ia., 1883, A.M., 1896; studied U. of Wis.; M.D., Coll. Phys. and Surg., Chicago, 1887; interne, Cook County Hosp., Chicago, 1887-89; studied Upsala, Prague, Berlin, 1890, 94, 95; M.D., ad eundem, Rush Med. College, 1896; hon. M.D., U. of Norway, 1911; Sc.D., U. of Mich., 1913, U. of Wis., 1916; U. of Chicago, 1940; LL.D., U. of Cincinnati, 1920, Western Reserve U., 1920, and Luther Coll., Decorah, Ia., 1936; m. Ellen Strandh, July 7, 1891; children—Aikyn (dec.), Josef Ludvig. Pathologist to Cook County (Ill.) Hosp., 1889-1903; lecturer pathology, Rush Med. Coll., 1890-92; physician to coroner's office, Chicago, 1890-94; prof. pathology, Coll. Phys. and Surg., Chicago, 1892-94; prof. morbid anatomy, Rush Med. Coll., 1895-98, prof. pathology, 1898-1933, prof. emeritus since 1933; prof. and head dept. pathology, U. of Chicago, 1901-32; dir. John McCormick Inst. for Infectious Diseases, 1902-39. Mem. Occupational Diseases Commission of Illinois, 1909-11. President Chicago Tumor Institute since 1938. Editor Journal of Infectious Diseases, 1904-40, Archives of Pathology, 1926-49. Chmn. div. of med. sciences, Nat. Research Council, 1924-25, 1926-27, 1929-30; chmn. Nat. Research Council, 1936-38; mem. Nat. Advisory Health Council, U.S. P.H.S., 1934-38; exec. dir. Nat. Advisory Cancer Council, U.S.P.H.S. 1937-1944. Received Centennial Award, Wis. State Medical Society, 1941, Distinguished Service medal, American Medical Association, 1942. Gold-headed cane, Association American Pathologists and Bacteriologists, 1944; Howard Taylor Ricketts award, U. of Chicago, 1949. Mem. National Acad. Sciences, Assn. Am. Phys., A.M.A., Chicago Med. Soc. (pres. 1919-21), Chicago Pathol. Soc. (pres. 1898-1902), Assn. Am. Pathologists and Bacteriologists (pres. 1901), Soc. Am. Bacteriologists (pres. 1929), Soc. Immunologists (pres. 1927), Inst. of Medicine of Chicago (pres. 1929), A.A.A.S. (v.p. 1909); hon. mem. Norwegian Med. Soc., Am. Soc. of Clinical Pathologists; mem. Norwegian Acad. of Sciences; honorary member Philadelphia Pathological Society, Swedish Medical Society (Stockholm), Norwegian Pathological Society, Vienna Microbiologie Society, American Society of Bacteriologists, Academy of Medicine, Washington, College of American Pathologists (honorary member). Decorated Order of St. Olaf (Norway). Club: University (Chicago, (Illinois). Author: Post-mortem Technique, 1894; Introduction to Study of Infectious Diseases. Editor: Durck's Pathologic Histology; Collected Works of Christian Fenger; Contributions to Medical Science, by Howard Taylor Ricketts. Co-editor and contributor to American Text-Book of Pathology, 1902; has written numerous articles on pathology, bacteriology and immunology. Co-compiler A Bibliography of Infantile Paralysis, 1789-1944, 1946. Home: 5650 Dorchester Av. Address: 21 W. Elm St., Chicago 10. Died July 5, 1951; buried Rosehill Cemetery, Chgo.

HELBURN, Theresa (Mrs. John B. Opdycke), stage dir. and producer; b. Julius and Hannah (Peyser) Helburn; A.B., Bryn Mawr, 1908; grad. student Radcliffe, 1908-09, Sorbonne, Paris, 1913-14; m. John Baker Opdycke (Oliver Opdyke), Jan. 13, 1920. Dramatic critic The Nation, 1918-19; exec. dir. Theatre Guild, 1919-32, adminstrv. dir., 1933—; exec. Columbia Pictures Corp., Hollywood, 1934-35. Staged Chrysalis, 1932, Mary of Scotland, 1933; produced (with Lawrence Langner) The Philadelphia Story, 1939; Oklahoma, 1943; Jacobowsky and The Colonel, 1944; Carousel, 1945; The Fatal Weakness, and The Iceman Cometh, 1946; Allegro, 1947; Silver Whistle, 1948; Come Back Little Sheba, 1950; As You Like It, 1950. Author: (plays) Enter the Hero, 1916; Allison Makes Hay, 1919; Denbigh, 1921; Other Lives (with Edward Goodman), 1921; A Hero Is Born, 1937. Contbr. verse and articles to Harper's, Century, New Republic, North American Rev., etc. Home: Weston, Conn. Office: 23 W. 53d St., N.Y.C. Died Aug. 18, 1959.

HELD, John, Jr., author, artist; b. Salt Lake City, Jan. 10, 1889; s. John and Anna (Evans) H.; m. Margaret Schuyler Janes, Jan. 1940; 1 dau., Judy. Began as cartoonist, 1907; writer, 1928—. Artist in res., Harvard U., 1940, U. of Ga., 1941. Served in U.S. Navy, World War. Democrat. Clubs: Coffee House, Century (New York). Author: Grim Youth, 1931; Women Are Necessary, 1931; The Flesh Is Weak, 1932; The Works of John Held, Jr., 1932; A Bowl of Cherries, 1933; Crosstown, 1934. Contbr. to mags. Home: 3106 Hurley Pond Rd., Belmar, N.J. Died Mar. 2, 1958.

HELFEN, Mathias, nat. pres. Catholic Dramatic Movement; b. Herforst, Germany, Jan. 29, 1889; s. Johann Mathias and Apollonia (Schommer) H.; grad. Strasbourg Coll., Alsace, 1910, Philos. Coll., Crefeld 1912, Cath. U., Fribourg, 1917. Ordained priest, R. C. Ch., 1917; asst. pastor Puettlingen and St. Wendel, Saar, 1917-20; asst. dir. St. Michael's Coll., Boppard, Rhineland, 1920-22. Came to U.S., 1922. Pastorates in Minn., 1922-27, in Wis., 1927—; pastor St. Catherine's Church, Oconomowoc, Wis., 1934-41; now retired from pastoral work to devote all time to theatre. Founder and organizer of Cath. Dramatic Movement, 1922, nat. pres., 1922—; founder and organizer of Cath. Dramatic Guild, 1926, nat. pres., 1926—; organized professional actors to create professional Cath. stage in all parts of the U.S., 1937; editor Practical Stage Work, 1926-32 and 1940—. Founder of Cath. Summer Sch. in Drama, Marquette U., 1938, now asso. with Sch. of Dramatics; with Lake Region Summer Theatre, 1941; author and director of annual Passion Play of Milwaukee, 1941—; organizer and dir. of Father Helfen's Children's Theatre, 1942—; founder and dir. The Players Guild of Milwaukee, 1942. Editor of Catholic Theatre Year Book, the mag. Practical Stage Work and of plays published by the Catholic Dramatic Movement. Honorary mem. Literary and Artistic Inst. of France. Author: The Staging of Passion Plays and Lenten Dramas, 1931; also over sixty plays sponsored by Cath. Dramatic Movement; Catholic Theatre Year Book, 1938—; author, director, producer of new version of Goethe's "Faust," 1945; In Search of Peace, His Lips Were Sealed, 1949-51. Lecturer on dramatics, Founder and supervisor Catholic Theatre Sch., Cath. Children; Theatre, Young Actors Guild, 1946, N.Y. City. Author: of 18 records on the Life of Christ, 1946, also The American Passion Play and Children's

Stories on Records. Address: Catholic Dramatic Movement, P.O. Box 1336, Milw. Died Mar. 24, 1955; buried Holy Cross Cemetery, Milw.

HELLER, George, fedn. exec. sec.; b. N.Y.C., Nov. 20, 1905; s. David and Frances (Heller) O.; student City Coll. of N.Y., 1923-25; m. Clara Mahr, June 3, 1934; children—Toni, Francesca. Actor with Neighborhood Playhouse, 1926-29; appeared in Broadway prodns.: Maya, 1928, Love Nest, 1928, Grand St. Follies, 1927-28-29, Three Penny Opera, 1931, Dark Hours, 1931, The Climax, 1931, Sailor Beware, 1933, Squaring the Circle, 1934; Till the Day I Die, 1935, Waiting For Lefty, 1935, You Can't Take It With You, 1936; exec. sec. N.Y. local of Am. Fedn. Radio Artists, 1937—, nat. exec. sec. 1946-50, national executive sec. Television Authority, 1946-50, merged orgn. Am. Fedn. TV and Radio Artists, 1950—; bd. mem. U.S.O. Camp Shows, Inc. Mem. Asso. Actors and Artists of Am. (1st v.p.); Am. Theatre Wing (5th v.p.). Democrat. Jewish religion. Home: Sunny Ridge Rd., Harrison, N.Y. Office: 15 W. 45th St., N.Y.C. Died May 30, 1955.

HELLER, Helen West, artist; b. Rushville, Ill.; d. Washington Miller and Edith (Harrington) Barnhart; ed. St. Louis Sch. of Fine Arts; scholarship, Art Students' League of N.Y.; m. Roger Paul Heller, Mar. 20, 1914. Works in mediums of oil painting, egg tempera, mosaic, wood engraving. Murals in tempera, Neponait Hosp., Brooklyn; works owned by Brooklyn Museum, N.Y. Public Library, Berkshire Museum, Pittsfield, Mass., Ill. State Museum of Art, Springfield, Chicago Municipal Art Gallery, Lindsborg, Kan. Art Gallery, Library of Congress, Washington, D.C., Smithsonian Institution, U.S. National Museum, permanent collection of Graphic Art of the Western Hemisphere, owned by the Internat. Bus. Machines Corp. Individual exhbns. in all mediums Brooklyn Museum of Art, 1932: Columbia U., 1933; Gallery Secession, 1935; paintings and mosaics, Artists' League of Am., 1948; retrospective of wood engravings, Wellman Hall, Springfield, Mass., 1948; 1st prize for engraving, Library of Congress, 1949. Included in American Abstractions, Whitney Museum, N.Y., 1935; Library of Congress Print Exhibition, 1944 (a Pennell prize); Pennell Fund purchase, 1948. A self-portrait, 1948, engraving, property of Nat. Acad. of Design, included in historic collection of members portraits. Hon. mem. Artists League of Am.; mem. Etchers, Gravers, Lithographers and Wood Engravers; asso..Nat. Acad. of Design. Author: Xiolographic, book of poems by the artist, Migratory Urge (first all-woodcut book pub. in U.S., text cut intaglio), poems previously pub. weekly in Chicago Evening Post Mag. of the Art World, 1925-26 and in poetry magazines, 1919-21, 1928. Woodcuts U.S.A. (deluxe edition of 20 designs) 1947. Home: 732 E. 6th St., N.Y.C. 9. Died Nov. 19, 1955; buried Rosehill Cemetery, Linden, N.J.

HELLMAN, George Sidney, author; b. N.Y. City, Nov. 14, 1878; s. Theodore and Frances (Seligman) H.; A.B., Columbia (Phi Beta Kappa), 1899, A.M., 1900; m. Hilda Emily Josephthal, June 2, 1903; children—Geoffrey Theodore, Rhoda; m. 2d, Irene Shuman Schafer, Aug. 15, 1939. Editor (with W. A. Bradley) East and West (monthly mag. of letters), 1899-1900. Mem. local sch. bd., N.Y. City, 1914-18. Dir. dept. of fine and applied arts, Army Ednl. Commn. Y.M.C.A., 1918-19; mem. Army Ednl. Corps, A.E.F., 1919; apptd. by Gen. Pershing dir. of instrn. Fine and Applied Arts, A.E.F., 1919; dir. (with Lloyd Warren) of A.E.F. Art Training Center, at Bellevue, nr. Paris, 1919; chmn. army com. on French and Am. relations, Beaune, Côte d'Or, 1919; mem. sub-prefect's com., French Homes; mayor's com. on memorial to French and Am. soldiers who died in the war, Beaune, 1919; dir. Coll. of Fine and Applied Arts, A.E.F. Univ., 1919; originated the idea for the American School of Art at Fontainebleau; Officer d'Académie, France, 1919; chmn. John Purroy Mitchel Memorial Com., Columbia U., 1919; chmn. com. on sculpture, Walt Whitman Memorial. Pres. The New Gallery, 1925-29. Independent Republican. Clubs: Author, Columbia Univ., Whist, Regency. Author: The Hudson and Other Poems, 1909: Original Drawings by the Old Masters, 1914; Esther (3-act drama), 1917; Applied Arts and Education, 1919; Art and the Citizen, 1919; Later Essayists (Cambridge History of Am. Literature), 1921; The Way It Ended, 1921; Washington Irving, Esq., 1925; The True Stevenson—A Study in Clarification, 1925; Lanes of Memory, 1927; Peacock's Feather, 1931, made into a screen picture under the title of "Night in Paradise," 1945; Persian Conqueror, 1935; Benjamin N. Cardozo—American Judge, 1940. Editor of Letters of Irving and Brevoort, 1807-43, 2 vols., 1915; Unpublished Poems by R. L. Stevenson, 2 vols., 1916; Mercy-Argenteau Memoirs, 2 vols., 1917; Journals of Washington Irving (with W. P. Trent), 3 vols., 1919; Unpublished Prose Pieces by R. L. Stevenson (with H. H. Harper), 1921; Poems by R. L. Stevenson (with W. P. Trent), 1921; The Seas Were Mine by Capt. Howard Hartman, 1935. Contbr. poems and stories, also contbr. on art, history and lit. to mags., and articles in cyclopedias and screen scenarios. Home: Monsey, N.Y. Died July 16, 1958.

HELM, Roy, judge; b. Cumberland Co., Ky., Aug. 22, 1888; s. George Alfred and Helen (Campbell) H.; A.B., So. Normal Sch., Bowling Green, Ky., 1907; student U. of Chgo.; A.B., U. of Fla., 1910, grad. student, 1910-11; B.A. and M.A., law, U. of Oxford, Eng.; m. Geta Sloss, Dec. 26, 1918; 1 dau., Rheta. Admitted to Ky. bar, 1914 and practiced until 1940; circuit judge 33d jud. dist. of Ky., 1940-46; judge, Ct. of Appeals of Ky. since 1948. Mem. Ky. Hist. Soc., Phi Delta Phi. Democrat. Mason. Rotarian. Clubs: Filson, Frankfort Country. Home: Hazard, Ky. Office: Court of Appeals, Frankford, Ky. Died Apr. 19, 1951.

HELM, William P(ickett), journalist; b. near Warrenton, Virginia, May 4, 1883; s. William Pickett and Agnes Harwood (Marshall) H.; grad. high sch., Warrenton, 1896; m. Selma White Snyder, October 29, 1921; children—Margaret Leslie (Mrs. John C. Phillips, Jr.), Meredith, Selma Snyder (Mrs. Martin J. Leader), Lewis Marshall. Began business career as reporter on Chattanooga (Tenn.) Times and other dailies, 1904-05; reporter, city editor, mng. editor Newark (N.J.) Morning Star, 1906-10; Associated Press corr., New York and Washington, D.C., 1911-17; asst. to v.p. Nat. Coal Assn., Washington, D.C., 1918-21; newspaper syndicate writer, 1921-41, and contbr. economic and financial articles to mags.; Washington corr. of daily newspapers, 1933-41; financial editor United States News Agency, 1941-46; editor and pub. William P. Helm's Washington News Letter, 1946-54; now newspaper correspondent and writer of articles on financial subjects. Director publicity so. div. Rep. Nat. Com., 1928. Editor weekly Washington Letter on bus. information. Author: The Truth About Taxes, 1924; History of the Anti-Saloon League (with Wayne B. Wheeler), 1926; The Federal Budget (with Gen. Herbert M. Lord), 1929; Washington Swindle Sheet, 1932; Harry Truman, a Political Biography, 1947; (with Daniel E. Casey) Slash Those Taxes, 1948. Contbr. to various mags. Collaborator in writing books. Contbg. editor Transport Topics. Home: 6111 44th Av., Riverdale, Md. Office: Colorado Bldg., Washington. Died Oct. 30, 1958; buried Rock Creek Cemetery, Washington.

HELMHOLZ, Henry Frederic, pediatrist; b. Chgo., Aug. 24, 1882; s. August C. and Elizabeth K. (Vogel) H.; B.S., U. Wis., 1902, D.Sc., 1943; M.D., Johns Hopkins, 1906; univs. of Berlin and Vienna, 1907-09; m. Isabel G. Lindsay, Dec. 30, 1907; children—Lindsay, Henry Frederic, August Carl, II, Margaret. Fellow Johns Hopkins, 1906-07; asst. prof. pediatrics Rush Med. Coll., Chgo., 1910-20; med. dir. Infant Welfare Soc., Chgo., 1910-20; mem. Ohio S. A. Sprague Meml. Inst. for Med. Research, 1912-20; now prof. pediatrics May Found., U. Minn.; head sect. pediatrics Mayo Clinic, Rochester, Minn., 1921-47, sr. cons. sect. on pediatrics, 1947-49; chief med. cons. for UN Internat. Childrens Emergency Fund in Europe, 1948. A vice-chmn. White House Conf. on Children in a Democracy, 1940; chmn. Subcom. on Child Health of Advisory Com. of Children's Bur.; pres. Fifth Internat. Congress of Pediatrics. Decorated Order of Carlos Findlay (Cuba). Asso. mem. Am. Urol. Assn.; mem. Am. Pediatric Soc. (ex-pres.), Am. Acad. of Pediatrics (ex-pres.. hon. mem. Latin div.) Am. Bd. Pediatric Examiners, Soc. for Research in Child Development, Am. Assn. Bacteriologists and Pathologists, Am. Soc. Pharmacology and Exptl. Therapeutics, Am. Physiol. Soc., Chi. Psi, Phi Beta Kappa, Sigma Xi, Alpha Omega Alpha; hon. mem. Bolivan, Cuban, Mexican, Colombian pediatric socs., Pediatric Soc. Brazil, Deutschen Gesellschaft für Kinderheilkunde; corr. Author: Diseases of the Genito-urinary System in Infancy and Childhood (with S. Amberg), 1930. Editor-in-chief Am. Jour. Diseases of Children, 1917-24, asso. editor, 1926—. Home: Rochester, Minn. Died Aug. 19, 1958.

HELMICK, Milton John, lawyer; b. St. Louis, Nov. 27, 1885; s. John and Ida (Wynkoop) W.; student Stanford U., 1905-06, 1907-08, U. Colo., 1906-07; LL.B., U. Denver, 1910; m. Mildred E. MacLanahan,, Jan. 29, 1916. Admitted to Colo. bar, 1911, N.M. bar, 1912; practiced in Socorro, N.M., 1912-17; asst. atty. gen. N.M., 1917; practiced in Albuquerque and atty. for N.M. Central Ry., 1919-23; atty. gen. of N.M., 1923-25; judge N.M. 2d Dist. Ct., 1925-34; judge U.S. Ct. for China from 1934 until abolition of extra territoriality, 1943; prof. Comparative Law Sch. of China since 1939; returned to U.S. on diplomatic exchange ship, Aug. 1942; mem. President's Bd. of Visa Appeals, 1944-45; special mission to Chungking for State Dept., 1944; counsel for Standard-Vacuum Oil Co. in China, 1945-51; attaché and consul, Am. Legation in Morocco acting as judge of consular courts at Tangier and Casablanca, 1952. Served with inf., U.S. Army, 1918. Mem. Royal Asiatic Soc., Sigma Alpha Epsilon, Phi Delta Phi. Democrat. Mason. Address: American Legation, Tangier, Morocco. Died Oct. 19, 1954.

HELMS, Elmer Ellsworth, clergyman; b. Ada, O., Nov. 8, 1863; s. Daniel and Elizabeth (Miller) H.; A.M., Ohio Northern U., 1888, Ph.D., 1894, LL.D., 1925, Litt.D., 1936, L.H.D., 1946; S.T.D., Syracuse University, 1925; D.D., University of Southern California, 1926; married Ora Hoy, July 26, 1888 (died May 12, 1894); children—Paul Hoy, Ruth (deceased); married 2d, Lois Stanbro, October 2, 1899 (deceased November 25, 1951). Superintendent of pub. schs., Hutchinson, Kan., 1888-90; traveling college sec. Y.M.C.A., 1890-91; ordained ministry Methodist Episcopal Ch., 1891; pastor Smethport, Pa., 1891-94, Central Park, Buffalo, N.Y., 1894-97, Springville, N.Y., 1897-99, again Central Park 1899-1902. Linwood Av. Ch., Buffalo, 1902-05, Plymouth Ch., Buffalo, 1905-11, Central Ch., Wilkes-Barre Pa., 1911-16, Calvary Ch., Phila., 1916-20 First Ch., Los Angeles, Calif., 1920-33 (built and financed church plant at cost of $1,500,000); raised 8 million dollars for churches and instns. Mem. Gen. Conf. M.E. Ch., 1924, 32, alternate, 1936; mem. Ecumenical Methodist Conf., Atlanta, 1931. Trustee U. of Southern Calif. Platform lecturer. Won first prize National Sermon Contest, 1904. Mem. Kappa Sigma. Republican. Clubs: Southern Calif. Auto, Los Angeles Country. Author: That Young Man, 1893; The Gate to the Gospel, 1913, 3d edit., 1925; The Living Bread, 1920; God in History, 1923; Forgotten Stories, 3d edit., 1924; Booze, Bootleggers, Beer, 1926; Men Who Made and Marred History, 1928; The Gospel of the Mediterranean, 1930; Life Stories, 1937; Trailing the Presidents, 1940; The President's Wives, 1941; Numerous and Humorous Stories of the Presidents, 1943; Kate Field, 1944; More Life Stories, 1947; also more than 30 booklets and pamphlets. Contbr. to The Upper Room, The Christian Advocate, Liberator, National Voice, Readers Digest, Upper Room Pulpit and other religious periodicals. Home: 3945 Ingraham St., Los Angeles 5. Deceased.

HELMS, Paul Hoy, corporation executive; b. Ottawa, Kan., Sept. 19, 1889; s. Rev. Elmer Ellsworth and Ora (Hoy) H.; grad. Lafayette High Sch., Buffalo, N.Y., 1908; A.B., Syracuse U., 1912; LL.D., 1948; m. Pearl E. Ellis, June 10, 1914; children—Paul Hoy, Elizabeth Jane, Lois M. Pres. Hall Baking Co., Buffalo, 1914-23; sec.-treas., Ward Baking Co., N.Y. City, 1924-25; pres. Gen. Baking Corp., N.Y. City, 1925-26, Helms Bakeries, Los Angeles, since 1931; dir. Los Angeles br. Fed. Reserve Bank of San Francisco; dir. and v.p. Smoke Tree Ranch, Palm Springs. Del. Rep. Conv., 1948-52. Dir. DeMille Found.; pres. Helms Found., Inc.; chmn. bd. dirs. Ford Fund for Adult Edn.; mem. bd. fellows Claremont (Cal.) Coll. Mem. So. Cal. Com. for Olympic Games (pres.), U.S. Olympic Assn. (dir.), Tennis Patrons Assn. (dir.), Amateur Athletic Union (dir.), Beta Theta Pi. Republican. Methodist. Mason. Clubs: California, Los Angeles Country. Home: 10401 Wilshire Blvd., Los Angeles 24. Office: 8800 Venice Blvd., Los Angeles 34. Died Jan. 5, 1957.

HELSER, Maurice David, college dean; b. Thornville, O., Mar. 29, 1890; s. David M. and Emma S. (Zartman) H.; B.S.A., Ohio State U., 1914; M.S., Ia. State Coll., 1916; student U. of Chicago, 1931, also student Harvard, 1934; m Elizabeth Stevens, Aug. 20, 1914; children—Carolyn Jane, Margaret Elizabeth. Teacher grade schs., Thornville, O., 1909-10; instr. State Agrl. Sch., Jonesboro, Ark., 1914-15; teaching scholar, Ia. State Coll., 1915-16, instr., asst. prof., asso. prof., prof. animal husbandry, 1916-32, dir. personnel, 1931—, dean junior coll, 1933—; chief in meat investigation Ia. Agrl. Expt. Sta., 1923-32. Supt. carcass div., Internat. Livestock Expn., 1918-31; asst. supt. sheep dept., Ia. State Fair, 1918-31; mem. Ames City Council, 1920-24. Mem. Ia. State Com. of Y.M.C.A. Mem. Am. Soc. of Animal Production, A.A.A.S., Ia. Acad. of Science, Am. Coll. Personnel Assn., Nat. Assn. of Deans and Advisers of Men, Cardinal Key, Phi Kappa Phi, Alpha Zeta, Gamma Sigma Delta, Alpha Gamma Rho, Alpha Phi Omega. Republican. Presbyn. Clubs: Saddle and Sirloin (Chicago); University (Des Moines); Rotary, Golf and Country (Ames). Author: Farm Meats, 1923; Essentials in the Selection of Meat (with Viola M. Bell), 1930; Market Classes and Grades of Livestock (with A. B. Caine), 1927. Home: 234 Hyland, Ames, Ia. Died Apr. 26, 1956; buried Iowa State Coll. Cemetery.

HEMINGWAY, Samuel Burdett, educator; b. New Haven, Sept. 8, 1883; s. Samuel and Minerva Lee (Hart) H.; A.B., Yale, 1904; A.M., 1905; Ph.D., 1908; m. Mary Jordan Dimock, June 15, 1918. Instr. in English, Yale, 1908-13, asst. prof., 1913-26, asso. prof., 1926-33, prof. English, 1933-50, prof. emeritus, 1950—, master of Berkeley Coll., 1937—. Trustee Mount Holyoke Coll. Clubs: Elizabethan, Senior Society of Berzelius (Yale); Yale, Century Assn. (N.Y.C.). Editor: 3 Vols. Yale Edition of Shakespeare, 1917-1921, 1924; New Variorum Edition of Shakespeare's Henry IV, Part I, 1937. Home: 42 Lincoln St., New Haven 10. Died Dec. 30, 1958; buried Grove Street Cemetery, New Haven.

HEMINGWAY, Walter Clarke, business exec.; b. New Haven, Conn., Sept. 11, 1887; s. Frederick Howard and Mary Terry (Clarke) H.; Ph.B., Sheffield Sci. Sch., Yale, 1909; m. Jane Elizabeth Ball, Apr. 10, 1915 (dec. Jan. 1931); 1 son, Richard; m. 2d, Mrs. Ruth Hutchinson Ball, May 5, 1933; stepchildren—Ernest Elijah Ball, Robert Hutchinson Ball. With Am. Bridge Co., 1909-17, draftsman, engr., Elmira (N.Y.), Ambridge (Pa.), Wilmington (Del.), also designer, N.Y. office, 1909-12, constrn. supt., Panama Canal Zone, 1912-14; with Fed. Shipbldg. and Dry Dock Co., 1917-48, engr., supt., 1917-27, v.p., gen. mgr., 1927-48, dir., 1927-48; pres., dir. Pittsburgh Steamship Co. since 1948. Mem. Soc. Naval Architects and Marine Engrs. (v.p.), Council of Am. Shipbuilders, Am. Bur. of Shipping, Lake Carriers Assn. (dir.). Republican. Conglist. Clubs: Mid Day, Kirtland, Country, Union (all Cleveland); Montclair Golf (N.J.); Duquesne (Pittsburgh). Home: Carpenter Rd., Gates Mills, O. Office: Rockefeller Bldg., Cleve. Died Mar. 21, 1951; buried Mount Hebron Cemetery, Upper Montclair, N.J.

HEMINGWAY, Wilson Linn, banker; b. Potosi, Mo., Dec. 2, 1880; s. Wilson E. and Helen (Gerault) H.; B.S., Vanderbilt U., 1900; m. Lois Roots, Mar. 1, 1905; children—Margaret, Helen, Miriam. Began as bank collector, Little Rock, Arkansas, 1900; secretary, Mercantile Trust Company, Little Rock, 1906-15, pres. 1915-19; v.p. Nat. Bank of Commerce, St. Louis, 1919-29; pres. Federal Commerce Trust Co., 1924-29; exec. v.p. Mercantile Commerce Bank & Trust Co., 1930-33, pres. Jan. 1933, chmn. bd., 1947; pres. Mercantile Commerce Co. since Jan. 1932; chmn. exec. com. Merc. Trust Co. since 1951; apptd. head St. Louis Loan Agency, Reconstruction Finance Corp., Feb. 1932; dir. Texas Pacific Ry. Pres. St. Louis Regional Inter-American Center. Chairman U.S. Inter-American council. Trustee Vanderbilt U., Washington U. Pres. Am. Bankers Assn., 1942; v.p. Inter Am. Council Commerce and Prodn., 1951-52. Republican. Clubs: Clubs: Noonday, St. Louis Country. Home: 4931 Lindell Blvd., St. Louis 8. Office: 721 Locust St., St. Louis 1. Died Sept. 22, 1954.

HEMPEL, Frieda, operatic soprano; b. in Saxony; d. of Emil H. and Augusta (Morler) Hempel; student Sterns Conservatory, Berlin, under Mme. Nicklass Kempner; m. William B. Kahn (div.). Début, Royal Opera House, Berlin in Merry Wives of Windsor; appeared in Schwerin Opera House; toured Europe, as principal guest soprano at Covent Garden, London, Grand Opera, Paris, Warsaw, Stockholm, Brussels, Ostende, San Sebastian, all other principal opera houses, orchestras throughout the Continent. One of five Imperial German Ct. Singers; prin. coloratura soprano, Royal Opera, Berlin, Germany, later coloratura soprano Met. Opera Co., N.Y. Principal rôles: Violetta in Traviata, Gilda in Rigoletto, Susanna in Figaro, Rosina in Barber of Seville, Eva in Meistersinger, Marie in Daughter of the Regiment, Marschallin in Rosenkavalier (which role she created in Berlin, N.Y.), Mimi in La Bohême, Margaret in Faust, about 70 other leading rôles in Italian, French, German operas; chosen to impersonate Jenny Lind in Hist. Centennial Concert, Carnegie Hall, N.Y., 1920; has since given many "Jenny Lind" concerts U.S., twice toured the British Isles. Decorated by Emperor of Germany, King of Belgium, Grand Duke of Mecklenburg-Schwerin, Duke of Anhalt, etc. Died Oct. 7, 1955; buried Heerestrasse Freidhof, Berlin, Germany.

HEMPHILL, Victor Herman, lawyer; b. Carlinville, Ill., Sept. 21, 1882; s. Robert S. and Mary J. (Ross) H.; B.S., Blackburn Coll., 1902, LL.D., 1936; LL.B., Washington U., 1905; m. Adele M. Loehr, July 21, 1915; children—Barbara (Mrs. James L. Henning), Robert. Instr., 1902-03; admitted to Ill. bar, 1905, since practiced in Carlinville; states atty. Macoupin Co., 1916-20, 28-32; mayor of Carlinville, 1922-28; circuit judge, 1933-45; taught Northwestern U. Law Sch., summer 1936, 38. Trustee Blackburn Coll., Carlinville. Mem. Am., Ill. bar assns., Phi Delta Phi. Democrat. Methodist. Mason. Author: Illinois Jury Instructions, Civil and Criminal (2 vol.). Home: 941 E. First N. Office: 126½ E. Main St., Carlinsville, Ill. Died Oct. 19, 1957.

HEMPSTEAD, Clark, co-chairman of the board of the Pillsbury Mills, Inc.; b. Galena, Ill., Oct. 29, 1873; s. William and Anna Jane (Clark) H.; A.B., U. of Minn., 1896; LL.B., Harvard, 1904; m. Clara A. Newhall, Aug. 21, 1906. Teacher, Shattuck Sch., Faribault, Minn., 1896-1901; admitted to Minn. bar, 1905, and then practiced in Minneapolis in office of Koon, Whelan & Bennett, 1904-07; mem. firm Koon, Whelan & Hempstead, 1908-21; sec. and gen. counsel Pillsbury Flour Mills Co., Minneapolis, 1921-36, pres., 1936-40, gen. counsel, 1940-46, co-chmn. of bd. Pillsbury Mills, Inc., since 1940. Episcopalian. Home: 1777 Dupont Av. S., Mpls. 5. Office: Pillsbury Bldg., Mpls. 2. Died June 29, 1952; buried Lakewood Cemetery, Mpls.

HENDERLITE, James Henry, clergyman; b. Marion, Va., Feb. 27, 1872; s. George Washington and Rachel Anna (Killinger) H.; B.A., and B.Litt., Hampden-Sydney Coll., 1891; student Columbia (S.C.) Theol. Sem., 1893-94; B.D., Louisville Presbyn. Theol. Sem., 1896; D.D., Davidson (N.C.) Coll., 1918; m. Nelle Crow, Mar. 25, 1903; children—Virginia (Mrs. Frank St. Elmo Jones), Rachel, James Henry. Ordained ministry Presbyn. Ch. in U.S., 1896; pastor Accomac, Va., 1896-1902, Henderson, N.C., 1902-07, Fredericksburg, Va., 1907-12, also teacher classes in philosophy and Bible, at Fredericksburg Coll.; pastor First Ch., Gastonia, N.C., 1913-—. Mem. bd. trustees Union Theol. Sem. (Richmond, Va.), Queen's-Chicora Coll. for Women (Charlotte, N.C.), Junior Coll. for Men (Maxton, N.C.); formerly mem. exec. com. of religious edn. and publ.. and of com. of stewardship and finance, Presbyn. Ch. in U.S.; rep. to Western sect. of Alliance of Ref. Chs., term, 1931-39; moderator Synod of N.C., 1923-24; mem. adv. com. of Christian edn. Presbyn. Ch. in U.S.; adv. mem. Va. Capitol Bicentennial Commn. (for the 200th Anniversary of the Founding of Richmond by Col. William Byrd). 1737-1937. Democrat. Mason (32°), K.P. Home: Gastonia, N.C. Deceased.

HENDERSON, Charles Belknap, former chmn. bd. Reconstruction Finance Corp.; b. San Jose, California, June 8, 1873; s. Jefferson and Sarah W. (Bradley) H.; g.s. Lewis Rice Bradley, 1st gov. of Nev.; family settled in Nev., 1872; student U. of Pacific, 1892; spl. course in history, Stanford U.; LL.B., U. of Michigan, 1895, LL.M., 1896; LL.D. (honorary), University of Nevada; married Ethel Smith, 1901; children—Wellington S., Charles J. Began practice at Elko, Nev., 1896; dist. atty. of Elko County, Nev., 1901-05; mem. Nev. legislature, 1905-07; regent U. of Nev., 1907-17; apptd. mem. U.S. Senate, Jan. 4, 1918, by Gov. Emmet D. Boyle, to fill vacancy until election, caused by death of Francis G. Newlands, elected Nov. 1918, for unexpired term ending 1921; pres. and dir., Elko (Nev.) Telephone & Telegraph Co.; dir. Western Pac. R.R. Co. Dir. R.F.C., 1934-47, chmn. bd., 1941-47. Democrat. Episcopalian. Was 2d lt. Troop M, 2d U.S. Vol. Cav., Spanish-Am. War, 1898. Mason (Shriner), Elk. Clubs: Pacific Union, Burlingame Country (San Francisco); Metropolitan (Washington, D.C.). Home: 1055 California St., San Francisco. Died Nov. 8, 1954; buried Elko, Nev.

HENDERSON, Daniel (MacIntyre), author; born Balt., May 27, 1880; s. Daniel MacIntyre and Alice Matilda (Ashcroft) H.; ed. pub. schs.; m. Bertie Corinne Askew, June 7, 1904 (dec.); 1 dau., Ruth (Mrs. H. Woodward McDowell); m. 2d, Ernestine Rauch, Jan. 14, 1937. On staff McClure's Mag., 1915-21; staff N.Y. Evening Post, 1921-22; asso. editor McClure's Mag. and People's Home Journal, 1922-24; staff of Hearst Magazines, Inc., 1924-48; ret., 1948. Trustee, Carnegie Fund for Needy Authors. Mem. Poetry Soc. Am., St. Andrew's Soc. of N.Y. (hist). Authors Guild, U.S. Naval Inst. Clubs: Authors, Coffee House. Author: Life's Minstrel—A Book of Verse, 1919; Great Heart—The Life Story of Theodore Roosevelt, 1919; Jungle Roads and Other Trails of Roosevelt, 1920; Boone of the Wilderness, 1921; Pirate Princes and Yankee Jacks (U.S. naval campaign with Barbary pirates), 1923; A Harp in the Winds (verse), 1924; Children of the Tide, 1926; The Golden Bees (biog. novel), 1928; A Crown for Carlotta (hist. novel), 1929; The Crimson Queen (Mary Tudor), 1933; Frontiers (verse), 1933; Ballads of American Trails; From the Volga to the Yukon; The Russian March to Alaska and California (history), 1944; Yankee Ships in China Seas; Americans in China (history), 1945; The Hidden Coasts: Life of Admiral Charles Wilkes, U.S.N., 1953; (with Burton Jesse Hendrick) Life of Louise Whitfield Carnegie, 1950; Lives and Times of Poets Alice and Phoebe Cary (with Ernestine Henderson) (posthumously); Book of Verse: Chant for Captain Kidd (posthumously); Louisiana Purchase and Western Expansion (posthumously). Editor Reveille: war poems by members of our Armed Forces (book), 1943. Contbr. to mags. Home: R.D. 1, Hampton, N.J. Died Nov. 12, 1955.

HENDERSON, Earl C., ins. exec.; b. Ingersoll, Ont., Can., Dec. 25, 1892; B.A., U. Toronto. Vice pres., actuary Conn. Gen. Life Ins. Co., Hartford, Conn. Fellow Soc. Actuaries. Home: 15 Birch Rd., West Hartford, Conn. Office: 55 Elm St., Hartford, Conn. Died Mar. 14, 1955; buried West Hartford, Conn.

HENDERSON, Elmer Lee, surgeon; b. Garnettsville, Ky., Mar. 23, 1885; s. Jonas and Henrietta (Lewis) H.; M.D., U. Louisville, 1909; m. Laura Bell Owen, April 4, 1911; children—William Owen, Henrietta Marie. In practice of gen. surgery, Louisville, 1911-—; mem. staff Ky. Bapt. Hosp., St. Joseph Infirmary; mem. cons. staff S. S. Mary and Elizabeth Hosp.; courtesy staff all other pvt. hosps., Louisville; spl. surg. cons. to air surgeon's office, U.S. Army, 1942-—. Chmn. 5th Service Command Com. Procurement and Assignment Service for Physicians, Dentists and Vets., 1942-46. Served from lt. to maj., M.C., World War I; with AEF, 9 mos.; lt. col. Med. R.C., 1919-20. Mem. bd. overseers U. Louisville. Mem. mission to Japan to make survey and recommendations on Social Security, med. edn., med. service, 1948. Mem. bd. govs. Kosair Crippled Children's Hosp.; bd. trustees Nat. Soc. Crippled Children and Adults. Diplomate Am. Bd. Surgery. Hon. fellow Societe Piedmontese Di Chirurgia, Internat. Coll. Surgeons, Japanese Med. Assn.; fellow A.C.S.; mem. Southeastern Surg. Cong. (pres. 1946-47, mem. exec. com., 1947-—), So. Med. Assn. (councillor from Ky., 1938-42; chmn. surg. sect. 1942-44; pres. 1946-47; trustee, 1947-—), A.M.A (bd. trustees, 1938—, chmn., 1947—), World Med. Assn. (mem. council, del. from A.M.A., 1948; pres., chmn. bd. U.S. Com. Inc.). Alumni Assn. U. of Louisville (pres. 1938-41), Ky. Med. Assn. (pres. 1941-42), Jefferson County Med. Soc. (pres. 1918), Am. Legion, Alpha Omega Alpha. Mason (33°, Shriner), De Molay. Clubs: Pendennis, Filson, Big Spring Golf (Louisville). Home: 87 Valley Rd. Office: 606 S. 4th St., Louisville. Died July 30, 1953.

HENDERSON, John Thompson; b. Belltown, Tenn., July 27, 1858; s. Benjamin Peck and Margaret Adaline H.; A.B., Carson Coll., 1933; A.M., 1895, LL.D., 1917; Columbian U., 1899-1900, m. Sophrona California Williams, May 14, 1883; children—Maude Lee (wife of Dr. J. Victor Henderson), Margaret Mata (dec.). Prof. mathematics, Carson Coll., 1883-93; pres. Carson and Newman Coll., 1893-1903. Va. Intermont Coll., Bristol, Va., June 1, 1903-14. Pres. Tenn. Bapt. Conv., 1891-1902, Bapt. Congress, 1896; v.p. Southern Bapt. Conv., 1898, 1917; elected corr. sec. of Bapt. State Mission Bd. of Tenn., 1902, but declined; pres. Bapt. Gen. Assn. of Va., 1907; gen. sec. Baptist Brotherhood of the South, July 1908-July 1938; retired, 1938. Home: Knoxville, Tenn. Deceased.

HENDERSON, Joseph W(elles), lawyer; b. Montgomery, Pa., Feb. 6, 1890; s. Samuel B. and Jean (Wells) H.; A.B., Bucknell U., 1908, A.M., 1913, D.C.L., 1944; LL.B., Harvard 1913; LL.D., Temple U., 1944; m. Anne K. Dreisbach, May 26, 1917; 1 son, J. Welles. Admitted to Pa. bar, 1913, began practice at Phila.; mem. firm Rawle & Henderson 1916-—. Spl. counsel on ins., Alien Property Custodian, 1918; spl. asst. to Atty. Gen., 1953-—. Dir. Nat. Traffic Bur. Mem. Nat. Adv. Council to Com. on Patents, Ho. of Rep. Mem. Pension Bd., Presbyn. Ch , 1945-48; mem. nat. council on Naturalization and Citizenship, 1946, War dept. Adv. Com. on mil. justice; mem. hearing bd. examiners for hearing examiner personnel, U.S. Civil Serv. Commn. Trustee Tabor Home for Children. Chmn. bd., trustee Bucknell U. Vice pres. Nat. Assn. of Legal Aid Orgn., dir. Phila. Legal Aid Soc. Mem. Am. Bar Assn. (pres. 1943-44; mem. gen. council, 1935; state del., 1936-37; mem. bd. govs., 1937-40; assembly del., 1940; mem. council, sect. legal edn., 1940-43); mem. council ins. sect., 1944; Phila. Bar Assn. (mem. bd. govs. 1936-39, chmn. 1939); Maritime Law Assn.; (mem. exec. com.); Pa. State Bar Assn. (chmn. com. to consider necessity for constl. conv., 1933, com. on Pa. Constitution 1937; chmn. Com. on War Work, 1940-43); chmn. internat. law com., 1944-45; Inter-Am. Bar Assn. (council 1944); hon. mem. of Canadian, Mont., Vt., Wash. bar assns. Mem. Harvard Law Sch. Assn. (v.p.), St. Andrew's Soc. of Phila. (pres.), Phi Beta Kappa, Phi Kappa Psi, Omicron Delta Kappa (hon.). Decorated Officer and Chevalier of Order of Crown of Italy. Republican. Presbyn. Clubs: Rittenhouse, Union League, Midday, Harvard, Sunnybrook. Mem. adv. bd. Editors Am. Bar Assn. Jour. Asso. editor Am. Maritime Cases, 1931-—. Home: 201 W. Gravers Lane, Chestnut Hill, Pa. Office: Packard Bldg., Phila. Died July 25, 1957; buried W. Laurel Hill Cemetery, Montgomery County, Pa.

HENDERSON, Melvin Starkey, orthopedic surgeon; b. St. Paul, Minn., Feb. 18, 1883; s. Melvin Brooks and Emily Grace (Starkey) H.; M.B., U. of Toronto, 1906. M.D., 1914; m. Mabel Christensen, Feb. 10, 1912; children—Edward Drewry, Melvin Starkey. Mem. staff of Mayo Clinic, Rochester, Minn., 1907-50; prof. orthopedic surgery, Mayo Foundation, U. of Minn., 1920-—. Fellow Am. Coll. Surgeons, Acad. Orthopedic Surgeons (pres. 1936); mem. Am. Orthopedic Assn. (pres. 1934), A.M.A., Am. Bd. Orthopedic Surgery (pres. 1934), Clin. Orthopedic Soc., Western Surg. Assn., Minn. Med. Assn. (pres. 1932), Southern Minn. Med. Assn. (pres. 1918), Minn. Acad. of Medicine, Pan-Am. Med. Assn., Internat. Orthopedic Assn., Societas Orthopedica Scandinavica, Société des Chirurgiens de Paris, Sigma Xi, Nu Sigma Nu. Episcopalian. Mason. Clubs: University (Rochester), University (St. Paul). Contbr. numerous articles to med. jours. Home: 801 9th Av. S.W., Rochester, Minn. Died June 17, 1954; buried Rochester.

HENDERSON, Philip Eldon, educator; b. Lynchburg, O., May 23, 1901; s. Herschel Nelson and Martha Mae (DeLaney) H.; A.B., U. of Colo., 1922; M.B.A., Harvard, 1926; m. Myrtle Hardaker, June 7, 1934; children—Philip Eldon, Cynthia Myrtle. High sch. tchr., Wyo., Mont., 1922-24; auditor H. C. Hopson and Co., N.Y.C., summers 1926-28; instr. Temple U., 1926-28; head dept. commerce Junior Coll. of Conn., 1928-29; asso. sec. Taylor Soc. for Sci. Mgmt., 1929-31; comptroller Mt. Holyoke Coll., 1931-34; traveling auditor, retail store supr. B. F. Goodrich Co., 1934-35; asst. mgr. Cocoa and Chocolate Code Authority, 1935-36; finance mgr. Farm Security Adminstr., 1936-37, asst. regional dir., 1936-37, regional dir., 1937-41; asst. to pres. Western Coll. for Women, Oxford, O., 1941-43, v.p., 1943-45, pres., 1945-51; chmn. dept. econs. and bus. adminstrn. Wilmington Coll. 1951-—; adminstrv. staff Summer Sch. for Am. Students U. Oslo, Norway,

1948. Mem. Nat. Assn. Foremen. Soc. Advancement Mgmt. Mason (32°). Clubs: Kiwanis (chmn. vocational guidance Ohio dist.), Harvard, University (Cin.). Home: Lynchburg, O. Office: Wilmington College, Wilmington, O. Died Apr. 25, 1955; buried Lynchburg, O.

HENDERSON, Robert, naval officer; b. Albany, N.Y., Oct. 15, 1878; s. William and Isabella (Simpson) H.; B.S., U.S. Naval Acad., 1902; LL.B., George Washington U., 1925; grad. U.S. Naval War Coll., 1920, U.S. Army War Coll., 1927; m. Margaret Tyson Ellicott, May 25, 1905; children—Robert Ellicott (U.S.N.R.), Carroll Ellicott (wife of Dr. Eilif C. Hanssen). Entered U.S. Navy, Spanish War, 1898, served successively through all grades to rear adm., 1947; ret. voluntarily, 1929; served in Spanish War, West Indies Revolution; comdr. troop transports to France, World War I; served on active duty in Alaska, India and Navy Dept., World War II. Vice pres., dir. So. Cal. Asso. Newspapers (a subsidiary of Copley Press) 1929—. Nominated Rep. candidate to Congress, 18th Cal. Dist., 1931; del. from Cal. to Cleveland Rep. Nat. Conv., 1936. Decorations: Navy Cross, Spanish War Service medal; World War I Service medal with service bars and stars for Battleship Fleet, W.I. Campaign, Army Armed Guard Service, Cruiser and Transports Force; World War II Service medal; Royal Norwegian Order of Saint Olaf (rank of commodore), Chinese Spl. Breast Order of Yun Hui with ribbon; Order of Polish Restituta Officers Cross; Czechoslovak medal of Merit First Class with silver star; War Dept. Letter of Commendation for World War I Services. Baptist. Clubs: Chevy Chase, Army and Navy (Washington); Yacht (N.Y. C.); Athletic (Los Angeles). Home: 126 S. Lucerne Blvd., Los Angeles. Office: 801 Moraga Dr., Bel Air, Cal. Died Feb. 5, 1956; buried Arlington Nat. Cemetery.

HENDERSON, Walter C.; b. Chelsea, Mass., July 6, 1876; s. William C. and Margaret (Robertson) H.; LL.B., Boston U., 1903; A.B., George Washington U., 1926; m. Margaret L. Orpin, Oct. 21, 1908 (dec.); 1 son, Fletcher O. (dec.). Practiced in Boston, 1903-07; dist. law officer of Forest Service, 1908-10; admitted to bar U.S. Supreme Court, 1910; asst. to solicitor of Dept. of Agr., Washington, 1910-16; asst. chief, Biol. Survey, 1916-26, asso. chief, 1927-40; asst. dir. Fish and Wildlife Service, 1940-—. Fellow A.A.A.S.; mem. Am. Ornithologists' Union, Am. Forestry Assn., Nat. Conservation Assn., Cooper Ornithol. Club, Am. Soc. Mammalogists, Biol. Soc. Washington, Nat. Assn. Audubon Socs., Epsilon Pi. Republican. Episcopalian. Mason. Clubs: Cosmos, Kenwood Golf and Country. Office: Fish and Wildlife Service, Dept. of Interior, Washington. Deceased.

HENDREN, Paul, naval officer; b. nr. Statesville, N.C., Nov. 10, 1889; s. John J. and Sarah Pearl (Linney) H.; B.S., U.S. Naval Acad., 1913; grad. U.S. Naval War Coll., 1932, U.S. Indsl. Coll., 1933; m. Elizabeth Bryson Pettit, Feb. 4, 1922; children—Constance Pettit (Mrs. H. M. Nicholson, Jr.), Paul M.; m. 2d, Emma B. Williamson, June 1, 1957. Commd. ensign U.S. Navy, 1913, advanced through grades to vice adm., 1949; participated in occupation Vera Cruz, Mexico, 1914, in World Wars I and II; commanded cruiser U.S.S. Philadelphia in invasion of N. Africa, of Sicily, and at Salerno, 1943; ret. Aug. 1949. Awarded Legion of Merit (3), gold star in lieu of 4th; Military medal 1st class; diploma from Chile; British Distinguished Service Order. Episcopalian. Clubs: Army-Navy (Washington); Army-Navy Country (Arlington, Va.); N.Y. Yacht; Cape Fear (Wilmington, N.C.). Contbr. articles to New York Times, Sat. Eve. Post, U.S. Naval Inst. Proc. Home: 616 Market St., Wilmington, N.C. Died Nov. 28, 1958; buried Arlington Nat. Cemetery.

HENDRICKSON, Homer O., educator, clergyman; b. Burlington, Ia., Feb. 20, 1890; s. Peter and Mary Lena (Schroeder) H.; student Ia. Wesleyan Acad., 1912; A.B., Ia. Wesleyan Coll., 1916; spl. student Boston U., 1917; B.D., Garrett Bibl. Inst., 1920; M.A., Northwestern U., 1920, Ph.D., 1932; spl. student U. Mich., 1938; m. Grace Iris Scholes, Dec. 25, 1917. Ordained to ministry Meth. Ch., 1916; pastor in Ia., Mass. and Ill., 1915-20; prof. econs. and sociology Ia. Wesleyan Coll., 1920-27; prof. polit. sci. and sociology U. Dubuque, 1927-28; prof. history and polit. sci. Albion (Mich.) coll., 1928-—, now Henry M. Loud prof. history and polit. sci., chmn. social sci. div., 1950-—, chmn. dept. history and polit. sci., 1951. Mem. City Council, Mt. Pleasant, Ia., 1924-27. Mem. Mich. Council Nat. Def., 1942-45. Mem. Midwest Polit. Sci. Assn., Miss. Valley Hist. Assn., Mich. Oil and Gas Assn., Pi Kappa Delta, Lambda Chi Alpha, Omicron Delta Kappa. Republican. Methodist. Mason. Home: 1109 Perry St., Albion, Mich. Died Feb. 2, 1958; buried Aspen Grove Cemetery, Burlington, Ia.

HENKLE, Charles Zane, banker; b. Chgo., Aug. 16, 1892; s. William H. and Mary F. (Zane) H.; student Cornell U., 1911-12; m. Rita J. Guignon, Nov. 11, 1922; 1 son, Charles Zane (dec.). Solicitor, Commonwealth Edison Co., Chgo., 1912-13; div. contract agt. Pub. Service Co. of No. Ill., Evanston, Ill., 1914-15; salesman Counselman & Co., investment bankers, Chgo., 1916-17, Ill. Trust & Savs. Bank, Chgo., 1920-21; municipal buyer, bond dept. Merchants Loan & Trust Co., 1922; corp. buyer, bond dept. Ill. Merchants Trust Co., 1923-29; 2d v.p. Continental Ill. Co., 1929-32; 2d v.p. Continental Ill. Nat. Bank & Trust Co., 1932-40, v.p. 1941-—. Served as 1st lt., 166th Inf., capt., 359th Inf., AEF, 1917-19; col., on active duty, dep. dir. personnel Gen. Staff Corps, hdqrs. 6th Service Command, 1942-44. Vice chmn. Chgo.-Cook County 6th War Loan Com.; treas., mem. nat. exec. com. Mil. Training Camps Assn. of U.S., 1944-49. Trustee Ravinia Festival Assn., 1940-49. Chmn. Red Cross Fund Chgo., 1948, chmn. Chgo. chpt. A.R.C., 1948-50. Mem. Am. Banking Inst., Mil. Order World War, Am. Legion. Republican. Clubs: Union League (pres. 1946-47), Commercial, Exmoore Country, Bankers, Caxton. Awarded Silver Star, Purple Heart, Army Commendation ribbon. Home: 17 Brittany Rd., Highland Park, Ill. Office: 231 S. LaSalle St., Chgo. 90. Died Oct. 3, 1949.

HENMON, Vivian Allen Charles, educator; b. Centralia, Wis., Nov. 27, 1877; s. Joseph Jonas and Minnie (Ekelund) H.; A.B., Bethany Coll., Kan., 1895, A.M., 1898; Ph.D., Columbia, 1905; m. Katharine Porter Vilas, June 9, 1914. Prin. schs., Lincoln, Mo., 1895-97; instr. pedagogy, 1898-1900, prof., 1900-05, Bethany Coll.; lectr. on psychology Columbia, 1905-07; prof. psychology, edn., 1907-10, acting dean Coll. Liberal Arts, 1909-10, U. Colo.; asso. prof. edn., 1910-13, prof., 1913-26, dir. Sch. of Edn., 1916-26, prof. psychology U. Wis., 1927-48, emeritus, 1948-—; prof. ednl. psychology Yale, 1926-27; prof. summer sessions, Columbia, Harvard, Yale. Adv. in ednl. psychology Modern Lang. Study, 1925-29; mem. Com. on Modern Langs., 1929-43. Supr. psychol. research, Civil Aeros. Authority, 1939-40. Pres. Aviation Exam. Bd., Syracuse, N.Y. Capt. Aviation Sect., Signal O.R.C., 1917-19; maj., 1919-31. Republican. Lutheran. Fellow A.A.A.S. (v.p. and chmn. sect. L, 1919); mem. Am. Psychol. Assn., Soc. Coll. Tchrs. Edn. (pres. 1926), Am. Edn. Research Assn., Soc. Advancement Edn., Phi Beta Kappa, Sigma Xi, Alpha Tau Omega, Phi Kappa Phi, Phi Delta Kappa. Home: 4205 Hillcrest Drive, Madison 5, Wis. Died Jan. 10, 1950.

HENN, Albert William, mfr.; b. New Britain, Conn., Jan. 26, 1865; s. Francis A. and Barbara (Wilhelmy) H.; student grammar sch.; m. Gertrude J. Bruce, 1889; children—Jessie (dec.), William (dec.), Edwin Charles, Howard Ralph, Jeannette Marie, Robert Bruce. Began with Acme Machine Screw Co., Hartford, Conn., subsequently with the Nat. Acme Mfg. Co., Cleve., now The Nat. Acme Co., Cleve., mfrs. automatic screw machines, of which is a director; now retired. Treas. and trustee Glenville Hosp.; trustee Cleveland Hosp. Service Assn. Republican. Episcopalian. Mason. Home: 23131 Lake Shore Blvd., Euclid, O. Died May 2, 1947.

HENNESSY, John Lawrence, hotel and restaurant exec.; b. Angola, N.Y., Jan. 8, 1886; s. John L. and Margaret (Ryan) H.; ed. in pub. schs. of N.Y.; m. Mary Ellen Hanson, Apr. 17, 1907. Began in hotel business as freight elevator operator, Hotel Iroquois, Buffalo, 1900, advancing to mail and information clerk; joined Court Inn, Buffalo, as room clerk and cashier, 1906; with Hotels Statler Co., Inc., 1913-48, became v.p., 1928, vice chmn. bd., 1938, chmn. bd., 1945, v.p. and dir. Statler Hotels Co., Del.; v.p. Hilton Hotels Corp.; dir. hotel operations Kirkeby Hotels, N.Y.C.; chmn. bd. Pitts. Hotel Co.; chmn. bd. Pitts. Hotels, Inc.; pres., dir. J. L. Hennessy Assos., Inc.; dir. Childs Co., Louis Sherry, Inc., Pitts. Hotels, Inc. Served during World War II as chmn. war food com. Am. Hotel Assn.; vice chmn. Restaurant Industry Adv. Com. to O.P.A.; spl. food cons. to Sec. of War; food cons. AEC, Los Alamos, 1952. Clubs: Metropolitan, N.Y. Skeeters (N.Y.C.); Deepdale Golf (Great Neck, N.Y.); North Hills Golf (Douglaston, N.Y.). Office: Hotel Statler, N.Y.C. Died June 2, 1955; buried Angola, N.Y.

HENNESSY, Michael Edmund, newspaperman; b. London, Eng., Oct. 24, 1866; s. Michael and Hanora (Martin) H.; brought by parents to U.S., 1875; ed. pub. schs., Boston, Eliot Acad., Jamaica Plain, Mass.; m. Catherine T. Sullivan, June 25, 1890; children—James Morgan (dec.), Grace (dec.), Michael E., Kathryn S., William Russell (dec.), Anna G., Walter J. (dec.). Mem. staff, Boston Globe, 1889-—, polit. reporter, 1900-—. Roman Catholic. Clubs: Newspaper, Clover (past-pres. and sec.), John Boyle O'Reilly (Boston). Author: Massachusetts Constitutional Conventions, 1917; Calvin Coolidge—From a Green Mountain Farm to the White House, 1924; Four Decades of Massachusetts Politics, 1935. Contbr. chpt. on politics and pub. events to Commonwealth History of Mass., 1900-28; writer Round About with M. E. Hennessy, editorial page feature, Boston Sunday Globe. Has known every pres. of U.S. since Pres. Cleveland; campaigned with McKinley, Bryan, Roosevelt, Taft, Wilson, Harding, Coolidge, Smith, Franklin D. Roosevelt, Landon, Willkie. Home: 46 Gardner St., West Roxbury, Mass. Office: 244 Washington St., Boston. Died May 12, 1955.*

HENNING, George Neely, univ. prof.; b. Washington, Apr. 10, 1871; s. George Custis and Susannah (Neely) H.; A.B., magna cum laude, Harvard, 1894, A.M., 1898; Litt.D., George Washington U., 1919; studied at Sorbonne, Paris, 1900-01; unmarried. Instr. French, Columbian Acad., Columbian Coll., 1894-97; instr. French, Harvard, 1899-1900; prof. Romance lang., 1901-39; prof. emeritus since 1939, dean Sch. of Graduate Studies, 1919-31, George Washington U.; sabbatical year, Paris, 1931-32. Mem. Inst. Français de Washington (administrateur), Phi Beta Kappa, Delta Phi Epsilon. Chevalier, Légion d'Honneur (France), 1934. Clubs: Federal Schoolmen's, Cosmos (Washington). Editor: La Question d'Argent, by A. Dumas, fils, 1898; Polyeucte, Martyr; tragédie Chrétienne, by Pierre Corneille, 1907; Representative French Lyrics of the Nineteenth Century, 1913, revised and enlarged, 1935; La Course du Flambeau, by Paul Hervieu, 1922; Representative Stories of Anatole France, 1924; Abeille at autres contes (by Anatole France), 1927. Contbr. articles on French lang. and lit. in Modern Lang. Notes, Romanic Rev., Books Abroad, French Rev., Harvard Alumni Bull., Modern Lang. Jour. Home: 3720 McKinley St., N.W., Washington 15. Died Dec. 30, 1950; buried Congressional Cemetery, Washington.

HENNINGS, E(rnest) Martin, artist; b. Pennsgrove, N.J., Feb. 5, 1886; s. Martin and Louise (Dunklau) H.; art edn., Art Inst. Chicago and Nat. Academy of Munich; married Helen Otte; one daughter, Helen Hennings Winton. Painter of Western landscapes, genre figure compositions and portraits. Represented in permanent collections of Preston Harrison Gallery, Los Angeles, Pa. Acad. Fine Arts, Phila., Mus. of Art, Houston, state collections Springfield, Ill. and Phoenix, Ariz., City Collection, Chgo., John H. Vanderpoel Collection, also H. J. L. Stark Collection, Orange, Tex. Awarded gold medal, Palette and Chisel Club, 1916; Englewood Woman's Club prize, Art Inst. Chicago, 1916, Clyde M. Carr prize, and Fine Arts Bldg. prize, same, 1922; Cahn prize, 1923; Lippincott prize, Pa. Acad. Fine Arts, 1925; Fine Arts Bldg. purchase prize ($500), 1926, and Frank prize, 1927, Art Inst. Chicago; Isidor medal, Nat. Acad. Design, New York, 1926; hon. mention, Paris Salon, 1927; 1st prize ($3,000) Tex. Wild Flower Competition, 1929; 1st prize, Acad. of Western Painters, Los Angeles, 1938. Mem. Assn. Taos Soc. Artists. Home: Taos, N.M. Died May 19, 1956; buried Meml. Park Cemetery, Evanston, Ill.

HENRICKS, Harold H., mfg. exec.; b. Pullman, Ill., July 11, 1889; s. Edward W. and Elikabeth (Van Winkle) H.; M.E., U. Ill., 1911; m. Florence Wilson, Sept. 18, 1926; children—Mary Patricia, Louise Ann. Joined Youngstown Steel Door Co., Cleve., 1925, pres. since 1949. Mem. Delta Kappa Epsilon. Republican. Roman Catholic. Elk. Clubs: Union (Cleve.); Youngstown, Youngstown (Ohio) Country. Home: 19101 Van Aken Blvd., Shaker Heights 22, O. Office: The Arcade, Cleve. 14. Died Nov. 1955.

HENRY, David W(atters), ret. univ. dean; b. New Canaan, Conn., Aug. 16, 1885; s. William and Margaret (Watters) H.; ed. Wyckoff Prep. Sch., New Canaan, Merrill Bus. Coll., Norwalk and Stamford, Conn.; diploma, State Normal Coll., Hyannis, Mass., 1909; A.B., State Teachers Coll., Emporia, Kan., 1911; M.A., Columbia U., 1916; diploma, U. of London (Eng.), 1937; m. Annis Lenore Canfield, Apr. 29, 1916; children—Marjorie Lee (Mrs. Leonard West), John McIntyre, David Watters, William Garrett, Robert James, Annis Katherine. Prin. North Center Sch., 1909-10, Rowayton Sch. (Norwalk), 1911-13; teacher Ethical Culture Sch., N.Y. City, 1913-14; asst. prof., edn. and psychology, U. of Toledo, 1914, asso. prof., 1915, dean, Coll. of Edn., 1920-55, ret. acting dean, college arts, 1929-32. Fellow A.A.A.S.; mem. Acad. Polit. Science, Coll. Teachers of Edn., A.A.A.S., N.E.A., American Acad. of Political and Social Science, Am. Assn. Univ. Profs., Am. Assn. Sch. Adminstrs., Ohio Teachers Assn., Ohio Supts. Assn., Phi Delta Kappa, Phi Gamma Mu, Kappa Delta Pi, Toledo chapter Internat. Torch Club. Home: 2538 Goddard Rd., Toledo. Died Oct. 12, 1955.

HENRY, Howell Meadors, educator; b. Newberry, S.C., Aug. 18, 1879; s. Hugh Pressley and Martha Harman (Boozer) H.; B.A., Newberry (S.C.) Coll., 1898; M.A., Vanderbilt U., 1908, Ph.D., 1913; m. Addie Fort, Aug. 28, 1913; children—Howell Kirkland, Hugh Fort. Tchr. pub. schs., S.C., 6 yrs.; fellow Vanderbilt, 1907-09, instr. in history, 1909-13; with Emory and Henry Coll., 1913-—, prof. history and econs., until 1924, prof. history and polit. science, 1924-—, dean, 1918-40. Mem. Am. Hist. Assn., Am. Polit. Science Assn., Tau Kappa Alpha, Pi Gamma Mu. Democrat. Methodist. Mason. Rotarian. Author: Police Control of the Slave in South Carolina, 1915. Home: Emory, Va. Died June 7, 1956; buried Emory.

HENRY, James McClure, missionary, educator; b. of Am. parents, Canton, China, Dec. 2, 1880; s. Benjamin C. (D.D.) and Mary Little (Snyder) H.; B.A., U. of Wooster, 1901, D.D., 1924; B.D., Union Theol. Sem., 1907; m. Natalie de Froideville, d.

President Francis Brown, of Union Theol. Sem., Oct. 11, 1909; children—Richard Morris, Mary Luise (Mrs. W. J. McFarland), James Francis Brown, Arthur G. (dec.), Natalie de Froideville (Mrs. R. A. Cordova). Missionary Am. Presbyn. Mission, Canton, China, 1909-19; with Lingnan U., 1919—, pres., 1924, provost, 1927-48, Am. dir., 1949-51; chief, overseas Chinese sect., Com. for Free Asia, 1951-52; dep. dir. U.N.R.R.A. Kwangtung Regional Office, 1945-47; adviser, Kwangtung Provincial Govt., 1948. Chmn. Canton Refugee Areas Relief Com., 1938-41. Attached to 14th Air Force Northern Kwangtung (Free China), 1944-45. Presented with keys to city and made hon. citizen, Canton, China, 1948; decorated by Chinese Government, Order of the Brilliant Star, 1949. Mem. Phi Gamma Delta, Delta Sigma Rho, Phi Beta Kappa. Republican. Mason. Gov. 96th Rotarian dist. 1938-41; mem. Nokomis Rotary. Interned at Canton by Japanese Govt. Repatriated 2d Gripsholm, 1943. Home: Nam Yuen, Nokomis, Florida. Office: Box 426, Nokomis, Fla. Died Dec. 18, 1958.

HENRY, Myron Ormell, surgeon; b. Minneapolis, Minn., Dec. 28, 1893; s. Wilson and Rose (Cannon) H.; B.S., U. of Minn., 1919, B.M., 1920; M.D., Harvard, 1922; m. Lucile Fisher, Apr. 14, 1920; 1 dau., Katherine. Interne, St. Mary's Hosp.; Mass. Gen. Hosp.; practice of medicine and surgery, Minneapolis, specializing in orthopedic surgery since 1922; faculty U. of Minn. Med. Sch., Minneapolis since 1924, as asst. in orthopaedic surgery. Fellow Internat. Orthopedic Soc., Am. Coll. Surgeons, Am. Orthopedic Assn.; mem. Hennepin Co. Med Soc., Minn. State Med. Assn., Clin. Orthopedic Soc. (past pres.), Am. Acad. Orthopedic Surgeons (pres.), Chi Psi, Nu Sigma Nu. Roman Catholic. Home: 4866 W. Lake Harriet Blvd., Minneapolis. Office: 401 Medical Arts Bldg., Mpls. 2. Died Aug. 31, 1953.

HENRY, Patrick, ex-congressman, lawyer; b. Madison Co., Miss., Feb. 12, 1843; ed. Miss. Coll., Clinton, Miss., Madison Coll., Sharon, Miss., and Nashville, Tenn., Mil. Coll.; left latter, 1861, to enter 6th Miss. inf., C.S.A.; served through war until surrendered, April 26, 1865; maj. 14th (conolidated) Miss. regt., m. Margie E. Cocke, Feb. 10, 1874. Farmed, 1866-73; since then in law practice at Brandon, Miss.; mem. Miss. legislture, 1878, 1890; del. at large to State Constitutional Conv., 1890; mem. Congress, 1897-1901, 7th Miss. dist.; mem. Miss. senate, 1903-07. Democrat. Address: Brandon, Miss. Died May 18, 1930.

HENRY, Sidney Morgan, shipping exec.; b. Staten Island, N.Y., Dec. 2, 1878; s. James B. and Louisa (Anderson) H.; B.S., U.S. Naval Acad, 1901; M.S., Mass. Inst. Tech., 1905; m. Julia B. Persons, Sept. 11, 1907 (dec. 1933); children—Sidney Morgan, Julia P. (dec.); m. 2d, Katherine E. Crabbs, Oct. 25, 1948. Commnd. naval cadet U.S. Navy, 1897, advanced through grades to capt., 1918; served in Spanish-Am. War and World War I; resigned, 1920; asst. to pres., later v.p. Balta Dry Docks & Shipbldg. Co., also v.p. Calvert Navigation Co., 1920-21; comml. mgr., later v.p. U.S. Shipping Bd Emergency Fleet Corp., 1921-25; with firm Edward P. Farley & Co., shipping, 1926-34; financial v.p. Munson Steamship Line, 1928; pres. J. B. Inderrieden Co., 1933-35; gen. mgr. for trustees Munson Steamship Line and affiliated cos., 1934-39; dir. Glen Falls Ins. Co., 1949-58. Asst. to dep. chief Office Procurement and Materials, Navy Dept., 1942-43. Decorated Spanish-Am. War medal, Sampson medal, Victory medal. Mem. Soc. Naval Architects and Marine Engrs., Chi Phi. Republican. Episcopalian. Clubs: Army and Navy, Chevy Chase (Washington); India House (N. Y.C.). Address: 35 Fifth Av., N.Y.C. 3. Died Mar. 16, 1959; buried U.S. Naval Acad. Cemetery, Annapolis, Md.

HENRY, Stuart, author; b. Clifton Springs, N.Y., Sept. 17, 1860; s. Oliver H. and Harriet (Hill) H.; A.B., U. Kan., 1881, A.M., 1893; studied 6 yrs. in Germany, Italy, Sorbonne, Paris; m. Nellie G. Thacher, 1889 (dec.); m. 2d, Georgia M. Johnson, 1895 (died 1936). Formerly sec., treas. Colo. Loan & Trust Co. and numerous allied irrigation and land cos., Denver; pres. N.Y. State Security Co., N.Y.C.; v.p. Autographic Register Co. of N.J. Pres. Phi Beta Kappa Alumni in N.Y.; treas. Carnegie Benevolent Fund for Authors. Republican. Clubs: Authors (treas.), Century (N.Y.). Author: Paris Days and Evenings, 1896; Hours with Famous Parisians, 1897; A Romance of a French Salon, 1903; The Nets (London), 1911; Villa Elsa, 1920 (only Am. novel discussed in regular session, French Acad.); French Essays and Profiles, 1921; Conquering Our Great American Plains, 1930. Former mem. editorial staff New Internat. Ency. Address: Century Club, N.Y.C. Died Feb., 1953.

HENSHAW, Albert Melville, educator; b. Cin., Mar. 6, 1879; s. Edward and Mary (Knight) H.; student Ohio Mil. Inst., Cin., 1892-97, U. Cin., 1902; m. Nancy Ely, June 8, 1908; children—Hugh Ely, Mary Katherine. Comdt. Ohio Mil. Inst., 1905-16, supt., 1916—; dir. G. Henshaw & Sons Furniture Co., Henshaw Realty Co. Dir. Belmont Coll. Republican. Episcopalian. Mason. Address: Ohio Mil. Inst., College Hill, Cin. Died June 20, 1950.

HENSON, John O'Neal, lawyer; b. Martinsburg, W.Va., Sept. 4, 1887; s. John O. and Annie (Harley) H.; student W.Va. U. Law Sch., 1906-08; m. Fay M. Miller, Nov. 1, 1913. Admitted to W.Va. bar, 1908, and since practiced in Martinsburg; asst. atty. gen. of W.Va., 1911-13; former pres., dir. Peoples Trust Co. Mem. State Bd. of Edn., 1929-33; mem. State of W.Va. Bd. of Law Examiners, 1919—, pres., 1935—. Mem. Am., W.Va. bar assns. Republican. Episcopalian. Clubs: Opequon Golf, Rotary (Martinsburg); Seaview County (Absecon, N.J.); Columbia Country (Washington). Home: "Red Hill." Office: Downey and Henson Bldg., Martinsburg, W.Va. Died Oct. 19, 1952.

HENWOOD, Berryman, judge; b. Hannibal, Mo., Apr. 23, 1881; s. George W. and Jennie (Dunham) H.; LL.B., cum laude, U. of Mo., 1904; m. Adele Tucker, Oct. 17, 1907 (died Mar. 23, 1937); children—Ethelyn (dec.), Virginia, Marion, Berryman (1st lt., U.S.M.C.R.; killed on Okinawa, July 2, 1945). Began practice of law at Hannibal, Mo., 1904; served as city atty., Hannibal, Mo., 1909-13; commr. Supreme Court of Mo., 1927-30; judge of Supreme Court, 1930-33; in practice at St. Louis, Mo., 1933-34. Jefferson City, Mo., 1935-52. Mem. State Eleemosynary Bd., 1935-37. Trustee in bankruptcy, St. Louis Southwestern Ry., Jan. 1936-Sept. 1947. Mem. Mo. Rep. State Com., 1912-16; chmn. Mo. Rep. State Conv., 1914; del. to Rep. Nat. Conv., 1916. Mem. Am. Bar Assn., Mo. State Bar Assn., Phi Delta Phi. Methodist. Mason, Elk. Home: 1116 Moreau Drive, Jefferson City, Mo. Retired 1952. Died Mar. 7, 1955. Buried Riverview Cemetery, Jefferson City, Mo.

HEPBURN, Frederick Taylor, investments; b. Corry, Pa., Apr. 26, 1873; s. Charles J. and Georgianna (Taylor) H.; C.E., Rensselaer Polytech. Inst., 1893; m. Mary McClelland Hepburn, Nov. 1, 1900; children—Mary McClelland (Mrs. Carlos Lazo), George, Rodman advancing to div. engr. Pa. R.R., 1893-1906; gen. mgr. Ohio Elec. Ry., 1906-10. Saginaw-Bay City (Mich.) Gas, Electric and Street Rys., 1910-11; pres. H. D. Walbridge & Co., N.Y. City, operating gas and electric companies, 1911-27; pres. Penn Pub. Service Co., 1912-25; partner Frederick T. Hepburn & Co., investment securities, N.Y. City, since 1927; pres. Automatic Nut Co.; v.p. Candlemas Collieries Co.; dir. Electric Power & Light Corp., United Gas Corp., Catalin Corp. of Am., Silver Brook Anthracite Co. Life trustee Rensselaer Polytech. Inst. Mayor Village of Lattington, Nassau County, N.Y. Life mem. Am. Inst. E.E., Am. Soc. C.E.; mem. N.Y. C. of C. Clubs: Engineers, India House, Creek. Home: Locust Valley, L.I., N.Y. Died June 15, 1956.

HEPBURN, William McGuffey, dean law sch.; b. Cin., Oct. 5, 1900; s. Charles McGuffey and Julia (Benedict) H.; A.B., Ind. U., 1921; LL.B., Yale, 1928; LL.M., Harvard, 1930; student Sorbonne, Paris, summer 1923; m. Helen Bridget, June 30, 1926; children—William McGuffey, Jr., Julia Ann, Mary Helen, Catherine Brook, Lucy Benedict, Andrew Moore. Teacher Linton (Ind.) High Sch., 1921-22; tutor and instr. in French, Ind. U., 1922-24; instr. New Haven (Conn.) High Sch., 1924; instr. in French, Yale, 1925-29; asst. prof. of law, U. of Ala., 1930-31, asso. prof., 1931-32, prof., 1932—, on leave, 1940-41, and 1943-44. dean School of Law, 1944-50; dean and prof. of law Emory University Sch. Law, Atlanta, 1950—; vis. prof. U. N.C., summer 1949, U. Chgo. Sch. Law, summer 1956. Mem. Nat. W.S.B., Washington, 1951-52. Associate sec. Am. Assn. of Univ. Profs., Washington, 1940-41. Pub. mem. and vice-chmn. regional War Labor Bd., 4th region, March 1943-June 1944, part-time public mem. June 1944-Dec. 1945; mem. Ala. Bd. Bar Examiners, 1944-50; mem. Judicial Council of Ala., 1944-50. Member Am., Ala., Ga. bar assns., Am. Assn. Univ. Profs. (pres. U. Ala. Chapter, 1934-37; mem. nat. council (1938-41); chmn. Labor-Management Advisory Council U.S. Conciliation Service, Region IV, 1946; member Phi Beta Kappa, Beta Theta Pi, Phi Delta Phi, Omicron Delta Kappa. Democrat. Episcopalian. Author: Cases on Torts, 3d edition, 1954. Contributed numerous articles to law reviews, etc. Speaker on legal and ednl. subjects. Home: 1388 Harvard Rd. N.E., Atlanta 6. Died Feb. 28, 1960.

HEPPENHEIMER, Ernest J., judge; b. Jersey City, N.J., Feb. 24, 1869; s. Frederick and Christine (Hofer) H.; ed. Peekskill (N.Y.) Mil. Acad. and Phillips Acad., Andover, Mass.; m. Ruth Norris, Apr. 18, 1914. Mem. F. Heppenheimer's Sons, lithographers, New York, 1889-96; cattle ranching in Tex., 1889-97; organizer Colonial Life Ins. Co. of Am., 1897, pres., 1906-43, chmn. bd., 1943—. Pres. Bd. of Aldermen, Jersey City, 1910-13, commr. of finance; Dem. presdl. elector, 1912; pres. N.J. Harbor Commn., 1912-13; apptd. judge Court of Errors and Appeals, by Gov. Woodrow Wilson, 1913; reappointed by Gov. Edge, 1919-25. Dir. Northern Valley Nat. Bank, Tenafly, N.J., now citizens Northern Valley Nat. Bank, Colonial Life Ins. Co. of Am. Trust Co., N.J., Provident Instn. for Savs. Jersey City. Episcopalian. Home: Tenafly, N.J. Died Jan. 23, 1955.

HEPPENSTALL, Thomas Earl, lumber exec.; born Wiarton, Ont., Can., Mar. 1, 1898; s. Robert and Mary Letitia (King) H.; student pub. schs. of Wiarton; m. Cecile Margaret Coughlan, Aug. 1, 1922; children—Robert Richard, Barbara Ann (Mrs. David Teague Parker). Asst. elec. supt. Internat. Nickel Co., 1918-22; with Long Bell Lumber Co., Longview, Wash., 1923—, v.p. in charge engring., 1951—; mem. adv. bd. Washington State Inst. of Tech. Profl. engr., Wash. Mem. Forest Products Research Soc. Roman Catholic. Clubs: Rotary, Country (Longview). Inventor of electronic process of measuring moisture content of lumber, cereal grains, etc. Home: 1604 Kessler Blvd. Office: Long Bell Lumber Co., Longview. Wash. Died Jan. 25, 1956; buried Longview.

HERBERT, F. Hugh, playwright, novelist, scenario writer; b. Vienna, Austria; s. Lionel Frederick and Paula (Knepler) H.; Gresham Sch. (Norfolk) England; B.S., Univ. of London; m. Mary Alice, May 12, 1927; children—Diana Patricia, Pamela Joan. Advt. copywriter; short story writer; novelist; scenario writer; playwright. Lieut., Royal Garrison Artillery (World War I). Author: There You Are; A Lover Would Be Nice; The Revolt of Henry; Kiss and Tell (play); Meet Corliss Archer (short stories); Quiet Please (play); Hit Me Again (play); The Poseur; For Love or Money (play); Growing Pains (verse); Sitting Pretty, The Moon is Blue; Girl Can Tell (play), 1953; Best House in Naples (play), 1956; Little Hut (screen play) 1957. Democrat. Home: 1108 Tower Rd., Beverly Hills, Cal. Address: care 20th Century-Fox, Los Angeles. Died May 17, 1958.

HERBERT, Frederick Davis, engineering; b. Brooklyn, N.Y., Oct. 16, 1873; s. Wilbur F. and Charlotte Amelia (Weekes) H.; M.E., Cornell U., 1897; m. Jane Whittlesey Mitchell, Sept. 16, 1903; children—Emily Whittlesey (Mrs. W. Almon Stopford), Charlotte Weekes (Mrs. Philip L. DuQuesnay), Frederick Davis, John Mitchell, Sidney Pembroke, Wilbur Fisk. Draftsman, Harlan & Hollingsworth Co., shipbuilders, Wilmington, Del., 1897-1900; editor Marine Engineering, 1900-04; with Allis Chalmers Co., 1904-07, Terry Steam Turbine Co., 1908-40; pres. Kearfott Engring. Co., Inc., N.Y. City, 1918-46; director Kearfott Mfg. Corp., since 1947; pres. Kearfoot Co., Inc., since 1946. Fellow American Society Mechanical Engineers; member Society of Naval Architects and Marine Engrs. (ex-council), Shipbuilders Council of America, Am. Soc. Naval Engrs., Montclair Soc. Engineers (past president), Instn. Naval Architecture (London), N.E. Coast Engrs. and Shipbuilders (Newcastle-on-Tyne), Maritime Assn. of N.Y., Propellers Club of U.S., Chamber Commerce, State of N.Y., Nat. Assn. Mfrs., U.S. Chamber of Commerce. Sigma Chi. Clubs: Cornell, Engineers, India House, Railway (New York); Appalachian Mountain (Boston); Upper Montclair County. Home: 27 Norwood Av., Upper Montclair, N.J. Office: Little Falls, N.J. Died Aug. 4, 1955; buried Highland Heath, West Milford, N.J.

HERBERT, J. Joseph, lawyer; b. Indianapolis, Aug. 26, 1894; s. Dr. Leo H. and Eugenia (Fechtdegen) H.; student Lafayette Coll., 1913; A.B., U. of Mich. 1915, LL.B., 1917; m. Imogene McLeod, Apr. 22, 1918; children—Catherine (Mrs. Ralph Ahlskog), Robin Harcourt, Mary Imogene. Admitted to Mich. bar, 1919 and since practiced in Manistique; mem. firm Herbert, Wood & Hood; legal advisor to Gov. of Mich., 1944-45; dir. Manistique Pulp & Paper Co., Manistique Light & Power Co., W.S. Butterfield Theaters, Inc., Butterfield Mich. Theatre Co. Dir. Regent U. of Mich. since 1940; trustee Nat. Music Camp at Interlochen since 1942. Citation from Mich. Health Council, 1954. Served with U.S. Army, France, 1917-19. Chmn. Conf. Governing Bds. of State Supported Instns. of Higher Edn. (Mich.), since 1950. Mem. Am. Bar Assn., Am. Judicature Soc., Am. Law Inst., Am. Acad. Polit. and Social Scis., Am. Legion (state comdr. 1925-26), Upper Peninsula Development Bur. (pres. Mich., 1942-43, mem. exec. com.), Chi Phi. Republican. Presbyterian. Clubs: Rotary; Detroit, University (Detroit); Lawyers (U. of Mich.). Home: 728 Range St. Office: 127 S. Cedar St., Manistique, Mich. Died July 28, 1956; buried Fairview Cemetery, Manistique.

HERDER, Ralph Barnes, newspaper pub.; b. St. John's, Newfoundland, Can., Aug. 10, 1894; s. William James and Elizabeth (Barnes) H.; student Meth. Coll., St. John's, Mt. Allison U., Sackville, N.B., Can.; m. Mary Rendell, June 4, 1924; children—Robert Rendell, Stephen Rendell. Pres. The Telegram Pub. Co., St. John's. Exec. Newfoundland div. Canadian Red Cross. Regent Mt. Allison Coll. Served from pvt. to lt., Royal Newfoundland Regt., World War I; overseas in Gallipoli and France. Mem. Canadian Press Assn. (dir.). Mason. Home: 3 King's Bridge Ct. Office: The Evening Telegram, Water St., St. John's, Newfoundland, Can. Died Jan. 1955.

HERGESHEIMER, Joseph, author; b. Phila., Pa., Feb. 15, 1880; s. Joseph and Helen Janet (MacKellar) H.; educated at a Quaker school, Philadelphia, and Pa. Acad. Fine Arts; m. Dorothy Hemphill, 1907. Author: The Lay Anthony, 1914; Mountain

Blood, 1915; The Three Black Pennys, 1917; Gold and Iron, 1918; Java Head, 1919; The Happy End, 1919; Linda Condon, 1919; San Cristóbal de la Habana, 1920; Cytherea, 1922; The Bright Shawl, 1922; The Presbyterian Child, 1923; Balisand 1924; From an Old House, 1925; Tampico, 1926; Quiet Cities, 1928; Swords and Roses, 1929; The Party Dress, 1929; The Limestone Tree, 1931; Sheridan, 1931; Berlin, 1932; Tropical Winter, 1933; The Foolscap Rose, 1934. Also contbr. to mags. Home: Stone Harbor, N.J. Died Apr. 25, 1954; buried Oakland Cemetery, West Chester, Pa.

HERLY, Louis, surgeon; b. Vienna, Ill., Aug. 11, 1881; s. Leopold and Regina (Popper) H.; student Coll. City N.Y., 1894-97; Columbia Coll., 1897-99; M.D., Columbia, 1903; m. Queenie Brown, Dec. 15, 1928; children—Irene Winifred (Mrs. Robert C. Wilson), Lillian Isabelle. Gen. surgery at St. Marks, Lincoln, Community, Lenox Hill, Flower, Sydenham, Flower-Fifth Av. Hospitals, N.Y. City, since 1908; staff mem. Fordham Med. Coll. Hosp. for Women since 1911; cancer research, Inst. for Cancer Research, Columbia U., Memorial Hospital, N.Y. City, since 1920; collaborated in cancer work at Radium Hemmet, Stockholm, and Radium Inst., Copenhagen, 1923; extensive study trips to European med. centers and research insts., 1904, 1913, 1922-23; asso. in cancer research, Columbia U., since 1946. Mem. N.Y. County and State med. socs., N.Y. Acad. Medicine, Am. Med. Assn., N.Y. Pathol. Soc., Am. Cancer Research Asso. Internat. Cancer Congress. Author articles including: A Critical Investigation of the Freund-Kaminer Reaction, 1920; Adenomyoma of the Uterus: Relation to Malignancy, 1924; Experimental Production of Tumor in White Rat, 1926. Studies in Selective Differentiation of Tissues by Means of Filtered Ultra-violet Light, 1944, A Simple Diagnostic Blood Test for Cancer, 1947. Early investigator of tar cancers in animals; discovered new method of diagnosing malignancy of breast tumors by means of filtered ultra-violet light; producted sarcoma in mice by means of sterile and cell free ascitic fluid; exhibited blood test for early cancer at 4th Internat. Congress of Cancer Research, St. Louis, 1947. Home: 440 West End Av., N.Y.C. Died July 14, 1952; buried Mount Pleasant Cemetery, Pleasantville, N.Y.

HERMAN, Henry Edson Todd, judge; b. Highland, Ill., Jan., 21, 1891; s. Henry and Nettie (Todd) H.; prep. edn., Smith Acad., St. Louis; LL.B., Washington U., 1912; m. Gladys Downing, Aug. 24, 1926; children—Nettie, Jane. Admitted to Wash. bar, 1912, began practice at Spokane; apptd. justice Supreme Ct., Wash., 1931-32; resumed practice of law at Spokane, 1933. Served as enlisted man, Inf., F.A., U.S. Army, Sept. 1917-Jan. 1919. Mem. Am. Law Inst., Am. Judicature Soc., Am., Wash. State bar assns. Republican. Elk, Moose, Eagle, Red Man. Clubs: Washington Athletic (Seattle); Univesgity-Union Club (Tacoma). Home: 845 W. Cliff Av. Office: Columbia Bldg., Spokane, Wash. Died Jan. 21, 1950; buried Riverside Park Cemetery, Spokane.

HERMAN, James R(ussell), business exec.; b. Edwardsville, Pa., Aug. 1, 1898; s. James O. and Margaret (Spangler)H.; A.M., Bucknell U., 1919; m. Ruth Reynolds, Aug. 9, 1924; children—Charles R., J. Russell. Tchr. mathematics Ridgewood (N.J.) High Sch., 1919-20; asso. with Met. Life Ins. Co., N.Y.C., 1920—, asst. actuary, 1927-39, asso. actuary, 1939-46; sec., 1946—. Fellow Actuarial Soc. Am. (mem. council), Am. Inst. Actuaries. Trustee Crozer Theol. Sem., Ridgewood YMCA. Republican. Presbyn. Home: 218 Phelps Road, Ridgewood, N.J. Office: Metropolitan Life Ins. Co., 1 Madison Av., N.Y.C. Died July 9, 1951.

HERMAN, Leon Emerson, newspaperman; b. Reed City, Mich., Sept. 21, 1887; s. Lewis E. and Melissa Jane (Cassidy) H.; ed. Detroit public and high school; m. Mary L. Maley, Aug. 1, 1914; 1 son, James Lewis. Began in newspaper work, 1905; successively in advertising work with Detroit Free Press, St. Louis Republic, Chicago Record Herald; advt. mgr. Indianapolis Sun, 1911-14; joined Scripps Howard Newpapers, 1914; advt. solicitor Cincinnati Post and Columbus Citizen, 1914-18; advt. mgr. Oklahoma City News, 1918-21; business mgr. Dallas Dispatch, 1921-22, Memphis Press, 1922-25; v.p. and business mgr. Akron Times Press, 1925-29; pres. and business mgr. Memphis Press Scimitar, 1929-40; pres. Buffalo Colorpress, Inc.; v.p., Greater Buffalo Press, Inc. Methodist. Home: Westbrook Hotel. Office: 1021-23 Marine Trust Bldg., Buffalo 5. Died Mar. 17, 1956.

HERMANNSSON, Halldor, educator; b. Völlur, Iceland, Jan. 6, 1878; s. Herm. E. and Ingunn H. Johnson; grad. Reykjavik Coll., 1898; Cand. Phil., U. of Copenhagen, 1899, studied there, 1901-04; Ph.D. (hon.), U. of Iceland, 1930. Curator of Fiske Icelandic Collection, Cornell U. Library, 1905-48; instr. Scandinavian langs. Cornell U., 1905-09, lecturer, 1913-20, asst. prof., 1920-24, prof., 1924-46, prof. emeritus, 1946—. Decorated Comdr. of the Order of the Iceland Falcon; hon. mem. Icelandic Lit. Soc.; corr. fellow Medieval Acad. Am. Author: Bibliography of the Icelandic Sagas, 1908; The Northmen in America, 1909; Bibliography of the Sagas of the Kings of Norway, 1910; The Ancient Laws of Norway and Iceland, 1911; Bibliography of the Mythical-heroic Sagas, 1912; Icelandic Authors of Today, 1913; Icelandic Books of the Sixteenth Century, 1916; The Periodical Literature of Iceland, 1918; Modern Icelandic, 1919; Bibliography of the Eddas, 1920; Icelandic Books of the Seventeenth Century, 1922; Icelanders in America (in Danish), 1922; Eggert Olafsson, 1925; Two Cartographers, 1926; Sir. Joseph Banks and Iceland, 1928; Icelandic Manuscripts, 1929; The Cartography of Iceland, 1931; Saemund Sigfússon and the Oddaverjar, 1932; Old Icelandic Literature, 1933; Introduction to Codex Frisianus, 1932; Icelandic Illuminated Manuscripts of Middle Ages, 1935; The Sagas of Icelanders, 1935; The Problem of Wineland, 1936; Sagas of the Kings of Norway and the Mythical-Heroic Sagas, 1937; Illuminated Manuscripts of the Jónsbók, 1940, Bibliographical Notes, 1942; also Catalogues of the Fiske Icelandic Collection, 1914, 27, 43; Catalogue of Runic Literature, 1918. Editor: The Story of Griselda in Iceland, 1914; An Icelandic Satire (Lof Lyginnar), 1915; Gisli Oddsson's Annalium in Islandia farrago and De mirabilibus Islandiae, 1917; Jon Gundmundsson and His Natural History of Iceland, 1924; Ari Thorgilsson's The Book of the Icelanders, 1930; The Icelandic Physiologus, 1938; The Vinland Sagas, 1944; The Saga of Thorgils and Haflidi, 1945; The Hólar Cato (posthumous), 1958. Address: Cornell University Library, Ithaca, N.Y. Died Aug. 28, 1958.

HERMS, William Brodbeck, prof. emeritus; born Portsmouth, O., Sept. 22, 1876; s. Carl Julius Herman and Rosa Emma (Brodbeck) H.; B.Sc., Baldwin-Wallace Coll., 1902, hon. D.Sc., 1935; studied Western Reserve U., 1905; Ohio State U., Lake Lab., Sandusky, Ohio, summers 1903, 04, 05; M.A., Ohio State U., 1906; Harvard, 1907-08; m. Lillie (Carrie) Magly, June 14, 1902; children—William Magly, Herbert Parker, George Walter. Head of Sch. of Commerce and prof. theory and practice of domestic commerce, 1902-05, instr. biology, 1904-05, Baldwin-Wallace Coll.; teaching fellow zoölogy, 1905-06, instr. exptl. zoölogy and invertebrate zoölogy, summer sessions, 1907-08, Ohio State U.; acting head dept. zoölogy, Ohio Wesleyan U., 1906-07; Edward Austin fellow in zoölogy, Harvard, 1907-08; asst. prof. parasitology, 1908-15, asso. prof., 1915-20, prof., 1920-46, prof. parasitol. emeritus, 1946; head div. entomology and parasitology, 1923-46; U. of Calif. visiting prof. med. entomol., Ohio State U., summer 1930. Officer in charge malaria investigations, Calif. Bd. Health, 1910-13; consulting entomologist and parasitologist, Calif. Bd. of Health, since 1913; made malaria-mosquito survey of Calif. Del. from Ohio Wesleyan U. to 7th Internat. Zoöl. Congress, Boston, 1907; from Calif. and U. of Calif. to Internat. Hygiene Exhibit, at Dresden, Germany, 1911; from U. of Calif. to Pan Pacific Food Conservation Congress, Honolulu, 1924; from U. of Calif. to 4th Internat. Congress of Entomology, Ithaca, N.Y., 1928. Capt. Sanitary Corps, U.S. Army, Feb. 5, 1918; maj., Aug. 14, 1918; attached to dept. lab., Fort Sam Houston, Tex., Feb. 18-April 17, 1918; thence to office of surgeon, Hdqrs. Port of Embarkation, Newport News, Va., Apr. 23, 1918-Feb. 20, 1919; in charge of malarial drainage operations, chief of insect control and asst. sanitary insp.; hon. disch., Feb. 20, 1919; lt. col., San. Res. Corps, Apr. 21, 1924-Sept. 22, 1940; Inactive Res. until called to active duty, Carlisle Barracks, Pa., Jan.-Sept. 1943. Investigated coconut pests of Fanning and Washington Islands, 1924. Awarded rank of Chevalier du Mérite Agricole (France), 1935; Benj. Ide Wheeler distinguished citizenship medal (Berkeley), 1937. Chmn. draft bd. No. 70, Calif., Oct. 1940-Jan. 1943. Fellow A.A.A.S.; fellow Calif. Acad. of Science, Entomological Soc. Am. (v.p. 1933, pres. 1941); hon. mem. Nat. Malaria Com. Helminthological Soc. Washington, Am. Assn. Econ. Entomologists (pres. 1928), Pacific Coast Entomol. Soc. (chmn. 1925-26), Western Soc. Naturalists, Am. Soc. Parasitologists (v.p. 1936), Am. Soc. Naturalists, Am. Soc. Tropical Medicine, Ohio Acad. of Science, Scabbard and Blade, Sigma Xi, Alpha Zeta, Phi Sigma, Delta Omega, Alpha Kappa Lambda, Am. Legion. Pres. Bd. of Edn., Berkeley, Calif., 1915-18 and 1921-25; pres. Berkeley-Contra Costa (Calif.) Area Council Boy Scouts Am., since 1928; dir. Am. Auto. Assn., 1946; pres. Calif. State Auto Assn., 1947. Republican. Mason. Clubs: Faculty, Lions. Author: Malaria, Cause and Control, 1913; Laboratory Guide to the Study of Parasitology, 1913; Textbook in Medical and Veterinary Entomology, 1915-23, 3d edit., 1939, 4th edit., 1949; Mosquito Control (with H. F. Gray), 2d edit.. 1944. Home at 2032 Del Norte St., Berkeley, Calif., sold, Apr. 1951. Died May 9, 1949; buried Sunset View Cemetery, Berkeley.

HERNDON, Charles Traverse, clergyman; b. Delaplane, Va., July 29, 1857; s. Rev. Thaddeus and Mary Frances (Gibson) H.; student Richmond (Va.) Coll., 1876-79, D.D., 1907; grad. So. Bapt. Theol. Sem., Louisville, 1881; m. Sarah Jennings Adams, Jan. 21, 1891. Ordained Bapt. ministry, 1881; pastor Leesburg and Hamilton, Va., 1881-1908 (organized and built chs. at both places); pastor Salem, Va., 1908-16, Warrenton, Va., May 1, 1916—. Mem. Beta Theta Pi. Democrat. Mason. Home: Warrenton, Va. Died 1936.

HERNDON, James B(aird) Jr., hotel exec.; b. Comanche, Tex., Nov. 27, 1898; s. James B. and Blanche (Dunkerley) H.; A.B., U. Mo., 1921; m. Sara Kesterson, Feb. 4, 1934 (died 1949). Asst. and nat. bank examiner, Dallas, 1921-24; dist. rep. Bank of America, N.Y. City, 1924-26; asst. branch mgr. Calif. Bank, Los Angeles, 1926-29; with Hilton Hotels, 1929—, v.p. and treas. Hilton Hotels Corp., N.Y. City, 1946—, exec. v.p. Mayflower Hotel Co., Washington, 1950—; treas. Hotel Waldorf-Astoria Corp., N.Y. City, 1949—, v.p. and dir. Hilton Hotels, Internat., N.Y. City, 1949—; dir. Jefferson Hotel Co. Served with O.T.C., 1918. Mem. Am. Hotel Assn. (1st v.p., 1950-51, pres., 1951-52); past pres. N.M. and Rocky Mt., Denver and Dallas hotel assns.; mem. Beta Theta Pi, Conquistadores del Cielo. Roman Catholic. Contbr. articles on hotel subjects. Collector books of G.A. Henty; books on hotels, foods, wines and gastronomical subjects. Address: Albuquerque. Died Jan. 4, 1953; buried Albuquerque.

HERNDON, John Goodwin, coll. prof.; b. Washington; D.C., Nov. 26, 1888; s. John Goodwin and Florence Early (Linton) H.; A.B., Washington and Lee, 1911, M.A., 1912; student U. of Wis., 1912-14, fellow in taxation, 1912-13; Ph.D., U. of Pa., 1931; student Harvard, 1929, U. of Geneva, Switzerland, 1930, U. of Mich., 1937; m. Grace Cordelia Middleton, Apr. 7, 1915; children—Dale Linton, Richard Middleton, Constance (deceased), Carol May (Mrs. Noble Burford, Jr.). With Wis. Tax Commission, in charge corporation income tax, 1912-14; expert, special agent, U.S. Bureau Labor Statistics, 1914-17; with personal income tax div., U.S. Bureau Internal revenue, 1917-18; tax consultant Nat. City Co., 1918, Guaranty Trust Co., Phila. and London brs., 1919-20; tax consultant, 1921-28; asso. prof. economics, Ursinus Coll., 1927-28; asst. prof. economics and govt., Haverford Coll., 1929-33, asso. prof., chmn., dept. govt., 1933-47; prof. pub. finance, 1947—; spl. lecturer Am. Inst. Banking, 1920-22, Haverford Coll., 1929, U. of Pa., 1931-33, Swarthmore Coll., 1937. Sec. Am. delegation to gen. meeting governmental experts on double taxation, Geneva, 1928; del. to San Francisco and London U.N. Conf. as tech. adviser, City of Phila., 1945. Commd. Ky. Col., 1952. Fellow Am. Soc. Genealogists (v.p., 1949—); mem. Hist. Soc. Pa., Va. Hist. Soc., Colonial Soc. Pa., Geneal. Soc. Pa. (v.p., exec. dir.), Pa. Soc. S.R., Pa. Soc. War 1812 (historian 1939-51), Soc. Colonial Wars (Pa.), Soc. Descs. Colonial Clergy, Phi Sigma Kappa, Phi Beta Kappa, Delta Sigma Rho, Pi Gamma Mu. Clubs: Penn, Franklin Inn (Philadelphia, Pennsylvania). Presbyterian. Author: Public Employment Offices in the United States, 1918; Relief from International Income Taxation, 1932; Your New Income Tax, 1932; Our New Federal Taxes, 1934; Federal Income Tax, 1941; Principles of Constitutional Interpretation, 1941; The Reverend John Thomson (circa 1690-1753), 1943; The Cunninghams of Cub Creek (Virginia), 1944; numerous articles for econ. and geneal. jours., etc.; as chief investigator, Bureau of Budget, Washington, 1936-37, prepared "A Study of the Federal Ownership of Real Estate and of Its Bearing on State and Local Taxation." Editor in chief, Winston Business Administration, 1935-51 and Winston Monthly Tax Digest, 1948-51; editor The Pa. Geneal. Mag., 1946—. Author: The Herndon Family of Virginia, Vol. I, 1947; Herndons of the American Revolution, Part I, 1950, Part II, 1951, Part III 1952, Part IV, 1953. Co-author Fighting for Freedom, 1947. Home: 1 College Lane, Haverford, Pa.; (summer) "Green Leges," Goshen, N.H. Office: 1300 Locust Street, Phila. 7. Died June 29, 1957; buried Glenwood Cemetery, Washington.

HERNON, William Seton, business exec.; b. Cortland, N.Y., June 16, 1891; s. William and Anna (Green) H.; student Cortland Normal Sch., 1909; B. S., U. of Pa., 1913; m. Edna MacMurray, Dec. 22, 1932; 1 dau., Anna Harriet. Chmn. exec. com. Ritter Co., Inc., Rochester, N.Y.; dir. Pub. Nat. Bank, Hernon Pearsall Co., Peter A. Frasse Co., Childs Co. Mem. N.Y. Stock Exchange. Republican. Roman Catholic. Clubs: University, Stock Exchange Lunch (N. Y.C.); Greenwich (Conn.) Country; Country, Genesee Valley (Rochester, N.Y.). Home: Zaccheus Mead Lane, Greenwich, Conn. Office: 120 Broadway, N.Y. C. Died Jan., 1952.

HEROY, James Harold, business exec.; b. N.Y.C., Aug. 18, 1881; s. William Ward and Helen Maria (Hoyt) H.; B.A., Columbia Coll., 1902; m. May Browning Fisher, June 2, 1909; children—William Ward, James Harold, Christina (Mrs. George Gunton Wilcox). Began as clerk, Pitts. Plate Glass Co., N.Y.C., 1902, asst. mgr. N.Y. warehouse, 1910-12, in charge of Brush Div., Balt., 1912, dir., 1924—, v.p. 1935—; pres. Glaces de Courcelles, Courcelles, Belgium, 1924—; sec., dir. So. Alkali Corpn. Southern Minerals Corp., Southern Pipe Line Corp., Corpus Christi, Tex., 1931—. Mem. S.R., Mayflower Soc., Huguenot Soc., Phi Beta Kappa. Republican. Episcopalian. Clubs: University, St. Andrew's Golf. Home: 580 Park Av., N.Y.C. 21. Office: Pittsburgh Plate

Glass Corp., 30 Rockefeller Plaza, N.Y.C. 20. Died Sept. 4, 1950.

HERRESHOFF, Charles Frederick, cons. engr., naval architect; b. Nice, France, May 28, 1876; s. James Brown and Jane Brown H.; student Glasgow (Scotland) U.; m. Edna M. Burt, 1912 (dec. 1937); m. 2d, Virginia Townsend, May 26, 1943. Chief engr. Am. & British Mfg. Co., Bridgeport, Conn., 1904-08; v.p. and chief engr., Herreshoff Motor Co., Detroit, 1908-09, pres., 1909-10, v.p. and gen. mgr., 1910-14. Invented an engine to run by superheated steam up to 800 degrees Fahrenheit; center control for automobile; electric switch for electric horn on steering gear of automobile, etc. A leader in originating improvements in automobiles and steam yachts; designer of Alabama, motor yacht champion of America, 1907, 08, 09; of Vim, winner interstate races, New York to Poughkeepsie, 1908, 09; of Chickadee, winner of Mass. Yacht Assn. cup; of Vivian, winner Hudson-Fulton Celebration races, etc. World's record holder for mile championship, U.S Navy Course, Hudson River, 1907; winner of Canad's cup, with Iroquois, etc. Herreshoff motor car won gold medal of Am. Automobile Assn., 1910, and same yr. won more prizes than any other car. Designer of Nevada, 65 Rater, 1901, winner of Glasgow, Scotland, internat. expn. races, also largest winner of any Am. designed yacht in foriegn waters. Mem. Soc. Automotive Engrs. Republican. Episcopalian. Home: 924 Scott St., Yacht Club Terrace, San Diego, Cal. Died Jan. 30, 1954.

HERRICK, Charles Judson, univ. prof.; b. Minneapolis, Oct. 6, 1868; s. Rev. Henry Nathan and Anna (Strickler) H.; B.S., U. Cin., 1891, Sc.D., 1926; M.S., Denison U., 1895, Sc.D., 1930; Ph.D., Columbia, 1900, Sc.D., 1931; m. Mary Elizabeth Talbot, Aug. 17, 1892; 1 dau., Ruth. Instr. natural sciences, Granville Acad., 1891-92; prof. natural sciences, Ottawa U., 1893-93; fellow in biology, 1893-95, instr., 1895-96, Denison U.; univ. scholar biology, Columbia, 1896; asso. in comparative neurology, Pathol. Inst. of N.Y. State Commn. in Lunacy, 1897-1901; prof. zoology, Denison, 1898-1907; prof. neurology, U. Chgo., 1907-34, emeritus in residence, 1934-37, emeritus 1937, chmn. dept. anatomy, 1933; visiting prof. anatomy, emeritus, U. Mich., 1942. Fellow A.A.A.S. (secretary zool. sect. 1902-07, chmn. 1908); pres. Ohio Acad. Science, 1903. Author many books and papers on biol. and neurol. subjects. Editor Journal Comparative Neurology since 1894. Commd. maj., Sanitary Corps, N.A., 1918. Mem. Nat. Acad. Sciences, Kon. Akademie von Wetenschappen te Amsterdam, Norwegian Acad. of Science and Letters; Royal Acad. Science of Sweden; honorary member American Neurol. Assn., Société Scientifique "Antonio Alzate," Mexico; corr. mem. Académie Royale de Medicine de Belgique. Home: 236 Morningside Drive, Grand Rapids 6, Mich. Died Jan. 29, 1960.

HERRICK, Cheesman Abiah, ret. coll. pres.; b. Redwood, N.Y., July 21, 1866; s. Delos and Sophonia (Curtis) H.; student Ill. State Normal U., 1887-89; Ph.B., U. Pa., 1894, Ph.D., 1899; LL.D., Lafayette, 1913, Muhlenberg, 1916, U. of Pa., 1930; m. Clara B. James, June 29, 1897 (dec. 1936). Taught ungraded country schs., Jefferson County, N.Y., Winnebago County, Ill., 1884-87; prin. town schs., at Hopedale and Minier, Tazewell County, Ill., 1889-92; asst. sec., lectr. Am. Soc. for Extension of Univ. Teaching, 1894-95; instr. in history, 1895-98, dir. 1898-1909, dept. of commerce, Central High Sch., Phila.; prin. William Penn High Sch., Phila., 1909-10; pres. Girard Coll., Phila., 1910-36; ret. 1936. Lecturer comml. geography, Harvard Summer Sch., 1904; spl. agt. in commerce and advisor for comml. edn. of Federal Bd. for Vocational Edn., 1917-19. Mem. dept. jury awards St. Louis expn., 1904; del. 8th Internat. Geog. Congress. Life mem. Am. Hist. Assn., Hist. Soc. of Pa., Pa. State Ednl. Assn. (pres. 1910); mem. N.E.A. (pres. bus. edn. sect. 1904), Am. Acad. of Polit. and Social Science, Nat. Soc. Promtion Indsl. Edn. (v.p. 1914-17, pres. 1917-18), Phila. C. of C. (chmn. edn. com. 1922-25; dir. and mem. exec. com., 1923-26), Phi Beta Kappa. Presbyn. Author: Commercial Education, 1900; The Meaning and Practice of Commercial Education, 1904; Reclaiming a Commonwealth, 1911; History of Commerce and Industry, 1917; Outstanding Days, 1920. Editor: Macmillan Commercial Series of Text-books; English Readings for Commercial Classes, 1921; Call Him Not Dead, 1922; Stephen Girard, Founder, 1923; First Things, 1924; White Servitude in Pennsylvania, 1926; History of Girard College, 1927; More First Things, 1936; School Prayer, 1936; Clara James Herrick—A Memoir, 1939; Death Life's Crown, 1947; Girard College Worthies, 1948. Address: 6733 Emlen St., Germantown, Phila. 19. Died Feb. 1956.

HERRICK, Everett Carleton, theologian; b. Livermore, Me., June 13, 1876; s. Joel Richardson and Mary Jessie (Chase) H.; A.B., Colby Coll., 1898, D.D., 1919; grad. Newton Theol. Instn., Newton Center, Mass., 1901; student Harvard, 1901-03; D.D., Brown U., 1927; LL.D., U. Me., 1929; D.D., Dartmouth, 1932; L.H.D., Boston U., 1939; m. Sarah Munroe Hall, Oct. 19, 1904. Ordained to ministry Baptist Ch., 1901; pastor Charlestown, Mass., 1901-14, Fall River, 1914-26; pres. The Newton Theol. Instn. (now Andover Newton Theol. Sch.), 1926-46; retired. Pres. Mass. Bapt. Conv., 1923-24. Mem. Am. Theol. Soc., Bd. Mgrs. No. Bapt. Bd. Edn. and Publ. Mason. Club: University (Boston). Home: 5 Ripley Terrace, Newton Center, Mass. Died Feb. 13, 1957.

HERRICK, James Bryan, physician; b. Oak Park, Ill., Aug. 11, 1861; s. O.W. and Dora E. (Kettlestrings) H.; A.B., U. Mich., 1882, A.M. (hon.), 1907, LL.D., 1932; Sc.D. (hon.), U. Chgo., 1938, Northwestern U., 1940; M.D., Rush Med. Coll. (U. Chgo.), 1888; m. Zellah P. Davies, 1889; children—Helen Powers (Mrs. George H. Gilbert, Jr.), John Origen. Intern Cook Co. Hosp., Chgo., 1888-89, instr. medicine Rush Med. Coll., 1890-94, adj. prof., 1894-1900, prof., 1900-27, now emeritus; attending physician Presbyn. Hosp., Chgo., 1895-1945. Mem. Assn. Am. Physicians, A.M.A. (Distinguished Service medal 1939), Ill. State, Chgo. med. socs., Inst. Medicine Chgo. (pres. 1925); hon. mem. N.Y. Acad. Medicine, Cardiac Soc. of Great Britain and Ireland. Author A Short History of Cardiology, 1942; Memories of Eighty Years, 1949. Contbr. to med. jours. articles in field. Republican. Clubs: University, Literary. Home: 70 Cedar St. Office: Peoples Gas Bldg., Chgo. Died Mar. 7, 1954; buried Dorset, Vt.

HERRIOT, Edouard Marie, govt. ofcl.; France; b. Troyes, France, July 5, 1872; s. Nicolas and Jeanne (Collon) H.; ed. Lycée de la Roche Sur-Yon Coll. Sainte Barbe, Ecole Normal Supérieure; m. Blanche Rebatel, Oct. 28, 1899. Mayor of Lyon, 1905—; formerly prof., Lycée de Nantes, Lycée de Lyon; senator, 1912-19; dep. 1919-42; pres. council of Ministers of Fgn. Affairs, 1924-26; pres. of Chamber, 1926-27; minister pub. instrn., 1932, of State, 1934-36; pres. Chamber, 1935-43. Arrested by Vichy pres. of Nat. Assembly 1947-53. Mem. Academie Française. Pres. com. of European Union, 1948. Author: Madame Récamier et ses amis, 1904; Impressions d'Amérique, 1923; Dans la forêt Normandie, 1925; La vie de Beethoven, 1929; Lyon n'est plus, 1938; Jadis, tome premier des mêmoires, 1948. Home: 1 cours d'Herbouville, Lyon, France. Office: Hotel de Ville, Lyon, France; also National Assembly, Palais Bourbon, Paris, France. Died. Mar. 1957.*

HERRIOTT, Irving, lawyer; b. Chgo., Oct. 10, 1886; s. David and Janet Irving (Richardson) H.; m. Juanita C. Howard, Nov. 29, 1909; children—Irving Howard, Janet, Martha. Admitted to Ill. bar, 1907; claims atty. Ill. Traction System, 1908-10; gen. atty. C.&N.W. Ry. Co., 1910-18; entered pvt. practice, 1918; mem. firm Montgomery, Hart, Pritchard & Herriott; gen. counsel, dir. Zenith Radio Corp., Athey Products Corp., The Rauland Corp. Mem. bd. govs. Henrotin Hosp. Mem. Am., Ill., Chgo bar assns. Clubs: Law, Union League, Beverly Country, Mid-Day, Tavern (Chgo.); Lawyers (bd. govs.) (N. Y.C.); American (Mexico City). Republican. Presbyn. Home: 210 E. Pearson St., also 10848 S. Hoyne Av. Office: 120 S. Las Salle St., Chgo. 3. Died Nov. 17, 1953.

HERRLE, Colin (hûrl), Am. Red Cross official; b. Washington, D.C., July 9, 1892; s. Gustave and Anna (Koch) H.; grad. Pace Inst. of Accountancy, 1914; student Southeastern U., Washington, D.C., 1916-18; m. Anne Theodora Brown, June 28, 1917; children—Theodora Patricia (Mrs. William McSherry Stock), Anne Theodora, Colin. Sec. and accountant, Am. Red Cross, 1910; treas. Chinese River Conservancy Commn., 1914; sec. Rockefeller Foundation War Relief Commn., 1914-15; exec. sec., Am. Red Cross, 1924-27, dir. disaster relief, Eastern U.S., 1928-40, dir. war relief production service since 1940, national adminstr. disaster relief, 1946-52, national disaster consultant since 1952. Decorated Grand Cross of Serbian Red Cross, 1915. Republican. Home: 19 Aspen Street, Chevy Chase, Maryland. Office: National Headquarters, American Red Cross, Washington. Died Dec. 16, 1952; buried Glenwood Cemetery, Washington.

HERRMANN, Ernest Edward, naval officer; b. Memel, Germany, July 17, 1896; s. Albert Edward and Friedrieka (Wiechmann) H.; came to U.S., 1897, naturalized, 1905; student Coll. City of New York, 1914-15; B.S., U.S. Naval Acad., 1918; m. Jean Simpson Stewart Hughes, June 8, 1918; 1 dau., Margot Jean. Commd. ensign U.S. Navy June 6, 1918, and advanced through grades to rear adm., March 4, 1944; on duty, Cruiser Transport Force, World War I; served in various capacities, chiefly gunnery, in Atlantic and Pacific Fleet ships, 1918-39; battle force gunnery officer, 1939-40, U.S. Fleet gunnery officer, 1940-41; instr. in ordnance and gunnery U.S. Naval Acad., 1924-26, 29-31, 34-37; coordinator for antiaircraft matters, Bur. of Ordnance, Navy Dept., Washington, D.C., 1941-43 dir. of plans, 1943-44; commanded heavy cruiser U.S.S. Boston, from Marianas campaign to beginning Okinawa campaign, 1944-45; chief, logistic plans, Office of Chief of Naval Operations, Navy Dept., 1946; comd. cruiser Div. 3, U.S. Pacific Fleet, 1947, Div. 13, 1948-49; supt. U.S. Naval Postgrad. Sch. since 1950. Awarded 3 Legions of Merit for service, World War II. Episcopalian. Author: Exterior Ballistics, 1926, 1930, 1935 (official text books on subject, U.S. Naval Acad.). Address: Supt. U.S. Naval Postgraduate School, Monterey, Cal. Died Nov. 19, 1952; buried Arlington Nat. Cemetery.

HERRON, John S(tanley), educator; b. Bordentown, N.J., Oct. 4, 1887; s. James and Mary E. (Carey) H.; grad. N.J. State Teachers Coll., Trenton, 1906; B.S., New York U., 1915, M.A., 1918; LL.D., Seton Hall U., South Orange, N.J., 1944; m. Alice I. Kearney, October 1912; children—Alice J. (Mrs. David C. Townsend), John S., Jr. Teacher and prin. in elementary schs. of Paterson, Newark, and Nutley, N.J., 1906-18; prin., Newark Schs., 1918-37, asst. supt. of schs., 1937-42, deputy supt. of schs., 1942-43, supt. schs., 1943-53; dean, sch. edn. Seton Hall U., South Orange, since 1953. Member board trustees Newark Public Library, Newark Museum, Newark Safety Council, Newark Welfare Fedn., Robert Treat council, Boy Scouts of Am. Received Alumni citation from N.J. State Teachers Coll., Trenton, June 1946. Mem. Am. Assn. of Sch. Adminstrs., N.E.A., Guidance and Personnel Assn. of Am., N.J. Edn. Assn., N.J. Dept. of Superintendence. Club: Kiwanis. Contbr. articles in various ednl. publs. Home: 583 Mt. Prospect Av., Newark 4. Office: Seton Hall U., South Orange, N.J. Died July 10, 1954.

HERSCHDORFER, Manuel, educator; b. Bklyn., Oct. 22, 1896; s. Alexander and Rosa (Ganzfried) H.; B.Sc., N.Y.U., 1935, M.Sc., 1937; Ph.D., Ukrainian Free U., Munich, 1951. Instr. mathematics Amherst Coll., 1945-46; prof. chmn. dept. mathematics Seton Hall U., 1946—. Mem. Am. Math. Soc., Am. Acad. Sci., Sherchenko Scientific Soc., Circolo Matematico di Palermo. Home: 67 Taylor Pl., South Orange, N.J. Died July 6, 1958.

HERSH, A(mos) H(enry), biologist; b. Lancaster, Pa., Nov. 2, 1891; s. George and Margaret (Rudy) H.; A.B., Franklin and Marshall Coll., 1914, A.M., 1915, Sc.D., 1946; student Princeton, 1915-16; Ph. D., U. of Ill. (fellow in zoology, 1919-22), 1922; m. Roselle Karrer, Aug. 19, 1922; children—Charles Karrer, Robert Tweed. Grad. asst. in biology Princeton, 1915-16; instr. in zoology Kan. State Coll., 1916-18; instr. in biology Marquette U., 1918-19: instr. in zoology U. of Mich., 1922-23; instr. biology Western Res. U., 1923-25, asst. prof., 1925-36, asso. prof., 1936-46, prof. biology, 1946—. Fellow Ohio Acad Sci., A.A.A.S.; mem. Am. Soc. Zoologists, Am. Soc. Naturalists, Genetics Soc. of Am., Am. Soc. Human Genetics, Soc. for Study Development and Growth; Am. Assn. U. Profs., Gamma Alpha, Sigma Xi, Phi Kappa Sigma. Contbr. articles on genetics and relative growth to sci. jours.; Blakiston's New Gould Medical Dictionary, 1949. Home: 1937 Parkway Dr., Cleveland Heights 18, O. Office: Western Reserve University, Cleve. 6. Died Aug. 28, 1955.

HERSHEY, Charlie Brown, educator; b. Gettysburg, O., Dec. 14, 1878; s. Adam Baer and Susan Mary (Brown) H.; A.B., U. of Ill., 1914, A.M., 1921; Ed.D., Harvard, 1923; LL.D., Colo. Coll., 1934; m. Zora Hope Faught, Aug. 20, 1907 (dec. Apr. 1938); m. 2d, Katherine Waters, July 29, 1941. Pres. Union Christian Coll., Merom, Ind., 1915-21; dean of men, prof. of edn. Colo. Coll., 1923-28, dean and prof. of edn., 1928—, acting pres., 1933-34, 43-45, dean emeritus and prof. edn., 1947—; prof. edn. Defiance (O.) Coll., summers 1922, 23, U. Rochester, summers 1926, 28, 29. Mem. park bd. Colorado Springs. Trustee Christian Pub. Assn., Dayton, O., 1912-25. Moderator Colo. Congl. Conf., 1940-41; pres. Rocky Mountain Radio Council, 1941-45. Mem. Phi Delta Kappa. Republican. Conglist. Clubs: Colorado Schoolmasters, Winter Night (sec.-treas. 1935-44; pres. 1944-45), Rocky Mountain Harvard (pres. 1928-29); El Paso, Rotary (pres. 1939-40). Author: Colorado College, 1874-1949, 1952. Address: Box 244, West End Station, Colorado Springs, Colo. Died Dec. 17, 1955; buried Colorado Springs.

HERSHEY, Paris N., banker; b. Florin, Pa., July 27, 1883; s. Jacob G. and Mary (Nissley) H.; student Millersville Tchrs. Coll., 1900-02; m. Cora Witmer, Feb. 21, 1907; children—Gladys, Harold, Elinor. Creamery operator Lebanon (Pa.) Creamery Co., 1905-14; dir. milk div. Hershey (Pa.) Chocolate Corp. since 1913; agrl. mgr. Hershey Estates since 1928; pres. Hershey Nat. Bank since 1946; dir. Fidelity Bldg. & Loan, Hershey Trust Co. Dir. Hershey Found. Mem. Lebanon C. of C. Clubs: Rotary, Hershey Civic, Lebanon Country, Hershey Country, Quentin Riding. Home: 310 Hathaway Park. Offices: Hershey Chocolate Corp., 10th and Elizabeth Sts., Lebanon, Pa. Died Dec. 30, 1956; buried Hershey (Pa.) Cemetery.

HERSHOLT, Jean, actor; b. Copenhagen, Denmark, July 12, 1886; s. Henry and Clara (Petersen) H.; ed. Knud School and College, Copenhagen; M.A., Bowdoin College, Brunswick, Maine; LL.D., U. Cal., 1953; Litt.D. (hon.) Ill. Wesleyan U.; m. Via Andersen, Apr. 11, 1914; 1 son, Allan. Came to U.S., 1913, naturalized, 1920. Began acting in Dagmar Theater, Copenhagen, 1904; continued on European stage until 1913; in Hollywood since 1913; under contract with Metro-Goldwyn-Mayer Film Corp.; played in more than 400 pictures, including Four

Horsemen, Greed, Stella Dallas, Old Heidelberg, Emma, Old Soak, Alias the Deacon, Men in White, Grand Hotel, The Country Doctor (Dr. Dafoe of Dionne quintuplets), Sins of Man, Reunion, Heidi. Starred as Dr. Christian in "Dr. Christian" radio series since 1937. Knighted by King Christian X of Denmark, 1946, for work as pres. Am.-Denmark Relief, Inc., during World War; awarded King's Medal of Liberation. Pres. Acad. Motion Picture Arts and Scis., 1945-49. Partner, mem. bd. dirs. Sol Lesser Productions, Inc., Hollywood. Hon. pres. Calif.-Denmark Home Foundation; pres. Motion Picture Relief Fund. Awarded Motion Picture Relief Fund Medallion, 1946; received plaque from Ind. Motion Picture Producers Assn., 1946; Look mag. industry-wide achievement award, 1949; Oscar award by Acad. Motion Picture Arts and Scis., 1939, 49, 50. Mem. Hollywood Bowl Assn. (pres.), Hollywood C. of C. (dir.). Mason. Elk. Clubs: University, Grolier (New York); Bohemian (San Francisco); Players (New York). Received degree Dr. of Humanities from Rollins College, Winter Park, Fla. Author: Complete Translation of Hans Christian Andersen's Fairy Tales; co-author (novel) Dr. Christian's Office. Home: 602 Rodeo Dr., Beverly Hills, Cal. Died June 2, 1956; buried Forest Lawn Meml. Park, Glendale, Cal.

HERSMAN, Hugh Steel, ex-congressman; b. Port Deposit, Md., July 8, 1872; s. William M. and Mary H. (Steel) H.; A.B., Southwestern Presbyn. U., Clarksville, Tenn., 1893; post-grad. work U. Cal., 1896-98. Pres. First Nat. Bank, Gilroy, Cal., 1914-18; chmn. organizing com. Cal. Prune and Apricot Growers, 1916; mem. 66th Congress, 8th Cal. Dist.; officer or dir. various corpns. Democrat. Presbyn. Home: Gilroy, Cal. Died Mar. 7, 1954.

HERTER, Albert, artist; b. N.Y.C., Mar. 2, 1871; s. Christian and Mary (Miles) H.; pupil of Carroll Beckwith, N.Y., J. P. Laurens and Cormon, Paris; m. Adele McGinnis, Apr. 5, 1893. Spltу. mural decoration; hon. mention, Paris Salon, 1890; medal, Atlanta Expn., 1895; Lippincott prize 1897; hon. mention, Nashville, 1897; Evans prize, Am. Water Color Soc., 1899; bronze and silver medals, Paris, 1900. A.N.A.; mem. Am. Water Color Soc., Soc. Mural Painters, Architectural League N.Y. (v.p.), N.Y. Water Color Club. Chevalier Legion of Honor (France), 1928. Club: Century. Home: East Hampton, L.I., N.Y. Died 1950.

HERTS, B(enjamin) Russell, writer, interior decorator; b. New York, May 27, 1888; s. Benjamin H. and Belle (Seligman) H.; A.B., Columbia, 1908; m. Erinna Gardes, Mar. 28, 1918. A founder, editor and mgr. "Moods" (mag.), 1908-09; editor The Forum, 1909-10. A founder and editor (with Richard Le Gallienne) The International magazine; publisher and editor (with Edwin Markham) The Younger Choir; editor The Intercollegiate Magazine; contbr. articles and verse to magazines; public lecturer for Board of Education, New York, since 1910; interior decoration editor Vogue and Vanity Fair, 1913; cons. decorator to Washington Square Players, 1915-16, to The Stagers, 1924-25; dramatic editor Los Angeles Life, 1923; v.p. Herts Bros. Co., decorators, 1908-15, pres. and general dir., since 1915; lecturer for New York School of Interior Decoration, 1923-25; also examiner for City of New York. Designed Interior of Court of Appeals Chamber, State House, Albany, New York, sets for William A. Brady, Grace George, and Arthur Hopkins; also interiors for hotels Sherry Netherlands, Delmonico, Madison-No. 1 Fifth Av., Beaux Arts, Victoria, etc.; dir. decoration Spence-Taylor Hotel chain since 1948. Mem. Fed. Grand Jury Panel. Mem. Poetry Soc. Am., Am. Inst. Interior Decorators, Inst. Beaux Arts Architects, Fabian Soc. (London, Eng.). Clubs: Cavendish, Art in Trades, Vagabonds (New York); Authors' (London). Author: A Female of the Species (prod. Berkeley Theatre, New York, 1914); Depreciations, 1914; The Decoration and Furnishing of Apartments, 1915; The Son of Man, 1917; (part author) Forum Stories, 1913; The Art and Business of Interior Decoration, 1922; Practical Hints on Interior Decoration, 1924; Expert Misbidding (in collaboration), 1932; Grand Slam (motion picture and novel), 1933. Compiler: W. B. Yeats Calendar, 1915. Home: 360 E. 55th St. Office: Ritz Tower Hotel, N.Y.C. 22. Died Nov. 3, 1954; buried Ferncliff Cemetery, N.Y.C.

HERTY, Charles Holmes, Jr., metallurgist; b. Athens, Ga., Oct. 6, 1896; s. Charles H. and Sophie (Schaller) H.; B.S., U. of North Carolina, 1918; M.S., Mass. Inst. Tech., 1921, D.Sc., 1924; m. Kathleen Malloy, Nov. 13, 1929; children—Dorothea, Charles H. III, Kathleen, Timothy. Research asso., Sch. of Engring. Practice, Mass. Inst. Tech., at Lackawanna plant of Bethlehem Steel Co., 1924-26; in charge ferrous metall. research, U.S. Bur. of Mines, 1926-31; dir. research Metall. Advisory Bd., Pittsburgh, Pa., 1931-34; research engr. Bethlehem Steel Co., 1934-42, asst. to vice pres. in charge of operations since 1942. Served as sergt. Ordnance Dept., U.S. Army, 1918-19. Mem. Am. Iron and Steel Inst., Am. Inst. Mining and Metall. Engrs. (Hunt medalist; Howe lecturer), Am. Soc. for Metals (Campbel lecturer, Saveur Award), Am. Chem. Soc., Nat. Acad. Sciences, Engineers Club of Lehigh Valley, Phi Beta Kappa, Sigma Xi, Delta Kappa Epsilon, Alpha Chi Sigma. Republican. Episcopalian. Author of about 81 tech. papers for various societies. Home: R.D. No. 1, Hellertown, Pa. Office: Bethlehem Steel Co., Bethlehem, Pa. Died Jan. 17, 1953; buried Nisky Hill Cemetery, Bethlehem, Pa.

HERVEY, Harry Clay, author, explorer; b. Beaumont, Tex., Nov. 5, 1900; s. Harry Clay and Jane Louise (Davis) H.; ed. Sewanee (Tenn.) Mil. Acad.; Ga. Mil. Acad.; grad. prep. sch. U. of the South, Sewanee, 1917; unmarried. Began writing for newspapers, 1916. Served as 2d lt. Jr. O.R.C., 3 mos., 1918. Democrat. Episcopalian. Author: Caravans by Night, 1922; The Black Parrot, 1923; Where Strange Gods Call, 1924; Ethan Quest, 1925; Congai, 1927; King Cobra, 1927; Red Ending, 1929; The Iron Widow, 1931; Red Hotel, 1932; Travels in French Indo-China, 1933; The Damned Don't Cry, 1939; School for Eternity, 1941; The Veiled Fountain, 1947; Barracoon, 1950; also Congai (play in collaboration with Carleton Hildreth), several motion pictures, including, Shanghai Express, Devil and the Deep, Road to Singapore; about 70 short stories, including, The Young Men Go Down, in The Best Short Stories of 1924, and articles and novelettes in mags. Traveled in Asia, Africa and Islands of the Pacific; led expdn. into Upper Indo-China, 1925, and discovered additional Khmer ruins. Address: care De Soto Hotel, Savannah, Ga. Died Aug. 12, 1951; buried Bonaventure Cemetery, Savannah, Ga.

HERVEY, Walter Lowrie, educator; b. Mt. Vernon, O., Sept. 28, 1862; s. Rev. Dwight B. and Mary Elizabeth (Reeder) H.; A.B., Princeton, 1886; A.M., 1889, Ph.D., 1892; m. Antoinette Bryant, July 14, 1887 (deceased 1945); one son Walter Bryant. Teacher of Latin and Greek in secondary schs., 1886-89; prof. history and institutes of edn., dean of faculty, New York Teachers Coll., 1889-91, pres., 1892-97; mem. Bd. of Examiners, Dept. of Edn., New York, 1898-1933; editor The Spoken Word, official organ of Good Speech Soc. of New York, since 1933; teacher of classes in the oral study of prose and verse, since 1933. Dean Chautauqua School of Pedagogy, 1894-99. Camp secretary of the Y.M.C.A., at Amherst, Nova Scotia, 1916, Camp McClellan, Anniston, Ala., 1917. Mem. Nat. Council of Edn.; chmn. ednl. com. West Side Y.M.C.A., 1901-25; member board managers Schools Branch, Y.M.C.A.; chairman advisory committee McBurney School; member executive bd. Religious Edn. Assn.; mem. New York Child Welfare Com.; chmn. advisory bd. Clarence H. White Sch. of Photography. Mem. Poetry Soc. America. Phi Beta Kappa. Author: Picture Work, 1896. Writer and lecturer on education. Editor of Horace Mann Readers, also Junior Literature. Home: 418 Central Park W., N.Y.C. Died Oct. 14, 1952.

HERVEY, William Rhodes, lawyer, banker; b. Somerville, Tenn., Mar. 26, 1870; s. William Blount and Joanna (Rhodes) H.; A.B., U. of Ark., 1890; LL.B., U. of Mich., 1894; m. Browning Clarke, June 1, 1907; 1 son, William Rhodes. Practiced in Los Angeles, 1894-1907; v.p. Am. Nat. Bank of Los Angeles, 1907-09; pres. Am. Savings Bank, 1908-11; judge Superior Court of Calif., 1909-11; v.p. Security-1st Nat. Bank, 1911-30; v.p. State Mutual Bldg. & Loan Assn.; dir. and trustee many corporations; sr. mem. firm of Hervey & Hervey, attys. at law. Mem. Am., Calif. State and Los Angeles bar assns. Republican. Episcopalian. Mason (33°, K.T., Grand Master Masons in Calif. 1917-18). Clubs: California, Los Angeles Country, Sunset. Home: 2267 Chiselhurst Dr. Address: 458 S. Spring St., Los Angeles Cal. Died Feb. 1, 1953.

HERZBERG, Max J(ohn), teacher, editor, author; born at New York City, New York, March 29, 1886; son of Leopold and Mary H.; A.B., Columbia, 1906; married Edna M. Newman, June 30, 1914; children—Richard A., Donald G. Head of English department Central High School, Newark, New Jersey, 1912-29; supervisor of English, pub. schs., Newark, 1929-33; instr. in English, Mercer Beasley Law Sch., 1925-27; instr. in extension courses, Rutgers U., 1927-29; at Montclair (N.J.) State Teachers Coll., 1943, 1944; lecturer on English education, N.Y.U., 1945, 1946; prin. Weequahic High Sch., Newark, 1933-51; literary editor of the Newark Evening and Sunday News, 1919-—. President Stephen Crane Association, 1924-30; was member committee that prepared syllabi in English for schools of N.J., 1926, 1942-49; adv. editor The English Jour., 1933-34; Town Meeting of Air adv. com.; pres. Nat. Council Teachers English, 1942-43, director of publications, 1951-—, chmn. radio committee; past president Newark Schoolmen's Club, N. J. Secondary School Principals Association; member N.J. Council National Youth Adminstrn., 1940-42; mem. Museum of Modern Art; charter mem. Assn. for Edn. by Radio. Author: Speaking and Writing English (with collaborator), 1925; Myths and Their Meaning, 1928; New Style-Book of Business English, 1928; Outline of Contemporary American and British Literature, 1928; Secretarial Procedure (with collaborator), 1929; Romance (with collaborators), 1932; American Literature (with collaborators), 1933; Off to Arcady—Adventures in Poetry, 1933; English Literature (with others), 1934; Mark Twain Omnibus, 1935; Classic Myths, 1935; Albert Payson Terhune Omnibus, 1937; Americans in Action (with collaborator), 1937; Situations in Which Citizenship Can Be Taught, 1940; series, For Better Reading (Quest, Venture, Rewards—with Austin M. Works and M. P. Paine), 1940; Radio and English Teaching, 1940; Insults: A Practical Anthology, 1941; Happy Landings, an aviation anthology (with collaborators), 1942; English at Command, 1943; Humor of America (with collaborator), 1945. Editor: Stories of Adventure, 1927; This Is America, 1951; (with collaborators) Better English, 16 vols., 1952; Dictionary of American Literature (posthumously); sch. edits. various works. Contbr. to Ency. Britannica; editor Word Study, a periodical for English teachers; editor Photoplay Guides, Nat. Council Teachers of English, 1934-35; chairman editorial committee Photoplay Studies. Department of Secondary Education of N.E.A., 1935-39; radio editor for mag., Education. Co-ordinator in English, Phi Delta Kappa Dictionary of Edn., 1944; editor, guide to Lawrence Olivier prodns. of Henry V., Hamlet; editor various publs.; chmn. selection com. of Teenage Book Club, 1945-—; mem. adv. com. of Young America, 1948-49. Contributor to mags.; broadcaster over radio stations; author of inscriptions on 14 bronze tablets erected by Schoolmen's Club of Newark to mark historical occasions; also tablets at Stephen Crane birthplace. Home: 135 Mercer Pl., South Orange, N.J. Office: Newark News, Newark 1. Died Jan. 21, 1958.

HERZOG, Anna Edes (hĕr'zŏg), Christian Sci. lect.; b. River Falls, Wis.; d. John W. and Helen M. (Smith) Bradshaw; C.S.B., Christian Sci. Bd. of Edn., 1928; m. John Seward Herzog, Jan. 20, 1904. Christian Sci. practitioner, 1916, tchr., 1928, lectr., 1942-46. Contbr. to Christian Sci. periodicals. Address: 921 Spahr Bldg., Columbus O. Died Sept. 28, 1955.

HESS, Frank L., geologist; b. Streator, Ill., Sept. 4, 1871; s. Jesse M. (M.D.) and Mary (Brown) H.; A.B. in geology and mining, Stanford, 1903; m. Eva Roseberry, May 25, 1903. With U.S. Geol. Survey, 1903-25, U.S. Bur. Mines, 1925-44, profl. work in Alaska, Bolivia, Burma, Can., Ceylon, Chile, China, Federated Malay States, India, Italy, Mex., and in nearly all the mining states of U.S., now ret., lectr. on geology U. Md., 6 yrs. Hon. custodian of rare earths and rare metals, U.S. Nat. Museum. Former mem. of Com. on Determination of Geologic Age, Nat. Research Council, A.A.A.S., Soc. Econ. Geologists, Washington Acad. Sciences, Geol. Soc. of Washington, Petrologist Club, Geol. Soc. Am. (fellow), Mineral. Soc., Phycol. Soc. of the Americas. Methodist. Author papers on rare metals and their deposits, pegmatites and other geol. subjects. Address: 5509 Roosevelt St., Bethesda, Md. Deceased.

HESS, Julius Hays, pediatrician; b. Ottawa, Ill., Jan. 26, 1876; s. Amson and Caroline (Oestricher) H.; M.D., Northwestern U., 1899; intern Alexian Bros. Hosp., Chicago, 1899-1900; post-grad. work, Johns Hopkins Univ. Hosp. and hosps. in Germany and Austria, 1900-01, and 1910, 13, 27; m. Clara E. Merrifield, Apr. 15, 1902; children—Mrs. Jean Merrifield Spencer, Mrs. Carol Lucille Saphir. Practiced in Chicago, Illinois, since 1902; specializing in diseases of children; pediatrician to Michael Reese Hosp.; professor pediatrics emeritus, University of Illinois Coll. of Medicine. Mem. A.M.A., Ill. State Med. Soc., Chicago Med. Soc. (pres. 1934-35), Am. and Chicago pediatric societies, American Academy of Pediatricians (Borden award 1952), A.C.P. Consulting pediatrician at Municipal Contagious Hospital, Chicago; member of advisory committee Children's Bureau, Department of Labor, Washington, D.C. Republican. Clubs: Standard, Adventurers. Author: Premature and Congenitally Diseased Infants, 1923; Feeding and the Nutritional Disorders of Infancy and Childhood (6 edits.); Infant Feeding, 1923; The Physical and Mental Development of Prematurely Born Children, 1934; Medical Care and Nursing Care of Premature Infants, 1941. Home: Hotel Windermere East, 1642 E. 56th St. Office: 104 S. Michigan Av., Chgo. Died Nov. 2, 1955.

HESS, Leslie Elsworth, mfr.; b. Beach Haven, Pa., Dec. 29, 1869; s. John I. and Almira (Everard) H.; student Wyoming Sem., Kingston, Pa.; m. Jennie Conover, June 18, 1896; children—Ruth, Dorothy, Helen, Eloise, Elizabeth. Began as telegraph operator and chief clerk to agt. D.,L.&W. R.R., Kingston, Pa., 1891; works mgr. J. G. Brill Co., 1932-35, exec. v.p., 1935-42, pres., 1942-—, dir., 1935-—. Home: 143 W. Bryn Mawr Av., Lansdowne, Pa. Office: 62d St. and Woodland Av., Phila. Died Oct. 7, 1952; buried Berwick, Pa.

HESS, Wendell Frederick, educator, research dir.; b. Troy, N.Y., Jan. 1, 1903; s. Wendell, Jr. and Anna Marie (Beiermeister) H.; E.E., Rensselaer Polytech. Institute, Troy, N.Y., 1925, Dr. Engring., 1928; m. Grace Eleanor Towne, Feb. 4, 1933; children—Wendell Towne, Eleanor Sylvia, Frederick W., John. Instr. Rensselaer Polytech. Inst., 1928-30, asst. prof. elec. engring. and physics, 1930-37; asst. prof. metall. engring., 1937-38; asso. prof. and head of welding lab., 1938-45; prof. and head welding lab., 1945-47, head department of metallurgical engring. 1947-—, dir. research, 1952-—, tchr. course in welding to U.S.N. Annapolis grads., sent by Bur. of Yards and Docks, 1929-47. Fellow Am. Inst. Elec. Engr.; mem. Am. Inst. Mining and Metall. Engrs., Am. Welding soc. (pres., hon. life mem.; Samuel Wylie Miller Meml. medallist, 1949), Am. Soc. for Engring. Edn., Am. Soc. Metals, Am. Soc. Testing Materials, Sigma Xi. Awarded Lincoln Gold Medal by Am. Welding Soc.; University Award of the Resistance Welder Mfrs. Assn., 1944, 1945, 1947, 1948; Am. Iron and Steel Inst. Medal, 1944; John Price Weatherill Medal of Franklin Inst., 1948. Home: 25 Hawthorne Av. Office: Rensselaer Polytechnic Inst., Troy, N.Y. Died Apr. 21, 1954; buried Oakwood Cemetery, Troy.

HESSE, Frank McNeil, steel corp. exec.; b. New Cumberland, W.Va., Oct. 19, 1894; s. Charles H. and Nell (McNeil) H.; ed. New Cumberland High Sch. and Bethany (W.Va.) Coll.; m. Mary Elizabeth Wylie; children—Barbara Jean, Elinor Gail, Frank McNeil, Jr., Brian Carl. Accounting dept. Weirton Steel Co., 1912, asst. auditor, 1921, auditor, 1923, asst. treas., 1925, treas., 1928; vice pres. and treas. Nat. Steel Corp. since 1929; v.p., sec. and asst. treas. Great Lakes Steel Corp., Mich. Steel Corporation, director, vice president, assistant sec. and asst. treas. Weirton Steel Co.; dir., v.p., sec. and asst. treas. The Hanna Furnace Corp.; dir., v.p. and sec. Hanna Iron Ore Co.; dir., v.p. and asst. treas. Beaver Creek Consol. Coal Co.; v.p., sec. and treas. Nat. Mines Corp., dir. v.p., sec. and treas. Weirton Coal Co., Oak Hill Supply Co., Nat. Steel Products Co.; vice president and assistant sec. Steel Framing & Bldg. Corporation; director, v.p. and treas. Weirton Improvement Co.; v.p., sec. and treas. Midwest Steel Corp.; dir. Bank of Weirton, Peoples Bank of Weirton, Edgewater Steel Co. Dir. West Virginia Mfrs. Assn. Trustee Bethany Coll. Mem. Am. Iron and Steel Inst., Controllers Inst., Kappa Alpha. Republican. Clubs: Duquesne, Pittsburgh Athletic Association (Pittsburgh); Williams Country. Home: 37 Woodland Dr., Pitts. 28. Office: 2800 Grant Bldg., Pitts. Died July 10, 1952; buried Homewood Cemetery.

HESSER, Frederic William, naval officer; b. Hinsdale, Mont., Dec. 2, 1904; s. William Hewey and Jessie Marie (Lemon) H.; B.S., U.S. Naval Acad., 1927; M.B.A., Harvard, 1932; grad. Army Indsl. Coll., 1938; m. Annah Clarke Day, Apr. 11, 1930; 1 dau., Joann Patricia. Commd. ensign, Supply Corps, U.S.N., 1927, advanced through grades to rear admiral, 1953; associate professor Harvard, 1943-45; exec. officer Navy Supply Corps Sch., 1942-45; staff supply officer Western Sea Frontier, 1945-48; fleet supply officer Pacific Fleet 1948-49; Gen. Stores Supply officer, Phila., 1949-53; dir. Navy Cost Inspection Service, 1953. Recipient Navy Commendation Ribbon. Clubs: University (Washington); Bohemian (San Francisco). Home: care H. D. Walter, 1275 Greenwich St., San Francisco 9. Office: Bur. Supplies and Accounts (OT), Navy Dept., Washington 25. Died Apr. 1, 1954; buried Arlington Nat. Cemetery.

HESTER, William John, sec. of U. of Miami; b. New York, N.Y., Sept. 13, 1902; s. Robert James and Regina (Sier) H.; B.S., U. of Pittsburgh, 1926; student Duquesne U.; LL.B., U. of Miami, 1934; grad. student in law, Mich. Univ.; m. Teresa Kerrigan, Oct. 4, 1927; 1 daughter, Mary Ann. Clerk, Mellon Nat. Bank, Pittsburgh, Pa., 1926; real estate salesman and sales manager, 1929-31; admitted to Florida bar, 1934, and practiced until 1939; asst. prof. of law, Univ. of Miami, 1937-40, associate, 1940-42; legal counsel for University, 1938-41, treas., 1941, sec., prof. of law since 1942. Consultant in the War Manpower Commn. since Feb. 16, 1943. Compliance commr. C.P.A., 1946-48. Mem. Dade County, Fla., and Am. bar assns., Am. Planning and Civic Assn., Am. Arbitration Assn., Phi Alpha Delta. Club: Riviera Country. Home: 239 Sarto Av., Coral Gables, Fla. Deceased.

HETERICK, Robert Hynton, med. dir. USPHS (ret.); b. Georgetown, O.; s. Robert Grant and Martha Bell (Cooper) H.; student U. Cin., M.D., Med. Coll. of Ohio, 1906; grad. U.S. Army Med. Sch., 1911; m. Frances Susan Felker, Feb. 8, 1908. Resident physician Ohio Maternity Hosp., 1906, Hosp. of Good Samaritan, Cin., 1907; commd. 1st lt., Med. Dept., U.S. Army, 1909; commd. asst. surgeon, US PHS, 1911, passed asst. surgeon, 1915, surgeon, 1923, sr. surgeon, 1931; served in Iloilo, Manila, Batan, P.I., 1912-15; instr. pub. health U. of Philippines, 1914-15; assigned to U.S. Naval Forces in European waters during World War I; med. dir., 3d Dist. U.S. Indian Service, 1935-36, commd. med. dir., 1937; formerly sr. med. officer Ellis Island Hosp., exec. officer Marine Hosps. at Chgo., Cleve. and San Francisco; former comdg. officer Vineyard Haven, Savannah and Louisville Marine hosps. and USPHS Hosp. 30, Chgo.; mem. surg. staff. San Pedro Gen. Hosp., Cal. Hosp., French Hosp., Cal. and Hollywood hosps., Los Angeles; chief quarantine officer, Port of Los Angeles, 1941-46; supr. ports of Hueneme, Port San Luis, Santa Barbara, Newport, San Diego, quarantine affairs; dist. med. officer, War shipping Adminstrn., Los Angeles Dist., 1944-45; cons. in pub. health and sanitation to port surgeon, U.S. Army, Los Angeles, to sr. med. officer of U.S. Naval Bases at San Diego and Terminal Island, 1941-45; cons. in pub. health to State of N.M., City of Albuquerque; lecturer in pub. health U. So. Cal. Med. Sch., U. of N.M. Recipient medal S.A.R., 1948; hon. mem. Indian Medical Service, third district. Fellow A.C.S.; mem. A.M.A., Med. Officers of World War Vets. Fgn. Wars of America, Assn. Mil. Surgeons, S.A.R., Wanderers and Sojourners, Omega Upsilon Phi. Mason (32°, Shriner). Author: articles on public health in various med. jours.; Health Hints for Primary Teachers, 1949. Also short stories for children. Address: 605 Ridgecrest Dr., Albuquerque, N.M. Died Sept. 14, 1957.

HETLER, Donald McK(inley), univ. prof.; born Osage City, Kan., Feb. 19, 1896; s. Thomas Jefferson and Katharine (Slusser) H.; A.B., Univ. Kan., 1918, A.M., 1923; Ph.D., Yale (Nat. T.B. Assn. fellow, 1924-26), 1926; m. Rossleene Merle Arnold, Jan. 1, 1928 (dec.); 1 d., Katharine Jane. Chemist Hercules Powder Co., Parlin, N.J., 1918-21; grad. asst., dept. chemistry, Univ. Kan., 1921-24; asst., Rockefeller Inst., 1926-28; instr., Washington Univ. Sch. Med., 1928-31, asst. prof., 1931-37; asso. prof., dept. bacteriology, Mont. State Univ., 1937-38, prof. and chmn., dept. bacteriology since 1938. Fellow A.A.A.S. Mem. Am. Chem. Soc., Alpha Chi Sigma, Sigma Xi, Phi Sigma, Acacia, Gamma Alpha. Republican. Methodist. Mason. Research work in field of chem. studies of bacteria, immune sera, bacteriophage, immunity in cancer. Home: 322 E. Beckwith Av., Missoula, Mont. Died Sept. 1, 1956.

HEUER, George J., surgeon; b. Madison, Wis., Feb. 6, 1882; s. George H. and Louisa (Zehnter) H.; B.S., U. Wis., 1903; M.D., Johns Hopkins, 1907; hon. LL.D., U. Cincinnati, 1932; m. Juanita Reid, July 18, 1925; children—George J., Reid. Intern Johns Hopkins Hosp., Baltimore, 1907, asst. resident surgeon, 1908-11, resident surgeon, 1911-14; asso. prof. surgery, Johns Hopkins, 1914-22; prof. surgery, U. Cincinnati, 1922-31, Cornell U. Med. Coll., 1931-47, prof. emeritus since 1947. Surgical dir. Cincinnati Gen. Hosp., 1922-31; surgeon in chief New York Hosp., 1931-47, now cons. surgeon. Served as major, Med. Corps, U.S., in France, June 1917-Feb. 1919. Fellow Am. Coll. Surgeons, A.A.A.S.; mem. A.M.A., Am. Surg. Assn., Soc. Clin. Surgery, So. Surg. Assn., Am. Soc. Thoracic Surgery, Neuro Surg. Soc., N.Y. Surg. Soc., N.Y. Acad. Medicine, Med. Soc. State of N.Y. (mem. com. med. research), Harvey Soc. of N.Y., Am. Genetic Assn., N.Y. Acad. Science, Osler Soc. of N.Y.; hon. fellow Chicago Surg. Soc.; hon. mem. Soc. of Univ. Surgeons; corr. hon. mem. Academy Science, Med., Physical and Natural, U. of Havana, Cuba. Mem. Founders Group, Am. Bd. of Surgery. Mem. adv. bd. Cushing Brain Tumor Registry of Yale U. Sch. of Medicine. Clubs: University (New York); Megantic Fish and Game (Quebec and Me.). Contbr. to surg. jours. and chapters on surgery of thorax to Keen's Surgery, Lewis's Surgery, Nelson's Loose Leaf Surgery. Home: 2900 N.E. Center Av., Fort Lauderdale, Fla. Died Dec. 15, 1950; buried, Fincastle, Va.

HEUSER, Emil (hoi'zĕr), educator, research asso.; b. Stralsund, Germany, Sept. 15, 1882; s. Karl Ludwig and Olga (Oborn) H.; student Tech. U. Munich, Germany, 1903-05, Tech. U., Karlsruhe, 1905-07, U. of Graz, Austria, 1907-09; Dr. Engring. Sci., Tech. Univ., Karlsruhe, 1909; m. Frieda Thiele, July 2, 1910; children—Heinrich, Dietrich, Klaus, Andreas. Came to Canada, 1926; naturalized British subject. Mill chemist various German and Austrian pulp and paper mills, 1909-12; prof. cellulose chemistry Tech. U., Darmstadt, 1912-23; dir. research Glanzstoff-Werke (rayon), Seehof nr. Berlin, 1923-26; dir. research Canadian Internat. Paper Co., Hawkesbury, Ont., Can., 1926-38; research asso. Inst. Paper Chemistry, Appleton, Wis., 1938-47, ret. Mil. service with Red Cross, 1916-18. Mem. govt. com. for utilization of cellulose waste (alcohol, furfural, fodder). Mem. Am. Chem. Soc. (chmn. cellulose div. 1937), Tech. Assn. Pulp and Paper Industry, Wis. Acad. Letters and Science. Sec. German Assn. Pulp and Paper Chemists and Engrs., 1918-26; hon. prof. cellulose chemistry, Tech. Univ., Berlin, Charlottenburg, 1923-26. Editor: Papierfabrikant, 1918-23; founder and editor: Cellulose-Chemie, 1920-26. Author: Das Farben des Papiers auf der Papiermachine (Berlin), 1913; Lehrbuch der Cellulose-Chemie (Berlin), 3d edit., 1927; translation into Russian (L. K. Lepin and N. A. Shilova), Moscow, 1923. Textbook of Cellulose Chemistry (translation C. J. West and G. J. Esselen), 1924; The Chemistry of Cellulose, 1944. Contbr. to sci. publs., Germany and U.S., and to sci. vols., chiefly on pulp and paper, cullolose, noncellulosic carbohydrates, lignin, and wood. Home: 339 Vista de la Playa, La Jolla, Cal. Died Dec. 24, 1953.

HEWE, Laurence Ilsey, civil engr.; b. Dover, N.H., Sept. 28, 1876; s. Horace Greeley and Helen Ilsley (Jones) H.; B.Sc., Dartmouth, 1898; Ph.D., Yale, 1901; m. Agnes Danforth June 1901; 5 children. With Mass. Hwy. Commn., 1897-99; prof. mathematics and engring. R.I. State Coll., 1901-05; instr. mathematics Yale, 1905-09; with U.S. Pub. Rd. Adminstrn., 1911—; successively chief of econs., dist. engn., gen. insp., dep. chief engr., chief Western Region Hdqrs., San Francisco. Cons. to government of Saudi Arabia, 1946-47. Chmn. Am. delegation Internat. Rd. Congress Munich, 1934. Mem. Am. Soc. C.E., Am. Assn. Highway Ofcls., Am. Math. Soc. (1901-31), Sigma Xi, Casque and Gauntlet; fellow A.A.A.S. Clubs: Cosmos (Washington), Commonwealth (San Francisco). Author: (with Prof. Jas W. Glover) Highway Bonds, 1913; (with Prof. H. L. Seward). Design of Diagrams for Engineering Formulas, 1924; American Highway Practice (2 vols.), 1941. Contbr. tech. articles in math. and engring. publs.; tech. and popular articles in World's Work, Nat. Geog. Mag., Collier's, etc. Home: 114 Edgewood Av. Office: Phelan Bldg., San Francisco. Died Mar. 2, 1950; buried Goodnoe Hills, Washington.

HEWES, Thomas, lawyer, cons.; born Balt.; s. M. Lewin and Virginia Sumter (Smith) H.; A.B., Yale University, 1910, LL.B., cum laude, 1912; m. Genevieve Chase, June 17, 1911 (dec.); children—Thomas, Helen Davis, Charles, Patricia Pierson; m. 2d, Harriet Hanlon, August 2, 1940. Admitted to Connecticut bar, 1912, and since in practice at Hartford, Connecticut and in Washington, D.C.; asso. with Robinson, Robinson & Cole, 1912-19; senior mem. Hewes, Phillips & Lindsey, 1919-29; mem. firm Robinson, Robinson & Cole, 1929-33; asst. sec. U.S. Treasury, 1933; special asst. to U.S. Sec. of State, 1934-35; chmn. Commn. to Reorganize State Departments of Conn., 1935-37; senior mem. Hewes, Prettyman and Awalt, and successor firms Hartford, Connecticut, New York City and Washington, 1935-52; now counsel Shepherd, Mortha and Merritt at Hartford. Chmn. committee of State Bar Association, to promote a state-wide system of aid to poor litigants, 1920-30. Served as 2d lieutenant, F.A., U.S. Army, during World War. Mem. Conn. Ho. of Rep., 1914-16, Conn. Civil Service Commn., 1917-21, Commn. to Revise Gen. Statutes, 1927-30; mem. Conn. Commn. to Recommend Form of Liquor Control; apptd. by Gov. treas. of State of Conn., Oct. 1937; coordinator of state and Fed. relief agencies following hurricane of Sept. 1938; col. staff of Gov. of Conn., 1931-38; mem. Park and Forest Commn of Conn., 1937-49, Jud. Council of Conn., 1932-40; with Adv. Commn. Council Nat. Defense, June-Nov. 1940; Adminstrn. of Export Control, Nov. 1940-June 1941. Conn. State adminstr. war savs. staff U.S. Treasury, 1943; chmn. Conn. War Finance Com., U.S. Treasury, 1943. Active in Dem. party since 1912; del. to many State conventions, Nat. Conv., St. Louis, 1916, Philadelphia, 1936, Chicago, 1940. Mem. Am. and Conn. bar assns., Scroll and Key. Episcopalian. Clubs: Yale, Century Association (N.Y.); Hartford. Author: Decentralize for Liberty, 1945-47, English edit., 1950, German edit., 1950. Home: Farmington, Conn. Died June 15, 1957; buried Farmington, Conn.

HEWITT, Clarence Horace, clergyman; b. Shrewsburg, Vt., Oct. 25, 1890; s. Rev. Harley W. and Ann Grace (Ackley) H.; B.Th., Aurora (Ill.) Coll., 1926, D.D. (hon.), 1943; A.M., U. of N.H., 1927; m. Flora Annetta Eaton, June 30, 1914; children—Clyde Eaton, Robert Clarence. Ordained to ministry of the Advent Christian Chs., 1912; pastor, Magnolia, Wis., 1914-15, Hudson Falls, N.Y., 1915-18, Peace Dale, R.I., 1918-22, South Vernon, Mass., 1922-23, Dover, N.H., 1923-27, Providence, R.I. since 1947; prof. of theology, Aurora (Ill.) Coll., 1927-42; exec. sec., Advent Christian Gen. Conf. of Am., Aurora, 1942-47, sec. of conf. since 1920; sec. Advent Christian Publication Soc. since 1947. Author: The Hope of the Apostles, 1924; Faith for Today, 1940; Class Book in Eschatology, 1942; Vital Atonement, 1946; The Seer of Babylon, 1948. Home: 36 Western Promenade, Cranston, R.I. Office: Advent Christian Church, Providence 9. Died Sept. 2, 1952.

HEWITT Edward Ringwood, engr., inventor, author; b. Ringwood Manor, N.J., June 20, 1866; s. Abraham Stevens and Sarah Amelia (Cooper) H.; g.s. of Peter Cooper; A.B., Princeton, 1889, A.M., 1892; U. of Berlin 1890-91; m. Mary E. Ashley Sept. 7 1892; children—Candace (Mrs. Gordon Stevenson), Ashley C., Lucy (Mrs. Guido Pantalconi), Abram. Chemist, Peter Cooper Glue Factory, 1901-02; designed automobiles, established one design, in Eng., known as the "Adams-Hewitt"; dir., engr. Metzger Motor Car Co.; built motor trucks under name of Hewitt Motor Co., which was absorbed by Internat. Motor Co., of which became cons. engr., dir. Mem. Am. Soc. M.E., Am. Assn. Auto Engrs. Clubs: Century, Anglers, Dutch Treat, Players, Tuxedo. Author: Secrets of the Salmon; Telling on the Trout; Trout Streams; Handbook of Stream Improvement; Handbook of Fly Fishing; Trout Raising and Stocking; Those Were the Days, 1943. Address: 48 Gramercy Park, N.Y.C. Died Feb. 1957.*

HEWITT, Harvey, univ. prof., musician; b. South Royalton, Vt., Apr. 27, 1885; s. John Harvey and Jane (Smith) H.; student Goddard Sem., Barre, Vt., 1905, New Eng. Conservatory of Music, 1910; studied with Carl Baermann, Boston, 1911, George Boyle,

Peabody Inst., Baltimore, 1914, Carlo Buonamici, Boston, 1915, Alfred DeVoto, Boston, 1917, Ernest Hutcheson, N.Y. City, 1920, Isadore Philipp, Paris, 1921; student Conservatoire Americaine, Fontainbleau, France, 1923, Cornell U., 1930, Columbia, 1936; m. Edith Weekes Say, June 29, 1929. Instr., Ohio Wesleyan U., 1910-29, asso. prof., 1929-32, prof., 1932-52, emeritus prof. since 1952, head dept. of music, 1921, 1932-36. Recipient Adam Poe medal, Founders award Ohio Wesleyan U., 1952. Member Pi Kappa Lambda, Phi Mu Alpha. Republican. Episcopalian. Home: 62 S. Liberty Av., Delaware, O. Died Nov. 3, 1954.

HEWITT, Theodore Brown, prof. German; b. Hanover, Germany, Dec. 5, 1881; s. of Am. parents, John Haskell and Mary Louisa (Downing) H.; prep. edn. pvt. sch., Berlin; B.A., Yale, 1902, Ph.D., 1917; M.A., Harvard, 1907; studied Freiburg and Marburg univs.; m. Berenice Amanda Fowler, Apr. 9, 1914 (died Mar. 13, 1938); children—John Hollis, Berenice Martha; m. 2d, Mrs. Amorette Field Rochester, Aug. 15, 1942. Instr. modern langs., Lawrenceville (N.J.) Sch., 1904-06; instr. in German, Phillips Acad., Andover, Mass., 1908-09, Williams Coll., 1909-16; asst. prof. German, Yale, 1917-18, Williams Coll., 1917-23; prof. German and head of dept., of the university of Buffalo, 1923-52, professor emeritus, 1952. Translator German documents, Department of Justice, 1917, Post Office Department Washington, 1918, F.B.I., 1943. Mem. Modern Language Association of America, American Association University Professors, American Association German Teachers (dir. Western N.Y. br.). Republican. Conglist. Club: Yale. Author: A Short Course in Practical German Composition, 1915; German for the American Soldier (with Prof. H. A. Farr), 1918; Paul Gerhardt as a Hymn Writer and His Influence on English Hymnody, 1918; Intermediate German Composition, 1923; Idiomatic German Composition, 1937. Editor: E. v. Keyserling's Abendliche Häuser, 1931, and his Dumala, 1934; Im Stillen Winkel und Andere Novellen, 1936. Contributor to modern language periodicals. Home: 1131 Delaware Av., Buffalo. Deceased.

HEWLETT, James Howell, educator; b. Morgan County, Ala., July 29, 1888; s. Thaddeus Plummer and Lou Emma (Arms) H.; A.B., Birmingham Southern Coll., 1912; A.M., Vanderbilt U., 1913; student Johns Hopkins, 1926-27; Ph.D., U. Chgo., 1931; m. Mary Spencer, May 30, 1914; 1 son, James Spencer. Prof., head dept. English, Ky. Wesleyan Coll., winchester, 1913-17, Olivet (Mich.) Coll., 1917-18, Drury Coll., Springfield, Mo. 1918-20; prof. English, head dept. Centre Coll., Danville, Ky., 1920—, dean of men, 1928-32, asso. dean of coll., 1932-36 dean of summer session, 1933—, acting pres. 1936-38, 1942-44, 46-47, dean of college, 1938—; prof. English, summer sessions, Berea College, 1921-23, U. Ky., 1924, U. of Louisville, 1928. Chmn. com. on non-mems. So. Assn. Colls. and Secondary Schs., Ky. Assn. Colls. and Secondary Schools, 1943-44, 1944—; pres. Assn. Ky. Registrars, 1944-45; v.p. Assn. Ch.-Related Colls., Ky., 1944-45. Mem. Modern Lang. Assn. Am., Am. Assn. Univ. Profs., Phi Beta Kappa, Omicron Delta Kappa, Kappa Phi Kappa, Pi Kappa Delta, Kappa Sigma. Democrat. Methodist. Clubs: Johns Hopkins Tudor Stuart (Balt.); Anaconda (Danville). Home: Danville, Ky. Died Dec. 27, 1948; buried Danville, Ky.

HEXTER, Joseph, bakery exec.; b. N.Y.C., Jan. 12, 1887; s. Berman and Julia (Peirrea) H.; student City Coll. N.Y., 1916-18; m. Georgia Lester, Nov. 10, 1932; children—Berman, Julian. With Ward Baking Co., 1911-23; formed Hexter Baking Co., 1923-32; pres. Columbia Baking Co. since 1932, dir. since 1932; dir. Ideal Packaging Co. since 1932. Mem. governor's staff State of Ga., 1941-53. Mem. bakers war com., World War II. Mem. Am. Bakers Assn. (mem. bd. govs.), So. Bakers Assn. (pres. 1942). Mason. Home: 36 Sutton Pl. So. N.Y.C. Office: 375 Highland Av. N.E. Atlanta 2. Died 1954.

HEYE, George Gustav (hī), b. N.Y. City, Sept. 16, 1874; s. Gustav and Marie Antoinette (Lawrence) H.; E.E., Sch. of Mines, Columbia U., 1896; Ph.D., U. of Hamburg, 1929. Formerly mem. firm Battles, Heye & Harrison, bankers. Started Am. anthropol. collection, 1903, which developed into the Heye Museum; founded the Museum of the American Indian, Heye Foundation, 1916, endowed it, turned over entire collection of nearly half a million specimens, and became its director. Hon. fellow Royal Anthrop. Inst. (London); hon. mem. Order of Indian Wars. Clubs: University, Lotos, Explorers (pres. 1923-30). Office: Museum of the American Indian, Heye Foundation, Broadway at 155th St., N.Y.C. 32. Died Jan. 20, 1957; buried Heye Mausoleum, Woodlawn Cemetery, N.Y.C.

HIATT, Walter Sanders, newspaper man; b. Jasper, Tenn., June 17, 1878; s. Hiram Roberts and Ellen Olivia (Mitchell) H.; student univs. of Ky., Paris and Berlin; m. Camille Buisson, France, Mar. 10, 1902; children—Guy, Roland (dec.), Robert McCulloch. Chief yeoman USN, Spanish-Am. War, 1898; began newspaper work with Morning Herald, Lexington, Ky., 1899; with editorial dept. New York Times, 1901-04; extensive contbr. to mags. on transportation subjects; wrote series of articles for Railway Age, from France and Italy, on transportation problems of the war; represented Associated Press with Italy Army. After the Armistice went to Vienna with the retreating Austrian Army and reported downfall of the empire; later spl. missions to Balkans, Near East, Russia, etc. Died June 1956.

HIBBARD, Benjamin Horace, prof. agrl. economics; b. Bremer County, Ia., Jan. 9, 1870; s. Alfred Alanson and Elizabeth Ann (Bazeley) H.; B.S.A., Ia. State Coll. Agr. and Mech. Arts, 1898; Ph.D., U. of Wis., 1902; Halle and Berlin, Germany, 1908; m. Daisy Jeannette Baker, Dec. 31, 1902 (died Apr. 6, 1925); 1 dau., Virginia Jeannette; m. 2d, Margaret M. Baker, June 12, 1926; 1 son, Howard. In charge department of economics, Ia. State Coll. Agr. and Mech. Arts, 1902, prof. agrl. economics, 1904-13; spl. agt. agrl. div. Bureau of Census, 1911; prof. agrl. economics, 1913, and head of dept., 1919-32, U. of Wis.; prof. emeritus since 1941. Taught in summer sessions of Utah Agrl. Coll., Colorado State Coll., Kansas State Coll., Garrett Biblical Inst.; also taught one semester at Okla. State Coll., 1940-41, Miss. State Coll., 1940-41, Mont. State Coll., 1941-42. Mem. Am. Econ. Assn., Am. Farm Econ. Assn., Amer. Acad. Polit. and Social Science, Phi Kappa Phi, Alpha Zeta, S.A.R. Conglist. Author: Effect of the Great War upon Agriculture (Carnegie Foundation publ.), 1919; Marketing Agricultural Products, 1921; A History of the Public Land Policies, 1924; Agricultural Economics, 1948; also many bulls. and articles. Home: 2227 Hollister Av., Madison 5, Wis. Died Aug. 11, 1955.

HIBBARD, Carlisle V., YMCA ofcl.; b. Oconomowoc, Wis., Aug. 12, 1876; s. Daniel Osmer and Ida F. (Brightman) H.; B.S., U. of Wis., 1900, post-grad. study in polit. science, 1907; m. Sue Eugenia Lowell, Aug. 1902; children—Esther Lowell, Carlisle (dec.), Russel. Student sec. Internat. Com. YMCA, Tokyo, Japan, 1902-04; field rep. of same with Japanese Army in Manchuria, 1904-05; with Tokyo City YMCA, 1905-07; asso. nat. sec. Internat. Com. YMCA, in Japan, 1909-14; in charge at New York, Internat. Com. YMCA, work for allied armies and prisoners of war, 1914-17; asso. gen. sec., in charge at New York of overseas div. Nat. War Work Council and Com. on Allied Armies and Prisoners of War, YMCA, 1917-20; asso. gen. sec. overseas div., Internat. Com. YMCA, 1920-24; sec. YMCA, U. Wis., 1924—. Mem. Phi Beta Kappa, Alpha Delta Phi. Conglist. Home: Shorewood Hills. Office: 740 Langdon St., Madison, Wis. Died Nov. 28, 1954; buried Janesville, Wis.

HIBBARD, Frank, wholesale hardware; b. Chicago, Ill., July 10, 1873; s. William Gold and Lydia Beekman (Van Schaak) H.; ed. Harvard Sch., Chicago; St. Paul's Sch., Concord, N.H.; King's Sch., Stamford, Conn.; m. Martha Harlan Johnson, July 15, 1897 (dec.); children—William Gold III (dec.), Lydia H. Holland; m. 2d, Dorothy Ford Robbins, Oct. 29, 1913. Entered employ of Hibbard, Spencer, Bartlett & Co., 1893, v.p., 1916-26, chmn. bd., 1926-46, now chmn. exec. com. Republican. Clubs: Chicago. Home: 1301 Astor St., Chgo. Office: 2201 Harvard St., Evanston, Ill. Died Nov. 3, 1957; buried Graceland Cemetery, Chgo.

HIBBARD, Frederick Cleveland, sculptor; b. Canton, Mo., June 15, 1881; s. David Moulton and Sarah Cleveland (Fiske) H.; ed. Christian U. (now Culver-Stockton Coll.), LL.D., 1929; U. of Mo.; Illinois Inst. Tech., Chicago; Art Inst., Chicago; m. Gladys E. Vance, Sept. 30, 1903 (died 1930); children—Frederick W. (dec. 1945), Eugene M., Cora Belle, Robert, Josephine; m. 2d, Elisabeth Haseltine, Mar. 18, 1932. Represented by statue of Mark Twain at Hannibal, Mo.; statue of General James Shields, Carrollton, Mo.; soldier memorials, Jackson, Mich., Winchester, Va., Forsyth, Ga., Pittsburgh, Pa., Great Bend, Kan., Princeton, Ill. and McConnellsville, O.; U.D.C. memorial, Shiloh Nat. Park, Tenn.; equestrian statue of Gen. U.S. Grant, Vicksburg, Miss.; statue of General Lawton, Fort Wayne, Indiana; Tom Sawyer and Huck Finn, Hannibal, Mo.; Champ Clark, Bowling Green, Mo.; Carter H. Harrison statue, Chicago; Col. Alexander Doniphan statue, Richmond, Mo.; Dr. G. V. Black, Chicago; Col. David N. Foster, Fort Wayne, Ind.; Dr. Willoughby Miller, Columbus, O.; Volney Rogers, Youngstown, O.; 2 bronze fountain groups, Lakeside, Michigan; 2 bronze fountain groups, Grant Park, Chicago; Pond memorial, Ft. Wayne, Ind.; memorial fountain, Hines Hosp., Maywood, Ill.; Senator Stone statue, Nevada, Mo.; Jefferson Davis statue, Capitol Bldg., Frankfort, Ky.; statue Speaker Henry T. Rainey, Carrollton, Ill.; fountain figure Lincoln Park Conservatory, Chicago; statue of Speaker David E. Shanahan, Capitol Bldg., Springfield, Ill.; statue Sen. Benjamin R. Tillman, Columbia, S.C.; statue Jefferson Davis, Montgomery, Ala.; David Wallach Fountain, Chicago (in collaboration with Elisabeth Hazeltine Hibbard); granite group of Mary Todd Lincoln and Abraham Lincoln, Racine, Wis.; portrait relief, Father Nebreda, Phoenix, Ariz.; Spanish-Am. War Memorial, Springfield, Ill.; portrait busts of Dr. Fred Koch, Wm. Farrar Newberry, Dr. Carl Johann Culver. Honorary Mention Art Institute, Chicago, 1913; Mrs. John C. Shaffer prize, Art Institute, Chicago, 1914; gold medal, Kansas City Art Institute, 1924. Mem. Art Inst. Chicago (life), Municipal Art League of Chicago (1st v.p.), Art Inst., Chicago Alumni Assn. (past pres.). Club: Cliff Dwellers. Home: 1201 E. 60th St. Studio: 923 E. 60th St., Chicago 37. Died Dec. 12, 1950.

HICKEY, Joseph Aloysious, clergyman, educator; b. Chicago, Ill., May 30, 1883; s. James J. and Margaret (Dawson) H.; grad. St. Gabriels' High Sch., Chicago; B.S., Villanova Coll., 1902, A.B., 1903, A.M., 1905; Ph.D., Internat. Coll., Rome, 1907, D.D., 1915; Dr. Canon Law, Appolinare U., Rome, 1908. Joined Augustinian Fathers (O.S.A.), 1903; ordained priest R.C. Ch., 1906; instr. St. Rita Coll., Chicago, 1908-10; prof. ethics and sociology, Villanova Coll., 1910-24, regent of studies, same, 1913-24, pres., Jan. 1925—. Mem. Catholic Edn. Assn. (v.p. and mem. commn. on standardization). Address: Villanova Coll., Villanova, Pa. Died July 9, 1955.

HICKMAN, Cuthbert Wright, univ. prof.; b. Marshall, Mo., Jan. 22, 1888; s. Cuthbert Henry and Mary Lee (Wright) H.; B.S., U. of Mo., 1913; M.S., U. of Ida., 1928; grad. student, U. of Neb., 1931; m. Teresa Keane, June 4, 1919 (dec. Aug. 8, 1950); children—Mary Catherine (Mrs. Todd H. Slade), Margaret Elizabeth (Mrs. James H. Meyer); m. 2d, Mildred Hall Reid, Nov. 25, 1953 (dec. Jan. 9, 1954); m. 3rd, Vaughan Prater Lattig. Instructor animal husbandry Pa. State Coll., 1913-14; prof. animal husbandry dept., U. Ida., 1914—, asst. dean Coll. Agr., 1942-46, acting dean, 1946-47. Councilman, Moscow, Ida., 1941-53. Member Chamber of Commerce, American Soc. Animal Production, Am. Suffolk Sheep Soc. (sec.-treas. Moscow), Alpha Zeta, Sigma Xi. Mason. Elk. Club: Rotary. Home: 615 Moore Av., Moscow, Ida. Died Apr. 21, 1956; buried Moscow.

HICKMAN, Herman Michael, athletic coach, television and radio performer, lectr., author; b. Johnson City, Tennessee, Oct. 1, 1911; s. Herman M. and Ossie Mae (Feathers) H.; A.B., U. Tennessee, 1932, m. Helen Clara Smith, June 16, 1932. Profl. football player, 1933-34; asst. coach Wake Forest (N.C.) Coll., 1935-36, N.C. State Coll., 1937-42, U.S. Mil. Acad., West Point, 1943-47; head coach Yale, 1948-52, football cons. since 1952; head coach Eastern Coll., All-Stars, 1949, Shrine North-South, 1948-51, All-Stars, Chgo., 1951; sports commentator N.B.C., N Y.C., 1950-51; member panel Celebrity Time TV show C.B.S., N.Y.C., 1950-51 condr. Herman Hickman TV show, Herman Hickman Pontiac Show, N.B.C. TV, 1952-56; regular columnist Sports Illustrated, Time, Inc.; daily program CBS, The Herman Hickman Show and CBS TV sports program, 1956—. Recipient Graham McNamee Memorial Award as the man who most benefited sports, 1950; The Golden Fleece Award, 1952; E. P. Dutton award best sports story of year, 1955; Banshees award for sportsmanship, 1956; N.Y. Touchdown Club award, 1956. Asso. fellow Branford Coll. (Yale); member Sigma Alpha Epsilon. Methodist. Clubs: St. Elmo, Torch, Graduate (New Haven). Author: The Herman Hickman Reader, 1953. Contbr. Sat. Eve. Post, Readers Digest, Family Circle, Better Homes and Gardens, others. Home: Pleasant Hill, Woodbridge, Conn. Died Apr. 1958.

HICKMAN, Norman, mfg. exec.; b. Kent, Eng., 1890; s. James and Pauline (Norman) H.; A.B., Yale, 1912; m. Mary Frances Gilbert, June 2, 1917; 1 son, Norman Gilbert. Came to U.S., 1909, naturalized, 1915. With Am. Metal Co., Ltd., N.Y.C., since 1916, v.p. since 1942; dir. Titan Metal Mfg. Co., Consol. Coppermines Corp., Lead Industries Assn. Episcopalian. Home: 1185 Park Av., N.Y.C. 28. Office: 61 Broadway, N.Y.C. 6. Died Mar. 9, 1953; buried Woodlawn Cemetery, N.Y.C.

HICKOK, Charles Thomas (hĭk'ŏk), college prof.; b. Bloomfield, O., Nov. 8, 1869; s. Dormer L. and Eliza O. (Merrill) H.; A.B., Western Reserve U., Cleveland, O., 1890, Ph.D., 1895; studied Johns Hopkins U., 1890-91; m. Nellie Alice Turner, Oct. 9, 1897 (dec.); children—Mary Louise (dec.), Eliza (Mrs. Carl Kesler). Prin. Marion (O.) High Sch., 1895-96, Western Res. Acad., 1897-1903; prof. econs. Coe Coll., 1905-40, now prof. emeritus. Conglist. Mason (32°). Author: The Negro in Ohio, 1895. Home: 2018 Fifth Av., Cedar Rapids, Ia. Died Sept. 1, 1958; buried Cedar Rapids, Ia.

HICKS, Frank M., railroad exec.; b. Jackson, Tenn., July 27, 1893; s. Robert Banjamin and Frances (Jones) H.; student pub. schs. of Tenn.; m. Olive Peale, May 16, 1914; children—Marianne, Frank M. With Gulf, Mobile & Ohio R.R. Co. Mobile, Ala., 1913—, was pres. and dir., now chmn. bd., also officer, dir. of four subsidiaries; director Mchts. Nat. Bank of Mobile, Protective Life Ins. Company. Member of the advisory council of the So. Research Inst., Birmingham, Ala. Clubs: Chicago (Chgo.); Bankers of Am. (N.Y.C.); Athelstan

(Mobile); Mobile Country (Spring Hill, Ala.); Lakewood Golf (Point Clear, Ala.). Home: 1907 Old Shell Rd. Office: 104 St. Francis St., Mobile, Ala. Died Feb. 12, 1959.

HICKS, Frederick Charles, librarian, educator; b. Auburn, N.Y., Oct. 14, 1875; s. William and Martha (Tailby) H.; Ph.B., Colgate U., 1898, Litt. D., 1922; LL.B., Georgetown Law Sch., 1901; A.M., Brown U., 1907, Yale, 1928; m. Susan A. M. Vars, Apr. 24, 1912; m. 2d, Mrs. Helen Richards, Apr. 14, 1927; 1 s., H. Morgan. Map div., Library Congress, 1898-1904; practiced law, Auburn, 1904-05; librarian, Naval War Coll., Newport, R.I., 1905-08; asst. librarian Bklyn. Pub. Library, 1908-09; supt. reading rooms Columbia, 1910-11, asst. librarian, 1911-15, law librarian, 1915-28, asso. prof. legal bibliography, 1921-28; prof. legal bibliography Yale, 1928-29, prof. law, 1929-44, law librarian, 1928-44, emeritus prof. law, 1944—, acting law librarian, 1944-46. Mem. adv. com. Pub. Affairs Information Service. Fellow Am. Library Inst.; mem. Am. Assn. Law Libraries, A.L.A., Delta Upsilon, Phi Beta Kappa; pres. South Wellfleet (Mass.) Neighborhood Assn., 1937-39. Clubs: Graduates, Elizabethan, Paint and Clay (New Haven). Author: Biography of Thomas Hutchins and reprint of his Topographical Description of Virginia, etc., 1778, 1904; The Equality of States and The Hague Conferences, 1908; Aids to the Study and Use of Law Books, 1913; Bermuda in Poetry, 1915; The New World Order, 1920; Men and Books Famous in the Law, 1921; Materials and Methods of Legal Research, 1923, 3d edit. 1942; Human Jettison, 1927; Organization and Ethics of the Bench and Bar, 1932; Unauthorized Practice of Law (with E. R..Katz), 1934; Yale Law School—The Founders and the Founders' Collection, 1935—From the Founders to Dutton, 1936—The County Court House Period, 1937—Twenty Years of Hendrie Hall, 1938; Yale Law Library Classification, 1939; William Howard Taft, Yale Professor of Law and New Haven Citizen, 1945. Editor Selected Official Documents of the South African Republic and Great Britain, 1900; Serials of an International Character, 1921; Famous American Jury Speeches, 1925; Arguments and Addresses of Joseph Hodges Choate, 1926; High Finance in the Sixties, 1929; Famous Speeches by Eminent American Statesmen, 1929; Yale Law Library Publs. 1935-46. Contbr. to law and other periodicals. Home: 75 Mill Rock Rd., New Haven 11. Died Apr. 30, 1956.

HICKS, Lawrence Emerson, biologist; b. Fredericktown, O., Oct. 22, 1905; s. Earl H. and Floy (Coe) H.; B.S., Otterbein Coll., 1928; M.S., Ohio State U., 1929, Ph.D., 1933; m. Thyra Jane Bevier, June 27, 1931; children—Jane Ann, Thomas Edward Deam. Biol. asst., Otterbein Coll., 1926-28; bot. asst. Ohio State Univ., 1928-30, instr., 1930-34; game ecologist Ohio Div. Conservation, 1929-31; forester and wildlife conservationist in charge Region 3, U.S. Soil Conservation Service, 1934-36; biol. U.S. Fish and Wildlife Service; asst. prof. zoölogy, entomol., and dir. Ohio Wildlife Research Sta., 1936-45; summers: New England Camps, U.S. Bur. Plant Industry, instr. field ecol. U. of Buffalo, N.Y. State Museum; ecol., Ohio Conservation Lab.; owner Buckeye Apiaries; dir. Ohio Apiaries Co-operative. Chmn. tech. com. Columbus Metropolitan Parks; U.S. del. to Internat. Ornithol. Congress, Rouen, France, 1938. Fellow Am Ornithol. Union (sec. 1937-45), A.A.A.S., Ohio Acad. Science; mem. Wilson Ornithol. Soc. (sec. 1931-36, v.p., 1937-39, pres. 1940-41), Inland Bird Banding Assn. (v.p.), Wheaton Club (pres.), Cooper Ornithol. Club, Ecol. Soc., Wildlife Soc., Am. Soc. Mammalogists, Biol. Soc. Washington, Limnol. Soc., Ohio Beekeepers Assn. (v.p.), Nat. Outdoors Writers, Sigma Xi, Gamma Alpha, Gamma Sigma Alpha, Theta Alpha Phi. Co-author: The Pheasant in North America (Am. Wildlife Inst., 1945; won Wildlife Soc. Award for 1945); author: Breeding Birds of Ohio (Ohio biol. survey, 1935), Ohio Game and Song Birds in Winter (Ohio div. conservation, 1931), numerous scientific papers; contbr. articles on natural hist. to newspapers and jours.; lecturer on animal and plant life; collector: biol. specimens and rare books on natural history, plant and animal specimens for Herbaria, museums and labs. Home: 8 Chatham Rd., Columbus 14, O. Died Jan. 20, 1957; buried Fredericktown, O.

HICKS, Thomas Holliday, ret. naval officer; b. Sept. 8, 1869; entered USN, 1892, and advanced through the grades to rear adm., 1925; retired 1933. Deceased.

HICKS, William Arthur, banker; b. Little Rock, Ark., Oct. 12, 1880; s. William Henry and Mary Oliia (Diehl) H.; ed. pub. schs.; m. Nellie Miller, Nov. 6, 1901 (dec. 1951); children—Marian, Nellie Louise. Stenographer, 1898-99; r.r. accountant, 1900-04; chief clk. and system organizer for Waters, Pierce Oil Co., 1905-06; credit and sales mgr. H. W. Johns-Manville Co., New Orleans, La., 1907-08; returned to Little Rock and engaged in banking business since 1913; now chmn. Peoples Nat. Bank. Mem. advisory com. Little Rock office. Reconstruction Finance Corp. Former pres. Ark. Children's Home Soc. (erected $200,000 free hosp. for crippled children); served on Liberty Loan drives, World War. Mem. Am. Bankers Assn. (exec. council), Ark. Bankers Assn. (pres. 1923). Democrat. Episcopalian. Mason. Home: 2404 State St. Office: Peoples Nat. Bank, Little Rock. Died June 22, 1952; buried Little Rock.

HICKS, Xenophon, ret judge; b. Clinton, Tenn., May 2, 1872; s. William R. and Lurana (Duncan) H.; A.B., Grant U., Athens, Tenn., 1891; LL.B., Cumberland U., 1892; LL.D., Chattanooga U., 1923; LL.D., Cumberland Univ., 1940; m. Effie May Sawyer, Oct. 22, 1896; children—Louise, Elizabeth. Began practice at Clinton, 1892; city atty., 1892-93; county atty. Anderson County, 1894-96; capt. 6th U.S. Vol. Inf., Spanish Am. War, 1898; alderman and mayor of Clinton; mem. Tenn. Senate, 1911; asst. atty. general 2d Circuit of Tenn., 1911-13; judge Criminal and Law Court, 1913-18; judge Circuit Court, 19th Circuit of Tenn., 1918-23; U.S. dist. judge, East and Middle dists. of Tenn., 1923-28; U.S. circuit judge, Sixth Circuit, since June 12, 1928, Presiding judge since 1938, chief judge since 1948. Mem. Beta Theta Pi, Phi Delta Phi. Republican. Methodist. Club: University (Cincinnati). Home: Clinton, Tenn. Address: Federal Bldg., Knoxville, Tenn. Died Nov. 2, 1952.

HIERONYMUS, William Peter (hi-rŏn'e-mŭs), educator; b. Mt. Olive, Ill., June 2, 1893; s. Willam and Augusta (Holtgreve) H.; A.B., Capital U., Columbus, O., 1917; grad. Theol. Sem., 1921; M.A., U. Neb., 1927; Ph.D., 1934; m. Loretta Renner, May 25, 1921; children—Virginia (wife of Rev. Ernest O. Baack, Jr.), Miriam, Carol. Instr. Woodville (O.) Normal Acad., 1919-20; pres. Hebron (Neb.) Jr. Coll., 1921-30; head dept. edn., dir. summer session, v.p. Augustana Coll., Sioux Falls, S.D., 1930-38; 1st dir. parish edn. Am. Luth. Ch., 1938-45; acting pres. Midland Coll., Fremont, Neb., 1945, pres., 1945-52; prof. edn. Wagner Coll., S.I., 1952—. Mem. state bd. examiners (Neb.) asso. state supt. office, 1927-30; sec.-treas. Neb. Junior Coll. Conf., 1927-30; chmn. or mem. nat. Luth. ednl. coms.; v.p. Nat. Luth. Ednl. Conf., 1929, pres., 1947. Mem. N.E.A., N.S.E.A., Soc. Advancement Edn., Phi Delta Kappa. Lutheran. Rotarian. Author: At the Feet of the Master Tchr., 1937. Contbr. articles to ednl. and religious mags. Home: 138 Beverly Av., Sunnyside, S.I. 1, N.Y. Died 1957.

HIESTAND, Jean Carter (hē'stand), ins. exec.; b. Van Wert, O., Sept. 19, 1893; s. William Henry and Mary Jane (McIntosh) H.; student Wooster U.; m. Helen Victoria Odaffer, Sept. 6, 1921; children—Jean Carter, William Charles. Chairman board, mem. bd. dirs. Ohio Farmers Ins. Co., and Ohio Farmers Indemnity Co.; mem. bd. dirs. Underwriters Adjusting Co., Underwriters Service Assn., Inc. Condr. Akron (O.) Area Boy Scout Band, Region 4 Boy Scout Band, U.S. World Jamboree Boy Scout Band, 1951 Awarded Silver Beaver, Silver Antelope by Boy Scouts Am. Mem. Ins. Fedn. Ohio (p. pres.), Ohio State Safety Council (p. pres.), Nat. Safety Council, Boy Scouts of Am. mem. nat. council, 4th regional exec. com.), Sigma Chi. Methodist. Mason (K.T., Shriner, 32°). Home: P.O. Box 125. Office: Ohio Farmers Insurance Co., Le Roy, O. Died Mar. 26, 1959.

HIGBEE, Irving Jackson, lawyer; b. Homer, N.Y., Nov. 11, 1881; s. Frederick Pratt and Anna Sarah (Darby) H.; LL.B., Syracuse U., 1903; m. Marguerite Spicer James, Aug. 2, 1905; children—Katherine Anna, Irving Jackson. Admitted to N.Y. bar, 1903, and since practiced in Syracuse; spl. asst. to the atty. gen., designated as hearing officer in conscientious objector cases, Selective Training and Service Act, 1942; U.S atty. for No. Dist. of N.Y., 1943-51; now in private law practice. Mem. Municipal Civil Service Commission of Syracuse, 1916-29 (pres. 1922-29). Member N.Y. State. Onondaga Co. (pres. 1948) bar assns., N.Y. State Title Assn. (v.p. 1947-48), Onondaga Co. Hist. Assn., Syracuse Law College Assn. Home: 119 Garfield Av. Address: 312 Gridley Bldg., Syracuse, N.Y. Died Apr. 9, 1955.

HIGBIE, Carlton M., financier; b. Chicago, 1890; s. Nathan Bradley and Corda E. Terwilliger (H.); ed. private schools of Chicago; m. Laura Butler, April 10, 1915; m. 2d Annette Phillips, July 1935; 9 children. With McClurg & Co., St. Louis, 1908-12, George H. Burr & Co., Chicago, 1912-15, Keane Higbie & Co., Detroit, 1915-28, Guardian Detroit Bank, 1928-33; pres. Carlton M. Higbie Corp., Detroit, since 1935; chairman board Higbie Mfg. Co.; dir. Square D Co., Avco Mfg. Corp. Clubs: Detroit, Bloomfield Country, Bloomfield Open Hunt, Metamora Hunt. Home: Bloomfield Hills, Mich. Office: Buhl Bldg., Detroit 26; also Higbie Mfg. Co., Rochester, Mich. Died Mar. 1, 1955.

HIGBY, Gilbert C., architect. Fellow Am. Inst. Architects since 1931. Office: 1060 Broad St., Newark, N.J.* Died Jan. 21, 1952.

HIGGINBOTTOM, Sam, missionary; b. Manchester, England, Oct. 27, 1874; s. Samuel and Jane (Baines) Higginbottom; came to United States, 1894; student Mt. Hermon (Mass.) Sch., 1894-99; student Amherst Coll., M.Sc. (hon.), 1928, D.L.H., 1940; B.A., Princeton, 1903, M.A., 1911, Dr. Philanthropy, 1925; B.Sc. in Agriculure, Ohio State U., 1911, D.Sc., 1952; LL.D., Western Reserve U., 1939; m. Jane Ethlind Cody, Oct. 28, 1904; children—Gertrude Cody, Sam Ashton, Elizabeth Baines, Henry Cody, Jane E., David Baines. Missionary, Presbyn. Church in U.S.A. to India, 1903-45; organizer Agrl. Inst.; pres. emeritus Allahabad Christian Coll.; lectured in U.S. and India; active in behalf of lepers and the blind. Moderator Presbyn. Church in U.S.A, 1939; president of Christian Service Tng. Center, Inc., 1949. Decorated Kaiser-I-Hind, gold medal by Indian Government, 1924, bar added, 1943; King George Silver Jubilee medal, 1935; Coronation medal, 1937, for service in India (wife also awarded same decorations); Am. Agrl. Editor's Assn. nat. award, 1952. Author: The Gospel and the Plow, 1921; What Does Jesus Expect of His Church, 1940; Sam Higginbottom. Farmer (autobiog.). 1949. Address: Cody Villa, Babson Park, Fla. Died June 11, 1958; buried Lake Wales Cemetery.

HIGGINS, Andrew Jackson, ship builder; b. Columbus, Neb., Aug. 28, 1886; s. John Gonigle and Anna Long (O'Conor) H.; student International Correspondence Schools; Creighton University, 1903-06, hon. LL.D., 1943; m. Angéle Colsson, October 16, 1908; children—Edmond C., Andrew J., Frank O., Angéle (Mrs. Charles S. Dana), Roland C., Dawn. Lumber mill owner and operator, Ala. and Miss., 1908-15; lumber broker and exporter, New Orleans, 1915-20; pres. Higgins Lumber and Export Co., New Orleans, 1920-30; pres. Higgins Industries, Inc., builders of motor boats, planes, engines, ship radios, etc., New Orleans, since 1930; pres. Higgins Aircraft Corp., Higgins Engine Co., Inc.; Higgins, Inc.; director La. Savings Bank and Trust Co. Served as lieutenant Neb. Nat. Guard. Inventor and patentee some 30 patents pertaining to amphibious landing craft and vehicles. Member New Orleans Levee Board, former member New Orleans Airport Commission. Member Soc. Am. Mil. Engrs., Soc. Am. Automotive Engrs., Am. Soc. Naval Architects and Marine Engrs., Nat. Aeronautic Assn., Army Ordnance Assn., U.S. Power Squadrons, Creighton U. Alumni Assn. Democrat. Unitarian. Mason. Office: Higgins, Inc., Plant No. 2, New Orleans. Died Aug. 1, 1952; buried Metairie Cemetery, New Orleans.

HIGGINS, Daniel Paul, architect; b. Elizabeth, N.J., Sept. 12, 1886; s. Patrick and Mary (Dowd) H.; ed. pub. schs. and bus. coll., Elizabeth, and Alexander Hamilton Inst.; m. Anna Dorothea Boll, Oct. 6, 1909; children—Daniel Paul, Patricia Dorothea Fitzgerald. With Office of John Russell Pope, 1905-22, associate 1922-37; partner firm of Eggers & Higgins since 1937; trustee and member executive com. Emigrant Indsl. savings Bank, N.Y. City; mem. bd. of real estate and mortgage management dept., Mfrs. Trust Co., N.Y. City. Chmn. bd. Catholic Youth Orgn.; member of the advisory council, School of Commerce, University of Notre Dame; mem. bd. dirs. Boys' Clubs of America, Police Athletic League (N.Y. City), Madison Square Boys' Club; mem. board Boy Scouts of America, the Greater New York Fund; mem. bd. govs. Greater N.Y. Fund. V.p. Nat. Inst. of Social Scis ; mem. board directors National Catholic Community Service; mem. Am. Inst. of Architects (treas. 1932-36), Archtl. League of N.Y. (treas. 1931-33), N.Y. Bldg. Congress, Assn. of Master Knights of Sovereign Order of Malta in U.S., Equestrian Order of the Holy Sepulchre of Jerusalem. Awards: 35 yr. medal for youth work; medal for youth work Boys Work Expn.; Club of Champions Award, Archdiocese of N.Y., 1948; medal of honor N.Y. chap. Am. Inst. of Architects; gold medal Archtl. League; winner Christian Herald nat. ch. bldg. competition. Works: University Club, Milwaukee; Union Gas and Elec. Bldg., Cincinnati; Constitution Hall for Daus. Am. Revolution (Washington), Syracuse Medical College; residence of Mrs. Graham Fair Vanderbilt; United States Line-S.S. American interiors; Indiana U. Music Hall, Bloomington, Ind.; Triboro Hosp., Queens, N.Y.; Bainbridge Naval Training Sta., Maryland; Air Support and Ferry Command Base, Memphis, Tenn.; Elmira Holding and Reconsignment Point, Horseheads, N.Y.; Junior League Bldg., Spence School, Frick Collection, interiors for 4 Grace Line ships, Cardinal Hayes Memorial High Sch. (all N.Y. City); Senate Office Bldg., Am. Red Cross Bldg., Washington: Archbishop Stepinae High Sch., White Plains, N.Y., designed interiors of the S.S. United States. Clubs: New York Yacht, Metropolitan. New York Athletic, Cornell (N.Y.); Gipsy, Engineers, Circus Saints and Sinners, American Horse Show Assn., Dutchess Valley Rod and Gun. Contbr. to professional jours. Home: 19 E. 88th St., New York 28; also Carmel, N.Y. Office: 100 E. 42d St., N.Y. C. Died Dec. 26, 1953.

HIGGINS, Edwin Werter, ex-congressman; b. Clinton, Conn., July 2, 1874; s. Werter Chapin and Grace Agnes (Taintor) H.; ed. Norwich Free Acad., LL.B., Yale, 1897; admitted to bar, 1897; m. Alice May Neff, Sept. 21, 1904. Mem. Conn. Gen. Assembly, 1899; corporation counsel of Norwich, Conn., 1901-02 and 1920-21; member Republican State Central Committee, 1900-06; county health officer, New London County, Conn., 1900-05; del. Rep. Nat. Conv.,

1904, 16; pres. atty. Norwich, 1905; elected to 59th Congress, Oct. 2, 1905, for unexpired term (1905-07) of F. B. Brandegee, elected U.S. senator; reëlected to 60th, 61st and 62d Congresses (1905-13), 3d Conn. Dist.; served on the judiciary com.; pres. Norwich Palace Theatre Corp. Pros. atty., Criminal Ct. of Common Pleas, 1932-46. Mem. Am. Bar Assn., S.A.R., Soc. of Mayflower Descendants, Phi Sigma Kappa. Home: 130 Union St. Office: 48 Broadway, Norwich, Conn. Died Sept. 24, 1954; buried Maplewood Cemetery, Norwich.

HIGGINS, Eugene, painter, etcher; b. Kansas City, Mo., Feb. 28, 1874; s. Thomas C. and Nora (O'Flaherty) H.; ed. L'Ecole des Beaux Arts and Julian Acad., Paris; m. Anita Rio, concert singer, Apr. 1919. Represented in Metropolitan Museum (New York City), New York Pub. Library; Congressional Library (Washington, D.C.); Brooklyn Inst. Arts and Sciences; Los Angeles Mus.; Milwaukee Art Inst.; British Museum (London); Bibliothèque Nationale (Paris); William and Mary Coll.; Springfield (Ill.) Inst. Library of Congress and Boston Pub. Library purchased entire lifetime output of etchings. Painted 3 U.S. Post Office murals for Fed. Arts Project, Washington, D.C. Awarded $1,000 Logan 1st prize, Grand Central Galleries, New York, 1928; Norman Waite bronze medal, Art Inst. Chicago, 1929; $1,000 Altman 1st prize and Ranger purchase prize, Nat. Acad. Design, 1931; $1,000 Shaw purchase prize Salmagundi Club, 1932; Nat. Arts medal, 1933; Diplome D'Honneur Exposition Internationale des Arts et des Techniques, Paris, 1937; $300 Carnegie award for best painting, Nat. Acad. Design, 1937, Altman prize, 1942, 1952. N.A., 1928; gold medal Nat. Arts Club, 1951; Gold Medal of Honor, Audubon Society, 1956. Fellow Met. Mus.; member Society Am. Graphic Artists Nat. Ins. Arts and Letters, Am. Water Color Soc., Lyme Soc. of Artists. Catholic. Clubs: Nat. Arts, Artists (life), Salmagundi. Home: 360 W. 22d St., N.Y.C. 11. Died Feb. 19, 1958; buried Calvary Cemetery, N.Y.C.

HIGGINS, John Clark, consul; b. Linden Hill, St. George's, Del., Aug. 17, 1838; s. Anthony Madison and Sarah Clark (Corbit) H.; Ph.B., Del. Coll., 1856; m. Elizabeth C. Reybold, Dec. 13, 1860. Farmer, a founder of vulcanized fibre industry, Wilmington; master Del. Grange, 1890-94, lectr., 1886-90; became consul at Dundee, Scotland, 1897. Rep. nominee for gov. of Del., 1896. Trustee Del. Coll. Mem. Am. Guernsey Breeders Cattle Club (founder). Home: Delaware City, Del. Died 1924.

HIGGINS, John Patrick, judge; b. Boston, Mass., February 19, 1893; s. Patrick and Winifred (Gilligan) H.; S.B., Harvard, 1917; ed. Boston U. Law Sch. and Northeastern Sch. of Law (LL.B., 1927); hon. LL.D., Mount St. Mary's College, Maryland; St. Michaels Coll., Vt., Northeastern U., Mass., Boston U.; m. Eleanor G. McNamara (dec.); 1 dau. Eleanor. Began as chem. engr., 1919; admitted to Mass. bar, 1927; in practice at Boston, since 1927; mem. Mass. Ho. of Rep., 1929-34; mem. 74th and 75th Congresses (1935-37), 11th Mass. Dist.; chief justice Superior Ct. of Mass., since 1937. Served as ensign Pay Corps, U S.N., World War I. Mem. Am. Chem. Soc., Am. Legion, Catholic Order of Foresters (former trustee), K.C. Democrat Home: 263 Pond St., Jamaica Plain, Mass. Died Aug. 2, 1955.

HIGGINS, William Lincoln, physician, ex-congressman; b. Chesterfield, Mass., Mar. 8, 1867; s. Martin Luther and Elizabeth Susan (Hayden) H.; M.D., U. City N.Y., 1890; m. Annah J. Clapp, Oct. 8, 1890 (died Feb. 2, 1943); children—Ruth Amelia (Mrs. Wm. A. T. Cassedy), Ruby Elizabeth (Mrs. LeRoy Carrier Brown); m. 2d, Mrs. Lillian A. Curley, Apr. 22, 1946. Began practice at Willington, Conn., 1890; removed to South Coventry, Conn., 1891; has served as med. examiner for several ins. cos.; med. examiner for coroner of Tolland County, Conn., 1891-1947. Sergt. Home Guard, South Coventry, and served as surgeon Student Tng. Corps, Conn. State Coll., World War I. First selectman, Coventry, 16 yrs.; county commr. Tolland County, 12 yrs. Mem. Conn. Ho. of Reps., 1905, 07, 17, 19, 21, 25, 27; mem. Conn. Senate, 1909-10; sec. of state, Conn., 2 terms, 1929-33; mem. 73d and 74th Congresses, 2d Conn. Dist. Ex-pres. Booth-Dimock Meml. Library. Mem. A.M.A., Conn. Med. Soc. (pres. 1906; legislative sec. 1937). Tolland County Med. Assn. (past pres.), S.A.R. Republican. Conglist. Mason (32°, K.T., Shriner), Elk; mem. Grange. Clubs: Fox and Coon, Men's Social. Home: South Coventry, Conn. Died Nov. 19, 1951.

HIGHLAND, Cecil Blaine, publisher, banker; b. West Milford, W.Va., Nov. 2, 1876; s. John E. and Lucinda E. (Patton) H.; grad. Lexington Coll., 1899; m. Ella C. Clark, Feb. 10, 1909; children—Virginia L. (Mrs. Richard U. Duerr), Cecil Blaine. Dep. county clk., Harrison County, W.Va., 1899-1904; Engaged in gas and oil bus., 1904—; purchased, developed Highland Park and Golf Plaza, 1912-18; purchased Wetzel (W.Va.) Republican, 1913, pub., 1913-46; pres., gen. mgr., dir., treas. Clarksburg Pub. Co. (W.Va.), 1940—; pres., dir. Empire Nat. Bank of Clarksburg, 1941—. Dep. sheriff Wetzel County, 1904-08; senator W.Va. Legislature, 1924-28. Mem. Clarksburg C. of C. Republican. Methodist. Mason (K.T.). Home: 245 Virginia St., New Martinsville, W.Va. Office: Empire Nat. Bank, Clarksburg, W.Va. Died Feb. 6, 1957; buried Greenlawn Meml. Cemetery, New Martinsville.

HIGHSMITH, J(ohn) Henry, educator; b. Sampson County, N.C., Oct. 5, 1877; s. Lewis Whitfield and Margaret (Tatum) H.; A.B., Trinity Coll., Durham, N.C., 1900, A.M., 1902; grad. scholar Tchrs. Coll. Columbia, 1904-06; LL.D., Catawba Coll., Salisbury, N.C., 1925; Ed.D., Wake Forest (N.C.) Coll., 1934; m. Lula V. Johnson, Aug. 21, 1907 (died Jan. 23, 1919); children—John Henry, Lula Belle; m. 2d, Kate Maude Herring, June 30, 1921; children—Katherine Herring, Louise Westbrook. Prin. grammar sch., Durham, N.C., 1901-04; prof. philosophy and Bible, Meredith Coll., Raleigh, N.C., 1906-07; prof. edn. and philosophy Wake Forest (N.C.) Coll., 1907-17 resigned; mem. State Bd. Examiners and Inst. Conductors, by apptmt. of Gov. Thomas W. Bickett, 1917-21; state high school supr., 1920-33; dir. Div. of Instructional Service of the State Dept. Pub. Instrn., 1932—; instr. Summer Normal School, Baton Rouge, La., 1906; prof. edn. State Normal Coll., Greensboro, N.C., summers 1912-16, State Coll. Agr. and Engring., Raleigh, summers 1917-34, Duke U., 1935—. Mem. State Bd. Examiners, N.C., 1915-17; dir. reorgn. of high schs., Okla., 1928, Miss., 1929; mem. N.C. State Bd. Commercial Edn.; chmn. com. on secondary edn. Southern Assn. Colls. and Secondary Schs., 1932. Pres. Bd. of Edn., Bapt. State Conv.; mem. exec. com. on coöp. study of secondary school standards; chmn. curriculum com. N.C. 12 yr. Program, 1942. Mem. N.E.A., Am. Assn. Sch. Adminstrs., N.C. Acad. Sci., N.C. Coll. Conf., Nat. Assn. High Sch. Suprs. (pres. 1929), N.C. Edn. Assn. (pres. 1939), So. Assn. Colls. and Secondary Schs. (vice pres., 1946), Omicron Delta Kappa, Phi Beta Kappa, Kappa Delta Pi. Democrat. Mason, Rotarian. Home: 832 Wake Forest Rd., Raleigh, N.C. Died May 8, 1953.

HIGLEY, Miles M., educator; b. Chatfield, Minn., Nov. 24, 1867; s. Francis Marion and Ella Elvira (Chamberlain) H.; grad. as Master Accts., Gem City Bus. Coll., Quincy, Ill., 1887; m. Mae F. Shields, Apr. 19, 1897; children—Florence L., Warren M. Pres. Pioneer Investment Co.; v.p. Fidelity Nat. Bank; mgr. and part owner Blair-Higley Bus. U. Past pres., mem. bd. dirs. Carnegie Library. Republican. Methodist. Mason (32°, Shriner), Elk. Clubs: Athletic, Advertising, Rotary (pres. 1922-23); gov. Rotary Internat., Dist. No. 1 (B.C., Alaska, Wash., Ore.). Home: 607 W. 14th Av. Address: Blair-Higley Business University, Spokane, Wash. Deceased.

HILD, Oscar F(rank), labor union exec.; b. Cincinnati, Feb. 15, 1901; s. Charles and Bertha (Zobel) H.; student Coll. Liberal Arts, U. Cincinnati, 1926-28, Coll. Medicine, 1929-30; Mus.D., honoris causa, Cincinnati Coll. Music, 1949; m. Shirley Rukin, Oct. 10, 1934; children—Dorothy Ann, Guy (Gerald Marvin), Allen Charles. Instrumental musician with various bands and orchestras, 1916-30, including Chicago Opera, 1919, and Cincinnati Symphony Orchestra, 1922; bus. agt. Cincinnati Union of Musicians, 1931, pres. since 1932. Rep. A.F. of L., 4th session UNESCO Gen. Conf., Paris, also spl. adviser U.S. delegation to the conf., Sept.-Oct. 1949. Mem. Internat. Exec. Bd. of Am. Fedn. Musicians since 1940. Mgr.-dir. Cincinnati Summer Opera since 1934 (which presents the only summer grand opera season in America). Democrat. Mason (K.T.). Home: 245 Baxter Av., Cincinnati 20. Office: Atlas Bank Bldg., Cincinnati 2. Died Apr. 24, 1950; buried Walnut Hills Cemetery, Cincinnati.

HILDEBRAND, Jesse Richardson, writer; born Smithsburg, Md., Feb. 3, 1888; s. Edwin Oswald and Melissa (Richardson) H.; grad. Central High Sch., Washington, D.C., 1907; attended George Washington U.; m. Marion Alice Hoyt, June 25, 1915; children—Jean, Harriet. Reporter and dramatic editor Washington Times, 1907-12; asso. editor New Britain (Conn.) Herald, 1912-14; feature and editorial writer Washington Times, 1914-17; reporter and feature writer Evening Star, Washington, 1917-19; editorial staff National Geographical Magazine since 1919, asst. editor since 1931, life trustee since 1946; lecturer on applied geography, School of Foreign Service, Georgetown Univ. Clubs: Nat. Press, Monday Evening (sec. 3 yrs.), Cosmos, Overseas Writers. Wrote: Man's Amazing Progress in Conquering the Air, 1924; The Columbus of the Pacific, 1927; The World's Greatest Overland Explorer, 1928; Trains of Today—and Tomorrow, 1936; California's Coastal Redwood Realm, 1939; The World's Foremost Fiber (Cotton), 1940; Our Most Versatile Vegetable Product (Rubber), 1940; Glass "Goes to Town," 1943. Contbr. mag. and numerous syndicated newspaper articles, etc. Home: 1409 31st St. N.W., Washington 7. Address: National Geographic Magazine, Washington 6. Died Sept. 18, 1951; buried Cedar Hill Cemetery, Washington.

HILDEBRANDT, Fred. H., ex-congressman; b. West Bend, Wis., Aug. 2, 1882; s. Charles F. and Mary (Straub) H.; student pub. schs., Waupun, Wis.; m. Mary Berner, Jan. 1, 1910. Railroad passenger condr. for many yrs.; mem. 73d to 75th Congresses, 1st S.D. Dist. Mem. Order Ry. Condrs. Democrat. Mason, Kiwanian. Home: Watertown, S.D. Died Jan. 26, 1956; buried Watertown.

HILDEBRANDT, Howard L(ogan), artist; b. Allegheny, Pa.; s. George H. and Christina (McComb) H.; student N.A.D.; Julian Acad., Paris, under Constant and Laurens; École des Beaux Arts, Paris; m. Cornelia Ellis (miniature painter), 1902. Portrait painter. Awarded Evans prize and 1st honor, Asso. Artists of Pitts., 1911; gold medal, Allied Artists of America, 1925; first prize, Salmagundi Club, 1925, Isadore prize, 1930. Represented in permanent collections of John Herron Art Inst., Indpls., Butler Art Institute, Youngstown, O. Mem. Nat. Acad. Design, Am. Water Color Club, Nat. Arts Club, New York Water Color Club. Clubs: Salmagundi, Lotos, Century (N.Y.C.); New Canaan Country. Home: 306 E. 51st St., N.Y.C.; (summer) New Canaan, Conn. Died Nov. 11, 1958.

HILDRETH, Melvin Davis, lawyer; b. Fargo, N.D., Sept. 18, 1890; s. Melvin Andrew and Luella (Davis) H.; A.B., Fargo Coll., 1913; LL.B., Columbia, 1916; m. Jean Calvert Tighe, Nov. 30, 1922; children—Jean Calvert, David Melvin, Richard, Robert Andrew. Admitted to the N.D. bar, Jan. 6, 1917; former gen. counsel, President's War Relief Control Bd.; past pres. of Robert H. Terrell Law School. Pvt., corpl., sergt., lt. F.A., A.E.F., 1918-19. In chg. of entire N.D. campaign for Wilson, 1916; exec. sec. Nat. Prog. League during 1932, 36, and 40 campaigns; dir. of Orgn. Nat. Ind. Com. for Roosevelt and Truman; D.C. del. Dem. Nat. Conv., 1936, 40, 44, 48, 52, 56. Chmn. com. grandstands and arrangements, Roosevelt inaugurals, 1933, 37, 41. Chmn. Truman-Barkley Inaugural Com., 1949. Democratic Nat. Committeeman for D.C.; mem. bd. dirs. Am. Assn. for U.N. Mem. bd. dirs. Chinese Community Ch. Mem. unofficial Am. delegation to the League of Nations, 1938, Commission to Study the Orgn. of Peace, D.C., Am. bar assns., Am. Legion, Phi Delta Theta. Nat. Capital Sesquicentennial Commn. (exec. vice chmn.), Past pres. Circus Fans Assn. America. Member Comite l'Honneur de St. Die; Officer de l'Ordre de la Sante Publique, France. Chevalier de la Legion D'Honneur; l'Ordre National Honneur et Merite, Haiti. Contbr. articles on internat. relations to jours. Home: 2500 Massachusetts Av. N.W., Washington. Address: 1420 New York Av. N.W., Washington 5. Died Dec. 23, 1959.

HILDUM, Clayton Edward, ry. official; b. Jamestown, N.Y., April 2, 1871; s. Edward Burke and Chloe Nichols (Wellington) H.; student Thiel Coll., 1893-95; A.B., Wittenberg Coll., 1897; m. Mary C. Schambs, of Mansfield, O., July 5, 1899; children—Mary Elizabeth, Edward Barkdoll, Frederick Wellington. Clk. with Erie R.R. Co., 1898-1905; auditor in various depts., 1905-13; mgr. accounting dept. U.S. R.R. Adminstrn., 1918-20; comptroller Lehigh Valley R.R., 1920-24, v.p., 1924-30, exec. v.p., 1930-38, special work for Lehigh Valley R.R. in coal region; pres. Coxe Bros. & Co., Inc., coal production; retired, Jan. 1, 1945. Served with U.S.N., Spanish-Am. War. Mem. Alpha Tau Omega. Republican. Clubs: Railroad, Traffic (New York). Home: 1152 Martine Av., Plainfield, N.J. Died Mar. 27, 1952.

HILL, Alferd J., lawyer; b. Memphis, Mo., July 8, 1881; s. Robert and Julia (Stevens) H.; LL.B., U. So. Cal., 1909; m. Rose Evelyn Huchendorf, July 8, 1909 (died Apr. 28, 1938); 1 dau., Marjorie Evelyn (Mrs. William W. Harvey); m. 2d, Alice Foster Harper, Aug. 15, 1948. Admitted to Cal. bar, 1909, since practiced in Los Angeles; sr. partner, Hill, Farrer & Burill; mem. faculty, law sch. U. So. Cal., 1914-22; dep. dist. atty. Los Angeles County, 1910-13, county counsel, 1913-23; pres. Sunset Ry. Co., 1938—, Three-Arch Bay Assn., 1951—. Mem. Los Angeles C. of C. (past dir.), Phi Delta Phi. Mason (32°, Shriner). Club: Wilshire Country. Home: 5 Alta Mira Three Arch Bay, South Laguna, Cal. Office: 411 5th St., Los Angeles 13. Died Jan. 30, 1953.

HILL, Bancroft, cons. engr.; Balt.; May 5, 1887; s. Charles Ebenezer and Kate Watts (Claymon) H.; student Johns Hopkins, 1906-07, B.S., Mass. Inst. Tech., 1911; m. Frances G. McCoy, May 5, 1915. Began as draftsman, 1915; successively civil engr., harbor engrs., pres. Harbor Bd. of Balt., engr. Port Development Commn., 1919-25; valuation engr. United Rys. & Electric Co., Balt., 1925-35; exec. v.p. Baltimore Transit Co., 1935-36, pres., 1936-45. Devoted last 8 yrs. life making appliances to aid crippled children. Author articles on costs, depreciation, valuation and earnings of pub. utilities. Home: 1812 Sulgrave Av., Mt. Washington, Balt. 9. Died Jan. 5, 1957; buried Druid Ridge Cemetery, Balt.

HILL, Bert Hodge, archæologist; b. Bristol, Vt., Mar. 7, 1874; s. Alson Collins and Carrie Emily (Hodge) H.; A.B., U. of Vt., 1895; A.M., Columbia, 1900; student Am. Sch. Classical Studies, Athens, Greece, 1900-03; L.H.D. (hon.), U. Vt., 1920; Ph. D. (hon.), U. Salonica, 1951; m. Ida Carleton Thallon, Aug. 15, 1924 (dec. Dec. 1954). Prin. Newport (Vt.) Acad., 1895-98; asst. curator classical antiquities, Mus. of Fine Arts, Boston, 1903-06; lecturer on Greek sculpture, Wellesley Coll., 1904-06; dir. Am. Sch. Classical Studies, Athens, Greece, 1906-26, also mem. mng. com.; acting vice chmn. and chmn. Greek Refugee Settlement Commn. (under League of Nations), 1927, 28; dir. U. of Pa. Mus. excavations, Cyprus, 1931-32 (Lapithos), 1934-54 (Kourion), hon. research fellow, 1955—. Norton lectr. Archaeol. Inst. Am., 1936-37. Dir. emeritus Am. Sch. Classical Studies at Athens since 1949; exec. officer U.S. Ednl. Found. in Greece, 1950-52. Fellow Am. Acad. Arts and Sciences; mem. Archaeol. Inst. America (vice president 1949), Am. Philol. Assn., Austrian Archæol. Inst., German Archæol. Inst., Greek Archæol. Soc. (hon.), Soc. for Promotion of Hellenic Studies of London (hon.), Phi Beta Kappa, Delta Psi. Methodist. Contbr. to archaeol. publs. of articles on ancient Athenian architecture, epigraphy. Address: 9 Plutarch St., Athens, Greece. Died Dec. 2, 1958.

HILL, Mrs. Caroline Miles; b. Pleasant Hill, O., July 20, 1866; d. Israel and Keturah (Pickering) Miles; A.B., Earlham Coll., 1887; Ph.D., U. Mich., 1892; m. William Hill, Jan. 24, 1895 (died 1920). Tchr. and social settlement worker; especially devoted to promotion of world peace. Mem. Ill. League Women Voters. Quaker. Clubs: Woman's City, Chicago Woman's. Compiler: World's Great Religious Poetry, 1923; Twentieth Century Love Poems, 1929. Home: 5802 Blackstone Av., Chgo. Died Aug. 21, 1951; buried in crypt First Unitarian Ch., Chgo.

HILL, Charles Leander, univ. pres.; b. Urbana, O., July 28, 1906; s. David Leander and Keren W. (Andrews) H.; A.B. magna cum laude, Wittenberg Coll., 1928; B.D., Hamma Div. Sch., 1931, S.T.M., 1933; grad. studies in philosophy and theology, U. of Berlin, 1931-32; Ph.D. in Philosophy, Ohio State U., 1938; D.D. (hon.), Morris Brown Coll.; LL.D., (hon.) David Payne Coll.; L.H.D. (hon.), Paul Quinn Coll.; m. Rosalie Lloyd Young, June 3, 1949. Dean, Turner Theol. Sem. of Morris Brown Coll., Atlanta, 1933-44; pastor Bethel A.M.E. Ch., Columbia, S.C., 1944-47; pres. Wilberforce U. since 1947; exchange prof. ancient langs. Atlanta Univ. System, 1937-42. Mem. Am. Philos. Assn., Am. Assn. Social Sci. Teachers, Am. Acad. Arts and Scis., Royal Inst. Philosophy, Am. Christian Com. on Palestine, A.A. A.S., Alpha Phi Alpha. Mason (32°). Author: Loci of Philip Melanchthon, 1945: A Critical Exposition of the Philosophy of Melanchthon; A Short History of Philosophy from Renaissance to Hegel; Works of Melanchthon on Hitherto Unpublished in English, 1955; Anthony William Amo; Black Philosopher of Guinea, 1955. Address: Shorter Hall, Wilberforce Univ., Wilberforce. Died Dec. 8, 1956; buried Oak-Dale Cemetery, Urbana, O.

HILL, Charles Lewis, farmer; b. Rosendale, Wis., Sept. 5, 1869; s. George Cook and Georgiana (Brainard) H.; ed. country sch. and short course in agr., University of Wisconsin; married Mina O'Neil, Nov. 11, 1891 (deceased September 3, 1957); children—Mrs. Anna Louise Gray, George O'Neil, Mrs. Margaret Muriel Orvis, Mrs. Jessie May Gates, John Dudley, Mrs. Walter S. Houston. Farmer and cattle raiser since 1888; mem. Charles L. Hill & Sons, importers and breeders of Guernsey cattle; has made 11 trips to Europe and imported over 2,000 cattle. Prohibition candidate for gov. of Wis., 1914, for U.S. Senate, 1916. Pres. Wis. State Bd. Agr., 1911; mem. State Bd. Edn., 1915-21; chmn. State Dept. Agr. and Markets, 1929-38; U.S. del. World's Dairy Congress, Copenhagen, 1931. Moderator Wis. Congl. Conf., 1929-30; del. Nat. Council Congl. Christian Chs., 1950. Trustee Ripon College. Mem. Nat. Dairy Assn. (pres.), Am. Dairy Fedn., Am. Guernsey Cattle Club (president 1912-14, Wisconsin Live Stock Breeders' Association (pres.), Wisconsin Dairymen's Assn. (pres.), Wis. Temperance Edn. Assn. (pres.). Treasurer Prohibition Nat. Com. Conglist. Author: The Guernsey Breed, 1917; History of Wisconsin Guernseys; The Descendants of Grandfather Hill. Home: Rosendale, Wis. Died June 1, 1957; buried Rosendale.

HILL, Claiborne Milton, theologican; b. Suisun, Calif., Nov. 16, 1857; s. Sterling and Sarah Russell (Joyce) H.; student McMinnville (now Linfield) Coll., D.D., 1889, LL.D., 1926; B.A., U. of Ore., 1881, M.A., 1884; grad. Rochester Theol. Sem., 1884; S.T.D., Pacific Sch. of Religion, 1937; D.D., Berkeley Baptist Div. Sch., 1937; m. Anna F. Pengra, Dec. 31, 1884; children—Amy Helen (Mrs. Paul K. Yost), Carey Sterling. Ordained Baptist ministry, 1884; pastor Eugene, Oregon, 1884-90; supt. missions, Am. Bapt. Home Mission Soc., for Ore., 1890-93; pastor 10th Av. Ch., Oakland, Calif., 1893-1904; pres. and prof. Bibl. and practical theology, Berkeley Bapt. Div. Sch., Oct. 1904-Aug. 1937, now pres. emeritus. Pres. Pacific Coast Bapt. Conf.; pres. Bd. of Edn. of Northern Bapt. Conv., 3 terms; mem. Foreign Mission Bd. of same, 8 yrs. Mem. Phi Beta Kappa. Republican. Club: City Commons of Berkeley (pres. 1933). Author: They Sought a Better Country; Arise and Build. Home: 2509 Hillegass Av., Berkeley, Cal. Died Jan. 27, 1950.

HILL, Claude Eugene, clergyman; b. Pike County, Mo., Jan. 11, 1874; s. Thomas V. and Keturah (Lewellyn) H.; ed. Chillicothe (Mo.) Normal Sch., 1892-93, U. of Chicago, 1901; hon. M.A., Christian U., Canton, Mo., 1912; D.D., U. of Chattanooga, 1921; m. Sallie Thomas, Sept. 25, 1895; children—Allene Thomas (Mrs. W. M. Marshall), Margaret Josephine (dec.), Claude E. (dec.), Mary Elizabeth (Mrs. John O. Brittain), Sallie Mildred (dec.). Ordained ministry Disciples of Christ Ch., 1896; pastor successively first Ch., Mobile, Valparaiso and Chattanooga, to 1923. First Christian Ch., Tulsa, 1923-48, emeritus; chaplain Hillcrest Memorial Hospital, Tulsa. Pres. Ala. Christian Endeavor, Union. 1905-07, nat. supt. Christian Endeavor, Disciples of Christ, 1906-18; trustee Internat. Soc. of Christian Endeavor, 1906-18; mem. exec. com. Internat. Conv., Disciples of Christ, 1923-26; chmn. Peace Commn., same denomination, 1926, mem. Commn. on Ministry, 1926-30; fraternal del. to Chs. of Christ, Gt. Briatin, 1932. Pres. Nat. Evangelistic Assn., 1932-33; dir. Christian Bd. of Publs., St. Louis; dir. German Evangelistic Soc.; chairman nominating com. National Convention Disciples, 1938-39; member Commission for Restudy of the Disciples; trustee Hillcrest Memorial Hospital, Tulsa; president Oklahoma Council of Churches, 1942; president Oklahoma Convention of Christian Churches, 1943. Democrat. Mason (K.T., Shriner; Grand Prelate, Grand Commandery, K.T. of Oklahoma, 1932). Clubs: Kiwanis, Men's Dinner (dir.), Knife and Fork Club, Tulsa Club. Author: Keeping the Faith, 1928; Plea of the Disciples of Christ for Christian Unity, 1931. Home: 1252 Hazel Blvd., Tulsa, Okla. Died Feb. 10, 1957.

HILL, David Spence, educator, psychologist; b. Nashville; s. Rev. Felix Robertson and Martha Ordalia (Mayes) H.; B.A., Randolph-Macon Coll., 1897; student Harvard, summer 1897, Washington U. Law Sch., 1901; Ph.D., Clark U., 1907; LL.D., U. Ky., 1916; LL.D., U. Ariz., 1920; m. Julia Payne, June 14, 1902. Instr. Smith Acad. of Washington U., 1897-1904; prof. psychology and edn. Peabody Coll. for Tchrs., Nashville, 1907-11; prof. psychology and edn. Tulane U., 1911-13; dir. div. ednl. research supported by Delgado Fund and Com. Council, New Orleans, 1913-16; prof., lectr. summers, U. Mont., 1913, Cornell, 1914, U. Cal., 1916, U. Minn., 1928, U. Wyo., 1929, Ind. U., Purdue, Detroit and Buffalo univs., 1932; prof. U. Wis., 1916-17, U. Ill., 1917-19; studied schs. and colls of Can. with respect to rehabilitation of disabled soldiers, under auspices of Red Cross and Fed. Bd. for Vocational Edn., 1918; pres. State U. N.M., 1919-27; fought successfully, 1926, the proposed constitutional amendment which would have deprived univ. of revenues from oil discovered on university lands; research prof. in edn. U. Ala., 1927-29; research asso. and acting dir. research, Nat. Adv. Com. on Edn., 1930-31; staff asso. Carnegie Found., N.Y.C., 1931-34; surveyed 269 libraries of Washington, for Am. Council on Edn. under grant under Carnegie Corp., 1934-35; research staff for higher edn. Regents' Inquiry into Edn., State N.Y., 1935-37, Brookings Instn., Washington, 1939-41. Hist. indsl. studies of Jeffersonville Quartermaster Depot, Indiana and U.S. Army, 1942-46 and cited by War Dept. for ingenuity and resourcefullness, 1946; vis. prof. psychology U. Louisville, 1946; ednl. survey, Linden, N.J., 1947-48. Pres. So. Soc. Philosophy and Psychology, 1915-16; hon. mem. Nat. Assn. State Univs.; life mem. Am. Psychol. Assn., Phi Beta Kappa. Elector Hall of Fame N.Y.U. Democrat. Presbyn. Mason. Author: An Experimental Study of Delinquent and Destitute Boys, 1913; Individual Differences in Children of the Public Schools, 1913; Public Schools of New Orleans in Relation to Vocation, 1914; Educational Research in Public Schools (joint author), 1915; Measurements in Elementary Education, 1915; Industry and Education—A Study of Manufacturing Establishments of New Orleans and of the Occupations of Boys and Men, 1916; Introduction to Vocational Education, 1920; Federal Relations to Education, Basic Facts (co-author), 1931; Economy in Higher Education (co-author), 1933; Control of Tax-Supported Higher Education (for the Carnegie Foundation), 1934; Libraries of Washington (for the Carnegie Foundation), 1937; Educational Survey of Montgomery County, Md. (for Brookings), 1941; 30 monographs for War Dept., 1942-46. Contbr. psychol. studies on retinal stimuli, correlation, mnemonics, etc., 1909-39. Home: 1424 St. James Court, Louisville. Died Nov. 11, 1951.

HILL, Edward Llewellyn, chemist; b. Carthage, Ill., Jan. 19, 1900; s. William Kuhns and Katharine (Griffith) H.; A.B., Carthage College, 1922, Doctor of Science (honorary), 1955; M.S., University of Ill., 1925 Ph.D., State U. of Ia., 1930; m. Mary Lucille Mullen. Aug. 15, 1935; children—Katharine Lucille, David Llewellyn. Instr., Carthage Coll., 1925-27, asst. prof., 1928-29, asso. prof., 1930-32, prof. and head chemistry dept., 1933-42; prof. chemistry, Augustana Coll., Rock Island, Ill., since 1947; research chemist, Armour Research Foundn., Ill. Inst. Tech., Chicago, 1942-47, supervisor organic chemistry research, 1945-47; exec. and research dir., Augustana Research Foundn. since 1947. Fellow A.A.A.S.; mem. American Society Heating and Ventilating Engrs., Am. Chem. Soc., Am. Oil Chemists Soc., Ill. Acad. Sci., Theta Chi Delta, Beta Beta Beta, Phi Lambda Upsilon, Sigma Xi. Contbr. to jours. organic chemistry. Home: 3909 8th Av. Office: 35th St. and 7th Av., Rock Island, Ill. Died June 6, 1958; buried Moss Ridge Cemetery, Carthage, Ill.

HILL, Edwin Conger, author, radio news commentator; b. Aurora, Ind., Apr. 23, 1884; s. Harvey Boone and Mary (Conger) H.; Ind. U., 1901; post grad. student Butler Coll.; m. Jane Gail, July 29, 1922. Reporter New York Sun, 1904-23; dir. Fox News Reel, 1923-24; scenario editor Fox Film Corp., 1925-26; feature writer New York Sun, 1927-32; radio broadcaster "Human Side of the News" and syndicate feature writer since 1932. Mem. Sigma Chi. Republican. Episcopalian. Clubs: Knollwood Country, Rockwood Hall Country, Westchester Country. Author: The Iron Horse, 1925; The American Scene, 1933; Human Side of the News, 1934. Office: 515 Madison Av., N.Y.C. Died Feb. 12, 1957.

HILL, Ernie, fgn. corr.; b. St. Louis, Dec. 28, 1908; s. Ernest M. and Nena (Berry) H.; student Washington U., 1928-29; B.A., U. Okla., 1935; Nieman fellow, Harvard, 1942-43; m. Christine Squire, Jan. 25, 1931; married second, Terry Crothers, Aug. 16, 1950; two stepsons—Pav and Jonathan. Editor alumni publs. U. Okla., 1933-36; political reporter, Okla. News, 1936-39, political writer, United Press, Okla. City. Washington, N.Y.C., 1939-42, Latin Am. writer, Time mag., 1943; Latin Am. columnist Miami (Fla.) Herald, 1944-45; fgn. corr. Chgo. Daily News, 1945—, covered Peron's 1st Argentine campaign, 1946, Rome (Italy) bur. mgr., 1948-49; UN corr., 1950, Middle East corr., 1952, Tokyo (Japan) bur. mgr., 1953, London (Eng.) bur. mgr. with spl. assignement to U.S.S.R., Spain, Morocco, 1953—. Mem. Sigma Chi, Sigma Delta Chi. Clubs: Harvard (Miami); Wooden Horse (London); American (Buenos Aires); Overseas Press (N. Y.C.). Home: 22 Cottesmore Ct., Stanford Rd., London, W.8, Eng. Office: care Chicago Daily News, 400 W. Madison St., Chgo. 6. Died May 19, 1958; buried Putney Vale, London, Eng.

HILL, Frederick Sinclair, business exec.; b. nr. Arcadia, N.C., Dec. 9, 1888; s. Joel and Julia Ida (Ragsdale) H.; student Guilford Coll., 1904-07: m. Lucretia Wilson, Dec. 8, 1920 (died 1937); children—Lucretia Wilson (Mrs. Robert W. Sills, Jr.), Frederick Sinclair, Thomas Joel; m. 2d, Lois Williams Sweeney, May 10, 1947. With Nat. Bank of Lexington (N.C.), 1907-08; accountant R. J. Reynolds Tobacco Co., Winston-Salem, N.C., 1908-27, asst. treas., 1927-37, treas., 1937—, dir., 1943—; dir. The First Nat. Bank of Winston-Salem. Mem. bd. trustees U. of the South, Sewanee, Tenn., 1943-46. Pres. Travelers Aid Soc.; chmn. court of review Boy Scouts Am., mem. Izaak Walton League. Democrat. Episcopalian (vestryman). Mason. Clubs: Twin City, Forsyth Country, Old Town, Civitan (Winston-Salem). Home: 363 Lynn Av., Winston-Salem 5. Office: Fourth and Min Sts., Winston-Salem 1, N.C. Died, Jan. 27, 1951.

HILL, Harry Granison, clergyman; b. Union City, Ind., Sept. 15, 1874; s. George R. and Elizabeth (Eichelbarger) H.; A.B., Bethany (W.Va.) Coll., 1897, A.M., 1900; post-grad. work U. of Chicago, Ind. U., Columbia; D.D., Austin Coll., Effingham, Ill., 1904; m. Katherine Elgin Ralston, June 22, 1897 (dec. Nov., 1958); children—Herbert, Paul, Dorothy Katherine. Ordained ministry Christian (Disciples) Ch., 1897; pastor successively at Hebron, Ind., Fergus St. Ch., Cincinnati, First Ch., Omaha, Neb. and Third Ch., Indianapolis, until 1912. also nat. sec. of edn. Disciples Ch.; Chautauqua lecturer; pres. Ind. Coll. Music and Fine Arts, Indianapolis; consulting psychologist; pastor New Thought Temple, Cincinnati, 1926-43; pastor The City Temple, nondenominational, since 1943; conducts Life Adjustment Clinic; Sunday services held in theater to accommodate crowds; often on radio programs. Mem. Delta Tau Delta. Mason (32°). Club: Torch. Author: Rational Religion, 1931; Paradox and Principle; Heart to Heart Talks. Contbr. philos., psychol. and religious articles. Home: 3932 Davenant Av., Cin. 13. Died Feb. 15, 1951; buried Spring Grove Cemetery, Cin.

HILL, Henry Albert, bus. exec.; b. Athens, Greece, April 24, 1896; s. Arthur and Evanthea Augusta (Toole) H.; ed. Europe, U. of Athens. law; m. Priscilla Capps, Dec. 9, 1933; 1 son, Henry Albert. Became U.S. citizen, 1943. Clerk U.S. consulate, Athens, 1914-17; vice-consul, 1917-19; asst. to U.S. del. Allied Financial Com., 1917-19; in bus., N.Y. City, 1919-20; opened Am. Express office, Athens, 1921; mgr. 1921-41; dir. Greek C. of C., Am. Relief Com., Athens Y.M.C.A., Greek War Relief; trustee, Athens Coll.; treas., St. Paul's Ch.; left Greece at German invasion; with Am. Express, Bombay, 1941-42; advisor, Near East Foundn., 1942; exec. vice pres., Greek War Relief, 1943; spl. asst. to U.S. ambassador to Greece and Yugoslavia, Am. econ. advisor to mil. liaison mission in Greece, 1943-45; gen. mgr. Am. Express Co., Paris, 1945-46, v.p., gen. mgr., 1947-58, N.Y.C., 1958—. Gov. Am. Hosp. Trustee Am. Sch. Classical Studies, Athens. Decorated Legion of Honor, 1949; comdr. of the Order of the Phoenix (Greece), 1954. Member of Paris C. of C. (v.p., 1947-48), dir. Am. Com.

Civilian Relief, Am. Aid Soc., Union Interalliee. Clubs: American, Propeller, Yachting (Athens), Athens Golf, Athens Automobile; St. Cloud Golf, St. Germain Golf, Travellers (Paris); Nassau (Princeton, N.J.). Home: 12 Boudinot St., Princeton, N.J. Office: American Express Co., 65 Broadway N.Y.C. Died June 20, 1959.

HILL, Henry Clarke, penologist; b. Hamilton, Ill., Feb. 1, 1877; s. Thomas Alexander and Ellen White (Lynde) H.; grad. high sch., Galesburg, Ill.; business college, Galesburg; m. Blanche Colville, Nov. 14, 1900; children—Philip Coville, Blanche Joan (Mrs. Richard Seidel). Began as postal clk., Galesburg, 1899; post office insp., 1905-09; European rep. of N.Y. Credit Men's Assn., 1909-12; asst. sales mgr. Thomas B. Jeffery Co., Kenosha, Wis., 1912-14; in charge automobile purchases for French War Dept., Paris, 1914-15; attending personal interests, 1916-29; warden Ill. State Penitentiary, 1929-32; warden U.S. Penitentiary, Lewisburg, Pa., 1932-40; supt. Pa. Industrial Sch., Camp Hill, Mar. 1, 1940-June 18, 1943; apptd. chmn. Pa. Board of Parole, June 18, 1943. Pvt. 1st Arty. Bn., Ill. Vols., Spanish-Am. War; 1st lt. and q.m. Arty Bn., Ill. Nat. Guard, 1900-04; maj. 10th Ill. Inf., Ill. Nat. Guard, 1917-20. Trustee National Probation and Parole Assn. Mem. S.A.R., Am. Prison Assn., Police Chiefs Assn. of S.E. Pa. (hon.), Kappa Sigma (hon.), Spanish Am. Veterans Assn., Vets. of Foreign Wars, Middle-Atlantic States Parole Conf., Pa. Assn. Probation and Parole, Pa. Citizens Assn. Health and Welfare, Pa. Chiefs of Police Association, Pennsylvania Society. Member of the Governor's commission to study state penal and correctional instns. Chmn. Gov's. Adv. Com. on prison construction. Baptist. Mason (32°, K.T., Shriner, Jesters), K.P., Modern Woodmen, Elk. Author: papers, pamphlets on penological subjects. Address: Pennsylvania Board of Parole, 2025 N. Front St., Harrisburg, Pa. Deceased.

HILL, James, Jr., chmn. dir. Sterling Drug, Inc.; b. Newman, Ky., Jan. 21, 1898; s. James and Alice (Greenwood) H.; student U. Ky., 2 years; grad. Bowling Green (Ky.) U., 1920; m. Mary Marlowe, Dec. 31, 1917; children—James III, Marjorie G. With Ernst & Ernst, accountants, 1920-22; U.S. Treasury Dept., 1922-29; accountant Sterling Products, Inc. (name changed to Sterling Drug, 1942), N.Y.C., 1929-33, treas., 1933-41, pres., 1941-55, now chmn. bd., chief exec. officer; dir. Irving Trust Co., Am. Ferment Co., Buffalo; dir. and other official positions in other Sterling Drug subsidiary companies. Apptd. mem. drug industry advisory com., WPB. Dir. Brand Names Found. Baptist. Clubs: Congressional (Washington, D.C.); Country; Union League (N.Y.C.). Home: Washington. Office: 1450 Broadway, N.Y.C. Died Jan. 1960.

HILL, James Brents, ry. pres.; b. Spencer, Tenn., Nov. 14, 1878; s. Jas. Anderson and Mary (Lowrey) H.; Licentiate of Instrn., George Peabody Coll. for Tchrs., Nashville, 1898; m. Grace Marion Cooper, Oct. 22, 1913; children—Mary Eleanor (dec.), Grace M. (Mrs. Ashton Harcourt), James B. Began as telegraph operator Nashville, Chattanooga & St. Louis Ry., 1898, continued in transportation dept., later treasury dept. and exec. offices, advancing to asst. to pres. and treas., pres., 1926-34; pres. L.&N. R.R. Co., 1934-50, ret., chmn. exec. com., dir., 1950—; dir. Commonwealth Life Ins. Co. Mem. bd. govs. Speed Art Mus. Dir. Assn. Am. R.R.'s, Citizens Fidelity Bank & Trust Co., Louisville. Trustee George Peabody Coll. for Tchrs. Mem. Christian (Disciples) Ch. K.P. Clubs: Pendennis, Louisville Country. Home: 2540 Ransdell Av. Office: 908 W. Broadway, Louisville. Died Mar. 31, 1952.

HILL, James Perminter, ret. judge; b. German, N.Y., Apr. 7, 1878; s. James and Ruth A. (Purdy) H.; student Cincinnatus Acad.; LL..D., Bklyn. Law Sch., St. Lawrence U., 1938; m. Florine Hall, 1907; 1 dau., Janet Wadsworth. Admitted to N.Y. bar, 1901; dist. atty. Chenango County, N.Y.. 1908-13; county judge, Chenango County, 1914-23; elected justice of the Supreme Court for term 1924-37, re-elected 1937; and designated asso. justice Appellate Div., 3d Dept. by Gov. Smith, 1927, presiding justice, appointed by Governor Lehman, 1933-49, ret. Republican. Episcopalian. Club: Norwich. Home: Norwich, N.Y. Died June 9, 1950; buried Mt. Hope Cemetery, Norwich.

HILL, James W., railroad executive; born Orient Ia., Jan. 22, 1895; s. William J. and Elizabeth S. (Schultz) H.; m. Ethelmae M. Clark, Oct. 18, 1919. Station helper, telegraph operator, station agt., train dispatcher. Rock Island Lines, 1910-20, traffic rep., 1920-22, gen. agt.-traffic dept., 1922-36, gen. freight agt., 1936-37, asst. freight traffic mgr., 1937-39, gen. freight traffic mgr., 1940-45, freight traffic officer, 1945-48, v.p. since 1948; gen. traffic manager D.&R.G.W. R.R. Co., 1939-40. Served with Signal Corps, 1917-19. Clubs: Traffic, Union League (Chicago); Denver; Traffic (New York). Home: 2600 N. Lakeview Av. Office: La Salle St. Station, Chgo. 5. Died Aug. 12, 1951.

HILL, John A(rthur), wool specialist; b. nr. Carrollton, O., June 10, 1880; s. James Ross and Mary (Marshall) H.; B.S., University of Wyoming, 1907, Doctor of Laws (hon.), 1948; m. Evelyn Corthell, June 30, 1911; children—Robert Morris, John Marshall, Ross Corthell, Nellis Eugene, Sally Evelyn. Special work in wool, Philadelphia Textile Sch., Philadelphia, 1907; wool specialist University of Wyoming Expt. Station since 1907; prof. textile industry, Wyo. Agrl. Coll. since 1912; dean Agrl. Coll. and dir. Expt. Sta., U. of Wyo., 1923-50; chmn. bd. of deans for adminstrn. purposes, 1941-50; v.p. U. Wyo., 1950-51; cons. in animal husbandry. U.S. Bureau Animal Husbandry, 1928-32; judge of wool at Chicago International Live Stock Exposition, 1932, 33, 34, and at San Francisco World's Fair, 1940, at American Royal Livestock Exposition, 1947, 48, mem. advisory com. to study Nat. Live Stock Marketing Conditions, 1940-45; mem. wool advisory board, U.S. Dept. Agriculture. Awarded medal, Casper (Wyo.) Kiwanis, for distinguished service to state, 1943; named Outstanding Livestockman of U.S. for 1949 by Am. Soc. Animal Prodn. and portrait hung in Saddle and Sirloin Club, Chicago. Served as captain 166th Depot Brigade, World War I; commd. in Infantry Sect. O.R.C., United States Army, since 1923, now lt. col. (retired since June 30, 1944). Mem. Wyoming State Board Agr., Am. Soc. Animal Production (Western v.p. 1930-31; pres. 1932), N.E.A., Colo. Wyo. Acad. Science, Wyo. Farm Bureau, Reserve Officers Assn., Wyo. Pioneers Assn., Am. Legion, Sigma Xi, Epsilon Sigma Phi, Phi Beta Kappa, Phi Kappa Phi, Lambda Gamma Delta, Alpha Zeta; fellow A.A.A.S. Republican. Club: Lions. Co-author: Range Sheep and Wool (with Fred S. Hultz), 1931. Writer and lecturer on wool production; contbr. to Nat. Wool Grower, Wyo. Stockman Farmer, Wyo. Wool Grower, etc. Mem. editorial bd. Jour. of Am. Soc. Animal Production, 1941-45. Home: 264 N. 9th St., Laramie, Wyo. Died Mar. 10, 1951; buried Laramie.

HILL, Leslie Pinckney, educator; b. Lynchburg, Va., May 14, 1880; s. Samuel Henry and Sarah Elizabeth (Brown) H.; A.B., Harvard, 1903, A.M., 1904; Litt.D. (honorary), Lincoln U.; LL.D., Morgan State Coll., 1939, Haverford Coll., 1951; Ed.D. (hon.), Rhode Island Coll. Edn., 1956; m. Jane Ethel Clark, June 29, 1907; children—Eleanor Taylor (Mrs. Clifford Valentine), Hermione Clark (Mrs. Thomas S. Logan), Elaine Serena (Mrs. Frank Snowden), Natalie DuBois (Mrs. Rosamond Nelson), Mary Dorothea (Mrs. Herbert Tucker). Teacher and head dept. of edn., Tuskegee Inst., Ala., 1904-07; prin. Manassas (Va.) Indsl. Sch., 1907-13; prin. Inst. Colored Youth (in 1920, name changed to Cheyney Training Sch. for Teachers), 1913-30; pres. Cheyney Training Sch. for Teachers (State Teachers Coll.), 1930-51, now pres. emeritus; coll. lectr. on gen. edn.; adminstr. Mercy-Douglass Hosp., Phila., 1953-56. Mem. United Service Orgn., Pa. Dept. of Welfare; mem. Del. County Bd. of Assistance; founder and pres. bd. dirs. West Chester Community Center; founder, pres. Pa. State Negro Council; chmn. adv. com. on work in colls. for Negroes, Nat. Council Student Christian Assns.; dir. Armstrong Assn. of Phila., Interracial Com., Phila., Delaware County Tb and Health Assn.; mem. state bd., Met. Phila. bd. YMCA; dir. Delaware County Health and Welfare Council; founder, pres. Camp Hope; mem. Citizens Council Delaware County; mem. Phila. Citizens Com. on City Policy; Bd. Presidents of Pa. State Teachers Colls.; mem. bd. Visitation of Del. Co.; Nat. Council Student Christian Assn., State Commn. on Study of Urban Colored Population; mem. Hoover Commn. on Reorganization Fed. Govt. Class orator, Harvard, 1903. Pres. Eastern States Assn. of Teachers Colleges and Professional Schools for Teachers. Mem. N.E.A., Am. Teachers Assn., Pa. Tchrs. Assn. (founder), Am. Assn. Sch. Adminstrs., Pa. Edn. Assn., Pa. Assn. Tecachers of Colored Children (a founder), Am. Acad. Polit. and Social Science, Phi Beta Kappa, Kappa Alpha Psi. Club: Harvard (Phila.). Author: Wings of Oppression (lyric), 1927; Toussaint L'Ouverture (drama), 1929. Co-author: What the Negro Wants, 1944. Address: 46 Lincoln Av., Yeadon, Pa. Died Feb. 1960.

HILL, Mabel Jones, orgn. exec.; b. Pinewood, Tenn., Apr. 9, 1884; d. Richard Wood and Jane (Coleman) Jones; student spl. courses in history, Peabody Coll.; m. Albert Ewing Hill, June 30, 1917 (died Jan. 1933); 1 son, Albert Ewing. Pres., Davidson County League of Women Voters, 1918-22; pres. Tenn. Baptist Missionary Union, 1920-23; pres. Tenn. Assn. Planned Parenthood, 1939-41; mem. Girl Scout Commn. for Nashville area, 1938-41; mem. Nashville Bd. Edn., 1933-38; sponsor Woman's Action Com. for Lasting Peace since 1944; dir. Nashville Assn. for U.N. Mem. Tenn. State Dem. Com. since 1938, Nat. Dem. Com. since 1940; del. to Nat. Dem. Com. (mem. resolutions com.), 1940-44; mem. adv. com. Tenn. Dept. of Labor. Mem. Ladies Hermitage Assn. Baptist. Clubs: Centennial, Wednesday Study, Golf, Lane Garden. Home: 2005 Linden Av., Nashville 4. Died Oct. 4, 1957; buried Mt. Olivet Cemetery, Nashville.

HILL, Pierre Bernard, clergyman, author b. Richmond, Va., Mar. 4, 1877; s. Robert and Evelyn Gay (Bernrad) H.; student Richmond Coll. (now U. Richmond); A.B., Hampden-Sydney Coll., 1902, D. D., 1919; B.D., Union Theol. Sem., 1905; LL.D., Austin Coll., 1935; Litt.D., Baylor U., 1950; m. Ella Lee Thraves, June 1, 1905; children—Samuel Bernard, John Pierre, Martha Evelyn, David Lee. Religious work in mountains and coal fields of Va. during student years; ordained ministry Presbyn. Ch. in U.S., 1905; pastor successively St. Elmo and Lookout Mountain Chs., Tenn.; Rivermont Ch., Lynchburg, Va.; West End Ch., Roanoke, until 1912; missionary in Korea, 1912-16; pastr, 2d Ch., Roanoke, and First Ch., Louisville, until 1921, First Ch., San Antonio, 1921-40, now pastor emeritus; rebuilt church at Louisville and made extensive improvements in First Ch., San Antonio, instituted a unique system of religious edn. of young people. Moderator Synod of Tex., Presbyn. Ch. in U.S., 1937-38. Served with YMCA, World War I; lectured at munition plants and railroad shops. Awarded Algeron-Sydney-Sullivan medallion, 1937, N.Y. So. Soc. for Outstanding Service. Former trustee Austin (Tex.) Presbyn. Coll. Capt. Tex. Ranger; hon. life mem. Tex Sheriffs Assn.; chaplian Tex. Identification Assn., U.S. Border Patrol, Tex. State Rangers, Tex. State Highway Patrol, Texas Police Assn., Tex. Pioneers, Old Freighters of Tex., 101 Ranch Assn., Old Trail Drivers of Texas. Mem. A.A.A.S., Texas Acad. Sci., Sojourners, Victoria Inst. of Great Britain, Indsl. Plant Protection Assn., Chi Phi; hon. mem. French Inst. Arts and Letters. Democrat. Mason (32°, Shriner); Past Grand Chaplain Grand Chapter R.A. Masons of Texas. Author: The Questionnaire (a method of enlisting members for service); Studies on Korea; The Truth About Evolution; Preparation for Church Membership; What Presbyterians Believe; Making a Home; Don't Worry; The Meaning of Death; Living For Jesus; Hand Book for Personal Workers; What Have You Done?; If You Believe; Where I Found God; The Men Who Lost the Star: A Morning Prayer and an Evening Prayer; Texas I Hear You Calling, and Other Poems, (War Song). Pioneer radio speaker, 1923—, Church In The Hills. Home: Hunt, Tex. Died Jan. 1958.

HILL, Ralph Waldo Snowden, lawyer, diplomatist; b. Washington, D.C., Aug. 20, 1882; s. Eugene F. and Minnie (Waldo) H.; student U. of Mo.; LL.B., U. of Va., 1909; post-grad. work in polit. science, George Washington U., and L'Ecole des Sciences Politiques, Paris; m. Katharine (Strickler) Wilcox, Aug. 18, 1941. Admitted to Mo. bar, 1909, later to D.C. bar; practiced in Mo. and D.C.; apptd. asst. solicitor Department of State, May 23, 1916, asst. legal adviser; Am. expert at Finance Ministers' Conf., Paris, Jan. 1925; served as Am. Observer, Reparation Commn., June 1, 1925-Feb. 1927; on spl. missions for State Dept., Berlin, July 1925, London, 1925, 27, 31, Canada Oct. 1939, Haiti, Apr. 1941; counsel for U.S. in matters before Internat. Joint Commn., U.S. and Canada; retired, Mar. 31, 1945. Mem. Soc. Colonial Wars. Clubs: Chevy Chase (Washington); Colonnade (Charlottesville, Va.); Valley (Montecito, Cal.). Address: 665 Buena Vista Rd., Santa Barbara, Cal. Died Aug. 1, 1954; buried Rock Creek Cemetery, Washington.

HILL, Randolph William, physician; b. Lexington, Va., Jan. 20, 1854; s. Gen. Daniel Harvey and Isabella (Morrison) H.; M.D., U. Louisville, 1876; post-grad. Bellevue Hosp. Med. Coll., N.Y.C., 1881. Practiced in N.Y.C., 1876-88; q.m. in charge U.S. Marine Hosp., San Pedro, Cal., 1888-97; mem. Cal. State Bd. of Health, 1897-1903 (pres. 1899-1903); practiced in Los Angeles, 1901—. Democrat. Presbyn. Mason. Club: Jonathan (Los Angeles). Home: 4031 Wilshire Blvd. Office: Byrne Bldg., Los Angeles. Died Nov. 19, 1926.

HILL, Reuben L(orenzo), coll. prof., chemist; b. Ogden, Utah, Mar. 24, 1888; s. George Richard and Elizabeth Nancy (Burch) H.; student Brigham Young U., 1908-11; B.S., Utah State Agrl. Coll., 1912; Ph.D., Cornell U., 1915; m. Mary Theresa Snow, Oct. 11, 1911; children—Reuben Lorenzo, Cornella (Mrs. Mac Novak), Richard Snow, Theresa Marie (Mrs. Donald Ashdown), Wesley Sherwin, Alwyn Spencer, Edward Eyring, Carl David. Instr. in biochem. Cornell U., 1914-16; biochemist, Bureau of Chemistry, U.S. Dept. Agr., Washington, 1916; biochemist Md. Agr. Expt. Sta., 1916-18; head dept. chemistry Utah State Coll. of Agr. since 1919, human nutritionist, expt. sta., 1919-41. Commd. 1st lt., San. Corps, U.S. A., 1918; in Med. Officers Training, Camp Greenleaf, 1918, 2 mos.; nutrition officer, Camp Upton, L.I., 1918-19, 6 mos.; capt. Gen. Res. Corp, U.S. Army, 1927-41; recalled to active duty as maj., U.S. Army, 1941; completed Army Nutrition course, Army Med. Center, Washington, 1941, 2 mos.; nutritionist and chief Nutrition Service, 5th Service Command, U.S. Army, 1941-44, 34 mos.; apptd. lt. col., San. Res. Corps, 1946. Mem. Am. Chem. Soc., Am. Assn. Univ. Profs., A.A.A.S., Utah Acad. Arts, Sci. and Letters, Res. Officers Assn., Sigma Xi. Republican. Mem. Ch. of Jesus Christ of Latter-Day Saints. Author of research papers and bulls. on milk secretion, soft curd milk. Holder patent on original equipment used in Hill Curd Test. Home: 645 N. 8th East St., Logan, Utah. Died Jan. 22. 1953; buried Logan (Utah) City Cemetery.

HILL, Robert E. Lee, ex-pres. Rotary Internat., univ. exec.; b. St. Charles, Mo., Sept. 29, 1890; s. Lewis Ely and Mary (Gough) H.; student Stephens Coll., Columbia, Mo.; grad. Culver Mil. Acad.; B.S. in Agr., U. Mo., 1912, M.S., 1913, student journalism, 1915-18; m. Gertrude Lyon, June 7, 1913; children—Mary Jane, Virginia Lee. Began as editor agrl. publ., 1913; adminstrv. office U. Mo., 1921; dir. alumni activities; editor and business mgr. alumni mag.; dir. Boone Savings & Loan Assn.; chmn. Federal Home Loan Bank of Des Moines, Mutual Savings Life Ins. Co. (St. Louis). Chmn. Outstate Mo. War Finance Com., pres. Mo. War Chest, Inc. Chmn. pub. relations com. U. Mo. Campaign; chmn. Mo. div. Am. Cancer Soc.; chmn. U.S. Savings Bond Div. (Mo.); Mo. chmn. Save the Children Fedn., Inc. Dir. Automobile Club of Mo. Mem. Mo. Bankers Assn. (sec. 1944—), Acacia, Kappa Alpha, Theta Nu Epsilon, Chi Chi Chi, Sigma Delta Chi, Alpha Delta Sigma. Democrat. Methodist. Clubs: Rotary Internat. (pres. 1934-35), Country (Columbia). Home: 706 Stewart Rd. Office: 15 S. 8th St., Columbia, Mo. Died Apr. 24, 1957.

HILL, Tom Burbridge, ret. naval officer; born Ft. Worth, Dec. 12, 1898; s. Benjamin Felix and Norma (Burbridge) H.; student Colo. Sch. of Mines, 1916-17; B.S., U.S. Naval Acad., 1922; student U.S. Naval Postgrad. Sch., 1927-28; M.S., U. of Mich., 1929; m. Lillian Jamison, Nov. 3, 1924; children—Thomas Burbridge, Emma Patricia (Mrs. Wm. Truman Smith), Norma Lillian (Mrs. John M. Redfield). Commissioned ensign United States Navy, 1922, and advanced through grades to vice admiral, retired; gunnery officer U.S.S. California and U.S.S. North Carolina, World War II; mem. staff of comdr. in chief Pacific, 1942-45; comd. U.S.S. Wyoming, 1945, U.S.S. Missouri, 1946-47; dep. dir., div. of atomic energy Office of Chief of Naval Operations, Washington, 1947-48, dir., 1949; mem. Mil. Liaison Com. to Atomic Energy Commn., 1949; amphibious task force commander Far East, 1951; chief of staff Pacific Fleet, 1952; superintendent naval gun factory, 1952; also comdt. Potomac River Naval Command, 1953. Awarded Legion of Merit, Bronze Star Medal, World War I Victory medal, American Defense medal with fleet clasp, Asiatic Pacific Area Campaign and World War II Victory medals. Member Naval Institute, Sigma Alpha Epsilon, Iota Alpha. Episcopalian. Clubs: New York Yacht; Army and Navy Country (Washington); Army and Navy. Home: 3803 Everett St., Kensington, Md. Died Oct. 21, 1957; buried Arlington Cemetery.

HILL, Vassie James (Mrs. A. Ross Hill): b. Kansas City, Mo., Mar. 29, 1875; d. John Crawford and Fanny (Shouse) James; A.B., Vassar Coll., 1897; m. Hugh Campbell Ward, Oct. 26, 1898 (died Aug. 15, 1909); children—Hugh Campbell, James Crawford, Frances, John Harris; m. 2d, Albert Ross Hill, Sept. 6, 1919 (died May 6, 1943). President of Ward Investment Company, 1909-39, founder and member board trustees Country Day School for Boys, Kansas City, 1910-26; a founder and president board Sunset Hill Sch. for Girls, Kansas City. First vice chmn. Mo. Div. Woman's Com. of Council Nat. Defense; first woman mem. for Mo. of Dem. Nat. Com.; mem. bd. trustees Vassar Coll., 1919-24; pres. Asso. Alumnae of Vassar Coll.; treas. Am. Assn. of Univ. Women, 1923-45; mem. adv. bd. Prog. Edn. Assn.; mem. Nat. Women's Com. of 1933 Mobilization for Human Needs, also of 1934; mem. advisory council of League of Nations Assn.; chmn. Adv. Com. K.C. School Social Work, Interviewer for Nat. Scholarship Com. of 7 women's colls. Del. to nat. conf. of U.S. Nat. Commn. for UNESCO, 1952. Mem. World Peace Council of Kansas City (vice president), Kansas City League of Women Voters (vice president and member committee of Campaign for Better Civil Service); trustee Sarah Lawrence College; honorary chairman Volunteer Service Bureau of Kansas City; formerly mem. adv. board WPA Nursery Sch. Project; mem. bd. sponsors Kansas City Women Volunteers for Nat. Defense; chmn. Coll. Contact Com. for WAVES, Kansas City Area; chmn. edn. sect. Mayor's Youth Conf. of Kansas City, 1948. Clubs: Cosmopolitan (New York); Woman's City, Kansas City Country; University Women's. Home: 800 W. 52d St., Kansas City 2, Mo. Died June 23, 1954.

HILL, Walter Newell, marine corps officer; b. Haverhill, Mass., Sept. 29, 1881; s. Edwin Newell and Lizzie Williams (Briggs) H.; student Noble and Greenough Sch., Boston; student Harvard, 1900-04; grad. Army War Coll., 1929; m. Mary Bainbridge Fitzpatrick, June 21, 1924 children—Leigh (Mrs. Dean R. Harbold), Walter Newell. Commd. 2d lt. USMC, 1904, advanced through grades to brig. gen., 1938; served in W. Indies, Philippines, China, France, World War I, Washington, World War II; ret. from active service, 1945. Decorated Navy Medal of Honor, Medaile Militaire (2), Haiti. Episcopalian. Clubs: Army Navy (Washington), Harvard (N.Y.C.); Noronton (Conn.) Yacht. Home: 222 E. 71st St., N.Y.C. 21. Died June 29, 1955; buried Nat. Cemetery, Arlington, Va.

HILL, Willam Austin, ch. ofcl.; b. Ellenburg, N.Y., May 2, 1873; s. Austin Stevens and Margaret May (Linihan) H.; student Colby Acad., New London, N.H., 1894-98; A.B., Brown U., 1902, D.D., 1927; A.M., Harvard, 1904; B.D., Newton Theol. Instn., 1906; m. Anne Louise Cranska, June 29, 1904; children—Margaret Linihan (Mrs. Cedric Hubbel Start), Ruth Albro (Mrs. Rumsey Miller McGregor), Deborah (dec.), William Austin. Ordained to ministry Bapt. Ch., 1904; pastor Trinity Bapt. Ch., Arlington, Mass., 1904-08, Woodland Park Bapt. Ch., St. Paul, 1908-14, 1st Bapt. Ch., Medford, Mass., 1915-17; joint dist. sec. Am. Bapt. Foreign Mission Soc., Am. Bapt. Home Mission Soc., Am. Bapt. Publ. Soc., 1917-19; sec. Missionary Edn. of bd. Edn., No. Bapt. Conv., also officer bd. edn., 1919—; now ret. Mem. bd. mgrs. Am. Bapt. Fgn. Mission Soc., 1916-17, Missionary Edn. Movement of U.S. and Can.; trustee bd. Colby Jr. Coll. for Women (formerly Colby Acad.), New London, N.H., Newton Theol. Instn., Internat. Soc. of Christian Endeavor; mem. Protestant Com., Boy Scouts of America. Mem. Vt. Legislature, 1943-44. Mem. N.E. Historic-Geneal. Soc., R.I., N.Y., Vt. hist. socs., Isle la Motte Hist. Soc., S.A.R., Phi Gamma Delta. Republican. Edited many books in the field of Christian lit. Contbr. to Americanna Annual and other mags. Home: Isle LaMotte, Vt. Died July 1951.

HILLAS, Robert M., mfr.; b. West Hoboken, N.J., Sept. 20, 1884; s. Robert John and Mary (Mulholland) H.; M.E., Stevens Inst. Tech., 1908; m. Bertha B., Apr. 6, 1926; 1 dau., Dorothy B. Benney. In automobile business, 1905-31. Chairman board of directors Columbian Carbon Co., 1933; director of Binney & Smith Co. Republican. Club: Blind Brook Golf. Home: Indian Harbor, Greenwich, Conn. Office: 380 Madison Av., N.Y.C. Died Feb. 9, 1956.

HILLEBRAND, Harold Newcomb (hĭl'lĕ-brănd), author, educator; b. Washington, Jan. 1, 1887; s. William Francis and Martha May (Westcott) H.; student Cornell U., 1905-06; A.B., Harvard, 1909, A.M., 1910, Ph.D., 1914. Sheldon traveling fellow Harvard, doing research work in London, 1911-12; asst. in English, Harvard, 1912-14; with U. Ill., 1914—, prof. English, 1931—, head dept. English, 1939-46. Served as 1st lt. inf. U.S. Army, 1917-18, capt., Camp Grant, Ill., and Camp Lee, Va., 1918-19. Unitarian. Author: Writing the One-Act Play, 1925; The Child Actors of the Sixteenth and Seventeenth Centuries, 1926; Edmund Kean, 1933; Troilus and Cressida, 1953. Editor New Variorum Shakespeare, 1946. Died Jan. 26, 1953.*

HILLER, Alfred, clergyman, educator; b. Sharon, N.Y., Apr. 22, 1831; s. John F. and Margaret (Houck) J.; student dist. schs. and acads.; grad. Hartwick Theol. Sem., 1857; D.D., Wittenberg Coll., Springfield, O., 1882; m. Henrietta Sophia Miller, Sept. 9, 1857. Licensed by N.Y. Ministerium (Luth.), 1957; began ministry at Fayette, N.Y.; pastor German Valley, Morris County, N.J., 1858-81; prof. systematic theology Hartwick Theol. Sem., 1881—. Wrote History of Lutheran Church in New Jersey, Luth. Quar. Rev., Jan.-Apr. 1898. Address: Hartwick Sem., Otsego County, N.Y. Died Jan. 27, 1920; buried Hartwick Sem. Cemetery.

HILLIARD, Benjamin Clark (hĭl'yärd), judge; b. nr. Osceola, Ia., Jan. 9, 1868; s. Albert George and Euphemia Ellen (Clark) H.; LL.B., State U. Ia., 1891; m. Tida Zimmerman, May 22, 1889; children—Loraine (widow of Judge Ralph E. Finnicum), Albert, Opal, Benjamin Clark, Bertha Tida (dec.). In practice of law at Kansas City, Mo., 1891-93; moved to Denver, 1893; former mem. firm Hilliard, Lilyard & Finnicum; mem. 64th-65th U.S. Congresses, 1st Colo. Dist.; justice Supreme Ct. of Colo., 1931—, chief justice, 1939-41, 49—. Mem. Colo. Ho. of Reps., 1902-03. Mem. Am., Colo., Denver bar assns. Democrat. Mem. Disciples of Christ Ch. Mason (past grand master), K.P., Woodman of the World. Home: 3132 Federal Blvd., Denver 11. Office: State House, Denver. Died Aug. 7, 1951.

HILLMAN, John Hartwell, Jr., corp. exec.; b. Trigg Furnace, Ky., Apr. 27, 1880; s. John Hartwell and Sallie Murfree (Frazer) H.; m. Juliet Cummins Lea, June 27, 1907 (dec.); children—John Hartwell, Margery Lea (Mrs. J. Merrill Wright, Jr.), Anne Elizabeth, Henry Lea, Mary Lea (Mrs. John Keating) also Patricia Polk Miller; married 2d., Dora Keen Butcher, Aug. 18, 1948; adopted children—Howard, Tatnall. Chmn. Texas Gas Transmission Co.; pres. Hillman Coal and Coke Co.; chmn. finance com. Pitts. Coke & Chem. Co.; officer, dir. many other cos. in coal, iron, steel, natural gas and banking. Clubs: University, Duquesne, Fox Chapel, Pittsburg Golf. Home: 5045 5th Av. Office: 330 Grant St., Pitts.; 120 Broadway, N.Y.C. Died Sept. 25, 1959; buried Homewood Cemetery, Pitts.

HILLS, Laura Coombs, flower painter; b. Newburyport, Mass., Sept. 7, 1859; d. Philip K. and Mary P. Hills; pupil Helen M. Knowlton, Cowles Art Sch. and Art Students' League, N.Y. Medal Art Interchange, 1895, Paris Expn., 1900; 2d prize Corcoran Art Gallery, Washington, 1901; silver medal Buffalo Expn., 1901; gold medal, St. Louis Expn., 1904; medal of honor, Panama P.I. Expn., 1915; 1st award of medal of honor, Pa. Soc. Miniature Painters, 1916, A.N.A.; mem. Am. Soc. Miniature Painters, Am. Soc. Artists, Boston Artists' Guild, Water Color Club. Painter of flowers in pastel. Home: Newburyport, Mass. Died 1952.

HILLS, Oscar Armstrong, clergyman; b. Union County, Ind., Dec. 13, 1837; s. Darwin Todd and Sarah (Anderson) H.; A.B., Wabash Coll., 1859, A.M., 1862, D.D., 1876; grad. Western Theol. Sem., Pitts., 1862; m. Miriam Wright, 1862 (dec. 1866); 2d, Louise Esther Freer, 1869 (dec. 1884); 3d, Ida Faust, Aug. 12, 1886. Ordained Presbyn. ministry, 1862; pastor Spruce Creek Ch., Pa., 1862-65, Central Ch., Cin., 1865-78, North Ch., Pittsburgh, N.S., 1878-81, 1st Ch., Santa Barbara, Cal., 1881-82, 1st Ch., San Francisco, 1882-83, Wooster, O., 1885-98, Westminster (Univ.) Ch., Wooster, O., 1898-1907, retired. Dir. Western Theol. Sem., 1878—; trustee U. of Wooster, 1885—. Author: Companion Characters, 1883; Carmina Subseciva, 1900; New Shafts in the Old Mine, 1906; The Testimony of the Witnesses, 1913. Address: Wooster, O. Died Jan. 9, 1919.

HILLYER, H(enry) Stanley, business exec.; b. East Orange, N.J., Jan. 14, 1887; s. James Rankin and Lillian Stanley (Smith) H.; preparatory Hoosac School; A.B., Williams Coll., 1908; married Louise Estelle Bernhardt, March 31, 1933; 1 son, Robert Couthouy William. With Deering Milliken & Co., A. S. Haight & Co., wholesale drygoods, N.Y. City, 1908-17; real estate salesman and exec. vice pres. Gaines, Van Nostrand & Morrison, 1920-29; organized H. Stanley Hillyer, Inc., real estate, N.Y. City, 1929, pres. since 1929; pres. Hillyer & Bell, Inc.; trustee West Side Savs. Bank, N.Y.C. Former mem. bd. govs. N.Y. Real Estate Bd.; mem. bd. mgrs. Greenwich House; dir. Washington Square Home for Friendless Girls; pres. Washington Square Assn.; v.p. Musicians Foundn., N.Y.C. Received award N.Y. Real Estate Bd. for most ingenious and beneficial real estate transaction for assembling site of N.Y. U.-Bellevue Med. Center, 1947. Served as 1st lt., aide to chief ordnance office, U.S. Army, World War I; with A.E.F.; munitions officer, Army Arty., 1st Army, Meuse-Argonne Offensive; capt. with Peace Commn. Mem. Delta Psi. Episcopalian (vestryman). Clubs: Bohemians, Williams (New York). Composer of art songs, and other music. Home: 10 W. 9th St. Office: 5. W. 8th St., N.Y.C. 11. Died Jan. 2, 1955; buried St. James the Less, North Phila.

HILSON, Edwin I., investment banker; b. N.Y. City, Apr. 16, 1895; s. Max and Minnie (Meinhard) H.; student Sachs Collegiate Inst., Phillips-Exeter Acad.; m. Mildred Stern, June 18, 1924; children—John S., Mary E. In cigar mfg. bus., Mt. Carmel, Pa., 1912-17, 1919-22; in investment banking since 1922, partner Wertheim & Co., N.Y. City, since 1932; dir. George A. Fuller Co., Gen. Realty & Utilities Corp., Punta Alegre Sugar Corp., Tanamo Sugar Corp., Compania Azucarera Tanamo de Cuba, Nat. Cuba Hotel Corp., Nedick's Stores, Inc., Blackstone Hotel, Inc., The Gotham, Hotel Beverly-Wilshire. Dir. N.Y. Eye and Ear Infirmary and Hosp. for Spl. Surgery. Served with U.S. Army, 1917-19. Republican. Clubs: Economic, Harmonie, Bankers of America, New York Stock Exchange Luncheon (New York); Century Country (Purchase, N.Y.); Havana (Cuba) Yacht. Home: 927 Fifth Av., N.Y. City; also Greenwich, Conn. Office: 120 Broadway, N.Y.C. 5. Died July 13, 1952.

HILTON, James, author; b. Leigh, Lancashire, Eng., Sept. 9, 1900; M.A., Cambridge U., 1922; married. Author: And Now Goodbye, 1932; Ill Wind, 1932; Lost Horizon, 1933; Goodbye, Mr. Chips, 1934; We Are Not Alone, 1937; Random Harvest, 1941; The Story of Dr. Wassell, 1943; So Well Remembered, 1945; Nothing So Strange, 1947; Morning Journey, 1951; Time and Time Again, 1953. Address: care Little, Brown Co., Boston. Died Dec. 20, 1954; buried Long Beach, Cal.

HILTON, Warren, psychologist, lawyer; b. St. Louis, Nov. 13, 1874; s. Manetho and Mary Eleanor (Block) H.; spl. study Harvard, 1892; A.B., Washington U., 1895; LL.B., St. Louis Law Sch., 1900; m. Kitty K. Rubey, Dec. 23, 1897; m. 2d, May F. Moore, May 6, 1920; m. 3d, Adele P. White, Nov. 1, 1932. Instr. in English, Washington U., 1895-96, Toensfeldt Inst., St. Louis, 1896-98; prin. Mt. Pleasant Sch., St. Louis, 1898-1900; practiced law, St. Louis, 1900-06; dealer in securities and financial adviser to various corps., 1906-20. Founder, 1911, organizer and pres. Soc. of Applied Psychology; has lectured on applied psychology in all parts of U.S. Mem. Nat. Inst. Social Sciences, Acad. Polit. Science (New York), Nat. Conservation Assn. (Washington), Sigma Alpha Epsilon. Republican. Conglist. Author: Psychology and Achievement, 1914; also (brochures), 1914-16. Making Your Own World; The Driving Power of Thought; The Trained Memory; Power of Mental Imagery; Initiative Psychic Energy; Mind Mechanicsm; Mind Mastery; The Technique of Success; External Efficiency Factors; Specific Applications of Psychology; Mental Processes and Personality. Home: "Hochelaga," Rockland Av., Victoria, B.C. Died Aug. 4, 1958; buried Forest Lawn Cemetery, Los Angeles.

HIMES, Charles Francis, physicist; b. Lancaster County, Pa., June 2, 1838; s. Wilviam D. H.; A.B., Dickinson Coll., 1955, A.M., 1858, LL.D., 1896; Ph.D., U. Giessen, 1865; m. Mary E. Murray. Prof. mathematics Troy (N.Y.) U., 1860-63; prof. natural sci. Dickinson Coll., 1865-85, physics, 1885-96, acting pres., 1888-89. Author numerous lectures and addresses on sci. and ednl. subjects; editor chem. textbooks. Has made specialty of photographic investigation. Address: Carlisle, Pa. Died Dec. 6, 1918.

HIMSTEAD, Ralph E(bner), educator, editor; b. Blue Mound, Ill., Jan. 31, 1893; s. Christopher and Carolyn (Ellrich) H.; A.B., U. of Ill., 1916; LL.B., Northwestern U., 1921, A.M., 1924, J.D., 1924; S.J.D., Harvard, 1929; LL.D., Cornell College, 1946; married Dorothy Scott, September 7, 1918; children—James (dec.), Scott. Teacher English, Central High Sch., Omaha, Neb., Jan.-June 1919; prof. pub. speaking, Cornell Coll., Mt. Vernon, Ia., 1919-23, professor political science, 1923-24; Harris fellow in political science, Northwestern University, 1922-23; prof. of law, Syracuse U., 1924-36; gen. sec. Am. Assn. Univ. Profs., Washington, D.C., since 1936; research fellow Harvard Law Sch., 1928-29; prof. polit. science, Pa. State Coll., summers, 1925, 26; prof. law, Northwestern U. Sch. of Law, summer 1927. Mem. U.S. Office of Edn. Wartime Commn., 1941-43; mem. U.S. National Commn. for UNESCO. Served as private, advancing to rank of 1st lieut., U.S. Army, 1917-19; instr. Central O.T.C. June-Dec. 1918. Mem. Am. Polit. Science Assn., Am. Soc. International Law, Am. Assn. Univ. Profs., Phi Delta Phi, Phi Kappa Phi, Delta Sigma Rho, Acacia. Methodist. Clubs: Cosmos, Federal Schoolmen's (Washington, D.C.), Manor Country (Norbeck, Md.). Author Elec. Utilities: The Crisis in Public Control (with W. E. Mosher); and articles and reports in edn. journals. Editor Bull. Am. Assn. Univ. Profs. since 1937. Home: 4110 Rosemary St., Chevy Chase, Md. Office: 1785 Massachusetts Av., Washington 6. Died June 9, 1955; buried Arlington Nat. Cemetery.

HINCKLEY, Allen Carter, singer; b. Boston, Oct. 11, 1877; s. Frederic Allen and Elizabeth S. (Carter) H.; student Amherst Coll., U. Pa.; studied under Carl Schachner, Phila., and Oscar Sanger, N.Y. C.; married. Taught harmony and counterpoint and directed a choral soc. of 50 voices; made début in Boston in Robin Hood, 1901; went to Hamburg, Germany, in 1903, first appeared in grand opera as King Henry, in Lohengrin, 1904; repertoire embraces the leading oratorios, 75 grand operas and hundreds of songs; sang at Hamburg, 6 yrs., Bayreuth, 3 seasons, London, 3 seasons, Met. Opera, 3 yrs., Chicago Opera, 2 yrs.; tour S. Africa and Australia, 2 yrs.; single performances Paris, Vienna, Berlin, Stockholm, etc. Head of vocal dept. Conservatory of Music, Kansas City, Mo., 1917-23; later teaching in N.Y.C.; condr. Village Light Opera group, N.Y.C. Mem. bd. govs. Kansas City Theatre. Mem. Am. Acad. Tchrs. Singing, Delta Kappa Epsilon. Unitarian. Clubs: Harmonie, Walsingham London. Died Jan. 28, 1954.

HINCKLEY, Frank Erastus, lawyer; b. Beardstown, Ill., Aug. 21, 1871; s. William H. and Abbie R. (Peck) H.; A.B., Beloit Coll., 1892, A.M., 1897 (Phi Beta Kappa); law course U. Cal., 1897-99, Columbia, 1904-06, Ph.D. in Internat. Law, 1905; student consular, colonial adminstrn. at Paris and London, 1899-1900; m. Flora Huggins, June 9, 1896. Admitted to bar by U.S. Court for China, 1907, Supreme Ct. Cal., 1913, Supreme Ct. U.S., 1917, U.S. Treasury and Tax Ct. U.S., 1941. Clk. U.S. Ct. for China, 1906-10, dist. atty., 1910-15; in practice at Shanghai, China, 1915, San Francisco, 1916-—; lectr. on internat. law sch. of jurisprudence U. Cal., 1921-33. Mem. Episcopal Diocese to Cal. Com. on Canons, 1941-—; dep. to Gen. Conv., 1943. Councillor Royal Asiatic Society, China, 1909-16; mem. Harvard Law Sch. Internat. Law Research Adv. Com., 1927-—. Mem. Am Soc. Internat. Law (charter; exec. council 1925-28), Am., Cal., San Francisco bar assns. Episcopalian. Clubs: Commercial, Faculty, Shanghai (life mem.). Author: American Consular Jurisdiction in the Orient, 1906. Home: 2750 Main Av., Berkeley 8, Cal. Office: Merchants Exchange, San Francisco 4. Died Oct. 1950*

HINCKLEY, Frank L(eonard), lawyer; b. Providence, Aug. 31, 1869; s. Herbert Frank and Elizabeth Davis (Clarke) H.; A.B., Brown U., 1891; LL. B., Harvard, 1894; m. Anita W. Baker, June 4, 1910; children—Anita Candler, Elizabeth Clarke, Francesca Leonard, Gladys Candler, Frank Leonard. Admitted to R.I. bar, 1895, since practiced in Providence; mem. Hinckley, Allen, Salisbury & Parsons, and predecessor, 1906-—; dir. or officer various corps. Mem. City Council of Providence, 1898-1900; R.I. Bd. Bar Examiners, 1900-27; rep. City Com., 1916-45, Commn. Revision Corp. Laws, 1918-20. Trustee Mary C. Wheeler Sch.; dir. Legal Aid Soc. of R.I. Mem. Am., R.I. bar assns., Assn. Bar City of N.Y., Am. Law Inst., Am. Judicature Soc., Harvard Law Sch. Assn., Alpha Delta Phi. Republican. Clubs: Hope, Art, Turks Head, Agawam Hunt (Providence); Brown University, University (N.Y. C.). Home: 72 Waterman St., Providence. Office: Industrial Bank Bldg., Providence 3. Died Sept. 8, 1959.

HINDMARSH, Harry Comfort (hind marsh), newspaperman; b. Bismark, Mo., Jan. 13, 1887 (parents Canadian citizens); s. Henry Frank and Etoile (Comfort) H.; B.A., U. Toronto, 1909; m. Ruth Atkinson, Nov. 27, 1915; children—Ruth (Mrs. N. A. Folland), John C., Harry A., Joyce (Mrs. A. E Armstrong). Reporter, Detroit News, 1907-08, Toronto (Ont.) Globe, 1909-10; sec. Erickson, Perkins & Co., brokers, Toronto, 1910-11; reporter Toronto Star, 1911-12, city editor, 1912-29, mng. editor, 1929-48; pres. Toronto Star, Ltd., 1948-—; sec.-treas. Toronto Star Realty, Ltd. Sec.-treas., trustee Atkinson Charitable Found. Mason (32°). Home: Shorewood, Oakville, Ont. Office: 80 King St. W., Toronto, Ont., Can. Died Dec. 20, 1956; buried Oakville, Ont., Can.

HINERFELD, Benjamin, textile mfg. exec.; b. N.Y. C., Sept. 10, 1896; s. Joseph and Rebecca (Blank) H.; A.B., Coll. City N.Y., 1916; m. Anne Blitz, June 27, 1925; children—Norman M., Robert E. Cashier Community Bank, N.Y.C., 1926-29; v.p. Internat. Madison Bank & Trust Co., 1929-31; spl. dep. supt. banks State of N.Y., 1934-46; pres. Purity Drug Co., Inc., Passaic, N.J., 1932-46; treas. Witty Bros., Inc., mfg. clothiers, N.Y.C., 1934-51; sec., treas. Hamilton Textile Mills, Inc., N.Y.C., 1946-—; pres. Hamilton Hosiery Mills, Inc., Hillcrest Factors, Inc., Empire State Bldg.; exec. v.p. Julius Kayser & Co., N.Y.C., 1954-—. Mem. Am. Legion. Mason. Home: 66 Park Av., N.Y.C. Office: 425 Fifth Av., N.Y.C. 16. Died Aug. 4, 1957.

HINES, Duncan, business man and author; b. Bowling Green, Ky., Mar. 26, 1880; s. Edward L. and Nela (Duncan) H.; ed. high school and business college; married Clara Wright Nahm, Mar. 22, 1946. With Wells-Fargo Express Co., Western U.S., 1898-1903; later with Green Copper Co., Cananea, Mexico; then entered printing and advertising business; has travelled extensively throughout U.S.; lives on a farm. Author: Adventures in Good Eating, 1936; Lodging for a Night; Adventures in Good Cooking; Vacation Guide; Duncan Hines' Food Odyssey. Died Mar. 15, 1959; buried Bowling Green.

HINES, Laurence Edward, physician; b. Livermore, Ia., June 8, 1896; s. Edward J. and Clara Helen (Knowles) H.; student Creighton Coll., Omaha, Neb., 2 yrs.; M.D., Northwestern Univ., 1919, B.S., 1925; m. Dorys Elizabeth Zinn, June 29, 1921; children—Laurence Edward, John Richard, David Winslow, James Jordan, Anne, George. Resident physician Michael Reese Hosp., Chicago, 1919, Cook County Hosp., 1920-21 research, John McCormick Inst. Infectious Diseases, 1921-24; dir. pathol. lab., St. Joseph Hosp., since 1922, pres. of staff, 1934; attending staff Passavant Hosp.; formerly attending physician Cook County Hosp.; prof. medicine Northwestern U. Licentiate Am. Bd. Internal Medicine; fellow Am. Coll. of Physicians; mem. Chicago Soc. of Internal Medicine, A.M.A., Chicago Med. Soc., Chicago Pathol. Soc., Inst. Medicine, Chicago, Sigma Xi, Nu Sigma Nu. Catholic. Clubs: University, Edgewater Golf. Contbr. to Archives Internal Medicine, Jour. Am. Med. Assn., Archives of Pathology. Home: 5322 Lakewood Av. Office: 104 S. Michigan Av., Chgo. Died May 13, 1955.

HINES, Ralph J., lumber; b. Chgo., June 22, 1900; s. Edward and Loretta (O'Dowd) H.; student Phillips Andover Acad., Yale; Ph.B., B.A., M.A., Oxford U., Eng. Sr. v.p. Edward Hines Lumber Co., 1925-32, pres. 1932-42, chmn. bd., 1942-—; pres., dir. Oregon & Northwestern R.R., Edward Hines Farm Land Co., Edward Hines Pacific Coast Lumber Co.; dir. Hines Land & Timber Co., Continental Coal Co. Joined Aviation br. USN, 1942. Clubs: Racquet and Tennis (N.Y.C.); Racquet, Shoreacres (Chgo.). Home: Crescent Rd., Lake Bluff, Ill. Office: 77 W. Washington St., Chgo. Died May 28, 1950.*

HINKLE, Beatrice M. (hing'k'l), psychiatrist; b. San Francisco, Calif., Oct. 10, 1874; d. B. Frederick Mores and Elizabeth (Benchley) Van Geisen; ed. pvt. schs. and under tutors; M.D., Cooper Med. Coll. (now med. dept. Stanford U.), 1899; m. Walter Scott Hinkle, 1892 (died Feb. 7, 1899); children—Walter Mills, Mrs. Consuelo Andoga Shepard. City phys., San Francisco, 1899-1905 (1st woman phys. to hold a public health position); moved to New York, 1905; associated in practice with Dr. Charles R. Dana several yrs.; specializes in psycho-analysis; opened the first psycho-therapeutic clinic in America, at Cornell Med. Coll., N.Y. City, 1908. Mem. A.M.A., Am. Neurol. Soc., New York Acad. of Medicine, Am. Assn. for the Advancement of Sci., Am. Psychiatric Assn., Nat. Inst. Social Sciences. Author: The Re-Creating of the Individual, 1923; also numerous monographs on psycho-analysis and psychol. subjects. Lecturer on psychol. subjects. Translator: The Psychology of the Unconscious (by C. G. Jung), 1916; The Living and the Lifeless (by Dirk Coster), 1929. Home: Roughlands, Washington, Conn. Office: 31 Gramercy Park, N.Y.C. Died Feb. 28, 1953.

HINKLE, Elmer Forry, business exec.; b. Columbia, Pa., Sept. 22, 1907; s. Samuel Wisler and Elziabeth Elmira (Forry) H.; student Franklin Marshall Coll., 1925-26; Ph.B., Phila. Coll. Pharmacy and Sci., 1930; m. Violet E. Myers Aug. 8, 1936; children—Mary Elizabeth, Susanne Forry. Profl. rep. Sharp & Dohme, 1930-32; dir. ednl. dept. Hershey Chocolate Corp., 1932-35, sales promotion mgr., 1935-47; dir. purchases Automatic Canteen Co. Am., 1947-48, v.p. in charge sales and purchases, 1948-50, pres., 1950-—, also dir.; pres., dir. Canteen Co., Elizabeth Candy, Inc., Automatic Canteen Co. of Can., Ltd. Mem. Kappa Psi. Republican. Lutheran. Mason (Shriner). Clubs: Union League, Executives, Merchants and Manufacturers, Rotary (Chgo.); Michigan Shores (Wilmette). Contbr. articles trade jours. Home: 1943 Greenwood Av., Wilmette, Ill. Office: Merchandise Mart Plaza, Chgo. 54. Died Nov. 1, 1957; buried Hershey, Pa.

HINKLE, Frederick Wallis, lawyer; b. Cin., Jan. 3, 1870; s. Thornton Mills and Helen F. (Sage) H.; A.B., Yale, 1892; LL.B., Cincinnati Law Sch., 1894; m. Susanna R. Walsh, Apr. 9, 1917. In practice, Cin., 1894-—; treas. Guardian Bank and Savings Co. (formerly Morris Plan Bank), 1918-—, v.p., 1937-—; instr. med. jurisprudence Pulte Med. Coll., Cin., 1896-1900; formerly hon. curator, arms and armour, Art Museum Assn.; rec. sec. Hist. and Philos. Soc. Ohio, 1913-31; sec. trustees Sinking Fund, Cin., 1906; dir. Young Men's Merc. Library Assn., 1895-—, pres. 1908; treas. Cin. Law Library Assn., 1921-—; chmn. exec. com. Cincinnati Assn. for Welfare of the Blind, 1920-23, sec., 1923-—; mem. Board of Health, City Cin., 1924, resigned; mem. Board Park Commrs., 1924-—; mem. City Planning Commn., of Cincinnati, 1926-—; chairman adv. bd. Good 1924-30; mem. Recreation Commn. of Cin., 1926-—; chmn. adv. bd. Good Samaritan Hosp., 1926-30; trustee Art Museum Assn., 1925-40, resigned; dir. Cin. Musical Festival Assn., 1924-44; mem. adv. bd. Cin. YMCA; mem. Ohio Revolutionay Memorial Commn., 1929-40; trustee Cin. Coll. Music, 1927-32; chmn. bd. Better Business Bur., 1937-—. Trustee Zoöl. Soc. Cin., 1933-—, Bethesda Hosp., 1938-44. Mem. Cin. Bar Assn., Lit. Club (sec. 1915-17, v.p. 1917, pres. 1918), Mil. Order Loyal Legion (registrar 1915-23, recorder 1923-26, jr. vice-comdr. 1926, sr. vice-comdr. 1927-29, comdr. 1929), Ohio State Archaeol. and Hist. Soc., S.R., U.S. Army Ordnance Assn. (pres. post 1929), Nat. Assn. Travelers Aid Socs. (dir. 1929-33), Travelers Aid Soc. Cin. (former pres.). Club: Cincinnati (v.p. 1925, pres. 1926). Home: Edwards and Walsh Rd., Cin. 8. Office: Union Trust Bldg., Cin. Died Dec. 4, 1950; buried Spring Grove Cemetery, Cin.

HINKLE, Ross Oel, lawyer; b. Fenton, Mich, Nov. 2, 1883; s. William H. and Lyla A. (Jones) H.; B.S., U. Mich., 1906; LL.B., Chgo.-Kent Coll. Law, 1912; m. Gladys Hallam, May 31, 1913; 1 son, William Hallam. Telephone engr. Western Electric Co., Chgo., 1906-12, mem. patent dept., 1912-16; admitted to Ill. bar, 1912; mem. firm Forse, Bain & Hinkle, Chgo., 1919-24, Williams, Bradbury, McCaleb & Hinkle, 1924-40, Williams Bradbury & Hinkle, 1940-46; with Hinkle, Horton, Ahlberg, Hansmann & Wupper, 1946-—. Mem. bd. edn. Riverside-Brookfield High Sch., 1934-42, pres., 1941-42. Mem. Am., Ill., Chgo. bar assns., Chgo. Patent Law Assn., Phi Delta Phi. Republican. Presbyn. Mason. Clubs: Union League. Home: 70 Woodside Rd., Riverside, Ill. Office: 141 Jackson Blvd., Chgo. 4. Deceased.*

HINMAN, Dale Durkee, army officer; b. Cherokee, Ia., Nov. 4, 1891; s. Frank Melvin and Ida Emerita (Durkee) H.; E.M., Colo. Sch. of Mines, 1915; grad. Command and Gen. Staff Sch., 1927, War Coll., 1934; m. Mrs. Elizabeth H. Kirkpatrick, Jan. 2, 1940; children (by 1st marriage)—Georgiana M., Frank M. Mining engr., 1915-16; commd. U.S. Army, Nov. 30, 1916, advanced through the grades to brig. gen. (temp.), 1941; comdg. gen. 38th Coast Arty. Brigade, 1941-42; Office of Chief of Coast Arty., 1942-—. Mem. Tau Beta Phi, Beta Theta Pi. Presbyn. Club: Army and Navy (Washington). Address: Office, Chief of Coast Artillery, War Dept., Washington. Died Dec. 26, 1949.*

HINMAN, Harold J., lawyer; b. Albany, N.Y., Feb. 22, 1877; s. Addison J. and Susan Mary (Hotaling) H.; Ph.B., Union Coll., 1899, A.M., 1924, LL.D., 1939; LL.B., Albany Law Sch., 1901; m. Lucy E. Warner, June 7, 1906; children—Mildred H. Straub, Martha H. Ellis, Edward Hawley (dec.). Practiced in Albany, 1901-18; justice Supreme Ct. of N.Y., 3d Jud. Dist., term 1918-32. Assigned to appellate div. 3d dept., 1922-32; ofcl. referee Supreme Court, 1933-40; now member of firm Hinman, Straub & Manning; dir. and mem. exec. com. Glens Falls Ins. Co. Mem. N.Y. Assembly, 1910-15 (chmn. judiciary com., 1912, minority leader, 1913, majority leader, 1914, 15); mem. Constl. Conv., 1915; dep. atty. gen., 1915-18; pres. Bd. of Edn., Albany, N.Y., 1918. Pres. bd. trustees Albany Law Sch.; v.p. bd. trustees Albany Public Library; life trustee Union Coll., Albany Med. Coll., Dudley Obs., Albany Acad. for Girls; pres. bd. govs. Union Univ. Mem. Alpha Delta Phi, Phi Beta Kappa. Clubs: University, Albany Country. Home: 292 State St. Office: 90 State St., Albany, N.Y. Died Feb. 21, 1955.

HINMAN, Harvey DeForest, lawyer; b. Pitcher, Chenango County, N.Y., Sept. 17, 1864; s. Edward and Eveline E. (DeBell) H.; prep. edn. Cincinnatus (N.Y.) Acad.; LL.B., Albany Law Sch. (Union Coll.), 1889; m. Phebe A. Brown, Nov. 27, 1901; 1 son, George L. Practiced in Binghamton, N.Y., 1891-—; dir. 1st Nat. Bank of Binghamton, Security Mutual Life Insurance Company, D.L.&W. Fuel & Supply Company, Inc., Binghamton Gas Works. Mem. N.Y. Senate, 1905-13; Rep. canidate for gov. of N.Y., 1914; sr. mem. firm of Hinman, Howard & Kaltell since Jan. 1, 1900. Presbyn. Mason. Home: 93 Chestnut St. Office: Security Mut. Bldg., Binghamton, N.Y. Died July 11, 1954.

HINSHAW, (John) Carl (Williams), congressman; b. Chicago, Ill., July 28, 1894; s. William Wade and Anna (Williams) H.; C.E., Princeton U., 1916; grad. student Sch. of Business, U. of Mich., 1916-17; m. Helen Frances Veeder, June 24, 1924 (died Jan. 12, 1929); 1 son, John Veeder; m. 2d, Wilberta Ripley, Jan. 1, 1932; 1 son, William Ripley. Began with Mercury Mfg. Co., Chicago, 1920-23; salesman Walker Vehicle Co., Motor trucks, Chicago, 1923-26; asst. dist. sales mgr., 1924-26; salesman Halsey-Stuart Co., investments, Chicago, 1927-28; with corp. buying dept. Continental Nat Co., investments, Chicago, May-Oct. 1928; real estate investments, Tucson, Ariz., 1928-29; real estate and insurance, Pasadena, Calif., and Hinshaw Huston Co., 1929-32, Morse-Hinshaw Co., 1932-39; mem. 76th and 77th Congresses (1939-43), 11th Cal. Dist., 78th to 84th Congresses from the 20th Cal. Dist.; mem. House Com. on Interstate and Foreign Commerce; mem. Joint Commn. on Atomic Energy; vice chmn. Congressional aviation policy bd. of 80th Congress. President 47th District. Republican Assembly, California, 1934; vice president Los Angeles County Republican Assembly, 1935-36; mem. Republican State Central Com., 1934, 36, 38; Rep. nominee for rep. in Congress, 1936; vice chmn. Rep. Nat. Congl. Com., 1945. Director, Pasadena Realty Bd., 1933-36; dir. Calif. Real Estate Assn. since 1935, exec. chmn. Arroyo-Seco-Parkway Assn. since 1934; v.p. Carmelita Civic Grandstand Assn., Inc., 1937-39; dir. Pasadena C. of C., 1938; mem. Pasadena Tournament of Roses Assn.; chmn. highway legislation coms., Calif. Chamber of Commerce. Served in U.S. Army, May 1917-Sept. 1919; commd. 1st lt., 16th Engrs. (Ry.); with A.E.F., 1 year; disch. as capt. Corps Engrs. Awarded Wright Brothers Meml. Trophy, 1953. Mem. Am. Legion, Vets. Fgn. Wars, World War Engrs. Assn., Soc. Automotive Engrs., S.A.R. (life); mem. American Soc. Civil Engrs.; mem. Inst. Aero. Scis., Astron. Soc. Pacific, Congl. Flying Club (dir. 1945), Princeton Terrace Club, Zeta Psi. Methodist. Mason (32°), Elk. Clubs: Columbia Country (Washington); Overland (Pasadena). Home: 1401 S. Oak Knoll Av., Pasadena, Cal. Office: 1511 House Office Bldg., Washington. Died Aug. 5, 1956.

HINSHAW, David, public relations counsel; born Emporia, Kansas, November 4, 1882; son Stephen Curtis and Hannah (Lee) H.; B.S., Haverford Coll., 1911; married Augusta Wiggam, July 1, 1916 (deceased 1949); children—Robert Y., Sarah. Field representative of the Progressive National Committee (Bull Moose), 1912-14; mem. personal staff of Herbert Hoover, Oct. 1927-Nov. 1928; served in various capacities in Republican Presidential campaigns since 1916; directed Latin-Am. pub. relations Standard Oil Co. (N.J.), 1938-41; v.p. Inst. of Pub. Relations 1942-48; Honnold lecturer, Knox Coll., Galesburg, Ill., 1933; conducted private pub. relations business many years. Vice pres. and trustee Oscar S. Straus Memorial Assn.; trustee, mem. exec. com. and v.p. Theodore Roosevelt Memorial Assn.; trustee, mem. Haverford College Corp., William Allen White Foundation; member at large, Am. Friends Service Com., Save the Children Fedn. Awarded Theodore Roosevelt medal, 1949; decorated Commander of Order of Lion (Finland), 1950. Republican. Quaker. Clubs: Union League, Nat. Republican, Rockefeller Center Luncheon (New York); University (Washington). Author: Stop, Look and Listen, 1932; Sowing the Wind, 1937; The Home Front, 1943; Journalism—Today's Third Estate, delivered at Pulitzer Sch. of Journalism, Columbia U., May 1943; Political Party Platforms, 1944; A Man From Kansas: The Story of William Allen White, 1945; An Experiment in Friendship, 1947; Take Up They Bed and Walk, 1948; Sweden: Champion of Peace, 1949; Herbert Hoover, American Quaker, 1950; Rufus Jones, Master Quaker, 1951; Heroic Finland, 1952. Home: Dunmow Farm, West Chester, Pa. Died Nov. 5, 1953.

HINSHAW, Virgil Goodman, prohibition worker; b. Woolson, Ia., Jan. 15, 1876; s. Ezra I. and Glaphrey (Shelley) H.; A.B., Penn Coll. Ia., 1900; LL.B., Law Dept., U. of Minn., 1908; m. Eva C. Piltz, Sept. 6, 1911 (died Jan. 28, 1923); children—Harold, Randall, Robert Patton, Virgil; m. 2d, Nettella Loy, Aug. 1924; children—Harvey Loy, Paul Milas. Traveling sec. Nat. Intercollegiate Prohibition Assn., 1900-06 and 1908-10 (traveled to 185 colls.); practiced law in Portland, Ore., 1910-12; chmn. Prohibition Party Nat. Com., 1912-24; founder and first pres. Prohibition Foundation, Inc., 1916; supt. Internat. Reform Federation, 1923-26; extension secretary same, 1926-30, and internat sec., 1930-43. Traveled and organized Prohibition movement in Austria, Germany and Czechoslovakia, 1921. Worked with D. A. Poling and allied forces in 33 states to save 18th amendment, 1931-33, concentrating in Calif. fall of 1932, all of 1933. Mem. Nat. Temperance Council and Nat. Legislative Conf. since their orgn.; served as extension sec. Meth. Bd. of Temperance, Prohibition and Pub. Morals, 1921-22. Organizer and mem. Calif. Drys, Inc. (orgn. for State prohibition amendment); chmn. Southern Calif. Prohibition Com.; chmn. Prohibition Education Foundation. Chmn. Calif. State Prohibition Com., 1944-46; candidate State Comptroller, 1946, 50; polled largest Prohibition Party vote in U.S. Quaker and Methodist; campaigned to save Kan. prohibition amendment, 1948. Home and office: 935 N. Oakland Av., Pasadena 6, Cal. Died Aug. 3, 1952; buried Mountain View, Pasadena.

HINSON, Noel Bertram, engr.; b. Evansville, Ind., Dec. 25, 1885; s. John Thomas and Sally Margaret (Vick) H.; grad. Los Angeles High Sch.; student Internat. Corr. Sch.; m. Ethel Florence Adland, June 20, 1911 (dec. Nov. 28, 1929); 1 dau., Barbara Jane (Mrs. Burton Cliffe Kaye); m. 2d Lois Myerhoff, June 18, 1931. With So. Calif. Edison Co. and its predecessor, Edison Electric Co., 1906-51, v.p., exec. engr., 1945-51, ret. Jan. 1, 1951. Mem. elec. power survey com. Edison Electric Inst., 1948-52; chmn. Pacific S.W. Power Interchange Com., 1943-52. Registered professional engineer, California. Fellow Am. Inst. E.E. (v.p. 1935-37, dir. 1949-53); mem. A.A.A.S., Astron. Soc. Pacific, Pacific Coast Elec. Assn., Tau Beta Pi (hon. mem.). Mason. Clubs: Univ., Electric (Los Angeles); Oneonta (South Pasadena). Contbr. articles population growth, planning electric utilities. Home: 1709 Marengo Av., South Pasadena, Cal. Died Apr. 16, 1958.

HINTON, Charles Louis, painter, sculptor; b. Ithaca, N.Y., 1869; s. Louis Josiah and Jane (Edwards) H.; student pub. schs., Clapham, Eng.; studied art, N.A.D., N.Y.C. (winner traveling scholarship); studied Julian Acad. and Ecole des Beaux Arts, Paris; m. Grace A. Boyce, Sept. 17, 1906; children—Charles Louis, Edgar Douglas, Susanne Jane. Tchr. drawing N.A.D., 1901-—, now dean N.A.D. Sch. of Fine Arts. Has exhibited paintings and small bronzes in numerous exhbns., N.Y. C.; painted life-size mural painting for Orphans' Court, City Court House, Wilkes-Barre, Pa.; 14 life size panels, mural, Second Nat. Bank, Wilkes-Barre; historic medals, Lincoln Medal, Lindbergh Medal. Nat. Academician; mem. Nat. Sculpture Soc. (ex-sec.). Illustrator: Under the Trees and Elsewhere. (by Hamilton Wright Mabie), 1893; Emmy Lou (by George Madden Martin), 1902; many illustrations in mags. Home: 74 Gard Av., Bronxville, N.Y. Office: 109th St. and Amsterdam Av., N.Y.C. Died Oct. 12, 1950.

HINTON, Harold B., author, journalist; b. Frederick, Ill., June 9, 1898; s. Harlan and Emma (Boaz) H.; grad. Sewanee Mil. Acad., 1914; A.B., U. of the South, 1917; A.M., Vanderbilt U., 1920; m. Eva Robertson, Nov. 23, 1920; 1 son, Harold Clendenin. Began in newspaper work, 1919; successively with New York World Washington Bur., Nashville Tennessean and N.Y. Times; mem. editorial staff N.Y. Times, Paris and London, 1923-32, assigned to Washington Bur., 1932; asst. to J. P. Kennedy at Am. Embassy, London, 1938; asst. to sec. of Def. James Forrestal, 1948-49. Enlisted Air Service, Apr. 1917; commd. 1st lt., 1918; served with A.E.F., 16 mos.; called to active duty with Air Corps, Apr. 28, 1941, and assigned as asst. intelligence officer, 3d Air Force, Tampa, Fla., with rank of major; asst. chief of staff, Intelligence, Hdqrs. 12th Air Force in Italy, as colonel; reverted inactive duty, March 28, 1946. Awarded Legion of Merit, Army Commendation Ribbon, Croix de Guerre, with Palm (France). Democrat. Episcopal. Clubs: Nat. Press (Washington), Chevy Chase. Author: America Gropes for Peace, 1937; Cordell Hull, 1942; Air Victory; The Men and The Machines, 1948. Articles on futility of "neutrality policy" which was written into law appeared in North American Review, New York Times Mag. and elsewhere, 1936-41. Home: 1425 34th St. N.W. Address: New York Times, 1701 K St. N.W., Washington. Died Mar. 12, 1954; buried Arlington Nat. Cemetery.

HINTON, Raymond J., dir. dependents claims, Veterans Adminstrn. Home: 1314 Hemlock St. N.W., Washington. Dir. Apr. 6, 1958; buried Arlington Nat. Cemetery.

HIRE, Cha(rle)s, prof.; b. Whitley Co., Ind., Dec. 1, 1887; s. Simon W. and Anna Catharine (Seymour) H.; A.B., Ind. U., 1915, M.A., 1917, Ph.D., 1927; m. Frances Willard Swain, June 13, 1920; children—Helen Margaret (Mrs. Herbert Neal Drennon), Eleanore Ann. Rural sch. teacher, Whitley County, Ind., 1907-08, 1909-10 high sch. prin., Churubusco, Ind., 1912-14; physics lab. asst., Ind. U., 1915-17, physics instr., 1919-23, asst. prof. physics, 1923-25, prof. physics, since 1943, supervisor physics instrn., A.S.T.P., 1943-44, acting chmn. dept. physics, 1944-45; head dept. phys. sciences, Murray State Coll., 1925-43, dir. summer session, 1931, dir. and coordinator civilian pilot training, 1940-43. Served as capt. ordnance dept. A.E.F., 1917-19. Fellow A.A.A.S.; mem. Am. Phys. Soc., Am. Assn. Physics Teachers, Am. Assn. Univ. Profs., Sch. and Soc., Sigma Xi. Republican. Methodist. Mason. Author: Laboratory Studies in College Physics, College Physics for General Education. Home: 215 E. 8th St. Office: Indiana University, Bloomington, Ind. Died Sept. 8, 1952.

HIRSCH, Gustav, cons. engr.; b. Columbus, O., Nov. 4, 1876; s. Leonhard and Charlotta (Meyer) H.; M.E. in Elec. Engring., Ohio State U., 1897; m. Aletta Kremer, Aug. 12, 1899; 1 dau., Irene Dorothea. Cons. engrs., builder or engr. of utility properties in all states, 1902-—; v.p. and dir. Conneaut Telephone Co.; pres., dir. Warren Telephone Co., Gustave Hirsch Orgn., Skyway Broadcasting Co.; v.p., dir. Mansfield Telephone Co., United Utilities, Inc.; dir. Elyria Telephone Co., Cosmo Investors Corp., Jaeger Machine Co. Dir. Ohio Mental Health. Served from pvt. to capt. O.N.G., 1893-96, 1899-1901; 2d lt., Signal Corps, U.S. Army, Spanish-Am. War; maj. and lt. col., Signal Corps, U.S. Army, 1917-19, now lt. col. U.S. Army retired. Decorated French Verdun medal. Registered engr., Ohio. Fellow Am. Geog. Soc.; mem. Am. Soc. M.E., Am. Inst. E.E., Am., Ohio socs. profl. engrs., A.A.A.S., Ind. Telephone Pioneers, Am. Legion, U.S. Veteran Signal Corps Assn., United Spanish War Vets. (dir.), Ohio Independent Telephone Assn., Independent Telephone Pioneers of America, Tau Beta Pi. Elk. Clubs: Columbus Athletic, Scioto Country, Columbus Riding (Columbus). Home: 2459 Tremont Rd. Office: 1347 W. 5th Av., Columbus 12, O. Died Jan. 7, 1959; buried Green Lawn Cemetery, Columbus.

HIRSHBERG, Herbert Simon, librarian; b. Boston, Mass., July 7, 1879; s. Simon and Eva (Warschauer) H.; A.B., Harvard, 1900; B.L.S., N.Y. State Library Sch., 1905; m. Blanche A. L. Lowe, June 16, 1910; children—Robert Lowe and Richard Lowe (twins), Herbert Simon, Walter Andrew. Cataloguer, Boston Pub. Library, 1902-03; asst. N.Y. State Library, 1904-05; asst. music div. Library of Congress, 1905-06; asst. and branch librarian, Carnegie Library, Pittsburgh, 1906-08; reference librarian, Cleveland Pub. Library, 1908-14; instr. Western Reserve U. Library Sch., 1909-14; librarian Pub. Library, Toledo, 1914-22; librarian, Ohio State Library, 1922-27; librarian Pub. Library, Akron, O., 1927-29; dean Sch. of Library Science, Western Reserve, 1929-43, dir. libraries, 1929-45; editorial consultant, Americana Corporation, 1945-—. Pres. bd. trustees, Pub. Library, Winter Park, Fla. Mem. A.L.A. Bd. of Edn. for Librarianship, 1925-30; camp librarian, A.L.A. at Great Lakes Naval Training Sta., Chicago, June-Oct. 1918. Fellow, Am. Library Inst. Life mem. A.L.A. (mem. council, 2d v.p. 1937-38); mem. Ohio Library Assn. (pres. 1917-18), Assn. Am. Library Schs. (v.p. 1939-40), Fla. Library Assn. Clubs: Rowfant, University (librarian), Winter Park (Winter Park, Fla.). Author: Subject Guide to Reference Books, 1942, 2d ed., 1952; Subject Guide to U.S. government publications (with C. H. Melinat), 1947. Home: Merrill, N.Y. and 788 Bonita Dr., Winter Park, Fla. Died Sept 15, 1955.

HIRTH, Emma P., gen. sec. Nat. Bd. of YWCA of U.S.A. Address: 600 Lexington Av., N.Y.C. Died May 8, 1951.

HITCH, Arthur Martin, educator; b. Cuba, Mo., Feb. 26, 1875; s. Charles R. and Ruth E. (Martin) H.; student Mo. Sch. Mines, Rolla, Mo., 1892-93; A.B., U. Mo., 1897, B.S. in Edn., 1907, A.M., 1934; LL.D., Westminster College, 1944; m. Bertha Johnston, June 27, 1908; children—Charles Johnston, Thomas Kemper. Began teaching, 1897; with Kemper Military Sch., 1899-—, v.p. and prin., 1907-27, supt. 1927-49, pres., 1934-—. Lt. col. O.R.C. Vice pres. N. Central Assn. Colleges and Secondary Schs., 1933-34; pres. Assn. of Mil. Colls. and Schs. U.S., 1932-33; pres. Am. Assn. Junior Coll., 1933-34. Regent Central Mo. State Tchrs. Coll., 1937-49, pres. bd., 1942-—. Mem. N.E.A. Republican. Presbyn. Mason, Rotarian (gov. 134th dist. internat. 1944-45). Author: Cadet Days of Will Rogers. Home: 601 3d St., Boonville, Mo. Died Feb. 20, 1956; buried Walnut Grove Cemetery, Boonville.

HITCHCOCK, Alfred Marshall, teacher, author; b. Troy, N.Y., May 7, 1868; s. Rufus Clark and Louisa (St. John) H.; A.B., Williams Coll., 1890, A.M. (hon.), 1921; A.M., Dartmouth, 1896; m. Harriet May Thompson, July 17, 1900. Teacher, Hartford Pub. High School, 1897-1924. Mem. Phi Delta Theta. Republican. Conglist. Clubs: Williams (New York); University, Twentieth Century (Hartford). Author: A Practice-Book in English Composition, 1906; Theme-Book in English Composition, 1910; Rhetoric and the Study of Literature, 1913; Composition and Rhetoric, 1913; New Practice-Book in English Composition, 1914; Over Japan Way, 1917; Junior English Book, 1920; High School English Book, 1923; Bread Loaf Talks on Teaching Composition, 1927; Study Plans for Novels, 1927; Bread Loaf Talks on Teaching Literature, 1928; Composition and Grammar, 1929; Sentence Craft (with Alfred A. Wright), 1931; A New England Boyhood, 1934; Lucy, Perhaps, 1935;

Drill. 1935. Editor: The Alhambra (Irving). 1899; Ivanhoe (Scott), 1900; Lady of the Lake (Scott), 1911. Home: 41 Woodrow St., West Hartford 7, Conn. Died Apr. 14, 1941; buried Simsbury, Conn.

HITCHCOCK, Frank Lauren, mathematician; b. N.Y.C., Mar. 6, 1875; s. Elisha Pike and Susan Ida (Porter) H.; A.B., Harvard, 1896, Ph.D., 1910; student U. of Paris, France, 1897-1903, U. Cin., 1906-07; m. Margaret Johnson Blakely, May 25, 1899; children—Lauren B., George B. Asst. in chemistry, Harvard, 1895-96; instr. chemistry, Milton (Mass.) Acad., 1896-97; prof. chemistry Fargo (N.D.) Coll., 1903-06; instr. chemistry, Franklin Sch., Cin., 1906-07; asst. prof. physics, Kenyon Coll., 1907-09; instr. mathematics, Mass. Inst. Tech., 1910-17, asst. prof., 1917-49, ret. 1949. Fellow Am. Acad. Arts and Sciences; mem. Internat. Soc. for Promotion Study of Quaternions and Allied Branches, Sigma Xi. Author: (with Clark S. Robinson) Differential Equations in Applied Chemistry. Conglist. Home: Hillside Terrace, Belmont, Mass. Died May 29, 1957.

HITCHLER, Theresa (Marie Therese Franziska), librarian; b. N.Y.C.; d. Peter and Katherine (Hanna) H.; student Hunter Coll., N.Y.C.; spl. student N.Y. State Library Sch., 1898. Head cataloger New York Free Circulating Library, 1899; supt. cataloging dept. Bklyn. Pub. Library, 1899—; instr. library science Simmons Coll., Boston, 1914. Riverside (Cal.) Summer Library Sch., 1916, 18, 21, 22; chief instr. summer sch. of the Ecole de Bibliothécaires, Paris, 1924; lecturer before library schs. Fellow Am. Library Inst.; mem. A.L.A. (exec. bd.), N.Y. Library Assn. (ex-pres.), N.J., Cal. library assns., L.I. Library Club (ex-pres.), N.Y. Library club (ex-pres.), N.E.A., City, State and Nat. library clubs; hon. mem. Mass. Library Club. Episcopalian. Clubs: Town Hall, American Woman's. Wrote: Cataloging for Small Libraries, Comparative Cataloging Rules; also articles for Library Jour. Home: 1036 Logan Av., N.Y.C. 61. Deceased.

HITCHLER, Walter Harrison, dean of law; b. Plymouth, Pa., Feb. 20, 1883; s. Adolph Frederick and Alice Carey (Harman) H.; B.L., U. of Va., 1905; D.C.L., Dickinson Coll., 1932; LL.D., Saint Francis Coll., Loretta, Pa., 1932, Muhlenberg Coll., 1939, Albright College, Reading, Pa., 1943. Editor Michie Pub. Co., Charlottesville, Va., 1905-06; tchr. Dickinson Sch. of Law, Carlisle, Pa., 1906-17; editor Statuatory Law of Pa., 1919-23; tchr. Dickinson Sch. of Law, 1919-30, dean of sch., 1930-54. Chmn. Pa. Liquor Control Bd., 1939-40; chmn. Alien Enemy Hearing Bd., U.S. Dept. of Justice, 1941—. Admitted to bars of Pa. and Va. Served as 2d lt. inf., U.S. Army, 1918-19; 1st lt. O.R.C., 1919-23, capt., 1923—. Mem. Am., Pa. bar aasns., Raven Soc. (U. of Va.), Am. Law Inst. Episcopalian. Mason. Clubs: Rotary, Carlisle Country; Penn Athletic (Phila.). Contbr. to Dickinson Law Review. Home: Sadler Curtilage, Carlisle, Pa. Died Feb. 5, 1959.

HITE, George E., Jr., partner, Milbank, Tweed, Hope & Hadley; born at Wheeling, W.Va., 1886, ed. Williams Coll., 1908, Columbia U. Law School, 1911, N.Y. City; chmn. bd. Arnold Constable Corp.; v.p. and dir. Faspray Corp.; dir. Northern Ins. Co. of N.Y., Assurance Co. of America. Home: Greenwich, Conn. Office: 15 Broad St., N.Y.C. Died Nov. 1, 1950.

HITER, Frank Ambrose (hī' ter), business exec.; b. Owensboro, Ky., Mar. 27, 1892; s. Forest Ashby and Fanny (Ambrose) H.; grad. Tenn. Mil. Acad., Sweetwater, 1910; m. Florence Dillon, Dec. 21, 1939. Automobile distbr., Louisville, 1912-15; retailer automobile accessories, 1915-18; asst. sales mgr. Alemite Corp., 1920-24, v.p., gen. sales mgr., 1924-33; v.p., gen. sales mgr. Stewart-Warner Corp., 1933-44, sr. v.p. since 1944, also dir.; dir. Williamson Candy Co., United Wallpaper, Inc. Served with 312th F.A., A.E.F., 1918-19. Presbyn. (bd. trustees). Clubs: Racquet, Tavern (Chgo.); Glen View Country (Golf, Ill.). Home: 1448 Lake Shore Dr., Chgo. 10. Office: 1826 Diversey Parkway, Chgo. 10. Died Apr. 9, 1955; buried Rosehill Cemetery, Chgo.

HOAG, Gilbert Thomas (hoig), coll. dean; b. Lewiston, Me., Sept. 20, 1899; s. Clarence Gilbert and Anna (Scattergood) H.; grad. Phillips Exeter, 1916; A.B., Haverford Coll., 1920; A.M., Harvard, 1925, Ph.D., 1937; m. Katharine Harris, June 25, 1927; children—Katharine Van Alen, Margaret Garrett, Elizabeth Thacher. Clk. Brown Brothers and Co., 1921-23; asst. mgr. bond dept. Parrish & Co., 1923-24; instr. English and tutor in div. of modern langs. Harvard, 1927-28; instr. English, Amherst Coll., 1928-38; dean and prof. English, Kenyon Coll., Gambirer, O., 1938-45, on leave as cons., meteorology program USAAF, 1942-43, coordinator mil. programs, 1943-44, on leave as dir. of training, later as asst. to exec. dir., overseas br. O.W.I., 1944-45; dean Haverford Coll., 1945—. Sherman Pratt Faculty Fellow in Scandinavia and Germany, 1935-36. Home: Haverford College, Haverford, Pa. Died Sept. 17, 1952.

HOAGLAND, Denis Robert (hōg'länd), prof. plant nutrition; b. Golden, Colo., Apr. 2, 1884; s. Charles Breckenridge and Lillian May (Burch) H.; A.B., Stanford, 1907; A.M., U. Wis., 1913; m. Jessie A. Smiley, May 1, 1920 (dec.); children—Albert Smiley, Charles Rightmire, Robert Charles. Asst. and instr. agrl. chemistry U. Cal., 1907-10, asst. prof. agrl. chemistry, 1913-20, asso. prof. plant nutrition, 1920-25, prof., 1927—, faculty research lectr., 1942, head div. of plant nutrition, 1921—, chmn. dept. botany, 1934-36, asso. chemist Agrl. Expt. Sta., 1920-25, chemist, 1925—; research chemist U.S. Dept. Agr., 1910-12. Received Stephen Hales prize Am. Soc. Plant Physiologists, 1930; joint recipient A.A.A.S. prize, 1940. Fellow A.A.A.S. (pres. Pacific div., 1941), Am. Acad. Arts and Scis.; mem. Western Soc. Soil Science (pres. 1924), Am. Soc. Hort. Science, Am. Soc. Agronomy, Internat. Soc. Soil Science, Nat. Acad. Science, Am. Chem. Soc., Am. Soc. Naturalists, Bot. Soc. Am., Am. Soc. Plant Physiologists (pres. 1932), Western Soc. Naturalists (pres. 1931). Club: Faculty (U. of Calif.). Cons. editor Soil Science; mem. bd. editors Ann. Rev. Biochemistry. Contbr. sci. articles on results of research on mineral nutrition on plants. Home: 839 Indian Rock Av., Berkeley, Cal. Died Sept. 5, 1949.

HOBART, Lewis Parsons, architect; b. St. Louis, Jan. 14, 1873; s. George Lewis and Virginia (Easton) H.; ed. U. of Calif., 1893-94, Am. Acad. at Rome, 1894-95, Beaux Arts Inst. of Design, Paris, 1900-02; m. Mabel Deming, Apr. 30, 1903; children—Lewis Deming, John Easton. Practiced in New York, 1904, San Francisco, 1906—. Works: Firemen's Fund Ins. Co. Bldg., U. Cal. Hosp., Wm. Taylor Hotel, Mills Tower, Grace Cathedral—all of San francisco; U.S Post Office Bldg., Portland, Ore.; Del Monte (Cal.) Hotel; Golden Gate Internat. Expn.; Bohemian Club; San Francisco Zoöl. Gardens. Elected first pres. Art Commn. City and County of San Francisco, 1932. Fellow A.I.A.; mem. Am. Acad. at Rome, Soc. Beaux Arts Architects. Episcopalian. Clubs: Pacific Union, Bohemian. Home: 2275 Broadway. Office: 525 Market St., San Francisco. Died Oct. 19, 1954.

HOBBIE, Henry Martin, merchant; b. Montgomery, Ala., Dec. 3, 1880; s. Henry M. and Leonora Elizabeth (Jackson) H.; student U. of Ala., 1897-98; m. Bessie Rogers, Jan. 18, 1911; children—Henry Martin, Ethel Leann. Began in mercantile bus., Montgomery, 1898; pres. Fourth Nat. Bank, 1919—; pres. H. M. Hobbie Grocery Co., Hobbie Elevator Co., Hobbie Motor Car Co.; v.p. All States Life Ins. Co.; v.p., treas. Home Bond & Mortgage Co. Served as agt. U.S. Treasury, 1916, 17, handling crop moving funds for orderly marketing; chmn. for State of Ala., War Finance Corp., 1921-23. Mem. Sigma Alpha Epsilon. Democrat. Methodist. Clubs: Rotary, Montgomery Country. Home: 618 S. Perry St., Montgomery, Ala. Died Feb. 22, 1944.

HOBBINS, James R(ussell), mining; b. Madison, Wis., Aug. 19, 1883; s. Joseph William and Mary Newton (Mears) H.; student U. Wis., 1900-01; m. Bertha May Bollinger, Aug. 3, 1908; 1 dau., Mary Alice. State and spl. agr. for fire ins., 1904-10; surveyor and constrn. engr., 1910-12; in comml. dept. Great Falls (Mont.) Power Co., 1912-16; mgr. No. Mont. div., also Mont. Power Co., 1916-22; asst. to pres. Anaconda Copper Mining Co., 1922-23, became v.p., dir., 1923, exec. v.p., 1936-40, pres., 1940—; pres. Butte Water Co., Andes Copper Mining Co., Chile Copper Co., Chile Exploration Co.; v.p., dir. Butte Anaconda & Pacific Ry. Co.; dir. Nat. City Bank of N.Y., Mines Investment Corp., Copper Export Assn., Am. Brass Co., Anaconda Sales Co., Internat. Smelting & Refining Co., Anaconda Wire and Cable Co. Mem. Kappa Sigma. Clubs: Butte Country (Butte); Montana (Helena); India House, City Midday, The Links, Recess, Canadian, Madison Square Garden (N.Y.C.); Sleepy Hollow Country (Scarborough, N.Y.). Office: 25 Broadway, N.Y.C. Died Nov. 14, 1949.

HOBBS, Franklin Warren, ret. textile exec.; b. Roxbury, Mass., Sept. 24, 1868; s. William and Mary Marland (Cogswell) H.; S.B., Mass. Inst. Tech., 1889; studied at Bradford (Eng.) Textile Coll., 1891; hon. M.Sc., Dartmouth, 1913; D.Sc., Middlebury College, 1942; D.Textile Sc., U. S.C., 1948; m. Jane Hallett Whitman, May 31, 1892 (dec.); children—Wm. Whitman, Marland Cogswell, Franklin Warren (died 1935), Rebekah. Instr. mech. engring. Mass. Inst. Tech., 1889-91; entered employ of Arlington Mills, 1891 (now div. William Whitman Co., Inc.); treas., pres. and exec. officer, 1902-46; Arlington Mills acquired William Whitman Co., Inc. (selling agents), changing name to William Whitman Co., Inc., 1946; chmn. bd. William Whitman Co., Inc., ret. 1952; dir. Arkwright Mutual Fire Ins. Co.; trustee Mt. Auburn Cemetery. Chmn. bd. dirs. Wentworth Inst.; life mem. Corp. Mass. Inst. Tech.; chmn. bd. Textile Found. Chmn. bd. Brookline, Mass. Sch. Com., 1904-15. Ex-pres. Nat. Assn. Cotton Mfrs.; sr. v.p., dir. Nat. Assn. Wool Mfrs.; mem. Am. soc. M.E., C. of C. Boston, Soc. Colonial Wars, S.R. Republican. Episcopalian (past pres. Mass. club). Clubs: Republican of Mass., Union, Commercial (ex-pres.), Country, Republican. Home: 192 Commonwealth Av. Office: 78 Chauncy St., Boston. Died June 16, 1955.

HOBBS, Gustavus Warfield, Jr., clergyman, editor; b. Washington, D.C., Aug. 29, 1876; s. Rev. Gustavus Warfield and Jeannette Dawson (Richardson) H.; A.B., Baltimore City Coll., 1896; D.D., U. of South; m. Augusta Richardson Kent, of Baltimore, Md., Oct. 18, 1902; children—Gustavus Warfield III, Mary Richard (Mrs. Wilfred B. Fry). City staff, Baltimore American, 1897; Spanish-Am. War corr., 1898-99; Washington corr., city editor, mng. editor, Phila. Pub. Ledger, 1903-16; art dir. Cyrus H. K. Curtiss Newspaper Publs., 1914-16; editor Baltimore Sunday Sun, 1916-23. Ordained deacon, 1923, priest, 1925, P.E. Ch.; editorial sec. Nat. Council P.E. Ch., 1923; editor The Spirit of Missions and Church at Work; exec. sec. dept. of Publicity Nat. Council, P.E. Ch., 1926; now retired; chaplain Md. chpt. Sons Colonial Wars. Capt. chaplain 107th Inf., Nat. Guard, New York. Club: Nat. Arts. Author: The Japan-Russian War, 1905; (with Dr. Ralph S. Tarr) The Geology of the San Francisco Disaster, 1906. Pen name, Sydney Tyler. Address: McKinsey Rd., Severna Park, Md. Died April 24, 1957; buried Loudon Park Cemetery, Balt.

HOBBS, Sam(uel) Francis, lawyer, ex-congressman; b. Selma, Ala., Oct. 5, 1887; s. Samuel Freeman and Frances John H.; A.A., Marion Mil. Inst., 1905; student Vanderbilt U., 1905-06; LL.B., U. of Ala., 1908, LL.D., 1949; m. Sarah Ellen Greene, Jan. 8, 1913; children—Samuel Earle Greene, Rosa Miller, Truman McGill. Practiced law, Selma, 1908-21; judge 4th Jud. Circuit of Ala., 1921, resigned to resume law practice, 1926; mem. 74th to 81st Congresses (1935-51), 4th Ala. Dist. (a mgr. in impeachment of Judge Halsted L. Ritter, 1936); mem. law firm Hobbs, Hobbs & Hobbs, Selma. Chmn. Music Shoals Commn., 1931; chmn. Ala. NRA Com., 1933, Patron Internat. Law Assn. Mem. Dallas County, Ala. State and Am. bar assns., Am. Judicature Soc., Delta Kappa Epsilon, Phi Delta Phi, Phi Beta Kappa. Democrat. Presbyterian. Mason. Kiwanian. Home: 329 Mabry St., Selma, Ala. Died May 31, 1952.

HOBBS, William Herbert, geologist; b. Worcester, Mass., July 2, 1864; s. Horace and Mary Paine (Parker) H.; S.B., Worcester Poly. Inst., 1883, D.Engring., 1929; fellow geology, Johns Hopkins, 1887-88, A.M., Ph.D., 1888; student U. of Heidelberg, 1888-89; LL.D., U. of Michigan, 1939; m. Sara K. Sale, June 23, 1896; 1 dau., Winifred (Mrs. J. N. Lincoln). Curator Geol. Mus., 1889-90, asst. prof. mineralogy and metallurgy, 1890-99, prof. mineralogy and petrology, 1899-1906, U. of Wis.; prof. geology and dir. Geol. Lab., U. of Mich., 1906-34, prof. emeritus since 1934; Russel lecturer, 1931. With U.S. Geol. Survey, 1886-1906; U.S. asst. geologist, 1896. Lectured on World War I, summer sch., U. of Pittsburgh, 1918; extended cruises to mandated Pacific Islands, 1921; exch. prof. Technische Hoogeschool, Delft, 1921-22. Dir. Greenland expdns., U. of Mich., 1926-31, hon. director 1932-33. Vice-pres. Internat. Glacier Com., 1930-36. Fellow A.A.A.S. (v.p. 1932), Geol. Soc. America (first v.p. 1922); mem. Am. Philos. Soc. (mem. council 1930), Assn. Am. Geographers (first v.p. 1917; pres. 1936), Mich. Acad. Science (pres. 1917). Chevalier Legion Honor, France, 1924. Club: Explorers (New York). Author: Earthquakes, 1907 (German transl. 1910); Characteristics of Existing Glaciers, 1911; Earth Features and Their Meaning, 1912; The World War and Its Consequences (with Introd. by Theodore Roosevelt), 1919; Leonard Wood Administrator, Soldier and Citizen, 1920; Earth Evolution and Its Facial Expression, 1921; Cruises Along By-ways of the Pacific, 1923; The Glacial Anticyclones, 1926; Exploring About the North Pole of the Winds, 1930; Peary, 1936; Explorers of the Antarctic, 1941; Fortress Islands of the Pacific, 1945; Glacial Studies of the Pleistocene of N. Am., 1947; (autobiography) An Explorer-Scientist's Pilgrimage 1952. Adv. mem. O.S.S., 1941-45. Designer project for combined open-cut and tunnel sea-level ship-canal across Tehuantepec Isthmus in Mexico, sea level ship-canal across Honduras, 1952. Home: 1005 Berkshire Road, Ann Arbor, Mich. Died Jan. 1, 1953.

HOCHBAUM, Hans Weller (hōk'boum), agriculturist; b. Chicago, Ill., July 20, 1881; s. John Ernst and Matilda (Weller) H.; B.S., Cornell U., 1905; m. Gertrude Schenck, Mar. 15, 1910; children—Hans Albert, Mary Elizabeth (Mrs. John Collins Leavitt), Gertrude Matilda. Prof. of agr., Colo. State Coll. of Edn., 1906-12, State Normal School, Los Angeles, Calif., 1912-13; county agrl. agent, Ada County, Ida., 1913-14; state leader county agents and vice-dir. of extension, U. of Ida., 1914-18; sr. agriculturist, extension service, U.S. Dept. Agr., 1918-34, prin. agriculturist in charge extension work Eastern states, 1934-39, also in charge subject matter specialists, 1938-39, chief div. of field coördination since 1939; chmn. U.S. Govt. Victory Garden Com., 1941-45. conducted summer term grad. courses for extension workers, Utah State Coll., Cornell U., U. of Vermont, Colo. State Coll. Mem. Alpha Zeta, Epsilon Sigma Phi. Unitarian. Mason. Author: bulls. and articles on extension work, gardening. Club: Comos (Washington, D.C.). Home: 7329 Blair Rd. N.W. Office: Extension Service, U.S. Dept. of Agriculture, Washington. Died 1952.

HOCKEMA, Frank C. (hŏk'ĕ mȧ), univ. vice pres.; b. Shadeland, Ind., Mar. 25, 1892; s. Henry T. and Elizabeth (Bush) H.; graduate Ind. State Teachers Coll., 1913; B.S. in M.E., Purdue, 1918, M.S. in M.E., 1923; Ph.D., Indiana Univ., 1947; m. Martha Kuipers, June 16, 1920; children—Max Wesley, Thomas Kuipers, David Franklin. Instructor mechanical engineering, Purdue, 1920-25, assistant professor, 1925-28, asso. prof., 1928-32, prof. mech. engring. and indsl. engring. since 1932, dir. Personnel, 1932-34, asst. to Pres., 1934-43, dir. summer session, 1934-37, sec. to bd. trustees since 1935, exec. dean since 1943, vice president since 1944; University rep. in charge veterans' affairs since 1942; consulting industrial engr., 1920-34; trustee Lafayette Savings Bank since 1938; trustee Lafayette Transit Co. since 1947. Served as 2d lt. C.A.C. and instructor artillery sch., Ft. Monroe, Va., 1918-19. Mem. City Council, 1929-38. Dir. Red Cross, Community Chest; sec.-treas. Christian Reformed Ch. Corp.; mem. ednl. adv. com. to state supervisor publ. instrn. Studied Am. Univs. for Carnegie Corp., 1940. Mem. Army Adv. Com., since Sept. 1946; mem. City Planning Commn., since 1945; mem. A.A.A.S. Am. Soc. M.E., Conf. of Higher Edn. (mem. exec. com. since 1945), Ind. State Ednl. Rev. Com. (chmn. com. on philos. of edn., since 1944), Soc. for Profl. Engring. Edn., Am. Soc. Engring. Edn. (com. indsl. relations colls.), Ind. Soc. of Chicago, Post War Planning Com., Scabbard and Blade, Tau Beta Pi, Pi Tau Sigma, Blue Key, Leather Medal of Sigma Delta Chi, Alpha Chi Rho. Mem. Christian Reformed Ch. Clubs: University, Reading, Garden, Country. Contbr. to ednl., engring. and scientific publs. Lecturer on ednl., industrial and business subjects. Home: 832 N. Chauncey, West Lafayette, Ind. Office: Purdue Univ. Lafayette, Ind. Died Feb. 3, 1956; buried Grand View, Cemetery.

HOCKENSMITH, Wilbur Darwin, bus. exec.; b. Irwin, Pa., Aug. 17, 1878; s. Franklin Cramer and Caroline (Davis) H.; student Alleghany Coll., Meadville, Pa. 1895-96; M.C., U. of Pittsburgh 1901; m. Mabel Cornelia Elderkin, Sept. 14, 1904; children—Wilbur Darwin, Mary Louise (Mrs. Charles W. Murdock), Franklin C., Cornelia Jane (Mrs. John P. McCune), Stanton Elderkin. Chief engr. Hockensmith Corp., Penn, Pa. 1905-12, vice pres. 1913-27, pres. and general manager since 1928, president of the board since 1949. Served as private, Spanish American War 1898. Trustee, University of Pittsburgh. Member Western Pa. Engrs. Soc. Republican. Methodist. Mason (life mem.). Club: Kiwanis (past pres.). Holder 3 patents on mine car wheels and mine cars. Home: Lincoln Highway, Irwin, Pa. Office: Hockensmith Corp., Penn, Pa. Died Aug. 19, 1951; buried Union Cemetery, Irwin, Pa.

HODGDON, Charles (hŏj'dŭn), architect; b. Boston, 1866; s. Charles F. and Sarah T. (Lynam) H.; grad. high sch., Weymouth, Mass.; m. Mary E. Mendum (died 1934); children—Frederick M., John M.; m. 2d, Elizabeth Rohrbach, May 7, 1940. Began practice at Boston; moved to Chgo., 1907; mem. Coolidge and Hodgdon 1914-30; firm architects of McKinlock Court, Art Inst. Chgo., Swift Hall, Joseph Bond Chapel, Wieboldt Hall and Med. Sch. and Hosp. of U. Chgo., Social Sci. Bldg., Bobs Roberts Meml. Hosp., 1st Presbyn. Ch., Clinton, Ia., Fountain St. Bapt. Ch., Grand Rapids, Mich., Tenth Church of Christ, Scientist, Chgo. Second Church of Christ, Scientist, Kalamazoo, Mich., Temple Sholem, restoration of Old Main, Knox Coll., as a nat. monument; 6 bldgs. for St. Olaf Coll., Northfield, Minn., br. libraries for City Chgo., many other churches and college bldgs., amd bldgs. for Great Lakes Naval Training Station, USN; mem. firm Charles Hodgdon & Son, 1930—. Unitarian. Club: Union League (Chgo.). Address: 240 N. Daroca St., San Gabriel, Cal. Died Nov. 21, 1953; buried Mountain View Cemetery, Altadena, Cal.

HODGE, Frederick Webb (hŏj), ethnologist; b. Plymouth, Eng., Oct. 28, 1864; s. Edwin and Emily (Webb) H.; brought to the U.S. at age of 7; ed. pub. schs. and Columbian (now George Washington) U. (non-grad.); D.Sc., Pomona Coll.; LL.D., U. of New Mexico; Litt.D., Univ. of Southern California; m. Margaret W. Magill, August 31, 1891; m. 2d, Zahrah E. Preble (died April 27, 1934); m. 3d, Gene P. Meany. In U.S. Geological Survey, 1884-86; secretary Hemenway Archæol. Expdn. which excavated ancient ruins in Ariz. and N.M., 1886-89; in July 1889, entered Bur. Am. Ethnology; made further researches among the Indians of Arizona and New Mexico in subsequent yrs. In Feb. 1901, became an executive official in the Smithsonian Instn.; transferred, July 1905, to Bur. Am. Ethnology, devoting spl. attention to the Handbook of American Indians, part 1 of which was published, 1907, part 2, 1910. Ethnologist-in-charge, Bur. of Am. Ethnology, 1910-18; with Museum of Am. Indian, New York, 1918-31; now dir. Southwest Museum, Los Angeles. Mem. advisory board Heard Museum, Phoenix, Ariz. Has conducted several archæol. and ethnol. expdns. in the Southwest; excavating ruins of Hawikuh, one of "Seven Cities of Cíbola," nr. Zuñi, N.M., 1917-23; founder, mem. council, and pres. Am. Anthrop. Assn.; ex-pres. Anthrop. Soc. Washington; mem. Nat. Research Council, 1921-23, 1927-30; trustee Sch. of Am. Research and Lab. of Anthropology; fellow A.A.A.S. (v.p. sect. H, 1916), Royal Anthrop. Inst. of Gt. Britain and Ireland; mem. Am. Antiquarian Society, Texas Historical Association, Historical Society of New Mexico, Death Valley '49ers, Archeol. Survey Assn. of So. Cal., Mus. No. Ariz.; Western Museums Conf. (pres. 1942-43), California Writers Guild (hon.), Société des Américanistes de Paris, Soc. Cientifica Antonio Alzate, Mexico; hon. companion Order of Indian Wars; Pasadena Society Artists (honorary); a founder and advisory editor Quivira Soc. for translation of rare Spanish documents on early Southwest. Clubs: Ends of the Earth (N.Y.); Westerners, Zamorano (Los Angeles). Author many monographs. Contbr. ethnol. and archeol. articles to scientific publs. Editor: Handbook of the American Indians North of Mexico, 1907-10; Narratives of Cabeza de Vaca and Coronado, 1907; Curtis's North American Indian (20 volumes); Falconer's Letters and Notes on the Texan Santa Fe Expedition, 1930; Indian Notes and Monographs (of the Museum of the American Indian); McKenney and Hall's Indian Tribes; and publications of Bureau of American Enthnology, the Southwest Museum; etc. Editor of the American Anthropologist, 1899-1910, 1912-14. Annotator (with C. F. Lummis) of Memorial of Fray Alonso Benavides, 1630, and (with G. P. Hammond and Agapito Rey) of the revised Memorial of 1634, 1945. Home: 1375 Lida St., Pasadena 3, Calif. Office: Southwest Museum, Highland Park, Los Angeles 42, Cal. Died Sept. 28, 1956.

HODGES, Brandon Patton, state ofcl.; b. Asheville, N.C., Sept. 6, 1903; s. Daniel Merritt and Clara (Patton) H.; student U. N.C., 1922-24, Wake Forest Coll., 1925-26; m. Genevieve Hare, July 17, 1932; children—Brandon Patton, Sarah Jane. Admitted to N.C. bar, 1926, practiced in Ashville, 1926-48; county atty., Buncombe County, N.C., 1936-46; mem. N.C. State Senate, 1943-47, chmn. com. on apprpriations, 1945, chmn. adv. budget commn., 1946; mem. commn. to revise ins. laws, 1944-45, mem. state sch. commn., 1947-48, chmn. state banking commn., 1949—, mem. state bd. edn., 1949—; exec. counsel to gov., 1947; state treas., 1948—; counsellor, asst. sec. Carolina div. Champion Paper & Fibre Co., Hamilton, O., 1953—. Chmn. bd. trustees Western Carolina Tchrs. Coll., 1947-48. Mem. Sigma Chi. Presbyn. Mason. Home: 354 Kimberly Av., Ashville, N.C. Office: State Capitol, Raleigh, N.C. Died Dec. 4, 1957.

HODGES, Gilbert Tennent, publisher; b. Monroe, Wis., June 29, 1872; s. Gilbert Tennent and Anna (Banks) H.; LL.B., U. of Wis., 1895; Master Commercial Science, Bryant Coll., 1931; m. Edith Martin, June 21, 1906. Admitted to Ill. bar, 1895, practiced at Chicago, 1895-1905; mem. advertising dept. Frank A. Munsey Co., Chicago, 1905-12; western advertising mgr., 1912-17; advertising mgr. New York Sun, 1917-18; advertising mgr. Frank A. Munsey Co., 1918-25; mem. exec. com. The N. Y. Sun since 1925, chmn., 1935-50; staff executive The Wall Street Journal since 1950; dir. Munsey Trust Company, Washington, Mohican Co. (N.Y.). Apptd. lt. col., U.S. Army Res., 1931, 36. Decorated French Legion of Honor, 1937, U.S. Selective Service Medal, 1946; recipient Award of Merit, N.Y. Alumni Assn. Wis. U., 1956; Award of Merit, Advt. Club of N.Y., 1956. Past pres. and chairman Advt. Fedn. of Am.; honorary member U. of Wis. Research Foundation; mem. Phi Delta Theta. Independent Republican. Clubs: Union League, University, Advertising, Economic, Sleepy Hollow Country. Sales Executives, Lawyers (N.Y.); Army and Navy (Washington); Seigniory (Quebec); Thirty of London (hon. mem.). Home: 29 Washington Sq., N.Y. City 11. Office: 44 Broad St., N.Y.C. 4. Died July, 1959.

HODGES, Leigh Mitchell, writer, lecturer, b. Denver, July 9, 1876; s. Charles H. and Elizabeth P. (Mitchell) H.; grad. high sch., Carthage, Mo., 1894; student Sch. of Fine Arts, St. Louis, 1 yr.; m. Nadine Converse Skinner, Apr. 22, 1903; children—Mitchell Converse, Mary Leigh (Mrs. Harold G. Beeson). Became reporter then city editor, the Daily Ledger, Mexico, Mo., 1895-96; reporter, Kansas City Star, 1897-99; editorial staff, Ladies' Home Journal, New York and Phila., 1899-1901; started "The Optimist" column in Phila. Times, 1902, which was transferred to The North American, Phila., same year, and appeared continuously in that paper until 1925; one of four persons initiating and founding Christmas Seal sales program for fight against TB, 1907; now in Evening Bulletin, Phila. (50th anniversary of The Optimist column, 1952, marked by contbns. from Ex-President Truman, Ex-President Hoover and many others); mem. editorial staff The North American, 1906-15, contbg. editor, 1915-25. Inaugurated first publicity campaign for Tb, Christmas Seals, 1907. Recipient 1952 Benjamin Rush Award by Bucks Co. Med. Soc. and also by Med. Soc. State Pa. Mem. Am. Fedn. for Physically Handicapped, Nat. Tb. Assn. (hon.), Pa. and Bucks Co. (past pres.) Tb. and health socs., Bucks Co. Hist. Soc., Nat. Roadside Council (gen. com.), Mo. Author's Guild (hon.), Internat. Mark Twain Soc. (hon. 1952). Author: The Great Optimist and Other Essays, 1903; The Life Worth While, 1904; The Worth of Service, 1905; The Great Encouragement, 1913; Bird Guardians, 1915; The Bard at Home (Shakespeare Tercentenary masque), 1916; "Processional" (poem read at Cathedral of St. John the Divine, N.Y., by Bishop Manning), 1933, A Boy from Kentucky, 1939; The People Against Tb., 1942. Compiler: Poems We Love, 1908. Contbr. to the New Yorker, Reader's Digest, London Times and others. Broadcasting program, "The Optimist," 1938-39. Corr. editor Revised Hymnal for P. E. Ch. in the U.S., 1940-41. Home: Doylestown, Pa. Died Apr. 4, 1954; buried Doylestown Cemetery.

HODGES, William Franklin, lawyer; b. Hiseville, Ky., Mar. 3, 1877; s. Edmund and Docia (Turner) H.; C.E., B.S., LL.B., Valparaiso (Ind.) U., 1904; m. Casandra Vernon Newberry, Jan. 3, 1901; children—Thomas Merle, Jennie Theodocia (Mrs. Burton B. McRoy). Admitted to Ind. bar, 1904; mem. Hodges, Ridgely & Davis, Gary, since 1916. Mem. Ind. State Senate, 1922-30; mayor of Gary, 1918-22. Mem. adv. bd. Salvation Army since 1920, chmn. bd. since 1935; pres. Gary Indsl. Found. Mem. Am., Ind., Gary bar assns., Gary C. of C. (pres.). Republican. Conglist. Mason (32°). Club: Com. of 100 (Miami Beach, Fla.). Home: 740 Fillmore St. Office: 607 Broadway, Gary, Ind. Died May 14, 1954; buried Calumet Park Cemetery, Gary, Ind.

HODGKINS, Alton Ross, educator; b. Newcastle, Me., Mar. 19, 1890; s. Daniel W. and Alice (Bartlett) H.; A.B., Bates Coll., 1911; A.M., Am. U., 1926; Ph.D., Johns Hopkins, 1929; m. Blanche Couessin, July 19, 1941. With U.S. Dept. of State, 1911-20; head dept. geography State Normal Sch., East Stroudsburg, Pa., 1922-23; asso. prof. economics U. Md., 1923-25; research asso. Inter-Am. High Commn., 1926; spl. advisor Legation of Guatemala, 1927-29; prof. economics and sociology Randolph-Macon Woman's Coll., 1929-41; bus. specialist Office Inter-Am. Affairs, 1941; asso. prof. economics, Tulane U., 1942-47; prof. and head dept. economics and bus. adminstrn., Centre Coll. of Ky. since 1947; vis. prof. econ., U. Chattanooga, summers, 1947, 48. Mem. Lynchburg Council Social Agencies, Little Theatre. Mem. S.W. Social Sci. Soc., Am. Econ. Assn., Phi Beta Kappa, Delta Sigma Pi. Democrat. Episcopalian. Author: (article) Consumption and the Good Life, 1945; Marine Insurance (monograph), 1926; contbr. articles. Home: 440 Smith St., Danville, Ky. Died Feb. 23, 1952; buried Newcastle, Me.

HODGSON, Morton Strahan, fertilizer mfr.; born Athens, Ga., April 23, 1889; s. Edward R. and Mary Virginia (Strahan) H., Sr.; B.S., U. of Ga., 1909, Princeton, 1911; m. Lydia Slye Hutchins, Oct. 18, 1911; children—Morton S., R. Hutchins, Mrs. Nell Hodgson Watt, Robert (Killed in action 1945). With Hodgson's, Inc., Athens, since 1911, salesman, 1915, sales mgr., 1915-30, v.p., 1930-38, pres. since 1938; dir. Ga. Power Co., Citizens and So. Nat. Bank. Dir. Salvation Army, Y.M.C.A. Mem. Nat. Fertilizer Assn. (dir.), Newcomen Soc. of England. Baptist. Club: Rotary. Home: 749 Cobb St. Office: 286 Oconee St., Athens, Ga. Died Dec 4, 1954.

HODGSON, William Roy, Australian govt. ofcl.; b. Kingston, Victoria, Australia, May 22, 1892; s. Robert Hodgson; ed. Sch. of Mines (Ballarat, Victoria), Royal Mil. Coll. (Duntroon, Australian Capital Terr.), U. Melbourne; LL.B.; m. Muriel Bruce McDowell, Oct. 1919; 1 son, 1 dau. Served with Australian Imperial Forces during World War I; severely wounded, Gallipoli landing; attached Gen. Staff, Army Hdqrs., Melbourne, tng. operations and intelligence sects., 1921-34; asst. sec. Dept. External Affairs, Commonwealth of Australia, Canberra, 1933-35, sec. 1935-45; apptd. temporary Australian high commr. to Can., Jan. 1945; apptd. minister to France, Oct. 1945; head Australian del. to Preparatory Commn. and 1st Assembly UN, London, 1945-46; rep. Australia on Security Council, New York, March 1946; del. Australia Peace Conf., Paris; rep. Australia Trusteeship Council, March 1947; Australian rep. Security Council, 1946, 47; rep. Australian Human Rights Commn.; Econ. and Social Council; Spl. Com. on Balkans; Spl. Assembly on Palestine; Australian Ambassador to France, 1948-49; Commonwealth rep. on Allied Control Council, Japan, 1949-52; Australian high commnr. to S. Africa, 1952-57; retired, 1957. Decorated Croix de Guerre with Palm. Address: care Dept. of External Affairs, Canberra, Australia. Died Jan. 24, 1958.

HOE, Robert, banker, mfr.; b. N.Y.C., Feb. 24, 1876; s. Robert and Olivia Phelps (James) H.; prep. edn., Lawrenceville (N.J.) Sch.; student Harvard, 1896-98; m. Mary Elliott Thompson, Jan. 15, 1918; children—Robert, Edward Livingston. With R. Hoe & Co., printing press mfrs., advancing to pres., 1899-1913; pres. Duplex Printing Press Co., Battle Creek, Mich., 1914-16; chmn. bd. Hoe Corp., Poughkeepsie, also chmn. First Nat. Bank, Poughkeepsie. Hon. chmn. N.Y. State Bridge Authority. Trustee Vassar Bros. Hosp. Member Am. Soc. M.E.,

Soc. of Cin. Cincinnati. Republican. Presbyn. Clubs: Grolier, Harvard, Quill (New York); Lake Placid (N.Y.); Surf (Miami Beach, Fla.). Patentee of improvements on printing presses and other machinery. Home: Poughkeepsie, N.Y. Died Feb. 1960.

HOEFELD, Norman, editor, writer; b. Chgo., Sept. 2, 1897; s. Albert and Sadie (Lelewer) H.; student U. Mich., 1915-17, U. Chgo., 1918, Northwestern, 1946; m. Alice Oberndorf, Jan. 2, 1926; children—Albert, Barbara. Editor-in-chief Am. Family Mag., Chgo., 1949-51; editorial research and surveys Consol. Book Pubs., Chgo., 1951—. Author articles and fiction popular mags. Home: 2440 Lake View Av., Chgo. 14. Office: 153 N. Michigan Av., Chgo. 1. Died Dec. 1956.

HOEFER, Charles Wenzel, newspaper pub.; b. Chgo., Apr. 30, 1891; s. Ernest and Leonore (Meyer) H.; ed. parochial and high schs., Ill.; m. Ethel Thorton Watson, Dec. 31, 1908; children—Charles Watson, Warren Watson. Adv. dir. Aurora (Ill.) Beacon-News, 1916-41, pub., 1941-51, ret.; v.p., dir. The Copley Press, Inc., 1941—. Dir. The Aurora Found.; pres. Ill. Daily Newspaper Markets, Inc. Mem. Aurora Chamber of Commerce, Aurora Hist. Soc. Clubs: Union League, Aurora Country, Phoenix (Aurora), Elk, Moose. Home: 803 Downer Pl. Office: 4-6 Main St., Aurora, Ill. Deceased.*

HOELZEL, John P., pres. and dir. Pittsburgh Screw & Bolt Corp., Gary Screw & Bolt Co.; dir. Pittsburgh Brewing Co. Home: 5611 Aylesboro Av. Office: 2719 Preble Av., Pitts. Died Dec. 26, 1950; buried Homewood Cemetery.

HOEY, Clyde Roark (hōō'ē), U.S. senator; b. Shelby, N.C., Dec. 11, 1877; son of Capt. Samuel Alberta and Mary Charlotte (Roark) Hoey; ed. law dept. U. of N.C.; LL.D., Davidson Coll., 1937, University of North Carolina, 1938, Duke University, 1938, Bob Jones University, 1951; married to Bessie Gardner, Mar. 22, 1900 (died February, 13, 1942); children—Clyde R., Charles A., Isabel Y. Began in printing office at 12, later editor county newspaper; admitted to N.C. bar, 1899; mem. N.C. Ho. of Rep., 2 terms, 1898-1902, Senate, 1902-04; asst. U.S. dist. atty., Western Dist. of N.C., 1913-19; elected to 66th Congress (1919-21), 9th N.C. Dist., Dec. 16, 1919, to fill vacancy caused by resignation of Edwin Y. Webb; declined renomination, and resumed practice of law, 1921, Democratic Presidential Elector-at-Large, 1928, gov. of N.C., 1937-41; again in practice of law since 1941; U.S. senator from N.C., since Jan. 1945. Mem. Omicron Delta Kappa, Sigma Chi. Methodist. Mason, Odd Fellow, K.P., Woodman of the World. Home: Shelby, N.C. Office: Senate Office Bldg., Washington. Died May 12, 1954; buried Sunset Cemetery, Shelby, N.C.

HOFFHERR, Frederic G(eorge), educator; b. Lyon, France, Oct. 16, 1887; s. Georges and Berthe (Frick) H.; student Univ. of Lyon; m. Antoinette Noel de la Houssaye, Aug. 1924. Came to U.S., 1919. Instr., Columbia, 1921, asst. prof. and chmn. dept. of French, 1927, asso. prof., 1932; asso. prof. and chmn. dept. of French, Barnard Coll., 1935-45, prof. of French and chmn. dept. of French since 1945. Gen. editor French Series, Harpers Bros. Mem. France-America (mem. bd. of dirs.). Decorated: Officier de la Légion d'Honneur, Médaille Militaire, Croix de Guerre, Officier d'Académie, Chevalier de Saint-Sava. U.S. del. to Rassemblement du Peuple Français. French Protestant. Club: Columbia Univ. Author: Esquisse de la France, 1946. Contbr. articles to French and American publs. Home: 375 Riverside Dr., N.Y. C. 25. Died Oct., 1956.

HOFFMAN, Abram (hŏf'măn), orthodontist, educator; b. Fort Plain, N.Y., Mar. 5, 1875; s. Abram and Caroline (King) H; student Clinton Liberal Inst., 1891-95; D.D.S., U. Buffalo, 1899; m. Lillian Bartels, Oct. 2, 1901; children—Burton Abram, Hester Elizabeth; m. 2d, Helen B. Bartron, July 16, 1932. Tchr. orthodontia, U. Buffalo, 1899-1907, asst. prof., 1907-10, prof., 1910-25; prof. orthodontia N.Y.U., 1925-27; prof. orthodontia Northwestern U., 1927-40, also dean of students Dental Sch. and head dept. of orthodontia, became prof. emeritus, 1940. Fellow Am. Coll. Dentists, 1924; certified by Am. Bd. of Orthodontia, 1929; mem. Am. Dental Assn., Am. Soc. Orthodontists, Federation Dentaire Internat., Internat. Orthodontic Congress, Xi Psi Phi, Omicron Kappa Upsilon. Clubs: University (Chgo.); Exmoor Country (Highland Park). Asso. in compilation of Black's Index to 1933. Home: Ft. Lauderdale, Fla. Died Feb. 1958.

HOFFMAN, Burton C(harles), book publisher; b. Weehawken, N.J., Aug. 4, 1911; s. Herman and Belle Rose (Steinhardt) H.; A.B., Syracuse U., 1932; m. Louise Winters, Aug. 6, 1937; 1 dau., Beatrice Carole. Book publisher and editor since 1933; pres. Dial Press, Inc., since 1936. Served as capt., U.S. Army, 1945. Mem. Am. Book Publishers Council, Sigma Alpha Mu. Awarded Bronze Star Medal. Ind. Democrat. Jewish religion. Club: Publishers' Advertising. Home: 205 W. 89th St. Office: Dial Press, Inc., 461 Fourth A., N.Y.C. Died Feb. 6, 1953.

HOFFMAN, Edward Richard, accountant and tax consultant; b. Dear Park, Md., Apr. 30, 1879; s. Richard Henry and Martha Sawyer (Tilson) H.; student Chesborough Sem., North Chili, N.Y., 1890-93, Drexel Institute, Phila., 1895; private tutor in engineering, 1898-99; married Theresa Sara Booker, February 6, 1904 (deceased February 7, 1949); children—Edward Richard, Jr., Elizabeth (Mrs. Mario Giannini). With Presbyn. Bd. of Publication, 1893); bookkeeper, John Wanamaker, Phila., 1894-98; N.Y. Shipbuilding Co., Camden, N.J., 1898-99; sec. Sun Electric Mfg. Co., Phila., 1899-1900; John Hines & Co., pub. accountants, Phila., 1900; Audit Co. of N.Y. at Phila., 1900-04; in charge of finances, William Knabe & Co., Baltimore, 1904-08; v.p. and dir., United Surety Co., Baltimore, 1904-10; gen. auditor, asst. to pres., in charge of finances, Am. Piano Co., 1908-09; pub. accountant, Price Waterhouse & Co., Barrow, Wade, Guthrie & Co., and others, 1910-18; associated with Miles M. Dawson, cons. actuary, in accounting and actuarial investigation, including investigations of N.Y. State Indsl. Com., Pa. State Dept. of Labor and Industry, Ins. for U.S. Shipping Bd., actuarial investigations for Ins. Dept. of Dist. of Columbia, 1918-23; pub. accountant and tax consultant, Edward R. Hoffman & Co., since 1923. Served as pvt. Co. A, 5th Regt., Md. Nat. Guard, 1905-08. Mem. Maryland Soc. (N.Y.), N.Y. Soc. Order of Founders and Patriots of Am. (gov. 1934-36; dep. gov. gen. court, 1937); chmn. bd. trustees Gen. Court of Patriotic Societies of Am., 1937; chmn. Patriotic Societies Com. of Thayer Sesquicentennial Celebration at West Point, 1936; mem. Sons of the Revolution, Soc. of Colonial Wars, Soc. of Mayflower Descendants, L.I. Hist. Soc., Soc. of Tammany of Columbian Order. Awarded Grand Cross, Order of Crown of Charlemagne. Grand Officer, Knights of the Holy Sepulchre; Commdr. Imperial Mil. Order of Constantine and Saint George. Member First Church of Christ Scientist of Boston. Mass. Mason (32°, K. T., Shriner); St. Paul's Conclave No. 12, Knights of the Red Cross of Constantine. Club: Long Island Country, Englewood Golf; Quill, Economic (N.Y.). Home: 782 West End Av. Address: 36 West 44th St., N.Y.C. 18. Died Nov. 24, 1953.

HOFFMAN, Harold Giles, ex-gov.; b. South Amboy, N.J., Feb. 7, 1896; s. Frank and Ada Crawford (Thom) H.; grad. high sch., South Amboy, 1913; m. Lillie Moss, Sept. 20, 1919; children—Ada Moss, Lillie Moss (dec.), Hope. Director N.J. Division of Employment Security since February 1938. Enlisted as pvt., 3d N.J. Inf., 1917; promoted through grades to capt. Hdqrs. Co., 114th Inf.; participated in Meuse-Argonne campaign; major, U.S. Reserve since 1925; active service United States Army 1942-46, lt. col. Transportation Corps; disch. colonel. Awarded the Legion of Merit and the Verdun Medal. Mem. N.J. Ho. of Assembly, 1923-24; mayor of South Amboy, 1925-26; mem. 70th and 71st Congresses (1927-31); 3d N.J. Dist.; commr. of motor vehicles, N.J., 1930-35; gov. of N.J., 3 yrs., 1935-37. V.p. Nat. Safety Council. Mem. Jr. Order U.A.M., Patriotic Sons America, Am. Legion, Vets. of Foreign Wars. Republican, Methodist. Mason, Elk, Eagle; mem. Royal Arcanum. Clubs: Lambs, Circus Saints and Sinners (pres.), N.Y. Athletic. Author: Mile a Minute Men; Getting Away with Murder; The Crime, The Case, The Challenge. Home: 178 Broadway, South Amboy, N.J. Office: Div. Employment Security, Trenton, N.J. Died June 4, 1954.

HOFFMAN, Hugh French T(homason), army officer; b. Van Buren, Ark., Nov. 27, 1896; s. Bert and Dora (Thomason) H.; B.S., U.S. Mil. Acad., 1918; grad. Cav. Sch., basic course, 1920, regular course, 1937, Command and Gen. Staff Sch., 1941; m. Winifred Gurney, July 19, 1924; childdren—Hugh French Thomason, Richard Gurney. Commd. 2d lt., U.S. Army 1918, advancing through grades to maj. gen., 1951; with Army of Occupation, Germany, 1919; with 13th Cav., 1920-24; academic instr. U.S. Mil. Acad., 1924-28; with 1st Cav., 1928-31, 12th Cav., 1931-36, 6th Cav., 1937-40, 5th Cav. (including Admiralties Campaign), 1940-44; comdg. 2d Cav. Brigade (7th and 8th Cav.), 1944-45, Japan, 1945-49; comd. 1st Cavalry Div., Luzon, 1945. Chief of Staff, 4th U.S. Army, Fort Sam Houston, Tex., 1949—. Address: Chief of Staff, Hdqrs. 4th Army, Fort Sam Houston, Tex. Died Apr. 19, 1951.

HOFFMAN, John Washington, univ. pres.; b. Noblestown, Pa., July 11, 1867; s. George Washington and Elizabeth (Haggarty) H.; B.A., Washington and Jefferson Coll., Pa., 1892, M.A., 1895, D.D., 1910, LL.D., 1917; LL.D., Temple U., 1923; studied Yale, 1892-93, Princeton, 1893-95; m. Anna W. Pugh, June 20, 1900. Ordained to M.E. ministry, 1897; pastor New Cumberland, W.Va., 1897-98, Sheridan, 1898-99, California Av. Ch., Pitts., 1900-06, Crafton, Pa., 1906-13, Duluth, Minn., 1913-16; pres. Ohio Wesleyan U., 1916-28, now pres. emeritus. Mem. Phi Gamma Delta, Phi Beta Kappa (Ohio Wesleyan U.). Republican. Mason (32°, K. T.). Home: San Marino, Cal. Died July 3, 1953; buried San Gabriel (Cal.) Cemetery.

HOFFMAN, Samuel David, lawyer; b. Bklyn., Jan. 1, 1900; s. Barnet and Sarah (Jelin) H.; A.B., Rutgers U., 1921, L.H.D., 1957; LL.B., N.J. Law Sch., 1922; m. Clara Kenarik, Feb. 19, 1933; children—Elaine (Mrs. David Martin Green), Barnett Elihu. Tchr. history and civics New Brunswick High Sch., 1921-22; admitted to N.J. bar, 1922, practiced law in New Brunswick, 1922-57; city commr. New Brunswick, 1935-38, local govt. commr., 1938-51, city atty., 1955-57; dir., counsel First Nat. Bank of Sayreville, N.J., 1955-57. Founder, mem. Jewish Social Service, 1925-57; cons., spl. counsel Redevelopment Agy., charge riverfront development, 1949-57 mem. planning bd. New Brunswick, 1935-38, vice chmn. housing authority, 1943-49; chmn. supreme ct. ethics and grievance com. Middlesex County, 1955-56; chmn. U.S.O.-Jewish Welfare Bd. com. for Central N.J., 1943-45. Dem. municipal chmn. New Brunswick, 1935-38; del. Dem. Nat. Conv., 1936. Trustee Rutgers U.; founder, 1st chmn. Rutgers Caravan, 1952-54. Trustee Middlesex Gen. Hosp. Recipient Theodore Rosen Meml. award Phi Epsilon Pi, 1952; Americanism award Jewish War Vets, 1957. Mem. Jewish Fedn. New Brunswick (founder, 1st pres.), Rutgers Alumni Assn. (pres. 1951-52), Phi Epsilon Pi (hon. supeior Lambda chpt. 1936). Author articles on housing planning, redevelopment. Home: 220 Lawrence St. Office: 83 Paterson St., New Brunswick, N.J. Died Oct. 15, 1957; buried Van Liew Cemetery, Ahavas Achim Plot, New Brunswick, N.J.

HOFFMAN, W(illiam) D(awson), author, newspaperman; b. Johnstown, Pa., July 11, 1884; s. William and Hannah (Dawson) H.; ed. pub. schs.; m. Zoe Parker, June 4, 1907; children—Wm. Parker, David Martin. Reporter, editor and mgr. El Paso Evening News, 1906-09; sec. internat. com., Rio Grande, 1907; editor, mgr. Albuquerque Tribune-Citizen, 1910-11; pres. Direct Legislation League of N.M.; corr. Madero Revolution of northern Mexico; corr. Associated Press, Tex. and N.M.; feature writer Chicago office Newspaper Enterprise Assn.; editor Tulare (Calif.) Advance; staff Arizona and Calif. dailies; Oakland Tribune; staffs Fort Worth Record, San Francisco Chronicle, Seattle Star, Los Angeles Tribune, Express, Daily News. Instructor Henry School of Social Science. Clubs: California Writers American Newspaper Guild, Los Angeles X-Club. Author: (novels) Gun Gospel; The Man From El Paso; Knights of the Desert; Westward to Paradise; The Range Defenders; Bravo Jim; The Saddle Wolf; Santone; Roarin' Rinconada; Boss of Thunder Butte; Tremaine of Texas; The Canyon of No Return; The Texas Tiger; Range Ghost; The Dude Deputy; Feudists of the Outlands; Law of the Lash; The Running M.; Hampton of the Water Guns, Tracker Teague of Texas, The Maverick Man; Hawk of the Mesquitals; Crimson Highwayman, 5 motion pictures. Home: 1648 Del Valle Av., Glendale, Cal. Died Mar. 10, 1952; buried Los Angeles.

HOFFMAN, William George, educator; b. Beacon Falls, Conn., Jan. 29, 1882; s. William George and Mary (Bomely) H.; student Providence Classical High Sch., 1896-1900; A.B., Brown U., 1904; m. Mabelle Corinne Hough, Feb. 18, 1909; children—Barbara Ruth (Mrs. Roger Eliott), Helen Elizabeth (Mrs. Ellard Purcell). Teacher of English, East Providence (R.I.) High School, 1908-10, high school, Malden, Mass., 1910-13, High Sch. of Commerce, Boston, 1913-20; instr. English, Boston U. Coll. Bus. Adminstrn., 1920-27, prof. English and pub. speaking, 1927—, chmn. English dept., 1942—. Mem. Am. Assn. U. Profs., Phi Beta Kappa, Beta Theta Pi, Delta Sigma Pi, Beta Gamma Sigma. Episcopalian. Mason. Author: Public Speaking for Business Men, 1923, rev. 1931, 49; The Public Speaker's Scrapbook, 1935; (with Roy Davis) Write and Speak Better, 1937; Public Speaking Today, 1940; The Speaker's Notebook, 1943; (with Ralph L. Rogers) Effective Radio Speaking, 1944; How to Make Better Speeches, 1948. Home: 21 Alameda Rd., West Roxbury 32, Mass. Died July 12, 1954; buried Puritan Lawn Cemetery.

HOFFMANN, Ernst, mus. educator; born Boston, June 18, 1899; s. Jacques and Paula (Schwitzer) H.; ed. Boston Latin Sch., 1910-13, A.B., cum laude, Harvard, 1914-18; student New Eng. Conservatory, Berlin Hochschule für Musik, 1921-22; m. Annemarie Hoffmann, May 14, 1924; 1 son, Clifford Joern. First violinist, Boston Symphony Orchestra, 1920-21; went to Germany to study conducting; asst. conductor, Breslau Opera House, 1922-24, regular conductor, 1924-34 (one of few Americans holding such a post in Germany); guest condr. Berlin, Vienna, Munich and Posen Symphony orchestras; returned to the U.S. in 1934; first appearance at the Lewisohn Stadium, New York; became head Commonwealth Symphony Orchestra, Boston; conductor, Houston Symphony Orchestra, 1936-47; now prof. Ind. U., mus. dir. philharmonic and opera; condr. Indpls. Philharmonic Orchestra; established Ind. U. Philharmonic, 1948. Condr. 121st Heavy Coast Artillery Band. Clubs: Kiwanis, Harvard (Houston). Home: 925 S. Highland, Bloomington, Ind. Died Jan. 3, 1956.

HOFMANN, Josef (Casimir) (hŏf'măn), pianist; b. Cracow, Poland, Jan. 20, 1876; father pianist, capellmeister and composer; learned piano under father, in infancy, and at age of 7 attracted attention of Anton Rubinstein; in 1887 came to U.S. where he was to give 80 concerts in one season, but after playing 42 concerts was compelled to abandon tour by interference of the Soc. for Prevention of Cruelty to Children; returned to Europe and studied under Urban, Moszkowski and Anton Rubinstin; Mus.D., U. Pa.; married; children—Josefa (by 1st marriage), Anton, Edward, Peter (by 2d marriage). Now retired as concert pianist. Has made many concert tours, Americas and Europe; dir., dean and instr. piano, Curtis Inst. of Music, Phila., 1925-38. Composer of concertos and piano pieces; also a symphony and orchestra suite. Writer on mus. topics. Address: 321 S. Occidental Blvd., Los Angeles 5. Died Feb. 16, 1957.

HOGAN, Bernard Francis, banker; b. Brooklyn, N.Y., Mar. 24, 1885; s. Thomas and Catherine (Dunleavy) H.; student pub. schs.; m. Sarah E. Rehm, May 17, 1925; 1 dau., Helene Marjorie. Employee and officer Title Guarantee Trust Co., 1902-20; pres. F. C. Sauter Agency, real estate and ins., 1920-26; with The Greater N.Y. Savings Bank since 1926, trustee, 1926, and pres. since 1934; organizer in 1933, and chmn. Group Five, Mortgage Information Bureau for Savings Banks of Kings and Queen Counties. Dir. Brooklyn Chamber of Commerce, mem. Chamber of Commerce, State of N.Y. Club: Cherry Valley (Garden City, N.Y.). Home: 114 Tenth St., Garden City, N.Y. Office: 451 Fifth Av., Brooklyn. Died Sept. 26, 1955.

HOGAN, Edward A., Jr. (hō'gȧn), law dean; b. Natick, Mass., June 12, 1908; s. Edward A. and Mary Ellen (O'Regan) H.; A.B., Boston Coll., 1930, LL.B., 1934, LL.D., 1955; LL.M., Harvard, 1935; LL.D., St. Mary's Coll., 1941; m. Mary Frances Cleary, Dec. 28, 1937; children—John, Edward, Mary, Ann, Peter, Paul, Virginia Margaret. Admitted to Mass. bar, 1934; in practice, law, Natick, Mass., 1934-35; asst. prof. law U. San Francisco, 1935-36, prof., 1936—, dean law sch., 1939-51; vice dean U. Cal. Hastings Coll. Law, 1951—; lecturer Am. Inst. of Banking, 1936—. Adviser Cal. Law Revision Com.; mem. Citizens Com. to Advise Atty. Gen. on Crime Prevention. Trustee Coro Found. Mem. Am. Law Inst. Club: Lawyers, Haravard, University. Home: 766 Third Av., San Francisco 18. Died Aug. 30, 1957.

HOGLE, James A., investment banker; b. Salt Lake City, Utah, Oct. 12, 1876; s. James and Ida Elizabeth (King) H.; Ph.B., Yale, 1899; Columbia U. School Mines, 1902; LL.D. (honorary), Westminster College; married Mary C. Copley, September 7, 1910; children—James E., George H., Mary Katharine. Assaying and sampliying, Anaconda Copper Mining Company, Anaconda, Montana, 1899-1900, engineer, Butte, Montana, office: 1900-02; independent mining engineer, 1902-15; stock and bond brokerage business, Salt Lake and Ogden, 1915; took over the Salt Lake City Branch of Logan & Bryan, 1917; took over Los Angeles office of Post & Flagg, 1941; Denver office of Sargent, Malo Company, 1942; sr. partner J. A. Hogle & Co., Salt Lake City, since 1924. Mem. Investment Bankers Assn. of Am., Am. Inst. M.E., N.Y. Stock Exchange Salt Lake Stock Exchange, Assn. Stock Exchange Firms, Chicago Bd. Trade, American Institute of Management. Trustee Westminster Coll. Hon. mem. Rotary Internat. Clubs: University, Alta, Commercial, Rotary. Home: 548 E. South Temple. Office: 132 Main St., Salt Lake City. Died Sept. 14, 1955.

HOH, Paul Jacob (hō), theol. sem. pres.; b. Reading, Pa., Sept. 20, 1893; s. Philip Jacob and Mary Ellen (Schick) H.; A.B., Central High Sch., Phila., 1911, U. of Pa., 1914; B.D., Luth. Theol. Sem. at Phila., 1924, S.T.M., 1930; D.D., Muhlenberg Coll., 1938; LL.D., Upsala Coll., 1945; m. Anna Moldenke, Sept. 18, 1919 (dec.); children—Philip Richard, Mary Elise (dec.); m. 2d, Marjorie Ecco Morgan, July 26, 1945. Instr. in English and mathematics, 1914; ordained to ministry of Luth. Ch., 1918; pastor St. Mark's Luth. Ch., Bethlehem, Pa., 1918-20, Holy Trinity Ch., Wildwood, N.J., 1920-21, Ascension Ch., Phila., 1921-30; editor Parish and Church Sch. Bd. of United Luth. Ch. in America, 1930-37; prof. practical theology, Luth. Theol. Sem., Phila., since 1937, pres. since 1945. Chmn. public panel War Labor Board, 1943-44. Member Phi Beta Kappa. Editor Luth. Church Review, 1926-27, Christian Life Course, 1930-36, Luth. Church Quarterly since 1943. Author: Little Children Come Unto Me, 1927; The Gospel According to St. Luke, A Study, 1936; Studies in First Corinthians, 1937; Parish Practice, 1944. Co-author: (with O. Fred Nolde) My Life, 1934; My Pupils, 1934; My Bible, 1935; My Work, 1935; My Preparation, 1935; My Materials, 1936; My Group Sessions, 1936; My Progress, 1937; (with Mabel Elsie Locker) Human Nature, 1935; (with Philip R. Hoh): Two Minutes with God, 1940. Home: 7318 Boyer St. Office: 7301 Germantown Av., Phila. 19. Died Jan. 20, 1952; buried Valley Forge Gardens, King of Prussia, Pa.

HOHLFELD, Alexander Rudolf, univ. prof.; born Dresden, Germany, Dec. 29, 1865; s. Karl Gottlieb and Helene (Libbert) H.; ed. Annen Real-Gymnasium, Dresden; Ph.D., U. of Leipzig, Germany, 1888; Litt.D., Middlebury (Vt.) Coll., 1937; teacher in England, 1888; student at Paris, 1889; m. Helen Voss, of Elgin, Ill., June 24, 1890; children—Ralph Alfred (dec.), Helen Minnie, Karl Voss (dec.), Rudolph L. (dec.). Instr. French, 1889-90, adj. prof. Romance languages, 1890-92, professor Germanic languages, 1892-1901, dean Acad. Department, 1900-01, Vanderbilt Univ.; prof. German, Univ. of Wis. 1901-36, emeritus, 1936—. Decorated Knight's Cross of the Order of Merit, German Federal Republic, 1955. Member of the Modern Lang. Association America (chmn. central div., 1904, pres. 1913), Am. Assn. Teachers of German (pres. 1933), Goethe-Gesellschaft in Weimar, Goethe-Verein in Vienna; hon. senator Deutsche Akademie (München, Germany). Author: Die altenglischen Misterienspiele, 1888. Editor of two stories by Marie von Ebner-Eschenbach, 1898. Editor-in-chief of Deutsches Liederbuch für amerikanische Studenten, 1906; editor Neues deutsches Liederbuch, 1931, and of The Goethe Centenary at the University of Wisconsin, 1932. Coauthor: Wortindex zu Goethe's Faust, 1940; Fifty Years with Goethe, 1952. Contbr. to Am. and German periodicals. Home: 1911 Vilas Av., Madison, Wis. Died Apr. 18, 1956; buried Madison, Wis.

HOIDALE, Einar, lawyer, ex-congressman; b. Tromso, Norway, Aug. 17, 1870; s. Andrew and Dorothea (Lund) H.; brought to U.S., 1879; LL.B., U. Minn., 1898; m. Martha Skjei, Mar. 7, 1912; children—Elsa, Sherwood, Jean. Began as newspaper pub., Dawson, Minn.; began practice of law at New Ulm, Minn., 1898; 73d Congress, Minn. at large. Judge advocate, maj. Minn. N.G., 1900-08. Mem. Theta Chi. Democrat. Club: Minneapolis Athletic. Home: Leamington Hotel. Office: McKnight Bldg., Mpls. Died Dec. 5, 1952.

HOKE, Travis Henderson, editor, author; b. St. Louis, Oct. 28, 1892; s. George Storer and Marie patricia (Henderson) H.; prep. edn. Manual Training School, Washington U.; student Washington U., 1913-14; special study N.Y.U., 1919; m. Ann Brill Shapiro, Mar. 27, 1918 (div. 1935); m. 2d, Alice Dickinson, Oct. 10, 1943. Reporter St. Louis Republic, 1909, Sport and Stage, St. Louis, 1910; asst. sec. St. Louis Civic League, 1911-12; field sec. Lakes-to-Gulf Deep Waterway Assn., 1913; editor Public Affairs, St. Louis, 1913; sec. Greater St. Louis Com., 1914-15; asso. editor The Dial, 1916-17; editor Reilly & Britton Pub. Co., Chgo., 1917-18; foreign trade editor Standard Statistics Co., N.Y. C., 1918-19; asso. editor Am. Weekly (Sunday mag. of Hearst newspapers), 1920-29; editor Popular Science Monthly, 1929-30. Served from cpl. to sgt., C.A., N.Y.G., 1918-19. Author: Weather (with E. E. Free), 1929; Marraige or Its Equivalent, 1934; The Short Story Builder (with Stewart Beach), 1935; also collaborator in med., mil. and hist. books. Contbr. to mags. State dir. for N.Y. City of Works Progress Adminstrn. Federal Writers' Projects, 1936-37. Address: 333 Riverside Dr., N.Y.C. 25. Died June 14, 1947.

HOLAHAN, Maurice Fenelon, corp. ofcl.; b. Waukon, Ia., July 3, 1873; s. James and Kathryn (Fenelon) H.; student pub. schs., Waukon, Ia., 1880-92; m. Margaret McMorrow, Oct. 2, 1902 (dec.); children—Maurice Fenelon, Margaret (Mrs. Frank R. Howard). With Deering Harvester Co. and Internat. Harvester Co., 1894—, repairs and sales, Nashville, 1894-1900, br. mgr., Atlanta, 1900-15; Springfield, Ill., 1915-19, successively dist. sales mgr., asst. sales mgr., sales mgr., v.p. in charge of sales, Chgo., 1919-35, became 1st v.p. and mem. bd. dirs. and exec. com., 1935, now dir. Republican. Roman Catholic. K.C. Clubs: Chicago, South Shore Country (Chgo.). Home: 5555 Everett Av. Office: 180 N. Michigan Av., Chgo. Died Nov. 19, 1957; buried Mt. Olivet Cemetery, Worth, Ill.

HOLBROOK, Elmer Allen, educator; b. Fitchburg, Mass., June 23, 1881; s. John Perry and Martha (Allen) H.; B.S., Mass. Inst. Tech., 1904, E.M., U. Ill., 1916; D.Sc., U. Pitts., 1948; m. Sarah Kirby, Aug. 15, 1905 (died 1907); 1 dau., Katherine; m. 2d, Edith L. Brookfield, 1912; children—John Brookfield, Dorothy Mary, E. Allen, Ruth Estelle. Supt. Gould (Mont.) Mines Co., 1904, Ruby Gulch Mining Co., 1905; gen. supt. Daily Reduction Co., Hedley, B.C., 1906-09; cons. practice, 1909-10; prof. mining N.S. Tech. Coll., Halifax, 1911-12; asst. prof. mining, U. Ill., 1913-14, prof. in mineral preparation, 1915-16; with U.S. Bur. Mines, 1917-22, asst. dir., 1920-22, also chief metal mining engr. and exec. officer of investigations br. of the Bur.; dean sch. of mines Pa. State Coll., 1922-27, also acting dean Grad. Sch., 1925-27; dean, Schs. of Engring. and Mines, U. Pitts., 1927-50, ret.; tech. adviser NRA in formation of the Bituminous Coal Code, 1933; mem. Pa. State Sanitary Water Bd., 1947—; commr. for Pa. on Ohio River Valley Interstate Water Sanitation Commn., 1948—. Nat. pres. Nat. Soc. Profl. Engrs., Am. Standards Assn., Phi Gamma Delta, Sigma Xi, Theta Tau, Sigma Tau, Sigma Gamma Epsilon, Phi Kappa Phi. Methodist. Club: University. Author articles on mining and engring. Home: 1543 Shady Av., Pitts. Died Feb. 1957.

HOLBROOK, Roland C., corp. exec.; Newport, Vt., Apr. 10, 1898; s. Jesse William and Kate M. (Stewart) H.; student Central Coll., Winnipeg, Man., Middlebury (Vt.) Coll.; m. Florence M. Leckie, Jan. 28, 1922 (dec.); 1 son, Richard Carlyle. With Liquid Carbonic Canadian Corp., Ltd., 1919—, pres. and gen. mgr., hdqrs. Montreal, 1939—; pres. Liquid Carbonic West Indies, Ltd., Imperial Oxygen, Ltd., Liquid Carbonic Venezolana, S.C.; v.p. Nat. Fire & Casualty Ins. Co.; dir. Liquid Carbonic Co., Ltd., London, Liquid Carbonic Corp., Chgo., Liquid Carbonic Industries, S.A., Brazil. Mem. Canadian Mfrs. Assn., Montreal Bd. Trade. Mason. Clubs: Engineers, Thistle Curling, Canadian, Royal Montreal Golf, Seigniory (Montreal). Home: 3980 Cote-des-Neigas Rd., Montreal. Office: 8400 Decarie Blvd., Montreal 16, P.Q., Can. Died July 29, 1956.

HOLCH, Arthur Everett, educator, plant ecologist; b. Gilman, Ill., Apr. 18, 1891; s. Frederick Godfrey and Mary Elizabeth (West) H.; B.Mus. with spl. honors, U. Ill., 1913; A.B., U. Colo., 1913, A.M., 1924; Ph.D., U. Neb., 1931; m. Hazeldean Shirley, June 8, 1915; children—Mary Shirley (Mrs. William L. Jacobs), Arthur Everett. Supt. schs., Cortez, Colo., 1913-14; prin., sci. instr. Cripple Creek (Colo.) High Sch., 1914-18; prin. Scottsbluff (Neb.) High Sch., 1918-19; asst. prof. biology, dir. band and orchestra Neb. State Tchrs. Coll., 1919-21, chmn. biology dept., 1921-32; instr. botany U. Neb., 1930-31; chmn. botany dept. Denver U., 1932—. Fellow A.A.A.S. (council 1931-32); mem. Ecol. Soc. Am., Brit. Ecol. Soc., Bot. Soc. Am., Neb. (pres. 1930-31), Colo-Wyo. acads. sci., Sigma Xi, Phi Delta Kappa, Kappa Delta Pi, Phi Sigma, Delta Sigma Rho, Pi Kappa Lambda, Pi Gamma Mu. Episcopalian. Contbr. articles profl. jours. Home: 140 Krameria St., Denver 20. Died Mar. 12, 1958.

HOLCOMB, Horace Hale, ry. ofcl.; b. Platteville, Wis., Oct. 12, 1865; s. Judson H. and Martha (Whitcher) H.; student Wis. State Normal Sch., Platteville; m. Mary Lee Bragg, 1888; children—Ruth (Mrs. Frank H. Eustis), Martha (Mrs. Goodwin Clark), Horace Hale. Began as clk. local freight office C.,B.&Q. R.R., 1889, trans. to gen. offices, 1898, chief clk., 1903, asst. gen. freight agt., Chgo., 1908, gen. freight agt., Omaha, 1912, asst. freight traffic mgr., Chgo., 1917, freight traffic mgr., 1920-29, v.p., 1929-39; retired. Mason. Clubs: Union League, Traffic (Chgo.); Hinsdale (Ill.). Home: 225 E. First St., Hinsdale, Ill. Office: 547 W. Jackson Blvd., Chgo. Died Oct. 19, 1955.

HOLDEN, Alice M., prof. polit. sci.; b. Worcester, Mass., Aug. 16, 1882; d. Charles S. and Emma L. (Morse) Holden; A.B., Smith Coll., 1905; A.M., Radcliffe Coll., 1916, Ph.D., 1924; student, U. of Mich., 1919-20, Acad. of Internat. Law, The Hague (Netherlands), 1937. Sec., dept. of econs., Harvard, 1906-11; bur. of research in municipal govt., Harvard, 1911-16; instr., polit. science, Vassar Coll., 1916-17; instr., history, Wellesley Coll., 1917-18; successively instr., asst. prof., associate prof., prof., Smith Coll., 1921-50, chmn., dept. of govt., 1940-50; director Smith Coll. Jr. Year in Geneva, 1946-47; chmn., Smith Coll. Emergency Council, 1942-45. Carnegie Fellow in internat. law, U. of Mich., 1919-20, Radcliffe Coll., 1920-21; mem. Am. Soc. of Internat. Law (exec. council, 1939-42), Am. Soc. of Internat. Law, Am. Polit. Science Assn., Am. Assn. of U. Women, Cath. Assn. of Internat. Peace, Phi Beta Kappa. Democrat. Catholic. Asso. editor, Nat. Municipal Rev., 1917-18; mem. bd. editors, Am. Polit. Science Rev., 1915-16. Contbd. articles to jours. Home: Smith College, Northampton, Mass. Died Dec. 25, 1951.

HOLDEN, Carl Frederick, naval officer; b. Bangor, Me., May 25, 1895; s. William F. and Mary Ellen (Riley) H.; B.S., U.S. Naval Acad., 1917; M.S. (elec. communication engring.), Harvard, 1924; m. Cordelia Folsom Carlisle, Nov. 27, 1919; children—Jean, Carl Frederick. Commd. ensign U.S. Navy, 1917, and advanced through grades to rear adm., 1945; duty in destroyers, Queenstown, Ireland and Brest, France, 1917-19, as exec. officer, navigator, engring. officer, 1919-22; on staff of comdr., destroyer scouting force, Atlantic, 1924-27; mem. U.S. Naval mission to Brazil, Rio de Janeiro, 1927-30; communication officer, U.S.S. Arizona, 1931-32; comdr. U.S.S. Tarbell, 1932-34; dist. communication officer, 14th Naval Dist., Honolulu, T.H., 1934-36; navigator U.S. S. Idaho, comdg. officer; U.S.S. Ramapo, 1936-38; in charge of radio shore activities, office of dir. of naval communications, U.S. Navy Dept., 1938-40; exec. officer, U.S.S. Pennsylvania, 1940-42; communication officer, U.S. Fleet, 1942, dir. of naval communications, 1942-43; comdg. officer, U.S.S. New Jersey, Task Force 38 and 58, Pacific, 1943-45; comdr. cruiser div., Pacific, 1945; comdr. training command, Atlantic fleet, 1946-52; comdr., U.S. Naval base, N.Y., 1948-52, ret. 1952; pres. Fed. Telecommunication Labs., Inc., 1952—. Awarded Legion of Merit with gold star in lieu of 2nd with V for combat, bronze star with gold star in lieu of 2nd with V for combat, victory medal with star, World War I, Occupation Germany Medal, World War I, China Service Medal, following World War II medals: Am. defense medal with star. Asiatic Pacific with 11 stars, Am. area, Victory, Naval occupation service, Philippine Liberation with 2 stars. Republican. Roman Catholic. Clubs: Army Navy, Army Navy Country (Washington), N.Y. Yacht, India House (N. Y. City), Racquet and Tennis (N.Y. City), Union (N.Y.C.). Home: Greenfield, N.H. Office: Federal Telecommunication Laboratories, Inc., 500 Washington Av., Nutley 10, N.J. Died May 18, 1953; buried Arlington Nat. Cemetery.

HOLDEN, Hale, paper manufacturer; b. Kansas City, Mo., Apr. 30, 1900; s. Hale and Ellen Mitchell (Weston) H.; grad. Hotchkiss Sch., Lakeville, Conn.; A.B., Yale, 1922; m. Josephine Bell Cotton, Aug. 4, 1923 (died Mar. 12, 1937); children—Joan Holden, Hale III; m. 2d, Margaretta Large Harrison, May 3, 1938; m. 3d, Carolyn McKay Stanton, Dec. 15, 1951. Draftsman Pullman Co., 1922-23, sales agt., 1923-30, asst. to pres., 1930-31, v.p., 1931-42; pres. and dir. Byron Weston Co., Dalton, Mass., May 1, 1942—; dir. Pittsfield Third Nat. Bank, City Savings Bank, Pittsfield, Mass., Berkshire Life Insurance Co.; treas. House of Mercy Hospital, Pittsfield, Mass. Served in U.S. Naval Reserve, active duty, Sept.-Dec. 1918, inactive duty, 1919-22. Republican. Episcopalian. Clubs: Yale (New York); Pittsfield Country, Waconah Golf; Rolling Rock (Ligonier). Home: 780 Holmes Road, Pittsfield, Mass. Office: 12 Main St., Dalton, Mass. Died June 30, 1954; buried Dalton.

HOLDEN, Thomas Steele, business exec.; b. Dallas, Tex., May 5, 1886; s. Thomas Steele and Mary Helen (Wylie) H.; A.B., U. of Tex., 1907, A.M. in Mathematics, 1911; B.S. in Architecture, Mass. Inst. of Tech., 1916; m. Anne Stratton, Aug. 17, 1922; 1 son, Clay Stratton. Mathematics instr., U. of Tex. and Mass. Inst. Tech., 1909-14; archtl. practice, Boston, Mass., and Akron, O., 1916-18; spl. econ. investigator, U.S. Dept. of Labor, Jan.-June 1919; with F. W. Dodge Corp., pubs. constrn. and archtl. information, New York, since 1919, chief statistician, 1919-27, v.p. in charge statistics and research, and dir. 1927-41, pres., 1941-53, vice chairman board, 1953—; member board dirs. First Federal Savs. and Loan Assn., New York. Hon. mem. Bus. Adv. Council for Dept. of Commerce; pres., gov. N.Y. Bldg. Congress, Inc., 1935-40; dir. Commerce and Industry Assn. N.Y.; v.p., dir. Regional Plan Assn., Inc.; v.p., trustee John B. Pierce Found., 1954—. Served as 1st lt. Engring. Div., Ordnance Dept., U.S. Army, 1918; capt. Ordnance Res. Corps, 1919-22. Mem. N.A.M., A.I.A. (hon. member nat. and N.Y. chapters). Archtl. League of New York, Phi Gamma Delta and Phi Beta Kappa. Episcopalian. Clubs: Century, Engineers (New York); Tokeneke (Darien, Conn.); Nat. Press (Washington, D.C.). Contbr. of articles on constrn. industry economics, housing, etc., to publs. Lecturer to real estate bds., trade assns. Home: Rock Meadow, 27 Tory Hole Rd., Darien, Conn. Office: 119 W. 40th St., N.Y.C. 18. Died Nov. 3, 1958.

HOLDER, Charles Adams, ex-fgn. service officer, ret. banker; b. N.Y.C., Nov. 2, 1872; s. Charles H. and Harriett (Hall) H.; student Columbia, 1890-92; M.D., Jefferson Med. Coll., Phila., 1897; m. Margaretta Bonsall Taylor, 1907 (died 1933); children—Margaretta (Mrs. Albert Graebner), Charles H., Richmond; m. 2d, Mrs. Dorothy Caruso, July 5, 1933 (div. 1940). Asst. demonstrator therapeutics Jefferson Med. Coll., 1897-1900; physician in chief children's dept. So. Dispensary, Phila., asst. physician Jefferson Hosp. Clinic, aslo asst. editor Progressive Medicine, 1898-1900; practiced at Colorado Springs, Colo., physician St. Francis Hosp., 1900-09; joined fgn. service, 1909, counsul at Roen, France, 1909-12, consul gen. to Norway, 1912-13, Cologne, Germany, 1913-14; vice consul London, 1914-15, consul gen., 1915; fgn. trade adviser to Dept. of State, 1915-19; became pres. Adia Banking Corp., vice v.p. Guaranty Trust Co. in charge fgn. dept., ret. 1927. Home: 200 E. 66th St., N.Y.C. Died Apr. 2, 1955.

HOLDER, Edward Perry, mfr.; b. Pluckemin, N.J., Mar. 4, 1892; s. John Childs and Anne Kennedy (Kershow) H.; grad. Phillips Exeter Acad., 1914; B.A., Yale Coll., 1918; m. Florence Fitzpatrick, May 28, 1931; 1 dau., Ann Kershow Pietrafesa. Pres. Vulcan Iron Works, Wilkes-Barre, Pa., 1940-43; pres. and dir. Wickwire Spencer Steel Co., 1943-45, The Colorado Fuel and Iron Corp., Am. Wire Fabrics Corp., Wickwire Spencer Aviation Corp., Wickwire Spencer Metall. Corp., Colo. and Wyo. Ry. Co., Colo. and Wyo. Telegraph Co., 1945-46; pres. and dir. Cenco Corp., Holder Foundation; chmn. bd. dirs. Am. Bosch Corp., Arma Corp., Central Scientific Co., Great American Industries, Inc., Rex Products Corp.; dir., and mem. exec. com., National Can Co.; dir. Calif. Wire Cloth Corp., Colo. Fuel & Iron Warehouse Co., 1945-46; dir. Cineflex Corp., Kropp Forge Co., Shields, Inc., Standard Silica Corp., Universal Boring Machine Co. Presbyterian. Clubs: Yale (New York); Lake Shore (Chicago); Glen Ridge (N.J.) Country; Split Rock (Phila.). Home: 10 Crestmont Rd., Montclair, N.J. Office: 347 Madison Av., N.Y.C. 17. Died Sept. 5, 1951; buried Immaculate Conception Cemetery, Fayetteville, N.Y.

HOLDING, Elisabeth Sanxay, author; b. Brooklyn, N.Y.; d. Charles Skeffington and Edith (Hollick) Sanxay; ed. Miss Whitcombe's Sch., Packer Inst., Miss Botsford's Sch., Staten Island Acad.; m. George E. Holding, Aug. 2, 1913 (died 1943); children Skeffington Quin Ardron, Antonia Sanxay Schwed. Protestant. Mem. P.E.N., Authors League. Author: Invincible Minnie, 1920; Rosaleen Among the Artists, 1921; Angelica, 1921; The Unlit Lamp, 1922; The Shoals of Honor, 1926; The Silk Purse, 1928; Miasma, 1929; The Death-Wish, 1934; Strange Crime in Bermuda, 1937; The Obstinate Murderer, 1938; No Harm Intended, 1939; The Girl Who Had to Die, 1940; Who's Afraid?, 1940; Speak of the Devil, 1941; Kill Joy, 1942; Lady Killer, 1942; The Old Battle-Ax, 1942; Net of Cobwebs, 1945; The Innocent Mrs. Duff, 1946; The Blank Wall, 1947; Miss Kelly (juvenile), 1947; Too Many Bottles, 1951; The Virgin Huntress, 1951; The Widow's Mite, 1953. Also short stories in mags. Address: care Peter Schwed, Simon and Schuster, 630 Fifth Av., N.Y.C. 20. Died Feb. 7, 1955.

HOLDING, Robert Powell, banker; b. Wake Forest, N.C., Dec. 31, 1896; s. Thomas Elford and Minta (Royall) H.; A.B., Wake Forest Coll., 1916, LL.B., 1917, LL.D., 1957; m. Maggie Browne, January 11, 1922; children—Robert, Lewis Royall, Frank Browne. Asst. cashier Bank of Morehead City (N.C.), 1917-18, First Nat. Bank, Smithfield, N.C., 1918-19; cashier, First and Citizens Nat. Bank, Smithfield, 1919-26, v.p., 1926-34, pres., 1934—, chmn. of the bd., pres., dir., First-Citizens Bank & Trust Co.; dir. Carolina Tel. & Tel. Co., Carolina Ins. Co. Seashore Transportation Co., Textron, Inc. Trustee Wake Forest Coll. Mem. N.C. State Banking Commn. Home: S. 3d St. Office: Market St., Smithfield, N.C. Died Aug. 26, 1957; buried Riverside Cemetery, Smithfield.

HOLL, Dio Lewis, math. prof.; b. North Canton, O., Jan. 7, 1895; s. of Samuel J. and Emma (Swartz) H.; ed. Canton (Ohio) high sch.; A.B., Manchester Coll., 1917; M.A., Ohio State U., 1920; Ph.D., U. of Chicago, 1925; m. Irma Nauman, Aug. 1924; children—Bruce R. William W., Barbara Elizabeth. High sch. principal, 1917; grad. asst., instr., dept. of math. Ohio State U., 1919-22; grad. fellow U. Chgo. dept. math., 1922-23; asst. prof. math. Ohio Wesleyan U., 1923-25; asst. prof. math. Iowa State Coll., 1925-30, asso. prof. math., 1930-34, prof. math., 1934—, now also head dept. math., research prof. applied math., 1937—. Abstractor of papers in applied elasticity for Zentrablatt fur Mechanik, 1934-39; in applied elasticity for Mathematical Reviews since 1940. Has published many research articles in applied mathematics. Soldier, U.S. Army, Base Hospital, Camp Sherman, Ohio, 1918-19. Mem. Am. Math. Soc., Am. Soc. M.E. (mechanics sect.), Delta Sigma Phi, Pi Mu Epsilon, Sigma Xi (sec.-treas. Iowa State Coll. chpt., 1936-41, pres. 1941-42). Presbyn. Contbr. articles to research publs. Home: 2323 Donald St., Ames, Ia. Died May 20, 1954; buried College cemetery, Ames, Ia.

HOLLADAY, Alexander Quarles, educator; b. b. Spottsylvania Co., Va., May 8, 1839; s. Hon. Alexander and P. Q. (Poindexter) H.; grad. Univ. of Va.; studied in Univ. of Berlin; studied law, Univ. of Va., and in Richmond, Va. (LL.D., Davidson Coll., N.C.); m. Virginia Randolph Bolling, Apr. 17, 1861 (died 1899). Served in Confederate army, 1861-65; State senator, Va., 4 yrs.; practiced law; educator 21 yrs.—pres. Stonewall Jackson Inst., Abingdon, Va., Fla. State Coll., and N.C. Coll. Agr. and Mech. Arts, 1899-1901; retired to farm. Fellow Soc. Sciences, Letters and Art, London. Democrat. Presby'n. Address: Warminster, Va. Died Jan. 4, 1949.

HOLLAND, Ernest O., ex-coll. pres.; b. Bennington, Ind., Feb. 4, 1874; s. Philip C. and Ann A. (Chittenden) H.; A.B., Ind. U., 1895, LL.D., 1937; fellow in edn. Columbia, 1909-10, Ph.D., 1912; LL.D., Whitman College, 1942; studied in Europe, summers 1905, 09, studied social and economic conditions there, 6 mos., 1923-24. Tchr. high schools, Ind., 1895-1900; head English dept., Boys' High Sch., Louisville, 1900-05; asso. prof. edn. Ind. U., 1905-07, jr. prof., 1907-08, prof. secondary edn., 1908-11; supt. schs., Louisville, 1911-16; pres. Wash. State College, Pullman, 1916-45, pres. emeritus, 1945—; lectr. on ednl. adminstrn. U. Cal., summer 1912, and on college and university adminstrn. Tchrs. Coll. (Columbia), summer 1926. Visited leading U.S. art centers to obtain paintings for Virginia and Charles Orton Collection, 1945-47; now conducting ednl. survey in Austria for USAF. Mem. Wash. Bd. Edn.; mem. Adv. Bd. Reconstrn. Ednl. Alliance; mem. Com. of Selection, Rhodes Scholarship Trust, 1927-32; elector Hall of Fame, 1928—; ex-sec. Soc. Coll. Tchrs. of Edn.; pres. Assn. Land-Grant Colleges and Univs., 1931-32; mem. Am. Acad. Polit. and Social Science, Acad. Political Science, League of Nations Assn., A.A.A.S., Phi Beta Kappa, Sigma Chi, Phi Delta Kappa, Phi Kappa Phi, Sigma Delta Chi; mem. various national and state war coms.; chmn. Com. of Twenty-two on Teachers' Annuities, Pub. Schs., State of Wash., 1945-47. Joint author: Coll. and Univ. Administration. Author: Written and Oral Composition (with Martin W. Sampson), 1907; The Pennsylvania State Normal Schools and Public Schools, 1912. Home: 305 Columbia St., Pullman, Wash. Died May 30, 1950.

HOLLAND, Laurier Fox-Strangways, mining engr.; b. London, Eng.; s. Lt. Col. F. Holland (Indian Staff Corps) and Lily Mary (Everett) H.; ed. King's Coll., London; Sch. of Mining, Queen's U., Ont., Can., 1898; m. Lillian Harris, Halifax, N.S. Was metallurgist of Black Eagle Mine, Ont.; mine capt., Belmont Mine, Ont.; mill supt., Waverley Mines, N.S.; mgr. Evangeline Gold Mine, N.S.; supt. of mines for Smuggler Union Mining Co., Telluride, Colo., 1905-13; also examining engr. New England Exploration Co.; research work in rare metals, especially molybdenum, to 1916; field engr. Consol. Ariz. Smelting Co., Humboldt, Ariz., 1916-17; cons. engr. Ariz. Mines & Reduction Co., Wickenburg, Ariz., and Rare Metals Refining Co., Pasadena, Cal., 1917-19; mgr. for U.S. Smelting, Refining & Mining Co. of the Crater Mining Co., Ariz., 1920-21; research work in flotation processes, 1924; micro-paleontologist for Cal. Petroleum Corp. and the Tex. Co. (Cal), 1925-29; pres. and gen. mgr. Golden Horseshoe Mining Corp., Ltd., to 1933; gen. mgr. Guildford Mine, Placerville, Cal., 1934; now gen. mgr., sec. Pacific Mines, Oregon Mine, Rose Mine, Texas Hill Placer, Harmon Mine, Excelsior, Epley Mine and the Missouri Flat Placer; sec. and treas. Placerville Gold Mining Co. (all at Placerville, Cal.); cons. engr. Mem. Am. Inst. Mining and Metall. Engrs., Am. Assn. Petroleum Geologists, Soc. Economic Paleontologists and Mineralogists, Legion of Honor of Am. Inst. Mining Engrs. Episcopalian. Mason. Clubs: Peter Pan Woodland (Cal.); Royal Socs. (London). Address: Placerville, Cal. Died Nov. 13, 1957; buried East Lawn Cemetery, Sacramento.

HOLLAND, Leicester Bodine, prof. fine arts; b. Louisville, Ky., May 23, 1882; s. James W. and Mary Boggs (Rupert) H.; grad. William Penn Charter Sch., Phila., 1898; B.S., U. of Pa., 1902, B.S. in Architecture, 1904, M.A., 1917, Ph.D., 1919; m. Louise Elizabeth Whetenhall Adams, Dec. 27, 1923; children—Barbara Adams, Marian Rupert, Lawrence Rozier. Architect and archtl. draftsman with Wilson Eyre, Jr., Cram, Goodhue & Ferguson, and mem. firm of Howell & Holland, Phila., until 1912; teacher architectural design and history of architecture, U. of Pa., 1913-18; asso. prof. architecture, Am. Sch. of Classical Studies at Athens, 1919-22; prof. fine arts, Vassar, 1925-27, U. of Pa. 1929-46, ret.; prof. architecture, also head department of architecture, University of Miami since 1948; also chief division of fine arts, Library of Congress, 1929-43; with office of Strategic Services, 1944. Architect with Corinth Excavations of American School in Athens, 1946-47. Fellow Am. Inst. Architects; mem. Archaeol. Institute of America, American Philos. Soc. (councillor). Clubs: Century Assn., Franklin Inn. Author: The Garden Blue Book, 1914; Traffic Ways about France in the Dark Ages, 1919; Ready Written Specifications (with Harry Parker), 1925. Contbr. Am. Jour. Archæology. Home: 415 W. Price St., Philadelphia 44, Pa. Office: Miami University, Oxford, O. Died Feb. 17, 1952; buried Leicester, Mass.

HOLLAND, Robert Allen, art dir.; b. Edgerton, Mo., May 6, 1868; s. Robert Elbert and Sarah Elizabeth (Bowring) H.; student DePauw U., Greencastle, Ind., 1889-94. Cincinnati Art Acad., 1901-02; m. Eliza A. Creek, 1892; children—Mrs. Lucile Mae Stohlman. Glen Allen, Mrs. Aithra Bence Shelton; m. 2d. Madeline Borggraefe, 1923. Clergyman M.E. Ch., 1889-93; acting dir. City Art Mus., St. Louis, 1912-13, dir. 1913-23; dir. Kansas City Art Inst., 1924-33; curator William Rockhill Nelson Gallery of Art and Mary Atkins Museum of Fine Arts, Kansas City, 1930-33. Art lecturer. Home: Castlewood, St. Louis County, Mo. Ded Feb. 12, 1959.

HOLLAND, Rupert Sargent, author; b. Louisville, Ky., Oct. 15, 1878; s. James William and Mary B. (Rupert) H.; A.B., Harvard, 1900; LL.B., U. of Pa., 1903; m. Margaret Currier Lyon, Aug. 19, 1918; children—Richard Lyon (deceased), Eleanor Sargent, David Thurston. Admitted to bar, 1903; chief atty. Legal Aid Soc., Phila., 1904-10; lecturer Am. Soc. for Extension of University Teaching. Mem. bd. mgrs. Apprentices' Library of Philadelphia, Philadelphia City Institute, Wayne Library. Club: Franklin Inn. Author: The Count at Harvard, 1906; Builders of United Italy, 1908; The Man in the Tower, 1909; Historic Boyhoods, 1909; Historic Girlhoods, 1910; The Boy Scouts of Birch Bark Island, 1911; Historic Inventions, 1911; Knights of the Golden Spur, 1912; Historic Poems and Ballads, 1912; Heart of Sally Temple, 1913; Historic Adventures, 1913; Historic Heroes of Chivalry, 1914; William Penn, 1915; The Boy Scouts of Snow-Shoe Lodge, 1915; Blackbeard's Island, 1916; Historic Events of Colonial Days, 1916; The Blue Heron's Feather, 1917; Lafayette, We Come, 1918; All 'Round Our House, 1919; Neptune's Son, 1919; The Man in the Moonlight, 1920; Refugee Rock, 1920; The Panelled Room, 1921; The House of Delusion, 1922; Peter Cotterell's Treasure, 1922; Lafayette for Young Americans, 1922; Crooked Lanes, 1923; The Mystery of the Opal, 1924; Minot's Folly, 1925; Pirates of the Delaware, 1925; Historic Ships, 1926; The Rider in the Green Mask, 1926; Historic Railroads, 1927; Red Beard of Virginia, 1927; Historic Airships, 1928; The Splendid Buccaneer, 1928; Drake's Lad, 1929; Sons of Seven Cities, 1929; The Pirate of the Gulf, 1929; The Dauntless Company, 1930; Mad Anthony, 1931; Yankee Ships in Pirate Waters, 1931; A Race for a Fortune, 1931; Captain Tsipp, 1932; Rescue, 1932; How Murder Speaks, 1933; Big Bridge, 1935; The Sea Scouts of Birch-Bark Island, 1936; Plays of the American Colonies, 1937; The Boy Who Lived on London Bridge, 1938; The Chateau of the Swan, 1939; Steadfast at Valley Forge, 1939; Secret of Blennerhassett, 1941; Wreckers Reef, 1941; Freedom's Flag, 1943; also mag. articles and stories. Home: 216 Walnut Av. Wayne, Pa. Died May 3, 1952.

HOLLAND, Ubert Cecil, univ. prof. and dean; b. Petrolia, Ont., Can., May 16, 1889; came to U.S., 1924, naturalized 1936; s. John and Mary Jane (McIntyre) H.; B. Applied Sci., U. of Toronto, 1920; M.E., U. of Pa., 1928; m. Dorothy Theresa Stevens, June 7, 1938; 1 son, Robert Stevens. Ins. munitions Imperial Munitions Bd., Toronto, 1915-16; purchasing agent Russell Motor Car Co., 1916-18; lecturer in machine design U. of Toronto, 1920-24; lecturer U. of Pa., 1924-31; designer of oil circuit breakers Gen. Electric Co., Phila., 1926-30; asst. prof. mech. engring. Rutgers U., 1931-35, asso. prof., 1935-38, asso. prof. engring. drawing, 1938-41, asst. coordinator civilian pilot training corps, 1940-41, head gen. engring. dept. and asst. to dean, 1941-46, prof. engring. drawing, 1942—, asst. dean, 1946—, acting dean, 1947-48. Served with Canadian Officers Training Corps, Eng., World War I. Mem. A.S.M.E., A.S. Engring. Edn., Tau Beta Pi. Holder patent on steel drafting table. Home: 105 Lincoln Av., Highland Park, N.J. Office: College of Engineering, Rutgers Univ., New Brunswick, N.J. Died Feb. 26, 1957; buried Franklin Meml. Park, New Brunswick.

HOLLENBECK, Don, radio analyst, writer, journalist; b. Lincoln, Neb., March 30, 1905; s. Clyde and Clara (Davey) H.; student Univ. of Neb.; m. Angélique Dean, Aug. 8, 1941; children—Zoë, Jessie. Home: 148 E. 48th St., N.Y. City 17. Office: 485 Madison Av., N.Y.C. 22. Died June 22, 1954.

HOLLIDAY, Robert Paul, editor, pub.; b. Norwalk, O., Apr. 22, 1894; s. Albert Clinton and Mary O'Minda (McGuckin) H.; grad. high sch., Norwalk, O., 1912; m. Mary Roller Carpenter, May 25, 1921. Began in newspaper business, 1912; editor and pub. Santa Monica, Calif., Evening Outlook, 1922-30; pub. San Francisco Call-Bulletin, 1930-35; now chairman West-Holliday Co. First lieut. of infantry, U.S. Army, World War; lt. col. of inf., Calif. N.G. Republican. Episcopalian. Mason. Home: Box 258, Hollister. Cal. Address: 625 Market, San Francisco 5, Cal. Died Jan. 1959.

HOLLIDAY, Wallace Trevor, ret. oil co. exec.; b. Cleve., Mar. 10, 1884; s. William Wallace and Mary E. B. (McDonald) H.; student Western Reserve U., 1901-04; A.B., Cornell U., 1905; LL.B., Harvard, 1908; LL.D., Rollins College, 1947; m. Nellie B. Stiers, Dec. 28, 1910; children—Samuel James, Margaret Louise; m. 2d, Mary A. Osborne, May 9, 1940. Began practice of law at Cleve. with Kline, Tolles & Goff, later Holliday, Grossman & McAfee; rep. Standard Oil Co. of Ohio as gen. counsel, 1917-28, pres., 1928-49, chmn. bd., 1949-50. Dir. Am. Petroleum Inst., Nat. Petroleum Assn.; pres. Great Lakes Exposition, 1937; mem. Petroleum Industry War Council, 1941-45, Nat. Petroleum Council; pres. Cleveland C. of C., 1943-44. Dir. N.A.M., 1932-43, regional v.p. 1939-42. Mem. exec. Council, World Federalists, U.S.A., mem. exec. com. United World Federalists; chmn. Greater Cleve. Hosp. Fund campaign, 1946-47. Trustee Berea Coll. Mem. Delta Upsilon. Republican. Episcopalian. Clubs: Rowfant, Union, Cleveland Athletic, Chagrin Valley Hunt. Home: Chardon, O. Office: Midland Bldg., Cleve. Died Nov. 7, 1950; buried Gates Mills Cemetery, Cleve.

HOLLINGSWORTH, Amor, paper mfr.; b. Boston, Oct. 18, 1880; s. Zachary Taylor and Ida (Hollingsworth) H.; A.B., Harvard, 1902, student law sch., 1902-04; m. Evelyn Knapp Parsons, Nov. 24, 1908; children—Amor, Evelyn Livingston, Schuyler. With Tileston & Hollingsworth Co., 1904—, pres., 1908-42, chmn. bd.; with Penobscot Chem. Fibre Co., Boston, 1904—, president, 1919—, chmn. board; pres. Penobscot Development Co., 1919—; dir. Boston Safe Deposit & Trust Co., Hollingsworth & Vose Company, Arkwright Mutual Fire Insurance Company. Clubs: Harvard, Brook (New York City); Somerset, Tennis and Racquet, Harvard (Boston). Address: 211 Congress St., Boston 10. Died Oct. 28, 1955; buried Miton, Mass.

HOLLINGWORTH, Harry Levi, psychologist; b. DeWitt, Neb., May 26, 1880; s. Thomas and Libbie (Andrews) H.; student Neb. Wesleyan U.; B.A., U. Neb., 1906; Ph.D., Columbia 1909; LL.D., U. Neb., 1937; m. Leta A. Stetter, Dec. 31, 1908 (died Nov. 27, 1939); m. 2d, Josefine Weischer, June 12, 1946. Asst. in psychology U. Neb., 1904-06; principal high school, 1906-07; asst. in psychology Columbia, 1907-09, instr., 1910-14, asst. prof., 1914-16, asso. prof., 1916-21, prof., 921-46, emeritus. Mem. Phi Beta Kappa, Sigma Xi, Alpha Tau Omega. Author: Inaccuracy of Movement, 1909; Influence of Caffein, 1912; Principles of Appeal and Response, 1913; Studies in Judgment, 1913; Outline for Experimental Psychology, 1914; Outlines for Applied and Abnormal Psychology, 1914; Advertising, Its Principles and Practice, 1915; Vocational Psychology, 1916; The Sense of Taste, 1917; Applied Psychology, 1917; Psychology of Functional Neuroses, 1920; Judging Human Character, 1922; Psychology of Thought, 1926; Mental Growth and Decline, 1927; Psychology, Its Facts and Principles, 1928; Abnormal Psychology, 1930; Educational Psychology, 1932; Psychology of the Audience, 1935; Psycho-Dynamics of Chewing, 1939; Leta Stetter Hollingworth, a Biography, 1943; Psychology and Ethics, 1949. Home: Montrose, N.Y. Died Sept. 17, 1956; buried Wyuka Cemetery, Lincoln, Neb.

HOLLIS, Allen (hŏl-Is), lawyer; b. Concord, N.H., Dec. 20, 1871; s. Abijah and Harriette Van Mater (French) H.; student Harvard Law Sch., 1892-93; hon. A.M., Dartmouth, 1906; m. Amoret Nichoson, Nov. 10, 1897; children—Allen (dec.), Franklin. Admitted to N.H. bar, 1893; pres. Concord Electric Co., Exeter & Hampton Electric Co.; dir. United Life & Accident Ins. Co. Dir. Class C and v. chmn. Federal Reserve Bank, Boston, 1914-36; also dir. Public Service Co. of N.H. and of other corps. Pres. N.H. Forestry Assn. Club: Union (Boston). Congregationalist. Mason. Home: 110 Centre St. Office: 17 Capitol St., Concord, N.H. Died Apr. 26, 1955.

HOLLIS, Henry Leonard, mining engr.; b. Boston, Feb. 17, 1866; s. John Henry and Esther (Harlow) H.; student Bklyn. Poly. Inst.; E.M., Sch. of Mines, Columbia, 1885; m. Jane Dustin Grannis, Nov. 9, 1892 (dec.); 1 dau., Mrs. Clara Hollis McLean. Profl. work, 1889—, has been examination and management of mining properties, and consultation work in connection with development and operation of mines, gas and petroleum properties and metall. plants; dir. Libby-Owens-Ford Co., Electric Bond & Share Co. Unitarian. Mem. Am. Inst. Mining and Metall. Engrs. Clubs: Chicago, Saddle and Cycle, Old Elm (Chgo.). Home: 1242 Lake Shore Dr. Office: 224 S. Michigan Av., Chgo. 4. Died Nov. 1958.

HOLLISTER, Fred H., banker; b. Rockton, Ill., Aug. 21, 1865; s. George Henry and Fannie E. (Hooker) H.; m. Lydia Belle Gifford; children—Helen (Mrs. J. Harvey Douglas), Mary (Mrs. Ronald N. Brown), Frances (Mrs. George Nelson). Banking, 1890—; chmn. bd. Northwest Security Nat. Bank, Sioux Falls, S.D.; pres., dir. Security State Bank, Tyndall, S.D., Security State Bank, Geddes, S.D.; dir. Girton-Adams Ice Co. Mason (Shriner). Club: Minnehaha Country (Sioux Falls, S.D.). Home: 221 E. 21st St. Office: Northwest Security Bank, Sioux Falls, S.D. Died Oct. 20, 1955.*

HOLLISTER, Joseph, newspaper man; b. Norfolk, Conn., Nov. 11, 1877; s. Charles Norman and Annie (Dempsey) H.; grad. Robbins Prep. Sch., Norfolk, Conn., 1896; studied classics and history under pvt. tutors; m. Helen Pauline Barrett, Sept. 20, 1899. Began newspaper writing in boyhood; asso. editor Berkshire Evening and Weekly Eagle, 1898—, contbg. daily column of verse, pleasantry and philosophy, under title of The Note Book; contbr. articles to New York Sun, etc.; wrote for Govt. signed editorials, dealing with thrift stamps, during war period. Mem. City Council, Pittsfield, 1904-05. Mem. Pittsfield Park and Playground Assn., Young Woman's Home Assn. (dir.), Berkshire br. Mass. Soc. for Prevention of Cruelty to Children. Republican. Conglist. Mason. Home: 81 Commonwealth Av. Address: 33 Eagle St., Pittsfield, Mass. Died 1946.

HOLLOWAY, William Grace, business exec.; b. San Francisco, May 17, 1886; s. William Edlin and Alice (Grace) H.; A.B., Harvard, 1908; m. Hilda Holmes, July 18, 1918; children—William Grace, Hilda (Mrs. Eben W. Pyne). Joined W.R. Grace & Co., N.Y. City, 1908, asst. mgr. San Francisco office, 1911-12, resident mgr., Peru, 1915-22, v.p., 1922-45, dir. since 1929, treas. 1936-48, chmn. bd. dirs. 1945-55, hon. chmn. bd. dirs., 1955—; chmn. Grace Bros. & Co., Ltd., London, 1923-29; mem. adv. com. to dirs. Chem. Corn Exchange Bank; director Grace Line. Trustee Village of Old Westbury (L.I.), 1935-47; treas. Lima (Peru) chpt. A.R.C., 1917-22. Founder, dir., treas. Brit. Am. Hosp., Lima, 1921-22; founder, dir. Am. Soc. Peru, 1917-22, pres. 1920-21; dir. Grace Inst., N.Y. City, Lillius Gilchrest Grace Inst., Tenant's Harbor, Me.; dir., pres. Iglenart Health Fund. Clubs: India House, Meadow Brook, Piping Rock, Racquet and Tennis (N.Y.C.); City of London; Nacional (Lima); Burlingame Country (San Francisco). Home: Foxland, Old Westbury, L.I. Office: 7 Hanover Sq., N.Y.C. 5. Died Jan. 7, 1959.

HOLLY, William H., ret. judge; b. Bellefonte, Pa., Sept. 19, 1869; s. Timothy R. and Margaret (McDonough) H.; student pub. and pvt. schs., Macomb, Ill.; m. Nell McClen, Dec. 19, 1894; 1 dau., Margaret. Admitted to Ill. bar, 1891, and began practice at Macomb; mem. Prentiss, Baily & Holly, 1891-92, Baily & Holly, 1892-99, Camp & Holly, 1899-1902; removed to Chicago, Sept. 1902; mem. Hall & Holly, 1906-12, Mills & Holly, 1912-14; asst. state's atty., 1914-16; resumed private practice, 1916; mem. Darrow, Sissman, Holly & Carlin, 1922-26; alone, 1926-30; later member Babcock, Holly, Worthy & Gilruth; apptd. spl. traction counsel City of Chicago, Sept. 1923; formerly atty. for Nat. Woman's Trade Union League, Am. Fed. of Teachers, Pub. Ownership League of America; judge U.S. Dist. Court, 1933-43, ret. Vice pres. Universalist Gen. Conv., 1917; mem. exec. com. Ill. Univeralist Conv., 1912-23, pres., 1912-15; mem. council Northwestern Settlement, 1912-22. Chmn. bd. trustees Lombard (mem. bd. mgrs. 1933) bar assns., Phi Delta Phi College, Meadville Theol. School, 1940-44; pres. Abraham Lincoln Centre. Mem. Am., Ill., Chgo. (mem. bd. mgrs. 1933) bar assns., Phi Delta Phi (hon.). Democrat. Mason (K.T.). Clubs: City, Chicato Literary (pres. 1945-46), Union League, Tavern. Contbr. to Life and Labor, and other mags. Home: 7301 Sheridan Rd., Chgo.; also Tucson, Ariz. Address: U.S. Court House, Chgo. Died Jan. 30, 1958.

HOLM, George Elmer, biochemist; b. Cokato, Minn., Jan. 20, 1891; s. John and Anna Sophia (Jonsson) H.; B.S., Carleton Coll., 1914; M.S., U. Minn., 1916, Ph.D., 1919; m. Julia M. Zanger, June 22, 1918; children—Helen Marie (Mrs. William W. Bedsworth), Julianne (Mrs. Lewis B. Timberlake). Principal of the high school in Dawson, Minn., 1914-15; instr. dept. agrl. biochemistry U. Minn., 1919, asst. prof., 1919-20; biochemist bur. diary industry U.S. Dept. Agr., 1920-42, head dairy products research div. since 1942. Ofcl. U.S. del. Internat. Dairy Congress, Berlin, 1937, Stockholm, 1949. Served as 1st lt. C.W.S., U.S. Army, 1917-19. Received Borden award Am. Chem. Soc., 1942, superior service award U.S. Dept. Agr., 1948. Mem. Am. Chem. Soc., Am. Dairy Sci. Assn., Washington Acad. Sci., A.A.A.S., Sigma Xi, Gamma Sigma Delta, Phi Lambda Upsilon, Alpha Chi Sigma, Gamma Alpha. Club: Cosmos (Washington). Contbr. articles profl. publs. Home: 3513 R St., Washington 7. Office: Bureau of Dairy Industry, U.S. Dept. of Agriculture, Washington. Died Nov. 11, 1955; buried Arlington Nat. Cemetery.

HOLMAN, Howard Francis, bus. exec.; b. Chicago, 1878, Chairman Diamond Match Co.; member finance com. and dir., First Nat. Bank (Ramsey, N.J.); pres. and dir., Mahwah (N.J.) Savings and Loan Assn. Home: 30 Armour Rd., Mahwah, N.J. Office: Diamond Match Co., 122 E. 42d St., N.Y. C. Died May 5, 1954.

HOLMAN, Jud McCarty (hōl'măn), wholesale grocer; b. Hemingway, Miss., Mar. 26, 1886; s. Dr. Isaac Judson and Annis (McCarty) H.; ed. Hemingway (Miss.) Pub. Sch., U. of Miss. and Soule Bus. Coll. (New Orleans); m. Charline Grant, Apr. 15, 1923; 1 dau., Carolyn. Began as retail grocer, 1910-19; in wholesale grocery business, 1919—; partner McCarty-Holman Co., wholesale grocers, Jackson, Miss., 1919—, sec.-treas. and dir. Jitney-Jungle, Inc., retail self-service; chmn. bd. Deposit Guaranty Bank and Trust Co.; dir. Standard Life Ins. Co. Chmn. Budget com. and dir. Jackson Community Chest; mem. bd. dirs. Jackson Y.M.C.A. Mem. Chamber of Commerce. Mem. First Christian Ch. (official bd.). Clubs: Exchange (past pres.), Jackson Country (Jackson, Miss.). Home: 120 Ridge Drive. Office: 451-455 N. Mill St., Jackson 117, Miss. Died Feb. 18, 1950.

HOLMAN, Rufus C., ex-senator; b. Portland, Ore.; s. Charles and Mary (Huntington) H.; grad. Portland High Sch., 1896; m. Gertrude Eleanor Watson, Apr. 15, 1903 (died Feb. 3, 1938); 1 dau., Eleanor Watson (Mrs. Harold Burkitt); m. 2d, Mrs. Norma Ward Lundeen, July 4, 1944. Began as farmer; successively teacher in district sch., steamboating, bookkeeping and accounting. Formerly member of firm Davis & Holman, Portland Paper Box Co.; U.S. senator from Ore., 1939-45. Formerly dir. Asso. Industries of Ore.; formerly pres. Pacific Coast Assn. Paper Box Mfrs.; pres. Stream Purification League of Ore.; mem. Portland Charter Commn.; chmn. Columbia River Interstate Bridge Commn.; pres. State Assn. of County Judges and Commrs.; pres. Mt. Hood Loop Rd. Assn.; dir. Portland Library Assn.; v.p. West Side Pacific Highway Assn.; mem. Port of Portland Commn.; formerly state treas. of Ore. Mem. Sons and Daughters of Ore. Pioneers (pres.). Republican. Episcopalian. Mason (Shriner, past potentate), Patron of Husbandry (7th degree). Clubs: Craftsmens (pres.), Anglers (pres.), Portland Rotary (dir.). Home: 2116 S.W. Montgomery Drive. Office: care Portland Paper Box Co., Portland, Ore. Died Nov. 1959.*

HOLMBERG, George C., ret. life ins. exec.; b. Mpls., Jan. 30, 1882; s. Nicholas A. and Anna (Smith) H.; U. Minn., 1903; widower; 1 dau., Georgia Elizabeth. Vice pres., dir. Security Nat. Bank, Sioux Falls, S.D., 1911-19; mem. examining bd. War Finance Corp., Washington, 1921, sec. Mpls. agy., 1923-25; v.p., treas., dir. Northwestern Nat. Life Ins. Co., Mpls., 1925—; mem. bd., finance com. Northwestern Fire & Marine Ins. Co., Twin City Fire Ins. Co.; mem. trust com. First Nat. Bank & Trust Co. Vice chmn. Mpls. adv. com. Reconstrn. Finance Corp. Mem. adv. bd. Home for Children and Aged Women. Asst. to dirs. R.F.C., Washington, 1932. Clubs: Minneapolis, Automobile, Inst. Fine Arts (Mpls.). Home: 4912 Arden Av., Mpls. 10. Died Aug. 9, 1953.

HOLMES, (Elias) Burton, travel-lecturer; b. Chicago, Ill., Jan. 8, 1870; s. Ira and Virginia (Burton) H.; ed. Allen Acad. and the Harvard Sch., Chicago; m. Margaret Elise Oliver, Mar. 21, 1914. First lecture in Chicago, 1890; since then in all principal Am. cities; presenting 58th annual series of illustrated travelogues, 1951. Has traveled in nearly all countries and lectured about them. Awarded Cavaliere Crown of Italy, Commendador Isabel La Catolica, Grand Star of Ethiopia, Golden Honor Cross Austrian Republic, Gold Medal from Chicago Geographic Soc. Clubs: Metropolitan, Explorers, Circumnavigators (hon. pres.), Lambs, Players (N.Y.); Chicago; Masquers (Hollywood). Home: Topside, 2020 Grace Av., Hollywood 28, Cal. Died July 22, 1958; buried Forest Lawn, Glendale, Cal.

HOLMES, Champneys Holt, physician; b. Macon, Ga., Jan. 30, 1894; s. John Champneys and Pearl (Lewis) H.; B.S., U. of Ga., 1915; M.D., Johns Hopkins U., 1919; m. Jacqueline Swift, Aug. 25, 1938. Began private practice of medicine, 1922; specialized in diseases of the chest, 1931—; mem. staff, Emory U. Med. Sch., 1922—. Mem. staff Atlanta Tb Assn., 1922—, pres., 1939—. Mem. Planning Council. Fellow A.C.P.; mem. A.M.A., Fulton County Med. Soc., Ga. State Med. Assn., Nat., So. Tb assns., Am. Coll. Chest Physicians (pres. 1938-39), Trudeau Soc., Phi Delta Theta, Phi Chi. Episcopalian. Club: Presidents, Piedmont Driving (Atlanta). Contributor many articles and editorials on chest diseases. Mem. editorial staff Diseases of the Chest. Died June 12, 1950.*

HOLMES, Edward Jackson, pres. Boston Museum of Fine Arts; b. Boston, Jan. 3, 1873; s. Edward Jackson and Henrietta Goddard (Wigglesworth) H.; A.B., Harvard, 1895, LL.B., 1899; L.H.D., Tufts College 1944, m. Mary Stacy Beaman, July 8, 1897. Treas. Elizabeth Peabody House Assn., 1907-21, Students' House Corp., 1914-35; trustee Boston Museum of Fine Arts, 1911-25, dir. 1925-34, pres., 1934—. Decorated Order of the Crown of Belgium, 1937. Mem. Am. Acad. Arts and Sciences, Order of The Cincinnati; hon. mem. Boston Soc. of Architects, Phi Beta Kappa. Republican. Unitarian. Clubs: Somerset, Harvard Travelers', Harvard (Boston); Harvard, Century Association (N.Y.C.). Home: Topsfield, Mass. Died May 29, 1950.

HOLMES, Frank G., designer; b. Pawtucket, R.I., Apr. 2, 1878; s. Frank Eugene and Jennie Elizabeth (Graham) H.; student R. I. Sch. of Design and New York Sch. of Art; married Marie Bolton, 1906; children—Graham, Bolton; m. 2d Louise Harford Alien, Sept. 20, 1928. Designed silverware, Howard Sterling Co., Providence, 1898-1901, Dominick and Haff, N.Y., 1901-05; designer and sec., Lenox, Inc., Trenton, N.J., 1905—, Lenox china (Holmes design, in the Nat. Mus. Sèvres, France). Apptd. by Herbert Hoover member Paris Expedition Commission, Decorative and Indsl. Art, 1925. Mem. bd. trustees Sch. Art League Bd. of Edn., N.Y.C., 1946—. Awarded Craftsmanship medal, Am. Inst. of Architects 1927, Binns medal, Alfred (New York) Univ.; awarded silver medal, Am. Designers Institute, 1943; Award for Excellence, Nat. Alliance Art and Industries, N.Y. City, 1932. Pres. bd. trustees, Sch. of Indsl. Art, Trenton, N.J. Mem. Modern Mus. of Art, N.Y. City. Republican. Protestant. Clubs: Salamagundi, Dutch Treat, Architectural League of N.Y. (N.Y. City). Home: 211 W. State St. Office: care Lenox, Inc., Trenton, N.J. Died Apr. 20, 1954; buried Ewing Church Cemetery, Trenton.

HOLMES, Frederick, business exec.; b. Chgo., Aug. 28, 1889; s. Marshall Fuller and Lillian (Hoppin) H.; Ph.B., U. Chgo., 1913; m. Gertrude Brintnall, May 17, 1917; children—Henry B., John H. With George L. Cragg (patent lawyer), Chgo., 1913; dir. Duncan Electric Mfg. Co., 1913—, meter, transformer tester, 1914, transformer design, 1915, sales, accounting depts., 1915, expediter, 1916-18, sec., 1918-19, asst. mgr., 1919-22, in charge mfg., sales, development, 1922-25, v.p., 1925-29, pres., 1929-50, chmn. bd., 1950—; dir. Holmes Radio Supply Co., Lafayette. Pres. community fund, 1933; dir. Tippecanoe Co. TB Assn., American Red Cross, Mental Health Assn., Mental Health and Achievement Center. Professional engineer, Indiana. Member Nat. Electric Mfrs. Assn. (sec., chmn. electric measuring instruments sect., chmn. watt-hour meter group), Ind. Mfrs. Assn. (dir.), C. of C. (dir.), Am. Inst. E.E., Alpha Delta Phi. Presbyn. (bd. trustees). Clubs: Sarasota Yacht; Maxinkukee Yacht; N.A. Yacht Racing Union; Columbia (Indpls.); Town and Gown. Home: 535 S. Seventh St. Office: Duncan Electric Mfg. Co., Lafayette, Ind. Died Jan. 15, 1958.

HOLMES, George Sanford, newspaperman; b. Pawtucket, R.I., Nov. 27, 1883; s. Frank Eugene and Jane Elizabeth H.; Ph.B., Brown U., 1904; m. Mrs. Hortense Belcher Hammond; 1 dau. (by previous marriage), Mrs. Herman E. Russell. Began as reporter, Providence Telegram, 1904; with Rocky Mountain News, Denver, Colo., 1908-28; mng. editor, 1925-28; Wash. corr. Scripps-Howard Newspaper Alliance, 1928-38; with Natl. Youth Adminstrn., 1938-40; with War Dept., Dec. 1940-July 1946; War Assets Adminstrn., 1946-49; Washington corr. Daily Sentinel, Grand Junction, Colo., and daily News, Lamar, Colo., 1949-50; information officer Defense Electric Power Adminstrn., 1951. Member Brown Alumni Assn., Alpha Tau Omega, Phi Beta Kappa. Mason. Clubs: Kiwanis (ex-pres.), Mile High (Denver); National Press, Cosmos (Washington). Author: The Story of Walter Scott Lenox, 1924; Yes, this is Washington, 1949. Home: 5104 Worthington Drive, Yorktown Village, Md. Died Aug. 21, 1955; buried Parklawn, North Washington Cemetery, Inc., Yorktown Village.

HOLMES, Harry Nicholls, coll. prof.; b. Lawrence County, Pa., July 10, 1879; s. John Pattison and Eliza (Nicholls) H.; B.S., Westminster Coll., New Wilmington, Pa., 1899, M.S., 1907; LL.D., 1941; Ph.D., Johns Hopkins, 1907; m. Mary V. Shiveley, July 15, 1909; children—Charles Shiveley, Richard Remsen. Prof. chem. Earlham Coll., Richmond, Ind., 1907-14; Oberlin Coll., 1914-45, prof. emeritus since 1945. Mem. Nat. Research Council, 1923-29 (chmn. sub-com. on chem. of colloids 1919-25); cons. NDRC, 1942. Recipient Kendall Award in colloid chemistry, 1954, James Flack Norris Award in teaching, 1955; Oberlin Alumni medal, 1945; gold medal American Institute of Chemists, 1951; Westminster Alumni medal, 1957. Fellow A.A.A.S., American Inst. Chemistry; mem. Am. Chem. Soc. (councilor at large, 1926-29, 1930-33, 1938-41, pres. elect, 1941, pres., 1942), Gamma Alpha, Sigma Xi, Alpha Chi Sigma, Phi Lambda Upsilon; hon. mem. Met. Chem. Inst. of South Africa, 1942. Conglist. Author: Outline of Qualitative Analysis, 1908-45; Laboratory Manual of General Chemistry, 1909, 30, 37, 49; General Chem., 1921, 30, 36, 41, 49; Lab. Manual of Colloid Chemistry, 1921, 28, 34; Bibliography Colloid Chemistry, 1923; Elements of Chemistry (with Louis W. Mattern), 1927; Introductory Coll. Chem. 1925, 31, 39, 46, 51; Out of the Test Tube, 1934, 37, 41, 43, 57; Have You Had Your Vitamins, 1938; Strategic Materials and National Defense, 1942; also 70 articles giving results of original chem. research. Home: 329 Reamer Pl., Oberlin, O. Died July 1, 1958.

HOLMES, Malcolm Haughton, music educator; b. Brockton, Mass., Aug. 2, 1906; s. Charles W. and Ethel M. (Holmes) H.; B.S., Harvard, 1928, grad. student, 1928-31. Instr. music faculty Wellesley Coll., 1933-43; faculty Berkshire Music Centre, 1940-41; mem. faculty New Eng. Conservatory, Boston, since 1944, dean since 1945; mem. faculty Greenwood Chamber Music Camp, Cummington, Mass., since 1947; condr. Harvard Orchestra, 1932-50, Radcliffe Coll. Orchestra, 1935-50, Harvard Band since 1942; guest condr. Boston Symphony Pops and Esplanade Concerts since 1938. Mem. Music Tchrs. Nat. Assn. (exec. com. 1947-50), Harvard Mus. Assn. (dir.), Delta Upsilon, Phi Mu Alpha Sinfonia, Pi Kappa Lambda, Tau Zeta Epsilon (hon.), Pierian Sodality of 1808. Club: Harvard (Boston). Author: Conducting the Amateur Orchestra, 1951; 2 publs. of music. Home: 69 Fox Hill Rd., Wellesley Hills, Mass. Office: 290 Huntington Av., Boston. Died June 16, 1953; buried Mt. Auburn Cemetery, Cambridge, Mass.

HOLMES, Pehr G., ex-congressman; b. Sweden, Apr. 9, 1881; s. John Jacob and Caroline (Johnson) H.; brought to U.S., 1886; student pub. schs., Worcester, Mass.; m. Frida Charlotte Johnson, May 26, 1903 (dec. Oct. 22, 1936); children—Wilfred Kenneth, George Everett. Organizer, 1909, and owner Holmes Electrotype Foundry; trustee Worcester Mechanics Savings Bank; dir. Guaranty Bank & Trust Co., Mutual Trust Life Ins. Co., Chgo. Trustee Fairlawn Hosp., Worcester. Mem. City Council, Worcester, 8 yrs., pres. Bd. of Aldermen, 1915-16; mayor of Worcester, 1917-19; mem. Governor's Council, Mass., 1925-28; mem. 72d to 80th Congresses, 4th Mass. Dist. Ex-pres. Mass. Hwy. Assn. Republican. Conglist. Mason, Odd Fellow, Elk, Red Man. Club: Worcester Country. Home: 27 Holden St. Office: 167 Commercial St., Worcester, Mass. Died Dec. 19, 1952; buried Old Swedish Cemetery.

HOLMES, Ralph Clinton, oil industry executive; b. Sharon Center, Pa., Aug. 24, 1874; s. Elba D. and Catherine L. (Dodge) H.; grad. high sch., Olean, N.Y., 1895; m. Dora May Hamilton, Apr. 20, 1904; 1 son, Frederic Hamilton. With Standard Oil Co. at Olean, 1895-1901; with Solar Refining Co., Galatea, O., 1901-02; with The Texas Co., 1902 until retired, beginning as mgr. refining dept., Beaumont, Tex., dir., 1906, v.p., chmn. mfg. and marketing com., 1913; became mem. exec. com. and pres. The Texas Co. of Mexico, 1920, pres. Texas S.S. Co., 1922; pres. The Texas Co. and The Texas Corp., and several subsidiary companies, 1926. Chmn. subcom. on refining, also mem. midcontinent sect. Nat. Petroleum War Service Com., and mem. priorities com. on refinery materials and tinplate, World War. Clubs: City. Houston (Houston); Bartlett Country, Essex Fox Hounds. Home: Shingle House, Pa. Died Dec. 1950.

HOLMES, Rudolph Wieser, physician; b. Chgo.; s. Edward Lorenzo and Paula (Wieser) H.; student Harvard, 1888-90; M.D., Rush Med. Coll., Chgo., 1893; postgrad. work hosps. at Vienna and Prague, 1900-01; m. Maria Baxter, May 5, 1898. Specialist in obstetrics and gynecology; prof. emeritus of obstetrics and gynecology Rush Med. Coll. at U. Chgo.; formerly asso. prof. obstetrics Northwestern U. Med. Sch.; chief dept. obstetrics Passavant Meml. Hosp. Dir. Am. Com. on Maternal Welfare, Inc.; former mem. adv. com. Childrens Bur. Treas. 1st Am. Congress on Obstetrics and Gynecology, Cleve., 1939. Fellow A.C.S., Inst. Medicine Chgo., Am. Gynecol. Soc., Central Assn. Obstetricians and Gynecologists (pres. 1931-32); mem. A.M.A., Ill., Chgo. med. socs., Chgo. Gynecol. Soc. (past pres.). Republican. Unitarian. Club: University. Home: University, Va. Died Apr. 25, 1953; buried Rosehill Cemetery, Chgo.

HOLMES, Thomas James, bibliographer; b. Newcastle, Staffordshire, Eng., Dec. 26, 1874; s. Elisha and Maryjane (Rhodes) H.; ed. in pub. schs. and evening schs.; Litt.D. (hon.), Trinity Coll., Hartford, 1941; m. Alice Mary Browning, Dec. 24, 1901; children—Thomas B., Alice Rosa, John B. Came to U.S., 1902, naturalized citizen. Apprenticed to David Dilworth, bookbinder, printer, bookseller and publisher, Newcastle, Eng., 1887; later with George Thomas Bagguley, inventor of color tooling process on vellum; mem. staff of Riviere and of Zaehnsdorf, London, 1895-99; with George Thomas Bagguley, 1899-1902; with Club Bindery, N.Y. City, 1902-09; editor bookbinding dept. The Progressive Printer, St. Louis, Mo., 1907-10; mgr., later salesman, Rowfant Bindery, Cleveland, O., 1909-13; part time asst. John G. White Collection of Folklore and Orientalia, Cleveland (O.) Pub. Library, 1916-20; librarian William G. Mather Collection, 1916-35; compiler and editor Mather Bibliographies, Am. Antiquarian Soc. Library, 1936-40. Recipient diploma and bronze medal for bookbinding, Paris Internat. Expn., 1900, Penton bronze medal, Cleve. Mus. of Art, 1919. Mem. Am. Antiquarian Soc., Bibliog. Soc. Am. Unitarian. Clubs: Rowfant, Cheshire Cheese, Library (Cleveland, O.). Author: Fine Bookbinding, 1912; Notes on Richard Mather's Church Government, 1923; Samuel Mather of Witney, 1674-1733, 1928; Bookbinding of John Ratcliff and Edmund Ranger, 17th Century Boston Bookbinders, 1928; Increase Mather—His Works, A Short-title Catalogue, 1930; English Ballads and Songs, an annotated list of collections (with Gordon W. Thayer), 1931; Increase Mather, A Bibliography of His Works (2 vols.), 1932; The Mather Collection at Cleveland, 1933; The Mather Bibliography, 1937; Cotton Mather, A Bibliography of His Works (3 vols.), 1940; The Minor Mathers, A List of Their Works, 1940; Autobiographical Letter to Prof. Lyon N. Richardson, with list of publs., 1956. Home: Burton, O. Died Feb. 7, 1959.

HOLT, Andrew Hall, prof. civil engring.; b. Sunderland, Vt., Aug. 23, 1890; s. Winfield Selah and Effie Ida (Andrew) H.; student Burr & Burton Sem., Manchester, Vt., 1904-08; B.S. in C.E., U. of Vt., 1912, C.E., 1922; M.S., State U. of Ia., 1920, J.D., 1931; m. Ruth E. Brownson, Jan. 1, 1915; children—Elisabeth Ursula, Barbara Ruth, Winfield Andrew, Nancy Fay. Began 1911, surveying and engring., summer work with Am. Bridge Co., Ia. Ry. & Light Corp., U.S. Dist. Engr. and others; engr. in chg. river improvements, Iowa City; instr. U. of Vt., 1912-14; instr. civil engring., State U. of Ia., 1914-17, asst. prof., 1919-21, asso. prof., 1921-34, prof., 1934-37; prof. civil engring. and head of dept. of civil engring., Worcester Poly. Inst., since 1937. Served as capt. engrs., U.S. Army, A.E.F., World War I; col., Corps Engineers, commanding 361st Engineer Regiment, Pacific and European Theaters, World War II; Colonel, Corps of Engineers Reserve, ret. Member Iowa, Massachusetts and Federal bars. Member Am. Soc. Civil Engrs., Am. Society for Engineering Edn., Soc. American Military Engrs., Worcester Society of Civil Engineers, Scabbard and Blade, Order of Coif, Phi Beta Kappa, Tau Beta Pi, Sigma Xi, Theta Tau, Alpha Tau Omega. Republican. Conglist. Mason. Author: Manual of Field Astronomy, 1916, 2d edit., 1927; (with B. J. Lambert) Elementary Structures in Steel and Concrete, 1929; also papers on surveying and the law of boundaries. Home: 10 Germain St., Worcester, Mass. Died Nov. 22, 1956; buried Ira Allen Cemetery, Sunderland, Vt.

HOLT, Edwin Bissell, psychologist; b. Winchester, Mass., Aug. 21, 1873; s. Stephen Abbott and Nancy Wyman (Cutter) H.; A.B., Harvard, 1896, Ph.D., 1901; A.M., Columbia, 1900. Instr. psychology, Harvard, 1901-05, asst. prof., 1905-18; vis. prof. psychology, Princeton, 1926-36. Author: The Concept. of Consciousness, 1914; The Freudian Wish,

1915; Animal Drive and the Learning Process, Vol. I, 1931. Home: Tenants Harbor, Knox County, Me. Died Jan. 25, 1946; buried Winchester, Mass.

HOLT, Hamilton, editor, educator; b. Bklyn., Aug. 19, 1872; s. Judge George Chandler and Mary Louisa (Bowen) H.; A.B., Yale, 1894; post-grad. studies in sociology and economics Columbia, 1894-97; LL.D., Ursinus Coll., 1915; Litt.D., Wooster Coll., 1916; LL.D., Wilberforce U., 1920, Oberlin Coll., 1921, Otterbein Coll., 1922, Baylor U., 1927; L.H.D., Boston U., 1928; D.Sc., U. Tampa (Fla.), 1948; D.H., Keuka (N.Y.) Coll., 1948; m. Alexina Crawford Smith, Feb. 8, 1899 (died Feb. 19, 1936); children—Beatrice (Mrs. Joseph H. Chadbourne), Leila (Mrs. Maurice E. H. Rotival), John Eliot, George Chandler. Mng. editor The Independent, 1897-1913, editor and owner, 1913-21, cons. editor, 1921; Dem. candidate for U.S. Senate, spl. election, Conn., 1924; pres. Rollins Coll., 1925-—, elector Hall of Fame. Pres. 3d Am. Peace Congress; ex-pres. Am. Scandinavian Found., Greek Am. Club; a founder Italy American Soc., League to Enforce Peace, Netherlands Am. Found., Friends of Poland, League of Nations Non-Partisan Assn.; trustee Ch. Peace Union; former exec. dir. Woodrow Wilson Found.; mem. Nat. Inst. Social Sciences, Simplified Spelling Bd. Visited battlefronts of allied armies as guest of various govts., 1918; went to Paris as head of League to Enforce Peace and was made liaison officer between Am. delegation and League to Enforce Peace; toured U.S., speaking for the League; visited Europe again, 1919, 20, 22, 27, 30, 37; attended 2d, 3d, 8th assemblies League of Nations, UN Conf., San Francisco, 1945. Decorated Comdr. Order of Sacred Treasure (Japanese), 1903; Officer Order of George I (Grecian), 1919; Officer Order Pub. Instruction, 1920, Knight Legion of Honor, 1921, Officer, 1935 (French); Officer Order of Crown of Italy, 1920; Knight Polonia Resituta (Polish), 1922; Knight of North Star (Swedish), 1923; Comdr. Order of St. Sava (Serbian), 1931; Pro Dania, 1946. Lecturer for Am. br. Internat. Conciliation, World Peace Found.; Weinstock lectr. U. Cal.; Isaac Bromley lectr. Yale. Mem. Order of Ahepa. Clubs: Century (N.Y.C.); Cosmos (Washington); University (Orlando and Winter Park, Fla.). Author: Undistinguished Americans, 1906; Commercialism and Journalism, 1909; Introduction to ex-President Taft's book, The United States and Peace, 1914. Lectures: The Rollins Adventure in Education; Accomplishments of the League of Nations; Japan; Personal Recollections of the Last Ten U.S. Presidents; The Charter of the United Nations. Established at Rollins Coll., 1916, "The Conference Plan of Study," designed to bring teacher and student into close discussion and contact. Home: Winter Park, Fla.; (summer) Woodstock, Conn. Died Apr. 26, 1951; buried Woodstock, Conn.

HOLT, Henry Chandler, banker; b. N.Y.C., Jan. 13, 1881; s. George Chandler and Mary (Bowen) H.; student Phillips Andover Acad.; B.A., Yale 1903; m. Margaret Carson, Oct. 20, 1919; children—Margaret Carson, Mary Bowen, Susanna Aspinwall. Yard clerk Southern Ry., Princeton, Ind., 1903-06; supr. stations D.L.&W. R.R., Hoboken, N.J., 1906-12; clerk Central Hanover Bank & Trust Co. (formerly Central Trust Co.), N.Y.C., 1912, asst. sec., 1913-20, v.p., 1920-46, retired since June 30, 1946; past pres. Central Hanover Safe Deposit Co. Formerly trustee Internat. Com. of YMCA, Vassar Coll. Istanbul Women's Coll.; dir., pres. Near East Coll. Assn.; dir. N.Y. Women's League for Animals, 42d St. Property Owners and Merchants Association. Trustee Woodstock Acad., Rollins Coll.; Grenfell Assn. of Am.; Roseland Park; trustee and chmn. bd. Internat. Grenfell Assn. Mem. Skull and Bones (Yale), Delta Kappa Epsilon. Republican. Mason. Clubs: University, Yale (N.Y.C.). All-American center, 1901-02. Home: Chandler Farms, Pomfret, Conn. Died Feb. 20, 1955; buried Woodstock, Conn.

HOLT, Lee Cone, chemist; b. Harlan, Ia., Feb. 19, 1880; s. Lee Elwood and Eva Boise (Collier) H.; B.S., Pomona Coll., Cal., 1901; Ph.D., U. Mich., 1905; grad. study, U. Berlin, 1907-08; m. Daisy Ellen Ben Oliel, June 18, 1907 (dec.); children—Florence Lee (dec.), Helen Agnes (dec.); Lee Elbert; m. 2d, Maud N. Rogers, July 1939. Instr. in chemistry Pomona Coll., 1901-02, Carnegie research asst., 1903-05; instr. in organic chemistry U. Mich., 1905-08, asst. prof., 1908-13, asso. prof., 1913-16; with Dow Chem. Co., Midland, Mich., 1916-17, Semet Solvay Co., Syracuse, N.Y., 1917-18; with Nat. Aniline & Chem. Co., Buffalo, 1918-29, in charge research and development work, 1921-29, v.p., 1922-29; with Jackson Lab. of Du Pont Co., 1929-45, retired, 1945-—. Mem. Am. Chem. Soc., Phi Beta Kappa, Sigma Xi. Republican. Contbr. articles to German and Am. chem. jours. Home: "Holthaven," Preston, Md. Died May 27, 1957.

HOLT, Lucius Hudson, author; b. Atchison, Kan., Jan. 16, 1881; s. Fred Park and Regina Miller (Hudson) H.; B.A., Yale, 1902, M.A., 1904, Ph.D., 1905; m. Katherine Beers, June 18, 1903; children—Guy Bryan, Roger Clerc. Instr. English, Yale, 1905-08; asst. editor Webster's Internat. Dictionary, 1908-10; prof. English and history, with rank of lt. col., U.S. Mil. Acad., May 11, 1910, rank of colonel since 1920, in charge dept. economics, govt. and history, 1919-26, prof. economics, govt. and history, 1926-30, acting dean, 1926-28; vice chmn. City Bank & Trust Co., Hartford, 1930-32; on editorial staff Webster's New Internat. Dictionary, 1932-34; mng. editor Webster's Dictionaries, 1934-46, ret. Col. O.R.C., A.U.S. Member American Geographical Society, Zeta Psi and Phi Beta Kappa fraternities. Clubs: Zeta Psi (New York City); Graduate, Elizabethan (New Haven, Connecticut); City (Springfield, Mass.). Author: Introduction to the Study of Government, 1914; Leading English Poets, 1915; History of Europe, 1862-1914 (with A. W. Chilton), 1917; Brief History of Europe, 1789-1815 (with A. W. Chilton), 1918; Military Correspondence, Reports and Orders, 1919; Elementary Principles of Modern Government, 1923; English Analysis and Exposition (with A. W. Chilton, 1923; Introduction to Ancient History, 1927; Economic Effects of Modern War, 1929. Translator: The Elene of Cynewulf, 1904. Compiler: Selections from Prose of Macaulay, 1916. Home: 35 Riverview Terrace, Springfield, Mass. Died Jan. 20, 1953.

HOLT, Rush Dew, ex-senator; b. Weston, W.Va., June 19, 1905; s. Dr. Matthew Samuel and Chilelia (Dew) H.; student W.Va. U., 1920-22; A.B., Salem Coll., 1924; LL.B., La Salle, 1943; m. Helen Froelich, June 19, 1941; children—Helen, Rush Jr. Teacher Bedford City (Va.) High Sch., 1924; instr., Salem (W.Va.) Coll.; athletic dir. St. Patrick's School, W.Va., 1925-28; became instr. Glenville (W.Va.) State Teachers Coll., 1927; mem. W.Va. House of Delegates, 1931-35, and 1943-47 (re-elected to 4th term by "write in" vote; elected 5th term with no opposition; elected 6th term on both Rep. and Dem. tickets); member U.S. Senate from W.Va., 1925-41. Mem. U.S. del. to Interparliamentary Conf., Oslo, Norway, 1931; U.S. del. to Moral Rearmament Conf., Calif., 1948; U.S. del. Internat. Moral Rearmament Conf., Switzerland, 1948. Mem. nat. council Boy Scouts Am. Mem. W.Va. Ho. of Delegates, 1954-—. Mem. bd. Meth. Ch. Mem. Am. Polit. Sci. Assn., Elbetee Legion, Sons of Revolution, S.A.R., W.Va. Hist. Soc.; hon. v.p. Am. Flag Day Society; past state pres. Moose Assn.; past pres. W.Va. State Soc. Elks. Methodist. Republican (cand. Congress 1950, gov. 1952). Editor W.Va. Taxpayer; author weekly column "Facts and Figures" in 75 papers. Conducted state wide, weekly radio news cast. Home: Weston, W.Va. Died Feb. 8, 1955.

HOLT, William Franklin, capitalist; b. Mercer County, Mo., Jan. 18, 1864; s. James and Nancy (Brantley) H.; student pub. schs.; m. Fannie Jones, Aug. 16, 1885. Engaged in merc., mfg. and banking bus., Mo., Colo. and Ariz.; moved to Redlands, Cal., 1900; built electric lighting plants in 5 towns, established 7 banks and installed water systems; pres. Holton Power Co., Holton Interurban Ry. Co., Imperial Valley Gas Co., Coachella Valley Ice and Electric Co., Seeley Townsite Co., Los Angeles Fire Ins. Co. Mem. Disciples Ch. K.T. Home: Redlands, Cal. Deceased.

HOLT, William Joseph (Dick), lawyer; b. Hillsboro, Tex., Aug. 14, 1891; s. Joseph J. and Katie (Glasgow) H.; student Cumberland U., 1909-10; LL.B., U. Mich., 1912; m. Carrie Lee Canuteson, June 12, 1920; children—William J., Jr., Martha A. (Mrs. George Taylor). Admitted to Tex. bar, 1916; gen. practice, Waco, Tex., 1916-23; dist. atty. office, Waco, McLennon County, 1923-30; atty. gen. dept., Austin, Tex., 1934-39; practice in Dallas, 1939-—; mem. firm Clark, Coon, Holt & Fisher. Organizer and 1st pres. Dallas chpt. Fed. Bar Assn. Enforcement Atty., U.S. Govt., 1942-45. Presbyn. Mason (Shriner), Odd Fellow. Home: 4041 Glenwick Lane, Dallas. Office: Republican Bank Bldg., Dallas 1. Died 1955.*

HOLTER, Norman B., merchant; b. Helena, Mont., Feb. 8, 1868; s. Anton M. and Mary Pauline (Loberg) H.; E.M., Sch. of Mines, Columbia, 1891; m. Florence Jefferis, June 27, 1900; children—Marian Holter Barbour (dec.), Richard Minor (dec.), Norman Jefferis. In merc. business, Helene, 1891-—; pes. A. M. Holter Hardware Co.; dir. Federal Res. Bank. Mpls., 1914-31; dir. Montana Power Co. (Butte). Chmn. Liberty and Victory loans, Mont. World War. Mem. Delta Psi. Republican. Episcopalian. Clubs: Montana (Helena); Los Angeles Country (Beverly Hills). Home: 520 Monroe Av., Helena, Mont. Died Feb. 8, 1957, buried Forestvale Cemetery, Helena.

HOLTON, Edwin Lee, educator; b. Scott County, Ind., Dec. 15, 1876; s. William Henry and Mary Hannah (Crist) H.; diploma Ind. State Normal Sch., Terre Haute, Ind., 1900; A.B., Ind. U., 1904; studied Columbia 1909-10 1916-17 Ph.D. 1927; studied U. Paris 1919; m. Anna Carr, Aug. 4, 1904 (died Aug. 1, 1908); 1 dau., Ruth; m. 2d, Lillian Beck, June 1, 1911; 1 dau., Mary. Prin. twp. high schs., Henryville and Lapel, Ind., and supt. schs., Holton, Kan., and Noblesville, Ind., until 1908; supr. Indsl. Schs., N.Y.C., 1908-09; prof. edn. and dean of summer school Kan. State Coll. of Agr. and Applied Science, 1910-—. Dir. of farm project instrn. U. Minn., 1925-26. Deputy commr. A.R.C. in France, 1918-19. was in charge reëducation and rehabilitation of the disabled soliders and sailors of U.S. in France; with assimilated rank of major in U.S. Army, rep. U.S. as mem. of Inter-Allied Com. on Reëducation and Rehabilitation of war-disabled men. Mem. N.E. A., Soc. Coll. Tchrs. Edn., Phi Beta Kappa, Phi Kappa Phi, Phi Delta Kappa, Pi Gamma Mu.; pres. Kansas State Tchrs. Assn., 1923. Republican. Methodist. Mason (32°). Clubs: Country, Rotary (dist. gov. internat. 1930-31) (Manhattan); Kansas Schoolmasters', Kansas Authors'. Author: (with Dr. W. E. Grimes) Modern Agriculture; Training Teachers of Vocational Agriculture. Home: Manhattan, Kan. Died July 7, 1950.

HOLTON, Jessie Moon (Mrs. Frederick Arthur Holton), educator; b. Ilion, N.Y., Sept. 16, 1866; d. Clinton Abner and Frances (Hawkins) Moon; Fairfield (N.Y.) Acad.; student Cornell U., 1883-86; m. Frederick Arthur Holton, July 29, 1891 (died Nov. 28, 1929). Founder, 1901, and prin. Holton Arms Sch., Washington. Trustee All Souls Ch. Unitarian. Home: 2125 S St., Washington. Died Aug. 15, 1951.

HOLTON, Winfred B., Jr.; b. Oct. 27, 1888; s. Winfred Byron and Lula C. (Glover) H.; A.B., Wesleyan U., 1910; m. Elizabeth Curran, Dec. 4, 1920; children—Nancy E. (Mrs. G. B. M. Walker), Patricia C. (Mrs. Claud Morris), Winfred B. III. With Bur. Municipal Research, N.Y.C., 1910-16, asst. dir., 1915-16; asst. dir. N.Y. State Budget Com., 1916; engaged in survey examinations and preparation of reports on pub. works and pub. utility projects and taxation in various states, municipal and provincial govtl. depts. in U.S. and Canada, 1912-17; mng. dir. San Francisco Bur. of Governmental Research, 1916-17; U.S.S.B. Emergency Fleet Corp., chmn. contracts, claims and cancellations bd. and acting v.p., 1918-19; pres. Holton, Richards & Co., Inc., 1920-49; pres. and chmn. exec. com. Walworth Co., mfrs. valves, pipe fittings and tools, 1935-51, chmn. bd., 1951-—; dir. Westcott Valve Co., Walworth Internat. and Cal. cos., Copper Recovery Corp. (subsidiary RFC Metals Reserve Corp.); trustee Susquehanna Silk Mills. Mem. valve mfrs. adv. com. WPB, 1941-45, prodn. cons., 1943-45; Valve and Fitting Industry, 1943-45. Served as capt. Ordnance, U.S. Army, 1917-18. Trustee Wesleyan U., 1935; hon. life mem. Wesleyan U. Alumni Council (chmn. 1926-31). Pres. and dir. Valve Mfrs. Assn., 1938-50; v.p. and dir. Pipe Fittings Mfrs. Assn., 1937-49; chmn. bd. trustees Navy Indsl. Assn., 1944-46. Mem. N.A.M., Am. Petroleum Inst., U.S. and N.Y. State C.'s of C., Psi Upsilon. Republican. Clubs: Pelham Country (pres. 1940-45, chmn. bd. govs. 1945-50, mem. bd., 1950-—), University, Uptown (N.Y.); Faculty (Middletown); Blind Brook (Portchester, N.Y.). Home: 98 Rockledge Dr., Pelham Manor, N.Y. Office: 60 E. 42d St., N.Y.C. Died July 12, 1957; buried Beechwood Cemetery, New Rochelle, N.Y.

HOLTZCLAW, Jack Gilbert, pub. utility exec.; b. Perry, Ga., Nov. 22, 1886; s. Robert Newsom and Evelyn West (Gilbert) H.; B.S. in E.E., Georgia School of Technology, 1907; m. Lyda L. Smathers, May 17, 1911; children—Adora Evelyn (Mrs. John Aaron Prevost), Josephine (Mrs. Calvin Houghland); married 2d, Mary Elizabeth Morris, June 30, 1951. Supt. Pensacola (Fla.) Electric Co., 1916-19, general manager, 1919-24; v.p. Gulf States Utilities Co., 1925-29; pres. Va. Electric & Power Co., 1929-—; dir. Lawyers Title Insurance Corp.; chmn. Indsl. Adv. Com., Federal Reserve Bank of Richmond. Mem. Sigma Alpha Epsilon. Democrat. Mason (32°). Clubs: Commonwealth, Hermitage, Country of Virginia, Farmington Country, Rotunda. Home: 209 Queen Charlotte Rd., Windsor Farms, Richmond. Office: Electric Bldg., Richmond, Va. Died Dec. 13, 1955.

HOLZER, Charles Elmer (hōl'zēr), surgeon; b. Sherwood, O., July 29, 1887; s. William Henry Frederick and Susan Frances (Kintner) H.; M.D., Ohio State U., 1909, hon. LL.D., 1945; post-grad. work, Polyclinic Hosp. (N.Y.), U. of Vienna, and Guy's Hospital, London, Eng.; D.Sc. from Rio Grande Coll.; m. Alma E. Vornholt, Oct. 1914; children—Charles Elmer, Jr., Alma Christine, Richard Vornholt, Maria Louise, Elizabeth Anne. Med. officer Ohio Hosp. for Epileptics, Gallipolis, O., 1909-10; founder, 1910, and surgeon, Holzer Hospital, Gallipolis. dir. Comml. and Savs. Bank of Gallipolis. Ex-pres. Bd. Edn. Central Tri-State Med. Soc.; ex-pres. bd. trustees Rio Grande Coll.; trustee Ohio State Archeol. and Historical Society; ex-president Friends of the Land. Fellow American College Surgeons; member A.M.A., Ohio State Med. Assn., Internat. Coll. of Surgeons, Gallia County Hist. Soc. (pres.). Republican. Methodist. Mason (K.T.), Elk. Club: Gallipolis Rotary. Home: Gallipolis, O. Died Nov. 1, 1956; buried Mound Hill Cemetery, Gallipolis, O.

HOLZINGER, Karl John, educator; b. Washington, Aug. 9, 1892; s. John Michael and Sara (Ritchie) H.; A.B., U. Minn., 1915, A.M., 1917; Ph.D. summa cum laude, U. of Chicago, 1922; grad. student U. of London with Karl Pearson and Charles Spearman, 1922, 1925; m. Marion Stone, June 17, 1917; children—Karl John, Jr., Ruth. Instr. math.

U. of Minn., 1917; mem. faculty U. of Chicago, since 1920, prof. statistics since 1929. Served with Psychol. Corps, U.S. Army, World War I. Mem. Am. Statis. Assn. (v.p., 1933), Psychometric Soc. (pres. 1941), Phi Beta Kappa, Delta Upsilon. Club: Quadrangle (Chicago). Author: Statistical Methods, 1928; Influence of Environment on Intelligence, Achievement and Conduct of Foster Children (with F. Freeman), 1928; Resume of Spearman Theory, 1930; Student Manual of Factor Analysis, 1935; Spearman-Holzinger, Preliminary Reports (1-9) on Factor Analysis, 1935-40; Factor Analysis: A Synthesis (with H. Harmon), 1941; Twins (with Freeman and Newman), 1937; Stability of A Bi-Factor Solution (with F. Swineford), 1939; Reliability of A Bi-Factory Solution (with F. Swineford), 1942; Books of Tables. Joint editor: Jour. Educational Psychology since 1949. Home: 5747 Dorchester Av., Chgo. 37. Died Jan. 15, 1954.

HOLZKNECHT, Karl J(ulius), (hōlz'knecht), prof.; b. Louisville, Ky., July 5, 1899; s. Gustave and Julia (Kern) H.; A.B., U. of Louisville, 1920; A.M., U. of Pa., 1921, Ph.D., 1923; m. Eleanore A. Butler, July 25, 1924. Reader in English, U. of Pa., 1920-21, George Leib Harrison fellow, 1921-23; asst. prof. English, U. of Louisville, 1923-26. asso. prof., 1926-28; instr. English Washington Square Coll., N.Y. U., 1928-29, asst. prof., 1929-35, asso. prof., 1935-45, prof. since 1945, head dept. Grad. Sch. since 1949, chairman div. langs. and lit., grad. sch., 1954; vis. lectr. U. Ia., summers 1926-27, West Tenn. State Teachers Coll., summer 1928, U. of So. Cal., summer 1948. Sec. Coll. Conf. English in Central Atlantic States, 1930-42, pres. 1945-47. 55; sec. local selective service bd., 1940-41. Recipient Sesqui-Centennial medal, U. Louisville, 1948. Mem. Modern Language Assn., Modern Humanities Research Assn., Shakespeare Assn., Bibliog. Soc. of America, Phi Beta Kappa. Clubs: Renaissance of New York City (president 1947). Author: Literary Patronage in the Middle Ages, 1923; Outlines of Shakespeare's Plays (with Homer A. Watt and Raymond Ross), 1935; Outlines of Tudor and Stuart Plays, 1497-1642, 1947; The Backgrounds of Shakespear's Plays, 1950. Editor: A Freshman Miscellany, 1929; Selected Plays of Shakespeare (with Norman E. McClure), 4 vols., 1936-41; Sixteenth Century English Prose, 1954; (with George K. Anderson) The Literature of England, 1953. General editor: Harper English Lit. Series. Compiler: A Literary Map of the British Isles, 1934; Children's Books of Long Ago (with Homer A. Watt), 1942. Contbr. articles to jours. and mags. Home: 20 Crow's Nest Rd., Bronxville, N.Y. Office: 100 Washington Sq. E., N.Y.C. 3. Died Mar. 24, 1956; buried Louisville.

HOMBERGER, Alfred William (hŏm'bûrg-ēr), prof. chemistry; b. Prairie du Sac, Wis., May 18, 1887; s. Robert and Anna (Schoenburg) H.; A.B., U. of Wis., 1905 (honors in chemistry); M.S., U. of Ill., 1908, Ph.D., 1910; studied U. of Göttingen and Columbia; m. Iva Lucille Ward, 1915. Instr. in chemistry, Rose Poly. Inst., Terre Haute, Ind., 1905-07; asst. prof. chemistry, Ill. Coll., Jacksonville, Ill., 1910-11; prof. chemistry, dir. of chemistry, Illinois Wesleyan U., 1911-18; prof. chemistry and head of department, U. of Louisville, 1918-42, prof. physiol. chemistry and nutrition and head of dept., School of Medicine, U. of Louisville 1942-52, ret. June 1952, prof. nutrition Sch. Dentistry. Mem. executive com. Louisville Presbyn. Seminary since 1950. Fellow A.A.A.S.; mem. Am. Chem. Society (councillor for Louisville sect.), 1920-45, Ky. Acad. Science (pres. 1939-40), American Association of University Professors, Alpha Tau Omega, Gamma Alpha, Sigma Xi, Phi Lambda Upsilon, Theta Chi Delta, Alpha Epsilon Delta. Contbr. papers on research. Home: 2368 Carlton Terrace, Louisville. Died Sept. 11, 1952.

HOMBERGER, Ludwig Maximilian, educator; b. Darmstadt, Germany, Oct. 21, 1882; s. Adolf and Emma (Strauss) H.; student U. Munich, 1901-03. U. Berlin, 1903-04, U. Leipzig, 1904; Dr. juris and rerum politicarum, P. Würzburg. 1906; m. Elizabeth Bertha Wagner, Apr. 9, 1913. Came to U.S., 1938, naturalized, 1944. Passed bar examination, 1908; employee Bavarian State Rys., 1909-20, German Nat. R.R., 1920-35, exec. v.p., mem. directorate, 1931-35; lectr. U. Adminstrn.-Berlin, 1928-38; vis. lectr., vis. prof., asso. prof. Am. U., Washington, 1939-45, prof. transportation, dir. transportation insts., profl. insts., 1945-—. Cons. transportation services Civil Def. of D.C., 1951-—. Writer sect. for transportation study Nat. Resources Planning Bd., 1940-41; with OSS 1942-45, chief transport sect., Europe Africa div., 1944-45; survey transportation West Germany, E.C.A. and German Govt., 1950. Recipient German Order of Merit, 1953. Mem. American Econ. Assn., Soc. Advancement Management, Acad. Polit. Sci., Am. Soc. Traffic and Transportation, Am. Assn. U. Profs., Lexington Group. Author: Wirtschaftsführung und Finanzwesen bei den englischen Eisenbahnen, 1928; Wirtschaftsführung und Finanzwesen bei amerikanischen Eisenbahnen, 1929; Wirtschaftsführung and Finanzwesen der Deutschen Reichbahn, 1934, also transportation articles mags. Home: 1830 N. Quintana St., Arlington 5, Va. Died Nov. 22, 1954.

HOMER, Sidney, composer; b. Boston, Dec. 9, 1864; s. George and Anna Maria (Swift) H.; Boston Latin Sch., Phillips Acad., Andover, Mass.; first mus. studies with George W. Chadwick; spent 5 yrs. in Germany, studied 3 yrs. at Royal Conservatory of Munich under Joseph Rheinberger: Dr. Music (hon.), Rollins Coll., 1939; Curtis Inst. Music, 1943; m. Louise Dilworth Beatty, Jan. 9, 1895 (dec. May 6, 1947); children—Louise (Mrs. Ernes t V. Stires), Sidney, Katharine (Mrs. Douglas Fryer), Anne Marie (Mrs. William M. Doerflinger) Hester Makepeace (Mrs. Robert E. Henry, Jr.), Helen Joy (dec.). Teacher harmony, counterpoint, Boston 8 yrs.; Mass., conducted lectures and classes in study of symphonies and Wagnerian music dramas. Mem. A.S. C.A.P. Composer (songs); Sweet and Low, and Thy Voice Is Heard (from Tennyson); A Woman's Last Word (from Browning), and The Last Leaf (from Oliver Wendell Holmes); Sing Me a Song of a Lad That Is Gone, Requiem, and Stormy Evening (from Stevenson's Underwoods); Dearest (from Henley's Hawthorn and Lavender); The Pauper's Drive; The Bandanna Ballads: The Song of the Shirt; Sheep and Lambs; General William Booth Enters Into Heaven (from Vachell Lindsay); The Everlasting Mercy; The Widow in the By Street (John Masefield); chamber music: 2 sonatas, violin and piano, 2 string quartets, trio and quintet, piano and strings; Sonata and Introduction and Fugue for organ; Chamber Music and Organ Sanata; also 17 children's songs from Christina Rossetti's "Sing Song." Author: My Wife and I (bigraphy), 1939. Address: 36 Gramercy Park, N.Y.C. Died July 10, 1953; buried Bolton on Lake George, N.Y.

HONNOLD, William Lincoln (hŏn'nōld), mining engr.; b. Oconee, Ill., Apr. 16, 1866; s. Rev. Robert and Sarah (Ernest) H.; Knox Coll., Galesburg, Ill., 1886-87, LL.D., 1927; U. Mich., 1887-88; E.M., Mich. Coll. of Mines, Houghton, 1895; D.Sc., Claremont Coll., 1936; D.Eng., Mich. Coll. Mining and Tech., 1937; m. Caroline Burton, Nov. 12, 1895. Successively foreman, supt., mgr. and cons. engr. of mines, in Minn. and Cal., 1895-1902; went to S. Africa, 1902, as cons. engr. Consolidated Mines Selection Co. (London) and subsidiary cos., becoming mng. dir., 1912, also chmn. Transvaal Coal Trust, Brakpan Mines, Springs Mines and The New Era Co.; retired from S. Africa, 1915. Was mem. Council of Edn. and v.p. Chamber of Mines, Johannesburg, S.A. Apptd. dir. in London of Commn. for Relief in Belgium, 1915; trans. to New York, as dir. in America, 1916, continuing until armistice; now dir. Commn. for Relief in Belgium, Ednl. Found. Spl. rep. in Europe of Guaranty Trust Co. of New York, 1919; dir. (permanent) Anglo-Am. Corp. of South Africa, Ltd. Trustee Cal. Inst. Tech., Claremont Colleges; hon. trustee Pomona Coll. Mem. Am. Inst. Mining and Metall. Engrs., Ming and Metall. Soc. Am. Decorated Comdr. Order of the Crown, Médaille Commemorative du Comite Nat. (Belgian); Médaille Reconnaissance Française (French). Mem. Phi Delta Theta, Tau Beta Pi, Phi Beta Kappa, Phi Beta Kappa Associates. Republican. Mason. Clubs: California, Los Angels Country, Bel-Air Country, Sunset (Los Angeles). Home: Bel-Air, Los Angeles 24. Office: Pacific Mutual Bldg., Los Angles 14. Died May 6, 1950; buried Oak Park Cemetery, Clearmont, Cal.

HONORÉ, Paul (ŏn-ŏr-ā'), mural painter; b. Crawford County, Pa., May 30, 1885; prep. edn., Cass Tech. High Sch., Detroit; art edn. Sch. of Fine Arts, Detroit, Pa. Acad. Fine Arts, Phila.; pupil of Frank Brangwyn; m. Kate Ethel York, Feb. 1, 1911; children—Paul York, Ethel Mary. Specialist on murals, also wood block decorations for books; former dir. fine arts Naval Tng. Center Bainbridge, Md. Represented by murals at Midland (Mich.) County Court House; Dearborn (Mich.) Pub. Library; 1st State Bank, Detroit; Highland Park (Mich.) High Sch.; Players Club, Detroit; Peoples Church, Lansing, Mich.; NRC, Washington; Mich. Bldg. at Century of Progress Expn., Chgo. (now at Lansing, Mich.); Midand Country Club; Dearborn (Mich.) High School; Southeastern High School, Detroit; painter prize poster for women's registration, World War II. Recipient Marvin Preston prize Mich. Artists Exhibit, Detroit Mus. of Art, 1917, Museum Founders prize, 1917; Walter Piper purchase prize Scarab Club, Detroit, 1928. Mem. Mural Painters Soc. N.Y., Authors League, Soc. Arts and Crafts, Founders Soc. of Detroit Mus. Art. Clubs: Scarab (Detroit); Nat. Arts (N.Y.C.); Washington Arts. Made wood block decorations for Heroes from Hakluyt, Tales from Silverlands, Tales Worth Telling, Romantic Rascals, Frontier Ballads, Winged Horse, Winged Horse Anthology, Seasoned Timber, etc. Founder Paul Honoré Fellowship, 1931. Dir. of fine arts Bainbridge Naval Training Center. Home-studio: 131 S. 22d St., Phila.; (summer) Port Deposit, Md. Died Apr. 12, 1956.

HOOD, George E., congressman; b. Wayne County, N.C., Jan. 27, 1875; s. Edward B. and Edith (Bridgers) H.; ed. pub. schs.; m. Julia Annie Flowers, Sept. 23, 1903. Admitted to N.C. bar, 1896, and practiced in Goldsboro; sec. Dem. Exec. Com., Wayne Co., 1896; treas. Wayne Co., N.C., 1897-9; mem. N.C. Ho. of Rep., 1901; mayor of Goldsboro, 1901-7; Dem. presdl. elector, 1912; mem. 64th and 65th Congresses (1915-19), 3d N.C. Dist. Capt. Co. B., N.C.N.G., 1901-5; lt. col., insp. general's dept., 1905-7; retired, 1909, rank of col. Mem. Goldsboro Bar Assn. Methodist. Home: Goldsboro, N.C. Died Mar. 1960.

HOOK, James William, engr.; b. near Hedrick, Ia., Jan. 9, 1884; s. James and Virginia (Eller) H.; B.M.E., Ia. State Coll., 1905, M.E., 1912; m. Hattie Rosamond Bechtel, Sept. 17, 1907; children—James William, Rose Virginia. Editor and pub Cody (Wyo.) Enterprise, 1905-06; sales engr. Globe Machinery & Supply Co., Des Moines, Ia., 1906-09; sales mgr. and later gen. mgr. C. A. Dunham Co., Marshalltown, Ia., 1909-16; pres. and dir. Allied Machinery Co. of America, New York, also dir. other corps. in New York, 1916-23; pres. and treas. Geometric Tool Co., New Haven, Conn., 1923-44; pres. and director United Illuminating Company of New Haven, Conn., 1939-42, chairman of Board, 1942-—; director Acme Wire Co., of New Haven. Mem. Connecticut Emergency Relief Commission, 1933-36; resident industrial advisor NRA, 1933; member Industrial Advisory Board NRA, 1934-35; vice chairman Durable Goods Industries Com. NRA, 1934-35; mem. Bd. of Edn., Tarrytown, N.Y., 1922-23; distribution com., New Haven Foundation; 1928-38; pres. N.E. Council, 1937-38; mem. President Hoover's Nat. Orgn. on Unemployment Relief, 1931-33; chmn. Conn. Unemployment Commn., 1931-33; awarded the Marston medal by Iowa State Coll., 1940, for achievement in engineering; mem. Bus. Adv. Council for the U.S. Dept. of Commerce, 1939-—. Trustee University of Connecticut, 1935-53, chairman, 1949-53; trustee New Haven YMCA (chmn.); member Citizens Action Commission of New Haven; mem. New England Regional Manpower Committee, 1943-44; v.p. Mfrs. Assn. of Conn., 1941-46. Member A.A.A.S., Am. Soc. M.E., Academy Political Science, Society of Colonial Wars, Tau Beta Pi, Kappa Sigma. Republican. Mason (32°). Clubs: University (New York City); Graduate, Quinnipiack, Lawn, Country (New Haven). Author: Industry's Obligation to the Unemployed, 1938. Co-author: The New Outlook in Business, 1940; wrote genealogies, James Hook and Virginia Eller, 1925; Judge Karl Bechtel, of Hanau, Germany, 1936; George Michael Eller and Descendents of His in America, 1957. Home: 56 Mulberry Hill St., Hamden 17, Conn. Office: 80 Temple St., New Haven 6. Died Oct. 21, 1957; buried Evergreen Cemetery, New Haven.

HOOPER, Ben W., ex-gov. Tenn.; b. Newport, Tenn., Oct. 13, 1870; grad. Carson and Newman Coll., Jefferson City, Tenn., 1890; m. Anna B. Jones, Sept. 25, 1901; children—Anna B., Ben Jones, Randolph, Janella, Lemuel W., Newell Sanders. Admitted to Tenn. bar, 1894; asst. U.S. atty. Eastern Dist. Tenn., 1906-10; gov. of Tenn., 1911-13, 13-15; resumed practice as mem. firm Hooper, Cate & Greer. Baptist. Rep. nominee for U.S. senator, 1916, 34; elected judge Chancery Ct., 1920, resigned, 1921; became mem. U.S. R.R. Labor Bd., Chicago, serving as chmn., 1922-26; mem. Great Smoky Mountain Park Commn., 1927-28, chief land buyer for park, 1928-29; became mem. law firm Hooper, Crawford & Hurd; now retired from law practice and chiefly engaged in writing and in dealing in mountain real estate. Vice pres., Constitutional Conv., 1953. Served as capt., Spanish-Am. War, 1898-99; served in Puerto Rico. Mem. Vets. Fgn. Wars. Clubs: Kiwanis, Ruritan. Address: P.O., Newport, Tenn. Died Apr. 18, 1957.

HOOPER, C. E., broadcast audience measurement; b. Kingsville, O., May 31 1898; s. Alfred E. and Clementia Charlotte (MacEwen) H.; A.B., Amherst Coll., 1921; M.B.A., Harvard, 1923; m. Emily Judson Reed, Sept. 7, 1927; 1 dau., Mary Stuart. Asst. mgr., Liberty Savings & Loan Co., Yakima, Wash., 1923-24; advt. mgr. Harvard Business Review, 1924-26; advt. mgr. Scribners Mag., New York, N.Y., 1926-29; account exec. Doremus & Co., New York, N.Y., 1929-31; in charge development of syndicated services, Daniel Starch, 1931-34; pres. Clark-Hooper, Inc., New York, N.Y., 1934-38; pres. C. E. Hooper, Inc., New York, N.Y., 1938-—. Served as pvt., Inf., U.S. Army, 1918. Mem. Am. Marketing Assn., Market Research Council, Delta Tau Delta. Clubs: Harvard, Players, Amherst (New York); Tavern, Chicago; Bohemian (San Francisco); Shore and Country (Norwalk, Conn); Tokeneke (Darien, Conn.); Fly Fishers (Roscoe, N.Y.). Author: (with M. N. Chappell) Radio Audience Measurement, 1944. Home: 343 Flax Hill, South Norwalk, Conn. Office: 10 E. 40th St., N.Y. City 16; Dry Hill, Norwalk, Conn. Died Dec. 15, 1954.

HOOPER, Frank Finley, educator; b. Holly Springs, Miss., Nov. 23, 1877; s. Wesley Watson and Mattie (Green) H.; A.B., U. Chattanooga, 1897; A.M., U. Wis., 1910; m. Marie Louise Steward, June 25, 1907. Prof. mathematics U. Chattanooga, 1904-—, dean Coll. of Arts, 1919-—, acting pres., 1920-21. Mem. So. Commn. on Accredited Schs. Mem. Assn. Colls. and Secondary Schs. of So. States, Tenn. Coll. Assn. (exec. com.), Math. Assn. America, Tenn. Acad. Science, Nat. Registrars' Assn.,

Kappa Sigma. Republican. Methodist. Clubs: Kiwanis, Chattanooga Golf and Country. Home: 521 Battery Pl., Chattanooga, Tenn. Deceased.

HOOPER, John William, banker, industrialist; b. N.Y.C., Oct. 4, 1896; s. Alfred Frederick and Sophie Dorothy (Schierholz-Freitag) H.; student Townsend-Harris Hall, City Coll., N.Y., Pace Coll., and other specialized courses in accounting, finance and comml. law; D.C.S., Gettysburg Coll., 1954; m. Mabel Kathleen Strachan, Sept. 7, 1925; children—John William (dec.), Janet Dorothy (Mrs. David Paine Osborn). Employed in municipal, real estate and constrn. work, 1914-17; mng. accountant Harris, Kerr and Cook, Chartered Accountants, London, and N.Y. C., 1918-25; practiced pub. accounting as C.P.A., 1925-49; comptroller, v.p. charge finance Am. Machine and Foundry Co. and affiliated cos., 1925-49, dir., 1930-54; trustee Lincoln Savs. Bank, Bklyn., 1943-—, exec. v.p., 1949, pres., 1950-—; dir. Mundet Cork Corp., N.J., Intertype Corp., Bklyn. Past chmn. local S.S.S.; former mem. panel War Labor Bd. Dir., former chmn. Bklyn. chpt. A.R.C.; dir. N.Y.C. Anti-Crime Com., Inc.; Bklyn. campaign chmn. Greater N.Y. Fund, 1952; trustee Savs. Banks Life Ins. Fund; trustee, mem. exec. com. Wagner Coll., S.I.; pres. Pestalozzi Found. Am., N.Y.; trustee Bklyn. Inst. Arts and Scis., Polytechnic Inst. Bklyn.; Bklyn. chmn. United Hosp. Fund, 1950. Recipient of Brotherhood award of Nat. Conf. of Christians and Jews, 1957. Mem. Savs. Bank Assn. N.Y. (chmn. Group V, mem. council adminstrn., budget, legislative commn.), Soc. C.P.A.'s Conn., Am. Inst. Accountants, Am. Inst. Banking (mem. adv. council, N.Y.), C. of C. (chmn. exec. com.). Republican. Mason. Clubs: Downtown, Economic, Union League (N.Y.C.); Rotary, Brooklyn, Municipal (dir.), Rembrandt, Apollo (dir.) (Bklyn.); Lake Placid. Home: one Pierrepont Street, Bklyn. 1; (country) South Salem, N.Y. Office: 531 Broadway, Bklyn. 6. Died Oct. 22, 1959; buried Lutheran Cemetery, Bklyn.

HOOPER, Robert P., cotton mfr.; b. Baltimore, Md., July 15, 1872; s. James E. and Sarah (Poole) H.; hon. LL.D., Jefferson Med. Coll.; m. Marion Baylies, 1896; pres. Wm. E. Hooper & Sons Co.; director of Lumbermen's Mutual Casualty Co. (Chicago), Nat. Retailers Ins. Co., Excess Ins. Co. (Chicago), Insurers (Pa.). Home: Chestnut Hill. Office: Broad and Arch Sts., Phila. 7. Died July 5, 1958.

HOOPER, Stanford Caldwell, rear admiral USN, ret., electronics consultant; b. Colton, Cal., Aug. 16, 1884; s. William Swayze and Mary (Caldwell) H.; B.S., U.S. Naval Academy, 1905; m. Margaret Nye, May 27, 1915; 1 dau., Elizabeth. Commd. ensign, USN, 1907, advanced through grades to rear adm., 1938; first U.S. Fleet radio officer, 1912; head of Radio Div., Navy Dept. during 3 tours of shore duty beginning 1915; comd. destroyer Fairfax during World War I; chief engr. Fed. Radio Commn., 1927-28; dir. Naval Communications, 1928-34; dir. Tech. Div., Naval Operations, and chmn. Naval Research Com., 1934-39; dir. Radio Liaison Div., 1940-43, ret. Hooper Trophy awarded annually to outstanding electronics div. USNR. Decorated World War I medal Navy Cross, Mexican Campaign medal (United States); Legion of Honor (France); awarded gold medal Institute Radio Engineers, 1934, Marconi Medal of Merit, 1939, Elliot Cresson Medal (Franklin Institute), 1945, U.S. delegate to International Radio Confs. at The Hague, Bucharest, Lisbon, Cairo, Chile. Episcopalian. Clubs: Army and Navy, Army and Navy Country, Chevy Chase, Sulgrave (Washington, D.C.); New York Yacht; Bath (Miami Beach, Fla.). Editor of Robinson's Manual of Radio Telegraphy and Telephony. Address: 4425 Garfield Street N.W., Washington; also 6320 Alton Rd., Miami Beach, Fla. Died Apr. 6, 1955; buried Arlington Nat. Cemetery.

HOOPINGARNER, Dwight Lowell, pub. relations counsel, industrial and commercial exec., author; b. Lincoln, Neb., Oct. 8, 1893; s. Noah Leander and Dora Emma (Stallsmith) H.; fellow in philosophy of edn., U. of Tex., 1911-13, A.B., 1913, A.M., 1915; fellow Columbia and Carnegie Inst. Tech., 1916-17; married to Iris Veda Huddleston, June 9, 1951. Instr. philosophy of Edn. U. of Tex., 1913-16; dir. employment and edn. Nat. Bank of Commerce, N.Y. City, 1917-18; exec. counsel on labor relations, Thomas L. Chadbourne, N.Y. City, 1919; lecturer on labor relations, Harvard Grad. Sch. of Business Adminstrn., 1919-20; instr. in same, Columbia, 1920; gen. practice as counsel on labor relations, 1920-22; exec. mgr. Cleveland (O.) Building Trades Employers Assn., 1922-23; exec. head American Construction Council, 1923-33; managing dir. New York Building Congress, 1924-26; head Dwight L. Hoopingarner Co., real estate and finance brokerage; pub. relations counsel Beneficial Indsl. Loan Corp., 1929-32. Chmn. Special Com. of Federal Bldgs., by appmt. Sec. of Interior, 1933-34; asso. dir. housing div. Federal Pub. Works Adminstrn., 1934-37; mem. of com. on seasonal occupations and industries, New York State Unemployment Ins. Law. Consultant on construction industries, labor production div., War Production Bd., 1942, chief of consultation and appeals branch, construction div., 1942-43, asst. to v. chmn. on industry operations, 1944-45; dir. Facilities and Constrn. Div. and planning specialist Nat. Security Resources Bd., 1948-51; mem. planning staff D.P.A., 1951, dep. dir. expansion goals staff, 1951-52; dir. facilities div., office prodn. resources Nat. Security Resources Bd., Exec. Office of the President, 1952. Exec. vice pres. Arthritis and Rheumatism Foundation of D.C., Inc. Mem. advisory committee on business research of Social Science Research Council, New York; mem. com. on slums and blighted areas, President's Conf. on Home Bldg. and Home Ownership. Head of employment management br. U.S. Shipping Bd. Emergency Fleet Corp., World War I. Mem. American Association for Labor Legislation, American Legion, Phi Beta Kappa, Phi Delta Kappa, Methodist. Clubs: Touchdown, Gyro International, Harvard. Author: Labor Relations in Industry, 1925; The Management of Labor, 1927. Writer of booklets for U.S. Shipping Bd. Emergency Fleet Corp.; Labor Loss in Terms of Production Hours, 1918; Handbook on Employment Management, 1918, 19. Spl. lecturer at Mass. Inst. Tech., Dartmouth, etc. Home: Upperville. Office: P.O. Box 26, Upperville, Va. Died Jan. 26, 1955.

HOOPINGARNER, Newman Leander, cons. business psychologist; b. University Place, Neb., May 1, 1891; s. Noah Leander and Dora Emma (Stallsmith) H.; A.B., U. of Tex., 1913, A.M., 1915; grad. study Columbia, Carnegie Inst. Tech. and N.Y.U.; m. Ethel Barron, June 24, 1917; 1 son, Newman Avery. Tutor in psychology and asst. to dir. extension dept., U. of Tex., 1912-15; instr. psychology and history of edn., Southwest Tex. State Teachers Coll., summer 1914; mgr. edn. exhibits and lecturer on sch. improvement, U. of Tex., 1915-17; major research fellow in applied psychology, Bur. of Salesmanship Research, Carnegie Inst. Tech., Pittsburgh, Pa., 1917-18; asso. prof. applied psychology and field rep. Bur. Personnel Research, same inst., 1919-20; dir. service methods, Bus. Training Corp., N.Y.C., 1920-21; lecturer on business psychology and management, N.Y. U., 1922-26, Brooklyn Edison Sch., 1922-25, Brooklyn Inst. Arts and Sciences, 1922-26; organizer, and dir. Bur. of Business Guidance, 1923-—; asst. prof. business psychology, Sch. Commerce, N.Y.U., 1926, asso. prof., 1927-31, prof., 1931-—. Personnel adj. Ordnance Training Camp, Camp Hancock, Ga., 1918-19; 2d lt., ordnance, Feb. 1, 1918, 1st lt., Nov. 1, 1918; capt., A.G.D., 1919-29. Mem. A.A.A.S., Winconna Assn., Inc. (dir.), Personnel Research Fed., Phi Delta Kappa, Pi Gamma Mu; fellow, American Geographical Society of New York. Methodist. Mason. Club: City. Author: (in collaboration) Modern Production Methods, 1921; Self Measurement Tests for Executive and Business Ability, 1923; Personality and Business Ability Analysis, 1927. Originated and developed a method of analyzing and developing personality which may be applied in education and in business; organized the first credit course in personality improvement offered in any college or university. Home: 14 Dartmouth St., Rockville Center, L.I., N.Y. Died Jan. 1958.

HOOTON, Earnest Albert (hōō'tŭn), anthropologist; b. Clemansville, Wis., Nov. 20, 1887; s. William and Margaret Elizabeth (Newton) H.; B.A., Lawrence Coll., Appleton, Wis., 1907, Sc.D., 1933; M.A. University of Wisconsin, 1908, Ph.D., 1911; also LL.D. (honorary), 1954; Rhodes Scholar at Oxford U., 1910-13, diploma in anthropology, 1912, B.Litt., 1913; m. Mary Beidler Camp, June 3, 1915; children —Jay Camp, William Newton, Emma Beidler. Instr. anthropology, 1913, asst. prof., 1921, asso. prof., 1927, prof. since 1930, Harvard. Asst. curator somatology, Peabody Museum, 1913-14, curator since 1914. Fellow A.A.A.S. (v.p. sect. H, 1923-24), Royal Anthropol. Inst., Am. Acad. Arts and Sciences; mem. Am. Anthropol. Assn., Am. Assn. Phys. Anthropol., Am. Genetic Assn., Am. Philos. Soc., Am. Soc. Naturalists, Nat. Acad. Sci., Phi Beta Kappa; hon. fellow Am. Acad. Dental Science. Author: Ancient Inhabitants of the Canary Islands, 1925; The Indians of Pecos, 1930; Up from the Ape, 1931; rev. ed., 1946; Apes, Men and Morons, 1937; Crime and the Man, The American Criminal, Vol. I, Twilight of Man, 1939; Why Men Behave Like Apes and Vice Versa, 1940; Man's Poor Relations, 1942; "Young Man, You are Normal," 1945; also papers on physical anthropology. Home: 13 Buckingham St., Cambridge, Mass. Died May 3, 1954; buried Mt. Auburn Cemetery.

HOOVER, Blaine, pub. adminstr.; b. Red Cliff, Colo., Jan. 23, 1893; s. Simeon Newhouse and Caroline Ida (Lowry) H.; student Beloit (Wis.) Coll., 1911-14, U. Chgo., 1914-15; m. Edith Johnson, 1916 (dec.); children—Blaine, Harwood, Elaine, Bruce; m. 2d, Eleanor Ann Louise Reese, Oct. 11, 1941. Supr. timekeeping and payrolls U.S. Steel Corp., 1910; sec. to exec. in charge personnel Franklin MacVeagh & Co., 1916-17; expert personnel and mgmt., U.S. Shipping Bd., 1918-19; mgr. employment and tng., The Shuman Co., 1920-28; mgr. Yale U. Press, 1929-33; state dir. of personnel Ill. Emergency Relief Commn., 1934; state dir. of employment Works Progress Adminstrn., 1935-36; supt. employment, sec. and mem. civil service bd. Chgo. Park Dist., 1937-47; mem. exec. council Civil Service Assembly of U.S. and Can., 1943-46, pres. 1945-48; chmn. U.S. Personnel Adv. Mission to Japan, 1946-47; chief Civil Service Div., adviser Japanese Civil Service System, Gen. Hdqrs. S.C.A.P., 1947-49. Served with Ill. N.G., 1917. Mem. Am. Soc. for Public Adminstrn., Nat. Civil Service League (mem. council), Am. Polit. Sci. Assn., Tau Kappa Epsilon, Phi Alpha Delta, Delta Sigma Rhl. Clubs: City, Illinois Athletic (Chgo.); American (Tokyo, Japan). Address: 649 Hinman Av., Evanston, Ill. Died Sept. 3, 1950.

HOOVER, Frank G(arfield), business exec.; born New Berlin, O., Apr. 4, 1883;. William Henry and Susan (Troxel) H.; ed. Oberlin Coll., 1900-01, Ohio State U., 1902-03; m. Edna Seiler, Sept. 18, 1907; children—Richard S., W. Henry, David C. with W. H. Hoover Co., and The Hoover Co., 1904-—, dir. The Hoover Co.; pres. N. Canton (formerly New Berlin), O., mfrs. vacuum cleaners, 1948-—. V.p. Nat. Council and chmn. Nat. Field Operations. Boy Scouts of America. Mason (33°). Home: 821 S. Main St. Office: The Hoover Co., North Canton, O. Died Dec. 3, 1954; buried North Canton Cemetery, North Canton.

HOOVER, George Pendelton, lawyer; trail atty. Teapot Dome litigation. Home: 15 W. Lenox St., Chevy Chase, Md. Office: Investment Bldg., Washington. Died Nov. 5, 1943.*

HOOVER, Harvey Daniel, teacher of theology; b. New Oxford, Pa., June 17, 1880; s. Samuel E. and Jane J. (Gable) H.; student Gettysburg (Pa.) Coll., 1894-96; Susquehanna Univ., Selinsgrove, Pa., 1896-1902, A.B., 1899, A.M., 1900, B.D., 1902; Ph.D., Ill. Wesleyan U., Bloomington, Ill., 1907; S.T.D., Gettysburg, 1918, D.D., Wittenberg College, Springfield, O., 1922; Litt.D., Carthage (Ill.) College, 1935; m. Miriam Grace Stock, June 17, 1902; 1 dau., Dorcas Grace (Mrs. Paul H. Ensrud). Minister at Friedens, Pa., 1902-04, East Pittsburgh, 1904-07; prof. sociology and philosophy, Susquehanna U., 1907-09; prof. philosophy and edn., and pres. Carthage (Ill.) Coll., 1909-26; prof. Pastoral Theology and Liturgies and Dean of the Seminary Chapel, Lutheran Theological Seminary, Gettysburg, 1926-52; prof. Phila. Lutheran Deaconess Sch., 1954-58. Instructor Nawakwa Training Camp, Adams County Leadership School, Baltimore Deaconess Training School; lecturer on popular educational, literature and sociol. topics. Vice pres. bd. govs. Council for Clinical Training (N.Y.); member migrant conv. Nat. Council of Chs. of U.S.A.; pres. of dirs. Nawakwa Training Sch, Member N.E.A., Am. Sociol. Soc., Religious Edn. Assn., Luth. Hist. Acad., A.A.A.S., Nat. Hoover Assn., Am. Geog. Soc., S.A.R. (state chaplain), Sigma Nu, Rural Sociol. Soc., Nat. Com. on Mental Hygiene, Pa. Welfare Conf., Ch. Social Workers, Am. Hymn Soc. (N.Y.), Hymn Soc. (London). Adams County Hist. Society, Phi Kappa Rho, Pi Gamma Mu. Sec. Common Service Book Com., United Lutheran Church America. Clubs: University (Chicago); Lions. Wrote: Master Mind; Lift Up Your Eyes; History of Carthage College; In His Presence. Editor Bible Reading Fellowship (monthly); also ed. of Light for Today and of 5 vols. of Nat. Luth. Edn. Assn. Home: Gettysburg, Pa. Died May 11. 1958; buried New Oxford, Pa.

HOOVER, Herbert William, manufacturer; b. North Canton, O., Oct. 30, 1877; s. William Henry and Susan (Troxel) H.; ed. high sch., North Canton, O.; student Hiram (O.) Coll., 1896-97; m. Grace Louise Steele, Dec. 15, 1905; children—Polly Louise (Mrs. L. E. Connelly), Jane (Mrs. E. Scott Hill), Herbert William, James Clary. Entered father's saddlery factory, 1898, became vice pres. when business was incorporated as The W. H. Hoover Co., 1903; an organizer, with father and others, Electric Suction Sweeper Co. (which immediately began production of Model O Hoover cleaners), 1908, gen. mgr., 1908-22; pres. The Hoover Co., 1922-48, chairman of bd., 1948-—; dir. Harter Bank & Trust Co. Dir. Canton (O.) Welfare Fedn. Chmn. bd. Community Christian Ch. Mem. Vacuum Cleaner Mfg. Assn., Am. Soc. Sales Execs., Nat. Assn. Mfrs. (arbitration bd.). Clubs: Surf, Indian Creek (Miami Beach, Fla.); Union (Cleveland); Canton, Brookside (Canton, O.); Touissant Shooting (Oak Harbor, O.). Address: The Hoover Co., North Canton, O. Died Sept. 16, 1954; buried North Lawn Cemetery, Canton.

HOOVER, Theodore Jesse, mining engr.; b. West Branch, Ia., Jan. 28, 1871; s. Jesse Clark and Huldah Randall (Minthorn) H.; A.B., Stanford, 1901; m. Mildred Crew Brooke, 1899 (died 1940); children —Louis Brooke (Mrs. William Havselt), and Mrs. Cornelius Willis, Mrs. Charles McLean, Jr. Manager of the consulting engineers of mines in Cal., Mex., Russia, Burma, Australia and Alaska, 1903-19; prof. mining and metallurgy Stanford, 1919-—, dean of engring., 1925-36, now dean of engring. emeritus. Mem. Am. Inst. Mining and Metall. Engrs., Cooper Ornithol. Club. Author: Concentrating Ores by Flotation, 3d edit., 1916; Economics of Mining, 1933; 3d ed., 1947; The Engineering Profession, 1941; 2d ed., 1947. Home: Rancho del Oso, Davenport, Santa Cruz County, Cal. Died Feb. 5, 1955.

HOOVER, William H., lawyer; b. Lodi, O., Apr. 20, 1889; s. Benjamin F. and Claudia I. (Crawford) H.; A.B., Wooster U., Wooster, O., 1909, LL.B., Harvard, 1913; m. Grace M. Young, June 15, 1915; 1

s., John M. (adopted). Admitted to Mont. bar, 1914, and in gen. practice Great Falls, Mont., until 1936; pres. First Nat. Bank, Great Falls, 1933-36; western gen. counsel Anaconda Copper Mining Co., 1936-43, gen. counsel, 1942, v.p. and gen. counsel 1943-49, pres. since 1949, dir. since 1947; gen. counsel Mont. Power Co., 1936. Served as a private in U.S. Army, World War I. Director of the National City Bank of New York, The First Nat. Bank of Great Falls, Mont. Power Co., Anaconda Wire & Cable Co., Andes Copper Mining Co., Butte, Anaconda & Pacific Ry. Co., Butte Water Co., Chile Copper Co., Chile Exploration Co., Chile Steamship Co., Inc., Green Cananea Copper Co., Internat. Smelting and Refining Company, The American Brass Company. Delegate to the republican National Covention, 1924. Mem. Great Falls C. of C. (pres.). Am. Bar Assn., Mont. Bar Assn., Nat. Assn. Mfrs. Clubs: Kiwanis International (dist. gov.). Home: 1039 W. Broadway, Butte, Mont. Address: 616 Henessy Bldg., Butte, Mont., and 25 Broadway, N.Y.C. Died June 6, 1952.

HOPE, Richard (John William), educator; b. Pueblo, Colo., Aug. 12, 1895; s. William and Martha (Festner) H.; student, Concordia Sem., St. Louis, 1913-16; A.M., Univ. Southern Calif., 1923; B.D., 1926; Ph.D., Columbia, 1930; m. Lydia Koepsel, June 21, 1923. Ordained to the ministry of the Luth. Ch., June 1916, and served pastorates in Univ. City, Mo., 1916-20, Los Angeles (Grace Ch.), 1920-26; prof. English and history, Concordia Coll. Inst., Bronxville, N.Y., 1926-28; lecturer in philosophy, Columbia, 1929-30; asso. prof. of philosophy, Univ. Pittsburgh, 1930-44, prof. of philosophy, 1944—, head dept., 1955—. Lectr. Germany, 1953-54. Mem. Am. Philos. Assn., Am. Assn. Univ. Profs.; Polygon, Philosophical Soc., Pittsburgh, Phi Beta Kappa, Sigma Xi, Phi Kappa Phi. Republican. Author: The Book of Diogenes Laertius 1930; A Guide to Readings in Philosophy, 1939; How Man Thinks, 1949; (translator) Aristotle's physics, 1952. Home: 515 S. Aiken Av., Pitts. 32. Died July 28, 1955; buried Allegheny Cemetery, Pitts.

HOPKINS, B. Smith, chemist; b. Owosso, Mich., Sept. 1, 1873; s. Loren Hopkins and Clara Sibley (Norgate) H.; A.B., Albion (Mich.) Coll., 1896, A.M., 1897, Sc.D., 1926; studied Columbia, 1900-01; Ph.D., Johns Hopkins, 1906; LL.D., Carroll Coll., 1940; m. Maude Childs, June 25, 1901; children—Harvey Childs, B. Smith; m. 2d, May L. Whitsitt, Dec. 17, 1942. Began with pub. schs., Menominee, Mich., 1897; prin. high school, 1898-1900, supt. schs., 1901-04; prof. chemistry Neb. Wesleyan U., 1906-09, Carroll Coll., Waukesha, Wis., 1909-12; with U. Ill., 1912—, prof. inorganic chemistry, 1923—, dir. sci. Gen. Studies Div., 1941-42, dir. chemistry teaching Army Specialized Tng. Program, 1942-43; spl. summer lectr. Northwestern U., 1910-11, Western Reserve U., 1929, emeritus, 1941. Pres. Urbana Bd. Edn., 1932-44. Fellow A.A.A.S.; mem. Am. Chem. Soc., Am. Electrochem. Soc., Ill. Acad. Science (pres. 1933-34), Central Assn. Science and Mathematics Tchrs., Am. Philos. Soc., Sigma Xi, Phi Beta Kappa, Phi Lambda Upsilon, Alpha Chi Sigma, Alpha Tau Omega. Conglist. Clubs: Exchange; Chaos (Chgo.). Author: Exercises in Chemistry (with W. A. Noyes), 1917, 19; Chemistry of the Rarer Elements, 1923; Laboratory Exercises in General Chemistry (with H. A. Neville), 1925, 26, 31; General Chemistry for Colleges, 1930 (rev. 1937, 42); Essentials of College Chemistry, 1932; with J. C. Bailar, Jr. 1945; Laboratory Exercises in General Chemistry (with M. J. Copley), 1937, (with M. J. Copley and F. B. Schirmer, Jr., 1942); (with T. Moeller and F. B. Schirmer, Jr., 1946). Co-author: Chemistry and You, 1939, 44, 49; chapters in Chemistry of Less Familiar Elements, 1940. With colleagues discovered element 61, named it illinium, 1926. Home: 402 W. Florida Av., Urbana, Ill. Died Aug. 27, 1952.

HOPKINS, Benjamin Franklin, industrialist; b. Cleveland, O., June 13, 1876; s. David J. and Mary J. (Jeffreys) H.; student Central High Sch., Western Res. Acad. and Adelbert Coll., Western Res. U.; m. Evelyn Lower, June 5, 1912; children—David Jeffreys, Benjamin Franklin, John Brooks. Began as worker in steel mills; in association with brother, developed and built Belt Line R.R. (now owned by N.Y.C. R.R.), Cleve., Belt & Terminal Realty Co.; founded Cleve. Graphite Bronze Co., 1919, pres., dir. 1919-48, now chmn. Mem. Soc. Automotive Engrs., Cleve. Engring. Soc. Clubs: Union, Country, Shaker Heights Country, Cleveland Athletic (Cleve.); Detroit Athletic. Home: 3107 Fairmount Blvd., Cleveland Heights, O. Office: 17000 St. Clair Av., Cleve. 10. Died Dec. 26, 1955; buried Knollwood Cemetery, Cleve.

HOPKINS, Fred Mead, editor, publisher; b. Epworth, Iowa, July 12, 1875; s. Timothy Mead and Augusta Amelia (Brown) H.; educated high school, 1891-92, U. of Ia. (law), 1893-95; m. Carolyn Constance Bertholet, Oct. 25, 1899; children—Constance B. (Mrs. Kenneth Rice), Edmond M., Virginia A. (Mrs. Warner Woodworth). Admitted to Ia. bar, 1895, and practiced in Dubuque, 1895-1903; Federal Court reporter, Toledo, O., 1903-04; city editor, asst. mng. editor Toledo (O.) Blade, 1904-12; mng. editor Toledo Times, 1912-13; editor and pub. Fostoria (O) Daily Review, 1913-43; purchased Fostoria Daily Times, August 1943, now publisher Review-Times. Served as mayor of Fostoria, 1920-23, postmaster, 1924-36; Republican publicity director for Ohio, campaign 1916; president Fostoria Chamber of Commerce, 1915-27. Apptd. by president mem. com. to select members Seneca County, O., draft bds., World War II; publicity dir. Civilian Defense; dist. adviser Boy Scouts. Served as 1st sergt. Co. A, 49th Ia. Inf., 1898-99; chairman Red Cross during World War I. Vice chairman postwar and Future Planning Council; apptd. mem. 5 board Federal Vets. Housing Com. Mem. Inland Dailies Assn., Nat. Editorial Assn., Ohio Newspaper Assn., Ohio Select List, Vets. Foreign Wars, Vets. Spanish-Am. War. Organized Ohio Hotel Greeters, 1903. Republican. Presbyterian. Mason (32°), Moose. Clubs: Rotary (past dist. gov. Rotary Internat.), Country, Fostoria. Compiled and edited History of 1895 Law Class of Univ. of Iowa, 1938. Home: 947 N. Main St. Office: 113-117 E. Center St., Fostoria, O. Died Dec. 15, 1954; buried Fountain Cemetery, Fostoria.

HOPKINS, John Jay, lawyer and business executive; born at Santa Ana, California, on October 15, 1893; son of Reverend John Thomas and May Irene (Hymer) H.; studied Occidental Coll., Los Angeles, 1911-14, LL.D., 1955; A.B., U. of Cal., 1915; LL.B., Harvard, 1921; married to Ruth Smith, June 26, 1917; one daughter Lianne (Mrs. Clement Conger). Practiced in offices of Cravath, Henderson, Leffingwell & de Gersdorff, N.Y. City, 1921-24, then under own name in N.Y. City; spl. asst. to Ogden L. Mills, secretary of Treasury, 1932-33; gen. counsel, and dir. Mayflower Associates, Inc., 1933-36; engaged in practice of law in N.Y.C., 1936-41; chmn. board, pres. Gen. Dynamics Corp.; chmn. bd., mng. dir. Canadair, Ltd.; mem. adv. com. 45th St. br. Chase Manhattan Bank; dir. Tide Water Asso. Oil Co., Lincoln Service Corp., Mfrs. Credit Corp. Mem. nat. adv. com. Case Inst. Tech.; trustee Com. Econ. Development, Grant Monument Assn., Lovelace Found., Albuquerque, N.M., Theodore Roosevelt Assn.; mem. governing bd. Nat. Indsl. Conf. Bd.; nat. campaign chmn. Arthritis and Rheumatism Found.; mem. armed services com. Nat. Council YMCA's. Del. Rep. Nat. Conv., 1928, 32. Enrolled as seaman 2d class, later commd. ensign USNRF, World War I. Decorated Comdr. 2d class Order White Rose Finland; recipient Horatio Alger award, 1953; named Industrialist of yr., Soc. Indsl. Realtors, 1955. Fellow Canadian Geog. Soc., mem. Am., N.Y. State, Cal. bar assns., Am. Enterprise Assn. (vice chmn., trustee, mem. exec. com.), Am. Mgmt. Assn., Nat. Aero. Assn., Nat. Aviation Club, N.A.M. (dir.-at-large, chmn. nuclear energy com.; del. 2d Internat. Conf. Mfrs., Paris 1954), Nat. Security Indsl. Assn. (past chmn. bd. and pres.; trustee, mem. exec. com.), Shipbuilders Council Am. (dir.). Soc. Naval Architects and Marine Engrs., Air Force Assn., Am. Ordnance Assn., Def. Orientation Conf. Assn. (past pres.), Mil. Order Loyal Legion U.S., Naval Hist. Assn., Navy League U.S. (dir.), Marine Hist. Assn., Naval Aviation Edn. Council, Nat. Inst. Social Scis., Peruvian-Am. Assn., Save Redwoods League, Soc. Medalists, English-Speaking Union U.S., Fgn. Policy Assn., Pan-Am. Soc. U.S., U. Cal. Alumni Assn., U.S., Internat. (Canadian council, dir. and del. 1955 Conv., Tokyo: mem. U.S. council) C.'s of C., Mexican C. of C. U.S., Audubon Soc., Soc. Colonial Wars, Soc. War 1812, Loyal Legion, S.R., Am. Legion, Newcomen Soc., Canadian Profl. Golfers Assn., Internat. Golf Assn., Inc., N.Y. (founder, chmn., pres.), Internat. Golf Assn., Ltd. (founder, chmn., pres.), Profl. Golfers Assn. Am. (vice chmn. adv. com.; mem. Ryder Cup and internat. matches com.), U.S. Srs. Golf Assn., Am. Horse Shows Assn. Inc., N.Y. Presbyn. Mason (32°, K.T.). Clubs: Burning Tree (Bethesda, Md.); Columbia Country (Chevy Chase, Md.); Garden City (N.Y.) Golf; Royal and Ancient Golf of St. Andrews (Fife, Scotland); Canadian, Laval-sur-le-Lac, Saint James (Montreal); Areo, Alfalfa, Metropolitan, Nat. Press, 1925 F St. (Washington); New London Tuna, Thames (New London, Conn.); Lotos, Propeller, Nat. Republican, Metropolitan (N.Y.C.). Author papers on U.S. Treasury fiscal matters. Home: 2800 Woodley Rd., Washington. Offices: 1001 Connecticut Av., Washington 6, also 445 Park Av., N.Y.C. 22. Died May 3, 1957; buried Forest Lawn, Glendale, Cal.

HOPKINS, Joseph Gardner, physician; b. Brooklyn, June 30, 1882; s. George Gallagher and Alice (Gardner) H.; student Adelphi Acad., Brooklyn, 1890-98; A.B., Columbia, 1902; M.D., Johns Hopkins, 1907; unmarried. Interne Johns Hopkins Hosp., 1907-08; resident pathologist St. Luke's Hosp., New York, 1908-10; bacteriologist, 1910-13; asst. instr. clinical pathol. Columbia, 1911-13, asso. in bacteriol., 1913-14, asst. prof. bacteriol., 1915-17, asso. instr. in dermatology, 1920-26; prof. dermatol., 1925-47, prof. emeritus since 1947; dir. Dermatology Vanderbilt Clinic, 1926-47, Presbyn. Hosp., 1936-47; practicing physician New York City since 1921. Served as bacteriol. Am. Red Cross Commn. to Serbia, 1915. Served as lt., capt. U.S. Army Med. Corps, 1917-19; investigator com. on med. research, Office Scientific Research Development, 1941-46, tech. observer, consultant Office of Field Service, 1945-46; civilian cons. to surgeon gen. (Army), 1945-46; cons. Veterans Hosp., Bronx, N.Y., since 1946. Mem. Am. Bd. Dermatol. and Syphilol., 1938-47. Mem. Am. Dermatol. Assn., Am. Acad. Dermatol., Soc. Investigative Dermatol., New York Dermatol. Soc., Am. Soc. Pathol. and Bacteriol., Soc. Am. Bacteriol., Am. Mycological Soc., Torrey Botanical, Soc. Pithotomists, Royal Soc. Medicine, Austrian Dermatol. Soc. (hon. mem.), Swedish Dermatol. Soc. (corr. mem.), Phi Beta Kappa, Alpha Omega Alpha. Republican. Episcopalian. Clubs: Century Assn., Columbia University. Home: 217 Haven Av., New York 33. Office: 102 E. 78th St., N.Y. City 21. Died Feb. 27, 1951; buried Washington St. Cemetery, Geneva, N.Y.

HOPKINS, Robert Milton, dir. Cane Ridge Preservation Project; b. Trenton, Ky., July 12, 1878; s. Alexander Campbell and Mary Louise (Broadhurst) H.; student Culver-Stockton Coll., Canton, Mo., 1894-96; A.B., U. of Mich., 1900; grad. study U. of Chicago, 1902, 04, 07; D.D., Culver-Stockton Coll., 1926, Birmingham (Ala.) Southern Coll., 1926, Boston U., 1932; LL.D., Translyvania Coll., 1930; m. Iva Helen Collins, Dec. 20, 1906; 1 son, Robert Milton. Ordained ministry Ch. of Christ (Disciples), 1896; pastor Chapin, Mich., 1899, Glendora, Mich., 1900; state sec. Ky. Christian Bible Sch. Assn., Louisville, 1900-10; sec. Bible Sch. dept. Am. Christian Missionary Soc., Cincinnati, 1910-20; gen. sec. religious edn., United Christian Missionary Soc., St. Louis, 1920-28; gen. sec. World's Sunday Sch. Assn. 1928-40; pres. United Christian Missionary Soc., 1939-46. Chmn. Internat. Council of Religious Edn., 1920-31; trustee, College of the Bible, International Council of Religious Edn., Crystal Beach Christian Assembly. Rep. of United Christian Missionary Society at headquarters of World Council of Churches, Geneva, Switzerland, 1946-47; pres. Golden Rule Found., 1949-52, exec. v.p., 1952-53; dir. Cane Ridge Preservation Project, 1953—. Democrat. Leader in merger Internat. S.S. Council of Evang. denominations with Internat. Council of Religious Edn., and in reorganization of World's S.S. Assn. at 9th World's Conv., Glasgow, Scotland, 1924; participated in world ecumenical ch. gatherings, Wash., 1910, Zurich, 1913, Glasgow, 1924, Los Angeles, 1928, Rio de Janeiro, 1932, Oslo, 1936, Oxford, 1937, Madras, 1938; Toronto, 1950; raised endowment for 1st Disceples of Christ chair of religious edn., Coll. of Bible, Translyvania Coll., Lexington, Ky., 1909. Cleared 20 year accumulated debt of United Christian Missionary Soc., 1942. Life mem. Am. Bible Soc. Club: Town Hall (N.Y.C.). Home: 508 E. Main Stt., Lexingtotn, Ky. Died May 9, 1955, buried Paris, Ky.

HOPKINS, Thomas Cramer, geologist; b. Center County, Pa., May 4, 1861; s. Isaac Cramer and Mary Ann (Glenn) H.; B.S., De Pauw U., 1881; M.S., 1890; A.M., Leland Stanford Jr. U., 1892; Ph.D., U. Chgo., 1900; D.Sc., Colgate U., 1923; m. Edistina Farrow, Jan. 8, 1890 (dec. May 1907); m. 2d, Elizabeth G. Hendrix, Mar. 31, 1909. Prin. high sch., Rising Sun, Ind., 1887-88; instr. in chemistry De Pauw U., 1888-89; asst. geologist Ark. Geol. Survey, 1889-92, Ind. Geol. Survey, 1895, 96, 1901; prof. geology Pa. State Coll., 1896-99, Syracuse U., 1900-32. Mem. Geol. Soc. America, Washington Geol. Soc., Sigma Xi, Phi Beta Kappa, Phi Kappa Phi, Phi Delta Theta. Republican. Methodist. Clubs: Faculty, Current Events, Onondaga, Geology. Author: Marble and Other Limestones, 1893; Brownstones of Pennsylvania, 1896; Clays and Clay Industries of Pennsylvania, 1898; Elements of Physical Geography (text-book), 1908; Laboratory Manual on Physical Geography, 1909; also numerous papers on geol. subjects pub. in tech. jours. and in various state reports. Home: 114 Victoria Pl., Syracuse, N.Y. Died Apr. 3, 1935.

HOPKINS, Walter Lee, lawyer; b. Rocky Mount, Va., Dec. 26, 1889; s. Wm. Leftwich Turner and Mary Ella (Hancock) H.; student William and Mary Coll., 1908-11; spl. work U. of Va., summer 1911; A.B., Washington and Lee U., 1912, LL.B., 1914. Admitted to Va. bar, 1914; editor and mgr. Franklin Chronicle, 1916-17; with Hairston, Woodrum and Hopkins, 1914-16; mem. Hopkins and Hopkins, Richmond, 1920—. In U.S. Army, 1917; commd. lt. inf. and assigned to 318th Regt., 80th Div.; in charge Cable Sect. Bur., War Dept., from Nov. 17, 1918, until hon. disch., Mar. 10, 1919; asst. chief atty. Board of Contract Adjustment, War Dept., 1919 (asso. mem. 1919-20); apptd. mem. staff of Gov. John Garland Pollard of Va., 1930, by Gov. Ruby Laffoon of Ky., 1933 (a.d.c. with rank of col.), Gov. Eugene Talmadge of Ga., June 5, 1934 (a.d.c. with rank of lt. col.), Gov. Wm. H. Murray, of Okla., May 28, 1934 (a.d.c. with rank of col.); commd. by Gov. J. M. Futrell, of Ark., in Ark. Res. Militia, with rank of col., May 25, 1934, and assigned as aide-de-camp on his staff; re-apptd. by Gov. Talmadge as mem. staff (a.d.c. with rank of lt.

col.), to rank from Jan. 16, 1935; apptd. to staff of Gov. James V. Allred of Tex., May 17, 1935 (a.d.c. with rank of lt. col.); commd. hon. col. in the Nat. Guard of U.S. and State of Miss., Aug. 23, 1935, by Gov. Sennett Conner; apptd. mem. of staff of Gov. Olin D. Johnston, of S.C. (a.d.c. with rank of lt. col.), 1938; reappointed mem. of staff of Gov. Johnston, Feb. 1, 1943; appt. mem. of staff of Gov. James H. Davis of La. (a.d.c. with rank of col.), Oct. 28, 1944; asst. adj. gen. U.C.V., 1927, 28, with rank of brig. gen.; apptd. judge adv. gen. on staff of comdr. in chief, U.C.V., 1935 (with rank of brig. gen.). Mem. Va. House of Dels., 1940—. Mem. or former mem. Am., Va. State and Richmond City bar assns., Va. State bar, Va. Society of Colonial Wars, S.R., S.A.R., La Société Nationale, 40 and 8, Am. Legion (post comdr. 1919; post adj. 1921; mem. state exec. com., 1920-22), Sons of Confederate Vets. (camp comdr. 1921-22; judge advocate in chief, 1921-22; state comdr. 1922-23; mem. nat. exec. council, 1923-24 and 1933-35; adj. in chief, 1923-33, 1935-44; comdr. in chief 1933-35); mem. Am. Acad. Polit. and Social Science, Am. Geog. Soc., Repeal Associates, Va. Commn. on Inter-racial Co-operation, Nat. Com. for Protection of Child, Family, School and Church (mem. exec. com.), Va. Hist. Soc., Phi Alpha Delta, Kappa Chi, Omicron Delta Kappa. Mem. bd. visitors R. E. Lee Camp, Soldiers' Home (pres.), Eightieth Div. Vets. Assn., Bd. Pension Commrs. of Richmond City (chmn.), Manassas Battlefield Foundation Com., Beauvoir, Jefferson Davis Memorial Home Com., Appomattox Hist. Park Assn. (v.p.; mem. bd. dirs.); Manassas Battlefield Confed. Park, Inc. (bd. dirs.), pres. bd. dirs. of R. E. Lee Camp Confed. Memorial Park; mem. bd. trustees, Booker T. Washington Birthplace Memorial (member executive committee). Democrat. Member State Central Democratic Committee and vice chairman third Congressional District Com. Episcopalian. Mason (32°, Shriner), Odd Fellow, Elk. Awards of S.C.V.; gold medal and Certificate of Distinction, "for unusual and extraordinary achievement in perpetuating the history of the South and Nation"; gold medal, Southland Star, "for distinguished and meritorious service in historical and patriotic work." Clubs: Westmoreland, Commonwealth. Author: Hopkins of Virginia and Related Families, 1931; Leftwich-Turner Families of Va. and Their Connections, 1932. Editor S.C.V. year book, 1926, 27. Contbr. various hist. publs. Home: 1017 Park Av. Office: Law Bldg., Richmond, Va. Died July 12, 1949.

HOPPER, Edna Wallace (Mrs. Albert O. Brown), actress; b. San Francisco, ed. Van Ness Sem., San Francisco; m. DeWolf Hopper, Jan. 28, 1893 (div. 1898); m. 2d, Albert O. Brown, Nov. 25, 1908. Debut as Mabel Douglas, in The Club Friend, at Star Theatre, N.Y.C., 1891; subsequently joined Charles Frohman's Stock Co. and appeared in numerous rôles; associated with DeWolf Hopper in musical comedy; appeared as Lady Holyrood, in Floradora, at Casino Theatre, N.Y.C., 1900, later as Wrenne, in The Silver Slipper, at Broadway Theatre; joined Lew Field Co., 1906; toured with Richard Carle, in Jumping Jupiter, 1911-12; starred as Lulu in Girl o' Mine, 1918; later in vaudeville; v.p. Edna Wallace Hopper Corp., beauty preparations. Died Dec. 1959.*

HOPPER, Franklin Ferguson, librarian; b. Eatontown, N.J., Sept. 17, 1878; s. Rulif Ferguson and Elizabeth Croxson (Wikoff) H.; A.B., Princeton, 1900, Litt.D., 1947; grad. Pratt Inst. Library Sch., 1901; m. Marion Stephens, Jan. 6, 1917 (died 1937); children—Elizabeth, Stephen Ferguson (died 1944), Ann. Cataloguer, Library of Cong., 1901-02; br. librarian Carnegie Library, Pittsburgh, 1903 order librarian same, 1904-08; librarian Tacoma, Wash., Pub. Library, 1908-14; chief order division, 1914-18, circulation department, 1919-41, dir., 1941-46, New York Public Library. Member Squadron A Cavalry, National Guard N.Y., 1918-20. Trustee Skidmore Coll., Saratoga Springs, N.Y. Trustee & vice president Am. Foundation for the Blind; trustee Fisk U., Nashville, Tenn., Pratt Institute. Mem. A.L.A. (exec. bd. 1925-29; v.p. 1935-36), N.Y. Library Assn. (pres. 1925-26), N.Y. Library Club (pres. 1923-24), Pacific Northwest Library Assn. (pres. 1913-14), Am. Assn. for Adult Edn. Awarded medal, 1st class, Order of White Lion (Czechoslovakia). Republican. Clubs: Princeton, Century (New York); Tiger Inn (Princeton U.). Home: 125 Hope St., Providence. Address: New York Public Library, N.Y. City. Died Nov. 29, 1950.

HOPPER, James Marie, writer; b. Paris, France, July 23, 1876; s. John J. and Victoire Blanche E. (Lefebyre) H.; came to America, 1887; Ph.B., U. Cal., 1898, student Law Sch., 1898-99; m. Mattie E. Leonard, Sept. 21, 1901; children—Elizabeth Marie, Maryan Halton, James Louis, Helene Victoire; m. 2d, Elayne Lawson, 1938. Reporter on San Francisco newspapers, 1899-1900; admitted to bar, 1900; instr. French, U. Cal., fall 1901; in ednl. dept., P.I., 1902-03; on staff McClure's Mag., 1903. War corr. for Collier's in France, 1914, to end of war. Mem. council Authors' League America, also pres. of Authors' Guild of Authors' League America, 1928-29, 30-31. Author: Caybigan, 1906; Goosie, 1910; The Freshman, 1912; What Happened in the Night, 1913; Medals of Honor, 1929; and over three hundred short stories pub. in leading mags. Co-author: "9009" (with F. R. Bechdoldt), 1908. Home: Carmel, Cal. Died Aug. 28, 1956.

HOPPING, Andrew Daniel, army officer; b. Lima, O., Jan. 3, 1894; s. Harvey Piatt and Carrie (Lockette) H.; A.B., Butler U., 1917; M.B.A., Harvard, 1935; grad. French Tank Sch., 1929, Q.M.C. Sch., 1931, Army Indsl. Coll., 1940; m. Gabrielle Decaux, Aug. 17, 1918; children—Andree Charlotte (wife of Lt. Peter P. Shills, Jr., U.S.M.C. Res.), Daniel Henri (officer U.S. Army), Gabrielle Louise (widow of Lt. George C. Oertel, Jr., killed in action, 1944), Harvey Charles, Mary Jane, Martha Caroline. Served with machine gun co., 151st Inf., Ind. N.G., 1917; commd. 2d lt., inf. U.S. Army, 1918; served with 38th Div., AEF, France; commd. 2d lt., U.S. Army, 1920, advanced through grades to brig. gen., 1945; with Army of Occupation, Germany, 1920-22; trans. Q.M.C., 1933; with supply div. War Dept. Gen. Staff, 1940-42; staff officer A.S.F., Washington, 1942-44; dep. q.m. gen. for supply planning and operations 1944-46; chief q.m. Philippines-Ryukus Command, Manila, P.I., 1946-47; q.m. Far East Comd., Tokyo, Japan, 1947—. Decorated Legion of Merit with oak leaf cluster. Mem. Q.M. Assn., Mil. Order of World War. Clubs: Army and Navy, Harvard Business School Alumni (Washington). Address: care Adjutant General's Office, Dept. of Army, Washington. Died Jan. 11, 1951.

HORACK, Frank Edward, political scientist; b. Belle Plaine, Ia., June 8, 1873; s. Frank J. and Katharyn (Mosnat) H.; Ph.B., State U. Ia., 1897, A.M., 1899; student univs. of Chgo., Halle and Berlin; Ph.D., U. Pa., 1902; m. Elizabeth Grace Collins, Sept. 6, 1905; 1 son, Frank Edward. Harrison fellow in polit. science U. Pa., 1901-02; instr. polit. sci. U. Ia., 1902, asst. prof., 1906, prof., 1915-43, prof. emeritus, 1943—. Mem. Am. Polit. Science Assn., Southwestern Polit. Science Assn., Am. Assn. Univ. Profs., State Hist. Soc. of Ia. (sec. 13 yrs.), Mo. Hist. Soc., Polit. Science Club (U. Ia.); mem. com. of Am. Political Science Association which issued report on the teaching of government, 1916. Unitarian. Clubs: Triangle (State University of Ia.), Rotary. Author: The Organization and Control of Industrial Corporations, 1903; The Government of Iowa, 1911, revised, 1921. Joint Author: Iowa Applied History Series (3 vols.); also numerous articles in the field of polit. science, 1912-45. Home: 329 Ellis Av., Iowa City, Ia. Died Nov. 14, 1956.

HORACK, Frank Edward, Jr., educator; b. Iowa City, Ia., May 2, 1907; s. Frank Edward and Elizabeth Grace (Collins) H.; A.B., State U. Ia., 1926, J.D., 1929; LL.M., Harvard, 1930, S.J.D., 1931; m. Helen Marie Sturgiss, 1940; children—Frank E. III, Sabra Franceise. Asst. prof. law W.Va. U., 1931-34; counselor to Governor's Com. on Efficiency and Economy, W.Va., 1933-34; legislative counsel to gov. of W.Va., 1934-35; spl. asst. to gen. counsel U.S. Treasury Dept., 1934-35; prof. of law Ind. U., 1935—, acting dean Law Sch., 2d semester 1948-49, dir. Office Mil. Information, 1942, coordinator war tng. programs, 1943-46. Mem. adv. council, Fed. Marketing Law Survey, 1938-40; adviser to gen. counsel FSA, 1939-42; Ind. commr. on uniform state laws since 1938; cons. Ind. Econ. Council; pres. City Plan Commn. Mem. Order of Coif, Phi Beta Kappa, Phi Delta Phi, Phi Kappa Psi. Democrat. Unitarian. Club; Columbia (Indpls.). Author: Cases and Materials on Legislation, 1940; Statutory Construction (3 vols.), 1943; (with Val Nolan, Jr.) Land Use Controls, 1955. Editor: Indiana Administrative Code, 1941. Contbr. to legal and polit. science jours. Editor Ind. Law Jour., 1940-47. Home: 819 S. Jordan Av., Bloomington, Ind. Died Nov. 25, 1957; buried Iowa City, Ia.

HORBERG, (Carl) Leland, educator; b. Cambridge, Ill., May 7, 1910; s. John August and Laura Amelia (Larson) H.; A.B., Augustana Coll., Rock Island, Ill., 1932; Ph.D., U. Chgo., 1938; m. Virginia Louise Bryan, May 30, 1942; children—Anders Lee, Bryan John. Asst. prof. geology Augustana Coll., 1935-37; instr. and asso. in geology U. Ill., 1938-42; asst. and asso. geologist Ill. Geol. Survey, 1942-46, geol. cons., 19 —; asst. prof. U. Chgo., 1946-48, asso. prof., 1948—; editor Journal of Geology, 1953—. Mem. Chgo. Acad. Sci. (sci. advisor), A.A.A.S., Geol. Soc. Am., Am. Geophys. Union, Ill. Acad. Sci. Author articles in geol. jours. Home: 5753 Drexel Av., Chgo. 37. Died Aug. 18, 1955; buried Rosedale Cemetery, Cambridge, Ill.

HORDYK, Gerard, artist painter; b. The Hague, Holland, Sept. 12, 1899; s. Hubertus and Sophia (Sillevis) Hordijk; B.Archtl.Engring., Delft U., 1927; student The Hague Art Acad., 1921-27; m. Margaret Mathews, Oct. 1, 1930; children—John Gerard, Marian (dec.). Came to U.S., 1940. Executed murals in Remonstrant Church, The Hague, Holland, 1928, Municipal Theatre, Amsterdam, 1937, Cité Université, Paris, 1938, Concertgebouw, 1940, Netherlands Information Bur., 1941, UN Information Bur., 1943 (N.Y.C.) also in pvt. homes Amsterdam, Eng., U.S. Designer stage productions for opera, ballet classic, period and modern plays, Amsterdam, 1935-40. Exhibited in one-man shows Amsterdam, The Hague, Rotterdam, Leiden bi-annual, 1926-40, Paris, 1930, 1932, London, 1934, N.Y.C., 1935, 40, 44, Washington, 1943, Los Angeles, Curacao, 1944. With group shows Bklyn., Springfield (Mass.), Chgo., Phila., Rio de Janeiro. Paintings purchased by mus., Rotterdam, The Hague, Batavia, N.E.I., Zagreb, Springfield, Mass., Phillips Meml., Washington. Home: Kromme Waal 17, Amsterdam, C, Holland. Address: care Contemporary Arts, 106 E. 57th St., N.Y.C. 22. Died Oct. 15, 1958; buried Westerveld, Velsen, Holland.

HORLICK, Alexander James, former pres. Horlick's Malted Milk Corp.; b. Racine, Wis., Oct. 3, 1873; s. William and Arabella R. H.; ed. public schs., Racine, 1884-90, Racine College, 1890-93; m. Bertha D. Hueffner, Feb. 16, 1898; children—Helen (Mrs. Harold S. Bond), Jeannette Arabella (Mrs. John F. Bowles, Jr.). Mem. Horlick's Malted Milk Corp., 1893—, pres. 1939, chmn. bd. (now ret.); dir. Racine Journal Printing Co., H. W. St. John & C., forwarders, N.Y. City, Mayor of Racine, 1907-11, Regent, U. of Wis., 1910-25; trustee St. Lukes Hosp., Alice Horlick Memorial Hosp., Racine. Served on Bd. of Appeals, Eastern Dist. Wis., during World War. Mem. Racine Mfrs. Assn., English-Speaking Union, Wis. C. of C., Am. Pharm. Assn. (life), Racine YMCA; hon. mem. Spanish War Vets. (Racine), Internat. Assn. Chiefs Police, Wis. Chiefs Police Assn. Republican. Episcopalian. Mason (32°), Elk, K.P., Sons of St. George. Clubs: Chicago, Union, Chicago Athletic (Chicago); Milwaukee, Press (Milwaukee); Downtown Athletic (New York); American (London); Racine Yacht, Racine Country, Somerset (Racine). Address: Racine, Wis. Died June 6, 1950.

HORMEL, Jay Catherwood, meat packing; b. Austin, Minn., Sept. 11, 1892; s. George A. and Lillian B. H.; ed. Shattuck Mil. Acad., Faribault, Minn., and Princeton U.; m. Germaine Dubois, May 19, 1922; children—George A., II, Thomas Dubois, James Catherwood. Workd in meat packing plant of Geo. A. Hormel & Co., Austin, Minn., during sch. vacations, continuously since, dir., 1914—, v.p., 1916-29, pres., 1929-45, chmn. bd., 1945—. Served as first lieutenant United States Army, 1917-18. Member American Legion. Elk. Clubs: Union League (Chicago); Minneapolis, Minneapolis Athletic; Princeton (New York); Rotary, Austin Country (Austin); Los Angeles Country. Address: Austin, Minn. Died Aug. 30, 1954; buried Austin.

HORN, Aaron Charles, business exec.; b. N.Y.C., 1876. Chmn. exec. com., dir. Sun Chem. Corp.; dir. contracting div. A.C. Horn Corp.; dir. A.C. Horn Co., Inc., A.C. Horn Co., Ltd., A.C. Horn Co. of Tex., Hudson Paint & Varnish, Inc., Mich. Research Labs., Inc., Retail Distbrs., Inc., Warwick Wax Co. Mason (Shriner). Home: Essex House, N.Y.C. Died Nov. 1952.

HORN, Nelson Paxson, coll. pres.; b. Tipton, Ia., May 23, 1890; s. Charlie C. and Ella F. (Paxson) H.; A.B., Mo. Wesleyan Coll., 1916; B.D., Garrett Biblical Inst., 1918, D.D., 1937; A.M., Northwestern University, 1919; LL.D., Baldwin-Wallace College, 1950; married Nell McGlumphy, June 30, 1915; children—Charles William, Roy Lester, Vera Nell (Mrs. Dale T. Hobson), Harold Eugene. Ordained to ministry Methodist Episcopal Church, 1917; pastor in Missouri Conference, M.E. Ch., 1913-21; dir. Inter-Ch. Sch. of Religion, Ia. State Coll., 1921-27; dir. of religious life, 1929-36; dir. insts. and life work, Bd. of Edn., M.E. Ch., 1927-29; pres. Baker U., 1936-56, ret. Mem. N.E.A. Clubs: Knife and Fork, Rotary. Author: Our Life Work, 1930. Contbr. religious articles. Home: 4062 Marian St., LaMesa, Cal. Died July 5, 1958; buried Oakwood Cemetery, Baldwin City, Kan.

HORNBECK, John Wesley, educator; b. Exeter, Ill., May 21, 1881; s. Levi L. and Laura (Wright) H.; B.Sc., Ill. Wesleyan U., 1906; A.M., U. Ill., 1909, post-grad., 1911-13, Ph.D., 1913; grad. student Cornell U., 1910-11; m. Frances C. Wolfe, June 10, 1915; children—Helen Frances (Mrs. Wilson P. Tanner), John Austin, Margaret Ann (Mrs. Harvey J. Lhost, Jr.). Prin. schs., Summer Hill., Ill., 1904-05; instr. mathematics Park Coll. Acad., Parkville, Mo., 1906-08; instr. physics U. Ill., 1911-12; asst. prof. physics Carleton Coll., Northfield, Minn., 1913-17, prof., 1917-25; research work Cornell U. (sabbatical leave), 1923-24; prof. physics Kalamazoo Coll., 1925—; mem. faculty Western Michigan College Edn., Kalamazoo, summers 1936, 40, 49. Recipient Oersted Medal for contbns. to teaching of physics, 1951. Fellow A.A.A.S.; mem. Am. Assn. of Physics Tchrs., Am. Physical Soc., Sigma Xi, Phi Kappa Phi. Club: Torch (pas tpres. Kalamazoo chpt.). Contbr. sci. mags. Address: 8 College Grove, Kalamazoo, Mich. Ded Feb. 27, 1951.

HORNE, Frederick Joseph, admiral; b. N.Y.C., Feb. 14, 1880; s. George Edward and Marguerite Agnes (Cooper) H.; grad. U.S. Naval Acad., 1899; m. Alma Beverly Cole McClung, Aug. 4, 1903.

Served on U.S.S. Texas and participated in battle of Santiago, Cuba, 1898; comd. ensign, 1901; advanced through grades to admiral; served as naval attache at Am. Embassy, Tokyo, Japan, 1915-19, receiving Navy Cross for distinguished and meritorious services during this period; became asst. to chief of Naval Operations, Navy Dept., Washington, D.C., 1941; apptd. vice chief of Naval Operations with rank of vice adm., 1942; promoted admiral, 1944; retired, 1946. Decorations: Navy Cross, Distinguished Service Medal, Army Legion of Merit, Navy Unit Commendation, Spanish Campaign, Santiago, Philippine Campaign, Comdr. of Legion of Honor (French); Grand Officer Order of Polonia Restituta (Polish); Grand Cordon Chinese Order Yellow Banner; Grand Officer Order Leopold with Palm, Croix de Guerre with Palm (Belgium); Brazilian Order of Naval Merit, Bank of Grand Cross; Knight Commander of Military Division of Order of British Empire. Club: Army and Navy. Home: 601 Margarita Av., Corondao, Cal. Died Oct. 1959.

HORNE, Joseph A., chmn. bd. Yale & Towne Mfg. Co.; b. England, 1869. Vice-pres. Citizens Savings Bank, Stamford, Conn.; dir. First Stamford Nat. Bank, Conn. Power Co. Mem. bd. trustees Stamford Hosp. Home: 237 Strawberry Hill Av., Stamford, Conn. Office: 405 Lexington Av., N.Y.C. Died Oct. 3, 1950.

HORNER, Wesley Winans, consulting engr.; b. Columbia, Mo., Sept. 22, 1883; s. William A. and Minnie (Winans) H.; B.S.E., Washington U., 1905, D.Eng. (hon.), 1952; post grad. deg. in C.E., 1909; m. Elinor Alice Hall, June 16, 1908; children—Frederic Winans, John Linscott, Richard William, David Alan. Asst. engr. 1905-19, engring. service City of St. Louis, chief engr., 1919-32, cons. engr. since 1932; in gen. personal cons. engring. practice, 1916-32; sr. partner Horner & Shifrin, cons. engrs., St. Louis, since 1933; faculty Washington Univ. as lecturer and prof. sanitary and hydraulic engring. 1934-42. Mem. tech. bd. of rev. P.W.A., 1933-35; water consultant and mem. nat. water com. Nat. Resources Planning Bd., 1936-43; bd. cons. engrs. Dept. of Agr., 1940-43, mem. adv. com. on research, 1952-55; mem. engring. adv. com. AEC, 1949-54. Mem. task force on water and power 2d Hoover Commn., 1953-55. Recipient Rudolph Hering Medal, Am. Soc. C.E., 1937. Mem. St. Louis C. of C. (com. chmn.), U.S. C. of C. (natural resources com.), Fedn. Civic Improveement Assns. (officer), Smoke Abatement League (pres.), State Bd. of Registration for Architects and Profl. Engrs. of Missouri, Am. Geophysical Union, Am. Pub. Works Assn. (past pres.), Am. Inst. Cons. Engrs., Am. Soc. C. E. (dir. 1933-35, pres., 1946). Sigma Xi, Tau Beta Pi, Sigma Chi. Clubs: Engineers, Missouri Athletic (St. Louis); Cosmos (Washington). Republican. Conglist. Contbr. to tech. pubs. Home: 64 Broadview Dr., Clayton 5, Mo. Office: 803 Shell Bldg., St. Louis 3. Died Sept. 22, 1958.

HORNEY, Karen, psychiatrist; b. Hamburg, Germany, Sept. 16, 1885; dau. Berndt and Clotilde (Von Ronzelen) Danielson; M.D., Univ. of Freiburg, Berlin, 1913; m. Oscar Horney, Oct. 1909; children—Brigitte (Mrs. K. Tschetwerikoff), Marianne (Mrs. W. von Eckardt), Renate (Mrs. F. Crevenna). Came to U.S., 1932, naturalized, 1938. Instr. Inst. for Psychoanalysis, Berlin, 1920-32; asso. dir., Chicago Inst. for Psychoanalysis, 1932-34; lecturer New Sch. for Social Research, New York City, since 1935; dean Am. Inst. for Psychoanalysis since 1941. Mem. Assn. for Advancement of Psychoanalysis, Am. Psychiatric Assn. Author: Neurotic Personality of Our Time, 1936; New Ways in Psychoanalysis, 1939; Self-Analysis, 1942; Our Inner Conflicts, 1945; Neurosis and Human Growth, 1950. Home: 240 Central Park South, N.Y.C. 19. Died Dec. 1952.

HORNEY, Odus Creamer, ret. army officer; b. Lexington, Ill., Sept. 18, 1866; s. James W. and Josephine (Creamer) H.; B.S., U.S Mil. Acad., West Point, N.Y., 1891; m. Kezia Bryan, July 29, 1891; children—Ruth (Mrs. T. G. M. Oliphant), Grace (Mrs. E. Louis Ford) (dec.), Esther (Mrs. Francis J. Gillespie), Odus C. With inf., U.S. Army, 1891-94; with ordnance dept., 1894-1930; ret. as brig.-gen.; designed, developed Springfield rifle, caliber 30; pioneered 16 inch rifle in U.S., built and put into operation pioneer Army Smokeless Powder Plant. Mem. Mil. Order of the World Wars, Nat. Sojourners. Mason (32°). Clubs: Engineers (Philadelphia), Army-Navy (Washington, San Francisco). Home: 452 Hillcrest Rd., San Mateo, Cal. Died Feb. 16, 1957; buried Presidio of San Francisco.

HOROWITZ, Louis Jay, ret. corp. ofcl.; b. Chenstochowa, Poland, Jan. 1, 1875; s. Salo A. and Anna (Cata) H.; ed. U. Chenstochowa; Sc.D., Union Coll., 1932; D.C.S., N.Y.U., 1950; m. Mary E. Decker, July 14, 1903. Came to U.S., 1892. Chmn. The Louis J. and Mary E. Horowitz Found., Inc. Dir. dept. fgn. relief A.R.C. Asst. to chief ordnance, dir. tank constrn. U.S. Army, World War I. Mem. Army Ordnance Assn. Clubs: Palm Beach (Fla.) Golf; Creek (Locust Valley). Home: Glen Cove, N.Y. Office: 60 E. 42d St., N.Y.C. 17. Died Dec. 2, 1956.

HORR, Alfred Reuel, banker; b. Wellington, O., July 14, 1875; s. Charles W. and Esther A. (Lang) H.; B.L., Cornell U., 1895; m. Charlotte L. Clement, Dec. 31, 1901. Admitted to Ohio bar, 1897, and practiced at Cleve. until 1899; claim agt. Erie R.R. Co., 1899-1900; mgr. Walker-Gordon Lab., 1900-01; asst. sec. Western Reserve Trust Co., 1901-03; asst. sec. Cleveland Trust Co., 1903-07, sec., later v.p., 1907-13, v.p., 1923—; treas., later v.p. Equitable Life Assurance Soc. of U.S., N.Y.C., 1913-22; v.p. Warner & Swasey Co. Trustee Oberlin Coll. Mem. Cleve. C. of C. (past pres.), Delta Upsilon. Clubs: Union, Cleveland Athletic, Mayfield Country; Union League (N.Y.C.). Author: Embarrassing Dollars, 1935; The Career of a Banker, 1945; History of the Court of Nisi Prius, 1946; The Log of the Schooner Bowdoin, 1947. Home: 1900 E. 30th St. Office: Cleveland Trust Co., Cleve. Died Nov. 1958.

HORR, Ralph A., ex-congressman; b. Saybrook, Ill., Aug. 12, 1884; s. Lewis Haines and Emma (Rock) H.; ed. U. Ill.; LL.B., U. Wash., 1911; m. Beulah Johnson, 1904 (dec.); m. 2d, Lenora Van Brocklin, Sept. 3, 1923; children—Lezern, Virginia Delta. Began practice at Seattle, Wash., 1911; served as chief dep. county treas., King County Wash.; mem. 72d Congress (1931-33), 1st Wash. Dist. Republican candidate for gov. of Wash., 1936. Served as 1st lt. inf., U.S. Army, World War. Chmn. Rep. County Com., King County, 10 yrs. Mem. Delta Tau Delta, Phi Delta Phi. Republican. Mason (Shriner), Elk, Moose, Eagle. Clubs: Washingtonians, Washington Athletic, Elks. Was grad. mgr. athletics, U. Wash. Home: 5127 Bangor St. Office: Smith Tower, Seattle, Wash. Died Jan. 1960.

HORRAX, Gilbert (hă'rŭx), neurosurgeron; b. Glen Ridge, N.J., Apr. 9, 1887; s. Edwin and Mary Alice (Gilbert) H.; A.B., Williams Coll., 1909, Sc.D., 1936; M.D., Johns Hopkins, 1913; m. Geraldine Kemmis Martin, June 29, 1921 (dec.); children—Trudeau Martin, Elizabeth Daintry; m. 2d, Helen Anne Pagenstecher (Mrs. S. S. Tregellas), July 19, 1938; 1 step-son, S. Staley Tregellas. House officer Peter Bent Brigham Hosp., Boston, 1913-14, neurol. resident, 1915-16, jr., later sr. asso. in neurol. surgery, 1919-32; Arthur Tracy Cabot fellow Harvard Med. Sch., 1914-15, successively asst., instr., faculty instr. and asst. prof. surgery, 1919-32, instr. in neurology courses for graduates, 1935-41; resident surgeon Mass. Gen. Hosp., 1916-17; neurosurgeon N.E. Deaconess and N.E. Bapt. Hosps., 1932—; in charge dept. neurosurgery The Lahey Clinic, Boston, 1932—; cons. to U.S. Vets. Hosp., W. Roxbury, Mass., 1944-46; cons. in neurosurgery Cushing Gen. Hosp., Framingham, Mass. Served from 1st lt. to maj. M.C., U.S. Army, France, 1917-19; USPHS Res., 1944—. Diplomate Am. Bd. of Surgery and Am. Bd. Neurol. Surgery. Fellow A. C.S.; mem. Soc. Neurol. Surgeons (pres. 1937-39), Am. Neurol. Soc. (v.p. 1940-41), Assn. for Research in Nervous and Mental Diseases (v.p. 1936), Am. Surg. Assn., N.E. and Boston surg. socs., Harvey Cushing Soc., Boston Soc. Psychiatry and Neurology (pres. 1939), Mass. Med. Soc., A.M.A., Royal Soc. of Med. (hon. mem. sect. of neurology); corrs. mem. Société de Neurol., France; hon. mem. La Societe de Neuro-chirurgie de la langue Française; mem. Phi Delta Theta, Gargoyle. Trustee Met. State Hospital (Waltham, Mass.), Lawrence Acad. (Groton, Mass.). Clubs: Harvard (Boston); Williams (N.Y. C.); The Country, Longwood Cricket (Brookline, Mass.); Orleans Fish and Game (Quebec, Can.). Contbr. numerous sci. articles to med. and surg. publs. Home: 30 Cedar Rd., Chestnut Hill, Mass. Office: 605 Commonwealth Av., Boston 15. Died Sept. 28, 1957; buried Forest Hills Cemetery.

HORSFORD, Cornelia, archaeologist; b. Cambridge, Mass., Sept. 25, 1861; d. Prof. Eben Norton and Phoebe (Gardiner) Horsford; student pvt. schs., Cambridge and Boston. Continued her father's archaeol. researches after his death, 1893; sent out archaeol. expdn. to Iceland, 1895, to examine ruins of the Saga-Time; also in British Isles, 1895, 96, 97, to examine ruins of open-airamphitheatres, forts, etc.; directed various researches among works of native races of N. America in connection with investigation of Norse discovery of America. Mem. N.Y. (life), Mass. hort. socs., Prince Hist. Soc.; hon. v.p. Viking Club of London; mem. Garden Club of America, Easthampton, Icelandic Antiq. Soc., Irish Texts Soc. Author: Graves of the Northmen, 1893; An Inscribed Stone, 1895; Dwellings of the Saga-Time in Iceland, Greenland and Vinland, Nat. Geographic Mag., 1898; Vinland and Its Ruins, Popular Science Monthly, Dec. 1899; Ruins of the Saga-Time. Historian Colonial Dames of Mass., 1917-23. Home: Sylvester Manor, Shelter Island, N.Y. Address: 27 Craigie St., Cambridge, Mass. Deceased.

HORTON, Herbert L(orenzo), banker; b. St. Charles, Ia., Dec. 15, 1893; s. Claude O. and Nellie (Bean) H.; grad. West Des Moines (Ia.) High Sch., 1911; m. Angelica Howden, Dec. 28, 1922. German Savings Bank, Des Moines, 1912-15; successively asst. cashier, cashier, asst. v.p., and v.p. Des Moines Nat. Bank, 1915-29; v.p. and dir. Ia.-Des Moines Nat. Bank and Trust Co., 1929-34, pres. since 1934; dir. Ia.-Des Moines Bldg. Co., Chicago, Rock Island & Pacific Co. Pres. Des Moines C. of C., 1936, Greater Des Moines Com., 1937; dir. Des Moines YMCA; chmn. for Iowa Com. for Econ. Development. Trustee Drake U., Hawley Welfare Found. Co-chmn. War Finance Com. for Iowa, World War II. Republican. Episcopalian. Clubs: Des Moines, Wakonda Country (Des Moines); Chicago. Home: 1708 Chacoma Pl. S.W., Albuquerque, N.M. Died Dec. 29, 1957; buried Albuquerque.

HORTON, Herman DeWitt, business exec.; b. near Columbus, Ga., Feb. 6, 1889; s. Henry Clay and Susan Caroline (Forest) H.; student South Ga. Coll., 1907, Ga. Bus. Coll., 1908; m. Daisy Eidson, Sept. 24, 1913; children—Henry Clay, Benjamin Stevens. Proprietor H. D. Horton Co., Charlotte, 1915-30; pres. Horton Motor Lines, Inc., 1930-40; chmn. bd. Associated Transport, Inc., Charlotte, N.C., since 1941. Bus. adviser of the govt. to Geneva, Switzerland, for Internat. Conf. of Internat. Labor Orgn., 1939. Mem. Am. Trucking Assns., Inc. (pres. 1949, chmn. bd., 1950). Mason (Shriner, potentate 1940). Clubs: Charlotte Country, Myers Park, City, Red Fez (Charlotte); Athletic (N.Y. City). Home: 352 Eastover Rd., Charlotte 7. Office: Associated Transport, Inc., Charlotte 8, N.C. Died May 1, 1959.

HORTON, Horace Babcock, business exec.; b. Rochester, Minn., Dec. 25, 1885; s. Horace E. and Emma (Babcock) H.; student pub. schs., Chgo., and Morgan Park Acad.; S.B., U. Chgo., 1907; postgrad. study in engring. U. Ill., 1906-07; Dr. Bus. Adminstrn. (hon.), Thiel Coll., Greenville, Pa.; m. Marjorie Jessy Mason, Sept. 15, 1909; children—Arthur Browning, Marjorie; m. 2d, Phyllis Fay, Oct. 6, 1919; children—Fay, John. Asso. with Chicago Bridge & Iron Co. since 1907, treas. and dir. since 1912, pres., 1945-56, chmn. bd., 1956—; dir. Chicago Bridge & Iron Co., Ltd., (Venezuela), John I. Hay Co. Mem. War Labor Bd., 1942-45. Mem. Western Soc. Engrs., Delta Kappa Epsilon. Republican. Clubs: Chicago, University, Tavern, South Shore Country, Flossmoor Country, Quadrangle, Central Illinois Hunting, Economic (Chgo.). Home: 1229 E. 56th St., Chgo. Office: 1305 W. 105th St., Chgo. 43. Died Sept. 1959.

HORVATH, Imre, Hungarian diplomat; b. 1901; student Technical U., Budapest. Counsellor, Hungarian Legation, Moscow, 1945-48; leader polit. mission, Berlin, 1948-49; minister to U.S., 1949-51, Gt. Britain, 1951-53; ambassador, Czechoslovakia, 1953-56; pres. Inst. Cultural Relations with Fgn. Countries, 1956; minister fgn. affairs, 1956—; mem. 11th Gen. Assembly UN. Address: Ministry of Foreign Affairs, Budapest, Hungary. Died Feb. 2, 1958.

HORWOOD, Murray Philip, pub. health engr.; b. N.Y.C., Dec. 31, 1892; B.S., Coll. City N.Y., 1913; S.M., Mass. Inst. Tech., 1916, Ph.D.. 1921; Harvard Tech. Sch. Pub. Health, 1917-18; m. Louise van Valkenburgh Peirce, Dec. 25, 1919; children—Louise van Valkenburgh (Mrs. Charles S. Alden), Charlotte Peirce, Sargent Peirce. Chemist, bacteriologist Bklyn. Sewage Expt. Station, 1913-15; Mass. Inst. Tech., 1916—, asso. prof., 1929-37, prof. bact. and pub. health, 1937-44, prof. sanitary science, 1944—; instr. advanced bacteriology Wellesley College, 1918-19; lectr. bacteriology, and public health, Boston U. Med. Sch., 1920-21; instr. hygiene Tufts Med. Sch., 1921-25, 1928-29. Conducted pub. health and Tb surveys in Me., Mass., R.I., Conn., N.J., Pa., Ind. and Okla.; dir. New England Health Surveys for Am. Child Health Assn., 1924; dir. investigation into bacteriology of household dusts, 1930; cons. in bacteriology, sanitation and biology for Atlantic Gelatin Co. (Gen. Foods Corp.), 1921-52; apptd. dir. M.I.T. Ednl. Project at College of Engring., U. Rangoon, Burma, 1952-54; cons. in pub. health engring. Boston Health Dept., 1941—; cons. for Salem Civic Action Com. on pollution of North River, 1944; dir. sanitation of Mass. Inst. Tech. dining services, 1944—. Author Sanitary Code, Arlington, 1937. Mem. bd. dirs. Housing Assn. Met. Boston, 1940-44; mem. exec. com. Mass. Tb League, 1942-48, Cambridge Tb and Health Assn. (pres. 1944-46); chmn. Health Com., Cambridge community Council, 1946-48; mem. adv. com. sch. hygiene, Boston Pub. Schs., 1927—; mem. nutrition com., Cambridge Red Cross, 1947-50. Apptd. WHO fellow, 1951. Fellow Am. Public Health Assn., A.A.A.S., Am. Acad. Arts and Sciences; mem. Am. Soc. Bacteriol., Boston Bacteriol. Club: Mass. Pub. Health Assn. (chmn. health officers sect. 1941-43; organizer and chmn., sect. on sanitation, 1944-45), Conf. Municipal Pub. Health Engrs., Inst. Food Technologists, Assn. Food and Drug Officials, Delta Omega, Sigma Xi. Author: Public Health Surveys, 1921; Sanitation of Water Supplies, 1932; Sedgwick's Principles of Sanitary Sci. and Public Health (with S. C. Prescott), 1935; Public Health in Burma, 1956; A Natural Scientist Looks at America's Foreign Economic Aid Program, 1957, also various papers on bacteriology, sanitation and pub. health. Home: 8 Craigie St., Cambridge 38, Mass. Died June 4, 1957.

HOSFORD, Charles Franklin, Jr. (hŏs'fôrd), lawyer, coal exec.; b. Bloomington, Ill., Apr. 26, 1887; s. Charles Franklin and Mary Emma (Reiber) H.;

A.B., Princeton, 1908; LL.B., Harvard, 1911; m. Jean Christie, June 20, 1916; children—Charles Franklin, Robert Christie, Jean Christie. Admitted to Pa. bar, 1911, practiced at Butler, 1911-23; pres. Butler Consol. Coal Co., 1923-31; dir. Coal Control Assn. of Western Pa., 1933-34; became mem. Coal Code Authority, Western Pa., 1933, and mgr., 1934; served about 2 years in Washington, on Bituminous pres., gen. mgr. Pa. Coal Products Co., 1938—; Coal Commn. as chmn., resiging Apr. 3, 1938; founded Nassau Chemicals, Inc., San Francisco, 1948. Democrat. Lutheran. Address: care Nassau Chemicals, Inc., San Francisco. Died Apr. 12, 1953.

HOSFORD, Willard Deere, farm machinery exec.; b. Clinton, Ia., June 13, 1882; s. Schiller and Floy Mabel (Chapman) H.; student Phillips-Exeter Acad., 1902; A.B., Yale, 1906; m. Mary Lee McShane, June 24, 1908. Vice pres. John Deere Plow Co. of Moline, Ill., since 1906; dir. Deere & Co., Fed. Res. Bank, Kansas City, Mo., Am. Res. Life Ins. Co., Northwestern Bell Telephone Co., Omaha, Union Stock Yards Co. Dir. Creighton Hall, Omaha. Mem. C. of C. Clubs: Omaha, Omaha Country. Home: 525 S. 37th St. Office: 912 Howard St., Omaha 8, Neb. Died Dec. 25, 1951, buried Omaha, Neb.

HOSFORD, William Fuller, business exec.; b. West Chicago, Ill., May 30, 1882; student pub. schs.; m. Marjorie Fraser, July 1913; children—Norman F., James A., William Fuller, Mrs. Herbert Smith, Mrs. Granger Bierwirth. With Western Electric Co. since 1900, engr. mfr., 1926-27, comptroller mfg., 1927-28, v.p., dir., 1928—; dir. Nassau Smelting & Refining Co., Bell Telephone Labs., Inc., Teletype Corp., Mfrs. Junction Ry. Co., Western Electric Co., Ltd., Can., Weco Corp. Westrex Corp., Northern Electric Co., Ltd., of Can. Mem. N.Y. Elec. Soc., Am. Soc. M.E. Clubs: Railroad-Mcahinery of New York; Canoe Brook Country (Summit, N.J.); Maplewood (N.J.), Country. Home: Blueberry Point, Arcadia Lake, Butler, N.J. Office: 195 Broadway, N.Y. C. 7. Died Jan. 1958.

HOSHOUR, Harvey Sheely (hŏsh'our), lawyer; b. Bellefonte, Pa., Aug. 2, 1890; s. Edward Everett and Mary Ellen (Sheely) H.; A.B., Gettysburg (Pa.) Coll., 1910, LL.D., 1938; LL.B., U. of Minn., 1914; m. Ruth Jesmore, Aug. 30, 1921; children—Barbara Ruth, Harvey Sheely. Admitted to Minn. bar, 1914, and practiced in Duluth, 1914-27, partner Fryberger, Fulton, Hoshour & Boyle; asst. to city atty., 1914-15; prof. law, U. of Minn., 1927-33; gen. solicitor Am. Telephone & Telegraph Co., N.Y. City, 1933-39; v.p., dir. and gen. counsel, N.E. Telephone and Telegraph Co., Boston, 1939-44; partner Morgan Chase, Headley & Hoshour, St. Paul, 1944-50; prof. law, U. of Minn. (part-time), 1946-49; prof. law U. of N.M. since 1950. Served as 1st lt. inf., U.S. Army, 1917-19. Mem. Am., Minn. State, N.M. bar assns., Phi Beta Kappa, Phi Delta Theta, Phi Delta Phi, Delta Sigma Rho. Author: Minnesota Annotation to Contracts' Restatement (with another), 1934; The Minnesota Business Corporate Act, in Minn. Statutes Annotated, 1947. Home: 804 Summit Av., Albuquerque, N.M. Died Oct. 9, 1951; buried Albuquerque, N.M.

HOSIC, James Fleming, educator; b. Henry, Ill., Oct. 11, 1870; s. James W. and Dorothy Ellen (Hervey) H.; grad. State Normal Sch., Peru, Neb., 1891; Ph.B., U. Chgo., 1901, Ph.M., 1902; Ph.D., Columbia, 1920; m. Nellie Augusta Lovering, Aug. 19, 1903; children—Grace Lovering (Mrs. Frank Otheman Reed), Virginia (Mrs. Harold J. Gibson). Principal of the high sch., Auburn, Nebraska, 1891-93; supt. schs., Arapahoe, Neb., 1894-96; head English dept. Neb. Normal Sch., 1896-1900; same dept. Chicago Normal Sch., 1902-21; spl. supr. Chgo. pub. schs., 1918-21; with Tchrs. Coll. (Columbia), 1921-36, prof. edn., 1924, emeritus since 1936; vis. prof. univs. Chgo., Pa., Cal., Syracuse, Kent State, Boston, and Rollins Coll. Asso. dir. Am. Jr. Red Cross, 1920-21. Life mem. N.E.A., Dept. Supervision and Curriculum Development (field sec.), Nat. Council Tchrs. English (a founder). Pres. University Club, Winter Park Fla., 1945-46. Author: Elementary Course in English, 1909; Practical English for High Schools (with W. D. Lewis), 1916, 26, 2d course, 1927; A Child's Composition Book (with C. L. Hooper), 1916, A Composition Grammar, 1916; Empirical Studies in Reading, 1921; Brief Guide to the Project Method (with Sara E. Chase), 1924; Pathway to Reading (with Bessie B. Coleman and Willis L. Uhl), 1926; Introductory Studies in Literature (with W. W. Hatfield), 1927; English for Junior High Schools (with Claudia E. Crumpton), 1928; American Language Series (with C. L. Hooper), 1931. Founder and editor English Journal, 1912-21, Educational Method, 1921-37; lectr. before ednl. and civic socs. Home: 1521 Highland Rd., Winter Park, Fla. Died Jan. 13, 1959; buried Winter Park.

HOSKINS, John Hobart, educator; b. Carmel, Ind., Jan. 17, 1896; s. John B. and Cicely (Lancaster) H.; B.S., Earlham Coll., 1919; M.S., U. Chgo., 1920, Ph.D. summa cum laude, 1924; m. Gertrude Louise Keller, June 18, 1931; children—John, William, Robert. Prof. biology Whittier Coll., 1920-22; fellow biol. sci. NRC, Eng., France and Belgium, 1924-25; vis. prof. U. Notre Dame, summers 1925-33; with dept. botany and bacteriology U. Cin., 1925—, head dept., 1928—; dir. The Valley Shopping Center. Dir. Lloyd Library and Mus., Cin.; trustee Cin. Country Day Sch., U. Cin. Research Found. Tng. specialist OQMG, World War II. Mem. A.A.A.S., Bot. Soc. Am. (past chmn. paleobot. sect.), Paleontog. Soc., Am. Phycol. Soc., Phytomorphol. Soc., Ohio, Ind. acads. scis., Phi Beta Kappa, Sigma Xi, Alpha Tau Omega. Club: Cincinnati Country. Editor paleobotany Am. Midland Naturalist, 1934 55; co-founder, asso. editor Lloydia, a Quarterly Jour. Biol. Sci., 1938—. Contbr. articles profl. jours. Home: 3566 Raymar Dr., Cin. 8. Died Feb. 7, 1957; buried Spring Grove Cemetery, Cin.

HOSKINS, John K., sanitary engr.; b. New Holland, Pa., July 12, 1884; B.C.E., Pa. State Coll., 1905, C.E., 1910; student U. Berlin, 1908-09; m. Mattie Sublette, Apr. 30, 1913. With cons. engrs. 1905-08, 10-13 water works design and constrn.; with USPHS as san. engr. principally in research activities relating to water supply and sewage disposal since 1913, in charge of stream pollution investigations sta. of the Service at Cin., 1924-40; head san. enging. activities of Service since 1940, asst. surgeon gen. USPHS, Washington, 1944-48, ret. 1948. Mem. bd. consultants Nat. Sanitation Found. Mem. bd. Washington Housing Assn., 1948. Former mem. Inst. Sewage Purification, Federal Sewage Research Assn. (pres. 1933-34), Fedn. Sewage Research Assn. (pres. 1945-46), Am. Pub. Health Assn. Home: 6318 Woodside Pl., Chevy Chase 15, Md. Died May 16, 1958; buried Arlington Nat. Cemetery.

HOSMER, Frank Alvin, clergyman; b. Seville, O., June 5, 1874; s. Stiles A. and Jane (Nelson) H.; Ph.B., Coll. of Wooster (O.), 1894, Ph.M., 1897, D.D., 1916; D.D., Jamestown (N.D.) Coll., 1916; m. Ada May Barling, June 30, 1903. Ordained ministry Presbyn. Ch. in U.S.A., 1900; pastor 2d Ch., Freeport, Ill., 1900-07, Central Ch., Chgo., 1907-19, 1st Ch., Greenwich, Conn., 1919-29, 1st Ch., Omaha, 1929-36, Benedict Meml. Ch., New Haven, 1936-44; Carnegie Peace Found. exchange preacher, British Isles, summers 1921, 25. Civilian chaplain S.A.T.C., Plattsburg, N.Y., July-Sept. 1918. Dir. Am. Tract Soc., Hastings (Neb.) Coll. Mem. Delta Sigma Rho, Phi Gamma Delta. Republican. Mason. Clubs: Lions, Professional Men's, University. Home: 12 Mt. View Terrace, Hamden, Conn. Died May 9, 1958; buried Forest Home Cemetery, Milw.

HOSTER, Herman Albert (hä'stẽr), univ. prof. (oncology); b. Columbus, O., Mar. 5, 1912; s. Herman Albert and Martha (Welle) H.; student Hill Sch., Pottstown, Pa., 1927-30; A.B., Yale, 1934; M.D., Johns Hopkins, 1938; m. Margaret Prentiss, March 23, 1938 (divorced); children—Frederick William, Albert Stanton; m. 2d, Miriam E. Shanley, Aug. 26, 1947. Interne, resident staff Jefferson Med. Coll. Hosp., Phila., June 1938-Sept. 1940; research fellow dept. biochemistry, Yale Sch. of Medicine, 1940-41; instr. medicine, Ohio State U. Coll. Med., 1941-44, asst. prof., 1944-46, asso. prof., 1946-47; prof. and coordinator oncology, prof. med., 1947; asso. dir. Div. Cancer Research since 1945; research dir. Ohio State Univ. Tumor Clinic and Columbus Cancer Clinic since 1947; pres. Hodgkin's Disease Research Found., Inc.; vice chmn. cancer com., Metropolitan Health Council (Columbus, O.) since 1947; vice chmn. and sec. of research Adv. Com. on Cancer, Ohio State U. Mem. Am. Assn. for Advancement Science, A.M.A., Ohio State Med. Assn., Columbus Acad. Medicine, Am. Assn. for Cancer Research, Am. Chem. Soc., Alpha Sigma Phi, Sigma Xi. Mem. Conglist. Ch., Columbus, O. Contbr. articles to scientific jours. Address: 2173 Bryden Rd., Columbus, O. Died May 14, 1951; buried Greenlawn, Columbus.

HOSTETLER, Joseph C., lawyer; b. Canal Dover, O., Aug. 8, 1885; s. Joseph H. and Caroline A. (Myers) H.; LL.B., Western Reserve Law Sch., 1908; m. Hazel Prior, Jan. 4, 1917. Admitted to Ohio bar, 1908, and began practice at Cleve. with Wm. R. Hopkins; asst. dir. of law, City of Cleve., 1910-16; mem. Baker (Newton D., ex-sec. war), Hostetler & Sidlo, 1916-31; Baker, Hostetler, Sidlo & Patterson, 1931-38, Baker, Hostetler & Patterson since 1938. Democrat. Unitarian. Clubs: Mid-Day, Union. Home: 13415 Shaker Blvd., Cleve. 20. Office: Union Commerce Bldg., Cleve. Died Dec. 2, 1958; buried Cleve.

HOTCHKISS, Clarence Roland, soldier, lawyer; b. Bradford County, Pa., June 5, 1880; s. Charles Frederick and Melissa (Taylor) H.; ed. acad., Owego, N.Y., Eastman Coll. of Bus. Administration (Poughkeepsie), 1903, Realty Inst. (New York), 1909; LL.B., U. of Ore., 1911; grad. various service schs., U.S. Army, including Tank Sch., 1930, War Coll., 1931; m. Grace Evangeline North, July 2, 1908. Organized C. R. Hotchkiss Co., Stewart-Hotchkiss Co., Realty & Mortgage Co., Portland, Ore., of which was pres., 1911-17; mem. Rep. Nat. Conv., 1916; presdl. elector and sec. Rep. State Central Com., Ore., 1920; U.S. marshal, District of Oregon, 1921-30. Admitted to Oregon bar, 1911, Federal Ct., 1928, U.S. Supreme Ct., 1937; practiced Portland, Oregon, 1911-17, 1920-21, 1938-41. Expediter and control supervisor Kaiser Shipbldg. Co., 1942-43; inventory auditor, Comml. Iron Works, 1944-45; counsel, National Mortgage & Bond Co., 1946. Served as pvt. 9th Pa. Inf., Spanish-Am. War; noncommd. officer, Co. A, 21st Inf. and Arty. Corps, U.S. Army, Philippine Insurrection; capt. and adj. 3d Ore. Inf., and dist. adj. on Mex. border; capt. Co. E, 162d Inf., World War, 30 mos., 20 mos. with A.E.F.; hon. disch. as maj., Oct. 1919; lt. col. Inf. Res., U.S. Army, 1923, col. 1932; mem. War Dept. Gen. Staff, 1933-37. Retired, 1948. Decorated D.S.M. Fellow Am. Geog. Soc., Am. Geneal. Soc.; mem. Fed. Bar Assn., Ore. State bar, Am. Legion, Vets. Fgn. Wars, United Spanish War Vets. (past camp comdr.; past dept. comdr.; nat. v-comdr.), Mil. Order World War (past chapter comdr.; state comdr.; mem. gen. staff), Reserve Officers' Assn. of U.S. (past state pres.; mem. nat. council Nat. exec. com.; awarded Armed Forces Res. medal with 4 hourglasses), S.A.R., Nat. Soc. of Puritan Descendants, Genealogical Soc. Colonial Wars, Founders and Patriots of America, Soc. War of 1812, Delta Theta Phi, Pi Gamma Mu, Scabbard and Blade. Conglist. Mason (32°, Shriner, K.C.C.H., Grotto, K.T., Sojourners), Clubs: Mazama Mountaineering (Portland); Army and Navy (Washington, D.C.). Author: Around the World As a Soldier, 1903; History of Third Oregon Infantry, 1914; England's Inns and Courts of Chancery (monograph), 1919; The Knight Hospitallers, 1933; Samuel Hotchkiss of the New Haven Colony and Some of His Descendants (booklet), 1933-39, 46. Editor Oregon Veteran, 1920-22. Home: 2632 S.E. Harrison St., Portland, Ore. Died Sept. 17, 1952; buried Arlington Nat. Cemetery.

HOTCHKISS, George Burton, author, educator; b. Naugatuck, Conn., Mar. 2, 1884; s. Edward Amos and Jane (Schofield) H.; B.A., Yale, 1905, M.A., 1906; Litt.D., N.Y.U., 1950; m. Margaret Woodbury, June 1, 1910; children—George Burton, Barbara, Jean, Margaret, Richards Woodbury, Mary. Instr. in rhetoric Beloit (Wis.) Coll., 1906-08; instr. in English N.Y.U., 1908-11, asst. prof. bus. English, 1911-14; reporter New York Evening Sun, 1909-10; with George Batten Co., advt. agy., 1912-1914; with N.Y.U., 1914—, as asso. prof. bus. English, 1914-15, prov. bus. English, 1915, prof. marketing, 1927, chmn. dept. marketing, 1915-28, 43-49, emeritus prof. marketing since 1950, Marketing consultant James F. Newcomb & Co., Inc., 1926-28. With War Trade Board (Bureau Imports), 1918; also Committee on Classification of Personnel until 1919, Silver Medal Annual Advertising Awards, 1947. Mem. Am. Marketing Assn., Alpha Kappa Psi, Beta Gamma Sigma, Alpha Delta Sigma, Alpha Phi Sigma. Conglist. Club: Authors' (London). Author: The Birthright (Yale Univ. poetry prize), 1906; Business Correspondence, 1909; Advertising Copy, 1924; Wheeler's Treatise of Commerce, 1931; An Outline of Advertising, 1933; Milestones of Marketing, 1938. Co-Author: Handbook of Business English, 1914; Advertising, 1914; Advertising—Its Principles and Practice, 1915; Business English, 1916; Principles of Advertising, 1919; Advanced Business Correspondence, 1921; Leadership of Advertised Brands, 1923; Measurement of Advertising Effects, 1927; Advertising Principles, 1927; New Business English, 1932. Home: Flushing, L.I. Office: 100 Washington Sq., N.Y.C. Died Mar. 28, 1953; buried Hillside Cemetery, Naugatuck, Conn.

HOTCHKISS, Willard Eugene, arbitrator, cons., educator; b. Amber, N.Y., June 20, 1874; s. Marcus Willard and Mary Eliza (Stewart) H.; Ph.B., Cornell U., 1897, Pres. Andrew D. White fellow, 1902-03, A.M., 1903. Pres. White traveling fellow, 1903-04, Ph.D., 1905; studied in France and Germany; LL.D., Northwestern, 1927; m. Irma Helen Schmelz, June 20, 1903; children—Willard Stewart, Helen (Mrs. Stanton Foster). Teacher, later asst. supt. George Jr. Republic, Freeville, N.Y., 1897-1900; instr. U. Pa., 1904-05; asst. prof. econs., Northwestern U., 1905-07, asso. prof., 1907-09, prof., 1909-17, 21-25, dean sch. commerce, 1908-17; prof. econs., dir. bus. edn. U. Minn., 1917-19; exec. dir. Nat. Indsl. Fedn. Clothing Mfrs., 1920-25; vis. prof. polit. sci., Stanford U., 1915-16, dean grad sch. business, 1925-32; pres. Armour Inst. of Tech., 1933-37; Maurice Falk prof. of social relations Carnegie Inst. Tech., 1938-44, dir. div. humanistic and social studies, 1941-44; prof. U. Cal., summer 1916; acting prof. industry U. Pa., 1931-32; lectr. N.Y.U., 1932-33; advisory com. U.S. Census, 1909; supr. of census, Cook County, Ill., 1910. Chmn. citizens' com. to investigate Juvenile Court of Cook County, 1911. Sec. Shipbuilding Labor Adjustment Bd., 1918-19; exec. sec. President's Industrial Conf., 1920. Ednl. adviser Inst. of Am. Meat Packers; investigaror U.S. Coal Commn., 1923; chmn. Calif. Econ. Research Council, 1926-29; Pacific Coast adviser, President's Emergency Com. for Employment, 1930-31; chmn. impartial wage bd., San Francisco bldg. industry, 1931, Gen. Code Authority, NRA, 1934; referee, Nat. R.R. Adjustment Bd., 1936; exec. dir. Allegheny Conf. on Community Development, 1944; panel chmn. Nat. War Labor Bd., 1943-45; public mem. Tenth Regional Bd., during 1945; pub. mem. and chmn. Enforcement Div., Nat. Wage Stabilization Bd., during 1946. Mem. Am. Econ. Assn. (v.p. 1913); bd. eds. Am. Econ. Rev., 1918-23; mem. Indsl. Relations Research Assn., Nat. Acad. Arbitrators, Soc. Advancement Mgmt. Author: Judicial Work of Comptroller Treasury, 1911; Higher Education and Business Standard, 1918. Compiler, Co-author Report on Juvenile Court and Care of Children in Illinois, 1911; History of the Shipbuilding Labor Adjustment Board (with H. R. Seager), 1921; Labor Relations in Coal Mining (with H. S. Dennison and J. H. Willits), 1923; Business in the New Era in "Man and his World" Series, 1929. Mechanization, Employment and Output per Man in Bituminous Mining (nat. Research Project), 1939. Editor and joint author of Stanford Conference on Business Education, 1927. Numerous arbitration decisions. Contbr. economic, business, and ednl. periodicals. Address: 107 Larkin Pl., Santa Monica, Cal. Died Sept. 18, 1956.

HOTCHKISS, William Horace, lawyer; b. Whitehall, N.Y., Sept. 7, 1864; s. Mason King and Rachel Amanda (Merriam) H.; A.B., Hamilton Coll., 1886, A.M., 1889, LL.D., 1929; m. Katherine Tremaine Bush, Apr. 25, 1895; children—Katherine (Mrs. Gordon T. Heard), Emily (Mrs. John S. Breckinridge, dec.). Practiced at Auburn, N.Y., 1888-90, Buffalo, 1890-1909, N.Y.C., 1912-—; organizer Am. Savings Bank, Buffalo. Active in drafting first primary election law in N.Y., 1892-98, first motor vehicle laws, 1903, important improvements to bankruptcy law, 1903; commr. for N.Y. on Uniform State Laws, 1907-09; supt. of ins. of N.Y. (under appmt. of Gov. Charles E. Hughes), 1909-12; referee in bankruptcy for Erie County (Buffalo), 1898-1909; mem. of New York State Insurance Bd., 1933-45. Lecturer many yrs. on bankruptcy law in Cornell U. Law Sch., New York Law Sch., and Buffalo Law Sch. State chmn. Prog. Party, 1912; signed call for nat. conv. to organize Prog. Party, Chgo., 1912. Mem. Am., N.Y. State bar assns., Bar Assn. Erie County (pres. 1908-09), Assn. Bar City N.Y. Phi Beta Kappa, Chi Psi Fraternity. Pres. N.Y. State Automobile Assn., 1904-06, Am. Automobile Assn., 1907-09. Presbyn. Clubs: Buffalo Lawyers (pres. 1905), Automobile of Buffalo (pres. 1903-04); Lawyers, University (N.Y.C.). Editor: Collier on Bankruptcy, 4th edit., 1903. Author of many monographs and articles on primary election laws, bankruptcy, insurance legislation, etc. Home: Lake Road, Rye, N.Y. Office: 150 William St., N.Y.C. 7. Died June 6, 1950.

HOTCHKISS, William Otis, coll. pres., geologist; b. Eau Claire, Wis., Sept. 17, 1878; s. Lyman Palmer and Almeda E. (Smith) H.; B.S. in Engring., U. Wis., 1903, C.E., 1908, Ph.D., 1916; D.Sc., Lafayette Coll., 1929; LL.D., Middlebury Coll., 1936; LL.D., U. Wis., 1937; D.Sc., Columbia, 1940; m. Edith Rachel Balsley, Sept. 20, 1904; children—Eugene Bishop, Edwin Lyman, Nancy (Mrs. Henry C. Boschen). Mining engr. Donora Mining Co., Duluth, 1902; exploration and geology work, Ontario, Can., 1903; cons. engr. Madison, 1904; inst. petrography and mineralogy U. Wis., 1904-07; exploration and geol. work, Cobalt, 1905; state geol. survey of Wis., 1906-08, in charge econ. geology, 1907; state geologist of Wis., 1909-25; dir., 1919-25, chmn., 1923-25, State Highway Commn.; pres. Mich. Coll. of Mining and Technology, 1925-35; pres. Rensselaer Poly. Inst. 1935-43, emeritus pres., 1945-—; cons. engr. N.J. Zinc Co., 1944-—. Dept. dir., brig. gen. Army Specialist Corps, June-Dec. 1942, in charge of Bureau of Engring. and Tech. Personnel. Started state hwy. work in Wisconsin and succeeded in having a hwy commn. formed. Mem. Science Advisory com. of Century of Progress Expn., Chgo., also chmn. geology subcom. Chmn. N.Y. State Regents Council on Apprentice Training. Fellow Geol. Soc. Am. (mem. council, treas.); mem. Assn. Am. State Geologists, Society Econ. Geologists (pres. 1946), Am. Inst. Mining Engrs., Am. Soc. C.E., Lake Superior Mining Inst., A.A.A.S., Wis. Acad. Sci., Arts and Letters, Wis. Hist. Soc., Sigma Nu, Tau Beta Pi, Sigma Xi, etc. Club: Cosmos (Washington). Author: Rural Highways of Wisconsin, 1906; Limestone Road Materials of Wisconsin (joint author); Mineral Lands of Northern Wisconsin; The Story of a Billion Years—in Century of Progress Science Series; Minerals of Might, 1945. Home: Two Tudor Lane, Scarsdale, N.Y. Died June 20, 1954.

HOUDE, Camillien, former mayor of Montreal; b. Montreal, Can., Aug. 13, 1889; s. Azade and Josephine (Frenette) H.; grad. Longueuil Coll., 1906; m. Mignonne Bourgie, 1913; children—Madeleine, Marthe (Mrs. J. L. Handfield); m. 2d, Georgianna Falardeau, June 23, 1919; 1 dau., Claire (Mrs. Marcel Thouin). Employed with Bank of Hochelaga (now Banque Canadienne Nationale), 1906-19; elected mem. Quebec legislature, 1923; elected mayor of Montreal, 1928, and since reelected, 1930, 34, 38, 44, 47, 50. Elected member of Parliament, Papineau Div., 1949. Decorated Knight of Legion of Honor (France), Comdr. of Order of British Empire, Comdr. Order of Crown of Italy. Home: 4455 St. Hubert St., Montreal, Can. Died Sept. 1958.

HOUGHTON, Edward Rittenhouse, publisher; b. Norristown, Pa., Mar. 13, 1871; s. James Clay and Grace Rittenhouse (Blackwell) H.; grad. Phillips Andover Acad., 1889; A.B., Amherst, 1893. With Houghton Mifflin Co., 1893-—, pres., 1922-39, chmn. bd., 1939-—. Republican. Episcopalian. Clubs: Union, Oakley Country, Milton Club. Home: 124 Canton Av., Milton, Mass. Office: 2 Park St., Boston. Died May 16, 1955; buried Mt. Auburn Cemetery, Cambridge, Mass.

HOUKOM, John Asbjorn (hou' kom), clergyman; b. Mekinock, N.D., Jan. 27, 1890; s. Olaf S. and Anna Marie (Glerum) H.; student Augsburg Acad., Minneapolis, Minn., 1909-10; B.A., Augsburg Coll., 1914; C.T., Augsburg Theol. Sem., 1917; m. Agnes Christine Adsem, May 15, 1918; 1 son, Leif Arnold. Ordained to ministry of Lutheran Ch., July 1, 1917; pastor Madelia, Minn., 1917-20, Blanchardville, Wis., 1920-34, Seattle, Wash., 1934-39, Ashland, Wis., 1939-—. Mem. bd. trustees Augsburg Coll. and Theol. Sem., 1933-48, pres., 1935-48. Served as Four-Minute Man, 1917-18; instr. civilian defense courses, Ashland, Wis., 1942. Mem. Am. Luth. Conf. (2d vice pres. 1942-46, 1st vice pres., 1946-—), Luth. Free Ch. (sec. English conf., 1920-22; pres. Rockford dist. 1922-26, 33-34; pres. Luther League Fedn., 1926-28; pres. Lutheran Ministers assn., Seattle, 1938; pres. Duluth dist. Luth. Free Ch., 1945-48; stewardship sec., 1939-—; sec. com. of efficiency and economy, 1930-35), Chequamegon Ministerial Assn. (pres. 1942-44), Norwegian-Am. Hist. Assn. Wis. State Hist. Soc. Progressive Republican. Mem. Kiwanis. Trans. (from Norwegian), Sanctification, Ludvig Hope, 1933; revised Explanation and Bible History by Urseth, 1934. Contbr. to various publs. Home: 216 Ninth Av., W., Ashland, Wis. Died Jan. 16, 1950.

HOURIGAN, John A., pub.; b. Wilkes-Barre, Pa., Dec. 7, 1872; s. Patrick and Bridget (Degnan) H.; ed. parochial, pub. schs., Wilkes-Barre, Pa.; m. Caroline G. Henderson, Jan. 17, 1905; children—John A., Carolyn G., Ruth (Mrs. Stuart E. Graham), Jane Mary (Mrs. E. J. Rowan). Composing Room Foreman, Circulation Mgr., Wilkes-Barre Record; purchased Wilkes-Barre Morning News, converted to Evening News, 1909; pub.; owner of News, 1909-39, when merged with Record and Times-Leader; chmn. of bd., Wilkes-Barre Pub. Co. (pubs. of the 3 papers), since 1939; v.p. and dir., Miners Nat. Bank, Wilkes-Barre; dir., Bertels Metal Ware, Kingston, Pa.; v.p. and dir., Walnut Park Plaza Apt. Hotel, Phila.; pres. and dir., Indian Springs Water Co. Served on 1st city planning commn., Wilkes-Barre, 1914. Mem. City Sch. Bd., 1919-27, pres., 1925-26; Civil Service Bd., City Fire Dept.; v.p. and dir., Wyo. Valley (Pa.) Community Chest. Mem. St. Mary's Cemetery Assn. (pres.); hon mem., Greater West Friendly Sons of St. Patrick. Republican. Roman Catholic. Clubs: Westmoreland, Rotary (charter mem. Wilkes-Barre). Home: 210 N. Main St. Office: 15 N. Main St., Wilkes-Barre, Pa. Died Nov. 5, 1951; buried St. Mary's Cemetery, Wilkes-Barre.

HOUSE, Joseph Warren, lawyer; b. Searcy, Ark., Oct. 29, 1886; s. Joseph Warren and Ina (Dowdy) H.; A.B., U. Ark., 1909; LL.B., Columbia Law Sch., 1912; m. Julia Clarke, Sept. 2, 1914; 1 dau., Ellen House Simpson. Admitted to Ark. bar, 1912; mem. law firm House & House, 1912-20; Coleman, Robinson & House, 1921-25; sr. mem. House, Moses & Holmes, 1926-—. Chmn. Dem. State Central Com., 1917-21. Mem. Am., Ark. State, Little Rock bar assns. Club: Country. Sigma Alpha Epsilon. Democrat. Presbyterian. Home: 2422 Broadway. Office: Boyle Bldg., Little Rock, Ark. Died Mar. 18, 1954.

HOUSER, Gilbert L(ogan), biologist; b. on farm, Lee County, Ia., July 9, 1866; s. David L(ogan) and Malvina (Saxe) H.; B.S., State U. Ia., 1891, M.S., 1892; studied U. Chgo., and Marine Biol. Lab., Woods Hole, Mass.; Ph.D., Johns Hopkins, 1901; m. Hattie Riggs, June 21, 1899; children—Arthur R., Harold S., Paul C., Ralph L., Mark R. Instr. animal biology State U. Ia., 1892-95, asst. prof., 1895-97, prof. and dir. Labs. of Aniamal Biology, 1897-—. Mem. biol. expdn. to W.I., summer 1893; investigator Marine Biol. Lab., Woods Hole, Mass., 4 seasons. Fellow A.A.A.S., Ia. Acad. Science (pres. 1910-11); mem. Am. Soc. Naturalists, Am. Soc. Zoölogists, Sigma Xi (corr. sec. Ia. chpt., and pres. 1917-18). Republican. Presbyn. Author of papers and articles on biol. science. Home: Iowa City, Ia. Died July 1951.

HOUSMAN, Laurence, author, playwright; b. Bromsgrove, Worcestershire, Eng., July 18, 1865; s. Edward and Sarah Jane (Williams) H.; student Bromsgrove Sch., 1876-82, Lambeth Sch. of Art, London, 1883-84, Nat. Art Training Coll., London, 1885-88; unmarried. Upon leaving sch., studied art and became book-illustrator; now author and playwright; art critic Manchester Guardian, 1899-1914; lecturer on lit. and social interests; dramatic reader of own plays. Mem. Soc. of Authors, League of British Dramatists, Dramatists Guild (U.S.), Peace Pledge Union; hon. fellow Royal Soc. of Literature. Socialist and Pacitist. Member Society of Friends. Author: (novels) Trimblerig, 1924; The Sheepfold, 1928; A Mod. Antaeus; King John of Jingalo; The Royal Runaway; The Duke of Flamborough; Uncle Tom Pudd; (tales) Moonshine and Clover, 1922; A Doorway in Fairyland, 1922; What O'clock Tales; Ironical Tales; Odd Pairs; What Next?; Strange Ends and Discoveries, 1948. (plays) Prunella (with H. Granville Barker), 1906; Little Plays of St. Francis, 1st series, 1925, 2d series, 1931; Victoria Regina, 1934; The Golden Sovereign, 1937; Bethlehem; The Chinese Lantern; Pains and Penalties; Cornered Poets; Palestine Plays; Samuel, the Kingmaker, 1944; (Anthology) Backwords and Forewords, 1945; (essays) Ploughshare and Pruning Hook; The Preparation of Peace; (poems) Collected Poems, 1937; The Family Honour, 1950 (play); The Kind and the Foolish, 1952; also many other books, etc. Contbr. articles, fiction and verse to mags. home: "Longmeadow," Street, Somerset, Eng. Died Feb. 20, 1959; buried The Friends' Meeting House, Street, Somerset, Eng.

HOUSTON, Charles Albert (hōō'stŭn), lawyer; b. N.Y. City, Mar. 14, 1881; s. Thomas Henry and Sarah Jane (Mountain) H.; B.A., Coll. City of New York, 1900; LL.B., New York U., 1903; m. Linda Priber, Mar. 10, 1909; children—Frederic Priber, Marie Luise, Linda Helen. Practiced at N.Y. City since 1903; mem. Otterbourg, Steindler & Houston. Asst. professor, College City of New York. Director, New York School for the Deaf. Treasurer Social Service Commission, New York Diocese; member standing committee of New York Diocesan Convention; secretary of the Church Publishing Association. Member New York State Bar Association, New York County Lawyers' Assn., Assn. Bar City of New York, Phi Delta Phi, Brotherhood of St. Andrew. Republican. Episcopalian. Clubs: Aldine, Scarsdale Golf, Manhattan, Am. Yacht. Author: Problems in Business Law (with J. H. Moore), 1920. Home: White Plains, N.Y. Office: 200 Fifth Av., N.Y.C. Died Oct. 16, 1951.

HOUSTON, Charles Hamilton, lawyer; b. Washington, Sept. 3, 1895; s. William LePre and Mary Ethel (Hamilton) H.; A.B., Amherst Coll., 1915; LL.B., Harvard, 1922, S.J.D., 1923; student U. Madrid, Spain, 1923-24; m. Margaret Gladys Moran, Aug. 23, 1924; m. 2d, Henrietta Williams, Sept. 14, 1937; 1 son, Charles Hamilton. Admitted to D.C. bar, 1924, practiced with father as Houston & Houston, 1924-39, Houston, Houston, Hastie & Waddy, 1939-50; vice dean, sch. of law Howard U., 1929-35; spl. counsel N.A.A.C.P., 1935-40, mem. nat. legal aid com., 1940-50; v.p. Am. Council on Race Relations, 1944-50; mem. President's Com. on Fair Employment Practice, 1944; gen. counsel Assn. Colored Ry. Trainmen & Locomotive Firemen, Internat. Assn. Ry. Employees. Mem. bd. edn. D.C., 1933-35. Served with U.S. Army, 1917-19, with AEF as 2d lt. 351st F.A. Mem. Nat. Bar Assn., Nat. Lawyers Guild, Am. Law Inst., Phi Beta Kappa, Alpha Phi Alpha. Home: 3611 New Hampshire Av. Office: 615 F St. N.W., Washington. Died Apr. 22, 1950; buried Lincoln Meml. Cemetery.

HOUSTON, Grant, surgeon; b. Ausable Forks, N.Y., Dec. 9, 1864; s. James and Margaret (Gibson) H.; Ph.G., S.D. State Coll., 1890, B.S., 1891; M.D., Hahnemann Med. Coll. and Hosp., Chicago, 1894; post-grad. work at Johns Hopkins, 1911, 13, U. of Vienna, 1909, London and Leeds, 1921; m. Anna Grace Dunlop, Sept. 15, 1897; 1 dau., Gertrude (Mrs. James D. Rogers). Practiced in Joliet, Ill., since 1894, specializing in surgery. Mem. governing com. Gorgas Memorial Inst. Fellow Am. Coll. Surgeons; mem. A.M.A., Will-Grundy Med. Soc. Joliet Assn. Commerce. Past pres. Joliet Sunday Evening Club. Republican. Methodist. Mason. Club: Rotary (Joliet). Address: 404 Buell Av., Joliet, Ill. Died Sept. 24, 1953.

HOUSTON, Henry A., ex-congressman, mcht.; b. nr. Millsboro, Del., July 10, 1847; student pub. and pvt. schs.; m. Eva Hickman, Oct. 5, 1882. Assisted his father on farm, 1869-72; lived in Mo., 1872-75; returned to Del.; taught sch., 5 yrs.; in 1882 succeeded his brother in merc. bus., in which he is still engaged. Mem. Sussex County Sch. Commn., 1898, twice reapptd.; mem. U.S. Congress, from Del., at large, 1903-05. Democrat. Address: Millsboro, Del. Deceased.

HOUSTON, Herbert Sherman, editor, pub.; b. Champaign, Ill., Nov. 23, 1866; s. Maj. Samuel and Emeline (Sherman) H.; Ph.B., U. S.D., 1888; studied U. Chgo., Boston U.; M.A., U. Pa., 1916; LL.D., U. S.D., 1917; m. Agnes L. True (died Dec. 5, 1936); m. 2d, Mrs. Carmen T. Calderon de Pinillos, Jan. 1, 1938. City editor of Sioux City Journal, 1890-92; with Chgo. Tribune, 1892-95, Outing Magazine, 1895-1900; mem. Doubleday, Page & Co., 1900-21 (v.p.); editor of Spanish edition of World's Work (La Revista del Mundo). Chmn. com. on information, and mem. exec. com., League to Enforce Peace, and mem. of com. that drafted platform of the League, at Independence Hall, Phila., June 1915; mem. Com. of C. of C. of U.S. on Economic Results of the War; pres. Asso. Advt. Clubs of the World, 1915-17; mem. Am. com. Internat. C. of C.; mem. Commn. on Internat. Justice and Good Will of Fed. Council of Chs. in America; formed internat. pub. co., 1921. Pub. Our World, 1921-24; founder, and pres. Cosmos Newspaper Syndicate, 1924-—; pres. Cosmos Broadcasting Co. to 1933. Delivered series of addresses in Japan, 1931; presented war debt settlement plan, Internat. C. of C., May 1931. Mem. Psi Upsilon (exec. council

1915-30), Phi Beta Kappa. Mem. U.S. Govt. Com. of Information during World War. Mem. Com. Walter Page Journalistic Fellowship; dir. Nat. Crusage against Illiteracy; mem. President Hoover's Nat. Advisory Com. on Illiteracy, Am. Child Health Assn., New York Child Welfare Soc., Student Internat. Union, Council on Internat. Relations; del. to Internat. C. of C., Paris, 1935, Berlin, 1937; commr. to Far East of N.Y. World's Fair, 1939; mem. com. for World Trade Center at N.Y. World's Fair representing Internat. C. of C.; chmn., 1941, The Institute for the Advancement of Visual Education and Vocational Training; v.p. Am. Plan for Med. and Surg. Care, 1941; mem. bd. dirs. World Education Service Council (chmn. com. World Friendship Hour for Schools of UN). Clubs: Century, Cosmos, The Pilgrims. Author: Blocking New Wars, 1918. Home: 4 W. 43d St., N.Y.C. Office: 70 5th Av., N.Y.C. Died May 14, 1955.*

HOUSTON, Persis Daniel, banker; b. Marshall Co., Tenn., Mar. 30, 1874; s. Persis Daniel and Medora Ann (Pickens) H.; student Haynes McLean Prep. Sch.; m. Margaret Louise Robinson, Oct. 24, 1894; 1 son, Persis Daniel. Chmn. bd., dir. So. Trust Co., Louisville, Mass. Mut. Life Ins. Co., Springfield; hon. chmn. First Am. Nat. Bank, Nashville; director Hermitage Hotel Co., Phillips & Buttorff Manufacturing Company. Chairman of Tennessee State Planning Commn. Member board directors, trustee Vanderbilt U.; trustee Fisk U. Mem. Am. Bankers Assn. (past pres.), Ry. Treasurers Assn. (past pres.). Home: Royal Oaks Apt. Office: First American National Bank, Nashville 3. Died Mar. 27, 1957.

HOUSTON, Samuel Frederic; b. Germantown, Phila., Aug. 30, 1866; s. Henry Howard and Sallie S. (Bonnell) H.; Ph.B., U. of Pa., 1887; hon. LL.D., 1939; m. Edith A. Corlies, Nov. 9, 1887 (died 1895); m. 2d, Mrs. Charlotte Harding Shepherd Brown (Chevalier Legion of Honor), Apr. 8, 1902 (died 1940). Chmn. of the board Real Estate Trust Company of Philadelphia. Trustee Univ. of Pa. Mem. Am. Acad. Polit. and Social Science, Am. Econ. Assn., Geog. Soc. Phila. Episcopalian; mem. standing com. Diocese Pa. and formerly of Nat. Council P.E. Ch. Mem. Pa. Hist. Soc., Church Hist. Soc. (vice-pres.), St. Andrews Society of Philadelphia (past president). Officier Legion of Honor, 1948; Soc., Colonial Wars, Mil. Order Fgn. Wars (hon. comdr. Pa. Commandery), Sons of the Revolution (v.p. Pa. soc.), War of 1812 (president gen.), Loyal Legion. Clubs: Rittenhouse, University, Church, St. Anthony, Union League, Corinthian Yacht, New York Yacht. Home: Chestnut Hill. Office: Real Estate Trust Bldg., Phila. Died May 2, 1952.

HOUSTON, William Cannon, ex-congressman; b. Bedford County, Tenn., Mar. 17, 1852; s. William and Elizabeth Clay (Morgan) H.; d. at Woodbury and Sweetwater, Tenn.; m. Lizzie Minor McLemore, Jan., 1899. Admitted to bar, 1878, and since in practice at Woodbury, Tenn.; judge 8th Jud. Circuit, 1894-1904. Mem. Tenn. Ho. of Reps., 1876, 80, 82; mem. 59th to 65th Congresses, 5th Tenn. Dist. Mem. Dem. State Exec. Com., 4 yrs.; presdl. elector, 1888. Mem. Christian (Disciples) Ch. Address: Woodbury, Tenn. Died Aug. 31, 1931.

HOUX, Frank L., ex-gov. Wyo.; b. Lexington, Mo., Dec. 12, 1860; s. George W. and Fannie (Price) H.; grad. Shaw's Bus. Coll., Lexington, 1884; m. Ida Mason Christy, Dec. 22, 1898. Asso. with W. F. Cody ("Buffalo Bill") in construction and settlement of first irrigated project under the Carey Arid Land Act in U.S.; sec. of State of Wyo., 1910, reëlected, 1914; became acting gov. of Wyo., succeeding John B. Kendrick, elected to U.S. Senate, 1917-19. Democrat. Presbyn. Mason. Clubs: Industrial (Cheyenne, Wyo.); Cody (Cody, Wyo.). Home: Cheyenne, Wyo. Decased.

HOVDE, Bryn(jolf) J(akob) (hŭv'dā), assn. exec.; b. Jersey City, May 17, 1896; s. Christian J. M. and Marie (Jacobson) H.; A.B., Luther Coll., Decorah, Ia., 1916; A.M., State Univ. of Ia., 1919, Ph.D., 1924; m. Theresse Arneson, Nov. 24, 1921; children—Christian Arneson, Ellen Margrethe, Carl Frederick. Instr. Norwegian and history, Luther Coll., 1919-23; asst. prof. history and polit. science, Allegheny Coll., Meadville, Pa., 1924-27; asso. prof. history, U. of Pittsburgh, 1927-37; dir. pub. relations office, Allegheny County (Pa.) Emergency Relief Bd., 1934-35; dir. dept. pub. welfare, City of Pittsburgh, 1936-38; adminstr. housing authority, Pittsburgh, 1938-44; acting dir. management div. U.S. Housing Authority, Washington, D.C., 1939-40; dir. Pittsburgh office Fed. Works Adminstrn., 1941; chief, div. cultural cooperation, U.S. Dept. of State, 1944-45; pres. New Sch. for Social Research, N.Y. City, 1945-50; Fulbright Research Scholar, Norway, 1950-51; visiting prof. U. of Wis., 1951-52; exec. director Pittsburgh Housing Assn., 1952—; tech. expert on staff Am. delegation to U.N. Conf., San Francisco, 1945; tech. sec. on staff Am. del. to London Conf. to establish United Nations Ednl., Scientific and Cultural Orgn., 1945. Served as 2d lt., C.A.C., U.S Army, 1918 Mem Allegheny County (Pa.) Bd. Pub. Assistance, 1936-39, planning commn. City of Pittsburgh, 1942-44; mem. bd. Nat. Pub. Housing Conference; member of the board of Oslo University Summer Sch. for American students. Awarded Guggenheim fellowship, 1930-31, American-Scandinavian Foundation fellowship, 1932. Mem. Am. Hist. Assn., Norwegian-Am. Hist. Assn., Am. Soc. Pub. Adminstrn., Nat. Assn. Housing Officials. Democrat. Club: Cosmos (Washington). Editor: The Evergreen House Report on Urban Planning, 1944. Author: Diplomatic Relations of the United States with Sweden and Norway, 1921; The Scandinavian Countries, 1720-1865, 1944. Home: 5825 Darlington Rd., Pitts. 17. Office: 200 Ross St., Pitts. 19. Died Aug. 10, 1954; buried Pitts.

HOVELL, Albert Armand, lawyer; b. Bklyn., 1877; student N.Y. Law Sch. Sr. mem. firm Hovell, Clarkson & Klupt, pres. and gen. counsel, Century Circuit Co., Inc.; pres. and dir. Charles H. Finch & Co., Argyle Holding Corp., Honack Constrn. Corp., Fourtown Realty Corp., Twain Realty Corp., and numerous other realty corps. Home: Cross Creak, Fla. Deceased.*

HOVER, William Adgate (hō'vẽr), mcht., banker; b. Mazomanie, Wis., Mar. 9, 1856; s. William Ulysses and Harriet (Harbaugh) H.; B.M.E., U. Wis., 1877; spl. student Sch. Mines (Columbia), 1877, 78; m. Marianna Vought, Sept. 1, 1886; children—William Tracy, Mary Throckmorton, Ruth Grandin, Dorothy Adgate, Harriet Harbaugh, Anne Vought, James Throckmorton Vought, Charles Stedman, Lloyd de Barberie. Assayer, Lake City, Colo., 1878; retail druggist, Denver, 1879-82; became wholesale druggist, Denver, title of W. A. Hover & Co., sr. partner, 1882-1937, chmn. bd., 1992; pres. U.S. Nat. Bank, 1904-08, 17-23, chmn. bd., 1908-17, now dir.; dir. Mountain States Tel. & Tel. Co. Pres. Bd. of Supervisors, City of Denver, 3 yrs.; pres. several terms Denver Traffic Bur., also as dir. Denver C. of C. and Comml. Assn. Mem. Nat. Wholesale Druggists' Assn. (pres. 1902-03), Mass. Soc. Mayflower Descs., Colo. Soc. S.R. (pres. 1909-10), Phi Kappa Psi. Republican. Episcopalian. Clubs: Denver, Denver Athletic, Pacific Coast; hon. life non-resident mem. Drug and Chemical Club of New York. Now retired. Home: 168 Glendora Av., Long Beach 3, Cal. Died Nov. 19, 1952; buried Fairmount Cemetery, Denver.

HOVEY, Rexford William, business exec.; b. N. Hatley, P.Q., Can., Nov. 10, 1892; s. Philip A. and Francis Jennie (Clapp) H.; B.S., McGill Univ., 1915, post-grad. work, 1915-19; m. Lesley Marion Duncalfe, May 29, 1916 (dec.); 1 son, Philip L.; m. 2d, Ruth A. Shearer, Dec. 24, 1949. Came to U.S., 1928, naturalized, 1944. Asso. with pulp and paper div. Forest Products Lab., and Imperial Munitions Bd., Montreal, Can., 1915-19; dir. research and tech. dir. Abitibi Power & Paper Co., Iroquois Falls, Ontario, Can., 1919-26; gen. mgr. Nashwaak Pulp & Paper Co., St. John, N.B., 1926-28; tech. dir. Oxford Paper Co., New York, N.Y., 1928-34, vice pres. in charge mfg., Oxford Paper Co. and Oxford Miami Paper Co., 1933-45, exec. v.p., 1948-56, vice chmn. bd., 1956—; also dir.; v.p. Nashwaak Pulp & Paper Co., 1947—; dir. Rumford Falls Power Co. Served on Imperial Munitions Bd., 1915-18; dir. paper div., War Prodn. Bd., Oct. 1943-44; spl. consultant, dir. Forest Products Bur. W.P.B., Jan.-Oct. 1945. Protestant. Clubs: Union League (New York); Seaview Country (Absecon, N.J.); Blind Brook, Inc. (Port Chester, N.Y.); Moraine Country (Dayton, O.); Mid-Ocean (Bermuda). Home: 6 Brooklands, Bronxville, N.Y. Office: 230 Park Av., N.Y.C. 17. Died July 7, 1957; buried Ferncliff, Hartsdale, N.Y.

HOVEY, William Simmons, pres. Fairbanks, Morse & Co.; b. Ithaca, N.Y., Nov. 23, 1875; s. Robert Moore and Laura (Stilwell) H.; M.E., Cornell U., 1897; m. Winifred Hayward, June 12, 1900. With Eastman Kodak Co., Rochester, N.Y., 1899-1902; with Fairbanks, Morse & Co., 1902—, pres., 1927—; dir. Municipal Acceptance Corp., Inland Utilities Co., Fairbanks-Morse Water Supply Co., Tennant Finance Co. Mem. Sigma Xi. Republican. Conglist. Clubs: University, Westmoreland Country, Barrington Hills Country. Home: 1507 Hinman Av., Evanston, Ill. Office: 900 S. Wabash Av., Chicago, Ill. Died Mar. 11, 1954.

HOWARD, A(lbert) T. (Bert), Rep. campaign dir.; b. Weeping Water, Neb., Apr. 6, 1893; s. Thomas Mentor and Deborah (Tompkins) H.; grad. Scottsbluff (Neb.) High Sch.; m. N. Antha Taylor, June 20, 1919 (dec. 1939); 1 son, William Reed; m. 2d, Emma Jane Veach, Dec. 18, 1940. Postal clk., asst. postmaster, 1910-17; sugar chemist, 1918-19; in grain, produce, machinery and livestock bus., 1920-24; traveling supt. Continental Oil Co., 1924-25; retail flower and gift shop bus., 1925-40; real estate broker, 1940—. Mayor, City of Scottsbluff, 1931-35; 1939-41; Neb. state senator, 1935-37; chmn., Rep. State Central Com., 1942—. Rep. Midwest State Chmns. Assn., 1946-48; midwest campaign dir., Rep. Nat. Com., 1948. Served as lt., U.S. Army F.A., World War I. Mem. Scottsbluff C. of C. (past dir.), Am. Legion, Vets. Fgn. Wars, Neb. Soc. for Crippled Children (v.p.). Republican. Conglist. Mason (Shriner). Club: Lions (Scottsbluff). Home: 202 E 17th St. Office: C. of C., Bldg., Scottsbluff. Neb. Died May 14, 1951; buried Fairview Cemetery, Scottsbluff.

HOWARD, Cecil de Blaquiere, sculptor; b. Niagara Falls, Can., Apr. 2, 1888; s. George Henry and Alice (Farmer) H.; ed. public school and high school, Buffalo, N.Y.; studied art, Buffalo Art Sch., and Julian's Academy, Paris, France; married Celine Coupet, 1916; children—Line, Noel Douglas. Lived and studied in Paris (France), 1905-40; overseas with O.S.S., 1944-45. Works include war memorials in France, works in museums and private collections in U.S., England and France. Chevalier de la Légion d'Honneur (France). Awarded 2 gold medals, Paris Exposition, 1937; George Widener Gold Medal, Philadelphia, Pa., 1944; Herbert Adams Memorial Award, National Sculpture Soc., 1953; Gold Medal, Architectural League, 1954. Fellow National Sculpture Soc. (pres. 1944-45). Mem. Societe des Beaux Arts, Salon d'Automne, Salon des Tuilleries (Paris), Nat. Ins. Arts and Letters, Nat. Acad. Design (U.S.), Century Assn. (N.Y.). Home: 40 W. 57th St., N.Y.C. 19. Died Sept. 1956.

HOWARD, Charles S., editor; b. Boston, July 9, 1865; s. Charles and Annie H.; student Boston pub. schs. Reporter, drama, music and movie editor Boston (Mass.) Daily and Sunday Globe, 1894—. Republican. Writer of plays and sketches. Home: 25 Park Vale Av., Allston, Boston. Office: Boston Daily and Sunday Globe, Boston. Died Mar. 2, 1951.

HOWARD, Claud, educator; b. Fannin Co., Tex., May 27, 1888; s. Henry H. and Sarah Alice (Merrill) H.; A.B., East Tex. State Tchrs. Coll., 1907; A.M., U. N.C., 1909, Harvard University, 1911; Ph.D., University of Chicago, 1922; m. Lula Frances Whitaker, Aug. 10, 1912; children—Elizabeth Alice (Mrs. K. G. Crawford), Rosamond (Mrs. Melvin Campbell), Lula Frances (Mrs. Harry R. Patrick), Helen Claud (Mrs. Heinz Lenz). Prin. Gober (Tex.) Pub. Sch., 1907-08; instr. English U. N.C., 1909-10; head dept. English Jacksonville (Ala.) Tchrs. Coll., 1911-19, Southwestern U., Georgetown, Texas since 1919. Author: The Dramatic Monologue: Its Origin and Development, 1910; Coleridge's Idealism in its Relationship to Kant and the Cambridge Platonists, 1924. Home: 1310 12th St., Georgetown, Tex. Deceased.

HOWARD, Clinton Norman, lecturer, reformer; b. Pottsville, Pa., July 28, 1868; s. Rev. Squire Benjamin and Clara Schenfelder (Nagle) H.; ed. under pvt. tutelage; m. Angeline M. Kellar, May 1, 1888; children—Ella Eva (dec.), Mrs. Winnifred Elizabeth Snider, John Gough (died in World War), Neal Dow, Mrs. Ruth Melody Hutchinson, Horace Greeley. Founder and pres. Prohibition Union Christian Men, 1890; began as lyceum and chautauqua lecturer, 1900; now supt. Internat. Reform Fed. Mem. Am. Civic Reform Union (advisory bd.), N.Y. Civic League, Nat. Temperance Soc. (v.p.), Am. Sabbath Assn., Internat. Lyceum Assn., etc. Baptist. Chmn. World Peace Commn., 1920-24, representing 41 nations, joined in call for world conf., Washington, D.C., 1925; in behalf of this commn. addressed Internat. Conf. for Limitation of Armament at Washington, D.C.; chmn. Nat. United Com. for Law Enforcement, 1924-36 (24 nat. bodies). Editor Progress (magazine). Address: 134 Constitution N.E., Washington. Died Apr. 25, 1955; buried Riverside Cemetery, Rochester, N.Y.

HOWARD, Dowell J., educator; b. Brookeville, Md., Aug. 11, 1897; s. Henry and Mary Florence (Jones) H.; B.S., Md. State Coll. (now U. of Md.), 1917; A.M., U. of Md., 1926, Sc. D. (hon.), 1950; student Va. Polytech. Inst., 1926; m. Mariel V. Gott, Jan. 31, 1920; children—Dowell J., Marianna V. Teacher vocational agr., Boyce, Va., 1919-24, prin., 1923-24; vocational agr. teacher, Practice Sch., Va. Polytech. Inst., 1924-25; dist. supervisor of agrl. edn. for Northern Va., 1925-35; asst. state supervisor of agrl. edn., 1935-42, state supervisor agrl. edn., 1942-46; asst. state supt. pub. instrn., Va. State Dept. Edn., 1946-49, acting state supt. public instrn., Sept. 1949-May 1950, state supt. public instrn., 1950—. Mem. bd. visitors Coll. of William and Mary U., Va. Mil. Inst., Va. Poly. Inst., Med. Coll. Va.; sec. to governing bd. Madison Coll., Longwood Coll., Va. State Coll., Va. State Sch.; mem. bd. Va. State Library, Va. Sch. for Deaf and Blind. Served with U.S. Army, World War I. Dir. food prodn. war training program, Va. State, 1942-46. Mem. Nat. Assn. State Dirs. Vocational Edn. (chmn. vets. training com.), Am. Vocational Assn. (life mem., mem. com. to revise constitution, mem. resolutions com.), Future Farmers of Am. (hon. state farmers degree; hon. Am. Farmers degree; nat. treas., mem. nat. bd. trustees; nat. treas., Future Farmers of Am. Found.; mem. bd. dirs.), Va. Assn. Future Farmers of Am. (advisor, exec. sec.), Am. Assn. Sch. Adminstrs., Va. Edn. Assn. (mem. publ. relations com.), Va. Vocational Assn. (past sec., past pres., past mem. exec. bd.), Sigma Nu, Phi Delta Kappa. Episcopalian (past mem. diocesan bd., mem. ch. sch. adv. com.). Club: Rotary Internat. (local pres., 1935-36, dist. gov. 186th Dist., del. Internat. Conv., Detroit and Havana; chmn. discussion group on youth service at Internat. Conv.,

Atlantic City). Home: 1617 Confederate Av., Richmond 27, Va. Died Feb. 23, 1957; buried Hollywood Cemetery, Richmond, Va.

HOWARD, Earl Dean, educator; b. Fayette, O., June 9, 1876; s. Albert John and Cora (Hoffman) H.; Ph.B., U. Chgo., 1902, Ph.M., 1903, Ph.D., 1905; student U. Berlin, 1904-05; m. Margaret Allen, June 19, 1907; children—Allen Carter, Mrs. Margaret Cooper, Claxton Edmonds. Instr. econs. U. Pa., 1905-07; asst. prof. and prof. econs. Northwestern U., 1907-41; on labor problems, Harvard, 1920-24, Stanford U., 1931; dep. U.S. fuel adminstr. for Ill., 1917. Sec. industrial relations com. C. of C. U.S.A.; v.p., dir. Hart, Schaffner & Marx, 1911-32; dep. adminstr., NRA, 1933-34; labor adviser City of Chgo., 1941-44; Chgo. area OPA rent dir., 1942-43. Director pre-legal div. John Marshall Law School. Club: University (Evanston). Author: Cause and Extent of the Recent Industrial Progress of Germany, 1905; Money and Banking (with J. F. Johnson), 1909; The Socratic Method for Developing Intelligence, 1923. Home: 411 Grove St., Evanston, Ill. Died July 14, 1956.

HOWARD, Edgar, ex-congressman; b. Osceola, Ia., Sept. 16, 1858; s. James Dakin and Martha (Daniel) H.; ed. Western Collegiate Inst., Ia. Coll. of Law (non-grad.); m. Elizabeth Paisley Burtch, Nov. 11, 1884. Reporter and city editor various papers until 1884; editor Papillion (Neb.) Times, 1884-1900; purchased, 1900, Weekly Telegram, of Columbus, Neb. (now a daily). Mem. Neb. Ho. of Rep., 1895; probate judge, Sarpy Co., Neb., 1896-1900; lt. gov. of Neb., 1917-19; mem. 68th to 73d Congresses (1923-35), 3d Neb. Dist. Mem. Neb. Press Assn. Democrat. Home: Columbus, Neb. Died July 19, 1951.

HOWARD, Ernest E(mmanuel), cons. engr.; b. Toronto, Can., Feb. 29, 1880; s. Rev. Henry Augustus and Emma (Skipp) H.; came to U.S. at early age; B.S., U. of Texas, 1900, C.E., 1900, Dr Engring. honoris causa, U. of Nebraska, 1939; D.Sc. (honorary), University of Missouri, 1952; married Josephine Tiernan, June 6, 1942. Instructor in engineering, University of Texas, 1901; bridge engineering. with J.A.L. Waddell and partners, 1901-14; partner successive firms, Harrington, Howard & Ash., 1914-28, now Howard, Needles, Tammen & Bergendoff; designers of bridges in 40 of the 48 States; various govtl. units and pvt. corps., incl. more than 20 railroads; Canada, Mexico, China, Russia, Etc. Work includes bridges across Mobile Bay, Fraser, Columbia, Willamette, Sacramento, Colorado, Neches, Mo. (15), Mississippi (9) (including bridges at Vicksburg, Natchez, Greenville, Miss., Rock Island, Ill., Dubuque, Ia., St. Mary's at Soo, O., Hudson, Delaware (incl. bridge being built at Wilmington) and other rivers and waterways; Welland Canal (18 bridges), Chesapeake & Delaware Canal (6 bridges), Harlem River and Bronx Kill spans of Triborough Bridge, N.Y.; Potomac River twin bridges at 14th St., Washington, D.C. (winner design competition); consultant service for New Jersey on Pulaski Skyway Viaduct and Raritan River Bridge; also various large viaducts; designer important bridge and viaduct structures for states of Del., Va., W.Va., Ala., Ark., Ill., Neb., Ky., Wis., Mo., Kan., Ia., Tex., and N.J.; engrs. for Maine Turnpike Express Highway, Denver-Boulder Turnpike, New Jersey Turnpike, bridges and express highways Akron and Toledo; cons. engineer Commission Renovation White House. U.S. war work, architect-engr. S.W. Proving Ground, Bluebonnet Ordnance Plant, Army Post Facilities, Ft. Riley, Internment Camp, Concordia; spl. design work for U.S. Engring. Bd.; compiled War Dept. Technical Manual TMS-286. Mem. Mo. State bd. of registration for architects and professional engrs., 1941-45. Received 5 of the 9 A.I.S.C. awards for the most beautiful bridges built in United States, 1942-48. Awarded Thomas Fitch Rowland Prize, A.S.C.E., 1921. Commd. Capt. Engrs. U.S. Army, 1918-19. Chmn. bd., U. of Kansas City since 1930. Fellow Am. Soc. M.E., A.A.A.S.; mem. Am. Inst. Cons. Engrs., Am. Soc. C.E. (dir., 1941-44, v.p., 1945-46, pres. 1950), Engring. Inst. Can., Am. Soc. Testing Materials Internat. Assn. Bdge. and Structl. Engrs. (U.S. del. 2d Internat. Cong., Berlin, 1926; chmn. Am. del. to 3d Cong., Liege, 1948, 4th Cong., Cambridge, London, 1952; U.S. rep. London Conf. Engring. Socs., 1948). Archaeological Institute of America, Military Order of World War, Tau Beta Pi, Phi Beta Kappa. Presbyterian. Clubs: Engineers, University, Country. Author: Documents Governing Bridge Construction, 1916; also tech. papers. Awarded Thomas Fitch Rowland prize, Am. Soc. C.E., 1921. Home: 5708 State Line Rd., Kansas City 2. Office: 1805 Grand Av., Kansas City 6, Mo.; and 99 Church St., N.Y.C. 7. Died Aug. 19, 1953; buried Kansas City, Mo.

HOWARD, Everette B., ex-congressman; b. Morgantown, Ky., Sept. 19, 1873; s. Addison A. and Adie P. (Harreld) H.; ed. pub. schs.; m. Hollis Hope, Dec. 4, 1895; 1 son, Paxton Howard. Settled at Tulsa, 1905, engaged as oil and gas producer; mem. and sec. State Bd. Pub. Affairs, Okla., 1911-15; state auditor of Okla., 1915-18; mem. 66th, 68th and 70th Congresses, 1st Okla. Dist. Democrat. Methodist. Made mem. Okla. Hall of Fame, 1941. Home: 1400 W. Illinois Av., Midland, Tex. Died Apr. 3, 1950.

HOWARD, Harvey James, ophthalmologist; b. Churchville, N.Y., Jan. 30, 1880; s. Charles William and Mary Jessie (Williamson) H.; A.B., U. Mich., 1904; M.D., U. Pa., 1908, A.M., Harvard, 1917; Oph.D., U. Colo., 1918; m. Maude Irene Strobel, June 25, 1910 (died May 3, 1948); children—Margaret Strobel (Jackson), James Howell, Martha Williamson Blake; m. 2d, Alice Tilson Eastes, Aug. 24, 1948. Resident physician Bryn Mawr Hosp., 1908; resident ophthalmic surgeon N.Y. Eye and Ear Infirmary, 1909, 10; head dept. ophthalmology U. Med. Sch., Canton, China, 1910-13; ophthalmologist Canton Christian Coll., 1912-15; ophthalmic surgeon Canton Hosp., 1912-15; fellow China Med. Bd. of Rockefeller Found. at Harvard, 1916-18, at Vienna U., 1923-24; ophthalmic asst. Harvard Post-Grad. Med. Sch., and Mass. Charitable Eye and Ear Infirmary, 1917-18; prof., head of dept. ophthalmology, Peking Union Medical Coll., 1918-27; med. adviser to Dept. Aeros., Chinese Govt., 1920-23; ophthalmologist to boy emperor of China, 1921-23; prof. ophthalmology Washington Univ. Sch. Medicine, 1927-33. Med. dir. Mo. Com. for the Blind, 1931-48. Certificate of Am. Bd. of Ophthalmic Examiners. Capt. M.C., U.S. Army, at Hazelhurst Field, Mineola, N.Y., 1918-19; col. Med. R.C., 1941; devised depth perception test for aviators for U.S. Army, Navy and Dept. of Commerce. Fellow A.C.S. and chmn. China br. of the Coll., 1926-28; mem. A. M.A., Am. Ophthal. Soc., Am. Acad. Ophthalmology and Otolaryngology, China Med. Assn., So. Med. Assn., Mo., St. Louis med. socs., Alpha Omega Alpha, Nu Sigma Nu, Alpha Tau Omega, Acacia, St. Louis Writers' Guild (pres. 1937), Soc. of St. Louis Authors (pres. 1941-45). Mil. decoration, Tiger, 5th class (Chinese), 1922. Held prisoner by bandits in Manchuria, summer 1925. Episcopalian. Mason (32°). Author: Ten Weeks with Chinese Bandits; also abt. 100 articles pertaining to ophthalmology. Address: 1725 Golf View Dr., Bellair Estates, Clearwater, Fla. Died Nov. 6, 1956.

HOWARD, Henry, chem. engr.; b. Jamaica Plain, Mass., July 5, 1868; s. Alonzo Potter and Emma (Babcock) H.; ed. Boston Latin Sch., Mass. Inst. Tech., 1885-89; m. Alice Sturtevant, Sept. 5, 1896; children—Katharine (Mrs. Charles Townsend), Henry Sturtevant, Thomas Clark, John Babcock, Robert Sturtevant (dec.). Became chemist 1889, supt. 1896, v.p., 1902-20, Merrimac Chem. Co., Boston, mfrs. of heavy chemicals; joined Grasselli Chem. Co., Cleveland, Ohio, 1920, and in charge of research and development work 6 years, now cons. chem. engr. Largely interested in public welfare; organized and directed dept. of U.S. Shipping Bd. which provided and trained personnel for new Am. Merchant Marine. Mem. Mfg. Chemists' Assn. of U.S. (pres. 3 yrs.; chmn. exec. com. 22 yrs.), Am. Inst. Chem. Engrs. (ex-pres.), Am. Chem. Soc. (mem. patent com.), Am. Electrochem. Soc. (past v.p.), Soc. Chem. Industry; mem. Joint Com. of U.S. and Canadian Chambers of Commerce. Republican. Episcopalian. Clubs: Union (Boston); India House, New York Yacht, Cruising Club of America; Club Nautico (San Sebastian, Spain; Porcupine (Nassau); Clambake, Spouting Rock Beach Assn. (Newport, R.I.). Home: Paradise Rd., Newport, R.I. Died Aug. 26, 1951.

HOWARD, James Raley, farmer; b. Marshall County, Ia., Mar. 24, 1873; s. Henry C. and Rhoda Jane (Adams) H.; Ph.B., Penn Coll., Oskaloosa, Ia., 1894, A.M., 1897; studied U. Chgo., 1899; m. Anna Pickerel, Dec. 27, 1900; children—Henry C., Robert P., John, Janet (Mrs. A. M. Patterson). Ednl. work, 1894-98; farmer and stockman, 1898-1904; bank cashier, 1904-09; farming and stock raising, 1909—. First pres. Marshall County (Ia.) Farm Bur., 1915-18; pres. Ia. Farm Bur. Fedn., 1918-19; pres. Am. Farm Bur. Fedn., 1919-23; mem. adv. com. Food Research Inst. of Stanford U., 1923; mem. St. Lawrence Waterways Commn., 1924; mem. bd. govs. Am. Agrl. Inst., 1923—; specialist in orgn. Federal Farm Bd., 1929. Republican. Quaker. Home: Homelands Farms, Clemons, Ia. Died Jan. 27, 1954. Buried Bangor Friends Cemetery, Union, Ia.

HOWARD, Joseph Henry, educator; b. Frankton, Ind., Feb. 26, 1860; s. John Anderson and Louisa Elvira (Plummer) H.; A.B., Ind. U., 1888, A.M., 1890; Ph.D., Stanford, 1899; m. Mary Ella Lowe, Sept. 4, 1888; children—Robert Lowe, Harold Porter. Tchr. dist., grade and high schs., and in coll. while student; asst. prof. Latin, Ind. U., 1894-1901; adj. prof. Latin, U. Neb., 1901-03; prof. Latin, U. S.D., 1903—. Prof. Latin, summers, U. Chgo., 1910, U. Colo., 1913-16. Mem. Am. Philol. Assn., Classical Assn. Middle West and South, Phi Beta Kappa, Beta Theta Pi. Democrat. Mem. Christian (Disciples) Ch. Author: Quantitative Reading of Latin Verse, 1898; Case Usage in Petronius' Satires, 1900; Selected Silvae of Publius Papinius Statius (pub. posthumously). Home: Vermilion, S.D. Died Aug. 31, 1949; buried Crown Hill Cemetery, Indpls.

HOWARD Kathleen, opera singer; b. Canada, of English parentage, naturalized citizen of U.S., d. George Henry and Alice A. (Farmer) H.; pupil of Oscar Saenger, New York, Jacques Bouhy, and Jean de Reszke, Paris, France; m. Edward K. Baird, 1916 (div. 1924). Began as ch. singer in N.Y.C.; operatic début in Metz, Germany, 1907, and at once gained recognition, continuing there 2 seasons; leading contralto Court Opera, Darmstadt, 3 seasons; sang prin. contralto parts at Wagner Festival; also in Royal Opera, at Covent Garden, London, with Nikisch conduting, season of 1913; leading contralto Century Opera Co., New York, seasons of 1913-14, 14-15; many concert and opera appearances in Great Britain, Germany, and countries of northern Europe; contralto Met. Opera Co., N.Y.C., 1916-28. Presented with imperial crown brooch by Czar of Russia. Now acting in motion pictures. Author: Confessions of an Opera Singer, 1918. Contbr. to mags. New York editor Harper's Bazaar, 1928-33; fashion editor Photoplay. Address: 5959 Franklin Av., Hollywood, Cal. Died Aug. 1956.

HOWARD, Leland Ossian, entomologist; b. Rockford, Ill., June 11, 1857; s. Ossian Gregory and Lucy Dunham (Thurber) H.; B.S., Cornell, 1877, M.S., 1883; Ph.D., Georgetown U., 1896; M.D. (hon.), George Washington U., 1911; LL.D., U. Pitts., 1911, U. Cal., 1929; Sc.D., U. Toronto, 1920; Rutgers U., 1930; m. Marie T. Clifton, Apr. 28, 1886; children—Lucy Thurber, Candace Leland (Mrs. Edward De Mille Payne), Janet Moore. Asst. entomologist Bur. of Entomology, U.S. Dept. Agr., 1878-94, chief of bur., 1894-1927, prin. entomologist, 1927-31, ret. Hon. curator dept. of insects, U.S. Nat. Museum, 1895—; cons. entomologist US PHS 1904—, sr. entomologist with grade of sr. surgeon in Res., 1919. Mem. com. on agr. Nat. Council Defense, 1917; chmn. sub-com. on med. entomology NRC, 1917. Trustee Cornell U., 1900-05. Permanent sec. A.A.S.S., 1898-1920; pres. Assn. of Econ. Entomologists, 1894, Biol. Soc. Washington, 1897-98, Cosmos Club, 1909, Washington Acad. Sciences, 1916, A.A.A.S., 1920; v.p. Internat. Congress of Agr., Paris, 1923; hon. pres. Internat. Conf. of Phytopathologists and Econ. Entomologists, Holland, 1923; chmn. Pan-Pacific Food Conservation Congress, Honolulu, 1924; pres. sect. econ. zoölogy Internat. Congress of Zoölogy, Budapest, 1927; pres. Internat. Congress Entomology, Ithaca, N.Y., 1929. Fellow Am. Acad. Arts and Scis.; mem. Am. Philos. Soc., Nat. Acad. Sciences; hon. mem. many fgn. sci. socs. Decorated Chevalier Legion of Honor, 1925, Officier, 1929, and Officier Order of Agricultural Merit (both of France), 1925; Medalist Holland Soc. of New York, 1924; 2d Capper award, 1931. Author: Mosquitoes—How They Live, Etc., 1901; The Insect Book, 1901; The House-Fly—Disease Carrier, 1911; monograph, Mosquitoes of North America, Carnegie Instn., 1912-17; History of Applied Entomology (Smithsonian Inst.). 1930; The Insect Menace, 1931; Fighting the Insects—The Story of an Entomologist, 1933. Home: 45 Pondfield Rd. W., Bronxville, N.Y. Died May 1, 1950.

HOWARD, Marion Edith, physician, editor; b. N. Y.C., Sept. 26, 1899; d. Gilmore and Eliza (Day) Howard; A.B., Barnard Coll., 1926; M.D., John Hopkins, 1931; m. Ashley W. Oughterson, Mar. 21, 1942. Instr. internal medicine Yale, 1936-41, asst. prof., 1941-47, asso. clin. prof. since 1947; asso. physician New Haven Hosp.; mem. faculty Med. Sch., Universidad Del Valle, 1957-59; editor Modern Drugs, also Modern Drug Ency. since 1948. Diplomate Am. Bd. Internal Medicine. Fellow A.C.P. Contbr. articles med. jours. Home: New Haven. Office: Universidal Del Valle, Cali, Colombia. Died Jan. 6, 1959; buried Cali, Colombia.

HOWARD, William Clyde, clergyman; b. Hamilton County, Ohio; s. William Rosecrans and Rhoda May (Ferris) H.; student U. of Cincinnati; grad. Lane Theological Seminary; D.D., Coll. of the Ozarks, 1923; LL.D. from Blackburn U., 1928; married Janie Spraul (dec.); children—Robert Clyde (dec.), James Denver (dec.), Jean, Clyde; married 2d, Elizabeth Kish, June 11, 1947. Ordained Presbyterian ministry; pastor successively Central Church, Houston, Tex., First Church, Independence, Kan., First Church, Oklahoma City, Okla., Second Church, Chicago, since 1926. Dir. of edn. (ch. and sch. depts.) Food Adminstrn., Tex., and lecturer at mil. cantonments, World War; spl. lecturer, colls., seminaries and civic clubs. Dir. McKinley Memorial Foundation, Champaign, Ill.; dir. Presbyterian Extension Bd. of Chicago, Presbyterian Home, Presbyterian Hosp.; mem. exec. com. of bd. of dirs. Presbyterian Theol. Sem. (Chicago); moderator Chicago Presbytery, 1931-32; moderator Presbyterian Synod of Ill., 1937; mem. bd. of trustees Sunday Evening Club of Chicago; pres. board Cedarville (Ohio) Coll.; mem. Ill. Relations Com. (Speaker's Bureau of Assn. of Commerce). Mem. Ohio Soc. (Chicago), Chicago Cleric Soc., S.A.R., (chaplain Ill. Chapter). Republican. Mason (K.T., Shriner). Clubs: Union League, Executives, Kiwanis (pres. 1931), Chicago Farmers. Home: 2343 E. 70 St., Chgo. 49. Died Sept. 23, 1953; buried Willow Cemetery, Toledo.

HOWARD, Willie (Levkowitz), actor; b. Neustadt, Germany, Apr. 13, 1886; s. Leopold and Pauline (Levkowitz); brought to U.S., 1886; ed. pub. sch., N.Y. City; m. Emily Miles, Feb. 15, 1920 (died Oct. 28, 1947). Began as boy soprano at age of 12; water boy at Proctor's; sang with Anna Held in The Little Duchess; appeared in vaudeville act known as Messenger Boys Trio; with brother Eugene, played as The Howard Brothers at Winter Garden, N.Y. City; appeared in George Whites Scandals, Ziegfield Follies; starred in Sky High, Girl Crazy. Crazy with the Heat; appeared in Priorities of 1942, N.Y.C., 1942; starred in Along Fifth Avenue. Died Jan. 12, 1949.

HOWE, Arthur, educator; b. South Orange, N.J., Mar. 3, 1890; s. Solomon Henry and Mabel Rose (Almy) H.; B.A., Yale, 1912; diploma, Union Theol. Sem., N.Y., 1916; LL.D., Tuskegee (Ala.) Inst., 1932; M.A., Yale, 1940; m. Margaret Marshall Armstrong, Aug. 16, 1916; children—Alice Armstrong, Harold, II, Arthur, Richard Armstrong, Sydney. Chaplain and teacher Loomis Sch., Windsor, Conn., 1916-18; asst. headmaster and chaplain Taft Sch., Watertown, Conn., 1918-27; asst. prof. citizenship, Dartmouth Coll., 1927-30; pres. Hampton Inst., 1931-40; mng. dir. Community Chest, Orange and Maplewood, N.J, 1941-49; pres., treas. Rockywold-Deephaven Camps, Inc., since 1949. Head coach Yale football team, 1912; dir. U.S. Boys' Working Res., State Conn., 1917-18; mem. sch. bd., Holderness, N.H. since 1952. Mem. bd. trustees Golden Rule Farm Boys Home, Tilton, N.H. Mem. Psi Upsilon. Ordained Presbyn. ministry. Home: 91 Highland St., Plymouth, N.H. Office: Rockywold Camp, Ashland, N.H. Died Mar. 28, 1955.

HOWE, Burton Alonzo, oil corp. executive; born Fairport, N.Y., Jan. 16, 1886; s. Charles Henry and Ella (Dennis) H.; B.A., Colgate U., 1909; m. Elizabeth Cooley, 1910; children—Burton A. (dec.), Elizabeth C., Mortimer C. (killed in action, U.S.S. Liscome Bay. 1943), Charles H.; m. 2d, Helen Armstrong, 1935. With Kelsey Brewer & Co., Grand Rapids, Mich., 1909-12; pres. Howe, Corrigan & Co., (Howe, Snow & Co.), 1912-29; v.p., E. H. Rollins & Sons, Inc., N.Y. City, 1929-35, chmn. bd. 1935-50; pres. Belleair Oil Corp., chmn. bd., 1950-54; dir. Blair, Rollins & Co., Inc., Blair Holdings Corp., Abercrombie & Fitch Co., Walworth Co. (N.Y.C.), Willys-Overland Motors, Inc. (Toledo). Mem. Delta Kappa Epsilon. Clubs: Wall Street, Bond (N.Y.C.); Round Hill (Greenwich, Conn.); Gulf Stream Golf (Delray Beach, Fla.); Indian Creek Country (Miami Beach, Fla.). Blind Brook (Port Chester, N.Y.). Home: Lake Av. Office: 281 Greenwich Av., Greenwich, Conn. Died Feb. 12, 1957; buried Putnam Cemetery, Greenwich, Conn.

HOWE, Edmund Grant, prof. polit. sci.; b. Hartford, Conn., Nov. 22, 1883; s. Daniel Robinson and Henrietta Atwood (Collins) H.; student, Jena U., 1907, Sorbonne (Paris), 1908, Leipzig U., 1907-08; Grenoble U. (France), 1908; A.B., Yale Coll., 1906; A.M., Harvard Coll., 1907; m. Eleanor Louise White, July 28, 1914; children—Daniel Robinson, William Emerson White. Instr., Marietta Acad., 1910-12; instr. U. of Pittsburgh, 1912-17; prof. U. of Ala., 1920-38; prof. Marietta Coll. since 1938; sec., State Council Nat. Defense, Hartford, Conn., 1916-17. Served as private, U.S. Army, Hosp. 16, New Haven, Conn., sgt., sanitary corps. Mem. Am. Polit. Assn., Phi Beta Kappa (past pres. U. of Ala., Marietta Coll.). Republican. Conglist. Author: Comments on Constitution of Alabama, 1923; essays on Iceland and Andorra, Chi Omega Magazine. Pub. speaker in Ala., Marietta, O. Home: Box 436 Tuscaloosa, Ala. Office: Marietta, Box 647, O. Died Aug. 20, 1950; buried Cedar Hill Cemetery, Hartford, Conn.

HOWE, Edward Leavitt, ret. banker; b. Princeton, N.J., Apr. 6, 1870; s. Edward and Hannah Tylee (Butler) H.; ed. Princeton U.; m. Isabel Charlotte Church, Dec. 8, 1916; m. 2d, Mrs. Dorothy Iona Campbell Hurd, Mar. 1, 1937, m. 3d, Adelaide H. Foster, Feb. 25, 1944. Became Banker, Princeton, 1888, now ret.; pres. Princeton Water Co.; dir. Princeton Bldg. & Loan Assn. Trustee Dorothea van Dyke McLane Assn. Mem. Am. Bankers Assn. (finance com.; exec. council; rep. of N.J.); mem. spl. currency commn. of Am. Bankers Assn. to confer with Congress in prepartation of Fed. Res. Act; mem. N.J. Bankers Assn., since orgn. (pres. 1910-11; chmn. com. on agrl. development; hon. v.p.). Asso. gen. dir. YMCA with Italian Army, 1918-19. Decorated Italian War Cross and Cavalier Crown of Italy. Mem. Am. Whig Soc. (Princeton). Republican. Presbyn. Club: Nassau (Princeton). Home: Upland Meadow. Office: 12 Nassau St., Princeton, N.J. Died Apr. 28, 1952; buried Princeton, N.J.

HOWE, Frederic William, educator; b. Westford, Mass., Sept. 30, 1872; s. Adonijah Woodbury and Martha Dunster (Butterfield) H.; student Worcester Poly. Inst.; B.S. in Chemistry, U. of N.H., 1894; spl. student Mass. Inst. Tech.; m. Flora Folger Haynes, June 21, 1900; children—Olive Haynes (Mrs. William G. Lossone, dec.), Elizabeth (Mrs. Wm. D. Middleton); m. 2d, Mrs. Jennie Barnard Bartlett (Tufts), Apr. 2, 1910. Asst. in chemistry Govt. Expt. Sta., Durham, N.H., 1894-95; chemist D. Whiting & Sons, Boston, Jan.-Oct. 1895; asst. in chemistry Mass. Inst. Tech., 1894-98; dir. Dept. of Chemistry and Dietetics, State Normal Sch., Framingham, Mass., 1898-1921; sci. dir., and dir. Walker Gordon Lab. Co., New York and Boston, 1902-41; dir. Food Lab. of Boston Floating Hosp., 1906-21, Food Lab. Infants' Hosp., 1907-21; dir. Sch. of Houshold Science and Arts of Pratt Inst., Bklyn., 1921-38; pres. Nat. Acilophilus Milk Coöp. Assn., 1923-43; Sewing Inst., Inc., mem. corp. Garland Sch. of Homemaking, Boston; trustee Geo. H. and Irene L. Walker Meml. Home for Children, St. Peter's Episcopal Church (Ogunquit, Me.). Mem. Food Conservation Commn., State of Mass., World War. Mem. White House Conf. on Child Health and Protection. Mem. 7th Internat. Mgmt. Congress. Fellow Am. Pub. Health Assn.; mem. New York Nutrition Council, Certified Milk Producers' Assn. of America. Republican. Episcopalian. Clubs: Church (dir.), Cliff Country of Ogunquit, Me. (dir.). Author of numerous papers read before sci. socs., also article in mags. Home: Ogunquit, Me. Died Nov. 27, 1957.

HOWE, Frederick Stanley, hosp. adminstr.; b. Cambridge, Mass., Nov. 28, 1885; s. Frederick Cutler and Evelyn Rebecca (Fessenden) H.; grad. Cambridge Latin Sch., 1904; A.B., Harvard, 1908; courses Harvard Bus. Sch., Mass. Inst. Tech., Columbia; m. Eleanor Stearns Wiggin, June 24, 1915; children—John Cutler, William Wiggin, Robert Stearns, Elizabeth Fessenden (dec.). Salesman and demonstrator Barrett Mfg. Co., Boston, 1907-10; asst. sec. and publ. agt. Am. Unitarian Assn., Boston, 1901-16; pvt. sec. to Mary M. Emory, Cin., 1916-18; asso. Charles T. Howe, export bus., N.Y.C., 1918-20; asst. bus. mgr. Rockefeller Inst. Med. Research, 1920-27; dir. Orange (N.J.) Meml. Hosp., 1927-50; adminstr. The Hosp. Center at Orange (consol. Orange Meml. and N.J. Orthopedic Hosps), Jan.-Sept. 1950, adminstr. cons. since Sept. 1950. Cons. in preparation plans for hosps. in Near East and on adminstrv. problems with instns. in U.S. Vice pres. Hosp. Council, Inc., N.J., since 1931; dir. Hosp. Bur. Standards and Supplies, N.Y.C.; trustee Hosp. Service Plan of N.J. (Blue Cross—an orgn., 1933-50), Victoria Found., Inc.; mem. bd. mgrs. N.J. Hosp. Licensing Bd. since 1949. Fellow Am. Coll. Hosp. Adminstrs. (mem. bd. regents 1946-48); mem. Am. (1st v.p., 1945-46), N.J. (pres., 1940) hosp. assns., Delta Upsilon. Republican. Unitarian. Editorial cons. Modern Hospital since 1935. Author numerous articles on hosp. topics. Home: 478 Fairview Av., Orange, N.J. Died Mar. 13, 1957.

HOWE, Gene Alexander, editor, newspaper pub.; b. Atchinson, Kan., Mar. 22, 1886; s. Edgar Watson and Clara L. (Frank) H.; student high sch., Atchison, 1899-1900; m. Gale Donald, Sept. 29, 1913; 1 dau., Jeanne. Printer and newspaper reporter, Kan., Ida. and Ore., 1900-07; reporter Atchison Globe, 1908-11; became editor Amarillo (Tex.) News-Globe, 1924, later pub. and sec. and treas. Amarillo News-Globe Pub. Co.; resigned as editor, 1936, but continues as writer of column under name of "Old Tack"; dir. Avalanche-Journal Pub. Co. Re-appointed mem. Tex. State Game and Fish Commn.; trustee of Ducks Unlimited. Dir. Presbyn. Children's Home, Amarillo. Democrat. Contbr. to professional and game conservation publs. Address: 1711 Harrison, Amarillo, Tex. Died June 25, 1952.

HOWE, George, architect; b. Worcester, Mass., June 17, 1886; s. James Henry and Helen (Bradford) H.; grad. Groton (Mass.) Sch., 1904; A.B., Harvard, 1908; grad. in architecture, Ecole des Beaux Arts, Paris, 1912; m. Maritje Patterson, July 18, 1907; children—Helen, Ann. Began practice in Phila., 1913; mem. Mellor, Meigs and Howe, 1916-28; architect for Phila. Savings Fund Soc. bank bldgs., Goodhart Hall of Bryn Mawr Coll., Coast Guard World War Memorial, Arlington Cemetery, 2 monuments in France for Am. Battle Monuments Commn., residences in Phila., etc.; practiced alone in Phila., 1928-29; member Howe & Lescaze, 1929-33. Architect for Oak Lane Nursery School, Philadelphia; Hessian Hills School, Croton-on-Hudson, New York; Philadelphia Saving Fund Society Office Building; numerous residences, etc.; in independent practice, 1933-42; architect for Phila. Evening Bulletin Bldg., Children's World, New York World's Fair; architet WCAU-TV and AM Broadcasting Station; residences, etc.; supervising architect Public Buildings Administration, 1942-44; deputy commissioner for Design and Constrn., 1944-45; now practicing in Phila.; Hoppin prof. and chmn. dept. architecture Yale, 1950-54, retired Hoppin professor emeritus, 1954—. Served as 1st lt., Corps of Interpreters, U.S. Army, overseas May 1917-Aug. 1919. Fellow Am. Inst. Architects (awarded gold medal Phila. chapter, 1922, 1939); mem. Archtl. League of New York, 1925. Episcopalian. Clubs: Philadelphia, Army and Navy. Author numerous articles on modern architecture. Mem. Archtl. adv. com. of Harvard, Princeton U., Calif. Inst. Tech., Mass. Inst. Tech. Pioneer in field of modern archtl. design. Home: Rittenhouse-Claridge, Phila. 3. Died April 16, 1955; buried Mt. Auburn Cemetery, Cambridge, Mass.

HOWE, James Lewis, chemist; b. Newburyport, Mass., Aug. 4, 1859; s. Francis A. and Mary F. (Lewis) H.; A.B., Amherst, 1880; A.M., Ph.D., Göttingen, 1882; hon. M.D., Hosp. Coll. of Medicine, Louisville, 1886; Sc.D., Washington and Lee Univ., 1946; married Henrietta Leavenworth Marvine, Dec. 27, 1883 (died October 11, 1943); children—Guendolen, Frances Ray (dec.), James Lewis. Prof. chemistry, Central University, 1883-86; scientist and lecturer, Polytechnic Society of Kentucky; 1886-94; professor chemistry and head department chemistry, Washington and Lee University, 1894-1938, emeritus prof. of chemistry and university historian, since 1938; also dean of School of Applied Science, 1921-32. Chmn. bd. Peoples Nat. Bank, Lexington, Va. Chairman Finance Com., Lexington (Va.) Town Council, Fellow A.A.A.S. (sec. chem. section, 1893, secretary council, 1894, gen. sec., 1895, v.p. chem. sect., 1900); mem. Am. Chem. Soc., Va. Acad. Sci. (pres. 1924), Nat. Inst. Social Science, Soc. Chem. Industry, Washington Acad. Sciences, Deutsche Chemische Gesellschaft, Chemical Society (London); mem. special committee on platinum, National Research Council, 1917. Recipient Herty Medal for advancement of chemistry in the Southeastern states, April 1937. Life trustee of United Society Christian Endeavor; moderator of Lexington Presbytery, 1945; Commissioner to General Assembly, Presbyterian Ch. United States, 1893, 1918, 25, 34, 39, 46, 47; member of advisory council, Simplified Spelling Bd., Va. Philatelic Federation; member, Phi Beta Kappa, Omicron Delta Kappa, Delta Kappa Epsilon. Mason (Knights Templar, Shriner); past lt. governor Kiwanis. Member Rockbridge County Defense Council. Author: A Bibliography of the Metals of the Platinum Group, 1897; Inorganic Chemistry According to the Periodic Law (with Francis Preston Venable), 1898, revised as Inorganic Chemistry for Schs. and Colleges, 3d edit., 1921; Brief History of Missions, 1913; (with staff of Baker & Co., Inc. A Bibliography of the Metals of the Platinum Group, 1749-1917, 1919; A Bibliography of the Metals of the Platinum Group, 1918-30 (with addenda to edit. of 1919), 1947; A Bibliography of the Metals of the Platinum Group (1931-40), 1953, (1941-50) (in press). Numerous papers in Jour. Am. Chem. Soc., Science, Virginia Mag. of History and Biography, etc. Translator. Home: 30 University Pl., Lexington, Va. Died Dec. 20, 1955; buried Lexington, Va.

HOWE, Stanley H(art), publicist; b. Howell, Mich., May 30, 1890; s. George Franklin and Eleanora (Hart) H.; A.B., Albion (Mich.) Coll., 1911; m. Helen Gregg, Jan. 31, 1913. Spl. investigator N.Y. Assn. for Improving Condition of Poor, 1911; organizer, and sec. Pub. Charities Assn. Pa., 1912; dep. commr. Pub. Charities under Mayor Mitchell N.Y.C., 1913-17; sec. N.Y. Pub. Welfare Com., 1917; exec. dir. Nat. Budget Com., which was largely instrumental in securing budget system for U.S. Govt. Served as capt., Q.M.C., U.S. Army, World War I; after armistice was with Ednl. Corps, AEF, Beaune, France. Vice chmn. finance com. Honest Ballot Assn., Actors' Nat. Meml. Fund Com.; organizer, v.p., sec. Home Community Corp. (for building moderate-priced homes under laws of State of N.Y.). Mem. Acad. Polit. Science, Nat. Conf. Social Work, Delta Sigma Rho, Sigma Nu. Republican. Clubs: City, Lions, New York Young Republican. Winner Nat. Intercollegiate Oratorical Contest, at Johns Hopkins U., 1911. Home: Otisville, Pa. Died Mar. 30, 1955.

HOWE, Walter Bruce, lawyer; b. N.Y.C., Nov. 18, 1879; s. Walter and Mary Bruce (Robins) H.; A.B., Yale, 1901; LL.B., Harvard, 1904; m. Mary Carlisle, Jan. 16, 1912; children—Bruce, Calderon, Mary. Began practice at N.Y.C., 1905; dept. asst. dist. atty., N.Y. County, 1906-09; practiced in Washington, 1912—; asst. U.S. atty., Washington, 1913; counsel to U.S. Senate Select Commn., Haiti and Dominican Republic, 1921-22, Am. Electoral Commn., Nicaragua, 1928, Commn. of Inquiry and Conciliation, Bolivia-Paraguay, 1929; arbitrator of Harrah Claim, U.S. vs. Cuba, 1929-30. Served as capt. inf. U.S. Army, 1917-19, sec. oprations sect. Gen. Staff, G.H.Q., AEF, 1918-19. Mem. Recorder Roberts Pearl Harbor Commn., 1941-42. Mem. Assn. Bar City N.Y. Republican. Protestant. Clubs: Metropolitan, Alibi (Washington); Racquet and Tennis (N.Y.). Home: Berry Hill, Newport, R.I. Office: 1819 H St. N.W., Washington 6. Died Feb. 20, 1954.

HOWE, William Francis, army officer; b. Dorchester, Mass., Dec. 16, 1888; s. William Francis and Alice (Tusley) H.; Ph.B., Yale, 1913; m. Margaret Allen, May 21, 1921; children—William F., Elizabeth, Margaret. Apprentice wool scouring and carbonizing plant, 1913, foreman, 1915-17; bond salesman, office mgr., 1920-37; asst. dir. Commonwealth Mass. Unemployment Compensation, 1938-41. Capt. F.A., 26th Div., commdg. battery C, 102d F.A., France, 1917-19; capt., Mass. N.G., 1920, advanced to brig. gen., 1939; in Federal Service 1941—; comdg. 51st F.A. Brigade, 26th Div., 1941-42; apptd. col., detailed as comdt. Army Schs., prof. mil. sci. and tactics Yale, 1943; asst. dir. Mass. Div. of Employment Security, 1948—. Decorated Croix de Guerre, 1918. Mem. St. Anthony, Delta Psi (Yale).

Clubs: Union Boat (Boston); Weston Golf, New Haven Lawn, Yale Graduate. Home: 38 Lincoln St., New Haven. Died Nov. 9, 1952.

HOWELL, Joseph A., business exec.; b. Troy, Ala., 1901. Pres. Tobacco By-Products & Chemical Corp.; pres., dir. Virginia Carolina Chemical Corp., Richmond, Va. Home: 47 Pocahontas Av., Richmond, Va. Died Feb. 16, 1960.

HOWELLS, John Mead, architect; b. Cambridge, Mass., Aug. 14, 1868; s. William Dean and Elinor (Mead) H.; student Mass. Inst. Tech.; A.B., Harvard, 1891; diploma Ecole des Beaux Arts, Paris; m. Abby McDougall White, Dec. 21, 1907; children—William White, John Noyes Mead. In practice as John Mead Howells, N.Y.C. Architect for Panhellenic Tower and Title Guarantee and Trustee Bldg., Daily News Building, N.Y.C., Tribune Tower, Chgo.; designed and erected bldgs. for Harvard, Yale and Columbia, for banking and fiduciary corps of New York, Chgo., San Francisco, Seattle, etc. Mem. Nat. Fine Arts Commn., Washington. Sent to Belgium, 1922, by Pres. Hoover's relief orgn. as commr. to lay out plans for U. of Brussels. Decorated Legion of Honor (French); Officer Order of Crown (Belgium). Fellow A.I.A.; mem. Nat. Inst. Arts and Letters, Soc. Beaux-Arts Architects (ex-pres.), Soc. Architects Diplomes, by French Govt. (ex-pres.). Clubs: Century, Harvard. Contbr. to Harper's, Century and other mags. Home: Kittery Point, Me. Office: 580 Park Av., N.Y.C. Died Sept. 22, 1959; buried Cambridge (Mass.) Cemetery.

HOWES, Benjamin Alfred (houz), engr.; b. Keene, N.H., Aug. 4, 1875; s. Benjamin Thomas and Maria Adelaide (Holt) H.; B.S., Mass. Inst. Tech., 1897; m. Ethel D. Puffer, Aug. 5, 1908; children—Ellen Dench (Mrs. J. A. R. Pimlott), Benjamin Thomas. With Frank Sprague, Sprague Multiple Unit System, N.Y., 1897-1900; mining equipment, design and constrn., with Randfontein Estates, S. Africa, and Thomas Robins, Paris and London, 1900-03; research and constrn., sand-lime brick, 1903-05; pvt. practice, N.Y., 1905-33; spl. problems, reinforced concrete, power plants, electro-metallurgy (including microanlaysis in such investigations), coal mining, oil prodn. and transport, power and pub. utilities, sch. and camp planning and operation; staff engr. Fed. Emergency Relief Adminstrn., 1934; sr. engr., chief of Materials Intake Sect., Resettlement Adminstrn., 1934-38; sr. engr., chief specifications and materials sect. U.S. Housing Authority, 1938-42; sr. archl. engr., chief materials sect., Fed. Pub. Housing Administrn.; developed specifications for 2½ billion dollars of govt. and war housing. Mem. Am. Soc. for Testing Materials, Soc. Am. Mil. Engrs., Nat. Soc. Profl. Engrs., Assn. Fed. Architects, Soc. Mass. Inst. Tech. Author: Building by a Builder, 1914; tech. articles on concrete bldg. construction. Home: 4911 V St., N.W., Washington 7. Died Jan. 9, 1952.

HOWES, Ernest Grant, v.p., dir. Howes Leather Co., Inc., Boston; b. Chatham, Mass., Oct. 5, 1871; s. Franklin and Mercy B. (Small) H. Trustee Boston U., New England Deaconess Hosp., Good Samaritan Hosp., West Palm Beach, Fla. Mem. exec. com. Palm Beach Civic Assn. Clubs: The Country (Brookline, Mass.); Algonquin (Boston); Metropolitan (N. Y. City); Old Guard Society of Palm Beach, Seminole Golf, Bath and Tennis (pres.), Gulf Stream Golf (mem. bd. govs.), Everglades (bd. govs. (Palm Beach, Fla.). Home: Jerusalem Rd., North Cohasset, Mass. Office: 321 Summer St., Boston. Died Oct. 7, 1956; buried Forest Hills Cemetery, Jamaica Plains, Mass.

HOWEY, Walter Crawford (hou'ē), editor, inventor; b. Ft. Dodge, Ia., Jan. 16, 1882; s. Frank Harris and Rosa (Crawford) H.; ed. Ft. Dodge pub. schs.; student Chicago Art Inst., 1899-1900; m. Elizabeth Board, 1900 (died 1935); m. 2d, Gloria Ritz, Sept. 1, 1936; 1 son, William Randolph. Reporter Ft. Dodge (Ia.) Messenger, 1902, Des Moines (Ia.) Daily Capital, 1902, Chicago American, 1904; city editor Chicago Inter Ocean, 1906-07, Chicago Tribune, 1907-17; editor Chicago Herald Examiner, 1917-22, Boston American, 1922-24; founder New York Mirror, 1924; assistant to William Randolph Hearst; editor Boston Record-American, 1939; editor Chicago Herald-American, 1942; supervising editor American Weekly, New York; Hearst newspapers, Boston and Chicago; president Internat. Research Laboratory, Lee Electric Company. Inventor of sound photo wire and radio transmission, photo electric engraving system, cold light photograph system, photo electric pantagraph and high speed code transmission. Home: The Eliot, 370 Commonwealth Av., Boston. Died Mar. 21, 1954.

HOWIE, Robert George, state ofcl.; b. Chgo., Dec. 3, 1890; s. Robert Wiley and Julia (Allen) H.; student pub. schs.; m. Blanche Elinor Buhler, Nov. 4, 1913; 1 dau., Jean Marjorie (wife George Brent Vivian, U.S. Army). Comd. 1st lt. U.S. Army, 1917, advanced through grades to col., 1942; assigned Mexican Border Service, 1916; co. comdr. 33d Div., France, World War I; served U.S., P.I., China, 1927-30; asst. comdt. Armored Force Sch., 1940-43; comdr. bases South Pacific, 1943-46; comdr. Fla. Mil. Dist., 1946-50, ret., 1950; apptd. state dir. civil def. Fla. since 1950. Bd. dirs. Duval Co. chpt. A.R. C. Decorated Silver Star, Legion of Merit, Bronze Star with oak leaf cluster, Bronze Star (Navy), Purple Heart, Order Brit. Empire; recipient Freedoms Found. first honor award for best state civil def. plan. Mem. Mil. Order World Wars. Mason (Shriner). Club: Timuquana Country (Jacksonville). Inventor Howie machine gun carrier. Home: 4981 Ortega Blvd., Jacksonville 5. Office: 2585 Riverside Av., Jacksonville, Fla. Died Aug. 1, 1954; buried Arlington Nat. Cemetery.

HOWLAND, Arthur Charles, educator; b. S. Danby, N.Y., Dec. 24, 1869; s. Charls and M. A. (Basset) H.; A. B., Cornell, 1893; studied Göttingen and Leipzig, 1894-95, Cornell U., U. Pa., 1895-97; Ph.D., U. Pa., 1897, Litt.D., 1940; m. Emily W. Berry, Sept. 3, 1902; children—Charles B., Arthur L., Emily H. Tchr. English, Wyo. Sem., Kingston, Pa., 1893-94; instr. European history U. Ill., 1897-98; teaching fellow U. Pa., 1898-99; instr. history, Tchrs. Coll. Columbia, 1899-1904; asst. prof. mediaeval history U. of Pa., 1904-11, prof., 1911-34, Henry Charles Lea prof. European history, 1934-40, prof. emeritus, curator of H. C. Lea Library, 1940—, lectr. history, 1942-43. Mem. Am. Hist. Assn., Medieval Acad., Delta Phi, Phi Beta Kappa. Editor, translator: Ordeals, Compurgation, Excommunication and Interdict, 1898; The Early Germans, 1899. Editor: Mommsen's History of Rome (abridged), 1906. Joint Author: World History in the Making, 1927; World History Today, 1927; Materials Toward a History of Witchcraft, 3 vols., 1939; Minor Writing of H. C. Lea, 1942; This Our World, 1946. Club: University. Home: 9 Guernsey Rd., Swarthmore, Pa. Died Mar. 28, 1952; buried West Laurel Hill Cemetery, Phila.

HOWLAND, Fred Arthur, ins. exec.; b. Franconia, N.H., Nov. 10, 1864; s. Moses N. and Sylvia Ann (Shipman) H.; A.B., Dartmouth, 1887, LL.D., 1933; LL.D., Middlebury Coll., 1943, U. Vt., 1943; studied law with Hon. W. P. Dillingham, Waterbury, Vt.; m. Rena Forbush, Sept. 24, 1894 (dec. Oct. 24, 1894); m. 2d, Margaret Louise Dewey, Feb. 1, 1899; children—Louise Dewey (Mrs. Edwin Clark), Sylvia Ann (Mrs. Paul Sample), Susan Griggs, Emily Shipman (Mrs. William C. Mansfield). Mem. Dillingham, Huse & Howland, 1892-1903; counsel for Nat. Life Ins. Co., 1903-09, v.p. 1909-16, pres., 1916-37, chmn. bd., 1937-43; dir. Central Vt. Ry., Barre & Chelsea R.R. Co., Nat. Life Ins. Co., Union Mutual Fire Ins. Co., Montpelier Nat. Bank, Rock of Ages Corp., Green Mountain Power Co., New England Electric System. Clk. Vt. Ho. of Reps., 1895; state's atty. for Washington County, Vt., 1896-98; sec. of state, 1898-1902; chmn. com. to revise banking laws of Vt., 1910; mem. State Bd. Edn., Vt., 1920-23; emergency commr. of finance, Vt., following flood of Nov. 1927. Trustee Dartmouth Coll., 1922-32, trustee emeritus; trustee Vt. State Library, Wood Art Gallery, Montpelier; pres. Kellogg-Hubbard Library, Montpelier. Chmn. Vt. delegation Nat. Rep. Conv., 1924. Clubs: St. Bernard Fish and Game (Can.); Tobique Salmon (New Brunswick). Home: 139 State St. Office: 131 State St., Montpelier, Vt. Died Mar. 30, 1953.

HOWLAND, Garth A(hyman), educator; b. Charles City, Ia., July 25, 1887; s. William Gordan and Harriet (Morean) H.; A.B., U. N.D., 1912; student Chgo. Sch. Civics and Philanthropy, 1912-13, Sorbonne, 1919, Harvard, 1922-23; A.M., 1930; m. Sarah Elizabeth Tracy, Nov. 21, 1926; children—Armand Tracy, William Garth. Asst. prof. fine arts U. Ind., 1923-27; head dept. fine arts Lehigh U., 1927—, dir. art gallery; mem. bd. examiners Bethlehem Palette Club; paintings on permanent exhibition: Raub Jr. High Sch., Allentown, Pa.; Liberty High Sch. Gallery, Bethlehem, Pa.; Lehigh U. Permanent Collection; also pvt. collections. Mem. Am. Vet.'s Soc. Artists, Coll. Art Assn., Lehigh Art Alliance (founder 1935), Phi Beta Kappa. Methodist. Author of articles on art. Home: 1415 Wood St., Bethlehem, Pa. Died Apr. 20, 1950; buried Bethlehem, Pa.

HOWLAND, Murray Shipley, clergyman; b. Wilmington, Del., Nov. 22, 1874; s. Charles S. and Mary C. (Shipley) H.; B.A., Yale, 1897, D.D., 1922; student Auburn Theol. Sem., 1897-99; grad. Union Theol. Sem., 1900; student U. Berlin, one semester, 1898, Oxford U., 1926; m. Margaret Merrill Granger, Aug. 3, 1909; children—Murray Shipley, Margaret Granger, Katherine, John Christopher. Ordained to ministry Presbyn. Ch., 1900; asst. pastor West End Ch., N.Y.C., 1900-02; pastor South Ch., Syracuse, N.Y., 1902-12, Lafayette Av. Ch., Buffalo, 1912-29, 1st Church, Binghamton, N.Y., 1929-48. Chmn. Social Survey of Syracuse, 1911; chmn. com. of Presbyterians that issued "The Affirmation," etc.; mem. Council of Synod of New York 2 terms, 1930-36; mem. editorial council and bd. dirs. Presbyterian Tribune. With YMCA in mil. camps, fall of 1917, in France, Feb.-Oct. 1918; cited in regtl. orders; recommended for Croix de Guerre. Trustee Binghamton Pub. Library, 1937-48. Apptd. by Gov. Lehman mem. Com. of 27 on Minority Groups and National Defense, 1940, reapptd. by Gov. Dewey, 1943; chaplain, Buffalo Gen. Hosp., 1947. Mem. Phi Beta Kappa. Republican. Mason. Clubs: Torch. Home: 233 Darwin Dr., Snyder (Buffalo), N.Y. Died Mar. 17, 1953.

HOYO, John Charles, lawyer; b. Weimar, Tex., July 20, 1891; s. George P. and Emma (Schmidt) H.; LL.B., U. Tex., 1916, Princeton U., 1919; m. Katherine Haensel, June 13, 1933; 1 son, John Charles. Tchr. Oak Grove Sch., Weimar, 1910-12; quiz master U. Tex., 1916; admitted to Tex. bar, 1916; city atty., Weimar, 1916-17; county judge, Colorado County, 1920-22; county atty., Guadalupe County, 1927-30; became sr. mem. firm Hoyo, Shelton & Haight, San Antonio, 1949; dist. judge 150th Jud. Dist. Ct., Bexar County, 1957-58. Mem. Tex. Legislature, Bexar County, 1941-47. Dir. Tex. Law Rev.; chmn. Taxpayers' League San Antonio. Served as ensign USN, 1917-19. Mem. Am., Tex., San Antonio bar assns., San Antonio Sci. Soc., Am. Legion, Nat. Sojourners. Democrat. Episcopalian. Mason (32°), Shriner); K.P. Home: 5203 Blanco Rd., San Antonio; (summer) Camp Alzafar, Boerne, Tex. Office: Majestic Bldg., San Antonio 5. Died Nov. 13, 1958.

HOYT, Creig Simmons, coll. dean; b. Auburn, N. Y., Feb. 27, 1894; s. Rev. Frank and Florence (Simmons) H.; ed. Unadilla (N.Y.) Acad.; B.S., Grove City Coll., 1913; A.M., Cornell U., 1917; Ph.D., U. Pitts., 1933; Sc.D., Grove City (Pa.) Coll., 1943; m. Matilda Thompson, July 22, 1915; children—Dr. Creig, Margaret. Successively instr. to prof. chemistry Grove City Coll., head dept. chemistry 1925—, dean, 1950—; cons. field of chemistry; mem. Grove City Bd. Edn., 1933-40; mem. Am Chem. Soc., Am. Inst. Chemists, Sigma Xi, Phi Lambda Upsilon. Mason, Rotarian. Author: numerous papers in field of chemistry. Prebyterian. Republican. Home: 631 S. Center St., Grove City, Pa. Died May 9, 1957; buried Grove City, Pa.

HOYT, Elton, II, sr. partner Pickands, Mather & Co.; b. Cleveland, O., June 13, 1888; s. James Humphrey and Jessie Proctor (Taintor) H.; grad. University Sch., Cleveland, 1906; A.B., Yale, 1910; HH.D. (hon.), Western Reserve University, 1951; LL.D. (hon.), John Carroll University, 1954; m. Cornelia Brown, Jan. 3, 1914; children—Nina (Mrs. Arnold Scruton), James Humphrey, II (died Aug. 1938), Elton, III. Began as iron ore salesman with Pickands, Mather & Co., operators and sales agents for iron ore, pig iron, coal, 1911, became partner, 1922, mng. partner, 1929, sr. partner, 1940; pres., dir. Mather Iron Co.; pres. Interlake S.S. Co.; dir. Youngstown Steel Door Co., N.Y.C. R.R., Interlake Iron Corporation. Served on War Chest and Liberty Loan campaigns and was mem. exec. com. Cleveland Red Cross during World War; member Iron and Steel Industry Advisory Committee. Chairman of the Alumni Board, Yale University, 1931-34. Trustee University Hosps. of Cleve., Cleve. Community Fund, Westminster School (Conn.), Western Reserve Historical Soc. Awarded Gary Meml. Medal, Am. Iron and Steel Inst., 1955. Mem. Psi Upsilon, Scroll and Key. Republican. Presbyterian. Clubs: Tavern (ex-pres.), Midday (ex-pres.), Union, Kirtland Country (Cleveland); Links (N.Y. City); Chicago (Chicago); Duquesne (Pittsburgh). Editor of Speeches and Papers of James Humphrey Hoyt, 1922. Home: Mentor, O. Office: Union Commerce Bldg., Cleveland, O. Died Mar. 16, 1955.

HOYT, Harold Wardwell, banker; b. Stamford, Conn., April 12, 1885; s. Clasen Wardwell and Elizabeth Adelaide (Smith) H.; Ph.B., Wesleyan Univ., 1905. Asst. sec. Title Guarantee & Trust Co., New York, 1916-23, asst. v.p., 1923-24, v.p., 1924-33, v.p., and general manager, 1933-36, pres., 1936-48, vice chmn. executive committee 1949—, trustee 1933-49; director City Real Estate Co., Municipal Mortgage Co., Long Island Safe Deposit Co., Title & Realty Safe Deposit. Trustee of Wesleyan Univ. since 1937. Mem. Delta Kappa Epsilon. Club: University (New York); Greenwich country, Indian Harbor Yacht (Conn.), Racquet and Tennis (N.Y.). Office: 176 Broadway, N.Y.C. Died July 9, 1953; buried Woodland Cemetery, Stanford, Conn.

HOYT, James Alfred; b. Columbia, S.C., July 16, 1877; s. James A. and Rebecca Caroline (Webb) H.; A.B., Furman U., Greenville, S.C., 1897; m. Clare Haynsworth Kinard, Mar. 8, 1904; children—Claire Kinard (Mrs. Charles C. Gaver), James Alfred III, Margaret Louise (Mrs. Charles L. Cogswell). Reporter, The Mountaineer, Greenville, 1897-99; reporter, editorial writer and news editor, The State, Columbia, 1899-1906; Columbia corr. News and Couier, Charleston, 1906-09; editor, pub. Daily Record, Columbia, 1909-12; clk. S.C. Ho. of Reps., 1909-15; elected to S.C. Ho. of Reps., 2 terms, speaker of house both terms until resignation, 1917; organizer, pres. Peoples Nat. Bank, Columbia, 1912-17; organizer, v.p. Homestead Bank (Morris Plan), 1913-17; v.p. and gen. mgr., later pres. Industrial Morris Plan Bank, Detroit, 1917-21; v.p. First and Old Detroit Nat. Bank (later First Nat. Bank), 1921-23; pres. Continental Bank, Detroit, 1924-25; pres. Morris Plan Corp. of America, 1925-28; organizer, pres. Industrial Banking Corp. of America, N.Y.C., 1928-30; in life ins. bus., New York and elsewhere, 1931-33; asst. gen. mgr., in charge finance and accounting dept. HOLC, 1933-35; asst. to dir. RFC, 1935-38; reporter decisions and librarian U.S. Court of Claims since 1938, Lt. col. staff gov. S.C., 1899. Mem. Chi Psi.

Democrat. Mason. Club: Cosmos (Columbia, S.C.). Contbr. to newspapers and mags.; author of articles on polit., econ. and hist. topics, The Phoenix Riot. S. Carolina Jurists on the Federal Bench, Ignoring the Facts, etc. Home: 1707 Columbia Rd., N.W. Address: U.S. Court of Claims, Washington. Died Apr. 1959.

HOYT, John Sherman, mfr., scout exec.; b. N.Y. City, July 29, 1869; s. Alfred M. and Rose E. (Reese) H.; grad. St. Paul's Sch., Concord, N.H., 1886; C.E., Columbia Sch. Mines, 1890, LL.D., 1930; m. Ethel P. Stokes, 1895. Director and member of the executive board of the Am. Car & Foundry Co. One of original founders, trustee v.p., Boy Scouts of Am. Conglist. Clubs: Down Town Assn., Union League (N.Y. City). Home: Darien, Conn. Office: care Boy Scouts of America, 2 Park Av., N.Y.C. 16. Died Mar. 30, 1954.

HOYT, W(illiam) Henry, author; b. N.Y.C., Jan. 10, 1884; s. Frederick Alphonsus and Florence Sarah (Murphey) H.; A.B., Fordham U., 1902; A.M., U. Vt., 1906; LL.B., Harvard, 1910. Admitted to bar, 1910, and since in practice N.Y.C., with Hawkins, Delafield & Longfellow. Mem. Lambda Iota (U. Vt.), Am. Hist. Assn., So. Soc. N.Y. Club: Harvard. Author: The Mecklenburg Declaration of Independence, 1907; The Murphey Papers: Being the correspondence and writings of Archibald Debow Murphey of North Carolina (1777-1832), 1914. Contbr. to The Biographical History of North Carolina, Vol. 4, 1906. Home: 52 Wall St., N.Y.C. 5. Died Sept. 6, 1957.

HSU, Mo (hsü), internat. judge; b. Soochow, China, Oct. 22, 1893; s. Hsiao-shih and Lan-ling H.; LL.D., Peiyang U., Tientsin, China, 1917; M.A., George Washington U., 1921; LL.D., Melbourne U., Australia; m. Hsu Chaoming, Aug. 3, 1916. Served in Chinese Embassy, Washington, 1920-22; attached to Chinese del., Wahhington Conf., 1921-22; prof. law and polit. silence, Nankai Univ., Tientsin, 1922-26; editor, Social Welfare, Tientsin, 1925; judge, later presiding judge, criminal chamber of Provisional Court, Shanghai, 1927; pres. Dist. Court, Chinkiang, 1927-28; successively served as counselor, chief, Internat. Affairs Dept.; chief, European-Am. Dept. and Asiatic Dept., Ministry Fgn. Affairs, 1928-31; special commr. fgn. affairs, Shanghai; vice minister, fgn. affairs, 1931-41; now dean, Sch. of Diplomacy, Central Polit. Inst.; minister to Australia, 1941-45; ambassador to Turkey, 1945-46; judge Internat. Court of Justice, UN, 1945-46; judge Internat. Ct. of Justice, The Hague, Netherlands, 1946. Home: Nanking, China. Address: International Ct. of Justice, The Hague, Holland. Died June 28,

HUBBARD, Charles J., explorer; b. Kansas City, Mo., June 25, 1902; s. Charles J. and Alice (Davis) H.; A.B. cum laude, Harvard, 1924, S.B. magna cum laude, 1925; m. Anna Fuller, 1925; 1 son, Charles J.; m. 2d, Dorothy Speare, 1934; m. 3d, Harriet Bissell, Jan. 18, 1943; children—Aries B., Hamal, Dana. Engr. Stone & Webster, Inc., 1925-28; v.p. George B. H. Macomber Co., Boston, 1929-31; made aerial surveys with N. Labrador Expn. of Forbes and Grenfel, 1931-35; freelance exploration and journalism, 1935-40; now chief Arctic Sect. U.S. Weather Bur., mng. U.S. interests in network internat. Arctic sci. stas. Served as lt. comdr. USNR, 1941-42; lt. col. USAAF, 1942-—. Condr. surveys and airfield construction in Greenland, N. Labrador, Hudson Bay area, etc., in development of northern airways through Greenland and eastern Canadian arctic for U.S. Army Air Transport Command; established first Arctic weather sta. network by airplane. Recipient medal, U.S. Dept. Agr., 1950. Mem. Am. Geographical Soc. Geophys. Inst. Clubs: Explorers, Cruising Club of America, Delphic, Varsity (Harvard). Contbr. articles and fiction to numerous popular mags. Navigator, aviator, comml. license. Office: Arctic Section, U.S. Weather Bureau, Washington. Killed in air crash at Alert, Ellesmere Island, July 31, 1950; buried Alert Ellesmere Island, N.W.T., Can.

HUBBARD, Charles Wells, mfr.; b. Newton, Mass., 1856; s. Charles Townsend and Elisabeth Blair (Wells) H.; A.B., Harvard, 1878; m. Anne L. Swann, June 3, 1889. Trustee of Ludlow Mfg. Associates (treas. 1887-1912); trustee Franklin Savings Bank of the City of Boston. Mem. corp. Mass. Inst. Tech. Republican. Unitarian. Clubs: Union, Country. Addres: Auburndale, Mass. Died May 27, 1933.

HUBBARD, Frederick A., former pres. Hanover Fire Ins. Co., 111 John St., N.Y.C. Died July 1956.*

HUBBARD, George David, geologist and geographer; b. Tolono, Champaign County, Ill., May 12, 1871; s. Linus Green and Helen Lorena (Stanard) H.; B.S., University of Illinois, 1896, M.S., 1898; A.M., Harvard, 1901; Ph.D., Cornell University, 1905; m. Edna Almira Rugg, Sept. 10, 1901; children—Ruth Marilla, Oscar Edwin, Dorothy Hope (dec.), Marjorie Helen. Fellow in science and acad. teacher of physics, University of Illinois, 1896-97; asst. in geology, same, 1897-1900; professor geography, Eastern Illinois State Normal School, 1901-03; instructor physiography, Cornell U., 1903-05; temp. asst. U.S. Geol. Survey, 1903-05; asst. prof. geology, Ohio State U., 1905-10; acting prof. geology, Oberlin Coll., 1910-12, prof., 1912-17, prof. geology and geography, 1917-36, emeritus, 1936-—; prof. geology and geography, Harvard Univ., summer, 1937, Berea (Ky.) College, 1941; visiting prof. geography, Univ. of Missouri, 1942-44 and 1946-48. Assistant geologist Ohio Geol. Survey, 1906-26; geologist S.D. Geol. Survey, summer 1945, 49. Fellow A.A.A.S., Geol. Soc. Am., Am. Geog. Soc., Assn. Am. Geographers, American Soc. Professional Geographers; member Academy Polit. Science, International Council of Religious Education. Ohio Acad. Sci. (pres. 1917), Sigma Xi. Republican. Conglist. Joint Author: Ednl. Bulletin (Ohio Geol. Survey), 1912; Columbus Folio (U.S. Geol. Survey), 1914. Author: Geography of Europe (Textbook), 1937; Geographical Influence of Gold and Silver Mining on United States, 1912. Contbr. about 100 papers on geol., geog. and ednl. subjects, also lecturer. Consulting practice. Home: 279 Oak St., Oberlin, O. Died June 11, 1958; buried in Oberlin.

HUBBARD, Giles Munro, public relations; born Camillus, N.Y., Mar. 30, 1887; s. Giles Humiston and Emma (Morse) H.; A.B., Colgate U., 1909; m. Elizabeth Gates, Sept. 26, 1913; children—Mrs. Jane H. Knox (dec.), John Merrill Hubbard. With Howe, Snow & Bertles, investment securities, Grand Rapids, Mich., 1912-19; v.p. J. G. White & Co., Inc., investment banking, N.Y. City, 1919-33; dir. The J. G. White Engring. Corp., chmn. bd., 1932-37; pres., dir. Doremus & Co., advt., N.Y. City, 1933-42; head of own public relations firm since 1942; director Gen. Reinsurance Corp., North Star Reinsurance Corp. President Community Chest, Pelham, N.Y., 1932-34. Mem. Phi Beta Kappa, Delta Kappa Epsilon. Republican. Baptist. Clubs: Bond (pres. 1931-32), University, Anglers, Downtown Assn. Home: 550 Park Av. Office: 120 Broadway, N.Y.C. 5. Died Dec. 30, 1953.

HUBBARD, John Charles, physicist; b. Boulder, Colo., Apr. 16, 1879; s. James Edwin and Rhoda Maude (Duke) H.; B.S., U. of Colo., 1901; Ph.D., Clark Univ., 1904; LL.D., Loyola Coll., Baltimore, 1938; m. Gertrude L. Pardieck, Feb. 9, 1929. Instr. in physics, at Simmons Coll., Boston, 1904 05; asst. prof. physics, New York U., 1905-06, Clark U., 1906-11; prof. physics Clark Coll., 1911-16; prof. and head of physics dept., N.Y. Univ., 1916-27; prof. same, Johns Hopkins Univ., 1927-46; physicist, Radiation Lab., Johns Hopkins Univ., 1946-47; research prof. physics, Catholic U. of Am., 1947-—. Dir. summer work in physics, New York Univ., 1906, U. of Colo., 1912, 14; research engr., Western Electric Co., summer, 1917. Commd. capt. Signal Corps, U.S.R., Div. Research and Insp., Sept. 29, 1917; active service in France, information sect. Office of Chief Signal Officer, A.E.F.; official historian, Signal Corps, A.E. F.; maj., Oct. 4, 1918; discharged, May 20, 1919. Awarded Mendal medal, Villanova College, 1946. Officier d'Académie Instruction Publique, 1919. Fellow A.A.A.S., Am. Acad. Arts and Sciences, Am. Physical Soc.; mem. Beta Theta Pi, Phi Beta Kappa, Sigma Xi; rep. of Am. Inst. of Physics on Am. Engring. Standards Com.; mem. at large Div. of Physical Sciences of Nat. Research Council, 1931-33; sec. member National Defense Research Committee. Clubs: Johns Hopkins (Baltimore); Andiron (New York). Author various papers giving results of original physical research. Asso. editor Physical Rev., 1933-35. Roman Catholic. Address: 4304 13th Place N.E., Washington. Died Aug. 2, 1954; buried Richmond, Ind.

HUBBARD, Nathaniel Mead, Jr., assn. exec.; b. Marion, Ia., Feb. 14, 1860; s. Nathaniel Mead and Katherine Wood (Hervey) H.; grad. U.S. Naval Acad., 1882; student Columbia La Sch., 1885-86; m. Alice Cooper (sculptor), 1905 (died 1937); children—Thanette (Mrs. Donald Joseph Hebert), Sarah Katherine (Mrs. Barnette I. Napier, Jr.), Natalys. Admitted to Ia. bar, 1886; asst. atty. for Ia. of C. & N.W. Ry., 1887-1906; v.p., gen. counsel Royal Union Mutual Life Ins. Co., Des Moines, 1906-27; retired from active law practice in 1927; since 1908 has operated a cattle ranch in western Colo. Served with USN 1882-84 (resigned 1884); reentered Navy in 1898 as ensign, promoted to lt. (j.g.); resgined 1899. Dir. Navy League of the U.S., 1922-—, v.p., 1932, pres., 1933, 36-—. Mem. U.S. Naval Inst., U.S. Naval Hist. Soc., Loyal Legion (by inheritance), Naval Order of Spanish-Am. War. Republican. Mason Club: Army and Navy (Washington). Contbg. editor to Sea Power. Home: Army and Navy Club. Office: Navy League of the U.S., Mills Bldg., Washington. Deceased.

HUBBARD, Walton, Christian Science lecturer; b. Manitowoc, Wis.; s. Harvey Fitzland and Anne Halsted (Warbasse) H.; student Rose Poly. Inst., Terre Haute, Ind., 1 yr.; M.D., Chicago Homœ. Med. Coll., 1901; C.S.B., Mass. Metaphys. Coll., 1913; m. Doris M. Long. Practiced medicine at Buckley, Wash., and Manitowoc, Wis., 1901-10; surgeon Tacoma Eastern Ry., 1901-03; Christian Science practitioner, 1910-16, lecturer, 1916-26 and 1937-40; practitioner and teacher, 1926-37, 1940-47, and since 1950; lectr., 1916-26, 1937-40, 1948-50. Mem. Sigma Nu, Phi Alpha Gamma. Mason. Home: 920 Moraga Dr. Office: 1146 Glendon Av., Westwood Village, Los Angeles. Died Nov., 1954.

HUBBART, Ralph (DeGolyer), business exec.; b. San Francisco, Feb. 28, 1881; s. Joseph and Kate (DeGolyer) H.; ed. pub. schs., Evanston, Ill.; m. Belle Sheridan Houston, Feb. 2, 1905; children—Mattiebelle (Mrs. A. R. Carman, Jr.), Charlotte (Mrs. Peter Fortune). Vice pres. John Burnham & Co., Chicago, 1910-32, Brailsford & Co., Chicago, 1938-39; pres. Allied Products Corp., Detroit, 1939-52, chairman of the board of directors since 1952, dir. since 1928; dir. The Detroit Bank, Vinco Corp., Zenith Radio Corp. Clubs: Detroit, Detroit Athletic. Home: The Whittier, 415 Burns Dr., Detroit 14. Office: 12677 Burt Rd., Detroit 23. Died Oct. 18, 1956; buried Meml. Park, Evanston, Ill.

HUBBELL, Clarence W., civil engr.; b. Cole County, Mo., Apr. 10, 1870; s. John James and Sarah Maria (Huntington) H.; B.S. in Civil Engring., U. Mich., 1893, C.E., 1904; m. Winifred Temperance Waters, Dec. 31, 1895; children—Theodore H., Mrs. Albert Huntington, Roger S., George E., Harriet W. Junior engr. on railroad location and constrn., 1887-93; chief draughtsman Detroit Water Works Dept., 1893-98, engr. in charge, 1898-1907; prin. asst. engr. water supply of Manila, P.I., 1907-09, city engr., Manila, 1909-10; chief engr. pub. works, P.I., 1910-13; cons. engr. Pub. Utilities Commn., P.I., 1913-14; returned to Detroit, 1915; cons. engr. on Detroit pollution, internat. boundary waters, 1915-16; city engr., Detroit, 1917-22; mem. engring. firm Hubbell, Roth & Clark, pres. 1915-47; mem. bd. cons. engrs. Detroit Sewage Collection and Treatment Project, 1925-37; cons. engr. Wayne County Sewage Treatment plant, 1937-40. Served as engr. on design and reconstruction of sewer system of Detroit, 1916-22, involving outlay of about $40,000,000; bd. engring. rev. San. Dist. Chgo., 1924-25; member Rapid Transit Commn., Detroit, 1925-40; mem. Bd. Review Sewage Treatment, Toronto, Ont., 1939. Mem. Am. Soc. C.E., Am. Assn. Engrs., Am., N.E. water works assns., Mich. (pres.), Detroit engring. socs. Recipient Norman medal, Am. Soc. C.E., 1902. Republican. Conglist. Mason (Shriner). Home: Hill Hollow, Milford, Mich. Office: Buhl Bldg., Detroit. Died Feb. 1, 1950; buried Benzonia, Mich.

HUBBELL, Frederick Windsor, pres. Equitable Life Ins. Co. of Ia.; b. Des Moines, Ia., Nov. 24, 1891, s. Frederick Cooper and Mary (Windsor) H.; A.B., Harvard, 1913; m. Helen L. Clark, June 19, 1915; children—Frederick Windsor (deceased), Helen Ann. Asst. treas. Equitable Life Ins. Co. of Ia., Des Moines, 1913, successively treas., v.p. and pres. since 1939. Served as capt. F.A., U.S. Army, 1918. Home: Route No. 6. Office: Equitable Bldg., Des Moines, Ia. Died Mar. 14, 1959.

HUBBELL, Grover Cooper, real estate; b. Des Moines, Ia., Feb. 3, 1883; s. Frederick Marion and Frances (Cooper) H.; student Culver (Ind.) Mil. Acad., 1898-1900, Lawrenceville (N.J.) Sch., 1900-02; Ph.B., Sheffield Scientific Sch. (Yale), 1905; m. Anna R. Godfrey, Sept. 27, 1905; children—Frances Cooper (Mrs. Hepburn Ingham), Helen Virginia (Mrs. Richard Barshell), Mary Belle (Mrs. James Windsor). In real estate business since 1905; v.p. F. M. Hubbell Son & Co. since 1920; v.p. Penrod Jurden Clark Co., Equitable Life Ins. Co. of Ia.; dir. Ia. Power & Light Co. Mem. bd. trustees Drake Univ. Clubs: Wakonda, Des Moines. Home: Terrace Hill, Des Moines. Office: Hubbell Bldg., Des Moines, Ia. Died Dec. 9, 1956.

HUBBELL, Raymond, composer; b. Urbana, O., June 1, 1879; s. Horace M. and Kate (Stone) H.; ed. pub. schs.; m. Estelle M. Persch, Aug. 15, 1912. Began as composer, 1898. Club: Lambs. Composer: Fantana; Knight for a Day; Poor Butterfly (song); Midnight Sons; Mexicano; The Kiss Burglar; The Runaways, 1903; The Jolly Bachelors, 1910; Yours Truly, 1927; also music scores for Ziegfeld Follies, 1911-17, 1923, 24; scores for New York Hippodrome, Hip Hip Hooray, 1915; The Girl From Cook's, 1927, The Big Show, Cheer Up, Happy Days, Good Times, Better Times; Three Cheers (for Will Rogers), 1929-30. Died Dec. 13, 1954.

HUBBERT, James Monroe, clergyman; b. Cassville, Mo., June 15, 1850; s. William and Nancy Ann H.; A.B., B.D., Cumberland U., Tenn., 1876; grad. Union Theol. Sem., N.Y.C., 1879; m. Minnie L. Brewster, Jan. 16, 1882. Ordained Cumberland Presbyn. ministry, 1875; pastor Lincoln, Ill., 1879-87, First Ch., Nashville, 1888-93, Lebanon, Tenn., and dean Cumberland Theol. Sch., 1894-1901, Marshall, Mo., and prof. homiletics, Mo. Valley Coll., 1902-06; stated clerk, Gen. Assembly Cumberland Presbyn. Ch., 1896-1906; asst. stated clerk, Gen. Assembly Presbyn. Ch. in U.S.A., 1907-21. Moderator Gen. Assembly Cumberland Presbyn. Ch., Kansas City, 1889; del. Pan-Presbyn. Councils, Belfast, Ireland, 1884, Washington, 1899, Liverpool, Eng., 1904. Address: Witherspoon Bldg., Phila. Died Oct. 6, 1934; buried Lincoln, Ill.

HUBBLE, Edwin Powell (hŭb'b'l), astronomer; b. Marshfield, Mo., Nov. 20, 1889; s. John Powell and Virginia Lee (James) H.; B.Sc., U. of Chicago, 1910, Ph.D., 1917; Rhodes scholar from Ill. at Oxford U., Eng., 1910-13, B.A. in Jurisprudence, 1912; honorary D.Sc., Oxford, 1934, Princeton, 1936, Brussels, 1937; LL.D., Occidental, 1936; U. of Calif., 1949; m. Grace Burke, Feb. 26, 1924. Admitted to Ky. bar, 1913; research work, Yerkes Obs., Univ. of Chicago, 1914-17; astronomer on staff Mt. Wilson Obs., Pasadena, Calif., since 1919; chmn. research com., Mt. Wilson and Palomar Observatories; Hitchcock Lecturer, Univ. of Calif., 1948; Silliman lecturer, Yale University, 1935; Rhodes Memorial lecturer, Oxford Univ., 1936. Student 1st O.T.C., Fort Sheridan, Ill., 1917; capt. inf., Aug. 1917; maj., Dec. 1917; comdr. 2 Batt., 343d Inf., 86th Div., U.S. Army, Sept. 1917-Nov. 1918; with A.E.F., Sept. 1918-Aug. 1919; hon. disch. at Presidio, San Francisco, Aug. 1919. Chief ballistician and dir. of Supersonic Wind Tunnels Lab., Ballistic Research Lab., U.S. War Dept., 1942-46. Awarded Medal for Merit, 1946. Fellow Royal Astronomical Soc., Eng.; mem. Astron. Soc., Astron. Soc. of Pacific, Nat. Academy Sciences, 1927, Am. Philos. Soc., 1929; Sigma Xi, Kappa Sigma. Awarded Barnard medal for scientific service, 1935; Bruce medal, 1938, Franklin medal, 1939. Royal Astronomical Soc. medal, 1940; hon. fellow, Queen's Coll., Oxford, 1948; membre de l'Institut, Academie de France. Trustee Huntington Library and Art Gallery. Clubs: Athenaeum, Sunset, Author: The Realm of Nebulae, 1936; The Observational Approach to Cosmology, 1937; The Nature of Science. Home: 1340 Woodstock Rd., San Marino, Cal. Office: Mt. Wilson Observatory, Pasadena 4, Cal. Died Sept. 28, 1953.

HUBER, Harvey Evert, educator; b. Bluffton, O., Mar. 19, 1884; s. Jacob Daniel and Nancy (Rayl) H.; B.S., Ohio Northern U., 1908, B.A., 1909; M.A., Yale, 1912; post-grad. work same univ. and U. of Wis.; m. Ida May Cotner, Aug. 6, 1913; 1 son, Max Nevin. Teacher in rural schs., 1902-05; teacher sci. high sch., Glenwood Springs, Colo., 1909-11; prof. biology, Ohio Northern U., 1913-18; field plant pathologist, Bur. of Plant Industry, U.S. Dept. Agr., 1918; prof. biology, Bluffton (O.) Coll., 1918-19; prof. biology and dir. premedical students, Ohio No. U., since 1919; dean Coll. of Liberal Arts 1920-52, dir. natural sci. div., head dept. biol., 1952—. also acting registrar, 1943-47. Mem. High School-College Relationship com. of Ohio Coll. Assn. 1941-50; nursing school committeeman, Memorial Hosp., Lima, O., since 1946. Faculty representative of the Armed Forces for Ohio No. U. during World War II. Former member School Bd., Ada, O. Fellow A.A.A.S., Ohio Acad. Science; mem. Am. Phytopathol. Soc., Ohio State Grange, Am. Genetic Assn., Sigma Phi Epsilon, Kappa Psi, Alpha Phi Gamma. Mem. Disciples of Christ Ch. Mason (32°, K.T.). Club: Torch. Home: 724 S. Union St., Ada, O. Died Apr. 21, 1953; buried Woodlawn Cemetery, Ada, O.

HUBER, Max, lawyer; ed. univs., Lausanne, Zurich and Berlin, D.C.L., Oxford U.; LL.D., Edinburgh; D.Phil., Geneva; D.D., D.Med., Zurich. Prof. constl. and internat. law, U. Zurich, 1902-21, later hon. prof.; served as judge, Permanent Court of Internat. Justice, 1921, pres. 1925-28, vice pres., 1928-30; pres. Internat. Red Cross Com., 1928-44. Author several books published in German, English and French. Address: 85 Muhlebachstrasse, Zurich, Switzerland. Died Jan. 1, 1960.

HUBER, Phil, business exec. Pres. and dir. Ex-Cello Corp. Address: 1200 Oakman Blvd., Detroit 6. Died Feb. 7, 1952.

HUBER, Ray Allen, newspaper pub.; b. Doylestown, O., Feb. 8, 1883; s. Nick and Carrie Ellen (Seidel) H.; student Buchtel Coll., Akron, 1900-01; m. Irene M. Vogt, Nov. 10, 1919. With Scripps-Howard Newspapers, 1901—; advt. solicitor Akron Press, 1901-04, advt. mgr., 1904-07, business mgr., 1907-21; business mgr. Cleveland Press, 1921-27; pres. Scripps-Howard Newspapers of Ohio, 1927-29; asst. gen. business mgr. Scripps-Howard Newspapers, 1929-31; pub. and v.p. New York World Telegram, 1931-38; exec. business dir. Scripps-Howard Newspapers, 1938-39, gen. bus. mgr. 1939, 49, mem. exec. com., 1949—; v.p. El Paso Herald-Post Pub. Co.; dir. Mem. exec. com. Scripps-Howard Supply Co.; dir. Allied Newspapers, E. W. Scripps Co., Scripps-Howard Investment Co. Clubs: Everglades (Palm Beach, Fla.); Blind Brook Country (Portchester, N.Y.). Home: 1056 Fifth Av., N.Y.C. 28. Office: 230 Park Av., N.Y.C. Died Feb. 3, 1958; buried Ferncliff, Hartsdale, N.Y.

HUBERT, Benjamin Franklin, coll. pres.; b. Mayfield, Ga., Dec. 25, 1884; s. Zack and Camilla (Hillman) H.; A.B., Morehouse Coll., Atlanta, 1909, A.M., 1928; B.S.A., Mass. State Coll., Amherst, 1912; grad. student U. Wis., 1913; LL.D., Allen U., Columbia, S.C., 1928; M.S., U. Minn.; grad. student Harvard, 1930-31, U. Minn., 1922-28, 37-38. Dir. agr. and agrl. extension service, S.C. State Coll., 1912-19; dir. agr. and supr. agrl. instrn. for State of Ala., 1920-26; pres. Ga. State Coll. since 1926; corr. Asso. Press. Founder of Log Cabin Community Country Life Center, Hancock County, Ga.; exec. dir. Assn. for Advancement of Negro Country Life; dir. pub. relations and chmn. nominating com. Savannah Negro Girl Scouts; chmn. Soldiers Social Service of Savannah. Supr. agrl. instrn. Negro Troops Army Ednl. Corps, France, 1919. Mem. Am. Teachers Assn., Am. Country Life Assn., So. Sociol. Soc., Am. Farm Econ. Assn., Ga. State Coll. Coop. Assn., Phi Beta Sigma; mem. Commn. on Interracial Cooperation. Baptist. Home: Georgia State College, Industrial College, Ga. Died Apr. 29, 1958.*

HUBSCHMAN, Albert, lawyer; b. N.Y.C., Sept. 12, 1899; s. Samuel and Martha (Greenfield) H.; student N.Y.U., 1919-21; student eve. sch. Emerson Inst., 1920-24; LL.B., George Washington U., 1928; m. Sarah Ann Turfler, Oct. 18, 1923; children—Ruth Elizabeth, George Harvey. Accountant Suffern & Compers Co., 1922-23; auditor U.S. Bur. Internal Revenue, 1923-29; admitted to D.C. bar, 1928, N.Y., 1935; pvt. practice law, 1929—; sec., dir. Realty & Indsl. Corp., Convent, N.J., 1935-53; pres. Roller-Smith Co., 1943-53, Elpeco Div. Roller-Smith Corp., Bethlehem, Pa., 1951-53; pres. Mann Homes; dir. Western Que. Mines, Ltd., Toronto, Snowshoe Mines, Ltd. Mem. Am. Bar Assn. Mason. Club: Democratic. Home: 470 E. Lincoln Av., Mt. Vernon, N.Y. Office: 70 Pine St., N.Y.C. Died Jan. 8, 1956; buried Mt. Pleasant Cemetery, Val Halla, N.Y.

HUDDLE, J(erome) Klahr; b. Bettsville, O., Mar. 25, 1891; s. Elvin Klahr and Emily Lora (Newcomer) H.; student Heidelberg U., Tiffin, O., 3 yrs., George Washington U.; m. Carolena Heiby, Apr. 5, 1921; 1 dau., Carolyn Lora (Mrs. Charles G. Wells, Jr.). High sch. prin., newspaper and comml. work, Ohio, until 1915; entered consular service, Apr. 19, 1915; attached to Am. Commn. to Negotiate Peace, Paris, 1918-19; with Am. Consulate Gen., Paris, 1919-20; with Am. Commn. to Germany, 1920; consul on spl. assignment, Warsaw, 1921; consul at Hamburg, Germany, 1921-23; spl. detail, Dept. of State, 1923-25; chief of Passport Div., 1925-27; consul at Cologne, Germany, 1927-30; consul gen. at Warsaw, Poland, 1930-35; became insp. Am. foreign service, 1935; assigned to Dept. of State, 1937; counselor of Legation, Bern, Switzerland, 1941; spl. detail, Dept. of State, 1946; 1st U.S. ambassador to Burma, Nov. 10, 1947; U.S. rep. UN Commn. for India and Pakistan (Jammu-Kashmir Dispute), 1948, also remaining ambassador to Burma, resigned both offices, 1950. Mem. Ref. Church in U.S. Mason. Home: 3434 Ashley Terrace, Washington 8. Died Mar. 16, 1959; buried Cedar Hill Cemetery, Suitland, Md.

HUDDLESTON, George, ex-congressman; b. Wilson County, Tenn., Nov. 11, 1869; s. Joseph Franklin and Nancy (Sherrill) H.; ed. pub. schs.; studied law, Cumberland U., Lebanon, Tenn.; m. Bertha L. Baxley, 1917; children—Mary, George, John, Jane, Nancy. Admitted to Ala. bar, 1891; practiced, Birmingham, 1891-1912 (retired); mem. 64th to 74th Congresses (1915-37), 9th Ala. Dist. Pvt. 1st Regt. Ala., Spanish-Am. War; 1st comdr. Ala. Vets. of Spanish-Am. War, 1899-1900. Democrat. Methodist. Grand Master of Odd Fellows for Ala., 1915. Home: Birmingham, Ala. Died Feb. 29, 1960.

HUDGINS, Edward Wren, judge; b. Buckingham County, Va., Jan. 17, 1882; s. Robert Henry and Lucy J. (Wren) H.; B.A., Richmond Coll., 1905, LL.B., 1908; Doctor of Laws, University of Richmond, 1948; married Lucy Morton, Mar. 16, 1910; children—Edward Morton, William Henry. Began practice at Chase City, Va., 1908; mem. McNeill, Hudgins & Ozlin, 1910-16, Hudgins & Ozlin, 1916-26; mem. Va. Ho. of Delegates, 1916-20; judge 34th Jud. Circuit, Va., 1926-30; justice Supreme Court of Appeals of Virginia, 1930-47, chief justice, since 1947; director Peoples Bank & Trust Company, Chase City. Chmn. Jud. Council for Va.; pres. Jud. Conf. of Va.; chmn. Conf. of Chief Justices (48 states), 1950-51. Y.M.C.A. sec. overseas, June 1918-Mar. 1919. Mem. Dem. Nat. Conv., 1924. Formerly pres. Va. Baptist Bd. of Missions and Edn.; mem. bd. trustees U. of Richmond, Fork Union Mil. Acad.; mem. Va. Hist. Soc. Mem. Va. and Am. bar assns, Sigma Phi Epsilon, Phi Beta Kappa, Phi Alpha Delta. Democrat. Baptist. Mason, Odd Fellow. Clubs: Commonwealth (Richmond); Mecklenburg Country (Chase City, Va.). Home: Chase City, Va. Office: Supreme Court of Appeals, Richmond, Va. Deceased.

HUDSON, Claude Silbert, chemist; b. Atlanta, Ga., Jan. 26, 1881; s. William James and Maude Celestia (Wilson) H.; B.S., Princeton, 1901, M.S., 1902, Ph.D., 1907; D.Sc. (hon.), 1947. Research asst. in phys. chemistry, Mass. Inst. Tech., 1903-04; instr. physics, Princeton, 1904-05; same, U. of Ill., 1905-07; assistant physicist, United States Geological Survey, 1907-08; assistant chemist, Bureau of Chemistry, United States Department Agriculture, and later chief of Carbohydrate Laboratory, 1908-19; chemist Bureau of Standards, United States Department Commerce, 1923-28; professor chemistry, U.S.P.H.S., 1928-51; mem. exec. com., editor Advance in Carbohydrate Chemistry. Councillor Internat. Union of Chemistry, 1930. Mem. Am. Com. on Organic Chem. Nomenclature, 1912. Mem. Am. Chem. Soc. (Nichols medal, 1916; Gibbs medal, 1929; Hillebrand prize, 1930; Richards medal, 1940; Borden award, 1941; chmn. organic div. of same soc. 1933), Nat. Acad. Sciences, German Acad. Natural Scientists (Halle), Acad. of Medicine (Washington, D.C.). Asso. editor: Journal of Am. Chem. Soc., 1938. Author: Collected Papers of C. S. Hudson, 2 volumes, 1946, 1948. Recipient Cresson medal, Franklin Institute, 1942. Recipient of $10,000 Grand Prize by Sugar Research Found., Inc., 1950, First Fed. Security Agency Distinguished Service Award, 1950, Distinguished Service medal, U.S.P.H.S., 1951. Died Dec. 27, 1952; buried Presbyn. Cemetery, Princeton, N.J.

HUDSON, Grant Martin, ex-congressman; b. Eaton Twp., Lorain County, O., July 23, 1868; s. Richard Martin and Mary (Still) H.; B.A., Kalamazoo Coll., 1894; m. Mildred Duncan Gilchrist, Oct. 4, 1894; (died May 13, 1921); children—Helen M., Richard G., Ruth M., Duncan G., Grant M., Winthrop S.; m. 2d, Mrs. Mary Edith Bloomer, June 28, 1930. Merce. business, 1896-1909; mem. State Industrial Accident Compensation Commn., 1920-21; mem. 68th to 71st Congresses, 6th Mich. Dist. Mem. Mich. Ho. of Reps., 1905-08. State supt. Mich. Anti-Saloon League, 1910-20; led forces that organized and carried Mich. "dry" by 68,000 majority, 1916; state mgr. Occidental Life Ins. Co. of Los Angeles. Field rep. State Tax Commn., 1939-42. Pres. Am. Bapt. Home Mission Soc., N.Y.; mem. exec. bd. No. Bapt. Conv.; pres. Mich. Bapt. Conv. Trustee Kalamazoo (Mich.) Coll., Storer Coll., Harpers Ferry, W.Va. Republican. Mason (K.T.), Odd Fellow, Rotarian. Home: Lansing, Mich. Died Oct. 26, 1955.*

HUDSON, Jay William, professor of philosophy, author, lecturer; b. Cleveland, O., Mar. 12, 1874; s. William Ingersoll and Emma (Pratt) H.; student Hiram Coll., 1893-95; Oberlin College, 1895; A.B., University of California, 1905; A.M., 1906; A.M., Harvard, 1907, Ph.D., 1908; m. May Bernard Small, August 11, 1909 (died 1915); m. 2d, Germaine Sansot, April 14, 1918. Assistant in philosophy, Univ. of California, 1904-06, Harvard, 1907-08; asst. prof. philosophy, U. of Missouri, 1908-11, asso. prof., 1912-13, prof., 1913-44, John Hiram Lathrop prof., 1930-44, prof. emeritus since 1944; lecturer, Insts. of Internat. Understanding for Rotary Internat., 1944-45; prof. Washington U., St. Louis, summer 1945; visiting professor, U. of Kansas City, 2d semester and summer, 1945-46; vis. prof., Stephens Coll., 1945-51, sabbatical year of philos. research in Europe, 1930-31. Dir. education department Massachusetts Peace Soc.; spl. lecturer American Sch. Peace League, 1914-15; prof. philosophy, George Peabody Coll. for Teachers, various summer quarters; speaker for Nat. Com. on Pub. Information and Mo. Council of Defense, 1917-18; commd. capt., Am. Red Cross in France, 1918. Mem. Nat. advisory bd., World Court League; mem. Nat. Com. on Food for the Small Democracies, Nat. Com. Friends of Democracy; mem. Am. Philos. Assn. (chmn. board of officers, 1939), Western Philos. Assn. (pres. 1939), Mo. Academy of Science, Am. Assn. Univ. Profs., Phi Mu Alpha, Phi Kappa Phi, Alpha Pi Zeta, Phi Beta Kappa (pres. Alpha of Mo. chapter, 1940; mem. 20th Triennial Council, united chapters, San Francisco, 1940). Mason (grand orator, grand Lodge of Mo., 1929, 44, 45). Clubs: Faculty, Rotary. Author: The Treatment of Personality by Locke, Berkeley and Hume, 1911; America's International Ideals, 1915; The College and the New America, 1920; The Truths We Live By, 1921; Abbé Pierre, 1922; Nowhere Else in the World, 1923; The Eternal Circle, 1925; Abbé Pierre's People, 1928 (awarded prize as best novel of 1928 by Catholic Press Assn.); Morning in Gascony, 1935; Why Democracy?, 1936; The Old Faiths Perish, 1939; Prayers of Aspiration, 1950; Life and Logic, 1950. Co-author: Religious Liberals Reply, 1947. Contbr. to philos. jours. Home: 216 Edgewood Av., Columbia, Mo. Died May 11, 1958; buried Columbia.

HUDSON, Millard Fillmore, naval med. officer; b. Madisonville, Tenn., Dec. 17, 1889; s. Millard Fillmore and Esther Ann (Magill) H.; Pharm. D., Univ. of Va., 1910; M.D., Vanderbilt Univ., 1917; m. Ollie Mae Sanford, March 6, 1918 (dec. Oct. 9, 1944); m. 2d, Helen O'Rourke, Feb. 19, 1946. Interne, U.S. Naval Hosp., Norfolk, Va., 1917; commd. lt. (j.g.), 1917, and advanced through grades to capt. 1941; specialized in internal medicine pres., med. examining bd., U.S. Navy, since 1947; mem. U.S. Navy Retiring Bd., also U.S. Navy Marine Corps Retiring Bd. Awarded various mil. decorations and commendation medals from Navy and Army, World Wars I and II. Diplomate Am. Bd. Internal Medicine. Mem. A.M.A., Kappa Psi. Democrat. Presbyterian. Home: 2480-16th St., N.W. Office: U.S. Naval Retiring Board, Washington 25. Died Mar. 29, 1951.

HUDSON, Richard Bradshaw, coll. dean.; b. Crawfordsville, Ind., Oct. 19, 1914; s. Cecil Paden and Louise (Morris) H.; A.B., Wabash Coll., 1936; A.M., U. So. Cal., 1938; postgrad. study Ind. U., 1938-39; Ph.D., Yale, 1945; m. Frances Elizabeth Martin, Sept. 3, 1939; children—Richard Bradshaw, David Michael, Daniel Benjamin. Teaching fellow in English, U. So. Cal., 1937-38; instr. English, Yale, 1942-43; teaching asst. to asst. prof. Ind. U., 1939-

53, dir. Writer's Conf., 1950-51, sch. letters, 1951-53; dean of coll., prof. English, Coe Coll., Cedar Rapids, Ia, 1953—. Served as lt., Naval Air Tng. Command, USNR, 1943-46. Mem. Modern Lang. Assn. Am., Phi Beta Kappa, Beta Theta Pi. Episcopalian. Clubs: Executives, Country (Cedar Rapids). Contbd. articles and revs. to mags. and learned jours. Home: 1570 Third Av. S.E., Cedar Rapids, Ia. Died Mar. 2, 1957.

HUDSON, Richard Furman, Jr., newspaper pub.; b. Montgomery, Ala., Feb. 11, 1916; s. Richard Furman and Lucile (Adams) H.; B.S., Ga .Sch. Tech., 1936; m. Anita Van de Voort, Feb. 7, 1939; 1 son, Richard Furman III. Reporter Montgomery Advertiser, 1936-38, editorial writer, asst. editor, 1938-41; asst. pub. The Advertiser-Jour., Montgomery, 1946-56, pub., 1956—; v.p., pub. The Advertiser Co. Served with USNR, 1941-45; comdr. res. Mem. Am. Soc. Newspaper Editors, Sigma Delta Chi. Episcopalian. Home: 3312 Bankhead Av. Office: Lawrence St., Montgomery, Ala. Died Sept. 1959.

HUGHES, Adella Prentiss, assn. exec.; b. Cleve., Nov. 29, 1869; d. Loren and Ellen (Rouse) Prentiss; A.B., Vassar, 1890; m. Felix Hughes, Oct. 5, 1904 (marriage dissolved). Organizer Cleveland Orchestra and its mgr., 1918-33; now v.p. and sec. Musical Arts Assn. Mem. Vassar Alumnae Assn., Phi Beta Kappa. Decorated, 1920, with Order of General Haller's Swords (Poland). Republican. Baptist. Club: Women's City. Author: Music is My Life (autobiography), 1947. Home: 2400 Kenilworth Rd., Cleveland Heights, O. Office: 11001 Euclid Av., Cleve. Died Aug. 23, 1950.

HUGHES, Charles Frank, editor; b. New York, N.Y., May 18, 1891; s. Charles Joseph and Louise (Travers) H.; student Coll. of St. Francis Xavier, 1908-11; A.B., Fordham U., 1912; m. Kathleen Sanders, Sept. 20, 1919. Edited The Xavier at Coll. of St. Francis Xavier, 1911; reporter New York Evening Sun, 1911, Daily Trade Record, 1912, New York Times, 1913-22; business editor, New York World, 1922-27; business news editor, New York Times, since 1927, also writer of The Merchant's Point of View, a Sunday column on business in New York Times. Served as lt. of inf., U.S. Army, 1917-18. Mem. The Silurians. Ind. Democrat. Author column N.B. Note Book for Nation's Business, 1944-50. Home: Shorefront Park, South Norwalk, Conn. Address: New York Times, N.Y.C. Died Dec. 24, 1951; buried Calvary Cemetery, Queens, N.Y.C.

HUGHES, Everett S., ret. army officer; b. S.D., Oct. 21, 1885; B.S., U.S. Mil. Acad., 1908; grad. Ordnance Sch. Tech., 1912, Sch. of the Line, 1922, Gen. Staff Sch., 1923, Army War Coll., 1928. Commd. 2d lt. F.A., 1908; 1st lt. Ordnance Dept., 1911; capt. F.A., 1916; major, Ordnance Dept., 1917, advanced through grades to maj. gen., 1943; became chief Equipment Div., Office of Ordnance, 1940; chief ordnance officer S.O.S.E.T.O., 1942, chief of staff, 1942; dep. chief of staff E.T.O., 1942; dep. theater comdr. N.A.T.O.U.S.A., 1943; spl asst. to theater comdr. E.T.O., 1944, inspector gen., 1945, chief of Ordnance, 1946; retired 1949. Decorated Comdr. Legion of Honor (France); Legion of Merit, D.S.M., Bronze Star (U.S.); Comdr. Nichan Iftikhas; Comdr. Order of Crown of Palm; Commander de l'Ordre de la Couroune avec Palm (France); Croix de Guerre (Russia). Address: The Westchester, Washington. 1940 avec Palm (France); Order of Fatherland Class Died Sept. 5, 1957; buried Arlington (Va.) Cemetery.

HUGHES, Gerald, lawyer; b. Richmond. Mo., July 8. 1875; s. Charles James (late U.S. senator) and Lucy (Menefee) H.; A.B., Yale, 1897; LL.B., Denver U., Law Dept., 1899; m. Mabel Y. Nagel, Apr. 3, 1908. Practiced law with father, 1899, until his death, 1911; then asso. with C. C. Dorsey, in firm of Hughes & Dorsey; chmn. bd. dirs. 1st Nat. Bank (Denver), Denver & Salt Lake Ry. Co.; also officer or dir. many other cos. Trustee Phipps Sanatorium. State senator, Colo., 1901-05. Democrat. Clubs: Denver, University, Country, Polo (Denver); Chevy Chase (Washington). Home: 1919 Alameda Av. Office: International Trust Bldg., Denver, Colo. Deceased.

HUGHES, Harold L(incoln), ret. v.p. U.S. Steel Corp.; b. Saugus, Mass., Nov. 2, 1879; s. James Riley and Laura Geraldine (Mansfield) H.; B.S. summa cum laude, Harvard, 1900; m. Jane Plunkett, Feb. 9, 1903 (died June 27, 1930); 1 dau., Mary Caroline. With U.S. Steel Corp. or its subsidiaries, 1901-50, beginning as draftsman Carnegie Steel Co., Pitts., 1901-03, in New York, 1903-05, Montreal, Can., 1905-07, Sydney, Australia, 1907-12, New York, 1913—; v.p. U.S. Steel Corp., 1937-50, ret. Treas. and dir. Am. Iron and Steel Inst. Republican. Clubs: Metropolitan, Harvard, India House (N.Y.C.); Duquesne (Pitts.). Home: Savoy-Plaza, N.Y.C. Died June 4, 1955.

HUGHES, Helen Sard, educator, writer; b. Chgo., July 9, 1882; d. John Bonner and Margart L. (Sard) Hughes; Ph.B., Ed.B., U. Chgo., 1910, A.M., 1911, Ph.D., 1917. Began career as teacher, 1903; dean grad. students Wellesley Coll., 1925-46, now prof. emeritus English literature. Author: The Gentle Hertford, 1940; (with R. L. Lovett and H. S. Hughes) The History of the Novel in England, 1932. Address: 10 Lovewell Rd., Wellesley, Mass. Deceased.

HUGHES, Hermann James, counselor A.R.C.; b. Balt., May 20, 1886; s. James Dixon and Teresa (Klatte) H.; A.B., Johns Hopkins ,1908; student U. of Munich, 1908-09; LL.B., Harvard, 1912; m. Janet Herron, Apr. 6, 1922; children—Cynthia H. Pyle, Jane Espy, Patricia Andrews, Penelope Davis. Practiced law in Balt., 1912-18; with A.R.C., Washington, since 1918, now counselor. Clubs: Baltimore Country, Harvard, Maryland (Balt.). Home: Glyndon, Baltimore County, Md. Office: Am. Red Cross, 17th and E Sts., Washington. Died July 22, 1953.

HUGHES, James H., ex-senator; b. Kent County, Del., Jan. 14, 1867; s. Eben and Rebecca Hurd; student Wilmington Conf. Acad., Dover, Del.; m. Caroline Taylor, Aug. 23, 1905; children—Caroline (Mrs. John P. Martin), Mary Adelaide (Mrs. W. Oakman Hay), James H. Admitted to Del. bar, 1890, practiced in Dover, 60 yrs.; sec. of state, State of Del., 1896-1901; U.S. senator from Del., 1937-43; dir. Farmers Bank of Del. Mem. Am., Del., Kent County bar assns., S.A.R. Democrat. Mason. Home: 46 S. State St., Dover, Del. Died Aug. 29, 1953; buried Lakeside Cemetery, Dover.

HUGHES, John H., army officer, ret.; b. N.Y.C., Feb. 4, 1876; s. Bernard and Catherine H.; grad. U.S. Mil. Acad., 1897; distinguished grad. Sch. of the Line, 1920; grad. Gen. Staff Sch., 1921. Commd. add. 2d lt. inf. U.S. Army, 1897, and advanced through grads to, maj. gen., 1936; retired 1940. Served in Cuba, Spanish-Am. War (wounded in action), Philippine Insurrection, in France, World War. Decorated D.S.M., Silver Star, Purple Heart. Mem. N.Y. Soc. Officers World War. Catholic. Clubs: Army and Navy, Army Navy Country (Washington); Army and Navy (Manila). Home: 1025 Connecticut Av. N.W., Washington. Died Aug. 1952.

HUGHES, Percy, univ. prof.; b. Peshawur, British India, Jan. 23, 1872; s. Thomas Patrick and Eliza (Lloyd) H.; Christ's Hosp., London, 1881-87; Diploma Teachers Coll. (Columbia), 1897; A.B., Alfred U., 1899; A.M., Ph.D., Columbia, 1904; m. Maude Williams, 1913; children (adopted)—Alfred Lloyd, Elizabeth Evelyn. Teacher in secondary schs., 1896-1901; instr. in philosophy, Alfred Univ., 1898-99; asst. in philosophy, Columbia, 1903-05; instr. in psychology and philosophy, U. of Minn., 1905-06; acting prof. philosophy and dir. extension courses, Tulane U., 1906-07; asst. prof. philosophy and edn., 1907-09, prof., 1909-21, prof. philosophy and psychology, dir. extension courses and summer sch., 1920-23, Lehigh U., 1921-31, Clara H. Stewardson prof. philosophy, 1931-42, prof. emeritus since Sept. 1942. Contbg. editor, Warren Jour., Belvidere, 1944. Fellow A.A.A.S.; mem. Am. Philos. Soc., Am. Assn. Univ. Profs., Am. Psychol. Assn., Sigma Xi. Presbyn. Author: The Concept Action in History and in Nat. Sciences, 1905; Introduction to Psychology, 1926. Home: Belvidere, N.J. Died Apr. 22, 1952.

HUGHES, Ray Osgood, educational author; b. Saxtons River, Vt., Nov. 13, 1879; s. Thomas Henry and Jennie Clara (Osgood) H.; grad. Vt. Acad., Saxtons River, 1896; A.B., Brown U., 1900; A.M., U. of Pittsburgh, 1924; L.H.D., Brown, 1941; m. Helene W. Hopkins, June 26, 1906. Instr., Williston Sem., Easthampton, Mass., 1900-01, Leland and Gray Sem., Townshend, Vt., 1901-02, Wellesley (Mass.) Boys' Sch., 1902-03, Keystone Acad., Factoryville, Pa., 1903-06, Westbrook Sem., Portland, Me., 1906-07, high sch., West Chester, Pa., 1907-11, 5th Av. High Sch., Pittsburgh, Pa., 1911-13; with Peabody High Sch., same city, 1913-29, vice-prin., 1926-29; dept. of curriculum study, Pittsburgh pub. schs., 1929-39, dir. of citizenship and social studies 1939-1945; instr. summer sessions Grad. Sch. of Edn., Harvard, 1926-30. Mem. A.A.A.S., Nat. Edn. Assn., Am. Hist. Assn., Am. Polit. Science Assn., Nat. Council for Social Studies (v.p. 1926-27, 34, 35; pres. 1936), Nat. Assn. Secondary Sch. Prins., Phi Delta Kappa. Baptist. Club: Unity. Author: Community Civics, 1917; Economic Civics, 1921; Elementary Community Civics, 1922; Problems of American Democracy, 1922; Textbook in Citizenship, 1923; New Community Civics, 1924; The Making of Our United States, 1927; American Citizenship Charts, 1929; Fundamentals of Economics, 1929; Workbook in Civics, 1930; Workbook in American History, 1931; Building Citizenship, 1933; The Making of Today's World, 1935; Workbook in World History, 1936; Building Citizenship Workbook, 1937; Good Citizenship, 1940; Today's Problems, 1942; Pennsylvania, Past and Present, 1944; Workbook for Today's Problems, 1948; Eastern Lands, 1954; Western Lands, 1954. Teachers' manuals to accompany various texts. Moderator, Junior Town Meetings, WWSW, 1944-47. Home: 5517 Beverly Pl., Pitts. Died Apr. 10, 1959.

HUGHES, Raymond Mollyneaux, coll. pres.; b. Atlantic, Ia., Jan. 14, 1873; s. Melancthon and Emily (Mollyneaux) H.; A.B., Miami U., 1893, LL.D., 1927; fellow in chemistry Ohio State U., 1895-97, M.Sc., 1897; Mass. Inst. Tech., 1897-98; LL.D., Coe College, 1928, Iowa State Coll., 1936; m. Ella Brainerd Rogers, July 11, 1901 (dec.); children—Thomas Rogers (dec.), Emily Mollyneaux (Mrs. Joseph C. Boyce); m. 2d, Helen Idsardi Richardson, 1938. Sci. tchr. Hamilton (O.) High School, 1893-95; prof. physics and chemistry Miami U., 1898-1904, chemistry, 1904-13, dean Coll. of Liberal Arts, 1908-11, acting pres., July 1, 1911, pres., 1913-27; pres. Ia. State Coll., 1927-36, now emeritus. Ednl. dir. S.A.T.C., Dist. 6, 1918. Sec.-treas. Assn. Am. Colls., 1918-21; sec. Commn. on Higher Edn. North Central Assn. of Colleges and Secondary Schs., 1923-26; sec. Am. Council on Edn., 1924-27, chmn., 1932-33; sec. Nat. Assn. State Univs., 1926-27; dir. Presbyn. Theol. Sem., 1939-42, mem. special com. on Board of Pensions of Presbyn. Ch., 1940-41. Mem. Delta Kappa Epsilon, Phi Beta Kappa. Republican. Presbyn. Author: A Manual for College Trustees, 1943; (with W. H. Lancelot) Education, America's Magic, 1946; A Study of American Graduate Schools Conferring the Doctorate, 1946. Home: Memorial Union, Ames, Ia. Died Sept. 22, 1958.

HUGHES, Robert M(orton), Jr., lawyer; b. Norfolk, Va., Apr. 24, 1880; s. Robert Morton and Martha L. (Smith) H.; A.B., William and Mary Coll., 1899, B.Litt., 1900; LL.B., U. Va., 1902; m. Caroline Wright Kennedy, Apr. 23, 1927; children—Robert Morton, Caroline Wright. Licensed atty., admitted to Va. bar, 1902, since practiced in Norfolk; sr. mem. Hughes, Little & Seawell since 1937; spl. asst. to Atty. Gen. U.S., acting as hearing officer for conscientious objectors to mil. service since 1942. Chmn. Citizens Trial Bd. to investigate charges against police anf fire divs. City of Norfolk, 1944; mem. Hampton Rds. Sanitation Dist. Commn. since 1945. Mem. Am., Va. State, Norfolk, Portsmouth (pres.) bar assns., Maritime Law Assn., Phi Beta Kappa, Kappa Alpha, Phi Delta Phi. Episcopalian (registrar). Clubs: Princess Anne Country, Va. Beach, Virginia, Civitan (past pres.), Townsmen's Soc. (past pres.) (Norfolk, Va.). Home: 418 Colonial Av., Norfolk 7. Office: 936 Wainwright Bldg., Bute and Duke sts., Norfolk 7, Va. Died Oct. 4, 1951.

HUGHES, Rowland Roberts, govt. ofcl.; b. Oakhurst, N.J., Mar. 28, 1896; s. Richard Roberts and Annie (Van Note) Hughes; Ph.B., Brown University, 1917, LL.D., (honorary), 1955; married to Dorothy Cowen, Dec. 4, 1918; children—Joy (Mrs. A. W. Zibart), Richard R., Barbara Anne (Mrs. D. Mihailoff), Mary Elisabeth (Mrs. W. N. Hall). Student of the College Training Class, National City Bank of New York, 1916, entered fgn. service branches at London, 1916-17, Shanghai, 1917-22, Bombay, 1922-26, Japan, 1926-27, returned to head office, 1927, served as insp. fgn. brs. in Europe, 1928-29, asst. comptroller, 1929-34, comptroller, 1934-51, vice president 1951-53; deputy director of the Bureau of the Budget, Washington, 1953-54, dir. 1954-56. Trustee Brown U. Mem. Associate Alumni Brown U., Beta Theta Pi. Mem. Com. Fed. Tax Policy (Tax Program for a Solvent America, published 1945, supplement published, 1947). Club: University. Address: 344 Via Hidalgo, San Rafael, Cal. Died Apr. 2, 1957.

HUGHES, Rupert, author; b. Lancaster, Mo., Jan. 31, 1872; s. Felix Turner and Jean Amelia (Summerlin) H.; brother of Felix Hughes; A.B., Adelbert Coll. (now Western Reserve Univ.), 1892, A.M., 1894; A.M., Yale U., 1899; Litt.D., Western Reserve U., 1936; m. 3d, Elizabeth Patterson Dial, Dec. 31, 1924 (died Mar. 23, 1945). Asst. editor Godey's Mag., Current Lit. and The Criterion; in London, May 1901-Nov. 1902, New York till 1905, with Ency. Britannica Co. Mem. Phi Beta Kappa, Delta Upsilon. Served pvt. to capt. N.G.N.Y., 1897-1908; capt., Mexican border service, 1916; asst. to adjutant general, N.Y., 1917; capt. Inf., Jan. 7, 1918; maj. Sept. 4, 1918; hon. disch. Jan 15, 1919; maj, Reserve Corps, Apr. 3, 1919; lieut. col., Mar. 10, 1928; active in formation of California State Guard, 1940; colonel commanding 2d Regiment, July 1, 1941, resigned Jan. 1943. Decorated with Order of Polonia Restituta (Polish), 1923. Author: The Lakerim Athletic Club, 1898; American Composers, 1900; Gyges Ring (verse), 1901; The Whirlwind, 1902; Live Affairs of Great Musicians, 1903; Zal, 1905; Miss 318, 1911; The Old Nest, 1912; What Will People Say?, 1914; Music Lovers' Cyclopedia, 1914; Empty Pockets, 1915; Clipped Wings, 1916; The Thirteenth Commandment, 1916; In a Little Town, 1917; We Can't Have Everything, 1917; Unpardonable Sin, 1919; Long Ever Ago (Irish stories), 1919; Cup of Fury, 1919; Fairy Detective (for children), 1919; What's the World Coming To?, 1920; Beauty, 1921; Momma, 1921; Souls for Sale, 1922; Within These Walls, 1923; Golden Ladder, 1924; Destiny, 1925; The Old Home Town, 1926; We Live but Once, 1927; The Patent Leather Kid, 1927; The Lovely Ducklings, 1928; Mermaid and Centaur, 1929; Ladies' Man, 1930; No One Man, 1931; Static, 1932; The Uphill Road, 1933; Love Song, 1934; The Man Without a Home, 1935; Stately Timber, 1939; City of Angels, 1941; Gyges' Ring and Other Verse, 1949; The Complete Detective, The Giant Wakes, 1950; The Triumphant Clay, 1951; The War of the Mayan King, 1952; other publs. include (biography) George Washington, 1926, 27, 30; Attorney for the People, the Story of Thomas E. Dewey, 1940; (plays) Alexander the Great (toured

U.S. 1903-04); All for a Girl (produced 1908); The Bridge (produced 1909, later revived as The Man Between); The Transformation (prod. 1909, later revised as Two Women); Excuse Me (prod. 1911; 4 cos. toured U.S., 1911-12, 2 cos. 1912-14, prod. in Australia, 1913, London, 1915); Uncle Zeb (prod. 1913); The Cat Bird (prod. 1910); (dramatizations) Tess of the Storm Country (prod. 1911); vaudeville sketches, including "Miss 318," 1912-14. Composed A Riley Album, "Cain," and other songs. Has written and directed many motion pictures; radio commentator, author, many radio sketches. Home: 204 N. Rossmore Av., Los Angeles 4. Died Sept. 9, 1956; buried Forest Lawn Meml. Park, Glendale, Cal.

HUGHES, William Leonard (hūz), educator; b. Edgar, Neb., Jan. 30, 1895; s. James Thomas and Amy (Wells) H.; A.B., Neb. Wesleyan U., 1919; M.A., Tchrs. Coll. Columbia, 1924, Ph.D., 1932; Sc.D., Boston U., 1949, Springfield (Mass.) Coll., 1956; m. Mary Elizabeth Cave, June 16, 1921; children—William, James; 1 adopted son, William M. Dir. phys. edn. Beatrice (Neb.) High Sch., 1919-23; asst. prof., coach Oberlin Coll., 1924-25; dir. health, phys. edn., athletics, and coach DePauw U., 1925-30; asso. Tchrs. Coll. Columbia, 1930-32, asso. prof. phys. edn., 1932-37, prof. phys. edn., 1937-45, acting chmn. dept., 1942-44; prof., dir. health and phys. edn. Temple U., 1945—. Chmn. nat. adv. bd., div. phys. fitness Office Civil Def., 1941-42; cons. div. phys. fitness Office of Edn., Fed. Security Agy., 1943; cons. research div. N.Y. Dept. Edn., 1944-47, Bd. Edn. Phila. Schs., Postwar Bldg. Program, 1944-45; mem. nat. com. and council U.S. Div. Phys. Fitness, 1943-45, cons. program for phys. tng. and athletics USAF Acad., 1955. Dir. Nat. Conf. Undergrad. Profl. Preparation in Health Edn., Phys. Edn. and Recreation, 1948, also moderator Nat. Conf. Grad. Study in Phys. Edn., 1948. Mem. Nat. Joint Com. on Phys. Fitness of Fed. Security Agy. and A.M.A., 1944-45; mem. nat. edn. com. Social Hygiene Assn.; mem. recreation com. Youth div. Community Councils N.Y.C. Mem. Bd. Edn., Leonia, N.J., 1941-45, Abington, Pa., 1949-51; mem. Abington Twp. Sch. Bldg. Authority, 1951-53. Mem. nat. council on health and phys. edn. YMCA. Served as 1st lt. inf. U.S. Army, World War I. Fellow Am. Assn. Health Phys. Edn. and Recreation (nat. bd. dirs. 1940-47, 52-55, pres. 1944-46), Am. Pub. Health Assn.; mem. N.E.A. Am. Assn. U. Profs., Am. Acad. Phys. Edn., Coll. Phys. Edn. Assn. (pres. 1934), Am. Recreation Soc., Am. Social Hygiene Assn., Am. Coll. Sports Medicine (treas. 1954-56), Phi Delta Kappa. Author: Administration of Health and Physical Education in Colleges, 1935, (with J. F. Williams) Athletics in Education, 1930, Sports—Their Organization and Administration, 1944; (with G. Killinger) Football, 1939; (with C. Murphy) Basketball, 1939; (with D. Jesse) Baseball, 1939; (with R. Conger) Track and Field, 1939; (with C. L. Brownell and J. F. Williams) Health Problems and How to Solve Them, 1942, Being Alive—Human Structure and Function, 1942, Youth Faces Maturity, 1942; (with Esther French) Administration of Physical Education, 1954. Editor, collaborator: The Book of Major Sports, 1939. Home: Homestead Lane, Horsham, Pa. Died Feb. 20, 1957; buried Whitemarsh Meml. Cemetery, Prospectville, Pa.

HUGO, Albert Carl, stock broker; b. Bklyn., Jan. 5, 1896; s. Albert Carl H.; student pub. schs. Bklyn.; m. Edith Kenwood, 1922. Began as runner A. M. Kidder Co., 1912; partner A. M. Kidder & Co., mems. N.Y. Stock Exchange, N.Y.C., 1927—. Mem. N.Y. Cotton Exchange, N.Y. Produce Exchange, N.Y. Coffee and Sugar Exchange, N.Y. Cocoa Exchange, Chgo. Merc. Exchange. Mason. Clubs: Country, Cherry Valley (Garden City, N.Y.); Atlantic Beach (L.I., N.Y.). Home: 109 Kilburn Rd., Garden City, N.Y. Office: 1 Wall St., N.Y.C. 5. Died June 25, 1957; buried Evergreen Cemetery, Bklyn.

HUGUELET, Guy Alexander, business exec.; b. Charleston, S.C., Jan. 1, 1891; s. George Arthur and Mamie (Melchers) H.; LL.B., U. of Ky., 1914; m. Mary Lovell Whitney, June 30, 1917 (dec.); children—Mary Whitney (Mrs. John B. Eversole III), Jacqueline (Mrs. Douglas S. Bradley); m. 2d, Angeline McCormick, Apr. 18, 1929; 1 son, Guy Alexander. With Southern Railway System, 1906-12; admitted to bar, 1914, practiced law Lexington, Ky., now of counsel law firm Stoll, Keenon & Park, Lexington; became organizer, gen. atty. and sec., Southeastern Greyhound Lines, 1926, president, chief exec. officer, 1928-54, chmn. bd., 1954—; pres. v.p., dir., of various subsidiary and affiliate motor carriers, which serve Ky., Tenn., Ala., Ga., Fla., Ohio, Ind., W.Va.; pres., dir. Keeneland Assn., Lexington; dir. First Nat. Bank & Trust Co., Lafayette Hotel Co., Lexington, and various other cos. Dir. Athletic Assn., chmn. exec. com., v. chmn. bd. trustees U. Ky., dir. Ky. Research Found.; dir. Ky. Tax Research Assn. Mem. U. Ky. Alumni Assn. (exec. com.), Am. Ky., Fayette County bar assns., Newcomen Soc., John Bradford Soc., Henry Clay Meml. Found. (life), Filson Club (Louisville), Ky. Hist. Soc., Huguenot Ch. Council (life), Sigma Nu. Ind. Episcopalian. Clubs: Lexington, Idle Hour Country, Lexington Country (Lexington); Pendennis (Louisville); Ponte Vedra (Fla.); Am. Yachtsmens Assn. (Washington); Thoroughbred of Am. Contbr. articles on motor bus transportation to various mags. Home: 220 Barrow Rd. Office: Short St. at Esplanade Lexington 6, Ky. Died July 23, 1955.

HUHNER, Leon (hû'nĕr), lawyer, historian and poet; b. Berlin, Germany, Sept. 18, 1871; brought to U.S., 1875; s. Edward and Minna (Jakmuss) H.; B.A., Coll. City of N.Y., 1890; A.M., Columbia, 1893, LL.B., 1893. Practiced law in N.Y.C., 1895—, specializes in surrogate's law. Mem. N.Y. County Lawyers' Assn. (chmn. Memorial com.), Am.. Hist. Assn., Am. Jewish Hist. Soc. (curator). Poetry Soc. Am., Phi Beta Kappa Alumni Assn., N.A. Relief Soc. (pres.), Phi Beta Kappa. Independent Democrat. Author: Judah Touro, a biography, 1946; (brochures or articles) Francis Salvador, Patriot of the Revolutionary War; The Jews of Georgia and of South Carolina in Colonial Times; Naturalization in New York Under the Act of 1740; Isaac de Pinto; The Struggle for Religious Liberty in North Carolina; The Jews of Ireland (London, 1908); David L. Yulee, Florida's First Senator; also numerous articles on early American, colonial and revolutionary history. Many of his poems have been included in several anthologies. Contributor in prose and verse to periodicals. During World War I, contbd. patriotic verse, particularly The Call to Arms and The Knitters; mem. Legal Advisory Bd.; official speaker in war work drives; mem. Mayor's Com. Nat. Defense, N.Y.C., At request of Mark Twain Assn., wrote sonnet on Centenary of Mark Twain, which was read at Hall of Fame at celebration of Centenary, Nov. 1935. Home: 140 W. 71st St. Office: 291 Broadway, N.Y.C. Died 1957.

HUIZINGA, Arnold van C(outhen) P(iccardt), theologian; b. Groningen, Netherlands, Sept. 10, 1876; s. Willem Jans and Trientje (Wieringa) H.; grad. Govt. Tng. Coll., 1894; B.S., Groningen U., 1896; came to U.S., 1900; B.D., Yale Div. Sch., 1904; Ph.D., Princeton, 1905; m. Faith Trumbull Mathewson, 1909; 1 dau., Faith T. Kelley. Prof. French, State U. Ia., 1905-06; prof. German, Trinity Coll., Conn., 1906-08; pastor Congl. Ch., Thompson, Conn., 1908-09; lit. work, traveling and lecturing 1909—, frequently appearing (unofficially) as spokesman for the Dutch in Am.; Dutch editor Govtl. Information Service, 1918-21. Pres. New Netherlands Assn. (N.Y.C.); mem. Netherland Abroad, etc.; counsellor of Netherland Emigration League; founder Science and Art Protective Soc. Author: Belief in a Personal God, 1910; American Philosophy Critically Considered in Relation to Present Day Theology, 1911; Authority of Might and Right, 1911; Authority—Its Function in Life, 1911; Theological Essays, 1917; Dutch Contributions to and Influence on America, 1924; Church and State, 1926; France, the Land of the Rights of Man; Calvinistic view of the State, 1933. Club: Princeton (N.Y.C.). Home: Thompson, Conn. Died Sept. 3, 1953.

HULBERT, Geroge Murray, judge, ex-congressman; b. Rochester, N.Y., May 14, 1881; s. Moses H. and Anna (Murray) H.; LL.B., N.Y. Law Sch., N.Y.C., 1902; m. Regina R. McNenney, June 6, 1906; 1 dau., Regina (Mrs. Joseph C. Kenney). Admitted to N.Y. bar, 1902, practiced in N.Y.C., 1902-34; apptd. judge U.S. Dist. Ct. for So. Dist. N.Y., June 6, 1934; mem. 64th and 65th Congresses, 21st N.Y. Dist.; resigned Jan. 1, 1918, to become corr. Dept. of Docks and dir. Port of City of N.Y.; elected pres. Board of Aldermen (vice mayor), N.Y.C., 1922-25; pres. Boston, Cape Code & New York Canal Co. Mem. Am. Bar Assn., Bar City New York, S.A.R. (v.p. gen. 1943-44; pres. Empire State Soc. 1944—); pres. Amateur Athletic Union, U.S. 1924-28; mem. exec. council Internat. Amateur Athletic Fedn. Trustee Elks Nat. Found., Alfred E. Smith Found. Grand Exalted Ruler, Elks, 1928-29. Democrat. Catholic. Club: New York Athletic. Home: 838 West End Av. Office: U.S. Court House, N.Y.C. Died Apr. 26, 1950; buried Gate of Heaven Cemetery, Hawthorn, N.Y.

HULEN, John Augustus, ry. ofcl.; b. Centralia, Mo., Sept. 9, 1871; s. Harvey and Fanny (Morter) H.; grad. Marmaduke Mil. Acad., Sweet Springs, Mo., 1891; m. Frankie L. Race, Feb. 14, 1893. In real estate and ins. business, Gainesville, Tex., 1891-98; city passenger agt. Frisco Lines, Houston, 1907-08, later gen agt. R.I.-Frisco Lines; apptd. gen. freight and passenger agt. Trinity & Brazos Valley R.R. Co., 1910, pres. and receiver, 1919, also pres. Galveston Terminal Ry. Co.; apptd. traffic mgr. Ft. Worth & Denver City and Wichita Valley ry. cos., 1920, v.p. of both, 1930-42; ret. Oct. 1, 1941; also retired as pres. Burlington, Rock Island R.R.; Co., Houston, Belt and Terminal Ry. Co., v.p. Union Terminal Co. Dallas, Ft. Worth & Denver Terminal Ry. Co. Dir. Ft. Worth Nat. Bank, Second Nat. Bank of Houston. Commd. lt. Tex. N.G., 1889, advanced to lt. gen. ret. 1935; served Philippine Insurrection, 1899-1901, comd. 6th Separate Brigade, Tex. border; served as brig. gen. U.S. Army, AEF, 1918-19 Awarded silver star "for gallentry in action," Philippine Insurrection; D.S.M. (U.S.); Croix de Guerre (France); recommended for Medal of Honor and twice for brevet maj. Mason (32°, Shriner), K.P. Clubs: Ft. Worth, River Crest Country (Ft. Worth). Home: Palacios, Tex. Died Sept. 13, 1957.*

HULEN, Rubey Mosley (hū'lĕn), judge; b. Hallsville, Mo., July 9, 1894; s. John W. and Lucy (Pollard) H.; grad. Kansas City Sch. Law, 1914; m. Anna English, June 11, 1919. Admitted to Mo. bar, 1915; engaged in practice of law, Centralia, Mo., 1915-17; elected pros. atty. Boone County, Mo., 1920; engaged in gen. pvt. practice, 1919-43; apptd. U.S. dist. judge for Eastern Dist. of Mo., 1943. Lecturer on Federal Jurisdiction and Procedure, law dept., Washington U., St. Louis. Entered O.T.C., 1917; commd. 2d lt., 1917; comdg. officer Co. A, 353d Inf., 89th Div., U.S. Army, at capture of Stenay, France, 1918; overseas 18 mos. Mem. Am., Mo., St. Louis bar assns. Home: 16 Southmoor, Clayton, Mo. Office: U.S. Court House, St. Louis. Died July 7, 1956.

HULETT, George Augustus, chemist; b. Will County, Ill., July 15, 1867; s. Frank Amos and Louise (Holmes) H.; Oberlin Coll., 1888-90; A.B., Princeton, 1892; Ph.D., U. of Leipzig, 1898; m. Dency Minerva, d. Dr. J. W. Barker, Aug. 15, 1904; 1 son, George Barker. Asst. in chemistry, Princeton, 1892-96; instr. phys. chemistry, 1899-1904, asst. prof., 1904-05, U. of Mich.; asst. prof. phys. chemistry, 1905-09, prof., 1909—, now emeritus, Princeton. Mem. U.S. Assay Commn., 1906; chief chemist U.S. Bur. Mines, 1912-13. Mem. Am. Chem. Soc., Am. Electro-chem. Soc., Am. Phys. Soc., Am. Philos. Soc., Nat. Acad. Sciences; mem. Nat. Research Council (vice chmn. division of chemistry and chem. technology, 1927-28; chmn. of div. at Washington, D.C., 1928-29). Clubs: Cosmos (Washington, D.C.); Chemists' (New York). Mem. foreign service com. of Nat. Research Council, 1917; spent 4 months, mostly at battle fronts of French and English, to study orgn. and development of scientific activities in connection with warfare; mem. N.J. Commn., Workman's Compensation for Occupational Diseases, 1923-24. Asso. editor Jour. Physical Chemistry, 1923-27. Home: 8 Greenholm, Princeton, N.J. Died Sept. 6, 1955; buried Princeton (N.J.) Cemetery.

HULICK, George Washington, lawyer, ex-congressman; b. Batavia, O., June 29, 1833; s. Lott and Rhoda (Dimmitt) H.; grad. Farmers' Coll., Ohio, July 9, 1855; m. Josephine W. Harrison Oct. 16, 1861. In charge Pleasant Hill Acad., 1855-8; studied law; admitted to bar Mar., 1857, practiced Batavia, O.; sch. examiner Clermont Co., O., 1856-9; Rep. candidate for pros. atty., 1858. Served capt. Co. E, 22d Ohio inf., Apr. 14 to Aug. 16, 1861; probate judge Clermont Co., 1864-7; mem. bd. ed'n Batavia, 9 yrs.; del. Rep. Nat. Conv., 1868; Hayes and Wheeler elector, 1876; mem. Congress, 6th Ohio dist. 1893-7. Republican. Address: Batavia, O. Died Aug. 13, 1907.

HULL, Alexander, composer; b. Columbus, O., Sept. 15, 1887; s. James Edward and Eva Jane (Hummer) H.; A.B., Muskingum Coll., 1906; B.M., U. of Pa., 1909; student piano, violoncello, voice, composition and orchestration pvtly.; m. Ruth Romig, Aug. 11, 1920; 1 son, Alexander. Teacher voice, Zanesville, O., 1907-08; head of music dept. Pacific Coll., Newberg, Ore., 1908-35; announcer and dir. Radio Sta. KOAC Sch. of the Air; instr. Portland Extension Center of U. of Ore. Mem. Authors' League America. Club: Portland Press. Composer: Ten Songs, 1913; also numerous songs, piano and orchestra pieces. Author: Shep of the Painted Hills, 1930. Contbr. 100 short stories to mags., among them "The Argosies" (O. Henry memorial award 1920). Radio advertising and production. Director Frederick and Nelson radio programs musical commentator Seattle Symphony Orchestra concerts, Seattle, Wash., 1939. Home: 7819 Dayton Av., Seattle. Died Mar. 4, 1953.

HULL, Clark Leonard, prof. psychology; b. Akron, N.Y., May 24, 1884; s. Leander G. and Florence L. (Trask) H.; grad. Alma (Mich.) Academy, 1905; student Alma College 2 years; A.B., U. of Mich., 1913; Ph.D., U. of Wis., 1918; m. Bertha E. Iutzi, 1911; children—Ruth Trask, Richard Hazard. Prin. pub. sch., Sickels, Mich., 1909-11; acting prof. psychology, Eastern Ky. State Normal Sch., Richmond, Ky., 1913-14; with U. of Wis. as instr. psychology, 1916-20, asst. prof., 1920-22, asso. prof. and dir. lab., 1922-25, prof., 1925-29; prof. psychology, Inst. Human Relations (Yale), 1929-47, Sterling professor of psychology, since July 1947. Fellow A.A.A.S.; member Am. Psychol. Assn. (council 1931-33, president 1935-36), Nat. Acad. Sciences, Am. Acad. Arts and Sciences, Sigma Xi. Club: University. Author: The Evolution of Concepts, 1920; Influence of Tobacco Smoking on Mental and Motor Efficiency, 1924; Aptitude Testing, 1928; Hypnosis and Suggestibility—An Experimental Approach, 1933; (with Hovland, Ross, Hall, Perkins and Fitch) Mathematico-Deductive Theory of Rote Learning, 1940; Principles of Behavior, 1943; Essentials of Behavior, 1951; A Behavior System, 1952. Contbr. to psychol. jours. Home: 888 Ridge Road, Hamden 14. Address: 333 Cedar St., New Haven. Died May 10, 1952; buried Willington, Conn.

HULL, Cordell, former sec. of state; b. Overton County (now Pickett), Tenn., Oct. 2, 1871; s. Wm. and Elizabeth (Riley) H.; student Nat. Normal U., Lebanon, O., 1889-90; B.L., Cumberland Univ. Law Sch., 1891; LL.D., U. of Notre Dame and George Washington U., Cumberland U., Columbia U., William and Mary, Williams Coll., 1934, Pa. Mil. Coll., University of Michigan, University of Wisconsin, 1935; L.H.D., Rollins Coll., 1935; m. Rose Frances Whitney, Nov. 24, 1917 (died Mr. 1954). Admitted to Tenn. bar, 1891. Mem. Tenn. Ho. of Rep., 1893-97; judge 5th Jud. Circuit, Tenn., 1903-07; mem. 60th to 66th Congresses (1907-21), 4th Tenn. Dist.; reelected 68th to 71st Congresses (1923-31), 4th Tenn., Dist., elected U.S. senator from Tenn. for term 1931-37, resigned, 1933; apptd. sec. of state, Mar. 4, 1933. Chmn. Dem. Nat. Com., 1921-24; chmn. Am. delegation Monetary and Econ. Conf., London, 1933; chmn. Am. delegation, 7th Internat. Conf. of American States, Montevideo, 1933; chmn. Am. delegation, Inter-Am. Conf. for Maintenance of Peace, Buenos Aires, 1936; chmn. Am. delegation, 8th Internat. Conf. of Am. States, Lima, 1938; chmn. Am. delegation to 2d Consultative Meeting of the Ministers of Foreign Affairs of the American Republics, Havana, Cuba, 1940. Capt. Co. H, 4th Tenn. Inf., Spanish-Am. War. Author of federal income tax system of 1913, revised act of 1916, and federal inheritance act of 1916. Resigned as Secretary of State on Nov. 27, 1944. Appointed delegate to United Nations Conference at San Francisco, Feb. 13, 1945. Awarded the Theodore Roosevelt Distinguished Service Medal, 1945; Nobel Peace Prize, 1945. Home: Carthage, Tenn.; also Wardman Park Hotel, Washington. Died July 23, 1955; buried Washington Cathedral.

HULL, George Ross, lawyer; b. Millersville, Pa., Oct. 13, 1888; s. George Washington and Anna Eliza (Hambleton) H.; student Millersville (Pa.) State Normal Sc., 1900-03, Franklin and Marshall Coll., 1903-06; A.B., Dickinson Coll., Carlisle, Pa., 1907; m. Margaret Rebecca Latham, June 15, 1914; children—George Ross, Anna Jeannette (Mrs. John C. Stevens), Harold Latham. Admitted to bar, 1913; dep. atty. gen. of Pa., 1920-22, 1st deputy, 1922-23; spl. asst. to atty. gen. of U.S., 1923-24; in pvt. practice of law since 1925; pres. and dir. The Harrisburger (hotel); dir. Pa. Power & Light Co., Capital Bank & Trust Co. (Harrisburg). Mem. procedural rules com. Supreme Ct. of Pa. since 1937. Mem. Am. Law Inst. since 1925. Mem. Am. and Pa. bar assns., Am. Acad. Polit. and Social Sci., Acad. Polit. Sci., Phi Kappa Sigma. Republican. Unitarian. Mason. Club: Union League (Phila.). Home: 1910 N. Second St. Office: 210 Walnut St., Harrisburg, Pa. Died Apr. 1, 1952.

HULL, Gordon Ferrie, physicist; b. Garnet, Haldimand County, Ont., Oct. 7, 1870; s. John and Jane (Moore) H.; A.B., U. Toronto, 1892, fellow in physics, 1892-95; fellow and asst. in physics U. Chgo., 1895-97, Ph.D., 1897; Cambridge U., 1905-06; studied at English and German univs., 1928-29; m. Wilhelmine Brandt, Sept. 5, 1911; 1 son, Gordon Ferrie. Taught in Hamilton Collegiate Inst., 1890-91; instr. physics U. Chgo., 1897-98, and summers 1898-99; prof. physics Colby Coll., Me., 1898-99; asst. prof physics Dartmouth Coll., 1899-1903, prof. 1903-40, prof. meritus, 1940—, active service, 1941-44; prof. physics Columbia, summer sessions 1909-15. Maj. Ordnance Dept., U.S. Army, 1918-19, head math. and dynamics sect., tech. staff Washington, and physics expert, tech. staff Ordnance Dept., 1919-20, cons. physicist, tech. staff, 1920—. Fellow Am. Acad. Arts and Sciences, A.A.A.S.; mem. Am. Phys. Soc., etc. Author: Survey of Modern Physics, 1936; Elementary Modern Physics, 1948. Contbr. various sci. jours. on radiation. Home: 5 Parkway, Hanover, N.H. Died Oct. 7, 1956.

HULL, Josephine (Sherwood), actress; b. Newtonville, Mass., Jan. 3, 1886; d. William Henry and Mary (Teksbury) Sherwood; grad. Radcliffe Coll.; studied dramatics with Kate Reignolds; m. Shelley Vaughn Hull (dec.). Joined Castle Square Stock Co., Beloit, toured with cos. in What Happened to Jones?, Why Smith Left Home, Way Down East, The Bridge, others; dir. Stock co. of Jessie Bonstelle, Detroit, 1922, Equity Players, N.Y.C., 1923; appeared in play Craig's Wife (winner Pulitzer prize 1926), play and motion picture After Tomorrow; played in You Can't Take it With You (winner Pulitzer prize 1937), Arsenic and Old Lace, 1941, also recreated role in motion picture by Warner Bros.; comedy player Harvey, 1944-48 (winner Pulitzer prize 1945); star The Golden State, 1950, Kin Hubbard, 1951, Whistler's Grandmother, 1952, Solid Gold Cadillac, 1953-54; TV appearance, 1955. Recipient Motion Picture Acad. award as best supporting actress (role in Harvey), 1951; Hollywood Fgn. Corr. award, 1951; Lambs award for noteworthy achievement in the theatre, 1956. Mem. Phi Beta Kappa. Address: care Actor's Equity Assn., 45 W. 47th St., N.Y.C. 19. Died Mar. 12, 1957; buried Newton Cemetery, Newtonville, Mass.

HULL, Merlin, congressman; s. George Miller and Hannah Bernice (Baker) H.; ed. Gale Coll., Galesville, Wis.; LL.B., De Pauw U., 1890; grad. study Columbian (now George Washington) U.; m. Jessie Matchette Robbins, Jan. 6, 1896; children—Perry Miller, Lois Margaret, Marion Bernice (Mrs. Leland I. Lamb). Admitted to Wis. bar, 1904, and began practice at Black River Falls; pub. Jackson County Journal 1904-26, Banner-Jour. since 1926. District atty., Jackson County, 1907-09; mem. Wisconsin Assembly, 1909-15 (speaker of House, 1913); sec. of state, Wis., 1917-21; mem. 71st Congress (1929-31), 7th Wis. Dist., and 74th to 82d Congresses (1935-53), 9th Wis. Dist. Republican. Methodist. Mason, K.P., Elk. Home: 515 Van Buren St. Office: 310 Main St., Black River Falls, Wis. Died 1953.

HULL, Nathan P.; b. Dimondale, Mich., Nov. 7, 1867; s. John and Sarah Jane (Pray) H.; student Mich. State Agrl. Coll., Olivet (Mich.) Coll.; m. Grace E. Bellows, June 30, 1897; children—Thelma, John W. Lecturer farmers' institutes 15 yrs.; overseer Mich. State Grange, 9 yrs., master 4 yrs.; lectr. Nat. Grange, 2 yrs.; pres. Grange Life Ins. Co., 20 yrs.; pres. Nat. Dairy Union, 18 yrs.; pres. Am. Dairy Farmers' Assn., 9 yrs.; pres. Nat. Cooperative Milk Producers Fedn., 8 yrs., Mich. Milk Producers Assn., 20 yrs.; dir. Peoples Finance Service, Inc.; v.p. and treas. Am. Annuity Savings Assn.; dir. Am. State Savings Bank, Central Trust Co. (both Lansing), Detroit br., Fed. Res. Bank of Chicago, 11 yrs.; co-partner Hull Bros. Silver Creek Farm. Mem. Grange. Republican. Presbyn. Mason, Elk. Author: Making the Dairy Pay, 1913. Home: 411 West St. Office: American State Bank Bldg., Lansing, Mich. Died Mar. 3, 1954.

HULT, Gottfried Emanuel, univ. prof.; b. Chicago, Mar. 14, 1869; s. Rev. Andrew and Charlotte (Hammarstrand) H.; A.B., U. of Minn., 1892, A.M., 1893; U. of Leipzig, 1896-99; U. of Chicago, 1899-1900; traveled and studied in Italy and Greece, 1906-07; Litt.D., from Beloit (Wis.) Coll., 1921; m. Florence Bowen, Dec. 2, 1894; 1 dau., Mrs. Florence Genevieve Spaulding. Prof. Greek lang. and lit., 1907-16, prof. classical langs. and lits. since Sept. 1916, Univ. of N.D. Mem. Am. Assn. Univ. Profs., N.E.A., Classical Assn. Middle West. Author: Reveries and Other Poems, 1909; Outbound, 1920; (verse dramas) Galileo; The Messiah; The Laughing Philosopher; Dion, The White Swan of Sicily. Translator (with critical introductions and notes) of 5 of Henrik Ibsen's dramas—Peer Gynt, Brand, Love's Comedy, The Pretenders, The Lady from the Sea; also translated all of Ibsen's lyrical works, with notes and introduction. A number of his plays have been produced in St. Paul Community Theatre, Pasadena Community Theatre, Vassar College Experimental Theatre, etc. Contbr. poems to Century, Forum, Independent, etc.; lectures on lit., esthetic and ethical subjects. Address: 1506 Rollin St., South Pasadena, Calif. Died June 28, 1950; buried Pasadena, Cal.

HUME, Alfred (hūm), educator; b. Beech Grove, Tenn., Dec. 1, 1866; s. William and Mary (Leland) H.; B.E., Vanderbilt U., 1887, C.E., 1888, D.Sc., 1890; LL.D., Miss. Coll., 1916, Westminster Coll. (Mo.), 1931, Southwestern (Tenn.), 1935; m. Mary Hill Ritchey, Dec. 23, 1891; children—Ben Hill (dec.), Annie Fulton, dec. (Mrs. H. M. Bryan), Leland, Myra (Mrs. J. H. Jones), Mary (Mrs. F. M. Kelton), Ritchey, Branham, William. Fellow and asst. in civil engring. Vandrbilt U., 1887-90; prof. mathematics, 1890-1926, acting prof. civil engring., 1900-02, dean College of Liberal Arts, 1905-20, vice-chancellor, 1905-24, chancellor, 1924-30; prof. mathematics and astronomy and acting chancellor U. Miss., 1906-07, chancellor, 1932-35, had dept. mathematics, chancellor emeritus, 1935—, acting chancellor, 1942-43; prof. mathmatics Southwestern U., Memphis, 1930-31; pres. Branham and Hughes Mil. Acad., Spring Hill, Tenn., 1931-32; mathematics, Summer Sch. of the South, Knoxville, 1903. Fellow A.A.A.S. (emeritus life mem.); mem. Soc. Promotion Engring. Edn., Engring. Assn. South (pres. 1914), Am. Math. Soc., Math. Assn. Am., Phi Beta Kappa, Beta Theta Pi. Democrat. Presbyn. Home: University, Miss. Died Dec. 25, 1950; buried St. Peter's Cemetery, Oxford, Miss.

HUME, Edgar Erskine, army officer; b. Frankfort, Ky., Dec. 26, 1889; s. Enoch Edgar (M.D.) and Mary (South) H.; B.A., Centre Coll., Ky., 1908, M.A., 1909; M.D., Johns Hopkins, 1913, Dr.P.H., 1924; D.M., U. Munich, 1914, U. Rome, 1915; 1st honor grad. Army Med. Sch., 1917; M.P.H., Harvard and Mass. Inst. Tech., 1921; D.T.M., Harvard, 1922; grad. U.S. Infantry Sch., 1928; hon. degrees from Centre Coll., U. Ky., Georgetown U., William and Mary, Hampden-Sydney, Washington and Lee, Transylvania U., Dickinson, Louisville, Washington and Jefferson, univs. of Naples, Rome, Florence, Bologna, Modena, Milan, Pisa, Siena, Chile, San Marcos (Peru), Paris, Madrid, and Leon (Nicaragua); grad. U.S. Army Medical Field Service Sch., 1936; m. Mary Swigert Hendrick, 1918 (deceased); 1 son, Edgar Erskine. Commd. 1st lt. Med. Corps, U.S. Army, 1916; promoted through grades to maj. gen., 1949. Staff Johns Hopkins Hosp., 1913-14; med. dir. Am. Relief Expdn. to Italy after earthquake, 1915; dir. dept. sociology, Disciplinary Barracks, Ft. Leavenworth, Kan., 1917; executive, Div. of Sanitation in Surgeon Gen.'s Office, 1917-18; comdg. officer U.S. Army Hospitals, with Italian Army; with Brit. Expeditionary Forces, 1918; at Meuse-Argonne, St. Mihiel and Vittorio-Veneto (wounded); chief med. officer (dir. typhus fever campaign) and Am. Red Cross Commr. for Serbia, 1919-20; in charge Army Lab. for N.E., Boston, 1920-22; editor Index Catalog Army Med. Library, Washington, 1922-26; med. insp. Infantry Sch., Ft. Benning, Ga., 1926-30; insp. Mass. and N.H. Nat. Guards, 1930-32; librarian Army Med. Library, 1932-36; dir. of adminstrn. Med. Field Service Sch., Carlisle, Pa., 1937-42; comdg. officer, Winter Gen. Hosp., Topeka, Kan., 1942-43; in African, Sicilian and Italian invasions (wounded); chief of public health, Sicily, 1943; chief Allied Mil. Govt., 5th Army, Italy, 1943-45; chief Mil. Govt. U.S. Zone, Austria, 1945-47; chief reorientation br. Dept. of Army, 1947-49; chief surgeon Far East Command, 1949-51, U.N., Korea, 1950-51; ret. for age, Dec. 31, 1951. Editor Mil. Surg., 1922; lectr. in med. history Georgetown Univ. and Univ. of Kan.; U.S. Army del. to Internat. Congress of Mil. Medicine, Paris, 1925, London, 1929, The Hague, 1931, Madrid, 1933, Brussels, 1935, Mexico, 1936, Bucharest, 1937, Washington, 1939, Basle, 1947, Stockholm, 1948 (nat. corr. for these congresses). Awarded D.S.M. (three), Silver Star (four), Legion of Merit, Purple Heart (four) Bronze Star (four), Soldier's Medal, Commendation ribbon (four), Air Medal (two), Typhus Medal (U.S.); also decorations from France, Gt. Britain, Belgium, China, Turkey, Philippines, Jugoslavia, Brazil, Russia, Bolivia, Sweden, Ecuador, Bulgaria, Tunis, Nicaragua, Denmark, Peru, Lithuania, Colombia, Norway, Haiti, Vatican, Esthonia, Cuba, Hungary, Chile, Netherlands, Finland, Venezuela, Latvia, Italy, Serbia, Panama, Poland, Spain, Greece, Czechoslovakia, Portugal, Montenegro, Luxembourg, Roumania, Korea; Bali Grand Cross of Sovereign Mil. Order of Malta; Sir Henry Wellcome prize, 1933; Oberlaender fellow to Germany, 1937; Gorgas Medal, 1948; hon. prof. U. Warsaw; hon. col. Royal Serbian Army; hon. cpl. French Army; hon. citizen of 40 Italian and Austrian cities. Mem. Soc. of Cincinnati (pres. gen.), Aztec Club (pres.), Kappa Alpha, Phi Beta Kappa, Sigma Xi, Alpha Omega Alpha, Delta Omega (founder; nat. pres. 1926), Omicron Delta Kappa, etc.; fellow Am. Acad. Arts and Sciences, Royal Soc. of Edinburgh, Royal Soc. Tropical Med. and Hygiene, Am. Coll. Surgeons, Am. Pub. Health Assn., Am. Coll. Physicians, Royal Italian Soc. Hygiene, Soc. Antiquaries of Scotland, academies of science of Spain, Mexico and Philadelphia, Assn. of Mil. Surgeons (pres.), academies of medicine of Rome, Washington (charter), Mex., Rio, Lima, Madrid, Swedish Soc. Anthropology, Royal Soc. of Naples, Accademia Pontiniana (Naples). Diplomate Am. bds. Neurology, Preventive Medicine and Internal Medicine. Clubs: Union (Tokyo, Japan); Army and Navy, Cosmos, Chevy Chase (Washington); Lambs, Metropolitan, Union, Explorers (N.Y.); Pithotomy (Baltimore); St. Botolph (Boston); Caccia (Rome); Cercle Militaire (Paris); Royal Soc. (London). Author of about 400 books and papers, including The Med. Book of Merit; Pettenkofer's Theory; Military Operations on the Italian Front (also Italian transl.); A Colonial Scottish Jacobite Family; Sanitation in War Planning; various papers on the Soc. of Cincinnati, Fighting Typhus Fever in Serbia; Preparation of Potable Water for Field, Heros von Borcke, Italy's Part in World War, Theodore O'Hara, Sandfly Fever, History and Work of Army Med. Library, Med. Service in Combined Army and Navy Operations, Med. Work of Knights Hospitallers, Ornithologists of Army Med. Corps, General Washington's Correspondence, Victories of Army Medicine, War and Medicine, Vesuvius Eruption of 1944, Medicine Goes to War, etc. Asso. editor Annals of Medical History. Contbr. to Ency. Brit., Ency. Am., Tice's Practice of Medicine, Dictionary of Am. Biography. Believed to be most decorated soldier in U.S. history. Home: Frankfort, Ky. Address: care Soc. of the Cincinnati, 2118 Massachusetts Av., Washington 8. Died Jan. 24, 1952; buried Arlington Nat. Cemetery.

HUME, Edward Hicks, educator; b. of Am. parents, Ahmednagar, India, May 13, 1876; s. Edward Sackett and Charlotte Elizabeth (Chandler) H.; B.A., Yale, 1897, hon. M.A., 1912; M.D., Johns Hopkins, 1901; grad. work, U. Liverpool, 1901-02; LL.D., Jefferson Med. Coll., 1923, U. Hongkong, 1925; m. Lotta Carswell, Sept. 24, 1903; children—Theodore Carswell (dec.) Charlotte Elizabeth, Margery (dec.), Edward Welch (dec.), Kathrina Joy. Acting asst. surgeon U.S.P.H.S., Bombay, India, 1903-05; sr. physician Yale Hosp., Changsha, China, 1906-23; dean Hunan-Yale Med. Coll., 1914-27, prof. medicine, 1916-23, clin. prof. medicine, 1923-27; pres. Colleges of Yale-in-China, 1923-27; exec. v.p. and trustee N.Y. Post-Grad. Med. Sch. and Hosp., 1928-33, dir., 1931-33. Founder and organizer Hosp. and Med. Coll. of Yale-in-China, Changsha. Chmn. Council Med. Edn. of China Med. Assn. 5 yrs., asst. editor China Med. Journal 9 yrs.; trustee Yale-in-China Assn.; trustee Lingnan U., Hua Chung Coll. Lectr. on Chinese medical history, Johns

Hopkins U. Spl. mem. Nat. Health Adminstrn. of China; spl. mem. Council on Med. Missions, China; sec. emeritus Christian med. council for Overseas Work; mem. program com. United China Relief; mem. bd. dir. Am. Bur. Med. Aid to China, Assoc. Bds. for Christian Colleges in China; mem. bd. mgrs. Am. Bible Soc. Fellow N.Y. Acad. Medicine; mem. Am. Oriental Soc., Chinese Medical Association, Am. Soc. Tropical Medicine, N.Y. Soc. Tropical Medicine, Am. Assn. of the History of Medicine, N.Y. Soc. for Medical History, N. China Br. Royal Asiatic Soc., Phi Beta Kappa, Psi Upsilon, Sigma Xi. Decorated by Chinese Govt. Order of Flourishing Grain, 3d class, 1926, Order of The Blue Jade, 1941. Presbyn. Clubs: Century (New York); Elihu (Yale). Author: The Chinese Way in Medicine, 1940. Doctors East, Doctors West, 1946 (winner W. W. Norton award). Doctors Courageous, 1950; Valiant Adventurer (Dr. W. W. Pettus), 1952. Home: 464 Riverside Dr., N.Y.C. 27. Died Feb. 9, 1957.

HUME, James Cleland, lawyer; b. Cin., May 22, 1862; s. James and Eliza (Cleland) H.; A.B., Hanover (Ind.) Coll., 1880, A.M., 1884; student U. of France, L'École de Droit, Sorbonne, Paris, 1881-82; LL.B. (prize essayist), U. Cin., 1884; m. Angie Hatton, June 25, 1890; 1 dau., Mary (Mrs. William Wallace). Practiced, Des Moines, since 1884, except 1921-22, when judge; 9th Jud. Sist. of Ia. Lecturer elementary law and equity jurisprudence, Iowa Coll. of Law, Des Moines, 1890-1900. Mem. Am., Ia., Des Moines (pres. 1914) bar assns., Phi Gamma Delta. Republican. Clubs: Des Moines, Prairie (pres. 1902-03). Writer of lectures, mag. articles and critical essays on law and internat. topics; also the Rougon-Macquart Series; Rossetti, the poet, Pierre Loti; Shaw and certain Shavian Plays; the Religion of Felix Adler; Jean Christophe; etc. Home: 13 34th St. Office: Youngerman Bldg., Des Moines, Ia. Deceased.

HUME, Omer Forest; Former Republican nat. committeeman from Ky.; in practice of medicine at Richmond for many years; regent Eastern Ky. State Coll., Louisville. Address: Richmond, Ky. Died Oct. 1959.*

HUMES, Augustine Leftwich, lawyer; b. Knoxville, Tenn., Nov. 16, 1874; s. Andrew Russell and R. Alice (Leftwich) H.; A.B., Princeton, 1896; LL.B. cum laude, Harvard, 1899; m. Elsa V. Portner, Apr. 2, 1919; 1 son, John P. In practice law, N.Y. City, since 1899; asso. in office Hornblower, Byrne, Miller & Potter, 1899-1907; member Byrne & Cutcheon, and successor firm, Taylor, Humes & Begg, 1907-19; mem. successor firms of Humes, Buck Smith & Stowell and Humes, Smith & Andrews, N.Y. City, since 1919; dir. Internat. Bus. Machines Corp.; advisor on Switzerland, War Trade Bd., Washington, 1918. Mem. Am. Bar Assn., Sons of Revolution, Society Colonial Wars, The Pilgrims, Assn. of the Bar of the City of N.Y. Republican. Episcopalian. Clubs: Union, Racquet, River, Tuxedo, Down Town Assn.(N.Y. City); Piping Rock (L.I.); Reading Room, Clambake, Spouting Rock (Newport, R.I.). Author articles in Harvard Law Rev. and Am. Bar Assn. Jour.; article, The Power of Congress over Combinations Affecting Interstate Commerce, reprinted in Selected Cases on Constitutional Law, 1938; editor, Harvard Law Rev., 1898-99. Home: 960 5th Av. Office: 50 Broadway, N.Y.C. 1. Died Sept. 25, 1952.

HUMMEL, George F., author; b. Southold, L.I., N.Y., Sept. 3, 1882; s. Gottlieb Friedrich and Anna H.; B.A., Williams Coll., 1902; M.A., Columbia, 1903, also post-grad.; m. Lillie Conrad Busch, 1914. Ranching in the Southwest and teaching in prep. schs., 1903-09; univ. scholar and alternate fellow Columbia, 1911; organizer business enterprises, 1912-16; organizer schs. of indsl. edn., 1916-21; exec. v.p. Horace Liveright, publishers, 1929-30. Mem. Phi Beta Kappa, Phi Gamma Delta. Club: Williams College (N.Y.C.). Author: After All, 1923; Subsoil, 1924; A Good Man, 1925; Evelyn Grainger, 1927; Lasy Isle, 1927; Summer Lightning, 1928; The World Waits, play, produced 1933; Heritage (novel), 1935; Tradition, 1936; Adriatic Interlude, 1938; Joshua Moore, American, 1943; The Eternal Mother, 1945; also short stories in mags. Home: 383 Central Park West, N.Y. C. Died Dec. 20, 1952.

HUMMEL, R. A., ret. chmn. Lone Star Cement Corp., director; dir. Am. & Fgn. Power Company, Inc., Carey-Baxter-Kennedy. Vice chmn. U.S. Inter-Am. Council; dir. Pan-Am. Soc. of U.S. Office: 100 Park Av., N.Y.C. 17. Died Aug. 6, 1959.

HUMMEL, William Grandville, educator, b. Roberts, Ill., Feb. 19, 1882; s. John and Sarah Matilda (Upson) H.; B.S., U. Ill., 1907; M.S. in Agr., U. Cal., 1912; m. Bertha Ella Royce, 1907. Asst. in farm mechanics Colo. Agrl. Coll., 1907-08; instr. agronomy N.M. Agrl. Coll., 1908-09; tchr. agr. Oxnard (Cal.) High Sch., 1909-10; head agrl. dept. Fresno (Cal.) High Sch. and Jr. Coll., 1910-11; instr. agrl. edn. U. Cal., 1911, asst. prof., 1912, asso. prof., 1915, prof. 1918; leave of absence as spl. agt. in agrl. edn., Fed. Bd. for Vocational Edn., 1917-20; asst. dir. for agrl. edn., 1918-19; apptd. dir. vocational edn. for State of Wash., Oct. 1919. Mem. Nat. Soc. for Vocational Edn., N.E.A., Phi Delta Kappa, Sigma Pi. Conglist. Author: Materials and Methods in High School Agriculture, 1913, bulls. Home: Olympia, Wash. Deceased.

HUMPHREY, Doris, choreographer; b. Oak Park, Ill., Oct. 17, 1895; d. Horace B. and Julia Ellen (Wells) Humphrey; Francis W. Parker School, Chicago; studied dance with Pavley and Oukrainsky, Josephine Hatlanek, Ruth St. Denis, Ted Shawn, Delcroze Sch.; m. Charles F. Woodford, June 10, 1932; 1 son, Charles H. Tchr., regisseuse, leading dancer Ruth St. Denis and Ted Shawn, touring U.S. and Orient, 1917-28; partner Charles Weidman, dancing studio, N.Y.C., 1928-45, with dancing co. toured U.S. playing colls. and univs., conducting tng. classes for tchrs. of dancing, retired from dancing, 1945; artistic dir., choreographer Jose Limon, 1942-—; dir. Dance Center, Y.M. and Y.W.H.A., N.Y.C., 1945-—; tchr. Conn. Coll. Sch. of the Dance, 1947-—; Guggenheim fellow, 1949; advisor dance prodns. at Palacio de Bellas Artes, Mexico City, 1950-51; mem. faculty Juilliard Sch. Music, N.Y.C., 1951-—; dir. and choreographer Juilliard Dance Theatre 1955-—. Pioneered in creation new dance technique, new method composition known as modern. Composed over 100 solos and ensemble dances in concert field. Choreographer shows and operas including School for Husbands, Run L'il Chillun, Lysistrata, Aida, Americana, Sing Out Sweet Land. Recipient of Capezio Annual Dance Award, 1954. Mem. Dance Panel of ANTA for U.S. Information Service, 1955-—. Revised dance terms Webster's Internat. Dictionary, 1931. Author: The Art of Making Dances, 1959. Home: 50 W. 72d St., N.Y.C. 23. Died Dec. 29, 1958; buried Forest Park, Ill.

HUMPHREY, Edward Frank (ŭm-frē), coll. prof., historian; b. at Winnebago, Minn., Apr. 22, 1878; s. John Gould and Louisa Maria (Hoyt) H.; A.B., U. Minn., 1903; A.M., Columbia, 1909, Ph.D., 1912; student U. Paris, France, 1910-11; m. Gertrude Warnock, Sept. 1, 1915; children—Mary Ann Ward, Christine Vera (dec.), John James (dec.), Gertrude Louisa. Supt. schs. Lake Benton, Minn., 1904-08; instr. history, Coll. City of N.Y., 1908-10, Columbia, 1911-15; Northam prof. history and polit. sci., Trinity Coll., Conn., 1915-48, emeritus prof., since 1948; vis. prof., Hillyer Coll., 1948-50; instr. history U. Ala., 1926, 29, U. Minn., 1928, Ohio U., 1931. Chmn. of High Sch. Com., Hartford, 1923-29. Lecturer N.Y. Pub. Lecture Bur. Pres. Mark Twain Library and Memorial Commn. Mem. Am. Hist. Assn., Am. Polit. Science Assn., Acad. Polit. Sci., Inst. of Politics, N.E. History Teachers' Assn., Conn. Hist. Soc., P.B.K., Sigma Alpha Epsilon, Acacia, S.A.R., Soc. of Mayflower Descendants in State of Conn. (gov.), Soc. of Desc. of Founders of Hartford (gov.), Pi Gamma Mu (nat. treas.). Republican. Conglist. Author: (thesis) Politics and Religion in the Days of Augustine, 1912; Nationalism and Religion in America, 1774 to 1789, 1924; An Economic History of the United States, 1931. Editor: George Washington on Religious Liberty and Mutual Understanding, 1932; Liberty Documents, 1936. Contbr. to Handbook for the Diplomatic History of Europe, Asia, and Africa, 1870-1914, Dictionary of Am. Biography, A Guide to Historical Literature (1936), also Am. Hist. Review, Polit. Science Quarterly, The Nation, History Teachers' Mag., etc. Home: 31 Whitney St., Hartford, Conn. Died Feb. 1960.

HUMPHREY, Harry Baker, plant pathologist; b. Granite Falls, Minn., Aug. 4, 1873; s. John Wadsworth and Adeline (Regester) H.; B.S., U. Minn., 1899; Ph.D., Stanford, 1907; m. Olive Agatha Mealey, June 10, 1901; children—Llewellyn Mealey, Robert Regester, Helen Wadsworth (Mrs. John M. McLernon), Isabel Estella (Mrs. G. H. Godfrey), Harry Bartholomew, John William David. Secondary sch. tchr. and prin., 1899-1903; instr. botany and grad. student, Stanford, 1903-07; instr. marine botany Hopkins Marine Sta., Pacific Grove, 1906-08 (summers); bot. editor Cree Pub. Co., 1907-08; prof. botany Wash. State Coll., 1908-13, vice dir. agrl. exptl. sta., 1912-13; instr. marine botany U. Wash., 1912 (summer); pathologist in charge cereal disease investigations Bur. Plant Industry, U.S. Dept. Agr., 1913-19, sr. pathologist, 1919-22, prin. pathologist 1922-43; retired, 1943; editor-in-chief Phytopathology, 1929-43. Fellow A.A.A.S.; mem. Can. Geog. Soc., Am. Phytopathol. Soc., Washington Bot. Soc., Wash. Biol. Soc., Wash. Acad. Sciences, Minn. Hist. Soc., Sigma Xi. Club: Cosmos. Author of several bot. papers: joint author of handbook of pisé de terre construction; contbr. bulls. and reports on researches of cereal diseases. Home: Cabin John, Md. Address: Cosmos Club, Washington. Died 1955.

HUMPHREY, William Francis, lawyer; pres. Tidewater Asso. Oil Co.; also officer and dir. many other corps. Received LL.B. from Univ. of Calif., 1895. Home: 1457 O'Farrell St. Office: care Tidewater Asso. Oil Co., 17 Battery Pl., N.Y.C. Died Feb. 3, 1960.

HUMPSTONE, Henry Judson, educator; b. Hampden, N.J., Mar. 29, 1870; s. William and Deborah Miller (Riddle) H.; student U. Rochester, 1889-92, A.B., 1906, A.M., 1912; student Fredonia (N.Y.) Normal Sch., 1903-05; Ph.D., U. Pa., 1917; m. Louise Rawson, (dec. 1908); m. 2d, Caroline E. Miles, June 7. 1923. Various positions, N.Y.C., 1892-99; editor Field and Stream, 1899-1900; half-time tchr. Fredonia Normal Sch., 1903-05; tchr. high sch., Westfield, N.Y., 1906-11, Western N.Y. Sch. for Deaf, 1911-13, East Liberty Acad., Pitts., 1913-14; instr. in psychology U. Pa., 1914-20; prof. psychology and head of dept. U. of N.D., since 1920; in charge N.D. Traveling Clinic. Fellow A.A.A.S.; mem. Am. Psychol. Assn., Am. Assn. U. Profs., Sigma Xi, Phi Delta Kappa, Delta Upsilon. Democrat. Baptist. Mason (K.T., Shriner). Home: 207 Division Av., Grand Forks, N.D. Died Apr. 20, 1952.

HUND, H. E., motor mfg. exec.; b. East Detroit, Mich., Oct. 7, 1888; s. George A. and Mathilde (Daniels) H.; student East Detroit pub. and high schs., 1894-1905; m. Emma Louise Madden; 1 son, James Madden, 1922. Clk., Am. Car and Foundry Co., 1905, Burnham Stoepel Co., 1907-09, Briggs Mfg. Co., 1909, asst. gen. mgr., 1912-17; supr. assembly plants, standardized truck div. for Q.M., U.S. Army, 1917-18; owner, H. E. Hund Co., 1919-22, sold to and became mgr. of Wilson Body Co., 1922-23; v.p., gen. mgr. Briggs Mfg. Co., 1929-1934; pres., gen. mgr. Reo Motors, Inc., 1940-49, now chmn. bd. Clubs: Athletic and Golf (Detroit); Country and Auto (Lansing). Home: 18652 Fairway Dr., Detroit 21. Office: Reo Motors, Inc., Lansing 20, Mich. Died Oct. 10, 1954.

HUNGERFORD, Samuel James, ret. ry. exec.; b. Bedford, Que., July 16, 1872; s. Samuel and Mary (Wilson) H.; student Bedford pub. schs.; Dr. Mech. Engring., U. Vt.; m. Mary Alberta DeMorest, Apr. 13, 1893; children—Stewart James, Alice M., Ethel (Mrs. W. B. Schon). Machinist apprentice South Eastern Ry., 1886-91; journeyman machinist, 1891-1903, successively master mechanic, supt. Winnipeg shops, 1903-10; supt. rolling stock, Can. Northern Ry., 1910-17, gen. mgr., Eastern Lines, 1917-18; asst. v.p. operating, maintenance and constrn. Can.-Nat. Ry., 1918-20, v.p., 1920-22, gen. mgr. Can. Northern Ry. System, 1922-23, v.p. operation and constrn., 1923-32, acting pres., 1932, pres. 1934, chmn. bd., 1936-41; resigned to become pres. Nat. Rys. Munitions, Ltd. Mem. Scientific Inst. of Studies of Communications and Transport, Engring. Inst. of Can. Decorated officer Order of British Empire, 1946. Clubs: Royal Montreal Golf, Laval sur le Lac Golf, Saint James' (Montreal); Nat. (Toronto). Home: 3025 Sherbrooke W., Montreal, Que., Can. Deceased.

HUNNEMAN, William Cooper, Jr., leather mfr.; b. Brookline, Mass., June 25, 1892; s. William C. and Helen L. (Richards) H.; B.S., Amherst Coll., 1915; m. Alyse Matthews, June 1, 1916; children—Alyse M. (dec.), Bruner R. (Mrs. George Strawbridge). Chmn. bd. William Amer Co., Phila., since 1935; pres. Lawrence-Johnson & Co., Inc., Phila., since 1940; dir. Penn Mut. Ins. Co., Girard Trust Corn Exchange Bank, Phila. Chmn. war fund A.R.C. (v. chmn. S.E. Pa. chpt. 1945). Mem. bd. Bryn Mawr (Pa.) Hosp.; chmn. Devon (Pa.) Horse Show. Home: 400 Caversham Rd., Bryn Mawr, Pa. Office: 215 Willow St., Phila. 23; also Land Title Bldg., Phila. 10. Died Jan. 23, 1958.

HUNNER, Guy LeRoy, ret. surgeon; b. Alma, Wis., Dec. 6, 1868; s. John and Eudora (Cooke) H.; B.S., U. Wis., 1893; M.D., Johns Hopkins, 1897; D.Sc., Dickinson Coll., 1913; m. Isabella Stevens, Sept. 10, 1902; children—Isabella Stevens (wife of Dr. John W. Parsons), Eudora Cooke (wife of J. D. Donovan); John Stevens (U.S. Army). Began practice surgery, Balt., 1902; adj. prof. emeritus of gynecology Johns Hopkins Univ. Med. Sch. Fellow ACS.; mem. Am., So. med. assns., So. Surg. Assn. (ex-pres.), Am. Gynecol. Assn., Am. Urol. Assn., Baltimore County Med. Soc., Baltimore City Med. Soc. (ex-pres.), Société Internationale d'Urologie, Phi Delta Theta. Democrat. Methodist. Contbr. chpts. to med. textbooks, also to med. jours. Home: Pasadena, Md. Died July 14, 1957.

HUNT, Albert Clarence, judge; b. Clarksville, Ark., July 30, 1888; s. William T. and Mattie (Rose) H.; grad. Mo. Mil. Acad., 1906; LL.B., Vanderbilt U., 1909; m. Essie Joel Hayden, Nov. 24, 1914; children—Elizabeth Hayden, Albert C., John W. Admitted to Okla. bar, 1909, and began practice at Wagoner; city atty., 1911-15; dist. judge 21st Jud. Dist., Okla., 1921-25; justice Supreme Ct. of Okla., 1925-31; dist. judge 7th Jud. Dist. Okla., 1941-55; justice Supreme Ct. 3d Dist. Okla., 1955-—. Chmn. State Election Bd. of Okla., 1936-41; mem. Jud. Council Okla., 1944. Mem. exec. bd. Boy Scouts Am., 20 years, pres. Last Frontier council, 1947-48. Pres. Okla. Conf. Dist. Judges, 1945-49. Mem. Am. Bar Assn., State Bar Okla. (v.p., gov.), Okla. Hist. Soc., Phi Delta Phi. Democrat. Methodist. Mason (32°, K.T., Shriner, K.C.C.H.). Clubs: Okla., Kiwanis (pres. 1921), Men's Dinner. Home: 439 N.W. 18th St. Office: State Capitol, Oklahoma City. Died Aug. 2 6, 1956; buried Rose Hill.

HUNT, Clara Whitehill, librarian; b. Utica, N.Y., 1871; d. Edwin and Mary (Brown) Hunt; grad.

Utica Free Acad., 1889, N.Y. State Library Sch., Albany, 1898. Pub. sch. prin., Utica, 1893-96; organized work with children in the Apprentices' Library, Phila., 1898, Newark Free Pub. Library, 1898-1902; supt. children's dept. Bklyn. Pub. Library, 1903-39. Mem. A.L.A., N.Y. Library Assn. Lectr. and contbr. to mags. on children's lit., library work with children, and related topics; compiler lists of children's books. Author: What Shall We Read to the Children?, 1915; About Harriet, 1916; Th Little House in the Woods, 1918; Peggy's Playhouses, 1924; The Little House in Green Valley, 1932. Address: Bloomfield, N.J. Died Jan. 10, 1958; buried South Sudbury, Mass.

HUNT, D. F., business exec.; b. Harvey, Ill., 1899; pres. and dir. United Stockyards Corp., Wilmington, Del.; vice pres. and dir. Portland Union Stockyards, St. Paul Union Stockyards, Sioux City Stockyards Co., Sioux City Terminal Ry., Peninsula Terminal Co., North Portland, Ore., Brighton Stockyards, Boston, Mass., St. Joseph (Mo.) Stockyards Co., Stockyards Ry.; dir. Union Stockyards Co. of Fargo, N.D. Home: 5555 N. Sheridan Rd., Chgo. 40. Office: 141 W. Jackson Blvd., Chgo. Died Apr. 12, 1959.

HUNT, Edward Eyre; b. Bellwood, Neb., Aug. 1, 1885; s. Edward Cassilly and Juliet Sears (Davis) H.; A.B., Harvard, 1910; m. Virginia Lloyd, d. Hugh Francis Fox, May 15, 1920; children—Edward Eyre, Virginia Lloyd (Mrs. Ralph J. P. Wedgwood). Secretary for apointments and assistant in English department Harvard, 1910-12; editorial staff American Mag., N. Y., 1912-14; war corr., Europe, 1914; Am. del. of Commn. for Relief in Belgium in charge Province of Antwerp, 1914-16; dir. of Publs. of Am. Red Cross, Washington, D.C., Mar.-Sept. 1917; head of economic rehabilitation work of Red Cross in France, 1917-18; dir. gen. civilian relief, Red Cross, Italy, 1917; labor manager clothing industry, New York, 1920; mem. Com. on Elimination of Waste in Industry, Federated Am. Engring. Socs., 1920, apptd. by Herbert Hoover; sec. of Conf. on Unemployment called by Pres. Harding, 1921; sec. U.S. Coal Commn.. 1922-23; American expert on scientific management, World Econ. Conf., 1927; mem. Com. on Recent Econ. Changes since 1928; sec. President's Emergency Com. for Employment, 1930-31, President's Research Com. on Social Trends, 1930-33; Am. mem. of World Economic Depression Inquiry, 1931; engaged in econ. and social surveys, Venezuela, 1939-40; chief indsl. economist, War Prodn. Bd., 1942-43; associate dir. field operations Office of Foreign Relief and Rehabilitation, U.S. Department of State, 1943. Chief of Italian Div., Fgn. Econ. Adminstrn., 1944., dir. Italian Div., Dept. State, 1945-46; chief Div. Protective Services, Dept. State, since 1947. Member Belgian-American Educational Foundation since 1920. Member Phi Beta Kappa and various engineering societies. Decorated Grand Officer, Order of the Crown (Italy), Chevalier, Order of the Crown (Belgium), Medal of Public Gratitude (France), gold medals of Antwerp, Malines, Belgian National Com., French Red Cross. Clubs: Cosmos (Washington, D.C.); Harvard (New York). Author: Sir Orfeo, 1910; War Bread—A Personal Narrative of the War and Relief in Belgium, 1916; Haj, 1916; Tales from a Famished Land, 1918; (with Herbert Hoover and others) Waste in Industry, 1921; (with others) Business Cycles and Unemployment, 1923; (with others) Seasonal Operation in the Construction Industries, 1924; Conferences, Committees, Conventions, and How to Run Them, 1925; An Audit of America, 1930; Greathouse, 1937. Editor: Scientific Management since Taylor, 1924; What the Coal Commission Found, 1925; Recent Economic Changes in the United States, 1929; The Power Industry and the Public Interest, 1944. Home: R.F.D. 3, Springfield, Ohio; and Riverside, Conn. Address: 27 W. 44th St., N.Y.C. Died Mar. 5, 1953; buried Oakdale Cemetery, Urbana, O.

HUNT, Graham Putnam, lawyer; b. Cin., Aug. 7, 1873; s. William Putnam and Margaret Graham (Hopper) H.; student Harvard, 1892-95, Cin. Law Sch., 1896-98; m. Frances Carlisle Mendenhall, June 20, 1905; children—Frances Mendenhall, Graham Putnam, Margaret Graham, Grace Mendenhall. Admitted to Ohio bar, 1898, began practice at Cin.; mem. firm Moulinier, Bettman & Hunt; dist. referce in bankruptcy, 15 yrs. Mem. Ohio Ho. of Reps., 1900; Dem. candidate for U.S. Senate, 1928. Mem. Am., Ohio, Cin. bar assns. Clubs: Harvard, Lawyers, Cincinnati Country. Home: 164 Glenmary Av. Office: First National Bank Bldg., Cin. Died Sept. 7, 1953.

HUNT, James Gallaway, clergyman, educator; b. Cambridge, N.Y., Aug. 9, 1870; s. John Legus and Mary Angeline (Gallaway) H.; grad. Cambridge Washington Acad., Cambridge, 1888; A.B., Monmouth (Ill.) Coll., 1893, D.D., 1906, L.H.D., 1946; Allegheny (now Pittsburgh-Xenia) Theol. Sem., 1897; studied Princeton, 1918; m. Florida Pattison, Aug. 17, 1897 (dec.); children—Charles Wishart, Arthur Alvan, Robert Cushman, John Legus, Mary Josephine (dec.), Howard Pattison. Ordained ministry U.P. Ch., 1897; missionary in Egypt, 1897-1917; prof. N.T. exegesis and lit. in Theol. Sem., at Cairo, 1908-17; in office of Bd. Fgn. Missions, Phila., 1919-20; prof. dept. missions and comparative religion Pitts. Theol. Sem., 1920-26; supply pastor McNaugher Meml. Ch.; prof. dept. of missions and comparative religion Coll. of Wooster, 1926-27; pastor of First Presbyn. Church, Mt. Vernon, O., 1927-40; supply pastor First Ch., Canton, O., 1942, First Ch., Cambridge, N.Y., 1942-43; pastor First Ch., Cambridge, N.Y., 1943-48. Teacher of the Bible at summer confs. and community Bible schools. Author: Foreign Missions Handbook, 1920; also numerous articles in religious mags. Home: Cambridge, N.Y. Died Dec. 8, 1949; buried family lot, Cambridge.

HUNT, Leigh, architect; b. Sioux City, Ia., July 22, 1881; s. William Henry and Emma Grace (Lawyer) H., private education; student Chicago Art Institute; m. 2d Elizabeth Augur Scott, 1922; 1 d., Betty Leigh; children by 1st marriage, Leigh Bryant, Willis Ashton (both dec.). Archtl. draftsman; with firms of Church & Jobson, Shepley, Rutan & Coolidge, James Gamble Rogers, W. Carbys Zimmerman, Solon Spencer Beman, Chgo.; in ind. practice since 1910. Past chmn. Milw. Housing Authority. Mem. Mayor's Interracial Relations Com. Fellow, past bd. mem. A.I.A. (past pres. Wis. chpt.); past sec.-treas. Wis. Architects Assn. Mason (32°, Shriner). Clubs: Cliff Dwellers (Chgo.); City (past pres.) (Milw.). Address: 3800 N. Humboldt Av., Milw. 12. Died May 27, 1959.

HUNT, Lester Callaway, U.S. senator; b. Isabel, Ill., July 8, 1892; s. William and Viola (Callaway) H.; student Ill. Wesleyan U., Bloomington, Ill., 1912-13; D.D.S., St. Louis U., 1917; post grad., Northwestern U., 1920; LL.D., University of Wyoming, 1950; married Emily Nathelle Higby, February, 3, 1918; children—Elise Nila, Lester Callaway. Dentist, Lander, Wyo., 1917-34; sec. of state, Wyo., 1935-43, gov., 1943-49, U.S. senator from Wyoming, January 1949—. Chmn. governor's conf., 1948-49. Served as first lieutenant, captain and major, Dental Corps., United States Army, 1917-19. Pres. State Bd. Dental Examiners, 1924-28. Dir. U. Wyo. Named Dentist of Year, 1951. Fellow International (hon.), Am. colls. dentists; mem. Pierre Fauchard Acad., Mem. Am. Dental Assn., State Dental Soc. (pres., 1927), Am. Legion, Psi Omega, Tau Kappa Epsilon. Mason (32°, Shriner), Elk, Eagle. Sponsor Wyoming Guide, 1941. Sponsor Wyoming Hist., Blue Book, 1946. Originated and designed Wyoming's unique "bucking horse" license plate, 1936. Home: 5105 Linnean. Office: 304 Senate Office Bldg., Washington. Died June 19, 1954; buried, Cheyenne, Wyo.

HUNT, Myron, architect; b. Sunderland, Mass., Feb. 27, 1868; s. Myron A. and Hannah (Miller) H.; ed. Northwestern Univ., Chicago, 1888-90; Mass. Inst. Tech., 1890-92; Boston and Chicago architects' offices, 1892-94; in Europe, 1894-96; m. Harriette Boardman, May 30, 1894 (died Oct. 27, 1913); children—William (dec.), Charles, Harriet, Hubbard, Robert; m. 2d, Virginia Pease, July 3, 1915. Practiced in Chicago 5 years; moved to Los Angeles, 1903; partner in Los Angeles for 5 yrs., with Elmer Grey; alone, 1908-20; partner with H. C. Chambers, firm name Myron Hunt and H. C. Chambers, 1920-47, H. C. Chambers and Lester Hibbard, since 1948. Architect for Occidental Coll., Los Angeles, and three other coll. groups; Rose Bowl, Pasadena; Pomona and Occidental Greek theatres; H. E. Huntington art gallery, residence and library; Santa Barbara and La Jolla art galleries; Pomona College Music Hall; Pasadena and Palos Verdes pub. libraries buildings; First Congl. Church, Riverside; Co. Nat. Bank and San Marcos Bldg., Santa Barbara; Los Angeles Ambassador, Flintridge and six other hotels; Pasadena, Riverside, Redlands, Uplands, White Memorial, Huntington Memorial, Hastings Memorial hosps.; Magan and Clough clinics; Pasadena and La Vina preventoria; La Vina Sanitorium; Boys and Girls Aid Orphanage; Magnin Bldg. and numerous other commercial and industrial bldgs., also residences and their landscaping; U.S. Army camps, Callan, Ft. Rosecrans, White, Pendleton; consultant San Diego Naval Training Base Library, Occidental Flagstone Hosp.; asso. with others on Hollywood Bowl, housing projects, hosps., and other important bldgs. Formerly chmn. Los Angeles County Govtl. Simplification Com., formerly mem. Internat. Hospital Assn. American Com.; mem. Architects Civic Center Com., City of Los Angeles. Fellow A.I.A.; mem. So. Calif. chapter A.I.A. (ex-pres.), Am. Hosp. Assn. S.A.R., State Assn. Calif. Architects (charter mem.), Sigma Chi. Clubs: University, Athenaeum (Pasadena). Holder Pasadena Noble Prize gold medal for 1928. Home: 200 N. Grand Av., Pasadena 3. Office: 124 W. 4th St., Los Angeles. Died May 26, 1952.

HUNT, Richard Carley, lawyer; b. Paris, France, Aug. 27, 1886 (parents U.S. citizens); s. Richard Howland and Pearl (Carley) H.; LL.B. cum laude, Yale, 1908; m. Elena Barron, Feb. 22, 1912 (div. 1923); children—Georgine (Mrs. Peter C. Wright-Clark) (dec.), Richard Barron; married 2d, Grace LeRoy, Dec. 11, 1948. Admitted to New York bar, 1910, and practiced before Federal and New York courts. Dir. Electrolux Corp., Emerson Radio and Phonograph Corp. P. R. Mallory and Co., Inc., Servel, Inc. Pres. Wenner-Gren Found. for Anthropol. Research; v.p., trustee Inst. for Crippled and Disabled. Mem. Assn. of Bar of City of N.Y., Yale Law Sch. Assn. (past pres.), Soc. of Colonial Wars, S.R., Pilgrims, Council on Fgn. Relations. Clubs: Down Town, Links, Creek, Century, Piping Rock, Racquet and Tennis, Anglers (New York); Flyfishers (London). Home: 141 E. 72d St., New York 21. Office: 70 Pine St., N.Y.C. 5. Died 1954.

HUNT, Westley Marshall, otolaryngologist; b. Auburn, Me., Sept. 1, 1888; s. Edward Everett and Ellen Matilda (Anderson) H.; B.S., Dartmouth, 1910, M.D., 1913; grad. St. Luke's Hosp. and S.I. Hosp., N.Y.C.; post-grad. study, Vienna; m. Emily H. Callaway, Feb. 27, 1920. Instr. N.Y.U. and Bellevue Med. Coll., 1920-22, lectr., 1922-25, clin. prof. otology, 1925-30; dir. dept. otolaryngology Fifth Av. Hosp., 1924-35; attending otolaryngologist and bronchopist St. Luke's Hosp., N.Y.C.; surgeon, director Manhattan Eye, Ear, and Throag Hosp.; cons. otolaryngologist Woman's Hosp., Huntington Hosp., S.I. Hosp., Nat. Hosp. for Speech Disorders, Ruptured and Crippled Hosp. Dir. Am. Bd. of Otolaryngology. Served as lt. (s.g.) USNRF, and maj. U.S. M.C., comdg. head surgery operating team, France, 1917-18. Past pres. New York League for the Hard of Hearing. Fellow A.C.S., N.Y. Acad. Medicine (past chmn. otolaryngology sect.); mem. A.M. A., Am. Laryngol. Assn., Am. Otol. Soc., Am. Broncho-Esophogological Assn. Am. Laryngol., Rhinol. and Otol. Soc. (v.p. eastern sect.), Clin. Research Soc. (pres. 1924), New York Bronchoscopic Club (pres. 1932), N.Y. Laryngol. Soc. (pres. 1942), Am. Acad. Ophthalmology and Oto-Laryngology, N.Y. Oto-Laryngol. Soc. (pres.), Soc. Colonial Ward (lt. governor), S.R., S.A.R., Mil. Order Foreign Wars, New York Soc. Mil. and Naval Officers World War, Assn. Mil. Surgeons of U.S., Order Founders and Patriots (past gov.), Soc. Mayflower Descendants of N.Y..(past gov.), Am. Legion (past comdr. Fiji Post), Alpha Kappa Kappa, Phi Gamma Delta. Republican. Conglist. Mason. Clubs: Quill (pres. 1942), Sleepy Hollow, Megantic Fish and Game. Home: Northport, L.I. Office: 907 Fifth Av., N.Y.C. 21. Died June 28, 1950; buried Cathedral St. John Divine, N.Y.C.

HUNTER, Aaron Burtis, sch. prin.; b. Phila., Apr. 26, 1854; s. John C. and Sarah Ann (Clark) H.; A.B., Amherst, 1876, D.D., 1916; grad. Union Theol. Sem., 1879; U. of Berlin, 1879-80; D.D., U. of the South, 1916; m. Sarah Lothrop Taylor, Jan. 19, 1888. Ordained to ministry P.E. Ch., deacon, 1881, priest, 1882; asst. to rector St. Luk's Ch., Germantown, Phila., 1881-2; rector St. Mary's, Hillsboro, O., 1882-84; chaplain Wolfe Hall, Denver, 1885-87; vice prin. St. Augustine's Sch., Raleigh, N.C., 1888-91, prin., 1891-1916. Mem. Delta Upsilon. Address: St. Augustine's Sch., Raleigh, N.C. Died July 12, 1933; buried Raleigh, N.C.

HUNTER, Jay Tyler, lawyer; b. Peoria, Ill., July 21, 1873; s. Thomas and Corlin (Sloan) H.; student Cornell University, Ithaca, N.Y., 1892-94; studied law privately; Ph.D., Bradley University, 1952; married Elizabeth A. Oakford, May 6, 1952; children—Thomas Oakford, Elizabeth Mary. Admitted to Ill. bar, 1899, and since practiced in Peoria; sr. partner Hunter, Kavanagh & McLaughlin; firm counsel for Pa. R.R. Co., Commercial Solvents Corp., Premier-Pabst Corp. and various ins. cos.; pres. Peoria Title & Trust Co.; vice president Toledo, Peoria & Western Railroad; dir. Commercial Merchants Nat. Bank & Trust Co. (Peoria), etc. Mem. Peoria Bd. of Edn. (pres. 1913-14); trustee Bradley University. Served on Exemption bd., World War. Mem. Am., Ill. State and Peoria County bar assns., Phi Delta Theta. Republican. Clubs: Creve Coeur, Peoria Country. Home: 304 Parkside Drive. Office: Commercial Bank Bldg., Peoria, Ill. Died Feb. 6, 1953.

HUNTER, John F., ex-congressman; b. Ford City, Pa., Oct. 19, 1896; s. Robert Bede and Annie (Feeney) H.; LL.B., St. John's U., Toledo, 1918. Admitted to Ohio bar, 1918, since practiced in Toledo and Washington; admitted to Va. bar, 1946; mem. Hunter & Friedman, Toledo. Mem. Ohio Ho. of Reps., 1933-34, Ohio Senate, 1935-36; mem. 75th to 77th Congresses, 9th Ohio Dist. Pres. Hunter Motors of Va. Mem. nat. council Boy Scouts of America. Served as private in World War, 1917-18. Mem. Am. Legion (comdr. Daly Post 1922-23), Vets. Fgn. Wars (hon.). Am. Bar Assn. Democrat. Address: 901 Prince St., Alexandria, Va. Died Dec. 1957.

HUNTER, Joseph Rufus, educator; b. Apex, N.C., June 6, 1865; s. Joseph Calvin and Piannetta (Beckwith) H.; grad. Wake Forest Coll., N.C., 1885, A.M., 1889; Ph.D., Johns Hopkins, 1895; unmarried. Taught in pvt. schs. N.C., 1885-88; prof. physics and mathematics, State Normal Sch., Oshkosh, Wis., 1891-93; prof. chemistry Richmond (Va.) Coll., 1895—, also former head of dept. Conbtr. articles in field. Has published articles on chem. subjects. Mem. Am. Chem. Soc., German Chem. Soc.; fellow A.A.A.S. Address: Raleigh, N.C. Died Mar. 1951.

HUNTER, Kent A., correspondent; b. Omaha, Neb., Feb. 7, 1892; s. William Howard and Anna May (White) H.; ed. Bellevue (Neb.) Acad., 1908-09; B.A., St. Thomas Coll., St. Paul, Minn., 1909-

12; m. Ruty Taylor, Apr. 11, 1953. Reporter Mpls. Tribune, 1912, Chgo. Inter-Ocean, 1913-15, Chgo. Examiner, 1915-17 and 1919-21, Los Angeles Examiner, 1921-24, Chicago Herald-American, 1924-28, N.Y. Journal-Am., 1928-41; corr. Washington bur., Hearst Newspapers. King Features Syndicate, 1945-51; special writer New York Journal-American; founded Facts, Evaluated, research service, 1954. Served as private to captain, 122d F.A., U.S.N.G., World War I; O.R.C., 1922-41; maj. to col., including staff Gen. Patton, in France, Luxembourg, Germany, World War II. Decorated Silver Star with 2 Oak Leaf Clusters, Bronze Star, Legion of Merit. Mem. Am. Legion, Mil. Order World Wars. Club: Army and Navy (Washington). Author of: Strategy and Tactics World Communist, Part 1, Senate Internal Security Committee, 1954; Symposium Soviet Total War, Vol. II, 1956; The Communist Drive for Africa, 1957. Home: 1026 16th St, Washington 6. Died Aug. 26, 1958; buried Arlington Nat. Cemetery.

HUNTER, Oscar Benwood, pathologist, educator; b. Cherrydale, Va., Jan. 31, 1888; s. Montgomery and Lillian Theresa (Edmonston) H.; M.D., George Washington U., 1912, A.B., 1916, A.M., 1917; m. Sidney Sophia Pearson, Dec. 26, 1914; children—Oscar Benwood, Frances Elizabeth, Mary Ellen, Margaret Pearson. Instr. in anatomy, George Washington U., 1912, prof. histology and embryology, 1913-16, prof. bacteriology and pathology, 1916-32, acting dean Dental Sch., 1918, asst. dean Med. Sch., 1918-32; pathologist George Washington U. Hosp. and Dispensary, 1916-32; pathologist The Doctors' Hosp., Sibley Memorial Hosp.; cons. pathol., Montgomery County Gen. Hosp.; prof. sanitary science, Central Training Sch. for Nurses, 1932-40; lecturer, Kober Foundation, Georgetown U., 1926; professorial lecturer Georgetown U., 1935-45; Am. U.; sec. Wash. Med. Bldg. Corp., Columbia Med. Bldg. Corp., Columbia Operating Corp., Doctors' Hosp., Maj. Med. Reserve Corps. Asso. Internat. Coll. Surgeons; fellow Am. Coll. Physicians, Coll. of Am. Pathologists; mem. Am. Hosp. Assn., Wash. Heart Assn., Wash. Acad. Scis., Wash. Acad. Med., Internat. Assn. Med. Museums, D.C. Rheumatism Soc., Diabetes Assn. of D.C., Inc., American Heart Association, A.M.A., American Association Anatomists, American Society Bacteriologists, American Society Pathologists and Bacteriologists, Am. Therapeutic Soc. (pres. 1938-39; sec. 1934-38 and since 1939), A.A.A.S., Southern Medical Association (vice pres., 1946-47, president-1948-49), Tri-State Medical Society, also Galen-Hippocrates Society, Medical Society D.C. (pres. 1928), Washington Medical Surg. Soc., George Washington U. Med. Soc. (pres. 1918-19, re-elected 1938-39; sec. since 1941), Am. Soc. of Clinic Pathologists, Am. Assn. for Study of Neoplastic Diseases, Miss. Valley Med. Soc. (hon.), Am. Assn. of University Profs., Assn. of Military Surgeons of U.S., Reserve Officers Assn. of U.S., Washington Soc. of Pathologists (pres. 1937-38), Am. Pub. Health Assn., Nat. Safety Council, Alpha Kappa Kappa; pres. Gen Alumni Assn. of George Washington U., 1928-29 and 1929-30. Republican. Roman Catholic. Clubs: University, Corinthian Yacht, Kiwanis of Washington (pres. 1941), Cosmos, Internat. Medical. Contbr. Washington Med. Annals, Am. Jour. Clin. Pathology, Jour. A.M.A., Jour. Lab. and Clin. Medicine, etc. Home: 3815 Bradley Lane, Chevy Chase, Md. Office: 915 19th St. N.W., Washington 6. Died Dec. 19, 1951.

HUNTER, R(obert) M(iller), prof. law; b. Champaign County, O., Feb. 28, 1895; s. Samuel McKendrie and Emma Jane (Atkinson) H.; A.B., Ohio Wesleyan, 1917; J.D., Ohio State, 1922; J.S.D., Yale, 1932; m. Mildred Huit, June 21, 1923; children—Robert Huit, Susan Jane, Phyllis Ann. Admitted to Ohio Bar, 1922; pvt. practice of law, Columbus, O., 1922-26; asst., coll. of commerce, Ohio State U., 1921-25, asst. prof., Coll. of Law, 1925-33, asso. prof., 1933-37, prof. and sec. Coll. of Law, Ohio State U. since 1937; spl. asst. to U.S. atty gen., Washington, D.C., 1941-45; spl. counsel Fed. Power Commn. May-Dec., 1945; mem. Zaibatsu mission to Japan for State and War Depts., 1946. Mem. Order of the Coif, Pi Sigma Alpha, Phi Delta Phi. Methodist. Author: Hunter's Cases on Ohio Trial Practice, 1938; revised forms in Bates Pleading Parties Practice and Forms (4th ed.) 1932. Contbr. articles to law revs. Home: 5100 Olentangy River Rd., Columbus 2. Office: College of Law, Ohio State University, Columbus 10, O. Died June 24, 1952; buried Mt. Tabor Cemetery, Champaign County, O.

HUNTER, Walter Samuel, psychologist; b. Decatur, Ill., Mar. 22, 1889; s. George and Ida (Weakley) H.; student Polytechnic Coll., Ft. Worth, Tex., 1905-08; A.B., U. of Tex., 1910; Ph.D., University of Chicago, 1912; honorary M.A., Brown University, 1943; married Katharine Pratt, January 1, 1913 (died Apr. 1, 1915); 1 dau., Thayer; m. 2d, Alda Barber, Aug. 1, 1917; 1 dau., Helen Barbara. Instructor philosophy, 1912-14, adjunct prof. psychology, 1914-16, U. of Texas; prof. psychology, U. of Kansas, 1916-25; G. Stanley Hall, prof. genetic psychology, Clark U., 1925-36; prof. psychology and dir. psychol. lab. Brown University, 1936—. Expert consultant to U.S. Sec. War, 1941-42; chief, applied psychology panel, N.D.R.C., 1943-45, mem. 1945-46; mem. Moe sub-com. for Bush Report, 1944-45; cons. Research and Development Bd., 1947—; mem. Undersea Warfare Committee N.R.C., 1946-51. Visiting prof. Tulane U., 1915, State U. of Ia., 1920, U. of Chicago, 1923, 30, U. of Calif. at Los Angeles, 1926, Northwestern U., 1927, Harvard, 1927-29 and 1932, U. of Minn., 1936. First lt., later captain Sanitary Corps, Psychology Div., U.S. Army, Sept. 8, 1917-Dec. 16, 1918. Awarded Presidential Medal for Merit, 1948. Fellow A.A.A.S. (vice pres. and chmn. Sect. I, 1932); mem. Am. Psychol. Assn. (council 1921-23, pres. 1931), Eastern Psychol. Assn. (pres. 1941), Soc. Exptl. Psychology, Internat. Congress Psychology (exec. sec. 9th congress, internat. com., 1929—), Am. Acad. Arts and Sci., 1933-47, Nat. Acad. Scis., Am. Philos. Soc., Phi Beta Kappa, Sigma Xi. Mem. Social Science Research Council, 1943-45; member div. anthropology and psychology, National Research Council, 1926-29, 1933-36 and 1939-42, chmn. same division, 1936-38. Member Research Board for Nat. Security, 1945, Sci. Advisory Group, Headquarters A.A.F., 1946-47. Author: General Psychology, 1919, 1923; Human Behavior, 1928. Asso. editor Psychology Bull., 1916-24, Jour. Animal Behavior, 1914-20, Jour. Comparative Psychology, 1921-25, Jour. Genetic Psychology, 1925-34, Genetic Psychology Monographs, 1926-34, Am. Jour. Psychol., 1940—; editor Behavior Monographs, 1922, Comparative Psychol. Monographs, 1922-27, Psychol. Index, 1925-36, Psychol. Abstracts, 1926-46. Contbr. on exptl. and theoretical psychology to scientific jours. Clubs: Art, Faculty. Home: 61 Prospect St., Providence. Died Aug. 3, 1954.

HUNTING, Fred Stanley, banker; b. East Templeton, Mass., Sept. 30, 1867; s. William and Mary (Day) H.; B.S., Worcester (Mass.) Poly. Tech. Inst., 1888; m. Harriett Alzina Sawyer, May 1, 1889 (died June 26, 1904); children—Ralph William, Lawrence Stratton, Harold Stanley; m. 2d Elma Pearl Balthis, June 10, 1907 (died Mar. 29, 1929); 1 son, William Fred. Draftsman, later asst. to chief engr., Ft. Wayne Electric Light Co., 1888-93, chief construction engr., 1893-99; treas. and sales mgr. Ft. Wayne Electric Works, 1899-1910, v.p. and treas., 1910-11; gen. mgr. Ft. Wayne Works of Gen. Electric Co., 1911-22; pres. and chmn. bd. Robbins & Myers Co., Springfield, O., 1922-27; retired from elec. business and spent much time in Calif., 1927-33; helped organize Ft. Wayne Nat. Bank, 1933, pres. to Jan. 14, 1941, chmn. of the Board since Jan. 14, 1941; dir. Lincoln Nat. Life Insurance Co. (mem. finance com.). Member Ft. Wayne Chamber Commerce (1st pres.). Mem. Allen County Council of Defense during World War. Fellow Am. Inst. Elec. Engrs.; hon. mem. Elec. Mfrs. Club of N.Y., Quest Club of Ft. Wayne. Republican. Conglist. Mason (33°). Clubs: Ft. Wayne Country. Home: Hotel Alms, Cincinnati. Office: Fort Wayne National Bank, Fort Wayne 2, Ind. Died Dec. 17, 1951; buried Lindenwood Cemetery, Fort Wayne.

HUNTINGTON, Archer Milton, author; b. New York, Mar. 10, 1870; s. Collis P. H.; private edn. in New York and Spain; hon. A.M., Yale, 1897, Harvard, 1904; Litt.D., Columbia, 1907; LL.D., Kenyon Coll., 1920, University of Madrid; m. Helen Manchester Gates, in London, England, August 6, 1895; m. 2d, Anna Vaughan Hyatt, March 10, 1923. Member Am. Geog. Soc. (ex-pres., mem. council), Am. Numismatic Society (honoary president), New York Chamber Commerce, Am. Acad. Arts and Letters, British Numismatic Soc., Royal Numismatic Soc. Royal Inst. Gt. Britain, British Inst. Philosophy, Royal Soc. of Arts, Bibliog. Soc., London Library, Phi Beta Kappa; founder The Mariners' Museum, Newport News, Va., also Brookgreen (S.C.) Gardens, 1930; corresponding mem. Spanish Acad., acads. of history, and of San Fernando, Ateneo of Madrid; member of Patronato of Museu Sorolla, 1941—, Fundaciones Vega Inclan, 1942—, Academy of Fine Arts, Palma, Mallorca; member college of electors, Hall of Fame of New York U.; founder and president Hispanic Society America; trustee American Museum Natural History, N.Y. Hist. Soc., Museum of the American Indian, Heye Foundation, Instituto Valencia de Don Juan, Casa del Greco, Casa de Cervantes. Received G. Melchers medal, Artists Fellowship, 1950; Knight Comdr. Order of Alfonso XII, Carlos III; Chevalier of Legion of Honor (France), 1927; Order of Carlos Manual de Céspedes (Cuba), 1937. Corr. mem. La Academia General de Ciencias de Cordoba. Clubs: Yacht, Grolier, National Arts, Authors', City, Yale University, India House, Columbia University, Harvard, Coll. Royal Societies, Authors. Author: A Note Book in Northern Spain, 1898; Lake Maker of Segovia (poems), 1928; The Ladies of Vallbona (poems), 1931; Youth, Torn Sails of Faith, Moraima's Tower, The Lady of Elche, America, Polvo, The Sea (poems), 1933; The Silver Gardens, Alfonso the Eighth Rides By (poems), 1934; Vela Venenosa, Rimas (poems), 1936; A Flight of Birds (poems), 1938; Spain and Africa (poems), 1943; Recuerdos (poems), 1949; Turning Pages, 1950; Tapestry, 1951; Tapestry II, 1952; Collected Verse, 1952; The Torch Bearers, 1955. Editor: Lady (Aulnoy's) Travels Into Spain (with intro), 1899; The Poem of the Cid, text, translation, and notes, 1897. Contributor articles to mags. Editor of Publications Hispanic Society of America. Presented, 1927 to Palace of Legion of Honor, San Francisco, art collection in memory of Collis P. Huntington, and to Yale University Museum, collection in memory of Arabella D. Huntington, art collection to Charleston (S.C.) Mus., 1931-32, the Archer and Anna Huntington Wild Life Forest Station to Syracsue U., 1932, building for Nat. Acad. of Design, New York City, 1940, also former residence and 500 acres to Palisades Interstate Park Commn., 1943, also to N.Y. State for State Teachers Coll. at Cortland, N.Y., Camp Pine Knot (198½ acres) as a memorial to Collis P. Huntington, 1949. Home: Box 245, Bethel, Conn. Died Dec. 11, 1955; buried Woodlawn Cemetery.

HUNTINGTON, Baldwin Gwynne, banker; b. Columbus, O., Jan. 13, 1879; s. Peletiah Webster and Frances (Sollace) H.; grad. Lawrenceville (N.J.) Sch., 1896; A.B., Princeton, 1900; m. Maybel Monypeny, Jan. 1904; children—Ann (Mrs. Carter Kissell), Frances Sollace (Mrs. Robert W. Wales), Lt. John Webster Perit, USNR; m. 2d Dorothy Seabury Briscoe, June 1936. Clk. Franklin Fire Ins. Co., 1900-02; with Huntington Nat. Bank, Columbus, since 1902, pres., 1931-49, chmn. bd. since Jan. 1949. Chmn. finance com. Midland Mutual Life Ins. Company. Republican. Presbyterian. Home: 292 S. Columbia Av. Office: Huntington National Bank, Columbus, O. Died Aug. 25, 1958; buried Greenlawn Cemetery, Columbus.

HUNTINGTON, Daniel Trumbull, bishop; b. Norwich, Conn., Aug. 4, 1868; s. Col. Robert Watkinson and Jane (Trumbull) H.; B.A., Yale, 1892; student Gen. Theol. Sem., 1892-93; grad. Berkeley Div. Sch., 1895, D.D., 1912; m. Virginia E. Haist, Dec. 7, 1916; children—Jane Trumbull, Mary Champion, Jonathan Trumbull, Elizabeth Catherine. Deacon, 1895, ordained priest, 1890, P.E. Church; missionary, Hankow, China, 1895-1900; went to Ichang, 1901, in charge of sch. and evangelistic work; opened a trade sch. for destitute boys, 1907; elected bishop of Wuhu (now Dist. of Anking), 1911; consecrated in Shanghai, 1912; retired, 1940. Mem. Psi Upsilon. Author: Chinese Primer, 1903; History of Diocese of Anking, 1943. Translated into Chinese: Practice of the Presence of God, 1905; Instructions for Baptism, 1924; Instructions for Confirmation, 1926. Address: 25 Kenilworth Rd., Wellesley 81, Mass. Died May 1, 1950; buried Woodlawn Cemetery, Wellesley.

HUNTINGTON, Edward Vermilye, mathematician; b. Clinton, Oneida County, N.Y., Apr. 26, 1874; s. Chester and Katharine Hazard (Smith) H.; A.B., Harvard, 1895, A.M., 1897; Ph.D., U. of Strassburg, Germany, 1901; hon. Sc.D., U. of San Marcos, Lima, Peru, 1925; m. Susie Edwards Van Volkenburgh, July 6, 1909. Instr. mathematics, Harvard, 1895-97, Williams Coll., 1897-99; in Europe, 1899-1901; instr. mathematics, 1901-05, asst. prof., 1905-15, asso. prof., 1915-19, prof. mechanics, 1919-41, emeritus since 1941, Harvard U. Western Exchange prof. from Harvard to Beloit, Carleton, and Knox Colls., 1925. Consultant, Nat. Defense Research Com. since 1942. Major, Gen. Staff, on statis. duty at Washington, 1918-19. Editor Annals of Mathematics, 1902-11. Fellow Am. Acad. Arts and Sciences (chmn. com. of pub., 1914-19), A.A.A.S. (vice pres. and chmn. section A, 1926), Am. Inst. of Math. Statistics; mem. Am. Philos. Soc., Am. Math. Soc. (v.p. 1924; rep. on National Research Council, 1923-26), Math. Assn. America (pres. 1918), Am. Statistical Assn., Am. Standards Assn. (mem. sectional com.; chmn. sub-committee on math. symbols, 1928), Assn. for Symbolic Logic, American Academy Political Science. Honorary member of Phi Beta Kappa. Author: Four-Place Tables of Logarithms and Trigonometric Functions, arranged for decimal division of the degree, 1907; Monograph IV on "The Fundamental Propositions of Algebra," in work entitled "Mathematical Monographs" (edited by J. W. A. Young), 1911; The Continuum and Other Types of Serial Order, 1917; Handbook of Mathematics for Engineers, 1918; chapters I and IV in "Handbook of Mathematical Statistics" (edited by H. L. Rietz), 1924; Survey of Methods of Apportionment in Congress (Senate Doc. No. 304), 1940. Contbr. to math. journals. Congregationalist. Devised the method of apportioning representatives in Congress which became law Nov. 15, 1941. Home: 48 Highland St., Cambridge 38, Mass. Died Nov. 25, 1952.

HUNTINGTON, George Herbert, educator; b. Gorham, Me., Apr. 12, 1878; s. Henry Strong and Mary Lawrence (Herbert) H.; B.A., Williams, 1900; B.D., Hartford Theol. Sem., 1907; student Teachers Coll., Columbia, and Union Theol. Sem., 1914-15 and 1922; D.D., Williams Coll., 1929; m. Elizabeth Wainwright, d. Cleveland H. Dodge, July 27, 1916. Instr., 1900, prof., 1907-37, prof. emeritus since 1937, v.p., 1917-37, and actg. pres., Mar. 1919-June 1920, Robert Coll., Istanbul, Turkey; also prin. Prep. Sch., 1907-27. Pres. bd. mgrs. Constantinople Y.M.C.A., 1915-24; dir. Am. Chamber Commerce for the Levant, 1923-33; mem. bd. mgrs. Am. Hosp., Constantinople. Conglist. Mem. Theta Delta Chi. Has traveled extensively in Asia and Europe. Address: (winter) Warm

Springs, Ga.; (summer) Prouts Neck, Me. Died Aug. 2, 1953.

HUNTINGTON, William Chapin, writer, editor; b. Des Moines, Ia., Apr. 13, 1884; s. Clarence Wm. and Edith (Chapin) H.; M.E., Columbia, 1907; Dr. Eng., Royal Tech. Coll., Aix-La-Chapelle, Germany, 1914; m. Frances A. Carpenter, Apr. 6, 1920; children—Joanna Carpenter (Mrs. Huntington Noel), Edith Chapin (Mrs. David Benton Williams). Metallurgist and metall. engr., U.S. Steel Corp., 1907-11; studied and traveled in Germany, Belgium and France, 1911-14, commercial agt. Chicago dist., U.S. Bur. Foreign and Domestic Commerce, 1914-16; commercial attaché, Am. Embassy, Petrograd, 1916-18; chief of Russian Div., Bur. Fgn. and Domestic Commerce, Washington, D.C., 1919-20; commercial attaché, Am. Embassy, Paris, Apr. 1920-Nov. 1922; cons. practice as industrial engr., 1923-24; research on Russian economic conditions, 1925—; lecturer Am. Univ., 1937-39. Editor Russian Translation Project, American Council of Learned Soc., 1944-49. Mem. Washington Literary Society. Episcopalian. Clubs: Cosmos, Chevy Chase (Washington, D.C.). Author: The Homesick Million—or Russia Out of Russia, 1933; Prospects of American Trade with the Soviet Union, 1935. Author many articles and book reviews. Address: 2101 Connecticut Av., Washington 8. Died Oct. 6, 1958.

HUNTRESS, Carroll Benton, coal sales exec.; b. Ogdensburg, N.Y., Nov. 25, 1885; s. Frank and Mary Elizabeth (Benton) H.; student St. Paul's School, Concord, N.H., 1900-03, Williams Coll., 1903-04, Harvard, 1905-06; m. Margery Gish, Nov. 3, 1908; children—Jack Benton, Douglas Knickerbocker, Marion, Carroll Benton; m. 2d, Geneve McClellan, Dec. 17, 1931. Newspaper reporter and editor, La Porte, Ind., 1907-12; exec. sec. Chamber of Commerce, La Porte, 1912-14, Marion, O., 1914-16, Allentown, Pa., 1916-19; Washington rep. Nat. Assn. Owners of R.R. Securities and other nat. assns., 1919-24; with Nat. Coal Assn., 1924-30, exec. sec., 1930-33; pres. and dir. Appalachian Coals, Inc., Cincinnati, a sales agency for 269 bituminous coal mines, 1933-36; v.p. Republic Coal & Coke Co. Chairman National St. Lawrence Project Conference in Opposition since 1947. Mem. Sigma Phi. Republican. Episcopalian. Clubs: Union League (Chicago); University (Washington); Whitehall (New York). Home: 119 Cottage Av., Mt. Vernon, N.Y. Office: Whitehall Bldg., 17 Battery Pl., N.Y.C. 4. Died Nov. 29, 1952; buried Salt Lake City.

HUNTRESS, Frank G., newspaper pub.; b. San Antonio, Tex., Feb. 24, 1870; s. Frank G. and Frances (Montes) H.; ed. high school, also spl. courses in English, adminstrn. and finance; m. Katherine Johnson, Dec. 1906. With San Antonio Express since 1884; passed through all depts., v.p. and gen. mgr., 1910, pres. and pub., 1911-54, chairman of the board and publisher, 1954—; director San Antonio Loan & Trust Co. Mem. Belknap Rifles Assn., Am. Newspaper Publishers Assn., Bureau of Advertising, Texas Daily Newspaper Association (ex-president), National Press Assn., Advertising Club of New York, Advertising Fedn. of America, Rotary Club. Awarded N. H. White trophy for civic welfare work, 1928 citation and trophy by Laredo (Tex.) civic leaders; co founder and pres.-emeritus, Bexar Co. chapter, Nat. Found. for Infantile Paralysis. Member Christian (Disciples) Church. Mason (32°, K.C. C.H., Shriner). Refused all political appointments offered to him. Home: Menger Hotel, San Antonio 5. Office: Express Pub. Co., San Antonio 6. Died July 30, 1955.

HUNZIKER, Otto Frederick, dairy scientist; b. Zürich, Switzerland, Dec. 25, 1873; s. Carl Otto and Louise (Pupikofer) H.; grad. agrl. sch., Zürich, 1892, Bryant & Stratton Bus. Coll., Providence, R.I., 1896; B.S.A., Cornell U., 1900. M.S.A., 1901; D.Sc., Purdue U., 1932; m. Florence Belle Burne, 1905; children—Thelma Belle, Florence Louise, Karl Otto (dec.), Walter Burne, Isabelle Mary, Otto Frederick. Came to U.S., 1893, naturalized citizen, 1904. Instr. in bacteriology, Cornell U., 1901-02; milk expert, Scranton Condensed Milk Co., 1902-05; prof. dairying, chief of dairy dept., Purdue U., and Ind. Expt. Sta., 1905-16; mgr. of mfrs. dir. research labs., Blue Valley Creamery Co. (23 factories) 1916-39. Dir. La Grange Fed. Savs. & Loan Assn., 1933-54. Del. U.S. Dept. Agr. to Internat. Dairy, Stockholm, 1911; London, 1928, Copenhagen, 1931. Berlin, 1937; Stockholm, Sweden, 1949, and The Hague, 1953; chmn. program com., Industry and Economics, World's Dairy Congress, Washington, 1923; mem. La Grange Bd. of Health (pres. 1926-27). Charter and life mem. Am. Dairy Sci. Assn. (pres. 1911-13), Nat. Dairy Council, Internat. Dairy and Food Sanitarians, Am.-Swiss C. of C., Sigma Xi, Gamma Alpha, Alpha Zeta. Winner Cornell-Ohio State U. essay contest, 1899; awarded Distinguished Service gold medal, Swiss Dairy Fedn., Berne, 1928. Protestant. Republican. Clubs: Cornell, Kiwanis. Author: Condensed Milk and Milk Powder, 1914, 18, 20, 26, 35, 46, 49; The Butter Industry, 1920, 27, 40. Dairy consultant, author and publisher dairy books, lectr. Invited to Australia and New Zealand, 1927, for investigations and recommendations as to dairy industry. Appointed dairy technologist by U.S. Dept. Agr. for dairy survey in Latin-Am. countries, 1942. Awarded diploma for sci. pubs., by Internat. Exposition, Milan, 1924. Home and Office: 103 Seventh Av., La Grange, Ill. Died Nov. 15, 1959.

HURD, Archer Willis, educator; b. LaCrosse, Wis., Jan. 7, 1883; s. Willis Warren and Elza (Millem) H.; student Lawrence Coll., Appleton, Wis., 1900-01; Ph.B., Hamline U., 1906; student U. of N.D., 1904-05; M.S., U. of Minn., 1924, Ph.D., 1928; student U. of Chicago, summers 1925, 26; m. Edith Leona MacMichael, Apr. 1, 1912; children—Everett Archer, Winston Willis. Teacher grade sch., Argyle, Wis., 1902, Darlington (Wis.) High Sch., 1903; with Tri-State Telephone Co., St. Paul, summer 1903; teacher Albert Lea (Minn.) High Sch., 1906-07, North High Sch., Mpls., 1907-26; exec. sec. com. on teaching of science, U. of Minn., and asst. dir. Bur. of Ednl. Research, 1926-29; research asso., Teachers Coll., Columbia U., 1929-34; asso. prof. edn., Northern Mont. Coll., 1935-36; prof. edn. and dean, Hamline U., 1937-43; organist and dir. of choir, 15 yrs.; dir. educational research and service, Med. Coll. Va., 1943—; instr. summers, U. Chgo., 1925-26, U.W. Va., 1935, 36, U. Mo., 1937, 39, 48, U. Ill., 1940. Mem. A.A.A.S., Va. Edn. Assn., Va. Acad. Sci., Int. Torch Club, Am. Assn. Sch. Adminstrs., Nat. Assn. Coll. Tchrs. Edn., N.E.A., Minn. Ednl. Assn., (sect. pres., 1927-28), Nat. Soc. Study Edn., Am. Ednl. Research Assn., Nat. Assn. Research in Science Teaching (pres. 1934-35), Soc. for Advancement of Edn., Phi Delta Kappa, Kappa Phi Kappa. Methodist. Club: Kiwanis (Havre, Mont.). Author: Work Text Book in High School Physics, 1931; Cooperative Experimentation, 1933; Teaching Unit in Science, 1934; Educational Psychology, 1940; Technic of Secondary School Teaching, 1941; Special Methods and Student Teaching, 1942; Educational Research and Nursing Education, 1945; Testing Program, 1946; Curriculum for Professional Schools, 1946; Course Within a Professional Curriculum, 1947; planning an Instructional program, 1948; Problems of Collegiate Success or Failure, 1949; Factors Influencing Student Success, 1950; Man and His Sociological and Psychological Environment, 1951; and others on sch. administrn. Contbd. over 100 research articles to educational journals. Home: 116 Bremner Blvd., Richmond 22, Va. Died Aug. 5, 1953.

HURIE, Wiley Lin (hū'rē), clergyman, educator; b. Petersburg, Ill., Mar. 17, 1885; s. John Solomon and Anna Maria (Houghton) H.; grad. Whipple Acad., 1902; A.B., Ill. Coll., Jacksonville, 1906; B.D., Union Theol. Sem., 1912; grad. study Columbia, 1911-12; D.D., Coll. of the Ozarks, 1919; LL. D., Cumberland U., 1939; m. Will-Ula Moores, Nov. 14, 1917; 1 dau., Mary Virginia (Mrs. Paul E. Parks). Ordained ministry Presbyn. Ch., 1911; acting pastor Christ Ch., N.Y.C., 1911, Ch. of The Covenant, N.Y.C., 1912; pastor Central Ch., Russellville, Ark., 1912-23; pres. Coll. of the Ozarks, Clarksville, Ark., 1923-49. Chmn. Pope County United War Work Com., 1918. Chmn. N.W. Ark. Housing Authority, 1941-50. Mem. Phi Beta Kappa. Democrat. Mason (32°). Rotarian. Home: Tallula, Ill. Died Nov. 28, 1954; buried Rock Creek Cemetery, Rock-Creek Community, Tallula.

HURLBUT, William N(athan), paper exec.; b. Chgo., July 4, 1889; s. William Daniels and Hattie (Deutsch) H.; student Cornell, 1908-10; m. Erna E. Hornig, Dec. 19, 1914; children—Erna (Mrs. L. A. White), Louise (Mrs. R. T. Parker), Marion (Mrs. H. P. Hargett), William D., Jean (Mrs. G. R. Compton). With Minn. & Ont. Paper Co., 1910, G.H. Mead interests, 1910-28; joined Internat. Paper Co., N.Y.C., 1928, v.p. since 1928, dir. since 1931. Republican. Episcopalian. Club: Pelham (N.Y.) Country. Home: 1362 Pelhamdale Av., Pelham Manor, N.Y. Office: 220 E. 42d St., N.Y.C. Died Feb. 4, 1956.

HURLEY, Edward Timothy, painter, etcher; b. Cin., Oct. 10, 1869; s. Timothy and Johanna (Dunlea) H.; studied Cin. Art Acad., with Frank Duveneck; m. Alice Irene Bishop, Aug. 17, 1908; children—Robert Edward, Alice Johanna. Has exhibited at Carnegie Inst., Pitts., Art Inst. Ch., Nat. Arts Club, N.Y.C., Herron Inst., Indpls., N.A.D., Cin. Mus., others; represented in permanent collections of Cin. Mus., Brit. Mus., London, New York Pub. Library, Congressional Library, The Nat. Gallery of Art, Washington, Detroit Museum of Art, Toledo Art Museum, Richmond (Ind.) Art Assn., Art Inst. Chgo., Bklyn. Mus., Cleve. Mus., The Nat. Gallery of Ireland (Dublin), Fine Prints of the Year, pub. 1934, 36, London and New York. Recipient gold medal, St. Louis Expn., 1904; Mr. and Mrs. Frank G. Logan medal for etching, Art Inst. Chgo., 1921; landscape prize, Columbus, O., 1921. Especially known for etchings of Cin. and vicinity. Rookwood pottery decorator. Has given illustrated lectures and practical demonstrations in etching. A.N.A. Mem. Ohio Poetry Soc., MacDowell Soc. (Cin.), Chgo. Soc. Etchers, Duveneck Society of Painters, Soc. Am. Etchers, Cin. Art Club, Crafters' Co. Cin., Soc. Profl. Artists, The Ohio Print Makers. Illustrator: The Town of the Beautiful River (31 etchings), 1915; Cincinnati (32etchings), 1916; For Old Acquaintance (32 etchings), 1917; Bridges and Byways (42 etchings), 1919; Impressions of Cincinnati (24 etchings), 1925; Streets and Spires (24 etchings), 1926; Old Mills and Covered Bridges (24 etchings), 1929; Familiar Scenes (24 etchings), 1937; Memories of Cincinnati (24 etchings), 1943. Home: 2112 St. James Av., Cin. 6. Died Nov. 29, 1950.

HURLEY, George, lawyer; b. Providence, R.I., Nov. 9, 1884; s. John and Mary (Donohue) H.; A.B., Brown U., 1907; Rhodes scholar from R.I. at Oxford, 1907-10; studied law Oxford, later Harvard, 1910-11; m. Marie Rose Walsh, Oct. 27, 1917; children—George, Constance. Admitted to R.I. bar, 1912, and practiced since at Providence. Dem. candidate for sec. of state, R.I., 1916; mem. Dem. State Central Com., R.I., 1920-28, chmn., 1921-22. Spl. asst. to Dept. of State, U.S., Oct. 6, 1917-June 30, 1919; attached to Am. Legation, at Copenhagen, Denmark, until June 1919; was rep. of War Trade Bd. at Copenhagen. Am. del. on Interallied Trade Com. for Denmark; spl. asst. to alien property custodian, 1919; asst. atty. gen. State of R.I., 1923-25. Dem. presdl. elector 1936. Chmn., Providence City Plan Commn., since 1944, Providence Family Welfare Soc. Mem. Criminal Law Advisory Commn. (R.I.), 1933-36; mem. R.I. Civil Service Commn.; mem. Am. and R.I. bar assns., Assn. of Am. Rhodes Scholars, Delta Upsilon, Phi Beta Kappa (Brown U.). K.C. Clubs: University, Catholic, Brown Univ. Home: 20 Adelphi Av. Office: Grosvenor Bldg., Providence. Died Mar. 10, 1954.

HURLEY, John Richard, mfr.; b. Wheaton, Ill., May 12, 1908; s. Edward N. and Florence (Amberg) H.; ed. Princeton; m. Gwendolyn Juergens, Dec. 12, 1933; children—Adrienne Lee, Gwendolyn Joan, Pauline Brooke. Pres., Thor Corporation; vice-pres. The Meadows Corp. Clubs: Chicago. Racquet, Chicago Golf, Princeton, Econ., University; Onwentia; Chevy Chase (Washington). Home: 1235 Astor St. Office: 2115 S. 54th Av., Chgo. 50. Died June 21, 1953; buried Calvary Cemetery.

HURLEY, Lawrence Francis, editor; b. Providence, R.I., Nov. 26, 1897; s. Thomas and Helena (Brennan) H.; A.B., Brown Univ., 1919; M.B.A., Harvard, 1922; m. Ann Blanche La Fond, Sept. 13, 1924. Entire career with National Business magazine, Washington, D.C.; circulation mgr., 1922-37, bus. mgr., 1937-41, asst. editor 1941-43, editor since 1943. Roman Catholic. Clubs: Metropolitan, Columbia Country, Chevy Chase (Washington); Harvard (New York). Home: 4944 Lowell St. N.W., Washington 16. Office: 1615 H St. N.W., Washington. Died Jan. 11, 1953.

HURLEY, Stephen Edward, lawyer; born Tenney, Minn., Dec. 31, 1892; s. Edward Joseph and Susan J. (Hopkins) H.; student St. Thomas Coll., St. Paul, 1909-11; A.B., Cath. U., 1913, A.M., 1914; LL.B., Georgetown U., 1914. Admitted to Ill. bar, 1915, and practiced in Quincy, 1915-16; asso. Defrees, Buckingham & Eaton, Chicago, 1916; mem. Defrees, Buckingham, Jones & Hoffman or predecessor firms, 1922-40; mem. Hurley & Simmons, 1940—; dir. The Oliver Corp. Coordinator Selective Service Adv. Bds., Cook Co., Ill., 1940-47; pres. Civil Service Commn., City of Chicago, 1947—. Served as officer, U.S. Army, 1917-19. Dir. Chicago Bar Assn. Found. Mem. Internat., Am. (ho. of dels., 1945, 1946-48, state del. Ill., 1948-51), Ill. and Chicago (pres. 1944-45) bar assns., Am. Law Inst., Am. Judicature Soc., Mediaeval Acad. Am., Mills Coll. Council, Am. Classical League, Acad. Polit. Sci., Chicago Natural History Mus., Ill. and Chicago hist. socs., Chicago Council on Fgn. Relations, Order of Coif (hon.). Clubs: Law (pres. 1947-48), Legal (pres. 1941-42), Chicago Literary (pres. 1947-48), Attic (gov. 1946-48), University, Caxton (council 1948-50) Wayfarers, Cliff Dwellers (Chicago); Lawyers (N.Y. City). Home: 222 E. Chestnut St., Chicago 11. Office: 135 LaSalle St., Chgo. 3. Died May 10, 1955; buried All Saints Cemetery, Des Plaines, Ill.

HURLEY, William E., ret. pub. ofcl.; b. Boston, Aug. 26, 1875; s. William and Ellen (McSorly) H.; student English High Sch. and Burdette Bus. Coll., Boston; m. Ella T. Cuddihy, Apr. 23, 1905. Began as substitute letter carrier, Boston, 1897; postoffice insp., 1907-15; asst. postmaster, Boston, 1915-18, 20-30, acting postmaster, 1918-20, 30, postmaster, 1931-35; treas. and receiver general Commonwealth of Mass., 1937-42. Mem. Boston C. of C., Charitable Irish Soc. of Boston. Catholic. Clubs: Boston City, Wollaston Golf, Algonquin Club. Home: St. Petersburg, Fla. Died Nov. 8, 1957.

HURSTON, Zora Neale, author; b. Eatonville, Fla.; d. Rev. John and Lucy Ann (Potts) H.; grad. high sch. deprtment, Morgan College, 1921; Litt.D., Morgan College, 1939; student Howard U., 1921-24; A.B., Barnard College, 1928. Research (with Dr. Franz Boas) and writing on folklore, Columbia, 1928-32 (private grant from Mrs. R. Osgood Mason and fellowship Rosenwald Foundation); Haiti and British West Indies (Guggenheim fellowship), 1936-

38; head drama dept. N.C. Coll. for Negroes (Durham, N.C.). Received Annisfield award ($1000) for "Dust Tracks on a Road," 1943, and Howard U. Alumni award for distinguished post-grad. work in literature, 1943. Mem. Am. Folklore Soc., Am. Anthrop. Soc., Am. Ethnol. Soc., Zeta Phi Beta. Pagan. Author: Jonah's Gourd Vine, 1934; Mules and Men, 1935; Their Eyes Were Watching God (also pub. Eng. and Italy), 1937; Tell My Horse (pub. London, 1939, as Voodoo Gods), 1938; Moses, Man of the Mountain, 1939; Dust Tracks on a Road (autobiography), 1942; The Voice of the Land, 1945. Compiled Collection of Bahamian Folk Songs (with composer William Grant Still). Contbr. short stories to Am. Mercury, Sat. Evening Post and other mags. Address: care Charles Scribner's Sons, 597 Fifth Av., N.Y.C. 17. Died Jan. 28, 1960.

HURWITZ, Wallie Abraham, mathematician; b. Fulton, Mo., Feb. 18, 1886; s. Harry and Emma (Mayfield) H.; A.B., B.S., A.M., U. of Mo., 1906; A.M., Harvard, 1907; Ph.D., Göttingen, 1910; unmarried. Asst. in mathematics, U. of Mo., 1905-06; instr. mathematics, Cornell U., 1910-14, asst. prof., 1914-24, prof., 1924—. Asso. editor Trans. Am. Math. Soc., 1914-26; editor Am. Math. Monthly, 1919-22; editor Bull. Am. Math. Soc., 1921-24. Fellow A.A.A.S.; mem. Am. Math. Soc., Math. Assn. America, Circolo Matematico di Palermo, London Math. Soc., Société Mathematique de France, Phi Beta Kappa, Sigma Xi. Jewish religion. Address: Cornell University, Ithaca, N.Y. Died Jan. 6, 1958.

HUSBAND, George Rosewall, educator; b. Cornwall, Eng., June 30, 1896; s. John and Elizabeth Ellen (Hollow) H.; brought to U.S., 1901, derivitive citizenship, 1908; A.B., U. Mich., 1923, M.A., 1927, Ph.D., 1932; m. Coral Lorene Sibilsky, Aug. 30, 1923; children—Robert George, John Andrew, Cheryl Joyce. Head comml. dept. Wyandotte (Mich.) High Sch., 1923-26; prof. U. Mich., 1928-29, 37-38, U. Cal., summer 1949, U. Wash., summer 1951; prof. accounting Wayne U., Detroit, 1926-28, 29-37, 1938-58; dept. chmn.; vis. prof. U. Istanbul, Turkey, 1955-56. Mem. nominations bd. Ohio State Accounting Hall of Fame. Mem. Am. Assn. U. Profs., Am. Accounting Assn. (v.p. 1946, pres. 1952), Phi Beta Kappa, Beta Gamma Sigma. Author: Principles of Accounting (with Olin E. Thomas), 1935; Introductory Accounting (with William J. Schlatter), 1949; Advanced Accounting (with Rufus Wixon and Arthur Bartholomew), 1951; Inadequacy of Orthodox Accounting Procedure in View of Fluctuating Price Levels, 1951; Accounting, Administrative and Financial, 1959; articles profl jours. Home: 16534 Huntington Rd., Detroit 19. Died Dec. 6, 1958.

HUSBANDS, Sam Henry, financier; born at Florence, South Carolina, February 14, 1891; son James Sam and Fannie (Heath) H.; grad. Florence (S.C.) High Sch., 1908; m. Teressa Dew, Nov. 25, 1923; children—Patricia Chappel, Sam Henry. With Peoples Bank (later 1st Nat. Bank), Florence, 1909-16 and 1919-32, advancing from runner to cashier; examiner R.F.C., 1932-33, asst. chief, 1933-36, chief of examining div., 1936-39, dir. R.F.C., 1939-46; mem. bd. dirs. Reconstruction Finance Corp. Mortgage Co., 1936-46; pres. Fed. Nat. Mortgage Assn., Washington, D.C., 1938-46; exec. vice pres. and dir. Transamerica Corp., San Francisco, 1946-49, pres. 1949-53, dir.; dir. Central Bank, Premier Ins. Co., Md. Casualty Co., Gen Metals Corp., Kaiser Steel Corp., Mfrs. Casualty Insurance Company, Mfrs. Fire Ins. Co., First Nat. Bank of Portland. Served with S.C. Nat. Guard on Texas border, 1916; 2d O.T.C., Oglethorpe, Ga., 1917; commd. 1st lt., field arty., U.S. Army, with A.E.F., 1918-19. Democrat. Baptist. Address: 211 Irving St., San Mateo, Cal. Died Nov. 1, 1955.

HUSE, Charles Phillips (hūz), ret. educator; b. Worcester, Mass., Mar. 3, 1883; s. Charles Archelaus and Irene (Phillips) H.; A.B., Harvard, 1904, A.M., 1905, Ph.D., 1907; m. Florence Bigalow Johnson, Jan. 31, 1911; children—Charles Phillips, Barbara, Thomas Johnson, George Bigalow (dec.). Instructor econs., Dartmouth, 1908-09, Harvard, 1909-11; asst. prof. econs., U. Mo., 1911-14; asst. prof. econs., Boston U., 1914-20, prof., 1920-53, ret. 1953. Assisted in establishing budget system, City of Columbia, Mo.; editorial work for Nat. Monetary Commn. 1910; helped direct war issues course, S.A.T.C., 1918, mem. Representative Town Meeting, Belmont, Mass., 1927—. Member of American Economical Association, Business Hist. Soc., Am. Assn. Univ. Profs., Phi Beta Kappa, Beta Gamma Sigma. Republican. Conglist. Author: The Financial History of Boston, 1916. Contbr. to bulls. and econs. publs. Home: 13 Pine St., Belmont 78, Mass. Address: 725 Commonwealth Av., Boston 15. Died July 13, 1958; buried Mount Auburn Cemetery, Watertown, Mass.

HUSE, Raymond Howard, clergyman; b. Woburn, Mass., July 24, 1880; s. John Smith and Mary Susan (Paine) H.; B.D., Drew Theol. Sem., 1928; D.D., Syracuse U., 1934; m. Mabel H. Ridgway, Sept. 1, 1906; 1 dau., Geraldine. Ordained ministry M.E. Ch., 1905; pastor Sanbornville, N.H., 1903-05, Exeter, 1906-09; dist. supt. Dover Dist., 1910-15; pastor Concord, 1915-24, Montpelier, 1925-26, Geneva, N.Y., 1926-35, Ithaca, N.Y., 1935-39; supt. West Dist. Central New York Conf., 1939-45; apptd. pastor, Skaneateles, N.Y., 1945. Del. Gen. Conf. M.E. Church, 1916, 32, 36; mem. Uniting Conf. of Methodism, 1939; Gen. Conf. of Meth. Ch., 1940, 44. Mem. Theta Chi Beta. Ind. Republican. Kiwanian. Author: The Soul of a Child, 1914; Letters on the Atonement, 1917; Teach Us to Pray, 1919; Theology of a Modern Methodist, 1920; Barefoot Days, 1922; The Christian Life, 1923; Be of Good Comfort, 1936; The Autobiography of a Plain Preacher, 1949. Contbr. to Zion's Herald, Boston. Lecturer on literary subjects, especially on Whittier. Address: Atkinson, N.H. Died Jan. 29, 1954; buried West Newbury, Mass.

HUSE, William (Woodman) (hūs), educator; born Rockford, Ill., May 25, 1898; s. William Woodman and Mary L. (Mosher) H.; A.B., Stanford, 1921; A.M., Princeton, 1928; m. Eleanor Markham Page, Dec. 26, 1932; 1 dau., Joan Markham. Instr. in English, Washington U., St. Louis, 1921-23; Princeton, 1923-24; asst. prof. of English, U. of Kan., 1927-29, Calif. Inst. Tech., 1929-38, asso. prof., 1938-47, prof. of English, 1947—; historian Office Sci. Research and Dev. Contract with Calif. Inst. for dev. of rockets and other ordnance, 1944-46. Mem. Modern Lang. Assn. of Am., Philol. Assn. of Pacific Coast, Am. Assn. U. Professors, Soc. Architectural Historians, Phi Beta Kappa. Author: Vitamins for Health (with Henry Borsook), 1941; chpts. XV-XXIV of Rockets, Guns and Targets, 1948. Editor: These United States; Contemporary Essays for Coll. Students (with Harvey Eagleson and Louis W. Jones), 1934. Contbr. miscellaneous articles and short stories to publs. Home: 3676 Yorkshire Rd., Pasadena 10, Cal. Died Jan. 24, 1958; buried Pasadena.

HUSKINS, C. Leonard, educator; b. Walsall, Eng., Nov. 30, 1897; s. William and Annie Clara (Darby) H.; student Sch. Agr., Olds, Alberta, 1915, 20; B.S.A., U. Alberta, 1923, M.S.A., 1925; Ph.D., U. London, Eng., 1927, D.Sc., 1934; m. Margaret Harman Villy, Aug. 18, 1923; children—Sheila Wijcot, Olwen Margaret, John Michael. Asso. prof. botany McGill U., Montreal Can., 1930-34, prof. genetics, 1934-45; prof. botany U. Wis., 1945—; prof. dept. botany U. Cal., 1938; Guggenheim fellow, dept. of zoology Columbia, 1942-43. Served with Canadian Inf., 1916; flying officer, pilot Royal Flying Corps and R.A.F., 1917-19. Fllow Royal Soc. Can.; mem. Genetics Soc. Am., Soc. for Study evolution, Am. Assn. U. Profs., Am. Naturalists. Contbr. research papers to various jours. Home: 965 University Bay Dr., Madison 5, Wis. Died July 26, 1953.

HUSS, Henry Holden, musician; b. Newark, June 21, 1862; s. George John and Sophia Ruckel (Holden) H.; grad. Royal Conservatory, Munich, Bavaria, 1882; m. Hildegard Hoffman, 1904. Appeared in concert, at N.Y. Philharmonic, Boston symphony concerts, Cin., Pitts., St. Paul and Detroit symphony concerts, Kneisel concerts, at Washington and elsewhere. Composer: Piano Concerto, Violin Concerto (both with orchestral accompaniment); Sanctus and Ave Maria for chorus and orchestra; Cleopatra's Death, for soprano solo and for orchestra; World Peace, anthem for mixed chorus; trio for piano, violin and 'cello; sonata, for violin and piano; sonata for 'cello and piano; 3 string quartettes; sonata for viola and piano; also mixed choruses, and male and female choruses, and many songs and piano pieces; also prize string quartette in B minor, etc. His compositions have also been performed in London, Paris, Hamburg, Munich and other European cities, and by Ysaye, Pugno, Zimbalist, Alma Gluck, Maud Powell, Franz Kneisel, Boris Hambourg, Christine Miller, Oscar Seagle, Louise Homer, Arthur Hartmann, David Bispham, Katherine Goodson, Rudolph Ganz, and others. Home: 144 E. 150th St., N.Y.C. Died Sept. 17, 1953.

HUSSEY, Raymond (hŭs'ĭ), physician; b. Greensboro, N.C., Dec. 26, 1883; s. John Bryant and Sue Ann (Mallard) H.; M.D., U. of Md., 1911; A.M., (hon.) Yale, 1927; m. Edith Woodward, June 14, 1917. Resident physician Municipal Tuberculosis Hosp., Baltimore, Md., 1911-12, Md. Tuberculosis Sanatorium, 1912-14; in gen. practice of medicine, Baltimore, 1912-15, also vol. asst., med. clinic, Johns Hopkins Hosp. Outpatient Clinic, 1914-15. med. clinic Phipps Tuberculosis Clinic, Johns Hopkins Hosp., Outpatient Clin. and dept. pathology, Johns Hopkins Med. Sch., 1915-16; asst. in pathology, Johns Hopkins Med. Sch., also resident pathologist, Baltimore City Hosps., 1916-17; associate in pathology and biophysics, Rockefeller Inst. Med. Research, New York, N.Y., 1919-22; asst. prof. pathology, Sch. of Medicine, Cornell U., 1922-24; asso. prof. pathology, Sch. of Medicine, Yale, 1924-27, prof., 1927-35; asst. attending physician, cardiology, Baltimore City Hosps., 1937-39, cardiologist, 1939-45; in practice of medicine, field of cardiac diseases, Baltimore, Md., also asso. prof. medicine, U. of Maryland, instr. medicine, Johns Hopkins Med. Sch., mem. visiting staff Union Memorial Hosp., Church Home and Infirmary, attending physician University Hosp. (Baltimore), 1937-45; physician in chief, St. Joseph's Hosp., Baltimore, 1940-41 (on leave from all civilian activities); dean, Sch. of Occupational Health, Wayne U., Detroit, Mich., 1945-49; sci. dir. Council on Indsl. Health, A.M.A., since 1950. Vice chmn. and acting chmn. div. med. sciences Nat. Research Council, 1918-19. Spl. investigator Md. Tuberculosis Commn., 1938-39; chmn. med. bd. adminstrn. of occupational disease law, Md., 1939-45. Served as lt., advancing to major, Med. Corps, U.S. Army, 1917-19; lt. col., Med. Reserve Corps, 1919-24; lt. col., Med. Corps, U.S. Army, 1943-45; assigned as sci. dir. Army Indsl. Lab., Baltimore, Md., Feb.-June 1943, comdg. officer and dir., 1943-45. Vice chmn. com. on blood transfusion Baltimore chapter Am. Red Cross, 1938-40, mem. bd. dirs. and mem. exec. com., 1939-44, chmn. Am. Red Cross Blood Donor Center, 1940-41. Mem. bd. govs., Am. Acad. Compensation Med., 1948. Mem. com. indsl. health Md. State Med. Soc., 1938-45, v. chmn., 1938-39, chmn., 1939-44; mem. med. com. Indsl. Hygiene Foundation America, Mellon Inst., Pittsburgh, Pa., since 1942; mem. professional adv. com. on physical restoration, Office Vocational Rehabilitation, Fed. Security Agency, since 1943. Fellow A.A.A.S., Am. Coll. Physicians, American Public Health Assn., Gerontological Society, Am. Med. Assn. (mem. council indsl. health since 1941); mem. Illinois State and Chicago med. socs., Am. Soc. Exptl. Pathology, Soc. Exptl. Biology and Medicine, Sigma Xi, Phi Sigma Kappa. Contbr. numerous articles to med. publs. Home: 105 E. Delaware Pl., Chicago 11. Office: 535 N. Dearborn, Chgo. 10. Died Apr. 15, 1953; Buried Balt.

HUSSLEIN, Joseph (hŭs'līn), clergyman, educator, editor; b. Milwaukee, June 10, 1873; s. George and Sophia (Dimler) H.; A.B., Marquette U., 1891; student philosophy, St. Louis U., 1894-97, theology, 1902-06, A.M., 1906; Ph.D., Fordham, 1919. Joined Soc. of Jesus (Jesuits), 1891; ordained priest R.C. Ch., 1905. Teacher St. Louis U., 1897-99, Jesuit Normal Sch., Florissant, Mo., 1899-1902, Jesuit Normal Sch., Brooklyn, 1907-08, John Carroll U., Cleveland, 1908-11, Fordham U., 1916-21; dir. dept. of sociology, St. Louis University, 1929-30, dean School of Sociology, 1930-33, dean Sch. of Social Service, 1933-40. Associate editor America, 1911-27; editor in chief Science and Culture Series since 1931; also editor in chief of Science and Culture Texts since 1933, and of Religion and Culture Series since 1933. Author: The Church and Social Problems, 1912; The Catholic Work in the World, 1917; The World Problem—Capital, Labor and the Church, 1918; Democratic Industry, A Catholic Social Platform, 1919; Evolution and Social Progress, 1920; Work, Wealth and Wages, published in 1921; also Bible and Labor, 1924; The Little Flower and the Blessed Sacrament, 1925; The Reign of Christ, 1928; The Mass of the Apostles, 1929; The Christian Social Manifesto, 1931; The Spirit World About Us, 1934. Editor: The Church and Labor (with Dr. John A. Ryan), 1920; Heroines of Christ, 1939; Social Wellsprings, 1940; Social Wellsprings II, 1942; The Golden Years, 1945; Our Great Devotions, 1951. Contbr. to mags. Address: St. Louis U., St. Louis. Died Oct. 19, 1952; buried Florissant, Mo.

HUSTON, Charles Lukens (hū'stŭn), mfr.; born Coatesville, Pa., July 8, 1856; s. Dr. Charles and Isabelle Pennock (Lukens) H.; A.B., Haverford Coll., Pa., 1875; m. Annie Stewart, July 23, 1895. Clerk and bookkeeper, Huston & Penrose, and Huston, Penrose & Co. (now Lukens Steel Co.), 1875-80; given charge of puddle mill, 1879, plate mills, 1882, built open hearth dept., 1891; became member Huston, Penrose & Co., 1879, and Charles Huston & Sons, 1881; 2d v.p. Lukens Steel Co. until 1897, works mgr. until 1925, v.p. since 1890; dir. Belmont Iron Works, etc. Dir. of poor for Chester County, Pa., 33 yrs.; v.p., dir. Montrose (Pa.) Bible Conf. Assn. Mem. Brit. Iron and Steel Inst.; asso. mem. Am. Soc. M.E.; mem. Am. Inst. Mining and Metall. Engrs., Franklin Inst. Presbyterian (elder). Home: 64 S. 1st Av., Coatesville, Pa. Died Mar. 14, 1951; buried Fairview Cemetery, Coatesville, Pa.

HUSTON, Claudius Hart; b. Harrison Co., Ind., Feb. 15, 1876; s. Columbus De Witt and Margaret Eleanor (MacRae) H.; Valparaiso U.; B.S., Chattanooga Normal University; married Grace Jordon, August 15, 1902 (died August 6, 1917); children—Eleanor, Katharine, Alice, Mildred. Began as coll. instr.; entered mfg. business at Chattanooga, 1901; chmn. Traanscontinental Oil Co.; also officer or dir. many other cos. Was pres. Chattanooga Mfrs. Assn., Chattanooga Chamber Commerce, Lee Highway Assn.; 1st v.p. Dixie Highway Assn.; chmn. 5th Liberty Loan Drive, Chattanooga territory. Chmn. campaign and advisory com. Rep. State Com. of Tenn., 1920; asst. sect. Dept. of Commerce, 1921-23; was chmn. Nat. Ways and Means Com. of Rep. Nat. Com.; chmn. Rep. Nat. Com., 1929. Chmn. exec. com. U. of Chattanooga. Presbyn. Mason (hon. 33°, Scottish Rite). Home: Wire Mill Rd., Stamford, Conn. Died Aug. 14, 1952; buried Forest Hills Cemetery, Chattanooga.

HUSTON, Howard Riggins, business exec.; b. Sweet Springs, Mo., July 29, 1892; s. Theodore F. and Elizabeth B. (Riggins) H.; A.B., Univ. of N.D., 1917, A.M., 1928; married Dorothy M. Gordon, July

3, 1920 (deceased); children—Virginia Harmony (Mrs. Eugene L. C. Laning), Felicity Sue (Mrs. Bruce Hill); married 2d, Janet McMillen Bingham, 1953. Chief of internal service (business manager), League of Nations, Geneva, Switzerland, 1919-30; asst. to pres. Am. Cyanamid Co., 1930-51, vice pres. since 1951, mem. bd. dirs. since 1952. U.S. del. Chem. Industries Com., International Labor Office; mem. adv. com. on occupational health Pub. Health Service. Served with 4th Div. as inf. officer and a.d.c. to Gen. E. E. Booth, 1917-18; sec. gen. staff, Am. Army in France, 1919. Mem. Phi Delta Theta, Delta Sigma Rho. Republican. Conglist. Mason. Club: University. Home: Truro, Mass. Office: 30 Rockefeller Plaza, N.Y.C. 20. Died June 8, 1955.

HUSTON, Ralph Chase, coll. dean; b. Fairfield, Ia., Mar. 10, 1885; s. John C. and Etta (Chase) H.; B.S., Parsons Coll. (Fairfield, Ia.), 1906, D.Sc., 1941; M.S., Iowa U., 1908, Ph.D., 1914; m. Mabel Moyer, Nov. 28, 1912; 1 dau., Margaret Esther (Mrs. Robert C. Williams). Tchr. Junction City (Kan.) High Sch., 1906-07; instr. Washington State Coll., 1909-11; asst. prof. Mich. State Coll., 1911-15, asso., 1915-25, prof. organic chemistry since 1925, dean of science, 1930-44, dean grad. studies, 1944-51, dean emeritus since 1951. Chmn. grad. council, Assn. Land Grant Univs. Fellow Am. Inst. Chemists, A.A.A.S.; mem. Am. Chem. Soc., Sigma Xi, Phi Kappa Phi, Alpha Chi. Sigma, Sigma Pi Sigma, Sigma Chi. Club: Walnut Hills Golf. Presbyn. Rotarian. Contbr. to profl. and sci. jours. Home: 4570 Chippewa Dr., Okemos, Mich. Died 1954.

HUTCHESON, William L., labor leader; b. Saginaw Co., Mich., Feb. 7, 1874; s. Daniel O. and Elizabeth (Culver) H.; ed. rural schools of Mich.; m. Jessie Tufts Sharon. Began as carpenter, 1890; became bus. rep., 2d, then 1st. gen. v.p. United Brotherhood of Carpenters and Joiners, gen. pres. since Oct. 8, 1915; 1st v.p. Am. Fedn. of Labor since Jan. 1940. Mem. War Labor Bd., 1917-19; charge of Labor Div., Nat. Rep. Party, 1932 and 1936. Dir. Home for Aged Carpenters, Lakeland, Fla. Mem. C. of C. Republican. Methodist. Mason (Scottish and York rites; Royal Order of Scotland, 33° So. jurisdiction), Odd Fellow. Clubs: Columbia, Highland Golf and Country (Indpls.). Died Oct. 20, 1953.

HUTCHINGS, John Richard, Jr., tobacco exec.; b. Durham, N.C., Feb. 1, 1893; s. John Richard and Lucille (Lea) H.; student pub. schs. of Greenville, N.C.; m. Helen Elizabeth Finnegan, June 5, 1924; 1 son, John Richard. Supt. T. A. Person & Co., Greenville, N.C., 1912; owner, propr. Tobacco Auction Warehouse, Johnsonville, S.C. and Sanford, N.C., 1913-16; tobacco buyer Am. Tobacco Co., Durham, 1916-30, now dir.; leaf buying supervisor purchases Am. Suppliers, Inc. (subsidiary of Am. Tobacco Co.), Durham, 1930-51, v.p. since 1951, dir. since 1951. Served as pvt. 1st class, 317th Ambulance Co., 80th Div., U.S. Army, 1917-19. Mason. Club: Hope Valley Country (Durham, N.C.). Home: 1519 Hermitage Court. Office: American Suppliers, Inc., Pettigrew and Blackwell Sts., Durham, N.C. Died June 21, 1958.

HUTCHINGS, Leslie Morton, univ. dean; b. Portland, Me., Sept. 13, 1915; s. Morton Belmont and Clare (Hammons) H.; B.S., U. Me., 1937, D.V.M., Mich. State Coll., 1940, M.S., 1942; Ph.D., Purdue U., 1947; m. Mary A. Bruce, July 1, 1939; children—Bruce Leslie, Alan M., John T. Asst. in pathology Mich. State Coll., 1937-40; research veterinarian, 1940-42; mem. faculty Purdue U. since 1942, head dept. vet. sci., 1950—, dean sch. vet. sci. and medicine, 1957—; cons. comml. concerns. Dir. Official Animal Disease Diagnostic Lab. of Ind.; mem. agricultural bd. NRC, 1957—; panel of experts on brucellosis World Health Orgn., Food Agr. Orgns. 1950—; chmn. nat. com. for eradication of hog cholera, 1951—; Ind. Veterinary examining bd. Voted Outstanding Young Man of Ind. by Jr. C. of C., 1947. Mem. Am. Vet. Med. Assn. (exec. bd. dist. III 1953—, council in education 1958—), United States Livestock Sanitation Assn., Ofcl. Conf. Research Workers in Animal Diseases in N.A., Ind. State Livestock San. Bd., Sigma Xi (recipient Research award, 1947). Club: Rotary. Home: 331 Hollowood Dr., West Lafayette, Ind. Office: Purdue U. Lafayette, Ind. Died July 22, 1959.

HUTCHINGS, Lester, automobile supplies; b. Excelsior Springs, Mo., Apr. 7, 1896; s. E. S. and Sarah (Overman) H.; high school, business coll.; m. Marguerite Duncan, Jan. 30, 1924. Certified public accountant, State of Mo., 1920-28; asso. with Western Auto Supply Co. since 1928, became 1st v.p. 1937, now pres.; dir. Central Surety & Ins. Corp., City Nat. Bank and Trust Co. (both Kansas City). Served in United States Navy, 1918-19. Mem. Soc. Pub. Accountants. Republican. Clubs: Kansas City (Kansas City); Mission Hills Country (Kan. City). Home: 2421 W. 65th St. Office: 2107 Grand Av., Kansas City, Mo. Died Feb. 12, 1951; buried Mount Moriah, Kansas City, Mo.

HUTCHINS, Frank Avery, librarian; b. Norwalk, O., Mar. 8, 1851; s. Allen Sabin and Henrietta Avery H.; student Wayland Acad., Beaver Dam, Wis., also Beloit Coll., 2 yrs. Librarian, Dept. of Edn., Wis., 1891-95; sec. Wis. Free Library Commn., 1895-1904. Address: Madison, Wis. Died 1914.

HUTCHINS, Jere Chamberlain; b. Carroll Parish, La., Oct. 13, 1851; s. Anthony W. and Mary B. (Chamberlain) H.; moved to Lexington, Mo.; student pvt. and pub. schs.; studied civ. engring.; m. Anna M. Brooks, 1881 (dec. 1900); m. 2d, Sarah R. Russell, 1903 (dec. May 1939). Began career in construction of Missouri, Gulf & Lexington Ry.; later constrn. engr. on Mo. railroads; reporter Waco (Texas) Examiner, 1874-80; returned to railroading, service 13 years with New Orleans & Pacific, Mo., Kan. & Tex., Louisville, New Orleans & Tex., and I.C. ry. cos.; mgr. Detroit Citizens Street Ry., 1894; worked for amalgamation of lines and was pres. Detroit United Ry., 1902-16, and chmn. bd., 1916-23, Detroit United Ry., owning, operating and controlling about 915 miles of electric ry. (purchased by City of Detroit 1922); now retired. Mem. Am. Soc. C.E. Clubs: Detroit, Yondotega, Country, Grosse Pointe (Detroit); Pelican (Boca Grande, Fla.). Home: 164 Provencal Rd., Grosse Pointe Farms, Mich. Office: Penobscot Bldg., Detroit. Died Feb. 24, 1943; buried Elmwood Cemetery, Detroit.

HUTCHINS, Lee Wilson, wholesale druggist; born Detroit, May 30, 1895; s. Lee Montgomery and Alice Kate (Wilson) H.; grad. Asheville (N.C.) Sch. for Boys, 1914; A.B., U. of Wis., 1918; m. Helen Elizabeth Bloomer, Sept. 25, 1923; children—Lee Helen (Mrs. Nicholas Rossano). With Hazeltine & Perkins Drug Co., Grand Rapids, Mich., since 1918, pres. and dir. since 1938; dir. Old Kent Bank, Am. Box Bd. Co., Consumers Power Co. Trustee Asheville Sch. for Boys, Foster Welfare Found., Grand Rapids. Mem. Alpha Tau Omega. Clubs: Kent Country, University, Peninsular (Grand Rapids); Lake Shore (Chicago). Home: 111 Lafayette St., Grand Rapids 3. Office: Hazeltine & Perkins Drug Co., Grand Rapids 2, Mich. Died June 17, 1956.

HUTCHINS, William J., college pres.; b. Brooklyn, N.Y., July 5, 1871; s. Robert Grosvenor and Harriet (James) H.; Oberlin Coll., 1888-90; B.A., Yale, 1892; Oberlin Theol. Sem., 1893-95; grad. Union Theol. Sem., 1896; D.D., Oberlin, 1920, Yale, 1921; LL.D., Marietta Coll., 1925, U. of Chicago, 1929, U. of Ky., 1939; L.H.D., U. of Louisville, 1937; m. Anna L. Murch, Aug. 5, 1896. Ordained Presbyterian ministry, 1896; pastor Bedford Ch., Brooklyn, 1896-1907; prof. homiletics, Oberlin Grad. Sch. of Theology, 1907-20; pres. Berea Coll., Ky., 1920-39, retired. Author: The Preacher's Inspirations and Ideals, 1917; The Religious Experience of Israel, 1919. Adviser to Danforth Foundation, 1940—. Home: Berea, Ky. Died Feb. 20, 1958.

HUTCHINSON, Ely Champion, indsl. exec. and cons. engr.; b. San Francisco, Feb. 10, 1882; s. Frederick Winslow and Ellen Cass (Tripler) H.; student pub. schs.; self-taught tech. edn.; m. Florence A. Grant, Sept. 26, 1906; 1 dau., Janet (Mrs. H. C. Alexander). Began work in the pattern shop and in the drafting room Union Iron Works, San Francisco, 1898; installing and operation hydro-electric plant in B.C., 1902-03; asst. mgr. mining dept. Union Iron Works, 1903-07; Pacific Coast rep. of Power & Mining Machinery Co., Cudahy, Wis., 1907-08; with Pelton Water Wheel Co., San Francisco, 1908-29, v.p., gen. mgr., 1922-26, prs., gen. mgr., 1926-29; editor Power (mag.), 1929-33; pres. Edgemoor Iron Co., 1933-34; exec. NRA, Washington, 1935, then under U.S. Dept. Commerce; cons. engr. J. G. White Engring. Corp.; mgr. Alco Products, Inc., 1936-39; cons. engr. indsl. orgn. and mgmt., 1940—; gen. mgr. Cambridge Div., Research Constrn. Co., Inc., 1941—. Became dep. dir. Office Prodn. Research and Development, WPB, 1944; chief indsl. research and development div., Office Tech. Services, U.S. Dept. of Commerce, Washington, 1945-48; chief gen. indsl. equipment sect., Office International Trade, Dept. Commerce, 1949. Inventor of numerous devices used in power plants. Chmn. N.Y. Com. Third Internat. World Power Confs. Fellow Am. Soc. M.E. (v.p. 1933-35; chmn. hydraulic prime movers power test code com., 1931-38); mem. Am. Soc. C.E., (chmn. bd. on honors, 1949), S.A.R. (life member California chapter); New York Committee Order Fgn. Wars. Clubs: Engineers (San Francisco); Engineers (N.Y.C.); Azted Club of 1847, Cosmos (Washington). Contbr. many tech. articles. Home: 4801 Connecticut Av., Washington 8. Died Nov. 12, 1955; buried St. Mathews Ch., Bedford, N.Y.

HUTCHINSON, George Alexander, prof. sociology; b. Jackson County, Ind., Dec. 20, 1876; s. Joseph and Elizabeth Ellen (McCleery) H.; A.B., Ind. U., 1906, A.M., 1908; Ph.D., Clarke U., 1910; post-grad. study same, 1917-18; m. Bertha McKinley, Oct. 30, 1917; children—Celia Gail, Beth Elaine. Teacher rural schs., 1896-99; prin. Twp. High Sch., Leesville, Ind., 1900-03; supt. schs., Wheatland, Ind., 1905-07; teaching fellow, Ind. U., 1907-08; fellow in psychology, Clarke U., 1908-10; prof. psychology and edn. Carnegie Inst. Tech., 1910-14, Drury Coll., Springfield, Mo., 1915-16; again fellow in psychology, Clarke U., 1917-18; prof. psychology, Grinnell (Ia.) Coll., 1918-19; prof. philosophy and sch. administration, U. of Ga., 1919-24, prof. sociology and dir. of extension div., 1925-28, prof. and head of dept. sociology and philosophy, 1928-31, prof. sociology and head of dept., 1931-41, prof. sociology, 1941-48; prof. emeritus since Sept. 1, 1948. Member Am. Assn. Univ. Profs., A.A.A.S., Phi Kappa Phi. Methodist. Mason. Home: 165 Hall St., Athens, Ga. Died Jan. 14, 1954; buried Oconee Hill Cemetery, Athens, Ga.

HUTCHINSON, Knox Thomas, govt. official; born Fayetteville, Tenn., Oct. 5, 1894; s. Thomas Levia and Mattie Lu (Beard) H.; B.S., George Peabody Coll. for Teachers, Nashville, Tenn., 1921, A.M., 1922, grad. student, 1924-26; grad. student U. of Tenn., 1922, Vanderbilt U., 1923; m. Stacie Mai Williams, June 7, 1919; children—Knox Thomas, Charles Milton, Norman Fenn. Teacher vocational agr. Davidson County Central High Sch., Nashville, 1919-27; dir. agrl. edn. State Teachers Coll., Murphreesboro, Tenn., 1927-36; also dir. research in agrl. edn. Peabody Coll., 1930; pres. Middle Tenn. Electric Membership Coöp., 1935-49, Tenn. Rural Electric Coöp. Assn., 1941-49; farmer 1936—; state senator, Tenn., 1939-40; asst. sec. of agr., 1949—. Trustee Sam Davis Memorial Soc., 1936-40. Mem. Tenn. State Grange (pres. 1944-49), Mid-South Cotton Growers Assn. (vice pres. 1946-49), Alpha Tau Alpha, Phi Delta Kappa. Democrat. Presbyterian. Home: 4313 Rawalt Dr., College Park, Md.; also Murfreesboro, Tenn. Office: Dept. of Agriculture, Washington. Died June 30, 1957; buried Evergreen Cemetery, Murfreesboro, Tenn.

HUTCHINSON, Myron Wells, Jr., naval officer; b. Bismarck, N.D., Dec. 29, 1892; s. Myron Wells and Gertrude G. (Griffin) H.; student Mich. State Coll., 1910-11; B.S., U.S. Naval Acad., 1915; M.S., Columbia, 1922; m. Heather P. Baxter, Apr. 20, 1918; children—Ronald B., David M., Kenneth F. Commd. ensign USN, 1915 advanced through the grades to commodore, 1946; chief of staff Hawaiian Sea Frontier and 14th Naval Dist., Pearl Harbor, T.H., 1945—. Decorated Bronze Star medal, Gold Star in lieu of 2d Bronze Star, spl. letter of commendation with ribbon and combat device, Victory medal, Am. Defense medal, China campaign medal, Haitian campaign medal, Am., European and Asiatic Theatre Medals. Mem. Am. Soc. Naval Engrs., Naval Inst., S.A.R. Presbyterian. Clubs: Army and Navy (Washington, D.C.). Home: Six Acton Pl., Annapolis, Md. Office: Chief of Staff, Hawaiian Sea Frontier and 14 N.D., Pearl Harbor, T.H. Died Oct. 1959.

HUTCHINSON, Paul, editor, author; b. Madison, N.J., Aug. 10, 1890; s. Charles X. and Annie M. (Petrie) H.; student Centenary Collegiate Inst., Hackettstown, N.J., 1907; Ph.B., Lafayette Coll., 1911, Litt.D., 1948; B.D., Garrett Bibl. Inst., 1915, D.D., 1930; D.D., De Pauw U., 1924; Litt.D., Ohio Wesleyan U., 1939, L.H.D., Ottawa U., 1947; m. Agnes Mitchell, June 24, 1915; children—Mitchell, Margaret, Martha, Barbara. Assistant editor Epworth Herald, Chicago, 1914-16; editor China Christian Advocate, Shanghai, China, 1916-21; exec. sec. China Centenary Movement (M.E. Ch.), 1920-21, also sec. Epworth League in China and chmn. China Christian Lit. Council; with publicity dept. M.E. Ch., in U.S., 1922-24; mng. editor The Christian Century, Chicago, 1924; editor, 1947; president Christian Century Foundation. Mem. Sigma Alpha Epsilon, Phi Beta Kappa (hon.). Author: Guide to Mission Stas. in Eastern China, 1919; The Next Step, 1921; The Spread of Christianity, 1922; The World Service of the Methodist Episcopal Church (part author), 1923; China's Real Revolution, 1924; The Story of Methodism (with H. E. Luccock), 1926; What and Why in China, 1927; The United States of Europe, 1929; Men Who Made the Churches, 1930; World Revolution and Religion, 1931; Storm Over Asia, 1932; The Ordeal of Western Religion, 1933; From Victory to Peace, 1943; The New Leviathan, 1946, also article, The Onward March of Christian Faith, 1955; The New Ordeal of Christianity. Club: University. Contributor to magazines. Home: 1028 Cherry St., Winnetka, Ill. Office: 407 S. Dearborn St., Chgo. Died Apr. 15, 1956; buried French Azylum, Pa.

HUTCHINSON, Robert Orland, educator; b. nr. Bedford, Ind., Jan. 15, 1889; s. Joseph and Elizabeth Ellen (McCleery) H.; student Marion (Ind.) Normal Coll., 1908-10; A.B., Ind. U., 1916; student U. Me., 1916-17; Ph.D., U. Chgo., 1923; m. Mona Marie Randolph, June 4, 1921. Tchr. Mecca (Ind) High Sch., 1908-10; prin. Walnut Grove (Ind.), 1910-11, Versailles (Ind.), 1911-13, Orleans (Ind.), 1914-16; instr. in physics and meteorology U. Me., 1916-17; research asst. Bur. of Standards, Washington, 1919; instr. in physics Miss. A. and M. Coll., 1919-20, asst. prof., 1920-21; teaching asst. U. Chgo., 1921-23; asst. prof. State Coll. Wash., 1923-25, acting head dept., 1925-26, asso. prof., 1926-28; prof. and head dept. mathematics Lincoln Meml. U., Tenn., 1929-31, registrar, 1930-31; prof., head dept. mathematics Tenn. Poly. Inst., 1931—, also coordinator Civilian Pilot tng., 1940-42. Served in Meteorol. Service, U.S. Army, with AEF, 1917-19. Fellow A.A.A.S.; mem. Math. Assn. Am., Nat. Council Tchrs. Mathematics, Am. assn. U. Profs., Tenn. Acad. Science, Sigma Xi, Phi Kappa Phi. Democrat. Conglist. Contbr. to sci. jours. Author: Introduction to Business Mathematics. Home: 530 N. Cedar St., Cookeville, Tenn. Died Oct. 22, 1950; buried Cookeville City Cemetery.

HUTCHINSON, William K., newspaper corr.; b. Reading, Pa., 1896. Began as newspaper reporter, Reading, Pa., 1913; served as reporter, telegraph and news editor on various newspapers in East and Middle West to 1920; with Internat. News Service since 1920, mem. Washington, D.C., staff since 1921, mgr. Washington bureau, 1939—, dean of Washington news service correspondents. Recipient of awards from U.S. Army, Navy and Air Force for outstanding patriotic civilian service, Sigma Delta Chi award, 1950. Mem. D.C. bar, Am. Legion, Gridiron Club. Author: Life and Works of William Borah, 1940; Ten Days That Changed the World, 1945. Home: 1603 Connecticut Av. N.W. Office: Pennsylvania Bldg., Washington. Died May 25, 1958; buried Arlington Nat. Cemetery.

HUTCHISON, Frederick William, artist; b. Montreal, Can., Mar. 14, 1879; s. John Henry and Elizabeth (Knox) H.; studied under William Brymner, Montreal Art Assn., William M. Chase, N.Y.C., Benjamin Constant and Jean Paul Laurens, Julian Acad. Paris. Came to U.S., 1905, naturalized, 1915. Instr. in art, Coll. City N.Y. Represented in permanent collections of Cleve. Mus., Toronto Mus., Quebec Nat. Gallery. Awarded 1st prize, Salmagundi Club Annual Auction Sale, 1933; Shaw prize, Salmagundi Club, 1935; Allen Butler Talcott meml. prize for landscape, Members Annual Exhibition, 1938. Academician, Nat. Acad., 1935; non-resident Academician Royal Canadian Acad., 1938; mem. Salmagundi Club of N.Y. (pres. 1937-38); Arts Club (Montreal). Died 1953.*

HUTCHISON, James Brewster, structural steel exec.; b. Rochester, N.Y., Feb. 6, 1913; s. Ernest James and Sarah Brewster (Smith) H.; student Union Coll., Schenectady, N.Y., 1931-32, Hobart College, Geneva, N.Y., 1932-33, Rochester (N.Y.) Bus. Inst., 1933, Rochester Institute of Technology, 1937; m. Marjorie Huntingdon Leach, Feb. 21, 1936; children—Thomas Jeffrey, John B. (dec.). Reporter, Rochester (N.Y.) Democrat and Chronicle, 1933; staff writer covering city, county and state courts, county government features, Rochester Times-Union, 1933-43; asst. chief Gannett News Service, Washington bureau of Gannett Newspapers, Washington, 1943-48; president. Leach Steel Co., Rochester, New York, since 1948; director Hutchison-Rathbun Co., builders supplies, Rochester, N.Y. Mem. 21st Regt., N.Y. Guard, 1942. Chmn. Rochester and Monroe County Publicity Com. for Salvaging War Materials, 1942-43. Mem. Press Gallery of U.S. Senate and Ho. of Reps.; accredited corr. United Nations. Mem. S.A.R., White House Corrs. Assn., Rochester Builders Exchange (v.p.), C. of C., N.Y. State Longspan Steel Truss Council (treas.), Circus Saints and Sinners, Kappa Alpha. Episcopalian. Clubs: Oak Hill Country (Rochester); Nat. Press (Washington). Home: 90 Knollwood Dr. Office: 80 Steel St., Rochester, N.Y. Deceased.

HUTCHISON, Stuart Nye, clergyman; b. Pleasant Plains, N.Y., May 20, 1877; s. Sylvanus Nye and Sarah Matilda (Seeley) H.; A.B., Lafayette Coll., 1900, A.M., 1903, LL.D., 1943; grad. Princeton Theol. Sem., 1903; D.D., Hampden-Sidney College, 1916; LL.D., Washington and Jefferson Coll., 1942; m. Mary Hall Thompson, Dec. 2, 1907; children—Janet (Mrs. David Evans), Stuart Nye, Richard Hall. Ordained to ministry Presbyn. Ch., 1903; asst. pastor South Park Church, Newark, 1903-04; pastor 1st Ch., Steubenville, O., 1904-06, 1st Ref. Ch., Newark, 1906-10, First Presbyn. Ch., Norfolk, Va., 1910-21, East Liberty Ch., Pitts., 1921-47; pres. ad interim The Western Theol. Sem., 1950-51. Moderator of Presbyn. Church, U.S.A., 1942-43; chmn. Presbyn. War-Time-Service Commn., 1942-44. Trustee Princeton Theol. Sem., Western Theol. Sem., Lafayette Coll., Grove City Coll., Maryville Coll. Mem. Presbyn. Bd. Pensions, 1923-47. Mem. Delta Upsilon. Clubs: Duquesne, Cleric. Author: The Soul of a Child, 1916; For the Children's Hour, 1918; Bible Boys and Girls, 1921; The Voice Within Us, 1932; Holy Ground, 1934. Contbr. to many religious publs. Home: 6112 Alder St., Pitts. Died Apr. 5, 1958.

HUTCHISON, William Easton, lawyer; b. Oxford, Chester County, Pa., July 14, 1860; s. William G. and Ann Eliza (Campbell) H.; A.B., Lafayette Coll., Pa., 1883, A.M., 1886, D.H.L. (honorary), 1951; LL.D., Coll. of Emporia, Kan., 1927; m. Reba Anderson, Aug. 6, 1895 (died 1929); foster-children—Rev. Ralph C., Dr. James E., Marian Hutchison Clements. Admitted to Pa. bar, 1886, Kansas bar, 1887, Kansas Supreme Court, 1889, United States Supreme Court, 1917; practiced in Ulysses, Kansas, 1887-92; county attorney, Grant County, Kansas, 1888-91; judge District Ct. 32d Jud. Dist. of Kan., 1892-1907; settled in Garden City, Kan., 1896; resumed practice there, 1907; mem. and sec. State Bd. of Bar Examiners of Kan., 1911-27; pardon atty. of Kan., 1925; asso. justice Supreme Court of Kan., 1927-39; again resumed practice of law; now mem. Hutchison, Vance, Hope & Fleming. Ex-pres. Garden City Bldg. & Loan Assn. Trustee Coll. of Emporia. Director Kansas Masonic Home Board (38 years). Mem. American Bar Assn., Kan. Bar Assn. (pres. 1911), Southwestern Kan. Bar Association (president 1945), Garden City Chamber Commerce (ex-pres.). Republican. Presbyterian. 33° Mason; Past Grand Master of Masons of Kan.; Grand High Priest, Grand Chapter, R.A.M., 1924; Grand Comdr. Grand Commandery K.T., Kan., 1928. Odd Fellow, K.P., Elk; mem. A.O.U.W. Club: Rotary of Garden City (ex-pres.). Home: Garden City, Kan. Died Apr. 5, 1952; buried Garden City, Kan.

HUTSON, Frederick Leroy, univ. prof.; b. Pittsburgh, Pa., Apr. 12, 1875; s. John Speed and Hannah Sophronia (Snyder) H.; A.B., Denison Univ., Granville, O., 1896; L.H.D., same university, 1935; Ph.D., U. of Chicago, 1907; m. Mrs. Sara Holmes Watts, Dec. 18, 1920; children—Holmes Leroy and (step-children) George Burghall Watts, William Wood Watts. Instr. classics, 1903-05, asst. prof., 1905-18 (leave of absence, 1906-07), prof. Greek and registrar, 1918-25 (leave of absence 1924-25), prof. classics, 1925-40, prof. of classics emeritus, 1940—, Princeton. Mem. Archaeol. Inst. America, Am. Philol. Assn., Phi Beta Kappa, Sigma Chi. Republican. Episcopalian. Club: Nassau (Princeton). Home: 42 Cleveland Lane, Princeton, N.J. Died Aug. 28, 1956; buried Princeton Cemetery.

HUTTON, William Edward, lawyer; b. Delavan, Wis., Aug. 10, 1872; s. John and Mary (Gaffney) H.; A.B., Harvard, 1895, LL.B., 1898; m. Alida Platt Lansing, June 29, 1899; children—John Lansing, Helen, Katherine (dec.), Charles (dec.). Admitted to Colo. bar, 1898, practiced since at Denver. Dir. Capitol Life Insurance Co., Independent Investment Co. Past chmn. bar com. Supreme Court of Colo. Dir. Denver YMCA. Mem. Denver (past pres.), Colo. (past pres.) bar assns., Phi Beta Kappa, Phi Delta Phi. Republican. Unitarian. Clubs: University, Harvard, Lincoln. Home: 836 E. 17th Av. Office: Capitol Life Bldg., Denver. Died Apr. 23, 1957; buried Denver.

HUTTY, Alfred, painter, etcher; b. Grand Haven, Mich., Sept. 16, 1877; s. Joseph Warren and Susan Browning (Squier) H.; ed. in art under Am. masters; m. Bessie Burris Crafton, Apr. 16, 1902; 1 son, Warren Crafton. Awarded gold medal, Scarab Club, Detroit Inst. of Art, 1923; Logan prize and medal Internat. Exhbn., Chicago Soc. Etchers, 1924; Shaw prize, Salmagundi Club, New York, 1924; Clark prize for etching Detroit Inst. of Art, 1925; landscape prize, New Haven Paint and Clay Club, 1925; Howe prize for etching, Detroit Inst. Arts, 1926. Represented in Art Inst. Chicago; Detroit Inst. of Art; Library of Congress; U.S. National Mus.; Art Gallery of Toronto; Honolulu Art Acad.; N.Y. Public Library; Cleveland Mus. of Art; Bibliotheque Nationale, Paris, France, John Herron Art Institute, Indianapolis, Ind.; Los Angeles (Calif.) Mus.; Gibbes Art Gallery, Charleston, S.C.; Municipal Gallery, Phoenix, Ariz.; Met. Mus. Art; Pasteur Inst.; British Mus., and other public collections, also in numerous private collections. Mem. Allied Artists of America, Soc. Am. Etchers, Chicago Soc. of Etchers, Printmakers of Calif., Prairie Printmakers, Southern Printmakers, Washington Soc. of Artists, Washington Water Color Club, Washington Arts Club, North Shore (Gloucester), Rockport, and Woodstock art assns., Am. Water Color Soc., Nat. Arts Club. Salmagundi, British Soc. Graphic Arts. Mem. Soc. Colonial Wars. Made associate plates for Am. Soc. College Print Collectors, Printmakers of Calif., North Shore Art Assn., Prairie Printmakers, Collectors of Am. Art. Clubs: St. Andrew's; Charleston (S.C.). Home and studio: Broadview, Woodstock, N.Y.; also 46 Tradd St., Charleston, S.C. Died June 28, 1954; buried Woodstock Society, Woodstock, N.Y.

HUXFORD Walter Scott, prof. physics; b. Neligh, Neb., Dec. 15, 1892; s. Herbert C. and Cora (Scott) H.; B.A., Doane Coll., Crete, Neb., 1917; M.S., U. of Neb., 1924; Ph.D., U. of Mich., 1928; m. Mary Bertha Whalen, Aug. 28, 1917; children—Sara May (Mrs. George Ball), Barbara Jane (Mrs. Joseph Nicol), Charles K., Mary Patricia. Engaged in elec. communications work, 1917-19; high sch. instr. physics, 1919-21; instr. later prof. physics Doane Coll., 1923-26 and 1928-29; physicist dept. of engring. research U. of Mich., 1930-32; asst. prof., later asso. prof. physics Northwestern U., 1932-39, professor since 1939; researches in gaseous electronics and infrared communication systems, methods of optical communications; director of research, Nat. Defense Research Council, 1943-45. Served as lt. 36th Inf., 12th Div., A.E.F., 1918-19. Awarded Army and Navy certificate of merit, 1947. Fellow Am. Phys. Soc.; mem. Optical Soc. Am., Ill. Acad. Sci., Sigma Xi. Conglist. Clubs: Physics, Chaos (Chgo.). Contbr. tech. articles profl. jours. Home: 3027 Thayer St., Evanston, Ill. Died Feb. 12, 1958; buried Meml. Park, Evanston.

HUXLEY, Henry Minor, patent lawyer; b. Newton, Mass., Jan. 21, 1880; s. Edward Charles and Alice Jane (Haley) H.; A.B., Harvard, 1899, A.M., 1902; LL.B., Chgo. Kent Coll. Law, 1911; m. Carroll Coleman, Apr. 16, 1913; 1 dau., Margaret Carroll (Mrs. Robert L. Deik). Operating dept. Am. Steel & Wire Co., Worcester, Mass., 1903-07; with Duplex Metals Co., N.Y.C., 1907-08, Brown & Williams, patent lawyers, Chgo., 1908-09, Linthicum, Belt & Fuller, 1909-14; admitted to Ill. bar, 1911; mem. firm Bell & Huxley, 1914-15, Wilkinson & Huxley, 1917-20, Wilkinson, Huxley, Byron & Knight, 1920-45; counsel Wilkinson, Huxley, Byron & Hume, Chgo., 1946—; pvt. practice, 1915-16; lectr. patent law Northwestern, 1928-29. Trustee Northwestern Mil. and Naval Acad., Seabury—Western Theol. Sem. dir. Freyn Engring. Co. Served as capt. 11th Ill. Inf., 1917, capt., maj. ordnance dept., Army U.S. 1918-19; 1st lt. inf. Ill. N.G., 1920-21, capt. tank corps, 1921-22; lt. col. ordnance dept., Army U.S., 1942-43; lt. col. hon. ret., 1947. Mem. Am. Bar Assn. (chmn. patent sect. 1928-30), Ill. State, Chgo. bar assns., Am. Patent Law Assn., Patent Law Assn. Chgo. (pres. 1932), Internat. Assn. Protection Indsl. Property (pres. Am. group 1931-32), Delta Upsilon, Delta Theta Phi. Republican. Episcopalian. Clubs: Law; Univ., Adventurers (Chgo.); Univ. (Evanston); Glen View; Chevy Chase; Farmington Country. Home: 1625 Judson Av., Evanston, Ill. Office: First National Bank Bldg., Chgo. 3. Died Aug. 19, 1954; buried Mt. Auburn Cemetery, Cambridge, Mass.

HYATT, Frank Kelso, ret. pres.; b. Chester, Pa., Nov. 19, 1885; s. Gen. Charles Eliot and Keziah West (Dyer) H.; father pres. Pa. Mil. Coll. many yrs.; student Gilbert's Acad., 1902, Swarthmore Prep. Sch., 1903; student Pa. Mil. Coll., 1903, LL.D., 1930; B.S. in Engring., Swarthmore Coll., 1907; m. Blanche L. Cramp, June 1, 1909 (dec. Oct. 1, 1950); 1 son (died in infancy); m. 2d, Mabel E. Cramp, Dec. 26, 1951. With Pa. Mil. Coll. since 1907, asst. prof. mathematics, 1909-12, prof., 1912-29, treas. since 1916, v.p., 1917-30, succeeded father as pres., 1930, also trustee, president emeritus since 1952. Organizer, and captain Troop G, Pennsylvania National Guard, 1910, lt. col. inf., 1917, col., 1930. Republican. Presbyterian. Mason (K.T.). Clubs: Union League, Pickering Hunt; (hon. mem.) Kiwanis (Philadelphia) Chester. Address: 701 E. 14 St., Chester, Pa. Died July 13, 1958.

HYDE, Charles Cheney, lawyer; b. Chicago, Ill., May 22, 1873; s. James Nevins and Alice Louise (Griswold) H.; A.B., Yale, 1895, A.M., 1898; LL.B., Harvard, 1898; LL.D., Northwestern U., 1924; m. Mary Paige Tilton, June 2, 1906 (died, July 13, 1937); children—James Nevins, Elizabeth Tilton. In law practice at Chicago, 1898-1923, Washington, D.C., 1920-23; mem. Hyde, Hennings, Thulin, Westbrook & Watson (Chicago and Washington), 1922; apptd. by President Harding solicitor for Dept. of State, Feb. 1923-June 30, 1925; prof. law, Northwestern University Law School, 1907-25; Hamilton Fish professor international law and diplomacy, Columbia, July 1, 1925-June 30, 1945, emeritus thereafter. Admitted to N.Y. bar, 1927, and since in practice at N.Y. City. Appointed, 1928, American mem. Permanent Commn. for Advancement of Peace, under treaty between U.S. and Venezuela; counsel for Guatemala in arbitration of boundary dispute with Honduras, 1931-32; lecturer internat law, Carnegie Endowment for Internat. Peace, summers, Ann Arbor, Mich., 1933-36. Lecturer U.S. Army Sch. of Mil. Govt., Charlottesville, Va., 1942. Pres. Am. Soc. Internat. Law, 1946-49. Named member Permanent Court of Arbitration at the Hague, May 1951. Member American Bar Association, Council Foreign Relations, International Law Association, Chicago Law Club, Mil. Order Loyal Legion, Delta Kappa Epsilon, membre de l'Institut de Droit Internat., Soc. Mayflower Descendants, Pilgrims of America, (corr.) Instituto Argentino de Derecho Internacional, Academia de Derecho Internacional of Universidad Catolica Bolivariana (Colombia). Republican. Reformed Episcopalian. Clubs: Century (New York); Metropolitan (Washington); University (Chicago). Author: International Law Chiefly as Interpreted and Applied by the U.S., 2 vols., 1922, 2d rev. edit., 3 vols., 1945 (awarded James Barr Ames prize by Harvard Law Sch. Faculty, 1947); also author of biography of Charles Evans Hughes as Sec. of State (Vol. X of The Am. Secs. of State and Their Diplomacy), 1929. Hon. mem. editorial staff Am. Jour. Internat. Law; contbr. to legal and other periodicals on matters relating to internat. law. Prepared monographs on internat. law printed by Dept. of State for confidential use of Am. delegates at Peace Conf., 1918-19. Author: Bombs, Super-Bombs and the Cost of Peace (Tex. Law Rev.), 1950. Home: 35 Claremont Av., N.Y. City 27; (summer) Prout's Neck, Me. Died Feb. 13, 1952; buried Newtown (Conn.) Cemetery.

HYDE, D(uncan) Clark, educator, economist; b. Quebec, P.Q., Can., Oct. 13, 1896; s. Alexander and Annie Carter (Brown) H.; A.B., McGill U., 1917; A.M., Harvard, 1918, Ph.D., 1921; m. Varina Moore Rhodes, Aug. 4, 1931 (dec. 1952). Came to U.S., 1929, naturalized, 1939. Instr. in econs. Harvard, 1920-21; asst. prof. econs. Knox Coll., Galesburg, Ill., 1921-22; prof. econs. Keio U., Tokyo, Japan, 1923-29; asso. prof. econs. U. Va., 1929-45, prof. econs., 1945—. Served as civilian lectr. Army Orientation Program, 1942. Mem. Am. Assn. U. Profs., Am., So. (pres. 1943-44) econ. assns., Econ. History Assn., Royal Econ. Soc., Beta Gamma Sigma, Delta Sigma Pi. Episcopalian. Club: Colonnade. Home: 1958 Thomson Rd., Charlottesville, Va. Died Feb. 1957.

HYDE, James Hazen, philanthropist; b. N.Y.C., June 6, 1876; s. Henry Baldwin and Annie (Fitch) H.; A.B., Harvard, 1898; A.M. (hon.), Princeton, 1903; Dr. honoris causa, Rennes U., France, 1920; LL.D., Skidmore College, 1956; 1 son, Henry Baldwin. Vice-pres. Equitable Life Assurance Soc. U.S., 1899-1905. Hon. pres., founder, dir. Fdn. Alliance Francaise in U.S. (1st pres.). Grand Croix Legion of Honor, France. Mem. Am. Soc. French Legion of Honor (exec. bd.), Am. Friends of Versailles, Inc. (mem. bd.), Académie des Sciences Marales et Politiques (Institut de France) since 1938. Organized Conried Met. Opera Co. (opened 1903); one of sponsors New Theatre, N.Y.C. (opened 1909). Mem. Harvard Romance langs. and lits. vis. com.; hon. trustee Am. Library, Paris; chmn. French Inst. Institute Francais de Washington; hon. mem. com. Am. Field Service Fellowships. Capt. and aide to High Commr., A.R.C., in Paris during World War I. Fellow Royal Soc. of Lit., Royal Soc. of Arts (London), Met. Mus. of Arts N.Y.C., N.Y. Hist. Soc., Am. Geog. Soc., Pierpont Morgan Library N.Y.C., Cleve. Mus. Art (life); mem. Am. Antiquarian Soc., France-America Soc. (v.p.). Clubs: Century, University, Knickerbocker, Meadowbrook, Ft. Orange (Albany), Troy, Mohawk, Schenectady, University (Albany); Union, Harvard (N.Y. C.). Address: Savoy-Hilton Hotel, N.Y.C. 22. Died July 26, 1959.

HYER, Frank Sidney, educator; b. Aztalan, Wis., May 28, 1869; s. Oliver Perry and Mary (Allerton) H.; grad. State Normal Sch., Milw., 1896; A.B., Ripon College, 1911; m. Hattie A. Broche, Sept. 1, 1896; children—Frank Perry, Harold Allen, Harriet Else, George Nelson. County supt. schs. Jefferson County, Wis., 1893-95; prin. ward sch., Sheboygan, 1896-97; supt. schs., Rhinelander, Wis., 1897-1900; prin. County Training Sch., Manitowoc, 1901-04; instr., head tng. dept. State Normal Sch., Stevens Point, Wis., 1904-19, pres., 1930-38; pres. State Teachers Coll., Whitewater, 1919-30. Chmn. A.R.C., Portage County, World War. Mem. N.E.A., Wis. Tchrs. Assn. (pres. 1922-23). Episcopalian. Mason, Kiwanian. Author: Laurel Readers, 1917. Lecturer and institute condr. Home: Stevens Point, Wis. Died Mar. 1, 1957; buried Forest Cemetery, Stevens Point.

HYLAND, Philip David, advertising executive; b. Chgo., May 16, 1899; s. John J. and Elizabeth (Flaven) H.; student pub. and parochial schs.; m. Ruth M. Kenefick, Jan. 30, 1926; children—Nancy Joy, Joy Ann, Marlana, Philip D. Vice pres. Hyland Bros. Co., Chgo., 1919-25; western advt. mgr. Your Home mag., Chgo., later advt. manager of mass market group for McFadden Publs., 1926-28; advt. mgr. Smart Set mag., N.Y.C., 1928-29; rep. Hearst's American Weekly, Chgo., 1929-31; rep. Liberty mag., 1931-54; advt. mgr., v.p. Macfadden Publs., N.Y.C., 1954—. Clubs: New York Athletic, Winged Foot Golf, Metropolitan Advt. Men's Golf (N.Y.C.); Coral Beach (Palm Beach, Fla.). Home: Penthouse 333 E. 43d St., N.Y.C.; also 208 Indian Rd., Palm Beach, Fla. Office: 205 E. 42d St., N.Y.C. 17. Died Mar. 17, 1958; buried Gate of Heaven Cemetery, Hawthorne, N.Y.

HYNES, John William (hīnz), educator; b. El Paso, Tex., June 24, 1886; s. Mark Joseph and Agnes (Kelley) H.; student St. Stanislaus Coll., Macon, Ga., 1901-06; A.B., St. Louis U., 1908, A.M., 1909; student Gregorian U., Rome, 1921-23, D.D., 1923. Joined Soc. of Jesus (Jesuits), 1901; teacher in high sch. dept. Coll. Immaculate Conception, New Orleans, La., 1909-12, Spring Hill Coll., Mobile, Ala., 1912-14, v.p., 1919-21; teacher of fundamental theology, St. Mary's Sem., Mundelein, Ill., 1923-27; regent of Loyola U., New Orleans, 1927-28, dean, 1928-31, pres., 1931-36; dean of Jesuit Philosophate, Spring Hill Coll., Mobile, Ala., 1937-39; dir. League of Laymen's Retreats since 1939. Mem. N.E.A., Nat. Cath. Edn. Assn., Southern Assn. of Colls. and Secondary Schs. (past v.p.), A.A.A.S., Phi Omega, Blue Key. Address: Jesuit Church, New Orleans, La. Died Feb. 4, 1953; buried Spring Hill Coll., Mobile, Ala.

HYPES, William Findley, sales exec.; b. Xenia, O., Feb. 11, 1861; s. Samuel Henry and Hannah (Van Brocklin) H.; student high sch., Xenia; m. Fanny E. Loomis, June 12, 1889. Began with Cooper, Hutchinson & Co., Xenia, 1876; became connected with Field, Leiter & Co., Chgo., 1880, and transferred to wholesale dept. Marshall Field & Co., 1881, gen. sales mgr., 1905—; dir. Towle & Hypes Co., Clinton, Ia. First pres. Chicago North Shore Music Festival; pres. Chgo. YMCA; trustee YMCA Coll., Chicago Sunday Evening Club. Republican. Presbyn. Clubs: Union League (past pres.); University (Evanston); Skokie Golf. Home: 1126 Michigan Av., Evanston, Ill. Office: 219 W. Adams St., Chgo. Died Aug. 25, 1935; buried Meml. Park, Evanston, Ill.

HYSLOP, James Augustus (hĭs'lŭp), entomologist; b. Chicago, Ill., July 7, 1884; s. Charles George and Mary Agnes (Garvey) H.; B.S., Mass. Agrl. Coll., 1908, Boston U., 1908; M.S., Washington State Coll., 1911; m. Grace Genevra Anderson, Oct. 7, 1911; children—Charles Douglas, James Anderson, Ryntha (Mrs. D. R. Geehring), Wynnifred (Mrs. R. J. Shields). In charge first gipsy moth eradication work in Conn., 1906; cotton boll weevil parasite work, U.S. Dept. Agriculture, 1907; cereal and forage insect investigation, Dept. Agr., 1908-17; entomologist in charge Div. of Insect Pest Survey and Information, Bur. of Entomology and Plant Quarantine, U.S. Dept. Agr., 1917-44; now retired. Fellow A.A.A.S., Am. Entomol. Soc.; mem. Am. Assn. Econ. Entomologists, Washington Acad. Science, Washington Entomol. Soc. Has specialized in Elateridae. Home: Stateside Dr., Silver Spring, Md. Died Jan. 16, 1953.

I

IBSEN, Heman Lauritz, prof. genetics; b. Chicago, Ill., Sept. 16, 1886; s. Oluf August Martin and Gemaliah (Larsen) I.; B.S. in Agr., U. of Wis., 1912; M.S., in Genetics, 1913, Ph.D., 1916; m. Elma Ruth Stewart, Dec. 22, 1927; 1 dau., Jane Ruth. Asst. in genetics, U. of Wis., 1913-17, in zoölogy, 1917-19; professor genetics, Kan. State College since July 1919. Member of American Society of Animal Production and of American Dairy Science Association. With Chemical Warfare Service, U.S. Army, 1918. Fellow A.A.A.S.; mem. Am. Society Zoölogists, Am. Society Naturalists, Am. Genetic Assn., Sigma Xi, Phi Kappa Phi, Gamma Sigma Delta, Alpha Zeta. Republican. Has specialized in research on inheritance and physiology of reproduction in guinea pigs, rabbits, cattle, and rats. Home: 1811 Laramie St., Manhattan, Kan. Died Jan. 29, 1955; buried Sunset Cemetery, Manhattan, Kan.

ICKES, Harold L. (ik'es), lawyer, writer; born Frankstown Township, Blair County, Pennsylvania, March 15, 1874; son of Jesse Boone Williams and Martha Ann (McEwen) I.; A.B., U. of Chicago, 1897, J.D., cum laude, 1907; LL.D., Washington and Jefferson Coll. and Lake Forest Coll., 1933, Berea, Pa. Mil. and Tufts colls. and Northwestern U., 1934, U. of Ala., 1935, U. of New Mexico, 1939; m. Anna Wilmarth Thompson, 1911 (died 1935); 1 son, Raymond Wilmarth; m. 2d, Jane Dahlman, May 24, 1938; children—Harold McEwen, Elizabeth. Began career as reporter with Chicago newspapers, 1897-1900; began law practice, Chicago, 1907. Became active in municipal reform politics, Chicago, in 1897; manager of the mayoralty campaigns of John M. Harlan, 1905, and of Charles E. Merriam, 1911; chmn. Progressive Co. Com., Cook Co., Ill., 1912-14; chmn., Ill. Progressive State Com., 1914-16; mem. Progressive Nat. Com. and Nat. Exec. Com., 1915-16; mem. Nat. Campaign Com. in charge of Charles E. Hughes' campaign for President, 1916. Chmn. Ill. State Council Defense Neighborhood Com., 1917-Apr. 1918; Y.M.C.A. work in France with 35th Div., A.E.F., Apr. 1918-Jan. 1919. Del. at large Prog. Nat. Conv., 1916, Rep. Nat. Conv., 1920, Dem. Nat. Convs., 1936, 1940 and 1944; pres. of People's Protective League, 1922; Ill. mgr. of Hiram W. Johnson presidential campaign, 1924; mgr. campaign of Hugh S. Magill, Independent Rep. candidate for U.S. Senator from Ill., 1926; became sec. of Interior in cabinets of Presidents Roosevelt and Truman, 1933-46; resigned Feb. 15, 1946; also administrator of public works, 1933-39, and oil administrator under NRA; became solid fuels adminstr. for war, Nov. 1941-Feb. 1946, and coordinator of fisheries, July 1942-Feb. 1946; also petroleum administrator, May 1941-Feb. 1946; coal mines administr., 1943-44; chmn. Nat. Resources Com., 1934-39; chmn. Nat. Power Policy Committee, 1934-Feb. 1946; mem. of National Defense Power Commn., 1938-39; chairman American delegation, Anglo-American Oil Treaty Negotiations, London, Sept. 1945; mem. Nat. Theodore Roosevelt Memorial Assn.; v.p. Roosevelt Memorial Assn. of Greater Chicago; mem. bd. advisers of Quetico-Superior Council until 1933; mem. Nat. Conservation Com.; chmn. People's Traction League, 1929-30. Chairman of the board of trustees, Roosevelt College, Chicago, Illinois, 1948-50. Awarded Louis D. Brandeis medal for service to humanity, 1940, Cornelius Amory Pugsley gold medal for distinguished park service in U.S. in 1941. Mem. Am. Bar Assn., Ill. Soc. S.A.R., Swedish Colonial Soc. (honorary), Chicago Press Veterans Assn., League of America, American Philatelic Society, Phi Delta Theta, Phi Delta Phi, Pi Gamma Mu (hon.). Clubs: University, Lake Shore Athletic (Chicago); Shawnee Country (Wilmette); Indian Hill (Winnetka); National Press (Washington, D.C.); Saints and Sinners (N.Y.). Author: The New Democracy, 1934; Back to Work, 1935; America's House of Lords, 1939; The Third Term Bugaboo, 1940; Not Guilty, 1940; Autobiography of a Curmudgeon, 1943; Fightin' Oil, 1943; My Twelve Years with F.D.R., 1948. Editor: Freedom of the Press Today, 1941. Home: Headwaters Farm, Olney, Md. Died Feb. 3, 1952; buried Sandy Spring, Md.

IDDINGS, Edward John, animal husbandman; b. Peru, Ind., Mar. 22, 1879; s. John Byron and Mary (Huber) I.; student Butler Coll., 1899-1901; B.S. in Agr., Colo. A.&M. Coll., 1907, M.S., 1922; LL.D. (honorary), University of Idaho, 1950; married Maud Augusta Rowell, June 24, 1908; children—Edward John (dec.), Catherine May (dec.). Spl. agt. Bureau of Plant Industry, U.S. Dept. Agr., 1906; asst. to dean of agr., Colo. A.&M. Coll., 1907-09; asst. in animal husbandry, same Coll., 1909-10; with U. of Idaho since 1910, prin. Sch. of Practical Agr. and asst. in animal husbandry, 1910-11, prof. animal husbandry, 1911-18, vice dean College of Agr., 1913-15, dean, 1915-18, dean of agr. and dir. Agrl. Expt. Sta., 1918-46; acting dir. extension service, 1923-24, emeritus since Nov. 1, 1946; on leave of absence director of extension, 1924-46; dean of agriculture on round-the-world tour, 1927, visiting leading farming and livestock producing countries; on sabbatical leave November 1, 1945-October 31, 1946. Fellow Am. Assn. for Advancement of Science, American Society of Animal Production, Delta Tau Delta, Alpha Zeta, Sigma Xi. Mason (K.T., Shriner). Author numerous bulletins and articles relating to live stock. Chosen Honor Grad., Colo. A. and M. Coll., 1947. Home: Moscow, Ida.; also San Jacinto, Cal. Deceased.

IDE, Charles Edward, utilities exec.; b. Brayton, Ia., Feb. 4, 1892; s. O. F. and Sarah Elizabeth (Cotton) I.; B.S., Ia. State Coll., 1914; m. Edith Lincoln Brown, Sept. 11, 1919; 1 son, Charles Edward. With Denver Gas & Electric Co., 1914; engr. Toledo (O.) Ry. & Light Co., 1915; with Henry L. Doherty & Co., N.Y. City, 1916; engr. Meridian (Miss.) Light & Ry. Co., 1917; asst. to gen. mgr. Cities Service Power & Light Co., 1922; v.p. and gen. mgr. Bristol (Tenn.) Gas & Electric Co. and Watauga Power Co., 1927; v.p. and gen. mgr. Tenn Eastern Elec. Co., Johnson City Traction Corp., Tenn. Realty Co., Tenn. Eastern Power Co., 1928; v.p. and gen. mgr., Erwin Electric Light & Power Co., 1929; pres. and gen. mgr. East Tenn. Light & Power Co., 1940-45; exec. v.p. and gen. mgr. The Toledo Edison Co., 1945-49, pres., 1949—; dir. O. Valley Elec. Corp., 1952—, Atomic Power Development Assos., 1955—; trustee Power Reactor Development Co., 1955. Pres. Toledo Community Chest, 1952; dir. Edison Elec. Inst. 1954—, Toledo Mus. Art. Profl. engr. Mem. Toledo (pres. 1949), Ohio (dir.) C.'s of C., Tau Beta Pi. Clubs: Toledo, Toledo Country, Inverness Country. Office: Edison Bldg., Toledo. Died Aug. 17, 1959.

IDELL, Albert Edward (ī-dĕll'), novelist; b. Phila., Pa., June 21, 1901; s. Albert Magilton and Melissa (Barr) I.; grad. Germantown High Sch., Phila., 1919; student Sch. of Indsl. Art, 1919-21; studied accounting at night sch.; m. Marguerite Bethulia Borgiano Cadwalader, December 30, 1926. Worked as grocery clerk, typist, truck helper, etc., while attending high sch.; sec. to dir. while attending art sch.; began in pub. accounting, 1921; working at accounting during winters and variously as harvest hand, railroad car repairer, laborer in packing house, short order cook in restaurant, etc., during summers; spent 6 months in Europe with group of artists, then hitchhiked through Germany and worked passage home on S.S. America; also spent 1926-27 in Sicily; began specializing in bldg. and loan and bank accounting, 1927; partner in mfg. fibre specialties, 1929; bank auditing, western N.C., 1931-32; study of restaurant accounting, also promoted prize fights in Asheville, N.C.; started a lending library, 1930; cons. in school lunch rooms, Phila. School Dist., 1932, became supervisor, 1933; conducted courses in restaurant management for Phila. Restaurant Assn.; writing since 1941. Awarded $1,000 Bookman's prize for best novel for one connected with book trade for novel Pug, story of prize fighter, 1941. Author books including: Pug, 1941; Cross in the Caribbean, 1941, Centennial Summer, 1943; Bridge to Brooklyn, 1944; The Sea is Woman, 1947; The Great Blizzard, 1948; Doorway in Antiqua, 1949; Stephen Hayne, 1951; The Corner Store, 1953; Rogers Folly, 1957. Editor, translator, The Bernal Diaz Chronicles, 1956, and others. Address: Box 84 N, West Palm Beach, Fla. Died July 7, 1958.

IDEMA, Henry, banker; b. Grand Rapids, Mich., Feb. 29, 1856; s. Henry and Frances (Van der Ploeg) I.; student pub. schs.; m. Annie Doornink, Feb. 3, 1880; children—Chester F., Walter D., Edward H. Mgr. Bradstreet's Mercantile Agency, Grand Rapids, 1882-93; chmn. bd. Old Kent Bank, Grand Rapids, Mich., 1908—; v.p. Mich. Trust Co.; treas. Metal Office Furniture Co., McKenzie River Timber Co.; dir. First National Bank, Holland, Mich., Tillamook Yellow Fir Co., Mich. Consolidated Gas Co. Trustee, treas. Isabella Home for Aged Women. Presbyn. Clubs: Peninsular, Kent Country. Home: 103 College Av. S.E. Address: Old Kent Blank, Grand Rapids, Mich. Died Jan. 5, 1951; buried Grand Rapuds.*

IGOE, William L., lawyer, ex-congressman; b. St. Louis, Oct. 19, 1879; s. Michael J. and Margaret (Hefferman) I.; pub. and parochial schs.; LL.B., Law Dept., Washington U., 1902; unmarried. Clerk and later asst. librarian, Mercantile Library, St. Louis. Mem. St. Louis Ho. of Dels., 1909-13 (resigned); member 63d to 66th Congresses (1913-21), 11th Mo. Dist.; now mem. Igoe, Carroll, Keefe & Doerner. Democrat. Catholic; Knight of St. Gregory. Home: 6226 Devonshire. Office: Boatmen's Bank Bldg., St. Louis. Died Apr. 20, 1953; buried Calvary Cemetery.

IHLDER, John (īl'dēr), civic work; b. Baltimore, Md., Mar. 8, 1876; s. John D. and Maude Anna (Mott) I.; grad. high sch., Yonkers, N.Y., 1896; B.S., Cornell U., 1900; m. Louise McLaren, Oct. 6, 1906; 1 son, Richard. Newspaper work and magazine writing, 1900-08; with Assn. of Commerce, Grand Rapids, Mich., 1908-10; field sec. Nat. Housing Assn., 1910-16; mng. dir. Phila. Housing Assn., 1917-20, also of Phila. Child Federation, and chmn. Social and Health Com., 1918-20; mgr. Civic Development Dept. U.S. Chamber Commerce, 1920-28; exec. dir. Pittsburgh Housing Assn., 1928-33; housing consultant to Nat. Capital Park and Planning Commn., 1929-34; exec. dir. Boston Housing Assn., 1931-34; executive Washington Committee on Housing, 1933-34; executive officer, Nat. Capital Housing Authority, 1934-52; consultant on housing Federal Defense Agencies, 1940-41. Chairman committee on types of dwellings, President's Conf. on Home Bldg., 1931. Mem. Phila. Zoning Commn., 1917-20; Philadelphia representative U.S. Housing Corp., 1918-19; chmn. U.S. Homes Registration Com., 1918-19; mem. bd. mgrs. Nat. Sch. Commercial and Trade Orgn. Executives, 1921-28; mem. City Planning and Zoning Advisory Com. of Federal Dept. of Commerce, 1921-34; mem. Commn. on Public Welfare Legislation, D.C. Mem. Inst. Planners (mem. bd. govs.), Washington Council Social Agencies (past pres.), Nat. Conf. Social Work, Internat. Federation for Housing and Town Planning (mem. of council), Nat. Assn. of Housing Officials (past v.p.); former pres. Middle Atlantic Regional Council; mem. interim com. during reorganization period of Community Chest and Council Social Agencies; mem. bd. dirs. Nat. Housing Conf. Mem. Phi Delta Theta. Unitarian. Club: Cosmos (Washington). Home: 2811 P St. N.W. Office: Washington. Died May 19, 1958.

IHLE, Leo (ealy), newspaper pub.; b. Cobden, Ill., Jan. 8, 1900; s. Charles A. and Caroline (Schelder) I.; m. Irene Johnston, June 13. 1922. Newspaperman, 1916—; bus. mgr. San Francisco Call-Bulletin, 1930-52, pub., 1953-55; v.p., dir. Hearst Publishing Co., Inc., Hearst Consolidated Publishers. Mem. Cercle de l'Union (dir.), Sigma Delta Chi. Comml. grower of cymbidium orchids, tuberous begonias, pelargoniums. Home: 267 Locust Av., San Rafael, Cal. Office: 860 Howard St., San Francisco 3. Died Sept. 2, 1956.

ILAK, Abdul, see ABDUL, Ilak Hashimi.

ILGENFRITZ, E.K., utilities exec.; b. Audubon, Ia., 1890; grad. Northwestern U. Sec., treas., dir. Ga. Power & Light Co., Valdosta, Ga.; v.p., treas., sec., dir. Fla. Power Corp. Home: 226 23d Av. N.E. Office: P.O. Box 4042, St. Petersburg, Fla. Died May 13, 1958.

ILLGES, John P(aul) (Il'jis), business exec.; born Columbus, Ga., May 4, 1881; s. Abraham and Mary L. (Barnett) I.; B.S., Ala. Poly. Inst., 1900; m. Dorothy Shannon, Jan. 19, 1905; children—John P., Norman S., Dorothy S. (Mrs. John W. Mayher). With Goldens' Foundry and Machine Co., Columbus, Ga., since 1900, became sec. and treas., 1915, pres., 1937, chmn. bd. since 1942; chmn. bd. and dir. Lummus Cotton Gin Co.; pres. and dir. Illges Securities Co.; dir. Columbus Bank & Trust Co., Muscogee Manufacturing Company, Swift Manufacturing Company, Swift Spinning Mills, Inc., Coca Cola Co. Memorial Foundn., Inc. Mem. Am. Camellia Soc. (vice pres. and dir.), Newcomen Soc. of Eng., Sigma Alpha Epsilon. Methodist. Mason. Club: Rotary of Atlanta. Organizer and chmn. A. and M. L. Illges Internat. Collector and propagater rare and unusual varieties of Camellia Japonica; sponsor Illges Medal for best seedling camellia introduced each yr. Home: "Plumfield," Columbus, Ga. Office: 1345 2d Av., Columbus, Ga. Died Dec. 27, 1957; buried Linwood Cemetery, Columbus.

ILLINGWORTH, Sir Cyril Gordon, commodore Cunard White Star Line; b. Kendal, Westmoreland, Eng., April 28, 1884; s. George R. and Ada (Oldfield) I.; ed. privately; m. Grace Watt, Nov. 9, 1917 (div. 1950); children—James, David; m. 2d, Marie Randall Caldwell, July 11, 1950. Cadet, the Sierra Line of squarerigger ships, 1901, served in sailing deep water ships 6½ years; with Cunard Line 1910-49, comd. Queen Mary 1942-49, comd. Queen Elizabeth; comd. Queens, Aquitania, Manretania, Laconia, Lancastria; commodore Cunard White Star fleet 1947-49. Served as capt. with Royal Navy Reserve, 1934, promoted commodore 2d class and commodore of Ocean Convoys, 1940. Knighted, 1949. Decorated Order Merit, Rank Comdr. U.S.A. 1949, Chevalier de L'Ordre, Maritime, France. Mem. Freeman of City of London, Honorable Co. of Master Mariners (freeman and livery-man). Clubs: Devonshire (London); Southampton Yacht. Home: Longwood Towers, Brookline, Mass. Office: Cunard White Star, Ltd., 25 Broadway, N.Y.C. Died Aug. 7, 1959.

IMAHORN, Albert Peter, banker; b. Mobile, Ala., Sept. 5, 1897; s. Albert Peter and Amelia (Hanlein) I.; student McGill Inst., Mobile, Ala., 1909-12, Spring Hill Coll., Mobile, 1913-14; m. Vera Nell Pearce, July 25, 1929. Became clk. People's Bank, Mobile, 1914; has been asst. nat. bank examiner, bank examiner State of Ala., examiner Fed. Farm Loan Bd., pres. Am. Nat. Bank & Trust Co., Mobile, mgr. loan agency R.F.C., New Orleans; pres. Hibernia Nat. Bank, New Orleans, 1933—. Mem. adv. com. R.F.C., New Orleans. Served as sgt. Q.M. Corps, AUS, World War. Democrat. Roman Catholic. Clubs: Boston, Louisiana, New Orleans Country (New Orleans). Home: 6126 St. Charles Av., New Orleans 15. Died May 21, 1949.

IMPERATORI, Charles Johnstone (ĭm-pĕr-ȧ-tō're), physician; b. N.Y.C., Jan. 20, 1878; s. Carlo and Sarah (Johnstone) I.; M.D., N.Y.U., 1899; m. Olga Gilbert, 1902; children—Charles Johnstone, Olga (Mrs. W. R. Wolfinbarger), Sarah (Mrs. William F. Farrell). Sub-externe Bellevue Hosp., 1899-1900, vis. surgeon, 1917-21, 30-35; prof. laryngology N.Y. Post-Grad. Med. Sch. and Hosp., Columbia, 1922-38; clin. prof. otolaryngology N.Y.U., 1932-35; cons. laryngologist Nyack (N.Y.) Gen. Hosp., Harlem Hosp., N.Y.; cons. bronchoscopist Manhattan Eye, Ear and Throat Hosp.; mem. div. med. scis. NRC, 1941-44. Served as lt. col., C.O. 309th Med. Regt., 84th Div., U.S. Army, 1917-19, AEF. Decorated Medaille D'Honneur Des Epidemies (France). Mem. Am. Laryngol. Assn. (pres. 1942-44), Am. Bronchoscopic Soc. (pres. 1928), N.Y. Acad. Med., Am. Rhinol. Otol. and Laryngol. Soc., A.M.A., A.C.S. (bd. govs. 1942-49), Alpha Delta Sigma, Phi Alpha Sigma. Republican. Episcopalian. Author: Diseases of Nose and Throat (with Dr. H. J. Burman), 1935, 2d edit., 1939, Spanish Am. edition, 1942. Address: Block House, Essex, N.Y. Died June 15, 1949.

INGALLS, Fay, business exec.; b. Cin., July 12, 1882; s. Melville Ezra and Abbie (Stimson) I.; grad. St. Marks Sch., 1900; A.B., Harvard, 1904, LL.B., 1907; m. Rachel Holmes, Sept. 21, 1908; children—Mary Holmes (Mrs. Calvin J. Haugh), Daniel H., Esther Abbie (Mrs. Kenneth T. Calder), Rachel (Mrs. David E. Hutchinson). Admitted to N.Y. bar, 1907; law clk. Strong & Cadwalader, 1907-08, Byrne & Cutcheon, 1908-11; mem. firm Holter, Ingalls & Guthrie, 1911-14; sec., gen. counsel, dir., mem. exec. com. Niles-Bement Pond & Asso. Cos., 1914-22; pres., treas. Va. Hot Springs, Inc., 1922—; propr. Homestead Hotel, Cascades Inn, also utilities and farms for community; v.p. Bath Co. Nat. Bank. Author: The Valley Road (story of Hot Springs). Contbr. column local weekly. Home: Hot Springs, Va. Died Nov. 23, 1957; buried Warm Springs (Va.) Cemetery.

INGALLS, Robert Ingersoll, chmn. bd. Ingalls Iron Works Co.; b. Huntsville, O., Oct. 27, 1882; s. Horace Putnam and Florence (Bimel) I.; student high sch., Bellefontaine, O., 1896-98, Ohio Northern U., 1898-1900; m. Ellen Gregg, Apr. 14, 1909; 1 son, Robert Ingersoll. Organized, 1910, since pres., chmn. bd. and dir. The Ingalls Iron Works Co.; pres., dir., Security Realty and Investment Co.; chmn. bd., dir., The Ingalls Shipbuilding Corp.; director Birmingham Tank Company, First National Bank of Birmingham. Pres. Birmingham Chamber Commerce 2 yrs. Democrat. Mason (32°). Clubs: Mountain Brook Country (Birmingham); Avoca Duck (New Orleans). Home: 2245 Crest Rd. Address: Ingalls Iron Works Co., Birmingham, Ala. Died July 12, 1951.

INGALLS, Walter Renton, cons. engr.; b. Lynn, Mass., Oct. 25, 1865; s. Jerome and Emma (Renton) I.; S.B., Mass. Inst. Tech., 1886; E.D., U. Mo., 1923; m. Ella Gordon, Oct. 26, 1898; children—Rosamond, Catherine (dec.), Hildegarde (dec.), Ursula. Mining and smelting, Leadville, Colo., 1886-89; asst. editor Engring. and Mining Jour., 1890-92; engr., supt. Pittsburgh & Mexican Tin Mining Co., Durango, Mex.; cons. mining engr., N.Y., 1893; mgr. Ill. Phosphate Co. (Ocala, Fla.), Brodie Gold Reduction Co. (Cripple Creek, Colo.), and metallurgist Gold & Silver Extraction Co., Ltd., Denver, 1894-95; supt. smeltery, Quien Sabe Mine, Durango, Mexico, 1896; asst. editor The Mineral Industry, 1897-99; acting editor Engring. and Mining Jour., part of 1897; metall. engr. Am. Zinc, Lead & Smelting Co., Columbia Lead Co., Laharpe Zinc Smelting Co., 1899-1904; chief commn. apptd. by Canadian govt. to report on zinc resources of B.C., 1905-06; editor Engring. and Mining Jour., 1905-19, The Mineral Industry, 1905-10. Cons. engr., N.Y.C., 1919-48. Dir. Am. Bur. Metal Statistics, 1920-47. Mem. Am. Inst. Mining and Metall. Engrs., Instn. Mining and Metallurgy (London), Mining and Metall. Soc. Am. (past prs.; elected hon. mem. 1946), Am. Inst. Weights and Measures (pres.). Clubs: Engineers, Lawyers. Author: Production and Properties of Zinc, 1902; Metallurgy of Zinc and Cadmium, 1903; Lead and Zinc in the United States, 1908; The Wealth and Income of the American People, 1922; Current Economic Affairs, 1923. Co-author: Report on the Zinc Resources of British Columbia, 1906; Notes on Metallurgical Mill Construction, 1906; Lead Smelting and Refining, 1906; Rules and Regulations for Metal Mines, 1915. Home: Ingaldsby, Boxford, Mass. Died Feb. 25, 1956; buried Pine Grove Cemetery, Lynn, Mass.

INGE, Francis Harrison (ĭnj), lawyer; b. Mobile Ala., May 20, 1902; s. Francis James and Ellen Mary (Harrison) I.; student Univ. Mil. Sch., Mobile, 1910-18; A.B., U. of Ala., 1922, LL.B., 1924; m. Alletta Turner, June 10, 1931; children—Waring, Ellen Ann; m. 2d, Sloss Whitaker Morris, September 22, 1956. Admitted to Ala. bar, 1924, and since practiced in Mobile; partner Inge & Bates, later Inge, Stallworth & Inge, later sr. partner in Inge, Twitty, Armbrecht & Jackson, now counsel; member of firm Inge & Twitty, 1956—; apptd. U.S. atty. for Southern Dist. of Ala., May 9, 1935, and 1939-43; dir. 1st Nat. Bank of Mobile (Ala.), Waterman Steamship Corp., Waterman Bldg. Corp., Title Ins. Company, Home Savs. & Loan Assn., Pan-Atlantic Steamship Corp., Gulf Shipbldg. Corp., L. Hammel Dry Goods Co.; mem. firm Inge & Twitty, Mobile, 1956—. Pres. Mobile County Tb Sanatorium. Trustee Mobile Infirmary Assn. Mem. Am. (del. of Ala. 1943-59), Ala. (pres. 1955-56), Mobile bar assn. (president 1939), Phi Beta Kappa, Delta Kappa Epsilon, Phi Delta Phi. Democrat. Episcopalian (vestryman Christ Ch.). Rotarian. Home: Cottage Hill Rd. Office: Merchants Bank Bldg., Mobile, Ala. Died Apr. 9, 1959.

INGE, Zebulon Montgomery Pike, lawyer; b. Greene County, Ala., Feb. 7, 1856; s. Maj. William B. and Elizabeth (Herndon) I.; A.M., So. U., Greensboro, Ala., 1875; studied law U. Va. and 1 yr. in office of Herndon & Smith, Mobile; m. Nona Johnston. Dec. 4, 1878. Admitted to Ala. bar, 1877; practiced, Mobile 1877—. Mem. Ala. Ho. Reps., 1884. Trustee Mobile city bond holders, 1885-1908. Mem. Ala. State Bar Assn. Democrat. Club: Mobile Commercial (ex-pres.). Home: 956 Government St. Office: City Bank Bldg., Mobile, Ala. Died Dec. 31, 1920; buried Mobile.

INGERSOLL, Leonard Rose, educator; b. N.Y.C., June 1, 1880; s. Hiram Day and Mary Augusta (Rose) I.; B.S., Colo. Coll., Colorado Springs, 1902; Ph.D., U. Wis., 1905; m. Barbara Ethel Smeigh, June 19, 1907 (died Apr. 3, 1917); children—Barbara M., Hugh D.; m. 2d, Helen (Flint) Wallace, Aug. 2, 1918; 1 son, Alfred C. Instr. physics U. Wis., 1905-08, asst. prof., 1908-10, asso. prof., 1910-25, prof., 1925—. Fellow A.A.A.S., Am. Phys. Soc.; mem. Wis. Acad. Sci., Arts and Letters, Phi Beta Kappa, Sigma Xi. Conglist. Mem. Smithsonian Expdn. to Mt. Wilson, Cal., for solar investigations, 1905, 06, 09. Author; (with O. J. Zobel) An Introduction to the Mathematical Theory of Heat Conduction, 1913; (with M. J. Martin) Experiments in Physics, 1942; (with O. J. Zobel and A. C. Ingersoll), Heat Conduction with Engineering and Geological Applications, 1948. Contbr. many articles to sci. jours., chiefly on subjects connected with electro-magnetic theory of light. Recipient of grants from Rumford Fund. Inventor glarimeter for measuring gloss of paper (adopted as standard govt. test, 1925). Club: University. Home: 1933 West Lawn Ave., Madison 5, Wis. Died Apr. 25, 1958.

INGHAM, Lucius Edwin, engineer; b. Oil City, Pa., Jan. 6, 1892; s. Phineas Staunton and Matie (Wilson) I.; student pub. schs.; m. Ann Brainard, Aug. 21, 1916; 1 dau., Janet Ann (Mrs. Sprengle). Engring. dept. United Natural Gas Co., 1910-23, Iroquois Gas Corp., 1923-30, Columbia Engring. Corp., 1931-36, Mich. Gas Transmission Co., 1936-39, v.p. Ky. Natural Gas Corp., 1939-47; v.p. operations, Tex. Gas Transmission Corp., 1947—, dir., 1947—; v.p. La. Natural Gas Corp., Shreveport, 1951—, Tex. No. Gas Corp., 1951—. Profl. engr., Ohio. Mason (32°). Home: 1922 Griffith Pl. E. Office: 416 W. Third St., Owensboro, Ky. Died Mar. 3, 1957; buried Oil City, Pa.

INGLEY, Fred (ĭng'lē), bishop; b. Staffordshire, Eng., Nov. 20, 1878; s. Albert and Mary (Bloomer) I.; brought to U.S., 1888; grad. Phila. Divinity School, 1906, S.T.D., 1921; D.D., Colorado College, 1928; m. Edith Mary Hansen, June 9, 1909; children—Fred, Hansen, Mary, Elizabeth, Ruth, Jane. Deacon, 1906, priest P.E. Ch., 1907; rector St. Mary's Ch., Braddock, Pa., 1906-08, St. Matthew's Ch., Kenosha, Wis., 1908-17, St. Mark's Ch., Denver, 1917-21; bishop coadjutor of Colo., 1921-38; bishop of Colo., 1938—; pres. of Province of the Northwest, 1929-35; provisional bishop of Wyoming, 1936. Dep. to Gen. Conv. P.E. Ch., 1916, 19; exec. chmn. Evergreen (Colo.) Conf. Pres. St. Luke's Hosp. and Church Home (Denver). Address: 1 So. Downing St., Denver 9. Died Feb. 15, 1951; buried Denver.

INGLIS, Richard, lawyer; b. Detroit, Mich., Nov. 23, 1880; s. Frank and Mary (Meginnity) I.; A.B., Harvard, 1903, LL.B., 1906; LL.D., Kenyon Coll., 1928; m. Marian Coale, Dec. 2, 1907; children—Richard, Jean (Mrs. Inglis Johnson) Marian (Mrs. Douglas S. Gibbs) (dec.). Admitted to Ohio bar, 1906, and became asso. firm Hoyt, Dustin & Kelley; atty. for Hocking Valley R.R. Co., 1908-09; mem. firm Bulkley & Inglis, 1910-15; partner in investment firm of Otis & Co., 1915-31; mem. law firm of Hauxhurst, Inglis, Sharp & Cull; pres. Inland Investors, Inc.; gen. counsel, v.p. and dir. Eaton Mfg. Co.; dir. Basic Refractories, Inc., Lamson & Sessions Co., Gabriel Co., prof. law of private corps., Western Reserve U., 1910-23. Trustee Kenyon Coll. Mem. Am., Cleveland and Ohio State bar assns. Republican. Episcopalian (trustee and chancellor Diocese of Ohio). Clubs: Nisi Prius, Harvard, Union, Tavern,

Kirtland Country (Cleveland); Harvard, Church (New York). Home: Lyndhurst, Cleveland 24. Office: 1501 Euclid Av., Cleve. 15. Died June 25, 1956.

INGRAHAM, William Moulton, lawyer; b. Portland, Me., Nov. 2, 1870; s. Darius Holbrook and Ella (Moulton) I.; A.B., Bowdoin, 1895, A.M., 1910; student Harvard Law Sch., 1895-96, and in office of Hon. Augustus F. Moulton, Portland; admitted to bar, 1897; m. Jessamine P. Damsel, June 1, 1901. Began practice in Portland, Nov. 1897; judge of Probate Court, Cumberland County, Me., 1907-15; mayor of Portland, 1915; asst. sec. of war, Washington, May 8, 1916-Nov. 8, 1917; surveyor of customs, Portland, Me., 1917-22. Trustee Portland (Me.) Savings Bank. Mem. Me. advisory bd. under Federal Pub. Works Act, 1933; elected mem. Me. Constitutional Conv. for repeal of the 18th Amendment, 1933. Democrat. Mem. Board of Overseers, Bowdoin Coll.; trustee Westbrook Jr. Coll., Monmouth Acad. Del. Dem. Nat. Conv., 1928. Pres. Me. State Soc. for Protection of Animals. Mem. Am. and Me. State bar assns., Me. Hist. Soc., Mayflower Descendants, Psi Upsilon, Soc. Colonial Wars, S.A.R. Episcopalian. Clubs: Lions, Cumberland, Portland Yacht, Country, Elks. Home: 79 High St. Office: Clapp Memorial Bldg., Portland 3, Me. Died Oct. 12, 1951; buried Evergreen Cemetery, Portland.

INGRAM, Jonas Howard, mfg. exec., ret. naval officer; b. Jeffersonville, Ind., Oct. 15, 1886; s. William Thomas and Anna I. (Howard) I.; student Culver (Ind.) Mil. Acad., 1902-03; B.S., U.S. Naval Acad., 1907; grad. U.S. Naval War Coll., 1940; m. Jean Fletcher-Coffin, July 14, 1914; children—William Thomas II, Mary-Birch (wife L. C. Hays, U.S.M.C.). Commd. ensign, U.S.N., 1909, advanced through grades to admiral, 1944; football coach U.S. Naval Acad., 1909-12, head coach, 1915-17, dir. athletics, dir. football, 1926-30; chief staff 9th Naval Dist., Great Lakes, Ill., 1921-23; comdr. U.S.S. Stoddert, 1924-26; exec., acting comdr. U.S.S. Pennsylvania, 1930-33; pub. relations officer Navy Dept., naval aide to sec. navy, 1933-36; comdr. Destroyer Sqdn. Six, U.S. Battle Fleet, 1936-37; capt. N.Y. Navy Yard, 1937-39; comdr. U.S.S. Tennessee, 1940, cruisers U.S. Atlantic Fleet, 1941, Allied Forces in South Atlantic, 1942; comdr.-in-chief Atlantic Fleet, 1944-46, ret. Apr. 1, 1947; commr. football, pres. All-Am. Football Conf., 1947-49; v.p., dir. Reynolds Metals. Co., Richmond, Va., since 1949; pres. Acme Fuel Co., Jeffersonville, since 1947; dir. summer schs. Culver (Ind.) Mil. Acad. 1952. Hon. mem. Princeton, 1915. Trustee U.S. Naval Acad. Alumni Assn., Inc. Clubs: New York (N.Y.) Yacht; Annapolitan (Annapolis, Md.); Racquet (Phila.); Army-Navy Country (Washington); Pendennis (Louisville); San Diego (commr.), University (San Diego, Cal.); Maxinkuckee Yacht (Culver, Ind.). Address: 330 Eighth St., Coronado 18, Cal. Died Sept. 10, 1952; buried Arlington Nat. Cemetery.

INGWERSEN, John Arthur, business exec.; born Chicago, Nov. 15, 1898; s. Emil Henry and Mary Lincoln (Harbeck) I.; A.B., U. of Ill., 1920; m. Mariann Bradt, Oct. 17, 1922; children—John, Elizabeth, Samuel, Mary, Joan, Deborah. Sports editor Rockford (Ill.) Morning Star, 1920-21; sports editor Middletown (O.) Journal, 1921-22, circulation mgr. and asst. treas., 1922-23; interviewer The Am. Rolling Mill Co. (now Armco Steel Corp.), 1923, chief interviewer, 1923-25, salesman, 1925-45, gen. mgr. sales, 1945-47, vice pres. in charge distbn. since 1947; dir. Sheffield Steel Corp. Mem. bd. trustees Middletown Civic Assn.; mem. Middletown Bd. Edn. Mem. Am. Iron and Steel Inst., Delta Kappa Epsilon. Republican. Presbyterian. Club: Moraine Country (Dayton). Home: 509 S. Main St. Office: 703 Curtis St., Middletown, O. Died Dec. 5, 1952.

INLOW, Richard Morehead (in'lo), clergyman; b. Palmyra, Mo., Mar. 2, 1867; s. Dudley Vardeman and Jane Elizabeth (Dowell) I.; A.B., William Jewell Coll., Liberty, Mo., 1890; Th.M., So. Bapt. Theol. Sem., 1896; D.D., Union U., 1911; m. Fannie Stokley, Jan. 7, 1891; children—Lura B., Ellis L., Lucile F., Eva R., Robert F. Ordained Bapt. ministry, 1896; pastor 1st Ch., Butler, Mo., 1896-98, 1st Ch., Harrisonville, Mo., 1898-1901, 1st Ch., Nevada, Mo., 1901-03; field sec. Bapt. S.S. Bd., Nashville, 1903-06; pastor 1st Ch., Joplin, Mo., 1906-09, 1st Ch., Nashville, 1909-13; pres. Union U., Jackson, Tenn., 1913-14; gen. sec. Ark. Bapt. State Conv., 1914-15; pastor Bellevue Bapt. Ch., Memphis, 1915-20, First Ch., Sedalia, Mo., 1920-26, Immanuel Ch., Oklahoma City, 1926——. Trustee Lexington (Mo.) Female Coll., Union U., Jackson, Tenn., Tenn. Coll., Murfreesboro; dir. Bapt. Meml. Hosp., Bapt. Bible Inst. (New Orleans); 1st v.p. So. Bapt. Conv. and ex-officio mem. of its bds., 1922-23; mem. exec. bd. Mo. Bapt. Gen. Assn., Chmn. com. home and fgn. missions. Mem. Home Mission Bd. So. Bapt. Conv.; mem. bd. mgrs. Okla. Bapt. State Conv.; moderator Okla. Bapt. Assn.; mem. exec. com. So. Bapt. Conv. Prohibitionist. Address: 3316 Wilway Dr., Albuquerque, N.M. Died July 22, 1952.

INMAN, Walker Patterson, business exec.; b. Atlanta, Aug. 21, 1894; s. William Henry and Nana-

line (Holt) I.; student pub. schs.; m. Georgia Polin, Mar. 24, 1951; 1 son, Walker Patterson. Dir. Duke Power Co. since 1947. Trustee Duke Endowment since 1945, Duke U. since 1949. Office: 30 Rockefeller Plaza, N.Y.C. Died Sept. 19, 1954.

INNES, George (in'ĕs), designer and mgr.; b. Grant Twp., Tama County, Ia., Feb. 8, 1873; s. James and Elizabeth (Munro) I.; grad. Tilford Collegiate Acad., Vinton, Ia., 1894; m. Edith Elizabeth Brainerd, Oct. 26, 1898; children—Brainerd Munro, John Sweet, Robert George, Donald Watson. Began as treas. Eagle Grove (Ia.) Electric Co., 1894; sold out and opened lumber business at Rushmore, and Magnolia, Minn., 1902; became cashier 1st Nat. Bank, Rushmore, 1905; pres., 1907——; in colonization business in Can., 1905-09. Made trip around the world, 1908-09, and from then until 1920 devoted mainly to promoting foreign missions. Made trip to Cairo, Egypt, 1914, to meet Lord Kitchener and through him to secure permission from Egyptian govt. to establish Am. Univ. at Cairo; spent summer, 1915, with Kitchener's successor, completing details for Christian Univ. in Egypt. Inventor Innes grain shocker, Innes grain pick up, Innes self baler and Innes window feeder, Innes bulk potato harvester, Innes flotation potato separator; chmn. bd. Innes Co. Address: 1704 Meadow Brook Rd., Altadena, Cal. Died June 27, 1953; buried Altadena, Cal.

INSKEEP, Annie Dolman, child psychologist; b. Gold Hill, Nev.; d. William Hickman and Christine Caroline (Hoerner) Dolman; B.L., U. Cal., 1893, M.L., 1896; Ph.D., U. Chgo., 1898; m. Lorenzo Dow Inskeep, June 11, 1895 (dec.); children—Lorenzo Dow, William Dolman. Asst. prof. psychology, Mills Coll., Oakland, Cal., 1903-05, acting head dept. philosophy, 1912-13; child psychologist, pub. schs., Oakland, 1919-21, Berkeley, Cal.; 1921-37; lectr. child psychology, U. Cal., summers 1925-27. Mem. Nat. League Am. Pen Women, Am. Assn. U. Women. Republican. Episcopalian. Club: University Women's. Editor Dolman Compendium. Author: Teaching Dull and Retarded Children, 1926; Child Adjustment, 1930. Contbr. ednl. articles and verse to mags. Home: 2037 Soledad Av., La Jolla, Cal. Died May 21, 1959.

INVERCHAPEL, Lord, Archibald John Kerr Clark Kerr, ex-ambassador; s. John Kerr and Kate Louisa (Robertson) Clark; m. Maria Teresa Diaz Salas, 1929. In British diplomatic service, 1906-48; E.E. and M.P. in Central Am. republics, 1925-28, Chile, 1928-30, Sweden, 1931-35; ambassador, Baghdad, 1935-38, China, 1938-42, Russia, 1942-46, U.S. 1946-48, Privy councillor, 1944——; created 1st baron, 1946. Knight Grand Cross St. Michael and St. George. Address: Lock Eck, Argyll, Scotland. Died July 5, 1951.

INVERFORTH, Lord, business exec.; b. April 24, 1865; m. Annie Dowie, 1889 (died 1941); children—1 son, 4 daus. Chmn., mng. dir. English, Scottish & Colonial Investment Co., Ltd.; chmn. Bank Line, Ltd., British Union Oil Co., Ltd., Forrestdale Trust, Ltd., G. D. Peters & Co., Ltd., United Baltic Corp., Ltd.; hon. pres. Cable & Wireless (holding), Ltd.; officer many other cos. Decorated D.S.M. (U.S.). Address: The Hill, Hampstead Heath, N.W. 3, and 31 St. Mary Av., London E.C. 3, Eng. Died Sept. 17, 1955.

IPSEN, Ernest Ludvig, artist; b. Malden, Mass., Sept. 5, 1869; s. Ludvig S. I.; studied art, Boston Mus. Fine Arts and Royal Acad., Copenhagen; m. Edith Boyden Crocker, 1908. Prin. works: Portraits at State House (Boston, and Trenton, N.J.), Johns Hopkins U., Hood Coll. (Frederick, Md.), Hotchkiss Sch. (Lakeville, Conn.), Mass. Inst. Tech., Butler Art Inst. (Youngstown); portrait of Dr. Maurice Francis Egan, presented to the King and Queen of Denmark; portrait Hon. Elihu Root, Century Club, N.Y.; Thomas W. Slocum, pres. Harvard Club, N.Y.; L. F. Loree, pres. D.&H. R.R.; Rutgers Coll.; Edwin Howland Blashfield, Pres. Nat. Acad. of Design, N.Y.; Dr. Cutler; John G. Agar; Dr. Henry van Dyke; late Dr. William F. Whitney; late Dr. Samuel J. Mixter; late Judge Henry A. M. Smith; Dr. Arthur McGiffert; late George A. Plimpton, Amherst Coll.; William Rutherford Mead; Dr. John Bates Clark; Dr. F. B. Giddings; Chief Justice William Howard Taft; Justice Charles W. Parker; Cass Gilbert; Irene Sutliffe; Annie Nathan Meyer; Samuel Hemingway; William Boyce Thompson; Rev. Dr. Edward Scribner Ames; Dean N. A. Pattillo; Henry S. Coffin; Brig. Gen. Stuart Heintzelman; Mr. and Mrs. Edward Lowe, Grand Rapids, Mich.; Dr. Edward D. Duffield for Prudential Ins. Co. of America, Newark, N.J.; John Blodgett, Grand Rapids; R. B. Hanson, Conservative leader, Can. House of Commons; Leo Hendrick Baekeland, Chemists' Club, N.Y.; Dr. Edgar Romig for West End Collegiate Ch., N.Y.; Pres. Chester A. Arthur for Union Coll., Schenectady, N.Y.; Dr. John Andrews, pres. Brown U.; Dr. E. D. Warfield, pres. Wilson Coll.; Gen. Robert E. Lee as supt. U.S. Mil. Acad. and Gen. Lee as Confederate Gen.; Prof. Walter Goodenow Everett for Brown U.; Dr. Frank Parker Day, former pres. of Union Coll.; Dr. Stanley King, pres. Amherst (Mass.) Coll.; Judge Henry Fields, Amherst Coll.; Dean Harry K. Fine, Fine Meml., Princeton,

N.J.; Miss May Margaret Fine, Fine Sch., Princeton, N.J.; former pres. of Amherst Coll.; Dr. George Olds, Olds Memorial Turner Hall, Amherst, Mass.; Dr. Frank Parker Day, for Union Coll., Schenectady, N.Y.; Dean Luther Phaler Eisenhart, Dean Robert K. Root, both for Princeton. Awarded Lippincott prize for "Mr. Lauth and Bottles," Pa. Acad. of Fine Arts Annual Exhbn., 1936; Proctor and Isaac N. Maynard prizes, N.A.D.; Nat. Arts Club prize, etc.; Century Assn. Art Com. Medal, best picture in professional exhbn., 1947-48. A.N.A., 1912; N.A., 1923; mem. Allied Artists Am., Nat. Arts Club, Century Assn. Home: 4040 Ventura Av., Cocoanut Grove, Miami, Fla. Died 1951.

IRBY, Nolen Meaders (ûr'bĭ), coll. pres.; b. Green Forest, Tex., July 27, 1887; s. Henry Wiley and Fannie Lou (Meaders) I.; A.B., U. Ark., 1916; A.M., George Peabody Coll. for Tchrs., Nashville, 1926, Ph.D., 1930; m. Nell Cole, Nov. 27, 1919; children—Nell Cole (wife of Major George A. Barron, Jr.), Mary Charles (Mrs. Lee Yarbrough). Supt. schs. Bearden, Ark., 1919-22; prin. North Little Rock High Sch., 1922-23; supt. schs., Marianna, Ark., 1924-27; prof. psychology Ore. State Coll., 1928-29; state agt. for rural schs. Ark., 1930-38; dir. field service U. Ga., 1938-41; pres. Ark. State Tchrs. Coll., Conway, Ark., 1941——. Served as capt. U.S. Army, 1918-19. Mem. Rural Com. Edn., A.E.R.A., Phi Beta Kappa, Kappa Delta Pi, Phi Delta Kappa. Rotarian. Home: 140 Donaghey Av., Conway, Ark. Died Nov. 1, 1958; buried Conway.

IRELAN, Singer B., business executive; b. Idaville, Ind., May 5, 1889; s. Claude and Abegail Irelan; B.S. in Electrical Engring., Purdue University, 1909, Dr. Engring. (honorary), 1951; married Lucy Welty, June 8, 1912 (now deceased); children—Nancy (Mrs. Wheeler Farish), Dorothy (Mrs. Jack Clarke), Betty (Mrs. James Cross); married 2d, Edith M. Fields, October 17, 1942. Cadet engineer Public Service Co., Denver, Colo., 1909-10; secretary Fremont Elec. Co., 1910-12; engr. H. L. Doherty & Co., 1912-14; vice pres. and gen. mgr. Bartlesville (Okla.) Gas & Elec. Co., 1914-16, City Light & Traction Co., Sedalia, Mo., 1916-17; Montgomery (Ala.) Light & Power Co., 1917-22; St. Joseph (Mo.) Ry., Light & Power Co., 1922-27; gen. mgr. securities and investment dept., H. L. Doherty & Co., 1927-33; spl. engr. and vice pres., Elec. Advisers, Inc., N.Y. City, 1933-44; pres. Cities Service Gas Co., Oklahoma City, 1944-52; pres., dir. Cities Service Oil Co. (Del.), Bartlesville, Okla., since 1952, Cities Service Oil Co., Ltd., Am. Gas Prodn. Co., Cities Prodn. Corp.; dir. Cities Service Co., Cities Service Petroleum, Inc., Cities Service Pipe Line Co., Empire Gas & Fuel Co., Great Lakes Pipe Line Co., Richfield Oil Corp., Lafitte Oil Traders, Inc., Texas-Empire Pipe Line Co., First Nat. Bank & Trust Co., Tulsa. Trustee Midwest Research Inst., Kansas City. Mem. Ind. Natural Gas Assn. Am. (dir.), Am. Petroleum Inst., U. Okla. Research Inst., Mid-Continent Oil & Gas Assn. (dir. Kan.-Okla. div.), Texas Mid-Continent Oil & Gas Assn. (dir.), Am. Gas Assn., U.S. C. of C. Doherty Men's Frat. (trustee, a founder), Delta Tau Delta. Clubs: Tulsa, Southern Hills Country, (Tulsa); Cherokee Yacht (Ketchum, Okla.); Hillcrest Country, Rotary, Bartlesville Gun, Bartlesville Skeet and Trap (Bartlesville, Okla.). Indiana Soc., Wing & Fin (Chgo.), Garden of the Gods (Colo. Springs); River (Kansas City); Fin'N' Feather (Dundee, Ill.). Home: 1423 Delaware. Office: Cities Service Oil Co., Cities Service Bldg., Bartlesville, Okla. Died June 18, 1956.

IRELAND, Merritte Weber, former surg. gen. U.S. Army; b. Columbia City, Ind., May 31, 1867; s. Martin and Sarah I.; M.D., Detroit Coll. Medicine, 1890; M.D., Jefferson Med. Coll. 1891. LL.D., 1919; A.M., U. Mich., 1920; LL.D., Gettysburg Coll., 1922, Wayne U., 1939; m. Elizabeth Liggett, Nov. 8, 1893; 1 son, Paul Mills. Apptd. asst. surgeon U.S. Army, 1891; capt. asst. surgeon, 1896; maj. surgeon 45th U.S. Inf., 1899; hon. disch. vols., 1901; maj. surgeon U.S. Army, and maj. M.C., 1903; lt. col., May 1, 1911; col., May 15, 1917; brig. gen. N.A., May 16, 1918; asst. surgeon gen. with rank of maj. gen. (temp.), Aug. 1918; surgeon gen., 1918-31 (ret.). Was in Santiago Campaign; in Philippines during insurrection; chief surgeon AEF in France until Oct. 12, 1918. Decorated D.S.M. (U.S.); Legion of Honor and Med. Epidemie (France); Order of the Bath (Gt. Britain); Polonia Restituta (Poland). Pres. A.C.S. Lutheran. Clubs: Army and Navy, Army and Navy Country. Address: War Dept., Washington. Died July 5, 1952.*

IRETON, Peter L. (ir'tŭn), bishop; b. Baltimore, Sept. 21, 1882; s. John Francis and Mary Ellen (Sheridan) I.; student St. Charles Coll., Catonsville, Md., 1895-1901; S.T.D., St. Mary's Sem., Baltimore, 1906; student Cath. U., 1906-07; LL.D., Mt. St. Mary's Coll., Emmitsburg, Md., 1934. Ordained priest, 1906; asst. St. Gregory's Ch., Baltimore, 1907-26; pastor St. Ann's Ch., Baltimore, 1926-35; appointed coadjutor bishop of Richmond, Va., Aug. 5, 1935; appointed bishop of Richmond, Va., April 14, 1945. Archdiocesan dir. Holy Name Soc., Baltimore, 1922-35; founder Holy Name Soc. Big Brother Assn.,

1923; trustee St. Mary's Industrial Sch. for Boys, 1910-35, v.p. and treas., 1922-35; trustee Cath. U. since 1930. Domestic Prelate to Pope Pius XI, Aug. 5, 1929; asst. at the Pontifical Throne, 1956—. Club: Press. Contbr. to ch. publs. Address: 800 Cathedral Pl., Richmond, Va. Died Apr. 27, 1958.

IRION, Theophil William Henry (I'rĭ-ŏn'), univ. prof.; b. Des Peres, Mo., Oct. 4, 1885; s. Christian Frederick and Meta Mathilda (Maschmeier) I.; Pd.B., Southeast. Missouri State College, Cape Girardeau, Missouri, 1904; A.B., B.S. in Edn., U. of Mo., 1911; A.M., Columbia, 1916, Ph.D., 1925; research student Stanford, 1923; m. Edith Grace Ham, May 30, 1916; 1 son, Arthur Lloyd. Teacher rural schs., 1904-06; teacher and prin. high sch., 1906-09; vice-pres. Stephens Coll., Columbia, Mo., 1911-12; prof. psychology and education, Southwest. Missouri State Coll., 1912-20; prof. ednl. psychology, Mich. State Normal Coll., Ypsilanti, Mich., 1920-26; prof. U. of Mich., summers, 1925, 26; prof. edn. U. of Mo. since 1926, dean of Sch. of Edn. and dir. Summer Sessions, 1930-45, prof. education since 1945. Editor American Schoolmaster, 1921-25. Member Missouri State Teachers' Association (pres. 1933), National Assn. of Colls. and Depts. of Edn. (pres. 1936-38), N.E.A., (mem. exec. com., 1944-45), Commn. on Defense of Democracy Through Edn., Society for the Advancement of Education, A.A.A.S., Am. Psychol. Assn., Phi Beta Kappa. Author: Comprehension Difficulties in the Study of Literature, 1925. Home: 117 Westwood, Columbia, Mo. Died Dec. 25, 1952; buried Valhalla, St. Louis.

IRISH, Fred Abbott, banker; b. Taylors Falls, Minn., Sept. 29, 1870; s. John S. and Emma Jane (Abbott) I.; student pub. schs. Moorhead, Minn.; m. Mila A. Brown, Oct. 22, 1903; 1 son, John F. Engaged in banking since 1890; chmn. bd. First Nat. Bank & Trust Co. of Fargo, N.D., 1944, now hon. chmn. dir. First Nat. Bank of Moorhead, Pioneer Mut. Life Ins. Co. Treas. N.D. Blue Cross, Greater N.D. Assn., Salvation Army, Fargo. Mem. S.A.R., Mayflower Soc., Newcomen Soc. (chmn. N.D.), Am. Automobile Assn. (treas. N.D.). Mason (Shriner), Elk, Kiwanian. Home: 709 S. 9th Av., Fargo, N.D. Died Mar. 4, 1959; buried Riverside Mausoleum, Fargo.

IRONS, Ernest Edward, physician; b. Council Bluffs, Ia., Feb. 17, 1877; s. Edward and Mary J. (Sharp) I.; B.S., U. Chgo., 1900, fellow, 1900-01, Ph.D., 1912; M.D., Rush Med. Coll., 1903; m. Gertrude Thompson, 1908; children—Edwin Newton, Spencer E. Practiced Chgo., 1903—; asst. in pathology and bacteriology, U. Chgo., 1902-04; clin. prof. medicine, emeritus, U. Ill. Med. Sch.; cons. physician Presbyn. Hosp. Mem. Nat. Adv. Health Council; hon. cons. USN. Mem. Assn. Am. Physicians, A.C.P. (pres.), Am. Assn. Pathologists and Bacteriologists, Am. Bd. Internal Medicine, Am. Soc. Bacteriology, A.M.A. (trustee; pres. 1949-50) Ill., Chgo. med. socs., Chgo. Pathol. Soc., Chgo. Soc. Med. History. Clubs: University, Chicago (Chgo.). Home: 5830 Stony Island Av. Office: 122 S. Michigan Blvd., Chgo. Died Jan. 18, 1959.

IRONSIDE, Henry Allan, clergyman; b. Toronto, Ont., Can., Oct. 14, 1876; s. John Williams and Sophia (Stafford) I.; brought by parents to U.S., 1886; ed. public schools; Litt.D., Wheaton (Illinois) College, 1930; D.D., Bob Jones College, 1942; m. Helen G. Schofield, Jan. 5, 1897 (died May 1, 1948); children—Edmund H., John S.; m. 2d, Mrs. Ann Hightower, Oct. 9, 1949. Began as preacher at age of 14 yrs. at Los Angeles, Calif., evangelist and Bible teacher since 1890; pres. Western Book & Tract Co. since 1912; prof. Biblical literature, Evang. Theol. Coll., Dallas, Tex., 1925-43; pastor Moody Memorial Ch., Chicago, 1930-48. Elected president of Africa Inland Mission, 1942. Author: Notes on Jeremiah, 1900; Minor Prophets, 1902; Notes on the Book of Proverbs, 1903; Ezra, Nehemiah and Esther, 1910; Lectures on Daniel the Prophet, 1914; Lectures on Revelation, 1917; Lectures on Romans, 1929; Things Seen and Heard in Bible Lands, 1936; In the Heavenlies, 1937; Lectures on I Corinthians, 1938; Lectures on II Corinthians, 1939; The Lamp of Prophecy, 1939; Changed By Beholding, 1940; The Way of Peace, 1940; Lectures on Galatians, 1941; Lectures on the Gospel of John, 1942; Lectures on the Acts of the Apostles, 1943; The Great Parenthesis, 1943; also many booklets. Editor Moody Church News. Died Jan. 15, 1951; buried Auckland, New Zealand.

IRVIN, Donald F(rederick), educator, clergyman; b. Rochester, Pa., Mar. 13, 1905; s. Fred S. and Bessie M. (Brinker) I.; A.B., Thiel Coll., Greenville, Pa., 1927, D.D., 1952; B.D., Phila. Luth. Sem., 1931; M.A., U. Pa., 1932, student sch. edn., 1945-52; grad. student Northwestern U., 1953-54; m. Margaret Abigail Jacobs, Jan. 20, 1933; children—Abigail Elizabeth (Mrs. Richard G. Radey), Margaret Catherine, Michael Jacobs. Ordained to ministry of Lutheran Ch., 1932; pastor Luth Ch. of Our Savior, Haddonfield, N.J., 1932-53; prof. Christian edn. Chgo. Luth. Sem., 1953—; mem. bd. Christian edn., dir. field work Ministerium of Pa., 1943-50, bd. parish edn. Luth. Synod of N.J., 1950-53, bd. publs. United Luth. Ch., 1950—. Mem. Phi Delta Kappa, Delta Sigma Phi. Author: Life of Jesus, 1951; Learning the Way, 1951; Teaching the Way, 1951, also church sch. texts. Home: 1618 S. 11th Av. Office: 1644 S. 11th Av., Maywood, Ill. Died May 14, 1955.

IRVIN, William Adolf; b. Indiana, Pa., Dec. 7, 1873; ed. public schools; m. Luella May Cunningham; children—Mrs. Frank Leitzell, Mrs. Herbert White, Mrs. Edward Hirsch, William Archibald, Mrs. J. Stephens; m. 2d, Mrs. Gertrude Whitman Gifford, 1910. Began as telegraph operator, Pa. R.R., 1888; became shipping clerk P. H. Laufmann Co., Apollo, Pa., 1895; asst. to vice pres., Am. Steel Tin Plate Co., 1904-24, vice pres. in charge operations, 1924-31; vice pres. U.S. Steel Corp., 1931, pres., 1932-38, vice-chmn. bd., 1938-39, now dir. Chmn. bd. trustees, Nat. Safety Council, 1942; pres. Pa. Soc. of New York, 1938-44; mem. bd. dirs. and exec. com., Willys Overland Motor Co., 1944. Clubs: Bankers, Union League, Blind Brook (N.Y.; mem. bd.); Duquesne (Pittsburgh). Office: 71 Broadway, N.Y.C. Died Jan. 1, 1952.

IRVING, Frederick Carpenter, physician; b. Gouverneur, N.Y., May 30, 1883; s. Andrew and Nina Frances (Carpenter) I.; grad. Phillips Exeter Acad., N.H., 1902; A.B. cum laude, Harvard, 1906, M.D. cum laude, 1910; m. Mary Amanda Chapman, June 25, 1912; children—Frances, Mary Brewster, Frederick Carpenter, Rebecca, Colin Franklin Newell. Began practice, Boston, 1910; William Lambert Richardson prof. Emeritus obstetrics, Harvard Med. Sch.; cons. obstetrician Boston Lying-In Hosp., Newton-Wesley Hosp.; cons. obstetrician and gynecologist Faulkner Hosp.; cons. surgeon N.E. Bapt. Hosp. Served from 1st lt. to maj. M.C., U.S. Army, France and Italy, World War I. Fellow A.C.S., Am. Gynecol. Soc. (v.p.); mem. Am. Bd. Obstetrics and Gynecology, A.M.A., Mass. Med. Soc., Boston Obstet. Soc.; hon. mem. Va. Obstet. and Gynecol. Soc., Sociedade Brasileira Gynecologia, So. Atlantic Obstet. and Gynecol. Soc., Mass. Charitable Fire Soc. Rep. Episcopalian. Club: Harvard (Boston, Mass.). Author: A Textbook of Obstetrics; The Expectant Mothers Handbook; Safe Deliverance, a Life-in-America Prize Book; also many articles med. jours. Home: 26 Edge Hill Rd., Brookline. Office: 1180 Beacon St., Brookline 46, Mass. Died Dec. 24, 1957.

IRWIN, Harry N., ret. univ. dean; b. Bellaire, O., Mar. 9, 1884; s. William David and Harriet (DeLong) I.; A.B., Wooster Coll., 1905; student U. Chgo., 1909-10, 15-18, A.M., 1910; m. Pauline Jackson, Sept. 8, 1917. Instr. Am. U. Beirut, 1905; asst. dean, Cleveland Sch. of Edn., 1920-25; dir. Sr. Teachers Coll., Cleveland Sch. of Edn., Western Reserve U., 1920-25; asso. dean Cleveland Sch. of Edn., 1925-28; asso. dean Sch. of Edn., Western Reserve U., 1928-33, asso. prof. edn., 1928-44; prof., 1944—, dean, 1933—, professor and dean emeritus, 1946—. Mem. Phi Delta Kappa. Presbyterian. Club: University (Winter Park, Fla.). Author: Outline of Elementary Grammar, 1911; Begining Lessons in English, 1911. Home: Woodsmere, Orlando, Fla. Died Jan. 27, 1955.

IRWIN, Robert Benjamin, welfare work; b. Rockford, Ia., June 2, 1883; s. Robert Payne and Hattie Edith (Chappell) I.; grad. Wash. State Sch. for Blind, 1901; B.A., U. Wash., 1906, Alumnus Summa Laude Dignatus, 1945; student Harvard, 1906-09, M.A., 1906; LL.D., Western Res. U., 1943; m. Mary Janet Blanchard, June 19, 1917; 1 son, Robert Benjamin (deceased). Supervisor classes for the blind, Cleveland pub. schs., 1909-23, also for classes for blind, and sight-saving classes for partially blind children in various cities and towns of Ohio, 1915-23; dir. Bur. of Research and Edn., Am. Found. for Blind, N.Y. City, 1923-29, exec. dir. from 1929, also mgr. Talking Book Studio; exec. dir. Am. Found. for Overseas Blind, N.Y. and Paris; exec. v.p. Nat. Industries for Blind; pres. Clear Type Pub. Com., Pompton Lakes, N.J. Fellowship John Simon Guggenheim Meml. Found. (2 yrs. at $4000 per yr.), 1951-52. Retired as cons. for life Am. Found. for Blind; cons. to U.N. on work for blind. Mem. N.J. State Commn. for Blind; pres. Am. Assn. of Workers for Blind, 1923-27; chmn. sub-com. on visually handicapped, White House Conf. on Child Health and Protection, 1930; chmn. orgn. com., N.Y. World Conf. on Work for Blind, 1931; chmn. Am. Uniform Type Com. which arranged with British authorities for adoption of a uniform braille code for blind of English-speaking world, 1932; chmn. adv. com. on the Blinded Veteran, U.S. Veterans Adminstrn., Am. Assn. Workers for Blind. Chmn. European Conf. on Welfare of the Blind, Oxford Univ., Eng., 1949; chmn. adv. com. on war blinded to surgeon gen. of Army, World War II. Decorated Chevalier Legion of Honor, France, 1947. Mem. Am. Assn. of Social Workers, Nat. Conf. of Social Work, Am. Public Welfare Assn. Club: Aldine. Unitarian. Editor of textbooks used in sight-saving classes in U.S.; author of monograph on blind relief legislation in the U.S., and other studies; also History of Work for Blind in the U.S. during the Past Fifty Years (in preparation). Home: "Bonshaw," R. 1, Box 135, Port Orchard, Wash. Died Dec. 12, 1951; buried Pompton Lakes, N.J.

IRWIN, Staford LeRoy (ûr'wĭn), army officer; b. Fort Monroe, Va., Mar. 23, 1893; s. Maj. Gen. George LeRoy and Maria Elizabeth (Barker) I.; B.S. U.S. Mil. Acad., 1915; grad. F.A. Sch., 1926, Command and Gen. Staff Sch., 1927, Army War Coll., 1937; m. Helen Hall 1921 (died 1937); 1 son, Francis LeRoy; m. 2d, Clare Moran, May 20, 1941; 1 son, Stafford D'Arcy. Commd. 2d lt., F.A., 1915, advanced through the grades to lt. gen., 1950; now comdg. gen. U.S. Forces in Austria. Mem. Army and Navy Country Club. Home: Asheville, N.C. Office: Hdqrs. USFA, Salzburg, Austria. Died Nov. 23, 1955.

IRWIN, Wallace, author; b. Oneida, N.Y., Mar. 15, 1875; s. David S. and Edith E. (Greene) I.; grad. Denver High Sch., 1895; student Stanford, 1896-99; m. Trace Luce, Mar. 22, 1901 (died 1914); m. 2d, Laetitia McDonald, Jan. 5, 1916; children—Donald McDonald, Wallace. Spl. writer, San Francisco Examiner, 1900; editor Overland Monthly Mag., 1902; revue writer Republic Theatre, San Francisco, 1903; writer topical verse, N.Y. Globe, 1904-05; on staff Collier's Weekly, 1906-07. Life hon. editor Harvard Lampoon, 1912. Mem. Com. Pub. Information, 1917-19. Hon. mem. Fijian Soc. Lt. comdr. USNR, 1926. Clubs: Players, Dutch Treat, Coffee House (N.Y.C.). Author: The Love Sonnets of a Hoodlum, 1902; The Rubaiyat of Omar Khayyam, Jr., 1902; Fairy Tales Up to Now; Nautical Lays of a Landsman; At the Sign of the Dollar, 1904; Chinatown Ballads, 1905; Random Rhymes and Odd Numbers, 1906; A Yankee Tourist (light opera, with Richard Harding Davis), 1907-08; Letters of a Japanese Schoolboy, 1909; Mr. Togo, Maid of All Work, 1913; Pilgrims into Folly, 1917; Venus in the East, 1918; The Blooming Angel, 1919; Suffering Husbands, 1920; Seed of the Sun, 1921; Lew Tyler's Wives, 1923; The Golden Bed, 1924; Mated, 1926; Lew Tyler and the Ladies, 1928; The Days of Her Life, 1931; The Julius Caesar Murder Case, 1935; Young Wife, 1936. Collaborator, Yankee Doctor in Paradise (with Dr. S. M. Lambert), 1940-41. Contbr. to mags. Home: (winter) Southern Pines, N.C.; (summer) 1 Summit Av., Larchmont, N.Y. Office: care Bankers Trust Co. 16 Wall St., N.Y.C. Died Feb. 14, 1959; buried Cave Hill Cemetery, Louisville.

ISAACS, Edith J(uliet) R(ich) (Mrs. Lewis Montefiore Isaacs) (I'zăks), editor; b. Milw., Mar. 27, 1878; d. Adolph W. and Rosa (Sidenberg) Rich.; graduate East Side High Sch.; A.B., Milw.-Downer Coll., 1897; m. Lewis Montefiore Isaacs, Nov. 28, 1904 (deceased, December 12, 1944); children—Marian Brody, Lewis Myer, Hermine I. Popper. Literary editor Milw. Sentinel, 1903; chief women's publicity, 2d Fed. Res. Dist., Liberty Loan campaigns, 1917-18; editor Theatre Arts Mag., quar., 1918-23, Theatre Arts Monthly, 1924-46. Former mem. Wis. Juvenile Court Commn. Mem. Authors' League Am., MacDowell Assn., Milw.-Downer Alumnae (ex-pres.), Am. Nat. Theatre and Acad. (v.p.), Phi Beta Kappa. Jewish religion. Clab: Cosmopolitan. Author: Theatre, 1927; Plays of American Life and Fantasy, 1929; Architecture for The New Theatre, 1935; The Negro in The American Theatre, 1947. Home: 24 W. 55th St., N.Y.C. 19. Died Jan. 10, 1956.

ISBRANDTSEN, Hans J., shipping exec.; born Dragoer, Denmark, 1891; m. Gertrude Mirus, 1921; children—Waldemar, Jakob, Neil (Mrs. Albert E. Rising, Jr.). Pres. and dir. Isbrandtsen Co., Inc., North Am. Transport Corp. Home: 87 Remsen St., Bklyn. 2. Office: 26 Broadway, N.Y.C. 4. Died May 13, 1953.

ISELIN, Ernest (īz'lĭn), b. New York, N.Y., Apr. 5, 1876; s. Adrian and Louise (Caylus) I.; A.B., Columbia University, 1898; married to Pauline Whittier, on April 6, 1904 (deceased 1946); children—Ernest, Louise. Began as banker, 1898; partner A. Iselin & Company, New York, New York; president and dir. Neptune Realty Co.; v.p. and dir. Adlin Corporation; treasurer and mem. board of dirs. Manhattan Storage and Warehouse Co., Manhattan Storage Safe Deposit Co.; chairman board Rochester & Pittsburgh Coal Company. Member board mgrs. Home for Incurables, New York, N.Y.; mem. advisory board New York Foundling Hospital, St. Vincent's Hospital. Member Psi Upsilon (Lambda Chapter). Decorated Chevalier Legion of Honor (France). Catholic. Clubs: New York Yacht, Down Town Association, Columbia University, University, Knickerbocker (New York); Travellers (Paris). Home: 943 Lexington Av. Office: 31 Nassau St., N.Y.C. Died Jan. 1954.

ISHAM, Ralph Heyward, collector books and manuscripts; b. N.Y.C., July 2, 1890; s. Henry Heyward and Juliet Calhoun (Marsh) I.; student Cornell U., 1908-09, Yale, 1910-11; married; children—Heyward, Jonathan Trumbull. Pres. Trumbull Securities Corp.; v.p. New England Water Power Co. Vol. British Army; served 3 yrs.; on staffs Field Marshal Sir William Robertson and Lord Haig, 1918-19. Decorated Comdr. Order British Empire, for war services; granted permanent rank of lt. col. Fellow Royal Geog. Soc. Clubs: Grolier, Union League, Garrick, Elizabethan (Yale), Royal Socs., Hurlingham (London). Owner large collection of books and manuscripts, acquiring in 1927 the "Boswell Papers." Office: 342 Madison Av., N.Y.C. Died June 13, 1955.*

ISLE, Walter Whitfield, educational adminstrn.; b. Brunswick, Mo., Feb. 27, 1889; s. John Wesley and Willie Ann (Fisher) I.; A.B., U. of Okla., 1915; A.M., Teachers Coll., Columbia U., 1919; Ed.D., Stanford U., 1942; m. Ruth Ann Bush, July 11, 1932; children—Walter Whitfield, Amy Elizabeth. High sch. principal, Pauls Valley, Okla., 1909-11; supt. Consolidated Sch., McLoud, Okla., 1911-14; high sch. prin., Mangum, Okla., 1915-16; supt. Consol. Sch., Ninnekah, Okla., 1916-17; supt. schs., Wewoka, Okla., 1917-21; special summer sch. instr., Central State Teachers Coll., Edmond, Okla., 1920-27; supt. city schs., Clinton, Okla., 1921-25, Duncan, Okla., 1925-27; high sch. prin., Ponca City, Okla., 1928-29, supt. city schs., 1929-35; pres. Southwestern State Teachers Coll., Weatherford, Okla., 1935-39; workshop asst. Stanford U., summer 1940; dir. study Stanford trained teachers, 1940-41; dir. research San Mateo (Calif.) Junior Coll., 1940-42; summer sch. instr., Colo. State Coll. Edn., 1941, Colo. State Coll., 1942; edn. services specialist, O.P.A., San Francisco region, 1942-45; pres. Eastern Washington Coll. of Edn., Cheney, Wash., since 1945. Served as pvt., F.A., U.S. Army, World War I. Mem. Okla. State Textbook Commn., 1935-39. Mem. Nat. and Wash. edn. assns., Okla. Edn. Assn. (bd. dirs.), Am. Assn. Sch. Adminstrs., Nat. Soc. Study Edn., Soc. Advancement Edn., Phi Gamma Delta, Kappa Delta Pi, Phi Delta Kappa (pres. Delta chapter). Mason. Author: A Follow Up Study of Stanford Trained Teachers, 1942. Home: President's Home. Office: Eastern Washington College of Education, Cheney, Wash. Died Jan. 10, 1951.

ISSEKS, Samuel Shepp (ĭs'sĕks), lawyer; b. N.Y.C., Apr. 17, 1900; s. Nathan and Mary (Goldstein) I.; B.A., Oberlin (O.) Coll., 1922; LL.B., Harvard Law Sch., 1925, S.J.., 1926; m. M. Wilma Nixon, Jan. 4, 1925; children—Janice Marilyn, Robert Dixon, William Watson, John Dixon. Admitted to N.Y. bar, 1927; agent in Treasury Dept. of U.S., 1926-27; asso. Root, Clark, Buckner & Ballantine, 1927-38; asst. atty. gen. State N.Y., 1938-39; spl. asst. to atty. gen. of U.S. (anti-grust div. Dept. of Justice), N.Y.C., 1939-43; mem. 3 man commn. apptd. by sec. of Army to investigate decartelization program in occupied Ger., Dec. 1948. Mem. law firm of Isseks, Laporte, Meyers and Verdon. Served in S.A.T.C., Oct.-Dec. 1918. Mem. Bar City N.Y., Am., N.Y. State bar assns., N.Y. County Lawyers, Phi Beta Kappa. Contbr. to legal jours. Home: 45 Fennimore Road, New Rochelle, N.Y. Office: 30 Broad St., N.Y.C. Died Jan. 20, 1951.

IVES, Charles E., composer; b. Danbury, Conn., Oct. 20, 1874; s. George E. Ives (musician) and Mary (Parmelee) Ives; studied music appreciation, harmony, counterpoint, instrumentation with his father; studied organ with Dudley Buck; B.A., Yale U., 1898; studied with Horatio W. Parker at Yale; m. Harmony Twichell, 1908; 1 dau., Edith (Mrs. George G. Tyler). Organist Cong. Ch., Danbury, 1887; organist St. Thomas Ch., New Haven, Conn., 1893-94, Centre Ch., New Haven, 1894-98; organist and choir master, First Presbyn. Ch., Bloomfield, N.J., 1898-1900, Central Presbyn. Ch., N.Y. City, 1900-02; clerk with Mutual Life Ins. Co., 1898-1906; formed ins. firm of Ives & Myrick and active, 1906-30; retired from business. Composer of songs, organ music, 4 symphonies, 4 violin sonatas, 2 piano sonatas, album of other piano music, 3 orchestral suites, 11 volumes of chamber music for various groups of instruments or chamber orchestras, also string quartets, trios, etc., choral music with and without orchestra, and instrumental groups, etc. Works include: Variations on America for organ, 1889; anthems, hymns, psalms and choral works, 1888-1904; songs (about 150), 1886-1928; Intercollegiate (march for mil. band), 1895; Harvest Festival (chorus, organ, trumpets, trombones), 1898; First String Quartet, Revival Service, 1896; First Symphony (D minor), 1898; Second Symphony, 1897-1902; First Piano Sonata, 1902-08; Third Symphony, 1911; Fourth Symphony, 1910-16; Symphony, Holidays: Washington's Birthday, 1913; Decoration Day, 1912; The Fourth of July, 1912-13; Thanksgiving Day, 1904; Set for Theater Orchestra, 1906-11; Browning Overture, 1905-12; The Unanswered Question —a Cosmic Landscape (orchestra), 1908; Second Piano Sonata: Concord, Mass., 1840-60, Emerson, Hawthorne, The Alcotts, Thoreau, 1911-15; for various groups of instruments or chamber orchestras (some with voices: Largo Cantabile, 1904; Adagio: The Innate, 1908; The Rainbow, 1914; The Pond, Halloween, From the Steeple and the Mountains, 1904-14; Gong on the Hook and Ladder—Firemen's Parade on Main Street, 1912; Calcium Light Night, 1897; Aeschylus and Sophocles, 1922; Over the Pavements, 1906-13; The Last Reader, 1911; Children's Day at the Camp Meeting, Fourth Violin Sonata, 1915; Quarter-tone Music; Chorales for Strings, 1913-14; a war march, They Are There, 1917; Three Tone Roads—on the way to Town Meetings, 1911-19; The Indians, 1912; On the Antipodes, 1915-23; works for chorus and orchestra; Lincoln, the Great Commoner, 1912; The Masses, 1915; An Election, 1920; General Booth's Entrance into Heaven, 1914; December, 1912; The New River, 1912; First Orchestral Set: Three Places in New England: Boston Common, Putnam's Camp, in Redding, The Housatonic at Stockbridge, 1914; Second Orchestral Set: An Elegy to Our Forefathers, The Rock-strewn Hills Join in the People's Outdoor Meeting, From Hanover Square North on a Tragic Day—a Theme of the People Again Arose, 1915. Elected mem. Nat. Inst. of Arts and Letters, 1945. Awarded Pulitzer Music Prize, May, 1947. Henry Hadley medal by Nat. Assn. for Am. Condrs. and Composers, June 1948. Home: West Redding, Conn. Died May 19, 1954; buried Wooster Cemetery, Danbury, Conn.

IVES, Frederick Manley, lawyer; b. Salem, Mass., Jan. 5, 1880; s. George Burnham and May Manley (Creamer) I.; A.B. magna cum laude, Harvard, 1901, LL.B., 1903; m. Charlotte Dwinell, June 23, 1906; children—Frederick M., Alice Creamer (Mrs. Charles J. Paine), Eleanor Dwinell (Mrs. Reginald B. Elwell), Charlotte (Mrs. John H. Bishop). Admitted to practice at Bar of Mass. Supreme Court, 1903, U.S. Supreme Court, 1910. Partner law firm Burdette, Wardwell & Ives, 1912-19; partner law firm Johnson, Clapp, Ives & Knight, Boston, 1919—; v.p. 1945-51, chmn. bd. 1951—, general counsel Boston Edison Co. 1919—. Director Boston Edison Co., Metropolitan Coal Co., Manhattan Market. Moderator Town of Winchester (Mass.), 1910-25. Mem. Am., Mass., Boston, and Essex County bar associaitions, Assn. of Interstate Commerce Commn. Practitioners, Beacon Soc., Bostonian Soc. Republican. Unitarian. Clubs: St. Botolph, Algonquin, Harvard (N.Y. and Boston). Home: 305 Highland Av., Winchester, Mass. Died Feb. 16, 1960.

IVES, Herbert Eugene, physicist; b. Phila., Pa., July 31, 1882; s. Frederic Eugene and Mary Elizabeth (Olmstead) I.; B.S., U. of Pa., 1905; Ph.D., Johns Hopkins, 1908; hon. Sc.D., Dartmouth and Yale, 1928, Pa., 1929; m. Mabel Agnes Lorenz, Nov. 14, 1908; children—Ronald Lorenz, Barbara Olmstead (Madame Charles Beyer), Kenneth Holbrook. Asso. with Ives Kromskop Company, Phila., 1898-1901; physicist, Bur. of Standards, Washington, 1908-09; physicist, Nat. Electric Lamp Assn., Cleveland, O., 1909-12, United Gas Improvement Co., Phila., 1912-18, Bell Telephone Laboratories, New York, 1919-47. Commissioned capt., Aviation Sect. Signal Corps, Jan. 1918, in charge exptl. work in airplane photography; discharged, 1919, and commd. maj. R.C. Contbg. editor Lightning Journal, New York, 1913-15; asso. editor Jour. of Optical Soc. America. Fellow A.A.A.S. (v.p. Sect. B, 1938), Am. Inst. E.E.; mem. Am. Philos. Soc., Am. Phys. Soc., Optical Soc. Am. (v.p. 1922-23, pres. 1924-25), Am. Astron. Soc., Franklin Inst., Am. Numis. Soc. (pres. 1942-47), Nat. Acad. Sciences, Phys. Soc. of London, Phi Beta Kappa, Sigma Xi; pres. Physics Club of Phila., 1917-18; v.p. Illuminating Engring. Soc., 1911-12; corr. mem. British Illuminating Engring. Soc. Section head, NDRC, 1941-46. Medals from Franklin Inst. for diffraction color photography, artificial daylight and studies of Welsbach mantle; John Scott medal and award, 1927, for electric telephotography and television; medal of the Optical Society for distinguished work in optics, 1937, U.S. Medal for Merit, 1948, Rumford Medal from Am. Acad. Arts and Sci., 1951. Inventor apparatus for testing visual acuity, various photometric instruments, illuminating devices, means for producing artificial daylight, relief pictures, electrical photoengraving, apparatus for transmission of pictures over telephone lines; in charge of experimental and development work culminating in first demonstration of television by wire and radio, 1927; developed scientific trichromatic palette for artists' use. De Forest lecturer, Yale, 1928; Lowell lecturer, Boston, 1932; Thomas Young orator Physical Society, London, 1933; Traill-Taylor memorial lecture, Royal Photographic Soc., 1933. Clubs: Cosmos (Washington); Century, (New York). Author: Airplane photography, 1920. Contbr. to scientific journals, Ency. Britannica, etc. Home: 32 Laurel Pl., Montclair, N.J. Died Nov. 13, 1953; buried Litchfield, Conn.

IVES, John Winsor, ex-fgn. service ofcr.; b. Elizabeth, Ill., Nov. 18, 1901; s. Fitch Howard and Sarah (McCormack) I.; student Randolph-Macon Acad., 1917-19, Ill. Wesleyan U., 1921-22, U. of Ill., 1923-24; m. Nischa Emmy Van Lempers, October 28, 1946. Am. vice consul, Mazatlan, Mexico, 1925-28; commercial agent Dist. Office of Bur. of Fgn. and Domestic Commerce, 1928-29; asst. trade commr., Bogota, Colombia, 1929; asst. trade commr., trade commr. and acting commercial attaché, Rio de Janeiro, 1930-39; consul, Lisbon, 1940-42; commercial attaché, Am. Legation, Lisbon, 1942-47; comml. attaché, Am. embassy, Guatemala City, May 1947; 1st sec. and Comml. attache, Am. embassy, Rome, 1950-53; State Dept., Washington, 1953-56, ret. 1956; sec. gen. U.S. C. of C. for Italy, Milan, 1956—. Mem. Sigma Chi. Author: Advertising in Brazil, 1937. Home: 240 S. Maple Av., Oak Park, Ill. Died Jan. 1, 1958; buried Warren, Ill.

IVEY, Joseph Benjamin, dept. store exec.; born Shelby, N.C., June 8, 1864; s. George Washington and Selina R. (Neal) I.; student Denver (N.C.) Sem.; m. Emma M. Gantt, Feb. 2, 1893; children—George M., Virginia (Mrs. C. R. Walker), Ella (Mrs. Oliver M. Litaker), Katherine (Mrs. Ervin Jackson); m. 2d Daisy Weatherly Smith, Oct. 8 1918. With Hoyle & Ivey, Belwood, N.C., 1880-93; head dept. store Henrietta (N.C.) Mills, 1893-1900; founded J. B. Ivey & Co., Charlotte, N.C., 1900; founder Ivey's, Inc., Asheville, N.C., Ivey-Keith Co., Greenville, S.C., Ivey's of Orlando, Ivey's of Daytona Beach, Ivey, Taylor Co., Raleigh, N.C. Formerly chmn. com. Bible teaching schs., dir. Y.M.C.A.; state chmn. Near East Relief. Methodist (steward; chmn. bd. trustees W. N.C. Conf.; trustee Meth. Home for Aged, Charlotte; delegate to 8 quadrennial Methodist conferences. Author: Successful Dahlia Raising in the South, 1931; My Memoirs, 1940. Home: 1638 E. Morehead St. Office: 31 N. Tryon St., Charlotte, N.C. Died Apr. 4, 1958.

IYENAGA, Toyokichi, publicist; b. in Japan, Yanagawa, 1862; s. Tatsunosuke and Noda, Ume I.; Ph.B., Oberlin, 1887; Ph.D., Johns Hopkins, 1890; m. Hiroi, Yui. Prof. polit. science, Waseda Univ. and Higher Commercial Coll., Tokyo, 1890-5; a sec. for Dept. of Foreign Affairs, 1895-7; commr. of Formosan Govt. to India, Persia, Turkey and China, 1898-9; professorial lecturer, polit. science, U. of East & West News Bur., 1914-22. Author: (with Kenoske Sato) Japan and the California Problem. Home: Sylvan Beach, N.Y. Died Dec. 29, 1936.
Chicago, 1901-20; lecturer Columbia U., 1913. Dir.

J

JACK, Frederick Lafayette, surgeon; b. Boston, Jan. 3, 1861; s. Lafayette and Sarah (Shaw) J.; prep. edn. Boston Latin Sch.; M.D., Harvard, 1884. House officer, 1884-86, aural surgeon, 1890-1913, surgeon-in-chief, 1913-19, Mass. Charitable Eye and Ear Infirmary; now cons. surgeon Mass. Eye and Ear Infirmary; instr. post-grad. Harvard Med. Sch. Hon. fellow Am. Otol. Soc. (sec. 1895-1908, pres. 1908-10); mem. Am. Laryngol., Rhinol. and Otol. Soc. (v.p. 1896-97, now emeritus mem.), Mass. Med. Soc., N.E. Otol. and Laryngol. Soc. (pres. 1906; hon. mem. since 1939), Boston Soc., Med. Improvement. Address: 215 Beacon St., Boston. Died May 3, 1951.

JACK, James Robertson, naval architect; b. Glasgow, Scotland, Mar. 30, 1866; student Dumbarton Sch. Sci. and Arts, 1883-87; spl. tutoring courses; spl. student Glasgow U. naval architecture (won 1st prize each term); m. Eleanor McNidder. Began as apprentice shipbuilder with Denny and Bros., Dumbarton, Scotland, 1882, drafting, 1884-89, chief designer, 1901, mgr., 1914; taught naval architecture, Dumbarton Sch. Sci. and Art, 1888-94; lectr. Royal Tech. Coll., Glasgow, 1894-1914; prof. Mass Inst. Tech., 1919-36 ret. Served in World War I, Curator (hon.) Nautical Mus., Mass. Inst. Tech. Awarded Order of British Empire, 1918, Crux del Merito Naval (Spain). Fellow Am. Acad. Arts and Scis.; mem. Instn. Naval Architecture, London, Inst. Engrs. and Shipbuilders Scotland, Soc. Naval Architects and Marine Engrs. (N.Y.), Theta Chi. Clubs: Propeller Club of Boston, N.E. Bot. (pres. 1928-32). Home: 24 Hillside Rd., Watertown, Mass. Died Jan. 6, 1952.

JACK, John George, dendrologist; b. Chateaugay, Que., Apr. 15, 1861; s. Robert and Annie Linda (Hayr) J.; m. Cerise Emily Agnes Carman, June 14, 1907 (died Aug. 29, 1935). Lecturer Arnold Arboretum, 1891-1908; lecturer landscape horticulture, Mass. Inst. Tech., 1899-1908; instr. forest botany Harvard, 1903-28, asst. prof. dendrology, 1928-35, asst. prof. emeritus, 1935—. Spl. agent U.S. Geol. Survey in Colo., 1898, U.S. Forest Service in Wyo., 1900; examiner and adviser Mass. Met. Water Bd., 1897-98. Fellow A.A.A.S., Am. Acad. Arts and Sciences; mem. Am. Forestry Assn., Soc. Am. Foresters, Mass. Hort. Soc., Boston Soc. Natural History, N.E. Bot. Club, Bot. Soc. Am., others. Home: East Walpole, Mass. Died May 20, 1949.

JACKLING, Daniel Cowan, mining; b. nr. Appleton City, Mo., Aug. 14, 1869; s. Daniel and Lydia Jane (Dunn) J.; ed. State Normal Sch., Warrensburg, Mo.; B.S., Mo. Sch. Mines, Rolla, 1892, Met.E., 1900, D.Eng., 1933; LL.D., U. Cal., 1940; D.Eng., U. So. Cal., 1940; D.S., U. Utah, 1942; m. Virginia Jolliffe, 1915. Asst. prof. chemistry and metallurgy Mo. chool Mines, 1891-93; chemist and metallurgist Cripple Creek Dist., Colo., 1894-95; in charge constrn. and operation metall. works of Mercur Gold Mines, 1896-1900; pres., dir. Mesabi Iron Co.; formerly pres. (retired), Utah Copper Co., Nevada Consolidated Copper Corp., Gallup Am. Coal Co., Bingham & Garfield Ry. Co., Nev. Northern Ry. Co.; Ray & Gila Valley Railroad Company; dir. (retired) Braden Copper Co., and dir. Mining Operations (retired), Kennecott Copper Corp. Col. on staff Governor J. H. Peabody, Colo., 1903-04, of Gov. William Spry, Utah, 1909-13; Utah commr. Alaska-Yukon-Pacific Expn., 1909. Dir. U.S. Govt. Explosives Plants,

1917, 18, 19; asst. to U.S. Dir. of Purchases, Storage and Traffic, 1918. Recipient active service gold medal, Colo. N.G., 1904; D.S.M., 1919: John Fritz medal, Engring. Socs. of N.Y., 1933. Mem. U. Mo. Adv. Council, 1933. Mem. Am. Inst. Mining and Metall. Engrs. (gold medalist 1930; dir. 1925-28, 1938-41; pres. 1938), Mining and Metall. Soc. Am. (gold medalist 1926; councillor 1939-44), Am. Chem. Soc., Am. Soc. M.E., Western Soc. Engrs. (Washington Award 1940), Am. Inst. Elec. Engrs., Mo. School of Mines Alumni Assn. (pres. 1932-33). Republican. Clubs: Engineers', Pacific Union (San Francisco); Menlo Country (Cal.); Alta (Salt Lake City), Mining (N.Y.C.). Address: Hobart Bldg., San Francisco 4. Died Mar. 13, 1956; buried Cypress Lawn Cemetery, Colma, Cal.

JACKMAN, Charles Lyman, corp. official; b. Concord, N.H., Aug. 4, 1871; s. Lyman and Sarah Freese (Tilton) J.; ed. Concord, N.H., pub. schs.; m. Mary E. Rolfe, May 17, 1900 (dec.); children—Margaret (Mrs. Carl G. Gesen), Roma Ann (dec.). Began as an office boy Capital Fire Ins. Co., 1888, pres. since 1912; pres. Underwriters Fire Insurance Company, Manufacturers & Merchants Mutual Insurance Company, and Phenix Mutual Fire Insurance Co., Northern Securities Co., Acquilla Co., Jackman & Lang, Incorporated, Page Belting Company, Corporation Trust of N.H. Republican. Conglist. Clubs: Wonolancet, Bow Brook (Concord). Home: 1 Auburn St. Office: 2 S. Main St., Concord, N.H. Died May 7, 1957; buried Concord, N.H.

JACKSON, Amos Henry, ex-congressman, mfr.; b. nr. Franklin, N.Y., May 10, 1874; s. George W. and Roxanna (Ripley) J.; ed. Gibson, Steuben Co., N.Y.; m. Mary Sharp, Nov. 28, 1872. Went west in 1866; soon after engaged in street-vending bus., which he followed until 1882; since then mfr. undergarments, factories at Fremont, Sandusky, Tiffin and Clyde, O.; also pres. Jackson Knife and Shear Co., Fremont, connected with other local enterprises and owner large real estate interests in Fremont; mayor of Freemont, 1897-1901; mem. Congress, 1903-05. Republican. Address: Fremont, O. Deceased.

JACKSON, Arthur C(harles), educator; b. Waitsfield, Vt., June 29, 1858; s. Alvin N. and Elizabeth (Scagel) J.; ed. U. Ill.; studied law under Gen. B. F. Butler and taught pub. schs., Boston for some yrs.; m. Isabella C. Stetson, Mar. 14, 1882. Traveler and lectr., 1880—; has crossed Atlantic 20 times; represented Fla. at various European expns. and at World's Fair, Chgo., 1893 (pres. state commn.); traveled over 1,000,000 miles in Europe and Am., lecturing on Fla. more than 1,000 times, designed and built Fla. Pavilion at Paris Expn., 1889, and Fla. State Bldg. at Chgo. Expn., 1893; established and personally installed 1st pub. libraries in Alaska; represented and lectured upon Alaska at five internat. expns., designed and built Alaska Bldg. at Buffalo Expn., 1901; New Hampshire Bldg., St. Louis Expn., 1904; built replica old Constn. House as Vt. Bldg.; replica of Longfellow birthplace as Me. State Bldg., at Portland, Ore., 1905. U.S. hon. commr. Antwerp Internat. Expn., 1894; del. London Geog. Congress, Paris Int. Ry. Congress (v.-p.), Congress Commerce and Industry, Internat. Geog. Congress; pres. Me. commn. Lewis and Clarke and Jamestown expns. Fellow Royal Geog. Soc.; Soc. Arts, Imperial Inst. London; pres. Alaska Geog. Soc., 1898, Internat. Longfellow Soc., 1906—, Nat. Good Roads Congress, 1908; pres. Nat. Good Roads Assn., 1908—; pres. Internat. Good Roads Congress, 1911, 13; ex-pres. Ill. State Good Roads Assn., Internat. Good Roads and Automobile Assn.; founder, 1st pres. Daniel Webster Birthplace Assn. Me. Prohbn. party nominee for U.S. senator, 1916. Founder, pres. The Longfellow U., Longfellow Meml. Libraries, Portland Hist. Soc., Longfellow U. Bible Coll., 1922—. Address: Longfellow Birthplace, Portland, Me. Deceased.

JACKSON, Chevalier, laryngologist; b. Pitts., Nov. 4, 1865; s. William Stanford and Katharine Ann (Morange) J.; student Western U. Pa., 1879-83; M.D., Jefferson Med. Coll., Phila., 1886; m. Alice Bennett White, July 19, 1899. Hon. prof. broncho-esophagology Temple U. Mem. A.M.A., Am. Laryngol. Assn., Am. Laryngol., Rhinol. and Otol. Soc., Pan Am. Med. Assn., A.C.S., Am. Bronchoscopic Soc., Am. Therapeutic Soc., Am. Assn. Thoracic Surgery, Am. Acad. Ophthalmology and Otolaryngology, Assn. des Medicins de Langue Francaise de l'Amerique du Nord, Phila. Co. Med. Soc., Penn. State Med. Soc., Coll. Physicians Phila., Phila. Laryngol. Soc., Phila. Pediatric Soc., Pitts. Acad. Medicine; hon. fellow Royal Soc. Medicine, Nat. Acad. Medicine Mexico, Swedish Med. Soc., Nat. Acad. Medicine Brazil, Scottish, French, Italian, Polish, Rumanian, Belgian and Spanish otolaryngol. socs. Decorated Officer Legion of Honor (France); Chevalier Order of Leopold (Belgium), Comdr. Order of Crown of Italy; Cross of Brazil. Clubs: Art and Rotary (Phila.). Author: Peroral Endoscopy and Laryngeal Surgery, 1914; Bronchoscopy, Esophagoscopy and Gastroscopy, 1934; Foreign Body in Air and Food Passages, 1934. Editor: (also contbr.) The Nose, Throat and Ear and Their Diseases, 1929; Bronchoscopy and Esophagoscopy. Contbr. Systems of Surgery and Medicine. Developed the method of removal of fgn. bodies from lungs by insertion of tubes through the mouth, also has contbd. to development of laryngeal surgery. Home: Schwenkville, Pa. Address: 3401 N. Broad St., Phila. 40. Died Aug. 16, 1958.

JACKSON, Dugald Caleb, elec. engr.; b. Kennett Square, Pa., Feb. 13, 1865; s. Josiah and Mary Detweiler (Price) J.; B.S. in Civil Engring., Pa. State Coll., 1885, C.E., 1888; grad. study in elec. engring. Cornell U., 1885-87; D.Sc., Columbia U., 1932; hon. D.Eng., Northeastern U., 1938; m. Mabel A. Foss, Sept. 24, 1889; children—Catharine Emma (Mrs. Philip L. Alger), Dugald Caleb. Vice pres., engr. Western Engring. Co., Lincoln, Neb., 1887-89; asst. chief engr. Sprague Electric Ry. and Motor Co., 1889; chief engr. central dist. Edison General Electric Co. 1890; cons. engr. 1891-1931, sr. mem. firm D. C. and Wm. B. Jackson 1902-18, Jackson & Moreland, 1919-30; prof. elec. engring. U. Wis., 1891-1907; prof. elec. engring. and in charge dept. Mass. Inst. Tech., 1907-35, prof. emeritus, 1935-51; lectr. Inst. E.E. of Japan, Iwadare Foundation, 1935; lectured on engring. edn. to univs. in China, 1936. Lt. col. engrs. in France, chief engr. Power Bd., AEF; chief engring. estimates Bd. to Estimate War Damage in Allied Countries, Am. Peace Commn., 1918-19, after disch., in recognition of war accomplishments, promoted to col. Engr. Res. Mem. internat. jury, Chgo. Expn., 1893, Buffalo Expn., 1901. Chmn. Research Com. on Indsl. Illumination, 1926-36; U.S. Govt. del. to World Engring. Congress, Tokyo, 1929; chmn. div. engring. and industrial research NRC, 1930-33; trustee Mass. Inst. Tech. Pension Assn., 1926-35; mem. Engrs. Council for Profl. Development, 1932-38; chmn. Engrs. Joint Com. on Ethics, 1940-50. Decorated Chevalier Legion of Honor (France); personal letter of commendation from Gen. Pershing; recipient Lamme medal of Soc. Promotion Engring. Edn. for tech. teaching, 1931; Edison medal of Amer. Inst. E.E., 1938. Fellow Am. Inst. E.E. (pres. 1910-11, hon. mem. 1944), Am. Academy Arts and Sciences (pres. 1937-39), A.A.A.S. (chmn. sect. M, 1932). Am. Phys. Soc., Am. Soc. M.E., (hon. mem. 1945); member Am. Philos. Soc., Am. Soc. C.E., Instn. E.E. (London), Société Française des Electriciens (Paris), Am. Soc. for Engring. Edn. (council 1902-03, 06-46, pres. 1905-06), Am. Inst. Cons. Engrs. (mem. council 1920-23, 1937, pres. 1938-40), Boston Soc. C.E. (pres. 1922-23), Newcomen Soc., Sigma Xi, Tau Beta Pi; hon. mem. Institut Scientifique d'Etudes des Communications and des Transports (Paris); hon. mem. Mass. Inst. Tech. Alumni Association. Author: Text-book on Electro-Magnetism and Construction of Dynamos, 1893; Electricity and Magnetism, a series of lessons, 1895; Alternating Currents and Alternating Current Machinery (joint author, 1896, rewritten and enlarged, 1913; An Elementary Book on Electricity and Magnetism and Their Applications (joint author), 1902, rewritten, 1919; Street Railway Fares, Their Relation to Length of Haul and Cost of Service (joint author), 1917; Engineering's Part in the Development of Civilization, 1939; Present Status and Trends of Engineering Education in the United States, 1939; Present-Day Salaries of Engineering Schools in the United States and Canada (with D. C. Jackson, Jr.), 1947; also about 180 papers on engring. and engring. edn. Patentee fields of electric rotating machinery and transformers, electric motors and instruments, electric motor starting devices, telephone equipment, train lighting. Home: 5 Mercer Circle, Cambridge 38, Mass. Died July 1, 1951.

JACKSON, Ed., ex-gov. Ind.; b. Howard County, Ind., Dec. 27, 1873; s. Presley E. and Elizabeth (Howell) J.; m. Lida Beaty. Admitted to Ind. bar, 1898, began practice at Newcastle; pros. atty. Henry County, Ind., 1903-05; apptd., 1909, by governor, judge Circuit Court of Henry County, to fill vacancy, and elected to same office; defeated for sec. of state, 1914, but elected 1916; resigned, 1917, to enter army; apptd. to fill vacancy as sec. of state, 1918, and elected to same office 1918, 20; gov. of Ind., 1925-28. Enlisted as pvt. U.S. Army, 1917; attended 2d O.T.C., Ft. Benjamin Harrison, Ind.; commd. capt., later maj. Republican. Home: Fairhill, Orleans, Ind. Died Nov. 20, 1954; buried Green Hill Cemetery, Orleans.

JACKSON, E(rnest) Hilton, lawyer; b. Front Royal, Va., Nov. 8, 1869; s. John Richard and Cornelia (Kerfoot) J.; A.B., Columbian U. (now George Washington U.), 1891, LL.B., 1892, LL.M., 1893, A.M., 1894, D.C.L., 1900; law student U. of Va. summer 1902 (pres. joint summer classes); m. Anne Wingfield, Nov. 8, 1900; children—Elizabeth Wingfield (Mrs. Paul F. Hannab), John Wingfield, Harriet Ann (Mrs. Samuel Cothran Young). Admitted to bar of the Dist. of Columbia and Virginia, 1895, bar of Supreme Court, 1906; associated with son in practice of law. Mem. inaugural com. of Pres. Wilson and Pres. F. D. Roosevelt; pres. George Washington Law Assn. (1934-37); chmn. bd. trustees, Baptist Home for children; chmn. joint conf. com. on public relations of Am. Baptist Conventions. Mem. Va., Am. and Dist. of Columbia bar assns., Am. Judicature Soc. Democrat. Mason. Club: Cosmos (Washington, D.C.). Author: Law Latin, 1897. Contbr. articles to law jours. Home: 112 Hesketh St., Chevy Chase, Md. Office: Woodward Bldg., Washington. Died July 16, 1950; buried Rock Creek Cemetery, Washington.

JACKSON, Frederick Mitchell, mfr.; b. Hamburg, Ala., Sept. 1, 1859; s. Robert D. and Sara (Mitchell) J.; ed. pvt. sch. and under tutors; m. Miriam Cory, Dec. 21, 1882. Formerly with Tenn. Coal, Iron & R.R. Co., Standard Coal Co., Ala. Consol. Coal & Iron Co.; chmn. bd. Employers Ins. Co. Ala., Perfection Mattress Spring Co., Jackson Securities & Investment Co.; pres. Jefferson Fed. Savs. & Loan Assn., Jefferson County Bldg. & Loan Assn.; dir. Birmingham Trust & Savs. Co. Chmn. campaign com. that secured prohibition amendment in Ala. legislature; chmn. exec. com. bd. trustees, Woman's Coll. Ala. (now Huntingdon Coll.); trustee, treas. Birmingham So. Coll.; ex-pres. Birmingham C. of C. Ind. Democrat. Meth. Mason. Home: 2800 Clairmont Av. Office: 213 N. 21st St., Birmingham, Ala. Died May 3, 1945; buried Birmingham.

JACKSON, George Pullen, musicologist; b. Monson, Me., Aug. 20, 1874; s. George Frederick and Ann Jane (Pullen) J.; student Royal Conservatory of Music, Dresden, 1897-98, Vanderbilt U., 1900-01; Ph.B., U. of Chicago, 1904, Ph.D., 1911; post-grad. work U. of Chicago, U. of Munich and U. of Bonn; m. Inez Emeline Wright, Dec. 23, 1906 (died 1918); children—Frances Helen, George Pullen, Jr.; m. 2d, Lois Diantha Barnes, Dec. 18, 1926 (died 1939). With Huston Biscuit Co., Birmingham, Ala., 1895-1900; teacher of German, Kan. State Agrl. Coll., Manhattan, 1905-06, Case Sch. Applied Science, Cleveland, O., 1906-07; spl. instr. German, U. of Chicago, 1908-10; instr. German, Oberlin Coll., 1910-12, Northwestern U., 1912-13; asst. prof. German, U. of N.D., 1913-18; prof. German, U. of Chicago, summer sessions, 1915, 16; asso. prof. German, Vanderbilt University, 1918-26, professor, 1926-43; emeritus since 1943. President University Philharmonic Society, Grand Forks, North Dakota, 1913-18; founder Nashville Symphony Orchestra, 1920, later Nashville Choral Club, Vanderbilt Singers; founder, hon. mem. Tenn. Music Teachers' Assn.; organizer, mgr. Old Harp Singers of Nashville; organizer Tenn. State Sacred Harp Singing Assn., 1939. Mem. Am. Musicol. Soc., Southeastern Folklore Soc. (pres. 1946); mem. bd. adv. editors Southern Folklore Quarterly; Southern Atlantic Modern Lang. Assn. (chmn. folklore sec. 1946, pres. 1948); Tenn. Folklore Soc. (pres. 1942), American Folklore Society (member of council), International Folk Music Council, Sigma Alpha Epsilon, Phi Beta Kappa. Wrote: The Rhythmic Form of the German Folk Songs (series in Modern Philology), 1916-17; White Spirituals in the Southern Uplands, 1933; Spiritual Folk-Songs of Early America, 1937; Down-East Spirituals, 1943; White and Negro Spirituals, 1943; Story of the Sacred Harp, 1944; also Another Sheaf of White Spirituals, 1952. Editor: Am. Folk Music for High School and other Choral Groups, 1947, Sing Brothers Sing, 1948; also author articles in Modern Language. Notes, Modern Philology, Am. Mercury, Va. Quarterly Review, World Today, Jour. Am. Folklore, So. Folklore Quarterly, Musical Quarterly, Ga. Rev., Grove's Dictionary of Music and Musicians. Address: 420 Royal Oaks Dr., Nashville 5. Died Jan. 19, 1953; buried Elmwood Cemetery, Birmingham, Ala.

JACKSON, Henry Hollister, ins. exec.; b. Barre, Vt., Aug. 30, 1884; s. J. Henry and Cora Augusta (Wood) J.; A.B., Yale, 1908, M.A., 1911; m. Carrie Carleton Bemis, June 15, 1909 (dec. July 28, 1944); married second time to Madine Johnson Rogers, June 26, 1946; children—Henry Hollister, Eleanor Alice, Robert Tilden. Educational work Spaulding High Sch., Barre, 1908-18, prin., 1915-18; with actuarial dept. Nat. Life Ins. Co., Montpelier, Vt., since 1918, asst actuary, 1920-25, asso. actuary, 1925-29, actuary 1929-43, v.p., actuary, 1943-50 v.p. since 1950. Author: Fragments, 1950. Contbr. tech. publs. Home: 20 S. Main St., Barre. Office: 131 State St., Montpelier, Vt. Died May 27, 1955.

JACKSON, Herbert Spencer, botanist; b. Augusta Center, N.Y., Aug. 29, 1883; A.B., Cornell U., 1905; Ph.D., U. of Wis., 1929; m. Eunice Edythe Doyle, Apr. 22, 1907; children—Kenneth Kendall, Dorothy. Asst. in mycology, Cornell U., 1904-05; asst. mycologist, and instr. botany, Delaware Coll. and Expt. Sta., 1905-08; Austin teaching fellow botany, Harvard, 1908-09; prof. botany and plant pathology, Ore. Agrl. Coll., 1909-15; chief in botany, Purdue U. Agrl. Expt. Sta., 1915-28; agt. Bur. Plant Industry, U.S. Dept. Agr., 1918-28; prof. of mycology, U. of Toronto, since 1929, head dept. of botany since July 1941; instructor botany, Harvard, summer, 1909; prof. plant pathology, Cornell U., summers, 1916, 17. Fellow A.A.A.S., Royal Soc. of Canada (pres. sect. V, 1944); mem. Bot. Soc. Am., Mycol. Soc. Am. (pres. 1934), Am. Phytopathol. Society (pres. Pacific div. 1915), Am. Soc. Naturalists, Can. Phytopathol. Soc., N.E. Bot. Club, Sigma Xi, Gamma Alpha, Phi Sigma. Republican. Presbyterian. Home: 75 Glenview Av., Toronto, Can. Died Dec. 14, 1951.

JACKSON, James Arthur, physician; b. Dansville, N.Y., May 4, 1864; s. James H. and Katharine J. J.; M.D., U. Buffalo, 1895. Mgr. The Jackson Sanatorium, sec. bd. dirs., physician on staff, 1895-1918. Address: Conesus, N.Y. Died Nov. 15, 1922; buried Dansville, N.Y.

JACKSON, John Gillespie, lawyer; b. Middletown, Conn., Feb. 12, 1880; s. Charles Eben and Evelyn (Quintard) J.; A.B., Columbia, 1901, LL.B., 1903; m. Grace Jewett Bunce, June 6, 1908; 1, son, John Gillespie. Admitted to N.Y. bar, 1903, asso. with Howard Taylor, N.Y., 1903-11; mem. firms Taylor, Jackson & Brophy, 1911-16, Taylor, Jackson, Brophy & Nash, 1916-24; mem. Jackson, Fuller, Nash & Brophy (now Jackson, Nash, Brophy, Barringer & Brooks), 1924—; dir. Press Pub. Co., Marine Midland Trust Co., Chemstrand Corp., Ketchikan Pulp Co.; gen. counsel, dir. Am. Viscose Corp. Trustee Home for Old Men and Aged Couples. Chmn. Com. Character and Fitness, Appellate Div., 1st Jud. Dept. Life trustee Columbia; mem. joint administrn. bd. Med. Center, 1946. Fellow Am. Bar Found.; mem. Am., N.Y. State (pres. 1941-42) bar assns., N.Y. County Lawyers Assn., N.Y. Law Inst. (chmn. exec. com.), Assn. Bar City N.Y. (v.p. 1941-42), Mass. Soc. Cin., St. Nicholas Soc., N.E. Soc., The Pilgrims (exec. com.), Am. Arbitration Soc. (dir.), St. George's Soc., Holland Lodge, Alumni Assn. Columbia U. Coll. and Law Sch., Soc. N.Y. Hosp., S.R., Delta Psi. Mem. exec. com. U.S. Golf Assn., 1929-38, pres., 1936-37; mem. U.S. Seniors Golf Assn. (pres. 1941-44; capt. team, 1945-49, hon. pres. 1956). Republican. Episcopalian (vestryman). Mason. Clubs: Union, Links, St. Anthony, Manhattan, Columbia University, Southampton, National Golf Links (gov.), Broad Street, Downtown, Royal and Ancient Golf of St. Andrews (Scotland); Walton Health Golf (England), The Church Club N.Y. Home: 164 E. 72d St. Office: 40 Wall St., N.Y.C. Died Apr. 27, 1959.

JACKSON, Joseph Henry, editor; b. Madison, N.J., July 21, 1894; s. Herbert Hallett and Marion Agnes (Brown) J.; prep. edn., Peddie Sch., Hightstown, N.J.; student Lafayette Coll., 1915-17; Litt.D. (honorary), U. So. Cal., 1950; m. Charlotte E. Cobden, June 21, 1923; 1 dau., Marion (Mrs. David Skinner). Asso. editor Sunset Mag., 1920-23, mng. editor, 1924-26, editor, 1926-28; lit. editor San Francisco Argonaut, 1929-30, San Francisco Chronicle since 1930; broadcaster of "Bookman's Guide," over Nat. Broadcasting Co., Pacific Coast network, 1924-43. Mem. bd. dirs. Book Club of Cal. Served with Ambulance Corps, U.S. Army, 1917-18; 2d lt. infantry, United States Army, 1918-19. Mem. Cal. Hist. Soc., Society of American Historians, Phi Kappa Psi. Democrat. Presbyterian. Clubs: Bohemian (San Francisco); University (N.Y.). Author: Mexican Interlude, 1936; Notes on a Drum, 1937; Tintypes in Gold, 1939; Extra! Extra! (with Scott Newhall), 1940; Anybody's Gold, 1941. The California Story, 1949; Bad Company, 1949; The Christmas Flower, 1951; My San Francisco, published in 1953; The Girl in the Belfry, published in the year 1955. Editor: Tale of Soldiers and Civilians, 1944; Continent's End, 1944; Portable Murder Book, 1945; San Francisco Murders, 1947; The Gold Rush Album, 1949; Western Gate: A San Francisco Reader, 1952. Contbr. to newspapers, mags., revs. Mem. bd. of judges O. Henry Memorial Award (short story annual) 1935, 1942, 1951 and of Harper Prize Novel Contest, 1947, 1949; mem. Pulitzer Prize fiction jury, 1949-51; mem. editorial bd. The Pacific Spectator. Home: 2626 Buena Vista Way, Berkeley, Cal. Office: San Francisco Chronicle, 5th and Mission Sts., San Francisco. Died July 15, 1955.

JACKSON, Katharine Johnson, physician; b. Sturbridge, Mass., April 7, 1841; d. Hon. Emerson Johnson; grad. Woman's Med. Coll. N.Y. Infirmary, 1876; since then associated in medical practice with her husband, Dr. James Hathaway Jackson at The Jackson Health Resort. Address: Conesus, N.Y. Died 1921; buried Dansville, N.Y.

JACKSON, Lambert Lincoln, author; b. Binghamton, N.Y., Apr. 14, 1870; grad. Cortland (N.Y.) State Normal Sch., 1891; A.B., U. Mich., 1897, A.M., 1899; B.Pd., Mich. Normal Coll., 1899; scholar Columbia, 1903-04, Ph.D., 1906; m. Grace Ford, Dec. 28, 1897 (died 1908); children—Lambert (dec.), Wendell Ford; m. 2d, Evelyn Seely, June 29, 1911; 1 son, Alan Seely. Asst. prof. mathematics, Mich. State Normal Coll., 1891-1900; prof. math., State Normal Sch., Brockport, N.Y., 1900-06; head of ednl. dept. D. Appleton & Co., 1906-12. Asst. supt. schs., Montclair, N.J., 1913-18; asst. commr. edn., State of N.J., 1920-28; 1st asst. supt. schs., Newark, N.J., 1928-35. Mem. Am. Math. Soc., N.E.A., A.A.A.S. Republican. Author: Educational Significance of 16th Century Arithmetic; Teachers' Manual to Beman and Smith's Higher Arithmetic, 1899; Teachers' Manual to Beman and Smith's Elements of Algebra, 1900; Teachers' Manual to Beman and Smith's Academic Algebra, 1903; Arithmetics for Grades (with J. W. A. Young), 1903-05; Elementary Algebra (with same), 1908; Plane Geometry (with same), 1916. Joint contbr. math. articles of New Internat. Ency., 1903-04; editor math. dept. New York Teachers' Monograph and N.J. Courses of Study. Address: Route 5, Box 301, Tucson. Died Mar. 28, 1952; buried Sleepy Hollow Cemetery, Tarrytown, N.Y.

JACKSON, Philip Ludwell, newspaper pub.; b. Portland, Ore., Oct. 18, 1893; s. Charles Samuel and Maria Foster (Clopton) J.; Litt.B., Princeton, 1915; M.B.A., Harvard, 1917; m. Alice D. Strowbridge, Mar. 15, 1922 (dec.); m. 2d, Ella R. Tenney, Nov. 21, 1931 (dec.); married 3d, Esma P. Ransom, June 11, 1951. Publisher of the Oregon Journal, Portland, Ore., since 1924; president of the Journal Publishing Co.; president KPOJ. Served as lt., Motor Transport Corps, U.S. Army, 1917-18, capt., 1918-19. Mem. bd. dirs. Chamber of Commerce (pres. 1934-35); pres. Pacific Coast div. Bur. Advt.; sec. Ore. Princeton Alumni Assn.; mem. Sigma Delta Chi. Democrat. Episcopalian. Clubs: University, Multnomah, Waverley Country, Portland Hunt, Racquet, National Press, Press Club of Oregon, Oregon Advertising; Princeton (N.Y.); Union League (San Francisco). Home: 11522 S.W. Riverwood. Address: Oregon Journal, Portland 7, Ore. Died Feb. 14, 1953.

JACKSON, Ralph LeRoy, educator; b. Edinburg, Pa., Aug. 13, 1888; s. Albert Matthews and Jennie B. (Simon) J.; ed. Western Military Acad., Alton, Ill., 1900-06; Shurtleff Coll., Alton, 1906-08; Litt. B., Princeton, 1911; grad. work, Harvard, 1913; m. Mary Prentiss Borden, June 17, 1914 (dec.); children—Albert Matthews (dec.), Ralph Borden, Charles Borden, William Andrew; married 2d Eve Mallory, August 16, 1948. Began as an instructor and coach, Western Mil. Acad., 1911; has served in every dept. of the sch., supt. since 1925, pres. of the corp. since 1930. Past pres. Private Schools Assn. of Central States; past pres. Assn. Mil. Colls. and Schs. U.S. Trustee Asso. Charities; past dir. Boy Scout Council. Democrat. Presbyterian. Rotarian (past president). Clubs: Princeton (St. Louis); Country (past pres.). Comdr. Civilian Defense, Alton area. Home: 2009 Seminary St., Alton, Ill. Died Aug. 14, 1952.

JACKSON, Richard Webber, business exec.; b. Detroit, May 23, 1912; s. Roscoe B. and Louise A. (Webber) J.; A.B., Yale, 1933; m. Margaret E. Keena, Dec. 1, 1934; children—Richard W., Linda Ellen. With Hudson Motor Car Co., Detroit, 1933—, vice pres., 1943—, dir., 1941—. Trustee or dir.; Children's Hosp. of Mich., Detroit U. Sch., Roscoe B. Jackson Lab. for Cancer Research (pres.), United Community Services, United Foundation (vice president), United Health and Welfare Fund of Mich. Clubs: Detroit Athletic, Economic (dir.), Detroit, County of Detroit; Grosse Pointe, Grosse Pointe Hunt. Home: 124 Merriweather Rd., Grosse Pointe Farms 30, Mich. Office: 12601 Jefferson Av., Detroit 14. Died Nov. 11, 1952.

JACKSON, Robert Houghwout, U.S. Supreme Ct. Justice; b. Spring Creek, Pa., Feb. 13, 1892; s. William Eldred and Angelina (Houghwout) J.; educated Albany (N.Y.) Law Sch. (Union U.); LL.D. (hon.), University of Brussels, Univ. of Warsaw, Dartmouth Coll., Syracuse Univ., and others; m Irene Gerhardt, Apr. 24, 1916; children—William Eldred, Mary Margaret. Admitted to N.Y. bar, 1913, and began practice at Jamestown. Appointed general counsel Bureau of Internal Revenue, 1934; asst. atty. gen. of U.S., 1936-38; solicitor gen. of United States, 1938-39; U. S. atty. gen., Jan. 1940-June 1941; asso. justice U.S. Supreme Ct., July 1941—. Apptd. by President Truman, 1945, to represent the U.S. in negotiating with Soviet Russia, United Kingdom and France on agreement for internat. trials of European Axis war criminals; also named as chief of counsel for U.S., to conduct prosecution of internat. trials of Goering, Ribbentrop and others. Trustee George Washington U., Albany Law School. Awarded Medal for merit by Pres. Truman, 1946. Elected hon. bencher Honourable Soc. of Middle Temple, London, 1946. Episcopalian. Mason (33°). Author: The Struggle for Judicial Supremacy, 1941; Full Faith and Credit-The Lawyers Clause of the Constitution, 1945; The Case Against the Nazi War Criminals, 1946; The Nurnberg Case, 1947; The Supreme Court in the American System of Government (Godkin Lectures prepared for delivery at Harvard), 1955. Author various articles for legal periodicals). Address: U.S. Supreme Court, Washington. Died Oct. 9, 1954; buried Frewsburg, N.Y.

JACKSON, Samuel Dillon, lawyer, atty. gen.; b. Allen County, Ind., May 28, 1895; s. Isaiah H. and Minnie (Whittenberger) J.; LL.B., Ind. Law Sch., 1917; m. Anna Fern Bennett, Dec. 26, 1914; children—James Woodrow, Robert Isaiah, Samuel Dillon. Admitted to bar, 1919; dir. and atty. First Fed. Savs. & Loan Assn., Fort Wayne, Ind.; pros. atty., Allen County, Ind., 1924-28; atty. gen. of Ind., 1940-41; U.S. senator, Jan. 28, 1944, Nov. 15, 1944. Mem. Ind., Allen County (past pres.) bar assns., Am. Legion (charter mem.). Democrat. Presbyn. (elder). Mason (33°); deputy for Indiana. Club: Quest. Home: 2503 West Drive. Office: 1335 Lincoln Bank Tower, Fort Wayne, Ind. Died Mar. 8, 1951.*

JACKSON, V(estus) T(wiggs), chemist; b. Sandersville, Ga., Jan. 29, 1889; s. Vestus and Jennie Irene (Beasley) J.; A.B., B.S., Mercer U., 1912; M.S., U. Chgo., 1916, Ph.D. cum laude, 1921; post-grad. work on photochemistry U. Wis., summer 1935; m. Josephine Louise Stenhouse, Sept. 12, 1918; 1 dau., Betty (Mrs. John Stanley Livingstone, Jr.). Asst. in physics Mercer U., 1910-11, asst. in chemistry 1911-12; instr. chemistry Okla. A. and M. Coll., 1912-16; chmn. research Lindsay Light Co., Chgo., 1916-19; 2d rank, chemistry dept. Catholic U. of Am., 1921-22; chem. research Western Electric Co., 1922-23; acting head, dept. chemistry Heidelberg U., Tiffin, O., 1924; asst. prof. chemistry U. Fla., 1924-27, asso. prof. 1927-35, prof., 1935—. Active duty tng., Ft. Benning, summer 1932; instr. chem. warfare, Ft. Bragg, summer 1936; Edgewood Arsenal, 1940; major (inactive) C.W.S., U.S. Army, Res. Officers Assn. Recipient Blalock Science medal (Mercer U.). Mem. Am. Chem. Soc. (past pres. Fla. sect.), Sigma Xi, Gamma Sigma Epsilon, Delta Sigma Phi, Phi Kappa Phi. Democrat. Club: Athenaeum (U. Fla.; past sec. and treas. and pres.). Author numerous articles on chem. subjects. Home: 515 Boulevard, Gainesville, Fla. Died Nov. 25, 1950; buried Oakwoods Cemetery, Chgo.

JACKSON, Wilfrid J(ames), physicist; b. Jacksonville, Nova Scotia, May 11, 1900; s. Capt. William G. L. (master mariner) and Helen E. (Musgrave) J.; student Sydney (N.S., Can.) Acad., 1914-17; B.A., Dalhousie Univ., 1921, A.M., 1923; A.M., Princeton, 1926, Ph.D., 1927; married Mabel E. Mott, June 21, 1932; children—Charles Wilfrid, Marilyn Mott. Came to U.S., 1923, naturalized, 1939. Demonstrator in physics, Dalhousie U., 1921-22; Macgregor teaching fellow, 1922-23; instr. of physics, Princeton U., 1923-25; James W. Queen fellow, physics, 1925-26, research asst., 1926-27; interim lecturer, mathematics, physics, King's Coll., Dalhousie Univ., 1927-28, spl. lecturer, univs. training, summer 1941; instr., physics, Rutgers, 1928-29, asst. prof., 1929-43; associate prof., 1943-46, prof. since 1946, chmn. dept. of physics, Douglass College, Rutgers State U., 1946—; vis. lecturer, Mass. Inst. Tech. ESMDT, 1941-42, radar sch., 1942-44, vis. asso. prof. radar sch., 1944-46; chief scientist N.Y. br. office, Office of Naval Research, 1950. Fellow American Association Advancement Science; mem. Am. Physical Society, American Inst. Physics, Am. Assn. Physics Teachers, Am. Assn. Univ. Profs. (pres. Rutgers chapter, 1946-47), N.B. Science Society, Sigma Xi (president of Rutgers chapter, 1954-55). Rotarian. Clubs: Dalhousie of N.Y.; Red Pine of N.B. (pres. 1948, 49). Contbr. articles in physics jours. Home: 250 Lawrence Av., Highland Park, New Brunswick, N.J. Died Mar. 13, 1959.

JACKVONY, Louis V., lawyer; b. Jan. 25, 1892; s. Antonio and Carmela (Grieco) J.; student pub. sch. and tech. high school Providence, also Boston U.; m. Clotilde Zambarano, Feb. 7, 1921; children—Louis V., Jacqueline J., Alma A. Admitted to bar, R.I. Supreme Court, 1917, and since in general practice, Providence; rep. from Providence in State General Assembly, 1921-22; asst. atty. gen. of R.I., 1925-30, atty. gen., 1939-40. Served with U.S. Army during World War I. Mem. nat. bd. dirs., exec. com. Camp Fire Girls, Inc. (treas. Narragansett council). Mem. Rep. State Central Com. Mem. Am. Legion. Home: 85 Gentian Av., Providence 8. Office: Turks Head Bldg., Providence 8. Died Dec. 24, 1950.*

JACOBI, Frederick (jȧ-kō'bĭ), composer, teacher of music; b. San Francisco, Calif., May 4, 1891; s. Frederick and Flora (Brandenstein) J.; ed. Ethical Culture Sch., N.Y. City, Hochschule für Musik Berlin, Germany; studied music with Paolo Gallico, Rubin Goldmark, Rafael Joseffy, Ernest Bloch; m. Irene Schwarcz, May 29, 1917; children—Maxine Emma (dec.), Frederick Arthur, Dorothea Rebecca. Asst. condr. Metropolitan Opera Co., 1913-17; teacher of composition, Julliard Graduate School, N.Y. City, 1936-50. Lectr. University of Calif., summer 1939. Mem. executive board League of Composers; charter member Am. Music Guild; mem. A.S.C.A.P. Received hon. mention Coolidge Competition, 1924; twice received award Society for Publ. of American Music. Jewish religion. Composer: Ode for Orchestra; Hagiographa; The Prodigal Son (opera); Indian Dances suite for orchestra; Three String Quartets; Sabbath Evening Service for the Synagogue; 2 Sabbath Evening Services for 10th anniversary Park Av. Synagogue, May 23, 1952; Concerto for Violin and Orchestra; Concertino for Piano and String Orchestra; Friday Evening Service Number 2; composer also many songs, violin, cello, and piano pieces. Compositions have been played by symphonies of San Francisco, Philadelphia, Chicago, Rochester, Boston and others Home: 5000 Independence Av., N.Y.C. 71. Died Oct. 24, 1952.

JACOBS, Edwin Elmore, college pres.; b. Congress, O., Feb. 19, 1877; s. Rev. Henry Stremmel and Elizabeth (Lindsey) J.; A.B., Wooster (O.) Coll., 1901; M.Sc., Mt. Union Coll., Alliance, O., 1906; Ph.D., Clark U., Worcester, Mass., 1917; studied at univs. of Chicago, Harvard, California; European travel, 1935; m. Mary Brown Cassel, June 25, 1907; children—Cassel H., Edwin, John Brown. Pres. Ashland Coll., 1918-35, pres. emeritus, 1935; instr. teachers' institutes; chautauqua lecturer. Fellow A. A.A.S., Ohio Acad. Science; mem. Am. Sociol. Soc.,

Pi Gamma Mu. Democrat. Mem. Brethren Ch., moderator Nat. Conv., 1928-29. Mason. Author: A Study in the Physical Vigor of American Women, 1920. Co-Author; Society Under Analysis. Contbr. to tech. mags. Home: Kingsburg, Cal. Died Oct. 31, 1953; buried Kingsburg Cemetery.

JACOBS, Harold Duane, govt. official; b. Paw Paw, Mich., Jan. 28, 1890; s. Fred Davis and Kate Hortense (Wilcox) J.; ed. high sch., Paw Paw; m. Marie Agnes Locey, June 10, 1916; 1 son, John Peter; m. 2d, Ethel Epstein Katz, May 15, 1941. Reporter Kalamazoo (Mich.) Telegraph, 1908, Bay City (Mich.) Tribune, 1909; reporter, later asst. city ed. Detroit (Mich.) Journal, 1910-12; telegraph editor Drovers' Journal, Chgo., 1913; became connected with United Press, Chgo., 1914, and mgr. successively at Milwaukee, Dallas and Detroit until 1917, also asst. mgr. at Chgo., 1918, cable editor, N.Y.C., 1918-19, mgr. at N.Y.C., 1920; mng. editor Washington (D.C.) News, 1921; a founder Baltimore Post, 1922, editor 1922-29; editor Pittsburgh Press, 1929-31; mng. editor New Bedford (Mass.) Standard-Times, 1931-34; editor Santa Barbara Press, 1934-37; mng. editor Santa Barbara News-Press, 1937-38; asst. administr. Wage and Hour Div., Dept. of Labor, 1938—; civilian advisor on pub. relations to War Dept. 1940—. Mem. Sigma Delta Chi, Alpha Phi Gamma. Club: Nat. Press. Home: Grey Rock, Pikesville, Md. Address: Wage and Hour Div., Dept. of Labor, Washington, D.C. Died July 1959.

JACOBS, Michel, sculptor, author, portrait and landscape painter; b. Montreal, Can., Sept. 10, 1877; s. Maurice and Esther (Jackson) J.; brought to U.S., 1885; educated École des Beaux Arts and Julian Acad., Paris, France; Nat. Acad., N.Y. Inventor new color theory. Has exhibited in Europe and U.S.; prin. works: portraits of Hon. William J. Bryan, Champ Clark, Joseph G. Cannon, U.S. Senator Oscar Underwood, 26 portraits in Baron de Hirsh Inst., Montreal, Can., Duchess Von Trackenberg, Princess Heinrich Von Schoenich-Carlath, Mischa Elman, Anna Pavlowa, Ossip Gabrilowitsch, Duc de la Chatre, Kathryn Goodson, Teressa Carenna, Gen. George C. Marshall, Maj. Gen. Blanton Winship (gov. gen. of P.R.), Lt. Gen. Robert Lee Bullard, etc.; sculpture—Rear Adm. Robert Peary, Fritz Kreisler, Rock of All Nations, Susan B. Anthony, etc. Enlisted U.S. Army, 1917, and advanced to col., World War I; participated in 6 maj. engagements; captured German gun, now on Boston Common; honorable discharge, 1919. Fellow Royal Soc. Arts (Eng.), 1936; mem. Gloucester Soc. Artists, Artists' Fellowship, Met. Color Guild (dir.), Am. Legion, Mil. Order World War, Soc. Am. Mil. Engrs. Clubs: Military and Naval, Salmagundi. Author: The Art of Color, 1923; The Study of Color, 1925; The Art of Composition; 30001 Color Combinations; Portrait Painting; Memoires. Address: Parmley Park, Rumson, N.J. Died Feb. 4, 1958; buried Arlington Nat. Cemetery.

JACOBS, Myrl Lamont, steel mfr.; b. Weldbank, Warren Co., Pa., May 16, 1885; s. Carl Bearse and Georgia A. (Truxel) J.; student Marietta Coll., 1902-1903; Mercersburg Acad., 1906; E.M., Lehigh U., 1910; m. Hermia Grace, Oct. 11, 1911; children—Barbara (Mrs. Robert Mayo), Carl Bearse. Asst. engr., Astoria Light, Heat and Power Co., N.Y. City, 1910; asst. engr., Mexican Light and Power Co., Hydro Elec. Tunnels and Dams, Mexico, 1912-13; asst. engr., N.Y. Municipal Railway, Brooklyn, N.Y., 1913-16; engr., F. H. Clement & Co., Bethlehem, Pa., 1916-20; gen. mgr. of quarries Bethlehem Mines Corp., 1920-34; gen. mgr., stone and slag div., Bethlehem Steel Co., 1934-39; asst. to v.p, Bethlehem Steel Co., 1939; v.p., Bethlehem Steel Co., 1940, and pres. of various Bethlehem subsidiary companies engaged in mining, 1940; dir. Bethlehem Steel Corp., Jan. 25, since 1940. Member, Am. Inst., Mining and Metall. Engrs., Am. Iron and Steel Inst., Newcomen Society. Republican. Episcopalian. Clubs: Metropolitan, Mining, University (N.Y. City), Bethlehem and Saucon Valley Country (Bethlehem, Pa.), Engrs. of Lehigh Valley. Home: 837 Tioga Av. Office: Bethlehem Steel Co., Bethlehem, Pa. Died Nov. 13, 1948.

JACOBS, Nathan Bernd, civil engr.; b. Pittsburgh, Pa., Dec. 18, 1891; s. Benjamin N. and Lottie (Pichel) J.; B.S. in san. engring., U. of Pittsburgh, 1914, San. Engr., 1917; m. Marie F. Oberndorf, Sept. 17, 1918; 1 dau., Emily Nan (Mrs. C. Morton Bachrach, Jr.). Assistant engineer Morris Knowles Incorporated, 1914-17, division engineer, 1917-21, assistant chief engr., 1921-32, pres. and chief engr. since 1932, now also treas. and dir.; mgr. Knowles-Main Appraisal Bureau, Pittsburgh and New York, since 1919; cons. engr. Maurice R. Scharff, N.Y., 1933-41; water cons. Dist. No. 2, Drainage Basin Study, Nat. Resources Planning Board; same, Interstate Commission on Delaware River Basin, 1936-39; consultant for the Office of Fgn. Economics Adminstrn.; consulting engineer Philadelphia Water Works; general manager Lewistown Water authority. Studied development of utilities for houses in Europe for President's (Hoover) Conference on Home Building and Home Ownership, 1931. Mem. bd. Emma Farm Assn. (pres. 1942-46), Maurice and Laura Falk Found. (v.p.), Irene Kauffman Settlement (pres. 1946-53), Ohio Valley Conservation and Flood Control Congress, Federation of Social Agencies, also Pittsburgh Housing Assn., Montefiore Hosp., Federal Jewish Philanthropies of Pitts., Rodef Shalom Temple, Am. Arbitration Assn. (Nat. Panel of Arbitrators), Jewish Welfare Bd. (Midwest sect.). Mem. American Institute Consulting Engineers, Am. Soc. Civil Engineers, Am. Water Works Association, Pa. Water Works Assn. (v.p.), Am. Soc. for Testing Materials, Nat. Soc. Professional Engrs., Am. Public Health Assn., Am. Soc. of Appraisers, Engineers Soc. of Western Pa., Pi Lambda Phi. Mason. Jewish religion. Clubs: Westmoreland Country (Export, Pa.); Civic Club of Allegheny County (pres. 1936-38); Engineers (Phila.); Concordia (Pittsburgh). Writer various tech. articles and speeches. Home: 6329 Bartlett St., Pittsburgh 17. Office: Park Bldg., Pitts. 22. Died Feb. 14, 1956.

JACOBS, Thornwell, educator; b. Clinton, S.C., Feb. 15, 1877; s. Rev. William Plumer (D.D.) and Mary Jane (Dillard) J.; A.B., Presbyn. Coll. of S.C., Clinton, 1894 (medalist and 1st honor), A.M., 1895, Litt.D., 1923; A.M., Princeton, 1899; grad. Princeton Theol. Sem., 1899; LL.D., Ohio Northern U., Ada, O., 1914; m. Maud Kistler Lesh, June 30, 1903. Ordained to ministry Presbyn. Ch., 1899; pastor Morganton, N.C., 1900-03; v.p. Thornwell Coll. for Orphans, 1903; former Westminster Mag., 1911, and in first issue (Jan. 1912) suggested plan for Pan Presbyn. Jubilee which met in Atlanta, May 1913; founder Oglethorpe U., Atlanta (elected pres. Jan. 21, 1915). Re-discovered burial place of Gen. James Edward Oglethorpe (founder of Ga.), 1923; Founder Crypt of Civilization, 1936. Mem. Grad. Council Nat. Alumni Assn. of Princeton. Author: Sinful Saddy, 1907; The Law of the White Circle (novel), 1908; Midnight Mummer (poems), 1911; The Oglethorpe Story, 1916; Life of William Plumer Jacobs, 1918; The New Science and the Old Religion, 1927; Islands of the Blest (poems), 1928; Oglethorpe Book of Georgia Verse, 1930. Editor: Diary of William Plumber Jacobs, 1937; William Plumber Jacobs Memorabilia, 1942. Author: Red Lanters on St. Michael's, 1940; Story of Christmas, 1941; Drums of Doomsday, 1942; Step Down, Dr. Jacobs, 1945. Address: Station C, Box 7142, Atlanta, also Clinton, S.C. Died Aug. 4, 1956; buried First Presbyn. Ch. Cemetery, Clinton, S.C.

JACOBS, Whipple, business exec.; b. Chicago, Feb. 2, 1897; s. William Vaughan and Mary (Whipple) J.; student public schools of Illinois; married Mary Latham, October 20, 1923; children—William Latham, Nancy, Ann; m. 2d, Christine Newcomb, May 19, 1941; 1 son, Christopher Newcomb. Cost clk., Belden Mfg. Co. (mfrs. elec. wires, cable, cordage), Chicago, 1914-17, purchasing agt., 1923-27, gen. sales mgr., 1927-30, v.p. in charge of sales, 1930-39, pres., 1939-49; pres. Phelps Dodge Copper Products Corp., N.Y. City, since 1949; dir. Central Republic Co., Chicago, Chicago Ry. Equipment Co. Trustee Ill. Inst. Tech. since 1943. Served with ambulance service, U.S. Army, 1917-19; with A.E.F., France, 1918-19. Mem. Ill. Mfrs. Assn. (dir. to 1948), Nat. Assn. Mfrs. (regional v.p. 1947-48, dir. 1946-50). Republican. Episcopalian. Clubs: Chicago, Commonwealth, Saddle and Cycle (Chicago); Wall Street, Cloud, River, Metropolitan (New York). Home: 450 E. 63rd St., N.Y.C. 21. Office: 40 Wall St., N.Y.C. 5. Died Aug. 19, 1952.

JACOBS, William States, clergyman; b. Clinton, S.C., Mar. 8, 1871; s. Dr. William Plumer and Mary Jane (Dillard) J.; B.A., Presbyn. Coll. of S.C., 1890, M.A., 1892; B.D., Columbia Theol. Sem., 1893; LL.B., U. S.C., 1893; M.A., Ph.D., Westminster Coll., Fulton, Mo., 1896; D.D., Austin (Tex.) Coll., 1909; m. Laura Harris, Nov. 18, 1896. Ordained to ministry Presbyn. Ch., 1893; pastor Edgefield, S.C., 1893-94, Columbus, Miss., 1894-99, Woodland St. Ch., Nashville, 1899-1906, 1st Church, Houston, 1906-32, Independent Ch., Houston, 1932—. Mem. Indsl. Commns. Tex., Govt. and Social Aspects Commn., Tex. Planning Bd., Southwestern Fardon and Parole Commn., Am. Brahma Breeders Assn. (v.p., dir.), Pan Am. Zebu Assn., Sociedad Univerode Agriculturo of Brazil. Radio lectr. and preacher of wide distinction; lectr. and writer on various phases of social justice and social security. Mem. Pi Kappa Alpha. Mason (32°, Shriner), K.P. Clubs: University, Riveroaks Country, Kiwanis, Campus, Salesmanship, Knife and Ford pres.), Houston Fram and Ranch (dir.), Beaumont Farm and Ranch (hon.). Home: 506 Lovett Blvd., Houston. Died Dec. 25, 1951; buried Forest Park Cemetery, Houston.

JACOBSON, Arthur Clarence, physician; editor, author; b. Brooklyn, N.Y., Sept. 28, 1872; s. John and Mary (Duggan) J.; desc. of Hendrick Jacobsen, from North Holland, who settled in New Amsterdam in 1649; M.D., L.I. Coll. Hosp., 1894; m. Catherine Heinrichs, Nov. 26, 1896; children—Mary Catherine (Mrs. Beverley Gnaedinger), Margaret Helena (Mrs. J. Arthur Cusick). Resident physician Brooklyn Hosp., 1894-95; med. inspector city schools, Dept. of Health, N.Y. City, 1899; physician, Dept. Pub. Welfare, N.Y. City, 1900-29; physician Dept. of Hospitals, N.Y. City, 1929-45; editor Medical Times, treasurer Romaine Pierson Publishers, Inc. Fellow A.M.A.; mem. A.A.A.S., Medical Library Assn., Medical Society State of New York and the County of Kings, Associated Physicians of Long Island, Alumni Assn. Brooklyn Hospital and Long Island College Hospital, British Soc. for Study of Addiction. Club: Authors' (London). Author: Genius—Some Revaluations, 1926. Address: 98 Montague St., Bklyn. 1. Died Oct. 15, 1958.

JACOBUS, David Schenck (jă-kō'bŭs), engineer; b. Ridgefield, N.J., Jan. 20, 1862; s. Nicholas and Sarah Catherine (Carpenter) J.; M.E., Stevens Ins. Tech., 1884 (Dr. Engring., 1906); spl. mech. engring.; m. Laura Dinkel, Apr. 5, 1899; children—David D., Laura C. (Mrs. Fred A. Muschenheim). Instructor, Stevens Institute Technology, 1884-97, prof. experimental mechanics and engring. physics, 1897-1906; adv. engr. The Babcock & Wilcox Co., 1906-41; now ret. Hon. mem. Am. Soc. Mech. Engrs., Boiler Code Com. (chmn. 1940-41); chmn. 1938, 1942 editions of American Welding Soc. Welding Handbook. Awarded Morehead medal by International Acetylene Assn. for year 1935 for leadership in formulation codes and procedures; awarded Miller medal by Am. Welding Soc., 1943; selected a Nat. Modern Pioneer by the Nat. Assn. Mfrs., 1940. Trustee Stevens Inst. Tech. Has written many papers and is an authority in steam engring. Hon. mem. Am. Soc. Mech. Engrs. (pres. 1916-17); mem. Soc. Naval Architects and Marine Engrs., Am. Inst. Mining and Metall. Engrs., Am Math. Soc., Am. Soc. for Engring. Edn., Am. Inst. Electric Engrs. (life), Am. Soc. for Testing Materials, Am. Soc. Refrigerating Engrs. (life), (pres. 1906-07), Am. Soc. Heating and Ventilating Engrs. (life), Am. Welding Soc. (hon.), pres. 1934-35, Petroleum Inst., American Society for Metals, Franklin Institute, Holland Soc. N. Y., Newcomen Soc. Eng.; fellow A.A.A.S. Club: Engineers, Stevens Metropolitan. Home: 93 Harrison Av., Montclair, N.J. Died Feb. 11, 1955; buried Montclair, N.J.

JACOBY, Henry Sylvester (jă-kō'bĭ), civil engr.; b. Springtown, Pa., Apr. 8, 1857; s. Peter Landis and Barbara (Shelly) J.; ed. Excelsior Normal Inst., Carversville, Pa., and pvt. instr.; C.E., Lehigh U., 1877, E.D., 1941; m. Laura Louise Saylor, May 18, 1880; children—John Vincent, Hurlbut Smith, Freeman Steel. Chief draughtsman U.S. Engr. Office, Memphis, 1879-85; instr. civil engring. Lehigh U., 1886-90; prof. bridge engring Cornell, 1890-1922, ret. Fellow A.A.A.S. (v.p. Sect. D., 1901; hon. mem. Am. Soc. C.E.; mem. Soc. Promotion Engring. Edn. (sec. 1900-02, v.p., 1913-14, pres. 1915-16), Am. Ry. Engring. Assn., Washington Acad. Scis., Religious Edn. Assn., Hist. Soc. Pa., Lehigh County Hist. Soc., Pa.-German Soc., Nat. Geneal. Soc. (pres. 1930-34), Geneal. Soc. Pa., Wasington Soc. Engrs. (hon.), Tau Beta Pi, Sigma Xi. Author: Notes and Problems in Descriptive Geometry, 1892; Outlines of Descriptive Geometry (3 parts), 1895-96-97; Text-Book on Plain Lettering, 1897; Text-Book on Roofs and Bridges (4 parts), 1890-98 (with Prof. Mansfield Merriman); Structural Details, or Elements of Design in Timber Framing, 1909; Foundations of Bridges and Buildings (with Prof. Roland P. Davis), 1914; Timber Design and Construction (with Prof. Roland P. Davis), 1929; The Jacoby Family Genealogy, 1930; Supplement, 1941; also numerous papers tech. jours. Genealogist of the Jacoby Family. Address: 3000 Tilden St. N.W., Washington 8. Died Aug. 1, 1955.

JAEGER, Alphons Otto (yā'gẽr), chemist; b. Bergzabern, Palatine, Germany, Oct. 14, 1886; s. Philip and Scholastica Adolphine Wilhemine (Stoecker) J.; student Inst. Tech. of Friedberg (Germany), 1906-07; U. Zurich (Switzerland), 1907; U. Basel (Switzerland), 1911, B.S., M.A., Ph.D., 1913; m. Hedwig Maria Wuermell, Sept. 9, 1920; children—Carl Heinz, Raymond Alphons, Marian Scholastica, Lucia Constancia. Came to U.S. 1923, naturalized, 1929. Research chemist Badische Anilin & Soda Fabrik, Germany, 1914-23; group leader research dept. Nat. Aniline & Chem. Co., Buffalo, 1923-25; cons. chemist, 1925-26; tech. dir. The Selden Co., Bridgeville, Pa., 1926-29, v.p., 1929-34; gen. mgr., research dir. Selden div. Am. Cyanamid & Chem. Corp., 1934-38, chmn. development com. Am. Cyanamid Co., 1938—; mem. new projects and process development coms.; dir. gen. tech. div. Mem. Am. Assn. Textile Chemists and Colorists, Am. Chem. Soc., Am. Soc. for Testing Materials, Internat. Soc. Leather Trades Chemists, Chem. Soc. (Eng.); hon. mem. U.S. Vets. Fgn. Wars (Overbrook Post). Republican. Roman Catholic. Club: Chemists (New York). Awarded numerous patents relating to apparatus and catalysts for Selden and Monsanto contact sulfuric acid processes, and with catalytic processes, apparatus, and catalysts for organic oxidations, oil cracking, catalysts, ammonia and Co oxidation catalysts, etc., dye intermediates and dyes, numerous organic acids, wetting agents and other Textile chemicals, leather and paper chemicals, paint, lacquer, varnishes, terpenes, Talloil etc. Contbr. tech. publs. Home: 1 Spring Rd., Milbrook, Greenwich, Conn. Office: 30 Rokefeller Plaza, N.Y.C. Died July 21, 1953.

JAFFRAY, Clive Talbot, ry. exec.; b. Berlin, Ont., Can., July 1, 1865; s. William and Agnes J.; student pub. schs. of Berlin, Ont.; m. Madeleine Palmer. Apr. 15, 1891. Came to U.S., 1885, naturalized, 1890. Began banking career, 1880; pres. First Nat. Bank, Mpls., 1917-24; pres. M.,St.P., & S.S.M. Ry., 1924-37, chmn. bd. 1937-44. now dir.; dir. Bank Stock Corp., Twin City Fire Ins. Co., Pillsbury Flour Mills, Northwestern Nat. Life Ins. Co., Northwestern Fire & Marine Ins. Co., First Nat. Bank of Mpls., Title Ins. Co., Minn. & Ont. Paper Co. Republican. Episcopalian. Clubs: Minneapolis, Minikahda (Mpls.). Home: 1616 Mt. Curve Av. Office: First National Bank Bldg., Mpls. Died Nov. 15, 1956.

JAGGAR, Thomas Augustus (jăg'gẽr), geologist; b. Phila., Jan. 24, 1871; s. Bishop Thomas Augustus and Anna Louisa (Lawrence) J.; Bach. of Arts, Harvard, 1893, A.M., 1894, Ph.D., 1897; D.Sc., Dartmouth Coll., 1938; LL.D., University of Hawaii, 1945; student at Munich Univ., 1894, Heidelberg Univ., 1895; m. Helen Kline, Apr. 15, 1903; children—Kline, Eliza Bowne; m. 2d Isabel P. Maydwell, Sept. 17, 1917. Instr. geology, Harvard U., 1895-1903, asst. prof., 1903-06; prof. geology, Mass. Inst. Tech., 1904-17, head of dept., 1906-12. Asst. geologist U.S. Geol. Survey, 1898-1904, in charge of work in S.D., Ariz. and Mass.; conducted volcano expdns. to Martinique, 1902, Vesuvius, 1906, Aleutian Isls., 1907, Hawaii and Japan, 1909, Costa Rica, 1910, Sakurajima, Japan, 1914, New Zealand, 1920; investigated Tokyo Earthquake, 1923, Alaskan volcanoes, 1927; leader of Nat. Geog. Soc. Pavlof Expdn., 1928; directed Aleutian expeditions 1929, 1931, 1932; geologist of U.S. Naval Obs. Eclipse Expdn. to Niuafoou, Tonga, 1930; established volcano experiment station, Hawaii, 1911; volcanologist in charge Hawaiian Volcano Obs., U.S. Weather Bur., 1919-24, U.S. Geol. Survey, 1924-35, chief of sect. of volcanology, 1926-35, with stations in Hawaii, Calif. and Alaska; volcanologist U.S. Nat. Park Service, 1935-40; retired; now research asso. in geophysics, U. of Hawaii. Awarded Burr prize for development amphibian vehicles, Nat. Geog. Soc., 1945. Dir. expeditions through research fellows of Hawaiian Volcano Research Assn., in Hawaii, also in Chile, 1929-30. Mem. Royal Soc. earthquake investigation, Montserrat, 1936. Fellow Am. Acad. Arts and Sciences, Washington Acad. Sciences (non-res. v.p., 1918). Author: Volcanology, 1931; Volcanoes Declare War, 1945; Origin and Development of Craters, 1947; Union through the ages, 1948; Steam Blast Volcanic Eruptions, 1949; Abrasion Hardness, 1950; My Experiments with Volcanoes, 1952. Contributor to memoirs of Geological Society of America, reports of U.S. Geological Survey, to scientific jours., reports and bulls. of Hawaiian Volcano Obs.; also editor of "Volcano Letter." Home: 34 Dowsett Av., Honolulu 17, T.H. Died Jan. 17, 1953.

JALLADE, Louis Eugene (zhȧ-lād'), architect; b. Montreal, Can., Feb. 16, 1876; s. Ettiene and Georgenia (Roger) J.; brought to U.S., 1877, naturalized, 1897; student New York Latin Sch., 1886-92, Met. Museum of Art Schs., 1892-96, Archtl. Ateliers of Beaux Arts Soc., 1896-99, Ecole des Beaux Arts, 1901-03; m. Eugenie M.-L. Pinquet, Feb. 2, 1901; children—Louis Eugene, 2d (dec.), Louis Eugene, 3d, John Henry. Architect, 1904—; asso. with Paul DuBoy, 1904, Allan & Collins, Boston, in charge of construction of Union Theol. Sem., N.Y., 1906; practiced alone, 1906 (designed Naval YMCA, Norfolk, Va., as first commission); tchr. architecture Columbia extension courses, 1906-09; bldg. consultant to nat. bd. YWCA, Soc. of Dirs. of Phys. Edn. in Colls., Playground and Recreation Assn., Russell Sage Found., Boys Club of America; cons. engr. for Dept. of Correction in remodeling Riders Island Penitentiary; dir. Staten Island Investment Service Corp., Upanin Hotels, Inc.; pres. Midridge Realty Corp.; now his 2 sons asso. with him. Works: YMCA bldgs. at Newport, R.I., West Side, New York, Roanoke, Va., Worcester, Mass., Allentown, Pa., McKeesport, Pa., also 124th St. and Lenox Av., N.Y.C., Hartford, Conn., Passaic, N.J., etc.; churches, Flatbush Congl., Bklyn., Broadway, Presbyn., N.Y.C., First Presbyn., Jamaica, N.Y., Mariemont (O.) Community, Metropolitan Temple, New York, etc.; colleges: Women's Coll. at U. Del., Recreation Bldg. at Skidmore, Skidmore Coll., Internat. House, New York, etc.; clubs: Town Hall and Phi Delta Gamma Club of New York, etc.; hospitals: Kings County Hosp., Addition, Red Hook-Gowanus Health Center, Hosp. Addition, Inst. Pediatry, N.Y., Coney Island Bklyn., Outpatient Dispensary Bldg. for Welfare Island, N.Y.C., Luch Hasting Hosp., Manchester, N.H.; also factory bldgs., hotels, garages, residences, schs., libraries, etc. Registered architect Conn., N.Y., N.J., Pa.; cons. engr. in N.Y. Served in N.Y. N.G., 1914-29, in all ranks from pvt. to maj., 11th Inf., and lt. col. 369th Inf.; brig. gen. N.Y. N.G. (ret.). Past pres. N.Y. Soc. Architects; mem. Archtl. League, Beaux Arts Soc., Beaux Art Inst. of Design. Ind. Republican. Episcopalian (former warden). Club: Army and Navy (Washington). Contbr. to profl. mags. Home: 22 E. 36th St. Office: 597 Fifth Av., N.Y.C. Died Feb. 26, 1957.

JAMES, Alfred Farragut, chmn. bd. Northwestern Nat. Ins. Co.; b. New York City, 1868. Dir. Northwestern Nat. Casualty Co., Ensign Ins. Co., Toronto, Dominion Fire Ins. Co., Toronto. Home: 1080 Thorne Lane, Milw. 11. Office: 526 E. Wisconsin Av., Milw. Died June 27, 1959.

JAMES, Alice Archer Sewall, author, artist; b. Glendale, O., 1870; d. Rev. Frank and Thedia (Gilchrist) Sewall; ed. pvtly.; studied in Europe and under Howard Helmick, Washington; m. at Washington, John H. James, 1899. Works have been exhibited in Paris Salon and various American exhbns. Author: An Ode to Girlhood and Other Poems, 1899; The Ballad of the Prince, 1900; The Torch—A Pageant, 1922; The Morning Moon, 1941; A Biography of Frank Sewall, 1952; also poems in magazines. Portraits in oil and pastel, 1930-50; religious murals and altar pieces for Urbana (O.) Chs. since 1946; The Last Supper, travelling altar piece, 1952. Address: care Miss Maud Sewell, 1514 17th St., Washington 6. Died Sept. 20, 1955.

JAMES, Bartlett Burleigh, educator; b. Cecilton, Md., Aug. 6, 1867; s. Edward Cornelius and Eliza (Patterson) James; A.B., Western Md. Coll., 1891, A.M., 1894; B.D., Westminster (Md.) Theol. Sem., 1892; Ph.D., Johns Hopkins, 1897, spl. courses in Dutch, 1894-95, in Tagalog, Arabic, Spanish, biology, botany, geology, 1900-01; grad. courses in psychology, 1911-12, 1913-14; m. Marietta Walsh, Apr. 27, 1898; children—Elizabeth Patterson, James. Entered Meth. Protestant ministry, 1892, ordained 1895; in Congl. ministry, 1898—; mem. Congl. com. of 15 to draft terms of union with Meth. Protestant and U.B. chs., 1903; prof. philosophy, Western Md. Coll., 1902-04; staff lectr. history, Am. Soc. Extension U. Teaching, 1904-05; chief editorial writer Balt. Am., 1905-20, prof. history and polit. sci., Western Md. Coll., 1920-25; prof. history, Am. U., 1925—. Spl. corr. Balt. Sun at various times, 1896-1900; dir. Current Comment, Jewish Ednl. Alliance, 1920-21. Staff lectr. Balt. Club Applied Psychology, 1921-22. Chautauqua lectr., 1923. Composed, pub. many sacred songs, librettos of sacred and children's cantatas. Mem. Am. Hist. Assn., Md. Hist. Soc., etc. Author: The Labadist Colony in Maryland, 1899; The Colonization of New England, 1904; The Revolution (asso. author), 1904; The Women of England, 1907. Editor: McSherry's History of Md., 1904; Jour. of Jasper Danckaerts, 1679-80, edited by Bartlett Burleigh James and J. Franklin Jameson, in Original Narratives of Early Am. History, 1913. Lectr., essayist. Lecture-recitalist. Home: 3617 Idaho Av. N.W., Washington. Died May 16, 1953; buried Washington.

JAMES, Edward Holton, author; b. Prairie du Chien, Wis., Nov. 18, 1873; s. Robertson and Mary Lucinda (Holton) J.; B.A., Harvard, 1896; m. Louisa Cushing, Dec. 27, 1899; children—Olivia (Mrs. Chanler A. Chapman), Mary, Louisa (Mrs. Alexander Calder). Practiced law at Seattle, Wash., 1898-1906; interned in Germany throughout the World War as polit. prisoner. European rep. of Unitarian Fellowship for Social Justice. Author: The Trial Before Pilate, 1909; Jesus for Jews, 1924; Crossroads in Europe, 1931; The Brown Man's Burden, 1931. Home: 26 Lexington Rd., Concord, Mass. Died Oct. 3, 1954.

JAMES, Edwin Leland, journalist; b. Irvington, Va., June 25, 1890; s. Alonzo and Sallie Elizabeth (George) J.; prep. edn., Chesapeake Acad., 1898-1906; A.B., Randolph Macon Coll., 1909; Doctor Humane Letters, Lehigh Univ., Oct. 1941; m. Simone Tremoulet, June 3, 1918; children—Claude, Michel, Monique. Reporter Baltimore Sun, 1910-12. Pittsburgh Dispatch, 1912-13, Albany Knickerbocker Press, 1913-14; with New York Times since Jan. 1, 1915, war corr., 1918-19, Paris corr., 1919-25, chief European corr., 1925-30, asst. mng. editor, 1931-32, mng. editor since Apr. 1932. Mem. Kappa Alpha, Phi Beta Kappa. Comdr. de la Legion d'Honneur and Officier de l'Instruction Publique (France). Methodist. Home: 79 E. 79th St. Office: 229 W. 43d St., N.Y.C. Died Dec. 3, 1951.

JAMES, Fleming, theologian; b. Gambier, O., Jan. 11, 1877; s. Fleming and Mary Ella (Duvall) J.; grad. Episcopal Acad., Phila., 1891; B.A., U. Pa., 1895, M.A., 1896, Ph.D., 1899; grad. Phila. Div. Sch., 1901; D.D., Berkeley Div. Sch., 1926, Theol. Sem., Va., 1941; S.T.D., Phila. Div. Sch., 1942; m. Rebecca Godwin, June 10, 1902; children—Fleming, Margaret Langhorst, Francis Godwin. Ordained deacon, 1901, priest, 1902, P.E. Church; charge St. Andrew's Ch., Phila., 1901-02; charge Am. congregation, Ch. of Our Saviour, Shanghai, China, 1902-06; charge St. Anna's Mission, Phila., 1906-12; rector St. Paul's Ch., Englewood, N.J., 1912-21. St. John's Ch., New Haven, 1932-35; prof. O.T. lit. and interpretation, Berkeley Div. Sch., 1921-40; dean, prof. O.T. Sch. Theology, U. of the South, 1940-47, exec. sec. O.T. sect., Rev. Standard Bible Com., 1947—. Editor Conn. Churchman, 1924-27. Mem. Soc. Bibl. Lit. and Exegesis, Nat. Assn. Bibl. Instrs., Phi Beta Kappa, Beta Theta Pi. Coauthor: The Beginnings of Our Religion, 1935. Author of Thirty Psalmists (Bohlen Lectures, 1936), 1938, and Personalities of the Old Testament (Hale Lectures, 1938), 1939. Home: North Haven, Conn. Died Sept. 11, 1959; buried Reisterstown, Md.

JAMES, Marquis, author; b. Springfield, Mo., Aug. 29, 1891; s. Houstin and Rachel (Marquis) J.; educated public schools of Enid, Oklahoma; m. Bessie Williams Rowland, June 25, 1914 (div.); 1 dau., Cynthia (Mrs. John Hugh Norwood); married 2d, Jacqueline Mary Parsons, Jan. 9, 1954. Began bus. career as reporter Enid (Okla.) Eagle, Kansas City (Mo.) Jour., St. Louis Globe-Democrat, Chicago Inter Ocean, St. Louis Republic, New Orleans Item, etc., 1909-13; copy reader, Chicago Tribune, 1914; asst. city editor Chicago Daily Journal, 1915; rewrite man, N.Y. Tribune, 1916; nat. dir. publicity, Am. Legion, 1919-23; member editorial staff of The New Yorker, 1925, American Legion Monthly, 1923-32. Was 1st lt., later captain infantry, United States Army, 19 mos. with A.E.F., France, 1917-19. Awarded Pulitzer prize for biography, 1930 and 1938. Member National Institute of Arts and Letters, Society of American Historians. Clubs: American Yacht (Rye, N.Y.); Nat. Press (Washington). Author: books including: A History of the American Legion, 1923; The Raven, A Biography of Sam Houston, 1929; Andrew Jackson, The Border Captain, 1933; They Had Their Hour, 1934; Andrew Jackson; Portrait of a President, 1937; Mr. Garner of Texas, 1939; Alfred I. duPont: The Family Rebel, 1941; Biography of a Business, 1791-1942 (a history of Insurance Co. of North America), 1942; The Cherokee Strip, 1945; The Metropolitan Life Insurance Co., 1947; The Texaco Story (history of the Texaco Co.), 1953; Biography of a Bank (with B. R. James), 1954. Contbr. to mags. and radio. Home: Rye, N.Y. Died Nov. 19, 1955; buried Greenwood Union Cemetery, Rye, N.Y.

JAMES, William Carey, clergyman; b. Plantersville, Tex., June 17, 1867; s. William Wellington and Annie Pedelia (Howell) J.; U. Tex., 1886-87; B.A., U. Richmond, Va., 1893, D.D., 1909; Th.D. magna cum laude, So. Bapt. Theol. Sem., 1905; m. Minnie L. Kennedy, June 20, 1894; 1 dau., Margaret Estelle. Prin., supt. schs., Tex., until 1901; instr. Baylor U., 1901-02; ordained Bapt. ministry, 1904; pastor Valley Station, Ky., 1904-05, Russellville, 1905-07, Grove Av. Ch., Richmond, Va., 1907-20; corr. sec. Edn. Bd. So. Bapt. Conv., 1920-24; pres. Bethel Coll., Russellville, Ky., 1924-28; pastor Williamsburs (Va.) Bapt. Ch., 1928-36. Mem. So., Va. Bapt. hist. socs., Beta Theta Pi. Democrat. Home: 2622 Idlewood Av., Richmond, Va. Died Jan. 23, 1958; buried Hollywood Cemetery, Richmond.

JAMES, William M(cGee), lawyer; b. Story City, Ia., May 13, 1901; s. Thomas Carson and Bertha Mahala (McCammon) J.; student U. Ia., 1920-21; LL.B., Chicago Kent Coll. Law, 1925; m. June Bernice Thrumston, Aug. 7, 1926; children—William McGee, John Carson. Admitted to Ill. bar, 1925; member firm Burke, James & Burke, 1934—; chmn. special committee drafted Ill. Probate Act, 1936-40; village attorney, Wilmette, Ill., 1935—; mem. faculty College Kent Coll. Law, 1926-47, v.p. bd. trustees, 1946—; gen. counsel First Fed. Savs. & Loan Assn., Wilmette; spl. asst. to Atty. Gen. U.S., 1954—. Mem. Am. (ho. of dels. 1947-48), Ill. (pres. 1947-48; chmn. sect. probate, trust law 1937-42; bd. govs. 1942-44) and Chicago bar assns., Am. Judicature Soc., Am. Legion, Delta Chi. Methodist. Author: Illinois Probate Procedure and Practice, 1934, Supplement, 1936; Illinois Probate Law and Practice, 1950; also legal articles. Editor-in-chief Ill. Probate Act. Annotated, 1940. Home: 909 Ashland Av., Wilmette, Ill. Office: 100 N. LaSalle St., Chgo. 2. Died Aug. 15, 1957; buried Memorial Park Cemetery.

JAMESON, Robert Willis, corp. official; b. Antrim, N.H., July 23, 1875; s. Nathan C. and Idabel B. (Butler) J.; ed. pub. schs. New York; m. Marie D'Arcy Buck, June 14, 1899; children—Caroline Mixer (Mrs. Joseph H. Currier), Isabel Butler (Mrs. William N. Chace). Began as clerk, 1890; was with Wm. Carroll & Co., New York, 1901-17; treas. and chmn. bd. Dominion Stores, Ltd., Canada, 1919-29; began with United Cigar Stores, 1929, pres., 1933-36; now dir. United Stores Corp., The Best Foods, Inc., Lorr Laboratories, Wilsil, Ltd. (Can.); chmn. exec. com., dir. McLellan Stores Company, McCrory Stores Corporation. Served with American Red Cross, overseas, 1918-19. Member Sons of Revolution. Democrat. Presbyterian. Mason. Home: Antrim, N.H. Office: 1107 Broadway, New York, N.Y. Died April 11, 1953.

JAMESON, Russell Parsons, educator; b. Mansfield, O., Jan. 5, 1878; s. Charles Bentley and Sarah (Parsons) J.; Ph.B., Oberlin (O.) Coll., 1900, A.M., 1906; D.L., U. Paris, 1911; post grad., Harvard and U. Paris; m. Florence Heath, Feb. 16, 1901; 1 dau., Marjorie Ruth (Mrs. Giulio C. Nardella). Began as library and club dir. Phelps, Dodge & Co. Mining Camp, Morenci, Ariz., 1900; instr., athletic coach, Oberlin Coll., 1904, instr. French and phys. edn., 1905, asso. prof. Romance langs., 1910-20, prof., head dept., 1920-44, prof. emeritus, 1944—; research on French history and Voltaire;

summer sessions courses, Ind. U., Western Res. U., Middlebury French Sch.; conducted extensive European tours (Temple Tours); lectr. Decorated Chevalier Legion of Honor. Mem. Nat. Commn. Cooperative Curriculum Planning; adv. mem. State Com. Evaluative Criteria. Mem. Modern Lang. Assn., Am. Assn. Tchrs. French, Council Am. Assn. U. Profs., Modern Lang. Sect. O. Coll. Assn. (past pres.), O. Council Modern Lang. Teaching, Tchrs. Central W. and S. (past pres.), Phi Beta Kappa. Republican. Conglist. Clubs: Philologues, Social Sciences, University (Winter Park, Fla.). Author: Montesquieu et l'Esclavage, 1911; Le Cercle Francais, 1932. Editor: Chants de France (with A. E. Heacox), 1922; Rire et Sourire, 1925. Home: 162 S. Cedar Av., Oberlin, O. and 539½ Chapman Av., Winter Park, Fla. Died June 2, 1954; buried Oberlin, O.

JAMIESON, Francis Anthony, newspaperman; b. Trenton, N.J., Nov. 8, 1904; s. William Michael and Mary Ellen (Crawford) J.; grad. Trenton (N.J.) High Sch., 1921; m. Charlotte Wiggin, Jan. 31, 1931; 1 dau., Joan Ellen (Mrs. Alexander Zucker); m. 2d, Linda Eder, December 5, 1940; 2 daus., Margaret, Frances. Legislative corr. Standard News Association, Jersey Observer, 1922-28; reporter, Trenton N.J. and N.Y. burs., Asso. Press, 1929-35; John Price Jones Corp., N.Y.C., 1935-40; pub. adviser, election campaign of Gov. Charles Edison (N.J.), 1940; with Office Coordinator of Inter-Am. Affairs, 1940-46; acting dir., 1945-46; associate Rockefeller Brothers; dir. Government Affairs Foundn., Inc. Internat. Basic Economy Corp. & Am. Internat. Assn., Econ., Social Development. Trustee Jackson Hole Preserve, Inc. Awarded Pulitzer prize for reporting, 1933. Mem. Century Assn. Club: National Press (Washington), Overseas Press. Home: 522 E. 86th St. Office: Room 5600, 30 Rockefeller Plaza, N.Y.C. Died Jan. 30, 1960.

JANE, Robert Stephen, indsl. chemist; b. Cornwall, Eng., Dec. 27, 1898; s. Alfred S. and Katherine (Hoskin) J.; B.A.Sc., U. B.C., Vancouver, 1922; M.Sc., McGill U., 1923, Ph.D., 1925; Wembley scholar U. London, 1925-27; D.Sc., honoris causa, McGill Univ., 1958; m. Ada Lois Pirie, Aug. 3, 1928; children—Dorothy Katherine, Margaret Frances. Plant chemist, later mem. plant research dept. Canada Carbide Co., Shawinigan Falls, Que., 1927-36 (merged with Shawinigan Chemicals, Ltd., wholly owned subsidiary of Shawinigan Water & Power Co.); research and development dept. Shawinigan Chemicals, Ltd., Montreal, 1936-43, v.p. charge research and development, 1946-54, dir., 1946—, exec. v.p., 1954-56, pres., 1956—; charge indsl. research dept. Shawinigan Water & Power Co., 1943-46, director, 1956—; president, director of the B.A.-Shawinigan, Limited, Montreal, St. Maurice Chemicals, Ltd., Montreal; vice pres., dir. Canadian Resins & Chemicals, Ltd., Montreal; dir. Shawinigan Products Corp. (N.Y.), Shawinigan Resins Corp. (Springfield, Mass.), Gelvatex Coatings Corp. (Anaheim, Cal.), Hedon Chemicals, Ltd. (Hull, Eng.). Dir. YMCA, Montreal. Fellow Chem. Inst. Can. (pres. 1952-53); mem. Soc. Chem. Industry (chmn. Montreal sect. 1941-42), Compressed Gas Mfg. Assn. Home: 6 Holmdale Rd., Hampstead, Que. Office: 600 Dorchester St. W., Montreal, Can. Died 1958.

JANIS, Elsie, actress; b. Columbus, O.; d. John E. and Janis E. Bierbower; descendant on paternal side from ancestors arriving in America in 1747 and who helped to build the first blockade at York, Pa., and fought under Washington; educated by private governess and teachers; m. Gilbert Wilson, Dec. 31, 1931. First appearance on state as Cain, in The Charity Ball, 1897; played vaudeville, 1898-1903; starred in The Belle of New York, 1904; later appeared in The Fortune Teller and The Duchess; starred in The Vanderbilt Cup, 1906-08; later starred under mgmt. of Chas. B. Dillingham, in The Hoyden, Fair Co-ed, and Slim Princess; starred in Elsie Janis and Her Gang (written by herself). Mem. D.A.R. Home: 614 N. Bedford Drive, Beverly Hills, Cal. Died Feb. 1956.

JANSEN, Ernest George, South African govt. ofcl. Rep. from Vryheid, Parliament of Union of South Africa, 1922-43, from Wolmaransstad, 1947; speaker of House, 1924-29, 1933-43; minister native affairs, 1929, 1948-50; gov. gen. Union of South Africa, 1950—. Address: Pretoria, Union of South Africa. Died Nov. 25, 1959.

JAQUA, Albert Roscoe (Bert), ednl. adminstr.; b. Reinbeck, Ia., Sept. 27, 1893; s. Albert and Mary Jane (Watson) J.; student Grinnell Coll., 1912-14; B.S., Ia. State Coll., 1917; m. Hildegarde Boudreau, Sept. 23, 1924 (dec. 1942); children—Denise (Mrs. S. J. Whitman), A. Richard; m. 2d, Esther Clark Reese, 1946. Salesman, 1923-28; editor ins. publs., 1928-45; dir. Ins. Inst., Purdue U., 1945-46, So. Meth. U., 1946—. Speaker UN and Atlantic Union. Served as 2d lt. AC, U.S. Army, 1917. C.L.U. Mem. Nat. Assn. Life Underwriters. Unitarian. Author: Basic Life Insurance, 1951; Formula Programming, 1955. Compiler tng. courses. Home: 6020 Swiss St., Dallas. Died June 16, 1957.

JAQUES, Charles Everett, mfr.; b. Chgo., Dec. 24, 1873; s. Frank F. and Abbie L. (Everett) J.; student Chgo. Manual Tng. Sch.; m. Annie C. Champlin, Aug. 9, 1899; children—Hallie M., Annie Laurie. Began with F. F. Jaques & Co., Kansas City, Mo., mfrs. K.C. baking powder; on organization, 1891, of Jaques Mfg. Co., became dir. and treas., and in 1895 moved to Chicago, in charge of Chgo. br., now the main office and factory of the co. Commd. by President Wilson maj. in Q.M. Corps, U.S.R., Oct. 30, 1916; on active duty at Plattsburg, N.Y., 1917; lt. col., U.S. Army, 1918-19; hon. discharged June 1919; now col., O.R.C. Republican. Mason (32°, K.T., Shriner). Home: 6314 Sheridan Rd., Chgo. Died 1955.

JARDINE, James Tertius (jär'dīn), agriculturist; b. Cherry Creek, Oneida County, Ida., Nov. 28, 1881; s. William and Rebecca (Dudley) J.; grad. Utah Agrl. Coll., 1905; studied U. of Chicago, summers 1905, 06; D.Sc. (hon.), Kansas Agrl. Coll., 1935; D.Sc. (hon.), Clemson Agrl. College, 1937; D.Sc. (hon.), Utah Agrl. College, 1946; married Gladys E. Carroon, Aug. 19, 1922; 1 son, James Carroon. Instr. in English, Utah Agrl. Coll., 1905-07; spl. agt. U.S. Forest Service, 1907-08; dep. forest supervisor, 1908-10; insp. grazing, in charge Nat. Forest Range, investigations and range surveys, 1910-20; dir. Ore. Agrl. Expt. Sta., 1920-31; insp. secretary's office, Dept. of Agr., Washington, D.C., June-Aug. 1924, insp. agrl. expt. stas. in Alaska; specialist in research, U.S. Office of Education, Dec.-Feb., 1927-28, and Sept. 1929-Mar. 1930; chief Office of Experiment Stations, U.S. Dept. Agr. 1931-46 (ret); dir. research, Dept. Agr., 1936-41. Special lecturer Yale Univ., 1914-16. Delegate Nat. Agrl. Conf., Jan. 1922. Fellow A.A.A.S.; mem. Washington Acad. Science, Phi Kappa Phi, Sigma Xi, Lambda Chi Alpha, Gamma Sigma Delta. Presbyterian. Club: Cosmos. Home: 4334 P St. N.W., Washington. Died Oct. 24, 1954; buried Logan, Utah.

JARDINE, John Earle, business exec.; b. N.Y. City, Dec. 7, 1871; s. John and Mary Elizabeth (Earle) J.; ed. private schs., N.Y. State; m. Mary C. Peck, Sept. 14, 1893 (dec.); m. 2d, Josephine Mary Christie, Sept. 16, 1952. Pres., gen. mgr., Pasadena (Calif.) Orange Growers Assn., 1902-03; v.p. William R. Staats Co., 1904, pres. 1920-47, chmn. bd., 1947 (co. became partnership, 1951, titled William R. Staats & Co.), partner, 1951—; director Consolidated Liquidating Corp., Union Oil Co. of Calif., Calif. Consumers Corp., Pacific Finance Corp., Calif. Inst. Associates. Trustee Southwest Museum; mem. finance com. Huntington Memorial Hosp. Mem. Soc. Colonial Wars, S.A.R. Clubs: California, Valley Hunt, Newport Harbor Yacht, Stock Exchange of Los Angeles. Home: 1445 S. Los Robles Av., Pasadena 5. Office: 640 S. Spring St., Los Angeles 14. Died Mar. 16, 1956; buried San Gabriel (Cal.) Cemetery.

JARDINE, William M., educator, ex-sec. of agriculture; b. Oneida County, Ida., Jan. 16, 1879; s. William and Rebecca J.; B.S. in agr., Agrl. Coll. of Utah, 1904; student, Grad. Sch. U. of Illinois, summer, 1906; LL.D., Agrl. College of Utah, 1925, Lafayette College, 1927, Kansas State College, 1938; m. Effie Nebeker, Sept. 6, 1905; children—William N., Marian, Ruth. Lived and worked on ranches, Ida. and Mont., until 20 yrs. of age; asst. dept. of agronomy, 1904, instr., 1905, prof., 1905, 06, Agrl. Coll. of Utah; asst. U.S. cerealist in charge of dry land grain investigations, 1907-10; agronomist Kan. State Agrl. Coll. and Expt. Sta., July 1910; lecturer Grad. Sch. of Agr., Mich. Agrl. Coll., 1912; acting dir. of Expt. Sta. and dean of agr., Jan. 1-Apr. 1, 1913, dir. of Expt. Sta. and dean of agr., 1913-18, and pres. 1918-25, Kan. State Agrl. Coll.; sec. of agriculture of U.S., 1925-29; E.E. and M.P. to Egypt, 1930-33; state treas. of Kansas, 1933-34; pres. of Municipal U., Wichita, Kan., 1934-49, emeritus since 1949. Pub. interest dir. Federal Home Loan Bank of Topeka; mem., Federal Savings and Loan Advisory Council; mem. bd. of dirs., National Safety Council. Council Federated Fruit and Vegetable Growers, Inc.; chmn. bd. Investment Corp. of America. Member and chairman agrl. production com. Kan. State Council Defense, 1917; pres. Internat. Dry-Farming Congress and Soil Products Expn., 1915-16, Am. Soc. Agronomy, 1916-17; mem. exec. bd. Nat. Research Council; adv. council Agrl. Commn. of Am. Bankers' Assn.; mem. President's Agrl. Conf. Fellow Am. Assn. Advancement of Sci.; mem. Am. Forestry Assn. (v.p.), Washington Acad. Sci., Kansas Acad. of Sci., Mass. Hort. Soc. Mem. Sigma Xi, Beta Theta Pi, Alpha Zeta, Phi Kappa Phi, Gamma Sigma Delta, Scabbard and Blade. Congregationalist. Mason. Rotarian. Club: Wichita Country (Wichita). Author of numerous papers and bulletins on farming, crop production, cooperative marketing and other phases of agriculture, economics and education. Owns and operates farms in Kansas and Idaho. Home: 408 Pike Rd., San Antonio. Died Jan. 17, 1955.

JARMAN, Lewis Wilson, coll. pres.; b. Covington, Ga., Aug. 10, 1880; s. Lewis Wilson and Mary (Loyd) J.; B.A., Emory Coll., 1899, M.A., 1901; graduate student Columbia University, 1925; LL.D., Hampden-Sydney (Va.) Coll., 1930; m. Laura Harris Martin, Dec. 25, 1903; children—Mary Isabel (wife of John English Nelson, U.S. Army), Margaret Loyd (Mrs. Margaret Jarman Hagood), Lewis Wilson, Jr. (U.S. Army), Laura Martin (Mrs. Rodolfo O. Rivera), Edward Boyce (USN), Alice Frances (USN), Mrs. Walter Gordon Browder). Prof. mathematics, Granbury (Tex.) Coll., 1899-1901, acting pres., 1901; farming and banking, Covington, 1903-23; prof. mathematics and astronomy, Chicora Coll., Columbia, S.C., 1924-27; prof. mathematics summers, Furman U.; v.p. Queens Coll., Charlotte, N.C., 1927-29; pres. Mary Baldwin Coll. 1929-46, pres. emeritus, 1946—. Mem. Phi Delta Theta, Phi Beta Kappa, Omicron Delta Kappa. Democrat. Presbyn. Kiwanian. Home: 905 Garden Dr., Garden Acres, Winter Park, Fla. Died Sept. 28, 1957; buried Palm Cemetery, Winter Park.

JARMAN, Pete, ex-ambassador; b. Greensboro, Ala., Oct. 31, 1892; s. Peter Bryant and Hunter Elizabeth (Gordon) J.; student So. Univ., Greensboro, Ala., 1907-11; A.B., U. of Ala., 1913; certificate, U. of Montpelier (France), 1919; LL.D., University of Melbourne, 1952; married Beryl Bricken, February 25, 1930. Chief clk. in Probate Office, Sumter (Ala.) County, 1913-17; asst. examiner of accounts State of Ala., 1919-31; sec. of State of Ala., 1931-35; asst. comptroller State of Ala., 1935-37; mem. 75th to 80th Congresses (1937-49), from 6th Ala. District; A.E. and P. of U.S. to Australia, 1949-53. Served as 2d lt., later 1st, 327th Inf., A.E.F., U.S. Army, World War; maj. Ala. N.G., 1922-24, lt. col., 1924-40. Mem. Am. Legion (comdr. dept. of Ala., 1927-28). Vets. of Foreign Wars, D.A.V.; Mil. Order of World War, Forty and Eight, Sigma Alpha Epsilon; Skulls, Key Ice (U. of Ala.). Democrat. Methodist. Mason. Home: Livingston, Ala. Died Feb. 17, 1955; buried Arlington Nat. Cemetery.

JARMAN, Sanderford, army officer (ret.); b. Boatner, La., Nov. 24, 1884; s. James Sanderford and Emily Amanda (Tullos) J.; student La. State U., 1901-04; B.S., U.S. Mil. Acad., 1908; m. Dorothy Donald, Apr. 20, 1910; children—Katharine Lea (Mrs. E. E. Clark, Jr.), Dorothy Schuyler (wife of Harvey Jablonsky. U.S. Army). Commd. 2d lt., C.A.C., U.S. Army, Feb. 14, 1908, and advanced through the grades to maj. gen., Oct. 1940; served as maj. of field arty. and lt. col. of coast arty. during World War I; mem. Gen. Staff, 1934-38; became comdr. 64th Coast Arty., Hawaii; organized and commanded Coast Artillery and Anti-aircraft Command, Panama Canal Zone, 1939-41; comdg. gen., Camp Stewart, Ga., Sept.-Dec. 1941, anti-aircraft Arty. Command, Eastern Defense Command, Dec. 1941-44, Saipan, 1944-45; ret., 1945. Decorated D.S.M. with 2 oak-leaf clusters (U.S. Army), D.S.M. (USN), Legion of Merit. Mason. Club: Army and Navy (Washington). Address: 3915 Oliver St., Chevy Chase, Md. Died Oct. 15, 1954.

JARRETT, William Ambrose, dean; b. Fiskdale, Mass., Dec. 3, 1886; s. Thomas Patrick and Hannah Sarah (Monahan) J.; Pharm.D., Mass. Coll. Pharmacy, 1913; B.S., Duquesne U., 1932; grad. work Duquesne U., 1933-35, Creighton U., 1936-37; married Alice Rooney, September 26, 1917; children—Betty Agnes (Mother Betty Jarrett, R.S.C.J.), Elinor Margaret (Mrs. Leo James Zents), Jane Mary (Mrs. Paul C. McGrath). Professor pharmacy and head dept., University of Maine, 1913-18, pharmaceutical research, Boston, 1918-20; owner retail pharmacy, Springfield, Mass., 1920-27; prof. pharmacy, U. of Fla., 1927-28, Conn. Coll. Pharmacy, 1928-29; prof. and head dept., Duquesne U., 1929-35; dean Coll. of Pharmacy, Creighton U., since 1935. Mem. Am. Pharmaceutical Assn., Neb. Pharm. Assn., Rho Chi, Phi Delta Chi, Omaha Chamber of Commerce. Contbr. numerous professional and ednl. articles. Home: 3918 Cass St., Omaha, Neb. Died Jan. 26, 1958; buried Calvary Cemetery, Omaha.

JASSPON, William Henry, business exec.; b. Charlotte, N.C., June 18, 1888; s. Max and Annie (Wolf) J.; ed. pub. schs. of Charlotte, N.C.; m. Ethel R. Reed, July 25, 1911; 1 dau., Miriam. Began career with Southern Cotton Oil Co., Charlotte, N.C., 1904-17; established own company, Memphis, Tenn., pres. Perkins Oil Co., Memphis, Tenn. since 1934, dir. since 1920. dir. (trustee) Univ. of Tenn. Research Corp. Knoxville, Tenn. Chmn. Fats, Oils and Feeds Com., Internat. Emergency Food Council, Washington, D.C., since 1943; director Fats and Oils Branch, Department Agr., Washington, D.C., June 1942-46. Mem. Memphis, Tenn. Bridge Commn. Home: 410 James Rd., R.F.D. 3. Office: 727 Beale St., Memphis, Tenn. Died May 6, 1951.

JASTRAM, Edward Perkins, (jăs'trăm), lawyer; b. Providence, R.I., Oct. 1, 1873; s. Pardon Sheldon and Julia Adie (Brown) J.; A.B., Brown, 1895; LL.B., Harvard Law Sch., 1898; m. Laura N. Whitney, Oct. 11, 1904; children—Edward P., Jr., Philip S. Admitted to R.I. bar, 1898, and since practiced in Providence; mem. Edwards & Angell, 1903—. Mem. R.I. Bar Assn. Republican. Unitarian. Clubs: University, R.I. Country, Agawam Hunt, Hope. Home: 104 Prospect St. Office: 15 Westminster St., Providence. Died July 22, 1954.

JASZI, Oscar (yä'sē), professor of political science; born in Nagy-Károly, Hungary, March 2, 1875; s. Francis (M.D.) and Rosa (Liebermann) J.; prep. education, pub. school and gymnasium, Nagy-Károly; Ph.D., U. of Budapest, 1896; m. Recha A. Wollmann-Rundt, Aug. 23, 1923; children—George, Andrew. Came to U.S., 1925, naturalized citizen, 1931. Official, State Dept. Agr., Hungary, 1898-1908; editor Twentieth Century (social science review), 1901-18; asst. prof. polit. science, U. of Kolozsvar, 1912-18; prof., U. of Budapest, 1918-19; minister for nat. minorities, Hungary, 1918-19; prof. polit. science Oberlin (O.) Coll., 1925-42, now retired. Visiting professor at Clark University, 1944-46. Member American Polit. Science Assn., American Historical Association; v.p. Soc. of Sociology (Budapest), 1913-18. Author: The State Philosophy of Historical Materialism (in Hungarian), 1903; Art and Morality (in Hungarian), 1904; Evolution of the Nation-States, 1912; Der Zusammenbruch des Dualismus, 1918; Revolution and Counter-Revolution in Hungary, 1924; Introductory Essays to Engelmann's Political Philosophy (with Karl F. Geiser), 1927; The Dissolution of the Hapsburg Monarchy, 1929; Propaganda and Dictatorship (co-author), 1936; Refugees (co-author), 1939; The City of Man, A Declaration on World Democracy (co-author), 1940; Czechoslovakia, Twenty Years of Independence (co-author) 1940; Democracy Is Different (co-author), 1941; Toward International Organization (co-author), 1942; Regionalism and World Organization (co-author), 1944; (with John D. Lewis) Against the Tyrant; Tradition and Theory of Tyrannicide, 1957. Editor La Hongrie Contemporaine, 1909. Contributor articles to The Nation, Foreign Affairs, The Yale Review, Slavonic Review, Social Research, The New Leader, Jour. of Central European Affairs, Freedom and Union and Encyclopedia of Social Sciences, also review, criticism, etc., to European periodicals. Home: 131 Forest St., Oberlin, O. Died Feb. 13, 1957.

JAY, Clarence Hollingsworth, petroleum exec.; b. St. Marys, O., July 21, 1886; s. Daniel Webster and Belle (Hollingsworth) J.; student Culver Mil. Acad., Univ. Sch., Cleve.; m. Queen I. Sutphen, Dec. 19, 1931; children—Robert Webster, Ann (Mrs. Gilbert G. Sykes), Patricia (Mrs. A. Guthrie Curtis). With Pure Oil Co. and Pure Transportation Co., Chgo., 1903—, sec. and treas., 1930—. Clubs: South Shore Country, Illinois Athletic, Sky-Line. Home: 675 N. Michigan Av., Chgo. 11. Office: 35 E. Wacker Dr., Chgo. 1. Died May 1957.

JAY, Mary Rutherfurd, landscape architect, author, lectr.; b. Fair Haven, Conn., Aug. 16, 1872; d. Rev. Peter Augustus and Julia (Post) Jay; archtl. study, Mass. Inst. Tech., 1906, Bussey Inst., Forest Hills, Mass., 1907. In practice of landscape architecture, N.Y.C., 1908—; landscape work in estates of Hon. George W. Wickersham, W. A. Rockefeller, I. N. Phelps-Stokes, Henry R. Mallory and others. Mem. Am. Com. for Devastated France, charge unit of famerettes working with U.S. Army Garden Service, Versailles, June 1918; with A.R.C., 1918-19. Fellow Royal Hort. Soc., London; mem. N.Y. Hort. Soc., Garden Club Am., Garden Club Orange and Dutchess Counties. Decorated Cross of Mercy (Serbia); silver medal (Am. Com. for Devastated France). Republican. Episcopalian. Club: Cosmopolitan. Author: The Garden Handbook, 1931; The Jay Family, a genealogical chart with over 900 names, 1935. Lectr. Royal Hort. Soc., Phila., Forum, Bklyn. Art Mus., garden clubs, etc. Home: "Rutherfurd Lodge," Drum Hill, Wilton, Conn. Address: 200 E. 78th St., N.Y.C. 21. Died Oct. 1953.

JEANMARD, Jules Benjamin, bishop; b. Breaux Bridge, La., Aug. 15, 1879; s. Jules and Frances Maria (Brown) J.; ed. St. Joseph's Sem. (Gessen, La.), Holy Cross Coll. (New Orleans), Kenrick Sem. (St. Louis), St. Louis Sem. (New Orleans). Ordained priest R.C. Ch., June 11, 1903; asst. at St. Louis Cathedral, New Orleans, 1903-06; sec. to archbishop of New Orleans, 1906-14; vicar gen. and chancellor Archdiocese of New Orleans, 1914-17; administrator Archdiocese of New Orleans, 1917-18; administrator newly erected diocese of Lafayette, La., Jan.-June 1918; apptd. 1st bishop of Lafayette, July 18, 1918; consecrated Dec. 8, 1918, and took possession of See, Dec. 12, 1918; ret. as bishop of Lafayette, Mar. 13, 1956; apptd. titular bishop of Bareta, Mar. 21, 1956; asst. to Pontificial Throne, Oct. 2, 1943. Decorated Comdr. de l'Ordre de la Legion d'Honneur (France). Address: 505 Cathedral St., P.O. Box 1126, Lafayette, La. Died Feb. 23, 1957; buried St. John's Cathedral, Lafayette.

JEANS, Philip Charles, prof. pediatrics; b. Hillsboro, O., Jan. 3, 1883; s. Frank Hibben and Anna Mary (Stafford) J.; A.B., U. Kan., 1904; M.D., Johns Hopkins, 1909; m. Grace Whittier Cushing, Dec. 22; 1914; 1 son, Robert Philip. Intern seven hosps., 1909-13; successively asst., instr., asso. prof. pediatrics Washington U., St. Louis, 1913-24; prof. and head pediatrics U. Ia., 1924-52, prof. emeritus, 1952. Midwest cons. on nutrition Pub. Health Service. Mem. com. Revision U.S. Pharmacopeia, 1951; mem. Steering com. and vice-chmn. food and nutrition bd., Nat. Research Council; mem. sci. adv. com. Nutrition Found., Inc. Fellow A.M.A. (mem. council on foods and nutrition since 1930, chmn. 1952), Am. Pediatric Soc. (governing council 8 yrs., pres. 1950-51); mem. Soc. for Exptl. Biol. and Med., Am. Inst. Nutrition, Soc. for Research in Child Development, Soc. for Pediatric Research, Nu Sigma Nu, Alpha Omega Alpha, Sigma Xi. Author: (with J. V. Cooke) Prepubescent Syphillis, 1930; (with W. Rand) Essentials of Pediatrics, 1934 (rev. edit. with W. Rand and F. Blake, 1946); Infant Nutrition (with W. M. Marriott) 1941 (rev. edit. 1947). Contbr. to many tech. articles. Sent to S.E. Europe 1921-22 by Red Cross for rehabilitation work with children; to Hawaii 1950 by U.S. P.H.S. for lectures on nutrition; to Central Am. 1952 by W.H.O. as nutrition consultant for Inst. Nutrition Central Am. and Panama. Home: 209 Black Springs Circle, Iowa City, Ia. Died Panama City, Oct. 22, 1952; buried Iowa City Cemetery.

JEFFERS, Henry William; b. Harford, Pa., Jan. 4, 1871; s. Watson and Betsey Milburn (Oakley) J.; grad. Wyoming Sem., Kingston, Pa., 1894; B.S., Cornell U., 1899; M.S. (hon.), Rutgers U., N.J. Agrl. Coll., 1927; m. Anna C. Adams, July 14, 1898; children—Emily Adams, Watson (dec.), Henry W., Louise E. Mgr. Walker-Gordon Lab. Co., 1898-1918, pres., 1918—; dir. First Nat. Bank, Princeton, N.J. Mem. adv. bds., U.S. Dept. Agr. and U.S. Food Adminstrn., World War; mem. N.J. State Bd. of Agr., 1916-27. Pres. Bd. Regents, N.J.; mem. bd. mgrs. N.J. Reformatory. Chmn. N.J. Rep. State Com., 1935-37. Conglist. Mason (32°, K.T., Shriner). Inventor of Jeffers bacteriology counter, Jeffers feed calculator, Rotolator. Home: Plainsboro, N.J. Died July 17, 1953.

JEFFERS, Katharine R(osetta), educator; b. California, Pa., Mar. 19, 1907; d. Samuel Allen and Anna Frances (Crabbs) Jeffers; B.A., U. Mo., 1927, M.A., 1928; Ph.D., Bryn Mawr Coll., 1932; student U. Berlin, 1929-30. Nat. Research fellow McGill U., 1933-34; instr. zoology Duke, 1937, asst. prof. zoology, 1939-47; dean of women, asso. prof. biology Coll. William and Mary, 1947-52; dean, prof. biology Jackson Coll., Tufts U., 1952—. Mem. Am. Soc. Zoologists, American Association Anatomists, National Assn. Deans Women, Am. Association U. Women, Phi Beta Kappa, Sigma Xi. Home: 72 Professors Row, Medford 55, Mass. Died May 15, 1959.

JEFFERS, William Martin, ry. official; b. North Platte, Neb., Jan. 2, 1876; s. William and Elizabeth (Gannon) J.; student high sch.; LL.D., Franklin and Marshall Coll., 1937, Creighton U., 1938, U. Wyo., 1939, Coll. of Idaho, 1941, Notre Dame U., 1942, Loyola U., Los Angeles, 1947; m. Lena A. Schatz, June 1900 (dec. Apr. 9, 1946); 1 dau., Eileen Kelliher Jeffers. Began as call boy U.P. R.R., 1890, successively clk. in operating and maintenance of way depts., agt. and telegrapher until 1898, train dispatcher, 1898-1900, chief dispatcher, 1900-05, trainmaster, 1905-08, asst. supt. Utah div., 1908-09, supt. Utah div., 1909-12, supt. Wyo. div., 1912-15, Neb. div., 1915, gen. supt., 1915-16, gen. mgr., 1916-28, v.p. operation, 1928-32, exec. v.p., 1932-37, pres., 1937-46, vice chmn. bd. dirs., Mar. 1946-Jan. 1953. Rubber dir. U.S. Govt., 1942-43. Knight of Malta. Club: California (Los Angeles). Home: Shamrock Cottage, Huntington Hotel, Pasadena, Cal. Office: Union Pacific Bldg., 422 W. 6th St., Los Angeles. Died Mar. 6, 1953.

JEFFERY, William Prentiss, lawyer; b. Brooklyn, N.Y., Feb. 24, 1878; s. Reuben and Emma (Lord) J.; student Denison U., 1896-98, N.Y. Law Sch., 1898-1900; m. Idelle Scott, Feb. 2, 1918; children—William Prentiss, Scott Wellington, Carleton, Janet Idelle. Admitted to N.Y. bar, 1901, and since practicing at New York; now member of Jeffery and Murray; director Container Corp. of America. Served as capt., later maj., Ordnance Dept., U.S. Army, World War. Formerly dir. and pres. Greenwich Country Day Sch. Formerly trustee Greenwich (Conn.) Acad. Mem. Am. Bar Assn., Assn. of Bar City of N.Y., Beta Theta Pi. Republican. Episcopalian. Clubs: Round Hill, Field (Greenwich). Home: 155 E. 72d St. Office: 50 Broadway, N.Y.C. 4. Deceased.

JEFFERYS, Charles William, artist; b. Rochester, Eng., Aug. 25, 1869; s. Charles Thomas and Ellen (Kennard) J.; student pub. schs., Toronto; LL.D., Queens U., Kingston, Ont.; m. Jean Adams (dec. 1899); m. 2d, Clara West, 1907 (dec. 1937); children—Mrs. C. A. Thompson, Mrs. E. Helm, Mrs. G. A. Fee, Mrs. H. Stacey, Mrs. O. W. Allen. Artist, N.Y. Herald, 1892-1900; Toronto Star, 1902-08; instr. in drawing and painting Sch. of Architecture, U. Toronto, 1909-32. Executed murals in Chateau Laurier (Ottawa), Manoir Richelieu (Murray Bay), Royal Ontario Museum (Toronto). Exhibited: Ontario Soc. of Artists, Royal Canadian Acad. of Arts, Canadian Soc. of Painters in Water Color, Graphic Arts Soc., Pa. Acad. of Fine Arts, Am. Water Color Soc., N.Y. Water Color Club. Represented in permanent collections of Nat. Gallery of Canada, Art Gallery of Toronto, and other pub. galleries. Hist. consultant on reconstruction of Habitation of Port Royal, N.S., of 1605, by Dominion Govt., 1938-39. Former pres. Graphic Arts Club, Can. Soc. Painters in Water Colors, Ont., Soc. of Artists, Royal Canadian Acad. of Arts, Arts and Letters Club (Toronto). Author: Dramatic Episodes in Canada's Story, 1930; Canada's Past in Pictures, 1934; The Picture Gallery of Canadian History, Vol. I (with T. W. McLean), 1942, Vol. II, 1945, Vol. III, 1950. Illustrator: Chronicles of Canada, Chronicles of America (asso. editor), Pageant of America. Contbr. of articles on history to various publs. Home: York Mills, Ont., Can. Died Oct. 8, 1951; buried St. John's Ch. Cemetery, York Mills.

JEFFRIES, Edward J., mayor; b. Detroit, Apr. 3, 1900; s. Edward J. and Minnie (Stotts) J.; A.B., U. Mich., 1920, LL.B., 1923; student Lincoln's Inn, London, Eng., 1923-24; m. Florence Bell, Jan. 24, 1930. Admitted to Mich. bar, 1923, and began practice in Detroit, 1924; gen. counsel The Maccabees, Detroit, 1929—. Mem. Common Council of Detroit, 1932-40; pres., 1938-40; mayor City of Detroit, Jan. 1940—. Mem. Delta Theta Phi. Clubs: Detroit Athletic, Detroit Golf. Home: 19241 Afton Rd., Detroit 3. Office: City Hall; and the Maccabees, 5057 Woodward Av., Detroit. Died Apr. 2, 1950.*

JEFFRIES, Walter Sooy, congressman; b. Atlantic City, N.J., Oct. 16, 1893; grad. Atlantic City Bus. Coll., 1909. Pres. Hotel Runneymede, Atlantic City. Mayor of Margate City, N.J., 1931-35; sheriff of Atlantic County, N.J., 1935-38; mem. 76th Congress, 2d N.J. Dist. Republican. Home: Margate, Atlantic City, N.J. Died Oct. 11, 1954; buried Laurel Meml. Park, Atlantic City.

JEFFS, Charles Richardson, naval officer; b. Bklyn., Jan. 20, 1893; s. Charles Frederick and Eliza (Boulton) J.; student Naval Acad. Post Grad. Sch., 1926-27; M.Sc., Columbia, 1928; m. Harriet Herring, Apr. 30, 1918; children—Charles R. (ensign U.S. Navy), Thomas Lee, Harriet Elizabeth. Entered U.S. Navy, 1911, commd. ensign, 1918, and advanced through grades to commodore, U.S.N., 1946; destroyer duty, U.S.S. Cushing, World War I; submarine service, 1922-31; asst. engr. then engr. officer battleship California, 1933-36; machinery supt., Mare Island Navy Yard, 1933-37; Yangtze patrol gunboats, 1938-41; staff Naval War Coll., 1942-43; comd. U.S.S. Appalachian, Guam, Leyte, Lingayen, 1944-45; dep. comdr. Naval Forces, Germany Land (State), Bremen, 1948-49; ret. as Rear Admiral, 1950; land commr. Bremen under High Commr. and Dept. of State, 1949—. Episcopalian. Home: 8186 San Gabriel Av., South Gate, Calif. Office: Deputy dir. Mil. Government Land Bremen, Bremen, Germany (A.P.O. 751). Died Oct. 1959.

JELKE, Ferdinand Frazier, internat. investment banker; b. Charleston, Ill., Feb. 5, 1886; s. John Faris and Louanna (Frazier) J.; student Phillips Acad., Andover, Mass., 1904; Ph.B., Yale, 1908; m. Clara Bartholomay June 19, 1907 (divorced Nov. 4, 1910); 1 son, Frazier Bartholomay; m. 2d, Eugenia Woodward, Dec. 19, 1930 (divorced May 24, 1934). Mem. New York Stock Exchange since 1919; sr. mem. Frazier Jelke & Co., internat. investment bankers, New York, London, Amsterdam and Toronto since 1919; pres. and dir. Comml. Chem. Co. since 1929; past vice pres. and dir. John F. Jelke Co.; past pres. and dir. George P. Braun & Co.; dir. Am.-Hawaiian Steamship Co.; past dir. Continental Nat. Bank & Trust Co. Enlisted U.S. Marine Corps, 1917; commd. 2d lt., 1918; attached to Am. Liaison Service under Col. Herman H. Harjes; attached to staff of French Lt. Gen. de L'Espee, comdg. 5th Mil. Region at Orleans. Decorated Chevalier Legion d'Honneur (French). Founded Frazier Jelke Foundation, Inc. (charitable orgn.), 1943, and since served as pres. and trustee. Past vice pres. and dir. Alliance Francais (N.Y.). Mem. Am. Soc. French Legion of Honor, Inc. (dir.). Mem. Soc. Colonial Wars, S.A.R., Soc. War of 1812, Mil. Order Fgn. Wars. Clubs: Racquet and Tennis, Turf and Field (New York); all Newport, R.I. clubs. Author: Letters from a Liaison Officer (pvt. pub.), 1919; An American at Large, 1947. Home: Eagle's Nest, Newport, R.I. Died Aug. 30, 1953.

JELLINGHAUS, C. L., ret. r.r. exec.; born New York, N.Y., Nov. 23, 1889; s. Adolph and Therese (Urchs) J.; ed., Friends Sem., New York, 1897-1903; Coll. of City of New York, prep., 1903-05, coll., 1905-07; m. Miriam Butler, Sept. 5, 1918; children—Barbara (Mrs. Orlando Scoppettone), C. Butler. Yard clerk, Long Island R.R., 1913; clerk New York Central R.R., 1914-16, office of gen. mgr., 1916-17, sec. v.p., 1917-18, spl. agt. Buffalo div., 1918-22, N.Y. terminal dist., 1922-23, insp. freight transportation, 1923-26, asst. to supt. property protection, 1926-36, supt., 1936-39, exec. sec. to pres., 1939-40, asst. to pres., 1940-44, mgr. freight transportation, 1944-46, v.p., gen. mgr., 1946-49, v.p. Detroit, resident v.p., asst. to pres., 1950, now ret.; dir., Great Lakes Engring. Works. Mem. Newcomen Soc. of England, Alpha Delta Phi. Clubs: Detroit Athletic, Traffic, (Detroit). Home: Bearsville, N.Y. Died Oct. 8, 1957.

JEMISON, David Vivian, clergyman; b. Marion, Ala., 1875; s. Perry and Tyresa (Carlyle) J.; D.D., Selma U., 1915, LL.D., 1937; m. Henrietta Phillips, June 18, 1902; children—David Vivian, E. Maurine, Irma Louise, Richie Pauline, Theodore Judson, Earl Lloyd. Ordained to ministry, Bapt. Ch.; pastor Tabernacle Ch., Selma, 1903-29, 36—; pastor St. Louis St. Ch., 1929-36. Pres. Ala. Bapt. Conv., 1916; pres. Nat. Bapt. Conv. U.S.A., 1940. Mem. Civic League. Democrat. Mason. Author: The Deplorable Conditions of the Visible Church, The Cause and The Remedy, 1931; The Minister and His Message, 1935. Home: 1605 Lapsley St., Selma, Ala. Died Feb. 20, 1954; buried Selma.

JENKINS, Alfred Alexander, Jr., bus. exec.; b. Cleve., Apr. 28, 1899; s. Alfred Alexander and Annabell (Hitchcock) J.; A.B., Western Res. U., 1923; m. Ruth Weber, Mar. 14, 1929; children—Sue, James. With ore dept. M. A. Hanna Co., 1927-29, salesman coal dept., 1929-35, asst. sales mgr., 1935-41, sales mgr., 1941-43, v.p. in charge sales, 1943-46; v.p. in charge sales Ohio coal div. Pitts. Consolidation Coal Co. since 1946. Served as pvt., U.S. Army, World War I. Mem. Cleve. Engineering Society, Phi Gamma Delta. Mason. Clubs: Westwood Country, Clifton (Cleve.); Ft. Henry (Wheeling, W.Va.). Home: 17829 Lake Rd., Lakewood 7, O. Office: Leader Bldg., Cleve. 14. Died June 13, 1959.

JENKINS, Charles Francis, publisher; b. Norristown, Pa., Dec. 17, 1865; s. Howard M. and Mary Anna (Atkinson) J.; ed. public schools; hon. A.M., Swarthmore Coll. (Pa.), 1926; hon. LL.D., Haverford Coll. (Pa.), 1938; U. of Pa., 1944; m. Maria G., d. Edward Cope, Feb. 12, 1890; children—Algernon Sidney, Mrs. Newlin T. Booth, C. Francis, Edward Cope. Pub. since 1883; chmn. Farm Journal, Inc.; dir. Provident Trust Co.; chmn. bd. Buck Hill Falls Co.; v.p. Deemer Steel Casting Co. Mem. bd. mgrs. Swarthmore Coll.; pres. bd. Ellis Coll. Mem. adv. com. Pa. Hosp.; mem. Pa. Museum, Jeanes Found. for Cancer Research. Pres. Fuel Savings Soc., Grandom Instn., Abolition Soc.; hon. pres. Germantown History Soc.; hon. mem. Phi Beta Kappa. Mem. Franklin Inst., John Bartram Assn. (mem. bd.), Am. Acad. Polit. and Social Sci., Am. Philos. Soc., English Speaking Union (v.p. Phila. branch since 1927), Soc. Am. Historians, Hist. Soc. of Pa. (councillor 1930-36; v.p. 1936-43; pres. since 1943), Friends Hist. Assn. (pres. 1928-35), (English) Friends Hist. Soc. (pres. 1922), N.Y. Bucks County, Chester County and Montgomery County Hist. Socs., Colonial Soc. Pa. (councillor 1919-21), Transatlantic Soc. Am. (pres. 1922-27), Geneal. Soc. Pa. (v.p. 1929-41). Clubs: Union League, Franklin Inn (Philadelphia). Mem. Soc. of Friends. Author: Quaker Poems, a collection of verse relating to the Society of Friends, 1893; Guide Book to Historic Germantown, 1902; Washington in Germantown, 1905; Jefferson's Germantown Letters, 1906; Lafayette's Visit to Germantown, 1911; Tortola, 1923; Button Gwinnett—Signer of the Declaration, 1926. Established Hemlock Arboretum, "Far Country," 1931. Home: "Far Country," Kitchen's Lane, Germantown 19, Philadelphia. Office: 230 W. Washington Square, Philadelphia 5. Died July 2, 1951; buried Upper Duhlin Friends Burial Ground, Ft. Washington, Pa.

JENKINS, C(laudius) Bissell, officer corps.; b. Summerville, S.C., June 3, 1865; s. Septimus Hamilton and Annie Manson (Gautier) J.; ed. Rockville Sch., Wadmawlaw Island, S.C.; m. Lula Thomas, June 25, 1889; 1 son, River T. Gen. mgr. Cameron & Barkley Co. at 20, vp. at 22, pres., 1898—; organizer Gen. Asbestos & Rubber Co., 1901, also pres. Formerly maj. Charleston Militia. Mem. Huguenot Soc. Am., N.E. Soc., S.C. Hist. Soc., St. Cecilia Soc., etc. Democrat. Presbyn. Mason. Clubs: Carolina Yacht, Wappoo Country. Home: 52 Boulevard. Office: 27 Cumberland St., Charleston, S.C. Died Jan. 21, 1940.

JENKINS, David Rhys, prof. elec. engring.; b. nr. Dover, N.J., Sept. 1, 1865; s. John Rhys and Mary (Griffith) J.; student Kan. State Agrl. Coll., 1881-83; B.S., in E.E., U. of Colo., 1904, E.E., 1907; m. Kate Belle Gordon, Aug. 12, 1892; children—Jane May (Mrs. Alfred C. Buck), Gordon Rhys. Teacher common schs. of Kan., 1883-86; editor, pub. newspaper at mining camp, Colo., 1891-96; prin. high sch., Coal Creek, Colo., 1896-1900; instr. in elec. engring., U. of Colo., 1905-08, asst. prof., 1908-19; became prof. elec. engring., Univ. of N.D., now retired. Mem. Am. Inst. E.E., Illuminating Engring. Soc., Inst. Radio Engrs., Soc. for Promotion Engring. Edn., A.A.A.S., Am. Assn. Univ. Profs., N.D. Soc. Engrs., Sigma Xi, Sigma Tau. Republican. Congregationalist. Mason. Club: Lions. Home: McDonald, Kan. Died Sept. 24, 1949; buried Grace Cemetery, McDonald.

JENKINS, J(ames) Caldwell, lawyer and steamship executive; b. Atlanta, Georgia, May 31, 1883; s. Judge James Caldwell and Susie (Scruggs) J.; g.s. Hon. William L. Scruggs, who served as U.S. minister to China, Venezuela and Colombia; LL.B., Georgetown U., 1914; m. Betty Maxey Chiles, Jan. 31, 1917; 1 dau., Betty. In U.S. Service, P.I., 1905-10; dir. of industrial relations and operations, U.S. Shipping Bd., 1918-26; v.p. U.S. Shipping Bd. Merchant Fleet Corp., 1926-31; v.p. Black Diamond Steamship Corp. and active in affairs of Am. Steamship Owners' Assn., 1931-37 (chmn. shipping information com.); chmn. N.R.A. Code Com.; mem. Labor Com., Legislation Com., Shipbuilding Wage Adjustment Com., Naviagation Laws Revision Com., President's Economic Liaison Com., President's Com. on Merchant Marine. Republican. Episcopalian. Author of several books and articles on industrial relations. Home: 3307 Cleveland Av. N.W., Washington 8, D.C.; also "Catoctin Farm," Waterford, Va. Died Oct. 28, 1956.

JENKINS, John Murray, ret. army officer; b. York, S.C., Nov. 5, 1863; s. Micah and Caroline Harper (Jamison) J.; grad. U.S. Mil. Acad., 1887, U.S. Inf. and Cav. Sch., Ft. Leavenworth, Kan., 1891; m. Lucretia Dwinelle Flower, Nov. 30, 1916. Commd. 2d lt. 5th Cav., 1887; promoted through grades to maj. gen., 1927; now ret. With Punitive Expdn., Mexico, 1916; organized and comd. trains, 2d Div., AEF; insp. 42d div. and 6th Corps; in campaigns, Champagne-Marne, Aisne-Marne, St. Mihiel; comd. 30th Inf., Meuse-Arganne (gassed); comd. 11th Cav., 1920-23; insp. gen., 1923. Decorated D.S.C. (U.S.) for extraordinary heroism in action near Cunel, France, Oct. 14, 1918; La Solidaridad (2d Class). Episcopalian. Home: The Dresden, 2126 Connecticut Av., Washington. Died Apr. 30, 1958; buried Arlington Nat. Cemetery.

JENKINS, Perry Wilson; b. Mt. Carmel, Ind., Apr. 5, 1867; s. Wilson Ragsdale and Susan (Smith) J.; A.B., Miami U., Oxford, O., 1890, A.M., 1891; student Ohio Law Sch., 1891; A.M., Columbia, 1900; fellow in astronomy, U. of Chicago, 1904-05; LL.D. (hon.), University of Wyoming, 1955; m. Eva C. Smith, June 24, 1897; children—Miriam A. (Mrs. Norman W. Barlow), Lois E., Helen V. (Mrs. John S. Kvenild), Ruth E. (Mrs. R. W. Wilson). Professor of mathematics, Tennessee Military Academy, Sweetwater, 1892-93, Amity College, College Springs, Iowa, 1893-96; professor of mathematics and astronomy Simpson Coll., Indianola, Ia., 1896-99; prof. applied mathematics and dir. Underwood Obs., Lawrence U., Appleton, Wis., 1900-04; irrigation engr. since 1905, ranchman, cattle raiser since 1908. Exec. mgr Green River Basin Development Co., Inc. Mem. Pub. Service Commn., World War I. Mem. Wyo. Ho. of Rep., 1919-25, Wyo. State Senate, 1929 (pres.); mem. Com. on Conservation and Administration of Pub. Domain (U.S.), 1929-32; pres. Wyo. Reclamation Assn., 1933-40; v.p. Nat. Reclamation Assn., 1933; v.p. Wyo. State Planning and Water Conservation Board, 1939; mem. Colo. River Commn., 1936-40, Named and founded Sublette County, Wyo. Originator of The Producer, nat. livestock mag., 1919. Awarded the Bishop medal "for meritorious public service," Miami U., 1940. Mem. Soc. Am. Engrs., Nat. Econ. League, Am. Nat. Livestock Assn., Nat. St. Lawrence Assn. (regional v.p. since 1946), Colo. River Water Users Assn. (pres. 1946), S.A.R. (pres. Utah soc., 1943), Phi Beta Kappa (life mem. of associates), Delta Kappa Epsilon. Republican. Presbyterian. Mason (32°); mem. Order Eastern Star. Contbr. tech. articles to mags. and newspapers. Home: Cora, Wyo. Office: 40 Virginia St., Salt Lake City 3. Died June 19, 1955; buried Pinedale, Wyo.

JENKINS, Thomas Albert, ex-congressman; b. Jackson County, O., Oct. 28, 1880; s. Samuel E. and Ann (Harris) J.; B.Sc., Providence U., Oak Hill, O., 1901; LL.B., Ohio State U., 1907; m. Mabel Wynne, Jan. 19, 1909. Admitted to Ohio bar, 1907 and began practice at Ironton; pros. atty. Lawrence County, O., 1916-20; mem. Ohio State Senate, 1922-24; mem. 69th to 85th Congresses, 10th Dist., Ohio; mem. Ways and Means Com. and Joint Com. on Atomic Energy; mem. Rep. Policy Com. for Ho. of Reps. Home: Ironton, O. Died Dec. 21, 1959.

JENKINS, Vernon Henry, ins. exec.; b. Wadsworth, Nev., Feb. 12, 1887; s. William and Maryann Alice (Eldred) J.; student Poly. Bus. Coll., Oakland, Calif., 1905-06; m. Emily Enloe Brierly, Dec. 18, 1909; children—Marion Elizabeth, Gordon Vernon. Co-owner and mgr. creamery, Bishop, Calif., 1906-09. of confectionery store, 1909-14; with Occidental Life Ins. Co. of Calif., Los Angeles, since 1914, salesman, 1914-21, field supervisor, 1921-24, co-mgr. home office agency, 1924-27, v.p. charge prodn., dir., 1931-46, sr. v.p., dir., 1946-51. vice chmn. bd. dirs. since 1951; v.p. Americommercial Corp., Bank of Am., Citizens Savs. and Comml. Bank of Alhambra, also pres. Union Brokerage Co., 1927-31. Mem. Health and Accident Underwriters Conf. (executive com.), Los Angeles Life Underwriters Assn. (pres. 1925). Mason. Clubs: Kiwanis (pres. 1925-26, Alhambra); San Gabriel (Cal.) Country; Athletic (Los Angeles); Commercial (San Francisco); Union League (Chicago). Home: 207 S. El Molino St., Alhambra, Cal. Office: 1151 S. Broadway, L.A. 54. Died Feb. 25, 1952; buried San Gabriel, Cal.

JENKINS, William J., coal co. exec.; b. Chicago, Feb. 5, 1873; s. William T. and Mary Jane (Voice) J.; ed. pub. schs., pvt. instrn.; m. Lilly Ellen Shoudy, Dec. 11, 1895; 1 son, Gerald Stuart. Asst. to gen. mgr. N.W. Improvement Co., Roslyn, Wash., 1896-1903; with Western Coal & Mining Co., Ill., Ark., Kan., Mo., Okla., 1903-13, gen. mgr., 1910-13; fuel agt. M.P.R.R. Co., 1903; with The Consol. Coal Co., St. Louis, since 1913, pres., gen. mgr. since 1922, The Consol. Power Co., Jefferson Oil & Gas Corp., Jefferson Southwestern R.R. Co.; chmn. bd. Mutual Bank & Trust Co. Mem. Am. Inst. Mining and Metall. Engrs., Am. Mining Congress, Nat. Coal Assn. Office: 716 Locust St., St. Louis 1. Died Jan. 12, 1953.

JENKINS, William Leroy, educator; b. Newark, Apr. 14, 1898; s. Edward Ephraim and Mary Booth (Gamewell) J.; B.S. in Chemistry, Bklyn. Poly. Inst., 1921; M.A., U. Mich., 1932, Ph.D., 1936; m. Lois Chichester, Apr. 12, 1926; children—Barbara Joan, Richard Bruce. Instr. Lehigh U., Bethlehem, Pa., 1935-38, asst. prof. 1939-45, asso. prof. 1946-47, prof. psychology, 1947—, head dept. psychology, 1955—. Fellow Am. Psychol. Assn.; mem. Am. Statis. Assn., A.A.A.S., Sigma Xi. Home: 1441 New Jersey Av., Hellertown, Pa. Office: Lehigh U., Bethlehem, Pa. Died July 25, 1957; buried Hellertown Union Cemetery, Hellertown, Pa.

JENKS, Albert Ernest, anthropologist; b. Ionia, Mich., Nov. 28, 1869; s. Stillman Leek and Sophia Parnell (Keeny) J.; B.S., Kalamazoo Coll., 1896; B.S., U. of Chicago, 1897; Ph.D., U. of Wis., 1899; Sc.D., Kalamazoo Coll., 1924; m. Maud Huntley, October 22, 1901 (deceased, June 1, 1950); 1 son, Clifford Huntley (deceased). Began career as economic editor Am. Thresherman, 1900-01; asst. ethnologist, 1901, ethnologist, 1902, Bur. Am. Ethnology, Washington; asst. chief Bur. Non-Christian Tribes, Manila, P.I., 1902; chief Ethnol. Survey P.I. (new name for Bur. Non-Christian Tribes), 1903-05; chief ethnol. dept., Philippine exhbn. of St. Louis Expn., 1904; asst. prof. of sociology, U. of Minn., 1906-07, prof. anthropology, 1907-38, chmn. Dept. Sociology and Anthropology, 1915-18, dir. Americanization training course, 1918-23, chmn. dept. anthropology, 1918-38, dir. archeological research fund, 1929-38, prof. of anthropology emeritus since 1938. Mem. Nat. Research Council, 1922-25 (chairman division anthropology and psychology 1923-24); lecturer University of California, Southern Branch, summers 1923, 25. Gold medalist La. Purchase Expn.; gold medal of honor from Philippine Govt. for ethnol. work. Investigation U.S. desert Indians, 1913-14, African desert Berber, Kabyl, Arab, 1914; visited European anthrop. collections and studied southern and eastern European emigration at its sources, 1914; spl. investigation ethnic amalgamation (Ojibwa Indian-White), 1915; studied methods of racial research, and prehistoric culture sites, in Europe, 1925; researches prehistoric Mimbres culture, New Mexico, summers 1928, 29, 31; researches prehistoric cultures northern Africa and Europe, spring and summer 1930; researches in prehistory of Minnesota and the Dakotas during 7 summers, 1932-38. Fellow A.A.A.S. (v.p., chmn. sect. H, anthropology, 1919-21); mem. Am. Anthropological Assn., American Genetic Assn., Society of Mayflower Descendants, Sigma Xi, Phi Sigma Kappa. Clubs: Six O'Clock, Campus. Baptist. Author: The Childhood of Jishib, the Ojibwa, 1900; The Wild Rice Gatherers of the Upper Lakes, 1901; The Bontoc Igorot, 1905; Ba-long-long, the Igorot Boy, 1907; Present Conditions and Future Needs of the Science of Anthropology (with W. H. R. Rivers and S. G. Morley), 1913; Indian-White Amalgamation, 1916; Chart of Prehistoric Man and Culture, 1927; Pleistocene Man in Minnesota, a Fossil Homo Sapiens, 1936; Minnesota's Browns Valley Man and Asso. Burial Artifacts, 1937; Sauk Valley Skeleton (with L. A. Wilford), 1938; (foreword in) Death Stalks the Philippine Wilds (Mand Huntley Jenks), 1951; contbr. to publs. Home: R.F.D. 1, Linden Shore, Mound, Minn. Office: Dept. of Anthropology, Ford Hall, U. of Minn., Mpls. 14. Died June 6, 1953; buried Lakewood Cemetery, Mpls.

JENKS, Orrin Roe, clergyman, educator; b. Rockford, Minn., Jan. 1, 1868; s. Cyrus Chase and Adelaide Margaret (Roe) J.; student U. Minn., 1892-93; B.D., Chgo. Theol. Sem., 1905; A.B., Mendota (Ill.) Coll., 1906; B.D., Divinity Sch. U. Chgo., 1908; D.D., Aurora (Ill.) Coll., 1920; m. Minnie Troxel, of Fort Ripley, Minn., Apr. 2, 1890 (died May 1897); children—Ethel Miriam (wife of Rev. Stanley Perry), Robert Wendell (dec.), Paul Stockman (dec.); m. 2d, Emma Minnie Dennin, Sept. 14, 1898; children—Ruth Dennin (Mrs. Chester M. Kearney), Margaret Prudence (Mrs. J. Allison Binford), Helen Marr (Mrs. Donald G. Lockward). Ordained to ministry of Advent Christian Church, 1885; pastor Fort Ripley, Minn., 1885-88, Magnolia, Wis., 1888-90, Sparta, Wis., 1890-92, Mpls., 1892-1900, Chicago, 1900-10; prin., theol. dept. Mendota Coll., 1894-1911; pres. Aurora (Ill.) Coll., 1911-33, pres. emeritus 1933—. Pres. Advent Christian Gen. Conf. of America, 1916-20. Asso. editor Our Hope, 1891-92; editor Gleams of the Morning, 1894-1901; western corr. World's Crisis, Boston, 1900-08; v.p. Ill. Federation of Colls., 1927-28, pres., 1928-29; midwest corr. Messiah's Advocate, Oakland, Cal., 1931—. Club: Union League (Aurora). Author: The Life and Times of Amos and Isaiah, 1908; The Last Prophets of Israel, 1909; Syllabus of the Life and Times of Jeremiah. Home: 231 Calumet Av., Aurora, Ill. Died June 17, 1951.

JENKS, William Jackson, ry. official; b. Wake County, N.C., Mar. 21, 1870; s. William S. and Retta (Baucom) J.; ed. pub. and pvt. schs.; m. Sallie C. Baldwin, 1891; children—Virginia Kyle (Mrs. P. D. Woods), Alice Retta (Mrs. H. S. Birchfield, dec.), Jack. Began ry. service as telegrapher, 1886; with N.&W. Ry. Co., 1887-1901; trainmaster and supt. S.A.L. Ry., 1901-08; with N.&W. Ry., 1908-—, chmn. car allotment commn., 1908-12, supt. and gen. supt., 1912-18, gen. mgr., 1918-24, v.p. in charge of operation, 1924-36, pres., 1936-46, chmn. of bd., 1946-54, director; dir. Virginia Holding Corp., Pocahontas Land Corporation, Winston-Salem Southbound Ry. Co., Frist Nat. Exchange Bank (Roanoke, Va.). Episcopalian. Clubs: Rotary, Shenandoah, Roanoke Country. Home: 2744 Jefferson St. S.E. Office: Norfolk & Western Ry. Co., Roanoke, Va. Died Jan. 17, 1960.

JENNINGS, David, merchant; b. Charleston, S.C., Mar. 1, 1882; s. Henry Burritt and Martha Glen (Reeves) J.; B.S., Clemson (S.C.) Coll.. 1902; m. Adelaide Gaston, Sept. 25, 1907; children—David (dec.), Adelaide Lee (dec.), Gaston. Operator of or selling agent for Textile Mills, 1907-—; mem. firm Reeves, Jennings & Co., selling agents, N.Y.C., 1919-20; pres. Aragon-Baldwin Cotton Mills, Chester, Rock Hill and Whitmire, S.C., 1929-30; asso. with 1921-49, and former dir. J. P. Stevens & Co., Inc., dry goods mchts., N.Y.C.; past dir. Marion Mfg. Co. (N.C.). Mem. So. Soc. of N.Y.C. Democrat. Episcopalian. Clubs: Princeton, Merchants, Arkwright (N. Y.C.); Siwanoy Country (Bronxville). Home: 21 Sagamore Rd., Bronxville, N.Y. Office: 44 Leonard St., N.Y.C. Died Feb. 17, 1955.

JENNINGS, John, Jr., lawyer; b. Jacksboro, Tenn., June 6, 1880; s. John and Julia (Forrester) J.; student Am. Temperance U., Harriman, Tenn., 1898-1900; B.S., U.S. Grant U., Athens, Tenn., 1902; m. Pearnie Ethel Hamby, Sept. 16, 1906; children—Ethel (Mrs. Martin S. Coykendall), Katherine (Mrs. Nowland Van Powell), Helen. Sch. tchr., 1897-1902; private practice, 1903-18, 1923-—; county supt. pub. instrn., Campbell County, Tenn., 1903-04, county atty., 1911-18; asst. atty. gen., U.S. Land Title Div., 1911-13; Chancellor 2d Chancery Div. Tenn., 1918-23; in practice law 1903-18, 22-—; mem. Jennings, O'Neil & Jarvis, Knoxville, 1930-—. Elected to 76th Congress, 2d Tenn. Dist., Dec. 1939, to fill unexpired term of J. Will Taylor, mem. 76th to 81st Congresses. Del. Rep. Nat. Convs. 1912, 36, 44. Mem. Am., Knox County, Tenn. bar assns. Republican. Bapt. Mason, Elk, Jr. Order Am. Mechanics. Home: 3945 Kingston Pike, S.W. Office: Mercantile Bldg., Knoxville, Tenn. Died Feb. 26, 1956; buried Highland Meml. Cemetery, Knoxville.

JENNINGS, Rudolph D., physician; b. Fremont, O., Nov. 21, 1852; attended Cornell Coll., Iowa.; received med. edn. at Chgo. Homoeo. Med. Coll. (1889), and at Kings Coll., London, England. Medical director and a member of The Dakota Springs Co. at Hot Springs, S. Dak., for 10 years; pres. and supt. S. Dak. State Bd. Health. Address: Hot Springs, S. Dak. Died July 10, 1916.

JENNINGS, Samuel Clemens, business exec.; b. Hillsboro, Tex., Jan. 28, 1867; s. Fountain Edward Pitts and Mary Jane (Ellis) J.; student pub. schs. Eureka Springs, Ark.; m. Louise May de Clercq, Aug. 1, 1894. With Western Bank Note Co., Chicago, Ill., 1891-1903; treasurer, and director Columbia Bank Note Company, Chicago, 1905-11, pres. 1911-45. Trustee University of Chicago. Republican. Baptist. Clubs: Union League (Chicago); Westmoreland Golf (Glenview, Ill.). Home: 2951 Grant St., Evanston, Ill. Office: 500 S. Ashland Av., Chicago, Ill. Died Dec. 23, 1952.

JENSEN, Elmer C., architect; b. Chgo., Mar. 18, 1870; s. John and Sabine (Petersen) J.; student pub. schs., also Art Inst. Chgo., 2 yrs.; m. Mary D. Nagel, June 27, 1900; 1 son, John C. Has been connected with office of the late William LeB. Jenney (who gained distinction by bldg. first skelton constrn. bldg. in America, Home Ins. Bldg., Chgo., 1884-85), 1885-—; grew up in business under Mr. Jenney and just prior to his death, 1907, organized, with M. B. Mundie, the firm of Jenney, Mundie & Jensen, firm name changed to Mundie & Jensen, 1913, to Mundie, Jensen, Bourke & Havens, 1936 to Mundie & Jensen, May 1, 1944, to Mundie, Jensen & McClurg, Apr. 1, 1946. Fellow A.I.A. (past pres. Chgo. chpt.); mem. Ill. Soc. Architects (pres. 1933-39), Chicago Bldg. Congress (pres. 1939). Republican. Episcopalian. Clubs: Cliff Dwellers, Union League. Office: 39 S. La Salle St., Chgo. Died Apr. 24, 1955.

JENSEN, Jens, landscape architect; b. Denmark, Sept. 13, 1860; s. Christian and Magdalen Sofia (Petersen) J.; ed. Agrl. Coll., Jutland, Denmark; Litt.D., U. of Wis., 1937; m. Anne M. Hansen, 1884 (died Nov. 4, 1934). Came to U.S., 1884; supt. Union and other small city parks, of the West Park System, Chicago, 1890-94; supt. Humboldt Park, 1894-1900; landscape architect and gen. supt. West Park System, 1906-09; cons. landscape architect same, 1909-20; pres. The "Clearing" (school), Ellison Bay, Wis.; mem. Chicago Special Park Commn., 1902-12, Chicago Met. Park Commn., 1903-04. Pres. Friends of Our Native Landscape; governing mem. Art Inst. Chicago (life); sec. Illinois Art Commn., 1906-14. Mem. Art Commn., Chicago; fellow A.A.A.S.; mem. Ill. Acad. Science. Club: Cliff Dwellers. Wrote: State Park and Forest Policy for Illinois; Landscape Report of Forest Preserves for Chicago, Ill.; Siftings; The Clearing. Address: The "Clearing," Ellison Bay, Wis. Died Oct. 1, 1951.

JENSEN, Johannes V(ilhelm), Danish writer; born Jutland, Jan. 20, 1873; s. Hans and Marie Jensen; Ph.D., U. of Copenhagen; Dr. Honoris Causa, U. of Lund, Sweden, 1929. Author of between 60 and 70 volumes, including novels, poetry and essays, since 1896. Awarded Nobel prize, 1944. Home: Kastelsvej 23, Copenhagen, Denmark. Died Nov. 25, 1950.

JENSEN, John Christian, educator; b. Utica, Neb., Oct. 19, 1880; s. Frantz Peter and Ellen (Jensen) J.; B.Sc., Neb. Wesleyan U., 1909; A.M., U. Neb., 1916, Ph.D., 1939; student U. Ia., summer 1916, U. Chgo., summer, 1921; m. Susan E. Allington, Aug. 25, 1909 (died Dec. 26, 1918); children—Robert Roderick, Margaret Ruth; m. 2d, Emma Wilhelmsen, Aug. 22, 1922. Instr. physics, Neb. Wesleyan U., 1907-09. prof., 1909-52, prof. physics and astronomy, 1939-—, dean men, 1934-36, 38-46; prin. Acad. Neb. Wesleyan U., 1939-43; vis. prof. Cornell Coll., 1952-53, Doane Coll., 1955-56. Registered profl. engr. Chief radio instr. War Tng. Unit, U. Neb., 1918; coordinator Civil Aeros. Adminstrn., Neb. Wesleyan U., 1939-43; research cons. Curtiss-Wright Corp., 1943-45. Fellow A.A.A.S., Inst. Radio Engrs. (rep. council A.A.A.S.), Am. Phys. Soc.; mem. Am. Geophysical Union, Am. Meteorol. Soc., Neb. Acad. Sci. (twice pres.), Inst. Radio Engrs., Am. Assn. U. Profs., Am. Optical Soc., Am. Interprofl. Inst., Sigma Xi, Sigma Pi Sigma, Phi Kappa Phi. Republican. Methodist. Has published research reports on relation of weather to radio reception, polarity of thunderclouds, ball lightning, and precipitation from local thunderstorms. Home: 4926 Leighton Av., Lincoln, Neb. Died Oct. 19, 1957; buried Wyuka Cemetery, Lincoln.

JENTE, Richard (jĕn'tē), univ. prof.; b. New Haven, Conn., Apr. 14, 1888; s. J. P. Hermann and Helene (Emmerich) J.; A. B., Yale Coll., 1910; M.A., Yale U., 1911; student U. of Jena, Germany, 1913-14; Ph.D., magna cum laude, U. of Heidelberg, 1917; m. Frances Augusta Hucke, Aug. 27, 1925; children—Richard Charles, Katherine Elizabeth. Instr. in German, Yale U., 1911-13, U. of Minn., 1917-18, and 1919-22, Washington U., 1922-23; asst. Prof., Washington U., 1923-27, asso. prof., 1927-37, acting head of dept., 1936-37; prof. of Germanic langs. and literatures, and head of dept. of German, Univ. of N.C., since 1937; visiting lecturer, U. of Chicago, summer, 1927. Translator for Com. on Pub. Information, Washington, D.C., 1918. Mem. Modern Lang. Assn., Linguistic Soc. of Am., South Atlantic Modern Lang. Assn., Am. Assn. of Teachers of German, Am. Folklore Soc., Alpha Sigma Phi. Protestant. Author: Die mythologischen Ausdrücke im altenglischen Wortschatz, 1921; Complete College German (with Erich P. Hofacker), 1939; German Composition and Conversation (in collaboration), 1943; Proverbia Communia, A Fifteenth Century Collection of Dutch Proverbs, 1943; Asso. editor of Studies in Philology; editor U. of N.C. Studies in Germanic Langs. and Lits. Pres. Am. Assn. of Teachers of German, 1945. Delta Phi Alpha (national vice-pres., 1943-46). Contbr. monogaphs and articles on proverb lore. Home: 2 Westwood Drive, Chapel Hill, N.C. Died Aug. 22, 1952, buried Chapel Hill, N.C.

JEPSON, Harry B(enjamin), educator; born New Haven, Aug. 16, 1870; s. Benjamin and Mary Louise (Wiswell) J.; A.B., Yale, 1893, Mus.B., 1895, A.M. (hon.), 1903; Mus.D., Colgate U., 1936; studied in Paris with Charles Widor and Alexander Guilmant; m. Mabel Preston Wyatt, Aug. 1, 1895. Mem. faculty Yale since 1895, prof. applied music and univ. organist emeritus 1939. Dir. Yale bur. U. Union, Paris, World War I. Clubs: Graduates, Elizabethan, Elihu, St. Wilfred. Author: University Hymns with tunes arranged for men's voices, cantata for men's voices, compositions for orchestra and many organ pieces including 3 sonatas. Home: New Haven. Office: Yale University, also 2d Nat. Bank, New Haven. Died Aug. 23, 1952.

JERNIGAN, Charlton C(oney), coll. pres.; born Dunn, N.C., Sept. 24, 1904; s. Bradley and Sarah (Giles) J.; A.B., Duke U., 1925, A.M., 1926 (univ. fellow in classics), Ph.D., 1935; student U. of Chicago, 1928-30; m. Margaret Ledbetter, Aug. 17, 1940; children—John Charles, Jerry Wyche. Head of English and Greek depts. Rutherford (N.C.), Coll., 1926-28; teaching asst. in English, U. of Chicago, 1928-30; univ. fellow in Greek, Duke U., 1930-33, instr. in Greek, 1933-35; prof. and head dept. of classics Woman's Coll., U. of N.C., 1935-49; head dept. of classics Fla. State U., 1949-51; pres. Queens Coll., Charlotte, N.C., since 1951. Member American Philol. Assn., Classical Assn. of Middle West and South, Am. Dialect Soc., Phi Beta Kappa. Democrat. Presbyterian. Mason (32°). Author: Comic Incongruity in Aristophanes, 1939. Contbr. various book revs. on classical scholarship in South Atlantic Quar. Address: 2300 Radcliffe Av., Charlotte, N.C. Died July 22, 1953; buried Sharon Meml. Cemetery, Charlotte.

JEROME, Brother (John B. Roese) (rōz), coll. pres.; b. Jamaica, N.Y., Oct. 17, 1896; s. John B. and Jeanette (Emerton) R.; B.A., St. John's U., 1929, M.A., 1931; LL.D., St. Bernardine of Siena Coll., 1952. Entered Franciscan Brothers, 1914; tchr. elementary schs., 1916-17; faculty St. Francis Prep. Sch., 1917-25, prin., 1925-35; prof. English St. Francis Coll., 1935, dean, 1936-43, 1949-52, pres. since 1952; gen. consultor Franciscan Brothers, 1928-43, superior gen., 1943-49. Trustee St. Francis Coll. since 1934, St. Francis Monastery since 1942. Mem. Nat. Cath. Ednl. Assn. K.C. Home: 41 Butler St., Bklyn. 31. Died June 1959.

JESSE, Richard Henry, coll. dean; b. Princess Anne, Md., Jan. 4, 1884; s. Richard Henry and Addie Henry (Polk) J.; A.B., U. of Mo., 1902; M.A., Harvard, 1907, Ph.D., 1909; m. Margaret Lucille Leyda; children—Richard Henry, William Leyda, Mary Margaret. Teaching fellow in chem., Harvard, 1908-09; instr. chemistry, U. of Ill., 1909-12, asso., 1912; prof. chemistry, U. of Mont., since 1912, dean of men, 1918-24, dean of faculty, 1924-45 and dean College Arts and Sciences, 1936-45, vice pres. since 1945. Member Am. Chem. Soc., Phi Beta Kappa, Sigma Xi, Phi Delta Theta. Democrat. Episcopalian. Rotarian. Contbr. chem. publs. Home: 610 University Av., Missoula, Mont. Died Dec. 23, 1955; buried Missoula.

JESSUP, Joseph John, civil engr.; b. New Providence, Ia., Dec. 18, 1856; s. Elias and Mary Jane (Morris) J.; grad. New Providence Acad., 1886; B.S., Penn Coll., Oskaloosa, Ia., 1891, M.S., 1892; post grad., U. Cal., 1900-02; m. Melissa Hammar, Aug. 23, 1892; children—Mildred, John Herschel, Mary Helen. Prof. mathematics and sci., Pacific Coll., Ore., 1891-96; pres. Whittier (Cal.) Coll., 1896-1900; instr. U. Cal., 1900-03; dep. city engr., Berkeley, 1903-08, city engr., 1908-18, cons. engr., 1918-30; city engr., Los Angeles, 1930-34; cons. civil and mining engr., 1934-57. Mem. (life) Am. Soc. C.E., Am. Assn. Engrs. and Architects. Republican. Mem. Soc. Friends. Home: 1977 N. New Hampshire Av., Los Angeles. Died Oct. 27, 1957.

JETER, Frank Hamilton (jē'tēr), agrl. editor; b. Santuck, S.C., May 2, 1891; s. Little Berry and Janie (Hamilton) J.; B.S., in Agr., Clemson Agrl. Coll., 1911, Sc.D., 1948; m. Irene Annie Albert, June 8, 1915; children—Frank H., Robert Vernon, Jane Gertrude. Asst. to dir. S.C. Expt. Sta., 1912-13; field man in fertilizer expts., German Kali Works, Atlanta, 1913-14; agrl. editor, N.C. State Coll., 1914-20, 22-—, dir. State Coll. News Bur., 1924-—; chmn. Bd. Student Publs., 1932-—; editor Soc. Fertilizer Assn., Atlanta, 1920-22; owner 376 acre farm in Union Co., S.C. Dir. farm programs, radio sta. WPTF, Raleigh. Pres. Kiwanis Club, 1925; chmn. Internat. Com. Agr., Kiwanis Internat., 1927-28, Torch Club, trustee Presbyn. Jr. Coll., 1943-—. Mem. Assn. Agrl. Coll. Editors (pres. 1919-20; has also served as sec.-treas., mem. exec. com., v.p.), Assn. So. Agrl. Workers (chmn. editorial sect. 1937-39), Alpha Zeta, Alpha Gamma Rho, Epsilon Sigma Phi, Phi Kappa Phi, Blue Key. Awarded many blue ribbons by Assn. Agrl. Editors for agrl. writing. Democrat. Presbyn. (elder). Clubs: Torch, Carolina Country. Contbr. agrl. articles to various mags. and newspapers, editor bulls., N.C. Agrl. Expt. Sta. Home: 304 Forest Rd., Raleigh, N.C. Died Sept. 16, 1955.

JEWELL, William Henry, mfg. exec.; b. Ishpeming, Mich., Dec. 26, 1892; s. Samuel and Susan (Bennett) J.; B.S., U. Mich., 1916; m. Elizabeth R. O'Brien, Feb. 1920 (dec. Feb. 1950); 1 dau., Cecile M.; m. 2d, Nora K. McMahon, April 1952. Plant engr. Ingersoll-Rand Co., 1919-30, asst. gen. mgr., 1930-39, gen. mgr., 1939-—, vice president, 1944-—. Member board of directors Robert Packer Hospital, Sayre, Pa., Hosp. Service Assn. Northeastern Pa., Wilkes-Barre. Mem. Am. Soc. Tool Engrs. Clubs: City, Country (Elmira); Canadian (N.Y.C.). Home: 611 N. Main St. Office: 101 N. Main St., Athens, Pa. Died Dec. 15, 1957.

JEWETT, Arthur Crawford, mech. engr.; b. Bath, Me., Aug. 26, 1878; s. Edwin Hale and Lizzie L. (Chapman) J.; B.S., Mass. Inst. Tech., 1901; m. Blanche Lind von Beseler, May 7, 1903 (dec.); children—Roger, Helen Hale (Mrs. Robert L. Lepper). Instr. mech. engring. U. Me., 1903-05, prof. mech. engring., 1905-14; engring. mgr. Bird & Son, East Walpole, Mass., 1914-16; supt. various depts. Winchester Repeating Arms Co., 1916-24; mem. research staff Nat. Indsl. Conf. Bd., N.Y.C., 1924-25; dir. Coll. Industries, Carnegie Inst. Tech., 1925-34. Exec. sec., Regional Labor Bd., 1933-35; supr. labor mgmt. Pa. dist. 15, Works Progress Adminstrn., 1935-36; cons. Indsl. Relations and Tng., 1936-41, U.S. Office Edn., 1941-47. Mem. Am. Soc.

M.E. Address: 905 Maryland Av., Pitts. Died July 27, 1957.

JEWETT, Frank Fanning, chemist; b. Newton Corner, Mass., Jan. 8, 1844; s. Charles and Lucy Adams (Tracy) J.; A.B., Yale, 1870, A.M., 1873; univs. of Göttingen and Berlin, Germany; m. Frances Gulick (q.v.). July 30, 1880. Tchr. Norwich Free Acad., later pvt. asst. to Dr. Wolcott Gibbs, of Harvard; prof. chemistry, Imperial U. of Japan, 1877-80; prof. chemistry and mineralogy Oberlin Coll., 1880-12, prof. emeritus, 1912. Trustee Oberlin Missionary Home Assn. Mem. Am. Chem. Soc., A.A.A.S., Deutsche Chemische Gesellschaft, Alpha Delta Phi. Author: Tables for Qualitative Chemical Analysis, 1883; Laboratory Manual of Inorganic Chemistry, 1885. Republican. Conglist. Address: Oberlin, O. Died July 1, 1926; buried Oberlin.

JEWETT, George Frederick, business exec.; b. St. Paul, Aug. 22, 1896; s. James Richard and Margaret (Weyerhaeuser) J.; A.B., Harvard, 1919, M.B.A., 1922; LL.D., Wash. State Coll., 1949; m. Mary Pelton Cooper, Sept. 12. 1925; children—George Frederick, Margaret Weyerhaeuser. Office mgr. Clearwater Timber Co., Lewiston, Ida., 1925; gen. mgr. Edward Rutledge Timber Co., 1928; pres. Potlatch Forests, Inc., 1946, chmn. bd., 1949—; dir. Northern Pacific Ry. Co. Served as ensign USNRF, 1917-21. Trustee Am. U., Cairo, Egypt; dir. Nat. Lumber Mfrs. Assn. Mem. com. to visit Harvard Forest, com. to visit Semitic and Egyptian Civilizations dept. Harvard. Asso. mem. Soc. Am. Foresters; mem. Western Forestry and Conservation Assn. (pres. 1936-43), N. Ida. Forestry Assn. (pres. 1935-44). Republican. Episcopalian (lay reader). Clubs: Harvard of N.Y., N.Y. Yacht; Harvard Faculty (Cambridge, Mass.). Home: W. 612 Sumner Av., Spokane 4; (summer) Woods Hole, Mass. Office: P.O. Box 1164, Spokane 10, Wash. Died Nov. 23, 1956; buried Coeurd Alene, Ida.

JEWETT, Harvey Chase, Jr., Rep. Nat. committeeman; b. Aberdeen, S.D., July 7, 1895; s. Harvey Chase and Kate (Kennedy) J.; A.B., Williams Coll., Williamstown, Mass., 1920; married Eleanor Katherine Porter, Oct. 10, 1921; (died Apr. 16, 1937); m. 2d, Laura A. Stowe, June 30, 1938; children—Harvey Chase III, Naval cadet Jack Porter (killed in airplane collision, 1950), Sarah Jane, Eleanor Katherine. Pres. Jewett Bros.; pres. Jewett Drug Co.; pres. Jewett Investment Co.; pres. Aberdeen Broadcast Co. since 1935; mem. Rep. Nat. Com. for S.D., 1936-July 1948 (mem. exec. com.); dir. Aberdeen Nat. Bank, Rushmore Mutual Insurance Co. (ret. 1949), Crippled Children's Hosp. (Sioux Falls, S.D.), So. Dakota Reclamation Assn. Served in Ambulance Service U.S. Army, with A.E.F., 1917-19. Mem. Aberdeen C. of C. (pres. 1929-30), Aberdeen Community Chest (pres. 1929-31), Am. Red Cross (chmn. Brown County). Mem. Am. Legion (adj. 1921), Beta Theta Pi. Roman Catholic. Elk. Clubs: Country, Promenade (Aberdeen); Minneapolis (Minneapolis). Home: 1206 N. Main St. Office: 1 N. Kline St., Aberdeen, S.D. Died Feb. 17, 1953; buried Cedar Hill Cemetery, Newark, O.

JEWETT, Nelson J., lawyer; b. Richland, Mich., Apr. 1872; s. Norman C. and Mary E. (Buell) J.; student Case Inst. Tech., 1893-94; B.P.E., Springfield Coll., 1925; LL.B., Georgetown U., 1908; M.L.P., George Washington U., 1909; m. Edith S. Dey, June 1902. Admitted to D.C. bar, 1908; landscape engr., Cleveland, 1895-96; phys. dir., Winnipeg, Can., 1901-04; examiner U.S. Patent Office, 1905-18; mem. Jewett, Mead, Browne & Schuyler, Washington, since 1919. Home: 4972 Rock Spring Rd., Arlington, Va. Office: Mungey Bldg., Washington. Died Sept. 30, 1951.

JIMENEZ (MONTACON), Juan Ramón (hē-mā'-nāth), poet; b. Monguer, Spain, Dec. 23, 1881; student U. Seville; m. Zenobia Camprubi, 1916 (dec. 1956). Author, poet, 1898—; after Spanish Civil War lived in various Central and South American countries, 1936-47; vis. prof. U. Md., 1947-51; vis. prof. Coll. of Humanities, U. Puerto Rico, Rio Piedras and Mayaguez, P.R., 1951—. Recipient Nobel prize in lit., 1956. Author numerous publs. in prose and poetry, most famous being, Paltero y Yo (Silver and I) (prose poems; trans. into several langs.), 1914, (English trans. pub. in U.S.) Platero and I, 1957; Selected Writings (pub. in U.S.), 1957. Home: 461 Pedro Berrios St., Floral Park, Hato Rey, P.R. Died May 29, 1958.*

JOANNES, Francis Y. (jō-ăn'ēs), architect; b. Green Bay, Wis., Sept. 27, 1876; s. William and Jane (Yeates) J.; student Art Inst. Chgo., Armour Inst., 1895-96; B.S. in Architecture, Cornell, 1900, grad. fellow, 1900-01; diplomé, Ecole des Beaux Arts, Paris, 1906; m. Augusta Connor Smith, Oct. 9, 1909; 1 dau., Frances Taft. Designer and office mgr. J. K. Peebles, Norfolk, Va., 1901-03; Senate and House additions to Va. State Capitol, Plan, Jamestown Expn., designer Francis H. Kimball, N.Y.C., 1906-12; office mgr. Donn Barber, N.Y.C., 1912-13; asso. Ross and MacDonald, Montreal, P.Q., 1913-15; Halifax Ocean Terminals, Toronto Union Station. Own practice, N.Y.C., 1916—. Works include: N.Y. State Hosp. for Defective Delinquents, Hilton Village, Va., Manhattan Storage & Warehouse Co., Calco Chemical Co.'s Plant, Bound Brook, N.J., YWCA bldgs., N.Y.C., Med. Center, Springfield, Mo. Dept. of Justice, also numerous fine residences; cons. architect large indsl. plants. Dir. Nat. Railway Pub. Co. Fellow A.I.A.; mem. Beaux Arts Soc., Diplomé Soc., Archtl. League, Sigma Xi, Delta Upsilon. Clubs: Cornell (N.Y.C.); Pine Orchard (Conn.). Republican. Episcopalian. Home: Pine Orchard, Conn. Died June 21, 1952.

JOEKEL, Samuel Levinson (yā'kĕl), clergyman, educator; b. Giddings, Tex., July 1, 1893; s. Herman Charles and Zipporah (Levinson) J.; B.A., U. Tex., 1913, M.A., 1916; B.D., Austin Presbyn. Theol. Sem., 1916; D.D., Austin Coll. and Trinity U. (Tex.), 1926; m. Dorothy Turner, June 26, 1918; children—Samuel Levinson (killed in action in New Guinea, Oct. 8, 1944), Robert Charles. Inst. ch. history Austin Presbyn. Sem., 1916; ordained ministry Presbyn. Ch. of U.S., 1916; pastor First Presbyn. Ch., Clarendon, Tex., 1916-17, Waxanachie, 1919-26, also prof. English Bible and philosophy Trinity U., 1920-26; prof. English Bible and religious edn., Austin Presbyn. Theol. Sem., 1926—. Instr. in Assn. of Religious Tchrs., U. Tex., 1926—. Frequent lectr. at summer confs. Presbyn. Ch. of U.S., at Kerrville, Tex., at Montreat (N.C.) Conf., and at Massanetta Springs (Va.) Bible Conf. Mem. local Red Cross and Liberty Loan Coms., 1917; army YMCA sec., Camp Travis, Tex., 1917-18; 1st lt. chaplain O.R.C., U.S. Army, Camp Zachary Taylor, Ky., 1918. Democrat. Mason (32°, Shriner). Clubs: Kiwanis (pres. Austin 1930; trustee Okla.-Tex. Dist. 1931), University. Author: While It Is Day, 1942 (ofcl. Home Mission Study Book of Presbyn. Ch. in U.S.); Fitly Framed Together, 1948. Co-author Understanding the Books of the Old Testament, 1950. Contbr. to Am. Pulpit Series, 1945. Home: 104 E. 27th St., Austin, Tex. Died Nov. 12, 1954; buried Giddings, Tex.

JOEL, George William Freeman, publisher; b. Syracuse, N.Y., Dec. 21, 1902; s. William and Rachel (Freeman) J.; student Colgate U., 1919-20, Syracuse Law Coll., 1924; m. Freda Bienstock, June 13, 1925; children—Nancy (Mrs. James Boring), Sue (Mrs. Barry Beere). Publicity dir. Brentano's Pub. Co., 1928-29, Covici-Friede, 1929-39; v.p., editor-in-chief Dial Press, N.Y.C., 1939-51, pres., 1951—. Dir. Am. Book Pubs. Council. Mem. Am. Arbitration Assn., Zeta Beta Tau. Club: The Players. Contbr. articles, lit. criticism various lit. publs. Home: 141 E. 88th St., N.Y.C. 28. Office: 461 Fourth Av., N.Y.C. 16. Died Apr. 28, 1959.

JOERG, W(olfgang) L(ouis) G(ottfried) (yĕrg), geographer; b. Brooklyn, N.Y., Feb. 6, 1885; s. Oswald and Denise (Coulin) J.; grad. Poly. Prep. Sch. of Brooklyn, 1899, Thomas Gymnasium, Leipzig, Germany, 1904; student U. of Leipzig, 1904, Columbia, 1904-06, U. of Göttingen, Germany, 1906-11; m. Hannah Heaton, Nov. 14, 1911; children—Oswald Heaton, Norton Coulin. Mem. scientific staff Am. Geog. Soc. 1911-37—asst. editor of Bull., 1911-15, asso. editor Geog. Review, 1915-20, editor research series, 1920-25, research editor, 1925-37; apptd. chief Div. of Maps and Charts, The Nat. Archives, 1937; member Federal Bd. of Surveys and Maps, 1937-42; mem. div. of geology and geography Nat. Research Council, 1924-27, and of exec. com., 1931-36, vice chmn., 1933-36; sec. U.S. nat. com. Internat. Geog. Union, 1931-37, chmn., 1937-39; mem. advisory com. U.S. Geog. Bd., 1931-34, Com. on Mapping Services of the Federal Govt., 1934; mem. U.S. Bd. on Geog. Names, 1937-47 (chmn. exec. com. 1938-47, com. on Antarctic names, 1943-47, adv. mem. since 1947; cons. prof. hist. geog., Univ. of Maryland, since 1947. Fellow A.A.A.S.; mem. Assn. Am. Geographers (v.p. 1928; pres. 1937), Am. Geophys. Union, Am. Soc. of Photogrammetry, Nat. Congress on Surveying and Mapping (charter mem. 1941), Arctic Inst. of North American (charter mem. 1948), Soc. Am. Archivists, Am. Assn. for State and local history; hon. mem. Geog. Soc. Neuchâtel (Switzerland). Unitarian. Club: Cosmos (Washington, D.C.). Author: Recent Geographical Work in Europe, 1922; Brief History of Polar Explorations since the Introduction of Flying, 1930; Work of the Byrd Antarctic Expedition of 1928 to 1930, 1930; and numerous papers on cartography, the regional geography of N. America and land utilization. Editor: Problems of Polar Research, 1928; Pioneer Settlement 1932; (with W. A. Mackintosh) Canadian Frontiers of Settlement, 9 vols. since 1934; contbg. editor Geographical Review since 1937. Home: 6302 Ridge Dr., N.W. Office: The National Archives, Washington. Died Jan. 7, 1952.

JOHN, William Scott, lawyer; b. Morgantown, W.Va., Jan. 10, 1878; s. Lemuel N. and Julia A. (Boyers) J.; A.B., W.Va. U., 1900, LL.B., 1902; m. Estelle Cox, Dec. 17, 1902. Admitted to W.Va. bar, 1902; instr. in law, W.Va. U., 1902-03; asst. clk. Supreme Court of Appeals, W.Va., 1903-05; mem. W.Va. Ho. of Rep., 1917, 18, 19 (minority floor leader 1917-18, majority leader 1919); of spl. counsel for W.Va. in Ohio and Pa. gas cases, Supreme Court of U.S.; of counsel W.Va. 1929 Water Power Act (held unconstitutional, 1931). Republican. Presbyterian. Member New Mexico and American bar assns. Author original "work or fight" law in United States (enacted by W.Va. legislature, Feb. 1919); also author of first law adopted by any legislature in U.S. against Bolshevism and the red flag (enacted Mar. 1919). Engaged in reorganization of various banks of W.Va. by plan which he formulated. Author articles on banking which appeared in Review of Reviews. Home: 1505 Ridgecrest Dr. S.E. Office: Sunshine Bldg., Albuquerque, N.M. Died May 18, 1954.

JOHNS, Clarence D(urward), educator; b. Auburn, N.C., Sept. 18, 1888; s. Thomas Jefferson and Mattie (Eccles) J.; A.B., Randolph-Macon Coll., 1908; A.M., U. Chgo., 1911; student Harvard, 1912-13, U. Chgo., 1913-14; m. Caroline Heezen, Sept. 1, 1926; 1 son, Richard Heezen. Asst. prof. history Wake Forest Coll., 1914-16; asst. prof. U. Richmond, 1916-17; prof. and acting head dept. history Randolph-Macon Coll., 1917-18; prof. history Baylor Coll., 1919-22; asst. prof. history U. Cin., 1922-23; prof. history Woman's Coll., U. N.C., 1923—, acting head dept., 1944-47, head dept., 1947—. Surveyed and catalogued the county archives of the State of Ill., under direction of Profs. E. B. Greene and Solon J. Buck, for Ill. Hist. Library, 1911-12. Mem. Am., So. hist. assns., Phi Alpha Theta, Sigma Phi Epsilon. Democrat. Home: 209 S. Chapman St., Greensboro, N.C. Died Aug. 7, 1950.

JOHNSON, Albert, editor; b. Springfield, Ill., Mar. 5, 1869; s. Charles W. and Anna E. (Ogden) J.; ed. high school; m. Jennie S. Smith, Aug. 16, 1904; 1 dau., Dorothy. Learned printer's trade; mng. editor New Haven Register, 1896-97; news editor Washington Post, 1898; editor Tacoma News, 1898-1906; editor, pub. Grays Harbor Washingtonian, Hoquiam, Wash., 1906-34; spl. writer Daily World, Wenatchee, Wash., 1937-39. Mem. 63d to 72d Congresses, 3d Wash. Dist. (chmn. Com. Immigration and Naturalization, 1919-31). Capt. C.W.S., U.S. Army, 1918. Mem. Wash. Press Assn. (pres. 1908-09), Loyal Legion, S.A.R. Republican. Mason (K.T.). Home: Hoquiam, Wash. Deceased.

JOHNSON, Albert Williams, judge; b. Weikert, Pa., Nov. 28, 1872; s. Alanson and Sarah Alice (Catherman) J.; student Central Pa. Coll., New Berlin; A.B. suma cum laude, Bucknell U., 1896 (M.A., D.C.L.); LL.D., Albright, Juanita and Lebanon Valley colls.; m. Dora Miller, Dec. 1893 (dec. Oct. 2, 1909); children—Miller A., Alice Susannah (Mrs. Carl Schug), Donald M., Albert Williams, Paul E.; m. 2d, Mary Cadman Steck, Dec. 13, 1913; children—Mary Louise, William Steck, David Cadman, Frederick Welty, John Van Wert, Diana Carl. Tchr. mixed and ungraded grammar and high schools at Laurelton, Union County (Pa.), and McEwensville, Northumberland County (Pa.), 1886-1901; admitted to Pa. bar, 1898; instr. in law Bucknell U., 1902-26; U.S. dist. judge Middle Dist., Pa., 1925—, for life term. Pa. Ho. of Reps., 1901-02; solicitor Borough of Lewisburg, also for Union County, 1908-12; pres. judge 17th Dist., Pa., 1912-22; solicitor Dept. of Edn., 1922-23. Trustee Bucknell U.; incorporator Dickinson Law Sch., Carlisle, Pa. Mem. P.O.S. of A. (state and nat. pres. 1927-29), Kappa Sigma. Lutheran. Odd Fellow, Modern Woodman; mem. Royal Arcanum. Home: Lewisburg, Pa. Died Mar. 22, 1957.

JOHNSON, Allan Chester, prof. classics; b. Loch Broom, N.S., Can., Aug. 11, 1881; s. Leander and Hannah (Creelman) J.; A.B., Dalhousie U., Halifax, Can., 1904, LL.D., 1929; Ph.D., Johns Hopkins, 1909; fellow Am. Sch. of Classical Studies, Greece, 1909-11; m. Laura Williamson, Aug. 14, 1912. Came to U.S., 1912, naturalized citizen, 1932. Tutor in classics, Dalhousie U., 1904-06; lecturer in Greek, U. of Alberta, 1911-12; asst. prof. classics, Princeton, 1912-22, asso. prof., 1922-23, prof. 1924-49; Musgrave prof. Latin, 1933-43, Andrew Fleming West professor of classics, 1943-49; visiting professor American Academy in Rome, 1933-34; visiting professor Stanford U., summer 1939. Trustee Am. Acad. in Rome, 1933-45; mem. mng. com. Am. Sch. of Classical Studies in Athens. Chmn. Am. School Classical Studies in Rome, 1940-45. Member American Philol. Assn., Phi Beta Kappa. Lecturer on T. S. Jerome Foundation, 1947, U. of Michigan; American Academy in Rome, 1948. Co-Author: (with Frank Frost Abbott) Municipal Administration in the Roman Empire, 1926. Edit.: (with H. B. Van Hoesen) Greek Papyri in the Princeton Collection, 1930; (with H. S. Gehman and E. H. Kase) John H. Scheide Biblical Papyri, 1937; (with S. P. Goodrich) Princeton Papyri Vol. IV, 1941; (with Louis C. West) Currency in Roman and Byzantine Egypt, 1944, Byzantine Egypt: Economic Studies, 1949. Author: Roman Egypt, 1936. Gen. editor: Princeton University Studies in Payrology, 1934—. Contbr. on Greek history to Am. Jour. Philology, Am. Jour. Archaeology, etc. Home: 3 College Rd., Princeton, N.J. Died Mar. 2, 1955; buried Princeton.

JOHNSON, Anna (Hope Daring), author; b. Bradford County, Pa., July 11, 1860; d. George T. and L. Jane (Van Vechten) Johnson; ed. Albion (Mich.) Coll. Taught dist. sch. several yrs. Mem. Nat. Fedn.

Press Women, Mich. Authors Assn. Author: (all under pen-name) To the Third Generation, 1901; Agnes Grant's Education, 1902; Entering Into His Own, 1903; The Furniture People, 1903; An Abundant Harvest, 1904; The Appointed Way, 1905; Madeline the Island Girl, 1906; Father John, 1907; A Virginian Holiday, 1909; Valadero Ranch, 1911; The Gordons, 1912; Paying the Price, 1914; Sowing and Reaping, 1922; Woods in the Home, 1928. Contbr. Juvenile and religious publs. Home: Hastings, Mich. Deceased.

JOHNSON, Arnold Milton, corp. exec.; b. Chgo., Jan. 11, 1907; s. Carl W. and Alma (Magnuson) J.; Ph.B., U. Chgo., 1928; m. Carmen C. Burr, Oct. 6, 1945; children—Wendy Alexis, Jeffrey Burr. Started with City Nat. Bank & Trust Co., 1932, v.p. 1945; owner, pres. Kansas City Athletics, Inc., Am. League baseball team, 1954—; vice chmn. bd. Automatic Canteen Co. Am., Chgo., 1953—, pres., dir., 1957—; chmn. bd. Northwestern Terra Cotta Corp., Chgo., Denver Terra Cotta Corp., Blakely Oswald Printing Co., Chgo.; dir. Henry Holt & Co. Inc. (N.Y.C.), H. M. Byllesby & Co. (mem. exec. com.), Mpls.-Moline Co. (mem. exec. com.), Western Tablet & Stationery Co., Dayton, Blomgren Bros., Chgo. Dir. Infant Welfare Soc. Served as lt. comdr. USN, 1942-46. Clubs: Kansas City (Mo.); Chgo. Athletic Assn., Saddle and Cycle, Post and Paddock, South Side Swedish (Chgo.); Fin'n Feather (Dundee, Ill.). Home: 1500 Lake Shore Dr. Office: 1430 Merchandise Mart, Chgo. 54. Died Mar. 10, 1960.

JOHNSON, Arthur Charles, editor; b. Ira, O., Oct. 10, 1874; s. Charles and Helen Frances (Cranz) J.; student Ohio U.; B.S., Buchtel Coll., Akron, O., 1897, M.S., 1900; LL.D., Bowling Green (O.) State U., 1946; m. Grace Reah, Dec. 31, 1902. Editor Buchtel Coll. publs., 1896-97; city editor Beacon Journal, Akron, 1897-1900; editorial staff Washington Post, 1901-02; city editor Columbus Evening Dispatch, 1902-12, editor in chief, 1912-23, asso. pub., 1923—. Served as regtl. sgt. maj. 8th Ohio Inf., Santiago Campaign, Spanish-Am. War. Life trustee Ohio U.; pres. Ohio Archaeol. and Hist. Soc.; pres. Rutherford B. Hayes Found., Fremont, O. Mem. Phi Delta Theta, Sigma Delta Chi. Republican. Methodist. Mason. Clubs: Rocky Fork Hunt, Dispatch Country. Home: 227 Preston Rd. Address: Columbus Evening Dispatch, Columbus, O. Died Nov. 11, 1950.

JOHNSON, Axel Petrus, writer, pub.; b. Gefle, Sweden, Sept. 24, 1878; s. Charles August and Hanna Christina (Hammer) J.; came with parents to U.S., 1888; ed. pub. schs., Minneapolis, and spl. student, U. of Minn., 1901-03; m. Augusta A. Holgerson, Dec. 2, 1902; 1 dau., Dorothea Evelyn. Reporter Minneapolis Tribune, 1900-03; adv. mgr. Minneapolis Times, 1903, Milwaukee Sentinel, 1905-06; business mgr. Chicago Record-Herald, 1906-12, gen. mgr., 1913-15; pub. and propr. Grand Rapids News, 1912-22; pres. A.P. Johnson Co., pubs. and printers since 1921. Mem. Co. I, 15th Regt., Minn. Vols., Spanish-Am. War. Mem. bd. of Library Commrs., Grand Rapids Pub. Library, 1926-42, president 1930-36; mem. national board Camp Fire Girls, 1928-34; trustee David Wolcott Kendall Memorial Sch. of Art, 1932-47 (pres. 1939-43); educational dir. Grand Rapids Furniture Expn., 1932-38. Republican. Scottish Rite Mason (33°). Clubs: Rotary (hon.), Torch (Grand Rapids). Compiler: Library of Advertising (6 volumes), 1912; Manual of the Furniture Arts and Crafts (with M. K. Sironen), 1928. Editorial writier on polit., econ. and philos. subjects for newspapers, etc. Author: One Wise Man (drama; with Dorothea Evelyn Johnson), 1939. Home: 356 Cherry St. S.E., Grand Rapids, Mich.; (summer) Scrub Oaks, Bitely, Mich. Died July 9, 1952.

JOHNSON, Bascom, assn. exec.; b. Washington, Jan. 17, 1878; s. Joseph Taber and Edith Maude Bascom J.; A.B., Yale, 1900; LL.B., U. Pa., 1903; m. S. Frances Adams, June 11, 1904; children—Bascom, Margaret, Joseph Taber. Admitted to Pa. bar, 1903 and in pracaice at Phila., 1903-09; law officer for Fed. Indian Bur., Washington, 1909-11; sec. Recreation Comms. of N.Y.C., 1912-13; with Am. Social Hygiene Assn., N.Y., 1913—, asso. dir., 1919—; spl. cons. for USPHS, 1938—; apptd. dir. Div. of Legal and Social Protection in the Office of the Coordinator of Health, Welfare, and Related Defense Activities, FSA, Washington, 1941; on project with state and local agys. of Cal. dealing with conditions of Panama Pacific Expn. and in City of San Francisco, 1915-17; dir. of investigations for the special body of experts, apptd. by the Council of the League of Nations, to study internat. traffic in women and children, 1924-27, chmn. Commn. of Three to make similar study in 20 countries of the Near, Middle and Far East; mem. Adv. Commn. on Protection and Welfare of Children and Young Persons, of the League of Nations, 1925—; cons. in N.M. for U.S. Indian Bur., 1935; an organizer and dir. campaign of pub. health edn. for San Antonio C. of C., 1937. Served as maj. San. Corps U.S. Army, 1917-19; assigned as dir. law enforcement division of Army and Navy Comms. of Tng. Camp Activities. Since 1941, dir. of legal and protective measures, Am. Social Hygiene Assn., and legal cons. of US PHS, temporarily assigned to 8th Service Command, U.S. Army, with hdqrs. at Dallas, 1941-45; resumed position as dir. of legal and protective services, Am. Social Hygiene Assn., ret. 1947. Called from retirement to rep. the Internat. Union Against Venereal Diseases, in orgn. citizen activities on both sides of Mexican border, Jan.-Apr. 1949. Mem. of Internat. Com. of Am. Social Hygiene Assn. and accredited representative of latter to ECOSOC. Home: 7 Clinton St., Pleasantville, N.Y. Office: 1790 Broadway, N.Y.C. Died Oct. 21, 1954.

JOHNSON, Ben, ex-congressman; b. Bardstown, Ky., May 20, 1858; s. William and Nannie (Crow) J.; ed. St. Mary's Coll., Ky. (A.M.); LL.B., Louisville Law U., 1882; m. Annie Cox Kouwenbergh, Oct. 12, 1886. Practiced law, 1882-91; pres. People's Bank, Bardstown, 1897—. Mem. Ky. Ho. of Reps., 1885-89 (speaker, 1887); collector internal revenue, 5th Ky. Dist., 1893-97; mem. Ky. Senate, 1905-06; mem. 60th to 69th Congresses, 4th Ky. Dist.; resigned to become chmn. Ky. State Hwy. Commn. Democrat. Home: Bardstown, Ky. Died June 4, 1950; buried Bardstown.

JOHNSON, Ben; b. Mansfield, Louisiana, Aug. 31, 1881; s. Walter and Sue (Roberts) J.; grad. La. State Normal Coll., Natchitoches, 1899; m. Irma Nabors, Mar. 23, 1909; children—Eleanor, Irma, Kathryn (deceased). Began as runner Bank of DeSoto, Mansfield, 1903, clerk, 1903-05, cashier, 1905-09, organizer 1909, v.p., 1909-10; pres., 1910-32, Bank of Commerce & Trust Co., Mansfield; president Commercial National Bank, Shreveport, La., 1921-32; v.p. Commodity Credit Corp., Washington, D.C., 1936-38. Trustee Export-Import Bank, 1936-38; special assistant R.F.C., 1932-38; pres. Pickering Lumber Corp., Kansas City, Mo., and Standard, Calif., 1938-46, chmn. bd., 1946-54; retired, 1954. Chmn. Am. Red Cross and Liberty Loan drives, DeSoto Parish, Louisiana, World War I; chmn. Fund Raising Campaigns Am. Red Cross, Tuolumne County, World War II. Democrat. Episcopalian. Mason (Shriner), Elk. Clubs: Sonora Golf, Sonora Lions, Commonwealth San Francisco. Address: 901 Monrovia St., Shreveport, La. Died Dec. 28, 1955; buried Mansfield, La.

JOHNSON, Carl W., business exec.; b. Red Wing, Minn., 1886. Sr. v.p., dir. Cleveland Graphite Bronze Co.; v.p. Blvd. Sport Shops; dir. Standard Products Co., Selected Securities Co., Parker Appliance Co., Ionia Mfg. Co., Paragon Aluminum Co., Ferro Enamel Corp. Home: 22401 Shaker Blvd., Shaker Heights 22. Office: 17000 St. Clair Avenue, Cleve. 10. Died June 5, 1956.

JOHNSON, Charles F. H., pres. Botany Worsted Mills; b. New York, N.Y., Sept. 5, 1880; s. Charles and Augusta E. (Hallenereutz) J.; m. Matilda K. Haeuser, Sept. 16, 1903; became asso. with Botany Worsted Mills, 1920, dir. since 1921, became asst. to pres., Mar. 1923, v.p., Nov. 1923, pres. since 1929. Former pres. Passaic Bd. of Trade; chmn. various civic activities; chmn. 2d, 3d, 4th and 5th Liberty Loans, Passaic. Served as maj. Air Service during World War I; col., Specialist Reserve, Air Service, since 1929; col., Air Service, assigned as advisor to director of Army Emergency Relief, June 1942; Legion of Merit, 1944. Director Erie Railroad, 1947; member other patriotic and civic organizations. Clubs: Army and Navy, Metropolitan, Congressional, National Press (Washington, D.C.); Lotos, Drug and Chemical, Military-Naval, Advertising, Manhattan, Univ. of Pa., Metropolitan (New York); Union League of N.Y.; City, Pennington (Passaic, N.J.). Office: 145 Dayton Av., Passaic, N.J. Died May 9, 1952; buried East Ridgelawn Cemetery, Delawanna, N.J.

JOHNSON, Charles F(rederick), Jr., shoe mfg. exec.; b. Binghamton, N.Y., Oct. 22, 1887; s. C. Fred and Ida (Bullock) J.; grad. Mercersburg Acad., 1905; LL.D., Colgate U., 1952; m. Jeannette Gaylord, July 17, 1909; children—Jeannette (Mrs. John Tunnicliff), Patricia (Mrs. William Luckie). Joined Endicott Johnson Corp., mfrs. and distbrs. leather, rubber, shoes, 1905, 1st v.p., gen. mgr., 1931-48, pres., gen. mgr., 1948-57, chmn. bd., 1957—; v.p., dir. Nat. Shoe Mfrs. Assn., N.Y.C.; dir. Marine Midland Trust Co. So. N.Y., Hohawk Airlines, Inc. Home: 335 Main St., Johnston City, Office: care Endicott Johnson Corp., Endicott, N.Y. Died Aug. 9, 1959; buried Riverhurst Cemetery, Endicott.

JOHNSON, Charles Spurgeon, univ. pres.; b. Bristol, Va., July 24, 1893; s. Charles Henry and Winifred (Branch) J.; A.B., Va. Union U., 1917, Litt. D., 1928; Ph.B., U. Chgo., 1918; L.H.D., Howard U., 1941; Litt.D., Columbia, 1947; LL.D., Harvard, 1948, U. Glasgow, 1952; m. Marie Antoinette Burgette, Nov. 6, 1920; children—Charles Spurgeon, Robert Burgette, Patricia Marie, Jeh Vincent. Dir. research and investigations Nat. Urban League, 1921; editor Opportunity, a jour. of negro life, 1923-29; dir. dept. social sci. Fisk U., 1928-47, pres., 1946—, also established Academic Development Program with headmasters and tutorial system plus closed circuit TV system; dir. Inst. Race Relations, Swarthmore Coll., 1933, co-dir., 1934-38. Am. mem. commn. apptd. by League of Nations to investigate forced labor in Liberia, 1930; sec. com. on negro housing Pres. Hoover's Conf. on Home Bldg. and Home Ownership, 1931; mem. sociology com. TVA, 1934; mem. exec. com. So. Commn. on Study of Lynching, So. Regional Council; mem. Pres.' Com. on Farm Tenancy, Tech. Com. on Tenancy, Commn. on Health Needs of Nation; mem. Nat. Manpower Council; mem. adv. bd. Nat. Youth Adminstrn. of Tenn., 1941; mem. exec. and planning com. White House Conf. on Children in a Democracy, 1940; dir. so. rural div. Negro Youth Study for Am. Youth Commn. and Council on Edn.; mem. Fulbright Bd. Fgn. Scholarships. Trustee Julius Rosenwald Fund, Nat. Urban League; dir.-at-large Bd. Home Missions Congl. Christian Chs.; del. 1st Assembly World Council Chs., Amsterdam, Holland; dir. race relations program Am. Missionary Assn., 1943-48; co-dir. race relations program Julius Rosenwald Fund, 1942-48; cons. John Hay Whitney Found., 1950-56. Mem. U.S. Edn. Mission to Japan, 1946; mem. exec. com. U.S. Commn. for UNESCO; mem. U.S. delegation to 1st UNESCO Conf., Paris, 1946; chmn. UNESCO Conf. on Race Relations in Paris, also lectr. for Am.-Scandinavian Found. at univs. of Stockholm, Oslo and Copenhagen, 1955; Am. corr. mem. UNESCO project for sci. and cultural history and mankind. Served as regtl. sgt. maj. inf. U.S. Army, AEF, World War I, participated Meuse-Argonne offensive. Recipient William E. Harmon gold medal for distinguished achievement among negroes in sci. for yr. 1930; cited for distinguished pub. service U. Chgo. Alumni Assn., 1945. Mem. Sociol. Research Assn. (sec.-treas. 1943-46), Am. Social Hygiene Assn. (v.p.), Nat. Tb Assn. (dir.), Am. Adult Edn. Assn. (v.p. 1956, chmn. 15th symposium on sci. philosophy and religion at Columbia), Am. (exec. com.), So. (pres. 1945) sociol. socs., Social Sci. Research Council, N.E.A., Nat. Planning Assn., Alpha Phi Alpha. Conglist. Author: The Negro in American Civilization 1930; Economic Status of the Negro, 1933; Shadow of the Plantation, 1934; Preface of Racial Understanding, 1936; The Negro College Graduate, 1936 (Anisfield award 1938); Growing Up in the Black Belt, 1941; Statistical Atlas of Southern Counties, 1941; Patterns of Negro Segregation, 1943; To Stem This Tide, 1943; Into the Main Stream, 1946; Education and the Cultural Crisis, 1951; (with others) The Negro in Chicago, 1922; Race Relations, 1934; The Collapse of Cotton Tenancy, 1935. Editor: Ebony and Topaz, 1927; Education and the Cultural Process, 1944. Co-editor: Race and Culture, 1950. Home: 1700 Meharry Blvd., Nashville. Died Oct. 29, 1956; buried Greenwood Cemetery, Nashville.

JOHNSON, Clarence S., business exec.; b. Chicago, July 21, 1892; s. Ole and Hilda (Brekke) J.; student Ark. State Teacher's Coll., George Peabody Coll.; m. Eva Y. Johnson, Apr. 28, 1914; 1 dau., Rozene (Mrs. Frank McClelland). Teacher, 1913-18; county agrl. agt., Logan and Bradley counties, Ark., 1918-26; product field man Ralston Purina Co., 1926-28, mgr. poultry dept., 1928-44, vice pres. in charge of products and research since 1944, mem. president's cabinet and mem. exec. com. Asso. dir. program of progress Presbyterian Church of U.S. Mem. bd. dirs. and exec. com. Am. Feed Mfrs. Assn. Republican. Club: Missouri Athletic. Home: 20 Frederick Lane, Kirkwood 22, Mo. Office: 835 S. 8th St., St. Louis 2. Died Mar. 20, 1952.

JOHNSON, Curtis Boyd, newspaper pub.; b. Knoxville, Tenn., Nov. 10, 1875; s. Jackson Selvidge and Belle (Biddle) J.; student Peabody and Hampden-Sydney schs., Knoxville, and Providence sch., Loudon County, Tenn.; m. Irving Harding McGeachy, May 2, 1942. Began newspaper career as advt. mgr. Knoxville Sentinel, 1900, becoming pub. and prin. owner, 1912; acquired partnership interest in Bristol (Tenn.-Va.) Courier and Chattanooga News; became prin. owner and pub. Charlotte (N.C.) Observer, 1916; propr. Semagraph Co.; owner Charlotte Engraving Co. Pres., founder Observer Fresh Air Camp; pres. Curtis B. Johnson Benevolent Assn.; past pres. So. Newspaper Pubs. Assn. Mem. Soc. of Davidson (N.C.) College, Omicron Delta Kappa. Democrat. Clubs: Charlotte Country, Executive. Home: Charlotte, N.C. Died Oct. 6, 1950.

JOHNSON, Earle Frederick, retired exec.; b. Moosic, Pa., Nov. 4, 1886; s. Frederick H. and Emma (Nichols) J.; C.E., Lehigh U., 1907; m. Mary Louise Thompson, Apr. 8, 1927; 1 son (by wife's previous marriage), Kent C. Thompson. Apprentice engr. McClintock-Marshall Constrn. Co., Pottstown, Pa., 1907-09; engr. and operating mgr. Du Pont Powder Co., Wilmington, Del., 1909-19; exec. in accessory mfg., Gen. Motors Corp., Detroit, 1919-30; retired, 1930-40; with War Prodn. Bd., Washington, 1940-42; v.p. Gen. Motors Corp. 1942-45; dir. Gen. Motors, January 1946—. Trustee Lehigh University. Member Newcomen Soc., Phi Sigma Kappa. Republican. Mason. Clubs: University, Links (N.Y. City); Detroit, Bloomfield Hills Country, Yondotega Country (Detroit); Los Angeles Country; Chevy Chase (Washington). Home: 8162 S. Jefferson Av., Detroit. Died July 24, 1958; buried Roseland Park, Detroit.

JOHNSON, Edith Christina, coll. prof.; b. Quincy, Mass., Jan. 10, 1891; d. John L. and Charlotte M. (Almquist) J.; A.B., Radcliffe Coll., 1916; M.R.E.,

Boston U., 1919; A.M., Radcliffe Coll., 1923, Ph.D., 1930; research and study in England, 1934-35. Teacher English and science, Keene (N.H.) High Sch., 1916-17; teacher English and history, Quincy (Mass.) High Sch., 1917-18; instr. religious edn. and chmn. dept., Bapt. Training Sch., Chicago, 1919-22; instr. English, Wellesley Coll., 1923-26, asst. prof., 1926-30, asso. prof., 1930-39, prof. since 1939, dir. of publicity, 1925-34. Sophie Hart Professor of English Composition since 1945; visiting professor of English, Upsala University, Sweden, for the first semester, 1948-49. Honorary fellow of American-Scandinavian Foundation. Member Friends of Boston Symphony Orchestra. Member Am. Assn. Univ. Women (pres. Boston br. 1944-46). Modern Language Assn. America (life), Am. Scandinavian Foundation, Soc. for Advancement Scandinavian Study, Coll. English Assn., Internat. Fedn. Univ. Women (delegate to conference Edinburgh, 1932, Stockholm, 1939), Phi Beta Kappa (pres. Iota chapter of Mass. 1938-41; del. and chmn. com. Triennial Council, San Francisco, 1940), English Assn. (London). Liberal Republican. Clubs: Boston Authors; Charles Lamb Soc. (London). Author: Lamb Always Elia, London, 1935; also articles and essays. Lectures on ednl. and lit. subjects. Home: 66 Dover Rd. Office: Wellesley College, Wellesley, Mass. Died Aug. 8, 1954; buried Milton (Mass.) Cemetery.

JOHNSON, Emsley Wright, lawyer; b. Augusta, Ind., May 8, 1878; s. Joseph M. and Mary (Wright) J.; A.B., Butler Coll., 1900; Ph.B., U. Chgo., 1901; LL.B., Ind. Law Sch., 1903; LL.D., Butler U., 1946; m. Katherine Griffin, Aug. 8, 1906 (dec. Jan. 29, 1918); children—Mardenna, Emsley Wright; m. 2d, Elizabeth Thompson, Aug. 2, 1920. Admitted to Ind. bar, 1903, and began practice at Indpls.; county atty. Marion County, Ind., 1916-21; was mem. Johnson and Elliott; now mem. Johnson and Zechiel; conducted prosecution of mayor of Indpls. and gov. of Ind.; v.p. New Augusta State Bank, Speedway State Bank. Mem. Park Bd., Indpls., 1924-26; mem. Bd. Public Works, Indpls., 1929-30. Mem. Selective Service Bd., World War; pres. Ind. Selective Assn. 3 yrs. Trustee Butler Coll.; vice chmn. bd. trustees Butler U.; v.p. bd. trustees Arthur Jordan Conservatory Music; v.p. Jordan Found.; mem. Indpls. Found., William E. English Found. Pres. Old Settlers Assn.; mem. Am., Ind., Indpls. (past pres.) bar assns., Lawyers Club (past pres.), Ind. Soc. of Pioneers (past pres.), Indiana Astron. Soc. (pres.), Sons of Vets., S.A.R. (mem. bd. mgrs. Ind. soc.). Republican. Presbyn. (pres. bd. trustees Tabernacle Ch.). Mason (32°, Shriner), Odd Fellow, Red Man. Clubs: Columbia, Meridian Hills Country. Home: 3447 Washington Blvd. Office: Peoples Bank Bldg., Indpls. Died Apr. 12, 1950; buried Crown Hill Cemetery, Indpls.

JOHNSON, Ernest Amos, coll. pres.; b. Ouray, Colo., Jan. 10, 1895; s. Nels and Anna Margaret (Wall) J.; A.B. in Bus. Adminstrn., Colo. Coll. 1918, LL.D., 1953; A.M., U. Denver, 1924; grad. work U. Chgo. and Northwestern U.; Ph.D., Northwestern U., 1933, D.Sc., Pace Coll., N.Y.C., 1956; D.C.L., Blackburn Coll., Carlinville, 1957; m. Edith Irene Glassford, Aug. 18, 1920; 1 son, Robert Willard. Asst. chief clk. in office dist. commercial supt. Western Union Telegraph Co., Denver, 1919-24; with Lake Forest Coll., 1924—, successively as instr. in economics until 1926, asst. prof. economics, 1926-27, associate professor, same, 1929-33, head of department, 1929-41, professor, 1933-41; acting president, Lake Forest College, 1941-43; president, Oct. 1, 1943—. Dir. First Nat. Bank, Lake Forest. Dir. McCormick Theol. Sem., Chgo. Served in A. U.S., 1918-19. Member American Econ. Assn., Presbyn. College Union, Phi Beta Kappa, Phi Delta Theta, Phi Eta Sigma. Republican. Presbyn. Clubs: University Economics, Executive (Chgo.); Onwentsia, Kiwanis (Lake Forest). Author series of articles on real estate securities. Home: 9 College Campus, Lake Forest, Ill. Died Apr. 13, 1959; buried Lake Forest.

JOHNSON, Franklin Winslow, coll. pres.; b. Jay, Me., Aug. 17, 1870; s. John Sullivan and Elizabeth Williams (Winslow) J.; grad. Wilton (Me.) Acad., 1887; A.B., Colby Coll., Me., 1891, A.M., 1894, L.H.D., 1916; LL.D., U. Me., Brown U., 1933; D.C.L., Acadia U., 1938; studied U. Chgo., Columbia; m. Carolyn May Lord, July 15, 1896; m. 2d, Imogene Donovan Hall, Nov. 9, 1929. Prin. Calais (Me.) High Sch., 1891-94, Coburn Classical Inst., Waterville, Me., 1894-1905, Morgan Park (Ill.) Acad., 1905-07; asst. prin. U. Chgo. High Sch., 1907-09, prin. 1909-19; prof. edn. Tchrs. Coll. (Columbia), 1919-29; pres. Colby Coll., Waterville, Maine, 1929-42, pres. emeritus, 1942—. Lectr. on secondary school adminstrn. U. Chgo., 1913-19; courses in secondary edn. Tchrs. Coll., 1916. Served as maj. San. Corps, U.S. Army, rehabilitation service, 1918-19. Mem. N.E.A., Religious Edn. Assn., Delta Kappa Epsilon, Phi Beta Kappa. Baptist. Mason. Club: University (Boston). Author: Problems of Boyhood, 1914; Administration and Supervision of the High School, 1925; also numerous articles on edn. in mags. Home: Mayflower Hill Dr., Waterville, Me. Died Feb. 19, 1956.

JOHNSON, Frederick William, attorney Land Management; b. Green River, Wyo., Mar. 11, 1881; s. William Adolphus and Ellen Charlotte (Larson) J.; A.B., U. of Neb., 1903, LL.B., 1905; m. Rose Gras, June 30, 1915; children—June Rose Marie, Rose Emily, Frederick William. Admitted to Neb. bar, 1905, Wyo. bar, 1906; in practice Rock Springs, Wyo., 1905-33; county atty., Sweetwater County, Wyo., 1914-20; city atty., Rock Springs, 1924-33; commr. U.S. General Land Office, 1933-48; now atty., Bur., Land Management, Dept. of Interior. Formerly mem. Wyo. State Bd. Law Examiners; western regional dir. Dem. Nat. Com., Salt Lake City, 1928. Mem. Theta Kappa Nu, Phi Delta Phi, Theta Nu Epsilon, Delta Kappa Epsilon. Democrat. Episcopalian. Elk. Home: Rock Springs, Wyo.; and 1701 16th St. N.W., Washington. Office: Bureau of Land Management, Dept. Interior, Washington. Died July 31, 1955.

JOHNSON, George W., corp. exec.; b. Plymouth, Mass., Mar. 25, 1880; s. George F. and Lucie (Willis) J.; ed. Worcester (Mass.) Acad. and Dean Acad., Franklin, Mass.; m. Lula Seagers, June 6, 1900; children—Marion Irma (Mrs. Joseph S. Young), Frank A., Wilma Margaret (Mrs. Brewster W. Smith). With Endicott Johnson Corp., Endicott, N.Y., since 1900, beginning as worker in tanneries, became supt. of tanneries, 1905, pres. of the corp., 1930-50, now dir. Address: 1102 Broad St., Endicott, N.Y. Died May 25, 1953.

JOHNSON, Grace Allen (Mrs. Lewis Jerome Johnson), educator; b. Maples, Ind., Sept. 29, 1871; d. Appleton Howe and Elizabeth Harriet (Bennett) Fitch; grad. Pratt Inst. Library sch., 1891; studied Northwestern U. and in Switzerland; m. Lewis Jerome Johnson, June 27, 1893; children—Jerome Allen, Chandler Winslow. State congl. chmn., Mass., and mem. Nat. Council Nat. Woman Suffrage Assn., 1915-17; chmn. bd. Mass. Woman Suffrage Assn., 1917; exec. sec. Mass. Woodrow Wilson Found., 1922, mem. council Mass. Fgn. Policy Assn., 1923-—; chmn. edn. com. for Mass., League of Nations Assn., 1926-33; pres. Garland Sch. of Home Making, 1930-37. Lecturer Boston U., Garland Sch. of Home Making, Wheelock Kindergarten Tng. Sch., Mass. Dept. Edn. Div. Univ. Extension and other instns. Public Forum leader under U.S. Dept. of Interior Office of Edn., Manchester, 1937. Testified before Congl. Committee on Prohibition, 1930. Del. to Progressive Party Nat. Conv., 1912. Name entered on honor rolls of Nat. Woman Suffrage Assn., 1920, Suffrage Pioneers of Cambridge, 1930; New England del. to Woman's Centennial Congress, 1940. Wrote: Dramatizaations of The Dispute Between Bolivia and Paraguay; The Case of the S.S. Lotus; (with Sir Herbert B. Ames, Kt.) The Case of China and Japan before the League of Nations; Text for a Model Council and a Model Assembly of the League of Nations; A Citizens' Guide. Home: 37 Kirkland St., Cambridge, Mass. Died Jan. 17, 1952.

JOHNSON, Harry Miles, psychologist; b. Nelson, Mo., May 16, 1885; s. Daniel H. and Virginia (Reeder) J.; A.B., Mo. Valley Coll., Marshall, 1909; fellow Johns Hopkins, 1911-12, Ph.D., 1912, LL.D., 1947; grad. study U. Chgo., 1911; m. Mary Ethel Johnston, Aug. 21, 1912. Asst. psychologist Nela Research Lab., Cleve., 1912-13, asso. psychologist, 1914-16, psychologist, 1916-18; research with B. F. Goodrich Co., Akron, 1920-21; lectr. psychology U. Minn., 1921-23; asst. prof. psychology Ohio State U., 1923-25; sr. fellow, Mellon Inst. U. Pitts., 1925-32; prof. psychology Grad. Sch., Am. U., Washington, 1931-36; asso. Hwy. Research Bd., NRC, 1936-38; prof. and chmn. dept. psychology, Tulane U., 1938-47, John Madison Fletcher research prof. psychology, 1947-50, prof. emeritus, research consultant indsl. psychology, 1950-—; vis. prof. summers, U. Va., 1932-33, 1935, U. Cal., Los Angeles, 1941, U. of N.C., 1947, Cornell, 1948, U. Pitts., 1949. Served from lt. to capt. San. Corps, U.S. Army, 1918-20, chief of psychology sect. AS Med. Research Lab., 1919-20. Mem. A.A.A.S., Am. Psychol. Assn., Nat. Inst. Psychology, Soc. Exptl. Psychology, Am. Assn. for Applied Psychology, Am. Statis. Assn., So. Soc. for Psychology and Philosophy (pres. 1931-32), Nat. Research Council (served as mem. various committees; chmn. com. on psychology of the highway, 1934-40). Democrat. Episcopalian. Author: Audition and Habit-formation in the Dog, 1913; Principles of Applied Psychology, 1951. Cooperating editor Am. Jour. Psychology. Contbr. many tech. articles to Am. psychol. jours. and popular sci. articles to Harper's Mag., Forum, Colliers, etc. Research on fatigue and sleep for Simmons foundation, on human causes of highway accidents, and on selection and training of aircraft pilots. Clubs: Cosmos, Round Table. Home: 7837 Freret St., New Orlans 18. Address: Tulane University, New Orleans 18. Died Aug. 15, 1953.

JOHNSON, Henry Mortimer, lawyer; b. Giddings, Lee County, Tex., Feb. 27, 1878; s. Lucian Campbell and Sallie Thomas (Renfrow) J.; ed. high schs. of Giddings, Tex., and Louisville (Ky.) and U. of Louisville Law Sch.; m. Ella-Monks Johnson, June 3, 1908; children—Henry Madison, Emory Gilbert, Samuel Meredith, Lucian Lyons. Admitted to Ky. bar, 1899, later to bar of Court of Appeals of Ky. and U.S. Supreme Court; practiced in Louisville and highest courts of Ky. and supreme court of U.S., since 1899; former pres. Am. Business Men's Research Foundation, Chicago; pres. Ky. Sunday Sch. Assn. since 1926; former director Louisville Y.M.C.A.; trustee Kentucky Female Orphan School, Midway, Kentucky; formerly president Churchmen's Federation, Louisville (now Louisville Council of Churches). Elder Douglass Blvd. Christian Church. Pub. speaker and leader in temperance cause. Home: 2346 Dundee Rd. Office: Louisville Trust Bldg., Louisville. Died Oct. 16, 1950; buried Cave Hill Cemetery, Louisville.

JOHNSON, Howard Cooper, lawyer; b. Camden, N.J., Jan. 18, 1876; s. George K. and Sallie Kaighn (Cooper) J.; student Eastburn Acad., Phila., 1885-92; B.L., Swarthmore (Pa.) Coll., 1896; LL.B., U. of Pa., 1899; m. Edith Lamb, Apr. 16, 1903; children—Robert E. L., Howard Cooper, Jr., George K. III. Admitted to Pa. bar, 1899; in gen. practice, Phila., 1899-1927; asso. counsel Penn Mutual Life Ins. Co., 1902-27; pres. Starr Savings Bank, 1924-29; vis-pres. gen. counsel Strawbridge & Clothier since 1927; dir. Benjamin Franklin Hotel Co.; pres. Jeanes Hosp., 1928-30; life engr. and pres. Swarthmore Coll. Mem. Phila. Com. of Pa. Economy League (chmn. 1935-40); pres. Central Soup Society; dir. Trustees of Philadelphia Yearly Meeting of Friends (pres. 1933-46); mem. Phila. Financial Adv. Commn.; mem. Committee of 15 on Philadelphia Finance and Economics, Philadelphia Highway Traffic Board; chmn. South Jersey-Phila. Rapid Transit Co.; mem. adv. com. Philadelphia Parking Authority; pres. Phila. Merchants Association (pres. 1935-40); dir. Family Service of Del. Country; Phila. Child Guidance Clinic, Delaware Co. Child Guidance Clinic. Dir. Phila. Credit Bureau (v.p. 1941-46); asso. dir. Wallingford chap., Am. Red Cross, Woman's Hospital of Philadelphia. Member American, Pa. State and Phila. bar associations, American Judicature Society, Law Academy of Philadelphia, American Philatelic Society, Zoological Soc. of Phila., Am. Geneal. Society, N.J. Soc. of Pa., Franklin Inst., Phila. Soc. for Preservation of Landmarks, Gen. Alumni Soc. of Univ. of Pa., Hist. Soc. of Pa. Congress Hall Law Soc., Academy of Political Sci., Delta Upsilon, Book and Key. Republican. Member Society of Friends. Clubs: Union League, Kiwanis, Swarthmore, Corinthian Yacht, Rose Tree Hunt (Phila.); Players (Swarthmore); Northeast Harbor (Me.) Fleet; Southwest Harbor (Me.) Country; Keystone Auto. Home: "Coleshill," Moylan, Pa. Office: 801 Market St., Phila. Died June 9, 1952.

JOHNSON, Jacob, ex-congressman; b. Alborg, Denmark, Nov. 1, 1847; brought to Am., 1854, naturalized, 1868; ed. pvt. schs., Cal.; married. Admitted to bar, 1877, since practiced in Utah; identified with mining and agr.; U.S. commr., Utah, 1881-93; was probate judge U.S. Ct., Sanpete County, 2 terms, by apptmt. of Presidents Cleveland and Harrison; asst. U.S. dist. atty., Utah Ty., 2 terms; county atty. Sanpete County, 1892-4; mem. Ho. of Reps., Utah Ty., 1893; judge 7th Jud. Dist., Utah, 1896-05; mem. 63d Congress, Utah at-large; Republican. Home: Spring City, Utah. Deceased.

JOHNSON, James McIntosh, chemist; b. Newberry, S.C., Aug. 15, 1883; s. William and Mary Eugenia (Kibler) J.; B.S., Newberry (S.C.) Coll., 1902, A.M., 1903; Ph.D., Johns Hopkins, 1908; m. Mabel Rebecca Earnshaw, Mar. 15, 1912; children—William Mercier, Mabel Eleanor, Phoebe Rebecca, Frances Lillian. Chemist, Johns Hopkins Hosp., 1908-09; chemist Bur. Chemistry, U.S. Dept. of Agriculture, 1910-18; research chemist Hygienic Laboratory (now Nat. Inst. of Health), U.S. Pub. Health Service, Washington, D.C., since 1918. Mem. Am. Chem. Soc. Democrat. Lutheran. Co-discoverer of present method of making sulpharsphenamine. Contbr. to scientific jours. Home: 1333 Spring Rd. N.W. Office: 1339 H St. N.W., Washington. Died Mar. 2, 1953.

JOHNSON, Jesse, theologian; b. Reynoldsburg, O., Apr. 12, 1863; s. W. W. and Sarah Jane, (Graham) J.; A.B., Muskingum Coll., 1887, A.M., 1890, LL.D., 1937; grad. Allegheny Theol. Sem. (now Pitts. Theol. Sem.), 1894; D.D., Grove City (Pa.) Coll., 1896; m. Maude M. Martin, July 24, 1890; children—Ray Martin, Leland Graham, Walter Wilson (dec.), Helen Margery (dec.), Jean Orr (dec.), William Wells. Mem. faculty Muskingum Coll., 1889-92, pres. coll., 1892-1902; ordained to ministry U.P. Ch., 1894; prof. ch. history and apologetics Xenia Theol. Sem., 1902-23, prof. ch. history, 1923-30, now prof. emeritus Pittsburgh-Xenia Theol. Sem.; pastor U.P. Ch., Mount Ayr, Ia., 1930-39; ret. Home: Reynoldsburg, O. Died Mar. 13, 1951; buried Xenia, O.

JOHNSON, Kenneth D(ewey), lawyer, educator; b. Quincy, Mass., Sept. 5, 1898; s. John Louis and Charlotte M(atilda) (Almquist) J.; A.B., Brown U., 1921; LL.B., Harvard, 1924; m. Ethel G. Mayo, Aug. 14, 1930; children—Mayo, Charlotte Dallas. Admitted to Mass. bar, 1924, and practiced as asso. firm of Goodwin, Proctor, Field & Hoar, Boston, 1924-30, individually, 1930-42; dean N.Y. Sch. of Social Work, Columbia, 1949-58, emeritus, 1958-—; judge,

Dist. Ct., Quincy, (also presiding judge Juvenile Ct.), 1930-38. Enlisted with Bn. C, 103th F.A., 26th Div., U.S. Army, Jan. 1917; with A.E.F., 1917-19; entered active duty with rank of maj., 1942, promoted col., 1945; chief labor officer, Signal Corps, Washington, 1942-45; chief, spl. labor mission to E. T.O., Jan. 1945; legal adviser to mil. govt., Germany, 1945-46; spl. asst. to sec. of war, 1946-47; gen. counsel Nat. Security Resources Bd., 1947-49. Mem. bd. of selectman, Milton, Mass., 1924-31, chmn., 1928-31; chief of rubber prodn. team, Office of Sec. of War, 1943-45; alternate mem. Pres.'s spl. commn. on employee loyalty, 1947-48. Recipient Silver star, Legion of Merit, Commendation ribbon with 2 clusters. Pres. Mass. Conf. of Social Work, 1936; pres. Habit Clinic for Child Guidance of Boston, 1936-41; dir. Citizens Com. on Children of N.Y.C., 1951—, chmn., 1954—; dir. National Travelers Aid Assn., 1950—, U.S.O., Inc., 1951—, Big Brothers Am., 1952—, N.Y. Chpt. A.R.C., United Neighborhood Houses, 1951—, Greater N.Y. Council for Fgn. Students, 1952—, pres., 1952-54; pres. N.Y. State Welfare Conf., 1956—; exec. gd. Internat. Social Service, 1949—; trustee Columbia U. Press, 1949—. Nat. Probation and Parole Assn., 1950—. Chmn. health and welfare adv. com. to AFL-CIO Community Services Com. Home: Barley Neck Rd., Orleans, Mass.; also 130 E. 75th St., N.Y.C. 21. Office: 2 E. 91st St., N.Y.C. 28. Died Nov. 6, 1958; buried Orleans, Mass.

JOHNSON, Lambert Dunning, business exec.; b. Elizabeth, N.J., Feb. 25, 1889; s. Edward Mead and Francine (Lambert) J.; A.B., Cornell U., 1911; m. Evelyn Lee Igleheart, Oct. 14, 1916. With Mead Johnson & Co., Evansville, Ind., 1911—, successively chemist, supt., mgr. prodn., sec., treas., vice-pres., gen. mgr., exec. v.p., and now pres. and chmn. bd.; pres., dir. Mead Johnson & Co. of Can., Ltd., Mead Johnson & Co. of Calif.. Mead Johnson & Co., Terminal Corp. Home: 2216 Lincoln Av., Office: Evansville, Ind. Died July 29, 1955; buried Oak Hill Cemetery, Evansville.

JOHNSON, Leighton Foster, otolaryngologist; b. Hingham, Mass., Nov. 30, 1891; s. Rev. Samuel F. and Dora Alice (Belcher) J.; M.D., Boston U., 1915; post grad. Harvard Med. Sch., 2 yrs.; m. Harriet Woodman, Nov. 28, 1917; children—Leighton Foster, David Stanton. Engaged in practice as physician, otolaryngologist, Boston, Mass., since 1923; prof. and head of dept. otolaryngology, Sch. of Medicine, Boston U., 1941-45; surgeon in chief, ear, nose, throat dept. Mass. Meml. Hosp., since 1941, pres. staff, 1952-53; consultant to Fitchburg, Natick, Norwood, Cape Cod, Marthas Vineyard and Nantucket hospitals; lecturer Wellesley College. Consultant to Guild for Hard of Hearing. Served as captain, Fourth Division, Medical Reserve Corps, United States Army, during World War I. Fellow American College Surgeons; mem. A.M.A. (pres. Norfolk Dist., 1935-36), Am. Bd. Otolaryngology, Am. Acad. Otolaryngology, Am. Bronchoscopic Soc., Am. Triological Soc., N.E. Otolaryngol. Soc. (pres.), Boston Surgical Soc., Am. Broncho-Aesophological Soc. (president elect), Psi Upsilon. Clubs: Algonquin (Boston); Wellesley (Mass.) Country; Wellfleet (Mass.) Country. Contbr. numerous articles to nat. sci. jours. Home: Longwood Towers, Brookline, Mass. Office: 203 Commonwealth Av., Boston. Died July 21, 1953.

JOHNSON, Lewis Jerome, civil engr., publicist; b. Milford, Mass., Sept. 24, 1867; s. Napoleon Bonaparte and Mary Tufts (Stone) J.; A.B. magna cum laude, Harvard, 1887; C.E., Lawrence Sci. Sch., 1888; student Federal Technische Hochschule, Zürich, 1888-89, and at École des Ponts et Chaussées, Paris, portion of 1889-90; m. Grace Allen Fitch, June 27, 1893 (dec.); children—Jerome Allen, Chandler Winslow. Instr. civil engring. Harvard, 1890-92; practiced at Chgo., 1892-94; instr. Harvard, 1894-96, asst. prof., 1896-1906, prof. civil engring., 1906-34, now prof. civil engring. emeritus; also prof. civil engring. Mass. Inst. Tech., 1914-19. Lectr. on applied econ. and polit. science Div. Univ. Extension, Mass. Dept. Edn., 1934—. Pres. Mass. Single Tax League, 1913-21, and of Nat. Single Tax League, 1918-20. Joint designer of Harvard Stadium. Fellow Am. Acad. Arts and Sciences; mem. Boston Soc. Civil Engrs., Am. Soc. C.E., Am. Assn. U. Profs., Proportional Representation Soc. (London), League of Nations Assn., Tau Beta Pi, Sigma Xi. Author: Statics by Algebraic and Graphic Methods, 1903; The Initiative and Referendum, An Effective Ally of Representative Government, 1909; The Cincinnati Plan (of city government) for American Cities, 1932; Undeveloped Possibilities of Democracy, 1932; Economic Taxes vs. Government Taxes, An Engineer's View of Taxation, 1934; other essays on generally overlooked fundamentals to polit. and econ. order. Joint author of proposed new charter (of 1911) for Cambridge, Mass.; collaborator with his son, Chandler, in the latter's drafting and securing the authorization of Plan E (Cincinnati Plan), optional for Mass. cities outside of Boston (chap. 378, Acts of 1938) and adopted by Worcester, Quincy, Medford and Revere. Contbr. to tech. jours. Home: 37 Kirkland St., Cambridge, Mass. Died Apr. 15, 1952; buried Milford, Mass.

JOHNSON, Ligon, copyright lawyer; b. Tuskegee, Ala., Jan. 20, 1873; s. Richard Allen and Emily Paine (Ligon) J.; student St. Mary's Coll., Belmont, N.C., 1887, Emory Coll., Oxford, Ga., 1888-89, U. of Ga., 1890, U. of Va. (law), 1891; m. Blanche Tindle Jones, Oct. 25, 1934. Admitted to Ga. bar, 1893, and began practice in Atlanta; spl. asst. to atty. gen. of Ga., 1902-06, and to U.S. atty. gen., 1906-15; practiced in New York since 1908; specialized in copyright law; participated in copyright legislation and hearings in U.S., Can., and Eng.; has one of the largest copyright reference libraries covering books, plays, motion pictures, etc., domestic and foreign; copyright and cons. counsel for Metro-Goldwyn-Mayer, 20th Century Fox, Warner Bros., First Nat. Pictures, etc.; consulting counsel to Alien Property Custodian on copyrights and literary property. Served as capt. Judge Advocate Dept. and on Gen. Staff during World War I. Mem. Am. Legion. Mason (Shriner). Club: Westchester Country (Rye, N.Y.). Home: Indian Chase Park, Greenwich, Conn. Office: 1619 Broadway, N.Y. City. Died Mar. 29, 1951; buried Oakwood Cemetery, Montgomery, Ala.

JOHNSON, Lincoln, business exec.; b. Waltham, Mass., Aug. 24, 1893; s. Frank Prescott and Helen Day (Perry) J.; Ph.B., Yale U., 1914; E.M., 1916; m. Virginia Hamill, Sept. 17, 1930; 1 dau., Barbara. Mining work Morocacha (Peru) Mining Co., 1916-17; mine exploration Andes Exploration Co., Peru and Chile, 1917-18; engr. Cosden Oil & Gas Co., Tulsa, 1919; asso. N.Y. Trust Co., 1919-28; with Estate of David Wolfe Bishop, 1929-31; v.p. Cortlandt Bishop, Inc., 1929-31; pres. Am. Art Assn., Anderson Galleries Inc., 1929-31; v.p. Mfrs. Trust Co., N.Y.C., 1931—. Mem. Fgn. Exchg. Com., N.Y.C.; arbitrator Am. Arbitration Assn., N.Y.C. Mem. Am. Inst. Mining and Metall. Engrs., Nat. Fgn. Trade Council, Inc. (governing mem.), Bankers Assn. Fgn. Trade, Phi Gamma Delta. Democrat. Unitarian. Club: Yale (N.Y.C.). Home: 200 E. 66th St., N.Y.C. 21. Office: 55 Broad St., N.Y.C. Died Sept. 2, 1957.

JOHNSON, Malcolm, pub. exec.; b. Chelsea, Mass., May 29, 1902; s. Ernest H. and Rachel A. (Goff) J.; S.B., Mass. Inst. Tech., 1923; m. Mathilde E. Whitridge, July 2, 1937 (div. 1953); children—Mathilde E., Malcolm W., Dallas G.; m. 2d, Mildred S. Young July 27, 1956. With Standard Oil Co. of N.Y., North China Div., 1923-27; mng. editor Atlantic Monthly Co., 1928-29; exec. v.p. Doubleday Doran & Co., 1937-43; exec. v.p. D. Van Nostrand Co.; chmn. bd. Franklin Publs., Inc. President Book Publishers Bur., 1941-44; mem. book pub. and mfg. industry adv. com. W.P.B., 1942-45. Dir. U.S. Internat. Book Assn., Inc., Editions for the Armed Services, Inc., 1942-46. Republican. Quaker. Clubs: Metropolitan (Washington); University, Players, Dutch Treat. Home: Bedens Brook Rd., Skillman, N. J. Office: 120 Alexander St., Princeton, N.J. Died Feb. 27, 1958.

JOHNSON, Melvin Maynard, Masonic official; b. Waltham, Mass., May 11, 1871; s. Hon. Byron B. and Louisa H. (Cutter) J.; A.B. and Ph.B., Tufts, 1892; LL.B., magna cum laude, Boston U. Law Sch., 1895; LL.D., U. Vt., 1936; L.H.D., Marietta College, 1941, Boston U., 1954; D.C.L., Illinois Wesleyan U., 1949; LL.D., Tufts Coll., 1949; m. Ina Delphene Freeman, Oct. 8, 1895 (died Dec. 9, 1947); children —Mrs. Dorothy J. Adams-Gagel (died, 1950), Melvin Maynard; married second, Eleanor Payzant, Aug. 14, 1954. Practiced with father under title of Johnson & Johnson, 1895-1902; mem. Rogers, North & Johnson, 1903-07, Johnson & North, 1907-39; gained internat. reputation in defense of LeBlanc-Glover murder case. Widely known as public speaker; prof. Boston U. Law Sch., 1918-35, dean, 1935-43, dean emeritus since 1943. Trustee Tufts Coll.; 1918-33, Fellow Am. Acad. Arts and Scis., A.A.A.S.; mem. Am. Law Inst., Am. Bar Assn. (life), Am. Psychiatric Assn. (hon.), Theta Delta Chi, Phi Beta Kappa, Phi Delta Phi. Republican. Episcopalian. Mason; Sovereign Grand Commander of Supreme Council 33° Northern Masonic Jurisdiction, U.S.A., 1933-54; Grand Master Masons in Massachusetts, 1913-16; dir. Grand Lodge Corp., mem. Bd. Masonic Relief; trustee Masonic Edn. and Charity Trust; pres. bd. trustees Supreme Council Corp., till 1954; honorary mem. many Masonic orgns. in U.S. and fgn. countries. Awarded Gourgap Medal (for notably distinguished service), of Supreme Council 33°, N.M.J., Distinguished Service Medals of Grand Lodges and Supreme Councils, R.I., Me., Conn., Mass., N.J., N.C., Nova Scotia, Czechoslovakia, Norway, Brazil, Uruguay, Argentina, France, Treiste, Canada, Chile, Italy, Belgium, Central Am., England, Mexico, Red Cross of Constantine, Grand R. A. chpt. Mass. and N.C. Clubs: Algonquin, Canadian (New York) Author: The Beginnings of Freemasonry in America, also author numerous mag. articles. Home: 124 Commonwealth Av. Office: Statler Bldg., Boston 16. Semi-retired. Died Dec. 18, 1957.

JOHNSON, Nels G., judge; b. Akranes, Iceland, Apr. 30, 1896; s. Gudbjartur and Gudrun (Olafsdottir) J., brought to U.S., 1900, naturalized, 1908; B.A., U. N.D., 1924, J.D., 1926; m. Ruth H. Hallenbeck; children—George Magnus, Grace Margot. Admitted to N.D. bar, 1926, and since in gen. practice law, Towner; states atty. McHenry County, N.D., 1929-37, 40-42; atty. gen. N.D., 1945-48; sr. mem. law firm Johnson and Rausch, 1948-54; judge Supreme Ct. N.D., 1954—. Served with 82d Div., U.S. Army, World War I. Mem. Sons of Norway, Phi Beta Kappa, Delta Sigma Rho, Coif, Pi Rho Chi. Republican. Presbyn. Mason. Home: 1110 1st St. N., Bismarck, N.D. Died Dec. 2, 1958.

JOHNSON, Nelson Trusler, foreign service officer; b. Washington, D.C., Apr. 3, 1887; s. Jeremiah and Salome (Trusler) J.; student at Sidwell's Friends School, Washington, D.C., 1900-06; attended George Washington Univ., 1906-07 (hon. LL.D.); m. Jane Thornton Beck, Oct. 10, 1931; children—Nelson Beck, Betty Jane. Appointed as student interpreter in China, 1907; vice and dep. consul gen. and interpreter, Mukden, 1909-10, at Harbin, Apr.-July 1910, Hankow, 1910-11, Shanghai, 1911-14; designated to have judicial authority in civ. and criminal cases; consul at Chungking, dec. 1914-Mar. 1915, Changsha, Mar. 2, 1915-July 30, 1918, Shanghai, Aug. 1-Nov. 1, 1918; assigned to Dept. of State, Div. Far Eastern Affairs, Dec. 11, 1918; expert asst. on Far Eastern Affairs to Am. commrs., Conf. on Limitation of Armament, 1921; apptd. consul gen. at large Nov. 23, 1921, and assigned to inspection Dist. of Eastern Asia; chief Div. of Far-Eastern Affairs, Dept. of State, 1925-27; asst. sec. of state, 1927-29; E.E. and M.P. to China, 1929-35, A.E. and P., 1935-41; E.E. and M.P. to Australia 1941-Mar. 31, 1946; sec. gen. Far Eastern Commn., 1946-52. Mem. N. China Br. Royal Asiatic Society, Delta Tau Delta. Clubs: Cosmos (Washington); Shanghai; Peking. Home: 4602 Van Ness St., N.W., Washington 16. Died Dec. 3, 1954; buried Rock Creek Cemetery, Washington.

JOHNSON, Osa Helen (Mrs. Martin Johnson), explorer, author, motion picture producer; b. Chanute, Kan., Mar. 14, 1894; d. William Sherman and Ruby Isabel (Holman) Leighty; grad. Chanute High Sch., 1910; D.Sc., Rollins Coll., 1941; m. Martin Johnson, May 15, 1910 (dec. Jan. 13, 1937). With husband made photographic expdns. to South Seas, 1912, Solomon Islands and New Hebrides, 1914, Borneo, 1917-19, making motion pictures of cannibals and head hunters and life of the savage tribes; made 5 expdns. to African jungles, 1921-34, Borneo, 1935-36, making motion pictures, some with sound, some from airplanes, of wild human and animal life; headed 20th Century-Fox expdn. into East Africa to make picture Stanley and Livingston, 1937; licensed air pilot; pres. Martin Johnson Pictures, Inc., Osa Johnson, Inc. Mem. Am. Mus. Natural History, Ninety Niners (women pilots), Soc. Women Geographers, Bus. and Profl. Women, Kansas Society; hon. mem. Girl Scouts Am., Beta Sigma Phi. Presbyn. Producer of motion pictures; Jungles Calling, 1937; I Married Adventure, 1940; African Paradise, 1941; Tulagi and the Solomons, 1943; (with Martin Johnson) Cannibaland, Cannibals of The South Seas, East of Suez, The Adventurous Orang, Trailing African Wild Animals, Simba, Across the World, Congorilla, Baboona, Borneo, Wonders of the Congo, Wings Over Africa, Three Boy Scouts in Africa. Author: Jungle Babies, 1930; Jungle Pets, 1932; Osa Johnson's Jungle Friends, 1939; I Married Adventure, 1940; Four Years in Paradise, 1941; Pantaloons, The Story of a Baby Elephant, 1941; Snowball, the Baby Gorilla, 1942; Bride in the Solomons, 1944; Tarnish, The True Story of a Lion Cub, 1945; (with Martin Johnson) Cannibal Land, 1921; Lion, 1929; Camera Trails in Africa, 1924; Safari—A Saga of the African Blue, 1928; Congorilla, 1931; Over African Jungles, 1934. Contbr. many articles to periodicals. Home: Bismarck Hotel. Address: Osa Johnson, Inc., 400 Park Av., N.Y.C. Died Jan. 7, 1953.

JOHNSON, Otis R., lumber exec.; b. Ft. Bragg, Cal., 1887; U. Cal., 1909. Pres., dir. Union Lumber Co., San Francisco; v.p. California Western R.R.; dir. Crocker Anglo Nat. Bank. Home: 1980 Vallejo St. Office: Crocker Bldg., San Francisco. Died July 1, 1957.

JOHNSON, Owen, novelist; born New York City, August 27, 1879; son Robert Wunderwood and Katherine (McMahon) J.; student Lawrenceville School, Yale University; married Gertrude Bovee, January 1926; children—Olivia (Madam Basile Pdekoff), Katherine Burnell, Robert U., Owen Denis, Patricia (J. Deely). Author (novels): Arrows of the Almighty, The Salamander, Wasted Generations, Children of Divorce, Sixty-First Second, Sacrifice, Coming of the Amazons; Lawrenceville stories: The Varmint, Tennessee Shad, Eternal Boy. Contbr. articles. Retired due to ill health, 1946. Home: Stockbridge, Mass. Died Jan. 27, 1952; buried Stockbridge, Mass.

JOHNSON, Palmer O(liver), univ. prof.; b. Eagl Grove, Ia., Sept. 13, 1891; s. Nels Andrew and Elizabeth Ann (Osmundsen) J.; A.B., U. Wis., 1912 B.S., U. Minn., 1921, M.S., 1926, Ph.D., 1928 research studies, Galton Lab., U. London, 1934-35 m. Hildegard Binder, Aug. 20, 1936; children—Gisela, Karin. Teacher and adminstr. in pub. schs. Minn. and Ill., 1913-16, 1921-25; asst. prof. edn U. Minn., 1928-34, asso. prof., 1934-36, prof. 1936—, chmn. dept. of statistics; vis. prof. U. W.Va. summer 1932. U. Tex., summer 1939; supt. anima breeding farms, 1917. Dir. Land-Grant Coll. Survey, Minn., 1928-30; specialist mem. survey commn. Higher Edn. Institutions, State of Ore., U.S. Office of Edn., 1929; prin. educationist and cons. Pres. Roosevelt's Adv. Com. on Edn., 1937-38; cons. Ednl. Policies Commn. since 1939; conferee research and statistics U.S. Office of Edn., 1947. Served as lt., Coast Arty., U.S. Army, 1918; coordinator and dir. Army Specialized Training Program of Exams, Minn., 1943-44. Fellow Am. Assn. Advancement of Sci. (v.p., chmn. Sect. Q, 1950), Am. Statistical Association (mem. council 1951-52); mem. Inst. of Math. Statistics, Psychometric Society, Biometric Society, Am. Ednl. Research Assn., Nat. Soc. for Study of Edn., N.E.A., Minn. Acad. Scis., Sigma Xi, Phi Delta Kappa, Gamma Sigma Delta, Alpha Zeta, Phi Kappa Sigma. Author: Curriculum Problems in Science, 1930; Aspects of Land-Grant College Education, 1934; (with O. L. Harvey) The National Youth Administration, 1938; (with others) The Effective General College Curriculum, 1937; (with others) An Evaluation of Modern Education, 1942; Statistical Methods in Research, 1949; (with others) Educational Research and Appraisal, 1953 (with R. W. B. Jackson) Introduction to Statistical Methods, 1953; Modern Statistical Methods: Inductive and Description (with R. W. B. Jackson), 1957; Modern Sampling Methods, 1959; articles profl., classical jours., yearbooks of national societies. Statistical editor Jour. of Exptl. Edn. Research in statis. methods and exptl. designs, measurement, higher edn., science education. Home: 3312 Edmund Blvd., Mpls. 6. Died Jan. 1960.

JOHNSON, Reginald Davis, architect; b. Westchester, N.Y., July 19, 1882; s. Joseph Horsfall and Isabel Green (Davis) J.; A.B., Williams Coll., 1907; B.S., Mass. Institute of Technology, 1910; married Kathleen Bushnell Leupp, June 9, 1910; children—Joseph Leupp, Ethel Murdock, Constance Davis. Trustee Haynes Foundation, trustee Hospital of the Good Samaritan (both Los Angeles); mem. exec. com. Los Angeles Co. Mus. Fellow American Institute of Architects. Chief Architect, Harbor Hills, Los Angeles Co., 1939; coordinating architect, Rancho San Pedro, City of Los Angeles, 1941; architect of Baldwin Hills Village, Los Angeles, with firm of Wilson, Merrill and Alexander as associates and Clarence Stein as consultant, during 1941; Awarded Exhibition Medal, A.I.A. for Residential Architecture, 1921; Medal, Architectural League of New York for design of Santa Barbara Biltmore Hotel, 1928; Medal, Better Homes in America for small house design, 1931. Mem. Los Angeles Co. Dem. Central Com. Home: 525 S. Grand Av., Pasadena 2, Cal. Died Oct. 28, 1952; buried San Gabriel (Cal.) Cemetery.

JOHNSON, Richard H., banker; b. Eastford, Conn., Feb. 18, 1855; s. Samuel A. and Mary C. (Carpenter) J.; B.S., U. Minn., 1882; LL.B., U. Mich., 1884; m. Mary M. Poole, July 17, 1889; children—Hartwell P., Mary Margery, Richard Watt, Beth Carpenter, Ward Kendall. An organizer, dir., cashier First Nat. Bank of Dickinson, N.D., 1890-1914, v.p., 1914—; pres. R. H. Johnson Ins. Co., Inc. Mayor of Dickinson, 1910-14; del. Rep. Nat. Conv., 1912. Mem. Chi Psi, Phi Delta Phi. Mason (Shriner), Elk. Home: Dickinson, N.D. Died Aug. 28, 1942; buried Dickinson Cemetery.

JOHNSON, Roger Bruce Cash, educator; b. Harbor Island, Bahamas, W.I., Jan. 13, 1867; s. Thomas William and Sarah Elizabeth (Cash) J.; A.B. magna cum laude, Princeton, 1887, fellow in philosophy, 1887-88, Ph.D. magna cum laude, 1900; m. Leontine Hamilton, Aug. 15, 1905. Prof. philosophy Miami U., Oxford, O., 1888-1905; preceptor in philosophy Princeton, 1905-10, prof., 1910-35, McCosh prof. philosophy, 1933-35, chmn. dept. philosophy, 1926-34, prof. emeritus, 1935—. Mem. Am. Philos. Assn., etc. Author: The Metaphysics of Knowledge, 1900. Home: Kittery Point, Me. Died July 7, 1946.

JOHNSON, (John) Rosamond, musician, composer; b. Jacksonville, Fla., Aug. 11, 1873; s. James and Helen Louise (Dillette) J.; began in music under mother at 4; student New England Conservatory of Music, and in Europe; piano with Charles F. Dennée, and Mme. Dietrich Strong, organ with George Whiting, harmony with Carl Riessman, and Davenport Kerrison, voice with William Dunham and Clarence B. Ashenden; A.M. (hon.) Atlanta J., 1917; m. Nora Ethel Floyd, July 3, 1913; 1 dau., Mildred Louise. Profl. début, Boston, 1894; supr. music pub. schs., Jacksonville, Fla., 1896-98; toured in vaudeville in U.S. and Europe; dir. music Hammerstein Opera House, London, 1912-13, Sch. Settlemnet for Colored People, N.Y.C., 1914—, also trustee same; dir. singing orchestra for Mrs. Emelie Hapgood's Colored Players, Garden and Garrick theatres, New York. Served as 2d lt. 15th Inf., N.Y.N.G., 1918. Mem. United Song Writers' Soc. America. Republican. Methodist. Mason. Club: Civic. Composer of music for Cole and Johnson's Shoo-Fly Regiment, Red Moon, Bert William's Mr. Load of Koal, also arrangements of Negro spirituals and over 300 popular songs. Joint composer of comic operas, Humpty Dumpty, Sleeping Beauty and the Beast; collaborated with Louis Hirsh in Come Over Here. Arranger of the Book of American Negro Spirituals. Made sub-chief Iroquois Indian Tribe, 1921. Home: 154 W. 131st St., N.Y.C. Died Nov. 11, 1954.*

JOHNSON, Silas, clergyman, coll. pres.; b. Baxley, Ga., June 13, 1889; s. Duncan Malcom and Mary Jane (Cleveland) J.; spl. student Emory Univ., Atlanta, Ga.; D.D., Fla. Southern Coll., 1943; D.D., Emory Univ., 1943; m. Helen Lee Douglas, June 21, 1910; 1 son, Douglas Marion. Ordained to ministry of Meth. Ch., Savannah, Ga., 1912; pastor Trinity Ch., Savannah, Ga., 1922-29, First Methodist Church Thomasville, Ga., 1929-33, Vineville Ch., Macon, Ga., 1933-37; dist. supt. Macon dist. Meth. Ch., hdqrs., Macon, Ga., 1937-40; exec. vice pres. Wesleyan Coll., Macon, Ga., 1941-42, pres. since 1946; pastor Mulberry St. Ch., Macon, Ga., 1942-46. Trustee Wesleyan Coll. since 1938, Candler Hospital (Savannah, Ga.), since 1930, South Ga. Conf. Meth. Ch. since 1939. Chmn. exec. com. Wesleyan Christian Advocate since 1937; mem. bd. pubs. since 1939. Club: Rotary (rep. club, Edinburgh, Scotland and Toronto conventions). Home: Wesleyan Coll., Macon, Ga. Died Oct. 25, 1951; buried Macon.

JOHNSON, Simeon Moses, lawyer; b. Cin., Mar. 18, 1859; s. Frederick A. and Julia (Moses) Johnson; LL.B., Cin. Law Sch., 1880; m. Gertrude Cohen, Dec. 7, 1893 (died Dec. 18, 1941); children—Ella Gertrude, Frederic William (dec.), George Harris. Practiced Cin., 1880—; Dem. nominee for judge of Common Pleas Ct., 1901; chmn. Dem. Campaign Com., Cin., 1907, 13, 21, 34; chmn. Hamilton County Dem. Exec. Com., 1920-48; vice mayor Cin., 1912-13; mem. Ohio State Commn. to investigate state jud. system, 1914; declined Dem. nom. for mayor, 1915; mem. Dem. Nat. Campaign Com., 1916; spl. asst. to atty. gen. of Ohio, 1917-18; del. to Dem. Nat. Conv., San Francisco, 1920, Houston, 1928; declined apptmt. as justice Supreme Ct. of Ohio, 1920. Trustee Cin. Law Library Assn. (pres.), Union Am. Hebrew Congregations (hon. exec. bd.). Mem. Am., Ohio (pres. 1912-13), Cin. (pres. 1918-19, 19-20) bar assns. Jewish religion. Clubs: Literary (pres. 1931-32), Cincinnati, Lawyers, Duckworth; Hyde Park Business Club. Home: 3427 Burch Av., Hyde Park. Office: 801 Atlas Bank Bldg., Cin. Died Apr. 8, 1957; buried United Jewish Cemetery, Cin.

JOHNSON, Theodore, business exec.; b. nr. Racine, Wis.; student pub. schs. of Racine. With J. I. Case Co., 1902—, asst. treas., 1918-24, sec., 1924-44, dir., 1924—, exec. v.p., 1944-48, pres. and dir., 1948-53, vice chmn. bd., 1953-55, ret. 1955; dir. 1st Nat. Bank & Trust Co. Home: 1344 Dean Blvd. Office: 700 State St., Racine, Wis. Died Feb. 4, 1956.

JOHNSON, Tillman Davis, judge; b. Rutherford County, Tenn., Jan. 8, 1858; s. Columbus Montgomery and Catherine (Davis) J.; Cumberland U., Lebanon, Tenn., 1876-80; m. Fannie McCall, July 27, 1881; children—Wade McCall, Ralph Montgomery, Ruth. Taught school in Tenn., 1880-85; prin. Govt. Indian Sch., Ft. Bennett, S.D., 1886-87, Ft. Hall, Ida., 1888-89; practiced law in Ogden, Utah, 1889-1915; judge U.S. Dist. Ct. for Utah, 1915-49. Mem. Utah Ho. of Reps., 1898-99. Dem. candidate for Congress, 1912. Baptist. Mason. Home: 105 East S. Temple St., Salt Lake City. Died Nov. 1, 1953.

JOHNSON, Walter Nathan, clergyman; b. Sampson County, N.C., Mar. 24, 1875; s. Calhoun Cornelius and Laura Ann (Alderman) J.; B.A., Wake Forest (N.C.) Coll., 1899, D.D., 1919; studied So. Bapt. Theol. Sem., Louisville, 1905, U. Chgo., 1911; m. Eva Coppedge, Aug. 15, 1900; children—Eva Foy, Martha Gladys, Laura Bruce, Falk Simmons. Ordained ministry Bapt. Ch., 1896; pastor in N.C. until 1904, Natchitoches, La., 1905-07; sec. of missions, Bapt. Com. La., 1907-09; pastor Wake Forest Coll., 1909-15; sec. missions N.C. Bapt. State Conv., 1916-20; establishing schs. of applied stewardship in Bapt. chs., 1920-25; former tchr. stewardship Mars Hill Coll., sec. Steward League Bapt. Ministers in So. States; now promoting adult Christian edn. in chs.; editor The Next Step (bull.). Author: (brochure) Southern Baptist Crisis, 1905; Stewardship Vitalized, 1926; Which—Dominate or Permeate?, 1929; (booklet) Spinal Adjustment. Home: Mars Hill, N.C. Died June 24, 1952; buried Wake Forest, N.C.

JOHNSON, William Arthur, mfr., contractor; b. Ord, Neb., 1885; s. William Benjamin and Sarah Frances (Freeman) J.; high sch., Riverside, Calif., 1903; m. Irene E. La Rue, 1908; children—Frances (Mrs. Winston R. Fuller), Margaret (Mrs. Earl G. Corkett). Contractor Riverside, California, 1903; changed name later to Johnson-Shea Co.; pres. Nat. Bank of Riverside, 1918-22; pres. Am. Pipe and Constrn. Co. and predecessor cos., 1922-52, chmn. bd., 1952—; chmn. bd. Amercoat Corp., Pipe Linings, Inc., 1952—; pres. Hall-Johnson Company, 1922-33; president Pacific Constructors, Incorporated (builders of Shasta Dam), Johnson, Inc., Southern Finance Service; vice president of Loma Vista Properties, Inc., Rose Hills, Inc.; Rose Hills Meml. Park Assn.; dir. Cal. Materials Co., Citizens Nat. Bank and Trust Co., Riverside, Calif. Johnson Western Constructors, Bartolo Co. First pres. Beavers, 1955-56. Trustee Pomona College. Clubs: California (Los Angeles); San Gabriel Country, Santa Ana Country, Newport Harbor Yacht. Home: 806 West Bay Av., Balboa. Office: 4635 Firestone Blvd., South Gate, Cal. Died May 10, 1956; buried Rose Hills Meml. Park, Whittier, Cal.

JOHNSON, William Burdett, ret. mfr.; b. Milw., June 7, 1875; s. Burdett J. and Sarah Y. (Gardner) J.; ed. in pub. schs. Milw.; m. Edith M. Remington, June 26, 1906 (died Feb. 1957); children—Dr. Frederick R., Norman B., Helen R. (Mrs. Jack B. Huntress). Began with B. J. Johnson Soap Co., 1895, this firm became Palmolive Co. of Del., 1917, and later Colgate-Palmolive-Peet Co., sec., dir., 1918-27, dir. since retirement from active bus. Mem. Evanston Hist. Soc. Republican. Christian Scientist. Mason (32°, K.T., Shriner). Clubs: Glen View, University, Evanston. Home: 5838 Starlight Way, Scottsdale, Ariz. Died July 20, 1959; buried Forest Home Cemetery, Milw.

JOHNSON, William C., mfr.; b. Birmingham, Ala., May 25, 1902; s. E. Judson and Ida (Hollingsworth) J.; ed. pub. sch. and high sch.; m. Dorothy Ann Hess, June 21, 1930; children—William Clifford, Nancy Ann, Eric Charles (dec.). Apprentice, Ala. Power Co., Birmimgham, 1920-24; with Allis-Chalmers Manufacturing Co. since 1924, field service and erection work, 1924-29, field rep., Atlanta, Ga., 1929-35 Chattanooga, Tenn., 1935-37, branch office mgr., Knoxville, Tenn., 1937-40, departmental sales mgr., Milwaukee, Wis., 1940-42, gen. sales mgr. gen machinery div., Milwaukee, 1942-44, vice pres. gen. machinery div., Milwaukee, 1944, became exec. vice pres. tractor and gen. machine div., 1951. Mem. N.A.M. (dir.), Engrs. Soc. of Milwaukee, Nat. Elec. Mfrs. Assn. (president), Newcomen Soc. of Eng., Milwaukee Assn. of Commerce. Mem. Vine St. Presbyterian Ch. Clubs: Executives, Athletic, Wisconsin, Milwaukee, Milwaukee Country (Milw.). Home: Elm Grove, Wis. Office: 1126 S. 70th St., Milw. Died July 25, 1951; buried Wis. Meml. Park.

JOHNSON, William Templeton, architect; b. Staten Island, N.Y., Aug. 31, 1877; s. Oliver Templeton and Caroline Sophia (Thomas) J.; ed. Staten Island Acad., 1893-96, Columbia, 1906-07, Atelier Laloux, École des Beaux Arts, Paris 1909-11; m. Clara Delafield Sturges, June 21, 1905 (divorced); children—Winthrop Templeton, Arthur Delafield, Alan Winthrop, Katharine Delafield; m. 2d, Helen Hayes Gleason, June 19, 1935. Began practice as architect at New York, 1911. Prin. works: Pub. Library and High Sch., La Jolla, Calif.; Fine Arts Gallery, Junipero Serra Museum, San Diego Trust & Savings Bank, San Diego Museum of Natural History (all San Diego, Calif.); 3 bldgs. for U.S. Govt., Iberian Am. Expn. (Seville, Spain); Bridges Music Auditorium, Claremont, Calif.; U.S. Post Office, San Diego, Calif., Administrn. Bldg. Consolidated-Vultee Aircraft Corp., San Diego, San Diego Pub. Library. Town planner, U.S. Shipping Bd., 1918. Mem. exec. com. Nat. Conf. on City Planning, 1912-16. Fellow Am. Inst. Architects (pres. San Diego Chapter 1931); mem. Fine Arts Soc. of San Diego. Democrat. Unitarian. Clubs: University, Cuyamaca, Century Assn. (N.Y.). Home: 4284 Jackdaw St. Office: San Diego Trust & Savings Bldg., San Diego, Cal. Died Oct. 14, 1957.

JOHNSON, Willis Ernest, college dean; b. Delano, Minn., Feb. 9, 1869; s. Jonas and Christine (Anderson) J.; student State Normal Sch., St. Cloud, Minn., 1890-94; Ph.B., Ill. Wesleyan U., 1900, M.A., 1907; B.A. and M.A., U. of Minn., 1918, Ph.D., 1919; LL.D., Dak. Wesleyan U., 1919; Sc.D., S.D. State Coll., 1923; m. Eunice Stanley, of Delano, Apr. 2, 1890; children—Willis Leslie, Arthur Lee, Stanley Clyde, Clarence Elbert, Aylesworth (dec.). Critic teacher, State Normal Sch., St. Cloud, 1894-95; prof. history and geography, State Normal Sch., Mayville, N.Dak., 1895-1902; prof. social sciences, 1902, v.p., 1905, pres., 1914-19, Northern Normal and Industrial Sch., Aberdeen, S.Dak.; pres. State Normal and Industrial Sch., Ellendale, N.Dak., 1913-14; pres. State Coll. of Agr. and Mechanic Arts, Brookings, S.D., 1919-23; professorial lecturer, U. of Minn., and prin. Univ. High Sch., 1923-24; dir. of edn., State Teachers' Coll., San Diego, Calif., from 1924 until retired. Served on staff ednl. survey of Va. and Ala. Mem. Phi Beta Kappa, Phi Delta Kappa, Kappa Delta Pi. Mason. Author: Mathematical Geography, 1907; South Dakota—A Republic of Friends, 1911; The State and Nation, 1917; Community Civics (with F. A. Ransom), 1922. Home: 2276 Hickory St., San Diego, Calif. Died Apr. 24, 1951; buried Brookings, S.D.

JOHNSTON, Alva, writer; b. Sacramento, Aug. 1, 1888; s. Alfred John and Luella (Buckminster) J.; ed. Sacramento (Calif.) High Sch.; m. Evelyn Colgan, Apr. 29, 1914; children—Elizabeth, Margaret (Mrs. Norman W. Erlandson). Began as reporter, Sacramento (Calif.) Bee, 1906; with New York Times, 1912-28, New York Herald Tribune, 1928-32; magazine writer, chiefly for New Yorker and Saturday Evening Post, since 1932. Awarded Pulitzer prize for reporting, 1922. Mem. A.A.A.S., Astron. Soc. of Pacific. Club: National Press. Author: The Great

Goldwyn, 1937; Wilson Mizner, the Legend of a Sport (privately printed), 1943; The Case of Erle Stanley Gardner. Home: 169 Bobolink Road, Yonkers, N.Y. Died Nov. 23, 1950.

JOHNSTON, Alvanley, labor exec.; b. Seeleys Bay, Leeds County, Ont., Can. (of Am. parents), May 12, 1875; s. David and Annie (Jarrell) J.; student pub. sch., Seeleys Bay, Can., 1882-88, Brockville (Ont.) Business Coll., 1890-91; came to United States, 1888; married Maud Ethel Forsythe, July 6, 1917 (died 1934); children—Anna Maud (Mrs.Harry Cecil Saddington), Marian Jean (Mrs. O. M. Kendall, Jr.). Began as railroad employee, 1892; locomotive engineer, Great American Rail Road, 1897-1909; gen. chmn. Brotherhood of Locomotive Engrs., Great Northern Ry., 1909-18; asst. grand chief engr. Brotherhood of Locomotive Engrs., Cleveland, O., 1918-25, grand chief engr. since 1925; pres. Park Lane Villa Hotel Co., and Brotherhood of Locomotive Engrs. Bldg. Ass'n. Mason (all bodies except 33°), Scottish Clans. Home: 3197 Warrington Rd., Shaker Heights, O. Office: Brotherhood of Locomotive Engineers Bldg., Cleve. Died Sept. 17, 1951; buried Acacia Meml. Park, Cleve.

JOHNSTON, Charles Eugene, ry. exec.; b. St. Elmo, Ill., Oct. 30, 1881; s. Alexander Morris and Mary Joseph J.; student pub. schs.; m. Ethel Irene Kirkpatrick, June 20, 1907; 1 son, Robert Kirk. Began in engring. dept. Chicago, Paducah & Memphis Ry. (now part of C.&E.I. R.R.), 1897; with StL.& S.W. Ry., 1897-98, C.&E.I. R.R., 1899; asst. engr. location, construction and maintenance, St.L.&S.F. R.R., 1900-03; resident engr. M.P. Ry., Feb.-June 1903; asst. engr. miantenance of ways. St.L.&S.F. R.R., 1903-06; locating engr. K.C.S. Ry., 1906-08, and continued with same road successively as office engr., 1908-09, div. engr., 1909-11, chief engr., 1911-17, gen. mgr., 1917-24, v.p., 1924-28, pres., 1928-38; chmn. Western Assn. Ry. Execs., Chgo., 1939-48; retired June 30, 1949. Mem. Am. Soc. C.E., Am. Ry. Engring. Assn. Republican. Home: 7955 Roseland Dr., La Jolla, Cal. Died July 10, 1951.

JOHNSTON, David Ira, lawyer; b. Indiana Co., Pa., Aug. 18, 1876; s. Robert Franklin and Lena Ann (Adams) J.; grad. Ind. (Pa.) State Teachers Coll., 1899; LL.B., U. Mich., 1903; m. Katherine F. Tullis; children—Elaine (Mrs. J. Hampton Tucker), David C., Lois (Mrs. Donald C. Smith). Began practice at Oklahoma City, 1903; mem. Lytle, Johnston & Soule. Past pres. Okla. Co. Bar Assn., Kendall Coll. (now U. Tulsa); former mem. State Bd. Edn. Chmn. Okla. Co. chpt. A.R.C., 1918-28. Mem. Am., Okla. bar assns., Nat. Assn. Mfrs. (nat. v.p.). Republican. Presbyn. Mason (32°). Clubs: Union League (Chicago), Men's Dinner, Lions, Okla. City Golf and Country, Oklahoma. Home: 300 N.W. 17th St., Oklahoma City. Died Oct. 22, 1958.

JOHNSTON, Frances Benjamin (jŏn'stŏn), photographer, author, lectr.; b. Grafton, W.Va., Jan. 15, 1864; d. Anderson Donophon and Frances Antoinette (Benjamin) Johnston; grad., Notre Dame, Govanston, Md., 1883; student, Julien Art Acad., Paris, 1883-85, Smithsonian Instn. Pioneer woman photographer. Travelled to Naples to interview, photograph Adm. Dewey after battle of Manilla Bay, 1899; recorded ednl. systems, U.S. Naval Acad. (Annapolis), West Point, Washington, Pub. Schs., insts. at Hampton, Va., Tuskegee, Ala., Carlyle, Pa., 1900-10; produced over 10,000 photographs for pictorial archives early Am. architecture, exhibited at Library of Congress. Work shown in leading art galleries of U.S. Mem. A.I.A. (hon.), D.A.R., Thornton Soc. (Washington). Republican. Decorated Officer d'Academia, Palmes Academiques, Gold Medal Expn., Paris; medals: Turin, Italy, Vienna and other awards. Clubs: Women's Nat. Press, Arts (Washington). Author: illustrator: Plantations of the Carolina Low Country. Illustrator: Colonial Churches in Virginia, Early Architecture of North Carolina, Mansions of Virginia. Home(winter): 1132 Bourbon St., New Orleans. Address: Arts Club of Washington, 2017 I St. N.W., Washington. Died May 16, 1952; buried Rock Creek Cemetery, Washington.

JOHNSTON, Gordon, educator; b. Fontanelle, Ia., July 26, 1903; s. William Ferguson and Sybil Cornelia (Gow) J.; student Grinnell (Ia.) Coll., 1921-22; A.B. magna cum laude, U. of Ia., 1925; George Washington Univ. Law Sch., 1926-27; LL.B., Yale, 1928; m. Marian Ellen Edman, Aug. 15, 1929; 1 dau., Susan Alison. Admitted to Colo. bar, 1928, Ill. bar, 1929; asso. with law firm, Hicks & Folonie, Chicago, 1928-32; mem. faculty, U. of Denver Coll. of Law, since 1932, dean since 1948; visiting prof., U. of Colo. Law Sch., 1934, 35, 39. Lt., U.S.N.R., 1942-45. Mem. Nat. (dir.), Denver (trustee, pres.) legal aid socs., Am. Bar Assn. (former acting adviser, sect. legal edn. and admissions to bar), Colo. (mem. bd. govs.), Denver bar assns., Am. Judicature Soc., Am. Law Inst., Central City Opera House Assn. (radio publicity dir. 1935-48), Phi Beta Kappa, Coif, Omicron Delta Kappa (nat. pres. 1951-55), Delta Tau Delta, Phi Delta Phi. Clubs: University, Law (past pres.) (Denver). Editor: Colorado Statutes and Cases on Wills and Estates (with Charles E. Works), 1948. Contbr. articles and book reviews in law jours. Home: 1497 S. Garfield St., Denver 10. Office: 1445 Cleveland Pl., Denver 2. Died Apr. 25, 1958.

JOHNSTON, Henry Alan, lawyer; b. Washington, D.C., Oct. 27, 1884; s. Robert and Minnie (Fuller) J.; A.B., Davidson (N.C.) Coll., 1903; A.M., Princeton, 1904; LL.B., U. of Va., 1909; m. Katharine H. Dickson, Jan. 27, 1914 (dec. 1947); children—William Dickson Mary Petty; m. 2d Helene Swatkowsky, Oct. 23, 1950. Admitted to Virginia bar, 1909, now mem. Clark, Carr & Ellis; dir. Industrial Bank Commerce of New York, Bankers Security Life Insurance Society. Legal advisor to United Kingdom-United States Steel Control Group, Duesseldorf, Germany. Director Barter Theatre of Virginia, Inc. Served as lt. U.S. Navy, chmn. U.S. Navy Bd. for Commandeering, 1917-19. Alderman, Norfolk, 1910-12. Director and vice pres. Thomas Jefferson Memorial Foundation. Member American Bar Association, Assn. Bar City New York, National Institute of Social Sciences, Phi Beta Kappa, Kappa Alpha, Phi Delta Phi, Delta Sigma Rho. Presbyterian. Mason. Clubs: Metropolitan (New York); Apawamis (Rye, N.Y.); Bankers Club of America. Author: What Rights Are Left, 1930. Contbr. to North Am. Review, Century Mag., Outlook, Independent, U.S. Law Review, Am. Bar Assn. Jour. Home: 40 E. 62d St. Office: 120 Broadway, N.Y.C. Died Aug. 1956.

JOHNSTON, James A.; b. Brooklyn, New York, Sept. 15, 1874; s. Thomas and Ellen (Walsh) J.; ed. pub. schs., Brooklyn, Spring Valley Sch. and Sacred Heart Coll., San Francisco, until 1889; m. Ida M. Fulton, Nov. 8, 1905; children—Nellie (dec.), Muriel, Fulton (dec.), Barbara. Admitted to Calif. bar by examination, 1919, and practiced at San Francisco; mem. Bd. of Supervisors, San Francisco, 1907-09; chmn. State Bd. of Control, Calif., 1911-12; warden Folsom Prison, 1912-13, San Quentin Prison, 1913-25 (resigned); v.p. American Trust Co., San Francisco, 1925-32; apptd. warden U.S. Penitentiary, Alcatraz Island, Calif., Jan. 1, 1934-Apr. 30, 1948; now asst. dir. Fed. Prison Bureau. Past pres. San Francisco Advertising Assn. Republican. Catholic. Clubs: Commonwealth (pres. bd. govs.), Rotary (past pres.), Olympic. Author: Prison Life Is Different; Alcatraz Island Prison and the Men who Live There, 1949; numerous pamphlets, and articles on prison work, on crime, penal instns., cost of crime, youth and crime, the indeterminate sentence, prison labor problem, etc. Chmn. Cal. Crime Commn., 1927-30; dir. penology in Governor's Council, 1929-30. Pres. Am. Prison Assn., 1940-41. Home: 2901 Pacific Av. Address: Post Office Bldg., San Francisco. Died Sept. 6, 1954.

JOHNSTON, John, chemist; b. Perth, Scotland, Oct. 13, 1881; s. James and Christina (Leslie)J.; B.Sc., Univ. Coll. (U. of St. Andrews), Dundee, Scotland, 1903; work in chemistry, Univ. Coll., 1903-05, U. Breslau, Germany. Prof. Abegg, 1905-07; research asso. in phys. chemistry Mass. Inst. Tech., 1907-08; D.Sc., U. of St. Andrews, 1908; M.A. (hon.), Yale, 1919; D.Sc. (hon.), N.Y.U., 1928, Lehigh, 1929; m. Dorothy Hopkins, July 17, 1909; children—Helen Leslie, John Murray, William Valentine. On staff of Geophysical Lab., Carnegie Instn. of Washington, 1908-16; in charge research dept. for Am. Zinc, Lead and Smeltijg Co., St. Louis, 1916-17, U.S. Bur. of Mines, 1917-18; sec. NRC, Washington, 1918-19; prof. chemistry, chmn. chemistry dept. Yale, 1919-27; dir. of research U.S. Steel Corp., 1927-46. Mem. Am. Chem. Soc., Franklin Inst., Am. Electrochem. Soc. (pres. 1933-34), British Iron and Steel Inst., Faraday Soc., Inst. Metals, Verein deutscher Eisenhüttenleute. Club: Century (New York). Address: Southwest Harbor, Me. Died Sept. 12, 1950; buried Southwest Harbor.

JOHNSTON, John Lawrence, exec.; b. Louisville, Ky., Apr. 23, 1887; s. John Thomas Morris and Florence (Brooks) J.; grad. Blees Mil. Acad., Macon, Mo., 1904; student Washington U., 1904-05; m. Ethel M. Brown, Sept. 9, 1908. Cashier Bass-Johnston Banking Co., Ashland, Mo., 1905-07; v.p. 1st Nat. Bank, Muskogee, Okla., 1907-10; cashier Nat. Reserve Bank, Kansas City, Mo., 1910-15; v.p. Liberty Bank, St. Louis, 1915-16, pres., 1916-20; pres. of Liberty Central Trust Co., 1920-25; v.p. Bond & Goodwin, Inc., 1925-28; president Lambert Company, 1928-49, now director; director Manufacturers Trust Co., Phillips Petroleum Co., Continental Can Company. Chairman of the Southwestern Division Red Cross Membership Drive, Dec. 1917 and same, 1918; also chmn. Red Cross drive, May 1918; and 4th Liberty Bond Campaign. Mem. Beta Theta Pi. Democrat. Baptist. Clubs: Racquet and Tennis, Links (N.Y.C.). Home: Cape Vincent, N.Y. Died July 14, 1958; buried Cape Vincent.

JOHNSTON, L(eon) S(anford), educator; b. Granger, Mo., Sept. 21, 1887; s. John Richard and Sarah Thorpe (Howard) J.; grad. Kirksville (Mo.) State Normal, 1907; B.S., U. Mo., 1916, A.M., 1918; postgrad. U. Chgo., 1924-30; m. Alice Helen Baker, Aug. 25, 1915; children—Sarah Alice (Mrs. J. C. Maycock), Harriet (Mrs. N. R. Arthur). High sch. mathematics tchr., Hannibwl, Mo., 1908-09, Richmond, Mo., 1909-11, Lingayen, P.I., 1912-13; instr. mathematics U. Philippines, 1913-14, head math. dept. Wis. State Normal, La Crosse, 1917-19; instr. mathematics U.S. Naval Acad., 1919-22; asst. prof. mathematics Pa. State Coll., 1922-26, asso. prof., 1926-28; asso. prof. mathematics U. Detroit, 1928-31, prof. mathematics, 1931; civil engr., maintenance of way, C.B.&Q. R.R., hdqrs. Chgo., summers 1918, 19, 20, B.&O. R.R., summer 1922; surveyor, 1913-14. Mem. Math. Assn. Am. (chmn. Mich. sect. 1934-35), Phi Delta Kappa, Sigma Xi. Democrat. Baptist. Author: Elements of Nomography, 1936; Differential Equations (with Dr. L. E. Mehlenbacher), 1947-48. Contbr. numerous articles to Am. Math. Monthly, 1929—. Home: 16509 Wildemere Av., Detroit 21. Died Feb. 18, 1955.

JOHNSTON, Oscar Goodbar; b. Jackson, Miss., Jan. 27, 1880; s. John Calvin and Emma Elizabeth (Goodbar) J.; grad. Ky. Mil. Inst., 1899; LL.B., Cumberland U., 1901; m. Martha Anderson, Feb. 21, 1905. Practiced law at Clarksdale, Miss., 1901-20; pres. Planters Nat. Bank, Clarksdale, Miss., 1921-26; removed to Memphis, Tenn., becoming identified with Delta & Pine Land Co., 1927; pres. Delta & ine Land Co., operating some 35,000 acres of farming land in Mississippi Delta, 1927-50; apptd. dir. of finance A.A.A., U.S. Dept. Agr., June 1, 1933, and v.p. CCC, Oct. 16, 1933; apptd. mgr. Govt. Cotton Pool, Jan. 8, 1934; asst. to sec. of the treasury, Jan. 1-July 1, 1935. Organized Nat. Cotton Council of America, 1939, pres., 1939-47, now chmn. bd.; dep. chmn., bd. dirs. Fed. Res. Bank of St. Louis, 1938-43; dir. Staple Cotton Coop. Assn., Greenwood, Miss., Staple Cotton Discount Corp., Greenwood, Ill. Central R.R., Chgo.; mem. Agrl. Adv. Council, U.S. Dept. Agr., 1939—. Mem. Miss. Ho. of Reps., 1908-18. Del. Dem. Nat. Conv., 1912, 1944, del.-at-large, 1916, 1940; mem. Dem. Nat. Com., 1920-24. Served as pvt. to 2d lt. Tank Corps, U.S. Army, 1918-19. Mem. Delta Kappa Epsilon. Methodist. Mason, Elk, Rotarian. Home: 1267 Fairview Av., Greenville, Miss. Died Oct. 1955.

JOHNSTON, Percy Hampton, banker; b. Lebanon, Ky., Jan. 1, 1881; s. William Johnston and Bluford (Oliver) J.; educated public schools; married Belle Rogers; children—Percy H., Jr., Dorothy Belle Ames. Began as clerk Marion National Bank, Lebanon, 1897; appointed national bank examiner, 1907, and became chmn. of examiners in states south of Ohio River and east of Miss. River, later one of nat. bank examiners at large; apptd. cashier Citizens Nat. Bank, Louisville, Ky., 1913; v.p., 1916; sr. v.p. Chem. Nat. Bank (now Chemical Corn Exchange Bank), N.Y.C., 1917-20, pres., 1920-35, chmn. bd. dirs., 1935-46, chmn. exec. com. and vice chmn. trust com., 1946, became hon. chairman, 1956; dir. New York Life Insurance Company. Dir. Bill of Rights Commemorative Society. Mem. board of govs. Federal Hall Memorial Associates, Inc. Mem. N.Y. State Bankers Assn. (chmn. com. on internat. monetary problems), Assn. of Reserve City Bankers (mem. com. on fed. fiscal policy), N.Y. State Chamber of Commerce (chmn. com. on corporate membership). Presbyn. Clubs: The Links, Southern Society (N.Y.). Home: 125 High St., Montclair, N.J. Office: 165 Broadway, N.Y.C. 15. Died Jan. 2, 1957.

JOHNSTON, Richard Holland, librarian; b. Windsor, Ont., Can., May 6, 1868; s. Rev. Hugh and Eliza (Holland) J.; B.A., U. Toronto, 1889; post-grad. in theology, Victoria Coll., 1889-92; m. Elizabeth Deborah, 1901; children—Hugh Libertus, Richard Holland, Mary Alice (Mrs. Wm. M. Conner). Librarian Victoria Coll., 1892-96; reference desk, Library of Congress, 1897-1910; librarian Bur. Ry. Econs. Library of Assn. Am. Rys. (spl. collection 300,000 items pertaining to rys.) 1910-1947. Fellow Am. Library Inst.; mem. A.A.A.S., A.L.A., Spl. Libraries Assn. (ex-pres.), Bibliog. Soc. Am. Author: Bibliography of Thomas Jefferson, 1905; Special Libraries, 1915, revised edit., 1931. Compiler: Railway Economics, 1912. Home: 727 Chesapeake Av., Silver Spring, Md. Died Jan. 2, 1955; buried Druid Ridge Cemetery, Balt.

JOHNSTON, William Greer, drug exec.; b. Chgo., Nov. 8, 1900; s. Thomas and Sara (Greer) J.; Ph.G., U. Ill.; m. Irene Smith, June 27, 1931; children—Betty Jean, Joy Rene, Bruce Arthur. Joined Walgreen Co., Chgo., 1923, v.p., 1942-45, dir., 1940-45; v.p. Rexall Drug Co., Los Angeles, 1946—, dir., 1947—; pres. Center Drug Co., 1952—; bd. dirs. Banner Gelatin Lab. Mason (Shriner). Home: 889 Linda Flora Dr., West Los Angeles 49. Office: 1 Windward, Venice. Died June 4, 1957; buried Forest Lawn Meml. Park, Glendale, Cal.

JOLIOT-CURIE, Frederic (zhô-lyō'kü-rē'), physicist; b. Paris, France, Mar. 19, 1900; s. Henri and Emilie (Roederer) Joliot; ed. Lycée Lakanal, Bourg-la-Reine; Ingénieur, Ecole de physique et de chimie industrielles de la Ville U. de Paris, 1923; Licencié (B.A.) in Sciences, University of Paris, 1927, Dr. Sciences, 1930; m. Iréne Curie, Oct. 9, 1926; children—Helén, Pierre, Asst., Faculty of Sciences, Univ. of Paris, 1932; maitre de Recherches, Caisse Nationale des Sciences, 1933; lecturer at the Sorbonne, 1935; prof., Coll. of France, 1937; dir. of lab. of atomic synthesis, Ivry, 1937; vice pres. Haut Comité des Recherches Scientifiques, 1938; mem. of commn. on atomic weights Union Internationale de la Chimie, 1938; dir. Centre National de la Recherche Scientifique, 1944; high commr. for atomic energy, 1946-50; prof. science University of Paris, also director Laboratoire Curie del' Institut du Radium, 1956—. Mem. com. Nat. Inst. Nuclear Scis. and Techniques. Became mem. Internat. Commn. on Standards for Radium, 1934, sec., 1936. Pres. Société de Chimie-physique de France, 1936-38. Comité de Gestion des Tables Annuelles de Constantes (com. of management of annual tables of constants), 1936; sec.-gen. Natl. Union of Intellectuals, 1945. Decorated Grand Croix de la Legion d'Honneur. Mem. Acad. of Medicine, Acad. of Sciences, Société Royale des Sciences de Liége, Acad. Royale des Sciences d'Amsterdam, Acad. des Sciences du Denmark, and many other scientific associations; president du Conseil Mondial de la Paix. Author: Le Noyau des Atomes (reports to Congrès de Leningrad), 1933; (With Mme. Joliot-Curie) Les Rayonnements des Atomes sous l'Action des Rayons Alpha (reports to Congrès de Physique Solvay), 1933; Le Neutron, Le Positron et la Radioactivité Artificielle; (brochures, in collaboration with Mme. Joliot-Curie) L'existence du neutron; l'électron positif; Radioactivité Artificelle; La Constitution de la Matiere et la Radioactivité Artificielle (Scientific Encyclopedia, Library of Teaching Technique), 1937; Prix Staline International. Address; 76 av. Le Nôtre à Antony (Seine), France. Died Aug. 14, 1958.

JOLIOT-CURIE, Irene (zho-lyō'-kü'rē), scientist, univ. prof.; b. Paris, France, Sept. 12, 1897; d. Pierre and Marie (Sklodowska) Curie; Licentiate in Physics and Math. U. of Paris, 1920, ScD., 1925; Dr. Honoris Causa, Edinburgh U., 1939. U. of Oslo, 1946, U. Cracow, 1951, es sciences physiques, Univ. de Sofia, 1948; m. Frederic Joliot, Oct. 9, 1926, children—Hélene, Pierre. Served as hosp. nurse in radiography during World War I. Asst. to Marie Curie at Inst. of Radium of Paris, 1918, head of studeis, 1932; head of research Caisse Nationale de la Recherche Scientifique, 1935; under-sec. of state for sci. research, June-Sept. 1936; lecturer, Faculty of Sciences of Univ. of Paris, 1937, prof. without chair, 1937; commr. atomic energy, prof. Faculty of Sciences, and dir. Laboratoire Curie, 1946. Mem. Internat. Commn. of Standards for Radium, 1934; mem. Com. of Management of Office of Astrophysical Research, 1936. Awarded Mateucci Medal by Italian Soc. of Sciences, 1932, Henri Wilde prize, 1933, and Marquet prize, 1934, by Acad. of Sciences of Paris, Nobel Prize for Chemistry, 1935 (all with Frederic Joliot-Curie), French Medal of Recognition, 1918, Medal of Soc. of Civil Engrs., 1937, Chevalier of Legion of Honor, 1935, Officer, 1939. Fgn. corresponding mem. Akademja Nauk Technieczynch w Warszawie, Acad. Royale de Medecine de Belgique; cor. mem. U.S.S.R. Acad. Scis., 1947, de l'academie des sciences de Berlin; mem. Am. Phys. Soc.; mem. (hon.) de l'Institute Grant Ducal du Luxembourg, 1947; de la Société Shimique des Indes, 1948, mem. (hon.), Edinburgh U. Women's Assn., 1947. Mem. sci. sect. Upper Council of French Radiodiffusion, 1936; mem. outside sect. Upper Council of Scientific Research, 1938. Author: Les Radioéléments Naturels; Propriétés; Preparation et Dosage, 1946. Home: 76 Avenue Le Notre, Antony (Seine), France. Office: Laboratoire Curie, 11 rue Pierre Curie, Paris, France. Died Mar. 17, 1956.

JOLLY, Robert Garland, hosp. supt.; b. Cave City, Ky., Mar. 27, 1885; s. James and Mildred Dee (Ford) J.; grad. Louisville Male High Sch., 1903; m. Lillie W. Burnett, Jan. 1, 1924. Clerk L. &N. R.R., 1903-06; evangelistic singer, 1906-13; mus. dir., bus. mgr. Gaston Av. Bapt. Ch., Dallas, 1913-17, First Bapt. Ch., Houston, 1917-19; supt. Meml. Hosp., Houston, 1919—. Vice pres. Am. Hosp. Assn., 1925, pres., 1934-35, chmn. com. employees' retirement, 1930-33; pres. Am. Protestant Hosp. Assn., 1931, Tex. State Hosp. Assn., 1931-32. Democrat. Baptist. Club: Rotary. Home: 2438 Stanmore Dr. Office: Memorial Hospital, Houston. Died May 14, 1952; buried Houston.

JOLSON, Al (Asa Yoelson) (jōl'sŭn), actor, singer; b. St. Petersburg, Russia, May 26, 1888; m. Henrietta Keller, 1906; m. 2d, Alma Osborne, 1922; m. 3d, Ruby Keeler, 1928 (div.). First appeared on stage as mem. of a mob in The Children of the Ghetto, at Herald Sq. Theatre, N.Y.C., Oct. 16, 1899; traveled with circuses, Dockstader's Minstrels, and appeared in vaudeville; played in La Belle Paree, at Winter Garden, N.Y.C., 1911, later in The Honeymoon Express, Robinson Crusoe, Jr., Sinbad, etc. Starred in talking pictures, The Jazz Singer, The Singing Fool, Say It With Songs; playing in own stage production Hold on to Your Hat, 1940-41. Sang for Jolson Story, Jolson Sings Again. Star of own radio program, Kraft Music Hall, NBC. Address: Beverly Hills, Cal. Died. Oct. 23, 1950.*

JOME, Hiram L. (jō'mĭ), prof. economics; b. nr. Sturgeon Bay, Wis., July 14, 1895; s. Knut O. and Karen (Riis) J.; A.B., St. Olaf Coll., Northfield, Minn., 1918; A.M., U. of Wis., 1920, Ph.D., 1925; m. Martha Fjelde, Dec. 20, 1920; children—Helen Marie (Mrs. James McPherson Houck), Florence Louise (Mrs. Frank Edward Donner). Asst. in economics, U. of Wis., 1920-23; asst. prof. econ., Denison U., Granville, O., 1923-25, prof. econ. and head of dept., 1925-31; engaged in statistical research, Ralph H. Jones Advt. Agency, Cincinnati, O., 1929; prof. econ. and head of dept., DePauw U., since 1931, Allen A. Wilkinson prof. social and bus. econs. since 1952; vis. tchr. in econ., U. Wis., 1925, West Va. U., 1926, U. of Mo., 1940; visiting teacher Indiana State Teachers Coll., 1950. Forum leader U.S. Bureau of Edn., Dayton, O., 1937; econ. cons. Ind. Tax Study Commn., 1952. Served with U.S.N.R., radio, World War I. Mem., Am. Finance Assn., Am. and Mid-West (past pres.) econ. assns., Am. Assn. Univ. Profs., Am. Legion. Methodist. Republican. Club: Kiwanis International. Author: Economics of the Radio Industry, 1925; Corporation Finance, 1948; Principles of Money and Banking, 1957. Home: 610 Highwood Av., Greencastle, Ind. Died Apr. 11, 1958; buried Forest Hill Cemetery, Greencastle.

JONAS, Maryla, concert pianist; b. Warsaw, Poland, May 31, 1911; d. Dr. Stainslaw and Regina (Barsky) J.; grad. Warsaw Conservatory, Lemberg (Poland) Conservatory, student of Paderewski, Turczynski, Sauer, Kreutzer; m. Dr. Ernest G. Abraham, Dec. 14, 1946. Debuted as soloist with Warsaw Philharmonic Orch., 1920, Germany, 1926; played series of Mozart recitals Salzburg, Bayreuth, 1927; asst. tchr. to Turczynski, Warsaw Conservatory; touring Denmark, Sweden, France, Holland, S.A., 1941-1946; debuted Carnegie Hall, N.Y.C., 1946; made annual tours of U.S. and Can. since 1946; recording artist for Columbia Records. Awarded Internat. Chopin prize, 1932, Internat. Beethoven prize, 1933. Hon. mem. Sigma Alpha Iota. Home: 952 Fifth Av., N.Y.C. 21. Address: care Columbia Artists Mgmt., Inc., 113 W. 57th St., N.Y.C. 19. Died July 1959.

JONAS, Ralph, lawyer, philanthropist; b. Brooklyn, N.Y., Nov. 7, 1878; s. Jacob and Bella (Mayer) J.; married; 4 children. Member firm Jonas & Neuburger, long active in philanthropic, ednl. and civic movements in Brooklyn and Greater New York; an organizer Brooklyn Chamber Commerce (of which was pres. 3 terms, developing it into the 2d largest chamber in the country), also an organizer Long Island Chamber Commerce; a leading factor in establishing the Bd. of Higher Edn. in City of New York, and mem. many yrs.; a leader in establishing a city maintained coll. in Brooklyn; founded Long Island University with a gift of $500,000; served as member Honorary Advisory City Plan Com. under three city administrations; member Governor's com. on cost of Pub. Edn. in State of N.Y., 1933; apptd. by Gov. Lehman, mem. Commn. on State Aid to Municipal Subdivisions, 1935. Hon. trustee Brooklyn Coll. Pharmacy; former trustee Brooklyn Inst. Arts, Sci. (life mem.) L.I. Coll. of Medicine; hon. dir. Jewish Hosp. of Brooklyn; former president Brooklyn Chamber of Commerce; founder mem. and mem. executive committee Society of Friends of Mexico; one of corporators New York World's Fair of 1939; mem. hon. com. Brooklyn Chapter Am. Red Cross. Mem. Am., N.Y. State (life) and Brooklyn bar assns., Assn. Bar City of New York, New York County Lawyers Assn.; asso. mem. Med. Soc. County of Kings, Museum of the City of New York (founder member), Mason. Clubs: Brooklyn (life); City (life), Lawyers (New York). Home: 15 Clark St., Brooklyn 2. Office: 115 Broadway, N.Y.C. 6. Died Apr. 29, 1952.

JONES, Allen Northey, investment banker; born Evansville, Ind., Feb. 27, 1896; s. Rev. W. Northey and Carrie L. (Clark) J.; A.B., Trinity Coll., Hartford. Conn., 1917, A.M., 1920; LLD., Hobart and William Smith colleges, 1956; m. Lillian Lovell, July 1, 1936; children—Sarah L. (Mrs. George C. Easter), Steven E. Statistician J. P. Morgan & Co., N.Y.C., 1919-35; v.p. Morgan Stanley & Co., Inc., New York City, 1935-41, partner, 1941—; director Conn. Gen. Life Ins. Co., J. I. Case Co., Doctors Hosp., N.Y. City. Trustee Trinity Coll. Chairman Newtown Republican Town Committee. Mem. Newtown bd. finance. Treas. Argentine-Am. C. of C. Clubs: University, Bond, Broad Street (N.Y. City); Chicago; Newtown Country; Hartford. Home: Newtown, Conn. Office: Two Wall St., N.Y.C. 5. Died Mar. 9, 1958.

JONES, Barton Mills, civil and hydraulic engr.; b. Parsons, Kan., Apr. 12, 1885; s. Robert Mills and Alice (Barton) J.; B.S. in Mech. Engring. and Elec. Engring., U. Cal., 1908; m. Mary Todd, June 2, 1914; children—Alice Barton (Mrs. Edward W. Burdge), Barton Mills II. Asst. engr. The Nevada California Power Co., 1904-05; part time draftsman Cory, Meredith & Allen, Pelton Water Wheel Co., and C. C. Moore, San Francisco, 1905-08; asst. engr. hydro-electric project on Rio Verde for Ariz. Power Co., 1908-10; chief engr., water power investigations, Boston-Colo. Power Co., 1910-12; hydraulice engr. Electric Bond & Share Co., New York, 1912-14; investigations and planning, also desigbing constrn. installations and equipment on flood control of Miami Valley, O., for Morgan Engring. Co. and Miami Conservance Dist., 1914-17, charge constrn. Lockington hydraulic fill dam, same, 1918-21; chief engr. flood control, Pueblo Conservancy Dist., Colo., 1921-26; pvt. cons. practice in irrigation, drainage, flood control, gold dredge mining, etc., 1926-29; oil field developmnt, Petroleum Reclamation Co., Bradford, Pa., 1930; head Antioch Industrial Research Corp. and dept. engring. Antioch Coll., Yellow Springs, O., 1930-33; constrn. engr. in charge planning and building Norris Dam, TVA, 1933-36, head design dept., embracing all projects, same, 1936-39. cons. design engr., 1939-41, head planning engr., 1941-42; Ingeniero-Director, Central Hidroelectric Del Cañon Del Pato, Peru, S.A., 1942-48; pvt. cons. engr. 1949; chief engr., gen. mgr. Miami (O.) Conservancy Dist., 1950-56; pvt. cons. practice, 1956—. Mem. Edison Pioneers, Am. Soc. C.E., Colo. Soc. Engrs., Tau Beta Pi. Presbyn. Mason (32°, Shriner). Club: Technical (Knoxville, Tenn.). Contbr. to tech. jours. Home: 1642 Brandon Av., Cin. 30. Died Oct. 14, 1957.

JONES, Bassett, elec. engr.; b. West Brighton, S.I., N.Y., Feb. 6, 1877; s. Bassett and Sarah Catherine (Oakley) J.; student Mass. Inst. Tech., 1896-99; m. Emma M. Starr, May 20, 1907 (dec.); m. 2d, Emily L. Warren, Mar. 11, 1922. Mem. Meyer, Strong & Jones, Inc., cons. engr., N.Y. City cons. on illumination N.Y. World's Fair, 1939. Fellow Am. Geog. Soc.; mem. Am. Standards Assn., (chmn. elevator standards com.; mem. elevator safety code com.; chmn. sub-com. on elevator safety research); Archtl. League New York, Am. Soc. M.E., Am. Statistical Assn., Soc. Am. Foresters. Clubs: Century, Explorers, Cruising Club of America. Received hon. degree of M.E. from Stevens Inst. Tech. Home: Nantucket Island, Mass.; and 101 Park Av., New York, N.Y. Died Jan. 25, 1960.

JONES, Bruce Carr, lawyer; b. Rockdale County, Ga., Aug. 5, 1877; s. George Salley and Martha Ruth (Carr) J.; student Law Sch., Mercer U., 1898-99; m. Mabel Frances Maxwell, Jan. 5, 1905; 1 dau., Lelia Ruth (Mrs. Harry N. Horton). With U.S. Commn. to Five Civilized Tribes, engaged in allotment of lands in Indian Ty. (now Okla.), in charge Cherokee Allotment Office, 1900-05; admitted to Indian Ty. (Okla.) bar, 1905; mem. Hardeman, Jones & Johnston (now Jones, Sparks, Benton & Cork), Macon, Ga., 1905—; v.p., dir. Macon Fed. Savs. & Loan Assn.; dir. First Nat. Bank & Trust Co. in Macon. Served in Ga. N.G., 1896-99. Mem. Central Ga. Council, Boy Scouts Am. Recipient Silver Beaver, Boy Scouts Am. Mem. Am., Ga. State, Macon bar assns., Soc. Ga. Archaeology, Ind. Democrat. Meth. Elk. (past exalted ruler and past state pres.), Mason (K.T.; 32°; Shriner, past potentate Al-Sihah Temple). Home: 1746 Forsyth St. Office: 1007-20 Persons Bldg., Macon, Ga. Died Feb. 8, 1959; buried Rose Hill Cemetery, Macon.

JONES, Carl H(enry), ret. naval officer; b. Jones Mill, Ala., June 17, 1893; s. Sidney Morgan and Mary Jane (Whittle) J.; B.S., U.S. Naval Acad., 1914; student Columbia, 1919-20; m. Elizabeth Stockton Dorsey, July 31, 1941. Commd. ensign USN, 1914, advanced through grades to rear adm., 1946, ret.; advanced to vice adm. on retired list. Commended for performance duty in action against enemy on Tarawa, Nov. 1943. Qualified to command submarine, 1917. Club: Army and Navy (Washington). Home: R.F.D. 3, Box 360, Annapolis, Md. Died Sept. 1, 1958; buried U.S. Naval Acad. Cemetery, Annapolis.

JONES, Carl Waring, newspaper pub.; b. Minneapolis, Minn., Aug. 24, 1887; s. Herschel V. and Lydia Augusta (Wilcox) J.; Litt.B., Princeton, 1911; m. Helen Thirza Winton, Oct. 29, 1921; children—Winton, Waring, Thirza (Mrs. C. Cleveland). Began in classified advertisnig department of the Minneapolis (Minnesota) Journal, 1913; copywriter, later mgr. copy, art and print dept. Lord & Thomas, advt. agency, Chicago, 1914-16; copywriter, Erwin, Wasey & Co., Chicago, 1916-18; advertising mgr. Minneapolis Journal, 1919-22, gen. mgr., 1922-28, pub. same, 1928-39, president and treasurer The Journal Printing Co.; chmn. board History Book Club, New York. With personnel operations division of General Staff, War Dept., Washington, D.C., Jan.-Dec. 1918; maj. Ordnance R.C. Dir. Minneapolis Inst. of Art, Minneapolis Sch. of Art, Minneapolis Orchestral Assn.; past vice pres., Soc. American Magicians; v.p., Internat. Brotherhood of Magicians. Decorated Knight, Order of St. Olav, for "contributions to a closer relationship between our peoples" (Norway), 1937. Republican. Presbyterian. Clubs: Minneapolis, Minikahda Club, Rotary Club, Automobile Club, Woodhill Country (Minneapolis, Minn.); University, Tavern (Chicago); The Players, Coffee House (N.Y.); Colonial (Princeton). Formulated program, 1919, for improving newspaper advertising and established committee on newspaper research, N.Y. City, which published, 1920, "Attainable Ideals in Newspaper Advertising." Awarded prize, 1927, by Am. Newspaper Pubs. Assn. for analysis of newspaper advertising. Editor: Greater Magic, 1939. Publisher: Expert Card Technique, 1940; Magical Ways and Means, 1941; Memoirs of Robert Houdini, 1944; Card Magic, 1945; Mental Magic, 1949; Pet Secrets, 1951; Modern Coin

Magic, 1952; The Oldest Deception, 1956; A Bibliography of Books on Conjuring in English from 1580 to 1850, 1957. Dep. dir. War Prodn. Bd., Region 12. Home: 1620 Mount Curve Av., Mpls.; also Wayzata, Minn. Died Jan. 5, 1957; buried Lakewood Cemetery, Mpls.

JONES, Carlton Allen, banker; b. Bainbridge, O., Mar. 16, 1879; s. Allen S. and Maria (Kern) J.; grad. Bainbridge High Sch., 1895; m. Edith Lea Carr, June 25, 1902; children—Dorothy Elizabeth (Mrs. John Franklin Clark), Carl A., Herbert Lea. Began as bank clk., 1895; cashier Dominion Nat. Bank, Bristol, Va., 1903-08; pres. Dixie Coca-Cola Bottling Co., 1908—; dir. Am. Bottlers of Carbonated Beverages, 1922-26, v.p., 1927-28, pres., 1929-30; dir. and chmn. H. P. King Co., Bristol, Tenn.; v.p. Washington Trust & Savings Bank, 1910—; mem. adv. com. First Nat. Bank, Bristol, Tenn.; pres., treas., co-pub. Johnson City (Tenn.) Press-Chronicle, 1934—; dir. New York Coca-Cola Bottling Co., N.Y.C. Democrat. Presbyn. Mason, Elk. Club: Country (past pres.). Home: "Scarhaven," Bristol, Va. Office: W. State St., Bristol, Va. Died July 23, 1950; buried Bristol, Tenn.

JONES, Charles Andrews, business consultant; b. Manassas, Virginia; s. George Bainbridge and Flora (Andrews) J.; student George Washington Law Sch., 1905-08; m. May Halliwell, Nov. 24, 1909; children—Doris, Barbara; m. 2d, Marie Seitz, Nov. 12, 1923 (dec.); m. 3d, Caroline M. Packard, Mar. 20, 1951. Clerk ins. office, 1899-1908; with Frank A. Munsey newspapers, 1908-11; in real estate business, 1911-33; gen. mgr. Home Owners Loan Corp., 1935-41; spl. asst. bd. of dirs. Reconstruction Finance Corp., 1941-43; president McPherson Corporation; senior associate Newmeyer-Associates. Served as capt. U.S. Army, 1918-19. Democrat. Club: Nat. Press (Washington). Home: 1921 Kalarama Rd. Office: 1000 Vermont Av., Washington 5. Died Aug. 22, 1958; buried Arlington Nat. Cemetery.

JONES, Cheney Church, social worker; b. nr. Elmore, Richardson County, Neb., June 13, 1880; s. James Francis and Susan Almira (Church) J.; grad. Crete Acad., 1900; A.B., Doane Coll., 1904, LL.D., 1932; grad. study, U. of Neb., summer 1905; LL.B., Yale, 1909; m. Nellie Bloom Knapp, Oct. 6, 1909; children—Frances Eleanor, Charlotte. Instructor in mathematics and science, Chadron (Neb.) Academy, 1904-05; prin. high sch., Fremont, 1905-06; spl. agt. Mass. Soc. for Prevention of Cruelty to Children, Boston, 1909-13; gen. agt. Cleveland Humane Soc., 1913-16; finance sec. Cleveland Welfare Federation, 1916; agt. War Dept. Commn. on Training Camp Activities, 1917; div. dir. civilian relief, later asst. div. mgr., Pa., Del. and N.E. divs., Am. Red Cross, 1917-22; gen. agt. and sec. Children's Protective Soc., Minneapolis, 1922-23; supt. N.E. Home for Little Wanderers, Boston, 1923-51, cons., 1951—; mem. faculty, Sch. of Edn., Boston U. and Sch. of Social Work, Simmons Coll. Editor The Little Wanderers Advocate, 1923-51. Mem. White House Conf. on Child Health and Protection, 1929-30; Mass. official del. White House Conf. on Children in a Democracy, 1939-40; pres. Child Welfare League of America, 1929-32; mem. advisory com. U.S. Children's Bur.; mem. Mass. Midcentury Com. on Children and Youth. Dir. Ella Lyman Cabot Found.; mem. supervisory bd. Am. Year Book. Mem. Mass. Bar, Nat. Com. for Mental Hygiene, Nat. Conference of Social Work (exec. com. 1939-42), Phi Delta Phi. Conglist. Clubs: Appalachian Mountain (Boston) Boston University Faculty. Contributor to Nat. Parent-Teacher and Social Work Year Book; mem. bd. dirs. American Year Book. Home: 22 Corning St., Beverly, Mass. Office: 201 Devonshire St., Boston. Died July 15, 1954; buried Central Cemetery, Beverly, Mass.

JONES, Clyde E., lawyer; b. Agency, Ia., Feb. 20, 1895; s. Edward R. and Harriett E. (Verdow) J.; B.A., U. Ia., 1917, LL.B., 1919; m. Verl E. Brown, Mar. 22, 1919; children—Barbara Jean, Margot Dean (Mrs. Kenneth D. Wingert). Admitted to Ia. bar, 1919, since practiced in Ottumwa; mem. firm Jones, White and Johnson, attys. Served with U.S. Army, World War I. Mem. Am. Legion, Am. (ho. of dels. 1955-58), Ia. (chmn. title standards com. 1945-47; gov. 1947-53; chmn. constitution and by-laws com. 1949-50; legal forms com. 1951-53; v.p. 1953-54, pres. 1954-55; chmn. probate com. 1955—) bar assns., Nat. Conf. of Bar Presidents (council mem., 1956-58), Ottumwa C. of C., Phi Beta Kappa, Order of Coif. Methodist (trustee). Mason, Elk; mem. Order Eastern Star. Club: Ottumwa Country (past pres.). Home: 147 Vogel Av. Office: 119 E. 2d St., Ottumwa, Ia. Died Sept. 5, 1959.

JONES, David Dallas, college pres.; b. Greensboro, N.C., Nov. 19, 1887; s. Sidney Dallas and Mary Jane (Holley) J.; B.A., Wesleyan U., 1911; student U. of Chicago, summers, 1912-13; M.A., Columbia, 1930; LL.D., Howard University, 1937, Syracuse University, 1954; married Susie P. Williams, June 21, 1915; children—David Dallas, Frances Estelle, Paul Maurice, Frank Sidney. Sec. Internat. Com. Y.M.C.A., 1911-14; exec. sec. Pine Street Y.M.C.A., St. Louis, Mo., 1914-23; with Commn. on Interracial Cooperation, Atlanta, Ga., 1923-25; pres. Bennett Coll., 1926—. Mem. bd. trustees of Commn. on Interracial Cooperation; mem. Nat. Boys Work Council, Y.M.C.A.; mem. Bd. of Edn. Meth. Ch.; chmn. bd. trustees Carnegie Library, Greensboro, N.C. Del. Gen. Conf. M.E. Ch., Atlantic City, 1932, Columbus, 1936; del. to Uniting Conf. Meth. Ch., Kansas City, 1939; del. Gen. Conf. Meth. Ch., Atlantic City, 1940, Kansas City, 1944, Boston, 1948 (mem. Commn. on rules); treas. Central Jurisdiction Meth. Ch., 1944-48. Mem. bd. dirs., Assn. American Colls., Southern Edn. Found. V.p. Nat. Assn. of Schs. and Colls. of the Methodist Ch. Mem. Phi Beta Kappa. Address: Bennett College, Greensboro, N.C. Died Jan. 24, 1956; buried Annie Merner Pfeiffer Chapel, Bennett College.

JONES, Dwight Bangs, editor; b. Devils Lake, N.D., Mar. 5, 1900; s. William David and Amy (Burgess) J.; student Staunton Mil. Acad., 1915-16; m. Tillie Noem, Oct. 4, 1920; 1 son, Donald Jay; m. 2d, Phyllis Gene Bambusch, May 29, 1945; children—Stephanie, Jacqueline, Kent Carroll. Newspaper work in Devils Lake, Grand Forks, N.D., Aberdeen, S.D., Miami, Jacksonville, Fla., Mpls., Duluth, Fairmont, Minn.; mng. editor St. Paul Pioneer Press. Handled publicity for Community Chest, Am. City Bur. of Chgo., 1928. Served as cpl., sgt. USMC, France, 1917-18. Mem. Am. Newspaper Guild, Am. Legion, Americans for Dem. Action. Home: 2098 Wellesley Av., St. Paul 5. Office: St. Paul Pioneer Press, St. Paul. Died Feb. 16, 1958; buried Ft. Snelling Nat. Cemetery.

JONES, Earl J., business exec.; b. Crescent, O., Jan. 19, 1893; s. William Newton and Eliza Jane (Hardesty) J.; educated in public schools; married Susie White, January 15, 1955; children (by previous marriage)—John William, Elizabeth Jane. Pres. and treas. Muskingum Coal Co., Zanesville, Ohio since 1937, Zanesville Investment Co., automobile financing, since 1940, Jones Motor Sales, Inc., Zanesville, since 1939; newspaper owner and pub. Earl J. Jones Enterprises, Inc., Zanesville, and Masillon, O., pres. and treas. since 1939; pres. Ring Realty Co. Republican. Presbyterian. Club: Athletic(Columbus, O.). Mechanized mining operations in U.S. First mine operator to use chain conveyors and belt conveyor for underground haulage system. Home: Riverside Drive. Office: P.O. Box 1071, Zanesville, O. Died 1957.

JONES, Edgar DeWitt, clergyman, author; b. Hearne, Tex., Dec. 5, 1876; s. DeWitt Clinton and Mary Virginia (Rumble) J.; U. of Mo., 1894-95, Ky. (now Transylvania) U., 1898-1900, D.D., 1934; D.D., Ill. Wesleyan U., 1915; LL.D., Lincoln Memorial U., 1932; Litt.D., Culver-Stockton, 1932, Bethany, 1937, Tex. Christian, 1938, Litt.D., Wayne U.; m. Frances G. Willis, Jan. 23, 1902; children—Edgar DeWitt, Mary Eunice (dec.), Dorothy Louise (Mrs. Thomas J. Sherrard), Frances Virginia (Mrs. John R. Walker), Willis Rumble, William Westbrooke. Abandoned study of law for ministry; ordained ministry Disciples of Christ, 1901; first pastorates, Bullettsville, Pt. Pleasant, Florence, and Petersburg, all of Ky.; pastor Erlanger, Ky., 1901-03, Franklin Circle Church, Cleveland, O., 1903-06, 1st Christian Ch., Bloomington, Ill., 1906-20, Central Ch., Detroit, Mich., 1920-26, Central Woodward Ch., Detroit, 1927-47, emeritus, 1947; summer lectr. on preaching Pacific Sch. Religion, 1953; exchange preacher to Scotland, 1932; apptd. mem. Judicial Council of Michigan, 1933, reappointed, 1939; apptd. mem. Mich. Corrections Commission, 1941. Editorial staff Detroit News, 1922-28; mem. staff of The Christian, 1926-32, and of the Christian Century, 1927—; contbg. editor to World Call, 1933. Del. to World's Missionary Conf., Edinburgh, 1910; del. Oxford and Edinburgh Confs., 1937; pres. Ill. Conv. Disciples, 1915-16; pres. Internat. Conv. Disciples, 1917-19; pres. Assn. for Promotion Christian Unity, 1931-41, Federal Council of Chs. of Christ in America, 1937-38. Pres. Detroit Council of Churches, 1944. Mem. Authors' League of America, Detroit Hist. Soc., Ill. Hist. Soc., Kappa Sigma, Internat. Soc. of Theta Phi. Mem. Nat. Council of Fifty Against Intolerance in America, Lincoln Foundation Advisory Group. Director of Abraham Lincoln Association. Democrat. Mason (32°). Clubs: Rotary, Wranglers, Detroit Athletic; Quill (New York); Authors' (London). Author: The Inner Circle, 1914; The Wisdom of God's Fools, 1916; Fairhope, The Annals of a Country Church, 1917; the Tender Pilgrims, 1917; Ornamented Orthodoxy, 1918; When Jesus Wrote on the Ground, 1924; Blundering Into Paradise, 1932; Am. Preachers of Today, 1933; The Pulpit Stairs, 1934; The Dogs of War, 1936; This Great Business of Preaching, 1936; Roses of Bethany, 1936; Lords of Speech, 1937; This Great Business of Being Christian, 1938; A Man Stood Up to Preach, 1943; Best Sermons of 1944; The American Pulpit Series, 1945; The Coming of The Perfect 1946; The Greatening of Abraham Lincoln, 1946; Lincoln and the Preachers, 1948; The Royalty of the Pulpit, 1951; The Influence of Henry Clay upon Abraham Lincoln, 1952; The Peace of Great Phantoms, 1953; Sermons I Love to Preach, published 1953. Edited: Best of John A. Hutton, 1949. Contributor to religious press and magazines; writer syndicated column Successful Living, 1939. Traveled in Ireland, 1923, writing series of articles. Toured Europe and Near East as corr. Detroit News, 1935. Student of Americana; lecturer on Lincoln, Jefferson, etc. Winner of W. J. Long prize for best Lincoln sermon, 1939. Home: 31 Elm Park Blvd., Pleasant Ridge, Mich. Address: 31 Elm Park, Pleasant-Ridge, Mich. Died Mar. 26, 1956; buried Bloomington, Ill.

JONES, Edward David, author; b. Orford, Wis., May 15, 1870; s. David O. and Elizabeth (Hield) J.; B.S., Ohio Wesleyan U., 1892, hon. M.A., 1907, LL.D., 1923; Ph.D., U. Wis., 1895; student univs. Halle and Berlin, 1893-94; m. Annabelle White, June 27, 1895. Instr. statistics and econs. U. Wis., 1895-98, asst. prof. econs. and comml. geography, 1900-01; prof. bus. adminstrn. U. Mich., 1902-19; in charge Foreman tng. courses, Harvard, 1919-20; v.p. Z. L. White Co., Columbus, O., 1921-22. Dir. employment mgmt. sect., War Industries Bd., civilian attache to com. on edn. and spl. tng. of Gen. Staff, and fed. agt. in employment mgmt. with Fed. Bd. Vocational Edn., 1918-19. Expert Dept. Edn. and Social Economy, U.S. Commn. to Paris Expn., 1899-1900, and mem. jury awards; mem. Internat. Congress of Arts and Scis., St. Louis Expn., 1903; holder diploma and bronze medal (hors concours), Paris Expn., and gold medal, for exhibits on indsl. conditions in U.S., at Buffalo Expn. Mem. Phi Delta Theta, Phi Beta Kappa. Clubs: Creighton, Players, University, Faculty. Author: Economic Crises, 1900; The Business Administrator, 1913; The Administration of Industrial Enterprises, 1916 and 1925; Investments, 1917; Bibliography of Employment Management, 1919. Vice pres. Columbus Gallery of Fine Arts; trustee Ohio Wesleyan U. Home: 162 Preston Rd., Columbua, O. Died Jan. 9, 1944; buried Oak Grove Cemetery, Delaware, O.

JONES, Edward E.; b. Harford, Pa., Nov. 25, 1867; s. Henry M. and Marietta L. (Blandin) J.; grad. Williston Sem., Easthampton, Mass., 1886; m. 3d, Kathryn B. O'Hara, 1922; children—Henry Sweet and Edward Jackson (by previous marriage). Mem. Pa. Ho. of Reps., 10 yrs., Senate 8 yrs.; mem. Farm Loan Bd., by appt. of President Harding, term 1923-31, resigned, 1927; registrar of the Treasury, 1929-33. Mem. Pa. Soc. of N.Y.C., Grange. Republican. Conglist. Mason, Odd Fellow. Known as "Good Roads Jones." Address: Harford, Pa. Died July 17, 1951; buried Harford.

JONES, Francis Ilah, govt. ofcl.; b. Blossburg, Pa., Nov. 29, 1864; s. Jacob and Rachel J.; ed. high sch. and bus. coll.; m. Margaret A. Evans, Apr. 23, 1890 (died 1915); children—Gwladys Webster, Francis Ilah, Clifford Ivor. Hardware bus. Blossburg, 1883-95, later postmaster; charge U.S. employment service, Pitts., during World War; dir. gen. U.S. employment service, Dept. of Labor, 1921—. Republican. Presbyn. Mason (32°, Shriner), Moose. Home: Ocean Grove, N.J. Address: Dept. of Labor, Washington. Deceased.

JONES, Frank Leonard, business exec.; b. nr. Kokomo, Ind., Feb. 25, 1872; s. John Henderson and Harriet (Harness) J.; B.S., Valparaiso (Ind.) U., 1890; A.B., Ind. U., 1898, LL.D., 1938; student U. Chgo., 1895; LL.D., Hampden-Sydney Coll., 1933; m. Rhoda Davis, June 12, 1917; 1 dau., Eleanor (Mrs. E. J. Jackson). Tchr. Manual Training High Sch., Indpls., 1895; supt. city schs., Tipton, Ind., 1896-99; state supt. public instrn., Ind., 1899-1903; with Equitable Life Assurance Soc. of U.S., 1906— as Ind. State mgr., 1906-28, Central Western supt., 1906-1920, v.p., 1928—. Pres. Greater New York Safety Council; chmn. Nat. Com. on Replacement. Served as dir. of ins. instrn. in AEF, 1918-19. Pres. Nat. Assn. Life Underwriters, 1925-26. Mem. Omicron Delta Kappa, Delta Tau Delta. Republican. Clubs: Columbia (Indpls.); North Hempstead Country (L.I.); Lake Placid (N.Y.); Everglades (Palm Beach, Fla.). Contbr. articles on ins. to mags.; lectr. on bus., ednl. and travel subjects. Home: 65 Woodedge Rd., Plandome, N.Y. Office: 393 7th Av., N.Y.C. Died Dec. 21, 1953; buried Young America, Ind.

JONES, Harold Wellington, physician, ex-army officer, editor; b. Cambridge, Mass., Nov. 5, 1877; s. Frank Henry and Elizabeth Cook (Towne) J.; ed. Mass. Inst. Tech., 1894-97; M.D., Harvard, 1901; Army Med. Sch., 1905-06 (honor grad.), Army Med. Field Service Sch., 1930; LL.D., Western Res. U., 1945; m. Eva Ewing Munn, Jan. 1, 1910 (died 1936); m. 2d, Mary Winifred Morrison, May 1, 1937; 1 dau., Helen (Mrs. Clifford M. Esler); 1 stepson, Frank A. McGurk. Physician, Boston, 1901; house surgeon Children's Hosp., Boston, 1902-03; practicing physician, St. Louis, 1903-05; asso. prof. orthopedic surgery St. Louis U. Med. Sch., 1904-05; entered M.C., U.S. Army, 1906, capt., 1909 (temp. col. and col., 1918-19), col., 1932; served in Philippines, 1906-08, 20-23; charge of ambulance and evacuation service, Mexican campaign, 1916; prof., sec. faculty Army Med. Sch., 1917-18; comdr. Beau Desert Hosp. Center, AEF, France, 1918-19; chief surg. service Gen. Hosp. 41, N.Y., 1920, Ft. Sam

Houston Hosp., 1927-33; comdg. officer Tripler Gen. Hosp., Hawaii, 1933-36; librarian Army Med. Library, Washington, 1936-43, dir., 1944-46. Sec. gen. 10th Internat. Congress Mil. Medicine, 1939; chief U.S. del. 9th Internat. Congress Mil. Medicine, Rumania, 1937; mem. Commn. Naval Experts revising Hague and Geneva Convs. (Red Cross), Geneva, 1937; v.p. Internat. Congress Air Relief, Budapest, 1937; hon. curator Osler Library, Montreal, 1936-46. Decorated Chevalier, Legion of Honor (Frence), 1918; Officer, l'ordre de la Sante Publique (France), 1939; Cross of Order of Merit (Poland), 1939; Rumania, 1940; Legion of Merit (U.S.) 1945; Philippine Insurrection, Mexican Expdn. and World War medals. Recipient Marcia C. Noyes award Med. Library Assn., 1956. Fellow A.C.S., A.A.A.S.; hon. fellow Cleve. Med. Library Assn., Beaumont Med. Club; hon. mem. Mexican Assn. Mil. Surgeons, Med. Library Assn. (pres. 1940, 41); mem. Boylston Med. Soc., A.C.S. (mem. com. on library). Unitarian. Clubs: Harvard (N.Y. C.); Army and Navy (Washington). Author: Green Fields and Golden Apples. Editor: Proceedings of 10th International Congress Mil. Medicine, 1939; Bulletin of Medical Library Assn., 1941-42; New Gould Medical Dictionary, 1946-56. Contbg., med. editor Ency. Americana. Contbr. about 600 articles to med. and hist. Jours. Mayo Found. lectr., 1942. Home: 1303 Chichester Av., Orlando, Fla. Died Apr. 5, 1958.

JONES, Harriot Hamblen, educator; b. Newton, Mass., Apr. 10, 1886; d. Ephraim Stone and Mary Homer (Linder) Hamblen; ed. Bigelow Sch. (Newton), Erasmus Hall High Sch. (Bklyn.), Perry Kindergarten Normal Sch. (Boston); m. Frank H. Jones, Aug. 16, 1917. Tchr. kindergarten, Newhall Sch., Waltham, 1908-10, Bemis Sch., Waltham, 1910-17; tchr. Perry Kindergarten Normal Sch., 1908-17, prin., 1917—. Mem. N.E.A., Asso. Childhood Edn., Pvt. Sch. Assn., Mass. State Kindergarten Assn., Council Adminstrv. Women. Rep. Episcopalian. Mem. O.E.S. Club: Hatherly Country. Home: 35 Chestnut Terrace, Newton Centre, Mass. Office: 25 Huntington Av., Boston. Died June 24, 1957.

JONES, Hilton Ira, chemist, lecturer; b. Mankato, Minn., May 9, 1882; s. Addison Sprague and Alice Nancy (Hilton) J.; A.B., Parker Coll., Winnebago, Minn., 1903; A.M., Drake Univ., 1904; Harvard Univ., 1906-08; fellow in chemistry, University of Chicago, 1908-09; Ph.D., University of South Dakota, 1916; Doctor of Science, Dakota Wesleyan University, 1948; married Blanche Pinkerton, June 16, 1908; children—Eugenia (Mrs. Clyde E. Peaster), Haydn, Llewellyn, Virginia (Mrs. R. W. Burrill), Joan (dec.), Ernestine Harriette (Mrs. Thomas C. Shaw), Florice (Mrs. Howard Dellard). Teacher of science, East High School, Des Moines, Ia., 1904-06; chemist for B. O. and G. C. Wilson, manufacturing pharmacists, Boston, 1907; professor chemistry, Central High School, Muskogee, Oklahoma, 1909-12; professor chemistry, Dak. Wesleyan University, 1912-18; professor chemistry and chem. engring., Okla. Agrl. and Mech. Coll., 1918-22; dir. of scientific research, The Redpath Bureau, 1922-29; dir. div. of edn. and research, The Nat. Selected Morticians, 1929-34; mng. dir. The Naselmo Corp., Chicago, 1934-37; mng. dir. Hizone Products (successor to Naselmo Corp.), 1937—. Registered pharmacist. Fellow A.A.A.S., Am. Inst. Chemists (past chmn. Chicago Chapt.), Chem. Soc. (London), Inst. Am. Genealogy; mem. Am. Chem. Soc., Am. Assn. Engrs., Isaac Walton League, Soc. Mayflower Descs., S.A.R., Order of First Crusade, Baronial Order Magna Charta, Sigma Phi Epsilon, Phi Kappa Phi, Pi Kappa Delta (diamond eye), Kappa Kappa Psi, Kappa Delta Pi. Meth. Mason (K.T., Scottish Rite), Elk, K.P. Clubs: Rotary, Engineers, Executives (Chicago). Contbr. to scientific publs.; sci. lecturer. Award of Merit Certificate, 11th editorial competition. Home: 1538 Forest Av., Wilmette. Office: Hizone Research Laboratory, 1211 Washington Av., Wilmette, Ill. Died May 2, 1955; buried Meml. Park Cemetery, Evanston, Ill.

JONES, J. Shirley, agrl. chemist; b. Garrett, Ind., Feb. 14, 1876; s. Sidney P. and Mary (Ditmars) J.; B.S., U. Cal., 1903; M.S. in agr., Cornell, 1914; m. Tillie Browning, Sept. 1906; children William Shirley. Chemist, asst. supt., Giant Powder Co., San Francisco, 1904-06; chemist Ida. Expt. Sta., 1906-14, chemist, dir., 1914-18; operating chemist, U.S. Nitrate Plant No. 1, Sheffield, Ala., for Ordnance Div. War Dept., 1918; prof. agrl. chemisty and expt. sta. chemist, Ore. Agrl. Coll., 1919—. Mem. Ida. Com. Indsl. Preparedness of Naval Cons. Bd. Mem. Am. Chem. Soc., Soc. Chem. Industry, A.A.A.S., Sigma Xi, Phi Lambda Upsilon. Presbyn. Mason. Home: Corvallis, Ore. Died Jan. 24, 1954.

JONES, Jesse Holman, former sec. of commerce; b. Robertson County, Tenn., Apr. 5, 1874; s. William Hasque and Anne (Holman) J.; student pub. schs.; LL.D., Southwestern U., 1925, So. Meth. U., 1927, A. and M. Coll. of Tex., 1936, N.Y.U., Temple U., 1937, John Brown U., 1938; Oglethorpe U., Washington and Jefferson Coll., 1941, Lafayette Coll., St. Lawrence U., Northwestern U., 1942; U. N.B., Can., 1948; m. Mary Gibbs, Dec. 15, 1920. Mgr., later gen. mgr. M. T. Jones Lumber Co., Dallas, 1895-1905; organized South Tex. Lumber Co., 1902; organized Tex. Trust Co., Houston, 1909 (now Bankers Mortgage Co.), of which was dir. and chmn. bd. at time of resignation, Apr. 28, 1932; v.p. Lumberman's Nat. Bank (now 2d Nat. Bank), 1907-15, Union Nat. Bank, 1910-18; chmn. bd. Nat. Bank of Commerce, Houston; owner and pub. Houston Chronicle; builder on a large scale and owner of important real estate in Houston and other cities. Dir. RFC, 1932-39, chmn. bd., 1933-39; chmn. exec. com., Export-Import Bank of Washington, 1936-43; adminstr. Fed. Loan Agency, 1939-45; apptd. sec. of commerce, Sept. 1940, resigned 1945. Mem. Nat. Emergency Council, 1933-39; mem. Econ. Def. Bd. (later Bd. Econ. Warfare), 1941-45; mem. Supply Priorities and Allocations Bd., 1941-42; mem. WPB, 1942-45; mem. Econ. Stblzn. Bd., 1942-45. Chmn. Tex. Commn., N.Y. World's Fair of 1939 and U.S. Golden Gate Expn., San Francisco, 1937-39. Hon. pres. San Jacinto Centennial Assn., Houston; dir. gen. Tex. Centennial Celebration, 1926-34. In recognition of services to State and Nation, The Texas legislature authorized the painting of his portrait, which was unveiled in the Capitol Bldg., at Austin, Oct. 7, 1935; decorated Order of Ching Hsin, Grand Cordon (China); Comdr. Royal Order of Vasa, King of Sweden, 1952; Knighthood in Order San Jacinto, 1954. Dir. gen. mil. relief A.R.C., Washington, 1917; mem. Red Cross War Council, 1918; del. with Henry P. Davison to Red Cross meetings in Paris, Cannes and Geneva, and assisted in organizing League of Red Cross Socs. of the World; mem. nat. adv. council, Girl Scouts; trustee George Peabody Coll. for Tchrs., 1929—, Tuskeegee Inst.; treas. Will Rogers Meml Commn.; ex-pres., treas., Woodrow Wilson Birthplace Found., Inc. Dir. of finance, Dem. Nat. Com., 1924-28; chmn. adv. finance com., 1928. Awarded regency in field of finance, 1935, by Soc. of Arts and Sciences; mem. Newcomen Soc. Methodist. Clubs: Nat. Democratic, Whist (N.Y.C.); Nat. Press, Metropolitan, Alfalfa, Jefferson Island Club (Washington); Bohemian (San Francisco); also many clubs and orgns. of Houston. Author: Fifty Billion Dollars, 1951. Home: Lamar Hotel. Office: Bankers Mortgage Bldg., Houston. Died June 1, 1956.

JONES, John George; b. Wales, Jan. 14, 1869; s. Humphrey and Lucy A. (George) J.; ed. University Coll. of Wales, Aberystwyth, Wales; m. Jemmie May Walden, Apr. 6, 1897. Came to U.S., 1888; engaged in newspaper work and mining in Mont. and Colo., 1888-97; orgn. salesmanship, sales mgmt. courses N. Y.U. Sch. of Commerce, 1913 (first sales mgmt. course ever given in a school of commerce); developed sales orgn. of Alexander Hamilton Inst. of which is treas. and vice president in charge of marketing. Spl. lectr. on marketing Case School of Applied Science, Cleve., 1915, 16; speaker before Nat. Assn. Life Underwriters, St. Louis, 1916, World Sales Congress, Detroit, 1917, etc. Chmn. com. on bus. methods and indsl. relations of Internat. Rotary Clubs, 1920-21; chmn. exec. com. Rotary Clubs' Prosperity Poster Campaign. Mem. Acad. Polit. Science, Nat. Fedn. Sales Execs. Club: New York Sales Managers (pres. 1932-33). Republican. Protestant. Mason, Elk. Author: Salesmanship and Sales Management, 1915; Sales Management, 1930. Speaker for Treasury Dept., 1917-18, and in war bond campaigns of World War II. Home: Bretton Hall Hotel, Broadway and 86th St. Office: 71 W. 23d St., N.Y.C. Died Aug. 1956.

JONES, Lester Martin, sociologist; b. Pickering, Mo., July 28, 1884; s. William Allen and Magdalene (Cline) J.; A.B., Baker U., Baldwin, Kan.; B.D., Union Theol. Sem., N.Y.C., 1913; A.M., Columbia, 1913; Ph.D., U. Wis., 1927; m. Nelle Roach, June 16, 1909; 1 son, Donald Wayne. Minister, Meth. Ch., Fillmore, Mo., 1909-10, Grace Meth. Ch., St. Joseph, Mo., 1913-16; prof. econs. and sociology, Mo. Wesleyan Coll., Cameron, 1916-20, dean, 1919-20; prof. econ. and sociology, Morningside Coll., Sioux City, Ia, 1920-27; prof. sociology, head dept. DePauw U., Greencastle, Ind., 1927—. Pres. Ind. Conf. Social Work; pres. Ind. Conf. Marriage and the Family; mem. adv. com. Nat. Conf. Family Relations. Mem. Ind. Acad. Social Scis. (pres. 1933), Ohio Valley, Am. sociol. socs. Club: Rotary (Greencastle). Author: Quakers in Action, 1929; Sociology of Poverty and Dependency—A Work Book, 1939. Home: 401 E. Seminary St., Greencastle, Ind. Died June 1954.

JONES, Lloyd E., army officer; b. Columbia, Mo., June 17, 1889; s. Dr. John Carleton and Clara Field (Thompson) J.; student U. of Mo., 1909-11; grad. Sch. of Fire, Ft. Sill, Okla., 1915, Army Center of Arty. Studies (A.E.F.), 1919, Command and Gen. Staff Sch., Ft. Leavenworth, 1924, Army War Coll., 1930; m. Elizabeth Herriot Rembert, May 17, 1919; children—Lloyd Edmonstone, John Carleton, Anne Iredell. Commd. 2d lt., Field Arty., 1911; promoted through grades to brig. gen. (temp.), May 1941; served as lt. col. (temp.) Regimental Exec., 5th F.A., with A.E.F.; mem. operations and training branch Gen. Staff Corps, 1930-34; exec. of tactics with rank of lt. col., Field Arty. Sch., 1935-38; prof. mil. science and tactics, U. of Mo., 1939-40; col., chief of staff, 1st Army Corps, Columbia, S.C., 1940-41; became comdr. 76th Field Arty. Brigade, Ft. F. E. Warren, Wyo., Apr. 1941; assumed comd., Cold Bay, Aleutian Islands, June 1942; directed occupation of Amchitka Island (Aleutians), Jan. 1943; trained 10th Mountain Div., Camp Hale, Colo., July 1943; duty A.G.F. War Coll., Dec. 1944; retired, Apr. 30, 1946. Awarded Distinguished Service Medal, Aug. 1943; Victory medal, 1919. Mem. U.S. Field Arty. Assn., Am. Legion, Beta Theta Pi, Scabbard and Blade. Mem. Knights of St. Patrick. Club: Army-Navy (Washington). Author: Field Artillery Applied Mathematics, 1922. Address: War Dept., Washington, D.C. Died Jan. 3, 1958.

JONES, Loyd Ancile, physicst; b. York, Neb., Apr. 12, 1884; s. Oscar Rodolph and Rocetha (Cottrell) J.; B.S. in E.E., U. of Neb., 1908, A.M., 1910; hon. D.Sc., Univ. of Rochester, N.Y., 1933; m. Lillian May Chaplin, Dec. 4, 1911. Lab. asst. in physics, Bur. of Standards, 1910-12; asst. physicist research lab., Eastman Kodak Co., 1912-16, head of physics dept., 1916—. Served as lt. Constrn. Corps, U.S. N.R.F., World War. Mem. Optical Soc. America (pres. 1929-31; Frederic Ives Medal, 1943), Soc. Motion Picture Engrs. (fellow; progress medal 1939; pres., 1923-26, engr. vice-pres., 1933-39, outstanding service award 1954), Illuminating Engineering Society, Am. Physical Soc., Royal Photo. Soc. (Hurter & Driffield Medal, 1949, progress medal, 1948), Photo. Society Am. (progress medal 1949, American Journalistic award), A.A.A.S., Sigma Xi. Contbr. to magazines. Home: 22 San Rafael Dr. Office: Kodak Park, Rochester, N.Y. Died May 15, 1954; buried Pittsford, N.Y.

JONES, Lynds, zoölogist; b. Jefferson, Ohio, Jan. 5, 1865; s. Publius Virgilius and Lavinia (Burton) J.; student Ia. Coll., 1888-90; A.B., Oberlin, 1892, Sc.M., 1895; Ph.D., U. Chgo., 1905; m. Clara Mabelle Tallman, Sept. 8, 1892; children—Lynds Leo, Theodore Burton (dec.), George Tallman, Beth, Harold Charles. Began asst. in zoology Oberlin Coll., before graduation, prof. animal ecology, 1922-30; also. curator Zoöl. Mus., ret. 1930; vis. lectr. Berry Coll., 1936-37, 39; tchr. summers, transcontinental automobile ecology classes. Fellow A.A.A.S., Am. Ornithol. Union; mem. Am. Soc. Zoologists, Am. Geog. Soc., Cooper Ornithol. Club, Wilson Ornithol. Club. Republican. Conglist. Author: Revised Catalogue of Birds of Ohio, 1903. Editor of The Wilson Bull., 1896-1924. Home: 352 W. College St., Oberlin, O. Died Feb. 11, 1951; buried Birmingham, O.

JONES, Marvin Fisher, physician; b. Spencer, N.Y., Mar. 10, 1889; s. George Edward and Sadie (Fisher) J.; M.D., U. of Buffalo, 1913; m. Jessie Hill, June 8, 1922; children—James McKernan, Beatrice Clair, Robert Marvin. Asst. surgeon, Lackawanna Steel Co., Buffalo, N. Y., 1913; resident surgeon eye, ear, nose and throat, N.Y. Post Grad. Sch. and Hosp., 1914; engaged in practice, specializing in otolaryngology, N.Y. City, since 1918; consulting otolaryngologist Welfare Island Hosp.; surgeon dir. otology and mem. bd. dirs. Manhattan Eye, Ear and Throat Hosp.; cons. otolaryngologist, Port Chester, N.Y., Tioga County Gen. Hosp. (Waverly, N.Y.), N.Y. Hosp. of Cornell Med. Center, N.Y. City; prof. otology N.Y. Post Grad. Med. Sch. and Hosp., 1927-31; prof. clin. otolaryngology Columbia, 1931-38. Served as 1st lt., Med. Corps, A.E.F., France and Italy (enlisted for overseas service with Base Hosp. No. 8) during World War I; 1st asst. to chief consultant otolaryngologist, Consultants Hdqrs., Neuf Chateau, France; in charge eye, ear, nose and throat, A.E.F., Italy; detached service Evacuation Hosp., Argonne. Fellow Am. Coll. Surgeons; mem. A.M.A., Am. Men of Science, N.Y. State Med. Soc. (past chmn. sect. otolaryngology), N.Y. County Med. Soc., Am. Acad. Ophthalmology and Otolaryngology (past mem. council), Am. Triol. Soc., Am. Otol. Soc., (pres., research fellow; mem. council; trustee otosclerosis research fund), American Laryngol. Soc., Acad. of Medicine (sect. of otolaryngology; past mem. council; past chmn.), N.Y. Otol. Soc. (past sec.), N.Y. Otolaryngol. Soc., Inc. (past pres.), N.Y. Laryngol. Soc. Protestant. Clubs: Salmagundi (New York). Mem. editorial bd. of Annals of Otolgoy, Quar. Rev. of Otolaryngology. Contbr. numerous sci. articles to med. publs. Home: 215 E. 79th St., N.Y. City. Office: 121 E. 60th St., N.Y. C. 22. Died May 26, 1952.

JONES, Millard Franklin, banker; b. Richmond, Va., Sept. 1, 1891; s. Richard Waring and Cora (Brown) J.; student pub. schs. of Richmond, Va.; m. Clyde Daughtridge, Mar. 27, 1917; children—Shirley Ann (Mrs. Benjamin Bunn Woodward), Shields Daughtridge (Mrs. Charles C. Harris, Jr.). Asst. to officers, later in credit dept. Mchts. Nat. Bank, Richmond, 1911-13, head discount dept., 1913-15; cashier Planters Nat. Bank (Planters Nat. Bank and Trust Co., 1929—), Rocky Mount, N.C., 1915-38, exec. v.p., 1938-44, pres., 1944—, dir., 1927—; v.p., dir. Planters Cotton Oil & Fertilizer Co., Rocky

Mount, N.C., 1921—; dir. Citizens Savings & Loan Assn., Rocky Mount, N.C., Atlantic Coast Line R.R. Co. of Va., Wachovia Bank & Trust Co., Winston-Salem, N.C., Security Life & Trust Co., Winston-Salem, N.C., Winston-Salem Southbound Ry. Co., Battleboro (N.C.) Oil Co., and mem. exec. com. Carolina Tel. & Tel. Co., Tarboro, N.C. Trustee State of N.C. Teachers' and State Employees' Retirement System. Chmn. region 2 N.C. War Finance com. (now war savings com.), Rocky Mount Civilian Def. Council during World War II. Hon. alumnus N.C. State Coll., Raleigh, N.C. Mem. Am. (exec. council 1930-32, 36-38, commerce and marine com., 1940-42, mem. at large Fed. legislation com., 1945—, mem. exec. com. of nat. bank div. 1948-51), N.C. (pres. 1934-35, research and bank conf. com., 1938—) bankers assns., Rocky Mount C. of C. (dir.), S.A.R. (N.C. chpt.), Sons Confederate Vets. (Stonewall Jackson Camp, Richmond, Va.). Democrat. Baptist. Mason (K.T. Shriner). Clubs: Benvenue Country, Kiwanis (Rocky Mount); Durant Island (Fort Landing, N.C.); Commonwealth (Richmond, Va.). Home: 627 Tarboro St. Office: care Planters Nat. Bank & Trust Co., Rocky Mount, N.C. Died Mar. 24, 1950.

JONES, Montfort, univ. prof.; b. Cambria, Wis., July 4, 1890; s. William Gabriel and Eunice (Evans) J.; student Beloit (Wis.) Coll., 1908-10; A.B., U. of Wis., 1912, A.M., 1914; m. Eleanor Lloyd, Aug. 2, 1916. On faculty, U. of Pittsburgh, since 1915, prof. of finance since 1924. Dir. Pittsburgh br. Fed. Reserve Bank of Cleveland; mem. faculty Grad. Sch. Banking, Am. Bankers Assn. Mem. Economists Nat. Com. on Monetary Policy. Mem. Am. Econ. Assn., Beta Gamma Sigma, Alpha Kappa Psi. Republican. Mason. Home: 6423 Kentucky Av., Pitts. Died May 17, 1954; buried Cambria, Wis.

JONES, Nellie Sawyer Kedzie (Mrs. Howard Murray Jones), home economist; b. Madison, Me., Aug. 2, 1858; d. Luke Folsom and Paulina Dinsmore (Gray) Sawyer; B.S., Kan. State Agrl. Coll., Manhattan, 1876; Ms., 1878; m. Robert F. Kedzie, Dec. 28, 1881 (died 1882); m. 2d, Howard Murray Jones, July 17, 1901. With Kan. State Agrl. Coll., 1882-97; tchr. Bradley Inst., Peoria, Ill., 1897-1901; lectured at many agrl. colls. Conglist. Contbd. numerous articles to The Country Gentleman, under title The Country Gentlewoman, also series entitled The Janet Letters. State leader of home demonstration agts. in Wis. during the war; state leader of home econs. extension work, Wis., 1918-33, ret. Address: Madison, Wis. Died Apr. 19, 1956; buried Forest Lawn Cemetery, Madison.

JONES, O(ssie) Garfield, prof. polit. sci.: b. St. Paris, O., Aug. 12, 1884; s. Caleb and Julia Ann (Goodwin) J.; B.S., O. Wesleyan U., 1912; student Cornell U., 1907-08; summer student O. State U., 1911, U. of Chicago, 1912 and 1913; student U. of Wis., 1912-13; Ph.D., U. of Calif., Berkeley, 1919; m. Nellie Clara Nixon, Dec. 1, 1916. Teacher and athletic coach, P.I., 1908-11; prof. polit. sci., and chmn. dept. polit. sci. U. Toledo, 1919—, prof. emeritus, 1954—. Served with U.S. Army, 1917-19; mine comdr. and comdr. 3d provisional bn., Corregidor, P.I. Awarded citation for efficiency in training mine command recruits, Corregidor, 1918; rated most efficient capt. in coast defense, Corregidor, 1919. Mem. Am. Polit. Sci. Assn., Nat. Municipal League, O. Coll. Assn. (pres. social sci. sect., 1941-42), Mid-Western Polit. Sci. Assn., Am. Assn. Univ. Profs., Nat. Assn. Parliamentarians, Am. Legion, Toledo C. of C., Toledo Municipal League. Methodist. Clubs: Sylvania Country, Torch Internat. (pres. Toledo Torch Club). Author several books on polit. sci., parliamentary procedure 1929-48; Senior Manual for Group Leadership, 1949; Parliamentary Procedure at a Glance. Contributor of numerous articles to various wellknown reviews and mags. Home: Walnut St., Paris, O. Died Feb. 19, 1957; buried Paris, O.

JONES, Paul Fouts, lawyer; b. Danville, Ill., Nov. 6, 1898; s. Oliver Morton and Emma (Fouts) J.; Northwestern U., 1917-19; LL.B., U. of Mich., 1922; m. Edith Fairfield, Jan. 23, 1924; children—John Morton, Don Paul. Admitted to Ill. bar, 1922, practiced at Danville; mem. Jones, McIntire & Jones, 1922-30; now Jones, Sebat & Swanson, Danville, Ill.; president National Casualty Company of Detroit; city atty., Danville 1924-25; U.S. dist. atty., Eastern Ill. Dist., 1931-35; dir. Dept. of Ins., Ill., 1941-44. Served as 2d lt. inf., U.S. Army, World War; capt. 33d Div. Ill. Nat. Guard, Judge Advocate Dept., Gen. Staff, 1930-39. Mem. Sigma Alpha Epsilon, Phi Delta Phi. Republican. Methodist. Elk. Home: 1517 N. Vermillon St., Danville, Ill. Office: Adams Bldg., Danville, Ill. Died Nov. 23, 1953.

JONES, Quill, oriental rug connoisseur; b. Indianapolis, Ind., Feb. 28, 1875; s. Charles and Cora (Sweetser) J.; ed. pub. schs. and in museums of Europe; unmarried. With various business concerns in Indianapolis until 1905; visited Oriental countries, 1905, to study rugs, and has since made 9 trips into the Orient, traveling 37,000 miles, 1917-19; traveled in Arabia, 1929, and was first Am. archaeol. collector ever to enter the Yemen; has since made many trips, collecting rugs, etc., Sabaean and Himyaritic antiquities, latter placed in Pa. U. Museum. Has given addresses before Columbia U., Pratt Inst., New York Sch. of Applied Design, etc.; also loaned exhibits to various instns. Address: 711 5th Av., N.Y.C. Died July 27, 1954.

JONES, Richard Hugh, utilities exec.; b Powell, S.D., Feb. 14, 1889; s. Richard Pritchard and Mary (Ferris) J.; student pub. schs.; m. Bessie Miers, July 30, 1924; children—Betsy Mae, Richard Hugh. With Utah Power & Light Co. since 1913, treas. since 1929, v.p. since 1943, also dir. Served as lt. A.C., U.S. Army, 1917-18. Mem. Salt Lake City C. of C. (dir.). Episcopalian. Mason (Shriner). Club: Salt Lake City Country. Home: 153 Virginia St. Office: Kearns Bldg., Salt Lake City. Died June 29, 1955; buried Mt. Olivet Cemetery, Salt Lake City.

JONES, Robert Edmond; b. Milton, N.H., Dec. 12, 1887; s. Fred Plummer and Emma Jane (Cowell) J.; A.B., Harvard Univ., 1910; m. Margaret Huston Carrington, June 21, 1933. Began designing for the theatre, New York, 1911; designer for "The Man Who Married a Dumb Wife"; "The Jest"; "Richard III"; "The Birthday of the Infanta"; "Macbeth"; "Redemption"; "Green Pastures"; "The Iceman Cometh"; began designing for color films in 1933, color designer of "La Cucaracha" and "Becky Sharp." Member National Institute of Arts and Letters. Clubs: Harvard, Players, Century. Author: Drawings for the Theatre; The Dramatic Imagination. Address: R.F.D. 1, Union, N.H. Died Nov. 26, 1954; buried Milton, N.H.

JONES, Robert Taylor, ex-gov. Ariz.; b. Rutledge, Tenn., Feb. 8, 1884; s. Samuel and Sarah (Legg) J.; m. Elon Armstrong; children—Albert Claud, Katherine. Began as engr.; served as state senator, Ariz.; gov. State of Ariz., 1938-41. Mason, Elk. Address: Phoenix, Ariz. Died June 11, 1958.*

JONES, Roy Bergstresser, independent oil producer; b. Virginia, Ill., Sept. 19, 1883; s. John Anthony and Ida Belle (Bergstresser) J.; student Ill. Wesleyan U., 1902-05; m. Martha Byrnes, Sept. 18, 1909; children—Courtney Brown, Roy Bergstresser. In ice cream and confectionery mfg. bus., 1905-12; gen. mgr. Colonial Refining Co. 1912-14; operated Jane Oil & Gas Co., 1913-14; real estate bus., Oklahoma City, 1914-15; pres., chmn. bd. dirs. Panhandle Producing & Refining Co. 1919-43; formerly pres., dir. Panhandle Producing & Refining Co., Panhandle Steel Products Co., Petroleum Bldg. chmn. bd., dir. Wichita Falls & So. R.R. Co.; v.p., dir. Faith Oil Corp.; v.p. Bond County Gas Co., Greenville, Ill.; dir. Wichita Engring. Co., Faith Oil Corp. Dir. Tex. Indsl. Conf. Office, Dallas. Internat. Petroleum Expn.; mem. Petroleum Industry War Council, 1941-43. Mem. Ind. Petroleum Assn. Am. (dir.), Am. Petroleum Inst. (dir.), N. Tex. Oil and Gas Assn. (dir.), Phi Gamma Delta. Republican. Presbyn. Mason (32°, K.T., Shriner). Clubs: Rotary, Wichita; Wichita Falls Country. Home: 406 Morningside Drive. Office: 204 Panhandle Bldg., Wichita Falls, Tex. Died 1948.*

JONES, Sullivan W., architect; b. N.Y.C., May 16, 1878; s. Bassett and Sarah Catherine (Oakey) J.; student Mass. Inst. Tech. to end of sophomore yr., class of 1900; m. Martha Gordon Waller, Apr. 30, 1902; children—Sally, Sullivan. With various archtl. firms until 1910; mem. Palmer, Hornbostel & Jones, 1910-14; supervising engr. in charge constrn. Naval Operating Base, Jamestown, Va., 1917-18; state architect of N.Y., 1923-28. Chmn. Nat. Constrn. Planning and Adjustment Bd., 1934-35; asst. coördinator for indsl. coöperation, 1935-36; chief housing br. WPB, 1941-42; cons. on Post War Housing Program, Cal. Reconstruction and Reemployment Commn., 1944; cons. on Veterans' Hosps. to chief of U.S. Engrs., 1946-47; chmn. A.S.A. Elevator Safety Com., 1921-48. Fellow A.I.A.; mem. Am. Engring. Standards Com., Nat. Research Council, Delta Upsilon. Democrat. Home: 325 E. 79th St., N.Y.C. Died Jan. 26, 1955.

JONES, W(elton) Paul, business exec., inventor, lecturer; b. Winslow, Ind., Oct. 25, 1901; s. Thomas Edward and Lydia Agnes (Welton) J.; student Oakland City (Ind.) Coll. (bus. and tech. sch.), 3 yrs.; m. Clesta Jean Walker, Jan. 16, 1925; 1 dau., Margaret Louise Theis. With Jones and Welton, cafe, Oakland City, Ind., while in college; service mgr. Frigidaire Corp., Indianapolis, 1920-23; sales mgr. Frigidaire Distributors A. F. Wood Co., Evansville, Ind., 1923-27; pres. and gen. mgr. Refrigeration Products Co., Evansville, 1928-29; ednl. dir. Servel, Inc., Evansville, 1929-30, advt. and sales promotion mgr., 1930-33, asst. gen. mgr. commercial div., 1933-34; exec. v.p. Fairbanks-Morse Home Appliances, Chicago, at Indianapolis, 1934-38; pres. Philco Refrigerator Co., Jan. 1939-Dec. 1940; p.v. Philco Corp., Phila., 1940-49, dir. 1942-49; dir. Kellett Aircraft Corp.; pres., gen. mgr., dir. Servel Inc., Evansville, Indiana, 1949-54, vice chmn. bd., spl. adviser, 1954—; pres. Kellett Aircraft Corp., 1954—. Inventor and patentee several developments and designs refrigeration methods and features; lecturer on sales principles, distribution economics and product design and adaptation. One of organizers and former trustee Nat. Sales Exec. Council; v.p. dir. Ind. Employers Assn., 1936-40; Indianapolis Chamber of Commerce, 1936-40. Former mem. W.P.B. elec. refrigeration industry adv. com.; chmn. O.P.A. industry adv. com. elec. refrigeration industry, 1942-46; mem. Am. Soc. Refrigeration Engineers. Mason. Methodist. Clubs: Huntington Valley Country, Union League (Phila.); Seaview Country (Atlantic City); Rotary, Country (Evansville). Home: R.R. 5, Hillsdale Rd. Office: 119 N. Morton Av., Evansville, Ind. Died Jan. 20, 1955; buried Oak Hill Cemetery, Evansville.

JONES, William Larimer, Jr., steel mfr.; b. Pittsburgh, Pa., Sept. 2, 1891; s. William Larimer and Leila (Dilworth) J.; ed. St. Paul's School, Concord, N.H.; Litt.B., Princeton U., 1915; m. Augusta Day Hall, Nov. 12, 1919; children—Anne Jones McGrail, Augusta Jones Richards, Leila Dilworth (dec.). Director Jones & Laughlin Steel Corp.; dir. Peoples First Nat. Bank & Trust Co. Dir. South Side Hosp. Served in U.S. Navy, Dec. 1917-May 1919; commd. ensign, May 1918; transport service, Sept. 1918-May 1919. Episcopalian. Clubs: Duquesne, Pittsburgh, Allegheny Country, Fox Chapel Golf, Edgeworth, Rolling Rock, H-Y-P (Pittsburgh); Princeton, University (N.Y.C.). Home: R.D. 2, Sewickley, Pa. Office: Park Bldg., Pitts. 22. Died Dec. 20, 1954; buried Homewood Cemetery, Pitts.

JONGERS, Alphonse, portrait painter; b. France, Nov. 17, 1872; s. Jean Jacques and Marie (de Schomberg) J.; Litt.B., U. of Paris, 1889; studied at École des Beaux Arts until 1892, in Spain, 1893-95; m. Louise McAllister, 1903. Came to U.S., 1897. Has exhibited at Paris Salon, Société des Artistes Français, etc.; works on permanent exhbn. at Met. Mus., N.Y., Nat. Gallery, Washington. Awards silver medal, St. Louis Expn., 1904; third medal, Paris Salon, 1906. Died 1945.*

JONSSON, Axel, business exec.; b. Gothenburg, Sweden, May 16, 1888; s. Axel and Ragnhild (Lundgren) J.; student Dresdener Kaufmannsche Höhere Handelsschule; m. Sigyn Janson, Mar. 23, 1914 (died Dec. 1934); children—Ingela (wife of Baron Göran von Essen), Aake, Ragnhild (wife of Comdr. Stig Broms), Maud (Mrs. Bertil Uhlén); m. Mrs. Joseph W. Wear, Nov. 17, 1949. Mng. dir. Swedish Am. Line, Gothenburg; dir. Angfartygs AB Tirfing, AB Broströms Linjeagentur, AB Bunkeroljor, AB Albatross, AB Motortank, Angfartygs AB Ferm, Hallands Angfartygs AB, Rederi AB Goteborg-Frederikshavnlinjen, Oceankompaniet, AB Coasting, AB Atlanttrafik, Rederi AB Svenska Lloyd, Göteborgs Bogsering & Bärgningsbolag, AB Götaverken, Eriksbergs Mek. Verkstads AB, Swedish Shipowners Assn., Sv. Angfartygs Assurans-Förening. Recipient Comdr. Italian Order of Crown, Royal Order of Vasa, Royal Order of Dannebrog, Vytautas, St. Olaf, St. Maurizio e Lazzaro, Finland's White Rose, Knight of Royal Order of North Star, Delaware Medal (1938), Danish Medal of Liberty (1946). Mem. bd. Swedish Tourist Traffic Assn., Gothenburg Tourist Assn., Lloyd's Register of Shipping, Sweden-Am. Foundn., Sweidsh Am. News Exchange, Swden Life Boat Assn. (pres.), Gothenburg Art Soc., Gothenburg Museum. Home: Saro, Sweden. Office: Swedish American Line, Broströmia, Gothenburg, Sweden. Died Jan. 11, 1950.

JOPSON, John Howard, surgeon; b. Phila., Dec. 28, 1871; s. William and Elizabeth S. (Thomas) J.; A.B., Phila. High Sch., 1888; Biol. Sch. U. Pa., 1890; M.D., U. Pa., 1893; m. Susanna B. Michener, June 7, 1909; children—Harry Gorgas Michener, Frances Leslie. Resident physician Univ. and Children's hosps., Phila., 1893-95; surgeon, Children's Hosp., 1900-29, Presbyn. Hosp., 1905-34; emeritus prof. surgery, Grad. Sch. Medicine, formerly clin. prof. surgery, Med. Sch., U. Pa.; cons. surgeon, Children's Hosp., Bryn Mawr Hosp. Maj. Med. R.C., 1917; lt. col., M.C., U.S. Army, Nov. 11, 1918. Fellow Am. Surg. Assn., A.C.S., Coll. Physicians Phila., Phila. Acad. Surgery (hon.); Soc. Clin. Surgery; Internat. Soc. Surgery. Author articles on Peritonitis, Intubation and Tracheotomy in Diphtheria, in Musser and Kelly's Handbook of Practical Treatment, 1911-12, 1917; also contbr. to Nelson's Loose-Leaf Surgery and med. jours. Home: Rutherfordton, N.C.; University Club, Phila. Died 1954.

JORDAN, Edward Benedict, univ. pres.; b. Dunmore, Pa., Dec. 17, 1884; s. Patrick Francis and Bridget (O'Hora) J.; B.S., St. Thomas Coll., Scranton, Pa., 1903; A.B., Mt. St. Mary's Coll., Emmitsburg, Md., 1905; S.T.D., Univ. of Propaganda, Rome, 1909. Ordained to priesthood, 1909; prof. biology, later edn., Mt. St. Mary's Coll., 1910-21, vice pres., 1918-20; lecturer in edn., St. Joseph's Coll., Emmitsburg, Md., 1915-21; instr. in edn., Cath. Univ., 1921-26, asso. prof., 1926, sec. Coll. Arts and Science, 1930-37, acting head dept. of edn., 1940, head, 1941-43, lecturer in edn., Trinity Coll., 1921-36; sec. Cath. Sisters Coll., 1921-36, dean, 1936-43, vice rector of univ. since 1943. Domestic Prelate, 1936. Mem. A.A.A.S., Nat. Cath. Edn. Assn., Soc. for the Advancement of Edn. Translator of DeHovre's Philosophy and Education, 1931; Catholicism in Education, 1934. Home: Catholic Univ. of America, Washington 17. Died July 19, 1951.

JORDAN, Edward Stanlaw, automobile mfr.; b. Merrill, Wis., Nov. 21, 1882; s. John and Kate (Griffin) J.; A.B., U. Wis., 1905; m. Charlotte Hannahs, Feb. 2, 1906; children—Jack Stanlaw, Jane, Joan. Worked way through college as newspaper reporter; learned salesmanship with Nat. Cash Register Co., Dayton, O.; entered automobile bus. with Thomas B. Jeffery Co., Kenosha, 1907; organized Jordan Motor Car Co., 1916, and since pres. Designated by student and alumni vote one of ten most distinguished alumni, U. Wis. Chmn. Advt. Com. and mem. Highways and Safety coms. Nat. Automobile Chamber Commerce; mem. Phi Gamma Delta. Republican. Mason. Clubs: Union, Mayfield Country, Pepper Pike Country, Mid-Day, Cleveland; University, Racquet (Chicago); Detroit Athletic. Home: 14923 Grandview Terrace. Office: 1070 E. 152d St., Cleve. Died Jan. 1959.

JORDAN, Riverda Harding, educator; b. St. Joseph, Mo., Apr. 12, 1873; s. William Amos and Clara (Harding) J.; B.A., Yale, 1893, M.A., 1913; Ph.D., U. Minn., 1919; A.M. (hon.), Dartmouth, 1919; m. Mary Vinette Hoover, Aug. 3, 1909; children—Richard Hollister, Hoover Harding. Bus. and clerical service until 1897; tchr. and dir. athletics Central High School, St. Joseph, 1897-1904; prin. Central High Sch. and dir. Normal Tng. Sch., St. Joseph, 1904-11; prin. West High Sch., Mpls., 1911-17; instr. rhetoric and edn. U. Minn., 1917-19; prof. edn. Dartmouth, 1919-21, also chmn. dept.; prof. edn. Cornell U., 1921-41, emeritus, 1941—, dir. summer session, 1924-34; extension lectr. Elmira Coll., 1922-23; vis. prof. U. Tampa, 1941-43. Instr. S.A.T.C., U. Minn., 1918. Dir. Cornell U. Christian Assn., 1922-35 (pres. 1935); mem. N.Y.C. Sch. Survey Com., 1924-25, Youngstown (O.) Survey, 1932. Fellow A.A.A.S., Am. Geog. Soc.; mem. Soc. Coll. Teachers of Edn. (mem. exec. com. 1926-29), Nat. Soc. Study of Edn., Nat. Assn. Summer Session Dirs. (sec. 1927; pres. 1931), Nat. Assn. of Colls. and Depts. of Edn. (v.p. 1929; chmn. exec. com. 1937-38), Am. Assn. U. Profs., S.R., Phi Kappa Phi, Phi Gamma Delta (chmn. nat. scholarship com. 1926-48), Phi Delta Kappa (an Honor Key); Kappa Phi Kappa (nat. pres. 1922-27; councilor 1928-39), Pi Gamma Mu, Alpha Kappa Delta; mem. Scholarship Commn. Nat. Inter-Fraternity Conf., 1931-32, chmn. com. on Chapter House Tutors, 1932-41; mem. N.Y. State Examination Bd., 1926-41; bd. dirs. Avon Park C. of C. (pres. 1947-49); mem. county draft board, 1948—; chmn. com. on cultural relations, Fla. Inter-Am. Center; nat. councilor, U.S. C. of C.; chmn. CED Avon Park. Methodist. Clubs: Rotary (pres. 1944-45), Phi Gamma Delta (New York). Author: Nationality and School Progress, 1921; Educational Measurements and the Classroom Teacher (with A. R. Gilliland), 1924, rev. edit. with F. S. Freeman, 1931; Extra-classroom Activities, 1928; Manual on How to Study, 1929, rev. edit., 1932; Junior High School Course of Study, 1930; Education as a Life Work, 1930. Contbr. to numerous periodicals; also some published verse. Mem. bd. editors Social Science. Address: Highland Lakes, Avon Park, Fla. Died Sept. 11, 1950; buried St. Joseph, Mo.

JORDAN, Samuel Martin, coll. pres.; b. Stewartstown, Pa., Jan. 6, 1871; s. James Cowden and Mary Rosanna (Mitchell) J.; A.B., Lafayette Coll., Easton, Pa., 1895, A.M., 1898, D.D., 1916; grad. study Princeton, 1895-98; grad. Princeton Theol. Sem., 1898; LL.D., Washington and Jefferson coll., 1935; m. Mary Woods Park, July 21, 1898. Ordained ministry Presbyn. Ch., 1898; missionary to Persia, 1898-99; prin. Am. High Sch. of Teheran (Persia), 1899-1925; pres. same since it became Alborz Coll. of Teheran, 1925. Mem. Acad. Polit. Science, Phi Beta Kappa. Awarded sci. medal, Dept. Edn., Persia. Republican. Contbr. to Missionary Review of World, Moslem Review, etc. Address: Alborz College of Teheran, Teheran, Iran (Persia). Died June 21, 1952.

JORDAN, Sara Murray (Mrs. Penfield Mower), physician; born Newton, Mass., October 20, 1884; d. Patrick Andrew and Maria (Stuart) Murray; A.B., Radcliffe Coll., 1904; Ph.D., U. Munich, Germany, 1908; M.D., Tufts Med. Sch., 1921; honorary D.Sc., Smith College, 1935; Tufts Coll. 1943, Wilson Coll., 1946; H.H.D., Suffolk U., 1954; D.M.S. (hon.), Woman's Med. Coll. Pa., 1956; m. Sebastian Jordan, Jan. 14, 1913; 1 dau., Mary (Mrs. Thomas H. Logan, Jr.) married 2d, Penfield Mower, Sept. 26, 1935. Engaged in practice of gastroenterology in Boston, 1922-58. In charge of gastroenterology, Lahey Clinic, 1923-58. Recipient Jane Addams medal, 1958. Fellow Am. Coll. Physicians; mem. Am. Gastro-Enterol. Assn. (pres. 1942-44; awarded Julius Friedenwald medal, 1952), American Med. Assn. (sect. gastroenterology, chmn. 1947-48), Mass. Medal Society, Phi Beta Kappa, Phi Beta Kappa Associates. Club: Cosmopolitan (N.Y.C.). Chmn. editorial board Gastroenterology, 1956-58. Author numerous articles on gastroenterological subjects. Home: 28 Foster St., Marblehead Neck, Mass. Died Nov. 1959.

JOSEPH, Lawrence Edgar, business cons.; b. Bellevue, O., Feb. 10, 1896; s. Fred Edgar and Rena (Kistler) J.; student Tutor Coll., 1911-17; m. Mary Hinds Ely, Dec. 4, 1919; children—Mary Louise, Doris Mae. Mech. engr. Blaw-Knox Co., 1919-25, industrial engr., 1925-35, management consultant, 1935-39, gen. mgr., 1939—, v.p. 1939-52; business management cons., 1952—. Served as 2d lt., U.S. Air Service (instr.), 1917-19. Mem. Iron and Steel Inst., Inst. of Steel Construction, Army Ordnance Assn., Nat. Planning Assn. Republican. Lutheran. Mason. Club: Pittsburgh Athletic, Duquesne, Pitts. Field. Home: Grandview Dr., Pitts. 15. Office: Farmer's Bank Bldg., Pitts. Died Oct. 28, 1954.

JOSS, John (Hubbard), govt. ofcl.; b. Indianapolis, Mar. 18. 1902; s. Frederick Augustus and Mary Quarrier (Hubbard) J.; A.B., Yale, 1926; LL.B., U. of Ariz., 1931; LL.M., George Washington U., Washington, 1946; m. Elizabeth Eleanor Taylor, July 1, 1931; children—Frederick Augustus, Mary Allen, Natalie Quarrier, Eleanor Wendy. Admitted to Ariz. bar, 1931, and practiced law, Mexico City, 1931-33, Indianapolis, 1933-37; 1st asst. counsel, Firestone Tire & Rubber Co., Akron, O., 1937-41; chief counsel, ration enforcement, O.P.A., 1942; spl. rep., U.S. Bd. of Econ. Warfare, Brit. E. Africa, 1942-43; asso. gen. counsel, War Assets Adminstrn., 1946-47; gen. counsel, 1947-49; commr. Liquidation Service, Gen. Services Adm.; mem. Renegotiation Bd., 1951—. Mem. Delta Kappa Epsilon, Phi Alpha Delta. Republican. Episcopalian. Mason (32°). All-American (football), Yale, 1925. Home: 3260 Nebraska Av., N.W., Wash. Office: The Renegotiation Board, Washington 25. Died Mar. 30, 1955; buried Crown Hill Cemetery, Indpls.

JOSSET, Raoul Jean (zhō-sā'), sculptor; b. Tours, France, Dec. 9, 1892; s. Edgar A. and Elisabeth (Lacomme) J.; student lycée of Lyons and Paris, France, 1906-14; B.Art, Beaux Arts Sch., Paris, 1915. Came to U.S., 1927, naturalized 1933. Sculptor since childhood; works in France include 15 war memls., and 1 Christ carved in concrete, 55 ft. high, at Jussy, Angels of Roupy; 200 war drawings, of which 3 were purchased by French govt.; sculpture and architecture in St. Quintin; etc. Works in U.S. include 40-ft. figures of Indians, carved in granite, on pylons of bridge, at Vincennes, Ind.; part of George Rogers Clark Memorial at Vincennes; works at Century of Progress Chicago, including figure 20 ft. high over main entrance to Federal Bldg., and eagles and seals on side entrances same building, also work on other modern bldgs. in Chicago; has reliefs, representing Navy, Army, Treasury and State; figures on Agrl. Bldg., etc.; decorations in many bldgs. of Chicago and other cities; commd. to work in Dallas, Texas, for State of Texas Centennial Expn., 1936; commd., 1936-37, by Tex. State Board of Control to execute the Refugio Memorial to King's Men, 30 feet high, bronze and Tex. granite, La Grange Memorial Wing statue, 20 bronze plaques for counties in State, Childress Memorial statue in Washington on the Brazos; 24 ft. statue N.Y. World's Fair; statue of Gen. Lafayette on grounds Phila. Museum of Art; taught sculpture 7 yrs. in Chicago; lectured with demonstrations Art Inst. of Chicago, Beloit Coll., Dayton Coll., Architectural Sketch Club of Chicago; teacher of sculpture Cooper Union, New York City, 1943-44; commissioned to execute bas relief for the Grand Lodge Masonic Temple, Waco, Tex., 1948. Awarded Beaux Arts prize, 1919; Salon medal, 1922; Chenavard prize, 1923; prize Salon scholarship, 1923; Societaire Salon d'Automme, 1924. Exhibited at Decorative Arts Exhbn., 1925. Fought at Verdun with French army and later served as interpreter A.E.F., World War I; was at Flirey and St. Mihiel. A.N.A. Address: 616 Exposition Av., Dallas 1. Died June 29, 1957; buried Calvary Hill Cemetery, Dallas.

JOST, Henry Lee (jōst), lawyer; b. N.Y., Dec. 6, 1873; s. Simeon and Lena (Bahr) J.; left an orphan in infancy; sent West from Mission House at Five Points, New York, and reared in Nodaway County, Mo.; ed. common schs.; studied law in office of S. E. Brown, Hopkins, Mo.; student Kansas City Law Sch., 1898-99; m. Alice Hanks, Aug. 1911; children—Mary E., Henry L. Admitted to Mo. bar, 1898; practiced Kansas City, Mo., 1899—; 1st asst. city counselor, resigned to become 1st asst. pros. atty., 1909-12; mayor Kansas City, 1912-16; asso. in practice with Frank Hagerman, 1916-20; mem. Hagerman and Jost, 1921-23. Lectr. on criminal law Kansas City Sch. Law, 1917-36. Mem. 68th Congress, 5th Dist. Mo.; now retired. Democrat. Episcopalian. Grand Master Workman A.O.U.W. for State of Mo., 1904-08. Mason (32°). Club: Kansas City. Home: R.F.D. No. 1, Belton, Mo. Died July 13, 1950.

JOSTES, Frederick Augustus (jōs'tēs), physician and surgeon; b. St. Louis, Mo., Aug. 14, 1895; s. Clemense and Appolonia (Niederberger) J.; B.S., Washington U., St. Louis, 1918, M.D., 1920; grad. student, orthopedic clinics, Eng., France, Germany, Austria, Switzerland, Ireland, Italy, 1925-26; m. Barbara Mary Donohoe, Dec. 4, 1945. Interne, Barnes Hosp., St. Louis, 1921, asst. resident surgeon, 1922, surgical pathologist, 1923; resident fellow, med. sch., Washington U., 1924; resident surgeon, orthopedics, Shriner Hosp. for Crippled Children, St. Louis, 1925; prof. clinical orthopedic surgery, U. of Mo., 1927-29; asst. prof. clin. orthopedic surgery, Washington U., since 1935; mem. staff Barnes, Childrens, Maternity, Deaconess, Jewish, City, County, Barnard Skin and Cancer hosps., St. Louis. Served with U.S. Navy, chief of surgery at Naval Air Station, San Diego, Calif., Jan.-July, 1942; exec. officer, Mobile Hosp. No. 2, July-Nov. 1942; sr. med. officer, U.S.S. Mt. Vernon, Nov. 1942-Feb. 1944; with bur. medicine and surgery, Office of Rehabilitation, Feb.-Sept. 1944; chief orthopedic surgery, U.S. Naval Hosp., St. Albans, Long Island, N.Y., Sept.-Nov. 1944; chief surgery and orthopedics, U.S. Naval Hosp., Great Lakes, Ill., Nov. 1944-Feb. 1946; dist. med. office, 12th Naval Dist., San Francisco; rank of capt., Naval Reserve. Member of the Baruch Committee on Phys. Medicine. Certified by Am. Bd. Orthopedic Surgery, 1934. Fellow Am. Coll. Surgeons; mem. St. Louis, Mo. State, Am. Southern and Miss. Valley med. assns., Clin. Orthopedic Assn., Am. Acad. Orthopedic Surgeons, Am. Orthopedic Assn., St. Louis Surg. Soc., Acad. Internat. of Medicine, La Societe Internationale de Chirurgie Orthopedique et de Traumatologie. Contbr. of articles to med. jours.; author chpts. in med. books. Home: River's Arm, St. Ferdinand de Fleurissant, St. Louis County, Mo. Office: 3720 Washington, St. Louis 8. Died May 19, 1952.

JOUHAUX, Leon (jōō-ō), French trade union leader; b. Paris, France, July 1, 1879. Began as asst. in office of match factory, Aubervilliers; Bourse du Travail, Angers, in sect. Bourses du Travail. Confédération Générale du Travail, 1906; sec. gen. Confedération Générale du Travail, 1909—; following World War I, served as labor del. of France to commn. to write Part XIII, Treaty of Versailles (International Labor Chart); then elected vice pres. Internat. Fed. of Trade Unions; also mem. workers group and vice president governing body, Internat. Labor Orgn.; active in League of Nations Conf. on Disarmament, particularly as to supression of private manufacture of arms and munitions; became head of movement against admission of totalitarian countries into Internat. Labor Orgn. Forced underground in 1940; arrested by French authorities, Dec. 1940; interned at Vals-les-Bains, later at Evaux-les-Bains; deported to Germany, Apr. 1943; liberated by U.S. Army, and reentered France, May 8, 1945. Became vice pres. World Fedn. of Trade Unions, 1945; pres. Econ. Council of Republic of France, 1947—; pres. Confédération générale du Travail Force Ouvriere, 1948—; v.p. Internat. Confederation of Free Trade Unions since 1949; del of France to all sessions Gen. Assembly, U.N. Recipient Nobel Peace Prize, 1951. Address: Confédération Générale du Travail Force Ouviere, 198 av. du Maine, Paris 14e, France. Died Apr. 28, 1954; buried Pére Lachaise Cemetery, Paris.

JOY, Charles Turner, naval officer; b. St. Louis, Feb. 17, 1895; s. Duncan and Lucy (Turner) J.; B.S., U.S. Naval Acad., 1916; M.S. (grad. work in explosive engring.), U. Mich., 1922; m. Martha Ann Chess, Oct. 16, 1924; children—Charles Turner, David Duncan, Mary Martha. Commd. ensign USN, 1916, and advanced through the grades to vice adm., 1949; served in U.S.S. Pennsylvania, 1916-20; exec. officer U.S.S. Pope, 1925-26; in U.S.S. California, 1928-31; comd. U.S.S. Litchfield, 1933-38; exec. officer U.S.S. Indianapolis, 1940-41; operations officer, staff of Vice Adm. Wilson Brown, 1941-42; comd. U.S.S. Louisville, 1942-43; on duty comdr. in chief hdqrs., 1943-44; comd. Cruiser Div. 6, 1944-45; comdg. Amphibious Group 2, 1945, Task Force 73 in Chinese waters, 1945-46; comdg. Naval Proving Ground, 1946-49; comdr. Naval Forces, Far East, 1949-52; sr. del. UN commd. delegation to Korean Armistice Conf., 1951-52; supt. U.S. Naval Acad., 1952—. Decorated Legion of Merit with 3 gold stars, Commendation Ribbon; D.S.C., D.S.M. (Army), D.S.M. (Navy) Bronze Star; Comdr. British Empire. Clubs: Chevy Chase (Md.); Army and Navy (Washington); New York Yacht (N.Y.C.). Address: U.S. Naval Acad., Annapolis, Md. Died June 1956.

JOY, James Richard, editor, librarian; b. Groton, Mass., Oct. 16, 1863; s. Richard Pickering and Mary (Hartwell) J.; B.A., Yale, 1885; M.A., 1891; Litt. D., Syracuse U., 1905; LL.D., Dickinson Coll., 1916; m. Emma Prentice McGee, Jan. 20, 1891 (died April 6, 1934); children—Helen, Alice, Gertrude. Asst. editor "Our Youth," 1885-99; S.S. editorial dept. Methodist Book Concern, New York, 1890-1904; asst. editor, 1904-15, editor, 1915-36, The Christian Advocate, New York, also chmn. editorial bd. retired, 1936; mem. editorial bd. Religion in Life. Librarian N.Y. Meth. Hist. Soc. 1936-52. Trustee Drew U. Delegate Methodist Episcopal Gen. Conference, 1908-36; sec. Class of 1885, Yale College. Clubs: Yale (New York), Phi Beta Kappa, Psi Upsilon, Scroll and Key. Author: The Greek Drama, 1887; Outline History of England, 1888; Grecian History, 1890, 1900; Rome and the Making of Modern Europe, 1892; Twenty Centuries of English History, 1898; Thomas Joy and His Descendants, 1900; Ten Englishmen of the XIVth Century, 1902; John Wesley's Awakening, 1937; The Joys of Joy Prairie, 1938. Editor: The Teachers of Drew, 1942. Home: 29

Perry St., New York 14, N.Y. Office: 150 5th Av., N.Y.C. Died July 1, 1957; buried Hillside Cemetery, Plainfield, N.J.

JOYCE, Adrian Dwight, mfr.; b. Sumner, Ia., Nov. 18, 1872; s. Moses and Ann (Hotham) J.; ed. pub. schs.; Dr. Engring. (hon.), Case Sch. Applied Sci., 1947; m. Anna Page, June 9, 1897 (died 1938); children—Marion (Mrs. John H. Lathe), Dwight P., Dorothy (Mrs. Clark P. Maxson), Phyllis (Mrs. John A. Duncan); m. 2d, Mrs. Mary D. Broughton, 1941. Chmn. bd. The Glidden Co.; pres. Durkee Famous Foods, Chem & Pigment Co., So. Pine Chem. Co.; dir. Wheeling & Lake Erie R.R., Cleve. Trust Co. Chmn. bd. trustees Cleve. Mus. Nat. Hist.; v.p. Coun. for High Blood Pressure Research; trustee Fenn Coll.; mem. bd of control Holden Arboretum. Republican. Unitarian. Clubs: Union, Mayfield, Mid-Day, City Club (Cleveland); Union League (Chicago); Seignory Club (P.Q., Can.). Home: 13515 Shaker Blvd. S.E., Shaker Heights, O. Office: Union Commerce Bldg., Cleve. Died Aug. 25, 1954; buried Lakeview Cemetery, Cleve.

JOYCE, James, congressman; b. Cumberland, O., July 2, 1870; LL.B., Cincinnati Law Sch., 1892; unmarried. In law practice at Cambridge, O., since 1895; mem. Ohio Ho. of Rep., 1895-9; del. Rep. Nat. Conv., Chicago, 1904; mem. 61st Congress (1909-11), 15th Ohio Dist. Address: Cambridge, O.

JOYCE, Kenyon Ashe, army officer; b. N.Y.C., Nov. 3, 1879; s. Charles Malcom and Norma McLeod (Kenyon) J.; distinguished grad. Infantry and Cavalry Sch., 1905; Army Staff Coll., 1906; Army War Coll., 1930; m. Helen E. Jones, Nov. 15, 1910 (dec. 1951); m. 2d, Mrs. Mary Kane Drury, March 27, 1953. Commd. 2d lt. cav., U.S. Army, 1901; advanced through grades to maj. gen. 1939. Participated in operations at Santiago, Cuba, Spanish-Am. War, 1898, in Northern Luzon and Cavite Province, Philippine Insurrection, 1900-01; operations against Ute Indians, Mont., 1906; during World War I served as chief of staff 87th, 83d divs., and Embarkation Center, Le Mans, France; participated in Meuse-Argonne offensive; on War Dept. gen. staff and gen. staff with troops; mil. attaché Am. Embassy, London, 1924-27; comdt. 3d U.S. Cavalry and Fort Myer, Va., 1933-36; comdr. 1st Cavalry Div., Fort Bliss, Tex., 1938-40; in command of Ninth Army Corps, Fort Lewis, Wash., 1941; comdg. 9th Service Command, 1943. Pres. Allied Control Commn. for Italy, 1943-44; ret. Nov. 30, 1943; mem. Cal. Crime Commn., 1947-50; mem. Pres. Com. Nat. Armed Forces Mus., 1957-60. Awarded D.S.M. on two occasions, Purple Heart (U.S.); Officer Legion of Honor and Croix de Guerre with palm (France); Knight Grand Cross, Order Crown of Italy; Order Aztec Eagle (Mexico). Clubs: Pacific Union, Burlingame, Bohemians (San Francisco); Army and Navy (Washington). Address: 1000 Mason St., San Francisco. Died Jan. 11, 1960; buried Arlington Nat. Cemetery.

JOYCE, Matthew M., judge; b. Emmetsburg, Ia., Apr. 29, 1877; s. Matt and Ella A. (Healy) J.; prep. edn., U. of Mich. Acad., 1895-97; law student, U. of Mich., 1898-1900; m. Annie Hughes Lewis, May 16, 1902 (dec.); 1 dau., Katherine Anne (died in infancy); m. 2d, Mary Isabel Daly, Nov. 23, 1910. Began practice of law at Missoula, Mont., 1900; moved to Fort Dodge, Ia., 1910; gen. atty. Minneapolis & St. Louis Ry., Minneapolis, Minn., 1917-19, gen. solicitor, 1919-21, gen. counsel, 1921-23, counsel for receiver, 1923-32; judge U.S. Dist. Court, Minn. Dist., since Feb. 1932. Mem. Am. Bar Assn., Minn. State Bar Assn., Phi Delta Phi. Republican. Catholic. Club: Minneapolis. Home: the Univ. of the South, 1944. Mem. Delta Tau Delta. Democrat. Mason. Rotarian. Home: 2228 1421 W. Franklin Av., Mpls. Deceased.

JOYCE, R. Edwin, distillery exec.; b. Washington, Nov. 10, 1897; s. Robert Edwin and Nellie (Beall) J.; LL.B., Georgetown U., 1922; m. Marguerite Eileen Cummings, Feb. 15, 1926. Entered govt. service as clk. Treasury Dept., 1917, Bur. Indsl. Alcohol, 1918-34, supervisor permits at Cin., 1930-34; dir. Fed. Alcohol Control Adminstrn., 1934; pvt. practice law, Washington, 1934-45; v.p. Nat. Distillers & Chem. Corp., 1945—; v.p. dir. Distilled Spirits Inst., Inc., 1946—; pres., dir. Licensed Beverage Industries, Inc.; v.p., dir. Montmorency Distillery, Ltd., Quebec, Can., 1952—; dir. W. & A. Gilbey, Ltd., Cin. Mem. Am. Bar Assn. Clubs: National Press, Kenwood Golf and Country (Washington); Union League (N.Y.C.); Country (Westhampton, L.I.). Home: 555 Park Av., N.Y.C. Office: 99 Park Av., N.Y.C. 16. Died Nov. 21, 1959; buried Washington.

JOYNER, James Yadkin, supt. of instrn.; b. Davidson County, N.C., Aug. 7, 1862; s. John and Sallie A. (Wooten) J.; Ph.B., U. N.C., 1881, LL.D., 1909; m. Effie E. Rouse, Dec. 1887. Prin. La Grange Acad., 1881-83; county supt. schs., Lenoir County, 1882-83; tchr. graded schs., Winston, N.C., 1884-85; lawyer in Goldsboro, N.C., 1886-89; chmn. Wayne Co. Bd. Edn., 1887-89; supt. Goldsboro graded schs., 1889-93; prof. English lang. and lit., State Normal and Indsl. Coll. of N.C., 1893-1902; supt. pub. instrn., N.C., 1902-19; resigned and engaged in framing. Alderman, Greensboro, N.C., 1899-1902; chmn. sub-text-book commn. of N.C., 1901. Pres. Assn. State Supts. of So. States, 1903-05; pres. N.E.A., 1909-10 (sec. trustees 1912—); mem. Rockefeller Sanitation Commn.; trustee U. N.C. Missionary Baptist. Pres. N.C. Tobacco Growers' Assn., 1921—. Democrat. Address: 304 E. Jones St., Raleigh, N.C.; R.F.D. 1, La Grange, N.C. Died Jan. 21, 1956.

JUCHHOFF, Frederick (ŭk'hŭf), educator; b. Enterprise, Kan., July 7, 1884; s. Rev. Henry and Henrietta L. (Gruen) J.; Ph.B., Kansas City U., 1906, Ph.D., 1912; M.A. in polit. science, Franklin & Marshall Coll.; LL.B., Ohio Northern U., 1908; LL.M., U. of Maine, 1913; LL.D., Lincoln U., 1936; grad. School of Commerce, Northwestern U.; grad. study, U. of Chicago and U. of Mich.; C.P.A., U. of Ill.; D.C.L., Chicago Law School, 1926; m. Edna Z. Collins, Sept. 12, 1908 (died Oct. 7, 1938). Instr. commerce, Berea (Ky.) Coll., 1906-08; asso. prof. commerce and finance, James Millikin U., Decatur, Ill., 1913-14; prof. law, Chicago Coll. of Law, 1914-17; prof. accounting, Toledo U., 1917-19; prof. economics and dir. Sch. of Finance and Adminstrn., Coll. of William and Mary, 1919-21, also acting dean Law Sch.; prof. business adminstrn., U. of Md., 1920-25; dean Grad. Sch. of Business Administration, Am. U., Washington, D.C., 1920-23, prof. and head dept. economics Grad. School same univ., 1923-28; editor world politics and constl. govt. dept., New Age Mag., since 1928; prof. economics, U. of Va., summers, 1915-20; lecturer in accountancy, U. of Pittsburgh, summer, 1922; professor economics Mich. State Teachers Coll., 1928-33; conducted survey Chicago pub. sch., situation under auspices Northwestern U. Law Sch., 1933-34; condr. weekly forum on economics and constl. government over radio station WWAE since 1932; condr. daily feature, "The Wall Streeter," WCFL, 1934-35, "The La Salle Streeter." Affiliated Broadcasting System, 1936; research in psychol. problems of legal edn., U. of Chicago, 1934-36; prof. constl. law and dean of law sch., Grand Rapids Coll. of Applied Science, 1936-39; prof. business adminstrn., Aurora Coll., 1940-46; prof. bus. adminstrn., Marquette U., 1946-50; vis. prof. bus. adminstrn. U. Wis., 1950; lectr. finance since 1950; lectr. finance Loyola U. since 1950. Nominee, atty. gen. of Ill., Prohibition party, 1944, 48. Editor, dept. of accountancy, Business Educator, 1923-24. Fellow Royal Econ. Soc. (British); mem. Am. Econ. Assn., Am. Assn. Univ. Profs., Am. Bar Assn., Phi Delta Kappa, Delta Sigma Pi, Sigma Mu Sigma (nat. pres. 1938-52); hon. mem. Société Academique d'Histoire Internationale (France). Mason (32°, Shriner). Club: City (Chicago). Home: 1511 E. 60th St., Chgo. 37. Died Dec. 13, 1953; buried Mt. Hope Cemetery, Chgo.

JUDD, Orrin Reynolds, banking; b. Kingston, N.J., Nov. 4, 1870; s. Orrin Bishop (Rev.) and Susanna (Reynolds) J.; B.C.S., New York U., 1902, LL.B., 1904; m. Bertha R. Grimmell, Oct. 4, 1905; children —Orrin Grimmell, Willard Reynolds (dec.), Hila Margaret (dec.). Began with Knickerbocker Ice Co., New York, 1883; certified pub. accountant, 1902; admitted to N.Y. bar, 1904; pres. Nassau Audit Co., 1904-10; with Knickerbocker Trust Co. and its successors by merger, Columbia and Irving Trust Co., successively asst. trust officer, 1909-14, trust officer, 1914-25, v.p., 1925-33; v.p. and trustee Kings County Savs. Bank, Bklyn., 1933-54. Treas. No. Baptist Conv., 1926-36; member Legal Advisory Board, City of New York, 1917-18; American Seamen's Friend Soc. (trustee since 1922, treasurer since 1934); trustee Colgate U., 1923-46; mem. council New York U. Meritorious service award, New York U., 1934. Mem. Am. Inst. Accountants, Soc. Colonial Wars, Alpha Kappa Psi, Delta Chi, Phi Delta Phi. Republican. Baptist. Clubs: Quill, New England Soc. (New York). Home: 275 Clinton Av., Bklyn. Died Mar. 5, 1955; buried Evergreen Cemetery, Bklyn.

JUDSON, Wilber, mining engr.; b. Lansing, Mich., July 26, 1880; s. James Bradford and Julia (Byrnes) J.; student Northwestern U., Evanston, Ill., 1897-98, U. of Mich., 1898-1900; S.B., Harvard, 1901; grad. study, Mich. Coll. of Mines, 1902-03; m. May E. Reynolds, Aug. 28, 1917. Began as mining engr., 1903; examining engr., mine and mill operations in U.S., Mexico and S.A., 1903-17; with W. B. Thompson interests, N.Y. City, as officer and dir. various mining and exploration projects, 1917-21; with Tex. Gulf Sulphur Co. since 1921, now v.p. and dir.; v.p., dir., Sulphur Export Corp.; dir. Mesabi Iron Corp. Member adv. com. on raw materials of U.S. Atomic Energy Commn.; mem. National Minerals Adv. Council. Mem. Am. Inst. Mining and Metallurgical Engineers. (ex-v.p.), Mining and Metallurgical Society of America (ex-v.p.). Clubs: Houston (Tex.); Union League, Harvard, University (all New York); Lawrence Beach; The Apawamis. Home: Newgulf, Tex. Office: 75 E. 45th St., N.Y.C. Died Aug. 9, 1951; buried Kinderhook, N.Y.

JULL, Morley Allan, poultry husbandry, teaching; b. Burford, Ont., Can., Aug. 26, 1885; s. John Henry and Ann Jane (Winskel) J.; B.S., U. of Toronto, 1903; M.S., McGill U., 1914; Ph.D., U. of Wis., 1921; m. Marion Louise Monkley, July 5, 1930; 1 son, Morley Allan. Came ti U.S., 1923, naturalized 1935. Asst. in poultry W.Va. Expt. Sta., Morgantown, W.Va., 1908-09; poultry commr., B.C. Dept. Agr., Victoria, B.C., 1909-11; head poultry dept. Macdonald Coll., McGill U., Montreal, Can., 1912-23; sr. poultry husbandman U.S. Dept. Agr., Washington, 1923-36; head poultry dept. U. of Md., 1936 until retirement, now prof. emeritus; poultry adviser with U.S. Overseas Mission. Rep. U.S. Govt. to 4th World's Poultry Congress, Ottawa, Can., 1927, 5th Congress, London, Eng., 1930. Oversees Mission Internat. Co-operation Adminstrn. with Egypt, Italy, Greece, Lebanon. Fellow A.A.A.S., Poultry Sci. Assn. (past pres.); teaching award 1952; adv. com. Am. Genetic Assn.; mem. Washington Acad. Sci., Am. Poultry and Hatchery Fedn., Phi Kappa Phi. Kappa Phi, Sigma Xi. Democrat. Methodist. Author: Poultry Breeding, 1952; Poultry Husbandry, 1951; Successful Poultry Management, 1951; Raising Turkeys, Ducks, Geese and Game Birds, 1947. Home: 6906 Pineway, University Park, Md. Office: U.S. Overseas Mission, American Embassy, Athens, Greece. Died Oct. 25, 1959; buried Fort Lincoln Cemetery, Bladensburg, Md.

JUNELL, John (jū-nĕl'), lawyer; b. Village of Indiana, Mich., May 10, 1886; s. John and Sophia (Anderson) J.; LL.B., U. Mich., 1907; m. Mary Derby Collester, Dec. 15, 1919. Admitted to Ill., Mich. bars, 1907; began practice Chgo.; practiced at Mpls., 1911—. Served in Aviation Div., U.S. Army, 1917; naval aviator, rank of ensign, 1918. Republican. Conglist. Clubs: Minneapolis, Minikahda. Home: 2727 E. Lake of Isles Blvd. Office: First Nat.-Soo Line Bldg., Mpls. Died Oct. 13, 1949.

JUNG, Carl Gustav (yoong), psychotherapist; b. Kesswyl (Thurgau), Switzerland, July 26, 1875; s. Paul and Emilie (Preiswerk) J.; M.D., U. Basel, 1900; honorary degree from universities of Calcutta, Allahbad, Geneva, Oxford, Harvard, Banaras Hindu University; married Emma Rauschenbach, February 26, 1903; children—Agathe Niehus, Gret Baumann, Franz, Marianne Niehus, Helene Hoerni. Interne Psychiatric Clinic, U. Zurich, 1900-04; head physician Psychiatric Clinic, 1905-09; lectr. in psychology U. Zurich, 1905-13; lectr. psychology Fed. Tech. U., Zurich, 1933-40; prof. med. psychology U. Basel, 1944-45; pvt. practice of medicine, specializing in psychotherapy, Küsnacht-Zurich, Switzerland, since 1909. C. G. Jung Institute Zurich (found. for research in analytical psychology) opened 1948. Fellow Royal Soc. Medicine (London); mem. Swiss Acad. for Med. Sci., Swiss Soc. for Psychiatry. Swiss Soc. for Practical Psychology, and many others. Author of numerous books, including the following, published in English: Collected Papers on Analytical Psychology, 1916; Psychology of the Unconscious, 1921; Psychological Types, 1923; Psychology and Religion, 1938; Essays on a science of mythology (with C. Kerényi), 1949; Psychology and Alchemy, 1953; Two Essays on Analytical Psychology, 1953; The Psychology of the Transference and Other Papers on the Analytical Process, 1953. Home: The Valley Vista, 2032 Belmont Rd., Washington 9. Died Nov. 28, 1955.

JURGATIS, John Paul, meat packer; b. Racine, Wis., Jan. 27, 1915; s. Adam and Emily (Stasilonis) J.; B.A., U. Wis., 1937, student law, 1936-38; m. Dolores Hinkel, Oct. 15, 1938; children—Mark, Susan. With Swift & Co., Chgo., 1938—, mgr. refinery dept., 1954-55, v.p., 1955—; v.p., dir. Derby Foods, Inc., Chgo., 1955—. Mem. Wis. Alumni Assn., Theta Chi. Home: 427 W. Franklin St., Wheaton, Ill. Office: Swift & Co., U.S. Yards, Chgo. 9. Died Oct. 20, 1958; buried Holy Cross Cemetery, Racine, Wis.

K

KABLE, Harry G., printing exec.; b. Lanark, Ill., July 15, 1880; s. John A. and Elizabeth (Speicher) K.; ed. Mount Morris (Ill.) Pub. Schs.; m. Edith Walkup, June 14, 1906; 1 son, Robert R. With Mount Morris News, Gospel Messenger (Mount Morris), 1896-98; with twin brother, Harvey J., purchased Mount Morris (Ill.) Index, Sept., 1898, inc., 1904; has specialized in printing of periodicals and mags. since 1905. Pres. Mount Morris Bldg. and Loan Assn., 1926-49, Kable Bros. Co., 1931-52. Mem. Ill. N.G., rank of 1st lt., 1923-28. Republican. Lutheran. Mason (Consistory, Shriner). Club: Kiwanis. Author: Mount Morris: Past and Present, 1937; War History of Mount Morris, 1948. Home: Sunset Hill Farm. Office: 404 N. Wesley Av., Mount Morris, Ill. Died July 2, 1952.

KADING, Charles August, ex-congressman; b. Lowell, Wis., Jan. 14, 1874; s. Charles and Elizabeth (Baganz) K.; student high sch., Horicon, Wis., summer sch., U. Wis.; LL.B., Valparaiso U., 1900; m. Elizabeth Holste, Nov. 7, 1900 (dec. July 31, 1925); 1 son, Charles Earl. Admitted to Wis. bar, 1900, and began practice at Watertown; practiced with wife as Kading & Kading until 1925, with son as Kading & Kading, 1929—; city atty. Watertown, 1905-12; dist. atty. Dodge County, Wis., 1907-13; mayor of Watertown, 1914-16; mem. 70th to 72d Congresses, 2d Wis. Dist. Mem. Wis., Dodge County bar assns. Republican. Conglist. Mason, K.P., Woodman, Elk. Home: Watertown, Wis. Died June 19, 1956; buried Oak Hill Cemetery, Watertown.

KAEMPFFERT, Waldemar Bernhard (kĕmpf'ĕrt), author; b. N.Y. City, N.Y., Sept. 1877; B.S., Coll City of New York, 1897; LL.B., New York U., 1904; D.Sc., Clarkson Poly. Inst., 1939; m. Carolyn Lydia Yeaton, Jan. 7, 1911 (died 1933). Was admitted to the New York bar in 1903; registered as a patent attorney; asst. editor of the Scientific American, 1897-1911, mng. editor, 1911-15; editor Popular Science Monthly, 1915-20; science editor N.Y. Times, 1927-28; dir. Mus. of Science and Industry, Chicago, 1928-31, science editor New York Times since 1931. Recipient Kalinga prize, 1954. Fellow Am. Soc. M.E. Club: Century (N.Y.C.). Author: History of Astronomy, 1910; New Art of Flying, 1911; Science Today and Tomorrow, 1939; Explorations in Science, 1953. Translator: Gas Engines and Producer-Gas Plants (by Rodolphe E. Mathot), 1905. Editor: A Popular History of American Invention, 1924. Contbr. to Am. and European scientific and engring. periodicals. Address: New York Times, 229 W. 43d St., N.Y.C. 23. Died Nov. 1956.

KAHLER, Harry Adams (kä'lĕr), banker; b. McConnellsville, O., Sept. 20, 1865; s. Francis Marion and Elizabeth (Adams) K.; student Ohio State U. 1882-85; m. Beulah Pace, Sept. 23, 1891; children—Mrs. Bruce Cole, Woodland. Began own account as mortgage broker, Dallas, 1897; organized O'Connor & Kahler, N.Y.C., 1899 succeeded by H. A. Kahler & Co., 1913 (dissolved 1918); pres. N.Y. Title & Mortgage Co., 1914-30; Am. Trust Co., N.Y.C., 1919-30. Formerly dir. Bank of Manhattan Co., Morris Plan Bank of N.Y., N.Y. Title Ins. Co., N.Y. Casualty Co. Caledonian-Am. Ins. Co.; trustee Am. Surety Co.; now ret. Republican. Clubs: Metropolitan, Bankers Everglades (Palm Beach). Home: 270 Pendleton Av. Palm Beach, Fla.; (summer) Littleton, N.H. Died June 5, 1959; buried Wheeler Hill Cemetery, Littleton.

KAHN, Howard, columnist; b. Bloomington, Ind., Jan. 30, 1886; s. Maurice and Celia (Hirsch) K.; A.B., Ind. U., 1908; m. Mary Moody. Began as reporter Cincinnati Enquirer, 1908; editor St. Paul Daily News, 1919-38; asso. editor St. Paul Dispatch and Pioneer Press, 1938-40, editorial columnist, 1940—; radio commentator, Station WMIN, St. Paul. Served as pvt. U.S. Army, on Mexican border, 1916; lt. French Army, France and Italy, 1916-18. Dir. St. Paul Preventorium, St. Paul chpt. Vols. America, St. Paul chpt. A.R.C. Mem. Sigma Chi. Decorated by French and Italian Govts. Club: St. Paul Athletic. Home: Route 4, Stillwater, Minn. Office: 55 E. 4th St., St. Paul. Died Mar. 27, 1951.

KAHN, Maurice Guthman, surgeon; b. Morrison, Ill., Mar. 27, 1873; s. Isaac and Hermina (Guthman) K.; M.D., cum laude, Harvard, 1898; m. Gertrude Berryman, Jan. 21, 1907. Practiced as surgeon, Denver and Leadville, Colo., 1900-14, Los Angeles, 1915—; instr. in anatomy, Denver and Gross Sch. of Medicine, 1903-04, U. So. Cal. Sch. of Medicine, 1918-19; surgeon Hosp. of Good Samaritan, Los Angeles, 1917—; surgeon-in-chief Cedars of Lebanon Hosp., Los Angeles, 1932—, prof. clin. surgery, U. So. Cal., Sch. of Medicine, 1931—. Trustee Federated Welfare Orgns. of Los Angeles, 1918-46. Served as mem. Med. Bd. of Appeals So. Cal. during World War. Fellow Am. Coll. Surgeons (founder), A.M.A., Am. Bd. Surgery (founder); mem. Western Surg. Assn., Pacific Coast Surg. Soc., Los Angeles Surg. Soc. Republican. Jewish religion. Mason (32°). Clubs: Jonathan, Harvard of Southern California, Hillcrest Country (Los Angeles). Contbr. to med. jours. Home: 450 N. Rossmore St. Office: 727 W. 7th St., Los Angeles. Died Sept. 12, 1950.

KAHN, Samuel, ry. official; b. San Antonio, Tex., Oct. 18, 1882; s. Achille and Clara (Josey) K.; student U. of Tex.; B.S. in E.E., Purdue, 1903, D. Engring., 1936; m. Rosalind Eleanor Weissbein, April 19, 1915; children—Barbara Clara (Mrs. Irvin B. Gardner), Rosalind Louise (Mrs. Lester H. Margolis), President Stockton Terminal and Eastern Railroad. Chairman of San Francisco Ordnance District of United States Army. Mem. Calif. Acad. Science. Republican. Jewish religion. Clubs: Concordia-Argonaut. Commonwealth, Stock Exchange Lunch. Address: 50 Baywood Av., San Mateo, Cal. Died Sept. 10, 1953.

KAIN, George Hay, lawyer; b. York, Pa.; Apr. 13, 1877; s. William Henry and Clara Maria (Hay) K.; prep. edn., York County Acad.; grad. York Collegiate Inst., 1893; B.S., Gettysburg (Pa.) Coll., 1897, M.S., 1900, LL.D., 1951; LL.B., Harvard, 1902; m. Cara Bahn Watt, Jan. 1, 1901 (died Apr. 21, 1938); children—George Hay, Richard Morgan, William. Instr. math., prep. dept. Gettysburg Coll., 1897-98; admitted to Pa. bar, 1902, and practiced since at York; mem. Cochran, Williams & Kain, 1912-30; Kain, Kain & Kain since 1937; v.p., director and counsel The York Water Co.; dir. and counsel The Farmers Fire Insurance Company. Trustee York County Academy. Member American, Pennsylvania State and York County bar assns., Phi Beta Kappa, Phi Delta Theta. Republican. Lutheran. Mason. (Dist. Dep. Grand Master, 1911-48; Grand Commander, K.T., 1941-42; 33°). Club: Lafayette. Home: 45 Springettsbury Pl. Office: 119 E. Market St., York, Pa. Died Feb. 1, 1958.

KAISER, Albert David (kī'zĕr), pediatrist; b. Phila., Pa., Nov. 20, 1887; s. Lewis and Sophia Caroline (Schnabel) K.; B.S., U. of Rochester, 1909; M.D., Harvard, 1913; m. Margaret Deland Dickinson, Nov. 4, 1915; children—Albert David, Margaret (Fisher). Practiced at Rochester since 1916; asso. prof. pediatrics, Univ. of Rochester, since 1930, professor child hygiene since 1945; consulting pediatrician Rochester General Hospital; assistant pediatrician Strong Memorial Hospital; has served as Health Officer for the City of Rochester, since 1945; attending pediatrician Convalescent Hospital for Children. Exec. Dir. Council Rochester Regional Hosp., 1946-1951. Mem. N.Y. State Health Preparedness Com. Mental Hygiene Council; Adv. Panel World Health Orgn. Capt. Med. Dept. U.S. Army, 1917-19, serving in France. Hon. pres. Rochester Tuberculosis and Health Assn. Trustee Rochester Chamber of Commerce. Director of Rochester Chapter American Red Cross. Awarded Civic Medal by the Rochester Museum, 1947. Trustee University of Rochester since 1939, Trudeau Sanitorium since 1946. Colgate Rochester Divinity School since 1947; director of the Eastman Dental Dispensary since 1947. Fellow American Acad. of Pediatrics; fellow Am. Pub. Health Assn.; mem. A.M.A. (past chmn., pediatrics section), Am. Pediatric Soc., Rochester Acad. of Medicine (past pres.), Rochester Museum Assn. (past pres.), Public Health Nursing Assn. (past pres.). Med. Soc. Monroe County (ex-pres.), Newcomen Soc. Phi Beta Kappa, Sigma Xi, Theta Chi, Baptist. Clubs: University, Country. Wrote: Children's Tonsils, In or Out. Home: 29 Buckingham St. Office: 44 Marshall St., Rochester, N.Y. Died Nov. 1, 1955.

KALB, Lewis Powell, corp. exec.; b. Bellefontaine, O., June 24, 1888; s. Edgar William and Alma Clementine (Powell) K.; M.E., Cornell U., 1910; m. Mary Louise Dial, Oct. 18, 1916; children—George Lewis, Louise Baldwin, William Parshall. Spl. apprenticeship Pierce Arrow Motor Car Co., Buffalo, N.Y., 1911-15; chief engr. Kelly Springfield Motor Truck Co., 1915-18, factory mgr., 1919-21; sales engr. Continental Motors Corp., 1921-24, asst. chief engr., 1924-30, chief engr., 1930-34, asst. to pres., 1934, factory mgr. Muskegon plant, 1934-40, vice pres., 1937, dir. since 1939, exec. vice pres., 1942-50; dir. Continental Aviation Engring. Corp.; exec. vice pres. and dir. Gray Marine Motor Co. Served as maj. motor transport corps, U.S. Army, 1918-19. Mem. Soc. Automotive Engrs. (mem. coms. for specifications and design of class B mil. truck and ordnance adv. com.; past v.p.), Beta Theta Pi. Republican. Episcopalian. Mason. Contbr. papers to S.A.E. Tech. meetings. Home: 547 Washington Rd., Grosse Pointe. Mich. Office: 710 Canton Av., Detroit. Died Dec. 28, 1957; buried Bellefontaine, O.

KALBFUS, Edward Clifford, naval officer; b. Mauch Chunk, Pa., Nov. 24, 1877; s. Daniel and Mary Electra (Jones) K.; grad. U.S. Naval Acad., 1899; m. Syria Florence Brown, May 13, 1905. Commd. ensign, USN, 1901; promoted through grades to rear adm., 1931; permanent rank of admiral on retired list, 1942. Participated in Spanish-Am. War, 1898, Philippine Insurrection, 1900-01, Cuba Pacification, 1905, Mexican occupation, 1914; capt. U.S.S. Pocahontas, World War I, later capt. U.S.S. Iowa, Trenton, California; mem. staff Naval War Coll., 1927-29; chief of staff Battleship Divs., Battle Fleet, 1930; dir. War Plans, Navy Dept., 1931; comdr. Destroyers, Battle Force, U.S. Fleet, 1931-34; pres. Naval War Coll., 1934-36, 39-42; vice adm., comdr. Battleships, Battle Force, U.S. Fleet, 1937; adm., comdr. Battle Force, U.S. Fleet, 1938-39, mem. Gen. Bd., 1942-45. Dir. of Naval History, 1944-45; mem. Am. Battle Monuments Commn., 1947-52. Mem. Military Order of Carabao. Episcopalian. Clubs: Army and Navy (Washington); hon. mem. Cruising Club of America. Home: Restmere, Newport, R.I. Died Sept. 6, 1954; buried Arlington Nat. Cemetery.

KALLOCH, Parker Cromwell (kăl'lŏk), surgeon; b. S. Norridgewock, Me., Mar. 27, 1856; s. Robert Mero and Olive Jane (Cromwell) K.; M.D., Jefferson Med. Coll., Phila., Pa., 1881; m. Florence Lawton, Oct. 25, 1893; children—Dudley C., Parker C., Loyer (wife of Dr. Solon McDaniel). Interne Jefferson Med. Coll. Hosp., 1881; in U.S. Pub. Health Service, 1881—. Mayor of Tularosa, N.M., 1924-25. Hon. mem. Am. Med. Assn. Episcopalian. Mason. Home: Tularosa, N.M. Deceased.*

KALMAN, Charles Oscar, corp. exec.; b. N.Y.C., May 9, 1872; s. Arnold and Sarah W. (Greve) K.; student Phillips Exeter Acad., 1889-90; Ph.B., Yale, Sheffield Scientific Sch., 1893; m. Margaret Rugg, 1900; m. 2d, Alexandra Robertson, Jan. 8, 1917. Clerk Union Bank, 1893; treas. and gen. auditor, C.G.W. Ry.; investment banking, 1908; pres. Kalman & Co., 1929-39; chmn. bd. Bliss and Laughlin, Inc., Globe Steel Tubes Co., Minneapolis Gas Co., pres. Alexandra Corp.; trustee Great Northern Iron Ore Properties; dir. First Trust Co. of St. Paul, First Bank Stock Corp., Gould-Nat. Batteries, Inc. Exec. v.p. The Orchestral Assn. of Mpls. Inc. Clubs: Minnesota, University (St. Paul), University (Chgo.). Office: Endicott Bldg., St. Paul 1. Died June 12, 1956.

KAMBESTAD, Howard S., business exec.; b. Kerkhoven, Minn., Jan. 13, 1910; s. Ole G. and Olive (Fjelstad) K.; student Brigham Young U., 1929, U. Wash., 1930-32; m. Muriel Easton, Jan. 19, 1933; children—Donald Ray, Sonia Dee. Auditor, office mgr. Nat. Biscuit Co., 1933-41; asst. gen. mgr. TWA Airlines, 1941-43; with Montgomery Ward & Co. since 1943, auditor, 1943-48, asst. controller, 1949-52, treas., 1952—, v.p., 1955—, acting controller, 1956—. Mem. Chgo. Crime Commn.; mem. budget committee Chicago. Community Fund. Mason. Home: 8211 W. Lake St., River Forest, Ill. Office: 619 W. Chicago Av., Chgo. Died Aug. 30, 1958.

KAMMERER, Percy Gamble (kăm'ĕr-ĕr), educator; b. Norfolk, Va., Nov. 17, 1885; s. Edward Percy and Mary Virginia (Gamble) K.; grad. Pomfret (Conn.) Sch., 1904; A.B., Harvard, 1908, Ph. D., 1920; m. Olivia Pattison Heminway, Nov. 4, 1916; children—Honora Harwood, Eleanor. Deacon, 1914, priest, 1916, P.E. Ch.; asst., St. Stephen's Ch., Boston, 1916-17, Grace Ch., Providence, 1917-18; Emanuel Ch., Boston, 1918-23; rector Trinity Ch., Pitts., 1923-28; dean Trinity Cathedral, 1928-30; provost Avon Old Farms Sch., Avon, Conn., 1930-40; asso. with British War Relief Soc., N.Y.C., 1940—. Club: Century (N.Y.C.). Author: The Unmarried Mother, 1918. Address: 7 W. 43d St., N.Y.C. Died Nov. 13, 1946.

KAMPER, Louis, architect; b. Rheinpfatz, Bavaria, Mar. 11, 1861; s. Peter and Maria (Esch) K.; educated technical schools, Germany; m. Emilie Kling, July 23, 1892 (died June 3, 1946); 1 son, Paul (deceased). Came to United States, 1882, naturalized citizen. Draftsman with McKim, Meade and White, N.Y. City, until 1889; mem. Scott, Kamper & Scott, Detroit, 1889-91, alone since 1892; dir. Indstl. Morris Plan Bank. Architect: Mich. Bldg., Buffalo (N.Y.) Expn., 1902; Providence Hosp., St. Mary's Hosp., Roseland Mausoleum, Cadillac Square Bldg., Book Bldg., Washington Blvd. Bldg., Eaton Tower, Book-Cadillac Hotel, Savoy Hotel, Industrial Bank Bldg., Bank of Detroit, Tappin Schs., Detroit Municipal Water Board Bldg. (all of Detroit); Huntington Bldg. and Roosevelt Hotel (both of Miami, Fla.); Westover Hotel, N.Y. City; Schaefer Bldg., Dearborn, Mich.; Saginaw Court House; etc. Mem. Am. Inst. of Architects, Mich. Soc. Architects, Detroit Engring. Soc. Presbyterian. Clubs: Detroit, Detroit Athletic, Detroit Country. Address: The Whittier Hotel, Burns Dr., Detroit 14. Died Feb. 24, 1953.

KANE, Francis Fisher, lawyer; b. Philadelphia, June 17, 1866; s. Robert Patterson and Elizabeth (Fisher) K.; A.B., Princeton, 1886, A.M., 1889; LL.B., U. of Pa., 1889; unmarried. Admitted to Pa. bar, 1889; formerly mem. Beck, Robinson & Kane, Phila., now practicing alone. Democratic nominee for Pa. Ho. of Rep., 1890; 1st asst. U.S. atty. Eastern Dist. of Pa., 1896-1900; nominee for mayor of Phila., 1903; U.S. atty. Eastern Dist. of Pa., by apptmt. of President Wilson, from Sept. 10, 1913-20, resigned. Served in Vienna as Am. rep. Friends' Relief Mission, 1923. Member Historical Society of Pennsylvania, Phila., Geog. Soc., Shakespeare Soc. of Phila., Phi Kappa Sigma. Episcopalian. Clubs: University, Univ. Barge. Recipient of the Philadelphia award of Bok Foundation, 1936, for his part "in establishing a voluntary defender for the helpless defendant in the criminal courts." Home: Peace Dale, R.I. Office: 1420 Walnut St., Phila. 2. Died May 27, 1955.

KANE, Paul V., army officer; b. Worcester, Mass., July 19, 1892; s. John and Johanna (Power) K.; student Mass. State Coll., 1911-12; B.S., U.S. Mil. Acad., 1916; grad. Army War Coll., 1937; m. Lillian Mary Reilly, Dec. 26, 1921; children—William Spooner, Walter Reilly, John Power. Commd. 2d lt., U.S. Army, 1916, advanced through the grades to brig. gen., 1942; assigned to 96th Inf. Div., 1942; left the 96th Div., 1944, was assigned to Hdqrs. III Army Corps; formerly at Camp Polk, La. under same assignment; comd. Task Force Frigid, Alaska; ret. 1949. Decorated Legion of Merit, Bronze Star, Silver Star, D.S.M. (U.S.); Legion of Honor (France); Distinguished Service Order (Gt. Britain); Croix de Guerre with palm. Club: Lions (Norman, Okla.). Home: P.O. Box 163, Forest Grove, Ore. Died July 1, 1959; buried Post Cemetery, West Point, N.Y.

KANTER, Charles Andrew, retired bank exec.; b. Detroit, Nov. 13, 1887; s. Henry L. and Marie (Carmichael) K.; B.A., Williams Coll., 1907; B.S. in Chem. Engring., U. Mich., 1911; m. Margaret E. Langley, Jan. 3, 1912; children—Elizabeth (Mrs. Arthur G. Reeves), Gretchen (Mrs. David W. Murray, Jr.), Adele (Mrs. David J. Luck), Henry, Sarah (Mrs. Richard H. Dick). Sr. v.p. and dir. Mfrs. Nat. Bank of Detroit, 1938-43, pres., 1943-49, chmn. bd., 1949-56, now mem. bd. dirs.; dir. Wayne Safe Deposit Co.; also dir. of the National Steel Corp. Served as capt. Ordnance, U.S. Army, 1917-19. Mem. Phi Beta Kappa. Presbyterian. Clubs: Rolling Rock (Pa.); Detroit; Grosse Pointe; Williams

(N.Y.). Home: 16805 Maumee Rd., Grosse Pointe 30, Mich. Office: 151 W. Fort St., Detroit. Deceased.

KANTZLER, George R(andolph), broker; b. Leadville, Colo., Oct. 20, 1897; s. Herman and Ada Jane (Cruickshank) K.; U. Wish., 1918; m. Eleanor Stone Ranlett, May 19, 1927. Fgn. Exchange banking, Far East, 1920-27; gen. broker securities and commodities, 1927—; partner E. F. Hutton & Co., general brokers, N.Y.C., 1942—. Mem. N.Y. Stock Exchange, N.Y and New Orleans cotton exchanges, N.Y. Coffee and Sugar Exchange, Chicago Bd. Trade. Clubs: Racquet, Tennis, Broad St., N.Y. Stock Exchange Luncheon (N.Y.C.). Home: 530 Park Av., N.Y.C. 22. Office: 61 Broadway, N.Y.C. 6. Died Nov. 1957.

KAPELL, William, concert pianist; b. New York, N.Y., Sept. 20, 1922; s. Harry and Edith (Wolfson) K.; student music with Dorothea Anderson La-Follette, 1932-37; Phila. Conservatory of Music; Juilliard Grad. Sch. of Music (fellowship), 1940; m. Rebecca A. R. Melson; children—David E., Rebecca. Winner, Naumburg contest, recital at Town Hall, N.Y. City, 1941; youngest winner Town Hall Endowment Series Award, 1942; made first appearance as soloist with N.Y. Philharmonic orchestra, summer, 1942; recital tour of U.S., 1942-43, Australia, S.A., summer 1945. Has appeared with majority of major symphony orchestras in U.S. since 1942. Home: 21 E. 94th St., N.Y. City. Address: care Columbia Concerts, 113 W. 57th St., N.Y. C. 6. Died Oct. 29, 1953.

KAPLAN, Eliezer, economist, statesman; b. Minsk, Russia, Jan. 27, 1891; s. Meir and Fruma (Shapiro) K.; Grad. Engr., Technical Coll., Moscow, 1917; m. Deborah Kaplan, July 19, 1921; children—Datia (Mrs. Ramati), Atara. Leader of Zionist Labour Movement in Russia until 1917, in Palestine since 1920; treas. and mem. of the exec. of the Jewish Agency for Palestine since 1933; reorganized finances of Jewish Agency and obtained loans from non-Jewish sources; head, dept. agrl. colonization of Jewish Agency until 1948. A founder of State of Israel, May 15, 1948, and since Minister of Finance; municipal councillor of Tel Aviv since 1925. Mem. exec. com. Gen. Fedn. Jewish Labour since 1923. Negotiator with British Govt. in London on solution of Palestine problem, 1946. Gov. bd. Anglo-Palestine Bank, Ltd., since 1934; dir. Palestine Development Co., Industrial Bank, Agricultural Bank. Mem. bd. War Econ. Adv. Council of Palestine, World War II. Mem. Palestine Assn. of Engrs. and Architects, Gen. Fedn. of Jewish Labour in Eretz Israel (Palestine). Mem. Palestine Labour Party. Jewish religion. Address: 6 Ben Maimon St., Jerusalem, Israel. Died July 13, 1952; buried Jerusalem, Israel.

KAPLAN, Frank R. S., exec.; b. May 26, 1886; s. Abraham and Bessie (Ezralet) K.; A.B., Washington and Jefferson Coll., 1907, A.M., 1912; LL.B., U. Pitts., 1910; m. Madeline May Roth, 1918; children—Irving M. J., Lois (Mrs. Finkel), Margery (Mrs. Auerbach). Admitted to Pa. bar, 1910, practiced in Pitts., 1910-49; dir. Copperweld Steel Co., 1915—, pres. 1949, chmn. bd., 1955—; dir. Sawhill Tubular Products Co; Pres. United Jewish Fund, Pitts., 1943-44; trustee Henry Monsky Found., Federation Jewish Philanthropies of Pitts. (pres. 1950-53), McKeesport Hosp., Montefiore Hosp., Pitts., Woodville State Hosp., Jewish Home for Aged, Hebrew Inst., Pitts., St. Vincent Coll., Latrobe, Pa. Mem. Pitts. Sch. Bd. Mem. Anti-Defamation League (mem. nat. commn.), Joint Def. Appeal (nat. com.), B'nai B'rith (past pres.), Tau Epsilon Rho, Phi Epsilon Pi. Jewish religion. Maosn. Clubs: Concordia, Westmoreland Country, Hundred (Pitts.). Home: 5251 Fair Oaks St., Pitts. 17. Office: Frick Bldg., Pitts. 19. Died Oct. 4, 1957; buried Westview Cemetery.

KAPPEL, Samuel, clothing chain exec.; b. Russia, 1889; wife, Minnie Kappel; children—Mrs. Muriel Rossow, Mrs. Doris Morrison, Mrs. Elaine Siris, Mrs. Joyce Sumberg, Joseph. Came to U.S., 1905. Engaged in clothing mfg. bus. in various capacities, 1905—; with Henry C. Marks founded clothing mfg. firm Kappel and Marks, 1916, Joseph Langerman added to partnership, 1924, later began retail operations as well, became Howard Stores Corp., Bklyn., 1944, now treas. and dir. Active Fedn. Jewish Philanthropies, Bklyn. Hebrew Home and Hosp. for Aged, Jewish Chronic Disease Hosp., Bklyn. Orphan Home. Fellow Brandeis U. Jewish religion. Club: Palm Beach Country. Home: 111 E. 56th St., N.Y.C.; also Larchmont, N.Y.; Palm Beach, Fla. Died Nov. 11, 1957.*

KARCHER, Walter Thompson (kär'chĕr), architect; b. Phila., Pa., Aug. 23, 1881; s. James Daniel and Marion Anna (Bullen) K.; B.S. in Arch., U. of Pa., 1901; student Am. Acad. in Rome, 1906; m. Mary Clark Turner, Oct. 28, 1914; children—Elizabeth Turner (Mrs. William Howard Nordstrom), Daniel Martin (lieutenant comdr., U.S.N.), Walter Thompson, Jr. (killed in line of duty, France, September 12, 1944). On design staff Louisiana Purchase Expedition, 1901-02; member firm Walter T. Karcher & Livingston Smith, Architects, since 1910. Principal designs of firm; U.S. Naval Hospital, Philadelphia; U.S. Naval Hospital, Annapolis, Md.; U.S. Army Hosp., Puerto Rico; bldgs. for Swarthmore Coll.; R.C.A. Victor Office Bldg., Camden, N.J.; Cooper Library, Camden, N.J., Bryn Mawr Presbyterian Church Group; Trinity Episcopal Ch. Group, Moorestown, New Jersey; Merion War Tribute House, Penn Valley Sch.; Field House; Lawrenceville School. Served as project supervisor, Housing and Transportation Division, United States Shipping Bd., World War I. Awarded Alumni travelling fellowship, U. of Pa., 1905. Trustee and sec. Meth. Orphanage, Phila. Fellow A.I.A.; mem. Merion Community Assn. (bd. of dirs.), Sigma Xi. Presbyterian. Home: The Fairfax, 43d & Locust Sts. Office: 1520 Locust St., Phila. Died Sept. 1953.

KARFIOL, Bernard, artist; born of American parents, Budapest, Hungary, May 6, 1886; son Benjamin and Kate K.; student Nat. Acad. of Design, 1900-01, Academie Julien, Paris, 1901-02; m. Marguerite Reuwée, May 7, 1906; children—Virginie Carolyn, George C. Reuwee. Represented in Met. Mus. of Art, Mus. of Modern Art, Whitney Mus., Baltimore Mus., Ft. Dodge (Iowa) Fedn. of Arts, Field Foundation, Brooklyn, Va. Mus. Art (Richmond, Va.), Lyman Allen Museum Art, New London, Conn., Addison Gallery, Andover, Mass.; Calif. Palace of Legion of Honor, Corcoran Gallery, Phillips Memorial Gallery, Dartmouth Coll., Detroit Inst. of Art, Los Angeles Mus., Newark (N.J.) Mus., Carnegie Inst. Mus., Wichita Art Museum (Kan.), Brooklyn Museum of Art. Awards: Pan-Am. Expn., 1925; Carnegie Inst., 1927 and 1929; William A. Clark prize and Corcoran gold medal, Washington, D.C., 1928; Fort Dodge Purchase Award, 1940; purchase award Va. Museum of Art, Richmond, Va. Mem. Soc. of Painters, Sculptors and Gravers (pres. 1935-36). Dir. Yaddo, 1946-52. Home: 44 W. Clinton Av., Irvington-on-Hudson, N.Y.; (summer) Ogunquit, Me. Studio: 54 W. 74th St., N.Y.C. Died Aug. 16, 1952.

KARIG, Walter (kăr'ĭg), ret. naval officer, author; b. N.Y.C.; ed. pvt. and pub. schs. of N.Y. and N.J.; art edn., N.Y. Sch. Fine and Applied Art, 1917; military scholarship student, Julian Academy, 1919; married to Eleanor Keating Freye, 1920; children—Patricia Mary (Mrs. Richard L. Ruffner, Junior), Keating Victoria (Mrs. Francis A. Carrier). Began as sports writer, Norfolk Virginian-Pilot, 1919; editor Elizabeth City (N.C.) Herald, 1920; editorial writer and artist Newark Evening News, 1921-42; chief editorial writer, 1933, chief of Washington bur. since 1934; mem. editorial bd. Liberty mag., 1938-42; U.S. Columnist London Star and Allied British newspapers, 1939-42; teacher journalism, Knights of Columbus Sch. for U.S. Vets., Newark, 1922. Served in French and Polish Armies; advanced from pvt. inf. to capt. motor transport, 1918-19; lt. comdr. U.S.N.R., 1942, comdr., 1944, capt., 1946; spl. asst. to Chief of Naval Operations, 1947-50; special deputy chief of information 1950; special assistant to the Secretary of the Navy, 1952-54; 1st v.p., del. to 1st Pan-American Press Congress, Mexico. Member bd. trustees, St. Agnes Episcopal Sch., Alexandria, Va. Mem. Military Order of Carabao, U.S. Naval Institute Mem. U.S. Mission to Philippines, 1935. Award Haller D.S.C. (Poland), Legion of Merit awarded by the United States Navy. Clubs: Nat. Press (bd. of govs. 1941-44), Overseas Writers, Gridiron, Cosmos. Author: (also illustrator): The Magic Acorn (with wife), 1928; Asia's Good Neighbor, pub. 1937; War in the Atomic Age, published 1946; The Fortunate Islands, History of Micronesia, 1948; novels, The Pig in the Parlor (with wife and daus.), 1949; Caroline Hicks, 1951; Battle Submerged (with Adm. Harley Cope), 1951; Neely, 1953; Don't Tread On Me, 1954; co-author "Battle Report," vol. I, 1944, vol. II, 1945; vol. III, 1945; vol. IV, 1948, vol. V, 1949; vol. VI, 1951; also author of four series of popular juvenile mystery stories. Home: Seminary Hill Post Office, Alexandria, Va. Died Sept. 30, 1956; buried Arlington Nat. Cemetery.

KARKER, Maurice Harmon, chmn. Jewel Tea Co.; b. Hyndesville, Schoharie County, N.Y., July 7, 1886; s. Frank A. and Melissa (Stevens) K.; ed. high sch., Cobleskill, N.Y.; m. Frances Adelaide Orr, July 19, 1907; children—Kathleen, Mary MacLaury. Served in U.S. Navy, 1905-23; advanced through grades to commander; served as asst. gen. storekeeper and accounting officer, Naval Station, Cavite, P.I., later gen. storekeeper, Brest, France, and officer in charge provisions and clothing depot, New York; resigned, 1923; with Jewel Tea Co., 1923-48, v.p., 1923-24, pres., 1924-42, chmn., 1942-48, ret. Chmn. Price Adjustment Bd., War Dept., July 1942-Sept. 1943. Received 3 citations, World War I; Medal for Merit, World War II. Clubs: Army, Navy (Manila); Cobleskill Golf and Country. Home: Anchorage Farms, Cobleskill, N.Y. Office: Jewel Park, Barrington, Ill. Died Nov. 19, 1951; buried Arlington Nat. Cemetery.

KARPINSKI, Louis Charles (kär-pĭn'skē), educator; b. Rochester, N.Y., Aug. 5, 1878; s. Henry H. and Mary Louise (Engesser) K.; grad. State Normal and Tng. Sch., Oswego, N.Y., 1897; A.B., Cornell U., 1901; Ph.D., U. Strassburg, Germany, 1903; m. Grace Maude Woods, Apr. 20, 1905; children—Robert Whitcomb, Mary, Louise, Ruth, Joseph Louis, Charles Elwin. Tchr. Berea (Ky.) Coll., 1897-99, Oswego Normal, 1903-04; in charge math. dept., Chautauquan Instn., Chautauqua, N.Y., 1905, 06, 07; Tchrs. Coll. fellow and univ. extension lectr., Columbia U., 1909-10; instr. mathematics, U. Mich., 1904-10, asst. prof., 1910-14, asso. prof., 1914-19, prof., 1919-48, emeritus. Mem. Am. Math. Soc.; Math. Assn. Am. A.A.A.S., Deutsche Mathematiker Verinigung, Comité Internat. d'Histoire des Scis. Democrat. Conglist. Author: The Hindu-Arabic Numerals (with David Eugene Smith), 1911; Robert of Chester's Latin Translation of the Algebra of Al-Khowarizmi, 1915; Unified Mathematics (with H. Y. Benedict and J. W. Calhoun), 1918; History of Arithmetic, 1925; The Arithmetic of Nicomachus (with M. L. D'Ooge and F. Robbins), 1926; Bibliography of the Printed Maps of Michigan, 1804-1880, with Atlas, 1931; Early Maps of Carolina and Adjoining Regions, Charleston, S.C., 1937; Bibliography of Mathematical Works Printed in America through 1850, 1940; Early Military Books in the University of Michigan Libraries (with Col. Thomas M. Spaulding), 1941. Collector of maps and early Americana; authority on early maps of Am. Expert authority on gas and electric rates. Home: 1315 Cambridge Rd., Ann Arbor, Mich.; (winter) Winter Haven, Fla. Died 1956.

KARPOVICH, Michael, educator; b. Tiflis, Russia, Aug. 3, 1888; s. Michael and Maria (Presniakov) K.; Candidate Hist. Scis., U. Moscow, 1914; Litt. D., Middlebury Coll., 1950; m. Tatiana Potapov, Nov. 4, 1923; children—Arseny, Natalia (Mrs. Oleg Anisimov), Sergei, Marina (Mrs. Lee M. Hydeman). Naturalized U.S. citizen, 1944. Asst. curator Hist. Mus. Moscow, Russia, 1914-15; sec. Russian Embassy, Washington, 1917-22; faculty Harvard, 1927—, prof. history, 1946-54, Curt Hugo Reisinger prof. Slavic langs. and lit., 1954-57. Served with War Dept., St. Petersburg, Russia, 1916-17. Trustee Humanities Fund, Inc., N.Y.C. Fellow Am. Acad. Arts and Scis.; mem. Am. Hist. Assn., Am. Assn. U. Profs. Greek Orthodox. Author: Imperial Russia, 1932. Co-author: Economic History of Europe. Editor: Outlines of Russian Culture (Paul Miliukov), 1942. Home: 516 Orange St., New Haven. Died Nov. 7, 1959.

KARTAK, Franz August, univ. dean; b. Oconomowoc, Wis., May 14, 1887; s. Charles Henry and Molly (Maurer) K.; B.S. in Elec. Engring., U. Wis., 1909, research fellow, 1909-11, E.E., 1911; m. Ella C. Mengel, June 22, 1911; 1 dau., Mary Frances. Instr. in elec. engring. U. Wis., 1911-13, dir. Standards Lab., 1913-19; prof. elec. engring. Sch. of Engring. of Milw., 1919-21, Marquette U., 1921-28, dean engring., 1928—. Fellow Am. Inst. E.E.; mem. Engrs. Soc. of Milw., Illuminating Engring. Soc., Soc. Promotion Engring. Edn., Tau Beta Pi, Eta Kappa Nu, Sigma Xi, Sigma Phi Delta. Roman Catholic. Home: 1940 N. 83d St., Wauwatosa, Wis. Address: 1210 W. Michigan St., Milw. Died Feb. 18, 1947.*

KARWOSKI, Theodore F(rancis) (car-vos-ski), educator; b. Odessa, Russia, Sept. 23, 1896; s. Joseph and Florence (Malinowska) K.; brought to U.S., 1901, derivative citizenship, 1912; Ph.B., U. Chgo., 1920; A.M., Columbia, 1923, grad. study, 1920-21; Ph.D., Harvard, 1928; m. Eila Kinghorn, June 12, 1943; step-children—Susan and Sally (twins). Instr. psychology U. N.D., 1923-25; Nat. Research fellow Harvard, 1927-29; research Technicolor, Inc., Boston, 1930; asst. prof. Dartmouth, 1930-36, prof. since 1936, chmn. dept. psychology, 1936-40, 51-55. Mem. Am. Psychol. Assn., Optical Society of Am. Author: Human Psychology, 1936; Color Music, 1938; Psychology, 1952. Home: 2 Tyler Rd., Hanover, N.H. Died Dec. 10, 1957; buried Hanover.

KASNER, Edward (kăs'nĕr), coll. prof.; b. New York, Apr. 2, 1878; B.S., Coll. City of New York, 1896; A.M., Columbia University, 1897, Ph.D., 1899, Doctor of Science (honorary), 1954; University of Göttingen, 1900; unmarried. Tutor mathematics, 1900-05, instr., 1905-06, adj. prof., 1906-10, prof, since 1910, Adrain prof. since 1937, Columbia U.; staff of trans. and bulletins, Am. Math. Soc., Revue Semestrielle des Mathématiques (Amsterdam). Speaker Internat. Congress of Arts and Sciences, St. Louis, 1904, Harvard, 1936; mem. Nat. Acad. Sciences, Am. Math. Soc. (v.p. 1908), A.A.A.S. (v.p. and chmn. Section Mathematics and Astronomy, 1909), Circolo Matematico di Palermo, Société Mathématique de France, Phi Beta Kappa. Mem. com. mathematics NRC. Author: Ivariants of the Inversion Group, 1900; Present Problems of Geometry, 1905; Differential-Geomeyric Aspects of Dynamics (Princeton Colloquium Lectures), 1913; Conformal Geometry, 1915; Einstein's Theory of Gravitation, 1920; Polygenic Functions, 1927; New Names in Mathematics, 1937; Isothermal Families (in Revista and Pastor vols.), 1943; (with James Newman) Mathematics and the Imagination, 1940, Swedish, Russian and Spanish trans. 1941, armed services edit 1945. Editor: Scripta Mathematics. Del. Internat. Mat. Congresses, Bologna and Zurich. Home: 430 W. 116th St., N.Y.C. 27. Died Jan. 7, 1955.

KASTEN, Walter, banker; b. Milw., Mar. 30, 1880; s. Frederick and Jane (Guy) K.; student Milw. U. Sch. and Culver (Ind.) Mil. Acad.; m. Anita Heinemann, Jan. 11, 1908; children—Gertrude Ann (Mrs. Everett G. Smith), George Frederick, Robert Walter; m. 2d, Elizabeth Elser Falk, Feb. 21, 1945. Began in banking business with Wis. Nat. Bank, Milw., 1898; pres. First Wis. Nat. Bank, 1924—; chmn. bd. First Wis. Trust Co.; trustee Northwestern Mutual Life Ins. Co.; pres. Wis. Bankshares Corp.; dir. Harnischfeger Corp., Briggs & Stratton Corp., Carnation Co., A. O. Smith Corp., Allis Chalmers Mfg. Co., Chain Belt Co., Concordia Fire Ins. Co., Title Guaranty Co. of Wis., Kimberly Clark Co., Milwaukee Mechanics Ins. Co. Treas. Columbia Hosp. Clubs: University, Wisconsin, Milwaukee, Milwaukee Athletic, Milwaukee Country. Home: 3365 N. Lake Drive. Office: First Wis. Nat. Bank, 743 N. Water St., Milw. Died Oct. 18, 1950.

KAUFFMAN, Ruth Wright (Mrs. Reginald Wright Kauffmann) (kouf'mȧn), author; b. N.Y.C.; d. Charles Keene and Harriet Butler (Hatch) Hammitt; ed. Misses Kirk's Sch., Bucknell Coll., Bryn Mawr Coll.; m. Reginald Wright Kauffman, 1909; children—Andrew John, Mary Barbara (Mrs. Jesse Zeldin), Gregory (dec.). Investigated woman's work in dept. stores, 1905, ins. offices, 1906, domestic service, 1906; Tchr. French, Latin, English, Misses Kirk's Sch., 1906-09; investigated "White Slavery," U.S., Europe, 1909-11; received Brit. Red Cross nursing certificate, nursed in English mil. hosps., 1914; war corr., 1914-18; sent abroad to report on woman's war work by N.Y. Tribune and for the Vigilantes, 1917. Organized publicity dept., "Waacs" (Woman's Auxiliary Army Corps), London, 1917; active service, publicity dept. A.R.C., 1918; YMCA publicity dept., 1919; tchr. rural sch., Me., 1939-40. Mem. Pi Beta Phi. Club: Shakespear (Bangor, Me.). Author: The Latter Day Saints (history, with Reginald Wright Kauffman), 1912; High Stakes (novel), 1914; Three Little Kittens, 1922; I-Don't-Want-To Series (for children), 1924; Route Barrée, 1925; Tigers and Things (with Andrew J. and Mary B. Kauffman), 1929; Stars for Sale (novel), 1930; Dancing Dollars (novel), 1931; To Paris With Aunt Prue (children's guide book), 1932; Tourist Third (novel), 1933; Sun Gold (novel), 1936; Narcotics, 1938; World of Women (pageant for Elmira Coll.), 1939. Contbr. to mags. With Woman Voters' Dept. Nat. Com. and compiler Harding Genealogy, 1920. Editor: Unfamiliar Quotations, 1949. Home: Rocky Top, Sebasco, via Bath, Me. Died Aug. 13, 1952; buried Mount Bethel Cemetery, Columbia, Pa.

KAUFFMAN, Alfred Otto (kawf'mȧn), former pres. Link-Belt Co.; b. Germany, Aug. 29, 1879; s. William K. and Louise Marie (Startz) K.; M.E., Pratt Inst., 1901; m. Mabel Frances Ulrich, June 9, 1915. Began as apprentice with Gen. Electric Co., Schenectady, N.Y., 1894; with Robert Hoe & Co., printing presses, 1895-98; with Link-Belt Co. 1901-42, successively draftsman, supt. constrn., sales engr., asst. to pres., mgr. Phila. plant, v.p. in charge Belmont plant and Dodge plant until 1924, pres. 1924-42; dir. Link-Belt Co., Gardner-Denver Co., La. Plant-Choate Co., Cardox, Co., Morden Frog and Switch. Clubs: Chicago, South Shore Country, Tavern (Chgo.). Home: 1648 E. 50th St., Chgo. 15. Died Aug. 7, 1959; buried Central Laurel Hill Cemetery, Phila.

KAUFFMANN, Rudolph Max, newspaper exec.; b. Washington, Dec. 22, 1882; s. Rudolph and Jessie (Kennedy) K.; A.B., Princeton, 1905,; m. Edith Charlotte Willis, Nov. 22, 1911; children—Rudolph II, Godfrey W., John Michael. Clk., Eve. Star, Washington, 1905, successively reporter, asst. to mng. editor, sec. and lit. editor, v.p. since 1949; v.p. Columbia Planograph Co. since 1928. Clubs: Cosmos, Metropolitan (Washington); Chevy Chase (Md.). Home: Greenacre, 1 W. Melrose St., Chevy Chase 15, Md. Died Nov. 29, 1956.

KAUFMAN, Paul D., educator; b. N.Y. City, Apr. 29, 1899; s. Philip and Emma (Hecht) K.; A.B., Coll. City of N.Y., 1919; J.D., N.Y.U., 1924. Admitted to N.Y. bar, 1925, and practiced with Hays, Podell & Shulman, N.Y. City, 1924-25, pvt. practice, 1925-31; sr. price atty., O.P.A., 1943; hearing officer and panel chmn. N.W.L.B., 1944-45; teacher DeWitt Clinton High Sch., N.Y. City, 1919-21; instr. Women's Law Class, Washington Square Coll., 1924-34; mem. faculty N.Y.U. Sch. Law since 1924, prof. of law since 1933. Mem. Am. Arbitration Assn. (arbitrator), Am. Assn. U. Profs., Phi Beta Kappa. Dir. Intramural Law Review since 1945. Contbr. to legal periodicals, and Ann. Survey of Am. Law. Home: 45 Hawthorne St., Brooklyn 25. Office: New York University, N.Y.C. 3. Died Feb. 8, 1952.

KAUFMAN, Ralph Odell, banker; b. Decatur, Ill., Mar. 3, 1879; s. Isaac Shellabarger and Claribel (Odell) K.; LL.B., U. Mich., 1906; m. Alice Fallon, Nov. 3, 1909; children—Alice Fallon, Ralph Odell. Began banking at Helena, Mont., 1906; v.p., cashier Union Bank & Trust Co.; dir. Helena Br. Fed. Reserve Bank of Mpls.; v.p. Northwest Bancorporation; pres. First Nat. Bank, Mt. Vernon, Ill., 1933—. State treas. A.R.C.; chmn. four-minute men, Mont., World War; past pres. Elkhorn Council Boy Scouts of Am. Mem. Delta Chi. Republican. K.C., Woodman, Elk. Home: Mt. Vernon, Ill. Died May 2, 1949; buried St. Mary's Cemetery, Mt. Vernon, Ill.

KAUFMANN, Edgar Jonas, merchant; b. Pittsburgh, Pa., Nov. 1, 1885; s. Morris and Betty (Wolf) K.; grad. Shadyside Acad.; student Yale, 1906; hon. D.Sc., U. of Pittsburgh, 1943; m. Liliane Sarah Kaufmann, June 22, 1909; son, Edgar J., Jr. Employed, Marshall Field Co., Chicago, 1 yr.; with Karstadt & Co., Hamburg, Germany, 1 yr.; in 1908 opened a small general store in Connellsville, Pennsylvania; in 1907, joined Kaufmann Stores, Inc., Pittsburgh, as asst. shipping clerk, where he continued in various capacities, becoming store manager; purchased interest and assumed active control of co., 1913; pres. until merger with May Dept. Stores, Oct. 1, 1946. Mem. bd. dirs. and vice president May Company; director of Liberty-Sixth, Incorporated. Service Engraving Co. Cons. to Leon Henderson, dir. O.P.A., Washington, 1943-45. Enlisted in United States Army, 1917; 1st lieutenant Field Artillery, stationed at Camp Taylor and later Camp Knox. Chairman board Research Bur. for Retail Training, U. of Pittsburgh. Dir. Allegheny General Hosp., Blue Cross Hosp. Service, Inc., Community Chest, Irene Kaufmann Settlement (Pittsburgh); dir. Salvation Army, United War Fund, United Jewish Fund, Emma Farm Assn., Pittsburgh Horticultural Soc.; mem. Pa. Highway Planning Commn., Urban Redevelopment Authority; hon. pres. Civic Light Opera Assn.; past pres. Y.M.H.A., Y.W.H.A. Pres. Retail Mchts. Assn., Labor Standards Assn. (Pittsburgh); hon. mem. Phi Lambda Phi, Delta Mu Delta, Omicron Delta Kappa, Eta Mu Pi. Clubs: Harvard-Yale-Princeton, Faculty, Concordia, Field, Westmoreland Country (Pittsburgh); Harmonie (N.Y.). Republican. Jewish religion. Homes: William Penn Hotel, Pittsburgh; Mill Run, Pa.; Palm Springs, Cal. Office: 400 Fifth Av., Pitts. Died Apr. 15, 1955; buried Bear Run, Fayette County, Pa.

KAUFMANN, Edmund I., merchant; b. Detroit, June 6, 1886; s. Aron and Jeannette (Marx) K.; student pvt. tutors, 1893-1908; m. Lillian Swope, Jan. 23, 1911 (dec. 1940); children—Joel Swope, Robert David, Aron Paul; m. 2d, Gertrude Dryfoos, June 14, 1946. Partner Finsterwalds, retail clothing, Toledo, 1910—, Kaufmanns Furniture, Reading, Pa., 1916—, Hadley Furniture, 1916—; pres. Kay Jewelry Stores (85 stores), founded 1916, Fairfax Distbg. Co., wholesale jewelry, founded 1924; chmn. American-Palestine Trading Corp. Former pres. Zionist Orgn. Am., pres. Jewish Fund for Med. Research; trustee Jewish Inst. Religion; pres. Leo N. Levi Meml. Hosp. Assn., Hot Springs, Ark.; dir. Dominican Republic Settlement Assn.; exec. dir. Joint Distbn. Com.; mem. adv. com. Jewish Chautauqua Soc.; pres. Chaim Weizmann Inst. of Science. Clubs: Woodmont Country (Washington); Harmonie, City Athletic (N.Y.C.). Office: Edmar Bldg., 702 H St., N.W., Washington. Died July 17, 1950.

KAUFMANN, Gordon Bernie, architect; b. London, Eng., Mar. 19, 1888; s. Gustav and Matilde (Cook) K.; ed. Whitgift Sch., Croyden, 1899-1904, Polytechnic, London, 1904-08; m. Eva Macfarlane, May 1911; children—Kenneth Macfarlane, Cecil St. Denis (Mrs. Thomas E. Dawson); m. 2d, Elsie Bryant Jenvey, Aug. 4, 1933. Came to U.S., 1914, naturalized, 1934. Partner Johnson, Kaufmann & Coate, architects, Los Angeles, 1920-24; practiced under own name 1924-42; Sr. partner Kaufmann, Lippincott, and Eggers, 1945-47; currently in partnership with J. E. Stanton; director of the Union Bank and Trust Company, Los Angeles. Works: newspaper plant of Los Angeles Times; Santa Anita race track, L.A. Turf Club; Scripps Coll., Claremont, Calif.; Dormitories and Athenæum, California Institute of Technology; Vultee Aircraft, Inc.; Consolidated Steel Company; Basic Magnesium, Inc. U.S. Army Chemical Warfare Service, Lt. Col., Col., 1942-45. Awarded Legion of Merit. Awarded Gold medal French Exposition, 1937. President Los Angeles Area Boy Scouts of America. Fellow American Institute Architects. Episcopalian. Club: California (Los Angeles); Bohemian (San Francisco); Cosmos (Washington, D.C.). Address: 627 S. Carondelet St., Los Angeles, Calif. Died Mar. 1, 1949.

KAUFMANN, Wilford E. (kôf'măn), chemist; b. Glenmont, O., Feb. 12, 1893; s. Christian and Eliza (Bohren) K.; student Houghton (N.Y.) Coll., 1913-16; A.B., Oberlin Coll., 1918, A.M., 1919; Ph.D., U. Ill., 1923; m. Selma Niedergesaess, June 14, 1924; children—Paul Edward, Ann Elizabeth, Donald. Research chemist Du Pont Co., Jackson Lab., Deepwater Point, N.J., 1919-21; grad. dept. of chemistry U. Ill., 1921-23; prof. chemistry Hiram (O.) Coll., 1923-24; research chemist, asst. dir. of research Du Pont Co., Newark, 1924-26; asst. prof. chemistry Williams Coll., Williamstown, Mass., 1927 ; head dept. chemistry Alma (Mich.) Coll., 1927-41, Carleton Coll., 1941-48; dean, v.p., Carroll Coll., Waukesha, Wis., 1948—; tchr. Mich. State Normal Coll., Ypsilanti, summer 1929; research chemist, organic lab. Dow Chem. Co., Midland, Mich., summers 1930, 31, 32, 33. Pres. Valley Trails council Boy Scouts Am., Saginaw, Mich., 1939-40. Served with 308th Inf., 77th Div., U.S. Army, 1918-19; with AEF, 1918-19. Mem. Am. Chem. Soc., A.A.A.S., Phi Lambda Upsilon, Sigma Xi. Republican. Presbyn. Club: Lions (Northfield, Minn.). Contbr. articles to Jour. Am. Chem. Soc. Home: 209 S. James St., Waukesha. Wis. Died Aug. 6, 1953.

KAULBACK, Frank S., business exec.; b. Sandy Creek, N.Y., July 19, 1878; s. George C. and Elivra Ann (Goodard) K.; prep. sch.; m. Elizabeth Flavia McGuire, Nov. 24, 1910; children—Frank S., Elizabeth Ann, Richard C. Vice pres., gen. mgr. Am. Radiator and Standard Sanitary Corp., Pitts., ret. 1948, dir. until 1956; v.p., dir. Standard Sanitary Mfg. Co. de Mexico, S.A., Mexico, D.F.; mem. exec. com. of finance com., director. Dir. Kewanee Boiler Corp., Heating & Plumbing Finance Corp., Standard Sanitary & Dominion Radiator, Ltd., Toronto, Can. Republican. Christian. Clubs: Duquesne (Pitts.), High and Country (Bellevue, Pa.); Butler (Pa.) Country. Home: 5834 Elmer St., Pitts. 6. Address: P.O. Box 1226, Pitts. 30. Died Dec. 20, 1956.

KAUTZKY, Theodore, artist; b. Budapest, Hungary, Oct. 20, 1896; s. Adolf and Sidonia (Stier) K.; grad. Royal U. Hungary, 1921; m. Ruth Carle, Dec. 19, 1925. Came to U.S., 1923, naturalized, 1929. Tchr. archtl. sketching and water color Pratt Inst., 1937-38; lectr. pencil sketching N.Y.U., U. Pa., U. Toronto; condr. own sch. pencil sketching and water color, 1936-37. Awarded hon. mention Chgo. Tribune Tower World Competition, 1922; Birch Burdette Long prize for archtl. illustration, 1937; Am. Water Color Soc. Medal of Honor, 1941, Obrig prize, 1949, Purchase prize, 1951; hon. mention for water color Allied Artists Am., 1943, Marine prize for water color, 1946, Gold medal, 1949; Salmagundi Club Laymember prize for oil, 1944, water color prize, 1948, oil prize, 1949, Auction prize and watercolor prize, 1952; Rockport Art Assn. water color prize, 1948, water color and popular prizes, 1950, 51; Balt. Water Club popular prize, 1949, 51; North Shore Arts Assn. popular prize, 1950; Hudson Valley Art Assn. watercolor prize, 1950; Naitonal Academy of Design Obrig prize, 1952; awarded gold medal of honor American Water Color Society (posthumously), 1954. Nat. academician Nat. Acad. Design; mem. Am. Water Color Soc., Allied Artists Am., Audubon Artists, Phila. Water Color Club, Rockport Art Assn., North Shore Arts Assn. Roman Catholic. Club: Salmagundi. Made Endl. motion picture film on pencil drawing for Ency. Brit. Films, Inc. Author: Pencil Broadsides (pencil sketching), 1941; Pencil Pictures (composition); Ways with Watercolor, 1949; Painting Trees and Landscapes in Watercolor, 1952. Home: 11 Marwood Lane, Yonkers 2, N.Y. Died May 18, 1953.

KAVANAGH, Francis Bernard (kăv'ăn-aw), lawyer; b. at Union City, Pa., August 14, 1879; s. John Francis and Mary Elizabeth (Kilroy) K.; LL.B., Baldwin U. (now Baldwin-Wallace Coll.), Berea, O., 1909; LL.M., Cleveland Law Sch., 1929; A.B., Western Reserve U.; m. Jean Woodford Wible, Jan. 21, 1928; children—Lawrence, Helen. Asst. supt. Cleveland City Farm Sch. for Boys, 1903-06; asst. gen. agent Cleveland Humane Soc., 1906-09; admitted to O. bar, 1909; atty. Cleveland Humane Soc., 1909-14; 1st asst. U.S. atty., 1914-19; spl. asst. to U.S. atty. for war prosecutions, Cleveland, 1918-19; 1st asst. U.S. atty., 1936-41; U.S. atty., 1941-42; spl. asst. U.S. atty. 1942-49, retired 1949; returned general practice of law 1949. Mem. Am., Ohio State and Cleveland bar assns., Federal Bar, American Judicature Soc., Veterans of Foreign Wars, Cleveland Chamber of C., Acad. Polit. Sci., Phi Beta Kappa, Delta Theta Phi. Democrat: Conglist. Mason (32°, Shriner). Club: City (Cleveland), Mid-Day, Koran Club. Author: New Jury Code for Ohio, together with Comments and Digest for New Jury Code (Page's edit.). Contbr. to Ohio Law Bull., Ohio Bar Reporter. Home: 120 Sunset Drive, Avon Lake, O. Office: Williamson Bldg., Cleve. Died Feb. 8, 1956.

KAVANAGH, James Edward (kăv'ăn-aw), ret. ins. exec.; b. Sharon, Ont., Can., Mar. 14, 1871; s. John and Elizabeth (Ryan) K.; student Owen Sound Collegiate Inst., 1893-95, Ont. Sch. of Pedagogy, 1895-96; m. Edith R. Shortly, Dec. 22, 1898; children—James Orville, Helen Weston, John Harold. Began as ins. agt., Met. Life Ins. Co., 1897; successively dist. mgr., 1902, supt. agencies, 1904, 4th and 3d v.p. in charge of group div., 1917, 19, respecitvely, 2d v.p. in charge div., 1924-36, v.p. in charge div. 1936-41, ret. Mem. War Savs. Com., World War I. Methodist. Mason. Club: Siwanoy Country (Mt. Vernon); Highland Park, Florida; Larchmond Shore. Home: Gramatan Hotel, Bronxville, N.Y. and Highland Park Club, Lake Wales, Fla. Office: 1 Madison Av., N.Y.C. Died Dec. 12, 1957.

KAVANAGH, Robert Vincent, clergyman, coll. pres.; b. Cokedale, Mont., Feb. 27, 1905; s. Robert Michael and Bridget Agnes (Gallagher) K.; A.B., Carroll Coll., 1926; M.A., U. So. Cal., 1927; S.T.B., Cath. U. Am., 1931; Ph.D., U. Wis., 1945. Ordained priest Roman Cath. Ch., 1931; staff mem. Carroll Coll., Helena, Mont., 1931-35, registrar, 1935-40, head English dept., 1944-51, pres. since 1951. Mem.

exec. bd. N.W. Assn. since 1951. Mem. Cath. Renascense Soc., Nat. Cath. Ednl. Assn., Delta Epsilon Sigma. K.C. Home: Carroll College, Helena, Mont. Died Apr. 1, 1957; buried Helena.

KAYE-SMITH, Sheila, novelist; b. Hastings, Sussex, Eng., Feb. 4, 1887; s. Edward and Emily Janet (de la Condamine) Kaye-Smith; student Hastings and St. Leonardo Coll., 1896-1905; m. Penrose Fry, Oct. 16, 1924. First novel published, 1908; best known works include: Sussex Gorse, 1916; Joanna Godden, 1921; The End of the House of Alard, 1923; Susan Spray, 1931; Tambourine, Trumpet and Drum, 1943; The Dardners and the Laurelwoods, 1947. Fellow Royal Soc. of Literature. Roman Catholic. Address: Little Doucegrove, Northiam, Rye, Sussex, Eng. Died Jan. 14, 1956; buried St. Teresa's Cath. Ch., Northiam, Sussex, Eng.

KAYN, Hilde B., artist; b. Vienna, Austria, 1903; became Am. citizen, 1926; studied art at Art Students League, N.Y.C., under George Bridgeman and George Luks. Mem. Nat. Acad. Design, Am. Water Color Soc., A.N.A., 1943. Died Aug. 29, 1950.*

KAYS, Donald Jackson (kāys), prof. agr.; b. Magnolia, Ill., Sept. 11, 1886; s. John A. and Mary Alice (Hartenbower) K.; ed. Northern Ill. State Normal Sch., 1903-06; B.S. in Agr., U. of Ill., 1912; m. Maud Mallin, June 15, 1914; children—John Mallin, Mary Lois, Marjorie, Donald J. Teacher, Rockford High Sch., 1906-08; farmed, 1908-10; teacher, animal husbandry dept., Ohio State U., 1912-14; prof., 1914-53, chmn. dept., 1940-51. Mem. A.A.A.S., Future Farmers America, Am. Soc. Animal Production, Alpha Zeta, Phi Kappa Phi, Gamma Sigma Delta, Alpha Delta Phi, Alpha Gamma Sigma, Delta Theta Sigma. Presbyterian. Democrat. Mason. Club: Faculty (Ohio State U.). Author: The Horse, 1953. Contbr. to agrl. jours. Home: 1493 Perry St., Columbus, O. Died Nov. 13, 1956; buried Walnut Grove Cemetery, Columbus.

KAZANTZAKIS, Nikos, author; b. Candia, Crete, Greece, Feb. 18, 1885; s. Michael and Maria (Christodoulaki) K.; student U. Athens; LL.D., Coll. of France, Paris; m. Eleni Samios, Nov. 10, 1945. Dir.-gen. Ministry Pub. Relief, 1919; minister without portfolio, Athens, Greece, 1945; dir. bur. translations of the classics UNESCO, 1948. Author: (translated into English) Zorba the Greek; Greek Passion; Freedom or Death; The Odyssee, 1957. Home: 8 Rue du Bas-Castelet, Antibes, Cote d'Azur, France. Died Nov. 26, 1957.

KEAN, Jefferson Randolph, ret. army officer; b. Lynchburg, Va., June 27, 1860; s. Robert G. H. and Jane Nicholas (Randolph) K.; g.g.s. Thomas Jefferson; student Episcopal High Sch., Bellevue H.S.; M.D., U. Va., 1883; studied New York Polyclinic; m. Louise Hurlbut Young, Oct. 10, 1894 (dec. 1915); children—Martha Jefferson, Robert Hill; m. 2d, Cornelia Knox, Mar. 24, 1919. Commd. lt. asst. surgeon, 1884; promoted through grades to col., 1914; retired, 1924; brig. gen. (temp.), 1918-19. Served on Western frontier 8 yrs.; took part in winter campaign of 1890-91 against the Sioux; then stationed 5 yrs. in Fla.; in Spanish War assigned to duty with 7th Army Corps; served in Cuba, 1898-1902, as dept. chief surgeon under Gen. Fitzhugh Lee and supt. dept. of charities under Gen. Wood; on return to U.S. in 1902 made asst. to surgeon-gen.; adviser dept. of sanitation for Provisional Govt. of Cuba, 1906-09; in charge sanitary div. surgeon gen.'s office, 1909-13. Author of laws organizing sanitary depts. of Cuba and P.R. and first Res. Corps, U.S. Army. Dir. gen. and organizer dept. of mil. relief of A.R.C., 1916-17; chief U.S. Ambulance Service with French Army, 1917-18; then deputy chief surgeon, AEF to end of war. Apptd. by President, mem. U.S. Commn. for construction of Nat. Expansion Memorial, at St. Louis, 1934, and mem. U.S. Commn. to erect Permanent Memorial to Thomas Jefferson, 1938. Pres. Assn. Mil. Surgeons of U.S., 1914-15 (sec. and editor same, 1924-34); mem. Phi Beta Kappa. Awarded D.S.M. (U.S.); Officer Legion d'Honneur; Grand Cross Order of Merit, Carlos J. Finlay (Cuba); awarded Gorgas medal by Assn. Mil. Surgeons of U.S., 1942. Home: 2804 N St. N.W., Washington 7. Died Sept. 4, 1950; buried Monticello, nr. Charlottesville, Va.

KEANE, Lee (Augustus), chem. mfg. exec.; b. Atwaters, N.Y., July 23, 1894; s. Austin Charles and Mary (Malley) K.; B.S., Cornell U., 1916; m. Florette Webb, Sept. 23, 1923; 1 son, Edward Webb. Chemist Goodyear Tire & Rubber Co., Akron, O., 1916-17, Faultless Rubber Co., Ashland, O., 1919-20, O'Bannon Corp., W. Barrington, R.I., 1920-24, Atlas Powder Co., Stamford, Conn., 1924-25, Proctor & Gamble, Memphis, 1925-27; v.p. U.S. Indsl. Chemicals, Inc., N.Y.C., 1936—. Served as lt. C.W.S., U.S. Army, World War I. Mem. Alpha Chi Sigma, Sigma Xi. Republican. Episcopalian. Clubs: New Canaan (Conn.) Country; Cornell, Union League, Uptown (N.Y.C.); Tokeneke (Darien, Conn.). Home: Rosebrook Rd., New Canaan, Conn. Office: 120 Broadway, N.Y.C. Died Feb. 7, 1958.

KEANE, Theodore John; b. San Francisco, Jan. 21, 1880; s. George Bernard and Theodosia Jane (Carter) K.; ed. Polytechnic High Sch., of San Francisco; studied art, Cal. Sch. Design. Sec. to Mayor Schmitz, of San Francisco, 1905; sec. Paul Elder & Co., book and art dealers, 1906-10; mng. dir. Mpls. Soc. Fine Arts, 1910-12; registrar Sch. of Art Inst. Chgo., 1912-14, dean, 1914—. Etcher of animals. Hon. mem. Attic Club Mpls., Chgo. Soc. Artists; mem. Art Students' League Chgo., Chgo. Soc. Etchers, Chgo. br. Archaeol. Inst. Am. (sec.), Independent Soc. Artists, Chicago. Clubs: National Arts (N.Y.C.); Cliff Dwellers, Palette and Chisel, South Side Tennis (Chgo.). Home: 5027 Dorchester Av., Chgo.

KEANE, William Edward, urologist; b. Detroit, Sept. 20, 1878; s. John and Maria E. (Ryan) K.; A.B., Detroit U., 1898, A.M., 1900, M.D., 1902, LL.D., 1927; m. Leontine N. D'Haene, Oct. 9, 1915; children—William E., Henry J., Leontine R., Mary Louise, Joseph P. Practiced in Detroit, 1902—; asst. in surgery Detroit Coll. Medicine (now Wayne U.), 1902-12, prof. urology, 1912—; cons. urologist Providence and Detroit Receiving Hosp. Fellow A.C.S.; mem. Am. Urol. Assn., A.M.A. Roman Catholic. K.C. Clubs: Detroit Athletic, Country Club. Home: 1007 Harvard, Grosse Pointe 30, Mich. Office: David Whitney Bldg., Detroit. Died Feb. 14, 1955; buried Mt. Olivet Cemetery, Detroit.

KEARNEY, Belle, lectr.; b. on plantation nr. Vernon, Miss.; d. Col. Walter G. and Sue (Owens) Kearney; ed. in Miss. Was engaged in teaching 6 yrs.; lectr., 1889—, chautauqua and lyceum platform; traveled extensively. Author: A Slaveholder's Daughter. Address: Flora, Miss. Died 1939.

KEARNEY, Raymond Augustine, bishop; b. Jersey City, N.J., Sept. 25, 1902; s. Joseph Peter and Nora Isabelle (Burke) K.; student Brooklyn Prep. Acad., 1916-19; A.B., Holy Cross Coll., Worcester, Mass., 1923, LL.D., 1948; D.D., N. Am. Coll., Rome, Italy, 1927; J.C.D., Cath. U. of Am., 1929; LL.D., St. Francis Coll., 1935, St. John's Univ., 1946. Ordained priest R.C. Ch., 1927; v. chancellor Diocese of Brooklyn, 1929-30, chancellor since 1930; auxiliary bishop of Brooklyn and titular bishop of Lysinia since Feb. 1935. Author: Principles of Delegation, 1929. K.C. Home: 378 Clermont Av. Office: 75 Greene Av., Bklyn. Died Oct. 1, 1956; buried Holy Cross Cemetery, Bklyn.

KEARNEY, Thomas Henry, botanist; b. Cin., June 27, 1874; s. Thomas H. and Lavinia A. (Miner) K.; student U. Tenn., 1889-91, Columbia (spl. course), 1893-94; LL.D., U. Ariz., 1920; unmarried. Asst. botanist Tenn. Agrl. Expt. Sta., 1892-93; asst. curator herbarium, Columbia, 1893-94; asst. agrostologist, 1894-97, asst. botanist, 1898-1900, asst. physiologist Bur. Plant Industry, U.S. Dept. Agr., 1900-02, physiologist, 1902, sr. physiologist, 1924-29, prin. physiologist, 1929-44 (retired June 30, 1944). Prin. work, study of the flora of Arizona. Fellow A.A.A.S. Cal. Acad. Sci.; mem. Bot. Soc. America, Washington Acad. Sciences, Bot. and Biol. socs., Washington, Cal. Bot. Soc. (pres. 1949). Club: Cosmos. Address: Cal. Acad. Sciences, San Francisco 18. Died Oct. 19, 1956; buried San Francisco.

KEARNS, John W., lawyer; b. Schenectady, N.Y., Apr. 21, 1904; s. John E. and Margaret E. (Wallace) K.; B.S.E., U. Mich., 1924; J.D., Northwestern, 1927; children—John W., Robert L., William S. Admitted to Ill. bar, 1927, and practiced as mem. firm of Burry, Johnstone & Peters, lawyers, Chicago, 1927-39; atty., The First Nat. Bank of Chicago, since 1939, v.p., law dept. since 1950; dir. Central Coal & Coke Corp. Mem. Am. and Chicago bar assns. Clubs: University (Chicago and Kansas City, Mo.), Chicago, Mid Day, Racquet, Glenview, Indian Hill, Law, Legal (Chicago). Home: 1320 North State Parkway. Office: 38 Dearborn St., Chgo. 90. Died Apr. 30, 1952.

KEATING, Anne C., librarian; formerly with Ind. State Tchrs. Coll. Library; librarian Ohio U., Athens, O., 1925-49. Died Sept. 21, 1952; buried Terre Haute, Ind.

KEBLER, Lyman Frederic, chemist, physician; b. Lodi, Mich., June 8, 1863; s. George John and Sophi G. (Gumpper) K.; Ph.C., U. Mich., 1890, B.S., 1891, M.S., 1892; spl. student Jefferson Med. Coll., Phila., 1898, Temple U., 1899-1903; M.D., George Washington U., 1906; m. Ida E. Shaw, Aug. 10, 1893; children—Mrs. Mabel Alice Kohr, Victor Lyman, Mrs. Ruth Wilhelmina Mercurio. Chief chemist for mfg. drug firm, Phila., 1892-1903; chief drug lab., Bur. Chemistry, Washington, 1903-07, chief, drug div., 1907-23, chief, spl. collaborative investigations, 1923-29; special adviser to Post Office Dept. in medical schemes, etc., to defraud, 1903-29; resigned from Govt. service to engage in pvt. work; chem.-med. cons. on foods, drugs, cosmetics, and mail order bus.; asst. prof. pharmacology and materia medica, Georgetown (D.C.) Coll., 1912-32. Instr. in chemistry, Ia. Agrl. Coll., 1888-89, U. Mich., 1891-92; mem. jury awards, Nat. Export Expn., 1898; mem. U.S. Pharmacopoeia Revision Com., 1910-20; sec. U.S. Pharm. Conv., 1920-30. Mem. Am. Chem. Soc. (v.p. 1917), A.M.A. (council pharm. chemistry, 1905-14), D.C. Med. Soc., Am. Pharm. Assn. (v.p. 1922, 23, 24; chmn. scientific sect. 1901-02; pres. Washington br. 1915; chmn. hist. sect. 1928-29), Kappa Psi, Theta Kappa Psi; fellow A.A.A.S.; hon. mem. Md. Pharm. Assn.; trustee Nat. Coll. Pharmacy, 1918-26; pres. chem. sect. Franklin Inst., Phila., 1902; pres. U. Mich. Alumni, Washington, 1917. Chmn. Employes Reclassification Com. Dept. Agr., 1920; formerly dir. of health, Columbia Heights Community Centre, Washington; mem. Business Men's Assn. and various civic bodies. Pres. Forum, Columbia Heights; mem. D.C. Drug Vets. Assn. Appeared many times before Congressional coms. and in court cases of P.O. Dept. Royal Arch Mason; Past Patron O.E.S. Club: Lions. Author: Eat and Keep Fit. Contbr. to chemical, food and medical subjects, on public welfare, drug habituation, analytical methods, adulteration of medicines and chemicals, harmful drugs, history of the tablet industry, variation of tablet medication, the use of the mails to defraud, etc. Home-Office: 1322 Park Rd. N.W., Washington. Died Mar. 4, 1955.

KECK, Charles, sculptor; b. N.Y.C.; s. Henry and Eliabeth (Camerer) K.; student N.A.D., Art Students' League, N.Y.C.; Master in Arts and Letters, Am. Acad. in Rome, 1904; m. J. Anne Collyer, June 3, 1923; children—James Collyer, Charles, John William. Asst. to Augustus St. Gaudens, 1893-98; 1st winner Prix de Rome, in open competition, 1899; gold medal for sculpture Archtl. League of New York, 1926; mem. Art Commn., N.Y.C., 1921-24. Prin. works: Monument to George Washington, Palermo Park, Buenos Aires; U.S.S. Maine meml. tablets for U.S. Govt.; Lewis and Clark, Charlottesville, Va.; equestrian monument of Stonewall Jackson, Charlottesville; Booker T. Washington, Tuskegee, Ala.; Friendship monument U.S. to Brazil, Rio Janeiro; Citizen Soldier, Irvington, N.J.; Soldiers' meml., Bklyn.; George F. Johnson monument, Binghamton, N.Y.; John Mitchell monument, Scranton, Pa.; Liberty monument, Ticonderoga, N.Y.; Montclair (N.J.) Soldiers' meml.; Lynchburg (Va.) Soldiers' meml.; Sesquicentennial medal, Souvenir Half-Dollar (State of Vt.); busts of Elias Howe, Patrick Henry and James Madison, Hall of Fame, N.Y.U.; bust of John Tyler, Capitol, Richmond, Va.; Shriners' peace monument, Toronto, Can.; meml. to Abraham Lincoln, Wabash, Ind.; Charles B. Aycock monument in the U.S. Hall of Fame, Washington; pediment for the Administration Building, Saratoga Springs, N.Y.; bas relief panels, Bronx County Building, New York, Nelson-Atkins Museum, Kansas City, Mo., Jackson County Court House, Kansas City, Mo.; equestrian monument to Andrew Jackson, Kansas City, Mo.; war meml., East Orange, N.J.; monument to 3 presidents from N.C.; sarcophagi of James B., Benjamin N., Washington Duke for Chapel of Duke U.; monument to James B. Duke, Durham, N.C.; Father Duffy monument, Times Square, N.Y.C.; Huey P. Long monuments, Baton Rouge, Washington; sarcophagus of Alfred I. duPont, Wilmington, Del.; Dr. Edmund A. Babler monument; St. Isaac Jogues monument, Lake George, N.Y.; Thomas Jefferson Rusk, Henderson, Tex.; Capt. Jones Monument, Gulfport, Miss.; Monument to Alfred E. Smith, N.Y.C.; bust of Harry S. Truman for Senate Wing containing vice-presidents. Mem. Am. Acad. in Rome, Nat. Sculpture Soc., Archtl. League of New York, Numismatic Soc., Art Commn. Assn., Beaux Arts Soc., Met. Museum, Century Assn. N.A., 1928. Episcopalian. Mason (32°). Home: Gipsy Trail Club, Carmel, N.Y. Address: 40 W. 10th St., N.Y.C. Died Apr. 23, 1951; buried Fishkill (N.Y.) Cemetery.

KEE, John, ex-congressman; b. Glenville, W.Va., Aug. 22, 1874; s. Jasper Newton and Louisa (Campbell) K.; student Glenville State Normal Sch., 1887-90, W.Va. U., 1898-99; m. Maude Elizabeth Frazier; children—James, Frances. In practice of law, Glenville, 1897-1900; with South Penn Oil Co., 1900-02; counsel for Virginian Ry. Co., 1902-10; practiced at Bluefield, W.Va., 1910-16, and 1918—; spl. legal work, Mexico, 1916-18. Mem. W.Va. State Senate, 1923-27; mem. 73d to 80th Congresses, 5th W.Va. Dist.; chmn. House Fgn. Affairs Com. Mem. Phi Sigma Kappa. Democrat. Episcopalian. Odd Fellow, K.P., Elk. Kiwanian. Home: Woodland Dr., Bluefield, W.Va. Died May 1951.

KEEFE, Frank B(ateman), congressman; b. Winneconne, Wis., Sept. 23, 1887; s. Thomas F. and Kathryn (Forscythe) K.; grad. Oshkosh (Wis.) State Normal Sch., 1906; LL.B., U. of Mich., 1910; m. Mildred Virginia Steele, Dec. 13, 1912; children—Virginia (Mrs. Charles F. Nolan), Jean Mary (Mrs. Edwin Rosten), Bateman. Teacher, 1906-07; admitted to Wis. bar, 1910 and began practice in Oshkosh; mem. 76th to 81st Congresses (1939-51), 6th Wis. Dist.; v.p. and dir. Oshkosh Bldg. & Loan Assn.; dir. Oshkosh Nat. Bank. Pres. Lake View Memorial Park. Mem. Am. and Wis. bar assns. Republican. Episcopalian. Mason (32°, Shriner). Elk. Eagle. Home: Oshkosh, Wis. Died Feb. 5, 1952; buried Lake View Meml. Park, Oshkosh.

KEEFE, John Hancock, ex-ry. exec.; b. Raub, Ind., Aug. 20, 1880; s. Thomas and Delia (Fife) K.; student Jesuit Coll., Galveston, Tex.; m. Edna Farrell, June 24, 1908; children—Mrs. Phillip S.

Deasy, Mrs. Sterling B. Price, John H. Started as office boy and messenger G.C.&S.F. Ry. Co., 1896-97, messenger, clerk, stenographer, Galveston, Tex., 1897-1902, chief clerk, 1902-05, asst. to 2d v.p. and gen. mgr. 1905-11, asst. gen. mgr., 1911-18; v.p., gen. mgr. Texas & Gulf Ry., 1906-10, pres. at Galveston, Tex., 1910-14; asst. dir., div. of operations U.S. R.R., Adminstrn., 1918-19; asst. to v.p. A.T.&S.F. Ry. Co., Chgo., 1919-22; pres., dir. S.E.F.I. and other affiliated cos., Chgo., 1922-44; v.p. A.,T.&S.F. Ry. Co., 1944-48; retired dir. Kansas City Terminal Ry. Co., Belt. Co. of Chicago, Chicago & Western Ind. R.R. Home: 3000 Sheridan Rd., Chgo. Deceased.

KEEFE, William J., judge; b. Clinton, Ia., Nov. 17, 1873; s. Thomas and Mary (Myles) K.; LL.B., U. Ia., 1894; m. Anna Belle Carroll, June 26, 1912; children—William Carroll, John Myles. Admitted to Ia. bar, 1895; practiced at Clinton, Ia., 1895-1933; county atty. Clinton County, 1902-10; judge U.S. Customs Ct., N.Y., 1933-47. Democrat. Roman Catholic. K.C., Elk. Home: 9 Tanglewylde Av., Bronxville, N.Y. Died Sept. 14, 1955.

KEEFER, Frank Royer, med. officer U.S. Army; b. Venango County, Pa., Oct. 10, 1865; s. John Brua and Caroline Rebecca (Royer) K.; Ph.B., Dickinson Coll., 1885, A.M., 1901, Sc.D., 1935; M.D., U. of Pa., 1889; m. Mary Cornelia Terrell, Feb. 18, 1903. Entered Army Med. Corps, 1890; advanced through grades to col. in 1916; brig. gen., asst. surg. gen., 1927, retired, 1929. Prof. Mil. Hygiene, U.S. Military Academy, 1910-14; comdg. mil. hosps., 1915-19; chief, med. div., Provost marshal gen. office, Washington, 1918; chief surgeon, Am. Forces in Germany, 1920-22; same, 2d Corps Area, N.Y. City, 1922-27; decorated officer French Legion of Honor. Chmn. D.C. Chapter Am. Red. Cross, 1930-42; now chmn. emeritus; fellow Am. Med. Assn. and Am. Coll. Surgeons. Mem. Chi Phi. Presbyterian. Clubs: Army and Navy; Chevy Chase; Army and Navy Country (Washington); University (Phila.). Author: Alcoholic Drinks and Narcotics; Military Hygiene and Sanitation. Address: 2800 Woodley Rd., Washington. Died May 15, 1954.

KEELER, Ralph Welles, clergyman; b. Bridgeport, Conn., Feb. 1, 1877; s. George Welles and Emily Clifford (Wells) K.; B.A., Wesleyan U., 1904, M. A., 1909; B.D., Drew Theol. Sem., 1907; M.A., Columbia, 1914; Master's Diploma in Edn., Teachers Coll., 1914; D.D., Baldwin-Wallace, 1913; Wesleyan, 1919; m. Ellen Martin Coughlin, July 11, 1906 (died June 30, 1944); children—Eleanor Elizabeth, Ralph Welles. Mem. N.Y. East Conf. Meth. Ch.; pastor Wethersfield, Conn., 1901-04, Goodsell Ch., Brooklyn, 1904-06, Bayville and Locust Valley, N.Y., 1906-07; ordained elder, 1907; pastor Cropsey Av. Ch., Brooklyn, 1908-11; sec. China Centennial Commn., Bd. Foreign Missions, 1907-09; exec. sec. Africa Diamond Jubilee Commn., 1909-10; publicity sec. Korea Quarter-Centennial Commn., 1910-11; asst. editor S.S. publs. M.E. Ch., 1911-14; asso. editor adult class publs. M.E. Ch. (Adult Bible Class Monthly, Home Dept. Quarterly, etc.), Cincinnati, 1914-17; dir. bureau of publicity, Bd. of Home Missions and Ch. Extension M.E. Ch., 1917-23; publicity sec. Joint Com. Foreign Lang. Publs., Home Missionary Council, Council of Women for Home Missions, and S.S. Council, 1920-23; dir. of publicity Com. on Conservation and Advance, Council of Bd. of Benevolence, M.E. Ch., 1920-23. Exec. sec. Gen. Conf. S.S. Exhibit and Inst., 1912; chmn. publicity com. Nat. Conv. Methodist Men, 1913; publicity sec. Home Mission Council, 1919-23. Dir. publicity, Gen. Conf. M.E. Ch., 1916, 20. Mem. editorial com. World Outlook, Missionary Review of the World, Missionary News, 1918-23; pastor Crawford Memorial Church, New York City, 1923-29, Goodsell Memorial Ch., Brooklyn, 1929-49; ret. 1949; interim pastor Reformed Ch., New Hyde Park, 1950-51, Community Congl. Ch., New Hyde Park, 1952. Recipient bronze medal for citizenship, Vets. Fgn. Wars, for 20 yrs. of outstanding service to vets., 1949; made hon. mem. Boy Scouts Am., 1951. Chmn. adv. editorial bd. Macfadden Publs., 1924-41. Counsellor in publicity Bd. of Hosps. and Homes of M.E. Ch., 1921-24; counsellor in publicity, annual meeting Am. Hosp. Assn., 1924; counsellor in publicity, N.E. Deaconess Assn., 1924-26; religious editor New York Evening Graphic, 1924-29. Vice-pres. and mem. of exec. com., Evangelistic Com., N.Y. City, since 1927; editor Physical-Religious Forum Mag., 1927-30. Republican. Mem. Veterans of Fgn. Wars of the U.S., Sons of Veterans of Civil War, Jr. Order of United Am. Mechanics, Beta Theta Pi, Phi Beta Kappa. Mason. Grand Chaplain, Grand Lodge of Masons, New York, Odd Fellow. Clubs: Beta Theta Pi, University. Co-editor: Militant Methodism, 1913; Wesleyan Verse (2d edit.), 1914. Joint Author: (with Ellen Coughlin Keeler) The Christian Conquest of America, 1918; A Centenary Survey of Methodist Episcopal Missions, 1919. Author: Chapter on Elective Courses for Adults in General Manual, Introduction and Use of the Graded Lessons, International Course; Heart Messages from the Psalms, 1917; Christian Democracy for America, 1919; Home Mission Graphics (The Call of the Country; The City's Challenge; Reconstruction in the U.S.A.; America's Obligations), 1919; The Reclamation of Men and Thinbs, 1919; Putting Hospitals and Homes in the Hearts and Minds of the People, 1921; Publicity for City Methodism, 1921; A Calendar of Prayer, 1922-23; Centenary Art Calendar, 1922, 23, 24; The Rural Nurse, 1923; The Executive Nurse, 1923; Publicity for Hospitals, 1923; The Physical Life in the Spiritual Conquest, 1926; Before Thine Altars, 1929; Through Cloud and Sunshine (verse), 1933; Along the Road From Yesterday, 1949; also hymns. Extensive contbr. short stories, prose and verse to religious and secular publs., also radio preacher. Home: care George Spann, Sundown Rd., Grahamsville, N.Y. Died Oct. 18, 1956; buried Cypress Hills Cemetery, Bklyn.

KEELER, Stephen Edwards, bishop; b. New Canaan, Conn., Apr. 16, 1887; s. Stephen Edwards and Annie Demarest (Husted) K.; prep. edn., Hoosac (N.Y.) Sch., 1902-06; A.B., Yale, 1910; B.D., Gen. Theol Sem., 1913, S.T.D., 1933; D.D., U. of South, 1948; D.D., Kenyon College, 1930; D.D., Seabury-Western Theological Seminary, 1954; married Eunice Daskam Stevens, June 2, 1915; 1 son, Stephen Edwards. Deacon, 1913, priest, 1914, P.E. Ch.; sr. curate St. Paul's Ch., Cleveland, O., 1913-15; rector St. Stephen's Ch., Pittsfield, Mass., 1915-23, St. Paul's Ch., Akron, O., 1923-29, St. Chrysostom's Ch., Chicago, 1929-31; elected bishop coadjutor P.E. Ch., Diocese of Minn., April 15, 1931; also bishop in charge of Hawaiian Islands, 1943; became bishop of Minnesota, Jan. 1, 1944; president Bishop and Directorate of Diocese of Minn., bishop in charge of Convocation of American Churches in Europe, 1954-—; and Chaplains in the United States Armed Forces in Europe, 1954-—. Director Wellesley Summer School and Conf., Wellesley, Mass., 1933-48. Pres. board of trustees Seabury-Western Theological Seminary (Evanston, Ill.), St. Mary's Hall for Girls, Shattuck School for Boys, St. James School for Boys, Bishopp Seabury Mission (all Fairbault, Minnesota), Breck School for Boys (St. Paul), Hoosac School for Boys. President of Gambier Summer Sch. and Conf. for Clergy and Ch. Workers, 1928, 29, 30; pres. Province of the Northwest, Episcopal Ch., 1935-39; provincial rep. Nat. Council of Episcopal Church, 1939-53; chmn. Nat. Commn. on Work among Coll. Students, 1939. Mem. Beta Theta Pi, Delta Sigma Rho. Republican. Club: University. Mem. intercollegiate debating teams, Yale, 1908-10; winner Ten Eyke Exhbn., 1909, De Forest gold medal, 1910. Home: 920 Mt. Curve Av. Office: 1409 Willow St., Mpls. 3. Died Sept. 25, 1956.

KEEN, Victor, newspaper corr.; b. Pueblo, Colo., June 9, 1898; s. Perry M. and Etta (Ford) K.; B.J., U. of Mo., 1922; m. Elizabeth Stein, Mar. 1, 1930; m. 2d, Alice Morgan, July 21, 1943; 1 dau., Morgan. Served in U.S. Coast Arty., Fort Logan, Fort Rosecrans, Fort Winfield Scott, 1918; on staff Pueblo Chieftain, 1919; United Press, Chicago, 1922; Omaha World-Herald, 1922-23; staff Japan Advertiser (Am. daily), Tokyo, also Japan corr. N.Y. Herald Tribune. Japan, 1923-28; Japan corr. Chicago Tribune, 1929; mgr. Far Eastern Bur., N.Y. Herald Tribune, headquarters Shanghai, Apr. 1929-June 1942; repatriated to U.S. on S.S. Gripsholm after 79 days imprisonment by Japanese in Shanghai, arriving in New York, Aug. 24, foreign cable desk, Herald-Tribune, New York, 1942-45; Far Eastern corr., New York Daily News, 1946, now on telegraph desk, Daily News. Member Phi Gamma Delta, Sigma Delta Chi, Kappa Tau Alpha. Clubs: American (Tokyo); Kobe, Kobe Regatta and Athletic, Kobe Lawn Tennis, Shioya Country (Kobe), American, Columbia Country (Shanghai). Address: 6 W. Wilson Circle, Red Bank, N.J. Died Jan. 30, 1955.

KEENAN, James R., corp. exec.; b. Harvard, Ill., May 30, 1891; s. Stephen and Elizabeth (McConnell) K.; student bus. adminstrn. Dixon Coll., 1910; m. Agnes Comiskey, June 30, 1920; 1 dau., Rosemary. Vice pres., dir. Consol. Foods Corp., Chgo.; dir. U.S. Products Corp., San Jose, Cal. Vice pres. Nat. Am. Wholesale Grocers Assn.; former pres. N.E. Wholesale Food Packers Assn. Clubs: Lakeside, Olympic Golf (San Francisco). Home: 50 Chumasero Dr. Office: Consol. Foods Corp., 230 California St., San Francisco. Died Oct. 26, 1957; buried St. Joseph Cemetery, Harvard, Ill.

KEENAN, Joseph Berry, lawyer; b. Pawtucket, R.I., Jan. 11, 1888; s. Bernard A. and Sarah (Berry) K.; A.B., M.A., Brown U., 1910; LL.B., Harvard, 1913; m. Charlotte Quigley, July 7, 1920; children—William Quigley, Joseph Berry, Betty Jean, John David. Admitted to Ohio bar, 1913, and since in practice at Cleve.; mem. firm Day, Day & Wilkin, 1919; apptd. spl. asst. to atty. gen. of Ohio to investigate crime, 1919; formed firm Keenan & Butler, 1930; apptd. spl. asst. to atty. gen. of U.S., to investigate crime, July 1933, asst. atty. gen. of U.S., in charge of criminal division of Dept. of Justice, Oct. 1933, asst. to the atty. gen., 1936-39; pvt. practice, Washington, 1939-—. U.S. chief of counsel for prosecution in trials of Japanese war criminals, Tokyo, Japan, 1946. Served with cav. Mexican border, 1916; with 137th F.A., AEF, 1917; commd. 1st lt. judge adv. gen.'s dept. Cited by Gen. Pershing "for meritorious service"; cited by French govt. "for distinguished service.' Mem. Am. Ohio, Cuyahoga County, Cleve. bar assns. Democrat. Roman Catholic. Home: 10 Hesketh St., Chevy Chase, Md. Office: Woodward Bldg., Washington. Died Dec. 8, 1954.*

KEENEY, Francis B., lawyer; b. Cambridge, Mich., Nov. 12, 1884; s. Alanson M. and Mary Jane (Dewey) K.; A.B., U. Mich., 1906, LL.B., 1908; m. Bernice Pearl Mitchell, May 30, 1910; children—Francis B., Ralph H. Admitted to R.I. bar, 1909; practicing lawyer, Providence, since 1908; v.p., dir. Chicago Stock Yards Co., F. H. Prince & Co., Inc.; trustee Brown & Sharpe Manufacturing Company Voting Trust. Member American, Rhode Island State bar assns., Phi Beta Kappa. Home: 97 Lorraine Av., Providence 6. Office: Turks Head Bldg., Providence 3. Died May 22, 1957.

KEENEY, Frederick Thomas, bishop; b. Fabius, N.Y., Feb. 9, 1863; s. Seabury B. and Melvina Esther (Andrews) K.; Ph.B., Syracuse U., 1886, Ph.M., 1889, D.D., 1900, LL.D., 1920; m. Georgia S. Smith, Aug. 3, 1886 (died May 8, 1929); 1 dau., Dorothea L. Ordained M.E. ministry, 1886; pastor Cincinnatus, N.Y., 1886-87, Tully, N.Y., 1888-89, Cazenovia, N.Y., 1890-92, Elmira, N.Y., 1893-98, Penn Yan, N.Y., 1898-99; presid'ng elder Auburn Dist., 1899-1901; pastor Elmira, 1901-04, Syracuse, N.Y., 1904-19; exec. sec. spiritual resource dept. Missionary Centenary, 1919-20; elected bishop, May 1920. Dir. Million Unit Fellowship Movement, 1936-40. Mem. Delta Kappa Epsilon, Phi Beta Kappa, Phi Kappa Phi. Home: 123 N.E. 97th St., Miami 38. Died Sept. 24, 1952; buried Oakwood Cemetery, Syracuse, N.Y.

KEENEY, Mrs. Ralph D., Rep. nat. committeewoman for Conn.; b. Hartford, Conn., Aug. 26, 1889; d. Normand Francis and Caroline White (Olmsted) Allen; ed. West Middle Sch., Hartford, Miss Dana's Sch., Morristown, N.J.; m. Ralph Denison Keeney, June 12, 1912. Mem. Conn. State Legislature, 1935-45. Club: Town and County (Hartford, Conn.). Home: Somersville, Conn. Died Apr. 13, 1959.

KEENEY, Russell Watson, congressman; b. Pittsfield, Ill., Dec. 29, 1897; s. Walter F. and Kittie Watson) K.; LL.B., De Paul U., 1919, LL M., 1921; m. Marge LaSchiavo, Nov. 18, 1950. Admitted to Ill. bar, 1919; practice law, Wheaton, Ill., 1919-53; state's atty. DuPage County, Ill., 1936-40; county judge DuPage County, 1940-53; circuit judge 16th Judicial Dist. Ill., 1953-56; mem. 85th Congress, 14th Dist. Ill. Mem. Am., Ill., DuPage County bar assns.; Ill. County and Probate Judges Assn. (past pres.), State's Atty.'s Assn. Ill. (past v.p.), DuPage County Farm Bur., DuPage County Tb Assn. (past pres.), Family Service Assn. DuPage County (v.p.), Wheaton (Ill.) C. of C., Am. Legion, 40 and 8; hon. mem. DuPage Bd. Realtors. Mason (32°, Shriner,), Moose, Elk. Home: 320 W. Seminary Av., Wheaton, Ill. Office: House Office Bldg., Washington 25. Died Jan. 11, 1958; buried Naperville (Ill.) Cemetery.

KEETON, Robert Wood, physician; b. West Point, Miss., July 7, 1883; s. James Madison and Georgia (Brown) K.; A.B., Cumberland U., 1903; student James Millikin U., 1903-05; A.B., U. Chgo., 1907, M.S., 1914; student U. Ill., 1910-12; M.D., Northwestern U., 1916; m. Emily Alcorn, Nov. 1, 1922. Taught chemistry, biology and physiology, Ill. and Tex., 1903-12; in practice internal medicine, Chgo., 1918-—; adj. prof. physiology and physiol. chemistry Albany (N.Y.) Med. Coll., 1912-14; asst. prof. pharmacology and therapeutics U. Ill., 1918-22; fellow Otho S. A. Sprague Meml. Inst., 1922-25; asso. prof. medicine Coll. Medicine, U. Ill., 1925-28, prof., 1928-51, prof. medicine emeritus, 1951, acting head of the department, 1933, head of the department, 1934-51. Chairman suburban Cook County tuberculosis sanitarium district, 1951-—. Diplomate Nat. Bd. Med. Examiners. Fellow A.C.P.; mem. A.M. A., Inst. Medicine, Am. Soc. Pharmacology and Therapeutics, Am. Physiol. Soc., Chicago Soc. Internal Medicine, Central Soc. Clin. Research, Am. Soc. Heating and Ventilating Engrs., Assn. Am. Physicians, Am. Bd. Internal Medicine, Soc. Exptl. Biology and Medicine, Miss. Valley, Ill., Chgo. med. socs., Central Interurban Clin. Club, Chgo. Heart Assn. (bd. govs.), Am. Diabetes Assn., Sigma Xi, Alpha Omega Alpha, Pi Kappa Alpha, Alpha Kappa Kappa. Presbyn. Clubs: University, Evanston Golf. Home: 1500 Hinman Av., Evanston, Ill. Office: 8 S. Michigan Av., Chgo. Died Jan. 22, 1957; buried Rosehill Cemetery, Chgo.

KEHOE, Joseph W. (kē-ō), judge; b. Portland, Ore., July 19, 1890; s. Joseph and Josephine (Thomas) K.; ed. Columbia U., Portland, Ore., 1905-09; LL.B., U. Ore., 1914; m. Katherine L. Southard, Feb. 9, 1916. Admitted to Ore. bar, 1915; in practice, Portland, 1915-17; admitted to Alaska bar, 1920; in practice, Juneau, 1920-24; U.S. commr., Ketchikan, 1924-29; in practice, Ketchikan, 1929-33; mem. Territorial Legislature, 1933 session; U.S. dist. atty. 3rd Div. Alaska, 1933-43, resigned 1943; mem. Territorial Legislature 1943 session. Spl. asst. to U.S. Atty. Gen., 1943-44; U.S. Dist. Judge, 2d Div., Alaska, 1944-51; sec. Alaska, 1951, 52. First lt. 347th F.A., U.S. Army, World War I. Mem. Am. Legion, Delta

Theta Phi. Democrat. Catholic. Elk. Address: Juneau, Alaska. Died Apr. 1959.

KEIGWIN, A(lbert) Edwin (kĕg'wĭn), clergyman; b. Clinton, Ia., July 21, 1869; s. Rev. Albert N. (D.D.) and Amanda L. (Bullock) Keigwin; A.B., Princeton Univ., 1891, A.M., 1894; Union Theol. Sem., 1894; D.D., Lafayette, 1906; LL.D., Ursinus Coll., 1928; m. Elizabeth Woodruff Gray, Apr. 18, 1911. Ordained Presbyn. ministry, 1894; pastor First Ch., Millville, N.J., 1894-1900, Park Ch., Newark, 1900-05, West End Ch., New York, 1905-46; also pres. Ursinus Coll., Pa., 1907-12. Pres. trustees Polytech. Inst. of Puerto Rico, Evangelical Sem., Rio Piedras, P.R. Mem. Presbyn. Board Home Missions, 1904-41 (pres. 1929-41); pres. Greater N.Y. Fedn. of Churches; mem. The Union League Club, Theta Delta Chi, St. David's Soc. (Welsh), S.A.R. Mason. Republican. Author: The Heart Side of the God, 1904; The Bethlehem of the Heart, 1905; The New Patriotism, 1914; The Greater Christmas, 1916; The Meaning of Life, 1923. Vice-moderator, Gen. Assembly Presbyn. Ch., U.S.A., 1937; del. from Presbyn. Ch., U.S.A., to World Conf. on Faith and Order, Edinburgh, 1937. Address: 340 Riverside Dr., N.Y. City. Died Sept. 21, 1951; buried Newton (N.J.) Cemetery.

KEIM, Franklin David, agronomist; b. Hardy, Neb., Sept. 10, 1886; s. Dennis and Jennie (Cramer) K.; ed. Bethany Coll. Acad., Peru State Normal; B. Sc., U. Neb., 1914, M.Sc., 1918; Ph.D., Cornell U., 1927; m. Alice Mary Voigt, June 12, 1914; children—Virginia (Mrs. William Honstead), Wayne Franklin. Tchr. in schs. of Nuckolls and Thayer Counties, 1905-08; prin. Chester (Neb.) High Sch., 1909-10; supt. schs., Blue Springs, 1910-11; mem. faculty U. Neb., 1914—, asst. in agronomy dept., 1914-16, extension specialist in agronomy, 1917-18, prof. agronomy, 1918—, acting chmn. dept. agronomy, 1930-32, chmn. 1932-52, ret.; chief agrl. sect. Biarritz Am. Army U., France, 1945. Dir. Union Nat. Ins. Co. (mem. exec. com.), Farmers State Bank. Received Plaque, Neb. Crop Improvement Assn., 1950; certificate of appreciation, 36 yrs. loyal service, U. Neb. Mem. C. of C., Farm House Frat., N.S.T.A., Nat. Geog. Soc., Am. Soc. Agronomy (past pres.), North Central Weed Com. (past v.p.), A.A.A.S. N.E.A., Neb. Writers Guild, Sigma Xi (past pres.), Gamma Sigma Delta. Mason (Shriner). Author numerous publs. on grass and weed research. Attended Grasslands Conf., Wales, summer 1937. Home: 1400 North 37th St., Lincoln 3, Neb. Died Mar. 7, 1956.

KEISER, George Camp, architect; b. Milwaukee, Nov. 2, 1900; s. George Edward and Mary Bigelow (Camp) K.; A.B., Harvard, 1924; B.Arch., Columbia, 1930; m. Nancy Hull, Sept. 16, 1938; children—Mary Damaris, Anne Blossom. Draftsman, John A. Rogers and David Hyer, Winter Park, Fla., 1934-36; designer Jas. Gamble Rogers, II, 1936-38; research in Islamic architecture and travel in Middle East, 1938; pvt. practice architecture, Winter Park, Fla., since 1938; founder The Middle East Inst., Washington, 1946, and since served as chmn. bd. govs.; pres. The George C. Keiser Found. since 1948; director Cuban Am. and Guantanamo sugar cos. Hon. dir. Florida Symphony Orchestra. Registered architect, Fla., Conn., D.C., National Council Archtl. Registration Bds. Mem. A.I.A., Fgn. Service Ednl. Found. (trustee), Am. Research Center in Egypt (trustee), Fla. Assn. Architects, Conn. Soc. Architects. Clubs: Metropolitan (Washington); Harvard (N.Y.C. and of Central Fla.); Century (N.Y.C.). Contbr. archtl. drawings and photographs to Archtl. Record; Moore, The Romans World; The Near East and the Great Powers, 1951. Home: 4344 Forest Lane, Washington; also 550 Via Lagano, Winter Park, Fla. Office: 1763 N St. N.W., Washington. Died Mar. 23, 1956.

KEITH, Allen Phelps, supt. schs.; b. Bridgewater, Mass., Dec. 18, 1872; s. Alfred Thomas and Mary B. (Phelps) K.; ed. State Normal Sch., Bridgewater, 1890-94; Ed.M., R.I. State Tchrs. Coll., 1929; m. Emma L. Harriman, June 26, 1900; children—Arthur Reginald, Doris, Allen Phelps. Began as tchr. Pascoag, R.I., 1894-95; supt. Burrillville 1895-1904, East Providence, 1904-06; prin. grade sch., New Bedford, Mass., 1906-08, supt. schs., 1908-42, ret. Bd. trustees Bristol County Agrl. Sch., 1914-38. Mem. N.E.A. (life), N.E. Supts. Assn., Mass. Supts. Assn. Republican. Conglist. Mason (K.T.). Rotarian. Home: 20 Locust St., New Bedford, Mass. Died Sept. 25, 1947.

KELCE, L. Russell, business exec.; b. Pittsburg, Kan., Aug. 5, 1897; s. David and Etta Emilene (White) K.; student pub. schs.; m. Gladys Agnes, Sept. 20, 1920; 1 son, Robert David. Joined Sinclair Coal Co., Kansas City, Mo., 1924, pres. since 1949, dir., 1930—; pres. Peabody Coal Co., 1955—, dir. (Peabody Coal Co. acquired the Sinclair group of coal cos. 1955); chmn., dir. C.G.W. R.R., Rail to Water Transfer Co.; president, dir. So. Coal Co., Sentry Royalty Co., Broken Aro Coal Co., Bevier Coal Co., Hume-Sinclair Coal Mining Co., Lynville Coal Co., No. Ill. Coal Corp., Pershing Coal Co., Portal Coals, Ltd., Power Coal Co., Rogers Co. Coal Co., Seminole Coal Corp., Sinclair Mines, Inc., Sinclair Mines (Can.) Ltd., Sunlight Coal Co., Tecumseh Coal Corp.; v.p., dir. Homestead Coal Co., Key Coal Co. Mem. Am. Inst. Mining Engrs. Mason (Shriner). Clubs: Kansas City, River, Rotary, Saddle and Sirloin (Kansas City, Mo.); Bohemian (San Francisco); Chicago. Office: 114 W. 11th St., Kansas City, Mo. Died June 30, 1957; buried Pittsburgh, Kan.

KELLAR, Chambers, lawyer; b. Memphis, Mar. 4, 1867; s. Andrew J. and Margaret Agnes (Chambers) K.; B.S., Vanderbilt, 1887; founder's medalist, class rep., fellowship in English, same univ., postgrad. work 1 year; LL.D., Dakota Wesleyan U., 1934; m. Florence Bullock, Feb. 19, 1902. City atty. Hot Springs, S.D., 1891; state's atty. Fall River County, 1892; gen. counsel Homestake Mining Co., 1904—; chmn. bd., dir. and atty. 1st Nat. Bank of Black Hills, Rapid City, S.D. Mem. S.D. (ex-pres.), Cal., Am. bar assns., Nat. Assn. Audubon Socs., Phi Delta Theta. Republican. Episcopalian. Mason (Shriner); charter mem. and organizer S.D. Soc. S.A.R. First to suggest adoption by the Govt. of the use of the shot gun in World War. Home: Lead, S.D. Died May 19, 1950.

KELLAR, Herbert Anthony, hist. assn. exec.; b. Hooper, Neb., Feb. 21, 1887; s. George and Mary Elizabeth (Summers) K.; U. of Chicago, 1909; grad. student Leland Stanford U., 1909-11, U. of Wis., 1911-13; LL.D. Augustana College, Rock Island, Ill., 1947; m. Dorothy Marion Alderton, Sept. 12, 1912; m. 2d, Lucile Edith O'Connor, Feb. 1, 1935; 1 dau., Alecea Summers. Teacher history and English, Manzanita Hall, Palo Alto, Calif., 1909-11; asst. in European history, U. of Wis., 1911-13; instr. medieval history, U. of Texas, 1913-14; instr. European and Am. History, U. of Minn., 1914-15; dir. McCormick Hist. Assn., Chgo., 1915-51, coordinator McCormick Collection, State Hist. Soc. Wis., 1951—, dir. exptl. division library cooperation, Library of Congress, 1941-42. Walter Lynwood Fleming lecturer on southern history, La. State U., 1939. Made survey of archives, State of Minn. for Am. Hist. Assn., 1914-15; in charge McCormick Centennial celebration, Va. Poly. Inst. and Washington and Lee U., 1931; dir. hist. restoration work, period 1800-31, Walnut Grove Plantation, Rockbridge County, Va., 1937-38. Chmn. nat. adv. com. of hist. records survey projects, W.P.A., 1940-42. Mem. com. on microcopying materials for research (copying hist. and cultural records in war zone), Am. Council of Learned Socs. 1940-46 (chmn. subcom. on selection of materials, 1941-46); member Chicago Metropolitan Library Council, 1945-46; mem. com. consultants in archives and history to Va. 350th Anniversary Commn., 1954-55; mem. adv. bd. Columbia Studies in History of Am. Agr., 1954-55. Mem. Am. Hist. Assn. (chmn. com. on historical source materials 1939-46, chairman com. on manuscripts, 1947-48), Miss. Valley Hist. Assn. (com. on policy 1944-47 pres. 1946-47), Southern Hist. Assn., Agrl. History Soc. (v.p. 1921-22, pres. 1922-24, sec.-treas. 1924-27), Soc. Am. Archivists (v.p. 1940-41, mem. council 1942-45, v.p. 1948-49); Council Econ. History Soc., 1941, Am. Assn. for State and Local History (mem. council, 1940-46); Am. Mil. Inst., Am. Documentation Inst., Oregon History Soc., Nat. Society Autograph Collectors, Historical Society Western Pa., Ill., La., Peoria (Ill.), Augustana and Rockbridge hist. socs., Philos. Soc. Tex., State Hist. Soc. Wis., Alpha Pi, Phi Gamma Delta. Clubs: Westerners, Civil War Round Table (Chicago); Milwaukee. Mem. bd. of editors Miss. Valley Historical Review, 1924-25, Agricultural History, 1929—. Compiler and editor: Solon Robinson, Pioneer and Agriculturist, 2 vols., 1936. Author: Memoranda on Library Cooperation, 1941. Contbr. to Crusade and Other Historical Essays, 1928; Dictionary of American Biography, 1928-37; also articles, documents, and reviews in hist. and library periodicals. Hist. advisor to moving picture Romance of the Reaper. Home: 973 University Bay Drive, Madison 5. Office: State Historical Society of Wisconsin, Madison, Wis. Died Oct. 8, 1955; buried Madison.

KELLEHER, Michael T(homas), business exec.; b. Cambridge, Mass., Jan. 30, 1897; s. Michael and Mary (Kilderry) K.; student Cambridge Latin Sch., 1909-14, Am. Inst. Banking, 1919-21; A.M. (hon.), Tufts Coll., 1948; LL.D., St. Anselms Coll., 1955; m. Mary Doyle, Oct. 9, 1929. Vice pres. Marsh & McLennan, Inc., Boston, 1938—; dir. Sheraton Plaza Hotel, Second Bank-State Street Trust Co., William Filene's Sons Co., Boston Mut. Life Ins. Co., Union Freight R.R. Co., Boston Garden-Arena Corp.; trustee Provident Instn. for Savs., Old Colony Charitable Trust; incorporator Greater Boston Charitable Trust, Mass. Bus. Development Corp. Mem. corp. Mass. Gen. Hosp., United Prison Assn. Mass.; vice chmn. Mass. Com. Catholics, Protestants and Jews. Trustee Boston Symphony Orchestra, Children's Hosp., Faulkner Hosp. Mem. com. pub. relations Boston U.; trustee, mem. com. on facilities Northeastern U. Chmn. exec. com. Nat. Cath. Community Service, Washington; pres. United Def. Fund, Inc., N.Y.C.; v.p., mem. exec. com. U.S.O. Dir. West End House, Boston Municipal Research Bur., Mass. Safety Council. Mem. Big Brother Assn. Boston, Boston Civic Improvement Com., Mass. Commn. Against Discrimination, Mass. Council for Pub. Schs., Mass. Soc. Med. Research, Nat. Fund. Med. Edn., Boston Maritime Assn., New Eng. Colls. Fund, Inc., New Eng. Council, United Negro Colls. Fund. Mem. Am. Irish Hist. Soc., Charitable Irish Soc., Bank Officers Assn., Ins. Brokers Assn., Cambridge C. of C., Newcomen Soc. N.A., English-Speaking Union, Bostonian Soc., Friends of Boston Symphony Orchestra, Am. Cancer Soc., N.A. A.C.P., United Fund Met. Boston, Forty Plus Club of New Eng., Navy League U.S., Am. Legion. Roman Catholic. Elk, K.C., Knight of Malta, Knight of Holy Sepulchre. Clubs: Gridiron, Commercial and Merchants, Aero, Clover (past pres.), Algonquin, Down Town, Boston Madison Square Garden, Cambridge, Y.D. (hon.), Press (hon.), Publicity (hon.). Home: 51 Beacon St. Office: 140 Federal St., Boston. Died 1958.

KELLER, Albert Galloway, educator; b. Springfield, O., Apr. 10, 1874; s. Jeremiah and Laura Stephenson (Smith) K.; A.B., Yale, 1896, Ph.D., 1899; m. Caroline Louise Gussmann, July 16, 1898; children—Caroline, Deane, Elsa. Instr. social science Yale, 1900-02, asst. prof., 1902-07, prof. science of society, 1907-42, prof. emeritus, 1942—. Served as capt. morale br. Gen. Staff, U.S. Army, Nov., Dec. 1918. Mem. Sigma Xi, Phi Beta Kappa. Author: Homeric Society, 1902, 1906; Queries in Ethnography, 1903; Cuestionario Etnográfico, México, 1907; Colonization, 1908; Physical and Commercial Geography (with H. E. Gregory and A. L. Bishop), 1910; Commercial and Industrial Geography (with A. L. Bishop), 1912; Societal Evolution, 1915, 32, 47, Japanese edit., 1919; Industry and Trade (with A. L. Bishop), 1918; Through War to Peace, 1918, 21; Evolution of Man (with others), 1922, 2d edit., as Evolution of the Earth and Man, 1929; Starting-Points in Social Science, 1923, 25, 47; (with W. G. Sumner) Science of Society, 4 vols., 1927; Man's Rough Road, 1932; Reminiscences of William Graham Sumner, 1933; Brass Tacks, 1938; Net Impressions, 1942. Editor: J. Scott Keltie's History of Africa, 1906; W. G. Sumner's War and Other Essays, 1911; Earth Hunger and Other Essays, 1913; The Challenge of Facts and Other Essays, 1914; The Forgotten Man and Other Essays, 1919; Selected Essays of William Graham Sumner (with M. R. Davie), 1924; Essays of William Graham Sumner (2 vols., with M. R. Davie), 1934; The Forgotten Man's Almanac, 1943; All of Us, 1944. Address: 55 Huntington St., New Haven 11. Died Oct. 31, 1956.

KELLER, Carl Tilden, accountant; b. Ft. Kearney, Neb., Aug. 26, 1872; s. Jasper Newton and Betty Scott (Henshaw) K.; student Boston Latin Sch., 1885-89; A.B., Harvard, 1894; m. Marian Mandell, Jan. 12, 1898 (dec. July 20, 1954). Clerk American Tel. & Tel. Co., N.Y.C., 1894, manager Mpls. and St. Paul offices, 1898; commercial agt. C.,R.I.&P. Ry., Denver, Colo. Springs and Cripple Creek, 1898-1901; supt. contract dept. N.E. Telephone & Telegraph Co., Boston, 1901-1907, gen. commercial supt., 1907-14, asst. gen. mgr., 1910-14; partner Lybrand, Ross Bros. & Montgomery, Boston, since 1915. Div. dir. of accounts, Am. Red Cross, World War. Dir. Boys' Clubs of Boston; vice chmn. and trustee Harvard-Yenching Institute; mem. visitors coms. Romance Language Dept., Library, Semitic and Egyptian Civilizations, University Press, Harvard; mem., trustee and treasurer of American Research Center in Egypt, Inc. Fellow A.A.A.S., Royal Geog. Society, Royal Asiatic Soc., Royal Central Asian Soc., Am. Geog. Soc.; East Asiatic Society, Am. Academy Arts and Sciences; mem. Middle East Inst., Am. Oriental Soc., Inst. of Pacific Relations, Archaeol. Inst. America, Newcomen Soc. Episcopalian. Clubs: University, Coffee House (New York); Odd Volumes, Union, Harvard, The Country (Boston); St. Maurice Fish and Game (La Tuque, Can.); Mount Royal (Montreal). Home: Peterborough, N.H. Office: 80 Federal St., Boston 10. Died May 13, 1955.

KELLER, Henry Jr., economist; b. Bellefonte, Pa., June 11, 1895; s. Harry and Anna Mary (Orvis) K.; B.S., Pa. State Coll., 1920; M.S., U. of Wis., 1921, Ph.D. in Agricultural Economics, U. of Wis., 1931; married Eleanor Schofield Parker, February 5, 1921 (dec. 1950); children—Henry Parker, Kenneth Parker; m. 2d Patricia R. Rhett, June 15, 1951. Asst., U. Wis., 1920-22; asst. prof. agrl. economics, Rutgers U., 1922-27, asso. prof., 1927-28, prof. agrl. economics since 1928. Enlisted in U.S. Army, Apr. 1917, commd. 2d lt., Inf. Corps, 1918; served in France, Apr.-Sept. 1918; disch. with rank of 1st lt., 1919. Wounded in action, Vesle River, Aug. 12, 1918. Mem. Am. Arbitration Assn. (nat. panel arbitrators), Am. Econ. Assn., Am. Statis. Assn., Am. Acad. Polit. and Social Science, Econometric Soc., Am. Farm Econ. Assn., Am. Geog. Soc. of New York. Presbyterian. Home: 1217 Cushing Rd., Plainfield, N.J. Died Nov. 22, 1954.

KELLER, Kent Ellsworth, ex-congressman; b. nr. Ava., Ill.; s. Phillip Jacob and Harriet Elizabeth (Bradley) K.; M.A., So. Ill. Normal U.; student Heidelberg U., Germany; had 5 yrs. mil. tng.; volunteered for mil. service, Spanish-Am. War, World War I and II; LL.B., St. Louis Law Sch.; m. Olive Robinson. Founder Ava Community High Sch. and teacher 5 yrs.; practiced law 1 yr.; gave up law practice on account of ill health and spent 12 yrs. in

Mexico, engaging extensively in mining; returned to Ill., 1912; mem. Ill. Senate from 44th Dist., 1913-17; mem. 72d to 76th Congresses, 25th Ill. Dist.; spl. asst. to U.S. ambassador to Mexico, 1945—. Known as campaign speaker, having appeared in 28 states under Dem. Nat. Com. Trustee School of Expression, Boston, 10 yrs.; v.p. for Ill. of Am. Rose Soc. Baptist. Author: Prosperity Through Employment; Strategy and the World War (I); An American School Army; Never Again (a book on deflation). Contbr. to mags. on preparedness and unemployment. Home: Ava, Ill. Died Sept. 3, 1954; buried Ava Evergreen Cemetery.

KELLETER, Paul Delmar (kĕl'lĕ-tĕr), forester; b. St. Louis, May 1, 1881; s. Carl and Pauline Josephine (Thomas) K.; grad. Central High Sch., St. Louis, 1899; A.B., Washington U., 1902; M.F., Yale, 1904; m. Lucy Taber Pool, Oct. 21, 1908; children—Helen, Paul. Forest supervisor Black Hills Nat. Forest, S. Dak., 1909-18; spl. rep. of sec. of agr. and chmn. bd. of exchange of 60,000 acres sch. lands with S.Dak., 1910-12; duty with dept. at Washington, 1918-23; dir. purchases and sales, Office Sec. of Agr., 1923-25; dir. extension, N.Y. State College Forestry, 1925-29; administrative asst., Federal Farm Bd., Washington, 1929; conservation dir. State of Wis., 1930-34; forest supervisor Huron Nat. Forest, Mich., 1934, Clark Nat. Forest, Mo., 1935-45; U.S. forest coordinator for State of Mo., 1945-46. Pres. Columbia Social Service Society, 1948-49. Mem. U.S. Dept. Agr. State War Board, 1940-46. Sec. Lawrence County (S.Dak.) Fuel and Food Adminstrns., 1917, 18, World War; pres. Sch. Bd., Deadwood, 1917; mayor of Kensington, Md., 2 terms, 1922-25. Mem. State Commn. of Resources and Development, 1943-45; state-wide com. on forestry for Mo. Sr. mem. Soc. Am. Foresters (sec. and mem. exec. council, 1919-20, 21), Mo. Assn. Social Welfare, State Hist. Soc. of Mo., Phi Kappa Phi, Kappa Phi Kappa, Alpha Xi Sigma, Robinhood, Naturalists Club. Republican. Episcopalian. Mason (32°, Shriner). Writer and speaker on forestry topics. Address: 1405 Pratt St., Columbia, Mo. Died Mar. 19, 1950; buried Glenwood Cemetery, Washington.

KELLEY, Augustine Bernard, congressman; b. New Baltimore, Pa., July 9, 1883; s. Abraham Francis and Mary Elizabeth (Kegg) K.; student parochial and pub. grade schs. and Greensburg (Pa.) High Sch. U.S. Mil. Acad.; studied mining engring. Internat. Corr. Schs., 1907-12, bus. adminstrn., Alexander Hamilton Inst., 1930-33; m. Ella Marie Bates, June 24, 1913 (Catholic Mother of America, 1944); children—Augustine Regis, Robert Vincent, Richard Bates, Jay Hilary, Paul Aloysius, Marcella Marie, Therese Eleanor, Katherine Anne, James Reeves. Member of scale, 1934-38, owner and operator of coal mines, Mammoth Coal Coke Co. (mines and coke ovens at Mammoth, Pa.), receiver, Lacosto Coal Co., and Fairfield Coal Co., 1924-26. Member 77th to 82d Congresses, from 27th Pa. Dist.; mem. 83d, 84th Congresses, 21st Pa. Dist. Mem. Am. Inst. Mining and Metall. Engrs., Assn. of Graduates of U.S. Mil. Acad. (life mem.), Army Athletic Assn., Pitts. Athletic Assn. Democrat. Clubs: Army and Navy (Washington), Kenwood Country Club. Home: 231 Westmoreland Av., Greensburg, Pa. Died Nov. 20, 1957.

KELLEY, Camille McGee, judge, lectr.; b. Trenton, Tenn.; d. Dr. John Preston and Virginia (Elder) McGee; acad. edn., also 2 yrs. in medicine; D.C.L. (Hon.) Southwestern University (Memphis), 1947; later studied law; m. Thomas Fitzgerald Kelley (now deceased); children—Lieutenant Comdr. Heiskell B. Gerald (deceased), Evelynn Camille (deceased). Judge Municipal Juvenile and Non-Support Court, Memphis, 1920— (2d woman juvenile court judge in U.S., 1st in the South); has handled 48,000 cases of human behavior involving children; lecturer on child welfare, behavior, crime prevention and citizenship. Appeared on many National radio and TV programs. Mem. Nat. Assn. of Juvenile Court Judges, Nat. Probation Assn., Y.W.C.A., Iota Tau Tau; member National and local Federation Bus. Profl. Women's Clubs (exec. staff), Am. Penwomen, Zonta Internat., Memphis and Shelby County Parent Teachers Assn. (charter mem.), Am. Platform Guild, Civil Air Patrol League of Am., Pilot International (hon. mem.), only woman member Internat. Optimists Club of Am. Received Scroll of Honor from Gen. Fedn. Women's Clubs, as one of 50 outstanding women of America, 1942. Named by Zonta Internat. one of Am.'s 5 greatest women. Selected as one of the 6 Most Wholesome Women of the World, by Women's Research Guild, N.Y., 1948, Outstanding Woman in Tenn. History, 1954; recipient achievement placque, men's civic clubs. Mem. conf. on Prevention and Control of Juvenile Delinquency, Nov. 1947. Democrat. Protestant. Author: "Delinquent Angels," 1947; Kelleygrams, 1948. Contbr. to mags. and ednl. publs. Home: 1688 Carruthers Av. Address Juvenile Court, 616 Adams Av., Memphis. Died Jan. 28, 1955; buried Forest Hill Cemetery, Memphis.

KELLEY, Cornelius Francis, lawyer; b. Mineral Hill, Nev., Feb. 10, 1875; s. Jeremiah C. and Hannah (Murphy) K.; LL.B., U. of Mich., 1898; D.C.S. (honorary), New York University, 1950; m. Mary Tremblay, June 2, 1903; children—Mrs. Katherine Florman (dec.), Mrs. Mary Dorothy Keresey (dec.), Mrs. Frances Theresa Keresey, Mrs. Cornelia Adrienne Hepburn, Mrs. Mary Tremblay Doubleday. Began practice at Butte, 1898; asst. county atty. Silver Bow County, 1899-1901; mem. Mont. Ho. of Rep., 1899-1901; candidate of Independent Dem. Party for Congress, 1900; entered legal dept. Anaconda Copper Mining Co., 1901, gen. counsel, 1908, v.p., 1911, pres. and dir., 1918-40, chmn. bd. dirs., 1940-55, retired but continues as a director; also dir. Andes Copper Mining Co., Chile Copper Co., Chile Exploration Co., Anaconda Sales Co., Butte, Anaconda & Pacific Railway Company, Anaconda Aluminum Co., Internat. Smelting and Refining Co., Mines Investment Corp., Santiago Mining Co., Am. Brass Co., Anaconda-American Brass Co., Ltd., Andes Exploration Co. of Me., Butte Water Co., Greene Cananea Copper Co., Guaranty Trust Co. of New York, Washoe Copper Company, Arizona Oil Co., Chile Steamship Company, Incorporated, Anaconda Export Co., Petrerillos Ry. Co., Anaconda Wire & Cable Company Pres.; trustee St. Patricks Cathedral. Mem. American Bar Assn., Montana State Bar Assn., Am. Mining Congress, Am. Inst. Mining and Metall. Engrs. Catholic. Clubs: Montana (Helena); Univ. of Mich.; The Links (New York); Gulf Stream (Fla.). Home: Shelter Rock Rd., Manhasset, L.I., N.Y. Office: Room 1800, 25 Broadway, N.Y.C. Died May 12, 1957.

KELLEY, Frank Harrison, naval officer (ret.); b. New Haven, Feb. 26, 1889; s. Frank Harrison and Jean (Richardson) K.; S.B., U.S. Naval Acad., 1910; m. Claire Parmelee, May 12, 1912; children—Janet Claire (Mrs. Joe S. Pearson), Frank Harrison, Edmund Parmelee, Archie Parmelee, Helen Patricia. Commd. ensign USN, 1912, advanced through grades to rear adm., 1946; served on all oceans and in all types naval ships; comdg. officer U.S.S. West Point, 1941-43; comdr. U.S. Naval Tng. Center, Farragut, Ida., 1943-46; ret. from active service, Dec. 1, 1946; pres., bd. dirs. Farragut Coll. and Tech. Inst., Sept. 1946—. Decorated Bronze Star Medal. Home: House 11-C-12, Farragut College and Technical Inst., Farragut, Ida. Died Nov. 19, 1953.

KELLEY, Phelps, mfg. exec.; b. Chgo., Sept. 7, 1901; s. William V. and Lilian (Phelps) K.; student Chgo. Latin Sch., Hotchkiss Sch.; B.A., Yale, 1924; m. Mary Louise Cotton, Oct. 25, 1924; children—Phelps Cotton, Brooks Mather, Cynthia Cotton. Corp. dept. Halsey Stuart & Co., 1925-35; dir., asst. to pres. Miehle Printing Press & Mfg. Co., Chgo., 1936-40, v.p., 1940-46, exec. v.p. 1946-57; exec. v.p., dir. Miehle-Goss-Dexter, Inc., 1957—; dir. DeFlorez Co., Mercury Engring. Co., Union Spl. Machine Co., Krim-Ko Co., Miehle Printing Press & Mfg. Co., Ltd. Trustee Council Technol. Development. Trustee Ill. Inst. Tech., Armour Research Found. Dir. Lyric Opera of Chgo. Episcopalian. Clubs: Shoreacres Attic, Chicago, Tavern, Onwentsia, Old Elm. Home: St. Mary's Rd. Libertyville, Ill. Office: 2011 Hastings St., Chgo. 8. Died Mar. 5, 1959; buried Lake Forest (Ill.) Cemetery.

KELLOGG, George Dwight, coll. prof.; b. St. Louis, Mo., June 28, 1873; s. Sanford Brown and Louise Parker (Allen) K.; A.B., Yale, 1895, Ph.D., 1898; fellow Am. Sch. Classical Studies in Rome, 1899-1900; studied in Germany, 1899, 1913; m. Anna Mary Collins, June 18, 1914; children—Helen Stewart (Mrs. Stanley Brampton Parker, Jr.), George Dwight. Asst. in Latin, 1896-97, instr., 1898-99, tutor, 1900-03, Yale; asst. prof. Greek and Latin, 1903-05, Williams Coll.; preceptor and asst. prof. classics, Princeton, 1905-11; prof. Latin lang. and lit., Union U., since 1911, acting prof. of American history, 1920-21, head Dept. of Ancient Classics since 1923, acting head Dept. of Philosophy, 1924-25, acting head Dept. of Econ., 1925-26; prof. emeritus, 1943-46. Lecturer in English. Visiting prof. of Latin, Univ. of Chicago, summer quarter, 1920; Syracuse University, summer sessions, 1926-28, 1930; Columbia University, summer sessions, 1931, 32. Mem. Am. Philol. Assn., Classical Assn. Atlantic States (v.p. 1906-10, 1911-12), British Classical Association, Society for Promotion of Byzantine and Modern Greek Studies, American Association Univ. Profs., Phi Beta Kappa (pres. of Alpha of N.Y., 1924-28); pres. Classical Sect. N.Y. State Teachers' Assn., 1917-19; etc. Republican. Presbyterian. Contbr. to Am. Jour. Philology, Classical Weekly, Proc. of Am. Philol. Assn., etc. Asso. editor Classical Weekly, 1925-35. Home: 1546 Wendell Av., Schenectady. Died Sept. 19, 1955.

KELLOGG, Gordon Hill, can mfg. exec.; b. Fairport, N.Y., Dec. 26, 1884; s. Myron J. and Mary (Hill) K.; grad. Colgate U., 1906; student Williams Coll.; m. Alice Richards Stringer, Oct. 2, 1909; children—Gordon Hill, L. Bradley. With Sanitary Can Co., Fairport, N.Y., 1907-08; with American Can Co., 1909—, mgr., Fairport, N.Y., 1909-12, dist. sales mgr., Rochester, N.Y., 1912-25, asst. gen. mgr. of sales, N.Y.C., 1926-32, gen. mgr. sales, N.Y.C., 1932-36, vice pres. in charge packers can sales, N.Y. C., 1936-40, v.p. in charge Central Div., Chgo., 1941—; dir. Crane Co. Pres. Canning Machinery and Supplies Assn., 1928, 29. Mem. Delta Kappa Epsilon. Republican. Presbyn. Clubs: Glen View, Chicago, Chicago Athletic Assn., University (Chgo.). Home: 1420 Lake Shore Dr., Chgo. 10. Office: 104 S. Michigan Av., Chgo. 3. Died Aug. 21, 1955.*

KELLOGG, Louise Phelps, historian; b. Milwaukee, Wis.; d. Amherst Willoughby and Belle M. (Phelps) K.; B.L., U. of Wis., 1897, Ph.D., 1901, Litt. D., 1926, for services to Wisconsin history; L.H.D., Marquette U., 1937; matriculated U. Paris and London School History and Economics. Asst. in history U. Wis., 1899-1900; fellow in Am. history, same, 1900-01; research associate State Hist. Society of Wis. 1901—; editorial asst. to Dr. R. G. Thwaites in early Western history, 1902-13. First sec. Woman's Com. Dane County Council Defense, 1917. Mem. Am. Hist. Assn., Miss. Valley Hist. Assn. (pres. 1930-31), Wis. Archaeol. Soc., Mo. Hist. Soc. (hon.), Am. Assn. University Women, League Women Voters, P.E.O., Am. Library Assoc.; former fellow Royal Historical Society of Gt. Britain. Awarded Lapham medal by Wis. Archeol. Soc., 1935. Episcopalian. Club: Madison Literary. Author: American Colonial Charter (Winsor Prize essay), 1904; The French Régime in Wisconsin and the Northwest, 1925; The British Régime in Wisconsin and the Northwest, 1935; Historic Wisconsin 1939. Editor: Frontier Advance on the Upper Ohio, 1916; Frontier Retreat on the Upper Ohio, 1917; Early Narratives of the Northwest, 1917; Charlevoix's Journal of a Voyage to North America, 1923; Juliette A. Kinzie Wau-Bun, 1932. Joint editor: (with Dr. R. G. Thwaites) Documentary History of Dumore's War, 1905; Revolution on the Upper Ohio, 1908; Frontier Defense on the Upper Ohio, 1912. Home: 511 N. Carroll St. Address: Wisconsin Historical Library, Madison, Wis. Died July 11, 1942.

KELLOGG, Morris W(oodruff), business exec.; b. Elizabeth, N.J., Jan. 16, 1873; s. James C. and Elizabeth (Woodruff) K.; student Stevens Inst. of Tech., Hoboken, N.J., 1890-94; m. Marie Winthrop, Oct. 6, 1910; children—Helen (Mrs. Maitland A. Edey), Beatrice (Mrs. Harvey C. McClintock). Pres. The M. W. Kellogg Co., N.Y. City, since 1905, chmn. of the bd. since 1946; pres. and dir. Canadian Kellogg Co., Ltd., since 1911; chmn. and dir. Kellex Corp., 1947-50; chmn. of the bd. Pullman, Inc., since 1950. Dir. and mem. exec. com. Am. Can Co., Guaranty Trust Co.; dir. Gasoline Products Co., Pullman, Inc., Polymerization Process Corp. Trustee New York Trade Sch. since 1937. Clubs: Links, Knickerbocker, Piping Rock, Links Golf, Racquet and Tennis. Home: Brookville, L.I., N.Y. Office: 225 Broadway, N.Y.C. 7. Died Feb. 22, 1952.

KELLOGG, Paul Underwood, editor; b. Kalamazoo, Mich., Sept. 30, 1879; s. Frank Israel and Mary Foster (Underwood) K.; spl. courses, Columbia, 1901-06, New York Sch. Social Work, 1902; hon. A.M., Amherst 1911; hon. Litt.D., Wesleyan U., 1937; m. Marion Pearce Sherwood, Oct. 5, 1909; children—Richard Patrick, Mercy Pearce; m. 2d, Helen Hall, Feb. 26, 1935. Reporter and city editor, Kalamazoo Daily Telegraph, 1898-1901; mng. editor of periodicals merged in The Survey, 1902-11; editor The Survey, 1912-42 (inc. Survey Graphic, 1921, Survey Midmonthly, 1923, merged 1949); dir. Pittsburgh Survey, 1907-10; one of founders of Survey Assos. Inc., 1911; chmn. com. on occupational standards Nat. Conf. Charities and Correction, 1910; sec. com. to secure U.S. Commission on Industrial Relations, 1911-12; mem. bd. Am. Union Against Militarism, 1914-17; dir. editorial and hist. bur., dept. civil affairs Am. Red Cross, Paris, 1917-18; mem. com. of inquiry on needs of refugees, Emergency Red Cross Commn., Italy, 1917; initiator (1918) and mem. bd. Foreign Policy Assn.; mem. advisory com. Penn Agrl. and Industrial Sch., St. Helena, S.C.; mem. bd. Nat. Federation of Settlements; mem. federal action com. Am. Assn. of Social Workers, 1932-33; vice chmn. advisory council, President's Com. on Econ. Security, 1934-35; chmn. advisory council N.Y. State Employment Service, 1934; mem. Am. Com. on Ethiopian Crisis, 1935; mem. bd. Am. Union for Concerted Peace Efforts, 1939; mem. Good Neighbor Com. on the Emigre and the Community, 1939; pres. Nat. Conf. of Social Work, 1939; mem. board Com. on Dem. Foreign Policy in 1942. Awarded medal for "distinguished and courageous journalism," N.Y. Evening Post Alumni Assn., 1935. Editor findings of Pittsburgh Survey (6 vols.). Joint Author: (with Arthur Gleason) British Labor and the War, 1918. Home: Henry Street Settlement, 265 Henry St., N.Y.C. Office: 112 E. 19th St., N.Y.C. Died Nov. 1, 1958.

KELLOGG, Robert James, philologist; b. North Fairfield, O., July 7, 1869; s. Theron Hotchkiss and Frances Esther (Penfield) K.; A.B., Cornell U., 1891, President White scholar in classics, and fellow in comparative philology same univ., Ph.D., 1896; studied U. Berlin, Harvard, U. Chgo.; Harrison research fellow in linguistic psychology U. Pa., 1922-23; m. Georgia Belle Houghton, June 27, 1895; children—Mrs. Carrie Frances Henderson, Mrs. Delora Belle Simons. Instr. modern langs. Ithaca (N.Y.) High Sch., 1895-96, in Greek, Colgate U., 1896-97; prof. Greek, Richmond (Va.) Coll., 1897-1901; instr. German, Cornell U., 1901-02; prof. modern langs. Millikin U., 1903-18, Denison U., Granville, O., 1918-

20; prof. modern langs. Okla. Bapt. U., 1920-23, prof. Greek and linguistics, 1923-25; prof. modern langs. and linguistics Ottawa U., 1925-30; oriental research at U. Kan., 1930-33. Mem. Modern Lang. Assn. America (life), Am. Philol. Assn. (life), Linguistic Soc. Am., Am. Oriental Soc. (v.p. Middle-West br., 1927, pres. 1927-28), Indogermanische Gesellschaft, Deutsche Morganländische Gesellschaft; Vorderasiatisch-Agyptische Gesellschaft, Soc. des Études Hitt. et Asianiques, Oriental Inst., Am. Sch. of Oriental Research, Egypt Exploration Soc., Phi Beta Kappa. Baptist. Mason. Author: Studies in Linguistic Psychology, 1912; Indo-European Coincidences in Hittite, 1925; Hittite Numerals, 1926. Contbr. to Collitz Festchrift, 1930; also articles and lectures on linguistic subjects. Address: 1401 N. Market St., Shawnee, Okla. Died Apr. 29, 1951; buried Shawnee.

KELLOGG, Walter Guest, lawyer; b. Ogdensburg, N.Y., Apr. 23, 1877; s. John Morris and Henrietta Powers (Guest) K.; student Union Coll., 1895-96; A.B., Columbia, 1899 (sr. class poet); student New York Law Sch.; LL.D., St. Lawrence U., 1917, Columbia University, 1929; Doctor of Letters, Union College, 1949; married Mary Peronne Hall, 1906; m. 2d, Agnes Lauriha, 1942. Practiced law, Ogdensburg, 1901—; special counsel General Electric Co., 1922—. Elected regent University of State of N.Y., 1914, reelected, 1916, for term of 12 yrs., resigned 1929; apptd. hon. fellow in English, Union Coll., 1934. Maj., judge adv. gen.'s dept., U.S. Army, 1918-19; apptd. by Sec. of War chmn. Bd. of Inquiry on Conscientious Objectors. Mem. Sigma Phi, Am. Legion. Republican. Episcopalian. Author: The Conscientious Objector, 1919; Parish's Fancy (novel), 1929. Contbr. to mags. Home: 10757 Weyburn Av., Los Angeles 24. Died June 22, 1956; buried Ogdensburg, N.Y.

KELLOGG, Wilbur Ralph, city mgr.; b. Indianapolis, Jan. 9, 1884; s. J. C. and Ellen (Elder) K.; m. Frances Frank, Jan. 1910; children—Frances K. Rippey, Eunice K. Langner. With engring. dept. Big Four R.R., 1905-12, real estate agt., 1912; real estate agt. Union Terminal Co. of Cincinnati, 1927-34, mgr., 1934; city mgr. Cincinnati since 1934. Methodist. Mason, Rotarian. Clubs: Queen City, Cincinnati, Kenwood Country. Address: 3717 Davenant Av., Cincinnati. Died Jan. 31, 1956.

KELLOGG, W(ill) K., mfr. food products; b. in Michigan; s. John Preston and Ann Jeanette K. Long identified with mfr. of Battle Creek cereal products; founder of the Kellogg Co. with plants located in Battle Creek, Mich. and Omaha, Neb.; also identified with other enterprises, including following: The Kellogg Australia Proprietary Co., Ltd., Kellogg Sales Co., Kellogg Co. of Canada, Ltd., and Great Britain, Ltd., Kellogg Co. of South Africa Proprietary Ltd. Formerly owner of W. K. Kellogg Arabian Horse Ranch, Pomona, Calif., now owned and operated by Calif. State Polytech. Coll. Founder, 1930, of The W. K. Kellogg Found. Donor of Wintergreen Lake Bird Sanctuary, Kellogg Experimental Farms and Reforestation Project, now owned and operated by Mich. State Agrl. Coll., Lansing. Home: Battle Creek, Mich. Died Oct. 6, 1951; buried Battle Creek.

KELLOR, Frances; b. Columbus, O., Oct. 20, 1873; d. Daniel and Mary (Sprau) Kellor; LL.B., Cornell Law Sch., New York, 1897; undergraduate and grad. work in U. of Chicago, 1898-1904, New York Summer Sch. of Philanthropy, 1901. Fellow Coll. Settlements Assn., 1902-04; sec., treas., N.Y. State Immigration Com., 1909; chief investigator, Bur. of Industries and Immigration, N.Y. State, 1910-13. Mem. New York Research Council, 1915; dir. of immigration, Transatlantic Steamship Passenger Confs., 1922. Pres. Am. Assn. Fgn. Lang. Newspapers, 1919-20; v.p. Publishers' Assn. of Am. Press, in Foreign Langs., 1920; 1st v.p. Am. Arbitration Assn. Author: Experimental Sociology, 1902; Out of Work, 1904, 1915; Straight America, 1915; Immigration and the Future, 1920; Federal Administration and the Alien, 1921; Security Against War, 1924; The United States Senate and the International Court, 1925; Arbitration in Action, 1941; Arbitration in International Controversy, 1945; American Arbitration, 1948. Office: care American Arbitration Assn., 477 Madison Av., N.Y. C. 22. Died Jan. 4, 1952; buried Greenwood Cemetery, Bklyn.

KELLS, Clarence Howard, army officer; b. Kennockee, Mich., Oct. 9, 1892; grad. Inf. Sch., Ft. Benning, Ga., 1925, advanced course, 1931; grad. Command and Gen. Staff Sch., Ft. Leavenworth, Kan., 1936, Q.M. Sch., Phila., 1937. Enlisted as private, C.A.C., 1917; commd. 2d lt. Inf., 1917, advanced through the grades to brig. gen., 1943; instr. 8th Inf., Chgo., 1933; adj. Hawaiian Q.M. Depot, Ft. Armstrong, Hawaii, 1937-39; instr.,Q.M. Sch., Phila., 1939-40; with Water Transport br. Transportation Div., Office Q.M. Gen., Washington, 1940-41, chief of br., 1941—. Address: Office of Chief, Transportation Service, War Dept., Washington. Died Mar. 24, 1954.*

KELLY, Edward Joseph, bishop; b. The Dalles, Ore., Feb. 26, 1890; s. James Leo and Henrietta (Wakefield) K.; ed. St. Mary's Acad., The Dalles, Columbia U., Portland, Ore., St. Patrick's Sem., Menlo Park, Calif., North Am. Coll., Rome, Italy; Ph.D., Propagation of Faith U., Rome, 1913, D.D., 1917; LL.D., U. of Portland (Ore.), 1935. Ordained priest R.C. Ch., 1917; missionary priest, Baker City (Ore.) diocese, 1917-19; sec. to Bishop McGrath and chancellor Baker City diocese, 1919-28; bishop of Boise (Ida.) diocese since 1928. Republican. Address: Boise, Ida. Died Apr. 21, 1956.

KELLY, Edward Joseph, ex-mayor of Chicago, consulting engineer; born Chicago, Illinois, May 1, 1876; son of Stephen and Helen (Lang) Kelly; educated in pub. and night schs., Chicago, and under pvt. tutors, LL.D., Notre Dame, 1928; m. Mary Edmunda Roche, Mar. 20, 1910 (died 1918); m. 2d, Margaret E. Kirk, Jan. 25, 1922; children—Edward Joseph (dec.), Joseph, Patricia, Stephen. Axman to chief engr. Sanitary Dist. of Chicago, 1894-1933; loaned to the State for work as Ill. Waterway commr.; appted. South Park commr. by Circuit Court, May 1922, re-apptd. commr., Mar. 1922, and re-elected president of bd. to which office was elected annually, 1924-34, when the consolidation of park districts sponsored by him for economy abolished all bds.; bd. had charge of 70 miles of parks and boulevards, including Lake Front and Michigan Blvd., south of Chicago River, calling for expenditure of $30,000,000; appointed mayor of Chicago to fill the unexpired term of A. J. Cermak, 1933, and elected, 1935, by vote of almost 800,000; re-elected, 1939 by similar high vote again re-elected April 1943. Served as v.p. of United States Conf. of Mayors, now pres. Directed the improvement of Grant Park; completion of Stadium; establishment of boulevards to relieve traffic; active in promoting bridge connecting outer drives at mouth of Chicago River; establishment of many parks, including one of 26 acres in colored district of Chicago; co-operated with officials of Century of Progress Exposition, Chicago, 1933, 34, securing re-opening of same, 1934; restoration of Fine Arts Bldg. in Jackson Park, as a convention hall and industrial museum; supervised as chief engineer 20 years program for Sanitary District to cost $120,000,000. A leader in fight for 10,000 cubic feet of water per second through the Main Drainage Canal; brought to successful conclusion Chicago's 50-year fight for subways and started $40,000,000 subway program in 1938; secured $100,000,000 superhighway program for Chicago, 1939; focused Congressional attention on municipal problems of housing, relief, transportation, city planning, education and taxation, 1933-39; organized the "Keep Chicago Ahead Com." of business men to stimulate comml. activities. Co-operated with state's atty. in drive against Chicago hoodlums, gangsters and racketeers; settled Chicago milk strike, 1934; organized Chicago's Own Christmas Benefit in 1933 to clothe needy children yearly, which in 7 years gave clothing and shoe outfits to approximately 448,000 needy children; established "Keep Chicago Safe" Committee; appointed Chicago Recreation Commission; U.S. Coordinator of Civilian Defense for Chicago Metropolitan Area; chiarman Chicago Commission on National Defense. Trustee Art Institute Chicago; ex-officio member Chicago Plan Commission. Elected Ill. Nat. Committeeman for the Dem. Party, 1940-44, 48. Mem. Am. Soc. Civil Engrs., Western Soc. Engrs., Chicago Assn. Commerce. Democrat. Clubs: Chicago, Chicago Athletic Assn., Beverly Country, Chicago. Home: 1301 N. State St. Office: 20 N. Wacker Drive, Chicago 6. Died Oct. 20, 1950; buried Mt. Calvary, Chicago.

KELLY, Eric Philbrook, author, educator; b. Amesbury, Mass., Mar. 16, 1884; s. Edward Lowell and Massalena Hadley (Philbrook) K.; A.B., Dartmouth, 1906, A.M., 1929; m. Katharine Collins Merrill, July 2, 1924. Reporter Westfield (Mass.) Times, 1906, Springfield Union, 1906-11, Hunterton Gazette, High Bridge, N.J., 1912, Boston Herald, 1914-18, Boston Transcript, summers 1922-24; instr. in Eng., Dartmouth, 1921-29, prof. journalism 1929-54, prof. emeritus, 1954—; lectr. and student (scholar Kosciuszko Foundation), U. Krakow, Poland, 1925-26. V.p. Paderewski Comn., New England, 1942-43. Sent to Mexico on mission for Office of Foreign Relief and Rehabilitation Operations, Dept. of State, 1943. Chmn. Pulitzer com. novel of the yr., 1951, 52, 54. Trustee Kosciuszko Foundation, Waynflete Academy, Portland, Me. Awarded John Newberry medal, 1928; Gold Cross of Merit (Poland); Chevalier Order Polonia Restituta, 1934, Commander, 1945; Gold medal, Kosciuszko Found., 1956, medal of achievement, 1957. Mem. of Modern Language Assoc. of Am., and other professional socs. Clubs: Polanie Club (Mpls.), Polish Arts, Polish Roman Catholic Union (Chgo.). Episcopalian. Author numerous books, 1924—, latest being: In Clean Hay, 1953. Editor Best Short Stories for Children, 1939; Life of Helena Modjeska (Series of Great Poles), 1941; also booklet The Hope of All Poles in the World, 1940; The Hand in the Picture (book), 1947; The Amazing Journey of David Ingram, 1949, and others. Co-editor Youngtown, Ariz. Record and Desert Call, 1959—. Summer home; Chebeague Island, Me. Winter home: Youngtown, Ariz. Died Jan. 1960.

KELLY, Francis Martin, bishop; b. Houston, Minn., Nov. 15, 1886; s. James C. and Ellen (Kelly) K.; grad. St. Thomas Acad., St. Paul, Minn.; Ph.B., Catholic U. of America, Washington, D.C., 1909; studied North Am. Coll., Rome, 1909-13; S.T.D., U. of Propaganda, Rome, 1913. Ordained priest R.C. Ch., 1912; appt. sec. to bishop of Winona, Minn., 1914; prof. philosophy, St. Mary's Coll. and Coll. of St. Teresa, Winona, 1913-26; chancellor diocese of Winona, 1920-22; vice rector St. Mary's Coll., 1918-26; consecrated titular bishop of Milasa and auxiliary bishop of Winona, June 9, 1926; apptd. bishop of Winona, Feb. 10, 1928. Home: 275 Harriet St., Winona, Minn. Died June 24, 1950; buried St. Mary's Cemetery, Winona.

KELLY, Fred C(harters), writer; b. Xenia, O., Jan. 27, 1882; s. Robert A. and Alice (Charters) K.; student U. of Mich., 1900-02; m. 2d, Marcelle van den Heuvel, 1938; children, Fred C., Jr. (by 1st marriage), Brian Booth, Jeanne Alice. Began as newspaper corr. at age of 14; conducted humorous column, Cleveland Plain Dealer, 5 yrs.; went to Washington, D.C., 1910, and for 8 yrs. wrote "Statesmen, Real and Near," the first daily Washington column ever syndicated; regular contributor of special articles to leading magazines. Served as special agent of the Federal Bureau of Investigation, for 18 months, World War I. Operated mile-square farm, Peninsula, Ohio. Clubs. National Press, Overseas Writers (Washington); Players (New York). Author: Human Nature in Business, 1920; The Fun of Knowing Folks, 1923; The Wisdom of Laziness, 1924; You and Your Dog, 1926; But On the Other Hand, 1928; Why You Win or Lose, 1930; How Shrewd Speculators Win (with Sullivan Burgess), 1932; How to Lose Your Money Prudently, 1933 (this book forced a change in Ohio banking laws within week of publication); One Thing Leads to Another (the growth of an industry), 1936; The Wright Brothers, a biography authorized by Orville Wright, 1943; David Ross—Modern Pioneer, 1946; George Ade—Warmhearted Satirist, a biography, 1947; The Permanent Ade (anthology), 1947; The Life and Times of Kin Hubbard (biography), 1952. Editor: Miracle at Kitty Hawk, 1951; How we Invented the Airplane (by Orville Wright), 1953. Home: Kensington, Md.; also Peninsula, O. Died May 23, 1959.

KELLY, Howard Charles, lawyer; b. New York, N.Y., Oct. 16, 1887; s. Lawrence and Agnes (Maxwell) K.; LL.B., New York Law Sch., 1910; m. Dorothy Cammell, July 23, 1937; children by previous marriage—Carol, Patricia. Admitted to Colo. bar, 1910, N.Y. bar, 1911, and since engaged in practice of law, New York, N.Y. Delegate to N.Y. State Constitutional Conv., drafting present provisions on social welfare, 1938. Chmn. bd. trustees City Club of N.Y. (civic organization), 1938-41, president 1941-44. Chairman, executive committee, Civil Service Reform Association since 1948; member national council, National Civil Service League since 1948. Member (trustee; chairman trusts and gifts committee) Bd. of Higher Education, New York, N.Y. Mem. Assn. Bar City of N.Y., N.Y. County Lawyers Assn., Am. Bar Assn., Lawyers Club. Democrat. Home: 22 E. 36th St., N.Y. City 16. Office: Kelly, Finn & Brisach, 150 Broadway, N.Y.C. 7. Died Dec. 15, 1952.

KELLY, Judith (Mrs. William D. English), author; b. Toronto, Can., Jan. 4, 1908; d. Henry Grattan and Gail Borden (Johnson) Kelly; student pvt. schs., Toronto and Boston; B.A., Vassar Coll., 1931; m. William D. English, June 29, 1933; children—Elissa Glenn Howe, W. D., Jr., Henry Kelly. Author: It Won't Be Flowers, 1936; Marriage Is a Private Affair, 1941 (awarded Harper prize); A Diplomatic Incident, 1949; miscellaneous short stories. Home: Beverly, Mass. Address: Houghton Mifflin Co., Boston. Died May 2, 1957; buried Mount Auburn, Cambridge, Mass.

KELLY, Monroe, naval officer; b. Norfolk, Va., July 30, 1886; s. William Armstead Lane and Alice (Reid) K.; student Norfolk Acad., 1902-04; B.S., U.S. Naval Acad., 1909; student U.S. Navy Post-grad. Sch., 1912-14; m. Lucy Winder Lamb, Sept. 23, 1914; children—Monroe, Lucy Lane. Commd. ensign USN, 1911, and advanced through the grades to rear adm., 1941; comdt. 3rd Naval Dist., 1944-48, ret. as vice adm.; served on U.S. naval mission to Brazil, 1927-31; U.S. naval attaché to the Netherlands, 1938-40; naval aide to Queen Wilhelmina, Aug. 1942; comdt. N.Y. Navy Yard, 1943-Nov. 1944. Decorated D.S.M. (Navy), World War I, Defense, N. Atlantic, and African Campaign medals; Grand Officer, Order of Orange-Nassau of the Netherlands. Comder. Order Brit. Empire; Commendador Orden Al Merito (Chile). Home: Landfall, Linkhorn Park, Virginia Beach, Va. Died Aug. 29, 1956; buried Forest Lawn Cemetery, Norfolk, Va.

KELLY, Paul (Michael), actor; b. Brooklyn, Aug. 9, 1899; s. Michael D. and Nellie Theresa (Murphy) K.; student St. Thomas Aquinias Acad., Brooklyn, 1912-13; private tutors; m. Dorothy MacKaye, Jan. 10, 1931 (dec.); m. 2d, Mardelle Zwicker, Jan. 23, 1941; children—Mimi Kathryn (adopted), Mary Mardelle Kirk (step-dau.). First appearance as actor, Grand Army Man, 1907; 1st motion picture for Vitagraph Co., Brooklyn, 1907; played first lead, Up The Ladder, by Owen Davis, Playhouse Theatre, N.Y., 1921; played Vina Delmar's Bad Girl, 1930; in first talking picture, Walter Winchell's Broadway Through a Keyhole, 1933; made 400 films; in Command Decision, on Broadway, 1947; continuing in motion pictures. Awarded for performance in Command Decision: Antoinette Perry Award (Theatre Wing's Award), Variety's Critic's Poll Award, Billboard's Donaldson Award. Republican. Roman Catholic. Died Nov. 6, 1956; buried Holy Cross Cemetery, Los Angeles.

KELLY, Robert Lincoln, educator; b. Tuscola, Ill., Mar. 22, 1865; s. Robert and Anna (Pearson) K.; Ph B., Earlham Coll., 1888; Ph.M., U. of Chicago, 1899, fellow in philosophy, 1899-1900; awarded fellowship, 1900-02; LL.D., DePauw 1907, Earlham Coll., Richmond, Ind., 1930, Alfred Univ., 1930, Marietta (O.) Coll., 1935, Tulane Univ., 1937, Univ. of N.M., 1940; L.H.D., Bates Coll., Lewiston, Me., 1932; m. Cecilia Rifner, Aug. 13, 1890; children—Agnes Rifner, Lois Anna, Robert Harper (col. U.S. Air Service, killed in action over France 1944). Sec. sch. prin., 1888-98; practical psychologist, Chicago Physiol. Sch., 1898-1900; in charge psychophysical measurements, Dewey Elementary Sch., Chicago, 1898-1900; acting pres., Penn Coll., Oskaloosa, Ia., 1900-01; dean, 1901-02, pres. 1902-17, Earlham Coll., Richmond. Ind.; exec. sec. Council of Ch: Bds. of Edn., U.S., 1917-35; pres. Assn. Am. Colls., 1914-16, permanent exec. officer, 1918-37, emeritus since June 1937. Lecturer on college adminstrn., Sorbonne, Univ. of Paris, 1924, Teachers Coll. Columbia, 1925-33, and New York Univ., 1927-29. Mem. Ind. State Bd. Edn., 1905-14; chmn. Bd. of Edn. of The Five Years' Meeting of Friends Ch. in America, 1903-17. Chairman colleges and universities section, 7th Biennial Conference of World's Edn. Assns., Tokyo, 1937. Mem. Am. Soc. of French Legion of Honor, Omicron Delta Kappa (hon.); mem. Nat. Conf. of Jews and Christians. Mem., Claremont Chapter Red Cross; dir. assignment of West Coast Am. Japanese citizens to Am. colls. War Relocation Authority; mem. bd. of Pilgrim Place for Ret. Missionaries, organizer, mem. Vis. Nurse Assn. (Claremont). Editor Christian Education, 1917-35, and Association American Colleges Bulletin, 1918-37. Chevalier de la Legion d'Honneur (French). Clubs: University (Chicago); Cosmos (Washington, D.C.); Faculty (Columbia U.); National Arts, Quill (New York City); University Club, (Claremont, California). Author of The Liberal College Curriculum, Theological Education in America, Tendencies in College Administration; The American Colleges and the Social Order. Editor The Effective College. Made many educational surveys. Congregational minister, lecturer. Home: 439 W. 8th St., Claremont, Calif. Office: 19 W. 44th St., N.Y.C. Died Dec. 12, 1954; buried Rose Hills Meml. Park, Whittier, Cal.

KELLY, William J., banker, consultant, mfr.; b. N.Y. City, Jan. 19, 1899; m. Grace Moir; 1 son, William J., Jr. Dept. head Chicago Trust Co., 1919, became 2d v.p., 1924. v.p. in charge banking dept., 1928; v.p. Nat. Republic Co., 1929, following merger of Chicago Trust and Nat. Bank of Republic; William Kelly & Co., management counsel, 1929-—; v.p. Kelly Steel Works, Inc., 1930-33, pres., 1933-46; pres. Machinery & Allied Products Inst., 1937-—; dir. Commonwealth Edison Co., Link Belt Company. Gen. sec. Chicago Assn. Commerce, 1924, dir., 1924-27, 1939-45, v.p., 1941; consultant to Donald M. Nelson, chmn. W.P.B., 1942-44; chmn. indsl. div. Navy Relief campaign, 1942; co-chmn. spl. gifts Community and War Fund, 1943, dir. 1943-45. chmn. bus. div., 1945; dir. Nat. Found. Infantile Paralysis Trustee Ill. Inst. Tech.; trustee, mem. exec. com. Armour Research Found.; trustee Chgo. Latin Sch., 1939-44; mem. Citizens Bd., U. Chgo.; mem. Northwestern U. Assos. Republican (asst. treas. Rep. Nat. Com. 1932). Clubs: Chicago, Racquet, Commercial, Attic, Casino Saddle & Cycle (Chgo.); Burning Tree, Metropolitan (Washington); Old Elm (Ft. Sheridan. Ill.); River (N.Y.C.); Glen View Golf. Home: 1448 Lake Shore Dr., Chgo. 10. Office: 120 S. LaSalle St., Chgo. 3. Died May 29, 1955; buried Rosehill Cemetery, Chgo.

KELLY, William Powers, educator; b. Troy, O., Dec. 30, 1865; s. David and Ellen E. (Powers) K.; grad. Troy High Sch., 1882; A.B., Dartmouth, 1886, A.M., 1890; post-grad. work Yale, 1906-07; m. Lilliam M. Lee, July 8, 1896; children—David William P. Tchr. Coes Northwood (N.H.) Acad., Worcester (Mass.) Acad., South Hadley (Mass.) High Sch., 1886-94; supt. schs., St. Johnsbury, Vt., Hudson, Mass., Attleboro, Mass., and Meriden, Conn., 1894-1911; headmaster Rutgers Prep. Sch., 1911-34. Mem. N.Y. Schoolmasters' Club, Theta Delta Chi, Phi Beta Kappa, and various ednl. socs. Address: Rutgers Preparatory School, New Brunswick, N.J. Died Mar. 28, 1953.

KELSER, Raymond Alexander (kĕlz'ĕr), bacteriologist and immunologist; b. Washington, Dec. 2, 1892; s. Charles and Josie Mary (Potter) K.; D.V.M., George Washington U., 1914; A.M., Am. Univ., 1922, Ph.D., 1923; diploma hon. asso. Royal Coll. Veterinary Surgeons, London; m. Eveline Harriet Davison, Sept. 5, 1914; 1 dau., Evelyn Rae (Mrs. John Andrew Allgair). Bacteriologist for H. K. Mulford Co., Glenolden, Pa., 1914, for U.S. Dept. Agr., 1915-18; served as lt. Veterinary Corps, U.S. Army, Mar.-Oct. 1918, capt., 1918-20; commd. capt. of same in regular army, 1920, maj., 1927, lt. col., 1933, col., 1939, brig. gen., 1942, retired 1946; chief of veterinary lab., Letterman hosp., San Francisco, 1918; comdg. officer Army Veterinary Lab., Philadelphia, 1919-20; chief Veterinary Lab. Sect. Army Med. Sch., Washington, 1921-24, instr. bacteriology same sch., 1922-24; mem. U.S. Army Med. Dept. Research Bd., Manila, P.I., 1925-28; chief of Veterinary Lab. Sect. and instr. bacteriology, Army Med. Sch., instr. in infectious diseases, serology and helminthology, Army Veterinary Sch., Washington, 1928-33; instr. in pathology and bacteriology, Grad. Sch. of Arts and Sciences, Am. Univ., 1930-33; research fellow in bacteriology, Harvard U. Med. Sch., 1933-35; mem. Army Med. Research Bd., Ancon, Canal Zone, 1935-38; director, Veterinary Div., Office of Surgeon Gen. U.S. Army, 1938-46. Professor bacteriology and dean of faculty, Sch. of Veterinary Med., U. Pa., Phila., 1946-52. Mem. A.A.A.S., Am. Acad. Tropical Medicine, Am. Pub. Health Assn. mem. Am. Vet. Med. Assn. (ex-v.p.), Am. Assn. Pathologists and Bacteriologists, Nat. Acad. of Sci., Soc. Am. Bacteriologists, Pa. State Vet. Med. Assn., Keystone Vet. Med. Assn., Am. Soc. Exptl. Pathology, Am. Soc. Tropical Medicine, Washington Acad. Sciences, Assn. of Mil. Surgeons of U.S., New York Academy of Science, Phi Zeta, Sigma Xi. Decorated D.S.M.; recipient of the Gorgas Medal; XII International Veterinary Congress prize; George Washington U. Alumni Achievement award. Methodist. Mason (32°). Clubs: Army and Navy (Washington); Army and Navy Country (Arlington County, Va.); Lenape (Phila.). Author: Manual of Veterinary Bacteriology, 1927; also articles. Discovered transmission of encephalomyelitis by mosquitoes, developed vaccine for rinderpest, resulting in eradication of worst stock plague in Philippines. Home: 268 Kent Rd., Wynnewood, Pa. Address: U. of Pa., 39th and Woodland Av., Phila. Died Apr. 16, 1952; buried Arlington Nat. Cemetery.

KELSEY, Albert, architect; b. St. Louis, Apr. 26, 1870; s. Albert Warren and Jeannette Garr (Washburn) K.; student U. Pa., 1896; studied in Paris, 1897-98 (traveling scholarship in architecture, U. Pa.); m. Henrietta L. Allis, Jan. 18, 1898; children—Albert Washburn, Charlotte Elizabeth, Charles Cashman; m. 2d, Mrs. Mary Erben Hamill, 1946. Practiced at Phila., 1894-—; architect for the Model City, St. Louis, 1903; designed plans for Pan-Am. bldgs., at Washington, in association with Prof. Cret; Carson Coll., bldgs. nr. Phila.; Sacred Heart Acad., Madison, Wis.; etc.; chmn. com. of experts for construction of Phila. Pkwy.; mem. various town planning commns.; an organizer Regional Planning Fed. of Phila. Tri-State Dist.; archtl. adviser Pan-Am. Union and dir. Columbus Meml. Lighthouse Competition, Santo Domingo. Decorated Comdr. of Isabella la Catolica by Alfonso XIII. Mem. bd. dirs. Fairmount Park Art Assn. Pres. Archtl. League America, 1908-09; fellow A.I.A.; mem. Archtl. League of New York, Pa. Assn. Architects (pres. 1916-17), Numismatic Soc. Democrat. Clubs: Franklin Inn, T-Square, University (Phila.). Home: Quoque, L.I.; also 2039 Delancy Pl., Phila. 3. Died May 6, 1950; buried Shirley, Mass.

KELSEY, Carl, educator; b. Grinnell, Ia., Sept. 2, 1870; s. James Carl and Mary Maria (Sutherland) K.; A.B., Grinnell Coll., 1890; student Andover Sem., 1892-95; grad. study U. Goettingen, 1896, U. Berlin, 1897; Ph.D., U. Pa., 1903, Litt.D., 1940; m. Gertrude Haldeman, Sept. 2, 1896. Social worker, Boston and Chgo., 1896-1901; Harrison fellow sociology U. Pa., 1901-03, asst. instr., 1903-04, asst. prof., 1904-06, prof. sociology, 1906-42; asst. dir. N.Y. Sch. Philanthropy, 1905-13, retired 1942. Dist. supt. War Risk Ins., 1918-19. Mem. Am. Acad. Polit. and Social Sci. (sec. 1906-12, v.p. since 1912). Author: Negro Farmer, 1903; Physical Basis of Society, 1916. Home: Mendenhall, Pa. Died Oct. 15, 1953.

KELSEY, Frederick Trowbridge, lawyer; b. Orange, N.J., Dec. 26, 1886; s. Frederick Wallace and Ella A. (Butts) K.; grad. Carteret Acad., Orange, N.J., 1903; A.B., Yale, 1907; LL.B., N.Y. Law Sch., 1909; m. Anna Welles Whitney, May 13, 1913 (dec. 1925); children—Whitney Trowbridge, Elinor Kelsey; m. 2d, Joan Skolnik, May 28, 1926; 1 son, Frederick Trowbridge; m. 3rd, Lucille T. Packer. Admitted to N.Y. bar, 1909, and since practiced in N.Y.C.; mem. McLean, Hayward & Kelsey, 1910-13, Lewis & Kelsey, 1913-25, Lewis, Garvin & Kelsey, 1925-33, Lewis & Kelsey, 1933-40, Kelsey, Waldrop, Spalding & Parker, 1940-41, Kelsey, Waldrop & Spalding, 1941-—. Chmn. bd. L. D. Seymour & Co.; dir. Colonial Trust Co., First Investors Corp., Namron Corp. Mem. Am., N.Y. State bar assns., Bar Assn. City of N.Y., County Lawyers Assn., Phi Beta Kappa, Ind. Republican. Episcopalian. Clubs: Bankers, Union League (N.Y.C.); Rock Spring (West Orange); Lake Placid (Essex County, N.Y.). Home: 200 E. 66th St., N.Y.C. 21. Office: 55 Liberty St., N.Y.C. Died Oct. 11, 1957.

KELSEY, Hugh Alexander, clergyman, educator; b. Berea, Kan., Feb. 10, 1872; s. Thomas Boston and Elizabeth (Cunningham) K.; A.B., Tarkio (Mo.) Coll., 1898; grad. Xenia Theol. Sem., 1903; student U. Chgo., 1920; D.D., Muskingum Coll., 1916; LL.D., Monmouth Coll., 1945; m. Luella T. Espy, Aug. 24, 1899; children—Hugh Espy, Mary Elizabeth, Margaret Mitchell, Alfred Alexander. Ordained to ministry U. P. Ch., 1903; pastor successively Unity, O., Altoona, Pa., E. Liverpool and Cambridge, O., until 1919; prof. Bible Muskingum College, 1919; pres. Sterling (Kan.) Coll., 1933-46, pres. emeritus, 1946-—. Trustee Ohio Anti-Saloon League, 1917-33. Spl. preacher in Army camps during World War; chaplain Ohio Sons of Vets., 1924. Nat. sec. Young Peoples Christian Union, 1914-15, mem. Nat. Com. 7 yrs.; moderator Ohio Synod, U.P. Ch., 1922, Synod of the Plains, 1947; vice moderator U.P. Ch., 1938; rep. Kan. Synod on Nat. Bd. of Adminstrn. U.P. Ch., 1945-47. Visited Emperor Haile Selassie I. of Ethiopia, Africa, upon invitation, 1927. Popular lectr. on Ethiopia. Club: Kansas Educators (pres. 1941-42). Contbr. to religious mags. Home: Sterling, Kan. Died Oct. 30, 1958.

KELSEY, Preston Telford, fire ins. exec.; b. St. Mary's, O., Oct. 4, 1867; s. Benjamin and Mary Adams (Gray) K.; ed. high sch., Indpls.; m. Laura Esther Halliday, Dec. 12, 1894; children—Martha (Mrs. R. A. Ashton), Lila (Mrs. Wallace C. Speers), Laura, Preston H. V.p. Marion Trust Co., Indpls., 1904; asst. mgr. Western dept., Chgo., Sun Ins. Office, 1904-13, mgr., 1913-19, became U.S. mgr. at N.Y.C., 1919; became pres. Patriotic Ins. Co., Am., N.Y.C., 1922; dir. Sun Indemnity Co.; ret. from active bus., 1928. Mem. Ind. N.G., 1885-92. Mem. S.R., Soc. of Mayflower Descs. Presbyn. Address: Southern Pines, N.C. Deceased.

KELSO, James Anderson, theologian; b. Rawal Pindi, India, June 6, 1873; s. Alexander P. and Louisa M. (Bolton) K.; A.B., Washington and Jefferson Coll., 1892, D.D., 1902, LL.D., 1943; B.D., Western Theol. Sem., 1896; student U. Berlin, 1896-97, U. Leipzig, 1899-1900, Ph.D., summa cum laude, 1900; LL.D., Coll. of Wooster, Ohio, 1919; Litt.D., Boston U., 1939; m. Wilhemina Wise, June 29, 1898. Ordained to ministry Presbyn. Ch., 1898; instr. Hebrew, Western Theol. Sem., 1897-1900, prof. Hebrew and O.T. lit., 1901-—, acting pres., 1908-09, pres., 1909-43, pres. emeritus 1944. Lectr. Am. Sch. Oriental Research, Jerusalem, 1922-23. Dir. Ministers Mutual Life Ins. Co. Mem. Bd. of Christian Edn., Presbyn. Ch., 1929-32; mem. bd. dirs. Presbyn. Ministers' Fund; trustee Presbyn. Hosp. Moderator Pitts. Presbytery, 1931, Synod of Pa., 1935; exchange preacher to Great Britain, 1938. Mem. Soc. Bibl. Lit. and Exegesis, Archeol. Inst. Am., Am. Oriental Soc.; found. mem. Phi Beta Kappa. Author: Die Klagelieder, Der Massorethische Text und die Versionen, 1901; Hebrew-English Vocabulary to the book of Genesis, 1917; A History of the Hebrews in Outline, 1921; The Hebrew Prophet and His Message, 1922. Contbr. to Hastings' Dictionary of Ethics and Religion, Hastings' Dictionary of the Bible, Standard Bible Dictionary. Contbr. to religious and secular press. Home: 515 S. Aiken Av., Pitts. 6. Died Nov. 3, 1951.

KELTON, Stanton Colt, chem. co. exec.; b. Columbus, O., Oct. 14, 1889; s. Frank C. and Isabelle Morrow (Coit) K.; student Ohio State U., 1907-08; A.B., Harvard, 1911, LL.B., 1914; m. Alice Gladden Twiss, Sept. 15, 1913; children—Helen Elizabeth (Mrs. John M. Cleary), Stanton Coit, Jane Gladden (Mrs. Charles Shoemaker), Franklin Crothers, George Twiss. Admitted to Mass. bar, 1914, practiced in Boston, 1914-16; sec., dir., counsel Rohm & Hass Co., Phila., 1916-—, also sec. subsidiaries in U.S., Can., 1920-—. Episcopalian (vestryman). Clubs: Martins Dam (a founder) (Wayne, Pa.); Racquet, Harvard (Phila.). Home: Rock Run, R.F.D. 1, Chester Springs, Pa. Office: 222 Washington Sq., Phila. 5. Died Dec. 24, 1956; buried St. Andrew's Cemetery, Glenmoore, Pa.

KEMMLER, Edward Albert, civil engr.; b. Columbus, O., 1867; s. William F. and Barbara K.; C.E., Ohio State U., 1888; m. Thecla Corzilius, Aug. 17, 1898. Asst. engr. U.P. Ry., locating new line in So. Utah and Ariz., 1889-91; asst. prof. civ. engring. Ohio State U., 1891-5; became constructing engr. city of Columbus 1895; dep. county engr., Summit County, 1938-40; ret. 1941; engring and planning dept., Akron, O., 1943-45, ret. Mem. Am. Soc. C.E., Ohio Soc. Profl. Engrs. (pres. 1900), Izaak Walton League, Columbus Maennerchor (pres. 1903-06). Mason (past master, 32°, Shriner). Contbr. to proc. engring. socs. Home: 85 Deshler Av. Office: Chamber of Commerce, Columbus, O. Died May 19, 1955.

KEMP, Alexander Nesbitt, bus. exec.; born San Francisco, California, son of Alfred Holmes and Elizabeth (Grigor) Kemp, ed. pub. schs., Oakland, Calif.; m. Madeliene Mary Haly, 1905; children—Phyllis (Mrs. Wallace Moir), Hale N. Began with Hongkong & Shanghai Banking Corp., London, 1900, jr. officer, N.Y. branch, 1903-05; with N. W. Halsey & Co., investment bankers, San Francisco, 1905-09; comptroller and v.p., Pacific Light & Power Co., San

Joaquin Light & Power Corp., Southern Calif. Gas Co., 1909-17; comptroller, later v.p. charge finances, Southern Calif. Edison Co., 1917-23, now dir. and mem. exec. and management coms.; exec. v.p. California Bank, 1923-28, now dir. and mem. exec. com.; pres. Pacific Mutual Life Ins. Co., 1935-42, chmn. bd., mem. exec. com. since 1942; war-time pres. Am. Airlines, 1942-45, now dir.; dir. Standard Oil Co. of Calif. (mem. finance com.). Republican. Clubs: Pacific Union, California, Los Angeles Country (Los Angeles), Bel-Air-Bay; Bohemian (San Francisco); Links, Economic (New York). Home: 10401 Wilshire Blvd., Los Angeles 24. Died Aug. 13, 1955.

KEMP, Harold Augustus, engr.; b. Frederick, Md., Apr. 27, 1894; s. Robert Augustus and Daisy Alice (Birely) K.; B.S., Va. Poly. Inst., 1917; short courses Rutgers U., 1930; m. Helen Virginia Work, Apr. 27, 1918; children—Helen Work (Mrs. Frank H. Whitney), Robert Augustus II (dec.), Virginia Bruyere (Mrs. William H. Holcombe, Jr.) Asst. master mechanic Westinghouse, Church, Kerr & Co., construction at Rock Island Arsenal, 1917-18; lt., Ordnance Dept., U.S. Army, asst. insp. Nitrate Plant No. 2, Muscle Shoals, Ala., 1918-19, supt. of service dept., 1919-20; steam engr. Dunlop, Am., Ltd., Buffalo, N.Y., constrn. power plant, pumping station, 1920-21; constrn. engr. Dupont Engring. Co., Buffalo, 1921-24; cons. engr. for sewage treatment plants, water supply, bridges, etc., with George C. Diehl, Inc., Buffalo, 1924-31; v.p., sec. Civic Research Corp., Buffalo, 1929-31; sr. engr. U.S. Engr. Office, chief of design, Ill. Waterways, Chgo., 1931-33, Upper Miss. River Project, St. Paul, 1933-34; gen. supt. design and constrn. sewage treatment plant and rebuilding pumping station, Washington, 1934-37; prin. engr. N. Atlantic Div. office, U.S. Army Engrs., flood control, 1937-38; chief engr. Dept. San. Engring., Washington, 1938-40; head engr., chief of airport sect., mem. of staff Bd. Engrs. for Rivers and Harbors, Office, Chief of Engrs., U.S. Army, Washington, 1940-44; dir. of san. engring. including supervision of water, sewer, refuse, pub. convenience and sewage treatment divs., D.C., 1944—; cons. engr., Office Civil Def. Planning, U.S., 1947-48; asst. dir. engr. services and coordinator, Utility Services D.C. Civil Def., 1951—. U.S. mem. apptd. by pres. Potomac River Basin Commn. 1941-44, D.C. mem., 1944—, chmn. 1950-51; mem. coordinating com. of Nat. Capital Park and Planning Commn., Washington Bd. Trade. Registered profl. engr. and land surveyor. Mem. Am. Soc. M.E., Am. Soc. C.E., Am. Pub. Health Assn, Soc. Am. Mil. Engrs., Am. Water Works Assn., Am. Pub. Works Assn., Md.-Del. Water and Sewerage Assn., Washington Soc. Engrs., Wash. Housing Assn., Am. Philatelic Soc., S.A.R., Frederick County (Md.) Hist. Soc., Am. Legion. Mason. Clubs: Engineers of Washington; Collectors and Washington Philatelic Soc. (Washington); Rotary. Prepared book, Estimating Data for Bridges and Miscellaneous Engineering Structures, for U.S. War Dept. Numerous articles on Potomac River. Home: 1721 N. Huntington St., Arlington 5, Va. Office: Govt. of D.C., Washington 4. Died Feb. 16, 1953; buried Mt. Olive Cemetery, Frederick, Md.

KEMP, Louis Wiltz, ret., Texas historian; b. Cameron, Tex., Sept. 4, 1881; s. Dempsey and Martha (Taylor) K.; student U. of Tex., 1901-03; L.H.D., Daniel Baker Coll., Brownwood, Tex., 1952; m. Violet Volz, Oct. 7, 1925; children—Charles Dempsey, Arthur Jeff. Asso. with Texas Oil Co., 1908, now ret. Served as lt., aviation sect. Signal Corps, U.S. Army, 1918-19. Mem. bd. Tex. State Library since 1937, former chmn.; chmn. bd. Tex. historians for Tex. Centennial, 1935-38; pres. San Jacinto Mus. of History. Historian gen. Nat. Soc. Sons American Revolution, 1946-47. Awarded diploma and medal of Reconnaissance Francaise, 1948; good citizenship medal, S.A.R., 1953. Mem. Houston Philosophy Soc., Tex. State Hist. Assn. (pres. 1941-45), Daughters Republic Tex. (hon.), Sons of Republic of Tex. (pres. San Jacinto chpt. 1946-47, pres. state chpt. 1948-49), Tex. State Philos. Soc., Newcomen Soc. Eng., Am. Hist. Assn., Chi Phi, Am. Legion. Democrat. Methodist. Mason. Club: Kiwanis. Co-editor and contbr.: Monuments Commemorating the Centenary of Texas, 1939; contbr. Handbook of Texas. Author: The Heroes of San Jacinto (with Sam Houston Dixon), 1932; Signers of the Texas Declaration of Independence, 1944. Home: 214 Westmoreland Av., Houston. Died Nov. 15, 1956; buried State Cemetery, Austin, Tex.

KEMPNER, Isaac Herbert, Jr., business exec.; b. Galveston, Tex., Oct. 1, 1906; s. Isaac Herbert and Henrietta Lenora (Blum) K.; student Asheville (N. C.) Sch., 1920-22, Morristown (N.J.) Sch., 1922-24; B.S., Harvard, 1928; m. Mary Josephine Carroll, Apr. 8, 1930; children—Isaac H., James Carroll. Asst. to pres. Texas Fig Co., Sugar Land, Tex., 1928-30; asst. to v.p. and gen. mgr. Imperial Sugar Co., Sugar Land, 1930-32; dir., v.p. and treas Imperial Sugar Co., Sugar Land, 1932-45, pres. and dir. since 1945; pres. and dir. Fort Bend Utilities Co. since 1938, City Stevedoring Co., Galveston, since 1940; dir. Imperial Bank & Trust Co., Sugar Land. Trustee Sugarland Industries, Harris and Eliza Kempner Fund. Served as lt. to comdr., U.S.N.R., 1942-45, in Atlantic Theatre. Legion of Merit. Member U.S. Cane Sugar Refiners Assn. (dir.), Am. Legion. Clubs: Bayou (Houston); Army-Navy (Washington); Lions (Sugar Land); Tejas. Home: 3688 Willowick Rd., Houston 19. Office: Imperial Sugar Co., Sugar Land, Tex. Died Oct. 20, 1953.

KENDALL, Elizabeth Kimball, educator; ed. Germany and France; 2d class in History Honor Sch., Oxford U., Eng.; LL.B. Boston U., 1892; A.M., Radcliffe Coll., 1899. Mem. history dept. Wellesley Coll., 1888-92, asso. prof., 1892-1902, prof. 1902-51. Fellow Royal Geog. Soc. Author: Source Book of English History, 1900; A Wayfarer in China, 1913. Co-author (with Katherine Coman; History of England, 1899, Short History of England, 1901. Address: Dorset, Vt. Died May 15, 1952; buried Somerset, England.

KENDALL, Harry R., ins. exec.; b. Ky. May 21, 1876; s. Preston B. and Adelia (Scearce) K.; ed. pub. schs. Louisville; Bryant and Stratton Bus. Coll.; LL.D. Harding Coll., 1950; m. Clara Kramer, May 2, 1934. Supt. Prudential Ins. Co., Louisville, 30 yrs.; pres. Fidelity Life and Accident Ins. Co., Louisville, 3 yrs.; chmn. bd. Washington Nat. Ins. Co., Chgo., 1926—. Trustee Lincoln Inst. of Ky. Methodist. Mason (32°, K.T., Shriner). Clubs: University (Evanston); Pendennis (Louisville); Executive, Chicago Farmers. Home: 2848 Sheridan Place, Evanston, Ill. Office: 610 Church St. Evanston, Ill. Died Apr. 3, 1958; buried Kane Hill Cemetery, Louisville.

KENDALL, Henry Plimpton, mfr.; b. Boston, Jan. 15, 1878; s. Rev. Henry L. and Clara Idella (Plimpton) K.; A.B., Amherst, 1899, A.M., 1934; LL.D., U. S.C., 1937; LL.D.; Amherst, 1949; D.T.I., Clemson Agrl. Coll., 1951; m. Evelyn Louise Way, Feb. 11, 1926; children—Henry Way, John Plimpton, Helen Louise. Chmn. bd. Kendall Co.; Mem. Mass. Commn. on Stabilization of Employment, 1931-33; mem. Bus. Adv. Council, U.S. Dept. of Commerce, 1933—, chmn. 1934-35; mem. Fed. Adv. Council, U.S. Dept. Labor, 1933-34. Mem. storage sect. War Industries Bd. of Council of Nat. Def., 1917; mem. Div. of Engring. and Indsl. Research, National Research Council, 1939-40; regional chmn., First Fed. Reserve Dist. Com. for Econ. Development, 1942-46; trustee, com. for Econ. Development, 1946-56, hon. trustee, 1956—. Awarded Taylor Key, Soc. for Advancement of Mgmt., 1944. Trustee Mount Holyoke Coll., 1923-46; trustee, Eastern States Exposition; trustee Deerfield Acad. Pres., Taylor Soc. Sci. Mgmt. 1929-31. Fellow Am. Acad. Arts and Scis.; mem. Am. Antiquarian Soc., Delta Kappa Epsilon. Repub. Clubs: Univ. (Chgo.); Univ., Odd Vols., Brookline Country, Union (Boston); Cosmos (Washington); Appalachian Mt. Author: Early Maps of Carolina and Adjoining Regions, 1930; Early Maps of Carolina, 1937. Joint Author: Profit Sharing, 1920; Profit Sharing and Stock Ownership for Employees, 1926. Home: Moose Hill Street, Sharon, Mass. Office: 140 Federal St., Boston 10. Died Nov. 3, 1959; buried Walpole, Mass.

KENDALL, John C., lawyer; b. Winona, Minn., Nov. 15, 1886; s. John J. and Ella E. (Catlin) K.; LL.B., U. Minn., 1910; m. Gertrude C. Walrath, May 28, 1920 (died 1933); 1 son, John W. Admitted to Ore. bar, 1910, and practiced in Coos Bay, 1910-21, Portland since 1927; partner Black and Kendal since 1940; circuit judge, 2nd Judicial Dist. of Ore., Coos Bay, 1921-27. Mem. Am., Ore., State and Mulnomah County bar assns., Fed. Communications Commn. Bar Assn. Republican. Episcopalian. Club: Arlington. Home: Club, Portland 5. Office: Cascade Bldg., Portland 4, Ore. Died Oct. 12, 1951.

KENDALL, Messmore, lawyer; b. Grand Rapids, Mich., Dec. 9, 1872; s. John Charles and Florence Helen (Messmore) K.; LL.B., Columbian (now George Washington) U., 1893, LL.M., 1894; L.H.D., Lafayette Coll., 1942; Litt.D., Tufts Coll., 1947; m. Maude E. Thomason, June 21, 1904; children—Elizabeth Ann, Messmore (dec.); m. 2d, Katherine G. Flynn, June 17, 1925; children—Florence Messmore, Messmore II, Sue Mason; m. 3d, Sepha Treble, Jan. 14, 1945. Admitted Mont. bar, 1894, N.Y. bar, 1897; mem. firm of Kendall & Herzog, 1905—; organized Braden Copper Co., Andes Copper Co., etc.; built Capitol Theatre, N.Y., 1917; organized Capitol Bus Terminal, 1928; v.p. George H. Doran Co., pubs., 1908-29; dir. Rinehart & Co., pubs.; pres. Moredall Realty Corp., Ladnek Realty Corp., Capitol Theatre Corp., Los Olmos Estates, Inc., Kendall Estates, Inc.; v.p., dir. Kenville Mines; dir. Metro-Goldwyn Pictures Corp., Capitol Bus Terminal, Quebec Gold Mining Corporation, Portrerillos Ry. Co., Pamour Porcupine Mines, Ltd., mem. adv. bd. Chem. Bank & Trust Co. (N.Y.C.); chmn. bd. Bank of Palm Beach & Trust Co.; pres. Playhouse Corp., Palm Beach, Fla. Capt. Signal Corps., U.S. Army, World War; col. staff of gov. of Ky. 1923. Chevalier of the Legion of Honor, 1950. Built and donated Washington Hall at N.Y. World's Fair. Candidate for rep. at large, N.Y. State, 1940. Mem. adv. bd. Salvation Army, N.Y.; trustee Children's Village, Dobbs Ferry, N.Y.; trustee Mus. City of N.Y.; chmn. Philipse Manor Hall Com.; chmn. com. to restore historic St. Paul's Church, Eastchester, N.Y. Former pres. gen. Nat. Soc. S.A.R.; mem. Am., N.Y. State bar assns., Assn. Bar City of N.Y., N.Y County Lawyers Assn., Am. Scenic and Historic Preservation Soc. (trustee) N.Y. Hist. Soc., Am. Inst. Mining and Metall. Engrs., Mil. Order Loyal Legion (comdr.), Order Founders and Patriots Am., St. Nicholas Soc., Gen. Soc. War of 1812, Am. Friends of Lafayette, (pres.), Soc. of Mayflower Descs. (gov.), Soc. Colonial Wars, Mil. Order Fgn. Wars. Republican. Episcopalian. Clubs: Metropolitan, Players, Twenty-Nine (N.Y.C.), Coffee House Deepdale, Illustrators and Writers, Everglades, Bath and Tennis, Coral Beach (Palm Beach). Author: Never Let Weather Interfere (autobiography), 1946. Has important collection of George Washington relics and theatrical collection. Home: Washington's Hdqrs., Dobbs Ferry, N.Y. Office: 1639 Broadway, N.Y.C. Died May 1, 1959.

KENDIG, Calvin Miles, chairman board, Hamilton Watch Co.; b. Conestoga, Pennsylvania, February 8, 1877; s. David Kussuth and Susan (Martin) Kendig; educated in common schools and special courses; married Blanche Fridy, June 10, 1909; children—Perry F., Susan F., Calvin F., John F. Accounting and asst. in credit dept. Follmer, Clogg & Co., 1894-98; office mgr. E. T. Fraim Lock Co., 1898-1902; with Hamilton Watch Co. since 1902, successively as credit mgr., cost accounting, purchasing agent and v.p., pres. and treas., 1939-48, chairman of the board, 1948-51; director Industrial Building & Loan Association. Member Mfrs. Association (dir.), Chamber of Commerce (dir.). Club: Hamilton. Home: Mountville, Lancaster County, Pa. Office: Hamilton Watch Co., Lancaster, Pa. Died Oct. 14, 1952.

KENDIG, H(arvey) Evert, univ. dean; b. Newville, Pa., Oct. 22, 1878; s. William Henry and Elizabeth J. (Christian) K.; student Pa. State Tchrs. Coll., Shippensburg, 1897; Ph.G., Medico-Chirurg. Coll., Phila., 1901, M.D., 1905; Pharm.D., Temple U., 1910; m. Agnes Charlton Royal, June 2, 1906; children—Agnes Elizabeth (Mrs. Richard W. Churchman), Janet Royal (Mrs. S. Logan Kerr), Catherine Lilian (Mrs. John W. Clegg, Jr.), Josephine Evert (Mrs. John N. Costello). Instr. pharmacy Medico-Chirurg. Coll., 1901-04, asst. prof., 1904-05; dean and prof. pharmacy Fla. Coll. Pharmacy, 1906-07; prof. pharmacy, Temple U., 1907—, dean and prof. public health Sch. Pharmacy, 1932—, asso. prof. pharmacology Med. Sch., 1914-22; prof. pharmacology and toxicology Women's Med. Coll. Pa., 1922-26. Served as major and adjutant, Temple U. Profl. Schs. Tng. Corps, World War; also examining physician Germantown Draft Bd., mem. Mayor's Com. on Home Defense (Phila.); became capt. Pa. N.G., 1920; maj. Med. Corps, State Fencibles (inf. regt.), Phila. Mem. Am. Pharm. Assn. (past pres. Phila. br.), Pa. Pharm. Assn. (chmn. com. on edn.; mem. A.Ph.A. com. on U.S. Pharmacopoeia, 1934-43; chmn. Nat. Steering Com. for Pharmacy Corps Bill), Am. Assn. Colls. of Pharmacy (pres. 1940-41; mem. nat. com. on edn. and defense 1940-43; chmn. joint com. on status of pharmacists in govt. services), 1934-43, Temple U. Gen. Alumni Assn. (bd. dirs.); hon. mem. Phila. Assn. Retail Druggists; hon. life mem. Ida., Md., N.D., Pa. and Utah pharm. assns.; charter mem. and mem. bd. dirs. Am. Found. on Pharm. Edn. Inc.; mem. Am. Council on Edn. for Pharmacy (mem. pharm. survey com.), Survey Organizer Nat. Scholarship Com., 1940; chmn. Am. Assn. Colls. of Pharmacy Com. on Scholarships, 1941 (chmn. com. on emergency problems). Am. Assn. Colls. Pharm. and Am. Pharm. Assn. rep. to Am. Council on Edn. Presbyn. (ruling elder, 1919—; treas. session funds, 1920—; former trustee —all First Presbyn. Ch. of Germantown). Com. on revision of Recipe Book III, 1934-43; adv. chmn. com. on status of pharmacists in govt. service, 1943. Remington medalist, 1944; medalist N.H. Pharm. Assn., 1946. Club: Union League (Phila.). Home: 8254 Crittenden St., Chestnut Hill, Phila. 18. Office: 3223 N. Broad St., Phila. 40. Died Apr. 18, 1950.

KENDRICK, W. Freeland, ex-mayor; b. Phila., June 24, 1874; s. William D. and Margaret K.; m. Mabel Bernard. Mayor of Phila., term Jan. 1924-Jan. 1928. Republican. Mason. Past Imperial Potentate A.A.O.N.M.S. Originator of idea of Shriners' hosps. for crippled children, now operating in various cities. Home: 5425 Woodbine Av., Phila. Died Mar. 20, 1953.

KENDRICKS, Edward James, air force med. officer; b. Alpena, Mich., May 27, 1899; s. George Washington and Mary (Lees) K.; student U. Mich., 1915-19; M.B., M.D., Northwestern, 1922; grad. U.S. Army Med. Sch., 1931, U.S. Army Med. Field Service Sch., 1932; flight surgeon U.S. Army Sch. Aviation Medicine, 1934; m. Wanda Hunt, May 5, 1942. Med. practice, Mich., 1923-30; surgeon U.S. Army Transport Republic, 1932-34; gen. flight surgeon duty, 1934-37; dir. dept. neuropsychiatry U.S. Army Sch. Aviation Medicine, 1937-42; surgeon 9th A.A.F., Middle East and E.T.O., 1942-45; surgeon personnel distbn. command, 1945-46; chief Aeromed. Lab., 1946-

49; dir. med. staffing and edn. Office Surgeon Gen., USAF, 1949-53; commandant of USAF School of Aviation Medicine, 1953—; promoted through ranks to brig. gen. Decorated Legion of Merit with oak leaf cluster, Soldiers medal, Bronze Stars, Presidential Unit Citation; various campaign medals (U.S.); Legion of Honor (France); Croix de Guerre (Belgium and Luxembourg); Kober Lecture award, 1951. Mem. A.M.A., Aeromed. Assn., Assn. Mil. Surgeons. Author articles in med. jours. Home: 163 First Av., Alpena, Mich. Office: Office of The Surgeon General, Hdqrs. USAF, Washington 25. Died Feb. 17, 1956; buried Arlington Nat. Cemetery.

KENGLA, Hannah M. Egan, educator; b. N.Y.C.; Nov. 25, 1891; d. John Joseph and Catherine (O'Leary) Egan; A.B., Hunter Coll., 1911; A.M., Columbia, 1913; Ph.D., Fordham U., 1922; m. Leo F. Kengla, Sr., July 8, 1946. Instr. of edn. Hunter Coll., 1911-23, asst. prof., 1923-28, asso. prof., 1928-34, prof. and dean of students, 1934-46, emeritus, 1946—. Mem. Nat. Assn. Deans of Women, Nat. Assn. Adminstrv. Women in Edn., Phi Beta Kappa. Roman Catholic. Clubs: Women's University. Home: 3007 143d St., Flushing, N.Y. Died Sept. 12, 1949.

KENKEL, Frederick P(hilip), sociologist; b. Chgo., Oct. 16, 1863; s. Henry and Albertine Voll (von Wallerstein) K.; student Northwestern Coll., Royal Acad. Mining, Freiberg, Saxony, pvt. study in Germany and Quincy (Ill.) Coll.; LL.D. honoris causa, St. Benedict's Coll., 1935; m. Eleanore von Kamptz, Nov. 15, 1892; children—Gerhard H., Anthony B., Fred H., Johanna, Gertrude, Marie Mercedes, Eleanore. Bookseller, pub., Chicago, 1885-95; journalist, 1896-1920, mng. editor Amerika (German lang. newspaper, St. Louis), 1905-20; dir. Central Bur. Cath. Central Verein Am., 1909—. Mem. bd. govs. United Charities, Inc., St. Louis. Mem. Cath. Assn. for Internat. Peace, Cath. Conf. on Indstl. Problems (ex-pres.), Nat. Catholic Charity Conf., Cath. Rural Life Conf., Cath. Charities of St. Louis (exec. com.), Cath. Anthropol. Conf. Decorated Knight of St. Gregory, 1914; Knight of Holy Sepulchre, 1926; recipient Laetare medal for 1930; posthumous citation for achievement in founding Central Bur. Library, St. Louis U., 1958. Democrat. Author: Schaedel des secundus arbiter, 1898. Editor Social Justice Review 1909—, Cath. Women's Union Bull., 1920—. Home: 3460 Itaska St. Office: 3835 Westminster Pl., St. Louis. Died Feb. 16, 1952; buried Resurrection Cemetery, St. Louis.

KENNA, Joseph Norris, judge; b. Charleston, W.Va., Jan. 10, 1888; s. Senator John Edward and Annie (Benninghaus) K.; law student U. Va., 1908-10; m. Louise Mountcastle, June 22, 1916; children—Nancy, Lee Mountclastle. Admitted to W.Va. bar, 1910; in office Chilton, McCorkle & Chilton, 1910-12; mem. Loeb & Kenna, 1912-19; asst. U.S. atty., So. Dist. W.Va., 1919-22; mem. Avis & Kenna, 1922-24; mem. W.Va. Ho. of Dels., 1931-32; judge Supreme Court of Appeals, W.Va., 1933—; re-elected to 2d twelve year term beginning Jan. 1, 1945. Mem. Phi Kappa Psi, Phi Delta Phi. Democrat. Presbyn. Mason (32°, Shriner). K.P. (past grand chancellor). Club: Edgewood Country. Home: 501 Swarthmore Av., Charleston, W.Va. Died Jan. 20, 1950; buried Sunset Meml. Park, South Charleston, W.Va.

KENNAMER, Charles Brents, judge; b. Kennamer Cove, Marshall County, Ala., Nov. 25, 1874; s. Seaborn F. and Nancy Elizabeth (Mitchell) K.; ed. pub. schs. and normal coll. (non-grad.); studied law at Georgetown U., 2 years; m. Birdie Hooper, Dec. 2, 1907; children—Charles B., Ralph, Seaborn A., Samuel Rexford, Mary Virginia (Mrs. George A. Harris). Began practice of law at Guntersville, Ala., 1903; held office of county solicitor Marshall County, Ala., 1905, 06; asst. U.S. atty. Northern Dist. of Ala., 1907-14, spl. asst. same, 1914-16; U.S. atty. Northern Dist. of Ala., 1922-31; resigned on appointment as judge U.S. Dist. Court, 1931. Alternate del. Rep. Nat. Conv., 1912, del., 1916, 20, 24, 28 (chmn. Ala. delegation 1920, 24, 28); Rep. candidate for Congress 7th Ala. Dist., 1906, 19, 20. Mem. Ala. State Bar Assn. Mem. Christian (Disciples) Ch. Mason. Home: Montgomery, Ala. Died June 3, 1955; buried Guntersville, Ala.

KENNEDY, Ambrose J(erome), ex-congressman; b. Balt., Jan. 6, 1893; s. Ambrose J. and Annie (McDonald) K.; student Calvert Hall Coll. and Poly. Inst., Balt.; m. Mary E. Dailey, Aug. 9, 1910; children—Mary B., Margaret A., Ambrose J., John D., Mildred, Jerome. Began as clk. Howard T. Williams & Co., ins. Balt., 1909; with Benson M. Greene & Co., 1915-24; in ins. business for self, 1924-32; v.p. Poor, Bowen, Bartlett & Kennedy, Inc., 1932—. Mem. Md. Ho. of Reps., 1918; mem. City Council, Balt., 1922-26; mem. Md. Senate, 1926; state parole commr., Md., 1929-32; mem. 73d to 76th Congresses, 4th Md. Dist. Dir. Balt. Cath. League. Roman Catholic. Elk. Club: Merchants. Home: 914 E. Biddle St. Office: 26 S. Calvert St., Balt. Died Aug. 29, 1950.*

KENNEDY, Annie Richardson (Mrs. H. D. Kennedy), evangelist, writer; b. Hopewell Hill, N.B., Can., Feb. 16, 1868; d. Ira and Hannah (Gross) Richardson; ed. high sch., business col., East Northfield (Mass.) Sch. and under pvt. tutors; m. H. D. Kennedy, evangelist and author, July 21, 1920 (dec.). Promoter, 1904—, and pres. Heartsease work for women and babies, N.Y.C. Mem. Interdenom. Assn. Evangelist, Winona Lake, Ind., v.p. Am. Tract Society. Naturalized citizen of U.S., 1917. Republican. Presbyterian. Author: The Heartsease Miracle, 1921; A Year in John's Gospel, 1923; The Footsteps of Faith; The Name; John's Epistles, 1933; Bethlehem's Babe, 1933; The Work of the Holy Spirit, 1940; also 28 religious tracts. Home: Elk Rapids, Mich. Address: 143 E. 51st St., N.Y.C. Deceased.

KENNEDY, Arthur Garfield, prof. English philology; b. Weeping Water, Neb., June 29, 1880; s. James Leroy and Helen (Hull) K.; A.B., Doane Coll., Crete, Neb., 1902, Litt.D., 1933; A.M., U. of Neb., 1905; Ph.D., Stanford U., 1914; m. Bertha Miller, July 20, 1910; children—James Miller, Katherine Mathilda. Teacher, Chadron (Neb.) Acad., 1902-04; teacher Latin and English, Norfolk (Neb.) High Sch., 1905-08; head of German, State Normal Sch., Spearfish, S.D., 1908-12; prof. English philology, Stanford University, 1914-45, professor emeritus since 1945. Member American Association of Univ. Profs., Bibliog. Soc. of America, Modern Lang. Assn. of America, Philol. Assn. of Pacific Coast, Am. Dialect Soc., Linguistic Soc. of America, Calif. Writers Club, Mediæval Academy of America, National Council of Teachers of English, College English Association, Phi Beta Kappa. Republican. Congregationalist. Author: The Pronoun of Address, 1915; Modern English Verb-Adverb Combination, 1920; Bibliography of Writings on the English Language, 1927; Concordance to Complete Works of Chaucer (with J. S. P. Tatlock), 1927; Anglo-Saxon Reader (with G. P. Krapp), 1929; Current English, 1935. Concise Bibliography for Students of English, 1940, 2d edit., 1945; English Usage, 1942. Contbr. to Am. Speech (bibliog. editor, 1925-35). Home: 1431 Arcadia Pl., Palo Alto, Cal. Died Apr. 21, 1954.

KENNEDY, Clarence Hamilton, entomologist; b. Rockport, Ind., June 25, 1879; s. Albert Hamilton and Emma Dorinda (Tennant) K.; A.B., Indiana U., 1902, A.M., 1903; A.M., Stanford, 1915; Ph.D., Cornell U., 1919; D.Sc. (honorary), Indiana University, 1950; married Lydia June Findley, March 16, 1927; children—Bruce Albert Hamilton, Mary Janet. Began as instr. in embryology, Ind. U. Biol. Sta., 1902; asst. in biology, Cornell U., 1915, instr. in limnology, 1916-17; instr. zoölogy, N.C. State Coll., 1918-19; instr. entomology, Ohio State U., 1919-21, asst. prof., 1921-30, asso. prof., 1930-33, prof., 1933-49, ret.; mng. editor Annals of Entomol. Soc. America, 1929-45; member editorial bd. ecol. monographs pub. by Ecological Soc. of America, 1934-40. Fellow A.A.A.S., Entomol. Soc. Am. (pres. 1935), Royal Entomol. Soc. of London, Ohio Acad. Sci.; mem. Am. Assn. Econ. Entomologists, Ind Acad. Sci., Ecol. Soc. America, Am. Soc. of Naturalists, Société Entomologique de France (Paris), Phi Delta Theta, Gamma Alpha, Sigma Xi (pres. Ohio Chapter 1926-27), Gamma Sigma Delta. Republican. Presbyterian. Club: Faculty (Ohio State U.). Author: Methods for the Study of the Internal Anatomy of Insects, 1933; Insects, Ency. Britannica, 1948; many articles in biol. jours. Home: 389 W. 10th Av., Columbus 1, O. Died June 6, 1952.

KENNEDY, Foster, neurologist; b. Belfast, Ireland, Feb. 7, 1884; s. William Archer and Hessie Foster (Dill) K.; ed. Queen's Coll., Belfast; M.D., Royal University of Ireland, 1906; married Katherine Caragol de la Terga; 1 daughter, Hessie Juana Dill and 1 daughter by previous marriage, Isabel Ann Foster. Resident med. officer Nat. Hosp., London, 1906; became chief of clinic New York Neurol. Inst., 1910; now prof. neurology Cornell U. Med. Coll., New York; consulting physician in neuropsychiatry, Bellevue Hosp.; consulting physician Neurol. Inst.; attending neurologist to New York Hosp.; cons. neurologist to Gen. Memorial, Lennox Hill, Women's, Monmouth (Long Branch, N.J.) Nassau (Mineola, L.I.), Vassar Bros. hosps. Chmn. com. neurology, National Research Council, Washington, D.C. Chairman Federal Medical Com., Ellis Island. Served médecinchef Hôp. Militaire, V.R. 76, France; commd. lt. Royal Army M.C., Brit. Army in France; promoted capt. and maj. and mentioned in dispatches. Fellow Royal Soc. Edinburgh, Royal Soc. of Medicine, London; mem. Am. Neurol. Assn. (past pres.), N.Y. Acad. Medicine, N.Y. Neurol. Soc. (pres.), N.Y. Command Brit. Great War Vets. Am. (past pres.); hon. mem. Neurol. Soc. of Paris, Hungary, Cuba, Mexico and Sweden. Decorated Confiere la condecoracion de la Orden Nacional de Merito, Carlos F. Finlay en el grado de Oficial, Cuba; Chevalier Legion of Honor (France). Protestant. Clubs: Century, River, Coffee House, Pilgrims. Contbr. to tech. jours. on neurol. and psychiat. subjects. Home: 14 Sutton Sq. Office: 410 E. 57th St., N.Y.C. 22. Died Jan. 7, 1952; buried Pendleton Hill Cemetery, R.I.

KENNEDY, Henry L., architect, engr.; b. Medfield, Mass., Aug. 15, 1897; s. John T. and Katherine (Davitt) K.; grad. Northeastern U., Boston, 1919; grad. student Beane U., France, 1920, Wentworth Inst., Boston, 1923; m. Helen S. Lake, Sept. 2, 1924; 1 dau., Dorothy Helen. Practicing architect, 1926-36, 40—; cons. architect, engr., 1925—; instr. constrn. course Wentworth Inst., 1926-36; lectr. cement and concrete tech. Harvard Grad. Engring. Sch., 1946-52; div. mgr. in charge concrete research Dewey & Almy Chemical Co., Cambridge, 1934—. Mem. corp. Belmont Hill Sch. Profl. engr., registered architect, Mass. Mem. Am. Soc. Mil. Engrs., Am. Concrete Inst. (past pres.), Am. Soc. Testing Materials, A.I.A., Am., Boston (Herschel award) socs. civil engrs. Clubs: Union League (Chgo.); Harvard Faculty (Cambridge, Mass.). Author: Cement and Concrete Technology (with Dr. R. F. Blanks), 1955. Home: 69 Radcliffe Rd., Belmont 78, Mass. Office: 62 Whittemore Av., Cambridge, Mass. Died Sept. 10, 1957; buried Medfield, Mass.

KENNEDY, John Thomas, educator; b. Phila., Pa., Dec. 24, 1883; s. John Thomas and Jane Matilda (Graham) K.; LL.B., George Washington U., 1907; grad. Washington Sch. of Accountancy, 1912; hon. Master Commercial Science, Benjamin Franklin U., 1926; m. Clephane Arnot, Mar. 5, 1921; 1 dau., Martha Jane. Admitted to D.C. bar, 1908; lecturer, Columbia U., 1915-16; head tech. dept., Pace Inst., New York, 1916-17; organizer and head training sch., U.S. Bur. Internal Revenue, Washington, 1918-19; admitted to Pa. bar, 1920; dean Pittsburgh Sch. Accountancy, 1921-26; pres. Benjamin Franklin U., Washington, 1925—, chmn. bd. trustees, 1926—. Stephen Girard Achievement award, 1955. Member of Am. Bar Assn., N.Y. County Lawyers Assn., Am. Accounting Assn., Am. Assn. Profs. Schools of Accountancy (pres.), Delta Sigma Rho. Republican. Presbyterian. Mason. Clubs: Accountants of America (New York); University, Arts (Washington). Author of several books dealing with Federal taxation, etc. Home: 3820 Reno Road N.W. Office: 1100 16th St. N.W., Washington. Died July 16, 1958; buried Nat. Presbyn. Ch.

KENNEDY, Joseph William, chemist; b. Nacogdoches, Tex., May 30, 1916; s. Joseph William and Mattie Baxter (Wade) K.; A.B., Stephen F. Austin State Teachers Coll., 1935; A.M., U. of Kan., 1937; Ph.D., U. of Calif., 1939; m. Adrienne Rushton Clark, Aug. 9. 1942; children—Joseph Wade, Burton Mack, Jill. Instr. chemistry U. of Calif., 1939-43; chemistry and metallurgy div. leader Los Alamos Lab., 1943-45; prof. chemistry, chmn. dept. Washington U., St. Louis, 46—; Priestley Lectr. Pa. State Coll., 1952; co-discoverer element 94 (plutonium), 1940. Awarded Medal for Merit, 1946, Jr. C. of C. award, 1948. Mem. Am. Chem. Soc., Am. Phys. Soc., Sigma Xi. Co-author: Nuclear Radiochemistry, 1949. Contbr. articles profl. jours. Office: Chemistry Dept., Washington Univ., St. Louis 5. Died May 5, 1957.

KENNEDY, Martin J., ex-congressman; b. N.Y. C., Aug. 29, 1892; s. Martin and Mary (Dean) K.; student pub. schs.; m. Elizabeth H. McNally, Feb. 10, 1923; 1 son, John. Engaged in insurance business; mem. State Senate, 1924-30; elected to 71st Congress, Mar. 1930, to fill vacancy and reëlected to 72d to 78th Congresses, 18th N.Y. Dist. Democrat. Roman Catholic. Home: 1349 Lexington Av. Office: 230 Park Av., N.Y.C. Died Oct. 1955.

KENNEDY, Raymond, author, educator; b. Holyoke, Mass., Dec. 11, 1906; s. John Aloysius and Ellen Louise (Curtin) K.; B.A., Yale, 1928, Ph.D., 1935; m. Ruby Jo Reeves, July 20, 1939; 1 dau., Ellen Reeves. Instr. Brent Sch., Baguio, P.I., 1928-29; field rep. General Motors Corp., Java and Sumatra, Dutch East Indies, 1929-32; instr. sociology Yale, 1935-40, asst. prof., 1940-43, asso. prof., 1943-47, prof., 1947—. Mem. Am. Anthropol. Assn. Am. Sociol. Soc., Far Eastern Assn., Phi Beta Kappa, Sigma Xi. Co-author: Jews in a Gentile World, 1942; The Science of Man In the World Crisis, 1945; Most of the World, 1948. Author: The Ageless Indies, 1942; Islands and Peoples of the Indies, 1943; The Islands and Peoples of the South Seas and Their Cultures, 1945; Bibliography of the Indonesian Peoples and Cultures, 1945. Home: 11 Burns St., New Haven. Died Apr. 27, 1950; buried Bandoeng, Java, Indonesia.

KENNEDY, Richard Oakley, business executive; b. Troy, N.Y., Sept. 12, 1885; s. Howard Samuel and Josephine Adelaide (Sharp) K.; ed. St. Paul's Sch., Garden City, N.Y., 1901-05; m. Sarah Klein, Feb. 6, 1907; children—Rev. Howard Samuel II, Richard Oakley, John Woodruff. Entered employ Cluett, Peabody & Co., Inc., Troy, as shipping clk., 1905, later foreman, supt., dir., 1917-41, v.p., 1927-44; associate, Ekholm Associates, Boston, Mass., 1945-46, Ginsberg Machine Co., Inc., 1946-49, cons., 1949—; partner Kennedy-Haight Associates, 1952—; director Ware River R.R. Co., Boston & Albany Railroad Co. Formerly captain N.Y. Guard, trans. to res. list, 1918. Trustee Troy Orphan Asylum, Troy Y.M.C.A., Troy Cemetery Assn., Marshall Sanitarium, Russell Sage Coll. Dir. Pittsfield and North Adams R.R. Mem. Newcomen Soc. of Eng. Republican. Methodist. Mason (32°, K.T.). Clubs: Troy. Home: 277 Park Av., N.Y. City. Office: 50 E. 42d St., N.Y.

C. Died Jan. 29, 1959; buried Oakwood Cemetery, Troy, N.Y.

KENNEDY, T(homas) Blake, judge; b. Commerce, Mich., Apr. 4, 1874; s. Thomas Bailey and Mary (Blake) K.; A.B., Franklin (now Muskingum) Coll., 1895, A.M., 1898; LL.B., Syracuse U., 1897; LL.D., Wyo. U., 1951; m. Anna H. Lyons, Feb. 8, 1906 (dec. Aug. 4, 1950). Practiced in Syracuse, N.Y., 1898-1901; moved to Cheyenne, Wyo., 1901, practicing there until 1921; referee in bankruptcy, 1903-13, 19-21; U.S. dist. judge Dist. of Wyo., 1921—. Chmn. Rep. State Com., Wyo., 1918-21; del. Rep. Nat. Conv., 1920. Presbyn. Mason (33°, hon.), Elk. Clubs: Rotary, Cheyenne Country. Home: 2512 Carey Av., Cheyenne, Wyo. Died May 21, 1957; buried Cheyenne.

KENNER, Albert Walton, army officer; b. Holyoke, Mass., Dec. 15, 1889; Ph.D., George Washington, U., 1910, M.D., 1915; grad. Army Med. Sch., Washington, 1917; m. Mlle. Raymonde Minard, Feb. 2, 1921 (dec. Apr. 1959); 1 son, Albert W. Commd. 1st lt. Med. R.C., 1916, regular army, 1917, and advanced through the grades to major gen., 1943; regimental surg., 26th Inf., 1st Inf. Div., World War I. Instr. U.S. Mil. Acad., West Point, N.Y., 1920-22. Gen. surg. service, Walter Reed Gen. Hosp., 1923-27; post surgeon Med. Field Service Sch., Carlisle Barracks, Pa., 1927-31; chief Surg. Service, Fort Banks, Mass., 1931; surgeon Harbor Def., Boston, 1931-32; chief surg. service, Ft. Banks, 1932-34; chief med. service, Sternberg Gen. Hosp., Manila, P.I., 1934-36; surg. duties, Ft. Myer, Va., 1936-37, post surgeon, 1937-41; Surgeon Armored Force, Fort Knox, Ky., 1941-42; chief surgeon Western Task Force Landing at Casa Blanca, Morocco, 1942; overseas, 1942-43; then with Army Group, Washington, 1942-43; chief of tng. inspections, Surgeon Gen. Office, Washington, 1943-49, ret. maj. gen.; chief med. officer S.H.A.E.F., European Theatre, 1944-45; chief surgeon for U.S. Forces, European Theatre, 1945-46; mem. sec. of War's personnel bd. 1946-49; med. dir. Columbia Hosp. for Women, Wash. Decorated D.S.C., D.S.M. with oak leaf cluster, Silver Star with two oak leaf clusters, Legion of Merit, Purple Heart (U.S.), Officer Legion of Honor, Croix de Guerre with palm, comdr. Order Sante Publique (France), Companion of the Bath (Gt. Britain), Grand Officer Assouam Alouette (Morocco), Comdr. Order of Crown, Croix de Guerre with palm (Belgium). Fellow Am. Coll. Surgeons. Club: Army-Navy (Washington). Home: 4925 Rodman St., Washington 16. Office: Columbia Hosp. for Women, 25th and L St. N.W., Washington. Died Nov. 12, 1959; buried Arlington Nat. Cemetery.

KENNON, William Lee, physicist; b. Columbus, Miss., May 3, 1882; s. Woodson Hughes and Sarah (Voigt) K.; B.S., Millsaps Coll., Jackson, Miss., 1900, M.S., 1901; Ph.D., Johns Hopkins University, 1906; married Emma Gerdine Sykes, Sept. 12, 1912; 1 son, Summerfield Sykes. Professor of chemistry and physics, Ky. Wesleyan Coll., 1901-03; univ. scholar, 1904-05; fellow in chemistry, 1905-06, Johns Hopkins; instr. chemistry, Williams, 1906-09; asst. prof. chemistry, 1909, acting prof. physics and astronomy U. Miss., 1911, prof., 1912—, chmn. dept., 1912-52. Alderman, Oxford, Miss., 1935-39. Kennon Obs., U. of Miss., named in his honor. Fellow American Assn. Advancement Science; mem. American Assn. Univ. Profs., Am. Physical Soc. (vice chmn. Southeastern Sect. 1935-36, chmn. 1942-43), Phi Beta Kappa, Omicron Delta Kappa, Kappa Alpha (Southern). Democrat. Mem. Meth. Ch. Author: Astronomy-a Textbook for Colleges, 1948. Home: 716 S. 8th St., Oxford, Miss. Box 116, University, Miss. Died Dec. 4, 1952; buried Greenwood Cemetery, West Point, Miss.

KENNY, Elizabeth (Sister Kenny), nurse; b. Warrialda, New South Wales, Australia, Sept. 20, 1886; d. Michael and Mary (Moore) Kenny; privately educated; grad. St. Ursulas Coll., Australia, 1902; unmarried. Nurse in Australian bush country, 1911-14; military nurse with Australian Army, 1914-18; research work in infantile paralysis since 1911; came to U.S., 1940, to present concept of the symptoms of the disease, infantile paralysis, to research institute. Author: Infantile Paralysis and Cerebral Diplegia, 1927; Treatment of Infantile Paralysis in Acute Stage, 1941; Kenny Concept of Infantile Paralysis and Its Treatment, 1942; And They Shall Walk (autobiography), 1943; Physical Medicine Concerning the Disease Infantile Paralysis, 1945; My Battle and Victory, 1951. Address: Toowoomba, Australia. Died Nov. 30, 1952; buried Toowoomba.

KENT, Frank Richardson, journalist; b. Baltimore, Md., May 1, 1877; s. Thomas Marine and Mary (Richardson) K.; ed. public and private schools; hon. M.A., U. of Md., 1911; awarded P.B.K. William and Mary Coll., 1934; Litt.D., Oglethorpe (Ga.) U., 1937; m. Minnie Whitman, Jan. 5, 1906 (died Apr. 28, 1910); 1 son, Frank R.; m. 2d, Elizabeth Thomas, 1916. Reporter Baltimore American, 1 yr.; began with Baltimore Sun, 1898, polit. reporter 10 yrs., Washington corr. 2 yrs.; sec., treas. Md. Agrl. Coll., 1910-11; mng. editor Balt. Sun, 1911-21, London corr., 1922-23; writer of syndicated column on politics in more than 100 papers. Member advisory board Pulitzer School of Journalism, Columbia U. Democrat. Episcopalian. Clubs: Maryland, Elkridge (Baltimore); National Press, Metropolitan (Washington, D.C.) Author: The Story of Maryland Politics, 1911; The Great Game of Politics, 1923; History of the Democratic Party, 1925; Political Behavior, 1928; Without Gloves, 1934; The Story of Alexander Brown & Sons, 1950. Home: Lombardy Apartments. Office: The Sun, Balt. Died Apr. 14, 1958.

KENT, Fred I., banker; b. Chicago, Ill., Feb. 12, 1869; s. Henry L. K.; ed. pub. schs., and Internat. Correspondence Schs., Scranton, Pa.; LL.D., Univ. of Southern Calif., 1930; m. Etta W. Williams, 1891. In banking, 1886; mgr. foreign exchange dept., 1st Nat. Bank, Chicago, 1905-07; became v.p. Bankers Trust Co., New York, 1909; dep. gov. Fed. Reserve Bank of New York, 1917-18; dir. div. of foreign exchange of Fed. Reserve Bd. until after Armistice; financial adviser to dir. of sales of War Dept. and rep. U.S. on Orgn. Com. of Reparations Commn. in Paris; dir. Bankers Trust Co. N.Y., Scarsdale Nat. Bank & Trust Co. (N.Y.); trustee, Councillor Nat. Indsl. Conf., Bd., Inc.; chmn. commerce and marine commn. of Am. Bankers Assn.; chairman council N.Y. U. Recipient Robert Dollar Annual award, 1945. Mem. Internat., U.S. C.'s of C., Commerce and Industry Assn. N.Y. (dir., mem. banking com.), American Institute of Banking, National Foreign Trade Council (dir.); mem. business adv. council U.S. Dept. of Commerce; dir. American Arbitration Association. Director and chairman Committee on Hoover Reorgn. Commn. Mem. exec. com. C. of C. State of N.Y. Mem. American Bankers Association, National Inst. Social Sciences, Met. Mus. Arts. Officer Legion of Honor (French); Comdr. Crown of Italy; comdr. Order of SS, Maurice and Lazarus (Italian). Protestant. Clubs: Union League, Scarsdale Golf, Bankers of America, Down Town Assn., Sleepy Hollow Country. Home: 70 Morris Lane, Scarsdale, N.Y. Office: 100 Broadway, N.Y.C. Died Oct. 25, 1954.

KENT, Robert Homer, prof. philosophy; b. Beck's Grove, Ind., Oct. 17, 1885; s. Webster and Susan (Lockman) K.; A.B., Franklin (Ind.) Coll., 1911, D.D., 1923; student Rochester Theol. Sem., 1911-14, B.D., 1921; studied U. of Chicago 6 summers; m. Myra Huckleberry, July 22, 1914; children—Robert Eugene, John Franklin, George Webster, Francis William. Ordained ministry Bapt. Ch., 1914; pastor Lebanon, Ind., 1915-18, Franklin, 1918-21; prof. philosophy, Franklin Coll., 1921-54, acting dean, 1929, acting pres., 1931-33, academic dean, 1946-51, acting pres., 1947-49. Lecturer on religious and ednl. subjects. Mem. exec. com. State Bd. Ind. Bapt. Conv. Mem. Ind. Hist. Soc., Ind. Philos. Assn., Kappa Delta Rho. Mason. Home: 159 E. King St., Franklin, Ind. Died Aug. 11, 1954; buried Green Lawn Cemetery, Franklin.

KENT, Roland Grubb, philologost; b. Wilmington, Del., Feb. 24, 1877; s. Lindley Coates and Anna (Grubb) K.; B.A., Swarthmore College, 1895 (Phi Beta Kappa, president of the chapter, 1912-15, vice pres., 1915-18, 1924-27), B.L., 1896, M.A., 1898; studied U. of Berlin, 1899-1900. Munich, 1900-91, Am. Sch. Classical Studies, Athens, 1900-02, U. of Pennsylvania, 1902-04, Doctor of Philosophy, 1903, Doctor of Letters, 1947; m. Gertrude Freeman Hall, July 12, 1904. Instr. Lower Merion High Sch., Ardmore, Pa., 1896-99; Harrison fellow in classics, U. of Pa., 1902-03. Harrison research fellow in classics, 1903-04, instr. Greek and Latin, 1904-09, asst. prof. comparative philology, 1909-16, prof., 1916-42, prof. Indo-European linguistics, 1942-47, emeritus, 1947; lectr. Sanskrit, Bryn Mawr Coll., 1910-14; prof. comparative philology, Ohio State U., summer 1921; delivered lectures at Sorbonne, Paris, June 1925; prof. comparative philology, Linguistic Institute, New Haven, Conn., summers, 1928, 1929, Ann Arbor, summer 1938, Chapel Hill, summers 1941, 1942. Decorated Chevalier Legion of Honor (France), 1934. Fellow Am. Acad. Arts and Sciences, 1934; mem. Am. Oriental Soc. (dir. 1917-20, 1924-27; v.p. 1923-24; pres. 1934-35), Am. Philol. Assn., Classical Assn. Atlantic States, Am. Assn. Univ. Profs. (charter mem.). Société de Linguistique de Paris, Oriental Club Phila. (sec.-treas. 1909-19; pres. 1919-20 and 1934-35); Classical Club Phila. (v.p. 1908-09; pres. 1909-10), Assn. Guillaume Budé (Paris; member of American committee), société des Études Latines (Paris), Linguistic Society America (founder, sec.-treas. 1925-40, pres. 1941), Philological Society of London (v.p. since 1941). Archaeol. Inst. of America. Volunteer helper Office of Strategic Services, 1943-45. Decorated Officer de l'Instruction Publique (French), 1926. Episcopalian. Author: Language and Philology (vol. 22 of Hadzsits and Robinson's Our Debt to Greece and Rome), 1923; The Textual Criticism of Inscriptions (monograph), 1926; The Sounds of Latin, 1932, 2d edition, 1940, 3d edition, 1945; The Forms of Latin, 1946; Old Persian Grammar, Texts, Lexicon, 1950. Editor of W. R. Newbold's The Cipher of Roger Bacon, 1928. Editor and translator of Varro de Lingua Latina, 2 vols., 1938. Contbr. to Am., English, French and German philol. periodicals. Home: 324 Aubrey Rd., Wynnewood, Pa. Died June 27, 1952; buried West Laurel Hill Cemetery, Phila.

KENTON, Edna, author; b. Springfield, Mo. 1876; d. James Edgar and Ruth (Rice) K.; A.B., U. Mich., 1897; unmarried. Contbr. short stories and articles to various mags. Author: What Manner of Man, 1903; Clem, 1907. Address: 240 W. 15th St., N.Y.C. Died 1954.

KEOGH, Andrew (kē'ō), librarian; b. Newcastle-upon-Tyne, Eng., Nov. 14, 1869; student Durham Coll. of Science, Newcastle-upon-Tyne; M.A., Yale, 1904; Litt.D., Univ. of Mich., 1928; Litt.D., Trinity College (Conn.), 1930; Litt.D., Middlebury (Vt.) College, 1937; m. Jessica Sherman Van Vliet, Aug. 6, 1900; children—Oswald Van Vliet, Cornelia Russell (dec.). Reference librarian, Newcastle Pub. Libraries, 1892-98; librarian Linonian and Brothers Library, Yale, 1899-1900; reference librarian, 1900-16, and university librarian, 1916-38, Yale U. Library, now emeritus; lecturer in bibliography, 1902-24, Sterling prof. bibliography, 1924-38. Yale U., now emeritus, also asso. fellow Trumbull Coll. Mem. A.L.A. (pres. 1929-30), Am. Library Inst. (ex-sec.), Am. Antiquarian Soc., N.Y. Hist. Soc., Conn. Acad. Arts and Sciences (ex-librarian), Conn. Hist. Soc., New Haven Colony Hist Soc. (dir.), Bibliog. Soc. of London, Oxford Bibliog. Soc., English Library Assn., Bibliog. Soc. America (pres. 1913-14), Elizabethan Club (trustee and ex-librarian), Acorn Club of Conn. (pres.), Beaumont Medical Club (Hon.). Club: Yale (N.Y.); Graduate, Elizabethan, Faculty (New Haven). Home: 49 Huntington St., New Haven 11. Died Feb. 13, 1953; buried Lake City, Minn.

KEOUGH, Austin Campbell, lawyer, motion picture exec.; b. N.Y.C., June 11, 1888; s. John J. and Jennie (Campbell) K.; A.B., Dartmouth, 1911; LL.B., Columbia, 1914; m. Katherine Upton, May 26, 1918. Admitted to N.Y. bar, 1917; asso. motion picture industry since 1919; legal dept. Famous Players-Lasky Corp., 1919-29; gen. counsel Publix Theatres Corp., 1932; sec., gen. counsel, dir. Paramount Publix Corp., 1932-35; v.p., sec., gen. counsel, dir. Paramount Pictures, Inc., 1935-49; v.p., gen. counsel, sec., dir. Paramount Pictures Corp. since 1950. Served as sgt., 104th Field Signal Bn., U S Army, 1918-19. Mem. Motion Picture Assn. Am (dir., chmn. law com.), Alpha Delta Phi. Roman Catholic. Clubs: University, Cherry Valley. Office, 1501 Broadway, N.Y.C. 18. Died Apr. 20, 1955; buried Williamstown, Mass.

KERBEY, Eric A., mfg. exec.; b. Rogers City, Mich., Oct. 8, 1898; s. Frank E. and Marie (Turno) K.; B.S. in mech. engring., U. Mich., 1921; m. Elizabeth G. Bell, Oct. 8, 1925; 1 dau., Barbara E. Design and sales engr. Am. Well Works, Aurora, Chicago, 1922-23; Chicago mgr. Payne Dean, Ltd., 1923-24; power plant equipment sales D.H. Skeer & Co., 1924-28; with Midwest Piping Company, Incorporated, 1928—, dir., 1943—, pres., 1955—. Mem. A.S. M.E., Am. Welding Soc., Tau Beta Pi, Les Voyageurs. Home: Conway Rd., Creve Coeur, Mo. Office: 1450 Second St., St. Louis 4. Deceased.

KERLIN, Robert Thomas, educator, author; b. Newcastle, Mo., Mar. 22, 1866; s. Thomas L. and Nancy (Jeffries) K.; A.M., Central Coll., Fayette, Mo., 1890; studied Johns Hopkins, 1889-90, U. Chgo., Harvard; Ph.D., Yale, 1906; m. Adeline K. Koster, July 10, 1907; children—Katharine Elizabeth, Elsa Adeline, Constance Lee. Prof. English, Mo. Valley Coll., 1890-94; in active ministry M.E. Ch., S., 1895-98; chaplain 3d Mo. Vols. in Spanish-Am. War; prof. English, Mo. Valley Coll., 1901-02, Southwestern U., 1902-03, State Normal, Warrensburg, Mo., 1903-06; instr. English, Yale, 1906-07; prof. lit., State Normal Sch., Farmville, Va., 1908-10, Va. Mil. Inst., Lexington, 1910-21, State Normal Sch., West Chester, Pa., 1922-27. Asso. editor of Arena, 1905-10. Lecturer on English lit., U. Vt. Summer Sch., 1911-17. Instr. AEF U., Beaune, France, 1919; lectr. in lit., Phila. Labor Coll., 1925-27; at Lincoln U., 1927; prof. English, Potomac State Coll., Keyser, W.Va., 1927-33. Lecturer in English lit. and European history, Western Md. Coll., 1933-40. Author: Mainly for Myself (poems), 1897; The Camp Life of the Third Regiment, 1898; The Church of the Fathers, 1901; Theocritus in English Literature, 1909; The Voice of the Negro, 1920; Negro Poets and Their Poems, 1923. Editor of Miltons Minor Poems in Johnson's English Classics. Home: 615 Memorial Av., Cumberland, Md. Dec Feb. 21, 1950.

KERN, Paul Bentley, bishop; b. Alexandria, Va., June 16, 1882; s. John A. and Margaret Virginia (Eskridge) K.; student Randolph-Macon Coll., 1897-99, D.D., 1919; B.A., Vanderbilt U., 1902, M.A. and B.D., 1905; D.D., Duke U., 1934, Victoria University (Toronto), 1938; LL.D., Emory U., 1936; Litt.D., Ohio Wesleyan, 1938; Doctor of Humane Letters, Willamette U., 1945; D.D., Wofford Coll., 1936; LL.D., Emory & Henry Coll., 1950; m. Lucy G. Campbell, June 11, 1907; children—Campbell, Virginia (Mrs. Julian M. Aldridge), Katherine (Mrs. Frank W. Buckner). Ordained ministry M.E. Ch., S., 1902; teacher Vanderbilt U., 1905-07; pastor Blakemore Ch., Nashville, 1907-10; Bellbuckle, Tenn.,

1910-12, Murfreesboro, Tenn., 1912-15; prof. ministerial efficiency, Southern Meth. U., Dallas, Tex., 1915-26, dean Sch. of Theology, 1920-26; pastor Travis Park Ch., San Antonio, Tex., 1926-30; elected bishop of M.E. Ch., S., assigned to Orient, 1930, in charge of confs. in Tenn. area, 1938-52, ret. Pres. Meth. Council of Bishops, also del. World Council of Churches, Amsterdam, 1948. Founder Summer Conf. for Christian Workers, Ovoca, Tenn., 1912. Fondren lecturer Southern Meth. U., Dallas, Tex., 1930; Cole lecturer Vanderbilt University, 1935; Jarrell lecturer Emory U., 1941; Peyton Lecturer Southern Methodist 1947-52. Member Kappa Alpha (Southern), Tau Kappa Alpha, Phi Beta Kappa. Author: (with Worth M. Tippy) A Methodist Church and Its Work, 1919; The Miracle of the Galilean, 1930; The Basic Beliefs of Jesus, 1935; Methodism Has a Message, 1941. Home: Lake Junaluska, N.C. Died Dec. 16, 1953; buried Mt. Olivet Cemetery, Nashville.

KERNER, Otto, lawyer; b. Chicago, Ill., Feb. 22, 1884; s. Karel and Josephine (Schejba) K.; LL.B., Lake Forest U., 1905; m. Rose B. Chmelik, July 27, 1907; children—Otto, Jr., Rose L., May R. Admitted to Ill. bar, 1905, and since practiced at Chicago; mem. Jones & Kerner; alderman 12th Ward, 6 yrs.; master in chancery, Circuit Court of Cook Co., 12 yrs.; elected judge Circuit Court, 1927, assigned to Appellate Ct., 1931; atty. gen. of Ill., 1933-38; circuit judge U.S. Court of Appeals, 7th Circuit. Mem. Am., Ill. State and Chicago bar assns. Dem. Mason (K.T., Shriner), Elk. Clubs: Bohemia, Iroquois, Ill. Athletic, Butterfield Country, Law Club, Legal Club. Home: 1031 Ashland Av., River Forest, Ill. Address: 1212 Lake Shore Drive, Chgo. Died Dec. 13, 1952; buried Bohemian Nat. Cemetery, Chgo.

KERNER, Robert Joseph, univ. prof.; b. Chicago, Ill., Aug. 26, 1887; s. Joseph A. and Rose (Veselak) K.; A.B., U. of Chicago, 1908, A.M., 1909; A.M., Harvard Univ., 1912, Ph.D., 1914; LL.D., U. of Omaha, 1937; Litt.D., Park College, Parkville, Mo., 1938; student Vienna, Berlin, Moscow, Paris, 1912-14; m. Frances Amelia Dorsey, May 31, 1917; children—Rose Maria (Mrs. Rose Kerner Shurtleff), Helen Dorsey (Mrs. Helen Kerner Bowker). Asst. hist. U. of Ill., 1908-09, Harvard, 1911-12; Rogers traveling fellow, Harvard, 1912-13, Ozias Goodwin fellow, 1913-14; instr. hist., U. of Mo., 1914, asst. prof. modern European history, 1916, asso. prof., 1918, prof., 1921-28, acting dean grad. sch., 1925-26; prof. modern European history, U. of Calif., 1928-41, Sather prof. of history 1941-54, emeritus, recalled to active service, 1954-57; director, Institute of Slavic Studies, emeritus, 1948-54, recalled to active service, 1954-57; lecturer on Eastern European history, Columbia, summer, 1920; lecturer world politics, U. of Chicago, summer, 1921, Inst. of Internat. Edn., 1921-23, U. of Ia., summer, 1924; visiting prof. Univ. of Hawaii, summer, 1935, Univ. of Colo., 1941; faculty research lecturer, 1942-43; mem. staff Col. House inquiry into terms of peace, 1917-18; staff Am. Peace Commn., Paris, 1918-19. Hon. mem. Hist. Soc. of Novy Sad (Jugoslavia); mem. Am. Hist. Assn., American Political Science Association (chmn. conference on Slavic studies 1956—), Alpha Pi Zeta, Delta Sigma Rho, Phi Beta Kappa. Assos.; corr. mem. Slavic Inst., Prague, Rumanian Acad., Bucharest, Internat. commn. for scientific and cultural history of mankind, UNESCO, Paris, France, 1952—; foreign mem. sect. of humanities and social sciences, Safarik Learned Soc. (Czechoslovakia); fgn. mem. Royal Bohemian Soc. of Letters and Scis.; Czechoslovak State Prize for Literature (1940); Author: The Foundations of Slavic Bibliography, 1916; The Jugo-Slav Movement, 1918; Slavic Europe (selected bibliography), 1918; Social Sciences in the Balkans and Turkey, 1930; Bohemia in the Eighteenth Century, 1932; The Balkan Conferences and The Balkan Entente (with H. N. Howard), 1935; Northeastern Asia (selected bibliography), 2 vols., 1939; (editor and co-author), Czechoslovakia: Twenty Years of Independence (1940); co-author) Poland (1945); (editor and co-author) Yugoslavia, 1949); The Urge to the Sea (Russia), 1942; The Russian Adventure, 1943; numerous articles. Contbg. editor Jour. of Internat. Relations, 1919-22; editor U. of Mo. Studies, 1925-27; mem. bd. editors Jour. Modern Hist., 1929-32, Am. Hist. Rev., 1949—. Gen. editor U.N. Series, 1940-50, 10 volumes; University of California Press; chmn. board editors of History Series, U. of Calif. Press, 1937-49. Editor: Northeastern Asia Series since 1937. Comdr. Order of the White Lion (Czechoslovakia); Officer Order of the Star of Roumania; Officer, Order of Leopold II (Belgium). Club: Bohemian (San Francisco). Home: 1320 Arch St. Address: University of California, Berkeley, Cal. Died Nov. 29, 1956.

KERNS, Shirley Kendrick, educator; b. Illiopolis, Ill., Oct. 16, 1872; s. Andrew Kendrick and Mary (Seeds) K.; A.B., U. Ill., 1897, Harvard, 1898; m. Jeanie Noyes Richardson, Dec. 26, 1905; children—Jeanie Noyes, Kendrick, Allen, Eleanor. Tchr. pub. sch., Rochester, Ill., 1894-95, prin., 1895-96; master Country Sch. for Boys of Balt., 1898-1900, acting headmaster 1900-01; sr. master Middlesex Sch., Concord, Mass., 1901-03, asst. headmaster, 1903-04; instr. in English, Noble and Greenough's Sch., Boston, 1904-06; founder, owner and headmaster Country Day Sch. for Boys of Boston, Newton, Mass., 1907-34, transferred ownership of sch. to bd. of trustees of which was treas. and mem. bd. Mem. Headmasters Assn., Country Day Sch. Headmasters Assn., Phi Beta Kappa. Republican. Club: Brae Burn Country. Home: 34 Waterston Rd., Newton, Mass. Died Apr. 13, 1950.

KERR, Charles William, clergyman; b. Slippery Rock, Pa., Apr. 2, 1875; s. Thomas A. and Margaret Annie (Miller) K.; grad. Slippery Rock State Normal, 1893; student Western Sem., Allegheny, Pa., 1895-97; grad. McCormick Theol. Sem., Chicago, 1898; D.D., Henry Kendall Coll. (U. of Tulsa), 1918; m. Annie Coe, Sept. 6, 1898; children—Margaret K. Hendrick, Hawley Coe. Pastor Presbyn. Ch., Edmond, Okla., 1898-1900, First Presbyterian Church, Tulsa, Okla., 1900-41, emeritus since Apr. 1, 1941. Trustee U. of Tulsa. Y.M.C.A. worker, 4-min. speaker, WW. Mem. Okla. Meml. Assn.; moderator Gen. Assembly of Presbyn. Ch., U.S.A., 1932-33, mem. Dept. on ch. Coöperation and Union, 1932-45; mem. Gen. Council of Presbyn. Ch., 1927-35; dir. Pioneers Assn. of Tulsa. Chaplain Hillcrest Hosp., Tulsa. Hon. mem. Pi Gamma Mu (Tulsa U.). Clubs: Knife & Fork (Tulsa); Tulsa Rotary (hon. mem.). Republican. Mason (32°). Rotarian. Home: 2404 Woodward Blvd., Tulsa. Died July 18, 1951; buried Rose Hill Cemetery.

KERR, Clarence D(ilworth), lawyer; b. Fairfield, Pa., Aug. 15, 1878; s. Thomas Bakewell and Clara (Dilworth) K.; grad. Lawrenceville Sch., 1897; A.B., Princeton, 1901; LL.B., Columbia, 1904; m. Janet Brinckerhoff, April 17, 1906; children—John Brinckerhoff, Harold Brinckerhoff, Clarence Dilworth, Mary Mason, William Dilworth. Admitted to N.Y. State bar, 1903; practiced with White & Case, N.Y.C., 1904-07, with Thomas W. Bakewell, 1907-09; mem. firm Fish, Richardson & Neave, N.Y.C., 1910—, specializing in patent law. Admitted to practice N.Y. Ct. of Appeals, 1903, U.S. Dist. and Circuit Cts., 1907, U.S. Supreme Ct., 1918. Served as capt. chem. warfare U.S. Army, 1918. With council Nat. Defense and War Industries Bd. later with gen. staff under Gen. Hugh Johnson, as $1 a yr. man, 1917-18. Pres. Englewood council Boy Scouts of Am., 1919-21; mayor Englewood, N.J., 1922-23; pres. Englewood Free Pub. Library, 1924-30; mem. bd. govs. Englewood Hosp. Assn., 1928—, pres., 1930-35; mem. bd. mgrs. Englewood Community Chest, 1936-42, chmn., 1939-41; pres. Lawrenceville Sch. Alumni Assn., 1926-27, mem. bd. trustees, 1927-47; pres. 1943-47; mem. Princeton Grad. council, 1921—, twice pres. Princeton Alumni Assn. No. N.J. Presbyn. Clubs: Commodore Clayton (N.Y.) Yacht, 1941-45, University, Down Town Assn., Princeton (N.Y.C.); Englewood, Englewood Field (Englewood, N.J.); Knickerbocker Country, Cap and Gown, Nassau (Princeton). Home: 217 Cedar St., Englewood, N.J. Office: 20 Exchange Pl., N.Y.C. 5. Died Sept. 20, 1957.

KERR, Henry H(amilton), utilities exec.; b. Ft. Worth, Jan. 11, 1892; s. Henry H. and Mary E. (Payne) K.; B.S. in electric engring. U. Colo., 1914; m. Helen J. Clancy, June 2, 1925; children—Mary Lucia, Barbara Anne. Joined Toledo Edison Company, 1929, v.p., 1946-53, v.p., 1953-58; ret. 1958; cons. Toledo Edison Commonwealth Assos., Jackson, Mich., 1958-59. Trustee Riverside Hosp. Fellow Am. Inst. E.E. (v.p. 1956-58); mem. Ohio Soc. Profl. Engrs., A.S.M.E., Toledo Mus. Art. Mason (Shriner) Clubs: Toledo, Inverness (Toledo). Home: 2365 Barrington, Toledo 6. Office: Edison Bldg., Toledo 4. Died June 13, 1959.

KERR, Hugh T., clergyman; b. Elora, Ont., Can., Feb. 11, 1871; s. William and Anne (Thomson) K.; B.A., U. Toronto, 1894, M.A., 1895, LL.D., 1937; student Knox Coll., Toronto, 1894-95; grad. Western Theol. Sem., 1897; D.D., Emporia Coll., Kan., 1908; D.D., U. Pitts., 1918, LL.D., 1934; LL.D., Washington and Jefferson Coll., 1920; D.D., Lafayette Coll., 1931; Dr. Humanities Bucknell U., 1948; m. Olive M. Boggs, June 12, 1901; children—Anna Boggs (Mrs. John Watson Harmeier), Hugh Thomson, Donald Craig. Ordained to ministry Presbyn. Ch., 1897; pastor Oakland Church, Pitts., 1897-1901, First Church, Hutchinson, Kan., 1901-07, Fullerton Avenue Ch., Chgo., 1907-13, Shadyside Presbyn. Ch., Pitts., 1913-46. Chmn. Alliance of Reformed Churches, 1947. Lectr. systematic theology and religious pedagogy, McCormick Theol. Sem., Chgo., 1910-11; Stone lectr. Princeton Sem., 1935; Moore lectr. San Francisco Theol. Sem., 1941. Exec. sec. The Pitcairn-Crabbe Found., 1947—. Pres. Presbyn. Bd. Christian Edn., 1923-41; moderator Gen. Assembly Presbyn. Ch., U.S.A., 1920-31. Corporator, Presbyn. Ch., U.S.A., 1920-31. Corpora- Pittsburgh, Western Pa. Sch. for Blind. Mem. bd. trustees U. Pitts., Washington and Jefferson Coll., Presbyn. Hosp. of Pitts., Pitts. Assn. for Improvement of Poor, Western Theol. Sem. Clubs: Duquesne, University, The Cleric. Author: Children's Story Sermons, 1911; Children's Missionary Story-Sermons, 1915; The Highway of Life, 1917; How to Teach the Life of Christ, 1917; From Port to Listening Post, 1918; How to Teach the New Testament, 1918; The Supreme Gospel, 1918; My First Communion, 1920; Children's Gospel Story-Sermons, 1921; Children's Nature Story-Sermons, 1923; The Gospel in Modern Poetry, 1926; Old Things New, 1931, children's Worship Story-Sermons, 1932; The Christian Mission in America, 1933; After He Had Risen, 1934; A God-Centered Faith, 1935; Faith and Life, 1937; Children's Everyland Story-Sermons, 1937; The Challenge of Jesus, 1939; Preaching in the Early Church, 1942, The Christian Sacraments, 1944. Home: Arlington Apts., Pitts. Died June 27, 1950; buried Homewood Mausoleum, Pitts.

KERR, John Hosea (kär), ex-congressman; b. Yanceyville, N.C., Dec. 31, 1873; s. Capt. John H. (C.S.A.) and Eliza Catherine (Yancey) K.; A.B., Wake Forest (N.C.) Coll., 1895, LL.D., 1945; m. Ella Foote, 1899; children—John Hosea, James Yancey. Began practice at Warrenton, 1895; solicitor 3d Dist. of N.C., 1905-16; judge Superior Ct. N.C., 1916-23; elected 68th Congress, 2d N.C. Dist., 1923, to fill unexpired term of late Hon. Claude Kitchin; mem. 69th to 82d Congresses, chmn. subcom. on appropriations. Father of the Roanoke River Flood Control and Power Project; dam at Buggs Island, Va., named by Congress the John H. Kerr Dam and Reservoir in his memory. Trustee U. N.C. Democrat. Baptist. Home: Warrenton, N.C. Died June 21, 1958; buried Fairview Cemetery, Warrenton, N.C.

KERRIGAN, James J., pharm. co. exec.; b. Bklyn., 1894. Pres., dir. Merck & Co., Rahway, N.J.; v.p., dir. Merck & Co., Ltd., Montreal, Que., Can., Mem. bd. govs., exec. com. Nat. Vitamin Found., Inc. Home: 11 Glendale Rd., Summit, N.J. Office: care Merck & Co., Rahway, N.J. Died Sept. 5, 1956; buried Gate of Heaven Cemetery, N.J.

KERRIGAN, Walter C., mfg. exec.; b. N.Y.C., 1892. 1 dau. Mrs. Joseph J. Cahill. Asst. to pres. Internat. Nickel Co. Mem. Am. Inst. Mining Engrs. Clubs: Mining, City Mid-day, Colonia Country. Home: 50 Woods Lane, Colonia, N.J. Office: 67 Wall St., N.Y.C. 5. Died July 16, 1957.

KERSHNER, Frederick Doyle, educator; b. Clear Spring, Md., Aug. 28, 1875; s. Andrew Jacob and Hannah (Lesher) K.; B.Litt., Ky. U., 1899; A.M., Princeton, 1900; studied in Europe, 1903, 1911; LL.D., Bethany Coll., 1913, Transylvania U., 1916; m. Pearl Archer, Aug. 25, 1909 (dec. Sept. 13, 1912); m. 2d, Elsie Martin, June 15, 1915; children—Frederick Doyle, Mary Eleanor, Beatrice Pearl. Dean, Kee Mar Coll., Hagerstown, Md., 1901-05, staff lectr. lit. and art Am. Soc. Extension Univ. Teaching, 1902-06; dean Am. U., Harriman, Tenn., 1906-08; pres. Milligan Coll., 1908-11, Texas Christian U., 1911-15; editor Christian Evangelist, St. Louis, 1915-17; editorial staff Christian Standard, 1918-19; prof. Christian doctrine Drake U., 1920-24; dean Sch. Religion, Butler U., 1924-44, dean emeritus and prof. Christian doctrine, 1944. Pres. Nat. Conv. Disciples of Christ, 1938. Mem. Am. Soc. Church History, Am. Theol. Soc., Indpls. Lit. Soc., Phi Kappa Phi, Theta Phi. Author: The Religion of Christ, 1912; Christian Baptism, 1913; How to Promote Christian Union, 1916; The Restoration Hand-book, 1918; Sermons for Special Days, 1921; The Christian Union Overture, 1923; Horizons of Immortality, 1926; The Spiritual Message of Great Art, 1928; Pioneers of Christian Thought, 1930; Those Gay Middle Ages, 1939; Stars, 1940. Staff contbr. to The Christian Evangelist, The Lookout. Home: 4257 Clarendon Rd., Indpls. Died Aug. 24, 1954.

KESCHNER, Moses (kĕsh'nẽr), neuropsychiatrist; b. Dobromil, Austria, Sept. 30, 1876; s. Leon and Lottie Taub K.; ed. Gymnasium, at Przemysl, Austria, Coll. City of N.Y.; M.D., Coll. Phys. and Surg. (Columbia), 1899; LL.B., New York Law Sch., 1909; m. Dorothea Jackson, Mar. 27. 1901; children—Myron, Sidney R., Harold W., Hortense. Practiced at N.Y. City, 1899—; visiting physician Dept. of Correction, New York, 1906-20; adj. neurologist Mt. Sinai Hosp., 1920-31; asso. neurologist Mt. Sinai Hospital, 1932-38; consulting neurologist Montefiore Hosp., Sydenham Hosp.; Beth Moses Hosp., Newark Beth Israel Hosp.; mem. med. advisory bd. National Jewish Hospital, Denver; former clinical professor neurology, Columbia University. Diplomate American Board Psychiatry and Neurology (1940). Fellow A.M.A., Am. Neurol. Assn., New York Acad. Medicine (chmn. of sect. neurology and psychiatry) Am. Acad. of Neurology; mem. Am. Assn. Advancement Sci., Med. Soc. State of N.Y., New York County Med. Soc., New York Neurol. Soc. (past president), American Psychiatric Association, Association for Research in Nervous and Mental Diseases, Eastern Medical Society (past president), Jewish Mental Health Society; New York Soc. for Clinical Psychiatry; mem. Grievance Com., Univ. of State of N.Y., 1926-1944; del. to Governor Lehman's Confs. on Crime. Cons. neuropsychiatrist, Induction Station, New York City, 1944-46. Democrat. Jewish religion. Contbr. of Dyskinesias, Tice's Practice of Medicine (Vol. X), Simulation and medicolegal aspects of injuries of skull, brain and spinal cord in Brock's Text Book, 1940. Home: 451 West End Av., N.Y.C. Died Aug. 31, 1956; buried Union Fields Cemetery.

KESSLER, Alfred August, Jr., army officer; b. Union Hill, N.J., Aug. 3, 1898; s. Alfred A. and Jane (Demorest) K.; B.S., U.S. Mil. Acad., 1922, M.S., Mass. Inst. Tech., 1932; grad. Air Service Primary Flying Sch., 1923, Advanced Flying Sch., 1924, Air Corps Engr. Sch., 1929, Tactical Sch., 1939; m. Polly Jane Crane, July 16, 1924; 1 son, Alfred A. III. Commd. 2d lt., U.S. Army, 1922; advanced through the grades to brig. gen., 1944; served with heavy bomber groups and as wing comdr. 8th Air Force, England, Apr. 1943-Mar. 1944; comdg. gen. Am. Air Force in Russia (shuttle bomber bases), Mar. 1944-Oct. 1944; wing comdr. 8th Air Force, England; mil. attache, Am. embassy, Stockholm, Sweden, Oct. 1944-47; dir. procurement and indsl. planning hdqrs., U.S. Air Force, Washington, 1947-50; deputy dir. maintenance, supply and services, 1950-51; director of supply and services, Washington, 1951-52; comdg. gen. 4th Air Force, September, 1952—. Decorated Legion of Merit, Silver Star, Distinguished Flying Cross, Air Medal with cluster. Distinguished Service Medal. Norwegian Order of St. Olav, Belgian Croix d'Guerre with palm, USSR Order of Suvorov, Swedish Silver Medal, Swedish Order of the Sword. Address: 1207 W. 4th St., North Platte, Neb. Died Nov. 30, 1956; buried The Presidio, San Francisco.

KESTEN, Paul W., business exec.; born Milw., Aug. 30, 1898; s. George H. and Lucy (Davies) K.; ed. U. Wis.; m. Joanne Kendall Gardner, September 22, 1946. Assistant advertising manager Gimbel Bros., Milw., 1916; account exec. McJunkin Advt. Agency, Chgo., 1918-19; advt. mgr. and v.p. Foreman & Clark Mfg. Co., 1919-26; fgn. travel and study, 1927-28; advt. writer Lennen & Mitchell, N.Y.C., 1929-30; advt. and sales promotion dir. C.B.S., 1930-35, v.p. and gen. mgr., 1936-40, exec. v.p. 1941-45, vice chairman board 1943-46, class A dir., 1937-46; co-founder and dir. War Advt. Council, 1941-46; chmn. exec. com. Cinerama Productions, 1952-54; dir. Cinerama, Inc., 1950—; 4711 Inc. 1951—; cons. C.B.S management, 1946—; dir. Free Europe Com., Inc., 1952—. Club: Lotos. Home: 860 5th Av., N.Y.C. Office: 111 E. 56th St., N.Y.C. Died Dec. 4, 1956.

KESTER, Frederick Edward, physicist; b. Eaton, O., Feb. 22, 1873; s. Henry and Wilhelmina (Kester) K.; M.E. in Elec. Engring., Ohio State U., 1895; A.M., Cornell, 1899, Ph.D., 1905; student U. Gottingen, 1903-04; m. Tamar Daker Whitmyre, June 8, 1907; children—Frederick Daker, Barbara (Mrs. Tom Page), William Henry, Elizabeth (Mrs. Robt. Holmer). Asst. in physics Ohio State U., 1895-98, instr., 1899-1901, asst. prof., 1901-07, asso. prof., 1907-09; prof. physics U. Kan., 1909—, chmn. dept. until 1941, emeritus, 1944. Fellow A.A.A.S. (emeritus life mem. 1948), Am. Phys Soc.; mem. Am. Assn. U. Profs., Am. Assn. Physics Tchrs., Kan. Acad. Science, Sigma Alpha Epsilon, Sigma Xi, Kappa Eta Kappa. Club: University (Lawrence, Kan.). Contbr. sci. jours. on investigations in physics. Home: 1612 Louisiana St., Lawrence, Kan. Died Mar. 31, 1954.

KETCHAM, Charles Burgess (kĕch'ăm), coll. pres.; b. Mechanicsburg, O., Dec. 4, 1889; s. Merrick Eugene and Ada Foote (Burgess) K.; A.B., Ohio Wesleyan University, 1913, D.D., 1932; B.D., Drew Theological Seminary, Madison, N.J., 1916; A.M., Columbia Univ., 1916; LL.D., Allegheny Coll., 1944; L.H.D., Baldwin-Wallace College, 1950; m. Lucile Brown, Apr. 8, 1918; children—Dorothy Jean (Mrs. Stuart Schaffner), Lucile Tipple (Mrs. John C. McIntosh), Charles Brown. Ordained M.E. ministry, 1916; director religious education, Trinity Church, Youngstown, Ohio, 1916-17; professor English Bible, Mt. Union College, 1917-18; instructor English Bible, Drew Theological Seminary, 1919-20; pastor Grandview Church, Columbus, Ohio, 1920-22, Parkwood-Asbury Church, Cleveland, 1922-23, M.E. Church, Oberlin, 1923-30. 1st Ch., Warren, 1930-37; dist. supt. Cleveland Dist., M.E. Ch., 1937-38; pres. Mount Union Coll., Alliance, O., 1938-53. Sec. Judicial Council of Meth. Ch., 1948-53; del. to Gen. Conf. Meth. Church, 1940, 44, 48, 52. Chaplain, U.S. Army, 1918-19; served in A.E.F. Sec. Warren Compliance Bd., NRA, 1933. Chmn. Stark County Bd. of Pub. Assistance, 1941-45. Chmn. bd. trustees Elyria Home for Aged, 1929-40; mem. N.E. Ohio Conf. (sec. bd. trustees; president bd. of education); mem. Judicial Council of Meth. Ch. (secretary since 1948); delegate Uniting Conference, 1939, and General Conference Meth. Ch., 1940, 1944. Mem. Ohio College Assn. (president 1946), Nat. Assn. of Schs. and Colls. of the Methodist Ch. (pres. 1946), Ohio Soc. of N.Y., Ohio Edn. Assn. Phi Beta Kappa, Pi Gamma Mu, Alpha Sigma Phi, Am. Legion, Rotary Club. Mason (33°). Contbr. religious articles. Home: 1304 S. Union Av., Alliance, O. Died Apr. 2, 1953; buried Spring Grove Cemetery, Cin.

KETTERING, Charles Franklin, engr., mgr., research cons.; b. nr. Loudonville, Ashland Co., O., Aug. 29, 1876; s. Jacob and Martha (Hunter) K.; E.E. in M.E., Ohio State U., 1904, E.D., 1929; honorary degrees from 29 other instns.; m. Olive Williams, August 1, 1905 (died, 1946); 1 son, Eugene Williams. Began with Star Telephone Co., Ashland, later with Nat. Cash Register Co., Dayton, O.; organized Dayton Engring. Labs. Co. (Delco) for mfg. own inventions; co-organizer The Dayton Metal Products Co. and Dayton-Wright Airplane Co., 1914; served for 27 yrs. as v.p. Gen. Motors Corp. and gen. mgr. research labs. div., now retired and serving as research cons. to co. and as dir.; dir. Nat. Cash Register Co., Ethyl Corp., Mead Corp., Moraine Development Co.; chmn. bd. Winters Nat. Bank and Trust Co., Flexible Co. Founded, 1927, and financed Charles F. Kettering Found., 1927, since served as chmn. of bd., giving active direction to researches in natural sciences, including work on chlorophyll and photosynthesis, artificial fever therapy, and cancer; pres. Thomas A. Edison Found.; dir. Sloan-Kettering Inst. for Cancer Research; co-founder Moraine Park Sch., Dayton; trustee Ohio State U., Antioch Coll., Coll. Wooster (O.), U. Miami (Fla.), So. Research Inst.; served as chmn. Nat. Inventors Council, Nat. Patent Planning Com., and Engring. and Indsl. Research Div., Nat. Research Council and as mem. Sci. Adv. Bd., Nat. Research Council; chmn. exec. com., Centennial of Engring., 1952. Fellow Nat. Acad. Scis.; pres. Soc. Automotive Engrs., 1918, A.A.A.S., 1945, member several other scientific and engring. socs. Scientific work includes invention of automotive starting, lighting, and ignition systems, electrified cash register, credit systems, and accounting machines; invented and marketed small generating unit for lighting farmhouses, etc.; originated and guided researches resulting in higher octane gasolines, including tetraethyl lead, extraction of bromine from sea water, high compression automobile engines, improved automobile finishes, nontoxic and noninflammable refrigerant, improved Diesel engines (applications of which include powering of railraods; contributor to or responsible for other developments of industrial importance. Home: Ridgeleigh Terrace, Dayton, O. Died Nov. 25, 1958; buried Dayton.

KEY, William Shaffer, oil investments; b. Dudleyville, Ala., Oct. 6, 1889; s. Callie R. and Hadassah (Fargason) K.; ed. high sch., Opelika, Ala., LL.B., Oklahoma City University, 1951; married Irene Davis, May 5, 1914; children—William Shaffer, Irene Genevieve (Mrs. Wm. Lee Harper), Robert Carleton. Began in hardware business, Wewoka, 1911; moved to Oklahoma City, 1927, and since engaged in oil bus.; pres. Key Bldg. Corp.; dir. Mutual Savs. & Loan Assn., Oklahoma Natural Gas Co. Works Progress Adminstr. for Okla., 1935-37. Candidate for Gov. of Okla., 1938. Was capt. infantry, U.S. Army, on Mexican border, 1916-17; successively capt., maj. and lt. col. U.S. Army, 17 mos. overseas. World War I; maj. gen. 45th Div., Nat. Guard of U.S.; in Federal service Sept. 1940-Nov. 1946; became provost marshal gen. of European Theater of Operations with hdqrs. in London, Oct. 1942. comdg. all U.S. troops in Iceland, June 1943-Dec. 1944; head U.S. Military Control Commn., Hungary, Dec. 1944-July 1946. ret. Oct. 1949. Civilian aide to Sec. Army in Oklahoma. Decorations: Distinguished Service Medal with Oak Leaf Cluster, Legion of Merit, Bronze Star Medal, Commendation Ribbon; Order of Bath (British); Order of Falcon (Icelandic), Distinguished Service Medal (Oklahoma). Warden Oklahoma State Penitentiary, 1924-27. Chmn. Oklahoma Pardon and Parole Board, 1928-1930. Trustee, Okla. City University. Pres. Oklahoma Historical Society, Masonic Foundation; member Supreme Council Scottish Rite. Mem. Am. Legion. Democrat. Baptist. Mason (33°). Clubs: Rotary, Men's Dinner. Comd. Okla. City Mil. Dist. during state-wide martial law, Sept.-Oct. 1923. Home: 600 Culbertson Dr. Office: Oklahoma Natural Bldg., Oklahoma City. Died Jan. 5, 1959; buried Oklahoma City.

KEYES, Charles Reuben (kēz), coll. prof.; b. Mt. Vernon, Ia., May 5, 1871; s. Marsden and Martha (Whittington) K.; B.Ph., Cornell Coll., Mt. Vernon, Ia., 1894; A.M., Harvard, 1898, Ph.D., 1923; studied univs. of Munich and Berlin, 1912-13; m. Sarah Naumann, Aug. 5, 1902; children—Catharine, Margaret. Prin. schs., Blairstown, 1894-97; instr. German, U. of Calif., 1900-03; prof. German lang. and lit., Cornell Coll., 1903-41; lecturer in anthropology since 1941. Research associate State Historical Society of Iowa since 1922; director Iowa State Archæological Survey since 1922; visiting research professor in anthropology, U. of Iowa, since 1944. Fellow Soc. for Am. Archæology, Ia. Acad. Sciences; mem. Central Sect. Am. Anthropol. Assn. (pres. 1926-27), Wis. Archaeol. Soc., Am. Assn. Univ. Profs., Cooper Ornithol. Club, Phi Beta Kappa. Methodist. Author: Prehistoric Man in Iowa; Antiquities of the Upper Iowa; Minott's Rock Shelter; and numerous articles and revs. on lit. and scientific subjects. Home: 323 10th Av. S., Mt. Vernon, Ia. Died July 23, 1951.

KEYES, Michael J., bishop; b. Dingle, Ireland, Feb. 28, 1876; s. Maurice and Mary (McKenna) K.; came to U.S., 1896, naturalized, 1921; student Christian Bros., Dingle, Ireland, 1882-93; S.T.L., J.C.L., Cath. U., Washington, 1911-22. Entered Soc. of Mary, 1901, ordained priest Roman Cath. Ch., 1907, consecrated bishop of Savannah, 1922, apptd. asst. to Pontifical Throne, 1935; ret.; Bishop of Areopolis, 1935. Home: Marist Coll., Washington 17. Died Aug. 1959.*

KEYS, Clement Melville, corporation officer; b. Chatsworth, Can., Apr. 7, 1876; s. George and Jessie Margaret (Evans) K.; B.A., Toronto U., 1897; m. Florence E. Hayes, June 15, 1905; children—Ethel Florence, Edith Margaret; m. 2d, Indiola Arnold Reilly, Oct. 23, 1924. Came to U.S., 1901, naturalized citizen, 1924. Teacher of classics, Ridley Coll., St. Catherine's, Ont., 1898-1900; reporter Wall Street Journal, New York, 1901-02, railroad editor, 1903-06; financial editor World's Work, 1906-11. Identified as officer or dir. for many years with aeronautical organizations, including Curtiss Aeroplane & Motor Corp., Curtiss-Wright Corp., Nat. Aviation Corp., North Am. Aviation, Inc., Transcontinental & Western Air, Inc., Sperry Gyroscope Co., B. F. Goodrich Co., Nat. Cash Register, and others; resigned from all aeronautical interests, 1932; founded, 1942, C. M. Keys Aircraft Service, Inc., and again active in aircraft and other industries; chmn. bd. Mackenzie Muffler Co., Youngstown, O., Montauk Beach Co., 1945; Clubs: Rockefeller Center, Wings. Home: 24 W. 55th St. Office: 551 Fifth Av., N.Y.C. Died Jan. 12, 1952.

KEYSER, Earl E(dward) (kī'ser), editor; b. York, Pa., June 5, 1903; s. William John and Lila Agnes (Landis) K.; student, Dickinson Law Sch., 1925-27. York Collegiate Inst., 1920-22; m. Thelma Gladys Hoke, June 5, 1927; children—Jack Edwin, Earl Edward. Reporter, York (Pa.) Gazette and Daily, 1920-25, Carlisle (Pa.) Sentinel, 1925-28; telegraph editor, Lancaster (Pa.) Intelligencer Jour., 1928-31, city editor, 1931-44, mng. editor, 1944-48, editor, since 1948. Mem. Lancaster Co. (Pa.) Dem. exec. com.; elceted for 1st seminar of Am. Press Inst., Columbia U., 1946. Mem. Am., Pa. (pres. 1953-54) socs. newspaper editors, Pa. Council Edn. in Journalism (v.p.), Asso. Press Mng. Editors' Assn., Inc., Sigma Alpha Epsilon, Sigma Delta Chi (pres. 1955). Democrat. Lutheran. Clubs: Rotary, Hamilton. Awarded Am. Legion Americanism medal. Home: 962 Edgemoor Ct. Office: 8 W. King St., Lancaster, Pa. Died May 11, 1955; buried Conestoga Meml. Park, Lancaster.

KEYSER, Ernest Wise, sculptor; b. Balt., 1876; s. S. and Helen (Wise) K.; gen. edn. in pub. and pvt. schs.; student Art Students' League, N.Y. and Academie Julian, Paris; m. Beatrice Oberndorf, Mar. 32, 1902; 1 dau., Ann Felicity. Made successive exhibits in Paris salons, has executed numerous portrait and mortuary and pub. meml. won in competition, including Enoch Pratt meml., Balt.; statue of Admiral W. S. Schley, in State House, Annapolis, Md.; Barry Meml., Frederick, Md.; bronze figure (Sir Galahad), for Harper Meml., Ottawa, Can.; Peter Fenelon Collier meml., N.Y.; Gahagan meml., Troy, Ohio; Leith Meml., Deal, N.J.; fountain figure, Newark (N.J.) Mus.; numerous fountains and garden sculptures. Awarded gold medal by N.Y. Soc. Architects for group "Mother and Child." Served as capt. 212th Coast Arty., N.Y. Nat. Guard, 12 yrs., retired. Mem. Architectural League of N.Y., Nat. Sculpture Soc., Beaux Arts Inst. of Design. Address: Atlantic Beach, Fla. Died Sept. 25, 1959.

KHARASCH, Morris Selig, educator; b. Kremenetz, Ukrania, Aug. 24, 1895; s. Selig and Louise (Kneller) K.; grad. Crane High Sch., Chgo., 1913; S.D., U. Chgo., 1917, Ph.D., 1919; m. Ethel May Nelson, June 24, 1923; children—Robert Nelson, Elizabeth Janet. Lecture asst. U. Chgo., 1916-17, chemist Sprague Meml. Inst., 1917-18, nat. research fellow in organic chemistry, 1919-22; asso. prof. organic chemistry U. Md., 1922-24, prof., 1924-28; asso. prof. organic chemistry U. Chgo., 1928-30, prof., 1930—, Carl William Eisendrath prof. chemistry, 1935—, now dir. Inst. Organic Chemistry, also Gustavus F. and Ann M. Swift distinguished service prof. In Gas Flame Div., U.S. Army, 1918; work on toxic gases at Johns Hopkins, later at Edgewood Arsenal; apptd. by sec. of war cons. to C. W. S., 1926; ofcl. investigator Nat. Def. Research Com., 1941; cooperative expert on thermochemistry for Internat. Critical Tables. Recipient Presdl. Merit Award, 1947; John Scott medalist for contbns. to Am. agr., 1948; Theodore Richards medalist, 1952. Mem. Am. Chem. Soc., Nat. Acad. Scis., Phi Beta Kappa, Sigma Xi. Club: Quadrangle (U. Chgo.). Awarded patents along pharm. lines and treatment of fungus diseases of small grains, isolation of active principle of ergot (ergotocine), Peroxide effect in organic reaction; atom mechanisms in organic reactions. Contbr. tech. articles in chem. jours. Home: 5750 Kenwood Av., Chgo. 37. Died Oct. 10, 1957.

KIBLER, A. Franklin, army officer; b. Stanton, Va., July 10, 1891; s. Green Markwood and Almira (Fishburne) K.; student Augusta Mil. Acad., Ft. Defiance, Va., 1906-08; B.S., Va. Mil. Inst., 1912; post grad. work U. Wis., 1914-15; grad. Signal Corps Sch., 1921, F.A. Sch., 1923, Command and Gen. Staff School, 1935, Army War College, 1938; married to Clara Fickel, September 23, 1918; children—Virginia Claire (Mrs. Samuel L. Obenschain), Robert Franklin. Commd. 2d lt., F.A., U.S. Army, Aug. 1917, and advanced through the grades to maj.

gen., 1944; comd. battery of F.A. during World War I; mem. President's Econ. and Social Mission to B. W.I., 1940; sr. Army mem. U.S. Mil. Mission to French W. Africa, 1942. Mem. War Dept. Gen. Staff, 1939-42; comdg. 78th Div. Arty., 1942-43; 13th Corps Arty., Sept., Oct. 1943; asst. chief of staff, G-3, 12th Army Group, 1943-45, chief G-3 Div., Theater Gen. Bd., ETO, 1945-46; dep. AUS rep. UN Mil. Staff Com., 1946-48; chief U.S. del. to Mil. Com. of the Western Union, 1948-49; dir. Joint Am. Mil. Adv. Group, Europe, 1949—. Decorated D.S.M. with oak leaf cluster, Legion of Merit, Bronze Star Medal, Army Commendation Ribbon (all U.S.); Officer Legion of Honor, Croix de Guerre with Palm (French); Comdr. Order of British Empire; Comdr. Order Orange-Nassau (Netherlands); Comdr. Order Leopold II, Croix de Guerre with Palm (Belgium); Comdr. with Crown, Order Civil and Military Merit of Adolph of Nassau, Croix de Guerre (Luxembourg); War Cross (Czechoslovakia). Mason. Club: Army and Navy (Washington). Address: 45 Orchard Rd., Staunton, Va. Died Jan. 24, 1955; buried Arlington Nat. Cemetery.

KIBLER, Thomas L(atimer), economist; b. Union, W.Va., Oct. 5, 1882; s. Rev. James Latimer and Rebecca (Arnold) K.; A.B., Randolph Macon Coll., 1904; A.M., George Washington U., 1908, Ph.D., 1913; grad. study U. Berlin, U. Heidelberg, Handelshochschule, U. Chgo.; m. Genevieve McClintic; children—Thomas L., Frank McClintic. Instr. in econs. U. Pitts.; 1911-12; asso. prof. econs. Agrl. and Mech. Coll. of Tex., 1913-14, prof., 1914-16; prof. transportation, dean, Sch. of Bus., Toledo U., 1916-18; capt. O.D., U.S. Army, 1918-19; prof. transportation, U. Wash., 1920-23, acting asst. dean Coll. of Bus. Adminstrn., 1921-23; prof. econs., U. of N.C., 1923-25; prof. econs., Ohio State U., 1925—; guest lectr. U. Hamburg, Germany, summer 1930. Mem. Am. Econ. Assn., Kappa Alpha, Delta Sigma Pi. Democrat. Methodist. Author: The Commodities Clause of the Interstate Commerce Act, 1916; Railroads of the Northwest (with others), 1923; Democracy in Transition (with others), 1937; World Politics, Americana Annual, 1932-50, other articles on econ. and finance (same pub.), and for Ency. Americana. Home: 1588 Waltham Rd., Columbus, O. Died 1957.

KIDD, Elizabeth (Bj), writer; b. Lancaster, N.Y., May 9, 1904; d. Samuel Fisher IV and Elizabeth Bradbury (Finch) Colt; student Miss Lockwood's, Chgo., 1915-17, U. Chgo., 1917-19, Chgo. Art Inst., 1919-21; m. Harry Kidd, 1924 (div. 1934). Fashion advt. dir. Strawbridge & Clothier, Phila., 1931-34; asso. copy dir. N.W. Ayer & Son, Inc., Phila., 1939-46; v.p. Lewis & Gilman, Inc., Phila., 1946-50. exec. cons.; contbg. editor Ladies Home Jour. until 1955; now with Internat. Playtex, N.Y.C. Received Josephine Snapp award (Chgo. Women's Advt. Club, for most outstanding work in advt. by a woman, 1946. Mem. Phila. Art Alliance. Club: Phila. of Advertising Women. Author: Just Like a Woman, 1945; Women Never Go Broke, 1948. Contbr. fiction and non-fiction to various mags., 1927—. Home: 5960 Drexel Rd., Phila. Died Feb. 17, 1958.

KIEB, Raymond Frances Charles (kēb), alienist; b. Lowville, N.Y., Aug. 24, 1881; s. Franklin Matthew and Mary Elizabeth (McGrath) K.; A.B., Cornell, 1902; M.D., Cornell U. Med. Coll., 1904; m. Harriett Marshall Brinckerhoff, Apr. 26, 1911. Physician N.Y.C. Charities Dept., Randall's Island hosps., 1904; med. intern. Matteawan State Hosp., Beacon, N.Y., 1905, asst. physician, 1905-10, med. supt. 1913-27, 31-40; 1st asst. physician Dannemora State Hosp., 1910-13; supt. Instn. for Defective Delinquents, 1940-42; ret. to become cons. neuropsychiatrist. Granted leave of absence to serve as commr. of correction in charge Dept. of Correction under reorganized scheme of state govt., N.Y., 1927-30; in charge of all prisons, reformatories, hosps. for criminally insane and instns. for defective delinquents, likewise Div. Probation, chmn. Bd. of Parole and State Correction Commn.; mem. Gov's. Cabinet. Pres., dir. George Gale Foster Corp.; dir. Bankers Comml. Corp., Am. Piano Corp., Mt. Beacon Ins. Co., Aeolian Am. Corp. Mem. A.M.A., N.Y. State, local med. socs., Am. Psychiatric Assn. Nat. Com. of Mental Hygiene, Mental Hygiene Com. of State Charities Aid Assn., N.Y. Soc. for Clin. Psychiatry, Soc. Med. Jurisprudence, Am. Civic Assn., Am. Prison Assn., Alpha Kappa Kappa. Nat. and state del. to Internat. Prison Congress, London, 1925, Prague, 1930, Berlin, 1935; del. Internat. Congress for Mental Hygiene, Washington, 1930, Paris, 1937. Clubs: Southern Dutchess Country; Amrita, Shawangunk Country. Home: Magnolia Manor, Beacon, N.Y. Died Mar. 1956.

KIEFHOFER, William Henry (kek ho-fer), economist; b. Forest Junction, Wis., Feb. 3, 1883; s. Rev. Gustavus and Christine (Gasser) K.; A.B., No. Central Coll., Naperville, Ill., 1904, LL.D., 1936; univs. London, Berlin, Leipzig, and Wis., 1909-13; Ph.D., U. Wis., 1913; m. Gladys Owen, June 24, 1916; children—William Henry Owen, Emilie Brace. Instr., prin. St. Peter (Minn.) and Arcadia (Wis.) high schs., 1904-09; instr. U. Wis., 1913-14, asst. prof., 1914-17, asso. prof., 1917-20, prof. since 1920, head dept. econs., 1916-31, chmn. grad. div. social scis., 1938-46; vis. prof. econs. U. Cal., summers 1917, 22; dir. 1st Nat. Bank, Madison. Chairman mediation and investigation com. Madison Bldg. Trades, 1921; mem., speaker U.S. Treasury War Finance Com. for Wis., 1942-46. Dir., trustee U. Wis. Y.M.C.A. since 1912, chmn. and speaker U.S. patriotic speaking campaign, 1917-18; chmn. hon. degrees com., 1939-41, gen. chmn. Centennial Celebration Com. Recipient U.S. Treasury award for Patriotic Service, 1941-45; Kiekhofer Meml. Fund to reward excellency in teaching at U. Wis., established by friends. Mem. Am. Econ. Assn. (executive com. 1924-30), Am. Polit. Sci. Assn., Am. Statis. Assn., Economists Nat. Com. on Monetary Policy (exec. com.), Am. Assn. U. Profs. (pres. Wis. br. 1944-45), Wis. Acad. Scis. Arts and Letters, Madison Lit. Club (pres. 1941-43), Phi Beta Kappa, Phi Kappa Phi (pres. Wis. br. 1938-39), Chi Phi, Artus. Conglist. Clubs: University (pres. 1927), Madison, Black Hawk Country. Author: An Outline of Economics, 7th edition, 1930; Syllabur of Economic Theory, 4th edit., 1951; Economic Principles, Problems and Policies, 1936, 3d edit, 1946; Problems in Economics, 1937; To Thee, Wisconsin, State and University, 1950. Editor: Century Studies in Economics, 16 vols. Home: 1919 Arlington Pl., Madison, Wis. Died Aug. 1, 1951; buried Forest Hill Cemetery, Madison.

KIERNAN, Peter D., ins. exec.; b. N.Y.C., Jan. 18, 1876; s. Frank J. and Jane (DeLacy) K.; ed. pub. schs., Albany; m. Carroll Guerin, Oct. 4, 1917. Began as an errand boy in ins. office at 12 yrs.; now mem. firm Rose & Kiernan, Albany; pres. Arkay Bldg. Co., Albany Comml. Co.; trustee Albany Home Bldg. Co. Trustee N.Y. State Hosp. for Treatment of Incipient Pulmonary Tb, Ray Brook, N.Y. Mem. Nat. Underwriters' Assn. (v.p.), C. of C. (pres.). Democrat. Catholic. Clubs: Albany, Albany Yacht, Wolfert's Roost Country. Home: 244 Clinton Av. Office: Arkay Bldg., Albany, N.Y. Died July 18, 1958.

KIHN, W(illiam) Langdon (kēn), artist; b. Brooklyn, N.Y., Sept. 5, 1898; s. Alfred Charles and Carrie Lowe (Peck) K.; ed. Art Students League, 1916-17, private teacher; pupil of Homer Boss, Winold Reiss; m. Helen Van Tine Butler, June 3, 1920; 1 dau., Phyllis. Painter, specializing in portraits of Indians. One-man exhibitions: Museum of N.M., Santa Fe, 1921; Milwaukee Art Inst., 1922; Denver Art Assn., 1922; U. of Okla., 1923; Los Angeles Museum of Art, 1923; San Francisco Museum of Art, 1923; U. of Wash., 1923; Corcoran Gallery of Art, Washington, D.C., 1925; Art Alliance of New York, 1925; House of Parliament, Ottawa, Can., 1925; Art Museum of Minneapolis, 1927; St. Paul (Minn.) Pub. Library, 1927; also many others in clubs, galleries, hotels, etc. Group exhbns.: Nat. Acad. Design and Archtl. League, New York; Brooklyn Museum of Arts; Chicago Art Inst.; Nat. Gallery of Can., Ottawa. Permanent exhbns.: Ohio State U., U. of Okla., Litchfield (Conn.) Museum, Provincial Museum of Brit. Columbia, McGill University, Montreal, Ottawa Nat. Museum, Vancouver Art Gallery, Royal Ontario Museum, Winnipeg Art Gallery, Thompson Memorial Mus.; pvt. collections; permanent collection 60 paintings given Wesleyan U., Middletown, Conn., by Edward Lyman Bill Found. Books illustrated: Beaver, Kings and Cabins (by Constance Lindsay Skinner); Dawn Boy of the Pueblo (by Lena Becker Scott); Desert Wife (by Hilda Faunce); Indian Days in the Rockies (by Marius Barbeau); When Red Men Ruled Our Forests, 24 paintings in Nat. Geog. Magazine, Nov. 1937; Red Men of the Southwest, 25 paintings in Nat. Geog. Magazine, Nov. 1940; Indians of Our Western Plains, 16 paintings in Nat. Geog. Mag., July, 1944; Totem Pole Builders, 16 paintings in Nat. Geog. Mag., Jan. 1945; First Familes of S.E. America, 8 paintings, Nat. Geog. Mag., Jan. 1946. Works also include portraits of Dr. Alexis Carrell, Ruth St. Denis, Ted Shawn, Ex-gov. Cross. of Conn. and Guy Wiggins. Mem. Conn. State Fine Arts Commn.; bd. dirs. Conn. Forest and Park Association. Fellow Am. Geog. Soc., Royal Soc. Arts (London); mem. Nat. Geog. Soc.; Arctic Inst. of North Am. Clubs: Explorers (hon. life), Salmagundi, Century Association (New York). Home: R.F.D. No. 1, East Haddam, Conn. Died Dec. 12, 1957; buried Hadlyne (Conn.) Cove Cemetery.

KILBORN, William T., mfr. metal products; b. Portland, Me., Sept. 23, 1897; s. James and Caroline (Goss) K.; student Phillips Andover Acad.; m. Marguerite Duttenhofer, Nov. 22, 1924. Asso. Flannery Mfg. Co., Bridgeville, Pa., 1933—, pres., dir., 1934—; pres., dir. Fort Pitt Mfg. Co., Pitts.; dir., mem. exec. com. Am. Broadcasting-Paramount Theatres, Inc., N.Y., Pitts. & W.Va. Ry. Co., Pitts.; dir. Canton Co., The Cottman Co., Balt., Nat. Union Fire Insurance, Pitts., The Pennroad Corp., Wilmington, Del. Served as 1st lt. F.A., France, World War I. Republican. Episcopalian. Clubs: Duquesne, Fox Chapel, Rolling Rock (Pitts.); Chicago (Chgo.); Cloud (N.Y.C.); Carlton (Washington); Racquet (Phila.). Home: Royal York Apts., Pitts. 13. Office: Bridgeville, Pa. Died Aug. 14, 1957; buried Abingdon Ch. Cemetery, Gloucester County, Va.

KILBRETH, John William, army officer; b. N.Y. City, Feb. 18, 1876; s. John W. and Mary (Culbertson) K.; grad. Westminster Sch., 1894; A.B., Harvard, 1898; grad. Arty. Sch., 1902; distinguished grad. Army Sch. of the Line, 1909; grad. Army War Coll., 1921; m. Mrs. J. Stevens Ulman, Feb. 27, 1923. Comnd. 2d lt. 4th Arty., Sept. 9, 1898; 1st lt. Arty. Corps, May 1901, capt., Apr. 1904; assigned to 6th Field Arty., June 1907; trans. to 5th F.A., Feb. 1915, to 1st F.A., Aug. 1915; maj. May 15, 1917; lt. col. (temp.), Aug. 5, 1917, col. (temp.), Feb. 7, 1918, brig. gen. (temp.), Oct. 1, 1918; retired Dec. 15, 1922; promoted brig. gen. on retired list, June 21, 1930. Served in Philippines in Light Battery F, 4th Arty., 1899-1901; instr. Sch. of Fire for Field Arty., Feb.-Aug. 1915, and Aug. 1917-May 1918; with 1st Army Arty., A.E.F., as chief of operation, June-Aug. 1918, as chief of staff, Aug.-Oct. 1918; comd. 55th F.A. Brigade, Oct.-Dec. 1918; at G.H.Q. from Dec. 1918; rejoined 55th Brigade, Feb. 1919. Mem. oversers visiting com. Dept. Mil. and Naval Science, Harvard. Awarded D.S.M., 1921. Clubs: Union, Church, Holland Lodge (New York); Pot and Kettle (Bar Harbor, Me.). Home: 907 Fifth Av. Address: Union Club, 791 Park Av., N.Y.C. 21. Died July 23, 1958; buried Spring Grove Cemetery, Cin.

KILENYI, Julio (kĭl'ā-nyē), sculptor; b. Arad, Hungary, Feb. 21, 1885; s. Joseph and Rosa (Pecsi) K.; ed. in Hungary; student Royal Arts Sch., Budapast, 1900-02, also studied in Germany and France, 1902-07. Came to U.S., 1916, naturalized, 1924. Active as sculptor in Argentina, S.A., 1907-16; represented by medallions and plaques on permanent exhbn. in Met. Mus. Art, Cleve. Mus. Art, Boston Mus. Fine Arts, Masonic Mus., U.S. War Dept., Newark Art Mus., Smithsonian Instn., N.Y. Hist. Mus., Oxford U. (Eng.), British Mus. and Victoria-Albert Mus., (London), The Franklin D. Roosevelt Library, Hyde Park, N.Y., Vatican Mus. (Rome), Columbia U.; Tercentenial medallian City N.Y.; 25 portraits Milw. Hall of Fame sports figures; 9 portraits Baseball Hall of Fame, Cooperstown; portraite of Pres. United Aircraft in Hartford; 50th Anniversary Boy's Club of Am. medallion, and others. Art director L. G. Balfour Company, Attleboro, Mass.; mem. Prezzi-Kilenyi Assoc., 1930—. Honorable mention Exhibition of Allied Artists Am., 1931; bronze medal 10th Olympiad Com., Los Angeles, 1932; Lindsey Morris memorial prize for basrelief, 1937. Fellow Am. Internat. Acad.; mem. Nat. Sculpture Soc. (life mem.), Archtl. League of N.Y. (hon. mem.), Am. Numismatic Soc., Allied Artists Am., Audubon Artists, Acad. Polit. Scientists, Am. Internat. Acad. (life), Internat. Soc. Am. (treas. 1952—), Bruckner Soc. Am. (v.p. 1935—). Home: 1 W. 67th St., N.Y.C. Died Jan. 29, 1959.

KILEY, John (Francis), business exec.; b. N.Y. C., June 21, 1908; s. William J. and Loretta (O'Hearn) K.; A.B., Holy Cross Coll., 1929; m. Marion A. Hanagan, Nov. 4, 1933; children—John, Richard, Dorothy. With Am. News Co., 1932-34, B. Altman & Co., 1934-37; joined Johnson & Johnson, New Brunswick, N.J., 1937, v.p. sales, 1951—, mem. mgmt. com., 1949—. Office: 501 George St., New Brunswick, N.J. Died Dec. 4, 1952.

KILEY, John Coleman, real estate exec. b. Boston, Mass., June 5, 1884; s. James and Mary (Coleman) K.; ed. Boston Latin Sch.; m. Bertha O'Connor, 1914; children—Jean (Mrs. David Wells), John C., Jr. Entered real estate business, 1910; operator of own real estate business since 1910; real estate adviser to Boston, 1910-14. Dir. New England Trust Company, Boston. Trustee, Provident Instn. for Savings in Town of Boston. Trustee Children's Hospital, Boston. Democrat. Roman Catholic. Club: Algonquin. Author: Changes in Realty Values in the 19th and 20th Centuries, 1941. Home: 285 Commonwealth Av. Office: 15 Bosworth St., Boston. Died June 3, 1952.

KILEY, Moses E. (kī'lē), R.C. bishop, Diocese of Milwaukee. Was head St. Vincent de Paul Soc. and Men's Mission, Chicago, 1918; later supt. Asso. Cath. Charities of Chicago Archdiocese and head of Holy Cross Mission; chmn. dirs. group Nat. Charities Assn., 1924-26; spl. adviser Am. College, Rome, Italy, 1926-34; consultore to Vatican's Russian Commn., 1929; bishop of Trenton, 1934-39; apptd. archbishop of Milwaukee, Jan. 1940. Address: 2000 W. Wisconsin Av., Milw. Died Apr. 15, 1953; buried St. John Cathedral, Milw.

KILGORE, Harley Martin, senator; b. Brown, W. Va., Jan. 11, 1893; s. Quimby and Laura Jo (Martin) K.; LL.B., W.Va. U., 1914; m. Lois Elaine Lilly, May 10, 1921; children—Robert Martin, Elinor Stuart (Mrs. Albert T. Young, Jr.). Admitted to West Virginia bar, 1914; in practice at Beckley, West Virginia, 1914-17 and 1920-32; became judge Criminal Court, Raleigh County, W.Va., 1932-40; mem. U.S. Senate, W.Va., 1940—; mem. special senate com. to investigate Nat. Def. Program, 1941-46, chmn.,

1946, chmn. Senate Judiciary Com. In 1st O.T.C., Fort Benjamin Harrison, Ind., 1917; successively 2d lt., 1st lt., capt., U.S. Army, 1917-20; officer W. Va. Nat. Guard, 1921-53, ret. col. Mem. Am. Polit. Sci. Assn., W.Va. Hist. Soc., S.A.R. Mem. Christian Ch. Democrat. Am. Legion, Mason, Moose, Elk, Delta Tau Delta. Address: 3834 Macomb St., N.W., Washington. Office: Senate Office Bldg., Washington. Died Feb. 28, 1956.

KILLIAN, John Allen (kĭl'ĭ-ăn), biochemist; b. Philadelphia, Pa., Jan. 4, 1891; s. Mark and Sarah Anne (Bradley) K.; A.B., Central High Sch., Phila., 1909, St. Joseph's Coll., Phila., 1913; A.M., Fordham U., N.Y. City, 1915, Ph.D., 1921; grad. study Columbia, 1915-16; m. Marie Frances Fitzpatrick, Sept. 1, 1917 (div.); children—Francis Mark, Joan Allen, Elizabeth Marie; m. 2d Josephine Gloria Castro; 1 son, Mark. Instr. chemistry, Fordham U., 1913-16; instr. in biochemistry, N.Y. Post Grad. Med. Sch. and Hosp., 1916-26, prof. 1926-33; established Killian Research Labs. for analytical and research work in biochemistry, bacteriology and pathology, 1933, pres. and dir. since 1933. Served as capt. Sanitary Corps, U.S. Army. Mem. Am. Chem. Soc., Am. Soc. Biol. Chemists, Soc. for Exptl. Biology and Medicine, Am. Gastro-Enterological Assn., Am. Urol. Assn., Am. Pub. Health Assn. Republican. Club: Chemists. Contbr. to tech. jours. Home: 425 E. 79 St. Office: 2 E. End Av., N.Y.C. Died Dec. 2, 1957.

KILMAN, Leroy Noble, writer; b. Drummondsville, Ont., Can., Mar. 26, 1878; s. Alva Hamilton and Ida M. (Noble) K.; ed. high sch.; LL.B., U. of Mich., 1905; m. Cecile Gauntlett, of Milan, Mich., July 26, 1910; children—Katherine, Julian. Came to U.S., 1898, naturalized citizen, 1904. Admitted to N.Y. bar, 1906; asst. U.S. atty. Western Dist. of N.Y., 1908-14; with Bur. of Naturalization, 1914—; dist. dir. of naturalization at Buffalo, N.Y., 1925—. Lecturer on the short-story, U. of Buffalo. Mem. Phi Delta Phi. Unitarian. Contbr. short stories to mags., 1912—; also articles on Americanization. Home: 200 Woodward Av. Office: Federal Bldg., Buffalo, N.Y. Deceased.

KILPATRICK, Harry Colman, banker; b. Philadelphia, Feb. 7, 1907; s. James Lester and Mary (Colman) K.; grad. Lehigh U., 1929; m. Barbara Park, Sept. 15, 1934; 1 dau., Barbara Gail. With Pease and Elliman, 1929-33; with Mfrs. Trust Co. since 1933, asst. vice pres., 1937-38, vice pres. in charge of mortgage dept., 1938-47, vice pres. and asst. to pres., 1947-50, exec. v.p. and dir. since 1950; pres. and dir. 261 5th Av. Corp.; dir. and mem. executive com. N.Y. Dock Trade Facilities Corp., N.Y. Dock Co.; dir. Bing and Bing, Inc., Interstate Dept. Stores Inc., New Yorker Hotel Corporation, 500 5th Avenue, Inc.; trustee Harlem Savings Bank. Served with Corps of Engrs., U.S. Army, advancing from capt. to lt. col., 1942-45; exec. officer to chief of engrs. Awarded Legion of Merit. Mem. Chamber of Commerce of State of N.Y. mem. Newcomen Soc. of Eng., Psi Upsilon. Clubs: Wall Street (New York); Apawamis (Rye, N.Y.). Home: 955 5th Av. Office: 55 Broad St., N.Y. City 15. Died Nov. 1, 1952.

KILPATRICK, William D., lecturer; b. Owosso, Mich.; s. William M. and Emma (Williams) K.; student Olivet (Mich.) Coll., 1892-95; LL.B., U. Mich., 1898; m. Lucy Lee Horsman, Nov. 9, 1898 (dec. Oct. 1950); children—Lucia Lee, Elizabeth, Martha. Practiced law at Owosso until 1900, at Washington, 1900-07; in land and timber business with Hon. J. W. Fordney, 1907-10; Christain Science lectr., 1917-44. Apptd. mgr. World Com. on Publ., First Church of Christ, Scientist, Boston, July 10, 1944. Mem. Sigma Alpha Epsilon. Republican. Home: Longwood Towers, Brookline 46, Mass. Office: 107 Falmouth St., Boston 15. Died Apr. 14, 1950.

KIMBALL, Charles Nathaniel, lawyer; b. Parkville, Mo., Sept. 20, 1872; s. Chester Frayer and Sarah Margaret (Boydston) K.; grad. Phillips Acad., Andover, Mass., 1899; student Harvard Law Sch., 1899; m. Mary Jane McGlinchey, July 3, 1904; children—Chester Frayer, Mary Boydston, Walter Sugden. Admitted to Pa. bar, 1894, to W.Va. bar, 1904; mem. Kimball & Sugden; active in organizing and operating gas and oil companies in W.Va., Okla., Ill., Kan., Ohio, Wyo. and Ky. since 1907; pres. Old Hundred Gold Mining Co. (Silverton, Colo.), Gen. Petroleum Engineers, Inc.; dir. Sistersville Tank & Boiler Works, First Tyler Bank & Trust Co. Dir. Sistersville Cemetery Association. Mayor Sistersville, West Virginia, 1 term: member West Virginia Rep. State Committee since 1916, state chmn., 1934-36; del. at large W.Va. to Rep. Nat. Conv., Cleveland, 1936; presdl. elector from W.Va. 4th Congl. Dist., on Rep. Nat. Ticket, 1940; alternate delegate-at-large, W.Va. to Republican National Convention, Chicago, Ill., 1944; del. from W.Va. to Progressive Nat. Conv., Chicago, 1916; alternate del.-at-large, to Rep. Nat. Conv., Phila., 1948. Chmn. Tyler County W.Va., Republican Exec. Committee 6 yrs. Mem. Pennsylvania Soc. of Order of Founders and Patriots of America, N.E. Historic Geneal. Soc. (life mem.), Mass. Soc. Mayflower Descs. (life mem.), Gov. and Company of Mass. Bay in New England (life mem.), Theta Nu Epsilon. Republican. Episcopalian. Mason, K.T., Shriner (life mem.), Elk (life mem.). Clubs: Country of Sistersville (dir.); Harvard of West. Pa. (Pittsburgh). Home: Sistersville, W.Va.; (summer) Chautauqua, N.Y. Office: Thistle Bldg., Sistersville, W.Va. Died May 9, 1956; buried Wellsboro, Pa.

KIMBALL, Dexter Simpson, univ. prof.; b. New River, N.B., Can., Oct. 21, 1865; s. William Henry and Jane (Paterson) K.; A.B., in engring., Stanford Univ., 1896, M.E., 1913; LL.D., from U. of Rochester, N.Y., 1926; D.Sc., Case School of Applied Science, 1930; Dr. of Engring., Kansas State Coll., 1933; Northeastern Univ., 1934, Lehigh U., 1939; m. Clara Evelyn Woolner, 1898; children—Isabella Jane, Dexter Simpson, George Norman. Apprentice and journeyman with Pope & Talbot, Port Gamble, Wash., 1881-87; in shops of Union Iron Works, San Francisco, 1887-93; in engring. dept. same, 1896-98; designing engr., Anaconda Mining Co., 1898; asst. prof. machine design, Sibley Coll. (Cornell U.), 1898-1901; works mgr. Stanley Electric Mfg. Co., 1901-04; prof. machine constrn., 1904-05, prof. machine design and constrn., 1905-15, prof. industrial engineering, 1915, Sibley Coll. of Cornell U. Actg. pres., July 1-Oct. 1, 1918 and Nov. 1929-Feb. 1930, dean Coll. of Engring., 1920-36, now emeritus, Cornell. Brackett lecturer, Princeton, 1929; lecturer on industrial orgn., Stanford Grad. Sch. of Business, 1930; lecturer, Grad. School, U.S. Naval Acad., 1943-52. Receiver for Ithaca Traction Corp., 1925; dir. McGraw-Hill Publ. Co., 1930-48; dir. Ithaca Savings Bank, 1932-42, 1st v.p., 1938-42; dir. Ithaca Enterprises, Inc., 1936. Mem. Council Indsl. Edn. N.Y. State Dept. Edn., 1911. U.S. fuel adminstr. for Tompkins Co., N.Y., 1917-18; dir. Training Schs. for Army Mechanics, 1917-18. Mem. bd. of visotors U.S. Naval Acad., 1922. Apptd. by Sec. of Commerce Hoover chmn. organizing com. 2d Pan-Am. Standardization Conf., 1927; chmn. Priority Com. on Machine Tools and Equipment, Office of Production Management, 1941, chief of priority section, Machine Tool Division, War Production Board, 1942-43. Mem. of staff Alexander Hamilton Institute, 1922, chmn. bd., 1930-35; chmn. bd. Internat. Accountants Soc.; chmn. Commn. on Rochester Mechanics Inst., 1927; pres. Ithaca Chamber Commerce, 1935-36. Mem. Soc. Promotion Engring. Edn. (v.p. 1922-23, pres. 1929), Am. Soc. Mech. Engrs. (pres. 1921-22), Federated Am. Engring. Soc. (vice president 1920-22), American Engring. Council (pres. 1926-28), Nat. Econ. League, A.A.A.S., Newcomen Soc., Kappa Sigma, Phi Kappa Phi (pres. Cornell chapter 1922-23), Sigma Xi, Tau Beta Pi (pres. 1922-23); hon. judge Fisher Body Craftsman's Guild. Honorary member Engineers Club of Philadelphia. Chmn. John Fritz Medal Bd., 1930, Hoover Medal Bd., 1930. Awarded Lamme medal by Soc. for Promotion of Engring. Edn., 1933; Worcester Reed Warner gold medal, Am. Society Mech. Engineers, 1933; H. L. Gantt gold medal American Management Assn. and Am. Soc. Mech. Engineers, 1943; Fred Winslow Taylor Key. Soc. for Advancement Management, 1948. Kimball Hall, Cornell U., named for him. Author: Elements of Machine Design (with John H. Barr), 1909; Industrial Education, 1911; Principles of Industrial Organization, 1913; Elements of Cost Finding, 1914; Plant Management; Industrial Economics, 1930; I Remember, 1952. Editor: The Book of Popular Science. Contbr. to scientific press. Home: Belleayre Apts., Ithaca. Died Nov. 1, 1952; buried Ithaca.

KIMBALL, Fiske, museum dir., architect; b. Newton, Mass., Dec. 8, 1888; s. Edwin Fiske and Ellen Leora (Ripley) K.; A.B. from Harvard, 1909, M. Arch., 1912; Ph.D., U. of Mich., 1915; Dr. Fine Arts, New York U., 1933, U. Pa., 1945; Litt.D., Temple U., 1951; married Mari Goebel, June 7, 1913. Assistant at Harvard, 1900-10; instr. U. of Ill., later asst. prof. architecture and fine arts, U. of Mich., 1912-19; prof. art and architecture, U. of Va., 1919-23; Morse prof. lit. of arts of design, in charge Dept. of Fine Arts, New York U., 1923-25; dir. Phila. Museum of Art, 1925—. Has served on editorial bds. of Art and Archaeology, Architectural Record. Art Bulletin, Gazette des Beaux-Arts and New England Quarterly; in charge Am. sect. of Allgemeines Künstler Lexikon, 1920-26; chmn. Va. Art Commn., 1920-23; mem. State Bd. for Examination of Engrs. and Architects, 1920-23, Thomas Jefferson Memorial Commission, 1935—; holder Sachs Research Fellowship, 1916-17; lecturer, Met. Museum, 1919-25, U. of Chicago, 1921, National Academy of Design, 1923-25, and at University of California in 1940. Architect of McIntire Amphitheatre, Gymnasium, University Apts., U. of Va.; and many other bldgs.; university architect New York U., 1924—. Engaged in restoration of important Am. Houses, among them Monticello, home of Thomas Jefferson, of Robert E. Lee, Stratford, Va., mansions of Fairmount Park, Phila., and on advisory bd. for restoration of Williamsburg, Va., advisory bd. for Rockefeller Center, New York, advisory board Nat. Park Service, 1935-51; mem. bd. dirs., Thomas Jefferson Memorial Foundation; mem. Jefferson Bicentennial Commn., 1940-43 (sec.); vice chmn. editorial bd. Papers of Thomas Jefferson. Fellow Am. Inst. Architects (past pres. Va. Chapter), Am. Assn. Museums (past pres.), Museum Council of Phila. (past pres.), Assn. Art Mus. Dirs., Am. Philos. Society, Phi Beta Kappa, Delta Upsilon; honorary correspondent member Royal Institute of British Architects; Philadelphia Award, 1951. Clubs: Century (New York); Rittenhouse, Art Alliance, T-Square (Phila.); Farmington Country (Va.). Author: Thomas Jefferson, Architect, 1916; A History of Architecture (with G. H. Edgell), 1918; Domestic Architecture of the American Colonies, 1922; American Architecture, 1928; Samuel McIntire, 1940; The Creation of the Rococo, 1943; Great Masterpieces of Painting in America (with L. Venturi), 1948. Editor Foundations of Classic Architcture, 1919. Frequent contbr. to literary and art magazines of Am. and Europe. Home: Lemon Hill, Fairmount Park. Office: Philadelphia Museum of Art, Parkway at 26th St., Phila. 30. Died Aug. 14, 1955.

KIMBALL, George Turner, hardware mfr.; b. Chicago, Ill., June 25, 1874; s. Penn Townsend and Helen Margaret (Gooch) K.; LL.B., Lake Forest Coll., 1899; m. Janette Thorson, June 30, 1902. Accountant, Linn & Dwight, Chicago, 1893-1906; lawyer and accountant, pvt. practice, 1906-13; auditor Am. Hardware Corp., New Britain, Conn., 1913-24, pres., 1924-45; now retired. Dir. New Britain Nat. Bank, Conn. Light & Power Co., Am. Hardware Corp. since 1945. Republican. Episcopalian. Mason (Shriner), Clubs: New Britain, Shuttle, Meadow. Home: 74 S. Burritt St. Office: 10 Franklin Sq., New Britain, Conn. Died Jan. 1, 1953.

KIMBALL, Harry Swift, indslist., b. Brockton, Mass., Jan. 14, 1875; s. Rufus Henry and Louise (Swift) K.; grad. U.S. Naval Acad., 1896; m. Adele C. Corner, Jan. 19, 1898. Resigned from U.S. Navy, 1896; pres. Am. Zinc, Lead & Smelting Co., Boston, 1902-16; pres. Remington Arms-Union Metallic Cartridge Co., 1916-20; v.p. and mgr. Gaston, Williams & Wigmore, Inc., N.Y.C., 1920-21; v.p., in charge finance, U.S. Shipping Bd. Emergency Fleet Corp., 1921-2; mem. firm Kimball & Co. Served as lt. comdr., USNR, Apr. 1917-Apr. 1921. Republican. Swedenborgian. Clubs: University, Union League, Bankers'. Home: Portchester, N.Y. Died Mar. 10, 1957.

KIMBALL, Justin Ford, educator; b. nr. Huntsville, Tex., Aug. 25, 1872; s. Justin A. and Elizabeth (Ford) K.; A.B. and A.M., Mt. Lebanon (La.) Coll. (now defunct), 1890; M.A., Baylor U., 1899, LL.D., 1920; studied U. Chgo., U. Mich.; m. Annie Lou Boggess, Apr. 12, 1905. Tchr. rural schs., La., 1890-92, high sch., Mexia, Tex., 1892-93; prin. high sch., Navasota, 1893-95, Temple, 1895-1900; supt. schs., Temple, 1900-02; practiced law, Waco, Tex., 1902-04; law clerk Dept. of Edn., Tex., 1904-05; supt. schs., Temple, 1905-14, Dallas, 1914-24; prof. edn. So. Meth. U., 1925-29; v.p. Baylor U., Dallas, 1929-39; lectr. on ednl. adminstrn. So. Meth. U., Dallas, 1924—; also lectr. various summers at Baylor U., U. Tex., Peabody Coll. for Teachers, Nashville. Mem. Dallas City Plan Commn.; dir. Kessler Plan Assn. of Dallas; pres. County Sch. Bd., Dallas. Mem. N.E.A., Tex. Tchrs. Assn. (past pres.); hon. life mem. Am. Hosp. Assn., as recognition of originating Am. plan of group hospitalization. Baptist. Mason. Clubs: Critic, Paideian. Author of various brochures on ednl. topics, etc. Home: 5431 Vickery Blvd., Dallas 6. Died Oct. 7, 1956.

KIMBALL, Marie Goebel (Mrs. Fiske Kimball), writer; b. N.Y. City; d. Julius and Kathryn (Vreeland) Goebel; private studies and at Radcliffe College, 1907-08; A.B., University of Illinois, 1911; Guggenheim fellow, 1945 and 1946; m. Fiske Kimball, June 7, 1913. Author: Thomas Jefferson's Cook Book, 1938; Martha Washington's Cook Book, 1940; The Furnishings of Monticello, 1940; Jefferson: The Road to Glory, 1943; Jefferson: War and Peace, 1947; Jefferson: The Scene of Europe, 1950. Contributor articles and fiction to North Am. Rev., Va. Quart. Review, Antiques, Am. German Review, Vogue, Ladies' Home Jour., Saturday Evening Post, N.Y. Times Mag., Good Housekeeping, etc. Editor: Rosegger, Das Holzknechthaus, 1913. Address: Lemon Hill, Fairmount Park, Phila. Died Mar. 2, 1955.

KIMBALL, Stockton, physician, univ. dean; b. Buffalo, N.Y., Aug. 17, 1902; s. Maulsby and Harriet (Stockton) K.; B.S., Harvard, 1924; M.D. cum laude, U. of Buffalo, 1929; m. Sylvia L. Becker, June 23, 1936; children—Caroline Stockton, Margaret Lund, Rosalind Sylvia. Interne, Buffalo General Hosp., Buffalo, N.Y., 1929-30; Guy's Hosp., London, England, 1931-32; Pathology Inst., Dr. L. Aschoff, Freiburg, Germany, 1932-33; assistant professor medicine, University of Buffalo School of Medicine, 1946—; asst. dean, 1944-46; dean, 1946—. Fellow A.C.P.; mem. Erie Co., N.Y. State, Am. Med. Assns., Am. Gastroenterol. Assn., Alpha Omega Alpha, Sigma Xi. Club: Saturn (Buffalo). Contbr. articles on gastrointestinal subjects to med. jours.; also contbr. chapters to Tice's Practice of Medicine, Nelson's Loose-leaf Medicine. Home: 215 S. Cayuga Rd., Williamsville 21, N.Y. Office: 3435 Main St., Buffalo 14. Died Feb. 7, 1958.

KIMBALL, Walter Gardner, banker; b. Canton, N.Y., Jan. 12, 1888; s. Solon Dexter and Jane (Loomis-Green) K.; student Holbrook's Mil. Acad.; B.S., St Lawrence U., Canton, N.Y., 1908; married, 1922 (divorced); 1 son, Dexter Hungerford; m. 2d, Elva Lavies, July 31, 1936. Chmn. bd., dir. Commercial Nat. Bank and Trust Co., N.Y.C.; pres., dir. Commercial Nat. Safe Deposit Co.; dir. Best & Co., Omnibus Corp. Trustee St. Lawrence U.; treas. Army Relief Soc. Served as lt. 9th U.S. Inf., 2d Div., 1917-19. Decorated D.S.C. (U.S.); Conspicuous Service Cross (N.Y. State), Croix de Guerre (France). Mem. S.R., Alpha Tau Omega. Presbyn. Clubs: University, Recess, Bankers (gov.) (N.Y.C.); Deepdale Golf. Home: 885 Park Av. Office: 46 Wall St., N.Y.C. Died Mar. 31, 1951; buried Canton, N.Y.

KINARD, James Pinckney, educator; b. Kinard, S.C., July 17, 1864; s. John Martin and Lavinia (Rook) K.; B.S., The Citadel, 1886, LL.D., 1930; Ph.D., Johns Hopkins, 1895; m. Lee Wicker, June 20, 1899; children—Lavinia Rook (Mrs. O. P. Smith), James Pinckney, Oscar Wicker (dec.), Katharine Madison (Mrs. Ben Strozier), Nelle McFall, Henry Harrison (dec.). Prof. English. Winthrop Coll., Rock Hill, S.C., 1895-1913, The Citadel, 1913-14; supt. schs., Newberry, S.C., 1916-17; prof. psychology, dean of Coll., Winthrop Coll., 1917-29; pres., 1929-34, pres. emeritus, 1934——. Pres. S.C. State Tchrs. Assn., 1917. Mem. Alpha Tau Omega. Democrat. Baptist. Rotarian (pres. 1927-28). Author: English Language and Literature, 1912; Our Language, 1927. Editor: Old English Ballads, 1902. Home: 704 College St., Rock Hill, S.C. Died June 1951.

KINCAID, Elbert Alvis (kĭn-kād'), economist; b. Palouse, Wash., Mar. 31, 1884; s. Alvis Atkins and Josephine (Davis) K.; A.B., Wash. State Coll., 1910; A.M., Harvard, 1911; Ph.D., U. Cal., 1922; m. Ethel Wexler, May 24, 1913; children—Olivia, Douglas. Dep. auditor Whitman County, Wash., 1911-13; asst. prof. econs. and history Wash. State Coll., 1913-16; instr. econs. U. Cal., 1916-22; asso. prof. finance U. Va., 1922-26, prof., 1926——; financial writer San Francisco Call., 1919-21; mem. Gov.'s Com. on Banking Legislation, Va., 1935; economist Fed. Reserve Bank of Richmond, 1937——, v.p., 1945-49; asso. dir. sch. bus. adminstrn. U. Va., 1952——. Mem. exec. com., adv. council on Va. Economy; mem. exec. com., Richmond Tax Study Commn. Mem. Va. Social Sci. Assn., Southern Econ. Assn., Am. Econ. Assn., Com. on Taxation and Gov., Va. C. of C.; Com. on Va. Bankers Conf., Va. Bankers Assn. Am. Staits. Assn., Raven Soc., Phi Beta Kappa, Beta Gamma Sigma, Alpha Kappa Psi, Omicron Delta Kappa, Alpha Tau Omega. Club: Colonnade. Lectr. Contbr. articles to profl. jours. Ex-mem. bd. of editors, Am. Econ. Review. Home: Rugby Rd. at Mason Lane, Charlottesville, Va. Died Jan. 16, 1958.

KINCHELOE, David Hayes, judge; b. Sacramento, Ky., Apr. 9, 1877; s. Robert M. and Lucy A. K.; B.S., Bowling Green (Ky.) Coll., 1898; m. Laura Stateler; 1 dau., Laura Imogene (wife of Comdr. James H. Davis, USN). Admitted to practice, Ky. bar, 1899; former mem. law firm Gibson & Kincheloe. Madisonville, Ky.; county atty., McLean County, 1902-06; mem. 64th to 71st Congresses, 2d Ky. Dist.; resigned, Oct. 5, 1930, to accept appointment as judge U.S. Customs Court. Dem. presdl. elector 2d Congl. Dist., 1912. Methodist. Home: 4935 Hillbrook Lane, N.W. Address: Dupont Circle Bldg., Washington. Died Apr. 16, 1950; buried Madisonville, Ky.

KIND, John Louis, educator; b. Portage, Wis., Dec. 6, 1877; s. Emil Frederick and Mary (Niess) K.; A.B., U. Neb., 1899, A.M., (scholar in German, 1899-1900, fellow in German, 1900-01), 1901; Ph.D., Columbia (Carl Schurz fellow, 1902-03), 1906; m. Elsbeth Veerhusen, Dec. 21, 1916. Tchr. German, Omaha (Neb.) High Sch., 1901-02; asst. in German, Columbia, 1903-05; instr. in German, U. Wis., 1905-08, asst. prof., 1908-16, asso. prof., 1916-19; held various exec. positions in industry, 1919-28; prof. Germanic langs. head dept. U. Tenn., 1928-49. Mem. Am. Assn. Tchrs. of German (mem. exec. council 1937, 38, 39, 46, 47, 48; chmn. program com., 1941-48; sec.-treas. Tenn. chpt. 1938——), Modern Lang. Assn., Geothe Soc. Am., Franklin Soc. (Switzerland), Tenn. Philol. Assn., Tenn. Ednl. Assn., E. Tenn. Ednl. Assn., U. Tenn. Philology Club, Phi Beta Kappa, Delta Phi Alpha, Delta Tau Delta. Presbyn. Club: Faculty. Author: Edward Young in Germany, 1906; Conversational Approach to German (with C. M. Purin and F. H. Reinsch), 1947. Editor: Grillparzer's Des Meeres und der Liebe Wellen, 1916, Grillparzer's Sappho, 1916; Durian's Kai aus der Kiste, 1936; Fröschel's Himmel, meine Schube, 1939. Contbr. to German Quar., Monatshefte, The Rainbow. Home: 314 Forest Park Blvd. N.W., Knoxville, Tenn. Died Oct. 30, 1958.

KINDLEBERGER, Jacob, mfr.; b. Roumback, Alsace Lorraine, Germany, Feb. 27, 1875; s. John and Matilda (Fraelich) K.; ed. Ohio Wesleyan U.; m. Lucinda Drucilla Faulkner, Dec. 7, 1905 (Died Nov. 17, 1954); 1 son, Joseph B. (dec.). Chmn. bd., Kalamazoo Vegetable Parchment Co., 1936——. Pres., Kalamazoo C. of C., 3 times. Trustee Bronson Methodist Hosp., Ohio Wesleyan U. Methodist (trustee). Rotarian. Home: 521 S. Riverview Dr. Office: Kalamazoo Vegetable Parchment Co., Parchment, Mich. Died Jan. 1, 1947; buried Riverside Cemetery, Kalamazoo, Mich.

KING, Alvin Olin, lawyer, ex-gov.; born Leoti, Kan., June 21, 1890; s. George Merritt and Bessie Brown (Stirling) K.; grad. Lake Charles High Sch., 1908, Parsons Bus. Coll., 1911; LL.B., Tulane, 1915; m. Willie Lee Voris, Jan. 29, 1916; children—Voris King, Alvin O. (dec.). Practiced law at Lake Charles, 1915; now mem. firm King, Anderson & Swift. Pres. King Corp.; chmn. bd. Powell Lumber Co., Weber-King Lumber Co., Inc., Farmers Land & Canal Co., Inc., Lake Charles Drug Stores, Inc., Am. Sulphur & Oil Co., Lake Charles Office Bldg. Co., Hayes Lumber Company, Kelly, Weber & Co., Inc., Farmers Rice Milling Co., Inc., Lake Charles Grain & Grocery Co., Lake Charles Feed Co., Inc., Farmers Land & Canal Company, Incorporated. Nat. councillor, U.S. C. of C., 1947-54; pres. Lake Charles Assn. Commerce, 1948; mem. La. Mineral Bd., 1948. Mem. council La. State Law Inst.; mem. Am. Law Inst. Mem. La. Senate, 14th Dist., 1924, reelected, 1928; pres. pro tem of Senate, May 1930; lt. gov. of La., Oct. 14, 1931; gov., Jan. 25, 1932. Chmn. Com. for draft of project for Exec. Dept. of new La. State Constn. Del. to Dem. Nat. Conv., 1932. Mem. Am., La. (bd. govs. 1949-53, pres. 1952-53), bar assns. Clubs: Pioneer, Lake Charles Country (Lake Charles, La.). Address: P. O. Box 865, Lake Charles, La. Died Feb. 21, 1958; buried Graceland Cemetery, Lake Charles.

KING, Arthur Dale, capitalist; b. Normandy, Tenn., Aug. 16, 1872; s. Robertson Jefferson and Mary Jane (Bramblette) K.; ed. pub. schs. Tenn. and Calif.; m. Florence Yoakum, Mar. 21, 1899 (dec. July 1958); children—Geraldine (Mrs. Winston Stuart Cowgill), Dale (Viscountess de Bonchamps). Cashier, 1st National Bank, Hanford, California, 1892-1903; organized King Lumber Co., 1903; president King Lumber Co., Kimble Oil Company; director The Charles Nelson Co.; director Wells Fargo Bank & Union Trust Co., Calif.-Western States Life Ins. Co. Mem. Seismol. Soc. Am., Astron. Soc. of Pacific, Calif. Hist. Soc. Republican. Episcopalian. Clubs: Pacific Union, Bohemian Press, Commonwealth, Commercial, Burlingame Country. Home: 835 Chiltern Rd., Hillsborough, Cal. Office: 111 Sutter St., San Francisco. Died May 10, 1952.

KING, Arthur S(cott), physicist; b. Jerseyville, Ill., Jan. 18, 1876; B.S., U. Cal., 1899, M.S., 1901, Ph.D., 1903; married. Asst. physics U. Cal., 1901-03, instr. physics, 1905-08; Whiting fellow Bonn U., 1903-04; Carnegie research asst. U. Berlin, 1904-05; supt. phys. lab. Mt. Wilson Obs., Carnegie Instn., 1908-43; physicist Cal. Inst. Tech., 1944-46; mathematician Naval Ordnance Test Sta., Pasadena, Cal., 1946-54. Civilian, Nat. Def. Research Com., 1944. Fellow Am. Phys. Soc., Meteoritical Soc. (pres. 1946-50); mem. Nat. Acad. Sci., Am. Optical Soc., Astronomers Soc., Astron. Soc. Pacific (pres. 1941). Home: 925 Topeka St., Pasadena 6. Office: Mount Wilson Observatory, Pasadena 4, Cal. Died Apr. 25, 1957.

KING, Campbell, army officer; b. Flat Rock, N.C., Aug. 30, 1871; s. Alexander Campbell and Mary Lee (Evans) K.; attended Charleston Coll.; hon. M.A., Harvard, 1920; distinguished grad. Inf., and Cav. Sch., 1905; grad. Army Staff Coll., 1906; grad. Army War Coll., 1911; grad. Gen. Staff Coll., 1920; m. Harriott Laurens King, December 19, 1907; children—Duncan Ingraham, Barbara. Private and corporal cavalry, July 1897-July 1898; commd. 2d lieut. 1st Infantry, July 9, 1898; promoted through grades to brig. gen., July 23, 1924; brig. gen. (temporary) during the World War; maj. gen., May 1, 1932; retired, 1933. Served in Cuba, Philippines, Hawaii, China, and on Mexican border; arrived in France with 1st Div., June 25, 1917; chief of staff, 1st Div., Dec. 1917-Sept. 1918; brig. gen. and chief of staff, 7th A.C. and 3d A.C., Oct. 1918-July 1919. Served in following sectors of the line in France: Somervillier, Ansauville, Montdidier, Saizerais and Vosges Mountains. Participated in following battles: Verdun, Aug. 1917, Cantigny, Montdidier-Noyon, Aisne-Marne, St. Mihiel, Meuse-Argonne. Took part in march to the Rhine and occupation of Coblenz bridgehead. Awarded D.S.M. (U.S.); Croix de Guerre with palm and silver star, Officer Legion of Honor (French); Comdr. Order of the Crown (Italian). Was first Am. officer, with Col. George B. Duncan, to receive French Croix de Guerre, awarded by Gen. Deville, comdg. 42d French Div., to which he was attached during French Verdun offensive, Aug. 1917. Home: Flat Rock, N.C. Died Oct. 16, 1953; buried Church of St. Johns in the Wilderness, Flat Rock.

KING, Charles Kelley, mfr. elec. supplies; b. Calais, Me., Dec. 7, 1867; s. George Gilman and Emeline Danforth (Kelley) K.; prep. edn., Calais Acad.; student spl. course, Johns Hopkins, 2 years. With Northwest Thompson Houston Co., St. Paul, Minn., 1889-90; sales engr. Ansonia Electric Co., Chicago, 1890-93; with Ohio Brass Co., Mansfield, since 1893, pres. and gen. mgr., 1928-46; pres., gen. mgr. Can. Ohio Brass Co., Ltd., 1928-46, now chmn. bd. both companies. Mem. National Elec. Mfrs. Assn. Republican. Episcopalian. Mason. Clubs: Elec. Mfrs., Westbrook Country. Home: Kingwood, Mansfield. Office: Ohio Brass Co., Mansfield, O. Died May 31, 1952; buried Mansfield Cemetery.

KING, D(onald) J(oseph), aviation exec.; born Sodus, Mich., Oct. 19, 1909; s. J. Edward and Gertrude (Bell) K.; A.B., Kalamazoo (Mich.) Coll., 1931; Naval Aviation, Naval Air Station, Pensacola, Fla., 1932; m. Ann Nichols, June 22, 1935. Flew with marine aviation, Quantico, Va., 1932-33; copilot United Airlines, Chicago, 1935-37; joined Northwest Airlines, 1937, chief pilot, Minneapolis, 1942-43, supt. no. region, Edmonton, Alta., Can., 1943-45, gen. mgr. eastern region, 1945-46, v.p. Orient region, Tokyo, Japan, 1946-53; capt. Northwest Airlines, 1953——. Baptist. Club: Minikahda (Mpls.). Home: 2256 W. Lake of the Isles Blvd., Mpls. Office: Northwest Airlines, 1885 University Av., St. Paul. Died Oct. 10, 1955; buried Crystal Springs Cemetery, Benton Harbor, Mich.

KING, Edward Postell, Jr., army officer (ret.); b. Atlanta, July 4, 1884; s. Edward Postell and Mary Montgomery (Edwards) K.; B.L., U. of Ga., 1903; grad. Sch. of Fire for Field Arty., 1912; Command and Gen. Staff Sch., 1923, Army War Coll., 1930, Naval War Coll., 1937; m. Elizabeth McLaws, Dec. 26, 1912 (dec. 1954); m. 2d, Pauline T. King Beutell, 1956. Commd. 2d lt., 6th Field Arty., U.S. Army, 1908, promoted through grades to maj. gen., 1941; instructor Command and Gen. Staff Sch., 1930-35, Army War College, 1937-40; retired 1946. Awarded D.S.M. with oak leaf cluster. Mem. Phi Delta Theta. Episcopalian. Mason. Clubs: Army and Navy (Washington); Army and Navy Country (Arlington, Va.); Savannah (Ga.) Golf. Prisoner of war of Japanese Govt.; released Aug. 1945. Address: Sea Island, Ga. Died Aug. 31, 1958, Brunswick, Ga. Buried Church Yard of St. John in the Wilderness, Flat Rock, N.C.

KING, Ernest Joseph, naval officer; b. Lorain, O., Nov. 23, 1878; s. James Clydesdale and Elizabeth (Keam) K.; grad. U.S. Naval Acad., 1901; student U.S. War College, 1932-33; hon. LL.D., College of William and Mary, 1942; LL.D., Columbia U., 1947; Princeton Univ., 1946, Miami Univ., 1946; D.Sc., Bowdoin College, Harvard Univ. and Northwestern U., 1945; D.C.L., Oxford University, 1945; m. Martha Rankin Egerton, October 10, 1905; children—Elizabeth Egerton (wife of Col. Oliver W. Van den Berg, U.S. Army), Eleanor Calvert (Mrs. Eleanor King Hempstead), Martha Stuart (wife of Lt. Gen. Frederic H. Smith, Jr., U.S.A.F.), Clara Clydesdale (Mrs. J. M. B. Howard), Florence Beverly, Mildred Wilson (Mrs. J. O. McReynolds), Ernest Joseph (lt. comdr. U.S.N.). Served as midshipman U.S.N., Spanish-American War; commd. ensign, U.S. Navy, June 6, 1903; advanced through grades to rear admiral, Nov. 1, 1933, admiral, 1941; asst. chief Bureau Aeronautics, 1928-29, chief, 1933-36; vice adm., comdg. Aircraft Battle Force, U.S. Fleet, 1938-39; mem. gen. bd., Navy Dept., 1939-40; then comdr. in chief, U.S. Atlantic Fleet; apptd. comdr. in chief U.S. Fleet, Dec. 1941, chief of naval operations, Mar. 1942-Dec. 1945. Apptd. Fleet Admiral, Dec. 17, 1944. Awarded Navy Cross, D.S.M., D.S.M. with 2 gold stars, Sampson medal, Spanish Campaign badge, Mex. Service medal, Victory Medal (1918) with bronze star, Am. Defense Service medal (1941), American Area Campaign medal, Order of Crown of Italy (Grand Ufficiale), Order Vasco Nunez de Balboa, Commander (2d degree) Panama, First Rank (Grand Cross) Moroccan Ouissam Alaouite Cherifian, French Morocco, Naval Order of Merit, 1st Class (Cuba, Am. Legion D.S.M., Star of Estrella Abdon Calderon, 1st Class, Ecuador, Order of Naval Merit (Gran Cruz) Brazil; Order of the Bath, Croix de Guerre, Grand Cross Legion of Honor (France), Order of Tripod (China); Grand Cross, Order George I (Greece), Knight Grand Cross, Order Orange Nassau (Netherlands), Order of Crown, Croix de Guerre (Belgium), Grand Cross, Mil. Order Italy, Gold Medal U.S. Congress. Clubs: Army and Navy, Army and Navy Country (Washington). Home: 2919 43d St. N.W., Washington. Died June 25, 1956; buried U.S. Naval Acad. Cemetery, Annapolis, Md.

KING, Helen Dean, zoologist; b. Owego, Tioga County, N.Y., Sept. 27, 1869; d. George Alonzo and Leonora Louise (Dean) King) A.B., Vassar, 1892; fellow in biology, Bryn Mawr, 1896-97, A.M., Ph.D., 1899; univ. fellow for research in zoölogy U. Pa.; unmarried. Student asst. in biology Vassar, 1894-95; tchr. sci. Baldwin Sch., Bryn Mawr, Pa., 1899-1907; asst. in anatomy Wistar Inst., Phila., 1909-10, asso., 1910-13, asst. prof. embryology, 1913-27, mem. same, 1927——. Fellow A.A.A.S.; mem. Am. Soc. Zoölogists (v.p. 1937), Am. Soc. Naturalists, N.Y. Acad. Science, Wistar Inst. (mem. adv. bd.), Soc. Exptl. Biology and Medicine, Am. Assn. Anatomists, Marine Biol. Lab. Assn. (Woods Hole, Mass.), Am. Genetic Assn., Phi Beta Kappa, Sigma Xi. Republican. Episcopalian. Contbr. on regeneration, sex determination, inbreeding, domestication, etc. Home: The Fairfax, Locust at 43rd St., Phila. Died Mar. 9, 1955.

KING, Henry Lord Page, army officer; b. Macon, Ga., Apr. 17, 1895; s. Richard Cuyler and Henrietta Dawson (Nisbet) K.; B.S. in E.E., Ala. Poly. Inst., 1916; m. Sarah Brumley Evans, Sept. 6, 1919; children—Henry Lord Page, May Lindsay (Mrs. Warren Duncan). Commd. 2d lt., June 9, 1917, and advanced through the grades to brig. gen., Dec. 1942; apptd. officer in charge, Mil. Personnel Div., Nov. 1941. Mason (Scottish Rite). Home: 1026 Crest Court, Neosha, Mo. Died Oct. 29, 1952.

KING, Horace Williams, engr.; b. Big Rapids, Mich., Feb. 10, 1874; s. Charles B. and Fannie L. (Williams) K.; C.E., U. of Mich., 1895; m. Mabel V. Jones, June 8, 1909. In gen. engring. practice, 1895-99; asst. engr., Nicaragua Canal surveys, 1899-1901; provincial supervisor Philippines, res. engr. Canton-Hankow R.R. and U.S. asst. engr. in charge constrn., Manila Harbor, 1901-04; engr. U.S. Reclamation Service, 1905-07; gen. practice, Ore., 1907-09; engr. in charge hydraulic dept., Arnold Co., Chicago, 1909-12; prof. hydraulic engring., U. of Mich., 1912-39, prof. emeritus since 1939. Republican. Mem. Am. Soc. C.E. (hon.), Sigma Xi; honorary member Mich. Engineering Soc., Chi Epsilon (Southern California chpt.). Author: Handbook of Hydraulics, 1917, 2d rev. edit., 1939; Manning Formula Tables, Vol. I, 1937; Vol. II, 1939; section, Irrigation and Drainage, Am. Civil Engineers Handbook, 5th edit., 1930; section on Hydraulics, Civil Engineers' Handbook, 1933, 2d edit., 1940. Co-Author: Elementary Hydraulics, 5th edit., 1948. Address: State Savings Bank Bldg., Ann Arbor, Mich. Died April 22, 1951; buried Pasadena, Cal.

KING, James H., physician, govt. ofcl.; b. Chipman, N.B., Jan. 18, 1873; s. Hon. George G. and Esther (Briggs) K.; student St. Martin's Acad., 1888-91; M.D., C.M., McGill U., 1895; LL.D. (hon.), Acadia U., 1923, Ottawa U., 1924; m. Nellie Sadler, Jan. 1, 1907 (deceased). Practiced medicine, Andover, St. John, N.B., 1895-98; dist. surgeon C.P. Ry., Crow's Nest Line, Cranbrook, B.C., 1898-1916. Rep., Cranbrook, B.C. Legislature, 1903-09, 1920; candidate Kootenay Ho. of Commons, 1911; elected to B.C. Legislature and reelected by acclamation at by-election, 1916; minister pub. works Brewster Govt., 1916, accepted portfolio pub. works Oliver Cabinet, 1918-22; minister of pub. works Dominion Govt., 1922-26; elected to Ho. of Commons, 1922, 1925, 1926; apptd. minister Dept. Health Soldiers' Civil Re-Establishment, 1926; mem. Canadian Senate since 1930, leader govt. and minister without portfolio, 1942, 45, speaker, 1945-49; del. World's Security Conf., San Francisco, 1945. Privy councillor; Knight of Grace, Venerable Order Hosp. of St. John of Jerusalem, St. John Ambulance Assn. Fellow A.C.S. (a co-founder, gov., 1913); mem. Grads. Soc. McGill U. Liberal. Baptist. Mason, Odd Fellow, K.P. Clubs: Union (Victoria, B.C.); Vancouver (B.C.); Country (Ottawa). Home: Devonshire Hotel, Vancouver, B.C. Office: The Senate, Ottawa, Can. Died July 14, 1955.

KING, James Harold, marine engring.; b. New Haven, July 17, 1892; s. John Joseph and Helen Josephine (Grady) K.; student N.Y. pub. schs., Yale, 1913; m. Dorothy MacIsaac, Dec. 7, 1918; children—James Harold, Doris E. (Mrs. Robert K. Coutlee). With The Babcock & Wilcox Co., 1914, assigned engring. sect. marine dept., 1917, asst. mgr. marine dept., 1928-31, mgr. dept., 1931, v.p., 1945, head boiler div., 1952, dir. 1953; dir. Diamond Power Specialty Co., Lancaster, O., Hooper Holmes Bureau, Inc., N.Y.C. Mem. Scarsdale (N.Y.) Planning Commn. Mem. Soc. Naval Architects and Marine Engrs. (pres. 1951-52), Inst. Marine Engrs. (v.p.), Am. Soc. Naval Engrs. (past council mem.), Am. Bur. Shipping, Engrs. Joint Council, Newcomen Soc., Alpha Chi Rho, Sigma Xi, Pi Tau Sigma. Republican. Roman Catholic. Clubs: India House, Cloud, Engrs., Yale (N.Y.C.); Met. (Washington); Winged Foot Golf. Author several tech. papers, articles. Home: 20 Bradford Rd., Scarsdale, N.Y. Office: 161 East 42d St., N.Y.C. 17. Died Nov. 1953.

KING, Julie Rivé, artist, concert pianist, composer; b. Cincinnati, Oct. 31, 1859; d. Léon and Caroline Rivé; her mother was a musician, and under her instruction Julie became so proficient that she played in concerts at 6; was a pupil of Liszt; m. Frank H. King, 1878. Well known in the musical world; has played over 200 concerts with Theodore Thomas, 80 with Seidl, and frequently with other eminent conductors in U.S. and Europe. Died July 24, 1937.

KING, Roy Stevenson, mech. engr.; b. Xenia, O., Sept. 10, 1876; s. William Harrison and Bertha Louise (Ritter) K.; M.E., Ohio State U., 1902; M.S., U. of Minn., 1907, U. of Chicago, 1914; Sc.D., U. of Ga., 1922; m. Estella Gertrude Peterson, Feb. 19, 1903. Constrn. foreman Aetna (Ind.) Powder Co., 1898-99; foreman Nat. Cash Register Co., 1902-03; instr. in mech. engring. dept., U. of Minn., 1903-05; asst. prof. exptl. engring., Ohio State U., 1905-07; gen. mgr. Hall-Cronan Co., Dayton, O., 1907-10; in engring. dept. Ind. Steel Co., Gary, 1910-12, engring. dept. Fairbanks, Morse & Co., 1912-14; asst. prof. mech. engring., U. of Ariz., 1914-17; prof. exptl. engring., Ga. Sch. Tech., Atlanta, 1917-23, head of mech. engring. dept. and supt. shops and power (plant), 1923-46; prof. emeritus mech. engring., Ga. Sch. Tech. since Sept. 1946; dir. Atlanta Fed. Savings & Loan Assn. Mem. Ga. State Board of Registration for Professional Engrs. and Surveyors. Chmn. Atlanta Smoke Abatement Bd.; vice pres. Ga. Soc. Professional Engrs., hon. mem. Ga. Engring. Soc. In engring. dept. picric acid plant, Picron, Little Rock, Ark., 1948. Fellow Am. Soc. M.E., mem. Am. Soc. Engring. Education (v.p. 1924-25), Newcomen Soc., Sigma Xi, Phi Kappa Phi, Pi Tau Sigma, Tau Beta Pi, fellow A.A.A.S. Methodist. Mason. Home: 1293 Oxford Rd. N.E., Atlanta 6. Died Oct. 12, 1956.

KING, Samuel Wilder, gov. of Hawaii; b. Honolulu, T.H., Dec. 17, 1886; s. James Anderson and Charlotte Holmes (Davis) K.; student pub. schs., Honolulu; grad. U.S. Naval Acad., 1910; m. Pauline Evans, Mar. 18, 1912; children—Charlotte K., Samuel Pailthorpe, Davis Mauliola, Evans Paliku, Pauline Nawahine. Mem. bd. supervisors city and county Honolulu, 1923-24; pres. Samuel W. King, Ltd. (real estate, ins.) since 1924; T.H. del. 74th, 75th, 76th congresses, 1935-41; governor of Hawaii until 1957, resigned in 1957. Served as lt. comdr. United States Navy, 1910-24. Member of Honolulu Realty Board, United States Naval Inst., U.S. Naval Acad. Grads. Assn., Order of Kamehameha, Am. Legion, Vets. Fgn. Wars. Republican. Club: Commercial. Home: Halekon, Kaneohe, Oahu, T.H. Office: Governor's House, Honolulu, Hawaii. Died Mar. 24, 1959.

KING, Stanley, coll. pres.; b. Troy, N.Y., May 11, 1883; s. Henry Amasa (judge Mass. Superior Court) and Maria Lyon (Flynt) K.; A.B., Amherst Coll., 1903; A.M., Harvard, 1906; LL.D., Dartmouth Coll., Colgate U., Wesleyan, 1932, Columbia U., 1933, Williams Coll., 1936, Hamilton Coll., 1938, Univ. of Rochester, 1939, Mass. State Coll., 1946; Amherst, 1946; m. Gertrude Louisa Besse, Dec. 12, 1906 (died April 10, 1923); children—Richard, Gertrude, Margaret (dec.); m. 2d, Margaret Pinckney Allen, July 23, 1927. Admitted to Mass. bar, 1906, and practiced in Boston; eastern mgr., dir. Internat. Shoe Co.; pres. Amherst Coll., 1932-46, pres. emeritus, 1946-51. Mem. com. on supplies, Council Nat. Defense, 1917; apptd. spl. asst. to Sec. of War, Oct. 4, 1917; mem. President's Industrial Conf., 1919-20; chmn. Mass. Commn. on Stabilization of Employment, 1931-34. Trustee Amherst Coll., 1921-46, trustee emeritus 1946-51. Trustee, Merrill Foundation, 1946-51, Mayhew Nevin Fund, 1946-51. Mem. Delta Kappa Epsilon, Phi Beta Kappa. Clubs: Union (Boston); Century (New York). Author: History of Endowment of Amherst College, 1950; Recollections of Folger Shakespeare Library, 1950; The Consecrated Eminence, 1951. Address: Amherst, Mass. Died Apr. 28, 1951; buried Monument in Wildwood Cemetery, Amherst.

KING, Steve M., lawyer; b. Mt. Enterprise, Tex., Aug. 30, 1878; s. Joseph Watts and Martha Caroline (Garrison) K.; student, Alexander Collegiate Inst., Jacksonville, Tex., 1898-99; m. Margaret Lloyd, June 14, 1905; children—Winnie Davis (Mrs. Raymond S. Mauk), Margaret (Mrs. Virgil R. Blanch), Katherine (Mrs. John W. Newton, Jr.). Gen. practice, 1904-07; mem. Ho. of Reps., Tex. Legislature, 1907-08, State Senate, Tex., 1915-17; asso. justice, 9th supreme Jud. Dist., 1917-18; gen. practice, 1919-36; U.S. atty., Eastern Dist. Tex., 1936-49. Vice-pres. U.S. Atty.'s Conf., 1942-43. With the law firm of King, Sharfstein, and Rienstra. Served in U.S. Army in Philippine Insurrection, 1901-02. Mason, Elk, Knight of Pythias. Clubs: Country, Rotary (Beaumont, Tex.). Home: 2298 McFaddin. Office: Perlstein Bldg., Beaumont, Tex. Died Apr. 24, 1958; buried Forest Lawn, Beaumont.

KING, Willard Vinton, banker; b. Brooklyn, N.Y., Nov. 3, 1868; s. William Vinton and Belle F. (Boyd) K.; A.B., Columbia, 1889; m. Mary Spingler van Beuren, Apr. 26, 1904. Began as messenger Produce Exchange Bank, New York, 1890, later with Continental Trust Co., of which became sec., 1898; v.p., 1901 (company merged with New York Security and Trust Co., 1904, later known as New York Trust Co.); pres. 1908-23, Columbia Trust Co., which absorbed Knickerbocker Trust Company; now retired; dir. Manati Sugar Co.; past dir. N.Y. Life Ins. Co.; direcotr United Artists Theatre Corp. Trustee Columbia U., Archaeol. Inst. Am. (chmn. bd.), Sch. Bus. Research, Museum of American Indian. Organized Columbia U. Alumni Fund. One of original com., N.Y. State Chamber Commerce (later Am. Arbitration Assn.; mem. com. on Comml. Edn. that developed Trade and Comml. Schs. of N.Y. Trustee (one of original) N.Y. Assn. for Blind. With assos., organized the Bowling Green Neighborhood Assn., chmn. until it becomes social center of Beekman St. Hosp. Mem. Phi Beta Kappa and Delta Upsilon fraternities. Protestant. Clubs: University, Columbia University. Author: Benefits and Evils of the Stock Exchange, 1913. Home: Convent, N. J. Died May 1, 1955; buried Evergreen Cemetery, Morristown, N.J.

KING, William Lyon Mackenzie, ex-Prime Minister of Canada; b. Berlin (now Kitchener), Ont., Dec. 17, 1874; s. John and Isabel Grace (Mackenzie) K.; B. A., U. Toronto, 1895, LL.B., 1896, M.A., 1897; post-grad., fellow in polit. economy U. Chgo., 1896-97; A.M., Harvard, 1898, Ph.D., 1909; fellow in polit. sci. Harvard, 1897-1900, including traveling fellowship abroad; LL.D., Queens, 1919, Toronto, 1922, Harvard, 1923, Edinburgh, 1923, Yale, 1924, Cambridge, 1926, McGill, 1929, Princeton, 1941, Columbia 1943, William and Mary College, 1948, U. London, (Eng.), 1948; D.C.L., Oxford, 1923; hon. fellow Royal Inst. Brit. Architects, 1944; hon. bencher of Gray's Inn, 1946; unmarried. Deputy Minister of Labor, Canada, and editor Labor Gazette, 1900-08; mem. Parliament (Liberal), North Waterloo, Ont., 1908-11, Prince, Prince Edward Island, 1919-21, North York, Ont., 1921-25, Prince Albert, Sask., 1926-45, Glengary, Ont., 1945—; Minister of Labor, Canada, 1909-11, pres. General Reform Assn. of Ontario, 1912-14; investigation of indsl. relations Rockefeller Found., 1914-17; mem. of nat. exec. Canadian Patriotic Fund, 1914-20; selected as leader of Liberal Party, Can., Aug. 1919; served to retirement, Aug. 7, 1948; leader of the Opposition, 1919-21, 30-35; Prime Minister, pres. Privy Council, sec. of state for external affairs, Canada 1921-30 (except June-Sept. 1926); resumed office as prime minister, Oct. 23, 1935, and continued after gen. election, Mar. 26, 1940, and after general election June 11, 1945 (Liberal adminstrn. sustained at both); retired as Prime Minister of Can., Nov. 15, 1948, relinquished portfolio External Affairs, Sept. 4, 1946. Rep. Can. at Imperial Confs., London, 1923, 26, 37, at meetings of Prime Ministers, London, 1944, 46; rep. Can. at Coronation of King George VI and Queen Elizabeth 1937; Minister in attendance on the King on visit of King and Queen to Can. and U.S., 1939. Concluded with President Roosevelt the Ogdensburg Agreement, Aug. 17, 1940 and the Hyde Park Declaration, April 20, 1941; signed the Washington Declaration on Atomic Energy with President Truman and Prime Minister Attlee, the White House, Washington, Nov. 14, 1945; chmn. Can. delegation to UN Assembly, Paris, 1948; rep. Can. at meeting of Prime Ministers, London, 1948. Rep. for Can. at signing of Multilateral Treaty for Renunciation of War, Paris, 1928; mem. council and v.p. assembly League of Nations, Geneva, 1928, 36; chmn. Canadian delegation to UN Conf. on Internat. Orgn., San Francisco, 1945, to Conf. of Paris, 1946. Companion St. Michael and St. George, 1906; Privy Council (Can.), 1909; Privy Council (United Kingdom), 1922. Received Order of Merit from His Majesty King George VI, 1948. Mem. l'Institut de France, 1948. Hon. mem. Canadian Legion. Presbyn. Author: The Secret of Heroism, 1906; Industry and Humanity—A Study in the Principles Underlying Industrial Reconstruction, 1918 (abridged edn. 1935), The Message of the Carillon and Other Addresses, 1927; Canada at Britain's Side, 1941; Canada and the Fight for Freedom, 1944. Address: Laurier House, Ottawa, Can. Died July 22, 1950.

KING, William Peter, clergyman; b. Franklin County, Ga., Feb. 27, 1871; s. George Lumpkin and Julia (Vaughter) K.; A.B., Emory U., Atlanta, 1893, A.M., 1895; studied theology Vanderbilt U. (founder medal for oratory); m. Mary Evans Harris, Jan. 17, 1900; children—George Harris, Ruskin, Julia, Howard La Prade, Fern. Ordained ministry M.E. Ch., S., 1898; pastor, Mo., 1898-1902, Ga., 1903—; pastor First Ch., Gainesville, Ga., 1922-26, also editor Wesleyan Christian Advocate, 1920-22; pastor First Ch., Athens, Ga., 1927-28. Del. to Gen. Conf. M.E. Ch., S., 1918, 22, 26, 30, 34, 38, Uniting Confs., 1939; del. Gen. Conf. Meth. Ch., 1941. Mem. Phi Beta Kappa, Kappa Alpha. Democrat. Editor: Humanism, 1931; Social Progress and Christian Ideals, 1931. Author: The Practice of the Principles of Jesus, 1926; Faith in the Divine Fatherhood; Right and Wrong: In a World of Confusion, 1939; Adventism, 1941; Motives for Christian Living, 1942; The Search for Happiness, 1946. Elected, 1928, book editor and editor Meth. Quar. Rev.; elected editor Nashville Christian Advocate, 1932. Compiler of book Behaviorism, 1930. Home: 1620 Linden Av. Address: 810 Broadway, Nashville. Died June 20, 1957; buried Woodlawn Meml. Park, Nashville.

KING, William Robert, clergyman; b. Brotherwood, Hawkins County, Tenn., Jan. 12, 1868; s. John Bell and Mary (Clark) K.; A.B., Washington (Tenn.) College, 1889, D.D., 1900; graduate Union Theological Seminary, New York, 1982; Ph.D., Wooster U., Ohio, 1900; LL.D., University of Tulsa, 1945; m. Florence Broyles, June 21, 1892; 1 son, William Robert. Ordained Presbyn. ministry, 1892; stated supply, Thalequah, Ind. Ty., 1892;93; synodical missionary Okla. and Ind. Ty., 1893-96; founder and pres. Henry Kendall Coll., Muskogee, Ind. Ty. (now Tulsa (Okla.) U., 1896-99; supt. Am. S.S. Union, for Southwest, 1899-1902; pastor 1st Ch., Monmouth, Ill., 1902-15, First Presbyn. Ch., St. Louis, July 1, 1915-July 1, 1919; sec. Presbyn. Bd. Nat. Missions, 1919-27, and exec. sec. Home Missions Council, 1927-38, retired. Made trip around the world, 1911-12, as mem. commn. of three sent out by Presbyn. Bd. Foreign Missions to study conditions and needs of mission fields. Joint author: Around the World Studies and Stories of Presbyterian Foreign Missions, 1913. Wrote: History of the Home Mission Council; also pamphlets on missionary subjects. Home: Church Hill, Tenn. Died Nov. 21, 1951; buried Oak Hill Cemetery, Kingsport, Tenn.

KING, William Wirt, clergyman, educator; b. Paint Bank, Va., Jan. 9, 1862; s. Rev. Francis H. J. and Rufina E. (Wilson) K.; grad. West Virginia State Normal School, 1881; B.A. from Scio College, at Scio, O., 1887; M.A., Ill. Wesleyan U., 1890, Ph.D., 1893; D.D., McKendree Coll., 1898, Ohio Wesleyan, 1922; S.T.D., Ia. Wesleyan, 1904; LL.D., Baker U., 1928; m. Alta Muse Ford, Oct. 2, 1889; 1 son, William Wirt. Ordained M.E. ministry, 1888; pastor 1st Ch., Huntington, W.Va., 1888-92, Trinity Ch., Lafayette, Ind., 1892-95, Lindell Av. Ch., St. Louis, Mo., 1895-1900, Grace Ch., Wilmington, Del., 1900-06, Central Av. Ch., Indianapolis, Ind., 1906-10, Grace Ch., St. Louis, 1910-16; dist. supt. Kansas City (Mo.) Dist., 1916-24; pres. Ozark Wesleyan Coll., Carthage, 1924-30, now emeritus; pastor emeritus, Grace Meth. Ch., St. Louis, since 1947. V.p. Bd. Home Missions and Ch. Extension M.E. Ch. Mem. Gen. Conf. M.E. Ch., 1920, 24; mem. Council of Bds. of Benevolence M.E. Ch., 1920-24; pres. Church Fedn., St. Louis, Mo., 1914-15, Kansas City, Mo., 1917-18. Republican. Mem. Beta Theta Pi. Mason (K.T., Shriner). Club: Rotary. Contbr. to various mags. on religious and ednl. subjects; author of chapters in "Out for Character," "The Optimist's Good Morning," and "God's Minute." Home: Walloon Lake, Mich. Died Sept. 2, 1957; buried Greenwood Cemetery, Petoskey, Mich.

KINGMAN, Russell Barclay, chmn. bd. Metal Textile Corp.; b. E. Orange, N.J., Dec. 17, 1884; s. Thomas Sewall and Anna Helena (Jenks) K.; desc. John Alden and David Barclay, Colonial gov. of N.J.; grad. Newark Academy, 1903; Litt.D., Upsala Coll., 1946; m. Ethel Kimberley Spencer, Dec. 17, 1908; children—Elsa (Mrs. F. Stark Newberry), Barclay Alden. Began learning the tanning trade, 1903; employed by firm of C. L. & R. E. Smith, 1903-05, Comstock Hoff Co., 1905-06; with Walton Advertising Agency, Boston, 1906-08; advertising mgr. Rogers & Wise Publications, 1908-11; New England representative Condé Nast Publications, 1911-13, Doubleday, Page & Co., 1913, Curtis Pub. Co., 1913-18; pres. Purity Cross, Inc., 1918-24; founder 1924, now chmn. bd. dirs. Metal Textile Corp.; chairman of board, Metal Textile Corp. of Canada, Ltd.; dir. Sinfra Corp. Created and produced emergency trench ration which was widely used in "No Man's Land" during World War I.; produced spl. high temperature aviation materials, radar products, etc., during World War II. Decorated Chevalier Legion of Honor (French), 1939; promoted to Officer de la Legion d'Honneur, 1947, Commandeur de la d'Honneur, 1952; recipient Gold Medal of Fedn. Francaise de Lawn Tennis, 1950; Medaille d'Or de l'Education Physique et des Sports (France), 1950 Founder, 1922, trustee N.J. Symphony Orchestra; hon. mem. Local 16, Musicians Union, A.F. of L.; chmn. adv. com. Friends of Griffith Music Found.; chmn. finance and adv. com. Casals Music Festival, France, 1950-52. Trutsee Hosp. Center at Orange. Mem. French Inst. in U.S., Soc. Mayflower Descs., Am. Inst. Graphic Arts; New England Soc. of the Oranges (v.p.), U.S. Lawn Tennis Assn. (pres., mem. Davis Cup com. of mgmt.), Alliance Francaise des Oranges (hon. pres.), Fédération de l'Alliance Francaise aux Etats-Unis et au Canada (exec. com.), Nat. Canners Assn. (hon.), N.J. Music Teachers Assn. (hon.), Internat. Lawn Tennis Fedn. (past pres., mem. com. mgmt.), Internat. Lawn Tennis Club U.S., France-Am. Soc., City of Orange Bd. Edn., Eastern Lawn Tennis Assn. (past pres.), Council Internat. Lawn Tennis Clubs (exec. com.), Internat. Lawn Tennis Clubs of France, Great Britain, Sweden, Belgium, Holland, Denmark, Argentina and Orange; mem. adv. bd. Eastern L.T.C. Republican. Episcopalian. Clubs: Rock Spring Country, Berkeley Tennis (pres.) (Orange); Bankers, The Bohemians (N.Y.C.); All England Lawn Tennis and Croquet (Wimbledon). Connoisseur of ancient printing; collector and player of ancient musical instruments; 'cellist, concertized coast to coast in America, and in Europe; 'cellist of Am. String Quartet. Inventor about 50 products and processes. Home: 382 Oakwood Av., Orange, N.J. Office: 647 E. First Av., Roselle, N.J. Died Mar. 12, 1959.

KINGSBURY, John A(dams), social worker; b. Horton, Kan., Aug. 30, 1876; s. John T. and Anna Gibson (Adams) K.; Wash. State Coll., 1900; U. Wash., 1903-06; B.S., Tchrs. Coll., Columbia, 1908; LL.D., Syracuse, 1931; m. Mabel Glass, Aug. 20, 1909; children—Jean Roberta, John Adams (dec.), Virginia Louise. Prin. schs., Prosser, Wash., 1899-1901; supt., Georgetown, Wash., 1901-04; prin. schs., Seattle, 1904-06; asst. sec. State Charities Aid Assn. of N.Y., 1907-11. Organized, 1910, Conf. of Mayors of State of N.Y.; orgn. New York Commn. of Safety, 1911; sec. N.Y. State Conf. Charities and Correction, 1911; mem. Gov. Sulzer's Pub. Health Commn., which revised health laws of N.Y. State, 1913; mem. Gov. Roosevelt's N.Y. State Pub. Health Commn., 1930-32; gen. dir. N.Y. Assn. for Improving the Condition of Poor, 1911-14; commr. pub. charities, N.Y.C., 1914-18, and ex-officio pres. of Bd. of Inebriety; sec. bd. ambulance service, and mem. bd. trustees, Bellevue and allied hosps.; sec. Milbank Meml. Fund, 1921-35; adminstrv. cons. Works Progress Adminstrn., 1935-36; mem. exec. com. N.Y. State Charities Aid Assn.; chmn. exec. com. Serbian Child Welfare Assn. America; sec. America-Jugoslav Soc., Inc.; chmn. Am. Council on Soviet Relations; mem. Council on Foreign Relations. Commd. maj. A.R.C., AEF; asst. dir., gen. relief in France, 1918; dir. dept. of citizenship, Ednl. Corps, AEF in France until discharge, July 8, 1919. Decorated Order of White Eagle and San Sava (Serbian); Reconnaissance Française (Fernch); presentation medal Nat. Inst. Social Sciences. Fellow Am. Pub. Health Assn.; asso. fellow N.Y. Acad. Medicine; mem. Nat. Conf. Social Work, Am. Meteors Assn., Amateur Astronomers Assn. Clubs: Players; Cosmos (Washington); Woodstock Country. Author: Red Medicine (with Sir Arthur Newsholme), Health in Handcuffs. Home: Lavorika, Shady, N.Y. Died Aug. 3, 1956; buried Woodstock (N.Y.) Meml. Cemetery.

KINGSTON, George Frederick, archbishop; b. Prescott, Ont., Can., Aug. 26, 1889; s. Richard and Elizabeth (Newman) K.; B.A., Trinity Coll., U. Toronto, 1913, M.A., 1914, Ph.D., 1923, D.D., 1940, LL.D., 1948; B.D., Univ. of Kings Coll., N.S., 1917, D.D. 1940; student Harvard Oxford U.; D.C.L., Bishops Coll., Lennoxville, 1945; D.D., Wycliffe, 1948; LL. D., Western U., 1948; m. Florence Belle Brown, Aug. 20, 1919; children—Elizabeth (Mrs. George E. Westman), Edith (Mrs. W. J. Orr), F. Temple. Prof. philosophy King's Coll., Windsor, N.S., 1920-22; prof. ethics Trinity Coll., 1922, dean of men students, 1926-40; canon St. James' Cathedral, Toronto, 1937; bishop of Algoma, 1940; bishop of Nova Scotia, 1944; archbishop of Nova Scotia and Primate of all Canada, 1947—. Bd. dirs. Edgehill Church Sch. for Girls; bd. govs. King's College Sch., King's College. Mem. Anglican Ch. of Can. Home: 402 Tower Rd. Office: 414 Barrington St., Halifax, N.S. Died Nov. 20, 1950; buried Trinity College Chapel, Toronto.

KINKEAD, Cleves (kĭn-kād'), playwright; b. Louisville, Ky., Mar. 4, 1882; s. Robert C. and Julia (Grinstead) K.; spl. studies, Centre Coll., Ky., later at Harvard (non-grad.); studied law, U. of Louisville; m. Kathleen Patch, Dec. 14, 1917. Formerly newspaper reporter with St. Louis Republic, New York Press, Louisville Post; practiced law, Louisville, 1905-13; mem. Ky. Ho. of Rep., 1908. Commd. 1st lt. inf., World War. Mem. Kappa Alpha. Mason. Clubs: Pendennis, Louisville Country, River Valley (Louisville); Players, Harvard (New York). Author: (play) Common Clay, first prod. Boston, Republic Theatre, New York, season 1915-16, pub. as novel, 1917. Address: Pendennis Club, Louisville 2. Died Oct. 1955.

KINNANE, Charles Herman (kĭn-năn'), educator; b. Bay County, Mich., Sept. 4, 1898; s. Thomas J. and Louise Marie (Senay) K.; B.S., U. of Ill., 1924, LL.B., 1924; J.S.D., Yale, 1926; m. Elizabeth Lucille Paullis, June 12, 1937; children—Thomas Francis, John Robert. Admitted to bars of Wyo., 1930, Ill., 1932, Calif., 1937; asst. prof. of law, U. of Wyo., 1924-27, dean of Sch. of Law, 1926-32, asso. prof., 1928-29, prof., 1929-32; practice of law and prof. of law, Loyola U., Chicago (part time), 1932-36; prof. and dean Sch. of Law, U. of San Francisco, 1936-39; prof. of law, De Paul U., Chicago, 1939-45 (on leave after Feb. 1943). Attorney U.S. Securities and Exchange Commn., Phila., Washington, 1943-48; prof. law, DePaul U., Chgo., since 1948. Served U.S. Army, 1917-19; with A.E.F. 20 months. Decorated Croix de Guerre (France), 1918. Mem. Am. Bar Assn., State Bar of Calif., Phi Alpha Delta; on nat. panel Am. Arbitration Assn. Author: A First Book on Anglo-American Law, 1932; contbr. various articles to legal periodicals. Home: 412 Mitchell Av., Elmhurst, Ill. Address: College of Law, DePaul Univ., 64 E. Lake St., Chgo. 1. Died Apr. 28, 1954; buried Mt. Carmel Cemetery.

KINNEY, Gilbert, senior vice-president, J. Walter Thompson Co.; b. New Haven, Conn., Mar. 20, 1884; s. Thomas I. and Cora Cornelia (Potvin) K.; grad. Hillhouse High Sch., New Haven, Conn., 1901; A.B., Yale, 1905; m. Anna Hart Jackson, Apr. 24, 1929; 1 son, Gilbert Hart. Office asst., J. Walter Thompson Co., 1905-07; v.p. Paul Block, Inc., 1907-17; sr. v.p., treas. J. Walter Thompson Co.; advertising since 1917; dir. Penick & Ford, Ltd., Inc. (mem. exec. com.), Scott Paper Co.; Nat. Outdoor Advertising Bur. Dir. Am. Assn. Advertising Agencies (chmn. 1938-39). Chairman Town Plan Commn., Greenwich, 1937-47; mem. Conn. Hy. Safety Commn. 1936-46; director (1943-49). N.Y. Hort. Soc., Assn. for Aid of Crippled Children (pres. since 1948), English-Speaking Union, Gramercy Boys' Club. Associate fellow Timothy Dwight Coll. of Yale U., 1938-48. Mem. executive com. Yale Alumni Bd.; dir. and chmn. Yale Alumni Fund, 1932-33; chmn. bd. Yale Alumni Publ.; mem. Elihu Club of Yale, Torch (honor soc.). Democrat. Catholic. Clubs: University, Yale; Round Hill (Greenwich); Pot and Kettle (Maine); Yeamans Hall (Charleston). Home: Old Mill Rd., Greenwich, Conn.; also 765 Park Av., New York, N.Y. Office: 420 Lexington Av., N.Y.C. Died Mar. 12, 1952.

KINNOCH, P. A., banker; b. 1888. Sr. vice pres. Am. Trust Co., San Francisco. Pres. Bankers' Assn. for Foreign Trade, 1946-47. Home: 47 Domingo Av., Berkeley, Cal. Office: American Trust Co., 464 California St., San Francisco. Died Jan. 25, 1951.

KINSEY, Alfred Charles, zoölogist; b. Hoboken, N.J., June 23, 1894; s. Alfred Seguine and Sarah Ann (Charles) K.; B.S., Bowdoin, 1916; Sc.D., Harvard, 1920; Sheldon traveling fellow, Harvard, 1919-20; m. Clara Bracken McMillen, June 3, 1921; children—Don (dec.), Anne, Joan, Bruce. Asst. in zoölogy, Harvard, 1917-18, in botany, 1918-19; asst. prof. zoölogy, Ind. U., 1920-23, asso. prof., 1923-29, prof., 1929—, also Waterman research asso.; in charge biol. exploration in Mexico and Central America, 1931-32, 1935-36; in charge study on human sex behavior, supported jointly by Indiana U., Rockefeller Foundation, and Nat. Research Council, 1942—. Member A.A.A.S., American Entomological Society, Association Economic Entomologists, Ind. Academy Science. Cambridge Entomol. Club, N.E. Bot. Club. Am. Soc. of Geneticists, Am. Soc. Naturalists, Am. Sociol. Soc., Am. Assn. Marriage Counselors, Acad. Natural Sci., Am. Zoöl. Soc., Am. Iris Soc., Zeta Psi, Phi Beta Kappa, Sigma Xi. Author: An Introduction to Biology, 1926; Field and Laboratory Manual in Biology, 1927; The Gall Wasp Genus Cynips—A Study in the Origin of Species, 1930; New Introduction to Biology, 1933 (revised 1938); Workbook in Biology, 1934; The Origin of Higher Categories in Cynips, 1936; Methods in Biology, 1937; Edible Wild Plants of Eastern North America (with M. L. Fernald), 1943; Sexual Behavior in the Human Male (with W. B. Pomeroy and C. E. Martin), 1948; Sexual Behavior in the Human Female (with W. B. Pomeroy, C. E. Martin and P. H. Gebhard), 1953. Home: 1320 E. First St., Bloomington, Ind. Died Aug. 25, 1956.

KINSMAN, Frederick Joseph, writer; b. Warren, O., Sept. 27, 1868; s. Frederick and Mary Louisa (Marvin) K.; grad. St. Paul's Sch., Concord, N.H., 1887, Keble Coll., Oxford, Eng., 1894; B.A., Oxon., 1894, M.A., 1899, D.D., 1911; S.T.D., Berkeley Div. Sch., Conn., 1909; LL.D., Wash. Coll., 1912, Seton Hall College, 1927. Deacon, 1895, priest, 1896, P.E. Ch.; master St. Paul's Sch., 1895-97; rector St. Martin's Ch., New Bedford, Mass., 1897-1900; prof. church history, Berkeley Div. Sch., 1900-03, Gen. Theol. Sem., 1903-08; bishop Del. 1908-19, resigned, to enter Catholic Ch. Author: Principles of Anglicanism, 1910; Catholic and Protestant, 1913; Prayers for the Dead, 1914; The Issues Before the Church, 1915; Outlines of Church History, 1916; Salve Mater, 1920; Trent, 1921; Americanism and Catholicism, 1924. Home: Lewiston, Me. Died June 19, 1944; buried Birchmere Tower Lot, Bryant Pond, Me.

KINSOLVING, Arthur Barksdale, clergyman; b. Middleburg, Va., Feb. 20, 1861; s. Rev. Ovid A. (D.D.) and Lucy Lee (Rogers) K.; grad. Episcopal High Sch., Alexandria, Va.; student U. Va., 1882-83; grad. Theol. Sem. of Va., 1886; D.D., Washington and Lee U., 1906; m. Sally Bruce, Feb. 5, 1895; children—Mrs. Magill James (dec. Apr. 14, 1947), Arthur Lee, Mrs. Beverly Ober, Mrs. Milton E. Gundersheimer, Mrs. John N. Brown, Herbert Leigh, Mrs. Egbert G. Leigh. First served as rector, Warsaw, Va.; rector Christ Ch., Bklyn., 1888-1906, St. Paul's Ch., Balt., 1906-42, St. John's Ch., Fishers Island, N.Y., summers, 1911-35. Dep. to Gen. Conv. of Episcopal Ch., 11 times; served as chmn. Nat. Com. on Christian Edn. Del. Pan-Anglican Conf. in Eng., 1906, Triennial Conv. of Episcopal Ch., Portland, Ore., 1922. Club: University (Balt.). Author: The Story of a Southern School, 1922; Texas George, A Life of the Right Reverend George Herbert Kinsolving, D.D., 1922; A Portrait Sketch of the Right Reverend Lucien Lee Kinsolving, 1946. Author pamphlets, including, A Short History of St. Paul's Parish, The History of St. Paul's School; also an article: The Catholicity of Christian Hymns. Home: 3003 N. Charles St., Balt. 18. Died Aug. 15, 1951.

KINZER, J. Roland, ex-congressman; b. Lancaster County, Pa., Mar. 28, 1874; A.B., Franklin andr Marshall Coll., 1896; m. Bertha Snyder. Admitted to Pa. bar, 1900, began practice at Lancaster; elected to 71st Congress Jan. 1930, to fill vacancy and was reëlected 72d to 79th Congresses, 10th Pa. Dist. Del. Rep. Nat. Conv., 1928. Home: Lancaster, Pa. Died July 25, 1955; buried Woodward Hill Cemetery, Lancaster.

KIPP, Orin Lansing, hwy. engr.; b. Wing, Ill., Feb. 18, 1885; s. Dyer Egbert and Mary E. (Basset) K.; B.S., Cornell Coll., Mt. Vernon, Ia., 1909; m. Leona B. Chapman, Feb. 11, 1913; children—Harriet (Mrs. Seth R. Fisher), Dorothy (Mrs. Randall R. Hunt), Mary (Mrs. Edward C. Nicholson), Ralph, Margaret (Mrs. A. N. Felice), Paul, Louise (Mrs. Roal Schneider) (deceased September 1, 1958. Engineer at Mitchell South Dakota, 1909-13; hwy. engr., Redwood Falls, Minn., 1914-16; constrn. engr. Minn. Hwy. Dept., 1916-35; constrn. engr., asst. chief engr., 1935-43, chief engr., asst. commr. hwys., 1943-55, hwy. engring. cons., 1955—. Exec. com. hwy. research bd. NRC. Mem. Am., Miss. Valley (pres.) assns. state hwy. ofcls., Minn. Engrs. and Surveyors Soc. (pres.), St. Paul Engrs. Soc. Methodist (ofcl. bd.). Home: 1685 Englewood St. Office: 1246 University St., St. Paul 4.

Died Feb. 17, 1958; buried Sunset Meml. Park, Mpls.

KIRBY, Daniel Bartholomew, ophthalmologist; b. Cleveland, O., Apr. 12, 1891; s. Daniel Bartholomew and Esther A. Robinson (Whitaker) K.; A.B., John Carroll University, Cleveland, Ohio, 1912, A.M., 1914, LL.D. (honorary), 1948; M.D., Western Reserve University, 1916; post-graduate student at Harvard Pa. University, Cornell University; m. Cecilia Katherine Hahn, June 9, 1923; children—Mary Elizabeth (Mrs. J. Dukes Wooters, Jr.), Mother Joan Kirby, Cecilia (Mrs. Peter Mullen), Janet Whitaker. Resident surgeon Bellevue Hosp., N.Y. City, 1921-23; asso. of Dr. John M. Wheeler, 1923-28; in private practice of ophthalmology since 1923; former surgeon in chief, Dept. of Ophthalmology, Bellevue Hosp., N.Y.; prof. emeritus department of ophthalmology, Coll. of Medicine, New York U.; cons. Surgeon in ophthalmology N.Y. Eye & Ear Infirmary and Manhattan Eye, Ear & Throat Hospital, New Rochelle Hospital. Served as lieut. (s.g.) Med. Corps, U.S. Navy, 1917-19. Former chairman American Board of Opthalmology. Mem. (hon.) Alumni Assn., N.Y. Eye and Ear Infirmary. Fellow N.Y. Acad. Med., Am. Coll. Surgeons; mem. A.M.A., N.Y. County & State med. societies, Am. and N.Y. ophthal. soc., Am Acad. Ophthal. and Oto-Laryngol. (research fellow in ophthal., 1923-29), Harvey Society, ophthal. socs. of Brazil, Argentina, Chile, Peru, Cuba, France, Greece. Awarded Schneider prize in ophthalmology. Roman Catholic (K.M., K.H.S.). Clubs: Union (N.Y.C.); Pelham Country; Lippincott (Phila.). Author of "Diseases of the Crystalline Lens" in Eye and its Diseases, edited by Conrad Berens, 1936; "The Crystalline Lens and Cataract" in Diseases of the Eye, edited by George Blumer, 1937; Surgery of Cataract, 1950; Advanced Surgery of Cataract, pub. 1955. Contributed many articles to ophthalmological and med. jours., including The Development of a System of Intracapsular Cataract Extraction in American Journal Ophthalmology, March 1942. Home: 76 Mount Tom Road, Pelham Manor, New York. Office: 780 Park Av., N.Y.C. Died Dec. 27, 1953; buried Gate of Heaven Cemetery, Hawthorne, N.Y.

KIRBY, Harold, educator; b. Tusket, N.S., Can., Feb. 2, 1900; s. Harold and Shirley (Sands) K.; B.S., Emory U., 1922; A.M., U. Cal., 1923, Ph.D. (James M. Goewey fellow 1924-25), 1925; m. Margaret Thomson, July 6, 1927; children—Janet Beaton, Roger Alan. Came to U.S., 1903, naturalized, 1933. Instr. biology Yale, 1925-28; asst. prof. zoology U. Cal., 1928-31, asso. prof., 1931-40, prof. zoology since 1940, chmn. dept. zoology since 1948; John Simon Guggenheim fellow, 1934-35; mem. expdns. C.A., Fanning Island, Africa, Madagascar. Fellow Calif., Acad. Scis.; mem. Am. Soc. Zoologists (editorial bd. Jour. Morph. since 1949), Soc. Protozoologists (v.p. 1952), Am. Soc. Parasitologists (v.p. 1946), Sigma Xi, Phi Beta Kappa. Club: Berkeley (Cal.). Contbr. chpts. in Protozoa in Biological Research, 1941; Materials and Methods in the Study of Protozoa, 1950; also articles sci. jours. Home: 1028 Cragmont Av., Berkeley 8, Cal. Died Feb. 24, 1952.

KIRBY, Rollin, cartoonist; b. Galva, Ill., Sept. 4, 1875; s. George Washington and Elizabeth (Maddox) K.; student pub. schs.; m. Estelle Carter, Nov. 6, 1903; 1 dau., Janet. Engaged as illustrator Collier's Mag., McClure's, Life, American, Harper's, etc., 1901-10; cartoonist on New York Mail, 1911, New York Sun, 1912, World, 1913 (series of social cartoons, under caption of Sights of the Town); polit. cartoonist of N.Y. World, 1914-31. World-Telegram, 1931-39, New York Post, 1939-42; Aug. 1942—, cartoons and editorials for Look mag.; cartoons for New York Times Sunday Magazine. Awarded Pulitzer $500 prize for cartoon, On the Road to Moscow, 1921, for cartoon, News from the Outside World, 1924, for cartoon, Tammany, 1928; writer verse, articles and sketches for the old Life, New Yorker and Vanity Fair. address: care Players Club, 16 Gramercy Park, N.Y.C. Died May 9, 1952.*

KIRCHNER, Henry Paul, mfr.; b. Buffalo, N.Y., Feb. 25, 1890; s. Hugo and Katherine (Bauer) K.; B.S. in Mech. Engring., U. of Pa., 1910; m. Marguerite Van Ormer, Sept. 3, 1919; 1 son, Henry P., Jr. Instr., U. of Pa., 1910-11; draughtsman, inspector, engr., asst. supt. Niagara Falls (N.Y.) and Canadian Niagara Power Cos., 1911-17; successively asst. works engr., works engr., supt. of maintenance, works mgr., v.p. Carborundum Co., Niagara Falls, and Canadian Carborundum Co., Ltd., 1919—, exec. vice pres., 1942-47, consultant vice pres., 1947—; ex-pres. Hutto Engineering Company; director Globar Corporation, Carborundum Company, Union Sandpaper Co., Australian Abrasives Pty. Ltd. Trustee Niagara County Savings Bank. Served in 10th Training Regt., Plattsburg, 1916; pvt. 1st sergt. Co. K, 309th Inf., U.S. Army, later 1st lt., capt. Ordnance Dept. (U.S. and fgn. service), 1917-19; maj. Ordnance Res. Corps, 1919-24. Asso. mem. Am. Inst. Elec. Engrs. Republican. Lutheran. Clubs: Niagara, Niagara Falls Country. Holder of many patents in abrasive field. Home: Hillcrest, Niagara Falls, N.Y. (summer) Kamambi, Paul Smith's, N.Y. Office: The Carborundum Co., Niagara Falls, N.Y. Died June 14, 1957; buried Riverdale Cemetery, Niagara Falls.

KIRK, Harris Elliott, clergyman; b. Pulaski, Tenn., Oct. 12, 1872; s. John Harvey and Katherine (McCord) K.; grad. Southwestern U., Memphis, Tenn., 1897, D.D., 1905, LL.D., 1925; LL.D., Davidson Coll., Davidson, N.C., 1937; m. Helen O. McCormick, June 24, 1897; children—Harris Elliott, Mary Louise (wife of Dr. Julius Lane Wilson), Helen Lucretia (Mrs. Harry J. Verner, Jr.). Ordained Presbyn. ministry, 1897; pastor Cottage Ch., Nashville, Tenn., 1897-99, 1st Ch., Florence, Ala., 1899-1901, Franklin St. Ch., Baltimore, Md., 1901—; ann. lecturer on historical Christianity, Princeton U., 1923-29, Goucher Coll., 1925-28; prof. Bibl. lit., Goucher, 1928—, lecturer Gen. Conf. Christian Workers, Northfield, 1917-26, mission confs. in China, summer of 1924; summer preacher Westminster Chapel, London, 1922-40; Sprunt lecturer Union Theol. Sem., Va., 1916; Carew lecturer Hartford Theol. Sem., 1916; spl. lecturer on homiletics and psychology, Hartford Sem., 1919-24; alumni lecturer New Brunswick Theol. Sem., 1920; faculty lecturer, McCormick Theol. Sem., 1922; university preacher Princeton, Yale, U. of Va., etc.; Shepard lecturer Bangor Theol. Sem., 1928; Reinicker lecturer P.E. Seminary in Va., 1929; Cole lecturer, Vanderbilt, 1930; Otts lecturer, Davidson Coll., 1930; McNair lecturer, Univ. of N.C., 1931; Rockwell Lectures, Rice Institute, Houston, Tex., 1939. Smith Lectures, Columbia Theological Seminary, 1946. Moderator Va. Synod, 1911; elected moderator Gen. Assembly Presbyn. Ch. in U.S., 1928; dir. Presbyn. Ministers' Fund for Life Ins., Phila.; v.p., trustee Peabody Inst. Mem. Phi Beta Kappa, Sigma Alpha Epsilon. Clubs: University, P. and L., Arts and Letters; Nat. Liberal (London). Author: The Religion of Power, 1916; The Consuming Fire, 1919; One Generation to Another, 1924; The Spirit of Protestantism, 1930; The Glory of Common Things, 1930; Stars, Atoms and God, 1932; A Man of Property, 1935; A Design for Living, 1939; also numerous articles in mags. Home: 502 Cathedral St., Balt. 1. Died Nov. 6, 1953; buried Greenmount Cemetery, Balt.

KIRK, Raymond Eller, chemist; b. Hamilton County, Neb., June 24, 1890; s. Joseph Alexander and Virginia Eads (Eller) K.; student Neb. State Normal, Kearney, 1910-13; B.S., U. of Neb., 1915; M.S., Ia. State Coll., 1917; Ph.D., Cornell, 1927; student U. of Chicago, summer 1919; m. Beth Sibley, June 30, 1920; children—Virginia, Josephine Alvira. Instr. in chemistry, Ia. State Coll., 1917-20; asst. prof. chemistry, U. of Minn., 1920-27, asso. prof., 1927-29; prof. and head dept. of chemistry, Mont. State Coll., and state chemist, 1929-31; prof. and head dept. of chemistry, Poly. Inst., Brooklyn, N.Y., 1931-55; dir. Shellac Research Bureau, 1936-42; also dean of the graduate school, 1944—. Served as civilian insp. Ordnance Dept. United States Army, 1917-18; captain Ordnance Reserve, 1923-30, major, 1930-42. Fellow Am. Inst. Chemists, A.A.A.S.; mem. Am. Chem. Soc., Am. Assn. Univ. Profs., Sigma Xi, Phi Lambda Upsilon, Alpha Chi Sigma, Phi Kappa Phi, Gamma Alpha, Delta Sigma Rho. Author: Laboratory Manual in Inorganic Chemistry (with M. C. Sneed), 1927. Co-editor Encyclopedia of Chemical Technology (15 volumes), 1947-56). Medical bd. editors Inorganic Synthesis, 1939. Contbr. to sci. jours. Home: 9269 Shore Rd., Bklyn. 9. Died Feb. 6, 1957.

KIRK, Waldorf Tilton, telephone exec.; b. Zanesville, O., July 11, 1897; s. Karl Tilton and Kate (Waldorf) K.; B.S., Washington-Jefferson Coll., 1923; m. Gretchen Stamats, Mar. 6, 1924; 1 dau., Jean M. (Mrs. Alan W. Meyer). With Mich. Bell Telephone Co., Detroit, 1923—, beginning as traffic student, successively dist. traffic supt. Grand Rapids, div. instrn. supt., Detroit, div. plant supt., Grand Rapids, gen. plant personnel supr., Detroit, asst. to v.p. and gen. mgr., gen. plant mgr., 1923-57, corporate sec., Detroit, 1957—. Pres. Telephone Pioneers Mich., 1956. Served as cpl., trench mortar bn., U.S. Army, 1916-19; AEF. Mem. Detroit Bd. Commerce, A.I.M., Am. Legion, S.A.R., Am. Soc. Corporate Secs., Engring. Soc. Detroit, Phi Kappa Psi. Presbyn. Club: Golf, Economic (Detroit). Home: 201 E. Kirby St., Detroit 2. Office: 1365 Cass Av., Detroit 26. Died Dec. 11, 1957.

KIRKBRIDE, Franklin Butler, trustee; b. Phila., Aug. 10, 1867; s. Thomas S. (M.D., LL.D.) and Eliza Ogden (Butler) K.; A.B., Haverford (Pa.) Coll., 1889; m. Lydia Brooks Bell; 1 son, David B. In charge Phila. office, Caledonia Mining & Mfg. Co., 1890-91, supt. U.S. mail equipment shops, Washington, 1891-93; asst. sec., sec., and sec. and treas. Pa. Co. for Insurances on Lives and Granting Annuities, 1893-1905; partner Alfred Booth & Co., mchts., N.Y.C., 1905-07; receiver of Rogers & Pyatt, Inc., 1908-09; pres. Eclipse Tanning Co., 1909-16; chmn. bd. Empire Cream Separator Co., 1912-22, S.K.F. Industries, Inc., 1916-22; dir. McIntosh & Seymour Corp., 1914-29; dir. and treas. 830 Park Av. Corp.; dir. Milbank Meml. Fund. Trustee Stevens Inst. Tech.; mgr. N.Y. Assn. for Improving Condition of Poor; mgr. Letchworth Village. Mem. Hist. Soc. Pa., Phi Beta Kappa. Republican. Presbyn. Clubs: Century, Down Town, Adirondack Mountain Reserve and Ausable (sec.). Author: (with J. E. Sterrett, C.P.A., and H. Parker Willis) The Modern Trust Company, 1905, 6th edit., 1925. Home: New Canaan, Conn. Office: 74 Trinity Pl., N.Y.C. Died Sept. 28, 1955.

KIRKLAND, James Robert, federal judge; b. Feb. 15, 1903; s. William J. and Margaret E. (Gardiner) K.; grad. Emerson Prep. Inst., Washington, 1923; graduate Pace Sch. of Accountancy, Washington, 1921-24, George Washington U., 1924-29, A.B., 1927, LL.B., 1928, LL.M., 1929; B.C.S., Benjamin Franklin U., 1930; LL.D., Southeastern U., Washington, 1947; m. Katherine Levison Kramer, June 1, 1937; children—Margaret Kramer, William Elliott, Carol Jean. Sec., U. S. P. H. S., 1921-22; asst. purchasing officer Bur. of Supply, Treasury Dept., 1922-25; asst. U. S. Dist. Atty., Washington, 1929-34; in pvt. law practice, Washington, since 1934; mem. Cromelin, Townsend & Kirkland, 1938-49; counsel, Senate D. C. Com., 1947-49; judge Dist. Ct. of U. S. for D. C., 1949—. Certified C.P.A., Del., 1933. Commander, U.S.N.R. Chmn. D.C. Jud. Conf., 1940; chmn. Washington Speakers Bur., 5th, 6th, 7th War Bond drives. Mem. Am. Bar Assn., D. C. Bar Assn. (past v.p.; chmn. Americanization com. 1942-43, Municipal Ct. of Appeals com. 1946; mem. Municipal Ct. disbarment com. 1945-46), Washington Bd. of Trade (chmn. com. on pub. utilities), Shepherd Park Citizen's Assn. (past pres.), Del. Bar, D.C. Bar, D.C. Inst. of C. P. A.'s (past dir.), Phi Delta Phi, Acacia. Republican. Episcopalian. Mason (Shriner), Rotarian. Home: 5226 Loughboro Rd., Washington 16. Office: U.S. Dist. Court for District of Columbia, Washington. Died Feb. 25, 1958; buried Rock Creek Cemetery, Washington.

KIRKLIN, Byrl Raymond, radiologist; b. Gaston, Ind., Sept. 22, 1888; s. John Walter and Sarah Lavina (McCreery) K.; B.S., Indiana U., 1926, M.D., 1914; m. Gladys Marie Webster, June 3, 1915; children—John Webster, Mary Webster. Radiologist Muncie (Ind.) Home Hosp. and private practice, 1916-25; radiologist Mayo Clinic, Rochester, Minn., 1926-54, chmn. sects. on Radiology, prof. radiology, Mayo Foundation, Univ. of Minn., 1936-54. Served as 1st lt., M.C., United States Army, World War I; col., M.C., U.S. Army, sr. X-ray consultant Office of Surgeon Gen., World War II; ret. col. M.C. Res; sr. cons. to surgeon gen., U.S. Army and to USAF. Past pres. Muncie Home Hosp. staff, Diplomate and mem. bd. trustees Am. Bd. Radiology (sec.-treas.); mem. adv. bd. med. specialties (sec.-treas.), Fel. Am. Coll. Radiology (pres. 1942-43), Am. Coll. Physicians, A.M.A., hon. fel. Internat. Coll. Surgeons; mem. Am. Roentgen Ray Society (pres. 1937-38), Radiol. Soc. North America, Minn. State and Olmsted County med. assns., Minn. Radiol. Soc. (pres. 1930), Am. Assn. Gastro-enterologists, Central Soc. Clin. Research, Am. Assn. Ry. Surgeons, Southern Minnesota Medical Association; corresponding mem. Academia Nacional de Medicina Republic de Colombia; hon. mem. Die Deutsche Röntgen-Gesellschaft (Germany), Royal Soc. Medicine (Eng.). Assn. Gastroenterologists of Paris (France), Soc. Colombiana de Radiologia, Soc. Mexicana de Radiologia y Fisioterapia, Soc. de Radiologia y Fisioterapia de Cuba, Chicago Roentgen Soc., St. Louis Med. Soc., Muncie Acad. Medicine (pres. 1921, 22), Dallas Southern Clin. Soc., Miss. Valley Med. Assn.; mem. Sigma Chi, Phi Rho Sigma, Sigma Xi. Republican. Methodist. Mason. Clubs: Univ., Rochester Country, Rotary (Rochester, Minn.); Army and Navy (Washington). Contbr. to med. jours. Home; 725 11th St., S.W. Office: Kahler Hotel Bldg., Rochester, Minn. Died Mar. 2, 1957; buried Rochester.

KIRKPATRICK, Blaine Evron, clergyman; b. Raub, Ind., Oct. 15, 1887; s. Truman and Emma (Shonkwiler) K.; B.A., Northwestern U., 1910, M.A., 1912; S.T.B., Garrett Bibl. Inst., 1912, D.D., 1925; D.D., Williamette U., 1923; m. Vernia Marks, June 26, 1912 (died June 30, 1937); children—Blaine Truman, Mary Esther, Virginia Lois; m. 2d, Lois Wentworth, July 18, 1938. Entered ministry M.E. Ch., 1911; successively pastor Trinity Ch., South Bend, Ind., First Ch., Crawfordsville and College Av. Ch., Greencastle, until 1920, First Ch., Salem, Ore., 1920-25; asst. sec., bd. edn. M.E. Ch., in charge Young People's Work, 1925-36; sec. Christian Coop. Fellowship, 1936-37; pastor Centenary Meth. Ch., Lebanon, Ind., 1937-41, Riverside Park Ch., Indpls., 1941-47, Monticello Ch., 1947-53; asso. minister 1st Ch., West Lafayette, Ind., also minister to students Wesley Found., Purdue U., 1953-57; pastor Wheeler (Ind.) Meth. Ch., 1957—. Dir. Wesley Found.; trustee DePauw U., 1917-20, 44-50, Williamette U., 1920-24. Mem. Joint Com. on United Youth Program, 1934-36. Mem. Ind. Christian Youth Council, 1939-43; chmn. adult div. Ind. Council of Chs., 1943-46. Mem. The Wranglers, Phi Beta Kappa. Author: Young People's Work for Young People, 1924; Adventures in Christian Leadership, 1930. Home: Wheeler, Ind. Died Jan. 23, 1959; buried Raub, Ind.

KIRKPATRICK, Carlos Stevens, railway official; b. Carrollton, Ark., Aug. 7, 1881; s. W. H. and Frances Ellen (Shipman) K.; grad. Carrollton Coll., 1899; m. Hazel Kirke Durnell, Nov. 11, 1907; 1 son, William Durnell. Began with Mo. and N.Ark. R.R., 1899, later with Houston&Tex.Central R.R. and Mo.& N.Ark. R.R.; with St.L.&S.F. R.R., 1903-04; in employ Guggenheim Exploration Co., 1904-05; with St.L.&S.F. R.R., 1905-13; chief engr. Cape Girardeau &Northern Ry., 1913-14; chief engr. Gulf Coast Lines, at Houston, Tex., 1916-25; chief engr. I.G.N. R.R. Co. and Gulf Coast Lines since 1925. Mem. Am. Soc. C.E., Am. Ry. Engring. Soc. Democrat. Home: 2405 Yupon Drive. Office: 641 San Jacinto Bldg., Houston. Died Mar. 1, 1957.

KIRKWOOD, John Gamble, chemist; b. Gotebo, Okla., May 30, 1907; s. John Millard and Lillian (Gamble) K.; student Calif. Inst. of Tech., 1923-25; S.B., University of Chicago, 1926, D.Sci. (hon.), 1954; Ph.D., Massachusetts Institute of Tech., 1929; Sc.D. (honorary), University of Brussels, 1959; m. Lillian Gladys Danielson, Sept. 5, 1930 (div. 1952); married 2d, Platonia P. Kaldes, March 11, 1958. 1 son, John Millard. Nat. research fellow Harvard, 1929-30; internat. research fellow, Leipzig and Munich, 1931-32; research asso., Mass. Inst. of Tech., 1930-31, 1932-34; asst. prof. of chemistry, Cornell, 1934-37, asso. prof., U. of Chicago, 1937-38; Todd prof. of chemistry Cornell, 1938-47; former Arthur Ames Noyes prof. chemistry, Calif. Inst. tech. Sterling Prof. and chmn. Dept. Chemistry, Yale, dir. division of science, 1956—; Lorentz professor theoretical physics, U. Leiden, 1959. Received Am. Chem. Soc. award in pure chem., 1936, Theodore William Richards medal of Am. Chem. Soc., 1950, Gilbert Newton Lewis Medal, 1953. Fellow American Academy of Arts and Sciences, American Phys. Society; mem. Am. Chem. Soc., Nat. Acad. Scis. (fgn. sec.), Am. Philos. Soc., N.Y. Acad. Sci., Sigma Xi, Sigma Chi. Contbr. articles to scientific jours. Address: Sterling Chemical Laboratory, 225 Prospect St., New Haven. Died Aug. 9, 1959; buried Grove St. Cemetery, New Haven.

KIROACK, Howard, orgn. exec., writer, lecturer; b. Bay City, Mich., May 21, 1888; s. Eugene and Marguerite (Brabau) Gilman; foster father George Kiroack; ed. pub. schs.; m. Emma M. Mallen, Jan. 9, 1936; 1 dau. by previous marriage, Jane (Mrs. Jane Cochran). A founder Laymen's Nat. Com., Inc. N.Y. City (non-profit, non-sectarian religious orgn. which founded and sponsors Nat. Sunday Sch. Week, Nat. Bible Week), and since served as exec. dir. Republican. Christian Scientist. Clubs: National Republican; Old Inlet; Bellport Bay Yacht. Home: South Howells Point Rd., Bellport, L.I., N.Y. Office: 204 Vanderbilt Hotel, N.Y. City 16. Died May 14, 1951.

KIRSCHBAUM, Arthur, anatomist; b. N.Y.C., Oct. 15, 1910; s. Morris Lyon and Etta (Rosenbloom) K.; B.S., N.Y.U., 1931; M.A., U. Minn., 1933, Ph.D., 1936, M.D., 1943; fellow anatomy Yale, 1937-38, 39-40; m. Nylene Elvira Eckles, Sept. 10, 1943; children—Lynn Arthur, Todd Bittner. Teaching asst. zoology U. Minn., 1931-34, teaching fellow anatomy, 1934-37, instr., 1941-42, asst. prof., 1942-45, asso. prof. anatomy, 1945-51; instr. anatomy Yale, 1938-39, 40-41; prof., head dept. anatomy U. Ill. Coll. Medicine, 1951-54; prof., chmn. dept. anatomy Baylor U. Coll. Medicine, 1954—, U. Tex. dental br., 1954—; cons. exptl. hematologist U. Texas M.D. Anderson Hosp and Tumor Inst., 1954—; cons. VA Hosp., 1956—. Cons. USPHS, 1951-55, 56—, VA, 1956—; consultant to committee on growth NRC, 1955-56; chmn. Gordon Cancer Conf., 1957—. Recipient Am. Cancer Soc. award, Minn., 1951. Mem. Am. Assn. Cancer Research (sec. S.W. sect. 1955—), A.A.A.S., Am. Soc. Exptl. Pathology, Soc. Exptl. Biology and Medicine, Am. Assn. Anatomists, Internat. Assn. Dental Research, Sigma Xi, Phi Beta Kappa. Mem. adv. editorial bd. Cancer Research, 1949—. Home: 4055 Tartan Lane. Office: M. D. Anderson Blvd., Houston. Died May 28, 1958; buried Houston.

KIRTLAND, John Copeland, educator; b. Trumansburg, N.Y., June 24, 1870; s. John Copeland and Cornelia Frances (Kellogg) K.; A.B., Hobart Coll., cum laude, 1890, A.M., 1893, L.H.D., 1915; grad. student Latin, Stanford, 1892-96; m. May Lemira Durham, Aug. 27, 1895 (dec.); children—Arthur (dec.), Paul, John Copeland (dec.), Cornelia Frances (Mrs. Edwin Olney Jones), Philip, Mary Louise (Mrs. Joseph Clifford Taylor), Edward Goodridge, Barbara (Mrs. Edward Augustine Koonnen), Lynn. Classical master in Washington College, Tacoma, 1890-92; asst. and instr. in Latin, Stanford U., 1893-96; acting prof. Latin, Hobart Coll., 1896-97; instr. Latin, 1897-98, Morison professor Latin, 1898-1939, emeritus since 1939, Phillips Exeter Academy, and chairman summer session faculty, 1919-29. Taught in summer session, Columbia University, 1918. Pres. Exeter Hospital Corp., 1926-39. Member American Philological Assn., Classical Assn. of England and Wales, Classical Assn. of New England (pres. 1938-39), N.H. Soc. Mayflower Descendants, Phi Beta Kappa. Chmn. Commn. on Coll. Entrance Requirements in Latin, 1908-10; asso. examiner in Latin, Coll. Entrance Exam. Bd., 1911-27 and 1936-39; chmn. com. on Latin word list, 1927; mem. Joint Com. on Grammatical Nomenclature, 1917, Com. on Ancient Lang. of Commn. on Reorganization of Secondary Edn., Gen. Curriculum Com. of Secondary Edn. Bd., Commn. on Revision of Definition of Requirements in Latin, 1915, 25 and 35; sec.-gen. Cum Laude Soc., 1911-29, regent, 1929-35, pres.-gen., 1935-38, regent at large since 1938. Sr. warden Christ Ch., Exeter, N.H., 1899-1938. Editor-in-chief Macmillan's Latin Series. Editor: Selections from the Correspondence of Cicero, 1898; Fabulæ Faciles, 1904, revised edit., 1932; Co-operative Latin Tests, 1933-39. Joint Editor: Orations of Cicero, 1906; An Introduction to Latin, 1914. Home: Exeter, N.H. Died May 9, 1951; buried Exeter, N.H.

KIRTLEY, James Samuel, clergyman; b. Saline County, Mo.; s. Major George R. and Harriett Elizabeth (Huey) K.; A.B., Georgetown (Ky.) Coll., 1883, D.D., 1894; student So. Bapt. Theol. Sem., Louisville, U. Chgo.; m. Mary Louise Kniffin, Mar. 2, 1897; children—George Sylvester, Mary Adelaide, Bess Harriett. Ordained to ministry Bapt. Ch., 1897; pastor Versailles, Ky., 1883-89, Delmar Av. Ch., St. Louis, 1889-96, Second Ch., Little Rock, Ark., 1896-99, Westport Ch., Kansas City, Mo., 1899-1903, First Ch., Elgin, Ill., 1903-08, First Ch., Duluth, Minn., 1908-10; Chautauqua, lyceum and union extension lectr.; acting pastor First Bapt. Ch., San Diego, Cal., 1917, Ninth St. Bapt. Ch., Cin., First Ch., Seattle, 1918-19. First Ch., Winnipeg, Can., 1919-21, First Bapt. Ch., Pitts., 1921; successively interim pastor Mt. Morris Ch., New York, First Ch., Dayton, Third Ch., St. Louis, Ch. of the Master, Cleve., First Ch., Phila., University Ch., Balt., First Ch., Oak Park, Ill., Ashland av. Ch., Toledo, Second Ch., Chgo., Calvary Ch., Mpls., First Ch., Springfield, Mass.; Mt. Auburn Ch., Cin., First Ch., Elmhurst, N.Y., First Ch., Grand Forks, N.D., Kenmore Ch., Akron, O., Temple Ch. Phila., First Bapt. Ch., Covington, Ky. Democrat. Mason. Author: The Young Man and Himself, 1903; Twenty-six Days with Jesus, 1906; That Boy of Yours, 1912; You and Your Church, 1920; His Last Thursday, 1934; also writer of Sunday School lessons for daily newspapers. Also article each Saturday for Cincinnati Enquirer, "Something for Today." Home: 45 Dixie Highway, Erlanger, Ky. Deceased.

KIRWIN, Thomas Joseph, urologist; b. Frederick, Md., 1891; s. James John and Margaret Mary (Surplus) K.; Ph.C., B.S., U. Mich., 1910; grad. student U. Wis. 1912-13; M.D., Tulane, 1916. Cornell, 1917; M.A. in anatomy, Columbia, 1923; M.S. in surgery, Yale, 1929; m. Margaret Hughes, Sept. 8, 1917; 1 dau., Ruth Ann (Mrs. William S. McLean). Instr. in urology, Cornell Med. Coll., 1920-22; instr. in embryology, histology, Columbia, 1921-23; chief of clinic, adjunct vis. urologist James Buchanan Brady Found., Dept. Urology, N.Y. Hosp.; attending genito-urinary surgeon, N.Y.C. Hosp., Welfare Island; cons. urologist Coney Island Hosp. (Bklyn.), Benedictine Hosp. (Kingston), Monmouth Meml. Hosp. (Long Branch, N.J.), South Nassau Communities Hosp.; prof. urology N.Y. Med. Coll.; dir. of urology Flower and Fifth Avenue Hosp., Met. Hosp.; dir. Bird S. Coler Hosp. Served as capt. M.C., U.S. Army, France, World War I (Arsne-Marne, Orse-Arsne, Saint Mihiel, Meuse-Argonne, Ypres-Lys). Certified by Bd. Urology. Fellow N.Y. Acad. Medicine, Am. Coll. Surgeons, Internat. Coll. Surgeons; mem. A.M.A., N.Y. State and County med. socs., Am. Urol. Soc., Italian Urol. Soc., Societa de Obstetrica Gynecology et Urology (Rumania), Internat. Urol. Soc., Societas Japonica Urologiae (hon.), Delta Tau Delta, Nu Sigma Nu, Sigma Zi. Clubs: University, Yale, University of Michigan (N.Y. C.). Author: (with Dr. O. S. Lowsley) Textbook of Urology, 1926, Urology for Nurses, 1936, Clinical Urology (2 vols.), 1940. Author Chpt. Oxford Loose Leaf Surgery; chpt., Diseases of the Ureter, in Ency. of Medicine; Diseases of the Ureter, in Cyclopedia of Medicine. Contbr. numerous articles on surg. subjects to sci. jours. Devised instruments known as the Kirwin vesical neck resector, Kirwin prostatic resector, Kirwin Lithotrite, Kirwin radon seed implanter, Kirwin measuring device for bladder tumor, Kirwin Automatic resectoscope, Kirwin cystoscope. Home: 21 E. 90th St., N.Y.C. 28. Office: 1 E. 63d St., N.Y.C. 21. Died Aug. 18, 1959.

KITCHEL, Lloyd, business exec.; b. N.Y.C., May 26, 1898; s. William Lloyd and Grace Welsh (Wheeler) K.; grad. St. Paul's Sch., Concord, N.H., 1916, Yale, 1920; m. Helen Renwick Weks, Oct. 29, 1921; children—Helen Lloyd (Mrs. S. McGill Gawthrop), William Lloyd II, Robert Weeks. Vice pres. Virginia Cellulose Co., Hopewell, Va., 1926-29; dir. and gen. mgr. Virginia Cellulose Dept., Hercules Powder Co., Wilmington, Del., 1929—. Republican. Episcopalian. Clubs: Wilmington Country, Wilmington (Wilmington, Del.); St. Andrews Golf (Hastings-on-Hudson, N.Y.); Coral Beach Tennis (Bermuda). Home: R.F.D. 1, Kennett Square, Pa. Office: care Hercules Powder Co., Wilmington 99, Del. Died June 30, 1950; buried Longwood Cemetery, Kennett Square.

KITCHIN, Thurman Delna, physician, educator; b. Scotland Neck, N.C., Oct. 17, 1885; s. William Hodge and Maria Figus (Arrington) K.; grad. Vine Hill Male Acad., Scotland Neck, 1902; A.B., Wake Forest (N.C.) College, 1905; student U. of N.C., 1905-06; M.D., Jefferson Med. Coll., Phila., 1908; LL.D., Duke U., 1931, U. N.C., 1933, Davidson College, 1947; spl. student in physiology Columbia, summer 1921; m. Reba Calvert Clark, Nov. 3, 1908; children—Thurman Delna, Irwin Clark, William Walton. Practiced at Lumberton, N.C., 1908; moved to Scotland Neck, N.C., 1910; prof. physiology Wake Forest Coll., 1917, pres., 1930-50, prof. physiology and hygiene, 1950—, dean Sch. of Medicine, 1919-30. Apptd. by Governor McLean mem. spl. com. to study problem of feebleminded in N.C., 1925; mem. bd. dirs. N.C. Sanatorium for Tb. Mem. Vets. Adminstrn. spl. com. on rehabilitation and edn. problems; mem. N.C. adv. council on Unemployment Compensation Commn.; chmn. N.C. Adv. Council for Employment Security Commn.; rep. of the Am. Assn. of Colls. Adv. Council on Med. Edn. Fellow A.C.P., A.A.A.S.; mem. A.M.A., So. Med. Dist. (pres. 1926-27), Wake County med. socs., Assn., Tri-State (president 1928-29) 6th District (president 1926-27), Wake County medical socs., Am. Gastroenterological Assn., Omicron Delta Kappa, Delta Kappa Epsilon, Phi Chi, Phi Beta Kappa. Democrat. Baptist. Mason. Author: Lectures on Pharmacology, 1929; The Doctor and Citizenship, 1934; Doctors in Other Fields, 1938. Home: Wake Forest, N.C. Died Aug. 28, 1955; buried Trinity Cemetery, Scotland Neck, N.C.

KITSON, Harry Dexter, psychologist; b. Mishawaka, Ind., Aug. 11, 1886; s. Clarence and Nellie (Hamblin) K.; A.B., Hiram (O.) Coll., 1909; A.M., U. Minn., 1913; Ph.D., U. Chgo., 1915; m. Angeline S. Freeman, June 14, 1922 (dec.); 1 son, Dexter Freeman (dec.). Asst. in psychology U. Minn., 1912-13; fellow U. Chgo., 1913-14, asso., 1914-15, instr., 1915-19; prof. psychology Ind. U., 1919-25; prof. edn. Tchrs. Coll., Columbia, 1925-1951. Served as 1st lt. CAC, AEF; on front with 53d Regt. CAC, staffs of ry. arty. brigades, 1st and 2d Armies. Mem. Am. Psychol. Assn., Sigma Xi, Alpha Tau Omega, Quadrangle Club (Chgo.). Author: How to Use Your Mind, 1916, 4th edit. 1951; Scientific Study of the College Student, 1917; Manual for the Study of the Psychology of Advertising and Selling, 1920; The Mind of the Buyer, 1921; The Psychology of Vocational Adjustment, 1925; Scientific Advertising, 1926; How to Find the Right Vocation, 1929, 3d edit. 1947; I Find My Vocation, 1931, 3d edit. 1947; Vocational Guidance for Those Out of School, 1936. Co-author Vocations for Girls, 1939, rev. 1951; Vocations for Boys, 1942; Helping People Find Jobs, 1950. Editor Kitson Careers Series. Home: 400 W. 119th St., N.Y. C. 27. Died Sept. 1959.

KITTELLE, Sumner Ely Wetmore (kĭ-tĕl'), Naval officer; b. Peekskill, N.Y., June 14, 1867; s. George Wetmore and Marie Louise (Geer) K.; grad. U.S. Naval Acad., 1889; m. Anna Lockwood, d. late Adm. Charles D. Sigsbee, Mar. 22, 1897; children—Anna Louise (wife of C. J. Moore, U.S. Navy), Elsa (dec.), Mary Sigsbee (wife of Lester A. Dessez, U.S. M.C.), Sumner Sigsbee, John, Nancy; m. 2d, Elizabeth R. Delaney (widow Gen. Delaney). Ensign, July 1, 1891; promoted through grades to rear adm., June 1921. Served on Dolphin, Spanish-Am. War, 1898; sec. Gen. Bd., Navy Dept., 1905-07; duty with the building of the Mississippi, 1907-08; served on Mississippi, 1908-09; exec. officer same, 1909-10; at Navy Yard, Boston, 1910-13; comd. Wheeling, 1913-14; at Naval War Coll., Newport, R.I., 1914; comd. Albany, 1914, Maryland, 1915; at Naval War Coll., 1915-17; apptd. comdr. Georgia, Jan. 5, 1917; sr. mem. Alaskan Coal Commn., 1919; mem. Bd. of Inspection and Survey, 1920; apptd. gov. of Virgin Island, by President Harding, Apr. 1921; comdr. Destroyer Squadrons of Scouting and Battle Fleets, 1922-24; comdt. Eighth Naval Dist., 1924; pres. Naval Examining Bd., 1925; comdt. Naval Dist. of P.I., 1926-28; comdr. Fleet Base Force, U.S. Fleet, 1928-29; pres. Bd. of Inspection and Survey, 1929-31, retired. Home: 2229 California St. N.W., Washington. Died Dec. 29, 1950.

KITTREDGE, Frank Alvah (kĭt'trĕj), U.S. Nat. Park Service; b. Glyndon, Minn., Mar. 29, 1883; s. Charles Brigham and Katherine (Forbes) K.; B.S. in C.E., U. Wash., 1912, C.E., 1915; m. Catharine Mears, Mar. 11, 1915; 1 dau., Catharine Jane (Mrs. Robert Andrews). With Alaska Central Ry., 1905-07; engr. in charge constrn., Wash. State Highway Commn., 1907-11; div. engr. Ore. State Highway Commn., 1913-15; sr. highway engr. Bur. Pub. Rds., 1917-27; chief engr. Nat. Park Service, U.S. Dept. of Interior, 1927-37, regional dir. Region Four, 1937-40, supt. Grand Canyon Nat. Park, 1940-41, supt. Yosemite Nat. Park, 1941-47, chief engr. U.S. Nat. Park Service, 1947-51. Served as 1st lt. Engr. Corps, U.S. Army, 1918; capt. Rd. and Bridge Engrs. in France, 1918-19. Mem. Am. Soc., C.E. (life mem.), Soil Conservation Soc., Wilderness Soc., Am. Planning and Civic Assn. Save the Redwoods League. Presbyn. Mason. Clubs: Sierra Mountaineers, Cosmos, American Legion. Address: 1951 Waverley St., Palo

Alto, Cal. Died Dec. 11, 1954; buried Alta Mesa, Los Altos, Cal.

KITTREDGE, Mabel Hyde, sociologist; b. Boston, Sept. 19, 1867; d. Abbott Eliot and Margaret Ann (Hyde) K.; ed. pub. and pvt. schs. Founder, 1901, and pres. Assn. of Practical Housekeeping Center, New York; inaugurated lunches in elementary schools of New York, 1908. Clubs: Cosmopolitan, Women's City. Author: Housekeeping Notes, 1911; Practical Homemaking, 1915; Home and Its Management, 1917. Home: Bass River, Mass. Died May 8, 1955.

KLAIN, Zora, univ. prof.; b. Norway, Me., Oct. 14, 1884; s. Maurice and Rose Rebecca (Harkins) K.; A.B., Clark Univ., 1912; A.M., Pa. State Coll., 1917; Ph.D., U. of Pa. (scholarship stipend, 1922, Harrison fellow, 1923), 1924; m. Mary Christine Dudley, Apr. 28, 1919; children—Priscilla Alden, Evangeline MacDowell, Dudley O'Sullivan. Instr., MacDonough (Md.) Sch., 1912-15; asst. prof. of German, Pa. State Coll., 1915-22; asst. prof. psychology and edn. U. of Rochester, 1924-25; chmn. dept. and prof. edn. Rutgers U. since 1925; prof. edn. Duke Univ., summers, 1923-25, U. of Pa., 1928, 29, 38. Mem. N.E.A., N.J. Edn. Assn., Am. Assn. Univ. Profs., Coll. Teachers of Edn., Phi Delta Kappa. Author: Quaker Contributions to Education in North Carolina, 1925; Educational Activities of New England Quakers, 1928. Contbr. articles to ednl. periodicals. Home: 10 Rutgers St., Stelton, N.J. Office: Rutgers Univ., New Brunswick, N.J. Died Nov. 6, 1952.

KLAMMER, Aloysius A., educator; b. Zamek, Poland, July 8, 1889; s. Philip and Marie (Ciesinska) K.; Reifezeugnis Royal Gymnasium, Culm, Germany, 1911; student Breslau U., 1911, Berlin Handelschochschule; Berlin U., 1911-14; Licencié és sciences commerciales, U. Fribourg, 1915, Ph.D., 1916; grad. study Columbia, summer 1922; m. Sophie A. Nadolony, May 15, 1915; children—Marie Theresa, Hedwig Ursula, Joseph Francis, Thomas Aloysius. Came to U.S., 1916, naturalized, 1922. Instr. modern langs. Ints. Sarinia, Fribourg, Switzerland, 1915-16; prof. modern lang. and lit. S.S. Cyril and Methodius Sem., Orchard Lake, Mich., 1917; prof. modern langs. Alliance Coll., Cambridge Springs, Pa., 1917-18 (and social scis.), St. John Kanty Coll., Erie, Pa., 1918-23; asst. prof. Creighton U., 1923-26, prof., 1926-—, dir. dept. modern langs., 1932-—. Mem. Omaha Welfare Bd., 1940-45. Dir. Am. Relief for Poland, 1942-46; 1st v.p. Polish Home, Inc., 1948-—; pres. Polish Welfare Club, 1932-34. Recipient Cross of Merit (Poland). Mem. Polish Nat. Alliance, Polish Am. Congress, Alliance Francaise, Polish Union U.S. of N.A. (sec. local chpt.), Neb. Modern Lang. Assn. (past pres.). Roman Catholic (past mem. Diocesan council). Editor-in-chief Western Star (Polish weekly 1926-45. Contbr. Polish, German newspapers. Home: 2520 S. 23d St., Omaha 9. Died June 8, 1953; buried Omaha.

KLAPPER, Paul, educator; b. Jassy, Rumania, July 17, 1885; s. Louis and Rachel (Halpern) K.; brought to U.S., 1892; A.B., Coll. City of N.Y., 1904; M.A., N.Y.U., 1907, Ph.D., 1909; student U. Wis, 1908; L.H.D., Yeshiva Coll., 1938; LL.D., Columbia, 1949; m. Flora Eydenberg, June 25, 1911; 1 son, Joseph Thomas. Formerly sec. Univ. Settlement Soc., New York; tutor, instr., asst. prof., prof. edn. Coll. City of N.Y., 1907-37, also dir. summer session, 1917-22, and dean sch. of Edn.; pres. Queens Coll., New York, 1937-48, emeritus; vis. prof. U. Chgo., 1949-50. Trustee State Univ. of N.Y., Brandeis U. Fellow A.A.A.S.; mem. N.E.A., New York Council of the State Commn. Against Discrimination, N.Y. State Commn. on Need for State Univ., Phi Beta Kappa, Kappa Delta Pi. Club: Town Hall. Author: Principles of Educational Practice, 1912; Teaching Children to Read, 1914; The Teaching of English, 1915; Modern English (with A. London), 1923; Teaching English in Elementary and Junior High School, 1924; Teaching of History, 1925; Contemporary Education, 1929; The Teaching of Arithmetic, 1934. Co-Author: Reading for Appreciation. Editor: College Teaching, The Appleton Series in Methods of Teaching. Home: 144-80 Sanford Av., Flushing, L.I. Office: 695 Park Av., N.Y.C. 21. Died Mar. 25, 1952.

KLAUBER, Edward; b. Louisville, Ky., Feb. 24, 1887; s. Morris and Ray (Forst) K.; ed. U. of Louisville, U. of Pa.; m. Gladys Gustafson, Feb. 23, 1925 (died 1943); m. 2d, Doris E. Larson, Apr. 1945. Reporter N.Y. World, 1912-16; reporter, editor New York Times, 1916-28; dir. pub. relations, Lenmen & Mitchell Advt. Agency, 1928-29; exec. v.p. Columbia Broadcasting System, 1930-42, became dir., May, 1937, chmn. exec. com., Mar. 1942, retired, 1943; associate dir. Office War Information, 1943-45. Club: Vineyard Haven (Mass.) Yacht. Home: 33 E. 70th St., N.Y.C. 21. Died Sept. 23, 1954.

KLEBERG, Edward Robert, lawyer; b. Cuero, Tex., Sept. 1877; s. Otto and Marie Otilie (Ploeger) K.; Litt.B., U. Tex., 1899; LL.B., 1900; unmarried. Admitted to Tex. bar, 1900, and became practice of law at Yorktown; removed to Corpus Christi, Tex., 1907; mem. firm Kleberg, Eckhardt, Mobley, Lockett & Weil; v.p. State Nat. Bank; v.p., dir. White Point Development Co.; v.p., counsel Guaranty Title & Trust Co.; dir., counsel Aransas Compress Co.; counsel Corpus Christi Nat. Bank, Nueces County Navigation Dist.; atty. Central Power & Light Co. Served as capt. in Army Service Corps, AEF, U.S. Army, World War. Mem. Sigma Chi. Democrat. Home: 309 Cole St. Office: Jones Bldg., Corpus Christi, Tex. Died Sept. 1, 1957.

KLEBERG, Richard Mifflin, ex-congressman; b. Corpus Christi, Nov. 18, 1887; s. Robert Justus and Alice Gertrudis (King) K.; gs. Richard King, founder of the King Ranch (1,250,000 acres); LL.B. and M.L., U. of Tex., 1911; m. Mamie Searcy, June 12, 1912; children—Mary Etta, Katherine Searcy, Richard Mifflin, Alice Gertrudis King. Began as foreman King Ranch, Kingsville, Tex., 1911; acting in management of same, 1913-24, chmn. bd., 1934-—; elected, 1931, to 72d Congress to fill vacancy caused by decease of Harry M. Wurzbach, term ending 1933, and reëlected from 73d to 78th Congresses (1933-45), 14th Tex. Dist.; mem. Tex. Game and Fish Commn., 1951-53. Dir. State Nat. Bank, Corpus Christi; trustee Estate of Mrs. H. M. King. Mem. exec. com. Tex. S.W. Cattle Raisers Assn., 1913-24; pres. same, 1927-29; mem. bd. dirs. Am. Nat. Live Stock Assn., 1924-32; organizer, 1928, and since pres. Tex. Federated Agrl. Assn.; mem. bd. Better Beef Assn. Former pres. board Tex. Coll. Arts and Industries. Mem. Phi Delta Phi, Sigma Chi. Democrat. Presbyn. Mason. Clubs: Corpus Christi Golf and Country; San Antonio Golf and Country; Kingsville Golf and Country; Congressional Country, Burning Tree Country (Washington). Home: King Ranch, Kingsville, Tex.; and Robert Driscoll Hotel, Corpus Christi, Tex. Died May 8, 1955; buried Chamberlain Cemetery, Kingsville.

KLECKNER, Martin Seler, surgeon; b. Allentown, Pa., Apr. 14, 1890; s. Francis and Amelia Isabella (Seler) K. B.S., Muhlenberg Coll., Allentown, Pa., 1910; M.D., Univ. of Pa., 1914; postgrad. study, Univ. of Pa., 1920-21, Postgrad. Hosp., N.Y.C., 1923-24, Cornell Med. Sch., 1926-28; m. Florence Street, Nov. 25, 1920; children—Martin Seler, Donald S., Francis S. Interne, chief resident German Hosp. (now Lankenau), 1914-16; surgeon Allentown Hosp., 1917-18; practice gen. surgery, Allentown, 1920-24, practice limited to diseases of the rectum and colon since 1924, cons. proctologist Sacred Heart Hosp., Allentown, St. Luke's Hosp., Bethlehem, Pennsylvania, Allentown State Hospital. Captain United States Army, World War I, 1918-20. Certified diplomate surgery and proctology. Fellow A.P.S., A.C.S. (counsellor State of Pennsylvania, 1934-38). Founder-fellow International College of Surgeons. Mem. A.M.A. (chmn. sect. gastro-enterology and proctology, 1946-47), Am. Proctologic Soc. (pres. 1939-40), Pa. State Cancer Commn. (chmn. 1946-49; pres. Lehigh Co. Unit since 1949), Wainwright Tumor Clinic Assns. (chmn. 1947, 1952, Pres., dir. 1951-52), Postgrad. and Phila. proctologic Socs. (p.p. both socs.), Lehigh Co. Med. Soc. (pres. 1950), Lehigh Valley Medical Association (president 1939), Am. Cancer Society (bd. dirs., Lehigh Co.). Invitation lectr. proctology, Univ. of Pa. Medical School. American Legion, Y.M.C.A. (director), Chi Phi, Alpha Kappa Kappa, Alpha Omega Alpha. Rep. Lutheran. Mason (Shriner), Elk. Clubs: Livingston, Lehigh Country, Maskenozha Hunting and Fishing; Union League (Phila.). Author articles on proctologic subjects and cancer in medical jours. Home: Dorneyville, 3110 Hamilton Blvd. Office: 202 N. 8 St., Allentown, Pa. Died May, 1958.

KLEIN, Frederick B., business exec.; b. Yonkers, N.Y., 1886. Pres., dir. Alexander Smith & Sons Carpet Co.; dir. Central Nat. Bank, Yonkers, Sloan-Blabon Corp., C. H. Masland & Sons. Trustee Alexander Smith Meml. Found., Carpet Inst. Am. Dir. St. John's Riverside Hosp. Home: 4 Delavan Terrace, Yonkers. Office: 225 Lake Av., Yonkers, N.Y. Died July 29, 1950.

KLEIN, Herman William, railroad exec.; b. Lathrop, Cal., Sept. 4, 1889; s. Conrad and Mary (Thielecke) K.; student pub. schs., Cal., Mo.; m. Queena M. Leithead, 1930. Mem. freight traffic dept. St. L.-S.F. R.R., 1906-09; joined S.P. Co., 1910, gen. freight and traffic mgr., rates and division, 1954-—. Mem. Pacific Traffic Assn. Pacific Railway. Mason. Clubs: Bohemian, Commercial (San Francisco). Home: 2677 Larkin St. Office: 65 Market St., San Francisco. Died Nov. 26, 1956.

KLEIN, John Warren (klīn), coll. pres.; b. Reading, Pa., Mar. 28, 1872; s. John and Sally (Custer) K.; B.A., Williamette U., 1897, M.A., 1898; D.D., Ursinus Coll., 1910; LL.D., Lebanon Valley Coll., 1934; Litt.D., Albright Coll., 1946; m. Anna Lanz, Nov. 24, 1898 (died 1946); children—Ruth Anna (Mrs. Herman DeMund), John Norman, Esther Adella (Mrs. Richard T. Williamson). Ordained ministry Evang. Ch., 1893, occupying various pulpits; head dept. of history Schuylkill Coll., Reading, Pa., 1918-23, v.p., treas., 1923-28; v.p., treas. Albright Coll., Reading, 1928-32, pres. 1932-38, pres. emeritus, 1938-—. Trustee Community Gen. Hosp., Albright Coll. dir. Tchrs. Protective Union (pres.); former mem. Reading City Planning Commn. Mem. N.E.A. Mason (Shriner). Clubs: University, Wyomissing, Kiwanis. Contbr. to religious and ednl. publs. Home: 223 Cherry Drive, Wyomissing, Pa. Died June 1957.

KLEINPELL, William Darwin, geologist; b. N.Y.C., Apr. 9, 1898; s. William Ernest and Alma (Wilke) K.; B.A., Stanford, 1921; m. Fay Baker, Dec. 1, 1927; children—Jean Fay (Mrs. C. Don Horton), Karoline Kay (Mrs. Harold Rosoff). Cons. petroleum geologist, 1932-—; dir. Kern County Land Co., San Francisco, 1948-—, Intex Oil Co., 1950-—. Mem. Am. Assn. Petroleum Geologists, Am. Inst. Mining and Metall. Engrs., Am. Geog. Soc., A.A.A.S. Home: 809 Oleander St. Office: Haberfield Bldg., Bakersfield, Cal. Died Apr. 1959.

KLEISER, George William, corp. exec.; b. Cloverdale, Cal., June 25, 1874; s. James A. and Elizabeth (Unferfate) K.; grad. U. Cal., Berkeley; D.D.S., Temple U., 1897; m. Maude H. O'Neil, Feb. 14, 1900; children—George William, John E. Founded The Foster and Kleiser Co., with W. F. Foster, in 1901; dir. Outdoor Advt., Inc., Outdoor Advt. Assn. of Am., Inc.; dir., chmn. bd. Foster & Kleiser Co. Republican. Episcopalian. Mason (Shriner, Jester). Club: San Francisco Golf; Wilshire Country, Los Angeles Country, California (Los Angeles). Home: 105 Baywood Av., San Mateo, Cal. Office: 1675 Eddy St., San Francisco 19. Died Nov. 30, 1952.

KLEISER, Grenville, author; b. Toronto, Can., July 15, 1868; s. Samuel Percival and Matilda Adelaide (Morley) K.; high sch. edn.; m. Elizabeth Margaret Thompson, July 5, 1894. For many yrs. instr. in pub. speaking; mem. Yale Div. Sch., 1902-04; founder, dir. Pub. Speaking Club in America, 1908, Great Britain, 1910. Author (or compiler): How to Speak in Public, 1906; Humorous Hits and How to Hold an Audience, 1908; How to Develop Power and Personality in Speaking, 1909; The World's Great Sermons, 1909; Personal Lessons in Public Speaking, 1910; How to Argue and Win, 1910; How to Develop Self-Confidence in Speech and Manner, 1910; Personal Lessons in Practical English, 1911; Great Speeches and How to Make Them, 1911; How to Read and Declaim, 1911; Personal Lessons in Business Success, 1913; Kleiser's Complete Guide to Public Speaking, 1915; Talks on Talking, 1916; Inspiration and Ideals, 1917; Fifteen Thousand Useful Phrases, 1917; How to Build Mental Power, 1917; How to Speak Without Notes, 1919; Something to Say—How to Say It, 1919; Successful Methods of Public Speaking, 1919; Model Speeches for Practice, 1919; The Training of a Public Speaker, 1919; How to Sell Through Speech, 1919; Impromptu Speeches, 1919; Word-Power, 1919; Christ, The Master Speaker, 1919; Vital English for Speakers and Writers, 1919; Similes and Their Use, 1925; Training for Authorship, 1925; Training for Power and Leadership, 1928; How to Improve Your Conversation, 1932; How to succeed in Life, 1933; Everyday Poems, 1941; Taking God Into Partnership, 1943; How to Chart Your Own Career, 1945; Grenville Kleiser's Scrap Book of Words You Should Know, 1946; The Bridge You'll Never Cross, 1948; Maek Your Life Worth Living, 1949. Address: 524 Fifth Av., N.Y.C. Died Oct. 1953.

KLEIST, James Aloysius, clergyman, educator; b. Silesia, Germany, Apr. 4, 1873; s. James and Barbara (Gierend) K.; student high sch. and coll.; entered Soc. of Jesus (Jesuits), 1891; studied asceticism, 1891-92; grad. Jesuit Normal Sch., Limburg, Holland, 1894; studied philosophy and gen. science, Valkenburg, Holland, 1894-97, divinity St. Louis U., 1902-06, and Prairie du Chien, Wis.; A.M., St. Louis U., 1914, Ph.D., 1919; student U. Berlin, 1926-27. Came to U.S., 1897; instr. Jesuit normal schs., Cleve., 1897-1902; tchr. classics Creighton U., Omaha, Neb., 1907-08, Campion Coll., Prairie du Chien, 1908-17, John Carroll U. of Cleve., 1917-28; prof. classical langs. St. Louis U., 1928-—. Specializes in Latin prose composition, N.T. Greek, and in translation of Classics. Mem. Archeol. Inst. of America, Mo. Acad. Science, Am. Philol. Assn., Linguistic Soc. America, Classical Assn. Middle West and South, Catholic Commn. on Intellectual and Social Affairs, Am. Cath. Bibl. Assn., Classical Philology Club of St. Louis. Chmn. St. Louis U. Center for Am. Mediaeval Dictionary Study; mem. com. on N.T. translation. Author: First Lessons in Greek, 1903; Advanced Lessons in Greek, 1904; Aids to Latin Prose Composition, 1912; Hints on Latin Style, 1912; Practical Course in Latin Prose Composition (2d edits.), 1914; The Memoirs of St. Peter, 1932; Gospel of St. Mark, 1936. Translator: The Dream of Scipio (Somnium Scipionis), 1915. Editor and translator: The Epistles of St. Clement of Rome and St. Ignatius of Antioch (Vol. I, Ancient Christian Writers), 1946; The Didache, Epistle of Barnabas, Epistles and Martyrdom of St. Polycarp, The Fragments of Popias, Epistle to Diognetus (also Ancient Christian Writers). Adapted A. Kaegi's Grammar of Classical Greek, for Am. schs., 1903. Address: St. Louis U., St. Louis. Died Apr. 28, 1949; buried St. Stanislaus Cemetery, Florissant, Mo.

KLEITZ, William L(ambert), banker; b. Highland Falls, N.Y., May 2, 1894; s. William and Albertina

(Isaksson) K.; A.B., Cornell U., 1915; m. Harriet Selby Gillette, Aug. 23, 1917; 1 dau., Virginia Gillette (Mrs. Spencer D. Moseley). Began with Imbrie & Co., N.Y.C., 1915; later with Hemphill White & Chamberlain, now Hemphill Noyes & Co., N.Y.C.; with Guaranty Trust Co. of N.Y., 1919—, asst. treas., 1920-23, asst. v.p., 1923-28, vice pres., 1928-46, dir., 1946-47, pres., 1947—; dir. Wilson & Co., Inc., Chgo., Inspiration Consol. Copper Co.; dir. in N.Y. and mem. of finance com. Royal Liverpool Ins. Group; dir. IBM World Trade Corp., W. T. Grant Co. Mem. N.Y. Community Trust (trustees com.), N.Y. State Banking Bd., Julliard Music Found. (treas., trustee), Presbyn. Hosp. (mem. corp.), Sarah Lawrence College (trustee 1940-47) dir. Met. Opera Assn. Served as 2d lt., inf., Res. Corps, U.S. Army, 1917; commd. 2d lt., inf., Regular Army, advancing through grades to capt., U.S. Army, 1917-19; enlisted as pvt., advancing to sergt., N.Y.N.G., 1922-25. Mem. Assn. Reserve City Bankers, Commerce and Industry Assn. of N.Y. (v.p., dir.), Am. Geog. Soc. (councillor), Cornell U. Alumni Assn. (pres. 1944-46), Assn. Ex-members Squadron A, N.Y. City, Pilgrims of U.S., Newcomen Soc. of Eng., Psi Upsilon. Republican. Episcopalian. Clubs: Apawamis, Manursing Island, Shenorock Shore (Rye, N.Y.); University; Racquet and Tennis, Cornell of N.Y., Madison Square Garden (N.Y.C.); Blind Brook (Port Chester, N.Y.); Chicago. Home: Boxwood Lane, Rye, N.Y. Office: Guaranty Trust Company of New York, 140 Broadway, N.Y.C. 15. Died Nov. 19, 1957.

KLEMIN, Alexander, aero. cons.; b. London, Eng. May 15, 1888; s. Albert and Dora (Clemens) K.; B.S., London U., 1909; S.M., Mass. Inst. Tech., 1915; LL.D., Kenyon College, 1934; D.Eng., N.Y.U., 1950; m. Ethel Murton, 1921; 1 dau., Diana. Came to U.S., 1913, naturalized, 1917. In charge aeronautics dept. Mass. Inst. Tech., 1916-17; officer in charge of Research Dept. Army Air Service, McCook Field, Dayton, O., during World War; cons. aero. engr., 1919-24; in charge Daniel Guggenheim Sch. of Aeronautics, N.Y.U., 1924-41; research prof. N.Y. U., 1942-44; lectr. aeros. Princeton, 1934-35; cons. engr. Aero. Br., Dept. of Commerce, 1927-29; designed first amphibian landing gear used in U.S., 1921. Mem. aerodynamics and rotation wing aircraft coms. NACA. Winner of army and navy airplane design competitions; Dr. Alexander Klemin ann. award established by Am. Helicopter Soc., 1951. Fellow Inst. Aero. Scis.; mem. Am. Soc. M.E., Soc. Automotive Engrs., Royal Aero. Soc., Am. Helicopter Soc. (pres. 1949-50). Helicopter editor Aero Digest; editor Handbook of Aeronautical Engineering. Episcopalian. Club: Wings. Author: Textbook of Aeronautical Engineering, 1918; If You Want to Fly, 1926; Simplified Aerodynamics, 1927; Airplane Stress Analysis, 1927; The Helicopter Adventure, 1947; (with A. T. McPherson) Engineering Uses of Rubber, 1956. Contbr. to tech. jours. Address: Anderson Road, Greenwich, Conn. Died Mar. 13, 1950; buried Arlington Nat. Cemetery.

KLEMME, Roland M., neurosurgeon; b. Belleville, Ill., May 17, 1896; s. G. D. and Margaret (Metzler) K.; M.D., Washington U., 1921; m. Virginia M. Knobeloch, Dec. 31, 1926; 1 son, Charles T. Rayhill (stepson). Intern Barnes Hosp., St. Louis, 1921-22; out-patient surgery, in charge surg. path. Barnes Hosp., 1911-24; fellow in neurosurgery Washington U., 1924; asso. with Dr. Ernest Sachs in neurol. surgery, 1925-34; instr. clin. neurol. surgery Washington U., 1927-41; pvt. practice of neurosurgery, 1934—; prof. surgery St. Louis U., 1942—, also head neurosurg. div.; cons. neurosurgeon several r.r. hosp. assns., state cancer hosp.; affiliated with St. Luke's, St. Louis City, St. Mary's, St. Louis County, St. John's, Jewish, DePaul Bethesda, Luth., St. Anthony's, Firmin Desloge, Shriner's, Mo. Bapt. hosps. (all St. Louis), Salinas Valley Meml., Monterey County hosps. (Salinas, Cal.), Monterey (Cal.) Hosp. Pres. Playgoers St. Louis, Inc., 1942-43; chmn. Contemporary Club, 1938-39. Diplomate Am. Bd. Neurology. Fellow A.C.S., Internat. Coll. Surgeons (treas. 1948-50; trustee); mem. A.M.A., Mo., St. Louis, Frisco, Mo.-Pacific, Mo.-Kan.-Tex., Monterey County, Mississippi Valley (life) med. socs., St. Louis Surg. Soc., Am., So., Cal., World, Western Indsl. med. assns., St. Louis Neurosurg. Soc., St. Louis Soc. for Crippled Children, Pan-Pacific Surg. Assn., Am. Assn. Ry. Surgeons, Internat. Soc. Gen. Semantics, N.Y. Acad. Sci., Acad. Polit. Sci., Southwestern Surg. Congress, Harvey Cushing Soc. (co-founder), Terre Haute Acad. of Medicine (hon.), Gorgas Soc. (hon.), AM. Assn. Industrial Physicians and Surgeons, Am. Soc. for Control of Cancer, Am. Assn. Anatomists; hon. mem. Soc. of Surgery of La Paz, Soc. of Medicine of Argentina, Surgical Soc. of Argentina; Societe de Chirurgie de Bordeauz, Sociedad de Chirugia de Madrid, Turkish, Am.-Soviet med. socs., and others; asso. mem. Assn. Med. Illustrators; fgn. member Soc. of Medicine and Surgery of Sao Paulo. Clubs: Racquet, University (St. Louis); Lotos (N.Y.). Author: Nursing Care of Neurosurgical Patients, 1949; 25 articles in profl. jours. Home: Carmel, Cal. Office: 45 W. Romie Lane, Salinas, Cal. Died Nov. 21, 1957.

KLEPPER, Frank B., ex-congressman, lawyer; b. Putnam County, Mo., June 22, 1864; s. Dr. T. G. and Mary E. (Hoyt) K.; student Baker (Kan.) U.; LL.B., U. Mo., 1898; m. Lela Madden, Nov. 30, 1893. Practice of law, Kingston, Mo., 1900-07, Cameron, Mo., 1907—; pros. atty. Caldwell County, Mo., 1900-04; mem. Congress, 3d Mo. dist., 1905-07; county atty. Clinton County, Mo., 1919-20. Trustee Mo. Wesleyan Coll., 1910-30. Republican. Address: 8th and Meade Sts., Cameron, Mo. Died Aug. 4, 1933; buried Evergreen Cemetery, Cameron.

KLIEN, Arthur Jay (klīn), educator; b. Sturgis, Mich., Dec. 10, 1884; s. John G. and Eva J. (McCradit) K.; B.A., Wabash Coll., 1906, LL.D., 1932; B.D. magna cum laude, Union Theology Sem., 1909; M.A., Columbia, 1909, Ph.D., 1916; m. Marian Annis Smith, July 2, 1912. Instr. history N.Y.U., 1909-10, Coll. City of N.Y., 1910-15; head dept. history and econs. Wheaton Coll., Norton, Mass., 1915-18; asst. dir. Service Bur., U.S. Com. on Pub. Information, 1918; capt. A.G.D., in charge orgn. of War Dept. Pub. Info. Services, Washington, 1918-19; asso. dir., Div. of Ednl. Extension, U.S. Bur. Edn., 1919; exec. sec. Nat. U. Extension Assn., 1919-20; exec. of Research and Development Service, U.S. Army Edn. and Recreation Div., Camp Grant, Rockford, Ill., 1920-21; ednl. advisor U.S. Army Corr. Courses, on mil. subjects, 1921-24; lt. col. O.R.C., staff specialist on active duty in Edn. and Schs'. Sect., Gen. Staff, U.S. Army, 1924-25; chief of Div. of Higher Edn., U.S. Bur. of Edn., 1926-30; dir. Survey of Land Grant Colls. and Univs. authorized by Congress; dir. survey of higher instns. Ore., survey of pub. higher edn., Ark., U.S. Office of Edn.; mem. staff, survey of U. Chgo., 1931-32; prof. of edn. Ohio State U., 1931-37, dean Coll. Edn. 1937-45, dean emeritus, 1945—; asso. dir. Survey Pub. Edn. in State of Wash., 1946; specialist in higher edn. in surveys of edn. in W.Va., 1945; Needs of Cal. in Higher Edn. (survey), 1947-48; Pub. Schs. of D.C., 1948; dir. survey O. Wesleyan U., 1947, U. Wyo., 1947-48. Mem. Ohio Citizens Council (dir.), Fgn. Policy Assn. Phi Beta Kappa. Presbyn. Author: Intolerance in the Reign of Elizabeth, Queen of England, 1916. Report on Survey of Rutgers U.; dir., editor Survey of Negro Colls. and Univs. Editor: Adventures in the Reconstruction of Education, 1941. Home: 6064 Olentangy River Rd., Worthington, O. Died June 1, 1957.

KLINCK, Arthur William, clergyman, educator; b. Elmira, Ont., Can., Jan. 19, 1900; s. George and Mary (Devitt) K.; brought to U.S., 1918, naturalized, 1937; B.D., Concordia Sem., 1924, S.T.M., 1925; Ph.D., U. Neb., 1935; m. Flora Buettner, 1925; 1 son, Robert George. Ordained to ministry Luth. Ch., 1925; pastor Our Redeemer Ch., North Platte, Neb., 1925-29, Calvary Ch., Lincoln, Neb., 1929-39; pres. Concordia Tchrs. Coll., River Forest, Ill., 1939-54; prof., chmn. dept. hist. theology Concordia Theol. Sem., St. Louis, 1954—. Chmn. bd. Christian edn. S. Neb. Dist. Luth. Ch., 1936-39. Mem. Am. Hist. Assn., Luth. Edn. Assn., Nat. Edn. Assn., Am. Inst. Archaeology, Lutheran Layman's League. Republican. Author: Old Testament History 1938; Instructors' Guide to Old Testament History (with Walter O. Kraeft), 1938; Home Life in Bible Times (also instrs. guide), 1947. Co-editor of Luth. Edn., ofcl. ednl. jour. Luth. Ch. (Mo. synod) 1939-54, contbr.; asso. editor Lutheran Witness, 1956—; mem., co-editor synodical com. Sunday Sch. Tchr. Tng., 1938—; chmn. Sunday Sch. tchr. tng. com. 1956—. Home: 21 Seminary Terrace, Clayton 5, Mo. Died Aug. 9, 1959; buried Our Redeemer Cemetery, St. Louis.

KLINE, I. Clinton, ex-congressman; b. Mt. Pleasant, nr. Sunbury, Pa., Aug. 18, 1858; s. Herman Garner and Mary (Bassett) K.; A.B., Lafayette Coll., 1893, A.M., 1897. Admitted to Pa. bar, 1894, since practiced at Sunbury; practiced for some time in Washington; made speaking tour of Pa. for Rep. Party, 1898, N.H., N.J., 1924; mem. 67th Congress, 17th Pa. Dist. Traveled through 8 countries of Europe, 1925, around the world, 1927. Mem. Delta Kappa Epsilon. Mason. Club: Masonic Temple. Address: 235 Market Sq., Sunbury, Pa. Deceased.

KLINE, John Robert, prof. mathematics; b. Quakertown, Pa., Dec. 7, 1891; s. Henry K. and Emma (Osman) K.; A.B., Muhlenberg Coll., Allentown, Pa., 1912, Sc.D., 1934; A.M., U. of Pa., 1914, Ph.D., 1916; Guggenheim fellow, U. of Göttingen, 1925-26; m. Anna B. Shafer, June 1, 1915 (deceased); 1 son, John Shafer; m. 2d Eunice Story Eaton, March 24, 1951. Instr. in math., U. of Pa., 1917-18, Yale, 1918-19; asso. in mathematics, U. of Ill., 1919-20; asst. prof. mathematics, U. of Pa., 1920-28, prof. since 1928, chmn. department of mathematics and Thomas A. Scott Professor of Mathematics since 1940; visiting professor, Bryn Mawr Coll., 1935-36, Swarthmore Coll., 1938-39; vis. prof. math. University of Colorado, summer 1949, U. Tubingen, Germany, first semester, 1952-53. Member board examiners mathematics College Entrance Examination Bd., mem. adv. council in mathematics Princeton since 1942. Sec. conf. for formation Internat. Math. Union, 1950; mem. div. mathematics Nat. Research Council, 1951. Mem. Am. Math. Soc. (asso. editor of bulletin; mem. council; sec.), A.A.A.S. (v.p. and chmn. Sect. A. 1938), Math. Assn. America, Am. Philos. Soc., Polish Math. Soc., Internat. Congress of Mathematicians (sec.), Soc. of Science and Letters of Warsaw, Alpha Tau Omega. Presbyterian. Mason. Contributor to Trans. Am. Math. Soc., Fundamenta Mathematicæ, etc. Asso. editor Trans. Am. Math. Soc., also of Am. Jour. Mathematics. Home: 529 Riverview Av., Swarthmore, Pa. Died May 2, 1955; buried Quakertown, Pa.

KLINEFELTER, Howard Emanuel, editor; b. Versailles, Ill., July 17, 1902; s. Emanuel and Norah (Gillis) K.; ed. pub. schs. of Versailles, Ill.; m. Milly Columbia Scrogum, July 2, 1923; children—Lenora (Mrs. W. L. Fitzgerald), Halmar Emanuel, James Andrew, Gloria Ann. Telegrapher, Wabash R.R. Co., Springfield, Ill., 1917-18; sec. Franklin Co. Farmers Assn., Union, Mo., June 1930-40; editor Missouri Farmer since 1940; mem. investment com., Mo. Farmer Assn. Mutual Ins. Co. since 1946; chmn. Mo. state adv. bd., Farm and Home Adminstrn.; mem. Mo. State Recreation Com. Recipient medal for patriotism, Fed. Govt., World War II. Mem. Mo. Farmers Assn. (sec. state legislative com., dir. information), Mo. Chamber of Commerce (state agrl. com.), Cooperative Editors' Association, hon. member Farm Writers Guild, hon. mem. Sigma Delta Chi. Mem. Christian Ch., Comd. Col., State of Mo., 1945. Home: Route 3, Columbia. Office: Missouri Farmers Association Bldg., Columbia, Mo. Died Oct. 27, 1956; buried Columbia Meml. Cemetery.

KLINGE, Ernest F., govt. ofcl.; b. Washington, Sept. 24, 1889; s. Henry E. and Katherine (Trueshelm) K.; student Cath. U., 1911-13, George Washington U., 1914-16; LL.B., M.P.L., Nat. U. Law, 1937; m. Edna Katherine Crandall, Apr. 26, 1915; children—Edna L. Ketchum, Mary A. Shorb. Orchestra condr., 1916-19; examiner U.S. Patent Office, Dept. of Commerce since 1918, now U.S. asst. commr. patents. Home: 9005 Fairview Rd., Silver Spring, Md. Office: U.S. Patent Office, Dept. of Commerce, Washington 25. Died May 4, 1952.

KLOCK, Mabie Crouse, real estate, mfg.; b. Syracuse, N.Y., Apr. 26, 1880; s. Frank Benjamin and Charlotte Lizzie (Crouse) K.; Ph.B., Yale, 1902; m. Nannie Clay Tenney, October 14, 1903 (died November 19, 1924); children—Marion (Mrs. George L. Scherrer), Laura Tenney (Mrs. Jay William Cronk), Frank Tenney, Nancy Crouse (dec.); m. 2d, Florence Taylor Greene, Mar. 16, 1926 (died July 21, 1930); m. 3d, Mary Baker Link, Aug. 1, 1931. Began as clk., 1902; in real estate and mfg. business since 1906; dir. and mem. exec. com. Crucible Steel Co. of America, First Trust & Deposit Co., Grinnell Corporation; director and sec. Onondaga Pottery Co.; trustee and mem. exec. com. Syracuse Savings Bank. Episcopalian. Mason. Clubs: University (New York); Century, University, Citizens (Syracuse). Home: 1052 E. Genesee Street, Syracuse 10, N.Y. Office: 200 W. Water St., Syracuse 2, N.Y. Died Mar. 11, 1955.

KLUGHERZ, John Anthony (klūg'herz), hotel exec.; b. Bklyn., Mar. 31, 1900; s. Charles William and Mary (Tynan) K.; student pub. schs., Bklyn.; m. Mary Anna Schag, Dec. 14, 1928; 1 dau., Mary Jean. Mail, information, and room clk. Hotel McAlpin, N.Y.C., 1921-28, office mgr., 1928-31; office mgr. Waldorf-Astoria, 1931-36, exec. asst. mgr., 1936-46; asst. mgr. and resident mgr. Hotel Plaza, 1946-52, gen. mgr. since 1952. Mem. N.Y. State, N.Y.C. hotel assns. Club: Bees. Address: Hotel Plaza, N.Y.C. 19. Died Aug. 29, 1953; buried St. Johns Cemetery, Queens, N.Y.

KLUYVER, Albert Jan, microbiologist; b. Breda, Netherlands, June 3, 1888; s. Jan Cornelis and Marie (Honigh) K.; Chem.E., Tech. U., Delft, Netherlands, 1910, Dr. Tech. Sci., 1914; student U. Vienna, 1911; D.Sc., Ia. State Coll., 1932; Dr. honores causa Univ. of Louvain (Belgium), 1953. Doctor Honores Causa Rutgers Univ., 1954; married Helena Johanna van Lutsenburg Maas, July 29, 1916; children—Antoinette, Jan Cornelis, Marie, Coenraad Theodore, Clasine Albertine. Asst. prof. tech. botany, Tech. U., Delft, 1910-16; indsl. adviser Netherlands Indian Govt., Buitenzorg, Java, 1916; chem. adviser Vegetable Oil Mill Concern, Bandoeng, Java, 1919-21; prof. microbiology Tech. U., Delft since 1921. Mem. Koninklyke Akademie van Wetenschappen Amsterdam, 1926; Ridder Orde Nederlandsche Leeuw, 1930; mem. Koninklyke Vlaamsche Academie van Wetenschappen (Belgium), 1938. Recipient Emil Christian Hansen gold medal (Copenhagen), 1946; Copley medal Royal Soc. (London), 1954. Fgn. mem. Academia Scientiarum Fennica (Helsinki), 1947; pres. Koninklyke Nederlandse Akademie van Wetenschappen, 1947-54; hon. member Soc. of Gen. Microbiology (Gt. Britain), 1948; hon. mem. Soc. Am. Bacteriologists, N.Y. Acad. Scis., 1949; fgn. asso. Nat. Acad. Scis., Washington, 1950; fgn. mem. Royal Soc., London. Fgn. hon. mem. Am. Acad. Arts and Scis. (Boston), 1953; corr. mem. Bot. Society of America, 1954. Member Netherlands Society Microbiology, Chem. Soc., Botanical Soc. Home: Nieuwe Laan 3. Delft. Office: Laboratorium voor Microbiologie, Technische Hogeschool, Delft, Netherlands. Died May 14, 1956.

KNABENSHUE, Roy, aëronaut; b. Lancaster, O., July 15, 1876; s. Samuel S (q.v.) and Salome (Matlack) K.; ed. at Toledo, O.; married. Has experimented with aërial navigation for several yrs.; made first airship flight in U.S. at St. Louis Expn., 1904; since then has made numerous successful flights in various parts of U.S. with airship constructed by himself. Address: 133 Melrose Av., Toledo, O. Died Mar. 6, 1960.

KNAPP, Arnold Herman (năp), ophthalmologist; b. N.Y.C., Aug. 20, 1869; s. Dr. Herman K.; A.B., Harvard, 1889; M.D., Coll. Phys. and Surg., Columbia, 1892, D.Sc., 1931; m. Julia Long, Apr. 14, 1909; children—Elisabeth, John, Ellen, Philip. Practiced in N.Y.C., 1896—; prof. ophthalmology Coll. Phys. and Surg., 1903-28; exec. surgeon Herman Knapp Meml. Eye Hosp., 1908-40. Editor: Archives Ophthalmology, 1909-49. Mem. A.M.A., Med. Soc. State of N.Y., Am. Acad. Ophthalmology and Oto-Laryngology, Am. Ophthal. Soc., N.Y. Ophthol. Soc. Republican. Unitarian. Clubs: University, Century. Author: Medical Ophthalmology, 1917. Address: 24 W. 55th St., N.Y.C. 19. Died Feb. 29, 1956.

KNAPP, Bliss, b. Lyman, N.H.; s. Ira O. and Flavia (Stickney) K.; A.B., Harvard U., 1901; C.S.B., Mass. Metaphysical Coll., 1903; m. Eloise Mabury, 1918. Christian Sci. practitioner, lectr., tchr.; elected a first mem. of The First Ch. of Christ, Scientist, Boston, 1901, pres., 1912-13, treas., 1917-18, first reader, 1923-26; mem. C.S. Bd. Lectureship, 1904-22, 27-30; lecture trip around world, 1912, 18-19; chmn. Bible Lesson Com., which prepares lesson sermons for use in all C.S. Chs., 1922-23. Author various lectrs. and contbns. to C.S. lit.; also Ira Oscar Knapp and Flavia Stickney Knapp, A Biographical Sketch, 1925; The Destiny of the Mother Church, 1947. Mem. N.H. Hist. Soc. Home: Longwood Towers, Brookline 46, Mass. Died Mar. 14, 1958; buried Mt. Auburn Cemetery, Cambridge, Mass.

KNAPP, Cleon Talboys, lawyer; b. Osceola, Wis., July 24, 1882; s. Benjamin and Adelaide (Talboys) K.; LL.B., U. of Minn., 1907; m. Ava Daratt, Apr. 2, 1908; children—Cleon T., Audrey. Admitted to Minn. bar, 1907, and began practice at Chisholm; moved to Bisbee, Ariz., 1913; city atty. Chisholm, 1911-13; mem. Minn. Ho. of Rep., 1911, 15; gen. atty. and v.p. Tucson, Cornelia and Gila Bend R.R. Co.; dir. Ajo Improvement Co., New Cornelia Coöp. Mercantile Co.; now mem. Knapp, Boyle, Bilby & Thompson. Mem. bd. of regents, U. of Ariz., 1940-53. Mem. Am., Ariz. and Calif. State bar assns., Delta Chi. Republican. Methodist. Mason (Shriner), Elk. Clubs: El Rio Golf, Old Pueblo Club, Tucson Country, Newcomen Soc. in N.A. Office: 907 Valley National Bldg., Tucson. Died June 8, 1953; buried Evergreen Cemetery.

KNAPP, Joseph Palmer, publisher; b. Bklyn., May 14, 1864; s. Joseph Fairchild and Phoebe (Palmer) K.; student Poly. Inst. Bklyn., Columbia, 1884; m. Margaret E. Rutledge; children—Joseph Fairchild, Claire Knapp Dixon. Chmn. bd. Publication Corp. Clubs: Columbia University, Racquet and Tennis, The Links, National Golf Links of America, Westminster Kennels, River. Home: 435 E. 52d St. Office: 580 5th Av., N.Y.C. Died Jan. 30, 1951.

KNAPP, Robert Talbot, educator; b. Loveland, Colo., Jan. 5, 1899; s. Herman and Almira (Talbot) K.; student Throop Coll. of Tech. (now Calif. Inst. Tech.), 1916-20; B.M.E., Mass. Inst. Tech., 1920; Ph.D., Calif. Inst. Tech., 1929; m. Pearl Gilliland, June 14, 1925. Instr. mech. engring., Calif. Inst. of Tech., 1922-30, asst. prof., 1930-36, asso. prof. 1936-50, dir. grad. research and major research projects in fields of applied mechanics, hydrodynamics and hydraulics, 1922-51, professor hydraulic engineering, 1951—; Clayton lectr. Instn. Mich. Engrs., London, Apr. 1952; Am. Soc. M.E. lecturer on Cavitation, 1953-55. Awarded Jr. Travel prize, Throop Coll. of Tech. (Alaska), 1919; John R. Freeman traveling fellowship in hydraulics, Europe, by Am. Soc. M.E., 1929; recipient Melville medal Am. Society M.E., 1955. Fellow American Physical Society; member of American Society M.E., American Soc. C.E., Am. Geophys. Union, Southwest Mus., Sigma Xi, Tau Beta Pi. Presbyn. Author numerous reports on research projects in field of fluid mechanics developed at Calif. Inst. Tech. Contbr. articles in engring. publs. Home: 1801 N. Country Lane, Pasadena 8, Cal. Died Nov. 7, 1957; buried Pomona, Cal.

KNEIP, Herbert Joseph (k'nip), pres. Nat. Comml. Bank & Trust Co.; b. Albany, N.Y., July 6, 1888; s. Joseph and Margaret (Herkenham) K.; student pub. schs., Albany; m. Katheryn L. B. Kane, Oct. 11, 1915; children—Margery J., Catherine M. Began as clerk Nat. Commercial Bank & Trust Co. of Albany, now pres.; pres. Commercial Safe Deposit Corp., Albany City Securities Corp.; trustee City & County Savings Bank of Albany; dir. Consolidated Car Heating Company, Albany Garage Co.; F.C. Huyck & Sons, S. Texas Development Co., D.&H. R.R. Corp., Trinity Inst.; mem. bd. govs. Albany Hosp. Treas. Child's Hospital. Roman Catholic. Clubs: Fort Orange, Country, University (Albany). Home: 37 Holmes Dale. Office: 60 State St., Albany, N.Y. Died Apr. 29, 1955.

KNICKERBOCKER, Fred Hugh, ry. ofcl.; b. Chgo., Dec. 10, 1875; s. A. E. and Agnes (McGowan) K.; ed. pub. schs.; m. Marion Knickerbocker, June 11, 1902; children—Marion Louise, Floyd. Began as stenographer to gen. freight agt., O.S.L. R.R., Mar. 16, 1897, and continued with same rd. consecutively as sec. to gen. supt. until 1902, sec. to v.p. and gen. mgr., 1902-09, asst. to gen. mgr., 1909-16, gen. supt., 1916-22; gen. mgr. Alaska S.S. Co. and Copper River & N.W. Ry., 1922-24; gen. mgr. L.A.&S.L. R.R. Co., 1924-37; asst. to pres. U.P. R.R., 1937—, retired S.A.R. Republican. Episcopalian. Mason. Clubs: Rainier, Washington Athletic (Seattle); Jonathan (Los Angeles). Address: Beverly Hills, Cal. Died May 26, 1955.

KNIFFIN, William Henry, banker, author; b. Kingston, N.Y., Oct. 29, 1874; s. William Henry and Mary E. (Hillyer) K.; ed. Kingston Acad.; m. Gertrude M. Griffin, Sept. 21, 1918; 1 son, William Vance. With Rondout Sav. Bank, Kingston, N.Y., 1890-1907; cashier Home Sav. Bank, Bklyn., 1907-12; treas. Onondaga County Sav. Bank, Syracuse, N.Y., 1912-14; v.p. First Nat. Bank, Jamaica, L.I., 1915-17; v.p. Bank of Rockville Centre, 1917—; instr. in finance N.Y. U. Mem. Am. Bankers Assn. (exec. sec. savs. bank sect.). Republican. Baptist. Mason. Author: The Savings Bank and its Practical Work, 1912; Practical Work of a Bank, 1915; Commercial Paper, 1917; The Business Man and His Bank, 1921; American Banking Practice, 1922; Commercial Banking, 1923. Home: Rockville Centre, L.I., N.Y. Died Feb. 28, 1951; buried Woodstock (N.Y.) Cemetery.

KNIGHT, Charles Robert, painter, sculptor, lecturer; b. Bklyn., Oct. 21, 1874; s. George Wakefield and Lucy Anne (Wilson) K.; student Bklyn. Poly. Inst.; art studies, Met. Museum, and Art Students' League, New York; m. Annie Hardcastle, May 9, 1901. Splty. animals and birds; illustrator for mags., and paintings and models of fossil creatures for U.S. Govt., Carnegie Museum, and Am. Museum of Natural History; portraits, large mural paintings, prehistoric men and animals, for Am. Museum Natural History, Los Angeles Museum, Chicago Natural History Museum, Carnegie Mus., Pitts., Nat. Mus., Washington, Carnegie Instn., Washington, Peabody Mus., New Haven, and many others; decorations for Hayden Planetarium, N.Y. City. Author: Before the Dawn of History; Life Through the Ages; Animal Anatomy and Psychology for Art Students; Prehistoric Man, The Great Adventurer. Lecturer: Life's Pageant Through the Ages and others. Address: 24 W. 59th St., N.Y.C. 19. Died Apr. 15, 1953; buried Middletown, Del.

KNIGHT, Edgar Wallace, univ. prof.; b. Northampton County, N.C., Apr. 9, 1886; s. John Washington and Margaret (Davis) K.; student Trinity Park Sch., Durham, N.C., 1902-05; A.B., Trinity Coll., 1909, A.M., 1911; Ph.D., Columbia University, 1913; D.Litt., Duke University, 1952; married Annie M. Turner, June 28, 1916; children—Anne (Mrs. Strother C. Fleming, Jr.), Jane (Mrs. James M. Ludlow). Asst. prof. of edn., 1913-16, prof., 1916-17, Trinity Coll.; supt. Wake County (N.C.) schs., July 1917-Sept. 1918; asst. ednl. dir. War Dept's. Com. on Edn. and Spl. Training, for Southeastern States, Sept. 1918-June 1919; prof. edn., Univ. of N.C., since 1919, Kenan prof. since 1934; dir. summer session, 1934-38; visiting prof. edn., Columbia, 1931-32. Lecturer in teachers' institutes and summer schs. Asso. editor High School Journal since 1919; advisory editor School Management. Mem. research staff of Laymen's Foreign Missions Inquiry on Edn. in China, 1930-31; mem. Ednl. Inquiry Commn. to Iraq, 1932. Mem. N.C. High School Textbook Commn., 1923; mem. N.C. Library Commn.; mem. bd. of trustees N.C. Coll. for Negroes. Member board of trustees, Louisburg College. Member N.C. Teachers' Assembly (president 1926-27). Nat. Soc. Coll. Teachers of Edn. (pres. 1935-36), Nat. Council of Education, Am. Hist. Assn., N.C. Lit. and Hist. Soc., N.E.A., Am. Acad. Polit. and Social Science, Am. Assn. of Univ. Profs., A.A.A.S., Soc. Am. Historians, Kappa Delta Pi (Laureate chpt.), Kappa Alpha, Phi Beta Kappa Phi Delta Kappa (Columbia); fellow Social Science Research Council, 1925-26. Consultant in gen. edn., War Plans Div., Gen. Staff, since June 1920; spl. collaborator U.S. Bur. Edn., 1920-21. Regional director Southeastern States, qualifying tests for civilians, Army and Navy College Training Program since 1943. Democrat. Methodist. Mason. Club: Hope Valley Country (Durham). Author: The Influence of Reconstruction on Education in the South, 1913; Some Principles of Teaching, 1915; Public School Education in North Carolina, 1916; Reconstruction and Education in Virginia, 1916; Reconstruction and Education in South Carolina, 1920; Public Education in the South, 1921; Training for Citizenship (with J. G. deR. Hamilton), 1921; The Making of Citizens (with same), 1922; Our Constitutions—National and State (with A. J. Clowd), 1924; Education in the South, 1924; Our State Government, 1926; Among the Danes, 1927; Notes on Education, 1927; Education in the United States, 1929 (rev. 1934, 41, 51); Reports on European Education, 1930; Education in Iraq (with others), 1932; China (with others), 1933; Culture in the South (with others), 1934; What College Presidents Say, 1940; Twenty Centuries of Education, 1941; Progress and Educational Perspective, 1942; The Graduate School, Research and Publication (with Agatha Boyd Adams), 1947; A Documentary History of Education in the South Before 1860, Vol. I, 1949, II, 1950, III, 1952, IV and V, 1953; Readings in American Educational History (with Clifton L. Hall), 1951; Fifty Years of American Education, 1952; Readings in Educational Administraton, 1953. Home: 623 E. Franklin St., Chapel Hill, N.C. Died Aug. 7, 1953; buried Chapel Hill Cemetery.

KNIGHT, Francis McMaster, banker; b. Wichita, Kan., Dec. 12, 1890; s. Newell Clark and Louise (Sloss) K.; A.B., Yale, 1912; Diplomé de l'Université de Poitiers, summer 1914; m. Helen Parkins, Oct. 6, 1921; children—Helen (Mrs. L. L. Stuart, Jr.), Robert, Margaret (Mrs. B. N. Rawdon), Nancy (Mrs. T. C. Fischer). Teacher French, Hotchkiss Sch., Lakeville, Conn., 1912-15; bond salesman Central Trust Co., Chicago, 1915-17, 1919-20, Ill. Trust & Savs. Bank, Chicago, 1921-22; successively asst. sales mgr., asst. mgr. and mgr., bond dept., Ill. Merchants Trust Co., 1923-28; v.p. Continental Ill. Co., Chicago, 1929-33; v.p. in charge U.S. Govt. securities dept. Continental Ill. Nat. Bank & Trust Co. Chgo. 1933—, sr. v.p. 1954-56, cons., 1956—. Mem. govt. borrowing com., 1946-56. Served as lt. (j.g.), USN, 1917-19. Mem. faculty Grad. Sch. of Banking, Rutgers U., 1943, Sch. of Banking, U. Wis., 1947-52; mem. bd. trustees Smith Coll., 1946-56. Pres. sch. bd. dist. 107, Highland Park, Ill., 1940-42; chmn. bd. dirs. Cent. Y.M.C.A. Coll., 1942-44. Chmn. 6th War Loan Drive, Chicago and Cook County. Treas. and mem. bd. trustees Chicago Symphony Orchestra; member board of trustees Ravinia Festival Assn. Mem. Investment Bankers Assn. (chmn. legislation com., 1931-33; mem. govtl. securities com., 1933—; mem. bd. govs. 1947-50; chmn. finance com. 1947-50), Am. Bankers Assn. (mem. research council; mem. com. on treasury war borrowing 1945, com. on govt. borrowing, 1946—; chmn. com. on Victory Loan drive 1945), U.S. C. of C. (com. on federal finance 1944-45), Phi Beta Kappa, Alpha Delta Phi. Clubs: Chicago, Commercial, University, Attic, Exmoor Country, Bond (pres. 1951) (Chgo.); Yale (N.Y.C.); Colony (Springfield, Mass.). Home: 160 Apple Tree Rd., Winnetka, Ill. Office: 231 S. LaSalle St., Chgo. 4. Died Aug. 3, 1958; buried Churchyard Winnetka Congregational Ch.

KNIGHT, Frank A., editor state del.; b. Chicago, Oct. 4, 1907; s. Charles E. and Charlotte (Stanmeyer) K.; student Wittenberg Coll., 1926; m. Orpha Regina Thomas, July 21, 1930; children—Frank, Thomas Albert. Sports writer Canton (O.) Daily News, 1926-29, Charleston (W.Va.) Gazette, 1929-36; pub. relations Carl Byoir & Assos., N.Y. City, 1936-37; promotion mgr., asst. pub. Charleston (W.Va.) Gazette, 1937—, editor and mng. editor, 1950—. Mem. W.Va. Ho. of Dels., 1940—. Mem. Nat. Newspaper Promotion Assn. (sec.-treas. 1947—), W.Va. State Newspaper Council (president 1951-52), W.Va. Asso. Press Assn. (state chairman 1951-52; now mem. bd.); mem. bd. Asso. Press Mng. Editors Assn.; mem. K.C., Elk. Club: Charleston Press. Home: 1643 Massey Circle, South Charleston. Office: 229 Hale St., Charleston, W.Va. Died July 6, 1956; buried Sunset Meml. Park, South Charleston.

KNIGHT, Grant Cochran, writer; b. Williamsport, Pa., Apr. 15, 1893; s. Levi Richard and Regina (Cochran) K.; student Lycoming County (Pa.) Normal Sch., 1907-10; Dickinson Sem., Williamsport, Pa., 1913-1914; A.B., Albright Coll., 1918, Litt.D., 1951; A.M., Gettysburg College, 1921; graduate study, Columbia University, 1926-27; married Ruth Martin Elliott, April 12, 1922—children—Emily Holladay, Dorothy Cochran. Instructor in English, Shippensburg (Pennsylvania) State Normal Sch., 1918-19, Gettysburg Coll., 1919-21; instr. in English, U. of Kentucky, 1921-23, asst. prof., 1923-25, asso. prof., 1925-39, prof. since 1939; visiting prof., Hunter Coll., summer, 1928; visiting professor New York University, summer 1950. Served as corpl. inf., U.S. Army, 10 mos., 1918-19. Mem. Shaw Soc. of London, Poetry Soc. of Am. Author: Superlatives, 1925; The Novel in English, 1931; American Literature and Culture, 1932; James Lane Allen and the Genteel Tradition, 1935; The Sealed Well (verse), 1943; The Critical Period in American Literature, 1890-1900, 1951; The Strenuous Age in American Literature, 1954. Editor: Readings from the American Mercury, 1926. Contbr. to mags. and to Dictionary of Am. Biography. Contbr. to Collier's Ency., 1950, and to Ency. Britannica. Home: Montclair, Lexington, Ky. Died Mar, 15, 1956; buried Williamsport, Pa.

KNIGHT, Harold Audas, journalist; b. Cazenovia, N.Y., Nov. 4, 1890; s. Nicholas and Anna May (Audas) K.; B.A., Cornell Coll., Mt. Vernon, Ia., 1913; B.Litt., Columbia Univ., 1914; married Helen Swift Brewer, July 15, 1916; 1 son, Lt. Richard Brewer (killed in action Dec. 18, 1944). Reporter Syracuse (N.Y.) Herald, 1914, Journal, 1915; asso. editor Am. Shooter (a du Pont-supported publ.),

1918-19; editorial staff Iron Age (N.Y. City), 1919-22, Journal of Commerce, 1922-40; asso. editor Steel Magazine, Cleveland, 1940-41; news editor of Materials and Methods, N.Y., 1941-48; asst. editor Journal of Metals—Technology and Practice, pub. by Am. Soc. Mining and Metall. Engrs., 1948-49; asso. editor publs. of Am. Chem. Soc., 1949——. Phi Beta Kappa. Clubs: University (Larchmont, New York); Shenorock Shore (Rye, N.Y.). Author series Purchasing on "Reading the Business Barometers," 1937; Materials Buying Manual, 1951; contbr. articles on metal situation. Home: The Brompton, Larchmont, N.Y. Office: Am. Chem. Soc., 60 E. 42d St., N.Y.C. 17. Died Nov. 2, 1954.

KNIGHT, Harry S., lawyer; b. Watsontown, Pa., Mar. 6, 1868; s. Frederick H. and Anna (Schoch) K.; ed. Wyoming Sem.; m. Mary B. Martin, June 16, 1897; 1 son, Frederick H.; m. 2d, Elsie I. Culp, June 18, 1947. Admitted to Pa. bar, since engaged in gen. practice of law; dir. U.S. Fidelity & Guaranty Co., Balt., First Nat. Bank of Sunbury. For many years active in Am. Bar Assn., past mem. exec. com., bd. govs., sec.; 1936-46, ex officio mem. bd. govs. and house of dels.; past pres. Pa. Bar Assn.; mem. Bar Assn. City of N.Y. Lutheran. Clubs: Rotary (past pres.); Susquehanna Valley Country (Sunbury); Union League (Phila.); Manufacturers (Milton); Country (Williamsport). Home: 103 Chestnut St. Office: Bittner Trust Bldg., Sunbury, Pa. Died Oct. 15, 1957.

KNIGHT, Jesse William, mining exec.; b. Payson, Utah, Aug. 20, 1874; s. Jesse and Amanda (McEwan) K.; grad. commercial course, Brigham Young U., 1894; m. Lucy Jane Brimhall, Jan. 18, 1899; children—Richard, Philip S. Began in mining business with father, at Eureka, Utah, 1897; pres. Big Hill Mining Co., Empire Minse Co., Great Western Mines Co., Dragon Consolidated Mining Co., Tintic Drain Tunnel Co.; v.p. Layton Sugar Co., Knight Ideal Coal Co., Ellison Ranching Co. Mem. Utah State Senate, 1918-22; Dem. candidate for gov. of Utah, 1908; mem. Utah State Tax Commn., 1933-39. Bishop of Church of Jesus Christ of the Latter Day Saints, Raymond, Alberta, Can., and counselor to pres. Taylor Stake, Alberta, 1903-05; counselor to pres. Stake of Utah, 1908-31; 2d counselor to pres. of L.D.S. Salt Lake Temple, 1944. Author: The Jesse Knight Family, 1941. Home: Canyon Blvd. Office: 8 W. Center St., Provo, Utah. Died Mar. 11, 1956; buried Provo City Cemetery.

KNIGHT, John, judge; b. Arcade, N.Y., Apr. 29, 1871; s. Andrew J. and Althea Elizabeth (Angier) K.; A.B., U. of Rochester, 1893; LL.D., Alfred U., 1931; m. Mary Fenner, Nov. 25, 1896; 1 dau., Althea Jane. Began law practice at Arcade, 1896; town clk., Arcade, 1892-96; federal referee in bankruptcy, 1899-1904; dist. atty., Wyoming County, N.Y., 1904-13; judge U.S. Dist. Ct., N.Y. Western Dist., since 1931. Mem. N.Y. Assembly, 1913-17; mem. N.Y. State Senate, 1916-31 (pres. pro tem, 1924-31). Mem. Delta Upsilon. Republican. Mason, Odd Fellow. Clubs: Buffalo Athletic; Silver Lake Country (Perry, N.Y.). Home: Arcade, N.Y. Address: U.S. Court House, Buffalo. Died June 15, 1955.

KNIGHT, Ryland, clergyman; b. Shelbyville, Ky., Feb. 20, 1876; s. Aaron Brightwell and Josephine (Ryland) K.; A.B. cum laude, Princeton, 1896; Th.M., So. Bapt. Theol. Sem., Louisville, 1899, Th. D., 1900; D.D., U. Richmond, Va., 1910; m. Julia Brooke Ryland, July 27, 1910 (dec. Dec. 8, 1923); m. 2d, Bess Acree, July 29, 1925. Ordained ministry So. Bapt. Ch., 1899; pastor successively, Dover Bapt. Ch., Shelby County, Ky., First Ch., Ashland, Ky., Calvary Ch., Richmond, Va., First Ch., Clarksville, Tenn., Immanuel Ch., Nashville, Delmar Ch., St. Louis, Second Bapt. Ch., Atlanta; pastor Second-Ponce de Leon Bapt. Ch., Atlanta, 1932-45, First Baptist Ch., Pulaski, Va., 1945——. Col. on staff gov. of Tenn., 1923-25. Pres. exec. bd. Tenn. Bapt. Conv., 1920-25; mem. Foreign Mission Board, So. Bapt. Conv., 1905-12, 35-45, Sunday Sch. Bd., 1918-25, Home Mission Bd., 1931-34; pres. Christian Council of Atlanta, 1941, 42; trustee U. of Richmond, Va. Democrat. Mason. Club: Pulaski Country. Office: 325 Randolph Av., Pulaski, Va. Died July 9, 1955.

KNIGHT, Walter David, clergyman; b. Marlboro, N.H., Sept. 4, 1891; s. Byron Charles and Clara S. (Nims) K.; B.S., Dartmouth, 1914; diploma Union Theol. Sem., 1917; m. Ruth Della Hubbard, May 24, 1917; children—Walter David, Paula Goodnow. Ordained to ministry Conglist. Ch., 1917; pastor's asst. Mount Washington Presbyn. Ch., 1915-18, pastor, 1920-37; religious work dir. East Side YMCA, N.Y.C., 1918-20; synod exec. N.E., Presbyn. Ch. U.S., 1937——. Instr. Presbyn. policy, history and usages Yale, Andover Newton Theol. Sch., 1938-58, Boston U., 1956-58, Harvard Div. Sch.; associate professor department of field service San Francisco Theological Seminary, 1958——; member War-Time Service Commission, Presbyterian Church USA (now Dept. Chaplains and Service Personnel), Dept. Ministerial Relations, 1951——. Trustee Baker Found. Protestant Work, Mass. Inst. Tech. Mem. Mass. Council Chs. (chmn. dept. research and strategy).

Author: Preparing Young People for Church Membership, 1938. Contbr. articles. sermons to religious publs. Address: 35 Waverly Rd., San Anselmo, Cal. Died Jan. 25, 1959.

KNIGHT, William Allen. clergyman; journalist; b. Milton, Mo., Oct. 20, 1863; s. Allen Anderson and Mary Ann (Robeson) K.; A.B., Hiram Coll., 1889; B.D., Oberlin Theol. Sem., 1900; A.M., Harvard, 1905; Litt.D., Bates Coll., 1908; D.D., Grinnell (Iowa) Coll., 1915; m. Maude Russell, Nov. 30, 1886; children—Sylvia (Mrs. Louis S. Headley), Gertrude (Mrs. Cleon Headley); m. 2d, Bertha Hastings Sanger, July 27, 1931. Ordained to Disciples ministry, 1886; pastor Columbus, O., 1886-89; Congl. pastor Cleve., 1890-94, First Congl. Ch., Saginaw, Mich., 1894-97, Central Ch., Fall River, Mass., 1897-1902, Brighton Congl. Ch., Boston, 1902-19, Plymouth Ch., Framingham, Mass., 1919-34; asso. editor Framingham News, 1934——. Author: The Song of Our Syrian Guest, 1904; The Love Watch, 1905; Saint Abigail of the Pines, 1905; The Signs in the Christmas Fire, 1908; The Shepherd of Jebel Nur, 1909; No Room in the Inn, 1910; Outside a City Wall, 1911; Peter in the Firelight, 1911; The Song of Our Syrian Guest, with Notes, 1911; At the Crossing with Denis McShane, 1912; On the Way to Bethlehem, 1912; To Little David of Smyrna, 1913; A Bedouin Lover, 1913; The Well by Bethlehem Gate, 1914; The Pictureland of the Heart, 1916; Wartime Over Here, 1918; A Lovely Find, 1943; Our Bethlehem Guests, 1944; After Forty Years (additions to Syrian Guest), 1945; A Christmas Secret, 1946; Fortieth Anniversary Edition of the Song of Our Syrian Guest (with new material), 1947; A Crisis In Morningdale, 1947. Home: 7 Church St., Framingham, Massachusetts; and N. Sutton, N.H. Office: News Bldg., Framingham, Mass. Died Feb. 11, 1957.

KNIPE, Emilie Benson, author, illustrator; b. Phila., June 12, 1870; d. Gustavus A. and Emilie Therese (Geisse) Benson; ed. pvt. sch., Phila.; Sch. Indsl. Art, and under Howard Pyle, Drexel Inst., Phila.; m. Alden Arthur Knipe, Nov. 29, 1902 (dec.). Illustrator for various mags., 1898——; invented and illustrated The Red Magic Book, 1910. Co-author (with husband): Little Miss Fales, 1910; The Missing Pearls, 1911; The Lucky Sixpence, 1912; Beatrice of Denewood, 1913; Remember Rhymes, 1914; Peg O' the Ring, 1915; A Maid of '76, 1915; Polly Trotter, Patriot, 1916; A Maid of Old Manhattan, 1917; The Lost Little Lady, 1917; Girls of '64, 1918; A Cavalier Maid, 1919; Vive La France, 1919; A Mayflower Maid. 1920; The Luck of Denewood, 1920; Diantha's Quest, 1921; The Flower of Fortune, 1922; A Continental Dollar. 1923; Powder Patches and Patty, 1924; Now and Then, 1925; The Shadow Captain (novel), 1925; Treasure Trove, 1927; Silver Dice (novel), 1927; Lost—A Brother, 1928; The Pirate's Ward, 1929; The Treasure House, 1930. Author: (novels; under pen name Therese Benson): The Unknown Daughter, 1929; The Go-Between, 1930. Strictly Private, 1931; Fools Gold, 1932; The Fourth Lovely Lady, 1932; Gallant Adventuress, 1933; Death Wears a Mask, 1935. Address: 30 Sutton Pl., N.Y. C. 22.; (summer) The Brick House, New Hartford. Conn. Died Oct. 25, 1958; buried New Hartford.

KNOLES, Tully Cleon, chancellor; b. Petersburg, Ill., Jan. 6, 1876; s. Thomas Stone and Laura Ellen (Hart) K.; A.B., U. S.C., 1903, A.M., 1908, D.D., 1919; LL.D., Coll. Pacific, 1927; DD., Pacific School of Religion, 1940; Doctor of Laws, Boston U., 1946; m. Emily Isabel Walline, August 23, 1899; children—Lorraine Isabel, Dorothy Ann, Peter Walline, Edith Eileen. George Harmon, Gordon Elbert, Tully Cleon, Leslie Gay. Head of history dept., U. S.C., 1909-19; pres. Coll. of Pacific, Stockton, Apr. 1, 1919-Oct. 22, 1946, chancellor, since Oct. 22, 1946. Member Cal. Annual Conf. Meth. Ch.; mem. Bd. of Edn. of Meth. Ch. Mem. N.E.A. (life), So. Cal. Hist. Soc., Am. Acad. Polit. and Social Science, Kappa Alpha, Phi Beta Kappa, Pi Gamma Mu, Phi Alpha Theta, Phi Kappa Phi. Mason. Rotarian. Club: Commonwealth (San Francisco). Address: College of the Pacific, Sotckton, Cal. Died Nov. 29, 1959.

KNOLL, Hans G. (nōl), mfr.; b. Stuttgart, Germany, Mar. 8, 1914; s. Walther C. and Maia (Vollmoeller) K.; student pvt., pub. schs.; m. Florence Schust. 1946. Came to U.S., 1938, naturalized, 1947. With Jantzen Knitting Mills, Brentford, Eng., 1933-35; propr. Plan. Ltd., London, 1935-37; propr. Hans Knoll Furniture Co., N.Y.C., 1939-41; pres. dir. Knoll Associates, Inc., N.Y.C., (also subsidiaries U.S., Germany, France, Belgium; dir. Bonnier's N.Y. C. Clubs: River (N.Y.C.); Arts (Chgo.). Home: 29 Sutton Pl. S. Office: 575 Madison Av., N.Y.C. 22. Died Oct. 8, 1955.

KNOTT, David H. (nŏt), hotel operator; b. Orange, Murray) K.; ed. pub. schs., N.Y. City, and Pedl-N.J., Oct. 22, 1879; s. James and Margaret (MacMac-die Sch., Hightstown, N.J.; m. Agnes Geekie (dec.) children—James. David H.. Robert G.. Margery; m. 2d, Daisy Gilchrest. Chmn. bd. The Knott Corp. (operators of hotels); dir. N.Y. City Omnibus Corporation; member board of directors N.Y. Board

Trade. Mem. N.Y. Assembly, 1913; sheriff of New York County, 1918-22; chmn. Dem. County Com., New York County. Mem. Vet. 7th Regt. N.G. N.Y. Chmn. bd trustees Peddie School (Hightstown, N. J.); mem. advisory board Salvation Army. Presidential Elector, 1936, 1940, 1944. Baptist. Clubs: Manhattan, Piping Rock; N.Y. Yacht; Camden (Me.) Yacht. Home: 43 Fifth Av., New York; and Glen Cove, L.I. Office: 575 Madison Av., N.Y.C. Died May 4, 1954.

KNOUS, William Lee, judge; b. Ouray, Colo., Feb. 2, 1889; s. John Franklin and Julia (Bain) K.; LL.B., U. Colo., 1911; LL.D., Colo. Coll. 1952, U. Denver, 1954; married Elsie Marie Grabow, July 1, 1915; children—William John, Robert Lee, Merle Ray. Admitted to Colo. bar, 1911, and became mem. firm Moynihan, Hughes & Knous; dept. dist. atty. Ouray County, 1913-18; rep. in Colo. Gen. Assembly, 1928-30, senator, 1930-36; pres. pro tem of Senate, 1935-36; mayor City of Montrose, 1926-30; asso. justice Colo. Supreme Court, 1937-46, chief justice, 1946-47; gov. of Colo., 1947-50; judge U.S. Dist. Ct. for Dist. of Colo., 1950-54, chief judge, 1954——. Mem. exec. com. Nat. Gov.'s Conf., 1947-49. Mem. 9th Regional War Labor Bd. Chmn. Nat. Sugar Panel of Nat. War Labor Bd., agent for Nat. War Labor Bd. in Montgomery Ward, Chgo., grievance cases; vice chmn. Meat Packing Commn., Daily Newspaper Commn. Pres. Rotary Club, Montrose, 1928-29. Mem. Western Colo. Bar Assn. (pres. 1932-34), Montrose C. of C. (pres. 1924-28). Order of the Coif, Phi Delta Phi, Kappa Delta Mu. Dem. Episcopalian. Mason (32°, Eljebel Shine). Elk. Clubs: Rotary, Democratic, Cherry Hills (Denver). Home: 615 Jersey St. Office: P.O. Bldg., Denver. Died Dec. 1959.

KNOWLES, Robert Bell, ret. lawyer; grad. Columbia U. Law Sch. Began practice of law, 1899, successively mem. of Taylor, Knowles & Hack, Taylor, Knowles, Hack & Armstrong, Knowles, Hack & Armstrong, Knowles & Hack; co-founder Chance Vought Corp. (later became a part of United Aircraft Corp.); formerly gen. counsel, Auditorium Conditioning Corp.; holder of basic for air-conditioning industry; former pres. John Waldron Corp.; former gen. counsel, treas. Ross Executors Corp. Home: 21 Essex Rd. Address: 382 Springfield Av., Summit, N.J. Died Dec. 4, 1958.

KNOWLSON, James S. (nōl'sŭn), corp. official; b. Chicago, Ill., June 29, 1883; s. James S. and Lulu S. (Howard) K.; M.E. and E.E., Cornell U., 1905; m. Norah Eustis, Sept. 30, 1914; children—Mary, James, Elizabeth, Barbara. Elec. engr. General Electric Co., Schenectady, N.Y., 1905-03; chmn. Stewart-Warner Corp.; dir. Erie R.R., First National Bank of Chicago, Peoples Gas Light & Coke Co. Chgo. Vice chmn. W.P.B., 1941-43; chmn. bus. adv. council, Dept. of Commerce, 1949-50. Awarded Medal of Merit, 1946. Mem. Sigma Psi. Republican. Episcopalian. Clubs: Chicago, University, Commercial (pres. 1944-45), Commonwealth (Chgo.). Home: 329 S. County Line, Hinsdale. Ill. Office: 1826 Diversey Parkway, Chgo. 14. Died Mar. 6, 1959.

KNOWLTON, Ansel Alphonse (nol'tun), educator; b. New Portland, Me., Oct. 12, 1875; s. Asa Ansel and Eliza (Hutchins) K.; A.B., Bates Coll., 1898; A.M., Northwestern U., 1903; Ph.D., U. Chgo., 1910; m. Gertrude Griffin, June 17, 1904; children—Harriet (Mrs. J. Warren Schroder), Kathleen (Mrs. B. L. Wilson), Ellen Cowan (Mrs. Kenneth C. Johnson). Instr. physics and chemistry Carleton Coll., 1899-1902; fellow Northwestern U. 1902-03; asst. prof. physics Armour Inst. Tech., 1903-07, asso. prof., 1908-09; asso. prof. physics U. Utah, 1909-15; prof. physics Reed Coll., Portland, Ore., 1915-48, ret. 1948; vis. prof. physics Bennington Coll., 1948-50. Received spl. award from Nat. Research Corp. Fellow Am. Phys. Soc.; mem. A.A.A.S., Am. Assn. Physics Tchrs. (v.p. 1939, 41, pres. 1942), Am. Assn. U. Profs., Sigma Xi, Sigma Phi Sigma, Pi Kappa Alpha. Republican. Unitarian. Mason. Clubs: University, City, Portland Golf and Country (Portland). Author: Physics for College Students, 1928, 2d ed., 1935; Laboratory Manual in Physics (with Marcus O'Day), 1930. Home: 125 S.E. 7th St., Beaverton, Ore. Died Jan. 9, 1957.

KNOWLTON, Philip Arnold, editor, writer; b. Providence, Aug. 8, 1887; s. Amos Arnold and Jennie Sinclair (Neil) K.; A.B., U. Wis., 1906, A.M., 1908; Litt.D., Middlebury (Vt.) Coll., 1934; m. Helyn Louise Protzman, Sept. 12, 1921; children—Gerald Neil, Thomas Roper, Phyllis (Mrs. Harry Foster). Tchr. Chico (Cal.) High Sch., 1908-09; instr. Stanford, 1909-12; sch. prin., Fairbanks, Alaska, 1912-14; with Alaska Engring. Commn., 1914-15; tchr. Calumet (Mich.) High Sch., 1916; with Macmillan Co., pubs., N.Y.C., 1916-51, 58, dir., 1928-51, ednl. editor, 1920-51; research dir. Profit-Sharing Research Found., 1951-53; with Houghton Mifflin Co., 1954-58. Mil. tng., 1917-18; 2d lt. Aviation corps, World War I. Mem. Alpha Delta Phi. Phi Beta Kappa. Club: Cosmos (Washington). Author textbooks, research reports, mag. articles. Address: 345 Marlborough St., Boston 15. Died Apr. 30, 1959.

KNOX, Mrs. Charles B. (Rose), gelatine mfg. exec.; b. Mansfield, O., Nov. 18, 1957; d. David and Amanda (Foreman) Markward; student pub. schs., Mansfield; m. Charles Briggs Knox, Feb. 15, 1883 (dec. June 1908), children—Charles Markward, James Elisha, Helen. Pres. Charles B. Knox Gelatine Co., 1908—; v.p. Kind & Knox Gelatine Co., 1930—. Mem. Asso. Grocery Mfrs. Am. (dir.), Fedn. Women's Clubs for Civic Improvement (pres.), Johnstown Hist. Soc., Daus. of Ohio in New York, Am. Woman's Soc. of N.Y., Aldine Soc. and Burroughs Club of Johnstown, Fedn. Women's Clubs (Johnstown), Fedn. of Women's Clubs of N.Y. State, Johnstown Bus. and Profl. Women's Club (hon.), Federated Garden Clubs of New York State, Inc., Life as a Fine Art. Republican. Presbyn. Club: Woman's Press. Author of many noted recipe books. Donor of Willing Helpers' Home for Women to City of Johnstown and Fulton County; an athletic field, stadium and field house, to Bd. of Edn. and City of Johnstown; swimming pool, to YMCA, Johnstown; set of chimes, to First Presbyn. Ch., Johnstown; set of chimes to St. Anthony's Slovak Co., Johnstown; an addition or Sunday school room to A.M.E. Zion Church, Johnstown. Home: 104 2d Av. Office: 13 Knox Av., Johnstown, N.Y. Died Sept. 26, 1950.*

KNOX, James E., business exec.; b. Johnstown, N.Y., Dec. 11, 1892; s. Charles B. and Rose Helen (Markward) K.; student Manlius, Haverford Coll., Wesleyan U.; m. Eleanor Williams Eckfeldt, Dec. 7, 1914; children—Mary Elizabeth K. Brumley, John Brooks, Nora K. Graham, Roseann K. Armstrong. Chmn. bd. Charles B. Knox Gelatine Co., Inc., Kind & Knox Gelatin Co., Camden, N.J. Home: 601 S. William St., Johnstown. Office: 13 Knox Av., Johnstown, N.Y. Died May 7, 1958; buried Johnstown Cemetery.

KNOX, Robert White, surgeon; b. Danville, Ky., Nov. 21, 1859; s. David A. and Martha H. (Maxwell) K.; A.B., Centre Coll., 1880, A.M., 1885; M.D., U. Va., 1882; m. Pearl H. Wallis, Nov. 11, 1892. Chief surgeon Atlantic div. S.P.R.R., 1902-30, ret. Ex-pres. Tex. State Med. Assn., 1919; ex-pres. S. Tex. Med. Assn. Fellow A.C.S.; mem. A.M.A., So. Med. Assn., So. Assn Ry. Surgeons; pres. Tex. Ry. Surgeons Assn., Am. Ry. Assn. Club: Houston. Home: 4018 Bute St. Office: Esperson Bldg., Houston. Died Sept. 27, 1942; buried Hollywood Cemetery, Houston.

KNOX, Rush Hightower, lawyer; b. Reed, Miss., Sept. 24, 1879; s. Isaac Nicholson and Martha Almarine (Hightower) K.; lit. course Miss. Coll., Clinton, 1901; LL.B., U. Miss., 1902; m. Florence F. Bigham, Nov. 2, 1904; children—Olivia May, Martha Elizabeth. Admitted to Miss. bar, 1902, and began practice at Houston; mayor of Houston, 1906-08; apptd. dist. atty. 3d Jud. Dist. of Miss., 1910, and elected to same office 1911, 15, 19; atty. gen. of Miss. 2 terms, 1924-32; mem. State Senate, 31st Senatorial Dist., 1936-44; now engaged in general practice of law. Pres. Houston Hosp.; trustee Miss. Bapt. Hosp., Jackson. Del. at large Dem. Nat. Conv., 1924. Mem. Am., Miss. bar assns., Sigma Chi. Baptist. Mason (K.T., Shriner), K.P., Woodman. Club: Lions. Home: 1413 Pinehurst. Office: Old Merchants Bank Bldg., Jackson, Miss. Died Nov. 14, 1946.

KNUBEL, Frederick Ritscher, clergyman; b. N.Y. C., Aug. 9, 1897; s. Rev. Frederick Hermann and Christine (Ritscher) K.; A.B., Gettysburg Coll., 1918 (salutatorian), D.D., 1937; grad. Luth. Theol. Sem., Phila., 1921, B.D., 1923; LL.D., Wagner College, 1945; L.H.D., Hartwick College, 1953; m. Alice Bark, April 30, 1929; children—Helen Alice, Dorothy Ann, Frederick Henry. Asst. pastor Evang. Luth. Ch. of the Reformation, Rochester, N.Y., 1921-27, pastor, 1927-44. Chmn. Church School Com., United Luth. Synod of N.Y., 1921-30; pres. Bd. of Edn. United Luth. Synod of N.Y., 1930-36; pres. Luth. Inner Mission Soc., Rochester, N.Y., 1933-38, Parish and Church Sch. Bd. United Luth. Ch., 1934-38; pres. Western Conf. of United Luth. Synod of N.Y., 1936-38; chmn. Commn. on Theol. Edn., United Luth Ch., 1938-40; v.p. Bd. of Edn., United Luth. Ch., 1938-48; mem. exec. bd. United Luth. Ch.; pres. United Luth. Synod of N.Y. and N.E., 1944—. Mem. R.O.T.C., 1917-18; served in F.A., Camp Zachary Taylor, Ky., Nov.-Dec. 1918. Mem. Phi Gamma Delta. Republican. Contbr. on religious subjects. Author: Pastoral Counseling, 1952. Home: 43 Rockland Pl., New Rochelle, N.Y. Office: 231 Madison Av., N.Y.C. Died Oct. 22, 1957.

KNUDSEN, Charles William, educator; b. Dawson, Ill., Dec. 9, 1890; s. Christian and Rintha May (Crawford) K.; student Eureka (Ill.) Coll., 1909-11; B.S., U. Ill., 1913, M.S., 1923, Ph.D., 1927; m. Ruth Whittier Jackson, Aug. 26, 1915. Chemist Ohio Agrl. Expt. Sta., Wooster, 1913-14, Armour & Co., Chgo., 1914-15; tchr. chemistry Carl Schurz High Sch., Chgo., 1914-15; prin. Twp. High Sch., Eureka, Ill., 1915-18; supt. of schs., Eureka, 1918-23; high sch. supr. U. Ill., 1923-27; asso. prof. edn. George Peabody Coll., Nashville, 1927-29, prof., 1929—; on leave, 1936-37, as lectr. in secondary edn., Harvard Grad. Sch. Edn.; instr. in edn. U. of Ill., summers, 1924-26; dir. Peabody Workshop in Junior Coll. terminal edn. courses, summer, 1941. Awarded Gen. Edn. Bd. fellowship for study abroad, 1931-32. Mem. Tenn. Edn. Commn., 1933-35. Coauthor: Social Studies—An Orientation Handbook for High School Pupils, 1935; An Introduction to Teaching, 1936; The Changing Curriculum, 1937. Author: Evaluation and Improvement of Teaching, 1932. Asso. editor Jour. Ednl. Research; mem. editorial bd., Ency. Ednl. Research. Home: Hampton Avenue, Nashville. Died Jan. 21, 1951; buried Woodlawn Meml. Park, Nashville.

KNUDSON, Albert Cornelius, theologian; b. Grandmeadow, Minn., Jan. 23, 1873; s. Asle and Susan (Fosse) K.; A.B., U. Minn., 1893; S.T.B., Boston U., 1896, Ph.D., 1900; studied Sch. of All Sciences, Boston U., 1896-97, univs. of Jena and Berlin, 1897-98; D.D., Allegheny Coll., 1906; Theol. D., U. of Berlin, 1923; LL.D., Lawrence Coll., 1926; m. Mathilde Johnson, July 7, 1899 (dec. Dec. 13, 1948). Prof. church history, Denver U., 1898-1900; prof. philosophy and English Bible, Baker U., 1900-02; prof. English Bible and philosophy Allegheny Coll., 1902-06; prof. Hebrew and O.T. exegesis Boston U. Sch. of Theology, 1906-21, prof. systematic theology, 1921-43, dean, 1926-38, dean emeritus, 1938—. Del. Gen. Confs., M.E. Ch., 1932-36, Edinburgh Conf. on Faith and Order, 1937, Uniting Conf. of Meth. Ch., 1939. Fellow Am. Acad. Arts and Sciences; mem. Am. Theol. Soc., Am. Philos. Assn., Delta Upsilon, Phi Beta Kappa. Author: The Old Testament Problem, 1908; The Beacon Lights of Prophecy, 1914; The Religious Teaching of the Old Testament, 1918; The Prophetic Movement in Israel, 1921; Present Tendencies in Religious Thought, 1924; The Philosophy of Personalism, 1927; The Doctrine of God, 1930; The Doctrine of Redemption, 1933; The Validity of Religious Experience, 1937; The Principles of Christian Ethics, 1943; The Philosophy of War and Peace, 1947; Basic Issues in Thought, 1950. Home: 18 Forest St., Cambridge, Mass. Died Aug. 28, 1953.

KNUDSON, John Immanuel, educator; b. Ruthven, Ia., Dec. 14, 1888; s. Christian and Mary (Mallenberg) K.; A.B., U. Chgo., 1919, A.M., 1920; student Ind. U., 1926-27; D.Sc. of Politics, U. Geneva, 1928. Prof. history and econs., Broadview Coll., La Grange, Ill., 1920-22; asso. prof. history, Franklin (Ind.) Coll., 1922-24, prof., 1924-26; prof. history and polit. sci., William Jewell Coll., Liberty, Mo., 1928-29; asst. prof. history and econs. Bklyn. Poly. Inst., 1929-32, Charles S. Baylis prof., head of dept., 1932—; Carnegie teaching fellow in internat. law, at Geneva, 1927-28. Decorated Chevalier Legion of Honor (France), 1935; elected to Académie Diplomatique Internationale (France), 1939. Chmn. dept. of history and polit. sci., Bklyn. Inst. Arts and Scis.; chmn. exec. com. Bklyn. Fgn. Affairs Forum; mem. exec. com. and dir. Am. Assn. UN; mem. Commn. to study Orgn. Peace. Trustee mem., mem. exec. and finance coms. Ch. Peace Union. Mem. Am. Acad. Polit. and Social Sci., Lambda Chi Alpha, Theta Alpha Phi, Pi Kappa Delta. Author: Methods of International Legislation (with reference to the League of Nations), 1928; A History of the League of Nations, 1938, (monograph) Reduction of Armaments by International Agreement (with W. E. Stephens), 1933. Lectr. internat. affairs. Home: Tuckahoe, N.J. Address: 99 Livingstone St., Bklyn. 1. Died Aug. 1959.

KNUTSON, Harold, ex-congressman; student common and agrl. schs., Minn. Learned printer's trade; formerly editor and pub. Royalton Banner, and Foley Independent; asso. editor St. Cloud Daily Journal-Press; mem. 65th to 80th Congresses, 6th Minn. Dist.; was Republican "whip" of House, chmn. Ways and Means Com.; chmn. joint com. on Internal. Revenue Taxation, joint com. on Reduction of Nonessential Fed. Expenditures. Former county chmn. Benton County (Minn.) Rep. Com. Past pres. No. Minn. Editorial Assn., Publisher Wadena Pioneer Jour. Home: Manhattan Beach, Minn. Died Aug. 21, 1953.

KOCH, Alfred (kōk), clergyman, educator; b. Arzheim-Palatinate, Oct. 19, 1879; s. Joseph and Margaret (Geier) K.; S.T.D., U. of Rome, 1911. Joined Benedictine Order (O.S.B.), 1916; ordained priest R.C. Ch., 1905; prof. Greek, Latin and French, Sem. of Sutri, Prov. of Rome, 1906-12; came to U.S., 1912; prof. Latin and German, Sacred Heart Mission House, Girard, Pa., 1912-16; prof. of exegesis, introduction and hermeneutics, St. Vincent Sem., Latrobe, 1917-30; archabbot of St. Vincent, 1930. Pres. Benedictine Soc. of Westmoreland County, Pa., since 1930. Address: St. Vincent Coll. and Seminary, Latrobe, Pa. Died Nov. 7, 1951; buried St. Vincent Cemetery, Latrobe.

KOCH, Elers (kōch), forester; b. Bozeman, Mont., Dec. 12, 1880; s. Peter and Laurentze Maria K.; B.S., Mont. State Coll., Bozeman, 1901; M.F., Yale, 1903; m. Gerda Heiberg-Jürgensen, Dec. 26, 1906; children—Stanley, Thomas Paul, Peter. Field asst. U.S. Forest Service, 1903-04, insp., 1905-06, forest supervisor, 1907-18, fire chief, 1919-20, asst. regional forester, 1921-41, chief div. of timber mgmt., 1921-43, ret. 1943. Fellow Soc. Am. Foresters. Republican. Presbyn. Contbr. articles on forestry subjects to periodicals. Home: 420 Beckwith Av., Missoula, Mont. Died Nov. 21, 1954.

KOCH, Julius Arnold (koh), chemist; b. Bremen, Germany, Aug. 15, 1864; s. Arnold and Amanda (Wenke) K.; came to America with parents in infancy; grad. Pitts. Coll. Pharmacy, 1884, Pharm.D., 1895; studied U. Munich, 1896, U. Heidelberg, 1897; Ph.D., Scio (O.) Coll., 1905; D.Sc., Washington and Jefferson coll., 1907; Ph.M., Phila. Coll. of Pharmacy and Sci., 1922; m. Albertine M. Strunz, Oct. 17, 1889 (died Feb. 28, 1900); children—Adele M. (dec.), Florence S., Elsa A.; m. 2d, Alice M. Cope, July 15, 1927. Entered drug bus. as apprentice, 1880, became propr., 1885, sold out bus., 1891; dean Pitts. Coll. of Pharmacy, 1891-1933, dean emeritus, 1933—; prof. pharmacy, 1891-99, prof. chemistry, 1899—; prof. chemistry, med. dept. U. Pitts., 1900-13. Chmn. exec. com. Am. Conf. Pharm. Faculties, 1908-20; ex-pres. Pa. Pharm. Soc.; pres. Am. Pharm. Assn., 1922-23; pres. Pitts. br. Am. Pharm. Assn.; mem. Deutsche Chemische Gesellschaft, Soc. Chem. Industry (London), Am. Chem. Soc., A.A.A.S. Author: Chemical Laboratory Tables, 1898; Laboratory Manual for Pharmaceutical Students, 1904. Reporter on the Progress of Pharmacy and editor Year Book of Am. Pharm. Assn. 1915-16; mem. Revision Com. U.S. Pharmacopoeia, 1910-20. Home: 921 East Laurel St., Ocala, Fla. Office: 1431 Blvd. of the Allies, Pitts. Died Feb. 10, 1956.

KOCH, Otto, oil exec.; chmn. treas., dir. Kendall Refining Co. Address: 684 E. Main St. Bradford, Pa. Died Oct. 12, 1948; buried Fredonia, N.Y.

KOCIALKOWSKI, Leo (kō-shâl-kow'skĭ), ex-congressman; b. Chgo., Aug. 16, 1882; s. Michael and Dorothy (Wendzinski) K.; ed. pub., bus. schs., Chgo. Engaged in tax appraisal and delinquent tax supervision County Treasury Bur., Cook County, Ill., 1916-32; mem. 73d to 77th Congresses, 8th Ill. Dist. Del. to Dem. Nat. Conv., 1928; ward committeeman, old Ward 33, present Ward 32, Chgo., 1930—. Clubs: Iroquois, Logan Square Athletic, Chicago Press. Address: 1421 N. Ashland Av., Chgo. Died Sept. 27, 1958; buried St. Adelberts Cemetery, Niles, Ill.

KOEHLER, Wilhelm Reinhold Walter, prof. fine arts; b. Reval, Esthonia, Dec. 17, 1884; s. Dr. Franz and Wilhelmine (Girgensohn) K.; came to U.S., 1934, naturalized 1944; student univs. Strasbourg, Bonn; Ph.D., U. Vienna, 1907; m. Margaret Bittkow, 1920; children—Lorenz (killed in action 1945), Andreas. Engaged as dir. State Mus., Weimar, Germany, 1913-18, prof. U. Jena, Germany, 1923-32; Kuno Franke prof. German art and culture, Harvard, 1932-34, prof. fine arts, 1934-53, William Dorr Boardman prof. of fine arts 1950-53, emeritus 1953; vis. prof. London U., 1954; sr. fellow in charge of research at Dumbarton Oaks, Washington, 1941-44. Corr. fellow British Acad. and Am. Mediaeval Acad. Home: 223 Marsh St., Belmont 78, Mass. Office: Fogg Art Museum, Cambridge, Mass. Died Nov. 3, 1959.

KOERNER, Theodor, Federal Pres. of Austria; b. Komorn, Austria, Apr. 24, 1873; s. Theodor and Karoline (Fousek) von K.; student Civilian lower coll., Reichenberg and Vienna, mil. upper coll., Mahrisch-Weisskirchen, War Acad. at Vienna; Dr. honoris causa, Technical Acad., Vienna; unmarried. Officer in the Austro-Hungarian Army, 1st in Pioneer Corps, then in Gen. Staff, 1894-1918; chief of Gen. Staff of Austrian Republic, then head of office in Ministry for Mil. Affairs, Supt. of Army, 1918 until ret. as gen., 1924. Socialdemocratic mem. Bundesrat (Upper House of Parliament), 1924-34, last chmn. 1934; imprisoned Feb.-Dec. 1934, also in 1944; mayor and governor of Vienna, 1945-51; Federal president of Austria, 1951—. Recipient numerous mil. decorations. Died Jan. 4, 1957; buried Presidential Vault, Central Cemetery, Vienna.

KOHLER, Herbert Calvin, editor; b. Muhlenberg Twp., Berks Co., Pa., Jan. 27, 1891; s. Alvin Deisher and Emma (Hill) K.; grad., Reading (Pa.) High Sch., 1909; m. Elsie Amanda Reeser, Apr. 24, 1913; children—Elizabeth Margaret (wife of Dr. Raymond Moyer), Grace Miriam (Mrs. Charles Wonderly, Jr.), Kathryn Emma May (wife of Rev. Frank E. Radcliffe), Marie Edna (Mrs. Fenwick Brown), Barbara Louise. Feature writer, gen. assignments and ct. reporter, Reading (Pa.) Herald, 1909-16; cost accountant, Bethlehem Steel Co., Pa., 1916-21; exec. editor, Allentown (Pa.) Record, 1921-23; city editor, Norristown (Pa.) Times-Herald, 1923; city editor, Reading Times, 1923-39, mng. editor, 1939—. Engaged in activities to end coal mine pollution and to clean Schuylkill River, also campaigned for and publicized Reading Pub. Museum and Art Gallery. Mem. Izaak Walton League of Am., Reading Y.M.C.A., Wyomissing Fire Co. No. 1, Rainbow Fire Co. Relief Assn., Reading and Berks Co. C. of C. Democrat. Lutheran. Mason (Consistory, 32°, Shriner). Clubs: Wyomissing, Automobile (both Reading); Lehigh (Allentown). Home: 1428 Garfield Av., Wyomissing, Pa. Office: 30 N. 4th St., Reading, Pa. Died Dec. 27, 1953; buried Charles Evans Cemetery, Reading.

KOHLER, Ruth DeYoung, journalist; b. Harvey, Ill., Aug. 24, 1906; d. Frederic Robert and Miriam (Cornell) DeYoung; A.B., Smith Coll., 1928; travel and study abroad, 1928, 37, 49, 52; LL.D., Ripon Coll., 1952; m. Herbert Vollrath Kohler, June 21, 1937; children—Herbert Vollrath, Ruth De Young, Frederic Cornell. Reporter Chicago Tribune, 1929-34, woman's editor, 1934-37; organized forum, Woman Congress, 1934-37; conducted weekly column Chicago Tribune, June 1940-Jan. 1941; also MBS weekly radio feature, Women World Wide. Chmn. Women's Div. of The Volunteers, 1936; commr. Kohler Girl Scouts, 1944-52; dir. Gen. Fedn. Women's Clubs, 1947-50; pres. Kohler Woman's Club; chmn. Better Homes for Kohler Village; dir. for Kohler Found. of Wade House Restoration, Greenbush, Wis. Dir. Kohler Found., Inc. Trustee Lawrence Coll. (Appleton, Wis.), Layton Sch. Art (Milw.), Westminster Choir Coll. (Princeton, N.J.). Chmn. Com. on Wis. Women, 1948, Wis. Centennial; curator, v.p. Wis. Hist. Soc.; founder, chmn. Women's Auxiliary Wis. Hist. Soc. Winner 1948 Theodora Youmans Citizenship award; citations from Wis. Hist. Soc., Am. Soc. on State and Local History, 1950. Established Ruth de Young Kohler scholarships for promising students at Smith Coll., 1950. Mem. Antiquarian Soc. Wis., Phi Beta Kappa. Republican. Episcopalian. Clubs: Fortnightly, Arts, Alliance of Business and Professional Women (Chgo.); Am. Legion Auxiliary; Woman's Club of Wisconsin (Milwaukee). Author: The Story of Wisconsin Women, Wisconsin's Historic Sites. Address: Kohler, Wis. Died Mar. 7, 1953; buried Kohler, Wis.

KOHN, Robert David, architect; b. Manhattan, N.Y., May 12, 1870; s. Theodore A. and Henriette (Frankfield) K.; student Coll. City of N.Y., 1884-86; Ph.B. in architecture, Columbia, 1890; École des Beaux Arts, Paris, 1891-95; m. Estelle J. I. Rumbold, Oct. 1905. Practiced in New York since 1895; architect of New York Evening Post Bldg., Ethical Culture Meeting House, bldgs. for the Montefiore and Mt. Sinai hosps., R. H. Macy & Co. Bldg., Temple Emanu-El, all N.Y. City; H. Black Co. and Lindner Co. bldgs., Cleveland; associated with Charles Butler and Clarence Stein, architects. Director Mt. Pleasant Cemetery Soc. Dir. housing div. of Pub. Works Adminstrn., 1933-34; v.p. N.Y. World's Fair 1939, mem. Bd. of Design; pres. Soc. for Ethical Culture, New York, 1921-44. Democrat. Fellow A.I.A. (pres. 1930-32); mem. New York Chapter A.I.A. (pres. 1913), Beaux Arts Soc. Home: Glendale Road, Ossining, N.Y. Office: 56 W. 45th St., N.Y.C. 19. Died June 1953.

KOHNSTAMM, Frank R. (kōn'stam), bus. exec.; b. Scranton, Pa., Aug. 29, 1896; s. Jacob M. and Fanny (Aswell) K.; m. Gerrtude Bissell, May 19, 1920; 1 son, Robert B. With Westinghouse Elec. Corp., 1917-42, sales mgr., merchandising div., Mansfield, O., 1939-42; exec. v.p., Van Der Horst Corp. of Am., Olean, N.Y., hdqrs. N.Y.C., 1942-44; with Baldwin Locomotive Works, 1944-47, mgr. testing equipment div., Phila., 1945-47; with Jack & Heintz, Inc., Cleve., 1947-—, v.p., 1947, sr. v.p., 1948, pres., 1949-—; dir. Tuffle & Kift, Inc., Chgo., Ferro Corp. Motch & Merryweather Machine Co., Cleve. Clubs: Country, Hermit, Pepper Pike (Cleve.); Wings (N.Y.C.); Everglades (Palm Beach, Fla.). Home: 13415 Shaker Blvd., Cleve. 20. Office: 17600 Broadway, Cleve. 1. Died Aug. 7, 1959.

KOINER, C. Wellington, engr., city mgr.; b. Augusta County, Va., May 16, 1870; ed. pub. and pvt. schs.; m. Katie M. Bragunier, Sept. 25, 1895; children—Carl W., Audrey Kathleen, Sara Marie, Virginia. Gen. mgr. Laurel Electric Light, Power & Heat Co., 1892-98; became gen. mgr. Oneida (N.Y.) Light & Power Co., 1898, when this co. was consol., forming Madison County Gas & Electric Co., 1901, was made supt., later pres., gen. mgr.; sec.-treas. Nat. Light & Imp. Co., St. Louis, 1905-07, in charge properties controlled by co. in Wichita, Kan., Ft. Worth, and Waco, Tex.; served as gen. supt., engr. Los Angeles Gas & Electric Co., 1907; engaged by City of Pasadena to build and manage its electric utility, 1908-21; cons. engr. to other cities; city mgr., Pasadena, 1921-25, 33-—; cons. practice, 1925-27; dist. mgr. So. Cal. Edison Co., Ltd. (South Bay terr.), 1927-33; dir. Pasadena Bldg. & Loan Assn. Past pres. Internat. City Mgrs'. Assn. Fellow Am. Inst. E.E., Am. Soc. Mil. Engrs. Presbyn. Mason, Elk, Kiwanian. Served as power expert, engring., staff U.S. Shipping Bd., Phila., for period during World War. Cons. engr. with power div. Pub. Works Adminstrn., Washington, 1935. Home: 1912 N. Fair Oaks Av. Office: City Hall, Pasadena, Cal. Died Sept. 29, 1947; buried Mountain View Cemetery, Altadena, Cal.

KOKATNUR, Vaman Ramachandra, cons. chemist; b. Athani, Bombay Presidency, India, Dec. 16, 1886; s. Ramachadra A. and Krishnabai K.; B.Sc., Bombay U., 1911; studied U. Cal., 1912-13; Shevlin fellow U. Minn., 1914-15, M.S., 1914, Ph.D., 1916; m. Helen Graber, Feb. 11, 1921; children—Urmila, Arvind. Came to U.S., 1912, naturalized, 1921. Chemist Ranade Indsl. Inst., Poona, India, 1911-12; research asst. U. of Minn., 1915-17; research chemist Matheison Alkali Works, 1917-18; chief of research dept. Niagara Alkali Co., 1918-20; asst. chief of vat dye group Nat. Aniline & Chem. Co., 1920-21; spl. chemist By-Products Steel Corp. and du Pont Co., 1921-22; cons. practice, 1922-—, covering research, engring., development, new processes, litigation, etc.; director of research Antoxygen, Inc., 1934-—, pres., 1942-—; in India as technical adviser and consulting manager of the Sri Shakti Alkali Works, Dhrangadhra, 1930-31; hon. tech. adviser to Am. Trade Commrs., India, 1930-33; cons. expert to Russia on 5 Year Plan reg. chlorine and caustic soda, 1928; faculty mem. Inst. of Chemistry, Am. Chem. Soc., Northwestern University, 1928; consulttant U.S. Navy, 1938. Holder of more than 30 chem. patents; first to make aeroplane dope solvent and vat dyes in Am.; inventor war gases; inventor M59 bomb and flame thrower. Served as capt. C.W.S., U.S. Army Res., active duty, 1942-44. Honored as outstanding inventor Sesquicentennial celebration, U.S. Patent Office, 1940; selected for Wall of Fame, New York World's Fair, 1940. Fellow A.A.A.S., Am. Inst. Chemists; mem. Am. Chem. Soc., History of Science Soc., Am. Electro-chem. Soc., Soc. Am. Mil. Engrs., Sigma Xi, Indian Science Congress. Unitarian. Club: Chemists. Home: 148-09 9th Av., Whitestone, L.I. Office: 114 E. 32d St., N.Y.C. Died Apr. 14, 1950.

KOLAR, Victor, conductor; b. Hungary. With N.Y. Symphony Orchestra, 1906-19; became asso. conductor Detroit Symphony Orchestra, 1919, later conductor; season conductor at Ford Gardens, Century of Progress Expn., Chgo., 1934; conductor Ford Sunday Evening Hour, radio broadcast. Now head of Orchestral Dept., Detroit Inst. Musical Art, condr. Detroit Women's Symphony Orchestra. Address: 1303 Hartwig, R.D. 3, Rochester, Mich. Died June 16, 1957.

KOLOWICH, George J., investment banker; b. Detroit, Feb. 1, 1897; s. Adolph and Kate (Nowak) K.; grad. Detroit Comml. Coll., 1912; m. Irene Acker, Feb. 1, 1917; children—George J., Hugh John, Frederic Raymond, Kaye Lois. Police judge, Detroit, 1921; pres. and dir. Griswold Bldg., Inc., 1943-47; dir. Detroit & Cleve Navigation Co., Detroit, 1943-47, now pres. Pres. and dir. Detroit Housing Corp., 1935-47, Nat. Bank Bldg. Co., Jackson, 1940-47; owner Detroit Towers, 1945-47, Whittier Corp., Detroit, 1943-47. Republican. Roman Catholic. Home: 408 Neff Rd., Grosse Pointe, Mich. Office: Griswold Bldg., Detroit 26. Deceased.

KOMAREWSKY, Vasili Ilyich, chemist; b. Moscow, Russia, Feb. 17, 1895; s. Ilya V. and Olga P. (Kindiakova) K.; grad. Moscow 9th Gymnasium, 1913; Ph.D., U. Moscow, 1925; m. Jessie Baxter, July 15, 1933. Came to U.S., 1932, naturalized, 1938. Research fellow Kaiser Wilhelm Inst., Berlin, 1926-30; research chemist Universal Oil Product Co., Chgo., 1932-41; prof. chem. engring., dir. catalysis lab. Ill. Inst. Tech., 1936-—. Mem. Am. Chem. Soc., Ill. Acad. Sci., A.A.A.S., Am. Soc. Engring. Edn., Sigma Xi, Alpha Chi Sigma, Phi Lambda Upsilon. Author: Isomerization of Pure Hydrocarbons, 1942; Techniques of Catalytic Reactions, 1956. Editor Advances of Catalysis, 1948-—. Patentee in field. Home: 5439 East View Park, Chgo. 15. Died June 21, 1957; buried New Milford, Ill.

KOMORA, Paul O(tto), health worker; b. N.Y. City, Aug. 24, 1891; s. Andrew and Sophia (Balogh) K.; ed. LaSalle Acad. and pub. high sch., N.Y. City, 1904-08; m. Mary Margaret Heffner, Aug. 9, 1924; children—Paul F., John G. Insurance business, 1908-16, health worker since 1917; with Nat. Com. for Mental Hygiene, 1917-42, successively ednl. asst., pub. dir., asso. sec.; asst. sec. N.Y. State Dept. Mental Hygiene, 1942-43, adminstrv. sec. since 1944. Served as sergt., Med. Dept., U.S. Army, World War I. Asst. sec. N.Y. State Mil. Hosp. Commn., 1920-21; chmn. Health Work Group, United Ednl. Program, Nat. Social Work Council, 1932; sec. Div. Ednl. Pub., Nat. Conf. Social Work, 1933-34; adminstrv. sec. Symposium on Mental Health, Sect. on Med. Scis., A.A.A.S., 1938; asst. sec., 1939-43, sec. since 1943, Am. Foundn. for Mental Hygiene; asst. sec., 1939-43, sec., 1943-48, Internat. Com. for Mental Hygiene; mem. Council Nat. Com. for Mental Hygiene, Am. Assn. Social Workers, Am. Assn. on Mental Deficiency, Nat. Health and Welfare Pub. Council. Author: State Hospitals in the Depression, 1934; co-author: Research in Mental Hospitals, Study No. 1, 1939, Study No. 2, 1942; co-author: Biography of Thomas W. Salmon, Psychiatrist (with Dr. Earl D. Bond), 1950; co-editor: Vol. X, Neuropsychiatry, Medical Dept. of U.S. Army, 1929; co-editor: Mental Health, Pub. No. 9, A.A.A.S., 1939; contbg. editor Mental Hygiene, 1933-42; contbr. to Ency. of the Social Sciences, 1933. Home: 36-A Weis Rd., Albany 3. Office: Governor Alfred E. Smith State Office Bldg., Albany, N.Y. Died July 18, 1950; buried Gate of Heaven Cemetery, Valhalla, N.Y.

KOMP, William H. Wood, entomologist; b. Yokohama, Japan, Mar. 16, 1893; s. Frederick and Carrie Joanna (Wood) K.; brought to U.S., 1895; derivative citizenship; student Mass. State Coll., 1911, N.Y. U., 1912; B.S., Rutgers U., 1916, M.S., 1917, D. Sc., 1955; fellow in agr. Cornell, 1917; m. Mildred Crowell, Sept. 1, 1914; 1 dau., Anita (Mrs. Harry M. Williams). Ensign, USPHS, 1918, advanced through grades to capt., 1944, malaria control; vis. staff mem. Gorgas Meml. Lab., Republic of Panama, 1931-47; traveling rep. Pan-Am. San. Bur., 1937; research in malaria, 1921-—; loaned to Rockefeller Found. Internat. Health Div. for research on yellow fever, Colombia, 1936; consultant to Creole Petroleum Co., Venezuela, 1936. United Fruit Co., tropical divs., 1924-30, Inst. Inter-Am. Affairs (consultant malaria), 1942-—. Chmn. com. on entomology Pan-Am. San. Conf., Rio, 1942. Fellow A.A.A.S., Am. Soc. Tropical Medicine and Hygiene; mem. Am. Mosquito Control Assn., Nat. Malaria Soc., Sociedad Venezolano de Ciencias Naturales (corr. mem.), Am. Acad. Tropical Medicine, Isthian Med. Soc. (Panama), Entomol. Soc. Wash., Washington Acad. Medicine, Chi Psi. Author: The Anopheline Mosquitoes of the Caribbean Region, bull., 1941; discovered Anopheles Darlingi (malaria mosquito) in Central Am., 1940. Home: 6906 Dartmouth Av., College Park, Md. Office: National Institutes of Health, Bethesda, Md. Died Dec. 7, 1955; buried Elmwood Cemetery, New Brunswick, N.J.

KOONTZ, Frederick Bowers, oil exec.; b. New Martinsville, W.Va., July 14, 1889; s. Henry and Jeanette (Bowers) K.; student Bethel Mil. Acad., Staunton Mil. Acad.; m. Marjorie Trude, Sept. 27, 1911; children—Pauline Annette Koontz Teale, Frederick Bowers. With Waters-Pierce Co. (subsidiary of Standard Oil of N.J.), Mexico, 1908-11; chemist Union Oil Co., Cal., 1911-14; chemist Shell Petroleum Corp., Cal., 1914-15, Standard Oil of Cal., 1915-17; with Mid-Continent Petroleum Corp., 1917-—, v.p., dir. in charge mfg. 1928-46, pres., 1946-48, vice chmn. bd., 1948-—. Dir. Mid-Continent Oil and Gas Assn., Am. Petroleum Inst. Mem. Tulsa C. of C. Episcopalian. Mason (32°), Elk. Clubs: Thoroughbred of Am., Tulsa, Oakhurst Country. 20-Year, University Tulsa Quarterback. Breeder of Hereford and Black Angus cattle and sheep on his Paulfred Farms near Tulsa and breeder (non-racing) of thoroughbred horses on his farms near Lexington, Ky. Home: 1703 S. Norfolk. Address: Box 381, Tulsa. Died Oct. 29, 1953.

KOONTZ, Louis Knott, prof. history; b. Shepherdstown, W.Va., Feb. 21, 1890; s. D. Frank and Virginia Harrison (Knott) K.; grad. Moler's sch. nr. Shepherdstown, 1904; A.B., Washington and Lee U., Lexington, Va., 1908; A.M., Johns Hopkins U., 1914, Ph.D., 1920; m. Ruth Cain Bell, Apr. 16, 1922; stepson, Gollin Burgess Bell and Lawrence Frye Bell. Instr. history and English, Frederick Coll., Frederick, Md. (now merged with Hood Coll.), 1908-09, pres., 1909-12; prof. of history and polit. science and dean, Davis and Elkins Coll., Elkins, W.Va., 1914-17, actg. pres., 1916; mem. editorial staff San Francisco Chronicle, 1921-22; since 1922 successively instr. history, asst. prof., asso. prof., now prof., U. of Calif. at Los Angeles; lecturer summer sessions, W. Va. U., 1927, 28, 31, Shepherd Coll. (W.Va.), 1930, 32, University of N.M., 1939, University of Ore., 1940, New York State Teachers Coll., 1941, U. of Ariz. 1945, U. of Va., 1949. Research tour Mediterranean countries and western Europe, 1935; visiting prof. colonial history, Coll. of William and Mary, 1937-38; mng. editor Pacific Hist. Review, 1936-47. Commd. 2d lieutenant Infantry, U.S. Army, at Plattsburg, N.Y., 1918; member historical staff Army War College, 1919, education section War Plans Division Gen. Staff, 1919-20; civilian ednl. adviser War Dept., Camp Grant, 1920, same in Philippine Islands, 1920-21. Mem. jury Frederick Bancroft award. Mem. Am. Hist. Assn., Southern Hist. Assn., Jefferson County Hist. Soc., Am. Assn. Univ. Profs., Phi Beta Kappa, Kappa Alpha, Pi Gamma Mu, Alpha Phi Omega, Omicron Delta Kappa. Conglist. Mason (K.T.). Author: The Virginia Frontier, 1754-1763, 1925; Robert Dinwiddie: His Career in American Colonial Government and Westward Expansion, 1941; also several hist. brochures and charts. Editor, Parish's The Persistence of the Westward Movement and Other Essays, 1943; Robert Dinwiddie Correspondence. 1947. Contbr. to hist. publs. Home: 10533 Kinnard St., Los Angeles 24. Died Aug. 6, 1951; buried Elmwood Cemetery, Shepherdstown, W.Va.

KOOP, William H., insurance exec.; ed. pub. schs. and Cooper Union, N.Y. City. Began with Great American Insurance Co., N.Y. City, 1894, dir. since 1927, pres., 1928-47, chmn. bd. dirs., 1944-47, chmn. exec. com. since 1947; chmn. exec. com., dir. of the following affiliated cos.; American Alliance Ins. Co., Am. Nat. Fire Ins. Co., Detroit Fire & Marine Ins. Co., Great Am. Indemnity Co., Mass. Fire & Marine Ins. Co., One Liberty Street Realty & Securities Corp., Rochester Am. Insurance Co.; pres. The Great American Corp.; mem. exec. com. Nat. Bd. Fire Underwriters; dir. Nat. Board of Fire Underwriters Bldg. Corp.. Sanborn Map Co. Has served as chmn. Explosion Conf. and pres. of the following: Am. Fgn. Ins. Assn., Eastern Automobile Conf., Nat. Bd. Fire Underwriters, N.Y. Fire Ins. Exchange. Address: One Liberty St., N.Y.C. Died Aug. 25, 1952.

KOPETZKY, Samuel Joseph (kō-pĕt'skĭ), surgeon; b. N.Y. City, Aug. 1, 1876; s. Joseph and Lena (Bernhardt) K.; student Coll. City of N.Y., 1894-96; M.D., Coll. Physicians and Surgeons (Columbia),

1898; m. Anah Doob, Apr. 2, 1903; children—Karl, Yvonne K. (Mrs. Robert Sterling). Prof. otology N.Y. Polyclinic Med. Sch. and Hosp. since 1920; cons. otolaryngologist, Beth Israel Hosp.; dir. of otolaryngology, United Israel Zion Hosp. (Brooklyn); cons. otologist Nyack (N.Y.) Hosp., Newark (N.J.), Beth Israel Hosp., Vassar Bros. Hosp. (Poughkeepsie, N.Y.). Served in Spanish-Am. War and World Wars I and II; colonel Med. Corps. Received the Legion of Merit and the Silver Star; Chevalier of the Legion of Honor (France). Fellow Am. Coll. Surgeons, A.M.A., New York Acad. Medicine, Am. Acad. Ophthalmology and Oto-laryngology, Am. Rhinol., Laryngol. and Otol. Soc. (pres. 1937-38), Med. Soc. of State of N.Y. (pres. 1941-42); corr. Société Laryngologie des Hospiteaux de Paris; formerly speaker House of Delegates, Medical Society State of N.Y. Author: Surgery of the Ear, 1908; Otologic Surgery, 1925, 2d edit., 1929; Deafness, Tinctus and Vertigo, 1948. Editor of New York Medical Week since its establishment, 1920-36; editor Surgery of the Ear. Home: 300 E. 57th St. Office: 30 E. 60th St., N.Y. City 21. Died Nov. 13, 1950.

KOPF, Carl Heath (kŭpf), clergyman; b. Buffalo, N.Y., Aug. 6, 1902; s. George Phillip and Viola (Heath) K.; B.S., Princeton, 1925; S.T.B., Boston U., 1930; D.D., Piedmont Coll., 1951, Princeton, 1956; m. Mary Fitz Randolph Chalfant, June 23, 1928; children—David Heath, John Randolph, Anne Elisabeth. Instr. history of Christianity, Princeton, 1925-26; ordained to ministry of the Congl. Ch., 1928; asst. pastor Eliot Congl. Ch., Roxbury, Mass., 1926-28; pastor Crombie St. Congl. Ch., Salem, Mass., 1928-33, Mount Vernon Congl. Ch., Boston, 1933-47, First Ch., Washington, since 1947; v.p. Am. Bd. Missions, 1946; president of Washington Fedn. of Churches, 1954-55. Author: Windows on Life, 1941; Personal Crisis, 1945; Fellowship of Prayer, 1952. Creator From a Window on Beacon St., 1938-47. Home: 3344 Runnymede Pl., N.W., Washington. Died July 4, 1958.

KOPPER, Samuel Keene Claggett, lawyer; born New York City, July 7, 1914; s. John Matthias and Sarah Genevieve (Claggett) K.; A.B., Princeton, 1937; LL.B., U. Va., 1940; grad. law student George Washington U., 1946-47; Diploma, Acad. de Droit Internat. de la Haye, 1953; m. Elizabeth Duke Lee, Sept. 1, 1941; children—Elizabeth Marshall, Samuel Keene Claggett, Richard Henry Lee, Robert Brooke. Law clk. Davies, Auerbach, Cornell & Hardy, N.Y.C., 1939; rsrch. sec. Fgn. Affairs Coun., Cleve., 1940-41; admitted to Ohio bar, 1941; asst. to counsel Lake Carriers Assn., Cleve., 1941; officer div. export controls Dept. of State, Washington, 1941; jr. exec. officer Bd. Econ. Warfare, 1941-42, staff office internat. security affairs, 1945-47, staff Bur. Nr. Eastern, S. Asian and African Affairs, 1947-49, dep. dir. Office of Near Eastern Affairs, 1950-52, resigned, 1952; dep. publicity dir. Nat. Volunteers for Stevenson, Chgo., Sept.-Dec. 1952; cons. to asst. secretary state for Near Eastern, S. Asian and African Affairs, 1953; counsel Arabian Am. Oil Co., 1953—, assistant to the chairman of the board, 1956—. Admitted to D.C. bar, 1953. Adviser to U.S. delegation UN Security Council, 1946-48, Gen. Assembly, 1947-49; rep. Internat. Law Assn. 18th-22 session UNEC OSOC Geneva; N.Y., 1954-56, 12th session UN Econ. Commn. Asia and Far East, 1956; rep. Nat. Assn. Mfgrs. to 11 session UN Econ. Commn. Europe, Geneva, 1956. Chmn. Men's Com., Mayor's UN Hospitality Com., 1956—; adv. council Dem. Nat. Com. Served as lt. comdr. USNR, 1942-45. Mem. Am. (chmn. com. on Nr. East law), Internat. (chmn. com. internat. restrictive bus. practices Am. br. 1954), D.C. bar assns., Am. Soc. Internat. Law (exec. council 1956—), Middle East Ins.t (bd. govs., 1956—), Am. Petroleum Inst., Société de Législation com paree, Fgn. Service Assn., Council Fgn. Relations. Episcopalian. Clubs: Princeton (N. Y.C.); Army and Navy (Washington); Farmington Country (Charlottesville, Va.), Larchmont Shore. UN corr. Middle East Jour., 1956. Author profl. articles. Home: 85 Willow Av., Larchmont, N.Y. Office: 505 Park Av., N.Y.C.; also Shoreham Bldg., Washington. Died June 1957.

KOPPLEMANN, Herman Paul, ex-congressman; b. Odessa, Russia, May 1, 1880; s. Henry and Jessie (Gitlin) K.; brought to U.S., 1882; student high sch., Hartford, Conn.; m. Adeline Greenstein, Mar. 23, 1902. Began as newsboy, Hartford, 1888; publisher's agent for various newspapers and mags. Mem. City Council, Hartford, 1904-12, pres., 1911; mem. Conn. Ho. of Reps., 1913-14; mem. Conn. Senate, 1917-18, 19-20; mem. 73d to 75th, 77th and 79th Congresses, 1st Conn. Dist. Mem. exec. bd. Mt. Sinai Hosp.; dir. United Jewish Charities; v.p. United Synagogue of America; mem. Met. Dist. Commn. Mem. Conn. Council of Defense, World War I. Hon. mem. V.F.W. Liberal Democrat. Mason, K.P. Clubs: Get Together, Tumble Brook Country. Home: 330 Laurel St. Office: P.O. Box 145, Hartford, Conn. Died Aug. 11, 1957.

KORBEL, Mario, sculptor; b. Osik. Bohemia, Mar. 22, 1882; s. Josef and Katherina (Dolezal) K.; studied art in Bohemia, Berlin, Munich and Paris, history of art, U. of Munich; m. Hilda Boyar, 1916; 1 son, Ivan Mario. Came to U.S., 1900. Principal works; a soldier's monument, erected by State of Ill., in Ga.; McPhee meml., Denver; Andante, Met. Museum, New York; Dancers, Detroit Museum; Alma Mater, U. of Havana, Cuba; dancing group Cleve. Museum; St. Therese, the Vatican, Rome; Sonata and Night, Mr. A. Huntington Gardens; President Mario Menocal (of Cuba); The Kiss group, in garden of William Ziegler of Noroton, Conn.; Sleeping Maiden, in garden of John Herbert of Fort Worth; Adolescence, in garden of George G. Booth, Detroit; portrait of late Senator Wm. Clark and family; portrait of Mrs. Brice Turner; medal for the Liberation of the Czechoslovak Republic; torso for Whitney Museum in New York. Awarded Goodman prize ($500), Grand Central Galleries, 1929. Mem. Am. Acad., French Legion of Honor, Nat. Sculpture Soc., Archtl. League of New York, Czechoslovak Art Club (N.Y.C. and Chgo.). Mem. Evang. Ch. Club: Embassy (N.Y.C.). Home: 28 E. 70th St., N.Y.C. Died Mar. 31, 1954.*

KORDA, Sir Alexander, motion picture exec.; born Turkeve, Hungary, Sept. 16, 1893; s. Henry and Ernestine Korda; ed. Reformist Coll. and Royal U., Budapest; m. Maria Farka, 1919; 1 son; m. 2d, Merle Oberon, 1939 (marriage dissolved); married 3d, Alexandra Irene Boycun, 1953. Began as newspaperman in Budapest; later became film producer, Budapest, Vienna, Berlin, Hollywood, Paris; chmn. London Film Prodns. (founded 1932), Alexander Korda Film Prodns. (founded 1939); former dir. United Artists Corp. of Am. Created Knight, 1942. Officer Legion of Honor (France). Address: 146 Piccadilly, London W. 1, Eng. Died Jan. 23, 1956.*

KOREN, William, Jr., fgn. service officer; b. Princeton, N.J., Apr. 8, 1909; s. William and Adelaide Louise (Thornell) K.; grad. Phillips Exeter Acad.; A.B., Princeton, 1930; B.S., Oxford U., 1933, B.Litt., 1934; M.A., Harvard, 1937; m. Isabelle Gilbert Johnston, May 4, 1935. Research staff Fgn. Policy Assn., 1934-35; instr. history Princeton, 1935-36, 39-41; asst. history Harvard, 1937-38; Social Sci. Research Council fellow for study in France, 1938-39; asst. to dir. research Office of Coordinator of Information (later OSS), 1941-42; div. asst. Dept. of State, 1942-43, research analyst, 1945-47, chief Western European sect. div. research for Europe, 1947-48; fgn. service officer, 1948—; 2d sec., consul, Paris, 1948-52, 1st sec., consul, 1952-53, detailed to NATO Def. Coll., Paris, 1951-52; 1st sec., consul, Teheran 1953—, with temp. rank of counselor, 1954—. Served from lt. (j.g.) to lt. USNR, 1943-45, ETO. Mem. Phi Beta Kappa. Home: 1419 36th St., Washington 7. Office: Dept. of State, Washington 25. Died Feb. 6, 1956; buried Princeton, N.J.

KORNGOLD, Eric Wolfgang, composer, conductor; b. Bruenn, Austria, May 29, 1897; s. Dr. Julius and Josephine (Witrofsky) K.; m. Luise von Sonnenthal, April 30, 1924; 2 sons, Ernest Werner, George Wolfgang; came to U.S., 1934. naturalized, 1943. Prof. Vienna State Academy for Music; condr. Opera House, Hamburg, Germany, and State Opera. Vienna; pianist, composer and conductor with many European orchestras. Composer, condr. of music for motion pictures; Anthony Adverse (Academy award), 1936; Adventures of Robin Hood (Academy award), 1938; Private Lives of Elizabeth and Essex, 1939; The Sea Hawk, 1940; The Sea Wolf, 1941; King's Row, 1941; The Constant Nymph, 1942; Devotion, 1943; Deception, Escape Me Never, 1946. Composer: (operas) Kathrin (first performed in Stockholm, Sweden, 1939); The Dead City (performed on eighty European opera stages, also Metropolitan Opera, New York City); The Miracle of Heliane; musci to Shakespeare's Much Ado About Nothing; symphonic works; Violin Concerto; Symphonic Serenade for Strings; Silent Serenade, OP. 39; Symphony in F. Sharp. OP. 40; Der Schneemnan; (operas) Der Ring des Polykates, Violanta; chamber and piano music; songs, etc. Home: 9936 Toluca Lake Av., North Hollywood, Cal. Died Nov. 29, 1957; buried Hollywood Meml. Cenetery.

KORNHAUSER, Sidney Isaac (kôrn'houz-ẽr), prof. anatomy; b. Cleveland, O., Nov. 3, 1887; s. Albert and Yetta (Goldberg) K.; A.B., U. of Pittsburgh, 1908; A.M., Harvard, 1910, Ph.D., 1912; student U. of Halle, 1912-13, U. of Würzburg, 1913-14; m. Anna Viola Marshall, Nov. 8, 1913; children—Albert Edward, Katherine, Edward Theodore. Instr. in biology, George Washington U., 1908-09, Austin fellow, Harvard, 1909-12, traveling fellow, 1912-14; asst. prof. of zoölogy, Northwestern U., 1914-17, asso. prof., 1917-18; prof. of zoölogy, Denison U., 1919-22; prof. of anatomy and head of department of anatomy, University of Louisville, 1922-58, prof. anatomy, chmn. emeritus, 1958—; exec. sec. Sch. of Medicine, U. of Louisville, 1928-48. Treas., sec., and v.p. Biol. Stain Commn., 1937-57, pres., 1957-59. Served as 2d lt. Sanitary Corps, U.S. Army, 1918-19; lt., later capt., Reserve Corps, since 1919. Fellow A.A.A.S.; mem. and exec. com. Assn. Am. Anatomists; mem. Am. Zoölogists, Am. Naturalists. Jefferson County Med. Soc., Alpha Omega Alpha (hon.). Author sci. contbns. to tech. jours. Died Jan. 1, 1959; buried Zachary Taylor Nat. Cemetery, Louisville.

KOSANOVITCH, Sava N., Yugoslav govt. ofcl.; b. Plaski, Lika, Yugoslavia, May 29, 1894; s. Nikola and Marica (Tesla) Kosanovic; grad. with law degree U. of Budapest, 1919. Began as journalist 1920; became sec. gen. Independent Democratic party, 1926; mem. Yugoslav parliament, 1927, senator, 1939, minister of supplies, 1941, minister of interior, social welfare and public health, 1944, minister of information, 1945; mem. of Presidium of Federal Peoples Republic of Yugoslavia, 1945, and 1950—; mem. parliament, minister of state; ambassador to U.S., 1945-50, Mexico, 1946. Del. to UN, London, 1946; mem. Yugoslav delegation to Ministers Confs., London and Paris, Peace Conf., Paris, UN, New York. Awarded Order of Merits to the People, 1st Class. Hon. mem. Yugoslav Newspapermen's Assn. Home: Jevremova 35/111, Belgrade, Yugoslavia. Died Nov. 1956.

KOSCINSKI, Arthur A., judge; b. Poland, Apr. 1, 1887; s. Anthony and Mary Lula K.; LL.B., U. Mich., 1910; m. Blanche Kruse, Sept. 3, 1913; children—Arthur J., Valeric M. (Mrs. Russell Rule), Philip A. Began practice of law in 1910; pub. adminstr. Wayne Co., 1923-36; U.S. dist. judge Eastern Dist., Mich. Mem. Detroit City Pension Commn., 1934-37, Mich. Pub. Trust Commn., 1937-38, Mich. Constnl. Revision Commn., 1941, Bd. of Wayne County Instns., 1942-43; govt. appeal agt., Selective Service Bd. 7, 1940-45. Trustee Sts. Cyril and Methodius Sem.; bd. trustees Alliance Coll., Cambridge Springs, Pa. Mem. Am., Mich. (grievance com. 1933—), Detroit bar assns., Am. Judicature Soc., Alumni Assn. of Sts. Cyril and Methodius Sem. (pres. 1927-42). Clubs: Economic, Advocates, Detroit Athletic, University of Michigan. Home: 679 Webb Av., Detroit 2. Office: Fed. Bldg., Detroit 26. Died Nov. 1957.

KOSMAK, George William (kŏs'măk), obstetrician, gynecologist, editor; b. New York, N.Y., July 24. 1873; s. Emil H. and Louise (Wack) K.; A.B., Columbia, 1894; M.D., Coll. Physicians and Surgeons, Columbia, 1899; m. Florence Fischer, Feb. 5, 1902; children—George William, Katherine Louise, Beatrice Florence. Physician, New York, 1902—; attending surgeon New York Lying-In Hosp., 1904-26; cons. obstetrician Caledonian, Woman's Infirmary, Fifth Av. and Nyack hosps.; med. dir. emeritus Booth Memorial; cons. Fed. Children's Bureau, New York State Dept. of Health; editor Am. Jour. Obstetrics, 1909-19; founder and editor Am. Jour. Obstetrics and Gynecology, 1920—; pres. Fischer Realty Co., editor N. Y. State Journal of Medicine. Chmn. med. bds of Maternity Center Assn., Visiting Nurses Association. Editor New York State Journal of Medicine. Hon. fellow Royal Coll. Obstetricians and Gynecologists; mem. American Medical Association, Am. Gynecol. Soc. (former pres.), Am. Assn. Obstetricians and Gynecologists, N.Y. Acad. Medicine, Med. Soc. State of N.Y. (treas. 1937-41; trustee), Theta Delta Chi. Clubs: Century, University (N.Y.C.). Author: Toxemia of Pregnancy, 1922. Contbr. to numerous med. jours. Address: 610 Park Av., N.Y.C. 21. Died July 10, 1954; buried Woodlawn Cemetery.

KOSTELLOW, Alexander Jusserand (kos'tĕl-lō), educator, painter, indsl. designer; b. Ispahan, Iran, Dec. 25, 1897; s. Alexander Jusserand and Beatrice (Mar-Jacques) K.; student U. of Berlin, 1912-16; Art Students' League, New York City, 1918-20, Nat. Acad., N.Y. City, 1921-22, Kansas City Art Inst., 1922-25; m. Rowena Reed, Sept. 26, 1921; 1 dau., Adele Beatrice. Came to U.S., 1917, naturalized, 1936. Art instr., Kansas City Art Inst., 1925-28; asso. prof., head dept. indsl. design, Carnegie Inst. of Tech., Pittsburgh, 1929-38; prof. of design, chmn. of design and structure curriculum, Pratt Inst., Brooklyn, 1940-47, chmn., dept. of indsl. design since 1945; dir. of product development and engring., U.S. Glass Co., Pittsburgh, 1936-39; v.p., product development and market research, Columbia Radiator Co., McKeesport, Pa., 1937-40; design consultant, Mine Safety Appliances, Pittsburgh, 1936-38, Pittsburgh Reflector Co., 1935-39; dir. A. J. Kostellow Associates, N.Y. City, since 1946. Regular exhibitor, Carnegie Internat., Whitney Mus., Modern Mus., Chicago Art Inst., Corcoran Art Gallery, Butler Mus., Nelson Mus. (Kansas City), Calif. and Chicago World Fairs. State Art Commr., Pa., 1937-40. Awarded portrait prize, Midwestern Exhibn., Kansas City, 1927; figure prize, Pittsburgh Associated Artists, 1932; hon. mention, Carnegie Internat., 1933. Fellow Am. Designers Inst. (nat. pres. and chmn. ednl. com., 1946-48); mem. Artists Equity of Am., Brooklyn Soc. of Artists, Pittsburgh Soc. of Artists (v.p., 1936-39); Tau Sigma Delta. Contbr. articles on curriculum structures, art and indsl. design. Home: 720 Burns St., Forest Hills, L.I., N.Y. Office: Pratt Institute, Bklyn. 5. Died Aug. 31, 1954.

KOSTER, Frederick Jacob (kŏs'tẽr), corp. exec.; b. San Francisco, Calif., Oct. 28, 1868; s. John L. and Berta Lisette (Wagener) K.; ed. high sch. and under pvt. tutors; m. Ida Louise Field, Mar. 12, 1908; children—Jane, Ann, Lisette, Louise. Began with Coos Bay Stave & Lumber Co., San Francisco, 1884; became supt., 1887, Calif. Barrel Co. (now Calif. Barrel Co., Ltd.), pres. since 1905. Chmn. Law and Order Com., San Francisco, 1916-18; pres. San Francisco Chamber of Commerce, 1916-18; mem exec. com. San Francisco War Camp Community Service, 1917-18; chmn. resources and conversion sect. War Industries Bd. (Calif., Nev. and Ariz.), 1917-18; mem. Nat. Foreign Trade Council, 1918-21; chmn. exec. com. and dir. Chamber Commerce of U.S., 1919-20; mem. European Relief Administration, 1921; chmn. San Francisco Endorsement Council, 1927-39; pres. Calif. Grape Control Bd., 1931-32; chairman Industrial Association of San Francisco; hon. chmn. Grape Advisory Council and of Wine Industry and Related Interests; pres. Calif. State Chamber Commerce, 1931-32; chmn. advisory board Y.W.C.A.; chmn. San Francisco Civil Defense Council; chmn. San Francisco Campaign for Armenian and Syrian Relief; dir. San Francisco Chapter of Am. Red Cross since 1926, chmn. 1937-43; chmn. San Francisco Conf. of Christians and Jews, 1940-44; dir. Golden Gate Internat. Expn.; pres. Calif. League of Progress, 1895; councillor of bd., Nat. Indusl. conf. Bd. Mem. California Historical Society. Trustee Calif. Coll. in China; dir. San Francisco Mus. Assn.; mem. Calif. Acad. Sciences. Republican. Clubs: Pacific Union, Bohemian (life), Olympic, San Francisco Commercial, San Francisco Golf and Country, Commonwealth Press (life) (San Francisco). Home: 1958 Vallejo St. (23). Office: 5933 Geary Blvd., San Francisco. Died Nov. 18, 1958; buried Holy Cross Cemetery, Colma, Cal.

KOUSSEVITZKY, Sergei (Alexandrovitch) (kōō'se-vĭt'skē), conductor; b. Russia, July 26, 1874; s. Alexander and Anne (Barabeitchik) K.; grad. Master of Free Arts, Conservatory of Moscow, 1894; hon. Mus. Doc., Brown U., 1926, Rutgers U., 1937, Yale, 1938, U. of Rochester, 1940; LL.D., Harvard, 1929; Mus.D., Williams Coll., 1943, Boston Univ., 1945; Litt.D., Princeton Univ., 1947; Dr. Humanities, Rollins Coll., 1949; Dr. Honoris Causa, U. Brazil, 1949; m. Nathalie Oushkoff, Sept. 8, 1905 (deceased); m. Olga Naumoff, Aug. 15, 1947. Prof. Conservatory of Moscow and as soloist (double bass) Imperial Theatre Orchestra; founder, 1910, and dir. until 1918, Koussevitzky Symphony Orchestra of 85 musicians, making extensive tours in Russia, also 3 journeys in chartered steamer on the Volga River (2,300 miles); founded the "Concerts Koussevitzky" in Paris, 1921, and at various times conducted orchestras in England, Germany, Italy, Spain, etc.; condr. Boston Symphony Orchestra since Sept. 1924. Founder "Musical Editions," for Russian composers, 1909. Initiator, 1938, and director since 1940 of Berkshire Music Center. Established in memory of wife, Koussevitzky Music Foundation, Inc., to assist composers and to further development of musical culture, 1942; founded Internat. Music Fund, 1948, under auspices UNESCO, to promote performance, recording, broadcasting of the music by living composers. Twice decorated by the Czar, 1903; Knight Legion of Honor (French), 1924, Officer, 1930, Comdr., 1936. Foreign hon. mem. Am. Acad. Arts and Sciences. Clubs: Tavern, Harvard (Boston); Lotos (New York). Composer: Concerto for Double Bass and Orchestra; many pieces for double bass and piano; transcriptions from classical works. Home: "Seranak," Lenox, Mass. Died June 4, 1951; buried "Church on the Hill," Lenox, Mass.

KOVACS, Richard (Ignatius) (kō'văch), physician; b. Nagybecskerek, Hungary (now Jugoslavia), May 5, 1884; s. Ignatius Marton and Irene (Korn) K.; student Kaiser Wilhelm U., Berlin, Germany, 1903-04; M.D., Royal Hungarian U., Budapest, 1901-03, 1904-06; m. Ina Claire Nickel, June 6, 1922. Came to U.S., 1909, naturalized, 1915. Interne, St. Rockus (City) Hosp., Budapest, 1907, 1st Mil. Hosp., Vienna, 1907; ship's surgeon Cunard Line, 1906 and 1909; clin. training U. of Vienna, 1907 and 1909; ship's surgeon Hamburg Am. Line, 1908; clin. asst. outpatient dept. Lenox Hill Hosp., New York, 1910-23, also Presbyn. Hosp., 1912-16; gen. practice of medicine, N.Y. City, 1910-20; phys. therapist Reconstruction Hosp., N.Y. City, 1920-29; adjunct prof. phys. medicine Polyclinic Med. Sch. and Hosp., N.Y. City, 1926-30, clin. prof., 1930-40, prof., 1940; attending phys. therapist Manhattan State Hosp. since 1929, Harlem Valley State Hosp., 1932, Dept. of Correction Hosp., 1938, Columbus Hosp., 1943; consultant Mary Immaculate Hosp., Jamaica, L.I., St. Charles Hosp., Pt. Jeffers, L.I., Alexian Bros. Hosp., Elizabeth, N.J., also Vets. Adminstrn., Branch No. 2, N.Y., surgeon gen. of the Army; U.S. del. to 5th Internat. Congress on Phys. Medicine, London, 1936; sec. Am. com. 5th and 7th Internat. Congress on Indsl. Accidents and Occupational Diseases. Vice chmn. Yorkville Dist. Charity Orgn. Soc., 1928-29. Examining physician Selective Service, World War I; instr. mil. postgrad. med. courses, World War II. Diplomate Am. Bd. Physical Medicine. Mem. Lenox Hill Neighborhood Assn., Hungarian Relief Soc. of N.Y. (dir.), Soc. Med. Jurisprudence (treas.), A.M.A. (consultant, council on phys. medicine), N.Y. Co. and N.Y. State Med. Soc., N.Y. Acad. Medicine (consultant, phys. medicine), Am. Therapeutic Soc., Am. Congress Phys. Medicine (sec., received Golden Key Award, 1948), N.Y. Soc. Phys. Medicine (past pres., treas.), Royal Soc. Medicine of London. Republican. Roman Catholic. Clubs: Internat. Med. of N.Y. (pres.), Liederkranz of N.Y. (trustee), Catholic of N.Y. Author: Electrotherapy and Light Therapy (Lea & Febiger, 1st edit. 1932, 6th revised edit. 1949), Manual of Physical Therapy (Lea & Febiger, 1935, 4th rev. edit. 1949); Nature—M.D. (Appleton-Century, 1934). Editor: Year Book of Physical Medicine, 1938-47; mem. editorial bd. Archives of Physical Medicine. Contbr. of numerous articles on phys. medicine. Home: 1150 Fifth Av. Office: 2 E. 88th St., N.Y. City 28. Died Dec. 29, 1950; buried Woodlawn Cemetery, N.Y.

KRACKE, Frederick J. H., asst. commr. agr. of N.Y.; b. N.Y.C., July 11, 1868; ed. at collegiate high school; in produce business with father in Washington market until 1896; since then asst. State commr. of agr. for dist. embracing the counties of N.Y., Kings, Queens, Suffolk and Richmond, and half of Westchester County N.Y. Mem. Rep. State Com.; pres. Tayntor Construction Co. Residence: 11 Kenmore Pl., Bklyn. Died Dec. 1952.

KRACKE, Roy Rachford, coll. dean; b. Hartselle, Ala., Dec. 5, 1897; s. Henry August and Carrie Camilla (Puryear) K.; student Ala. Poly. Inst., 1913-14; B.S., U. Ala., 1924; M.D., U. Chgo., 1927; m. Virginia Carolyn Minter, Oct. 17, 1925; children—Roy Rachford, Rachel Rebecca, Henry Minter, William Gunter, Robert Russel, Virginia Carolyn. Instr. in pathology U. Ala., 1925-26; successively instr. in pathology, asst. prof., asso. prof. and prof. of pathology, bacteriology and lab. medicine Emory U., 1926-44; pathologist Emory U. Hosp., 1930-44; now dean and prof. medicine (hematology), U. Ala. Sch. Medicine. Served with Hosp. Corps, USN, 1917-21; lt. (j.g.) M.C., USN, 1927-28; lt. M.C., USNR, 1928-38. Recipient certificate of merit by A.M.A. for med. research, 1934; gold medal by Am. Soc. Clin. Pathologists, 1935. Mem. Am. Bd. Pathology, A.M.A. (chmn. sect. of pathology 1938), So. Med. Assn. (chmn. sect. of pathology 1940), Med. Assn. of Ala., Jefferson County Med. Soc. of Ala., Am. Soc. Clin. Pathologists (past pres.), Sigma Xi, Phi Beta Pi, Phi Beta Kappa, Alpha Omega Alpha. Democrat. Presbyn. Club: Rotary. Author: Diseases of the Blood and Atlas of Hematology, 1937, 2d edit., 1941. Editor: Textbook of Clinical Pathology, 1938, 2d edit., 1940; Laboratory Manual of Bacteriology, 4th edit., 1941; Color Atlas of Hematology, 1947. Contbr. articles to med. jours. Address: Medical College of Alabama, 620 S. 20th St., Birmingham, Ala. Died June 27, 1950; buried Oak Hill Cemetery, Birmingham.

KRAEMER, Casper John, Jr. (krăm'ĕr), prof. classics; b. Union Hill, N.J., May 10, 1895; s. Casper J and Katharine Louise (Muendell) K.; A.B., N.Y.U., 1917, A.M., 1918, Ph.D., 1922; m. Ruth Isabelle Kuhlmann, June 10, 1920. Ogden Butler classical fellow N.Y. U., 1917-18, instr. English, 1918-19, Latin, 1919-22; asst. ancient history, Cornell U., 1922-23; instr. classics, N.Y. U., 1923-24, asst. prof. classics, 1924-27, asso. prof., 1927-30, prof., 1930—, chmn. dept., 1930-48; exchange prof. classics, U. Cal., Los Angeles, 1940; prof. classics, Columbia, summer 1932, spring 1934, U. Pa., summer 1935; dir. Colt Archeol. Inst. Fellow Am. Geog. Soc.; mem. Am. Numismatic Soc., Am. Philol. Assn., Archaeol. Inst. Am., Classical Assn. Atlantic States, N.Y. Classical Club, Andiron Club, Phi Beta Kappa. Author: Greek Papyri in the Library of Cornell Univ. (with W. L. Westermann), 1926; Complete Works of Horace, 1936; Early Fourth Century Hoard from Egypt (with T. Miles), 1952. Co-editor (with W. F. Albright) Scientific Publications of the American Foundation for the Study of Man. Editor Prentice Hall Classical Series. Excavations at Nessana, Volume III, 1958. Contbr. to ednl. and learned periodicals. Appearing on N.Y. U. telecasts WCBS-TV. Home: 14 Washington Pl., N.Y.C. Died Nov. 5, 1958.

KRAFFT, Walter A., business exec.; b. Meriden, Conn., July 14, 1889; s. Adalbert and Mary (Brown) K.; Grad. and Registered Pharmacist, Northwestern U., 1910; postgrad. Lake Forest (Ill.) Coll., 1914; m. Julia Clark Steven, June 25, 1939; 1 dau., Virginia S. Gen. mgr. and pres. Buck & Rayner Drug Stores, Chicago, 1912-1928; pres. Emporium World Millinery Co., Chicago, since 1929; dir. Aldens, Inc., Diana Stores Corp. Pres. Cancer Research Found., U. of Chgo. Mem. Citizens bd. U. of Chgo. since 1947. Lutheran. Clubs: Ill. Athletic, Chicago Athletic Assn., Rotary (past v.p.) (Chicago); Oak Park Country; Four Seasons (Pembine, Wis.); Fin 'n Feather (Dundee, Ill.). Home: 199 Lake Shore Dr., Chgo. 11. Office: 36 S. State St., Chgo. Died Jan. 6, 1959; buried Rosehill Cemetery.

KRAFT, James Lewis; b. Stevensville, Ont., Can., Dec. 11, 1874; s. George Franklin and Minerva (Tripp) K.; ed. common schs.; m. Pauline Elizabeth Platt, June 2, 1909; 1 dau., Edith Lucile. Came to U.S., 1903, naturalized citizen, 1911. Settled in Chicago, 1905, and became identified with cheese business; organized corporation, 1909; now chmn. bd. Kraft Foods Corp., Chgo. (became div. Nt. Dairy Products Corp.), v.p., dir. Invented pasteurizing process as applied to cheese industry. Trustee Baptist Theol. Sem., Chgo. Recipient of Horatio Alger award. Republican. Baptist. Clubs: Mid-Day, Lake Shore Athletic. Home: 1426 Chicago Av., Evanston, Ill. Office: 500 Peshtigo Court, Chgo. Died Feb. 16, 1953; buried Meml. Park Cemetery, Evanston, Ill.

KRAMER, Hans (krâ'mêr), cons. engr.; b. Magdeburg, Germany, Dec. 12, 1894; s. Adolf and Toni Kramer; came to U.S., 1902, naturalized, 1913; student U. Mich., 1912-13; B.S., U.S. Mil. Acad., 1918; grad. Engr. Sch., 1927, 1929; M.S., U. Pa., 1928; D.Eng., Tech. U. of Dresden, Germany, 1932; m. Alice Elizabeth Harvey, May 20, 1939; 1 son, Hans Harvey. Commd. 2d lt. C.E., U.S. Army, 1918, advanced through grades to brig. gen., 1942, ret. from service, 1945; now in practice as cons. engr. Recipient Freeman Travelling Scholarship, Am. Soc. C.E., 1930-31. Mem. Soc. Am. Mil. Engrs., Am. Soc. C.E., Permanent Internat. Assn. Nav. Congresses, Am. Geophys. Union, Am. Inst. Cons. Engr., Internat. Assn. Hydraulic Structures Research, Tau Beta Pi. Rep. of U.S. on Ark. River Compact between Colo. and Kans.; mem. bd. of cons. engrs. for the Panama Canal. Author: Modellgeschiebe und Schleppkraft, 1932. Address: 462 Nevada Av., San Mateo, Cal. Died Feb. 16, 1957; buried Golden Gate Nat. Cemetery, San Bruno, Cal.

KRAMER, Raymond Charles, corp. exec.; b. Phila., Pa., May 25, 1901; s. Dominick and Margaret K.; A.B., Pa. State Coll., 1922; m. Mildred Heyner, Oct. 10, 1933. Chmn. bd. Belding Heminway Co., Interstate Department Stores; director Allied Stores Corp.; mem. bd. dirs. Gimbel Bros., The Barden Corporation. Overseas in U.S. Army 1942-45. Awarded D.S.M., Legion of Merit. Chmn. Internat. Refugee Orgn., Mdse. Adv. Com. Mem. Am. Australian Soc. (dir.), Japan Soc. (v.p., dir.). Home: 32 E. 74th St. Office: 119 W. 40th St., N.Y.C. Died Jan. 24, 1957.

KRAMER, Rudolph Jesse, lawyer; b. Mt. Carmel, Ill., Feb. 28, 1872; s. Henry and Martha (Calverley) K.; ed. common schools and Hayward Collegiate Inst., Fairfield, Ill.; m. Mary I. Morrison, May 10, 1898; children—Corinne (Mrs. Kenneth L. McCurdy), Lucille (Mrs. John C. Roberts), Helen (Mrs. Wallace A. Thomas). Admitted to Ill. bar, 1896; now mem. Kramer, Campbell, Costello & Wiechert; apptd. dist. atty. B.&O. R.R. Co., 1904; apptd. div. counsel Southern Ry. Co., 1905; dir. First Nat. Bank of East St. Louis. Democrat. Senior counsellor Illinois State Bar Assn. Mason. Home: 601 N. 14th St. Office: First Nat. Bank Bldg., East St. Louis, Ill. Died Jan. 8, 1954.

KRAMMES, Emma Ruess (Mrs. Benaiah B. Krammes); b. Tiffin, O., Apr. 22, 1864; d. Anton J. and Caroline (Bloom) Ruess; B.S., Heidelberg Coll., 1882; m. Benaiah B. Krammes, May 22, 1884; 1 son, Russell Ruess. Pres. Woman's Missionary Soc., Tiffin Classis, Ref. Ch. in U.S., 1897-1903; pres. Woman's Missionary Union, Golden Jubilee, 1910-12; editor woman's sect. Outlook of Missions, 1910-13; pres. Woman's Missionary Soc., Ohio Synod Ref. Ch. in U.S., 1911-14; corr. sec. Woman's Missionary Soc. Gen. Synod Ref. Ch. in U.S., 1902-20, pres., 1920-26, 1st v.p., 1926-32, also trustee; rep. corr. to Interdenom. Missionary Fed. and Council, 1914-20; rep. to Conf. Foreign Missions Bds. in U.S. and Can., Fed. of Woman's Bds. Fgn. Missions in U.S. and Can., also to Council of Women for Home Missions, and Council for Home Missions; mem. Joint Com. on Indian and Negro Welfare, and Joint Com. of United Missions in Mesopotamia. Leader, tchr. mission study classes at denom. summer confs., insts. and interdenom. City Mission fedns. Mem. Pi Gamma Mu. Author of pageant, Famous Women of the Reformed Church; etc. Home: 14 Clinton Av., Tiffin, O. Died Sept. 5, 1956; buried Greenlawn Cemetery, Tiffin.

KRANZ, Leon George, university prof.; b. Columbia, Pa., Feb. 8, 1895; s. Lewis George and Margaret (Weimer) K.; grad. high sch., Coatesville, Pa., 1913; B.S., Springfield Coll., 1917; M.S., Northwestern Univ., 1932; m. Margaret Schultz, June 16, 1923; 1 dau., Greta Lee. Instr. in physical edn., Northwestern Univ., 1921-22, asst. prof., 1922-24, asso. prof., 1924-33, prof. and chmn. of dept., 1933—. Served as 2d lt. Air Service, 1917-19; flying instr. at Ft. Worth, Tex. Pres. Council Social Agencies of Evanston, 1946-47, 47-48. Mem. N.E.A., Am. Legion, Nat. Assn. Health, Phys. Edn. and Recreation (life mem.; mem. exec. com.), Mid-West Phys. Education Assn. (pres. 1947-48). Republican. Episcopalian. Mason. Clubs: Evanston (pres. 4 years), Kiwanis, University. Author: Personal Hygiene, 1932; Kinesiology Manual. Helped organize and conduct World Seminar at Olympic Games, Helsinki, Finland, 1952. Home: 2010 Orrington Av., Evanston, Ill. Died Sept. 29, 1956.

KRASCHEL, Nelson George (krăsh'ĕl), ex-gov. Ia.; b. Macon, Ill., Oct. 27, 1889; s. Fred K. and Nancy Jane (Poe) K.; m. Agnes Johnson, Apr. 2, 1913; children—Frederick, Dick (killed in service), James (killed in service). Live stock auctioneer, 1910-30; has conducted live stock sales in 22 states and Can., selling more than $50,000,000 worth of agrl. property; served as lt. gov. of Ia., 1933-37; elected gov. of Ia. for term 1937-38; gen. agt. Farm Credit Adminstrn., Omaha, Neb., 1943-49. Democrat. Methodist. Mason. Clubs: Des Moines; Omaha (Neb.) Athletic. Home: Harlan, Ia. Died Mar. 15, 1957; buried Harlan.

KRASS, Nathan, rabbi; b. Odessa, Russia; s. Paul and Rebecca (Lempart) K.; B.L., U. Cin.; B.H.L., Hebrew Union Coll., Cin., 1899, rabbi, 1903; post-grad. Harvard, U. Chgo.; Litt.D., Owensboro, (Ky.) Coll., 1909; D.D., Hebrew Union Coll., Cin., 1943; DD., Jewish Inst. of Religion, N.Y.C., 1946; m. Eda Keller, June 21, 1906; children—Mrs. Edward Popper, Mrs. Arnold Loewenheim. Pastorates, Donaldsville, La., 1899. Muncie, Ind., 1900-03, Owensboro, Ky., 1903-07, Lafayette, Ind., 1907-08, Rochester, N.Y. 1908-10. Temple Israel, Bklyn., 1910-18, Central Synagogue, N.Y.C., 1918-23; became rabbi Temple Emanu-El, N.Y.C., 1923, now rabbi emeritus. Prof. homiletics Jewish Inst. of Religion, N.Y.C.; lectr. for Pond Lyceum Bureau, Chautauqua, Bklyn. Inst. Arts and Sciences, also before colleges and societies on religious, ednl. and civic themes. Chmn. ednl. bd. Hebrew Ednl. Soc., Bklyn.; dir. Juvenile Probation Assn.; founder and head of Brownsville Forum. Mem. Central Conf. Am. Rabbis, Jewish Hist. Soc., N.Y. City Liberal Ministers' Assn. Toured U.S. in behalf Liberty bond sale, 1917-18; toured country as only rabbi among group of 100 in behalf of the Hebrew Union Coll., 1920; traveled in France, Austria, Roumania, Bessarabia, Bukovina, Poland, Russia, 1919-21; studied pogrom and food problems as spl. del. and exec. mem. Joint Distbn. Com.; exec. mem. Am. Jewish Relief Com. Toured U.S. on behalf Jefferson Meml. Fund, 1923. Dep. mem. adminstrv. com. Jewish Agency for Palestine, 1930-—. Mem. Soc. Am. Magicians, Jewish Publ. Soc. Am. (bd. mem.). Club: City Athletic. Home: 30 E. 71st St., N.Y.C. Died Nov. 22, 1949.

KRAYBILL, Henry Reist, biochemist; b. Mount Joy, Pa., May 1, 1891; s. Samuel Snyder and Mary Garber (Reist) K.; B.S., Pa. State Coll., 1913; M.S., U. of Chicago, 1915, Ph.D., 1917; m. Ruth Grove, June 9, 1916; children—Henry Lawrence, Richard Reist, Robert Grove (killed in action serving in South Pacific area), Donald Philip. Assistant chemist Pa. State Coll. Agrl. Expt. Sta., 1913-15; instr. in agrl. chemistry, Pa. State Coll., 1915-17; teaching fellow, U. of Chicago, 1916-17; asst. physiologist U.S. Dept. Agr., 1917-19; prof. agrl. chemistry and head of dept., Univ. of N.H., 1919-24; also state chemist, N.H., 1919-24; biochemist, Boyce Thompson Inst. for Plant Research, 1924-26; prof. agrl. chemistry, Purdue, 1926-43 and head of dept. of agrl. chemistry, 1934-43; also state chemist and seed commr. of Indiana, 1926-43. Scientific adviser to Frasch Foundn. Research in Agrl. Chemistry, 1939-47; dir. research and edn. Am. Meat Inst. Found., 1947-55, vice president and director research and education, 1955-—, also director dept. scientific research, 1941-—; professorial lectr. dept. of biochem., U. of Chgo., since 1941; cons. E.C.A. Mission to Greece, 1949. Fellow A.A.A.S., Am. Inst. Chemists; mem. Am. Inst. of Nutrition, Am. Chem. Soc. (div. of agr. and food chemistry 1934-35, chmn, 1936-38), Bot. Soc. America, Am. Soc. Plant Physiologists (sec.-treas. 1928-29; pres. 1930; v.p. 1933), Am. Soc. Hort. Science, Assn. Official Agrl. Chemists (vice-pres. 1937; pres. 1938), Am. Assn. Feed Control Officials (pres. 1932), Institute of Food Technologists, American Association Cereal Chemists, American Oil Chemists Society, American Society of Biological Chemists, Ill., Ind. acads. sci., Am. Assn. U. Profs., Am. Dietetics Assn., Am. Pub. Health Assn., Am. Soc. Animal Prodn., Am. Soc. Naturalists, Am. Soybean Assn., Assn. Food and Drug Ofcls., Fed. Am. Soc. Exptl. Biology, Nat. Assn. Commrs. Agr., Nat. Farm Chemurgic Council, Nat. Research Council, Soc. Chem. Industry, Soc. Exptl. Biology and Medicine, Alpha Zeta, Sigma Xi, Phi Kappa Phi, Alpha Chi Sigma, Phi Lambda Upsilon, Phi Tau Sigma, Gamma Sigma Delta. Baptist. Mason. Clubs: Quadrangle, Chaos, Chicago Chemists. Contbr. on agrl. biochemistry. Home: 5720 Woodlawn Av. Address: Am. Meat Inst. Found., U. Chgo., Chgo. Died Sept. 30, 1956; buried Mt. Joy (Pa.) Cemetery.

KREBS, William Samuel, prof. accounting; b. Albert Lea, Minn., Nov. 28, 1889; s. William Samuel and Adelaide Adele (Simms) K.; A.B., U. of Ill., 1913; A.M., U. of Wis., 1914; grad. student, Yale, 1914-16; m. Margaret Bowen, Aug. 24, 1916; 1 son, William Samuel. Merchandise accountant, Marshall Field & Co., Chicago, 1908-09; foreign exchange accountant, Guaranty Trust Co., New York, 1917; asst. prof. of economics, U. of Me., 1916-17, U. of Mich., 1917-18; asso.-prof. of accounting, Washington U., 1918-19, prof., 1919-—; visiting prof., summers, U. of Mich., 1918, U. of Minn., 1919, U. of Chicago, 1921-28, U. of Calif., 1922; dir. Teachers Nat. Loan Assn., 1925-40; official cons. accountant City of St. Louis. Recipient Alpha Kappa Psi National award, 1956. Nathaniel Currier fellow, Yale, 1914-16. Mem. Am. Accounting Assn. (v.p. 1924-26; pres. 1927), Am. Assn. Univ. Profs., Artus, Beta Gamma Sigma, Alpha Kappa Psi, Pi Gamma Mu. Author: Outlines of Accounting, Vol. 1, 1923, Vol. 2, 1927; Accounting Laboratory Manual, 1924; Types of Utility Rate Bases, 1945. Mem. staff The Accountants Handbook. Contbr. to prof. jours. Home: 7340 Forsythe Blvd. Office: Washington University, St. Louis 5. Died Jan. 3, 1958; buried Lebanon Cemetery, St. Louis.

KREGER, Edward Albert (krē'gẽr), army officer, lawyer; b. nr. Keota, Ia., May 31, 1868; s. William and Johanna H. K.; B.Sc., Iowa State College, 1890; studied law, State University of Iowa, and Iowa Coll. of Law, Drake U.; graduate of U.S. Inf. and Cav. Sch., 1905; grad. U.S. Army Staff Coll., 1906; m. Laura Mae Roddis, 1891; 1 dau., Vera Mae (wife of Colonel J. Huntington Hills, U.S. Army). High school prin., 1891-93; supt. schools, Cherokee, Ia., 1894-96; admitted to bar of Ia., Jan. 1897; D.C., 1930; Hawaii, 1932; U.S. Supreme Court, 1912. Began practice of law at Cherokee. Cadet, private through grades to major, Ia. State Coll. Cadet Corps, 1887-90; capt. and maj., Iowa N.G., 1893-98; capt. 52d Ia. Vol. Inf., Apr.-Oct. 1898; 1st lt. and capt. 39th U.S. Vol. Inf., 1899-1901; commd. 1st lt. inf., U.S. Army, Feb. 2, 1901; promoted through grades to col., June 4, 1920; brig. gen. (temp.), Feb. 1918-June 1920; apptd. maj. gen., judge adv. gen., U.S. Army, Nov. 16, 1928; retired from active mil. service Feb. 28, 1931. Served with 39th Inf. in Luzon, Philippine Islands, 1899-1901; with 28th Inf. in Luzon and Mindanao, 1901-04; instr. law, U.S. Army Staff Coll., 1906-08; asst. supervisor, Dept. of State and Justice, and chief Bureau of Elections, Provisional Govt. of Cuba, 1907-09; judge advocate, Dept. of Colo., 1909-11; assistant in judge advocate general's office, War Department, 1911-14; professor law, U.S. Military Academy, 1914-17; assistant provost marshal gen. of U.S., May 1917-Feb. 1918; acting judge advocate gen. for A.E. F. in Europe, Mar. 1918-Mar. 1919; acting judge advocate gen., U.S. Army, Mar. 1919-Oct. 1921; asst. judge advocate gen., U.S. Army, 1921-24; judge advocate 3rd Corps Area, 1924-25; legal adviser, Am. Delegation, Plebiscitary Commn., Tacna-Arica Arbitration. S. America, 1925-27; judge advocate 2d Corps Area, 1927-28; judge advocate gen., U.S. Army, 1928-31. Drafted the Electoral Law of Cuba, 1908. Compiled Cases on Martial Law, 1910; supervised preparation of Manual for Courts-Martial, U.S. Army, 1920, and Military Laws of the United States, Annotated, 1921. Contbr. to National Encyclopedia, 1932. Decorated D.S.C. "for extraordinary heroism" in action nr. Bay, Laguna, P.I., Mar. 10, 1900; D.S.M. "for exceptionally meritorious and distinguished services" as acting judge advocate gen., A.E.F., World War. Mem. Am. Bar Assn., Fed. Bar Assn., Am. Mil. Inst., State Hist. Soc. of Ia., Am. Soc. Internat. Law. Presbyterian. Clubs: Army and Navy, Congressional Country (Washington, D.C.). Address: 405 Geneseo Rd., San Antonio. Died May 24, 1955; buried Fort Sam Houston Nat. Cemetery, San Antonio.

KREHBIEL, Edward (Benjamin), b. Summerfield, Ill., Nov. 16, 1878; s. Christian and Susanna (Ruth) K.; A.B., U. Kan., 1902; studied at Harvard, and École des Chartes, Paris; Ph.D., U. Chgo., 1906; m. Mary L. Billings, Apr. 14, 1905; children—Christine, Martha, Susannah Ruth. Asso. and instr. U. Chgo., 1906-09; asso. prof. European history, 1909-12, prof., 1912-21, Stanford; prof. same, Columbia U. Summer Sch., 1911-12, 1914-16, at Summer School U. So. Cal., 1917, 19; research work at Washington, 1915-16. Investigator with "The Inquiry," 1917-18; dir. speakers' bur., and historian, U.S. Food Adminstrn. for Cal., 1918; publicity mgr., 1919-21, mdse. mgr., 1921-25, Weinstock, Lubin & Co., Sacramento, Cal.; N.Y. mdse. mgr. of J. L. Hudson Co., Detroit, 1925-26; retail stores mgr. Gorham Co., N.Y., 1926-29; gen. mgr., treas. Gorham, Inc., 1929-48, retired. Chmn. Retail Jewelers Code Com., 1933-34. Dir. Nat. Better Business Bur.; mem. Phi Beta Kappa (Kansas 1902, Chgo., 1906), Phi Gamma Delta. Clubs: Blind Brook, New York Sales Managers Club, Century Association, 24 Carat Club of New York (pres. 1941). Author: The Interdict, 1909; Syllabus of Lectures on International Conciliation (with David Starr Jordan), 1912; Nationalism, War and Society, 1916; Geographic Influences in British Elections, 1916. Translator of Luchaire's Social France at the Time of Philip Augustus, 1912. Home: 33 Main St., Ridgefield, Conn. Died June 15, 1950.

KREIDER, Charles Daniel (krī'dẽr), educator, editor; b. Lancaster, Pa., Dec. 29, 1867; s. William Eugene and Mary Josephine (Demuth) K.; A.B., Moravian Coll. and Theol. Sem., Bethlehem, Pa., 1892; m. Emily Augusta Hammer, June 29, 1898 (dec.); children—Alice Hammer (dec.), Josephine Hammer, Albert Hammer (dec.). Instr. Nazareth Hall, 1890-96, instr. Moravian Coll., Moravian Sem. and Coll. for Women, Bethlehem, 1896-97; asst. prin. Linden Hall Sem., 1897-98, prin., 1898-1912, also treas.; pastor Schoeneck Moravian Congregation, Nazareth, 1912-14; editor The Moravian, ofcl. organ, 1913-38; vice prin. Nazareth Hall, 1914-18; exec. sec. Denominational U.S. Service (war) Commn., 1918-20; pastor V. Moravian Congregation, Phila., 1918-20; rec. sec. Provincial Elders' Conf. (governing bd. Moravian Ch. Am., No. Province), 1922-41; sec. Soc. for Propagating the Gospel (oldest inc. missionary soc. in U.S.), 1922-41, also editor annual vol. of Proceedings; sec. Synod and editor jour., Eastern Dist., No. Province, Moravian Ch., Am. 1924; sec. Synod and editor jour., No. Province (U.S. and Can.), 1925, 30; editor The Moravian Missionary (monthly), 1926-40, bus. mgr., 1938-40; sec. bd. Moravian Coll. and Theol. Sem., 1926-41. Deacon, 1898, presbyter, 1908, Moravian Ch. Republican. Sec.-treas. Moravian Ednl. Assn., 1911-18; pres. local Dickens Fellowship, 1914-18. Author papers and contbns. on ednl. and hist. subjects. Pub. U.S. Service edit., 187th ann. vol. Moravian Daily Texts. Home: Nazareth, Pa. Died June 26, 1953.

KRESEL, Isidor Jacob, lawyer; b. Austria, Nov. 17, 1878; s. Sydney and Rebecca (Rice) K.; came to U.S., 1890; grad. Horace Mann High Sch., N.Y.C., 1897; LL.B., Columbia, 1900; m. Edna G. Herbst, June 6, 1904. Practiced at N.Y.C., 1900-—; asst. dist. atty. New York County, 1902-10; counsel of legislative com. investigating ins. complaints, 1911-12; counsel to bd. of N.Y. Assembly in impeachment of Gov. William Sulzer, 1913; spl. asst. to atty. gen. of U.S. in charge of proceedings against the packers, 1919-21; counsel to Chem. Foundation in suit of U.S. against it to recover the German dye and chem. patents, 1922-23; sr. mem. Kresel & Meyerson; chief counsel Seabury Investigation; head of ambulance chasing investigation. Home: 299 Park Av. Office: 15 Broad St. Died July 9, 1957.

KRESS, C(hristian) Adam, clergyman; b. N.Y. C., Oct. 20, 1879; s. Casper and Elise (Meyer) K.; grad. A.M. Chesbrough Sem. (now Roberts Wesleyan Coll.), North Chili, N.Y., 1900; student Temple U., 1908-09, Bibl. Sem., N.Y.C., 1917, Drew Theol. Sem., 1922-23; Ph.B., Kansas City U., 1911; Th.B., Eastern Bapt. Theol. Sem., 1927, B.D., 1928; m. Jessie Laura Thompson, June 16, 1903; children—Mildred Pauline (Mrs. Orland M. Conklin), Miriam Ruth (Mrs. George W. Crump). Ordained to Free Meth. Ministry, 1906; pastor in Alexandria, Va., Phila., Allentown, Newark, Bklyn.; dist. supt. Wilkes Barre Dist., 1912-16, N.Y. and Windsor dists., 1933-37, N.Y. and New England districts, 1940-44, Wilkes Barre Dist., 1944-48; instr. Latin and homiletics, Chesbrough Sem., 1918-19. Sec. N.Y. Annual Conf. of Free Meth. Ch. of N.A., 1912-19, 26-47; pres. Bd. of Examiners Conf., a course of study for ministerial candidates, 1939-—; mem. Gen. Conf. com. on revision of ministerial course of study, chmn., 1943; mem. Commn. on Christian Edn., 1943-47; sec. gen. Conf., also Bd. of Adminstrn., 1947-1951; mem. editorial com. Free Meth. Discipline; mem. adv. council Am. Bible Soc., 1935-—; chmn. Interdenominational Holiness Assn. Bklyn., 1942-—. Mem. Prohibition Party. Home: 73 Park St., Palmer, Died Aug. 3, 1955.

KRESS, George Henry, M.D.; b. Cincinnati, O., Dec. 23, 1874; s. Henry and Selma (Kern) K.; B.S., U. of Cincinnati, 1896; M.D., Med. Coll. of Ohio (U. of Cincinnati), 1899; post-grad. work Phila., Berlin, London and Vienna; m. Elizabeth Hamilton Hill, June 16, 1903. Asst. surgeon Nat. Soldiers' Hosp., Dayton, O., 1900-03; removed to Los Angeles, 1903; formerly specialized in diseases of eye, ear, nose and throat; dean Los Angeles Med. Dept. U. of Calif., 1914-38; was chief staff Graves Memorial Dispensary, and eye clinician; chief of the eye staff, Los Angeles County Hosp., 1910-38; was sec. faculty and prof. hygiene, University of Southern Calif. Coll. Medicine; emeritus prof. ophthalmology, Coll. of Med. Evangelists; sr. surgeon, U. of Southern Calif., S.A. T.C., World War I; ex-chmn. Los Angeles County Health Department Board; was member of Calif. State Bd. of Health; was chmn. Eye and Ear Com., Los Angeles City Schs.; was mem. Exec. Med. Group, Major Disaster Council, City of Los Angeles. Ex-president Calif. State Commn. to Investigate Tuberculosis of Calif. and Los Angeles tuberculosis assns., Los Angeles Acad. Ophthalmology and Oto-laryngology. Fellow Am. Coll. Surgeons, A.M.A. (past v.p.); mem. Los Angeles County Med. Assn. (past pres., past sec.-treas.), Calif. Med. Assn. (sec.-treas.; past pres.), Am. Acad. Ophthalmology and Otology, Pacific Coast Eye and Ear Soc., So. Calif. Hist. Soc., Calif. Hist. Soc., Sigma Alpha Epsilon (past honorary president), Phi Rho Sigma. Mason (32°). Clubs: The Family (San Francisco), Scribes (Los Angeles); Authors (Hollywood, California). Author: Historical Manual of Sigma Alpha Epsilon Fraternity, 1903; A History of the Medical Profession of Southern California, 1910. Editor Calif. and Western Medicine, 1927-1946. Historian, Calif. Med. Assn.; sec'y, Med. Soc. State of Calif. Editor Jour. of Phi Rho Sigma. Home: 131 South Rampart Blvd., Los Angeles 4. Died Jan. 18, 1954; buried Forest Lawn, Los Angeles.

KRESS, Samuel Henry, merchant; b. Cherryville, Pa., 1863; s. John Franklin and Margaret Dodson (Connor) K.; ed. high sch.; unmarried. Began as schoolteacher then entered retail mercantile bus., Nanticoke, Pa., 1887, wholesale stationery business, Wilkes-Barre, Pa., 1890, these dveeloped into the present S. H. Kress & Co., 5, 10 and 25c stores, now 264 stores in 29 states; chmn. S. H. Kress & Company. President Samuel H. Kress Foundation; trustee Metropolitan Museum of Art (New York), National Gallery of Art (Washington), Georgia Warm Springs Foundation. Member Military Order Loyal Legion of U.S., S.R., S.A.R. Republican. Lutheran.

Mason. Over a period of years acquired a collection of paintings and sculpture, particularly of the Italian school. This collection, practically intact, was presented as a gift to the National Gallery of Art, also paintings and sculptures presented to various museums, galleries and instns. Address: 1020 Fifth Avenue, N.Y.C. 28. Died Sept. 22, 1955; buried Woodlawn Cemetery, N.Y.

KRETSCHMER, Herman Louis (krĕtsh'mẽr), urologist; b. Chicago, Apr. 22, 1879; s. Benjamin H. and Louise (Schaefer) K.; M.D., M.C.L., Northwestern U. Medical Sch., 1904; hon. D.Sc., Marquette Univ., 1943; Ph.G., Northwestern Univ., 1900; hon. D.Sc., Northwestern, 1944; m. Lucy Barnett, Nov. 17, 1910 (died April 26, 1942); m. 2d Marion Ellen Hicks, Mar. 3, 1946. Practiced in Chicago since 1904; urologist Presbyn. Hosp.; consulting urologist Children's Memorial Hosp.; clin. prof. surgery (genito-urinary) Rush Med. Coll. (U. of Ill., formerly U. of Chicago). Ex-pres. Am. Bd. of Urology, Inc. Mem. Am. Med. Assn. (formerly treas. and chmn., sec. section on urology; pres. 1943-45); Interstate Post-grad. Assn. of North Am. (pres. elect); Editorial Bd. Am. Jour. of Urology (chmn.); Bd. of Honorary Consultants to Army Med. Library; Am. Bd. of Urology (ex-pres.). Mem. bd. trustees, Inst. of Medicine, former pres. bd. trustees Harris Schs. Fellow Am. Coll. Surgs.; mem. Chicago Med. Soc. (ex-pres.), Chicago Urol. Soc. (ex-pres.), Am. Urol. Assn. (ex-pres.), Am. Assn. Genito-Urinary Surgeons (ex-pres.), Clin. Soc., Genito-Urinary Surgeons (ex-pres.); International Urol. Assn., Western Surg. Assn.; mem. (hon.) Miss. Valley Med. Soc. Mem. Interstate Postgrad. Med. Assn. of N. America. Corr. mem. German and Hungarian urol. socs. Pres. Internat. Post Grad. Med. Assembly. Clubs: Athletic, University, Billings, Chicago (Chicago); Klinger Lake Country (Sturgis, Mich.). Contbr. on genito-urinary surgery. Mem. editorial bd. Jour. of Urology. Home: 200 E. Pearson St. Office: 122 S. Michigan Blvd., Chicago. Died Sept. 23, 1951; buried Rosehill Cemetery, Chicago.

KRIBBEN, Earl, dept. store exec.; b. St. Louis, July 2, 1903; s. Bertram Delafield and Mary (Kellogg) K.; B.S., U. Minn., 1924; m. Eleanor Cushman Kimball, June 20, 1940; children—Arthur Kellogg, Delafield. Stockroom clk., later asst. buyer, sec. to chmn. and pres. Marshall Field & Co., Chicago, 1925-32, sec.-treas. 1938-46, treas. 1946-52, asst. to the pres., 1952-53, v.p., 1954-—; sec. to chairman and manager tax and ins. depts. Commonwealth Edison Co., Chicago, and Pub. Service Co. of No. Ill. and various subsidiaries, 1932-38. Served as maj. and lt. col. Ordnance Dept., Washington, 1942-45. Asst. adminstr. Surplus Property Bd., 1945; dir. Ft. Dearborn Project, Central Bus. Dist. Commn.; trustee of the Civic Federation, Orchestral Association of Chicago, Taxpayers Fedn. Ill., Met. Housing and Planning Council, S. Side Planning Bd.; pres. and trustee Sprague Meml. Inst. Mem. Chicago Association Commerce and Industry (director), Delta Upsilon. Clubs: Chicago, Commonwealth, Tavern, Onwentsia, Casino, Commercial (Chgo.). Home: 1320 N. State Pkwy., Chgo. 10; (summer; R.D. 1, Mundelein, Ill. Office: 25 E. Washington St., Chgo. 2. Died May 31, 1959; buried Lake Forest, Ill.

KRICK, Edwin Vernon, banker; born Wabasha, Minn., Nov. 10, 1881; s. William H. P. and Carrie E. (Wyatt) K.; student high schs. and spl. courses; m. Sarah C. Adams, Aug. 12, 1906. Teller Mechanics Savs. Bank, San Francisco, 1906-12; teller, Savs. Union Bank & Trust Co., San Francisco, 1912-17; name changed to Am. Trust Co., 1927; asst. cashier, 1917-23, asst. v.p., 1923-25, cashier and treas., 1925-26, v.p., cashier and treasurer, 1926-44, sr. v.p., cashier and treas., 1945-49, sr. v.p. and treas. since 1950. Mem. San Francisco Ladies Protective and Relief Soc. Mem. Am. Inst. Banking (pres. San Francisco chpt., 1918, nat. orgn., 1924), Calif. Bankers Assn. (pres. 1938-39), Am. Bankers Assn., San Francisco Tuberculosis Assn. (dir.), Community Chest (council mem.). Mason. Clubs: Commercial, Commonwealth, Presidio, Bohemian. Home: 145 Laurel St., San Francisco 18. Office: 464 California St., S.F. 20. Died May 4, 1952.

KRIDL, Manfred, literary historian, educator; b. Lwow, Poland, Oct. 11, 1882; s. Edward and Zalenska (Victoria) K.; student U. of Lwow, 1904-07, Ph.D., 1909; student U. of Fribourg, 1907-08, U. of Paris, 1908-09. Came to U.S., 1940. Asst. prof. Polish lit. U. of Warsaw, 1922-29; prof. Slavic langs. and lit. U. of Brussels, 1929-33, prof. Polish lit. and lit. theory U. Wilno, 1933-39; prof. Slavic langs. Smith Coll., 1940-48; Adam Mickiewicz prof. Polish studies Columbia, 1948-—. Awarded Professeur agréé ã l'Université Libre de Bruxelles, 1933; Commdr. de l'ordre de la Coursnne (Belgian), 1933. Mem. Warsaw Learned Soc. Arts and Soc., Modern Lang. Assn. Am. Author: Mickiewicz and Lamennais, 1909; Criticism and Critics, 1922; Mickiewicz and Slowacki, 1925; History of Polish Literature of the Nineteenth Century, 1925-31; Adam Mickiewicz et la France, 1929; Introduction to the Study of Literary Works, 1936; Literary Essays, 1939; Adam Mickiewicz, Poet of Poland, 1951; History of Polish Literature, 1945; A Survey of Polish Literature and Culture, 1956; An Anthology of Polish Literature, 1957. Home: 423 W. 120 St., N.Y.C. 27. Died Feb. 4, 1957.

KRIEBEL, William F. (krē'bl), banker; b. Montgomery Co., Pa., Mar. 16, 1890; s. Jacob A. and Emma K.; student Peirce Sch., Phila., Pa., and Temple U.; m. Mabel Burtt, 1916; children—William Burtt, Howard B., John A. Asso. with The Pennsylvania Co. for Insurance on Lives and Granting Annuities (now The First Pennsylvania Banking & Trust Co.), Phila., since starting as clk., 1911, mgr. fgn. dept., 1920-26, cashier until 1932, vice pres. and treasurer, 1932-50, sr. v.p., 1950-—, director. Member of the Association of Reserve City Bankers (director 1939-42, vice pres., 1943); v.p. and dir. Phila. C. of C.; sec. Group I of Pa. Bankers Assn.; chmn. bank operations com. of Phila. Clearing House Assn.; dir. Eastern Div. of Investment Bankers Assn. of Am., 1944-48; mem. publicity and pub. relations com. of Phila. Stock Exchange. Mem. Pa. Soc. of N.Y.; Phila. Yearly Meeting of Friends. Clubs: Aronimink Golf, Racquet of Phila. Home: Possum Hollow Rd., Moylan-Rose Valley, Pa. Office: 15th & Chestnut St., Phila. Died Sept. 30, 1956.

KROEHLER, Peter Edward, mfg. exec.; b. Mound Prairie, Minn., 1872. Chmn. bd. and dir. Kroehler Mfg. Co. Home: Riverside, Ill. Office: Naperville, Ill. Died Aug. 15, 1950.

KROOS, Oscar August, company exec.; b. Sheboygan, Wis., Dec. 24, 1880; s. Max and Emma (Limprecht) K.; student parochial and pub. schs. of Sheboygan. Accountant, Sheboygan Brick & Tile Co., 1897-98; joined Kohler (Wis.) Co., 1899, accountant, clk., 1899-1908, sec., 1909-27, sec.-treas., 1927-37, v.p., 1937-40, exec. v.p., 1940-—, dir., 1913-—; dir. Kohler Co., Ltd., London, Eng.; v.p. Mountain States Supply Co., Salt Lake City, 1940-—, dir., 1925-—; sec.-treas., dir. Kohler Found., Inc., 1940-—; v.p., dir. Sheboygan Athletic Park Holding Co., 1923-—. Pres., dir. Sheboygan Baseball Assn., 1916-—; v.p., dir. Sheboygan Kiddies Camp Found., Inc., 1947-—. Mem. State Hist. Soc. Wis. (life), Friendship House, Inc. Clubs: Sheboygan, Country, Yacht (Sheboygan, Wis.); Chicago, Traffic (Chgo.). Home: 1425 N. 12th St., Sheboygan, Wis. Office: Kohler Co., Kohler, Wis. Died Sept. 3, 1957.

KRUCKMAN, Arnold, b. at sea, Nov. 13, 1880; s. Rudolph Godlove and Anna (Muller) K.; ed. pub. and pvt. schs. and by travel; m. Margaret Merry, June 1904 (died, 1946); m. 2d, Margaret Holden Naylor, Nov. 10, 1949. Corr. Spanish-Am. War, Russo-Jap. War, World War I; served on staff St. Louis Republic and Star; co-founder International News Service; musical editor Burr-McIntosh Monthly, 1907-11; first aero. editor, staff N.Y. World, first newspaper writer so apptd. to any newspaper staff in the world; aero. expert for Hearst pubs. for 3 years; organized the cross-country flights in U.S. prior to 1914; U.S. commr. at large, San Francisco Expn., 1915, chief of aeronautics same, vis. most of the countries of the worls in the interests of the expn.; conceived, organized the plan for the first 'Round-the-World Flight; an organizer, sec.-treas. League of the Southwest (8 states), which planned and brought into being Boulder Dam; dir. gen. Pacific S.W. Expn., 1928, D. C. George Washington Bi-Centennial Commn., 1932; organized Div. of Information, Research, Reference and Library, TVA, 1933; organized Am. Newscasting Assn., pioneer news distrbg. service, for radio stas., 1934; operates Kruckman News Service; Washington corr. for Glass Digest. Fellow Am. Geog. Soc.; mem. Am. Acad. Polit. and Social Sci., White House Corr. Assn., Imperial Japanese Aero. Soc. (hon.), Nat. Conf. Bus. Paper editors. Club: Overseas Writers. Author: Pageant of Flowers; Pageant of Freedom; The Colorado River Riddle; America (pageant); The Ozarks (novel); Personalities and Landmarks (Radio sketches). Contbr. to mags. and newspapers. Adopted into Hopi clan of the Coyote, 1928. Address: Benjamin Franklin P.O. Box 226, Washington 4. Died June 30, 1959.

KRUEGER, William Conrad, brewer; b. Newark, Nov. 10, 1888; s. Gottfried and Bertha Johanna (Laible) K.; student Newark Acad., Wallerstein Inst.; m. Georgina Morrison Jewett, Aug. 15, 1940; children—Tanis, William Conrad. Pres. G. Krueger Brewing Co., Newark, since 1926, Paramount Realty Co. since 1926, Krueger Beverage Co. since 1935. Mem. N.J. Brewers Assn. (v.p. since 1935). Episcopalian. Clubs: Essex County Country (West Orange); Down Town, Orange, Lawn Tennis (Orange, N.J.). Home: Llewellyn Park, West Orange, N.J. Office: 75 Belmont Av., Newark. Deceased.

KRUGER, Frederick Konrad (krü'gẽr), author, lecturer; b. Kottbus, Germany, 1887; s. Frederick John and Elizabeth (Zippel) K.; preparatory education, Royal Friedrich Wilhelm Gymnasium, Kottbus; student U. of Berlin, 1907, 08; A.M., U. of Neb. 1908; Ph.D., U. of Tübingen, Germany, 1910; grad. study, Columbia, 1912; m. Gertrude M. Jaeggi, 1913; children—Gerhard, Helen Gertrude. Came to U.S., 1907; naturalized citizen, 1930. Fellow and lecturer, U. of Calif., 1912-15; prof. polit. science, Midland Coll., Fremont, Neb., 1915-16, U. of Omaha (Neb.), 1919-23; asso. prof. polit. science, Wittenberg Coll., Springfield, O., 1923-25, prof., 1925-43; Am. exchange prof., U. of Göttingen, Germany, 1927-28; Am. guest prof. in Berlin, winter semester, 1934-35; prof. sociology, Valparaiso (Ind.) U., since 1945. Lutheran. Author: Brannkohlenindustrie der Niederlausitz, 1911; Government and Politics of the German Empire, 1915; Editor: An Undiplomatic Diary (The Bandholtz Diary), 1933. Contbr. articles on German govt., etc., Encyclopedia Americana. Home: 4 Locust St., Valparaiso, Ind. Died June 27, 1953.

KRUSE, E. T., chmn. of bd. The San Francisco Bank. Address: 526 California St., San Francisco. Died 1947.

KUCERA, Louis Benedict (kŭch'ẽr-å), bishop; b. Wheatland, Minn., Aug. 24, 1888; s. John W. and Mary (Skulzacek) K.; student St. John's U., 1903-05; A.B., College of St. Thomas, St. Paul, 1911, LL.D., 1933; A.M., Columbia Coll., Dubuque, Ia., 1917. Litt. D., Loras College, 1948. Ordained priest Rom. Cath. Church, 1915; assistant pastor Tama, Ia., 1915-16; dean of discipline, Columbia Academy, Dubuque, Ia., 1916-25; pastor Holy Trinity Ch., Protivin, Ia., 1925-30; consecrated bishop of Lincoln, Neb., Oct. 28, 1930. Address: 514 S. 18th St., Lincoln, Neb. Died May 9, 1957; buried Calvary Cemetery, Lincoln.

KUHN, Arthur K. (kūn), lawyer; b. Phila., Pa., Nov. 11, 1876; s. Herman and Caroline (Loeb) K.; A.B., Columbia, 1895, A.M., 1896, LL.B., 1897; Ph.D., 1912; post-graduate studies, U. of Zürich, Switzerland, 1904, École de Droit, Paris, 1905; m. Joan Schoenfeld, Mar. 24, 1903; 1 son, Kenneth Caro. Began practice, N.Y. City, 1898; mem. teaching staff, law dept., Columbia, 1909-11, 1915-17; spl. lecturer U. of Zürich, 1914; auxiliary lecturer, U. of Pa. Law Sch., 1926-32; counsel League to Enforce Peace, at Peace Conf., Paris, 1919. Del. 2d and 8th Pan-Am. Scientific Congresses, Washington, D.C., 1915, 1940; con. leader, Inst. of Politics, Williamstown, Mass., 1924, 26; prof. Acad. of Internat. Law, The Hague; mem. Institut de Droit International; adviser Harvard Research in International Law. Field director Am. Red Cross during World War. Mem. Internat. Law Assn. (mem. council; pres. Am. Br. 1939-40, mem. exec. com.), Am. Society International Law (mem. exec. council, v.p.), Am. Bar Assn., Bar Assn. City of New York, New York State Bar Assn. (com. on internat. law), N.Y. County Lawyers Assn. (mem. com. on international law), Academy of Political and Social Science, Council on Foreign Relations, American Foreign Law Association (pres. 1941-43), Pan-American Society, Phi Beta Kappa. Mason: chief commissioner of appeals Grand Lodge of Masons of N.Y. Club: Lawyers of New York. Author: International Civil and Commercial Law, 1905; Comparative Study of the Law of Corporations, 1912; Gundzüge des Englisch-Amerikanischen Privat und Prozessrechts, Zürich, 1915; Principes du Droit Anglo-American, Paris, 1924; Effets de Commerce en Droit International 1926; Conception du Droit Internat. Privé aux Etats-Unis, 1929; Comparative Commentaries on Private International Law or Conflict of Laws, 1937; Pathways in International Law, 1953; author of 1st systematic discussion of aerial law pub. in the U.S., 1908. Contbr. to legal publs. Mem. bd. editors Am. Jour. Internat. Law. Home: 465 Park Av. Office: 500 Fifth Av. N.Y.C. 36. Died July 8, 1954; buried Beth-El Cemetery, Bklyn.

KUHN, Ferd William, r.r. exec.; b. Belleville, Ill., Oct. 20, 1893; s. William and Ellanora (Pflaesterer) K.; student pub. schs.; m. Elizabeth Conlin, Sept. 17, 1921; children—William, Edward, Ferd. Local office L.&N. R.R., Belleville, Ill., 1913-16; transportation office Swift & Co., Nat. Stock Yards, East St. Louis, Ill., 1916-17; traffic dept. C.,I.&L. Ry., Chgo., 1917, freight traffic agt., 1920-23, gen. agt., Pitts., 1923-29, gen. freight agt., Chgo., 1929-46, freight traffic mgr., 1946-53, v.p. charge traffic, 1953-—. Served with AEF, U.S. Army, 1917-19. Mem. Nat. Freight Traffic Assn., Am. Legion. Clubs: South Shore Country, Union League, Traffic (Chgo.); Traffic (N.Y.C.). Home: 2112 N.E. 3rd Way, Winfield Park, Boca Raton, Fla. Office: 608 S. Dearborn St., Chgo. 5. Died Feb. 21, 1957; buried St. Marys Cemetery, Chgo.

KUIZENGA, John E., clergyman, educator; b. Muskegon, Mich., Dec. 20, 1876; s. Eildert and Johanna K. (Soldaat) K.; A.B. with highest honors, Hope Coll., Holland, Mich., 1899, D.D., 1916; grad. Western Theol. Sem. of Ref. Ch. in America, Holland, 1904; Morris fellow in philosophy U. Mich., 1914-15, A.M., 1915; studied U. Chgo. Div. Sch.; m. Anna J. Mulder, 1901; 1 dau., Marion Ruth; m. 2d, Elsie Conover Foster, Mar. 2, 1944; 1 dau., Donna Elsie. Tchr. English, Northwestern Classical Acad., Orange City, Ia., 1900-03; ordained ministry Ref. Ch. in America, 1904; pastor Ref. Ch., Graafschap, Mich., 1904-06; prof. Bible and philosophy Hope Coll., 1906-15; prof. practical theology Western Theol. Sem. of Ref. Ch. in America, 1915-28, prof. systematic theology, 1928-30, also pres., 1924-30; Stuart prof. apologetics and Christian ethics Princeton Theol. Sem., 1930-41; Charles Hodge prof. systematic theology, 1941-47, prof. emeritus, 1947—; guest lectr. U. of Dubuque, Ia., 1948, Western Theol. Sem., 1948, Hope Coll., 1948-49. Delivered lectures on apologetics and religious edn. at various theol. sems.; mem. faculty Winona Summer School Theology for several years; also mem. summer confs., etc. Pres. Gen. Synod Ref. Ch. in America, 1924-25. Mem. Am. Theol. Soc. Republican. Author of series of Bible lessons for children and young people and articles in theol. jours. Editor The Leader, a Reformed Church weekly, for about ten years. Lecture Religion and Life Seminars, Presbyn. Ch. U.S.A., 1948-49. Home: 1172 Beach Dr., Holland, Mich. Died July 8, 1949.

KULAS, Elroy John, (kōōl'ăs), steel fabricator; b. Cleveland, O., Mar. 21, 1880; s. Frank and Margaret (Hoffer) K.; ed. pub. schs., Cleveland, O.; Dr. of Commercial Science, Baldwin-Wallace Coll., 1939; m. Fynette H. Hill. President, director Midland Steel Products Company; dir. Pittsburgh & W. Va. Ry. Co., Wheeling & Lake Erie R.R., N. Am. Coal Corp. Mfr. cartridge cases for Italian, French and British, later for U.S., World War I. Mason (32°). Trustee of Baldwin-Wallace College, Berea, O. Clubs: Union, Mid-Day, Mayfield Country (Cleveland). Home: Gates Mills, O. Office: The Midland Steel Products Co., P.O. Box 6386, Cleve. 1. Died May 13, 1952.

KULP, Clarence Arthur, educator; b. Chalfont, Pa., August 23, 1895; s. Jacob Slifer and Katie Wolf (Stauffer) Kulp; B.S. in economics, Wharton Sch., U. of Pa., 1917; A.M., Grad. Sch., U. of Pa., 1921, Ph.D., 1924; m. Naomi Benner Alderfer, Feb. 16, 1918; children—Robert Alderfer, Donald Alderfer. With U. of Pa., 1919—, as instr. in economics, 1919-20, instr. in insurance, 1920-24, asst. prof., 1924-28, prof. of insurance, 1928—, chmn. department of ins., 1952-55, chmn. pension research council Wharton Sch., dean Wharton School Finance and Commerce, 1955—; lecturer in econs. Columbia U., 1937-50; cons. Social Security Administration, 1937—; consultant R.R. Retirement Board, 1942—; mem. sr. research staff, Social Security Com. of Social Science Research Council, 1935-38; lecturer in economics and finance Am. Inst. of Banking, Phila., 1920-35; research asso., dept. indsl. research U. Pa., 1930-32. Mem. federal adv. council United States Dept. Labor. Chmn. Pa. Com. on Workmen's Compensation, 1933-34; mem. for Pa. on Com. on Unemployment Ins., 1931-32; tech. advisor Pa. Com. on Unemployment Reserves, 1933; statis. editor Dept. of State, Pa., 1924-26; dir. N.H. Conf. on Unemployment Compensation, 1939, Vt. Conf., 1940, Mass. Conf., 1941. With U.S. Army, 1917-19; with A.E.F. 9 mos. Mem. bd. Family Service, Phila. Trustee, v.p. Thomas S. Harrison Found. Fellow Casualty Actuarial Soc. (edn. committee; asst. editor Proc.), Am. Assn. of Univ. Teachers of Ins. (past pres.), Am. Acad. Polit. and Social Sci. (vice pres.), Beta Gamma Sigma, Delta Sigma Phi. Mem. United Presbyn. Ch. Club: Lenape (Phila.). Author: Discounting of Dividends by Stock Market, 1924; Casualty Insurance, 3d edit., 1956; Social Insurance Coordination, 1938. Editor: Social Insurance, Vol. 170, Annals of Am. Acad. Polit. & Social Science, 1933. Contbr. to professional jours. Home: 413 Netherwood Rd., Upper Darby, Pa. Died Aug. 20, 1957; buried Zion Hill, Pa.

KUMM, Einar Axel, assn. exec.; b. Enköping, Sweden, July 24, 1901; s. Axel W. and Wilhelmina (Lindborg) K.; student pub. schs. Enköping; tech. and bus. courses Uppsala and Stockholm, Sweden, 1918-24; bus. course Chicago Central Coll. Commerce, 1930; m. Ruth Nilsen, Feb. 12, 1935; 1 son, Paul Per Axel. Came to U.S., 1927, naturalized, 1943. Sales rep. Carl Lamm Co., Stockholm, 1924-25; books importer, Chicago, 1928-29; circulation mgr. and N.W. editor Svenska Tribunen-Nyheter, Chicago and Minneapolis, 1930-31; student Swedish-Am. trade, Los Angeles, 1932-34; participant in orgn. Swedish Small Mfrs. Export Coops., 1935, Am. mgr., 1936-37; founder, pres. Products-from-Sweden Inc., N.Y. City, 1938-50; pres. Products Sales Assn., Inc., import-export, N.Y. City, 1947-50; mem. Swedish C. of C. of U.S.A. since 1936, dir., 1943-50, mng. dir., sec. since 1950. Home: 83 Shoreview Rd., Manhasset, N.Y. Office: 45 Rockefeller Plaza, N.Y.C. 20. Died Mar. 3, 1952.

KUNHARDT, Kingsley, business exec.; b. N.Y. C., Jan. 11, 1897; s. Henry R. and Mabel A. (Farnham) K.; student Browning Sch., 1905-14; B.S., Columbia, 1918; m. Marion G. Gilford, June 17, 1926; children—Alethea (Mrs. Harry W. Walker, II), Zella (Mrs. H. T. Van Ingen). With Kunhardt & Co., Inc., N.Y. City, 1919-22; joined Guaranty Trust Co. of N.Y., 1922, v.p., 1933-59, ret. 1959; dir., chmn. finance com. Carpenter Steel Co.; dir., mem. exec. com., chmn. finance com. Royal McBee Co.; trustee Diocesan Investment Trust, N.Y.C. Dir. Community Council of Greater N.Y.; mem. governing body Nat. Indsl. Conf. Bd., N.Y.C.; dir. Peabody Home, Fedn. Protestant Welfare Agencies, N.Y.C. Mem. Conn. Spaniel Field Trial Assn. (dir., sec.), S.R. Republican. Episcopalian. Clubs: Round Hill (Greenwich, Conn.); Church. Home: Meads Point, Greenwich, Conn. Office: 140 Broadway, N.Y.C. 15. Died Nov. 1, 1959.

KUNIANSKY, Max, foundry exec.; b. Russia, 1899; grad. Ga. Inst. Tech., 1919. Exec. v.p., gen. mgr. Lynchburg Foundry Co. Home: 3739 Woodside Av. Office: Peoples Nat. Bank Bldg., Lynchburg, Va. Died July 21, 1953; buried Fort Hill Burial Park, Lynchburg.

KUNIYOSHI, Yasuo (kōō-nĭ-yō-shĭ), artist; b. Okayama, Japan, Sept. 1, 1893; s. Ukichi and Itoko K.; student Los Angeles Sch. of Art, 1908-10, Nat. Acad. of Design, 1912, Independent Sch. of Art, New York, 1914-16, Art Students League, 1916-20; m. Sara Mazo, July 1, 1935. Instr. Art Students League and New Sch. of Social Research. President of Artists Equity Association since 1947. Represented in Columbus (O.) Museum, Newark Museum (N.J.), Philips Memorial Gallery, Detroit Museum, Portland (Ore.) Museum, Library of Congress, Art Inst. Chicago, Metropolitan Museum of Art, Whitney Museum of Am. Art, Modern Museum, Addison Gallery of Am. Art, Albright Art Gallery, Brooklyn Museum, Univ. of Nebraska art galleries, Arizona Museum, Va. Museum of Arts, Baltimore Mus., Santa Barbara Mus. of Art. Norton Art Gallery, Cranbrook Academy of Art, Walker Art Center, Cleveland Mus., Honolulu Art Mus., Ency. Britannica. Awarded Guggenheim fellowship, 1935-36; hon. mention Carnegie Inst., 1931, 2d prize, 1939; Temple gold medal, 1934; 1st prize Golden Gate Expn. (American section), 1939, J. Henry Scheidt memorial prize, Penn Academy of Fine Arts, 1944, 1st prize, Carnegie Institute, 1944, Norman Wait Harris prize, Chicago Art Institute, 1945, La Tausca $500 prize, 1947. Mem. Painters, Sculptors and Gravers, American Group, Inc., Artists Equity (hon. pres.), Am. Etchers Soc., Woodstock Artists Assn.; hon. asso. Nat. Inst. Arts and Letters. Home: 118 Waverly Pl., N.Y.C. 11. Address: 30 E. 14th St., N.Y.C. 3. Died May 14, 1953; buried Woodstock, N.Y.

KUNKEL, Frank Henry, lawyer; b. Cincinnati, O., Feb. 27, 1874; s. Frank and Anna (Kesslery) K.; LL.B., Cincinnati U., 1895; m. Mayme C. Clasgens, Sept. 7, 1898; children—Martha (Mrs. Robert A. Cline), Raymond J., Paul C. Admitted to Ohio bar, 1895, and since practiced in Cincinnati; mem. firm Kunkel & Kunkel; dir. and chmn. exec. com. The Globe Wernicke Co.; dir. J. & H. Clasgens Co., King Bag Co., Conservative Savs. & Loan Co. Asst. corp. counsel and mem. charter commn., City of Cincinnati; trustee Coll. of Music of Cincinnati. Mem. Am., O. and Cincinnati bar assns. K.C. Clubs: Cincinnati Country, Queen City, Cincinnati. Home: 2945 Wold Av., E. Walnut Hills, Cincinnati. Office: 505 Walnut St., Cin. 2. Died 1950.*

KUNKLE, Bayard Dickenson, corp. official; b. Steelton, Pa., Oct. 30, 1882; s. William Samuel and Leah Rebecca (Peck) K.; student Harrisburg Acad., 1900-02; B.S., Pa. State Coll., 1907, E.E., 1908; m. Frances Ethel Miller, Feb. 10, 1909; 1 dau., Mary Leah (Mrs. Donald Sunderlin). Plant electrician, United Electric & Valley Traction Co., 1908-10; engr. in coil and insulation sect. Westinghouse Electric & Mfg. Co., 1910-16; supt. and chief engr. Caskey-Dupree Co., Marietta, O., 1916-22; asst. supt. automotive elec. equipment Westinghouse Electric & Mfg. Co., East Springfield, Mass., 1922-25; supervisor Klaxon Horn Div., Remy Electric Co., Anderson, Ind., 1925-26, transferred to Delco-Remy plant, Dayton, O., 1926-27; supt. Frigidaire Corp., 1927-29; asst. gen. mgr. Delco Products Corp., Dayton, 1929-30, pres. and gen. mgr., 1930-34; asst. to v.p. Gen. Motors Corp., 1934-37, dir. mfg. sect. of operating staff, 1937-39, v.p. in charge accessory divs., 1939-40, v.p. in charge personnel staff, 1940-42, vice pres. in charge mfg., 1942-43, vice pres. in charge group 5, 1943-48, dir. 1948. Director General Motors Corp., Nylok Corp. (N.Y.), Growth Companies, Inc. (Phila.). Chmn. mfrs. com. Grenade Assn., World War. Commended by head of Trench Warfare Engring. Div. for work with Grenade Assn. Mem. Soc. Automotive Engrs., Delta Upsilon (life). Rep. Presbyterian. Club: Detroit Athletic. Occasional contbr. to industrial mags. Address: 700 Seward Av., Detroit 2. Died Sept. 14, 1953.

KUNTZ, Albert (kōōntz), professor of anatomy; b. Batesville, Ind., Mar. 19, 1879; s. Andrew and Barbara (Butz) K.; A.B., Morningside Coll., Ia., 1904; Ph.D., State U. of Ia., 1910; M.D., St. Louis U. Sch. of Medicine, 1918; m. Emma S. Magdsick, August 28, 1912; 1 daughter, Elizabeth Louise (Mrs. R. Hollis Hamstra). Professor science, Charles City (Ia.) College, 1905-08; fellow State Univ. of Ia., 1909-11, instr. in animal biology, 1911-13; asst. prof. anatomy, St. Louis U. Sch. of Medicine, 1913-16, asso. prof., 1916-19, prof. anatomy, 1919-30, prof. microanatomy, dir. of dept., 1930-46; professor anatomy, director of department since 1946. Mem. A.A.A.S., Am. Soc. Zoölogists, Am. Assn. Anatomists, Soc. Exptl. Biology and Medicine, Sigma Xi, Alpha Omega Alpha, Pi Gamma Mu; associate member American Neurological Society. Presbyterian. Author: The Autonomic Nervous System, 1929, 4th edit., 1953; Neuro-Anatomy, 1931, 5th edit., 1950; The Neuroanatomic Basis of Surgery of the Autonomic Nervous System, 1949; Visceral Innervation and Its Relation to Personality, 1951. Contbr. to med. jours. Home: 7355 Pershing Av., University City, Mo. Office: 1402 S. Grand Blvd., St. Louis. Died Jan. 19, 1957; buried Charles City, Ia.

KUNZIG, Louis A., army officer; b. Altoona, Pa., Jan. 6, 1882; grad. U.S. Mil. Acad., 1905, Sch. of Line, Ft. Leavenworth, Kan., 1922, Command and Gen. Staff Sch., 1926, Army War Coll., Washington, 1931. Commd. 2d lt. Inf., 1905, advanced through the grades to brig. gen., 1942; with 12th Inf., Ft. Washington, Md., 1931-34; 3d Corps Area, hdqrs., Balt., 1934-37; commd. 11th Inf., Ft. Benjamin Harrison, Ind., 1937-40; prof. mil. sci. and tactics U. Pa., 1940; with Inf. Replacement Center, Spartansburg, S.C., 1940-41; commd., Camp Blanding, Fla., 1941-44; ret. as brig. gen., 1944; bus. mgr. Mich. Liquor Control Commn., 1944—. Awarded Legion of Merit. Address: Michigan Liquor Control Commission, Lansing, Mich. Died Aug. 7, 1956.

KURCHATOV, Igor V(asil'evich), nuclear physicist; b. Russia, 1903; grad. Crimean U., Simferopol; student Baku Polytechnical Inst. Joined staff Physico-Technical Inst., Acad. Scis. of USSR, 1925, dir. nuclear physics lab. Physico-Technical Inst., supervised building of cyclotrons; research elec. relations in materials which possess quality of spontaneous polarization; observed nuclear fission provoked by neutron bombardment, 1933; research spontaneous fission of uranium. Became mem. Communist Party, 1948, elected to Supreme Soviet, 1950. Dir. Atomic Energy Inst., Acad. Scis. USSR. Decorated Order of Lenin; recipient Stalin prize. Mem. Acad. Scis. of USSR (presidium of the acad.). Author: Splitting the Atomic Nucleus, 1935. Address: care Academy of Sciences of USSR, B. Kaluzhskaya 14, Moscow, Russia. Died Feb. 1960.*

KURRELMEYER, William, educator; b. Osnabrück, Germany, Jan. 17, 1874; s. Eberhard and Bernhardine (Veditz) K.; A.B., Johns Hopkins, 1896, Ph.D., 1899; m. Carrie May Herrmann, June 18, 1902; children—Bernhard, Carrie May. Prof. modern langs. Franklin and Marshall Coll., 1899-1900; instr., asso., asso. prof. and prof. Johns Hopkins, 1900—, head dept., 1927, prof. emeritus, 1944. Mem. Modern Lang. Assn. America; hon. pres. Goethe Soc. of Md. and D.C.; pres. Soc. for History of Germans in Md. Editor: H. von Kleist's Michael Kohlhaas, 1902; Die erste deutsche Bibel, 10 vols., Tübingen, 1904-15; Wielands Gesammelte Schriften (vols. 6, 9, 11-15, 21, 22), Berlin, 1928-57; Hesperia, Schriften zur germanischen Philologie. Author: Die Doppeldrucke in ihrer Bedeutung für die Textgeschichte von Wielands Werken, 1913; Index to Publications of the Mod. Lang. Assn., 1919. Contbr. to philol. jours. Co-Editor: Modern Language Notes. Home: 1529 Linden Av. Balt. 17. Died Oct. 9, 1957; buried Woodlawn Cemetery, Balt.

KURTH, Wilfred, ins. exec.; b. New Britain, Conn., Sept. 24, 1875; ed. pub. schs., New Britain; m. Ethel A. McLean, July 31, 1901. With U.S. Branch (Hartford) Scottish Union and Nat. Ins. Co., 1891-1902; mgr. Canadian bus. Home Ins. Co., N.Y., 1902-16, sec. of co., 1916-20, v.p., sec., 1920-29, elected dir., 1925, pres., 1929-37, chmn. bd., 1937-41, now chmn. finance com.; pres. Franklin Fire Ins. Co. of Phila., City of N.Y. Ins. Co., Gibraltar Fire Ins. Co., New Brunswick (N.J.) Fire Ins. Co., Carolina Ins. Co., Homestead Fire Ins. Co., Ga. Home Ins. Co., Nat. Liberty Ins. Co. of Am., Balt. Am. Ins. Co. of N.Y., Paul Revere Fire Ins. Co. of N.Y., The Home Indemnity Co. of N.Y., Home Fire Securities Corp., Interzone Corp. (chmn. bd.); ex-pres. Nat. Bd. Fire Underwriters; U.S. mgr. Halifax Fire Ins. Co.; past pres., trustee Am. Foreign Ins. Assn.; mem. Ins. Soc., N.E. Soc., N.Y. C. of C. Clubs: Union League, Drug and Chemical, Blue Goose, Ridgewood Country, Arcola Country, Down Town Assn., The Recess, Bankers, Turf and Field, Terrace, Home: Ridgewood, N.J. Office: 59 Maiden Lane, N.Y.C. Died June 1959.*

KURTZ, Benjamin Putnam (kûrts), prof. English; b. Maui, Hawaiian Ty., Dec. 12, 1878; s. Benjamin Calhoun and Mary Du Bois (Flint) K.; grad. Horton Sch., Oakland, Calif., 1897; A.B., U. of Calif., 1901, Ph. D., 1905; m. Barbara Judith Hirschler, June 20, 1933. Mem. faculty, U. of Calif., since 1903, as instr. English, 1903-08, asst. prof. English, 1908-16, lecturer in extension div., 1908-10, asso. prof. English, 1916-19, prof., 1919-49, specializing in criticism, poetry and middle English lit. Mem. (from time to time) Modern Lang. Assn. America, Modern Humanities Research Assn. (Eng.), Am. Philol. Assn., Am. Folk-Lore Soc. Awarded gold medal by Commonwealth Club, San Francisco, 1934. Democrat. Club: Faculty. Author: Studies in the Marvelous, 1910; Essays in Exposition (with others), 1914; Methods and Materials of Literary Criticism (with C. M. Gayley), 1920; English Poetry, Its Principles and Progress (with C. M. Gayley and C. C. Young), 1920; Twelve Andamanese Songs, 1922; From St. Anthony to St. Guthlac, 1926; Gifer the Worm, 1929; The Pursuit of Death, a Study of Shelley's Poetry, 1933; New Letters of Mary Wollstonecraft (with C. C. Autrey), 1937; William Caxton, 1938; Charles Mills Gayley, a Biography, 1943. Editor: All the Way, Poems by A. W. Truesdell, 1913; Complete Poetical Works of Shelley, 1933. Contbr.

articles and book reviews to learned publs. Home: 59 Santa Clara Av., Oakland 10, Calif.; (summer) Glen Alpine, Lake Tahoe, Calif. Address: University of California, Berkeley, Calif. Died Oct. 18, 1950.

KURTZ, Ford, civil engr.; b. East Stroudsburg, Pa., Feb. 23, 1885; s. Nathaniel Pearson and Hannah (Morgan) K.; C.E., Cornell U., 1907; m. Gladys Chappell, June 28, 1917; 1 son, Peter. Aide, U.S. Coast and Geodetic Survey, 1907-09; asst. to hydraulic engr. J.G. White & Co., Inc., 1910-12, 1914-15, hydraulic design engr., successor firm J. G. White Engring. Corp., 1920-22, chief hydraulic design engr., 1923-27, hydraulic engr. since 1928, engring. mgr. 1940-49, member board of directors, 1948—, vice president in charge engring., 1949-53, president, 1953—; resident engr. Parr Shoals Power Company, Parr, S.C., 1913-14; resident engr. Caibarien-Remedios Waterworks Co., Caibarien, Cuba, 1916-17, dir., 1931-42, sec. 1933-42; designing engr. Langley Field, Hampton, Va., 1917-18; resident engr. U.S. Nitrate Plant No. 2, Muscle Shoals, Ala., 1918-19. Exec. mem. U.S. com. on large dams World Power Conf. Awarded Fuertes Medal for highest scholastic record in civil engring. Cornell U. Mem. Am. Soc. C.E., S.R. Presbyn. Clubs: Cornell (N.Y.); India House. Licensed profl. engr., N.Y., Pa. Home: 8876 Crestwood Av., Hollis 23, N.Y. Office: 80 Broad St., N.Y.C. 4. Died Aug. 9, 1956; buried Rosemont Cemetery, Newberry, S.C.

KURTZ, Thomas Richardson, naval officer; b. Mpls., Oct. 31, 1881; s. Thomas Croft's Wright and Anna Zehring (Richardson) K.; B.S., U.S. Naval Acad., 1901; m. Irene Van Arsdale, Sept. 16, 1908; children—Thomas Richardson, Irene Virginia (Mrs. William Scott Von Stein). Commd. ensign, USN, 1901, and advanced through the grades to commodore, 1945; retired from navy at own request, 1929; recalled to active duty, Feb. 1942; serving as chief of staff Eastern Sea Frontier. Mgr. of operations, Shell Oil Co., 1930-41. Decorated Navy Cross, Office Legion of Honor Clubs: Chevy Chase (Md.); Army and Navy (Washington and New York); Bay Head (N.J.) Yacht. Home: 350 W. 86th St., N.Y.C.; also Bayhead, N.J. Office: 90 Church St., N.Y.C. Died Mar. 1956.

KUTAK, Robert I(ngersoll) (kū'tŏk), sociologist; b. Chgo., Nov. 11, 1899; s. Frank Jerry and Anna (Hruby) K.; student U. Neb., 1919-21; A.B., Western Res. U., 1923; A.M., Columbia, 1925, Ph.D., 1933; m. MRosemary Norris, June 30, 1931; 1 dau., Elizabeth Louella. Research asst. Bd. of Edn., Cleve., 1923-27, head social sci. dept., John Adams High Sch., 1927-28; instr. social sci. Lawrence Smith Sch., N.Y.C., 1928-30; asst. dept. of sociology Columbia, 1930-31; asst. prof. of sociology U. Louisville, 1931-36, asso. prof., 1935-38, prof., head dept. sociology, 1938—. Served with 16th inf. 1st div. U.S. Army, 1917-19. Decorated Purple Heart, Cantigny, France, 1918. Vice chmn. Council of Social Agencies, Louisville, 1941-45; chmn. com. on research of Health and Welfare Council, Louisville; chmn. Family Living Inst. Mem. Am. Acad. Polit. and Social Sci., Am. Assn. Univ. Profs., Am., So. (mem. commn. on teaching sociology, 1944-46, v.p. 1950-51, sec.-treas. 1951-53) sociol. socs., A.A.A.S., Gerontological Soc., Nat. Council Family Relations (adv. com.), Common Council for Am. Unity, Ky. Conf. of Social Work (pres. 1937), Lambda Chi Alpha, Alpha Kappa Psi. Democrat. Episcopalian. Mason. Author: The Story of a Bohemian-American Village, 1933; The Possibilities of a Permanent Peace, 1953. Co-author: Principles of Police Work with Minority Groups, 1950. Editor: Manual of Cleveland, 1927. Home: 2622 Landor Av., Louisville 5. Died Jan. 28, 1959.

KYNE, Peter Bernard, author; b. San Francisco, Oct. 12, 1880; s. John and Mary (Cresham) K.; student pub. sch. and bus. coll.; m. Helene Catherine Johnston, Feb. 2, 1910. Began as clerk gen. mdse. store, later in wholesale lumber and shipping offices; lumber broker, newspaper man. Enlisted in Co. L, 14th U.S., Inf., 1898; mem. 3d expdn. to P.I.; vet. of Spanish-Am. War and Philippine Rebellion; capt. 144th F.A., World War. Republican. Clubs: Bohemian, Army and Navy. Author: Three Godfathers, 1913; The Long Chance, 1914; Cappy Ricks, 1916; Webster—Man's Man, 1917; The Valley of the Giants, 1918; The Green Pea Pirates, 1919; Kindred of the Dust, 1920; The Pride of Palomar, 1921; The Go-Getter, 1922; Never the Twain Shall Meet, 1923; The Enchanted Hill, 1924; The Understanding Heart, 1926; They Also Served, 1927; Tide of Empire, 1928; Parson of Panamint, 1936; Jim the Conqueror, 1929; Golden Dawn, 1930; Outlaws of Eden, 1930; Gringo Privateer, and Island of Desire, 1931; Two Make a World, 1932; Comrades of the Storm, 1933; Cappy Ricks Comes Back, 1934; Cappy Ricks Special, 1935; Soldiers, Sailors and Dogs, 1936; Dude Woman, 1940. Address: 2351 Bay W., San Francisco 23. Died Nov. 25, 1957.

KYRK, Hazel, educator; b. nr. Delaware, O., Nov. 19, 1886; d. Elmer Ellsworth and Jane (Benedict) Kyrk; Ph.B., U. Chgo., 1910, Ph.D., 1920; unmarried. Instr. econs. Wellesley Coll., 1911-12; instr., asst. prof. econs. Oberlin Coll., 1914-21; mem. statis. staff Am. Shipping Mission, London, Eng., 1918-19; research asso. Food Research Inst., Stanford, 1923-24; prof. econs. Ia. State Coll., 1924-25; asso. prof. home econs. and econs. U. Chgo., 1925-41, prof., 1941—. Chmn. consumers adv. com. OPA, 1943-45. Mem. Am. Econ. Assn., Am. Home Econs. Assn., Am. Assn. U. Profs., Am. Assn. U. Women, Phi Beta Kappa. Author: A Theory of Consumption, 1923; Economic Problems of the Family, 1933; The American Baking Industry (with J. S. Davis), 1925; Food Buying and Our Markets (with others), 1938; various monographs. Contbr. articles in periodicals. Home: 5717 Kimbark Av., Chgo. 37. Died Aug. 5, 1957; buried Ashley, O.

L

LABAREE, Mary Schauffler (Mrs. Mary S. Platt), ret. missionary, educator; b. Constantinople, Turkey, Mar. 19, 1868 (parents Am. citizens); d. Henry Albert and Clara Eastham (Gray) Schauffler; B.Litt., Oberlin Coll., 1888; m. Rev. Benjamin Woods Labaree, Sept. 13, 1893 (died 1904); children—Leonard W., Clara G.; m. 2d, Frederick G. Platt, 1915 (died 1932). Missionary of Presbyn. Bd. Fgn. Missions at Urumia, Persia, 1893-1905; traveling sec. Student Vol. Movement for Fgn. Missions, 1906-08; supt. New Britain (Conn.) City Mission (38 nationalities), 1909-14; also instr. in missionary practice Kennedy Sch. of Missions, Hartford Sem. Found., 1912—. Mem. Conn. Soc. Social Hygiene, Conn. Fedn. Chs. (immigration com.). Clubs: Commonwealth, Woman's. Author: The Child in the Midst, 1914. Lectr. on missions. Died Jan. 22, 1954

LABBERTON, John M(adison), prof. cons. engr.; b. nr. Hillsboro, N.C., Apr. 22, 1893; s. Herman H. and Mary (Efland) L.; B.S., U. of N.C., 1913; m. Mary Holton, 1917; 1 dau., Mary Holton; m. 2d, Victoria Dittler, 1938. Elec. mech. engr. Westinghouse Elec. Corp., 1913-35; mech. and marine engr., U.S. Navy, 1935-37; prof. N.Y. Univ. since 1937; cons. engr. for mfrs. of elec. and mech. apparatus since 1937. Civil Service examiner, N.Y. City. Lt. comdr., U.S.N.R. Mem. Am. Soc. M.E., Am. Soc. Naval Engineers, Society of Naval Architects and Marine Engineers. Mason. Member of Phi Beta Kappa, Tau Beta Pi, Sigma Xi, Pi Tau Sigma. Author of many tech. papers and articles; many patents in elec. and mech. field. Author: Marine Engineering, 1943. Editor-in-chief Marine Engineers Handbook, 1946. Home: 114 W. 183d St., N.Y.C. 53. Died Oct. 6, 1953.

LABELLE, J. Edouard, lawyer; b. Sorel, Que., Can., Sept. 24, 1883; s. Albert and Louise (Armstrong) L.; student Coll. de Montreal, U. Laval, Montreal; m. Jeanne de Kermarec, Jan. 29, 1912; children—René, Marguerite (wife of Dr. Lucien Perron), Arthur (M.D.). Called to bar of Que., 1908; created King's Counsel, 1919; asso. Elie Beauregard, 1908-28; now partner with son, Rene Labelle (Queen's Counsel). Pres. Provincial Bank of Can., Canadian Vickers, Ltd., Montreal Dry Docks, Ltd.; mem. bd. dirs. Société d'Administrn. et de Fiducie, La Prevoyance Assurance Co., Eastern Steel Products, Ltd., Orange Crush, Ltd., Laura Secord Candy Shops, Internat. Paint, Ltd.; dir. Canadian Nat. Rys., 1930-34, trustee, 1934-36. Recipient Order Brit. Empire, 1948. Mem. Montreal Bar Assn. (trustee 1930-31). Home: 55 Riverside Dr., St. Lambert, Que. Office: 159 Craig St. W., Montreal, Que., Can. Died Sept. 25, 1957.

LACASSE, Gustave (lȧ kăs), physician; b. Sainte Elisabeth, Que., Feb. 7, 1890; s. F.X.O. and Annie (Gernon) L.; B.A., Montreal Sem., 1909; M.D., U. of Laval, 1913; m. Marie-Anne St. Pierre, Apr. 15, 1915; children—Fernand, Hubert, Helene (Mrs. Lucien Guibord), Maurice, Aline (Mrs. Louis Bezaire), Yvon, Georgette, Hector, Annette, Jean-Louis, Lucien; m. 2d Rose Sasseville-Guilmant, Oct. 2, 1948. Practice, Tecumseh, Ont., 1914-51; med. health officer, Sandwich East, 1914-44. Pres. Maple Leaf Pub. Co., Ltd., Tecumseh, 1931-51. Dir. La Sauvegarde, Montreal. Mayor Tecumseh, 1928-30; mem. Senate Can., 1928-51. Chmn. Separate Sch. Bd. Tecumseh, 1927-28. Mem. La Société des Artisans, Med. Health Officers Ont., Can. Order of Foresters, L'Union Saint Joseph du Can., Ottawa Med. Soc., Assn. des Medecins de Langue Francaise du Can. Editor: La Feuille d'Erable, 1931-51. Home: Tecumseh, Essex County. Office: Tecumseh, Ont., Can. Died Jan. 18, 1953.

LA CAVA, Gregory (lä-kä'vä), motion picture producer; b. Towanda, Pa., Mar. 10, 1892; s. Pascal Nicholas and Eva (Wolz) LaC.; ed. in public and parochial schools of Towanda (Pa.) and Rochester, N.Y.; student Art Inst. of Chicago; m. Grace Garland, March, 1941; 1 son (by previous marriage), Billy. Began career as newspaper cartoonist; was pioneer in animated cartoon field; writer for motion pictures (Torchy comedies), 1922; became dir. of motion pictures (Womanhandled first important assignment); producer-dir. of Stage Door, My Man Godfrey, Primrose Path, Unfinished Business (1941). Ret. 1942. Home: Malibu Beach, Calif. Office: Universal City, Cal. Died Mar. 1, 1952.

LACKEY, Henry Ellis, naval officer; b. Norfolk, Va., June 23, 1876; s. Oscar Hamilton and Clara Caroline (Stone) L.; student Potomac Acad., Alexandria, Va., 1889-93; grad. U.S. Naval Acad., 1899; m. Katherine Peck, July 20, 1901; children—Anne Lockwood (Mrs. Augustus Lowell Putnam), Katherine de Montalant, Caroline Hamilton. Served as naval cadet, U.S.S. New York, Spanish-Am. War; commd. ensign, 1901, advanced through grades to rear adm., 1932. Decorated Sampson Medal, Navy Cross (U.S.); Spanish Order Naval Merit; Greek Order of Savior. Club: Army and Navy (Washington). Deceased.*

LACOUR-GAYET, Jacques, French economist; b. Paris, Oct. 26, 1883; s. Georges and Janet (Cecile) Lacour-G.; student Ecole Normale Supérieure, 1902-05; m. 1914; children—Jacqueline, Michel, Denise. Expert on staff League of Nations, 1928; mem. gen. council Bank of France, 1939-40; mem. bd. Nat. Council French Employers, 1946—; pres. Centre d'Études du Commerce, 1946—; v.p. Nat. Council Commerce, 1947—; pres. Nat. Fedn. Dept. Stores and Variety Chain Stores, 1937—; hon. chmn. Comité d'Action et d'Expansion économique, 1951—; vice chmn. Bd. Radio-Luxembourg, 1932—. Decorated grand officer Legion of Honor (France); Crown of Oak (Luxembourg); Mil. Cross (Gt. Britain); comdr. Mérite Commercialé, Crown of Belgium, Étoile noire du Bénin, Ouissan Alouite, Nicham Ifthikar; Gold medal Am. Legion (hon. col. U.S.A. 5th Div.). Mem. Académie des Sciences morales et politques (Inst. France), 1945—. Author: Chemins de fer de l'Algérie, 1912; Chemins de fer du Canada, 1912; La réforme Douanière, 1925; Commerce Jear et Économie dirigee, 1942; L'Ordonnance du Roi sur les prix et les métiers, 1944; Platon et l'Économie dirigée, 1944; Propos d'un libéral, 1948; De Platon á la Terreur, 1949; supervisor Histoire du Commerce, 1950-53 (6 vols.). Home: 37 Av. Charles Floquet, Paris VII. Office: 11 Rue Saint Florentin, Paris VII. Died Aug. 8, 1953.

La CROIX, Morris Felton, investment banker; b. Lynn, Mass., Mar. 15, 1888; s. Edward Wilton and Edith Lee (Morris) L.; A.B., Harvard, 1910, M.E., 1911; E.D. (hon.), Mich. Coll. Mining and Tech., 1954; m. Esther Humphrye Paine, Oct. 4, 1919; children—William Paine (dec.), Ruth Ward (Mrs. Nelson J. Darling, Jr.), Jeanne (Mrs. Bigelow Crocker, Jr.), Susanne (Mrs. Richard D. Phippen), and Edith Morris. Mining engineer with the Cleveland Cliffs Iron Co., Ishpeming, Mich., 1911-16; mining and investment banking since 1919, as partner firm Paine, Webber, Jackson & Curtis; chairman board directors Gen. Telephone Corp.; pres. and dir. Copper Range Co., Big Sandy Co., White Pine Copper Co., Copper Range R.R.; v.p., dir. Sunflower Petroleum Products; dir. Crown Cork Internat. Co., Internat. T. & T. Corp.; trustee Crocker, Burbank & Co., Association; also dir. and trustee various other corps. and trusts. Trustee Smith Coll., Belmont (Mass) Hill Sch., Roscoe B. Jackson Meml. Lab., Free Hosp. for Women, Boston, Mus. of Sci., Boston, Sarah Sargent Paine Meml. Library, Painesdale, Mich. Served as major engineer, U.S. Army with A.E.F. in France, 1917-19; with American Commission to Negotiate Peace, Paris, 1919. Mem. Am. Inst. Mining and Metall. Engineers, American Association Petroleum Geolgs., Soc. Am. Mil. Engineers, American Geog. Soc., Am. Legion. Republican. Clubs: Harvard (Boston); Harvard, Wall St. (New York); The Attic (Chicago); Country (Brookline, Mass.); Eastern Yacht (Marblehead, Mass.); Myopia Hunt (Hamilton, Mass.). Home: 34 Spooner Rd., Brookline, Mass.; (summer) Beach Bluff Av., Swampscott, Mass.; Sun Valley Farm, New Boston, N.H. Office: 24 Federal St., Boston 10. Died July 28, 1955.

LACY, George Carleton, bishop; b. Foochow, Fukien, China, Dec. 28, 1888; s. William Henry and Emma (Nind) L.; A.B., Ohio Wesleyan U., 1911, D.D., 1928; B.D., Garrett Bibl. Inst., 1914, D.D., 1928; M.A., Northwestern U., 1914, Columbia, 1938; student Nanking U., 1914-15, Boston U., 1920-21, Union Theol. Sem., 1928-29; m. Harriet Lang Boutelle, June 26, 1918; children—Creighton Boutelle, Eleanor Maie. Ordained to ministry Meth. Ch., 1914; pastor Tracy Meth. Ch., Detroit, 1912, Somers, Wis., 1912-13; dist. supt., Kiangsi, China, 1916-17, 1919-20; pres. William Nast Coll., Kiukiang, 1918-19; agy. sec. Am. Bible Soc. in China, 1921-41; sec. China Bible House, 1933-41; bishop Meth. Ch. in Foochow, Fukien Province, China, 1941—. Mem. Wis. Annual Conf., 1912-14, Kiangsi Conf., 1914-41. Mem. exec. com. Nat. Christian Council of China. Trustee Soochow U.; mem. bd. mgrs. Fukien Christian U., Hwanan Coll., Nanking Theol. Sem., Fukien Union Theol. Coll. Mem. Alpha Sigma Phi, Delta Sigma Rho. Pres. Foochow Rotary Internat., 1943-45. Club: American University (Shanghai). Author: The Great Migration and the Church in West China, 1940; The Great Migration and the Church Behind the Lines, 1941; The Book of Revelation and the Message of the Old Testament Prophets (in Chinese), 1944. Address: Methodist Church, Foochow, Fukien Province, China. Died Dec. 11, 1951; buried Foochow, Fukien, China.

LACY, Thomas Norman, business exec.; b. Lititz, Pa., Sept. 23, 1885; s. Mark and Ella A. (Bachman) L.; student Franklin and Marshall Acad., Lancaster, Pa., 1901-02; E.E. Lehigh U., 1906; m. Helen E. Steen, Apr. 7, 1915; children—Ruth (Mrs. William H. Decker Jr.). Engaged in various positions in long lines dept., Am. Tel. & Tel Co., Phila. and N.Y.C., 1906-12, div. plant engr., Atlanta, and N.Y.C., 1912-19, div. plant supt. Atlanta, 1919-25; div. plant supt. Mich. Bell Telephone Co., Detroit, 1925, chief engr., 1925-34, v.p., gen. mgr., 1934-46, pres., 1946-50, chmn., 1950, dir., 1934-—, ret. Dir. Community Chest of Met. Detroit, 1946. Pres. Telephone Pioneers of Am., 1949-50. Fellow Am. Inst. E.E.; mem. Detroit Engring. Soc. Presbyn. Clubs: Economic (dir.), Athletic, Detroit. Home: 415 Burns Dr., Detroit 14. Died Mar. 31, 1954.

LADD, Jesse A., ret. army officer; b. Bradner, O., Sept. 21, 1887; s. Jonathan Elmore and Adda (Jennings) L.; B.S., U.S. Mil. Acad., 1911; m. Florence Von Kanel, Oct. 21, 1913; children—Jesse A. (dec.), Jonathan Frederic, James Von Kanel. Commd. 2d lt., Inf., 1911, promoted through grades to brig. gen., 1941; assigned Port Richardson, Alaska, 1941, later comd. 9th Inf. Div. in Germany, ret. 1947. Mason. Home: 316 W. Wooster St., Bowling Green, O. Died Dec. 14, 1957.

LADD, John W., pres., dir. Cherry-Burrell Corp., Chgo. Home: 257 Woodstock Av., Kenilworth, Ill. Office: 427 W. Randolph St., Chgo. 6. Died 1951.*

LADENBURG, Rudolf Walter (lä'dĕn-bûrg), prof. physics; b. Kiel, Germany, June 6, 1882; s. Albert and Margarete (Pringsheim) L.; Ph.D., U. of Munich, 1906; post. grad. work, Cambridge, Eng., 1906-07; m. Else Uhthoff, Aug. 15, 1911; children—Margarete (Mrs. Fritz Eichenberg), Kurt, Eva Marie (Mrs. Ewald Mayer). Came to America, 1931. Univ. instr. and prof. at Breslau, 1908-25; scientific honorary mem. Academy Goettingen, at U. of Berlin, 1925-31; Brackett research prof. physics, Princeton U., 1931-50. Contbr. scientific books and articles. Home: 55 Princeton Av. Address: Palmer Physical Laboratory, Princeton, N.J. Died Apr. 3, 1952.

LADNER, Albert H., mem. U.S. Employees Compensation Commn.; b. Phila., Oct. 21, 1882; s. Albert H. and Emma S. (Konzelmann) L.; student Central High Sch. and Temple Coll., Phila.; m. Lillian Guenthoer, Apr. 14, 1909; children—Albert H., III, Robert A. Admitted to Pa. bar, 1906; practiced as mem. firm Ladner & Ladner, Phila.; now mem. U.S. Employees Compensation Commn. Supreme dictator, Loyal Order of Moose, 1929. Mason. Lutheran. Address: Social Security Bldg., 4th and Independence S.W., Washington. Deceased.*

LADNER, Grover C(leveland), lawyer; b. Phila., Jan. 8, 1885; s. Albert Henry and Emma S. (Konzelman) L.; LL.B., U. Pa., 1906; m. Mary C. Davis, 1907 (dec.); 1 dau., Kathryn Helen (Mrs. J. J. Carter). Admitted to Pa. bar, 1906, also U.S., Pa. supreme cts., fed. cts.; practice of law, mem. Ladner & Ladner, Phila., 1906-37; member Clark, Ladner, Fortenbaugh & Young since 1952; mem. commn. to codify, revise banking laws of Pa., 1917-19; special counsel pollution and water litigation, Phila., 1928-29; mem. fed. commn. to report on advisability fed. control stream pollution, 1934-36; dep. atty. gen., Pa., 1935-37; presdl. elector, Pa., 1936; member commn. for negotiation interstate compact between states of Ohio River basin, 1936; judge Orphan's Ct., Phila. Co., 1937-50; adj. prof. real estate, conveyancing law, Temple U., 1941-50; mem. water commn., Phila., 1945-46; justice Supreme Ct., Pa., 1950-52. Awarded Governor's medal for work on conservation, 1939; conservation award Pa. Fedn. Sportsmen's Clubs, 1940; Pa. State Game and Fish Assn. medal for services as pioneer crusader pure streams, 1945; Pa. Gardens Clubs citation, dedication meml. tree, 1947; Optimist Club citation for service in cause of pure streams, 1949, Reciprocity Club citation, 1949, United Businessmen's Assn. citation, 1950. Member Am., Pa. State, Phila. bar assns., Mil. Order Loyal Legion, Patriotic Order Sons Am., Izaak Walton League Am. Inc. (natl dir.), Schuylkill River Restoration Assn. (pres.), Pa. Fedn. Sportsmen's Clubs (hon. pres.). Moose. Clubs: Camp and Trail (pres.), Racquet, Penn Athletic (Phila.). Author: Ladner on Conveyancing in Pa. (rev. edit.), 1941; articles on abatement stream pollution. Home: 1520 Spruce St., Phila. Office: 1510 Chestnut St., Phila. 2. Died May 26, 1954.

LA DU, Dwight B., civil engr.; b. Van Buren, N. Y., 1876; s. J. Sears and Julia E. (Warner) La D; ed. pub. schs. Began with the engring. dept. State of N.Y., 1896, advanced to resident engr., 1911; apptd. dir. engr. Eastern div., laster spl. dep. state engr. in charge all canal and terminal work in the state of N.Y., resigned, 1918, engaged in contracting and as cons. engr.; state engr. of N.Y., 1923, 24. Mem. N.Y.-N.J. Bridge and Tunnel Commn., supervising constrn. Holland Tunnel; mem. Albany Port Comm., 1928-45, named chmn. 1934. Mem. Am., Eastern, Albany socs. Civil Engrs. Democrat. Mason (K.T., Shriner). Clubs: Ft. Orange, Albany Country, Wolferts Roost Country (Albany); Rochester (Rochester); Scranton Country. Home: 399 State St., Albany, N.Y. Died Aug. 16, 1954.*

LADUE, Laurence Knight, army officer; b. Mo., June 14, 1903; B.S., U.S. Mil. Acad., 1924; grad. Cav. Sch., troop officers course, 1930, advanced equitation course, 1931, Command and Gen. Staff Sch., 1941. Commd. 2d lt., U.S. Army, 1924, advanced through the grades to brig. gen., 1945. Address: War Dept., Washington 25. Died May 24, 1951.

LAESSLE, Albert (lĕs'lĕ), sculptor; b. Phila., Pa., Mar. 28, 1877; s. Henry Christian and Caroline Louise (Metzger) L.; grad. Spring Garden Inst., Phila., 1896, Drexel Institute, Phila., 1897; graduate in art, Pa. Acad. of Fine Arts, 1901; studied with Michel Béquine, Paris, 1904-07; m. Mary Prudden Middleton, June 7, 1905 (died Aug. 4, 1944); children—Albert Middleton, Paul; m. 2d, Albertine C. de Bempt, Oct. 6, 1946. Instr. Pa. Acad. Fine Arts, 20 yrs.; resigned 1939. Awarded Stewardson prize, 1902, Cresson traveling scholarship, 1904-07(both Pa. Acad. Fine Arts); bronze medal, Buenos Aires, 1910; gold medal, San Francisco Expn., 1915; Fellowship prize, Pa. Acad. Fine Arts, 1915; first prize for sculpture in "Americanization through Art" exhbn., Phila., 1916; George D. Widener memorial gold medal, Pa. Acad. Fine Arts, 1918; fellowship gold medal, same acd., 1923; gold medal, Sesquicentennial Exposition, Phila., 1926; hon. mention, Art Inst. of Chicago, 1920; James E. McClees prize, Pa. Acad. Fine Arts, 1928; 2d prize for best decorative group for garden, park or other outdoor placement, 1928; Sanford Saltus medal, Am. Numismatic Soc., N.Y., 1951. Represented in permanent collections Pa. Acad. Fine Arts, Phila. Art Club, Met. Museum (New York), Carnegie Inst. (Pittsburgh), Peabody Inst. (Baltimore), Calif. Palace of Legion of Honor, Reading (Pa.) Museum of Art, Johnson Square, Camden, N.J.; the bronze "Billy," placed in Rittenhouse Sq., Phila., 1919, bronze "Penguins" in Phila. Zool. Garden, 1918; "Bronze Turkey" acquired by University Club of Pa., 1940; Pennybacker Meml., Logan Circle Parkway, Phila., 10th issue medal for Society of Medalists; gardens of R. K. Mellon, Pitts.; Huntington Collection Am. Sculpture, Brookgreen Garden. Fellow American Numismatic Soc. of N.Y.; mem. Nat. Sculpture Society, Fellowship Pennsylvania Academy Fine Arts (hon. v.p.), Nat. Inst. of Arts and Letters; mem. Internat. Inst. Arts and Letters; asso. mem. Lindau, Bodenses, Switzerland, member of honor Academia Culturale Adriatica, Milan, National Academician, 1932. Home: 6142 S.W. 42d St., Miami, Fla. Died Sept. 4, 1954; buried Abington Friend's Graveyard, Jenkintown, Pa.

La FARGE, Christopher (lȧ-färj'), author; b. New York, N.Y., Dec. 10, 1897; s. Christopher Grant and Florence Bayard (Lockwood) La F.; grad. Groton Sch., 1916; A.B., Harvard, 1920; B.S., in Architecture, Pa. Sch. of Architecture, 1923; m. Louisa Ruth Hoar, 1923 (died 1945); children—Christopher Grant Champlin, William Ellis Rice; m. 2d, Violet Amory (Loomis), 1946; 1 son, Thomas Sergeant. Practiced architecture, 1924-32, first as designer with McKim, Mead & White then as partner in firms of La Farge, Warren & Clark and La Farge & Son; writing since 1932; lived in Eng., 1932-34. Chmn. exec. com. of writers com. of Com. to Defend America by Aiding the Allies; mem. Writers' War Bd.; mem. Writers' World Govt. Bd. Enrolled in Plattsburgh Camp, 1915, 1916, R.O.T.C., Plattsburgh, 1918; commd. 2d lt., Sept., 1918; disch., Dec., 1918. Mem. Poetry Soc. America, P.E.N. Club, Authors Guild (pres. 1945-47), Nat. Inst. Arts and Letters (v.p. 1948-49), Delta Psi, Phi Beta Kappa. Clubs: Spee, Signet Society (Harvard); Century, Coffee House (N.Y. City). Republican. Author: Hoxsie Sells His Acres, 1934, Each to the Other (A. C. Benson Silver Medal, Royal Soc. of Lit., England, 1942), 1939; Poems and Portraits, 1940; The Wilsons, 1941; East by Southwest, 1944; Mesa Verde, 1945; The Sudden Guest, 1946; All Sorts and Kinds, 1949; Beauty for Ashes, 1953. Contributor and author of poems and short stories to Atlantic Monthly, Harper's, American, New Yorker, etc. Works have appeared in several anthologies. Exhibited water colors at Ferargil Galleries, 1930, Wildenstein Galleries, 1931. Home: The River Farm, Sounderstown, R.I. Died Jan. 5, 1956.

LaFLECHE, Leo Richer, govt. ofcl. Can.; b. Concordia, Kan., Apr. 16, 1888 (parents Brit. subjects); ed. by pvt. tutors; m. Jean Brady, June 15, 1920; 4 sons, 1 dau. Mem. Purchasing Commn., Can., 1930; mem. Pensions Appeal Ct., 1931-32; dep. minister of nat. defense, 1932-42; Canadian mil. attaché to France; dep. minister nat. war services, Ottawa, 1940-42; mem. Privy Council and minister nat. war services, 1943-45; ambassador to Greece, 1945-49; now high commr. for Can. to Australia. Served with Canadian army, 1914-19. Address: Canberra, Australia. Died Mar. 7, 1956.*

La FOLLETTE, Robert Marion, Jr., ex-senator; born Maidon, Wis., February 6, 1895; s. Robert Marion and Belle (Case) LaF.; LL.D., University of Wisconsin, 1938; m. Rachel Wilson Young, Sept. 17, 1930; children—Joseph Oden, Bronson Cutting. Sec. to Senator Robert M. LaFollette 6 years; elected to U.S. Senate to fill unexpired term of father, Sept. 29, 1925, for term expiring Mar. 3, 1929, reëlected 3 times, last term expired Jan. 3, 1947. Author, economic cons. Received Colliers Mag. 1946 award. Clubs: Cosmos, Metropolitan, Congressional Country (Washington); Maple Bluff Country. Home: Maple Bluff Farm, Madison, Wis. Office: Nat. Press Bldg., Washington 4. Died Feb. 24, 1953; buried Forest Hill Cemetery, Madison, Wis.

La FORGE, Laurence (lä-fôrj), geologist; b. N.Y. City, Sept. 17, 1871; s. Abiel Teeple and Margaret Swain (Getchell) L.; A.B., Harvard, 1899, A.M., 1900, Ph.D., 1903; m. Fannie Agnes Carryer, June 28, 1893 (died July 13, 1924); 1 dau., Helen Grace (Mrs. Henry Gilmore Brousseari); m. 2d, Kate Louise Harbaugh, Sept. 8, 1930. Began as astronomer, 1894; instr. astronomy, Alfred Univ., 1896-97; Austin teaching fellow, Harvard, 1902-03; geologist U.S. Geol. Survey, 1901-05, 1914-27; aid in geology, U.S. Nat. Museum, 1905-08; research asso., Harvard, 1932-38; prof. geology, Suffolk Univ., 1939-40; prof. of geology, Teachers Sch. of Science, 1934-48; also professor of geology, Tufts Coll., 1942-45; cons. geologist, 1908-14, and 1927-—. Fellow American Geog. Society, N.Y. Acad. Sciences; mem. Am. Geophys. Union, Am. Forestry Assn., Nat. Geog. Soc., Geol. Soc. of Boston, A.A.A.S., U.S. Infantry Assn., Soc. Am. Military Engrs., Am. Museum of Natural History, Boston Mineral Club, Mt. Washington Observatory. Republican. Conglist. Clubs: Harvard Faculty (Cambridge). Home: 8 Shepard St., Cambridge, Mass. Died May 29, 1954; buried Newton (Mass.) Cemetery.

LAFOUNT, Harold Arundel (lȧ-fount'); b. Birmingham, Eng., Jan. 5, 1880; s. Robert A. and Emily Ethel (Hewitt) L.; came to U.S., 1893; ed. Utah State Agrl. Coll.; m. Alma Robison, Oct. 28, 1903 (died Sept. 8, 1938); children—Elsie Evelyn (Mrs. Karl Richards), Lenore (Mrs. George Romney), Constance (Mrs. John Scowcroft), Ruth (Mrs. Harry G Colby); married 2d Gladys MacDonald, September 6 1939 (died June 14, 1943). In retail hardware business with father at Logan, 1900-10; mgr. Pacific Land & Water Co., Salt Lake City, 1910-20; receiver Sevier River Land & Water Co., Salt Lake City, 1923-27; mfr. radio equipment. Salt Lake City, 1925-27; federal radio commr., 1927-35; pres. Atlantic Coast Network, Inc., (N.Y.), Broadcasting Service Organization, Inc. (Boston); vice pres., Wodaam Corp., Greater New York Broadcasting Corp., Fifty-Forty-Sixth Corp. (N.Y.). Also engaged in construction and development of real estate and housing projects. Mem. Salt Lake City Chamber of Commerce. Pres. Nat. Independent Broadcasters. Bishop, Ch. of Jesus Christ of Latter Day Saints, 1919-25. Republican. Home: P.O. Box 2287, Salt Lake City. Office: 565 Fifth Av., N.Y.C. Died Oct 21, 1952; buried Salt Lake Meml. Mausoleum.

LAFRENTZ, Ferdinand William (lȧ-frĕntz'), corp official; b. Island of Fehmarn, Germany, Mar. 25, 1859; s. Franz and Doris L.; came to U.S., 1873; ed. pub. and pvt. schs.; hon. Litt.D.; Doctor of Commercial Sci. N.Y. University; D. Litt., Lincoln Memorial University; married Emma Louisa Poole, Feb. 26, 1885; children—Elsbe Kate (dec.), Olga Lydia, Arthur Ferdinand, Hazel Rosaline. Instructor Bryant & Stratton College, Chicago, later Am. sec. Swan Land & Cattle Co., Cheyenne, Wyo., and practiced as public accountant, Ogden, Utah; admitted to Utah bar, 1893; with American Surety Co. of New York, 1893-—, formerly pres., now chmn. bd.; chmn. American Surety Co., Surety Fire Insurance Company; director Canadian Surety Co., Cia Mexicana de Garantias, Guardian Life Ins. Co. of America; trustee Central Savings Bank; head of F. W. Lafrentz & Co., certified pub. accountants; pres. American Audit Company. Mem. Wyo. Territorial Legislature (introduced Memorial petitioning Congress for statehood), 1888 Pres. Isabella Home, N.Y. City, German Soc. City of N.Y., Germanistic Society of America; chmn. bd. dirs. Lincoln Memorial University; chmn. Am. Pioneer Trails Assn.; dir. Oregon Trail Memorial Assn.; mem. Am. Inst. of Accountants (ex-pres.), New York State Soc. Certified Public Accountants. Lutheran. Clubs: Bankers, Montauk (Brooklyn, N.Y.); Maidstone, Devon Yacht (East Hampton); Wickyup (Me.); Piping Rock (Locust Valley, L.I.); Mountain Lake (Fla.). Author: Nordische Klänge, 1881; Cowboy Stuff, 1928. Home: 125 Eighth Av., Bklyn. Office: 100 Broadway, N.Y.C. 5. Died July 15, 1954; buried Greenwood Cemetery, Bklyn.

La GORCE, John Oliver (lȧ-gôrs), editor; b. Scranton, Pa., Sept. 22, 1880; s. of Gabriel Hauteville and Elizabeth Cecilia (Oliver) LaG.; A.M., Georgeton U.; Litt.D., George Washington U.; D.Sc., S.D. Sch. of Mines; D.Sc., U. Tampa, Tampa, Florida; D.Sc., U. Miami; married, Spl. writer, newspapers and mags., 1903-05; asst. sec. Nat. Geog. Society, 1905-07, pres., 1954-57, ret., now vice chmn., life trustee, 1917; asst. and assoc. editor, former editor Nat. Geographic Mag. Fellow of the Royal Geographic Society (Eng.); hon. mem. Geographical Soc. Peru; delegate U.S. Govt. to 3d Pan

Am. Scientific Congress, Lima, Peru, 1925; dir. Riggs National Bank. Trustee Corcoran Gallery of Art, Washington, D.C. Appointed postmaster Little America, Antarctica, 1933. Decorated Officer Légion d'Honneur. Member Nat. Geographic Society, Washington. Clubs: Cosmos, National Press, University, Army & Navy, Chevy Chase, Country (Washington), The Surf, La Gorce Country Club (Miami Beach). Author: The Warfare on Our Eastern Coast; Devil Fishing in the Gulf Stream; Food Fish of North Atlantic; Book of Fishes; Flight at the Timberline; Puerto Rico, the Gateway of Riches; Jamaica, Isle of Many Rivers; Penn's Land of Modern Miracles. Contbr. many travel articles. Home: 2120 Kalorama Rd., Washington. Died Dec. 1959.

LAHEY, Frank Howard (lā'hē), surgeon; b. Haverhill, Mass., June 1, 1880; s. Thomas and Honora Frances (Powers) L.; M.D., Harvard, 1904; hon. Sc.D., Tufts, 1927, Boston University, 1943, Northwestern U., 1947; LL.D. (honorary) University of Cincinnati 1951; m. Alice Wilcox, Apr. 15, 1909. Surgeon Long Island Hosp., 1904-05, Boston City Hosp., 1905-07; resident surgeon Haymarket Sq. Relief Sta., 1908; instr. in surgery, Harvard Med. Sch., 1908-09, 1912-15; asst. prof., later prof. surgery, Tufts Med. Sch., 1913-17; prof. clin. surgery, Harvard Medical School, 1923-24; surgeon in chief N.E. Baptist hospitals; director of surgery The Lahey Clinic, Boston. Served as major, Medical Corps, U.S. Army, World War; dir. surgery Evacuation Hosp. No. 30, A.E.F.; now hon. consultant to Medical Dept., U.S.N. Fellow Am. Coll. Surgeons (bd. govs.); honorary fellow Royal Coll. of Surgeons, England; mem. Am. and Internat. surg. assns., Am. Assn. for Study of Goitre, A.M.A. (pres. 1942), Société des Chirurgiens de Paris, Theta Delta Chi. Republican. Mason. Clubs: Harvard, Algonquin. Author of Lahey Clinic Number (Surg. Clinics of N. America), pub. yearly. Contbr. numerous articles on surg. subjects. Chmn. Procurement and Assignment Service for Med. Personnel for the Armed Forces. Home: 118 Bay State Rd. Office: 605 Commonwealth Av., Boston. Died June 27, 1953.

LAING, John Albert (lāng), lawyer; b. Albany, N.Y., Nov. 14, 1883; s. John Collier and Euphemia Taylor (Cochran) L.; A.B., Dartmouth, 1905; LL.B., Columbia, 1908; m. Ruth Elizabeth Fuller, June 1, 1910 (died Oct. 16, 1932); children—James Fuller, Helen Fuller (died Feb. 15, 1941), John Collier; m. 2d, Barbara Mackenzie Macleay, May 12, 1939. Admitted to N.Y. bar, 1907; began practice with Wherry & Morgan, N.Y.C., 1908; with Simpson, Thacher & Bartlett, 1909-10; with Pacific Power & Light Co. and Portland (Ore.) Gas & Coke Co., 1910-36, v.p., counsel to Feb. 1936; now mem. Laing Gray & Smith, gen. counsel for Pacific Power & Light Co., Portland Gas & Coke Co., Mountain States Power Co., and gen. practice; dir. Portland Gas & Coke Co. Pres. City Planning Commn., Portland, 1931-35; pres. Portland Rose Festival, 1930; mem. bd. regents, trustee Reed Coll., Portland; chmn. bd. regents, 1931-46; pres. Portland Symphony Soc., 1937-48. Am. Bar. Assn., Portland C. of C., Portland Art Assn., Dartmouth Assn. Ore. (pres., 1935-52), Phi Beta Kappa, Delta Tau Delta, Phi Delta Phi. Republican. Clubs: University, City, Arlington, Multnomah Amateur Athletic (pres. 1925-27). Organizer, sec. Portland Civic Stadium; mem. Ore. Adv. Commn. Liquor Control, 1933; chmn. adv. com. on travel promotion, Ore. State Hwy. Commn. Home: 12526 S.W. Edgecliff Rd. Office: Public Service Bldg., Portland 4, Ore. Died May 13, 1953.

LAISTNER, Max Ludwig Wolfram (läst'nĕr), educator, historian; b. London, Eng., Oct. 10, 1890; s. Max and Lisette Caecilia Katharina (Weber) L.; B.A., Cambridge, 1912, M.A., 1920, Litt.D., 1944, Craven student, Cambridge, for research in Greece, 1912-13; British School of Archaeology student, Athens, 1913-14. Asst. lectr. classics, Birmingham (England) U., 1914; lecturer history and archaeology, Queen's U., Belfast, Ireland, 1915-16; in mil. and govt. service, May 1916-Aug. 1919; lectr. classics, Manchester U., 1919-21; asst. prof. ancient history, U. London, 1921-25; prof. ancient history, Cornell U., 1925-40, John Stambaugh prof. history 1940—; Sather prof. classical literature, U. Cal., 1946; James W. Richard lectr. U. Va., 1950. Hon. fellow Jesus Coll., Cambridge; fellow Royal Hist. Society; corr. fellow Mediaeval Acad. Am. (councillor 1938-41, v.p. 1945-48); mem. Am. Hist. Assn. (mem. bd. of editors Am. Hist. Rev., 1942-47), English Classical Assn., English Hist. Assn., Soc. for Promotion Hellenic Studies, Phi Beta Kappa. Club: Authors' (London). Author: Greek Economics, 1923; Survey of Ancient History, 1929; Thought and Letters in Western Europe, A.D. 500-900, rev. edit., 1957; Greek History, 1932; A History of the Greek World from 479-323 B.C., 1936; The Greater Roman Historians, 1947; Christianity and Pagan Culture in the Later Roman Empire, 1951. Editor: The Philoxenus Glossary, 1926; Isocrates, De Pace and Philippus, 1927; Bedae Venerabilis Expositio Actuum Apost. et Retractatio, 1939; A Handlist of Bede MSS, 1943; The Intellectual Heritage of the Early Middle Ages, 1957 (edited by C. G. Starr). Contbr. articles and reviews of Classical Review, Harvard Theol. Review, Am. Hist. Review, Am. Economic Review, etc. Home: 216 Wait Av., Ithaca, N.Y. Died Dec. 10, 1959.

LAIT, Jacquin L. (Jack Lait) (lāt), writer; b. N.Y. City, Mar. 13, 1883; s. Leon and Anna (Rosenthal) L.; grad. Lewis Inst., Chicago, Ill., 1901; m. Laura Belle Leusch, Mar. 6, 1906; children—George, Jack, Mrs. Lois C. King. Newspaper reporter, critic and war corr., 1901-08; theatrical mgr., 1908-10; writer daily "Novelette" and "Gus the Bus" series, Chicago Herald and asso. syndicate papers, 1915-16; was on staff Chicago Tribune. Lecturer on journalism, Lewis Inst. Mem. Alpha Kappa. Jewish religion. Clubs: Press (Chicago), Overseas Press (N.Y.). Author: Help Wanted, 1914; Short Stories, 1916; One of Us, 1919; Beef, Iron and Wine, 1919; Gus the Bus, 1920; The White Way, 1921; Spice, 1922; Broadway Melody, 1928; The Big House, 1929; Put on the Spot, 1931; Gangster Girl, 1931; The Beast of the City, 1932; The Hook-Up, 1935; Our Will Rogers, 1935; Will Rogers' Wit and Wisdom, 1937. Co-author: New York: Confidential, 1948; Chicago: Confidential, 1949; Washington: Confidential, 1950; U.S.A.: Confidential, 1952. Editor Hearst Syndicates, 1921. N.Y. Daily and Sunday Mirror since 1936. Home-Office: 235 E. 45th St., N.Y.C. 17. Died Apr. 1, 1954; buried Hollywood (Cal.) Cemetery.

LAKE, Fred Wrightman, business exec.; b. Clinton, Mo., Mar. 12, 1888; s. Edwin J. and Abigail J. (Wrightman) L.; student Spaulding's Bus. Coll., Kansas City, Mo.; m. Lena Bixman, June 5, 1911 (dec.); children—Fred W. (killed in action, Oct. 15, 1943), John Paul, Mary Jane (Mrs. Fred V. Giffith, Jr.); m. 2d, Arline Margaret Atkinson, Jan. 24, 1942. Stenographer, A.D. Fish Commn. Co., Bd. Trade, Kansas City, Mo., 1904-08; bookkeeper, office mgr., J. R. Tomlin Grain Co., Bd. Trade, Kansas City, Mo., 1908-10; stenographer-bookkeeper, Hall-Baker Grain Co., Bd. Trade, Kansas City, Mo.; mgr. milling wheat dept.; v.p. Farmers Nat. Grain Corp., 1930, pres. to 1935; v.p. Continental Grain Co., Kansas City, Mo., 1935-43; exec. v.p., The Colo. Milling & Elevator Co., Denver, 1943-44, pres., 1944—. Republican. Christian Scientist. Clubs: Kansas City, Mission Hills Country (Kansas City, Mo.); The Chicago (Ill.); Denver Country, Cherry Hills Country (Denver). Home: 21 Crestmoor Dr., Denver 7. Office: Equitable Bldg., Denver 2. Died Dec. 1955.*

LAKE, John, missionary; b. Edgefield County, S.C., June 11, 1870; s. Capt. George Blocker and Rosa Florence (Jones) L.; LL.D., The Citadel, Charleston, S.C., 1930; student State Military College, class of 1891; Columbia Theological Seminary, 1891-93, Southern Baptist Theological Sem. (Louisville, Ky.), 1899-1902; m. Pearl Hall Williams (widow of Rev. S. T. Williams of China), 1907 (deceased); m. 2d, Carrie Elford Bostick (teacher in America and China), 1909 (deceased); m. 3d, Virginia Barclay Lake, dau. Prof. J. L. Lake, June 27, 1933; children—Virginia Austin and Rosa Florence. Y.M.C.A. secretary (city, county and state), 1891-1903; ordained to the ministry of the Baptist Church, 1893; pastor, school teacher and editor; missionary to China, 1903-35, missionary emeritus since 1939; founder Tai-Kam Island Leper Hosp. and Colony; pres. John Lake, Inc., for more than 10 years, and until at his request, it was dissolved and work merged with Foreign Mission Bd. and S. China Conv. Several missionary journeys around the world. Author of several volumes in verse. Has written several books and booklets on missionary work, in English and Chinese, edited and contributed to various jours. in both langs. Address: 3924 Baltimore Av., Kansas City, Mo. Deceased.

LAKE, Mack Clayton, mining co. exec.; b. Brodhead, Wis., Apr. 29, 1890; s. William and Amanda (McNich) L.; B.S., U. of Wis., 1914; m. Vera Alice Langdon, Oct. 20, 1915 (died Dec. 1946); children—William Joseph, James Langdon, Mack Clayton; m. 2d Edna Louise Moorehead, Dec. 1947. With M. A. Hanna Co., Cleveland, O., as cons. geologist and mining engr., 1915-49; v.p. and dir. Chapin Exploration Co., 1929-49, Arisota Corp., 1941-46; pres. and dir. Calmich Mining Co., 1940-42; dir. Consol. Copper Mines Co., 1932-38; v.p. and dir. Manganese Ore Co., 1942-45, Hanna Development Co., 1945-49; cons. geologist Oliver Iron Mining Co.; engaged in Venezuelan iron ore exploration, 1945-49; pres. and dir. Orinoco Mining Co., subsidiary U.S. Steel Corp., N.Y. City, since Jan. 1950. Mem. Am. Inst. Mining and Metall. Engrs., Soc. Econ. Geologists, Lake Superior Mining Inst., Mining and Metall. Soc. Am. Mason (Shriner). Clubs: Engineers (San Francisco); Claremont Country (Oakland, Calif.); Duquesne (Pittsburgh); Kitchi Gamma (Duluth); India House (N.Y. City); Siwanoy Country (Bronxville); Caracas (Venezuela) Country. Contbr. articles to profl. jours. Home: 1655 Plymouth Av., San Francisco 12; also 710 Park Av., N.Y. City. Office: 25 Broad St., N.Y.C. 4. Died Nov. 9, 1954.

LAKE, Marshall E(dgar), exec. engr.; b. Washington, Nov. 26, 1900; s. Marshall Beverly and Eleanor Gibson (Harper) L.; B.S., U. of N.C., 1922; m. Mabel Lina Foster, June 12, 1924; children—Mary (Mrs. James Austin), Eleanor (Mrs. Russell Garrison), John. With Westinghouse Elec. Corp., E. Pitts. summers 1920, 21; indsl. power sales engr. Duke Power Co., 1922-44, mgr. indsl. power sales program since 1944, supervision of comml. power sales since 1948, member board of directors, 1946—, vice president, 1954—. Member Bd. Sch. Commrs., Charlotte, N.C., 1941-46, chmn. bd., 1945-46; dir. Charlotte Y.M.C.A., 1936-41; dir. Salvation Army, Charlotte, 1949—. Head Mecklenburgh County, N.C., Civilian Defense Utilities Div., World War II. Registered professional engineer. Member of the American Inst. E.E. (co-organizer and sec. N.C. sect., 1929; sect. chmn. 1938), N.C. Soc. Engrs. (dir. 1945-46), Phi Beta Kappa. Baptist. Clubs: Engineers (pres. 1938), Rotary (Charlotte). Home: 926 Henley Pl., Charlotte 7. Office: 422 S. Church St., Charlotte 2, N.C. Died Nov. 16, 1958; buried Ever Green Cemetery Charlotte.

LAMADE, Howard John (la'-ma-dy), publisher; b. Williamsport, Pa., Jan. 15, 1891; s. Dietrick and Clara Anne (Rhen) L.; grad. Wenonah Mil. Acad.; B.S. in Chemistry, Pa. State U., 1912; B.J., U. Mo., 1913; m. Muriel Ruth Bird, Apr. 12, 1920; children—Howard John, Clara Anne (Mrs. D. R. L. Robison). With Grit Publishing Co., 1913—, beginning as clk., sec., v.p., dir., 1920—; chmn. bd. Williamsport Hotels Co., 1954—; dir. West Branch Bank & Trust Co., Williamsport Fed. Savs. & Loan Co., Little League, Inc. Trustee, mem. exec. bd. Pa. State U., 1939-56. Mem. Williamsport Community Trade Assn. (dir.), Phi Delta Theta, Sigma Delta Chi, Alpha Chi Sigma. Mason (33°), Kiwanian (past pres.). Home: 270 Grampian Blvd. Office: Grit Publishing Co., Williamsport, Pa. Died May 15, 1958.

LAMB, Albert Richard, prof. emeritus; b. Waterbury, Conn., Apr. 22, 1881; s. George Burton and Idabelle (Johnson) L.; prep. edn., Taft Sch., Watertown, Conn., 1895-99; A.B., Yale, 1903; M.D., Coll. Physicians and Surgeons, Columbia, 1907; m. Helen Foster, Jan. 4, 1910; children—Mary Nightingale, Albert Richard, Priscilla Foster, Helen. Interne Presbyn. Hosp., N.Y.C., 1908-10, resident bacteriologist, 1910-11, resident pathologist, 1911-13, chief of out patient dept. and asst. visiting physician, 1913-17, visiting physician since 1918; instr. of medicine, Coll. Physicians and Surgeons, 1913-18, became prof. clin. medicine, 1918, now prof. emeritus; pres. med. board Presbyn. Hosp., 1940-46; now consulting physician; cons. physician Englewood (N.J.) Hosp. Chmn. Med. Adv. Bd. No. 22, N.Y.C.; mem. emergency med. service Office Civilian Def., N.Y. Served as maj., M.C., U.S. Army, World War; attached to Am. Commn. to Negotiate Peace. Recipient D.S.M., Columbia U., 1956. Fellow A.C.P.; mem. A.M.A., Soc. Internal Medicine, N.Y. Acad. Medicine, N.Y. State Med. Soc., N.Y. Clin. Soc., Cosmopolitan Med. Club, Psi Upsilon, Skull and Bones. Republican. Episcopalian. Club: Century. Home: Pine Orchard, Conn. Office: Presbyn. Hosp., 622 W. 168th St., N.Y.C. Died Nov. 1959.

LAMB, Arthur Becket, prof. chemistry; b. Attleboro, Mass., Feb. 25, 1880; s. Louis Jacob and Elizabeth Camerden Townsend (Becket) L.; A.B., A.M., Tufts, 1900, Ph.D., 1904, D.Sc., 1922; A.M., Harvard, 1903, Ph.D., 1904; univs. of Leipzig, 1904, Heidelberg, 1905; m. Blanche Anne Driscoll, Dec. 27, 1923. Instr. Electrochemistry, Harvard, 1905-06; asst. prof. chemistry, N.Y.U., 1906, asso. prof., 1907, prof., 1909-12, also dir. Havemeyer Chem. Lab.; asst. prof. chemistry, Harvard, 1912-20, prof., 1920-48, prof. emeritus, 1949-52, dir. chem. lab., 1912-47, dean Grad. Sch. Arts and Sciences, 1940-43. Editor Jour. Am. Chem. Soc., 1917-49. Served as lt. col. Research Div. Chem. Warfare Service, U.S. Army, 1918-19, in charge defense chem. research; mem. U.S. Fixed Nitrogen Mission, 1919; dir. Fixed Nitrogen Research Lab., Washington, 1919-21. Awarded Am. Chem. Soc., Nichols Medal, 1943, Priestly Medal, 1949, Austin M. Patterson Award, Dayton Sect., 1951; Ballou Medal, Tufts Coll., 1944. Hon. Fellow The Chem. Soc. London, 1951. Fellow A.A.A.S. (v.p. 1933); mem. Am. Chem. Soc. (pres 1933), Am. Acad. Arts and Scis., Am. Philos. Soc., Am. Electrochem. Soc., Washington Acad. Scis., Nat. Acad. Sci., Deutsche Chemische Gesellschaft, Deutsche Bunsen-Gesellschaft, Delta Upsilon, Phi Beta Kappa, Alpha Chi Sigma, Phi Lambda Upsilon. Clubs: Faculty (Cambridge, Mass.); Harvard (Boston); Chemists (N.Y.); Country (Brookline). Home: 121 Colbourne Crescent, Brookline, Mass. Died May 15, 1952; buried Attleboro, Mass.

LAMB, Ella Condie, artist; b. N.Y.C.; d. James and Ellen (Harrison) Condie; studied in N.Y. under William M. Chase, Walter Shirlaw, and C. Y. Turner; in Eng. under Hubert Herkomar, R.A.; in Paris under R. Collin; m. Charles Rollinson Lamb; children—Richard C. (dec.), Karl B., Katharine S., Donald W., J. Condie. Specialty portrait and decorative painting; among important examples of mural work are paintings in Flower Meml. Library, Watertown, N.Y.; Governor Baldwin Meml., St. John's Ch., Detroit; Sage Meml., Cornell U.; reredos in St. Mary's Ch., Wayne, Pa.; Russell Meml., Wells Coll.; Hobart Meml., Briarly Sch., N.Y.C., others. Recipient Dodge prize N.A.D., 1889; hon. mention, Chicago

Expn., 1893, Buffalo Expn., 1901; gold medal, Atlanta Expn., 1895. Life mem. Art Students' League N.Y.; artist life mem. Nat. Arts Club; mem. Art Center, Nat. Soc. Mural Painters. Studio: Lambs Lane, Cresskill, N.J. Died Jan. 23, 1936.

LAMB, Hugh Louis, bishop; b. Coatesville, Pa., Oct. 6, 1890; s. Matthew J. and Anna (Coyle) L.; grad. high sch., Coatesville, 1907; grad. Overbrook Theol. Sem., Phila., 1912; S.T.D., Am. Coll., Rome, Italy, 1915; studied Catholic U., Washington, 1916-17. Ordained priest R.C. Ch., 1915; asst. rector Annunciation Ch., Phila., 1915-17, Ch. of the Holy Child, Phila., 1917-18; prof. Overbrook Theol. Sem., 1918-21; sec. to Cardinal Dougherty, 1921-23; asst. supt. Diocesan Schs., Phila., 1923-26; chancellor Archdiocese of Phila., 1926-36; made domestic prelate by Pope Pius XI, 1927; protonotary apostolic, 1929; auxiliary bishop of Phila. and vicar general, Phila., 1936-52; bishop of Greensburg since 1952. Address: 723 E. Pittsburgh St., Greensburg, Pa. Died Dec. 1959.

LAMB, Robert Scott, ophthalmologist; b. Washington, D.C., Oct. 15, 1876; s. Daniel Smith (M.D.) and Elizabeth (Scott) L.; M.E., Cornell U., 1894; M.D., Howard U., 1898; m. Sarah Keen, Feb. 5, 1901; children—Robert Keen, Elizabeth Scott. Has practiced at Washington since 1902; formerly asso. surgeon Episcopal Eye, Ear & Throat Hosp.; ophthalmologist Emergency, Gallinger and Doctor's hosps. Dir. research, trustee Ednl. Found. of Nat. Med. Soc. Mem. Med. Adv. Bd. No. 3, World War. Fellow Am. Coll. Surgeons; mem. A.M.A., Southern Med. Assn., Med. Soc. D.C., A.A.A.S., Am. Acad. Ophthalmology and Otolaryngology, Am. Ophthalmol. Soc., Am. Assn. for Study Endocrinology, Am. Genetic Soc., Am. Tuberculosis Assn., Am. Social Hygiene Assn., Am. Optical Soc., Social Hygiene Soc. of D.C. (pres. emeritus), Am. Civic Assn., Washington Bd. of Trade, S.A.R. (pres. 1946-47), Sons of Natives D.C. Mason. Clubs: Cornell (pres. 1937-38), University, Racquet, Washington Golf and Country, Torch. Home: University Club. Office: 711 Stoneleigh Ct., Washington. Deceased.

LAMB, William Frederick, architect; b. Brooklyn, N.Y., Nov. 21, 1883; s. William and Mary Louise (Wurster) L.; A.B., William Coll., 1904, D.Sc., 1932; grad. work Columbia U. Coll. of Architecture, 1904-06, Litt.D., 1943; Architect Diplomé par le Govt. Francais, Ecole des Beaux Arts, Paris, 1911; m. Cuthbert Dufour, July 29, 1926; 1 son, William Rhett. Mem. firm Shreve & Lamb, 1924-29; mem. firm Shreve, Lamb & Harmon, New York, since 1929. Work of firm includes Empire State Bldg., Standard Oil Bldg., Bankers Trust Bldg., Gen. Motors Bldg., N.Y. Times Bldg. (all N.Y. City), N.Y. Times Bldg., (all N.Y.C.), R. J. Reynolds Tobacco Co. Bldg., N.Y. Times Bldg., Mut. Life Ins. Co. (N.Y.C.), R. J. Reynolds Tobacco Co. Bldg., Winston Salem, N.C., Acacia Mut. Life Ins. Co., Washington, labs. for Johns-Manville Corp., R.C.A. Lab. additions and others; Newfoundland and Ferry Command bases for U.S. Army Engr. Corps; work for USCG, New London, Conn., Naval Tng. Sta., Sampson, N.Y., for Bur. of Yards and Docks; also bldgs. Hunter Coll., Conn. Coll. for Women, Williams Coll., Cornell U., Wesleyan U. Recipient Fifth Avenue gold medal, 1930, 31, 39; Architectural League of New York medal, 1931, medal honor Am. Inst. Architects N.Y. chpt. 1932, grand prix Paris Expn., 1937. Member of Art Commn. of City of New York, 1932-36; member Federal Commn. of Fine Arts, 1937-45. Co-ordinator of design, New York Worlds Fair, 1939. Fellow A.I.A.; mem. Beaux Arts Inst. of Design, Archtl. League of N.Y., Soc. Beaux Arts Architects (vice president 1939), American Institute of Arts and Letters. Clubs: Century Assn., University, Williams (New York); New Canaan Country. Home: 55 E. 72d St. Office: 11 E. 44th St., N.Y.C. Died Sept. 8, 1952.

LAMBERT, Byron James, civil engr., educator; b. Argyle, Wis., Apr. 25, 1874; s. Furniss and Mary Wasley (Reynolds) L.; B.Di., State Teachers Coll, Cedar Falls, Ia., 1896, M.Di., 1897; Ph.B., State U. of Ia., 1900, B.S. in C.E., 1901, C.E., 1906; m. Helen Leavitt Davison, Nov. 8, 1902; children—James Leavitt, Robert Davison, Mary Louise, Richard Hooker, Edward Reynolds. City engr. Cedar Falls and Waterloo, Ia., 1899-1901; chief engr. Waterloo, Cedar Falls & Northern Ry. during constrn., 1901-02; successively instr., prof., and head dept. civ. engring., State U. of Ia., 1902-50, acting dean of Engring. Coll., 1935-36. Cons. practice also gen. contractor; cons. engr. Moline Airport, Ia. City Municipal Swimming Pool. Major of engrs., U.S. Army, Nov. 1917; comdg. officer 3d Batt., 23d Engrs., in France, Mar.-Dec. 1918; engr. of bridges with 1st Army; hon. discharged, Jan. 6, 1919; lt. col. Engr. O.R.C. Mem. Am. Soc. C.E., Ia. Engring. Soc., Am. Soc. Military Engineers, Society Promotion Engineering Education, Iowa City Engrs.' Club, Scabbard and Blade, Sigma Xi, Tau Beta Pi, Sigma Tau, Chi Epsilon, etc. Republican. Methodist. Mason. Clubs: Triangle, Rotary. Joint author of Lambert and Holt's Elementary Structures in Steel and Concrete. Author: High Masonry Dams, Airport Engineering. Contbr. on engring. topics. Invented and patented all-steel stadium, 1923 and 1939. Course supervisor "Airport Engineering" in Nat. Defense Training, 1941. Home: 4 Melrose Circle, Iowa City, Ia. Died Oct. 29, 1952.

LAMBERT, Charles Irwin, psychiatrist; b. Argyle, Wis., Dec. 6, 1877; s. Furniss and Mary Wasley (Reynolds) L.; M Di., Ia. State Tchrs. Coll., Cedar Falls, 1897; B.S., State U. Ia., 1901, M.A. and M.D., 1903; grad. study Harvard and Munich; m. Bess Ann Coomer, Oct. 9, 1907; children—John Pierce, Robert Reynolds, Elizabeth Ann; m. 2d, Florence B. Gilpin, April 29, 1940. Instr. pathology Coll. of Medicine, State U. of Ia., 1904; asst. in neuropathology N.Y. State Psychiatric Inst., 1905-13; pathologist Manhattan State Hosp., 1910-13; asst. dir. Bloomingdale Hosp., 1913-22; chief of Vanderbilt Clinic (psychiatric dept. Columbia U.), 1922-28; asso. prof. psychiatry Coll. Phys. and Surg., 1922—; prof. psychiatric edn. Tchrs. Coll. (Columbia); med. dir. Four Winds Sanitarium, Katonah, N.Y. Served in World War as advisory psychiatrist in Draft Service, and sr. asst. psychiatrist Bloomingdale Hosp., designated as receiving hosp. for AEF, officers suffering neuro-psychiatric disabilities. Mem. A.M.A., Am. Psychiatric Assn., New York Psychiatric Soc., Sigma Xi. Republican. Presbyn. Clubs: Faculty (Columbia U.); Scarsdale (N.Y.) Golf. Home: "Spy Rock," Mt. Kisco, N.Y. Office: 13 E. 77 St., N.Y.C. 21. Died Apr., 1954.

LAMBERT, John S., jurist; b. Johnsonville, N.Y., Feb. 4, 1851; ed. pub. sch. and Greenwich (N.Y.) Acad.; studied law in office; m. Winnifred Phillips. Admitted to N.Y. bar, 1877; practiced law, Maysville, N.Y., 1877-8, and at Fredonia, N.Y., 1878-89. Mem. bd. supervisors Chautauqua Co., 1880-1; county judge Chautauqua Co., 1882-9; justice Supreme Court N.Y., since Jan. 1, 1890; Republican. Address: Fredonia, N.Y. Died July 16, 1936.

LAMBERTSON, William Purnell, ex-congressman; b. Fairview, Kan., Mar. 23, 1880; s. William Franklin and Ida (Brown) L.; student Ottawa (Kan.) U., 1898-1901, Law Sch. U. Chgo., 1902-04; m. Floy L. Thompson, Nov. 26, 1908; children—Alonzo Stagg, Elise, Edwina Floy, Milan Ward. Engaged in farming since youth; v.p. Kan. Farmers Union; dir. local telephone and elevator cos. Attended 2d O.T.C., Fort Sheridan, Ill., 1917. Mem. Kan. Ho. of Reps., 4 terms between 1909 and 1921 (speaker pro tem, 1911; speaker 1919); mem. Kan. Senate, 1913, 15; chmn. Kan. State Efficiency and Economy Commn., 1917; minority mem. Kan. Bd. of Adminstrn., 1923-25; candidate for Rep. nomination for gov., 1922, for Congress, 1924, 26; mem. 71st to 78th Congresses, 1st Kan. Dist. Mem. Phi Alpha Delta, Alpha Tau Omega. Baptist. Mason (32°, K.T., Shriner), Odd Fellow. Author: The Cloakroom. Home: Fairview, Kan. Died Oct. 26, 1957; buried Sabetha (Kan.) Cemetery.

LAMBETH, William Arnold, clergyman; b. Thomasville, N.C., Oct. 5, 1879; s. Frank Simmons and Ella (Arnold) L.; A.B., Trinity Coll. (now Duke U.), 1901; grad. study Vanderbilt, 1901-03; B.D., Yale, 1904; A.M., Harvard, 1905; D.D., Emory and Henry Coll., 1924; Duke, 1941; Litt.D., Fla. Southern Coll., Lakeland, Fla., 1929; m. Evelyn Elizabeth Walker, Oct. 14, 1913; children—Frances Walker (Mrs. Hal Kearns Reynolds), Elizabeth Walker, William Arnold. Admitted to ministry M.E. Ch., S., 1905; pastor Holmes Memorial Church, Salisbury, 1905-06, Spring Garden Church, Greensboro, 1906-07, Love's Church, Walkertown, 1907-09, West End Church, Winston-Salem, 1909-13, Main St. Church, Reidsville, 1913-16, 1st Church, Salisbury, 1916-18, Wesley Memorial Ch., High Point, 1918-22, Main Street Ch., Gastonia, 1922-24 (all in N.C.), Mount Vernon Place Ch., Washington, D.C., 1924-30, Trinity Ch., Durham, N.C., 1930-31, Central Ch., Asheville, 1931-33, and 1940-44, Wesley Memorial Ch., High Point, 1933-36; dist. supt. Winston-Salem Dist., Western N.C. Annual Conf., 1936-40; mem. Uniting Conf., Kansas City, 1939; Gen. Conf., Birmingham, 1938, Atlantic City, 1940; Southeastern Jurisdictional Conf., Asheville, N.C., 1940; Columbia, S.C., 1948; pres. Lake Junaluska Assembly, Inc., 1938-1944; dist. supt., Greensboro Dist., Western N.C. Annual Conf., 1944-49, ret. 1949. Mem. Phi Beta Kappa, Omicron Delta Kappa, Sigma Alpha Epsilon. Club: Rotary. Home: 1801 Shepard St., Morehead City, N.C. Died Nov. 20, 1952.

LAMBRIGHT, Edwin Dart, newspaper editor; b. Brunswick, Ga., May 21, 1874; s. Joseph Edward and Julia Sarah (Dart) L.; student Emory Coll., Oxford, Ga., 1890-92; Litt.D., Emory U., Atlanta, Ga., 1936; m. Cannie Rebecca Finch, Feb. 10, 1903; 1 dau., Mary Wallace (Mrs. M. M. Frost). Began as reporter on Brunswick Times, 1893; city editor, 1894, editor, 1895-99; city editor Tampa (Fla.) Tribune, 1899-1901, mng. editor, 1901-12, editor, 1912-17 and since 1923; postmaster, Tampa, 1917-23, Del. to Dem. Nat. Conv., 1912, 24 (chmn. delegation, 1924). Chief yeoman Ga. Naval Res., Spanish-Am. War; chmn. War Savings Stamp Campaign, four-minute man and publicity chmn. Liberty Loan Campaigns, World War. Mem. Fla. State Planning Bd., 1934-35. Fla. mem. Nat. Council of Nat. Economic League. Trustee Tampa Pub. Library, 1915-26. Chmn. Tampa United Service Orgns. Council 1941-45; pres. Emory U. Alumni Assn. Chmn. 116th Field Arty. Boxing Commn. 1942-45; pres. Tampa Civic Music Association. Mem. Am. Society Newspaper Editors, Nat. Aeronautic Assn., Phi Delta Theta, Sigma Delta Chi. Democrat. Methodist. Elk. Club: Rotary (pres. 1917-18), Tampa Executives (pres. 1941-42). Home: 828 S. Willow Av. Office: care The Tribune Co., Tampa, Fla. Died Dec. 1959.*

LAMM, Lynne M., correspondent; b. Phila., Feb. 6, 1890; s. I. L. and Dollie (Meinhold) L.; student pvt. schs.; m. Edna Wakeham, May 13, 1913; 1 son, Donald Wakeham. Reporter Washington Post, 1910-15; Washington corr. for newspapers and trade papers 1915—. Christian Scientist. Club: Nat. Press. Author: Tariff History of the Paper Industry of the U.S. Contbr. to mags. Home: 2408 California St., N.W. Office: National Press Bldg., Washington. Died May 14, 1949.

LA MONTE, John Life, educator; b. Columbus, O., Oct. 10, 1902; s. Charles Ludwig and Lillian (Shannon) L.; A.B., Ohio State U., 1922, A.M., 1923; A.M., Harvard, 1924, Ph.D., 1929; m. Marguerite Sisson, June 20, 1923; 1 son, Robert Ellis; m. 2d, Katherine Richardson, Aug. 14, 1929. Instr. history Ohio State U., 1925-27; instr. U. of Neb., 1917-29; lectr. history U. Minn., 1930-31; asst. prof., asso. prof. U. Cin., 1931-40; asso. prof. U. of Pa., 1940-47, Henry C. Lea prof. of medieval history, 1947—; summer lectr. U. Tex., 1940, U. So. Cal., 1948, Harvard, 1949; fellow Social Sci. Research Council, 1929-30, J. S. Guggenheim found., 1937-38. Served as lt. USNR, 1942-44. Fellow Royal Hist. Soc., London; mem. Medieval Acad. of Am. (council), Am. Hist. Assn., Soc. for Byzantine Studies, Am. Assn. U. Profs., Phi Beta Kappa, Sigma Nu, Phi Alpha Theta. Club: Franklin Inn (Phila.). Author: Feudal Monarchy in the Latin Kingdom of Jerusalem, 1932; The Wars of Frederick II in Syria and Cyprus, 1936; The Crusade of Richard Lionheart (with M. J. Hubert), 1941; The World of the Middle Ages, 1949. Editor: The History of the Crusades; University of Pennsylvania Translations and Reprints; Centers of Civilization (series). Contbr. to profl. jours. Address: 4014 Pine St., Phila. 4. Died Oct. 2, 1949.

LAMPE, William Edmund, ofcl. Evang. and Ref. Ch.; b. Frederick, Md., May 23, 1875; s. Christian Lewis Charles and Mary Eva (Babel) L.; grad. Frederick (Md.) Acad., 1892; A.B., Princeton, 1896, A. M., 1898, Ph.D. magna cum laude, 1908, grad. Theol. Sem. Ref. Ch., Lancaster, Pa., 1899; LL.D., Catawba College, Salisbury, N.C., 1937; D.D., Ursinus College, 1943; m. Anna Lenora Thomas, Dec. 28, 1899; children—Mary Elizabeth, William Thomas, Mrs. Grace Evelyn Morrison, Harold Christian, John Edmund, Carl Anspach, Anne Kathryn. Ordained to ministry Ref. Ch. in U.S., 1900; missionary, Sendai, Japan, 1900-07; also tchr. English, Greek and N.T. theology North Japan Coll., 1900-05, and chmn. Foreign Community of Sendai, 1903-07; organizer, 1908, sec., 1908-16, Laymen's Missionary Movement of Ref. Ch.; rec. sec. World's Sunday Sch. Assn., 1916-24, Fgn. Missionary Conf. N.A., 1917-22, 28, 29; sec. United Missionary and Stewardship Com., Ref. Ch. 1914-26; sec. Exec. Com. of Gen. Synod Reformed Ch. in U.S., 1926-34; now sec. of the Evang. and Reformed Ch. and its General Synod and General Council. Pres. United Stewardship Council Churches of Christ, 1933. Mem. Fed. Council Chs. (mem. exec. com., and commn. on Internat. Justice and Good Will). Gen. Commn. on Army and Navy Chaplains, Religious Publicity Council. Am. Acad. Polit. and Social Science, Temperance League of Pa. and America, Am. Whig Society (Pirnceton), Phi Beta Kappa, Lambda Chi Alpha (hon.). Republican. Clubs: Overbrook Assn. (ex-pres.), Penn Athletic. Author: The Japanese Social Organization, 1910. Contbr. to religious jours. Home: 5004 Pine St., Phila. 43. Office: 1505 Race St., Phila. Died Aug. 16, 1950; buried Frederick, Md.

LAMPLAND, Carl Otto, astronomer; b. Dodge County, Minn., Dec. 29, 1873; s. Ole Helleckson and Beret (Skartum) L.; B.S., Valparaiso (Ind.) Univ., 1899; A.B., Indiana U., 1902, A.M., 1905, LL.D., 1930; m. Verna Basil Darby, Feb. 8, 1911. Prin. Bloomfield (Ind.) High Sch., 1902; astronomer Lowell Obs., Flagstaff, Ariz., since 1903; member Lowell Obs. Eclipse Expdn. to Kan., 1918, also solar eclipse expdn. to Ensenada, Mexico, 1923. Was asst. to late Dr. Percival Lowell in visual observations of the planets Venus, Mars, Jupiter and Saturn; has given much attention to development of photography of delicate detail on planetary surfaces; prin. work of recent yrs. photographic observations of planets, satellites, comets, nebulae, novae, and star fields; has discovered many variable stars, and changes in nebulae; measurements of radiation from planets and determination of planetary temperatures (early work with W. W. Coblentz, continued and extended in recent years with the assistance of V. D. Lampland); transmission of the earth's atmosphere (with A. Adel); investigations in connection with trans-Neptunian planet Pluto. Exchange professor astronomy, Princeton, 1929. Fellow Am. Acad. Arts and

Sciences, A.A.A.S.; mem. Am. Astron. Society (council), Internat. Astron. Union (com. on planets and nebulae), Astron. Soc. Pacific, Société Astronomique de France, Astronomische Gesellschaft, Am. Physical Soc., Math. Assn. America, Am. Philos. Soc., Am. Math. Soc., Soc. for Research on Meteorites, Northern Ariz. Soc. of Science and Art (v.p. and trustee), Sigma Xi, Phi Beta Kappa; hon. mem. Sociedad Astronomico de Mexico. Medalist Royal Photographic Soc. of Grt. Britain, 1907. for photographs of planet Mars. Contbr. to astronomical journals. Address: Lowell Observatory, Flagstaff, Ariz. Died Dec. 14, 1951; buried Fairview Cemetery, Hayfield, Minn.

LAMPMAN, Ben Hur, editorial writer; b. Barron, Wis., Aug. 12, 1886; s. Herbert Hathaway and Viola Victoria (Emmons) L.; ed. pub. schs.; honorary M.A., University of Oregon, 1943; honorary LL.D., University of Portland, May 25, 1947; m. Lena McEwen Sheldon, June 1, 1906; children—Caroline Sheldon Cooper, Hope Hathaway Fiske. Founder, 1905 and pub. The Arena, Michigan City, N.D.; editor, and pub. Gold Hill (Oregon) News, 1912-1916; joined staff of The Oregonian, 1916, and editorial writer same since 1919, asso. editor since 1939. Apptd. poet laureate State Ore. by gov., 1951. Republican. Author: How Could I Be Forgetting?, 1929; The Tramp Printer, 1934; Here Comes Somebody, 1935; At the End of the Car Line, 1942; The Coming of the Pond Fishes, 1946; The Wild Swan, 1947. O. Henry Memorial Short Story Award, 1943, 1945. Home: 4 S.E. 84th Av. Address: The Oregonian, Portland, Ore. Died Jan. 24, 1954; buried Lincoln Meml. Park.

LAMPREY, Louise, author; b. Alexandria, N.H., Apr. 17, 1869; d. Rev. Henry Phelps and Ellen Selomy (Hardy) Lamprey; student Concord (N.H.) High Sch., 1884-85, Mt. Holyoke Coll., 1891. Editorial writer The Capital, Washington, 1894-98, Washington Times, 1896-1904, and in Rep. Nat. campaign of 1904; mag., newspaper and office work, N.Y.C., Washington and London, Eng., 1904-14; with World Book Co., Yonkers, N.Y., 1916-18. Spent summers, 1912-19, at a children's camp, East Berkshire, Vt., story telling, teaching handicraft, writing and staging impromptu plays. Author: In the Days of the Guild, 1918; Masters of the Guild, 1920; Days of the Discoverers, 1921; (with Mara Chadwick) The Alo Man, 1921; Children of Ancient Britain, 1921; Days of the Colonists, 1922; Children of Ancient Rome, 1922; Days of the Commanders, 1923; Children of Ancient Greece, 1924; Days of the Pioneers, 1924; Days of the Leaders, 1925; Children of Ancient Egypt, 1926; Days of the Builders, 1926; Wonder Tales of Architecture, 1927; Children of Ancient Gaul, 1927; The Treasure Valley, 1928; Natalia and Nikolai (with Varia Klenova), 1928; All the Ways of Building, 1933; The Tomahawk Trail, 1934; History of Limerick, Maine, 1937; Limerick Pageant, 1937; The Story of Weaving, 1939; The Story of Cookery, 1940; Building an Empire, 1941; Building a Republic, 1942. Contbr. articles on architecture and primitive dwellings to Jr. Ency. Britannica, 1935. Hoke: Limerick, Me. Died Jan. 13, 1951; buried Blossom Hill Cemetery, Concord, N.H.

LANCASTER, Chester L(eland), mfg. exec.; born Hamilton, O., 1904; s. James G. and Ora (Lancaster L.; Chem.E., U. Cin., 1929; m. Frieda Meier, Aug. 31, 1929; children—Nancy Helen, Patricia Ann. With Electric Auto-Lite Co., Sharonville, O, since 1928, chemist-plating supervisor, 1929-35, electroplating engr., 1935-38, gen. mgr. Buckeye Bumper div., Springfield, O., 1938-46, gen. mgr. Sharonville, O., 1946-50, v.p. since 1950. Mem. American Electroplaters Soc., Engring. Soc. Cin. Methodist. Home: 6501 Brackenridge, Ridgewood, Cin. 13. Died June 26, 1957; buried Hamilton, O.

LANCASTER, Ellsworth Gage, educator; b. Dixfield, Me., June 18, 1861; s. Benjamin Franklin and Aurora Deborah (Norcross) L.; A.B., Amherst, 1885, A.M., 1888; B.D., Andover (Mass.) Theol. Sem., 1889; Ph.D., Clark U., 1897; LL.D., Colo. Coll., 1905; m. Bertha A. Chase, July 17, 1889 (died, 1899); m. 2d, Elizabeth Tyler, June 25, 1907. Ordained Congl. ministry, 1889; pastor Ashby, Mass., 1889; prin. acad. at Eureka, Kan., 1890-5; prof. psychology and pedagogy Colo. Coll., 1897-1904; pres. Olivet (Mich.) Coll., 1904-15; head academic dept. Ky. Mil. Inst., London, Ky., 1921-23; prof. child and adolescent psychology U. Fla., Gainesville, 1930—. Mem. Internat. Congress Edn. and Protection of Children Within the Home. N.E.A. (pres. child study sect., 1904-5). Author: Psychology and Pedagogy of Adolescence, 1897; also mag. articles. War work for YMCA, 1917—. Address: Maine St., Gaines-North Conway, N.H. Died Nov. 14, 1934; buried Dixfield, Me.

LANCASTER, Henry Carrington, univ. prof.; b. Richmond, Va., Nov. 10, 1882; s. Robert Alexander and Williamine Cabell (Carrington) L.; B.A. and M.A., U. of Va., 1903; Ph.D., Johns Hopkins, 1907; hon. M.A., Amherst, 1912; Dr. hon. causa, Algiers, 1944, Paris, 1946; L.H.D. (honorary), Tulane Univ., New Orleans, 1950; married Helen Converse, daughter John Bates Clark, June 11, 1913; children—John Huntington (dec.), Helen Carrington (Mrs. Paul Rand), Maria Dabney (Mrs. Donald Churchill Cameron), Henry Carrington, Robert Alexander (dec.). Instructor of Romance languages at Amherst College, 1907-08, associate professor, 1908-10, professor, 1910-19 professor French lit. Johns Hopkins University, 1919-52, research professor since 1952, chmn. dep. Romance langs., 1919-47; visiting prof., New York University, 1930-41, Tulane University, New Orleans, 1950; Walker Ames professor, University of Wash., 1941; summer session, Univ. of Chicago, 1916, 24; asso. editor Modern Lang. Notes, 1919-28, editor in chief since 1928; editor Johns Hopkins Series in Romance lits. and langs.; corr. Rev. d'histoire litt. de la France since 1921. Dir. Foyer at Lizy-sur-Ourcq and Am. ednl. dir. of Foyers du Soldat, France, Dec. 1917-Dec. 1918. Dir. Am. Univ. Union (Paris); Hyde exchange lecturer in French univs., 1924-25. Chevalier Legion of Honor (France), 1932; Officer, 1948. Pres. Brit. Humanities Research Assn., 1947. Democrat. Presbyn. Mem. Modern Language Assn. of America (exec. council, 1920-23, 30, 1934-37; v.p. 1931, 38; pres. 1939), Am. Philos. Soc., Am. Acad. Arts and Sciences, Société des anciens textes français, Société des textes français modernes, American Assn. of Univ. Profs. (v.p. 1942-43), Delta Tau Delta and Phi Beta Kappa fraternities. Author: The French Tragi-Comedy, 1907; Pierre Du Ryer, Dramatist, 1912; Le Mémoire de Mahelot et d'autres décorateurs de l'Hôtel de Bourgogne et de la Comédie Française, 1920; La Calprenède, Dramatist, 1920; Jean Mairet, Chryséide et Arimand, 1925; A History of French Dramatic Literature in the Seventeenth Century (9 vols., 1929-42); Du Ryer, Alcionée, 1930; Saül, 1931; Five French Farces, 1937; Comédie Française, 1680-1701, 1941; Adventures of a Literary Historian, 1942; Sunset, a Hist. of Parisian Drama in the last years of Louis XIV, 1945; French Tragedy in the Time of Louis XV and Voltaire, 1950; The Comedie Francaise 1701-74, 1951; French Tragedy in the Reign of Louis XVI, 1953; Actors Roles at the Comédie Française, 1953; First French Tragedie Bourgeois Silvie, 1954. Editor: Racine, 1934; Index, Modern Language Notes, 1946. Clubs: University, Johns Hopkins. Home: 3938 Cloverhill Rd., Balt. Died Jan. 29, 1954; buried Richmond, Va.

LANCASTER, Walter B., ophthalmic surgeon; b. Newton, Mass., May 11, 1863; s. Charles Bartlett and Mary Elizabeth (Brackett) L.; A.B., magna cum laude, Harvard, 1884, M.D., 1889; grad. work, Vienna, London, Edinburgh; D.Sc. (hon.), Dartmouth Coll., 1939; m. Emma Winter, Dec. 15, 1885; 1 dau., Julia Elizabeth. Practice ophthalmology, Boston, Mass., since 1890; ophthalmic surgeon, Mass. Eye and Ear Infirmary, Mass. Gen. Hosp., Boston City Hosp.; chief staff eye clinic Dartmouth Coll., 1940-42; teacher med. sch. Harvard since 1898. Exec. officer, Ophthal. Study Council. Clerk, Foundation for Vision, Inc. Awarded ophthalmic research medal A.M.A., 1941, 5th De Scheinitz lecture Coll. Physicians, Phila., 1942, Leslie Dana medal for prevention of blindness, 1943; International Ophthalmic Medal of A.O.S., 1944; Lucien Howe Medal by American Ophthal. Soc., 1945. Served as major in the medical corps United States Army Air Force, 1918-19, in charge ophthalmology, research lab., Mineola. Mem. Am. Orthoplic Council; chmn. Am. com. on optics and visual physiol., since 1930. A founder, Lancaster course in ophthalmol. for graduate students. Mem. and past pres. Am. Ophthal. Soc., Am. Acad. Ophthal. and Otol., New England Ophthal. Soc., Am. Bd. Ophthal., A.M.A. (sect. on ophthal.); mem. A.A.A.S., A.C.S., Assn. Research in Ophthal. (mem. council); del. Internat. Congress Ophthal., 1929. Contbr. 75 papers to med. jours. Home: 374 Commonwealth Av. Office: 520 Commonwealth Av., Boston. Died Dec. 9, 1951.

LAND, Frank Sherman, orgn. founder; born Kansas City, Mo., June 21, 1890; s. William Sherman and Elizabeth L. (Sampson) L.; ed. pub. schs., St. Louis and Kansas City, Kan. City Art Inst., L.H.D., Indiana Technical College, Ft. Wayne, 1954. Merchant, 1910-14; dir. Columbia Nat. Bank, Kansas City, Mo. Mem. exec. com. Nat. Security Com., Washington. Sec. social service, Kansas City Scottish Rite, 1914-20; founder, 1919, since sec. general of Supreme Council, Order of De Molay, boy's orgn. of Masonic Order; pres. bd. trustees De Molay Dormitory Assn. of U. of Mo.; past potentate Ararat Temple, Kansas City; dep. imperial potentate of Shrine for North America, 1953, imperial potentate, 1954-55; trustee of the Harry S. Truman Library Corp.; past sovereign Red Cross of Constantine, grand standard bearer, Imperial Council, Red Cross Constantine of United States. Founder, 1927; Young Men's Civic Forum International; co-founder, 1930, Metro Clubs. Member American Advisory Council Yenching U., Peiping, China; mem. Nat. Youth Week Com. for U.S.; dir. Kansas City Zool. Soc.; mem. Native Sons of Kansas City, Mo., Mo. Hist. Soc.; life mem. Kansas City Conf. of Social Work. Hon. mem. Grand Chapter Royal Arch Masons of Mich.; hon. mem. Order of Sciots (Los Angeles); hon. mem. Grand Lodge, AF&AM, Mont., Grand Chpt. R.A.M., Mich. Grand Cross Ct. Honor, Supreme Council, 33°, A&ASR, SJ, 1955. First Internat. Gold Royal Arch Medal, Gen. Grand Chpt., Royal Arch Masons, 1951. Christian Scientist. Odd Fellow. Clubs: Chicago; Carriage, Kansas City. Presented Achievement Medal of City of Toledo, O., 1932. Home: 420 E. Armour Blvd. Office: 210 E. Armour Blvd. Kansas City 2, Mo. Died Nov. 8, 1959.

LANDES, Herbert Ellis, urologist, educator; b. Greencastle, Ind., Oct. 5, 1894; s. Albert and Mary Louise (Ellis) L.; A.B., De Pauw U., 1917; M.S., U. Chgo., 1919; M.D., Rush Med. Coll., 1922; grad. study U. Vienna, 6 mos. 1930, Johns Hopkins Hosp., 1930-32; m. Wyota Ann Ewing, Sept. 4, 1918; children—Mary Louise, John Ewing. Intern Presbyn. Hosp., 1921-22; clin. prof. urology, sch. medicine Loyola U., 1932, prof. 1934—, chmn. dept. urology, 1939—; sr. attending urologist Mercy Hosp., 1932, chmn. dept. urology, 1939—; cons. urologist Chgo. Municipal TB Sanitarium, Elgin (Ill.) State Hosp., Little Co. of Mary Hosp., Chgo., Burlington R.R., Lewis Meml. Hosp., Chgo. Diplomate Am. Bd. Urology. Fellow A.C.S.; mem. A.M.A., Ill. State Med. Soc., Inst. Medicine, Am., Chgo. urology assns., Sigma Xi, Phi Beta Kappa, Nu Sigma Nu, Phi Gamma Delta, Alpha Omega Alpha. Clubs: South Shore Country, University (Chgo.). Contbr. textbooks on urology; also articles. Home: 6901 Oglesby Av. Office: 30 N. Michigan Av., Chgo. Died Sept. 24, 1959.

LANDFIELD, Jerome (Barker), b. Newark Valley, N.Y., May 7, 1871; s. Jerome B. and Helen (Rogers) L.; A.B., Cornell U., 1894; grad. student Cornell and in St. Petersburg, Russia, 1894-97; m. Princess Louba Lobanoff-Rostovsky, Mar. 3, 1907. Mining exploration in Kirghiz Steppes, 1898, Ural Mountains, 1899, eastern Siberia, 1907; instr. in European History, U. Cal., 1902-06. Adv. Russian affairs, Dept. of State, 1918. Asso. editor The Weekly Rev., 1920-21, The Ind., 1921-23; sec. advisory bd. Columbia U. Sch. Journalism, 1925-28. Lectr. and writer. Fellow Royal Geog. Soc.; mem. Am. Hist. Assn., Am. Inst. Mining and Metall. Engrs., Russian Imperial Geog. Soc., Delta Upsilon, Phi Beta Kappa. Club: Bohemian (San Francisco). Editor, translator, Prisoner of the OGPU (by George Kitchin), 1935. Author: California—America's Vineyard, 1945; The Story of Wine, 1945; The Verdiers and the City of Paris—a Century in San Francisco, 1949. Home: Bohemian Club, San Francisco. Died Nov. 1954.

LANDIS, Harry DeWitt, judge; b. Sterling, Ill., July 17, 1878; s. Elam Hershey and Alice Narcissa (Eshleman) L.; B.S., U. of Neb., 1899, LL.B., 1901, J.D., 1919; m. Alice Mabel Cattle, June 27, 1907 (died Oct. 2, 1932); children—Harry DeWitt, Walter Elam, John Cattle, Frank Eshleman, Alice Mabel, George Edward. Admitted to Neb. bar, 1901, and practiced at Seward until 1925; mem. Norval Bros., 1919-25; acting county judge, Seward County, 1914-19; judge Dist. Court, 5th Neb. Dist., since 1925. Member Governor's Penal Investigating Committee. State chmn. 4-minute men, chairman Seward County 4-minute Victory speakers, and chmn. War Savings Stamps drive, Seward County, World War; lt. col. Judge Advocate Gen. Res. Regent U. of Neb. since 1917 (pres. bd. 1923, 28); trustee Hastings Coll., U. of Neb. Foundation; dir. Neb. Tuberculosis Assn.; pres. Social Welfare Soc., 1917-20; pres. Neb. Council for Crime Prevention. Mem. Am. and Neb. State bar assns., Res. Officers Assn., Civil Legion, Heroes of '76, Phi Delta Phi, Sigma Chi, Innocents (U. of Neb.), Pi Gamma Mu. Presbyterian. Mason, O.E.S., Odd Fellow, Elk; mem. Sons of Hermann. Clubs: University (Lincoln); Rotary, Sojourners. Home: 34 Lincoln St. Office: Court House, Seward, Neb. Died Apr. 23, 1956; buried Seward.

LANDOWSKA, Wanda, musician; born Warsaw, Poland, July 5, 1879; d. Marjan and Eva (Lautenberg) Landowski; student of piano at age of 4; grad. Warsaw Cons. of Music, 1893; Mus.D. (honoris causa), J. Hart College Music, 1953; m. Henry Lew, 1900. In U.S., 1941—; French citizen. Mem. faculty Schola Cantorum, Paris, 1900-13; founded School of Ancient Music, St. Leu la Foret, France, 1927, teacher, 1927-40; Am. debut, with Phila. Orchestra, 1923; holds classes for advanced musician, N.Y. City; concertized widely throughout Europe, Asia, Americas, Africa appearing as harpsichordist and piano soloist with major orchestras. Decorated Chevalier de la Legion of Honeur; Officer Polonia Restituta. Author: Music of the Past, 1909. Composer; recorded numerous compositions (RCA). Recorded all Bach's Forty-Eight Preludes and Fugues of the Well Tempered Clavier; recorded also many other compositions for piano and clavier. Responsible for renaissance of the harpsichord and true interpretation of 17th and 18th Century Music. Home: P.O. Box 313, Lakeville, Conn. Died Aug. 16, 1959; inurned Taverny, France.

LANDMAN, Louis W., business exec.; b. Waynetown, Ind., 1869. Pres. and dir. Parmalee Transportation Co., Chicago; dir. Gen. Transportation Casualty & Surety Co. Home: 1225 Park Av., N.Y. City. Office: 300 N. Desplaines St., Chgo. Died Aug. 15, 1952.

LANE, Arthur Bliss; b. Bay Ridge, Long Island, N.Y., June 16, 1894; s. James Warren and Eva Metcalf (Bliss) L.; prep. edn., Browning Sch., N.Y.

City, and École de l'Ile de France; A.B., Yale, 1916; m. Cornelia Thayer Baldwin, June 19, 1918; 1 dau., Margaret Bliss (Mrs. Albert E. Ninde) (deceased). In United States diplomatic service since 1916; private secretary Am. ambassador to Italy, 1916; 3d sec. of Embassy, Rome, 1917-19; 2d sec. of Embassy, Warsaw, 1919, London, 1920-22; sec. U.S. delegation to Supreme Council, Paris, 1921; sec. of Legation, Berne, Switzerland, 1922-24; asst. to undersec. of state, 1924; 1st sec., Mexico City, 1925-28, chargé d'affaires, part of 1926, 30, and 33; chief of Div. of Mexican Affairs, 1927-30; counselor of embassy, Mexico, 1930-33; minister to Nicaragua, 1933-36; E.E. and M.P. to Estonia, Latvia and Lithuania, 1936-37, Yugoslavia, 1937-41; minister to Costa Rica 1941; ambassador to Colombia, 1942-44; apptd. Ambassador near Polish Govt. in London, Sept. 1944; ambassador to Polish Govt., Warsaw, July 1945-47. Served as chmn. exec. com. Am. Foreign Service Assn., 1928-29, pres. 1930-31; chmn. Am. Com. to investigate the Katyn Massacure, Inc., 1949-52, Paderewski Testimonial Fund, 1948-51; mem. Nat. Com. for a Free Europe, 1949-51, Com. for a United Europe, Council on Fgn. Relations; coordinator of Fgn. Language Groups of Rep. Nat. Com., 1952 campaign. Mem. Connecticut National Guard, 1915-16. Mem. Diplomatic and Consular Officers Ret. (pres. 1954—), Zeta Psi. Clubs: Metropolitan, Alibi (Washington, D.C.); Racquet and Tennis, Yale, India House (New York); St. James (London). Author: Conquest in Yugoslavia, 1941; How Russia Rules Poland, 1947; I Saw Poland Betrayed, 1948. Lectures: The Folly of Appeasement, 1948; Time is Running Out, 1949. Home: 2442 Massachusetts Av. N.W., Washington 8. Died Aug. 12, 1956.

LANE, Chester T(evis), lawyer; b. London, Eng., June 7, 1905; s. Elmer Bloomfield and Julia Anthony (Tevis) L. (parents U.S. citizens); ed. Westminster Sch., London, 1917-22; A.B., Harvard, 1926, LL.B., 1930; m. Persis McClennen, Sept. 12, 1927; children—David, Julia Ann (Mrs. Eugene Lane Tarchar, Jr.), Dinah, Chester Tevis, Jr. Instr. and tutor in classics, Harvard, 1926-28, Radcliffe Coll., 1927-28; admitted to N.Y. bar, 1931; practiced with Milbank, Tweed, Hope & Webb (now Milbank, Tweed, Hope & Hadley, N.Y., 1930-35; with Securities & Exch. Commn., Wash., 1935-42, mem. staff gen. counsel, 1935-37, asst. gen. counsel, 1937-38, gen. counsel, 1938-42; asso. in pub. law, N.Y.U., 1941-42; spl. asst. to atty. gen., 1942-45; asso. chief spl. war policies unit, war div., Dept. of Justice, 1942-43; chmn. War Dept. Civilian Legal Personnel Com. (in charge of recruitment and approval of civilian attys. in War Dept.), 1942-46; sr. cons. Army-Navy liquidation commr., 1945; Lend-Lease adminstr. and dep. fgn. liquidation commr., 1946-47. Gen. practice law with Greenman, Shea, Lane, Sandomire & Zimet, 1947-49; now with Beer, Richards, Lane, Haller & Buttenwieser; cons. U.S. Civil Service Commn., 1948-49; lectr. N.Y. U. Sch. Law, 1949. Pres. Rockland Found., 1953-55. Recipient War Dept. Meritorious Civilian Service Commendation, 1945. Decorated Comdr. Order Orange-Nassau (Netherlands). Mem. Am. Bar Assn. (mem., vice-chmn., chmn. various coms., 1952—), Assn. Bar City N.Y. (chmn. adminstrv. law com. 1955—, mem. fed. legislative com. 1948-51, chmn. sect. adminstrv. law and procedure, post-admission legal edn. com. 1954-57, mem. adminstrv. law com. 1953-58, chmn. 1955-58, mem. bill rights com. 1958—), Phi Beta Kappa. Democrat. Clubs: Harvard (N.Y.); Chatham (Mass.) Yacht; Upper Nyack Tennis, Heights Casino. Home: Broadway, Upper Nyack, N.Y. Office: 150 Broadway, N.Y.C. 38. Died Mar. 12, 1959; buried Evergreen Cemetery, East Harwich, Mass.

LANE, Clarence Guy, physician; b. Billerica, Mass., Oct. 21, 1882; s. Albert Clarence and Estella Josephine (Davis) L.; A.B., Harvard, 1905, M.D., 1908; m. Mary Rivers McHarry, May 31, 1919; 1 son, Robert. Intern Worcester City Hosp., 1908-10; in gen. practice, Woburn, Mass., 1910-14; specializing in dermatology, Boston, 1914—; mem. dept. dermatology Mass. Gen. Hosp., 1920-47, chief of dept., 1936-47, teaching in dept. dermatology Harvard Med. Sch., 1922-47, head of dept., 1936-47; clin. prof. dermatology, 1939-47, emeritus, 1947—. On editorial bd. N.E. Jour. of Medicine, Archives of Dermatology and Syphilology; cons. in dermatology at a number of hosps. Served from lt. to capt. M.C., U.S. Army, 1918-19. Awarded Cutter medal, Phi Rho Sigma, 1948. Mem. A.M.A. (mem. council on planning and chemistry), Am. Bd. Dermatology and Syphilology (dir. and sec., 1932-43; pres. 1944-45; sec. Adv. Bd. for Med. Specialties 1941-43), Nat. Com. on Indsl. Dermatoses, Am. Dermatol. Assn. (dir. 1927-35, pres. 1935, sec. 1925-30), N.E. Dermatol. Soc., N.Y. Acad. of Medicine. Republican. Protestant. Mason (K.T., Shriner). Clubs: Harvard (Boston); Faculty. Editor: Vol. X of Practitioners Medical Library, 1935; contbr. about 70 articles to med. jours. Lecturer on dermatology A.M.A., 1949. Home: 220 Marlborough St., Boston. Died Mar. 12, 1954; buried Mt. Auburn Cemetery, Cambridge, Mass.

LANE, Clement Quirk, newspaperman; b. Chgo., July 7, 1897; s. John and Mary (Quirk) L.; m. Angela Lavery, Apr. 28, 1923; children—Rosemary, Clement Quirk (AUS), John Joseph, Robert Casey, Sheila. Reporter, Daily Press, Pontiac, Mich., 1921; reporter Chgo. Daily News, 1924-38, began Oxie O'Rourke column, 1938, city editor, 1942—; lectr. journalism Loyola U., 1937—. Served as corpl. Corps Engrs., U.S. Army, 1918-19. Roman Catholic. Home: 7443 N. Hoyne Av. Office: 400 W. Madison St., Chgo. Died Oct. 1958.

LANE, Elbert Clarence, clergyman; b. Jackson, Mich., July 19, 1870; s. Joshua Smith and Myra A. (Knight) L.; B.S., Adrian (Mich.) Coll., 1893, A. B., 1894, D.D., 1926; postgrad. U. Mich., 1894-95, U. Chgo., 1922-23, U. of Berlin, 1923; B.D., Hartford (Conn.) Theol. Sem., 1912; m. Ida Jane Haley, Aug. 8, 1894. Instr. in Latin, Adrian Coll., 1893-94; prin. high sch., Riverside, Ill., 1895-96; pastor Meth. protestant chs., Springdale, Pa., 1897-99, Amity, 1899-1903, Pitts., 1903-05, New Brighton, 1905-09, Community Ch., Wilson, Conn., 1909-21; instr. in Hebrew and Greek, Hartford Theol. Sem., 1912-21, asso. prof., 1921-26, prof., 1926-39, prof. emeritus, 1939—, acting dean, 1938; hon. lectr. Am. Sch. Oriental Research, Jerusalem, 1935; lectr. in N.T., Hartford Sch. Religious Edn., 1943-44; lectr. Near East Sch. Theology, Beirut, Syria. Trustee Adrian College, 1922-31. Mem. Soc. Bibl. Lit. and Exegesis, Nat. Assn. Bibl. Instrs., Archaeol. Soc., Fgn. Policy Assn., Sigma Alpha Epsilon. Republican. Conglist. Club: Connecticut Congregational. Contbr. to New Standard Bible Dictionary, 1926, co-editor 3d edit., 1936. Home: 69 Tremont St., Hartford 5, Conn. Died Aug. 26, 1950.

LANE, Robert Porter, social work exec.; b. Fort Wayne, Ind., Apr. 7, 1891; s. Chester Taylor and Caroline (Bloomfield) L.; A.B., Univ. of Mich., 1913, A.M., 1915; spent summers in grad. work, Univ. of Chicago, 1930-31-32; m. Bess B. Edwards, Sept. 2, 1913; children—Elizabeth Bobette (Mrs. Monroe C. Beardsley), Robert Edwards. Asst. sec. to Governor of Mich., sec. to Mich. Board of Pardons, 1911-12; instructor in rhetoric, Univ. of Mich., 1913-15, instr. political science, 1915-17; asst. mgr., Subscription-Agency Division, Curtis Publishing Co., 1917-19; asst. dir. of publicity, American Red Cross, 1919-20; European dir., American Junior Red Cross, 1920-23; special lecturer on economic and political conditions in Europe for Inst. of Internat. Education, 1923; asst. nat. dir., Junior Red Cross, 1923-25; vocational dir., Curtis Pub. Co., 1925-29; asst. prof. of indsl. society, Dartmouth Coll., 1929-34; special supervisor, Bureau of Labor Statistics, 1934; exec. sec., Com. on Labor Statistics, Central Statistical Board, Washington, 1934; exec. dir., Welfare Council, New York, 1934-46. Visiting prof. sociol., Harvard Univ., spring 1949. Dir. Community Survey, Kansas City, Kans., 1946; Springfield, Mass., 1947; New London, Conn., 1947, Greater Boston, 1947-49, Elizabeth, N.J., 1950; consultant to bd. dirs. Allegheny Co. Community Chest, 1949, exec. dir., 1950. Mem. Am. Assn. Social Workers, Nat. Conf. Social Work, Phi Beta Kappa. Home: Schenley Apts., 4014 Fifth Av., Pittsburgh 13. Office: 519 Smithfield St., Pitts. 22. Died Mar. 30, 1953.

LANG, Charles B., steel exec.; b. Thornton, Ill., Sept. 17, 1887; s. John M. and Kathryn (Kanarr) L.; student pub. schs. Ill.; m. Marion Bradley Flett, June 4, 1914; 1 son, John Austin. With Brownell Improvement Co., Chicago; various positions steel cos., Chicago, 1916; mgr. Peck Rolling Mills Ltd., Montreal, Can., 1916-18; works mgr. Dominion Steel & Coal Corp., Ltd., Montreal, 1918, gen. mgr., 1919, v.p., mng. dir., 1930, v.p., dir., 1946, exec. vice president, 1947, president, 1948, now chairman of the board and chief executive officer. Member Montreal Board Trade, Can. Manufacturers Assn., Can. Engring. Standards Assn., Am. Iron and Steel Inst., Iron and Steel Inst. (Eng.), Army Ordnance Assn. Clubs: Mt. Royal, St. Jame's, Beaconsfield Golf, St. Maurice Fish and Game, Forest and Stream, Ste. Anne's Curling, Halifax (Halifax); Rideau (Ottawa) Engineers. Home: 538 Lakeshore Rd., Beaurepaire. Office: Canada Cement Bldg., Montreal, Que, Can. Died Feb. 1958.

LANGENBERG, Harry Hill, business exec.; born St. Louis, Oct. 2, 1879; s. Henry F. and Martha Letitia (Haynes) L.; student Princeton, 1900; m. Alice Morton, Apr. 21, 1908; children—Henry F., Oliver M. Formerly pres. Langenberg Bros. Grain Co.; dir. 1st Nat. Bank, St. Louis Union Trust Co., Gen. Am. Life Ins. Co. Clubs: St. Louis Country, Noonday, Deer Creek (St. Louis). Home: 49 Westmoreland Pl. Office: Security Bldg., St. Louis. Died Apr. 29, 1958; buried Bellefontaine Cemetery, St. Louis.

LANGER, Charles Heinrichs, accounting educator; b. Hameln, Germany, Aug. 7, 1876; brought to U.S., 1882; Ph.B.; C.P.A by exam., Ill., 1911. Lectr. on accounting Northwestern U., 1909-12; now pres., ednl. dir. Walton Sch. Commerce, Chgo.; former mem. Walton, Joplin, Langer & Co., C.P. A.'s. Mem. Am. Inst. Accountants, Am. Accounting Assn., Ill. Soc. C.P.A.'s. Phi Theta Pi. Clubs: Chicago Athletic, South Shore Country. Author: Constructive Accounting; Cost Accounting; Office Procedure and Practice; Advanced Accounting and Auditing; Municipal Accounting; Stock Brokerage Accounting. Co-Author: Mathematics of Acounting and Finance. Home: 4950 S. Chicago Beach Dr. Office: 109 N. Wabash Av., Chgo. Died Feb. 20, 1952.

LANGER, William, senator; b. Everest, N.D., Sept. 30, 1886; s. Frank J. and Mary (Weber) L.; LL.B., University of North Dakota, 1906; A.B., Columbia, 1910; m. Lydia Cady, Feb. 26, 1918; children—Emma Bulkley (Mrs. J. Peter Shaeffer), Lydia Langer (Mrs. D. King Irwin), Mary Erskine (Mrs. Franklyn Gokey), Cornelia Lyndon (Mrs. Kenneth Noland). State's atty. of Morton County, North Dakota, 1914-16; atty. general 1916-1920; legal advisor, Council of Defense, World War; on N.D. campaign committee, Robert M. La Follette for President, each time he was a candidate, and co-manager of Hiram Johnson for President com.; Rep. nominee for gov. in 1920; gov. of N.D., 1933-July 17, 1934, when he was removed by the Supreme Court of N.D.; only person ever to be arrested in any English-speaking country for filing an affidavit of prejudice against a judge; again governor, 1937-39; U.S. senator, 1941—. Mem. Sigma Chi. Home: Wheatland, R.F.D. 1 (Bismarck), N.D. Address: Senate Office Bldg., Washington. Died Nov. 8, 1959.

LANGERMAN, Joseph, v.p., sec., dir. Howard Stores Corp. Address: 170 Tillary St., Bklyn. 1. Deceased.*

LANGFELD, Herbert Sidney (lăng'fĕld), psychologist; b. Phila., Pa., July 24, 1879; s. Charles and Flora R. L.; A.B., Central High Sch., Phila., 1897; student Haverford Coll., 1897-98; Ph.D., Berlin, 1909; Dr. de l'Univ., University of Montreal, 1954; m. Florence Hoffman Purdy, Oct. 6, 1904; m. 2d, Mary Brita Bergland, June 11, 1932. Sec. naval attaché, Am. Embassy, Berlin, 1902-03; research fellow, Harvard, 1909-10, instr., 1910-15, asst. prof., 1915-22, asso. prof., 1922-24, acting dir., Psychol. Lab., 1917-19, dir., 1919-22; prof. and dir., Psychol. Lab., Princeton U., 1924-47; Stuart prof. of psychology, 1937-47; Stuart prof. of psychology emeritus, 1947—. Fellow A.A.A.S. (v.p. 1931); member Am. Psychol. Assn. (sec. 1917-19, pres. 1930, hon. pres. New York branch, 1935-36. Research sec. Y.M.C.A., in France, 1918. Sec. gen. Internat. Congress Psychology, 1945-50, Internat. Union Scientific Psychology, 1950-54; v.p. sect. exptl. psychology Internat. Union Biology, 1955—. Fellow N.Y. Acad. Scis.; chairman committee on international relations division anthropology and psychology, Nat. Research Council. Mem. Pontifical Acad. Sciences, Phi Beta Kappa, Sigma Psi. Republican. Episcopalian. Clubs: Nassau, Springdale (Princeton); Harvard (N.Y. City). Author: On the Psycho-physiology of a Prolonged Fast, 1914; An Elementary Laboratory Course in Psychology (joint author), 1916; The Aesthetic Attitude, 1920; Problems of Personalities (joint author and editor); Psychology, A Factual Textbook (joint author and editor), 1935; A Manual of Psychological Experiments (joint author and editor), 1937; Introduction to Psychology (joint author and editor), 1939; Psychology for the Fighting Man (joint editor), 1943; Psychology for the Armed Services (collaborator), 1945. Co-editor: Foundations of Psychology, 1948; History of Psychology in Autobiography, 1952. Editor Psychol. Monographs, 1931-34; editor Psychol. Review, 1934-47. Home: 100 Elm Road, Princeton, N.J. Died Feb. 25, 1958.

LANGFORD, George W., contractor, ins., real estate; b. Logansville, Ga., Oct. 12, 1886; s. David C. and Rosalee (Clemmons) L.; ed. pub. schs.; m. Oct. 11, 1913. Sr. partner George W. Langford Co., Miami, gen. contractors; pres. Langford & Ledbetter, ins., Miami, Dallas Park Hotel, Miami. Served as mem. and chief examiner, Miami Civil Service Bd., Miami. Mem. S.A.R., Committe of 100, Miami Beach Methodist. Mason (32°, Shriner). Clubs: Pendennis (Louisville, Ky.); Miami Country. Home: Dallas Park Hotel, Miami; summer: Weissinger Gaulbert Apts., Louisville, Ky. Office: 127 S.E. Third St., Miami, Fla. Died July 28, 1952.

LANGLEY, Ernest Felix, educator; b. Toronto, Can., Feb. 27, 1874; s. Henry Anderson and Annie (Booth) L.; B.A., U. of Toronto, 1894, grad. fellow, 1894-95; student U. of Leipsig, 1895-96, U. of Heidelberg, 1896; A.M., Harvard, 1900, Ph.D., 1909; grad. student Istituto di Studi Superiori, Florence, Italy, 1905-06, Sorbonne, 1906 and 1927-28, Centro de Estudios Historicos, Madrid, 1927, summer courses at Paris, Geneva, Bagnères de Bigorre; m. Carrie F. Porter, July 17, 1901 (dec. Dec. 7, 1946); children—Frances (Mrs. John S. Martin), Marion (Mrs. John W. Stanley), Winifred (Mrs. L. L. Seeman). Came to U.S., 1896, naturalized, 1920. Instr. French, Dartmouth, 1896-1902, asst. prof. Romance langs., 1902-10; prof. French in charge instrn. in Romance langs. Mass. Inst. Tech., 1910-30; prof. Romance langs. in charge of dept. of modern langs. Mass. Inst. Tech., 1930-44, prof. emeritus, lecturer Modern languages, 1944-45; lectr. Romance langs. Harvard, 1924-39. Mem. Modern Lang. Assn. America, Am. Acad. Arts and Sciences, Am. Assn. U. Profs. (former mem. council), N.E. Modern Lang. Assn., Dante Soc. (v.p.), Balzac Society of America, Alpha Delta Phi. Awarded Governor General's medal, Toronto, 1938. Clubs: Technology Faculty, Harvard Faculty, Harvard Musical Assn. (Boston). Author: The Poetry of Giacomo da Lentino, 1915; Victor Hugo, Les Travailleurs de la Mer, 1911; Beaumarchais, Le Mariage de Figaro, 1917; Jules Sandeau, Mlle. de la Seiglière, 1923; Romantic Figures in Pen and Color, 1935; various articles and reviews in Publs. of Modern Lang. Assn., Harvard Studies in Philol. and Lit., The Romanic Review, etc. Home: 2 Potter Park, Cambridge 38, Mass. Died Sept. 23, 1954.

LANGLOIS, Ubald, bishop of Grouard. Address: McLennan, Alberta, Can. Died Sept. 18, 1953; buried Grouard, Alberta, Can.

LANGMUIR, Irving, chemist; b. Brooklyn, N.Y., Jan. 31, 1881; s. Charles and Sadie (Comings) L.; Met. E., Columbia Sch. of Mines, 1903; Ph.D., U. of Göttingen, 1906; D.Sc., Northwestern, 1921, Union U., 1923, Columbia, 1925, Kenyon Coll., 1927, Princeton, 1929, Lehigh U., 1934, Harvard, 1938, Oxford, 1938, Rutgers, 1941, Queen's Coll. (Canada), 1941; D.Ing., Tech. Hochschule, Berlin, 1929; LL.D., Edinburgh, 1921, Johns Hopkins, 1936, U. of Calif., 1946; m. Marion Mersereau, Apr. 27, 1912; children—Kenneth, Barbara. Instr. chemistry, Stevens Inst., Hoboken, N.J., 1906-09; physical chem. research, Research Lab. of Gen. Electric Co., Schenectady, N.Y., since 1909, now consultant of Research Lab.; engaged in development of gas filled tungsten lamps, electron discharge apparatus, condensation high vacuum pump, atomic hydrogen welding, work on monomolecular films and surface chemistry, cloud physics, including weather modification, etc.; also in 1917-18, on devices for submarine detection at Naval Exptl. Sta., Nahant, Mass. Lecturer, London, 1938, Hitchcock Foundation lecturer, U. of Calif., 1946; mem. bd. trustees, State U. of N.Y., Sept. 1948-50. Fellow A.A.A.S. (president 1941), Am. Physical Soc., Indian Acad. Sci. (hon.); mem. Am. Philosophical Soc., Am. Chemists Society (pres. 1929), Nat. Acad. Sciences, Am. Acad. Arts and Sciences, Royal Soc. Upsala, corresponding mem. Académie des Sciences, Paris, 1951, Tau Beta Pi, Phi Lambda Upsilon, Sigma Xi; also hon. mem. Royal Instn., Chem. Soc. of London, Royal Soc. (London), Royal Physiog. Soc. (Lund), Academia Brasileria de Sciencias (Brazil), Société de Chimie Industrielle. Was awarded Nichols medal by N.Y. sect. of American Chem. Soc. for researches on chem. reactions at low pressures, 1915; Hughes medal, Royal Soc. London, for researches in molecular physics, 1918; Nichols medal for researches on atomic structure, 1920; Rumford medal, Am. Acad. Arts and Sciences, for researches on thermionic phenomena, 1920; Cannizzaro prize, Royal Acad. of Lincei (Rome), 1925; Perkin medal, 1928; Sch. of Mines medal, Columbia U. in recognition of achievements in science and invention, 1929. Chandler medal, 1930; Willard Gibbs medal, 1930; Popular Science Monthly prize, 1932; Nobel prize in Chemistry, 1932, for work in surface-chemistry; Franklin medal by the Franklin Institute, 1934; Holly medal, by American Society of Mech. Engrs., 1934; award under John Scott Medal Fund, 1937, by Board of City Trusts, Phila., Egleston medal Columbia Engring. Schs. Alumni Assn., 1939; Nat. Pioneer award Nat. Assn. Mfrs., 1940; Faraday Medal award Elec. Engrs. of Gt. Britain, 1943; Medal for Merit, U.S. Army and Navy, 1948; John Carty Medal Nat. Acad. Scis., 1950. Clubs: Chemists (N.Y.); Mohawk. Contbr. to jours. Home: 1176 Stratford Rd., Schenectady. Died Aug. 17, 1957.

LANGWORTHY, Herman Moore, lawyer; b. Fairmount, Leavenworth, County, Kan., Dec. 16, 1880; s. Simon Burton and Mary (Moore) L.; prep. edn. high sch. and business coll., Leavenworth; B.A., U. of Kan., 1902, M.A., 1903; LL.B., Columbia, 1907; m. Minnie Leach, Aug. 5, 1908; children—Herman Moore, Dorcas Emlin, Robert Burton. Practiced in Kansas City, 1907—; mem. Warner, Dean, McLeod & Langworthy, 1913-23, Langworthy, Spencer & Terrell, 1923-36, Langworthy, Spencer, Terrell and Matz, 1936-39, Langworthy and Matz, and Langworthy, Matz & Linde, 1939—; chairman Charter Commission of Kansas City, 1924-25; receiver Kansas City Joint Stock Land Bank, 1928-31; dir. Fed. Res. Bank of Kansas City, 1932-33; counsel for Kansas City Agency, R.F.C., 1932-33; dir. exec. com. Union Nat. Bank; dir. Bowman-Hicks Lumber Co., Badger Lumber Company, K.C. Central Paper Box Company lecturer on insurance Kansas City School of Law, 1934-36. Director of Sch. District of Kansas City, Mo., 1935-36. Mem. Chamber of Commerce of U.S., Kansas City C. of C.; mem. Board of Election Commrs., Kansas City, 1941-45; mem. advisory council U. of Kansas City; mem. Rep. State Com., Mo., 1926-28; del. to Rep. Nat. Conv., Cleveland, 1936, chmn. resolutions com.; del. to Rep. Nat. Conv., Phila., 1940. Mem. Am., Mo. State, and Kansas City bar assns., Lawyers Assn., Phi Beta Kappa, Phi Delta Phi, Alpha Tau Omega. Republican. Presbyterian. Mason (Shriner). Clubs: University, Kansas City, Mission Hills Country, Kansas City Country. Home: 1021 W. 68th Terrace. Office: Union National Bank Bldg., Kansas City, Mo. Died Aug. 22, 1956; buried Forest Hill Cemetery, Kansas City, Mo.

LANHAM, Henderson Lovelace, congressman; b. Rome, Ga., Sept. 14, 1888; s. John Henderson and Julia (Thompson) L.; A.B., U. of Ga., 1910, B.L., 1911; A.M. Harvard, 1912; m. Anne White Phinizy, Sept. 1, 1915; 1 dau., Julia Anne (Mrs. Thomas Goulding Slappey, Jr.). Chmn. Rome (Ga.) Bd. of Edn., 1919-20; represented Floyd County in Ga. legislature, 1929-34, 36-39; solicitor gen. (pros. atty.) Superior Court, Rome Jud. Circuit, 1941-46; mem. 80th to 85th Congresses, 7th Ga. Dist. Mem. Sigma Chi, Phi Beta Kappa. Democrat. Methodist. Mason, Odd Fellow. Address: Rome, Ga. Died Nov. 10, 1957; buried Myrtle Hill Cemetery, Rome, Ga.

LANIER, Powless William, lawyer; b. Fulton, Tenn., Mar. 7, 1885; s. Isaac Hill and Ellen (Cooper) L.; LL.B., Cumberland U., 1908; m. Mary Louise Roberts, Dec. 28, 1910; children—Dorothy Louise, Powless William. Admitted to Tenn. bar, 1908, practicing at Covington, 1908-11; mem. Tenn. Ho. of Rep. (chmn. judiciary com.), 1911-12; judge juvenile and city ct., Memphis, 1913-15; practiced law, Jamestown and Fargo, N.D., 1923; now mem. law firm Lanier, Lanier, & Knox, Fargo; del. Dem. National Conv., 1928, 32 (mem. resolutions com. 1928); candidate for U.S. senator, 1932; U.S. dist. atty. State of N.D., 1933—; spl. asst. to U.S. atty. gen., Feb.-May, 1954. Dem. candidate Congress, N.D., 1954. Mem. Kappa Sigma. Democrat. Methodist. Mason. Author: We Desegregation Desegate the South, 1957. Home: 1108 4th Av. S. Office: Gate City Bldg., Fargo, N.D. Died Oct. 12, 1958; buried Riverside Cemetery, Fargo.

LANING, Jay Ford, ex-congressman; b. New London, O., May 15, 1853; s. John S. and Caroline (Wood) L.; A.M., Baldwin U., Berea, O., 1895; m. Caroline E. Sheldon, June 19, 1875; 1 son, Sheldon R. Admitted to bar 1875; practiced law, 1875-85; pub., 1885—. Mem. Norwalk (O.) City Council, 1884-8; mem. Ohio Senate, 1894-8; mem. 60th Congress (1907-9), 14th Ohio Dist. Del. Rep. Nat. Conv., 1904. Editor: Laning's Ohio Criminal Law, 1895; The Laning Ohio Rev. Statutes (3 vols.), 1905; The Laning Ohio Cyclopedic Digest (8 vols.), 1906; Laning's Ohio Business Corporations, 1906; Laning's Appellate Procedure, 1896. Author: Laning's Ohio Civil Government, 1896; Growth and History of Ohio, 1897. Address: Norwalk, O. Died Sept. 1, 1941.

LANIUS, James Andrew, educator; b. Louisiana, Mo., July 12, 1846; s. Rev. Jacob and Nancy (Tong) L.; ed. Central Coll., Mo.; m. Eleanor Bird, July 9, 1872; children—Ann Bird, Emily Bond, Rosella, Carol Vincent, Tudor. Tchr. Mo. and Ill. 62 yrs.; vice prin. Smith Acad., St. Louis, 1874-84; prin. Centenary Acad., Palmyra, Mo., 1884-91, 1898-1913; pres. St. Charles (Mo.) Coll., 1891-95; tchr. Latin and Greek, Pritchett Coll., Glasgow, Mo., 1895-98, also tchr. Latin, Palmyra High Sch.; ret. 1925. Originator plan for Correlation of Meth. Ch. Schs. in Mo., adopted 1899. Home: Palmyra, Mo. Died Apr. 12, 1930; buried Palmyra.

LANNON, James Patrick, naval officer (ret.); b. Alexandria, Va., Oct. 12, 1878; s. John and Johanna Valentine (Reddy) L.; B.S., U.S. Naval Acad., 1902. Commd. ensign U.S. Navy, 1904, advanced through grades to rear adm., 1942; served at sea and shore stas., U.S., Europe, Asia, 1902-45; ret. from active service, 1937. Awarded Congressional Medal of Honor, Navy Cross, Purple Heart, Navy War Cross (Italy). Roman Catholic. Address: Chevy Chase Club, Chevy Chase 15, Md. Died Mar. 13, 1953; buried Arlington Cemetery.

LANSDELL, Rinaldo Addison, clergyman, educator; b. McDuffie County, Ga., June 4, 1875; s. Edwin Erwin and Anna Augusta (Cody) L.; A.B., Mercer U., 1901; Th.M., So. Bapt. Theol. Sem., Louisville, 1904; post-grad. work U. Wyo., 1905-07; D.D., Union U., 1920; m. Ruth Kilpatrick, Jan. 29, 1902; children—Cyrus Hudson, Mrs. Anna L. Walker, Mrs. Ruth L. Henderson, Mrs. Lillian L. McElmurray, Emily Kilpatrick, Rinaldo Addison, Joseph Truett. Ordained Bapt. ministry, 1904; pastor Victor Coll., 1904-05, Laramie, Wyo., 1905-09; asso. pastor Immanuel Ch., Salt Lake City, 1909-10; financial sec. Bessie Tift Coll., Forsyth, Ga., 1910-13; field sec. Fgn. Mission Bd. So. Bapt. Conv., 1913-16; financial sec. U. Richmond, Va., 1916-20, 26-29, ret.; pres. Bluefield Coll. (jr. coll. for boys), 1920-26, also a founder. Mem. Sigma Nu. Democrat. Mason (32°, Shriner). Club: Rotary. Address: Hephzibah, Ga. Died Feb. 3, 1937.

LANSING, Ambrose (lăn'sĭng), Egyptologist and museum curator; b. Cairo, Egypt, Sept. 20, 1891; s. Joseph McCarrell and Isabella (Strang) L.; came to U.S., 1904, citizen by birth; A.B., Washington Jefferson Coll., 1911; student Leipzig (Germany) U., summers 1912-14; L.H.D., Bowdoin, 1948; m. Caroline Cox, Feb. 27, 1923; 1 son, Cornelius. With Met. Mus. Art, N.Y.C., 1911—, field archeol. in Egypt, 1911-22, asst. curator Dept. Egyptian Art, 1922-26, asso. curator, 1926-39, curator Dept. Egyptian Art, 1939—. Mem. vis. com. Semitic and Egyptian Civilization, Harvard. Fellow Am. Acad. Arts and Scis.; mem. Am. Oriental Soc., Oriental Inst. Chgo., Archeol. Inst. Am. Egypt Exploration Soc., Am. Museums Assn., Lambda Chi Alpha. Republican. Episcopalian. Club: Century (N.Y.). Author: Egyptian Expdn. Reports (supplements to the Bulletin of Metropolitan Mus. of Art), 1917-36; contbr. articles to Bull. of Met. Mus. Art. Address: Kings Ranch, Apache Junction, Ariz. Died May 28, 1959; buried Mesa, Ariz.

LANSING, John Ernest, chemist; b. Brookline, Mass., June 3, 1878; s. John Arnold and Florence (Stetson) L.; A.B., Harvard, 1898, A.M., 1900; traveled in Europe, 1898-99; m. Lucy Caroline Wells, June 27, 1907 (died Oct. 14, 1916); m. 2d, Josephine Camp Belcher, July 3, 1918; children—John Belcher, Edward Stickney, Marion Frances. Instr. natural sciences, Phillips Acad., Andover, Mass., 1901-05; asst. prof. chemistry, 1905-06, prof., 1906—, Hobart Coll., also registrar, 1914-21, acting pres., 1941-42. Mem. Am. Chem. Soc. Republican. Presbyn. Author: Laboratory Experiments in Chemistry, 1908, revised, 1944; A Short Course in Qualitative Analysis, revised, 1948; retitled Lansing's Qualitative Analysis, revised, 1958. Home: Geneva, N.Y. Died Sept. 28, 1958.

LANZA, Mario (born Alfredo Arnold Cocozza), tenor; b. South Phila., Jan. 31, 1921; s. Antonio and Maria (Lanza) Cocozza; ed. high sch.; studied voice with Irene Williams (Phila.), Grant Garnell and Enrico Rosati; scholarship at Tanglewood (Mass.) Festival, 1942; m. Betty Hicks, 1945; children—Colleen, Elissa, Damon, Mark. Singer, Spl. Services, U.S. Army. World War II, appearing in On the Beam and Winged Victory; soloist Grant Park, Chicago, 1946, Hollywood Bowl, 1947; contract with M-G-M, 1947; motion pictures: That Midnight Kiss, 1949; The Toast of New Orleans, 1950; played Caruso in The Great Caruso, 1951; Because You're Mine, 1952; Student Prince, 1954; Serenade, 1956; Seven Hills of Rome, 1958; For the First Time; radio, concert and record artist. Home: Hollywood, Cal. Office: 360 N. Camden Dr., Beverly Hills, Cal. Died Oct. 7, 1959.

LANZETTA, James J., ex-congressman; b. N.Y.C., Dec. 21, 1894; s. Luigi and Giovina (Lanzetta) L.; M.E., Columbia, 1917; LL.B., Fordham, 1924; unmarried. Mech. engr., 1919-21; in practice of law, N.Y.C., 1925—. Served with Engr. Corps and Air Service Mechanics, U.S. Army, 1917-19. Mem. Bd. of Aldermen, N.Y.C., 1932-33; mem. 73d and 75th Congresses, 20th N.Y. Dist.; now in pvt. practice of law. Democrat. Roman Catholic. Home: 318 E. 116th St. Office: 2 Lafayette St., N.Y.C. Died Oct. 1956.*

LAPHAM, J(ack) H., rancher, oil exec.; b. N.Y.C., July 4, 1885; s. Lewis H. and Antoinette (Dearborn) L.; B.A., Williams Coll.; m. Lucy Jane Thomas, Nov. 11, 1940; children—David, John, Julie, Jean. Dir., mem. exec. com. Texas Co., 1907—; co-owner Park Mo-tel, San Antonio, Flying L Ranch, Bandera, Tex.; pvt. pilot, 1926—. Served as maj., F.A., U.S. Army, World War I; col. AAF, 1942-45. Mem. Sportsmen's Pilot Assn., Nat. Soc. Arts and Letters, Alpha Delta Phi, Order of Alamo. Clubs: Country, Meadowbrook, Matagorda, Williams (San Antonio). Address: 333 E. Summit Av., San Antonio. Died Aug. 2, 1956; buried New Canaan, Conn.

La PORTE, William Ralph, physical edn.; b. Adario, O., Apr. 1, 1889; s. Wallace Bruce and Susanna W. (Kirk) L.; A.B., U. of Southern Calif., 1913, A.M., 1915; grad. study, U. of Southern Calif. Med. Coll., 1914-15. Princeton, 1918, Teachers Coll., Columbia, 1924-25; LL.D., George Pepperdine Coll., 1954; m. Lura E. Adams. Aug. 19, 1913; children—Dorothy Ruth, William Bruce. Dir. athletics, Page Mil. Acad., Los Angeles, Calif., 1910-13; prof. physical edn. and dir. of dept., U. of Southern Calif., 1913—, dir. mil. tactics, 1917-18; dir. recreation courses, So. Calif. Summer Sch. of Religious Edn., 1921-22. Dir. Sch. Physical Edn., Pacific Palisades Chautauqua, 1922-23; vis. prof. in charge dept. physical edn., U. of Calif., summer 1925; visiting prof., U. of Wash., summer 1937, Utah State Coll., summer 1940. Chmn. bd. dirs., U. So. Calif. Mutual Benefit Assn., 1934-52. Served as 2d lt. inf., personnel officer, United States Army, World War I. Recipient Luther H. Gulick award, 1951. Fellow Am. Acad. Phys. Edn. (chmn. com. on internat. relations 1931-36); mem. N.E.A., Am. Assn. for Health, Physical Edn. and Recreation, Dept. N.E.A. (chmn. com. research monographs 1930-31, chmn. constitution com. 1931-35, pres. southwest dist., 1934-36, chmn. dist. com. on professional student organization; chmn. state com. on professional standards and advancement; hon. fellow), Coll. Phys. Edn. Assn. (pres. 1930; vice president, 1929; chmn. curriculum research committee, 1928-53), Pacific Coast Society Directors Physical Education in Colleges (secretary 1928-33), American Association Univ. Profs. (pres. Southern Calif. Chapter 1930-31), Am. Student Health Assn. (chmn. com. on hygiene of phys. edn. activities, Nat. and Pacific Coast), Phi Beta Kappa, Kappa Alpha, Phi Delta Kappa, Sigma Delta Psi, Sigma Alpha, Phi Epsilon Kappa; rep. Nat. Collegiate Athletic Assn. (mem. council; ex-v.p.), Pacific Coast Inter-Collegiate Athletic Conf. (ex-pres.), Amateur Athletic Fed. America (ex-pres. Calif.

Div.). Republican. Methodist. Author: Handbook of Games and Programs, 1922; Recreational Leadership of Boys, 1926; Good Times for Boys, 1926; How Do You Stand?, 1927; The Physical Education Curriculum—A National Program, 1937, 4th edit., 1947; The Tumbler's Manual (with Al Rennef), 1938; Hygiene and Health, 1939, 4th edition 1945; (with J. W. Clemensen) Life Goes on, 1942, Your Health, 1942 and Your Health and Safety, 1942, revised edition, 1946; Teaching Safety Education in Secondary Schools (with Hunt and Eastwood), 1942. Author and director physical education motion pictures. Contbg. editor Jour. of Health and Physical Edn. and Research Quarterly. Contbr. physical edn. jours. Home: 801 via Somonte, Palos Verdes Estates, Cal. Died Jan. 14, 1955.

LA PRADE, Arthur Thornton (lá-präd'), lawyer; b. Winslow, Ariz., Mar. 3, 1895; s. Fernando Thornton and Lizzie (Dover) La P.; high sch. course, Ariz. State Teachers Coll., Flagstaff, 1909-13; A.B., U. of Calif., 1917, J.D., 1920; m. Lucile Hooper, Aug. 31, 1918; children—Arthur Thornton, Loren Hooper, Janice, Paul Whitmer. Began practice at Phoenix, Ariz., 1920; asst. county atty. Maricopa County, Ariz., 1923-24, county atty., 1925-26; asst. atty. gen. of Ariz., 1929-32, atty. gen., 1933-34; judge of Superior Court, 1939-44; judge of Arizona Supreme Court since 1945. Served as 2d and 1st lt. cavalry, U.S. Army, Aug. 1917-Dec. 1918. Mem. Delta Chi. Democrat. Presbyn. Club: Phoenix Country. Home: 330 E. Coronado Rd. Office: Capitol Building, Phoenix. Died June 30, 1957; buried Greenwood Meml. Park Mausoleum, Phoenix.

LAPRADE, Lloyd Stone, editor; b. Franklin County Va., Feb. 22, 1902; s. George Washington and Mary Elizabeth (Muse) L.; student Lynchburg Coll., 1919-22; A.B., Duke U., 1925; studied U. of Va. and Duke U., summer, 1926-27, Duke U. Law Sch., 1 term; m. Rhoda Kathleen Thomas, Aug. 8, 1936. Teacher Orlando (Fla.) High Sch., 1925-26, Maury High Sch., Norfolk, Va., 1926-27; reporter Durham (N.C.) Herald, 1929-31; legislative corr. Asso. Press, Jan.-May 1931; reporter Durham Herald, 1931-32, editor, 1932-43. Tech. editor USPHS, Atlanta Editorial Branch. Served as maj. U.S. Army, A.M.G. service, Dec. 1943-Sept. 1946. Decorated French Croix de Guerre with Palm, Belgian Croix de Guerre with Palm. Democrat. Mem. Christian (Disciples) Ch. Club: Kiwanis. Home: 105 Kathryn Av., Decatur, Ga. Office: John Silvey Bldg., Atlanta. Died Nov. 5, 1953; buried Woodlawn Cemetery, Ocala, Fla.

LARDNER, Henry Ackley, engr.; b. Oconomowoc, Wis., Oct. 1, 1871; s. Richard and Catharine (Breck) L.; B.S. in E.E., U. of Wis., 1893, E.E., 1895; m. Ethel Anne Elmore, Sept. 17, 1902; children—Dorothy Ann, Richard Penn. V.p. J. G. White Engring. Corp., N.Y. City. Mayor of Montclair, N.J., 1924-28. Past pres. N.J. State League of Municipalities, Montclair Community Chest, United Engineering. Trustees, 1939-41. Fellow Am. Inst. E.E., Am. Soc. M.E.; mem. Montclair Soc. Engrs. (pres. 1930-31), S.A.R., Sigma Chi. Episcopalian. Club: Lawyers (New York). Home: 9 Bradford Av., Upper Montclair, N.J. Office: 80 Broad St., N.Y.C. 4. Died Dec. 27, 1952.

LARDNER, John, writer; b. Chgo., May 4, 1912; s. Ring W. and Ellis (Abbott) L.; grad. Phillips Acad., Andover, Mass., 1929; student Harvard, 1929-30; m. Hazel Cannan, 1938; children—Susan Elizabeth, Mary Jane, John Nicholas. Reporter N.Y. Herald Tribune, 1931-33; sports columnist, N.Am. Newspaper Alliance, 1933-48; columnist and corr., Newsweek, 1939-57; critic and reviewer New Yorker, 1957-—; accredited war correspondent, U.S. Army, 1942 (made trip to Australia and Southwest Pacific Islands, 1942; N. Africa, 1943; Italy, 1943-44; Pacific campaigns, Iwo Jima and Okinawa, 1945, including war corr. New Yorker, Newsweek and N.A.N.A. Episcopalian. Club: Players. Author: The Crowning of Technocracy, 1933; Southwest Passage; the Yanks in the Pacific, 1943; It Beats Working, 1947; White Hopes and Other Tigers, 1951; Strong Cigars and Lovely Women, 1951. Home: 59 W. 12th St., N.Y.C. 11. Office: 152 W. 42d St., N.Y.C. 18. Died Mar. 24, 1960.

LARK-HOROVITZ, Karl (lärk'hôr'ō-vitz), prof. physics; b. Vienna, Austria, July 20, 1892; s. Moritz and Adelle (Hofmann) Horovitz; Ph.D., U. of Vienna, 1919; m. Betty Friedlaender, July 26, 1916; children—Caroline Betty, Karl Gordon. Came to U.S., 1925, naturalized, 1936. Asst. teacher of physics, U. of Vienna, 1919-25; internat. research fellow, U. of Toronto, 1925-26, U. of Chicago, 1926, Rockefeller Inst., 1926-27, Stanford U., 1927-28; prof. physics, Purdue U., since 1928, dir. Phys. Lab. since 1929, head dept. of physics since 1931. Served in Austrian Army, 1914-18. Fellow Am. Phys. Soc., A.A.A.S. (chmn. co-op. com. 1947-51, gen. sec. 1948-51); mem. Am. Assn. Physics Teachers, Sigma Xi, Sigma Pi Sigma, V.A.A.U.P., S.P.E.E. Lutheran. Contbr. articles to scientific jours. Home: 509 Lingle Av., Lafayette, Ind. Died Apr. 14, 1958.

LARKIN, Fred Viall, educator, industrial management engr.; b. Verona, Wis., April 2, 1883; s. Edwin Newcomb and Eudora (Viall) L.; B.S., U. of Wisconsin, 1906, M.S., 1915; Dr. Engring., Stevens Institute, 1948; married Nell Grant Wright, June 30, 1910; children—Franklin Jonathan, Richard Newcomb. Engr. and supt. Telluride (Colo.) Power Co., 1906-09; asst. and supt. Bargn Canal Contract No. 60, Empire Engring. Corp., N.Y. City, 1909-11; engr. Terry & Tench Co., N.Y. City, 1911-12; instr. later asst. prof. mech. engring., Lehigh U., 1912-15, prof. mech. engring. and head dept., 1919-27, dir. indsl. and mech. engring., 1927-48; asst. gen. supt. Harrisburg (Pa.) Steel Corp., 1915-19; cons. engr., 1919—. In charge plant producing army-navy ordnance, 1915-18; lecturer indsl. management, U.S. Naval Acad., 1942, cons. engr. Army Odnance Dept., 1944—. Mem. Am. Soc. M.E. (mem. publ. com. council, relations colls. com.), Am. Management Assn., Soc. Promotion of Engring. Edn. (mem. council, vice pres.), Newcomen Soc. of Eng. (vice chmn. com.), Pi Tau Sigma (nat. vice pres.), Tau Beta Pi, Sigma Xi, Lambda Chi Alpha. Republican. Methodist. Clubs: Rotary, Chemists (N.Y.), Saucon Valley Country. Contbr. to tech. publs. 2 patents granted 1933. Visited colleges and industries in Orient and Europe on trip around the world, 1932-33. Retired, 1948. Home: 135 Wall St. Office: Lehigh U., Bethlehem, Pa. Died May 23, 1954.

LARNED, John Insley Blair, bishop; b. Chgo., Oct. 5, 1883; s. Walter Cranston and Emma Locke (Scribner) L.; prep. edn. Lake Forest (Ill.) Acad. and Hill Sch., Pottstown, Pa.; B.A., Harvard, 1905; postgrad. Mass. Inst. Tech., 1905-08; B.D., Episcopal Theol. Sch., Cambridge, Mass., 1911; D.D., Trinity College, Hartford, Conn., 1935; LL.D., Hobart Coll., 1946; m. Elizabeth Virginia Jenkins, June 11, 1914; children—Emma Elizabeth, Frances Virginia, John Insley Blair. Deacon, 1911, priest, 1912, P.E. Ch.; curate St. John's Ch., S.I., N.Y., 1911-13; rector St. John's Ch., Globe, Ariz., 1913-16, Kingston, N.Y., 1916-18; dean Pro Cathedral of the Nativity, Bethlehem, Pa., 1918-22; rector St. John's Ch., Yonkers, N.Y., 1922-25; gen. sec. field dept. Nat. Council P.E. Ch., 1925-29; suffragan bishop of L.I., 1929-46; bishop in charge of Am. Episcopal Chs. in Europe, 1947—. Clubs: Harvard (N.Y.); Richmond County Country (S.I.). Address: P.O. Box 222, Bklyn. 1. Died Dec. 3, 1955.

LaROE, Wilbur, Jr., lawyer; b. Westfield, N.J., Sept. 25, 1888; s. Wilbur and Araminta (Sanson) LaR.; A.B., Princeton U., 1909; LL.B., N.J. Law School, 1912; LL.D., Dubuque University, 1947, Centre College, 1949; married Bertha Jennings, September 15, 1914; 1 daughter, Dorothy L. (Viera). Taught high school in Westfield, New Jersey, 1909-12; N.J. Law School, 1912-13; atty., examiner and chief examiner for Interstate Commerce Commn., 1914-20; pvt. practice, 1920—; sr. partner LaRoe, Winn & Moerman. Member Bd. of Parole, District of Columbia, 1934-46; Elder Chevy Chase Presbyn. Church, 1926—; mem. bd. of trustees, Princeton Theol. Sem., 1944—; mem. Gen. Council, Presbyn. Church U.S.A., 1945-50; Nat. Protestant co-chmn. Nat. Conf. Christians and Jews, 1949-53; moderator, Gen. Assembly. Presbyn. Ch., U.S.A., 1947. Awarded plaque Washington Fedn. Chs., outstanding work in field of civic affairs, 1938; awarded scroll by Corrections Div., Washington Council of Social Agencies, for work in field of criminology, 1947. Mem. of Assn. of Interstate Commerce Practitioners (treas.). Clubs: Cosmos, Columbia Country (Washington). Author: Parole with Honor, 1939; Lawyer-Moderator, 1948; The Church We Love, 1953. Home: 3900 Connecticut Av., Washington 8. Office: Investment Bldg., Washington 5. Died Apr. 12, 1957; buried Cedar Hill Cemetery, Washington.

La ROQUE, O(scar) K(ent) (lå-rōk), ret. bank ofcl.; b. Kinston, N.C., Mar. 20, 1883; s. Walter Dunn and Annie P. (Mewborne) La R.; ed. pub. schs. of Kinston, student Massey Bus. Coll., Richmond, Va.; m. Nora Lois Albritton, July 20, 1904; children—Oscar Kent, Richard West. Bank commr., S.C., 1917-18; nat. bank examiner, 1919-25; deputy ins. commr., N.C., 1928-35; pres. Fed. Home Loan Bank, Winston-Salem, N.C., 1935-48; mem. Home Loan Bank Bd., Washington, 1948-51, ofcl. in Greensboro, N.C., 1951-53; now retired. Democrat. Christian. Club: Rotary. Home: Kinston, N.C. Died May 2, 1956.

LARSEN, Lewis A(ugustus), corporation exec.; b. Ridgeway, Ia., July 17, 1875; s. Lewis H. G. and Mary (Christoffersen) L.; student Upper Iowa U., Fayette, Ia., 1893-95, St. Paul (Minn.) Coll. of Law, 1898-99, Northwestern U., 1901-02; m. Ellouise Baker, June 20, 1906; children—Julia Louise (dec.), Laurence Henry, William George. With Chicago Great Western Ry., 1895-1903, Oelwein, Ia., 1895-97, St. Paul, Minn., 1897-1903; chief clerk to supt. motive power Northern Pacific Ry., St. Paul, 1903-07; asst. to vice pres. of mfg. Am. Locomotive Co., New York, 1907-17, asst. comptroller, 1917; asst. to pres. Lima Locomotive Works, Inc., Lima, O., 1917-18, sec. and treas., 1918-20, v.p. and treas., 1920-44, sr. v.p., 1944-48, dir., 1918-48; pres. Superior Coach Corp., Lima, O., 1943-48, chmn., 1948-51; dir. 1923-51, cons. since 1951. Dir. Ohio C. of C. since 1935; v.p. Lima Y.M.C.A. since 1920; pres. Lima Library Bd., 1922-31. Mem. Beta Theta Pi. Republican, Methodist. Clubs: New York Traffic, Bankers (New York); Lima, Shawnee Country (Lima, O.). Home: 750 W. Market St. Office: E. Kibby St., Lima, O. Died Aug. 25, 1954.

LARSEN, Lewis P., pres., dir. Reeves MacDonald Mines, Ltd., Vancouver, B.C.; Pend Oreille Mines & Metals Co. Home: East 2314 Altamont Blvd. Office: Old National Bank Bldg., Spokane, Wash. Died July 14, 1955; buried Spokane.

LARSON, Carl W., dairy technologist; b. St. Ansgar, Ia., May 29, 1881; s. Henry and Minnie (Hansen) L.; B.S. in Agr., Ia. State Coll., 1906; M.S., Pa. State Coll., 1911; Ph.D., Columbia U., 1916; m. Nellie C. Wallace, Sept. 7, 1911; 1 dau., Eileen (Mrs. Charles A. Brady). Studied creamery and cheese factory methods in Minn. and Wis., 1906-07; instr. dairy husbandry 1907-11, asst. prof., 1911-13, prof. in charge dairy husbandry dept., Pa. State Coll., 1913-15; asst. prof. agr. and agrl. economics, Columbia, 1916-17; was with Dairy Div. Bur. Animal Industry, U.S. Dept. Agr., as dairy expert, asst. chief of Dairy Div., chief of Dairy Div., later chief of new Bureau of Dairy Industry; mng. dir. Nat. Dairy Council, 1928-29, Gen. Ice Cream Corp., 1930-36; pres. Whiting Milk and Bushway-Whiting Ice Cream Co., Boston, 1936-41; pres. and gen. mgr. The Bryant and Chapman Milk Co. and R. G. Miller & Sons, Hartford, Conn., 1942-44; mgr. and dir. West. N.Y. div. Gen. Ice Cream Corp., Buffalo, N.Y., 1944-46; sec. and mng. dir. Dairy Prod. Improve, Inst., Inc., 1947-53. Sent by Red Cross to France, 1918, to develop and improve milk supplies for hospitals. U.S. del. Internat. Dairy Fedn., Stockholm, 1911; official del. Internat. Dairy Congress, London, 1928. Fellow A.A.A.S.; mem. Am. Dairy Science Assn., Alpha Zeta, Sigma Psi, Gamma Sigma Delta. Republican. Lutheran. Clubs: Cosmos, Rotary, Athletic. Author: Principles and Methods of Milk Cost Accounting, 1916; Dairy Cattle Feeding and Management (part author), 1916. Home: Tudor Plaza Apt., 731 W. Ferry St., Buffalo 22. Died June 13, 1954; buried Mount Olivet Cemetery, Kenmore, N.Y.

LARSON, George Victor, educator; b. New Haven, Conn., Mar. 22, 1895; s. Otto C. and Agnes (Landin) L.; ed. pub. schs., Booth Prep. Sch. to 1910, and under pvt. tutors; m. Olga Hertha Kasperson, June 28, 1919; 1 son. James H. Clerk law firm of Townsend & Pitkin, New Haven, 1910-17, also studied law, court reporter and conducted pub. stenographer's office; devoted evenings to tutoring, and in 1911 founded the Larson Tutoring Sch.; expanded sch. to include day and evening sessions, 1916; has devoted entire time since 1917 to Larson Junior Coll., pres., Feb. 1935-47; president Larson College, since 1947. President New Haven Council of Churches, 1950-51. Fellow American Geographic Society; member Academy Political Science, New Eng. Assn. Colls. and Secondary Schs., Conn. Business Educators Assn., Eastern Commerical Teachers Assn., Commercial Edn. Assn. of New York, Founders Soc. Am., Vt. Hist. Soc., New Haven Chamber of Commerce, League of Nations Assn., Am. Assn. of Sch. Adminstrs., Phi Theta Kappa (hon.), Alpha Pi Epsilon (nat. pres. 1940—). Episcopalian (licensed lay reader and vestryman St. Paul's Ch.). Mason (K.T., 32°). Clubs: New Haven Automobile, New Haven Historical, New Haven Kiwanis, Hamden Music, Church Club of the Diocese of Conn. (pres. 1944-46), Vermont, American-Swedish Historical Foundation. Home: 1370 Whitney Av., Hamden, Conn. Died Apr. 10, 1952; buried East Lawn Cemetery, East Haven, Conn.

LARSON, Gustus Ludwig, cons. engr.; born Werpinge, Lund, Sweden, June 30, 1881; s. Ole and Ingrid (Sjostrom) L.; came to U.S., 1890, naturalized, 1902; B.S. in elec. engring., U. of Ida., 1907; M.E., U. of Wis., 1915; m. Marion Frances Anthony, June 30, 1914; children—Dorothy Alida, Foster Anthony. Test engr. Gen. Elec. Co., Schenectady, N.Y., 1907-09; asso. prof. mech. engring., U. of Ida., 1909-11, prof., 1911-14; with U. of Wis., 1914-51, as asst. prof. of steam and gas engring., 1914-15, asso. prof., 1915-20, prof. and chmn. dept. mech. engring., 1920-43; cons. engr. U. of Wis. and other clients in Wis. since 1915. Apptd. by Wis. Indsl. Commn. to assist in drafting heating and ventilating code for State of Wis., 1925, also air conditioning, 1936; mem. Pres. Roosevelt's Conf. on Home Bldg. and Ownership, Washington, D.C., 1931; mem. advisory com. 12th Nat. Expn. of Power and Mech. Engring., New York, 1936, 13th, 1937. Grad. mgr. athletics, U. of Ida., 1909-14. Served as cons. engr. Ordnance Div., U.S. War Dept., 1917-18. Mem. Am. Soc. Mech. Engrs. (chmn. Rock River Valley Sect., 1939), Am. Soc. Heating and Ventilating Engrs. (mem. council 1929-33; chairman, Committee on Research, 1932, and 1933; v.p. 1934-36; pres. 1936; chmn. exec. com. 1937), Engring. Soc. of Wis. (pres. 1933), Soc. for Promotion Engring. Edn., Am. Assn. Univ. Profs., Nat. Assn. Power Engrs., Engrs. Soc. of Milwaukee, Tech. Club of Madison, Tau Beta Pi, Sigma Xi, Pi Tau Sigma (nat. pres. 1926-29), Phi Kappa Phi, Gamma Alpha, Phi Delta Theta, Triangle. Republican. Presbyterian (elder; trustee Presbyn.

Student Center). Contbr. articles to Trans. Am. Soc. Heating and Ventilating Engrs.; editor of Heating, Ventilating and Air Conditioning Guide, 1936. Designed heating, ventilating and air conditioning for many bldgs. in Wis. including Union Bldg. and Field House (U. of Wis.), Wis. Gen. Hosp., Wis. Power & Light Bldg. (Madison), high schs. in Madison, Stevens Point, Janesville, Beloit, etc. Home: 1213 Sweet Briar Rd., Madison, Wis. Died Aug. 16, 1953.

LARSON, Lars Moore, educator and founder, 1885, and since then supt., New Mexico School for the Deaf; b. Vernon Co., Wis., Aug. 20, 1856; lost hearing in infancy; grad. Wis. School for the Deaf, Delavan, 1876; also at Gallaudet College at Washington, 1882; taught in Chicago deaf-mute day schools until 1884; m. 1893. Cora Gunn. Address: Santa Fe, N. Mex. Deceased.

LA RUE, Carl Downey, botanist; b. Williamsville, Ill., April 22, 1888; s. Abraham Chronister and Charlotte Parthena (Bates) La R.; B.S., Valparaiso U., 1910, A.B., 1911; A.B., U. of Mich., 1914, A.M., 1916, Ph.D., 1921; research, Harvard, 1936-37; m. Evelina Brown Forman, June 1, 1914; children—Adrian Jan Pieters, Anna Virginia, Charlotte Evelina, Carl Forman. Instr. botany, Syracuse U., 1916-17, botanist, Hollandsch-Amerikaansche Plantage Maatschappij, Sumatra, 1917-20; instr. botany, asst., asso. prof., U. of Mich., 1920-44, prof., 1944—; mem. Mich. Biol. Sta. staff, 1925-50; research Fed. Expt. Sta., Puerto Rico, 1951; specialist, rubber investigation, in charge S. American rubber expdn., U.S. Dept. Agr., 1923-24; specialist, co-dir., Ford Motor Amazon-Tapajos Expdn., 1926-27; agent, rubber investigations, in charge expdns., Bolivia, Nicaragua, Mexico, U.S. Dept. Agr., 1940-41, prin. specialist, U.S. Dept. Agr., 1943-44. Fellow A.A.A.S., Mem. Am. Soc. Naturalists, Bot. Soc. Am., Sullivant Moss Soc., Torrey Bot. Club, Mich. Acad. Sci., Arts, Letters (sec., 1923), Sigma Xi. Author: Agrl. Dept. bulls.; contbr. tech. articles to bot. jours. Home: 2940 Fuller Rd., Ann Arbor, Mich. Died Aug. 19, 1955.

La RUE, John W., mng. editor Cincinnati Enquirer. Address: Cincinnati Enquirer, Cin. Deceased.*

LASH, James Hamilton, clergyman; b. Athens, O., June 18, 1872; s. John Beal and Nancy (Coyle) L.; A.B., Hillsdale (Mich.) Coll., 1900, D.D., 1919; B.D., Hillsdale (Mich.) Theol. Sem., 1903; student Union Theol. Sem., 1904 to 1905; m. Frances Rebecca Colyer, Aug. 29, 1906; 1 dau., Barbara Frances. Ordained to ministry Free Bapt. Ch., 1901; pastor Free Bapt. chs., Ind. and Minn., 1901-05; pastor Congl. Ch., Rialto, Cal., 1905-08, Lake Av. Congl. Ch., Pasadena, 1908-17, Hollywood (Cal.), Congl. Ch., 1917—; moderator and pres. bd. dirs. So. Cal. Congl. Conf., 1914-15, dir., 1932—. Chmn. Community Chest, 1929-31; pres. Assn. of Ministers of Los Angeles and Vicinity, 1934. Mem. Delta Tau Delta. Republican. Conglist. Mason (grand chaplain, Grand Lodge of Cal., 1945-46, Knights Templar), K.P. Clubs: Hollywood Rotary (pres.), Clerical (Los Angeles). Traveler and lecturer. Home: 1768 N. Sycamore Av., Los Angeles. Died Dec. 17, 1949.

LASHAR, Walter B., chmn. bd. Am. Chain & Cable Co., First Nat. Bank & Trust Co.; pres. Dominion Chain Co., Ltd., Am. Fabrics Co.; dir. Bridgeport Hydraulic Co., N.Y., New Haven & Hartford R.R.; trustee Bridgeport-Peoples Savings Bank. Home: Fairfield, Conn. Address: Bridgeport, Conn. Died Nov. 5, 1955.

LASHLEY, K(arl) S(pencer), psychologist; b. Davis, W.Va., June 7, 1890; s. Charles Gilpen and Margaret Blanche (Spencer) L.; A.B. in Zoology, W.Va. U., 1910; M.S. in Bacteriology (teaching fellow 1910), U. Pitts., 1911, D.Sc., 1936; Ph.D. in Genetics (fellow 1913, Bruce fellow 1914), Johns Hopkins, 1914, Johnston scholar, 1915-16, LL.D., 1953; M.A. (hon.) Harvard, 1942; D.Sc., U. Chgo., 1941, Western Res. U., 1951, U. Pa., 1955; m. Edith Ann Baker, 1918 (dec. 1948); m. 2d, Dr. Claire Imredy Schiller, 1957. Instr. psychology U. Minn., 1917-18, asst. prof. psychology, 1920-21, asso. prof., 1921-24, prof., 1924-26; investigator U.S. Interdepartmental Social Hygiene Bd., 1919-20; acting prof. psychology U. Chgo., summer 1925, prof. psychology, 1929-35; acting prof. psychology Columbia, summer 1926; research psychologist Behavior Research Fund of Inst. for Juvenile Research, Chgo., 1926-29; lectr. univs. London, Berlin, Moscow, 1932; prof. psychology Harvard, 1935-37, research prof. neuropsychology, 1937-55, emeritus, 1955-58; dir. Yerkes Labs. of Primate Biology, 1942-55, emeritus, 1955-58. Hughlings Jackson Meml. lectr. Montreal Neurol. Clinic, 1937; Vanuxem lectr. Princeton, 1952. Recipient Howard Crosby Warren medal in psychology Soc. Exptl. Psychologists, 1937; Daniel Giraud Elliot Medal in zoology Nat. Acad. Scis., 1943; William Baly Medal in physiology Royal Coll. Physicians, 1953. Mem. Nat. Acad. Scis., Am. Philos. Soc., Am. Acad. Arts and Scis., Am. Psychol. Assn. (pres. 1929, pres. eastern br. 1937), Soc. Am. Naturalists (pres. 1947), Am. Soc. Zoologists, Am. Physiol. Soc., Soc. Exptl. Psychologists, Am. Soc. Human Genetics, NRC (div. anthropology and psychology 1927-30, 32-35), Fla. Psychol. Assn.; hon. mem. Am. Neurol. Assn., Harvey Soc., N.Y. Acad. Scis., Brit. Assn. Study Animal Behavior; fgn. mem. Royal Soc. London, Brit. Psychol. Assn. Author more than 100 articles and monographs (including Brain Mechanisms and Intelligence, U. Chgo. Press, 1929) on the Structure and functions of the brain, comparative psychology, animal behavior, instincts of birds and primates, learning, and genetics. Home: 3936 McGirts Blvd., Jacksonville 10, Fla. Died Aug. 7, 1958.

LASHLY, Arthur Valentine, lawyer; b. Randolph County, Ill., Feb. 14, 1880; s. George Washington and Cora (Woolford) L.; LL.B., St. Louis U., 1911; m. Leotta Marie Cochran; children—Ralph Cochran, Lawrence Hilton, George Clyde, Arthur Jacob, Robert Barnett. Began practice of law St. Louis, 1911; pros. atty. St. Louis County, 1913-15; mem. faculty St. Louis U. Law Sch., 1918-22; mem. Constl. Conv. of Mo., 1922-23; dir. Mo. Crime Survey for Mo. Bar Assn. and citizens' com., 1925-26; spl. asst. atty. gen. of Mo., St. Louis grand jury investigations, 1926; dir. Ill. Crime Survey (for Ill. Bar Assn. and Chicago Industrial Club), 1927-28; judge Circuit Court, 13th Mo. Dist., 1929-31; now mem. Lashly, Lashly and Miller. Mem. Am., Mo., St. Louis bar assns. Methodist. Democrat. Author: Reports of Missouri Crime Survey, 1926; Illinois Crime Survey, 1929. Contbr. articles to newspapers, etc. Home: 245 Blackmer Pl., Webster Groves, Mo. Address: 705 Olive St., St. Louis. Died Jan. 30, 1957.

LASKER, Albert Davis (lăs'kẽr), advtg. expert; b. of Am. parents, Freiburg, Germany, May 1, 1880; s. Morris and Nettie (Davis) L.; brought to U.S. in infancy; grad. high sch., Galveston, Tex., 1896; m. Flora Warner, June 9, 1902; children—Mary (Mrs. Leigh B. Block), Edward, Frances (Mrs. Sidney F. Brody); m. 2d, Doris Kenyon Sills Hopkins, Oct. 28, 1938 (div. June 9, 1939); m. 3d, Mary Woodard Reinhardt, June 21, 1940. With Lord & Thomas, advtg. agency, 1898-1942, becoming owner of company in 1908, and liquidating the company upon retirement from active business, Dec. 1942; apptd. special asst. to Sec. of Agriculture Houston by President Wilson, 1917; asst. chmn. Rep. Nat. Com., 1918-20; apptd. chmn. U.S. Shipping Bd. by President Harding, 1921, resigned June 10, 1923. Apptd. trustee Univ. of Chicago, 1937, resigned 1942. President Albert and Mary Lasker Foundation. Mem. Am. Jewish Com. of U.S. As part owner Chicago "Cubs" devised Lasker Plan for complete reorganization baseball which resulted in election of Commr. Landis, 1920. Home: 29 Beekman Place, New York 22. Office: Chrysler Bldg., N.Y.C. 17. Died May 30, 1952; buried Sleepy Hollow Cemetery, Tarrytown, N.Y.

LASKY, Jesse L., motion pictures; b. San Francisco, Calif., Sept. 13, 1880; s. Isaac and Sarah (Platt) L.; grad. high sch., San Francisco; m. Bessie Ginzberg, Dec. 1909. Formerly reporter on San Francisco newspaper, gold hunter, Nome, Alaska, leader Royal Hawaiian Band, Honolulu; began theatrical career as mgr. of Hermann, the magician; associated with B. A. Rolfe, as Lasky, Rolfe Co., 1902, in producing vaudeville acts; with Henry B. Harris in building and operating the Follies Bergere, New York, 1911; organizer, 1914, and later pres. Jesse L. Lasky Feature Play Co., with studios at Hollywood, Calif.; formerly v.p. Paramount Publix Corp. and produced independently for Fox Film Corp.; formerly pres. Pickford-Lasky Productions, Inc.; asso. producer RKO Radio Pictures, Inc. Originator "Gateway to Hollywood" radio program. Produced for Warner Bros.: Sergeant York; Adventures of Mark Twain; Rhapsody in Blue. Organized Jesse L. Lasky Prod. Inc.; produced for R.K.O. Radio Pictures, Inc., Without Reservations, The Miracle of the Bells; coproduced: Great Caruso (MGM). Address: California Studios, Hollywood, Cal. Died Jan. 13, 1956.

LASSER, Jacob Kay, pub. accountant; b. Newark, Oct. 7, 1896; s. Morris and Rebecca L.; student N.Y.U., 1915-17; B.S., Pa. State Coll., 1920, I.E., 1923; m. Terese Reuben, Jan. 1, 1924; children—Donald Judd, Barbara Ann. Mem. J. K. Lasser & Co., N.Y.C., 1923—; chmn. Fed. Tax Inst., N.Y.U., 1942-53, adj. prof. taxation, 1949-53; chmn. Inst. on Taxation Pa. State Coll., 1947-50; lectr. U. Miami Tax Conf., 1946-49; dir. Tax Inst., Inc., 1944-51, pres. 1949; editor Tax Clinic, Jour of Accountancy, 1943-53. Trustee Bard Coll., 1947-51. Served in USN, 1917-18. C.P.A., N.J., N.Y., Cal., Ill. Mem. Am. Inst. Accountants, N.Y. (v.p. 1949), N.J. socs. C.P.A.'s, Nat. Assn. Cost Accountants. Clubs: Engineers (N.Y.C.); High Ridge Country (Stamford, Conn.). Author: Federal Securities Act Procedure (with J. A. Gerardi), 1934; Your Income Tax, 1939-53; Your Corporation Tax, 1941-46; Handbook of Accounting Methods, 1943; How to Speed Up Settlement of Your Terminated War Contract, 1945; Business Executives Guide, 1945; How to Run a Small Business, 1945; Business Tax Guide, 1948; How Tax Laws Make Giving to Charity Easy, 1948; Corporate Accumulations and Section 102 (with Robert S. Holzman), 1949; Farmer's Tax Handbook, 1950; Estate and Gift Taxes, 1951; Managing Your Money (with Sylvia F. Porter), 1953. Editor: Excess Profits Tax Handbook, 1947; Handbook of Cost Accounting Methods, 1949; Handbook of Tax Accounting Methods, 1951; Handbook of Tax Techniques, 1951; Estate Tax Handbook, 1951; Handbook of Auditing Methods, 1953; Business Management Handbook, 1953; J. K. Lasser Reports on Taxes (newsletter). Office: 1440 Broadway, N.Y.C. 18. Died May 11, 1954.

LASSITER, Herbert Carlyle, rear adm. USN. Address: care Bureau of Naval Personnel, Dept. of Navy, Washington. Died 1950.*

LASSITER, William, army officer; b. Petersburg, Va., Sept. 29, 1867; s. D. W. and A. H. Lassiter; grad. U.S. Mil. Acad., 1889, Arty. Sch., 1894; m. Jeannette Johnson, Oct. 5, 1935. Commd. add. 2d lt. 4th Arty., 1889; promoted through grades to col., 1916; brig. gen. Nat. Army, 1917; maj. gen., 1918; from brig. gen. to maj. gen. regular army, 1920-22. Served with battery at attack and capture of Santiago, Cuba, July 1898; asst. instr. tactics, U.S. Mil. Acad., 1898-1901; comd. 7th Battery, F.A., Ft. Riley, Kan., 1901-03; on Bd. Prep. F.A. Drill Regulations, 1903-08; duty Office Inspector Gen. U.S. Army, 1908-09; duty Gen. Staff, 1911-13; duty as mil. attaché Am. Embassy, London, Eng., 1916; apptd. comdr. 51st F.A. Brigade, Boston, 1917; chief arty., 1st Corps, May 1918 (Aisne-Marne offensive), 4th Corps, Aug. 1918 (St. Mihiel offensive), 2d Army, Oct. 1918 (Toul sector); comdg. 32d Div., Nov. 20, 1918-Apr. 19, 1919 (march to Rhine and occupation of Coblentz bridgehead); chief arty., 3d Army. Apr. 19, 1919; returned to U.S. Aug. 6, 1919, assigned as col. to Gen. Staff Corps; comdr. Camp Knox, Ky., Sept. 1920-Sept. 1921; asst. chief staff in charge operations and tng., 1921-23; appt. comdr. Panama Div., 1923, Panama Dept., 1924; succeeded Gen. Pershing as head Tacna-Arica Plebiscite Commn., 1926; comd. 6th Corps Area, hdqrs., Chgo., 1927-28; comd. Philippine Dept., Apr.-Oct. 1928; comd. 8th Corps Area, 1928-30; comd. Hawaiian Dept., Sept. 1920-31, ret. 1931. Decorated D.S.M. (U.S.); Knight Comdr. Order of St. Michael and St. George (British); Comdr. Légion d'Honneur; Croix de Guerre, 2 palms (French). Address: 174 Miramar Av., Santa Barbara, Cal. Died Mar. 1959.

LATCHAW, John Roland Harris, coll. pres.; b. Venango Co., Pa., Sept. 7, 1851; s. Samuel and Ann (Ross) L.; A.B., Hillsdale (Mich.) Coll., 1881, A.M., 1884, D.D., 1891; post-grad., U. Chgo., 1895-6; m. Zella Amanda Kimball, Apr. 27, 1875. Ordained Christian ministry, 1878; founded, 1881, mgr., 1881-84, Barkeyville (Pa.) Acad.; pres., lectr. psychology and theology, Findlay Coll., 1884-93; pastor First Bapt. Ch., Zanesville, O., 1893-5, Bethel Bapt. Ch., Chgo., 1895-6, First Bapt. Ch., Defiance, 1896-7, Christian Assembly (Independent), Defiance, 1897-1902; pres. Defiance (O.) Coll., 1896-1902, Palmer U., (Ind.), 1902-3, became pres. Wilton Coll., Ia., 1907; pastor Christian Church, Romeo, Mich. Editor, and pub. The Truth Seeker; joint editor Unity Herald. Author: The Problem of Philosophy, 1881; The American College—Its Essential Features, 1887; Outline Lectures in Theology, 1893; Theory and Art of Teaching, 1893; Citizenship in Northwest Territory, 1894; Inductive Psychology, 1905; also sermons, addresses and popular lectures. Address: Romeo, Mich. Died 1928; buried Findlay, O.

LATHEM, Abraham Lance, clergyman; b. Hanover Twp., 30 miles west of Pitts., May 26, 1866; s. Robert and Eliza (Lance) L.; B.A., Washington and Jefferson Coll., 1890, D.D., 1915; student Western Theol. Sem., Allegheny, Pa., 1891; grad. Princeton Theol. Sem., 1893; Ph.D., Wooster U. (now Wooster, Coll.), 1901; m. Elizabeth McKeag, May 16, 1893; children—Lance B., Helen G. (Mrs. John C. Taber), Elizabeth A., Evangeline (Mrs. E. L. Buysse). Ordained to ministry Presbyn. Ch., 1893; pastor Martinsburg and Duncansville chs., Blair County, Pa., 1893-95, N. 10th Street Ch., Phila., 1895-1904, 3d Ch., Chester, Pa., 1904-39; organized Bible Presbyn. Ch. of Chester (unaffiliated), 1939, and has since been pastor; prof. pastoral theology Faith Theol. Sem., Wilmington, Del., 1937—. Started summer Bible School movement in Chester, Pa., 1911, which has extended through U.S. and into foreign countries; pres. and dir. Summer Bible School Assn. Prohibitionist. Author: The Way of Life, 1911; The Gospel by John (a study), 1927; Character Building, 1928; The Acts (a study), 1934; Sunrise, 1937; also various booklets pertaining to the Bible. Home: 412 E. 19th St., Chester, Pa. Died Feb. 21, 1955; buried Chester Rural Cemetery.

LATHROP, Alanson P., corp. ofcl.; b. Norwich, Conn.; s. Jabez S. and Julia (Backus) L.; student Norwich Acad.; m. Eleanor Farquhar, Nov. 18, 1890; children—Grayson Farquhar (dec.), Mrs. Gertrude L. Starring. Former dir. Am. Light & Traction Co., N.Y.C. Mem. Soc. Colonial Wars (N.Y.); New Eng. Soc. in the City of N.Y. Home: Savoy-Plaza Hotel. Office: 165 Broadway, N.Y.C. Died Apr. 1950.

LATHROP, Austin Eugene, business man; b. Lapeer, Mich., Oct. 5, 1865; s. Eugene and Maria (Parsons) L.; student pub. schs.; unmarried. Began as bldg. contractor, Ashland, Wis., 1882; contractor, Seattle, 1889-96; successively engaged in transportation, theatre, coal and gold mining and newspaper business, Alaska, 1896-—; theatre proprietor, 1912-—; coal operator, 1924-—; radio station owner, 1939-—. Pres. First Bank of Cordova, Bank of Fairbanks, Midnight Sun Broadcasting Co. (Station KFAR), Fairbanks, KENI, Anchorage, Alaska, Tanana Pub. Co., Healy River Coal Corp., Lathrop Co. (operating theatres and apt. houses); dir. Olympia Brewing Co., Olympia, Wash., Pacfiic Nat. Bank, Seattle. Mem. bd. regents U. Alaska. Mem. Rep. Nat. Com., 1928-33. Home: Anchorage, Alaska; and Fairbanks, Alaska. Died July 26, 1950.

LATHROP, Palmer Jadwin (lā'thrŏp), business exec.; b. Scranton, Pa., Nov. 24, 1909; s. Henry Ridgway and Charlotte Hope (Jadwin) L.; student Brooklyn Poly. Prep., 1921-23, Hotchkiss Sch., Lakeville, Conn., 1924-27; A.B., Princeton, 1931; m. Caroline Marsha Kinsey, Feb. 3, 1933; 1 son, James Palmer. Various positions with Bristol-Myers Co., N. Y. City, 1931-48; prodn. mgr., mfg. plant, Hillside, N.J., 1935-48, vice pres. in charge prodn., 1948; asst. to pres. Cameron Machine Co., Brooklyn, 1948-49, president since 1949, dir. and member executive com. since May 1947. Served with U.S. A.F. as glider pilot, later with Alaskan Division, Air Transport Command; disch. rank of major, 1945. Mem. Summit (N.J.) Bd. of Health. Mem. Soc. for Advancement of Management. Republican. Presbyterian. Clubs: Cap and Gown, Triangle (Princeton, N.J.); Baltusrol Golf (Summit, N.J.). Home: 77 Hillcrest Av., Summit, N.J. Office: 61 Poplar St., Bklyn. 2. Died Dec. 26, 1953.

LATIMER, Clyde Burney, judge; b. McLeansboro, Ill., Dec. 28, 1890; s. Sylvanus R. and Elizabeth (Bennett) L.; A.B., McKendree Coll., Lebanon, Ill., 1915; LL.B., Westminster Law Sch., 1927, LL.D., 1950; m. Ruby Robinson, Sept. 7, 1910; children—Cathryn Louise (Mrs. V. W. Horn), Richard L., James Joseph. School teacher, intermittently, 1910-24; admitted to Kentucky bar, 1927, and since practiced law, Glasgow, Ky.; judge Court of Appeals of Ky. since Oct. 1944; dir Glasgow Ry. Co. Mem. Ky. Workmens Compensation Bd., July-Oct. 1944. Del to Rep. Nat. Conv., Chicago, 1932. Past pres. Lions Club, Glasgow. Mem. Sigma Nu Phi. Home: 127 St. Marys Court, Glasgow, Ky. Office: 307 W. 3d St., Frankfort, Ky. Died Sept. 28, 1952; buried Frankfort.

LATIMER, Wendell Mitchell, chemist; b. Garnett, Kan., Apr. 22, 1893; s. Walter and Emma (Mitchell) L.; A.B., U. of Kan., 1915; Ph.D., U. of Calif., 1918; m. Bertha Eichenauer, Aug. 1, 1917; 1 son, Walter R.; m. 2d, Glatha Hatfield, June 16, 1926; children—Eleanor Ann, Robert Milton. Lecturer and demonstrator in chemistry, U. of Calif., 1918-21, asst. prof., 1921-23, asso. prof., 1924-31, prof., 1931-—; asst. dean Coll. Letters and Science, U. of Calif., 1923-24, dean College of Chemistry, 1941-50, associate director radiation laboratory, 1949-—. Official investigator National Defense Research Com., 1942-43; mem. War Dept. Mission to England, 1943; mem. div. 10 com., Nat. Defense Research Com.; technical observer and sci. expert G.H.Q., Southwest Pacific Area, 1944. Director Manhattan Eng. District Contract on Chemistry of plutonium, 1943-47. Member Chemical Corps Research Council, 1947-51, Commn. of Electrochemistry of Internat. Union of Pure and Applied Chemistry. Academy Polit. Sci., National Academy Sciences, American Chemistry Society, A.A. A.S., Electrochem. Soc., Sigma Xi, Alpha Chi Sigma. Guggenheim Foundation fellow, Munich, 1930. Recipient, Distinguished Service Award, Univ. of Kansas, 1948, Presidential Certificate of Merit, 1948, Nichols award N.Y. sect. Am. chem. Soc., 1955. Clubs: Bohemian, Orinda Country, Faculty. Author: A Course in General Chemistry (with W. C. Bray), 1923; Referennce Book of Inorganic Chemistry (with J. H. Hildebrand), 1929; Oxidation Potentials, 1938. Contbr. to chem. publs. Editor of Prentice-Hall chemistry series. Asso. editor Jour. Chem. Phys., 1933, Chem. Review, 1940. Home: 810 Euclid Av., Berkeley 8, Cal. Died July 6, 1955; buried Woodlawn Cemetery, Kansas City, Kan.

LATOURETTE, Earl C., state justice; b. Oregon City, Ore., Feb. 10, 1889; s. Charles David and Sedonia (Shaw) L.; A.B., U. Ore., 1912; children by previous marriage—Anne (Mrs. Kevin Cooke), Jeanne (Mrs. Kenneth Linklater), Earl C.; m. 2d, Eleanor Marshall. Admitted to Ore. bar, 1913; mem. firm C. D. Latourette, D. C. Latourette and Earl C. Latourette until 31; circuit judge Clackamas County, Ore., 1931-51; asso. justice Supreme Ct. Ore., 1951-—, chief justice, 1953-55. Mem. Am., Ore. bar assns., Kappa Sigma, Phi Delta Phi. Clubs: University, Arlington, Waverley Country (Portland). Home: 1650 John St. Office: Supreme Court Bldg., Salem, Ore. Died Aug. 18, 1956.

LATOURETTE, Howard Fenton (lă-tōō-ĕt'), lawyer; b. Oregon City, Ore. Sept. 4, 1883; s. Charles David and Sedonia Bird (Shaw) L.; B.L., U. Ore., 1905; m. Eleanor Rothermel, Nov. 16, 1910 (dec.); children—Allene (dec.), Nancy. Admitted to Ore. bar, 1905, and since practiced at Portland; mem. Latourette & Latourette, Portland, Ore., 1908-—. Speaker Ore. Ho. of Reps., spl. session, 1935; elected Dem. Nat. committeeman for Ore., 1936, reelected, 1940. Elk. Club: University (Portland). Home: University Club. Office: Corbett Bldg., Portland, Ore. Died June 29, 1957; buried Portland Meml. Cemetery.

LATTA, Robert Edward, dentist; b. Camden, S.C., June 3, 1894; s. William Herbert and Sarah Cason (Francis) L.; D.D.S., Emory U., 1917; student in Paris, London, Berlin, Mexico City; m. Mary Stewart Hewlett, July 15, 1933. Formerly tchr. Emory U., chief dental surgeon Child's Bur.; founder dental clinic Home for Incurables; dir. Churches Homes for Bus. Girls; chmn. bd. trustees Southeastern U.; chmn. bd. Am. Rescue Workers. Served as maj., Dental Corps, U.S. Army, World War I. Recipient president's pin, also bronze medal, Men's Garden Club of Am., 1951. Pres. Bapt. Young Peoples Union, chmn. No. Dist. Div. Founder Fulton County Dental Assn.; mem. Am., Ga. (life), No. Dist. dental assns., Fifth Dist. Dental Soc., Nat. Rehabilitation Assn., C. of C. (dir.), Ga. Dahlia Soc., Ga. Rose Soc. (pres.), Xi Psi Phi. Democrat. Presbyn. Clubs: Atlanta Burns (pres., sec.), Three Points (pres.), Atlanta Men's Garden (pres., sec.), East Lake, Atlanta Athletic, Speaker's (pres.). Author booklets on gardening. Contbr. to profl. mags. Home: 365 Peachtree Battle Av. N.W. Office: Medical Arts Bldg., Atlanta 3. Died Apr. 8, 1956.

LATTIG, Herbert Elmer, univ. dean; b. Anita, Ia., Jan. 28, 1892; s. Elmer Fritchie and Martha (Kirkham) L.; B.S., Univ. Ida., 1915, M.S., 1925; m. Vaughan E. Prater, Nov. 10, 1928. Rancher, 1915-22; teacher vocational agr., 1922-26; prof. agrl. edn., Univ. Ida., 1926-35, asst. dean, coll. agr., 1935-42, acting dean of men, 1942-46, dir. student affairs and dean of men since 1946. Coordinator Army Training Program, 1942-45. Mem. Am. Vocational Assn., Alpha Zeta, Sigma Nu. Author: Practical Methods in Teaching Vocational Agriculture, 1932; series of 6 booklets on Selecting, Fitting and Showing Livestock and Poultry (with J. E. Nordby), 1936. Home: 615 Moore-Av., Moscow, Ida. Died Nov. 26, 1953; buried Morris Hill Mausoleum, Boise, Ida.

LATTRE de TASSIGNY, Jean Joseph Marie Gabriel de, French army officer; b. Mouilleron-en-Pareds, Vendee, France, Feb. 2, 1889; s. Roger and Anne (Henault) Lattre de T.; student Coll. Jesuits, also St. Cyr; Dr. honoris causa, U. Montpellier, also U. Strasbourg; m. Simonne Calary de Lamaziere, March 21, 1927; 1 son, Bernard (dec. May 30, 1951). Vol. mil. service, 1908; sous-lt. 12th Regt. of Dragoons; comdr. batn. 93d Inf. Regt., Moroccan Campaign, 1921-25, chief batn., 1926; Sch. of War, 1927; mil. staff officer to v.p. High Council of War; col., comdg. 151st Inf. Regt., 1935-37; chief staff to mil. gov. gen. of Strasbourg, comdr. Army of Alsace, 1938; gen. brigade, 1939; comdr. 14th Inf. Div., Jan. 1940; gen. div., high comdr. troops, Tunicia, Tunis, 1941; gen. Corps of Army, comdg. 16th Mil. Div., Montpellier, 1942; sentenced to 10 years in prison, Nov. 11, 1942, escaped, Sept. 2, 1943; left France on Royal Air Force plane, Oct. 17, 1943; service with Free French Forces; gen., comdr.-in-chief 1st Army of France, 1944-45, France, Germany and Austria, Aug. 15, 1944; insp. gen. ground army, chief staff gen. Army, May 8, 1945; v.p. High Council of War, June 2, 1947; insp. gen. Armed Forces, Mar. 1, 1948; comdr.-in-chief Grand Forces of Western Europe, Oct. 5, 1948; presently high commr. of Fr., Indo-China, comdr.-in-chief Far East; named Marshall of France posthumously. Decorated: Medaille Militaire, Grand Croix of Legion of Honor (France), Compagnon de l'Ordre de la Liberation, Medaille des Evades, D.S.M., chief Comdr. Legion of Merit, Medaille d'or de l'Am. Legion G.C.B. de l'Ordre de Bain, Mil. Cross, Grand Coix de Grace Magistrale de l'Ordre de Malte. Clubs: Cercle Interallie (Paris); Cavalry (Pondon). Author: Histoire de la Premiere Armes Francaise (Rhine and Danube), 1949. Home: 4 Place Rio de Janeiro, Paris VIII°. Office: 4 bis, Blvd. des Invalides, Paris VII°. Died Jan. 11, 1952; buried Mouilleron-en-Pareds (Vendée).

LATZER, John A. (läts'ĕr), condensed milk co. ofcl.; b. Highland, Ill., Nov. 11, 1876; s. Louis and Eliza (Luehm) L.; B.S., U. Ill., 1899, M.S., 1900; m. Louise Briggs, Nov. 21, 1906; children—John B., Thomas F., Margaret L. Began in manufacture of condensed milk, 1900; pres. Pet Milk Co., St. Louis. Republican. Mason. Clubs: Missouri Athletic Assn., Bellerive Country. Home: 28 Brentmoor Pl. Office: Arcade Bldg., St. Louis. Died June 31, 1952.

LAUBENGAYER, Robert J. (lou'bĕn-gā-ĕr), newspaper pub.; b. Ann Arbor, Mich., Dec. 15, 1884; s. Jacob and Amelia (Weimer) L.; grad. high sch., Ann Arbor; student U. of Mich., 1906-07; m. Jessie Lee Stremning, Oct. 15, 1916; children—Betty Lee (Mrs. Betty L. Dieter), Barbara Amelia (Mrs. Barbara Macdonald). Began as reporter Detroit Tribune and Detroit News, Ann Arbor, 1900; pub. Salina (Kan.) Jour., 1925-50; v.p. Farmers Nat. Bank; pres. Country Club Development Co.; dir. Kan. Power & Light Co., Topeka; Daily News Hays, Consol. Printing & Stationery Co., Dunn Sulphite Paper Co. (Port Huron, Mich.); pres. KSAL, radio sta.; adv. bd. Kan. Live Stock Assn., v.p., 1937-38; mem. Kan. Unemployment Bd., 1930-32; mem. State Planning Bd., 1932-36; mem. Econ. Policy Com.; mem. com. of three that wrote wheat plan of AAA for 1933-34; mem. Wheat Crop Ins. Cons. Com. for Fed. Crop Ins. Co.; mem. Farm Security Adv. Com., 1939-40. Rep. Mason (32°, Shriner, Jester). Clubs: Salina Country, Michigan Union. Home: Country Club Heights, 413 Country Club Rd. Address: Salina Journal, Salina, Kan. Died Dec. 26, 1958.

LAUGHLIN, Gail, lawyer; b. Robbinston, Me., May 7, 1868; d. Robert Clark and Elizabeth Porter (Stuart) Laughlin) B.A., Wellesley, 1894; LL.B., Cornell U., 1898; founder The Agora; winner Cornell U. debate prize and leader Cornell U. collegiate debate team, 1898; unmarried. Editorial writer New York Commercial, 1898-99; practice of law, N.Y.C., 1899-1902; expert agt. U.S. Indsl. Commn., 1900-02; lectr. Nat. Woman Suffrage Assn., 1902-06; practiced law, Denver, 1908-14, San Francisco, 1914-24, Portland, Me., 1924-—; admitted to bars of N.Y., Colo., Cal. and to practice before U.S. Supreme Court. Dir. Cumberland Savs. and Loan Assn. Mem. Me. legislature, 1927-31, 33-35; mem. Me. Senate, 1937-41; apptd. reporter of court decisions, 1941. Mem. Colo. Bd. of Pardons, 1911-14; mem. Mayor's Advisory Council, Denver, 1912. Sec. state exec. com. Prog. party, Colo., 1912-14; state vice chmn. Prog. party, Colo., 1913-14; vice chmn. Nat. Woman's party; mem. Rep. State Central Com. of Cal., 1920-22. A founder and dir. Cal. br. Nat. League for Woman's Service; vice chmn. San Francisco County Women's Council of Defense; four-minute man, World War. Mem. Women's Lawyers' Assn., Am., Me., Cumberland County bar assns., Woman's Lit. Union of Portland (pres. 1927-29); a founder and first pres. Nat. Fed. of Bus. and Profl. Women's Clubs, 1919-20; pres. Cal. Civic League, 1918-20. Mem. Kappa Beta Pi. Clubs: Lincoln; Business and Professional Women's; Western Maine Wellesley. Unitarian. Writer on tariff and other econ. questions. Author of law making women eligible for jury service in Cal. and successfully defended constitutionality of the law. Home: 65 Revere St., Portland 5, Me. Died Mar. 13, 1952; buried Brooklawn Meml. Park, Portland.

LAUGHLIN, Samuel Ott Jr., business exec.; born Cleveland, Oct. 11, 1891; s. Samuel Ott and Mary (Magruder) L.; student Linsly Inst., Wheeling, W. Va., 1906-10; A.B., Washington and Lee U., 1914; m. Elizabeth Stone Rownd, June 16, 1928; children—Samuel Ott, III, Wm. Philip, David R. Laborer then foreman, 1915-17, Wheeling Tile Co., Wheeling W.Va., supt. then vice pres., 1920-29; pres., gen. mgr. and dir. Wheeling (W.Va.) Tile Co. since 1930; dir. mem. exec. and trust coms., Wheeling Dollar Savings and Trust Co.; dir. Fostoria Glass Co., Stone & Thomas, Wheeling Stamping Company. Served as 2d lt., 339th Machine Gun Bn., A.E.F., 1st lt. and adjutant, U.S. Army, 1917-19; overseas 12 mos. Dir. Ohio Valley Hosp. Mem. Tile Mfg. Assn. (past pres.), Greenwood Assn. (dir.), Pi Kappa Alpha Corp. (dir. and v.p.), Am. Newcomen Soc. of England, Omicron Delta Kappa. Rep. Presbyn. (trustee). Clubs: Rotary, Fort Henry, Wheeling Country. Home: Kenwood Pl. Office: Wheeling Tile Co., Wheeling, W. Va. Died July 29, 1957.

LAUTERBACH, Richard E(dward), journalist; b. N.Y. City, June 18, 1914; s. Morton Edgar and Hazel Augusta (Kronthal) L.; B.A., Dartmouth Coll., 1935; Nieman fellow, Harvard, 1946-47; m. Elisabeth Stuart Wardwell, July 25, 1935; children—Jennifer Wardwell, Ann March, David Stuart. Mng. editor, Golf mag., 1938-40, asso. editor, Life mag. (both at New York), 1941-42; war corr. Middle East for Life, 1943; chief, Time and Life Bureau, Moscow, U.S.S.R., 1943-44, fgn. editor Life, N.Y. City, 1945, roving editor in Far East for Time and Life, 1945-46; editor in chief, The Magazine of the Year, 1947; sr. editor, New York Star, 1948. Lecturer on Russia and Far East at universities sinie 1945. Mem. bd. trustees Downtown Community Sch., New York. Mem. bd. dirs. China Aid Council. Mem. Soc. Nieman Fellows, Council of Author's Guild, Phi Beta Kappa. Club: Dartmouth. Democrat (exec. dir. Young voters div. Dem. State Campaign, N.Y., 1938). Author: These Are the Russians, 1945; Through Russia's Back Door, 1947; Danger from The East, 1947. Contbr. to History in the Writing edited by Gordon Corvallo. Contbr. to leading mags. Home: 142 E. 18 St., N.Y.C. 3. Died Sept. 20, 1950.

LAVENDER, Harrison Morton, mining engr.; b. Scotland, S.D., Oct. 31, 1890; s. Albert Webster and Mary (Edgar) L.; E.M., Colo. Sch. of Mines, 1916; m. Florence T. Brush, July 3, 1941; children by previous marriage—Harrison Morton, Caroline (Mrs. William S. Chandler). Mining engr. in Ariz., Utah, Colo. and Mexico, 1916-23; chief mining engr. Calumet and Ariz. Mining Co., Bisbee, Ariz., 1926-31; mine supt. Copper Queen Branch, Phelps Dodge Corp., Bisbee, Arizona, 1932-35, asst. to vice-pres. and gen. mgr., Douglas, Ariz., 1936-37, gen. mgr., 1937-46, vice president and gen. mgr. since 1946, dir. Phelps Dodge Corporation, since 1949; pres., director Tucson, Cornelia & Gila Bend R.R. since 1940; dir. Apache Power Co., Curtis, Ariz., since 1937. Awarded Medal for Distinguished Achievement, Colo. Sch. of

Mines, 1948. Served with Engr. Corps, A.U.S., 1917-19. Mem. Am. Inst. Mining and Metall. Engrs., Am. Mining Congress. Republican. Episcopalian. Mason. Clubs: Arizona, Phoenix Country, Old Pueblo, California. Home: 910 E. Av. Office: Phelps Dodge Corp., Douglas, Ariz. Died Mar. 21, 1952.

LAVERY, Urban A(ugustin) (lā'very), lawyer; b. Lavery, Pa., Jan. 6, 1885; s. Sylvester and Elizabeth (Tracy) L.; B.S., U. Pa., 1906, M.A., 1907; student Columbia, 1907-08; J.D., U. Chicago, 1910; m. Grace Mary Donohue, June 30, 1925; children—Ann Elizabeth (Mrs. James K. Tyson), Mary Nealis (Mrs. Stuart Broad), Sylvia Joan. Admitted to Ill. bar, 1910; partner several law firms, Chgo., 1910-33; law editor West Pub. Co., St. Paul, 1934-39; mng. editor Am. Bar Assn. Jour., 1939-42; individual practice, specializing in Fed. law matters, 1942——; asst. to atty. gen. of U.S. in anti-trust matters, 1944-46; won noted Children's Case in 1946. Legislative draftsman Ill. Constl. Conv., 1919-21; pub. mem. War Labor Bd., Ill., 1942-45. Served as 1st lt., A.E.F., France, 1918. Mem. Am., Ill. and Chgo. bar assns., Phi Delta Phi. Democrat. Roman Catholic. Club: Law (Chgo.). Author: (standard law books) Federal Administrative Law, 1952; Ill. Revenue Act of 1939; Ill. Election Code of 1944. Contbr. legal jours. Home: 2332 Bryant Av., Evanston, Ill. Office: First National Bank Bldg., Chgo. Died Aug. 20, 1959; buried All Saints Cemetery, Des Plaines, Ill.

LAW, Frederick Houk, author; b. N.Y. City, Sept. 7, 1871; s. John Masseker and Jane Rachel (Houk) L.; grad. Oxford (N.Y.) Acad., 1891; A.B., Amherst, 1895; A.M., Columbia, 1896; studied Brown U. and New York U., Ph.D. from latter, 1914; m. Mary Kenniston Thorp, June 30, 1896 (died 1907); m. 2d, Carrie Ramsey Shields, June 29, 1912; children—John, Margaret (Mrs. Henry Mills), Janet (Mrs. Richard H. Amberg), Frederick, Robert. Instr. in English and French, Centre Coll., Danville, Ky., 1897-98; head dept. of English, high school, Pawtucket, R.I., 1898-1904, Stuyvesant High School, N.Y. City, 1904-42; editor ednl. dept. Reader's Digest, 1942-52. Formerly lecturer, N.Y. Free Public Lecture System; lecturer English lit., New York U., N.Y.; instr. English and pedagogy, Notre Dame Coll., Staten Island; president, High School Teachers' Association, N.Y. City, N.Y.; mem. exec. com., Joint Com. of Teachers Orgns., N.Y. City; First Assistants Association; N.Y. City Assn. High School Teachers of English; exec. bd. Nat. Commn., Defense of Democracy Through Edn. Fellow A.A.A.S.; mem. N.E. A. (former state dir. N.Y.), Nat. Council Tchrs. English, Sons Vets., Chi Phi. Republican. Conglist. Mason (32°, K.T., Shriner). Club: Adventurers (New York, sec.). Author numerous books since 1938; latest: Great Lives, 1951; Great Americans, 1953; Adventure, 1954; Patriotic Americans, 1955; editor various books, 1914——. Has traveled extensively in Arctic regions, Yukon, Labrador, South Sea Islands, South America, Cape to Cairo, Africa, China, Korea, Japan. Home: 472 Argyle Rd., Bklyn. 18. Died Sept. 7, 1957; buried Oxford, N.Y.

LAW, James Richard, architect, ex-mayor; b. Madison, Wis., Apr. 1, 1885; s. James and Amelia (Kindschi) L.; student spl. course architecture, U. of Pa., 1907-09; m. Susan Campbell, June 27, 1911; children—Lucia DeEtte, Susan Margaret. Began as architect, 1904; pvt. practice, Madison, 1914-32; pres. Law, Law & Potter, Madison, since 1914; dir. Wis. Life Ins. Co. Mayor of Madison, 1932-44; now chmn. Wis. State Highway Commn. Awarded St. Olav's medal by King Haakon VII of Norway, 1939. Mem. The Newcomen Society of England, Acacia. Republican. Conglist. Mason (Consistory, Shriner), Elk. Clubs: Madison, Maple Bluff Country (Madison). Home: 2011 University Av. Office: State Office Bldg., Madison 5, Wis. Died Mar. 14, 1952.

LAWLOR, Daniel J., editor; b. Lincoln, R.I.; s. Daniel O'Connell and Margaret (Stack) L.; ed. pub. sch. Cumberland, R.I.; special courses Brown U. and Boston U.; m. Julia L. Cunningham, Oct. 6, 1913. With Pawtucket (R.I.) Times since 1905, successively as reporter, state house corr., state political editor, telegraph editor, managing editor, and since 1927, editor; editor Pawtucket Times Anniversary Mag., Oct. 1921 (250th anniversary of founding of Pawtucket); A.P. corr., 1925-35. Roman Cath., K.C. Mem. R.I. Hist. Soc. Address: 23 Potter St., Pawtucket, R.I. Died Dec. 25, 1950; buried Forest Glade Cemetery, Wakefield, Mass.

LAWLOR, William F., educator; b. Paterson, N.J., s. James and Honorah (Ryan) L.; student Mt. St. Mary's Coll., Emmitsburg, Md., 1904-06, LL.D., 1952; A.B., Seton Hall Coll., 1908, A.M., 1910, LL.D., 1924, Villa Nova Coll., 1941; L.H.D., Seton Hall U., 1958. Ordained priest in Roman Catholic Ch., 1912; asst. supt., Newark (N.J.) Archdiocesan Schs., 1914-21, supt., 1921——; Archdiocesan Consultor. Former nat. pres. Cath. Sch. Supts.; trustee Seton Hall U., Archdiocesan Seminary, Seton Hall Coll., So. Orange, and Union Jr. Coll., Roselle, N.J. Recipient of Protonotary Apostolicship from Rome. Member Nat. Cath. Ednl. Assn. Author: Geography of State of New Jersey, 1926; Geography of State of New York, 1929. Home: 326 Avenue C., Bayonne, N.J. Office: 31 Mulberry St., Newark, N.J. Died June 21, 1959.

LAWRANCE, Charles Lanier, aircraft engr.; born Lenox, Mass., Sept. 30, 1882; s. Francis Cooper and Sarah Eggleston (Lanier) L.; A.B., Yale, 1905, hon. A.M., 1927; grad. École des Beaux Arts, Paris, 3 yrs.; hon. D.Sc., Tufts, 1928; hon. A.M., Harvard, 1929; m. Emily M. G. Dix, 1910; children—Emily, Margaret, Francis Cooper. Engaged in engineering since 1915, with special interest in development of aircraft engines; founder, 1917 and pres. until 1923, Lawrance Aero Engine Corp., N.Y. City; corp. merged with Wright Aeronautical Corp., 1923, pres., 1925-28, v.p., 1928-30; organized Lawrance Engineering & Research Corp., pres. and chief engr. until 1944; chmn. bd. of dirs. and dir. of engine research, 1944-46; now chief engineer and chmn. of board, Power Industries, Inc., N.Y. City; pres. C. L. Lawrance Corp. (realty); dir. and pres. Nitralloy Corp. Ensign N.Y. Naval Militia, 1916-17; assigned by Navy Dept. to aeronautical research, World War I. Fellow Royal Aeronautical Soc., Eng.; fellow Inst. of Aeronautical Sciences (pres. 1934-35); member Society Automotive Engrs., Aeronautical Chamber Commerce of America (pres. 1931-32), Sons of the Revolution, Society of the Cincinnati. Decorated Chevalier Legion of Honor (France). Awarded Collier trophy, 1928. Pres. Emergency Shelter, N.Y. City. Republican. Episcopalian. Clubs: Yale, Brook. Home: 151 E. 63d St., N.Y. City 21; and East Islip, L.I., N.Y. Office: Power Industries, 22 E. 42d St., N.Y. City 17. Died June 24, 1950; buried Locust Valley Cemetery.

LAWRENCE, Carl Gustavus, educator; b. Madison, Wis., Jan. 12, 1871; s. Ole H. and Marie (Hull) L.; B. Litt., U. of Wis., 1894, post-grad. work in history; A.M., U. S.D., 1919; LL.D., Yankton (S.D.) College, 1930; m. Gunda Jacobson, Aug. 22, 1900; children—Ernest Orlando, John Hundale. Prof. Latin and history Augustana Coll., Canton, S.D., 1894-98; supt. schs., Canton, 1898-1907; county supt. schs., Lincoln County, S.D., 1907-11; state supt. pub. instr., 2 terms, 1911-15; supt. schs., Canton, 1915-19; pres. Southern State Normal Sch., Springfield, S.D., 1919-33; Northern State Teachers Coll., Aberdeen, S.D., 1933-39, pres. emeritus, July 1, 1939——. Mem. State Bd. of Edn., 1925-32, Berkeley City Library Bd., Oct. 1946——. Pres. S.D. Edn. Assn., 1929-30. Lutheran. Mason. Rotarian. Home: 2441 Haste St., Berkeley, Cal. Died Aug. 26, 1954; buried Chapel of Memories, Oakland, Cal.

LAWRENCE, Edwin Gordon, author, teacher; b. Phila., Pa., Nov. 1, 1859; s. Prof. Philip and Mary E. (Maver) L.; ed. Friends Sch., Phila., public schools of New York, and by pvt. tutors; m. Sadie Secord, Mar. 14, 1891 (divorced June 25, 1903); children—Edwina Gordon, Olga Kelsey, Valdemar Philip, Eleanor Mary. Began in Madison Sq. Theatre, New York, 1879; starred as Osip in The Danicheffs, touring U.S., 1881-82; starred in For Her Sake, 1896-98. Succeeded father as dir. Lawrence Sch. Elocution and Acting, New York, upon his death, 1882; served in Europe, under Herbert Hoover, with Commn. for Relief in Belgium, 1915; asso. editor Athol (Mass.) Chronicle, 1919-20; editorial writer Miami (Fla.) Herald, 1921, spl. feature writer for newspapers, 1922; asso. editor, Palm Beach Times, West Palm Beach, Fla., 1923-25; now engaged in lit. work. Republican. Unitarian. Club: Shakespeare (Stratford-on-Avon, Eng.). Author: The Power of Speech, 1909; The Lawrence Reader and Speaker, 1911; Speech-Making, 1911; How to Master the Spoken Word, 1913; How to Improve the Memory, 1913; How to Speak, 1917, revised and enlarged; Sidelights on Shakespeare, 1918, revised and enlarged; Aids to Business, 1920; Rudiments of Speech, 1923; Homespun Verse (collected poems), 1932; How to Talk to People and Make an Impression, 1938; also newspaper serials, "A Thought for Today," "Tales of a Traveler," "The State of the Country," "Pause for a Moment," "Autocracy, Mobocracy—Or What?", "How Fares the Nation," "Promise Versus Performance," "In Behalf of Constitutional Representative Government." Contbr. verse to Boston Post and other publs. Spl. rep. of N.H. to Centennial Commemoration of the Fall of the Alamo, San Antonio, Mar. 6, 1936. Home: 4404 Montana St., El Paso, Tex. Died Nov. 22, 1950.

LAWRENCE, Ernest Orlando, prof. physics; b. Canton, S.D., Aug. 8, 1901; s. Carl Gustavus and Gunda (Jacobson) L.; student St. Olaf Coll., Northfield, Minn., 1918-19, A.B., U. of S.D., 1922; A.M., U. of Minn., 1923; student U. of Chicago, 1923-24; Ph.D., Yale, 1925; Sc.D., U. of S.D., 1936; Princeton, Yale, Stevens Inst. Tech., 1937, Harvard, U. of Chicago, Rutgers U., 1941, McGill U., Montreal, Can., 1946; LL.D., U. of Mich., 1938, U. of Pa. 1942 Sc.D., Univ. B.C., 1947, U. So. Cal., 1949, University San Francisco, 1949; LL.D., U. Glasgow, 1951; m. Mary Kimberly Blumer, 1932; children—John Eric, Margaret Bradley, Mary Kimberly, Robert Don, Barbara Hundale, Susan. Nat. Research fellow, Yale University, 1925-27, assistant professor physics, 1927-28; associate professor physics, U. of Calif., 1928-30, prof., 1930——, dir. Radiation Lab., 1936——. Awarded Elliott Cresson medal, Franklin Inst., 1937; Research Corp. prize and plaque, 1937; Comstock prize, Nat. Acad. Sciences, 1937; Hughes medal, Royal Soc. (Eng.), 1937; Nobel prize in physics, 1939; Duddell medal, The Phys. Soc., 1940; William K. Dunn award, American Legion, 1940; Holley Medal, American Society of Mechanical Engineers, 1942; Medal for Merit, 1946; Medal of Trasenster, 1947; Officier de la Legion d'Honneur, 1948; Faraday Medal, 1952; Annual award Am. Cancer Society, 1954. Board Foreign Scholarships, 1947. Mem. Solvay Conf., Brussels, 1933; mem. (hon.) U.S.S.R. Acad. Scis., 1943, Royal Swedish Acad. Scis., 1952, Royal Irish Acad., 1948. Mem. bd. of trustees, Carnegie Institution of Washington, 1944. Fellow American Physical Society, A.A.A.S., American Acad. of Arts and Sciences; Hon. Fellow Royal Soc. of Edinburgh, The Phys. Soc., Indian Acad. Sci.; mem. Nat. Acad. Scis., Am. Philos. Soc., Phi Beta Kappa, Sigma Xi, Gamma Alpha. Clubs: Faculty, Bohemian (hon.). Contbr. to Proc. Nat. Acad. Scis., Physical Review, Research in nuclear physics and applications of physics to biology and medicine. Home: 111 Tamalpais Rd., Berkeley, Cal. Died Aug. 27, 1958.

LAWRENCE, Frank Pell, business exec.; b. Newark, New Jersey, Oct. 18, 1886; s. Isaac Savage and Isabelle Pell (Moore) Lawrence; student Lehigh U.; m. Isabel R. Gregory, 1911; children—Elizabeth, Robert Gregory. Entered employ Bell Telephone System, 1912 as engr. for Southwestern Bell Telephone Co., St. Louis; various positions in Kansas City, Topeka, Oklahoma City; plant supt., St. Louis, 1924; gen. plant mgr. Upstate Area, N.Y. Telephone Co., Albany, 1929-33; gen. plant mgr. N.Y. City, 1933-34; v.p. and gen. mgr., Upstate Area N.Y. Telephone Co., 1934-39; v.p. and gen. mgr., Manhattan, N.Y. Telephone Co., 1939-41; v.p. Am. Telephone and Telegraph Co., Long Lines Dept., Jan. 1, 1941, now ret. Mem. bd. mgrs. Montclair Savings Bank. Inst. Elec. Engrs., Sigma Chi. Club: Montclair (N.J.) Golf. Home: 160 Eagle Rock Way, Montclair, N.J. also Little Brook, Califon, N.J. Died May 27, 1957.

LAWRENCE, Gertrude, actress; b. London, Eng., July 4, 1902; d. Arthur Lawrence and Alice Louise (Banks) Klasen; Dr. Fine Arts (hon.), Ithaca (N. Y.) College, 1948; student Convent of the Sacré Coeur, Streatham, Eng.; studied dancing under Madam Espinosa and acting under Italia Conti; married 2d, Richard Stoddard Aldrich (commander United States Naval Reserve), July 4, 1940. Made début in "Babes in the Wood," London, 1908; child chorister in "The Miraele," London, 1911; appeared in many plays in England until 1923; made Am. début in "Charlot's Revue of 1924"; played in "Oh, Kay," N.Y. City, 1926, London, 1927; "Icebound," London, 1928; "Treasure Girl," N.Y. City, 1928; "Candle Light," London and N.Y. City, 1929; "Private Lives," London, 1930, N.Y. City, 1931; "Take Two from One" and "Can the Leopard?," London, 1931; "Behold We Live," London, 1932; "This Inconstancy," and "Nymph Errant," London, 1933; "The Winding Journey," and "Moonlight Is Silver," London, 1934; "Hervey House," London, 1935; with Noel Coward in "Tonight at 8:30," London and N.Y. City, 1936; starred in "Susan and God," 1937-38; "Skylark," 1939-40; "Lady in the Dark," 1941, 42, 43; Tonight at 8:30 (revival), N.Y. and on tour, 1947-48; September Tide, 1948-49; The King and I, 1951; motion picture The Glass Menagerie, 1950; professor of drama Columbia University, 1952. Entertained armed forces, European theater, for E.N.S.A., 1944; entertained armed forces Pacific for U.S.O., 1945; "Pygmalion," 1945-46-47. First vice president American Theatre Wing War Service, Inc.; pres. Am. Branch E.N.S.A.; dir. British Actors Orphanage; mem. Red Cross Staff Assistance Service. Col. U.S. Auxiliary Ambulance Corps. Clubs: Tavern, Cosmopolitan, Press. Author: A Star Danced, 1945. Home: 17 W. 54th St., New York 19, and Dennis, Mass. Address: 36 W. 44th St., N.Y.C. 18. Died Sept. 6, 1952.

LAWRENCE, James Earnest, newspaper editor; b. Beatrice, Neb., July 4, 1889; s. James Grenville and Laura (Pheasant) L.; LL.B., U. Neb., 1911; married Helen Hamilton Graves, Dec. 11, 1912; 1 dau., Helen Elizabeth. Reporter Lincoln Star, 1907-11, city editor, 1911-14, mng. editor and editor since 1914; asso. prof. journalism, U. Neb., since 1918. Mem. adv. bd. for Neb., U.S. Pub. Works Administrn.; pres. Neb. State Hist. Society and Foundation; mem. Neb. Judicial Council. Collaborator: Autobiography of a Liberal, by George W. Norris. Presbyn. Mason. Clubs: Round Table, Lincoln Country. Home: 1315 S. 21st St. Office: Star Pub. Co., Lincoln, Neb. Died Sept. 16, 1957; buried Wyuka Cemetery, Lincoln.

LAWRENCE, Joseph Stagg, economist; b. Budapest, Austria-Hungary, Oct. 19, 1896; s. Joseph Schmalz and Elizabeth (Stumpf) L.; brought to U. S., 1903; grad. Masten Park High Sch., Buffalo, N.Y., 1915; student U. Genoble, France, Mar.-June 1919; grad. Princeton U., 1923; m. Ann Werner, Feb. 2, 1919 (div. Apr. 15, 1940); children—Mary Josephine, Joseph Stagg; m. 2d, Frances Bennett, Sept. 3, 1940; children—Bruce Bennett, Larry Jay, Dean Stagg, Guy Bedell. Teacher Princeton U., 1924-26, 1927-29,

N.Y.U., 1926-27; Am. Gen. Corp., Morris Plan Corp. of Am., Morristown Trust Co.; dir. Gen. Reinsurance Corp., North Star Reinsurance Corp.; v.p. Empire Trust Co. (author Empire Trust Letter). Enlisted as pvt. inv., U.S. Army, at outbreak of World War; served in three major engagements in France; hon. discharged as 1st lt. Fellow Inst. of Economics, 1929-30; mem. Economic Policy Commn., Am. Bankers Assn.; mem. Am. Econ. Assn., Phi Beta Kappa. Club: Princeton. Author: Stabilization of Prices, 1928; Wall Street and Washington, 1929; Banking Concentration in the United States, 1930; Understanding Money, 1932. Contbg. editor The Iron Age. Home: Lafayette, N.J. Died Aug. 25, 1950.

LAWRENCE, Victor H(enry), business exec.; b. Mayville, Wis., Apr. 29, 1897; s. Judge Frank M. and Lydia (Ruedebusch) L.; student, Lawrence Coll., 1915-17, Carnegie Inst. Tech., 1920-21; m. Vera Margaret Prochnow, June 3, 1920; children—Patricia Margaret, Shirley Ann. Civil engr., metallurgist, steel plant operator Minn. Steel Co., Northwestern Iron Co., Jessop Steel Co., Alan Wood Steel Co., 1926-41; asst. to pres. Otis Steel Co., 1941-42; gen. supt. Otis Works, Jones and Laughlin Steel Corp., 1942-47, v.p., planning and control, 1947, mmem. bd. dirs., mem. exec. com., v.p. indsl. relations, 1954—; v.p. Woodlawn Water Co. Mem. Am. Iron and Steel Inst., Iron and Steel Inst. Gt. Brit., Am. Soc. Metals. Republican. Episcopalian. Clubs: Duquesne, Pittsburgh Athletic (Pitts.). Holds patents, U.S. and Canadian on low alloy-high strength corrosion resisting steels. Home: 4584 Middle Rd., R.D. 3, Allison Park, Pa. Office: 401 Liberty Av., Gateway Center, Pitts. 30. Died Dec. 3, 1958; buried Mayville, Wis.

LAWRENCE, William Henry, educator; b. Boston, Sept. 4, 1868; s. Charles Henry and Isabel Matilda (Restieaux) L.; grad. English High Sch., Boston, 1887; B.S., Mass. Inst. Tech., 1891; m. Alice Gertrude Emerson, Sept. 7, 1921. Instr. in architecture Mass. Inst. Tech., 1891-1901, asst. prof., 1901-09, prof., 1909—, head dept. drawing, 1920-38, charge course in archtl. engring., 1927-38, prof. emeritus, 1938—, mem. faculty Lowell Inst., 1912-43, curator, 1921-53; lectr. on archtl. constrn. Harvard, 1924-25. Fellow A.A.A.S.; mem. A.I.A. (emeritus). Home: 811 Centre St., Jamaica Plain 30, Mass. Died June 12, 1958.

LAWRENCE, William Witherle, educator; b. Bangor, Me., May 29, 1876; s. Franklin Muzzy and Lucy Moulton (Witherle) L.; A.B., Bowdoin Coll., 1898, Litt.D., 1917; student U. Leipzig, 1898-99; A.M., Harvard, 1900, Ph.D., 1903. Instr. in German, Harvard, 1900-03; asso. prof. English lit., U. Kan., 1903-05; instr. English, Columbia, 1905-07, adj. prof., 1907-10, asso. prof., 1910-16, prof. English, 1916-36, prof. emeritus, 1936—. Ofcl. speaker and a Four Minute Man, World War I. Trustee Portland Pub. Library, Am. Scandinavian Found. Decorated Royal Order of Vasa, 1st class (Sweden), 1930. Overseer Bowdoin Coll., 1921-23, trustee, 1923—. Fellow Medieval Acad. Am.; mem. Modern Lang. Assn. Am., Portland Soc. Art (trustee), Phi Beta Kappa, Psi Upsilon. Episcopalian (vestryman). Clubs: Century Assn. (N.Y.C.), Faculty (Harvard), Men's Faculty (Columbia), Portland (Me.). Author: Medieval Story, 1911; Beowulf and Epic Tradition, 1928; Shakespeare's Problem Comedies, 1931; Chaucer and The Canterbury Tales, 1950. Editor: Much Ado, 1912; Goethe on the Theater, 1919. Contbr. to philol. periodicals. Home: 14 Bowdoin St., Portland 4, Me. Died July 29, 1958; buried Evergreen Cemetery, Portland.

LAWS, Bolitha James, chief judge; born in Washington, D.C., August 22, 1891; son of Bolitha James and Mary A. (Menefee) L.; LL.B., from Georgetown University, 1913, LL.M., 1914, LL.D., 1950; m. Nancy MacLeod; children—Nancy Lee, Bolitha James, III, Ileita Margaret, Mary Elizabeth. Admitted to D.C. bar, 1913; asst. U.S. atty. for D.C., 1914-20; pvt. practice with firm, Root, Clark, Buckner and Ballantine, New York, 1920-21; litigation counsel and asst. gen. counsel, U.S. Shipping Bd. Emer. Fleet Corp., 1921-22; law partner Paul B. Cromelin, 1922-38; judge, Dist. Court of U.S. for D.C., since 1938; designated judge of U.S. Emergency Court of Appeals, June 1943; apptd. chief judge Dist. Ct. of the U.S., for Dist. of Columbia, 1945. Mem. Am. Bar Assn., District of Columbia Bar Assn. (pres. 1937-38). Methodist. Mason. Club: Barristers. Home: 7 Oxford St., Chevy Chase, Md. Died Nov. 1958.

LAWSON, Alfred William, pioneer aircraft editor and mfr.; b. London, Eng., Mar. 24, 1869; s. Robert Henry and Mary (Anderson) L. Interested in aeronautics since 1907; founded, edited and published Fly, first popular aeronautical mag., Phila., Nov. 1908; editor Aircraft, N.Y. City, 1910-14; aircraft mfr., Green Bay, Wis., 1917-18; elected 1st v.p. Aeronautical Mfrs. Assn. of America, 1912; designed 26-passenger airplane and built it in Milwaukee, 1919; flew with this plane carrying passengers to Chicago, Toledo, Cleveland, N.Y. City, Washington, D.C., and back to Milwaukee, Aug.-Nov. 1919 (carried a total of 400 passengers and proved commercial aviation could be profitable). Awarded first air mail contract, 1920; believed first mfr. to build airplane cabin free of truss wires, first to equip cabins with sleeping berths. After retiring from aircraft manufacture, time devoted to writing books and articles. Reg. contbr. to The Benefactor; now Supreme Head of The Humanity Benefactor Foundation, Inc., The Direct Credits Society, Inc., and the Des Moines Univ. of Lawsonomy, Inc. Organized and inc. Lawsonian Religion, 1948, apptd. First Knowlegian, Supreme Head; started construction 1000 Lawsonian churches, 1950. Author: Aircraft History (copyrighted), 1947; Lawsonian Religion, 1949. Address: care Humanity Benefactor Foundation, 600 Woodward Av., Detroit 26, Mich., and Des Moines Univ., Des Moines, Iowa. Died Nov. 29, 1954.

LAWSON, Andrew Cowper, geologist; b. Anstruther, Scotland, July 25, 1861; s. William and Jessie (Kerr) L.; A.B., U. of Toronto, 1883, A.M., 1885; Ph.D., Johns Hopkins, 1888; D.Sc., U. of Toronto, 1923; LL.D., U. of Calif., 1935; D.Sc., Harvard, 1936; m. Ludovika von Jantsch, Nov. 30, 1889 (died Dec. 25, 1929); children—Andrew Werner, William Eric, Ludovico (dec.), James Albert (dec.); m. 2d Isabel R. Collins, Jan. 5, 1931. Geologist Geol. Survey of Can., 1882-90; prof. mineralogy and geology, 1890-1928, and dean Coll. of Mining, 1914-18, U. of Calif., retired 1928. Del. Geol. Congress, London, 1888, St. Petersburg, 1897, Toronto, 1913, Madrid, 1926; chmn. Calif. Earthquake Investigatin Commn., 1906; chmn. geol. and geog., Nat. Research Council, 1923. Hayden medalist, Acad. of Natural Science, 1935. Fellow Geol. Soc. America (pres. 1926; Penrose medalist 1938), Soc. Econ. Geologists, A.A.A.S., American Acad. Arts and Sciences; pres. Seismol. Soc. America, 1909-10; mem. Nat. Acad. Sciences, Am. Philos. Soc.; hon. mem. Am. Assn. Petrol. Geologists, Sierra Club. Author of numerous geol. papers and monographs. Home: 1555 La Vereda, Berkeley, Cal. Died June 16, 1952.

LAWSON, George (McLean), univ. prof.; b. Middle Haddam, Conn., May 26, 1898; s. George Newton and Ida Louise (McLean) L.; student Bates Coll., Lewiston, Me., 1915-19; M.D., Yale, 1924; D.P.H., Harvard (fellow in bacteriology, Nat. Research Council, 1924-26; Rockefeller fellow in public health, 1932), 1933; m. Gladys Holmes, May 6, 1922; 1 son, David Herbert Otis. Interne and asst. resident, pediatrics, Yale, 1923-24; mem. commn. for the Study of Whooping Cough, Boston, 1924-28; bacteriologist, Mass. Gen. Hosp., 1927-29; instr., bacteriology, Harvard Med. Sch., 1927-29; prof. of bacteriology, Univ. of Louisville Med. Sch., 1929-32, prof. of public health and bacteriology, 1932-37; epidemiologist and vital statistician, Louisville Health Dept., 1932-37; prof. of preventive medicine and bacteriology, Univ. of Va. since 1937. Chmn. bd. health, Charlottesville and Albemarle County since 1940. Served as pvt., Inf., U.S Army, 1918-19. Fellow Am. Public Health Assn. (mem. com. on whooping cough); mem. Soc. Am. Bacteriologists (sec. Va. br.), Soc. Pediatric Research, A.A.A.S., Va. Acad. Sci. (sec. bacteriology sect.), Albemarle County Med. Soc., Albemarle T.B. Assn. (bd. dirs.), Visiting Nurses Assn. (bd. dirs.); Alpha Omega Alpha, Delta Omega, Sigma Xi. Episcopalian. Author: Sect. on whooping cough, in "Diagnostic Procedures and Reagents" (with P. Kendrick, J. Miller), 2d. ed., 1945. Contbr. articles in field of bacteriology and communicable disease control in 42 publs. Home: Box 1113, Univ. Sta. Office: U. of Va. Medical Sch., Charlottesville, Va. Died Sept. 20, 1951.

LAWSON, George Benedict, educator; b. Brooklyn, N.Y., Aug. 11, 1867; s. Albert Gallatin and Eliza (Knight) L.; grad. Poly. Inst. of Brooklyn, 1884; A.B., Colgate, 1888, A.M., 1891, D.D., 1912; grad. study Hamilton Theol. Sem., 1888-89, Union Theol. Sem., 1889-91; m. Kate P. Lewis, Feb. 3, 1892 (died 1916); children—Margaret Louise, Elizabeth Knight; m. 2d, Margaret E. Holstein, June 8, 1927; 1 son, George Benedict. Ordained Bapt. ministry, 1892; successively pastor Delhi, N.Y., Bennington, Vt., Pleasant Street Church, Worcester, Mass., Brattleboro, Vt., until 1908; principal Vt. Acad., Saxtons River, 1908-16; prof. edn. and philosophy, Pa. Coll. for Women, Pittsburgh, 1916-22; prof. philosophy, Bucknell U., 1922-40; retired June 1940. Chaplain Vt. N.G., 1900-10; 1st lt. Tank Corps, U.S. Army, 1918. Mem. A.A.A.S., Am. Assn. Univ. Profs., Phi Beta Kappa, Delta Kappa Epsilon. Home: Lewisburg, Pa. Died Feb. 13, 1952; buried Lewisburg.

LAWSON, Laurin Leonard, army officer; b. St. Peter, Minn., Mar. 11, 1876; s. Magne and Hannah L.; ed. pub. schs., LaCrosse, Wis.; m. Mabel Shaw Halliday, May 10, 1906. Pvt. cos. D and B, 1st Wash. Inf., 1898-99; commd. 1st lt. 39th U.S. Inf., 1899; hon. mustered out 1901; 2d lt. Arty. Corps, U.S. Army, 1901, 1st lt., 1903; assigned to 3d F.A., June 6, 1907; capt. 4th F.A., Aug. 12, 1907; maj., May 15, 1917; lt. col. (temp.), Aug. 5, 1917; col. Nat. Army, Feb. 6, 1918; brig. gen. (temp.), Oct. 1, 1918. Served in Philippines thrice; at Vera Cruz, Mexico, 1914; with punitive expdn. into Mexico, 1916; comdt. Sch. Fire for Field Arty., Ft. Sill, Okla., 1918; comd. 15th F.A. Brigade, at Camp Stanley, Tex., 1919. Address: War Dept., Washington. Died Jan. 28, 1938.

LAWSON, Martin Emert, lawyer; b. near Mercersburg, Pa., May 15, 1867; s. Simon Frederick and Sarah Jane (Blair) L.; student Gem City Business Coll., Quincy, Illinois, 1886-87; studied law privately; LL.D., William Jewell College, 1945, Central Coll., Mo., 1951; m. Kate Riley, Oct. 10, 1894 (deceased October 30, 1949); children—James Enoch, Nancy (Mrs. Paul M. Jones). Admitted to Mo. bar, 1890, and since in practice at Liberty; also member of the bar U.S. Supreme Court; mem. firm Lawson, Hale & Colberd; vice pres. First National Bank, 1915—. President Liberty Board Edn., 1912-14; member Bd. Pub. Works, Liberty, 1905-13. Elected to each Gen. Conf. of the M.E. Ch., South, 1910-34; mem. com. to prepare constitution for the Ch., 1922-30, on unification with the M.E. Ch., 1926-30; mem. Gen. Bd. of Lay Activities, 1922-34, pres., 1926-30; pres. Jud. Council of M.E. Ch., South, 1934-39; v.p. Judicial Council Meth. Ch., 1939-48, mem. 1948-52; pres. Mo. Conf. Bd. of Ch. Extension, 1917-34, lay leader, 1919-34; mem. continuation com. Ecumenical Conf. of Methodism, 1931-52. Curator Woodson Institute, Richmond, Mo. (merged into Central Coll., Fayette, Mo.), 1896-99. Awarded plaque Wm. Jewell Coll. for 50 years as Gen. Atty. Mem. Am. and Mo. State bar assns., Mo. Heart Assn. (dir.). Dem. Mason (Shriner). Club: Liberty Rotary (pres. 1939, 40). Home: 456 Arthur St. Office: First National Bank Bldg., Liberty, Mo. Died Jan. 9, 1957.

LAWSON, Paul Bowen, coll. dean; b. Sitapur, India, Aug. 18, 1888; s. James Chapell and Ellen (Hoy) L.; came to U.S., 1903; student, Oberlin, 1905-06; B.S., John Fletcher Coll., University Park, Iowa, 1909; M.S., University of Kansas, 1917, Ph.D., from same university, 1919; married Sarah Alice Cooper, July 20, 1910 (deceased); children—Lois Marguerite (Mrs. Purdy F. Meigs), Lila Alice (Mrs. Charles E. Smith); m. 2d, Elizabeth C. Rupp, June 16, 1941. Instructor in biology, John Fletcher College, 1910-15; instr. entomology, U. of Kan., 1916-20, asst. prof., 1920-21, asso. prof., 1921-22, prof. and asst. dean, 1922-29, prof. and asso. dean, 1929-33, prof. and acting dean, 1933-34, dean since 1934. Fellow Entomol. Soc. America; mem. Kan. Acad. of Science, Phi Beta Kappa, Sigma Xi. Presbyterian. Clubs: Kiwanis. Editor of Jour. of Kan. Entomol. Soc. Home: 2215 Vermont St., Lawrence, Kan. Died Mar. 30, 1954; buried Oak Hill Cemetery, Lawrence.

LAWSON, Robert, illustrator; b. N.Y.C., Oct. 4, 1892; s. William Bethel and Elma Cecilia (Bowman) L.; student Montclair (N.J.) High Sch., 1907-11, N.Y. Sch. of Fine and Applied Art, 1911-13; m. Marie Abrams, Sept. 6, 1922. Illustrator, 1914—, etcher, 1929—; illustrator of Wee Men of Ballywooden (Mason), 1930; Unicorn with Silver Shoes (Young), 1932; Hurdy Gurdy Man (Bianco), 1933; Treasure of the Isle of Mist (Tarn), 1934; Golden Horse Shoe (Coatsworth), 1936; Wind of the Vikings; Story of Ferdinand; Swords and Statues; In Secret Service; Under the Tent of the Sky; Miranda is a Princess; Four and Twenty Blackbirds; Story of Jesus; I Hear America Singing; The Prince and the Pauper, 1937; and others. Author and illustrator: Ben and Me; Watchwords of Liberty; Country Colic; I Discover Columbus; Mr. Wilmer; Mr. Twigg's Mistake; They Were Strong and Good; Rabbit Hill; Robbutt. Awarded John Taylor Arms prize Soc. of Am. Etchers, 1931; Caldecott medal by A.L.A., 1941, also Newberry medal for prose writing. Served in camouflage sect., U.S. Army, World War. Home: Rabbit Hill, Westport, Conn. Died May 26, 1957.

LAWSON, Thomas R., educator; b. Wheeling, W.Va., Dec. 24, 1873; s. Joseph and Sarah Eliza (Brice) L.; C.E., Rensselaer Poly. Inst., 1898; m. Mary Agnes Lawrence, Aug. 23, 1899; children—Margaret Elizabeth (wife of Dr. D. A. Calhoun), Mary Virginia. With Rensselaer Poly. Inst., 1898—, prof. rational and tech. mechanics, 1908—, also head dept. of civil engring., 1921—; cons. practice along lines of water supply and sanitary and structural engring. Ex-pres. Clay Products Inst. of America, Am. Soc. for Testing Materials, Soc. of Engineers of Eastern New York. Associated with research com. on welding rail joints. Am. Bur. of Welding and Am. Ry. Engring. Assn.; mem. adv. com. to Indsl. Bd. of State of N.Y. on revision of State Standard Building Code; mem. Harbor and Dock Commn., Troy; chmn. com. paving brick standardization, Dept. Commerce. Mem. Am. Soc. C.E., Am. Soc. for Testing Materials, Am. Concrete Inst., Am. Welding Soc., A.A.A.S., Theta Xi, Tau Beta Pi, Sigma Xi. Republican. Presbyn. Home: Hotel Troy, Troy, N.Y.. Died Mar. 1953.

LAWSON, William C., vice pres. Brunswick-Balke-Collender Co.; b. London, Eng., Aug. 31, 1903; s. James William and Annie E. (Brooks) L.; grad. Cass Tech. High School, Detroit, 1922; married Mae Lear, September 15, 1922; 1 daughter, Iole Mae. Came to U.S., 1921, naturalized, 1929. Cabinet maker, later city salesman, Brunswick-Balke-Collender Co., Detroit, 1922, territory rep. in Mich., 1922-33, mgr. Detroit branch, 1934-37, mgr. Chicago home office, billiard and bowling div., 1937-41, dir. of company since 1939, v.p. since 1941. Home: 221 Woodstock, Kenilworth, Ill. Office: 623 S. Wabash Av., Chgo. Died Apr. 10, 1954; buried Cin.

LAWTON, Frederick, judge; b. Lowell, Mass., May 10, 1852; s. James and Sarah Stearns (Priest) L.; A.B., Harvard, 1874; m. Helen Spalding Mack, June 15, 1880. Admitted to Mass. bar, 1880; practiced at Lowell; mem. Mass. Senate, 1893; justice Superior Ct. of Mass., 1900-—. Trustee Lowell Textile Sch., Rogers Hall Sch. Address: Lowell, Mass. Died Apr. 1941.

LAY, Charles Downing, landscape architect; b. Newburgh, N.Y., Sept. 3, 1877; s. Oliver Ingraham and Hester Marian (Wait) L.; student Sch. of Architecture, Columbia, 1896-1900; S.B. in Landscape Architecture, Harvard, 1902; studied art with Mahonri Young, Allen Tucker, Gifford Beal; m. Laura B. Gill, Oct. 1, 1904; children—Oliver Ingraham, Alice Julia, David, George Cowles, Laurence (dec.). Mem. Lay & Wheelwright, 1911-14; associated, 1910, with Prof. H. V. Hubbard and R. Wheelwright, as Lay, Hubbard & Wheelwright, and founded Landscape Architecture (quar. mag.), editor and mgr. same until 1921; landscape architect Dept. of Parks, City of New York, 1913-14; made plans for improvement, of Albany, N.Y.; planner for U.S. Housing Corp.; designer of Marine Park, Bklyn.; landscape architect for many parks, subdivisions, private estates, gardens, etc. Consultant on landscape architecture N.Y. World's Fair, 1939. Received Oberlaender Trust grant for study of public recreation in Germanic countries, 1934, silver medal for plans Marine Park (Bklyn.), XI Olympiad (Berlin), 1936. Mem. Nat. Acad. Design, pres. Assoc. of the Arts Comn. Fellow am. Soc. Landscape Architects; mem. Am. Inst. of Planners, A.I.A., Art Students League of N.Y., Delta Upsilon. Republican. Unitarian. Clubs: Century Assn., Nat. Arts. Author: A Garden Book for Autumn and Winter, 1924; A Park System for Long Island, 1925; Studies for Albany (with A. W. Brunner), 1914; The Freedom of the City, 1926; also articles in mags. and newspapers. Also painter and etcher; work on exhbn. in Metropolitan, Whitney and Brooklyn museums, Phillips Gallery (Washington). Home: Stratford, Conn. Office: 141 E. 44th St., N.Y. C. 17. Died Feb. 14, 1956; buried Putney Cemetery, Stratford, Conn.

LAY, Frank Morrill, mfr.; b. Kewanee, Ill., Sept. 14, 1869; s. Hiram T. and Martha (Morrill) L.; student Prep. Knox Acad.; A.B., Amherst Coll., 1893; LL.D., Yankton College, 1937; m. Fannie Phelps Poole, June 24, 1896 (dec. 1948); 1 son, Edward Poole (dec.). Started with Boss Mfg. Co. as sec.-treas. in 1895, pres., 1932-35, chmn. bd. of dirs., 1935-48, dir., 1894-51; dir. Peoples Bank, Kewanee Mfg. Co., Kewanee Air Ports. Trustee Knox Coll., 1923-54, chmn. bd. 1940-54; trustee Yankton Coll., 1917-—. Mem. bd. of edn. in Kewanee for 6 yrs. Mason, Elk. Mem. Beta Theta Pi. Clubs: Midland Country of Kewanee (Ill.); Union League (N.Y.C.); University (Chgo.); Wilshire Country, California (Los Angeles); White Lake Golf of Michigan (dir.). Has attended every Nat. Republican Conv. for 44 yrs. Home: 103 W. Prospect St. Office: Kewanee, Ill. Died June 21, 1957; buried Pleasant View Cemetery, Kewanee.

LAYMAN, Waldo Arnold; b. Smithton, Mo., Oct. 27, 1869; s. Morgan and Rhoda C. (Arnold) L.; B. S., Rose Poly. Inst., Ind., 1892, M.S., 1894, E.E., 1899, Eng.Dr., 1933; m. Laura E. Toms, June 8, 1896; children—Edith (Mrs. Edward F. Deacon), Mary Arnold (Mrs. G. Donald Gibbins), Laura Arnold (Mrs. Keene N. Brundage), Grace Wilson (Mrs. Henry G. Isaacs). Entered employ of Wagner Electric Mfg. Co., St. Louis, 1892, successively draftsman, asst. supt., 1895, asst. mgr. and treas., 1898, gen. mgr. and dir., 1902, v.p. and mgr., 1910, pres. and chmn. bd., 1912-26; spl. partner N.Y. Stock Exchange firm, Nash, Cloud & Isaacs, 1929-30; partner firm Layman & Isaacs, 1930-31; now retired. Chmn. St. Louis Contemporary Club, 1911-13; pres. Nat. Metal Trades Assn., 1913-14; mem. bd. Nat. Soc. for Promotion of Indsl. Edn. several years; mem. adv. bd. David Rankin Jr. Sch. of Mech. Trades, St. Louis, 10 years; mem. Corp. Bd. of Washington U., St. Louis, 1916-26; trustee Rose Poly. Inst., Terre Haute, Ind., 4 years; pres. St. Louis Elec. Bd. of Trade, 1925-26; fellow Am. Inst. E.E. Ind. Republican. Conglist. Club: Engineers of St. Louis (pres. 1906). Home: The Gray Moss Inn, Clearwater, Fla. Died Oct. 25, 1950.

LAYNE, J(oseph) Gregg, historian; b. Huntington, W.Va., June 13, 1885; s. Jesse Martin and Susan (Gregg) L.; student Los Angeles High Sch., 1900-03; m. Artemisia Stose, June 14, 1906; children—Joseph Gregg (dec.), James Gregg, Dagny, Janice, Harriet Sue. Rep. Kueffel & Esser Co., engring. instruments, in So. Cal., 1903-19, of Taylor Instrument Cos. of Rochester, N.Y., in Cal. and the South, 1919-34; civic hist. commr. City of Los Angeles, 1933-34. Mem. library bd. Southwest Mus.; research under Rockefeller Found., Henry E. Huntington Library, 1944-47; historian Dept. Water & Power, Los Angeles, 1947-52; cons. in Western Americana, Library of U. Cal. at Los Angeles; dir. Library of Architecture and Allied Arts; lectr., collector Western Americana, owner over 4,000 vols. on the Southwest (his collection of Californiana purchased by U. Cal. for their spl. collections 1953). Mem. Hist. Soc. So. Cal. (dir. since 1925, pres. 1931-32, 1942-—), Cal. Hist. Soc. San Francisco, S.R., The Scribes (pres. 1947), Cooper Ornithol. Club, E Clampus Vitus, N.G.H., 1933. Republican. Presbyn. Mason (33°, Shriner). Clubs: Town and Beach, Rotary, Zamorano Book. Author: Los Angeles in 1850; Los Angeles—From the Founding through the first Decade of American Occupation; The Ghost Towns of the Mother Lode; The Books of California; Annals of Los Angeles, 1935; The First Census of the Los Angeles District, 1936; The Lincoln-Roosevelt League: Its Origin and Accomplishment, 1943; A Short History of the University of California at Los Angeles, 1943. Contbr. Hist. Soc. Quarterly, So. Cal. Hist. Soc. Quarterly. Co-author: The Zamorano Eighty—A California Bibliography, 1945. Editor of Quarterly of Hist. Soc. So. Cal., 1935-—, The Brand Book, Los Angeles, 1947, 48 editions; Western Wayfaring, published in 1954; also author article on Los Angeles, World Book. Chmn. in charge of translation of old Spanish archives of Los Angeles. Home: 1016 Selby Av., Westwood Hills, Los Angeles 24. Died Aug. 16, 1952; buried Pomona Cemetery, Pomona, Cal.

LAYTON, Frank Davis, fire insurance executive; b. at South Norwalk, Conn.; s. Jacob M. and Mary (Gardner) L.; ed. pub. schs., South Norwalk; m. Ethel Savory Keep. Began as an insurance agent with father's firm, J. M. Layton & Co., South Norwalk, spl. agent at N.Y. City for N.Y. and New Eng. for Nat. Fire Ins. Co. of Hartford, 1902-08, gen. agt., Hartford, 1908-09, asst. sec., 1909-18, sec., 1918-19, vice-president, 1919-28, elected dir., 1921, pres., 1928-48, chmn. bd., 1948-55; director Nat. Fire Ins. Co., Mechanics and Traders Ins. Co., Transcontinental Ins. Co., Franklin National Insurance Co. of N.Y. and United Nat. Indemnity Co. (New York), Phoenix Mutual Life Ins. Co., Connecticut Bank & Trust Co., Arrow-Hart & Hegeman Electric Co., Dime Savs. Bank (Hartford). Former maj. and brigade inspector, Conn. N.G., brevet lt. col. Former pres. and mem. exec. com. Nat. Bd. of Fire Underwriters; trustee Am. Ins. Assn. and chmn. Endowment Com. Hartford YMCA; dir. Hartford Hospital, Conn. Inst. for Blind. Mem. Conn. and Hartford Chambers of Commerce. Republican. Conglist. Mason (Shriner). Clubs: Hartford, Automobile, Wampanoag Country (Hartford); Seaview Country (Absecon, N.J.); Bankers (New York); Military-Naval Club of N.Y. Home: 26 Fernwood Rd., West Hartford 7, Conn. Office: care Nat. Fire Ins. Co., Hartford 15, Conn. Died Oct. 24, 1956.

LAZAR, Benedict Joseph, banker; b. Feb. 24, 1884; s. Joseph and Rebecca (Feldman) L.; grad. Am. Inst. Banking, St. Louis, 1914; m. Juliette Schwarz, Apr. 11, 1920; children—Elizabeth, Louise. Office boy, later auditor Mechanics Am. Nat. Bank of St. Louis, 1900-14; engaged in mortgage loan bus., 1915-17; audit clerk Fed. Res. Bank Cleve., 1918-20; cashier Fed. Res. Bank of Cleve., Cin. br., 1920-35, mng. dir., 1935-42; v.p. Fed. Res. Bank of Cleve. in charge Cin. br. (service retirement). Life mem. Am. Inst. Banking (Cin. chpt.), Cin. Assn. Credit Men, Cin. Numis. Assn., 1949. Mason. Clubs: Bankers, Rotary. Address: 750 E. Mitchell Av., Cin. 29. Died Dec. 4, 1955; buried Cin.

LAZAROVICH-Hrebelianovich, Princess (lä-zä'rō-vich rĕ-bĕ-lĭ-än'ō-vĭch), author; b. Eleanor Calhoun, at Visalia, Calif.; d. Judge Ezekiel Ewing (g. nephew John C. Calhoun) and Laura (Davis) Calhoun; ed. State Normal Sch., San Jose, Calif., and in London and Paris; m. in London, 1903, Prince Lazarovich-Hrebelianovich (Eugene de Czernucki-Lazarovich, Prince Hrebelianovich), civil engr.; children—Zora (dec.), also Doushan, Stevan, and Mara (step-children). Formerly acted Juliet, Rosalind, Portia, Cleopatra, Lady Macbeth, etc., in London, and modern leading roles in Haymarket Theatre (Theatre Royal), London, and in French in star parts, Racine and Shakespeare, with Paul Mounet-Sully and Coquelin, in Odéon National Theatre, Paris, Comédie Parisienne and Theatre d'Orleans. Originated pastoral plays in forest, with nature only for scenery, producing "As You Like It," Coombe Wood, Surrey, Eng., playing Rosalind with Lady Archibald Campbell as Orlando. Left stage upon marriage to share in husband's efforts for Balkan freedom; representations to Alexander Smith Cochrane, 1908, resulted in financing of the Danube-Aegean Waterway Project, and also in London, the underwriting by Sir Ernest Cassel of a loan of five million pounds to Sultan of Turkey connected with husband's plan of Agrarian Tax collecting and settlement for European Turkey in interest of Christian population. Co-author (with husband) of a memorandum looking to Serb victory and a justly constructive Fedn. of all South Slavs into a unified Yugoslav State (submitted at first Yugoslav conv., Chgo., Mar. 1915, organized by Dr. Potochniak and Dr. Smodlaka; paper distbd. by conv. and pub. verbatim in Novi Hrvat, New York, Mar. 1915); prior to crystallization of an afterwar South Slav State, formulated (with husband) Platform for a Yugoslav Republican Party of State (submitted to the Cleve. conv. of Yugoslav-Republican Alliance, Sept. 1919); gave to President Wilson (during his short visit home from Paris Peace Conference), in the State Department, Washington, the American Yugoslav Resolution of 16 February 1919, New York Yugoslav Mass Meeting, showing natural Yugoslav borders with demarcation of line down mid-Adriatic North-South, and which President Wilson accepted for the Paris Peace table. Author: The Serbian People—Their Past Glory and Their Destiny (with husband), 1910; Pleasures and Palaces (book of European memoirs), 1915; (play) The Way, Christ and Evolution, 1926; The Organic Character of Christ and Democracy. Writer and lecturer on cultural and polit. subjects. Ex-pres. Woman's Chamber of Commerce of New York. Originated and submitted to Federal Govt. and state govs., a triple co-ordinate program to eliminate and prevent unemployment destitution. Mem. of Pi Gamma Mu; hon. Officer of Old Guard of Ga., decorated with its jewelled Gold Cross of Honor by Gov. Gordon of Ga. at review of troops in presence of distinguished members of Calhoun family and other ofcls. Home: 3 E. 84th St., N.Y.C. Died Jan. 9, 1957.

LAZRUS, S. Ralph, watch company exec.; b. N.Y.C., July 25, 1898; s. Israel and Ella (Cohn) L.; student pub. schs. of N.Y.C., m. Rose Tobias, July 25, 1924; children—Eleanor Ann, Nancy Jane. With bros. formed partnership in Benrus Watch Co., Inc., New York City, 1945, treasurer, 1946-47, director, 1946-—, pres., 1954-56, chmn. bd., 1956-—. Chmn. bd. Five Towns Community Chest (Lawrence, N.Y.), 1944-45; trustee Village of Lawrence, 1943-—. Vice pres. Jewish Hosp. of Bklyn., Woodmere Acad., 1940-—; mem. bd. Adelphi Coll., Chicago Med. Sch.; v.p. United Palestine Appeal (N.Y.C.), 1945-—; mem. bd. United Jewish Appeal, 1945-—. Mem. Nassau Co. Bd. Edn., 1951-—. Served in, USN, 1917-18. Mem. Am. Watch Assn., Inc. (pres. 1945-46, 52-54, exec. com. 1955-—). Home: 291 Ocean Av., Lawrence. Office: 50 W. 44 St., N.Y.C. 36. Died Sept. 1959.

LEA, Fanny Heaslip, author, playwright; b. New Orleans, Oct. 30, 1884; d. James John and Margaret (Heaslip) Lea; B.A., H. Sophie Newcomb Memorial Coll., Tulane U., 1904; grad. work in English, Tulane, 2 yrs.; m. Hamilton Pope Agee, May 11, 1911 (divorced, 1926); 1 dau., Anne Worthen. Episcopalian. Mem. Phi Beta Kappa, Authors League of America. Author: Quicksands, 1911; The Jaconetta Stories, 1912; Sicily Ann, 1914; Chloe Malone, 1916; With This Ring, 1925; The Dream-Maker Man, 1925; With or Without, 1926; Wild Goose Chase, 1929; Lolly (play), 1930; Happy Landings, 1930; Good-Bye Summer, 1931; Take Back the Heart (poems), 1931; Half Angel, 1932; Summer People, 1933; Dorée, 1934; Anchor Man, 1935; The Four Marys, 1936; Crede Byron (play), 1936; Once to Every Man, 1937; Not for Just an Hour, 1938; There Are Brothers, 1939; Sailor's Star, 1944; Devil Within, 1948. Address: care Harold Obe, 40 E. 49th St., N.Y.C. Died Jan. 13, 1955.

LEA, Robert Wentworth, mfr., banker; b. Woodville, Wis., Jan. 18, 1886; s. William Wentworth and Jennie (Stiles) L.; student Hillside Prep. Sch., Hillside, Wis., 1899-1903; A.B., U. of Wis., 1907; m. Anna R. Sircom, Mar. 24, 1931; children—Catherine (Mrs. Allen Seiffert), Albert Lea. Began career at Otis Elevator Co., Moline, Quincy, Chicago, 1907-11; v.p. Moline Plow Co., 1911-17; v.p. and gen. mgr., Stephens Motor Car Co., Freeport, Ill., 1919-24; pres. and gen. mgr., Moline (Ill.) Implement Co., 1924-29; pres. and gen. mgr., Lea Fabrics, Inc., Newark, N.J., 1929-30; with Continental Ill. Nat. Bank & Trust Co., Chicago, Ill., 1931-33; became asst. adminstr. NRA, Washington, D.C., 1933; pres. and gen. mgr., Hammond Lumber Co., Hammond Shipping Co., and Hammond & Little River Redwood Co., (San Francisco), 1934-36; pres. and gen. mgr., West Va. Coal & Coke Corp., The Ohio River Co., and Junior Mercantile Co. (Cincinnati), 1937-39; v.p. for finance Johns-Manville Corp., 1939-46, pres. 1946-51, dir., 1940-—; member board mgrs., Del., Lackawanna & Western R.R. Co. (N.Y.C.); v.p., dir. Olin Industries, Inc., 1951-54, Olin Mathieson Chemical Corp., 1954-—; dir. Curtiss-Wright Corp., Universal Pictures Co., Inc. Col., AUS, div. purchase, storage and traffic, World War I. Mem. Phi Kappa Psi, Beta Gamma Sigma. Episcopalian. Clubs: Metropolitan, Rockaway Hunting, (New York); University (Chicago); Bohemian (San Francisco). Home: 1 Beekman Pl., N.Y.C. 22. Office: 460 Park Av., N.Y.C. Died Nov. 13, 1956; buried Eau Claire, Wis.

LEACH, George E., ex-mayor Mpls.; b. Cedar Rapids, Ia., July 14, 1876; s. William Benton and Mary Cook (Hammond) L.; student U. Minn., 1894-95; m. Ella Van Vorous, Oct. 9, 1903; m. 2d, Anita M. Churcher, Jan. 22, 1923. Insurance business at Mpls., 1898-—. Mayor of Mpls., 1921-29, elected to 5th term, 1937, 6th term, 1939. Pres. N.G. Assn. of Am., 1937. Served in World War as col., 151st Regiment, F.A., 67th Brig., 42d Div., 1st A.C., AEF; participated in 5 major engagements; served as brig. gen. in comd. 59th F.A. Brigade, Minn. N.G.; apptd. chief N.G. Bur., War Dept., 1931, with rank of maj. gen. for 4 yrs., ret. as maj. gen., comdg. 34th Div., 1941; now pres. George E. Leach, Inc. Decorated D.S.C., D.S.M. (U.S.); Legion of Honor, Croix de Guerre with 3 palms and star (France); Comdr. Crown of Italy; Medal of Merit (Minn.). Club: Army and Navy; Minneapolis Athletic. Home: 2101 W. Franklin Av. Office: 605 8th Av. S., Mpls. Died July 17, 1955; buried Ft. Snelling Meml. Cemetery.

LEACH, Howard Seavoy librarian; b. Penobscot, Me., May 14, 1887; s. George Elmer and Hattie Gertrude (Grindle) L.; A.B., Wesleyan U. Conn., 1913; 1918; asst. librarian Camp Meade, and librarian Camp der Dr. E. C. Richardson, 1913-15. Sgt. U.S. Army, A.M., Princeton, 1915; library tng. Princeton U. un-Lee; librarian U.S.S. George Washington, 1919; referance librarian Princeton U. Library, 1919-24; librarian Lehigh U., 1924-—. Mem. A.L.A., Pa. Library Assn.. Archaeol. Inst. Am. (pres. Bethlehem chpt. 1938), Am. Bibliog. Soc. Republican. Methodist. Clubs: Bethlehem, Sigma Chi. Author: List of Collections of English Drama in American Libraries, 1916; An Essay Towards a Bibliography of the Published Writings and Addresses of Woodrow Wilson (Mar. 1917-Mar. 1921), 1923; Bibliography of Howard Crosby Butler, 1924; Bibliography of Woodrow Wilson (1875-1924); Wilson—Public Papers, 6 vols.; (with R. M. Smith) The Shakespeare Folios and the Forgeries of Shakespeare's Handwriting in the Lucy Packer Linderman Memorial Library. Bethlehem, 1927. Home: Bethlehem, Pa. Died Nov. 17, 1948.

LEAHY, Edward L(awrence) (la'hē), U.S. senator; b. Bristol, R.I., Feb. 9, 1886; s. John and Anne (Murphy) L.; student Brown U., 1904-05; LL.B., Georgetown U., 1908; m. Fern Dixon, Jan. 15, 1913; children—Edward Lawrence (lt. U.S. Navy, lost in active service World War II), Ann (Mrs. Robert Rulon-Miller), Virginia (Mrs. Adrian Berwick). Admitted to R. I. bar, 1908, Master in Chancery, Superior Ct.; judge Probate Ct., Bristol, 1910-39; elected mem. R. I. Ho. of Reps., 1911; as mem. Tax Commn. and head State Tax Div., adminstr. of state taxes, 1919-48; dir. Dept. Revenue and Regulation, 1939; dir. finance, mem. State Sinking Fund Commn. and mem. State Retirement Bd., 1942-46; adviser to Dept. of Finance, 1948-49; U.S. senator from R.I. since 1949. Pres. R.I. Child Service, 1946-49, now mem. bd. dirs. and exec. com. of successor agency R.I. Children's Friend and Service Soc.; dir. Bristol Dist. Nursing Assn.; pres. Bristol Hist. Soc.; pres. Bristol Shade Tree Assn.; chmn. Bristol Zoning Com. Served as 1st lt., Judge Adv. Gen.'s Dept., U.S. Army, World War I; capt. Officers Reserve Corps. Mem. Am. Legion, Bristol Train of Artillery, Am. Forestry Assn. Democrat. Roman Catholic. Knight of Columbus, Rotarian. Club: Bristol Yacht. Home: 42 High St., Bristol, R. I. Office: Grosvenor Bldg., Providence; also Senate Office Bldg., Washington. Died July 22, 1953.

LEAHY, Lamar Richard (lā'hē), ret. naval officer; b. Buffalo, Feb. 11, 1880; s. Michael and Elizabeth (King) L.; ed. U. Buffalo Law Sch., 1897-98; B.S., U.S. Naval Acad., 1903; Naval War Coll., 1927-28; m. Margery Hamilton Clinton, Sept. 17, 1919. Commd. ensign USN, 1905, advanced through grades to rear adm., 1939; served in Cuban pacification and Mexican occupation; comd. U..S. Noma, operating off French Coast, during World War; Naval attache, Am. Legation, The Hague, 1925-27; ret. 1939; dir. Internat. Hydrographic Bur., Monte Carlo, Monaco, Apr. 1939-41; returned to active duty, U.S. Navy, Sept. 1941. Decorations: Cuban Pacification, Mexican Occupation, Victory Medal, Navy Cross, Order of Brit. Empire, Legion of Honor (France), Comdr. Order of White Lion (Czechoslovakia), Comdr. Order of Orange Nassau (Netherlands), Mil. Order, 2d class (Mexico), Comdr. Knights of Order Polonia Restituta . Trustee Woods Hole Oceanographic Inst., Mus. City of N.Y., Marine Mus. of City of N.Y. Mem. Am. Geog. Union. Clubs: Union, University, New York Yacht, Knickerbocker (N.Y.C.); Tuxedo (Tuxedo Park, N.Y.); Army and Navy, Chevy Chase (Washington); University (Buffalo); Newport Reading Room. Address: 910 Park Av., N.Y. C. Died Oct. 10, 1958.

LEAHY, William D., fleet admiral; b. Hampton, Iowa, May 6, 1875; s. Michael Arthur and Rose (Hamilton) L.; grad. high sch., Ashland, Wis., 1892; grad. U.S. Naval Acad., 1897; m. Louise Tennent Harrington, Feb. 3, 1904 (died April 21, 1942); 1 son, William Harrington. Commissioned ensign, U.S. Navy, 1899; and advanced through the grades to capt., July 1, 1918; chief bur. of ordnance, rank of rear adm., 1927-31; rear adm., Apr. 6, 1930; comdr. Destroyers Scouting Force, 1931-33; chief of Bureau of Navigation, 1933-35. Vice admiral commanding battleships of Battle Force, 1935-36; admiral commanding Battle Force, 1936-37; admiral, chief of Naval Operations, 1937-39; retired Aug. 1, 1939; apptd. gov. of Puerto Rico, 1939; ambassador to France, 1940-42; chief of staff to the Commander-in-chief of the Army and Navy of the U.S. 1942-49. Apptd. Fleet admiral of the U.S. Navy, Dec. 15, 1944. Served in Spanish-Am. War, Philippine Insurrection, Boxer trouble; chief of staff, Nicaraguan Occupation, 1912, Haitian campaign, 1916; command of U.S.S. Dolphin, Mexican Punitive Expdn., 1916; served as comdr. World War I. President Navy Historical Found., 1950-—. Awarded D.S.M., Navy Cross, also Santiago, Spanish Campaign, Philippine Service, Nicaraguan Campaign, Dominican Campaign, Mexican Campaign, Victory, American Defense Service, American Area Campaign medals, Comdr. Mil. Order of Aviz (Portugal), Estrella de Abdon Calderon, 1st class (Ecuador), Cravat Tripod Medal, Special Class (China), Knight Grand Cross of Polonia Restituta (Poland), Grand Cross of Legion of Honor, Croix de Guerre with Palms (France); the Knight Grand Cross Military Division Order of Bath (Britain); Grand Cross Order of Vasco Nunez de Balboa (Panama); Grand Cross, Order of Merit (Chile); Grand Cross Order of Naval Merit (Brazil); Knight Grand Cross Order of Orange-Nassau (Netherlands); Grand Cross Order of Crown with palm, Coix de Guerre with palm (Belgium); Grand Cross Military Order of Italy. Club: Army and Navy. Author: I Was There, 1950. Address: Main Navy Bldg., Constitution Av., Washington 25. Died July 20, 1959; buried Arlington Nat. Cemetery.

LEAHY, William Edward, lawyer; b. Monson, Mass., July 11, 1886; s. David Daniel and Bridget (Power) L.; grad. Monson Acad., 1903; A.B., Holy Cross Coll., Worcester, Mass., 1907, A.M., 1922, LL.D., 1947; LL.B., Georgetown U., 1912, LL.M., 1913, LL.D., 1943; LL.B., Gonzage College, D.C., 1923; m. Miriam Kramer, Nov. 26, 1913. Tchr. Williamstown High Sch., 1907-09; admitted to D C. bar, 1912, since practiced in Washington; instr. Georgetown U. Law Sch., 1916-22; instr. Columbus U. Law Sch., 1926-32, dean, 1926-32, pres., 1932-—; asst. U.S. atty., Washington, 1915-19; spl. U.S. atty., 1921, spl. asst. atty. gen. U.S., 1925-47. Chmn. bd. of appeal D.C. Selective Service System, 1940-41, state dir., 1941-47, reapptd. 1948; apptd. President's Commn. on Internal Security and Individual Rights, 1951, civilian aide to Sec. of Army for D.C., 1947, 56, Citizens' Adv. Council, 1952, chmn., 1953, Personnel Security Review Bd. AEC, 1952. Dir. Nat. Tb Assn., 1952; pres. Tb Assn. D.C., 1948-50. Mem. Pres.' Council Georgetown U., 1952. Recipient John Carroll award Georgetown U., 1952; citations Convocation Monson Acad., 1951, Am. Legion D.C., 1950, D C. Bar Assn., 1951. Mem. Am., D.C. bar assns., Sigma Nu Phi. K.C. Clubs: Lawyers, Cosmos, Rotary, Metropolitan, Alfalfa, Columbia Country (Washington); Lawyers (N.Y.C.). Home: 3325 Garfield St., Washington 8. Died June 5, 1956; buried Rock Creek Cemetery, Washington.

LEAKE, Eugene W(alter), lawyer; b. July 13, 1877; s. Thomas W. and Caroline (Veyrassat) L.; educated Phillips Acad., Andover, Mass., and N.Y. Law Sch.; m. Marion Bancroft Paige, Oct. 6, 1907. Admitted to N.J. bar, 1897, to N.Y. bar, 1907, and since in practice in N.Y.C. Mem. Congress 9th N.J. Dist., 1907-09; gen. counsel Adams Express Co., 1927-32; chmn. bd. Am. Ry. Express Co., 1931; trustee Paramount Publix Corp., 1933-35; chmn. of Loew's Retirement Plan Com. Democrat. Home: 425 E. 5th St. Office: 1540 Broadway, N.Y.C. Died Aug. 23, 1959; buried Cedar Lawn Cemetery, Paterson, N.J.

LEAMY, Frederick Walter (lē'mē), railroad exec.; b. West Rutland, Vt., Nov. 3, 1886; s. James and Catherine (Clark) L.; ed. Rutland Inst.; widower; children—William H., George A. Secretary to president, later assistant to president Delaware & Hudson Co., 1908-28, vice pres. since 1928, dir. since 1938, v.p. and treas. since 1947; sec. exec. com., asst. sec. Wheeling & Lake Erie Ry. Co., 1917; v.p., treas., dir., mem. exec. com., Chateaugay and Lake Placid Ry. Co., Cooperstown & Charlotte Valley R.R. Co., Cooperstown & Susquehanna Valley R.R., Greenwich & Johnsonville Ry. Co., Northern Coal & Iron Co., Ticonderoga R.R. Co.; vice pres., director, member executive com. Troy Union R.R. Co.; v.p., treas., dir. Del. and Hudson R.R. Corp., Hudson River Estates, Inc., Nortern N.Y. Development Co., Wilkes-Barre Connecting R.R. Co.; v.p., treas. Napierville Junction Ry. Co. Mem. Newcomen Soc. Roman Catholic. Clubs: Metropolitan (N.Y. City); Pomonok Country Club (Flushing, N.Y.). Home: 944 Park Av. Office: 230 Park Av., N.Y.C. 17. Died Dec. 11, 1951; buried West Rutland, Vt.

LEAR, Fred(erick) Roy, prof. emeritus, architect; b. Corning, N.Y., Dec. 2, 1882; s. Henry Washington and Josephine (Knapp) L.; B. Arch., Syracuse U., 1905; diploma, Beaux Arts Sch. of Architecture, 1911-14. Feb.-June, 1919; m. Lillian Huntley Congdon, Aug. 29, 1906; children—Ruth Winifred (Mrs. J. Leonard Mowery), Roma Aloise (Mrs. Bernard Loren), Cordelia Lillian (Mrs. Eldon W. Buell). Archtl. faculty, 1905-46, instr. 1905-08, asst. prof. 1908-14, prof. 1914-46, prof. emeritus, 1946-—; color consultant Onondaga Litholite Co., Syracuse, N.Y., 1930-36; exhibited 3 water color paintings Salon de Artiste Francais, Paris, France, 1913; designer: Univ. Ch., Syracuse, N.Y. (with Fred Revels), 1922, Grace Meth. Ch., Corning, New York, 1925-28, Lafayette Methodist and Lutheran Church of Atonement, Syracuse, 1928, memorial for Vice Admiral Peary in Arlington, Va.; numerous memorials cemetery structures, also houses. Served with ednl. corps U.S. Army, 1919; lecturer, aviation cadets on camouflage and camouflage detection, World War II. Registered Architect, N.Y., 1916. Mem. Museum Fine Arts, Architects of Syracuse, N.Y. State Assn. Architects, Am. Inst. Architects, Phi Kappa Phi, Tau Sigma Delta. Republican. Methodist. Mason. Clubs: Syracuse Alumni, East Gage (pres. 1930-45). Home: 862 Ackerman Av., Syracuse, N.Y. Died June 20, 1950; buried Hope Cemetery, Corning, N.Y.

LEARNED, Arthur Garfield (lĕr'nĕd), etcher, artist; b. Chelsea, Mass., Aug. 10, 1872; s. George Grant and Elizabeth (Tent) L.; ed. pub. schs., pvt. tutor in drawing and in art schs. of Munich and Vienna; studied in Paris, 1907-08; m. Leila Helen Sprague, 1900; 1 son, Bruce. Art staff Boston Herald, 4 yrs.; illustrated 8 volumes Breviary Treasurers, edited by Nathan Haskell Dole; also various books for Boston publishers; drawings for Life, Ladies' Home Journal, St. Nicholas, Town and Country, Harper's Magazine, etc. Exhibited portraits in N.Y. C., Phila., Worcester, Boston. Produced etchings of Edgar Allan Poe, Tennyson, Grieg, MacDowell, John Alexander, Paul Helleu and many others; also produced original concept of the Buddha, and St. Francis of Assisi; many symbolic drawings of spiritual realities. Painted portrait of Panchen Lama for Jacques Marchais Tibetan Mus.; also portrait of Dr. George Washington Carver for Bethune-Cookman Coll. Creates decorative panels, screens, friezes for rooms, etc. Address: Hillcrest Park, Stamford, Conn.; (winter) Daytona Beach, Fla. Died Dec. 1959.

LEARY, Frederick (John), banker; b. Greene, N. Y., Feb. 21, 1882; s. Humphrey and Mary A. (Normile) L.; grad. high sch.; m. Margaret E. Hayes, June 1, 1911; children—Frederick J., Dorothy C., Robert H. With Mutual Alliance Trust Co., N.Y.C., 1902-13, Central Hanover Bank & Trust Co., N.Y.C., 1913-47, ret.; dir., mem. finance com. Am. Smelting & Refining Co., U.S. Hoffman Machinery Co.; dir. John G. Paton Co. (N.Y.C.). Republican. Roman Catholic. Clubs: Garden City, Garden City Golf (Garden City, N.Y.). Home: 320 Park Av., N.Y.C. 22. Died Nov. 1953.

LEARY, Herbert Fairfax, ret. naval officer; b. Washington, May 31, 1885; s. Rear Adm. Richard Philipps and Augusta Neville (Irwin) L.; B.S., U.S. Naval Acad., 1905; m. Marion Barnes Bryant, Apr. 28, 1909; children—Herbert Fairfax, Neville Carlysle (Mrs. George K. Crozer, III). Commd. ensign USN, 1905, advanced through the grades to rear adm., 1938, vice adm., 1942; has served as gunnery officer, Battle Force; staff Naval Hdqrs., London; mem. Allied Naval Armistice Commn., naval attaché, Paris; liaison officer French Fleet; dir. fleet tng., naval operations; comdr. Eastern Sea Frontier, 1945; ret. Jan. 16, 1946; supt. N.Y. State Maritime Coll., 1946-51, ret. Decorated Navy Cross, Victory and Cuban campaign medals (U.S.), Legion of Honor (France). Episcopalian. Clubs: Chevy Chase Country (Chevy Chase, Md.); New York Yacht (N.Y.C.). Address: Villanova, Pa.; also Jamestown, R.I. Died Dec. 3, 1957.

LEARY, Lewis Gaston, clergyman; b. Elizabeth, N.J., Aug. 3, 1877; s. George S. and Joanna (Gaston) L.; B.Sc., Rutgers, 1897; M.A., N.Y.U., 1900, Ph.D., 1905; student Union Theol. Sem., 1897-99; grad. McCormick Theol. Sem., Chgo., 1900, postgrad. work, 1903-04; D.D., U. Vt., 1927; m. Beatrice E. Knight, December 15, 1904; children—Lewis, George Knight, Mary Emily (Mrs. Horace S. Peck), William Gillett. Ordained Presbyn. ministry, 1900; instr. Am. U., Beirut, Syria, 1900-03; pastor Blauvelt, N.Y., 1904-07, Huguenot Meml. Ch., Pelham Manor, N.Y., 1907-28, West Milford, N.J., 1935-—. Hon. asso. pastor Reformed Church, Verdun, France. Prof. Biblical literature, Vassar Coll., 1921-22; conducted People's Radio Vespers, 1927. Lecturer and contbr. numerous articles connected with O.T., Palestine, remote parts of Europe, and young people's problems. Mem. Phi Beta Kappa. Clubs: Clergy, Theta; Pinecliff Lake (West Milford). Author: The Christmas City, 1911; The Real Palestine of Today, 1911; Andorra, the Hidden Republic, 1912; Syria, the Land of Lebanon, 1913; Problems of Protestantism, 1933. Editor: From the Pyramids to Paul, 1935. Compiler: The Bible When You Want It, 1932; For Them That Mourn, 1938; The Service Book of Scripture and Prayer, 1941 (over three million copies distributed among armed forces). Address: West Milford, N.J. Died May 27, 1951.

LEARY, Timothy, pathologist; b. Waltham, Mass., May 10, 1870; s. Timothy and Catharine (Rooney) L.; prep. edn. Waltham High Sch.; M.D., Harvard, 1895; hon. A.M., Tufts Coll., 1907; m. Adelaide Olga Cushing, Sept. 17, 1901; children—Olga Cushing, Deborah, Timothy. Resident asst. pathologist Boston City Hosp., 1895-97; asst. prof. pathology and bacteriology Tufts Coll. Med. and Dental Schs.,

1897-1900, prof., 1900-29, now emeritus; med. examiner Suffolk County. Acting asst. surgeon Spanish-Am. War, 1898, serving in P.R. and Cuba and as comdg. officer U.S.A. Gen. Hosp., Ponce, P.R. Mem. Assn. Am. Pathologists and Bacteriologists, Internat. Assn. Geog. Pathology, A.A.A.S., A.M.A., Mass. Med. Soc., Soc. Am. Bacteriologists, Mass. Medico-Legal Soc. (pres. 1919-21), Mass. Soc. Examining Physicians (pres. 1926), Boston Med. Library Assn., Alpha Kappa. Catholic. Home: 44 Burroughs St. Office: 784 Massachusetts Av., Boston. Died Nov. 1954.

LEARY, William Henry, law educator; b. Hatfield, Mass., June 5, 1881; s. John and Ellen (Coleman) LL.D., U. Utah, 1944; m. Alice Marie Lynch, June 19, 1912 (died 1919); m. 2d, Catherine M. Flanagan, Oct. 29, 1921 (died 1927). Began law practice, Salt Lake City, 1909; prof. law, U. Utah, 1914-—, also dean Law Sch.; chmn. adv. council Dept. Employment Security of Indsl. Commn. of Utah; mem. Utah Bd. Commrs. for Promotion of Uniformity of Legislation in U.S.; pub. mem. 9th Regional War Labor Bd.; mem. State Council Def. World War I; chmn. labor com. State Council of Def., World War II. Mem. Am., Utah State (sec.) bar assns., Phi Gamma Delta, Phi Alpha Delta, Order of Coif. K.C. Home: 150 S. 13th East St., Salt Lake City. Died Apr. 6, 1957.

LEAVELL, Richard Marion, educator; b. Newberry Dist., S.C., Aug. 1, 1838; s. James and Emily A. (Worthington) L.; A.B., U. Miss., 1859; m. Annie Simpson Brown, Sept. 12, 1902. Served lt. and capt., 2d Miss. Inf., C.S.A., 1861-5; prin. Verona (Miss.) Male Acad., 1865-70; prof. English lang. and lit., Miss. Coll., Clinton, 1882-89; prof. English and belles lettres U. Miss., 1889-90, prof. philosophy and polit. economy, 1890-1908, prof. emeritus, 1908-—. Mem. Miss. Legislature, 1872-3. Mem. Am. Acad. Polit. and Social Science. Baptist. Democrat. Contbr. ednl. periodicals. Address: 310 N. 16th St., Oxford, Miss. Died Aug. 18, 1918; buried St. Peter's Cemetery, Oxford.

LEAVELLE, Arnaud Bruce (luh-vĕl), educator; b. Los Angeles, July 19, 1914; s. Arnaud Bruce and Elizabeth (Bryan) L.; B.A., U. Cal., 1937, M.A., 1939, Ph.D., 1940; m. Nancy Morgan, Dec. 25, 1944; children—Elizabeth Morgan, Katharin Olwen, Ardele B. Instr. polit. sci. Swarthmore (Pa.) Coll., 1939-40, 41-42, asst. prof., 1943-46; instr. U. Ill., 1942-43; asst. prof. Stanford, 1946-49, asso. prof., 1949-54, prof., 1954-—; Fulbright research scholar, Oxford U., Eng., 1952-53; vis. prof. Salzburg Seminar, Austria, 1953. Mem. Am. (exec. council 1953-55), No. Cal. (pres. 1956-57) polit. sci. assns., Am. Assn. Univ. Profs., Acad. Social and Polit. Sci., Phi Beta Kappa, Pi Sigma Alpha, Pi Kappa Delta, Pi Gamma Mu. Democrat. Baptist. Home: 274 Searsville Rd., Stanford, Cal. Died Oct. 22, 1956; buried Alta Mesa Meml. Park, Palo Alto, Cal.

LEAVITT, Ashley Day (lev'it), clergyman; b. Chgo., Oct. 10, 1877; s. Burke Fay and Lucina Maria (Day) L.; B.A., Yale, 1900; B.D., Hartford Theol. Sem., 1903; D.D., Bowdoin, 1918; m. Myrtle R. Hart, Sept. 7, 1904; children—Hart Day, Julia. Ordained Congl. ministry, 1903; asst. to Dr. E. P. Parker, S. Ch., Hartford, Conn., 1903-04; pastor Willimantic, 1904-08, S. Ch., Concord, N.H., 1908-13, State St. Ch., Portland, Me., 1913-19, Harvard Ch., Brookline, Mass., 1919-49, emeritus, 1949-—; Congl. Nat. council preacher, 1934. Chmn. Prudential Com. A.B.C.F.M., 1926-38; pres. Greater Boston Fed. Chs., 1926-28, 1944-46. Gates lectr. Grinnell (Ia.) Coll., 1938. Mem. Psi Upsilon. Skull and Bones (Yale). Republican. Clubs: Congregational (pres., 1929-30), Yale (pres. 1928). Author: Jesus and the Jury, 1925; Just A Moment. Home: 35 Waverly St., Brookline 46, Mass. Died Jan. 22, 1959.

LEAVITT, Roger, banker; b. Waterloo, Ia., June 25, 1860; s. John Hooker and Caroline Clark (Ware) L.; A.B., Beloit (Wis.) Coll., 1882, A.M., 1885; m. Alice S. Windsor, Oct. 29, 1885 (died 1890); 1 son, John Windsor; m. 2d, Katharine S. Townsend, June 21, 1892; children—Roger Townsend, Edward Townsend, Mary Louise, Charles Townsend, Ruth Townsend; m. 3d, Mary Larson, Aug. 25, 1925. Cashier Grundy County Nat. Bank, Grundy Center, Ia., 1885-88; dir. Cedar Falls (Ia.) Nat. Bank (now Cedar Falls Trust & Savs. Bank); pres. Marcus Lumber Co.; v.p. Cedar Falls Nat. Co.; sec. Cedar Valley Bldg. & Loan Assn. Former trustee Beloit Coll., Grinnell Coll., Chgo. Theol. Sem., Ia. State Bd. Edn. Mem. S.A.R. (ex-pres. Ia. chapter), Beta Theta Pi, Phi Beta Kappa. Republican. Conglist. Home: Cedar Falls, Ia. Deceased.

LEAVY, Charles Henry (lĕ'vē), U.S. dist. judge; b. York, Pa., Feb. 16, 1884; s. Jacob and Elizabeth (Miller) L.; student State Normal Sch., Warrensburg, Mo., 1902-03, State Normal Sch., Bellingham, Wash., 1907-08, Kansas City Law Sch., 1905-06; m. Pearl Williams, Aug. 1, 1912; children—Charles Williams, James Irving. School teacher in Mo., 1903-06, in Wash., 1906-13; admitted to Wash. bar, 1912, and began practice in Newport, Wash.; pros. atty. Pend Oreille Co., 1914-18; asst. U.S. dist. atty. for E. Wash., 1918-21; pros. atty. Spokane County, 1922-26; superior court judge, 1926-36; mem. 75th to 77th Congresses, 5th Wash. Dist.; judge U.S. Dist. Ct. Western Dist. of Washington, 1942-52, retired. Mem. Am. Bar Assn., Wash. State Bar Assn. Washington State Prosecuting Attorneys (pres. 1924). Mem. Central Valley Sch. Bd. 1923-27; Presidential Elector, Democratic Ticket, 1924. Democrat. Lutheran. Odd Fellow, Eagle, K.P. Clubs: Kiwanis, University-Union (Tacoma). Home: 4141 Madrona Way, Tacoma 7, Wash. Died Sept. 25, 1952; buried Mountain View Cemetery, Tacoma.

Le BARON, William, editor, playwright, producer; born Elgin, Illinois; son John K. and Mary (Bundy) Le B.; student University of Chicago, 1901-03, New York U., 1903-04; m. Mabel H. Hollins, June 26, 1909. Mng. editor Collier's Weekly, Jan. 1918-July 1919; dir. gen. Cosmopolitan Productions, 1919-24; asso. producer, Famous Players-Lasky Corp., 1924-27; v.p. Film Booking Office Studio, 1927-28; v.p. in charge production R.K.O. Productions, 1929-31; in charge of production, Paramount Studios, 1931-40; producer 20th Century-Fox Film Corp. since 1941. Mem. Authors' League America, Am. Soc. of Dramatists and Composers, Am. Soc. Composers, Authors, Pubs., Psi Upsilon. Author: (plays) The Echo; The Very Idea; Her Regiment (with Victor Herbert); Back to Earth; I Love You; Apple Blossoms (with Fritz Kreisler and Victor Jacobi); Nobody's Money; The Scarlet Man; The Love Letter; The Yankee Princess; Moonlight. Producer of pictures, Humoresque, Beau Geste, Cimarron, She Done Him Wrong, Kiss the Boys Good-bye, Week End in Havana, Song of the Islands, Springtime in the Rockies, Stormy Weather, The Gang's All Here, Pin-up Girl, Greenwich Village, Carnegie Hall. Address: 2024 Camden Av., Los Angeles 25. Died Feb. 9, 1958.

Le BLOND, Charles Hubert, bishop; b. Celina, O., Nov. 21, 1883; s. Charles McGinley and Anne Marie (Brennan) Le B.; prep. edn., Cathedral Sch. (Cleve.), 1889-97, St. Ignatius High Sch., 1897-1901; studied John Carroll U. and St. Marys Sem., until 1909. Ordained priest R.C. Ch.; became curate St. John's Cathedral, Cleve., 1909; was dir. Catholic Charities, Cleve.; consecrated bishop. Home: 718 N. 7th St., St. Joseph, Mo. Died Dec. 1958.

LEBOLD, Foreman M., business exec.; b. Chgo., Jan. 7, 1895; s. Nathan F. and Florence G. (Foreman) L.; B.S., E.M., Mich. Coll. Mining and Tech., 1915; m. Peggy Peterson, Feb. 24, 1936. With Morris Paper Mills since 1916, sales, 1916-29, pres. since 1929; pres. Timberline Dredging Co. since 1936. Trustee Michael Reese Hosp., Chgo., 1928-43; trustee Lincoln Meml. U., Harrogate Tenn. Served as 1st lt. U.S. Army, 1917-19. Mem. Am. Inst. Mining and Metallurgical Engineers, Chicago, Illinois historical societies, also Sigma Rho. Jewish religion. Clubs: Tavern, Mid-Day, Standard, Lake Shore Country. Home: 257 E. Delaware St. Office: 135 S. LaSalle St., Chgo. 3. Died Nov. 11, 1953.

LEBOUTILLIER, George (lĕ-bōō-tĭl-lēr'), ry. exec.; s. James L.; grad. U. of Cincinnati, 1895; m. Ilse M. Crawford. Chairman of the board Harborside Warehouse Co., Incorporated; chmn. adv. bd. Chem. Bank & Trust Co. (Brooklyn Branch). Mem. adv. council Regional Plan Assn. of N.Y.; dir. Jersey City C. of C. Clubs: New York Railroad, Ohio Soc. of New York, Metropolitan (New York); Railroad-Machinery of New York, Engineers, Metropolitan; Racquet (Phila.); Piping Rock (Locust Valley, L.I.). Home: 911 Park Av., N.Y. City 21. Office: Room 391, Pennsylvania Station, N.Y.C. 1. Died Oct. 5, 1952.

LE CLERC, J(oseph) Arthur (lĕ-klâr), chemist; b. Ware, Mass., 1873; s. John B. and Lucy (Chicoine) L.; B.Sc., Worcester Polytechnic Institute, 1895; Ph.D., University of Halle-Wittenberg, 1903; m. Emma V. Hall, 1895; married 2d, Yona Buchanan, 1937; m. 3d, Helen G. Davis (Helen Randle), 1943. On the staff of the United States Bureau of Chemistry, 1903-19, in charge of lab. of plant chemistry; chief chemist Miner-Hillard Milling Co., Wilkes-Barre, Pa., 1919-20; spl. trade commr. to Europe; spl. agent of Dept. of Commerce, specializing on grains and grain products, 1922-28; sr. chemist Bur. of Agrl. Chem. and Engring., U.S. Dept. of Agr., 1928-43; retired. Mem. Internat. Jury of Awards, Paris Expn., 1900, St. Louis, 1904, San Francisco, 1915. Decorated Chevalier du Mérite Agricole, France, 1907. Mem. Am. Chem. Soc. (pres. Washington sect. 1912), Washington Acad. Sciences, Am. Soy bean Assn., Am. Inst. Chemists, Am. Assn. Cereal Chemists, Food Technologists. Translator: L'Industrie des Cyanures (by R. Robine and M. Lenglen), 1905. Home: Friendship Pl., Kingsley Lake, Starke, Fla. Died Nov. 16, 1956; buried Magnolia Cemetery, Varnville, S.C.

LEDERER, Charles (lĕd'ĕr-ĕr), lawyer; b. Chicago, Ill., Apr. 22, 1877; s. Sigmund and Resie (Klausner) L.; Ph.B., U. of Chicago, 1898; LL.B., Northwestern U., 1901; m. Florence Freiler, Mar. 28, 1911; 1 son, Philip Charles. Admitted to Ill. bar, 1901; mem. Ill. legislature, 1908-10; mem. Lederer, Livingston, Kahn and Adsit; counsel for Sears, Roebuck & Co. Mem. Am., Ill. State and Chicago bar assns. Republican. Mason (32°, Shriner). Home: 5454 South Shore Drive. Office: 120 S. La Salle St., Chgo. Died Apr. 30, 1954.

LEDERER, Norbert Lewis, ret. chem. engr., author; b. Vienna, Austria, Dec. 28, 1888; s. James and Cecile Weller (O'Brien) L.; parents U.S. citizens; student high school and coll., Melk (Austria), 1897-1905, U. Vienna, 1905-09, Sorbonne, Paris, 1912-13; m. Elsie Zeisler, April 30, 1914 (div.); m. 2d, Lillian Day, Nov. 1, 1946, 1 stepdau., Renee (Mrs. Hugh Snelson). Chemist Scheidemandel-Motard Werke, Berlin, 1909-12; mgr. Sté. Ane. d'Industrie Chimique, Paris, 1912-14; mgr. O. Murray & Co., London, 1914-17; with C.E., U.S. Army, AEF, 1917-19 (served at Peace Conf.); mgr. chem. dept. J. Aron & Co., N.Y.C., 1919-22; U.S. rep. Scheidemandel-Motard Werke, 1922-39, export mgr. M. Golodetz & Co., N.Y.C., 1940-49; sec. Victor M. Calderon Co., Inc., 1949-52. Chmn. bd. trustees Authors Club-Carnegie Fund, N.Y.C.; tournament dir. U.S. Chess Fedn. Democrat. Episcopalian. Club: Authors (treas.). Author: Tropical Fish and Their Care, 1934; (with Lillian Day) Murder in Time, 1935; Death Comes on Friday, 1936. Contbr. articles on chess, music and criminology to mags. Home: 18 West 86th St., N.Y.C. 24. Office: 99 Hudson St., N.Y.C. Died Nov. 1955.

LEDERER, Richard M., business exec.; b. Chicago, 1887; s. Arthur and Sophia L.; student City Coll. of N.Y., Packard Bus. Coll., Am. Inst. Banking; m. Marguerite Kern, Dec. 12, 1915; children—Richard M., Jr., Dolly L. Maass. Served apprenticeship with M. Morgenthau, Jr., 1903-98; took over family banking and fgn. exchange bus. known since 1882 as Lederer's Banking House, 1912, incorporated as Standard Bank of N.Y., 1919, merged with Mfrs. Trust Co., 1927, became dir. and v.p. until 1929; organized Standard Nat. Corp., bldg. constrn. loan bus., 1923; purchased control of Woodside Nat. Bank in Queens County, N.Y., 1937, name changed to Standard Nat. Bank of N.Y., 1942, sold to Mfrs. Trust Co., 1942; organized Reredel Assos., family partnership to manage family investments, 1943. Was pres. Authorized Bankers Assn. State of N.Y.; v.p. Am. S.S. Ticket Agts. Assn. Am., N.Y. State bankers assns., Am. Bus. Congress, Am. Arbitration Assn., Commerce and Industry Assn., Fifth Av. Assn., Fedn. Jewish Charities, United Jewish Appeal, Anti-Defamation League, Am. Jewish Com., Joint Def. Appeal, N.Y. Guild for Jewish Blind, Nat. Conf. Christians and Jews, Mt. Vernon Community Chest, Freedom House, Mt. Vernon Y.M.H.A., Nat. Soc. Autograph Collectors (pres. 1950-51), N.Y. and Nantucket hist. socs., Bibliog. Soc. Am., Early Am. Industries, Am. Assn. State and Local History, Clements Library Assos. Clubs: Sales Execs., Advt. of N.Y., Harmonie, Fairview Country. Address: 111 E. 56th St., N.Y.C. Died July 24, 1952.

LEE, Algernon, journalist; b. Dubuque, Ia., Sept. 15, 1873; s. James and Jane (Emmerson) L.; student U. Minn.; m. Blanche Knappen, 1899 (died 1900); m. 2d, Dr. Matilda Sinai, 1907. Actively identified with Socialist movement, 1895-—; editor Socialist papers, 1898-1909; ednl. dir. Rand Sch. of Social Science, 1909-—. Del. Social Internat. Conf., 1904, 07, 16. Elected to Bd. of Aldermen, N.Y.C., 1917. Home: 1186 Madison Av. Office: 7 E. 15th St., N.Y.C. Died Jan. 1, 1954.

LEE, Archie Laney, business exec.; b. Monroe, N.C., Sept. 17, 1888; s. George Samuel and Mary (Laney) L.; A.B., Duke U. (Trinity Coll.), 1908; m. Beatrice Lodge Thomas, Nov. 21, 1925; children—Georgia Mepham (Mrs. Peter Bakewell), Alexander Laney. Newspaper reporter Atlanta Georgian, 1909-17; with D'Arcy Advt. Co., St. Louis, since 1919; copywriter, 1919-25, account exec. and dir., chmn. bd. dirs. since 1945. Dir. Coca-Cola Bottling Co., St. Louis, Coca-Cola Bottling Plants, Inc., Portland, Me. Independent. Clubs: St. Louis Country, Noonday. Owns and operates Ozark farm devoted to wildlife and conservation. Home: Eight Fordyce Lane, Clayton 5, Mo. Office: Mo. Pacific Bldg., St. Louis 3. Died Dec. 22, 1951; buried Bellefontaine Cemetery, St. Louis.

LEE, Canada (real name Lionel Cornelius Canegata), actor; b. N.Y. City, Mar. 3, 1907; s. James Cornelius and Lydia (Whaley) C.; student pub. schs., N.Y. City; m. Juanita Waller, Dec., 1925; 1 son, Carl Vincent; divorced Jan. 1942; m. 2d Frances Pollack, Mar. 1951. Studied violin, age 7 to 14; ran away to become jockey, at 14; rode until 16, then exercised horses until 18; went into boxing at 19; won Met. Inter-city and Jr. Nat. championships; turned professional at 20 and became leading contender for welterweight championship; eyes failed at 23; stopped fighting at 26; organized a band, playing for dances and at theaters; became interested in theater and secured part in Meek Mose. Stevedore at 28; played in Orson Welles' Negro Macbeth; with Rex Ingram in Haiti, doing Christophe; season with Ethel Waters doing Drylon in Mamba's Daughters; later narrator on "Flow Gently, Sweet Rhythm" program with John Kirby and Maxine Sul-

livan, Columbia Broadcasting System; selected for part of Bigger Thomas in Native Son, dir. by Orson Welles on Mercury Productions; appeared in Anna Lucasta, The Tempest, On Whitman Ave. (star and co-producer), The Dutchess of Malfi, Set My People Free; (films) Lifeboat; Body and Soul; Cry The Beloved Country. Baptist. Home: 235 W. 4th St., N.Y.C. Died May 9, 1952; buried Woodlawn Cemetery.

LEE, Frank Hood, congressman; b. Johnson County, Kan., Mar. 29, 1873; s. Daniel Marion and Lucy (Howard) L.; ed. pub. sch., Virgil City, Mo.; m. Allie King, Nov. 25, 1902; children—Dorothy E. (Mrs. Earl Steinert), Katherine B., Alfred King, Marion S., Harold H., Frank H., Mary Virginia. Successively newsboy, bootblack, livery stable worker, salesman; admitted to Mo. bar; became justice of the peace, 1894; mem. Mo. Ho. of Rep., 1915, 17; mem. 73d Congress (1933-35), Mo. at large. Democrat. Methodist. Elk. Office: 40½ Main St., Joplin, Mo. Died Nov. 20, 1953.

LEE, Frederic Edward, economist; b. Cowley County, Kan., Sept. 24, 1886; s. Frank Herbert and Susana Rodgers (Smith) L.; B.A., U. of Kan., 1911; M.A., Yale, 1912, B.D., 1914, Ph.D., 1916; studied Harvard, 1915-16; diploma Tokyo Sch. Foreign Langs., 1918; studied 2 yrs. London School of Economics; m. Edna Stewart, July 16, 1914; children—Frederic Edward, James Stewart, Robt. Andrew. Fellow and asst., Yale, 1914-15; prof. sociology and econ., Sei Gakuin Coll., Tokyo, 1916-18; economist in charge econ. intelligence sect., Russian Bur., War Trade Bd., 1918-19; regional economist for Eastern Asian region, Fgn. Trade Advisers' Office, Dept. of State, 1919-20; economist consul of U.S. for China, at Shanghai and Peking, 1920-22; dean, coll. arts and Sciences, prof., head dept. econ. and sociology, U. of Md., 1922-27, exec. dean of Univ., 1925-27; expert consultant in Far Eastern finance, Dept. of Commerce, 1923-27; Am. financial trade commr., Am. Embassy, London, 1927-29; one of Am. observers with Young Commn., Paris, 1929; prof. economics, U. of Ill., since 1929; dir. of research and consultant com. on banking research, Ill. Bankers Assn., 1937-38. Mem. Am. Econ. Assn., Economists' Nat. Com. on Monetary Policy, Am. Consular Assn., Asiatic Society, Japan. Conglist. Club: Union (Shanghai). Author: The Russian Co-operative Movement, 1920; Currency Banking and Finance in China, 1925; Participating Shares in British Investment Trusts, 1928; Banking and Trade Financing in the United Kingdom, 1929. Co-Author: United Kingdom—A Commercial, Industrial and Financial Handbook, 1930. Contbr. to mags. and periodicals; financial feature writer for Commercial and Financial Chronicle, Barron's Banking, etc. Home: 3102 50th St. S, Gulfport, Fla. Died Sept. 4, 1952.

LEE, George Cabot, banker; b. Chestnut Hill, Newton, Mass., Feb. 2, 1871; s. George Cabot and Caroline (Haskell) L.; A.B., Harvard, 1894; m. Madeline Jackson, Nov. 17, 1898; children—George C., James J., Nelson B.; m. 2d, Mrs. Gertrude C. Bartlett, July 8, 1926. Pres. Lee Higginson Safe Deposit Co.; trustee Revere Sugar Refinery, Mass. Fire & Marine Ins. Co., United Fruit Co. (exec. com.), U.S. Smelting & Refining Co., others. Assisted in sale of Allied loans and in raising funds for Allies, for A.R.C., K.C., others. Decorated Cross of St. Sava (Serbian). Home: Westwood, Mass. Office: 201 Devonshire St., Boston. Died Oct. 28, 1950.*

LEE, Gertrude Adams (Mrs. George Madison Lee); b. Sparta, Kent Co., Mich., Dec. 9, 1871; d. Marcellus and Fannie Adams; grad. high sch., Sparta; m. George Madison Lee, of Denver, Colo., July 19, 1893. Sec. Minimum Wage Commn., Colo., since July 23, 1917. Active in politics since 1893; v. chmn. Dem. State Central Com., Colo., 1910-13, chmn., 1913-14; Dem. presdl. elector, 1912; asso. mem. Dem. Nat. Com. since 1918. First woman to serve as state chmn. of polit. party and first woman elected presdl. elector. Home: Briggsdale, Colo. Address: State Capitol, Denver, Colo. Died Sept. 1959.

LEE, Graham, missionary; b. Rock Island, Ill., June 2, 1861; s. Mylo and Margaret Rhoda (Conklin) L.; A.B., Princeton, 1889; Hartford Theol. Sem., 1889-90; grad. McCormick Theol. Sem., 1892; m. Blanche Webb, Jan. 10, 1894. Ordained Presbyn. ministry, 1892; missionary, Pyengyang, Korea, 1892-12; pastor, Concord, Cal., 1912—. Address: Gilroy, Cal. Died Dec. 2, 1916; buried Gilroy.

LEE, James P., pres., dir. Omaha & Council Bluffs St. Ry. Co.; dir. United Benefit Life Ins. Co. Address: 360 Aquila Court, Omaha, Neb. Died Oct. 17, 1955.*

LEE, Jennette (Barbour Perry), novelist; b. Bristol, Conn., Nov. 10, 1860; d. Philemon F. and Mary (Barbour) Perry; A.B., Smith Coll., 1886; m. Gerald Stanley Lee, June 26, 1896 (died 1944); 1 dau., Geraldine. Tchr. English, Vassar, 1890-93; head dept. English, Coll. for Women, Western Res. U., 1893-96; instr. English Smith Coll., 1901-04, prof. English lang. and lit., 1904-13; dir. (with Gerald Stanley Lee) Training Sch. for Balance and Coördination, N.Y.C., 1926-33, Northampton, Mass., 1933—. Author: Kate Wetherill, 1900; A Pillar of Salt, 1901; The Son of a Fiddler, 1902; Uncle William, 1906; The Ibsen Secret, 1907; Simeon Tetlow's Shadow, 1909; Happy Island, 1910; Mr. Achilles, 1912; Betty Harris (English edition), 1912; The Taste of Apples, 1913; The Woman in the Alcove, 1914; Aunt Jane, 1915; The Symphony Play, 1916; Unfinished Portraits, 1916; The Green Jacket, 1917; The Air-Man and the Tramp, 1918; The Rain-Coat Girl, 1919; The Other Susan, 1921; The Mysterious Office, 1922; Dead Right, 1925; If You Must Cook, 1926; also numerous sketches and stories. Home: 88 High St., Northampton, Mass. Died Oct. 10, 1951.

LEE, John Clifford Hodges, army officer; b. Junction City, Kan., Aug. 1, 1887; s. Charles Fenlon and John Clifford (Hodges) L. (mother givern her father's name); B.S., U.S. Mil. Acad., West Point, N.Y., 1909; student Army Engring. Sch., U.S. Army Staff Coll., France, 1918, Army War Coll., Washington, D.C., 1931-32, Army Indsl. Coll., 1932-33; hon. LL. D., Bristol University; Sc.D. (hon.), Des Moines College Osteopathy and Surgery; m. Sarah Ann Row, Sept. 24, 1917 (died Aug. 25, 1939); 1 son, Colonel John Clifford Hodges, Jr.; married 2d, Eve B. Ellis, Sept. 19, 1945 (dec. 1953). Commd. 2d lt. C.E., U.S. Army, 1909, advancing through ranks to lieut. general (temp.), 1944; permanent major general, 1945; served, Panama Canal, 1909-10; 3d Battalion Engrs., 1911-13; mil. survey of Guam, 1913-14, of Luzon, 1914-15, Ohio River improvement, 1915-17; on staff Gen. Leonard Wood, 1917-18, 1919-20; with 89th Div., A.E.F. in France and Germany, 1918-19; Gen. Staff Corps (6th Corps Area and Philippine Dept.), 1920-23; in Office Chief of Engrs., 1923-26; dist. engr., Vicksburg, 1926-31; with Civic Works Authority, and dist. engr., Washington, D.C., 1934; mem. bd. engrs. for rivers and harbors, 1934-35; dist. engr. Phila., 1934-38; div. engr. N. Pacific Div., 1938-40; temp. duty, Air Corps, May-Aug. 1939; comd. San Francisco Port of Embarkation, Ft. Mason, Calif., 1940-41; comd. 2d Inf. Div., Nov. 1941-May 1942; comdg. Services of Supply and Communication Zone, E.T.O., May 1942-Jan. 1946; dep. theatre comdr., Jan. 1944; comdg. Mediterranean Theatre Operation, Jan. 1946-Sept. 1947; ret. at lt. gen. for disability, Dec. 31, 1947. Awarded Distinguished Serv. Medal (Army and Navy), Silver Star, Croix de Guerre; Grand Officer Legion of Honor; Knight Comdr. British Empire; also Belgian, Luxembourg and Italian decorations. Mem. Soc. Am. Mil. Engineers, Society of the Cincinnati, Scabbard and Blade. Episcopalian. Clubs: Army-Navy (Washington). Author: Manual for Topographers, 1915. Home: 182 Highland Rd., Southwood Hills. Address: Brotherhood of St. Andrew, 709 W. Market St., York, Pa. Died Aug. 30, 1958; buried Arlington Nat. Cemetery.

LEE, Jordan G., Jr., dean; b. Farmersville, La., Oct. 29, 1885; s. Henry Marshall and Emma Octavia (Lee) L.; B.S., La. State U., 1906, M.S., 1929; student U. of Mo., summer 1928, Ia. State Coll., 1930-31; m. Genevieve L. Barber, Sept. 6, 1909; children—Genevieve and Jordan Grey III. In charge livestock experiments, La. Expt. Station, 1906; organized and filled position with dept. of agr., Southwestern La. Inst., Lafayette, La., 1909-18; prof. and head vocational agr. div., La. State U., 1918-31, dean of agr., in charge expt. stations, agr. extension and resident teaching, since 1931. Major on governor's staff, 1916-20. Mem. nat. advisory com. on Inter-Am. Agrl. Edn., 1940-42; bd. dirs. Farm Credit Adminstr. Recipient of plaque for distinguished service to agr. in Ia. by Epsilon Sigma Phi, 1940; recd. plaque from U.S. Treasury for sale of U.S. Savs. Bonds, named Man of the Year in Agriculture for La. by Progressive Farmer, 1943. Mem. Assn. Southern Agricultural Workers (pres. 1949-50), Phi Kappa Phi, Omicron Delta Kappa, Alpha Zeta, Alpha Tau Alpha, Kappa Delta Phi, Kappa Sigma. Mason. Co-author: Farm Crops, 1925; Southern Field Crop Enterprises, 1928. Home: 439 State St. Office: Louisiana State U. and Agr. and Mech. Coll., Baton Rouge. Died Apr. 26, 1956; buried Greenoaks Meml. Park, Baton Rouge.

LEE, Paul Wayne, lawyer; b. Xenia, O., Nov. 26, 1876; s. Abel Thomas and Mary E. (Kyle) L.; A.B., University of Colorado, 1899; LL.B., University of Denver (Colorado), 1901; married Florence M. Moore, Aug. 22, 1906 (deceased 1949); children—Richard M., Margaret (Mrs. Paul A. Murphy), Barbara (Mrs. St. George Gordon). Mem. Lee, Bryans, Kelly and Stansfield, gen. counsel Pub. Service Co. of Colo. Member American, Colorado State and Denver bar associations, American Law Inst., Phi Gamma Delta. Republican. Clubs: Denver, Cactus, City. Home: 402 S. 4th St., Lamar, Colo. Office: Gas & Electric Bldg., Denver. Died Nov. 29, 1954; cremated Fairmount Cemetery, Denver.

LEE, Raymond Eliot, ex-army officer; b. St. Louis, Mar. 26, 1886; s. Joseph Milton and Emma Susan (Lowe) L.; B.S. in Civil Engring., U. Mo., 1909; grad. Command & Gen. Staff Sch., 1923; Army War Coll., 1927; m. Jeanette Baker, July 7, 1923; 1 dau., Susan Jenifer. Commd. 2d lt. U.S. Army, 1909, advanced through grades to brig. gen. (temp.), 1940; served Mexican Border, 1917, 2d Regular Div., 15th Field Artillery, World War, 1917-18, War Dept., 1918-22, P.I., 1923-26, Gen. Staff Corps, 1928-32; mil. attaché, London, 1935-39, 40-41; ret. Feb. 28, 1946. Decorated D.S.M. Mem. Beta Theta Pi. Episcopalian. Clubs: Chevy Chase, Army and Navy, Metropolitan (Washington). Home: 1344 30th St., N.W., Washington and St. Brandans, Paris, Va. Died Apr. 7, 1958.

LEE, Robert C(hurch), business exec.; b. Rochester, N.Y., Feb. 9, 1892; s. William Brewster and Alive (Ives) L.; A.B., Princeton, 1913; m. Nathalie Williams, Dec. 2, 1916 (div. Oct. 1941); children—Robert Church, Mary Brewster, Warren Williams; m. 2d, Oriana Stephens Newell, Apr. 4, 1944. Vice pres. Guardian Trust Co., Cleve., 1926-33; v.p., treas. White Motor Co., Cleve., 1936—; dir. White Motor Co. of Canada, Ltd., Montreal. Republican. Presbyn. Clubs: Princeton (N.Y.C.); University (Cleve.); Kirtland Country. Home: 2613 Derbyshire Rd., Cleveland Heights 6., O. Office: The White Motor Co., 842 E. 79th St., Cleve. 1. Died Mar. 10, 1951; buried Lakeview Cemetery, Cleve.

LEE, Robert H(arris), investment banker; b. Atlantic City, Mar. 30, 1904; s. Edward Sprogell and Mary Oliver (Harris) L.; student Haverford (Pa.) Coll., 1920-21; A.B., Princeton, 1924; student law sch. U. Pa., 1924-25; m. Florence Addams Fell, Apr. 3, 1934; children—Robert Harris, Joan Fell, Mary Oliver. Asso. Drexel & Co. since 1925, partner since 1942; dir. Mead Corp. Served with U.S.N., 1942-45. Mem. Phi Beta Kappa. Republican. Episcopalian. Club: Rittenhouse (Phila.). Home: Mt. Moro Rd., Villanova, Pa. Office: 1500 Walnut St., Phila. 1. Died Apr. 3, 1956; buired Laurel Hill Cemetery.

LEE, Samuel Todd, consular service; b. Leeds (Farnley), Eng., May 30, 1876; s. Thomas and Betsy (Todd) L.; came to America at 8 yrs of age; ed. pub. and high schs., Ann Arbor, Mich.; studied law U. of Va., modern langs. at La Universidad de Santo Tomás, Manila, P.I.; m. Emily Griggs Parker, of W. Rutland, Vt.; children—John Parker, Charles Todd, Thomas Bailey. Served in U.S.A. during war with Spain, and Philippine insurrection, in U.S., Cuba and P.I., 1898-1900; div. supt. pub. instrn., P.I., 1902-04; with Isthmian Canal Commn., at Ancon, Panama, 1905-06; with Dept. of State, Washington, 1906-07; Am. consul at Nogales, Mex., 1907-09, San Jose, Costa Rica, 1909-16, Rio Grande du Sul, Brazil, July 1916-June 1918, Porto Alegre, Brazil, 1918-23, Nottingham, Eng., 1923-25; consul gen. and foreign service insp., 1925-28; consul gen. at Lisbon, Portugal, 1928-31, at Rio de Janeiro, Brazil, 1931-36, retired. Home: Box 268, West Rutland, Vt. Died May 11, 1958.

LEE, Umphrey, university chancellor; b. Oakland City, Ind., Mar. 23, 1893; s. Rev. Josephus and Esther (Davis) L.; A.B., Trinity U., Tex., 1914, D.D., 1928; A.M., Southern Methodist U., Dallas, Tex., 1916; studied Columbia, and Union Theol. Sem., 1916-17, 1921-22, Columbia, 1928-29, Ph.D., 1931; Litt.D., Southwestern U., 1940, LL.D., Ohio Wesleyan U., 1942, Oklahoma City U., 1951; m. Mary Margaret Williams, Dec. 29, 1917; 1 son, Umphrey. Ordained ministry M.E. Ch., S., 1918; pastor Cisco, Tex., 1918-19; dir. Wesley Bible Chair, Austin Tex., 1919-21; pastor Ennis, Tex., 1922-23, Highland Park Meth. Ch., Dallas, 1923-36; prof. of homiletics, Sch. of Theology, Southern Meth. U., 1927-32; dean, School of Religion, Vanderbilt U., 1936-39, Drucilla Moore Buffington professor church history, 1937-39; president Southern Methodist University, 1939-54, chancellor, 1954—. Cole lecturer, Vanderbilt Univ., 1946; Quillian lecturer, Emory Univ., 1947; Alexander Gustavus Brown lectures, Randolph-Macon Coll., 1953, Willson lectr., Southwestern U. and Oklahoma City U., 1956; Willamette lecturer, Willamette U., 1956; Fondren lectr. So. Meth. University, 1957. Member General Conf. M.E. Church South, 1934; mem. Uniting Meth. Conf., 1939; mem. gen. conf. Meth. Ch., 1940, 44, 48; delegate Methodist Ecumenical Conf., 1946, 1951. President Southern University Conference, 1948. Mem. Civic Fed. of Dallas (pres. 1930-36). Mem. Mediæval Acad. of America, Wesley Historical Society (England), Am. Soc. Ch. History, Phi Beta Kappa. Clubs: Thirteen, Town and Gown (Dallas). Author: Jesus the Pioneer, 1926; Short Sketch of the Life of Christ, 1927; The Lord's Horseman—John Wesley, 1928; The Bible and Business, 1930; Historical Backgrounds of Early Methodist Enthusiasm, 1931; John Wesley and Modern Religion, 1936; The Historic Church and Modern Pacifism, 1943; Render Unto the People, 1947; A Short History of Methodism (with William Warren Sweet), 1956; Our Fathers and Us, 1958. Contbr. on religious subjects. Address: Southern Methodist University, Dallas. Died June 23, 1958.

LEE, Warren Isbell, ex-congressman; b. Bartlett, New York; s. Arthur D. and Nettie (Isbell) L.; Ph.B., Hamilton College, 1899, A.M., 1902; LL.B., New York Law School, 1901; married Mira Porter. Began practice at N.Y. City, 1901, member firm Lee, Bond, Hussey & Deitz; counsel and director Flatbush National Bank for 18 years prior to its merger; vice pres. Lamont Corporation. Mem. New York Assembly, 1906-10 and 1920; asst. dist. atty., Brooklyn, 1912-14; first dep. comptroller N.Y. State, 1915-16; of counsel to Pub. Service Commn., N.Y. City, 1917, 19; mem. 67th Congress (1921-23), 6th N.Y. Dist.; delegate to Republican State Convention various times. Trustee Hamilton Coll. (elected 4 year term). Member Delta Kappa Epsilon (past nat. pres.). Republican. Baptist. Mason (K.T., Shriner). Apptd. hon. Col. on staff of Gov., Virgin Islands, 1946. Elected Hamilton Coll. analyst for 1949. Club: Municipal. Writer and lecturer on current topics; author of History of Tau Chapter of Delta Kappa Epsilon. Collector of canes. Home: 441 Ocean Av., Bklyn. Office: 92 Liberty St., N.Y.C. Died Dec. 25, 1955; buried Greenwood Cemetery, Bklyn.

LEE, William Erwin, govt. ofcl.; b. Madison County, N.C., Jan. 27, 1882; s. Reuben Francis and Althea (West) L.; A.B., U. of Ida., 1903; studied law, U. of Wash., 1903-04; LL.B., Nat. U. Law Sch., 1906; m. Mary Madeline Shields, July 1, 1914; children—William Shields, Richard McGowan, Mary Madeliene, Flavia Ann, Charles Steele. Clerk to U.S. senators and congressmen during parts of each yr., 1904-08; admitted to Ida. bar, 1905, and began practice at Moscow; mem. firm Orland & Lee, 1913-23; asso. justice Supreme Court, Ida., 1923-26, chief justice, 1926-30; mem. Interstate Commerce Commn. 1930—, chmn., 1934. Capt., Idaho Nat. Guard, 1911-13; capt., Q.M.C., U.S. Army, 1918-19. Mem. Phi Beta Kappa, Phi Delta Theta. Republican. Elk. home: 5422 Moorland Lane, Edgemoor, Bethesda, Md. Office: Interstate Commerce Commn., Washington. Died Dec. 5, 1955; buried Arlington (Va.) Cemetery.

LEECH, (Lewis) Harper, newspaperman; b. Charlotte, Tenn., Nov. 19, 1885; s. Herbert Norvell and Margaret Morris (Harper) L.; M.A., Vanderbilt U., 1906; m. Lucille Pittman Collier (Dec. 1946); children—John Thornton, Herbert Pittman, Alfred Buckner. Reporter on Memphis Press, 1911, and in 1 year became mng. editor, continuing to 1916; Washington corr. for Scripps Newspapers, 1916-19; editor Denver Express, 1919-21; publicity sec. U.S. Railroad Labor Bd., Chicago, 1921-23; writer on economic subjects (under pen name of "Scrutator") for Chicago Tribune, 1923-28; chief editorial writer Chicago Daily Times, 1931-33; exec. editor Memphis Commercial Appeal, 1936; columnist and editorial writer Chicago Daily News since 1937. Capt. Gen. Staff Corps, cable press censorship, New York, 1918. Mem. Kappa Sigma. Democrat. Methodist. Club: Cliff Dwellers. Author: (with John C. Carroll) What's the News?, 1926; The Paradox of Plenty, 1932; Armour and His Times (with John C. Carroll), 1938; also articles for Encyclopaedia Britannica and Britannica Year Book. Home: 5410 N. Lakewood Av., Chicago 40. Office: 400 W. Madison St., Chicago. Died May 22, 1951.

LEECH, J. Russell, judge, The Tax Ct. of U.S.; b. Ebensburg, Pennsylvania, November 19, 1888; student Mercersburg Academy, 1905-07; A.B., Washington and Jefferson Coll., 1911; LL.B., U. of Pa., 1915; m. Amanda Mary Taylor; children—Mrs. Andrew R. Bird, Jr., Pamelia, Nancy T. Admitted to Pa. bar, 1915, began practice at Ebensburg; member 70th, 71st, 72d Congresses (1927-33), 20th Pa. Dist.; resigned from Congress, Jan. 1932, upon appmt. as mem. U.S. Bd. of Tax Appeals, reapptd., June 2, 1934, reapptd. June 2, 1946. Republican. Served as 2d lt. 64th Inf., U.S. Army and 7th Ammunition Train, 7th Div., AEF, World War I. Home: Curtis Court, Chevy Chase, Md. Office: 12th St. and Constitution Av., Washington. Died Feb. 2, 1952; buried Ebensburg, Pa.

LEEDS, Jules C., business exec.; b. Dec. 1, 1872; s. Lewis Levy (partner Manhattan Shirt Co.); m. Children—Robert L., Mrs. Merrill G. Weiler, Jr. Became v.p. Manhattan Shirt Co., N.Y.C., 1912, pres., dir., 1929, chmn. bd., 1949—. Served as head of men's apparel div. U.S.O. War Fund Drive, World War II. Home: Sherry Netherlands. Office: 444 Madison Av., N.Y.C. 22. Died Nov. 1952.

LEEDS, Morris Evans, mfr.; b. Phila., Mar. 6, 1869; s. Barclay R. and Mary (Maule) L.; ed. Westtown Boarding Sch., 1883-86; B.S., Haverford Coll., 1888, LL.D., 1946; studied U. of Berlin, 1892-93; Dr. of Engring., Brooklyn Polytechnic Inst., 1936; m. Hadassah J. Moore, June 10, 1926; children—Esther Hallett, Mary Maule. Pres. Leeds & Northrup Co., 1903-39; chmn. of bd. since 1939. Inventor of elec. and temperature measuring instruments. Mem. corp. and bd. mgrs. Haverford Coll. since 1909, pres., 1928-45; mem. Bd. of Public Edn. of Phila., 1931-49 (pres. 1938-48). Mem. Indsl. Adv. Bd. of NRA, 1933-35; mem. bus. adv. council Dept. of Commerce, 1933-39. Fellow Am. Inst. E.E., A.A.A.S.; mem. Am. Phys. Soc., Acad. Natural Sciences, Am. Soc. Steel Treating, Franklin Inst.; Assn. Scientific Apparatus Makers of U.S. (pres. 1920-26), Metal Mfrs. Assn. of Phila. (pres. 1924-30), Am. Philosophical Soc., Am. Acad. of Arts and Sciences, Phi Beta Kappa. Awarded Edward Longstreth medal of merit, Franklin Inst., 1920, for invention of Leeds & Northrup recorder; awarded Henry Laurence Gantt medal by Inst. of Management, "for distinguished achievement in industrial management as a service to the community," 1936, A.S.M.E. Medal by Am. Soc. Mech. Engrs., 1946, Edison Medal by Am. Inst. Elec. Engrs., 1949. Mem. Soc. of Friends. Clubs: Engineers, Univ., Philadelphia Cricket (Philadelphia); Cosmos (Washington). Co-author of "Toward Full Employment." Home: 1025 Westview St., Mt. Airy, Philadelphia 19. Office: 4901 Stenton Av., Phila. 44. Died Feb. 8, 1952; buried Friends Southwestern Burial Ground, Phila.

LEEDS, Paul, clergyman; b. Berrien County, Mich., Dec. 9, 1869; s. Alexander Brown and Susan Tabitha (Armstrong) L.; grad. high sch., Berrien Springs, Mich., 1887; m. Besse Allen, May 1, 1907. Ordained Congl. ministry, 1895; began home mission work among Creoles and Koasati Indians in Calcasieu Parish, La., and logging camps, 1893; served continuously in same field; lived in logging camps and homes of Creoles 9 yrs.; pastor, Welsh, La., 15 mos., 1906-07; now pastor at Kinder, La. Pres. Y.P.C.E. State Union, 1905-06. Recipient Rural Minister of year from La. award from Emory U., 1958. Address: Kinder, La. Died Oct. 15, 1958; buried Kinder.

LEEMING, Tom, lawyer; b. Chicago, Dec. 20, 1896; s. John and Margaret Eldridge (Sibley) L.; student St. Albans Sch., Knoxville, Ill., 1910-13, Howe (Ind.) Sch., 1913-14; A.B., U. Ill., 1919; student U. Chicago Law Sch., 1919-20; LL.B., Chicago Kent Coll. Law, 1922, LL.M., 1922; m. Dorothy Brewster, Apr. 6, 1927; children—John Brewster, Joyce. Law clk. Vose & Page, Chicago, 1920-21, Miller, Gorman, Wales & Noxon, 1922-23; admitted to Ill. bar, 1921; asso. Eckert, Peterson & Leeming since 1924, now partner; sec. and dir. The Book House for Children, Tallman, Robbins & Co., Lanteen Labs., Inc. Pres. bd. edn. Dist. 107, Lake Co., Ill., 1943-44. Served with U.S.N.R.F., World War I. Mem. Am., Ill. and Chicago bar assns., Art Inst. (life mem.), Sigma Chi, Phi Delta Phi. Clubs: Chicago Law, Illinois Athletic Association (life), Chicago Athletic Association (past pres.) (Chicago); Exmoor Country (Highland Park, Ill.). Home: 2119 Sheridan Rd., Highland Park, Ill. Office: 135 S. LaSalle St., Chgo. 3. Died June 1, 1953.

LEESMAN, Elmer Martin, lawyer; b. Chgo., Ill., Sept. 14, 1884; s. Charles and Martha E. (Von Farra) L.; grad. Northwest Division High Sch., Chgo.; LL.B., Northwestern U., 1909; m. Julie Bartholdy, Dec. 31, 1910. Admitted to Ill. bar, 1909 and began practice with Alfred W. Craven, Chgo.; mem. firm of Jordan & Leesman, 1916-17, Busch, Leesman & Roemer, 1917-23, Leesman & Roemer, 1923-27, Leesman, Roemer & Schnell, 1927-30, Leesman & Roemer, 1930-31; atty. Chgo. Title and Trust Co., 1931-40, Friedlund, Levin & Friedlund since 1949; prof. law, Northwestern U., 1927-50; now prof. emeritus. Mem. com. on character and fitness, Supreme Court of Ill., 1925-31, (chmn. of com., 1929-31). Mem. Am., Ill. State and Chgo. Bar Assns., Order of the Coif. Democrat. Author of articles in various law reviews and other periodicals. Home: 1794 Berkeley Rd., Highland Park, Ill. Office: 31 S. Clark St., Chgo. 3. Died July 26, 1959.

LEESON, Robert Ainsworth, business exec.; b. Newton, Mass., Feb. 12, 1877; s. Joseph Robert and Georgia (Harriman) L.; A.B., Harvard, 1899; m. Mildred Carruth Dix, Apr. 9, 1902 (dec.). Chmn. Universal Winding Co., Boston, Mass., 1938—; dir. New England Trust Co. Home: 390 Commonwealth Av. Office: 10 High St., Boston. Died Nov. 22, 1953.

LEETE, Frederick DeLand, bishop; b. Avon, N.Y., Oct. 1, 1866; s. Rev. Menzo Smith and Amelia (DeLand) L. (8th generation from Gov. Wm. Leete of New Haven and Conn. colonies, and Philip DeLand, French Huguenot refugee to Mass. before 1650); A.B., Syracuse U., 1889, A.M., 1891, D.D., 1903, L.H.D., 1921; grad. work, Syracuse U. and Rochester; LL.D., Albion Coll., 1912, Ohio Northern U., 1923, Southern Methodist U., Dallas, 1936; m. Jeanette Gertrude Fuller, July 28, 1891; children—Helen DeLand (Mrs. W. D. Keefer), Jeanette Fuller (Mrs. J. M. Mullin), Frederick DeLand, Jr.; married second, Zoe North Morrison, 1953. Ordained M.E. ministry, 1891; pastor Dryer Meml., Utica, N.Y., 1888-91; gen. sec. YMCA, 1891-94; pastor Little Falls, N.Y., 1894-98, Monroe Av., Rochester, 1898-1903, Univ. Ch., Syracuse, 1903-06, Central, Detroit, 1906-12; elected bishop 1912; charge, Ala., Ga., S.C., Fla., 1912-20; resident bishop, Ind., 1920, Ind. and southern Ill., 1924, Ia. and Neb., 1928-36. At various times trustee Chattanooga, Clark, DePauw and Neb. Wesleyan univs., Cornell Coll.; pres. Wesley Founds. of Ind. and Ia. univs.; pres. trustees Evansville Coll., 1924-26; mem. commn. Revision of Hymnal, 1928 to completion of new Hymnal, 1936; mem. bds. of Home and Fgn. Missions, 1912-36; pres. Ecumenical Meth. Council, Methodisms of Ams. and Orient, 1931-44; mem. bd. edn., M.E. Ch., 1924-28, 32; mem. War Bd., Bd. Bishops, 1917-18; pres. Council Benevolences, M.E. Ch., 1920-24; mem. Commn. Interdenom. Relations, 1916-24, 1928-36; chmn. Commn. Evangelism, 1932-36; mem. Commn. Central Confs., 1932-36; Ecumenical Meth. Conf., Toronto, 1911, London, 1921, Atlanta, 1931, mem. Ecumenical Meth. Council, Am. and Orient; del. to Irish Meth. Conf., 1927, Presbyn. Gen. Assembly, 1932, Meth. Protestant, 1936, Aldersgate Commemoration (Great Britain), 1938. Fellow Royal Soc. Arts (Eng.); mem. Nat. Assn. Bibl. Instrs., Nat. Inst. Social Scis., Am. Hist. Assn. (life mem.), Ind. Soc. War 1812 (charter mem.), A.A.A.S., Pi Gamma Mu, Phi Beta Kappa, Delta Kappa Epsilon, Phi Kappa Phi, S.A.R. (chaplain Fla. and Jacksonville chapters); dir. many yrs. Maxwell Fund, now N. Am. Holding Corp. Author: Every Day Evangelism, 1909; Christian Brotherhoods, 1912 (Japanese transl. by Kagawa and Uchiyama); The Church in the City, 1915; Francis Asbury, Itinerant, 1916; Christianity in Science, 1928; Palestine, Land of the Light, 1932; The Philosophy of Christian Education, 1933; Palestine, Its History, Peoples and Scenery, London, Eng., 1932; Pictures of Jesus (Lucknow), 1935; Skyward, 1936; New Testament Windows, 1939; The DeLand Family in America, 1943; The Methodist Bishops, A Bibliography and Quotations, 1948; Adventures of a Traveling Preacher, 1952. Founder The Methodist Hist. Library, Inc. Address: 1120 7th St. N., St. Petersburg, Fla. Died Feb. 16, 1958; buried Oakwood Cemetery, Syracuse, N.Y.

LEFEBVRE, Gordon, pres. and gen. mgr. Cooper-Bessemer Corp.; b. Richmond, Va., Jan. 27, 1889; s. William Clayton and Martha Harvey (Gordon) L.; student Va. Poly. Inst., 1910-13, U.S. Mil. Acad. 1907-10; m. Kathleen Clark, May 1913; children—Gordon, Kathleen. Machinist Norfolk & Western R.R., Roanoke, Virginia, 1913-15; mech. supt. E. I. duPont, Hopewell, Va., 1915-19; production engr. Chevrolet div., Gen. Motors Corp., Detroit, 1919-25, v.p. and gen. mgr. Canadian div., 1925-27, v.p. in charge operations Pontiac div., Pontiac, Mich., 1927-30; cons. engr. Detroit, 1930-37; mgr. Diesel div., Am. Locomotive Co., Auburn, N.Y., 1937-41; v.p., gen. mgr. Cooper-Bessemer Corp. 1941-Apr. 1943, pres. and gen. mgr. since 1943. Apptd. consultant Labor Div., WPB 1942; alternate chmn. Joint Canadian-Am. War Prodn. Com., 1941. Mem. Am. Soc. M.E., Soc. Naval Architects and Marine Engrs. Episcopalian. Mason. Home: New Delaware Rd., R.F.D. 5. Office: Cooper-Bessemer Corp., Mt. Vernon, O. Died June 27, 1957.

LEFFLER, George Leland, educator; b. Maryville, Mo., Jan. 11, 1899; s. Charles David and Adelaide Viola (Reeves) L.; A.B., U. of Kan., 1927; A.M., U. of Wis., 1930, Ph.D., 1931; m. Vada Morris, Sept. 8, 1932. In employ Irving-Pitt Mfg. Co., Kansas City, Mo., 1927; on research staff, U. of Wis., 1928-32, instr. economics, 1930-32; statisitician, various depts., State of Wis., 1931-32; asst. prof. finance, U. of Toledo, 1932-34, asso. prof., 1934-37; dep. county auditor, Toledo, 1935 and 1937; prof. economics, Pa. State U. and asst. dir., Pa. Bus. Survey, 1942-48, prof. finance, editor Pa. Bus. Survey, 1948—, asst. dean Coll. Bus. Adminstrn., 1956—. Served as pvt., inf., U.S. Army, 1918. Mem. Am. Economic Assn., Phi Beta Kappa, Alpha Kappa Psi, Pi Gamma Mu. Republican. Presbyn. Writer business monographs; contributing staff, Ency. Americana. Author: Industrial Trends in Pennsylvania, 1914—, 1941; The Stock Market, 2d edit., 1957; Your Bank, 1952; Using Your Bank, 1956. Home: 405 Arbor Way, State College, Pa. Died Feb. 14, 1958; buried Centre County Meml. Park, State College.

LEGGE, Barnwell R. (lĕg), army officer; b. Charleston, S.C., July 9, 1891; s. Claude Lascelles and Elizabeth Judd (Hutchinson) L.; B.S., Citadel, 1911; m. Phyllis B. Gray; 1 son, Barnwell Ingraham. Commd. 2d lt., 1916; lt. col., 1st Div., World War I, 1917-20; comdg. 1st Bn., 26th Inf.; adjt. 1st Div., Grad. Inf. Sch., 1923; Ecole Superieure de Guerre, 1925; hist. sec., Army War Coll., 1927-29; student Comd. and Gen. Staff Sch., 1929; mem. Inf. Bd., 1929-31; in comd. 3d Bn., 15th Inf., Am. Barracks, Tientsin, China, 1933-35; Army War Coll., 1936; instr. Comd. and Gen. Staff Sch., 1936-39; became U.S. mil. attaché, Bern, Switzerland, 1939. Advanced to brig. gen., May, 1942. Decorated D.S.C., D.S.M., Silver Star with 3 oak leaf clusters, Legion of Merit, Purple Heart, French Croix de Guerre with two palms, French Legion of Honor, Comdr. of Brit. Empire. Mem. Kappa Alpha (Southern). Address: American Legation, Berne, Switzerland. Died June 7, 1949.

Le GRAND, Abraham, clergyman; b. Milwaukee, Wis., Jan. 28, 1869; s. Adrian and Maria (Christiaansen) L.; prep. edn., Wayland Acad., Beaver Dam, Wis.; A.B., Brown U., 1896 (Phi Beta Kappa); studied U. of Chicago, 1905; D.D., Central Coll., Pella, Ia., 1910; m. Ella P. Chase, Nov. 3, 1897 (died Dec. 10, 1926); 1 son, Adrian James; m. 2d, Mabelle Rae McVeigh, June 2, 1928. Was ordained Baptist ministry, 1896; pastor successively at Bangor, Omro and Appleton (Wis.), Pella (Ia.), Quincy (Ill.), Central Ch., Kansas City, Mo., until 1921; exec. sec. Wis. Bapt. State Conv., 1921-39; v.p. Wayland Jr. Coll. and Acad., 1938-44; Pacific Coast rep. of Wayland Junior Coll. and Acad.; guest preacher, lectr. Declined presidency of Central College, 1910, Sious Falls Coll., 1915. Trustee Wayland U., mem. bd. dirs. Valhalla Mausoleum Assn., Milwaukee. Mem. Nat. Indian Assn. Vanguard Fellowship (Pasadena, Cal.). Mason (32°). Rotarian. Adopted into Winnebago Tribe and given name Ha-ta-sha-manigah (He who walks with the light). Home: 1019 N. Michigan Av., Pasadena, Cal. Deceased.

LEHMAN, Allan S., investment banker; b. N.Y. City, Jan. 7, 1885; s. Sigmund Mayer and Harriet (Lehman) L.; student Sachs Collegiate Inst., 1892-1902; A.B., Cornell, 1905; m. Evelyn Schiffer, Nov. 25, 1912; children—Ellen (Mrs. Richard McCluskey), Orin; m. 2d, Ann M. Roche, Aug. 3, 1948. Employe Lehman Bros., New York, 1905-08, gen. partner since 1908; dir. Gen. Realty & Utilities Corp., New York, The Studebaker Corp., South Bend, Ind., Southern States Land & Timber Corp., New Orleans, The Lehman Corp., New York. Served as 1st lt. motor transport corps, U.S. Army, 1918. Clubs: Cornell University, Harmonie, Sands Point Golf. Home: Picket Farm, Jericho Turnpike, Westbury, L.I. Office: 1 William St., N.Y.C. 4. Died Nov. 8, 1952.

LEHMAN, Edwin Partridge, surgeon; b. Germantown, Pa., June 9, 1888; s. Benjamin N. and Emily (Partridge) L.; B.A., Williams, 1910; M.D., Harvard, 1914, John Harvard fellow, 1913-14; m. Margaret Maxwell, Oct. 1, 1921; children—Richard, Lois Ann. Surgical house officer, Peter Bent Brigham Hosp., Boston, 1914-15; asst. resident surgeon, Barnes Hosp., St. Louis, Mo., 1915-16; asst. in surgery, Washington U. Sch. of Medicine, St. Louis, 1916-20, instr. in surgery, 1920-21, instr. clin. surgery, 1921-26, asst. prof., 1926-27, asso. prof., 1927-28, also in charge of lab. of surg. pathology, 1916-17; resident surgeon, Barnes Hosp., 1919-20, asst. surgeon, 1922-28; asst. surgeon St. Louis Children's Hosp., 1924-28, St. Louis Jewish Hosp., 1927-28; cons. surgeon, St. Louis Maternity Hosp., 1927-28; surgeon, St. Louis City Hosp., 1920-27 (chief surgeon Unit No. 1, 1926-27); surgeon to out-patients, Washington U. Dispensary, 1920-28; prof. surgery and gynecology, dir. dept., U. of Virginia, 1928-50, prof. surgery, dir. dept. since 1950; chief surgeon and gynecologist U. Va. Hosp., 1928-50, chief surgeon since 1950. Maj. G. Seelig lecturer, Washington U., St. Louis, 1949; William J. Mayo lecturer Univ. Mich., 1951. First lt. M.C., B.E.F., 1917-19. Dir. Virginia Cancer Foundn., 1940-44; dir. Am. Cancer Soc. (v.p. 1944-45, pres. 1947-48). Certified mem. founders' group Am. Board Surgery. Fellow American Surgical Association (vice president 1946), Southern Surg. Assn. (v.p. 1936, pres. 1948), Internat. Surg. Soc., A.C.S. (chmn. cancer com.), Soc. Univ. Surgeons (hon.), American Association for the Surgery of Trauma; member A.M.A., Southern Medical Association (vice chairman sect. on surgery 1931, chairman, 1933; vice chmn. Section on Med. Edn., 1943, chmn. 1944), St. Louis Assn. of Surgeons, St. Louis Med. Soc. (hon.). Pres. Charlottesville and Albemarle Community and War Fund, 1943 and 1944. Phi Beta Kappa, Alpha Omega Alpha, Sigma Xi. Contbr. to med. publs., author various monographs, articles covering lab. investigation, clinical observation, etc. Address: U. of Virginia, Charlottesville, Va. Died May 27, 1954.

LEHMAN, Linwood, univ. prof.; b. Suffolk, Va., Mar. 9, 1895; s. Nathan and Henrietta (Bottigheimer) L.; A.B., Univ. Va., 1915, A.M., 1917, Ph.D., 1920. Instr. in Latin, Univ. Va., 1915-20, asst. prof., 1920-26, asso. prof., 1926-30, prof. of Latin since 1930. Mem. Am. Philol. Assn., Va. Classical Assn., Photographic Soc. of Am., Phi Beta Kappa, Raven Soc., Zeta Beta Tau. Democrat. Reformed Jewish. Club: Colonnade (mem. bd. govs., 1927-29). Author: Quantitative Implications of the Pbyrrhic Stress, 1920. Editor: Un jeune homme presse, 1923; Correspondence between Thomas Jefferson and Pierre Samuel du Pont (with Dumas Malone), 1930. Contbr. articles in learned publs. Specializes. in classical prosody, vulgar Latin. Exhibitor in various nat. and internat. salons. Home: "Lehmanor," Minor Rd., Charlottesville, Va. Died Jan. 22, 1953.

LEHNERTS, Edward M., educator; b. Winona, Minn., Mar. 29, 1873; B.S., U. Pa., 1902; A.M., U. Minn., 1908; m. Wilhelmina H. Busch, 1908; 1 dau. Frances. Instr. geography Minn. State Normal Sch., Winona, 1896-98, prof. 1898-1907, asst. prof. geography, geology, 1907-18; instr. geography, geology Columbia U., 1917-22, geography Tchrs. Coll. Columbia, 1918-24; asso. prof. natural scis. Hunter Coll., 1920-21, founder, head dept. geology and geography, asso. prof., 1921-29, prof., 1929-42, prof. emeritus. Presented with Lehnerts Rock Garden as living meml. by faculty and student Hunter Coll., 1940. Dir. Am. Bur. Geography. Co-founder and editor Journal Geography, 1902-05. Founder and editor Bull. of Am. Bur. Geography, Physical and economic geography of the Upper Mississippi Valley, Geography of Minnesota, Physical and Commercial Geography, The Teaching of Geography, Geology of Northern New York. Address: Hunter College, 695 Park Av., N.Y.C. Died Dec. 21, 1953.

LEHR, John Camillus (lâr), former U.S. dist. atty.; b. Monroe, Mich., Nov. 18, 1878; s. Adam and Catherine (McCadden) L.; LL.B., U. Mich.; 1900; m. Anna F. Ryan, Apr. 17, 1907; children—Mary Virginia, Marjorie Catherine, John Camillus, Thomas Adam, James Thornton, Jeanne Rosemary. In practice of law at Monroe, 1900—. Circuit Ct. commr., Monroe County, 5 times; city atty., Monroe, 3 terms; former mem. Bd. of Edn. (10 yrs.) and Port Commn. of Monroe; mem. 73d Congress 2d Mich. Dist.; U.S. atty. Eastern Dist. of Mich. at Detroit, 1936-47. Pres. The Maccabees. Mem. Am., Mich., Monroe County bar assns. Democrat. Catholic. Mem. K.C. (former dist. dep.), Maccabees (Great Comdr. Mich. trustee). Former editor Mich. Hibernian. Home: 621 S. Monroe St. Office: 204 Maccabees Bldg., Detroit. Died Feb. 1958.

LEIDING, Harriette Kershaw (Mrs. Herman G. Leiding), writer; b. Sewanee, Tenn., June 1878; d. John and Susan (De Saussure) Kershaw; m. Herman G. Leiding, June 18, 1902; children—Joseph B. Kershaw, Richard B. Grant, Catharine (Mrs. Oswald L. Keller), Caroline, Jane Leiding—all relatives, adopted. Was state chmn. health and recreation, Council Def., S.C., during the World War; also chmn. publicity, Charleston chpt. A.R.C. for S.C.; 1st chmn. War Work of Charleston YWCA; dist. chmn. Serbian Relief; state chmn. Com. on Protection of Women Under Internat. Law; sec., treas. Charleston County br. Unemployment Com.; mem. Hist. Commn. Charleston, 1933-34; mem. Publicity Com., NRA drive; mem. Charleston Br. League Nations Assn., S.C. Hist. Assn. Mem. Gibbes Art Gallery, Charleston; hon. mem. Spanish-Am. War Vets. Democrat. Episcopalian. Clubs: Civic (past pres.), Tuesday (v.p.), Pen, Sketch. Author: Street Cries of a Southern City, 1911; A Walk Around Ye Old Historic Charleston, 1912; Historic Houses of South Carolina, 1921; Charleston Historic and Romantic, 1931; Folklore (play). Lectr. ednl., hist. and other subjects. Contbr. newspapers. Home: 10 Murray Boul., Charleston, S.C. Died Mar. 20, 1948; buried Magnolia Cemetery, Charleston.

LEIGH, Randolph (lē), author; b. Memphis, Tenn., Sept. 21, 1891; s. A. C. and Lura (Jones) L.; A.B., U. of the South, 1913; A.M., Columbia U., 1915; m. Lucy Helm Tillman, Nov. 30, 1915; children—Randolph, Armistead Claiborne III; m. 2d, Frida T. Frazer, Oct. 24, 1932; m. 3d, Marcelle Gervais, Aug. 26, 1948 (died November 1, 1953); one son, Richard. Publisher of the Cheyenne (Wyoming) State Leader and Sheridan (Wyo.) Enterprise, 1916-20; editorial writer Los Angeles Times, 1920-23; organizer Calif. Oratorical Contest, 1923; organizer, 1924, and later dir. gen. Oratorical Contest (later Internat. Oratorical Contest); organizer, 1925, and later dir. Nat. Intercollegiate Oratorical Contest. Served as lt. col. A.U.S., overseas in European Theatre of Operations as army historian, 3 yrs., World War II; now col. Mil. Intelligence Res. U.S. Army. Mem. Phi Beta Kappa, Kappa Alpha. Author: The Citadel of Freedom, 1924; Oratory, 1927; The Constitution in 1787 and Today, 1931; Conscript Europe, 1938; Forgotten Waters, 1941. Organized Randolph Leigh Expdn. to the Gulf of Calif., 1940-41. Wrote "American Enterprise in Europe" for U.S. Army Historical Sect. also 48,000,000 Tons to Eisenhower, 1945. Home: Fairfax County, McLean, Va. Died Nov. 1, 1953; buried Arlington (Va.) Cemetery.

LEIGH, William Robinson, artist, author; b. Falling Waters, W.Va., Sept. 23, 1866; s. William (USN) and Mary W. (Colston) L.; ed. pvt. tutor; studied art Md. Inst., Balt., under Hugh Newell, 1880-83, Royal Acad., Munich, under Raupp, 1883-84, Gysis, 1885-86, Von Loefftz, 1887, Von Lindenschmit, 1891-92; m. Anna Seng, 1898; 1 son, William Colston; m. 2d, Ethel Traphagen, June 4, 1921. Painted in Europe six cycloramas, including Battle of Waterloo, Bay of Naples, and Crucifixion of Christ, 1890-95; returned to U.S. 1895; works: three portraits for Washington & Lee U., Va.; The Poisoned Pool, Jones collection; The Great Spirit, Todd Gallery; Custer's Last Fight, The Lookout, Navaho Fire Dance, Pocahontas, Visions of Yesterday, Westward Ho!, Frank Phillips' Woolaroc Mus., Bartlesville, Okla.; Grand Canyon, Newark Mus.; Panning Gold, Buffalo Bill Mus., Cody, Wyo.; Stampede and Boomerang Throwers, Heckscher Art Mus., Huntington, L.I., N.Y.; Maya Historian, Heckscher Found., N.Y.C.; Writing the Epitaph, Dept. of External Affairs, Iveagh House, Dublin, Ireland; Argument With the Sheriff, Roundup, Bear Hunt in Wyoming, Up Where the Big Winds Blow, Portrait of an Indian Chief, Indian Sports, and Buffalo Mother, Thomas Gilcrease Inst. of Am. History and Art, Tulsa; Ready and Waiting and Struggle for Existence, IBM Corp. collection; The Roping, C. R. Smith collection, N.Y.C.; Double Crosser, Joslyn Art Mus., Omaha, Neb.; Buffalo Drive, Dr. C. Campbell Stiles, Short Hills, N.J.; The Master Hand, Huntington Hartford, N.Y.C.; Buffalo Hunt and bronze sculpture of Am. Buffalo, Stanford U., Palo Alto, Cal. as gift of Alfred E. Clegg, San Francisco; Sanctity of Motherhood, State of Conn. Connor Found.; Home Sweet Home, Best in the Bunch, Water Pockets, Hopi Courtship, and The Mystic, Jack Frye, Ft. Worth; Land of His Fathers, Dr. A. D. Pierce, Greenfield, Mass.; Grand Canyon, Cliff Dwellers, Italian Boy, Harold McCracken, Douglaston, L.I., N.Y.; Gorilla Sanctuary, owned by His Majesty, the late King Albert of Belgium; Navaho Pony, owned by H.R.H. Duke of Windsor; Midnight Ride of Paul Revere, used in fund raising drive to restore Old North Church Steeple, 1954; mag. illustrations, portraits, landscapes, figure and animal compositions; mem. Carl Akeley expdn. to central Africa, 1926-27, Carlisle-Clark expdn. to East Africa, 1928, both for Am. Mus. Natural History, N.Y.C.; master painter of backgrounds for animal groups in Akeley African Hall of Am. Mus. Natural History, 1932-35. Nat. Academician; pre-eminently distinguished for paintings of Am. S.W.; designated America's Sagebrush Rembrandt in article in Collier's Mag., Nov. 11, 1950. Recipient bronze medals, Royal Acad., Munich, 1884, 85, 86, 87, silver medals, 1891, 92; hon. mention, Paris Salon, 1892; first medal Appalachian Expn., Knoxville, Tenn., 1911; N.Y.C. Fedn. Women's Clubs award, 1950-51; Kappa Pi nat. art frat. citation, 1951; Benjamin West Clinedinst medal for outstanding achievement in fine arts, 1953; 60th Anniversary, cyclorama Einsiedeln, Switzerland citation, 1953; alumni honor medal, Md. Inst., Balt., 1954; Nat. Life Conservation Soc. award, 1954; Hudson Valley Art Assn. gold medal of honor awarded posthumously 1955 for painting Sanctity of Motherhood. Mem. N.A.D., Allied Artists of Am. (a founder), Authors League, Art Students League (instr.), Am. Artists Profl. League, Am. Watercolor Soc., Grand Central Art Galleries. Clubs: Salmagundi, Adventurers. Author: Clipt Wings, 1930; The Western Pony, 1933, Frontiers of Enchantment, 1938; short stories for magazines. Invented artists' campstool (patented 1918). Studio: 200 W. 57th St. Office: 1680 Broadway, N.Y.C. 19. Died Mar. 11, 1955; buried Oak Hill Cemetery, Nyack, N.Y.

LEIGHTON, Joseph Alexander, educator; b. Orangeville, Ont., Can., Dec. 2, 1870; s. James and Jane (Speers) L.; A.B. (Gov. Gen.'s medal), Trinity Coll., Toronto, 1891; Ph.D., Cornell, 1894; S.T.B., Episcopal Theol. Sem., Cambridge, Mass., 1896; univs. of Tubingen, Berlin and Erlangen, 1896-97; LL.D., Hobart Coll., 1913; Ohio State U., 1948; m. Victoria Elizabeth Paul, Apr. 4, 1899 (died Nov. 11, 1931); children—Paul Alexander, Reginald Frederick (died March 5, 1946); m. 2d, Helen Gager Brown, Nov. 23, 1932. Prof. philosophy and chaplain, Hobart Coll., Geneva, N.Y., 1897-1910; prof. philosophy, head dept., Ohio State U., 1910-41, emeritus; acting prof. philosophy, Stanford U., 1925; vis. prof., U. Cal., 1928, 37, U. So. Cal., 1928-29, U. Utah, 1932. Univ. preacher, Cornell, 1900, 02, 05, 07. Fellow A.A.A.S.; mem. Phi Beta Kappa, Am. Psychol. Assn., Am. Philos. Assn. (pres. Western Div., 1937-38). Chmn. com. univ. govt. Am. Assn. U. Profs.; mem. program com. Internat. Congress Philosophy, 1926. Author: Typical Modern Conceptions of God, 1902; What Is Personality?, 1903; Jesus Christ and the Civilization of Today, 1907; The Field of Philosophy, 1918, 5th edit., 1939; Educational Problems in Colleges and Universities (in collaboration), 1921; Man and the Cosmos. 1922; Religion and the Mind of Today, 1924; The Individual and the Social Order, 1926; Individuality and Education, 1928; Social Philosophies in Conflict, 1937; The Diversities of Cultures and the Unity of Mankind, 1949; also numerous articles on philosophy, religion, edn. and ethics. Contbr. Philosophical Essays in Honor of J. E. Creighton, 1917; Kant Bi-Centenary Vol., 1925; Contemporary American Philosophy, 1930; Contemporary Idealism in America, 1932. Home: 817 Oxford St., Worthington, O. Died June 17, 1954.

LEIGHTON, Kathryn Woodman (Mrs. Edward Everett Leighton), artist; b. Plainfield, N.H., Mar. 17, 1876; d. Alfred and Maria Thomas (Gallup) Woodman; grad. Kimball Union Acad., Meriden, N. H., 1895; grad. Mass. Normal Art Sch.; m. Edward Everett Leighton, Dec. 19, 1900; 1 son, Everett Woodman. Painter of Am. Indians, especially Blackfeet of Mont.; paintings exhibited in galleries throughout U.S. and in London and Paris. Mem. Profl. Artists League of Am., Cal. Art Club (dir.), D.A.R. Republican. Baptist. Clubs: Friday Morning (Los Angeles); Fine Arts (San Diego). Home: 1633 W. 46th St., Los Angeles. Died July 1, 1952.

LEIGHTON, Marshall Ora, engineer; b. Corinna, Me.; s. Llewellyn Morse and Annie Hinkley (Stone) L.; B.S., Mass. Inst. Tech.; m. Maud Augusta Hawkins, of Portland, Me. Resident hydrographer, 1902, chief div. hydro-economics, 1903-06, chief hydrographer, 1906-13, U.S. Geol. Survey; practiced as consulting engr. since 1913. Advisory hydrographer, U.S. Inland Waterways Commn., 1907-09, in which capacity he rendered report on flood control by reservoirs, pioneering present flood control program of U.S.; mem. Northern N.J. Flood Commn., 1903-04, Passaic River Dist. Flood Commn. (N.J.), 1905-06, Florida Everglades Engrg. Commn., 1913; chmn. Nat. Service Com. Engring. Council, 1915-20; pres. Nat. Public Work Dept. Assn., 1920-21; organized U.S. hydrographic surveys in Hawaii, 1909; explorations, Mexico and Andes of S.A., for hydro-electric power, 1923-24; v.p. and chief engr., E. Tennessee Development Co., 1925-27; dep. chief pub. works, Washington Met. Dist. Civilian Defense, 1941-43. Life mem. Am. Soc. C.E. Clubs: Metropolitan, Chevy Chase. Author: U.S. Govt. reports, treating of water supplies and water power, and numerous articles, essays and addresses. Home: Cape Elizabeth, Me.

Office: 910-17th St., N.W., Washington. Died Aug. 29, 1958.

LEINDECKER, John Philip, business exec.; b. Keokuk, Ia., 1889. Chmn. bd., dir. Western Tablet and Stationery Corp. Mason (Shriner). Home: 301 Volusia Av., Dayton 9. Office: Hulman Bldg., Dayton 2, Ohio. Died Aug. 15, 1958.

LEINEN, Raymond F., banker; b. Rochester, N. Y., May 26, 1890; s. Joseph Peter and Elizabeth A. (Schueler) L.; m. Frances Connor, Oct. 15, 1914. With Lincoln Rochester (N.Y.) Trust Co., 1905—, exec. v.p., 1930—; dir. Curtice Bros. Co., Stecher-Traung Lithograph Corp., Dollinger Corp., Rochester Button Co., Haloid Co., Buffalo branch Fed. Res. Bk. of N.Y., Bausch & Lomb Optical Co. Mem. Catholic Courier, Rochester Community Chest, Rochester Conv. and Publicity Bur. Roman Catholic. Clubs: Rochester, Genesee Valley, Oak Hill Country (Rochester, N.Y.). Home: 430 Yarmouth Rd. ,Rochester 10. Office: 183 Main St. E., Rochester 3, N.Y. Died Mar. 29, 1951.

LEISENRING, Edward Barnes (lī'sĕn-rĭng), coal operator; b. Nice, France, Jan. 12, 1895; s. Edward Barnes and Annie (Wickham) L.; brought to U.S., 1895; ed. Hotchkiss Sch., Lakeville, Conn.; B.S., Yale, 1917; m. Margaret Patterson Pierce, May 26, 1917; children—Ann Wickham, Mary Pierce, Carolyn Bertsch, Edward Barnes. Associated with engring. corps, Hazle Brook Coal Co., and became mine supt., v.p., 1923-26, pres., 1926-28; chmn. bd. Stonega Coke & Coal Co.; pres. Westmoreland Coal Co., Wentz Corp., Va. Coal & Iron Co.; v.p. Gen. Coal Co.; bd. mgrs. Lehigh Coal & Navigation Co.; mem. bd. of dirs. Whitehall Cement Mfg. Co., Girard Trustee Company, Western Saving Fund Soc. of Phila., Ins. Co. of N. Am. Seaman, 2d class, U.S.N.R.F., later ensign and lt. j.g., 1917-19. Mem. Delta Psi. Republican. Clubs: Philadelphia, Racquet (Philadelphia); Gulph Mills Golf; Merion Cricket; Radnor Hunt. Home: 320 Fishers Rd., Bryn Mawr, Pa. Office: Fidelity-Philadelphia Trust Bldg., Phila. Died June 16, 1952.

LEISERSON, William Morris (lī'sēr-sŭn), economist; born Esthonia, Apr. 15, 1883; son Mendel and Sarah (Snyder) L.; brought to United States, 1890; B.A., Univ. of Wis., 1908; Ph.D., Columbia, 1911; LL.D., Oberlin, 1947; m. Emily Nash Bodman, June 22, 1912; children—Avery, Lee, Sarah Eleanor (Mrs. David M. LaMar), Ruth Bodman (Mrs. Albert G. Sims), Charles Frederick (naval aviator, dec. Sept. 20, 1943), Mark Whittlesey, Philip Day. Expert on unemployment, New York Commn. on Employers' Liability and Unemployment, 1909-11; deputy industrial commr. Wis., 1911-14; asst. dir. research of the U.S. Commn. on Industrial Relations, 1914-1915; prof. economics and polit. science, Toledo U., 1915-18; chief of the division of labor administration, U.S. Dept. of Labor, 1918-19; chmn. Labor Adjustment Bd., clothing industry, of Rochester, N.Y., 1919-21; chmn. Bd. of Arbitration, men's clothing industry, of New York, 1921-23, Baltimore and Chicago, 1923-26; prof. economics, Antioch Coll., 1925-34. Secretary National Labor Board of NRA, 1933; chairman Petroleum Labor Policy Board, 1934; chairman National Mediation Board, 1934-39; member National Labor Relations Bd., 1939-43; chmn. Nat. Mediation Bd., 1943-44. Visiting prof. Johns Hopkins Univ., 1944-47; dir. labor organization study, 1947-49; mem. Pres.'s Commn. on Migratory Labor, 1950-51; labor relations consultant and arbitrator since 1951. Member American Econ. Assn., American Political Sci. Assn., Soc. for Public Adminstrn., Indsl. Relations Research Assn., Phi Beta Kappa. Club: Cosmos. Author: Unemployment in the State of New York, 1911; Adjusting Immigrant and Industry, 1924: Right and Wrong in Labor Relations, 1938; American Trade Union Democracy, 1959; and articles in various periodicals. Home: 3210 34th St. N.W., Washington; (summer) Salem, Conn. Office: 1129 Vermont Av. N.W., Washington. Died Feb. 12, 1957; buried family cemetery Moss Wood Glen, Salem.

LEITCH, Mary Sinton (lēch), author; b. N.Y. City, Sept. 8, 1876; d. Charlton Thomas and Nancy Dunlap (McKeen) Lewis; prep. edn., Miss Dana's Sch. (Morristown, N.J.) and Ossining (N.Y.) Sch.; student Smith Coll., 1894, 95, also in France and Germany; spl. courses, Columbia, 1898, 99; m. John David Leitch, steamship broker, Oct. 17, 1907; children—Charlton Lewis, Barbara McKeen, John David. Formerly insp. women's prisons, N.Y. State; asst. editor Historians, History of the World, 1904; traveled to different parts of world in sailing ships and tramp steamers, to study languages and customs of various nationalities; contbr. to Harper's Monthly, New York Herald, New York Evening Post, etc.; chmn. com. for securing Juvenile Court, Norfolk, Va., 1914-15. Mem. Poetry Soc. Am., Poetry Soc. of Va. (pres. 1933; co-pres. 1944, 45), Norfolk Poet's Club, Phi Beta Kappa. Asso. editor "The Lyric," 1927. Dem. Presbyterian. Author: The Wagon and the Star (verse), 1922; The Unrisen Morrow (verse), 1926; The Coming of the Cross (hist. pageant), 1927; The Black Moon (drama), 1929; Spider Architect (verse), 1937; From Invisible Mountains (verse), 1943. Translator: The Love Letters of Bismarck, 1901; Himself and I (Memoirs), 1950; Nightingale on the Moon, 1952. Editor: Lyric Va. Today (an anthology of verse). Home: "Wycherley," Lynnhaven. Bayside P. O., Va. Died Aug. 20, 1954; buried Old Donation Church, Bayside, Va.

LEITH, Charles Kenneth (lēth), geologist; b. Trempealeau, Wis., Jan. 20, 1875; s. Charles A. and Martha E. (Gale) L.; B.S., U. of Wis., 1897, Ph.D., 1901, LL.D., 1956; LL.D., Kenyon Coll., 1926; D.Sc., Lawrence Coll., Appleton, Wis., 1930, Columbia U., 1940, Stevens Institute of Technology, 1943; m. Mary E. Mayers, January 6, 1898; children—Kenneth, Andrew. Asst. geologist, U.S. Geol. Survey, 1900-05; asst. prof. geology, U. of Wis., 1902-03, prof. 1903-45. Professorial lecturer pre-Cambrian geology, U. of Chicago, 1905-17. Mineral adviser to Shipping and War Industries bds., Washington, 1918, to Am. Commn. to Negotiate Peace, Paris, 1919. Chmn. The Mineral Inquiry, 1929-38; leader of round tables on mineral resources, Institute of Politics, Williamstown, Mass., 1925 and 1926, British Institute of International Affairs, London, 1926, Inst. of Internat. Relations, Portland, Ore., 1932, Council on Foreign Relations, New York, 1933; mem. Science Advisory Bd., 1933-35; mem. Business Adv. and Planning Council for Dept. of Commerce, 1933-40; v. chmn. Planning Com. for Mineral Policy, 1934-37; chmn. Mineral Adv. Com. Army and Navy Munitions Bd., 1928-40; consultant on minerals, Nat. Def. Commn., O.P.M.; W.P.B. 1940-45. Chief Metals and Minerals Br., off. Prod. Research and Developmt. of W.P.B., 1942-45. Cons. Security Resources Bd., 1948-50, Research and Development Bd., since 1948. Atomic Energy Commn., since 1945. Hon. mem. Geol. Soc. of London. Fellow American Acad. Arts and Sciences, Geol. Soc. America (v.p. 1927; pres. 1933; Penrose medalist 1942); mem. Am. Inst. Mining and Metall. Engrs., A.A.A.S. (v.p. 1920), Wis. Acad. Sciences, Arts and Letters, Wis. Hist. Soc., Nat. Acad. of Sciences, Am. Philos. Soc., Soc. of Economic Geologists (president 1925), Mining and Metall. Soc. of America, Canadian Mining Inst., British Inst. of Mining and Metall. (hon.). Clubs: Cosmos, Chevy Chase (Washington); University (New York); University, Madison (Wis.). Author of books and articles on pre-Cambrian metamorphic, structural, economic geology, and on world minerals in their internat. relations. Latest book "World Minerals and World Peace," 1943. Asso. editor Journal of Geology and Economic Geology. Home: Sheraton Park Hotel, Washington 8. Died Sept. 13, 1956; buried Madison, Wis.

LEITZELL, Charles Wilson, clergyman; b. Churchville, Pa., Feb. 12, 1870; s. Daniel W. and Anna Amelia (Love) L.; ed. Edinburgh (Pa.) State Normal Sch., Susquehanna U.; A.B., Gettysburg Coll., 1893; A.M., Lutheran Theol. Sem., Gettysburg, 1896; D.D., Hartwick (N.Y.) Sem., 1913, LL.D., 1943; m. Mary C. Mumper, Mar. 2, 1895; children—Madalyn Love, Helen Ormsby (Mrs. G. Franklin Mosher), Walter Edgar, Ralph Newton. Entered Luth. ministry, 1895; pastor successively at Murphysboro, Ill., Newton, Ia., and Johnstown and Albany, N.Y., until 1920; sec. Luth. Y.P. Soc. Christian Endeavor 6 yrs.; pres. Synod of N.Y., United Luth. Ch. in America, 1920—; pres. Hartwick Coll., Oneonta, N.Y., 1929—. Chaplain N.Y. State Assembly, 1914-18. In charge N.Y. State for Nat. Commn. United Luth. Ch., World War; speaker for Red Cross, Liberty Loan campaigns, etc. Trustee Hartwick Sem., 1914-27, pres. bd., 1927-30. Mem. Phi Delta Theta. Republican. Mason; Grand Chaplain Grand Lodge of N.Y., 1918-19. Home: Oneonta, N.Y. Died Apr. 24, 1950.

LeLONG, Lucien, couturier, cosmetician; b. Paris, France, Oct. 11, 1889; s. Arthur and Valentine (Lambelet) LeL.; student Hautes Etudes Commerciales, 1911-13; m. Nelle Audey, 1919; 1 dau., Nicole; married second Princesse Nathlale Paley; married third, Sanda Dancovici; 1 dau., Christine. Established Maison Lucien LeLong, courture, 1919, Societe des Parfums Lucien LeLong, 1924. Decorated Knight Legion of Honor (France), 1926. Hon. pres. Chambre Syndicale de la Couture Parisienne. Mem. Paris C. of C. Roman Catholic. Address: Domaine de Courbois Angelet, Biarritz, Basses Pyrénées, France. Died May 11, 1958; buried Cemetery of Anglet, Basses, Pyrenees.

LELY, Nicholas George, fgn. diplomat; b. Athens, Greece, July 23, 1887; s. George and Antiope (Tambacopoulo) L.; grad. U. Athens Law Sch., 1916. Began diplomatic career, 1917; attaché Greek Legation, Rome, 1918; vice consul, Alexandria, 1919, acting consul gen., 1920; charge d' affairs, Cairo, 1921, sec. Legation, 1922; sec. Ministry Fgn. Affairs, Athens, 1923; sec. Greek Legation, Berlin, 1924, Belgrade, 1925, Prague, 1925, Berlin, 1926; chief div. in Ministry Fgn. Affairs, Athens, 1926; gov. Mt. Athos, Greece, 1927-29; again chief div. in Ministry of Fgn. Affairs, Athens, 1930; acting consul gen., Greece, London, 1930-31; 1st sec. Greek Legation, Washington, 1931-35, counselor, 1935-38, consul gen., N.Y.C., 1938-44; Greek Minister of Information in U.S., 1944—. Decorated Silver Cross of the Redeemer, Gold Cross of Valor, Comdr. Order of Phoenix (Greece); Gold Cross of Holy Sepulchre (Jerusalem); Comdr. of the Nile (Egypt). Author: Epinikion or Victorial Poems a book of poetry translated in English by Joseph Auslander. Home: Ritz Carlton Hotel. Office: R.C.A. Bldg., 30 Rockefeller Plaza, N.Y.C. Died Aug. 1958.

LEMAN, Beaudry, banker; b. Montreal, P.Q., Can., Jan. 2, 1878; s. Dr. Joseph and Polyxene (Beaudry) L.; B.S., U. of Lille, France, 1899; C.E., McGill U., 1900; D.C.S., U. of Montreal, 1934; m. Caroline Beique, May 12, 1908; children—Line (Mrs. Paul LaRoque), Jean, Paul, Andre. Resident engr. Shawinigan Water & Power Co., Shawinigan Falls, P.Q., 1900-07; cons. engr. City of Montreal underground elec. conduits and for several hydro-electric power developments, 1907-12; with Banque Canadienne Nationale, Montreal, since 1912, gen. mgr., 1914-33, v.p., 1933-34, pres., 1934-47, chmn. bd. since 1947; v.p. Gen. Trust of Can. since 1931; dir. Consol. Bakeries of Can., Montreal Tramways Co., Napierville Junction Ry. Co., Ogilvie Flour Mills Co., Shawinigan Water & Power Co. Trustee Sch. of Higher Comml. Studies. Mem. French Legion of Honor. Roman Catholic. Clubs: Montreal, Mount Royal, Cercle Universitaire (Montreal); Laval-sur-le-Lac, Segniory (Montebello); Rideau (Ottawa). Home: 597 St. Catherine Rd., Outremont, Montreal. Office: 112 St. James St., Montreal 1, P.Q., Can. Died Apr. 9, 1951.

LEMKE, William (lĕm'kē), congressman; b. Albany, Minn., Aug. 13, 1878; s. Fred and Julia (Kleir) L.; B.A., U. of N.D., 1902; studied law, U. of N.D. and Georgetown Law Sch.; LL.B., Yale, 1905; m. Isabelle McIntyre, Apr. 16, 1910; children—William, Robert, Mary. Began practice at Fargo, 1905; mem. nat. exec. com. Nat. Non-Partisan League, 1917-21; chmn. Rep. State Com., 1916-20; atty. gen. of N.D., 1921-23; mem. 73d to 76th Congresses, N.D. at large; mem. 78th to 81st Congresses, N.D. at large. Union Party candidate for President, 1936. Author Frazier-Lemke Re-Finance Bill, Frazier-Lemke Moratorium. Had charge of preparing laws establishing indsl. program of N.D. Mem. Phi Delta Theta, Eugene Field Soc. Author: You and Your Money. Home: 1222 9th St., South, Fargo, N.D. Died May 30, 1950.

LEMKIN, Raphael, lawyer; b. Bezwodne, Poland, June 24, 1900; s. Joseph and Bella (Pomeranz) L.; student Gymnasium in Bialystok, Poland; LL.D. (J. D.), U. Lwow, Poland, Sec. Court of Appeals, Warsaw, Poland, 1926-29, pub. prosecutor, 1929-34; prof. law Tachkemoni Coll., 1927-39; gen. practice law, Warsaw, 1934-39; lectr. U. Stockholm, 1940-41, Duke U., 1941-42; chief consultant Bd. Econ. Warfare and Fgn. Econ. Adminstrn., Washington, 1942-44, adviser on fgn. affairs, Dept. of War, 1945-47; mem. prosecution staff, U.S. Army as chief prosecutor Axis Criminality in Neuremberg, 1945-46; prof. law, Yale, 1948—. A founder World Movement to Outlaw Genocide (coined the word genocide and transformed it into internat. treaty); prin. adviser to U.N. on genocide conv. Mem. Am. Soc. Internat. Law. Jewish religion. Address: Yale University Law School, New Haven. Died Aug. 28, 1959.

LEMMEL, William Hugo (lĕm-mĕl'), supt. of schs.; b. Hope, Mo., Nov. 15, 1896; s. John and Emma (Ulrich) L.; B.Ped., Mo. State Teachers Coll., Cape Girardeau, 1916; A.B., U. of Ia., 1922, A.M., 1928; Ed.D., Teachers Coll., Columbia, 1940; m. Pansy King, Dec. 31, 1917; 1 son, Charles Rex. Supt. of schs. and teacher Ellsinore, Mo., 1917-18, Birmingham, Ia., 1918-19, Morning Sun, Ia., 1919-21; supt. schs., New London, Ia., 1921-24, Caruthersville, Mo., 1924-28, Flat River, Mo., 1928-36, Quincy, Ill., 1936-38, Highland Park, Mich., 1938-42, Wilmington, Del., 1942-46, Baltimore, Md., since 1946. Former Mo. County Red Cross Chmn., relief and reconstrn. bd. chmn., 1932-36. Recipient honor as citizen of Wilmington, Del. for outstanding service in "fortifying democracy," 1946. Mem. N.E.A. (mem. ethics com.), Commn. for Internat. Ednl. Reconstrn., Am. Assn. Sch. Adminstrs., Am. Soc. for Control of Cancer, Horace Mann League (mem. bd. dirs.), Army Adv. Com., Md. State Teachers Assn., Md. Soc. for Mental Hygiene, Md. Tuberculosis Assn., Baltimore Safety Council; Phi Delta Kappa. Independent. Presbyterian. Club: Rotary. Author: Development of Administrative and Non-Teaching Salary Schedules in Highland Park, Mich., 1942; How to Get Better Teachers for Our Schools, Town Meeting, 1946; contbg. author: Suggested School Health Policies, 1946. Mem. adv. com. School Executive mag. since 1945; mem. bd. consultants, Educator's Washington Dispatch, since 1947. Home: Ambassador Apts. Office: 3 E. 25th St., Board of Edn., Balt. Died Jan. 29, 1953.

LEMMON, Dal Millington, U.S. Circuit judge; **b. Newton, Kan., Oct. 29, 1887; s. Allen Bosley and Clara (Millington) L.; A.B., Stanford Univ., 1908; Doctor of Laws, McGeorge School of Law; married May Alice Dunn, Aug. 19, 1915; children—John V., Richard M., Maryalice, Donald D. Admitted to Calif. State Bar, 1909, and practiced law in Sacra**mento, 1910-33; judge of Superior Ct., Sacramento Co., 1933-47; apptd. judge, U.S. Dist. Ct., Northern dist. Cal., 1947, U.S. Circuit Judge, 9th Circuit, 1954. Mem. Am., Sacramento (pres., 1930-33) bar assns., Cal. Jud. Council (1943-47), Kappa Alpha. Elk. Clubs: Lions, Rotary (pres. 1930), Del. Paso Country, University, Sutter, Commonwealth, Pacific Union (San Francisco). Home: 3418 Brockway Ct. Office: Post Office Bldg., Sacramento. Died Apr. 26, 1958; buried St. Mary's Cemetery, Sacramento.

LEMON, Luther Orange, advt. exec.; b. Richmond, Ind., Nov. 10, 1900; s. Everett Roy and Harriet Hammond (Barber) L.; student Howe (Ind.) Mil. Sch., Earlham Coll., 1920-22; B.S., Columbia, 1924; m. Hortense Alice Bleker, June 20, 1940. With J. Walter Thompson Co., 1924—, successively asst. to treas., asst. treas., comptroller, treas., 1946—, dir., 1947—. Mem. Controllers Inst. Am., Beta Gamma Sigma. Episcopalian. Clubs: University, Church (N.Y. C.). Home: R.F.D. 1, Mount Kisco, N.Y. Office: 420 Lexington Av., N.Y.C. 17. Died Feb. 28, 1957.

LEMON, Willis Storrs, physician; b. Villa Nova, Ont., Feb. 8, 1878; s. George and Jane (Honey) L.; M.B., U. Toronto Faculty of Medicine, 1905; m. Ethel M. Haines, June 29, 1909; children—Katherine Ethel (wife of Dr. George A. Lord), Janette Louise (dec.), Dr. Willis Edward. Came to U.S., 1909, naturalized, 1917. Intern Toronto Gen. Hosp., 1905-06, Parry Sound Hosp., Ont., 1906-07; demonstrator in pathology and therapy U. Toronto, 1906-07; practice of medicine, Toronto, 1907-08; asso. physician Canadian Nat. Sanatorium for Tb, Gravenhurst, Ont., 1908-09; practiced in La Grange, Ill., 1909-17; asst. in sect. in div. of medicine Mayo Clinic, Rochester, Minn., 1917-18, head of sect., 1918-46; prof. medicine Mayo Found of U. Minn., 1934-46. Served as 1st lt. Minn. Home Guard, 1917-19. Recipient gold medal on graduation, George Brown Meml. research scholarship, Daniel Clark prize in psychiatry, all U. Toronto, 1905; gold medal (with Dr. S. W. Harrington) for exhibit at meeting of A.M.A., 1935. Mem. A.M.A., Minn., So. Minn. med. socs., Minn. Trudeau Med. Soc. (past pres.), Central Interurban Clin. Club (v.p. 1935), Minn. Soc. Internal Medicine, Assn. Am. Physicians, Am. Soc. for Clin. Investigation, Am. Assn. for Thoracic Surgery, Alpha Omega Alpha, Sigma Xi. Conglist. Contbr. chpt. The Nature of Postoperative Pulmonary Diseases, Prophylactic Measures and Treatment to (book) The Stomach and Duodenum by Eusterman and Balfour; also numerous articles to med. jours. Home: 930 7th Av. S.W., Rochester, Minn. Deceased.

LENFESTEY, Nathan Coggeshall (lĕn-fĕs'tē), banker; b. Marion, Ind., Mar. 1, 1890; s. William Lomax and Sarah (Coggeshall) L.; student De Pauw U., 2½ yrs.; B.S., Dartmouth, 1913; M.C.S., Amos Tuck School of Administration and Finance (Dartmouth), 1914; m. Jeannette Hazen Ricketts, Feb. 14, 1919; children—William Richard, John Francis, Virginia, Janet. Began banking bus. at Marion, 1907; now exec. v.p. and cashier Nat. City Bank, N.Y.; dir., v.p., sec., treas. Internat. Banking Corp.; dir., sec., treas. Nat. City Safe Deposit Co., dir., v.p., sec. treas. Nat. City Realty Corp. Mem. Phi Beta Kappa, Phi Kappa Psi. Methodist. Clubs: Union League, Bankers, Dartmouth, Phi Kappa Psi. Home: Summit, N.J. Address: 55 Wall St., N.Y.C. Died Aug. 8, 1954; buried Rosedale, Orange, N.J.

LENIHAN, Mathias Clement, archbishop; b. Dubuque, Ia., Oct. 6, 1854; s. Edmund and Mary (Donovan) L.; student St. John's College, Wis., 1870-73, St. Joseph's Coll., Dubuque, Ia., 1873-76, Grand Sem. (conducted by Sulpitians). Montreal, Can., 1876-79. Received minor orders from Bishop Hennessy, Dubuque; ordained deacon by Archbishop Bourget, Montreal, priest by Bishop Lefèvre, Montreal; consecrated bishop of Great Falls, Mont., 1904, now archbishop. Home: 305 W. Locust St., Dubuque, Ia. Deceased.

LENIHAN, Michael Joseph (lĕn'ihăn), ret. army officer; b. Hopkinton, Mass., May 2, 1865; s. James and Catherine (Granger) L.; grad. U.S. Mil. Acad., 1887, Inf. and Cav. Sch., 1891, Army War Coll., 1917, Naval War Coll., 1921; LL.D., Holy Cross Coll., Mass., 1925; m. Mathilde O'Toole, 1891 (died Aug. 29, 1934); children—Eleanora (Mrs. Douglass Taft Greene), Catherine (Mrs. Paul James Halloran); m. 2d, Mina Ward, 1938. Commd. add. 2d lt. 25th Inf., 1887, promoted through grades to col. 1917; brig. gen. Nat. Army, 1917, brig. gen. regular army, 1925. Prof. mil. sci. and tactics, Seton Hall Coll., South Orange, N.J., 1893-97; in Cuba, 1899, Philippines, 1899-1902; mem. Gen. Staff Corps, 1906-10; in Hawaii, 1913-16; at Army War Coll., 1916-17; comdr. 83d Inf. Brig., 1917; comdr. 153d Inf. Brig., 1918; in France, 1917-19; Army instr. Naval War Coll., 1921-24; comd. 3d Div., 1928-29; ret. 1929. Decorated Comdr. Legion of Honor and Croix de Guerre with 3 palms (French); Order of the Purple Heart with Oak Leaf Cluster. Home: Hopkinton, Mass. Died Aug. 13, 1958.

LENNEN, Philip Weiting (lĕn'ĕn), advt. exec., ret.; b. Syracuse, June 30, 1887; son Philip H. and Caroline Adele (Daniels) L.; student Trinity Chapel Preparatory School, New York City; m. Beth Marie Guilfoyle, March 18, 1919 (died Jan. 17, 1945); 1 dau., Patricia E.; m. 2d, Thelma Beatrice Attebery, March 1, 1946; 1 son, Ralph Attebery. Jr. copywriter, mail sales department, A. W. Shaw Company, Chicago, sales manager, 1907-10; vice president Royal Tailors, Chicago, 1911-23, Erwin-Wasey Co., Inc., Chicago, 1923-24; with J. T. H. Mitchell founded advertising firm Lennen & Mitchell, New York, 1924, v.p., 1924-30, pres., 1930-47, chmn. bd. since 1948, name changed to Lennen & Newell, Inc., Oct., 1952, retired 1954. Director Am. Assn. Advt. Agencies, 1944-48. Member St. Nicholas Society, Society of Colonial Wars. Episcopalian. Clubs: Metropolitan, Players, Madison Square Garden (New York); Piping Rock (Locust Valley, L.I., N.Y.); Turf and Field (Belmont, L.I., N.Y.). Home: Carlton House, 680 Madison Av., N.Y.C. 21. Died Dec. 25, 1955.

LENNOX, Edwin, pres. Am. Colortype Co. of N.J.; b. 1878; ed. Purdue U., 1899. Pres. Am. Colortype Co. of Ill., Lead Mould Electrotype Co.; v.p. and dir. Am. Art Works; dir. Samuel Gabriel Sons & Co. Clubs: University, Tavern. Home: 3240 Lake Shore Dr. Office: 1151 Roscoe St., Chgo. 13. Died July 1956.

LEON, Maurice, lawyer; b. Beirut, Lebanon Territory, June 29, 1880; s. R. A. and Emma R. L.; ed. in Paris schools; later in New York by his stepfather, Prof. Richard J. H. Gottheil, of Columbia; emigrated to America, 1894; admitted to N.Y. bar, 1903; married Frances Juliana Webster Goodrich, September 1, 1910 (divorced 1934); children—Goodrich (dec.), Elizabeth Goodrich (Mrs. E. L. Lawler), Frances Webster (Mrs. Morris Swadesh), Maurice. Member Choate, Byrd, Leon & Garretson, N.Y. City and predecessor firms, since 1919. Secured for French Government its first war loans in United States, $10,000,000, November 1914, and $25,000,000, April 1915, first allied war bonds on American market. Suggested and organized observance in U.S., beginning Sept. 6, 1915, of double anniversary of birth of Lafayette and Battle of Marne; organized Am. participation in Centenary of Marcelin Berthelot and foundation of Maison de la Chimie and memorial to Berthelot; director Maison de la Chimie, Paris, France. Decorated Cross of Legion of Honor (French), 1918; Officer Legion of Honor, 1923. Mem. Westchester County Commn. on Govt., 1934-36. Mem. Am. and N.Y. State bar assns., Assn. Bar City of N.Y., Am. Soc. Internat. Law, Chamber of Commerce State of N.Y. Clubs: India House, Sleepy Hollow Country, National Republican (mem. nat. affairs com.) (New York); University (Washington); Interallied (Paris). Author: How Many World Wars? The Warning of Foch, 1942, The Problem of Aggression, 1943. Contbr. to press, radio, mags. on world affairs, 1914-45. Home: Irvington on Hudson, N.Y. Office: 44 Wall St., N.Y.C. 5. Died Oct. 9, 1952.

LEONARD, Alton William, ret. pub. utility exec.; b. Monmouth, Me., Apr. 8, 1873; s. Frederick Alton and Elizabeth Ann (Parker) L.; ed. pub. schs., Mass.; m. Anne A. Keith, Apr. 8, 1898; children—Olive Elizabeth (Mrs. Thos. M. Green, Jr.), Richard Keith, Pamele Frances (Mrs. S. W. McElhone), Constance Mary (Mrs. E. S. McCord). Formerly pres. Puget Sound Power & Light Co., etc.; ret. 1931. Republican. K.P., Eagle. Clubs: Seattle Press Club, Yacht, Seattle Gun, University, Golf. Home: 1220 21st Av. North, Seattle 2. Died Mar. 11, 1959.

LEONARD, Clifford Milton, civil engr.; b. Chicago, Ill., Dec. 24, 1879; s. Arthur Gustavus and Clara C. (Yarnall) L.; B.S. in C.E., Mass. Inst. Tech., 1900; m. Flowerree K. Grey, Dec. 22, 1909; children—Fleury, Hope, Clifford. Engring. and construction business, Chicago, since 1905; chmn. board Leonard Construction Co. Was formerly dir. First Nat. Bank of Chicago, Continental Ins. Co. of N.Y., Colonial-Beacon Oil Co., Boston, War Finance Corp., Washington, D.C. Mem. Am. Soc. C.E. Clubs: Chicago, University, Onwentsia, Racquet (Chicago); Racquet and Tennis (New York). Home: Lake Forest, Ill., and Camden, S.C. Office: 37 S. Wabash Av., Chgo. Died Sept. 9, 1956.

LEONARD, Nellie Mabel (Fay Stuart), writer; b. Brookville, Mass., Oct. 31, 1875; d. Charles Melvin and Mary E. (Hobert) L.; ed. pub. schs. Extensive contbr. to mags., under pen name, 1895—, stories appearing in S.S. and other periodicals. Baptist. Author: The Graymouse Family, 1916; Uncle Squeaky's Vacation, 1917; Limpytoe's Attic Home, 1918; Granddaddy Whiskers, M.D., 1919; Uncle Squeaky's Country Store, 1920; The Mouse Book, 1926. Home: 997 S. Franklin St., Brookville, Mass. Died Mar. 11, 1956; buried Wendell Cemetery, Brookville.

LEONARD, Russell Henry, mfg. exec.; b. Somerset, Mass., Oct. 4, 1888; s. Henry B. and Annie A. (Hood) L.; A.B., Harvard, 1910; m. Helen Elizabeth Case, Sept. 19, 1911. Field agent, U.S. Tariff Bd., 1911; asst. to agent, Ludlow Co., 1912-13; treas. Wampanoag Mills, Fall River, Mass., 1914-22; treas. Ipswich Mills, Boston, 1922-26; pres. and treas. Pepperell Mfg. Co., Boston, 1924—; dir. First Nat. Bank. Clubs: Harvard (Boston); Harvard, Merchants (New York). Home: 145 Lee St., Brookline, Mass. Office: 160 State St., Boston. Died Nov. 5, 1949; buried Taunton, Mass.

LEOVY, Frank A (lē-ō'vĭ), chmn. bd. Gulf Refining Co.; vice chmn. bd. Gulf Oil Corp. of Pa.; pres. Western Gulf Oil Co., Venezuela Gulf Oil Co., Mexican Gulf Oil Co., Gulf Exploration Co., Am. Internat. Fuel & Petroleum Co., Gulf Research & Development Co. Home: 1165 Beechwood Blvd. Office: Gulf Bldg., Pitts. Died June 1949.*

LERCH, Alice Hollister, bibliographer and curator; b. Washington, D.C.; d. Milton J. and Mary Ashby (Hollister) Lerch. Began as librarian, Library of Congress, 1900; with Library of Congress, 1900-10, and 1923-48; served as chief bibliographer, Rare Book Collection; in library of Hispanic Society of America, 1910-17, N.Y. Pub. Library, 1917-30; librarian Rollins Coll., 1930-31; Folger Shakespeare Library, 1931-33. Mem. Bibliog. Soc. (Eng.), Bibliog. Soc. of Am., A.L.A., Dist. of Columbia Library Assn. Contbr. to Bibliographical Essays: A Tribute to Wilberforce Eames, 1924, author of A Printer Soldier of Fortune, 1936, and also bibliog. subjects. Home: 2205 California St., Washington. Died Oct. 8, 1951.

LERNER, Joseph J., business exec.; b. Phila., Pa., Jan. 23, 1887; s. Charles and Sophia Lerner; ed. Boys High School, Brooklyn, N.Y.; student Pa. Dental Coll., 1906-09; children—Richard Martin, Allan Jay, Robert Warren. Began career as a dentist; one of the organizers and founders in 1917 of Lorraine Stores Corp., name later changed to Lerner Stores Corp., now chmn. board. Member Westchester Country Club. Home: 249 Ocean Blvd., Golden Beach, Fla. Office: 354 4th Av., N.Y.C. Died Oct. 29, 1954.

LERNER, Samuel A., founder, chmn. bd. Lerner Stores Corp. Office: 354 Fourth Av., N.Y.C. Died Dec. 6, 1956.*

LERRIGO, Charles Henry (lĕr'rĭ-gō), physician, author; b. Birmingham, Eng., Sept. 12, 1872; s. George and Mary Olive (Watkins) L.; pub. schs., Eng.; came to U.S., 1886; M.D., Homoe. Med. Coll. of Mo., St. Louis, 1900; m. Annabel Barry, Apr. 16, 1895; children—Marion Olive, Ruth Annabel, Frank Charles, George Angus. Practiced in Topeka since 1900. First lt., capt. and maj. M.C., U.S. Army, Aug. 1917-May 1919. Mem. Kan. State Bd. of Health, 1905-24 (pres. 1909-10); state registrar of vital statistics for Kan., 1919-22; exec. sec. Kan. State Tuberculosis Assn., 1922-48, sec. emeritus, 1948. Health editor, Capper Farm Press. Fellow American Pub. Health Assn., A.M.A., Am. Geriatrics Soc.; hon. mem. Nat. Conf. Tuberculosis Workers, American Trudeau Society. Author: Doc Williams, 1913; The Castle of Cheer, 1916; The Boy Scout Treasure Hunters, 1917; Boy Scouts to the Rescue, 1919; Boy Scouts on Special Service, 1922; Boy Scouts of Round Table Patrol, 1924; The Merry Men of Robin Hood Patrol, 1927; The Kidnapped Doctor, 1929; The Sea Is His, 1932; A Son of John Brown, 1937; The Better Half of Your Life, 1951. Address: 1403 Fillmore St., Topeka, Kan. Died Dec. 4, 1955; buried Mt. Hope Cemetery, Topeka.

LERRIGO, Peter Hugh James; b. Birmingham, Eng., Oct. 6, 1875; s. George and Mary (Watkins) L.; came to U.S., 1886; M.D., N.Y. Homoe. Med. Coll. and Hosp., 1898; M.D., Medico-Chirurg. Coll., Phila., 1902; post-grad. Post-Grad. Sch. Medicine, N.Y.C., 1910; D.D., Franklin (Ind.) Coll., 1923; D.D., Bates Coll., Lewiston, Me., 1932; m. Edith Mary Dowkontt, Aug. 20, 1902 (died Dec. 18, 1941); children—George Dowkontt (dec.), Hugh D. (dec.), Edith Mary, Florence Lillian; m. 2d, Mabel Hannah Brown, Aug. 16, 1944. Served in Philippines as med. missionary of Am. Bapt. Fgn. Mission Soc., 1902-13; joint sec. for N.E., Fgn. and Home Mission Soc. and Publn. Soc., 1914-15; exec. sec. Five Yr. Program No. Bapt. Com., 1916-18; candidate sec. Fgn. Mission Soc., 1919-21; home sec., med. dir., sec. for Africa, Fgn. Mission Soc., 1921-40; exec. sec. World Relief Com., No. Bapt. Com., 1940-41; ret. 1941; reentered active service as sec. Christian Med. Council for Overseas Work, Jan. 1943; exec. sec. Fgn. Missions Conf. of N. A., 1943-45 (completed re-organization of headquarters staff and work, 1945); bd. dirs., chmn. archtl. com. Pilgrim Pl., Claremont, Cal., 1947-50; pres. Central Philippine Coll., Iloilo, P.I., 1950—. Opened mission to Capiz, P.I., 1903; built Emmanuel Hosp., Capiz, P.I., 1909; sent to Belgian Congo, 1920, 28, 35, to report work of Fgn. Mission Soc.; chmn. Com. Reference and Counsel, Fgn. Missions Conf. N.A., 1928, 29, pres. conf., 1932; mem. Internat. Missionary Council, 1935; missionary inspection tour, Japan, China, Philippines, Burma, India, Assam, 1930-31. Author: Stature of a Perfect Man, 1920; Rock-Breakers, 1922; God's Dynamite, 1924; Anita, a Tale of the Philippines, 1924; The World Thrust of Northern Baptists, 1928; Northern Baptists Rethink Missions, 1933; Omwa? Are You Awake?, 1936; Home: 777 Berkley Av., Claremont, Cal. Died Mar. 24, 1958; buried Claremont.

LERSNER, Victor Alexander, vice chmn. exec. com. Bowery Savings Bank, New York City. Home: 277 Park Av. Office: 110 E. 42d St., N.Y.C. Died Mar. 25, 1949.*

LESCOHIER, Alexander William (lĕs-kō'hĕr), pres. Parke, Davis & Co.; b. Detroit, Mich., June 27,

1885; s. Alexander and Minnie (Judge) L.; M.D., Wayne U., Detroit, 1909, hon. D.Sc., 1937; m. Eva Clare Lindabury, June 12, 1913; children—Ralph W., Donald H. Asso. with Parke, Davis & Co., pharm. and biol. products, surgical dressings, 1909—, mem. research staff, 1909-18, asst. dir. research and biol. lab., 1918-25, dir. exptl. medicine, 1925-28, asst. to pres., 1928, gen. mgr., 1928-38, dir., 1929—, pres., 1938—. Dir. Research Found. Wayne U. Coll. of Medicine. Mem. A.M.A., Wayne County Med. Soc. Club: Detroit. Home: 663 University Pl., Grosse Pointe 30, Mich. Died Nov. 17, 1951; buried Woodlawn Cemetery.

LESINSKI, John (lĕ-sĭn'skĭ), ex-congressman; b. Erie, Pa., Jan. 3, 1885; ed. St. Cyril and Methodius Sem., Detroit, Mich., and Detroit Bus. U.; m. 3d, Estelle Geisinger, June 1938; 2 children by present marriage. Began in bldg. and real estate bus., 1903; founder Hamtramck Lumber & Supply Co., First State Bank of Hamtramck, Dearborn (Mich.) Lumber Co. Mem. 73d to 81st Congresses, 16th Mich. Dist. Democrat. Home: 7420 Oakman Blvd., Dearborn, Mich. Died May 27, 1950; buried Mt. Olivet Cemetery, Detroit.

LESLIE, Frank Elliott, physician; b. Woburn, Mass., July 21, 1873; s. Freeman Francis and Sarah Jane (Russell) L.; prep. edn. Ayer (Mass.) High Sch., and Winthrop (N.Y.) Acad.; student Mass. Coll. Pharmacy, Boston, 1893-94; M.D., Med. Sch. Me. (Bowdoin), 1901; m. Nellie Vitella Ripley, June 2, 1903. Hosp. steward, Marine Hosp. Service, 1894-97; began gen. practice medicine, Andover, Me., 1901; mgr. Glenellis Sanitarium, Andover, 1905; mgr. VA Facility, Northampton, Mass., 1933-39, Mendota, Wis., 1939-43; psychiatrist USPHS, 1919-43. Served as maj. M.C., U.S. Army Med. Res.; ret. Aug. 1, 1943. Diplomate Am. Bd. Psychiatry and neurology. Mem. A.M.A., Me Med. Soc., Am. Psychiatric Assn., N.E. Soc. Psychiatry, U.S. Mil. Surgeons, Mil. Order World War. Unitarian. Mason. Club: University (Winter Park, Fla.). Home: Eastland Hotel, Portland, Me. (winter) St. Petersburg, Fla. Died Mar. 27, 1951; buried Arlington Nat. Cemetery.

LESLIE, Norman Henry, coast guard officer; b. Chicago, Aug. 25, 1898; s. Henry T. and Myrtie (Oliver) L.; B.S., U.S. Coast Guard Acad., New London, Conn., 1918; m. Unis Frazier, Sept. 25, 1926. Enlisted Coast Guard as ordinary seaman, June 1918, hon. discharged, July 1918; appointed cadet, Aug. 1918; commd. ensign, 1921, and advanced through grades to rear adm., 1950; served on ships: Seneca, N.Y. City, 1921; Tuscarora, Milwaukee, 1921; Unalga, Juneau, Alaska, 1922-26; Seneca, 1927; Ericsson, New London, Conn., as exec. officer, 1927-28; comd. Fanning, New London, Conn., 1928-30; assigned to Coast Guard Depot, Curtis Bay, Md., 1930-33; comd. Cahokia, Eureka, Calif., 1933-35; comd. Base Six, Fort Lauderdale, Fla., 1935-39; personnel officer and res. dir., Jacksonville (Fla.) Dist., 1939-41; comd. Haida, serving escort duty in Aleutians, 1941-42; chief of staff to dist. Coast Guard officer, 8th Naval Dist., New Orleans, 1942-44; dist. Coast Guard officer, New Orleans, 1944-45; dist. Coast Guard officer, 17th Naval Dist., Ketchikan, Alaska, 1945-46, comdr., 1946-47; comdr. 7th Coast Guard dist., Miami, 1947-49; chief office of personnel, Coast Guard Headquarters, Washington, 1949-51; comdr. 13th Coast Guard Dist., Seattle, since 1951. With international ice patrol (Seneca), 1921, Bering Sea Patrol (Unalga), 1922-26, (Haida) 1941. Served as dep. U.S. Marshal in Alaska while on Unalga; U.S. Commr. in Alaska while on Haida. Awarded Victory Medal without clasp for participation in World War I; commended for assistance rendered to crashed Navy Airship Akron, 1933; commended for assistance with establishment and conduct of Mounted Beach Patrol, 8th Naval dist., New Orleans; received commendation ribbon for war service on Haida. Mason (Shriner). Clubs: Propeller, Rainier, Arctic, Seattle Yacht. Home: 110 W. Highland Dr. Office: 618 2d Av., Seattle. Deceased.

L'ESPERANCE, Elise Strang, physician; b. Yorktown, N.Y.; daughter Albert Strang, M.D., and Kate (Depew) Strang; M.D., Woman's Medical Coll. of N.Y. Infirmary for Women and Children, 1901; D.Sc., Woman's Med. Coll., Pa.; LL.D., Lindenwood Coll.; asst., dept. of pathology, Cornell U. Med. Sch., 1910-12, instr., 1912-20, asst. prof., 1920-32, asst. prof., dept. preventive medicine, 1944-50, professor emeritus since 1950. Mary Putnam Jacobi Fellow for research in tumor pathology, Munich, Germany, 1914. Resident, Babies Hospital, New York City, 1901-02; pathologist, also dir. lab., New York Infirmary for Women and Children, 1910-44; dir. Strang Tumor Clinic since 1937; pathol., New York, Harlem, and Manhattan Maternity Hosp.; bacteriologist and asst. pathol. Memorial Hosp., also dir. Strang Cancer Prevention Clinics, 1940-50; staff, Memorial Hospital and New York Infirmary, 1937-50; attending physician in preventive medicine Memorial Hospital 1948-50. Received Lasker Award, Am. Pub. Health Assn., 1951. Fellow N.Y. Academy Medicine; member Westchester Co. N.Y. County and New York State med. socs., New York Pathology Society, American Assn. Pathol. and Bacteriol., Am. Assn. Immunologists, Am. Radium Soc., Harvey Soc., Am. Cancer Soc., Woman's, Am. Med. Woman's and Am. med. assns., (hon.) Am. Radiologists Soc. Cons. editor: Jour. Am. Med. Woman's Assn. Address: 535 Pelham Manor Rd., Pelham, N.Y. Died Jan. 21, 1959.

LESSENGER, Waldo Emerson (lĕs'ĕn-jĕr), educator; b. Irwin, Ia., July 6, 1898; s. William Arthur and Margaret (Roberts) L.; A.B., State U. Ia., 1919, M.A., 1922, Ph.D., 1925; m. Edna Louise Houser, July 27, 1923; children—Nancy Lee, Susan. Supt. pub. schs., Radcliffe, Ia., 1920-24; instr. in edn. Detroit Tchrs. Coll., 1925-26, asst. prof., 1926-28, asso. prof., 1928-30, prof., ednl. adminstrn. and research, 1930-31, dean, 1931— (now Coll. of Edn., Wayne U., Detroit). In 4th O.T.C., U.S. Army, World War. Mem. N.E.A., Mich. Edn. Assn., Nat. Assn. Coll. Tchrs. Edn., Am. Assn. Colls. for Teacher Edn. (pres. 1951), Mu Sigma Pi, Phi Delta Kappa. Home: 2300 Edison Av., Detroit 6. Deceased.

LESTER, Clarence Brown, librarian; b. Providence, R.I., May 7, 1877; s. John Erastus and Mary Jane (Brown) L.; A.B., Brown U., 1900, A.M., 1902; fellow in polit. science, U. of Wis., 1905-06; m. Maude Aldrich, Aug. 29, 1907 (died July 12, 1942); children—John Aldrich, Elizabeth, Jane (Mrs. Risto P. Lappala), Barbara (Mrs. Robert C. Smith), Margaret (Mrs. Walter H. Hansen). Instr. mathematics, Brown University, 1900-02, Rhode Island School of Design, 1901-02; submaster Monson Academy, 1902-05; organized, 1906, and in charge, 1906-08, legislative reference dept. Ind. State Library; head of legislative reference sect., N.Y. State Library, 1908-13; chief, pub. service training, 1913-20, sec., 1920-49, Wis. Free Library Commn. Wis. state dir. of library publicity and of exhibits for U.S. Food Administration, World War; adviser, Brit. Columbia Library Survey, 1928, survey of Am. Merchant Marine Library Assn., 1936, survey (with Paul Noon) of Tex. State Library, 1940. Pres. Nat. Assn. of State Libraries, 1923-24; pres. League of Library Commns., 1927-29. Fellow Am. Library Inst. (mem. research bd.); chmn. library extension bd. A.L.A., 1925-36; mem. Wis. Hist. Soc., Appalachian Mountain Club. Phi Beta Kappa, Delta Upsilon. Episcopalian. Mason (33°). Kiwanian. Home: 1931 Rowley Av., Madison 5, Wis. Died Dec. 8, 1951; buried Forest Hill Cemetery, Madison.

LESTER, James A., ret. army officer; b. Prosperity, S.C., Oct. 13, 1891; s. Allen and Rosaline Imogene (Ridgell) L.; B.S., The Citadel, Charleston, S.C., 1911; B.S., U.S. Mil. Acad., 1915; grad. F.A. Sch., 1926, Command and Gen. Staff Sch., 1927, Ecole de Guerre, France, 1929, Army War Coll., 1940; m. Mildred Minor White, July 1, 1925. Commd. 2d lt., U.S. Army, 1915, and advanced through the grades to maj. gen., 1945; served with A.E.F., France, 1918, with Army of Occupation, Germany, 1919; asst. mil. attaché, Paris, 1932-36; asst. comdt. F.A. Sch., 1941-42; comdr. div. arty., 1942-53; overseas Pacific theater, 1942-48; comd. 24th Div., Arty., Hollandia operaton, XIV Corps Arty., Bougainville, Luzon, Manila; on Gen. MacArthur's staff, Philippines, as provost marshal gen., 1945, and comdg. gen. Philippine Constabulary to Dec. 1945; comdg. 24th Inf. Div., Japan, 1945-48; comdg. gen. San Francisco port embarkation, 1948-53, ret. 1953. Decorated D.S.M. (U.S.); Officer Legion of Honor (France). Home: 2710 Preston St., Columbia, S.C. Address: Fort Mason, Cal. Died Mar. 10, 1958; buried Arlington Nat. Cemetery.

LESTER, Oliver Clarence, physicist, educator; b. Morris County, Kan., Nov. 3, 1873; s. John Augustus and Mary Virginia (Watts) L.; A.B., Central Coll., Fayette, Mo., 1897, A.M., 1898; AM., Yale, 1902, Ph.D., 1904; LL.D., Colo. Coll., 1941; m. Pynk Johnson, Sept. 8, 1897; children—Katherine Wheeler (Mrs. H. Laurence Humbley), Oliver Clarence, John Augustus. Prof. Latin and Greek, Hendrix Coll., Conway, Ark., 1897-98; asst. prof. Latin and Greek, Central Coll., 1898-1901; asst. in physics Yale, 1901-04, Loomis fellow in physics, 1903-04, instr. physics, 1904-07; prof. physics U. Colo., 1907—, dean Grad. Sch., 1919—, v.p., 1931—, also acting pres., 1922-23, 32-33, retired 1942, with titles of dean, prof., and v.p. emeritus; prof. physics U. Ind., 1942-43; prof. physics, U. of Colo., 1943-49, ret. 1949; physicist Colo. State Geol. Survey, 1914-18; dir. research Carnatite Products Co. (Vanadium Products Co.), Boulder, Colo., 1919-22; cons. in geophysics Midwest Refining Co., 1925-30, Gen. Petroleum Co., 1926-28; dir. First Nat. Bank in Boulder, United Am. Life Ins. Co. Fellow A.A.A.S. (pres. S.W. div. 1933-34), Am. Phys. Soc., Am. Assn. Sci. Workers), Am. Geog. Soc.; mem. Am. Soc. Engring. Edn., Am. Geophysical Union, Colo.-Wyo. Acad. Science (pres. 1929-30), Am. Assn. Physics Tchrs., Colo. State Hist. Soc. (life), Sigma Xi, Sigma Nu, Tau Beta Pi, Alpha Chi Sigma, Sigma Pi Sigma. Club: Boulder Golf. Author: The Integrals of Mechanics, 1909; also various scientific papers. Home: 1061 11th St., Boulder, Colo. Died Sept. 28, 1951.

LESTER, Orrin Clifford, banker; b. Beaver Co., Pa., May 8, 1878; s. William and Lucinda (Kuhn) L.; student Beaver (Pa.) Coll., 1899, Geneva Coll., Beaver Falls, Pa., 1903-06; spl. work in edn., Harvard, 1907; m. Lilian Vernon Feyler, July 2, 1907; children—Katherine, Charlotte, John Andrew. Teacher Pa. county schs., 1900-03; prin. Rochester (Pa.) High Sch., 1907-08, supt. pub. schs., Rochester, 1909-15; lecturer, 1915-17; dir. Nat. Speakers Bur. Am. Red Cross, 1917-18; asso. dir. Savings div., U.S. Treasury Dept., 1919-20, dir., 1921; dir. Civic League of Cleveland, 1922; v.p. Bowery Savings Bank, 1923—. Mem. Federal Commn. on Economic Edn.; sec. Mortgage Conf. of N.Y. Mem. East Side Chamber Commerce (chmn. bd.), Nat. Assn. Mutual Savings Banks (chmn. econ. edn. com.). Democrat. Club: Westchester Hills Golf (White Plains, N.Y.). Home: 1 Clubway, Hartsdale, N.Y. Office: 130 Bowery, New York, N.Y. Died Feb. 25, 1958.

LESTER, (Thomas) William, musician, composer; b. Leicester, Eng., Sept. 17, 1889; s. Thomas William and Mary Ann (Harvey) L.; ed. high sch., Keokuk, Ia.; studied piano under Jane Carey, composition and piano under Adolf Brune, organ under Wilhelm Middelschulte, voice under Sandor Radanovits; hon. Dr. Fine Arts, Beloit (Wis.) Coll., 1931; m. Margaret Ann Smith (soprano), Jan. 15, 1913; 1 son, Thomas William. Came with parents to U.S., 1902, naturalized citizen, 1916. Organist Memorial Ch. of Christ, Chgo., 1909-13, 2d Ch. of Christ, Scientist, Chgo., 1913-16, First Bapt Ch., Evanston, Ill., 1916-21, First Congl. Ch., Chgo., 1921-50; dir. Lyric Ensemble and St. Cecilia Chorus, of Aurora, Ill.; dir. Galien Valley Community Chorus (Three Oaks, Mich.), United Mother Singers (Chgo.); teacher of voice, piano, organ and theory Sch. of Music, De Paul U.; lecturer on musical history and appreciation of music Lewis Inst.; condr. South Bend (Ind.) Choral Soc., Mid-City Concert Orchestra. Mem. Am. Guild Organists (dean Ill. chpt. 1927-29), Art Inst. Chgo., Chgo. Artists Assn., Pro Musica, Sinfonia, Phi Mu Alpha. Conglist. Mason. Composer: Everyman (opera); Manabozo (opera); Se-a-wana (operetta); The Golden Syon (oratorio); The Tale of the Bell (cantata); Sacajawea (dramatic cantata), 1932; Virtue Is Its Own Reward (opera), 1949; The Minuet (opera), 1950; organ and piano works, songs, part songs, anthems, chamber music and orchestral compositions. Music review for Diapason. Home: Apple Tree Farm, R.F.D. 2, Berrien Springs, Mich. Studio: 64 E. Lake St., Chgo. Died Dec. 4, 1956.

LETCHWORTH, Edward Hance (lĕch'wûrth), lawyer; b. Buffalo, Mar. 24, 1881; s. William C. and Laura (Cutter) L.; A.B., Harvard, 1902, A.M., 1903, LL.B., 1905; m. Ruth B. Abbott, June 20, 1906; children—Edward H., George C. Admitted to N.Y. bar, 1905, began practice, Buffalo; mem. Kenefick, Letchworth, Baldy, Phillips & Emblidge, 1911-18, 22—; v.p. and gen. counsel Marine Trust Co., Western N.Y., 1919-21; pres. Nichols Sch., Buffalo, 1915-29; former dir., gen. counsel Marine Trust Co., now mem. sr. adv. bd.; dir. Maine Midland Corp.; Kleinhans Music Hall Mgmt., Inc., Niagara Share Corp., Marine Midland Trust Co. N.Y., Dunlop Tire & Rubber Corp., Hewitt-Robins, Inc., Messer Oil Corp. Mem. N.Y. State Bd. Law Examiners, 1919-21; pres. Buffalo Joint Charities and Community Fund, 1932-35; chmn. governing com. Buffalo Found.; vice chmn. N.Y. State, U.S. Def. Bonds Div., Treasury Dept. Awarded Chancellor's Medal by U. Buffalo, 1952. Fellow Am. Bar Found. Mem. Am., N.Y., Erie County bar assns., Assn. Bar City N.Y., Soc. Mayflower Descendants, Soc., Colonial Wars, S.A.R., Founders and Patriots, Delta Upsilon, Children's Aid and S.P.C.C. of Erie County (pres. 1919-21; dir.). Republican. Unitarian. Mason (32°). Clubs: Buffalo, Saturn, Thursday, Harvard of New York. Home: 728 Lafayette Av., Buffalo 22; (summer) Brunswick Pl., Niagara-on-the-Lake, Ont., Can. Office: Marine Trust Bldg., Buffalo. Died Oct. 22, 1958; buried Forest Lawn Cemetery, Buffalo.

LEUPP, Harold Lewis (lo͞op), librarian; b. N.Y.C., Oct. 11, 1877; s. Francis Ellington and Ada (Murdock) L.; A.B., Cornell, 1902; student N.Y. State Library Sch., Albany, N.Y., 1902-03, 03-04; m. Beulah Louise Cross, Sept. 1, 1906; children—Gordon Dodge, Alice Murdock, Constance Ann, Francis Lewis, Graham Murdock. Asst. reference librarian John Crerar Library, Chgo., 1904-06; supt. retail and library depts., U. Chgo. Press, 1906-09, supt. library dept., and librarian Hist. Group Library, 1909-10; asso. librarian U. Cal. Library, 1910-19, librarian, 1919-45, library cons., 1945, librarian emeritus, 1945—; chief of sect. Library Depot, Hqrs. Sixth Army, Presidio, San Francisco, 1946-50. Attended Business Man's T.C., Monterey, Cal., 1916, and 1st R.O.T.C., San Francisco, 1917; commd. 2d lt. Inf., N.A., 1917; served with 166th Depot Brigade, Camp Lewis, Wash.; discharged as capt. inf., 1918; commd. maj. Inf., O.R.C., 1919. Life mem. A.L.A., Cal. Library Assn. Home: 1838 San Juan Av., Berkeley 7, Cal. Died Feb. 11, 1952.

LEUSCHNER, Armin Otto (loish'nẽr), astronomer; b. Detroit, Jan. 16, 1868; s. Otto Richard and Caroline (Humburg) L.; grad. Royal Wilhelms-Gymnasium, Cassel, Germany, 1886; A.B., U. Mich., 1888, Sc.D. (hon.), 1913; grad. student Lick Obs., U. Cal., 1888-90; Ph.D., Berlin, 1897; hon. Sc.D., U. Pitts., 1900; LL.D., U. Cal., 1938; m. Ida Louise Denicke, May 20, 1896 (died Nov. 15, 1941); children—Erida Louise, Richard Denicke, Frederick Denicke (died Dec. 8, 1941). Instr. mathematics U. Cal., 1890-92, asst. prof., 1892-94, asst. prof. astronomy and geodesy, 1894-98, asso. prof., 1898-1907, dir. Student Obs., 1898-1938, prof. astronomy and chmn. dept., 1907-38, dean Grad. Sch., 1913-18, 20-23, prof. of astronomy and dir. Students Observatory, emeritus, 1938—. Mem., sec. Cal. Earthquake Commn., 1906-10. Spl. expert U.S. Shipping Board, 1917; in charge U. Cal. Naval Tng. activities, 1917-18; chmn. scientific com. and com. on occupational selection Cal. Council of Defense, 1918; maj. C.W.S., U.S. Army, 1918-19. Awarded Watson gold medal, Nat. Acad. Sciences for researches in astronomy, 1916; Knight Order of the North Star (Sweden), 1924; Bruce gold medal, Astron. Soc. Pacific, 1936; Rittenhouse medal, 1937. Halley lectr. U. Oxford, 1938. Fellow Cal. Acad. Scis., A.A.A.S. (pres. Pacific div. 1931-32), Seismol. Soc. Am., Internat. Geophys. Union, Astron. Soc. Pacific (pres. 1908, 36, 43); mem. Nat. Acad. Sciences, NRC, Am. Philos. Soc., Am. Math. Soc., Astronomische Gesellschaft, Am. Astron. Soc., Washington Acad. Scienes, Am. Assn. U. Profs. (pres. 1923-25), Delta Tau Delta, Sigma Xi, Phi Beta Kappa; fgn. asso. Royal Astron. Soc. of London; foreign mem. Royal Physiographical Soc., Lund, Sweden. Exec. sec. Nat. Research Council and acting chmn. div. of physical sciences, 1919; chmn. com. on comets and minor planets, Internat. Astron. Union, 1919-38, hon. chmn., 1938—. Clubs: University (San Francisco); Faculty (Berkeley); Cosmos (Washington); Authors' (London). Special field of investigation, theoretical astronomy; also perturbations of the Watson asteroids; improvement in the methods of determining preliminary orbits of comets and planets; perturbations of the Hecuba group of minor planets. Author: Beitrage zür Kometenbahnestimmung, Berlin, 1897; Short Methods of Determining Orbits from Three Observations; Tables of Minor Planets Discovered by James C. Watson; Research Surveys of 1091 Minor Planets; also papers on astron. subjects. Died Apr. 22, 1953.

LEUTWILER Oscar Adolph (lūt'wi-lẽr), mech. engr.; b. Highland, Ill., Feb. 16, 1877; s. Adolph and Selina (Seeger) L.; B.S. in Mech. Engring., U. Ill., 1899, M.E., 1900; m. Elise Kaeser, Sept. 5, 1901; children—Lester Glen, Kathryn Elizabeth. Instr. dept. mech. engring., Lehigh U., 1901-03; asst. prof. machine design, 1903-15, prof., 1915-21, prof. mech. engring. design, U. Ill., since Sept. 1921, head dept. mech. engring. since July 1934; Prof. mech. engring. design emeritus, 1945—. Mem. Am. Soc. M.E., Soc. Automotive Engrs., Soc. Promotion Engring. Edn. Am. Gear Mfrs. Assn., Sigma Alpha Epsilon, Sigma Iota Epsilon, Tau Beta Pi, Sigma Xi, Pi Tau Sigma, Theta Tau. Author: Elementary Machine Design, 1906; Mechanics of Machinery, Part I, 1907, Part II, 1908; Notes on Power Plant Design, 1913, rewritten and enlarged, 1947; Elements of Machine Design, 1917; Problems in Machine Design, 1923. Home: 710 Pennsylvania Av., Urbana, Ill. Died May 31, 1953; buried Mount Hope Cemetery, Urbana.

LEVAND, Louis, publisher; b. Russia, Jan. 25, 1887; s. Benjamin and Lena (Bornstein) L.; student pub. schs.; m. Irene Feltus, Aug. 25, 1929. Came to U.S., 1900, naturalized, 1906. Pub. Wichita Beacon since 1928. Clubs: Bankers (N.Y.C.), Wichita, Nat. Press (Washington). Home: 404 Courtleigh Dr., Wichita, Kan. Died July 24, 1953.

LEVAND, Max M. (lē-vănd'), pres. pub. co.; b. Cincinnati, O., May 28, 1892; s. Benjamin and Lena (Bornstien) L.; m. Lillian Eppstein, June 28, 1916; children—Elliott A., Jack B., Marvin H. With Denver (Colo.) Post, 1901-15, Kan. City (Mo.) Post, 1915-23, Casper (Wyo.) Herald, 1923-26, and St. Joseph (Mo.) Gazette, 1926-27; pres., gen. mgr., Beacon Newspaper Corp., Inc. (pub. of Wichita Beacon), Wichita, Kan., 1928—. Mem. Wichita C. of C. Mason (Shriner). Club: Rotary (Wichita). Home: 151 Courtleigh Dr. Office: Box 2082, Wichita 1, Kan. Died Mar. 22, 1960.

LEVER, (Richard) Hayley (lē'vẽr), artist; b. Adelaide, S. Australia, Sept. 28, 1876; s. Albion William and Catherine (Hayley) L.; ed. Prince Alfred College, Adelaide; studied in Paris, London, New York and St. Ives, Cornwall, Eng.; m. Aida Smith Gale, Dec. 28, 1905 (dec. 1949); 1 son, Richard Hayley. Came to U.S., 1912; art instructor Art Students' League, New York, since 1920. Hon. mention, Internat. Exbn., Carnegie Inst., Pittsburgh, 1913; silver medal, Nat. Arts Club, 1914; Carnegie prize, Nat. Acad., 1914; gold medal, San Francisco Expn., 1915, Nat. Arts Club, 1916; Sesnan gold medal, Pa. Acad. Fine Arts, 1917; Phila. Water Color Club prize, 1918; 4th prize, N.A.C., 1922; Temple gold medal, Pa. Acad., 1926; medal Montclair (New Jersey) Art Museum; Newark Art Club prize, Tercentary Exhibition; Edwin Palmer marine award of $500, 1936; bronze medal, Sesquicentennial, Phila., Pa.; Edwin Palmer marine prize of $600, Nat. Academy, 1938; Flower Painting prize, National Arts Club, 1940; New Rochelle Art Assn., N.Y., medal, 1941; Westchester Arts Craft Award, 1945, 1946, 1952; honorary mention, International Water Color Exhibition, Chicago, 1940. Represented in Sydney and Adelaide galleries, Bklyn. Mus., Pa. Acad. Fine Arts, Corcoran Art Gallery, Ft. Worth Mus., Detroit Inst. Arts, Des Moines Art Mus., Balt. Mus., Dallas Mus., Telfair Mus. (Savannah), U. Mus. (Lincoln, Neb.), Duncan Phillips Meml. Mus. (Washington), Whitney Mus. Am. Art, 1931, in White House, Washington (yacht Mayflower painted for Pres. Coolidge), St. Louis Art Mus., Montclair (N.J.) Art Mus., Syracuse (N.Y.) Art Mus., Nat. Arts Club, Los Angeles Mus., Duquesne Club Gallery, Pitts., Memphis Art Mus., Met. Mus. N.Y., Perth Amboy (N.J.) Pub. Library; Salt Lake U. Mus., also many pvt. collections. Mem. Nat. Arts Club (life), Nat. Acad., Whitney Studio Club, Royal British Artists, Royal Inst. Oil Painters, Royal West Eng. Acad., Art Students League (hon. life), Conn. Acad. of Fine Arts, Am. Painters and Engravers; Mt. Vernon Art Assn. (hon. life); A.N.A., 1926, N.A., 1933. Address: Nat. Arts Club, 19 Gramercy Park, N.Y.C. Died 1958.

LEVERICH, Henry Priestley, fgn. service officer; b. New Orleans, Aug. 12, 1907; s. Henry and Rachel (Bosworth) L.; student Taft Sch., Watertown, Conn., 1923-26; A.B., Princeton, 1930; m. Katharine S. Bingham, Apr. 29, 1932; children—Nancy Bingham, Bingham Bosworth, John B. (dec.). Apptd. fgn. service officer Dept. of State, 1931, vice consul, Geneva, 1931-32, vice consul, sec. Embassy, Berlin, 1933-40, sec. of legation, Lisbon, 1941-43, counselor of legation, Bucharest, 1947-48; to staff Dept. of State, asst. chief Central European Div., 1943-45, chief Area Div. V, 1946-47, with Office of European Affairs, Div. of Information Policy since 1949; in charge of Balkan Affairs, U.S. Dept. of State, 1952-56, dep. dir. Office Eastern European Affairs, 1956-59, dir. Eastern European Affairs 1959—. Office: care Dept. of State, Washington 25. Died Aug. 12, 1959.

LEVERONE, Louis Edward, corporation exec.; b. Wakefield, Mass., Apr. 29, 1880; s. Robert and Rose (Fosser) L.; B.S., Dartmouth, 1904; student John Marshall Law Sch., 1912; LL.D., Bradley University, 1951; married Florence M. Hanson, January 8, 1914. With Western Electric Co., Chicago, 1904-05; western salesman, Page Belting Co., Concord, N.H., 1905-09; sales mgr. Colonial Leather Co., Chicago, 1909-12; sales mgr. Stein, Hirsh and Co., Chicago, 1912-20; v.p., gen. mgr. Stein-Hall Mfg. Co., Chicago, 1920-42, and dir., dir. Stein, Hall & Co., Ltd. of Canada, 1931-42; chmn. bd. Automatic Canteen Co. of America, 1929-35, president, 1944-50, vice chairman and director, 1950-52; partner, Canteen Co., 1939—; general manager Canteen Food Service, 1942-45, pres. Nationwide Food Service, Inc., 1945—; director Nu Enamel, 1949—; owner Leverone Nursery, Half-Day, Ill.; chmn. bd., dir. Midway Air Lines; chmn. bd., pres. Nationwide Food Service, Ltd., Toronto; dir. Frontier Air Lines. Pres. Northwestern U. Settlement, 1940-43, dir., 1936-43; chmn. bd. Ill. Citizenship Conf., 1938—; mem. Ill. Chamber of Commerce (dir. 1937-41, chmn. legisl. com. 1939-41, pres. 1941-42, chmn. bd. 1942-43, chmn. aviation com. 1943-45); gen. chmn. Nat. Aviation Clinic; co-chmn. exec. com., Fifth Annual Aviation Clinic, Springfield, Ill., 1947; co-chmn. 6th Annual Aviation Clinic, Detroit, Oct. 1948; councillor for Ill., Nat. Aero. Assn., 1946-48, dir. and pres., 1948-52; v.p., 1952—. Insp., Ill. Aero. Commn., 1945—; pres. Ill. Aviation Conf., 1942—; chmn. sub-com. Air Transportation, Gov. Green's Ill. Postwar Planning Commn., 1944-48. Dir. Lustron Corp., Columbus, O., 1947; v.p. and director Property Investment Co., Eau Claire, Wis.; chmn. bd., dir. Perma-Metal Homes, Houston, Tex.; dir. and v.p., Homes of Distinction, Inc., Chicago, 1948. Mem. bd. mgrs. Nat. Air Council, 1948; adv. com. Nat. Safety Council, Chgo., 1948, mem. aviation com., 1949. Hon. chmn. Ill. Council Mgrs. Com.; mem. Council of Social Agencies of Chicago; mem. Am. Arbitration Assn., Ill. Development Council; mem. Defense Savings Com. for State of Ill., 1942-44; chmn. Civilian War Service Com., 1943-44; trustee, Union League Foundn. for Boys' Clubs, 1945—. Mem. adv. com. The Armed Forces Officers Club; mem. sponsoring com., Am. Bible Soc.; mem. Chicago Assn. Commerce (former mem. exec. com., former chmn. food products div.); mem. N.Y. State C. of C. Nat. Restaurant Assn., Am. Forestry Assn.; mem. adv. com. Nat. Safety Council, Chicago, 1948—. Founder, Phi Gamma Delta Vocational Bur., 1923; founder, Dartmouth Coll. Vocational Guidance Com. 1937; pres. Dartmouth Alumni Assn., Chicago, 1931-32; mem. Dartmouth Coll. Alumni Council, 1931-37. Mem. Collier Trophy com., 1948—; chmn. Inds. Panel Air Coordinating Com., 1948—; mem. John Jeffries Award, Inst. Aero. Scis., Inc.; hon. mem. Aero clubs of France, England, Belgium and Italy. Mem. bd. mgrs. Nat. Air Council, 1948—. Trustee, Dr. Godfrey Lowell Cabot-Wright Brothers Memorial Fund. Mem. Phi Gamma Delta (councilor, 1931-36, treas., 1936-43, pres., 1943-46). Mason. Clubs: University, Wings, Dartmouth (N.Y.); Univ., Union League, Exmoor Country, Executives (Chgo.); Everglades. Author various articles on bus., aviation and vocational training. Home: 620 N. Lake Rd., Lake Forest, Ill. Office: 18 South Michigan Av., Chgo. 3. Died Mar. 15, 1957; buried Hanover, N.H.

LEVESON GOWER, William Spencer (lōō-son gōre), Fourth Earl Granville, gov. N. Ireland; b. London, Eng., July 11, 1880; s. Earl Granville and Castalia Rosalind (Campbell); ed. at Wixenford and H.M.S. Britannia; m. Rose Contance Bowes-Lyon, May 24, 1916; children—Lady Mary Leveson Gower, Granville James (Maj. The Lord Leveson). Naval cadet Jan. 1894, midshipman, 1896, sub-lt., 1900, lt., 1902, comdr., 1913, capt., 1918, rear adm., 1929, vice adm. (ret.) 1935—; lt. gov. Isle of Man, 1937-45; gov. No. Ireland, 1945—. Chmn. Lilleshall Co. Decorated Knight Comdr. Victorian Order, Companion of the Bath, Knight of Justice of St. John, Distinguished Service Order. Mem. Brit. Amateur Fencing Assn. (pres.). Mem. Ch. of England. Clubs: All England Fencing (pres.), United Services, London Fencing, Sabre, Epée (London); also various gold clubs. Address: Government House, Hillsborough, Northern Ireland. Died June 25, 1953.

LEVIERO, Anthony Harry (lĕ-vē'ro), newspaperman; b. Bklyn., Nov. 24, 1905; s. Anthony Faustino and Thomasina (Lepore) L.; student Columbia, 1926-27, Coll. City of N.Y., 1927-28; m. Fay Harrison, Aug. 29, 1936; 1 dau., Toni Harrison. Office boy, clk., auditor maritime ins. and steamship firms, 1925-26; police reporter N.Y. American, 1926-28; gen. assignments reporter Home News, Bronx, N.Y., 1928; mem. reportorial staff N.Y. Times since 1929; covered crimes, criminal, civil and constl. litigation, mil. activities, U.S. Congress, White House. Enlisted 106th Inf., N.Y. N.G., 1923; 2d lt., M.I. Res., 1935; capt., A.U.S., G-2, E.T.O., G-2 Eastern Assault Force and AFHG, North Africa, 1942-43; GSC, M.I. Div., War Dept. Gen. Staff, 1943-45, advancing from maj. to lt. col.; also chief publs. br., G-2, WDGS. Recipient War Dept. Commendation Medal, 1946. Awarded Pulitzer prize for reporting nat. affairs, 1951. Mem. White House Correspondents Assn. (pres. 1954), Nat. Audubon Soc., Audubon Soc. D.C. Club: National Press (Washington). Home: 2445 Porter St., Washington 8. Office: 1701 K St. N.W., Washington 6. Died Sept. 3, 1956; buried Arlington Nat. Cemetery.

LEVIN, Leonard S., lawyer; b. Pittsburgh, Pa., July 20, 1874; s. Samuel and Mary (Leavitt) L.; grad. Duquesne Coll.; studied law in office of Joseph Stadtfeld, and University of Pittsburgh Law School; married Stella May Fink, Mar. 1, 1906; children—Mary Levin Buxbaum, Robert Fink, Lenore, Levin Wolbarsht. Practiced, Pittsburgh, from 1902; assistant city atty. under mayors Hays and Guthrie, 1903-09, assistant solicitor Allegheny County, 1936-42. Co-pub. Kit-Kats, monthly philos. mag.; editor and pub., The Politican (weekly, devoted to municipal and state govt.). Pres. Jewish Welfare Bd., Pittsburgh, World War I. Mem. legislative com., Credit Assn. Western Pa. (mfrs. and jobbers); acting pres. Nat. Assn. Jr. Republics (succeeding the late Thomas Mott Osborne, noted prison reformer); 1st v.p. Nat. Fedn. Temple Brotherhoods; pres. Redef Shalom Temple Men's Soc. 8 yrs. (life mem., exec. com.); mem. exec. com. (life mem.) Jewish Home for Aged, Pittsburgh; bd. dirs. Irene Kaufman Settlement, Montefiore Hosp., Fedn. Jewish Philanthropies, Young Men's Hebrew Assn. (all at Pittsburgh); bd. dirs. Home for Friendless Children (Erie, Pa.); Allegheny Co. Soc. for Crippled Children (Pittsburgh). Mem. U. of Pittsburgh Law Sch. Alumni Assn. (pres.); mem. gen. com., B'nai B'rith for Pa., N.J. Del. and W. Va. Author: Pa. Bulk Sales Act and other legislation; Trial of Jesus. Home: 76 Strathmore Rd., Brookline, Mass. Died Mar. 27, 1952; buried Sharon Meml. Park, Sharon, Mass.

LEVINGER, David, business exec.; b. Delta, Ida., Aug. 27, 1887; s. Louis and Rosa (Grutzmacher) L.; student Chicago Tech. Coll.; m. Clara Schuemann, Oct. 11, 1911; children—Ruth (Mrs. J. W. Peoples), Donald. Book clerk, A. C. McClurg & Co., Chicago, 1907; with Internat. Harvester Co., 1907-10; with Western Electric Co., Inc., Chicago, 1910—; vice pres., 1942, bd. dirs., 1931-52, ret. 1952; bd. dirs. and mem. exec. com., Chicago Title & Trust Co., 1947—; bd. dirs. Crane Co., Pheoll Mfg. Co. Mem. bd. trustees Ill. Inst. Tech. Mem. Am. Inst. Mining and Metall. Engrs., Am. Soc. M.E., A.A.A.S., Am. Soc. for Metals Chgo. Clubs: Union League, Economic, Chicago, Commercial (Chgo.); LaGrange (Ill.) Country. Home: 245 S. Park Road, LaGrange, Ill. Died Dec. 9, 1956.

LEVINGER, Elma Ehrlich (Mrs. Lee J. Levinger) (lĕv'in-jẽr), author; b. Chicago, Ill., Oct. 6, 1887; d. Samuel and Sarah (Fernberg) Ehrlich; student U. of Chicago, 1907-08, Radcliffe Coll., Cambridge, Mass., 1911-12; m. Lee J. Levinger, June 15, 1916; children—Samuel Harold (dec.), Leah Judith, Joseph Solomon. Teacher rural schools, Iowa and Illinois; dramatic dir. for Junior Drama League, Chicago, 1912; director entertainment Bureau Jewish Education, New York, 1913-15. Mem. Nat. Council of Jewish Women, Hadassah. Author: Jewish Holy-day Stories, 1918; The New Land, 1920; Playmates in Egypt (transl. into German), 1920; In Many Lands, 1923; Jewish Festivals in the Religious Schools, 1923; The Tower of David, 1924; Bible Stories for Very Little People, 1925; Through the School Year, 1925; Tales Old and New, 1926; Great Jews Since Bible Times, 1926; (with husband) The Story of the Jew, 1928; Wonder Tales of Bible Days, 1929; With the Jewish Child in Home and Synagogue, 1930; Entertaining Programs for the Assembly, 1930; Grapes of Canaan, 1931; Benjamin's Book About His Family, 1933; Bread for Beauty, 1935; More Stories of the New Land, 1938; Pilgrims to Palestine, 1940; Great Jewish Women, 1940; (with husband) Folk and Faith, 1942; The Beautiful Garden: Fighting Angel, the Story of Henrietta Szold, 1945; The Golden Door, 1947; Fathers of Israel, 1949; Albert Einstein, a biography, 1949; Galileo, 1952; They Fought for Freedom, 1953; Leonardo da Vinci, 1954; Jewish Adventures in America, 1955; Elijah, Prophet of the One God, 1956; also many plays and dramas, Winner of two national prizes of the Drama League of America, a national contest offered by Sinai Center (Chicago), also national contest for novel, "Grapes of Canaan."; Jewish Book Council Am. awards, 1957. Editor of The Jewish Child (mag.), 1914-15. Address: P.O. Box 884, Los Altos, Cal. Died Jan. 27, 1958.

LEVINSON, Abraham, physician; b. Aug. 25, 1888; s. Yehudah and Rebecca (Kreuger) L.; M.D., U. of Ill., 1911; postgrad. work U. of Vienna, 1914; B.S., U. of Chicago, 1917; studied Vienna and Berlin, 1923, 28, 30, 33; m. Ida Perlstein, 1912; children—Myrtle, Judith, Julian. Began practice, Chicago, 1911; child specialist; sr. attending pediatrist Michael Reese and Mt. Sinai hosps.; attending pediatrist, chief staff, children's div., Cook County Hosp.; v.p. staff Michael Reese Hosp., 1932-34; professor pediatrics Northwestern U. Med. Sch.; prof. pediatrics Cook County Grad. Sch. Medicine; dir. Dr. Julian Levinson Research Found. Pediatric Neurology. Ceritfied Am. Bd. Peditarics. Mem. A.M.A. (certfiicate honor, class 1, exhibit on cerebro-spinal fluid, 1932), Ill. Med. Soc. (certificate of merit for exhibit of original sci. research 1936, 1940; chmn. com. on mental hygiene), Chicago Med. Soc., Chicago Pediatric Soc. (v.p. 1934-35; pres. 1935-36), Am. Acad. Pediatrics, Inst. of Medicine, Am. Assn. Med. History, Sigma Xi, Phi Delta Epsilon. Recipient gold medal emblematic grand sci. award Phi Lambda Kappa for outstanding contbns. to sci. medicine, 1940, orator key of History of Medicine Soc. of Tulane U., 1942. Author: Cerebro-spinal Fluid in Health and Disease, 1919, 3d edit., 1929; Tobias and His Work, 1924; Examination of Children, 1924, 2d edit., 1927; Textbook on Pediatric Nursing, 1925, 3d edit., 1944 (Hebrew translation, 1933); Pioneers of Pediatrics, 1936, 1943; The Mentally Retarded Child, 1952; also numerous articles for med. jours. pertaining to children's diseases, chapters for various Systems of pediatrics, also translated German chapters on pediatrics. Condr. research in biochemistry and pediatrics. Home: 2933 Sheridan Rd. Office: 30 N. Michigan Av., Chgo. Died Sept. 17, 1955.

LEVINTHAL, Bernard Louis (lĕv'in-thawl), rabbi; b. Vilna, Russia, May 12, 1865; s. Rabbi Abraham and Sarah L.; ed. in Russian schs.; grad. High Rabbinical Insts. of Kovno and Wilna, Russia, 1888; D.D. (hon.) Yeshivah U., 1942; D.H.L. (hon.) Jewish Inst. Religion, 1948; m. Minna Kleinberg, Mar. 1886 (died 1929); m. 2d, Sarah B. Zizling, 1935; children—Israel H., Louis E., Abraham A. Came to U.S., 1891; minister United Orthodox Hebrew Congregations of Phila., 1891-48, ret. Founder Hebrew Free Schs., Free Burial Soc., Kohsher Meat Assn., and other Hebrew assns. of Phila.; founder and now pres. Orthodox Rabbinical Assn. of America, Hebrew Talmudic Inst., Phila.; founder and prin. Hebrew High Sch., Phila.; mem. Am. Jewish Com.; hon. v.p. Federation of Am. Zionists; mem. bd. of delegates of civil and religious rights of Jews; organized Council of Jewish Clubs of Phila.; mem. delegation of Am. Jewish Congress to Peace Conf., Paris. Mem. faculty, Rabbinical Coll. of America, New York. Address: 716 Pine St., Phila. Died Sept. 23, 1952.

LEVITT, Robert Daniels, publisher; b. N.Y.C., July 10, 1910; s. Israel Abraham and Naomi Rose (Daniels) L.; student N.Y.U., 1926; A.B., Rollins Coll., 1931; student Columbia Law Sch., 1931-33; m. Ethel Merman, Oct. 15, 1941 (div.); children—Ethel Merman, Robert Daniels; m. 2d, Sherry Shadburne, July 10, 1952. Reporter, feature writer, columnist N.Y. Jour., 1933-38; advt. promotion mgr. N.Y. Jour.-Am., 1938-39, promotion dir., 1939-40; asst. to circulation dir. Hearst Newspapers, 1941-42; dir. Hearst Promotion Enterprises, 1946-51; asso. pub. The Am. Weekly, also Puck-The Comic Weekly, 1951-53, pub., 1953-55; v.p., dir. Hearst Consol. Newspapers, Inc., Hearst Pub. Co., Inc.; dir. nat. sales Screen Gems, TV subsid. Columbia Pictures, 1956; v.p., gen. mgr. California Nat. Prodns., film subsidiary NBC, 1956-57, pres., 1957—. Served from capt. to lt. col. AUS, 1942-45. Mem. Inter-Am. Press Assn., Omicron Delta Kappa. Episcopalian. Mason. Club: Overseas Press. Home: 405 E. 54 St. Office: 663 5th Av., N.Y.C. 22. Died Jan. 27, 1958.

LEVY, Austin T., company exec.; b. N.Y. City, Dec. 16, 1880; s. Theodore and Joanna (Oppenheim) L.; student pub. schs. N.Y. City; m. June Rockwell, Nov. 10, 1915. Pres. Stillwater Worsted Mills, Harrisville, R.I., 1909-42, The Harrisville (R.I.) Co. since 1942. Republican candidate U.S. Senate, 1950. Author social-econ. articles, pamphlets. Address: Harrisville, R.I. Died Nov. 24, 1951.

LEVY, Irving J(acob), lawyer; b. N.Y.C., July 24, 1904; s. Dr. Maurice and Ida (Ratner) L.; B.S., Coll. City N.Y., 1924; LL.B., Columbia, 1929, LL.M., 1930; m. Dora Glesin, June 30, 1930; children—Susan, John. University fellow and research asst. Columbia, 1930-31; admitted to N.Y. bar, 1930; D.C. bar, 1937; in practice of law with Max D. Steuer, N.Y.C., 1931-34; supervising atty. NRA, Washington, 1934-35; asst. gen. counsel Resettlement Adminstrn., Washington, 1935-37; div. chief, solicitor's office Dept. Agr., 1937-38; asst. gen. counsel Wage and Hour Adminstrn., 1938-40; asst. solicitor Dept. Labor, 1940-42, asso. solicitor, 1942-43, acting solicitor, 1942-43; spl. asst. to atty. gen. of U.S., 1943-46; pvt. practice of law, Washington, 1946—; mem. Rauh & Levy, 1947—; gen. counsel United Automobile Workers (UAW-CIO), 1947—; lectr. Washington Coll. of Law, 1947—. Mem. D.C. Bar Assn. Contbr. articles to legal jours. Home: 3140 Highland Pl., Washington 8. Office: 1631 K St., Washington 6. Died Feb. 16, 1951.

LEWIS, Allen, artist; b. Mobile, Ala., Apr. 7, 1873; s. Seth Francis and Ida (Clark) L.; ed. pub. schs., Buffalo; studied Buffalo Art Students League, under George Bridgman; École des Beaux Arts, Paris, under Gérôme; m. Bessie Jayne, May 2, 1917. Exhibited at various salons and at Paris Expn., 1900, under name of Arthur Allen Lewis; returned to U.S., 1902; teacher wood engraving and color printing, etching, and illustration Art Students League, N.Y.C., 1924-32; teacher of wood engraving and etching New Sch. for Social Research, N.Y.C., 1932-34. Awarded Logan prize Chgo. Soc. of Etchers, 1916; Noyes prize Bklyn. Soc. of Etchers, 1917; bronze medal St. Louis Expn., 1904; gold medal San Francisco Expn., 1915; silver medal for woodcut Sesquincentennial Expn., Phila., 1926; Nathan I. Bijur prize Soc. Am. Etchers, 1928; John G. Agar prize Nat. Arts Club, 1928. Works on permanent exhbn. Harvard U. Library, Met. Mus. of Art; N.Y. Pub. Library; Bklyn. Mus. Arts and Sciences; Art Inst. Chgo.; Cleve. Mus.; Detroit Mus.; British Mus.; Bibliothéque Nationale, Paris; Allen Lewis collection Columbia University Library. Nat. Academician. Mem. Bklyn. Soc. of Etchers (1st pres.), Am. Inst. Graphic Arts (v.p. 1928-29). Republican. Presbyn. Illustrated: Undine; Journeys to Bagdad; Diverse Proverbs; Paul Bunyan; Short Stories (by Walt Whitman); Calico Bush; Hepatica Hawks; Once at Woodhall; Society Faces the Future; Ivanhoe; Longfellow's Poems; Made in India. Home: 97 N. Maple Av., Basking Ridge, N.J. Died Mar. 22, 1957; buried Florida, N.Y.

LEWIS, Arthur R(aymond), Jr., steamship exec.; b. N.Y. City, Mar. 6, 1909; s. Arthur Raymond and Fanny Gunver (Rungsted) L.; student Riverdale Country Sch., 1919-28; B.S., Yale, 1932; m. Beverly Kraft, Apr. 26, 1935 (divorced 1938); m. 2d, Marie Mahoney, Apr. 1, 1939. With Seas Shipping Co., Inc., and American-Cuban Steamship Line, Inc., N.Y. City, since 1932, inaugurated Atlantic and Great Lakes S.S. Co. service from Boston to Chicago, 1933, v.p., dir. Seas Shipping Co., 1933, pres., dir. since 1934, established regular freight and passenger service from U.S. North Atlantic ports to South and East Africa under trade name Robin Line, 1935; pres., dir. 39 Cortlandt St. Corp. since 1934. Mem. adv. bd. Chase Nat. Bank. Mem. Am. Bur. Shipping. Operated 60 ships for U.S. Govt., World War II. Mem. Maritime Assn. Port N.Y. (director), Am. Merchant Marine Conf. (dir.), Soc. Naval Architects and Engrs. Clubs: New York Athletic, Yale, Whitehall, Westchester Country, Wee Burn, Woodway. Home: 721 Hollow Tree Ridge Rd., Darien, Conn. Office: 39 Cortlandt St., N.Y.C. 7. Died Mar. 16, 1954.

LEWIS, David John, ex-congressman; b. nr. Osceola, Pa., May 1, 1869; s. Richard Lloyd and Catharine (Watkins) L.; never attended sch.; learned to read in Sunday sch.; m. Florida M. Bohn, Dec. 19, 1893. Employed in coal mine from age of 9 to 23; studied law and Latin; admitted to bar, 1892, and since in practice at Cumberland. Mem. Md. Senate, 1902-04; Dem. nominee for 61st Congress, 1908; elected 62d to 64th and 72d to 75th Congresses, 6th Md. Dist.; mem. U.S. Tariff Commn., 1917-25. Mem. Nat. Acad. of Sciences (physics sect.). Home: Cumberland, Md. Died Aug. 12, 1952; buried Cumberland.

LEWIS, Edward McElhiney, pub. relations ofcl.; b. St. Louis, Jan. 26, 1884; s. Edward Simmons and Pattie (Cooke) L.; ed. Smith Acad, St. Louis; Yale, 1902-04; m. Katherine Richardson, Aug. 19, 1919. Customers' man, stock broker's office, 1905; farmer on own irrigated farm nr. Santa Maria, Tex., 1907-13; polit. reporter, St. Louis Star, 1914-21; Washington corr., The Am. Legion, 1922-36; Rep. Congl. Com., 1936; with VA, 1937—, now dir. pub. relations. Enlisted U.S. Army 1917, attended 1st officers T.C., commd. 1st lt., promoted capt., hdqrs. troop, 10th div., staff Maj. Gen. Wood; disch., 1919. Mem. Book and Snake Soc. (Yale), Nat. Press Club Post, Am. Legion, S.R., War of 1812, Colonial Wars. Club: National Press (Washington). Home: 3133 O St., Washington 7. Office: Veterans Administration, Vermont and H St., Washington 25. Died Aug. 8, 1954; buried Arlington Cemetery, Washington.

LEWIS, Elijah Banks, ex-congressman; b. Dooly Co., Ga., Mar. 27, 1854; ed. pub. schs.; engaged in banking and mercantile bus., Montezuma, Ga. Mem. Ga. Senate, 1894-5; mem. 55th to 60th Congresses, 3d Ga. Dist. Democrat. Address: Montezuma, Ga. Deceased.

LEWIS, Elizabeth Foreman, author; b. Balt.; May 24, 1892; d. Joseph Francis and Virginia D. (Bayly) Foreman; student Tome Sch., 1906-09, Md. Inst. Fine Arts, Balt., 1909-10, Bryant and Stratton Secretarial Sch., Balt., 1916-17; studied Bibl. Sem. of N.Y., 1917; m. John Abraham Lewis, Jan. 28, 1921 (died 1934); 1 son, John Fulton. Asst. treas. Woman's Fgn. Missionary Soc., Shanghai, 1917-18; tchr. dist. schs., Chungking, W. China, 1918-19, Boys' Acad., Nanking, 1919-21. Methodist. Author: Young Fu of the Upper Yangtze, 1932 (awarded John Newbery Medal, A.L.A. 1933); Ho-Ming, Girl of New China, 1934; China Quest, 1937 (previous books now appear in Braille and many European langs); Portraits from a Chinese Scroll, 1938; preceding books were also pub. in Eng.); Test Tubes and Dragon Scales (with Dr. Geo. C. Basil), 1940; When the Typhoon Blows, 1942 (pub. in Eng.; transl. into Portuguese, Russian and Italian; recorded for Jr. League radio programs); also short stories in juvenile and adult mags. and anthologies. Home: Briar Cliff-on-Severn, Arnold, Md. Died Aug. 7, 1958.

LEWIS, Eugene W., banker; b. Belle Vernon, Pa., Sept. 6, 1870; s. Thornton F. and Margaret E. (Evans) L.; student pub. schs., New Castle, Pa., Curry U., Pitts.; m. Margaret M. Mellinger, June 3, 1902. Began as clk. Raney & Berger Iron & Steel Co., New Castle; with various cos., Pa., O.; gen. mgr. East Ohio Gas Co.; v.p. J. H. McLain Co., Canton, O.; pres. Canton Incandescent Light Co.; an organizer, v.p., treas. Timken-Detroit Axle Co.; organized Lewis Bonbright & Co., 1920, also new co., Lewis and Co. Inc.; an organizer, dir., Northwest Airways; an organizer, dir., v.p., Nat. Air Transport, Inc.; chief of prodn. br. Gen. Staff, War Dept., Washington, during war; pres., chmn. bd. Industrial Nat. Bank; dir. Sea Island Co. Apptd. by Sec. of State Kellogg as one of eight U.S. dels. to Internat. Congress on Pub. Works and Constrn., Paris, France, June 1925. Trustee Detroit Bur. Governmental Research, Detroit Tb. Sanatorium. Dir. Better Bus. Bur. Detroit; an organizer, dir., Detroit Citizens League; an organizer Detroit Boys' Club; organizer, dir. Community Fund. Mem. Am., Mich. bankers assns., Detroit Dist. Golf Assn. (bd. govs.), Childrens' Aid Soc. (pres., organizer), Frontier Nursing Soc. (nat. dir.). Republican. Mason (Shriner). Clubs: Detroit, Detroit Boat, Detroit Athletic (an organizer, founding dir.), Detroit Automobile; Grosse Point, Country (Grosse Point); Automobile of Mich. (dir., chmn. com. to investigate, report on plan for ins. of cars), Aero of Mich. (founding dir.). Originator of plan for indsl. relief, based upon 30 per cent of amount needed from fed. govt., 30 per cent from state govt., 25 per cent from employers, 15 per cent from employees. Author: Motor Memories, 1947. Home: 17040 E. Jefferson Av., Grosse Point 30, Mich. Dec. Oct. 2, 1954; buried Elmwood Cemetery.

LEWIS, Fletcher, lawyer; b. Highland Twp., Ind., Jan. 8, 1879; s. Samuel Brenton and Edith May (Sparks) L.; A.B., U. Mich., 1905, J.D., 1911; m. Sylvia Ware Ireland, Mar. 25, 1913 (dec. Feb. 25, 1926); m. 2d, Elizabeth Judd, July 9, 1930; children—Elizabeth Ann, Nancy Jane. High sch. tchr., athletic coach, Dubuque, Ia., also Seattle, 1906-10; admitted to Wash. bar, 1911, Ill., 1917; asso. George H. Walker, Seattle, 1911-17; asso. Butler, Lamb, Foster & Pope, Chgo., 1917-19, mem. firm, and successor firms, 1919-34; sr. partner Lewis & Carson, specializing corp. law, 1936-43; mem. firm McDermott, Will & Emery, 1944—; corporate, labor counsel various corps.; dir. Ottawa Silica Co., Mich. Silica Co. Mem. Am., Ill. State, Chgo. (chmn. drafting com. Ill., Chgo. bar assns. which prepared present Ill. Corporation Act) bar assns., Phi Alpha Delta. Republican. Methodist. Clubs: Univ., Mid Day (Chgo.). Author articles on corporate legal subjects. Home: 821 Kimball Rd., Highland Park, Ill. Office: 111 W. Monroe St., Chgo. 3. Died Mar. 14, 1955; buried Hopewell Cemetery, Vermillion County, Ind.

LEWIS, Franklin Allan, sports editor; b. Lafayette, Ind., Jan. 18, 1904; s. John Ralph and Mae (Armacost) L.; Purdue U., ex-1926; m. Helen Virginia Palmer, Dec. 8, 1939. Editorial work Miami

(Fla.) Daily Tab. 1925; sports editor Daytona Beach (Fla.) News-Jour., 1927-29, also lifeguard, Daytona Beach; press agt.-juvenile, touring Tab museum shows, 1929-30; asst. sports editor Cleve. Press, 1931-37, sports editor, sports columnist since 1939; sports editor radio sta. WGAR, Cleve., 1937-39. Mem. U.S. Attorney Gen's. Com. to Combat Juvenile Delinquency. Mem. Phi Kappa Sigma, Sigma Delta Chi. Author: The Cleveland Indians, 1949; (popular songs) My Virginia Rose, 1932; My Baby's Comin' Home, 1933; Sweetest Hour of All, 1935. Contbr. mags. Home: 3644 Norwood Rd., Shaker Heights. 22, O. Office: Cleveland Press, Cleve. 14. Died Mar. 12, 1958.

LEWIS, Franklin Fillmore, ret. coll. pres.; b. Indpls., Dec. 1, 1877; s. Benjamin and Martha (Lovings) L.; A.B., DePauw U., 1904, D.D., 1926; S.T.B., Boston U., 1906; A.M., Harvard, 1908; m. Cynthia Meyer, Oct. 5, 1910; children—Florence Ruth, Martha Katherine, Arnold Meyer, Franklin Lyman. Ordained to ministry M.E. Ch., 1908; pastor at Indpls., 1908-12, Watertown, S.D., 1912-17, Janesville, Wis., 1917-22, Ottawa, Kan., 1922-25, Kansas City, Mo., 1925-26; supt. St. Louis Dist., 1926-32; exec. sec. Bd. of Financial Review, St. Louis Conf. of M.E. Ch., 1932-35; became pres. Central Wesleyan Coll., Warrenton, Mo., 1935, was also trustee; pastor St. Paul's Meth. Ch., St. Louis, 1942-48, ret. 1948; pres. gen. mgr., organizer Lewis Constrn. Co. Trustee Mo. S.S. Council of Religious Edn. (mem. exec. com.), Wesley House (St. Louis), Anti-Saloon League: mem. exec. com. Internat. Council Religious Edn. Mem. Nat. Conf. Social Work; pres. bd. trustees St. Louis Conf., Meth. Ch. Mem. Assn. Coll. Presidents, Pi Gamma Mu, Delta Sigma Rho. Club: Osage Hills Country. Composer words and music of Good Bye Dear Homeland (war song). Established Lewis Sermon award DePauw U., 1954. Home: 555 W. Glendale Rd., Webster Groves, Mo. Died May 21, 1957.

LEWIS, Fred Justin, dean engring.; b. Blandford, Mass., Dec. 24, 1890; s. William Henry and Julia Freeland (Boise) L.; B.S. in C.E., U. of Me., 1914; M.S. in Hydraulic Engring., Pa. State Coll., 1923; C.E., U. of Me., 1922; m. Maude Ethel Hills, June 23, 1917; 1 dau., Alice Elizabeth (Mrs. Glenn Dixon Henderson). Instr. civ. engring., and asst. to boro engr., Pa. State Coll., 1914-16; valuation div., C.B. &Q. Ry. and M.P. R.R., 1916-17; asst. engr., City of Springfield, Mass., 1917-18, U.S. Army, 1918-19; instr. and asst. prof. civ. engring., Lehigh U., 1919-25; asso. prof., prof. civil engring., Vanderbilt University, 1925-33, dean School of Engineering since 1933; consultant in municipal and sanitary engineering. Member C. of C., Engring. Assn., Nashville (past president), American Society Civ. Engrs., Soc. Promotion Engring. Edn., Am. Pub. Health Assn., Am. Water Works Assn., Kappa Sigma, Phi Kappa Phi, Tau Beta Pi, Omicron Delta Kappa. Baptist. Club: Rotary (Nashville) (pres.). Home: Castleman Drive, Nashville, Tenn. Died Jan. 4, 1959; buried Woodlawn Cemetery, Nashville.

LEWIS, Frederic Thomas, educator; b. Cambridge, Mass., Mar. 18, 1875; s. Charles Sanford and Nettie Farnum (Brown) L.; A.B., Harvard, 1897, A.M., 1898, M.D., 1901; m. Ethel May Stickney, July 30, 1904; 1 son, Thomas Lothrop. Austin fellow in histology and embryology Harvard Med. Sch., 1901-02, instr., 1902-06, asst. prof., 1906-15, asso. prof. of embryology, 1915-31, prof. of comparative anatomy, 1931-41, prof. emeritus, 1941—. Fellow American Academy Arts and Scis., Fellow of Royal Microscopical Society, A.A.A.S.; member American Assn. Anatomists (v.p. 1914-16; pres. 1936-38), Boston Soc. Natural Hist. (v.p. 1926-29), Phi Beta Kappa. Author embryol. papers and of an arrangement of Stöhr's Lehrbuch der Histologie upon an embryol. basis. Demonstrator of 14-hedral shape of plant and animal cells. Home: 538 Chestnut St., Waban 68, Mass. Died June 2, 1951.

LEWIS, George Francis, lawyer; b. New York, N.Y., Nov. 21, 1885; s. Francis Cornelius and Sarah Elizabeth (Kelley) L.; student Mt. Hermon (Mass.) Boys Sch., 1902-04; LL.B., Cornell U., 1907; m. Elizabeth Lofgren, Mar. 2, 1912; children—Robert Gibson, George Francis. Admitted to N.Y. bar, 1907; mem. firm Lewis & MacDonald; v.p. and counsel Technicolor, Inc., Technicolor Motion Picture Corp.; counsel Heyden Chem. Corp., Am. Aniline Products Corp. Mem. Am. and N.Y. state bar assns., Delta Chi. Mason. Clubs: Downtown Athletic, Cornell, Lawyers, Union League. Home: 220 Madison Av. Office: 15 Broad St., N.Y.C. Died Nov. 17, 1953.

LEWIS, Harry Herbert, b. Miss., Mar. 16, 1891; s. William T. and Mary Nora (Joyce) L.; m. Lillian Miller, Aug. 19, 1917. Law enforcement officer, 1927-35; pub. relations, 1935-41; regional dir. Fed. Mediation Service, Seattle since 1941. Served in inf. and tank corps, U.S. Army, 1917-19. Mem. Am. Legion. Mason (K.T.). Home: 2034 E. 110, Seattle 55. Office: Republic Bldg., Seattle 1. Deceased.*

LEWIS, Henry Steele, business exec.; b. Pittsburgh, Pa., May 25, 1900; s. George Harding and Regina (Steele) L.; student Norfolk Acad., 1915, Episcopal High School, Alexandria, Va., 1916-18; B. in Chemistry, Cornell U., 1923; m. Virginia Syer, Oct. 22, 1930; 1 son, Henry Steele. With Dunlop Tire & Rubber Co., Buffalo, N.Y., 1923-24; asst. treas. Norfolk (Va.) Ledger Dispatch, 1926-34; sec.-treas. Norfolk Newspapers, Inc. (pub. Ledger Dispatch and Norfolk Virginian Pilot), 1934-35, bus. mgr. and sec.-treas., 1935-46, president since 1946, dir. since 1933; sec.-treas. and dir. WTAR Radio Corp., Norfolk, 1932-46, vice pres. and treas. since 1946; treas. and dir. Ledger Dispatch Corp. since 1946; dir. S. L. Slover Corp., Seaboard Citizens Nat. Bank. Mem. S.A.T.C., Cornell U., 1918, director, Richmond Newspapers, Incorporated. Mem. Chi Phi. Ind. Democrat. Episcopalian. Clubs: Virginia, Norfolk Country (Norfolk); Princess Anne Country (Virginia Beach, Va.). Home: W. 61st St., Virginia Beach, Va. Office: care Norfolk Newspapers, Inc., Norfolk, Va. Died Oct. 24, 1954.

LEWIS, Howard, lawyer; b. Caldwell, O., Oct. 18, 1877; s. Charles Thomas and Dora (Glidden) L.; Denison Univ., 1900; Harvard Law, 1903; m. Caroline Melvin Palmer, Apr. 20, 1910; children—Howard, Melvin Palmer. Admitted to Ohio bar, 1904, and began practice at Toledo; became mem. Doyle & Lewis, 1913, now Doyle, Lewis & Warner. Mem. Am., Ohio State and Toledo bar assns., Sigma Chi. Republican. Baptist. Mason. Clubs: Toledo, Toledo Country. Home: Perrysburg, O. Office: 1633 Nicholas Bldg., Toledo 2. Died Dec. 10, 1950.

LEWIS, Howard Bishop, educator; b. Southington, Conn., Nov. 8, 1887; s. Frederick A. and Charlotte R. (Parmelee) L.; B.A., Yale, 1908, Ph.D., 1913; m. Mildred L. Eaton, June 15, 1915; children—Charlotte Barber, Elizabeth Parmelee. Asst. in physiol. chemistry, Yale, 1911-13; instr. physiol. chemistry, U. of Pa., 1913-15; asso. in physiol. chemistry, U. of Ill., 1915-17, asst. prof., 1917-19, asso. prof., 1919-22; prof. and head dept. of biol. chemistry, Univ. of Mich., 1922—, also dir. College of Pharmacy, 1933-47; John Jacob Abel univ. prof. biol. chemistry, 1947—. Henry Russell lectr. U. of Mich., 1948-49. Mem. National Board of Med. Examiners, 1935-50. Mem. Council on Foods and Nutrition, A.M.A., 1936—. Elected mem. Nat. Acad. Scis., 1949. Fellow A.A.A.S.; mem. Am. Chem. Soc., American Institute Nutrition (council 1941-42; v.p. 1942-43; pres. 1943-44). Am. Pharm. Assn., A.M.A. (associate), Am. Physiol. Soc., Am. Soc. Biol. Chemists (sec. 1929-33, v.p. 1933-35; pres. 1935-37, council 1937-40, 41-42), Soc. Exptl. Biol. and Med. (ed. bd. 1927-38), Alpha Omega Alpha, Phi Beta Kappa. Alpha Chi Sigma, Phi Kappa Phi, Phi Lambda Upsilon, Phi Sigma, Sigma Xi, Rho Chi. Democrat. Episcopalian. Contbr. to scientific jours. on subjects of nutrition and physiol. chemistry. Beaumont lecturer Wayne County Med. Soc., 1932; Harvey Society lecturer, 1941. Mem. editorial bds., Physiol. Reviews, 1935-39, Jour. of Nutrition, 1935-39, 1940-45; Chem. Reviews, 1938-40, Jour. Biol. Chem., 1938—. Home: 1714 Wells St., Ann Arbor, Mich. Died Mar. 7, 1954.

LEWIS, Howard Corwin, publisher; b. New York, N.Y., Oct. 9, 1890; s. James Henry and Sara Electra (Evans) L.; m. Florence Carlson, Nov. 18, 1922; children—John Morgan, Sara Sue. With Dodd, Mead & Co., Inc., publishers, N.Y. City, since 1913, dir. since 1928, president since 1942; vice president and director Dodd, Mead & Co. (Canada), Ltd., Toronto, Ontario. Served with 112th Heavy Field Artillery, Army of United States, Camp McClellan, Alabama, 1917, with A.E.F., France, 1918-19. Dir. Council on Books in Wartime, 1943. Dir. Nat. Assn. Book Pubs., 1932-40 (pres. 1939). Republican. Episcopalian. Clubs: Century Assn., Players (treas. 1939-44), Dutch Treat, Coffee House (N.Y. City); St. Andrews Golf. Home: 1010 Fifth Av. Office: 432 Fourth Av., N.Y.C. Died Oct. 2, 1952; buried Grace Ch., N.Y.C.

LEWIS, J. Wilbur, banker; b. Irvington, N.J., Oct. 9, 1892; s. John R. and Alice Anne (Spear) L.; m. Marion S. Williams, Aug. 2, 1920 (died Sept. 1945); children—Jane A. (Mrs. Marshall Belding), John W.; m. 2d, Ruth Crogan Farrington, Oct. 18, 1946; step-dau., Mrs. John L. Reiss. Connected with Union Dime Savs. Bank, 1911—, becoming asst. sec., 1924, asst. treas., 1934, treas. 1935, trustee 1936, v.p. 1937, pres. 1948; dir. Bank of N.Y., Met. Life Ins. Co.; past pres. Savs. Bank Assn. State N.Y.; dir. Institutional Investors Mut. Fund, Inc., Savs. Banks Trust Co. Republican. Mason. Clubs: Rock Spring (W. Orange, N.J.); Union League (N.Y.C.); Baltusrol Golf (Springfield, N.J.). Home: 181 Hartshorn Dr., Short Hills, N.J. Office: 1065 Sixth Av., N.Y.C. Died May 20, 1959; buried Rosedal Cemetery, Bloomfield, N.J.

LEWIS, James Malcolm, army officer; b. Moundsville, W.Va., Feb. 17, 1898; s. Edgar Malcolm and Marie (McClune), L.; B.S., U.S. Mil. Acad., 1920; grad. F.A., Basic Sch., Fort Knox, Ky., 1921, Command and Gen. Staff Sch., 1936. Commd. 2d lt. F.A., U.S. Army, 1920, advanced through grades to maj. gen., 1954. Decorated Legion of Merit, Bronze Star. Home: 515 Tenth St., Moundsville, W.Va. Office: care, The Adjutant General's Office, War Dept. Washington 25. Died Apr. 19, 1954.

LEWIS, James Ogier, petroleum engr.; b. San Jose, Calif., Jan. 21, 1886; s. Edward B. and Belle (Montgomery) L.; A.B. in Geology, Stanford U., 1917, as of 1909; m. Hazel A. McPike, July 3, 1910; children—Vesta Evadne, Beatrice May, Donald DeWitt. Geologist in Calif., Can., Tex. and Mont., 5 yrs.; with U.S. Bur. Mines 6 yrs., 1916-21, in charge petroleum div. 2 yrs.; built Bartlesville Petroleum Expt. Sta.; now cons. engr., Houston, Tex. Mem. Am. Inst. Mining and Metall. Engrs. (recipient of Anthony F. Lucas Medal, 1946), Am. Assn. Petroleum Geologists. Home: 3340 S. MacGregor. Office: 1552 Mellie Esperson Bldg., Houston. Died June 15, 1954; buried Mountain View Cemetery, Oakland, Cal.

LEWIS, Jesse Willard, retired exec.; b. Fenton, Mich., Nov. 19, 1880; s. Leslie and Etta (Wolfrom) L.; student pub. and night schs., N.Y.C.; m. Florence Smith, Mar. 17, 1910. Clk., runner, office boy Continental Pub. Co., 1896-97; stenographer, sec., clk. motive power and rolling stock dept., maintenance of way dept., engring. dept. N.Y.C. R.R., 1897-1901; bookkeeper, auditor, accountant, statistician Am. Locomotive Co., 1901-10; chief statistician Gen. Electric Co., 1910-21, asst. comptroller, 1921-23, asst. to pres., 1923-36, treas., 1936-47, ret. 1947. Clubs: Mohawk (Schenectady, N.Y.); Bankers (N.Y.C.). Home: 1088 Park Av., N.Y.C. 28. Died Feb. 26, 1957.

LEWIS, John Henry, sch. adminstr., clergyman; b. Americus, Ga., Mar. 8, 1884; s. Sim and Hattie (Smith) L.; A.B., Morris Brown Coll., Atlanta, Ga., 1905; B.D., Yale, 1913; A.M., Univ. of Chicago, 1914; LL.D., Wilberforce (O.) U., 1936; m. Eva Brown Walker, Nov. 8, 1916 (deceased); children—John H., Jr., James W., Milton D., Anita A.; m. 2d, Urnestnie Bell, Aug. 12, 1931; 1 son, David Levering. Ordained to ministry of African Meth. Episcopal Ch., 1915; pastor 1st A.M.E. Ch., Pasadena, Calif., 1918-19; pastor Union A.M.E. Ch., Little Rock, Ark., 1939-40; pres. Morris Brown Coll., 1920-28, 51-58; prin. Dunbar High Sch. and Jr. Coll., Little Rock, Ark., 1929-43; pres. Shorter Coll., North Little Rock, Ark., 1943-44; dean Payne Theol. Sem., Wilberforce U., Wilberforce, O., 1944-51. Mem. N.E.A., Nat. Urban League, Nat. Assn. Advancement of Colored People; Alpha Phi Alpha, Sigma Pi Phi Boule. Republican. Home: 601 University Pl., N.W., Atlanta. Died Oct. 3, 1958; buried South View Cemetery, Atlanta.

LEWIS, Kemp Plummer, textile exec.; b. Raleigh, N.C., Sept. 12, 1880; s. Dr. Richard H. and Cornelia Viola (Battle) L.; A.B., U. N.C., 1900; m. Lottie Hays Sharp, Apr. 16, 1912; children—Ann (Mrs. E.S. Orgain), Margaret (Mrs. H.C. Bridgers), Lottie (Mrs. Charles T. Woollen), Martha (Mrs. David S. Stanley). Sec. to pres. Erwin Mills, Inc., Durham, N.C., 1900-16, asst. sec., treas., 1916-25, sec., treas., 1925-32, pres., treas., 1932-49, chmn. bd. since 1949; v.p. Oxford Cotton Mills, 1932-46, Erwin Yarn Co., 1932-45, Bank of Harnett, 1932-52; dir. Fidelity Bank, Durham & So. Ry. Trustee U. N.C. Mem. Am. Cotton Mfrs. Inst. (pres.), Nat. Assn. Mfrs. (dir.), Phi Beta Kappa. Clubs: Merchants (N.Y.C.); Princess Anne Country (Virginia Beach, Va.); Biltmore (N.C.) Forest Country; Hope Valley Country (Durham). Home: 418 S. Duke St. Office: Erwin Mills, Inc., West Durham Station, Durham, N.C. Died June 1952.

LEWIS, Lloyd Griffith, surgeon; b. Remsen, N.Y., Nov. 10, 1902; s. John Griffith and Nettie (Griffith) L.; A.B., Hamilton Coll., 1924; M.D., Johns Hopkins, 1928; m Lois Falconer, Aug. 16, 1930 (div. Feb. 3, 1959); 1 son, John Richard; m. 2d, Frances Carter Frick, Feb. 14, 1959. Intern, asst. res., resident urology Johns Hopkins Hosp., 1928-33; instr., asst., asso. prof. Johns Hopkins, 1930-46; associate prof. urology med. sch. Georgetown U., 1946-48, prof. urology, 1948-53, prof. clin. urology, 1953; staff Doctors Hosp., Georgetown University Hosp.; consultant urology Walter Reed Army Hosp., Nat. Inst. Health, Bolling Field United States Air Force Hosp. Served as maj. to col., med. corps U.S. Army, 1942-46; chief sect. urology Walter Reed Gen. Hosp. Trustee of Hamilton College. Diplomate American Board of Urology. Member of Am. Medical Assn., Am. Urological Assn. (chmn. com. visual edn.). Contbr. med. jours. Address: Kennedy-Warren Apts., Washington. Died Mar. 2, 1959; buried Arlington Nat. Cemetery.

LEWIS, Lucy May, librarian; b. Traer, Ia., Feb. 5, 1879; d. James Henry and Emmeline (Carmichal) Lewis; student Pomona Coll., 1899, 1902-04; A.B., U. Ill., 1905, B.L.S., 1906; hon. Dr. Library Sci., Ore. State Coll., 1945. Librarian N.M. Coll. A. and M. Arts, 1906-11; asst. librarian, cataloger Ore. State Coll., 1911-18, asst. and reference librarian, 1918-20, librarian, 1920-45; dir. libraries Ore. State System Higher Edn., 1932-45, dir. emeritus, 1945—. Mem. A.L.A. (chmn. 2 groups, mem. exec. bd., mem. coms.), Pacific N.W. (pres. 1936-37; mem. bibliog. center com. 1939—), Ore. library assns., Am. Assn. U. Women, P.E.O., Zeta Kappa Psi, Phi Kappa Phi, Kappa Delta. Republican. Presbyn. Mem. Order of Eastern Star. Club: Zonta.

Co-author: Library Practice for Freshmen, 1922. Contbr. tech. publs. Home: Hotel Benton. Office: Oregon State College Library, Corvallis, Ore. Died Dec. 5, 1951.

LEWIS, Marion L., publisher; b. Valparaiso, Ind.; s. Sylvester A. and Marie (Hansford) L.; student Valparaiso U.; m. Mabel E. Mosher, 1905; children—Bruce Mosher, Koradine (Mrs. Sanford Liftell Smith). Taught sch. Ind. and Kan.; served as dep. treas. Porter County, Ind.; entered publishing bus. traveling through many states of U.S.; organized (as outgrowth of Lewis Pub. Co., Chgo) the Lewis Historical Pub Co., in N.Y. in 1907, has since served as pres. this and subsidiary companies, including The Am. Hist. Co., Inc., Dominion Pub. Co., Ltd.; pres. First Nat. Bank of Nutley, N.J.; dir. Guarantee Title and Mortgage Co., Bank of Nutley, Nutley Mortgage and Title Guaranty Co. Former trustee Valparaiso U.; trustee Centenary Junior Coll., Hackettstown, N.J.; pres. bd. trustees Nutley Free Pub. Library. Methodist (pres. bd. trustees, treas. ofcl. bd.). Mem. C. of C. State N.Y. Home: Nutley, N.J. Office: 80 Eighth Av., N.Y.C. 11. Died Jan. 1, 1951.

LEWIS, Sinclair, author; b. Sauk Centre, Minn., Feb. 7, 1884; s. Edwin J. (M.D.) and Emma (Kermott) Lewis; A.B., Yale University, 1907, Litt.D., 1936; m. Grace Livingstone Hegger, April 15, 1914; 1 son, Wells (killed in World War II); m. 2d, Dorothy Thompson, May 14, 1928; 1 son, Michael. Formerly a reporter, New Haven Journal and Courier, San Francisco Bulletin, Associated Press, etc.; successively asst. editor or editor Transatlantic Tales, Volta Review, Frederick A. Stokes Co., Adventure, Publishers' Newspaper Syndicate, and editor George H. Doran Co., to 1916. Mem. Am. Acad. of Arts and Letters. Author: (novels) Our Mr. Wrenn, 1914; The Trail of the Hawk, 1915; The Job, 1917; The Innocents, 1917; Free Air, 1919; Main Street, 1920; Babbitt, 1922; Arrowsmith, 1925; Mantrap, 1926; Elmer Gantry, 1927; The Man Who Knew Coolidge, 1928; Dodsworth, 1929; Ann Vickers, 1933; Work of Art, 1934; It Can't Happen Here, 1935; Prodigal Parents, 1938; Bethel Merriday, 1940; Gideon Planish, 1943; Cass Timberlane, 1945; Kingsblood Royal, 1947; World So Wide, 1951; plays, Hobohemia, N.Y., 1919; Jayhawker (with Lloyd Lewis), N.Y., 1934; It Can't Happen Here (in collaboration), produced Federal Theatre, with twenty-one companies, 1936; Angela Is Twenty-Two (in collaboration with Fay Wray, prod. on the road, 1938-39, with author playing star role for a time), Plays in bookform: Jayhawker, and Dodsworth (with Sidney Howard), 1935; It Can't Happen Here, 1938. Contbr. short stories to mags. Nobel prize in literature, 1930. Died in Rome, Italy, Jan. 10, 1951; buried Sauk Centre, Minn.

LEWIS, Spearman, newspaperman; b. Appleton, Wis., Aug. 15, 1879; s. Alexander Richard and Gertrude (Spearman) L.; student Wheaton (Ill.) High Sch., Mich. Mil. Acad.; m. Camille Hincher, Mar. 27, 1906 (died 1928); m. 2d, Virginia Louesa Glenn, June 22, 1930. Began as newspaper reporter, New Brunswick, N.J., 1899; while acting dir. Chgo. Tribune fgn. news service, during peace negotiations at Paris, France, obtained and sent to U.S. a secret copy of the peace treaty which was made public through the U.S. Senate, June 9, 1909; this exploit frequently referred to as the world's greatest scoop. Mayor of Surfside, Fla., 1935-37. Vol. USN, Spanish-Am. War, 1898, aboard U.S.S. Scorpion, dispatch boat for the Flying Squadron; dir. various patriotic drives, World War I; head of publicity bur., Camp Grant, Ill., later with TMCA in France. Roosevelt Republican. Episcopalian. Mason. Home: Surfside, Fla. Died Feb. 4, 1954; buried Hillside Cemetery, Plainesfield, N.J.

LEWIS, Spencer Steen, naval officer; b. Calvert, Tex., Jan. 8, 1888; s. James Berry and Mary Elizabeth (Meredith) L.; B.S., U.S. Naval Acad., 1910; m. Jensy Yerger Loop, 1914 (died 1942); children—Mary Meredith (Mrs. William C. Rodgers), Harriette Loop (Mrs. Arkie C. Hauck); m. 2d, Amy Joan Micklam, 1944. Commd. ensign USN, 1910, advanced through grades to rear adm., 1942; ret. vice adm. 1947, Decorated Navy Cross, D.S.M., Legion of Merit (U.S.); Companion of the Bath (Gt. Britain); Legion of Honor, Croix de Guerre (France). Episcopalian. Clubs: Army and Navy, Army-Navy Country (Washington). Home: Calvert, Tex. Office: Navy Dept., Washington 25. Deceased.

LEWIS, Theodore Leonard, coll. pres.; b. Springfield, Mo., Feb. 15, 1903; s. James William and Frances L. (Alderson) L.; Ph.B., Wheaton (Ill.) Coll., 1931; B.D., No. Bapt. Theol. Sem., 1937, Th.D., 1941; D.A.O., Staley Coll., 1950; L.H.D., Western New England College, 1958; married Mattie Barclay, Dec. 5, 1925; children—Grace Elaine (Mrs. Robert MacKerron), James Barclay, John Stacy. Ordained to ministry, 1928; pastor Harrison St. Ch., Oak Park, Ill., 1929-41; prof. theology No. Bapt. Theol. Sem., 1941-44; pastor First Bapt. Ch., Hammond, Indiana, 1942-44; pres. Gordon Coll. Theology and Missions 1944—. Mem. Nat. Assn. Evangelicals, Evang. Theol. Soc., Phi Alpha Chi. Home: Chebacco Rd., Hamilton, Mass. Office: Box E, Beverly Farms, Mass. Died Mar. 12, 1959.

LEWIS, William Luther, pres., sec., treas. and dir. Chicago Pneumatic Tool Co., N.Y.C. Home: Pleasantville Rd., Briarcliff Manor, N.Y. Office: 6 E. 44th St., N.Y.C. 17. Died June 28, 1952; buried Kensico Cemetery, Valhalla, Westchester County, N.Y.

LEWISOHN, Ludwig (lōō'ī-zōn), author; b. Berlin, Germany, May 30, 1883; s. Jacques and Minna (Eloesser) L.; brought to America, 1890; B.A., M.A., Coll. of Charleston, S.C., 1901, Litt.D., 1914; M.A., Columbia, 1903; m. Louise Wolk, February 8, 1944; one son, James Elias. Member editorial staff Doubleday, Page & Co., 1904-05; mag. writer, 1905-10; instr. German, U. of Wis., 1910-11; prof. German lang. and lit., Ohio State U., 1911-19; dramatic editor, The Nation, 1919. Asso. editor of same, 1920-24. Jewish religion, Zionist. Editor of The New Palestine, 1943-48; now professor at Brandeis University, Waltham, Mass. Author: The Broken Snare, 1908; The Modern Drama, 1915; The Spirit of Modern German Lit., 1916; The Poets of Modern France, 1918; The Drama and the Stage, 1922; Upstream, 1922; Don Juan, 1923; The Creative Life, 1924; Israel, 1925; The Case of Mr. Crump, 1926; Cities and Men, 1927; Roman Summer, 1927; Island Within, 1928; Adam, 1929; Mid-Channel, 1929; Stephen Escott, 1930; Last Days of Shylock, 1931; The Golden Vase, 1932; Expression in America, 1932; This People, 1933; The Permanent Horizon, 1934; An Altar in the Fields, 1934; Trumpet of Jubilee, 1937; For Ever Wilt Thou Love, 1939; The Answer, 1939; Renegade, 1942; Breathe Upon These, 1944; Anniversary, 1948; Among the Nations, 1948; Goethe: The Story of a Man (2 vols.), 1949; The Magic Word, 1950; The American Jew, 1950; In a Summer Season, 1955; also Theodor Herzl, 1955. Editor: A Book of Modern Criticism, 1919; Creative America, 1933; Rebirth—A Book of Modern Jewish thought, 1935. Translator of many works of Hauptmann, Wassermann, Rilke, Werfel, etc. Address: Brandeis Univ., Waltham, Mass. Died Dec. 31, 1955; buried Sharon (Mass.) Meml. Park.

LEWISOHN, Margaret S., ednl. dir.; b. N.Y. City, Feb. 14, 1895; d. Isaac Newton and Guta (Loeb) Seligman; grad. Miss Masters Sch., Dobbs Ferry, N.Y., 1912, Inst. Musical Art, 1914; post-grad. work teaching; m. Sam A. Lewisohn, Feb. 2, 1918; children—Dr. Marjorie G., Joan (Mrs. Sidney Simon), Elizabeth A. (Mrs. Julian Calvert Eisenstein), Virginia M. (Mrs. Ernest Kahn). Teacher of music, settlements, ungraded classes, New York City, 1914-17; chmn. Women's City Club Education Committee, 1930-36; member Mus. Modern Art Edn. Com., 1936-44; chmn. bd. trustees, Little Red Schoolhouse, 1936-40; mem. bd. trustees, Pub. Edn. Assn., N.Y. City, 1941—, professional dir., 1941-46, chmn. bd. trustees, 1946—. Trustee, Bennington Coll., 1939-46, Vassar Coll., 1946—. Mem. adv. bd. on vocational edn. of N.Y. City Bd. Edn.; mem. adv. bds. Child Study Assn., Vocational Service for Juniors, Playschools. Clubs: Women's City, Cosmopolitan, Westchester Country. Author articles in ednl. mags.; lecturer, on pub. edn. Home: 45 East End Av., N.Y.C. 28. Office: care Pub. Edn. Assn., 20 W. 40th St., N.Y.C. 18. Died June 14, 1954; buried Salem Fields Cemetery, Bklyn.

LEWISOHN, Sam A., mining, banking, civic, ednl. work; writer on econ. and indsl. subjects; b. N.Y.C., Mar. 21, 1884; s. Adolph and Emma M. (Cahn) L.; A.B., Princeton, 1904; LL.B., Columbia, 1907; m. Margaret V. Seligman, Feb. 2, 1918; children—Marjorie Greta, Joan Emma, Elizabeth Anne, Virginia. Mem. firm Lewisohn & Co.; pres., dir. Miami Copper Co., Gen. Development Co., Kerr Lake Mining Co., S.A. Gold & Patinum Co.; chmn. bd. Tenn. Corp.; dir. City and Suburban Homes Co., Equitable Life Assurance Soc. Trustee, v.p. Museum of Modern art; trustee N.Y. Found., Fedn. for Support of Jewish Philanthropic Socs. of N.Y., Jewish Child Care Assn. of N.Y.; hon. chmn., treas. Stadium Concerts, Inc.; treas. Acad. Polit. Sci.; past pres. Am. Mgmt. Assn.; pres. Am. Prison Assn.; dir. Prison Assn. N.Y. Former mem. N.Y. State Commn. for Correction; dir. Fed. Prison Industries Corp.; dir. Youth Counsel Bur.; employer del. to Internat. Labor Conf., 1935; apptd. mem. distbn. com. of N.Y. Community Trust, 1938; mem. municipal Art Commn., 1948. Mem. Assn. Bar City N.Y., State Bar Assn. Clubs: City, Players, Princeton, Recess, Harmonie, Century Country, Mining. Author: The New Leadership in Industry, 1926; Painters and Personality, 1937, 48; Human Leadership in Industry, 1945. Co-author: Can Business Prevent Unemployment?, 1925. Home: 115 E. 73d St. Address: 61 Broadway, N.Y.C. Died Mar. 13, 1951.

LEWTON, Frederick Lewis, technologist; b. Cleve., Mar. 17, 1874; s. George Washington and Annie Louise (Taylor) L.; student Rollins Coll., Winter Park, Fla., 1887-90; grad. Drexel Inst., Phila., 1895; A.B., George Washington U., 1922; D.Sc., Rollins Coll., 1930; m. Emilie Marie Hempel, June 29, 1899; children—Lilian Louise (Mrs. J. B. Hopkins), Myrtle Hempel (Mrs. H. I. Rothrock), Rhoda (Mrs. J. Jennings), Norma (Mrs. P. Michaelson); m. 2d, Blanche Banister Clark, July 24, 1930. Instr. chemistry Drexel Inst., Phila., 1895-1904; econ. botanist Phila. Comml. Mus., 1896-1900, curator, 1900-04; sci. asst., Bur. Plant Industry, U.S. Dept. Agr., 1904-08, asst. botanist, 1908-12; curator div. crafts and industries U.S. Nat. Mus., 1912-46, research associate in crafts and industries, 1946—. Archivist, Rollings College since 1954. Director Northwestern Fed. Savs. & Loan Assn. Mem. Washington Acad. Scis. Phila. Acad. Natural Scis. Presbyn. Author numerous papers on botany of econ. plants and history of inventions; contbr. to Century Dictionary, Bailey's Ency. Horticulture, Book of Rural Life. Home: 1911 Englewood Rd., Winer Park, Fla. Died Feb. 21, 1959.

LEY, Frederick Theodore, contractor, realtor; b. Springfield, Mass., Apr. 22, 1872; s. Frederick William and Martha (Hollistin) L.; student Springfield pub. schs.; m. Mignon Casseday, Apr. 27, 1902; children—Frederic, Theodore, Mrs. Gordon Regan. Pres. and Founder Fred T. Ley & Co., Inc., constrn. co., organized in 1893, builders bridges, dams, ships, hydro-electric systems, cantonments, factories, comml. and apt. bldgs., U.S. and fgn. countries, including Chrysler Bldg., N.Y.C. Chmn. Liberty Loan campaigns, pres. War Chest Assn., Springfield. Mem. Mass. Militia, 1891-98; ensign Naval Brigade, Spanish-Am. War. Mem. Real Estate Bd. of N.Y., Inc., Commerce and Industry Assn. N.Y. Conglist. Club: Union League (N.Y.C.). Home: 280 Park Av. Office: 30 E. 40th St., N.Y.C. Died July 13, 1958; buried Ferncliff Cemetery, Ardsley, N.Y.

LEY, Harold Alexander, ins. exec.; b. Springfield, Mass., May 28, 1874; s. Frederick C. and Martha H. L.; student pub. schs. of Springfield; m. Anne Kingsley, Feb. 15, 1899; m. 2d, Beatrice McComb Doyle, Sept. 20, 1933. Founder, 1913, and chmn. bd. Life Extension Inst.; dir. Case, Pomeroy & Co., Mass. Mut. Life Ins. Co., Bush Terminal Bldgs. Co.; mem. N.Y. adv. bd. Liberty Mutual Ins. Co. Mason. Clubs: Union League (N.Y.C.); Bald Peak Colony of Melvin Village, N.H.; Blind Brook (Port Chester, N.Y.). Home: Melvin Village, N.H. Office: 11 E. 44th St., N.Y.C. Died May 11, 1956; buried Melvin Village.

LEYENDECKER, Joseph Christian (lī'ěn-děk'ẽr), artist; b. Montabour, Germany, Mar. 23, 1874; s. Peter and Elizabeth L.; Chgo. pub. schs., Art Inst. Chgo., Académie Julian, Paris. Exhibited at Salon Champ de Mars, Paris, 1897; illustrator many mags. and advertisements, covers for Sat. Eve. Post, Collier's, others. Home: 48 Mount Tom Rd., New Rochelle, N.Y. Died July 25, 1951.*

LEYSEN, Ralph J(ames) (lī'sěn), newspaper editor; b. Muscatine, Ia., June 23, 1888; s. Jacob P. and Jane (Cassidy) L.; ed. Muscatine schools; m. Ann Gault-Witcher, Dec. 1, 1934; 1 dau., Jancey Witcher (Mrs. Walter D. Stockly). Began as reporter on Muscatine Journal, 1905, became city editor and mng. editor; mng. editor Daily Times, Davenport, Ia., since 1922. Mem. Davenport Library Bd., Davenport Chapter of Am. Red Cross; mem. board of dir. C. of C.; mem. bd. Salvation Army; mem. Am. Soc. of Newspaper Editors. Republican. Clubs: Contemporary, History Round Table, Davenport, Outing (Davenport, Ia.); National Press (Washington). Home: 2721 Middle Rd. Office: Daily Times, Davenport, Ia. Died May 28, 1951; buried Oakdale Mausoleum, Davenport.

L'HEUREUX, Hervé Joseph (lẽr-rẽr), foreign service officer; b. Manchester, N.H., Mar. 6, 1899; s. Rodolphe and Desneiges (Pichette) L'H.; A.B., George Washington U., 1925; LL.B., U. of Detroit, 1935; m. Jeannette Blum, June 21, 1927; children—David Eugene, Jeanne Rose (Mrs. John J. Schwab, Jr.), George Hervé. Vice consul, Windsor, Ont., Can., 1927-35, consul, 1935; consul, Stuttgart, Germany, 1936-39, Antwerp, Belgium, 1939-41, Lisbon, Portugal, 1941-42, Algiers, 1943-44; also became sec. North African Economic Bd., and exec. officer Civil Affairs section Allied Forces Hdqrs., Algiers, May 1943, also chief of civil adminstrn. for North and West Africa, Dec. 1943; Am. consul gen. Marseille, France, 1944-47; chief of the visa division, Dept. of State, 1947-52; supervising consul general for Western Germany, 1952-55, also exec. director U.S. High Commn. for Germany; consul gen., Montreal, Can., with personal rank of minister, 1955-57; career minister in Fgn. Service confirmed posthumously by Congress, July 11, 1957. Secretary fo United States senator in Washington, D.C., 1919-26; admitted to New Hampshire bar; counselor Supreme Court of U.S. Served with 26th Div., U.S. Army, 1917-19. Decorated Silver Star, Originator of the Prayers-for-Peace movement. Mem. Society of American Legion Founders, New Hampshire and American bar assns., Yankee Div. Vets. Assn., Am. Legion, Post Mortem Club, La Société Des 40 Hommes et 8, Chevaux, Delta Theta Phi, Last Man's Club. Rotarian. Home: 123 Riley Av., Manchester, N.H.; also 5201 38th St., Washington 15. Address: care Department of State, Washington 25. Died July 9, 1957; buried Arlington Nat. Cemetery.

LIAUTAUD, Andre (lē-ō-tō'), ex-Haitian diplomat; b. Port-au-Prince, Haiti, Oct. 1, 1906; B.L., Inst. St. Louis de Gonzague, Port-au-Prince, 1924; B.S., Tchrs. Coll., Columbia U., 1930; student Ecole Centrale D'Agriculture, 1924-25; m. Ghyslaine Brandt, May 21, 1941; children—Frantz, Claude-Hervé Andre; children by former marriage—Gerard, Colette, Jacqueline. Farm sch. tchr., 1925-28; asst. dir. rural edn., 1928-38; commr. gen. for agrl. colonies, 1938-41; dir. rural edn., 1941-42; undersec. finances, commerce, nat. economy, June-Nov. 1942; E.E. and M.P. to U.S., 1942-43, A.E. and P. Decorated Grand Officer Haitian Honneur et Merite, officer Haitian order Petion-Bolivar. Mem. Haitian Lodge Coeurs Unis. Club: Cercle Port-au-Princien. Author: Une Année De Colonisation Agricole, 1939; collaborator: Geographie Locale (Livre 1), 1930; L'Enseignement de la Lecture par La Méthode Globale, 1935; Geographie D'Haiti, 1942. Home: Port-au-Prince, Haiti. Died July 25, 1951; buried Port-au-Prince.

LIBBY, Orin Grant, educator; b. Hammond, Wis., June 9, 1864; s. Asa and Julia (Barrows) L.; grad. Wis. State Normal Sch., River Falls, Wis., 1886; B.L., U. Wis., 1892, M.L., 1893, fellow in history, 1893-95, Ph.D., 1895; m. Eva Gertrude Cory, Sept. 12, 1900; children—Margaret Eva, Charles Cory. Instr. history, U. Wis., 1895-1902; prof. Am. history U. N.D., ret. 1945. Pres. State Library Commn. of N.D., 1909. Reorganized, 1903, sec. State Hist. Soc. N.D. to 1945; organized, 1903, pres., 1903-09, State Audubon Soc. N.D. Mem. Miss. Valley Hist. Assn. (pres. 1909-10), State Hist. Soc. N.D. Phi Beta Kappa, Alpha Pi Zeta, Sigma Alpha Epsilon. Mason. Author: Geographical Distribution of the Vote of the Thirteen States on the Constitution in 1787-88, 1894; also numerous hist. monographs and mag. articles. Editor of Historical Collections, State Hist. Soc. N.D., vols. I-VII and N.D. Hist. Quarterly, vols. I-X. Home: Grand Forks, N.D. Died Mar. 29, 1952.

LIBBY, Warren Edgar, lawyer; b. Lisbon, Me., Apr. 8, 1888; s. Warren Leland and Rachel Ann (Woodrow) L.; A.B., Bates Coll., Lewiston, Me., 1909; student George Washington U. Law Sch., 1910-12; m. Elsie Pomeroy, June 30, 1913. Teacher and athletics coach, Goddard Sem., Barre, Vt., 1909-10; admitted to Calif. bar, 1912, and practiced at San Diego until 1923 and at Los Angeles since 1923; chief counsel of Pickwick Stages System, 1913-32, when merged with Pacific Greyhound Lines, Inc.; organizer The Pickwick Corp., 1923, gen. counsel, v.p. and dir., 1923-36; gen. counsel, Pickwick Hotels, Pickwick Nitecoach Corp.; counsel Pacific Greyhound Corp.; mng. editor Pickwick Papers, 1928-30; organizer, 1932, gen. counsel Columbia Pacific Nitecoach Lines, 1932-42, Los Angeles Shipbuilding & Drydock Corp., 1942-44. Mem. bd. of legal advs. of U.S. Civil Serv. Com., 1941-44; chmn. Four-Minute Men, San Diego County, Calif., World War I. Mem. Local Draft Baord, World War II, 1942-45. Chairman advisory board, Little Theatre of Beverly Hills, 1932-34. Mem. Am. Bar Assn., Am. Law Inst., State Bar of Calif., (mem. com. to revise corporation laws, 1928-33; mem. legislative com.; chmn. conf. of delegates, 1943-45; chmn. Co. Courts Com. 1942-50; mem. bd. govs. 1947-50); mem. Los Angeles Bar Assn., (chmn. judiciary com., 1933-35, legis. com., 1935-37); San Diego Bar Assn., (dir. 1923). Rep. Christian Scientist (first reader 1920-23). Mason (33°). Club: Men's of Beverly Hills (pres. 1933). Home: 718 N. Camden Dr., Beverly Hills, Cal. Office: Spring Arcade Bldg., Los Angeles. Died Dec. 22, 1955.

LICHTENBERGER, James Pendleton, sociologist; b. Decatur, Ill., June 10, 1870; s. Conrad H. and Elizabeth (Nesbit) L.; A.B., Eureka (Ill.) Coll., 1893; A.M., Hiram (O.) Coll., 1902; fellow N.Y. Sch. of Philanthropy, 1908-09; Ph.D., Columbia, 1909; m. Martha A. Cantrell, June 29, 1892; children—Muriel E. (Mrs. J. B. Leopold), Yolande V. (Mrs. J. V. Pequignot). Minister Disciples of Christ; pastor Canton, Ill., 1896-99, Buffalo, N.Y., 1899-1902, N.Y. City, 1902-08; prof. sociology, U. of Pennsylvania. 1909-40, retired. Mem. American Academy Polit. and Social Science since 1909, secretary since 1912; member Am. Sociol. Society, Beta Gamma Sigma. Republican. Author: Development of Social Theory, 1923; Divorce—A Social Interpretation, 1931. Home: 71st St. at Greenhill Road, Phila. Died Mar. 17, 1953.

LIDDELL, Donald Macy (lĭd-dĕl'), engr.; b. Lawrenceburg, Ind., Feb. 28, 1879; s. Oliver Brown and Josephine (Major) L.; A.B. (chem. and phys. course), Johns Hopkins, 1900; m. Edith Stabler, Dec. 2, 1905; children—Donald M., Jr., Edith Jordan (Twiss). With Detroit Copper Mining Co., Morenci, Ariz., 1900-01, Balt. Copper Smelting & Rolling Co., 1901-05, U.S. Metals Refining Co., Chrome, N.J., and Grasselli, Ind., 1905-10; asso. editor, mng. editor Engring. and Mining Jour., N.Y.C., 1910-16; cons. engr. with Merrill, Lynch & Co., 1916-17; partner firm Weld & Liddell, cons. engrs., 1919-36; pres. Homewood Apartment Co. Balt.; dir. Nat. State Bank, Elizabeth, N.J.; dir. Compañia Minera del Sur. Cuba trustee Nat. State Corp. Capt. A.S., O.R.C., active service, Feb. 2, 1918-May 20, 1919; with Res., July 6, 1919-Sept. 22, 1924; comd. maj. Res., Sept. 22, 1924, lt. col., Nov. 20, 1930; on active duty with Prodn. Engring. Br., Air Corps, July 15, 1942-Oct. 10, 1943; chief engr. War Credits Bd., Dec. 2, 1917-Apr. 25, 1918. Mem. Mining and Metall. Soc. Am., Am. Inst. M.E., Mil. Order Loyal Legion, Mil. Order Fgn. Wars, Beta Theta Pi, Phi Beta Kappa. Republican. Clubs: Army and Navy (Washington); (hon. mem.) Mining (London); Mining (pres.), Univ. (N.Y.C.). Author: Metallurgists and Chemists Handbook, 1916; Handbook of Chemical Engineering, 1922; Handbook of Non-Ferrous Metall., 1926, revised 1945; The Uncommon Metals, 1949; also numerous articles tech. jours. Co-author: International Control of Mineral Resources, 1926; The Principles of Metallurgy, 1932; Mineral Resources of the United States and Its Capacity to Produce, 1934; Chessmen, 1937. Originated selenium recovery methods in use for many years in most Am. copper refineries; several waterproofing methods for stucco work; first successful commercial watermix method for magnesium-oxichloride stucco. Home: 30 E. 55th St., N.Y.C. Office: 33 Rector St., N.Y.C. Died Aug. 16, 1958.

LIEB, Charles, ex-congressman; b. Flehingen, Germany, May 20, 1852; Bryant & Stratton's Bus. Coll., Louisville; m. Katherine Mohr, 1877. Pres. Farmers Bank, Rockport, Ind.; mfr. hardwood lumber and contractor. Mem. City Council, Rockport, several terms; apptd. postmaster, Rockport, by Pres. Cleveland; mem. Ind. Ho. of Rep., 1907-08, 11-12; mem. 63d Congress, 5th Ind. Dist, 64th Congress, 1st Dist.; Democrat. Home: Rockport, Ind. Deceased.

LIEB, Charles Christian (lēb), pharmacologist; b. N.Y.C., Apr. 19, 1880; s. Charles Adam and Magdalena (Stephan) L.; student Columbia Inst., 1893-98; A.B., Columbia Coll., 1902, M.D., Coll. Phys. and Surg., 1906; post-grad. London U., 1908-09, Utrecht U., 1929; m. Henrietta Haaker, June 25, 1908. Instr., Coll. Phys. and Surg., Columbia, 1909-10, asst. prof. pharmacology, 1910-21, asso. prof., 1921-23, prof., 1923-29, Hosack prof. 1929-44, Hosack prof. emeritus, 1944—. Mem. Physiol. Soc. (London), Am. Physiol. Soc., Soc. of Pharmacology and Exptl. Therapeutics, Soc. Exptl. Biology and Medicine, A.M.A., Phi Delta Theta, Phi Beta Kappa, Sigma Xi, Alpha Omega Alpha. Presbyn. Clubs: University, Columbia University, Columbia Faculty. Home: 1 W. 72d St. Office: 630 W. 168th St., N.Y. C. Died April 1956.

LIEDER, Frederick William Charles (lee'der), educator; b. N.Y.C., Nov. 7, 1881; s. William Jacob August and Agnes (Betz) L.; A.B., Cornell Univ., 1902, A.M., 1903; Ph.D., Harvard, 1907; m. Margaret Lewis Bailey, June 19, 1926. Fellow in German, Cornell U., 1903-04; teaching fellow in German, Harvard, 1904-06, instr., 1906-20, asst. prof., 1920-28, asso. prof. 1928-48, emeritus prof. Germany, 1948—, chmn. dept. Germanic langs. and lits., 1932-35. Mem. Modern Lang. Assn. Am., N.E. Modern Lang. Assn., Am. Assn. Tchrs. German, Soc. for Advancement of Scandinavian Studies, Am. Assn. U. Profs. Clubs: Faculty (Cambridge); Harvard (Boston); Cornell of New England; Harvard Musical Assn. Translator: The Reichsbank, 1910. Editor: Schiller's Don Carlos, 1912; Moser's Der Bibliothekar, 1913; Goethe's Hermann und Dorothea, 1917; Manual of Military German (with R. W. Pettengill), 1918; German Poems and Songs, 1929; First German Reader (with G. M. Howe), 1930; Popular German Stories, 1931. Contbr. reviews and articles. Gen. editor of Harper's German Series (20 vols.) 1935—. Home: 18 Brown St., Cambridge, Mass.; (summer) Harwichport, Mass. Died July 30, 1953. Buried Mt. Auburn Cemetery.

LIEDER, Paul Robert, prof. English; b. Brooklyn, N.Y., Sept. 18, 1889; s. William J. A. and Agnes (Betz) L.; A.B., Harvard, 1910, A.M., 1912, Ph.D., 1915; unmarried. Instr. of modern langs., Mass. Inst. Tech., 1912-15; instr. of English, Smith Coll., 1915-17, asst. prof., 1917-20, asso. prof., 1920-25, prof., 1925-54, emeritus, 1954, chmn. dept. English, 1926-37; lecturer in English, Mt. Holyoke Coll., 1920, 22-23, Columbia, summer, 1925. Served as ensign, U.S.N.R.F., 1918. Member Modern Language Association America, American Dialect Assn., Am. Assn. Univ. Profs., Soc. for Advancement of Scandinavian Studies, Facsimile Text Soc., Northampton Historical Soc., Phi Beta Kappa, D. U. Club (Harvard). Clubs: Northampton, Northampton (Mass.) Country; South Shore (Harwichport). Author: Scott and Scandinavian Literature, 1920. Editor: Poems of Tegnér, 1914; (with Brander Matthews) Chief British Dramatists, 1924; (with Robert Morss Lovett and Robert Kilburn Root) British Poetry and Prose, 1928, rev. 3 vols., 1938, 49; (with same) British Drama, 1929; Eminent British Poets of the Nineteenth Century, 2 vols., 1938; (with Robert Withington) The Art of Literary Criticism, 1941. Editor: Northampton Poets, 1948—. Home: 18 Brown St., Cambridge, Mass. Died May 14, 1956.

LIGHT, Charles Porterfield, ret. hotel mgr.; b. Berkeley County, W.Va., Dec. 21, 1871; s. John Hanson and Emma Florence (Heyser) L.; ed. pub. and pvt. schs., W.Va., and high sch., Hagerstown, Md.; m. Margaret Hunter Harlan, June 6, 1900; 1 son, Charles Porterfield. Mem. W.Va. State Bd. of Agr., 1905-09; state highway commr. W.Va., 1909-11; sec. American Highway Assn., 1911-16; a founder of the Am. Assn. of State Highway Officials, organized Dec. 12, 1914 (25th reunion held on Oct. 9, 1939, in Washington, where it was organized); mgr. D.C. office Fidelity Mutual Life Insurance Co., 1916-18; rep. in Dist. of Columbia Nat. City Co. of N.Y., 1918-32; with management Willard Hotel Co., 1933-46; mem. exec. staff Mayflower Hotel 1946-51. Secretary of 3d Liberty Loan Conv., Washington, D.C., 1918. Trustee Washington (D.C.) Y.M. C.A., 1921-28. Mem. Sons of the Revolution (sec. Washington Society, 1920-30), Democrat. Mason. Presbyterian. Clubs: Alfalfa (hon. pres.) University. Home: 305 Jackson Av., Lexington, Va. Died Mar. 14, 1955; buried Falling Waters Presbyterian Churchyard, Berkeley County, W.Va.

LIGHT, Evelyn, publisher; b. N.Y.C., January 6, 1904; d. Wellington James and Minnie E. (Malone) Light; student pub. schs. N.Y.C.; m. Richard R. Smith, May 15, 1946. Asso. editor Plain Talk Mag., 1928-30; sec. to Theodore Dreiser, 1930-34; with coll. dept. Am. Book Co., 1934-36; revision asst. ency. Volume Library, 1936-38; free lance editing, 1938-41; tech. writer Fairchild Aviation Corp., 1942, adminstrv. officer, 1942-43; mem. N.Y. Bd. Film Review, Fed. Office of Censorship, 1943-45; editor Richard R. Smith, 1945-48; pres. Richard R. Smith Pub., Inc., since 1948. Author: Ways and Means to Successful Retirement (under pen name Evelyn Colby), 1952. Address: Topside, West Rindge, N.H. Died June 5, 1958.

LILIENTHAL, Joseph Leo, Jr., physician; b. N.Y. City, Nov. 1, 1911; s. Joseph Leo and Edna (Arnstein) L.; B.S., Yale, 1933; M.D., Johns Hopkins, 1937; m. Katherine Arnstein, June 25, 1937; children—Julia. Nina. Clinical Clerk, National Hospital, Queen's Square, London, England, 1937; house officer Presbyterian Hospital, New York City, 1938-40; resident physician Johns Hopkins Hospital, 1940-42, physician since 1946; asso. prof. medicine Johns Hopkins, since 1946, prof. environmental medicine since 1950; research neuromuscular and respiratory physiology. Cons. Nat. Science Found.; mem. com. aviation medicine and com. naval med. research Nat. Research Council. Mem. med. bd. Nat. Muscular Dystrophy Assn. Cons. to Sec. of Def., Research and Development Bd., 1948-53. Office of Naval Research, 1951—. Surgeon Gen. Dept. Army, 1950-53, clin. center Nat. Inst. Health. Mem. Nat. Bd. Med. Examiners, chmn. medicine test com. Physiol. Study Sect. Nat. Inst. Health USPHS, 1953—. Served as lt. comdr., U.S. N.R., 1942-46. Fellow N.Y. Academy Sci.; mem. Am. Institute Biological Sciences, American Clinical Climatological Association, Society of Medical Consultants to Armed Forces, Association of American Physicians, Am. Soc. Clin. Investigation, Am. Physiol. Society, Society Exptl. Biology and Medicine (mem. nat. council), Interurban Clinical Club, American Federation Clinical Research, Sigma Xi, Phi Beta Kappa, Alpha Omega Alpha, Phi Gamma Delta. Club: 14 W. Hamilton St. Home: 6203 Blackburn Lane, Baltimore 12. Office: Johns Hopkins Hospital, Balt. 5. Died Nov. 19, 1955.

LILIENTHAL, Samuel, corp. exec.; b. San Rafael, Cal., Aug. 1, 1884; s. Ernest R. and Bella (Sloss) L.; U. Cal., ex 1905; m. Alice Haas, Nov. 3, 1909; children—Ernest R., Elizabeth Gerstley, Frances M. Pres. Haas Bros., Inc., S.F., since 1928; dir. Wells Fargo Bank, Cal. Ins. Co. Office: 3d and Channel Sts., San Francisco. Died Jan. 20, 1957.

LILLIE, Harold Irving, surgeon; b. Grand Haven, Mich., May 6, 1888; s. Walter Irving and Harriett Ellen (McGrath) L.; A.B., U. Mich., 1910, M.D., 1912; m. Oda Kittredge, Sept. 10, 1913; children—John Canfield, Jean. Instr. U. Mich. Med. Sch., 1913-15; instr. Rush Med. Coll., Chgo., 1915-17; head ear, nose, throat sect., Mayo Clinic, 1917-51, sr. cons. medicine, 1951-53, emeritus, 1953—; professor otolaryngology and rhinology Mayo Found. Grad. Sch., U. Minn., 1921-53. Served as 1st lt. M.C. during World War, assigned as essential tchr. Diplomate Am. Bd. Otolaryngology, Inc. (pres. 1949). Mem. Minn. State, S. Minn., med. socs., Zumbro Valley Med. Assn., Internat. Coll. Surgeons, A.C.S., A.M.A., Am., Minn. acads. opthalmology and otolaryngology, Am. Rhinol., Laryngol. and Otol. Soc. (pres. 1939), Am. Otol. Soc., Am. Laryngol. Assn. (pres. 1945-46), Internat. Coll. Surgeons, U. Mich. Union (life), Alpha Omega Alpha, Phi Beta Pi, Sigma Xi. Republican. Catholic. Clubs: University, Rochester Golf and Country. Home: Midfields, Route 1, Rochester, Minn. Died Aug. 27, 1957; buried Oakwood Cemetery, Rochester.

LILLIE, Ralph Stayner, biologist, educator; b. Toronto, Can., Aug. 8, 1875; s. George Waddell and Emily Ann (Rattray) L.; B.A., U. Toronto, 1896, hon. Sc.D., 1936; grad. student U. Mich., 1896; Ph.D., U. Chgo., 1901; m. Helen Eva Makepeace, June 2, 1906; children—Frank Rattray, Walter Makepeace. Asst. in physiology Harvard, 1901-02, instr.

physiology, 1905-06; instr. and adj. prof. physiology U. Neb., 1902-05; research asst. Carnegie Inst. Zoöl. Sta., Naples, Italy, 1904-05; Johnston scholar Johns Hopkins, 1906-07; instr., asst. prof. physiology and exptl. zoölogy U. Pa., 1907-13; prof. biology Clark U., 1913-20; biologist Nela Research Lab., Cleve., 1920-24; prof. gen. physiology U. Chgo., 1924-40, prof. emeritus, 1940—; instr. and investigator general physiology Marine Biol. Lab., Woods Hole, Mass., 1902—. Fellow Am. Acad. Arts and Sciences, A.A.A.S.; mem. Am. Physiol. Soc., Am. Soc. Biol. Chemists, Am. Soc. Naturalists, Soc. Exptl. Biology and Medicine, Am. Soc. Zoölogists, Am. Philos. Soc., Phi Beta Kappa, Sigma Xi. Trustee Marine Biol. Lab., Woods Hole, Mass. Spl. researches in fundamental properties of living substance and physiology of stimulation, growth, cell-division, radiation effects, philosophical aspects of biology. Home: 5545 Kenwood Av., Chgo. 37. Died Mar. 19, 1952.

LILLY, Richard C., banker; b. St. Paul, Minn., Nov. 4, 1884; s. Donald W. and Mary Catherine (Enright) L.; graduate St. Paul (Minn.) Coll. Law, 1909; m. Rachel Cunningham, Sept. 28, 1910 (dec.); children—Richard C. (deceased), John C., David M. Messenger, later clerk, Merchants National Bank, St. Paul, Minn., 1900-10, assistant cashier 1910-13, v.p., 1913-18, pres. 1918-29; pres. First Nat. Bank (merged with Mchts. Nat. Bank), 1929-45, chmn. bd., 1945-54, now dir.; chmn. bd. dirs., Toro Mfg. Corp., Minneapolis since Jan. 1946; dir. Archer-Daniels-Midland Co., Great Northern Ry. Co., J. L. Shiely Co., St. Paul, Brown and Bigelow. St. Paul. Trustee St. Paul Seminary. Catholic. Clubs: Minnesota, Somerset, Athletic (St. Paul); Minneapolis, Minikahda (Mpls.). Home: 2155 Delaware Av. Office: First National Bank, St. Paul. Died Oct. 23, 1959.

LILLY, Thomas Jefferson, ex-congressman; b. Flat Top, W.Va., June 3, 1878; s. Joseph Lilburn and Martha J. (Cox) L.; student law dept. McKinley U., Chgo.; m. Roxie May Lilly, Sept. 10, 1898. Tchr. country schs.; farmer; admitted to W.Va. bar, 1911; mem. 68th Congress, 5th W.Va. Dist. Democrat. Baptist. K.P., Woodman, Workman, Red Man, Elk. Home: Hinton, W.Va. Died Apr. 2, 1955; buried Restwood Cemetery, Hinton.

LINCOLN, Azariah Thomas (lĭng'kŭn), chemist; b. Montfort, Wis., June 25, 1868; s. Joseph Hollis and Margaret (Laird) L.; B.S., U. Wis., 1894, M.S., 1898, fellow, 1898-99, Ph.D., 1899; m. Jennette Emeline Carpenter, June 30, 1904. Instr. chemistry, U. Cin., 1900-01; instr. chemistry U. Ill., 1901-03, asst. prof., 1903-08; asst. prof. chemistry Rensselaer Poly. Inst., 1908-12, prof. phys. chemistry, 1912-21; prof. chemistry; Carleton Coll., 1921-23, chmn. dept. chemistry, 1923-39, prof. emeritus, 1939—. Mem. Am. Chem. Soc., Am. Electro-Chemical Soc., Soc. Chem. Industry, A.A.A.S., Sigma Xi, Phi Lambda Upsilon, Alpha Chi Sigma. Republican. Conglist. Author: Elementary Quantitative Analysis (Lincoln and Walton), 1907; Textbook of Physical Chemistry, 1918. Translator: (with David H. Carnahan) Theoretical Principles of the Methods of Analytical Chemistry, Based upon Chemical Reactions (from the French), 1910; General Chemistry, 1927. Home: 203 Maple Av., Northfield, Minn. Died Mar. 31, 1958; buried Lancaster, Minn.

LINCOLN, Charles Monroe, newspaper exec.; b. Bath, Me., Mar. 15, 1866; s. George Mitchell and Frances Lucretia (Berry) L.; m. Annie Palmer Fisher, 1892 (died 1941); children—Mrs. David Paige, Mrs. James Van Dyk, Mrs. Wyllys Ames. Mem. staff of N.Y. Herald, filling exec. positions, including that of editor of Paris edit., with periods with James Gordon Bennett, 1895-1906; mng. editor N.Y. World, 1910-20; mng. editor N.Y. Herald, 1920-24; mem. editorial staff N.Y. Times as specialist in internat. affairs, 1926-44; retired, 1944. Pres. James Gordon Bennett Memorial Corp., 15 yrs.; hon. pres. Silurian Soc. (N.Y. City); mem. Soc. Mayflower Descendants, S.A.R. Club: The Rowfant (Cleveland). Explored for Jas. Gordon Bennett, route of proposed canal between Caribbean and Pacific, reporting in favor of Panama; collaborated with Marconi in proof of feasibility of wireless telegraphy, 1899; collaborated with Glenn Curtiss in demonstration meaning of airplane, use in war, 1910. Home: 93 Cooper Av., Montclair, N.J. (legal residence); 380 Oak Knoll Av. N.E., Warren, O.; also Orrs Island, Me. Died Dec. 22, 1950; buried Mt. Hebron Cemetery, Upper Montclair, N.J.

LINCOLN, Edmond E(arl), economist, business cons.; b. near McCook, Neb., Feb. 5, 1888; s. Charles Sanford and Christiana (Bayless) L.; B.A., O. Wesleyan U., 1909; selected from Ohio as Rhodes Scholar to Oxford U., 1908 (Lincoln Coll.); B.A., Honor Sch. of Modern History (Oxford), 1910; M.A., Oxford, 1914; Ph.D., in banking, finance and public utilities, Harvard, 1917; m. Edith Walker, Aug. 14, 1915; children—Elinore (Mrs. Edward K. Bachman), Robert Edmond; m. 2d, Mary Margaret Lynch, Sept. 2, 1948; children—Edmond Lynch, Mary Anna. Engaged variously in farming, manufacturing, contracting and building, 1902-08; teacher in Ohio public schools, 1903-04; prof., head of English dept., Mt. Union Coll., 1911-12; prof., head dept. history and economics, St. John's Coll., 1912-14, sec. of faculty, 1913-14; on faculties of Harvard economic dept. and Grad. Sch. Bus. Adminstrn. 1914-22, specializing in finance, pub. utilities, econ. history, and applied economics; lectr. indsl. and financial courses U. Extension and Radcliffe Coll.; traveled widely abroad; winner first prize ($1,000) Hart Shaffner & Marx economic essay contest, 1917; chief statistician and economist, Western Electric Company, Inc., New York, 1922-27; economist, acting commercial manager, and special asst. to pres. Internat. Tel. & Tel. Corp., 1927-31; economist E. I. duPont de Nemours & Co., 1931-53; cons. Investors Diversified Services, Inc.; dir. Cleve. Cliffs Iron Co., Ventures, Ltd., Falconbridge Nickel Mines Limited (Can.), Brightwater Paper Co. Expert spl. agt. U.S. Dept. Commerce, in charge of report on central electric light and power stas. in U.S., 1918-20; Am. econ. corr. for Benn Bros. Syndicate, London, 1919-20; mem. com. on bus. finance, Boston C. of C., 1920-21, com. on pub. utilities, 1921-22; mem. Commerce and Industry Assn. N.Y. (com. on city transit 1924—; chmn., 1926-27; and various other coms.); mem. com. on costs of distribution, C. of C. of U.S., 1925-26, and of finance dept. com., 1929-31); mem. Econ. Policy Com., mem. C. of C. of State of N.Y. (past chmn. com. on taxation), exec. com. on Fed. Finance and Fed. Expenditures, Nat. Council of State C. of C., Wilmington C. of C. (com. on legislation). Trustee Mount Union Coll.; mem. council Harvard Found. for Advanced Study and Research, Harvard Bus. Sch. Assos.; dir. Harvard Alumni Assn. Fellow Am. Geog. Soc.; mem. Am. Finance Assn., English Speaking Union, Am. Mgmt. Assn. (past dir., v.p. finance, hon. life mem.), Nat. Assn. Mfrs. (various coms.), Nat. Indsl. Conf. Bd. (various coms.), Acad. Polit. Sci., Am. Acad. Polit. and Social Sci., A.A.A.S., Am. Assn. for Labor Legislation, Am. Chem. Soc., Am. Econ. Assn. (life), Nat. Tax Assn., Am. Mus. Natural History, Am. Statis. Assn. (life), Econ. Club of N.Y., Economist's Nat. Com. on Monetary Policy, Fgn. Policy Assn., Nat. Bur. Econ. Research, Nat. Farm Chemurgic Council, Oxford Soc. (life), Pan-Am. Soc., Population Assn. Am., Royal Econ. Soc. (Eng.), Tax Inst., Citizens Com. for Hoover Report, Phi Beta Kappa (asso.). Mason. Clubs: Harvard, Bankers of America, Lotos (New York); Wilmington, Wilmington Country; Met. (Washington); Harvard of Del. (past pres.); Sunday Breakfast (Phila.). Author: The Results of Municipal Electric Lighting in Massachusetts, 1918; Central Electric Light and Power Stations (1917), 1920; References in the Economic History of Europe and of the United States, 1920; Problems in Business Finance, 1921 (3d edit., 1924); Applied Business Finance, 1922 (5th edit., 1941); Steps in Industry, 1926; Testing Before Investing, 1926 (2d edit., 1930); Applied Economic History, 1932. Translator Monetary Inflation in France, 1790 (by Pierre Samuel duPont), 1950. Address: 907 Westover Rd., Wilmington, Del. Died May 14, 1958.

LINCOLN, Gatewood Sanders, naval officer; b. Liberty, Mo., Aug. 5, 1875; s. James Edwin and Margaret Pixley (Bird) L.; student William Jewell Coll., Liberty, Mo.; grad. U.S. Naval Acad., 1896; m. Enfield C. Stogdale, June 20, 1900. Served from ensign to capt. USN, 1898-1918; on New Orleans in Adm. Sampson's fleet, off Santiago, Cuba, and in West Indies, Spanish-Am. War, 1898; engr. officer Navy Yard, Mare Island, Cal., 1912-14; comd. Dolphin, 1915; head Dept. Elec. Engring. and Physics, U.S. Naval Acad., 1915-17; comd. Powhatan, transporting troops to France, 1917-18, St. Louis, escorting troop convoys to English Coast, Sept.-Nov. 1918, and comd. U.S.S. St. Louis until Oct. 1919. Mem. Am. Soc. Naval Engrs., Kappa Alpha. Episcopalian. Club: N.Y. Yacht. Address: Navy Dept., Washington. Died Oct. 15, 1957.

LINCOLN, John Cromwell, elec. mfr.; b. Painesville, O., July 17, 1866; s. William E. and Louisa (Marshall) L.; E.E., Ohio State U., 1888; D.Sc. (honorary), Arizona State College, 1958; m. Myrtie Humphreys, 1891; children—Louise L. Kerr, John G.; m. 2d Mary Dearstyne Mackenzie, 1914; m. 3d Helen Colvill, 1918; children—Lillian C. (Mrs. Lillian Howell), Joseph C., David C. Supt. constrn. Short Electric Co., 1889-93; partner Elliott-Lincoln Electric Co., 1893-94; organized Lincoln Electric Co., Cleve., 1895, inc., 1905, pres., 1905-28, chmn. bd., 1928-54, hon. chmn. bd., 1954—; organized Lincoln Electric Mfg. Co. (now Reliance Electric Mfg. Co.), 1904, developed many inventions; pres. Bagdad (Ariz.) Copper Corp.; Built Camelback Inn on Ariz. Desert, 1936; pres. Camelback Inn Co., 1932—; chmn. bd. Universal Wire Spring Co.; organized Lincoln Bonding Co., 1914. Pres. Henry George Sch. Social Sci.; dir. Desert Mission Y.M.C.A., Good Samaritan Hosp., John C. Lincoln Hosp. Mem. Sigma Xi, Tau Beta Pi. Home: 4701 Cholla Lane. Office: Camelback Inn, Phoenix. Died May 24, 1959.

LINCOLN, Julius, clergyman; b. Lindsborg, Kan. Sept. 20, 1872; s. Andrew and Anna C. (Johnson) L.; A.B., Bethany Coll., Lindsborg, 1891, A.M., 1894, L.H.D., 1941; was graduated from Augustana Theol. Sem., Rock Island, Ill., 1893; Yale, 1895-96; D.D., Wittenberg College, Springfield, Ohio, 1910, Thiel Coll., 1910; m. Gertrude Dunn, 1918. Ordained Luth. ministry, 1893; asst. pastor Bethany Ch., Lindsborg, and prof. Greek, Bethany Coll., 1893-95; pastor Swedish Luth. Ch., Meriden, Conn., 1895-96, 1st Ch., Jamestown, N.Y., 1896-1918, Swedish Luth. Angelica Ch., Los Angeles, Calif., 1918-20. Mem. Bd. of Edn., Jamestown, 1898-1907 (pres. 1903-07); mem. Bd. Park Commrs., 1908-10; mem. Bd. Hosp. Commrs., 1909-10; alternate del. Rep. Nat. Conv., 1904; presdl. elector, 1908; mem. N.Y. Assembly, 1911-12. Pres. N.Y. Conf. of Swedish Luth. Augustana Synod; pres. Calif. Conf.; v.p. Luth. Hosp. Soc. of Southern Calif. Apptd. mem. spl. commn. of Federal Food Adminstrn. to study food conditions in the allied countries, Nov. 1917-Jan. 1918; dir. of publicity and support Swedish Nat. Sanatorium for Tuberculosis, Denver, Colo., 1921-25; exec. sec. Brotherhood of Augustana Synod, 1925-28; mem. bd. Augustana Coll., Rock Island, Ill., 1926-30; dir. pub. relations Augustana Hosp., Chicago, 1934-39; pastor Trinity Luth Ch., Chicago, 1939—. Sec. Am.-Swedish Hist. Foundation, 1926-40, pres., 1940—; sec. Sedish-Am. Ter-Centenary Assn., 1936-38. Decorated Knight Royal Order of Vasa (Sweden), 1930, King Gustaf V "New Sweden" medal and diploma, 1938. Translator: Sven Hedin's A Conquest of Tibet. Address: 410 Evergreen Av., Chgo. 10. Died July 20, 1954; buried Jamestown, N.Y.

LINCOLN, Leroy Alton, chmn. bd. Metropolitan Life Ins. Co.; b. Little Valley, N.Y., Aug. 18, 1880; s. Charles Zebina and Lusette (Bonsteel) L.; A.B., Yale, 1902; legal edn. Albany (N.Y.) Law Sch., 1902-03; m. Mary S. Moore, Sept. 6, 1905 (died 1908); m. 2d, Marie Louise Baer, June 14, 1913 (died 1928); children—Charles Waters, Thomas Ridgely; m. 3d, Hilda F. Deyoe, Aug. 1, 1930. Admitted to N.Y. bar, 1904; practiced in Buffalo, 1904-15; counsel N.Y. State Ins. Dept., 1915-17; practiced in N.Y. City as partner Rumsey & Morgan, 1917-19; with Met. Life Ins. Co., 1918—, gen. atty., 1918-27; gen. counsel, 1927-29, 1st v.p. and gen. counsel, 1929-30, v.p. and gen. counsel, 1930-36, pres., 1936-51, now chmn. bd. Del. N.Y. State Constitutional Conv., 1915. Mem. Am. and N.Y. State bar assns., Assn. Bar City of N.Y., past pres. Chamber of Commerce of the State of New York; v.p., Empire State Assn. of Commerce, Inc.; member Commerce and Industry Association (N.Y. City). Republican. Presbyterian. Clubs: University, The Links, Huntingdon Valley Country (Phila.); Pine Valley Golf (N.J.); Saucon Valley Country (Pa.). Home: 770 Park Av. Office: 1 Madison Av., N.Y.C. Died May 9, 1957; buried Mt. Hope Cemetery, Hastings-on-Hudson, N.Y.

LINDAHL, Oscar Nathanael, bus. exec.; b. Sweden; s. Andrew and Emma Lindahl; ed. pub. and pvt. schs., Chicago; m. Fannie Stevens Treloar, Sept. 25, 1911; 1 dau., Ruth Fannie (Mrs. Walter M. Urbain). With Butler Bros., wholesale gen. mdse., Chicago, 1900-07, Ill. Steel Co., 1907-11; comptroller, sec. and dir., Universal Portland Cement Co. (now Universal Atlas Cement Co.), 1911-41; v.p. in charge finance, dir., Carnegie-Ill. Steel Corp., Pittsburgh, 1941-49; exec. dir. gen. state authority, exec. dir. state highway and bridge authority of Pa. since 1949; dir. American Window Glass Company; former mem. faculty Chicago Law Sch. Alderman, Brewyn, Ill., 1913-17, sec. bd. local improvements, 1914-17; dir., v.p., Carnegie Libraries of Braddock, Homestead and Duquesne (all Pa.); dir. U.S. Steel and Carnegie Pension Fund; mem. Pittsburgh Regional Hosp. Planning Com. Mem. Pa. State C. of C. (dir., exec. com.), Pittsburgh C. of C. (chmn. com. of Inst. on Bus. and Econ. Problems in a Pvt. Enterprise Economy), Chicago Assn. of Commerce, Nat. Assn. Cost Accountants (dir. 1928-30, mem. research com.), Ill. Mfrs. Costs Assn. (pres. 1920-21, adv. com. since 1921), Controllers Inst. of Am. (pres. 1939-40, bd. dirs., 1939-41, adv. council 1940-46, chmn. postwar controllship problems com. 1943, com. on war contracts termination policies and procedures 1944-47, chmn. com. on fed. taxation since 1934; trustee and mem. exec. com. Controllership Found., Inc.), Nat. Assn. Mfrs. (govt. finance com. 1940-47, tax adminstrn. com. since 1940), Am. Iron and Steel Inst., Internat. Accountants Soc. (mem. adv. bd.). Republican. Clubs: Union League, Economic, Kiwanis (pres. 1928) (Chicago); Pennsylvania Soc. (N.Y.); Duquesne, Univ., Athletic Assn. (Pittsburgh). On bd. of editors of 3d ed. of Financial Handbook. Contbr. articles to mags. Lecturer on financial subjects. Home: Schenley Apts., Pittsburgh. Office: 18th and Herr Sts., Harrisburg, Pa. Died May 6, 1952; buried Chaple Hills Garden West, Elmhurst, Ill.

LINDBERG, Irving Augustus, financial adviser, banker; b. Cherokee, Ia., Feb. 14, 1887; s. Rev. Charles and Hannah (Nystrom) L.; Ia. State Coll., 1904; A.B., U. of Ill., 1910; grad. student Washington Coll., Law and Accounting, 1912; LL.D., Universidad de Santiago de Leon de los Caballeros, 1944; married Bertha Betty Buettner, November 28, 1947; children (by previous marriage)—Irving Augustus, Charles David. Connected with railway and newspaper work until 1907; economist, President Taft's Economy and Efficiency Commission, Washington, D.C., 1911-12, mem. N.G. Naval Reserve, Washington, 1911-12; with commission from U.S. to reorganize fiscal system of Nicaragua, 1912; collector of customs and captain, Port of Bluefields, Nicaragua, with rank of col., 1913-41, also customs officer, Atlantic Coast of Nicaragua; col. Nicaraugua Secret Service, World War; dep. collector-gen. and auditor Customs Service, Republic of Nicaragua, 1918-51; collector-gen. of customs and Am. high commr., Republic of Nicaragua, 1928-—; pres. bd. control of prices and trade, 1944; mem. bd. of control Nicaragua Foreign Exchange, 1931-—; mem. bd. to supervise expenditures from $1,500,000 loan, 1932; dir. gen. Nicaragua Petroleum Monopoly, 1932; mem. Nicaraguan sect. Inter-Am. High Commn.; chmn. Am. Red Cross, Nicaragua, Nicaraguan del. as foreign trade adviser Foreign Trade Conv., San Francisco, 1920; inspector gen. Nicaraguan consulates in U.S., 1925; Nicaraguan del. to 4th Pan. Am. Commercial Conf., Washington, D.C., 1931; on financial missions to U.S. and Europe, with rank of E.E. and M.P., 1931, 32, 33, 34, 35, 36 and 37; E.E. and M.P. of Nicaragua to Germany, Italy and Sweden, 1931-37; insp. Nicaraguan consulates and legations in Europe, 1937; apptd. financial agent at London with rank E.E. and M.P. to attend coronation representing Nicaragua; apptd. consul gen. of Norway to Nicaragua, 1938; pres., chmn. bd. dirs. Dairyland State Bank, Bruce, Sheldon and Exeland, Wis.; member advisory bd. The F. A. Gomez & Cia, Ltd., Nicaragua. Accompanied President, General Anastasio Somoza on visit to U.S., 1939; honorary minister of customs, 1940; commd. col., apptd. mem. Gen. Staff, Nicaraguan Army, 1942, brigadier general for life, 1946. Awarded President's Medal of Merit by President Anastasio Somoza for 30 years continous service in Customs (copy of the citation pub. in U.S. Congressional Record). Registered Certified Public Accountant, Nicaragua. Apptd. trustee fiscal agent for liquidation Nicaragua's frozen comml. debt, 1938; pres. bd. control prices and trade, controller gen. rationing throughout Republic, 1944-45; mem. commn. regulate trade, 1945; adviser to Nicaraguan del. at Allied Nations World Security Conf.; permanent adviser. Nicaraguan delegation UNO, 1946. Nicaraguan del. to Internat. Trade Cong., New Orleans, 1946; chief Nicaraguan del. Internat. Statistical Congress, Washington, D.C., 1947; treasurer of Nicaragua Relief for Volcano Victims, 1947. Mem. Coordination Com. for Nicaragua, 1942-—; Nicaraguandel. Coffee Conf., 1948; econ. adv. Republic of Nicaragua and Nicaragua Nat. Bank, 1944-48; chmn. bd. govs. Am. Library of Nicaragua, pres. 1945-46. Donated Cordobas $5,000 interest from fund used for annual prizes for schoolboy or girl submitting best essay on Nicaragua, 1942; given $40,000.00 residence in Nicaragua by President Somoza for long faithful loyal services; presented painting of President Roosevelt, by Professor Fernandez, Spanish artist, to American library in Managua. Mem. Byrne, Lindbergh and Byrne, accountants and auditors; press correspondent. Member Assn. of the Consular Corps of Nicaragua, Am. Soc. of Nicaragua (exec. com., 1947). Mason (32°, Shriner). Clubs: Theta Delta Chi (New York); Nejapa Country, Metropolitan (Washington, D.C.); life member University Club of Leon, American Officers (permanent mem. bd. govs., 1927-33; Mawanda (Ill.); International House (New Orleans). Author: The Statistical Services and Activities of Nicaragua, 1940. Contributor articles and reports on Nicaragua, reports of collector-gen. of customs and high commission, 1928-—. Awarded Medal of Merit by Nicaraguan Customs Service, several citations and awards, 1947-51; Chevalier of the First Class of the Royal Order of St. Olav by his majesty King Haakon of Norway, 1946. Home: Bruce, Wis. Office: care Brown Brothers, Harriman & Co., 59 Wall St., N.Y. C. Died Apr. 8, 1957.

LINDEBERG, Harrie Thomas, architect; b. Bergen Point, N.J., Apr. 10, 1880; s. Theodore and Eleanor Augusta (Osterlon) L.; ed. 6 yrs. in offices of McKim, Mead & White; m. Eugenie Lee Quinn, June 14, 1906 (died Nov. 1906); m. 2d, Lucia Hull, July 8, 1914; children—Linda, Lytle Polk; m. 3d, Angeline Krech James, Aug. 12, 1937. Practiced at N.Y.C., 1906-—; architect North Coll., Wesleyan U., Middletown, Conn.; Ontwentsia Club, Lake Forest, Ill.; Asheville (N.C.) Country Club Bldg.; R. T. Vanderbilt Laboratory, East Norwalk, Conn.; Astor Memorial Bldg., Rhinebeck, N.Y.; Doubleday & Co. Pub. Plant, Hanover, Pa.; S. Wing, Country Life Press, Garden City, L.I., and residences, including those of P. D. Armour, Lake Forest, Ill.; John S. Pillsbury, Mpls.; Michael N. Van Buren, Newport, R.I.; Eugene du Pont, Wilmington, Del.; James Stillman, Pocantico Hills, N.Y.; Horace Havemeyer, Islip, L.I.; Hon. Cameron Morrison, Charlotte, N.C.; William Farish, Houston, Tex. Apptd. cons., adv. State Dept. on fgn. bldgs., 1935, for Consulate, Shanghai; Legation, Helsingfors; commd. Feb. 1934 by U.S. Govt. to design Embassy bldgs. in Moscow, U.S.S.R. Academician Nat. Acad. Design, Archtl. League N.Y., Beaux-Arts Inst. Design, 1949; mem. A.I.A., Am. Soc. Swedish Engrs., John Ericsson Soc., Assn. Ex-Members of Squadron A, Nat. Inst. Arts and Letters. Clubs: Coffee House, River, Piping Rock (N.Y.C.); Onwentsia (Chgo.). Homes: 277 Park Av., N.Y.C.; also Locust Valley, L.I. Office: 277 Park Av., N.Y.C. Died Jan. 10, 1959.

LINDEGREN, Alina M. (lĭn'dĕ-grĕn), ednl. specialist; b. Vasa, Finland, Jan. 9, 1887; d. Charles Frithiof and Hilda Marie (Bjorn) L.; naturalized 1895; diploma, State Tchrs. Coll., Superior, Wis., 1906, B.Ph., U. Wis., 1921, M.A., 1922, Ph.D., 1928. Tchr. Superior, Wis., 1906-20; asst. dept. history U. Wis., 1921-25; prof. Oxford Coll. for Women, Ohio, 1925-28; history tchr. Superior State Tchrs. Coll., 1928-31; specialist in Western European Edn., U.S. Office Edn., Washington, 1931-42, acting chief Div. Comparative Edn., 1942-45; specialist in European Edn., Div. Internat. Edn., 1945-53, specialist in Comparative Edn., Europe and the British Commonwealth, 1953-—. Mem. Am. Hist. Assn., Am. Acad. Polit. and Social Sci., N.E.A., Nat. Council Social Studies, Pi Gamma Mu. Author: Education in Germany; Education and Service Conditions of Teachers in Scandinavia, the Netherlands and Finland; also a series of 3 bulls. on higher edn. in each of Sweden, Norway, and Denmark; articles and a bull. on edn. in other countries. Home: 3601 Connecticut Av. N.W., Washington 8. Office: U.S. Office of Edn., Washington. Died Jan. 25, 1957; buried Graceland Cemetery, Superior, Wis.

LINDEMAN, Eduard Christian, tchr., author; b. St. Clair, Mich., May 9, 1885; s. Frederick and Frederika Johanna (von Piper) L.; B.S., Mich. Agrl. Coll., 1911; hon. H.M., Springfield Coll., 1937; LL. D. Wagner Meml. Luth. Coll., 1942; hon. LL.D., Rockford Coll., 1947; m. Hazel Charlotte Taft, Aug. 29, 1912; children—Doris Eleanor (Mrs. Robert Gessner), Ruth Christine (Mrs. Donald O'Neil), Elizabeth Taft (Mrs. George D. Leonard), Barbara. Worked as laborer until 21; editor The Gleaner, Detroit, 1911-12; social work, Lansing, 1912-14; teacher and extension worker, Mich. Agrl. Coll., 1915-17; tchr. YMCA Coll., Chgo., 1918-19, N.C. Coll. for Women, 1919-21, N.Y. Sch. of Social Work of Columbia U. 1924; lectr. New Sch. for Social Research, N.Y.C., 1925-27, Pendle Hill, 1933-34, Temple U., 1934-35, U. Cal., 1936, 38, Columbia, 1941-42, Stanford U., 1941; U. Wis., 1943; Walter Rauschenbush lecturer Colgate-Rochester Divinity Sch., 1943. Trustee New School for Social Research, 1943, Editorial Staff, Penguin Books, Inc.; mem. exec. com. Am. Youth for World Youth, Am. Assn. for Adult Edn., Pub. Edn. Assn. (dir. 1941), Progressive Edn. Assn.; cons. Nat. Council of Parent Edn., 1929-33; mem. Council World Assn., for Adult Edn., Inst. of Pacific Relations. Dir. of research for workers, Ednl. Bur. America, 1926-27; dir. Dept. of Community Organization for Leisure, Works Progress Adminstn., Washington, 1935-38; planning cons. for profl. and service div., 1939, pres. N.J. State Conf. of Social Work, 1934; chmn. N.J. Library Planning Com. and N.J. Social Planning Com., 1934; adviser National Housing Assn. 1933-—; chmn. ednl. com. N.Y. council on Housing; mem. exec. com. N.Y. Council on Adult Edn. 1933-—. Chmn. Survey Com. Nat. Council for Conservation of Human Resources, 1937; chmn. Hunterdon County Library Commn., 1927-40; adviser Inst. for Propaganda Analysis, 1937, pres., 1938-39; mem. bd. Council Against Intolerance; mem. com. on research and edn. Fed. Council of Chs.; dir. Service Bur. for Intercultural Edn., 1939-40. Adv. editor Rural America; advisor to the Nat. Forum, 1939-—, Mem. adv. com. White House Conf. on Children in Democracy, 1939; chmn. sub-com. on leisure of President's Interdepartmental Com. for Reorganizing Federal Govt., 1938, 39; pres. Good Neighbor Com., 1942-— (mem. planning bd.); mem. exec. com. Pioneer Youth of America; dir. Am. Civil Liberties Union 1941-—; dir. Am. Labor Edn. Service, 1940-—; mem. U.S. Com. on Ednl. Reconstruction, 1943; chmn. advisory com. Wm. C. Whitney Found.; chmn. Nat. Bd. Nat. Share-Croppers Fund, 1942-43; chmn. bd. Nat. Child Labor Com., 1944-—; chmn. bd. Union for Dem. Action, N.Y.C. br., 1945; mem. bd. Citizens Com. for Children, 1945. Mem. bd. N.Y. Assn. of Day Nurseries, 1945. Trustee Briarcliff Junior Coll., Adelphi Coll., Nat. Child Labor Com., Internat. Community Center, Nat. Gallery for Indian Art, Nat. Urban League, Hudson Guild. Mem. Nat. Conf. of Social Work, Internat. Conf. of Social Work. Dir. Am. Assn. on Indian Affairs, 1940-—, treas. 1942-—; fellow mem. Am. Sociol. Soc., American Academy of Physical Education; American Country Life Assn., Academy Political Science, Social Service Employees Union, Am. Assn. Social Workers, Friends of Am. Democracy (mem. advisory com.), Council on Family Relations. Conglist. Clubs: City, Franklin Inn. Author: College Characters (essays and verse), 1912; The Community, 1921; Social Discovery, 1924; The Meaning of Adult Education, 1926; Urban Sociology, 1928; Dynamic Social Research, 1933; Social Education, 1933; Wealth and Culture, 1935; Leisure: A National Issue, 1939. Contbg. editor, Youth Service Digest, Edited: Emerson, the Basic Writings of America's Sage, 1947. Home: 235 E. 22d St., N.Y.C. Died Apr. 13, 1953.

LINDER, Frederick M., business exec.; b. Newark, Apr. 1892; s. Frederick and Catherine L.; student pub. schs. of Newark; m. Catherine Keil. With Jacob Ruppert, N.Y.C., 1911-—, now pres. Pres. Brewery Found.; dir. Met. Brewery Inst. Served as capt. U.S. Army, Mexican Border campaign, also World War I. Clubs: N.Y. Athletic, Westchester Country. Home: 1 Rahnays Dr., Mt. Vernon, N.Y. Office: 1639 3d Av., N.Y.C. 28. Died Oct. 1956.

LINDERSTROM-LANG, Kaj, educator; b. Frederiksberg, Copenhagen, Denmark, Nov. 29, 1896; s. C.F. and Ellen (Bach) Linderstrom-L.; C.E., Denmark's Tech. High Sch., 1919, Dr. Techn. (hon.), 1954; Ph.D., U. Copenhagen, 1955, U. Oslo, 1956; M.D. (hon.), U. Ghent, 1948, Karolinska Inst., 1948; D.Sc., U. Libre de Bruxelles, 1948, Cambridge U., 1949, N.Y.U. 1955; m. Gerda Kyndby, Mar. 25, 1922; children—Birte (Mrs. Knud Max Moller), Carl Ulrik. Chem. engr. Carlsberg Lab., Copenhagen, 1919, asst. chem. dept., 1919-38, head chem. dept., 1938, prof., 1938-—; Dunham lectr., 1939; Lane med. lectr., San Francisco, 1951; Herter lectr., Balt., 1951; pres. bd. Nordisk Insulin Lab., 1939-56; president Danish Academy Tech. Sci.. 1956; mem. Finsen Inst. Recipient prize of Tech. Funds, Copenhagen, 1955, Alfred Benzon prize, 1954, H.C. Orsted medal, 1941, Thunberg award, 1954; decorated Knight Order of Dannebrog, 1948. Mem. N.Y. (hon.), Norwegian, Nat., Royal Danish acads. scis., Acad. Tech. Scis. Copenhagen, Harvey Soc. (hon.), Societe Chimique de Belgique (hon.), Vetenskaps Societeten Uppsala (hon.), Am. Acad. Arts and Scis. (hon.), Am. Philos. Soc., Societe Belge de Biochimie (hon.), Societe de Biologie (corr. mem.), Finska Vetenskaps Societeten, Internat. Union of Biochemistry (pres. 1958). Address: 10 Gamle Carlsbergvej, Copenhagen, Valby, Denmark. Died May 25, 1959.

LINDLEY, Erasmus Christopher, lawyer; b. Dublin, Ind., Oct. 23, 1870; s. Osmond and Achsah (Wilson) L.; B.L., U. Mich., 1895, LL.B., 1896; m. Clara Ann Hill, 1917 (died 1947). Asst. state's atty. Cook County, Ill., 1903, 04; atty. Sanitary Dist. of Chgo., 1905-06; gen. atty. C.,R.I.&P. Ry. Co., 1907-10; v.p., gen. counsel G.N. Ry. Co., 1916-22; now practicing alone. Joined Ill. Naval Militia, 1898; with USN, Spanish-Am. War. Mem. Ill., N.Y., Minn. bar assns. Republican. Clubs: University, Midday, Tuxedo (N.Y.C.). Home: Tuxedo Park, N.Y. Office: 50 Broadway, N.Y.C. Died July 13, 1957.

LINDLEY, Walter C., judge; b. Neoga, Ill., July 12, 1880; s. Alfred W. and Irena (Carey) L.; A.B., University of Illinois, 1901, also LL.B., 1904, J.D., 1910, Doctor of Laws, 1956; married Louise Dewey Brown, April 30, 1913; children—Mary Aletta Byrne, Louise Dewey Morgan, Walter C. Practiced at Danville, Illinois, as member of firm, Lindley, Penwell & Lindley, 1904-22; master in chancery, U.S. Court, 1912-18; member Board of County Commissioners of Vermilion County, 1916-20; mem. Bd. of Edn., Danville; judge U.S. Dist. Court, Eastern Dist. of Ill., appointed by Pres. Harding, 1922; appointed judge U.S. Circuit Ct. of Appeals, Chicago, Sept. 1949. Appointed mem. of U.S. Emergency Court of Appeals 1944. Mem. Am., Chicago and Ill. State bar assns., Phi Beta Kappa, Phi Gamma Delta, Phi Delta Phi, Order of the Coif. Rep. Presbyterian. Mason (32°, Shriner), Elk. Clubs: Danville Country (ex-pres.), Union League, Midlothian, Tavern, Standard (Chgo.). Home: 1212 Logan Av., Danville, Ill. Died Jan. 3, 1958.

LINDNER, Clarence Richard, newspaper pub.; b. N.Y.C., Jan. 4, 1890; s. Walter and Minnie (Bachman) L.; grad. DeWitt Clinton Hish Sch., N.Y.C., 1908; m. Gladys Dudley, Feb. 13, 1925; 1 son, Dudley. Asso. editor Judge and Leslie's Weekly, 1909-11; successively adv. mgr. Cleve. News Leader, Detroit Times, Toledo Blade and Newark Star Eagle until 1921; pub. Detroit Times, 1921-27, N.Y. American, 1927-29, San Francisco Examiner, 1929-—; asso. prof. of journalism Stanford; v.p., dir. Hearst Consolidated Publications. Served as pvt. F.A. U.S. Army, World War I. Mem. bd. dirs. Yenching U., Peiping, China. Home: San Francisco. Office: Hearst Bldg., San Francisco. Died Jan. 7, 1952.

LINDQUIST, Robert John (lĭnd'kwĭst), executive; b. Sycamore, Ill., Dec. 26, 1902; s. John J. and Christine (Lindstrom) L.; B.S., C.P.A., U. of Ill., 1923; m. Vernal Mae Hughes, Sept. 1, 1924; 1 son. Rubert John, Jr. Pub. accountant Gray, Hunter & Co., Quincy, Ill., Arthur Andersen & Co., Chicago, 1923-30; gen. auditor Chicago Joint Stock Land Bank, 1930-32; chief auditor, R.F.C., Washington, 1932-41; v.p. and dir. Defense Plant Corp., Washington, 1940-41; dir. Rubber Reserve Co., Washington, 1940-41; v.p. and dir. Reynolds Metals Co., Richmond, Va.; v.p. and dir. U.S. Foil Co., Fulton Sylphon Co., Bridgeport Thermostat Co., Inc., Eskimo Pie Corp., Reynolds Corp., Reynolds Fiscal Corp., Reynolds Mining Corp., American Thermometer Co., Inc., Grayson Heat Control, Ltd., Reynolds Alloys Co., Richmond Radiator Co., Robertshaw Thermostat Co.; dir. Reynolds Research Corp., Arlette Inc., 1941-43; v.p., comptroller and dir. of Curtis-Wright Corp., 1943-45; financial vice pres. of Standard Oil Co. (Ind.), since 1945, dir. since June 1946; dir. Martin & Schwartz, Inc., Salisbury, Md., Pan American Petroleum Corp., New Orleans. Mem. Beta Gamma Sigma, Beta Alpha Psi, Theta Alpha. Lutheran. Mason. Clubs: Evanston Golf (Evanston, Ill.); Chicago (Chicago). Home: 1350 Astor St., Chicago 10. Address: 910 S. Michigan Av., Chicago. Died May 5, 1951; buried Elmwood Cemetery, Sycamore, Ill.

LINDSAY, Arthur Oliver, publisher; b. Decatur, Ill., Dec. 14, 1878; s. John and Edna (Nicholson) L.; ed. Whipple Acad., Jacksonville, Ill.; B.S., Ill. College; and LL.D. (honorary), Illinois College, 1953; m. Roberta Hawkins, Dec. 30, 1908 (dec. 1954); 1 son, Arthur. With Birmingham (Ala.) News, 1903-08, asst. bus. mgr., 1905-08; asst. bus. mgr., Birmingham Ledger, 1908-15; pres. and gen. mgr., Whig Co., pub. Quincy (Ill.) Whig, 1915-20, Quincy Whig-Journal, 1920-26; pres., Quincy Newspapers, Inc. (pub. of Herald-Whig and Journal), 1926—; dir., Quincy Broadcasting Co. (operator of radio sta. WGEM), 1948—. Pres., Anna Brown Home for Aged, Quincy, 1929-40; mem., Lay Adv. Com., Quincy Coll., 1947-48; member citizens' committee U. of Ill., 1953—. Mem. Inland Daily Press Assn. (dir., v.p., pres. and chmn. of bd., 1929, 30, 31, 32, 33), Ill. Daily Newspaper Markets (pres., 1939-40), Quincy C. of C. (pres., 1943-44), Ill. State C. of C. (dir., 1945-46). Club: Quincy Country. Home: 1805 Maine St. Office: Herald-Whig Square, Quincy, Ill. Died Nov. 16, 1956; buried Woodland Cemetery, Quincy, Ill.

LINDSAY, Samuel McCune, univ. prof.; b. Pittsburgh, Pa., May 10, 1869; s. Daniel Slater and Ella (England) L.; Ph.B., U. of Pa., 1889, LL.D., 1909; post-grad. courses at univs. of Pa., Halle, Berlin, Vienna, Rome and Paris, 1889-94; Ph.D., U. of Halle, 1892; hon. LL.D., San Marcos Univ., Lima, Peru; m. Anna Robertson Brown, Apr. 9, 1896; children—Mrs. Flora Lindsay Magoun, Daniel England, Mrs. Eleanor Lindsay Whiteleather. Served as special agent of U.S. Senate Finance Com. to report on wholesale prices in Europe, 1892; expert agent of U.S. Industrial Commn. to report on railroad labor, 1899-1900; commr. of edn., P.R., 1902-04. Was prof. sociology, Univ. of Pennsylvania, 1896-1907, then prof. social legislation, Columbia, until July 1, 1939, now emeritus. Chmn. emeritus Nat. Child Labor Committee. Fellow Royal Economic Society, Great Britain, A.A.A.S.; mem. Am. Acad. Polit. and Social Science (pres. 1900-02), Am. Econ. Assn.; pres. Acad. Polit. Science, New York, 1910-30; pres. Am. Assn. for Labor Legislation, 1918-19; hon. mem. Masaryk Acad., Prague, Czechoslovakia; corr. mem. Museo Social Argentino, Buenos Aires. Clubs: Century, Town Hall; Cosmos (Washington). Author: Die Preisbewegung der Edelmetalle, Jena, 1893; Social Aspects of Philadelphia Relief Work, 1895; Railway Labor in the United States, 1902; reports on Education in Porto Rico, 1903-05; Reports on Child Labor, 1904-07; Financial Administration of Great Britain (with W. W. and W. F. Willoughby), 1917; chapter on social insurance, in Democracy and Reconstruction, 1919; Economic Aspects of Emergency Housing Legislation in New York, 1921, 23; (joint author) Educational Survey, Porot Rico, 1925. Contbr. to Ency. Britannica, and various encyclopedias, revs. and mags. Home: 5417 Sherrier Pl. N.W., Washington 16. Died Nov. 11, 1959.

LINDSEY, Harry W(ilson), Jr., lawyer; b. Dayton, O., Aug. 6, 1889; s. Harry W. and Minnie (Sloan) L.; LL.B., Ohio State U., 1911; m. Margaret Burkhard, Mar. 20, 1916; 1 dau., Patsy. Admitted to Ohio bar 1911, Ill. bar 1940; patent dept. Nat. Cash Register Co., 1913-17; patent counsel Willys Overland Co., 1917-21; practiced law, specializing in patent law, Chgo., since 1921; partner Davis, Lindsey, Hibben & Noyes, and predecessors since 1921. Mason. Club: University (Chgo.); Westmoreland (Willmette, Ill.). Home: 120 Abingdon Av., Kenilworth. Office: 332 S. Michigan Av., Chgo. 4. Died Dec. 1959.

LINDSEY, Sterling Paul, Jr., govt. ofcl., banker; b. Corning, Ark., Feb. 14, 1902; s. Sterling Price and Anna A. (Jordan) L.; ed. State Agrl. and Mech. Coll., Jonesboro, Ark.; m. Bernice Aarah Wilcoxson, Feb. 7, 1926; children—Susanna Pauline, Prudence Louise, Priscilla Loraine, Paula Anice, Phyllis. Asso. with Nat. Stock Yards (Ill.) Nat. Bank, 1923-25; vice pres. Peoples State Bank, Colchester, Ill., 1928-29; vice pres., cashier Edinburg, Ill., State Bank, 1930-33; vice pres. Cabool (Mo.) State Bank, since 1934; asst. treas. Prodn. Credit Corp., St. Louis, Mo., 1933; asst. to prodn. credit commr., Farm Credit Adminstrn., Washington, 1934-36, asst. dir. crop and feed loan div., 1936-37, dir., 1937-46, vice pres., Regional Agrl. Credit Corp., dir., 1943-46; dep. adminstrn., Farmers Home Adminstrn., since 1946; pres. Security State Bank, Brookfield, Mo., since 1950. Mason (K.T., 32°, Shriner). Club: Exchange (Ill.) (vice pres., 1933-34). Home: 612 W. 59th St., Kansas City 2, Mo. Office: Room 5012 S. Bldg., U.S. Dept. Agriculture, Washington. Died Nov. 1950.

LINDSLEY, Herbert Kitchel (lĭndz'lē), banker, ins. exec.; b. Delaware County, Ind., June 21, 1874; s. Aaron Kitchel and Elizabeth (Buckles) L.; ed. pub. schs., Sterling, Kan.; m. Jessie Piper, June 16, 1909; children—Robert Kitchel, Herbert Piper. Began as clk. in country store, 1888; agt. Pacific Express Co., Sterling, Kan., 1892-96; dealer in broom corn since 1896; pres. Am. Warehouse Co. (said to be largest handlers of broom corn in world) since 1904; dir., mem. exec. com. Farmers & Bankers Life Ins. Co.; dir. 1st Nat. Bank (Wichita), Central States Fire Ins. Co., Chandler Nat. Bank, Lyons, Kan. Mem. Kan. Ho. of Rep., 1925-28, Kan. State Senate, 1929-33. Mem. President's Econ. Com., 1932. Mem. Kan. Hist. Soc. Past pres. Am. Life Conv., now mem. exec. com. Republican. Mason (32°, K.T., Shriner), Odd Fellow, Elk. Clubs: Wichita Business, Wichita Country. Home: 120 So. Pershing Av. Office: Farmers, Bankers Life Bldg., Wichita, Kan. Died Oct. 30, 1951.

LINEN, James A., Jr., exec.; b. Scranton, Pa., Oct. 11, 1884; s. James Alexander and Anna (Blair) L.; grad. Lawrenceville Sch., 1902; A.B., Williams Coll., 1907; m. Genevieve Tuthill, Oct. 22, 1908; children—James Alexander, Harriet Tuthill, Mary, Sally Strong. Receiver for Scrapton (Pa.) Steam Pump Co., 1910-13; v.p. and treas. Scranton Pump Co., 1913-16; treas. United Service Co., 1920-23; pres. Lincoln Trust Co., 1923-38; chmn. bd. Internat. Corr. Sch. and affiliated instns., 1928-37; pres. Internat. Ednl. Pub. Co., 1937-51; now chmn. Internat. Correspondence Schs. World Ltd., Inc.; chmn. bd. Internat. Correspondence Schs. Ltd., London, Capetown, Cairo, Bombay, Australasia, New Zealand; dir. Centro Espanol; de Ensenanza por Correspondencia, S.A., Madrid; Internat. Schs. Co. Latin Am., Argentine Co., Escuelas Internaciolales de la America del Sud; Women's Inst. Domestic Arts and Scis., Ltd., Haddon Craftsmen, Wessel Mfg. Co., Internat. Correspondence Schs. Can., Ltd., Internat. Textbook Co., Internat. Correspondence Schs. World, Ltd., Inc.; Conservator Union National Bank, Pennsylvania, 1933. Member Scranton City Council, 1913-16, president, 1915-16; chairman Red Cross Flood Disaster Drive, Lackawanna County, 1936; chairman Scranton chapter American Red Cross, 1938-41; pres. Scranton Community Chest, 1932-33, incorporator and mem. original bd. of dirs. Charities Assn. of Pennsylvania, Lackawanna County Chief of Emergency Welfare Service, Citizens Defense Corps, 1942-45. Served as 2d lieut., 13th Pa. Inf., Mexican Border, 1916-17; capt. and personnel adjutant, Machine Gun Training Center, U.S. Army, 1917-19. Member U.S. council International C. of C., 1950-54; trustee Scranton Keystone Jr. Coll. Mem. Nat. Com. for Marshall Plan to Aid European Recovery, 1947-48. Mem. Sigma Phi. Republican. Presbyterian. Clubs: Williams (N.Y.); Scranton (Scranton). Home: Waverly, Pa. Office: International Correspondence Schools, Scranton, Pa. Died Dec. 5, 1957; buried Hickory Grove Cemetery, Waverly, Pa.

LINFIELD, Frederick Bloomfield, agriculturist; b. Twillingate, Newfoundland, July 18, 1866; s. Samuel and Rachel (Patten) L.; B.S.A., Toronto U., 1891; m. Mary A. Mahoney, Dec. 26, 1892; children—Frederick Bertil, Mrs. Rachel Azalea Sager, Mrs. Leila Mary Nye. Asst. in dairy dept. Ontario Agrl. Coll., 1891-93; prof. animal industry and dairying Utah Agrl. Coll., Logan, 1893-1902; prof. agr. Mont. State Coll., 1902-13; dean div. agr., 1913-37; dir. Mont. Agr. Expt. Sta., 1904-37, dir. emeritus, 1937-42, ret. Methodist. Home: 721 3d Av. S., Bozeman, Mont. Died Sept. 23, 1948; buried Sunset Hills, Bozeman.

LINFORD, Leon Blood, univ. prof.; b. Logan, Utah, July 8, 1904; s. James H. and Mary Hooper (Blood) L.; B.S., Utah State Agrl. Coll., 1923, A. M., 1925; Ph.D., U. of Calif., 1930; m. Imogene Kesler, June 20, 1936; children—Lawrence Leon, Rulon Kesler. Asso. prof. mathematics Utah State Agrl. Coll., 1932-35, head dept., 1933-36, prof. physics and head dept. 1935-41; staff mem. radiation lab. Mass. Inst. Tech., 1941-46; physicist Naval Research Lab., Boston Field Sta., 1946; prof. physics and head dept. U. Utah, 1946—, dir. Upper Air Research Project, USAF, 1947-57. Mem. U.S. Commn. III, Internat. Sci. Radio Union, 1954. Fellow Am. Phys. Soc., A.A.A.S.; mem. Am. Assn. Physics Tchrs., Am. Assn. U. Profs., Utah Acad. Scis. Arts and Letters, Sigma Xi, Sigma Pi Sigma, Phi Kappa Phi. Author of articles on moisture relations in porous media and on photoelectricity. Mem. editorial bd. Mass. Inst. Tech. Radiation Lab. Series. Home: 1584 Glen Arbor, Salt Lake City 5. Died Mar. 12, 1957; buried Salt Lake City Cemetery.

LINGELBACH, Anna Lane (lĭng'ĕl-băk); b. Shelbyville, Ill., Oct. 10, 1873; d. Oscar F. and Mary E. Lane; A.B., Ind. U., 1895; studied U. of Chicago, Sorbonne, Paris; Ph.D., U. of Pa., 1916; m. William E. Lingelbach, 1902; children—William E., Anna, Robert Lane. Lecturer in history, Bryn Mawr Coll., 1918-19; prof. history Temple U., 1922-52. Officer of United Service Club, 1917-20 (club used by 250-000 enlisted men); mem. Phila. Bd. Pub. Edn., 1920-50, v.-p., 1938-48; mem. Presbyn. Bd. of Christian Education, 1923-48, vice-president, 1943-48; pres. Philadelphia Federation of Women's Clubs and Allied Organizations, 1933-35; chairman Department of International Relations, State Fedn. of Pa. Women, 1934-38 (chmn. of resolutions 1938-41); pres. W. Phila. Women's Com. for Phila. Orchestra, 1934-45; del. Anglo-Am. Hist. Conf., 1931, 36; dir. Crime Prevention Assn.; mem. Emergency Aid of Pa. Mem. Pa. Soc. Colonial Dames (chmn. Sulgrave Manor Endowment Fund Com., 1923-24), Am. Hist. Assn., Hist. Soc. Pa., Swedish Colonial Soc., Geneal-Soc. Pa., Kappa Kappa Gamma, Phi Beta Kappa; mem. exec. bd. Repub. Women Pa. Clubs: New Century (pres. 1925-29), Acorn, Temple U. Women's. Contbr. articles to Am. Hist. Rev., Dictionary Am. Biography, Current History and other publs. Home: 4304 Osage Av., Phila. Died July 14, 1954; buried West Laurel Hill, Phila.

LINGENFELTER, Mary Rebecca (lĭng'ĕn-fĕlt-ẽr), librarian, writer; b. Philipsburg, Pa., Jan. 5, 1893; d. Stewart B. and Annie J. (Brown) Lingenfelter; certificate, Drexel Inst. Library Sch., Phila., 1914; B.S. in Edn., U. of Pa., 1929; M.S., Columbia U., Sch. of Library Service, 1932; summer session, Oxford U., England, 1928; grad. study U. of Chicago, 1939-43; unmarried. Cataloger, Drexel Inst. Library, 1914-16; independent organizer sch. and coll. libraries, 1916-17, and 1925-29; librarian Ardmore (Pa.) Free Library, 1917-19; hosp. librarian, A.L.A., War Service, 1919-20; librarian, U.S. 4th Naval Dist., 1920-22, U.S. Vets. Hosps., Phila. and N.Y. City, 1922-25; librarian, Ohio State U., Bur. of Ednl. Research, 1929-31; head dept. edn., Enoch Pratt Free Library, Baltimore, 1932-35; associate librarian, Teachers College, Columbia, 1935-39; library cons. RCA Victor Division of Radio Corporation of America, 1943-46, special libraries consultant, since 1946; instructor in library science, Johns Hopkins University, summers, 1927, 29; same, Ohio State University, summers, 1930, 31; writing and research in visual edn., since 1939; organized library, Postgrad. Sch., U.S. Naval Acad., 1947; econ. editor Women's Bur., U.S. Dept. Labor, 1948. Carnegie fellowship, 1931-32. Mem. A.L.A., Spl. Libraries Assn., Nat. Vocational Guidance Assn., Phi Delta Gamma. Republican Methodist. Club: Soroptimist (West Chester, Pa). Spl. libraries mission to Scandinavian countries, fall 1946. Author: Vocations in Fiction; Books on Wheels; Wartime Jobs for Girls; (with May B. Van Arsdale) Manners Now and Then, 1940; (with H. D. Kitson) Vocational Guidance Through the Library: Vocations for Girls (2d edition, 1951); Vocations for Boys; Jobs for G.I.'s series, 1945-47; Gus, the Trailer Parrot. Compiler of bibliographies; contributor of articles and book reviews to magazines. Home: 208 E. Essex Av., Lansdowne, Pa. Died May 8, 1953.

LINGHAM, Fred J. (lĭng'ăm), retired flour mill exec.; b. Belleville, Ont., Can., Oct. 31, 1875; s. Thomas and Lydia (McTaggart) L.; came to U.S., 1893; ed. high sch. and business coll.; m. Lucia L. Pike, June 6, 1898; children—Charles Frederick, Lucia. Began as clk. witr Anchor Milling Co., Superior, Wis., 1893; treas. Federal Milling Co., Lockport, N.Y., 1907-20; pres. N.Y. State Millers Assn., 1911-12; chief of flour milling div. of U.S. Food Administration (dollar a year man), 1917-18; pres. Federal Mill, Inc., Lockport, 1920 until ret.; adv. dir. Marine Trust Co. of Western N.Y. Was instrumental in securing passage in Congress of Grain Standard Act, 1916, for Federal supervision of inspection of grain; mem. Com. on Agr., U.S. Chamber of Commerce, 1922-24; pres. Millers Nat. Federation, 1918 and 1933-34; chmn. Wheat Flour Milling Code Com. and Authority, 1933-34; mem. Business Advisory Planning Council, Dept. of Commerce, 1933-34; dir. and chmn. arbitration com. Buffalo Corn Exchange; mem. Com. on Industrial Economics of Nat. Assn. of Mfrs. Mem. Nat. Com. on Business Welfare, U.S. Chamber of Commerce; mem. bd. dirs. Lockport Y.M. C.A.; mem. exec. com. Millers Nat. Fedn. (hon. mem. 1943); chmn. Nat. Com. on Flour Ceilings and Subsidies. Awarded gold medal by War Administrator Herbert Hoover for war services. Republican. Episcopalian. Mason (32°). Clubs: Town and Country (Lockport). Home: Lockport, N.Y. Died Oct. 10, 1954.

LINGLE, Bowman Church, co. dir.; b. Chgo., Sept. 30, 1876; s. Samuel B. and Jennie M. (Church) L.; A.B., U. Chgo., 1896; m. Bertha Kendall, June 30, 1908. With N. W. Harris & Co., 1896; v.p. Harris Trust & Savs. Bank, Chgo., 1912-46; dir. Central and S.W. Corp. (sec. bd. dirs., 1947—), N.A. Light & Power Co., Pacific Spruce Co. Mem. Ill. area bd. Y.M.C.A. Presbyn. (trustee). Clubs: Chicago, University, Old Elm, Saddle and Cycle. Home: 900 N. Michigan Av., Chgo. 11. Office: 111 W. Monroe St., Chgo. 3. Died July 1, 1959; buried Oakland Cemetery, Princeton, Ill.

LINGLE, Walter Lee (lĭng'g'l), clergyman; b. Rowan County, N.C., Oct. 3, 1868; s. Wilson Alexander and Martha Jane (Lynch) L.; A.B., and A.M. Davidson Coll., N.C., 1892, D.D., 1906; LL.D., Southwestern Presbyn. U., 1920, Duke, 1932, U. N.C., 1933; grad. Union Theol. Sem., Va., 1896;

post-grad. U. Chgo., 1896; m. Alice Merle Dupuy, Jan. 2, 1900; children—Louise Denton, Nan Russell, Walter Lee, Caroline Dudley (Mrs. Frederick Lester). Ordained to Presbyn. ministry, 1897; instr. Union Theol. Sem., 1896-98, pastor Dalton, Ga., 1898-1902, Rock Hill, S.C., 1902-07, 1st Ch., Atlanta, 1907-11; McCormick prof. Hebrew lang. and S.S. work, 1911-14, prof. ch. history and missions, 1914-24, Union Theol. Sem.; pres. Presbyn. Gen. Assembly's Tng. Sch. for Lay Workers, Richmond, Va., 1924-29; pres. Davidson (N.C.) Coll., 1929-41, pres. emeritus, 1941—. Editor-in-chief of the Union seminary Review, 1912-22; mgr. So. Presbyn. Conf., Montreat, N.C., 1910-24; pres. trustees Davidson Coll., 1906-29; moderator Presbyn. Synod of N.C., 1915; mem. Internat. S.S. Lesson Com., 1914-23. Elected moderator Gen. Assembly Presbyn. Ch. in U.S., 1920. Democrat. Mem. Beta Theta Pi, Phi Beta Kappa, Omicron Delta Kappa. Author: Presbyterianism—A Heritage and a Challenge; Presbyterians—Their History and Beliefs; The Bible and Social Problems; Why I Believe in the Deity of Christ; Memories of Davidson College (1888-1946) Contbg. editor Christian Observer, Louisville, 1931—. Home: Davidson, N.C. Died Sept. 19, 1956; buried Davidson.

LINK, Henry Charles, psychologist; b. Buffalo, N.Y., Aug. 27, 1889; s. George and Martha (Kraus) L.; student Northwestern (now North Central) Coll., 1908-10; A.B., Yale Univ., 1913, A.M., 1915, Ph.D., 1916; m. Carolyn Crosby Wilson, May 2, 1917; children—James Wilson, Robert Frederick, Anne Luise. Psychologist since 1917; with U.S. Rubber Co., 1919-23, Lord & Taylor, New York, 1923-28, Gimbel's, Pittsburgh, 1928-30; sec.-treas., The Psychol. Corp., 1931-41, vice president and director since 1941; director Psychol. Service Center, New York, 1931-41; originator of the "P.Q." or Personality Quotient, 1936. Originator, 1932, since dir., Psychol. Barometer (poll of public opinion and buying habits by 10,000 quarterly interviews). Member Yale Artillery Battery, 1916. Dir. Vocational Adjustment Bur., New York. Mem. Am. Psychol. Assn., Assn. of Consulting Psychologists, Men of Science, Phi Beta Kappa. Club: Yale (New York). Author: Employment Psychology, 1919; Education and Industry, 1923; The New Psychology of Selling and Advertising, 1932; The Return to Religion, 1936; The Rediscovery of Man, 1938; The Rediscovery of Morals, 1947; The Way to Security, 1951. Home: Scarsdale, N.Y. Office: 522 Fifth Av., N.Y.C. Died Jan. 9, 1952.

LINK, Samuel Albert, educator; b. nr. Lebanon, Tenn., July 10, 1848; s. William B. and Amanda (Randolph) L.; grad. Ewing Coll., Ill., A.M., 1882; B.Litt., U. Nashville, 1891; was coll. editor and coll. poet at Ewing; read law, but did not enter practice; m. Sallie A. Deboe, 1875 (died 1892). Engaged in teaching, 1874—; was supt. Tenn. Sch. for Blind, 7 yrs.; later pres. Tenn. Female Coll., Franklin; Latin tchr. City High Sch., Nashville. Mem. Tenn. Hist. Soc. Author: Sketch of Paul H. Hayne, 1890 M12; Pioneers of Southern Literature (2 vols.), 1899, 1900 M12; also various booklets on So. poets, 1895-8 M12, and on Great Americans, 1901-2. Contbr. Meth. Quarterly and Christian Advocate, Nashville. Pres. Link Sch. Address: Thomasville, Tenn. Deceased.

LINK, William W., ex-congressman; b. Poland, Feb. 12, 1884; s. John and Cecelia (Moneczkowski) L.; came to U.S., 1887; student Lewis Inst.; m. Frances Susanna Wisniewski, June 1, 1910; children—Robert Kasmir, Helen S. (Mrs. John Buchinger), Oren Raymond, Genevieve Susanna (Mrs. Irving Palluth), Chester Valentine. Pres. Imperial Japanning and Enameling Co., 1912-32; pres. bd. local improvements, City of Chgo., 1932-36, v.p., 1936—; mem. Cook County Civil Service Comm., 1942-44; mem. 79th Congress, 7th Ill. Dist.; dir. Milwaukee Avenue Nat. Bank. Sec. Policy Am. Dem. Orgn. Ill., 1930—. Mem. Chgo. Soc. Polish Nat. Alliance. Polich Roman Catholic Union. Democrat. Address: 5104 N. Mango Av., Chgo. 30. Died Sept. 23, 1950.

LINN, William Alexander, author; b. Sussex, N.J., Sept. 4, 1846; s. Dr. Alexander and Julia (Vibbert) L.; A.B., Yale, 1868; admitted to N.Y. bar, 1883; m. Margaret A. Martin, 1871 (died 1897). Reporter, asst. city and night editor N.Y. Tribune, 1868-71; on editorial staff N.Y. Evening Post, 1871-1900, except that he edited Troy (N.Y.) Morning Whig, 1872-73; pres. Mut. Bldg. & Loan Assn., Hackensack, N.J., 1887— People's Nat. Bank of Hackensack, 1903-15, First Nat. Bank of Ridgefield Park, N.J., 1910-13. Mem. commn. appt. by gov. of N.J., 1899, to report on preservation of Palisades, which framed and secured passage of the law under which Interstate Commn. (of which was mem. until 1912) was apptd., which has rescued the Palisades from destruction. Trustee Johnson Pub. Library. Author: The Story of the Mormons, 1902; Rob and His Gun, 1902; Horace Greeley, 1903. Contbr. agrl. and hort. jours. Address: Hackensack, N.J. Died Feb. 23, 1917.

LINN, William Bomberger, judge; b. Ephrata, Pa., Dec. 20, 1871; s. Valentine and Mary (Bomberger) L.; LL.B., U. Pa., 1897, LL.D., 1948; LL.D., Franklin and Marshall Coll., 1934; D.C.L., Hahnemann Coll., 1939; m. Josephine Stewart Wood, June 4, 1902; children—Anne Wood, Mary Bettina. Admitted to Pa. bar, 1897, and practiced in Phila., 1897-1919; judge Pa. Superior Ct., 1919-32; justice Pa. Supreme Ct., 1932—. Pres. Athenaeum of Phila.; pres. Library Company of Phila. (founded by Benjamin Franklin, 1731); trustee, mem. bd. dirs. Free Library of Phila. Episcopalian. Club: Union League (Phila.). Author numerous articles on legal subjects. Home: 6374 Overbrook, Phila. Office: City Hall, Phila. Died June 13, 1950.

LINSCHEID, Adolph (lĭn'shīd), ex-coll. pres.; b. nr. Mannheim, Germany, Dec. 24, 1879; s. Philipp and Elizabeth (Ewy) L.; brought by parents to U.S., 1881; grad. Springfield (Mo.) Normal Sch., 1903; B.S., Fremont (Neb.) Coll., 1912; A.M., U. Okla., 1920; Ph.D., Columbia, 1928; m. Hazel Audrey Thompson, 1906; children—Stewart Philip, Billy Adolph. Tchr. rural schs., Minn., 1896-99; supt. schs., Prague, 1903-08, Okemah, 1909-10, Bristow, 1910-11; prof. English, Southeastern State Normal Sch., Durant, Okla., 1912-19; pres. East Central State Tchrs. Coll., Ada, Okla., 1920-49. Mem. Am. Assn. Tchrs. Colls., Okla. Edn. Assn. (pres. 1931-32), Presidents of Tchrs. Colls. (chmn. Okla. Council 1929-31). Democrat. Mason (32°). Clubs: Lions, Commercial. Author: In-Service Improvement of the State Teachers College Faculty, 1928. Lctr. Active in religious work; has taught a large men's Bible class continuously, 1920-45. Home: Ada, Okla. Died Dec. 28, 1949; buried Ada.

LINTON, Ralph, anthropologist; b. Phila., Pa., Feb. 27, 1893; s. Isaiah Waterman and Mary Elisabeth (Gillingham) L.; B.A., Swarthmore Coll., 1915; M.A., U. of Pa., 1916; Ph.D., Harvard, 1925; m. Adelin M. Hohlfeld, Aug. 31, 1934; 1 son, David Hector. Field work in archæology, N.M., 1912, 17; Guatemala, 1913, N.J., 1915, Ill., 1916, Colo., 1919, Marquesas Islands, 1920-21, Ohio, 1924, Wis., 1932-33; in ethnology, Polynesia, 1920-22, Madagascar, 1925-27, South Africa, 1928, Okla., 1934. Asst. curator of ethnology, Field Museum of Natural History, 1922-28; prof. anthropology, U. of Wisconsin, 1928-37; prof. anthropology, Columbia, U., 1937-39; chmn. dept. of anthropology, 1939-43; Sterling prof., anthropology, Yale U. since 1946. Editor Am. Anthropologist, 1939-44. Corpl. Battery D, 149th F.A., U.S. Army, Rainbow Div., 1917-19. Awarded Viking medal, 1952; Huxley Meml. medal, 1954. Mem. Am. Anthrop. Assn. (pres. 1946), A.A.A.S. (v.p. 1937), National Academy Sciences (chmn. div. anthropology 1949-51), Phi Beta Kappa, Sigma Xi, Alpha Kappa Delta; honorary member Académie Malgache. Hon. fellow Royal Anthrop. Inst. Gt. Britain. Mem. Nat. Research Council, 1931-32, 1940-45; mem. Social Science Research Council, 1932-39, American Council of Learned Societies, 1947-50. Quaker. Author: The Material Culture of the Marquesas Islands, 1924; Use of Tobacco Among North American Indians, 1924; The Archæology of the Marquesas Islands, 1925. Guide to the Polynesian and Micronesian Collections, Field Museum, 1925; The Tanala, A Hill-Tribe of Madagascar, 1932; The Study of Man, an Introduction, 1936; Acculturation in Seven American Indian Tribes, 1940; Cultural Background of Personality, 1945; editor, The Science of Man in the World Crisis, 1945; The Tree of Culture, 1955. Editor: Most of the World, 1949. Address: Dept. of Anthropology, Yale Univ., New Haven. Died Dec. 24, 1953.

LINTOTT, Edward Barnard (lĭn'tŏt), artist; b. London, Eng., Dec. 11, 1875; s. Edward Stephen and Georgiana (Hawley) L.; student Académie Julien Sorbonne U., Ecole de Beaux Arts, Paris, 1900-10; m. Kate Elizabeth Jane Smith, Jan. 1, 1901; 1 dau., Phyllis Marjorie; m. 2d, Marie Walther Sterner, Aug. 25, 1931. Came to U.S., 1927. Examiner in art to Bd. of Edn., London, Eng., 1920-27. Represented in Contemporary Art Soc., Lond; Imperial War Museum, London, Musee de Ghent, Belgium; Nat. Gallery of New South Wales, Australia; Aberdeen Art Gallery, Scotland; Victoria and Albert Museum, London, British Museum; Bklyn. Mus., Boston Museum; Haggin Meml. Gallery, Cal., Andover Art Gallery; fgn. sect. of the Louvre, Paris; Hackley Art Gallery, Muskegon, Mich.; Canajoharie Museum, British Museum, Joselyn Memorial Museum, Omaha; Coué Collection, Balt., Smithsonian Instn. In British Diplomatic Service, 1915-19. Mem. Nat. Soc. Portrait Painters (Eng.), Internat. Soc. of Painters, Sculptors and Gravers. Clubs: Art (London); Lotos (N.Y. C.). Author: The Art of Water Color Painting, 1920; also book of drawings of the 107 members of the New York Philharmonic Symphony Orchestra, 1939. Address: 147 W. 55th St., N.Y.C. Died Mar. 12, 1951

LIONBERGER, Isaac H. (lī'ŭn-bĕr-gẽr), lawyer; b. Boonville, Mo., Aug. 30, 1854; s. John R. and Margaret (Clarkson) L.; student Washington U., St. Louis, to 1870; A.B., Princeton, 1875; studied in St. Louis Law Sch.; m. Louise Shepley, June 9, 1886. Admitted to bar, 1877; asst. atty. gen. U.S. 1896; prof. law of corpns. St. Louis Law Sch., 1892-1907. Chmn. pub. welfare com. on charter revision, St. Louis, 1901; sec. Com. Pub. Safety, 1892; govt. del. Universal Congress Lawyers and Jurists, St. Louis, 1904. Mem. Am., St. Louis (pres. 1899-1900) bar assns., Mo. Hist. Soc. (pres. 1929—). Democrat. Clubs: University (pres. 1900), Country, Noon-Day. Author: Law of Corporations (Missouri); The Felicities of Sixty Years, 1920; The Meaning of Property, 1921. Home: 37 Westmoreland Pl. Office: Security Bldg., St. Louis. Died Sept. 12, 1948.

LIPMAN, Clara, actress; b. Chgo.; d. Abraham and Josephine Lipman; m. Louis Mann. First played ingénuses with Mme. Modjeska, afterwards appeared with A. M. Palmer's Co.; created ingénue part in Incog and played in German and English companies in classical drama; starred jointly with Louis Mann in Girl From Paris, The Telephone Girl, Girl in the Barracks, Red Kloof, All on Account of Eliza, Strange Adventures of Miss Brown, and her own comedy, Julie Bon Bon, and The French Lady. Author: (plays) Pepi; Julie Bon Bon; Lady from Westchester; His Protégé, Billy with a Punch; The Italian Girl; Marie de Fleury; Work or Fight; The Fiddler; Wolf at the Door. Co-author: (plays) Elevating a Husband; Nature's Nobleman; Children of Today; The Hunted Lady; Depends on the Woman; Flames and Embers, Royal Maid; Honor Thy Children; Two Sweethearts; The Good-for-Nothing; Exemption; Right or Wrong; Some Warriors; Great Billy's Gost; Hardest Job. Wrote dialogue of moving picture Sins of the Children. Home: 839 Riverside Dr., N.Y.C. Died 1952.

LIPMAN, Frederick Lockwood, banker; b. San Francisco, Feb. 21, 1866; s. Charles Frederick and Frances Caroline (Kellogg) L.; student pub. schs.; m. Edith Law, July 25, 1891; children—Edward Crossley, Robert Lookwood, Mary Edith Jensen. In stockbroker's office, 1878-83; with note dept. Wells Fargo & Co. Bank, San Francisco, 1883; chmn. bd. Wells Fargo Bank & Union Trust Co. (formerly Wells Fargo Nev. Nat. Bank), now ret. Mem. Am. Econ. Assn. Republican. Untarian. Clubs: Pacific Union, Bohemian. Home: 2943 Avalon Av., Berkeley, Cal. Office: Wells Fargo Bank & Union Trust Co., San Francisco. Died May 11, 1950.

LIPPINCOTT, Richard H(amilton), business exec.; b. Brooklyn, June 11, 1901; s. Charles and Anna (Hamilton) L.; ed. pub. schs. of Brooklyn; m. Agnes Chamberlin, Sept. 21, 1929; children—Sue, Richard H., Patricia. Office boy Equitable Life, N.Y., 1919-22; salesman Sealkap Co., 1922-28; salesman Holeproof Hosiery Co., 1928-31, asst. sales mgr., 1931-38, v.p., gen. salesmgr. Milw., 1935-56; salesmgr. John F. Long Co., Phoenix, 1956—; dir. Brand Names Found. Mem. Wis. Apparel Assn. (chmn. bd., pres.), Wis. Mens Golf Assn. Republican. Episcopalian. Club: Wisconsin Men Apparel (past pres.), Milwaukee Athletic, Oconomowoc Golf, Oconomowoc Lake. Address: Sundown Ranch, Scottsdale, Ariz. Died Feb. 18, 1957.

LIPPMANN, Julie Mathilde, author, dramatist, critic; b. Brooklyn, N.Y.; d. Adolph and Marie Sophie L.; ed. in pvt. schs. Began writing at very early age; contbr. to Century, Harper's, Atlantic and other mags. Author: Jock o' Dreams, 1891; Miss Wildfire, 1897; Dorothy Day, 1898; Sweet Ps., 1902; Dearie, Dot and the Dog, 1903; Del's Debt, 1903; Everyday Girls, 1904; Martha By-the-Day, 1912 (dramatized and prod. 1914; pub. in Braille); Making Over Martha, 1913; Martha and Cupid, 1914; Burkes' Amy, 1915; Governess, 1916; Mannequin, 1917; Interlopers, 1917; Flexible Ferdinand, 1918; Guest Detective; (plays) A Fool and His Money, 1897; Cousin Faithful, 1897; The Facts in the Case, 1897; Rubber Stamp, 1915; First Person Singular, 1920; Fool's Hill, 1926; Deadgame Sport, 1928; Jessup, Jr., 1930. Active in work of Vigilantes, a patriotic assn. of authors and illustrators for counteracting enemy propaganda, World War I; actively asso. with Theatre Wing, World War II (awarded citation for unusual vol. work). Home: 3731 Earls Court View, Cin. 26. Died Apr. 10, 1952; buried Greenwood Cemetery, N.Y.C.

LIPSCOMB, William H., business exec.; b. Manassas, Va., July 23, 1888; s. William N. and Mary Dabney (Weir) L.; student Univ. of Va., 1906-11; m. Frances Rebecca Ross, 1922 (dec. 1933); children—Helen Ross, Samuel Ross. Engr. Pub. Service Ry. of N.J., Elizabeth, N.J., 1911-12, Dublex Metals Co., New York, N.Y., 1912-13, Richmond Power & Light Co., 1913-14; engr. and salesman U.S. Steel Corp., New York, N.Y., 1914-17, 1919-25; pres. Habirshaw Cable & Wire Corp., New York, N.Y., 1926-28, Dubilier Condenser Corp., New York, N.Y., 1929-30, B. & R. Inc., Huntington Terrace Corp., Washington, D.C., 1931-41; dir. Potomac Electric Power Co., Barber & Ross Co., Washington, D.C., since 1931 White Sulphur Springs Corp. since 1946; dir. and mem. exec. com. C. & O. Ry., since 1942. Episcopalian. Clubs: Rolling Rock (Ligonear, Pennsylvania), Chevy Chase (Maryland). Home: 2101 Connecticut Avenue N.W., Washington, D.C. Office: American Security Bldg., Washington, D.C. and Raspberry Plain, Leesburg, Va. Died July 29, 1957.

LIPTON, Sir Thomas Johnstone, tea and provision mcht.; b. in Glasgow, Scotland, of Irish parents,

Chmn. Lipton Limited tea and provision mchts., London, and principal towns of Great Britain and Ireland; owns tea estates in Ceylon; pres. Thomas J. Lipton Co., pork packers, Chgo.; owner Lipton Refrigerator Car Lines, Chgo.; makes frequent business visits to U.S. Created Knight Comdr. Victorian Order, 1901, Baronet, 1902. Owner of steam yacht Erin and sailing yachts Shamrock I and Shamrock II, contested the America's Cup in 1899, 1901, 03. Address: Osidge, Southgate, Middlesex, Eng. Died 1933.

LISCHER, Benno Edward (lĭsh'ĕr), orthodontist; b. Mascoutah, Ill., June 27, 1876; s. Christopher and Caroline (Freund) L.; D.M.D., Washington U., 1900; m. Mary Louise Huber, Sept. 1, 1901; children—Grace, Carl Edward, Mary Louise. Prof. orthodontics, Washington U., 1902-24; non-resident lecturer on orthodontics, U. of Mich., 1925-29; prof. orthodontics, U. of Calif., 1930-33; dean and prof. orthodontics Washington Univ. Sch. of Dentistry, 1933-45, now dean emeritus. Hon. pres. Internat. Orthodontic Congress, N.Y. City, 1926; presiding chmn. orthodontics, 7th Internat. Dental Congress, Phila., Pa., 1926. Mem. Am. Soc. Orthodontists (president 1912-13), Am. Assn. Dental Schs. (pres. 1942-43), Am. Assn. Dental Editors (president 1941), American Dental Assn., Am. Med. Assn., St. Louis Dental Soc., Mo. State Dental Association; fellow A.A.A.S., International Assn. Dental Research. Club: Town and Gown. Author: Elements of Orthodontia, 1909; Principles and Methods of Orthodontics, 1912. Translator: Simon's Dental Anomalies, and Simon's On the Norm-Concept in Orthodontics, 1926. Home: 313 N. Rockhill Rd., Webster Groves 19, Mo. Died Oct. 10, 1959.

LISTER, Charles Baynard, editor; b. Wilmington, Del., July 4, 1898; s. James Whittington and Florence (Carson) L.; student pub. schs. Wilmington, Del.; m. Frances Lynette Harper, Oct. 22, 1919; 1 dau., Frances Lynette. With mil. sales div. E. I. du Pont de Nemours, Wilmington, Del., 1916-21; writer for Nat. Rifle Assn. of America, Washington, 1921-—, now exec. dir.; editor The American Rifleman, 1939-—. Mem. nat. council, nat. com. health and safety Boy Scouts Am.; bd. dirs. Boys Clubs of Washington. Served in U.S. Army, 1917-19. Mem. Am. Ordnance Assn., U.S. Olympic Assn., U.S. Naval Inst., Am. Museum Natural History, Nat. Geog. Soc., Optimist Internat. (life), Washington Criminal Justice Assn. (mem. bd. dirs.). Clubs: National Press, Columbia (Washington); University, Jefferson Island, Blue Ridge Rod and Gun. Author of tech. and instrn. manuals pertaining to small arms, ballistics and training methods. Editor: The N.R.A. Book of Small Arms (2 vols.). Home: 6608 32d Pl., Washington 15. Office: 1600 Rhode Island Av., Washington 6. Died May 14, 1951; buried Arlington Nat. Cemetery.

LISTON, H(ardy) Sr., coll. pres.; b. Fairfield County, S.C., Mar. 30, 1889; s. Huey Lord and Maggie (Davis) L.; A.B., Biddle U. (now Johnson C. Smith U.), Charlotte, N.C., 1911; B.S., U. Chgo., 1925, A.M., 1928; Ped.D., Johnson C. Smith U., 1937; LL.D., Maryville Coll., 1952, Lincoln U., 1953; m. Estelle Hoskins, June 28, 1916; children—Hugh Hoskins, Hardy, Sara Margaret (Mrs. Royal Spurlark), Estelle Simmons (Mrs. Charles Muse), Aurelia Blanche, David Julian. Prin. and tchr. Carrier St. Sch., Spartanburg, S.C., 1912-13; adminstrv. asst., tchr. mathematics Kittrell Coll., N.C., 1913-15, Slater State Normal Sch., N.C., 1915-25; dean Winston-Salem Tchrs. Coll., 1925-31, Knoxville (Tenn.) Coll., 1931-43; exec. v.p. Johnson Smith U., 1943-47, pres., 1947-—. Mem. commn. on instns. of higher edn. Assn. Colls. and Secondary Schs. for Negroes, 1935-43, chmn., study com.; mem. com. on structure, orgn. and functioning of the ch. Presbyn. Ch., U.S.A. Mem. exec. com. N.C. Council Chs., 1954-56; pres. N.C. Negro Coll. Conf., 1954-55. Mem. Assn. Collegiate Deans and Registrars in Negro Schs., 1931-43 (v.p. 1942, pres. 1943), Alliance of Ref. Chs. throughout the World holding The Presbyn. System (western section), Alpha Phi Alpha, Beta Kappa Chi, Alpha Kappa Mu. Presbyn. Author: Study of Work of Jeanes Supervising Teachers for Negro Rural Schools, 1928; co-author: Study of Community Life of Negro Youth, 1941. Editor, Quarterly Review of Higher Edn. Among Negroes, 1943-—. Contbr. article on Qualitative Requirements for Coll. Graduation to Proceedings of Nat. Assn. of Collegiate Deans and Registrars in Negro Schs., 1934. Home: Johnson C. Smith U., Charlotte, N.C. Died Oct. 20, 1956; buried West Pinewood Cemetery, Charlotte.

LITCHFIELD, Electus Darwin (lĭch'fēld), architect; b. New York, Apr. 25, 1872; s. William Backus and Emily (Pope) L.; grad. Brooklyn Poly. Inst., 1889; M. E. Stevens Inst. of Tech., 1892; m. Elizabeth B. Rodman, Oct. 6, 1906; children—Elizabeth Burnham, William Burnham. With Carrère & Hastings, architects, 2 yrs.; associated, and then mem. Lord & Hewlett, architects, 1901-08; mem. firm Tracy, Swartwout & Litchfield, 1908-13, alone, 1913-19, firm Electus D. Litchfield & Rogers, 1919-26; in practice under own name 1926-—. Architect. U.S. Post Office and Courthouse, Denver; St. Paul Pub. Library; James J. Hill Reference Library, St. Paul; proposed Nat. Armory, Washington; Bklyn. Masonic Temple; City Club; Tuberculosis Pavilion, Riverside Hosp., N.Y.; architect, town planner Yorkship Village, a permanent industrial town of 1,700 houses built during war for Emergency Fleet Corp., N.Y. Shipbuilding Co.; 800 Park Av., other apts.; The Astoria Column, Astoria, Ore., other monuments. Cons. architect U.S. Post Office, Courthouse and Customhouse, Albany, N.Y. Mem. N.Y. Com. on City Plan, 1927; mem. Building Code Revision Commn., N.Y., 1906-07; a winner in competition for design of N.Y. City slum clearance projects and apptd. an architect for Red Hook project; in assn. with Louis Allen Abramson architect for reconstrn. of Bellevue Hosp. Fellow A.I.A. Mem. Architectural League of N.Y., Municipal Art Soc. (ex-pres.), N.Y. Fine Arts Fedn., Beaux Art Inst. Design, Citizens Housing Council (dir.), N.Y. Bldg. Congress (founder; chmn. orgn. com. 1921), Soc. Colonial Wars of N.Y. (ex.-gov.), Gen. Soc. Colonial Wars (ex-deputy gov. gen. from N.Y.), The Pilgrims, Tau Beta Pi. Democrat. Episcopalian. Clubs: City, Church. Home: 171 E. 73d St. Office: 80 Fifth Av., N.Y.C. 11. Died Nov. 27, 1952.

LITCHFIELD, Paul Weeks, corp. official; b. Boston, Mass., July 26, 1875; s. Charles M. and Julia (Weeks) L.; B.S., Mass. Inst. Tech., 1896; m. Florence Brinton, June 23, 1904; children, Mrs. Howard L. Hyde, Mrs. A. Wallace Denny. Began with Goodyear Tire and Rubber Co., supt., 1900-15, v.p., 1915-26, pres., 1926-40, chmn. bd., 1930-58, now hon. chmn.; chmn. Goodyear Aircraft Corp., etc. Formerly mem. bd. Mass. Inst. Tech.; dir. U. Akron. Mem. Mass. Inst. Tech. Alumni Assn. (ex-pres.). Mem. Nat. Exec. Bd. of The Boy Scouts of Am., former vice chmn. Region Four, Boy Scouts of America, former chairman Region Four, Senior Scouting, Boy Scouts America. Decorated Order Cruzeiro do Sul (Brazil); Order del Sol (Peru); Royal Order of Vasa (Sweden); Order of Adolphe of Nassau (Luxemburg); Order Indsl. Merit. Mem. Soc. Automotive Engrs., Nat. Assn. Mfrs., Nat. Air Council, Navy League. Mason (33°). Clubs: University, City, Portage Country, Wings, Inc., Arizona, Union (Cleve.); Automobile Old Timers, Inc. Writer of "Autumn Leaves," Indsl. Republic; Indsl. Voyage (autobiography of P. W. Litchfield); magazine articles. Leader in development work of lighter-than-air craft. Home: 1010 Merriman Rd. Office: 1144 E. Market St., Akron, O. Died Mar. 18, 1959.

LITTELL, Clarence Guy, former pres. R. R. Donnelley & Sons Co.; b. in Ill., 1882; s. Willis Ruthven and Nancy Dana (McGee) L.; grad. U. Ind.; m. Neva Penny, 1901; children—Hugh Ruthven, Willis Harrison, Nancy Jane. Started with R. R. Donnelley & Sons Co., Chgo., 1903, retired as pres. 1945. Republican. Home: Winnetka, Ill. Died Oct. 1958.

LITTELL, Frank Bowers, astronomer; b. Scranton, Pa., Feb. 21, 1869; s. Henry Woolsey and Marie Antoinette (Bowers) L.; Ph.B., Wesleyan, 1891, Sc.D., 1919; A.M., Columbian (now George Washington) U., 1894; m. Josephine La Monte Mercereau, Apr. 9, 1902; children—Marion Mercereau, Charles Henry. Computer Naval Obs., 1891-96; teacher mathematics, Scranton High Sch., 1896-97; computer, 1897-98, asst. astronomer, 1898-1901, Naval Obs.; prof. mathematics USN, 1901-33, when retired. Mem. U.S. eclipse expdns. to Barnesville, Ga., 1900, Solok, Sumatra, 1901, Porta Coeli, Spain, 1905, Los Angeles (airship), 1925, expdn. to Sumatra, 1926; mem. U.S. party to determine Washington-Paris longitude, using radio signals, 1913-14; variation of latitude by the photographic zenith tube, 1915-33; determination of World longitudes by radio, San Diego (Cal.) sta., 1926. Made catalogue of 23,521 stars (with W. S. Eichelberger); vertical circle observations made with the 5-inch altazimuth, 1898-1907, and 1916-33 (pub. 1939); Washington-Paris longitude by radio signals (with G. A. Hill). Fellow A.A.A.S., Royal Astron. Soc. (Eng.); mem. Philos. Soc. Washington, Am. Astron. Soc. (councillor 1928-31), Washington Acad. Sciences, Sociedad Astronomica de Mex., Soc. Astron. de France, Internat. Astron. Union, Am. Geophys. Union Astron. Soc. of Pacific, Phi Beta Kappa. Spl. editor on astronomy, Webster's New Internat. Dictionary and World Book Ency. Annual. Home: 3704 Porter St., Washington 16. Died Mar. 28, 1951; buried Arlington Nat. Cemetery.

LITTEN, Frederic Nelson, educator, author; b. Chicago, May 26, 1885; s. Nelson L. and Mary (Chapin) L.; student mech. engring., Ill. Tech. (Lewis Inst.); m. Ella Mendsen, 1909; 1 son, Frederic Chapin. Foreman, asst. supt., pub. utility plants, 1904-07; constrn. engr., operating engr., power and pub. utility plants, 1907-26; began writing, 1926; asst. editor Am. Boy mag., 1937-38; became asso. prof. of creative writing, Medill Sch. of Journalism, Northwestern U., 1938, chmn. fiction dept. since 1946; book reviewer for Chicago Sun. Writings included in Best Stories for Boys, 1927; Blue Ribbon Stories, 1928; Am. Boy Stories, 1929; Storyland, 1929; Best Air Stories, 1930; Good Reading for High Schs., 1931; Sports Anthology, 1932; Story Hits of 1932; Reading is Fun, 1934; Collection for High Schs., 1941; Best Flying Stories, 1941; Portraits, 1942; People and Progress, 1943. Mem. Chicago Fiction Guild, Authors League of Am., Midland Authors. Mem. adv. bd. Midwestern Writers Conf. Assn. Clubs: Arts, The Cliff Dwellers (Chicago). Author: Rhodes of the Flying Cadets, 1928; Sunup on the Range, 1928; Brooks of the Valley Airways, 1930; Rhodes of the 94th, 1932 (Jr. Lit. Guild selection for 1936); Rhodes of the Leathernecks, 1934; Pilot of the High Sierras, 1936; Pilot of the North Country, 1938; Air Trails North, 1939; Transatlantic Pilot, 1940; Pilot of the High Andes, 1941; Airmen of the Amazon, 1942; Air Mission to Algiers, 1943; Sinister Island Squadron, 1944; Rendezvous Over Mindanao, 1945; Kingdom of Flying Men, 1946; Short Story Writing (text book), 1946; Code of a Champion, 1950; Air Mission Red, 1951. Four of his books have been pub. in Braille; five have Brit. publ. Also author of about 600 short stories, novelettes, serials in 41 nat. mags. Home: 402 Prospect Av., Lake Bluff, Ill. Office: Medill Sch. of Journalism, Northwestern U., Wieboldt Hall, 335 E. Chicago Av., Chicago. Died July 26, 1951.

LITTICK, Orville Beck, newspaper pub.; b. Zanesville, O., July 2, 1890; s. William Oliver and Laura Priscilla (Beck) L.; A.B., Ohio Wesleyan U., 1912; m. Anna Sophia Holzmiller, July 20, 1916; children—Marie Annette (Mrs. Tobin), William Orville. Asst. football coach Ohio Wesleyan U., athletic dir. and football coach Centre Coll. in Ky. and Beloit (Wis.) Coll., 1912-20; newspaper work, Zanesville, 1920-26; owner and editor Daily Independent, Murphysboro, Ill., 1926-30; gen. mgr. Zanesville Pub. Co. since 1930, pres. since 1941; v.p. radio sta. WHIZ since 1946; bd. dirs. Citizens Nat. Bank. Gen. chmn. Zanesville Community Fund, 1934; pres. Zane Trace area Boy Scouts Am., 1935-36; sec.-treas. Abbott Home for Aged Men. Member of Ohio Select List Daily Newspapers (past pres.), Ohio (past pres.) and Muskingum (past pres.) socs. for crippled children, C. of C. (dir.), Beta Theta Pi, Sigma Delta Chi. Presbyn. (past pres. bd. trustees). Club: Rotary (past pres.; dist. gov. So. Ohio 1940-41). Home: 427 Harding Rd. Office: 34 S. Fourth St., Zanesville, O. Died Sept. 2, 1953.

LITTLE, Chauncey B., ex-congressman; b. Olathe, Kan., Feb. 10, 1877; s. John T. and Mary W. (Bundy) L.; ed. Kansas State Agrl. Coll. and U. Kan.; LL.B., U. Kan., 1898; m. Nellie B. Sherman, Oct. 3, 1903; children—Maxine (dec.), Loraine. Admitted to Kan. bar, 1898, and began practice at Olathe; city atty., Olathe, 1901-06; county atty. Johnson County, Kan., 1909-13; mem. 69th Congress, 2d Kan. Dist. Candidate for gov. of Kan., 1928. Democrat. Episcopalian. Mason, Elk, Eagle, Odd Fellow. Home: Olathe, Kan. Died Oct. 1952.

LITTLE, David M(ason), educator; b. Marblehead, Mass., July 27, 1896; s. David Mason and Clara Bertram (Kimball) L.; A.B., Harvard, 1918, A.M., 1922, Ph.D., 1935; m. Helen L. Crocker, Sept. 27, 1917 (dec.); children—Priscilla Alden (Mrs. F. A. Webster), David Mason, Jr., Adams Crocker, Katharine Kimball (Mrs. Harold T. Blake), married 2d. Rosamond T. (Bennett) Sturgis, May 26, 1949. Assistant in English, Harvard University, 1920-25, assistant in history, 1921-22, asst. dean Harvard Coll., 1922-24, tutor in div. of modern langs., 1924-26, instr. in English, 1925-26, instr. in English and tutor in div. of modern langs., 1929-30, sec. to the univ. since 1936, master of Adams House since 1938, mem. faculty of arts and sciences since 1938, mem. bd. freshmen advisers since 1938, curator of theatre collection, 1933-40, asst. dir. tercentenary celebration, 1936; exec. sec. Harvard Endowment Fund, 1921-26. Served as ensign, U.S.N.R., during World War 1. Trustee Middlesex Sch., Concord. Chmn. service div. Greater Boston United War Fund, 1945. Member Phi Beta Kappa. Clubs: Harvard (member board govs.) (Boston); Harvard (New York); Faculty (Cambridge). Editor and part author: The Education of the Modern Boy, 1925. Author: Pineapples of Finest Flavor, 1930. Home: Apthorp House, Linden St., Cambridge 38, Mass. Died Apr. 25, 1954; buried Salem, Mass.

LITTLE, William Augustus, judge; b. Talbot County, Ga., Nov. 6, 1838; s. Dr. William G. and M. A. L.; student U. Ga.; A.B., Oglethorpe U., 1859; pvt. to capt. C.S.A., 1861-5. Admitted to bar, and began practice at Talbotton, Ga.; now at Columbus, Ga. Asst. sec. Ga. Senate, 1871-2; solicitor-gen. Chattahoochee Circuit, 1872; mem. Ga. Constl. Conv., 1877; Ho. of Reps., 1882-88 (speaker 1884-88); asst. atty.-gen., 1891-92, atty.-gen. of Ga., 1892-94; asst. atty.-gen. of U.S., 1896; asso. justice Supreme Ct. of Ga., 1897-1903. Democrat. Address: Columbus, Ga. Died Feb. 27, 1924.

LITTLEDALE, Clara Savage, editor; born at Belfast, Maine, January 31, 1891; daughter Reverend John Arthur and Emma (Morrison) Savage; A.B., Smith College, 1913; m. Harold Aylmer Littledale, Dec. 20, 1920; children—Rosemary, Harold Aylmer. Reporter and editor of the woman's page of the New York Evening Post, 1913-14; press chairman National American Woman Suffrage Assn., 1914-15; asso. editor Good Housekeeping, 1916-18, fgn. corr., 1918-19; free lance writer, 1919-26; editor Parents' Mag. since 1926. Mem. N.Y. League of Women Voters, Child Study Assn. of Am., Am. Assn. for Adult Edn.,

Nat. Com. on Parent Edn. women's conf. group, U.S. Children's Bur. Commn. on Children and Youth. Contbr. articles to mags. Home: 5 Sniffin Court, New York 16. Address: Parents Mag., 52 Vanderbilt Av., N.Y.C. Died Jan. 9, 1956.

LITZINGER, Marie, prof. mathematics; b. Bedford, Pa., May 14, 1899; d. Rush and Katherine (O'Connell) Litzinger; A.B., Bryn Mawr Coll., 1920, M.A., 1922; student U. of Rome, Italy, 1923-24; Ph.D., U. of Chicago, 1934. Teacher, Devon (Pa.) Manor Sch., 1920-22, Greenwich (Conn.) Academy, 1924-25; instr. Mt. Holyoke Coll., South Hadley, Mass., 1925-28, asst. prof., 1928-37, chmn. dept. mathematics since 1937, asso. prof., 1937-42, prof. since 1942, prof. mathematics John Stewart Kennedy Foundn. since 1948. Mem. Am. Math. Soc., Math. Assn. of Am., Conn. Valley Sect. Assn. Teachers of Mathematics in New Eng. (pres. 1940-41), Sigma Xi. Democrat. Author: (article) A Basis for Residual Polynomials in N Variables (Transactions of the Am. Math. Soc., Vol. 37, No. 2, 1935). Home: Bedford, Pa. Office: Mt. Holyoke College, South Hadley, Mass. Died Apr. 7, 1952.

LIVERMORE, Russell B., lawyer; b. Yonkers, N. Y., Mar. 22, 1894; s. Arthur L. and Henrietta J. (Wells) L.; A.B., Dartmouth Coll., 1915; LL.B., Columbia, 1921; m. Josephine S. Lanier, Aug. 2, 1928. Admitted to N.Y. bar, 1922; partner law firm Livermore & Lanier, chmn. exec. com. and dir. Link Belt Co. Mem. N.Y. State Assembly, 1922-23. Served as 1st lt., A.E.F., World War I; col., A.A.F., Office of Strategic Services, World War II. Awarded Distinguished Service Cross, Silver Star, Legion of Merit, Purple Heart. Clubs: Union League (New York); Dartmouth College. Home: 455 E. 51st St. Office: 501 Fifth Av., N.Y.C. Died May 21, 1958, buried Arlington Nat. Cemetery.

LIVERSIDGE, Horace Preston (lĭv'ẽr-sĭj), pub. utility exec.; b. Norristown, Pa., Sept. 29, 1878; s. Thomas and Elizabeth (Preston) L.; graduate Drexel Inst., Phila., 1897, grad. study in elec. engring., 1897-98; hon. Dr. of Engring., Stevens Inst. of Technology, 1940; hon. ScD., in Commerce, Drexel Inst. Tech., 1943; m. Sara B. Moore, Oct. 14, 1902; children—Preston Moore, Robert Passmore, Thomas Kinnard. With Edison Electric Light Co. (Phila. Electric Co. since 1902) since 1898, beginning as inspector, advancing through engring. and operating depts. to supt. electric plant constrn., supt. generating plant, assistant chief engineer, until 1924, vice pres. and assistant chief engineer 1924-26, vice pres. and general manager, 1926-38, director since 1936, pres. 1938-47, chairman board since June 1947; dir. several Phila. Electric Company subsidiaries. Director Insurance Co. of North America and subsidiaries; dir., mem. exec. com., Fidelity Mut. Life Insurance Co.; dir. Benj. Franklin Hotel Co., Central-Penn. Nat. Bank, James Lees & Sons Co. Chairman of board Drexel Inst. (co-chmn. expansion program); trustee Jefferson Med. Coll. and its Hosp.; mem. bd. mgrs. University Museum; member of the advisory board of Salvation Army; director Community Chest, Phila.; v.p., mem. exec. com. United Fund; adv. bd. Philadelphia Council Churches; trustee Nat. Safety Council, Thomas Alva Edison Found., Inc. Mem. adv. com. Edison Electric Inst.; Member of Assn. Edison Illuminating Cos. (ex-pres.), A.S.M.E., Am. Inst. E.E., Illuminating Engring. Soc., Electric Assn. Phila. (bd. govs.; ex-pres.), James H. McGraw Com. of Awards for Elec. Men. Granted James H. McGraw award for cooperation, 1932, Murrell Dobbins Pioneers of Industry Award, 1944; Edward Powell award for outstanding contbns. to bus. life of Phila., 1951; William Penn award for outstanding contbns. to bus. and econ. life of the nation, 1952; National Human Relations award The National Conference of Christians and Jews, 1955. Republican. Presbyterian. Clubs: Union League, Engineers, Midday, Racquet, Philadelphia Country (Philadelphia); Seaview Country (Absecon, N.J.); Gulph Mills Golf (Gulf Mills, Pa.), Kennebunk River, Cape Arundel (Kennebunkport, Me.). Home: Lafayette Rd. and Stony Lane, Bryn Mawr, Pa., and Kennebunkport, Me. Office: 1000 Chestnut St., Phila. 5. Died Dec. 8, 1955; buried West Laurel Hill Cemetery, Bala-Cynwyd, Pa.

LIVINGSTON, George, government official; born Union City, O., Sept. 14, 1886; s. Adam and Mary (Thomas) L.; B.S., Ohio State Univ., 1909; studied Cornell Univ., 1913, Univ. of Halle, 1914; m. Inez Van Sickle, June 7, 1911; children—Mary Jane, Robert James. Instr. farm crops, Ia. State Coll. Agr. and Mechanic Arts, 1909-10; asst. prof. agronomy in charge instrn. in field crops, Ohio State U., 1911-14; acting chief dept. of agronomy, same univ., and asso. agronomist Ohio Agrl. Expt. Sta., 1914-15; specialist in grain marketing, 1915-19, chief, 1919-21, Bur. of Markets, U.S. Dept. Agr.; dir. Livingston Econ. Service; exec. v.p. Millers Nat. Fedn., 1929-39; dir. food supply, advisory commn. to the Council of Nat. Defense, 1940; consultant on food supply, Bur. of Indsl. Conservation, WPB, 1941-42; chief, food and agrl. supplies, Office of Fgn. Relief and Rehabilitation, U.S. State Dept., 1943; chief, compliance div., Great Lakes area, War Food Adminstrn., 1943. Commodity Exchange Supervisor, 1944—. Mem. Alpha Zeta. Unitarian. Club: Union League (Chicago). Author: Laboratory Manual of Cereals and Forage Crops, 1913; Field Crop Production, 1914. Home: 303 Elmwood Rd., Champaign, Ill. Office: Board of Trade Bldg., Chgo. Died June 15, 1954.

LIVINGSTON, Goodhue, architect; b. N.Y.C., Feb. 23, 1867; s. Robert Edward and Susan M. C. (dePeyster) L.; A.B., Columbia, 1888, Ph.B. in Architecture, 1892, M.A. 1914; m. Louisa Robb, Apr. 8, 1896; children—Goodhue, Cornelia Thayer. Practiced in N.Y.C., 1896—; architect of Chem. Nat. Bank Bldg., Bankers Trust Bldg., St. Regis Hotel, Knickerbocker Hotel, Ardsley Club, B. Altman & Co.'s Bldg., J. P. Morgan & Co.'s Bldg., N.Y. Stock Exchange addition (all N.Y.C.); Rickers Island Penitentiary; Palace Hotel (San Francisco); Bank of America, Equitable Trust Co. Bldg. (N.Y.C.); Mitsui Bank & Trust Co. (Tokyo, Japan); U.S. Post Office and Court House Bldg., and Gulf Bldg. (Pitts.); Haden Planetarium; Capitol of the State of Ore.; etc. Trustee (N.Y.C.); Dispensary. Fellow A.I.A.; mem. Archtl. League N.Y. (medal of honor), St. Anthony, Nat. Inst. Social Sciences, Delta Psi. Republican. Episcopalian. Mason. Clubs: Brook (gov.), Racquet and Tennis, Century, Knickerbocker, (N.Y.C.); Meadow (pres.), Shinnecock Hills Golf, of Southampton. Home: 38 E. 65th St. Office: 101 Park Av., N.Y.C. Died June 1951.*

LLEWELLYN, William H. H., lawyer; b. Monroe, Wis., Sept. 9, 1854; s. Joseph Howard and Louisa (Fry) L.; Tabor (Ia.) Coll.; studied law 3 yrs., Omaha, Neb., and 4 yrs. Las Cruces, N.M.; m. Ida M. Little, Mar. 9, 1878. Admitted to N.M. bar, 1886; mem. law firm Rynerson, Wade & Llewellyn, 1886-93, Bonham & Llewellyn, 1901-04, Llewellyn & Llewellyn, 1908-10, Llewellyn & Medler, 1911—; dir., atty. several mining and other cos.; atty. Western Union Telegraph Co. for N.M. U.S. Indian agt. for Apache Indians of N.M., 1881-5; mem. N.M. Territorial Ho. of Reps., 1897, speaker 1901, 03, chmn. Judiciary Com. both sessions; mem. 1st State Legislative Assembly, N.M., 1912—; territorial atty., 3d Dist., 1901-5; U.S. atty., 1905-08; spl. asst. to U.S. atty.-gen., 1908—, in prosecutions of violations of neutrality laws of Congress and smuggling Chinese persons into U.S. from Mexico; also dist. atty. 8th Dist., 1909—. Prosecuted for U.S. A.F.&S.F. Ry. Co. and Colo. Fuel & Iron Co. for violation of Sherman law, 1906. Capt. Troop G, 1st U.S. Vol. Cav. (Roosevelt's Rough Riders), 1898, Spanish-Am. War; promoted maj. in field, siege of Santiago de Cuba, July, 1898; on Gov. Otero's staff 5 yrs. and Gov. Hagerman's staff about 2 yrs., to 1906, with rank of col. and judge advocate-gen. N.M. N.G. Del. Rep. Nat. Conv., 1884, 96, 1900, 04, 08. Episcopalian. Mason (K.T., Shriner). Home: Las Cruces, N.M. Deceased.

LLOYD, Bolivar Jones (loid), pub. health worker; b. Bryan, Tex., May 10, 1872; s. David Stoax and Mary (Benson) L.; M.D., U. Tex., 1897; m. Josephine Gomez, Jan. 26, 1910; children—Edmund Henry, Bolivar Joseph, Roger Milton. Joined USPHS, 1900, ret. 1938, asst. surgeon gen. Div. San. Reports and Statistics, radio service, publicity, also edited Pub. Health Reports, 1922-26. Served as pres. and dir. Spl. San. Commn., Guayaquil, Ecuador, 1908-09; nat. dir. health, Republic Ecuador, 1909-10; physician to pres. of Ecuador, 1907-10; san. adv.-insp. USN, 1917-19. U.S. del. First Pan Am. Conf. Dirs. of Health, Washington, 1926; asst. dir. Pan Am. San. Bur., 1926-38. U.S. del. 8th Pan Am. San. Conf., Lima, Peru, 1927, 9th Conf., Buenos Aires, Argentina, 1934. Mem. Nat. Acad. Medicine (Lima, Peru), A.M.A., Am. Pub. Health Assn. Republican. Mason (K.C.C.H.). Clubs: Nat. Sojourners (ex-pres. Washington chpt.). Has specialized in control of plague, yellow fever and smallpox. Decorations: Order el Merito, Comdr., Ecuador, Order, Finlay, Cuba. Address: 4342 Warren St. N.W., Washington. Died May 28, 1955; buried Fort Lincoln Cemetery, Washington.

LLOYD, Edward, VIII, naval officer; b. Balt., July 20, 1857; s. Edward VII and Mary Lloyd (Howard) L.; ed. Bishop's Sch., Easton, Md.; grad. U.S. Naval Acad., 1878; m. Elizabeth Robinson, Oct. 12, 1887; 1 son, Edward IX. Commd. ensign USN, 1878, advanced through grades to commodore, 1911, ret. 1911. Club: Officers' (Annapolis, Md.). Home: Wye Lodge, 203 Prince George St., Annapolis, Md. Deceased.

LLOYD, Edward Lester, corp. ofcl.; b. Patton, Pa., Dec. 15, 1903; s. William Robert and Lydia (Edwards) L.; B.Sc., U. Pitts., 1927; Ph.D., State U. Ia., 1935; m. Martha Hall, Sept. 6, 1930; children—Roger Hall, Lydia Althea. Asst. dean U. Pitts., 1926-27; with Oldsmobile div. Gen. Motors Corp., 1927-30; asso. prof. Okla. A. and M. Coll., 1930-36; instr. State U. Ia., 1933-34; chief market data sect. U.S. Bur. Fgn. and Domestic Commerce, 1935-39; exec. v.p. A.C. Nielsen Co., Chgo., 1939-58; vice chmn. A. C. Nielsen, Ltd., Australia, mng. dir., vice chmn., Oxford, Eng.; vice chmn. A. C. Nielsen (Switzerland) S.A.; dir. A. C. Nielsen (Belgium) S.A., A. C. Nielsen Co., G.M. B.H., Frankfort, Germany. Mem. Am. Marketing Assn., Am. Statis. Assn., Am. C. of C. (dir. in London), Sigma Chi. Presbyn. Club: American (London). Contbr. articles profl. jours. Home: Pawhuska, Okla.; also Oxford, Eng. Died Mar. 30, 1959. buried Pawhuska, Okla.

LLOYD, E(dwin) Russell, geologist; b. Lloydsville, W.Va., Nov. 3, 1882; s. Nimrod Wesley and Mary Magdalene (Bender) L.; grad. W.Va. Conf. Sem., 1901; A.B., Ohio Wesleyan U., 1905; elected Rhodes scholar from W.Va., at Oxford U., 1905, B.A., 1908; Burdett Coutts scholar, same, 1908-09; grad. student and fellow U. of Chicago, 1909-11; m. Helen Burnett Gardner, Jan. 7, 1920 (died Jan. 11, 1934); children—Anne Gardner, Edwin Russell (dec.). Asst. and associate geologist U.S. Geol. Survey, Washington, D.C., 1911-17, in charge coal land classification, 1915-16; geologist Sinclair-Central Am. Oil Co., 1917-18; again asso. geologist U.S. Geol. Survey, 1918-19; chief geologist Sinclair-Wyo. Oil Co., Casper, Wyo., 1919-21, Mid-Kansas Oil & Gas Co., Mineral Wells, Tex., 1921-23, Argo Oil Co., Denver, Colo., 1923-24; cons. practice, also chief geologist New York Oil Co., Denver, 1924-26; dist. geologist Roxana Petroleum Corp., Roswell, N. M., 1927; cons. practice, Denver and Midland, Tex., 1928-32; dist. geologist, Superior Oil Co., Midland, Tex., 1932-36; cons. practice since 1936. Fellow Geol. Soc. America; mem. Am. Assn. Petroleum Geologists (hon. mem., asso. editor), Am. Geophysical Union, Sigma Xi, Gamma Alpha. Address: Midland, Tex. Deceased.

LLOYD, Frank S., educator, adminstr., coll. and U.S. govt.; b. London, Eng., Jan. 27, 1900; s. George Grant and Elizabeth (Pocock) L.; B.P.E., Springfield Coll., 1923; A.M., Clark U., 1924; Ph.D., N.Y.U., 1933; m. Eleanor Daley; children—Judson, William, Virginia, June. Capt. Brit. Army 1914-19; senior dir. physical edn., Yorkshire, Eng., 1920-21; prof. physical edn. and psychology, Southwestern Coll., Kan., 1924-26; instr. in edn. N.Y.U., 1926-28, asst. prof. edn., 1928-30, asso. prof. edn., 1930-35, prof. edn., 1935-44; prof. hygiene and chmn. dept. Coll. City N.Y., 1944—. Asst. dir. recreation, office defense health and welfare services Fed. Security Agency, 1941-42; chief physical fitness sect., 1942-43; exec. dir. com. on physical fitness, 1943-44. Dir. studies on safety in colleges, secondary schs. and elementary schs. for N.Y.U.; research adviser in physical edn.; mem. White House conf. on child health and protection; mem. Regents adv. council on health and physical edn., N.Y. State; mem. curriculum revision com. State N.Y.; mem. research com. soc. coll. dirs. phys. edn.; mem. nat. exec. council, YMCA; examiner, bd. edn. N.Y.C.; mem. spl. commn. for evaluation physical fitness program, of Navy, Norfolk Naval Tng. Sta., Va.; chmn. commn. on post war planning for U.S. govt. com. on physical fitness. Chmn. water safety and accident prevention com. N.Y. chpt. A.R.C.; mem. bd. dirs. War and Peace Memorial Com., N.Y.C., Guiding Eyes, Inc. Fellow Am. Acad. Phys. Edn. (chmn. awards com.), Police Athletic League (dir.), Am. Assn. for Health, Physical Edn. and Recreation, Pi Delta Kappa, Pi Gammu Mu. Author: Safety in Secondary Sch. Physical Edn. (Nat. Bur. Casualty and Surety Underwriters), 1932; Safety in Athletics (W. B. Saunders), 1936; contbr. Interpretations of Physical Education (A. S. Barnes); contbr. Wingate Memorial Lecture Services; contbg. editor to Research Quarterly and other jours. Home: R.F.D. Patterson, N.Y. Office: The City College of N.Y., 138th St., and Convent Av., N.Y.C. 31. Died Jan. 1957.

LLOYD, Frank T., lawyer; b. Middletown, Del., Oct. 29, 1859; s. Horatio G. and Caroline E. (Newell) L.; grad. Middletown Acad., 1875; studied law privately; LL.D., N.J. Law Sch., 1936; m. Mary Pelouze, Feb. 22, 1887; children—Mrs. Ethel Lea Davis, Frank T., Mrs. Mary P. Davis. Admitted to Pa. bar, 1882, N.J. bar, 1897, counsellor, 1900; mem. N.J. legislature, 1896-97; prosecutor of pleas, Camden County, N.J., 1899-1906; judge Circuit Court of N.J., 1906-24; asso. justice Supreme Court of N.J., 1924-38; now mem. Starr, Summerill & Lloyd, Camden, N.J. Pres. Camden County Library Assn. Mem. Am., N.J., local bar assns., Am., English socs. for psychial research, Am. Acad. Polit. and Social Science. Republican. Presbyn. Home: Merchantville, N.J. Office: 330 Market St., Camden, N.J. Died Nov. 22, 1951.

LLOYD, Ralph Bramel, corp. official; b. Neosho, Mo., Feb. 28, 1875; s. Louis Marshall and Sarah Elizabeth (Bramel) L.; student Ventura (Calif.) Grammar Sch., 1887-92, Berkeley (Calif.) High Sch., 1892-95, U. of Calif., 1895-98; m. Lulu Nettie Hull, Jan. 28, 1904 (dec.); children—Eleanor (Mrs. Mark Justin Dees), Edna Elizabeth (Mrs. William Thomas Davis), Ida Hull (Mrs. Homer Daniel Crotty), Lulu May (Mrs. Richard Ronald Von Hagen); married 2d Edith Louise Nattkemper, Feb. 22, 1949. Began as supt. ranching interests in Calif., 1898; v.p. and gen. mgr. Pacific Tank & Pipe Co., 1904-11; took over management of Ventura Land & Water Co. (owned by Lloyd family), 1911; organized, 1926, and since pres. Lloyd Corp., Ltd., formed to handle affairs of family, including oil lands, oil development, city and timber properties, bldgs., banking, farming, citrus growing, livestock raising; dir. Security First Nat. Bank, Los Angeles, U.S. Nat. Bank of Portland (Ore.). Mem. Emergency Com. of 48 of oil industry, 1932-33; chmn. State Regulatory Com. of the Oil Industry of State of Calif. under NRA, 1933-35; sec. Govs. Conf., Washington, 1933; mem. Petroleum Industry War Council 1941-45, Nat. Petroleum Council, 1946-48. Trustee Calif. Inst. of Technology; mem. Assos. of U. of Calif. Past president and director Western Oil and Gas Assn.; mem. dir. Oil Producers Agency of Calif., Independent Petroleum Assn. of America, American Petroleum Institute; member Am. Inst. Mining & Metall. Engrs. (asso.), Los Angeles, Hollywood, Ventura, Ventura County, Portland, State of Calif, and U.S. chambers of commerce, Delta Upsilon. Methodist (pres. bd. trustees Wilshire Ch.). Mason. Clubs: California, Univ., Los Angeles Country (Los Angeles); Arlington (Portland, Ore.). Home: 962 N. Alpine Drive, Beverly Hills, Calif. Office: 9441 Olympic Blvd., Beverly Hills, Cal. Died Sept. 9, 1953.

LLOYD, Samuel, lawyer; b. East Orange, N.J., July 9, 1897; s. Dr. Samuel and Adele Ferrier (Peck) L.; A.B., Princeton, 1921; student Harvard Law Sch., 1921-23, Yale Law Sch., 1923-25; m. Ruth Lapham, Sept. 4, 1924 (div. 1950); children—Samuel, Ruth (Mrs. Kenneth M. Scott), Adele Ferrier (Mrs. Leo Hagan), Christopher; m. 2d, Julie P. Spermo, July 8, 1950; one daughter, Barbara Jean. Admitted to New York bar, 1926 and the Connecticut bar, 1932; partner Lloyd, Decker, Williams & Knauth, 1935-54; director and general counsel Seaboard Shipping Corporation, 1939-51; dir. Am.-Hawaiian S.S. Co., 1935-50; general counsel American Otol. Soc., Inc. Served as sergt. 1st class, U.S. Army Med. Res. Corps, 1917-18; lt., Field Artillery, 1918-20. Mem. Am. and N.Y. bar assns., Bar Assn. City of N.Y. Republican. Episcopalian. Clubs: Ox Ridge Hunt (Darien, Conn.); Woodway Country (Springdale, Conn.); Uptown (N.Y.C.). Address: Goodhill Rd., Weston, Conn. Died May 9, 1959; buried Lakeview Cemetery, New Canaan, Conn.

LLOYD, Stewart Joseph, prof. chemistry; b. Hamilton, Ont., Can., Sept. 12, 1881; s. Joseph and Sage (Peregrine) L.; B.A., U. of Toronto, 1904; M.Sc., McGill U., 1906; Ph.D., U. of Chicago, 1910; m. Edith Marian Dawson, Dec. 27, 1911; children—Frances Valentine, Virginia Edith, Edith Vane. Prof. chemistry and metallurgy, U. of Ala., 1909—; also dir. of lab. and dean Sch. of Chemistry, Metallurgy and Ceramics; cons. chem. engr. Ala. Power Co.; asst. state geologist, 1930—; acting State geologist of Ala., 1939-45. Mem. Am. Inst. Chem. Engrs., Am. Chem. Soc., Soc. Chem. Industry, Am. Inst. Chemists, Electrochem. Soc., Canadian Inst. Chemistry. Episcopalian. Home: University, Ala. Died Aug. 1959.

LLOYD, Walter Hamilton, Jr., editor; b. Chgo., Apr. 29, 1896; s. Walter Hamilton and Ida May (Riley) L.; grad. high sch., Valparaiso, Ind., 1914, Purdue U., 1918; m. Lorraine Fort Hughes, Aug. 11, 1917; children—Hugh Wm., Margaret Lorraine, Lorraine Margaret, Walter Hamilton. With The Ohio Farmer, 1920-42, editor, 1922-35, editor, mgr., 1935-42; marketing specialist, Transportation and Storage br. War Food Adminstrn., 1942-44; dir. Kraft Foods Co. Dairy Farm Service, 1944—. Served with 214th Field Signal bn. U.S. Army, Camp Custer, Mich., 1918-19. Sec. Am. Agrl. Editors' Assn., 1930-38; pres., 1938-39; dir., Class C, Fed. Res. Bank of Cleve., 1941-42. Mem. Am. Soc. Agrl. Engrs., Nat. Grange, Alpha Gamma Rho, Alpha Zeta, Sigma Delta Chi. Episcopalian. Chmn. ofcl. Ohio Com. 7th World's Poultry Congress and Expn., 1938-39. Home: 1207 Elmwood Av., Evanston, Ill. Office: Kraft Foods Co., P.O. Box 1163, Chgo. 90. Deceased.

LOBECK, Armin Kohl (lō'bĕk), prof. geology; b. New York City, Aug. 16, 1886; s. Adolph Christian and Elmire Celeste (Voullaire) L.; A.B., Columbia, 1911, A.M., 1913, Ph.D., 1917; m. Bertha Merrill, Dec. 25, 1917; children—Elmire, Merrill. Instructor Phila. Coll. Pharmacy, 1911-14; asst. prof. U. of Wis., 1919-24, asso. prof., 1924-29; prof. geology, Columbia, 1929-54, emeritus prof. Bd. govs. Nature Conservancy, 1954—. Founder, 1922, now pres., dir. Geographical Press. Mem. geog. sect., Am. Commn. to Negotiate Peace, Paris, World War I. Consultant War and State Depts., World War II. Neil Miner Medal, Assn. Geology Tchrs., 1956. Fellow A.A.A.S., N.Y. Acad. Science; mem. Geol. Soc. of America, Assn. of Am. Geographers, Sigma Xi. Independent. Presbyterian. Club: Men's Faculty (Columbia U.). Author: Block Diagrams, 1924; Guide to Geology of Allegany State Park, 1927; Geology of Mammoth Cave National Park, 1928; Airways of America, 1933; Geomorphology, 1939; Military Maps and Photographs (with Maj. W. Tellington, U.S. Army), 1944; physiographic descriptions of Europe, Asia, Africa, N. Am.; Geological Diorama of U.S. Trustee, Nat. Parks Assn., 1944-50; Things Maps Don't Tell Us, 1956. Contbr. maps, block diagrams, guides and articles to geol. astronomy and geog. publs. Home: 251 Sunset Av., Englewood, N.J. Died Apr. 26, 1958.

LOBENSTINE, Edwin Carlyle (lō'bĕn-stēn), missionary, clergyman; b. Leavenworth, Kan., Jan. 18, 1872; s. William Christian and Rose (Bayha) L.; grad. Phillips Exeter Acad., 1891; A.B., Yale, 1895, D.D., 1936; student Union Theol. Sem., 1895-98, Auburn Theol. Sem., 1898; m. Rose Hoffman, June 5, 1904 (dec.); 1 dau., Rose Hoffman (Mrs. Robert E. O'Bolger; m. 2d, Susan Clark, June 2, 1914; children—James Clark, Susan Clark McKeever. Ordained to ministry Presbyn. Ch., 1898, missionary service in China with Bd. Fgn. Missions Presbyn. Ch. U.S.A., 1898-1937, church and adminstrv. work, Anhwei Province, 1898-1911; mem. China Council Presbyn. Mission, 1906-11; supt. Famine Relief, Anhwei Province, 1910-11; hon. exec. sec. Central China Famine Relief Com., 1911-12; sec. continuation com. Nat. Christian Conf., Shanghai, 1913-22; sec. Nat. Christian Council of China, 1922-35, sec. China Christian Edn. Assn., 1924-35; mem. Internat. Missionary Council, 1919, 28, 32 and 35; mem. Nat. Flood Relief Commn., 1931-32; mem. China Internat. Famine Relief Commn., 1932-35. Mem. bd. dirs. U. Nanking, 1912-35, Ginling College, 1931-35, mem. bd. founders U. Nanking, 1935—, Ginling Coll., 1935-40, Hauchung U., 1935—; trustee Peiping Union Med. Coll., 1929-36; chmn. China Med. Bd., Inc., N.Y.C., 1936-45; pres. Yale-in-China Assn., 1935-44, trustee, 1936—. Mem. intercollegiate br. bd. YMCA of City of N.Y., 1943-46. Mem. Phi Beta Kappa. Clubs: Century, Yale (N.Y.). Mem. editorial bd. China Mission Yearbook, 1916-35. Home: 1148 Fifth Av., N.Y.C. 28. Died July 1958.

LOBRANO, Gustave S., editor; b. New Orleans, July 24, 1902; s. Domnick and Mary Frances (Stubbs) L.; LL.B., Cornell, 1925; m. Jean Flick, Apr. 15, 1927; children—Dorothy Jean, Alexander Flick. With New Yorker Mag., 1937—, mng. editor, 1941—; bd. dirs. The New Yorker Mag., Inc., 1951—. Home: 325 Bedford Rd., Chappaqua, N.Y. Office: 25 W. 43d St., N.Y.C. 36. Died Mar. 1, 1956; buried Hammond, La.

LOCKE, Alain LeRoy (lŏk), prof. philosophy; b. Phila., Pa., Sept. 13, 1886; s. Pliny Ishmael and Mary (Hawkins) L.; A.B., Central High Sch., Phila., 1902; grad. Phila. School of Pedagogy, 1904; A.B., Harvard, 1907; Rhodes scholar from Pa., at Oxford U., 1907-10; studied U. of Berlin, 1910-11; Ph.D., Harvard, 1918; unmarried. Asst. prof. philosophy and edn., Howard U., Washington, 1912-16, became prof. philosophy, now ret.; vis. prof. Univ. of Wis., 1945-46, New School of Social Research, 1947, College of the City of New York, 1948. Statistician N.J. Semi-Centennial Commn. of the Negro, 1912-14. Personnel officer and instr. war aims, Howard U.S. A.T.C., 1917-18. Mem. Am. Ethnol. Soc., Am. Negro Acad., Negro Soc. for Hist. Research, Phi Beta Kappa, Sigma Psi Phi, Theta Sigma, Phi Beta Sigma; corr. mem. Académie des Sciences Coloniales (Paris). Episcopalian. Club: Civic (New York). Author: Race Contacts and Inter-racial Relations, 1916; The New Negro, 1925; The Negro in America, 1933; Frederick Douglass, a Biography of Anti-Slavery, 1935; The Negro and His Music, 1936; Negro Art—Past and Present, 1937; The Negro in Art, 1941; (with Bernhard Stern) When Peoples Meet: A Study in Race and Culture Contact, 1941. Editor of Plays of Negro Life, 1927; Bronze Booklet Series—Associates in Negro Folk Education, 1937. Contributing editor, Survey Graphic; Inter-American Exchange professor to Haiti, 1943. Home: 12 Grove St., N.Y.C. Died June 1954.

LOCKE, Bessie, kindergarten promotor, assn. exec.; b. West Cambridge, Mass.; d. William Henry and Jane M. (Schoulder) Locke. Was pastor's asst. All Souls Ch., Bklyn., 2 yrs.; organized East-End Kindergarten Union of Bklyn.; mem. gen. com. Bklyn. Free Kindergarten Soc., 1896-1923, financial sec.; financial sec. N.Y. Kindergarten Assn.; secured endowments in perpetuity for five mission kindergartens in Greater N.Y.; founder, organizer, dir. and exec. sec. Nat. Kindergarten Assn., 1909—; chif of Kindergarten Div., U.S. Bur. of Edn., Washington, 1913-19; dir. Nat. Council of Women, 1910-46, hon. v.p. 1946; chmn. kindergarten extension Nat. Congress of Parents and Tchrs., 1913-22; mem. governing bd. Nat. Coll. Edn., 1920—; cons. Ednl. Policies Commn., Washington. Mem. Daus. of Founders and Patriots of Am.; life mem. Internat. Council of Women, Assn. for Childhood Edn. Christian Scientist. Home: 360 Central Park West. Office: 8 W. 40th St., N.Y. C. Died Apr. 9, 1952.

LOCKE, Walter, editor; b. St. Marys, W.Va., Mar. 16, 1875; s. Francis Marion and Sarah Jane (Shields) L.; educator pub. schs.; L.H.D. from Antioch College, 1948; married to Annette Elizabeth Philbrick, Sept. 10, 1910; 1 son, Francis Philbrick. Began as reporter Nebraska State Journal, Lincoln, Neb., 1903, asso. editor, 1904-26; editor Dayton Daily News, 1927-53, sr. editor, 1953—; editorial contbr. Springfield News, Atlanta Journal Miami News. Trustee Antioch College. Member American Society of Newspaper Editors. Unitarian. Mason. Clubs: Engineers, Discussion (Dayton); Town and Gown. Author: A Cash Transaction, 1930; Whistling Post, Ohio (essays), 1934; John Halcyon's Father, 1945; Halcyon Days, 1949; This World My Home, 1957. Home: Bri-

arlock, 5824 Brantford Rd., Dayton 14. Died Oct. 23, 1957.

LOCKETT, Andrew M., contracting engr.; b. Marion, Ala., Sept. 4, 1865; s. Powhatan and Martha Jane (Moore) L.; student Howard Coll. (Marion), U. Tenn., Stevens Inst. Tech.; m. Anne Waddell, Jan. 29, 1895; children—Andrew M., Elizabeth W. (Mrs. J. Norton Stewart). In employ of Henry R. Worthington, contracting engr., 1887; with Comegys & Lewis, contractors, 1888; again with Henry R. Worthington, engring. dept., 1888-93, mgr. St. Louis office, 1893-95, Atlanta office, 1895-98, asst. gen. sales mgr., N.Y.C. 1898-99; pres. A. M. Lockett & Co., Ltd., New Orleans, 1899—; also agt. of Henry R. Worthington and Babcock & Wilcox Co., N.Y.; mem. indsl. adv. com. 6th Dist. Fed. Res. Bank. Chmn. for State of La., Bd. of Engrs. on Indsl. Inventory; asso. mem. Naval Cons. Bd.; pres. New Orleans C. of C., 1930-31. Mem. Am. Soc. M.E., La. Engring. Soc., Chi Psi. Democrat. Episcopalian. Clubs: Boston, Automobile, Country. Home: 322 Hillary St., New Orleans, and Pass Christian, Miss. Office: Whitney Bank Bldg., New Orleans. Deceased.

LOCKHART, Burton Wellesley, clergyman; b. Lockhartville, Kings County, N.S., Jan. 24, 1855; s. Nathan Albert and Elizabeth Ann (Bezanson) L.; A.B., Acadia Coll., N.S., 1878, A.M., 1882; grad. Newton Theol. Instn., Newton Centre, Mass., 1882; D.D., Dartmouth, 1894; m. Fanny Mary Upson, Dec. 24, 1883. Licensed to preach by Bapt. Ch. of Gaspereaux, N.S., 1876; minister Lockeport, N.S., 1878-79; ordained Bapt. ministry, Suffield, Conn., 1882; pastor, Suffield, 1882-83, 3d Congl. Ch., Chicopee, Mass., 1888-93, Franklin St. Congl. Ch., Manchester, N.H., 1893-1921, now emeritus. Republican. Club: Winthrop (Boston). Home: Manchester, N.H. Died Feb. 13, 1937; buried Westfield, Mass.

LOCKHART, Clinton, educator; b. Lovington, Ill., Feb. 21, 1858; s. George Washington and Harriet (Hostetler) L.; A.B., Transylvania U., 1886, A.M., 1888, LL.D., 1908; Ph.D., Yale, 1894; m. Mollie Smith, June 23, 1885; 1 dau., Naomi (Mrs. Spearman Webb). Ordained Disciples ministry, 1901; pastor Millersburg and Columbia, Ky., and Monticello, Mo.; prof. Bible chair, Ann Arbor, 1893-94; pres. Columbia Coll., Ky., 1894-95, Christian U., Canton, Mo., 1895-1900; prof. Semitic and Bibl. lit., Drake U., 1900-05; pres. Tex. Christian U., 1906-11, prof. O.T. and semitics, 1906-43, dean, 1916-20, emeritus, 1943-51. Pres. Southwestern Soc. of Bibl. Study and Research, 1931-32. Author: Laws of Interpretation, 1890; Principles of Interpretation, 1901; Messianic Message of the Old Testament, 1905; Old Testament Life and Literature, 1925; Apostolic Christianity, 1925; Apples of Gold (poems of religion and nature), 1938. Lecturer on Bibl. subjects; retired 1943. Home: 3115 University Dr., Ft. Worth. Died June 11, 1951; buried Greenwood Cemetery, Ft. Worth.

LOCKHART, Gene (Eugene), actor, writer, stage director; b. London, Ont., Can.; s. John Coates (Scottish tenor) and Ellen Lockhart; ed. St. Michael's Sch., De La Salle Inst. (Toronto), Brompton Oratory Sch. (London, England); pvt. tutors; m. Kathleen Arthur, actress and musician; 1 dau., June. As a child appeared as a Scottish dancer with the 48th Highlanders Regiment Kiltires Band of Can.; appeared as Gustave in The Riviera Girl, New Amsterdam Theatre, N.Y. City, 1917; wrote and directed revue, The Pierrot Players; wrote (with Deems Taylor) and played in musical fantasy Heigh Ho, 1921; joined Boston Opera Co. presenting Gilbert & Sullivan repertoire, 1922; played on Broadway, 1923-26; wrote, directed and played in his revue, The Bunk of 1926, 1926; toured with Kathleen Lockhart in their original Recital Revue, 1927-30; lecturer on stage technique, Juilliard Inst. of Music, N.Y. City, 1931-34; toured own revue, How's Your Code, 1932; on N.Y. stage intermittingly; played Willy Loman, Death of a Salesman, 1949-50; under contract to Metro-Goldwyn-Mayer, 1934, and since appeared in over 70 pictures; appeared as Regis in Algiers (nominated for Academy award for performance), 1938; Bob Cratchit in A Christmas Carol, Stephen Douglas in Abe Lincoln in Illinois (twice honored with 1st place for best supporting performances in the Hollywood Critics Monthly Preview); appeared in Going My Way, 1944, Miracle on 34th St., 1947, I'd Climb the Highest Mountain, 1950. Has produced over 400 sketches; writer for radio, including Broadway Varieties, Lazy Dan, Abroad with the Lockharts. Contbr. articles in theatrical mags. Wrote lyrics for The World is Waiting for the Sunrise. Mem. Am. Soc. of Composers, Authors and Publishers, Acad. of Motion Picture Arts and Sciences, Screen Actors Guild (past bd. mem.). Clubs: The Players, Dutch Treat (N.Y. City), Authors (Hollywood). Address: care of Authors Club, 6525 Sunset Blvd., Hollywood, Cal. Died Mar. 31, 1957.

LOCKLEY, Fred (lŏk'lē), author; b. Leavenworth, Kan., Mar. 19, 1871; s. Frederic and Elizabeth Metcalf (Campbell) L.; student Ore. Agrl. Coll.; B.S.D., Willamette U., 1895; m. Hope Gans, June 16, 1897 (dec.); children—Frederick Llewelyn (dec.), Lawrence Campbell, Hope (dec.); m. 2d, Laura Simpson, Feb. 19, 1930. Part owner E. Oregonian, Pendleton, 1901-05; gen. mgr. Pacific Monthly Mag., Portland, 1905-10; editorial writer, columnist Ore. Jour., 1911—. With A.E.F., Nov. 1917 till Armistice; was war corr. Ore. Jour., also wrote for Paris edit. N.Y. Herald, and Stars and Stripes; YMCA sec. charge front line work, at Abbeville, Amiens, etc., on Brit. front. Mem. Alaska Yukon Sourdough Assn., Sigma Delta Chi. Republican. Presbyn. Mason. Author: Vigilante Days in Virginia City; Sol Tetherow, Wagon Train Master; Across the Plains by Prairie Schooner; To Oregon by Ox Team in '47; Hist. of the Columbia River Valley; Oregon Folks; Oregon's Yesterdays; Oregon Trail Blazers; Edwin Markham. Specializing on Pacific Northwest History. Home: 4227 S.E. Stark St. Office: Oregon Journal, Portland, Ore. Died Oct. 15, 1958.

LOCKMAN, DeWitt McClellan, artist; b. Bklyn., July 30, 1870; s. Jacob K. and Mary Taintor (Abbe) L.; pupil of James H. Beard, N. A., Nelson N. Bickford and William Sartain; studied in Europe, 1891-92, 1901-02; m. Evelyn Clair Walker, Feb. 18, 1946. Represented in permanent collections of N.A.D., Yale, Phillips Exeter Acad., Soc. of Cincinnati (Washington), Art Commn. City N.Y., Ft. Ticonderoga (N.Y.) Mus., N.Y. Hist. Soc., Pa. Acad. Fine Arts, West Point Mil. Acad., Mt. Vernon (N.Y.) City Hall, Washington and Jefferson Coll., Met. Mus. N.Y., numerous other pub. and pvt. collections. Recipient silver medal Panama Pacific Expn., 1915; Lippincott prize Pa. Acad. Fine Arts, 1918; Isaac N. Maynard portrait prize N.A.D., 1922; gold medal N.Y. Hist. Soc., 1933; gold medal Allied Artists Am., 1936. Served in Office of Naval Intelligence, 3d Naval Dist., 1917-18. Mem. Art Commn., N.Y.C., 1925-29; mem. bd. control Artists Fund Soc., 1917-20. Trustee Sch. Art League N.Y.C. (mem. bd. 1928-39); chmn. civilian adv. com. on Art, U.S. Mil. Acad. N.A., 1921; mem. Nat .Assn. Portrait Painters (council 1923-26, chmn.), Allied Artists Am., Inc. (pres. 1945-46, trustee, 1946—), Municipal Art Soc. (chmn. on painting), Nat. Inst. Arts and Letters, Fine Arts Fedn. N.Y., Am. Artists Profl. League (mem. nat. exec. com. 1933), Am. Fine Arts Soc. (life), Art Commn. Asso. (pres. 1948, 49), N.Y. Hist. Soc. (mem. art com.; rec. sec.), Nat. Commn. to Advance Am. Art (mem. bd.), N.A.D. (pres. 1949), St. Nicholas Soc. (life). Episcopalian. Clubs: Century, Ends of the Earth, Brook, Lotos. Address: 222 Central Park South, N.Y.C. 19. Died July 1, 1957.

LOCKRIDGE, Ross Franklin, writer; b. Miami County, Ind., Oct. 26, 1877; s. Brenton Webster and Charlotta A. (Wray) L.; A.B., Ind. U., 1900, LL. B., 1907; Litt.D., Lincoln Meml. U., 1938; m. Elsie Lillian Shockley, July 23, 1902; children—Robert Bruce (dec.), V. Shockley, Lillian Louise, Ross Franklin (dec.). Tchr. pub. schs., Ind., 1895-1903; prin. high sch., Peru, Ind., 1903-05; librarian Ind. U. Law Sch. Library, 1905-06; asst. instr. in pub. speaking Ind. U., 1906-07, head pub. speaking dept., sec. extension div., 1913-14, extension lectr., 1917-22, dir. historic site recital course, summer sessions, 1930-32, dir. Hoosier hist. insts., summer sessions, 1946-50; admitted to Okla. bar, 1907, practiced at Shawnee, 1907-13; sec. Citizens League of Ind. and editor The Citizen, 1914-17; employment mgr. and welfare dir. Wayne Knitting Mills, Ft. Wayne, Ind., 1917-22; Ind. rep. World Book Co., 1922-34; state supervisor gen. adult edn., Ind. Emergency Edn. Div., 1934-35; Ind. dir. Fed. Writers' Projects, 1935-37; dir. of Hoosier Historic Memorial Activities under the Ind. U. Found., 1937-50; chmn. New Harmony Meml. Commn., 1937-39; dir. New Harmony State Meml., 1939-43; mem. Benjamin Harrison Meml. Commn., 1940. Extension Instr. in Hist. Methods, Edn. No. 490, Ind. State Tchrs. Coll., 1943-50. Police judge, Shawnee, 1909-11; county Judge, Pottawatomie County, Okla., 1911-13; public defender, Oklahoma, 6 months 1913. Mem. Miss. Valley Hist. Assn., Ind. Hist. Soc., Soc. Ind. Pioneers, Phi Beta Kappa, Phi Gamma Delta, Phi Delta Phi. Democrat. Methodist. Clubs: Rotary, The Filson, Indiana Schoolmen's. Author: How Government Functions in Indiana, 1918; George Rogers Clark, 1927; A. Lincoln, 1930; The Hoosier Township Trustee, 1930; LaSalle, 1931; The Old Fauntleroy Home, 1939; Theodore F. Thieme—A Man and His Times, 1941; The Labyrinth of New Harmony, 1941; The Story of Indiana, 1951. Home: 1000 S. High St., Bloomington, Ind. Died Jan. 12, 1952; buried Lindenwood Cemetery, Fort Wayne, Ind.

LOCKWOOD, Charles Clapp, lawyer; b. Bklyn., Sept. 2, 1877; s. James Knox Polk and Katharine (Marshall) L.; LL.B., N.Y. Law Sch., 1900; m. Patricia M. Bleiler, Apr. 18, 1906. Clk. to ex-Supreme Ct. Justice Jasper W. Gilbert until his death, 1898, and to Hon. Henry D. Hotchkiss, late justice Supreme Ct.; admitted to N.Y. bar, 1903, and practiced with late William Seward Maddox and William Thurston Gilbert; practiced alone, 1908—; mem. N.Y. Assembly, 1914, Senate 4 terms, 1915-22; Rep. and Coalition candidate for comptroller City of N.Y., 1921. Chmn. for 4 years of Senate com. to Investigate rents, housing and combinations in restraint of trade, mem. com. to investigate finance, City of N.Y.; 8 years chmn. Senate Com. Pub. Edn.; mem. N.Y. Transit Commn. (now Met. Div. of Pub. Service Commn.), under appointment of Gov. Alfred E. Smith, term 1926-29; reapptd. by Gov. Roosevelt; elected justice Supreme Ct. of N.Y., 1931, reelected 1946; apptd. ofcl. referee of Supreme Ct., 1948. Rep. nominee for lt. gov. State of N.Y., 1928. Mem. Am., N.Y. State, Bklyn. bar assns. Mason. Clubs: Nat. Republican, Union League, Montauk, Brooklyn. Home: 60 Remsen St., Bklyn. 1. Died Sept. 21, 1958; buried Evergreens Cemetery, Bklyn.

LOCKWOOD, Charles Davenport, lawyer; b. Stamford, Conn., Nov. 11, 1877; s. Henry and Helen (Davenport) L.; Ph.B., Yale, 1900, LL.B., cum laude, 1903; m. Gertrude Bell, Oct. 13, 1906; children—Charles Davenport, Walter Bell, Mrs. Barbara L. Bunker. Admitted to Conn. bar, 1903, to N.Y. bar, 1904; dep. asst. dist. atty. N.Y. County under William Travers Jerome, 1903-06; practiced in Stamford since 1906; judge probate court, Stamford, 1907-13; joined Homer S. Cummings, former U.S. atty. gen., in firm of Cummings & Lockwood, 1909, now senior partner; director and member executive committee American News Co.; dir. Union News Co. Mem. lower house, Connecticut General Assembly, 1913; del.-at-large Dem. Nat. Conv., 1916, 20; chmn. bd. Citizens Savings Bank, Stamford Water Co.; dir.; First-Stamford Nat. Bank & Trust Co.; dir., mem. exec. com. Seymour Mfg. Co., Am. Crucible Co., Naugatuck Valley Co. Chmn. Stamford Exemption Bd., State Council of Defense, World War I. Del.-at-large to Conn. Constitutional Conv., 1933; Presidential elector at large for Roosevelt and Garner and chmn. of Electoral Coll. which met in Hartford. Formerly member State Board of Finance and Control. Formerly judge advocate, 2d Co., Gov.'s Foot Guard, New Haven. Mem. Am., Conn. State and Stamford bar assns., Berzelius, Phi Delta Phi, Sigma Xi. Democrat. Episcopalian. Mason, Elk. Clubs: Stamford Yacht, Woodway Country; Yale (New York). Home: 34 Saddle Rock Rd. Office: 1 Atlantic St., Stamford, Conn. Died Dec. 12, 1949.

LOCKWOOD, Ira Hiram, physician; b. Storm Lake, Ia., Nov. 29, 1885; s. Eli and Adelia (Day) L.; B.S., Buena Vista College, Storm Lake, Iowa, 1905, Doctor of Laws, 1956; student at the Univ. of Iowa, 1905-07; M.D., General Med. Coll. of Chicago, 1909; m. Jessie King, June 8, 1915. Interne and resident, Flower Hosp., N.Y. City, 1909-11; engaged in med. practice, Lincoln, Neb., 1911-17 and 1919-24; in practice of radiology, Kansas City, Mo., since 1924; dir. radiology Research Hosp., Kansas City; radiologist and dir. Research Clinic; cons. radiologist Kansas City Municipal hosps. 1 and 2; radiologist Children's Mercy Hosp., Fitzgibbon Memorial Hosp. (Marshall, Mo.), Olathe Community Hosp., Kan., Cushing Meml. Hosp., Leavenworth, Kan., Bothwell Meml. Hosp., Sedalia, Mo., Smithville Community Hosp., Miss., Kelling Clinic, Waverly, Mo. Served as maj. Med. Corps U.S. Army, during World War I; chief of X-ray dept. Evacuation Hosp. No. 1, A.E.F.; later head of X-ray service II army, A.E.F. Pres. Research Clinic, Blue Shield (Kansas City, Mo.); commn. mem. Dist. 9 Blue Shield Med. Care Plans; area cons. V.A. Trustee Am. Bd. Radiology (president); chairman board chancellors, Am. Coll. Radiology (gold medal award, pres.). Trustee Blue Cross-Blue Shield (Kansas City, Missouri), Frederick C. Narr Fellowship Foundation. Diplomate Am. Bd. Radiology. Fellow International College of Surgeons, American College of Radiology; mem. Am. Roentgen Ray Soc., Radiol. Soc. of N.A. (recipient award of merit for original sci. investigation or roentgenol. examination of the breast; past pres.), A.M.A., So. Med. Association American Radium Society (honorary), Am. Legion, Vets. Fgn. Wars. Clubs: Kansas City, Rotary (Kansas City, Mo.). Contbr. of numerous articles on radiol. subjects to sci. publs. Home: 4607 Jefferson. Office: Argyle Bldg., Kansas City, Mo. Died July 28, 1957; buried Forest Hill Abbey, Kansas City.

LOCKWOOD, John Salem, surgeon; b. Shanghai, China, Oct. 2, 1907; s. William Wirt and Mary Rebecca (Town) L.; A.B., De Pauw U., 1928; M.D., Harvard, 1931; Med. Sc.D., Coll. of Phys. and Surg. Columbia, 1937; m. Dorothy E. Tufts, Oct. 1, 1932; children—Elinor Towne, Marcia Robinson, Dorothy Tufts. Intern in surgery Presbyn. Hosp., N.Y.C., 1932-34, jr. and sr. fellow in surgery, 1934-37; instr. in surgery and fellow in surg. research U. Pa. Sch. of Medicine, 1937-39, asst. prof. surg. research, acting dir. dept., 1942-44; asso. in surgery and dir. tumor clinic Hosp. of U. Pa., 1940-42; prof. surgery Yale, also asso. surgeon New Haven Hosp., 1944-46; prof. surgery Columbia U. and attending surgeon Presbyn. Hosp., 1946—. Chief div. surgery, com. on med. research OSRD, Washington, 1944-46; mem. com. on surgery and com. on chemotherapy NRC, and surgery study sect. Nat. Adv. Health Council, USPHS, Washington. Civilian mem. com. on med. scis. Nat. Research and Development Bd., Nat. Mil. Establishment, 1948—. Recipient Presdl. Certificate of Merit, 1948. Mem. Am., N.Y. County med. assns., Soc. U. Surgeons (pres. 1948), Am. Soc. for Clin. Investigation, Am. Surg. Assn., Soc. of Clin. Surgery, Phila. Coll. Physicians, N.Y. Surg. Soc., A.C.S., N.Y. Acad. Medicine, Harvey Soc., Am. Assn. for Cancer Research, Phi Kappa Psi, Alpha Kappa Kappa, Sigma Xi. Contbr. articles to med. jours. Mem. editorial bd. Christopher's Textbook of Surgery, Annals of Surgery. Home: 170 Lincoln St., Englewood, N.J. Office: 630 W. 168th St., N.Y.C. Died June 16, 1950.

LOCKWOOD, Luke Vincent, lawyer, author, antiquarian; b. Bklyn., Feb. 1, 1872; s. Luke A. (LL. D.) and Mary Louise (Lyon) L.; A.B., Trinity, 1893, A.M., 1895, L.H.D., 1927; LL.B., N.Y. Law Sch., 1895; m. Alice Gardner Burnell, Nov. 16, 1897; children—Luke B., Dr. Jane. Admitted to N.Y. bar, July 19, 1895. Formerly mem. Bd. of Estimates and Taxation and chmn. Hwy. Commn., Town of Greenwich, Conn.; pres. Greenwich Trust Co., 1921-23, now chmn. Mem. governing com. Bklyn. Mus.; v.p. Marrine Mus., Am. Mus. Assn. (treas.); dir. Greenwich Hosp., pres., 1916-32, Brooklyn Inst. Arts and Scis., Mus. of City of New York (v.p.), Woman's Hosp. (pres.). Chmn. Draft Exemption Bd. No. 15, Fairfield Co., Conn., 1917-18. Fellow Royal Society of Art, London, England., Mem. Am. Bar Assn., Assn. Bar City of New York, Am. Antiquarian Soc., S.C., Conn., N.Y. hist. socs., Acad. of Polit. Science, Soc. Colonial Wars, Walpole Soc., New Eng. Soc., Phi Beta Kappa; hon. life fellow Metropolitan Museum of Art; hon. mem. Nat. Soc. Mural Painters; mem. of Art Commn., City of New York, 1918-21, mem. and sec., 1935-37, sec., 1940—, now pres.; pres. Art Commn. Associates; mem. art commn., Greenwich, Conn.; dir. Fine Arts Federation; trustee Antiquarian and Landmark Soc., Soc. for Preservation New Eng. Antiquities. Clubs: Century, Union, Down Town Association, Pilgrims, Nat. Arts, Grolier, Field (Greenwich), Alpha Delta Phi. Author: Colonial Furniture in America, 1901, revised and enlarged, 1913; The Pendleton Collection, 1905; A Collection of English Furniture of the Seventeenth and Eighteenth Centuries, 1907; Furniture Collectors' Glossary, 1913; also articles on furniture collecting and colonial silver. Home: 281 Lake Av., Greenwich, Conn. Office: 165 Broadway, N.Y.C. Died Jan. 23, 1951.

LOCKWOOD, Preston, bus. exec., lawyer; b. St. Louis, Oct. 28, 1891; s. George Robinson and Anna (Davis) L.; A.B., Wash. U., St. Louis, 1912; A.B. (Rhodes Scholar), Oxford U., 1917; LL.B., Columbia, 1922; m. Frances Castles Francis, Dec. 31, 1932; step-children—Pomeroy T. Francis, John C. Francis, Elizabeth Francis (Mrs. H. K. Hudson). Reporter N.Y. Morning World, 1913, N.Y. Times, London, Eng., 1915; instr. Sch. of Journalism, Columbia, 1920-22; weekly correspondent (Law) Time Magazine, 1923; admitted to N.Y. bar, 1924; asso. White & Case, N.Y.C., 1922-25; partner Davisson & Manice, 1925-30, Pynchon & Co., 1930-31, Davisson, McCarty & Lockwood, 1932-42; dir. Consol. Aircraft Corp., 1929-41; sec., asst. gen. counsel Brewster Aeronautical Corp., 1942, dir., 1943, pres., 1944—; chmn. Preferred Stockholders Com., Pub. Service Corp. of N.J. Served in A.F.S., 1915-16, French Army, 1917; 1st lt. F.A., U.S. Army, 1917-19. Trustee Am. Field Service Fellowship Fund. Mem. Am., City of N.Y. bar assns., Assn. Ex-mem. Sqdn. A. Acad. Polit. Sci., Inst. Aero. Scis., S.A.R., Phi Delta Theta. Episcopalian. Clubs: Racquet and Tennis, University, Bankers (N.Y.C.). Author: Henry James First Interview; Underwriting Contracts (with S. A. Anderson), and other articles. Home: 1075 Park Av., N.Y.C. 28. Office: 40 E. 40th St., N.Y.C. 16. Died Mar. 30, 1951.

LOCKWOOD, Thomas Dixon, patent lawyer, elec. expert and engr.; b. Smethwick, Staffordshire, Eng., Dec. 30, 1848; s. John F. and Mary (Dixon) L.; ed. common schs. there; tech. knowledge of elec. engring. and patent law, self acquired; m. Mary Helm, Oct. 20, 1875; children—Arthur George Frederick, Stanley Dixon (dec.). Learned and practiced machinists' trade in Eng., 1859-65, telegraphy in Can., 1866-67; made paper, Lee, Mass., 1868-69; made plate glass, Ind., 1869-71; worked on rys., Mass., Conn., N.J., telegraph operator, ticket agt., locomotive engr., 1871-75; in service Am. Tel. and Tel. Co. and predecessors, 1879—. Patent atty., expert in elec. inventions before patent office and U.S. cts.; authority on telephony and telegraphy, ret., 1919. Mem. Instn. Elec. Engrs., London; fgn. life fellow Imperial Inst., London; life fellow Am. Inst. E.E.; hon. mem. Nat. Elec. Light Assn., Old Time Telegraphers and Hist. Assn.; hon. mem. Telephone Pioneers Am. Clubs: Exchange, Algonquin, City (Boston). Author: Information for Telephonists, 1881; Electrical Measurements, 1883; Electricity, Magnetism and the Electric Telegraph, 1885. Translator, reviser of Ohm's Law, 1890. Contbr. to elec. and other jours. Home: 83 Bellevue Av., Melrose, Mass. Deceased.

LOEB, Carl M. (lōb); b. Frankfort-on-the-Main, Germany, Sept. 28, 1875; s. Adolph and Minna L.; m. Adeline L. Moses, Nov. 12, 1896; children—Mrs. Margaret Kempner, John L., Carl M., Henry A. Came to U.S., 1892, naturalized citizen, 1897. Became connected with Am. Metal Co., 1892, made mgr. St. Louis office, 1895, called to New York, 1905, and served as v.p., later pres.; retired from presidency, June 30, 1929; sr. partner Carl M. Loeb, Rhoades & Co., internat. bankers and brokers, since 1931. Mem. coms. on coppers, spelter and lead, War Dept., World War I. Hon. chmn. Home for Aged and Infirm Hebrews; trustee Valeria Home. Mem. C. of C. of the State of New York. Mason. Clubs: Harmonie, Metropolitan Opera. Home: 910 Fifth Av. Office: 61 Broadway, New York, N.Y.; and Lincoln Av., Harrison, N.Y. Died Jan. 1955.

LOEB, Howard A., banker; b. Philadelphia, Pa., July 25, 1873; s. August B. and Mathilde (Adler) L.; ed. Friends Central Sch., Phila.; B.S., U. of Pa., 1893, M.E., 1894. Practiced engring., 1894-1907, as officer and dir. Francis Bros. & Jellett, Inc.; became v.p. Tradesmens Nat. Bank, Phila., 1907, elected pres., 1915, and on merger with Guarantee Trust & Safe Deposit Co. and Chelten Trust Co., 1928, elected chmn. Tradesmens Land Title Bank and Trust Co., 1953; dir. Tradesmens Bank & Trust Co.; dir. South Chester Corp., South Chester Tube Company, Chester Tidewater Terminal, Incorporated, Horn & Hardart Company, Liberty Mutual Insurance Company (Pa. advisory bd.); The Warner Company (Phila.); dir. Phila. Clearing House Assn., 1941-49 (pres.). Mem. bd. mgrs. Fife-Hamill Memorial Health Center for S.E. Phila., Travelers Aid Soc., Phila. Tuberculosis and Health Assn. Mem. Am. Acad. Polit. & Social Science, Acad. Natural Sciences, Phila. Museum Art, Phila. Art Alliance, Old York Road Hist. Soc., Hist. Soc. of Pa., Foreign Policy Assn., Franklin Inst. Clubs: Down Town, Midday, Bank Officers', Locust (Phila.); U. of Pa. Club: Bankers (New York). Office: Room 512, Land Title Bldg., Broad and Chestnut Sts., Phila. Died Nov. 3, 1955.

LOEB, Isidor, univ. prof.; b. Roanoke, Mo., Nov. 5, 1868; s. Bernhard and Bertha (Myer) L.; U. of Mo., 1881-82, 1884-87, 1891-93, B.S., 1887, M.S., LL.B., 1893, LL.D., 1933; LL.D., Washington U., 1953; university fellow in jurisprudence, Columbia Univ., 1894-95, Ph.D., 1901; U. of Berlin, Germany, 1899-1900; m. Carrie Lengsfield, Apr. 6, 1915 (dec. Nov. 11, 1951); children—Mrs. Fannie L. Barker and Mrs. Bertha L. Wallbrunn (twins), Benjamin Lengsfield. Tutor in history, 1892-94, asst. professor, 1895-99, professor political science and public law, 1899-1925, dean university faculty, 1910-16, acting president, 1923, dean faculty of business and public administration, 1916-25, University of Mo.; professor polit. science, 1925-39, and dean Sch. of Business and Pub. Adminstrn., Washington U., 1925-40, emeritus since 1940. Special investigator, National War Labor Board, 1941-42; State price officer, Eastern Missouri Office of Price Administration, 1942-43. Director Wohl Foundation, 1941. Member Missouri State Tax Commission, 1906. Mem. State Hist. Soc. of Mo. (pres. 1944-47), Am. Polit. Sci. Assn. (pres. 1933), Am. Econ. Assn., Phi Beta Kappa, Beta Gamma Sigma, Phi Delta Phi, Order of Coif. Author: The Legal Property Relations of Married Parties, 1900; Government in Missouri, 1912; Syllabus of American Citizenship, 1920; also articles and reviews in various publications. Co-editor Journal Missouri Constitutional Convention (1875), 1920, also Debates Missouri Constitutional Convention (1875), 1930-44. Clubs: Town and Gown. Home: 105 Arundel Pl., St. Louis 5. Died June 4, 1954.

LOEB, Leo (lěrb), pathologist; b. Germany, Sept. 21, 1869; s. Benedict and Barbara (Isay) L.; educated at Gymnasium; studied natural science and medicine, univs. of Heidelberg, Berlin, Freiburg, Zurich, 1889-96; research fellow, McGill U., 1903; Sc.D. (hon.), Washington U., 1948; m. Georgiana Sands, Jan. 3, 1922. Asst. prof. exptl. pathology, U. Pa., 1904-10; dir. dept. pathology, Bernard Skin and Cancer Hosp., St. Louis, 1910-15; prof. comparative pathology, Washington U., 1915-24, prof. pathology, 1924-37, and emeritus prof. since 1937. John Phillips memorial prize, Am. Coll. Physicians, 1935. Fellow A.A.A.S.; mem. Am. Assn. Pathologists and Bacteriologists (pres. 1914-15), Am. Physiol. Soc., Soc. of Cancer Research (pres. 1911), Internat. Assn. for Cancer Research (v.p.), Soc. Exptl. Medicine and Biology, Assn. Am. Physicians, Am. Philos. Soc., A.M.A., Washington Acad. Science; Am. Association for the study of Goitre, Nat. Acad. Sciences; hon. mem. French Soc. of Endocrinology. Author: The Venom of Heloderma (with collaborators), 1913; Edema, 1923; The Biological Basis of Individuality, 1945. Contbr. chiefly on tissue and tumor growth, tissue culture, psychiology of generative organs, pathology of circulation, venom of Heloderma, analysis of experimental ameobocyte tissue, internal secretions, biological basis of individuality, etc. Home: 40 Crestwood Drive, St. Louis 5. Died Dec. 28, 1959.

LOEWY, Edwin, textile mfg. exec.; b. N.Y. City, Sept. 8, 1893; s. Leopold and Caroline (Eschelbacher) L.; ed. pub. schs. of N.Y. City; m. Flora Schoenfeld, June 11, 1931; 1 dau., Betty Ann (Mrs. Hans Wertheimer). Began as apprentice, Textile Importing Co., 1908; became salesman; associated with A. Sterzelbach & Co., 1919-22; established own bus. under name of Edwin Loewy Co., N.Y. City, 1923, and served as pres., 1923-26; became dept. mgr., Cohn Hall Marx Co., 1926, vice pres. since 1946, dir. since 1945; vice pres. and dir., Union (S.C.) Mfg. & Power Co., since 1946; treas. United Merchants Indsl. Fabrics Corp., 1944; v.p. United Merchants & Mfrs., Inc., since 1952; dir. Aiken Mills, Inc., Associated Textiles of Canada, Ltd., The Seminole Mills. Served with U.S. Army, 1917-19. Trustee Lexington Sch. for the Deaf. Treas., Textile Distributors Inst., Inc.; mem. com. of Ednl. Found. for Apparel Industry. Mem. Nat. Conf. of Christians and Jews (com. mem.), Fedn. of Jewish Philanthropies (com. mem.). Clubs: Sunningdale Country (Scarsdale, N.Y.); Harmonie (N.Y. City). Home: 930 Fifth Av., N.Y. City 21. Office: 1407 Broadway, N.Y.C. Deceased.

LOEWY, Erwin, hydraulic engr.; b. Becow, Sept. 18, 1897; s. Leopold and Charlotte (Sekeles) L.; student Charles U., Prague, 1914-15, Kings Coll., London, 1924; m. Margaret Zander, May 10, 1912; 1 dau., Brigitte Dolores. Came to U.S., 1940, naturalized, 1947. Banker, Eng., 1921-24; pres. indsl. enterprises, France, 1925-28; gen. sales mgr. Schloemann Engring. Co., Germany, 1928-36; v.p. Loewy Engring. Co., Ltd, London-Bournemouth-Paris, 1936-40; founder, pres. Loewy-Hydropress, Inc., N.Y.C., 1940-56, Loewy Constrn. Co., Inc., 1941—, Sintercast Corp. Am., 1947—; v.p., dir. Baldwin-Lima Hamilton Corp.; cons. USAF, 1945-51. Chmn. City Symphony Orchestra of N.Y. Served as capt. Austrian Army, 1915-18. Mem. Inst. Metals (London), Iron and Steel Inst., Naval Engrs. Soc., Iron and Steel Engrs. Home: 25 Central Park W., N.Y.C. 23. Office: 111 Fifth Av., N.Y.C.; also 19 Bradford St., Lake Placid, N.Y.; Paschall P.O., Phila. 42. Died July 13, 1959.

LOFTIN, James Otis (lŏf'tĭn), coll. pres.; b. Thornton, Tex., July 19, 1887; s. Sam R. and Lila (McLellan) L.; student N. Tex. State Normal Coll., Denton, 1905-07; A.B., S.W. Tex. State Teachers Coll., San Marcos, 1925; A.M., Colo. State Coll., Greeley, 1927; m. May Cotton, July 5, 1922 (dec.); children—James, Patsy; m. 2d Matilda Glidden Fuller, Dec., 1950. Teacher history, Seymour (Tex.) High Sch., 1907-08, McLean High Sch., 1908-09; supt. Floydada High Sch., 1909-11; supt. Estacado Schs., 1911-12; teacher math. and science, Corpus Christi High Sch., 1912-15; prin. of elementary and high schs., San Antonio, 1915-34; pres. Tex. Coll. of Arts and Industries, Kingsville, Tex., 1934-1941; pres. San Antonio College since 1941. Civilian Pilot Training Coordinator, 1942-43. Mem. Tex. State Teachers Assn. (pres. 1933-34), N.E.A., Kingsville Chamber of Commerce, Phi Delta Kappa. Democrat. Baptist. Mason (Scottish Rite, Shriner). Clubs: Rotary (past pres.), Kiwanis (past pres.). Address: 126 Sharon Dr., San Antonio. Died Dec. 31, 1955; buried San Antonio.

LOFTIN, Scott Marion, lawyer; b. Montgomery, Ala., Sept. 14, 1878; s. William Marion and Loreta C. (Thomason) L.; student, Washington & Lee U., 1898-99, LL.D., 1934; D.C.L., U. of Fla., 1935; LL.D., Temple U., 1935, Stetson U., 1952. Admitted to Fla. bar, 1899, began practice at Pensacola; apptd. gen. solicitor Flagler corps., hdqrs. Jacksonville, Fla., Nov. 1917, gen. counsel, 1921, v.p. and gen. counsel since 1925; mem. Loftin & Wahl, Jacksonville, Loftin, Anderson, Scott, McCarthy & Preston, Miami, Florida; president the Atlantic & East Coast Terminal Co., University of Florida, Endowment Corporation, St. Augustine Historical Preservation and Restoration Assn.; gen. counsel and dir. Fla. East Coast Hotel Co., Fla. East Coast Car Ferry Co., West Palm Beach Water Co., Model Land Co., Perrine Grant Land Co., Gulf Life Ins. Co., Ft. Dallas Land Co., Chuluota Land Co.; receiver Fla. East Coast Ry., 1931-41; trustee Fla. East Coast Ry. since 1941; mem. Southern Regional R.R. Coordinating Com.; v.p. and gen. counsel P.&O.S.S. Co.; dir. Atlantic Nat. Bank (Jacksonville), Fla. Publishing Co., Railway Express Agency, Fruit Growers Express, Florida State Chamber of Commerce; vice-president Jacksonville Terminal Company, U.S. senator from Fla. to fill unexpired term of late Senator Trammell, May 26-Nov. 3, 1936. Mem. Fla. Ho. of Rep., 1903; county solicitor Escambia County, Fla., 1904-17. Mem. Am. Bar Assn. (pres. 1934-35), Am. Law Inst., Am. Judicature Soc., Fla. Bar Assn., Jacksonville Bar Assn. (ex-pres.), Alpha Tau Omega, Omicron Delta Kappa, Phi Beta Kappa, Phi Delta Phi, Blue Key; mem. com. apptd. by Supreme Court of U.S. to revise rules of practice and procedure in federal courts, 1935; mem. U.S. atty. general's advisory com. on crime, 1935. Democrat. Mason (32°, Shriner); Past Grand Chancellor K.P. Clubs: Seminole, Kiwanis (past dist. gov.), Timuquana Country, Fla. Yacht. Home: 1536 Riverside Av. Office: Graham Bldg., Jacksonville, Fla. Died Sept. 22, 1953.

LOFTUS, Clarence James, lawyer; b. West Union, Ia., June 15, 1887; s. William and Katherine (Nugent) L.; LL.B., Drake U., Des Moines, Ia., 1908; spl. studies at Drake and with leading professionalists; m. Eleanore Marie Mathers, Apr. 22, 1918. Admitted to Ia. bar, 1908, and practiced in Des Moines, 1908-14; admitted to Ill. bar, 1914, and since practiced in Chicago; mem. Parkinson & Lane, specialists in patent, trade-mark, unfair competition cases, 25 yrs.; sr. member Loftus, Lucas & Hammand, counselors in patent causes, since 1945; appeared before Fed. courts and U.S. Supreme Ct. since 1914. Mem. Am., Ill. and Chicago bar assns., Chicago Patent Law Assn., Am. Patent Bar Assn. of Washington, Cath. Lawyers Guild of Chicago, Am. Judicature Soc. Roman Catholic. Clubs: Mid-Day, University, Press, Drake University, Executives (Chgo.); Evanston (Ill.) Golf. Author articles on patents and patent law. Home: 850 Lake Shore Dr., Chgo. 11. Office: 135 S. La Salle St., Chgo. 3. Died May 11, 1953; buried Rosehill Cemetery, Chgo.

LOGAN, Robert Fulton, artist; b. in Canada; s. Robert Tremaine and Maria Martin (DeWinton) L.; ed. Art Inst. of Chgo. Sch. of Boston Museum Fine Arts; m. Rosamond Conant, June 23, 1928; 1 dau., Rosamond. Awarded Logan medal, Chgo. Soc. Etchers, 1922; Josephine Hancock Logan prize, 1939. Works on permanent exhibition: (paintings) "Les Molineaux-Billancourt," Luxembourg Gallery, Paris; "Spanish Iris," Art Soc., Hartford, Conn.; (portrait) Ambassador Eustis, Am. Embassy, Paris; (etchings) Met. Museum Art, New York; Library of Congress, Washington, D.C.; Avery Mem. Art Museum, Hartford, Conn.; Art Inst. Chicago; British Museum, London; Fitzwilliam Museum, Cambridge, Eng.; Bibliothéque Nationale and Luxembourg Museum, Paris, and Musée de Blerancourt, Musée de St. Denis, France; New York Pub. Library; Ann Arbor (Mich.) Art Assn.; Detroit Art Institute, Brooklyn Art Museum, Boston Museum of Fine Arts, Smithsonian Institute, Nat. Gallery (Wash.), Yale Mus. of Fine Arts, Lyman Allyn Mus., New London. Head of Dept. of Fine Arts, Conn., Coll., New London, Mem. U.S.N.R.F., 1918; asst. dir. Atelier of Painting, Bellevue Art Training Center, A.E.F. Member American Artists Professional League, Chgo. Soc. Etchers, The Society of Am. Etchers, Société Internationale Gravure Originale en Noir (Paris), Paris Salon Nationale des Beaux Arts, Conn. Acad. Fine Arts, Mystic Art Assn., Coll. Art Assn. Address: 939 Pequot Av., New London, Conn. Died Dec. 1959.

LOGAN, Thomas Dale, clergyman; b. Pitts., Jan. 29, 1851; s. John T. and Henrietta (Bryan) L.; A.B., Lafayette Coll., Pa., 1869, D.D., 1895; grad. Western Theol. Sem., Pa., 1874; m. Caroline B. Mahoney, Mar. 22, 1877. Ordained Presbyn. ministry, 1874; pastor 2d Ch., Meadville, Pa., 1874-88, 1st Ch., Springfield, Ill., 1888-13. Stated clk. Springfield Presbytery; chmn. home mission com. Synod of Ill., 1899-11. Dir. McCormick Theol. Sem., Blackburn Coll., Carlinville, Ill. (pres. bd.). Republican. Mem. Sigma Chi. Home: 430 S. 2d St., Springfield, Ill. Died Mar. 29, 1921; buried Allegheny Cemetery, Pitts.

LOHMANN, Carl Albert, univ. exec.; b. Akron, O., Aug. 9, 1887; s. Albert Carl and Grace Tod (Perkins) L.; student St. Paul's Sch., Concord, N. H., 1902-06; B.A., Yale, 1910, M.A. (hon.), 1926, L.H.D., 1953; studied music in Berlin, 1910-11; m. Helen Macgill Andrews, Mar. 25, 1918; children—John, Ann, Sarah Tod. With B. F. Goodrich Co., Akron, 1912-17; with Country Life Press, Garden City, L.I., N.Y., 1920; treas. Inst. Music and Music Sch. Settlement, Cleve., 1921-25; sec. alumni adv. bd. Yale, 1925-27, sec. univ., 1927-53, ret., curator of prints, 1926-30, 46—. Trustee U. Rochester, 1938-48. Served as lt. Constrn. Corps, USN, 1917-19. Republican. Episcopalian. Clubs: Yale (N.Y.C.); Elizabethan, Graduate (New Haven). Home: 176 St. Ronan St., New Haven. Died May 19, 1957; buried Grove St. Cemetery, New Haven.

LOHNES, Horace L. (lō'nĕs), lawyer; b. Donnelsville, O., Apr. 24, 1897; s. George C. and Hager Shobe (Frantz) L.; student Ohio State U., 1917-18; LL.B., George Washington U., 1924, LL.M., 1925; M.P.S., Am. U., 1927; m. Thelma Marie Foley, Oct. 4, 1919; 1 dau., Roberta Lee. Admitted to D.C. bar, 1924, and since practiced in Washington; partner Dow, Lohnes and Albertson since 1930. Mem. Am., Fed. Communications and D.C. bar assns., Radio Pioneers Am., Delta Theta Phi (past nat. chancellor; past pres. Delta Theta Phi Found., Inc.; Horace L. Lohnes Senate established at Columbus U. Sch. Law, 1948), Geo. Washington Law Sch. Alumni Assn. (president 1951). Mason (Shriner). Clubs: National Press, University. Home: Twin Oaks, R.F.D. 4, Vienna, Va. Office: Munsey Bldg., Washington 4. Died Dec. 23, 1954.

LOICHOT, Raymond William, banker; b. Canton, O., Dec. 13, 1891; s. L. A. and Philamena (Piero) L.; student Georgetown Prep. Sch.; A.B., Georgetown U., 1913; m. Rozell Green, 1935; children—Louis (dec.), William, Mary, Suzanne, Armonde, Elizabeth. With First Nat. Bank of Canton, 1931—, v.p., 1931-46, pres., 1946—, dir., 1925—; dir. Bonnot Co., Ohio Ferro Alloys Corp., Hercules Motors Corp., Atlantic Register Co. Home: 235 23d St. N.W. Office: First National Bank, Canton, O. Died Aug. 27, 1957; buried St. John's Cemetery, Canton.

LOKEY, Eugene, corp. exec.; b. Guntersville, Ala., July 29, 1892; s. Jefferson Davis and Ada (Gilbreath) L.; student Howard Coll., Birmingham, 1908-10; m. Mary Ellen Todd, June 9, 1913; children—Eugene M., Mary Ellen (Mrs. John Andrew Geddes). Newspaper reporter Birmingham, Atlanta, Savannah, N.Y.C., 1910-23; with N.Y. Tribune, 1923, N.Y. Herald-Tribune, 1923-26, N.Y. Times, 1926-35; dir. pub. relations N.Y. Stock Exchange, 1935-39, v.p. 1939-50; v.p. Curtis-Wright Corp. since 1951. Cons. 2d Commn. on Orgn. Exec. Br. Govt., 1955—. Democrat. Conglist. Home: 114 E. Taylor St., Savannah, Ga. Died Jan. 31, 1956; buried Bonaventure Cemetery, Savannah, Ga.

LOMAS, Alfred Jackson, railways exec.; b. Spondon, Derbyshire, Eng., Feb. 17, 1886; s. John and Elizabeth (Jackson) L.; student pub. schs. of Spondon, Meth. Sch., Derby; m. Marie Hartigan, Nov. 26, 1913; children—John Arthur, Margaret, Joan. Baggageman Canadian Nat. Rys., Lake Joseph, Ont., 1909, successively clk., dock agt., chief clk., yard agt., agt., yardmaster, fuel supervisor various locations Central region, 1909-30, acting asst. supt., Hornepayne, 1930, alternated positions of acting asst. supt. and yardmaster at Capreol and Gravenhurst, 1930-37, asst. supt., Hornepayne, 1937-38, at Capreol, 1938-40, supt., 1940-42, Toronto Terminals, 1942-44. gen. supt. Montreal dist., 1944-48, gen. mgr., Toronto, 1948-49, became v.p. Central region, Toronto, 1949, now ret. Mem. Toronto Bd. Trade. Clubs: Rotary, National (Toronto); Mt. Stephen (Montreal). Home: 174 Alexandra Blvd., Toronto, Ont., Can. Died Sept. 11, 1954.

LOMBARDI, Cornelius Ennis, lawyer; b. Houston, Oct. 3, 1888; s. Cesar and Caroline G. (Ennis) L.; A.B., Yale, 1911; LL.B., Harvard, 1914; m. Adele E. Volk, May 16, 1923; children—Leonard Volk, Cornelius Ennis, Richard Ennis. Admitted to N.Y. bar. 1915; practiced N.Y. City, 1915-16; atty. A. H. Belo & Co., pubs. The Dallas News, 1919-22: asso. Baker, Botts, Parker & Garwood, Houston, Kansas City, Mo., 1922-35; partner Lombardi, Robertson, Fligg & McLean, and Lombardi, Fligg, McLean & Slagle, Kansas City, Mo., 1936—; dir. Long-Bell Lumber Co., Long Bell Lumber Corp., Kan. City, Mo., 1937—. Chmn. Land Clearance for Redevelopment Authority of Kansas City, 1953-55. Served from 2d lt. to 1st lt., 149th F.A., 42d Div., 1917-19. Awarded Citation by Gen. Pershing, Silver Star, Purple Heart. Member Kansas City, American, Missouri bar associations, K.C. Lawyers Assn. (president 1949), Phi Beta Kappa. Episcopalian. Home: 5310 Belleview Av., Kansas City 2. Office: R. A. Long Bldg., Kansas City 6, Mo. Died Feb. 12, 1956; buried Dallas.

LONARDI, Eduardo, Pres. of Argentina; b. Argentina, Sept. 7, 1896; grad. mil. coll.; m. Mercedes Villada Achavel; five children. Entered army service as lt. of arty. and advanced through grades to maj. gen.; ret., 1951. Following armed forces revolution of 1955, which deposed Juan Peron from the presidency, became pres. of Argentina, Sept. 23, 1955. Address: Buenos Aires, Argentina. Died Mar. 22, 1956.*

LONG, Augustine V., judge; b. Lake City, Fla., May 14, 1877; s. Thomas T. and Annie Mariah (Pemberton) L.; ed. pub. schs., and Fla. Agrl. Coll., about 2 yrs.; studied law in attorneys' offices 3 yrs.; m. Ruby May Brownlee, Sept. 12, 1899; children—Ella May (Mrs. F. A. Canova), Augustus C., Annie E. (Mrs. Marcus Conant). Admitted to bar, 1898, and began practice at Starke, Fla.; admitted to practice before Supreme Ct. Fla., 1899, and later before Supreme Ct. U.S.; mem. Fla. Ho. of Reps., 1903; apptd. state's atty., 1907, and state's atty., 8th Jud. Circuit, 1910. serving until 1921; judge Circuit Ct., 1921-34; judge U.S. Dist. Ct. for No. Dist. Fla., 1934—. Served in Fla. N.G., 15 yrs., ret. as capt.; 1st lt. vols., Spanish-Am. War. Democrat. Presbyn. Mason. Home: Gainesville, Fla. Address: U.S. District Court, Gainesville, Fla. Died May 20, 1955; buried Gainesville.

LONG, Breckinridge, ex-govt. ofcl., lawyer; b. St. Louis, May 16, 1881; s. William Strudwick and Margaret M. (Breckinridge) L.; A.B., Princeton, 1904, A.M., 1909; student St. Louis Law Sch. (Washington U.), 1905-06; hon. LL.M., Washington U., 1920; LL.D., Lincoln Meml. U. (Tenn.), 1945; m. Christine Alexander Graham, June 1, 1912; 1 dau., Christine Wilcox. Admitted to Mo. bar, 1906; began practice in St. Louis, 1907; 3d asst. sec. of state, by appmt. of Pres. Wilson, 1917-20; Dem. nominee for U.S. Senate from Mo., 1920; del. Dem. Nat. Conv., 1928 (mem. com. on platform resolutions); then practicing internat. law. Spl. asst. to atty. gen., 1933; A.E. and P. to Italy, 1933-36; ambassador on spl. mission to Brazil, Argentina and Uruguay, 1938; apptd. mem. Commn., under treaty with Italy, for Advancement of Peace, 1939; spl. asst. to sec. of state, in charge of problems arising from the war, 1939-40, asst. sec. of state 1940-44. Mem. War Communications Bd., 1941-44, U.S. delegation to Dumbarton Oaks Conf., 1944. Trustee Princeton, 1937-41; bd. dirs. Jefferson Meml. Found. (v.p.); Am. Peace Soc.; bd. trustees Corcoran Gallery Art. Mem. Commn. on Revision of Judical Procedure, Mo., 1914. Mem. Jefferson Bicentennial Commn., 1941-43, U.S. Govt. Princeton Bicentennial Commn., 1946-47. Presbyn. Clubs: Metropolitan, Jefferson Islands, (Washington). Author: Genesis of the Constitution of the United States, 1925. Home: Montpelier Manor, Laurel, Md. Died Sept. 26, 1958; buried Crypt of Nat. Cathedral, Washington.

LONG, George C., Jr., ret. ins. co. exec.; m. Winnie Flateau; 2 daus. Former pres. Phoenix Ins. Co.; pres. Conn. Fire Ins. Co., Reliance Ins. Co. of Can.; v.p. Mpls. Fire & Marine Ins. Co.; dir. Hartford Nat. Bank & Trust Co., Central States Fire Ins. Co., Phoenix Mut. Life Ins. Co., Holyoke Water Power Co., Great Eastern Fire Ins. Co.; trustee Mechanics Savs. Bank. Ret. 1951. Address: 30 Trinity St., Hartford, Conn. Died July 15, 1958.*

LONG, George Edward, business exec.; b. Rock Island, Ill., 1886. Chmn. bd., dir. Koehring Co., Milw.; dir. Kwik-Mix Co., Port Washington, First Wis. Nat. Bank, Milw., First Wis. Trustee Co., Wis. Bankshares Corp. Home: 7227 N. 115th St. Office: 3026 W. Concordia Av., Milw. 18. Died Jan. 21, 1957.

LONG, Geo;ge Shannon, congressman; b. Tunica, La., Sept. 11, 1883; s. Huey Pierce and Caledonia (Tison) L.; student Mt. Lebanon (La.) Coll., 1897-99; married to Jewell Irene Tyson, on May 11, 1953. Practice of dentistry, 1904—, in Okla., 1904-35, Monroe, La., 1935-40, Pineville, La., 1940-52; supt. La. Colony and Tng. Sch., Pineville, 1948-50; lawyer; founder, dir. Dr. George S. Long Corp., advisor to Gov. Earl K. Long, 1951; mem. 83d-85th Congresses, 8th Dist. La.; mem. house vet.'s affairs and adminstrn. coms. Mem. Okla. State Legislature, 1920-22, chmn. banking commn.; del. Dem. Nat. Conv., 1948; candidate U.S. Ho. of Reps., 1948-50. Mem. Pineville C. of C. (past pres.), Okla. Bar Assn., La. State Dental Assn. Baptist. Mason (32°, Shriner). Kiwanian. Home: 1121 Milam St., Pineville, La. Office: House Office Bldg., Washington. Died Mar. 22, 1958; buried Greenwood Meml. Park, Pineville.

LONG, Haniel (Clark), writer; b. Rangoon, Burma, Mar. 9, 1888; s. Samuel Parker and May (Clark) L.; came to U.S., 1891; parents Am. citizens; A.B., Harvard, 1910; m. Alice Lavinia Knoblauch, Aug. 12, 1912 (dec. 1956); 1 son, Anton. Reporter N.Y. Globe and Commercial Advertiser, 1909-10; instr. English, Carnegie Inst. of Tech., Pittsburgh, 1910-15, asst. prof., 1915-20, asso. prof., 1920-26, part time prof., 1926-29. Moved to Santa Fe, N.M., 1929. Organizer Writers' Editions (non-profit, cooperative pub.), 1933, exec. dir., 1935-39. Mem. Delta Upsilon, Phi Beta Kappa. Author: Poems, 1920; Notes for a New Mythology, 1926; Atlantides, 1933; Pittsburgh Memoranda, 1935, rev., 1937; Interlinear to Cabeza de Vaca, 1936; Walt Whitman and the Springs of Courage, 1938; Malinche (Doña Marina), 1939; Piñon Country, 1941; Children, Students and a Few Adults, 1942; The Power Within Us, 1943; The Grist Mill, 1945, rev. 1946; A Letter to St. Augustine, 1950; Spring Returns, 1958. Compiler: Carnegie Tech. War Verse, 1918; The Soldier's Progress, 1918. Contributor Rocky Mountain Cities, 1949. Address: care Haniel Long Fund, Naples, N.Y. Died Oct. 17, 1956; buried Lakewood Cemetery, Mpls.

LONG, Howard Hale, educator, coll. dean; b. News Ferry, Va., Mar. 4, 1888; s. Thomas and Ann (Vassar) L.; B.S., Howard U., 1915; M.A., Clark U., 1916; Ed. D. (Austen scholar), Harvard, 1932; m. Ollie Mae Guerrant, Dec. 22, 1917 (dec.). Instr. psychology Howard U., 1916; dean Paine Coll., Augusta, Ga., 1919-23; head dept. edn. Knoxville Coll., 1923-24; instr. Miner Normal Sch., Washington, 1924-25; asso. supt. charge ednl. research D.C. pub. schs., 1925-48; dean of the coll. Central State Coll., Wilberforce, O., 1948—. Research asst. to sub-com. on instrn. Ohio Sch. Survey Com., 1954-55; Nat. cons. and evaluator, Phelps-Stokes Project. Mem. nat. council, national dir., mem. exec. com. YMCA. Diplomate and fellow Am. Bd. Examiners in Profl. Psychology. Fellow Am. Psychol. Assn.; mem. Am. Assn. U. Profs., A.A.A.S., Am. Assn. Examiners and Adminstrs. Ednl. Personnel, N.E.A., Ohio Valley Philosophy of Edn. Soc. (pres.), Miami Valley Psychol. Assn. (pres.), Am. Tchrs. Assn. (treas.). Contbr. articles profl. jours. Address: Central State College, Wilberforce, O. Died Feb. 21, 1957.

LONG, Joseph Harvey, pub.; b. near Jonestown, Pa., May 21, 1863; s. Edward Christian and Sarah (Roebuck) L.; student pub. schs. and high sch., Pittsburgh, Pa.; hon. LL.D., Marshall Coll., 1936; m. Cora Hildreth Thompson, June 12, 1884 (dec.); children—Luther Thompson (dec.), Virginia (dec.), Paul Walker, Edward Harvey (dec.). In employ Wheeling Sunday Leader, 1881-82, Erie Dispatch, 1882-84, Oswego (N.Y.) Palladium, 1884-86, Wheeling (W.Va.) Register, 1886-90; joined in orgn. Wheeling Evening News, 1890, sold interest, 1893; purchased Huntington (W.Va.) Herald, 1893, sold Herald, 1895 and purchased the Advertiser, Huntington, W.Va.; with three sons and Mr. Gideon, acquired Huntington Herald Dispatch; chmn. bd. Huntington Publishing Co., 1927—; director of First Huntington National Bank. Served as postmaster Huntington, West Virginia, 1916-21. Col. on staff of gov.; mem. Governor's Tax Com., 1925. One of four state dels. to Dem. Nat. Conv., Chicago, 1932. President of Huntington C. of C., 1936-41. Democrat. Conglist. Mason (K.T.). Clubs: Guyan Country, Gypsy (Huntington). Home: 835 Park Hills. Office: Cor. 5th Av. and 10th St., Huntington, W.Va. Died Dec. 28, 1958; buried Spring Hill Cemetery, Huntington.

LONG, Lewis Marshall, ex-congressman; b. Gardner, Ill., June 22, 1883; s. William Henry and Lucy Adeline (Ward) L.; grad. Plano (Ill.) High Sch., student U. Ill., 2 yrs.; LL.B., John Marshall Law Sch., Chgo., 1929; m. Genevieve A. Rice, Oct. 26, 1911. Telegraph operator, sta. agt. Burlington R.R., Sandwich, Ill., 1904-30; admitted to Ill. bar, 1930, and practiced at Sandwich; alderman Sandwich, 1922-24, mayor, 1935-36; mem. 75th Congress, Ill. at large. Mem. Sandwich Twp. High Sch. Bd. Edn., 1930-36. Democrat. Presbyn. Mason. Eastern Star. Home: 120 Elmood Pl., Sandwich, Ill. Died Sept. 9, 1957.

LONG, Mitchell, lawyer; b. Pulaski, Tenn., Nov. 15, 1889; s. W. B. and Eliza (McGoldrick) L.; legal study under Gen. Charles T. Cates, Jr., 1911-1914; m. Kathrine Lockett, Feb. 20, 1923; 1 son, Mitchell Long (dec.). Admitted to Tenn. bar, 1914; pvt. practice of law, Knoxville, Tenn., since 1914. Dir., chmn. bd. and gen. counsel Sterchi Bros. Stores, Inc.; dir. and gen. counsel Jefferson Woolen Mills; gen. counsel Hamilton Nat. Bank; mem. Cates, Smith & Long, 1921-45; Cates, Fowler, Long & Fowler, since 1945. Chairman State Democratic exec. com., 1937-38; del. State-at-Large to Dem. Nat. Convs., 1928, 1944. Served as capt. 114th field arty. A.E.F., World War I. Mem. commn. uniform state laws, 1930-49; Tenn. constitutional revision commn., 1945-46. Mem. Am. Bar Assn. (house dels. 1940-48; bd. govs. 1945-48; chmn. com. on aeronautical law, 1941-42), Tenn. and Knox Co. bar assns., Am. Law Inst. Presbyterian. Club: Cherokee Country. Home: 2704 Kingston Pike, Knoxville 16. Office: Hamilton National Bank Bldg., Knoxville 2, Tenn. Died Apr. 2, 1953.

LONG, Orie William, educator; b. Millersburg, Ky., May 25, 1882; s. James Riley and Armilda (Cheatham) L.; student Millersburg Mil. Inst., 1897-1900; A.B., Centre Coll., 1903, Litt.D., 1943; A.M., Harvard, 1911, Ph.D., 1913; student U. Berlin, 1906, U. Munich, 1914; m. Sally Rayen Davis Leake, June 20, 1934; 1 dau., Mary. Instr., Corsicana (Tex.) High Sch., 1904-06; prof. modern langs. Tex. Christian U., 1906-10, Worcester Poly. Inst., 1913-16; instr. German Mass. Inst. Tech., 1912-13; mem. faculty Williams Coll., 1916—, prof. German, 1932-48, William Dwight Whitney prof. German lit., 1948-50, emeritus prof., 1950—; lectr. U. Chicago, summers 1918, 1922. Mem. Am. Assn. U. Profs., Eng. Goethe Soc., Modern Humanities Research Assn., Modern Lang. Assn. Am. (exec. council 1943-47, v.p. 1948, editorial bd., 1947-51), N.E. Modern Lang. Assn., Williamstown Welfare Assn. (pres.), Kappa Alpha, Conglist. Author: Thomas Jefferson and George Ticknor, 1933; Literary Pioneers, 1935; Frederic Henry Hedge, A Cosmopoltian Scholar, 1940. Contbr. articles and revs. to profl. jours. Home: 139 Maon St., Williamstown, Mass. Died Sept. 14, 1955; buried Williams Coll. Cemetery.

LONG, Percy Waldron, univ. prof.; b. Boston, Sept. 21, 1876; s. William Mann and Annie Florence (Waldron) L.; A.B., Central High Sch., Phila., 1893; A.B., Harvard, 1898, A.M., 1900, Ph.D., 1906; studied U. of Pa., 1898-99; m. Florence Maie, d. J. J. Enneking, June 30, 1903; children—Enneking Waldron, Eliot Stuart, Norton Enneking, Donald Mann; m. 2d, Mary V. McDonald, June 25, 1938. Specialist editor Webster's New Internat. Dictionary, 1903-09, and 1925-33; instr. in English, Harvard, 1909-19, Radcliffe, 1909-13, Wellesley, 1912-16; head of English, Commonwealth of Mass., Dept. University Extension, 1916 23; asso. prof. New York Univ., 1934-39, prof., 1939-47; editor Dialect Notes, 1912-30; editor Publ. of Modern Lang. Assn., 1932-47, pres. 1948 and sec. of the Association Adjutant R.O.T.C., Harvard, 1917-18; personnel officer S.A.T.C., 1918-19. Member Am. Dialect Soc. Republican. Author: Studies in the Technique of Prose Style, 1915; French for Soldiers, 1917; Military English, 1918; Comparison, 1921; The Greek Element in English, 1931. Reorganized authority on poet Edmund Spenser, discovered origin of the English novel, "From Troilus to Euphues." Address: 3829 Veazey St., Washington 16. Died Oct. 2, 1952; buried Arlington Nat. Cemetery.

LONG, William Joseph, clergyman; b. North Attleboro, Mass., Apr. 3, 1866; s. Denis and Catherine (Burke) L.; grad. Bridgewater (Mass.) State Normal Sch., 1887; A.B., Harvard, 1892; grad. Andover Theol. Sem., 1895; M.A., Ph.D., Heidelberg, 1897; univs. of Paris and Rome, 1897-98; m. Frances Marsh Bancroft, Sept. 5, 1900; children—Lois Bancroft, Frances Kittredge, Brian Bancroft. Ordained to Congl. ministry, 1899; pastor First Ch., Stamford, Conn., 1899-1904; pastor at large, 1904—; lectr.

on nature, animal life, and lit. Made notable defense of ministerial liberty at Cambridge (Mass.) Council, 1898. Author: The Making of Zimri Bunker, 1898; Ways of Wood Folk, 1899; Wilderness Ways, 1900; Beasts of the Field, 1901; Fowls of the Air, 1901; Secrets of the Woods, 1901; School of the Woods, 1902; Following the Deer, 1903; A Little Brother to the Bear, 1903; Northern Trails, 1905; Brier Patch Philosophy, 1906; Whose Home Is the Wilderness, 1907; History of English Literature, 1909; American Literature, 1913; How Animals Talk, 1919; Wood Folk Comedies, 1920; America—History of Our Country, 1923; Mother Nature, 1923. Home: Stamford, Conn. Deceased.

LONGACRE, Charles Smull, editor; b. Valley Forge, Pa., Dec. 1, 1871; s. Henry Wise and Elizabeth Bergey (Smull) L.; grad. Keystone State Normal Sch., Kutztown, Pa., 1895; A.B., Battle Creek (Mich.) Coll., 1898; B.A., Emmanuel Missionary Coll., Berrien Springs, Mich., 1916; M.A., George Washington U., 1918; m. Florence Martha Hughes, June 7, 1899; children—Ethel Elizabeth (Mrs. Harold B. Hannum), Clarence Hughes (dec.). Tchr. pub. schs. 4 yrs.; evangelist 10 yrs.; prof. Bible exegesis and history 5 yrs., Atlantic Union Coll., S. Lancaster, Mass., pres. of coll. 4 yrs.; editor Liberty (quarterly mag.), Washington, 1913-42, now asso. editor; gen. internat. sec. Religious Liberty Assn., 1913-41, now asso. sec.; has lectured throughout U.S. and in Europe; gen. sec. Am. Temperance Soc., 1933-46; asso. sec., 1946—; del. from Seventh Day Adventist denomination to Internat. Conf. on Calendar Reform, League of Nations, Geneva, 1931. Republican. Seventh Day Adventist. Author: Freedom, Civil and Religious, 1920; The Church in Politics, 1926; Studies on Religious Liberty and Civil Government, 1929; Roger Williams—His Life, Work and Ideals, 1939; The Temperance Bulletin, 1943; also many pamphlets on religious liberty, Sunday laws, churches in politics, etc. Home: 102 Park Av., Takoma Park. Office: 6840 Eastern Av. N.W.. Washington. Died Oct. 23, 1956.

LONGCOPE, Warfield Theobald (lŏng'kōp), physician; b. Balt., Mar. 29, 1877; s. George von S. and Ruth (Theobald) L.; A.B., Johns Hopkins, 1897; M.D., Johns Hopkins, 1901; LL.D., St. John's Coll., 1934, Johns Hopkins U., 1951; D.Sc., U. Rochester, 1941; Docteur "honoris causa," U. Paris, 1945; m. Janet Percy Dana, Dec. 2, 1915; children—Barbara, Duncan, Mary Lee, Christopher. Resident pathologist of Pa. Hosp. Phila., 1901-04; dir. Ayer Clin. Lab., same, 1904-11; asst. prof. applied medicine, U. Pa., 1909-11; asso. prof. practice of medicine, 1911-14, Bard prof., 1914-21, Columbia; asso. vis. physician, 1911-14, dir. med. service Presbyn. Hosp., N.Y., 1914-21; prof. medicine Johns Hospkins Med. Sch. and physician in chief Johns Hopkins Hosp., 1922-46. Commd. maj., Med. O.R.C., 1917; on active duty med. div., Office of Surgeon Gen. U.S. Army, Washington, Aug. 1917-July 1918; col., Medical Corps, U.S. Army, A.E.F., July 1918-Jan. 1919. Fellow (hon.) Coll. Physicians (Phila.). Mem. Assn. Am. Physicians, A.M.A., Soc. Exptl. Biology and Medicine, Am. Soc. Clin. Investigation, Am. Soc. Exptl. Pathology, A.A.A.S., N.Y. Acad. Medicine, N.Y. Clin. Soc., Am. Clinic and Climatological Soc., Harvey Soc., Medico Chirurg. Faculty of Med., Balt. City Med. Soc., Nat. Acad. Scis.; fellow Am. Coll. Phys., Am. Acad. Arts and Scis.; hon. mem. Royal Soc. of Medicine, Société des Hôpital, Paris, Hon. Fellow Scandanavian Congress for Int. Med. Extensive investigations in clin. medicine and in pathology. Home: "Cornhill Farm," Lee, Mass. Died April 25, 1953.

LONGINO, Olin Harrington (lŏn'jĭ-nō), army officer (ret.); b. Atlanta, June 27, 1887; s. Thomas Dick and May (Harrington) L.; B S. in Elec. Engring., Ga. Sch. Tech., 1907; student Coast Arty. Sch., 1914, Command and Gen. Staff Sch., 1925-26, Army War Coll., 1934-35; m. Lila Evans, Aug. 28, 1913; children—Frances May (wife of Lt. Col. Edw. Sigerfoos, U.S. Army), Thomas Dick, II. Commd. 2d lt. U.S. Army, 1908; promoted through grades to brig. gen., 1941; sailed for france, 1917, as capt., comdg. H Battery, 8th Regt., Coast Arty.; participated in St. Mehiel and Meuse-Argonne offensives; returned to U.S. as lt. col., 1919; served in Eng. and Alaska, also comd. anti-aircraft tng. centers, Camp Edwards, Mass., Ft. Sheridan, Ill., during World War II; ret. 1945. Home: College Park, Ga. Died Sept. 7, 1955.

LONGLEY, Clifford Boles, (lŏng'lē) lawyer; b. Chicago, Ill., Nov. 25, 1888; s. William Hey and Isabelle Maud (Smoot) L.; student Lewis Inst., Chicago, 1904-07; LL.B., U. of Mich., 1913; m. Harriet Lawrence, Sept. 16, 1916; children—James Lawrence, Mary Frances. Admitted to Mich. bar, 1913, and began practice at Detroit; with firm Choate, Robertson & Lehman, 1913-17; associated with Ward N. Choate, 1917-19; legal dept. Ford Motor Co., 1919-21, counsel, 1921-41; counsel Manufacturers Nat. Bank of Detroit and Detroit, Toledo & Ironton Railroad Co., Estate Edsel B. Ford, Estate of Henry Ford, Estate of Clara J. Ford; mem. Bodman, Longley, Bogle, Armstrong & Dahling. Pres. and trustee Nat. Training Sch. for Pub. Service; chairman of the board of trustees Citizens Research Council; dir. American Red Cross; mem. Citizens Com. for Better Govt. in Mich. Member American, Michigan and Detroit bar associations. Republican. Clubs: Detroit Club, Detroit Athletic, Yondotega, Country of Detroit. Home: 8120 E. Jefferson Av., Detroit 14; also 40755 Ten Mile Rd., Farmington, Mich. Office: Buhl Bldg., Detroit 26. Died July 15, 1954; buried Woodlawn Cemetery, Detroit.

LONGMAN, (Mary) Evelyn Beatrice (Mrs. Nathaniel Horton Batchelder), sculptor; b. Winchester, O.; d. Edwin Henry and Clara (Adnam) Longman, student Olivet Coll., Mich., 1896-98; Art Inst. Chgo., 1898-1900, degree with honors, 1900; asst. in studio of Daniel Chester French for several yrs.; hon. M.A., Olivet, 1906; m. Nathaniel Horton Batchelder, June 28, 1920. In N.Y., 1900-20. Silver medal, St. Louis Expn., 1904, Panama Expn., San Francisco, 1915; Shaw meml. prize, Nat. Acad., 1918; W.M.R. French gold medal, Art Inst. Chgo., 1920; Widener gold medal, Pa. Acad., Phila., 1921; Watrous gold medal from N.A.D.. 1923; Charles Noel Flagg prize, Conn. Acad., 1925; Shaw Meml. prize, Nat. Acad. Design, 1926. Executed bronze doors to chapel, U.S. Naval Acad.; bronze doors to library, Wellesley Coll.; colossal statue of Victory, dome of Festival Hall, St. Louis Expn.; Allison Monument, Des Moines, Ia.; Fountain of Ceres, in Ct. of Four Seasons, San Francisco Expn.; statue of Spirit of Communication, Am. Tel. & Tel. Bldg., N.Y.C.; sculpture on Centennial Monument, Chgo.; sculpture on War Meml., Naugatuck, Conn.; Williams Meml., All Souls Ch., N.Y.C.; sculpture on facade of Employers Liability Bldg., Boston; Spanish War Meml. Hartford, Conn.; memls. to Gen. William Jackson Palmer in Hampton (Va.) Inst., Union Station (Denver), Mexico City, Salt Lake City, Colo. Coll. (Colorado Springs, Colo.); war meml. and meml. early settlers, Windsor, Conn.; monument to pioneers of industry, Hartford, Conn.; bust of Thomas A. Edison, Deutsches Mus., Munich; relief on facade of Post Office and Fed. Bldg., Hartford, Conn.; Benson Family Meml. Titusville, Pa.; Pennypacker Meml., Harvard. Portrait A. Lawrence Lowell, Harvard, F. W. Taussig, Harvard, Pres. Thomas S. Gates, U. Pa., Loomis Sch. Meml. of World War II. Represented in Met. Mus. (N.Y.), Art Inst. Chgo., Toledo Mus. Art, St. Louis Art Mus., Cin. Art Mus., Cleve. Mus. Art, John Herron Art Inst. (Indpls.), Wadsworth Atheneum (Hartford, Conn.). A.N.A., 1909, N.A., 1919; mem. Am. Fedn. Arts, Nat. Sculpture Soc., Am. Numismatic Soc., Archaeol. Inst. Am., Conn. Acad. Fine Arts. Club: Nat. Arts. Home: Osterville, Mass. Died Mar. 1954.

LONGMAN, (Mary) Evelyn Beatrice (Mrs. Nathaniel Horton Batchelder), sculptor; b. Winchester, O.; d. Edwin Henry and Clara (Adnam) Longman, student Olivet Coll., Mich., 1896-98; Art Inst. Chgo., 1898-1900, degree with honors, 1900; asst. in studio of Daniel Chester French for several yrs.; hon. M.A., Olivet, 1906; m. Nathaniel Horton Batchelder, June 28, 1920. In New York, 1900-20. Recipient silver medal St. Louis Expn., 1904, Panama Expn., San Francisco, 1915; Shaw memorial prize Nat. Acad., 1918; W.M.R. French gold medal Art Inst. Chgo., 1920; Widener gold medal Pa. Acad., Phila., 1921, Watrous gold medal N.A.D., 1923; Charles Noel Flagg prize, Conn. Acad., 1925; Shaw Meml. prize Nat. Acad. of Design, 1926. Executed bronze doors to chapel, U.S. Naval Acad., to library Wellesley Coll.; colossal statue of Victory, dome of Festival Hall, St. Louis Expn.; Allison Monument, Des Moines, Ia.; Fountain of Ceres in Court of Four Seasons, San Francisco Expn.; statue of Spirit of Communication, Am. Tel. & Tel. Bldg., N.Y.C.; sculpture on Centennial Monument, Chgo.; sculpture on War Memorial, Naugatuck, Conn.; Williams Meml., All Souls Ch., N.Y.C.; sculpture on façade of Employers Liability Bldg., Boston; Spanish War Meml. Hartford, Conn.; memorials to Gen. William Jackson Palmer in Hampton (Va.) Inst., Union Station (Denver), Mexico City, Salt Lake City, Colo. Coll. (Colorado Springs, Colo.); war memorial and memorial to early settlers, Windsor, Conn.; monument to pioneers of industry, Hartford, Conn.; bust of Thomas A. Edison, Deutsches Museum, Munich, also Naval Research Laboratory, Washington; relief on façade of Post Office and Federal Bldg., Hartford, Conn.; Benson Family Meml., Titusville, Pa.; Pennypacker Memorial, Harvard; portrait of A. Lawrence Lowell, Harvard; portrait of F. W. Taussig, Harvard; portrait of Pres. Thomas S. Gates, U. Pa.; Loomis Sch. Memorial of World War II. Represented in Met. Mus. Art, Art Inst. Chgo., Toledo Mus. Art, St. Louis Art Mus., Cincinnati Art Mus., Cleve. Mus. Art, John Herron Art Inst. (Indpls.), Wadsworth Atheneum (Hartford, Conn.). A.N.A., 1909, N.A., 1919. Mem. Am. Fedn. Arts, Nat. Sculpture Soc., Am. Numismatic Soc., Archaeol. Inst. America, Conn. Acad. Fine Arts. Club: Nat. Arts. Home: Osterville, Mass. Died Mar. 10, 1954.

LONGWELL, Oliver Henry, coll. pres.; b. Connersville, Ind., Dec. 22, 1855; s. Lewis Genung and Mary Ann (Pattison) L.; A.B., No. Ind. Normal (now Valparaiso) U., 1880, A.M., 1885, Ph.D., 1894; m. Mary D. Stalker, Sept. 16, 1882. Pres. So. Ia. Normal Sch., Bloomfield, 1880-4. Western Normal Coll., Shenandoah, Ia., 1884-90, Highland Park Coll., Des Moines, Ia., 1890-1913. Republican. Presbyn. Author: Complete English Grammar, 1893; Elementary English Grammar, 1902. Home: 641-19 St., Des Moines, Ia. Died Jan. 13, 1921; buried Glendale Cemetery.

LONGYEAR, Edmund Joseph, mining engr.; b. Grass Lake, Mich., Nov. 6, 1864; s. Isaac and Roanna (Davis) L.; student U. Mich., 1883-86; E.M., Mich. Coll. Mines, 1888; m. Nevada Patton, Apr. 16, 1890; children—Clyde Stanley, Robert Davis, Philip Owen, Margaret (Mrs. Ralph H. Lutz), Richard Patton, Edmund Joseph. With location party, Marquette, Houghton and Ontonagan Ry., 1886-87; with J. M. Longyear, Marquette, Mich., 1887, 88-91. Mich. State Geol. Survey, 1888; pioneered in diamond drilling operations Mesabe Range, 1890, active in development of the mining area thereafter; cos. which later included mfg. cos. also, were organized under name of E. J. Longyear Co., hdqrs. Hibbing, moved to Mpls. 1911; served as pres. to 1924, v.p., dir. 1924—; operations included many areas in U.S., Can., Cuba, Mexico, numerous European, Asian and African countries; retired 1924. Sec. Hibbing sch. Bd., 1897-98; pres. Village of Hibbing, 1898-99; mem. budget and distbn. com. Community Fund, 1918-24, chmn. 1918; mem. bd. dir. YMCA, 1913-25; dir. Elliot Park Neighborhood House, 1919-24. Mem. Ulster County Hist. Soc., N.E. Hist.-Geneal. Soc., N.Y. Geneal. and Biog. Soc., Soc. Mayflower Descs., S.R. Republican. Baptist Clubs: Minneapolis, Lafayette. Address: 454 S. Bedford Dr., Beverly Hills, Cal. Died Dec. 4, 1954; buried Forest Lawn Meml. Park, Glendale, Cal.

LOOFBOUROW, John Robert, prof. biophysics; b. Cin., Nov. 1, 1902; s. John Wilson and Henrietta (Botts) L.; A.B., U. Cin., 1923; Sc.D., U. Dayton, 1936; m. Dorothea M. Gano, July 6, 1926; 1 son, John Wiltshire. Instr. physics U. Cin., 1925-29, research asso., 1929-35; prof. biophysics U. Dayton, 1935-36; research prof. Institutum Divi Thomae, 1935-40; asso. prof. Mass. Inst. Tech., 1940-45, prof. biophysics and exec. officer biol. dept., 1945—. Exec. sec. radar div., NDRC, 1942-46; pres. Cheviot Theatre Corp., 1931-40; cons. Crosley Radio Corp., 1924-34; chmn. spl. adv. bd. AEC, 1947-48. Fellow A.A.A.S., Am. Phys. Soc., Am. Acad. Scis.; mem. Chem. Soc. (London, Eng.), Physical Soc. (London), Biochem. Soc. (London), Faraday Soc., Optical Soc. Am., Beta Theta Pi. Contbr. sci. jours. Home: 68 Sparks St. Office: Mass. Inst. Tech., Cambridge, Mass. Died Jan. 22, 1951; buried Mount Auburn Cemetery, Cambridge.

LOOMIS, Charles Wheeler, bag mfg. exec.; b. Parkersburg, W.Va., Sept. 25, 1891; s. Charles Wheeler and Miriam (Nye) L.; S.B., Mass. Inst. Tech., 1917; m. Helen Margaret Clark, June 7, 1917; children—Charles Clark, Robert Nye. With Bemis Bros. Bag Co., St. Louis, 1919-57, mgr. Memphis plant, 1931-47, dir. personnel, 1947, v.p., 1949-57, dir., 1952-57, ret. Jan. 1957. Served as capt. C.E., U.S. Army, Eng. and France, 1917-19. Mem. Beta Theta Pi. Clubs: Noonday, University, Bogey, Algonquin Golf (St. Louis); Oyster Harbors (Osterville, Mass.). Home: 816 S. Hanley Rd., Clayton 5, Mo. Office: 408 Pine St., St. Louis 2. Died Dec. 19, 1957.

LOOMIS, Louise Ropes, educator, ret.; b. of Am. parents, Yokohama, Japan, May 3, 1874; d. Henry and Jane Hering (Greene) Loomis; B.A. Wellesley, 1897; A.M., Columbia, 1902, Ph.D., 1906. Inst. Greek and history, Whitman Coll., Walla Walla, Wash., 1898-1901; lectr. history, Barnard Coll., N.Y.C., 1903-05; warden Sage Coll., lectr. history Cornell U., 1905-09, Barnard Coll., 1920-21; prof. history Wells Coll., 1921-40. Fellow Royal Hist. Soc.; mem. Am. Hist. Assn., Am. Soc. Ch. History, Medieval Acad., Am. Civil Liberties Union, Phi Beta Kappa. Socialist. Author: Medieval Hellenism, 1906; The Book of the Popes, 1916; The See of Peter (with James T. Shotwell), 1927. Editor: Five Dialogues of Plato, 1942; Readings in Aristotle, 1943, Homer's Iliad, 1944. Home: 92 Livingston St., New Haven 11. Died Jan. 2, 1958.

LOOMIS, Madeleine Seymour, Braille expert and instructor; b. Hartford, Conn.; d. Archibald Gilbert and Ellen Seymour (Hanson) Loomis; grad. Mary C. Wheeler Sch., Providence; Certificate, Nat. Inst. for Blind, London, 1931. Began study of Braille in 1918; teacher Braille and dir. Braille, Chicago chapter Am. Red Cross, 1919-27, organized and taught Braille classes, Providence (R.I.) chapter, 1919, New York chapter, 1922; mem. faculty and teacher Braille, Teachers Coll., Columbia U., since 1935; worked on Braille system for Turkish language with rep. from Turkey. Counselor Comié de Unificación del Braille of Del Primer Congreso Tiflológico Pan-Americano. Vice regent Mary Washington Colonial chapter D.A.R. Mem. Internat. Council for Exceptional Children. Republican. Episcopalian. Author: Grade One-and-a-Half Braille and How to Learn It in Ten Lessons, 1922; Standard English Braille in Twenty Lessons, 1934; Sequence and Syllabication, 1936; A Guide to Rule 34, 1937; (with P. C. Mitchell) Braille Chemical Notations and How to Use Them, 1939; You Can Learn to Read Braille, 1939; The Writing of Braille Mathematical Notation, 1941; The Braille Reference Book, 1942; The Writing of Grade Three Braille, 1944; Which Grade of Braille Should be Taught First?, 1948. Contbr. articles to professional jours. Home: 12 E. 97th St., New York 29. Office: Teachers College, Columbia University, N.Y. City 27. Died Aug. 16, 1950; buried Cedar Hill Cemetery, Hartford, Conn.

LOOMIS, Ruth, ex-coll. dean; b. North Manchester, Conn., Aug. 11, 1864; d. Rev. Henry and Frances Elizabeth (Craft) L.; A.B., Vassar, 1885; studied La Sorbonne and École Normale Supérieure, Sèvres, Paris, France, 1892; Litt.D., Colo. Coll., 1917. Instr. English, Vassar, 1886-95; dean of women Colo. Coll., Colorado Springs, 1896-1917. Mem. League Nations Assn., Nat. Soc. Colonial Dames in State of N.Y., Phi Beta Kappa. Home: 211 Private Way, Lakewood, N.J. Died 1957; buried Poughkeepsie, N.Y.

LOOPER, Edward Anderson, otolaryngologist; b. Silver City, Ga., Dec. 16, 1888; s. John Anderson and Jennie (Stewart) L.; M.D., U. of Md., 1912; Emory U., 1908-10; Ophthal.D., U. of Colo., 1913; m. Lola Patenall, Jan. 15, 1920; children—Edward A., Lola Elise, Sybil Ann. Began practice as specialist in eye, ear, nose and throat, Baltimore, Md., 1913; prof. diseases of nose and throat, U. of Md., since 1921: laryngologist, Univ. Hosp. since 1921; surgeon, Baltimore Eye, Ear and Throat Hosp., since 1930; mem. exec. com. and mem. staff Woman's Hosp. since 1931; oto-laryngolist Md. State Sanatorium for Tuberculosis since 1922; otolaryngologist, Eudowood Sanatorium for Tuberculosis since 1920; laryngologist, Md. Gen., St. Agnes, Franklin Square, West Baltimore Gen., and Nurses and Child's Hosps.; mem. staff, Union Memorial and Mercy Hosps.; cons. laryngologist Kernan Hosp. for Crippled Children; bronchoscopist and esophagoscopist, University Hosp. and U.S. Marine Hosp.; cons. otolaryngologist, Provident Hosp.; otolaryngologist Baltimore City Hosps. for Tuberculosis, Edward McCready Memorial Hosp., Crisfield, Md.; and Havre de Grace Hosp., Md. Served as 1st lt. Med Reserve Corps, U.S. Army, 1918; instr. and capt., Ft. Oglethorpe; in France 2 yrs.; maj., Med. Reserve Corps. Fellow Am. College Surgeons (mem. advisory council com. for otolaryngology); mem. American Bronchoscopic Society (vice-pres.), Am. Rhinol., Laryngol. and Otol. Soc., Am. Acad. Ophthalmology and Oto-Laryngology, Am. Laryngol. Assn., Internat. Coll. of Surgeons (past state regent) Med. and Chirurg. Faculty of Md., Baltimore City Med. Soc., Southern Med. Soc. (past councillor); asso. mem. Am. Coll. Chest Physicians. Democrat. Baptist. Clubs: Baltimore Country, Gibson Island Country. Author: The Diagnosis and Treatment of Laryngeal Tuberulosis, 1937; also about 30 articles related to subjects in specialty. Home: 504 Overhill Rd., Roland Park, Baltimore. Office: 104 W. Madison St., Balt. Died Jan. 14, 1953.

LOPEZ, Pumarejo Alfonso, diplomat; born Honda, Columbia, Jan. 31, 1886; educated privately and pvt. schs., Bogotá; student in polit. economy and finance in London, and U.S. Entered the coffee business, 1903; became bank mgr., newspaper owner, rep. of investment houses and utility cos.; co-founder and v.p. Am. Mercantile Bank of Colombia, pres., 1918. Entered politics; elected Liberal deputy for Tolima Assembly, 1915; minister to London, 1933; Colombian del., London Economic Conf., 1933; chmn. Colombian delegation to 7th Pan-Am. Conf., Montevideo, 1933; lecturer at Sorbonne, Paris, 1933; pres., Colombia, 1934-38, re-elected, 1942; chmn. delegation of Colombia at U.N.; Ambassador to Britain 1959—. Contributed to establishment of Bogotá's "University City." Co-founder newspaper, The Liberal, 1910; editor The National Daily; contributor to The Republican, and to revs. Author: Official Politics, Messages, Letters and Discourses, of President López (5 vols., 1934-38); International Politics, and International Series of Discourses, Messages, Cablegrams and Other Documents of Pres. López. Address: London, Eng. Died Nov. 20, 1959.*

LORD, Chester Bradford, banker; born Dedham, Mass., Dec. 5, 1875; s. William H. and Mary Augusta (Endicott) L.; ed. high school; m. Amy Lester, June 16, 1908. Vice pres. in sales orgn. Endicott Johnson Corp., 1901-27; pres., dir. First Nat. Bank, Binghamton, 1928-53, chmn. bd. dir., 1954—; dir. Endicott Trust Co. Dir., treas. Blind Work Assn., Inc., Sheltered Workshop for the Disabled. Chmn. trustees Y.W.C.A. Club: Binghamton. Home: 67 Riverside Dr. Office: First Nat. Bank, Binghamton, N.Y. Died Oct. 2, 1958.

LORD, Daniel Aloysius, clergyman; b. Chicago, Ill., Apr. 23, 1888; s. George Douglas and Iva Jane (Langdon) L.; A.B., Loyola U., Chicago, 1909; Litt.D., Creighton U., 1936, Boston Coll., 1937. Entered Soc. of Jesus, St. Stanislaus Sem., Florissant, Mo., 1909; for classical studies; science and philos., St. Louis U., 1914-17; prof. English, St. Louis U., 1917-20; co-founder, St. Louis U. Sch. Edn. and extension courses; ordained to priesthood, Roman Catholic Ch., 1923; dir. nat. hdqrs. of Sodality of Our Lady, dir. The Queen's Work, Inc., St. Louis, 1925-48; editor the Sodality publs. Founder and dir. Summer Sch. of Catholic Action, 1931-48; dir. Jesuit Inst. Social Order, 1944-47; nat. dir. Knights and Handmaids of Blessed Sacrament. Mem. Acad. of Gallery of Living Cath. Authors, 1940. Author (books): Armchair Philosophy, My Mother, Religion and Leadership, Guidance of Youth, Guidance of Parents, The Glorious Ten Commandments, and other books; some fiction and detective novels; author of over 200 pamphlets with circulation of 17,000,000, transl. into some 20 fgn. langs.; author and dir. pageants: Mother of Youth (St. Louis U. Centennial); Jamaica Triumphant (Nat. Pageant of Jamaica, B.W.I.); The Restless Flame (Marquette U.); numerous musical plays, dramas; dir. Canadian Martyrs' pageant, Salute to Canada, 1949. Lectr. on lit., current events, philos., etc. Home: 4970 Oakland Blvd. Address: 3115 S. Grand Blvd., St. Louis. Died Jan. 15, 1955; buried St. Stanislaus Seminary, Florissant, Mo.

LORD, Frederic W., constrn. engr.; b. Brooklyn, N.Y., July 3, 1871; s. Joseph and Mary (Archer) L.; ed. private schs., Brooklyn Poly. Inst., Mass. Institute Tech.; m. Mrs. Alice K. Garrison, Sept. 29, 1906; children—Anne (Mrs. Wolcott Andrews), Mrs. Mary Reed, Ellen (Mrs. Robert Pierce), (stepchildren) Lloyd K. Garrison and Mrs. Carl Binger. Founder, 1895, and chief exec., Lord Electric Co., Inc., New York, Boston, Pittsburgh, to 1948. Introduced bill in Congress, 1943, for awarding contracts on a merit basis rather than competitive. Received citation for "long and useful service and helpful suggestions for improving the procedures for letting of contracts," Nat. Elec. Contractors Assn., 1942. Author: Ethics of Contracting, 1918; Selective Method of Letting Contracts, 1938; also articles and papers same subject. Clubs: Racquet and Tennis, Engineers, Uptown, Mid-day, Mass. Inst. Tech. (New York). Democrat. Home: 238 E. 68th St. Address: 10 Rockefeller Plaza, N.Y.C. 20. Died. Dec. 31, 1951.

LORD, Kenneth Prince, army officer, ret.; b. Rockland, Me., Dec. 11, 1888; s. Brig. Gen. Herbert Mayhew and Annie Stuart (Waldo) L.; B.Sc., Tufts Coll., 1929; grad. Field Arty. Sch., Battery Officers' Course, 1922, advanced Course, 1928, Command and Gen. Staff Sch., 1930, Army Indsl. Coll., 1931; m. Helen Elizabeth Cooper, Sept. 6, 1913; children—Kenneth Prince, Herbert Mayhew, II. Commd. 2d lt., Cavalry, U.S. Army, Dec. 30, 1911; transferred to Field Arty., July 1, 1920; promoted through grades to brig. gen., U.S. Army, Oct. 3, 1941; retired, 1946. Served with Punitive Expdn. in Mexico; participated in Aisne-Marne, St. Mihiel and Meuse-Argonne offensives and with Army of Occupation in Germany, World War I; chief of staff, Eastern Defense Comd. and First Army; comdg. gen. Eastern Defense Comd., World War II. Awarded Silver Star Citation for Gallantry in action in Meuse-Argonne Offensive, 1918; Legion of Merit with Oak Leaf Cluster, and Army Commendation Ribbon. Rep. Christian Scientist. Mason. Home: Rockland, Me. Office: 100 Beech St., Rockland, Me. Died Apr. 28, 1957.

LORD, Louis Eleazer, coll. prof.; b. Ravenna, O., July 14, 1875; s. Eleazer and Mary (Lewis) L.; A.B. and A.M., Oberlin, 1897; A.M., Harvard, 1900; Ph.D., Yale, 1908; L.H.D., Illinois College, Jacksonville, 1929; Litt. D., College of Wooster, Wooster, O., 1940; studied U. of Berlin, 1908-09; m. Frances Partridge (A.B., Oberlin, 1899), 1900; 1 dau., Priscilla. Prof. Latin and Greek, Pritchett Coll., Glasgow, Mo., 1898-99; instr. Latin and Greek, 1903-08, asso. prof., 1908-12, prof., 1912-41, emeritus prof. of classics since 1941; Oberlin Coll. Visiting prof. of classics, Univ. of Illinois, 1942-43; Martin Classical lecturer, Oberlin Coll., 1943; prof. ancient history and classical lit., Scripp Coll., 1944-49; president Bureau of University Travel 1946-56. Pres. bd. trustees Oberlin Kindergarten Training School, 1912-33; trustee Oberlin-Shansi Memorial Association 1931-48; president board trustees Oberlin Village Improvement Soc., 1915-40; dir. Peoples Banking Co., 1926-40; director summer school, Bur. University Travel, 1922-25; annual prof. Latin, Am. Acad. in Rome, 1923-24; annual prof. Greek, American School of Classical Studies, at Athens, 1928-29, visiting prof., 1936-37; dir. summer session of same, 1931-50. Asso. dir. of personnel, Am. Red Cross, 1918-19. Special consultant Office of Price Administration, 1942. Mem. Archaeol. Inst. America (pres. 1932-37), American School of Classical Studies, at Athens (exec. com.; chmn. mng. com. 1939-50; member board trustees since 1939; commn. for the excavation of the Agora at Athens since 1939) Athens Coll., Greece (bd. trustees), Am. Philol. Assn., English Classical Assn., Classical Assn. Middle West and South (sec. 1915-20; pres. 1922-23), Ohio Classical Conf. (pres. 1922-23), Soc. for Promotion of Hellenic Studies, Soc. for Promotion of Roman Studies, the American Classical League, Phi Beta Kappa, Eta Sigma Psi (hon.). Hon. member Greek Archæological Society, 1939. Decorated Chevalier Order of the Redeemer (Greece); Officer Order of George I (Greece); Commendatore della Corona d'Italia; Officer Royal Order of the Phoenix, Greece. Alumni Medal, Oberlin Coll., 1948. Conglist. Author: Aristophanes (Our Debt to Greece and Rome series), 1925; The Roman Historians, 1927. Editor Oberlin Alumni Magazine, 1904-15, Anacreon, 1928. Translator: Orfeo of Politian, Aminta of Tasso, 1931; 7 of Cicero's Orations for Loeb Classical Library, 1927; Latin Third Year (with Loura Woodruff), 1939; Thucydides and the World War (Martin Classical Lectures), 1945. History of The American School of Classical Studies at Athens, 1947. Home: 3 Concord Av., Cambridge, Mass. Address: 11 Boyd St., Newton, Mass. Died Jan. 24, 1956; buried Oberlin, O.

LORD, Pauline, actress; b. Hanford, Calif., Aug. 8, 1890; d. Edward and Sarah (Foster) L.; m. O. B. Winters, 1929 (div. 1931). First appeared on stage with the Belasco Stock Co., San Francisco, as the made in "Are You a Mason?", 1903; toured in repertory with Nat Goodwin, 1905, and played in his co. in New York; subsequently appeared as Ruth Lenox in The Talker; later in On Trial, The Deluge, The Harvest, Samson and Delilah, Anna Christie; played Amy in They Knew What They Wanted, 1924; also starred in Distant Drums, Ethan Frome, Sleep My Pretty One; appeared in movie Mrs. Wiggs of the Cabbage Patch, 1935. Address: 55 Park Av., N.Y.C. Died Oct. 11, 1950.

LORD, Robert Howard, clergyman; b. Plano, Ill., July 20, 1885; s. Frank Howard and Julia Marie (Custin) L.; student Northwestern U., 1902-03; A.B., Harvard, 1906; A.M., 1907; Ph.D., 1910; student univs. Vienna, Berlin and Moscow; Ph.D. (hon.), U. Lwow, Poland, 1921; student St. John's Sem., Brighton, Mass., 1926-29. Instr. history Harvard, 1910, advancing to prof., 1924-26; ordained priest Roman Cath. Ch., 1929; curate St. Cecilia's Ch., Boston, 1929-30; prof. ch. history St. John's Sem., Brighton, 1930, vice rector, 1933; pastor St. Paul's Ch., Wellesley, Mass., since 1944; Papal domestic prelate with title Rt. Rev. Monsignor, 1950. Trustee Boston Pub. Library. Mem. Am., Mass. and Am. Cath. hist. socs., Acad. Polit. Sci. (N.Y.), Cath. Commn. for Intellectual and Cultural Affairs. Author: The Second Partition of Poland, 1915; Some Problems of the Peace Conference (with Prof. C.H. Haskins), 1920; The Origins of the War of 1870, 1924; Archibald Coolidge, Life and Letters (with Harold J. Coolidge), 1932; History of the Archdiocese of Boston, 3 vols. (with Frs. John E. Sexton and Edward T. Harrington), 1944. Address: 502 Washington St., Wellesley 81, Mass. Died May 22, 1954.

LORENZ, Joseph, lawyer; b. Phila., Feb. 26, 1893; s. Carl and Rose (Wurtemburg) L.; student Perkiomen Sch., Pennsburg, Pa., 1907-10; A.B., Harvard, 1914, LL.B., 1916; student U. of Rennes, Brittany, France, 1919; m. Katherine M. Broderick, Sept. 12, 1930; 1 son, Joseph P. Admitted to N.Y. State bar, 1917, and practiced as asso. firm of Rushmore, Bisbee & Stern, 1916-18 and 1919-21; mem. firm Lorenz, Finn & Lorenz since 1921, specialist in corporate reorgn. since 1935; instr. in govt. and sociology City Coll. of New York, 1929; instr. Fordham Univ. Sch. of Law, 1922-24, asso. prof. of law, 1924-28. Receiver and trustee Richard Whitney & Co.; counsel for trustee of Childs Co. in reorgn. and mem. bd. dirs. following reorgn. Dir. Reid, Collins & Company, Inc.; Paul M. O'Neill International Detective Agency, Incorporated, Herma Products Corporation, C. J. Reid & Co., Inc., Smokador Mfg. Co., Inc. Served with 81st and 80th divs., U.S. Army, France, 1918-19. Mem. N.Y. State Bar Assn., Bar Assn. of City of N.Y., N.Y. County Bar Assn. Mem. Dutch Reformed Ch. Clubs: Harvard, Bankers, The Pilgrims (New York); Ketchaboneck Country (Westhampton, L.I.). Home: 655 Park Av., N.Y. City 21. Office: 165 Broadway, N.Y.C. 6. Died 1958.

LORENZ, Keith, lawyer; b. Philadelphia, May 2, 1890; s. Carl and Rose (Wurttemburg) L.; A.B., Harvard, 1912; LL.B., Columbia, 1916; student Balliol Coll., Oxford, 1919; m. Helen W. Laimbeer, Feb. 14, 1931; children—John Laimbeer, Keith, Jr. Asso. Shearman & Sterling, attys., prior to and shortly after 1st World War; asst. U.S. Atty., So. Dist. of N.Y., 3 yrs.; mem. law firm, Lorenz, Finn & Lorenz since 1923; apptd. mem. N.Y. State Labor Relations Bd. for six yr. term by Gov. Dewey, 1945, and designated as chmn. Bd. by the Gov., 1949, reappointed and redesignated chmn. bd. 1951. 2d lt., 304th F.A., 77th Div., during 1st World War. Active on the Emergency Com. Military Training Camp Assn.; attended the Business and Professional Men's Military Training Camp at Plattsburg, N.Y., 1940. Chief of the Legal Division and mem. of the Board of Awards, N.Y. Ordnance Dist., War Dept., 1942. Mem. Nat. Assn. for the Prevention of Blindness (dir., mem. exec. com.). Mem. 304th Field Artillery A.E.F. Assn., Bar Assn. City of N.Y., Am. and N.Y. State bar assns., Balliol Soc., Oxford Soc., The Pilgrims. Republican. Presbyn. Mason. Club: Harvard (N.Y. City). Home: 25 East 83rd St., N.Y.C. 28. Office: 165 Broadway, N.Y.C. 6. Died July 25, 1952; buried Woodlawn Cemetery, N.Y.

LORENZ, William Frederick, psychiatrist; b. N.Y. C.; Feb. 15, 1882; s. Herman and Elise (Kuenzlen) L.; student N.Y.U., 1898-99; M.D., Bellevue Hosp. Coll., 1903; m. Ada Holt, May 21, 1915; children

—Adrian Holt Vanderveer, William Frederick, Thomas Holt, Paul Kuenzlen, Joseph Dean. Med. interne Gen. Hosp., N.Y.C., 1903-05; med. staff Manhattan State Hosp., 1906-10; clin. dir. Wis. State Hosp., 1910-14; spl. expert, research investigation of Pellagra, USPHS, 1914-15; dir. Wis. Psychiat. Inst., 1915—; prof. psychiatry, U. Wis., 1915—. Pres. Wis. Service Recognition Bd., 1921-24; mem. Med. Council U.S. Vets.' Bur., 1923—; pres. Wis. State Bd. Control, 1923-25; pres. Wis. Rehabilitation Bd., 1925; chmn. State Bd. Mental Hygiene, 1938—. Served in Spanish-Am. War 7 mos., 1898; maj. in comd. Field Hosp. Co. 127, with 32d Div., AEF, 1919-19. Decorated D.S.M.; citation by Gen. Pershing. Mem. A.M.A., Am. Psychiat. Assn., Assn. Research in Nervous and Mental Diseases, Central Psychiat. Soc., Milw. Neuro-psychiat. Soc., Sigma Xi, Phi Alpha Sigma, Sigma Delta Chi, Alpha Omega Alpha. Republican. Mem. Christian Ch. Contbr. new remedies for treatment of syphilis of central nervous system (with Dr. A. S. Loevenhart), 1920-25. Notable work in promoting rehabilitation of disabled ex-service men; also investigations in use of carbon dioxide gas in treatment of psychoses. Col. M.C., Wis. N.G. and U.S. Res. Home: Route 2, Madison 5, Wis. Died Feb. 18, 1958; buried Forest Hill Cemetery, Madison.

LORENZEN, Ernest Gustav, educator; b. Russee-Kiel, Germany, Apr. 21, 1876; s. Joachim and Caroline (Busch) L.; came to America, 1892; Ph.B., Cornell U., 1898, LL.B., 1899; École de Droit, École Libre des Sciences Politiques, Paris; univs. of Heidelberg and Göttingen; J.U.D., maxima cum laude, Göttingen U., 1901; hon. M.A., Yale, 1917; m. Charlotte Bruck. Practiced law, N.Y.C., 1901-03; prof. law, U. Me., 1903-04; prof. law, 1904-11, dean, 1910-11, George Washington U.; prof. law, U. Wis., 1911-14, U. Minn., 1914-17, Yale U., 1917—. Mem. Am. Bar Assn., Societe de Legislation Comparée (Paris), Internat. Law Assn., Phi Beta Kappa, Delta Chi. Author: Die wesentlichen Bestandteile des gezogenen Wechsels, 1901; Cases on the Conflict of Laws, 1909, 2d edit., 1924; The Conflict of Laws Relating to Bills and Notes, 1919. Contbr. legal articles to Am. and European revs. Address: Yale Univ., New Haven, Conn. Died Feb. 12, 1952.

LORING, Augustus Peabody, Jr., trustee; b. Boston, Mass., Apr. 16, 1885; s. Augustus Peabody and Ellen (Gardner) L.; A.B., Harvard, 1908; student Harvard University Law School, 1909-11; Boston University Law Sch., 1911-12; married Rosamond Bowditch, June 22, 1911 (dec.); children—Mary (Mrs. Nathaniel Dudley Clapp), Rose (Mrs. Townsend Heard), Augustus P., 3d, Ellen Gardner (deceased), Elizabeth (Mrs. Augustus H. Fiske, Jr.), William Caleb, Jane Gray. Trustee at Boston, Massachusetts, since 1912; pres. Galveston-Houston Co.; chmn. bd. Plymouth Cordage Co.; trustee Suffolk Savings Bank for Seamen and Others, Baystate Corp.; dir. N.E. Trust Co., Fall River Gas Co., Mass. Hospital Life Ins. Co., Haverhill Gas Co., Ft. Worth Transit Co., Boston & Maine R.R. Co., Houghton Mifflin Co.; pres., dir. Loring Coolidge Service Corp. Served in Mass. Nat. Guard; Capt. Mass. State Guard. Member Massachusetts Republican State Commn., 1929-31, Beverly, Mass., Republican City Commn., 1909-30, Beverly, Mass., Bd. Aldermen, 1910-18; chmn. Beverly, Mass., Sch. Com., 1921-40. Pres., bd. trustees, Farm and Trade Sch.; trustee Boston U. Mem. council Colonial Soc. (pres.), Mass. Hist. Soc. (treas.), American Antiquarian Soc., Grange, Charitable Irish Soc. (Boston), Wine and Food Soc. (dir.). Pres., trustee Peabody Mus., Salem; dir. Essex Inst. (Salem), Bostonian Soc., Indsl. Sch. for Crippled and Deformed Children. Dir. Am. Neptune, Inc.; trustee and vice pres. Boston Atheneum. Republican. Mason, Odd Fellow, Elk. Unitarian (moderator), treas. trustee 1st Ch. in Boston). Clubs: Somerset, Odd Volumes (pres.), St. Bourtolph, Union, Cruising Club of America (Boston); Tavern; Grolier (N.Y.). Home: 573 Hale St., Beverly, Mass., and 2 Gloucester St., Boston. Office: 35 Congress St., Boston, Mass. Died Oct. 1, 1951.

LORING, Emilie (Mrs. Victor J. Loring), author; b. Boston; d. George M. and Emily Frances (Boles) Baker; student pvt. schs.; m. Victor J. Loring; children—Robert Melville, Selden Melville. Contbr. short stories and serials to mags. Author: For the Comfort of the Family, 1915; The Mother in the Home, 1917; The Trail of Conflict, 1922; Here Comes the Sun!, 1924; A Certain Crossroad, 1925; The Solitary Horseman, 1927; Gay Courage, 1928; (play) Where's Peter?, 1928; Swift Water, 1929; Lighted Windows, 1930; Fair Tomorrow, 1931; Uncharted Seas, 1932; Hilltops Clear, 1933; We Ride the Gale!, 1934; With Banners, 1934; It's a Great World!, 1935 (first two books pub. under pen name of Josephine Story); Give Me One Summer, 1936; As Long As I Live, 1937; Today Is Yours, 1938; High of Heart, 1938; Across the Years, 1939; There Is Always Love, 1940; Where Beauty Dwells, 1941; Stars in Your Eyes, 1941; Rainbow at Dusk, 1942; When Hearts Are Light Again, 1943; Keepers of the Faith, 1944; Beyond the Sound of Guns, 1945; Bright Skies, 1946; Beckoning Trails, 1947. Died Mar. 1951.‡

LORING, Ralph Alden, univ. prof.; b. Natick, Mass., June 16, 1897; s. Henry Everett and Florence Lindsay (Keith) L.; B.S., Dartmouth Coll., 1920; A.M., Harvard, 1927; Ph.D., Ohio State U., 1932; m. Louise Adele Russell, Aug. 21, 1925; children—Elizabeth Louise, David Henry, Judith Adele. Instr. in mathematics, Dartmouth Coll., 1920-22; asst. in physics, Harvard, 1922-26, instr., 1926-27; instr. in physics, Northwestern U., 1927-31; hon. research fellow in physics, Ohio State U., 1932-34; asst. prof., U. of Louisville, 1934-37, asso. prof. physics, 1937-43, prof. since 1943, head of dept. physics since 1934; research with AEC, Oak Ridge, Tenn., 1952. Mem. Am. Phys. Soc., A.A.A.S., Am. Assn. Physics Tchrs., Phi Beta Kappa, Sigma Xi. Contbr. articles on spectroscopy to physical jours. Home: 1212 Wolfe Av., Louisville 13. Died Dec. 31, 1952; buried Hingham, Mass.

LOTSPEICH, Roy Nicholas (lots-peech); s. William Alexander and Alice (Susong) L.; ed. pub. schs. and Carson Newman Coll.; m. Ethel Moore; 1 daughter, Ethel (Mrs. Charles H. Smith, Jr.). Founder Appalachian Mills Co., Knoxville, pres. and treas. until 1938; pres. and pub. Knoxville Journal; pres. and treas. Lotspeich Realty Co. Mem. Am. Newspaper Pubs. Assn., Southern Newspaper Pubs. Assn., Nat. Assn. Mfrs. (dir. 1934-35), Am. Cotton Mfrs. Assn., Am. Cotton Textile Inst., Am. Knit Goods Mfrs. Assn., Tenn. Mfrs. Assn., U.S. C. of C. Episcopalian. Clubs: Cherokee Country, Holston Hills Country (Knoxville); Everglades (Palm Beach, Fla.). Home: 3150 Kingston Road. Office: 614-620 S. Gay St., Knoxville, Tenn. Died Sept. 8, 1951; buried Highland Meml. Cemetery, Knoxville, Tenn.

LOTT, Charles H., hotel exec.; b. Thornville, O., Jan. 28, 1876; s. George W. and Lorena J. (Martin) L.; student Ohio State U.; m. Anna B. Branson, Mar. 7, 1931. Pres., treas. Lott Hotels, Inc., 1909-27; treas., gen. mgr. Detroit Leland Hotel, 1931—; pres. Indian Village Manor, 1949—. Address: Detroit Leland Hotel, Cass and Bagley Avs., Detroit 26. Deceased.*

LOTZ, Oscar, physician; b. Milwaukee, Wis., June 23, 1880; s. Louis and Frya (Dorestan) L.; spl. course in biology, U. of Pa., 1902, M.D., 1905; m. Gertrude Knowlton, Apr. 18, 1918; children—Margaret, Barbara. Practiced at Milwaukee, 1907; mem. State Board of Med. Examiners, 1918-24 (pres. 1922); chmn. com. on health Milwaukee County Council of Defense, 1918; Medical Advisory Board, Selective Service, 1917-18; mem. State Bd. Nursing Edn., 1925-33; cons. Milwaukee Children's Hosp., Maple Crest Sanatorium, Whitelaw; mem. staff Columbia Hospital; exec. sec. Wis. Anti-Tuberculosis Assn. Pres. Miss. Valley Tuberculosis Conf., 1948-49. Fellow A.M.A., Am. College Physicians; diplomate Am. Board Internal Medicine; mem. Wis. State Med. Soc. (1st v.p. 1918), Milwaukee County Med. Soc., Milwaukee Acad. Medicine (pres. 1924), Nat. Tuberculosis Assn., Am. Trudeau Society, Phi Alpha Sigma. Club: University. Home: 2320 East Newton Av., Shorewood 11. Office: 1018 N. Jefferson St., Milw. 2. Died Jan. 15, 1953.

LOUCKS, William Dewey, lawyer, corp. ofcl.; b. Albany, N.Y., Sept. 25, 1879; s. William and Mary De Ette (Brimmer) L.; A.B, Union Coll., Schenectady, N.Y., 1900; m. Jane A. Myers, Apr. 25, 1917; 1 son, William Dewey. Admitted to N.Y. Bar, 1902; mem. Loucks, Cullen & Loucks, 1929—; dir. Aeolian Am. Piano Corp., Roosevelt Field, Inc., Pittston Co., Clinchfield Coal Co. Presbyn. Mason. Clubs: Metropolitan, Bankers (N.Y.C.); American Yacht (Rye, N.Y.). Home: Park Lane Hotel, N.Y.C.; (summer) Scarsdale, N.Y. Office: 230 Park Av., N.Y.C. Died Sept. 1957.

LOUDERBACK, George Davis (loud'ẽr-băk), geologist; b. San Francisco, Apr. 6, 1874; s. Davis and Frances Caroline (Smith) L.; A.B., U. Cal., 1896, Ph.D., 1899, LL.D., 1946; m. Clara Augusta Henry, Oct. 3, 1899. Asst. in mineralogy U. Cal., 1897-1900; prof. geology and mineralogy U. Nev., 1900-06; research asst. Carnegie Inst., 1903-05; asst. prof. geology, U. Cal., 1906-07, asso. prof., 1907-17, prof., 1917-44, prof. emeritus, 1944—, dean College Letters and Science, 1920-22, 30-39, faculty research lectr., 1940. In charge geol. expdn. interior of China for Standard Oil Company of N.Y., later for Chinese Govt., 1914-16. Chmn. com. on geology and mineral resources State Council Defense, 1917-19; in charge coöp. war mineral investigation in Cal., for U.S. Geol. Survey, U.S. Bur. Mines and State Council Defense, 1918-19; mem. Pacific Coast sub-com. geology of NRC, 1917-19. Mem. Cal. Commn. on St. Francis Dam Failure, 1928, other state cons. bds. on safety of dams, 1929—. Fellow A.A.A.S., Geol. Soc. Am. (ex-sec. Cordilleran sect., chmn. 1919-22; v.p. 1936); mem. Seismol. Soc. Am. (sec. 1907-10, pres. 1914, 29-35), Am. Inst. Mining and Metall. Engrs., Cal. Acad. Sciences, Washington Acad. Sciences, Am. Geog. Soc., Mineral. Soc. Am., Soc. Econ. Geologists (v.p. 1939), Am. Petroleum Geologists, Am. Geophysical union, Am. Soc. Oceanography and Limnology, Phi Kappa Sigma, Theta Tau (nat. pres. 1919-25), Phi Beta Kappa, Sigma Xi, Phi Lambda Upsilon, Tau Beta Pi. Clubs: Faculty (pres. 1939-46), City-Commons (pres. 1935-36) (Berkeley); Athenian-Nile (Oakland); Commonwealth, Engineers, Sierra, Bohemian (San Francisco). Contbr. on geol. and mineral topics, especially on basin range struc. and west coast stratigraphy, faultlines and earthquakes; discoverer of Benitoite and other minerals. Del. to Pacific Science Congress, Java, 1929, San Francisco, 1939. Editor Bulletin of Seismol. Soc. of America, 1935—. Home: 107 Ardmore Rd., Berkeley 7, Calif. Office: Bacon Hall, U. of California, Berkeley 4, Cal. Died Jan. 27, 1957.

LOUDON, A(lexander), sec. gen. Permanent Ct. of Arbitration; born The Hague, June 5, 1892; son of Alexander and Henriette Francoise (Eschauzier) L.; Litt.D., Union Coll., 1942; LL.D., Hope College, Tufts College, 1940, Rutgers College, Rensselear Poly. Inst., Central College, 1942, University of Leiden, U. So. Cal., 1945; m. Beatrice C. Cobb, Aug. 10, 1935; children—Henriette, Alexander. Entered Netherlands diplomatic service, 1916; served as attache at Netherlands legation, London; 2d sec., legation, Buenos Aires, and legation at Wash., D.C.; became 1st sec., legation, Madrid, 1926; became counselor in Lisbon as charge d'affairs, 1932; became E.E. and M.P., 1934; minister, Bern, Switzerland, and permanent Netherlands' rep. at League of Nations; apptd. minister to U.S., Dec. 1938, ambassador, 1942-July 1947; mem. Council of State, Dec. 1947-May 1951; apptd. sec. gen., Permanent Ct. of Arbitration, The Hague, June 1951. Mem. Omicron Delta Kappa. Address: Waalsdorper weg 72, The Hague, Netherlands. Died Feb. 4, 1953.

LOUGH, James Edwin (lō), psychologist; b. Eaton, O., June 24, 1871; s. William Henry and Ester Green (Stubbs) L.; A.B., Miami U., 1891, A.M., 1894, hon. Pd.D., 1913; A.B., Harvard, 1894, A.M., 1895, Ph.D., 1898; m. Dora Albonetta Bailey, June 27, 1900; children—Edwin Bailey, Barbara Esther, Richard Colburn, Dorothea. Teacher pub. schs, Ohio, 1891-93; instr. psychology, Radcliffe Coll., 1894-98; Wellesley, 1897-98, Harvard, 1896-98; prof. psychology, State Normal School, Oshkosh, Wis., 1898-1901; prof. exptl. psychology and method, Sch. of Edn., New York U., 1901-27; Sec. Sch. of Pedagogy, 1902-17, and of the Washington Square Collegiate Div., 1903-13, New York U. (originator, 1903, of collegiate div.), dir. Summer Sch., 1902-22, and dean of Div. for Extramural Teaching, 1908-26. Originated and organized Univ. World Cruise, actg. pres. on first cruise, 1926-27, educational dir. since 1926; pres. Am. Floating Univ. since 1932. Presbyterian. Fellow A.A.A.S., Am. Geog. Soc.; mem. Am. Psychol. Assn., Am. Philos. Soc., Am. Assn. Univ. Profs. (charter mem.), Phi Beta Kappa, Delta Kappa Epsilon (council, 1909-10, 1919), Phi Delta Kappa. Clubs: Harvard (New York); Rotary International. Author: Outline of Psychology for Teachers, 1902; Analyzing Yourself, 1916; Psychology for Teachers (with Benson, Skinner and West), 1926. Home: 2260 Pelham Av., Los Angeles 25. Died June 3, 1952.

LOUGHRAN, John T. (lôr'ĕn), judge; b. Kingston, N.Y., Feb. 23, 1889; s. Bernard and Margaret (Coffey) L.; LL.B., Fordham U., 1911; LL.D., 1925; LL.D., St. John's University, 1934, Syracuse University, 1946, Hobart and William Smith College, Siena College, 1948, Manhattan College, 1952; m. Cornelia Brodhead, June 15, 1915 (died Aug. 7, 1938); 1 son, John Brodhead. Admitted to N.Y. bar, 1911; in practice at Kingston, 1911-22, at New York, 1922-30; justice of Supreme Ct. of N.Y., 1930-34; judge New York Court of Appeals, term 1934-48, apptd. chief judge, Sept. 28, 1945, elected for full term Nov. 5, 1946. Democrat. Catholic. Clubs: Manhattan (N.Y.C.); Fort Orange (Albany). Home: 12 John St. Address: Ulster County Court House, Kingston, N.Y. Died Mar. 1953.

LOUIS, John Jeffry, advt. counsel; b. Indpls., Mar. 3, 1895; s. Lyman W. and Rosa (Hodge) L.; m. Henrietta Johnson, June 18, 1924; children—John Jeffry, Herbert Johnson, Michael William. With Needham, Louis and Brorby, Chgo., 1929-57; advt. counsel Pure Oil Co., 1957—; dir. Abbott Labs.; chmn. Ariz. Broadcasting Co., dir. State Bank & Trust Co. of Evanston, S. C. Johnson & Son (Racine, Wis.); dir. Am. Inst. Fgn. Trade, Phoenix. Trustee, Northwestern U., Deerfield (Mass.) Assn.; chmn. bd. Evanston Hosp. Served as 1st lt. World War I; chmn. selective service, World War II; pres. army council U.S. Army. Awarded Purple Heart World War I. Clubs: Glenview Country, Commercial, Old Elm, Chicago, Attic; Los Angeles Country, Phoenix Country, Paradise, Valley, Ariz. Country (Ariz.); Chevy Chase (Washington). Home: 2703 Euclid Park Pl., Evanston, Ill. Office: 135 S. LaSalle St., Chgo. 3. Died Feb. 19, 1959.

LOUNSBURY, Charles Edwin (lounz'bûr-ĭ), newspaperman; b. Denver, Colo., Apr. 5, 1898; s. George Fenner and Alice May (Williams) L.; ed. pub. schs., Denver, 1905-16; attended Colorado Coll., Colorado Springs, Colo.; m. Florence Carlson, Apr. 7, 1924; children—Jeanne Zoe, Patricia Ann. Reporter Denver News-Times, 1919-21, Denver Post, 1921-26; with Scripps-Howard Newspapers since 1926; editor Denver Rocky Mountain News, 1931-36, Register-Tribune Syndicate since 1940. Mason (32°, K.T., Shriner).

Clubs: Denver Press (pres. 1929), Des Moines. Home: 4337 Pleasant St. Office: Register-Tribune Bldg., Des Moines, Ia. Died Nov. 2, 1952.

LOUNSBURY, George Fenner, newspaper man; b. Mound City, Ill., Aug. 22, 1872; s. George Edgar and Helen (Aldrich) L.; ed. pub. schs., Denver, and under pvt. instrn.; m. Alice Williams, 1895 (dec.); 1 son, Charles Edwin; m. 2d, Ethel Wyatt, 1902 (dec.); m. 3d, Margaret Seyler, Sept. 27, 1932 (dec.). Began as reporter, Denver Republican, 1890; dramatic editor Evening Wis., 1905-08; editorial writer Milw. Sentinel, 1908-12, asso. editor, 1919-21, 30-37, editor, 1921-30, chief editorial writer, 1937—; mng. editor Milw. Daily News, 1913-14. Head Press Bur. War Finance Central Com., Milw., 1917-19; editor Wis. Freemason, 1944—. Mason (33°, K.T., Shriner; Grand Master in Wis. 1939-40). Republican. Clubs: Milwaukee Press (pres. 1911); Professional Men's (pres. 1942); Wisconsin. Home: Hotel La Salle. Office: 123 W. Michigan St., Milw. Died 1958.

LOUTHAN, Henry Thompson, Bapt. minister, educator; b. Melrose, Va., Nov. 5, 1866; s. Carter McKim and Mary Ella (Brown) L.; A.B., U. Chgo., 1909; A.M., 1912; student Richmond Coll., 1886-91, U. Va., 1893-94, So. Bapt. Theol. Sem., 1895-98; m. Elizabeth Rowland Hurt, Mar. 25, 1903; children—Mary Tyler, Carter Thomas. Instr. Coll. of William and Mary, 1903-04; adjunct prof., 1904-10; head dept. history and econs., Mercer U., 1912-14; prin. Edmund Pendleton High Sch., Va., 1914-18; instr. history, Staunton Mil. Acad., 1918-25; head dept., 1925-32. First lt., Caroline Co. Home Guard, Va., 1917-18. Mem. S.A.R., Sons Confederate Vets., Phi Beta Kappa, Sigma Phi Epsilon, Pi Gamma Mu. Mason. Author: The Congressional Career of William Cabell Rives of Va., 1911. Editor: The Am. Bapt. Pulpit, 1903. Contbr. William and Mary Coll. Quarterly, The Standard, Richmond Dispatch, The Confederate Veteran. Home: Retreat, Duane, King William County, Va. Died July 20, 1953; buried Hollywood Cemetery, Richmond, Va.

LOUTTIT, Chauncey McKinley (lout'it), psychologist; b. Buffalo, N.Y., Oct. 9, 1901; s. William Henry and Susan (Bruman) L.; B.S., Hobart Coll., Geneva, New York, 1925; Ph.D., Yale Univ., 1928; married Laura Talcott, August 23, 1926; children—Robert Irving, Richard Talcott. Research fellow, Training Sch., Vineland, N.J., 1925; instr., Yale, 1925-28; research asso., psychol. clinic, U. of Hawaii, 1928-30; asst. prof., Ohio U., 1930-31; asst. prof. psychology, Indiana University, 1931-38, asso. prof., 1938-40; director psychological clinic, 1931-40; with United States Naval Medical School, 1940-41; asst. chief of psychology div., Office of Coordinator of Information, 1941-42; asst. officer in charge, quality control section, training div., Bureau of Naval Personnel, 1942-44; comdg. officer Naval Training Sch. (indoctrination), Camp Macdonough, Plattsburgh, N.Y., Feb.-Oct., 1944; comdg. officer, service sch. command, Naval Training Center, Bainbridge, Md., 1944-45; prof. psychology, Ohio State University, 1945-46; dean of faculty, Sampson College, 1946-47; exec. dean, Galesburg Undergrad. Div., U. of Illinois, 1947-49, assistant to the provost 1949-54. Visiting professor University of Oregon, summer of 1937, Ohio State U., 1939; professor chairman department psychology, Wayne U., 1954—. Mem. Ind. Society Mental Hygiene (bd. dirs., 1939-41; pres. 1941), Ind. State Conf. Social Work (bd. dirs., also exec. com., 1937-40). Fellow A.A.A.S., Am. Psychol. Assn. (mem. council, 1943-46); mem. Am. Assn. for Applied Psychology (exec. sec., 1940-42; pres., 1943; chmn. mil. psychology sect.), Phi Beta Kappa, Sigma Xi, Lambda Pi. Author: Bibliography of Bibliographies in Psychology, 1900-1927, 1928; Handbook of Psychological Literature, 1933; Clinical Psychology, 1936, rev. edit., 1947. Editor: Directory of Applied Psychology, 1st edit., 1941, 2d edit., 1943; Psychological Abstracts, 1947; Professional Problems (with R. S. Daniel), 1953. Address: 631 W. Oakridge, Ferndale, Mich. Died May 24, 1956.

LOVE, Charles Everts, bus. exec.; b. Burdett, N. Y., Jan. 20, 1910; s. David and Winifred (Chase) L.; A.B., Hobart Coll., 1932; m. Louise Cornman, Aug. 12, 1934; children—Charles Everts, David Farnsworth. Student salesman to v.p. charge sales, Bus. Machines Corp., 1932-50; exec. v.p., dir. Comml. Controls Corp., Rochester, N.Y., 1950—; dir. Comml. Controls Can., Ltd., Toronto. Trustee Hobart and William Smith Coll., 1950—. Served as lt., U.S.N.R., 1944-46. Mem. Nat. Sales Execs. (treas., dir.), Office Equipment Mfrs. Inst., Rochester C. of C., Newcomen Soc. England. Presbyn. Clubs: Rochester; Sales Execs. (dir.), Genesee Valley (Rochester). Home: 1180 Clover St., Rochester 10. Office: 1 Leighton Av., Rochester 2, N.Y. Died Sept. 27, 1955; buried Glenwood Cemetery, Watkins Glen, N.Y.

LOVE, James Lee, educator, textile mfr.; b. Gastonia County, N.C., Dec. 30, 1860; s. Robert Calvin Grier and Susan Elizabeth (Rhyne) L.; Ph.B., U. N.C., 1884; student Johns Hopkins, 1884-85; A.M., Harvard, 1890; m. June James Spencer, Dec. 23, 1885 (died 1920); children—Cornelia Spencer, James Spencer; m. 2d, Mary Elizabeth Satterfield, Aug. 22, 1923; children—Mary Elizabeth (Mrs. Charles Orth), Jean Lee (Mrs. John Albert). Instr. in English and history U. N.C., 1883-84, asso. prof. mathematics, 1885-89, sec. of faculty, 1885-89, librarian, 1887-89; Morgan fellow, Harvard, 1889-90; instr. mathematics Lawrence Sci. Sch, Harvard and Annex (now Radcliffe Coll.), 1890-1901, asst. prof., 1901-11, mem. adminstrv. bd. Lawrence Sci. Sch., 1895-1907, sec. and exec. officer, 1900-07, acting dean, 1904, 1906-07, head mathematics Lawrence Sci. Sch. and Summer Sch., 1891-1909; mem. and sec. of faculty on summer courses in arts and scis., Harvard, 1900-06, chmn., 1906-09; dir. Summer Sch. Arts and Scis., 1900-09; sabbatical leave, 1909-11; sec. and treas. Saxony Spinning Co., Lincolnton, N.C., 1909-10; asst. to dir. summer session, Columbia, 1910-11; dir. Provident Teachers Agency, Boston, 1911-18; pres. Gastonia Cotton Mfg. Co., 1919-23; sec.-treas. Southern Dyeing Co., 1925-27, pres. and mgr., 1927-33; dir. Burlington Mills Corp., 1933—. Served as sergt., Mass. State Guard, 1917-19. Mem. A.A.A.S., Am. Math. Soc., S.A.R., Beta Theta Pi, Phi Beta Kappa. Liberal Democrat. Presbyn. Mason. Clubs: Kiwanis, Mathematics and physics (Harvard U. and Mass. Inst. Tech.). Author: Outlines of Plane Trigonometry, 1894; Differential and Integral Calculus, 1899; 'Tis Sixty Years Since, A Story of the University of North Carolina in 1880's; R. C. G. Love, A Builder of the New South, 1949; (booklets) Reprinted of a Harvard Report, 1944, The Lawrence Scientific School in Harvard University, 1944. Home: 610 Fountain Pl., Burlington, N.C. Died May 6, 1950.

LOVE, John W(illis), newspaperman; b. Shelby, O., Dec. 18, 1892; s. Matthew T. (M.D.) and Luella (Bloom) L.; A.B., Oberlin (O.) Coll., 1914; m. Margaret McRoberts, 1924; children—Janet (dec.), Robert, Duncan. Editor Shelby Citizen, 1914; with The A. I. Root Co., Medina, O., 1915; reporter Cleveland (O.) Plain Dealer, 1916-20, business column writer, 1922-30; editor survey of criminal justice for Cleveland Foundation, 1921; column writer, Cleveland Press, since 1931. Seminar instr. in history, Mather Coll., Western Reserve U., 1937-39; advisor, Com. on Pub. Debt Policy; industrial development committee, Ohio C. of C. since 1946. Served as second lieut. infantry, 137th Depot Brigade, U.S. Army, Camp McClellan, Ala., 1918. Trustee, Oberlin (O.) College. Member American Legion, American Statis. Assn., Econ. History Assn., C. of C., Phi Beta Kappa, Delta Sigma Chi. Clubs: City, Mid-Day, Advertising, Row-Fant; National Press (Washington). Scripps-Howard writer and magazine contbr. on business and econ. subjects. Home: 12425 Fair Hill Rd. Office: Cleveland Press, Cleve. Died Sept. 21, 1958.

LOVE, Thomas J., educator, clergyman; b. Phila., Apr. 18, 1891; s. Thomas and Sarah Regina (Porter) L.; A.B., Woodstock (Md.) Coll., 1916, M.A., 1919; Ph.D., Gregorian U., Rome, Italy, 1939; LL. D. Villanova Coll., 1943. Prof. physics Loyola Coll., Balt., 1916-18; prof. physics, radio and aeros. Georgetown U., 1918-20; prof. physics Canisis Coll., Buffalo, N.Y., 1924-26; head dept. physics Loyola Coll., 1927-38, dept. mathematics, 1931-38; head dept. physics Georgetown U., 1938-39, 1944-53; pres. St. Joseph's Coll., Phila., 1939-44; rector and superior Old St. Joseph's Ch., Phila., 1953—. Mem. Assn. Coll. Pres.' Pa., Am. Acad. Polit. and Social Scis., Am. Assn. Jesuit Scientists, Alpha Sigma Nu. Roman Catholic. Home: Old St. Joseph's Church, Phila. Died Jan. 2, 1955*

LOVELAND, Gilbert, book editor; b. Hamburg, Ia., Aug. 22, 1892; s. Frank and Madge Agnes (Burkholder) L.; B.A., Northwestern U., 1914, M.A., 1915; m. Marjorie Ella Grantham, June 20, 1917; children—Hugh Frank, Joan deGrau, Mary Grantham. Mem. commn. on finance, M.E. Church, 1915; sec. to chief, Bd. Fgn. Missions, M.E. Ch., 1916-17; supt. missionary edn., Bd. S.S., M.E. Ch., 1918-23; took orders during this period, resigned same, 1924. Sec. Great Basin Oil Co., 1923-27; with Henry Holt & Co. since 1927; editor religious books, 1927-33, mgr. sch. div. since 1934, gen. editor, 1942-45; sec., 1932-41; v.p. 1936-53; editor Am. Book Co., 1954—. Mem. Phi Beta Kappa. Democrat. Conglist. Publications: Training World Christians, 1912; also articles. Home: 4 E. 10th St., N.Y. City 3. Office: 55 Fifth Av., N.Y.C. 3. Died Apr. 27, 1956.

LOVEMAN, Amy, editor; b. New York City, May 16, 1881; d. Adolph and Adassa (Heilprin) Loveman; student Horace Mann Sch.; A.B., Barnard Coll., 1901; Litt.D., Wheaton Coll., 1950, Wilson College, 1950; unmarried. Began as book reviewer, 1914; asso. editor, N.Y. Evening Post Lit. Review, 1920-24; asso. editor, Saturday Review of Lit., 1924— (sec. and dir.); head editorial dept. Book-of-the-Month Club, 1938-51; member of the board of judges, 1951—. Member of Phi Beta Kappa. Author: I'm Looking for a Book, 1936. Co-author: Saturday papers, 1921; Designed for Reading, 1934. Judge M.G.M. Annual Novel Award, 1944, 45, 46; cons., 1947-48. Awarded Columbia U. medal for excellence, 1945; Constance Lindsay Skinner Achievement Award of Women's Nat. Book Assn., 1946. Home: 210 E. 73rd St. Office: 25 W. 45th St., N.Y.C. Died Dec. 11, 1955; buried Fairmount Cemetery, Chatham, N.J.

LOVERIDGE, Earl W(inchester), forester; b. Oil City, Pa., Nov. 25, 1890; s. Melvin E. and Mina (Ellis) L.; B.S., Pa. State Coll., 1912; m. Mildred St. Louis, Dec. 1, 1916; 1 son, Melvin Earl. Tech. asst., forest ranger and various supervisory positions, U.S. Forest Service, Fla. and Ark., 1913, Ariz. and N.M., 1914-26, Washington, 1927-33; asst. chief, 1934-54; department of state attaché, Bogota, Columbia, 1955-57; forestry cons. to Govt. of Yugoslavia, 1958—; head dept. public adminstrn. Grad. School, Dept. of Agr.; adv. Puerto Rico on reorganization of forests, 1951; Venezuela, 1952. Received the United States Department of Agriculture Distinguished Service award, 1951. Mem. Soc. Am. Foresters, Soc. Pub. Adminstrn., Orgn. of Profl. Employees (U.S. Dept. of Agr.). Author: Job-Load Analysis and Planning of Executive Work in Nat. Forest Adminstrn., 1922; co-author: Washington-Field Relationships in Fed. Service, 1942. Contbr. articles to Jour. of Forestry. Author forestry plans, natural resources program for various govts., survey reports on major forest regions of U.S. Home: 6101 16th St., Washington 11. Died May 26, 1959.

LOVETT, Edgar Odell, educator; born at Shreve, O., Apr. 14, 1871; s. Z. and M. E. (Spreng) L.; A.B., Bethany (W.Va.) Coll., 1890; M.A., Ph.D., U. of Va., 1895; Ph.D., Univ. of Leipzig, 1896; LL.D., Drake U., 1898; Tulane Univ., 1911, Baylor U., 1920, Bethany Coll., 1934; Princeton, 1954; Sc.D., Colorado College, 1927; m. Mary Ellen Hale, 1897; children—Adelaide (Mrs. W. Browne Baker), Henry Malcolm, Ellen Kennedy (dec.), Laurence Alexander. Prof. mathematics, West Ky. Coll., 1890-92; instr. astronomy, U. of Va., 1892-95; stud. Leipzig and Christiania, 1895-96; fellow by courtesy, Johns Hopkins, 1897; lecturer mathematics, univs. of Va. and Chicago, 1897; instr. mathematics, 1897, asst. prof., 1898-1900, prof., 1900-05, prof. astronomy, 1905-08, Princeton; first president Rice Institute, Houston, Texas, 1908-46, president emeritus since 1946. Decorated Officier Legion d'Honneur (France), 1938. Member American Philos. Society, Am. Astron. Soc., Belgian-Am. Ednl. Foundation; Fellow R.A.S., A.A.A.S. (v.p. sect. A, Baltimore meeting, 1908); mem. Am. (sometime mem. council and asso. editor Bulletin), France and London, math. socs., Phi Beta Kappa, Sigma Xi, Beta Theta Pi. Contbr. on geometry, mechanics and math. astronomy to various Am. and foreign jours. Address: P.O. Box 1892, Houston 1, Died Aug. 13, 1957; buried Greenwood Cemetery, Houston.

LOVETT, Robert Morss, teacher, editor; b. Boston, Mass., Dec. 25, 1870; s. Augustus S. and Elizabeth (Russell) L.; A.B., Harvard, 1892; m. Ida Mott-Smith, June 4, 1895; children—Robert Morss (killed in Belleau Wood, France), Beatrice Russell, Ruth. Asst. in English, Harvard, 1892, instr., 1893; instr. rhetoric, U. of Chicago, 1893, asst. prof. English, 1896-1904, asso. prof., 1904-09, prof., 1909-36, dean in junior colls., 1903-07, dean of junior colleges, 1907-20. Govt. secretary Virgin Islands, 1939-43. Vis. prof. of Eng., Univ. of Puerto Rico, Rio Piedras P.R. 1944. Mem. National Inst. Arts and Letters. Clubs: University, Tavern (Chicago); Harvard (New York). Author: A History of English Literature (with W. V. Moody), 1902; Richard Gresham (novel), 1904; A First View of English Literature (with W. V. Moody), 1905; A Winged Victory (novel), 1907; Cowards (play), prod. Fine Arts Theatre, Chicago, 1914, pub. in "Drama," Aug. 1917; Edith Wharton (criticism), 1925; Preface to Fiction, 1930; History of the Novel in England (with Helen Sard Hughes), 1932. Compiler: (anthology) British Poetry and Prose (with R. K. Root and Paul R. Lieder), 1928; Selected Poems of William Vaughn Moody, 1930; A College Reader (with Howard Mumford Jones), 1937; All Our Years (autobiography), 1948. Editor of The Dial, 1919; editorial bd. The New Republic, 1922-30. Home: 800 S. Halsted St., Chgo. Died Feb. 8, 1956.

LOW, Abraham Adolph, physician, psychiatrist; b. Baranow, Poland, Feb. 28, 1891; s. Lazar and Blossom (Wahl) L.; student U. Strasbourg, 1910-13; M.D., U. Vienna, 1919; m. Mae Willett, June 18, 1925; children—Phyllis Kay, Marilyn Carroll. Came to U.S., 1921, naturalized, 1927. Intern Allgemeines Krankenhaus, Vienna, Austria, 1919-20; practice medicine, N.Y.C., 1921-23, Chgo., 1923-25, neurology, 1925-30, psychiatry, 1931—; instr. neurology, med. sch. U. Ill., 1925-31, asst. prof. psychiatry, 1931-40 asst. dir. psychiat. inst., 1931-40, asso. prof. psychiatry, 1940, acting dir. psychiat. inst., 1940-41; asst. state alienist Ill., 1933-41; founder, med. dir. Recovery, Inc., 1937—. Served with M.C., Austrian Army, 1914-18. Fellow A.M.A., Am. Psychiat. Assn.; mem. Ill. Psychiat. Soc., Chgo. Neurol. Soc., Central Neuropsychiat. Assn., Am. Group Psychotherapy Assn. Author: Studies in Infant Speech and Thought, 1936; Techniques of Self-Help in Psychiatric After-Care (3 vols.), 1943; Mental Health Through Will-Training, 1950. Contbr. articles profl. publs. Home: 215 Davis St., Evanston, Ill. Office: 30 N.

Michigan Av., Chgo. 2. Died Nov. 17, 1954; buried Memorial Park Cemetery, Evanston.

LOW, Mrs. Marie Dickson, mem. Dem. Nat. Com. Address: 1748 Parkham Rd., Warren, O. Died Apr. 26, 1953. Buried Mt. Calvery Cemetery, Stelibenville, O.*

LOWDEN, Isabel (lou'dĕn), pres. Music Edn. League; b. Point Pleasant, Ia.; d. Lorenzo Orren and Nancy Elizabeth (Breg) Lowden; A.M., Stuttgart Coll., Ark.; student Oberlin Conservatory of Music, 1 year, and Florence Adams Sch. of Expression, Chgo., 1 yr. Taught music in Little Rock, Ark., 5 years, also soloist Episcopal Cathedral; owned school of expression, Omaha, Neb., 5 years; music critic Chicago Daily News, 1913-14; dir. speakers' bur. N.Y. chpt. A.R.C., during World War I; founded Music Edn. League, New York, 1923, since served as pres. and dir. (League is devoted to ednl. work, 500,000 children participating in benefits); founder Tempo (mag. sponsored by Music Edn. League), 1934, editor, 1934—. Has written and produced benefit pageants, New York: Memorial Festival in honor of those who have died in the cause of Freedom, produced in 1919, 20, 21; The Spirit of Service, for the Red Cross Roll Call, 1920; America, for the first Victory Ball, 1921; A Norse Romance, in which Sonja Henie made her American debut as a skater at Madison Square Garden, 1930, for the benefit of the Music Edn. League. Episcopalian. Home: 157 W. 57th St. Office: 119 W. 57th St., N.Y.C. 19. Died Nov. 5, 1957; buried Iowa Falls, Ia.

LOWE, John Smith, ret. clergyman; b. Watertown, N.Y., 1878; s. Leonard S. and Mary M. (Kimball) L.; St. Lawrence U., Canton, N.Y., 1898-1903, grad. Canton Sch. of Theology, 1903; D.D., Lombard Coll., Galesburg, Ill.; m. Adelaide E. Bouck, July 1, 1903; 1 son, John Smith 2d. Ordained to ministry Universalist Ch., 1901; pastor LaCrosse, Wis., 1903-10, Ch. of the Mediator, Providence, R.I., 1910-17. Elected gen. supt. Universalist Chs. of America, 1917; minister 2d Ch. of the Redemption, Boston, 1928-34, Ch. of Immanuel, Rockland, Me., 1934-53; summer minister Round Pond, 25 yrs. Chaplain CAC, U.S. Army, 1910-17. Mason. Rotarian (past pres.). Address: Rockland, Me. Died Mar. 23, 1954; buried Achorn Cemetery.

LOWE, Titus, bishop; b. Bilston Eng., Dec. 17, 1877; s. William Henry and Anna (Scribbins) L.; came to U.S., 1892; B.A., Ohio Wesleyan U., 1900, M.A., 1908; Western Theol. Sem., Allegheny, Pa., 1900-02; D.D., Neb. Wesleyan U., 1916, Ohio Wesleyan U., 1920; LL.D., Neb. Wesleyan U., 1926; L.H.D., Coll. of Puget Sound, 1931; m. Anna Bessie Creed, Oct. 18, 1901 (died Apr. 4, 1911); children —Madelyn, Evelyn, Titus (dec.); m. 2d, Edith Eglantine Egloff, Jan. 6, 1913; 1 dau., Anna Jane. Ordained M.E. ministry, 1900; pastor Fourth St. Ch., Braddock, Pa., 1900-03, Thoburn Ch., Calcutta, India, 1903-08, South Fork, Pa., 1908-09, First Ch., Cedar Falls, Ia., 1909-13, First Ch., Omaha, Neb., 1913-21; corr. sec. Bd. Foreign Missions, 1921; elected bishop, May 22, 1924; assigned to Singapore area of M.E. Ch., 1924-28, to Portland (Ore.) area, 1928-39; bishop Meth. Ch., Indianapolis, since 1939. Pres. Indianapolis Meth. Hosp., 1942, pres., gen. commn. on World Service and Finance, 1944; pres. com. on Interdenominational Relations, 1944; pres. of Council of Bishops, 1946-47. Lecturer under Internat. Com. Y.M.C.A., in France, 6 mos., 1917-18. Mem. Gen. Conf., M.E. Ch., 1916, 20, 24. Mem. Sigma Chi. Mason (33°, hon. K.T.). Office: Underwriters Bldg., Indianapolis 4, Ind. Died Nov. 27, 1959.

LOWELL, Orson, painter, cartonnist, illustrator; b. at Wyoming, Ia., Dec. 22, 1871; s. Milton Horace and Frances M. (Kinney) L.; grad. Chicago Schools, 1887; studied art at Chicago Art Inst., 1887-93; m. Jessica M. Hawley, Oct. 20, 1898. In New York since 1893; illustrated many books, much mag. text and has done covers for many periodicals, also advertising drawings and posters; social cartoonist for Life, 1907-15, for Judge, 1915-23; with Erickson Advt. Agency, 1921-29; cartoonist George Matthew Adams Service, 1937-38; on staff The American Girl, 1935-45; cartoonist The Churchman, 1943-46. Member Guild Free Lance Artists (pres. 1924-25), Soc. of Illustrators (life mem.), Authors' League Am., Iowa Press and Authors' Club, New Rochelle Art Assn. (life.). Trustee New Rochelle Public Library, 1930-44. Club: Dutch Treat (N.Y.). Home and Studio: Rochelle Park, New Rochelle, N.Y. Died Feb. 1956.

LOWEN, Charles Jules, Jr., govt. ofcl.; b. Denver, June 15, 1915; s. Charles J. and Bernice T. (Duffy) L.; student U. Colo., 1934-38; m. Helen Muriel Stokes; children—Carol M., Barbara E., Charles S., Ellen C. Propr. base operation for chartering and selling of aircraft, 1938-42; dir. overseas, asst. dir. domestic operations, Capital Airlines, 1946-48; dir. aviation City and County of Denver, 1948-51, mgr. safety and excise, 1954; dealer automobiles, Lowen-Thomson-Brown, Denver, 1951-54; dep. adminstr. CAA, 1955, adminstr., 1955—. Served as maj. USAAF, 1942-45; exec. officer Air Transport Command Group. Mem. Am. Legion, Vets. Fgn. Wars, Chi Psi. Clubs: Denver, Denver Country, Denver Athletic, Mile Hi, Cactus, Press (Denver); Nat. Aviation (Washington). Home: 2630 E. Cedar Av., Denver; also 4801 Dexter Terrace, Washington. Office: Civil Aero. Adminstrn., 16th and Constitution Av., Washington 24. Died Sept. 5, 1956; buried Mt. Olivet Cemetery, Denver.

LOWENSTINE Mandel, mfg. exec.; b. Chgo., 1882. Chmn. and pres. Central Steel & Wire Co., Chgo. Mason, Elk. Home: 1000 Lake Shore Dr., Chgo. 11. Office: 3000 W. 51st St., Chgo. 80. Died May, 1957.*

LOWIE, Robert Harry (lō' ē), ethnologist; b. Vienna, Austria, June 12, 1883; s. Samuel and Ernestine (Kuhn) L.; brought to U.S. at age of 10; A.B., Coll. City N.Y., 1901 (Phi Beta Kappa); Ph.D., Columbia U., 1908; Sc.D., U. Chgo., 1941; m. Luella W. Cole, Aug. 23, 1933. Asst. dept. anthropology Am. Mus. Natural History, 1908-09, asst. curator, 1909-13, asso. curator, 1913-21; lectr. Columbia U., 1920-21; asso. prof. anthropology U. Cal., 1917-18, 21-25, prof., 1925-50; vis. prof. Yale, 1937; faculty research lectr. U. Cal., 1949; anthrop. expdns. to No. Plains Indians, 1906-14, 16, 31, Lake Athabaska, 1908, plateau tribes, 1914-15, Hopi, 1915, 16. Viking Fund medalist, 1947; Thomas H. Huxley Meml. lectr. and medalist, 1948. Fellow Am. Ethnol. Soc. (sec. 1910-20; pres. 1920-21), Royal Anthrop Inst. (hon.); mem. Nat. Research Council (chmn. div. anthropology and psychology 1931-32), Nat. Acad. Scis., Am. Philos. Soc., Am. Anthrop. Assn. (pres. 1935), Am. Folk-Lore Soc. (pres. 1916-17), German Ethnol. Soc. (hon.), Bavarian Acad. Scis. (corr. mem.), Société des Americanistes de Paris (corr. mem.), Phi Beta Kappa, Sigma Xi. Author: The Assiniboine, 1909; Social Life of the Crow Indians, 1912; Societies of the Crow, Hidatsa and Mandan Indians, 1913; The Sun Dance of the Crow Indians, 1915; The Age-Societies of the Plains Indians, 1916; Culture and Ethnology, 1917; Myths and traditions of the Crow Indians, 1918; Primitive Society (French, Chinese, and Japanese trans.), 1920; Primitive Religion, 1924; The Origin of the State, 1927; Are We Civilized?, 1929; Intro. to Cultural Anthropology (French trans.), 1934, 40; The Crow Indians, 1935; The History of Ethnological Theory, 1937 (Spanish translation); The German People, 1945; Social Organization, 1948; Toward Understanding Germany, 1954; Indians of the Plains, 1954; A Practical Handbook for Planning a Trip to Europe (with Luella Cole), 1957; Robert H. Lowie, Ethnologist (Autobiography); Crow Texts; Dictionary of the Crow Language; Lowie's Selected Papers. Club: Faculy (Berkeley). Home: 2521 Benvenue Av., Berkeley, Cal. Died Sept. 21, 1957; buried Berkeley.

LOWREY, Lawson Gentry, psychiatrist; b. Centralia, Mo., Dec. 23, 1890; s. Ernest (M.D.) and Eupha Orme (Sappington) L.; student Bethany Coll., Lindsborg, Kan., 1905-07; A.B., U. of Mo., 1909, A.M., 1910; M.D. cum laude, Harvard University, 1915. Pathologist at the Danvers State Hospital, 1914-17; 1st asst. physician and chief med. officer, Boston Psychopathic Hosp., 1917-20; asst. dir. Psychopathic Hosp., U. of Ia., 1920-23; dir. demonstration child guidance clinic (in Dallas, Mpls., St. Paul, Cleve.), Nat. Com. for Mental Hygiene, 1923-27; dir. Inst. for Child Guidance, N.Y., 1927-33; attending physician N.Y. Neurol. Inst., 1932-37; psychiatrist, pediatric dept. New Rochelle (N.Y.) Gen. Hosp., 1933—; cons. in psychiatry Grasslands Hosp., 1930-44; psychiatrist Clinic for Gifted Childrens, N.Y.U., 1933-35, Bklyn. Hebrew Orphan Asylum, 1937-44; dir. Mental Hygiene Research Unit, Vocational Adjustment Bur., 1937-39; psychiatrist Traveler's Aid Soc., 1938-42; dir. Bklyn. Child Guidance Centre, 1940-45; asso. attending psychiatrist Vanderbilt Clinic, 1945—; asst. in anatomy U. Mo., 1909-10, asst. prof. anatomy, 1911-12; 1909-10; prof. anatomy and histology U. Utah, 1910-11; teaching fellow in histology and embryology Harvard, 1912-14, James Jackson Cabot research fellow neuropathology, 1915-16, fellow neuropathology, 1916-18, instr. in neuropathology, 1918-20, in psychiatry, 1918-20, in psychology, 1919-20; asst. and asso. prof. U. Ia., 1920-23; lectr. So. Meth. U., 1923; lecturer in psychiatry, U. Minn. Med. Sch., 1923-24, Smith Coll. Sch. of Social Work, 1926-36, N.Y. Sch. of Social Work, 1930-36; N.Y.U. Sch. Edn., 1933-35, Hunter College, 1937; asst. clin. prof. psychiatry Columbia Coll. Phys. and Surg., 1945—. Mem. White House Conf. on Child Health and Protection, 1930; mem. program com. Internat. Congress on Mental Hygiene, 1930; exec. com. Internat. Com. Mental Hygiene, 1947—; mem. China Aid Council, 1943—; cons. many orgns.; qualified psychiatrist in the State of N.Y. Mem. Assn. of Anatomists, Assn. Pathologists and Bacteriologists, N.Y. State Med. Assn., A.M.A., Am. Psychiatric Assn. (chmn. program com. 1928-31), A.A.A.S., Boston Soc. Neurology and Psychiatry, N.E. Psychiatric Soc., N.Y. Neurol. Soc., N.Y. Acad. Medicine, N.Y. Acad. Sciences, Acad. Polit. and Social Science, Am. Orthopsychiatric Assn. (pres. 1928-30, editor, 1930-48, N.Y. City Com. for Mental Hygiene (chmn. 1930-35), Am. Psychopathol. Assn., N.Y. Psychiatric Soc., Westchester County Mental Hygiene Assn. (pres. 1946), Sigma Xi, Alpha Omega Alpha, Pi Kappa Alpha, Phi Beta Pi (supreme officer, 1918—, moderator, 1931—). Independent Democrat. Mason (32°). Author: Report of Kindergarten Project, 1937-39; Psychiatry for Social Workers, 1946. Editor: Monograph Series of American Orthopsychiatric Assn.; Institute for Child Guidance Studies. Editor of Am. Jour. Orthopsychiatry, 1930-48. Office: 25 W. 54th St., N.Y.C. 19. Died Aug. 1957.

LOWRY, D.R., pres., dir. Ingersoll-Rand Co., Canadian Ingersoll-Rand Co., Ltd.; dir. Corn Exchange Bank Trust Co. Address: 11 Broadway, N.Y. C. 4. Died Aug. 9, 1955.

LOWRY, Frank J(acob) (lou'rĭ), ret. naval officer; b. Cresco, Ia., Feb. 15, 1888; s. Jacob John and Jennie (Mullen) L.; student St. Johns Mil. Acad., Delafield, Wis., 1905-06; B.S., U.S. Naval Acad., 1911; Naval War Coll., 1925-26; m. Julia Kessel, Dec. 18, 1940. Promoted through grades to vice adm., 1950, ret.; served with task force participating in Battle of Coral Sea, Battle of Midway; comd. Moroccan Sea Frontier Forces, 1943, later the 8th Amphibious Forces at Anzio (Italy) and Toulon (France) landings; also participated in Operations Crossroads, the first test of the atom bomb at Bikini atoll. Decorated Navy Cross, D.S.M., Legion of Merit and Gold Star (U.S.); Campanion Order of the Bath, Oak Leaf (British); Legion of Honor, Croix de Guerre with Palms (French); Grand Officer, Ouissam Alaouite Cherifien (Morocco); Grand Officer, Nichan Iftikar (Tunisia). Campaign medals; Nicaraguan (1912), Mexican, Victory, American Defense, Asiatic-Pacific, European-African, American. Clubs: Army and Navy (Washington), Columbia Country (Chevy Chase, Md.). Mason (K.T.). Home: 5134 Coombsville Rd., Napa, Cal. Died Mar. 27, 1955.

LOWSLEY, Oswald Swinney (lō'slē), urol. surgeon; b. Santa Barbara, Calif., Sept. 4, 1884; s. Vincent and Willie Ann (Swinney) L.; A.B., Stanford, 1905; M.D., Johns Hopkins, 1912; grad. Bellevue Hosp., N.Y., 1915; children—Lydia Ann, David William, Martha Winifred, Oswald Swinney; married 3d, Celeste Nocito, Aug. 29, 1949; married 4th, Winifred Atherton, Jan. 17, 1953. Practiced in N.Y. City since 1915; cons. urol. surgeon to Ruptured and Crippled Peekskill, Monmouth Memorial, Nassau County and Bloomingdale hosps., also to Stamford Hosp., St. Luke's Hosp. (Newburgh, N.Y.), Jamaica Hosp., Fitkin Memorial Hosp. (Spring Lake, N.J.), Norwalk (Conn.) Hosp., Flushing Hosp., St. Agnes Hosp. (White Plains, N.Y.) Englewood (N.J.) Hosp., Nat. Jewish Hosp. (Denver, Colo.), Kings Hosp. (Bay Shore, L.I.). St. Clare's Hosp., N.Y. Hosp. (N.Y.C.), Jersey City Med. Center; pres., dir. Oswald Swinney Lowsley Found. urology; a pioneer in surgery of genito-urinary organs under local and regional anesthesia. First director of the dept. urology, James Buchanan Brady Foundation of N.Y. Hosp. and St. Clare's Hospital. Served as private California N.G., 1905-07, 2d lt., 1907-08; lt. s.g. U.S. Navy, 1917-18; hon. consultant to Med. Corps, U.S. Navy, since 1942. Diplomate Am. Bd. Urology. Fellow A.C.S., Internat. Coll. Surgeon, New York Academy Medicine; mem. A.M.A., Am. Urological Assn. (pres. 1941-42), International Urol. Assn., Barcelona Urol. Society, New York State, New York County, Costa Rican, Mexican, Venzuelan, Uruguayan medical societies, Osler Soc. N.Y., Soc. Alumni of Bellevue Hosp. (treas. 1919-36, v.p. 1937, pres. 1938), Societa de Obstetrica, Ginecologie et Urologie (Rumania); corr. mem. Deutsche Gesellschaft für Urologie Assn. Française d'Urologie, Magyar Urolgiai Tarsasag Türk Urologi Cemiyet, Royal Soc. of Medicine of Great Britian, Sociatá Italiana di Urologia, Societá Piamontese di Chirurgia, Internat. Soc. of Urology, Venezuela Urol. Assn.; hon. urologist Mil. Hosp., Guatemala; Socio Honorario, La Assiaciòn Medica Hondurana; Socio Honorario, La Juventud Medica de Guatemala; hon. prof. U. of Haiti; hon. fellow Accion Medica del Peru; hon. mem. Sociedad Peruana de Urologia y Venereologia, Pan-American Confederation Urologists, Pan-Am. Med. Assn.; life-mem. Stanford Alumni Assn. Decorated Officier l'Ordre d'Honneur et Merite (Republic d'Haiti); Al Merito (Ecudor); Commendodore Order Merit John Pablo Duorte (Dominicon Republic); Creszzire do Sul, (Brazil). Dem. Episcopalian. Mason. Clubs: Johns Hopkins, Stanford, Stanford Associates, Adventures, Physicians, University, N.Y. Athletic, Tokeneke Club, Wee Burn Country. Author: Embryology of the Prostate, 1912; A Textbook of Urology (with T. J. Kirwin), 1926; Urology for Nurses (with T. J. Kirwin), 1936; Clinical Urology (with T. J. Kirwin), 1940, 2d edit., 1943; also many articles on urol. subjects; operative treatment of the kidney and the embryology, anatomy, morphology, pathology and surgery of the prostate gland, tuberculosis of kidney, diverticulitis of bladder and urethra, and lesions of the ureter. Editor of Oxford Urological Surgery and Yearbook of Urology. Originator of Lowsley ribbon gut method of kidney operations and of operation for relief of impotence, also a new operation for hypospadias. Inventor of many operative instruments and tables. Home: 860 5th Av., N.Y.C. 21. Office: 111

E. 71st St., N.Y.C.; also 727 W. 7th St., Los Angeles. Died June 4, 1955; buried Fishkill, N.Y.

LOWSTUTER, William Jackson (lō-stūt-ẽr), theologian; b. Brownsville, Pa., Oct. 19, 1871; s. Jacob and Margaret (Coatsworth) L.; A.B., Allegheny Coll., 1898, A.M., 1908, D.D., 1915; S.T.B., Boston U. Sch. Theology, 1908; Ph.D., Boston U., 1911; studied Berlin and Marburg; m. Lida Vance Moore, Sept. 15, 1903 (died Sept. 21, 1941); m. 2d, Mrs. Anna B. Taylor, Jan. 9, 1946. Ordained to M.E. ministry, 1898; prof. N.T. lit. Iliff Sch. Theology, Denver, 1911-18; prof. N.T. lit. and interpretation Boston U. Sch. Theology, 1918-41, registrar, 1918-42, ret. Mem. Phi Beta Kappa, Phi Delta Theta. Mason. Home: 1115 18th Av. N., St. Petersburg, Fla. Died Feb. 11, 1958; buried Dawson, Pa.

LOWSTUTER, William Jackson (lō-stūt-ẽr), the-Knight, O.; s. Robert Alexander and Alma (Sears) L.; B.A., summa cum laude, Syracuse U., 1902, D.D., 1920, S.T.D., 1942, baccalaureate preacher, 1942; B.D., Union Theol. Sem., 1907; studied Columbia; m. Marguerite Cornell Dickson, Feb. 21, 1903; children—Robert Dickson, Carolyn Fulton, Hugh Sylvester, Marguerite. Ordained ministry M.E. Ch., 1906; asso. pastor Washington Sq. Ch., N.Y., 1906-07, St. Stephen's Ch., N.Y., 1907-13; with Bd. Edn. M.E. Ch., 1913-14; pastor 1st Ch., Covington, Va., 1914-16, 1st Ch., St. Mary's, W.Va., 1916-18, 1st Ch., Morgantown, W.Va., 1918-21, 1st Ch., Wichita, Kan., 1921-25, 1st Ch., Oakland, Cal., 1925-31, Temple Ch., San Francisco, 1931-46; Ch. of Petaluma, Cal., 1946-54, ret. Four-minute man, pres. Pleasant Co. (W.Va.) Chpt. A.R.C., World War; del. Internat. Kiwanis Conv., Atlanta, 1923, Denver, 1924. Am. organizer, 1st pres. Wichita Commn. on Week Day Religious Edn. Mem. bd. Goodwill Industries of San Francisco; mem. No. Cal. Commn. to Study Orgn. Peace; regional sponsor No. Cal. Council World Citizenship; bd. trustees Coll. of the Pacific, Stockton, Cal.; del. to Gen. Conf. of M.E. Ch., Atlantic City, 1932; Columbus, 1936; del. Western Jurisdictional Conf. Meth. Ch., 1940; mem. bd. dirs. Civil Liberties Union (North Cal. br.), Cal. Temperance Fedn.; mem. Petaluma Ministerial Union (pres.) Ecumencial Meth. Council (Western sect.); mem. San Francisco br. Nat. Council Jews and Christians; mem. Pacific Coast Com. World Alliance for Internat. Friendship Through the Chs.; mem. Deputation on Evangelism to Seattle, Portland, Spokane, 1945; mem. U. Christian Mission to Wash. State Coll., 1946. Mem. Phi Beta Kappa, Phi Kappa Psi. Democrat. Mason (32°), Odd Fellow. Clubs: Lions, Commonwealth, San Francisco Torch (founder, 1st pres.), Petaluma Loyal Knights of the Round Table International (charter mem., life mem., chaplain emeritus). Co-author: Christian Objectives in Education, The Music of the Gospel, Great Sermons on Evangelism; Render Unto Caesar; The Road Aheao, 1956. Contbr. Christian Century Pulpit. Address: 402 Grand Av., Oakland 10, Cal. Died Oct. 10, 1957; buried Mt. View Cemetery Mausoleum, Oakland.

LOWTHER, Hugh Sears, educator; b. Morgan County, O., Nov. 10, 1877; s. Rev. Robert A. and Alma (Sears) L.; prep. edn., Walkill Acad., Middletown, N.Y., 1892-95; winner state scholarship, Cornell U., 1895; A.B., summa cum laude, Syracuse U., 1899; Harrison fellow in classical langs., U. Pa., 1902-04, Ph.D., 1904; student Alliance Francaise, Paris, summers, 1901-08; m. Maria López, June 17, 1920. Instr. Latin and Greek, Genesee Wesleyan Sem., 1899-1901; instr. French, Friends Sch., Wilmington, Del., 1901-02, and of Classical and Romance langs., Coll. City of N.Y., 1904-20, 22-24; prof. French, U. So. Cal., 1920-22; acting head dept., 1921-22; prof. classical langs., chmn. div. fgn. langs., Occidental Coll., 1924-45. Lectr. classical archaeology Bd. Edn., N.Y.C., 1905-10; travel and research in archaeology and philology in Europe, various periods, 1901-28; traveling in Hawaii, South Seas, 1934, Mexico, 1937, 48. Mem. Archeol. Inst. Am., Am. Assn. U. Profs., Classical Assn. Pacific States (pres. 1926-28), Am. Philol. Assn. (Pacific Coast br.), Am. Classical League, So. Cal. Modern Lang. Assn. (v.p. 1929-30), S.R., Phi Beta Kappa, Phi Kappa Phi, Phi Eta, Phi Kappa Psi, etc. Author: Notes on Syntax of Martial, 1904. Contbr. philol. jours. Home: 330 South Santa Anita St., San Gabriel, Cal. Died June 16, 1959.

LOY, Sylvester K(line), chemist; b. Hamburg, Pa., Aug. 18, 1879; s. Walter S. and Hettie M. (Kline) L.; grad. Keystone State Normal Sch., Kutztown, Pa., 1899; A.B., Franklin and Marshall Coll., 1905; Ph.D., Johns Hopkins, 1910; m. Ella May Nash, Aug. 13, 1912. Tchr. pub. schs., 1899-1901; prof. physics and chemistry Keystone State Normal Sch., 1907-08; instr. chemistry Simmons Coll., Boston, 1910-11; asst. research chemist Colgate & Co., Jersey City, N.J., summer, 1911; research chemist U. Wyo. Agrl. Expt. Sta., 1911-13, prof. chemistry and dir. lab., 1913-18; chief chemist The Midwest Refining Co., 1918-21, Casper Plant, Standard Oil Co. (Ind.), 1921—; cons. chemist U.S. Bur. Mines (shale oil), 1920—. Mayor of Casper, Wyo., 1923. Mem. Am. Soc. Testing Materials. Home: Casper, Wyo. Deceased.

LUCAS, Arthur Fletcher, economist; b. Dover-Foxcroft, Me., Dec. 24, 1896; s. Herbert A. and Marian (Fletcher) L.; A.B., Bates Coll., 1920; Ph.D., Princeton, 1925; m. Agnes Page, 1921; children—Elizabeth Anne, Frances Stanhope. Instr. Princeton, 1920-22, 24-26; asso. prof., later prof. Clark U. since 1926, dir. div. bus. adminstrn. since 1946; cons. Harvard Grad. Sch. Bus. Adminstrn., 1937-39; vis. lectr. Wellesley Coll., 1940; prin. adminstrv. analyst U.S. Bur. Budget, 1943-46, cons., 1946-48; economist com. small bus. U.S. Ho. of Reps. since 1950. Mem. Am. Econ. Assn., Am. Assn. U. Profs., Phi Beta Kappa, Delta Sigma Rho. Episcopalian. Author: Legal Minimum Wage in Massachusetts, 1927; Industrial Reconstruction and Control of Competition, 1937. Contbr. to bus. and econ. jours. Home: 54 Morningside Rd., Worcester, Mass. Office: 129 House Office: Bldg., Washington 25. Died July 7, 1953; buried Wilmington, Vt.

LUCAS, Noah, banker; b. Norwich, Conn., July 26, 1887; s. Noah Everett and Sarah A. (Bunting) L.; student Norwich Free Acad., 1901-05; m. Clara L. Worth, Apr. 22, 1914; children—Mary Louise (Mrs. Richmond T. Crolius), Robert Worth. With Dime Savings Bank, Norwich, 1905-10, Thames Loan & Trust Co., 1910-13; with Savings Bank of New Britain (Conn.), 1913— as clerk, 1914, asst. treas., 1922, treas., pres., 1937—; dir. Am. Hardware Corp., Landers, Frary & Clark, Skinner Chuck Co., New Britain Trust Co. Dir. New Britain Gen. Hosp., trustee Jerome Home (pres. bd.), Y.M.C.A. Republican. Conglist. Mason. Clubs: Shuttle Meadow, New Britain (New Britain). Home: 84 Dover Rd. Office: 178 Main St., New Britain, Conn. Died Nov. 21, 1956; buried Fairview Cemetery, New Britain.

LUCAS, Oliver G.; pres. Nat. Bank of commerce; dir. Wesson Oil and Snowdrift Co., Inc., So. Cotton Oil Co., Federal Reserve Bank (New Orleans br.), New Orleans Agency RFC. Address: 210 Baronne St., New Orleans. Died July 4, 1950.*

LUCAS, William Cardwell, lawyer, banker; b. Osceola, Mo., Oct. 10, 1877; s. John H. and Nannie Taylor (Cardwell) L.; A.B., U. of Mo., 1900, LL.B., 1901; m. Margaret Dorsey, Jan. 20, 1900 (died June 18, 1921); 1 son, John H.; m. 2d, Beulah Stevenson, Dec. 16, 1926; 1 son, William Cardwell. Practiced law at Osceola, Mo., 1901-09; mem. Johnson & Lucas (firm now Johnson, Lucas & Bush), Kansas City, Mo., 1909—; gen. counsel Kansas City Power & Light Co., 1921-47, ret. 1947; chmn. bd. and gen. counsel, Osceola Bank, Lowry City Bank, Citizens Bank (Appleton City, Mo.), St. Clair Investment Co., Osceola Abstract Co., Tri-County State Bank (Eldorado Springs, Mo.), Humansville (Mo.) Bank; dir. Kansas City Trust Co., Mo. Abstract & Title Ins. Co., Shenandoah Dives Mining Co. Mem. Am. Bar Assn., Mo. State Bar Assn., Kansas City Bar Assn. (ex-pres.), Phi Delta Phi, Sigma Alpha Epsilon, Theta Nu Epsilon. Democrat. Methodist. Clubs: University, Kansas City. Home: 7541 Terrace St. Office: Bryant Bldg., Kansas City, Mo. Died Sept. 22, 1954; buried Forest Hill Cemetery.

LUCE, Edgar Augustine (lōōs), lawyer; b. San Diego, Cal., May 20, 1881; s. Moses A. and Adelaide (Mantania) Luce; A.B., Stanford U., 1905; m. Carma Coppard, Nov. 17, 1923; children—Edgar Arthur, Gordon Coppard, Sylvia Marilyn. Admitted to Cal. bar, 1905; mem. Luce, Sloane & Luce, San Diego, 1905-11, Luce & Luce, 1911-19, Luce & Swing, 1925-28, Stearns, Luce & Forward, 1928-39, Luce, Forward, Lee & Kunzel, 1939-48, Luce, Forward, Kunzel & Scripps, 1948—; v.p., dir. San Diego El Cortez Co.; dir. San Diego Trust & Savings Bank. Dep. city atty., San Diego, 1909-10; state senator, Cal., 1914-18; judge Superior Ct., San Diego, Cal., 1919-25; mem. Bd. Govs., Cal. State Bar, 1933-36. Served as 2d lt., Air Service, U.S. Army, World War I. Mem. Zeta, Psi, Phi Delta Phi. Republican. Clubs: University, Cuyamaca, San Diego Rowing (San Diego). Home: 3543 3d Av., San Diego 3. Office: San Diego Trust & Savings Bldg, San Diego 1, Cal. Died Aug. 27, 1958; buried Greenwood Meml. Park, San Diego.

LUCE, Harvey Gardner, business exec.; b. Grand Rapids, Mich., Sept. 10, 1900; s. Hiram Gardner and Belle (Parsons) L.; student U. Mich., 1919-21; m. Lois Wickerts, Aug. 13, 1926. Joined MacManus, John & Adams, Inc., 1935, exec. v.p., 1947—, also asst. to pres. Served as maj. M.I. Div. WDGS, 1944-45. Home: Box 163. Office: MacManus, John & Adams, Inc., Bloomfield Hills, Mich. Died Nov. 24, 1955.

LUCEY, Thomas Elmore, lyceum entertainer, actor, author; b. nr. Monroe, N.C., Jan. 15, 1874; s. William D. and Hannah Cornelia (Moore) L.; ed. in country newspaper offices; took profl. course in Perry Sch. of Oratory and Dramatic Art, St. Louis; pvt. instr'n., Chgo.; unmarried. Entered office Russellville (Ark.) Democrat at 13, to learn trade; in 10 yrs. acquired half interest; went to Atlanta, to assume interest in Alkahest Mag.; poet Tri-State Press Assn., 1898. Appeared at several So. Chautauquas in author's readings; had experience on dramatic stage, playing roles ranging from farce-comedy to the classics. Character actor and make-up artist; has toured all U.S. and Can. Known as "Poet-Entertainer of the Ozarks." Mem. Christian (Disciples) Ch. Democrat. Mem. Ark. Press Assn., Atlanta Symphony Club (charter mem.); helped found Chgo. Social Guild; charter mem. Internat. Lyceum Assn. Author: Etchings by an Optimist, 1894; Through Prairie Meadows (poems), 1004; At the Altar of Atonement (a drama); also poems and sketches in current periodicals. Address: Eurkea Springs, Ark. Died June 1, 1947; buried Meml. Park, Berryville, Ark.

LUCKE, Balduin (lōō kä), pathologist; b. Oedinghausen, Hesse, Germany, Nov. 3, 1889; s. Frederick and Helene (Rommel) L.; grad. Gymnasium, Kassel, 1906; M.D., U. of Pa., 1912, Dr.P.H., 1916; m. Marion Hague Rea, Mar. 2, 1917 (died Nov. 1, 1946); 1 son, Balduin; m. 2d Helen Hughes Norris, Nov. 15, 1947. Came to U.S., 1906, naturalized, 1915. Intern, Phila. Gen. Hosp., 1912-14; asst. instr. pathology, U. of Pa., 1914-17, instr., 1919-20, asst. prof., 1920-27 asso. prof. 1927-32, prof. pathology 1932—, chmn. dept., 1947—; Guiteras lectr., Buffalo, 1940. Gross lectr., Phila., 1944, Fenger lectr., Chicago, 1945, Mütter lectr., Phila., 1948. Served as lt., med. corps U.S. Army, 1917-19; mem. Med. Res., 1919-42; lt. col., med. corps active service, 1942-46, dep. dir. Armed Forces Inst. Pathology; ret. as col., 1946. Awarded Legion of Merit. Mem. bd. hon. consultants Army Med. Library; sci. adv. bd. Armed Forces Inst. Pathology (chmn. 1946); div. med. scis. Nat. Research Council, 1943—, subcom. on oncology, 1948— (chmn., 1951—); Fellow Coll. Physicians of Phila.; mem. Am. Soc. for Exptl. Pathology (pres., 1942-46), Assn. Am. Phys., Soc. Exptl. Biol. and Med., Corp. Marine Biol. Lab., Am. Assn. for Cancer Research, A.A.A.S., Sigma Xi, Alpha Omega Alpha. Clubs: Cosmos (Washington); Merion Cricket (Haverford, Pa.). Mem. editorial bd. Cancer Research. Author articles in profl. publs. Home: 623 Rose Lane, Bryn Mawr, Pa. Office: U. of Pennsylvania, Phila. 4. Died Apr. 26, 1954; buried Arlington Nat. Cemetery.

LUCKE, Charles Edward (lŭk'ē), cons. mech. engr.; b. N.Y.C., June 20, 1876; s. John Franklin and Sarah Frances (McGrury) L.; B.S., Coll. City N.Y., 1895; M.S., N.Y.U., 1899; Cornell U., 1899; Ph.D., Columbia, 1902, Sc.D., 1929; m. Ida M. Becker, Mar. 24, 1904. Prof. mech. engring. Columbia, 1906-41, head dept., 1908-41, Stevens prof. emeritus, 1941—; mech. engring. cons. Served in USN, World War I, comdr. USNRF. Mem. Am. Soc. M.E., Am. Soc. Refrigerating Engrs., Soc. Automotive Engrs., Am. Soc. Heating and Ventilating Engrs., Soc. Naval Architects and Marine Engrs. Clubs: Engineers', Columbia University. Author: Gas Engine Design, 1905; Power, 1911; Engineering Thermodynamics, 1912; also about 80 papers on profl. subjects. Holder more than 120 U.S. patents. Home: 88 Morningside Drive. Office: Pupin Bldg., Columbia U., N.Y.C. 27. Died Mar. 27, 1951.

LUCKENBACH, John Lewis, shipping exec.; b. Kingston, N.Y., Nov. 19, 1883; s. Edward and Henrietta (Weber) L.; grad. cum laude Holbrooks Mil. Acad., 1902; grad. Princeton, 1906; student night courses in engring. Pratt Inst., Bklyn.; m. Kate Isobel McGregor, Jan. 26, 1916. In charge maintenance and repair of Luckenbach ships, Pacific Coast, 1912-15; in charge design and constrn. new ships, Luckenbach fleet, N.Y.C., 1915-18; in charge building some 35 ships in Japan and 4 in China, U.S. Shipping Bd., 1918-20; v.p. in charge maintenance, repair and operation of vessels Luckenbach S.S. Co., 1920-25, retired 1925. Exec. v.p. Am. Bureau of Shipping, 1927-32, acting pres., 1932-33, pres., 1933—. Chmn. Am. Merchant Marine Conf. Com., 1936—. Pres. bd. trustees Webb Inst. Naval Architecture. Mem. adv. com. Daniel Guggenheim Sch. of Aeronautics, N.Y.U. Apptd. mem. Senate tech. com. on safety at sea, 1935, chmn. structural efficiency com. Del. to Internat. Conf. Naval Architects and Marine Engrs. (London), Engring. Congress (Glasgow, Scotland), 1938. Rep. Am. Bureau of Shipping at 1st Congress of Classification Societies, Rome, Italy, 1939; mem. U.S. delegation to Internat. Conf. on Safety of Life at Sea, London, 1948. Received Distinguished Public Service Award, USN, 1943. Mem. Navy League U.S. (N.Y. council), Soc. Naval Architects and Marine Engrs. (v.p., mem. council), Inst. Naval Architects London (v.p.), Inst. Marine Engrs. (London), N.E. Coast Instn. Engrs. and Shipbuilders (Newcastle-on-Tyne), Am. Soc. Naval Engrs., Princeton Engring. Assn., Newcomen Soc., Ins. Soc. of N.Y., C. of C. of U.S., N.Y. C. of C. Clubs: India House, Princeton, New York Yacht (N.Y.C.); Metropolitan, Cedar Creek; Beaver Dam Winter Sports, Seawanhaka Corinthian Yacht. Home: Crescent Beach Rd., Glen Cove, L.I., N.Y. Office: 45 Broad St., N.Y.C. 4. Died 1951.

LUCKEY, Henry Carl (lŭk'ē), ex-congressman; b. East St. Louis, Ill., Nov. 22, 1868; s. Frederick and Louise (Kruhoeffer) L.; A.B., U. Neb., 1911, LL.

B., 1912, M.A., 1914; student Columbia, 1914-15, m. Hattie Caroline Franke, Oct. 7, 1893; children—Anna Louise (Mrs. Charles E. Paul), Helen Marguerite (Mrs. Kaho Daily). Engaged in farming in Neb., 1894-1900, 02-09; realtor and builder, Lincoln, Neb., 1915-34; mem. 74th and 75th Congresses, 1st Neb. Dist. Trustee Midland Coll., 1919-25. Jeffersonian Democrat. Lutheran. Author: Reform of Judicial Procedure, 1914; Eighty-Five Amerian Years (autobiography). Home: El Cerrito, Cal. Died Dec. 31, 1956.

LUCKHARDT, Arno Benedict (lŭk'härt), physiologist; b. Chgo., Aug. 26, 1885; s. Gustav Adolph and Aurelia (Weber) L.; student Conception (Mo.) Coll., 1897-1903, LL.D., 1933; B.S., U. Chgo., 1906, M.S., 1908, Ph.D., 1911; M.D., Rush Med. Coll., 1912; Sc.D., Northwestern U., 1934; m. Luella Catherine LaBolle, Apr. 24, 1912; children—Hilmar Francis, Paul Gregory, Mary Aurelia. Asst. in bacteriology U. Chgo., 1908-09, in physiology, 1909-11, asso., 1911-12, instr., 1912-14, asst. prof., 1914-20, asso. prof., 1920-23, prof., 1923-41, chmn. dept. physiology, 1941-50, Dr. William Beaumont Distinguished Service prof. in physiology, 1947-50, now Distinguished Service prof. physiology emeritus; now research cons. J. B. Roerig & Co., of the Pharm. House of Chas. Pfizer & Co., Inc., of N.Y.C. Mem. bd. dirs. Dr. William Beaumont Found., Inc., Prairie du Chien, Wis. Fellow A.M.A., Soc. for Exptl. Biology and Medicine, Internat. Coll. of Anesthetists, Internat. Soc. Dental Research, hon. fellow Am. Coll. of Dentists; hon. mem. German Med. Soc. Chgo., St. Louis Med. Soc.; mem. Internat. Anesthesia Research Soc., Order of Bookfellows, Am. Psychol. Soc. (past pres.), Inst. Traumatic Surgery Fedn. Am. Socs. for Exptl. Biology (pres. 1933-35), Gorgas Soc., Walter Reed Soc. (life), A.A.A.S., Ill. Med. Soc., Am. Dental Assn. (council on therapeutics), Kaiserlich Deutsche Akademie der Naturforscher, Phi Beta Pi, Sigma Xi, Phi Beta Kappa, Gamma Alpha, Alpha Omega Alpha, Theta Nu Epsilon, etc. Clubs: University, B.M.C. (pres. 1939-40), Chicago Literary Club (past pres.). Recipient Alpha Omega medal, 1938; Callahan Memorial Award medal, Ohio Dental Society; Phi Beta Pi "Man of the Year" citation, 1948; certificate of award Water Reed Society, 1952. Discoverer, with J. Bailey Carter, of ethylene gas as an anesthetic agent with properties superior to nitrous oxide, commonly known as "laughing gas"; researches in physiology of the parathyroid glands, gastric and pancreatic secretion, and in the history of physiology, dentistry and medicine. Home: 5216 Greenwood Av., Chgo. Died Nov. 6, 1957; buried Somonauk, Ill.

LUDEWIG, Jos(eph) W(illiam) (lŭd-wig), ret. naval officer, educator; b. Washington, June 2, 1904; s. Joseph Gottlieb and Louise (Zimmerman) L.; B.S., U.S. Naval Acad., 1925; M.S., Carnegie Inst. Tech., 1933; student, U.S. Naval Postgrad. Sch., 1931-32, 33-34; mem. Minerva Lorraine Damon, May 12, 1928. Commd. ensign U.S. Navy, 1925, and advanced through grades to rear adm., 1947; served in cruisers, destroyers, gunboats, battleships and on U.S. Fleet and Task Force staffs; combat duty Nicaraguan campaign, 1928, and World War II; progress officer, U.S. Naval Gun factory, Washington, 1943-44; ret. as rear adm., Jan. 1, 1947; asso. prof. dept. metal. engring., Carnegie Inst. Tech., 1947—. Awarded Legion of Merit combat order, (twice), Bronze Star (combat), Pacific and World War II campaign medals, Nicaraguan campaign medal. Mem. U.S. Naval Inst., Am. Soc. Engring. Edn., Am. Soc. Metals, Mil. Order World Wars, Phi Kappa Phi. Republican. Episcopalian. Clubs: Army-Navy Country (Washington), Butler Country, Univ. (Pitts.). Home: Stonecrest, Middle Rd., Glenshaw, Pa. Office: Carnegie Inst. of Technology, Pitts Died Mar. 17, 1958.

LUDLOW, F(rank) Milton, utility exec.; b. Newark, N.J., Aug. 8, 1896; s. William Edward and Florence E. (Keller) L.; student Newark Inst. Arts and Scis., 1914-18, also U. Newark; m. Hazel H. Weinrich, May 18, 1921 (dec., 1955); children—Lorraine (Mrs. W. Merritt Colehamer), Bernice Ruth; married second, Margaret Wheeler Hawkins, May 3, 1958; one step-son, Thomas L. Hawkins III. Stock transfer agt. Pub. Service Corp. of N.J. and all subsidiary cos., 1917-26, asst. treas., 1926-44, chmn. welfare com., 1944-48; chmn. welfare com. Pub. Service Electric & Gas Co. and all subsidiary cos., 1948—, corp. sec., 1953—. State treas. Emergency Relief Adminstrn. N.J., 1931-33, dep. state dir., 1934-36; first chmn. Combined Selective Service Bds., Newark, 1941-45; mem. bd. mgrs. Home for Disabled Soldiers, N.J., 1944-47. Mem. exec. and finance com. A.R.C., 1940—, chmn. bd., 1943-44; trustee, mem. exec. com. N.J. Blue Cross, 1945-57, v.p., 1957—; gen. chmn. Welfare Fedn., Newark, 1945, trustee, mem. exec. com., 1946-48; trustee, chmn. exec. com. Presbyn. Hosp., N.J., 1944-56; trustee of United Hospitals of Newark, 1957—. Served as cpl., drill instr., USMC, 1918-19. Mem. Am. Legion (post comdr. 1923, co. comdr. 1932, state finance officer N.J. 1933-34), Forty and Eight, Am. Soc. Corporate Secs., Lambda Tau. Republican. Mason. Presbyn. Clubs: Essex (Newark), Rotary. Home: 75 Prospect St., East Orange, N.J. Office: 80 Park Pl., Newark. Died Jan. 18, 1959.

LUDLOW, Louis Leon (lŭd'lō), ex-congressman; b. Fayette County, Ind., June 24, 1873; s. Henry Louis and Isabella (Smiley) L.; grad. high sch., Connersville, Ind., 1892; LL.D., Butler U., 1940; m. Katherine Huber, Sept. 17, 1896; children—Margery (Mrs. Elmer Louis Kayser), Blanche (Mrs. Ralph Hoskins Hudson), Virginia (Mrs. John Frederick Hudson), Louis. Reporter on Indpls. Sun, 1892-95; reporter Indpls. Sentinel, 1895-99, Washington corr., 1901; polit. reporter Indpls. Press, 1899-1901; Washington corr., Star League of Ind., 1903-13, Columbus (O.) Dispatch and Ohio State Jour., Columbus, 1913-29; mem. 71st and 72d Congresses, 7th Ind. Dist. and 73d to 77th Congresses, 12th Ind. Dist. (first corr. in U.S. to go from press gallery to Congress). Mem. Soc. Ind. Pioneers, Phi Gamma Dalta. Democrat. Methodist. Clubs: Indiana Democratic (Indpls.); National Press (Washington, pres. 1927). Author: From Cornfield to Press Gallery, 1924; In the Heart of Hoosierland, 1925; Senator Solomon Spiffledink, 1927; America Go Bust, 1933; Hell or Heaven, 1937. Home: Colonnade Apts., 843 N. Meridian St., Indpls. Died Nov. 28, 1950; buried Rock Creek Cemetery, Washington.

LUDLOW, William Orr, architect; b. New York, N.Y., May 24, 1870; s. Rev. James Meeker and Emma (Orr) L.; M.E., Stevens Inst. Tech., 1892; m. Abbie Hartwell, June 10, 1902; children—David Hartwell, William Hartwell. Engaged as archtl. draftsman with Carrere & Hastings, architects, N.Y. City, 1892-95; sr. mem. firm Ludlow & Valentine, architects, 1895-1909; sr. mem. firm Ludlow & Peabody, 1909-35, Ludlow & Ludlow, Summit, N.J., since 1935; work includes 40 coll. bldgs., 30 chs. and large number banks, hosps. and wide variety of bldgs. (more than 400 in all); architect for office bldg. of New York Times, the Johns-Manville Bldg., and 48-story Chase Tower, also bldgs. in India and Greece. Gov. New York Building Congress (chmn. com. for recognition of craftsmen, 15 yrs.; v.p. 7 yrs.). Mem. Am. Red Cross (chmn. Com. on Accident Prevention Madison-Chatham Chapt., cited for Meritorious Personal Service, 1946). Fellow Am. Inst. Architects (nat. chmn. Com. on Public Information). Mem. N.J. Soc. of Architects, Washington Soc. N.J., Madison Hist. Assn., Delta Tau Delta, Tau Beta Pi. Presbyn. (elder). Home: Midwood Terrace, Madison, N.J. Office: Commercial Bldg., Summit, N.J. Died Jan. 21, 1954.

LUDLUM, Seymour DeWitt, physician, psychiatrist, neurologist; b. Goshen, N.Y., Aug. 1, 1876; s. John Frank and Loisa May (Minturn) L.; B.S., Rutgers University, 1897, Sc.D., 1951; M.D., Johns Hopkins U., Baltimore, Md., 1902; 1 son, Seymour D. (by previous marriage; married 2d, Mabel Stewart, October 9, 1920 (deceased). Began chief on staff, neuro-psychopathic dept., Philadelphia General Hospital, 1910-47, active consultant, since 1947; medical director and owner, Gladwyne Colony, private sanitarium for mental and nervous disease, Gladwyne, Pa., since 1912, dir. Gladwyne Research Lab. for Mental Research, 1912—; prof. neurology, University of Pennsylvania Graduate Sch. of Meicine, 1920, professor psychiatry, 1922-53. Member of the Am. Psychiatric Assn., Am. Neurological Assn., A.M.A., Am. Chem. Soc., Phila. County Med. Soc., Johns Hopkins Medical Soc., Assn. Research Nervous and Mental Diseases, Eugenic Research Assn., Am. Therapeutic Assn. Republican. Presbyterian. Clubs: University, Philobiblon, Medical of Phila. Author of about 50 articles on research in mental and nervous diseases. Home and Office: Gladwyne Colony, Gladwyne, Pa. Died Dec. 2, 1956.

LUDY, Llewellyn V. (lū'dĭ), educator; b. Millgrove, Ind., Jan. 26, 1875; s. George Washington and Martha Letitia (Wood) L.; B.S. in M.E., Purdue, 1898, M.E., 1900; m. Ruth Henderson Miller, June 22, 1929. Asst. to Dean W. M. M. Goss, Purdue, 1898-99, instr. mech. engring., 1899-1901, prof. mech. engring., 1901-11, prof. exptl. engring., 1912-45, emeritus 1945; prof. steam and gas engring., U. Wis., 1911-12; cons. mech. engr.; expert Bur. Forestry, Washington, summer, 1900; insp. Carnegie Steel Co., summer, 1901. In charge spl. tng. of soldiers, Purdue, 1918; local rep. U.S. Shipping Bd., Emergency Fleet Corp., World War. Presbyn. Republican. Mem. Am. Soc. M.E., A.A.A.S., Am. Assn. U. Profs., Ind. Acad. Sci., Soc. Promotion Engring. Edn., Ind. Engring. Council, Sigma Xi, Sigma Phi Epsilon, Pi Tau Sigma, Tau Beta Pi. Rotarian. Author: Air Brakes, 1915; Locomotive Boilers and Engines, 1916; Steam Engines, 1916; Steam Engine Indicators, 1916; Valve Gears, 1916; Mechanical Engineering Laboratory Notes, 1942; Researches in Steam and Gas Engineering. Home: 600 Russell St., West Lafayette, Ind. Died Nov. 8, 1952; buried Hartford City, Ind.

LUECKE, John, ex-congressman; b. Escanaba, Mich., July 4, 1889; s. Frederick and Marie Suzanna (Lange) L.; ed. pub. graded schs., Escanaba; m. Rose Margaret Jaeger O'Callaghan, June 27, 1927; children—Conrad John, (stepdau.) Helen Lily O'Callaghan (Mrs. Ray LaPorte). Paper mill worker; mem. City Council, Escanaba, 1934-36; Mich. State Senate, 1935-36; mem. 75th Congress (1937-39), 11th Mich. Dist. With Fed. Mediation and Conciliation Service, 13 yrs. Served as pvt., Punitive Expeditionary Force, Mexico, 1916-17; sergt. 1st class with A.E.F., 1917-19. Democrat. Presbyn. (elder). Home: 814 S. 14th St., Escanaba, Mich. Died Mar. 21, 1952; buried Lakeview Cemetery.

LUEDDE, William Henry (lüd'dĕ), ophthalmologist; b. Warsaw, Ill.; s. Henry J. M. and Emilie M. (Naumann) L.; M.D., Washington U., St. Louis, 1900; vol. asst. eye clinic Royal U., Kiel, Germany, 1904-05; student Laboratoire d'Ophthalmologie, Sorbonne, Paris, 1906; m. Nettie B. Shryock, Mar. 24, 1909 (died Nov. 2, 1946); children—Philip S., Fullerton W., Henry W.; m. 2d, Irene E. Garbarino, Jan. 2, 1948. Asst. to Drs. Green, Post and Ewing, 1901-04; in pvt. practice, St. Louis, 1906—; asst. surgeon, Eye Clinic, Washington U., 1908-12; ophthalmic surgeon, St. Louis Eye, Ear, Nose and Throat Infirmary, 1912-16; prof. ophthalmology St. Louis U., 1921—; ophthalmologist in chief Firmin Desloge Hosp., St. Mary's Hosp. and Infirmary; oculist Mo. Bapt. Sanitarium; attending ophthalmologist U.S. Marine Hosp.; cons. in ophthalmology St. Louis City, St. Louis County and St. Johns hosps. Recipient Gill prize (disease of children) by Washington U., 1900, Leslie Dana medal (prevention of blindness), 1933. Served from capt. to maj. M.C., U.S. Army, World War I; col. AUS, 1931-41. Dir. St. Louis Society for the Blind. Fellow A.M.A., A.A.A.S.; mem. many national, internat. and fgn. med. and ophthal. assns., S.R., Alpha Omega Alpha. Conglist. Mason (K.T.). Club: University. Home: 139 N. Tunbridge Dr., Stoneleigh Towers, St. Louis County 24. Office: 256 Hampton Village, Medical Center, St. Louis. Died Mar. 19, 1952.

LUEDER, Arthur Charles, former Chgo. postmaster, ex-state auditor; b. Elmhurst, Ill., Mar. 12, 1876; s. John and Juliana (Brumund) L.; student Elmhurst Coll., 1885-90, Chgo. Law Sch., 1899-1902; m. Martha R. Mueller, Apr. 6, 1904 (died 1956); children—Roland G., Ruth (Mrs. Wardecker). Entered real estate bus. 1899. Postmaster, Chgo., 1921-33; state auditor, 1940-48, ret. Rep. candidate for mayor of Chgo., 1923. Was mem. 1st Regt., Ill. N.G.; sgt. Co. D, 1st Ill. Vol. Inf., Spanish-Am. War, 1898. Mem. Nat. Assn. Real Estate Bds., Real Estate Assn. of Ill., Chgo. Real Estate Bd., Cook Co. Real Estate Bd., Chgo. Mortgage Bankers Assn., Nat., Ill. assns. postmasters, Federal Business Assn., Chgo. Hist. Soc., Art Inst. Chgo., Field Museum, N.A.U., Nat. Union, Royal League, Nat. Aeronautical Assn., Soc. Army of Santiago de Cuba, Spanish War Vets. Lutheran. Mason (32°, Shriner), Moose. Clubs: Hamilton, Medinah Country, German (v.p.), Chicago Rod and Gun. Home: 67 N. Lincoln St., Lombard, Ill. Died May 7, 1957.

LUEDKE, August J(ohn), steel exec.; b. Milwaukee, May 18, 1884; s. H. August and Emma (Pritzlaff) L.; student U. of Wis., 1908; m. Anita Goll, Feb. 15, 1915; 1 daughter, Mrs. Margaret Anita Luedke Sensenbrenner. Sec.-treas. Milwaukee Corrugating Co.; Milcor Steel Co., Milwaukee, 1906-38; now dir., mem. exec. com., Concordia Fire Ins. Co., Milwaukee Mechanics Ins. Co., Marine Nat. Exchange Bank, Old Line Life Ins. Co.; dir. Inland Steel Co., Firemens Ins. Co., Commercial Casualty Ins. Co., Girard Fire & Marine Ins. Co., Nat. Ben Franklin Fire Ins. Co. Home: 2716 Newberry Blvd., Milw. 11. Died Apr. 2, 1954; buried Forest Home Cemetery, Milw.

LUFKIN, Garland, glass co. exec.; b. Salem, Mass., Sept. 5, 1896; s. Olvin Horace and Cora Archer (Ballard) L.; B.S., Mass. Inst. Tech., 1920; m. Roma Helen Reilly, July 10, 1926; 1 dau., Ann. Mech. engr. A. H. Kerr & Co., Okla., 1920-21; draftsman, furnace foreman, chief draftsman, chief engr., Ill. Glass Co., Alton, Ill., 1921-29; chief engr. Owens Ill. Glass Co., 1929-31, plant mgr., 1931-37, gen. mgr. Closure div., 1937-41, v.p. and gen. mgr. Glass Container div., 1941-43, v.p. gen. mgr. packaging and process research dept., 1943-47, v.p. analysis special mgmt. problems, 1947—. Served as pvt. to 2d lt., 101st Engrs., 26th Div., U.S. Army, 1917-19, with AEF., Sept. 1917 to July 1919. Mem. Am. Soc. M.E. Clubs: Toledo; Inverness, Country (Toledo, O.). Home: 4205 Brookside Rd., Toledo 6, O. Died Oct. 23, 1950.

LUFKIN, Willfred Weymouth, Jr., business exec.; b. Essex, Mass., Feb. 3, 1903; s. Willfred Weymouth and Adelaide (Stapleton) L.; grad. Gov. Dummer Acad., 1921; B.S., U. N.H., 1925; student Lowell Textile Sch., 1925-26; m. Thada Benbrook, June 20, 1943; children—Deborah, Susan, David, Amy, Lucy. Started as assistant treasurer with the company of Ipswich Mills, 1927; dir., v.p. gen. mgr. Ipswich Mills, Inc., 1928-29; mdse. mgr. Spool Cotton Co., N.Y.C., 1930-31; mgr. textile div. U.S. Tariff Commn., Washington, 1931-33; mem. Barrington Assos., management cons., N.Y.C., 1944-46; with Dan River Mills, Inc., N.Y.C., 1946-50, v.p., dir., gen. sales mgr., 1949-50; with Wellington Sears Co., N.Y.C., 1950—, dir., pres. mem. exec. com.; v.p. Celanese Corp. Am.; pres. Fgn. Celanese; pres., dir. Worth Street, Inc., Dixie Mills, Inc., Equinox Mill, Columbus Mfg. Co., Cabin Crafts, Inc.; mem. br. adv. com., Hanover Bank. Mem. Nat. Panel, Am. Arbitration Assn. Clubs: Merchants, Union League, Baltusrol, Short Hills. Home: Colebrook, Conn. Office: 65 Worth St., N.Y.C. 13. Died Apr. 12, 1957; buried Essex, Mass.

LUHRSEN, Julius G. (lōōr'sĕn), labor ofcl.; b. Desplaines, Ill., Apr. 1, 1877; s. Henry William and Louise C. (Henningsmeier) L.; student pub. schs.; m. Josephine C. Cross, Dec. 23, 1900 (died Feb. 25, 1958); children—Alice Wray (Mrs. Edmund F. Becker), Josephine L. (Mrs. Robert H. Stevenson). Worked on farm and studied telegraphy at night, 1892; railroad telegrapher, 1893-98; comml. telegrapher and corr. Chgo. Bd. of Trade, 1899-1900; returned to railroad as telegrapher and promoted to train dispatcher, 1901, subsequently chief dispatcher, night chief dispatcher and chief clk. trainmaster's office until 1917; organized Am. Train Dispatchers' Assn., Spokane, 1918, pres., 1918-35, now hon. pres. (on leave of absence); exec. sec.-treas. Ry. Labor Executives Assn., 1945-50. Apptd. mem. Mgmt.-Labor Policy Com., War Manpower Commn., Policy Com., OPA; mem. Office of Defense Transportation Com., U.S. R.R. Retirement Bd., Nat. del. Rep. Conv., 1920 (mem. labor platform com.). Club: Kenwood Golf and Country (Washington). Home: 2456 W. Estes Av. Office: 844 N. Rush St., Chgo. Died Oct. 16, 1956; buried Tuscola, Ill.

LUKA, Milo (lōō'kä), baritone; b. Prague, Czechoslovakia, Aug. 9, 1890; s. Vaclav and Pauline (Kolar) L.; ed. in Prague; m. May Gotthart, Nov. 19, 1916. Sang in principal opera houses of Europe; came to U.S., 1920; joined Chgo. Civic Opera Co., 1923. Prin. roles in Rigoletto, Aida, Barber of Seville, Pagliacci, Othello, Il Trovatore, Tannhauser. Home: 621 Melrose St., Chgo. Deceased.

LULL, Richard Swann, paleontologist; b. Annapolis, Md., Nov. 6, 1867; s. Capt. Edward P. (USN) and Elizabeth F. (Burton) L.; B.S., Rutgers U., 1893, M.S., 1896, hon. D.Sc., 1918; Ph.D., Columbia, 1903; hon. M.A., Yale, 1911; m. Clara Coles Boggs, July 2, 1894; 1 dau., Dorothy. With div. entomology U.S. Dept. Agr., 1893; asst. and asso. prof. zoölogy Mass. State Coll., 1894-1906; asst. prof. vertebrate paleontology Yale, 1906-11, prof., 1911-23, prof. paleontology, 1923-27, Sterling prof. paleontology, 1927-36, now emeritus. Asso. curator of vertebrate paleontology Peabody Museum, Yale, 1906-20, curator vertebrate paleontology, 1920-26, hon. curator, 1932—, dir., 1922-36, acting dir., 1937-38, now emeritus; asso. fellow Jonathan Edwards Coll., Yale; lectr. on paleontology U. Cal., summers 1925, 35, 37, Harvard, 1939. Instr. seamanship USN Tng. Unit, Yale, 1917-18. Fellow Am. Acad. Arts and Sciences, Geol. Soc. America, Paleontol. Soc. (treas. 1911-24, pres. 1925); mem. Soc. Vertebrate Paleontology, Am. Museum Natural History (hon. life), Chi Psi, Sigma Xi, Phi Beta Kappa. Recipient Elliot medal, Nat. Acad. Sciences for 1933; Society of Colonial Wars. Episcopalian. Author: Organic Evolution, and other books and memoirs. Editor Am. Jour. of Science, 1933-49. Home: 200 Livingston St., New Haven 11. Died Apr. 22, 1957; buried Evergreen Cemetery, New Haven.

LUM, Ralph Emerson, lawyer; b. Chatham, N.J., Apr. 21, 1877; s. Frederick Harvey and Alice Elizabeth (Harris) L., prep. edn., St. Paul's Sch., Garden City, L.I., 1893-96; A.B., Columbia, 1900; post-grad. study, New York U., 1900-01; m. Sylvia Swinnerton, August 21, 1902 (died May 13, 1945); children—Philip Livingston Swinnerton, Ralph Emerson, Mary de Peyster; married Mary Tison Page, May 26, 1950. Began practice of law, 1900. State chmn. (N.J.) World Ct.; chmn., Morris County (N.J.) Rep. Com.; dir. Community Chests and Councils; ex-pres. Newark Welfare Fedn.; v.p. Newark Safety Council. Dir. Newark Museum. Trustee St. Barnabas Hosp., Pawling (N.Y.) Sch. Mem. Am. Bar Assn., N.J. Bar Assn. (ex-pres.), Newark Music Foundation (v.p.), N.J. Soc. of the Order of the Founders and Patriots of America, Phi Kappa Psi, Phi Delta Phi. Mason (33°); past grand master Masons of N.J. Clubs: Essex (Newark); Canoe Brook Country (Summit, N.J.); Columbia Univ. (N.Y. City); Hollywood Adirondack (N.Y.). Home: 145 Fairmount Av., Chatham, N.J. Office: 605 Broad St., Newark 2, N.J. Died Mar. 21, 1952.

LUMLEY, Frederick Elmore (lŭm'lē), prof. sociology; b. Iona, Elgin County, Ont., Can., June 7, 1880; s. Moses Willey and Dama Edith (Williams) L.; grad. Coll. of the Disciples, St. Thomas, Ont., 1901; student McMaster U., 1901-03, M.A., 1907; A.B., Hiram (Ohio) Coll., 1905; B.D., Yale, 1909, Ph.D., 1912 (DeForest scholar); m. Margaretta Sewell, Oct. 4, 1905; 1 son, Frederick Hillis (dec.). Ordained ministry Disciples of Christ Ch., 1901; minister, Toronto, Can., 1901-03; prin. Sinclair Coll., St. Thomas, 1905-07; minister Congl. Church, Northford, Conn., 1908-12; hon. fellow and asst. in dept. of sociology, Yale, 1910-12; prof. sociology, Coll. of Missions and Butler Coll., Indianapolis, Ind., 1912-20; same, Ohio State University, 1920—, chairman of the department, 1932-40, now professor emeritus; visiting professor sociology, Yale, 2d semester, 1924, Northwestern U., summer 1924, Syracuse U., summer 1929, Western Reserve, summers 1931, 32. Mem. Sherwood Eddy Seminar for Foreign Study, 1923. Elected asso. Internat. Inst. Sociology, 1934. Mem. City of Columbus Planning Commn., 1942-46. Member Am. Sociol. Soc., A.A.A.S., Fgn. Policy Assn., Ohio Valley Sociol. Soc. (pres. 1937-38), Am. Assn. Univ. Profs., Alpha Kappa Delta, Phi Beta Kappa (honorary). Adviser to local draft board. Clubs: Faculty (president 1939), Crichton, Torch Club. Author: Means of Social Control, 1925; Principes of Sociology, 1928, 2d edit., 1934; Ourselves and the World (with B. H. Bode), 1931; The Propaganda Menace, 1933. Editor The Ohio Valley Sociologist, 1930-44. Contbr. sociol. articles. Home: Union, Ont., Can. Died July 26, 1954.

LUND, Lawrence Henry, business exec.; b. Brooklyn, N.Y., Apr. 8, 1897; s. Hans A. and Oline (Kvam) L.; ed. public schools, Brooklyn; m. Marie V. Daly, Sept. 7, 1925; children—Joan Marie, Lawrence Henry, Robert John. Sec. credit div., Wholesale Shoe House, N.Y., 1914-15; statistician Paramount Pictures Corp., N.Y., 1915-17; traveling auditor Triangle Film Corp., N.Y., 1917-18. Bookkeeper Automatic Typewriter Co., N.Y., 1919-21; auditor Westinghouse Electric Internat. Co., N.Y., 1921-37; asst. treas., asst. sec. and credit mgr. Westinghouse Electric Corp. (formerly Westinghouse Electric & Mfg. Co.), Pittsburgh, 1937-41, treas. and asst. sec., 1941-45, v.p. and treas. since 1945; treas. and dir. Turtle Creek & Allegheny River R.R. Co., East Pittsburgh; treas. and asst. sec. The Westinghouse Co., Pittsburgh, Westinghouse Radio Stas., Inc., Phila.; dir. Westinghouse Electric Internat. Co., Compania Westinghouse Internacional, Compania Westinghouse Electric de Cuba, Westinghouse Electric Co. of India, Westinghouse Electric Co. of South Africa, Ltd., Westinghouse Electric Co. of Brazil, Westinghouse Electric Co., S.A., Westinghouse Electric Co., Ltd., Electric Ry. Equipment Securities Corp., Phila. Served as corpl., U.S. Army, 1918-19. Awarded Westinghouse Award of Merit, 1942. Mem. Pittsburgh C. of C., Controllers Inst. of Am. Lutheran. Mason. Clubs: Duquesne, University, South Hills Country (Pittsburgh). Home: 1361 Terrace Dr., Pittsburgh 16. Office: 306 Fourth Av., Pittsburgh 30. Died Mar. 14, 1949.

LUND, Robert Leathan, industrialist; b. Louisville, Ky., June 14, 1875; s. Harry Majendie and Sarah Ann (Stephenson) L.; C.E., Vanderbilt U., Nashville, 1896, M.S., 1897; D.Sc. (honorary), St. Louis Coll. Pharmacy; m. Minnie Cowden Yowell, Aug. 16, 1899; children—Robert Leathan, Joel Yowell, William Rector, Dorothy Talbot (Mrs. Austin Porter Leland). Instr. in engring. Vanderbilt U., 1895-97, adjunct prof., 1897-1903; cons. engr., Little Rock, Ark., 1903-05; dept. mgr., mem. bd. dirs. International Shoe Co., St. Louis, 1906-15; organized Lund-Mauldin Co. (later Lund Williams Shoe Co.), St. Louis, 1915, pres., 1915-25; officer mem. board of directors Lambert Pharmacal Co., St. Louis, 1925-44; exec. v.p. and v.p. Lambert Co., N.Y. City, 1932-44, mem. bd. dirs. to 1944; dir. Majestic Mfg. Co., St. Louis; pres. Nat. Assn. Mfrs., 1932-33, chmn. bd., 1934-35, hon. v.p. and dir. for life; mem. and graduate, mem. business advisory council U.S. Dept. Commerce, 1933—; Chemical Warfare, Adv. Bd., U.S. Army; mem. St. Louis Ordnance Dist. Adv. Bd.; mem. advisory com. U.S. Patent Office, 1934—. Chmn. St. Louis Com. on Relief and Employment, 1932; mem. indsl. adv. bd. N.R.A.; dir. Associated Industries of Mo., St. Louis C. of C.; pres. Downtown Y.M.C.A., 1933; mem. exec. com. Proprietary Assn.; mem. Nat. Indsl. Conf. Bd.; mem. U.S. Com. Inter-Am. Council of Commerce and Industry; mem. bd. trustees Culver-Stockton Coll., Canton, Mo.; pres. St. Louis Coll. Pharmacy; nat. pres. Jr. Achievement, Inc. 1940-48, hon. pres.; pres. America's Future, Inc., N.Y.C.; v.p. Am. Enterprise Assn., N.Y.; trustee Nat. Council for Community Improvement. Mem. Am. Fedn. Pharm. Edn., Newcomen Soc. Eng., Acad. Polit. Sci., Phi Beta Kappa, Tau Beta Pi, Delta Kappa Epsilon. Mem. Disciples Ch. Clubs: University, Noonday, Bellerive Country. Co-author: (with Howard Coffin) The Truth About the New Deal: (with other industrialist) The New Outlook in Business. Contributor economic articles. Home: 5968 Cabanne Pl., St. Louis. Died Mar. 9, 1957; buried Bellefontaine Cemetery, St. Louis.

LUNDBERG, Alfred J(ulius), banker; b. San Francisco, Feb. 9, 1890; s. Laurits J. and Emilie M. (Bruus) L.; student Heald's Bus. Coll.; m. Claire F. Richards, Aug. 27, 1946. Sec. to pres. Anglo & London-Paris Nat. Bank, San Francisco, 1911-12; clk. J. Barth & Co., stock and bond brokers, 1912-25, partner, 1926-33; pres. Key System Transit Lines, 1927-46. Oakland Title Ins. & Guaranty Co., 1949-53; dir., mem. exec. com. Bank of Am., N.T.&S.A.; dir. Sherwood Swan & Co., Ltd., Manning Tank Lines, Inc., Lang Transportation Co. President San Francisco Stock Exchange Inst., 1925-26. Mem. Cal. Transit Assn. (pres. 1933, 40), Am. Transit Assn. (exec. com. 193-46, pres. 1939), Cal. State C. of C. (pres. 1940-42), Oakland C. of C. (pres. 1940-42), Cal. Acad. Sci., A.A.A.S., East Bay United Fund (pres. 1952). Clubs: Pacific Railway; Commonwealth of California; Athens Athletic (Oakland, Cal.), Home: 596 Haddon Rd., Oakland 6, Cal. Died June 14, 1956.

LUNDEBERG, Harry, labor union exec.; b. Oslo, Norway, Mar. 25, 1901; s. Karl and Allette (Koffeld) L.; student pub. schs., Norway. Came to U.S., 1919, naturalized, 1933. First connected with Australian Seamens Union; trans. to Sailors Union of Pacific, 1923, sec.-treas., 1936—; founder Seafarers Internat. Union of N.A., A.F. of L., 1938, pres. 1938—; v.p. Cal. Fedn. Labor, 1938—; president Maritime Fedn. of Pacific, 1935-36; pres. Maritime Trade Dept., AFL-CIO, 1955—. Served as mcht. seaman, World War I. Republican. Lutheran. Office: Seafarers International Union, 450 Harrison St., San Francisco. Died Jan. 28, 1957; buried Olivet Meml. Park, South San Francisco.

LUNDELL, Gustav Ernst Fredrick (lŭn-dĕl), govt. ofcl.; b. Bklyn., Jan. 11, 1881; s. Ernst Oscar and Johanna Ulrica (Bergstrom) L.; A.B., Cornell, 1903, Ph.D., 1909; D.Sc., Fordham, 1941; m. Helen Marguerite Drake, Sept. 7, 1910; children—Helen Frances, Ernst Drake. Instr. Northwestern U., 1903-06, Cornell, 1906-11, asst. prof., 1911-17; chemist Nat. Bureau Standards, 1917-35, chief chemistry div., 1935—. Received Hillebrand award Chem. Soc. of Washington, 1932; fellow Am. Ceramic Soc., 1941. Mem. Am. Soc. for Testing Materials (pres., 1941-42, v.p., 1939-41), Am. Chem. Soc., Optical Soc. America, Wash. Acad. Sciences. Episcopalian. Republican. Co-author: Applied Inorganic Analysis, 1929; Chemical Analysis of Irons and Steels, 1931; Outlines of Methods of Chemical Analysis, 1938. Home: Chevy Chase, Md. Died June 8, 1950.

LUNDQUIST, Harold Leonard (lŭnd'kwist), clergyman, educator; b. Minneapolis, Minn., Nov. 1, 1894; s. Andrew Gustaf and Ida Caroline (Anderson) L.; LL.B., U. of Minn., 1917; student Moody Bible Inst., 1920-21, and 1922-23, Princeton Theol. Sem., 1921-22; D.D., Wheaton Coll., 1938; m. Beatrice Elizabeth Anderson, Sept. 12, 1922; children—Patricia Marguerite, Beatrice Ruth, James Harold. Admitted to the Minn. bar, 1917; legal and credit work, 1917-18; ordained ministry, 1925; with Moody Bible Inst. as asst. to the dean, later asst. dean, 1924-32; dean of Ednl. Div., 1932-41; prof. of English Bible and asso. editor Moody Monthly, 1941-47; pastor First Evang. Free Church, Chicago, 1947-52; exec. dir. Evangelical Welfare Agy., 1952-57; pastor First Mission Covenant Church, Chicago., 1958—. Served in U.S. Army, 1918-19. Republican. Presbyn. Author: Can America Be Saved, 1939; Why Study Prophecy, An Appraisal of Its Dangers and an Appreciation of Its Blessings, 1940; Dynamic Christian Living, 1943; Leadership for Christ, 1946; Out of the Question Box, 1958. Also writer of numerous Sunday School lessons for Moody Monthly; also writer of newspaper syndicated lessons pub. in about 2700 papers in America, 1936-47. Home: 2443 Wilson Av., Chicago 25. Office: 6558 N. Artesian Av., Chgo. 45. Died Mar. 1959.

LUNKEN, Eshelby F., pres. Lunkenheimer Co.; b. Cin., Dec. 10, 1890; s. Edmund H. and Edith I. (Hodgson) L.; student pub. schs., Denver; m. Helen C. Pattison, Mar. 9, 1910. Dir. Lunkenheimer Co., Cin., 1912—, pres., 1919—; dir. The Central Trust Co. Clubs: Queen City, Cincinnati Country, Camargo. Home: 3524 Holly Lane, East Walnut Hills, Cin. Died 1949.*

LUNT, William Edward, college prof.; b. Lisbon, Me., Jan. 13, 1882; s. Edward Henry and Katherine Garcelon (Flagg) L.; A.B., Bowdoin, 1904; A.M., Harvard Univ., 1905, Ph.D., 1908, traveling fellow of Harvard in Europe, 1907-08 and 11; hon. L.H.D., Bowdoin College, 1929, Haverford Coll., 1952; Litt. D. (honorary), Princeton University, 1950; m. Elizabeth Elliott Atkinson, Dec. 5, 1910; children—William Edward, Jr., Robert Henry (dec.). Asst. in govt., Harvard, 1905-07; instr. history, U. of Wis., 1908-10; Thomas Brackett Reed prof. history and polit. science, Bowdoin, 1911-12; prof. English history, Cornell U., 1912-17; Walter D. and Edith M. L. Scull prof. English constl. history, Haverford Coll., 1917-52. Chief of Italian div. of Am. Commn. to Negotiate Peace, Paris, 1918-19. Overseer, Bowdoin Coll. Fellow Mediaeval Acad. of Am. (council 1932-35; v.p. 1936-39; clerk 1945-48, pres. 1951-54); corr. mem. Royal Historical Soc.; mem. Am. Hist. Assn., Am. Soc. Ch. History, Zeta Psi, Phi Beta Kappa. Author: The Valuation of Norwich, 1926; History of England, 1928, 2d edit., 1945; Papal Revenues in the Middle Ages, 1934; Financial Relations of the Papacy with England to 1327, 1939 (awarded Haskins medal); Collectors of Clerical Subsidies, in The English Government at Work, 1327-1336, vol. II, 1947; asso. editor Am. Hist. Review, 1945-47; also articles on the history of mediaeval papacy, etc. Home: 5 College Lane, Haverford, Pa. Died Nov. 10, 1956; buried Chebeague Is., Me.

LURTON, Douglas Ellsworth, editor, publisher, writer; b. Monticello, Minn., June 29, 1897; s. Dr. Freeman E. and Alice Howe (Babbitt) L.; student U. of N.D., 1916-18; m. Helen Grace Leo, July 1, 1925; children—Grace Elizabeth, Margaret Mary. Drama editor, city editor, Minneapolis Daily News, 1920-21; night editor Grand Forks (N.D.) Herald, 1922-24; asst. city editor Minneapolis Daily Star, 1925-26, city editor, 1927; supervising editor Golfer and Sportsman, Hollywood, Modern Mechanix, Radioland, Screen Book, Screen Play, 1932-36, Motion Picture, Movie Classic, 1935-36; mng. editor The Literary Digest, 1936-37; v.p. and business mgr., Kingsway Press, Inc., Your Health Publications, Inc., since 1937; Yourself Publications, Inc., since 1939; Publications Management, Inc., since 1941; Woman's Life Publications, Inc., since 1942; Wilfred Funk, Inc., 1942-50; pres. and bus. mgr. Basic Publications, Inc., since 1945; originator, pub. and editor Your Life since Oct. 1937, Your Personality since Jan. 1939, Your Health since Mar. 1939, Woman's Life since 1942, Success Today since 1946, Marriage Mag. since 1948; pubs. cons. since 1941. Mem. Soc. Mayflower Descendants, Phi Delta Theta, Phi Delta Phi, and Sigma Delta Chi. Mason. Clubs: Players, Scarsdale Golf. Author: Life and Morals of Jesus, 1940; My Mother's Bible (anthology), 1941; collator of Roosevelt's Foreign Policy, 1933-41, 1942; Make the Most of Your Life, 1945; The Power of Positive Living, 1950; Complete Home Book of Money-Making Ideas, 1954. Contbr. to numerous mags. Home: 238 Mamaroneck Rd., Scarsdale, N.Y. Office: 270 Park Av., N.Y.C. 17. Died Aug. 27, 1956; buried Wadena, Minn.

LUSK, Clayton Riley, lawyer, ex-state senator; b. Lisle, N.Y., Dec. 21, 1872; s. Samuel R. and Clara M. (Root) L.; grad. Portland State Normal Sch., 1895; LL.B., Cornell, 1902; m. Anna Lee Mix, June 1904; 1 dau., Elinor M. (Mrs. J. Henry Stagg, Jr.). Mem. Davis & Lusk, Cortland, 1902-15, now mem. firm of Lusk, Buck & Folmer; firm changed to Lusk, Folmer, Ryan & Fenstermacher. Judge Cortland 2 terms, 1904-09; mem. N.Y. Senate 3 terms, 1919-24 (elected pres. pro tem. and majority leader, Jan. 1921, minority leader, Jan. 1923); acting lt. gov. and acting gov. for portion 1922. Mem. Phi Delta Phi. Republican. Presbyn. Mason, Odd Fellow, Elk. Clubs: Nat. Republican, Cornell (N.Y.C.) Cortland Country. Home: Cortland, N.Y. Died Feb. 14, 1959.

LUSTIG, Alvin, designer; b. Denver, Colo., Feb. 8, 1915; s. Harry and Jeannette (Schamus) L.; student Los Angeles City Coll., 1933-34, Art Center Sch., 1934-35, study with Frank Lloyd Wright, 3 months, 1935, travel and independent study, 1935-36; m. Elaine Firstenberg, Dec. 19, 1948. Art dir., Westways, monthly mag. pub. by Automobile Club of So. Calif., 1933-34; free-lance designer, operator own typographic and printing business, 1936-40; free-lance designer, 1940-44, 1944-46, 1946-51, Los Angeles, N.Y. City since 1951; visual research dir. Look mag., N.Y. City, 1944-46; vis. critic in design, Yale, since 1951; teacher Black Mountain Coll., summer art inst., 1945, Art Center Sch., Los Angeles, 1946-48, Calif. Sch. Art. 1949, U. So. Cal., 1950-51, U. Ga. as design adviser, 1951; dir. exptl. workshop graphic design, co-sponsored by Yale and Mus. Modern Art; art dir. Art Digest since 1953; lectr. Portland Art Mus., Dallas Mus. Art, Walker Art Center, Furman U., Modern Inst. of Art, Los Angeles, Calif. Inst. Tech., U. Ga., U. Calif. Exhibits: A-D Gallery, N.Y. City, 1950 (one man show—comprehensive showing of all phases of work; showing at various mus. and colls.); Art Directors Club 24th Annual Advt. exhibit; Book Jacket designers Guild exhibition, 1948, 49, 50, 51; Detroit Institute of Art Modern Living exhibit, 1949; Fifty Books of the Year exhibit, 1947-50; Metropolitan Museum of Art Book Jacket Collection; Mus. of Modern Art Graphic Art Collection, Museum of Modern Art, Modern Art in Your Life Exhibit, 1949; O.W.I. Exhibit, Cairo, Egypt, graphic work by selected Am. designers; Printing for Commerce exhibit, Am. Inst. Graphic Arts, 1949; Soc. of Contemporary Designers First Annual Exhibit Stockholm Nat. Museum, "Eight America Designers", 1947; Victoria and Albert Museum, England, Internat. Book Jacket exhibit, 1949; exhibit Museum of Modern Art, N.Y.C., 1955. Recipient awards: Fifty Books of the Year, 1949, 50, 53; Award of Merit, Inst. of Graphic Arts, 1948, 49, 50; Good Design Show, Mus. of Modern Art, chair design selected. Mem. Soc. Contemporary Designers (mem. exec. bd.), Am. Inst. Graphic Arts. Articles and works published in various nat. publs. Home: 625 Park Av., N.Y.C. 22. Office: 132 E. 58th St., N.Y.C. 22. Died Dec. 4, 1955.

LUTHRINGER, George Francis (lōōth'rĭng-ēr), economist; b. Petersburg, Ill., Feb. 17, 1904; s. George F. and Pearl Alnutt (Sampsell) L.; student Staunton (Va.) Mil. Acad., 1920-21; Phillips Exeter, 1921-22; B.S., Princeton, 1926, Ph.D., 1932; m. Winifred Jutten, June 18, 1930; children—Janet Irene, David George. Instr. and asst. prof. economics and finance, Princeton, 1930-38; financial adv. to joint prep. com. on Philippine Affairs, State Dept., Washington, D.C., 1937-38; divisional asst., econ. adv. office, State Dept., 1938-41; asst. chief div. financial affairs, State Dept., 1941-43; served as financial expert, Office of High Commr, to Philippine Is., Feb.

1943-May 1944; chief div. Financial Affairs, State Dept., May 1944-46; dir., Office Financial and Development Policy, State Dept., May-July 1946; attended Bretton Woods and Savannah monetary confs. as tech. adv. to U.S.; mem. U.S. del. of Allied Commn. on Reparations Moscow, 1945; apptd. U.S. alternate exec. dir. Internat. Monetary Fund, July 1946; dep. dir. research dept., 1948; dep. dir. Far and Middle East and Latin Am. Dept., 1950, dir. Latin Am., Middle and Far Eastern dept.; 1952-53, dir. western Hemisphere Dept., 1953—; rep. Fund, London Preparatory meeting of Internat. Conference on Trade and Employment, Oct.-Nov. 1946. Mem. Am. Econ. Assn. Democrat. Episcopalian. Club: Princeton (Washington). Author: The Gold Exchange Standard in the Philippines, 1934; (with L. V. Chandler and D. C. Cline) Money, Credit and Finance, 1938; (with B. Dell), Population, Resources and Trade, 1938. Home: 1417 34th St., N.W., Washington 16. Office: Internat. Monetary Fund, 1818 H St. N.W., Washington. Died Mar. 11, 1955.

LUTZ, Samuel G., ry. ofcl.; b. Maryland, Ill., Dec. 8, 1868; s. J. M. and Sara (Garber) L.; grad. Albion (Ia.) Sem.; A.B., Western Coll., Toledo, Ia., 1887; m. Cora B. Foreman, Apr. 21, 1892; children—Vera F. (Mrs. Emerson Cole Ward), Jeanette. Entered freight traffic dept. Ia. Central R.R., Marshalltown, Ia., 1890, apptd. chief clk. freight traffic dept., 1894, asst. gen. freight agt.; 1898; asst. gen. freight agt. M.&St.L. R.R., hdqrs at Peoria, Ill., 1904-08; freight traffic mgr. M.&St.L. R.R. and Iowa Central Ry. cos., Mpls., 1908-09; gen. freight agt. C.&A. and Toledo, St. Louis & Western, M.&St.L. R.R. and Ia. Central Ry., Chgo., 1909-10; traffic mgr., Mpls. & St. Louis and Ia. Central Ry. cos., Mpls., 1910-14; apptd. gen. traffic mgr. C.&A. R.R., Chgo., 1914, v.p. in charge of traffic, 1917, holding that position at time roads were taken over as a war measure by the Fed. Admin-strn., Jan. 1, 1918, and then apptd. traffic mgr. under the federal mgr. for the C.&A., C.P.&St.L., P.&P.U. R.R. and P.R.T. Co. Mem. Chgo. Traffic Com. under director gen. of railroads from June 1, 1918, to end of federal control. Resumed duties as v.p. in charge of traffic of C.&A. R.R., Mar. 1, 1920; apptd. to similar position on Peoria Ry. Terminal Co., 1920; apptd. chief traffic officer for the receivers of Peoria Ry. Terminal Co., 1922, and same year apptd. chief traffic officer for receivers of C.& A. R.R., retaining position as v.p. in charge of traffic of C.&A. Corp.; chief traffic officer C.&A. R.R. Co., retired 1931; dir. Joliet Union Depot Co., Miss. River Bridge Co. Republican. Conglist. Mem. Western Traffic Exec. Com., Western Trunk Line Com, Ill. Freight Assn., U.S. C. of C., Chgo. Assn. Commerce. Clubs: Union League, Traffic, Evanston Golf. Address: Sebring Fla. Died 1956.

LYETH, J. M. Richardson (leeth), lawyer, corp. exec.; b. Strong City, Kan., Apr. 13, 1886; s. John Chester and Dolly (Richardson) L.; A.B., Harvard, 1907, A.M., 1908, LL.B., 1910; m. Judith Longyear, Feb. 14, 1911 (dec. 1924); children—J. M. Richardson, Munro Longyear; m. 2d, Helen Gloyd, Oct. 7, 1931. Admitted to N.Y. bar, 1911, and since practiced at N.Y. City; sr. partner Lyeth & Voorhees 1947-54; counsel Maclay, Morgan and Williams; dir. Longyear Realty Corp., Acro Manufacturing Company. Served as ensign, United States Navy, 1918. Clubs: Knickerborcker, Down Town, Harvard, St. Andrews Golf, Sleepy Hollow Country. Home: 4663 Waldo Av., N.Y. City 71. Office: 76 Beaver St., N.Y.C. 5. Died Dec. 23, 1957.

LYFORD, Oliver Smith, exec. and cons. engr.; b. Cleve., Mar. 21, 1870; s. Oliver Smith and Lavinia A. (Norris) L.; Ph.B., Yale, 1890; post-grad. Cornell U.; m. Frances Lyman Meigs, Jan. 1896; children—Mrs. Margaret Sheldon, Olive Meigs. Chief engr. Westinghouse Electric & Mfg. Co., 1897-99, v.p., gen. mgr. Siemens & Halske Electric Co., 1899-1901; cons. engr., mng. engr. Westinghouse, Church, Kerr & Co., 1902-12; pvt. practice, 1913-16; v.p. Finance & Trading Corp., 1919-22; pvt. practice, 1923; v.p., gen. mgr. Lawrence Investing Co., and Lawrence Park Heat, Light & Power Co., 1924-26; v.p. Brooklands, Inc., 1927—; v.p. Santa Clara Lumber Co. Served from maj. to lt. col. Ordnance Dept., U.S. Army, 1917-18. Fellow Am. Inst. E.E.; mem. Berzelius soc. (Yale), Kappa Alpha (Cornell). Republican. Presbyn. Club: Yale (N.Y.C.). Home: 54 Dana Pl., Englewood, N.J. Died Mar. 5, 1952; buried Delhi, N.Y.

LYMAN, David Russell, physician; b. Buffalo, Mar. 8, 1876; s. Henry Leslie and Jane Ellen (Newman) L.; grad. Jones U. Sch., Charlottesville, Va.; M.D., U. Va., 1899; hon. A.M., Yale, 1916; hon. D.Sc., Wesleyan U., 1942; m. Virginia Scott Cocke, Oct. 12, 1905; children—Clara Pollard, Jane Leslie. Instr. histology, U. Va., 1898, in anatomy, 1899; asst. resident, Johns Hopkins Hosp., 1900-01, Adirondack Cottage Sanatorium, 1901-03; med. supt. Gaylord Farm Sanatorium, Wallingford, Conn., 1903-53; mem. Conn. State Health Council, 1929-47; dir. 1st Nat. Bank, Wallingford. Asso. fellow Branford Coll., Yale U. Served with A.R.C., France, 1917-18;

mem. commn. for prevention tb in France, 1917-18. Mem. Conn. State Tb Commn., 1914-18. Mem. council Henry Phipps Inst. of U. Pa. Recipient Gold Medal award, New Haven Advt. Club, 1954. Fellow A.M. A.; mem. Conn. State Med. Soc. (ex-pres.), New Haven County Med. Soc. (ex-pres.), Am. Climatol. and Clin. Assn. (pres. 1926), Am. Sanatorium Assn. (pres. 1926), Nat. Tb Assn. (pres. 1918; Trudeau Medal, 1943), Soc. Colonial Wars, Phi Beta Kappa, Alpha Omega Alpha. Episcopalian, Elk. Clubs: Rotary (hon. mem.), Wallingford Country, New Haven Country, Graduate (pres. 1947-49), Inquisitors, Social Science (New Haven); Colonnade (U. Va.). Raven. Home: 228 Edwards St., New Haven. Address: Gaylord Farm, Wallingford, Conn. Died Oct. 15, 1956; buried Cedar Hill, Hartford, Conn.

LYMAN, Frank Hubbard, lawyer; b. Greggsville, N.Y., Sept. 1, 1863; s. Elihu Hubbard and Martha (Collins) L.; student Olivet (Mich.) Coll., 1882-86; m. Edith Watrous, Nov. 15, 1906. Admitted to Mich. bar, 1889, began practice at Grand Rapids; county atty. Maricopa Co., Ariz., 1912-15; judge Superior Ct., Ariz., 1915-22; judge Supreme Ct. of Ariz., 1922-25; in gen. practice, Phoenix, 1925—. Mem. Am., Ariz. State bar assns. Democrat. Presbyn. Mason, Odd Fellow, Elk. Clubs: Arizona, Phoenix Country. Home: 8550 N Ramona Rd. Office: Luhrs Tower, Phoenix. Died Jan. 1, 1957; buried Greenwood Cemetery, Phoenix.

LYMAN, George Dunlap, pediatrician, author; b. Virginia City, Nev., Dec. 12, 1882; s. Dean Briggs and Anna Louise (Dunlap) L.; A.B., Stanford U., 1905; M.D., Coll. Phys. and Surg. Columbia, 1909; post-grad. univs. of Munich, Vienna and Berlin, 1912-14; m. Dorothy Quincy VanSicklen, Dec. 28, 1911; children—Dorothy Quincy (Mrs. J. Wm. Beatty), Elizabeth Ann (Mrs. David Potter). Intern Bellevue Hosp., N.Y.C., 1910-11; practiced in San Francisco, 1914—; mem. faculty of medicine, Stanford, now emeritus; mem. vis. staff Stanford U. Hosp. and St. Mary's Hosp. Fellow Am. Acad. of Pediatrics; mem. Am., Cal. med. assns., Cal. Acad. Medicine, Soc. Am. Historians, Sigma Alpha Epsilon, Omega Club (Coll. Physicians and Surgeons). Republican. Clubs: Bohemian, P.E.N. (San Francisco). Author: Care and Feeding of the Infant, 1915, 2d edit., 1922; John Marsh, Pioneer, 1930; Wierzbicki—The Book and the Doctor, 1933; Saga of the Comstock Lode, 1934 (awarded Commonwealth Club gold medal, 1934); Ralston's Ring, 1937; A Friend to Man, 1938. Owner of over 6,000 vols. of Californiana; mem. Cal. adv. com. of Stanford U. Press. Home: 3673 Jackson St. Office: 384 Post St., San Francisco. Died July 26, 1949; buried Mountain View Cemetery, Oakland, Cal.

LYMAN, Rufus Ashley, educator; b. Table Rock, Neb., Apr. 17, 1875; s. William Graves and Sophie Lee (Allen) L.; A.B., U. Neb., 1897, A.M., 1899, M.D., 1903; m. Carrie Day, July 1, 1899; children Esther, Caroline (dec.), Elizabeth, Louise, Rufus Ashley, Edwin Day. Prof. pharmacology Coll. of Medicine, U. Neb., 1904-08, organizer, 1908, and dean Coll. of Pharmacy, 1908-46, also dir. dept. of student health 1919-45, became dean emeritus 1946; dir. Sch. of Pharmacy, U. Ariz., 1947, dean Coll. of Pharmacy, 1949-50. Editor in Chief, American Pharmacy, 1944—. Mem. com. to formulate program for Pharmacy Unit of S.A.T.C., 1918. Fellow A.A.A.S.; mem. Am., Neb. med. assns., Am., (hon. pres. 1952-53), Neb. pharm. assns., Am. Assn. Colls. of Pharmacy, Am. Assn. Sch. Physicians, Am. Pub. Health Assn., Am. Student Health Assn., United Provinces Pharm. Assn. of India (hon.), Am. Council on Edn. (vice chmn. 1929-30; also member Commonwealth Fund Com., making a study of pharm. edn. and practice for natl. application), Am. Inst. History of Pharmacy (v.p. 1941), Sigma Xi, Phi Delta Chi, Omega Beta Pi, Delta Sigma Phi, Rho Chi. Republican. Presbyn. Remington Medalist for distinguished pharmaceutical service, 1947. Founder and editor Am. Jour. Pharm. Edn., 1937—. Home: 1649 S. 21st St., Lincoln 2, Neb. Died Oct. 12, 1957.

LYMAN, Theodore, physicist; b. Boston, Nov. 23, 1874; s. Theodore and Elizabeth (Russell) L.; A.B., Harvard, 1897, Ph.D., 1900. Instr. physics Harvard, 1902-07, asst. prof., 1907-17, dir. Jefferson Physical Lab., 1910-47, prof. physics, 1917-26, Hollis prof. emeritus, 1926—. Capt. Aviation Sect., Signal R.C., 1917; maj. Engr. Corps, U.S. Army, 1918; service with AEF, flash and sound ranging, 1917-19. Recipient Rumford medal Am. Acad. Arts and Scis.; Elliott Cresson medal Am. Philos. Soc.; Frederick Ives medal Optical Soc. Am. Fellow Am. Acad. Arts and Sciences (past pres.), A.A.A.S., Royal Geog. Soc.; mem. Nat. Acad. Sciences, Am. Phys. Soc. (past pres.). Unitarian. Club: Somerset (Boston). Discoverer Lyman series. Home: 105 Heath St., Brookline, Mass. Died Oct. 11, 1954.

LYNCH, Clyde Alvin, coll. pres.; b. Harrisburg, Pa., Aug. 24, 1891; s. John Henry and Carmina Blanche (Keys) L.; prep. edn. Lebanon Valley (Pa.) Acad.; A.B., Lebanon Valley Coll., 1918, A.M., 1925, D.D., 1926; B.D., Bonebrake Theol. Sem.,

1921; A.M., U. Pa., 1929, Ph.D., 1931; LL.D., Albright Coll., 1937; m. Edith L. Basehore, June 30, 1914; children—Rose Eleanor, John Howard. Ordained to ministry United Brethren in Christ, 1916; pastor successively Centerville Circuit Chamber Hill and Ebenezer, Linglestown and Rockville (all Pa.) until 1918; pastor Antioch and Pyrmont, O., 1918-21. Ephrata, Pa., 1921-25, 2d Ch., Phila., 1925-30; del. to Gen. Conf., 1933, 37, 41, 45; asst. instr. psychology U. Pa., 1929-30; prof. homiletics and practical theology Bonebrake Theol. Sem., Dayton, O., 1930-32; pres. Lebanon Valley Coll., Annville, Pa., 1932-—. Pres. So. Conv. Dist., Pa. State Edn. Assn., 1931-38, mem. exec. com., 1938-39, 1948, del. to N.E.A. Conv., 1938, pres. dept. higher edn., 1948; mem. exec. com. Pa. YMCA. Mem. Fed. Council Chs. of Christ in America (alternate mem. exec. com.; mem. com. of research and edn., com. on town and country); mem. Bd. of Christian Edn. of Evangelical United Brethren Ch.; mem. com. on edn., Pa. Sabbath Sch. Assn.; mem. exec. com. Pa. Council of Churches, chmn. of dept. of Social Relations. Mem. State Commn. on Area Colleges and chmn. Area 2; chmn. State Commn. on Displaced Persons; mem. executive com. Pa. Assn. Colleges and Universities. Chmn. Selective Service Bd. No. 3, Lebanon County, Pa., 1940-41; mem. Pa. com. Thomas Jefferson Bicentennial Commn. Mem. A.A.A.S., Am. Psychol. Assn., Pa. Acad. of Science, Dept. Sch. Administrs. N.E.A., Lebanon C. of C. (mem. airport com.; mem. com. on edn. and industry). Republican. Mason (33°, Shriner), Grand Chaplain, Grand Lodge of Pa.; Supreme chaplain of Supreme Forest, Tall Cedars. Clubs: Lebanon Rotary (pres.); Torch, Executives (Harrisburg). Chmn. Bd. mgmt., Army U.S.O. Bldg., Lebanon, 1942-45. Contbr. to ch. publs. Lecturer on religious, civic and ednl. subjects. Home: 103 E. Main St., Annville, Pa. Died Aug. 6, 1950; buried Grandview Meml. Park, Annville.

LYNCH, Florence (Mrs.), Dem. nat. committeewoman; b. LeMars, Ia., Feb. 17, 1891; d. Fred and Catherine (Willmes) Coddington; ed. public schools, LeMars, Ia., Seattle, Wash.; grad. LeMars High Sch.; m. William Lynch, June 1, 1910 (died Dec. 10, 1944). Engaged in business as jobber and retailer since 1915; pres. William Lynch Tobacco Co. since 1915. County chmn. Dem. County Central Com., 1930-44, committeewoman 8th Congl. Dist., 1930-48; sec. Dem. State Central Com., 1936-40, state vice chmn., 1940-44, Dem. nat. committeewoman for Ia. since 1944; del. to Dem. Nat. Conv., since 1944. co-chairman credentials for 1952 convention. President Lynch Lumber Company; v.p., dir. Pacific Paperboard Co., v.p. Pacific Converters Co., Longview, Wash.; sec., treas. Pacific Material Co., Portland. Chmn Nat. Foundation for Infantile Paralysis, Plymouth County, 7 years. Chmn. volunteer services Am. Red Cross (Plymouth County), 10 yrs., mem. executive committee, 25 yrs.; sec. 8th Congl. Dist. United Service Orgns. since 1943. Mem. Business and Professional Womens Club (Washington). League of Women Voters. Home: Box 428, LeMars, Iowa. Died Apr. 29, 1953.

LYNCH, Frederick J., physician; b. Cambridge, Mass., Nov. 13, 1889; s. Albert Edward and Mary Elizabeth (Carty) L.; B.S., Bowdoin Coll., 1915; M.D., Harvard, 1919; m. Hope Anne Mahaney, Nov. 25, 1925. Surgeon-in-chief for obstetrics and gynecology Boston City Hosp., Cambridge City Hosp., Symmes-Arlington Hosp., Arlington, Mass.; asst. obstetrician Mass. Gen. Hosp.; former prof. obstetrics, chmn. dept. Tufts Coll. Med. Sch.; former asst. in gynecology, Med. Sch., Harvard; obstetrician-in-chief Mt. Auburn Hosp., Cambridge; cons. obstetrics Lawrence Meml. Hosp., Medford, Beth Israel Hosp. Mem. A.M.A., Mass. Med. Soc. (chmn. sect. obstetrics and gynecology, 1931-32), Am. Assn. Gynecologist, Obstetrician and Abdominal Surgeon, N.E. Obstet. and Gynecol. Soc. (pres. 1944-45), Boston Obstet. Soc., Am. Bd. Obstetrics and Gynecology, Alpha Delta Phi, Alpha Kappa Kappa, Alpha Omega Alpha. Clubs: Abraxus, Harvard (Boston); Winchester Country. Home: 56 Watertown St., Lexington, Mass. Office: 475 Commonwealth Av., Boston 15. Died July 8, 1957; buried Mt. Auburn Cemetery, Cambridge, Mass.

LYNCH, Jerome Morley, surgeon; b. Ireland; s. Daniel and Jane (Browne) L.; student Queen's Coll., Cork, Edinburgh U.; M.D., Rush Medical Coll., Chgo., 1895; m. Harriet Louise Husted; Jan. 1, 1901. Chief surgeon St. Bartholomew's Hosp., N.Y.C.; prof. proctology N.Y. Polyclinic Hosp.; cons. surgeon Doctor's Hosp., N.Y.C. Served as lt. comdr. USN, 1917; surgeon at Naval Hosp., Bklyn., and at sea, U.S.S. America. Diplomate Am. Bd. Surgery. Fellow A.C.S., Royal Society of Medicine (honorary); member A.M.A., New England Proctologic Soc., Am. Gastroenterological Assn., Am Proctologic Soc. (pres. 1917-18), Mil. Order Fgn. Wars. Author: Diseases of Rectum and Colon, 1914; Tumors of Colon and Rectum, 1925; Know Your Patient, 1943. Contbr. to Johnson's Surgery, Woods Hand Book of the Medical Sciences, Tice's Practice of Medicine. Clubs: Union (N.Y.C.); Author's (London, Eng.). Home: Carmel, Cal. Died Apr. 22, 1951.

LYNCH, Joseph Patrick, bishop; b. St. Joseph, Mich., Nov. 16, 1872; s. John V. and Veronica J. (Botham) L.; grad. St. Charles' Coll., Ellicott City, Md., 1891, St. Mary's Sem., Baltimore, 1895, Kenrick Sem., St. Louis, 1900; LL.D., St. Edwards Univ., Austin, Tex., 1930; ordained R.C. priest, June 9, 1900; asso. rector, Cathedral, Dallas, Tex., 1900-02; pastor St. Stephen's Ch., Weatherford, Tex., 1902-03; built St. Rita's Ch., Hanley, Tex., 1909, St. Edward's Ch., sch., rectory, Dallas, 1903-10; consecrated bishop of Dallas, July 12, 1911. Procurator fiscalis, 1905-10; apptd. vicar-gen. Diocese of Dallas, June 19, 1910; apptd. administrator of Diocese, "sede vacante," Aug. 6, 1910; apptd. asst. to Papal throne by Pope Pius XI, July 12, 1936 (25th Anniversary of Episcopal Conservation). Founded and built St. James' Ch., 1933, St. Mary's Ch., and Christ the King Ch. and parish, Dallas, 1941. Address: 4946 Swiss Av., Dallas 6. Died Aug. 19, 1954; buried Calvary Hill Cemetery, Dallas.

LYNCH, Walter A., ex-congressman; b. N.Y.C., July 7, 1894; s. Joseph B. and Katherine (Joyce) L.; ed. Fordham Prep. Sch., 1907-11; A.B., Fordham Coll., 1915; LL.B., Fordham Law Sch., 1918; m. Claire R. Mitchell, Oct. 16, 1920; children—Walter A., John J. Admitted to N.Y. bar, 1918; asso. Olcott, Bonynge, McManus & Ernst, 1915-25; mem. McManus, Ernst & Ernst, 1925-28, McManus, Ernst, Ernst & Lynch, 1928-32; mem. Glass & Lynch, N.Y.C., 1932-—. Temp. magistrate, N.Y.C., 1930. Mem. 76th to 81st Congress, 23d N.Y. Dist. Del. N.Y. State Constl. Conv., 1938. Mem. Am. Bar Assn., N.Y. County Lawyers Assn. Assn. Bar City N.Y., Bronx County Bar Assn. Democrat. Catholic. K.C. Clubs: Manhattan, New York Athletic, Catholic of New York, Lawyers (N.Y.C.). Home: 295 Alexander Av. Office: 170 Broadway, N.Y.C. Died Sept. 1957.

LYNCH, Warren J., steel mfr.; b. Ogdensburg, N.Y.; s. John S. and Elizabeth (Warner) L.; student pub. schs. Cleve.; m. Clara Hughes Spining. Began railway service with the "Big Four," at Cleve., as clerk in auditing dept., later in passenger dept., until line was consolidated, 1889, with the C.,C.,C.& St.L. Ry. Co., with which continued in charge of advt. dept., 1889-93, chief clerk to passenger traffic mgr., 1893-96, asst. gen. passenger agt. at St. Louis, 1896-97, asst. gen. passenger and ticket agt. at Cin., 1897-99, gen. passenger and ticket agt., 1899-1905; passenger traffic mgr. N.Y. Central lines, 1905-10, asst. v.p. in charge operations, lines west of Buffalo, 1910-11; v.p. Am. Steel Foundries, 1911-40, dir., 1928-47; ret. Home: Gramatan Hotel, Bronxville, N.Y. Died Aug. 1950.

LYNCH, Willard A., investment banker; b. N.Y.C., Dec. 7, 1893; s. Morris W. and Mary Ann (Brosnan) L.; m. Helen Bowen, June 26, 1940; children—Willard A., Richard M. Joined W.C. Langley & Co., 1915, partner 1927; dir. Am. Water Works Co. Mem. N.Y. Stock Exchange. Attached to Gen. Staff, Washington, 1917-18. Clubs: Metropolitan, Union League, Manhattan, Lawyers, New York Athletic, Bankers (N.Y.C.). Home: 1130 Park Av., N.Y.C. 28. Office: 115 Broadway, N.Y.C. 6. Deceased.

LYNCH, William Orlando, prof. history; b. on farm nr. Delphi, Ind., Sept. 10, 1870; s. Isaac Newton and Frances Jane Berniece (Connelly) L.; graduate of Indiana State Normal School, 1896; A.B., Indiana U., 1903; A.M., U. of Wis., 1908; Austin scholar, Harvard, 1911-12; m. Bertha Thomas, June 27, 1894; 1 dau., Mary Bernice (Mrs. Alfred L. Spurlock). Teacher in rural schs., Ind., 1890-93; prin. village schs., 1893-95; teacher, high sch., Elkhart, Ind., 1896-1901, 1903-07; asst. prof. history, Ind. State Teachers Coll., Terre Haute, 1908-13, prof. 1913-18; prof. history, Ball State Teachers Coll., Muncie, Ind., 1918-20, and at Indiana University, 1920-41, professor emeritus, 1941-—; visiting prof. history, University of Alabama, summers, 1925, 27, U. of Tenn., summer, 1930. Regional dir. Survey of Federal Archives for Ind., 1936. Del. to Ind. Progressive State Conv., 1912, 14. Life mem. Am. Hist. Assn., Miss. Valley Hist. Assn., (pres. 1938-39); mem. Ind. Hist. Soc. (pres. 1946-50); Southern Hist. Assn., Am. Assn. Univ. Profs. Presbyn. Club: Exchange. Democrat. Author: Fifty Years of Party Warfare (1789-1837), 1931; History of Indiana State Teachers College, 1946. Contributor various historical papers. Member bd. editors Miss. Valley Hist. Rev., 1925-29, of Jour. of Southern History, 1936-40. Editor Indiana Magazine of History, 1928-41; acting editor Miss. Valley Hist. Rev. July-December, 1946. Contbr. Dictionary of Am. Biography and Dictionary of Am. History. Columnist Delphi Citizen, 1937-41, Star-Courier, Bloomington, Ind., 1945-—. Home: Box 187, Brownstown, Ind. Died Mar. 29, 1957; buried Rose Hill Cemetery, Bloomington, Ind.

LYNE, Daniel Joseph (līn), lawyer; b Boston, Apr. 3, 1889; s. Eugene and Julia A. (Crowley) L.; A.B. magna cum laude, 1910, LL.B. cum laude, 1912; m. Susan M. O'Brien, June 18, 1923; children—Eugene, Daniel Joseph, Austin Francis, Susan Markham, Kerry Richard, Sheila Ann. Admitted to Mass. bar, Circuit Ct. Appeals, Dist. Ct., 1912, U.S. Supreme Ct., 1921; practice of law, Boston, since 1912; partner Lyne, Woodworth & Evarts since 1919; sec., dir. Thomson Electric Welder Co. since 1916; asst. dist. atty., Suffolk Co., 1927; mem. Mass. Bd. Probation, 1927-37, mem. Spl. Crime Commn., 1933; gen. counsel First Nat. Stores, Inc., since 1940, dir since 1947; gen. counsel, sec. La Touraine Coffee Co., Inc., Kenedy & Co., Inc., since 1941; dir. Trimount Coop. Bank, 1926-38; trustee Suffolk Savs. Bank since 1942; dir. Old Colony Trust Co., Boston Mut. Life Ins. Co. Dir. Boston Legal Aid Soc. since 1927; treas. Voluntary Defenders Com., Inc., since 1935; dir. Greater Boston Community Fund, 1938-49, v.p., 1939-41; gen. counsel, exec. com. Greater Boston Development Com. since 1944, vice chmn. since 1947; dir. Greater Boston United War Fund, 1941-45, gen. counsel, 1945; mem. Mass. Com. Pub. Safety, 1941-45. Trustee Perkins Instn., Mass. Sch. for Blind, since 1937, George Robert White Fund, 1941-42. Mem. Am., Mass., Boston (chmn. grievance com. 1931-33, v.p. 1937-41, pres. 1941-42) bar assns., Boston C. of C. (dir. 1933-36), Mass. Civic League (v.p. 1936-40), Community Fedn. Boston, Boston Latin Sch. Assn. (pres. 1941-44), Internat. Friendship League (dir. since 1947). Clubs: Clover (pres. 1939-1940), Harvard (Boston, N.Y.C.); Longwood Cricket, Eire Soc. (pres. 1946-47). Home: 130 Beacon St., Chestnut Hill, Newton 67, Mass. Office: 75 Federal St., Boston 10. Died Oct. 2, 1957; buried Holyhood Cemetery, Newton, Mass.

LYNETT, Elizabeth Ruddy (lī'nĕt), newspaper pub.; b. Scranton, Pa., June 23, 1902; d. Edward James and Ellen A. (Ruddy) Lynett; student St. Cecelia's Acad., Scranton, 1915-19; A.B., Trinity Coll., 1923. With The Scranton Times since 1923, reporter, 1923-46, partner-publisher, 1946-—. Incorporator and subscriber Lackawanna United Fund. Mem. Nat. Council of Cath. Women (past chmn. com. on indsl. problems), Pa. Tuberculosis and Health Society (member of the board). Democrat. Roman Catholic. Clubs: Century, Scranton, Country. Prepared series of newspaper articles on sweatshop conditions and poor wage scales of women and children in local factories and mills, based on personal employment, 1933. Pulitzer prize awarded The Scranton Times for most distinterested and meritorious public service rendered by any Am. newspaper during yr. 1945 Home: 841 Clay Av., Scranton 10. Office: Times Bldg., Scranton 1, Pa. Died Apr. 2, 1959.

LYNN, Charles J(ackson), drug exec.; b. Indianapolis, Jan. 17, 1874; s. William C. and Harriet N. (Kellogg) L.; student pub. schs. Indianapolis; Doctor of Laws, Wabash College, 1953; married Celestia McEachren, March 31, 1900 (dec. 1942); m. 2d Dorothy J. Black, Oct. 2, 1945. Employee Daniel Stewart Co., Indianapolis and Lord, Owen & Co., Chicago, wholesale druggists, 1889-95; with Eli Lilly & Co., Indianapolis, 1895-—, sales mgr., Indianapolis, 1906, gen. mgr., 1907-32, sec., 1909, mem. bd. dirs., 1913, v.p., 1932-—, retired from active service, 1940. Member of the board of directors Western Tax Council. Asso. chief sect. med. ind. War Industries Bd., 1918. Mem. bd. trustees Purdue, Long Coll. for Women of Hanover Coll., Methodist Hosp. (Indianapolis); pres. bd. trustees Hanover Coll., and Indpls. Y.M.C.A; mem. bd. dirs. Am. Red Cross (Indianapolis chpt.); pres. bd. dirs. English-Speaking Union (Indianapolis br.); mem. bd. dirs. English-Speaking Union of U.S.; mem. bd. grants Am. Found. Pharm. Edn. Mem. Am. Drug Mfrs. Assn. (pres., 1916-18), Am. Shorthorn Breeders Assn. Indiana Horse and Mule Breeders Assn. (director), S.A.R., Soc. Ind. Pioneers. Presbyn. (board trustees 2d Presbyn. Ch. Endowment Fund). Clubs: Saddle and Sirloin (Chicago), Columbia, Athletic, Univ., Contemporary (Indpls.). Home: 5600 Sunset Lane, Indpls. 8. Office: Eli Lilly & Co., Indpls. 6. Died Sept. 22, 1958.

LYNN, Harry Hudson, safe mfr.; b. N.Y.C., June 19, 1885; s. James William and Sarah Mary (McCormack) L.; student engring. Columbia, 1903-07; m. May A. Huntington, Feb. 3, 1910; children—Virginia Huntington (Mrs. E. A. Dickson), Amy Huntington (Mrs. Francis D. Walker). Bridge and structural engr., 1907-12; successively factory engr., sales mgr., br. mgr. Mosler Safe Co., Hamilton, O., 1912-27, v.p., treas., gen. mgr., 1927-46, exec. v.p., 1946-52, chmn. bd. since 1952; v.p., treas. Mosler Lock Co., Covington, Ky.; treas. Guardian Metals Co., Hamilton; v.p. Protectall Safe Co., Syracuse, N.Y. Mem. Ohio, Hamilton C.'s of C., Safe Mfrs. Nat. Assn. (president), Bank and Security Vault Mfrs. Assn. (past pres.), Sigma Xi, Tau Beta Pi. Republican. Roman Catholic. Home: 27 Jewett Dr., Wyoming, O. Office: 320 Fifth Av., N.Y.C. 1; also Mosler Safe Co., Hamilton, O. Died Feb. 1, 1956.

LYNN, Robert Henry, clergyman, educator; b. Grand Pass, Mo., Jan. 13, 1892; s. William Franklin and Susan Elizabeth (Williams) L.; A.B., Ottawa (Kan.) U., 1920; Colgate-Rochester Div. Sch., 1920-21; A.M., Div. Sch. U. Chgo., 1922, postgrad., 1922-24; Th.M., Berkeley Bapt. Div. Sch., 1940, Th.D., 1945; postgrad. Pacific Sch. Religion, 1939-40; m. Margaret Anna White, Sept. 18, 1923; children—Robert Merrifield, Arthur Whiting, Elizabeth Anne,

Margaret Mallory, David Northrup. Ordained to ministry Bapt. Ch., 1918; pastor Osawatomie, Kan., 1919-20, Conesus, N.Y., 1921, First Ch., Woodstock, Ill., 1922-24; acting pres. Colo. Woman's Coll., Denver, 1925-26; pastor Sixth Av. Ch., Tacoma, Wash., 1926-30, head dept. of religion U. Redlands, Cal., 1931—. Served in U.S. Army, 1918. Mem. Pi Kappa Delta. Democrat. Home: 122 The Terrace, Redlands, Cal. Died Oct. 13, 1949; buried Redlands.

LYON, Frank, rear adm. (ret.). Address: care Bureau of Naval Personnel, Dept. of Navy, Washington. Deceased.*

LYON, Gideon Allen, journalist; b. Saginaw, Mich., Sept. 23, 1867; s. Gideon Allen and Emma Frances (Ward) L.; grad. Washington High Sch., 1885; m. Florence Louise Russell, Apr. 21, 1893; children—Emma Louise (Mrs. Casper Morris Thompson), Rowland. Joined staff of Evening Star, Washington, 1887, and assigned to White House and adjacent govt. depts.; on staff N.Y. Recorder 18 mos., 1892-93; returned to Star and assigned to U.S. Senate; detailed to editorial writing, 1896; asso. editor Evening Star-Sunday Star 1908-48, acting editor during absence of chief. Mem. Lit. Soc. Washington, Overseas Writers. Episcopalian. Clubs: Arts (pres. 1924-25); Cosmos. Contbr. several series of travel letters, from England, 1911, Belgium, France and Italy, 1914, Porto Rico, 1925, Japan and China, 1929, Egypt, 1931, Mexico, 1938, Hawaii, 1939. Home: 209 Rosemary St., Chevy Chase, Md. Died Jan. 8, 1951.

LYON, Hastings, lawyer, author; b. East Longmeadow, Mass., Aug. 9, 1876; s. Solon and Mary (Carter) L.; student Harvard; A.B., Dartmouth, 1901; LL.B., Harvard Law Sch., 1905; m. Sarah Henderson, Dec. 27, 1937; 1 step-dau., Lillian (Mrs. Hainon Miller). Staff Springfield (Mass. Republican, 1901-02, Hartford Times, 1904; spl. writer Boston Transcript, 1902-03; investment banking, with Dominion Securities Corp., Toronto, Montreal and London, 1906-08; connected with same business, New York, 1909-11; prof. finance, Dartmouth, 1912-14; asso. prof. finance, Sch. of Business, Columbia, 1916-42 (now retired); practiced law, New York, 1914-39, formerly mem. Haskell, Lyon & Block. Member of Phi Beta Kappa. Republican. Club: Faculty of Columbia University. Author: Corporation Finance, 1912; Principles of Taxation, 1914; Investment, 1926; The Constitution and the Men Who Made It, 1936; Life of Edward Coke (with Herman Block), 1929; Corporations and Their Financing, 1938; Determinants of the Rate of Interest, 1942; Risk, Profit and Loss, 1943; Dictatorship of the Proletariat in the United States, 1943; Living on the Public Debt, 1944; The Economy and Its Money, 1947. Home: Morningside Heights, 435 W. 119th St., N.Y.C. Died Apr. 26, 1953; buried First Congl. Ch. Cemetery, Ludlow Center, Mass.

LYON, James Alexander, cardiologist; b. Broome County, N.Y., Feb. 28, 1882; s. Henry and Catherine (Murray) L.; student pub. schools and pvt. tutoring, Ohio U., Syracuse U.; M.D., Md. Med. Coll., Balt., 1906; grad. study Harvard Med. Sch., Univ. Coll. Hosp. and Nat. Hosp. for Disease of Heart (London), U. Vienna; m. Irene Elizabeth Moore (dec.); 1 dau., Elizabeth Moore. Intern Bay View Hosp., Balt., 1906-07; asst. physician Loomis Sanatorium, Liberty, N.Y., 1907-09; asst. supt. and sr. physician Mass State Hosp. for Tb, Rutland, Mass., 1909-16; prof. clin. cardiology Georgetown U, 1929-40; cardiologist and mem. cardiac com. The Doctors Hosp., Inc.; cons. cardiologist and mem. med. bd. Children's Hosp.; cons. cardiologist Homeopathic, and Columbia hosps.; asst. physician Out-Patient Dept. Johns Hopkins' Hospital, 1925-26; attending cardiologist and chief of cardiac clinic, Emergency Hosp., 1929-40; post grad. study, Nat. Hosp. for Diseases of Heart, London, 1923, U. of Vienna, 1924, Mass. Gen. Hosp., Boston, 1926. Mem. bd. dirs. Washington Loan and Trust Co., Inter-Am. Horse Show Assn., Inc., Community Chest of D.C.; mem. medical advisory board Civilian Defense Met. Area, D.C.; mem. nat. med. council U.S. Veterans Bureau. Served from lt. to maj. M.C., U.S. Army, 1916-25; Mexican border service, 1916-17; joined AEF, 51st brig., 26th Div., 1917; organized and commanded Camp Hosp. No. 4. Neufchateau, France, 1917, Evacuation Hosp. No. 19, Soisson Sector (French), 1918; grad. U.S. Army Sanitary Sch., Longue, France, 1918; bn. surgeon 104th U.S. Inf., 26th Div., 1918-19; asst. chief med. service U.S. Base Hosp., Camp Devens, Mass.; chief med. service Base Hosp., Camp Shelby, Miss., and Gen. Hosp. No. 8, Otisville, N. Y., 1919; asst. to attending surg. U.S.A. Dispensary, Washington, 1919-23; detached service Med. Dept., U.S. Army, London and Vienna, 1923-24; post surgeon, Fort Wayne, Detroit, Mich., 1924-25; resigned 1925, to enter pvt. practice in Washington. As bn. surgeon 104th U.S. Inf., participated in battles, Champagne-Marne, Aisne-Marne, Meuse-Argonne, St. Mihiel, Ile de France, Lorraine, defense of Toul; citations: French Army Corps, Army of the East (Verdun), and in gen. orders Nos. 28 and 74, 26th Div., U.S. Army (Aisne-Marne, Meuse-Argonne. Decorated Croix de Guerre with Gold Star, Grande Guerre, Victoire Apparaint Chateau Thiery, Verdun; Abdon Caldern (Ecuador); Purple Heart, Silver Star, Victor Medal with 5 campaign clasps, Mexican Border Service Campaign medal (U.S.); Mil. Order of Carabao (U.S.). Diplomate Am. Bd. Internal. Medicine. Fellow A.M.A., A.A.A.S., N.Y. Acad. Medicine, Am. Coll. Physicians (life mem.); mem. D.C. Med. Soc., So. Med. Soc., Am. Therapeutic Society (ex-pres.), Am., Washington (ex-pres. and sec.) heart assns., Assn. Mil. Surgeons U.S., Mil Order Fgn. Wars (surgeon gen. of Nat. Commandery; past comdr. Washington Commandery), Pan-Am. Med. Assn. (trustee; mem. regional adminstrs.; ex-pres. Washington chapter. Internat. Med. Soc. (ex-treas.; mem. bd. dirs.), Am. Inst. Banking, Washington Med. and Surg. Soc., Mil. Order of Purple Heart, Am. Assn. History Medicine, Mil. Order World War (life mem., Mil. Order of Carabao, Nat. Sojurner's, Heroes of '76, Am. Legion, George Washington Post No. 1, Soc. Am. Legion Founders (Paris, 1918, life member nat. adv. council), 104th U.S.A. Inf. Regt. Vets. Assn.; ex-mem. Gen. Staff, Nat. Commandery, ex-comdr. D.C. Commandery), Nat. Geog. Soc., The Hippocrates-Galen Society of Washington, Ohio U. Alumni Assn., (D.C. chapter), Syracuse U. Alumni Assn. (D.C. Chapter), English-Speaking Union (dir., mem. exec. com. D.C. chapter), Phi Delta Theta (nat.; ex-pres. D.C. alumni club), Phi Chi. Clubs: Army and Navy (ex-mem. bd. govs.), Metropolitan, Chevy Chase, Woodmont (Md.) Rod and Gun (mem. bd. govs.). Home: Glenview Farm, Baltimore Blvd., Rockville, Md.; also 1028 Connecticut Av., Washington, D.C. Office: Washington Med. Bldg., 1801 I St. N.W., Washington. Died Aug. 4, 1955.*

LYON, Leverett Samuel, economist and executive; b. Will Co., Ill., farm, Dec. 14, 1885; s. Edward Payson and Charlotte (Rose) L.; student Beloit (Wis.) College, 1906-07 L.H.D., 1953; Ph.B., U. Chgo., 1910; LL.B., Kent College of Law, 1915; A.M., University of Chicago, 1919, Ph.D., 1921; LL.D., Ill. Inst. Tech., 1950, Northwestern U., 1951; m. Lucille Norton, June 26, 1915; children—Richard Norton, David Mansfield. Head department civic science, Joliet Township High School, 1910-14, 1915-16; admitted to Illinois bar, 1916; assistant in economics, University of Chicago, 1916-17, instr. 1917-19, asst. prof., 1919-23, asso. prof., 1923; dean Sch. Commerce and Finance, prof. economics and head dept., Washington Univ., 1923-25; lecturer on bus. adminstrn., Columbia University, summer, 1925, University of Denver, summer, 1931; professor economics, Robert Brookings Grad. Sch. of Economics and Govt., 1925-29; mem. research staff, dir. ednl. activities and pub. relations Brookings Instn., 1929-32, exec. v.p., 1932-39; chief exec. officer Chicago Association Commerce and Industry, 1939-54, chairman of the executive com., 1954—; chmn. Chgo. Home Rule Commn., 1953-55; exec. dir. N. Eastern Ill. Met. Area Govtl. Services Commn., 1956-57; dept. asst. adminstr. for trade practice policy, NRA, 1934, U.S. delegate to Internat. Congress on Bus. Edn., Amsterdam, 1929, London, 1932. Editorial asst. U.S. Food Adminstrn., World War I. Mem. Chgo. Com. on Nat. Defense, World War II; member Governor's Committee on Taxation, 1941; member executive council Chicago Civil Defense Corps. Mem. State Commn. to Survey Higher Edn., 1943-44. Trustee Brookings Instn., Beloit Coll.; trustee Howard U., 1935-39. Recipient citation for pub. service U. Chgo., 1941. Mem. Chicago Bar Assn., Am. Econ. Assn., Acad. of Polit. Sci. Am. Statis. Assn., Am. Marketing Assn. (pres. 1933), Newcomen Society, Phi Beta Kappa, Phi Kappa Psi (national president 1936-38), Delta Sigma Rho, Phi Delta Phi, Beta Gamma Sigma, Alpha Kappa Psi. Clubs: Chevy Chase (Washington, D.C.); Executives, Union League, Rotary, Mid-Day, Commercial, Economic (Chicago, Illinois). Author or co-author: Elements of Debating, 1913; Eight Lessons (Bull. of Nat. and Community Life), 1917; A Survey of Commercial Education in the Public High Schools of the United States, 1919; A Functional Approach to Social Economic Data, 1920; Our Economic Organization, 1921; Education for Business, 1922, 2d edit., 1923, 3d edit., 1931; Business Cases and Problems, 1925; Making a Living, 1926; Salesmen in Marketing Strategy, 1926; Vocational Readings, 1927; Hand-to-Mouth Buying, 1929; Some Trends in the Marketing of Canned Foods, 1930; Advertising Allowances, 1932; The Economics of Free Deals, 1933; The ABC of the NRA, 1934; The National Recovery Administration—An Analysis and an Appraisal, 1935; The Economics of Open Price Systems, 1936; A Preliminary Analysis for a Program of Economic Education, 1937; Government and Economic Life, Vol. I, 1939, Vol. II, 1940; Your Business and Postwar Readjustment, 1944; Great Lakes-St. Lawrence Seaway and Power Project, 1951; Modernizing a City Government, 1954; Nothing but Nonsense (verse), 1954. Co-editor: Textbooks in the Social Studies (11 vols.); Prospects and Problems in Aviation, 1945; Governmental Problems in the Chicago Metropolitan Area, 1957. Contbr. numerous articles profl. jours. and encyclopedias. Home: 1358 Harbin Dr., Sarasota, Fla. Died Sept. 7, 1959.

LYONS, Lucile Manning (Mrs. John F.); b. Raymond, Tex., Sept. 11, 1879; d. John W. and Charlie Ella (Burton) Manning; grad. as Licentiate of Instruction, Peabody Normal Coll., Nashville, 1899; B.A., U. Nashville, 1900; m. John F. Lyons, Oct. 23, 1901; children—Burton, John F., Jr. Organized Harmony Club, Ft. Worth, 1904; organized, 1st pres. Tex. Fedn. Music Clubs, 1915; sec. Nat. Fedn. Music Clubs, 1915, pres., 1921-25; mgr. mus. and dramatic attractions, Fort Worth and Dallas; lectr. mus. subjects. Regional dir. fed. music project under Works Projects Adminstrn., states of Tex., Ark., Miss., La., Okla.; state dir. fed. music project under Works Projects Adminstrn. for state of Tex. Mem. Sigma Alpha Iota. Democrat. Presbyn. Mem. Order Eastern Star. Clubs: Harmony, Nat. Federation of Music Clubs. Home: 900 Southland Av., Ft. Worth. Died Sept. 25, 1958; buried Greenwood Cemetery.

LYTELL, Bert, actor, dir.; b. N.Y.C., Feb. 24, 1887; s. William H. and Blanche (Mortimer; L.; student Upper Canada Coll., Toronto; m. Grace Menken, Mar. 16, 1930. Early tng. in stock cos., Albany and Rochester (N.Y.), San Francisco; first Broadway appearance with Marie Dressler; played in Mary's Ankle; motion pictures include The Lone Wolf, Boston Blackie, Alias Jimmy Valentine, The Right of Way; starred in vaudeville in The Valiant; returned to Broadway in Brothers, The Church Mouse; The First Legion (also producer); Margin for Error, Lady in the Dark, The Wind is 90, I Like it Here; master of ceremonies Philco TV theater; was original Father Barbour in TV show One Man's Family. Served in central inf., Officers Camp McArthur, Waco, Tex., World War I. Mem. U.S.O. Camp Shows, Am. Theatre Wing; Actors Equity Assn. (pres. 1942-45, hon. pres.). Episcopalian. Club: Lambs. Home: 145 W. 58th St., N.Y.C. Died Sept. 28, 1954.*

M

MAASKE, Roben J(ohn) (mäs′kē), coll. pres.; b. Bertrand, Neb., Oct. 31, 1903; s. Frank H. and Minnie (Ross) M.; student Doane Coll., Crete, Neb., 1921-22; B.A., University of Neb., 1927; M.A., U. of Ore., 1936; Ph.D., U. of Minn., 1938; m. Iola A. Solso. Teacher, 1-room rural school near Bertrand, Neb., 1922-23; prin. Ewing High Sch., 1924-25; supt. Irrigon, Ore. Pub. Sch., 1927-29; supervisor Portland (Ore.) Pub. Schs., 1929-31; dep. state supt. Ore., 1931-36; prof. sch. adminstrn, U. of N.C., and editor The High School Journal, 1937-39; pres. Eastern Ore. Coll. Edn., La Grande, 1939-50; pres. Ore. Coll. Edn., Monmouth, 1950—; vis. prof. summer sessions, U. S.D., 1937, U. N.C., 1940, U. Colo., 1941-42, U. Chgo., 1945, U. Ida., 1946-47, U. So. Cal., 1949-51. Mem. Ore. Acad. of Science, N.E.A., Adult Edn. Assn., Pacific Northwest Assn. of Adult Edn., Am. Ednl. Research Assn., Oregon Educational Association, A.A.A.S., American Academy of Political and Social Science, Phi Delta Kappa, Kappa Delta Pi, Pi Kappa Phi. Presbyterian. Independent Republican. Elk, Mason, Rotarian, Grange. Author numerous booklets, brochures and articles. Home: 395 College St., Monmouth, Ore. Died Feb. 19, 1955; buried Bertrand, Neb.

MAASS, Herbert Halsey, lawyer; b. San Francisco, Mar. 2, 1878; s. Julius and Celia (Redlich) M.; LL.B., New York U., 1898, LL.M., 1899; L.H.D., (hon.) Case Inst. of Technology, Cleveland; m. Hannah Lowenstein, Apr. 27, 1905; children—Dorothy (Mrs. Elson Guiterman), Joan (Mrs. Victor Oristano), Herbert H., Jr. Admitted to N.Y. State bar, 1899, and since practiced in N.Y.C.; mem. Maass, Davidson, Levy & Friedman; dir. and counsel Consol. Cigar Corp., Pershing Square Bldg. Corp., Murray Hill Operating Co. Chmn. bd. of trustees Inst. for Advanced Study, Princeton, N.J., 1942—. Mem. Am. and N.Y. State bar assns., N.Y. County Lawyers Assn., Assn. of Bar of City of N.Y. Jewish religion. Mason. Clubs: Harmonie (N.Y.); Ocean Beach (Elberon, N.J.). Home: Sherry Netherland Hotel, N.Y.C. 22. Office: 100 Park Av., N.Y.C. 17. Deceased.

MABIE, Edward Charles (mā′bē), coll. prof., play producer; b. La Crosse, Wis., Oct. 27, 1892; s. Fred Lincoln and Emma (Viner) M.; B.A., Dartmouth, 1915, M.A., 1916; Dr. Fine Arts, Illinois Wesleyan University, 1952; m. Grace Francis Chase, June 15, 1916; 1 dau., Priscilla Ann. Instr. in public speaking, Dartmouth, 1915-16; prof. rhetoric and oratory, Ill. Wesleyan Coll., Bloomington, Ill., 1917-18; asst. prof. English, U. of Ky., 1918-20; with State U. of Ia. since 1920, prof. speech and head of dept. since 1925, dir. gen. Studies, College of Liberal Arts, 1947, director university theatre; regional director Federal Theatre Project, 1935-36. Vice-president Nat. Theatre Conf.; pres. Nat. Assn. Teachers of Speech, 1926; pres. Am. Ednl. Theatre Assn., 1937. Mem. Delta Sigma Rho, Phi Beta Kappa (hon.). Conglist. Mason (32°). Wrote: Plays for High Schools, 1921. Editor: University Debater's Annual, 1915, 16. Author, director: Never Ending Frontier. Home: 2 Woolf Av. Ct., Iowa City, Ia. Died Feb. 9, 1956.

MABIE, Louise Kennedy, writer; b. Cleve.; d. James H. and Mary Gillen (Pierce) Kennedy; student

Horace Man Sch., New York, and by pvt. tutelage in langs., history and music; 1 dau., Mary Louise (Mrs. J. M. Ellis). Conglist. Author: The Wings of Pride; The Lights Are Bright. Contbr. short stories to Saturday Evening Post, Collier's, Cosmopolitan, Ladies' Home Journal. Address: care Brandt & Brandt, 101 Park Av., N.Y.C. 17. Died Nov. 10, 1957.

MABON, Thomas McCance (mă'bon), physician; b. Pitts, Aug. 11, 1890; s. John Steele and Jane Hearst (McCance) M.; B.S., Princeton, 1913; M.D., Harvard, 1917; Master of Public Health, U. of Pittsburgh, 1953; m. Marjorie Arnold, Dec. 28, 1921; 1 son, Thomas McCance. House pupil Mass. Gen. Hosp., Boston, 1917-18, indsl. clinic, 1921; immunologist Singer Meml. Research Lab., Pitts., 1918-19; asst. prof. dept. hygiene and preventive medicine, U. Pitts., 1922-27, asso. prof., 1933-41, prof. since 1941, instr. medicine, sch. medicine, 1924-28, asst. prof., 1928-48, asso. prof. medicine since 1948, sr. staff Falk Clinic; sr. staff Presbyn. Hosp., Pitts. Served as 1st lt. M.C. A.U.S., 1918-19. Diplomate Am. Bd. Internal Medicine, founders group Am. Bd. Preventive Medicine and Pub. Health Fellow A.M.A., A.C.P., Am. Pub. Health Assn., Am. Diabetes Assn.; mem. Allegheny Co. Med. Soc. (pres 1948-49), Med. Soc. Pa., Am. Heart Assn., Am. Psychomatic Soc., A.A.A.S., Pitts. Acad. Medicine (sec. 1927-46, pres. 1946-47). Clubs: Princeton (N.Y.), Harvard (Boston); Harvard-Yale-Princeton, University (Pitts.). Home: 5446 Kipling Rd., Pitts. 17. Died 1958.

MacALISTER, Sir Ian, ret. orgn. exec.; b. Liverpool, Eng., Apr. 1, 1878; s. Sir John and Elizabeth (Batley) MacA.; Found. scholar, St. Paul's Sch., London, 1892-97; M.A., Merton Coll., Oxford U., 1901; m. Dorothy Seaton, Jan. 7, 1909; children—Joan (Mrs. Spowart), Elizabeth (Mrs. Divine), John, Dorothy (Mrs. McNeill), Peter, Anthony, Helen (Mrs. Ambrose). A.D.C., pvt. sec. to Earl of Dundonald, 1902-04; journalist Times, Morning Leader, Westminster Gazette, 1904-07; sec. Royal Inst. Brit. Architects, 1908-43. Served as a lieutenant in Royal Defense Corps, 1916-19, Q.M. Home Guard, 1940-44. Created Knight, 1934. Member Athenaeum, Royal Empire Soc., Royal United Service Instn.; hon. asso. Royal Inst. Brit. Architects; hon. mem. A.I.A. Home: Little Gables, Tonbridge, Kent, Eng. Died June 10, 1957.

MacARTHUR, Charles, author, playwright; b. Scranton, Pa., Nov. 5, 1895; s. Rev. William T. and Georgiana (Welstead) MacA.; ed. Wilson Memorial Acad., Nyack, N.Y.; m. Helen Hayes, Aug. 17, 1928; children—Mary (dec.), James. Reporter Chicago Herald and Examiner, Chicago Tribune and N.Y. American, 1914-23; spl. writer Hearst's Internat. Magazine, 1924; writer and produced motion pictures and plays, 1929—. Vice pres. Lancaster & Chester Railroad. Served as trooper 1st Ill. Cav., Mexican Border, 1916; pvt. 149th F.A. (Rainbow Div.) A.E.F., 1917-19; assistant to Chief of Chem. Warfare Service, Washington, D.C., with rank of Lt. Col., 1942-45. Clubs: River, Coffee House; The Tavern (Chicago). Author: War Bugs, 1926; (plays) Lulu Belle (with E. Sheldon), 1926; Salvation (with S. Howard), 1927; The Front Page (with Ben Hecht), 1928; Twentieth Century (with Ben Hecht), 1933; Ladies and Gentlemen (with Ben Hecht), 1939; Johnny on the Spot, 1941; Swan Song (with Ben Hecht) 1946; also numerous motion pictures. Contbr. fiction. Home: Nyack, N.Y. Died Apr. 21, 1956; buried Oak Hill Cemetery, Nyack, N.Y.

MACARTHUR, John R(obertson), educator; b. Winnipeg, Manitoba, Can.; Mar. 31, 1874; s. Duncan and Catharine (Robertson) M.; B.A., U. Manitoba, 1892; Ph.D., U. Chgo., 1903; unmarried. Came to U.S., 1898, naturalized, 1906. Instr., Manitoba Coll., 1893-98; head dept. English, N.M. State Coll., 1903-10, and dean, 1911-13; agt. Internat. Com., Y.M.C.A., Ellis Island, 1910-11; prof. English, Kan. State Coll., 1914-20; asso. prof. English, Cal. Inst. Tech., 1920-23, prof. langs., 1923-45, dean of freshmen, 1923-36, acting dean of freshmen 1943-45; prof. emeritus of languages, 1945—; made Deacon Episcopal Church, 1928, ordained priest, Episcopal Ch., 1945; vicar Ch. of Good Shepherd, Bonita, Cal., 1954-57. Mem. Phi Beta Kappa Assos., Phi Kappa Phi, Sigma Phi Epsilon, Pi Kappa Delta (nat. sec. 1920-22, nat. pres. 1922-26, editor 1922-28). Episcopalian. Club: Athenaeum (Pasadena). Author: First Part of Sir John Oldcastle, 1907; Biblical Literature and Its Backgrounds, 1936; Ancient Greece in Modern America, 1943. Home: 183 3d Av., Chula Vista, Cal. Died Jan. 31, 1960.

MACARTNEY, Clarence Edward Noble (mâ-kärt'-nē), clergyman; b. Northwood, O., Sept. 18, 1879; s. J. L. (D.D.) and Catherine (Robertson) M.; B.A., Univ. of Wis., 1901; M.A., Princeton, 1904; graduated Princeton Theological Seminary, 1905; D.D., Geneva College, 1914, Litt.D., same college, 1933; LL.D., Washington and Jefferson Coll., 1939; LL.D., Coll. of the Ozarks, 1939; D.D., University of Pittsburgh, 1953; unmarried. Ordained Presbyterian ministry, 1905; pastor 1st Church, Paterson, N.J., 1905-14, Arch St. Ch., Phila., 1914-27; First Church, Pittsburgh, 1927-53. Dir. Westminster and Princeton theol. seminaries; moderator Presbyn. Ch. in U.S.A., 1924-25. Stone Foundation lecturer, Princeton Theol. Sem., 1928; Ott lecture, Davidson Coll., 1934; Macartney lecture, Phila., 1928, 35, 46; Davis lecture, Hiram College, 1937, Smythe lectures, Columbia Theol. Sem., 1939; John S. Bussing lectures, Western Theol. Sem., Holland, Mich.; lectures at Wittenburg Coll., 1943, Princeton Inst. of Theology, 1944, 45, Ala. Bible Society, 1945. Author of 57 books in field of history, biography and religion since 1913; latest publs.: Mountains and Mountain Men of the Bible, 1950; Strange Texts But Grand Truths, 1953; Chariots of Fire, 1950. Grant and His Generals, 1953; Faith Once Delivered, 1953; The Woman of Takoah, 1955; Mr. Lincolns' Admirals, 1956. Address: Fern Cliffe, Geneva Coll., Beaver Falls, Pa. Died Feb. 19, 1957; buried Grandview Cemetery, Beaver Falls, Pa.

MACAULEY, Alvan, automobile mfr.; b. Wheeling, W.Va., Jan. 17, 1872; student Lehigh U., 1888-90; George Washington U., 1890-92; m. Estelle Littlepage, Nov. 20, 1895; children—Alvan, Mary (Mrs. Henry Whiting), Edward. Was admitted to bar in Ohio, 1897; practiced in Washington, 3 yrs.; with Nat. Cash Register Co., Dayton, O., 1895-1901; gen. mgr. Burroughs Adding Machine Co., Detroit, 1901-10; gen. mgr. Packard Motor Car Co., 1910-34, v.p., 1913-16, pres. 1916-39, chmn. bd., 1939-48. Pres. Automotive Council for War Prodn. Mem. Detroit Bd. Commerce, Automobile Mfrs. Assn. (pres.). Clubs: Old, Detroit, Detroit Golf, Country, Yondotega. Address: 735 Lake Shore Drive, Grosse Pointe Shores 30, Mich. Deceased.

MacBRAYNE, Lewis E., author; b. New Britain, Conn., Nov. 1, 1871; s. William S. and Mary S. (Slate) M.; grad. Lowell High Sch.; traveled in Europe; m. Sarah E. Thurlow, Aug. 27, 1903; children—Elinor, Thurlow, Elizabeth, Frances. With Lowell (Mass.) Courier-Citizen as reporter and editor 27 yrs. Regional dir. for State of N.Y. on spl. war work with Dept. of Interior, 1918-19; field sec. Mass. C. of C. in 1919. Gen. mgr. Mass. Safety Council, 1921; state dir. safety, Federal Works Projects, 1934-36. Republican. Conglist. Author: The Men We Marry, 1910; One More Chance (with James P. Ramsay), 1916; An Engaging Position (play). Contbr. to mags. Home: 45 Glendale Road, Belmont, Mass. Office: 80 Federal St., Boston. Died Dec. 29, 1954; buried Lowell, Mass.

MacBRIDE, D.S., business exec.; b. Oakland, Cal., 1893; B.S. Civil Engring., U. Pa., 1956. Pres., dir. American Cement Corp.; dir. Portland Cement Asso., Rogers & Baldwin Hardware Co., Springfield, Mo. Home: 1109 Brynllawn Rd., Villanova, Pa. Office: 1530 Chestnut St., Phila. 2. Died Mar. 9, 1959.

MacCAUGHEY, Vaughan (mâ-koi'), educator; b. Huron, S.D., July 7, 1887; s. William Franklyn and Matilda (Vaughan) MacC.; B.S.A., Cornell U., 1908; post-grad. work University of Chicago, 1916-17; B.Ed., San Francisco State College; married Janet H. Brooker, Nov. 25, 1909; children—Hamilton, Matilda, Horace, Patricia, Nancy, Phoebe-Jean. Asst. Cornell U., 1905-08; head dept. natural science and v.p. Territorial Normal Sch., Hawaii, 1908-09; prof. botany, Coll. of Hawaii, 1910-19; supt. pub. instrn. for H.T., 1919-23. Visiting prof. U. of Calif., summer, 1911, Cornell U., summer, 1912; prin. Mid-Pacific Inst. Mills Sch., 1913. Chautauqua Instn., 1906, 07, 14, 15, 16; 8 continental lecture tours; dir. Territorial Summer Sch., Kilauea Volcano, Hawaii, 1919; biol. explorations, H.I.; extension staff U. of Calif. since 1923; mem. Nat. Council Boy Scouts of America, spl. field commr. Calif., dir. edn. Region 12; dean San Francisco Training Sch. for Scout Officers; dir. Pacific Coast Survey of Race Relations, N. Calif., 1924. Mem. Hosp. Corps, 1st Inf. Nat. Guard, Hawaii, 1909-12, Co. B 1st Inf., 1913-15. Supt. Bible Sch. Central Union Ch., 1913-16. Pres. Honolulu Ad Club, 1919-21; dir. for Hawaii, N.E.A., 1916-23; mem. Nat. Editorial Council, N.E.A., 1922-23; del. World Conf. on Edn., San Francisco, 1923; chmn. exec. com. Pan-Pacific Ednl. Conf., 1921; del. Pan-Pacific Scientific Conf., 1919; joint founder and pres. Agassiz Club of Cornell. Joint founder and editor Hawaiian Educational Review, 1913-16; editor Sierra Educational News, 1923-52, ret.; dir. Audubon Camp of Cal., 1952-53; Pacific Coast rep. Nat. Audubon Soc. since 1952. Fellow A.A.A.S.; mem. S.A.R., Sigma Xi, Phi Gamma Mu. Republican. Conglist. Mason. Author: The Natural History of Chautauqua, 1917; The Schools of Hawaii; Race-Mixtures in Hawaii. Contbr. more than 200 papers to scientific and ednl. jours. Home: 726 Cragmont Av., Berkeley 8, Calif. Office: 693 Sutter St., San Francisco 2. Died Mar. 24, 1954.

MacCHESNEY, Nathan William, lawyer, jud. officer, diplomat, soldier; b. Chgo., June 2, 1878; s. Alfred Brunson (M.D., lieutenant colonel United States Army) and Henrietta (Milsom) MacChesney; brother of Chester M. MacChesney; A.B., Coll. of Pacific, 1898; spl. student Stanford, 1896-99; student instr., U. of Ariz., 1898-99; student Northwestern Law Sch., 1899-1900; LL.B., U. of Mich., 1902; LL.M., Northwestern Univ., 1922; hon LL D., Coll. of Pacific, 1926, U. of Mich., 1934; m Lena Frost, Dec. 1, 1904; children—Alfred Brunson III, Gordon. Senior member MacChesney & Becker, Chicago; special assistant attorney general of United States, 1911-12; special asst. state's atty., 1912; spl. asst. atty. gen., Ill., 1913-33; spl. counsel City of Chicago, 1924; gen. counsel Nat. Assn. Real Estate Bds.; apptd. U.S. minister to Canada by President Hoover, 1932-33; high commr. for Canada, Century of Progress Exposition, Chicago, 1933-34; consul general for Thailand (Siam), 1924—; appointed U.S. referee in bankruptcy, 1943. Life member National Conference Commissioners on Uniform State Laws (president 1922-25); of counsel for United States Senate in investigation of U.S. War Vets. Bur. and of Rent Control in D.C. and for War Dept. in U.S. Supreme Court, 1914-17; counsel Nat. Child Labor Com. and draftsman many acts for social, uniform and progressive legislation; lecturer U. of Ill., 1908-16; mem. exec. com. Chicago Plan Commn.; mem. Air Bd. of Chicago; mem. Chicago Crime Commn.; trustee Northwestern U., 1913-48, life trustee, 1948—; trustee Nat. Alumni Council U. of Mich., Carson Long Inst., Pub. Health Inst.; chairman Bd. Salvation Army, life mem. Com. 15. Served in Ill., Calif. and Ariz. N.G., 1893-1917 and as judge advocate gen. of Ill., 1911-17; served with 33d and 86th divs. and sec. of War in U.S., and 33d Div. and G.H.Q., A.E F in France on staffs of Sec. of War Baker, Gens. Crowder, Ansell, Carter, Barry, Wood, Kreger, Bell, Bethel and Pershing, 1917-19; assigned active duty, U.S. Army, June 27, 1917; dep. judge advocate, Central Dept. U.S. Army, 1917-18; judge advocate, G.H.Q., A.E. F., in France, brig. gen. Ill. N.G., col. U.S. Army. Presented with commemorative sabre; recommended for D.S.M.; awarded citation by Gen. Pershing "for exceptionally meritorious and conspicuous services, A E.F." Mil. Order of Purple Heart and Victory Medal with citation (U.S.); also U.S. Army Commendation medal with 2 stars; United Nations and French Commemorative medals; Comdr. Order of the White Elephant conferred by King of Siam; Chevalier Order Crown of Italy; Officer French Legion of Honor. On active duty with United States Army, 1942-43. Mem. American Bar Assn. (v.p. 1925-26; chmn. sect. Internat. and Comparative Law, 1934-35; chmn. sect. Real Property, Probate and Trust Law, 1936-38; House of De's. 1939); mem. Ill. State Bar Assn. (life; pres. 1915-16), Chicago Bar Assn. (bd. mgrs., 1943-45), Association Bar City of New York, Conference of Bar Association Delegates (chmn. 1926-27), Am. Law Inst. (charter mem.), Am. Inst. Criminal Law and Criminology (pres. 1910-11), Am. Soc. Internat. Law, S.A.R., Soc. War of 1812 (pres. 1912-14, Sons of World Wars (past comdr.), Phi Kappa Psi, Phi Beta Kappa, Pi Gamma Mu, Phi Delta Phi, Order of the Coif (nat. pres. 1910-13), Northwestern U. General Alumni Assn. (president 1922-24, awarded Alumni Medal, 1947), Northwestern University Foundation (pres. 1926-28); honorary member Chicago Council of Foreign Relations; English-Speaking Union; member Alliance Francaise (treas., director), Italy-American Society, hon. life mem. Chicago Hist. Soc.; hon. mem. Md., Neb., Iowa, Minn., Ohio, Pa., Tex., Tenn. state bar assns., Chicago Assn. Commerce. Mem. exec. com. Rep. Nat. Conv., 1908-20; active in Theodore Roosevelt, 1912, and Leonard Wood, 1920, campaigns; dir. organization bur., Hoover, Rep. Nat. Com., 1928-32. Pres. Nat. Rep. Lawyers League, 1928-40. Presbyterian. Mason. Clubs: University, Chicago, Union League, Chicago Law, Chicago Literary, Knollwood, Michigan Union, Lawyers (Ann Arbor); Metropolitan (Washington). Author: (or editor) Abraham Lincoln, The Tribute of a Century, 1909; The Significance of the War of 1812; Uniform State Laws; Challenge to American Ideals; French Contribution to American Life; Military Policy and Laws of the U.S.; Principles of Real Estate Law; Law of Real Estate Brokerage. Home: 710 Lake Shore Drive, Chicago; (summer) Riverhill Farm, Belvidere Rd. and Desplaines River, Libertyville, Lake County, Ill. Office: 225 S. Clark St., Chgo. Died Sept. 25, 1954; buried Oak Woods Cemetery, Chgo.

MacCONNELL, John Wilson, surgeon, educator; b. McConnellsville, S.C., Jan. 11, 1878; s. John Daniel and Sarah Amanda (Jaggers) MacC.; B.S., Davidson (N.C.) Coll., 1902, M.A., 1906; M.D., U. Md., 1907; studied Columbia, U. Edinburgh; m. Agnes Haig Doyle, July 28, 1909 (dec.); 1 son, John Courtney. Resident surgeon Presbyn. Hosp., Balt., 1907-08; practiced at Davidson, 1908—; organized dept. of biology Davidson Coll., prof. biology, 1908-19, prof, physiology and hygiene, dir. student health service, now emeritus; dir. Bank of Davidson. Served as 1st lt. M.C., U.S. Army, Mexican border, 1916; capt. Base Hosp., Camp Jackson, 1917; maj. to lt. col. AEF, 1918-19, col., 1925; hon. disch. 1919; retired 1929, as lt. col. E.O.R. Sec. N.C. Bd. Med. Examiners; surgeon So. Ry. Fellow A.M.A.; mem. Med. Society State of N.C., Tri-State, So. med. assns., Nat. Fedn. Medical Bds. (v.p.), Am. Legion, Mil. Order of World War, Sigma Alpha Epsilon, Nu Sigma Nu, Phi Beta Kappa, Omicron Delta Kappa. Democrat. Presbyn. Mason, K.P. Home: Davidson, N.C. Died Sept. 26, 1950; buried Davidson, N.C.

MacCULLOUGH, Gleason Harvey, educator; b. Sawyerville, Que., Sept. 9, 1895; s. Robert and Florence (Harvey) MacC.; B.S., Worcester Poly. Inst., 1918; M.S., 1931; Sc.D., U. Mich., 1932. Came to U.S., 1901, naturalized, 1918. Faculty Worcester Poly. Inst. since 1918, instr., asst. prof. mech. engring., 1918-32, prof. engring. mechanics, head dept. mech. engring. since 1949. Mem. Mathematics Assn. Am., A.S.M.E., Am. Soc. Engring. Edn., Soc. Exptl. Stress Analysis, Sigma Xi, Tau Beta Pi, Sigma Phi Epsilon. Republican. Baptist. Clubs: Economic. Torch. Author: Elements of Strength of Materials (with S. Timoshenko). Contbr. articles profl. publs. Home: 61 Monadnock Rd., Worcester, Mass. Died Oct. 15, 1956; buried Hope Cemetery, Worcester, Mass.

MacCUTCHEON, Aleck (mā-kŭch'ŭn), cons. elec. engr.; b. Stockport, N.Y., Dec. 31, 1881; s. Samuel J. and Janet L. (McBurney) MacC.; grad. Albany State Normal Coll., 1901; E.E., Columbia, 1908; m. Caroline S. Sheffer, Dec. 23, 1908; children—Samuel M., Richard H. Elec. engr. Crocker-Wheeler, 1909-14; elec. engr. Reliance Electric and Engring. Co., Cleve., 1914, v.p., 1922-46, ret.; dir. Engring. Co. (Cleve.). Served as lt. USN, 1917-19. Received Lamme Medal awarded by Am. Inst. E.E., 1948. Mem. Am. Inst. E.E. (pres. 1936-37), Am. Standards Assn., Assn. Iron and Steel Engrs., Phi Kappa Sigma, Tau Beta Pi, Eta Kappa Nu. Conglist. Clubs: Columbia U. (N.Y.C.); Canterbury, Lost Lake Woods. Home: 3104 Woodbury Rd., Shaker Heights, Cleve. Died Mar. 3, 1954; buried Germantown, N.Y.

MACDONALD, Angus Lewis, Can. govt. official; b. Dunvegan, N.S., Aug. 10, 1890; s. Lewis and Veronica (Perry) M.; B.A., gold medalist, St. Francis Xavier Univ.; LL.B., Dalhousie Univ.; honorary LL.D.; student Columbia Univ.; S.J.D., Harvard; LL.D., Univ. of Ottawa; LL.D., Queen's University; m. Agnes Mary Foley, June 17, 1924; children—Aileen Veronica, Angus Lewis, Jr., Coline Foley, Una. Admitted to N.S. bar, 1921; King's counsel, 1936; read law with Donald MacLennan, Inverness, N.S., 1919-21; asst. dep. atty.-gen., Halifax, 1921-24; lecturer, Dalhousie Law Sch., Halifax, 1922-24, prof. of law, 1924-29; associate editor Dominion Law Reports, 1929-30; elected mem. N.S. Assembly for Halifax South, Aug. 1933, re-elected, 1937; elected premier of N.S. and Provincial sec. and treas., Sept. 1933; apptd. minister of nat. defense for Naval Services, July 1940, resigned 1945; premier of Nova Scotia, since Sept. 8, 1945. Served as lt., 25th Btn., capt., 185th Batn., World War I. Roman Catholic. Mem. Liberal Party. Clubs: Halifax (Halifax); Ashburn Golf and Country. Home: "Winwick," Marlboro Woods, Halifax, N.S. Office: Province House, Halifax, N.S. Died Apr. 13, 1954.

MacDONALD, Betty (b. Anne Elizabeth Campbell Bard), author; b. Boulder, Colo. Mar. 26, 1908; d. Darsie Campbell and Elsie Tholimar (Sanderson) Bard; ed. Roosevelt High Sch., Seattle; student U. Wash.; m. Robert E. Heskett, 1927 (div.); children—Ann Elizabeth, Joan Sydney; m. 2d, Donald Chauncey MacDonald, Apr. 24, 1942. Labor adjuster NRA, 1931-33; with procurement div. U.S. Treasury Dept.; supr. publicity N.Y.A., 1939-42; asst. purchasing agt. U.S. Office Emergency Mgmt.; chief clerk West Constrn. Co., Seattle. Author: The Egg and I, 1945; Mrs. Piggle-Wiggle, 1947; The Plague and I, 1948; Mrs. Piggle-Wiggle's Magic, 1949; Anybody Can Do Anything, 1950; Nancy and Plum, 1952; Onions in the Stew, 1955; Mrs. Piggle-Wiggle's Farm, 1954; Onions in the Stew, 1955. Mem. Theta Sigma Phi. Home: P.O. Box 3, Carmel Valley, Cal. Address: care J. B. Lippincott Co., East Washington Sq., Phila. Died Feb. 7, 1958.

MacDONALD, Byrnes, petroleum exec.; b. N.Y. City, Jan. 1, 1908; s. George and Belle (Byrnes) MacD.; student Newman Sch., Lakewood, N.J., 1918-25, Hill Sch., 1925-28; A.B., Princeton, 1932; m. Aleta Morris, Feb. 2, 1935; 1 son, George Morris. With N.R.A., 1935; dep. police commr., N.Y. City, 1936-37, dep. commr. Dept. Welfare, 1938-39, sec. to mayor, 1939-41; asst. to pres. Sinclair Oil Corp. since 1946. Mem. bd. Andrew Freedman Home; mem. nat. exec. bd. Boy Scouts Am. since 1934. Served as lt. comdr. U.S.N.R., 1941-45, Pacific Theatre. Mem. Florence Crittenton League, Girls Service League, Irish Hist. Soc., Am. Legion, Mil. Order Fgn. Wars, Navy League. Roman Catholic. Elk, Knight of Malta, Knight of Holy Sepulchre. Clubs: Newport Country, Reading Room, Spouting Rock (Newport, R.I.); Meadowbrook (Westbury, L.I.); The Brook, Racquet and Tennis (N.Y.C.); Links, U. Cottage (Princeton). Author: Italo-Vatican Accord, 1932. Home: 895 Park Av., N.Y.C. 21; (summer) Chepstow, Narragansett Av., Newport, R.I. Office: 600 Fifth Av., N.Y.C. 20. Died Oct. 1959.

MACDONALD, George Everett, editor; b. Gardiner, Me., Apr. 11, 1857; s. Henry and Asenath Chase (Hussey) M.; ed. pub. schs.; m. Grace Dayton Leland, July 20, 1888; children—Eugene Leland, Putnam Foote. Printer's apprentice Truth Seeker (weekly), N.Y.C., 1875, later foreman and asst. editor; newspaper work in Cal. and Wash., 1887-93; asst. editor Truth Seeker, 1893-1909, editor, 1909-36; pres. Truth Seeker Co. Republican. Freethinker. Author: Fifty Years of Freethought. Home: Upper Montclair, N.J. Office: Truth Seeker Co., N.Y.C. Died July 21, 1944.

MacDONALD, Henry, lawyer; b. Wilkes-Barre, Pa., Jan. 24, 1890; s. Michael and Mary (Barrett) MacD.; LL.B., Yale U., 1911; m. Charmian Gordon Campbell, Aug. 20, 1938; children—Catherine, Gerald, Joseph. Admitted to N.Y. bar, 1912, since in practice of law, specializing in corporate and estate work; general counsel for Nassau & Suffolk Lighting Co. and other public utilities since 1915; pres. Public Service Corp. of L.I.; Mamargil Realty & Development Corp., N.Y.C., Hemnord Realty Associates, N.Y.C. Dir. Gen. Mayor's Com. on Nat. Defense, N.Y.C., World War; served as ensign U.S. Naval Reserve, World War. Decorated Knight Order of Dannebrog (Denmark); Comdr. Crown of Italy (Italy); Chevalier Legion of Honor (French); Grand Cross of Order of Holy Sepulchre, Grand Cross Order of St. Lazare, Knighthood Sovereign Mil. Order of Malta (Papal decorations). Trustee, sec. and treas. Newman Sch., Lakewood, N.J.; pres. Occupational Research Found.; v.p. Catholic Youth Orgn.; exec. sec. Catholic Big Brothers; chmn. Center Com. on Business and Industries. Mem. Am. Acad. Polit. Science, Am., N.Y. State and N.Y. Co. bar assns., Nat. Geog. Soc., Mus. of Natural History, Italy-Am. Soc., Franco-Am. Soc. Japan Soc., Friendly Sons of St. Patrick (life), Met. Mus. Art, Am. Irish Hist. Soc., St. Paul's Guild, Am. Soc. Royal Italian Orders, Calvert Associates, Yale Law Sch. Assn., Museum of French Arts (life), Am. Legion. Clubs: Yale, University, Piping Rock, Bankers, West Side Tennis, Down Town Assn., Down Town Athletic (founder member), Everglades (Palm Beach, Fla.); The Pilgrims, (N.Y.C.); Interalliée (Paris, France). Author: New York City Committee on National Defense, 1919. Home: 778 Park Av., N.Y.C. Office: 85 Liberty St., N.Y.C. 6. Died Apr. 23, 1956; buried Gate of Heaven Cemetery, Hawthorne, N.Y.

MacDONALD, Thomas Harris, engr.; b. Leadville, Colo., July 23, 1881; s. John and Elizabeth (Harris) MacD.; student Ia. State Tchrs. Coll., Cedar Falls, 1899-1900; B.C.E., Ia. State Coll. Agr. and Mech. Arts, Ames, 1904; D.Eng. (hon.), Ia. State Coll., 1929; m. Bess Dunham, Mar. 7, 1907 (dec. 1935); children—Thomas Harris, Margaret Elizabeth (Mrs. Charles William Weidinger); m. 2d, Caroline L. Fuller, Nov. 24, 1953. Began with engring. dept. C.G.W. Ry.; chief engr. Ia. State Hwy. Commn., 1904-19; chief U.S. Bur. Pub. Rds., Dept. of Agr., 1919-39; became commr. pub. rds., charge pub. rds. adminstrn. Fed. Works Agy., 1939, ret. from U.S. service, 1953; head hwy. research center Tex. A. and M. Coll., 1953—. Decorated Medal of Merit (U.S.); Cross Legion of Honor (France); Knight 1st class Order of St. Olav (Norway); fgn. mem. Masarykova Akademie (Czechoslovakia). Recipient Marston Medal for achievement in engring. Ia. State Coll., 1939. Mem. Am. Assn. State Hwy. Ofcls. (exec. com.), Beta Theta Pi, Tau Beta P. Presbyn. Club: Cosmos (Washington). Author papers on hwy. engring., adminstrn. and finance. Home: 1000 Puryear Dr., College Station, Tex. Died Apr. 7, 1957; buried Cedar Hill Cemetery, Washington.

MacDOUGAL, Daniel Trembly (măk-dōō'găl), botanist and author; b. Liberty, Ind., Mar. 16, 1865; s. Alexander and Amanda MacD.; B.S., DePauw U., 1890, A.M., 1894, LL.D., 1912; M.S., Purdue U., 1891, Ph.D., 1897; student Tübingen and Leipzig, 1895-96; LL.D., U. Ariz., 1915; m. Louise Fisher, Jan. 24, 1893. Agt. U.S. Dept. Agr. on explorations in Ariz. and Ida., 1891-92; instr. plant physiology U. Minn., 1893-95, asst. prof., 1895-99; dir. labs. and asst. dir. N.Y. Bot. Garden, 1899-1905; dir. Dept. Bot. Research and Laboratory for Plant Physiology, Carnegie Inst. of Washington, 1905-33. Fellow Cal. Acad. Science; life mem. Bot. Soc. America, Am. Soc. Plant Physiology, A.A.A.S., Torrey Bot. Club; mem. Am. Philos. Soc., Cal. Bot. Soc.; fgn. mem. Hollandsche Maatschappe d. Wetenschappen, Societé Nationale D'Acclimatation de France; hon. mem. Bot. Soc. of Edinburgh; corr. mem. Czechoslovak Bot. Soc.; pres. Am. Soc. Naturalists, 1910; gen. sec. A.A.A.S., 1920-25. Clubs: Century (N.Y.C.); Old Pueblo (Tucson). Author: Influence of Light and Darkness Upon Growth and Development, 1903; Botanical Features of North American Deserts, 1908; The Water-Balance of Succulent Plants, 1910; Conditions of Parasitism in Plants, 1910; Alterations in Heredity Induced by Ovarial Treatment, 1911; The Salton Sea, 1913; Hydration and Growth, 1919; Growth in Trees, 1921, 1924; Hydrostatic System of Trees, 1926; The Green Leaf, 1930; Pneumatic System of Plants, Especially Trees, 1933; Studies in Tree Growth by the Dendrographic Method, 1935; Tree Growth, 1938. Editor: Species and Varieties (De Vries); contbr. Sci. Am. Hon. pres. 7th Internat. Bot. Congress, Stockholm, 1952, 8th, Paris, 1954. Home: R.F.D. No. 1, Box 185, Carmel, Cal. Died Feb. 22, 1958.

MacDOUGALD, Dan (măk-dōō'găld), lawyer; b. Russell County, Ala., Mar. 31, 1883; s. William Alexander and Emily Caroline (Fitten) MacD.; LL.B., U. of Ga., 1910; m. Jessie St. John Adams, Apr. 14, 1917; children—Gilmer Adams, Dan. Admitted to Ga. bar, 1910, and practiced in own name at Atlanta, 1910-14; mem. firm King & Spalding (later Spalding, MacDougald & Sibley), Atlanta, 1914-35; then mem. firm Colquitt, MacDougald, Troutman & Arkwright (now MacDougald, Troutman, Sams & Schroder); gen. counsel, Ga. Power Co. (chmn. bd. dirs.), South-Eastern Underwriters Assn., Cotton Ins. Assn., counsel for other corporations; direction The Southern Company, Southern Services, Incorporated. Served in F.A., O.T.C., Camp Taylor, 1918; commd. 1st lt., U.S. Res., 1918. Dir. U. of Ga. Athletic Assn. Mem. U. of Ga. Alumni Soc. (pres. 1932-33), Am., Ga., and Atlanta bar assns., Am. Law Inst., Newcomen Soc., Phi Delta Phi, Sigma Alpha Epsilon. Democrat. Presbyterian. Mason (Shriner). Clubs: Lawyers, Capital City, Piedmont Driving, Peachtree Golf (Atlanta). Home: 48 Peachtree Circle. Office: 1607 William-Oliver Bldg., Atlanta. Died Apr. 13, 1953; buried Westview Cemetery, Atlanta.

MacDOUGALL, Edward Archibald, real estate; b. Bklyn., July 16, 1874; s. Thomas Archibald and Virginia Antoinette (Randolph) M.; ed. pub. schs., New York; m. Lilian Victoria Randall, June 18, 1893; children—Viola (Mrs. Charles W. Adams, Jr.), Albert Edward (dec.), Robert Archibald, Lilian (Mrs. Leland H. Emery, dec.), Audrey (Mrs. Archie R. Giroux), Kathryn (Mrs. J. Lawrence O'Neill). In real estate business, 1903—; with Paris-MacDougall Co., 1907-09; pres. The Queensboro Corp. (owners and developers of Jackson Heights, N.Y.C.) ,1909—. Chmn. Borough Pres. Harvey's Spl. Com. to Study Proposed Revision of Assessment Procedure; chmn. on Bridges, Tunnels and Ferries of Queens Plannin N.Y.C. Mayor's Com. on Taxation; mem. City Plan-Com. on Bridges, Tunnels and Ferries of Queens Planning Com., v. chmn. sub-com. on sources of revenue ning and Zoning Com. of President Hoover's Conf. on Home Bldg. and Home Ownership, 1930; mem. Mayor's Housing Conf. Com., 1920, Mayor's Com. on Housing, Zoning and Distribution of Population, 1928; dir. Nat. Assn. Real Estate Bds. (chmn. housing com.), N.Y. State Assn. Real Estate Bds. (chmn. com. city and suburban planning), Real Estate Bd. N.Y. (chmn. mortgage com.; mem. bd. of govs.), Regional Plan Assn., Inc. (dir. adv. com.), L.I. Real Estate Bd., N.Y. State Chamber of Commerce, Mchts. Assn. N.Y. (com. bldg. laws and regulations), L.I., Queensboro C.'s of C., Charity Orgn. Soc. N.Y. (tenement house com.). Republican. Clubs: Transportation, Uptown (N.Y.C.); Bald Peak Country; Madison (Conn.) Beach Yacht. Home: Jackson Heights, L.I., N.Y.; (summer) Wolfeboro, N.H. Office: 8120 37th Av., Jackson Heights, L.I., N.Y. Died Sept. 1, 1944; buried Kenview Cemetery, N.Y.

MacDOWELL, Charles Henry, ex-pres. Armour Fertilizer Works; b. Lewistown, Ill., Oct. 21, 1867; s. John Ross (M.D.) and Ella (Burgett) MacD.; high school edn.; shorthand course, Wesleyan U., Bloomington, Ill.; hon. D.Sc., U. of Pittsburgh, 1921; m. Janet, d. Dr. Matthew W. Borland, Oct. 25, 1892 (died 1929); m. 2d, Claire Leavitt, Oct. 27, 1934. With Armour & Co. since 1887; personal stenographer and sec. to Philip D. Armour, 1888-93; organized, 1894, the fertilizer dept., now Armour Fertilizer Works, of which was pres. 1910-32; pres. Tenn. Chemical Co.; dir. Armour & Co., 1919-33, v.p., 1923-32. Unofficial advisor U.S. Dept. of State, 1910, in German potash controversy; developed, with colleague, 1915, alunite potash mine at Marysvale, Utah (first producing potash mine in America); mem. Chemicals Com., Nat. Council of Defense, summer, 1917; organized chemicals div. of War Industries Bd., 1917, and served as its dir. during war period; went to Paris, 1919, as asso. econ. advisor to Am. Commn. to Negotiate Peace and served as chmn. many meetings between Allied and German experts at Versailles. Del. and speaker Pres. Harding's Agrl. Conf., Washington, 1921; chmn. Am. sect. trade and industry group, Internat. Chamber of Commerce Conf., Rome, 1923; del. and speaker Dept. of Agr. Nat. Conf. on Utilization of Forest Products, Washington, 1924. Conf. and Round Table leader, "Fertilizer Raw Materials and Their Political Significance," at Williamstown Inst. of Politics, 1926; speaker First Congress Internat. Soc. of Soil Science, Washington, 1927; chmn. Am. Com. on Internat. Ententes, Internat. Chamber of Commerce Congress, Stockholm, 1927, del. at Amsterdam, 1929. Speaker 2d Internat. Bituminous Coal Conf., Carnegie Inst., Pittsburgh, 1928. Mem. U.S. Chamber of Commerce nat. resources prodn. com., 1928-30, and nat. water policy com., 1929-30. Pres. Chicago Better Business Bureau, 1932-33. Mem. advisory bd. Chemical Warfare Service, 4th Procurement Div., U.S. Army; apptd. mem. Nat. Research Council (div. engring. and indsl. research), 1937. Mem. bd. Davis Mus. of Natural History, Rollins College (chmn. 1944-45). Mem. industrial committee Florida State C. of C. V.p. Winter Park C. of C., 1946. Fellow A.A.A.S., Am. Geog. Soc., Ill. Acad. Science, Chicago Academy of Science, Royal Society of Arts, British Institute Philosophical Studies; honorary life mem. Nat. Fertilizer Assn. (pres. 1904-05, 1921-22);

mem. Am. Forestry Assn. (vice president, 1925), American Arbitration Association, Field Museum of Natural History (life), Am. Chem. Soc., Western Soc. Engrs. (pres., 1921), Am. Mil. Engrs., Newcomen Society, Business Men's Art Club (pres. 1936-37), Am. Soc. French Legion of Honor, Belgian League of Honor in the U.S., Fla. Acad. of Science, Pi Gamma Mu; mem. exec. bd. Am. Engring. Council, 1922-23. Awarded D.S.M. (U.S.); Officer Legion of Honor (French); Comdr. Crown of Belgium; Knight Crown of Italy. Clubs: University, Glenview Golf (pres., 1928-29); University (Winter Park, Fla.). Wrote: German and Other Sources of Potash; Significance of Yorktown; The Problems of Muscle Shoals; also tech. and econ. articles. Editor: Armour's Farmers Almanac, 1898-1932. Home: 1300 College Point, Winter Park, Fla. Died Mar. 4, 1954, buried Winter Park, Fla.

MacDOWELL, Mrs. Edward (Marian Griswold Nevins); b. N.Y. City, Nov. 22, 1857; d. David N. and Cornelia (Perkins) Nevins; musical edn. received under aunt, Mrs. Roger Perkins, and Edward MacDowell, then prof. pianoforte, Darmstadt Conservatary, Germany; Litt.D., N.J. State Coll. for Women, 1938; Mus.D., N.H. State Univ., 1930; Litt.D., Middlebury College, Middlebury, Vermont, 1939; Mus. D. (honorary), Chicago Musical College, 1949; m. Edward MacDowell, July 21, 1884 (died Jan. 23, 1908). Founded, with others, MacDowell Peterborough Colony (The Edward MacDowell Assn., Inc., Peterborough, N.H.), for fostering creative talent in all arts, exec. dir., 1908-47, also hon. pres. Concertized many years U.S. and Canada for benefit of assn. activities. Awarded Pettee medal, Univ of N.H., 1940; Henry Hadley medal for outstanding service to music, 1941. Author: Random Notes, 1950. Home: Peterborough, N.H.; also Los Angeles. Died Aug. 23, 1956; buried Private Cemetery, MacDowell Colony, Peterborough, N.H.

MacEACHERN, Malcolm T. (măk-ĕk'ĕrn), physician; b. Argyle, Victoria County, Ont., Can., Aug. 27, 1881; s. Hector G. and Ann (Smith) MacE.; M.D., C.M., McGill U. Med. Sch., Montreal, 1910; D.Sc., Marquette, 1926; LL.D. (hon.), McGill, 1950; m. Fannie C. Brandon, Aug. 31, 1915; 1 dau., Frances Isobel. Came to U.S., 1923, naturalized. School teacher, 1902-06; resident physician Montreal Maternity Hosp., 1910-11, med. supt., 1911-13; gen. supt. Vancouver (B.C.) Gen. Hosp., 1913-22; dir. gen. Victorian Order of Nurses for Can., 1922-23; asso. dir. and dir. Hosp. Activities, Am. Coll. of Surgeons, 1923-50, chmn. of administrative bd., 1923-50; mem. adv. edit. bd. Hosp. Management, 1924-50; mem. edit. bd., The Modern Hosp., 1926-50; prof. and dir. hospital adminstrn., Northwestern U. since 1943; member editorial council of Hosps.; mem. Joint Committee on Education, Am. Coll. Hosp. Adminstrs. and Am. Hosp. Assn.; chmn. Tri-State Hosp. Assembly. Pres. Am. Hosp. Assn., 1924-25, dir. of professional relations since 1950. Fellow A.C.P., A.C.S. (hon.), Am. Coll. Hosp. Administrators (hon.), Am. Med. Assn.; diplomate Am. Board Obstetrics and Gynecology, Western Hospital Assn. (honorary president since 1928), Inter-American Hosp. Assn. (honorary president since 1941), International Hospital Assn. (pres., 1938-41), College of Physicians and Surgeons (Ont. and B.C.), Chicago Medical Society (president, 1946-47), Alpha Kappa Kappa, Alpha Omega Alpha. Presbyterian. Rotarian. Recipient, Award of Merit from Am. Hosp. Assn., 1939; Golden Key of Merit, Am. Congress on Physical Therapy, 1940. Author: Hospital Organization and Management; Medical Records in the Hospital. Clubs: Lake Shore, Rotary. Contributor numerous articles to hosp. publs. Home: 2440 Lake View Av. Office: 18 E. Division St., Chgo. Died Feb. 3, 1956; buried Fenelon Falls, Ont., Can.

MACELWANE, James B(ernard) (măk'ĕl-wān), geophysics; b. nr. Port Clinton, Ottawa County, O., Sept. 28, 1883; s. Alexander and Catherine Agnes (Carr) M.; student St. Stanislaus Coll. and John Carroll U., Cleveland, until 1907; A.B., St. Louis U., 1910, A.M., 1911, M.S., 1912; Ph.D., U. of Calif., 1923; D.Sc. (honorary), Saint Norbert College, 1949; LL.D. (honorary), Washington University, 1953; D.Sc. (honorary), John Carroll University 1954. Joined Society of Jesus (Jesuits), 1903; ordained priest R.C. Ch., 1918. Instr. in mathematics, St. John's Coll. High Sch., Toledo, 1907-08, in physics, St. Louis U., 1912-13; asst. prof. physics, same univ., 1913-15, 1918-19; asst. prof. geology, U. of Calif., 1923-25; prof. geophysics and dir. dept., St. Louis Univ., since 1925, prof. geophysical engring. since 1949, dean Graduate School, 1927-33, dean Inst. Tech. 1944—. Recipient Jackling Lecturer award, Am. Inst. Mining and Metall. Engrs. Mem. Nat. Science Board. Fellow A.A.A.S. (past v.p.), Geol. Soc. America, Am. Geog. Soc.; mem. Am. Physical Soc., Seismol. Soc. America (ex-pres.), Jesuit Seismol. Assn. (pres.), Am. Meteorol. Soc. Am. Geophys. Union (president, sect. of seismology), Am. Inst. Mining and Metall. Engrs., Mo. Acad. Sciences (ex-pres.), St. Louis Acad. Sciences (ex-pres.), Optical Soc. America (asso.), Nat. Research Council, Nat. Acad. Scis., Societa Sismologica Italiana, Societa Meteorologica Italiana, Soc. Exploration Geophysicists, Am. Assn. Petroleum Geologists, Sigma Xi. Democrat. Received Bowie Medal of Am. Geophys. Union, 1948. Author: Loose Leaf Manual of Laboratory Experiments in Coll. Physics, Parts I, II, III, IV, V (with J. I. Shannon), 1914; Theoretical Seismology, Vol. I, Geodynamics, 1936, new edition, 1949; When the Earth Quakes, 1947; also more than 100 papers and articles, alone and with others, on seismology and other subjects. Editor and joint author of Bull. of Nat. Research Council on Seismology, 1933. Co-author: Internal Constitution of the Earth, 1939; Compendium of Meteorology, 1951. Home: 221 N. Grand Blvd., St. Louis 3. Office: 3621 Olive St., St. Louis 8. Died Feb. 15, 1956; buried St. Stanislaus Seminary, Florissant, Mo.

MACFADDEN, Bernarr (măk-făd'ĕn), physical culturist; b. nr. Mill Springs, Mo., Aug. 16, 1868; s. Wm. R. and Elizabeth (Miller) M.; ed. pub. schs.; m. 2d, Mary Williamson, 1912 (div.); children—Helen, Byrnece, Beulah, Braunda, Beverly, Berwyn, Brewster; married 3d, Joni Lee. Founder in 1898, and Pub. Physical Culture Magazine, True Story (mag.), 1919, True Romances, 1923, Dream World, Love and Romance, 1924, True Detective Mysteries Mag., 1925, Master Detective Mag., 1929; formerly publisher Liberty Weekly, Photoplay, Movie Mirror, True Detective, etc.; formerly pres. and chmn. bd. Macfadden Publications, Inc. Founder of "Physcultopathy" (healing through physical culture), Macfadden Institute of Physical Culture, Am. Inst. for Phys. Education, and of Bernarr Macfadden Foundation Inc. (with sponsored Loomis Sanatorium, Liberty, N.Y.), Castle Heights Mil. Acad., Lebanon, Tenn., Physical Culture Hotel, Dansville, N.Y., Macfadden-Deauville Health Hotel, Miami Beach, Fla., Bernarr Macfadden Foundation School for Children, Briarcliff Manor, and Tarrytown, N.Y. Inaugurated Cosmotarianism, the Happiness Religion, 1947. Mem. Italy-American Soc., Nat. Aeronautic Assn., Com. of One Hundred (Miami Beach, Fla.). Unitarian. Clubs: N.Y. Athletic, Congressional Country. Author of Ency. of Physical Culture, and numerous health books. Office: 220 E. 42d St., N.Y.C. 17. Died Oct. 12, 1955; buried Woodlawn Cemetery.

MACFARLAND, Charles Stedman, clergyman and author; b. Boston, Dec. 12, 1866; s. Daniel and Sarah Abigail (Crafts) M.; B.D., Yale, 1897, Ph.D., 1899; D.D., Ursinus and U. of Paris: S.T.D., Geneva; LL.D., Elon; m. Mary Perley Merrill, Mar. 9, 1904; children—Charles S., James M., Lucia M. Hogan; m. 2d, Genevieve Dayton, Jan. 22, 1938. Gen. mgr. T. O. Gardner & Co., Mfrs., Boston and New York, 1885-92; gen. sec. Y.M.C.A., Melrose, 1892-93; asst. pastor Maverick Congl. Ch., E. Boston, 1893-94; student Yale U., 1894-99; instr. 1900; ordained Congl. ministry, 1897; lecturer Yale Univ., 1908-10, minister Maplewood Ch., Malden, Mass., 1900-07; pastor S. Norwalk, Conn., 1906-11; social service sec., 1911-12, general sec., 1912-31, now gen. sec. emeritus, Federal Council of the Churches of Christ in America. Lecturer on philos., scientific and theological subjects; book review editor The Federal Council Bulletin; editor of Corpus Confessionum; lecturer univs. of Berlin, Prague, Paris, Athens, Strasbourg, also at Rollins College, Winter Park, Florida. National field scout commr. Boy Scouts of America. Chaplain (lt. col.) O.R.C., U.S. Army, V.p. Universal Christian Conference on Life and Work; Am. mem. Central Bur. European Chs., Geneva; chmn. Huguenot-Walloon-New Netherlands Commn., 1924; trustee of Church Peace Union; Golden Rule Foundation; pres. Mountain Lakes Historical Society; custodian, borough records, Mountain Lakes; pres. Evang. Alliance of U.S. Mem. Phi Beta Kappa. Decorated Officer Legion of Honor (France); Order of Leopold (Belgium); Order of Phoenix (Greece); Chevalier of the Order of the Holy Sepulchre (Jerusalem). Clubs: Yale (New York); University (Winter Park, Florida); Graduates (New Haven, Conn.). Author: The Spirit Christlike; The Infinite Affection; Jesus and the Prophets; Spiritual Culture and Social Service; Christian Service and the Modern World; The Great Physician; The Progress of Church Federation; International Christian Movements; Christian Unity in Practice and Prophecy, 1933; The New Church and the New Germany, 1934; Chaos in Mexico, 1935; Contemporary Christian Thought, 1936; Across the Years, 1936; Trends of Christian Thinking, 1937; Steps Toward the World Council, 1938; The Christian Faith in a Day of Crisis, 1939; I Was in Prison, 1939; Current Religious Thought, 1941; A Digest of Christian Thinking, 1942; A Survey of Religious Literature, 1943; Peace Through Religion, 1945; Lyman P. Powell: Pioneer in Education and Religion, 1946; Religion through the Ages, 1948; Christian Unity in the Making, 1949. Editor, part author: The Christian Ministry and the Social Order; The Churches of the Federal Council; Christian Unity at Work; The Churches of Christ in Council; The Church and International Relations, 2 vols.; The Church and International Relations—Japan; Christian Coöperation and World Redemption; The Churches of Christ in Time of War; The Churches of America and France; The Old Puritanism and the New Age. Contbr. to mags. Home: Mountain Lakes, N.J. Office: 297 Fourth Av., N.Y.C. Died Oct. 26, 1956.

MacFARLAND, Frank Mace, educator; b. Centralia, Ill., June 10, 1869; s. Dr. Parker Moore and Sarah Elizabeth (Mace) MacF.; Ph.B., DePauw, 1889; A.M., Stanford, 1893; univs. of Wurzburg, Germany and Zurich, Switzerland, 1894-96; Ph.D., Würzburg, 1896; m. Olive Knowles Hornbrook, Aug. 27, 1902. Prof. biology and geology Olivet (Mich.) Coll., 1889-93; instr. histology Stanford, 1892-94, asst. prof., 1894-97, asso. prof., 1897-1909, prof., 1909-34, emeritus prof., 1934—. In charge Marine Biol. Lab., Pacific Grove, 1910-13; co-dir. Hopkins Marine Station, Pacific Grove, Cal., 1915-17. Fellow A.A.A.S., Cal. Acad. Sciences (corr. sec. 1926-32; 1st v.p., 1932-34, pres., 1934-46; hon. mem., 1946—, acting dir. of mus. and Steinhart Aquarium, 1934-38); hon. life mem. Nat. Geog. Soc.; corr. mem. Malacol. Soc. London; mem. Am. Assn. Anatomists, Western Soc. Naturalists, Am. Malacological Union, Delta Kappa Epsilon, Phi Beta Kappa, Sigma Xi. Club: Commonwealth. Home: 775 Santa Ynez St., Stanford University, Cal. Died Feb. 21, 1951; buried Alta Mesa Cemetery, Palo Alto, Cal.

MacFARLANE, David Laing, coll. pres.; b. Dundee, Scotland, Mar. 13, 1893; s. John and Margaret (Laing) MacF.; A.B., Northwestern, 1916; S.T.B., Garrett Bibl. Inst., 1917; Ph.D., U. of Edinburgh, Scotland, 1931; m. Mildred Scott, June 26, 1918; 1 dau., Jean Scott. Ordained to ministry M.E. Ch., 1916; pastor Clifton, Ill., 1917-18, Sibley, Ill., 1919-22; prof. history and polit. science, Southwestern Coll., 1922-35; prof. history, Kan. State Teachers Coll., Emporia, 1935-43, dean of men, 1936-43, president since 1945. On college leave—chairman State Board of Social Welfare, 1943-45. Second lieutenant infantry, U.S. Army, World War. Member Kansas Educators Club, Am. Legion, Delta Tau Delta, Pi Gamma Mu. Mason. Rotarian (past gov. dist. 123). Author: Wesleyanism in Scotland, 1931. Home: 1501 Berkeley Road, Emporia, Kan. Business Address: Kansas State Teachers College, Emporia, Kan. Died Jan. 3, 1953; buried Meml. Lawn Cemetery, Emporia, Kan.

MACFARLANE, John C., business exec.; b. Ashton, Ont., Can., Aug. 7, 1889; s. Rev. Alex H. and Annie (Howie) M.; B.A., Queens U., 1911, M.A., 1912; student Osgoode Hall Law Sch., 1915; D.C.L., Mt. Selison U., 1949; m. Mildred A. Courtig, June 21, 1919; 1 dau., Audrey S. (Mrs. Stewart E. McDonald). Vice pres. Canadian Gen. Electric, 1941—, dir., 1942—; chmn. Tech. Service Consul, Ont., 1947—; pres. Canadian Radio Patents Ltd.; dir. Canadian Nat. Exhbn. Councillor Royal Canadian Inst.; trustee Queens U. King's Counsel, Province of Ont., 1934. Mem. Canadian Mfrs. Assn. (pres. 1944-45, treas., 1949—), Gen. Alumni Queens U. (pres. 1936-38), Canadian Bar Assn. Mason. Clubs: Lawyers, Granite, Royal Canadian Yacht, Ontario (past pres.) (Toronto). Home: 51 Ava Rd., Forest Hill Village, Ont. Office: 212 King St. W., Toronto, Ont., Can. Died Jan. 8, 1954.*

MacFARLANE, Peter, supt. gospel mission; b. Northcote, Minn., Apr. 12, 1884; s. John and Annie (MacEdward) MacF.; student Macalester Coll., 1905-08, D.D., 1957; D.D., N.W. Theol. Sem., 1943; m. Nelle Nelson, Oct. 24, 1934; 1 son, John Murdoch. Supt. Union Gospel Mission, St. Paul, 1909—, expanded mission from no property to one of the largest missions in United States, including main bldgs., 6 brs., 2 boys clubs, fresh-air camp; organizer new missions throughout U.S. and Can., evangelistic and Bible conf. worker, 1919—, pioneer worker for under privileged children in gospel mission field. Mem. Internat. Union Gospel Missions (pres., 1931-35, chmn. exec. com., 1942—). Republican. Presbyn. Home: 853 Mound St. Office: 235 East 7th St., St. Paul. Died Apr. 3, 1958; buried Hallock, Minn.

MacGREGOR, Clarence, ex-congressman, judge; b. Newark, N.Y., Sept. 16, 1872; s. James W. and Harriet (Cratar) MacG.; student U. Rochester. Admitted to bar, 1897, began practice at Buffalo, N.Y.; mem. N.Y. Assembly, 1908-12 inclusive; mem. 66th to 70th Congresses, 41st N.Y. Dist; justice Supreme Court State of N.Y., 1929-43, ofcl. referee, 1943—. Republican. Baptist. Mem. Psi Upsilon, Past Grand Chancellor K. of P. of N.Y. Home: Buffalo Athletic Club 8, Buffalo, N.Y. Died Feb. 18, 1952; buried Forest Lawn Cemetery, Buffalo.

MACGREGOR, David Hutchison, economist; born Angus, Scotland, May 10, 1877; s. Robert and Lilias (Hutchison) M.; ed. George Watsons Coll., Edinburgh, Univ. Edinburgh, Trinity Coll., Cambridge; hon. LL.D., Edinburgh, 1948; m. Claire Nelson. Prof. economics, Leeds Univ., 1909-19, Manchester Univ., 1919-21, Oxford Univ., 1922-45. M.C., 1917. Author: Industrial Combination, 1906; Evolution of Industry, 1911; Enterprise Purpose and Profit, 1934; Public Aspects of Finance, 1939; Economic Analysis and Policy, 1949. Home: Three Lucerne Rd., Oxford. Office: All Souls Coll., Oxford, Eng. Died May 5, 1953.

MacHARG, John Brainerd (må-kärg'), prof. history; b. Rome, N.Y., July 11, 1873; s. John Brainerd and Susan Lucretia (Noble) MacH.; C.E., Cornell U., 1893; A.B., Hamilton Coll., 1900, A.M., 1909;

studied Leipzig U., 5 semesters, 1909-11, 1913-14; Ph.D., Columbia U., 1917; hon. A.M., Lawrence Coll., Appleton, Wis., 1937; L.H.D. (honorary), Hamilton College, 1953; m. Alice Lee Fleniken, June 21, 1928. Engaged in mfg. fishing tackle, 1893-1900; teacher Greek and history, Auburn (N.Y.) High Sch., 1900-09; dir. Leipzig Am. Sch., Leipzig, Germany, 1909-14; asst. prof. modern lang. and history, Hamilton Coll., 1911-13; asst. in English history, Leipzig U., 1913-14; asst. in history, Columbia, 1916-17; prof. history, Lawrence Coll., Appleton, Wis., 1917-37, emeritus, 1937—; sold to Eastman Kodak Co., Ready Mount Kodaslide idea; consultant with firm, 1937-41; lecturer, consultant upon visual method of teaching. Mem. Am. Geog. Soc., Nat. Geographical Soc., Rochester Museum Assn., Nat. Hist. Soc., Wis. Archaeol. Soc., Wis. Hist. Soc., Archaeol. Soc. of N.M., Cornell Engring. Assn., Psi Upsilon, Phi Beta Kappa. Episcopalian. Clubs: Rome, Teugega, Colorado Mountain. Author Outline Maps Greek and Roman History, 1907; Outline Atlas for the Study of English History and Literature, 1907; Visual Representations of the Trinity, 1917; A System of Notes for the Study of American History, 1923; Old Ironsides, 1927; A Picturol Life of Abraham Lincoln, 1931; History of U.S. in Outline, 1933; also 20 outline lecture manuals with film-strip illustrations. Contbr. to mags. Home: 318 N. George St., Rome, N.Y. Died Oct. 31, 1954; buried Rome Cemetery.

MacHARG, William (Briggs), author; b. Dover Plains, N.Y., Sept. 18, 1872; s. William Storrs and Frances Eunice (Briggs) MacH.; student U. Mich., 1892-95. Reporter, asst. Sunday editor and Sunday editor Chgo. Tribune, 1899. Mem. Phi Kappa Psi. Club: Dutch Treat. Author (with Edwin Balmer); The Achievements of Luther Trant, 1910; Surakarta, 1913; The Blind Man's Eyes, 1916; The Indian Drum, 1917; Peewee, 1921; The Affairs of O'Malley, 1940. Contbr. to Sat. Eve. Post, Colliers and other mags. Home: Goin Lane, Alpine, N.J. Address: care Brandt & Brandt, 1010 Park Av., N.Y.C. 17. Died Feb. 21, 1951; buried Rosehill Cemetery.

MACHEN, Arthur Webster (mā'chĕn), lawyer; b. Baltimore, Mar. 18, 1877; s. Arthur Webster and Mary Minnie (Gresham) M.; student U. Sch. for Boys, Baltimore, 1888-93; A.B., Johns Hopkins, 1896; LL.B., Harvard Univ., 1899; m. Helen Chase Woods, Dec. 1, 1917; children—Mary Gresham, Arthur Webster, Elizabeth Hall (Mrs. C. Harvey Palmer, Jr.). Admitted to Maryland bar, 1899, and since practiced in Baltimore (with father to 1915); mem. Armstrong, Machen & Allen, later Armstrong, Machen, Allen & Eney, now Armstrong, Machen & Eney since 1925; special assistant to atty. gen. of U.S., 1914, 15. Chmn. Tax Revision Commn. of Md., 1929. Mem. Am. and Baltimore bar assns., Md. Bar Assn. (pres. 1939-40), Phi Kappa Psi, Phi Beta Kappa. Democrat. Presbyterian. Clubs: Maryland, Merchants (Baltimore). Author: Modern Law of Corporations, 1908; Federal Corporation Tax Law of 1909, 1910. Home: Ruxton, Md. Office: O'Sullivan Bldg., Baltimore. Died May 27, 1950.

MACHLETT, Raymond R. (măk'lĕt), business exec.; b. N.Y.C., July 31, 1900; s. Robert Herman and Paula (Hoering) M.; student Cornell U., 1922; m. Alice M. Titchener, Nov. 1, 1924; children—Alice F., Raymond R., Paula S. Engr. E. Machlett & Son, 1922, pres., 1924-28; chief engr. Rainbow Light, Inc., neon lights, 1926-31; organized Machlett Labs., Inc., mfrs. electron tubes, 1931, pres., dir., 1931—; dir. Machlett X-Ray Tubes (Gt. Briatin), Ltd., High Voltage Engring. Corp., Cambridge, Mass. Trustee Cornell chpt. Alpha Delta Phi. Recipient Stevens Inst. Honor Award, 1945. Author of tech. papers in X-ray and other tech. jours.; also holder of numerous patents. Home: New Canaan. Office: 1063 Hope St., Springdale, Conn. Died Jan. 7, 1955.

MACHMER, William Lawson (măch'mer), dean, prof. mathematics; b. Moselem, Pa., Jan. 30, 1883; s. Alfred and Louisa (Adam) M.; B.E., Keystone State Normal Sch., 1901; A.B., Franklin and Marshall Coll., 1907, A.M., 1911, L.H.D., 1948; Ed.D., Am. Internat. Coll., 1936; LL.D., University Massachusetts, 1952; m. Olive Bonine, Aug. 30, 1911; children—Gretchen Bonine, Katharine Louise (Mrs. Philip O. Carr), Jane Elizabeth (Mrs. Eugene Fubini), William Lawson. Teacher Pa. pub. schs., 1901-04; head dept. of mathematics, Franklin and Marshall Academy, 1907-11; instr. mathematics, Massachusetts State Coll., 1911-15, asst. prof., 1915-19, asso. prof., 1919-20, prof. mathematics and asst. dean, 1920-24, dean, 1924-47, head dept. mathematics, 1935-40; became dean U. of Mass. 1947, now dean emeritus. Chmn. Amherst Sch. Com., 1921-36. Staff mem. for Federal survey of Land Grant Colleges and Universities, 1928. Mem. New England Coll. Entrance Certificate Bd. (sec.), Eastern Assn. Deans and Advisers of Men (pres. 1940), Nat. Geog. Soc., New England Assn. Colls. and Prep. Schs., New England Assn. Mathematics Teachers, Phi Beta Kappa, Phi Kappa Phi, Pi Gamma Mu, Alpha Sigma Phi. Conglist. Mason. Clubs: State Coll. Faculty (Amherst), Franklin Harvest. Home: 151 Amity St., Amherst, Mass. Died May 25, 1953; buried Amherst.

MACIEJEWSKI, Anton Frank (mä-chĕ-yĕs'kĭ), ex-congressman; b. Anderson, Tex., Jan. 3, 1893; s. Frank and Frances (Ciesielski) M.; ed. pub. schs., Cicero, Ill., and Lewis Inst., Chgo.; m. Anna Kosobucki, Nov. 19, 1913. Organized Eagle Coal Co., wholesale and retail coal, Cicero, 1916; asst. Cook County agent in charge of relief, 1925-28; supr. and treas., Cicero, 1932-39; mem. 76th and 77th Congresses, 6th Ill. Dist. Trustee Sanitary Dist. of Chgo., 1943-46, pres., 1946; organized Blvd. Manor Defense Homes Corp., 1942. Mem. Cicero, Ill. and Nat. Dem. coms.; del. to Nat. Conv., Houston, 1928; organized Cicero Bd. of NRA. Mem. Polish Roman Cath. Union, Polish Nat. Alliance, Polish Falcons, Polish Cavalry, Chgo. Coal Mchts. Assn., Garfield Park Business Men's Assn., Hawthorne Business Men's Assn., St. Vincent de Paul Soc. (treas.). Democrat. Roman Catholic. K.C., Moose, Elk, Woodman. Clubs: Cicero Lions; Illinois Athletic (Chgo.). Home: 5037 W. 31st Place, Cicero, Ill. Died Sept. 25, 1949.

MACK, A(rthur) B(laine), business exec.; b. Joliet, Ill., Mar. 24, 1884; s. John Jewell and Voisa (Brownson) M.; student Joliet pub. schs.; m. May Lewis, May 9, 1909; children—John H., Janet L., Jeanne H. Clk. accounting, operating depts. Elgin, Joliet & Eastern Ry., Joliet, Chgo. Junction Ry., West Hammond, Ill., Ind. Harbor Belt R.R., Ind. Harbor and Gibson, Ind., 1902-12; auditor, gen. freight agt. Lakeside & Marblehead R.R., Cleve., 1916-22; asst. gen. mgr. Kelley Island Lime & Transport Co., 1922-28, v.p., 1928-45, dir. since 1935, exec. v.p. since 1945, mem. exec. com. since 1946; dir. Cleve. Quarries Co. since 1948. Mason. Clubs: Union, Mid-day. Home: 15404 Edgewater Dr., Lakewood 7, O. Office: Leader Bldg., Cleve. 14. Died Aug. 30, 1954.

MACK, Connie (Cornelius McGillicuddy), baseball mgr.; b. East Brookfield, Mass., Dec. 23, 1862. Began as catcher on East Brookfield baseball team, 1883; catcher on professional team, Meriden, Conn., 1884; catcher, Hartford, Conn., team (New England League), 1885, Washington, D.C., team (Nat. League), 1886-89; Buffalo, N.Y., team (Brotherhood League), 1890; mgr. Pittsburgh team (Nat. League), 1891-96; catcher mgr. Milwaukee team (Western League), 1897-1900; mgr. Phila. Athletics (Am. League), 1901-54. Won Am. League pennants, 1902, 05, 10, 11, 13, 14, 29, 30, 31; won World Series, 1910, 11, 13, 29, 30. Awarded Bok prize for distinguished service to Phila., 1929. Died Feb. 8, 1956.

MACK, Edward, theologian; b. Charleston, S.C., July 16, 1868; s. Rev. Joseph Bingham and Harriet Hudson (Banks) M.; A.B., Davidson Coll., N.C., 1886, A.M., 1887, later LL.D.; Columbia Theol. Sem., 1887-88; grad. Princeton Theol. Sem., 1889; U. of Berlin, 1890-91; D.D., Hampden-Sydney Coll., 1899; Ph.D., U. of Cincinnati; m. Mary Ashley Kirby, June 22, 1892; children—Edward, Mary G. (wife of Capt. T. T. Patterson, U.S.N.), Rev. Joseph Bingham, George Kirby; m. 2d Lenore Tinsley, June 4, 1918; 1 son, Tinsley. Ordained Presbyn. ministry, 1889; supply First Ch., Charlotte, N.C., 1889, 1892-93; pastor Central Ch., St. Louis, 1893-97, First Ch., Norfolk, Va., 1897-1901, First Ch., Shreveport, La., 1901-04; prof. O. T. lang. and lit., Lane Theol. Sem., Cincinnati, 1904-15; McCormick prof. O.T. Lit., Union Theol. Sem., Richmond, Va., 1915-39; prof. emeritus since 1939. Lecturer on L. P. Stone Foundation, Princeton Theol. Sem., 1923; Milton Stewart Foundation lecturer in China, 1925. Moderator Synod of La., 1903, Synod of Va., 1935; Moderator Gen. Assembly Presbyn. Ch. in the U.S., 1939-40. Mem. Soc. of Mayflower Descendants, S.R., Sigma Alpha Epsilon, Phi Beta Kappa. Author: Teaching Values of the Old Testament; Theology of Hosea and Amos; Early Puritans of Virginia; The Preacher's Old Testament; Office of the Deacon; The Christ of the Old Testament; The Hebrew Looks Up to God; and of other mag. and encyclopedia articles. Home: Berrybrook, Orange, Va. Died Sept. 25, 1951; buried Hollywood Cemetery, Richmond, Va.

MACK, John E., lawyer, corp. exec.; b. Poughkeepsie, N.Y., June 10, 1874; s. Daniel and Margaret (Hefferman) M.; grad. high sch., 1892; m. Wilhelmina B. Immekus, Oct. 25, 1899; children—Margaret M., John E., Edward J., Mary C. Began law practice at Poughkeepsie, 1896; justice of the peace, Poughkeepsie, 1900-07; dist. atty., Poughkeepsie, 1907-12; justice Supreme Court of N.Y., 1930; chief counsel Joint Legislative Com. to Investigate Pub. Utilities, 1934-36; pres. General Aniline & Film Corp., 1941; v.p., dir. Fallkill Nat. Bank. Democrat. K.C., Elk. Home: 110 Fulton Av. Office: 234 Main St., Poughkeepsie, N.Y. Died Feb. 22, 1958.*

MACK, Russell Vernon, congressman; b. Hillman, Mich., June 13, 1891; s. Cornelius W. and Lucy (Deacon) M.; student Stanford U., U. of Wash.; m. Laura E. Prohaska, Jan. 26, 1947. Reporter to mgr., the Aberdeen (Wash.) World, 1914-32; owner and pub., the Hoquiam Washingtonian, 1934—. Member 80th-86th Congresses from the 3d District of Washington. Past Pres. Northwest Rivers and Harbors Congress. Republican. Episcopalian. Mem. Am. Legion (past post commander), Washington State Elks Association (past state president). Home: Emerson Apts., Hoquiam, Wash. Died Mar. 28, 1960.

MACK, Warren Bryan, coll. prof.; b. Flicksville, Pa., Jan. 18, 1896; s. Oscar and Anna Maria (Lockard) M.; Ph.B., Lafayette Coll., Easton, Pa., 1915, hon. Sc.D., 1946; B.Sc., Pa. State Coll., 1921; M.Sc., Mass. Agrl. Coll., 1924; Ph.D, Johns Hopkins, 1929; m. Pauline Gracia Beery, Dec. 27, 1923. Teacher of science, Manasquan (N.J.) High Sch., 1915-18; tester, N.Y. Edison Co., 1919; instr. in pomology, Mass. Agrl. Coll., 1921-23; instr. horticulture, Pa. State Coll., 1923, instr. vegetable gardening, 1924, asst. prof., 1924-26, asso. prof., 1926-30, prof. vegetable gardening, 1930-44, head dept. of horticulture since 1937, prof. horticulture since 1944. Mem. bd. dirs. American Horticultural Council, Inc. Commd. 2d lt., F.A., U.S. Army, 1918. Exec. sec. state victory garden com. Pa. State Council of Defense, 1942-45. Fellow A.A.A.S.; mem. Am. Soc. Hort. Science (pres., 1944-46), Am. Soc. Plant Physiologists, Bot. Soc. America (physiol. sect.), Pa. Hort. Soc., Audubon Artists, Society American Etchers, Gravers, Lithographers and Woodcutters, Alpha Zeta, Phi Beta Kappa, Phi Beta Kappa Associates, Sigma Xi, Phi Kappa Phi. Club: Salmagundi (New York). Contributor papers and articles to professional and tech. jours. since 1922. Engaged in graphic art (wood engraving) as avocation since 1927. Represented in Baltimore Art Museum, N.Y. Pub. Library, Fogg Museum, Library of Congress, Glasgow U. Associate Nat. Acad. of Design (graphic sect.). Awarded Warren H. Manning Purchase Prize, 1938, Appalachian Museum Purchase Prize, 1940 (Southern Print-makers Soc.), 2nd prize Nat. Exhbn. of Prints made during current year, 1943; 3rd prize, same exhbn., 1946 (Library of Congress); Marvin F. Jones Purchase Prize, Salmagundi Club, 1948. Warren Mack Arts Exhibit founded by Soc. Am. Graphic Artists at Pa. State U., 1955. Home: Old McKinney Rd., R.D. 2, Denton, Tex. Died July 6, 1952; buried Centre Country Meml. Park, State College, Pa.

MACKALL, Paul, executive; b. Alexandria Co., Va., May 15, 1886; s. James McVean and Evanina F. (Evans) M.; M.E., Lehigh U., 1907. Asso. with Bethlehem Steel Co. since 1907, mgr. sales Chicago and St. Louis, 1907-15, Western sales rep., Chicago, 1916, asst. gen. sales agent, 1916, gen. mgr. sales, 1927, vice pres. since 1928, director since 1932 Mem. War Industries Board, Inter-Allied Munitions Quarters (London, Paris, Rome), head of Steel Section, Allied Munitions Council, World War I; mem. advisory com. W.P.B., World War II. Mem. Steel Production Advisory Com., Office of Industry Cooperation, Dept. of Commerce. Mem. Am. Iron and Steel Inst. Republican. Epis. Clubs: The Cloud, Link Racquet and Tennis, India House, Nat. Golf Links of Am., University, Chicago, Racquet, Philadelphia, Travelers, Paris, Bethlehem, Saucon Valley Country. Home: Windy Way Farms, R.F.D. 4. Office: Bethlehem Steel Co., Bethlehem, Pa. Died 16, 1954; buried Oak Hill Cemetery, Georgetown, Washington.

MacKAY, Henry Squarebriggs, Jr. (mă-kī'), lawyer; b. Boston, Mass., Oct. 7, 1891; s. Henry Squarebriggs and Robena (MacKay) M.; academic and legal edn., U. of Va., 1909-14; m. Katharine P. Flint, dau. U.S. Senator Flint, of Los Angeles, Calif., Oct. 6, 1914; 1 son, Flint. Admitted to Calif. bar, 1914, to Federal and U.S. Supreme Courts; practiced in Los Angeles, 1914—; partner Flint & MacKay and predecessors; v.p., mem. exec. com., dir. Hearst Publ. Co., v.p., mem. exec. com., dir., gen. counsel Hearst Consol. Publs., Inc.; v.p., dir. The Hearst Found., Inc.; v.p. Hearst Corporation; co-exec Estate of William Randolph Hearst (deceased); chmn. advisory com. on earthquake rehabilitation and flood relief loans, R.F.C., 1933-35; chmn. NRA activities for Los Angeles County, 1933, Civil Works Administration wage scale bd., 1934, business advisory council, 1934, Los Angeles Better Housing Campaign, 1934-35, Federal Emergency Relief Administration Wage Scale Bd., 1935; mem. Gov. Merriam's Citizen's Unified Highway Com., 1935-36; mem. Gov.'s Com. on Taxation, 1936-38; former dir. Los Angeles Chamber of Commerce, Automobile Club of Southern California and Pacific Mutual Life Ins. Co.; del. Nat. Dem. Conv., 1932. Served as 2d lt. United States Inf. Reserve (machine gun section), 1918, World War I; lt. commander U.S. Nat. Reserve Force, 1935-41 (retired). Mem. Am., Calif. State, Los Angeles bar assns. Mem. Am. Legion, Phi Delta Theta, Tau Nu Epsilon, Phi Delta Phi. Episcopalian. Mason (32°, Shriner). Clubs: California (Los Angeles, Calif.); Newport Harbor Yacht (Balboa); Bay, Mesa Gun, Balboa Angling. Dir. Tenth Olympiad Committee of the Games of Los Angeles, U.S.A., 1932; dir. All Year Club of Southern Calif., 1931. Dir. Community Development Assn., Los Angeles Turf Club, Inc. Home: 2130 E. Balboa Rd., Balboa, Cal. Office: Rowan Bldg., Los Angeles. Died July 5, 1954.

MACKAYE, Percy (mă-kī'), poet-dramatist; b. New York, Mar. 16, 1875; s. Steele and Mary Keith (Medbery) M.; A.B., Harvard, 1897; hon. A.M.,

Dartmouth, 1914; hon. Litt.D., Miami U., 1924; studied as matriculated student, U. of Leipzig, 1899-1900; m. Marion Homer Morse, Oct. 8, 1898; children—Robert Keith, Arvia, Christy Loring. Traveled in Europe, 1898-1900, residing successively at Rome, Brunnen (Switzerland), Leipzig and London; taught in pvt. sch., New York, 1900-04; joined Cornish (N.H.) Colony, 1904. Lectured at Harvard, Yale, Columbia and many other univs., on the theatre, 1906-13; delivered address on "The Worker in Poetry" before Am. Acad. and Nat. Inst., New Theatre, New York, 1911; delivered Harvard Phi Beta Kappa poem, 1908, and commemorative poems on many leaders and public events since 1903; dir. of his own community masques; was apptd. to 1st Am. fellowship in poetry and drama at Miami U., 1920; held seminar class in poetry and Am. folk-backgrounds, Rollins Coll., winter terms, 1929-31; joined MacDowell Colony, Peterborough, N.H., summer 1930; apptd. mem. bd. govs., Cambridge Sch. of Drama, Harvard, 1930. Mem. Nat. Inst. Arts and Letters, Poetry Soc. America; hon. mem. Harvard Phi Beta Kappa; mem. Dramatists' Guild of Authors' League America, Society Am. Dramatists and Composers, Nat. Econ. League, Soc. Mayflower Descs., P.E.N. Clubs: Players, Harvard, MacDowell (New York); Cosmos (Washington, D.C.), Garrick of London (hon.). Translator many classics. Author (plays, poems and books): The Canterbury Pilgrims, comedy, 1903; Fenris the Wolf, tragedy, 1905; Jeanne d'Arc, tragedy, 1906; Sappho and Phaon, tragedy, 1907; The Scarecrow, 1908; Lincoln Centenary Ode, 1909; Mater, comedy, 1908; The Playhouse and the Play, essays, 1909; Poems, 1909; A Garland to Sylvia, comedy, 1910; Anti-Matrimony, satirical comedy, 1910; To-morrow, play, 1911; Yankee Fantasies, 1-act plays, 1912; The Civic Theatre, 1912; Uriel, and Other Poems, 1912; Sinbad the Sailor, a lyric drama, 1912; Sanctuary, a bird masque, 1913; St. Louis, civic masque, with 7,500 actors, 1914; The Immigrants, lyric drama, 1915; A Thousand Years Ago, comedy, 1914; The Present Hour, poems, 1914; The New Citizenship, civic ritual, 1915; A Substitute for War, essay, 1915; Poems and Plays, 2 vols., 1916; Caliban, community masque, 1916; The Canterbury Pilgrims, opera, 1917; American Consecration Hymn, 1917; Community Drama, essay, 1917; The Evergreen Tree, Christmas masque, 1917; The Roll Call, masque of the Red Cross, 1918; James Russell Lowell centenary poem, 1919; Washington, ballad-play, 1919; The Will of Song (with Harry Barnhart), 1919; Rip Van Winkle, folk-opera, 1920; The Pilgrim and the Book, 1920; Dogtown Common, narrative poem, 1921; This Fine-Pretty World, folk-comedy, 1923; The Skippers of Nancy Gloucester, narrative poem, 1924; Kinfolk of Robin Hood, play for children, 1924; Untamed America (with wife), 1924; April Fire, Concord Battle poem, 1925; Tall Tales of the Kentucky Mountains, 1926; Napoleon Crossing the Rockies, play, 1927; Winged Victory, poem on Lindbergh's return, 1927; Epoch—The Life of Steele MacKaye (memoir in 2 vols.), 1927; The Gobbler of God, narrative poem, 1928; Kentucky Mountain Fantasies, folk-plays, 1928; The Sphinx, comedy, 1929; Songs of a Day, 1929; Weather-goose-Woo, 1929; William Vaughn Moody—20 Years After, poem to E. A. Robinson, 1930; Exeter Stream (with Keith MacKaye), poem for Phillips Exeter Acad. Sesquicentennial, 1931; Wakefield, George Washington Bicentennial Folk-Masque, 1932; Bernard Shaw-Henderson Festival Address, 1933; The Faith of Poetry, World Fellowship of Faiths, Chicago, 1933; Edmund Clarence Stedman, centenary tribute, 1933; The National Theatre of Regionalism, U.S. Congress address, 1935; American Theatre-Poets (1904-1910), edited, introd. to Wm. Vaughn Moody's Letters to Harriet, 1935; In Another Land (poems inter-translated with Albert Steffen, Swiss folk-poet), 1936; The Far Familiar (poems), 1937; Robert Burns (with Marion Morse Mackaye), 1939; Poesie Religio, 1940; My Lady Dear, Arise!, 1940; What Is She?, 1942; What We Will (mystery play), 1943; I Met God Walking Leisurely, 1943; Poog's Pasture, The Mythology of a Child, 1951; (and sequel) Poog and the Caboose-Man, 1952. Editor: Plays of Steele Mackaye, 1941; Emma: A Play, by Marion Mackaye, 1941. Elected advisory editor Folk-Say (nat. mag. of Am. folklore), 1929. Assembled Mackaye Collection Dartmouth Coll. Library, with bibliography, Annals of an Era—1826-1932. Founded Marion Morse-Percy Mackaye Collection, Harvard Library, 1943. Vis. prof. creative aspects of the drama, Sweet Briar Coll., Va., 1932-33; dir. folk-tales, White Top (Va.) Folk Festival, 1933; made folk-researches, Appalachian Mts., Fla. 1933-35, Switzerland, Eng., Scotland and Ireland, 1936-37; enacted role of James McNeil Whistler in Sir Henry Irving Centenary Festival, London, 1938. Elected founder mem. Phi Beta Kappa Assos., 1941. Received Shelley Meml. prize award for poetry, 1942; elected pres. Pan-Am. Poets' League of N. Am., 1943. Given nat. testimonial on 70th birthday, announcing his Tetralogy for the Theatre; The Mystery of Hamlet, King of Denmark, comprising the four plays: The Ghost of Elsinore, The Fool in Eden Garden, Odin Against Christus, The Serpent in the Orchard, 1945. Received $5000 Fellowship Award of Acad. of Am. Poets, 1948, for Hamlet cycle of plays, produced by Pasadena Playhouse at Shakespeare's Birthday Festival, 1949. Edited The Journal (1898-1939) of Marion Morse MacKaye, 1946; The Goal, Harvard Class of 1897; Fiftieth Anniversary poem, 1947; Intimations, poems, 1947; William Butler Yeats, A New Portrait, published in 1947; also A Sequestered Shrine, 1950; Discoveries and Inventions (1901-50), Poems of public events, 1950. Home: Cornish, N.H., P.O., Windsor, Vt. Office: 16 Gramercy Park, N.Y.C. 3. Died Aug. 31, 1956.

MacKEE, George Miller, dermatologist; b. Jersey City, Sept. 19, 1878; s. Horace Elber and Jennie Amanda (Updyke) MacK.; M.D., N.Y.U.-Bellevue Hospital Medical College, 1899; married Katherine M. Sullivan. Private practice, New York City, 1900-Post-grad. Med. Sch. and Hosp.; prof. emeritus dermatology Columbia U.; formerly dir. div. of dermatology and syphilology, N.Y. Skin and Cancer Unit, N.Y. Post-Grad. Med. Sch. and Hosp., Columbia; dermatologist Welfare Hosp.; cons. dermatologist N.Y. Post-Grad., St. Luke's and St. Vincent's hosps., N.Y. Skin and Cancer Unit. Fellow N.Y. Acad. Medicine, N.Y. Dermatol. Soc., Manhattan Dermatol. Soc., N.Y. Roentgen Soc., A.A.A.S.; corr. mem. British Assn. Dermatology and Syphilology; mem. A.M.A., Am. Acad. Dermatology and Syphilology (past pres.), Am. Dermatol. Assn. (past pres.), Am. Roentgen Ray Soc., Am. Radiol. Soc., Radium Soc., Am. Coll. Radiology, Radiol. Soc. N.A.; hon. mem. Cuban Dermatol. Soc., Argentine Dermatol. Soc. Author: X-Ray and Radium Treatment in Diseases of Skin, Cutaneous Cancer and Pre-Cancer; Skin Diseases in Children. Contbr. to med. jours. Address: Haviland Rd., Stamford, Conn. Died May 8, 1955.

MacKEEVER, John C., printing exec.; b. Steubenville, O., Feb. 3, 1885; s. John C. and Luella (Simeral) McK.; ed. pub. schs.; m. Betty Gertrude Williams, May 27, 1914; children—Betty (Mrs. E. F. Dow), Harry F. Salesman, Shredded Wheat Biscuit Co., 1903-05; dist. sales mgr., Arbuckle Bros., 1905-08; mgr. premium dept. and asst. advt. mgr. Procter & Gamble, Cincinnati, 1908-14; sales mgr. and later pres., Knapp Co., N.Y. City, 1914-23; v.p. and sales mgr., Gerlach-Barklow Co., Joliet, Ill., 1923-33, pres., dir., since 1933, Dir. United Printers & Publishers, Inc., Joliet, since 1933, pres. 1949-54; dir. Artographic Corp., Greetings, Inc., P. F. Volland Co.; Rust Craft Publishers, Elgin, Joliet & Eastern R.R.; v.p. Alexander Mfg. Co., Bloomington, Ill., 1949—; chmn. bd. Western Lithograph Co., Los Angeles, 1953. Pres. Ill. Mfrs. Assn., 1944-45, mem. adv. bd., 1946-53, dir. since 1946. Director Joliet-Will Co. Community Chest, Inc.; exec. chmn. Will Co. chpt. Ill. Div. Am. Cancer Soc., 1948-52, Ill. div., 1951-52; mem. nat. adv. com. Stephens Coll., Columbia, Mo. Hon. vice president Rainbow Council Boys Scouts of America, Joliet. Kentucky Colonel since 1950. Director of The Sportsmans' Club of Am. Clubs: South Shore (Chicago); Rotary, Joliet Country (Joliet). Address: 600 E. Second St., Los Angeles 54. Deceased.

MACKENZIE, Donald Hector, educator; b. Rossland, B.C., Aug. 12, 1901; s. Murdoch and Catherine (McShannon) M.; B.B.A., M.B.A., U. Wash., 1925; m. Mary Catherine David, Dec. 26, 1943; children—Mary Ann, Catherine Emily, Donald David. Came to U.S., 1920, naturalized, 1937. Clk. G.N. Ry., Rossland, 1918-19; mines accountant Cons. Mining & Smelting Co. of Can., Trail, B.C., 1926-27; accountant William Baker & Co., Rossland, 1927; teaching fellow U. Wash., 1927-29, instr., 1929-34, asst. prof., 1934-39, asso. prof., 1939-44, prof. accounting and statistics, 1944—, chairman dept., 1946—; advt. work, 1929—; vis. lectr. grad. sch. bus., Harvard, 1940; dir. Hunter Bros., Ltd. Examiner Nat. War Labor Bd., 1942. Mem. Seattle Transit Commn., 1952-56, chmn. 1954. C.P.A., State Wash., 1933. Mem. Soc. Advancement Mgmt. (mem. adv. editorial bd., 1940-48), Am. Arbitration Soc., Am. Accounting Assn., Wash. Soc. C.P.A., C. of C. Author: Mathematics of Finance, 1937; Fundamentals of Accounting, 1949. Contbr. profl. and trade jours. Home: 6020 Wellesley Way, Seattle. Died Aug. 27, 1955.

MacKENZIE, William Ross, brewery exec.; b. Halifax, N.S., Dec. 2, 1885; s. Alexander and Jane T. (Ross) MacK.; student pub. schs. of Halifax; m. Stella Maud Webster, June 11, 1910; 1 dau., Katharine (Mrs. A. K. Hill); m. 2d, Cathlene Anderson, Jan. 12, 1949. Pres., chmn. Western Canada Breweries, Ltd., Vancouver, 1950—; v.p. Moore's Restaurant, Ltd., Reliance Securities Corp., Ltd.; dir. Carling Breweries (Alberta), Ltd., The Carling Breweries (B.C.), Ltd., Carling Breweries (Sask.), Ltd., Carling Brewering (Manitoba), Ltd., O'Keefe Brewing Co. (Sask.), Ltd., O'Keefe Brewing Co. (Manitoba), Ltd., Brewery Products, Ltd., Kiewel Brewing Co., Ltd., Pelissier's Brewery, Ltd., B.C. Forest Products Co., Ltd. Presbyn. Clubs: Capilano Golf, Shaughnessy Heights Golf (Vancouver); Manitoba (Winnipeg); Assiniboia, Wascana Golf (Regina); Saskatoon. Home: 6312 Carnarvon St., Vancouver 13. Office: 2790 Vine St., Vancouver, B.C., Can. Died Jan. 8, 1960.

MACKENZIE, William Roy, educator; b. River John, N.S., Can., Feb. 14, 1883; s. Archibald and Sarah Archibald (Eaton) M.; A.B., Dalhousie U., 1902, LL.D., 1950; Ph.D., Harvard, 1910; m. Mary Ethel Stuart, Oct. 3, 1906. With Washington U., 1910-1952, asso. prof. English until 1918, prof. and head of dept., 1918-49; lectr. at summer sessions Harvard. Mem. Modern Lang. Assn. Am., Am. Folklore Soc., Am. Philol. Assn., Mediaeval Acad. Am., English-Speaking Union, Phi Beta Kappa, Pi Epsilon Delta, Omicron Delta Kappa. Clubs: University, Harvard, Round Table, Burns, Town and Gown. Author: The English Moralities, 1914; The Quest of the Ballad, 1919; Ballads and Sea Songs from Nova Scotia, 1928; also monographs on The English Moralities and on Shakespeare's Hamlet. Address: Washington University, St. Louis. Died Sept. 27, 1957; buried Nova Scotia.

MACKEOWN, Samuel Stuart (măk kŭ'ĕn), univ. prof., cons. engr.; b. New York, N.Y., Dec. 3, 1895; s. Joseph James and Dora (Chancellor) M.; A.B., Cornell U., 1917, Ph.D., 1923; m. Littie B. Uhrlaub, March 21, 1928 (died Oct. 8, 1948); 1 dau., Littie M. (Mrs. Littie Mackeown Hicks). Assistant physicist, United States Bureau Standards, 1919; instr. physics, Cornell U., 1920-23; Nat. Research Fellow in physics, 1923-26; asst. prof. elec. engring., Calif. Inst. Tech., Pasadena, 1926-29, asso. prof., 1929-41, prof. since 1941; cons. engr. and patent expert for Gen. Electric Co., Am. Telephone & Telegraph Co., Metro-Goldwyn-Mayer, Technicolor, Standard Oil of Calif., etc. since 1929. Served as 2d lt., S.C. (Radio Development Sect.), U.S.A., 1918-19; lt. comdr., U.S.N.R. since 1938. Fellow Inst. Radio Engrs. (mem. bd. editors), A.A.A.S.; mem. Am. Inst. Elec. Engrs., Am. Assn. Univ. Profs., Sigma Xi, Tau Beta Pi. Republican. Presbyterian. Clubs: Athenaeum, University, Valley Hunt (Pasadena); Cornell (New York). Home: California Club, 538 S. Flower St., Los Angeles 13. Died May 29, 1952.

MACKIE, Thomas Turlay, coll. prof., physician; b. Great Barrington, Mass., May 10, 1895; s. David Ives and Isabel (Turlay) M.; A.B., Harvard, 1918; M.D., Columbia, 1924; D.T.M. and Hygiene, London Sch. of Hygiene and Tropical Medicine, London, 1931; m. Carolyn B. Van Cortlandt, May 31, 1921 (divorced 1941); children—Mrs. Wm. H. Savage, Madame Philippe Bouriez; married second, Janet Welch, March 5, 1942 (divorced 1951); married third time Helen Holme Warnock, Dec. 19, 1951. Asst. in medicine Columbia, 1926-29; instr., 1933-33; research asso. Pub. Health and Preventive Medicine, Cornell U. Med. Coll., 1933-35, asso., 1935-46; asst. clin. prof. medicine Columbia, 1938-46; prof. preventive medicine and head of dept. Bowman Gray Sch. of Medicine, Wake Forest Coll., 1946-51; dir. Inst. of Tropical Medicine, 1947—; asst. physician. Presbyterian Hosp., N.Y. City, 1929-33; asst. attending physician Fifth Av. Hosp., 1932-35; attending physician Roosevelt Hosp., 1936-46; cons. physician Beekman St. Hosp., N.Y. Infirmary for Women and Children, Fairview Hosp., Great Barrington, Mass., 1946. Cons. in tropical medicine to U.S. sec. of war, 1940-42, Vets. adminstr. Branch 4, 1946-49; cons. in internal medicine and tropical medicine, Atlanta area, Vets. Adminstrn., 1949—; spl. cons. epidemiology div. U.S.P.H.S.; mem. subcom. on tropical diseases Nat. Research Council, 1940-42 and, 1947—; mem. health com. Office for Relief and Rehabiliation, Dept. of State, Army Bd. for Investigation of Influenza and other Epidemic Diseases 42; cons. VA Hosp., West Haven, Conn., Norwalk (Conn.) and Stamford (Conn.) hosps., Roosevelt Hosp., N.Y.C. Chmn. bd. Am. Found. for Tropical Medicine. Fellow A.C.P., Royal Soc. Tropical Medicine and Hygiene; Mem. Am. Clinical and Climatol. Assn., A.A.A.S., Am. Soc. Tropical Medicine, Am. Acad. Tropical Medicine, American Gastro Enterol. Assn., A.M.A., N.Y. Acad. Medicine, Alpha Omega Alpha. Recipient Duncan Medal, London School of Tropical Medicine, 1931; Legion of Merit, 1946. Episcopalian. Co-author: Manual of Tropical Medicine. Home: North Av., Westport, Conn. Died Oct. 5, 1955; buried Great Barrington, Mass.

MacKINNON, Eugene, newspaper editor; b. Helena, Mont., Feb. 17, 1898; s. Hugh Angus and Sarah Elizabeth (Cronin) MacK.; Mt. St. Charles Coll., 1914-17; U. of Mont., 1920-22; m. Anne Jones, Jan. 19, 1934; children—Sally Anne, Mary Jean. Began newspaper career as reporter for Daily Missoulian, Missoula, 1920; city editor Livingston Enterprise, 1921; telegraph editor Great Falls Leader, 1922; news editor Yakima (Wash.) Herald, 1923-24; Northwest editor Portland (Ore.) Telegram, 1924-25; news editor Great Falls (Mont.) Tribune, 1925, Anaconda Standard, 1926-28, Montana Standard (Butte), 1928-29; editor Billings Gazette, 1929-36; gen. mgr. Salt Lake Tribune and Telegram, since 1947; chmn. spl. standing com. Am. Newspaper Pub. Assn., 1936-42; mgr. Newspaper Publishers Assn. of Phila., 1942-46; asst. gen. mgr. Evening Bulletin, 1946-48; gen. mgr. Salt Lake Tribune and Telegram, 1948. Master engr. sr. grade Engr. Corps, U.S. Army, 18 mos., World War. Mem. Sigma Nu, Sigma Delta Chi. Clubs: Poor Richard, Salt Lake Country, Alta, Rotary. Home: 1446 East South Temple. Office: 143 S. Main St., Salt Lake City 1. Died Aug. 8, 1951.

MacKINNON, James Angus, Can. senator; b. Port Elgin, Ont., Can., Oct. 4, 1881; s. James and Margaret (Tolmie) MacK.; student Port Elgin and Kincardine, Ont.; LL.D., U. Alberta, 1948; m. Annie Irene Sharp, June 28, 1911 (dec. 1944); 1 dau., Keltie (Mrs. Denis Flattery). Reporter, Edmonton (Alberta) Bulletin, 1903-04; founder, pres. James A. MacKinnon Co., Ltd., Edmonton, 1911-—; mgr. Can. Credit Men's Trust Assn. of Central and Northern Alberta, 1921-—; dir. Dairy Supplies Ltd., Edmonton, Catelli Food Products Ltd., Montreal and Lethbridge Can.-Mont. Pipe Line Co., Clgary, International Bus. Machines Co., Ltd., Toronto. Elected to Canadian House of Commons, 1935, re-elected 1940, 45; mem. Privy Council and apptd. minister without Portfolio, 1939, minister trade and commerce, and resources, 1948-49; mem. Can. Senate, 1949-—. Liberal. Presbyn. Clubs: Rideau, Country (Ottawa); Mayfair Golf and Country, Country (Edmonton); St. James' (Montreal). Home: 10064 Jasper Av., Edmonton, Alberta. Address: The Senate, Ottawa, Can. Died Apr. 18, 1958.

MACKLIN, W(illiam) A(lexander) Stewart, ret. naval officer; b. Illchester, Md., July 23, 1897; s. Capt. Charles Fearns and Emily Slaughter (Stewart) M.; B.S., U.S. Naval Acad., 1917; m. Eleanor Keith, Sept. 15, 1920 (div. July 1932); m. 2d Mary Margaret Allen, Nov. 5, 1933; children—Margaret Ann, Stewart Allen. Cmmd. ensign USN, 1917, advanced through grades to rear adm., 1947; served in U.S.S. Virginia, 1917, U.S.S. O'Brien, 1918-19; instr. U.S. Naval Acad., 1923-25, 28-30; exec. officer gunboat Asheville, Central Am. and China coast, 1930-33; comd. gunboat Oahu, Yangtze river, 1933-35; attached to Navy Dept. Hydrographic Office, 1935-37; navigator U.S.S. Idaho, 1937-38; exec. officer U.S.S. Dobbin, 1938-39; dist. intelligence officer 5th Naval Dist., Norfolk, Va., 1939-41; comdr. destroyer div. 62, North Atlantic, and escort comdr. for convoys between Can. and Eng., 1941-42; comdr. Eastern Sea frontier escort vessels, 1942-43; comdr. U.S.S. Richmond, North Pacific, 1943-44; exec. officer, U.S. Naval Tng. Sta., Newport, R.I. 1944-46; retired, 1947. Decorated Legion of Merit with combat citation. Home: Wolford P.O., Md. Died Oct. 5, 1957; buried Arlington Nat. Cemetery.

MacKNIGHT, Dodge, artist; b. Providence, Oct. 1, 1860; s. John W. and Phoebe (Davenport) M.; studied with Fernand Cormon, Paris; m. Louise Queyrel, 1892 (dec.); 1 son, John Eugene (dec.). In France and Spain until 1897; has traveled and painted in Utah, Ariz., Ore., Newfoundland, Mexico, Morocco and Canada; paintings on permanent exhbn. in Boston Mus. Fine Arts, Fenway Court; Fogg Mus., Cambridge; Worcester Museum, etc. Home: East Sandwich, Mass. Deceased.

MACKY, Eric Spencer, artist, pvt. coll. pres.; b. Auckland, N.Z., Nov. 16, 1880; s. Joseph and Kate (Spencer) M.; grad. Nat. Gallery Sch. of Painting, Melbourne, Australia, 1905; Julien Acad., Paris, 1910; LL.D., Cal. Coll. Arts and Crafts, 1952; m. Constance Jenkins, Aug. 20, 1912; children—Donald, Joseph. Came to the U.S. 1911, naturalized, 1938. Artist, portrait painter; dean of faculty Cal. Sch. Fine Arts, San Francisco, 1917-44, prof. painting and drawing, 1919-—; pres. Cal. Coll. Arts and Crafts, Oakland, 1944-—. Mem. San Francisco Art Assn. Clubs: Bohemian, Faculty (U. Cal.); Rotary (Oakland). Paintings represented in numerous pub. and pvt. art collections. Home: 3973 16th St., San Francisco 14. Office: 5212 Broadway, Oakland 18, Cal. Died May 5, 1958; buried Berkeley, Cal.

MACLACHLAN, John Miller, b. Jackson, Miss., Oct. 9, 1905; s. John Miller and Lucy Holt (Harrison) M.; grad., Texas Mil. Inst., 1924; A.B., Millsaps Coll., 1919; A.M., Univ. of N.C., 1932, Ph.D., 1937; m. Emily White Stevens, Sept. 3, 1931; children—John Bruce Stevens, Morgan Douglas, Alan Stuart. Research asst. Inst. for Research in Social Science, Chapel Hill, N.C., 1931-34; asst. prof. agricultural economics and rural sociology, N.C., State College, 1934-35; Julius Rosenwald Fund, 1935-37; vis. prof. of sociology, North Texas State Teachers Coll., 1937, 1938; asst. prof. of sociology, Univ. of Miss., 1937-38; asst. prof., U. of Fla., 1938-40, asso. prof. and acting head of dept., 1940-41, prof. and head of dept., 1941-—, asst. dean, College of Arts and Sciences, 1946, asso. dean, 1946-48, head dept. sociology and anthropology, 1948-—; chief of staff Fla. Med. Center Study, 1952-53. Member bd. dirs. Fla. Blue Cross, Mem. Fla. Tb. and Health Assn. (bd. dirs.), Sigma Upsilon, Pi Gamma Mu, Alpha Kappa Delta, Phi Kappa Phi, Delta Chi. Democrat. Episcopalian. Club: Seminole (Jacksonville). Author: Florida's Doctors, 1954; People and Health in Florida, 1954; Florida's Hospitals, 1954; This Changing South, 1956. Contbr. to books, also articles and reviews to profl. jours. Home: 1908 N.W. 7th Lane, Gainesvile, Fla. Died Sept. 1, 1959.

MACLAURIN, William Rupert, economist; b. Wellington, New Zealand, July 25, 1907; s. Richard Cockburn and Alice (Young) M.; A.B., Harvard, 1929, M.B.A., 1932, D.C.S., 1936; m. Elfriede Carter, Sept. 2, 1933; children—Katharine Adams, Robert Campbell, Joan, Nancy Hadfield. Fiske scholar, Trinity Coll., Cambridge, England, 1929-30; Sheldon Travelling Fellow (Harvard) to Australia, 1934-35; Guggenheim Fellow, 1950-51; instructor Harvard Graduate School of Business Adminstrn., 1935-36; asst. prof. economics, Mass. Inst. Tech., 1936-40, asso. prof., 1940-42, prof. since 1942; dir. Indsl. Relations Sect., 1937-45, and since 1948; sec. Bowman Com. on Science and Pub. Welfare, Office of Scientific Research and Development, Washington, D.C., 1945. Mem. Am. Acad. Arts and Sciences, Am. Econ. Assn., Economic Hist. Assn. Author: Economic Planning in Australia, 1929-36, 1937; The Movement of Factory Workers (with Charles A. Myers), 1943; Invention and Innovation in the Radio Industry, 1949. Contbr. numerous professional articles to various periodicals. Home: Trapelo Rd., South Lincoln, Mass. Office: Industrial Relations Section, Mass. Inst. of Technology, Cambridge, Mass. Died Aug. 17, 1959.

MACLAY, William Walter, civil engr.; b. N.Y.C., Mar. 27, 1846; s. Dr. Archibald and Julia Anne (Walker) M.; grad. U.S. Naval Acad., 1863; A.M., N.Y.U., 1868, C.E., 1872; m. Marian Bensel, Sept. 16, 1874. Commd. ensign, 1863; master, 1865, advanced through grades to lt. comdr., 1868; participated in both attacks on Ft. Fisher; after war made cruise of 3 yrs. around the world with Commodore John Goldsborough, as his navigating officer; apptd. by Japanese govt. to survey and designate sites for light houses, 1868; apptd. acting fleet capt. to Commodore Goldsborough, comdg. U.S. Asiatic Squadron, 1868; asst. prof. mathematics U.S. Naval Acad., 1868-69; resigned from Navy to study civil engring., 1871; asst. engr. and 1st asst. engr. N.Y. dept. of docks, 1873-93; now cons. engr.; pres., mgr. Glens Falls Portland Cement Co., 1893-1905. Mem. Inst. Civil Engrs., London, Am. Soc. C.E. (Norman gold medal, 1877), Internat. Soc. for Testing Materials; corr. mem. N.Y. Hist. Soc. Club: University (N.Y. C.). Author: Notes and Experiments on the Use and Testing of Portland Cements, 1877; Portland Cement for Engineering Works, 1892. Home: Lee, Mass. Office: 220 W. 57th St., N.Y.C. Deceased.

MACLEAN, Alexander Tweedie, ins. exec.; b. Glasgow, Scotland, July 8, 1887; s. Hugh and Isabella (Brotherton) M.; ed. in schools and by tutors in Scotland; m. Amy Catherine Hodgson, July 8, 1916. Came to U.S., 1910, naturalized, 1920. Began career with City of Glasgow Life Ins. Co., Glasgow, Scotland; asst. actuary Home Life Ins. Co., N.Y.C., 1916; asst. actuary Mass. Mutual Life Ins. Co., 1916-27, became actuary, 1927, v.p., 1936, pres., 1945-—, dir., 1936-—. Fellow Faculty of Actuaries (Scotland), Actuarial Soc. Am. Mem. exec. com. Am. Life Conv. Chmn. British War Relief for Western Mass., 1943-46. Mem. Pilgrims Society. Episcopalian. Clubs: Colony (dir.) (Springfield); Longmeadow (Mass.); Metropolitan (N.Y.C.). Home: 216 Overbrook Rd., Longmeadow, Mass. Office: 1295 State St., Springfield, Mass. Died May 15, 1950.

MACLELLAN, Robert J., ins. exec.; b. St. John, N.B., Can., Mar. 26, 1874; s. Thomas and Helen (Jardine) M.; m. Cora Llewellyn, Nov. 22, 1905. With Citizens Bank & Trust Co., Chattanooga, 1893-98, Richmond Cotton Oil Co., Chattanooga, 1898-1905; sec. Provident Life & Accident Ins. Co., 1905-16, pres., 1916-53, chmn. bd. since 1953; dir. Am. Trust & Banking Co. Trustee U. Chattanooga; dir. Maryville (Tenn.) Coll. Served with C.E., U.S. Army, 1892-93. Clubs: Mountain City, Chattanooga Golf and Country, Fairyland, Fairyland Golf, Lookout Mountain. Home; 28 Bluff View. Office: Provident Bldg., Chattanooga, Tenn. Died June 7, 1956; buried Forest Hills Cemetery.

MACMILLAN, Cyrus, educator, mem. Can. Parliament; b. Belfast, Prince Edward Island, Sept. 12, 1882; s. Hector and Isabel (Fraser) M.; student Prince of Wales Coll.; B.A., M.A., hon. LL.D., McGill U.; M.A., and Ph.D., Harvard; m. Margaret Neilson Brower, Aug. 15, 1916. Head English dept. McGill U., dean faculty arts and sci.; minister fisheries Can. Cabinet, 1930; mem. Can. House Commons; Parliamentary asst. to Minister Nat. Defense for Air; mem. Royal Commn. Maritime Claims, Atlantic Fisheries; chmn. Royal Commn. Edn. Prince Edward Island; chmn. Parliamentary Commn. Soldiers Pensions; chmn. Vets. Land Act, Soldiers' Honours and Awards, Social Security. Served as comdg. officer, 6th Can. Siege Battery, World War I. Club: University (Montreal). Author: McGill and Its Story; Canadian Wonder Tales: Canadian Fairy Tales; Glooskap's Country. Home: Hillsborough House, Charlottetown, Prince Edward Island, Can. Died June 29, 1953; buried Sherwood Cemetery, Charlottetown.

MacMILLAN, Hugh R., mfg. exec.; b. N.Y.C., Dec. 9, 1903; s. Hugh R. and Laura E. (Seckler) MacM.; grad. U. Mo., 1927; m. Mary Lee Lipscomb, Jan. 29, 1944; children—Betsy Ann, Robert Hugh. Employee Procter & Gamble Co., 1930-40; indsl. engr. Colgate-Palmolive-Peet Co., 1941, supt. Jersey City plant, 1941-43, domestic prodn. supt., 1943-45, gen. domestic supt., 1945-46, v.p. in charge prodn., 1946-—, dir., 1955-—. Mem. Kappa Sigma. Republican. Presbyn. Home: 22 Joanna Way, Short Hills, N.J. Office: 300 Park Av., N.Y.C. 22. Died Oct. 6, 1957.

MacMILLAN, John Alwyn, founder, director and consultant, Dayton Rubber Company; born on farm, Prince Edward Island, Canada; son of Alexander and Elizabeth (Robertson) MacM.; ed. pub. sch. and Prince of Wales College; married 2d Patricia P. Baker. Taught school on Prince Edward Island then moved to Denver, Colo., where he lived for 15 years during which time he was asso. gen. mgr. of Equitable Life Assurance Soc. of U.S. for several western states, and also officially connected with W. C. Lothrop & Co., and the Brinkhaus Investment Co., both large cos. engaged in real estate subdivision development and home bldg.; moved to Dayton; founded Dayton Rubber Company, becoming gen. mgr., pres., 1916-36, chmn. bd., 1936-46. Mem. Citizens Relief Com. following Dayton flood. Pres. and treas. Second Street Properties Co.; pres. Dayton Chamber of Commerce; director Ohio Chamber of Commerce, National Assn. Mfrs.; dir. Miami Valley Hosp., Dayton War and Community Chest, Y.M.C.A., Ohio Public Expenditure Council, Nat. Junior Achievement, Inc. Mem. Soc. Automotive Engrs. Baptist. Clubs: Canadian (New York); Engineers, Moraine Country, Rotary (ex-pres.). Home: "Far Hills Estate," Dayton, O. Died June 7, 1952; buried Mausoleum Woodland Cemetery, Dayton.

MacNIDER, William de Berniere, pharmacologist; b. Chapel Hill, N.C., June 25, 1881; s. Virginius St. Clair and Sophia Beatty (Mallett) M.; U. N.C., 1898-1903, M.D., 1903; student U. Chgo.; spl. student Western Res. U.; hon. D.Sc., Med. Coll. Va., 1933; LL.D., Davidson (N.C.), Coll., 1934; m. Sarah Foard, Jan. 23, 1918; 1 dau., Sarah Foard. Kenan prof. of pharmacology U. N.C., 1905-—, Kenan research prof. of pharmacology, 1920, dean med. sch., 1937-40; Harvey Soc. lectr., 1928-29; Chandler Meml. lectr. Columbia U.; Smith-Reed-Russell lecturer George Washington U. Sch. of Medicine, 1938; Brown-Sequart lectr. Med. Coll. Va., 1938; Mayo Foundation lecturer, 1939; formerly special lecturer in pharmacology, Duke U. Med. Sch.; physician in chief pro tem. Peter Bent Brigham Hosp., Apr. 1925; cons. on gerontology Nat. Inst. of Health; mem. Nat. Bd. Med. Examiners (chmn. examination com.). Mem. NRC com. on nutritional aspects of ageing; chmn. Am. div. Internat. Club for Research on Ageing. Recipient Kober medal Assn. Am. Physicians, 1941. Fellow A.A.A.S., Am. Acad. Arts and Sciences, A.C.P.; mem. Am. Soc. for Pharmacology and Exptl. Therapeutics (pres. 1932-34, mem. council), A.M.A. (chmn. sect. of pharmacology and therapeutics, 1927), Med. Soc. N.C. (pres. 1925-26), Am. Physiol. Soc., Am. Assn. Pathologists and Bacteriologists, Am. Assn. Biol. Chemists, Soc. Exptl. Biology and Medicine (pres. 1941-42), Am. Assn. U. Profs., Am. Soc. Exptl. Pathology, Assn. Am. Physicians, Am. Assn. Anesthetists, Nat. Anaesthesia Research Soc. (research com.), Internat. Anaesthesia Research Soc. (pres. 1934-35), Elisha Mitchell Sci. Soc. (pres.), Am. Assn. Hist. Medicine, N.C. Acad. Science, Nat. Research Council (mem. com. on cellular physiology; mem. exec. com. med. div.), Nat. Acad. Sciences, N.Y. Acad. Sciences, Am. Soc. Naturalists, Am. Philos. Soc., Harvey Soc. (hon.), Pathological Soc. Great Britain and Ireland, Brit. Physiol. Soc. (asso. fgn. mem.), Gerontol. Soc. (chmn. council), Sigma Xi (pres. U. chpt.), Phi Chi, Sigma Nu, Phi Beta Kappa, Alpha Omega Alpha. Democrat. Episcopalian. Club: Cosmos (Washington). Asso. editor of proceedings Soc. for Exptl. Biology and Medicine; asso. editor the Quarterly Journal of Alcohol Study, Journal of Pharmacology and Experimental Therapeutics. Contbr. many articles to medical and biological jours. setting forth results of original pharmacol. investigations; research on production of acute and chronic nephritis; toxicity of the general anaesthetics for kidney with methods for protection; stability of acid-base equilibrium of blood in nephritis and in animals of different age periods; toxaemias of pregnancy. Research papers on Toxic Action of Alcohol, Uranium and Chloroform on the Liver, Liver Regeneration, The Resistance of atypical Regenerated Liver Cells to the Above Mentioned Toxic Agents, The Influence of Liver Degeneration and Repair on the Acid Base Equilibrium of the Blood, also papers dealing with acquired resistance of fixed tissue cells. Awarded Gibbs prize for med. research, 1930-31, by New York Acad. Medicine; Research medal, Southern Med. Assn., 1933. Delivered convocation address Am. Coll. of Physicians, 1942. Home: Chapel Hill, N.C. Died May 31, 1951; buried Chapel Hill Cemetery.

MACOMBER, Alexander (mă kŭm'bẽr), cons. engr.; b. Newton, Mass., May 21, 1885; s. James and Mary Elizabeth (Simmons) M.; B.S., Mass. Inst. Tech., 1907; m. Alfrieda Terry, Aug. 15, 1929. Elec. engr. No. Cal. Power Co., 1907-10; engr. with Chas. H. Tenney & Co., mgrs. pub. utilities, 1910-17; mem. Macomber & West, cons. engrs. and mgrs. pub. utilities, 1920-50; pres. Nantucket Gas & Elec. Co., Manchester Elec. Co., Gas Service, Inc.; mng. dir. Portland Gas Light Co., Community Pub. Service Co., Northeast Gas Transmission Co. Pres. Franklin

Found. Commr. Port of Boston Authority. Served as Gas Div. W.P.B., Washington, 1942-46. Served as maj. C.E., U.S. Army, 1917-19. Trustee Old South Church, Boston. Mem. Am. Gas Assn., Alpha Tau Omega (nat. treas.). Republican. Conglist. Club: Union, Algonquin, Engineers (Boston), Nashua Country, Peterbough Country (N.H.). Contbr. to tech. publs. Home: 401 Beacon St. Office: 110 State St., Boston. Died Mar. 14, 1956; buried Mount Auburn Cemetery, Cambridge.

MACOMBER, John R. (māk'ŭm-bẽr), corp. official; b. Framingham Centre, Mass., Nov. 1, 1875; s. John F. and Helen A. (Hunt) M.; ed. Chauncey Hall Sch., Boston, 1893; Mass. Inst. of Technology; honorary A. M., Tufts Coll., 1920. Began business career with N. W. Harris & Co., Boston, 1894, pres. Harris, Forbes & Co., Inc., Boston, 1916-31; chmn. board Chase Harris Forbes Corp., 1930-33; chmn. bd. First Boston Corp., 1934-47, now dir.; dir. U.S. Smelting, Refining & Mining Co. (Boston), Bird & Son, Inc. (East Walpole, Mass.), United Shoe Machinery Co. Director Mass. Soc. for Prevention of Cruelty to Animals, American Humane Education Society; trustee, N.E. Conservatory of Music, Boston; pres. Massachusetts General Hospital; life member corp. Mass. Inst. Tech. Unitarian. Clubs: Union, Country (Brookline); Longwood Cricket, Turf and Field, Nat. Steeplechase and Hunt Annual, Millwood Hunt, Am. Thoroughbred Breeders Assn. Algonquin; Links, Recess (N.Y.C.). Home: Salem End Rd., Farmingham, Mass. Office: 75 Federal St., Boston. Died May 11, 1955; buried Farmingham Center, Mass.

Mac PHERSON, Earle Steele, engr., motor vehicle mfg. exec.; b. Highland Park, Ill., July 6, 1891; s. Arthur Grant and Emma (Eckhardt) Mac P.; B.S. in Mech. Engring., U. Ill., 1915; m. Florence Lucille Jones, Mar. 11, 1941; 1 dau., Sandra Lucille. Exptl. lab. engr. Chalmers Motor Co., 1915-17; asst. chief engr. Liberty Motor Car Corp., 1919-22; design engr., asst. chief engr. Hupp Motor Car Co., 1930-34; asst. to v.p. engring., chief engr. Chevrolet-Cleveland, chief engr. product study 6, Gen. Motors Corp., 1935-47 (all Detroit); exec. engr. Ford Motor Co., Dearborn, Mich., 1947-49, chief engr., 1949-52, v.p. engring., mem. adminstrn. com., 1952—. Served as capt., A.S., A.E.F., 1917-19; engr. Bolling Mission, France. Mem. Soc. Automotive Engrs., Inc., Engring. Soc. of Detroit, Coordinating Research Council, Inc., Phi Delta Theta, Tau Beta Pi. Mason. Clubs: Detroit Athletic; Red Run Golf (Huntington Woods, Mich.). Home: 8775 Lincoln Dr., Huntington Woods. Office: Ford Motor Co., Dearborn, Mich. Died Jan. 28, 1960.

MACPHERSON, Walter Henry, clergyman; b. Delaware, Ont., Can., Sept. 27, 1877; s. William and Elizabeth (Heard) M.; brought to U.S., 1889; student U. Chgo., 1903-07; L.H.D., Lombard (Ill.) Coll., 1925; S.T.D., Tufts, 1936; m. Cecelia Clifford, June 26, 1906. Asst. pastor Congl. Ch., South Chicago, 1903-06; ordained ministry Universalist Ch., 1907; asst. pastor St. Paul's Ch., Chgo., 1907-11; pastor The Universalist Ch., Joliet, Ill., 1912—; pres. Universalist Gen. Conv., 1935-39. Regional dir. War Camp Community Service, 1917-19. Founder Kenmore Play Sch., Chgo., 1910. dir., 1910-16; trustee Ryder Divinity Sch., U. Chgo. Mem. Inst. World Affairs. Universalist; mem. Internat. Assn. Religious Liberals. Rotarian. Lecturer. Author: The Golden Past Still Lives. Home: 621 W. Marion St. Office: 156 N. Chicago St., Joliet, Ill. Deceased.*

MacPHIE, Elmore I., business exec.; b. Springfield, Mass., Oct. 21, 1888; B.S., Tufts Coll., 1911; married Etta Marion Phillips, September 4, 1915; children—Franklin W., Walter P. Science teacher, Blake School, Minneapolis, Minn., 1911-12; dist. sales mgr. Washburn Crosby Co., Minneapolis, Minnesota, 1912-17; pres. Otis Allen & Son Co., Lowell, Mass., 1917-27; vice pres. and treas. Atlas Plywood Corp., 1927-35. pres., dir. since 1935; chmn. bd., director of Davidson Plywood & Lumber Company, Los Angeles, Plywood Inc., Trenton, New Jersey; president and dir. Marvil Package Co., Robinson Hardware Co., Laurel, Del., Nansemond Co., Suffolk, Va.; dir. Northwestern Veneer & Plywood Corp., Gladstone, Mich., Rockland-Atlas Nat. Bank, Boston, Plywood, Inc., Detroit, Snow Hill (Ala.) Lumber Co., Yuba Consol. Gold Fields (Boston and San Francisco), Liberty Mutual Insurance Co., Boston, Butts & Ordway Co., Cambridge, Mass. Director and treas., Mt. Pleasant Home, Boston; dir. Newton YMCA; trustee Newton-Wellesley Hosp., Newton, Mass., Tufts Coll. Mem. Delta Tau Delta. Mason (32°, K.T., Shriner). Clubs: Braeburn, Webhannet; second, Algonquin (Boston). Home: 48 Prince St., West Newton, Mass. and Kennebunk Beach, Me. Office: Statler Bldg., Boston. Died Mar. 22, 1955; buried Lowell (Mass.) Cemetery.

MacQUIGG, Charles Ellison (māk-kwĭg'), college dean; b. Ironton, O., Jan. 19, 1885; s. Charles Bridwell and Rosa (Ellison) MacQ.; E.M., Ohio State U., 1909; hon. Eng.D., Clarkson Coll. of Tech.; m. Lillian Rodgers, Dec. 25, 1912; children—Rodger Ellison, Charles Harrison, David Ellison. Civil engr. Santa Fe Ry., 1909-10; asst. engr. of tests Anaconda Copper Mining Co., 1910-12; head dept. metallurgy, Pa. State Coll., 1912-17; research and development work Union Carbide and Carbon Co., research labs., 1919-37; dean Coll. Engring., Ohio State U., since 1937; dir. Engring. Expt. Sta. of Ohio since 1937; dir. and nat. councillor Ohio State U. Research Found.; mem. Ohio Water Resources Bd. Morehead medalist, Internat. Acct. Assn. Capt Ordnance Dept. U.S. Army, 1917-19; now lt. col. ordnance, O.R.C. Mem. Am. Inst. Mining and Metall. Engrs.; mem. Am. Soc. for Engring. Edn. (pres. 1947-48), Am. Soc. Mech. Engrs., Ohio Acad. Science (fellow), Newcomen Soc., Am. Assn. Advancement of Sci., Am. Soc. for Metals, Sigma Xi, Tau Beta Pi. Republican. Episcopalian. Mason. Contbr. tech. articles to jours. Home: 393 W. 8th Av., Columbus, O. Died Apr. 24, 1952; buried Ironton, O.

MacRAE, Elmer Livingston, artist; b. N.Y. City, July 16, 1875; s. Charles and Mary Jane (Rogers) MacR.; ed. pub. and pvt. schs. and 1 yr. Fordham Coll.; studied art, Art Students' League, under Twachtman, Beckwith, Blum and Mowbray and 2 seasons in summer classes under Twachtman, at Cos Cob, Conn.; m. Constant Holley, Oct. 16, 1900; children—(twins) Constant (Mrs. H. Smith) (dec.), and Clarissa (Mrs. Manuel Velasquez). Painter in oil, pastel and water color of marines, landscapes, figures and portraits, also woodcarving. Exhibitor in current exhbns. An organizer, trustee and treas. Am. Painters and Sculptors; an organizer, sec. and treas. The Pastellists; mem. New York Water Color Club; sec. Greenwich Soc. of Artists. Conglist. Home: Cos Cob, Conn. Died Apr. 2, 1953.

MacRAE, Harry B., Christian Science lecturer; b. Dollar Bay, Mich., Feb. 14, 1891; s. James and Emma Sophia (McKernan) MacR.; student Univ. of Minn., Univ. of Cincinnati,; C.S.B., Bachelor of Christian Science, Mass. Metaphysical Coll., conducted by Board of Edn., 1937; m. Gerda Siljan, Dec. 10, 1919. Mem. Mother Church of Christ Scientist since 1923; first reader, pres., and mem. of the bd. of trustees, First Church of Christ Scientist, Dallas, Tex.; primary class instrn. in Christian Science, 1931; lecturer, Christian Science Bd. of Lectureship, Mother Church, since 1947. Served with U.S.A. Air Force as lt., 1917-19. Mem. Reserve Officers Assn. of the U.S., Delta Tau Delta. Mason. Contbr. of articles to Christian Science periodicals. Home: 4447 Westway Av., Dallas 5. Office: Kirby Building, Dallas 1. Died Jan. 9, 1958.

MACVANE, Silas Marcus, educator; b. Bothwell P.E.I., Aug. 14, 1842; s. Alexander and Emily (Macdonald) M.; A.B., Acadia Coll., N.S., 1865, Ph.D. (hon.), 1895; studied U. Berlin; A.B., Harvard, 1873; m. Emily Grace de Mille, 1873; children—Edith Elizabeth, Emily Dora, Dorothy Alice. Instr. in polit. economy Harvard, 1875-78, history, 1878-83, asst. prof. history, 1883-6, McLean prof. ancient and modern history, 1887-1911, emeritus, prof., 1911-14. Fellow of the American Academy of Arts and Sciences. Author: The Wages Question; Austrian Theory of Value; Working Principles of Political Economy; The South African Question; Translation of Seignobos' History of Europe since 1814. Address: 16 Quincy St., Cambridge, Mass. Died Rome Italy, Jan. 19, 1914.

MacVITTY, Karl de G., fgn. service officer; b. Nashville, Feb. 27, 1883; s. Frank Dow and Katheryn (deGiers) MacV.; prep. edn. Garrett Mil. Acad., Nashville, and Jarvis Hall, Denver; studied abroad under pvt. tutor, 2½ yrs. Engaged in newspaper reporting and private business till 1917; appointed vice consul, at Genoa, Italy, 1917; trans. to Belfast, Ireland, then to Nassau, Bahama Islands, 1919; became consul, consul assigned to Saigon, French Indo-China, 1920, Sydney, Australia, 1921, Auckland, 1921; fgn. service officer, 1924; assigned Teheran, 1925, Stockholm, Sweden, 1926, Leghorn, Italy, 1928, Malta, 1929, again to Leghorn, 1929; consul at Nairobi, Kanya Colony, E. Africa, 1930-32, at Cape Town, 1932-33, Panama, 1933-34; 2d sec. of Legation, Panama, 1934-35; 1st sec. of Legation, 1935-36; charge d'affaires Am. Legation, Sofia, Bulgaria, 1936-37, 1st sec., 1937-38; consul Amoy, China, 1938-41, consul gen., Noumea, New Caledonia, 1941; consul gen., Alexandria, Egypt, 1943-44; retired from U.S. Foreign Service, 1944. Fellow Royal Philatelic Soc. (London). Episcopalian. Clubs: Army and Navy, National Press (Washington). Home: Nashville. Address: Berkeley, Cook Rd., Hermitage, Tenn. Died Feb. 6, 1959; buried Nashville.

MACY, Carleton, corp. ofcl.; b. White Plains, N.Y., Oct. 14, 1872; s. Josiah H. and Jennie (Carpenter) M.; m. Helen Lefferts, Dec. 11, 1900 (died Oct. 7, 1936); m. 2d, Winifred E. Lefferts, Oct. 30, 1947. Vice-pres., dir. Deed Realty Corp.; dir. Anchor Hocking Gass Corp., Chilton Pen Co., Gen. Pub. Service Corp., Hudson Corp., Henrietta Mill, Martel Mill, Inc., Mellwood Corp. Mem. Soc. Colonial Wars, St. Nicholas Soc. Clubs: Union, Rockaway Hunt. Home: Hewlett, L.I., N.Y. Died Jan. 1949.

MACY, Edward Warren, welfare exec.; b. Fitchburg, Mass., Aug. 7, 1893; s. Edward Jenkins and Helen Elizabeth (Macy) M.; student Worcester Acad.; Mass. Inst. Tech., ex-1916; M.A. hon., Coll. Ozarks. 1932; m. Edith Dewing, Aug. 24, 1914; children—Edward Arthur, Molly Edwina (dec.). Sociologist Swarthmore Child Guidance Clinic, 1915-17; gen. sec. Savannah Social Service Fedn., 1922-24; exec. asst. Nat. Child Labor Com., 1924-26; dir. A.R.C. Disaster Relief (Ill. cyclone, 1927, N.J. fires, 1930, Conn. flood, 1936); dir. pub. dept. Marts & Lundy, Inc., philanthropic financing, 1926-31; gen. dir. Bklyn. Children's Aid Soc., 1931-48; now director orgn. L.I. Symphony Society. Licensed minister Am. Evangelical Church, 1956. Director N.Y. Heart Assn., 1949-50, Sister Elizabeth Kenny Found., 1950-54, United Def. Fund-U.S.O., 1952-54. Formerly: asso. judge Juvenile Ct., Savannah; pres. Ga. Assn. Family Welfare Agencies; mem. Ga. State Commn. on Dependent, Neglected and Disabled Children; sec. So. Regional Child Welfare Conf.; mem. bd. dirs. Child Welfare League Am.; com. member Nat. Conf. Social Work and Welfare Council of N.Y.C. Mem. com. which reorganized childrens div. N.Y.C. Dept. of Welfare. Served as maj., then col. Inf., U.S. Nat. Army, 1917-18; field dir. A.R.C., 1919-21; Commander USCG Reserves, World War. II, captain USCG Auxiliary, 1948-56. chaplain, 1956—. Decorated French Commemorative, French Victory, Verdun, St. Mihiel, Chateau Thierry medals, World War I; Am. Def. award, Atlantic Theatre medal, Navy Commendation (2 citations), World War II. Awarded 3d prize seascape painting, 1951 (one-man shows Art League of Nassau Co., L.I. Hist. Soc. 1951). Mem. French War Vets. (hon. life), Vets. Fgn. Wars (past comdr.), Am. Assn. Social Workers, Army and Navy Union U.S.A., Mil. Order Indian Wars, U.S. Soc. War 1912, Sons of Union Vets., Am. Legion, Alpha Delta Tau. Rep. Episcopalian. Clubs: Art League of Nassau County. Author various articles newspapers and mags. Built, operated one of the 1st wireless stas., 1907; built, flew one of the 1st heavier than air machines, 1910. Home: 128 Willow St., Bklyn.; also Oceanside, L.I., N.Y. Died Oct. 29, 1958.

MACY, George, book publisher; b. N.Y.C., May 12, 1900; student Columbia U., 1917-21; m. Helen Kaplan, 1927; children—Linda Winokur, Jonathan George. Editor quar. Zeta Beta Tau, 1922-28. gen. sec., 1923-28; founder, pres. The Limited Editions Club, 1929—, The Heritage Press, 1935—; mng. dir. The Nonesuch Press, London, 1936; founder, pres., The Readers Club, 1940—. Recipient Accolade for best frat. pub., three times, 1923-28; spl. exhbn. Salle d'Honneur of the Bibliotheque Nationale in Paris, 1948; spl. exhbn. in King's Library of Brit. Mus., 1952; Gold Medal by Inst. Graphic Arts, 1953; Zeta Beta Tau Man of the Year, 1954. Decorated Legion of Honor, Comdr. Companions of Medoc (France). Author: The Collected Versus of George Jester. Editor: A Soldier's Reader, 1943; A Sailor's Reader, 1943. Office: 595 Madison Av., N.Y.C. 22. Died May 20, 1956.

MACY, Nelson, retired engr. and exec.; b. N.Y.C., Oct. 2, 1869; s. Francis H. and Mary (Nelson) M.; student pvt. schs., Greylock Inst., S. Williamstown, Mass., Stevens Inst. Tech., Hoboken, N.J.; M.E., Cornell U., 1894; m. Katherine J. Burchell, June 6, 1899 (dec.); m. 2d, Edith Brander Mathews, Apr. 30, 1906 (dec.); children—Frances H. (dec.), Nelson, Alice, Macy Buckner. Began as machinist for Southwark Foundry & Macine Works, Phila., 1892; engring. exec. for Rathbone Sard & Co., Aurora, Ill., 1892-93, for Otto Gas Engine Works, Phila., 1894-97, for Deutz Lithographing Co., N.Y.C., 1897; pres. Corlies Macy & Co., N.Y.C., ret. as chmn. bd., 1928; past pres. Navy League of U.S. Engr. U.S. U.S. Cruiser Topeka, Spanish-Am. War, apptd. naval aide to gov. of Conn., 1941. Recipient Santiago and Spanish Campaign medals. Mem. Chi Phi. Episcopalian. Clubs: Players, N.Y. Yacht (N.Y.C.); Field (Greenwich, Conn.). Former editor: Sea Power. Home: Glenville Rd., Greenwich, Conn. Office: 441 Pearl St., N.Y.C. Died Apr. 7, 1957; buried Putnam Cemetery, Greenwich, Conn.

MADDON, John W., ex-congressman; b. Chattooga County, Ga., June 3, 1848; ed. common schs.; entered C.S.A. at 15 and served as pvt. to end of war. Admitted to bar, 1877; practiced at Summerville, Ga., 1877-86; county commr., 1878-80; mem. Ga. Ho. of Reps., 1880-84, Senate, 1884-86; judge Superior Ct., 1886-92; mem. 53d to 58th Congresses, 7th Ga. Dist.; mayor of Rome, Ga., 1906, 07; judge Circuit Ct., 1909-11; judge Superior Ct., 1911-13; became pres. State Mut. Life Ins. Co., 1913. Comdr. Confed. Vets. Assn., 1912. Address: Rome, Ga. Died 1922.

MADDOX, Louis Wilson, army officer; b. Lamar Mo., Apr. 22, 1891; s. John Walter and Judith M.; grad. high sch., 1908; Inf. Sch., 1927; Coast Arty. Sch., 1928; Army Finance Sch., 1934; m. Naomi Barnhouse, July 17, 1922; 1 dau., Jean. Commd. 2d lt. U.S. Army, 1917, advanced through grades to brig. gen., 1945; fiscal dir. Hdqrs. Gen. MacArthur. Decorated campaign and battle stars for World Wars I and II, D.S.M. Mason, Elk. Home: 1558 Hamilton Av., Palo Alto, Cal. Died July 1, 1956; buried Presidio Cemetery, San Francisco.

MADDUX, Parker Simmons, lawyer, banker; b. Dixon, Solano County, Calif., May 29, 1880; s.

Lafayette Jackson and Mary Blythe (Simmons) M.; grad. U. of Calif., 1902; Harvard Law Sch., 1905; LL.D., St. Mary's Coll., 1940; m. Edith Marion Walker, 1905 (died Jan. 1932), children—Jackson, Meredith; m. 2d, Grace Helen Butler, Aug. 1933. Admitted to Calif. bar, 1905; law practice, San Francisco, 1905-10; asst. U.S. atty. for Northern Dist. of Calif., 1910-12; apptd. atty. for Savings Union Bank & Trust Co., San Francisco, 1913, dir. and v.p. 1919; v.p. Mercantile Trust Co. of San Francisco (a consolidation of Savings Union Bank & Trust Co. and Mercantile Nat. Bank of San Francisco), 1920, then elected dir. of Mercantile and of its successor Am. Trust Co., resigned as dir. and v.p. May 1, 1930; exec. vice pres. The San Francisco Bank, 1930-33, pres. 1933-53, chmn. bd., 1953, dir. 1930—; dir., officer of 18 banking, other corps., 1920-30. Mem. bd. govs. Internat. Bank for Reconstruction and Development; mem. Nat. Com. of 13, Nat. Citizens (com. for reorgn. exec. branch of govt., Pacific Coast Adv. Council and San Francisco Adv. Council of Crusade for Freedom. Mem. Regional Loan Com., Reconstrn. Finance Corp., Loaning Agy.; mem. finance com. of the Mayor of San Francisco in connection with the United Nations Conf.; park commr. city and county of San Francisco, 1935-43, fire commr., 1943-44. Nat. dir. Greek War Relief Inc.; treas. Nat. Foundation for Infantile Paralysis of N. Calif.; trustee San Francisco Soc. for Prevention of Cruelty to Animals; trustee De Young Museum, Californians, Inc.; United Seamen's Service, San Francisco Port Area; dir. Golden Gate Internat. Exposition, 1939-40. Pres. Tanforan Charities Foundation; treasurer, Recreation for the Blind, Inc., Clark Moore Johnson Memorial Fund, Variety Club Blind Babies Found. N. Calif.; mem. bd. dirs. San Francisco branch Am. Cancer Soc.; treas. Texas City Disaster Fund; dir. Columbia Park Boys Club. Recipient National Citizenship Award by Veterans of Foreign Wars, 1944. Member Calif. Acad. Scis., Calif. Hist. Soc. (patron mem.), Alpha Tau Omega. Clubs: Pacific Union, Commercial, Press (San Francisco); Bankers (N.Y.C.); St. Francis Yacht. Roman Catholic. Home: 2868 Vallejo St. Office: The San Francisco Bank, 526 California St., San Francisco. Died Oct. 31, 1953; buried Holy Cross Cemetery, San Francisco.

MADISON, Charles C., lawyer; b. Corning, Ia., Oct. 10, 1878; s. William S. and Lavina E. (Doyle) M.; ed. pub. schs., Independence, Mo.; LL.B., Kansas City Sch. Law (U. of Kansas City), 1900; m. Emma L. Locke, Jan. 20, 1909; children—Martha (Mrs. Edgar J. Bumsted), Charles L., Pelide L. Began practice at Kansas City, Mo., 1900; asst. atty. for Mo., C.&A. R.R., 1900-08; city counselor, Independence, 1907-09; mem. Rep. State Com., 1906-12; del. Rep. Nat. Conv. (Mo. mem. rules com.), 1916; chmn. Jackson County Rep. Com., 1918-20; U.S. atty. Western Dist. of Mo., 1921-26; Rep. nominee judge Supreme Ct. of Mo., 1936. Mem. Lawyer's Assn. of Kansas City and Mo. State bar assns. Presbyterian. Home: 1264 W. Gregory. Office: Commerce Bldg., Kansas City, Mo. Died Aug. 31, 1957; buried Woodlawn Cemetery, Independence, Mo.

MADISON, Harold Lester; b. Warwick, R.I., Sept. 23, 1878; s. George Warren and Fannie Louise (Spink) M.; grad. East Greenwich (R.I.) Acad., 1897; Ph.B., Brown U., 1901, A.M., 1902; m. Florence A. Ball, Aug. 20, 1905. Asst. in biology Brown U., 1903-04, instr., 1905; prof. biology Union U., Jackson, Tenn., 1905-08; curator Park Museum, Providence, 1908-21; curator of edn. Cleve. Museum Natural History, 291-39, acting dir., 1928-31, dir., 1931-39; now field exec. R.I. Audubon Soc. Sec., asst. treas. Am. Assn. Museums, also councilor and editor Museum Work, 1918-22. Fellow A.A.A.S.; mem. Ornithologists Union, Am. Soc. Mammalogists. Republican. Conglist. Mason. Author: Key to Rhode Island Wild Flowers, 1915; Trees of Ohio, 1922; Mound Builders, Indian Homes, 1926; Florida Fishes, 1936; Wild Flowers of Ohio, 1938. Home: 1235 Narragansett Blvd., Edgewood, R.I. Deceased.

MAENNER, Theodore Henry, mem. Rep. Nat. Com.; b. St. Paul, Mar. 3, 1891; s. Louis T. and Freda (Frech) M.; B. Arch., Wash. U., St. Louis, 1914; m. Gladys Robertson, Jan. 8, 1919; children—Mary (Mrs. W. Russell Bowie Jr.), Elizabeth (Mrs. Mallory Kountze), John R. Pres., treas. T. H. Maenner Co., Omaha, Neb., 1920—; chmn. Neb. Power Co., 1944-46; pres. T. H. Maenner, Inc., City Nat. Bank Bldg. Co., City Nat. Vaults, Court Realty Co., Maenner-Built, Inc., Maenner Corp.; partner Maenner-Cullingham Co., N.W. Contractors; dir. Panama Canal Co. Counselor Ak-Sar-Ben, 1933-46; pres. YMCA, 1948-51. Dir. Omaha Pub. Power Dist., 1948-50; chmn. 2d Congl. Dist. Neb. Republican Party, 1942-46; treas. Douglas County Central Com., 1934, chmn. Finance Com., 1952-55; mem. Rep. Nat. Com. 1956—. Mem. Omaha Real Estate Bd. (past pres.), Neb. Real Estate Assn. (past pres.), Nat. Assn. Real Estate Bds. (past pres.), Mortgage Bankers Assn. Am., Home Builders Assn. Omaha, Omaha Assn. Bldg. Owners and Mgrs. Home: 5678 Marcy St. Office: City National Bank Bldg., Omaha, Neb. Died Jan. 17, 1958.

MAGER, Charles Augustus (Gus Mager) (mā'gẽr), painter, comic cartoonist; b. Newark, Oct. 21, 1878; s. Charles Augustus and Lina Christianna (Vollmer) M.; ed. pub. schs. Newark; m. Matilda Stunzi, Jan. 30, 1907; 1 son, Robert Augustus. Comic cartoonist N.Y. Jour., N.Y. World, McNaught Syndicate; freelance cartoonist for Popular Sci. Mag., Outdoor Life, United Nature Cartoons, Feature Syndicate. Creator currently running comics, Hawkshaw the Detective, Groucho the Monk and 6 other characters, Game Gimmicks and Un-Natural History. Represented by paintings in Met., Newark and Whitney Museums; painting authority for N.Y. World's Fair. Mem. Artists of N.J., Artists of Today. Address: 334 White Oak Ridge Rd., Short Hills, N.J. Died July 1956.

MAGILL, Frank Stockton (mā-gĭl), ret. sch. adminstr.; b. Lewistown, Ill., July 15, 1875; s. John Fulton and Ellen S. (McCabe) M.; B.A., Parsons Coll., Fairfield, Ia., 1896; M.A. magna cum laude, Washington and Jefferson Coll., 1906, LL.D., 1935; m. Anne Nelson, Oct. 27, 1910; children—M. Margaret, Frances H., T. Nelson, John F., Anne N. Tchr. English, Purdue U., 1904-06; acting dean, Wilural History, 1921-39, acting dir., 1928-31, dir., Penn Hall Sch. for Girls, Chambersburg, Pa., 1910-47, ret.; sec.-treas. Penn Hall Co. Mem. Pa. legislature, 1918-21. Mem. Univ. Assn. Am., Pi Gamma Mu, Phi Kappa Phi. Republican. Presbyn. Address: Chambersburg, Pa. Died Nov. 14, 1952; buried Chambersburg.

MAGILL, George Paull, coll. pres.; b. Lewiston, Ill., Nov. 20, 1867; s. John Fulton and Ellen (McCabe) M.; A.B., Parsons Coll., 1890, A.M., 1895; grad. McCormick Theol. Sem., 1893; D.D., Buena Vista Coll.; m. Olive Ogilvie, Dec. 13, 1895; children—James Fulton, Mrs. Margaret Fread. Ordained to ministry Presbyn. Ch., 1893, pastor Cabery, Ill., 1893-96, Owatonna, Minn., 1896-1903, Oliver Ch., Minneapolis, 1903-08, Central Ch., Des Moines, Ia., 1908-13; pres. Highland Park Coll., Des Moines, 1912-18; pastor Wilmette, Ill., 1918-28. Mem. Phi Kappa Sigma. Republican. Mason. Club: Wilmette Optimist (founding mem.; pres. 1928-29). Address: 1011 Lake Av., Wilmette, Ill. Died Oct. 4, 1954.

MAGILL, Hugh Stewart; b. Auburn, Ill., Dec. 5, 1868; s. Hugh S. and Charlotte (Richmond) M.; A.B., Ill. Wesleyan U., 1894, LL.D., 1913; non-resident grad. work, U. of Chicago; m. Amina Foster, July 24, 1894 (died April 22, 1955); one son, Roswell Foster. Principal of the Auburn (Illinois) High School, 1894-98, Converse Sch., Springfield, Ill., 1898-1900; asst. prin. Springfield High Sch., 1900-04; prin. Princeton (Ill.) Twp. High Sch., 1904-13; supt. schs., Springfield, Ill., 1913-17; dir. gen. Ill. Centennial Celebration, 1917-18; field sec. Nat. Edn. Assn., 1919-22; gen. sec. Internat. Council Religious Edn., 1922-34; pres. Am. Fedn. Investors, Inc., 1934-43; now retired from active business. Mgr. Hall of Religion, Century of Progress Expn., Chicago, 1933-34. Mem. Ill. Senate, 1911-15; author Ill. woman suffrage law, also ednl. and reform laws. Mem. bd. trustees Ill. Wesleyan U., and numerous other bds. Served as sec. Ill. State Art Commn. Russell Colgate citation, Distinguished Service in Christian Edn. in N.A. by Nat. Council of Chs., 1951. Member Ill. Centennial Commn.; pres. Ill. State Teachers Assn., 1914; life mem. N.E.A. Ind. Republican candidate for U.S. senator from Illinois, 1926. Writer and lecturer on public questions. Methodist. Mason (32°, K.T., Shriner). Home: 603 W. Jefferson St., Auburn, Ill. Died Oct. 2, 1958; buried Auburn.

MAGINNIS, Charles Donagh, architect; b. Londonderry, Ireland, 1867; s. Charles and Bridget (McDonagh) M.; Cusack's Acad., Dublin; winner Queen's prize in mathematics, So. Kensingtoon, London, 1883; LL.D., Boston Coll., 1921, Holy Cross Coll., 1925; D.H.L., Tufts Coll., 1931; Dr. Arts, Harvard, 1949. Came to America in 1885; m. Amy Brooks, 1907 (dec.); children—Alice Maria, Charles D., John (dec.), Elizabeth, Paul. Began practice, Boston, 1886; mem. firm of Maginnis & Walsh; especially devoted to ecclesiastical architecture. Member Municipal Art Commission, Boston, 1909-17; member Massachusetts State Art Commission, 1911-20, chairman, 1916-20; trustee Boston Museum of Fine Arts. Appointed pres. Internat. Congress of Architects by U.S. Government. Member visiting con. Architectural School, Harvard, 1935—. Fellow A.I.A. (pres. 1937-40); mem. Boston Soc. Architects, Am. Academy Arts and Sciences; hon. corr. mem. Royal Inst. of British Architects; honorary member Am. Society of Landscape Architects, hon. mem. Archtl. Assn. of Chili; member National Academy of Design, Acad. Arts and Letters, Boston Archtl. Club, Saturday Club, Examiner Club. Master of Arts and Crafts Soc., Bostonian Soc., Am. Fedn. of Arts, Knight of the Order of Malta. Laetare medalist, 1924; firm awarded gold medal for ecclesiastical architecture, A.I.A., 1925; J. Harleston Parker gold medal, 1925; Washington C. of C. bronze medal, 1926; diploma of honor, Budapest, 1930, Gold Medal, Am.-Irish Hist. Soc.; Gold Medal, Erie Soc., Boston; Gold Medal, Am. Inst. Architects, 1948; Benjamin West Clinedinst Gold Medal, 1948. Clubs: St. Botolph, Tavern, Union (all of Boston), Century (N.Y.). Author: Pen Draw'ng, 1898. Writer on architecture and pen illustration, for professional magazines. Lecturer on ecclesiastical art. Home: 219 Dean Rd., Brookline. Office: 126 Newbury St., Boston. Died Feb. 15, 1955; buried Holyhood Cemetery, Chestnut Hill, Mass.

MAGISTAD, Oscar Conrad (măg'ĭs-tăd), soil chemist; b. Forestville, Wis., Sept. 8, 1900; s. Gilbert and Marie (Hovi) M.; B.S., U. of Wis., 1922, M.S., 1923, Ph.D., 1924; m. Lila A. Simon, Aug. 4, 1926. Soil chemist, United Fruit Co., Tela, Honduras, 1924-27; asso. prof. agrl. chemistry and asso. agrl. chemist, U. of Ariz., 1927-30; chemist Pineapple Expt. Station, Honolulu, T.H., 1930-35; dir. Hawaii Agrl. Expt. Station, 1935-38; dir. U.S. Regional Salinity Lab., U.S. Dept. Agr., 1938-40, and 1942-45; asst. chief Bur. Plant Industry, 1940-41; dir. research Libby McNeill & Libby, Hawaii, since 1945. Mem. Am. Chem. Soc., A.A.A.S., Am. Soc. Plant Physiology, Am. Soc. Horticulture, Am. Soc. Agronomists, Am. Soc. Soil Scientists, Geophysiol. Union, Hawaiian Bot. Soc. (pres. 1938), Hawaiian Acad. Science (pres. 1938), Western Soc. Soil Scientists (v.p. 1942-43), Engring. Assn., Alpha Zeta, Phi Lambda Upsilon, Phi Kappa Phi, Sigma Xi. Presbyn. Mason. Club: Representatives. Contbr. to scientific jours. Home: 2721 Puubonua St., Honolulu, Hawaii. Died May 6, 1953; buried Forestville, Wis.

MAGLIN, William Henry, army officer; b. N.Y.C., May 4, 1898; s. Jeremiah Joseph and Margaret (Hock) M.; B.S., U.S. Mil. Acad., 1924; m. Kathryn Swint, May 9, 1950. Served as pvt. and corpl. Troop L, 5th U.S. Cav., 1917-18; commd. 2d lt. Inf., 1924, advanced through grades to maj. gen., 1953; provost marshal Allied Forces N. Africa, 1942-43, organizer, dir. Korean Nat. Police, 1945-47, apptd. provost marshal gen., U.S. Army, 1953; retired 1957. Awarded Legion of Merit with oak leaf cluster, Army Commendation ribbon and campaign medals, Korean Military Order of Taeguk, 1953, Distinguished Service medal, 1957; William Freeman Snow medal for distinguished service to humanity, Am. Social Hygiene Assn., 1956 Refereed amateur and professional boxing, New York City and Honolulu, 1934-37; asso. coach U. Md. Boxing team, 1937-39. Home: Route 1, Box 202-B, Pelican Dr., Melbourne Shores, Melbourne, Fla Died Jan. 11, 1958; buried Arlington Nat. Cemetery.

MAGNIER, Anthony Aloysius, merchandising exec.; b. Jersey City, Apr. 2, 1898; s. Michael J. and Beatrice (Coleman) M.; student Drake Bus. Coll., 1915-17; m. Margaret B. Costello, June 30, 1924; children—Marjorie (Mrs. Daniel P. Nugent), Madeline (Mrs. Edward H. Schollmeyer), John T., James J., Anthony A., Anne Marie. With J. C. Penney Co., 1917—, successively stenographer, tax accountant, asst. sec., 1917-56, sec., 1956-58, ret. Mem. Nat. Retail Dry Goods Assn., Nat. Assn. Assessing Officers, Am. Legion. K.C., Elk. Home: 384 Grove Rd., South Orange, N.J. Died Feb. 6, 1959.

MAGOR, S. F., (mā'gor), engring. and sales exec.; b. Troy, N.Y., Mar. 1, 1888; s. John Fabian and Christina Jane (Darling) M.; stunent Rensselaer Poly. Inst., Troy, N.Y., 1908-12; m. Jewell Bell, Jan. 18, 1922; children—Laura Jean (Mrs. Stanley Doughty). In oil and gas bus., 1913—; with United Fuel Gas Co., subsidiary of Columbia Gas and Electric Co., 1922-29, became v.p.; now v.p. and dir. Superior Oil Co. of Calif., Los Angeles. Address: 15604 Woodfield Pl., Sherman Oaks, Cal. Died Oct. 11. 1957; buried Forest Lawn Meml. Park, Hollywood Hills, Cal.

MAGOUN, Herbert William, author, educator; b Bath, Me., Feb. 17, 1856; s. Thomas P. I. and Maria (Littlefield) M.; A.B., Ia. (now Grinnell) Coll., 1879, A.M., 1882; Ph.D., Johns Hopkins, 1890; m. Martha Roberts Mann, June 8, 1892; children—Marion (Mrs. C. S. Gillett), Frederick Alexander, Harold Ives. Asst. prin., high sch., Oskaloosa, Ia., 1879-80; prin. grammar sch., Bath, Me., 1880-81; tutor Ia. Coll., 1881-84; life ins. business, 1884-85; student Greek at Johns Hopkins U., 1885-87, fellow in Sanskrit, 1887-88, fellow by courtesy, 1888-89, acting physical dir., 1889-90, clerical work, 1891-92; acting prof. Greek, Colo. Coll., 1890-91; acting prof. Greek, then Latin, Oberlin Coll., 1892-95; research work, 1895-98; licensed to preach, Congl. Ch., 1899; prof. Latin and didactics, then Latin and Greek, Redfield Coll., 1898-1904; research work, 1904-22; pres. Mass. Coll. of Osteopathy, 1921-26; lit. work, 1927—; lectr.; asso. editor Bibliotheca Sacra, 1908-32, Bible Champion, 1916-22, Christian Faith and Life, 1938-39. Mem. Am. Oriental Society (life), Am. Philol. Assn. (life), Phi Beta Kappa, Boston Congregational Club. Author: Volts from a Layman's Dynamo (series beginning 1927). Redactor: Mexican Linguistics, and the Asuri-Kalpa, a Sanskrit witchcraft text. Has written over 250 monographs and papers on metrical, philological, Oriental, religious, critical, scientific, psychol., and other subjects including Biblical exegesis, also various editorials, notes, book revs., and (under pen name) parabolic sketches. Home: 89 Hillcrest Rd., Belmont 78, Mass. Died Jan. 8, 1956; buried Mt. Auburn Cemetery, Cambridge, Mass.

MAGOWAN, Sir John Hall, mem. British fgn. service; b. Armagh, Northern Ireland, Oct. 5, 1893; s. William Hall and Sara Ann (Irvine) M.; ed. Royal Sch., Armagh, 1906-11; B.A., Trinity Coll., Dublin, 1915; m. Winifred Isabel Ray, June 22, 1917; children—Ann Isabel (wife of G. S. Young), William Andrew, David John. Entered foreign service Sept. 1919; vice consul in Germany, 1920-28; chargé d'affaires, British Legation in Haiti, 1929-31; comml. sec. British Embassy, Washington, 1931-34, comml. counsellor, Berlin, 1937-39; at Treasury, Whitehall, 1939-40; dep. comptroller gen. Export Credits Guarantee Dept., London, 1940-42; minister, British Embassy, Washington, 1942-48; ambassador to Venezuela since 1948. Served in Royal F.A., 1915-18. Decorated Companion of the Order of St. Michael and St. George; Knight Commander of the Order of the British Empire. Address: British Embassy, Caracas, Venezuela. Died Apr. 5, 1951; buried Mountnorris Co., Armagh, N.I.

MAGRADY, Frederick W. (mȧ-grā'dĭ), lawyer; b. Pottsville, Pa., Nov. 24, 1863; s. William and Isabel (McConaghy) M.; B.E., Bloomsburg State Normal Sch., 1890, M.E., 1892; LL.B., Dickinson Sch. Law, 1909; m. Mary Kiefer. Began practice at Mt. Carmel, Pa., 1909; mem. 69th to 72d Congresses, 17th Pa. Dist.; past pres. Shamokin and Mt. Carmel Transit Co.; pres. Ashland & Shamokin Transit Co.; secy.-treas. Pemberton Coal & Coke Co.; dir., solicitor First Nat. Bank (Mt. Carmel), Mt. Carmel Water Co.; pub. speaker in drives, World War; dir. Four Minute Men. Mem. and legal adviser Selective Service Bd. No. 5, Mt. Carmel, 1942-—, mem. Selective Service Bd., No. 5, Northumberland County, Pa. Mem. Am., Pa., Northumberland County bar assns. Mason (K.T.), Old Fellow (grand master Pa. 1924-25), P.O. Sons of America (state pres. 1921-22). Republican. Home: Mt. Carmel, Pa. Died Aug. 27, 1954.

MAGRATH, William, artist; b. Cork, Ireland, March 20, 1838; came to America, first time, in 1855. N.A., 1876; mem. Soc. Painters in Water Colors, New York. Died 1918.

MAGRUDER, Bruce (mȧ grōō'dẽr), army officer; b. in D.C., Dec. 3, 1882; grad. advance course, Inf. Sch., 1923; grad. Command and Gen. Staff Sch., 1927. Enlisted as pvt. CAC, 1904; commd. 2d lt., Inf., 1907, advanced through grades to maj. gen., 1940; served as lt. col. Inf., 1918-20; comdg. 1st Armored Div., 1940; comdg. officer Inf. Replacement Training Center, Camp Wolters, 1942-45, ret. Decorated D.S.M., Legion of Merit. Address: Orlando, Fla. Died July 23, 1953.

MAGRUDER, Frank Abbott, educator; b. Woodstock, Va., May 6, 1882; s. John Williams and Lucretia (Donaldson) M.; B.A., Washington and Lee U., 1905; Ph.D., in Polit. Sci., Johns Hopkins, 1911; L.H.D., 1945; League of Nations Library, Geneva, Switzerland, summer 1921; m. Louise Southgate Taylor, Sept. 1, 1915 (dec. 1929); children—Mary Elizabeth, Margaret Louise; m. 2d, Clara Taylor Gainor, 1930. Prin. pub. school, in S.C., 1 yr.; later taught in mil. acad., Ky., 2 yrs.; instr. politics Princeton U., 1911-17; prof. polit. science Ore. State Coll., 1917-—; ad-interim head of dept. of polit. science, U. Md., 1935-36. Mem. Am. Polit. Science Assn., Phi Beta Kappa (Johns Hopkins), Phi Kappa Phi. Methodist. Author: Recent Administration in Virginia, 1911; The American Government (text book), 33d edit., 1949; National Governments and International Relations, 15th edition, 1949; Our Nation's Government (in collaboration), 8th edit., 1939, Moral Teachings of the Bible, 1925; The Constitution (in collaboration), 1933; The American National Government Today (in collaboration), 1936; Our Government at Work, 10th edit., 1949. Active in civic and religious boards, chairman mf com. operating all-year camp for 300 youths, Camp Magruder for Youth, dedicated 1947. Home: 2323 Monroe St., Corvallis, Ore. Died Dec. 2, 1949.

MAGRUDER, John, ret. army officer; b. Woodstock, Va., June 3, 1887; s. John Williams and Mary Louise (nee Donaldson) M.; student Massanutten Acad., 1903-05; B.S., Va. Mil. Inst., 1909; distinguished grad. Command and Gen. Staff Sch., 1926; grad. Army War Coll., 1931; m. Helen Schurman, Mar. 4, 1922; children—Barbara, Malcolm, Munro. Commd. 2d lt. inf. U.S. Army, 1910; transferred to field arty., 1911; advanced through grades to brig. gen., 1940. Served in P.I., 1913-15; with AEF in France, 1918-19; asst. mil. attaché, Peking, China, 1020-24, mil. attaché 1926-30; comdt. Va. Mil. Inst., 1932-35; mil. attaché, Bern, Switzerland, 1935-38; chief Intelligence Br., War Dept. Gen. Staff, 1938-41; comd. arty., 1st Div., 1941; chief Mil. Mission to China, 1941-42; dep. dir. OSS, 1943-45, dir. Strategic Services, Unit W.D. 1945-46. Home: 1061 Thomas Jefferson St., Wasington 7. Died Apr. 30, 1958; buried Arlington Nat. Cemetery.

MAGSAYSAY, Ramon (măg-sī-sī), Pres. of Rep. of the Philippines; b. Iba, Zambales, P.I., Aug. 31, 1907; s. Exequiel and Perfecta (del Fierro) M.; student Coll. Liberal Arts, U. Philippines, 1927-31, Coll. Engring., 1927-28, LL.D., 1955; B.S.C., José Rival Coll., 1933; LL.D., Quezon College, 1951, Fordham University, 1952, Nat. University, 1954; E.D. (hon.), Featí Inst. of Technology, 1954; L.H.D. (hon.), Far Eastern U., 1954; D.S.P.H., (hon.), Manila Central U., 1954; married Luz Banzon, June 10, 1933; children—Teresita, Milagros, Ramon. Engaged in automotive work until Dec. 1941, becoming branch mgr., later gen. mgr., Yangco Transportation Company, 1941; worked in motor pool, 31st Inf., 31st Div., U.S. Army, 1941-42; joined in orgn. Western Luzon Guerilla Forces, of which commd. capt., 1942; hdqrs. exec. officer, later comdr., Sawang, San Marcelino, Zambales, 3 yrs.; became comdg. officer Zambales Mil. Dist., Jan. 1945; this force supported 38th Div., U.S.: Army, at Battle of ZigZag Pass and in operations in mountains, 1945; apptd. by U.S. Army, mil. gov. Zambales, and promoted maj., 1945; disch. from service, 1946; rep. Zambales to Congress of the Philippines, 1946-50; chmn. Vets. Mission to Washington, 1948; one-man mission to U.S. to secure mil. aid, 1950; sec. nat. def., Sept. 1950-Mar. 1953 (resigned); pres. Rep. of Philippines since Nov. 1953. Reorganized and retrained army (which absorbed Philippine Constabulary) to fight against Huks (Peoples Liberation Army), 1951; initiated program to subdue Moro outlaws, 1952. Formerly chmn. bd. and gen. mgr. Manila R.R. Recipient Philippine Legion of Honor, Philippine Merit Medal; Bronze Star Medal, Legion of Merit, Presdl. Citation (U.S.); also numerous other awards. Clubs: Manila Polo, Baguio Country, Army and Navy, Casino Español, Manila Yacht, Manila (hon. life), Rotary, Lions. Home: Castillejos, Zambales; also Malacañang, Manila, P.I. Died Mar., 1957.

MAHAN, Bryan Francis, ex-congressman; b. New London, Conn., May 1, 1856; LL.B., Albany Law Sch. (Union U.), 1881. Began practice, New London, 1881; mem. Conn. Ho. of Reps., 1882-83; mayor, New London, 1904-06, 1909-13, again elected, 1913; mem. State Senate, Conn., 1910-11; mem. 63d Congress, 2d Dist. Conn. Democrat. Home: New London, Conn. Died Nov. 16, 1923.

MAHER, Aldea, physician; b. New Orleans, Oct. 7, 1892; dau. Thomas Francis and Joseph Anne (Rupert) Maher; B.A., Newcomb Coll., 1913, Tulane U., 1935; M.A., Tulane, 1914, student in advanced chemistry, 1915; M.D., Tulane U. Sch. Medicine, 1919. Interne Charity Hosp. New Orleans, and Mass. Gen. Hosp. (Boston) dept. biochemistry, 1920; pathol. New Orleans Dispensary for Women, 1919-20; established dept. of metabolism and chem. Hotel Dieu Hosp., 1920, asso. pathol. and biochem., 1920-39, mem. staff, 1920-—, cardiol., 1933-39, acting dir. dept. pathol., Jan.-July 1934, established dept. cardiol., 1934, mem. exec. com., 1939-33, chmn. and mem. committees, 1922-45; established own clinicopathol. lab., 1936; establ. dept. biochem. Charity Hosp., 1924, dept. biochem. Loyola U., 1929, dept. biochem. research, grad. dept. Loyola, 1929; dir. Pan-Am. Lab., 1923-40; pathol. Nix Clinic, 1930-45; supervising dir. lab. Nix Med. Bldg., 1945-—. Instr. dept. clinical med. Tulane U., 1919-20, dept. pathology, 1920-23; teacher high sch. chem. Dominican Convent, 1921-23; teacher chem. Charity Hospital School of Nurses, 1921-23, Hotel Dieu Hosp. Sch. Nursing, 1931-39; prof. biochem. Loyola U., 1929-39, spl. lecturer biochem. Loyola U. Dental Sch., 1939-—; dir. hosp. training and prof. med. technol. Loyola Sch. Med. Technol., 1935-—. Served as sanitary insp., U.S. Pub. Health Emergency Service, 1918; jr. med. officer, U.S. Civil Service Commn., 1936, sr. med. officer, 1940-41. Accredited clin. pathol. and pathologic anatomist by Am. Bd. Pathol., 1937; accredited by Am. Assn. of Life Ins. Med. Dirs. of America, 1944. Recipient Radio Award in Radio History, U.S. Radio Commn., Washington, 1922. Special mention, med. art, La. State Med. Soc., 1928; 2d prize pastel portrait, Chgo., Am. Physicians Art Assn., 1944; medal of award oil portrait, Atlantic City, 1947. Fellow Am. Soc. Clin. Pathol., Coll. Pathol., Coll. Cardiol.; mem. La. Milk Commn., 1920-—; mem. com. New Orleans Grad. Assembly, 1941-49 (chmn. pathol. committee 1941); member Louisiana division Am. Cancer Society (chmn. 1936-39, exec. com. 1937-38, bd. dirs. 1948-57); mem. Am. Med. Assn., Orleans Parish Med. Soc., La. Med. Soc., So. Med. Soc., Am. Soc. Clin. Pathol., La. Pathol. Soc., La. Heart Assn., Catholic Physicians Guild, Am. Physicians Art Assn., Pan-Am. Alliance, Nat. Women's Med. Assn., La. br. Women's Med. Assn., New Orleans Symphony and Symphony Guild, Little Theatre, Art Assn., Opera Assn., Opera Guild, Philharmonic Soc., Pop Concert (all at New Orleans); mem. Mid-Winter Sports Assn., New Orleans Soc. Stars and Bars (hon.), Am. Acad. Sciences, Beta Epsilon Upsilon (hon.), Alpha Omega Alpha, Alpha Epsilon Iota (founder and 1st pres. Tulane U. 1919-21). Roman Catholic. Clubs: Orleans, Quota. Author: numerous articles in tech. med. jours. Home: 5665 West End Blvd., New Orleans 24. Office: 1110 American Bank Bldg., New Orleans 12. Died Nov. 20, 1959.

MAHIN, Edward Garfield (mā'hĭn), ret. prof.; b. Lafayette, Ind., Aug. 16, 1876; s. Charles Wesley and Mary (Ogden) M.; B.S., Purdue Univ., 1901, M.S., 1903, Doctor of Science honoris causa, 1950; Ph.D., Johns Hopkins University, 1908; m. Margaret Parsons, June 10, 1903; children—Marjorie Felicia (Mrs. W. J. Berwanger), William Edward, Mary Elizabeth (Mrs. J. J. Dunnigan), Carol Dorothea (Mrs. J. L. Ockert). With Purdue U., as asst., instr., asso. prof., prof. of analytical chemistry, 1901-25; with U. of Notre Dame, 1925-49, professor metallurgy, 1925-32, prof. and head dept. of metallurgy, 1932-49; metallurgist, U.S. Naval Engring. Expt. Sta., summers, 1917, 18. Mem. Am. Soc. for Metals (chmn. Com. on Constitution and By-laws, 1938-39; member publs. com. 1941-43, chmn. 1943-44), American Institute Mining and Metall. Engrs., American Foundrymen's Assn., Am. Soc. of Engineering Edn., Ind. Acad. Science (fellow, pres. 1928-29), Iron and Steel Inst. (Brit.), Inst. of Metals (Brit.), Tau Beta Pi, Phi Lambda Upsilon, Sigma Xi, Phi Beta Kappa. Republican. Methodist. Author: Quantitative Analysis, 1914, 4th edit., 1932; Quantitative Agricultural Analysis (with R. H. Carr), 1923; Introduction to Quantitative Analysis, 1929; Elementary Physical Metallurgy, 1948. Contributor to various technical jours. Research in hardness, carburization and inclusions in steel. Home: 206 Wakewa Av., South Bend 17, Ind. Died Feb. 2, 1952; buried St. Joseph Valley Meml. Park, South Bend, Ind.

MAHON, Russell C., chmn. bd. R. C. Mahon Co. Home: 415 Burns Dr., Detroit 14. Office: 6565 E. Eight Mile Rd., P.O. Box 4666, Detroit 34. Died Mar. 24, 1956.

MAHONEY, George William (mȧ hō'nē), oculist; born Lawton, Mich., Dec. 31, 1860; s. Michael and Honoria Marie (Davis) M.; student U. Mich., 1885-87; M.D., Bellevue Hosp. Med. Coll.-N.Y.U., 1888; m. Julia Garvy, Oct. 21, 1908; children—Mrs. Miriam M. McDevitt, George J. Began practice at Decatur, Mich., 1888; moved to Chgo., 1893; prof. ophthalmology and dir. Loyola U. Sch. Medicine; cons. oculist St. Vincent Infant Asylum, House of the Good Shepherd; oculist Mercy, Henrotin, U.S. Marine and St. Mary of Nazareth hosps. Commd. by Gov. Altgeld, 1896, capt. and asst. surgeon 7th Regt., Ill. N.G., 1896-1904, resigned; mustered into vol. service of U.S. in spring of 1898; served through Spanish-Am. War; held rank of capt. and asst. surgeon; detached from 7th Regt. during summer of 1898 and placed in charge of hosps. corps of 2d Army Corps. Fellow A.C.S.; mem. A.M.A., Ill., Chgo. med. socs., Chgo. Ophthal. Soc., Am. Bd. of Ophthalmology. Democrat. Catholic. Home: 605 Central Av., Wilmette, Ill. Office: 30 N. Michigan Blvd., Chgo. Deceased.

MAHONEY, John Friend (mȧ-hō'nē), retired US PHS officer; born Fond du Lac, Wisconsin, Aug. 1, 1889; s. David and Mary Ann (Hogan) M.; M.D., Marquette U., 1914; m. Leah Ruth Arnold, Sept. 29, 1926; children—Janet Ann, John Friend. Interne Milwaukee County and Chicago Lying-In Hosps., 1914-16; commd. officer in U.S.P.H.S., Sept. 1917; dir. Venereal Disease Research Lab., U.S. Marine Hosp., Staten Island, July 1929-Dec. 1949; commissioner of health of City of N.Y., 1950-53; gen. dir. Bur. Labs., N.Y.C. Dept. Health, 1954-—. Fellow A.M.A., Am. Pub. Health Assn.; mem. N.Y. Acad. of Medicine, N.Y. Acad. of Sci. Club: Richmond County Country (Staten Island, N.Y.). Winner of the A.P.H.A. Lasker Award, 1946. Home: 32 Valley St., S.I. 5, N.Y. Office: Dept. of Health, 125 Worth St., N.Y.C. Died Feb. 23, 1957; buried Arlington Nat. Cemetery.

MAHONY, Walter Butler (mā'ō-nē), corp. official; b. Columbus, O., Dec. 16, 1877; s. Walter Augustus and Ella Janette (Morgan) M.; g.-s. of Carey Allen, and lineal desc. of Wm. White of Mayflower; B.A., cum laude, Amherst, 1898; LL.B., New York U., 1903; m. Mary Murray Butler, Feb. 17, 1909; children—Janet Morgan (Mrs. Robert W. Wilson), Mary Murray (Mrs. Leland S. Brown), Walter Butler, Jr.; married 2d Mrs. Edith Bell Phyfe, May 17, 1951. Admitted to N.Y. bar 1903, and began practice at N.Y. City; formerly with Emerson McMillin & Co., pub. utilities, later dir. and counsel U.S. Rubber Plantations, Inc., and affiliated cos.; editor and pub. North Am. Review Oct. 1926-Mar. 1935; dir. First Nat. Bank (Ossining), U.S. Rubber Co.; formerly dir. and mem. exec. com. Goodyear Tire and Rubber Co., Seiberling Rubber Co. Pres. bd. mgrs. N.Y. Inst. for Edn. of the Blind. Trustee First Presbyn. Ch. of N.Y., Roosevelt Hosp. Mem. Am. Geog. Soc., Am.-Irish Hist. Soc., Acad. of Polit. Science, English Speaking Union, Delta Kappa Epsilon (ex-mem. exec. council), Phi Delta Phi. Republican. Congregationalist. Clubs: Century, University, Amherst, Delta Kappa Epsilon (ex-gov.), Phi Delta Phi, Sleepy Hollow Country (ex-gov.), New York Yacht, The Pilgrims, Society of Mayflower Descendants, "Ends of the Earth." Traveled around the world, 1907, 16, 20. Writer on finance and topics connected with rubber industry. Home: 510 Park Av., N.Y.C. 22. Died Jan. 9, 1954.

MAHURAN, Stuart Ansala (mȧ-hū'răn), editor; b. Colwich, Kan., July 15, 1892; s. John Andrew and Cora (Martin) M.; B.A., Upper Ia. U., 1931, Litt.D., 1938; M.A., State U. of Ia., 1932; Ph.D. in Journalism, State U. of Missouri, 1940; m. Marie Gerstenberger, June 25, 1917; children—Betty Vivian (dec.),

Kathleen Marie, Madeline Louise, Elaine Agnes. Supt. schs. Hazleton, Ia., 1914-16; news editor Creston Advertiser, 1917-18; city editor Mason City Globe, 1922-23; editorial writer Dubuque Telegraph-Herald, 1925-27, Evansville (Ind.) Jour., 1927-30; city editor Clinton (Ia.) Herald, 1930-32; editor Dubuque Telegraph-Herald, 1932-35; prof. of journalism since 1935, and acting dir. 1936-38, dir. since 1938, Sch. of Journalism, Creighton U., Omaha; prof. of journalism Pa. State College since 1941. Served as instructor Arty. Officers T.C., Ft. Zachary Taylor, Ky.; hon. disch. Dec. 3, 1918; 1st sergt. Ia. Nat. Guard, Mason City, 1920. Editor: The Nebraska Style Book, 1936-39; Pennsylvania School Press Exchange. Editor: The National Echo. Home: 545 West Ridge Av., State College, Pa. Died Feb. 9, 1953; buried Centre County Meml. Park, State College, Pa.

MAIER, Guy, pianist; b. Buffalo, N.Y.; s. John Maier and Eva (Fetzer) M.; grad. N.E. Conservatory of Music, Boston, Mass., 1913; studied in Berlin, Germany, 1913-14; hon. Dr. of Music, Chicago, 1940; m. Lois Auten Warner, June 1, 1921; children—Robert Auten, Theodore Charles. Début as concert pianist, Boston, 1914; has appeared throughout U.S., Europe and Australia; originator of concerts for young people; prof. of piano, U. of Mich. Sch. of Music, 1924-31; mem. faculty Juilliard Sch. of Music, N.Y. City, 1935-42, asst. nat. dir. Federal Music Project, 1935-38. Editor Teacher's Round Table and Technic Pages, Etude Magazine, 1935-46, Pianists Page since 1946; lecturer on music, Univ. of Calif. (Los Angeles) since 1946; consultant on music, Stephens Coll., Columbia, Mo., since 1946; summer music courses for teachers, Virginia Intermont Coll., Bristol, Va., Sherwood Music Sch., Chicago, MacPhail Coll. of Music, Minneapolis. Served with Y.M.C.A. in France, 1917-19, World War I. Member U.S. Coast Guard Reserve, 1944-45. Author of textbooks on piano playing: Pastels, Etudes for Every Pianist, Chopin, 25 Preludes with Study Analyses, Thinking Fingers, Children's Technic Book. Composer, arranger and editor. Contbr. to musical mags.; writer on topics in field of mus. edn. Home: 1048 14th St., Santa Monica, Cal. Died Sept. 24, 1956; buried Buffalo.

MAILLIARD, John Ward, Jr. (my-ärd), mfr. agt.; b. San Francisco, Mar. 25, 1891; s. John Ward and Lizzie (Page) M.; student Taft Sch., Watertown, Conn.; Yale U.; m. Kate Peterson, Sept. 20, 1913; children—John W., III, William, James. With Mailliard & Schmiedell, mfrs. agts., importers, San Francisco, since 1910, pres. since 1932, dir. since 1923; dir. S.O.S. Co., Fireman's Fund Ins. Co., Calif. Pacific Title Ins. Co., Western Pacific R.R. Co., Assn. Director Institute for Philosophical Research. Clubs: Bohemian, Pacific Union, San Francisco Commercial (San Francisco). Home: 3375 Jackson St., San Francisco 18. Office: 601 Montgomery St., San Francisco 11. Died July 11, 1954.

MAINWARING, William Bernard, newspaper pub.; b. Gotham, Wis., Feb. 21, 1897; s. William and Rose (Bailey) M.; B.S., Ore. State Coll., 1920; Litt.D., Coll. Ida., 1953; m. Jennie Lewis, Jan 29, 1934; children—William Lewis, Ruth Helen. Pub. Hermiston (Ore.) Herald and Milton (Ore.) Eagle, 1921-23; with Tillamook (Ore.) Herald, McMinnville (Ore.) News-Reporter and Albany (Ore.) Herald, 1923-25; co-pub. Baker (Ore.) Democrat-Herald, 1925-53; pub. Ida. Free Press, Nampa, Ida., 1937-53, Salem (Ore.) Capital Jour., 1953—; dir. Fed Home Savings & Loan Assn. Mem. Oregon State Board of Higher Education. Trustee College Ida. Pres. United Fund, Indsl. Development Council. Served with Inf., U.S. Army, World War I. Mem. C. of C. (dir.), Pi Kappa Alpha, Sigma Delta Chi. Presbyn. Mason (Shriner, K.T.), Kiwanian (past pres.). Home: 2660 Doughton St. Office: 280 N. Church St., Salem, Ore. Died Jan. 19, 1957; buried City View Cemetery, Salem.

MAIRS, Samuel, chairman board Archer Daniels Midland Co.; b. Hastings, Minn., Aug. 26, 1879; s. Samuel and Abbie (Gardner) M.; student Univ. of Minn.; m. Mary Goodell, June 6, 1912 (dec.); children—George, Robert, Thomas, Mary Anne; m. 2d, Mrs. Graves. Chmn. bd. Archer-Daniels Midland Co. since Nov. 1947. Home: 5 Heather Pl., St. Paul. Office: 600 Roanoke Bldg., Mpls. Deceased.

MALAKIS, Emile, univ. prof.; born Bagdad (of Greek parents), Sept. 14, 1897; s. Dionysius and Victoria (Paduan) M.; came to U.S., 1913, naturalized, 1920; A.B., U. of Pa., 1917, Ph.D., 1925; student U. of Paris, 1920-22, Jusserand travelling fellow, 1920-21, U. of Pa. travelling fellow, 1930-32; m. Marian Porter Moore, June 4, 1924. Instr. Romance langs. U. of Pa., 1918-24, asst. prof., 1924-36; asso. prof. French lit. Johns Hopkins, 1936-48, prof. French lit. and chmn. dept. Romance languages 1948—. Officier d'Academie, France, 1935; Chevalier Legion d'Honneur, 1950. Member Modern Language Association of America, American Assn. Univ. Profs., Am. Assn. Teachers of French, Modern Humanities Research Assn., Foreign Policy Assn., Societe Chateaubriand (Paris), Institut Francaise de Washington, Phi Beta Kappa. Democrat. Orthodox Ch. Author: Le Francais du Commerce, 1923; French Travellers in Greece, 1925; Intermediate French Grammar, 1928; co-author: Toc, Toc, Toc, Douze Petites Pieces de theatre, 1929; French by Reading, 1932; Petite Histoire de la Civilisation Francaise, 1935. Critical editor; Chateaubriand, Itinéraire da Paris a Jérusalem, 2 vol., 1946. Adv. editor Modern Lang. Notes since 1936. Contbr. articles to scholarly jours. Home: 1123 N. Eutaw S ., Balt. 1. Died June 20, 1954.

MALAN, Daniel Francois, ex-prime minister Union S. Africa; b. Riebeek West, Union S. Africa, May 22, 1874; s. David Francois M.; M.A., Victoria Coll. and Theol. Sem., Stellenborch, Union S. Africa; D.D., Utrecht U., Holland; m. Martha Sandberg, June 16, 1926; m. 2d, Maria Ann. Ordained to ministry of Dutch Reformed Ch.; minister Dutch Reformed Ch., 1905-15; editor daily newspaper, Die Burger, Cape Town, Union S. Africa, 1915-24; mem. Parliament, Calvinia, Union S. Africa, 1919; minister Interior, Edn. and Pub. Health, 1924-33; chancellor U. Stellenborch; prime minister Union S. Africa, 1948-54. Mem. Nationalist Party. Home: Capetown, Union S. Africa. Died Feb. 7, 1959.

MALCOLM, D(ougal) O(rme), mining corp. exec.; b. Poltalloch, Kilmartin, Argyll, Aug. 6, 1877; s. William Rolle and Georgina (Wellesley) M.; student Eton Coll., 1890-95; M.A., Oxford (fellow All Souls Coll., 1899), 1899; m. Claire Stopford, 1910 (died 1920); m. 2d Lady Evelyn Farquhar, 1923. Mem. British Civil Service, 1900-12; mem. exec. com. dirs. British South Africa Co. since 1913, pres. bd. since 1937; chmn. Rhodesia Rys. Trust, Limited, 1939—; member board of directors of New Consolidated Gold Fields, Limited, Standard Bank of S. Africa, Ltd., DeBeers Consol. Mines, Ltd. K.C.M.G. Clubs: Brooks, Beefsteak. Author: Nuces Relictae, The British South Africa Co., 1889-1939, also articles in various mags. Home: 53 Bedford Gardens, London W. 8. Office: 11 Old Jewry, London, E. C. 2, Eng. Died Aug. 30, 1955.

MALLERY, Earl Dean (măl'ēr-ĭ), municipal adminstrn.; b. Alliance, Neb., Oct. 7, 1889; s. John Amos and Idella Belle (Round) M.; student Neb. Jr. Normal Coll., 1906-07, U. of Neb., 1907-09; m. Kathryn Underhill Willis, June 24, 1913 (died 1942); children—Ruth Elizabeth (Mrs. Frank M. Headley), Bruce Willis; married 2d, Priscilla Thomas, July 20, 1946. Began as clerk in mercantile business, 1910; mem. State Child Welfare Commn., 1913-14; city mgr., Alliance, Neb., 1932-36; mgr. Washington Office, Am. Municipal Assn., 1936-39; mem. local planning com. Nat. Resources Bd., 1938-39; mem. airport advisory com. Civil Aeronautics Authority, 1938; mem. Neb. State Planning Bd., 1934-35; mem. U.S. Civilian Defense Board, 1942; consultant N.S. R.B., 1950; civil defense officer, Federal Civil Defense Administration. Member Nebraska House of Reps., 1913-15, Neb. State Senate, 1915-17; del. Rep. Nat. Convs., 1916, 20; mayor Alliance, Neb., 1929-32. Mem. com. on highway organ. and administrn., Highway Research Bd. pub. works adv. com., Fed. Works Agency, bd. dirs. Pub. Administrn. Service. Member American Municipal Association, American Committee for International Union of Local Authorities, International City Mgrs. Assn., Am. Soc. for Pub. Adminstern., Alpha Tau Omega. Club: Nat. Press (Washington). Editor of Washington News Letter and State League Notes, American Municipal News. Author of reports, articles and pamphlets on municipal adminstrn. Home: Dorchester House. Office: Federal Civil Defense Administration, Cafritz Bldg., Washington. Died July 27, 1952.

MALLERY, Otto Tod (măl'ēr-ĭ); b. Willets Point, N.Y., April 27, 1881; s. Major John Conrad (grad. U.S. Mil. Acad., 1867) and Anna Louise (Winslow) M.; A.B., Princeton, 1902; post-grad. work, U. of Pa. and Columbia; m. Rosamond Robinson Junkin, Nov. 2, 1910 (died 1915); children—Dr. Otto Tod, Rosemary (Mrs. H. H. Gregg); married 2d, Louise Marshall, 1918; children—Bayard, David. Field secretary Recreation Association of Philadelphia, 1908, treas., 1910, pres., 1926-48; pres. Public Education Assn. of Phila., 1911-14; sec. Bd. of Recreation, Phila., 1912-15, pres. 1915-16; mem. Pa. State Indsl. Bd., 1915-23; nat. exec. com., dir. War Camp Community Service, 1918; staff War Labor Policies Bd., 1918; staff of Arthur Woods, asst. to sec. of war, as chief of Federal Aid and Works Sect., War Dept., 1919; exec. sec. Pa. Emergency Pub. Works Commn., 1917-23. Member President's Conference on Unemployment (member econ. advisory com. and executive secretary public works Committee, 1921; American observer at Canadian govt. Unemployment Conference, Ottawa, 1922; spl. investigator of industrial relations for U.S. Coal Commn., 1923; mem. Nat. Com. on Seasonal Operations in the Construction Industries, 1923; sr. business specialist U.S. Dept. Commerce, 1930; co-sponsor of Fed. Employment Stabilization, Oct. 1931; mem. state advisory com. of Nat. Youth Administrn., 1936-40; mem. Pa. State Planning Bd., 1936-38; mem. Phila. City Charter Commn., 1937; consultant Nat. Resources Planning Bd., 1939-43; econ. advisor to U.S. delegation to Internat. Labor Office and reporter of Public Works Com., Geneva, 1937; econ. advisor to employers delegation to Conf. of Am. States Members of Internat. Labor Office, Havana, 1939; del.-at-large on U.S. National Commn. of UNESCO, 1956-59. Trustee Am. Acad. Polit., Social Sci.; pres. bd. of trustees, Carson Coll. for Orphan Girls; chairman board of dirs. Nat. Recreation Assn.; chmn. Interdependence Council. Clubs: Franklin Inn (Phila.); Cosmos (Washington). Author: Economic Union and Durable Peace, 1943, More than Conquerors, 1947; (with others) Declaration of Interdependence, proclaimed in Independence Hall, Phila., 1956. Contbr. articles in field to various publs. Address: 9006 Crefeld St., Phila. 18. Died Dec. 16, 1956.

MALLON, Paul (Raymond) măl'lŭn), writer; b. Matton, Ill., Jan. 5, 1901; s. John Bernard and Mary (MacDonough) M.; student U. Louisville, 1918-19, U. Notre Dame, 1919-20; Litt.D., Marquette U.; LL.D., College of Holy Cross, U. Notre Dame, 1946; m. Viola Jane Wingreene, June 29, 1929. Began as reporter Louisville Courier-Jour., 1918, later with Herald-Post, Louisville, and South Bend (Ind.) News-Times; with United Press, 1920-32, in New York, and as political writer, Washington, 1923-32; originated Washington Column, News Behind the News, then published in about 300 newspapers, 1930-47. Published 2 secret Senate roll calls, 1929, resulting in abolition of secret Senate sessions for consideration of nominations to federal office. Roman Catholic. Club: Belle Haven Country. Books: Practical Idealism, 1944; The Ease Era, 1945. Home: Belle Haven, Alexandria, Va. Died July 30, 1950.

MALLON, Winifred, writer; b. North Evans, Erie County, New York, November 30, 1879; d. Robert Patrick and Carrie L. (Morsman) Mallon; ed. public grade and high schools, Washington, D.C.; unmarried. Writer for newspapers and mags. since 1902; with Chicago Tribune on part-time basis, Washington bureau, 1905-17, asst. Washington corr., 1917-25; with N.Y. Times on special assignments, 1925-29, mem. Washington staff, 1929-49. Member American Press Society (board of governors 1937), Theta Sigma Phi. Club: Womens National Press (pres. 1935-36). Contbr. fiction and articles to Red Book, Liberty, and other mags. Home: 2311 Connecticut Av., Washington. Died Apr. 4, 1954; buried Congressional Cemetery, Washington.

MALLORY, C(assius) C(hester), ret. S.S. exec.; b. Heppher, Ore., Oct. 18, 1890; s. William Luther and Mary (Yerkes) M.; student pub. schs. of Heppher, Ione and Portland, Ore.; m. Lenore Amanda Bredull, Mar. 4, 1921; children—William P., Susan C. (Mrs. Robert Cremin). Clk. Bank of Ione, 1906-08; bookkeeper, timekeeper Smith & Jones Contractors, 1908-09; bookkeeper Pacific Tel. & Tel. Co., 1909-10; chief clk. Spokane, Portland and Seattle Ry., 1910-19; asst. comptroller U.S. Shipping Bd., 1919-21; asst. auditor Pacific Mail S.S. Co., 1921-25; asst. gen. mgr., treas.-gen. mgr., v.p. Panama Inc., 1934-52, president, dir., 1953-55, chmn. bd., 1955-57, ret.; was pres., dir. various subsidiaries. Mail S.S. Co., 1925-34; v.p., treas., dir. Grace Line, Mem. Am. S.S. Owners Protective Assn. (dir.). Clubs: Propellor (dir.) (N.Y.C.); India House, Larchmont Shore, Skytop. Home: Lake Wales, Fla. Died Jan. 2, 1959.

MALLORY, Tracy Burr, pathologist; b. Boston, 1896; s. Frank Burr and Persis (Tracy) M.; M.D., Harvard, 1921; m. Edith Brandt, June 6, 1925; children—Kenneth Brandt, Jean Roberts (Mrs. William J. Childs). Moseley Travelling fellow Harvard, 1925-26, instr. bacteriology med. sch., 1923-26, instr. pathology, 1926-35, asso., 1935-37, asst. prof., 1937-48, prof. pathology since 1948; chief lab. pathology and bacteriology, Mass. Gen. Hosp., Boston since 1926; cons. pathology Regional Area I, Vets. Adminstrn. Served with Med. Corps., U.S. Army, as maj. to lt. col. 1943-45. Decorated Legion of Merit. Mem. Am. Assn. Pathologists and Bacteriologists (pres., 1950-51), Coll. Am. Pathologists (sec.-treas., 1948-51), A.M.A., Am. Soc. Exptl. Pathologists, Am. Cancer Soc. Author articles sci. jours. Asst. editor of Am. Jour. Pathology, 1941-43, mem. editorial bd. since 1943; editor case histories of Mass. Gen. Hosp. New Eng. Jour. Pathology since 1926. Contbr. to Medical History of U.S. Army in World War II. Home: 178 South St., Needham 92. Office: Mass. General Hospital, Boston. Died Nov. 11, 1951.

MALONE, Dudley Field, lawyer; b. New York, June 3, 1882; s. William C. and Rose (McKenny) M.; A.B., St. Francis Xavier, 1903; LL.B., Fordham U., 1905; m. 2d, Doris Stevens (writer, economist and mem. exec. com. Nat. Woman's Party), Dec. 1921; m. 3d, Edna Louise Johnson, Jan. 29, 1930. Began practice in New York, 1905; apptd. city atty., 1909; 3d asst. sec. of state, Apr. 21-Nov. 1913; collector Port of New York, Nov. 24, 1913-Sept. 7, 1917; resigned as public protest against failure of President Wilson and his administration to urge and pass the Woman Suffrage Amendmant. Jr. lit. U.S. Navy and served in overseas transportation service, 6 months, 1918. Liberal in politics and thinking; long advocated recognition of Russian Soviet Republic. Asso. with Clarence Darrow for the defense in evolution trial in Tenn. which was prosecuted by William Jennings Bryan. In co-operation with Capt.

William H. Staton, founder of Assn. Against the Prohibition Amendment, made first nat. speaking coast to coast tour for the repeal of prohibition. Died Nov. 5, 1950.*

MALONEY, John Philip, prof. law; b. Northampton, Mass., June 7, 1881; s. Jeremiah and Margaret (Gleason) M.; B.S., Amherst Coll., 1903; LL.B., N.Y.U., 1911; LL.D., St. John's U., 1931; m. Edna G. Goll, Aug. 1, 1917; children—John Philip, Gerald T. Prin. Mystic (Conn.) High Sch. 1903-05; instr. Staunton (Va.) Mil. Acad., 1905-07; admitted to N.Y. bar, 1912, practiced in N.Y.C., 1912-25; prof. law St. John's U. Sch. of Law, 1925—, vice dean 1927—. Arbitrator, Am. Arbitration Assn.; mem. Bd. Legal Examiners, U.S. Civil Service Commn. Mem. Am. Bar Assn., Acad. Polit. Science, N.Y. State Hist. Soc., Am. Acad. Polit. and Social Science, Phi Gamma Delta, Phi Delta Phi. Roman Catholic. Author: Cases on Real Property, 1927; Cases and Materials on Mortgages, 1928, rev. edit., 1940; (with Chaffee and Simpson) Cases and Materials on Equity, 1939, Cases on Equity, 2d edit. 1946, 3d edit. 1950; (with McNiece), Materials on Security Transactions, 1947; (with others) American Law of Real Property, 1951. Home: 319 Hillside Av., Leonia, N.J. Died Oct. 23, 1950; buried St. Mary's Cemetery, Northampton, Mass.

MALONEY, William J(oseph) M. A., neurologist; b. Edinburgh, Scotland, Oct. 16, 1882; s. Bernard Joseph and Isabella (McNees) M.; M.B. and Ch.B., U. of Edinburgh, 1905, M.D., 1907; LL.D., Fordham U., 1923; studied univs. of Paris, Munich and London until 1909; m. Margaret, d. late Charles F. McKim, architect, May 3, 1913 (dec.). Holder of Ettles, Holdsworth and other scholarships, at Edinburgh U.; came to U.S., 1911; formerly prof. nervous and mental diseases Fordham U., and adj. prof. nervous and mental diseases Post-Grad. Hosp. and Med. Sch., New York; now cons. neurologist, City Hosp., New York. Served in British Army, Aug. 1914-16; mentioned in dispatches, Apr. 25 and June 4, 1915; discharged with rank of capt., 1916, "permanently incapacitated as result of wounds." Awarded mil. cross, Mons Star, and other medals. Fellow Royal Soc. of Edinburgh. Roman Catholic. Author: Hydrotherapy and Balneology (sect. in System of Therapeutics, edited by Billings), 1913; Meningitis (sect. in Modern Treatment of Nervous Diseases, edited by White and Jelliffe), 1914; Locomotor Ataxia, 1918; The Forged Casement Diaries, 1936. Translator: The Nursling, 1907; Poliomyelitis (by Wickman), 1914. Address: 38 East 73d St., N.Y.C. Died Sept. 3, 1952; buried Rosedale Cemetery, Orange, N.J.

MALOTT, Clyde A(rnett) (má'lŏt'), geologist; b. Atlanta, Ind., Sept. 10, 1887; s. John Franklin and Alice (Fippen) M.; A.B., Ind. U., 1913, A.M., 1915, Ph.D., 1919; m. Mary Orda Clayton, July 30, 1911; children—Alice, Roland Floyd. Tchr. pub. schs., Ind., 1909-15; instrnl. staff, dept. geology, Ind. U., 1916-24, prof. geology 1924-47, acting head dept. geol. and geography, 1941-45; engaged in geol. research in Ind., 1947—; mem. staff Okla. Geol. Survey, summer 1916, Ind., 1919-21; geologist Empire Gas & Fuel Co., summers 1918, 23; geologist Pure Oil Co., 1924; acting prof. geology Williams Coll., 1st semester 1929-30; mem. staff, Ill. Geol., summer 1930; cons. Sun Oil Co., 1938-40. Mem. A.A.A.S., Geol. Soc. Am., Ind. Acad. Sci. (v.p. 1937, pres. 1944), Nat. Speleological Soc., Phi Beta Kappa, Sigma Xi. Recipient of award for distinguished publ. paper, Proc. Ind. Acad. Sci., 1948. Author: Physiography of Indiana, 1922; author of 40 or more publ. sci. papers and many pvt. reports chiefly on Indiana geology, etc.; studies in Indiana Caverns a specialty. Republican. Baptist. Home: 708 S. Woodlawn Av. Office: Indiana University, Bloomington, Ind. Died Aug. 26, 1950.

MALTBY, Ralph B., paper exec. Vice pres., dir. St. Regis Paper Co., N.Y.C., St. Regis Paper Co. (Can.), Ltd., Eastern States Corp., Taggart Corp.; exec. v.p., dir. St. Regis Sales Corp.; pres., dir. Bates Valve Bag Corp. of Brazil, Cia. Argentine de Productos de Papel; dir. Norwood & St. Lawrence R.R., Conn. Valley Logging & Driving Co., St. Regis Timber Co., Ltd. Home: 31 Masterton Rd., Bronxville, N.Y. Died Oct. 1952.

MANCE, Grover Cleveland (măns), geologist; b. Pine Bush, N.Y., Feb. 5, 1883; s. Eli Dewitt and Mabel Edith (Barroclough) M.; B.S., Colgate U., 1906; A.M., 1913, Ph.D., Ind. U., 1915; m. Martha Blanche Nelson, Sept. 1, 1906; children—Donald Roscoe, Caryl Hope. Prof. chemistry Rochester (Ind.) Coll., 1906-08; high sch. tchr., 1908-12; teaching fellow Ind. U., 1913-15; geol. investigator, Ind., 1913-16; prin. high sch., Maysville, Ky., 1916-17; prof. geology St. Lawrence U., Canton, N.Y., 1917-22; prof. geography Syracuse U. Summer Sch., 1921; prof. geography and geology Winthrop Coll. (S.C. Coll. for Women), Rock Hill, S.C., 1922-33; cons. geologist and mineralogist, Rock Hill, S.C., 1933-41; dean sch. science Oglethorpe U., 1942; dean of Oglethorpe U., 1943-44; prof. chemistry N.W. Jr. Coll., Orange City, Ia., 1943-45, also Union Coll., Barbourville, Ky., 1946-48, Lander Coll., Greenwood, S.C., 1951-53. Fellow A.A.A.S., S.C. Acad. Sci. (founder, 1st pres.; sec. 1925-34); mem. Sigma Xi, Beta Theta Pi. Presbyn. Mason (K.T.). Writer and lecturer on geol. and ednl. subjects. Address: 302 Aiken Av., Rock Hill, S.C. Died May 24, 1955; buried Woodlawn Cemetery, Hamilton, N.Y.

MANCHESTER, Earl Northup, librarian; b. Factoryville, Pa., July 12, 1881; s. Walter N. and Louisa A. (Northup) M.; A.B., Brown U., 1902; student N.Y. State Library Sch., 1902-03; post-grad. work, Brown U., 1903-04; m. Alice A. Wood, Jan. 14, 1914; 1 son, John Wood. Second asst. librarian, Borwn U., 1903-05; reference librarian, same, 1905-11; head of reader's dept. U. of Chicago Library, 1911-21; dir. libraries, U. of Kan., 1921-28; dir. of libraries, Ohio State U., 1948-52, dir. libraries and prof. library adminstrn. emeritus, 1952; dir. S. Cornelia Young Library Daytona Beach, Fla., 1953-54. Entered war service with A.L.A., Jan. 1918; camp librarian, Camp Cody (N.M.), Camp Grant (Rockford, Ill.); port representative Base Sect. 2, Bordeaux, Fr., Jan.-Sept. 1919. Mem. A.L.A. (council), Kan. Library Assn. (pres. 1925), Ohio Library Assn. (pres. 1933-34), Phi Beta Kappa, Phi Gamma Delta; pres. Chicago Library Club, 1921. Episcopalian. Clubs: Faculty, Torch. Home: 29 N. Oleander Av., Daytona Beach, Fla. Died Nov. 11, 1954.

MANDEVILLE, William Hubert, lawyer; b. Elmira, N.Y., Apr. 16, 1893; s. Hubert C. and Mary F. (Stoops) M.; B.E., Union Coll., 1915; student, Columbia Univ. Law Sch., 1915-17; m. Ruth C. Buck, Oct. 6, 1917; 1 son, David C. Admitted to N.Y. State bar, 1920, since practiced in Elmira; mem. firm of Mandeville Buck Teeter & Harpending and predecessor firms; chmn. exec. com., vice pres. and dir. Thatcher Glass Mfg. Co., Inc., since 1943; dir. Hardinge Bros., Inc., Chemung Canal Trust Co., Le-Valley McLeod, Inc., Elmira Floral Products Inc. Trustee Elmira Savings Bank. Served as capt., U.S. F.A., A.E.F., 1917-20. Mem. bd. edn., Elmira, 1924-32, pres., 1930-32. Life trustee Union Coll.; trustee Elmira Coll. Mem. Am., N.Y. State and Chemung County (pres., 1949) bar assns., Assn. of Bar of City of New York, Psi Upsilon. Republican. Episcopalian. Clubs: University (New York City); City, Golf. Home: 670 Hoffman St. Office: Robinson Bldg., Elmira, N.Y. Died Mar. 21, 1954.

MANGUM, Willis Lester (măn'gŭm), air brake mfr.; b. Nephi, Utah, Nov. 27, 1873; s. James Harvey and Amy Lorette (Bigler) M.; student Brigham Young U.; m. Jennie Pearl Knight, Sept. 6, 1905; children—Gloria K. (Mrs. U. Lynn Miller), Max K., Beth K. (Mrs. Ben B. Johnson), Dixie K. (Mrs. Wm. J. Snow, Jr.), Jessie K. (Mrs. Adam Y. Bennion), William Lester, John Knight. Sec.-treas. mining and smelting cons., woolen mills, live stock and agrl. cos. U.S. and Can., 1905-21; an organizers, 1926, since pres. Internat. Air Brake Co.; dir. Twentieth Century Mining Co., Knight Investment Co., Big Hill Mining Co. Now retired. Mem. Bd. Edn., Provo Pub. Schs. (ex-pres.) 8 yrs. Republican. Mormon. Home: 381 E. Center, Provo, Utah. Died June 24, 1949.

MANKIEWICZ, Herman J(acob) (man-key-witz), writer; b. N.Y. City, Nov. 7, 1897; s. Frank and Johanna (Blumenau) M.; A.B. with honors, Columbia, 1916; m. Sara Aaronson, July 1, 1920; children—Donald Martin, Frank, Johanna. Mng. editor, Am. Jewish Chronicle, N.Y. City 1916-17; dir. Am. Red Cross News Service, Paris, 1919-20; fgn. corr., reporter N.Y. World, 1920-23; with dramatic dept. N.Y. Times, 1923-26; dramatic critic The New Yorker, 1925-26; silent title writer, writer silent and talking motion pictures, including Citizen Kane, (Acad. Award, 1941); producer Million Dollar Legs, Monkey Business, Horse Feathers, and others since 1926. Author: (plays) The Good Fellow (with Geo. S. Kaufman), 1926; The Wild Man of Borneo (with Marc Connolly) 1927; The Meal Ticket, 1937. Contbr. to Vanity Fair, Life. Sat. Eve. Post, Saturday Rev. Flying cadet, U.S. Army, 1917-18; pvt. 1st class, 5th Marines, 2nd div., A.E.F., 1918-19. Home: 1105 Tower Rd., Beverly Hills, Cal. Died Mar. 6, 1953.

MANLEY, John Ellis, former gen. sec. Nat. Council YMCA and of Internat. Com. YMCA's; b. nr. Lawrence, Kan., Jan. 25, 1879; s. George Fletcher and Annie Elizabeth (Reed) M.; student Kan. Agrl. Coll., 1901-02; spl. student Washburn Coll., Topeka, Kan., various periods; grad. YMCA Coll., Chgo., 1908; H.M., Internat. YMCA Coll., Springfield, Mass., 1934; m. Elizabeth Harris, Sept. 1, 1909; children—John Carmack, Mary Elizabeth, Suanna Harris. Country sch. tchr., 1899-1901; asst. sec. YMCA, Topeka, Kan., 1902-06, state sec. Kan., 1908-16, budget dir. Internat. Com., 1917-27, met. gen. sec. Pitts., 1928-32; gen. sec. Nat. Council YMCA's of U.S.A., 1933-40, ret.; called back into service as exec. dir. War Prisoner Aid Com. Ex-pres. Employed Officers Assn. of YMCA's of U.S. and Can. Mem. various nat. coms. responsible for organizing U.S.O. for Nat. Defense. Now regional dir. San Francisco development program Mass. Inst. of Technology. Conglist. Contbr. to publs. of YMCA. Home: Alexander Hamilton Hotel, 631 O'Farrell St. Office: 111 Sutter St., San Francisco. Deceased.

MANLY, Basil, economist; b. Greenville, S.C., Mar. 14, 1886; s. Charles and Mary Esther Hellen (Matthews) M.; student U. Mo.; A.B., Washington and Lee U., 1906; fellow dept. polit. sci. U. Chgo., 1909-10; m. Marie Merriman Bradley, Dec. 15, 1912; 1 dau., Laura Bradley (Mrs. W. O. Briggs, Jr.). Expert U.S. Bureau of Labor Statistics, 1908-12; dir. research and investigation U.S. Commn. on Industrial Relations, 1913-15; econ. expert Newspaper Enterprise Assn., 1915-17; spl. asst. to Francis J. Heney, spl. atty. for Fed. Trade Commn., 1918; joint chmn. Nat. War Labor Bd., 1918-19; dir. Scripps Econ. Bureau, 1919-20; dir. People's Legislative Service, 1921-27; spl. corr. N.Y. Evening World, Bklyn. Daily Eagle, Newark Evening News and other papers, 1928-29; spl. counsel U.S. Senate Com. on Campaign Expenditures, 1931 (prepared report of com. and drafted new Corrupt Practices Act); Washington rep. Power Authority of State N.Y., 1932-33; mem. Fed. Power Commn., 1933-45, vice chmn., 1933-36, 42-44, chmn., 1944-45, resigned; v.p., dir. So. Natural Gas Co., 1945—. Designated commr. in charge Nat. Power Survey, authorized by Exec. Order, 1933, and Electric Rate Survey, authorized by Cong. Joint Resolution, 1934; supervised plans and reports of both these pioneer undertakings. Apptd. by President Roosevelt, vice chmn. Nat. Defense Power Co., 1938; chmn. Com. on Generation and Distribution, Nat. Assn. R.R. and Utilities Commrs., 1939. Planned and supervised publ. of National Electric Rate Book, 1940. Supervising commr. War Power Contracts, 1942-45, Natural Gas Investigation, 1944. Commd. by Gov. of Wis. to study European agrl. and econ. conditions, 1923. Mem. Am. Planning and Civic Assn., Am. Acad. Polit. and Social Science, Phi Beta Kappa, Phi Gamma Delta. Clubs: Cosmos, Columbia Country (Washington). Author: Wages and Working Conditions in the Steel Industry, 4 vols. (U.S. Bur. Labor Statistics), 1912; Increase in Prices of Anthracite Coal, 1913; Report of Basil M. Manly, Director Research and Investigation (U.S. Commn. on Industrial Relations), 1915; Summary, Report on Meat Packing Industry (Federal Trade Commn.), 1918; Are Wages Too High?, 1921; The Bread Tribute, 1924; The Farmer's Tax Burden, 1930; World Barriers to Peace and Prosperity, 1931; Regional Coordination and Intergration of Electric Utilities—The Federal Point of View, 1936; Wanted—An Industrial Armistice, 1947. Contbr. on econ. topics. Home: 5059 Sedgwick St. N.W. Office: Southern Bldg., Washington 5. Died May 11, 1950; buried Fort Lincoln Moseleum, D.C.

MANLY, Robert Emmet, lawyer; b. Rushford, Minn., July 6, 1869; s. Anthony Andrew and Catherine (Mulcahy) M.; Valparaiso U.; B.S., U. of Minn., 1890, LL.B., 1896; unmarried. Enlisted in N.D. Vols., Apr. 26, 1898, and went with regt. to P.I., June 1898; mustered out (P.I.) July 31, 1899; in practice in Philippine Islands, 1899—, also a planter, lumberman and mine operator. Del. Dem. Nat. Conv., 6 times between 1912 and 1932; mem. Dem. Nat. Com. for P.I., 1912—. Mem. Am. Bar Assn. Vet. Army of Philippines, Spanish War Vets. Clubs: Elks, Circumnavigators. Home: Naga, Camarines Sur. P.I.

MANN, Conrad Henry, organizer, financier; b. Butler Twp., Scott County, Ia., Jan. 7, 1871; s. John and Catherine Virginia (McCausland) M.; student prep. sch. and U. Marburg, Germany, 1883-91, bus. coll., Davenport, Ia., 1892-93; m. Emma Werle, Sept. 11, 1902. Began as farm hand, 1893; with U.S. Express Co., 1894-97; organizer Modern Woodmen America, 1897, Order of Mut. Protection, 1899, Columbian Knights, 1903; grand sec. Fraternal Order of Eagles, 1907-11, now financial dir.; sec., treas. and gen. mgr. Kansas City (Mo.) Breweries Co., 1909-19; pres. Down Town Garage Co., Standard Savings & Loan Co., Associated Industries of Mo.; dir. Empire Storage & Ice Co., First Nat. Bank (Mercedes, Tex.). Dir. Horner Kansas City Conservatory, Kansas City Convention Hall. Pres. Kansas City C. of C. Republican. Catholic. K.P., Eagle, Elk, etc. Clubs: Kansas City, Kansas City Athletic, Hillcrest Golf, etc. Home: The Walnuts, 5049 Wornall Rd. Office: Commerce Bldg., Kansas City, Mo. Deceased.

MANN, Ellery Wilson, mfr.; b. Bklyn., May 25, 1890; s. Henry and Emma (Lindstrom) M.; grad. pub. schs.; m. Marion Edna Berrian, Mar. 25, 1915; children—Marion Edna (wife Dr. Stuart Hakes), Emma Christina (Mrs. Henry D. Williams), Ellery Wilson. Office boy Standard Oil Co., 1907-10, advt. dept., 1910-11; with H. K. McCann Co., 1911-25, v.p., 1915-25; pres. Zonite Products Co., 1925-35, Tampax, Inc., 1936—; former pres. Bellerose (L.I.) Nat. Bank. Former mayor, Bellerose; mem. Nassau County Charter Commn. Mem. C. of C. Clubs: Metropolitan, Cloud, Lotus (N.Y.C.); Wheatley Hills Golf; American (London). Home: 24 Cathedral Av., Garden City, L.I., N.Y. Office: Chrysler Bldg. East, N.Y.C. 17. Died Jan. 15, 1956.

MANN, Frank Hurt, gen. sec. Am. Bible Soc.; b. Petersburg, Va., May 8, 1883; s. Edwin Murray and Pattie (Cowles) M.; preparatory edn. Hoge Memorial

Mil. Acad., Blackstone, Va.; A.B., Hampden-Sidney College, Virginia, 1903, B.Litt. and M.A., 1904; Litt. D., Moravian College, 1953; married Anna C. Rogers, May 10, 1919; children—Roger Cornwell, William Hodges. Conducted mission school in mountains of Va., sub-prof. Hampden-Sidney (Va.) Coll., later asst. sec. Y.M.C.A., Havana, Cuba; sec. com. on tuberculosis, Charity Orgn. Soc. of N.Y. City, 1905-18; sec. Am. Bible Soc., 1919-24, later vice-pres. and chmn. of finance com., now general secretary; former president and director Union Guarantee & Mortgage Co., Union Mortgage Co., Roslyn Estate, Inc., Suburban Brokerage Corp., Macaba Corporation, United Equities, Inc.; former treasurer Federal Council Churches of Christ in America; prominent in S.S. and mission work in N.Y. City; was v.p. 8th Av. Mission; past pres. Presbyn. Social Union of N.Y. City. Served in Field Arty., Camp Zachary Taylor, Ky., advancing to 1st lt. Mem. Pi Kappa Alpha. Democrat. Presbyn. (elder Rye Presbyn. Ch.). Clubs: Manursing Island, Shenorock Shore, Camp Fire of America. Home: Rye, N.Y. Office: 450 Park Av., N. Y.C. 22. Died Oct. 1954.

MANN, Heinrich Ludwig (män), writer; b. Lubeck, Germany, Mar. 27, 1871; s. Thomas Heinrich and Julia (Bruhns) M.; student pub. schs., Lubeck, U. Berlin; m. Nelly Kroeger, Sept. 9, 1939. Left Berlin, Feb. 1933; lived in France, 1933-40; came to U.S., 1940. Began as a novelist, 1893 and continued writing novels, short stories, essays and plays. Pres. Prussian Acad., Sect. of Lit., Berlin, 1937-39. Lutheran. Club: Pen (London, N.Y.C.). Author of 16 novels, 4 vols. of short stories, 6 vols. of essays and 8 plays (all pub. in Germany); translated from the German: The Little Town, Professor Unrat (The Blue Angel), Young Henry of Navarre, Henry, King of France. Home: 264 S. Doheny Drive, Beverly Hills, Cal. Died Mar. 12, 1950.*

MANN, Joseph F., lawyer; b. Bloomfield, N.J., Dec. 2, 1890; s. Joseph McElroy and Fannie (Carter) M.; A.B., Princeton, 1911; LL.B., New York Law School, 1913. With Masten & Nichols, N.Y. City, 1913-17, McKinstry, Taylor and Patterson, N.Y. City, 1917-21, Clark, Carr & Ellis, N.Y. City (mem. of firm), since 1921; asst. gen. counsel, U.P. R.R. Co., 1940-42, general counsel, since 1942; director U.P. Railroad Company and subsidiaries. Merchant-Sterling Corp., Sterling Iron & Ry. Co., Cushman & Wakefield, Inc. Trustee Mary W. Harriman Charitable Trust. Mem. Bar Assn. of City of New York, Phi Beta Kappa. Home: 33 Hillside Av., Montclair, N.J. Office: 120 Broadway, N.Y.C. Died Nov. 4, 1951.

MANN, Klaus, author; b. Munich, Germany, Nov. 18, 1906; s. Thomas (author) and Katja (Pringsheim) M.; ed. schools of Munich; student Heidelberg U.; unmarried. Came to U.S., 1936, naturalized, Sept. 1943. First book published in Germany, 1925; novelist, playwright, actor, critic, journalist in Germany, to 1933; actively opposed Hitlerism and expatriated by Nazis, 1934; editor refugee mag. Die Sammlung, Amsterdam, 1933-35; writer and lecturer, U.S. since 1936; editor lit. rev., Decision, N.Y. City, Jan. 1941-Feb. 1942. Served in U.S. Army, Dec. 1942-Oct. 1945. Mem. Internat. P.E.N. Lutheran. Author: (books pub. in English) The Fifth Child, 1927; Alexander, 1930; Journey into Freedom, 1935; Pathetic Symphony (a Tschaikovsky novel), 1936; (with Erika Mann) Escape to Life, 1939; (with Erika Mann) The Other Germany, 1939; The Turning Point (Thirty-five Years in This Century), 1942; André Gide: And The Crisis of Modern Thought, 1943. Contributor to Atlantic, Esquire, Town and Country, Tomorrow, The Nation, American Mercury, etc. Address: 1550 San Remo Drive, Pacific Palisades, Cal. Died May 21, 1949.

MANN, Lester Bradwell, lawyer; b. Long Pond, Ga., Sept. 30, 1886; s. Zachary Taylor and Ida Clementine (McGregor) M.; student S. Ga. Coll.; B.S., Ga. Sch. Tech., 1907; M.P.L., Georgetown U., 1915; m. Helen Moore, Nov. 10, 1920; children—John McGregor, Helen Louise (Mrs. John Masters), Douglas, Donald. Admitted to D.C. bar, 1915, Ill. bar, 1939; asst. commr. patents, Washington, 1920-21; pvt. practice, Chgo., 1921—; sr. mem. Mann, Brown & Hansmann, and predecessors, 1938—, specializing in patent law. Counselor Boy Scouts Am. Trustee Hinsdale (Ill.) Pub. Library. Served as capt., U.S. Army, World War I. Mem. Am., Ill. State, Chgo. bar assns., Am. (bd. mgrs.), Chgo. (pres. 1943) patent law assns., Western Soc. Engrs. Mason (K.T., Shriner). Clubs: Union League, Engrs. (Chicago); Hinsdale (Ill.) Golf; Three Lakes (Wis.) Rod and Gun. Home: 344 N. Radcliffe Way, Hinsdale, Ill. Office: 53 Jackson Blvd., Chgo. 4. Died Mar. 27, 1954; buried Hinsdale.

MANN, Rowena Morse, clergyman, lecturer, author; b. Ithaca, N.Y.; b. Benjamin and Sarah (Fitchette) Morse; B.S., State U. Ia., 1891; studied Cornell U., U. Chgo. Div. Sch., 1898-1900, U. Berlin, 1900-03; Ph.D., U. Jena, Germany, 1904 (tablet unveiled there in her honor, 1933, as the tablet unveiled there in her honor, 1933, as the first woman to receive a doctor's degree from that univ.); m. Rev. Newton Mann, Aug. 20, 1912 (dec.). Ordained to Unitarian ministry, 1906; pastor Geneva, Ill., 1905-06, Keokuk, Ia., 1906-10, Third Ch., Chgo., 1910-25; dir. Western Unitarian Conf., 1912-16. First woman to occupy the pulpit (1921) at Harvard U.; professorial lectr. in philosophy Jena U., 1933 (first woman to lecture in philosophy in any German U.). Mem. Am. Assn. U. Women (dir. Chgo.), Am. Psychol. Assn., Am. Philos. Assn., Am. Sociol. Soc., UN Assn. for Peace. Clubs: University Woman's (hon.), Chicago Woman's (hon.), Lecturer on art and ethical subjects; official lecturer Assn. for League of Nations. Lectured extensively on World Fedn. for Peace, 1906; for League to Enforce Peace, 1912; Democracy or Dictatorship, 1934; for Assn. of Nations Against War, 1943-44. Spoke over Leipsig, Germany, radio, on Peace the Better Way, 1933; U. Berlin, Against Militarism, 1933; U. Warsaw. World League for Peace, 1933, U.S. Tours on U.N.A. or World Final Catastrophy, 1945-46; ofcl. lectr. for UN Assn. Author: Theories of Knowledge, 1904; Moral Education and the Scientific Method, 1925. Translator of Pfleiderer's Ethik, 1924; The Revolution in Philosophy, 1933. Contbr. to periodicals. Home: 5741 Kenwood Av., Chgo. Died Mar. 3, 1958.

MANN, Stanley, mfg. exec.; b. New Brighton, Pa., Jan. 29, 1876; s. James H. and Sara (Rebout) M.; ed. pub. schs. New Brighton; m. Helen Hook, July 23, 1927; 1 dau., Natalie Jean. Credit mgr. Standard Chain Co., Pitts., 1903-17, Am. Chain & Cable Co., Inc., Bridgeport, Conn., 1917-29, comptroller, 1929-43, asst. treas., 1943-46, treas., dir., 1946—; dir. Dominion Chain Co., Ltd., Canada. Treas., dir. William T. Morris Found., Inc., N.Y. Home: 931 Riverton Terr., Stratford, Conn. Office: 929 Connecticut Av., Bridgeport, Conn. Died Aug. 20, 1958; buried Mountain Grove Cemetery, Bridgeport.

MANN, Thomas, author; b. Lübeck, Germany, June 6, 1875; s. Heinrich and da Silva-Bruhns M.; hon. D.Litt., Harvard, Columbia, Princeton, Yale, and other univs.; m. Katja Pringsheim, 1905; children—Erika, Klaus Heinrich, Angelus, Monika, Elizabeth, Michael. Apptd. lecturer, Princeton U., 1938. Winner Nobel prize for literature, 1929; Cardinal Newman award, 1937. Formerly mem. Prussian Acad. of Arts; life mem. Am. Acad. Arts and Letters; elected member of Nat. Inst. of Arts and Letters. Author: Buddenbrooks, 1901; Fiorenza (play), 1906; Death in Venice, 1912; Royal Highness, 1916; A Man and His Dog, 1918; Bashan and I, 1923; The Magic Mountain, 1924; Children and Fools, 1928; Three Essays, 1929; Mario and the Magician, 1929; Past Masters, 1933; Joseph and His Brothers, 1934; Stories of Three Decades, 1936; Freud, Goethe, Wagner, 1937; Joseph in Egypt, 1938; The Coming Victory of Democracy, 1938; The Beloved Returns (novel), 1940; The Transposed Heads, (a legend of India), 1941; Joseph the Provider (novel), 1944; Essays of 3 Decades, 1947; Doctor Faustus (novel), 1948; The Holy Sinner, 1951. Contributor to various magazines. Received Goether National Award, Goethe Committee, at Weimar, 1949; Goethe Award, Frankfurt, 1949. Address: 1550 San Remo Dr., Pacific Palisades, Cal. Died Aug. 12, 1955.

MANNES, David (măn'nĕs), violinist, music sch. dir.; b. N.Y.C., Feb. 16, 1866; s. Henry and Natalie (Wittkowsky) M.; pub. sch. edn.; studied music N.Y.C., Berlin and Brussels; Mus.D., Oberlin Coll., 1942; m. Clara Damrosch, June 4, 1898; children—Leopold D., Marya Mannes Clarkson. Concertmaster N.Y. Symphony Soc., 1902-11; dir. Music School Settlement and organizer Music School Settlement for Colored People until 1915; sonata recitals with Mrs. Mannes in pub. and pvt. series, N.Y.C., Boston, London, and other cities. Founder 1916, and co-director of the Mannes Music Sch.; co-editor with Mrs. Mannes and Louis Untermeyer, New Songs for New Voices; condr. for 30 yrs. of free concerts at Met. Decorated Knight of the Crown of Italy; Officer of Public Instruction (French). Author: Music Is My Faith (autobiography), 1939. Home: 120 East 75th St. Studio: 157 E. 74th St., N.Y.C. 21. Died Apr. 25, 1959; buried Woodlawn Cemetery, N.Y.C.

MANNEY, Charles Fonteyn, composer; b. Bklyn., Feb. 8, 1872; s. Charles Palmer and Henrietta (Meserole) M.; pvt. edn., followed by course at Bklyn. Poly. Inst.; was not grad.; boy soprano soloist and chorister in St. Paul's and Ch. of the Redeemer, Bklyn.; studied theory of music in New York with William Arms Fisher; later moved to Boston; studied harmony and counterpoint under J. Wallace Goodrich, and form and composition with Dr. Percy Goetschius. Composer of many songs, anthems and piano pieces, song cycle, A Shropshire Lad, and two sacred cantatas: The Resurrection; The Manger Throne. Mem. Harvard Mus. Assn., Am. Soc. of Composers, Authors and Pubs. Home: 52 Gramercy Park, N.Y. C. 10. Died 1951.

MANSFIELD, Frederick William, lawyer, ex-mayor Boston; b. East Boston, Mar. 26, 1877; s. Michael Read and Catherine (McDonough) M.; LL.B., Boston U., 1902, LL.D., 1938; m. Helena Elizabeth Roe, June 29, 1904. Admitted to Mass. bar, 1902, now practicing in Boston. Dem. nominee for gov. of Mass., 1910, 17, 18; treas. of Mass., 1914; mayor of Boston, 1933-37. Mem. Mass. State Bar Assn. (pres. 1929-31), Am. Law Inst. (charter mem.), United Spanish War Vets., Vets. Fgn. Wars, Kearsage Assn. K.C. Chancellor Equestrian Order of Holy Sepulchre of Jerusalem. Home: 96 Bay State Rd. Office: 18 Tremont St., Boston. Died Nov. 6, 1958.

MANSFIELD, William Douglass, editor, publisher, banker; b. Elizabeth Twp., Pa., Mar. 6, 1878; s. James MacDonald and Helen Mar (Douglass) M.; student Douglas Business Coll., McKeesport, 1895-96; m. Margaret Alice Butler, Feb. 15, 1908 (died 1934); 1 son, William Douglass. Real estate and insurance broker, 1900-27; mem. Pa. State Senate, 1923-35 (chmn. com. on edn., 1925-33); county commr., Allegheny County, Pa., 1932-36; pres. Daily News Pub. Co., McKeesport, Pa., since 1925, editor Daily News since 1927; chmn. of the bd. First Nat. Bank of McKeesport (Pa.), 1937-41; pres. First Nat. Bank since Apr. 1941. Chmn. McKeesport (Pa.) Housing Authority since 1937; president of McKeesport Chamber of Commerce. Trustee of McKeesport Hosp., McKeesport Y.M.C.A. Republican. Methodist. Mason. Clubs: Youghiogheny Country (McKeesport); Amen Corner, Bankers' (Pittsburgh). Home: 540 Sixth Av. Office: Daily News Bldg., McKeesport, Pa. Died Oct. 6, 1952; buried Mt. Vernon Cemetery, McKeesport.

MANSON, Richard, newspaper exec.; b. N.Y.C., Apr. 21, 1901; s. Harry and Ann (Manson) Rozoff; B.A., Columbia, 1921, Publisher, 1927-34; joined staff New York Post 1934, asst. to gen. mgr., 1946-47, asst. mng. editor, 1947-49, asst. to pub., 1949-51, gen. mgr. since 1951; dir. N.Y. Post Corp. since 1949, N.Y. Post Found. since 1951. Served with F. A., 12th Armored Div., A.U.S., France and Germany, 1942-46, advancing to 1st lt. Recipient Bronze Star Medal. Mem. Phi Beta Kappa. Home: 13 E. 63d St., N.Y.C. 21. Office: 75 West St., N.Y.C. 6. Died Aug. 27, 1954; buried Ferncliff, Greenburg, N.Y.

MANSS, Harvey McKnight, advt. exec.; b. Cin., Apr. 24, 1886; s. Louis and Phoebe (Renner) M.; student Cin., 1905-07; A.B., U. Mich., 1909; m. Alice Kelsall, Nov. 21, 1911. Mgr. H. Walter Thompson Co., Cin., 1909-20; advt. mgr. Andrew Jergens Co., 1920-30; merchandising mgr. Sterling Products, Inc., N.Y.C., 1930-37; pres. The Bayer Co., Inc., 1937-41; v.p., dir. Sterling Drug, Inc., 1941—; v.p. Dancer-Fitzgerald-Sample, Inc. Mem. Nat. Assn. Retail Druggists, Theta Delta Chi. English Lutheran. Club: Winged Foot Golf. Home: 37 Bonnie Briar Lane, Larchmont, N.Y. Office: 170 Varick St., N.Y. C. 13. Died May 1959.*

MANUILSKY, Dmitry Zakharavish, ex-UN del.; b. 1883; ed. U. St. Petersburg (now Leningrad), the Sorbonne, Paris, France. Lived abroad, 1907-17, as exile for having participated in Kronstadt uprising of 1906; mem. Revolutionary Com. of the Ukraine, 1920-21; elected mem. Presidium of Comintern, 1924; became Minister Fgn. Affairs, also dep. chmn. Council of People's Commissars, Ukrainian S.S.R., 1944; chmn. Ukrainian Delegation, San Francisco Conf., 1945, chmn. Com. 1 (Preamble, Purposes and Principles) to Preparatory Commn. of UN, of which was elected v.p., and to Gen. Assembly, London; became UN charter mem. and chief del. from the Ukraine. Mem. Acad. of Scis. USSR. Address: United Nations, Lake Success, N.Y. Died Feb. 22, 1959.*

MANWARING, A(lbert) Homer II (mănwäring), elec. mfg. exec.; b. Phila., July 14, 1912; s. Roy A. and Ruth (McDowell) M.; student Haverford Sch., 1930; B.S., Pa. State Coll., 1934; m. Esther H. Fitzgerald, Sept. 19, 1936; children—Albert H., John L., Barbara R. Cadet engr. Phila. Electric Co., 1934-36, mem. indsl. sales dept., 1936-38; sales engr. Phila. Elec. & Mfg. Co., 1938-40, sales mgr., sales and engineering, 1940-42, executive vice pres. and gen. mgr. since 1942, mem. bd. dirs. since 1939. Served as lt. U.S.M.C. Res., 1934-36. Sec. Phila. War Prodn. Pool, 1942-44. Mem. Nat. Elec. Mfrs. Assn., Am. Inst. E.E., Illuminating Engring. Soc. (pres. 1953-54), S.A.R., Pi Kappa Alpha Presbyn. Clubs: Union League, Huntingdon Valley Country (gov.); Engineers (Phila.); Racquet. Home: 1422 Hopeland Rd., Wyncote, Pa. Died Nov. 11, 1956; buried West Laurel Hill Cemetery, Phila.

MARBLE, John Putnam, research geochemist; b. Worcester, Mass., May 30, 1897; s. J(oseph) Russel and Emily Greene (Chase) M.; A.B., Williams Coll., 1918; student Clark U., 1919; A.M., Harvard, 1928, Ph.D., 1932; m. Adelaide Holme Maghee, May 21, 1921; children—Katharine Chase Bejnar, Richard Almy, Rosamond Weis, John Putnam, Jr. With J. Russel Marble & Co., Marble-Nye Co., drysaltery bus., Worcester, 1919-26; independent geochem. research under auspices Nat. Research Council, Washington, since 1931 (at U.S. Geol. Survey, 1931-35, U.S. Nat. Mus. since 1935, asso. in mineralogy of Mus. since 1945); tech. aide and spl. asst. Nat. Defense Research Com. of Office Sci. Research and Development, 1942-46; vice chmn., com. on measurement of geologic time, Div. Geology and Geography, Nat. Research Council, 1936-46, chmn. since 1946; part author reports of com.; sec.-treas. Am. Geol.

Inst. 1950-52. Del. to 17th and 18th International Geologic Congresses, 1937, 48, 10th session Internat. Union Geodesy and Geophysics, 1954. Fellow A.A. A.S., Geological Soc. America, Mineralogical Soc. America, Meteoritical Soc.; mem. Am. Chem. Soc., Electrochem. Soc., American Geophysical Union (general sec. 1953—), Wash. and N.Y. acads. of sci., Geol. Soc. Wash., Sons of the Revolution (Mass. soc.), Phi Beta Kappa, Alpha Chi Sigma, Gamma Alpha. Club: Petrologist, Harvard, Cosmos, Chevy Chase (Washington); Williams (N.Y. City); University (Boston); Harvard Faculty (Cambridge); Worcester (Worcester, Mass.); Nantucket (Mass.) Yacht. Home: 3221 Macomb St., Washington 8. Office: U.S. National Museum, Washington 25. Died June 6, 1955; buried Arlington Nat. Cemetery.

MARBLE, Thomas Littlefield, judge; b. Auburn, Me., Dec. 24, 1876; s. Henry (M.D.) and Mercy (Littlefield) M.; A.B., Bowdoin College, 1898, LL.D., 1926; LL.B., Harvard U., 1904; m. Harriet E. Fuller, Aug. 15, 1906. Prin. Gorham (N.H.) High Sch., 1899-1901; admitted to N.H. bar, 1904; mem. firm of Rich & Marble, Berlin, 1905-17; asso. justice Superior Court of N.H., 1917-25; asso. justice Supreme Court of N.H., 1925-43; apptd. by gov. N.H. mem. of commn. to unify, codify and amend the pub. laws of N.H., 1939; chief justice Supreme Court of N.H., 1943-47; law cons. to law firm Morse & Grant, Concord, N.H., since 1947. Del. to N.H. Constitutional Conv., June 1948. Mem. New Hampshire Bar Association (pres. 1926-27), Phi Beta Kappa, Delta Kappa Epsilon. Republican. Universalist. Mason (K.T.). Home: Concord, N.H. Died Oct. 23, 1952; buried Gorham, N.H.

MARBURGER, Ralph E(merson), lawyer; b. Commercial Point, O., Nov. 28, 1894; s. Jacob A. and Nora L. (Beavers) M.; student Bliss Bus. Coll., 1911-12; Ohio State U., 1922; m. Marthena DuMont, Aug. 13, 1924. Admitted to Ohio bar, 1922; practicing lawyer, Columbus, 1922-26, partner Bricker, Marburger, Evatt & Barton, since 1944; gen. atty. Ohio Bell Telephone Co., Cleveland, 1926-31, v.p. in charge pub. relations, 1931-37, v.p., gen. mgr., 1937-44; dir. Lima (O.) Telephone & Telegraph Co., Newark (O.) Telephone Co.; solicitor Pa. R.R. Trustee Franklin U. Served as corpl. 329th Inf., 1918-19. Mem. Better Bus. Bur. of Columbus (pres., 1941-44), Am. Ohio State, Columbus bar assns., Am. Judicature Soc., Phi Alpha Delta. Clubs: Rotary, University, Columbus Country (Columbus); Ohio Society of New York. Home: 1445 E. Broad St., Columbus 5. Office: 50 W. Broad St., Columbus 15, O. Died July 25, 1954.

MARCANTONIO, Vito, ex-congressman; b. N.Y. City, Dec. 10, 1902; s. Samuel and Angelina (De Dobitis) M.; LL.B., N.Y.U. Law Sch., 1925; m. Miriam A. Sanders, May 20, 1925. Mgr. campaign of F. H. La Guardia for Congress, 1924-32; admitted to practice in N.Y. State, 1926; asst. U.S. dist. atty., 1930-31; mem. 74th and 76th to 81st Congresses (1935-37 and 1939-51), 18th N.Y. District. Mem. N.Y. Co. Lawyers Assn. Catholic. Home: 231 E. 116th St. Law Office: 11 Park Pl.; Congressional Office: 1484 1st Av., N.Y.C. Died Aug. 9, 1954; buried Woodlawn Cemetery, N.Y.C.

MARCH, Peyton Conway, ret. gen. U.S. Army; b. Easton, Pa., Dec. 27, 1864; s. Francis Andrew and Mildred Stone (Conway) M.; A.B., Lafayette Coll., 1884, A.M., 1887, LL.D., 1918; LL.D., Union Coll., 1918, and Amherst Coll., 1919; Dr. of Mil. Science, Pa. Mil. Coll., 1934; B.S., U.S. Mil. Acad., 1888; grad. Arty. Sch., Ft. Monroe, 1898; m. Mrs. Josephine (Smith) Cuningham, July 4, 1891 (died Nov. 18, 1904); children—Mrs. Mildred Millikin, Mrs. Josephine Swing, Peyton Conway (dec.), Mrs. Vivian Frank (dec.), Lewis Alden (dec.); m. 2d, Cora V. McEntee, Aug. 25, 1923. Add. 2d lt. 3d Arty., June 11, 1888; 2d lt., Nov. 30, 1888; 1st lt., Oct. 25, 1894; maj. 33d Vol. Inf., July 5, 1899; lt. col., June 9, 1900; hon. discharged vols., June 30, 1901; capt. Arty. Corps, U.S. Army, Feb. 2, 1901; maj., Jan. 25, 1907; assigned to 6th F.A., June 6, 1907; lt. col., Feb. 8, 1912; col. 8th F.A., Aug. 26, 1916; brig. gen., June 17, 1917; maj. gen., Nat. Army, Aug. 5, 1917; maj. gen. U.S. Army, Sept. 23, 1917; gen. May 20, 1918. Comd. Astor Battery, 1898 (mountain battery presented to government by Col. John Jacob Astor); comd. Am. forces in action at Tilad Pass, Luzon, P.I., Dec. 2, 1899, in which Gen. Gregorio del Pilar was killed; during same expdn. Gen. Venancio Concepcion, chief of staff to Aguinaldo, surrendered to Maj. March; in charge mil. and civil govt. in district Lepanto-Bontoc and southern half Ilocus Sur, Feb.-June 1900; Province of Abra, to Feb. 1901; commissary-gen. of prisoners, P.I., to June 30, 1901; mem. Gen. Staff, 1903-07; mil. attaché to observe Japanese Army in Russo-Japanese War, 1904; army arty. comdr. A.E.F. in France, 1917; apptd. actg. chief of staff U.S. Army, Mar. 4, 1918; gen. and chief of staff, May 20, 1918; retired, 1921. Nominated for bvt. Mar. 20, 1902, "for distinguished gallantry in action," capt. U.S. Army (for action nr. Manila, Luzon, Aug. 13, 1898), lt. col. U.S.V. (for actions nr. Porac, Sept. 28, and at San Jacinto, Luzon, Nov. 11, 1899), col. U.S.V. (for actions at Tilad Pass, Dec. 2, and Cayan, Luzon, Dec. 5, 1899). Recipient Thanks of Congress by resolution, 1953; decorated Silver Star medal (4 oak-leaf clusters) for participation in these engagements; D.S.C. "for distinguished gallantry in action"; D.S.M., 1918, for "exceptionally meritorious and distinguished services"; Grand Cross Order of St. Michael and St. George (Eng.); Grand Officer Legion of Honor (France); Grand Cross Order of George the First (Greece); Grand Cordon Order of Crown (Belgium); Grand Cross Order Crown (Roumania); War Cross (Czechoslovakia); Grand Cordon of the Chia Ho (China); Grand Cordon of the Polonia Restituta (1st class); Grand Cross Order of St. Maurice and St. Lazarus (Italy); Grand Cross Order of the Rising Sun (Japan). Mem. Soc. of the Cincinnati (Va.) Descendants of Signers of Declaration of Independence, Army and Navy Union, Phi Beta Kappa, Delta Kappa Epsilon. Clubs: Army and Navy (Washington, D.C.); Union League (New York). Author: The Nation at War, 1932; also various newspaper articles. Home: 1870 Wyoming Av. N.W., Washington. Died Apr. 13, 1955; buried Arlington Nat. Cemetery.

MARCHANT, Trelawney E., ret. army officer; b. Lexington County, S.C., May 11, 1887; son of Julian M. and Addie (Senn) M.; grad. Draughons Bus. Coll. (Columbia, S.C.), 1911; Command and Gen. Staff Sch., 1939-40; Inf. Sch., 1940; m. Lila Cave, 1919; children—Trelawney E., Julian M., Nancy C. Engaged in banking 1911-40 less time in active Army service. Service N.G. of U.S., 1905-43; active service Mexican Border 1916-17, World War I 1917-19, World War II 1940-43; ret. 1943 disability incurred in line of duty, rank Brig. Gen., Infantry. Home: 2329 Blossom St., Columbia, S.C. Died June 2, 1950; buried Mt. Hebron Meth. Ch., Lexington County, S.C.

MARCOTTE, Henry (mär'kŏt), clergyman; b. Negaunee, Mich., Apr. 10, 1870; s. Joseph and Harriet (Robart) M.; B.A., Lake Forest (Ill.) Coll., 1893, D.D., 1913; grad. McCormick Theol. Sem., 1896 (honor man); m. Nora Nickerson, Feb. 4, 1901 (died Jan. 31, 1912); children—Harriet Eleanor, Mary Isabel; m. 2d, Mary Wiggins, Sept. 16, 1913; children—Jean M., Ann. Ordained Presbyn. ministry, 1896; pastor First Ch., Astoria, Ore., 1896-1903, Westminster Ch., Portland, 1903-16, Second Ch., Kansas City, Mo., 1916-24; mem. Bd. of Christian Edn., 1924-26; pastor Grace Memorial Ch., Evansville, Ind., 1926, First Presbyn. Ch. (union of Grace Memorial and Walnut Street Chs.). 1926-35; now supply pastor. Mem. Bd. of Nat. Missions, Presbyn. Church, U.S.A., 1931; moderator of Synod of Ind., 1932-33. Republican. Address: 2815 N.E. 41st Av., Portland, Ore. Died Apr. 28, 1955; buried Portland Meml. Cemetery.

MARCUS, Ralph, educator; b. San Francisco, Aug. 17, 1900; s. Moses and Selma (Neufeld) M.; B.A., Columbia, 1919, M.A., 1920, Ph.D., 1927; fellow div. sch. Harvard, 1925-27; m. Alice Rubin, Apr. 8, 1928; children—Daniel Robert, Philip Selmar. Lectr. Semitic langs. Columbia, 1927-43; instr., asst. prof. Semitic philology Jewish Inst. Religion, 1927-34, prof., 1934-43; asso. prof. Hellenistic culture U. Chgo., 1943-50, prof., 1950—. Author: Law in the Apocrypha, 1927; Josephus, vols. 5, 6, 7, 8, 9, Philo, Questions on Genesis and Exodus, 1953 (both Loeb Classical Library). Asso. editor Classical Philology, Rev. of Religion, Jewish Social Studies, Jour. Bibl. Lit. Office: Oriental Institute, U. of Chicago, Chgo. 37. Died Dec. 25, 1956.

MARGIOTTI, Charles Joseph (mär-jĭ ŏt'ĭ), lawyer; s. Joseph and Fortunata (Reca) M.; grad. Ind. State Teachers Coll., 1912; LL.B., U. of Pa. Law Sch., 1915; Litt.D., St. Francis Coll., Loretto, Pa., 1934; m. Denise Wery, Feb. 5, 1918; children—Juliette Charlotte, Charles Joseph. Began at 11 as water boy, later laborer in brick yards; worked way through teachers coll. and law sch.; began practice at Punxsutawney, 1915; has appeared before courts in 46 counties in Pa. and in 12 different states; atty. gen. of Pa., 1935-38, 1950-51. President Denise Coal Company; vice president Old Dominion Turnpike Corp. of Va.; sec., treas. Rend-Mar Coal Co.; treas. Capitol Engineering Corp., Dillsburg, Pa. Mem. Allegheny Co. Bar, Jefferson County Bar, Nat. Aeronautic Assn., Amen Corner, Univ. of Penn. Gen. Alumni Assn. Chmn. Bd. Govs., St. Francis Coll., Loretto, Pa.; Member American and Pa. State bar assns., Phi Sigma Pi Eta, Phi Alpha Zeta. Elk. Member K. of C., Eagles, Moose, Foresters of America. Clubs: Pittsburgh Athletic, Railway (Pitts.). Home: 4130 Bigelow Blvd. Address: Grant Bldg., Pitts. Died Aug. 25, 1956; buried Punxsutawney, Pa.

MARIN, John (măr'ĭn), artist; b. Rutherford, N.J., Dec. 23, 1872; s. John C. and Annie Louise (Currey) M.; student Stevens Inst. Tech.; art edn. Pa. Acad. Fine Arts, Art Students League of N.Y., also in Paris, France; A.F.D., Yale, 1950, Univ. of Maine, 1950; m. Marie H. Hughes, Apr. 1914; 1 son, John C. Water colorist and painter in oils. One-man shows of sea and landscapes, annually, N.Y.C., since 1909, including one-man show at Mus. Modern Art, 1936. Represented in Met. Museum of Art, Bklyn. Mus. of Art, San Francisco Mus. of Art, Phillips Memorial Gallery (Washington, D.C.), Museum of Modern Art (N.Y. City), Art Inst. of Chgo., and several other museums; also in private collections. Received Fine Arts Medal of Am. Inst. Architects, 1948. Home: Addison, Me. Died Oct. 1, 1953; buried Fairview (N.J.) Cemetery.

MARIO, Queena (mä'rē-ō), soprano; b. Akron, O., Aug. 21, 1896; d. James and Rose (Carewe) Tillotson; student Ogontz (Pa.) Sch., 1907-08, Plainfield (N.J.) High School, 1908-10; m. Wilfred Pelletier, Nov. 23, 1925 (divorced Aug. 1936). Debut as Antonia in Tales of Hoffman, with San Carlo Opera Co., 1918, continued with that company until 1921; then with Scotti Opera Co., 1921 22, Ravinia Opera Co., summer, 1922, with Met. Opera Co., 1922-39; sang with the Italian Opera Co., in Paris, 1925, San Francisco Opera Co., 6 seasons between 1923 and 1933, Ravinia Opera Co., 1928-31; vocal tchr. Curtis Inst. of Music, Phila., 1931-34; pvt. studio, N.Y.C., 1934—; tchr. voice and operatic acting Juilliard Grad Sch., N.Y.C.; tchr. singing; writer; dir. Queena Mario Group. Hon. mem. Mu Phi Epsilon, Sigma Alpha Iota; mem. D.A.R. Author: Murder in the Opera House, 1934; Murder Meets Mephisto, 1942, Death Drops Delilah, 1944. Home: 205 W. 57th St., N.Y.C.; also Bethel, Conn. Died May 28, 1951; buried Woodlawn, N.Y.

MARJERISON, Howard Mitchell (mär-jĕr'ĭ-sŭn), dentist; b. Lawrence, Mass., Nov. 19, 1895; s. Isaiah D. and Lillie (Mitchell) M.; D.M.D., Tufts Coll., 1916, Sc.D. (hon.); m. Beatrice Temple, 1917; children—Barbara, Mitchell, Janice. Intern Forsyth Dental Infirmary for Children, 1916-17; practice of dentistry, part time, 1917-40; instr. prosthetic dentistry Tufts Coll. Dental Sch., 1917-23, asst. prof., 1923-29, asso. prof. and head of dept. of partial prosthodontics, 1929-33, acting dean and asso. prof. prosthetic dentistry, 1933-34, dean and asso. prof., 1934-39, dean and prof., 1939-40; dean and prof. dentistry U. Ill. Coll. Dentistry, 1940-44; asso. dir. Forsyth Dental Infirmary, 1944-50, dir., 1950—; lectr. on preventive dentistry, Harvard U. Chmn. com. on dentistry NRC. Trustee Forsyth Dental Infirmary for Children. Served as 1st lt. Dental Res. Corps, U.S. Army, 1918. Mem. Am. Dental Assn., Mass., New Eng. dental socs., Am. Acad. Dental Sci., Robert R. Andrews Hon. Soc., Internat. Assn. Dental Research, A.A.A.S., Am. Pub. Health Assn., Fédération Dentaire Internat., Sigma Xi, Delta Sigma Delta, Omicron, Kappa Upsilon, Phi Beta Pi. Trustee, Forsyth Dental Infirmary for Children. Mason. Home: 5 Fernald Dr., Cambridge 38, Mass.; also Old Comers Rd., Chatham, Mass. Office: 140 Fenway, Boston 15. Died Sept. 4, 1955.

MARK, Clarence, business exec.; b. Chicago, Oct. 13, 1882; s. Clayton and Anna (Griffith) M.; B.S., Harvard, 1906; m. Frances Tracy, Apr. 8, 1908; children—Anna, Alice (Mrs. Edward Friedel), Clarence Griffith, William Killian; m. 2d, Victoria St. George Joyce, Feb. 6, 1924; children—Victoria (Mrs. Guilford Peters), Joyce (Mrs. Horace Bouvier), Gordon St. George, John. Chmn. bd. Clayton Mark & Co., Evanston, Ill., 1936-48, pres.; pres. G. Washington Coffee Co., 1943-46; v.p., dir. Am. Home Foods, 1943-46; exec. com. First National Iron Bank, Morristown, N.J. Dir. All Souls Hospital; member Harvard Engring. Society. Republican. Roman Catholic. Clubs: Harvard (New York); University (Chicago); Morris Co. (N.J.) Golf; Yacht, Sankaty Head Golf, Pacific (Nantucket, Mass.). Home: Normandy Parkway, Morristown, N.J. Died Sept. 6, 1955; buried Nantucket, Mass.

MARK, Kenneth Lamartine, educator; b. of Am. parents, Leipzig, Germany, Aug. 27, 1874; s. Edward Laurens and Lucy Thorp (King) M.; A.B., Harvard, 1898, A.M., 1900, Ph.D., 1903; m. Florence Louise Wetherbee, June 19, 1907. Asst. in chemistry Harvard, 1900-03; instr. chemistry Simmons Coll., 1903-07, asst. prof., 1907-13, asso. prof., 1913-15, prof., 1915-41 (emeritus), dir. Sch. Science, 1915-41. Fellow Am. Acad. Arts and Sciences; mem. Am. Chem. Soc., Delta Upsilon. Republican. Author: Laboratory Exercises in General Chemistry, 1916; Laboratory Exercises in Inorganic Chemistry, 1922; Delayed by Fire, being the Early History of Simmons College, 1945. Capt. Sanitary Corps U.S. Army, 1918. Home: 200 Riverway, Boston 15. Died Jan. 12, 1958.

MARKEL, Samuel A., ins. exec.; b. Elizabeth, N.J., Apr. 3, 1885; s. Andrew Markel; children—Lewis C., Irvin S., Stanley B., Milton L. Chmn. Am. Fidelity & Casualty Co., Inc., Richmond, Va., also Markel Service, Inc. Office: Insurance Building, Richmond 22, Va. Died Feb. 18, 1954; buried Richmond.

MARKELL, Charles, lawyer, judge; b. Baltimore, Md., Dec. 16, 1882; s. John and Elizabeth Charlton (Harris) M.; A.B., Johns Hopkins Univ., 1902; LL.B., Univ. of Md., 1904; m. Jeannette Jones, June 16, 1909 (died Feb. 26, 1923); children—Charles, Jeannette (Mrs. Charles G. Page), Ann Elizabeth. Admitted to Md. bar, 1904, gen. practice of law, Baltimore, Md., 1904-45, partner Cook & Markell and predecessor firms, 1907-45; mem. commn. on Judiciary Article of Md. Constn., 1941-43; apptd. judge Md. Ct. of Appeals, 1945, elected 1946, chief judge, 1952. Dir., counsel Samuel Kirk & Son, Inc., 1923-45, Pemco Corp., 1943-45. Mem. reorgn. com. Seaboard

Airline Ry. receivership, 1943-45. Mem. Am., Md. State (pres. 1941-42), Baltimore City bar assns., Am. Law Inst., Am. Judicature Soc., Phi Beta Kappa. Episcopalian (vestryman). Republican. Clubs: University, Merchants, Hamilton Street, Baltimore Country. Home: 100 W. University Pkwy. Office: Court of Appeals of Md., Annapolis, Md.; also Court House, Balt. Died Feb. 24, 1955.

MARKERT, Frederic Schaefer, mfg. exec.; b. East St. Louis, Ill., July 22, 1901; s. George Henry and Dorothy (Schaefer) M.; B.S., U. Ill., 1924; Profl. Ceramic Engr., 1933; m. Francine MacDowell, June 4, 1927; children—Dorothy Mae, James MacDowell. Ceramic engr. Belleville (Ill.) Enameling & Stamping Co., 1924-26; with Ferro Corp., mfrs. porcelain enamels, frits and glazes, Cleveland, 1926—, asst. gen. mgr., dir., v.p., 1936-47, exec. v.p., gen. mgr. and dir., 1947—. Mem. Triangle, Keramos. Republican. Methodist. Mason. Home: 21341 Aberdeen Rd., Rocky River, O. Office: 4150 E. 56th St., Cleve. 5. Died Mar. 30, 1954; buried Lakewood (O.) Park Cemetery.

MARKEY, Lawrence Morris (mär-kē), author; b. Alexandria, Va., Jan. 10, 1899; s. Isadore Girard and Helen Shepherd (Morris) M.; student John Marshall High Sch., Richmond, Va., 1913-16; m. Helen Turman, Oct. 18, 1921; 1 dau., Sue. Reporter successively for Atlanta Journal, Newark Ledger, N.Y. Daily News, N.Y. World, 1920-25; on staff The New Yorker, 1925-33; writer for mags., 1923—. Served with A.R. C., France, World War I; Navy war corr., convoy from N.Y. to Casablanca and PTO, Carrier Essex, World War II. Recipient ofcl. commendation Sec. James Forrestal. Democrat. Author: The Band Plays Dixie, 1927; That's New York, 1927; This Country of Yours, 1932; Manhattan Reporter, 1935; Well Done!, 1945; Unhurrying Chase, 1946; Dr. Jeremiah, 1950. Contbr. articles and short stories to mags. Home: Halifax, Va. Died July 10, 1950; buried Oakland Cemetery, Scottsburg, Va.

MARKHAM, Edward M. (märk'ȧm), ret. army officer; b. Troy, N.Y., July 6, 1877; s. Cornelius and Margaret (Carney) M.; M.A., C.E., U.S. Mil. Acad., 1899, hon. B.S., Rensselaer Polytechnic Inst., 1934; m. Grace S. Markham, Jan. 27, 1904; children—Edward M., Harrison S., Grace K. (Mrs. W. J. Natteson). Commd. 2d lt., Engrs., 1899, advanced through grades to maj. gen., chief of engrs., 1933; retired ad maj. gen., 1938; commr. of public works, N.Y.C., 1938; pres. Great Lakes Dredge & Dock Co., Chicago, 1938-45; ret. 1945. Clubs: Army-Navy (Washington); Chicago Athletic Assn. (Chgo.); Home: 59 Manning Blvd., Albany, N.Y. Died Sept. 14, 1950.

MARKHAM, R(euben) H(enry), journalist; b. Twelve Mile, Kan., Feb. 21, 1887; s. Lucius C. and Maggie (Benjamin) M.; A.B., Washburn Coll., Topeka, 1908; B.D., Union Theol. Sem., N.Y. City, 1911; A.M., Columbia, 1912; m. Mary Gall, Aug. 31, 1909; children—Eleonora, Helen, Jordan. Missionary for Am. Mission Bd. of Boston, Bulgaria, 1912-18, as acting dir. Am. Boys' Sch., 1914, Am. Girls' Sch., 1917 (witnesses 1st and 2d Balkan wars and several revolutions); sec. Y.M.C.A., Archangel, Russia, 1918, later with Russian prisoners in France; returned to Bulgaria under Mission Bd., 1920-26, as head Mission publ. work, founded monthly mag., The Seed, editor church paper, The Morning Star; founded weekly, The World, printed in Bulgarian lang. (discontinued after 2 yrs.); with Christian Science Monitor, 1926-49, as Bulgarian and Balkan corr., and for Central and S.E. Europe; covered Ethiopian War, 1935, in Bible Land, 1936, Socialist uprising, Austria, 1934, Hitler's entrance into Vienna, 1938; staff writer in U.S., 1939-42 and 1946-49; in Europe to report from Balkan countries, 1945, expelled from Romania and other Russian controller countries, 1946; on leave as dep. chief work for Balkans, O.W.I., in New York, Washington and Mediterranean Area, 1942-44; spl. cons. to U.S. Govt., 1949; resigned to do free lance writing; lectr.; feature writer for various mags. Conglist. Mason. Author: Bulgaria, Today and Tomorrow, 1931; Meet Bulgaria, 1931; The Wave of the Past, 1941; Tito's Imperial Communism, 1946; Rumania Under the Soviet Yoke, 1948; Protestants Awake, 1949; Communists Crush Churches in Eastern Europe, 1950. Home: 18 Fairfield St., Boston 16. Died Dec. 29, 1949; buried Twelve Mile Cemetery, Smith Co., Kan.

MARKHAM, Reuel Finney, educator; b. Kensington, Kan., Sept. 18, 1891; s. Henry F. and Corie (Sherman) M.; A.B., Washburn U., 1916; postgrad. Oberlin Coll., 1917; B.D., Yale, 1920; A.M., Columbia, 1928. Ed.D., 1946; m. Evangeline McNaughton, Aug. 4, 1919; children—Eleanor Jean, Barbara Ann. Asst. dir., dir. Am. Collegiate Inst., Istanbul, Turkey, 1920-32; dean and acting pres. Aleppo (Syria) Coll., 1932-37; prof. edn. Washburn U., 1938-44, acting dean coll., 1941-42, dean of students, 1942-44; adviser of students City Coll. N.Y., 1945-46; dean coll. letters and sci. St. Lawrence U., 1946-49; temporary head guidance center Am. U., 1950; supr. counseling Coll. of William and Mary of Norfolk, also Va. Poly. Inst., 1950—, also prof. edn. Vet. of World War I. Ednl. dir., gen. dir. Topeka Civil Def. Mem. Va. Assn. Guidance and Personnel Workers, Am. Personnel and Guidance Assn., Inc., So. Coll. Personnel Assn., Hampton Roads Vocational Guidance Assn., Phi Delta Kappa, Kappa Delta Pi. Conglist. Clubs: Rotary, Kiwanis, Torch. Home: 1650 W. 49th St., Norfork, Died Jan. 5, 1957.

MARKHAM, Thomas F., bishop; b. Mar. 22, 1891; s. James and Nora (Hickey) M.; A.B., Holy Cross Coll., 1913, LL.D., 1951; S.T.D., D.C.L., Rome. Ordained priest Roman Cath. Ch., 1917; pastor Sts. Peter and Paul Ch., S. Boston, Mass., 1940-42, St. Peter's Ch., Lowell, 1942; became rural dean, N. Middlesex County, Mass., 1942; domestic prelate, 1945, protonotary apostolic, 1946; consecrated titular bishop of Acalissus and auxiliary bishop of Boston, 1950. Home: 327 Gorham St., Lowell, Mass. Died July 4, 1952.

MARKHAM, William Hugh, lawyer; b. Independence, Wis., Dec. 13, 1888; s. Arthur Augustus and Rose Camilla (Bishop) Markham; student Lawrence College, Appleton, Wisconsin, 1907-08; LL.B., University of Minn., 1911; m. May Alice Spencer, June 28, 1915 (died 1950); children—Spencer Augustus, Rosemary Margaret Reuschlein, Patricia Ruth Reese; m. 2d Alice M. Spencer Smith, Mar. 26, 1950. Admitted to Minn. bar, 1911, and began practice at Winona; moved to Horicon, Wis., 1913. Served in 46th Training Battery, F.A. Corps, O.T.S., Camp Taylor, Ky., 1918. Spl. municipal judge, St. Charles, 1912-13; city atty., Horicon, 1914-23, and 1942-48, mayor, 1926-34, 1936-38, 1940-42, member City Council, 1923-26; member Wisconsin State Senate, 1926-30; Circuit Court Commr., 1929—. Rep. candidate for U.S. Senate, Wisconsin, 1928. Pres. Nat. Rep. Club of Wis. Mem. American Bar Assn., Wis. and Dodge County bar assns., Izaak Walton League, Chamber of Commerce, Am. Legion. Presbyterian. Odd Fellow, Grand Master 1947-48. Grand Rep., 1948-51, Aide to Gen. Com., Patriarchs Militant, 1945-54. Eagle, Elk. Clubs: Dodge County Skat League (pres.); Wis. Skat League (pres. 1952-55), Nat. Skat League (pres. 1954), Horicon Lions (pres.). Author: Book of Poems and Odes (nome de plume The Bard of Horicon), 1956; also treatise America's Problem Child. Author of Wis. legislation to restore Horicon Marsh as a wild life refuge. Home: 306 Palmatory St., Horicon, Wis. Died Jan. 31, 1958; buried Oak Hill Cemetery, Horicon.

MARKLEY, Edward Anthony, lawyer; b. Jersey City, Dec. 8, 1891; s. Albert E. and Kate (Engelhardt) M.; LL.B., N.Y. U., 1911; LLM., 1913; m. Edna Sauer, Sept. 5, 1934; children—Inez, Barbara, Audrey. Admitted to N.J. bar, 1911, since practiced in Jersey City; mem. firm of Markley & Broadhurst since 1918; pres. John Marshall Coll., 1928-50. Mem. Am., N.J. State, and Hudson Co. (pres. 1928) bar assns. Home: 40 Grosvenor Rd., Short Hills, N.J. Office: One Exchange Pl., Jersey City. Died June 2, 1952.

MARKS, Laurence Mandeville, partner Laurence M. Marks & Co.; b. Brooklyn, N.Y., Mar. 4, 1892; s. Alexander Drummond and Caroline (Mandeville) M.; grad. Hotchkiss Sch. (Conn.), 1910; A.B., Yale U., 1914; married Mrs. Marjorie G. Martin, Sept. 30, 1946. Started career with Lee, Higginson & Co., investment bankers in N.Y.C. After World War I returned to the company. Resigned in July, 1932, and organized investment banking firm of Laurence M. Marks & Co. in N.Y.C. with branch office in Albany, N.Y. Dir. Air Products, Inc., N.Y., Divco Corp., Detroit, Mich., Nat. City Lines, Inc, Chicago, Ill. Shamrock Oil & Gas Corp., Amarillo, Tex. Gov. Assn. of Stock Exchange Firms, 1945-48. Trustee Brooklyn (N.Y.) Sav. Banks. Served in Mexican Border Campaign with Squadron A, N.Y. Nat. Guard, 1916-17. At outbreak of World War I joined U.S. Army and was assigned to First Reserve Officers Training Camp at Plattsburg Barracks, N.Y. Was commd. 2d lt., Field Artillery, First Div., served with 5th F.A., A.E.F., from Dec. 1917-May 1919. Promoted to 1st lt., Sept. 1918 and made capt. in Mar. 1919. Was awarded Croix de Guerre and received various citations for bravery while in action. Mem. Governing Com. N.Y. Stock Exchange (1934-38). Gov. Investment Bankers Assn. of Am., 1939-40 (pres. 1951), Nat. Assn. Securities Dealers, 1940-43. Treas. N.Y. State Rep. Com., 1936-37. Chmn. Citizens Family Welfare Com., 1936. Dir. Brooklyn and Queens Y.M.C.A.; Brooklyn Bureau of Charities; Brooklyn Hospital; Travelers Aid Soc. Mem. Phi Beta Kappa, Alpha Delta Phi, Wolf's Head (Yale). Clubs: Union (gov. 1942-46); Yale; Links; Heights Casino (gov., 1938—); Wall St. (gov. 1940-43); Bond of New York, (pres. 1932-33, gov. 1930-34); Piping Rock. Home: 775 Park Av. Office: 49 Wall St., N.Y.C. Died Aug. 25, 1958.

MARKS, Lionel Simeon, engr.; b. Birmingham, Eng., Sept. 8, 1871; s. Samuel Edward M.; student Mason Coll., Birmingham, 1888-92, engring. diploma, 1891; B.Sc., London U., 1892; arrived in America, 1893; M.M.E., Cornell U., 1894; m. Josephine Preston Peabody, June 21, 1906 (died Dec. 4, 1922); children—Alison Peabody, Lionel Peabody. Instr. mech. engring., Harvard U., 1894-1900, asst. prof., 1900-09, prof. 1909-40, prof. emeritus, 1940; also prof. Mass. Inst. Tech., 1914-18. Fellow Am. Acad. Arts and Sci., A.A.A.S., Am. Soc. M.E. (nat. lecturer 1944-46). Mem. Old Cambridge Shakespeare Assn. (pres.), Phi Beta Kappa, Sigma Xi (nat. lecturer 1942; pres. Harvard chapt. 1946-47), Tau Beta Pi. Consltng. engr. science and research div., Bureau of Aircraft Prodn., 1918; chmn. section on prime movers, engring. Div., Nat. Research Council, 1918. Clubs: Harvard of Boston; Faculty of Cambridge; Harvard of New York; University, Mexico City. Author: Steam Tables and Diagrams (with H. N. Davis), 1900; The Airplane Engine, 1922; Axial-Flow Fans (with C. Keller), 1937. Editor: Mechanical Engineers' Handbook. Home: 19 Garden St., Cambridge, Mass. Died Jan. 6, 1955.

MARKS, Percy, author; b. Covelo, Cal., Sept. 9, 1891; s. Henry and Sarah (Lando) M.; B.L., U. Cal., 1912; A.M., Harvard, 1914; m. Margaret Ellen Gates, Dec. 17, 1927; 1 dau., Sally Jean. In ednl. work, 1914-24, successively supr. edn. State Infirmary, Tewksbury, Mass.; instr. in English, Mass. Inst. Tech., Dartmouth College, Brown U. and Conn. U. Served as 2d lt. Inf., World War I. Club: High Lane. Author: The Plastic Age, 1924; Martha, 1925; Which Way Parnassus?, 1926; Lord of Himself, 1927; A Dead Man Dies, 1929; The Unwilling God, 1929; Craft of Writing, 1932; Better Themes, 1933; Tree Crown Straight, 1936; And Points Beyond, 1937; What's a Heaven For, 1938; The Days Are Fled, 1939; No Steeper Wall, 1940; Between Two Autumns, 1941; Full Flood, 1942; Knave of Diamonds, 1943; Shade of Sycamore, 1944; The College Writer (with Adolphus J. Bryan), 1945; Blair Marriman, 1949. Address: 147 Thornton St., Hamden 17, Conn. Died Dec. 27, 1956.

MARKWOOD, Michael Edward, orgn. exec.; b. Hagerstown, Md., Sept. 27, 1914; s. Robert David and Nora Cecilia (Loar) M.; student U. Ga. Evening Sch.; m. Louise Margaret Rarick, July 2, 1934; children—George Edward, Marsha Eileen, Michael Edward. Messenger Bur. Biol. Survey, Dept. Agr. (later Bur. Fish and Wildlife Service, Dept. Interior), 1934-39, sr. clk. Fish and Wildlife Service, Albuquerque, N.M., 1939-42, adminstrv. asst., Atlanta, 1942, adminstrv. officer, 1943-45, Boston, 1945-46, chief br. finance and procurement, 1948-52; nat. rep. Nat. Fedn. Employees, 1946-48, pres., 1955—; dep. comptroller Materiel Command, Chem. Corps. Dept. Army, 1952-55. Recipient award for superior achievement Dept. Interior. Mem. Soc. Personnel Adminstrn., Am. Soc. Pub. Adminstrn., Am. Acad. Polit. and Social Sci., Soc. Advancement Mgmt., Civil Service Assembly U.S. and Can. Contbr. articles on personnel profl. publs. Home: 9809 26th Av., Hyattsville, Md. Office: 1729 G St., Washington 6. Died Jan. 27, 1957; buried Mt. Olivet Cemetery, Washington.

MARLATT, Charles Lester (mär-lăt), entomologist; b. Atchison, Kan., Sept. 26, 1863; s. Washington M. (one of founders and first prin. Blue Mont Coll., now Kan. State Coll.) and J. A. (Bailey) M.; B.S., Kan. State Coll., Manhattan, Kan., 1884, M.S., 1886, D.Sc., 1921; m. Florence L. Brown, Dec. 1, 1896 (died Oct. 28, 1903); m. 2d, Helen Stuart Mackay Smith, July 5, 1906; children—Florence, Virginia, Charles Lester (dec.), Helen, Dorothy, Constance. Asst. prof. Agricultural Coll., Manhattan, Kan., 2 yrs.; asst. entomologist, U.S. Dept. Agr., 1889-94, 1st asst. and asst. chief entomologist, 1894-1922, asso. chief, 1922-27, chief Bur. of Entomology, 1927-33; engaged in hist. and geneal. work, 1933—. Directed, 1909-12, effort to secure a national law to prevent importation of infested and diseased plants into U.S., resulting in the Plant Quarantine Act of Aug. 20, 1912; chmn. Federal Hort. Bd. to supervise enforcement of this act, 1912-28; responsible for reorganization and assembling from other bureaus of Dept. of Agr., of all plant quarantine and regulatory work, under a new office, created by the sec. of agr. of Plant Quarantine and Control Adminstrn., chief of this office, July 1, 1928-Dec. 1, 1929. Mem. editorial com. Jour. of Agrl. Research, 1919-26. Fellow A.A.A.S.; pres. Entomol. Soc. Washington, 1897-98, Assn. Econ. Entomologists, 1899; mem. Washington Acad. Sciences, Biol., Archaeol. and Geog. socs., Phi Kappa Phi. Clubs: Cosmos, Chevy Chase, Metropolitan (Washington). Author: An Entomologist's Quest, 1953; also many papers and bulletins on systematic and economic entomology and on plant quarantine; also 16 volumes of service and regulatory announcements, recording 68 foreign and domestic plant quarantines, the regulations thereunder and explanatory papers, 1914-1929. Home: (legal) 1521 16th St., Washington; also Wild Cliff, Seal Harbor, Me. Died Mar. 3, 1954.

MARLEY, James Preston, ret. army officer, educator; b. nr. Slayden, Tex., Nov. 20, 1882; s. Thomas Jefferson and Mary Eudora (Powell) M.; student U. Tex., 1901-02; B.S., U.S. Mil. Acad., 1907; hon. grad. Gen. Service Schs., 1923; grad. Army War Coll., 1928, Naval War Coll., 1929; m. Anne Augusta Bonner, June 10, 1909. Commd. 2d lt. F.A., U.S.

Army, 1907, promoted through grades to brig. gen. major gen. (temp.), 1941; served various army stations at posts in the U.S., P.I., and Panama Canal Zone; comd. 8th Motorized Div., U.S. Disciplinary Barracks; retired; now head math. dept. Columbian Prep. Sch. Decorated Mexican Border medal, Victory medal, Am. Campaign Medal, World War II Medal. Mason (K.T., Shriner). Club: Army Navy Country (Arlington, Va.). Home: 3514 Quebec St., N.W. Washington. Died Nov. 27, 1952; buried Arlington Nat. Cemetery.

MARLOWE, Julia (Sarah Frances Frost), actress; b. Caldbeck, Cumberlandshire, Eng., Aug. 17, 1866, came to U.S. with parents at 5 yrs. of age; lived in Kan. 2 yrs.; moved to Ohio, locating finally in Cincinnati; attended pub. schs. until 12th yr.; then joined juvenile opera co., which gave Pinafore, Chimes of Normandy and other light operas; in juvenile co. was called Frances Brough (the latter a family name); later played a child's part in Rip Van Winkle, and, the next season, played small parts in co. which gave classic dramas in West; retired temporarily from stage and studied 2 yrs. N.Y.C.; m. Robert Tober; m. 2d, Edward Hugh Sothern, Aug. 17, 1911 (died Oct. 28, 1933). Metropolitan début as Parthenia in Ingomar; starred from 1888 in Shakespearean and other tragic and romantic rôles; retired, 1924. Address N. Y.C. Died Nov. 12, 1950.

MARMER, Harry Aaron, tidal engr.; b. Proskurof, Ukraine, June 21, 1885; s. Isaac Baer and Rechoma (Segal) M.; came to U.S., 1889; grad. Woodbine (N.J.) Agrl. Sch., 1901; B.Sc., Rutgers, 1907, M.S., 1930; m. Hazel Ellison Dakin, Nov. 16, 1916 (dec.); children—Kalmon Elias, Nancy Jane. Asst. engr. Cape May Real Estate Co., 1907; tidal computer, U.S. Coast and Geodetic Survey, Washington, D.C., 1907-20; asst. chief, Div. of Tides and Currents, same, since July 1920. Received Agassiz Medal in oceanography, 1951. Fellow A.A.A.S.; mem. Philos. Society of Washington, Assn. Am. Geographers, Am. Geophys. Union, Am. Soc. C.E. Club: Cosmos. Author: Tides and Currents in New York Harbor, 1925; The Tide, 1926; Coastal Currents Along the Pacific Coast of the U.S., 1926; Tidal Datum Planes, 1927; The Sea, 1930; Chart Datums, 1930. Contbr. to scientific and tech. publs. of articles dealing with tides, currents and gen. oceanography; contbg. editor Geog. Rev. Home: 7106 7th St. N.W., Washington. Deceased.

MARONEY, Frederick William, ret. physician and coll. dean; b. Springfield, Mass., Jan. 10, 1884; s. Bernard and Ellen (Sullivan) B.; M.P.E., Normal Coll., Am. Gymnastic Union, 1906; M.D. cum laude, Tufts Coll., 1918; m. Bernice Gallagher, Aug. 18, 1921; 1 dau., Sheila Alice. Instr. in health edn. Lawrencheville (N.J.) Sch., 1906-10; head dept. health edn. Newark Acad., 1910-13; lectr. Harvard, summers, 1911-16, coach gymnastic team, 1914-18; gymnasium team and fencing team coach Bowdoin Coll., 1913-14; lectr. Battle Creek (Mich.) Normal Sch., summers 1917-18; dir. dept. of health edn. State Teachers Coll., Wis., 1918; dir. health and phys. edn. State Dept. Edn., N.J., 1918-21; lectr. Rutgers U., summers 1919-24; dir. health edn. Atlantic City (N.J.) pub. schs., 1921-30; lectr. U. Ill., summers 1925, 26; pres. Arnold Coll. for Phys. Edn., New Haven, 1930-31; lectr. U. So. Cal., summers, 1927, 28, Tchrs. Coll. Columbia, summers 1929-44; asso. prof. phys. edn., 1931-41; dean students and chmn. dept. personnel service, Bklyn., 1944-54, dean emeritus, 1954. Served as 1st lt. M.C., U.S. Army, 1918. Mem. N.J. Phys. Edn. Assn., N.J. State Athletic Assn. Am. Assn. for Health, Phys. Edn. and Recreation (past pres. Eastern Dist. Soc.), Nat. Assn. Health, Phys. Edn. and Recreation (past pres.). Democrat. Roman Catholic. Author: Physical Education Manual, 1939; co-author Health, Happiness and Success, series of health edn. texts, 1940. Recipient fellowship N.J. Phys. Edn., 1938, Am. Assn. for Health, Phys. Edn. and Recreation, 1941; Ling medal for service to sch. children of Cal., 1928. Mem. White House Conf. on Child Health and Protection, secondary sch. com. on health and recreation, 1940. Mem. Nat. Civilian Adv. Com. for Phys. Fitness, Naval Personnel, 1942. Address: 3111 Glenwood Rd., Bklyn. 10. Died Oct. 4, 1958; buried St. Charles Cemetery, L.I.

MARQUART, Edward John (mär-kwärt), naval officer (ret.); b. Valparaiso, Ind., Mar. 11, 1880; s. Peter Anton and Anna Catherine (Miller) M.; B. S., U.S. Naval Acad., 1902; m. Marie T. Scannell, June 3, 1916 (dec. Mar. 1937); m. 2d Helen Holbert, Apr. 19, 1938. Commd. ensign U.S. Navy, 1904, and advanced through grades to rear adm., 1936; served in U.S.S. Ore., Asiatic sta., 1902-03, U.S.S. Frolic, Philippine insurrection, 1903-06, U. S.S. Illinois, Cuba, 1906-07; U.S.S. New York (later U.S.S. Rochester), 1909-10; comdr., U.S.S. Cuttlefish, 1907-09; ordnance asst. to mgr., N.Y. Navy Yard, 1910-12; engr. officer, U.S.S. Mississippi and Ohio, 1912-14; gunnery officer, U.S.S. Arkansas, Mexican service, 1914-15; with Naval Gun Factory, Washington Navy Yard, 1915-19; comdr. submarine div. and submarine base, Canal Zone, 1919-20; exec. officer, U.S.S. Wyoming, 1921-22; sr. asst. aide for Navy Yards, U.S. Navy Dept., 1922-24; comdr., submarine div., Asiatic fleet, 1925-27; with Office of Naval Operations, Navy Dept., 1927-30; tech. adviser to Sec. of Navy, 1930-31; comdr., U.S.S. Louisville, Pacific, 1931-32; dir. of fleet maintenance, Office of Naval Operations, 1932-35; comdt., 16th Naval Dist. and Navy Yard, Cavite, P.I., 1935-37; comdr., Yangtze patrol, 1937-38; comdr. mine craft, battle force, 1939-41; comdt., Navy Yard, N.Y., 1941-43, 3d Naval Dist., 1942-44; ret. from active service, Apr. 1, 1944. Mem. of Hepburn Bd. apptd. by Sec. of Navy to investigate and report upon need for nat. defense, 1938-39; mem. Naval Examining Bd., 1939. Awarded letter of commendation, U.S. Navy Dept., World War I; Legion of Merit, World War II; Spanish campaign medal, Philippine campaign medal, Cuban pacification medal, Mexican service medal, Victory medals (both World Wars), Yangtze service medal, Am. Defense service medal, fleet clasp; officer of Legion of Honor (France); hon. comdr., Order of Brit. Empire. Protestant. Home: 755 South El Molino Av., Pasadena 5, Cal. Died Nov. 4, 1954; buried National Cemetery, Arlington, Va.

MARRIAGE, E(dward) Charles D(acre), librarian; b. Colchester, Eng., Oct. 6, 1881; s. E. Burgess and Rebecca R. (Lynch) M.; grad. Leighton Park Sch., Reading, Eng., 1899; M.A., Clare Coll., Cambridge, Eng., 1903; E.M., King's Coll., London, 1904; m. Evelyn Frances Graham, Nov. 24, 1922; children—Edward Graham, Charles Burgess. Came to U.S., 1904, naturalized, 1909. Mining engr., Pioche, Nev., 1905-22, prop. Pioche (Nev.) Assay Office, 1911-22; ore purchasing agt., Am. Smelting and Refining Co., 1918-22; mining editor Pioche (Nev.) Record, 1920-23; founded Caliente (Nev.) Herald, 1923-24; justice of peace, Caliente, Nev., 1924-35; Nev. State librarian, Carson City, since 1935. Served on draft bd., World War I, state chmn. Victory Book World War II. Mem. A.L.A., Nev. Library Assn. (past pres.), Nev. Press Assn., Nev. Area Council Boy Scouts of Am. (v.p.). Democrat. Mem. Soc. of Friends. Elk. Oddfellow (grand master Nev., 1933-34). Club: Rotary (pres.). Contbr. to engring. and mining jours., World Book Ency., Ency. Britannica, Year Books and gen. edit. Statesman's Year Book, Nat. Ency., Colliers Year Books and gen. editions. Home: 311 E. Proctor. Office: State Library, Carson City, Nev. Died Aug. 13, 1950; buried Lone Mountain Cemetery, Carson City.

MARRINER, Robie D., business exec.; b. Belmont, Me., Aug. 3, 1901; s. Fred A. and Nettie B (Alexander) M.; student Bates Coll., Lewiston, Me., 1923, U. Chgo.; m. Norma MacDonald, June 26, 1934 (dec. June 1956). Supt. schs., Guilford, Me., 1927-35; agt. Am. Book Co., hdqrs., Auburn, Maine, 1935-43, gen. sales mgr., New York City, Aug. 1943-Feb. 1946, pres. Am. Book Co., New York, N.Y., since Feb. 1946; pres. Audio Education, Inc. Mem. N.E. A., Me. Teachers Assn. Mem. Universalist Ch. Mason. Home: 51 Shepley St., Auburn, Me. Office: 55 5th Av., N.Y.C. Died Aug. 18, 1956.

MARRIOTT, Arthur C., dir. DuPage Title Co., Wheaton, Ill.; v.p., dir. Wheaton Trust & Savings Bank; ret. v.p. Chgo. Title & Trust Co.; dir Lombard (Ill.) Bldg. & Loan Assn., Kane County Title Co., Geneva, Ill., and Lake County Title Co., Crown Point, Ind.; pres., dir. McHenry County Title Co., Woodstock, Ill. Home: 285 Cottage Hill Av., Elmhurst, Ill. Office: DuPage Title Co., Wheaton, Ill. Died Oct. 1957; buried Wheaton Cemetery.

MARRIOTT, Ross W. (măr'ĭ-ŏt), mathematician; b. Paxton, Ill., Dec. 30, 1882; s. Joshua H. and Elizabeth (Kelley) M.; B.S., Valparaiso (Ind.) U., 1904; A.B., Ind. U., 1906; A.M., Swarthmore, 1907; Ph.D., U. Pa., 1911; m. Marian Redfield Stearne, Sept. 8, 1915; 1 dau., Alice Elizabeth. Instr. mathematics Swarthmore, 1907-10, asst. prof., 1910-22, asso. prof., 1922-27, prof., 1927—. Mem. Swarthmore Coll. Eclipse Expdns., Mexico, 1923, New England, 1925, 32, Sumatra, 1926, 29; mem. U.S. Naval Obs. Eclipse Expdn., 1930. Research ballistician on spl. aircraft ammunition, E. I. du Pont de Nemours & Co., 1918. Fellow A.A.A.S., Royal Astron. Soc.; mem. Am. Astron. Soc. Am. Math. Soc., Math. Assn. Am., Sigma Xi. Republican. Quaker. Contbr. research papers on astron. subjects. Home: 213 Lafayette Av., Swarthmore, Pa. Died Oct. 19, 1955; buried North Cedar Hill Cemetery, Phila.

MARSH, Joseph Franklin, coll. pres.; b. Toll Gate, W.Va., Jan. 29, 1877; s. Jefferson and Angelina (Cunningham) M.; B.Pd., W.Va., Wesleyan Coll., 1901, Pd.D., 1927; A.B., W.Va. 1907, A.M., 1912; m. Florence Catharine Keller, May 29, 1922; 1 son, Joseph Franklin. Began teaching, 1894; supt. schs. Harrisville, W.Va., 1902-05; prin. Fairmont High Sch., 1908-09; asst. state supt. schs., W.Va., 1909-15; sec. State Bd. of Regents, 1915-19; sec. State Bd. of Edn., and dir. vocational edn., 1919-29; pres. Concord State Tchrs. Coll., 1929-45, pres. emeritus, 1945—. Exec. sec. W.Va. Food Adminstrn., World War, also four-minute man. Mem. Am. Commn. to Study Cooperation in Europe, 1913. Recipient Silver Beaver award S. W.Va. council Boy Scouts Am., 1941. Mem. N.E.A., Am. Vocational Assn. (life), W.Va. Edn. Assn. (bldg. com.), W. Va. Athletic Assn. (eligibility com.), Phi Beta Kappa. Republican. Methodist. Mason. Clubs: Rotary (Princeton, W.Va., dist. gov. internat. 1947-48); Mountain (Morgantown). Author: The Teacher Outside of the School, 1928; also various brochures and bulls. Editor W.Va. School Journal, 1921-25. Home: Athens, W.Va. Died Jan. 15, 1949; buried Resthaven Meml. Park, Princeton, W.Va.

MARSH, Reginald, painter, engraver, etcher; b. Paris, France, Mar. 14, 1898; s. Fred Dana and Alice (Randall) M.; A.B., Yale, 1920; pupil K. H. Miller and Jacques Maroger, N.Y. City; m. Felicia Meyer, January 2, 1934. Instuctor Art Students League, New York City and Moore Institute, Philadelphia. Painter of contemporary life subjects: represented in collections: Metropolitan Museum of Art, Whitney Mus. Am. Art (New York), museums in Chicago, Boston, Philadelphia and other cities in U.S., Library of Congress; works include: frescoes in Custom House, N.Y. City and Post Office, Washington, D.C. Artist war-corr. Life mag., fall of 1943. First W. G. Clark Prize, $2,000 and Corcoran gold medal, Corcoran Biennial, Washington, 1945; Salmagundi Club purchase prize, $1,000, 1945; Dana medal Pa. Acad. Fine Arts; J. Watson Blair prize Art Inst. of Chicago. Served in O.T.C. U.S. Army, 1918. Fellow Royal Soc. Arts (London); mem. Nat. Acad., Soc. Am. Etchers, Nat. Inst. Arts and Letters. Author: Anatomy for Artists, 1945. Home: 240 E. 15th St. Studio: 1 Union Square, W., N.Y.C. Died July 3, 1954; buried Dorset, Vt.

MARSH, Robert McCurdy, lawyer; b. Paterson, N.J., Jan. 8, 1878; s. Elias Joseph and Sarah Lord (McCurdy) M.; A.B., Harvard, 1899, A.M., 1900; LL.B., Columbia, 1903; m. Charlotte Delafkeld, June 1, 1921; 1 dau., Charlotte Prime (Mrs. Donald Eldredge). Admitted to N.Y. State bar, 1903; asso. Guthrie, Cravath & Henderson, 1903-06, Howland, Murray & Printice, 1906-09, Sullivan & Cromwell, 1909-15; practiced alone, 1915-17; mem. Marsh, Emgree & Pfeiffer, and successor Marsh & Pfeiffer, 1919-29; partner Delafield, Thorne, Burleigh & Marsh, N.Y.C., and successors Delafield, Thorne & Marsh, Delafield, Marsh, Porter & Hope, now Delafield, Marsh & Hope, 1929—. Served as capt., F.A., U.S. Army, World War I; maj. and lt. col., F.A., U.S. Army Res. Corps, 1919-33. Mem. N.Y. Legislature, 1916-17. Mem. War Dept. Claims Bd., Spl. adviser to sec. of war, 1919-20, Justice Supreme Ct. of N.Y. (by appt. of gov.), 1922. Pres. N.Y. Sch. for the Deaf 1937-47. Fellow American Bar Found. Member of the New York County Lawyers Association (pres. 1940-42), Am. Bar Assn. (mem. ho. of dels. 1942-46); N.Y. State Bar Assn., Assn. Bar of City of N.Y., War Com. of Bar of City of N.Y., 1942-46. Compliance commr., WPB, for N.Y. State and Northern New Jersey, 1942-44. mem. appeals bd. of Motion Picture Arbitration Tribunals, 1943-49. Mem. Board of Health, City of N.Y., 1945-54; pres. Church Club of N.Y., 1945-48; v.p. Protestant Council of N.Y., 1944-56; del. gen. assembly, 1952—, mem. gen. bd. Nat. Council Chs., 1954—. Republican. Episcopalian. Clubs: Union, University, Nat. Republican, Downtown (N.Y.C.); Long Island Country (Eastport, L.I.). Contbr. profl. journals. Home: 570 Park Av., N.Y.C. 21; (country) Old Lyme, Conn. Office: 15 William St., N.Y.C. 5. Died Sept. 9, 1958.

MARSHALL, Albert Edward, cons. chem. engr.; b. Liverpool, Eng., May 18, 1884; s. Edward and Marie (Sheppard) M.; student Liverpool Inst., 1896-1900; B.S., University Coll., Liverpool, 1900-04; external student South Kensington, London, 1905-06; m. Ruth Marriott Hildebrandt, Nov. 29, 1919; children—Albert Edward, Richard Sheppard. Came to U.S., 1911, naturalized citizen, 1932. Research chemist United Alkali Co., Eng., 1904-07, asst. mgr. Fleetwood Works, Eng., 1907-10; asst. mgr. Thermal Syndicate, Newcastle-on-Tyne, 1910; mgr. Thermal Syndicate, N.Y. City, 1912-16; works mgr. Davison Chem. Co., Baltimore, 1916-21; consulting chem. engr., Baltimore and New York, 1921-38; pres. Rumford (R.I.) Chem. Works, 1938-48; vice pres. Heyden Chemical Corporation, 1948-50; v.p. Gen. Aniline & Film Corp., N.Y. City, Mar.-Dec. 1942; dir. Investors Trust Co., Providence, Rhode Island Hosp. Trust Co., Providence. Pres. New England Indsl. Research Foundation, dir. New England Council; mem. corp. Northeastern U.; v.p. Coffin Sch., Nantucket, Mass.; member adv. council, Dept. of Chem. Engring., Princeton U.; mem. adv. council, R.I. State Coll. Engr. Expt. Station. Mem. Am. Inst. Chem. Engrs. (v.p. 1932-33; pres. 1934-35; dir. 1940-43), Society of Chem. Industry (chmn. 1933-34), Providence Engring. Soc. (dir. since 1941), Am. Chem. Soc., Am. Inst. Mining and Metall. Engrs., Inst. of Food Technologists, Optical Soc. of America, Royal Soc. of Arts (London). Episcopalian. Clubs: Chemists (New York); Turks Head, University (Providence); Squantum Assn. (Barrington, R.I.); Nantucket Yacht (Nantucket, Mass.). Home: 730 Elmgrove Av., Providence, R.I. Office: 603 Industrial Trust Building, Providence, R.I. Died Sept. 15, 1951; buried Providence.

MARSHALL, Arthur Lawrence, army officer; b. St. Louis, Apr. 9, 1900; s. Jacob Magruder and Lula

May (Moore) M.; student Drake Bus. Coll., Jersey City, 1915-16; m. Maude Eloise Adams, Aug. 23, 1937 (div. 1954). Cotton broker M. F. Jones, Lawton, Okla., 1920-30; ice mfr. Anderson Ice Co., Oklahoma City, 1930-36; commd. 2d lt., ORC, 1924, advanced through grades to maj., 1941; commd. lt. col., AUS, 1941, advanced through grades to maj. gen., 1954, brig. gen., U.S. Army, 1955; camp comdr., dist. comdr. Dist. Q.M., Civilian Conservation Corps, 1937-40; utilities officer, post engr. Ft. Sam Houston, Tex., 1940-42; chief of repairs, utilities, dep. to div. engr. N.E. div. Corps Engrs., Boston, 1942-43; exec. to chief engr., Caribbean Def. Command, Panama. Canal Zone, 1943-44; chief engr., asst. chief of staff, G-4, Caribbean Def. Command, 1944-46; spl. asst. to budget officer War Dept. Army Gen. Staff, Washington, 1946; budget officer, chief fsical div. O.Q.M.G., Washington, 1946-51, comptroller, dep. for adminstrn., 1951-53; comdg. gen., Q.M. Depot, Jeffersonville, Ind., 1953-54; comdg. gen., hdqrs. Q.M. Market Center System, Chgo., 1954—. Decorated Legoin of Merit. Mem. Q.M. Assn. Mason. Clubs: Union League, Illinois Athletic (Chgo.). Home: 1645 E. 50th St., Chgo. Office: 226 W. Jackson Blvd., Chgo. 6. Died Oct., 1956.

MARSHALL, Bernard Gay, author; b. North Easton, Mass., Aug. 23, 1875; s. Francis F. and Helen F. (Doten) M.; ed. high sch., Easton, and by pvt. study; m. Ida M. Conklin, July 1903; 1 dau., Harriet C. Club: Writers' Dinner (San Francisco chpt. P.E.N.). Author: Cedric the Forester, 1921; Walter of Tiverton, 1923; The Torch Bearers, 1923; Redcoat and Minute Man, 1924; Old Hickory's Prisoner, 1925, also short stories in mags. Home: 2374 Eunice St., Berkeley, Cal. Died Dec. 14, 1945.

MARSHALL, Carrington Tanner, lawyer, ex-judge; b. Zanesville, O., June 17, 1869; s. John Wesley and Rachel Ann (Tanner) M.; LL.B., Cin. Law Sch., 1892; LL.D., U. Cin., 1925, Wilmington (Ohio) Coll., 1926; m. Dora Foltz, June 1900; 1 dau., Constance (Mrs. James T. Lowe). Practiced law at Zanesville, 1892-1920, Columbus, 1933—; chief justice Supreme Court of Ohio, 1921-32. Chmn. Com. of Direction for Study of Jud. Adminstrn. in Ohio. Mem. Am. Bar Assn. (chmn. jud. sect.), Am. Law Inst. (nat. adv. com.), Ohio Judicial Council (pres.), Delta Theta Phi. Presbyn. Clubs: Athletic (Columbus); Civitan (internat. pres.). Author: A History of Courts and Lawyers of Ohio; New Divorce Courts for Old; Liberty under Law in America; Law Reforms and Law Reformers; (with Ex-Sen. Roscoe C. McCulloch) The United Nations Charter and the Constitutional Voice (pamphlet). Presiding judge U.S. Mil. Tribunal No. 3 Trial of War Crimes, Nuremberg, Germany. Home: 218 N. Parkview Av. Office: 63 S. High St., Columbus, O. Died June 28, 1958; buried Zanesville, O.

MARSHALL, George Anthony, business exec.; b. Plattsville, Ont., Can., June 19, 1892; s. Ralph and Maria (Hanthorne) M.; Faculty of Edn., Queens U., 1911; m. Alicita Gonzalez Reimundis, June 23, 1941; children—Elaine, Arminda, Donald. Salesman No. Aluminum Co., Toronto, 1912; tchr. Galt (Ont.) Collegiate Inst., 1913-15; salesman Nat. Cash Register Co., Ltd., Toronto, Can., 1920-27, mgr. The Cuba Co., Havana, 1928, mng. dir. London, Eng., 1929-33, v.p. overseas operation Nat. Cash Register Co., 1933—. Served as lt. CEF, 1915-19. Mem. Inc. Sales Mgrs. Assn., Am. Assn. Clubs: Canada, American, Highgate Golf (London); Moriane Golf (Dayton, O.). Home: Courtenay House, Courtenay Av., Highgate, London, N. 6. Office: The Nat. Cash Register Co., Ltd., London, N.W. 1, Eng. Died July 15, 1958.

MARSHALL, George Catlett, army officer; b. Uniontown, Pa., Dec. 31, 1880; s. George Catlett and Laura (Bradford) M.; student Va. Mil. Inst., 1897-1901; hon. grad., U.S. Inf.-Cav. Sch., 1907; grad. Army Staff Coll., 1908; D.Sc., Washington and Jefferson Coll., 1939; Dr. Mil. Science, Pa. Mil. Coll., 1940, Norwich U., 1942; LL.D., William and Mary Coll., 1941, Trinity Coll., 1941, Columbia U., 1947, Princeton, 1947, Harvard, 1947, Amherst Coll., 1947, Brown U., 1947, McGill Univ. (Can.), 1947, Lafayette Coll., 1947, U. of Calif., 1948; Dr. Civil Law, Oxford U., 1947; married Elizabeth Carter Coles, February 11, 1902 (died 1927); m. 2d, Katherine Boyce Tupper Brown (October 15, 1930; stepchildren—Molly B. Winn, Clifton Stevenson (dec.), Lt. Allen Tupper (killed in action Italy, May 29, 1944). Commd. 2d lt. inf., Feb. 2, 1901; promoted through grades to maj. gen., 1939; served in the Philippines, 1902-03, 1913-16 instr. Army Staff Coll., 1908-10; with A.E.F., 1917-19, Gen. Staff 1st Div., chief of operations 1st Army, chief of staff 8th Army Corps; participated in Battle of Cantigny, Aisne-Marne, St. Mihiel and Meuse-Argonne operations; a.d.c. to Gen. John J. Pershing, 1919-24; served in China, 1924-27; instr. Army War Coll., 1927; asst. comdt. Inf. Sch., 1927-32; comdr. 8th Inf., 1933; sr. instr. to Ill. Nat. Guard, 1933-36; comdg. general 5th Brig., U.S. Army, 1936-38; chief war plans div. Gen. Staff, July-Oct. 1938; deputy chief of staff U.S. Army, Oct. 1938-July 1, 1939; acting chief of staff, July 1-Sept. 1939; chief of staff with rank of general, Sept. 1939-Nov. 1945; General of the Army, Dec. 1944. Chief mil. mission to Brazil, May-June 1939. Apptd. spl. rep. of the Pres. to China with personal rank of Ambassador, Nov. 1945. Council of Fgn. Ministers, Moscow and London, U.N. Gen. Assembly, N.Y., 1947. Appointed secretary of state, Jan. 1947, resigned Jan. 1949; restored to active army list at own request, 1949; secretary defense, September 1950-51; pres. A.R.C., 1949-50. Chmn. U.S. delegation Coronation Queen Elizabeth, 1953. Awarded thanks of Congress with Gold Medal, D.S.M. with oak leaf cluster Silver Star, Victory Medal with 5 bars (U.S.); Croix de Guerre with Palm, Silver Medal of Valor (Montenegro); Grand Croix Legion of Honor (Fr.), Officer Order of Saints Maurice and Lazarus, and Officer Order of the Crown (Italy); Order of La Soledaridad (Panama); Grand Comdr. Order of Merit (Brazil); Star of Aldon Calderon (Ecuador); Gran Oficial del Sol del Peru (Peru); Grand Cross of Ouissam Alaouite (Morocco); Military Order of Merit, 1st Class (Cuba); Order del Merito (Chile); Knight Grand Cross, Order of the Bath (Brit.), Order of Suvarov, 1st Degree (USSR). Received the Theodore Roosevelt Distinguished Service Medal of Honor for 1945; Varieties clubs Humanitarian Award, 1947, Freedom House Award, 1947, Nat. Planning Assn. Gold Medal, 1949, Nat. Civic Service Award, Order Eagles, 1949; N.Y. Bd. Trade Award for distinguished service and contribution to American Way, 1949; U.S. Conf. of Mayors Award for Distinguished Pub. Service 1949; Disabled Am. Veterans, N.Y. Chpt. Citizenship Award, 1950; Distinguished Service Medal, American Legion, 1951; Four Freedoms Foundation, Award, 1952; recipient of the Nobel peace prize, 1953. Member Society of the Cincinnati, Kappa Alpha. Episcopalian. Clubs: Army and Navy, Alibi (Washington); Army and Navy Country; Army and Navy (San Francisco); Metropolitan (N.Y.). Home: Leesburg, Va.; Liscombe Lodge, Pinehurst, N.C. Office: The Pentagon, Washington. Died Oct. 16, 1959; buried Arlington Nat. Cemetery.

MARSHALL, Henry Wright, newspaper pub.; b. near Springfield, O., Jan. 29, 1865; s. Solomon Huffman and Sarah A. (Wright) M.; ed. public schools and business college; LL.D. (honorary), Purdue University, 1931; m. Laura Van Natta, February 18, 1891 (died December 1948); one son, Henry Wright. Pres. Lafayette Bridge Co., 1889-98; pres. Western Paving & Supply Co., Chicago, Milwaukee and Indianapolis, 1900-03; was also pres. Western Constrn. Co., Pub. Utilities Co., Evansville, Ind., and v.p. Evansville & Southern Ind. Traction Co. Purchased Lafayette Morning Journal, 1914, Lafayette Daily Courier, 1919, consolidated, 1920, as the Journal and Courier, of which is pres. and editor in chief; acting pres. Purdue U., 1921-22, pres. bd. trustees and chmn. exec. com., 1923-27; pres. Montmorenci Elevator Co. Mem. Ind. House of Reps., 1899-1905 (speaker 1903-05); v.p. Ind. Commn. to St. Louis Expn., 1904; chmn. bd. Internat. Live Stock Expn. of Chicago. Republican. Methodist. Elk. Club: Columbia (Indianapolis); Saddle and Sirloin (Chicago). Home: 514 Calvert Lane. Address: Sixth and Ferry Sts., Lafayette, Ind. Died Jan. 31, 1951; buried Montmorenci (Ind.) Cemetery.

MARSHALL, James A. K., banker; b. London, Eng., 1890; s. James and Mary G. M.; student pub. schs.; m. Katharine Hitchcock, 1924; children—Frank Hitchcock, James LeRoy, Mary Hitchcock, Katharine K. Mem. firm Wood Struthers & Co., N.Y. City; dir. Putnam Trust Co., Am. Surety Co., Nat. Ry. Publs., Hans, Rees Sons, Inc. Mem. N.Y. Stock Exchange. Rep. Town Meeting, Greenwich, Conn. Home: Greenwich, Conn. Office: 20 Pine St., N.Y.C. Died Nov. 4, 1951.

MARSHALL, John Noble, steel exec.; b. Pittsburgh, May 21, 1897; s. Charles D. and Dora (Noble) M.; B.S. in Civil Engring., Lehigh U., 1920; m. Marian Deutsch, Sept. 29, 1924; children—Dr. James Smith, Nancy (Mrs. Guy S. Forcier). Engaged with McClintic-Marshall Construction Company, Pittsburgh, Pa., 1920-31; Bethlehem Steel Corp., 1931-49; chmn. bd. Granite City (Ill.) Steel Company, Aug. 1, 1949—, pres., 1950-56, chmn. bd., chief exec. officer, 1956—; dir. Granite City (Ill.) Steel Co., Hughes-Foulkrod Co., Phila., Am. Zinc, Lead & Smelting Co., St. Louis, American Iron & Steel Inst., dir. 1st Nat. Bank, St. Louis Union Trust Company, St. Louis Shipbuilding and Steel Co., Federal Barge Lines, Incorporated, Granco Steel Products Co. Republican. Episcopalian. Clubs: Rolling Rock (Ligonier, Pa.); Duquesne (Pitts.); Union League (N.Y.C.); Racquet, University, Bogey, Noonday (St. Louis). Home: 625 S. Skinker Blvd., St. Louis. Office: Granite City Steel Co., Granite City, Ill. Died Apr. 15, 1958.

MARSHALL, M. Lee, business exec.; b. Marshall, Mo., June 17, 1884; s. Charles and Annie Lee (Willis) M.; ed. pub. schs., Kansas City, Mo.; LL.D. (hon.), Franklin & Marshall Coll., Lancaster, Pa.; m. Anna McCluer, Nov. 30, 1907; 1 son, Lee McCluer. Began as office boy, H. P. Wright Investment Co., Kansas City, Mo., 1901; stenographer and salesman, Swift & Co., 1903-04; mdse. broker, 1905-06; flour broker, 1907-14; v.p. Campbell Baking Co., 1915-21; United Bakeries Corp., 1922-35; president Bakeries Service Corp., 1925-35; v.p. Continental Baking Corp., 1926; chmn. bd. since 1927, pres., 1934-Jan. 1943; also chmn. all subsidiary companies; chief, Shipping Procedure Br., Services of Supply, U.S. Army, April-Sept. 1942; consultant on food to chmn. of War Prodn. Bd., Sept. 1942-May 1943; deputy adminstr., War Food Adminstrn., May-Nov. 1943; dir. Food Distrbn. War Food Adminstrn., Jan. 1944-Jan. 1945; also for same period, chmn. Requirements and Allocation Com., War Food Adminstrn.; U.S. mem. Combined Food Board; v.p. and dir. Commodity Credit Corp.; pres. and dir. Federal Surplus Commodity Corp.; chmn. U.S. Agencies Indsl. Feeding Com.; dir. and organizer, Office of Supply, and Office Marketing Services, War Food Adminstrn., Jan.-Feb. 1945. Dir. and treas., Am. Inst. of Baking; gov. Am. Bakers Assn.; exec. dir., Emergency Food Collection, 1946; trustee and treas., Am. Bakers Foundation. Trustee Mo. Valley Coll., Marshall, Mo., 1949. Mem. Christian (Disciples) Church. Mason (32°, K.T., Shriner). Clubs: Union League, New York Bakers, New York Athletic, The Pilgrims, New York Southern Society (New York); Anawamis, Golf (Rye, N.Y.); Saddle and Sirloin (Kansas City). Home: 1095 Park Av. Office: 630 Fifth Av., N.Y. City 20. Died Aug. 1, 1950.

MARSHALL, Rembert, lawyer; b. Buena Vista, Ga., Sept. 22, 1892; s. Charles Absalom and Ella (Holton) M.; B.A., Vanderbilt U., 1915; student law Vanderbilt U., 1914-15, Cumberland U., 1915; m. Harriet Smiley McDaniel, Oct. 5, 1921; 1 son, Sanders McDaniel. Admitted to Tenn. bar, 1916, and practiced law in that state until 1918; asso. with father in furniture business, Nashville, Tenn., 1919-22; asso. with law firm, McDaniel & Neely, Atlanta, Ga., 1922-28; mem. firm McDaniel, Neely & Marshall, 1928-34, Neely, Marshall & Greene, 1934-51, Marshall, Greene, Baird and Neely, 1952-54, Marshall, Greene and Neely, 1954—; division counsel for State of Georgia of Southern Railway Company, since 1934; standing master in chancery, Atlanta Div., Northern Dist. of Ga., U.S. Dist. Court, since 1928; dir. Walton Cotton Mill Co., Monroe, Ga. Served with U.S.Army, 1918. Trustee Vanderbilt U. Mem. Am. Bar Assn., Ga. Bar Assn. (past pres.), Atlanta Bar Assn., Lawyers' Club of Atlanta (past pres.), Internat. Assn. Insurance Counsel, Soc. Colonial Wars in State of Ga., Am. Law Inst., Beta Theta Pi, Phi Delta Phi. Democrat. Episcopalian. Mason. Clubs: Capital City, Piedmont Driving, Peachtree Golf (Atlanta). Home: 875 W. Pace's Ferry Rd. N.W. Office: 1040 Hurt Bldg., Atlanta 3. Died Dec 28, 1957.

MARSHALL, Rosamond Van der Zee, writer; b. N.Y.C., Oct. 17, 1902; d. Charles Hull and Florence (Hudson) Botsford; ed. Miss Eaton's Sch., Pasadena, Cal., private tutors, Lycee de Jeunes Filles, Dijon, France, Real-Gymnasium, Vienna, and U. Munich; m. 2d, Albert Earl Marshall; 1 dau., Alexandre Marshall. Ardent alpinst, having 21 new routes with amateurs to her credit in Swiss and Italian Alps and in Tatra Mountains, Poland. Mem. Alpine clubs of Switzerland and Italy. Author: L'Enfant du Cirque, 1930; La Main d'Acier, 1931; Plaisirs D'Amour, 1932; Le Vaisseau Fantôme, 1933; Vengeance du Sheik, 1934; Mystères de Chinatown, 1934; Mystères de Londres, 1935; None But the Brave, 1942. Winner N.Y. Herald Tribune $200 prize for best book in group for older children. 1942. Address: Houghton Mifflin Co. 2 Park St., Boston 7. Died Nov. 13, 1957.

MARSHALL, Thomas Worth, civil engr.; b. Economy, Ind., Mar. 24, 1872; s. Swain and Cynthia M.; B.C.E., Purdue U., 1894; m. Kathleen C. Huff, Oct. 4, 1897. In practice as civil engr., 1895—; mem. firm of Sample & Marshall, cons. engrs., 1904—. Author: Logarithmic Tables of the Measures of Length Extending from 0 to 50 Feet at Intervals of One-sixteenth of an Inch, 1902 E 15. Home: 223 Blair Rd., Takoma Park, D.C. Died Mar. 28, 1952.

MARSHALL, William Gilbert, retired electrical corporation official; born Pittsburgh, on March 17, 1888; the son of David W. and Agnes (Wallace) M.; A.B., Washington and Jefferson College, 1911, LL.D., 1942; LL.B., University Pitts., 1914; m. Belle Vance McClymonds, Dec. 9, 1914. Law dept. Pitts. Railways Co., 1916-26; dir. personnel Phila. Co., 1926-29; asst. to v.p. Westinghouse Electric & Mfg. Co., 1929-34, v.p. indsl. relations, 1954-51; retired. Apptd. chmn. labor-mgmt. policy com. WPB, 1942. Dir. Electric Building and Loan Assn.; pres., dir. Wilkinsburg Bank; adv. com. Ligonier office Mellon Nat. Bank & Trust Co. Trustee Washington and Jefferson Coll. Pres. East Boroughs Council Boy Scouts of Am. Certified tree farmer Am. Tree Farm System. Mem. Allegheny County Bar Assn. Western Pa. Safety Council, Pitts. Personnel Assn., Wilkinsburg C. of C., Kappa Sigma (Beta Delta chpt.), Phi Delta Phi. Mason. Clubs: Rotary, University, Duquesne, Rolling Rock (Pitts.). Home: Laughlintown, Pa. Died July 8, 1957; buried Homewood Cemetery, Pitts.

MARSHUTZ, Joseph H(unter), lawyer; b. Shelbyville, Ill., Aug. 10, 1877; s. William B. and Ellanora (Hunter) M.; A.B., U. Ill., 1898; LL.B., Harvard, 1902; m. Jessie Burnham, Jan. 15, 1908; 1 dau., Josephine M. (Mrs. Maurice D. James). Admitted to Wis. bar, 1902, since practiced in Milwaukee; mem. Marshutz, Hoffman & Hallows and predecessors, 1908-—; v.p., dir. Greusel Distributing Corp., 1940-—; sec., dir. Van Horne-Kaestner Leather Co., 1939-—; dir. Courteen Seed Co., Northwestern Acceptance Co., Louis Allis Co., Milsco Mfg. Co., H. Niedecken Co. Mem. Citizens' Govtl. Research Bur., Inc., Am. and Wis. bar assns., Sigma Chi. Republican. Conglist. Clubs: The Milwaukee, Milwaukee Country (Milwaukee); The Madison (Wis.). Home: 1224 No. Prospect Av. Office: 324 E. Wisconsin Av., Milw. 2. Died Nov. 20, 1956; buried Forest Home Cemetery, Milw.

MARSTON, Anson (mär'stŭn), civil engr.; b. Seward, Ill., May 31, 1864; s. George W. and Sarah (Scott) M.; grad. West Rockford (Ill.) High Sch., 1883; studied Berea Coll., 1884; C.E., Cornell, 1889; Eng.D., U. Neb., 1925, Mich. State Coll., 1927; m. Alice Day, Dec. 14, 1892; children—Morrill Watson, Anson Day. Engr. Mo.P. Ry. on location and constrn., 1889-92; in charge constrn. Ouachita River Bridge, 1891-92; prof. civil engring. Ia. State Coll., 1892-1920, dean and dir. engring. div., 1904-32, senior dean, 1932-37, dean emeritus, 1937-—. Mem. Ia. Hwy. Commn., 1904-27, chmn. 1913-15. Commd. maj. C.E., 1917, lt. col., 1918; comd. 97th Engrs. till demobilization, 1918; col. Reserves to 1944. Mem. Engring. Bd. of Review, Sanitary Dist. Chgo., 1924, 25; cons. engr. Miami, Fla., sewerage, 1925-27; mem. (Fla.) Everglades Engring. Bd. of Rev., 1927; mem. Interoceanic Canal Bd., to advise on Nicaragua Canal and enlargement Panama Canal, 1929-32; mem. Mississippi River Engring. Board Review, 1932, 33; chmn. Iowa Merit System Council, 1939-—. Mem. NRC (rep. Am. Soc. C.E.), 1919. Recipient Chanute medal Western Soc. Engrs., 1903; Fuertes medal Cornell U., 1904; Lamme medal Soc. for Promotion of Engring. Edn., 1941. Mem. Am. Soc. C.E. (dir. 1920-22, v.p. 1923-24, pres. 1929), Am. Soc. for Testing Materials, Ia. Engring. Soc. (pres. 1900), Soc. Promotion Engring. Edn. (treas. 1906-07, pres. 1914-15), Land Grant Coll. Engring. Assn. (pres. 1913-14), Am. Assn. of Land Grant Colls. and Univs. (pres. 1929), S.A.R. Mason (32°, K.T.). Club: Cosmos (Washington). Author: Sewers and Drains, 1907; Engineering Valuation (with T. R. Agg), 1936. Contbr. engring. jours. and trans. Home: Ames, Ia. Died Oct. 21, 1949; buried Ia. State Coll. Cemetery, Ames.

MARTELL, Eldred Roland, forester; b. Romeo, Mich., Sept. 4, 1901; s. Leonard Roland and Grace Mae (Eldred) M.; B.S.F., U. of Michigan, 1925, M.S.F., 1926, Ph.D., 1932; m. Ruth Ann Whittier, Oct. 21, 1925. With U.S. Forest Service in Ala., Va., Ga., Ariz. and Washington, D.C., 1926-29; teacher of forestry Pa. State Coll., 1932-35; teacher forestry and asst. dean Sch. of Forestry, U. of Idaho, 1935-40; teacher forestry, head dept. of forestry and conservation, Purdue U., since 1940. Chmn. Ind. Timber Marketing Bd.; sec.-treas. O.P.A. industry advisory com. N.C. Hardwood Lumber Region. Mem. Soc. Am. Foresters (sr. mem.; chmn. div. edn.; chmn. inland empire sub-sect.; chmn, central states sect.), Am. Forestry Assn., Sigma Xi, Xi Sigma Pi, Gamma Alpha. Contbr. articles on forest edn. and in field of research to professional publs. Home: 1958 Summit Drive, West Lafayette, Ind. Died Sept. 27, 1957.

MARTIN, Anne Henrietta, writer, feminist; b. Empire City, Nev., Sept. 30, 1875; d. William O'Hara and Louise (Stadtmuller) Martin; A.B., U. Nev., 1894; A.B., Leland Stanford Jr. U., 1896, A.M., 1897; LL.D., U. Nev., 1945; studied Columbia, univs. of London, Leipzig, 1899-1901; student Chase's Art Sch., N.Y.C., 1899-1900. Head dept. history U. Nev., 1897-1901; lectr. art history, 1901-03. Asso. with Emmeline Pankhurst in British suffrage movement, 1909-11. Pres. Nev. Equal Franchise Soc., 1911-14, organized and conducted campaign which won woman suffrage in Nev., 1914; apptd. by the gov. mem. Nev. Ednl. Survey Commn., 1915. Mem. exec. com. Nat. Am. Woman Suffrage Assn.; elected nat. chmn. Nat. Woman's Party, at 1st Woman's Party Nat. Conv., Chgo., 1916; chmn. nat. legislative com. same, 1916-18. First woman candidate for U.S. Senate, running as Ind. from Nev., 1918, 20; through mag. and newspaper articles and work in Congress, 1919-20, initiated passage of Sheppard-Towner law for protection of maternity and infancy. Western regional dir. Women's Internat. League for Peace and Freedom, 1926-31; mem. nat. bd. same, 1926-36; del. to World's Congress, same, Dublin, 1926, Prague, 1929 (chmn. commn. on Future Work). Author: Story of Nevada Woman Suffrage Campaign, 1948; also articles on polit. econ. and feminist subjects pub. in Am., Eng. publs., also articles in Ency. Britannica. Mem. Am. Hist. Assn., Kappa Kappa Gamma, Phi Kappa Phi. Clubs: Lyceum, Am. Women's (London); Nat. Arts (N.Y.C.); Women's City (San Francisco). Home: Carmel-by-the Sea, and Reno. Died Apr. 15, 1951; buried Reno.

MARTIN, Charles Fletcher, author, army officer; b. Indian Bay, Ark., Oct. 25, 1876; s. Micajab David and Sarah (Radman) M.; B.S., U.S. Mil. Acad., 1900, École Supérieure de Guerre, Paris, France, 1921; grad. advanced course Cav. Sch., 1922; spl., advanced courses Field Arty. Sch., 1923; distinguished grad. Command, Gen. Staff Sch., 1924; grad. of Army War Coll., 1929; m. Mabel G. Wood, Aug. 28, 1903; 1 dau., Kelsey Loftus (wife of Col. John W. Mott, U.S. Army). Commd. 2d lt. cav., 1900; advaned through grades to col., 1929; col. (temp.), World War I. Served in Philippines, 1901-03, 14-16, 30-33; asso. prof. modern langs. U.S. Mil. Acad., 1917-18; duty with 5th sect. Gen. Staff, AEF, in France, 1918-19; on Gen. Staff, 1924-28, chief of staff, Philippine Div., 1930-33; comdg. 7th U.S. Cav., 1929-30, 13th U.S. Cav., 1933-36; assigned to Office of Insp. Gen., Washington, 1936; exec. Office of Insp. Gen., 1937-40; ret., 1940; recalled to active status and on duty at Army War Coll., Washington, 1942-46. Additional duty as mem. The Army Ret. Bd., Washington, 1943-—. Clubs: Army and Navy (Manila, P.I., West Point, N.Y.C., Washington); Army-Navy Country (Arlington, Va.). Author: the French Verb, Conjugation and Idiomatic Use; Essentials of French Pronunciation; At West Point, French Composition (with George M. Russell); Winning and Wearing Shoulder Straps; Your Boy and the Other One in Universal Training (with Col. P. S. Bond); Medical Service in Modern War (with Col. P. S. Bond); also short stories, spl. articles. Address: care Riggs' Nat. Bank, Washington. Died May 16, 1949; buried Arlington Nat. Cemetery.

MARTIN, Charles Irving, soldier, lawyer; b. Ogle County, Ill., Jan. 25, 1871; s. William H. and Mary (Nettleton) M.; grad. Ft. Scott (Kan.) Normal Sch., 1892; LL.B., U. of Kan., 1907; m. Lou Ida Ward, Nov. 28, 1894; 1 dau., Mrs. Lillia Mae Markley. Clerk Dist. Court, Bourbon County, Kan., 1901-05; mem. Kan. Senate, 1905-09; admitted to Kan. bar, 1907, and practiced in Ft. Scott, Topeka and Wichita, Kansas; admitted to bar of Supreme Court, U.S., 1923. Enlisted as private Co. F. 1st Inf. K.N.G., Aug. 26, 1890; 2d lt. 1st Inf., Apr. 6, 1893; capt., Aug. 1894; capt. 20th U.S. Vols., Apr. 30, 1898; maj. 20th Kan. Vol. Inf., July 22, 1899; participated in 27 engagements in P.I.; col. insp. gen., K.N.G., Mar. 4, 1907; brig. gen., Apr. 29, 1909; adj. gen. of Kan., 1909-17, 1919-23. Brig. gen. U.S. Army, Aug. 5, 1917; comdg. 70th Inf. Brig., 35th Div., A.E.F.; observer with British troops in front line trenches, May 1918; comd. sector in front line trenches, July 20-Sept. 1, 1918; participated in St. Mihiel offensive; hon. discharged, Dec. 1, 1918; brig. gen. Ken. Nat. Guard, comdg. 69th Inf. Brig., 1921-32, major general commanding 35th Division, National Guard troops Kansas, Missouri and Neb., 1932-35; retired; mgr. Veteran Administration Facility, Wadsworth, Kansas, 1927-41; now assistant adjutant general of Kanas. President Adjutants General Association of U.S., 1912-23; former pres. Nat. Guard Assn. U.S.; mem. Philippine Vets., Spanish War Vets, Am. Legion, Forty and Eight, Sojourners, Mil. Order of the World War, etc. Republican. Methodist. Mason, etc. Club: Rotary. Address: 3416 Moore Av., Cheyenne, Wyo. Died May 8, 1953; buried Wadsworth Nat. Cemetery.

MARTIN, Clarence Eugene, lawyer; b. Martinsburg, W.Va., Mar. 13, 1880; s. Morgan W. and Ella Genevieve (Mulligan) M.; LL.B., U. W.Va., 1899, LL.D., 1933; LL.M., Cath. U. Am., 1901, LL.D, 1951; LL.D., Dickinson, 1933; m. Agnes G. McKenna, Sept. 28, 1904; children—Morgan V., Clarence E. (both lawyers). Admitted to W.Va. bar, 1901, and began practice at Martinsburg; city atty., 1904-06; member Martin & Seibert. Pres. W.Va. Constitutional Convention to ratify 21st Amendment, 1933. Trustee Catholic University of America; West Virginia member Conf. of Commrs. on Uniform State Laws, 1925-41; mem. W.Va. Judicial Council from 1933-41, 52-—; chmn. Housing Authority City Martinsburg, 1938-41; resigned last three to accept appointment to the U.S. Senate by Gov. Holt in 1941, to succeed Senator Neely, who resigned to become gov. of W.Va.; refused seat by two votes in favor of appointee of Gov. Neely. Mem. W.Va., Judicial Council for term ending 1958. Delegate Democratic National Convention, 1944. Member American Bar Assn. (pres. 1932-33), Am. Soc. Internat. Law (exec. com. 1934-37), Am. Judicature Soc., W.Va. (pres. 1924) and Berkeley County (pres.) bar assns., Am. Law Inst. (charter mem.), Am. Hist. Association, American Cath. Hist. Assn. (pres. 1927), Am. Acad. Polit. and Social Science. Apptd. Knight Comdr. of St. Gregory by Pope Pius, 1929. Col. on staff of gov. of Ky. Democrat. Clubs: Rotary (hon.), Opequon Golf. Home: 418 S. Queen St. Office: People Trust Bldg., Martinsburg, W.Va. Died April 24, 1955; buried Rosedale Cemetery, Martinsburg.

MARTIN, Edgar, architect; b. Burlington, Ia., February 26, 1871; s. Daniel and Celia Jane (Black) M.; advanced mathematics and mechanics of engring., Paris, 2 years.; drawing from life, Académie Colarossi, Paris; m. Berthe Eugéne Parcot. Member Schmidt, Garden & Martin, 1906-26, Pond & Pond and Edgar Martin, 1926-39. State architect of Illinois, 1917-24; supervisory architect in charge of rehabilitation of the physical plant of the Chicago Bd. of Edn., 1924-25. Architect of Centennial Memorial Bldg., Springfield, Ill.; Clin. Hosp. of U. of Ill., Chicago; Main Building, Surgical and Psychopathic bldgs., Cook County Hospital, Chicago; General Hosp., St. John, New Brunswick; Passavant Meml. Area Hosp., Jacksonville, Ill.; many other important hospitals; Sch. of Tropical Medicine, San Juan, Puerto Rico; hospital architect and consultant to the Texas Co. in the Barco Concession Development, Colombia, S.A.; consultant architect for Clinical Hosp. of U. of Venezuela, and asso. architect and engr. for the Clinico Medico, Caracas, Venezuela; Order of Maccabee's Bldg., Port Huron, Mich.; Royal Neighbors Bldg., Rock Island, Ill. The Underwriters Lab., Chicago, indsl. plants for Montgomery Ward Co., Bunte Bros., Am. Snuff Co., Acme Steel Co., Peterson Linotype Co., Chicago. Armories for the Nat. Guard at Chicago, Peoria, Danville and Kankakee, Ill. Mem. Am. Soc. C.E., A.I.A., Am. Hosp. Assn. Clubs: Arts, Chicago Athletic. Home: 76 E. Walton Pl. Office: 206 S. Michigan Av., Chgo. Died Sept. 17, 1951.

MARTIN, Edwin Manton, lawyer, industrialist; b. Washington, D.C., July 20, 1902; s. Charles Edwin and Emma (Entenman) M.; student George Washington U., 1920-21; LL.B., Georgetown U., 1925; m. Chase Black, Dec. 31, 1932; children—Chase Edwina, Mary Joan, Wm. P. Admitted to U.S. Supreme Ct., D.C. Supreme Ct., N.Y. Supreme Ct., Indiana Supreme Ct., U.S. Patent Office, U.S. Fed. Dist. Ct., Ct. of Customs and Patent Appeals. Practiced Washington, D.C., 1925-30; patent counsel Am. Locomotive Co., 1930-35, Hazeltine Corp., N.Y. City, 1935-39; sec. and gen. counsel Farnsworth Television & Radio Corp., Ft. Wayne, Ind., 1939-45, v.p., mem. board dirs., 1945-48; chmn. bd. dirs. Am. Bosch Corp., Springfield, Mass., 1947, 48; v.p. and sec., mem. bd. dirs. Farnsworth Research Corp., 1940-48, Thomasville (N.C.) Furniture Corp., 1946-48; chmn. bd. Standard Electronics Corp., Martin Investment Corp., 1949-55; gen. patent counsel Hughes Aircraft Co., 1955-—. Spl. Asst. to Atty. Gen. U.S., 1943-46, hearing officer Enemy Alien Hearing Bd., 1943-46. Mem. Patent Law Assn. Los Angeles, Ind. Supreme Ct., N.A.M. (exec. com. on patents and research), Ind. Soc. Chgo., Sigma Nu Phi. Episcopalian. Clubs: Metropolitan (N.Y.C.); Nashua Country. Address: 1414 San Remo Dr., Pacific Palisades, Cal. Died Nov. 21, 1956; buried Woodlawn Cemetery, Santa Monica, Cal.

MARTIN, Floyd A., physician, univ. prof.; born El Dorado Springs, Mo., Aug. 16, 1888; s. William Segal and Eula Ann (Logan) M.; A.B., U. of Mo., 1906-12, A.M., 1912; M.D., Johns Hopkins, 1914; m. Margaret Norman, Nov. 14, 1936. Instr. pathology, U. of Mo., 1914-15; bacteriol. Detroit Clinical Lab., 1916-22; gen. practice, 1923-42; asso. prof. pathol. and bacteriol., U. of Mo., 1942-45, medicine, 1945-47, prof. bacteriol. and preventive medicine, 1947. Mem. Am. Assn. Univ. Profs., Soc. Am. Bacteriol., Am. Pub. Health Assn., Mo. State Med. Soc., Sigma Xi, Phi Beta Pi. Republican. Home: 1319 Anthony, Columbia, Mo. Died June 2, 1954; buried El Dorado Cemetery, El Dorado Springs, Mo.

MARTIN, Frank, lawyer; b. White County, Ark., Jan. 1, 1864; s. Benjamin Franklin and Jane (Adams) M.; A.B., U. Ore., 1885; LL.B., U. Mich., 1892; m. Ella L. Hall, Dec. 27, 1893; children—Frank, Jr., Homer E. Admitted to Ida. bar, 1892, since practiced in Boise; sr. partner Martin & Martin, his sons being partners; atty. gen. Ida., 1901-02; mem. bd. regents State U., 1897-99, Ida. Code Commn., 1899-1900, Ida. State Bar Commn., 1925-27, Ida. State Jud. Council. Presdl. elector, 1912, 16, 32; Dem. candidate for U.S. senator, 1924. Mem. Am., Ida. State (twice pres.) bar assns., Sigma Delta Kappa. Democrat. Odd Fellow (grand sire of the order, 1928-29). Home: 323 Franklin St. Office: Idaho Bldg., Boise, Ida. Died May 22, 1943; buried Pioneer Cemetery, Boise.

MARTIN, Frederick LeRoy, ret. army officer; b. Liberty, Ind., Nov. 26, 1882; s. John Charles and Nancy Jane (Abbernathy) M.; B.S. in Mech. Engring., Purdue U., 1908; grad. Air Corps Tactical Sch., 1925, Command and Gen. Staff Sch., 1926; Army War Coll., 1935; m. Grace Margaret Griffiths, June 26, 1912; 1 son, John Robert. Commd. 2d lt. CAC, U.S. Army, 1908; transferred to Air Service, 1920; advanced through the grades to temp. rank brig. gen., 1937; wing comdr. 3d Wing, G.H.Q., Air Force, 1937; temp. rank major gen., 1940; comdg. gen., Hawaiian Air Force, 1940-41; comdg. gen., 2d Air Force, U.S. Army, 1942; comdg. gen. 2d Dist., Army Air Forces, Central Tech. Tng. Command, 1942-44, ret. 1944. Awarded D.S.M. and Legion of Merit. Mason. Club: Adventurers (Chgo.). Home: 641 Lorna Lane, Los Angeles. Address: War Dept., Washington. Died Feb. 24, 1954.

MARTIN, F(rederick) O(skar), engr., geologist; b. Mittweida, Saxony, Germany, Aug. 20, 1871; s. Frederick August and Anna Emmeline (Heyne) M.; Realschule, Mittweida, Saxony; Columbian Univ., D.C., 1900-02; studied Harvard and Catholic U.; m. Agnes Elizabeth Riese, Aug. 13, 1908; children—

—Anna Elisabeth (deceased), Agnes Fritzi, Mrs. Margareth Martin Hamer. Was engaged in mining and prospecting in Alaska, California, Idaho, Washington and Montana, 1894-1900; asst. in soil survey and scientist, Bur. of Soils, U.S. Dept. of Agr., 1901-05; asst. engr. Panama Canal, div. of meteorology and river hydraulics, 1905-06; engring. work and ry. contractor, 1906-09; mineral insp., U.S. Dept. Interior, 1909-19, principally in Calif. oil fields; geologist, Union Oil Co. of Calif., 1919-30, principally in Colombia, S.A.; later in private practice; mining engineer, Division of Investigations, U.S. Department Interior, 1933-41; now in private practice. Hon. consul for Austria at Los Angeles, 1932-33. Del. to Internat. Geol. Congress, Madrid, Internat. Congress de Forage, Paris, 1929. World Engring. and Power Congress, Tokio, 1929. Fellow Royal Geog. Soc., Am. Geog. Soc., Pacific Geog. Soc.; mem. Am. Inst. Mining and Metall. Engrs., Am. Assn. Petroleum Geologists, Pi Gamma Mu. Author: Explorations in Colombia, South America. Home: 2038 Pine St., South Pasadena, Cal. Died June 30, 1951.

MARTIN, Frederick Roy; b. North Stratford, N.H., Nov. 17, 1871; s. John Douglas and Caroline T. (Thompson) M.; A.B., Harvard, 1893; M.A. (hon.), Brown, 1902; LL.D., R.I. State Coll., 1925; m. Anna F. Wayne, Sept. 9, 1909 (died 1940); 1 dau., Nancy. On staff Boston Jour., 1893-98; asso. editor Providence Jour., 1898-1904, editor, 1906-12; dir. Asso. Press, 1912, asst. gen. mgr., 1912-20, acting gen. mgr., 1920-21, gen. mgr., 1921-25; dir. D. Appleton-Century Co., Bronxville Trust Co. Mem. bd. overseers Harvard, 1925-27, 40-46. Mem. S.A.R., Soc. Colonial Wars. Decorated Officer Legion of Honor (France); Knight of the Northern Star (Sweden). Clubs: Harvard (pres. 1938-41), Century (N.Y.C.). Home: 6 Brooklands, Bronxville 8, N.Y. Died Apr. 27, 1952; buried Kensico Cemetery, Valhalla, N.Y.

MARTIN, George Whitney, lawyer; b. Rochester, N.Y., Dec. 17, 1887; s. Edward Sandford and Julia (Whitney) M.; student Groton Sch., 1900-06; A.B., Harvard, 1910; m. Agnes Wharton Hutchinson, Jan. 29, 1916; children—Amy Pemberton (Mrs. Robt. W. Chapin), Julia Whitney (Mrs. F. Sargent Cheever), Agnes Wharton (Mrs. Ridley Whitaker), George Whitney, Fanny Alice (Mrs. Thomas M. Connelly). Admitted to N.Y. bar, 1913, practiced with Byrne & Cutcheon, N.Y.C., 1912-13; mem. Emmet, Marvin & Martin, N.Y.C., 1923—. Pres. Brearley Sch., 1923-45. Served as 1st lt. U.S.F.A., 1917-19; col. 104th N.Y. Inf., comdg. officer; brig. gen. 5th N.Y. Arty. Brigade, World War II. Decorated Silver Star. Democrat. Episcopalian (vestryman). Clubs: Century, Harvard, Down Town, Somerset (Boston). Contbr. popular mags. Home: Wilton, Conn. Office: 48 Wall St., N.Y.C. 5. Died Jan. 5, 1959.

MARTIN, Glenn L., airplane mfg.; b. Macksburg, Ia., Jan. 17, 1886; s. Clarence Y. and Minta (DeLong) M.; ed. Kan. Wesleyan Univ., D.Sc., 1933; hon. D.Eng., U. of Md., Case Sch. of Applied Sci., 1945; hon. D.Sc., Brown U., 1941, University of Omaha, 1945, University of Southern California, 1949; unmarried. Began in 1907 to build gliders; designed and built pusher type airplane, 1908, taught self to fly; established one of first airplane factories in U.S., 1909; constructed airplanes of various types, including monoplanes and water aircraft; held speed, altitude and endurance records, 1909-16; gave many exhibition flights in U.S. and Can., qualified for F. A.I. Aviators' Certificate, Aug. 9, 1911; holds Aviation Certificate No. 56, and Expert Aviator's Certificate No. 2, Aero Club Am.; inc. Glenn L. Martin Co., Santa Ana, Cal., 1911; moved factory to Los Angeles, 1912; built airplanes for exhbn. flying and sport use until 1913, when first order was received from War Dept. for Model TT, which was later adopted by Army for tng. purposes; produced several new models for U.S. Army, and built for the govts. of Holland and Netherlands, East Indies, 24 airplanes; factory was employing about 150 men constructing aircraft; in 1917 merged interests with Wright Co., resulting in the Wright-Martin Aircraft Corp. of New York; withdrew from Wright-Martin Co., 1917, and organized The Glenn L. Martin Co. of Cleve.; designed the first Am. designed airplane for Liberty engines and built Martin bombers; new plant completed at Cleve., 1918, co producing Martin bombers for U.S. Army, Navy and Mail planes; plant relocated at Middle River, Balt., 1929; between 1929 and 1945 built the China Clipper, Hawaiian Clipper, Philippine Clipper, B-10, British Maryland, British Baltimore, B-26 Marauder, PBM and Mars airplanes, currently producing planes for the Army and Navy and 3 types of commercial air transports; president of The Glenn L. Martin Company, 1907-49, chmn. bd., 1949-52, hon. chmn. bd., 1952—; dir. Balt. Co., 1929-33; dir. Indsl. Corp. 1933-46. Pres. East End Mfrs. Assn. of Cleve. 1924-26. Former trustee Am. Forestry Assn.; trustee N. Am. Wild Life Found., Inc.; spl. adv. bd. YMCA; former dir. Ducks Unlimited (Can.); former v.p., trustee Ducks Unlimited, Inc. Fellow Royal Aeronautic Soc. London; hon. fellow Inst. Aero. Scis., Inc. (past pres.); mem. Nat. Aero. Assn. (Ohio gov., pres. Cleve. chpt. 1924-26, life mem.), asso. mem. Soaring Soc. Am.; hon. mem. Rotary of Am., Middle River, Md., Santa Ana, Cal., and Johnstown, Pa.; mem. Soc. Automotive Engrs. (Wright Bros. Com.), Izaak Walton League Am., Md. State Game and Fish Protective Assn., Orange County Coast Assn., Am. Athletic Union (life mem.), Ak-Sar-Ben Soc., Tau Beta Pi (Md. Beta Chapt.), Delta Sigma Phi. Pres. Aircraft War Prodn. Council, 1943; pres., mem. bd. dirs. Aircraft War Prodn. Council East Coast; mem. bd. regents, U. of Md., 1945-48. Dir. Cleveland C. of C., 1924-26, Md. Commn. on Post War Planning and Development; chmn. The Alaskan Com. of Outdoor Writers Assn. of Am.; chmn. bd. dirs., All Am. Amateur Baseball Assn.; life mem. Daniel Guggenheim Medal Board of Awards; pres. League of Maryland Sportsmen. Clubs: Los Angeles Athletic, Vermejo (Los Angeles); Baltimore Country, Early Birds Maryland Flying, Annapolis Yacht, Merchants of Baltimore, The Wings, Inc., Marco Hunting and Fishing (hon.), Md. Flying, Touchdown of Washington. Recipient two medals for overocean flight from Newport to Catalina (Cal.), 1912; bars added May 10, 1927, commemorating 25th anniversary of this flight which was re-enacted in the China Clipper, designed and built by The Glenn L. Martin Co.; Collier Trophy by President Roosevelt, for greatest achievement in aeronautics in America in 1932; Civic award Advt. Club of Baltimore for business achievement in 1937; Daniel Guggenheim medal Inst. Aero. Scis. for contbn. to aero. development and prodn. of many types of aircraft of high performance, 1941; Lord and Taylor Annual Am. Design Award for 1942; Sports Afield Trophy for 1943 for America's Most Outstanding Conservationist; Forbes Mag. award as one of America's 50 foremost bus. leaders, 1947; President's Certificate of Merit for meritorious service in aiding U.S. during prosecution of World War II, 1948; Officer of French Legion of Honor, 1949. Delivered Wright Memorial Lecture before Royal Aeronautic Society, London, 1931, Van Rensselaer lecture before Drexel Inst., Phila., 1938. Founded Glenn L. Martin Coll. of Engring. and Aeronautical Sci., U. of Md., 1945. Home: 3703 Greenway. Office: Mercantile Trust Bldg., Balt. 2. Died Dec., 1955.

MARTIN, Harry Brownlow, writer; b. Salem, Ill., May 26, 1873; s. Thompson George and Jennie L. (Wren) M.; student Vincennes (Ind.) U., 1889-92; m. Susie Fuller Flanders, Dec. 3, 1900; children—Gould Bond, Doris Brownlow (Mrs. Robert V. Parks). Writer and cartoonist since 1893; with St. Louis and New York newspapers, 1893-1925; sr. mem. Martin News Service since 1925; pres. Martin Publs., Inc., since 1922. Republican. Methodist. Mason (K.T., Shriner). Mem. U.S. Golf Assn. (mus. com.). Clubs: Press, Writers and Artists, Shawnee; Westchester Country. Author: Pictorial Golf, 1927; What's Wrong with Your Game?, 1929; Golf Made Easy, 1930; Golf for Beginners, 1931; Great Golfers in the Making, 1932; Graphic Golf, 1935; Fifty Years of American Golf, 1936; St. Andrews Golf Club, 1938; Broadway—Story of a Street, 1941. Contbr. articles and drawings to newspapers and gen. mags. Creator of the Weather Bird St. Louis Post-Dispatch in 1901—Oldest of all daily newspaper features. Home: 50 Park Av., N.Y.C. 16. Died Apr. 15, 1959; buried St. Louis.

MARTIN, Harry Leland, A.R.C. exec.; b. Hollandale, Miss., Oct. 28, 1908; s. Harry Leland and Beatrice Mae (Cockroft) M.; A.B. with distinction, Miss. Coll., 1928; married June 1930 (div. July 1940); 1 son, Hal III. Internat. v.p. Am. Newspaper Guild, 1938-43, pres., 1947-53; v.p. Internat. Orgn. of Journalists, 1948-49; alternate pres. and N.A. v.p. Internat. Fedn. Journalists, 1952-54; U.S. del. to UN Freedom of Information Conf., Geneva, 1948; ofcl. cons. UN subcommn. on Freedom of Information, 1948; labor information dir. and advisor to ECA central office, Paris, 1948-52, Mut. Security Agency, 1952-53; mem. CIO exec. bd., 1950-53; nat. dir. pub. information nat. A.R.C., 1955—. Mem. Internat. Confederation Free Trade Unions Internat. Cons. Com. for Profl., Comml. and Supervisory Employees, 1951-53. Served as vol. enlisted man USN, 1942-45. Mem. Pub. Relations Soc. Am., Am. Acad. Polit. and Social Sci., Nat. Publicity Council of Health and Welfare Agencies (dir.), French-Italian Cultural Assn., Newspaper Film Critics Am. (past pres.), Memphis Newspaper Guild (founder, 1st pres.). Baptist. Clubs: American (Paris); National Press. Home: 945-M Arlington Towers, Arlington, Va. Office: Dir. Office Pub. Information, Am. Nat. Red Cross, 1730 E St., Washington 13. Died Dec. 23, 1958; buried Family Grounds, Stanton, Tenn.

MARTIN, J. H. Thayer, lawyer; b. Woodbridge, N.J., Mar. 22, 1875; s. J. H. T. and Lillie (Freeman) M.; A.B., Harvard, 1896, LL.B., 1898; student Columbia Law Sch., 1897-98; m. Edna Boice, Feb. 28, 1906; children—Carol (Mrs. Charles R. Prichard), Doris (Mrs. Gerry Keene). Admitted to N.Y. bar, 1898, N.J. bar, 1899; law clk. Lindabury, Depue & Faulks, Newark, 1898-99, Frederick F. Guild, 1900; jr. partner Guild & Martin, Newark, 1900-16; pvt. practice law, 1916-25; partner Martin & Reiley, Newark, 1925—; pres., dir. Morris & Essex R.R. Co., 1942-45. Tax commnr. of N.J., 1931-41. Twp. atty., Woodbridge, 1900-02, 11, 17-24; atty. bd. edn., 1917-53; mem. N.J. House of Assembly, 1904-05; bd. edn. City of Newark, 1950-53. Mem. Nat. Assn. Tax Administrs. (pres. 1936), Am., N.J., Essex County, Middlesex County bar assns. Home: 62 Concord St., Nashua, N.H. Office: 744 Broad St., Newark 2. Died June 26, 1958.

MARTIN, James Lawrence, investment banking; b. Boston, Mass., Jan. 28, 1878; s. James Lawrence and Lucy Jane (Black) M.; student pub. schs. Melrose, Mass.; m. Ruth Judson Hall, June 4, 1902 (dec.); children—Katherine (Mrs. Katharine Martin Shanley), Mrs. John Barker Wing. Started as clerk William Basset, Boston, Mass., 1894-96; asst. cashier Estabrook & Co., 1896-1917; mgr. Hartford office, 1907, Chicago office, 1910; est. James L. Martin & Co., Chicago, Ill., 1917, owner 1917-21; partner Pynchon & Co., N.Y. City, 1921-31; agent N.Y. Life Ins. Co., Chicago, 1933-43; now associated with Glore Forgan & Co., Investment Bankers; chmn. bd. Ashland Oil & Refining Co. 1935-45, vice-chmn. since 1945, dir. since 1919, chmn. exec. com. since 1951; cons. Ames Emerich & Co., Inc.; dir. Ashland Oil & Transportation Co., North Shore Gas Co., Birtman Electric Co. Episcopalian (sr. warden, Trinity Ch., Highland Park, Ill.). Clubs: Attic of Chicago (pres. and dir); Exmoor Country (Highland Park, Ill.). Address: 105 S. La Salle, Chgo. Died May 21, 1954.

MARTIN, James MacDonald, clergyman; b. Orange, N.J., Aug. 1, 1875; s. James and Helen Frances (Macdonald) M.; B.A., Rutgers, 1899, M.A., 1902; B.D., New Brunswick Theol. Sem., 1902; m. Hattie Belle Matthews, June 17, 1902 (died 1944); children—Paul Matthews (dec.), Elizabeth Helen, James Dean, Donald Maynard, Palmer Luther, Charles Matthews; married 2d, Gertrude Augusta Lovejoy, 1946. Ordained ministry Ref. Ch. in America, 1902; pastor North Paterson, N.J., 1902-05, Spring Valley, N.Y., 1905-08, Broadway Ch., Paterson, N.J., 1908-15, Hudson, N.Y., 1915-21, Third Ch., Holland, Mich., 1921-34, Church of the Master, N.Y. City, 1934-44, Manor Ch., N.Y.C., 1944-53, Winfield, Woodside, L.I., 1945—. Permanent clk. Gen. Synod Ref. Ch. in Am., 1920-54; pres. Particular Synod of N.Y., 1920-21; stated clk. Classis N.Y., Reformed Ch. in Am., 1935-54; pres. Bronx Clergy Assn., 1941-42, Ref. Ministers Clergy Club, 1953—. Home: 42-11 67th St., Woodside, L.I. N.Y. Died Nov. 9, 1956.

MARTIN, John, coll. prof., lectr.; b. Lincoln, Eng., May 13, 1864; s. John and Ann (Winch) M.; student Nat. Normal Sch., London, 1883-84; B.Sc., London U., 1889; LL.D., Rollins Coll., Winter Park, Fla., 1936; m. Prestonia Mann, Sept. 1, 1900. Came to U.S., 1898, naturalized, 1903. Tchr. London pub. schs., 1885-94; prof. East London Tech. Coll., 1894-99; lectr., dir. League for Polit. Edn., N.Y.C., 1900-02; free lance writer, traveling lectr., 1903-15; lectr., cons. Internat. Relations, Rollins Coll., 1930—; dir. City Housing Corp., N.Y.C. Mem. N.Y. Bd. of Edn., 1908-16. Dir. League Polit. Edn. N.Y. Mem. London Fabian Soc. (mem. exec. com.). Democrat. Club: University (Winter Park, Fla.). Author: Democracy and Dictators Today, 1935. Home: Genius Dr., Winter Park, Fla. Died Apr. 6, 1956.

MARTIN, John C(unningham), ex-congressman; b. Salem, Ill., Apr. 29, 1880; s. Benjamin Estill and Florida Ann (Cunningham) M.; ed. Salem pub. schs., Ill. Coll., Jacksonville, Ill.; m. Margaret Bills, May 16, 1914; children—Mary Ann, John, Barney. Pres. Salem Nat. Bank 1933—; dir. Fed. Res. Bank, St. Louis, 1922-32, State treas. of Ill., 1933-35, 1937-39; chmn. Ill. State Tax Commn., 1935-36; chmn. Ill. Emergency Relief Commn., 1935-38; mem. 76th Congress, Ill. at large. Democrat. Home: Salem, Ill. Died Jan. 1952.

MARTIN, John Wellborn, ry. exec., ex-gov. Fla.; b. Plainfield, Fla., June 21, 1884; s. John Marshall and Willie Martin (Owens) M.; student pub. schs.; m. Lottie Wilt Pepper, Jan. 30, 1907. Admitted to Fla. bar, 1914; practice of law, Jacksonville, 1914-23; mayor, Jacksonville, 1917-23; gov. Fla., 1925-29; trustee Fla. East Coast Ry., 1942—. Mason (32°, Shriner). Clubs: Florida Yacht, Timuquana Country. Home: 3664 Richmond St., Jacksonville 4. Office: Florida Title Bldg., P.O. Box 1259, Jacksonville 1, Fla. Died Feb. 22, 1958.

MARTIN, Joseph I., ret. army officer; b. Chicago, Feb. 1, 1894; s. George William and Justine (David) M.; M.D., Chicago Hosp. Coll. of Medicine, 1918; grad. Army Med. Sch., 1925, (hon.) Med. Field Service Sch., 1926, Inf. Sch., advanced course, 1928, Command and Gen. Staff Sch., 1934, Army War Coll., 1940; m. Margaret Anna Schander, Apr. 17, 1914; children—Justine Estelle (Mrs. Paul R. Smith), George William, Dolores Amanda (wife of Lt. Col. Orville Tackett), Joseph Ignatius, Robert Edward. Physician and surgeon, 1918—; commd. 1st lt., U.S. Army, 1918, advancing through the grades to maj. gen., 1949; served as med. officer at Ft. Riley, Kan.; Camp Grant, Ill.; Sternberg Gen. Hosp., Manila, P.I.; Ft. Sam Houston, Tex.; Army Med. Center, Washington, D.C.; Carlisle Barracks, Pa.; Ft. Snelling, Minn.; Ft. Des Moines, Ia.; Ft. Benning, Ga.; Ft. Leavenworth, Kan.; Ft. Sherman, also

Quarry Heights, Canal Zone; Army War Coll., Washington, D.C.; 6th Corps Area, Chicago; with 5th Army overseas; Service World War II; (est. med. dept. Replacement Training Center, Camp Grant, Ill., 1940; chief surgeon, 5th Army in Africa and Italy, 1943-45, Western Pacific, 1945, Gen. Hdqrs., Pacific, 1946; commandant Med. Field Service Sch., Ft. Sam Houston, Tex. 1947-53; chief surgeon U S Army, Europe, 1953-55, ret. Decorated Victory Medals, World War I, II, Am. Legion of Merit, Pre-Pearl Harbor, Am. Defense, European-North African, Pacific, Japanese Occupation, Typhus Commn., Distinguished Service Medal; Comdr. (British Empire); Croix de Guerre (France); Italian Silver Star, Royal Order of the Crown (Italy); Brazilian Medal of War; Polish Order Crossed Swords; Czechoslovakian Order Mil. Cross. Mem. A.M.A., Assn. Mil. Surgeons U.S. (pres.). Moose, K.C. Home: 2244 Juliet Dr., Santa Rosa, Cal. Died Apr. 13, 1957; buried Arlington, Va.

MARTIN, Lester, textile mfr.; b. Wills Point, Tex., Aprl 7, 1907; Samuel and Sarah (Arkin) M.; m. Sylvia Hur, Nov. 6, 1932; children—Jane L. (Mrs. Ginberg), Robert M., Alana. With Consolidated Textile Co., Inc., 1942-—, pres., dir., 1950-—; with Bates Mfg. Co., 1955-—, pres., 1957-—; pres., chmn. Mojud Co., Inc., N.Y.C., 1957-—. Home: 1185 Park Av. Office: 112 W. 34th St., N.Y. City. Died Apr. 1959.

MARTIN, Mabel Wood, writer; b. Toronto, Can.; d. William and Ann Amelia (Loftus) Doyle; due to death of parents in her childhood, raised by uncle, Henry Holden Wood, name changed to Wood; desc. on maternal side of Loftus family of England, of which the Marquis of Ely is head; ed. by governess at home, in San Francisco, Calif., and trained as writer under Ambrose Bierce; m. Col. Charles F. Martin, U.S. Army; 1 dau., Kelsey Loftus (wife of Col. John W. Mott, U.S. Army). Contbr. short stories to Scribner's, McClure's, Everybody's, Smart-Set, Cosmopolitan, Collier's Weekly, etc.; traveled widely in China, Japan and in Europe. Protestant. Author: Sentinel at the Western Gate (serial novel), 1915; The Green God's Pavilion (novel), 1920; The Lingering Faun (novel), 1927. Clubs: Sulgrave, Woman's Nat. Democratic (Washington). Address: The Riggs Nat. Bank, 1503 Pennsylvania Av., Washington. Died June 13, 1956; buried Arlington Nat. Cemetery.

MARTIN, Mellen Chamberlain, lawyer; b. Three Oaks, Mich., July 26, 1886; s. Moses Mellen and Mary (Pierce) Martin; LL.B., Univ. of Mich., 1912; m. Clara Trueblood, Aug. 22, 1914; children—Edward Trueblood, Marilyn (Mrs. Philip Mallen). Admitted to Mich. Bar, June 1912, Ill. Bar, Oct. 1912; asso. with law firm of Kirkland, Fleming, Green, Martin & Ellis, Chicago, since 1912, active partner since 1918; dir. and gen. counsel Lake Shore Nat. Bank since 1920. Served as legal adviser Exemption Bd. Selective Service, Chicago, 1917-18; mem. Chicago Nat. Guard Commn. and of Civic and Social Commn., 1920. Mem. Am., Ill., and Chicago bar assns., Chicago Law Inst., Theta Delta Chi. Republican. Conglist. Clubs: Legal, Law, Chicago, University, Mid-Day, Tavern, Commonwealth (Chicago); Lawyers (Univ. of Mich.); Indian Hill Country (Winnetka, Ill.); Golf and Tennis, Riding and Hunt (Tryon, N.C.). Home: 190 E. Pearson St., Chicago 11. Office: 33 N. La Salle St., Chgo. 2. Died May 6, 1952; buried Meml. Park Cemetery.

MARTIN, Motte, missionary; b. Marlin, Tex., Jan. 1, 1879; s. John Alfred and Alla (Slater) M.; A.B., Austin Coll., Sherman, Tex., 1900, D.D., 1911; B.D., Union Theol. Sem. Richmond, Va., 1903; m. Bess Lilley Sentell, Dec. 31, 1908; 1 son, George Motte. Ordained to ministry Presbyn. Ch. South, 1903; missionary of Presbyn. Ch. to Luebo, Kasai Dist., Kongo Free State (now Congo Belge), Africa, 1903-—. Pres. Congo Protestant Council, 1938, 39. Active in stopping natives rebellion during World War. Escort to King Albert and Queen Elizabeth of Belgium at official opening of Congo branch of Cape-to-Cairo Ry., 1928. Decorated Chevalier d l'Ordre Royal du Lion, 1925, Medaille Commemorative for distinguished service, 1930, by King Albert; Chevalier d l'Ordre de la Couronne, 1935, by King Leopold III of Belgium. Contbr. to church papers in English and Buluba-Lulua. Address: Box 330, Nashville. Died Sept. 15, 1946; buried Luebo, Belgian Congo, Africa.

MARTIN, Riccardo (Hugh Whitefield), operatic tenor; b. Hopkinsville, Ky., Nov. 18, 1881; played violin as a child; began music study at early age in Germany and Italy; later studied composition and orchestration under Edward MacDowell at Columbia; studied singing under Sbriglia and Escalaïs, Paris, under Lombardi, Florence, Italy. Début as Faust, at Nantes, France, 1904; sang Andrea Chénier, Verona, Italy, 1905, at Milan, 1906; made initial appearance U.S. as Canio, in Pagliacci, French Opera House, New Orleans; touring U.S., 1906-07; mem. Met. Opera Co., 1907-15, Boston Opera Co., 1915-17; sang 3 grand seasons 1910, 11, 20), Royal Opera, Covent Garden, London; Centennial season, Mexico City, 1910; mem. Chgo. Opera Co., 1920. Composer of songs, choruses, also several pieces for orchestra. Has made several concert tours as recitalist. Mem. Nat. Inst. Social Scis. Address: care Harry and Arthur Culbertson, 33 W. 42d St., N.Y.C. Died Aug. 11, 1952.*

MARTIN, Royce George, corp. official; b. June 7, 1884, Clint, Texas; s. George W. and Frances Ann (Boyd) M.; ed. St. Patrick's Academy, St. Aloysius Acad.; m. Doris C. Brown (deceased); children—Louise, Doris. Began in production dept., Western Electric Co., 1905; later associated with Felt & Tarrant. Pres. and gen. mgr. Automobile Mortgage Corp. of Texas, 1914-21; pres. and gen. mgr., Safe-T-Stat Corp., 1922. President The Electric Auto-Lite Co., 1934-—; pres. and chmn. bd., 1944-—. Clubs: Inverness, Carranor Hunt, Polo, Toledo Country (Toledo); Cloud, Twenty-one (New York); Detroit Athletic (Detroit); Stoner Creek, Elkhorn Beagles (Kentucky); Bath, Old Guard Soc. of Palm Beach Golfers, Indian Creek Country (Florida). Address: P.O. Box 931, Toledo 1. Died May 1, 1954; buried Cincinnati.

MARTIN, Santford, newspaper editor; b. Hamptonville, N.C., May 30, 1886; s. Asbury Jackson and Victoria (Brown) M.; grad. Yadkinville (N.C.) Normal Sch., 1906; A.B., Wake Forest (N.C.) Coll., 1909, grad. law course, 1910; Litt.D. (hon.), Western Carolina College, 1954; m. Ava Michael Poole, Oct. 2, 1910; children—Edwina, Santford. Admitted to N.C. bar, 1910; editor Winston-Salem Journal, 1912-52, Sunday Journal since 1952, Twin City Sentinel, 1927-52, editorial page, 1952-54, editor emeritus Winston-Salem Jour. and Sentinel newspapers, 1954-—; pvt. sec. Gov. of N.C., 1917-20. N.C. state dir. Four-minute Men, 1917-18; mem. N.C. State Dept. Conservation and Development, 1926-43; chmn., 1941-43; chmn. N.C. State Bd. Edn., 1954-—. Mem. Winston-Salem Found. Com.; trustee N.C. Bapt. Hosp., 1947-51. Mem. Internat. Press Inst., Am. Soc. Newspaper Editors, N.C. Press Assn. (honorary life member). Democrat. Baptist. Mason. Author: Letters and Papers of Governor Thomas Walter Bickett, 1921. Winner N.C. Press Assn. annual award for best editorial written in North Carolina, 1942. Home: 831 Roslyn Rd. Office: Journal and Sentinel, Marshall St., Winston-Salem, N.C. Died Apr. 14, 1957.

MARTIN, Thomas Paul, physician; b. Shippensburg, Pa., Oct. 30, 1864; s. Joab and Louie (Olivia) M.; student State Normal Sch., Shippensburg; M.D., Coll. Phys. and Surg., Balt., 1887; m. Janet Wilson, Jan., 1896. Practiced at Pitts., 1887-88, since at Taos, N.M. Sec. Territorial Bd. of Health, N.M., 1896-1904. Mem. A.M.A., N.M. Med. Soc., S.A.R. Republican. Mason (32°), Elk. Home: Taos, N.M. Deceased.

MARTIN, T(homas) T(heodore), evangelist; b. Smith County, Miss., Apr. 26, 1862; s. Matthew Thomas and Annie (Strickland) M.; A.B., Miss. Coll., Clinton, 1886; Th.M., So. Bapt. Theol. Sem., Louisville, 1896; m. Ivy Manning, June 1, 1905; children—Thomas Todd, Bessie Ivy, Dixie May, Martha Ray, Theodore K. Prof. natural sciences Baylor Female Coll., Belton, Tex., 1886-88; ordained to Bapt. ministry, 1888; pastor Glenview, Ky., 1890-91, Leadville, Colo., 1891-93, Canon City, Colo., 1894, Glenview, Ky., 1895-96, Beattyville, 1896, Cripple Creek, Colo., 1897-1900; in evangelistic work 1900; dean School of Evangelism, Union U., Jackson, Tenn., 1919-30; founder at Cooke Springs, Ala., 1930, Am. Sch. Evangelism. Prohibitionist. Author: Gems from the Sick Room, 1897; The Conversion of Ruth Wyatt, 1898; God's Plan with Men, 1912; Redemption and the New Birth, 1913; The New Testament Church, 1917; The Second Coming of Christ, 1921; Married Life, Its Present Day Dangers and Evils, 1921; Going to Hell in Droves, 1921; Heaven, Hell, and Other Sermons, 1923; Hell and the High Schools, 1923; The Evolution Issue, 1923; Evolution or Christ°, Christ or Hell, 1924; The Inside of the Cup Turned Out, 1932; The Communist Party, 1932. Home: Blue Mountain, Miss. Died May 23, 1939; buried Gloster, Miss.

MARTIN, V(erey) G., coll. prof.; b. Miss., Jan. 14, 1891; s. Henry Edmund and Fannie Catherine (Lofton) M.; A.B., Miss. Coll., 1912; grad. student agr., Miss. Agr. and Mech. Coll., 1912-13; M.S., Cornell U., 1927; m. Eva Myrtle Jones, May 11, 1917; children—Verey G., Nancy Davis (Mrs. Bernhard Francis McAvoy, Jr.), Eva Jean (Mrs. Robert Whittaker Jones), Elizabeth Patricia (Mrs. Donald Lee Garey). Engaged as teacher of agriculture high sch., 1914-20; county agrl. agent, 2 yrs.; asso. prof. agrl. edn., Miss. State Coll., 1920-23, prof., head agrl. edn. dept., since 1923, dean sch. of edn., dir. summer session, 1935-37; vis. prof. agrl. edn., Colo. State Coll., summer 1938, La. State U., summer 1940, vis. prof. Okla. Agr. and Mech. Coll., summer 1951. Teacher training rep., Southern Region Com. on Responsibilities and Relationships in Teacher Training and Supervision; mem. Nat. Com. on Objectives in Vocational Agr.; spl. editor, Evening Schs., Agricultural Education Mag., 1934-39; consultant on study, Pub. Edn. in Miss., 1926; consultant nat. study, Negro Land-Grant Colls., 1947-50; edn. specialist, A.A.A., Southern Region, summers 1934, 36-38; chmn. Nat. Com. on Tchr. Edn. in Agrl. Edn., 1954; mem. nat. bd. trustees Future Farmers Am. Found., 1956-57. Mem. Am. Vocational Assn., Miss. Edn. Assn., Phi Delta Kappa, Alpha Zeta, Alpha Tau Alpha. Ind. Democrat. Meth. Mason. Co-author: (play) Mr. Farmers Meets the Tariff. Compiler: Digest of a Nat. Study on Instrn. on Food Conservation under the Food Prodn. War Training Program, 1947. Contbr. articles to agrl. edn. and agrl. jours. Address: State College, Miss. Died Mar. 7, 1956; buried Antioch Cemetery, Rankin County, Miss.

MARTIN, Walton, surgeon; b. S.I., N.Y., Feb. 4, 1869; s. Kingsley and Clementine Walton (Allen) M.; Ph.B., Sheffield Sci. Sch. (Yale), 1889; M.D., Coll. of Physicians and Surgeons (Columbia), 1892; m. Charlotte Hunnewell, Jan. 28, 1921. Practiced, N.Y.C., 1895-—; asst. demonstrator anatomy, Coll. of Phys. and Surg., Columbia, 1895-1901, instr. surgery, 1901-09, asso. in surgery, 1909-13, prof. clin. surgery 1913-—, asso. prof. surgery 1919-—. Fellow A.C.S., Am. Surg. Assn.; mem. N.Y. Surg Soc., Am. Soc. Thoracic Surgery. Established hosp., Juilly, France, 1914-15. Clubs: University, Century Association. Author: Quiz Compend of Chemistry, 1899. Reviser: Green's Pathology, 1897. Translator: Vol. on Surgery of the Head (from Van Berman's Surgery), 1903. Contbr. article on infection in relation to surgery, in Nelson's and in Lewis's Surgery, 1944. Home: Cornwall, Conn. Office: 230 E. 49th St., N.Y. C. Died June 18, 1949; buried Cornwall, Conn.

MARTIN, William Logan, lawyer; b. Scottsboro, Ala., Feb. 20, 1883; s. William Logan and Margaret (Ledbetter) M.; B.S., U.S. Mil. Acad., 1907; LL.B., U. of Ala., 1908; married Thelma C. Sloss, June 24, 1954. Commissioned second lieutenant U.S. Army, June 14, 1907; resigned Aug. 15, same yr.; admitted to Ala. bar, 1908, and practiced in Montgomery; asso. in practice with brother, Thomas W. Asst. pros. atty., Montgomery County, 1909-10; asst. atty. gen. of Ala., 1911-15, atty. gen. term 1915-19 (resigned); apptd. judge 15th (Montgomery) Jud. Circuit, Feb. 3, 1919; settled at Birmingham upon expiration of term, Nov. 18, 1920; mem. firm Martin & Blakey; dir., gen. atty. Ala. Power Co. Commd. maj. aviation sect., Signal Corps, U.S. Army, 1917, trans. to F.A., 1918; hon. disch., 1919. Mem. Am. (state del. 1937-—, gov. 1943-46, chmn. com. employment and social security 1946-49, v.p. Assn. Endowment 1953-—), Ala. (pres. 1946-47), Birmingham bar assns., Assn. Bar City N.Y., Assn. Grads. U.S. Mil. Acad. (trustee 1954-—), S.A.R., Soc. Colonial Wars (dep. gov. Ala. 1956-57), Phi Delta Theta, Theta Nu Epsilon, Phi Delta Phi. Presbyterian. Clubs: Mountain Brook, Army and Navy (Washington). Author publs. including: Political Parties; The Amending Power. Home: 2500 Lanark Rd. Office: 600 N. 18th St., Birmingham 3, Ala. Died Feb. 25, 1959.

MARTIN, William McChesney, banker, atty.; b. Lexington, Ky., July 2, 1874; s. Thomas L. and Hettie (McChesney) M.; A.B., Washington and Lee U., 1895; LL.B., St. Louis Law Sch. (Washington U.), 1900; m. Mary Rebecca Woods, Nov. 21, 1905; children—William McChesney, Malcolm Woods. With L. &N. R.R., St. Louis, 1896-99; with Mississippi Valley Trust Co., 1900-14, advancing to v.p.; chmn. and fed. reserve agt. Federal Reserve Bank, St. Louis, 1914-29, gov., 1929-36, president, 1936-41; now member law firm Martin, Peper & Martin. Chmn. dist. com. on capital issues, Federal Reserve District No. 8, World War I. Trustee Washington and Lee University. Member American, Missoui and St. Louis bar associations. Phi Beta Kappa. Clubs: Noonday, Bogey, Inc. Author: Modern Banking and Trust Company Methods, 1920; also various pamphlets on banking, banking law and the federal reserve system. Home: 525 Clara Av. Office: 407 N. 8th St., St. Louis. Died Feb. 28, 1955; buried Bellefontaine Cemetery, St. Louis.

MARTIN, William Thompson, lawyer; b. Glasgow, Ky., Mar. 25, 1823; s. John Henderson and Emily Monroe (Kerr) M.; grad. Centre Coll., Ky., 1840; m. Margaret Dunlop Conner, Jan. 5, 1854. Studied law in father's office, Vicksburg, Miss.; admitted to bar, 1844; dist. atty., 1st jud. dist., Miss., 1845-49. Whig in politics prior to Civil war. Served from capt. to maj. gen. Confederate States Army, 1861-63; in siege of Yorktown, battle of Williamsburg (wounded), Seven Pines, 7 days' battles nr. Richmond, Antietam; ordered west after Md. campaign, was in battles at Spring Hill, Tenn., Shelbyville, Chickamauga, Clinch River, Maryville, siege of Knoxville, Fair Garden and Mossy Creek; with Gens. Johnston and Hood from Dalton to the fall of Atlanta; surrendered with Gen. Dick Taylor's command, May, 1865. Del. to State Constitutional Conv., 1865; elected to Congress from 1st Miss. dist., 1868, but was denied the seat; del. Dem. Nat. convs., 1868-1880; mem. State senate, 1882-94. Trustee State U., 1876-88; v.p. for Miss. So. Hist. soc.; pres. bd. trustees Jefferson Coll. (Miss.), 1880-88; mem. State Constitutional Conv., 1890. Completed in 1884, as sole pres. of the co., the N.J.&C. R.R. from Natchez to Jackson. Home: Monteigne, Natchez, Miss. Died Mar. 9, 1910; buried Natchez.

MARTIN DU GARD, Roger, writer; born Paris, France, 1881. Author: (books) Devenir, 1907; Jeau Barois, 1913; Les Thibault (9 vols.), 1922-39; La Confidence Africaine, 1931; Vieille France, 1933; Recollections of André Gide, 1953; Postman, 1954; (plays) Le Testament du Père Lebeu, 1914; La Goufle, 1928; Un Taciturne, 1932. Awarded Nobel prize for lit. 1937. Home: Bellême, Orne, France. Died Aug. 1958.

MARTINU, Bohuslav (mär'tē-nōō), composer; b. Policka, Czechoslovakia, Dec. 8, 1890; s. Ferdinand and Karolina (Klimes) M.; student Conservatory of Prague; m. Charlotte Quennehen, Mar. 21, 1932. Came to U.S., Mar. 1941. Vis. prof. in composition, Princeton U., until 1953; now lives in France. Among his later compositions: (for orchestra) Prelude en forme de Scherzo; Fantaisies Symphoniques (Symphony No. 6.); Toccata et Due Canzoni; Sinfonietta Giocoas (piano and orchestra); Sinfonietta La Jolla Violin Concerto- Rhapsody Concerto (viola and orchestra); Double Violin Concerto; for chorus: Five Czech Madrigals; three sacred and three secular Czech Madrigals; chamber music: Trio No. 2 (violin, cello and piano); Quartet (oboe, violin, cello and piano); String Quartet No. 7; for two pianos: Three Czech Dances; operas: The Marriage; What Men Live By; Comedy on the Bridge (Award 1951); Greek Passion; La Locandiera (Goldoni text); symphonies: Julietta (G. Neveus) three acts; Symphonies I to VI, Military Marches. Recipient N.Y. Critics Circle award, 1955. Address: care Boosey & Hawkes, 30 W. 57th St., N.Y.C. 19. Died Aug. 1959.

MARVEL, Josiah, ex-ambassador, lawyer; b. Wilminton, Del., Nov. 26, 1904; s. Josiah and Mary (Jackson) M.; A.B., Yale, 1927, LL.B., Harvard, 1931; m. Gwladys Hopkins Whitney, Feb. 22, 1943; children—Josiah, Jr., Jonathan Hopkins. Partner, firm, Marvel & Morford, Wilmington, 1932-49, Logan, Marvel & Boggs, Wilmington, 1950-—; McNutt, Marvel & Dudley, Washington, 1950; sec. of State, Del., 1938-41; apptd. E.E. and M.P. to Denmark, 1946; apptd. A.E. and P. to Denmark, 1947; chmn., Internat. Claims Commn., Dept. of State, 1950-53. Enlisted as pvt. in Army and advanced through ranks to capt., Southwest Pacific, 1945. Clubs: Wilmington (Del.); Harvard (N.Y.C.); Metropolitan (Washington). Editor: Marvel on Delaware Corporations, 1932. Home: Greenville, Del. Office: Continental American Bldg., Wilmington, Del.; also Barr Bldg., Washington. Died Dec. 29, 1955; buried Centreville, Del.

MARVIN, George, editor; b. Brewster, N.Y., July 31, 1873; s. Samuel W. and Susan (Decker) M.; A.B., Harvard, 1899; Harvard Law Sch., 1902-03; unmarried. Master Groton (Mass.) Sch., 1900-02, 04-07; asst. instr. in English, Harvard, 1902-03; with U.S. Consular Service, China, 1907-08; in service Chinese Govt., 1908-10; sec. syndicate of N.Y. banks organized for Chinese loans, 1909; with U.S. Embassy, Paris, France, 1910; editorial writer N.Y. Press, at times, 1911-13; with World's Work, 1914, now Washington editor same, and editor in chief Spanish World's Work (quarterly). Fellow Royal Geog. Soc.; mem. Asiatic Soc., Delta Kappa Epsilon, Phi Delta Phi, etc. Republican. Presbyn. Clubs: Harvard, Metropolitan, National Press, Chevy Chase (Washington); Harvard (N.Y.C.); Varsity, Delta Phi (Cambridge, Mass.). Contbr. to mags. Home: 1718 H St. N.W., Washington. Died Dec. 22, 1955

MARVIN, Henry Howard, prof. of physics; b. Grinnell, Ia., Aug. 14, 1884; s. Francis Park and Martha (Longley) M.; B.S., Grinnell Coll., 1906; Ph.D., Columbia, 1912; m. Alma Ethel Wright, Sept. 9, 1911; children—Margaret Jane (dec.), Burton Wright, James Francis, Jean Alice (Mrs. Harold T. Amrine), David Keith, Henry Howard, Ruth Janet. Teacher Grinnell (Ia.) High Sch., 1906-08; instr. in physics, Columbia, 1911, Mass. Inst. Tech., 1911-12; asst. prof. of physics, Tufts Coll., 1912-17, prof., 1917-19; prof. physics, U. of Neb., since 1919, chmn. dept. 1922-49; lecturer in physics, U. of Minn., 1941-42. Mem. A.A.A.S., Am. Physical Soc., Am. Physics Teachers Assn., Neb. Acad. of Sciences (pres. 1930), Phi Beta Kappa, Sigma Xi. Home: 5310 Colby St., Lincoln 4, Neb. Died July 24, 1954.

MARVIN, Langdon Parker, lawyer; b Albany, N.Y., Sept. 16, 1876; s. Selden Erastus and Katharine Langdon (Parker) M.; grad. The Albany Acad., 1894; A.B. magna cum laude, Harvard, 1898, A.M., 1899, LL.B. cum laude, 1901 (editor Harvard Law Review); m. Mary Eliot Vaughan, Dec. 9, 1916; children—Diana Gibson, Langdon, Jr. sec. to Justice Horace Gray, Supreme Court, U.S., 1901-02; to Hon. Elihu Root while mem. Alaskan Boundary Tribunal, London, 1903; asso. with Carter & Ledyard and Carter, Ledyard & Milburn, N.Y.C., 1902-07; mem. Rand, Moffatt & Webb, 1908-09, Jerome & Rand, 1910, Marvin, Hooker & Roosevelt (Franklin D.), 1911-20, Emmet, Marvin & Roosevelt, 1920-24, Emmet, Marvin & Martin, 1924-—; dir. Met. Life Ins. Co. Mem. Plattsburg Mil. Tng. Camp, 1915; maj. dep. commr. A.R.C. Commn. for Gt. Britain, A.E.F., 1918; thereafter maj. M.I., O.R.C., U.S. Army. Trustee Boys' Club, N.Y. Mem bd. overseers Harvard, 1913-19, 1921-27, 1938-44. Mem. Harvard Fund Council, 1925-30. 1933-39. Mem. Mil. Tng. Camps Assn., U.S. (exec. com., past sec.), Asso. Harvard Clubs, (pres. 1922-23), Harvard Alumni Assn. (pres. 1927-28), Harvard Law Sch. Assn. N.Y.C. (pres. 1930-31), Soc. of N.Y. Hosp. (gov., pres. 1942-46) English-Speaking Union (dir.), The Pilgrims of the U.S. (exec. com.), Am. Bar Assn., N.Y. State Bar Assn., Assn. Bar City N.Y. (vice-pres. 1929-31), Am. Soc. Internat. Law, Am. Law Inst., Phi Beta Kappa (v.p. Harvard chpt., 1932-34; pres. 1934-36), Mil. Order Loyal Legion of U.S. Nat. Vet. of Fgn. Wars. Republican (com. N.Y. County). Episcopalian Warden, Church of the Epiphany, N.Y.C.; mem. vestry St. Mary's-by-the-Sea, North East Harbor, Me. Clubs: Harvard (sec., 1907-17, vice pres., 1929-32; pres., 1932-36), Knickerbocker, Downtown (N.Y.C.); Metropolitan (Washington); Harvard (Boston); Faculty (Cambridge, Mass.); Pot and Kettle (Bar Harbor). Home: 133 E. 64th St., N.Y. City 21. Office: 48 Wall St., N.Y.C. 5. Died Oct. 14, 1957.

MARVIN, Thomas O., ex-tariff commr.; b. Portsmouth, N.H., Dec. 10, 1867; s. Thomas E. O. and Anne Maria (Lippitt) M.; prep. edn. Portsmouth High Sch.; B.D., Tufts Coll., 1888, later post-grad. course; m. Flora Myrick Sugden, Nov. 15, 1894; children—Marion (Mrs. Charles M. Dale), Mrs. Marjorie M. Hartford. Minister of Universalist chs. at Albany, N.Y., Spencer, Mass., until 1894; engaged in newspaper work, lit. editor Boston Journal, editorial writer; sec. Home Market Club, Boston, 1911-21; editor The Protectionist, 1911-21; mem. U.S. Tariff Commn., 1921-30, vice chmn., 1921, chmn., 1922-30. Trustee Tufts Coll. Mem. Hist.-Geneal. Soc. of Mass., Bostonian Soc., N.H. Hist. Soc., S.R., Theta Delta Chi. Republican. Club: National Press (Washington). Home: Portsmouth, N.H. Died Aug. 21, 1952; buried Marvin Family Cemetery, New Castle, N.H.

MARX, Alexander, educator; b. Elberfeld, Germany, Jan. 29, 1878; s. George and Gertrud (Simon) M.; grad. gymnasium, Koenigsberg, 1895; studied Koenigsberg U., Berlin U., and Rabbiner-Seminar; Ph.D., Koenigsberg, 1903; D.H.L., Jewish Institute of Religion, 1938, Hebrew Union College, 1945; D.Litt., Dropsie College, 1948; married Hanna Hoffmann, June 27, 1905; children—Rosie Sarah, Jakob Benjamin. Came to U.S., 1903; prof. history Jewish Theol. Sem , 1903-—, dir. of libraries. Mem. publ. Com. of Jewish Pub. Soc. America; pres. Kohut Memorial Foundation. Fellow American Academy of Jewish Research, Medieval Academy America; mem. Am. Jewish Historical Society (vice pres.); corr. mem. Jewish Hist. Soc. of Eng. Author: Seder Olam (nach Handschriften und Druckwerken), 1903; Untersuchungen zum Siddur des Gaon R. Amram, 1908; The Correspondence between the Rabbis of Southern France and Maimonides about Astrology, 1926; A History of the Jewish People (with Max L. Margolis), 1927; Zunz's Letters to Steinschneider. 1934; The Scientific Work of Some Outstanding Mediaeval Jewish Scholars, 1938; Studies in Jewish History and Booklore, 1944; Essays in Jewish Biography, 1947. Editor of Berliner, Gesammelte Schriften, I (with A. Freimann and M. Hildesheimer), 1913; M. Steinschneider, Gesammelte Schriften, I (with H. Malter); Jewish Studies in Memory of George Alexander Kohut (with S. Baron); Festschrift für Aron Freiman (with H. Meyer). Contbr. numerous articles to Jewish mags. and revs. in Am., Europe, and Israel. Home: 90 Morningside Dr., N.Y.C. Died Dec. 26. 1953; buried Union Field Cemetery, Long Island, N.Y.

MARX, Guido Hugo, educator; b. Toledo, Mar. 29, 1871; s. Joseph E. and Johanna Eleanora (Pulster) M.; grad. Toledo High Sch., including course in Scott Manual Tng. Sch., 1887; M.E., Cornell, 1893; m. Gertrude Van Dusen, June 6, 1895; children—Eleanor (dec.), Guido Van Dusen (dec.), Sylvia (dec.), Barbara. With Gleason Works, Rochester, N.Y., 1893-94, Bement, Miles & Co., Phila., 1894-95; at Stanford U., 1895-—, prof. machine design, 1908-36, emeritus prof., 1936-—; cons. on tech. edn., San Jose State College, 1943. Assisted in organizing Progressive movement in Cal. and del. Progressive Nat. Conv., 1912. Pres. Cal. Fedn. Tchrs., 1936-37. Fellow A.A.A.S.; mem. Am. Acad. Polit. and Social Science, Sigma Xi, Delta Upsilon. Club: Commonwealth (San Francisco). Author: (with A. W. Smith) Machine Design, 1905. Contbr. on phases and trends of higher edn., and on researches in machine elements, particularly gearing. Home: 356 Lincoln Av., Palo Alto, Cal. Died Sept. 10, 1949.

MARZALL, John Adams (mär-zäl') patent lawyer; b. Chicago, Mar. 8, 1896; s. George A. and Anne (Adams) M.; LL.B., St. Louis U., 1925; LL.M., De Paul U., Chicago, 1936; M.P.L., John Marshall Law Sch., 1942, LL.D., 1952; m. Catherine Dwyer, July 4, 1919. Civil engr. C.M.&St.P. Ry., asst. engr., Chgo. Union Station Co., Chgo., 1916-19; civil engineer and district manager, 1919-25; admitted to Missouri bar, 1925, Illinois, 1927, D.C., 1936; since practiced patent law in Chicago; senior member Marzall, Johnston, Cook & Root; commissioner of patents of U.S. Patent Office, 1949-53. Recipient Dept. of Commerce gold medal for distinguished service; 1952. Served as ensign, U.S. Navy, 1918-19; lieutenant (junior grade) Naval Reserves since 1920. Mem. Am., Ill. and Chicago bar assns., Am. Patent Law Assn., Chgo. Patent Law Assn. (v.p., chmn. legislative com. 1957-—), Fed. Bar Assn., Delta Theta Phi, Delta Sigma Phi. Christian. Clubs: University, Lincoln Park Gun; Army and Navy (Washington); Edgewater Golf (Chgo.). Home: 1120 Lake Shore Dr., Chgo. 11. Office: 135 S. La Salle St., Chgo. Died Jan. 1, 1959.

MASCUCH, John Thomas (mă-shōō'), business exec.; b. Newark, N.J., Aug. 6, 1899; s. Ferdinand and Julia (Kopko) M.; ed. Central High Sch., Newark, N.J., 1914-17; m. Elizabeth A. Hanschka, Oct. 23, 1926; children—Joan Elizabeth, Ann Barbara. Began as draftsman, 1916; dir. and officer, Cox Corp., Wilkes-Barre, Pa., 1923-26; dir. and pres. Breeze Corps., Inc., Newark, N.J., since 1926; dir. Federal Laboratories, Pittsburgh, Pa.; pres., dir. Anderson Stove Co., Foundry Ser Co., Anderson, Ind., Aldrich Company, Wyoming, Ill., Essex Tool & Die Co. Served with A.E.F., 1918-19. Decorated Victory Medal. Mem. Army Ordnance Assn, N.A.C., Army Signal Assn. Home: The Gateways, Normandy Heights, Morristown, N.J. Office: Breeze Corporations, Inc., 41 S. 6th St., Newark, N.J. Died Oct. 25, 1951.

MASENG, Sigurd (mäs' eng), Norwegian consul; b. Kristiania, Norway, Mar. 1, 1889; s. Carl Olsen and Karoline Gustava (Christensen) M.; student U. Oslo, 1907, Handelshochschule der Borcse, 1913; m. Borghild Mathilde Kjaerstad, Jan. 31, 1922; children—Kari (Mrs. John H. Hanson), Peer. Comml. and indsl. prodn., overseas export, 1909-18; entered Royal Norwegian Service as mem. State Dept., 1918-24; v. consul Antwerp, Belgium, 1925; 1st sec. Norwegian Legation, Moscow, 1925-28; mem. State Dept. Eastern Europe div., 1928-32, dir., 1932-36; consul, Chicago, 1936-47, consul gen. since 1947. Mem. Norwegian Olympic Com., 1924-36. Decorated Comdr. Order Brit. Empire (Gt. Britain); Knight Order of St. Olav, St. Olav Medal (Norway); Knight Polonia Restituta (Poland); Knight Golden Cross of Austria. Mem. Internat. Rifle and Pistol Union (past pres. Norwegian div.), Ski Assn. Norway, Norway and Am. rifle assns. Clubs: Norske, Swedish, Tavern, Lake Shore, Adventurers (Chicago). Home: 1411 N. State Parkway, Chicago 10. Office: 360 N. Michigan Av., Chgo. 1. Died Apr. 20, 1952.

MASON, Bernard Sterling, author; born Warren, Mich., June 2, 1896; son Jesse and Annie L. (Tharrett) M.; ed. Purdue U., 1914-15, U. of Mich., A.B., 1920, Ohio State U., A.M., 1929, Ph.D., 1931. Sec. Y.M.C.A., Ann Arbor, Mich., 1915-18, Fairmont, W.Va., 1918-19; Boy Scout exec., Toledo, O., 1920-21, Columbus, O., 1921-24; instr. in sociology and social adminstrn., Ohio State U., 1925-33; free lance author and lecturer since 1933; editor Camping Mag. 1935-43; director Camp Kooch-i-ching, International Falls, Minnesota. Served as pvt. F.A., United States Army, World War I. Presbyn. Author: Rope Spinning, 1928; Camping and Education, 1930; The Theory of Play (with E. D. Mitchell), 1934; Social Games for Recreation (with E. D. Mitchell), 1935; Active Games and Contents (with E. D. Mitchell), 1935; Primitive and Pioneer Sports, 1937; Necatos Games and Contests, 1937; Drums, Tomtoms and Rattles, 1938; Woodcraft, 1939; Roping, 1940; Jud Goes Camping, 1941; Democracy in the Summer Camp, 1941; The Junior Book of Camping and Woodcraft, 1943; Dances and Stories of the American Indian, 1943; The Book for Junior Woodsmen, 1945; The Book of Indian-Crafts and Costumes, 1946; Cabins, Cottages and Summer Homes, 1947. Contbr. articles to mags. Lecturer; specialist in Indian dancing, whip cracking, woodcraft and campcraft. Home: 2530 Salem Av., Cin. 8. Died Apr. 11, 1953.

MASON, Daniel Gregory, musician; b. Brookline, Mass., Nov. 20, 1873; s. Henry and Helen Augusta (Palmer) M.; A.B., Harvard U., 1895; Litt.D., Tufts, 1929; Mus.D., Oberlin Coll., 1931, U. of Rochester, 1932; studied music in Boston, New York and Paris; m. Mary Lord Taintor Mason, October 8, 1904. Prof. emeritus, music, Columbia U. Composer: Elegy (piano), 1901; Sonata for Violin and Piano, 1912; Pastorale for Violin, Clarinet and Piano, 1913; Country Pictures (piano), 1914; Quartet for Piano and Strings, 1914; First Symphony, 1915; "Russians," 1917; String Quartet on Negro themes, 1918; Prelude and Fugue (piano and orchestra), 1919; Silhouettes (piano), 1923; Songs of the Countryside, 1926; Chanticleer Overture, 1929; Second Symphony, 1931; Serenade (for string quartet), 1931; Suite after English Folk-songs, 1933; Third Symphony ("Lincoln"), 1936; etc. Author: From Grieg to Brahms, 1902; Beethoven and His Forerunners, 1904; The Romantic Composers, 1906; Contemporary Composers, 1918; Artistic Ideals, 1927; The Dilemma of American Music, 1928; Tune In, America, 1931; The Chamber Music of Brahms, 1933; Music in My Time, 1938; The Quartets of Beethoven, 1947. Mem. Am. Soc. of Composers, Authors and Publishers, Nat. Inst. of Arts and Letters. Home: 68 E. 86th St., N.Y.C. Died Dec. 4, 1953.

MASON, George Allen, lawyer; b. Chgo., June 25, 1870; s. Daniel Webster and Martha Frances (Gould) M.; A.B., Williams Coll., 1891; LL.B., Northwestern

U., 1894, LL.M., 1926; m. Elizabeth Leavitt Norcross, June 15, 1898; children—Paul Norcross (dec.), George Allen. Admitted to Ill. bar, 1894, since practiced in Chgo.; asst. corp. counsel, Chgo., 1907-11; city atty. Highland Park, 1909-11, Lake Forest, Ill., 1911-12. Trustee Seabury-Western Theol. Sem., Kemper Hall Alumni trustee of Northwestern U., 1924-32. Mem. Am., Ill., Chgo. bar assns., Chgo. Law Inst., Legal Club, Law Club, Delta Kappa Epsilon. Republican. Episcopalian. Clubs: University, Exmoor Country, Highland Park. Author: Special Assessments—Illinois, 1931. Home: 180 Hazel Av., Highland Park, Ill. Office: 69 W. Washington St., Chgo. Deceased.

MASON, George Grant, capitalist; b. Millburn, Ill., Sept. 16, 1868; s. Thomas and Margaret (Smith) M.; Sheffield Sci. Sch. (Yale), 1885-88; Stevens Inst. Tech., 1888-89; m. Marion Peak, June 7, 1897. Began with C.,M.&St.P. Ry., 1889; now dir. Erie Ry., City and Suburban Homes Co. Republican. Presbyn. Mason. Clubs: Metropolitan, University, Union, Tuxedo (N.Y.C.); University (Chgo.). Home: Tuxedo Park, N.Y. Office: 2 Rector St., N.Y.C. Died Apr. 30, 1955.

MASON, George W(alter), mfr.; b. Valley City, N.D., Mar. 12, 1891; s. Simon and Annie (Simons) M.; B.S., Univ. of Mich., 1913; children—John Kay, George Walter, Carolyn J., Barbara J. With mfg. div. Studebaker Corp., 1913-14; layout and production Dodge Bros., 1914-15; purchasing agent Am. Auto Trimming Co., Detroit, 1915, Wilder Tanning Co., Waukegan, Ill., 1916; in charge bus. extension, Irving National Bank, N.Y., 1919-21; in chg. mfg., Chrysler Corp., 1921-26; pres. Copeland Products, Inc., 1926-28; pres. and chmn. bd. Nash-Kelvinator Corp. until merger as Am. Motors Corp. of which was chmn. bd., and pres. Mem. Automobile Mfrs. Assn. (pres.) Society of Automotive Engineers, Phi Kappa Sigma. Republican. Mason. Clubs: Detroit, Detroit Athletic, Detroit Golf. Home: 18600 Fairway Drive. Office: American Motors Corp., Detroit, Mich. Died Oct. 8, 1954; buried White Chapel Mausoleum, Bloomfield Hills, Mich.

MASON, Guy, retired government official; born Sept. 10, 1880, Princeton, Ind.; son Morris W. and Mary E. (Wheeler) M.; LL.B., LL.M., National U. (Washington, D.C.), 1915-17; m. Louise Urquhart Burges, June 27, 1906; 1 daughter, Louise Urquhart (Mrs. Humphrey Peake Harnsberger). Reporter various newspapers including Washington Post, St. Louis Globe Democrat, Washington Herald, New York World and London Daily Telegraph, 1906-17, admitted to District of Columbia bar, 1917, and since practiced in Washington; mem. law firm of Mason, Spalding and McAtee; mem. Plaza Commn., 1914-15, first D.C. rent commn., 1919; apptd. D.C. commissioner, July, 1941-51. ret. Served U.S. Army, Spanish-Am. War, Philippine Insurrection. Mem. Am. Bar Assn., Am. Judicature Soc., D.C. Bar Assn., Sigma Nu Phi. Democrat. Episcopalian. Mason (32°; Shriner). Clubs: National Press, Burning Tree Golf, Metropolitan (Washington). Home: 4545 Connecticut Av. N.W., Washington 8. Died July 10, 1955; buried Arlington Nat. Cemetery.

MASON, James Orley, mfg. exec.; b. Glens Falls, N.Y., Feb. 27, 1883; s. John Shubel and Catherine (Barrett) M.; student pub. schs. of Glens Falls; m. Florence Batcheller, Sept. 1907; children—Orley Batcheller, Florence Mary, Cora Catherine, Martha Elizabeth. Operating mgr. Laurentide Paper Co., Grand Mere, P.Q., Can., 1916-29, Canada Power & Paper Co., 1929-31; mfg. mgr. Consolidated Paper Co., 1932-33; became v.p. Mead Corp., Chillicothe, O., 1936, exec. v.p., dir., 1948, now cons. Baptist. Home: Bell's Hill, P.O. No. 92. Office: Chillicothe, O. Died Oct. 2, 1958; buried Chillicothe.

MASON, Julian Starkweather, newspaper man; b. Chgo., July 8, 1876; s. Edward Gay and Julia Maria (Starkweather) M.; A.B., Yale, 1898; m. Florence Grey, June 1, 1908; children—Grey, Barbara. With Chgo. Record Herald, 1902, Chgo. Tribune; mng. editor Chgo. Evening Post, 1916-22; mng. editor N.Y. Tribune, now Herald Tribune, 1922-26; editor in chief New York Evening Post 1926-33. Mem. Psi Upsilon. Republican. Presbyn. Address: Old Brookville, N.Y. Died Nov. 8, 1954.

MASON, Maud M., artist; b. Russellville, Ky., Mar. 18, 1867; d. Damascus K. and Sarah S. (Ryan) M.; pupil of William M. Chase, Arthur W. Dow, Henry B. Snell, N.Y., Frank Brangwyn, of London. Recipient gold medal (ceramics) San Francisco Expn., 1915; bronze medal Nat. Arts Club, 1921; 1st prize Nat. Assn. Women Painters and Sculptors, 1922; medal for paintings Tenn. State Fair, 1929. Mem. Nat. Assn. Women Painters and Sculptors (pres. 1912-18), Master Craftsmen, Southern States Art League, League Profl. Artists, N.Y. Soc. Ceramic Arts (past pres.), Allied Artists Am., N.Y. Water Color Soc., Soc. of Painters N.Y. Asso. Nat. Acad. Design, 1934. Clubs: Nat. Arts (life), Pen and Brush (hon.). Left all her paintings to Brooks Meml. Art Gallery, Memphis, which dedicated and named a room for her. Address: Nat. Arts Club, 15 Gramercy Park, N.Y.C. Died Aug. 28, 1956; buried Kensico Cemetery, N.Y.C.

MASON, William Clarke, lawyer, business exec. Sr. partner law firm Morgan, Lewis & Bockins, Phila.; dir. Scott Paper Co. Recipient Am. Bar Assn. medal, 1957. Office: 123 S. Broad St., Phila. 9. Died Nov. 19, 1957.

MASSEE, Edward Kingsley (măs'ē), lawyer, retired army officer; b. Alma Center, Wis., July 26, 1871; s. Rev. William and Laura Jane (Davenport) M.; student Hamline U., 1889-91; honor grad. Inf.-Cav. Sch., 1904; grad. Army Staff Coll., 1905; LL.B., U. of Minn., 1908; m. Therese Lyons, Aug. 27, 1902. Served as pvt., corpl., sergt., arty., 1892-95; sergt., later 1st lt. and bn. adj. 3d Wis. Inf., 1898-99; pvt., later regtl. sergt. maj. U.S. Vols., 1899-1901; 2 d lt. U.S. Inf., 1901, advancing through grades to maj., judge adv., June 12, 1917; retired with rank lt. col., July 1, 1920. Decorations: Legion of Merit, 1944. Campaign ribbons: Spanish-American War, Puerto Rican Occupation, Philippine Campaign (1900-01), Mexican Border, World War I (France, 3 stars). Judge, 1st Circuit Court, Territory of Hawaii, Mar. 1926-Feb. 1929; judge, U.S. Dist. Court, Hawaii, 1929-35. Engaged in voluntary war work, Dec. 8, 1941-44. Mem. Am. Bar Assn., Bar Assn. Hawaii, C. of C., Am. Legion, Mil. Order World Wars. Home: 1919 N.E. 21st Av., Portland 12, Ore. Died Feb. 15, 1960.

MASSEY, Richard W(alter), financier; b. Sumterville, Ala.; s. Rev. R. A. and Emma A. M.; student Baylor U., 1886-87; m. Bessie Spencer, 1891; 4 children. Organizer, 1887, and for 50 years pres. Massey System of Business Colls., Birmingham, Ala., Richmond, Va., Louisville, Houston, Columbus, Ga., Montgomery, Ala., Jacksonville, Fla.; asst. organizer, 1907, 25 yrs. v.p. Protective Life Ins. Co. Organizer, pres. 2 years, Anchor Building & Loan Co.; pres. Bessrich Investment Co.; owner Massey Office Bldg.; other bldgs. and large real estate holdings. Chmn. Birmingham chpt. A.R.C., 1917. First pres. Gen. Forrest Highway; ex-pres. Ala. Good Roads Assn.; v.p. Birmingham C. of C., 1910, pres., 1911. Trustee Ala. Inst. for Deaf and Blind, 1918-21. Methodist. Clubs: Surf (Miami Beach). Author and pub. Massey's Modern Bookkeeping, Massey's Commercial Law and various books on business subjects. Home: 3000 Mountain Brook Parkway, Birmingham, Ala.; also (winter) Miami Beach, Fla., and (summer) Lake George, N.Y. Died Aug. 5, 1949.

MASTER, Henry Buck, clergyman; born Elizabeth, N.J., Oct. 28, 1871; s. George Buck and Esther Maria (Coxe) M.; A.B., Princeton, 1895, A.M., 1897; B.D., Princeton Theol. Sem., 1898; D.D., Hanover Coll., 1917, Lafayette Coll., 1930; LL.D., James Millikin and Dubuque univs., 1922; Litt.D., Coll. of Emporia, Kan., 1928; m. Lucy Olmsted, Oct. 21, 1902; children—William Olmsted, John Redman Coxe, Henry B., George Olmsted (dec.). Ordained Presbyn. ministry, 1898; pastor's asst., 1st Ch., Buffalo, N.Y., 1898-1900; acting pastor, same, 1900-03; pastor 1st Ch., Ft. Wayne, Ind., 1905-19; gen. sec. Board of Pensions, Presbyn. Ch. in U.S.A., 1919-37, mem. of Board, chmn. investment com., 1937-40. Initiated creation and operation of Service Pension Plan in Presbyn. Chs. in U.S.A.; mem. Layman's Com. which raised $15,000,000 fund to cover accrued liabilities. Moderator Gen. Assembly of the Presbyn. Ch. in U.S.A., Syracuse, N.Y., 1936. Mem. bd. dirs. Presbyn. Hosp., Phila., since 1938 (chmn. religious work com.; member finance com.). Y.M.C.A. secretary in France, in charge of hut at Gievres 4 mos.; transferred to entertainment work; attached to Field Hosp. 3, during St. Mihiel drive. Am. sec. Alliance Ref. Chs. Throughout the World Holding the Presbyterian System for twenty years; v.p. Alumni Assn., Princeton Theol. Sem.; hon. mem. Lawton-Wayne Post Spanish War Veterans. Republican. Mason (32°, past grand master Emanuel Chapter Rose Croix). Clubs: Princeton, University, Union League, Midday (Phila.); Princeton, City (New York); Country (Phoenix, Ariz). Retired 1937. Home: 116 Glenn Rd., Ardmore, Pa. Died May 18, 1955.

MASTERS, Frank Meriro, educator; b. Franklin County, Tex., July 28, 1870; s. Basil Earl and Mary Ellen (Penn) M.; A.B., Calhoun Coll., Kingston, Tex., 1893; Th.M., So. Bapt. Theol. Sem., Louisville, 1897, grad. study, 1897-98; D.D., Okla. Bapt. U., 1920; m. Lillie White Randolph, June 9, 1898; children—Catharine Chamberlain (Mrs. Roy Rosser), Earl Randolph, Courtland Kerfoot, Frank Meriro, Julian Penn. Tchr. pub. sch., Tex., 1893-94; ordained to ministry Bapt. Ch., 1894; pastor Clifton Ch., Louisville, 1896-98, First Ch., San Angelo, Tex., 1898-1902, First Ch., Weatherford, Tex., 1902-05, College Av. Ch., Ft. Worth, 1905-10, First Ch., Ardmore, Okla., 1910-15; pres. Okla. Bapt. U., Shawnee, 1914-19; field sec. Bapt. Gen. Conv. of Ark., 1919-22; corr. sec. Bapt. State Mission Bd. of Ark., 1922-28; pastor First Ch., Sturgis, Ky., 1928-31; pres. Bethel Coll., Russellville, Ky., 1931-33; adviser of adminstrn. Georgetown (Ky.) Coll., 1934; pastor Burkesville, Ky., 1935-40; pastor Second Ch., Princeton, Ky., 1942-46; dean and teacher Old and New Testament, W. Ky. Bapt. Bible Inst., Clinton, Ky., 1950. Mem. State Mission Bd., Bapt. Gen. Conv. of Tex., 1908-10, of Okla., 1910-15; mem. Foreign Mission Bd., So. Bapt. Conv., 1913-15; pres. Bapt. Pastors Conf., Okla., 1913-15; mem. Board of Missions in Ky., 1928-31; v.p. Ky. Bapt. Hist. Soc., 1941, 50. Democrat. Rotarian. Writer series of articles Alexander Campbell Movement; Studies of Christ's Return; History of Bethel Bapt. Assn. in Ky.; History of Baptists in Kentucky, 1949. Contbr. to ch. publs. Home: 719 N. 13th St., Mayfield, Ky. Died Apr. 3, 1959; buried Clinton (Ky.) Cemetery.

MASTERS, Howard Russell, neuropsychiatry; b. Fredericksburg, Va., July 2, 1894; s. John William and Ada Byron (Chisholm) M.; grad. Randolph-Macon Acad., Front Royal, Va., 1912; student Randolph-Macon Coll., 1912-15, LL.D. (honorary), 1955; M.D., Medical Coll. of Virginia, 1919; m. Bealmear Dare Linthicum, Oct. 25, 1921; children—Bealmear Dare, Howard Russell; married 2d, Sarah Elizabeth Huneycutt, May 1950; children—Elizabeth Chisholm, Sarah Kathryn. Interne Johnston-Willis Hospital, Richmond, Virginia, 1919-20, N.Y. Neurol. Inst., 1920; resident physician Tucker Sanatorium, Richmond, 1921; studied endocrinology St. Louis, 1921; asst. in surg., Med. Coll. of Va., 1919-20, instr. nervous and mental diseases, 1920-25, asso. in neuropsychiatry, 1925-39, asso. prof. since 1939; lecturer in normal and abnormal psychology, Coll. of William and Mary (Richmond div. Sch. of Social Work), 1927-29; lecturer in psychiatry, same, 1927-32; lecturer Med. Coll. of Va. in normal and abnormal psychology, 1932; asso. chief of staff, Tucker Hospital, Richmond; visiting physician Hosp. Div. Med. Coll. of Va., Crippled Children's Hosp., Sheltering Arms Hosp.; attending neurologist Johnston-Willis Hosp., Richmond; mem. staff Richmond Meml. Hosp. Mem. Gov.'s Adv. Bd. on Mental Hygiene, Richmond, 1926—; mem. bd. Meml. Guidance Clinic, 1933—, v.p., 1943-44, pres., 1945-50. Elector for N.Y.U. Hall of Fame. Mem. Med. Res. Corps, United States Army, Dec. 1917-July 1919. Diplomate Am. Bd. Psychiatry and Neurol.; mem. Am. and So. med. assns., Va. Neuropsychiatric Assn. (exec. com. 1936, 37), Neuropsychiatric Soc. of Va. (pres. 1942; executive com., 1942-43), Am. Psychiatric Assn. (mem. com. on pub. edn. since 1941), Med. Soc. of Va., Tri-State Med. Assn. (pres. 1937), Mental Hygiene Soc. of Va. (exec. com. 1936, 37; pres. 1938-40), Richmond Acad. Medicine, Assn. for Study of Internal Secretions, Soc. of Alumni Randolph-Macon Coll. (pres. 1932-34), Kappa Sigma, Phi Chi, Omicron Delta Kappa. Democrat. Methodist. Club: Commonwealth. Contbr. mags. Home: 24 Tapoan Rd. Office: 212 W. Franklin St., Richmond, Va. Died Jan. 27, 1959; buried Confederate Cemetery, Fredericksburg, Va.

MASTERS, John Volney, univ. prof.; b. Joplin, Mo., May 5, 1884; s. John H. and Mary C. (Brown) M.; A.B., Indiana U., 1908, A.M., 1920, LL.B., 1921, S.J.D., Harvard, 1931; m. Estella Keith, Mar. 22, 1902; 1 son, Keith; m. 2d, Lea Cowles, Dec. 1952. Teacher, Hall (Ind.) High Sch., 1902-03; supt. schs., Trafalgar, Ind., 1907-09, Oaktown, Ind., 1909-11; head history dept. Lafayette (Ind) High Sch., 1911-15; prin. Greencastle (Ind.) High Sch., 1915-16; head history dept. Central High Sch., South Bend, Ind., 1917-22; instr. history Ball State Teachers Coll., Muncie, Ind., summer 1922; mem. faculty Sch. of Law, U. of Ala., 1922— (on leave 1930-31); mem. faculty Sch. of Law, Vanderbilt U., summer 1927, U. of Kan., 2d semester, 1933-34. Mem. Delta Chi, Phi Alpha Delta. Republican. Methodist. Mason. Mem. Civitan Club of Tuscaloosa, Ala. (organizer, 1st pres., dist. gov. Ala. dist. Civitan Internat.). Home: 1609 University Av., Tuscaloosa, Ala. Died Oct. 7, 1954; buried Tuscaloosa.

MASTERS, Victor Irvine, clergyman; b. Anderson County, S.C., Mar. 4, 1867; s. Priestley A. and Martha Amelia (Burriss) M.; A.B., Furman U., Greenville, S.C., 1888, A.M., 1889, D.D., 1913; Th.M., Southern Bapt. Theol. Sem., 1893; m. Lois Eunice Wickliffe, July 19, 1893; children—W. Wickliffe, Victor Irvine. Ordained Baptist ministry, 1889; past Rock Hill, S.C., 1893, 94, Pocahontas, Va., 1894-96; asso. editor Bapt. Courier, Greenville, S.C., 1896-1905; editor and owner Bapt. Press, 1905-07; asso. editor Religious Herald, Richmond, Va., 1908-09; ednl. sec. and supt. publicity, Southern Bapt. Home Mission Bd., Atlanta, Ga., 1909-21; editor Home Field (official mission mag. of Southern Baptists), 1909-17; editor Western Recorder, Louisville, 1921-1942. Mem. Kappa Alpha, Iota Chapter, Furman U., 1888. Author: The Home Mission Task, 1912; Baptist Home Missions, 1914; Baptist Missions in the South, 1915; Country Church in the South, 1916; Call of the South, 1918; Making America Christian, 1921; Re-Thinking Baptist Doctrines, 1937. Address: Box 1445, De Soto City, Fla. Died June 30, 1954; buried Pinecrest Cemetery, Sebring, Fla.

MASTERSON, Patrick J(oseph), clergyman; born N.Y. City, Feb. 2, 1910; s. Francis and Joan (Dorgan) M.; student Holy Name Sch., N.Y. City, 1916, Saint Francis Xavier High Sch. N.Y. City, 1924, Fordham Coll., 1928; A.B., Saint Joseph's Sem., 1929.

Ordained priest Roman Cath. Ch., June 8, 1935; served as asst. priest in several parishes, N.Y. City, 1935; advocate in matrimonial tribunal Archdiocese of N.Y., 1937-42; asst. exec. sec. Nat. Legion of Decency, 1942-47, exec. sec. since 1947. Served with Chaplain Corps, U.S. Navy, 1943-46; commd. lt. (j.g.), 1943, promoted lt., 1945; served as chaplain P.T.O., 1945. Home: 110 E. 12th St. Office: 453 Madison Av., N.Y.C. 22. Deceased.

MASTON, Robert H(ayden), banker; born Brazil, Ind., Apr. 16, 1897; s. Charles Edwin and Elizabeth (Farrow) M.; B.S., U. of the South, 1919; m. Constance Reynolds Ivy, June 12, 1928; children—Robert Hayden, Constance Ivy, Clerk Guaranty Bank & Trust Co., Memphis, Tenn., 1919-22; nat. bank examiner, N.Y. City, 1922-25; cashier Union Planters Nat. Bank & Trust Co., Memphis, 1925-27, vice pres. and cashier, 1927-29; asst. cashier Nat. City Bank of N.Y. City, 1929-37, asst. vice pres., 1937-46, v.p., 1946—. Served as pilot naval aviation, 1917-18, World War I. Mem. Southern Soc. of New York, Tenn. Soc. of New York, Am. Inst. Banking (pres. Memphis chpt., 1927-28), Pelham Manor Assn. (pres. 1944-47, dir., 1942—). Episcopalian. Clubs: Pelham Country; Huguenot Yacht (New Rochelle, N.Y.); Union League (N.Y. City); The Boston (New Orleans). Home: 684 Esplanade, Pelham Manor, N.Y. Office: 55 Wall St., N.Y.C. Died Apr. 5, 1957.

MATAS, Rudolph (măt'ăs), surgeon; b. Bonnet Carre, nr. New Orleans, La., Sept. 12, 1860; s. Dr. N. Hereu and Teresa (Jorda) M.; ed. Paris, Barcelona, Brownsville (Tex.), Soule's Coll. (New Orleans); grad. Lit. Inst. of St. John, Matamoros, Mexico, 1876; M.D., Tulane, 1880; LL.D., Washington U., 1915, U. of Ala., 1926, Tulane, 1928; Sc.D., U. of Pa., 1925, Princeton, 1928; M.D., honoris causa, Nat. U. of Guatemala, 1934; widower. Began practice at New Orleans, 1880, specializing in surgery since 1895; prof. surgery, Tulane Med. Dept., 1895-1927, emeritus since 1928; sr. surgeon Charity Hosp., 1894-1928, consultant since 1928; chief sr. surgeon Touro Infirmary, 1905-35, hon. chief surgeon, 1935-—; cons. surgeon Eye, Ear, Nose and Throat Hosp.; etc. Mem. La. Council Nat. Defense, 1915-18; organizer and dir. Base Hosp. 24 (Tulane Unit) for service in France, 1916-17; maj., dir. New Orleans Sch. for Intensive Surg. War Training, M.O.R.C., 1917-18. Fellow Am. Coll. Surgeons (v.p. 1913, 20; pres. 1924-25), A.A.A.S., Havana Acad. Medical Sciences; mem. A.M.A. (chmn. sect. surg. 1908; v.p. 1920, 32-33), Am. Surg. Assn. (pres. 1909), So. Surg. Assn. (pres. 1911; hon. fellow 1927), Am. Assn. Thoracic Surgeons (pres. 1920), La. State Med. Soc. (pres. 1894-95), New Orleans Med. and Surg. Assn. (pres. 1886), Am. Soc. Clin. Surgery (v.p. 1908-10), Orleans Parish Med. Soc., Am. Assn. Cancer Research, Am. Soc. Control Cancer, Am. Assn. Exptl. Medicine, Am. Assn. Anatomists, Nat. Assn. Study and Prevention Tb, Am. Assn. Endocrinology, Assn. Mil. Surgeons U.S. Army, Nat. Inst. Social Sciences, Am. Assn. Friends of Med. Progress, Nat. Econ. League, Am. Museum Natural History, La. Hist. Soc., So. Art League, Art Assn. New Orleans, New Orleans Zoology, Soc., La. League of Civil Service Reform; hon. fellow Royal Coll. of Surgeons, Eng., 1927; pres. internat. Soc. of Surgery, 1936-38; hon. mem. New Orleans Acad. Scis., La. State Pharm. Assn., Ill. Central and Miss. Valley R.R. Surgeons, Am. Assn. Traumatic Surgery, Acad. Medicine (N.Y.), Am . Soc. Regional Anesthesia, Boston Surg. Soc., Am. Soc. History of Medicine, Phila. Acad. Surgery, Hon. pres. Pan-Am. Med. Congress, Washington, 1895, v.p. for La., 1896; mem. and rapporteur arterial surgery (surg. sect.) Internat. Med. Congress, London, 1913; mem. Assn. Française de Chirurgie (rapporteur by invitation, and hon. pres. 1922); mem. Soc. Internat. de Chirurgie (rapporteur by invitation); hon. pres. Internat. Surgical Congress, Warsaw, 1929; hon. mem. Royal Acad. Medicine (Rome), Assn. Polish Surgeons, Soc. Ital. Physicians in America; corr. mem. Peruvian Surg. Soc., Cuban Surgical Society, Société Nationale de Chirurgie (Paris), Med. Soc. Copenhagen (Denmark), Surg. Soc. Madrid; corr. fellow Royal Acad. Medicine (Madrid); hon. fellow Royal Acad. Medicine, and Catalonian Acad. Med. Sci. (Barcelona), Royal Acad. Medicine (Belgium); hon. pres. Surgical Society (Barcelona); mem. Soc. Internat. pour l'Histoire de la Med. (Paris); hon. surgeon Eye, Ear, Nose and Throat Hosp., New Orleans; asso. mem. French Nat. Acad. Medicine; hon. mem. 12th Congress Internat. Soc. Surgery, London, 1947; hon. fellow Am. Soc. Anesthesiologists, Royal Belgian Acad. Sci.; hon. mem. Belgian Surg. Soc., Greek Nat. Soc., Surg. Soc. Lyons, La. State Acad. Sci., Am. Soc. Univ. Surgeons, American Soc. Vascular Surgeons, La. Surg. Society; hon. mem. 50 yr. Club La. State Med. Soc., Miss. State Med. Soc.; hon. pres. emeritus past pres.' adv. council La. Med. Soc. Ofcl. del. from City of New Orleans to Nat. Finlay Celebration, Havana, 1941. Honor guest, City of Havana, Municipal medal, 1941; Finlay medal Cuban Med. Fedn., 1941; Officer Order Public Instruction (Venezuela), 1925; Knight Civil Order of Alfonso XII of Spain, 1929; Chevalier Legion of Honor (France), 1932; Knight Order of Isabella the Catholic (Spanish), 1934; comdr. Nat. Cuban Order of Carlos Finlay, 1936; officer Order of Leopold, Belgium, 1939. Recipient first distinguished service medal A.M.A., 1938. Mem. Italian-Am. Soc., Stars and Bars of Tulane (pres. 1922), Nu Sigma Nu (president hon. council, 1936; merit medal, 1942), Alpha Omega Alpha, Kappa Delta Phi, hon. fellow Alpha Zeta Circle, Omicron Delta Kappa. Clubs: Boston, Round Table, Young Men's Business (honorary), Lions (hon.). Editor New Orleans Med. and Surg. Jour., 1883-85. Henry Bigelow medalist of Boston Surg. Soc., 1926; Times-Picayune award for community service, 1940. Chmn. Violet Hart Com. Award Matas Medal Vascular Surgery. Hon. 1934. Author of many treatises and monographs on surg. subjects, specially vascular surgery, and frequent contbr. to med. jours. and text books. Home: 2255 St. Charles Av., New Orleans. Died Sept., 1957.

MATHER, Elmer James, business exec.; b. Philadelphia, Pa., Nov. 12, 1889; s. James and Mary Emma (Baldwin) M.; ed. Phila. pub. schs., Banks Bus. Coll.; m. 2d, Elinor H. Burch, Dec. 2, 1942; 1 son (by previous marriage) David James. Sales mgr. Breyer Ice Cream Co., Phila. and N.Y. City, 1915-29; gen. sales mgr. Nat. Dairy Products Corp., N.Y. City, 1929-30, dir., 1926-56, v.p., 1942-56; dir. So. Dairies, Inc., Washington, 1930—, pres., 1930-42, chairman board, 1942-55. Treas., dir. Milk Industry Found.; treas. Dairy Industry Com.; v.p., dir. Dairy Remembrance Fund. Member National Dairy Council (dir.), Internat. Assn. Ice Cream Mfrs. (dir.). Republican. Methodist. Mason. Clubs: Miami Shores Country (Miami, Fla.); Columbia Country, University (Washington). Home: 6919 Woodside Pl., Chevy Chase 15, Md. Office: 60 M St., Washington 13. Died Apr. 15, 1958; buried Cedar Hill Cemetery, Suitland, Md.

MATHER, Frank Jewett, Jr. (măth'ẽr), professor art; b. Deep River, Conn., July 6, 1868; s. Frank Jewett and Caroline Arms (Graves) M.; A.B., Williams, 1889, L.H.D., 1913; Ph.D., Johns Hopkins, 1892; studied U. Berlin, École des Hautes Études, Paris; m. Ellen Suydam Mills, Feb. 20, 1905; children—Margaret (Mrs. Louis A. Turner), Frank J. Instr. and asst. prof. English and Romance langs., Williams College, 1893-1900; editorial writer N.Y. Evening Post, asst. editor the Nation, 1901-06; art critic N.Y. Evening Post, 1905-06, 10-11; Am. editor Burlington Mag., 1904-06; joint editor Art Studies, 1923-—; prof. art and archaeology Princeton, 1910-33 (emeritus); dir. Univ. Art Mus., 1920-48. Mem. Nat. Inst. Arts and Letters, Am. Acad. Arts and Sciences, Am. Acad. Arts and Letters, Hispanic Soc. Am. (corr. mem.), Am. Philos. Soc., Dante Soc., Delta Psi. Ensign USNRF, 1917. Clubs: Century, Authors (N.Y.C.). Author: Homer Martin, Poet in Landscape, 1912; The Collectors (short stories), 1912; Estimates in Art, 1916; The Portraits of Dante, 1921; A History of Italian Painting, 1923; Ulysses in Ithaca, 1926; Modern Painting, 1927; The American Spirit in Art, in The Pageant of America, 1927; Estimates in Art, series 2, 1931; Concerning Beauty, 1935; Venetian Painters, 1936; Western European Painting of the Renaissance, 1939; also several lit. and philol. monographs. Home: 3 Evelyn Pl., Princeton, N.J. Died Nov. 11, 1953; buried Deep River, Conn.

MATHER, Gordon Macdonald, founder, bd. chmn. Mather Spring Co.; b. St. James, La., Sept. 24, 1868; s. Joseph and Mary (Lyons) M.; attended private schools; m. Charlotte Bope, Feb. 23, 1911. With Cleveland Axle Mfg. Co., Cleve., 1886, moved with company to Canton, O. in 1891; organized Mather Spring Co., Toledo, 1911, was pres. and gen. mgr., now bd. chmn.; dir. Mather Spring Co., Toledo Trust Co., Gordon Mfg. Co., Hercules Motors Corp. (Canton, O.). Mem. Toledo C. of C., Toledo Zool. Society. Clubs: Toledo, Country, Carranor Hunt and Polo. Home: Dixie Highway, Perrysburg, O. Office: Castle Bldg., Toledo 10. Deceased.*

MATHER, Rufus Graves; b. Morristown, N.J., Mar. 16, 1874; s. Frank Jewett and Caroline Arms (Graves) M.; direct desc. of Rev. Richard Mather, father of Increase Mather, 1st colonial pres. of Harvard; B.A., Williams Coll., 1895; m. Winifred, d. of Henry Holt, November 16, 1922. Engaged in business in New York; went abroad, 1906, during art research in Italy; vol. office mgr., Roman district, Am. Red Cross in Italy, 1917-18; founder and hon. v.p. (with Miss Holt, afterward wife) Light House No. 8, Italian nat. orgn. for prevention of blindness in Italy, under patronage of King and Queen; cofounder (with wife) Light House No. 10, Canton, China, 1929, also edn. campaign to prevent blindness in Egypt, 1928, in Shanghai, China, 1929; promoted prevention of blindness in Palestine, Syria, Greece, Straits Settlements; Java, Norway, Sweden, Denmark, Czechoslovakia, Brazil, Argentine, Chile, Peru, Cuba, Porto Rico, Bermuda, Trinidad, Hungary and Austria; lectured on prevention of blindness, 1935, before members of governments of Ireland, Greece, Turkey, Bulgaria, Jugoslavia and Austria, also before royalty and at universities, resulting in fresh efforts in behalf of the blind; in 1936 with wife lectured in Japan on prevention of blindness and justice for the blind and present at inauguration of first "Lighthouse" for blind in Osaka which was result of their visit in 1929; in China lectured and started a nat. "Lighthouse" movement under the presidency of Madame Chiang Kai-shek. Lecturer on art archive research, Harvard, Johns Hopkins, Princeton, Columbia, Am. Acad. in Rome, etc. Contbr. articles relating to document of the Della Robbia, L'Arte (Rome, Italy) and Am. Jour. Archæology; compiler geneal. information now in Brit. Museum and Coll. of Arms, London. Advanced at the request of the King Emperor from the rank of Cavaliere Ufficiale to Commendatore of the Crown of Italy. Mem. Delta Psi. Clubs: The Pilgrims, Williams, Century (New York). Author: Excavating Buried Treasure; Archive Research, Its Nature and Yield, 1945. Home: 3 Evelyn Pl., Princeton, N.J. Office: 111 E. 59th St., N.Y.C. 22. Died Apr. 27, 1952; buried Morristown, N.J.

MATHER, William Gwinn, iron and steel mfr.; b. Cleve., Sept. 22, 1857; s. Samuel Livingston and Elizabeth Lucy (Gwinn) M.; A.B., Trinity Coll., Conn., 1877, M.A., 1885, LL.D., 1932; LL.D., Kenyon Coll., 1924; L.H.D., Western Res. U., 1937; m. Mrs. Elizabeth R. Ireland, May 18, 1929; 1 stepson, James D. Ireland. Has been with Cleveland-Cliffs Iron Co., 1878-—, pres., 1890-1933, chmn., 1933-47, hon. chmn., 1947-51; chmn. Lake Superior and Ishpeming R.R. Co.; dir. Republic Steel Corp., Kelley Island Lime & Transport Co., Medusa Portland Cement Co., also several mining cos. Pres. Cleve. Museum of Art; mem. bd. trustees Trinity Coll., Kenyon Coll., U. Hosps., Western Reserve U. Mem. Am. Antiquarian Soc., Bibliog. Soc. London, Bibliog. Soc. Am. Western Reserve Hist. Soc. (trustee), Colonial Soc. Mass., Soc. Colonial Wars, Psi Upsilon. Republican. Episcopalian (vestryman, sr. warden; also president of trustees and treasurer of the Diocese of Ohio). Clubs: Union, Kirtland, Rowfant, Country, Tavern, Chagrin Valley Hunt (Cleve.); University (Chgo.); Grolier (N.Y.C.). Home: 12407 Lake Shore Blvd. Office: Union Commerce Bldg., Cleve. Died Apr. 5, 1951; buried Lakeview Cemetery, Cleve.

MATHERLY, Walter Jeffries (măth'ẽr-lĭ), univ. dean; b. Mackville, Ky., May 3, 1888; s. George and Martha (Lawson) M.; A.B., William Jewell Coll., Liberty, Mo., 1915, hon. LL.D., 1940; M.A., Washington U., 1916; fellow in economics, U. of Minn., 1916-17; m. Enid Putnam, Apr. 12, 1919; children—Eleanor Putnam, Walter J. II. Asst. in polit. economy, U. of Chicago, 1917-18; prof. economics, Georgetown (Ky.) Coll., 1919-20; asso. prof. business adminstrn., U. of N.C., 1920-23, prof., 1923-26; prof. economics and dean Coll. of Business Adminstrn., U. of Fla., since 1926, acting dean General Coll., 1935-37, 1943-44, chmn. faculty com., Inst. Inter-Am. Affairs, University of Florida, 1930-44. Mem. bd. of directors Citizens Bank of Gainesville; mem. bd. dirs. Jacksonville branch Federal Reserve Bank of Atlanta (chmn. 1944 and 1947). Served as 1st lt. and chaplain U.S. Army, World War I. Specialist in land-grant college curricula, U.S. Office of Edn., summer 1929. Mem. Fla. Citizens Finance and Taxation Com., 1930; chmn. Merit System of Florida State Bd. Health, and Crippled Children's Commn., 1940-43; pres. Alachua Co. Council Health and Welfare, 1940-41; state campaign mgr., Field Army of Fla., Am. Cancer Soc.; pres. Fla. State-wide Pub. Health Com., 1940-43; dir. health and physical fitness, State Defense Council of Fla., 1942; dir. Citizens Service Corps, Alachua County Defense Council, 1941-44; part-time pub. mem. Regional War Labor Bd., Dist. V, 1943-44; county chairman of sponsoring committee of Children Home Society of Florida; chairman executive board Gainesville Little Theater 1928-45; Florida state campaign chairman for March of Dimes, 1954, 55. Fellow A.I.M.; member American Assn. Collegiate Schs. of Business (pres. 1935-36), Am. Economic Assn., Southern Econ. Assn. (v. pres.; past pres.), Social Science Research Council (Southern regional com. 1930-34), Florida State Chamber Commerce (dir.). U. Fla. Athletic Assn., Inc. (president), Sigma Nu, Alpha Kappa Psi, Phi Kappa Phi, Tau Kappa Alpha, Beta Gamma Sigma, Florida Blue Key, Pi Gamma Mu. Democrat. Episcopalian. Elk (v.p. Fla. State Elks Assn. 1946-47, pres. 1950-51; dist. dep. grand exalted ruler, 1950-51; chmn. operating com., mem. endowment fund bd. trustees Harry-Anna Crippled Childrens Home. (Mason (grand orator, Fla., 1950-51). Club: Rotary (pres. 1942-43; dist. gov. 1944-45). Author on Bus. Edn. in the Changing South. Contbr. on econ. and bus. subjects. Home: 620 Boulevard, Gainesville, Fla. Died Sept. 25, 1954; buried Evergreen Cemetery, Gainesville, Fla.

MATHES, James Monroe, advt. agy. exec.; b. Dover, N.H., 1889; s. Valentine and Mary (Pendexter) M.; grad. Dartmouth, 1911; m. Ruth French Dearborn, Mar. 16, 1916. Pres., dir. J. M. Mathes, Inc., N.Y.C., 1933-—; dir. Canada Dry Ginger Ale, Inc., Canada Dry Internat., Inc., G. B. Seely's Sons, Inc., Chelmsford Co., Durez Plastics & Chemicals, Inc., Emory Air Freight Corp. Active Jr. Achievement. Clubs: University, Cloud, Union League (N.Y.C.); North Hempstead Country; Round Hill; Field; York (Me.) Country. Home: 20 Church St., Greenwich, Conn. Office: 260 Madison Av., N.Y.C. 16. Died Apr. 28, 1957.

MATHESON, George Wilson (măth'ĕ-sŭn), law sch. dean; b. Glasgow, Scotland, June 10, 1894; s. Donald and Catherine Jimeson (Wilson) M.; brought by parents to U.S., 1897; A.B., Columbia, 1914; LL.B., St. Lawrence U. Law Sch., 1917; LL.D., St. John's Univ., Brooklyn, N.Y., 1926; m. Constance M. de Pool, Nov. 19, 1936. Admitted to N.Y. bar, 1917, and began practice at Brooklyn; prin. Y.M.C.A. Prep. Sch., Brooklyn, 1914-17; prof. of law, Brooklyn Law Sch., 1917-25; dean St. John's Univ. School Law, 1925, now emeritus; supervising dean St. John's Univ., Borough Hall Div., 1929-41; co-founder (with Judge Philip A. Brennan) St. John's Univ. Sch. of Law; St. John's Univ. Borough Hall Coll. (now Univ. Coll.); St. John's Univ. Sch. Commerce; St. John's Univ. Coll. Pharmacy. Mem. Selective Service Appeals Bd. No. 14, N.Y. State. Arbitrator Am. Arbitration Assn. Served U.S. Navy, 1917-18; lt. comdr. U.S.N.R. (retired). Mem. Am. Bar Assn., Brooklyn Bar Assn., Am. Law Inst., N.E. A. (dept. of higher education), N.Y. State Bar Assn., Joint Conf. on Legal Edn. of New York State, Phi Kappa Psi, Phi Delta Phi; hon. member Delta Mu Delta, Sigma Delta Kappa, Iota Theta; member board of directors Alumnae Assn. of Phi Delta Phi. Member Society of Older Grades of Columbia University. Presbyn. Mason (32°, Shriner). Clubs: Columbia Univ., Cherry Valley Club; Pinehurst Country (N.C.); St. Andrews Society. Author: Principles of Law of Agency, 1921; Cases on Law of Agency, 1922. Cases on Law of Damages, 1922; Cases and Materials on the Law of Evidence (Matheson and Prince), 1949. Home: Duncraig Manor, Southern Pines, N.C.; also: 7 Harvard Rd. S., Garden City, N.Y. Office: 96 Schermerborn St., Bklyn. 2. Died Apr. 29, 1957; buried Evergreen Cemetery, Bklyn.

MATHESON, Robert, educator; b. West River, N.S., Can., Dec. 20, 1881; s. Walter Alexander and Mary (Anderson) M.; prep. edn. Pictou Acad.; student N.S. Sch. of Science; B.S., Cornell U., 1906, M.S., 1907, Ph.D., 1911; m. Margaret Katherine Macpherson, Aug. 25, 1911; 1 son, Robert Macpherson. Prof. entomology S.D. State Coll., 1907-09; prof. zoology, N.S. Coll. Agr., 1912-13; prof. entomology (med. entomology and parasitology) Cornell U., 1914-49; cons. health sect. TVA. Fellow A.A.A.S., Entomol. Soc. Am.; mem. Am. Soc. Parasitologists (v.p. 1940; mem. editorial bd.), Am. Assn. Econ. Entomologists, N.S. Inst. Science, Am. Soc. Tropical Medicine, Washington Acad. Sciences, Phi Kappa Phi, Phi Kappa Sigma, Sigma Xi, Gamma Alpha; corr. mem. Venezuelan Soc. Natural Sciences, Acad. of Natural Sciences of Chile, Phila. Acad. Natural Sciences. Republican. Presbyn. Handbook of the Mosquitos of North America, 1929, rev. edit. 1945; Medical Entomology, 1932; Laboratory Guide in Entomology, 1939; Entomology, 1944, rev. edit. 1951; also many articles in jours. and experiment station publs. Home: 204 Parkway, Cayuga Heights, Ithaca, N.Y. Died Dec. 14, 1958.

MATHEWS, Albert Prescott (măth'ūz), physiol. chemist; b. Chicago, Ill., Nov. 26, 1871; s. William Smith Babcock and Flora E. (Swain) M.; S.B., Mass. Inst. Tech., 1892; studied biology, Cambridge, Eng., Naples, Italy, and Marburg, Germany, 1895-97; Ph.D., Columbia, 1898; hon. D.Sc. Institutum Divi Thomae, 1940; m. Jessie Glyde Macrum, Feb. 7, 1895; 1 dau., Mrs. Noreen Macrum Koller. Asst. in biology, Mass. Inst. Tech., 1892-93; fellow, 1893-95, hon. fellow, 1897-98, Columbia; asst. prof. physiology, Tufts Coll. Med. Sch., 1899-1900; instr. physiology, Harvard Med. Sch., 1900-01; asst. prof. physiol. chemistry, 1901-04, asso. prof., 1904-05, prof., 1905-18. and chmn. dept. of physiology, 1909-16, U. of Chicago; prof. biochemistry, U. of Cincinnati, 1918-—, prof. emeritus, 1940-—. Known for original investigations in parthenogenesis, upon the nature of nerve impulse, in pharmacology and chem. biology; trustee Marine Biol. Lab., Woods Hole, Mass. Fellow A.A.A S.; mem. Am. Chem. Soc., Am. Physiol. Soc., Biochem. Soc., Soc. de chimie biologique, Biochemical Soc. (British), Soc. Exptl. Biology Great Britain; foregin mem. Academia Nationale dei Lincei, Rome. Commd. capt., Quartermasters Corps, Feb. 1917, and on active duty, Aug. 1917-Nov. 1918, at hdqrs. Central Dept. Author: Text Book of Physiological Chemistry (6th edit.); The Nature of Matter, Gravitation and Light; Gravitation, Space-Time and Matter, 1934; Principles of Biochemistry. Contbr. to scientific jours. Home: 1237 Glenwood Blvd., Schenectady 8. Died Sept. 21, 1957; buried Allegheny Cemetery, Pitts.

MATHEWS, Basil Joseph, educator, editor, author; b. Oxford, Eng., Aug. 28, 1879; s. A. H. and Emma (Colegrove) M.; M.A., Oxford U., 1904; LL.D. (hon.), Univ. of British Columbia, 1949; m. H. Anne Passmore, 1905 (died 1939); m. 2d, Winifred Grace Wilson, 1940. Began as private sec. to Principal Fairbairn, of Mansfield Coll., Oxford, 1899; mem. lit. staff Christian World, 1904-10; editorial sec. London Missionary Soc., 1910-19, etc.; also sec. and chmn. lit. com., Ministry of Information, British Govt., 1917-19; dir. Press Bur. of Conf. of Representatives of British Missionary Socs., 1920-24; internat. lit. sec. World's Com. of Y.M.C. Assns. (boys' work), Geneva, Switzerland, 1924-29; prof. Christian world relations, Boston U. and Andover-Newton Theological Institution, 1932-44; released for service as deputy dir., Am. Div., Ministry of Information, British Government, 1939-40; prof., Christian world-relations, Union Coll. affiliated to U. of British Columbia, Vancouver, Can., 1944-49. Clubs: Athenaeum, P.E.N. Author: The Splendid Quest, 1911; Livingstone, the Pathfinder, 1913; John Williams, the Shipbuilder, 1914; The Secret of the Raj, 1915; Paul, the Dauntless, 1916; Three Years' War for Peace, 1917; Dr. Wardlaw Thompson, 1918; The Riddle of Nearer Asia, 1918; The Ships of Peace, 1919; Christian Fellowship in Thought and Prayer (with Rev. H. Bisseker), 1919; The Argonauts of Faith (Mayflower Pilgrims), 1920; The Clash of Colour, a Study of the Race Problem, 1924; Wilfred Grenfell, the Master Mariner, 1924; Black Treasure, 1925; Young Islam on Trek, 1926; The Spirit of the Game, 1927; Roads to the City of God, 1928; Jesus and Youth, 1929; The Clash of World Forces, a Study of Nationalism, Bolshevism and Christianity, 1931; A Life of Jesus, 1931; A Little Life of Jesus, 1933; John R. Mott—World Citizen, 1933; World Tides in the Far East, 1934; Consider Africa, 1935; There Go the Ships, 1935; Shaping the Future, 1936; India Reveals Herself, 1937; The World in Which Jesus Lived, 1937; The Church Takes Root in India, 1938; Through Tragedy to Triumph, 1939; Supreme Encounter, the God of History in the World of Today, 1940; We Fight for the Future, the British Commonwealth in the World of Nations, 1940; Pattern for Living, 1942; United We Stand, The Peoples of the United Nations, 1943; The Adventures of Paul, 1944; Unfolding Drama in South East Asia, 1944; Booker T. Washington, 1948; Foward Through the Ages (U.S.A. ed.) Disciples of all Nations: The Story of Christian Expansion (British ed.), 1951. Address: Triangle Cottage, Old Boar's Hill, Oxford Eng. Died Mar. 29, 1951.

MATHEWS, John Elie, justice; b. Gray's Landing, Ga., July 19, 1892; s. John Wilcox and Ophelia McNatt (Hall) M.; B.S., Emory U., 1913; m. Alice Schumpert, Nov. 24, 1914; children—Alice (dec. 1919), John Elie, William Hugh, Helen Bryan (wife of C.F. Harding, U.S.N.). Admitted to Ga. bar, 1914, Fla. bar, 1916; prin. Eastman (Ga.) High Sch., 1913-15; practiced with W.H. Bostwick, Jacksonville, Fla., 1916-19, under own name, 1919-48; partner with son as Mathews & Mathews, 1949-51; justice Supreme Court of Florida, 1951-—, chief justice, 1955-—; attorney for Duval County, Florida, 1922-30. Mem. ho. of reps. Fla. State Legislature, 1929-33; mem. Fla. State Senate, 1942-50. Mem. Fla., Jacksonville (pres. 1937) bar assns., Civic Round Table (pres. 1937). Democrat. Methodist (trustee 1928-48). Mason (33°, Shriner). Club: Ponte Vedra (Jacksonville). Home: 1207 Siminole Dr. Office: Supreme Court Bldg., Tallahassee. Died Apr. 30 1955; buried Evergreen Cemetery, Jacksonville, Fla.

MATHEWS, William Hooker, mfg. exec.; b. Creston, Ia. Jan. 29, 1890; s. St. Elmo and Rose (Hooker) M.; student Simpson Coll., Indianola, Ia.; m. Louise Bodeker, Dec. 23, 1913; children—William H., Jr. (dec.), Marjorie Louise, Jane Rose. Supt. records and returns U.S. Vets. Bur., Wasington, 1918-20; mgr. nat. and govt. accounts dept. Am. Kardex Co., Tonawanda, N.Y., 1921, v.p. in charge gen. sales and advt., 1921; midwest divisional mgr. Remington Typewriter Co., Chgo., 1921; v.p., gen. sales mgr. Remington Rand, Buffalo, N.Y., 1923, v.p. asst. to the pres., also dir. advt. and machine maintenance, v.p., gen. mgr. typewriter and supplies div., v.p., N.Y.C., v.p., gen. sales mgr. shaver div., Bridgeport, Conn., v.p. and chmn. gen. sales com. New York, to 1939; dir. Remington Rand subsidiaries; vp., dir. and mem. exec. com. Devoe & Reynolds Co., Inc., 1938-49; pres. Southern Pacific Milling Co., Santa Barbara, Cal., 1949-—. Past mem. Nat. Office Equipment Mfrs. Assn.; past mem. steering and advt. coms. Nat. Paint, Varnish & Lacquer Assn., past mem. exec. com. N.Y. Paint, Varnish & Lacquer Assn. Elk. Clubs: Montecito Country, University, Channel City, Rancheros Visitadores, Santa Barbara, Santa Barbara County Riding, Santa Barbara Trail Riders, Inc. (Santa Barbara); Santa Maria (Cal.). Home: 1400 Hillcrest Rd. Office: 735 State St., Santa Barbara, Cal. Died Feb. 15, 1959.

MATHIAS, Robert David (mȧ-thī'ȧs), banker; b. Kansas City, Kan., May 15, 1897; s. G.U. Grant and Bertha (Wise) M.; student Rice Inst., Houston, 1914-15, Centre Coll., Danville Ky., 1915-17; m. Virginia Gertrude Grassell, Oct. 26, 1922; children—John Grant, Margaret Jane (Mrs. Kenneth Haynie), Robert David. With Depositors State Bank, Chgo. 1920-32; pres., dir. First Nat. Bank, Elkhart, Ind., 1932-35; v.p., dir. Old Nat. Bank, Evansville, Ind., 1935-48, pres., dir., 1940-48; pres. Chgo. Nat. Bank since 1948, also dir.; dir. C.& E.I. R.R., Gen. Bottlers, Inc., Chgo., Pepsi-Cola Co., Chgo., Wilson Steel & Wire Co., Chgo. Mem. Ind. Bankers Assn. (pres. 1947-48). Presbyn. (trustee). Clubs: Chgo., Union League (Chgo.); Glen View; Swan Lake. Home: 3260 Lake Shore Dr., Chgo. 13. Office: 120 S. LaSalle St., Chgo. 3. Died June 22, 1953.

MATISSE, Henri, French artist; b. Le Cateau, Nord, France, Dec. 31, 1869; student in lycée and faculty of law U. Paris; studied art Ecole des Beaux Arts, and atelier Gustave Moreau; m. Amelie Noellie Parayre, 1897; children—Jean, Pierre, Marguerite. First exhbn. works Soc. Nationale des Beaux Arts, 1893; 1st Am. exhbn., N.Y.C., 1908; 1st retrospective show, Paris, 1910; exhibited in 1st and 2d Post-Impressionist exhbns., London, 1910-11 and 1912; designed curtain scenery and costumes for Diagheliev ballet, Le Chant du Rossignol, 1920; 1st Am. retrospective show, N.Y.C., 1927. Received 1st prize Carnegie Internat. Exhbn., 1927. Represented in museums and other pub. and pvt. collections of Europe and U.S. Home: Nice, Alps Maritimes, France. Died Nov. 3, 1954.*

MATSON, Robert H(ayden), banker; b. Brazil, Ind., Apr. 16, 1897; s. Charles Edwin and Elizabeth (Farrow) M.; B.S., U. of the South, 1919; m. Constance Reynolds Ivy, June 12, 1928; children—Robert Hayden, Constance Ivy. Clerk Guaranty Bank & Trust Co., Memphis, 1919-22; nat. bank examiner, N.Y.C., 1922-25; cashier Union Planters Nat. Bank & Trust Co., Memphis, 1925-27, v.p., cashier, 1927-29; asst. cashier Nat. City Bank of N.Y. City, 1929-37, asst. v.p., 1937-46, v.p., 1946-—. Served as pilot naval aviation, 1917-18. Mem. So. Soc. N.Y., Tenn. Soc. N.Y., Am. Inst. Banking (pres. Memphis chpt. 1927-28), Pelham Manor Assn. (pres. 1944-47, dir. 1942-—). Episcopalian. Clubs: Pelham Country; Huguenot Yacht (New Rochelle, N.Y.); Union League (N.Y.C.); The Boston (New Orleans). Home: 684 Esplanade, Pelham Manor, N.Y. Office: 55 Wall St., N.Y.C. Died Apr. 1957.

MATSON, Theodore Malvin, univ. prof., traffic engr.; b. Denver, Mar. 17, 1903; s. Thomas and Alice (Swanson) M.; A.B., Stanford, 1923, E.E., 1925; m. Naomi Robinson, Aug. 14, 1926; 1 dau., Mary Jane. Electrical research asst. to Frank G. Baum, cons. engr., 1925; asst. engr. Pacific Gas and Electric Co., 1926; resident engr. San Francisco Traffic Survey Com., 1926-29; chief engr. City-wide Traffic Com. of Kansas City, Mo., 1929 30; asst. traffic engr. City of Phila., 1930-33, traffic engr., 1933-36; research asso. Bur. for Street Traffic Research, Harvard; dir. San Francisco City-wide Traffic Survey, 1935-37. research asso., 1937-38; research asst., asst. prof. Bur. for Street Traffic Research, Yale, 1938-43; dir., prof. Bur. Highway Traffic, Yale, since 1943; cons. Eno Foundn. for Traffic Control; sec. Com. on Transportation, Yale; traffic cons. to engr. bd., U.S. War Dept. Dir. Inst. Traffic Engring., 1939-41; mem. nocturnal logistics committee, Nat. Defense Research Council, 1943-45; traffic cons. for pub. and private agencies. Mem. Inst. Traffic Engrs., Highway Research Bd., Sigma Xi. Clubs: Yale (New York); Graduate (New Haven). Author: Market Street Traffic Control Plan, 1928; Street Traffic Control Plan of San Francisco, 1927; (with Miller McClintock) Report to San Francisco Traffic Survey, 1927; (with Miller McClintock) Traffic Control Plan for Kansas City, 1930; Principles of Traffic Signal Timing, National Safety Council Transactions, 1929; (with T. W. Forbes) Measurement of Overtaking and Passing Distances, 1940; (with L. Williams) Elements of Intersection Redesign, 1940: War Worker Transportation, 1943; Traffic Engineering, 1954. Home: 255 Ridgewood Av., Hamden, Conn. Died Dec. 15, 1954; buried St. Mary's Cemetery, Mount Carmel, Conn.

MATTERN, David Earl, educator; b. Colfax, Ia., Dec. 11, 1890; s. Jacob Asbury and Dora (Ogg) M.; B.M., Bush Temple Conservatory of Music, Chicago, 1911; student Chicago Conservatory of Music, 1908-10; A.B., Cornell, 1915; student Eastman Sch. of Music, U. of Rochester, 1923-25; M.Ed., U. of Mich., 1932; studied violin with Ludwig Becker (Chicago), Ottakar Sevcik and Paul Stoeving (Ithaca, N.Y.), Vladmir Resnikoff (Eastman Sch. of Music); studied conducting with Albert Coates and Eugene Goossens (Eastman Sch. of Music); m. Viola Smith, Apr. 21, 1924; 1 dau., Shirley (Mrs. Haldon Smith). Played professionally in Chicago, also teacher Bush Temple Conservatory, 1906-11; teacher of music edn., Cornell, summers 1915-20, Westchester (Pa.) Normal Sch., summers 1922-25, Eastman Sch. of Music, 1921-26; supervisor of music, Grand Rapids, Mich., schs., 1926-29; prof. music edn. and head dept. music edn., U. of Mich., since 1929; first violinist, Rochester (N.Y.) Philharmonic Orchestra, 1922-26; conductor Schubert Club, Grand Rapids, 1926-29, Men's Glee Club, U. of Mich., 1931, 47, U. of Mich. Extension Orchestra, Detroit, since 1945. Mem. Music Educators Nat. Conf. (mem. various coms.), Music Teachers Nat. Assn. (chmn. music edn. com. 1945-48), Michigan Music Educators Assn. (pres., 1945-47), Phi Delta Kappa, Phi Mu Alpha, Lambda Chi Alpha. Presbyn. (mem. of session). Club: Rotary International. Contbr. articles in music jours. Home: 3081 Dover Pl., Ann Arbor, Mich. Deceased.

MATTESON, Herman Howard (măt'tĕ-sŭn); born Grundy County, Ill., Mar. 17, 1875; s. John Richardson and Nelly Lenore (McAllister) M.; B.S., U. of Minn., 1896, M.A., 1897; M.D., Wis. Eclec. Med. College, 1899; m. Mellissa Norton Whitbeck, 1900 (dec.); m. 2d, Valentine Beck, 1936. Acted as surgeon of exploring parties in Central America, ship's surgeon, surgeon to federal penitentiaries. Dir. of research, Nat. Nutrition Found., Los Angeles. Mem. Authors League America, Pi Gamma Mu, Free Lances. Clubs: University of Minnesota, Deauville Club (Santa Monica, Calif.). Author: The Trap, 1921; also short stories and serials in mags.; many sociol. articles on prison system and nat. lecturer on the same theme; author and dir. motion picture depicting aboriginal life of Puget Sound and Alaska. Originator, writer and broadcaster of radio program known as The Family Doctor, travel stories and simplified health talks. Home: 129 N. Oxford. Office: 4350 Beverly Blvd., Los Angeles. Died Mar. 18, 1951.

MATTHAI, Joseph Fleming, ins. exec.; b. Balt., Nov. 24, 1889; s. William H. and Alice B. (Jones) M.; M.E., Cornell, 1912; m. Emily Schoolfield, Nov. 16, 1931; children—Joseph Fleming, Robert S. Lane (stepson). With Beaver Dam Marble Co., 1912-15; with U.S. Fidelity & Guaranty Co., 1915—, dir., 1940—, v.p., 1940, exec. v.p., 1945—, chmn. bd., 1955—; v.p., dir. Del Mar Co.; dir. Balt. Nat. Bank (now Fidelity-Balt. Nat. Bank & Trust Co.), Fidelity Insurance Co. of Can., Fidelity & Guaranty Ins. Co., Savs. Bank of Balt. Dir. U.S. C. of C., 1947-49; pres. Assn. Casualty and Surety Companies, 1950-52. Clubs: Maryland, Merchants, Elkridge. Home: 3901 Greenway, Balt. 18. Office: U.S. Fidelity & Guaranty Co., Calvert and Redwood Sts., Balt. 3. Died May 24, 1955; buried Druid Ridge Cemetery, Balt.

MATTHES, Gerard Hendrik, civil and hydraulic engr.; b. Amsterdam, Holland, Mar. 16, 1874; s. Willem Ernst and Johanna (van der Does) M.; B.S. in Civil Engring., Mass. Inst. Tech., 1895; m. Mary M. Bewick, Mar. 3, 1904; 1 dau., Florence B. (Mrs. H. E. Stephens). Came to U.S., 1891, naturalized, 1896. Instrument man and draftsman, 1895-97; asst. hydrographer U.S. Geol. Survey, 1897-1902; engr. asst. supervising engr. U.S. Reclamation Service, 1902-07; designing engr., resident engr., and supt. constrn. Colo. Power Co., 1907-11; prin. engr. hydro-electric dept. Am. Water Works and Guaranty Co., on constrn. of power development in W.Va., 1911-13; div. engr. for State Water Supply Commn. of Pa., in charge of flood problems, 1913-15; hydraulic engr. Miami Conservancy Dist. on flood control, 1915-20; U.S. asst. engr. War Dept., Chattanooga, Tenn., charge survey of Tenn. River and tributaries which include first aerial photog. survey of rivers undertaken by war dept., 1920-23; con. engr., N.Y., specializing aerial surveys and hydro-elec. power projects, 1923-28; with War Dept. as sr. hydro-elec. engr. and later prin. engr. charge comprehensive studies relating to water power, flood control, and nav. improvements in southeastern states, 1929-32; prin. engr., head engr. and cons. to pres. Miss. River Commn. on flood control of lower Miss. River, 1932-45; also head engr. and dir. U.S. Waterways Expt. Sta., 1942-45; pvt. cons. practice specializing river, harbor and irrigation projects, N.Y.; cons. to sec. hydraulic resources, Mexico, 1948-50; cons. Associated Navigation Companies, Colombia, S.A., on improvement Magdalena River, 1952. Member astronomic expedition to Sumatra sent by Mass. Inst. Tech., 1901; cons. to Nat. Resources Bd. for lower Miss. River, 1934, for War Dept. on Conchas Dam, N.M., 1935-37; mem. spl. cons. bd. on flood control for T.V.A., 1936; charge geol. investigation of alluvial valley of Miss. River for Miss. River Commn., 1941-45. Recipient citation and award for exceptional civilian service from War Dept., 1944. Mem. Am. Soc. C.E. (chmn. com. on floods 1934-41; hon. mem. 1943; Norman medalist 1949), American Geophys. Union, Engineers Club. Inventor tetrahedral block revetments for river banks; designer of topographic slide rule for use in plane-table surveying. Author and illustrator: River Engineering pub. in American Civil Engineering Practice, Vol. II, 1956; also articles and reports. Address: Broadway Central Hotel, 673 Broadway, N.Y.C. 12. Died Apr. 8, 1959; buried Oak Creek Canyon, Prescott, Ariz.

MATTHEWS, Burrows, newspaper editor; b. Buffalo, N.Y., Jan. 27, 1893; s. George Edward and Mary Elizabeth (Burrows) M.; grad. St. Lukes Sch., Wayne, Pa., 1911; m. Edith Peter, June 1, 1916 (died Mar. 6, 1947); one son, James Newson; married 2d, Anne M. McIlhenney. Reporter for the Buffalo Express, 1911, legislative corr. at Albany, N.Y., 1914-15, city editor, 1916-17, Sunday editor, 1919-23, mng. editor, 1923-26, pres. and gen. mgr., 1926; pres. and editor Buffalo Courier-Express, merger of Express and Courier, 1926-30, v.p. and editor, 1930—. Served as 1st lt., later capt. inf., U.S. Army, 1917-18; entered the service Aug. 1943 as major; promoted lt. col., 1944; attached Pub. Relations Div. of SHAEF; spl. adv. Gen. Ridgway, Far East Command, 1952, later at SHAPE. Awarded Bronze Star. Pres. N.Y. State Publs. Assn., 1939; mem. Am. Soc. Newspaper Editors, Sigma Delta Chi, dir. Buffalo Soc. of Natural Scis., Republican. Presbyn. Clubs: Saturn, Country, Pack, Pytonga Fish and Game. Home: 224 Summer St. Address: 787 Main St., Buffalo, N.Y. Died Dec. 30, 1954; buried Forest Lawn Cemetery, Eden, N.Y.

MATTHEWS, Francis Patrick, govt. ofcl.; b. Albion, Neb., Mar. 15, 1887; s. Patrick Henry and Mary Ann (Sullivan) M.; A.B., Creighton U., 1910, A.M., 1911, LL.B., 1913; LL.D., Marquette U., 1940, John Marshall Coll., Jersey City, N.J., 1943; LL.D., Villanova Coll., Phila., 1950, Loyola U., 1950, Holy Cross Coll., Creighton U., U. Notre Dame, 1951; m. Mary Claire Hughes, Nov. 24, 1914; children—Mary Claire (Mrs. John E. Dwyer), Kathleen (Mrs. J. R. O'Connell), Francis P. Jr., Patricia (Mrs. William Rosser), Marian (Mrs. D. Howard), Marguerite (Mrs. Robert G. Schneider). Admitted to Nebraska bar, 1913; consul Reconstruction Finance Corp. Nebraska and Wyo., 1933-49; chmn. bd. and dir. Securities Acceptance Corp.; pres. 1st Fed. Savings and Loan Association of Omaha; director radio station WOW, Inc.; director and member executive committee Northwestern Bell Telephone Co. Chmn. Douglas Co., Neb., Dem. Central Com., 1932-36; dir. for Dept. of Finance, U.S. Chamber of Commerce, 1941-51, chmn. com. on Socialism and Communism; mem. bd. dirs. Omaha Chamber of Commerce, 1937-41; pres., 1938-39; mem. citizens com. Community Chests of America; mem. bd. govs. Omaha Community Chest, 1930-40, pres. 1938-39, chmn. 1936 campaign; mem. bd. dirs. Father Flanagan's Boys' Home, Boys Town, Neb., mem. bd. regents Creighton U.; dir. Duchesne Coll. and Convent of the Sacred Heart; past chmn. Met. Utilities Dist. Omaha, Omaha Public Library Board.; vice president National War Fund (mem. bd. and exec. com.); mem. exec. com., Nat. Conf. of Catholic Charities, 1931-34; v. chmn. United Defense Fund; v.p. U.S.O. (mem. bd., exec. com. and incorporator); chmn. exec. com., Nat. Catholic Community Service; member board American Overseas Aid, Sept. 1948; member board, sec., War Prisoners Aid; mem. President's Com. on Civil Rights, 1947; secretary of Navy, May 1949-July 1951; served as U.S. ambassador to Ireland,, 1951-53. Awarded Medal for Merit, 1946. Decorated Knight, Order of St. Gregory, 1924, Knight Comdr., 1938, Knight Comdr. with Grand Cross, 1942; Knight Comdr. with Grand Cross of Knights of Holy Sepulchre, 1944; designed Secret Papal Chamberlain with Cape and Sword by Pope Pius XII, 1944; awarded Catholic Action Medal, St. Bonaventure's Coll., N.Y., 1943. Spl. rep. of Cath. Adminstr. Bd. of Bishops to visit England, Ireland and Scotland, 1943, various countries in Europe and Middle East, 1944, in connection with welfare services for U.S. armed forces and relief for peoples of liberated areas. Member Am., Neb., Omaha and Fed. Commns. bar assns., Irish-Am. Hist. Soc. of N.Y. Nebraska State Historical Soc. Democrat. Roman Catholic. K.C. (Neb. state dep. 1923-24; supreme board directors, 1924-33; deputy supreme knight 1933-39; supreme knight 1939-45). Clubs: Rotary, Omaha Athletic; Metropolitan of N.Y. National Press, hon. Army-Navy (Washington). Home: 3920 Dewey Av. Office: Omaha Nat. Bank Bldg., Omaha, Neb. Died Oct. 18, 1952; buried Calvary Cemetery, Omaha, Neb.

MATTHEWS, Harry S(loan), Jr., business exec.; b. Stretford, Eng., June 17, 1902 (parents U.S. citizens); s. Harry S. and Gertrude B. (Gleason) M.; student pub. schs., U. Pitts., class 1924; m. Myrtle Swormstedt, Mar. 28, 1929; 1 son, Harry Sloan, III. With Pitts. Consolidation Coal Co. since 1927, v.p. in charge sales since 1949; dir. North Western-Hanna Fuel Co. Home: 450 Maple Av., Edgewood, Pitts. 18. Office: Koppers Bldg., Pitts. Died Dec. 19, 1954.

MATTHEWS, Isaac George, clergyman; b. Middleville, Ont., Can., May 29, 1871; s. Jacob and Jeanette (Anderson) M.; A.B., McMaster U., Ont., 1897, A.M., 1898; B.Th., McMaster Theol. Sem., 1903; Ph.D., U. Chgo., 1912; studied Marburg U., Germany; m. Nina Blanche Foreman, Sept. 4, 1905; children—Jean Doris, Jackson Kenneth. Ordained Bapt. ministry, 1898; pastor Jackson Av. Ch., Vancouver, 1898-1900, New Westminster, B.C., 1900-03; prof. O.T. lang. and lit. McMaster U., 1904-19; pastor 1st Bapt. Ch., New Haven, 1919-20; lectr. Yale Div. Sch., 1919-20; prof. O.T. lang. and lit. Crozer Theol. Sem., 1920-42; prof. history Christian Ch., Bapt. Inst., Phila., 1921-26; annual prof. Am. Sch. Oriental Research, Jerusalem, 1930-31. Mem. Soc. Bibl. Lit. and Exegesis, Am. Oriental Soc., Oriental Club of Phila. Republican. Author: The Jewish Apologetic to the Grecian World in the Apocryphal and Pseudepigraphical Literature, 1914; How to Interpret Old Testament Prophecy, 1919; Old Testament Life and Literature, 1923, revised, 1934; Commentary I and II Samuel, 1929; Commentary Haggai and Malachi, 1935; Commentary Ezechiel, 1937; The Religious Pilgrimage of Israel, 1947. Address: 173 Owen Av., Lansdowne, Pa. Died Mar. 26, 1959.

MATTHEWS, Paul, bishop; b. Glendale, O., Dec. 25, 1866; s. Stanley and Mary Ann (Black) M.; A.B., Princeton, 1887, D.D., 1916; B.D., Gen. Theol. Sem., N.Y.C., 1890, S.T.D., 1916; D.D., Seabury Div. Sch., 1915. Trinity and Univ. of South; m. Elsie Procter, May, 1896 (died 1946); children—Charlotte Elizabeth (Mrs. H. S. van Buren), Thomas Stanley, Mary Ann (Mrs. William Mode Spackman), Harriet Procter (dec.), Margaret (Mrs. Walter Flinsch), Dorothea (Mrs. D. M. Dooling). Deacon, 1890, priest, 1891, Protestant Episcopal Ch.; asst. Ch. of Advent, Walnut Hills, Cin., 1890-91; entered Associate Mission, Omaha, in charge St. Paul's and St. John's chs., 1891-95; rector St. Luke's Cin., 1896-1904; dean St. Paul's Cathedral, Cin., 1904-13; elected bishop coadjutor of Milw., 1905, but declined; dean of Cathedral, Faribault, Minn., and prof. Seabury Div. Sch., 1913-15; consecrated bishop of N.J., 1915, retired, 1937. Home: Merwick, Princeton, N.J.; also Winter Park, Fla. Died Jan. 17, 1954; buried Princeton Cemetery.

MATTHEWS, Velma Dare, biologist; b. Burlington, N.C., Aug. 3, 1904; d. Joseph Marvin and Cora (Moore) Matthews; A.B., Woman's Coll. of Univ. of N.C., 1925; A.M., Univ. of N.C., 1927, Ph.D., 1930; research Allegany Sch. Natural History, summer 1931, Univ. of N.C., 1932-34, U. of Va., summer 1935; unmarried. Prof. of biology, Ark. Agr. and Mech. Coll., Monticello, 1930-31; prof. of biology and head dept., Coker Coll., Hartsville, S.C., since 1935; visiting prof. of mycology, Mt. Lake Biol. Sta. of U. of Va., summer, 1936. Mem. S.C. Acad. Science (v.p. 1941-45, pres. 1946-47), N.C. Acad. Science, Bot. Soc. Am., A.A.A.S., Mycol. Soc., Am. Fern Soc., Torrey Bot. Club, Am. Assn. Univ. Women, Sigma Xi. Author: Studies on the Genus Pythium, 1931; Saprolegniales, North American Flora, Vol. II, 1937. Contbr. to scientific jours. Address: Coker Coll., Hartsville, S.C. Died Jan. 7, 1958.

MATTHIAS, Edward Shiloh (mȧ-thī'ȧs), judge; b. Gilboa, O., Apr. 6, 1873; s. Albert C. and Eleanor P. (Harris) M.; A.B., Ohio Northern Univ., 1893, hon. LL.D., 1925; LL.D., Miami University, 1952; married Mary F. Crouch, April 23, 1898; children—Edward D., John Marshall, Mrs. Mary Ellen Dawson, Mrs. Alice Helen Jacoby, Mrs. Florence Howe Merkel. Admitted to Ohio bar, and began practice in Van Wert, O., 1895; city solicitor, Van Wert, 1896-1900; judge Court of Common Pleas 3d Judiciary Dist. of Ohio, 1904-14; judge Supreme Court of Ohio since Jan. 1, 1915. Served as capt. Co. D, 2d Ohio Vol. Inf., Spanish-Am. War, Apr. 23, 1898-Feb. 10, 1899. Dept. comdr., Dept. of Ohio, United Spanish War Vets., 1927-28, comdr. in chief, 1930-31. Mem. bd. of trustees Ohio Northern U. Mem. Am. and Ohio bar assns., Delta Theta Phi. Clubs: University, Optimist. Republican. Presbyterian. Mason (32°). Home: 2135 Iuka Av., Columbus, O. Died Nov. 2, 1953.

MATTHIESSEN, Francis Otto, teacher, writer; b. Pasadena, Cal., Feb. 19, 1902; s. Frederic William and Lucy Orne (Pratt) M.; student Hackley Sch., Tarrytown, N.Y., 1914-18; A.B., Yale, 1923; B. Litt., Oxford U., 1925; A.M., Harvard, 1926, Ph. D., 1927; D.Litt., Princeton, 1947. Instr. Yale, 1927-29; instr. and tutor, Harvard, 1929-30, asst. prof., 1930-34, asso. prof., 1934-42, prof., 1942—, chmn. bd. of tutors in history and lit., 1931-48, sr. tutor, Eliot House 1931-33; mem. editorial bd. New England Quarterly, 1937-40; Alexander lectr. U. Toronto, 1944; vis. prof. Charles U., Prague, fall term, 1947; sr. fellow Kenyon Sch. English, 1948—. Mem. nat. exec. com. Progressive Citizens of Am.; Mass. del. at large, Progressive Party; trustee Samuel Adams Sch. of Social Studies, 1944-48; mem. exec. com. Mass. Civil Liberties Union; pres. Harvard Tchrs. Union, 1940-42, 46-47. Mem. Nat. Inst. Arts and Letters, Am. Fedn. Tchrs., Phi Beta Kappa, Signet Soc. (Harvard), Psi Upsilon, Skull and Bones, Elizabethan Club (Yale). Episcopalian. Author: Sarah Orne Jewett, 1929; Translation: An Elizabethan Art, 1931; The Achievement of T. S. Eliot, 1935 (new and enlarged edition), 1947; American Renaissance: Art and Expression in the Age of Emerson and Whitman, 1941; Henry James: The Major Phase, 1944; Russell Cheney; A Record of His Work, 1947; The James Family, 1947; From the Heart of Europe, 1948; Theodore Dreiser, 1950; The Responsibilities of the Critic, Essays and Reviews, 1952. Editor: Stories of Writers and Artists by Henry James, 1944; Selected Poems of Herman Melville, 1944; The American Novels and Stories of Henry James, 1947; The Notebooks of Henry James (with Kenneth B. Murdock), 1947; The Oxford Book of American Verse, 1950. Home: 87 Pinckney St., Boston. Office: Harvard U., Cambridge, Mass. Died Apr. 1, 1950.

MATTHISON, Edith Wynne (Mrs. Charles Rann Kennedy) (măth'ĭ-sŭn), actress; b. Birmingham, Warwickshire, Eng.; d. Henry and Kate (Wynne) Matthison; student King Edward's Grammar Sch. and Midland Inst., Birmingham; hon. M.A., Mt Holyoke Coll., 1927; Litt.D., Rutgers Coll. and Oberlin Coll., 1932, Russell Sage Coll., Troy, N.Y., 1934; m. Charles Rann Kennedy, July 19, 1898. Naturalized U.S. citizen, 1917. Began in music comedy and since appeared in Greek plays, Everyman (in which she created the title rôle), Mysteries, Shakespearean and other Elizabethan plays, old English comedies, and modern plays. Played Portia and Rosamund with Sir Henry Irving, Andromache in the Troades and Elektra in the Elektra of Euripides in Court Theatre, London; played Auntie in The Servant in the House and played Herdisa in the Winterfeast; appeared as Sister Beatrice (Maeterlinck), Hermione and Mrs. Ford (Shakespeare), also in The Blue Bird, The Piper, The Terrible Meek, The Necessary Evil; part of Andromache in the Granville Barker rivals of The Trojan Women of Euripides at the Am. univs. In motion pictures, starred in The Governor's Lady, as Queen Katherine, in Henry VIII, with Sir Herbert Beerbohm Tree, last American tour; as Light, in Maeterlinck's The Betrothal; then toured own company in husband's plays, The Chastening, The Admiral, The Salutation, Old Nobody, Crumbs, Flaming Ministers. Also in Greek plays; starred in annual Greek play at Bennett Jr. Coll., Milbrook, N.Y., of which was until 1940 a trustee, and head of the drama dept. Recipient gold medal for best stage diction, Am. Acad. Arts and Letters, 1927. Home: 10678 Rochester Av., West Los Angeles 24, Cal. Died Sept. 23, 1955; buried Inglewood Park Cemetery, Inglewood.

MATTILL, Henry Albright (măt-tĭl'), biochemist; b. Glasgow, Mo., Nov. 28, 1883; s. Henry and Emma (Fryhofer) M.; A.B., Adelbert Coll. (Western Reserve U.), 1906; A.M., 1907; Ph.D., U. of Ill., 1910; S.Dc. (honorary), Western Reserve Univ., 1952; m. Helen Isham, Dec. 31, 1912; 1 son, John Isham. Asst. in chemistry, U. of Ill., 1906-08, fellow in biochem., 1908-10; assistant professor physiol. and physiol. chemistry, U. of Utah, 1910-11, asso. prof., 1911-12, prof., 1912-15; asst. prof. nutrition, U. of Calif., 1915-18; prof. biochemistry, U. of Rochester, 1919-27; prof. of biochemistry and head of department, University of Iowa since 1927. Captain and maj. Sanitary Corps, Div. of Food and Nutrition, Army U.S. and A.E.F., 1918-19. Recipient Iowa medal Am. Chemical Society, 1950. Fellow A.A.A.S.; mem. Am. Soc. of Biol. Chemists (sec., 1933-38; council 1938-44; edit. com., 1944—; v.p. 1951, pres. 1952), Am. Physiological Soc. (edit. bd. Physiol. Rev. since 1948), Soc. Exptl. Biology and Medicine, Am. Chem. Soc., Am. Inst. of Nutrition, A.A.U.P., Iowa Acad. Sci., Phi Beta Kappa, Sigma Xi, Gamma Alpha, Phi Lambda Upsilon, Alpha Chi Sigma, Alpha Omega Alpha. Unitarian. Home: 358 Lexington Av., Iowa City, Ia. Died Mar. 30, 1953.

MATTINGLY, Barak Thomas (măt'ing-lĭ), lawyer; b. Eureka Springs, Ark., Mar. 15, 1901; s. Hunter and Hallie (Beam) M.; A.B., Marvin Coll., Fredericktown, Mo., 1917; student St. Louis U., 1920-21; LL.B., LL.M., City Coll. Law, St. Louis, 1924; m. Melba Schmidt, Dec. 30, 1922. Admitted to Mo. bar, 1924, since practiced in St. Louis, sr. partner, Lowenhaupt, Mattingly, Charnoff & Stolar; chmn. bd. Ozark Airlines; chmn., v.p. Accounts Supervision Co., Parliament Loan Co.; chmn. The Bank of Ferguson; pres. The Underwriters Co.; dir., v.p. Nat. Hotel Enterprises, Inc., City Bus. Terminal, Inc.; dir. Am. Transit Corp., Nat. Warehouses, Inc. Chmn. Mo. Rep. Com., 1937, 38, 39; mem. Rep. Nat. Com., 1940-46. Served as pvt. 6th Regt., USMC, 2d Div., AEF, 1917-19. Dir. Central Hosp. Mem. Am., Mo. State, St. Louis bar assns., Am. Judicature Soc., Am. Legion (chmn. comdrs. conf.), Soldier Meml. Commn. (vice chmn.), Marine Corps League, Purple Heart Soc. Republican (mem. and counsel nat. com.). Presbyn. Mason (32°, Shriner). Clubs: Ambassador, Balboa Bay, Capitol Hill, John Marshall, Nat. Republican. Columbia. Home: 2 Chambers Rd., St. Louis 15. Office: 209-408 Oliver St., St. Louis 2. Died July 18, 1957; buried Hiram Cemetery.

MAUDE, Cyril Francis, actor, mgr.; b. London, Eng., Apr. 24, 1862; s. Capt. Charles Henry and Hon. Georgiana Hanbury Tracy M.; studied for the stage; m. Winifred Emory (actress), June 20, 1888 (died 1924); 1 son, 2 daus.; m. 2d, Mrs. P. H. Trew, 1927. Went to Can., 1882, on account of ill health, and worked as farm hand; début as the servant in East Lynne, Denver, 1884; returned to Eng. same yr. and appeared as Mr. Pilkie in The Great Divorce Case, Criterion Theatre, London, 1886; played in various theatres in London for 10 yrs., as a comedian; with Frederick Harrison managed Haymarket Theatre, London, 1896-1905; mgr. The Playhouse, 1907—. Prin. rôle: Major Bingham, in The Second in Command; Lord Meadows, in Toddles; James Cottenham, in Tantalizing Tommy; the Red Gavin Dishart, in The Little Minister; Sir Peter Teazle, in The School for Scandal; Doctor Pangloss, in The Heir-at-Law; Richard Lascelles, in The Flag Lieutenant; etc. Made tour of U.S. and Can., 1913-14. Ex-pres. Nat. Managers' Assn., Actors Orphanage. Mason. Clubs: Garrick, Beefsteak, Ranelagh (London); Players (N.Y.C.). Home: Torquay, Eng. Died Feb. 20, 1951.*

MAURER, Oscar Edward, clergyman; b. Garnavillo, Ia., Jan. 22 1878; s. Jacob D. and Loretta E. (Wirkler) M.; B.A. magna cum laude, Beloit (Wis.) Coll., 1903, D.D., 1912; M.A., Yale, 1906, B.D. cum laude, 1906; m. Marion Elizabeth Spooner, July 25, 1905; children—William Spooner, Oscar Edward, Eric Wirkler, Marion. Ordained to Congregational ministry, 1906; pastor Great Barrington, Mass., 1906-09, Center Ch., New Haven, 1909-43, pastor emeritus, 1943-50; interim pastor Central Union Ch., Honolulu and Union Church, Wailuku, Hawaii, 1943-45, United Church, Bridgeport, Conn., 1946-47, First Ch., St. Petersburg, Fla., 1947-48, First Ch., Branford, Conn., 1948. Mem. 2d Regt. Wis. N.G., 2 yrs.; chaplain 2d Co. Governor's Foot Guard of Conn. with rank of capt. Trustee of Home for Aged Women; chmn. bd. trustees Talladega (Ala.) Coll.; dir. New Haven Pub. Library; mem. Pilgrim Fund Commn.; mem. exec. com. Am. Missionary Assn.; dir. Congl. Home Board; rec. sec. Am. Bd. Commrs. for Fgn. Missions; dir. Conn. Temperance Found.; hon. v.p. New Haven Family Soc.; dean Conn. Congl. Young People's Summer Conf., 1924-27; mem. Congl. Commn. on Missions; moderator Gen. Council Congl. and Christian Chs. of the U.S., 1938-40; sec. YMCA, Camp Meade, Md., 1917, in France, 1917-18. Mem. Assn. Congl. Ministers, Beta Chapter Phi Beta Kappa (Wis.), Beta Chapter Delta Sigma Rho (Wis.), Phi Kappa Epsilon (Yale), Pi Gamma Mu. Clubs: Lions, Graduate, Friars. Author: Brotherhood of the Burning Heart, 1915; Pilgrim Principles, 1920; A Puritan Church, 1938. Three Early Hawaiian Christians, 1944. Editor Yale Divinity Quarterly, 1905-06. Editor, Daily Devotions, 1946-50. Home: 90 Avon St., New Haven 11. Died Nov. 30, 1950; buried New Haven.

MAURO, Philip (mou'rô), author, lawyer; b. St. Louis, Jan. 7, 1859; s. Charles G. and Charlotte E. (Davis) M.; ed. Columbian U., Washington; m. Emily J. Rockwood, 1882; children—Margaret F., Isabel R. (Mrs. Charles S. French). Author: From Reason to Revelation; Man's Day, 1908; Life in the Word, 1909; The Number of Man, 1911; God's Gift and Our Response, 1914; God's Gospel and God's Righteousness, 1914; God's Love and God's Children, 1914; Looking for the Savior, 1914; The World and Its God, 1917; After This—The Church, The Kingdom and The Glory, 1918; God's Present Kingdom, 1919; Ruth, the Satisfied Stranger, 1920; Our Liberty in Christ, 1920; A Kingdom Which Cannot Be Shaken, 1921; Evolution at the Bar, 1922; Chronology of the Bible, 1922; The Seventy Weeks and The Great Tribulation, 1923; James—The Epistle of Reality, 1923; The Patmos Visions, 1925; How Long to the End, 1927; The Gospel of the Kingdom, 1928; The Hope of Israel, 1929; Of Things Which Soon Must Come to Pass, 1932; The Four Horsemen of the Apocalypse; Short Exposition of the Seventy Weeks Prophecy, 1933; The Church, the Churches and the Kingdom, 1936. Home: 713 Blue Ridge Av., Culpeper, Va. Died Apr. 7, 1952.

MAURY, Antonia Caetana de Paiva Pereira (maw' rĭ), astronomer; b. Cold Spring-on-Hudson. N.Y., Mar. 21, 1866; d. Mytton and Virginia (Draper) M.; A.B., Vassar, 1887. Asst., Harvard Obs., 1889-95, research asst., 1917-35, ret. 1935; work instr. physical sci. Gilman Sch., Cambridge, Mass., 1891-94, on classification of stellar spectra and spectroscovic binaries. Mem. Am. Astron. Soc., Audubon Soc., New Eng. Wild Flower Preservation Soc., Am. Scenic and Historic Preservation Soc. Author of Classification of Spectra of Bright Northern Stars, pub. as Harvard Annals, Vol. XXVIII, Part 1, 1897; Spectral Changes of Beta Lyrae, 1933. Home: 407 S. Broadway, Hastings on Hudson, N.Y. Deceased.

MAVERICK, Maury (măv'rĭk), lawyer; b. San Antonio, Tex., Oct. 23, 1895; s. Albert and Jane Lewis (Maury) M.; ed. Va. Mil. Inst., 1912-13, U. of Tex., 1913-16; m. Terrell Louise Dobbs, May 22, 1920; children—Maury, Terrelita (Mrs. Sam Houston Clinton, Jr.). Admitted to bar, Tex., 1916, Cal., 1917; practiced in Tex., Los Angeles, Calif., and Washington, D.C. Dir. Govt. Div. of War Prodn. Bd., Washington, D.C., 1941-43; vice chmn. W.P.B., 1943-46; chmn. Smaller War Plants Corp. (govt. war agency), 1943-46. Mem. 74th and 75th Congresses (1935-39), 20 Tex. Dist. Mayor San Antonio, Tex., 1939-41; as mayor reorganized city depts., including health, police and fire; also built numerous projects, including "Villita," restoration old Spanish Village, the Pan-Am. Center. Leader in Ho. of Reps. in fight for Tenn. Valley Authority, conservation natural resources and power legislation; proponent of slum clearance and pub. works; proposed in Congress, 1938, 50,000 planes and 100,000 trained mil. pilots; early advocate of big navy, air force and mechanized army. Served with 157th Inf., Camp Kearney, Calif.; 1st lt., 28th Inf., 1st Div., A.E.F., France; wounded Oct. 4, 1918. Awarded Silver Star, Purple Heart, Citation for "gallantry in action." On two special presdl. missions to Europe during World War II, including all Allied Nations and Japan. Mem. Am. Legion, D.A.V., S.A.R., Vets. Fgn. Wars, Legion of Honor (France), Sigma Chi, Sigma Delta Chi. Democrat. Episcopalian. Clubs: National Press, Army and Navy (Washington, D.C.). Contbr. mags. Author of "A Maverick American" and "In Blood and Ink." Home: 2422 Hillcrest Dr. E. Address: Transit Tower, San Antonio. Died June 7, 1954; buried San Jose Cemetery, San Antonio.

MAWHINNEY, Robert James, ex-solicitor U.S. Treasury; b. Phila., Oct. 1, 1859; s. Robert and Rosanna (Hunt) M.; ed. pub. schs. and pvt. acad.; LL.B., Nat. U., Washington, 1901, LL.M., 1902; m. Mary Suttill, Apr. 16, 1884; children—Joseph J., Raymond J., Marie A. (Mrs. Leo I. Kavanagh), Robert F., John A. Entered Govt. service as telegraph operator and stenographer, 1883; apptd. law clk. in office of solicitor of U.S. Treasury, 1906, chief clk. and chief law clk., 1918; apptd. asst. solicitor of the Treasury, 1921, solicitor, 1926-33. Mem. Treasury Dept. Com. to draft important banking laws, 1907-08. Republican. Catholic. Author of Digest of Opinions of the Solicitor of the Treasury (1880-1910), 1910, (1911-12), 1912, and of Laws of the United States Concerning Money, Banking and Loans (1778-1909), 1910—all Govt. publs. Home: Kensington, Md. Office: Munsey Bldg., Washington. Died Nov. 18, 1954.*

MAXIMOS, Demetrios, ex-prime minister of Greece; b. Patras, Greece, July 6, 1873; s. Epaminondas and Aspasia (Londos) M.; ed. in Greece; m. Irene Manussi, Jan., 1915. Vice gov. and gov. Nat. Bank of Greece, 1914-23; senator, minister fgn. affairs and prime minister, Greece, 1932-47. Decorated crosses Kingdoms of Norway, Belgium, Italy, Yugoslavia, Roumania, Ethiopia, others. Orthodox Greek. Address: 3 Rue Lykiou, Athens, Greece. Died Oct. 15, 1955.

MAXSON, Willis Edward, ret. ry. exec.; b. Mapleton, Kan., Oct. 18, 1864; s. Daniel Webster and Louise M.; student Baker U., Baldwin, Kan., 1882-83; m. Isadora Rich, Nov. 1884 (dec.); children—Harry, Meta Maxson Robertson, Willis Edward, Jr.; m. 2d, Antoinette Gooch, Oct. 1917. With A.T.&S.F. R.R. Co., 1884-97, as station clerk, 1884-85, surveying, 1885-86, agent and operator, 1886-89, relief agent, 1889-91, joint agent with Gulf, Colo. & Santa Fe, 1891-97; with Gulf, Colo. & Santa Fe Ry. Co., 1897-1939, as agent and terminal supt., 1897-1901, supt., 1901-06, gen. supt., 1906-18 (gen. mgr. Federal R.R. Adminstrn. 1918-20), asst. gen. mgr., 1920-36, v.p. and gen. mgrs., 1936-39; also v.p and dir. 9 subsidiaries; v.p., dir. Santa Fe Tie & Lumber Co.; pres., dir. Houston Belt & Terminal Co., Ft. Worth Union Depot, Galveston Union Passenger Dept. Co.; dir. Dallas Union Passenger Terminal Co., Texas City Terminal Co.; retired Sept. 1, 1939. Mem. Galveston, Houston, Dallas and Ft. Worth Chambers of Commerce. Republican. Episcopalian. Mason. Clubs: Galveston Country; Lake Polk Country (Temple, Tex.). Home: 2720 Christopher Dr., Galveston, Tex. Died Jan. 16, 1952.

MAXWELL, Evelyn Croom, judge; b. Ala., July 27, 1863; s. Augustus Emmet and Julia Hawks (Anderson) M.; grad. normal dept. U. Nashville, 1882; m. Wilhelmina Thornton, Feb. 1, 1894. Admitted to bar, 1885; judge Criminal Ct. Escambia County, 1892-96; judge 1st Jud. Circuit of Fla., 1896-1901; Supreme Ct. commr., 1901; justice Supreme Ct. of Fla., 1902-04, resigned; now practicing law. Address: Pensacola, Fla. Deceased.

MAXWELL, Ralph Lester, state supreme ct. justice; b. Nashville, Ill., Apr. 9, 1905; s. Ira E. and Laura (Reidelberger) M.; A.B., U. Ill., 1931, LL. B., 1932; m. Beulah House, June 10, 1925; 1 dau., Madalyn. Admitted to Ill. bar, 1932; gen. practice of law, Nashville, 1932-36; states atty., Washington-Co., Ill., 1936-45; circuit judge, Third Circuit, Ill., 1945-51; Supreme Court Justice, Ill., 1951—. Mem. Am. Judicature Soc., Am. and Ill. bar assns. Home: 310 W. Main St., Nashville, Ill. Office: Supreme Ct. Bldg., Springfield, Ill.; 115 A. East Main St., Nashville, Ill. Died Aug. 29, 1956.

MAY, Andrew Jackson, congressman; b. Langley, Ky., June 24, 1875; s. John and Dorcus (Conley) M.; LL.B., 1898; m. Julia Grace Mayo, July 17, 1901; children—Olga May (Mrs. Clifford B. Latta), Andrew J., Robert V. Teacher, country schs., Floyd and Magoffin counties, Ky., 5 years; admitted to Ky. bar, 1898; in practice at Prestonsburg, 1900—; county atty., Floyd County, 1901-09; later spl. judge Circuit Court, Johnson and Martin counties; pres. Beaver Valley Coal Corp. Mem. 72d Congress (1931-33), 10th Ky. Dist., and 73d Congress (1933-35), Ky. at large, and 74th to 78th Congresses (1935-45), 7th Ky. Dist.; chmn. House Com. on Mil. Affairs since Feb. 1938. Democrat. Baptist. Mason (K.T.). Mem. Rotary Internat. Home: Prestonsburg, Ky. Died Sept. 6, 1959.

MAY, Samuel Chester, educator; born in Portland, Ore., Dec. 7, 1887; s. Emanuel and Amelia (Selling) M.; student Yale, 1908-10; LL.B., Yale Univ. Law Sch., 1912; M.A., Columbia Univ., 1920; m. Eleanor Ownsworth Parkin, Feb. 19, 1913 (died May 30, 1935); children—Randolph Parkin, Kenneth Ownsworth; m. 2d, Bernice Hubbard, Dec. 12, 1940. In practice of law, Portland, 1913-17; instr. in polit. science, Dartmouth, 1920-21; asst. prof. polit. science, U. of Calif., 1921-25; asso. prof., 1925-30, prof., 1930-55, emeritus, dir. Bur. of Pub. Adminstrn., 1930-55. 2d lit., U.S. Army, 1918. Mem. City Council, Berkeley, Calif., 1923-25; mem. com. on cost of crime, Nat. Commn. on Law Observance; consultant Calif. City Mgrs. Assn., Calif. Conf. of City Planning; U.S. del. to Union of Cities, Paris, France, 1925; U.S. del. to Internat. Congress of Local Authorities, London, 1932, Berlin, 1934, 36; U.S. del. Internat. Inst. Administrative Sciences, Warsaw, 1936, Bucharest, 1938; trustee Berkeley Library, 1935-40; mem. Berkeley Personnel Bd., 1940—; mem. Calif. Commn. on Local Home Rule; mem. Calif. Crime Problem Advisory Com.; dir. research, Commonwealth Club of California, 1925-40, Calif. State Advisory Com. on Pub. Service Training, 1938;

chairman California State Planning Board, 1939-43; chmn. Tech. Review Com. Calif. Reconstruction and Reemployment Commn., 1943-45; exec. sec., Western Governmental Research Assn., 1937-40, pres. 1947-48; sec.-treas. Social Science Research Conf. of the Pacific Coast, 1940-41; mem. exec. com. Calif. State Council of Defense, 1940-43, exec. vice-chmn., 1940-41; State rep. to San Francisco Bay Region Met. Defense Council 1941-45; member of American Soc. for Public Adminstrn.; mem. Am. Acad. Polit. and Social Science, Am. Polit. Science Assn., Calif. Acad. Science, National Municipal League, Western Governmental Research Assn., Social Science Research Council (mem. com. on pub. adminstrn. 1928-29), Internat. City Mgrs. Assn. (mem. research com.), Alpha Kappa Lambda, Pi Sigma Alpha (Nat. v.p.); hon. mem. Inst. Pub. Adminstrn. (Great Britain), membre titulaire Institut Internat. des Sciences Administratives. Mason (32°). Clubs: Faculty, Sierra. Contbr. to Nat. Municipal Review, Am. Polit. Science Rev., etc. Home: 16 Roble Rd., Berkeley 5, Cal. Died Sept. 30, 1955; buried Sunset Mausoleum, Berkley, Cal.

MAYBANK, Burnet Rhett, U.S. senator; b. Charleston, S.C.; grad. Porter Mil. Acad. and Coll. of Charleston; m. Elizabeth de Rossett Myers (died 1947); children—Burnet, Roberta, Elizabeth; m. 2d, Mrs. Mary Randolph Pelzer. Cotton exporter; alderman, City of Charleston, S.C., 1927-31; mayor of Charleston, 1931-38; governor of S.C., 1939-41; elected to fill unexpired term of U.S. Senator James F. Byrnes, 1941, re-elected for term ending 1949, present term expires 1955. Served in S.C. Naval Militia and U.S. Navy, World War I. Mem. Soc. Colonial Wars, Am. Legion, Vets. of Foreign Wars, Junior Order, Alpha Tau Omega. Episcopalian. Mason, Elk. Address: Senate Office Bldg., Washington. Died Sept. 1, 1954; buried Magnolia Cemetery, Charleston, S.C.

MAYER, Andre, U.N. official, prof.; b. Paris, France, Nov. 9, 1875; M.D., Faculty of Medicine, U. of Paris, 1900, L.D.S., Faculty of Sci., 1904; Litt.D., Middlebury, 1942, LL.D., U. of Glasgow, 1947; Hon. Dr. U. of Liége, 1956; m. Jeanne Weill, Apr. 7, 1919; children—Jean, Genevieve. Prof., U. of Strasbourg, 1919-22, Coll. de France, Paris, since 1922; dir. Inst. Physiochemical Biology; v.p., Coll. de France, 1929-47; sec. Council for Sci. Research, Paris, 1935-40; chmn., Food and Agr. Orgn., U.N., 1945-—. Mem. Nat. Acad. Medicine, France; Fedn. of Natural Science Socs. (pres., 1929-31); Acad. of Sciences (Institut de France). Address: 47 Rue De Vaugirard, Paris, France. Died May 27, 1956.

MAYER, Hy. (Henry), caricaturist; b. Worms-on-Rhine, July 18, 1868; s. Hermann M., Sr., and Helen (Loeb) M.; ed. in Eng. and Germany; grad. Gymnasium, Worms, 1885; m. Alice McKenna, Jan. 31, 1924. In business, London, where his father was established as vanilla importer in 1862; came to U.S., 1886; spent 1 yr. in Mexico. Began as artist at Cincinnati, 1887; N.Y.C. since 1893; illustrator for Fliegende Blaetter (Munich), Figaro Illustré, Le Rire (Paris); weekly page of cartoons of current events in Black and White (1898-1900), Pick-Me-Up, Pall-Mall Mag., Punch (London), Life (Worms-eye views), Judge, Truth, Harper's, Century, Collier's, etc.; cartoonist New York Times, in weekly page entitled "Impressions of the Passing Show," 1904-14; editor in chief of Puck, New York, 1914, and contbg. editor 1915. Author: Autobiography of a Monkey, 1896; In Laughland, 1899; Fantasies in Ha-Ha, 1899; A Trip to Toyland, 1900; Adventures of a Japanese Doll, 1901; Alphabet of Little People, 1901. Illustrator: The Real New York; The Top of the World; The Tumble Man, 1913; Puck Album of Caricatures, 1915. Mem. Salmagundi Club, The Lambs. Originated hand in motion drawing, creating cartoons under eye of camera. Weekly cartoons in Animated Weekly, 1909-16; released about fifty motion pictures, "Travelaughs," caricaturing his travels; creator of "Tissme, Doll," 1906. Presented by Emperor of Japan, 1906, with two original Cloisonné vases bearing imperial crest. Etcher and painter. Home: 1 Flax Hill Gardens, South Norwalk, Conn. Died Sept. 27, 1954.

MAYER, Joseph Bell, public utilities; b. Freiburg, Baden, Germany, Jan. 4, 1849; s. Jay A. and Eugiene (Walm) M.; grad. high sch., Freiburg; m. Belle F. Falck, 1874 (died 1919); children—Mrs. Robert H. Grim, J. Arthur. Came to U.S., 1868, naturalized citizen, 1872. Engaged in mercantile business until 1892; organizer and mgr. syndicates purchasing and improving large tracts of land in Buffalo and vicinity, 1892-95; organizer, 1895, later v.p. and gen. mgr. Buffalo Traction Co.; organizer Lima (O.) Ry. Co., Lima Electric Light & Heat Co., Louisville (Ky.) Lighting Co., Ft. Wayne (Ind.) Lighting Co.; asso. with Widener-Elkins Phila. syndicate in consolidation of 600 miles of rys. in Ohio; effected consolidation of Western N.Y. & Pa. Traction Co.; organized and financed Buffalo & L.E. Traction Co., 1902-06; established Erie Lighting Co., and supervised erection of high tension transmission lines in Western N.Y. and Northern Pa., in connection with Niagara Falls power; now pres. Olean Electric Light & Power Co.; v.p. Bradford Electric Co.; dir. Olean, Bradford & Salamanca R.R. Co., Erie Lighting Co. Civil service commr. for N.Y., 1895; mem. N.Y. Commn. to San Francisco Expn., 1915. Del. Dem. Nat. Conv., Chicago, 1896, and St. Louis, 1904. Mason. Clubs: Manhattan, City Midday, Automobile, Lido Country (New York); Buffalo, Country (Buffalo); City (Olean, New York). Home: 270 Park Av., N.Y. City. Died Apr. 5, 1951; buried Woodlawn Cemetery, N.Y. City.

MAYER, Louis Burt (mā'ĕr), motion picture producer; b. Minsk, Russia, July 4, 1885; s. Jacob and Sarah (Meltzer) M.; educated pub. schs., St. John, N.B., Can.; LL.D., U. N.B., 1939; m. Margaret Shenberg, June 14, 1904 (div.); children—Edith (Mrs. William Goetz), Irene (Mrs. David O. Selznick); m. 2d, Lorena L. Danker, Dec. 4, 1948. Naturalized citizen of U.S., 1912. In ship and indsl. plant salvaging business until 1906; began in motion pictures as operator of theatre, Haverhill, Mass., 1907, later controlling all theatres at Haverhill; controlled New Eng. rights for D. W. Griffith's Birth of a Nation; former propr. Am. Feature Film Co., film booking agency, New Eng.; an organizer and v.p. Metro Pictures Corp.; producer of motion pictures, as Louis B. Mayer Pictures Corp., until merged with Metro Pictures Corp., 1924, which merged with Goldwyn Co. becoming Metro-Goldwyn-Mayer Corp., of which became 1st v.p. in charge prodn.; also chief prodn. mgr. Loew's, Inc. Del. to Rep. Nat. Conv., 1928; vice chmn. Cal. Rep. State Central Com. Trustee Los Angeles Jewish Orphans Home. Mem. C. of C., U.S., Los Angeles C. of C., Community Welfare Fedn. Los Angeles (mem. bd.), Nat. Housing Com. for Congested Areas, Comml. Bd. of Los Angeles. Decorated Officer Legion of Honor, 1937; Cross of White Lion, Czechoslovakia, 1938. Jewish religion. Mason (Shriner). Clubs: Hillcrest Country; All Year Club of Southern California. Home: 625 Ocean Front, Santa Monica, Cal. Died Oct. 29, 1957.

MAYER, Oscar F., meat packer; b. Bavaria, Mar. 29, 1859; s. Ferdinand and Wilhelmina Mayer; student pub. schs., Germany; came to U.S., 1873; married Louise Greiner, May 12, 1887 (died, 1931); children —Oscar G., Frieda (Mrs. Edward Collins), Louise (Mrs. George L. Schein), Elsie (Mrs. Joseph T. Steuer), Eugenie (Mrs. Adolph C. Bolz). Started with George Weber, Detroit, Michigan, 1873-76; founded Oscar F. Mayer & Bro., Chicago, 1883; now chmn. bd. Oscar Mayer & Co., packers, Chicago, and Madison, Wis. Democrat. Lutheran. Home: 5727 Sheridan Rd. Office: 1241 Sedgwick St., Chgo. 10. Died Mar. 11, 1955; buried Rosehill Cemetery, Chgo.

MAYERS, Lawrence Seymour, corp. ofcl.; b. N.Y. C., Oct. 29, 1890; s. Morris and Pauline (Herzig) M.; student Columbia, 1911; m. Rena Ullman, July 4, 1918; children—Lawrence S., Nancy P. (Mrs. Edward H. R. Blitzer). Founder, partner L.&C. Mayers Co., 1912-29, L.&C. Mayers Co., Inc., 1929-—, treas., 1929-—; pres., 1950-56, now also chairman Cons. WPB, 1942, Fgn. Econ. Adminstrn., 1944. Candidate for congress 20th Congl. Dist. N.Y., 1944. Mem. Fed. Grand Jury Assn. (dir. So. Dist. N.Y.). Sponsor national international essay and editorial contests on subject of world peace. Home: 605 Park Av., N.Y.C. 21. Died Dec. 3, 1956.

MAYHAM, Ray Edwin (mā'ăm), banker; b. Jersey City, N.J., Apr. 3, 1882; s. Thomas Creighton and Mary Adaline (Lawyer) M.; attended Friends Sch., Rahway, N.J.; grad. Centenary Collegiate Inst., Hackettstown, N.J., 1899; student Am. Inst. of Banking and spl. coll. courses in banking; children—Grace (Mrs. Gerald L. Goodstone), Ray Edwin, Robert Terrill. Clerk Equitable Trust Company, New York City, 1899-1910; asst. treas. Union Trust Co. (now Hudson Co. Nat. Bank), Jersey City, 1910-12; state bank examiner, N.J., 1912-20; comptroller and trust officer West Side Trust Co., Newark, N.J., 1920-24, dir. since 1922, v.p., 1924-28, pres. since 1928; v.p. South Side Nat. Bank and Trust Co., Newark, 1925-28, dir., 1925-34, pres., 1928-34; v.p. Peoples Nat. Bank, Newark, 1926-28, dir., 1926-34, pres., 1928-34 (South Side Nat. Bank and Trust Co. and Peoples Nat. Bank merged with West Side Trust Co., 1934); pres. and director West Side Securities Co., 1929-33. Served as capt. and finance officer Gas Defense Division, C.W.S., U.S. Army in World War I. Treas. Essex Co. (N.J.) Bankers Assn., 1932-33, v.p., 1933-34, pres., 1934-35; treas. Newark Clearing House Assn., 1924-31, mem. Clearing House com., since 1931, vice president, 1938-41 and 1946-48, president, 1941-44; chairman committee on Federal Reserve relations for Northern N.J. of N.J. Bankers Assn., 1935-41; dir. N.J. State Chamber of Commerce, 1928-44; served as chmn. com. on banking and currency, Newark Chamber of Commerce, and mem. loan com., National Credit Corporation; member State of N.J. Banking Advisory Board 1942-46; chairman Newark War Savings Banking and Finance Committee, 1942-43. Trustee Centenary Collegiate Institute 1933-44, vice president board 1935-44. President League of Dem. Clubs of N.J., 1908-12; mem. Union County Dem. Com., 1909-11, 1922-36; pres. Rahway Dem. Club, 1909-11; pres. Westfield Dem. Club, 1922-36; elected N.J. Dem. pres. elector, 1940. Finance Com. Chmn. N.J. Ind. Voters for Roosevelt, 1944. Mem. Sons of Am. Revolution; historian West Fields Chapter, 1921-41, pres., 1928; treas. N.J. Soc., S.A.R., 1929-32, 1935-39. Mem. Acad. Polit. Science, Am. Inst. Banking, Am Legion (comdr. Martin Wallberg Post, Westfield, N.J., 1922-23), N.J. Audubon Soc., N.J. Hist. Soc., Reserve Officers Assn. of U.S., Newark Reserve Officers Assn. (pres. 1941), Royal Arcanum, Schoharie County (N.Y.) Hist. Soc., S.C. Hist. Soc., Scottish Rite Soc., Union County (N.J.) Hist. Soc., N.Y. State Hist. Assn. Mason, Elk. Clubs: Bond of N.J.; Athletic, Down Town, Baltusrol Golf. Writer and speaker on banking and business question. Address: Diamond Spring Rd., Denville, N.J. Died Sept. 13, 1952; buried Hillside, N.J.

MAYNARD, Harold Howard, university prof.; b. Janesville, Ia., May 31, 1889; s. Jesse Dana and Anna (Green) M.; A.B., Ia. State Teachers Coll., 1912; A.M., U. of Ia., 1915, Ph.D., 1922; A.M., Harvard, 1919; m. Adda Belle Forbes, Aug. 10, 1918; children—Robert, Eleanor (Mrs. Erchinger). Public sch. teacher, prin., 1912-14; instr. Vanderbilt U., 1919-20; asst. prof. business orgn., State Coll. of Wash., 1920-23; prof. business orgn., Ohio State U., since 1923, chmn. dept. since 1928. Served as pvt., sergt. and 2d lt., Quartermaster Corps, U.S. Army, 1917-19. Mem. American Marketing Assn. (dir. 1947-48), American Economic Assn., National Assn. of Teachers of Marketing (pres. 1930), Acacia, Beta Gamma Sigma, Delta Sigma Pi. Republican. Methodist. Mason. Kiwanian. Co-Author: An Introduction to Business, 1925; Principles of Marketing, 4th ed., 1946; An Introduction to Business Management, 1933 and 1939; Retail Marketing and Merchandising, 1938; Sales Management, 1940; Drug Store Management, 1941. Author: Marketing Northwestern Apples, 1923; Sales Management, rev., 1957; Principles of Marketing, rev., 1957. Home: 1780 Ardleigh Rd., Columbus 21, O. Died Mar. 13, 1957.

MAYNARD, John William, editorial writer; b. Newark, Nov. 14, 1877; s. William (M.D.) and Amelia (Kolp) M.; m. Alma Smith, June 19, 1901 (dec.); 1 dau., Dorothy S. Reporter Newark News, 1894-1912, mng. editor, 1912-24, asso. editor, 1924-27, editorial page staff, 1933-57. Vice pres., dir. Franklin Capital Corp. of Newark, 1928-32. Pres. N.J. Welfare Council, 1948-51; trustee Newark U.; dep. dir., then dir. Emergency Relief Newark. Home: 334 Grove St., Montclair, N.J. Died Sept. 26, 1957; buried East Ridgelawn Cemetery, Delawanna, N.J.

MAYNARD, Poole, cons. geologist and technologist; b. Baltimore, Feb. 15, 1883; s. Albert and Emma Dorsey (Poole) M.; A.B., Johns Hopkins Univ., 1905, Ph.D., 1909; married; children—Mary Cary, Albert. Student asst. in economic geology, Johns Hopkins, 1905-09; mem. Md. Geol. Survey and Va. Geol. Survey, 1905-09; spl. employment U.S. Geol. Survey, 1907; asst. state geologist, Ga. Geol. Survey, 1909-12; cons. geologist Central of Ga. Ry., 1912-24; industrial geologist, Atlanta, Birmingham and Coast R.R. since 1925, Atlantic Coast Line R.R. since 1938; vice pres. Maynard Furniture Co., Belton, S.C.; adviser in non-metallics to U.S. Bur. of Mines since 1939, also cons. engr.; established bus. as cons. geologist, 1912, particular reference to industrial processes in non-metallics; orginated patents for manufacture heavy clay vitrified products from slag and clay. Coloring of burned clay granules by precipitation of colors; collaborator in patents and processes for concentration of bauxites, for mfr. of magnesia and other chem. products from dolomite; first to recover potash commercially from shales and to locate in Ga. bentonites, roofing slates. Some time fellow Geol. Soc. of America, A.A.A.S.; mem. Am. Inst. Mechanical Engineers, Paleontol. Soc. America, Society of Economic Geologists, mem. various mining, chem. and ceramic socs., Kappa Alpha (Southern). Democrat. Episcopalian. Author of more than 100 geol. bulls. and papers. Address: 759 Myrtle St. N.E., Atlanta, Ga. Died Aug. 22, 1952; buried West View Cemetery, Atlanta.

MAYNARD, Theodore, author, lecturer; b. Madras, India, November 3, 1890; son Reverend Thomas Henry and Elizabeth Anthony (Teague) M.; in U.S., 1909-11, and since 1920; naturalized citizen, Feb. 1941; A.B., Fordham U.; A.M., Georgetown U.; Litt.D., Marquette U.; Ph.D., Catholic U. of America; m. Sara Katherine Casey, June 8, 1918 (deceased); children—Michael Felix Antony, Rosemary Joan, Paul Francis, Philip Austin Theodore, Christine Mary, Mary Theodora Clare, Kevin Peter Desmond; m. 2d, Kathleen Sheehan, October 19, 1946; received in Roman Catholic Church, 1913; professor English literature Dominican College, San Rafael, California, 1921-25, at St. John's Coll., Brooklyn, N.Y., 1925-27, at Grad. Sch., Fordham U., 1927-29, Georgetown U., 1929-34, Mt. St. Mary's Coll., Emmitsburg, Maryland, 1934-36. President The Catholic Poetry Soc. America. Author numerous books since 1915; latest publs.: The Long Road of Father Serra, 1954; St. Ignatius and the Jesuits, 1956; Great Catholics in American History, 1957. Address: 3 N. Court, Port Washington, N.Y. Died Oct. 18, 1956.

MAYO, Earl Williams, editor, writer; b. Springville, N.Y., May 5, 1873; s. Capt. William L. and Clarinda (Williams) M.; grad. Griffith Inst., 1890;

Cornell U., 1894; m. Marie Susanne Thill, 1901; 1 son, Earl Willims, Jr. (lt. comdr. USNR); m. 2d, Alva Stewart Morrison, 1952. Instr. English, Cornell, 1894-95; staff N.Y. Sun, 1895-96; editor McClure's Syndicate, 1898; Sunday staff N.Y. Herald, 1899; spl. traveling corr. in Europe and America for McClure's, Outlook, World's Work, American and other mags. Founder and editor magazine Sugar and (with Russell Palmer) World Petroleum. Travel in connection with activities of trade and tech. orgns. and in promotion of indsl. cooperation with Latin America and Europe, 1930-39. Editorial dir. internat. mag. group (English and Spanish). Mem. Latin Am. Inst., Am. Petroleum Inst., World Petroleum Congress, Acad. Polit. Sci., Silurians, Inst. du Petetroles du Sud America. Clubs: Pipeline; Cornell (N.Y.C.); City, National Press, Nomads. Author: Cape Cod Folks (play); A Border Rivalry (serial); The Land of the Loon (with F. K. Scribner); Big Battles Against Disease. Home: New Canaan, Conn. Office: 604 Fifth Av., N.Y.C. Died Oct. 10, 1957; buried Springville, N.Y.

MAYO, Nelson Slater, veterinarian; b. Calhoun County, Mich., Nov. 16, 1866; s. Perry and Mary Ann (Bryant) M.; B.S., Mich. State Agrl. Coll., 1888, M.S., 1890; D.V.S., Chicago Vet. Coll., 1889; grad. work, Cornell U., 1897-98; honorary degree University of Havana, Cuba, 1944; m. Mary Lucy Carpenter, July 30, 1890; children—Marguerite, Donald (dec.), Dorothy (dec.), Robert, Mary Louise. Asst. veterinarian Mich. Agrl. Expt. Sta., 1888-90; prof. veterinary science, Kan. State Agrl. Coll., 1890-97, Conn. Agrl. Coll., 1897-1901, Kan. State Agrl. Coll., 1901-04; vice dir. Cuban Agrl. Expt. Sta. and chief Dept. Animal Industry, Republic of Cuba, 1904-09; prof. animal husbandry and vet. science, Va. Poly. Inst., Blacksburg, 1909-13; mgr. vet. dept. Abbott Labs., Chicago, 1913-30, now retired. Mem. Am. Vet. Med. Assn. (sec. 1913-15), Phi Delta Theta. Episcopalian. Mason. Clubs: Illinois, Spanish American (Chicago). Author: Diseases of Animals, 1903. Devised and introduced an arsenical solution for destruction of cattle ticks. Home: 600 Mulberry Pl., Highland Park, Ill. Died July 5, 1958; buried Lake Orion, Mich.

MAYS, Floyd Rosenbaum, ret. ry. ofcl.; b. Crockett, Va., Aug. 28, 1879; s. John Saunders and Susan (Groseclose) M.; ed. high sch. and business coll., Roanoke, Va.; m. Fannie Louise McClain, May 14, 1913; 1 son, Floyd Randolph. Apprentice and machinist N.&W. Ry., 1895-1901; machinist Y.&M. V. R.R., 1901, locomotive fireman, 1901-03, locomotive engr., 1903-11, instr. on transportation rules, 1911, traveling engr., 1911-12, asst. trainmaster, 1912-13, trainmaster, 1913-17, supt. New Orleans div., 1917-23, gen. supt. at Memphis, 1926-29; supt. Ill. div. I.C. R.R., at Champaign, Ill., 1923-26, gen. supt. of equipment, Chgo., 1929-39, gen. mgr., 1939-40, v.p., gen. mgr., 1940—; pres., dir. Chgo. Produce Terminal Co.; dir. Birmingham Belt R.R. Co., The Belt Ry. Co. of Chgo., Gulf and Ship Island R.R. Co., So. Ill. and Mo. Bridge Co., Peoria & Pekin Union Ry. Co. Club: Flossmoor (Ill.) Country. Home: 6900 Oglesby Av. Office: 704 Sixth Av., Cleveland, Miss. Died Aug. 18, 1953.*

McADAMS, Thomas Branch, banker; b. Richmond, Va., Nov. 12, 1879; s. George Brockenbrough and Sarah Reed (Branch) M.; B.A., Richmond Coll. (now U. of Richmond), 1897, M.A., 1898; LL.D., U. of Richmond, 1924; m. Edna Harris McLure, Oct. 9, 1906; children—Sarah Read (dec.), Edna Wylie (Mrs. J. S. Davenport III), Louise (Mrs. B. F. Deford Jr.), Thomas B. (dec.), Juliet Gill (Mrs. C. G. Carey), George Brockenbrough. Began as clk. Merchants Nat. Bank, 1898; with Thomas Branch Co., 1899-1904; with Merchants Nat. Bank, 1904, sr. v.p. until 1925, also partner Scott & Stringfellow until 1925; exec. v.p. State & City Bank & Trust Co., 1925-26; exec. mgr. State-Planters Bank & Trust Co., 1926-33; president Union Trust Company, Baltimore, 1933-47, chairman, 1947—, now director; director United States Fidelity & Guaranty Co. (Balt.). Was colonel on staffs Govs. Swanson and Mann; state dir. Nat. War Savings Campaign, and mem. Liberty Loan Exec. Com., World War. Trustee U. of Richmond. Mem. Am. Bankers Assn. (pres. 1921-22), Va. Bankers Assn. (pres. 1912), Assn. Reserve City Bankers (president 1918), Richmond Clearing House Assn. (pres. 1921). Am. Acceptance Council (exec. com. 1921-24), Phi Beta Kappa, Phi Kappa Sigma (grand alpha, 1926), etc. Mason (K.T., 32°, Shriner), Soc. of the Cincinnati, etc. Democrat. Episcopalian. Clubs: Maryland, Elkridge Hunt, Merchants; Commonwealth, Rotary (ex-pres.). Home: 100 W. University Parkway. Office: Union Trust Co. of Md., Balt. 3. Died Dec. 31, 1957; buried Hollywood Cemetery, Richmond, Va.

McADOO, Henry Molseed (măk'ȧ-dōō), pres. U.S. Leather Co.; b. Phila., June 7, 1880; s. William and Margaret Anne (Campbell) McA.; grad. Friends Central Sch., Phila., 1898; m. Margaret Gaulbert Nice, Apr. 26, 1911; children—William Nice, Henry Molseed, Richard Budd. Began as clerk, McAdd & Allen, leather, Phila., 1898; pres. U.S. Leather Co., 1935—; dir. C. C. Collings & Co., Nice Ball Bearing Co., Empire Electric Brake Co. Mem. raw materials div. Council Nat. Def., 1940-41. Served as capt. Q.M. Dept., U.S. Army, World War I. Republican. Episcopalian. Clubs: Union League, Phila. Cricket, Bachelors' Barge (Phila.). Home: Skippack Pike, Fort Washington, Pa. Office: 27 Spruce St., N.Y.C. 8. Died June 4, 1951.

McALESTER, Andrew Walker, Jr. (măk-ăl'ĕs-tẽr), ophthalmologist; b. Columbia, Mo., Feb. 19, 1876; s. Andrew Walker and Sallie (McConathy) M.; Christian Coll., Columbia, Mo.; B.Litt., U. of Mo., 1897, A.B., 1903, M.D., 1905; certificate, Royal London Ophthalmic Hosp., London, 1905; m. Tillie Hall Bedford, Oct. 21, 1899; 1 son, Andrew Walker. Prin. Mo. Sch. for Blind, 1898-1900; practice of ophthalmology, Kansas City, Mo., since 1906; attending oculist Menorah, St. Luke's, Research Hosp.; chief of eye service, Kansas City General Hosp.; prof. ophthalmology, Med. Sch. U. of Kan., 1908-12. Oculist for Chicago, Burlington and Quincy Railroad, M.-K.-T. R.R., Milwaukee R.R., U.S. Compensation Com. Democrat. Fellow Am. Coll. Surgeons; mem. A.M.A. (House of Dels., 1909-15), Mo. State Med. Assn. (sec. 1907-09, pres. 1944), Jackson County Med. Soc., Am. Acad. Ophthalmology and Oto-Laryngology, Beta Theta Pi, Phi Beta Pi. Was maj., Med. Corps, U.S. Army, attached to Air Serice, A.E.F., in France. Clubs: University, Mission Hills Country. Home: 5509 Mission Drive, Kansas City. Office: Bryant Bldg., Kansas City, Mo. Died Aug. 17, 1954.

McALISTER, Alexander Worth, ins. exec.; b. Asheboro, N.C., Mar. 21, 1862; s. Alexander C. and Adelaide (Worth) McA.; A.B., U. N.C., 1882; m. Sarah Little, Apr. 11, 1894; children—Frank Little, John Worth, Lacy Little, Jean Colvin, Alexander Worth, Flax Reid. Began in ins. bus., Greensboro, 1891; chmn. bd. Pilot Life Ins. Co. Fuel adminstr. N.C., World War I. Vice chmn. N.C. State Bd. Charities and Pub. Welfare; ex-pres. N.C. Conf. Social Service; 1st pres., organizer Greensboro Council Catholics, Jews and Protestants. Mem. Phi Beta Kappa, Phi Kappa Sigma. Democrat. Originator county unit system of pub. welfare as adopted by N.C. Home: 700 Country Club Dr. Office: Pilot Life Insurance Co., Sedgefield, Greensboro, N.C. Died Nov. 20, 1946.

McALISTER, Heber Lowrey, educator and military leader; b. Pontotoc Co., Miss., Sept. 18, 1882; s. William Monroe and Annie (Garrett) McA.; B.S., Miss. Coll., 1906, M.A., 1916; LL.D., Quachita Coll., 1932; m. LaNora O'Baugh, May 18, 1909. Asst. in mathematics, Miss. Coll., 1906, prof. mathematics and dean of Ouachita Coll., Arkadelphia, Ark., 1907-16; dean of Bryan (Tex.) Acad., 1916-17; dir. extension, Ark. State Teachers Coll., 1919-30, pres., 1930-41; commr. Athletics Ark. Inter-Collegiate Conf. since 1948. Maj., inf., U.S. Army 1917-19; lt. col., inf., Nat. Guard 1921, col., 1922, brig. gen., Adj. Gen'ls Dept. 1924-26; col. inf. 1928; col. U.S. Army, 1940-43; brig. gen. Adj. Gen.'s Dept. 1945-51, ret. 1951. Mem. N.E.A., Ark. Edn. Assn., N.G. Assn. Democrat. Baptist. Rotarian. Home: Conway, Ark. Died Dec. 22, 1956; buried Conway, Ark.

McALISTER, Hill, ex-gov.; b. Nashville, Tenn., July 15, 1875; student Vanderbilt U., 1893-97; m. Louise Jackson, Nov. 27, 1901; children—Mrs. Hamilton Love and Mrs. D. U. Bathrick. Began law practice at Nashville, Tenn., 1897; city attorney, Nashville, 1905-09; mem. Tenn. State Senate, 1911, 13; state treas. of Tenn., 1919-27 and 1931-33; gov. of Tenn., 1933-37. Dem. presdl. elector, Tenn. at large, 1916; chmn. Tenn. State Dem. Exec. Com., 1918-20. Mem. Christian Ch. Address: Nashville, Tenn. Died Oct. 1959.

McALL, Reginald Ley, organist, cons. hymns in ch. worship; b. Bocking, Essex County, Eng., Aug. 20, 1878; s. Rev. Robert and Elizabeth (Lonsdale) McA.; ed. schs. of Tonbridge and Weymouth, Eng.; A.B., Johns Hopkins, 1900; student Peabody Conservatory of Music, Baltimore; Doctor of Music, honorary, Hanover (Ind.) College, 1943; married Sarah A. Burwell, June 23, 1903 (deceased, August 29, 1950); children—Sarah Burwell (Mrs. Ralph de Someri Childs), Robert Lonsdale, Lewis Wardlaw (deceased); m. 2d, May deForest Payne, February 2, 1952. Came to U.S., 1897, naturalized, 1923. Organist St. John's Ch., Georgetown, D.C., 1901-02; representative and organ expert, Estey Organ Co., New York, 1903-17; organist Ch. of the Covenant, New York, 1902-50; founder, 1924, and dir. Training Sch. in Church School Music, New York. Mem. com. on worship Fed. Council of Chs.; member Nat. Assn. of Organists (chmn. exec. com. 1920-26, pres. 1926-29, v.p. 1930), Hymn Soc. of America (pres. 1931-33; chmn. exec. com., 1934-41; chmn. hymn festival com. since 1935; executive sec. since 1941), Am. Guild of Organists (mem. council, 1935-37). American representative with McAll Mission, Paris, France, 1917 (pres. N.Y. Auxiliary Am. McAll Assn. since 1948); served in Y.M.C.A., with French Army, 1917-18; financial sec. American Seamen's Friend Soc., 1919-31; supervisor seamen's dept. Central Registration Bur., 1931; asst. to dir. Bur. of Homeless and Transients, New York, 1934; consultant on seamen's policies in transient relief, 1935; sec. Nat. Association of Seamen's Welfare Agencies, 1937-45. Republican. Presbyn. Clubs: Quill, St. Wilfrid, National Arts. Author: Practical Ch. School Music, and many articles and pamphlets on musical subjects, also research pamphlets on merchant seamen. Home: 15 Gramercy Pk., N.Y.C. 3. Office: 297 4th Av., N. Y.C. 10. Died July 9, 1954; buried Mt. Hope Cemetery, N.Y.C.

McALLESTER, Samuel Jackson, lawyer; b. Chattanooga, Aug. 7, 1884; s. Andrew J. and Martha J. (McNabb) McA.; B.S., U. Tenn., 1905; B.L., Chattanooga Coll. Law, 1911, M.L., 1936; m. Marguerite Spears, Apr. 8, 1913 (dec. Aug. 1922); children—Samuel Jackson, Spears. Admitted to Tenn. bar, 1911, since practiced in Chattanooga; mem. firms Cooke, Noll & McAllester, 1912-16, McAllester, Harris & McAllester, 1940-46, McAllester & McAllester, 1946—; U.S. referee in bankruptcy U.S. Dist. Ct., Eastern and So. divs., 1924-42. Pres. B. Mifflin Hood Co., Daisy, Tenn., 1946—; v.p. McAllester Hosiery Co.; v.p., sec. Moccasin Bushing Co.; dir. Pioneer Bank Chattanooga. Mem. Hamilton County (Tenn.) Bd. Edn., 1919-22, Tenn. Bd. Edn., 1929-38; U. trustee Tenn., 1949—; pres. Erlanger and Children's Hosp., 1930-42. Served with U.S. Army, World War I. Mem. Hamilton County (pres.), Am., Tenn. bar assns. Presbyn. (tchr. Bible class). Clubs: Civitan (pres.), Mountain City (Chattanooga); Fairyland. Home: 616 E. Brow St., Lookout Mountain, Chattanooga. Office: James Bldg., Chattanooga 2. Died Dec. 9, 1957.

McALLISTER, Charles Eldridge, clergyman; b. Providence, R.I., Oct. 10, 1893; s. Charles Edward and Mary Elizabeth (Greene) McA.; B.A., Bard Coll., Columbia U., 1914, M.A., 1917; B.D., Gen. Theol. Sem., 1917; Litt.D., St. John's Coll., 1930; D.D., U. of Md., 1930; LL.D., University of Nevada, 1949; m. Clutha Elizabeth Ralyea, June 26, 1918; children—Lt. Charles Ralyea (deceased), Virginia (Mrs. John Snoddy). Ordained ministry P.E. Ch., 1917; curate St. Michael's Ch., N.Y. City, 1917-18; vol. chaplain Pelham Bay Naval Base, 1917-18; fellow and instr. Greek, Gen. Theol. Sem., 1917-18; rector St. Matthew's Parish, Hyattsville, Md., 1918-22, St. John's Ch., Hampton, Va., 1922-26; gen. sec. Field Dept., Episcopal Church, 1926-28; rector Church of St. Michael and All Angels, Baltimore, 1928-30, St. Luke's, Evanston, Ill., 1930-32; dean Cathedral of St. John the Evangelist, Spokane, since 1932. Del. Gen. Convention P.E. Ch., 1928, 34, 37, 41, 43, 46. Pres. Assn. Governing Bds. of State Univs. and Allied Instns. Regent for State Coll. of Wash.; trustee Lakeside Sch. for Boys, Seattle, Arboretum Foundation of U. of Wash. Chmn. Council of Advice Missionary Dist. Spokane; dir. Wash. State Mental Hygiene Soc., Wash. State Social Hygiene Assn., Spokane branch of the English-Speaking Union. Mem. Phi Beta Kappa, Sigma Alpha Epsilon. Mason. Clubs: Spokane City, University, Spokane Country Club; Coeur d'Alene Country. Author of plan for introduction of motion pictures in the work of the Church; Sermon outlines, the Every-Member Canvass, Before, During and After. Author: Inside the Campus, Mr. Citizen Loooks at His Universities. Home: 214 E. 13th Av. Address: Cathedral of St. John the Evangelist, Spokane 10, Wash. Died Apr. 16, 1952.

McALLISTER, Henry, lawyer; b. Phila, Pa., Feb. 28, 1872; s. Henry and Elizabeth (Cooper) McA.; B.L., Swarthmore Coll., 1892; LL.D., Colo. College, 1940; studied law in office of Horace G. Lunt, Colorado Springs, Colo.; m. Phebe H. Ketcham, June 24, 1896 (died 1944); children—Townsend Sherman, Henry (died 1936). Began practice at Colo. Springs, 1894; asst. dist. atty. 4th Dist., Colo., 1895-97, dist. atty., 1898-1900; moved to Denver, 1906; mem. firm Vaile, McAllister & Vaile, 1908-16; since in gen. practice alone; gen. counsel D.&R.G. R.R. Co, and successors, 1916—; dir., general counsel to the D.&R.G.W. R.R. Co., 1947—. Mem. Am., Colo. and Denver bar assns.; associate mem. Assn. Bar City of New York. Republican. Clubs: Denver, University, Mile High, Denver Country. Home: 1880 Gaylord St. Office: Equitable Bldg., Denver, Colo. Died July 20, 1954.

McALPINE, William H(oratio), cons. engr.; b. Lawrence, Mass., Aug. 22, 1874; s. William Taylor and Caroline (Lothrop) McA.; B.S., Mass. Inst. Tech., 1896; m. Mary Dudley Gray, Mar. 3, 1906 (dec.); 1 dau., Carolyn Lothrop (Mrs. Joseph Neave Field); m. 2d, Regina Walsh, Aug. 31, 1943. With U.S. Corps of Engrs., 1902-54, chief engring. div., 1934-44, spl. asst. to chief of engrs., 1944-54, ret. 1954; cons. engr. Recipient award for exceptional civilian service, U.S. War Dept., 1946. Mem. Am. Soc. C.E. (hon.), Soc. Am. Mil. Engrs., Permanent Internat. Assn. Navigation Congresses. Address: 4607 Connecticut Av., Washington 8. Died Nov. 1, 1956; buried Mount Olive Cemetery, Washington.

McANDLESS, Alva John, pres. Lincoln Nat. Life Ins. Co.; b. Capac, Mich., Oct. 23, 1890; s. William E. and Elizabeth (Copeland) McA.; B.A., U. of Mich., 1917; m. Maurine Gordon, 1923; 1 son, Hugh. Began as actuary Grange Life Ins. Co., 1917; actuary Detroit Life Ins. Co., 1918; asst. sec. Lincoln Nat. Life Ins. Co., Ft. Wayne, Ind., 1919, sec., 1926, v.p., 1930, 1st v.p. and dir., 1934, exec. v.p., 1936, president since 1939; director Ft. Wayne Nat. Bank,

Life Insurance Association of Am., Magnavox Co. Member actuarial advisory committee V.A. Pres. American Life Convention, 1942. Fellow Society of Actuaries; mem. Phi Beta Kappa. Clubs: Tavern (Chicago), Country, Quest (Ft. Wayne); Sr. Actuaries. Home: 1417 Hawthorne Rd., Ft. Wayne 6, Ind. Office: 1301 S. Harrison St., Ft. Wayne 1, Ind. Died Jan. 24, 1954; buried Ft. Wayne.

McANENY, George (măk'â-nĕn-ĭ), ret. banker, publicist; b. Greenville, N.J., Dec. 24, 1869; s. George Francis and Katherine (Dillaway) McAneny; grad. Jersey City High School, 1885; LL.D., Hobart Coll., 1914; m. Marjorie Jacobi, Jan. 4, 1900; children—Mrs. Ruth Loud, Mrs. Elizabeth Harrison, Herbert, Arnold, Ernest, David. On staff N.Y. newspapers as reporter and corr., 1885-92; asst. sec. Nat. Civil Service Reform League and New York Civil Service Reform Assn., 1892-94, sec., 1894-1902, pres., 1927-36; sec., exec. officer N.Y. Municipal Civil Service Commn. under Mayor Low, 1902; co-author Rev. N.Y. State Civil Service Law, 1899; drafted and revised Civil Service rules for N.YC. in effect, 1902-—; read law with Edward M. Shepard, 1903-06; pres. City Club, New York, 1906-09; incorporator Bur. of Municipal Research, 1907; mem. com. apptd. by Gov. to revise N.Y.C. Charter, 1908, and adviser to later City Charter commns.; elected, on Fusion tickets, pres. Boro of Manhattan, 1910-13, and pres. bd. of Aldermen, 1914-Jan. 1916 (acting mayor of New York several months); chmn. Transit Com. of City Govt. which, with Pub. Serv. Commn., developed City's Dual Subway System, representing investment, city and operating companies of $600,000,000, 1911-13; chmn. Com. on the City Plan, for comprehensive planning and zoning of New York (zoning ordinances adopted 1916, first in America); medal of Société des Architectes Diplômes par le Gouvernement Français (Paris), for services to city planning and architecture, 1913; later decorated Chevalier Legion of Honor (France); received medal Archtl. League of N.Y., 1915, joint medal of archtl., engring., and landscaping societies, 1939, and medal of Fine Arts Fedn., 1940; honorary mem. New York Chapter of A.I.A., Archtl. League; lecturer on municipal govt. at Yale, 1914 (Dodge Foundation), Union Coll., 1924 (Day Foundation); exec. mgr. New York Times, 1916-21; v.p. Am. Newspaper Publs. Assn., 1920-21; mem. com. 3 pubs. under War Trade Bd., to regulate consumption of newsprint paper, World War, 1917-19; v.chmn., 1906, chmn., 1917, Carl Schurz Memorial Com.; mem. editorial com. on publ. Speeches, Correspondence and Political Papers of Carl Schurz, 1913; chmn. bd. Trustees Coll. of City of N.Y., 1916-25; chmn. State Transit Commn., 1921-26; mem. Russell Sage Foundation Com., 1922-29, to prepare plans for development N.Y.C. and met area upon which Found. and pvt. funds expanded $1,500,000; pres., 1930-—, of body organized to carry on this project, the Regional Plan Assn.; reorganized City's Sanitation Dept., 1933; City comptroller for unexpired term, to Dec. 31, 1933; chmn. commn. apptd. by Gov. on State Grants-in-Aid to Municipalities, 1935; chmn., Commn. apptd. by Pres. of the U.S., on Fiscal Relations of U.S. Govt. and D.C., 1936; pres., Title Guarantee & Trust Co., 1934-36, chmn. bd., 1936 until retirement; dir. Met. Life Ins. Co., Bowery Savings Bank, Home Ins. Co., City of N.Y. Ins. Co., City Real Estate Co., Title and Realty Safe Deposit Co., Ritz Carlton Hotel Corp. of N.Y. and (pres.) Ritz Carlton Hotel Corp. of Boston; organized movement for holding World's Fair in N.Y. in 1939; serving as pres. Fair Corp. first year, to May 1936, and since as chmn. bd.; chmn. bd. govs. Fed. Hall Memorial Assos. (N.Y. City), 1940. Mem. Reformed Dutch Ch. Democrat. Clubs: Century, Union, City, Bankers, Pilgrims of U.S. Home: 252 Bayard Lane, Princeton, N.J. Office: Title Guarantee & Trust Bldg., 176 Broadway, N.Y. C. Died July 29, 1953.

McARTHUR, Lewis Linn, Jr., banker; b. Chgo., Ill., Jan. 30, 1898; s. Dr. Lewis L. and Mamie (Walker) McA.; A.B., Yale, 1919. Asso. with Northern Trust Co., Chgo., 1919-—, v.p. 1931-—. Served with A.E.F., 1918-19. Pres. and trustee Chgo. Home for Incurables; treas., trustee St. Luke's Hosp. Assn.; trustee Eleanor Assn. Mem. Soc. Colonial Wars, Descendants of Mayflower Soc., Orchestral Assn. of Chgo. Clubs: Chgo. U., Cliff Dwellers (Chgo.); Wawashkamo (Mackinac Island). Home: 230 E. Delaware Pl., Chicago. Office: 50 LaSalle St., Chicago 50. Died Feb. 10, 1960.

McAULIFFE, Daniel J., ex-newspaper man, ret. ins. exec.; b. St. Louis, May 30, 1874; s. Daniel and Bridget (Cleary) M.; A.B., St. Louis U., 1893; m. Mary Agnes McCartin, June 12, 1905 (dec.); children—Mrs. Lucille M. G. Goletz, Jane Marie. Reporter, St. Louis Republic, 1897, becoming city editor, mgr. St. Louis Semi-Weekly Republic and Farm Progress, and mng. editor Republic, 1906-13; resigned to engage in gen. contracting business; later established ins. bus. which he sold on retirement, 1940; v.p. Mountain Valley Water Co., N.Y.C. Mem. Silurians. Club: Missouri Athletic. Editor Oil Trade Jour., N.Y.C. Home: 45 LaSalle Av., Rye, N.Y. Died Mar. 19, 1957.*

McAULIFFE, Eugene (măk-aw'lĭf), ret. coal co. exec.; b. Maidstone, Kent, Eng., Oct. 3, 1866; s. John and Mary (Williams) McA.; brought by parents to U.S., 1872; ed. pub. and pvt. schs.; D.Eng., U. Mo., 1927; m. Nell Shuler, June 17, 1896; children—Kathleen, Mary Jean (Mrs. Charles C. Tucker), Rosemary (dec.). In motive power dept. various rys. of U.S. and Mexico, 1886-1903; fuel agt. Frisco Lines, 1903-08; gen. coal agt., 1910-17; gen. coal agt. Rock Island Lines, 1908-10; pres. Brazil Block Coal Co., 1908-10, Union Colliery Co., 1917-23; pres. The Union Pacific Coal Co., 1923-44, chmn. bd. trustees, 1944-47, ret.; pres. Wash. Union Coal Co., So. Wyo. Utilities Co., Union Pacific Water Co. 1923-45. Mgr. fuel conservation sect. U.S. R.R. Administrn., 1918-20. Mem. Am. Inst. Mining and Metall. Engrs. (dir. 1929-34, v.p. 1933-35, pres. 1942), Newcomen Soc. Eng.; hon. mem. Brit. Instn. Mining Engrs. Episcopalian. Mason (K.T.). Clubs: Engineers, Omaha (Omaha); Union League (Chgo.). Author: Railway Fuel, 1927; Romance and Tragedy of Coal, 1931; When Can Their Glory Fade, 1952. Home: 5610 Farnam St., Omaha 3, Neb. Died June 2, 1959; buried Forest Lawn Cemetery, Omaha.

McBAIN, James William, chemistry; b. Chatham, N.B., Can., Mar. 22, 1882; s. James Afleck Fraser (D.D.) and Mary Morrison (Quin) McB.; B.A., U. of Toronto, 1903, M.A., 1904; student U. of Leipzig, 1904-05; Ph.D., U. of Heidelberg, 1906; hon. D.Sc., Brown U., 1923, U. of Bristol, England, 1928; m. Mary Evelyn Laing, Jan. 1, 1929; children—Janet Quin, John Keith. Lecturer in physical chemistry, U. of Bristol, 1906-19, Leverhulme prof. in physical chemistry, 1919-26; visiting prof., U. of California, 1926; professor of chemistry, Stanford, 1927-47, professor emeritus, 1947-—. Awarded Davy medal, Royal Society, 1939. Director National Chemical Laboratory, Poona, India, 1949-52. Fellow Royal Society, Royal Institute Chemistry; member American Chem. Soc. (Counselor at large Calif. sect.), Am. Assn. Univ. Profs., Nat. Inst. Social Sciences, Chem. Soc. (British), Bunsen Gesellschaft, Faraday Soc. (hon. life mem., v.p. 26-29), Soc. of Rheology (v.p. 1946), Association of University Teachers of Great Britain (pres. 1922-23), Bristol University Alumni Assn. (pres. 1923-26), Rotary Internat (pres. Palo Alto club 1933, Poona Club 1952), Sigma Xi, Alpha Chi Sigma, Phi Lambda Upsilon (hon.), Gamma Alpha. Presbyn. Mason. Clubs: Commonwealth, Bohemian (San Francisco). Editor, Journal of Colloid Science; assisted O.S.R.D., N.A.C.A. and W.P.B. (Rubber Reserve) during World War II; invited guest from U.S.A. to 220th Anniversary celebration of the Acad. of Scis. of U.S.S.R. Author: The Sorption of Gases and Vapours by Solids, 1931; Textbook of Colloid Science, 1949. Contbns. to chem. jours. Home: Stanford University, Cal. Died Mar. 12, 1953; buried Palo Alto, Cal.

McBRIDE, F(rancis) Scott, minister; b. Carroll County, O., July 29, 1872; s. Frank and Harriet (Miller) McB.; B.S., Muskingum Coll. (New Concord, O.) 1898, D.D., 1915; grad. Pittsburgh Theol. Sem., 1901; m. Geraldine Van Fossen, July 10, 1901; children—Christine Harriet (Mrs. Lewis Watt), Geralda Pearl (Mrs. Arthur Armstrong; now deceased), John Van Fossen (deceased). Teacher 4 years; ordained to ministry of the United Presbyterian Church, 1901; pastor Kittanning, Pennsylvania, 1901-09, 9th Av., Ch., Monmouth, Ill., 1909-11; dist. supt. Anti-Saloon League of Ill., Springfield, 1911-12; state supt. Ill. Anti-Saloon League, Chicago, 1912-24; general supt. Anti-Saloon League of America, 1924-36; superintendent of Pa. Anti-Saloon League, 1936-43, interim pastor Somonauk (Ill.) U. P. Ch., 1944-45. Supt. Emeritus of Anti-Saloon League of Am., 1946-—. Mem. World League against Alcoholism (exec. com.). Moderator Synod of Ill., United Presbyn. Ch., 1944-45. Vice-moderator United Presbyterian Ch., 1934-35. Mem. Federal Council Chs. of America, Pi Gamma Mu. Editor Illinois Issue, 1912-15; Pennsylvania Issue, 1936-44. Home: 128 Walnut St., Barnesville, O. Died Apr. 23, 1955; buried Westerville, O.

McBRIDE, Karl R., Sr., business exec.; b. Sadie Rooke; children—Karl R., Mrs. A. E. Van Wirt, Mrs. Henry L. Ryer, Jr., Mrs. William R. Forbes. Organized color div. Imperial Paper and Color Corp., 1915, pres., 1931-53, chmn. bd., 1953-—. Dir. Glen Falls (N.Y.) Nat. Bank and Trust Co., Queensbury Hotel. Home: 156 Ridge St. Office: Imperial Paper and Color Corp., Glen Falls, N.Y. Died Aug. 19, 1957.*

McCAFFERTY, Thomas Bowles, food mfg. exec.; b. Sharpsburg, Pa., May 1, 1898; s. Ernest Dair and Florence (Bowles) McC.; A.B., Allegheny Coll., 1920; m. Helen Thoburn, June 21, 1923; 1 dau., Betty Jane. With H. J. Heinz Co., Pittsburgh, since 1920, asst. to dir. mfg., 1923, asst. to v.p. and sec., 1938, asst. sec., 1942, dir. and sec. since 1945; dir. Am. Telephone and Telegraph Co. since 1952. Trustee Allegheny Coll.; trustee, sec. and treas., Eden Hall Farm Found. Presbyn. (vice chmn. bd. trustees). Clubs: Duquesne, Civic. Home: Mt. Royal Blvd., Allison Park, Pa. Office: 1062 Progress St., Pitts. 12. Died Mar. 30, 1954.

McCAHAN, David (mă-kā'han), insurance educator; b. Huntingdon, Pa., Aug. 26, 1897; s. Albert Johnson and Amanda Mabel (Settle) McC.; B.S. in Econ., U. of Pa., 1920; M.A., 1922, Ph.D., 1928; post-grad. work, George Washington U., 1922-26; C.L.U., Am. Coll. Life Underwriters, 1929; m. Rebekah Finley Morse, June 22, 1927; children—Patricia Morse, David, Elizabeth, John Finley. Instr. statistics, Wharton Sch. (U. of Pa.), 1920-22, asst. prof. of ins., 1926-34, asso. prof., 1934-36, prof. since 1936; asst. mgr. ins. dept. Chamber Commerce of U.S., 1922-26; sec., asst. dean Am. Coll. Life Underwriters, 1929-34, dean, 1934-51, executive v.p., 1951-52, president since 1952 (trustee); director Fire Association, Philadelphia, Reliance Insurance Co. Mem. Bd. of Corporators of the Presbyn. Ministers Fund, 1936-46 (dir. 1940-45); exec. dir., S. S. Huebner Foundation for Insurance Edn.; president Swarthmore Bd. of Sch. Dirs., 1947-52; member bd. of trustees, Am. Institute for Property and Liability Underwriters, Inc., College Retirement Equities Fund; member Nat. Com. on Family Financial Security Education; member executive com., trustee Teachers Insurance and Annuity Assn. of Am., 1944-48. Served as ensign U.S. Naval Flying Corps during World War I. Member American Academy Political and Social Science, American Association University Professors, Am. Assn. Univ. Teachers of Ins. (pres. 1940, 41), Am. Econ. Association, Am. Soc. of Chartered Life Underwriters (secretary 1930-45), Beta Gamma Sigma, Lambda Chi Alpha. Republican. Presbyterian. Author: State Insurance in the United States, 1929; Life Insurance as Investment (with S. S. Huebner), 1933. Special insurance editor of Webster's New International Dictionary. Editor of Huebner Found. lectures; Life Insurance: Trends and Problems, 1943; The Beneficiary in Life Insurance, 1948; Life Insurance Trends at Mid-Century, 1950; Investment of Life Insurance Funds, 1952. Contbr. numerous articles in profl. and ins. jours. Significant Developments of War Period," monographs (4 volumes), Am. Coll. of Life Underwriters, 1945. Home: 607 Strath Haven Av., Swarthmore, Pa. Office: Dietrich Hall, U. Phila. Died June 28, 1954; buried Greenwood Cemetery, Bklyn.

McCAIG, William Dougal (MacKi), accountant railroad exec.; b. Mount Carmel, Pa., Jan. 18, 1874; s. Arthur and Jane (McIlwaine) McC.; ed. high school and Richmond Bus. Coll., Savannah, Ga.; m. Henrie Emma Walker, Oct. 16, 1907 (died Jan. 31, 1935); children—Emma Lawson (Mrs. Walter Garland Edwards), Jean (Mrs. Ferdinand Badger Johnson, Jr.), Arthur Walker (dec.), Martha (Mrs. George Brainerd Chapman); m. 2d, Willie Mae Key, Jan. 3, 1942. Stenographer C. of Ga. Ry., 1891-93; stenographer Plant System of Railways (now A.C.L. R.R.), 1893-99, travling auditor, 1899-1901; traveling auditor A.C.L. R.R. Co., 1902-05, auditor station accounts, 1906-10, asst. auditor freight receipts, 1911-16, asst. comptroller, 1917-12, comptroller, 1924-43, v.p. accounts and frieght claims, 1943-—; comptroller Charleston & Western Carolina Ry., Winson-Salem Southbond Ry. Co.; dir. Wilmington Savings & Trust Co. City commr. City of Wilmington, N.C., 1916-22. Chmn. gd. govs. Community Hosp.; dir. James Walker Meml. Hosp., 1925-—; dir. Flora MacDonald Coll., Red Springs, N.C., 1933-—. Mason. Clubs: Cape Fear, Cape Fear Country, Carolina Yacht (Wilmington, N.C.). Home: 1711 Princess St. Office: A.C.L. R.R. Bldg., Wilmington, N.C. Died Jan. 1, 1951; buried Oakdale Cemetery, Wilmington.

McCAIN, Charles Simonton, banker; b. Pine Bluff, Ark., Jan. 18, 1884; s. William Simonton and Eliza Catherine (Chesnutt) McC.; prep. edn., high sch., Little Rock, Ark.; student Erskine Coll., Due West, S.C.; A.B., Yale, 1904; m. Frances Walker, June 6, 1917; children—William Simonton, Charles Simonton, Grace McCain Durrell. In banking business, Little Rock, 1899, and advanced to pres. Bankers Trust Co.; v.p. Nat. Park Bank, New York, 1925-27, pres., 1927-29; became pres. Chase Nat. Bank, 1929, later chmn. bd.; pres. United Light & Power Co., Chicago, 1934-39; pres. Dillon, Read & Co. Inc., N.Y., 1939-51, now dir.; B. F. Goodrich Co., American Viscose Corporation, National Cash Register Company, Corn Products Refining Company, Congoleum-Nairn, Inc., International Paper Company. President of Little Rock Clearing House, 1920-21. Served as chairman of Pulaski County War Savings committee, chairman Jewish Relief Campaign, New York City Citizens Committee, Navy Relief Soc. Campaign; mem. exec. com. Am. Red Cross and Liberty Loan Drives and treas. Jewish Relief and Salvation Army drives, State of Ark. Mem. Am. Bankers' Assn. (exec. council, 1920-23), Alpha Delta Phi, Phi Beta Kappa. Clubs: Links, Yale, Recess, Piping Rock. Democrat. Presbyn. Home: 10 Gracie Square. Office: 46 William St., N.Y.C. Died Dec. 13, 1957.

McCALL, Arthur G(illett), soil scientist; b. Buena Vista, O., Nov. 11, 1874; s. Moses D. and Elizabeth (Gillett) McC.; B.S., Ohio State U., 1900; Ph.D., Johns Hopkins, 1916; m. Harriett M. Flower, Dec. 1896; children—Herbert F., Elizabeth L., Dorothy H., Harriett A. Scientist, Bur. of Soils, U.S. Dept.

Agr., 1901-04 chief, 1927, chief soil investigations, 1927-36; prof. agronomy and head dept., Ohio State U., 1904-16; prof. geology and soils, U. Md., 1916-27; in charge soil investigations, Md. Expt. Sta., 1916-27; with Soil Conservation Service, 1936—, ret. 1944, but continuing in Govt. Service in cons. capacity. Served with Army Ednl. Corps, U.S. Army, France, 1919. Exec. sec. 1st Internat. Congress Soil Sci. Fellow A.A.A.S., Am. Soc. Agronomy (ex-pres); mem. Assn. Ofcl. Agrl. Chemists, Sigma Xi, Alpha Zeta, Phi Kappa Phi, Gamma Sigma Delta, Alpha Gamma Rho; corr. mem. Czechoslovakian Acad. Soil Sci. Conglist. Club: Cosmos. Author: Physical Properties of the Soil, 1908; Broom Corn Culture, 1912; Studies of Soils, 1915; Studies of Crops, 1916. Home: College Park, Md. Address: 4707 Calvert Rd., College Park, Md. Deceased.

McCALL, Oswald Walter Samuel, clergyman; b. Melbourne, Australia; s. Thomas and Sarah (Sterritt) McC.; ed. pvt. colls. and U. Melbourne; D.D., Pacific Sch. Religion, Berkeley, Cal., 1924; Litt.D., Marietta Coll., 1941; m. Florance May Jones, Mar. 27, 1914 (died June 1956); children—Betty May, Mary Estelle, Margaret Beverley, Patsey (dec.); m. 2d, Dolly Adeline Cannamela, Aug. 1, 1957. Ordained ministry Meth. Ch. Australia, 1912; pastorates Australia, 1912-17, 19-21; came to U.S., 1921; pastor 1st Congl. Ch., Berkeley, Cal., 1922-39; pastor 1st Congl. Ch., Chgo., 1939-43; pastor St. Andrew's-Wesley United Ch., Vancouver, B.C.; now pastor Devon Union Ch., Milford, Conn.; lectr. religion and internat. affairs at various univs. and colls., U.S.; radio preacher, Chgo.; instr. pub. speaking, Pacific Sch. Religion, 1924; prof. homiletics Presbyn. Theol. Sem., Chgo., 1940-41. Moderator, No. Cal. Congl. Conf., 1934-35. Made tour of Africa, British Isles and Europe, 1914; spl. preacher, lectr. Australian Imperial Forces, Egypt, Eng., France, World War. Hon. mem. Eugene Field Lit. Soc. Study, travel, British Isles, 1936-37; mem. seminar for development devotional lit., 1935-39. Dir. Congl. Union, Chgo.; v.p. Chgo. Congl. Club; pres. Kobe Coll. Corp. Author: Cardinals of Faith, 1924; The Stringing of the Bow, 1928; Christ's Shining Way, 1931; The Uses of Literature in the Pulpit, 1931; The Gods of Men, 1934; The Fulfillment (a choralogue), 1939; The Hand of God, 1940; In Such a Night as This, 1947; also articles, short stories and sketches. Earl lectr. Berkeley, The Continuing Reformation, 1949. Address: 6 Devol St., Milford, Conn. Died June 1959.

McCAMIC, Charles (mă-kăm'ik), lawyer; b. Wellsburg, W.Va.; s. Nathan Stanton and Frances (Dowden) McC.; LL.B., Yale, 1899; LL.D., West Virginia Wesleyan University, 1925; m. Anna F. Smith, Apr. 9, 1902 (deceased); 1 dau., Frances Smith (Mrs. W. R. Tinker, Jr.); m. 2d, Elizabeth McCoach Taylor, Mar. 15, 1943; step son, John Taylor. Admitted Conn. and W.Va. bars, 1899, and to Supreme Court of U.S., 1911; practiced Moundsville, W.Va., 8 years, Wheeling, 1907—; member McCamic & Clarke. Pres. Interstate Bridge Co., Bellaire, O.; dir. Sehon-Stevenson Co.; dir. and past pres. American Bridge, Tunnel and Turnpike Assn. Member W.Va. House of Representatives, 1905. Served as captain, World War, 1917-18; ret. lieut. col. J.A.G., Res. member American Bar Assn., W.Va. Bar Assn. (sec. 10 yrs.; Am. Gas Assn. chmn. war effort com.), Am. Law Inst., Internat. Law Assn., W.Va. Hist. Soc. (past pres.), Newcomen Soc., Va. S.A.R., Res. Officers Assn., Am. Legion (1st adj. state orgn.), Johnson Soc., Lichfield, England; Soc. Am. Legion Founders, Military Order Foreign Wars United States 27th Division Association, Kappa Alpha, Phi Alpha Delta, Phi Beta Kappa, Scabbard and Blade, Order of Coif, Phi Beta Kappa (asso.). Director in associates of Phi Beta Kappa. Episcopalian (mem. vestry). Mason. Clubs: Grolier, Yale (New York); Ft. Henry, Wheeling Country, Metropolitan (Washington); Rowfant (Cleve.); Virginia Seniors Golf Assn. Author: Doctor Samuel Johnson and the American Colonies, 1925. Home: Hawthorne Court, Wheeling. Office: Wheeling, W.Va. Died Jan. 13, 1957.

McCANDLESS, Robert Buchanan, govt. official; b. Montezuma, Ia., Nov. 1, 1855; s. John and Kate (Buchanan) McC.; grad. Sheldon (Ia.) High Sch., 1902; student Grinnell (Ia.) Coll., 1905; m. Clara Lanning, July 15, 1908 (dec.); 1 son, George (dec.). Engaged in banking, 1907-24; with Bur. of Comptroller of the Currency, Apr. 1924—, serving as receiver, later supervising receiver; apptd. dep. comptroller, July 1941. Mason. Home: 5420 Connecticut Av. N.W., Washington 15. Office: Treasury Bldg., Washington. Retired. Died Mar. 11, 1958; buried Sheldon, Ia.

McCANN, Charles Mallette, newspaperman; b. Washington, Mar. 23, 1893; s. Charles Mallette and Helen (Smith) McC.; student pub. schs., Washington; m. Judith Shackelford, June 29, 1940. Reporter Washington Herald, 1911; with United Press Assns., 1915—, beginning as corr., Washington, successively corr., London, N.Y.C., night cable editor, day cable editor, 1915-54, fgn. news commentator, 1954—. Served as sgt. 312th Machine Gun Battalion, 79th Div., U.S. Army, World War I. Recipient citation for excellence Overseas Press Club, N.Y.C., 1957. Episcopalian. Home: 35 E. 35th St., N.Y.C. 16. Office: 220 E. 42d St., N.Y.C. 17. Died Mar. 6, 1959; buried Arlington Nat. Cemetery.

McCANTS, E(lliott) Crayton (măk-kăntz), educator; b. Ninety Six, S.C., Sept. 2, 1865; s. Nathaniel S. (M.D.) and Ettie E. (Poole) M.; B.S., S.C. Mil. Acad. (Citadel), Charleston, S.C., 1886; Litt. D., U. of S.C., Columbia, S.C., 1927; m. Tressa L. Lipscomb, Sept. 19, 1889; children—Elliott L., Mattie, Edwin C., Tressa, Mary, Nell, Robert C., Thomas C. Teacher pub. sch., Abbeville, S.C., 1886-87; commandant cadets, Greenwood Male High Sch. (with rank of capt. S.C. Militia), 1887-88; editor Greenwood (S.C.) Tribune (weekly), 1888; farmer, 1889; teacher Sardis (Miss.) pub. sch., 1890-91; prin. pvt. sch. for girls, Arcadia, La., 1892-93; prin. Normal Sch., Stuart, Va., 1892-93; prof. mathematics, Danville (Va.) Coll. for Young Ladies, 1893-95; prin. secondary sch., McEwen, Tenn., 1895-96; prin. pub. sch., Augusta, Arkansas, 1896-98, Blackville, S.C., 1898-1900; instr. in advanced mathematics, City High Sch., Anderson, S.C., 1900-07; superintendent of city schools, Anderson, S.C., 1907-45; superintenden temeritus, 1945—. Instructor in county summer normal schs. for teachers, 1900—. Raised company for Ark. regt., Spanish-American War, of which was capt., but was not mustered into service. Mem. State Teachers Assn. of S.C. (sec. 1910-13; pres. 1920-22). Retired July 1, 1945. Mem. M.E. Ch., South. Independent Democrat. Clubs: Country, Rotary. Author: In the Red Hills, 1904; One of the Gray Jackets, 1909; Stories and Legends of South Carolina, 1927; White Oak Farm, 1928; Ninety Six, 1930. Contbr. fiction to mags. Home: Anderson, S.C. Died Oct. 23, 1953; buried Silverbrook Cemetery, Anderson.

McCARDELL, Claire (mc cärdell), designer; born Frederick, Md., May 24, 1905; d. Adrian Leroy and Eleanor (Clingan) McCardell; student Parsons School Design, 1926, 28, Paris, 1927; m. Irving Drought Harris, Mar. 10, 1943. Designer for Townley Frocks, N.Y.C., since 1932, v.p. since 1952; designer outdoor and sports styles. Awarded Citation of Honor, Am. Fashion Critics award in 1942 and 1943; Hall of Fame Award, 1958 (Posthumous); award, 1943; Neiman Marcus award, 1948; Womens Nat. Press Club award, 1950. Trustee Parson's Sch. Mem. bd. govs., v.p. Fashion Group. Author: What Shall I Wear, 1956. Home: 151 E. 79th St. Office: 550 7th Av., N.Y.C. Died Mar. 22, 1958.

McCARRAN, Patrick A. (măk-kăr'răn), senator; b. Reno, Nev., Aug. 8, 1876; s. Patrick and Margaret (Shea) M.; A.B., U. of Nevada, 1901, A.M., 1915, hon. LL.B., 1945; hon. LL.B. Georgetown U., 1943. m. Martha Harriet Weeks, Aug. 10, 1903; children—Mary, Margaret, Norine, Mrs. Patritia Taylor, Samuel. Engaged in farming and stock raising in Nev.; mem. Nev. Legislature, 1903; admitted to Nev. bar, 1905; practiced in Tonopah and Goldfield during the mining booms of those places; dist. atty. Nye County, 1907-09; resumed practice in Reno, 1909; asso. justice Supreme Court of Nev., 1913-17, chief justice, 1917-18; mem. U.S. Senate, 1933—. Chairman Senate Judiciary Com. 1943-46, 1949-53; chmn. special subcom. on Foreign Economic Coop., 1950-52. Member State Pardon Board and State Pardon Parole Bd., 1913-19; chmn. State Bd. of Bar Examiners, 1931. Rep. of Nev. to Nat. Irrigation Congress, 1904; pres. Truckee River Water Users Assn., 1921-22. State chairman Four-Minute Men, World War. Mem. American Bar Assn., Nev. State Bar Assn. Home: 401 Court St., Reno; 4711 Blagden Av., Washington. Office: Senate Office Bldg., Washington. Died Sept. 28, 1954; buried Mountain View Cemetery, Reno.

McCARTER, Thomas Nesbitt, ret. utility exec.; b. Newark, Oct. 20, 1867; s. Thomas N. and Mary Louise (Haggerty) McC.; A.B., Princeton, 1888, A.M., 1891; Rutgers U., 1937, Newark U., 1938, John Marshall College, 1938; studied law in father's office, and at Columbia, 1889-1900; m. Madeleine G. Barker, Feb. 9, 1897; children—Mrs. Nelson Doubleday, Thomas N., Uzal H., Mrs. Carlos D. Kelly. Mem. law firm McCarter, Williamson & McCarter, 1891-99, then practiced alone; judge 1st Dist. Court of Newark, 1896-99 (resigned); mem. N.J. Senate from Essex County, 1900-1902; apptd. atty. gen. of N.J. by Governor Murphy, 1902, for term of 5 years; resigned, 1903, to become pres. of Public Service Corp. of N.J., of which was the principal organizer (this corp., through its subsidiaries, controls and operates nearly all the important gas, electric and transportation utilities of the state); continued as pres. to 1939, chmn., 1939-45, sr. exec. officer 1903-45, ret. since 1945; chmn. bd., chmn. exec. com., dir. Fidelity Union Trust Co., Newark, retired 1947; dir., exec. com. Chase National Bank 1925-46, pres. American Electric Ry. Assn., 1911-12. Dir. Am. Gas Assn., 1918-22, 1927-29; trustee Edison Electric Inst., 1933-42 (pres. 1934-36), Newark Coll. Engring., Tech. Sch. of City of Newark, 1929-43, Rutgers U., 1938-42. Hon. mem. Newark C. of C. Clubs: Essex (Newark); Princeton (N.Y.C.); Ivy (Princeton); Rumson Country, Seabright Beach; Mountain Lake (Fla.). Author: District Court Practice of N.J., 1898; one Phase of a Jerseyman's Activities, 1933, supplementary vol., 1939, final vol. 1946. Recipient Letter in Life as alumnus by Pingry School, Elizabeth, N.J., commencement, 1939. Home: Rumsonhill, Rumson, N.J.; (winter) Mountain Lake, Lake Wales, Fla. Died Oct. 23, 1955; buried Rumson, N.J.

McCARTHY, Daniel J., neurologist; b. Phila., June 22, 1874; s. Daniel and Rebecca M.; M.D., U. Pa., 1895; married. Practiced in Phila., 1899—; prof. med. jurisprudence, U. Pa.; neurologist Phila. Gen. Hosp (Blockley); cons. neurologist State Hosp. for Insane, Norristown; dir. med. and sociol. investigation Municipal Ct. Phila. Asso. trustee U. Pa. Mem. A.M.A., Med. Soc. State Pa., Phila. Med. Soc., Am. Neurol. Assn., Phila. Neurol. Soc., Am. Medico-Psychol. Assn., Pathol. Soc. Phila. Catholic. Editor: Reese's Medical Jurisprudence and Toxicology (8th edit.). Author: The Prisoner of War in Germany, 1917. Co-author Medical Treatment of Mental Disease, 1956. Address: 107 S. Suffolk Av., Ventnor, N.J. Died Oct. 9, 1958.

McCARTHY, Frank Jeremiah, r.r. ofcl.; b. Indpls., May 14, 1905; s. Frank and Margaret (Rogers) McC.; student U. Notre Dame, 1921-24; LL.B., Ind. U., 1944; m. Agnes Larmore, May 17, 1930 (dec. May 19, 1935); children—Anne (Mrs. John J. Ring), Alice (Mrs. Patrick J. Donahue), Mary Catherine, Frank E.; m. 2d, Frances Patricia Bilderback, Feb. 3, 1945; children—James, Kevin, Frances, David, Kathleen. Chief clk. traffic dept. N.Y. C. R.R., Indpls., 1926-30, chief clk., city passenger agt., 1930-38; vice chmn. Asso. Railways of Ind., 1938-42, chmn., 1942-45; spl. asst. legal dept. Pa. R.R., Washington, 1945-51, asst. v.p., 1951-55, v.p., 1955—. Adv. council Law Sch., U. Notre Dame. Decorated Knight Comdr. Equestrian Order Holy Sepulchre of Jerusalem. Clubs: Congressional Country, Metropolitan, Carlton (Washington). Home: 4925 Lowell St., Washington 16. Office: Pennsylvania Bldg., 425 13th St., Washington 4. Deceased.

McCARTHY, James E., univ. prof.; b. Holyoke, Mass., Oct. 9, 1896; s. Daniel Charles and Katherine Veronica (O'Connor) M.; m. Dorothy Teresa Hoban, June 8, 1927; children—James Brian, Edward Desmond, Teresa Mary, Kevin. Dean Emeritus, Coll. of Commerce, Notre Dame U.; v.p. Northeast Broadcasting Co.; management consultant, dir. Assos. Investment Co., First Bank & Trust Co., South Bend, Indiana, Gerity-Mich. Corp., Adrain, Mich. Roman Cath. Author: The Physical Assets of the State of Indiana and the Earnings and Distribution of Income of Indiana Corporations, 1939. Home: 1154 E. Colfax Av., South Bend, Ind. Died July 11, 1958.

McCARTHY, Joseph Edward, bishop; b. Waterbury, Conn., Nov. 14, 1876; s. Eugene and Johanna (Colloty) McC.; A.B., Holy Cross Coll., Worcester, Mass., 1899; Catholic U. of America, 1899-1900, Seminaire de Saint Sulpice, Paris, 1900-03. Ordained priest R.C. Ch., 1903; with St. Thomas Sem., Hartford, Conn., 1903-08 and 1928-32; priest Sacred Heart Ch., Wauregan, Conn., 1910-13, All Hallows Ch., Moosup, Conn., 1913-28; bishop of Portland 1932-48, ret. Address: 307 Congress St., Portland, Me. Died Sept. 8, 1955; buried Waterbury, Conn.

McCARTHY, Joseph R(aymond), U.S. senator; b. Grand Chute, Outagamie County, Wis., Nov. 14, 1908; s. Timothy Thomas and Bridget (Tierney) McC.; LL.B., Marquette U., 1935; m. Jean Kerr, Sept. 29, 1953. Farm worker and grocery store employe during early years until 1929; practiced law, Waupaca, Wis., 1935-36; mem. firm Everlein & McCarthy, Shawano, Wis., 1936-39; elected circuit judge, 1939, 1945; U.S. senator from Wis., 1946— (vice chmn. Joint Com. on Housing, also mem. Banking and Currency Com. 1947-48; mem. Com. on Expenditures in Exec. Depts. 1947-52, Spl. Com. to Investigate Nat. Def. Program 1949-51, Appropriations Com. 1951—, Rules and Adminstrn. Com. 1952—, Com. on Govt. Operation (chmn.) (also chmn. Permanent Investigations sub-com. 1953-54) 1953—, Joint Com. on Library (chmn. 1953—). Served from pvt. to capt. USMC, 1942-45; assigned to marine aviation as ground officer; tail gunner (17 missions in S. Pacific). Recipient D.F.C., Air Medal with four gold stars; citation for extraordinary achievement as marine intelligence officer. Mem. Vets. Fgn. Wars, Am. Legion, Amvets. Republican. K.C., Lion, Elk, Eagle. Author: America's Retreat from Victory, The Story of George Catlett Marshall, 1951; McCarthyism, The Fight for America, 1952. Home: 514 Story St., Appleton, Wis. Office: Senate Office Bldg., Washington. Died May 2, 1957.

McCARTHY, Kathryn O'Loughlin, ex-congresswoman; b. Hays, Kan., Apr. 24, 1894; d. John and Mary Ellen (McIntosh) O'Loughlin; B.S. in Edn., Fort Hays State Coll., 1917; J.D., U. of Chicago, 1920; m. Daniel M. McCarthy, Feb. 4, 1933. Admitted to bar, Kan., 1921, Ill., 1923; with law firm Ekern, Meyers, Janisch, Chicago, 1921-23; asst. legislative counsel Am. Mut. Alliance, Chicago, 1923-26; atty. Legal Aid Bur., United Charities of Chicago, 1926-27; mem. law firm McCarthy & McCarthy, Hays, Kan. Mem. Kan. Ho. of Rep., 1931; mem. 73d Congress (1933-35), from the 6th Kansas Dist.

(1st congresswoman from Kansas). Mem. Am. Assn. Univ. Women, Kappa Beta Pi (former nat. pres.), Daughters of Isabella. Democrat. Catholic. Club: Business and Professional Women's. Home: 220 W. 12th St. Office: 127 W. 11th St., Hays, Kan. Died Jan. 16, 1952; buried Catholic Cemetery, Hays.

McCARTHY, Leighton Goldie, business exec.; b. Walkerton, Ont., Dec. 15, 1869; s. John Leigh Goldie and Frances Olivia (Irwin) McC.; ed. Barrie (Can.) public and grammar schools; LL.D., Univ. of Toronto, 1941; LL.D., Western University (London), 1942, Queens U. (Kingston), 1943; married Muriel Drummond Campbell, June 2, 1900; children—Leigh Hamilton (Mrs. Brookes Gossage), Zina Hope (Mrs. Ernest Howard), Nancy Manners (Mrs. Brooke Bell), Jean Goldie (Mrs. Rodney Northey), John Leighton Campbell. Barrister and solicitor, Can., 1892, King's counsel, 1902; mem. Can. House of Commons, 1898-1908; minister to U.S., 1941-43; apptd. ambassador 1943; resigned Dec. 31, 1944. Director Canada Life Assurance Co.; chairman board, National Trust Co., Ltd.; vice president and director Central Canada Loan & Savings Co., chmn. bd. Toronto Savings & Loan Co.; dir. Aluminum, Ltd.; vice president and director Union Carbide Company of Canada, Ltd., Canadian Nat. Carbon Co., Ltd., Prest-O-Lite Co. of Canada, Ltd., Dominion Oxygen Co., Ltd., Electro Metall. Co. of Canada, Ltd. Trustee Ga. Warm Springs Found. Mem. Anglican Ch. Mason. Clubs: York, Toronto, University, Golf (Toronto); Hunt, Ontario; Rideau (Ottawa). Home: 45 Walmer Rd., Toronto 4, Can. Died Oct. 5, 1952.

McCARTHY, Wilson, lawyer, ry. pres.; b. American Fork, Utah, July 24, 1884; s. Charles and Mary (Mercer) McC.; LL.B., Columbia U., 1913; m. Minerva Woolley, June 22, 1910, children—Dennis, Kathleen (Mrs. W. W. Riter), Patricia (Mrs. S. S. Sumner), Mary (Mrs. R. A. Kimball), Geraldine (Mrs. V. P. White). Began as rancher, 1900; admitted to bar, Oct. 1913, practiced at Salt Lake City; asst. county atty., Salt Lake Co., 1914-16; dist. atty., 3d Utah Judicial Dist., 1916; apptd. judge same dist., 1918; resigned fall 1919 to enter private practice; elected state senator Salt Lake County, 1926; appointed western dir. Reconstruction Finance Corp., 1932; mem. law firm of McCarthy, Richards & Carlson, Oakland, California, 1933; pres. Denver & Salt Lake Ry. Co., Dec. 1934-Apr. 1947; apptd. co-trustee D. & R.G. R.R. Nov. 1935 and elected pres. reorganized D. & R.G.W. R.R., Apr. 1947; dir. Mountain States Telephone & Telegraph since 1935, First Nat. Bank of Denver since 1936, First Security Corp., Ogden, Hotel Utah, Salt Lake City, since 1948, Fed. Res. Bank (Denver br.), 1937-42; dir. Holly Sugar Corp., 1953—, Ideal Cement Co., 1953—. Dir. Assn. American Railroads, 1941-46; pres. National Western Stock Show since April 1941. Regent University of Utah, 1926-32. Democrat. Mem. Church of Latter Day Saints. Clubs: Denver Country, Denver, Rotary (Denver); University (Salt Lake City); Athenian-Nile (Oakland, Calif.); Newcomen Society. Address: 2408 Haven Lane, Salt Lake City. Died Feb. 12, 1956; buried Wasatch Lawn Cemetery, Salt Lake City.

McCARTY, Dan, governor; b. Ft. Pierce, Fla. Jan. 18, 1912; s. Daniel Thomas and Frances (Moore) McC.; B.S.A., U. Fla., 1934; m. Olie Brown, Sept. 21, 1940; children—Daniel T., III, Michael Samuel, Frances Lela. Citrus grower, packer, rancher; rep. St. Lucie Co., Fla. State Legislature, 1937-43, house speaker, 1941; governor of Fla. since 1953. Chmn. adv. com. on edn. St. Lucie Co., 1946-47, 50-51; chmn. fund drive, community library; state campaign chmn. Am. Cancer Soc., 1949-50; mem. citizens tax com., 1947. Served as battery comdr. Battery B., 172d F.A., U.S. Army, 1941-45, advanced to col. U.S. VII Army. Decorated Legion of Merit. Bronze Star, Purple Heart (U.S.); Croix de Guerre (France). Mem. Jr. C. of C. (past pres.), Sr. C. of C. (past pres.), Presidents' Round Table, Ft. Pierce Vol. Firemen's Assn. (chmn.), Am. Legion, Vets. Fgn. Wars, Blue Key, Sigma Phi Epsilon. Episcopalian (sr. warden). Mason (Shriner), Odd Fellow, Elk (lodge trustee), Woodmen of the World, Moose. Club: Ft. Pierce Rotary (past pres.). Home: Fort Pierce, Fla. Office: Governor's Office, Tallahassee. Died Sept. 28, 1953; buried Fort Pierce, Fla.

McCARTY, Richard Justin, railway ofcl.; b. Clarksburg, Va. (now W.Va.), Mar. 12, 1851; s. Joseph Cresap and Ann (McCally) M.; student Soule U., Chapel Hill, Tex., 1865-68; grad. in pure mathematics U. Va., 1871, in applied mathematics, 1875; m. Mary Louise Allen, June 24, 1877. Axman, rodman, transitman I.G.N. R.R., Tex., 1871-74; with Kan. Rolling Mill, Kansas City, Mo., 1875-79; in accounting dept. Kansas City, Ft. Scott & Memphis R.R., 1879-84; gen. mgr., chief engr. Met. St. Ry. Co., Kansas City, 1888-96; auditor Kansas City, Pitts. & Gulf R.R. Co. (now K.C.S. Ry.), 1900-03, 05-06; v.p. K.C.S. Ry. and affiliated cos., 1907—, also chmn. valuation com. Mem. Am. Soc. C.E., Am. Soc. M.E., Royal Socs. Club (London, Eng.), Beta Psi. Author: Federal Valuation of Railroad Property, 1915. Home: 3820 Warwick Blvd. Office: Kansas City Southern Ry. Bldg., Kansas City, Mo. Deceased.

McCASKEY, Charles Irving, ret. financial adminstr.; b. Ft. Snelling, Minn., Aug. 7, 1877; s. Maj. Gen. William Spencer and Eleanor Forsythe (Garrison) McC.; ed. Yeates Inst. (Lancaster, Pa.), St. Thomas Hall (Holly Springs, Miss.), Kan. A. and M. Coll., U. Kan. (non-grad.); m. Selden Fant, May 22, 1905; children—Selden Fant, Chas. Irving, Eleanor, Mary Clayton. Served as examiner, chief clk., chief of insp.' div., dep. surveyor, acting surveyor of customs, at Manila, P.I., and insp., acting dep. surveyor of customs, N.Y.C., collector of customs, Corinto, Nicaragua, also as mgr. branches Banco Mercantil Americano de Colombia at Cartagena, Cali, Manizales and Medellin, Colombia, S.A., and mgr. br. of Compania Mercantil de Ultramar, at Cartagena, Colombia; asst. to W. Morgan Shuster, treas. gen. of Persia, 1911-12; accompanied A. C. Millspaugh to Persia, 1922; treas. gen. of Persia, 1922-27; dir. Imperial Persian Mint, 1923-27; dir. Bank-i-Iran, 1923-24, of Gen. Supply Service of Persian Govt., 1926-27, and of the Imperial Persian Govt. Pawnbroking Instn., 1927. Supr. Internal Revenue, Supr. of Customs, 1928-32; acting financial adviser, 1930-32, financial adviser, 1935-38, Republic of Liberia, West Africa, with station at Monrovia. Sec. to gov. of P.R., 1934-35, ret. Mem. Beta Theta Pi, The Philippine Club (N.Y.C.), The Loyal Legion of the U.S. (Washington). Republican. Episcopalian. Decorated Grand Commander with Star, Order of the Star of Africa. Home: 1239 Irwin Street, San Rafael, Cal. Died Mar. 16, 1954; buried San Rafael.

McCASKEY, John Piersol, mayor; b. nr. Gordonville, Pa., Oct. 9, 1837; s. William and Margaret Eckert (Piersol) M.; student Boys' High Sch., Lancaster, Pa.; m. Ellen Margaret Chase, Aug. 8, 1860. Tchr. Lancaster Boys' High Sch., 50 yrs., prin. 40 yrs., resigned, 1906; mayor of Lancaster, 1906-10; sec. Lancaster Watch Co. 18 yrs. Sec. Pa. State Ednl. Assn., 1870—. Episcopalian. For many yrs. a leader in Pa. in Arbor Day observance. Editor, pub. Pa. Sch. Jour., 1880—, asst. editor, 1866—; editor many compilations of favorite songs and hymns, including Treasury of Favorite Song, 3 vols., and of Lincoln Literary Collection; pub. Lincoln Art Series, etc. Writer on ednl. subjects, especially good memory work in lit. McCaskey High Sch., Lancaster, named in his honor. Address: Lancaster, Pa. Died Sept. 19, 1935.

McCASKILL, Oliver LeRoy (măk-kăs'kĭl), prof. law; b. Taylorville, Ill., Dec. 6, 1877; s. Daniel and Harriet H. (Robinson) McC.; Ph.B., U. of Chicago, 1901, J.D. cum laude, 1905; m. Fannie Bell, Oct. 1, 1912; children—Margaret Jane (Mrs. Richard Marsh), Daniel. Practiced, Chicago, with father, as member McCaskill & McCaskill, 1905-14; was lecturer on bankruptcy, Univ. of Chicago Law Sch.; prof. law, W.Va. U., 1914-16, Cornell U., 1916-26, U. of Ill. 1926-46; Hastings College of Law, since 1946; spl. counsel for Cornell University, 1916-26; member summer faculty Columbia School of Law, 1921, University of Colorado School of Law, 1930, University of Southern California Law School, 1938; spent four months visiting and studying operation of N.C., Va., New York and English courts, 1937. Chairman Wage Stabilization Enforcement Commission for Cal., Nev. and Ariz., 1951-52. Member American and Illinois bar associations, Phi Gamma Delta, Phi Delta Phi, Phi Kappa Phi, Order of the Coif. Republican. Methodist. Mason. Club: Bohemian. Author articles in legal publs.; mem. drafting com. Ill. Civil Practice Act (tech. adviser), 1933; editor-in-chief Illinois Civil Practice Act Annotated, 1933; editor Ill. Civil Practice Annotated supplement, 1936. Home: 2319 Green St. Office: 515 Van Ness Av., San Francisco. Died Jan. 13, 1953; buried Cypress Lawn, San Francisco.

McCASLIN, Robert Horace (măk-kăs-lĭn), clergyman; b. Sweetwater, Tenn.; s. Joseph Henry and Margaret Ella (Magill) McC.; B.S., Sweetwater Mil. Coll., 1900; A.B., Maryville (Tenn.) Coll., 1903; student Union Theol. Sem. in Va., Richmond, 1906; D.D., Richmond Coll., 1910; m. Grace Nelson Pollard, June 7, 1906 (deceased); m. 2d, Corrie Boineau Wilson, 1954; children—Susie Virginia, Robert H. (dec.). Ordained Presbyn. ministry, 1906; pastor 1st Ch., Cleveland, Tenn., 1906-08, 1st Ch., Bowling Green, Ky., 1908-13, 1st Ch., Montgomery, Ala., 1913-22, Riverside Ch., Jacksonville, Fla., 1922-32, Second Presbyterian Church, Memphis, Tenn., 1932-42, Park Lake, Orlando, Florida, 1942-53, pastor emeritus 1953—; pastor Windermere Union Ch., 1954—. Mem. Gen. Assembly Presbyn. Ch. in U.S.; del. Pan Presbyn. Alliance, Pittsburgh, 1921, Cardiff, Wales, 1925, Belfast, 1933; mem. Home Mission Bd., Presbyn. Ch. U.S. (exec. com.); moderator Synod of Florida, 1929. Director of Columbia (S.C.) Theol. Seminary, Southwestern Presbyn. U.; mem. State Edn. Commn., apptd. by Gov. Kilby to make general survey of state's ednl. interests. Life mem. Y.M.C.A.; colonel and chaplain Confederate Veterans Assn.; chmn. of War Camp Community Service Bd. World War I. Mem. Internat. Council Religious Edn.; member Defense Service Council Presbyterian Ch. Mem. Sons of American Revolution, Tenn. Soc., Civil Legion, Pi Gamma Mu. Democrat. Mason (K.T.), Shriner. Clubs: Rotary, University, Orlando Country Club. Author: Things That Count; Things Worth While; History Presbyterianism. Home: 1713 Lakeside Dr., Orlando, Fla. Died July 12, 1958; buried Greenwood Cemetery, Orlando.

McCAUGHAN, Russell Craig (măk-kăn'), exec. sec. Am. Osteopathic Assn.; b. Monroe County, Ind., July 19, 1889; s. James Zwingle Alexander and Mary Jane (Craig) McC.; grad. high sch., Kokomo, Ind., 1907; student Indiana U., 1909-11; D.O., Am. Sch. of Osteopathy, Kirksville, Mo., 1914; hon. Ph.D., Phila. Coll. of Osteopathy, 1935; hon. D.Sc., Coll. of Osteopathic Phys. and Surgeons, Los Angeles, 1940; hon. D.Sc., Kirksville Coll. of Osteopathy and Surgery, 1942; m. Bessie Alice Loop, Nov. 24, 1914. Teacher pub. schs., Howard County, Ind., 1908-10; instr. in chemistry, Am. Sch. of Osteopathy, 1910-14; practiced in Kokomo, 1914-31; exec. sec. Am. Osteopathic Assn., 1931-56 exec. sec. emeritus. Mem. Am., Indiana and Chicago osteopathic assns. Republican. Methodist. Mason. Clubs: South Shore Country, Chicago Rotary, Executives. Home: 190 E. Chestnut St. Office: 212 E. Ohio St., Chgo. 11. Died Mar. 21, 1957; buried Kokomo, Ind.

McCAULEY, Clayton M. (măk-kaw'lē), orthodontist; b. Hustberg, Tenn., Nov. 15, 1876; s. George D. and Nancy (Albright) McC.; B.S., Valparaiso U., 1898; D.D.S., U. Ill., 1901; m. Blanche Ramsey, Oct. 11, 1899; children—Dallas R., Elmer. Practiced at Chgo., 1901-04; adjunct prof. operative technics U. Ill. Coll. Dentistry, 1902-04; removed to Tex., 1904; formerly practiced Los Angeles; head dept. orthodontia Orthopedia Hosp., Los Angeles. Co-organizer, dir. Guaranty Bank & Trust Co., Dallas; co-organizer, sec. Golden State Securities Co., Los Angeles; builder, owner The Outlook and Dental Research Lab., Vista, Cal. Commd. maj. Dental Res. Corps, U.S. Army. Formerly pres. Nat. Assn. Dental Examiners; pres. Tex. State Dental Assn., chmn. dental com., Rotary Internat.; pres. Tex. State Bd. Dental Examiners; pres. Pacific Coast Soc. Orthodontists; mem. Am. Dental Assn., So. Cal. Dental Soc., Am. Soc. Orthodontists, Neb. Dental Assn. (hon.); del. Nat. Dem. Conv., 1908. Home: 2395 Araby Dr., Palm Springs, Cal. Died May 7, 1957; buried Inglewood (Cal.) Park Cemetery.

McCAULEY, James Wayne, army officer; b. Jedsonia, Ark., Sept. 24, 1902; s. James Allen and Rose Mae (Best) McC.; student U. Ark., 1921-22; A.B., Ouachita Coll., 1925; grad. Brooks Field AAF Pre-Flight Sch., 1928, Kelly Field AAF Basic Flying Sch., 1929, Maxwell Field AC Tech. Sch., 1929; m. Ruth Frair, Feb. 12, 1934; children—James Wayne, John Milton. Commd. 2d lt. inf. U.S. Army, 1923, trans. AC, advanced through grades to brig. gen., 1944; comdg. officer Seattle Air Def. Wing, fighter group in command air defenses of N.W., 1942; comdr. Fighter Wing, Eng., 6 mos., as comdr. of wing participated in Normandy offensive, June 6, 1944, and established Am. Air Force Hdqrs. on continent, June 7, 1944; also participated fighter bomber operations during campaigns in France and Belgium; comdg. gen. Hdqrs. 70th Fighter Wing, USAAF, Germany; now vice comdr. eastern air def. force, Stewart Air Force Base. Decorated Air Medal, Legion of Merit (U.S.); Legion of Honor (France). Mem. Phi Delta Kappa. Home: 135 E. Merrick St., Shreveport, La. Died Mar. 9, 1958.

McCAW, Henry, meat packing exec.; b. St. Paul, Oct. 29, 1893; s. William and Roberta (Leck) McC.; m. Ruth Tucker, June 30, 1917; 1 dau., Harriet (Mrs. Warren E. Yaap). With Swift & Co., Chicago, since 1911, v.p. since 1950, Union Stock Yards since 1920. Mem. Chicago Bd. Trade. Home: 9048 S. Laflin, Chicago 20. Office: 4115 Packers Av., Chgo. 9. Died Sept. 14, 1952; buried Mt. Hope Cemetery, Chgo.

McCLARAN, John Walter (măk-lâr'ĕn), naval officer; b. Wooster, O., Oct. 1, 1887; s. John Cook and Elisabeth (Deer) McC.; student Wooster Acad., 1901-04, Wooster U., 1905-06, U.S. Naval Acad., 1907-11; m. Stephana Prager, Nov. 25, 1925; children—Stephen, Ann, Patricia. Commd. ensign USN, 1911; promoted through grades to rear adm., 1941; served in P.R. uprising, 1912, Mexican occupation, 1914, World War, 1917-18; asst. naval attaché Tokyo, 1920-22; staff comdr., Yangtze Patrol, 1922-24; established bases for 1st round-the-world flight in Kurile Islands and Japan, 1924; staff comdr. Battle Force, 1928-30; comdr. Mine Div., 1933-35; comd. Flagship Mine Force, 1937-39; laid first submarine nets in Puget Sound and San Francisco Bay, 1937; assisted in establishing advance base, Midway Islands, 1938-39; ret. because phys. disability, 1941. Awarded D.S.C., Mexican Campaign medal, Victory medal, etc. Mem. Phi Gamma Delta. Clubs: Chevy Chase (Md.); Army and Navy Country (Washington); Goofy Gooney (Midway Island). Home: 1138 Mission Ridge Rd., Santa Barbara, Cal. Died Mar. 28, 1948.

McCLAVE, Charles Rowley, milling and grain exec.; b. Bath, N.Y., Feb. 8, 1873; s. Michael H. and Eliza (Rowley) McC.; grad. Elmira (N.Y.) Free Acad.; m. Daisy Allston Green, Sept. 24, 1902; children—Elizabeth, Charles Green. Sheep rancher, 1901-04; entered flour milling and grain bus., 1904; organizer Mont. Elevator Co., Moore, Mont., 1904, mgr., 1904-48, chmn. bd., 1948—; organizer Mont. Flour Mills Co., Great Falls, Mont., 1911, mgr., 1911-48, chmn. bd., 1948—. Active on bds. trade orgns., bds. trustees hosps. and schs., vestryman on ch. bds. Mem. Newcomen Soc. Mason (Shriner), Elk, Rotarian. Address: care Mont. Flour Mills Co., Great Falls, Mont. Died Aug. 26, 1956; buried Highland Cemetery, Great Falls, Mont.

McCLELLAN, William (măk-klĕl'lăn), engring. exec.; b. Phila., Nov. 5, 1872; s. John and Margaret (Marshall) McC.; B.S., U. Pa., 1900, Ph.D., 1903, E.E., 1914; m. Caroline May Stroup. Instr. physics U. Pa., 1900-05, dean Wharton Sch., 1916-19; with Phila. Rapid Transit Co., 1900-05; engr. Westinghouse, Church, Kerr & Co., 1900-05; engr. Westinghouse, Church, Kerr & Co., 1905-07; dir. Campion McClellan Co., 1907-15; mem. Paine, McClellan & Campion, 1915-20, McClellan & Junkersfeld, 1922-29; v.p. Stone & Webster Engring. Corp., 1929-33; pres. William McClellan & Co., Ltd., 1930-33, Potomac Electric Power Co., 1933-39; pres. Washington Ry. & Electric Co., 1935-40, chmn., 1940-43; pres. Union Electric Co. of Mo., 1939-41, chmn., 1941-46; chmn. bd. Steam Motive Power, Inc.; dir. Riggs Nat. Bank, Capital Transit Co., Potomac Electric Power Co., Research Corp. N.Y.; cons. engr., Public Service Commn., 2d dist. N.Y., 1911-13; v.p. Cleveland Electric Illuminating Co., 1919-21; mem. President's Commn. on Muscle Shoals, 1925. Dir. gen. Alumni Soc. U. Pa., 1921; past trustee U. Pa.; trustee Lingnan U. Former dir. Nat. Symphony Orchestra Assn., pres., 1938-39. Fellow Am. Inst. E.E. (pres. 1921-22); mem. Am. Soc. M.E., Am. Engring. Council (pres. 1938-39), Council Fgn. Relations; past pres. Asso. Pa. Clubs. Dir. Washington Board of Trade, 1939. Trustee, Com. for Economic Development. Mem. Alpa Chi Rho, Phi Beta Kappa, Sigma Xi, Beta Gamma Sigma. Republican. Episcopalian. Clubs: University, Univ. of Pa. of New York (ex-pres.); University, University of Pa. Varsity (Phila.); Cosmos, Metropolitan, Chevy Chase (Washington). Contbr. to tech. mags. and tech. socs. Home: Burgundy Farm, Alexandria, Va. Died Nov. 14, 1950; buried Ivy Hill Cemetery, Alexandria.

McCLELLAND, George William, educator; b. Dobbs Ferry, N.Y., June 18, 1880; s. Charles Paul and Meta Janet (Babcock) McC.; grad. Westminster Sch., Simsbury, Conn., 1898; A.B., U. Pa., 1903, Ph.D., 1916, LL.D., 1931; L.H.D., Ursinus Coll., 1944; LL.D., U. Pitts., 1945, Dickinson Coll., 1946; D.H.L., Dropsie Coll., 1947; m. Mildred I. Child, Nov. 4, 1916; children—George Bryant, Marion Child. Instr. English and Latin, Coll. City of N.Y., 1905-11; instr. English, U. Pa., 1911-17, asst. prof., 1917-25, prof., 1925—, dir. admissions, 1921-26, v.p., 1925-39, provost 1939-44, pres. 1944-48, chmn., 1948-51. Sec. Assn. Colls. and Secondary Schs. of Middle States and Md., 1912-39, pres. 1940; mem. Am. Philos. Soc., Modern Lang. Assn. Am., St. Andrews Soc., Phi Beta Kappa, Beta Gamma Sigma, Kappa Sigma. Presbyn. Club: University (Phila.); Lenape. Home: 730 S. Latches Lane, Merion, Pa. Died Aug. 20, 1955; buried West Laurel Hill, Bala-Cynwyd, Pa.

McCLELLAND, James Farley, mining engr.; b. Poughkeepsie, N.Y., Mar. 3, 1878; s. James Farley and Mary (Vincent) McC.; E.M., Columbia, 1900; A.M. (hon.), Yale, 1910; m. Jane Adams Kearney, Dec. 7, 1912; children—Jean K. (Mrs. Julian S. Barrett), James F., George K., Vincent (killed in service USN World War II). Instr. geology and mining U. Wyo., 1900-01; with Indiana Gold Dredging Co., Oroville, Cal., 1901-02; instr. in mining, Columbia, 1902-05; in gen. mining practice, Tonopah, Nev., 1905-08; prof. mining Leland Stanford Jr. U., 1908-10; prof. mining engring. Sheffield Sci. Sch. (Yale), 1910-17; editor-in-chief, specification sect. Signal Corps, 1917-18; chief prodn. engring. Bur. Aircraft Prodn., 1918-19; cons. engr. Liberty Nat. Bank, N.Y.C., 1919-20; v.p. Liberty Industrial Corp., 1921-22; asst. v.p. New York Trust Co., 1922-28, v.p., 1928-29; v.p. Chemical Nat. Bank and Trust Co. and Chemical Nat. Co., 1929-31; v.p., dir. Phelps Dodge Corp., 1931-47, ret., now dir. and mem. exec. com. Mem. Am. Inst. Mining and Metall. Engrs. Clubs: Century, Union League, India House (N.Y.C.). Home: Mead's Point, Greenwich, Conn. Office: 40 Wall St. Died May 6, 1955.

McCLELLAND, Silas Edward, oculist, aurist; b. Decatur, Macon County, Ill., Jan. 13, 1860; s. Joseph Edgar and Margery (Wheeler) McC.; M.D., Rush Med. Coll., 1884; post grad. work, same, 1889, New York Post-Grad. Med. Sch., 1894-95, 97, Royal London Ophthal. Hosp., 1902; hon. D.Sc., James Millikin U., 1938; m. Sarah Rose Armstrong, Nov. 1884 (died 1889); m. 2d, Margaret Ellen Baird, May 6, 1891 (died 1935). Became registered pharmacist in Illinois, 1883; chmn. bd. trustees James Millikin Estate; trustee Anna B. Millikin Estate; pres. Union Iron Works, Decatur; chmn. bd. Millikin Nat. Bank, Decatur; dir. Millikin Trust Co. Pres. bd. mgrs. Decatur Coll. and Industrial School of James Millikin U., 1907-14. Mem. Ill. State and Macon County med. socs., Decatur Med. Soc. (ex-pres.). Republican. Presbyn. Mason (K.T.). Home: 904 W. Williams St. Office: Millikin Bldg., Decatur, Illinois. Died Mar. 7, 1953.

McCLINTOCK, Miller; traffic cons.; b. Cedar Rapids, Neb., June 13, 1894; s. George Henry and Elizabeth Ann (Miller) McC.; A.B., Stanford, 1918, A.M., 1920; A.M., Harvard, 1922, Ph.D., 1924; D.Sc., Tufts, 1938; m. Hazel Barton, Sept. 4, 1917; children—Thomas Miller, John William. Instr. in English, Stanford, 1918-21; asst. prof. municipal govt. U. Cal., 1924-26; dir. Bureau Street Traffic Research, Harvard, 1925-38, Bur. Municipal Research, 1926-38; dir. Bur. for Street Traffic Research, Yale, 1938-42; cons. on traffic and transportation to various cities, states and Fed. Govt., 1925; chief exec. Traffic Audit Bur., Inc., 1933-42; dir. Advertising Research Found., 1939-41; adviser Can Mfrs. Inst., 1941-42; exec. dir. Advertising Council, Inc., 1942; pres. MBS, 1943-44, Instructional Films, Inc., 1948-51, Sound Book Press Soc., Scarsdale, N.Y., 1951—; member bd., cons. Ency. Brit. Films, Inc., 1945-46; mem. bd. Asso. Musak, 1945-46, Unicef, 1957—. Member Inst. Traffic Engrs., Am. Polit. Science Assn., Soc. Automotive Engrs. Episcopalian. Clubs: Yale (N.Y.C.); Shenorock Shore (Rye, N.Y.); Chevy Chase (Washington). Author books on traffic and transport, advertising and marketing subjects. Home: Scarsdale, N.Y. Died Jan. 1960.*

McCLOSKEY, John Francis (măk-klŏs'kē), coll. dean; b. Johnstown, Pa., May 19, 1894; s. Hugh Francis and Mary Ann (McDevitt) McC.; B.B.A., Tulane U., 1925, M.B.A., 1942; student Loyola U., New Orleans, 1933-35; m. Mildred Louise Lambert, June 3, 1930; children—John Francis, Elinor Mae, Dennis Vincent. Began as drug clerk, 1911; registered pharmacist, 1926; retail drug store owner, 1927-35; professor business administration, Loyola University, 1928-32, dean College of Pharmacy, 1933—. Mem. bd. advisers Hotel Dieu Hosp. Served as 1st lt., Infantry, 1917-18, with AEF, 18 months. Decorated Purple Heart; Black Star; Legion of Honor. Distinguished service citation, Loyola U., 1954. Mem. Royal Photog. Soc. of Great Britain, Am. Pharm. Assn., La. State Pharm. Assn., Am. Assn. Colls. Pharmacy (president elect 1958), New Orleans Acad. of Science, Nat. Assn. Retail Druggists, American Society Hospital Pharmacists, Alpha Sigma Nu Honor Society; New Orleans Assn. of Commerce, American Legion, D.A. Veterans; Blue Key, Sigma Phi Epsilon, Rho Xi, Theta Beta, Epsilon Kappa Sigma, K.C.; Last Man's Club (New Orleans, La.). Co-founder Hist. Pharmacy Mus.; Mem. City of N.O. Committee on Pharmaceutical Museum. Author: Working Hours and Delivery in Retail Drug Stores, Study Methods in Pharmacy, 1942. Contbr. articles to drug jours. Editor La. Pharmacist, monthly jour., 1943—. Home: 2935 Calhoun St., New Orleans 18. Died Dec. 9, 1957; buried Metairie Cemetery, New Orleans.

McCLOUD, Bentley Grimes, bank director, business executive; born in Portsmouth, Ohio, August 19, 1884; s. Charles L. and Nellie (Bentley) McC.; student pub. schs.; m. Florence Olmsted, November 1, 1910. Started with the First Nat. Bank of Chicago as clerk, 1903; asst. clearing house bank examiner, Chicago Clearing House, 1911; cashier and subsequently asst. gov. Federal Reserve Bank of Chicago, 1915; v.p. Union Trust Co. of Chicago, 1921; v.p. First Nat. Bank of Chgo., 1929, pres., 1945-50, dir., 1933—; dir. Dayton Rubber Co., Miehle Pring Press & Mfg. Co., Standard Oil Co. (Ind.), Rudolph Wurlitzer Co. Life trustee Northwestern U. Home: 263 Chestnut St., Winnetka, Ill. Office: 38 S. Dearborn St., Chgo. Died May 10, 1956.

McCLOUD, Earl, C.S. lectr.; b. nr. Greenville, O.; s. Joseph and Margaret Jane (Martin) McC.; ed. pub. schs., Celina and Piqua, O.; m. Gladys Marian Heilig, Aug. 6, 1913; children—Patty Lou, Peggy Jane (twins). Asso. with Piqua Leader, 1901-02, Wellsville (O.) Record and Canton (O.) News-Democrat, 1902-03, St. Louis Globe-Democrat, 1904-08; editor Western Ins. Review, 1903-08; telegraph editor St. Louis Star, 1908-10, San Antonio Express, 1911-12; asst. city editor San Antonio Light, 1912-17; Christian Science camp welfare worker, 1918-19, practitioner 1919—, became Christian Science tchr., 1928, Normal Class of Mass. Metaphysical Coll.; apptd. to Christian Science Bd. of Lectureship, The First Ch. of Christ, Scientist, Boston, 1941. Has lectured in all parts of continental U.S., Mexico and Canada. Home: 111 Eleanor Av., San Antonio. Died Oct. 3, 1949.

McCLOY, Charles Harold, univ. prof.; b. Marietta, O., Mar. 30, 1886; s. William Alexander and Emma Maria (Langley) McC.; Ph.B., Marietta Coll., 1907, M.A., 1910; student Harvard U., summers 1905, 06, 07, Johns Hopkins Med. Sch., 1911-13, Ohio State U., 1919-20; Ph.D., Columbia Univ., 1932; D.Sc., Marietta College, 1947, Grinnell, 1955; Litt.D., George Williams Coll., 1957; P.E.D., Ottawa Univ., 1958; m. Anna Florence Fisher, Dec. 20, 1907; children—Emma (Mrs. James Walter Layman), William Ashby, Robert Winston, Amanda Ruth (Mrs. Edward Kilbourn Capen), George Edward. Instr. physical training, Marietta Coll., 1905-07; dir. physical edn. and acting head dept. of biology, Yankton Coll., 1907-08; physical dir. Y.M.C.A., Danville, Va., 1908-11; instr. physical edn., Pub. Athletic League, Baltimore, 1911-13; sec. Dept. of Physical Edn., Nat. Council of Y.M.C.A., China, 1913-21; dir. Sch. of Physical Edn., Nat. Southeastern U., Nanking, China, 1921-26; sr. instr. health edn., Detroit Teachers Coll., 1926-27; sec. for research in physical edn., Nat. Council Y.M.C.A., N.Y. City, 1927-30; lecturer, Teachers Coll., Columbia U., 1928-29; research prof. anthropometry and physical edn., State U. of Ia., 1930—. Expert consultant U.S. War Dept., 1941—; mem. civilian adv. com. for Navy's Physical Fitness Program and Joint Army and Navy Com. on Welfare and Recreation; Testing—Ground Forces, Air Forces of the Army. Fellow Am. Acad. Physical Education (secretary-treas. 1941-46, president 1947), Am. Assn. for Health, Physical Edn. and Recreation; mem. Am. Assn. Physical Anthropologists, Psychrometric Soc., Phi Beta Kappa, Sigma Xi, Phi Tau Phi (Chinese). Recipient Research Award, Am. Acad. Physical Edn., 1938; Gulick award, 1944; Hetherington award, Am. Acad. Phys. Edn., 1956. Mason. Club: Triangle (State U. of Ia.). Author: (in Chinese) Gymnastic Nomenclature, 1915; The Physiology of Exercise, 1915; Track and Field Athletics, 1915; Calisthenics, 1915; A Syllabus of Anthropometry, 1917; An Outline of Kinesiology, 1917; A Manual of Marching, 1917; Soccer Football, 1918; Calisthenics, A Manual for Teachers, 1919; Muscular Action, A Syllabus for Kinesiology, 1919; Biology and Physical Education, 1921; A Textbok of Physical Examinations, 1923; Graded Apparatus Work, 1925; Syllabus of Physical Education, 1921; (in English) The Measurement of Athletic Power, 1932 Appraising Physical Status; The Selection of Measurements, 1936; Appraising Physical Status: Methods and Norms, 1938; Tests and Measurements in Health and Physical Education, 3d ed., 1949; Philosophical Bases for Physical Education, 1940; A Laboratory Manual for Tests and Measurements in Health and Physical Eucation (with Aileen Carpenter), 1941. Gen. editor for physical edn. series. Contbr. to Chinese, Latin Am. and Am. ednl. jours. Home: 620 Holt Av., Iowa City, Ia. Died Sept. 18, 1959.

McCLUNG, George Harlan, clergyman; b. Ottumwa, Ia., Oct. 31, 1879; s. Henry Clay and Alice Catherine (Harlan) McC.; Knox Coll., Galesburg, Ill., 1898-99; A.B., Heding Coll., Abingdon, Ill., 1903; Garrett Bibl. Inst., Evanston, Ill., 1903-04; D.D., Ill. Wesleyan U., 1916; m. Blanche Davis, Aug. 15, 1906; children—Marjorie, George Harlan. Worked on Miss. River steamboats and as printer. Ordained ministry Meth. Ch., 1903; pastor Bradley, Ill., 1903-04, Terre Haute, Ill., 1904-09, Tonica, Ill., 1909-12, Dwight, Ill., 1912-17, Kankakee, Ill., 1917-26, Grand Rapids, Mich., 1926-35, Central Park Ch., Buffalo, N.Y., 1935-38, Asbury Ch., Watertown, New York since 1938; dean of the Jefferson County Ministerium. Mem. Gen. Conf. Meth. Church, 1924 and 1932; mem. World Service Commn., 1924-28; mem. various coms. and councils of Northern N.Y. Conf. and Council of Chs.; del. to Jurisdictional Conf., 1944. Hon. life mem. Am. Fed. of Musicians; hon. mem. Theta Beta Chi (Syracuse U.). Republican. Mason (32°). Club: Watertown Rotary (past pres.). Home: Watertown, N.Y.; (summer) Epworth Hts., Ludington, Mich. Died Oct. 9, 1952.

McCLUNG, Will Clinton, clergyman; b. Johnson County, Tex., Dec. 18, 1886; s. William Israel and Tabitha (Proctor) McC.; student Tex. Bapt. U., 1907-08; Th.B., Southwestern Bapt. Sem., Fort Worth, 1915; grad. Chaplains Tng. Sch., Louisville, 1918; A.B., N. Tex. State Tchrs. Coll., 1922; D.D., Howard Payne Coll., Brownwood, Tex., 1929; m. Hazel Lewis, Dec. 25, 1910; children—Will Clinton, Hazel, Herbert Ward (dec.). Ordained to ministry Bapt. Ch., 1910; pastor 1st Bapt. Ch., Alvord, Tex., 1915-17, Comanche, Okla., 1918-19, Denton, Tex., 1920-30, Wichita, Kan., 1931-37, Immanuel Bapt. Ch., Little Rock, Ark., 1937—. Chaplain, rank of 1st lt. U.S. Army overseas 13 mos.; participated battle of Argonne; with Army of Occupation, Germany, 6 mos. Trustee Ottawa (Kan.) U. Mem. state bd. Tex. Bapt. Conv. 8 yrs.; pres. Pastors' and Laymen's Assn., 1928; pres. Alumni Assn. Southwestern Bapt. Sem., 1929-30. Mason (K.T.). Study and research in Europe, Syria, Egypt and Palestine, 1923. Contbr. religious publs. Address: Immanuel Bapt. Ch., Little Rock, Ark. Died Nov. 27, 1937.

McCLUNG, William H., lawyer; b. Plum Tp., Allegheny Co., Pa., Nov. 22, 1854; s. Rev. Samuel M. and Nancy Cowan (Gilchrist) McC.; grad. Pitts. High Sch., 1873, LL.D., Western U. Pa.; unmarried. Admitted to Pa. bar, Dec. 16, 1876. Mem. Am., Pa. bar assns., etc.; del. Universal Congress Lawyers and Jurists, St. Louis, 1904. Address: University Club, 123 University Pl., Pitts. 15. Died Mar. 9, 1936; buried Allegheny Cemetery, Pitts.

McCLURE, Charles Freeman Williams, anatomist; b. Cambridge, Mass., Mar. 6, 1865; s. Charles Franklin and Joan Elizabeth (Blake) McC.; A.B., Princeton University, 1888, A.M., 1892, E.M. fellow in biology, 1888-89; student College Physicians and Surgeons (Columbia), 1890-91; univs. of Berlin, 1893, Kiel, 1895, Würzburg, 1897; hon. Sc.D., Columbia, 1908; m. Grace Latimer Jones, Aug. 25, 1921. Instr. biology, Princeton U., 1891-95, asst. prof., 1895-1901, prof. comparative anatomy, 1901-34, now prof. emeritus. Mem. Peary Relief Expdn., 1899. Mem. Am. Soc. Naturalists, Am. Zoöl. Soc., Assn. Am. Anatomists (v.p., 1910-11, exec. com., 1912-16, pres., 1920-21), Am. Philos. Soc., Anatomische Gesellschaft, Phi Beta Kappa, Sigma Xi; fellow A.A.A.S. Clubs: Ivy, Nassau (Princeton). Author of numerous papers on the anatomy and development of the vascular system, œdema, etc. Formerly editor Anatomical Record. Home: Princeton, N.J. Died July 23, 1955.

McCLURE, James Gore King, farmer; b. Lake Forest, Ill., Oct. 28, 1884; s. James Gore King and Annie (Dixon) McC.; grad. of Lake Forest (Ill.) Acad., 1900; B.A., Yale, 1906, hon. M.A., 1939; studied New Coll., Edinburgh, Scotland, 1906-07, McCormick Theol. Sem., 1908-09, universities of Tübingen, Jena and Berlin, 1909-10; hon. D.Sc., Berea (Ky.) College, 1929; hon. M.A., Harvard, 1941; hon. LL.D., U. of North Carolina, 1942; m. Elizabeth Skinner Cramer, Mar. 29, 1916; children—James Gore King III (dec.), Elizabeth (Mrs. James Clarke). Farming in N.C., 1916—; pres. Farmer's Federation, Inc. (organized to develop markets and stimulate production of farmers in Western N.C.; originator Lords Acre movement); president Farmers Loan Corporation; editor Farmers Federation News; president Appalachian Mutual, Incorporated, Treasurer Chest Mutual Cooperative. President Am. Forestry Assn., 1937-41; member North Carolina Conservation and Development Bd., 1925-33. Pub. dir. Home Loan Corp., 1937-40; pres. Skyline Coop. Dairies; v.p. N.C. Symphony Assn.; chmn. Citizens Com. for Better Schs., Ashville, 1952-54. Trustee Berry Schs., Rome, Ga. Awarded gold medal, Inst. Social Sciences, 1944. Mem. N.C. Forestry Assn. (dir.), Soc. Mayflower Descendants (elder for State of N.C.), Ashville Civic Music Assn. (pres.), Nat. Citizens Committee for Public Schools. Republican. Minister Presbyn. Ch. Clubs: Pen and Plate, Civitan, Bilmote Forest; Yale, Century (N.Y.C.). Home: Hickory Nut Gap Farm, Fairview, N.C. Address: Asheville, N.C. Died June 17, 1956.

McCLURE, Robert A., ret. army officer; b. Mattoon, Ill., Mar. 4, 1897; s. George and Harriet Julia McC.; student Ky. Mil. Inst., Lyndon, 1912-15; Inf. Sch., 1923-24; Cav. Sch., 1925-36; Command and Gen. Staff Sch., 1930-32; Army War Coll., 1935; m. Marjory Leitch, Nov. 11, 1918; children—Robert Dugald, Richard Alexis. Commd. 2d lt., 1916; promoted through the grades to maj. gen., 1955; served in P.I., China, Japan, N. Africa, Eng. France: instr. Inf. Sch., 1926-30, Army War Coll., 1935-40; mil. attaché, Am. Embassy, London, 1941-42; chief Intelligence, European Theatre, 1942; Allied Force Hdqrs. 1942-43; chief psychological warfare Div., S.H.A.E.F., 1944-45; director, Information Control Div. of Military Govt., Germany, 1945-47; chief Psychol. Warfare Div., 1950-53; chief U.S. Mil. Mission with Iranian Armed Forces 1953-56, ret. Address: Shalimar, Fla. Died Jan. 1, 1957.

McCLURE, Robert Owen, coll. pres., churchman; b. Henderson, Ky., Aug. 5, 1885; s. William Preston and Elizabeth Jane (Cottingham) McC.; A.B., Asbury Coll., Wilmore, Ky., 1904, M.A., 1908; student Garrett Biblical Institute, 1920, D.D., 1921; D.D., Taylor University, 1920; student Northwestern University, summers 1921, 1922; LL.D., Lincoln Memorial U., 1931; m. Esther Adelaide Hardy, June 4, 1908; children—Bruce Hardy, Esther Adelaide. Pres. Belle City Coll., Lake Charles, La.; pastor St. Charles Av. Meth. Ch., New Orleans, 1914; supt. Athens Dist., Ohio Conf., 1930-31, Chillicothe Dist., 1931-36; minister Epworth Meth. Ch., Toledo, O., 1936-41; superintendent of Lima Dist., 1941-43; became president of the Ohio Northern University, 1943, now retired; three months study Mediterranean Area, 1932. Trustee White Cross Hosp., Columbus, O., Flower Hosp., Toledo. Mason (Scottish Rite, Shriner). Clubs: Torch (Toledo); Rotary (Lima). Home: Winter Park, Fla. Deceased.

McCLURE, Roy Donaldson, surgeon; b. Bellebrook, O., Jan. 17, 1882; s. James Albert (M.D.) and Ina Hester (Donaldson) McC.; A.B., Ohio State U., 1904, hon. D.Sc., 1936; M.D., Johns Hopkins, 1908; hon. D.Sc., Washington and Jefferson Coll., 1944; studied U. of Prague, Bohemia, 1906; m. Helen Keene Troxell, March 4, 1916; children—Mary Keene Stearns, Roy Donaldson, M.D., Douglas Templeton. Assistant to Dr. Alexis Carrel, Rockefeller Inst., 1907-08; house surgeon New York Hosp., 1909-11; resident surgeon Johns Hopkins Hosp., 1912-16, also instr. in surgery, Johns Hopkins Univ.; an organizer and surgeon in chief Henry Ford Hosp., Detroit, since 1916; dir. med. dept. Ford Rubber Plantation, Brazil, 1928-46; chief surgeon D.T.&I. R.R.; extra-mural lecturer in post-grad. medicine, U. of Mich.; Guest speaker Congrès Français de Chirurgie, Paris, 1937. Trustee Henry Ford Hospital since 1938. Mem. sub-com. on surg. infections, sub-com. on burns, 1940-45; committee on prosthetic devices, 1945-46, committee on artificial limbs since 1946, of National Research Council. Regional rep. coms. on admission, Johns Hopkins and Duke University Med. Schools. Chmn. Mich. Med. Advisory Bd. No. 3, World War I, 1917, same, World War II; mem. Detroit committee on Foreign Relations. Member blood procurement com., Detroit, Am. Red Cross. Maj. Med. Corps, U.S. Army, 1918-19; served as comdg. officer Evacuation Hospital No. 33, A.E.F. Member of the board of trustees of the Michigan Foundation for Medical and Health Edn. since 1946. Fellow Am. College Surgeons (gov.), Am. Surg. Assn.; member Southern Surg. Assn., Am. Med. Assn., Société Internationale de Chirurgie, Am. Coll. Surgeons (bd. govs. 1935-38), Ohio State Univ. Assn. (pres. 1925-27), Central Surg. Assn. (founder and first pres. 1940-41), Detroit Acad. of Surgery (pres. 1929), Detroit Acad. Medicine (pres. 1945-46), Johns Hopkins Med. and Surg. Assn. (act. pres. 1946), Phi Beta Kappa (Ohio State; pres. Detroit Assn. 1939-42), Sigma Xi, Delta Upsilon, Nu Sigma Nu. Republican. Presbyterian. Clubs: Detroit, Economic (bd. dirs.) Newcomen Soc., Grosse Pointe Country. Author of numerous papers giving results of studies and experiments, alone and with others. Mem. adv. bd., Annals of Surgery, also editorial bd., Am. Jour. Surgery. Home: 1490 Iroquois Av. Address: Henry Ford Hospital, Detroit 2. Died March 31, 1951.

McCLURE, W(illiam) Frank, advt. exec.; b. Warren, O., Apr. 22, 1877; s. William Anderson and Agnes (Scott) McC.; ed. pub. schs.; hon. B.C.S., Central YMCA Schs., Chgo., 1922; m. Stella May Ward, Aug. 25, 1897; children—Lawrence Francis, Katherine Agnes (dec.). Editor Ashtabula (O.) Record, 1898; reporter Cleve. Press, and Cleve. Plain Dealer, 1899; contbr. to mags., 1901-08; advt. mgr. Redpath Lyceum Bur., Chgo., 1910-17, Ft. Dearborn Bank, 1917-20, Am. Bond & Mortgage Co., 1920-22; v.p., Chgo. mgr. Albert Frank & Co., 1922-31; v.p. Carroll Dean Murphy, Inc., 1931-35; exec. v.p. Critchfield & Co., 1935-40; exec. v.p. Smith, Benson & McClure, Inc., 1940-48; v.p. Carroll Dean Murphy, Inc., 1948—; dir. Bills Realty Co.; dir. Central Howard Assn. Founder, 1914, since pres. Wilmette Sunday Evening Club, enlarged to New Trier Sunday Evening Club, combining four communities, 1935, and to North Shore Sunday Evening Club, 1940; founder adv. council Chgo. Assn. Commerce, 1919, pres. 5 yrs.; chmn. Nat. Adv. Commn., 1917-27; sec. Advt. Fedn. Am., 1928-29; founder and 1st pres. Chgo. Federated Advt. Club, 1934-35; dir. Chgo. Better Business Bur., 1932—; hon. trustee Chautauqua Instn., Chautauqua, N.Y.; trustee at large Chgo. Ch. Fedn., 1939—; trustee Advertising Foundation of Northwestern U., former pres. State Advertising Clubs of Ill. Republican. Conglist. Club: Union League (life mem.; chmn. entertainment com. 11 yrs.). Home: 219 Broadway, Wilmette, Ill. Office: 39 S. LaSalle St., Chgo. Died Jan. 3, 1951; buried Meml. Park, Evanston, Ill.

McCLURE, William L., surgeon; b. Goldendale, Wash., Dec. 24, 1880; s. Edward P. and Mary L. (Davis) McC.; Wash. State Normal Sch.; M.D., Northwestern U., 1909; m. Joy L. Massey, July 11, 1911; 1 dau., Nancy Joy. Began practice at Yakima, Wash., now retired; former mem. staff St. Elizabeth's Hosp.; mem. Sch. Bd., Yakima. 1915-28. Served in M.C., U.S. Army, 1917-19, advancing to lt. col. Fellow A.C.S.; mem. Am., Wash. med. assns., Yakima County Med. Soc., Phi Beta Pi, Alpha Omega Alpha. Republican. Mason (32°). Clubs: Lions, Elks (Yakima); University (Seattle). Home: 301 N. 41st Av. and Avalanche, Yakima, Wash. Died Oct. 7, 1949; buried Terrace Heights Cemetery.

McCLURKIN, Robert, pres. Matthiessen & Hegeler Zinc Co. Address: LaSalle, Ill. Died Mar. 29, 1949.

McCLURKIN, Robert J. G., govt. ofcl.; b. Lisbon, N.Y., Dec. 8, 1911; s. Rev. Walter C. and Morna G. (McWilliams) McC.; A.B., U. Pitts., 1931, M.A., 1932; grad. study U. Pa., 1936-40; m. Mary Julia Shelton, Dec. 24, 1935; children—Megan Joan, Peter, James. Grad. asst. history U. Pitts., 1931-33; master Perkiomen Sch., Pennsburg, Pa., 1934-38; grad. asst. U. Pa., 1938-40, instr. econs., 1941-42, Muhlenberg Coll., Allentown, Pa., 1940-41; asst. chief air transport div. and aircraft div. Bd. Econ. Warfare and Fgn. Econ. Adminstrn., 1942-45; asst. chief, later chief aircraft div. Office Fgn. Liquidation Commr., 1945-46; asst. dir. (internat.), later dir. Econ. Bur., Civil Aero. Bd., 1946-51; dep. dir. Office N.E. Asian Affairs, Dept. State, 1951-54, dir. 1954-56; Imperial Def. Coll., London, Eng., 1956. Mem. Am. History Assn. Home: 3016 Homewood Pkwy., Kensington, Md. Office: Dept. of State, Washington 25. Died May 6, 1956.

McCOACH, David, Jr., army officer; b. Phila., Jan. 27, 1887; s. David and Clara (Kelly) McC.; student U.S. Mil. Acad., 1906-10, Engr. Sch., 1911-12, Sch. of the Line, 1921-22, Command and Gen. Staff Sch., 1922-23, Army War Coll., 1927-28; m. Anna C. Black, June 26, 1911; 1 son, David, III. Commd. 2d lt. Engring. Corps, U.S. Army, 1910, advanced through grades to major gen., 1943; engr. commr., D.C., 1938-41; Office of Chief of Engrs., Washington, 1941; in charge Montgomery Ward, Chgo., 1944-45. Mem. Am. Soc. C.E., Am. Soc. Mil. Engrs. Presbyn. Mason (32°). Clubs: Army-Navy, Army and Navy Country, Chevy Chase Country (Washington). Home: Wardman Park Hotel, Washington. Died Dec. 15, 1951; buried Arlington Nat. Cemetery.

McCOLLESTER, Parker, lawyer; b. Detroit, Sept. 5, 1890; s. Lee S. and Lizzie (Parker) McC.; student Phillips Exeter Acad.; A.B., Tufts Coll., 1911; LL.B., Harvard, 1914; m. Dorothea Baldwin, Sept. 7, 1921; children—Roger Sherman, Duncan Lee, Ann Parker (Mrs. John B. Emerson). Admitted to Mass. bar, N.Y. bar; asso. Brandeis, Dunbar & Nutter, Boston, 1914-16; asst. gen. solicitor N.Y.C. R.R., 1916-17, 1919-26; partner Lord, Day & Lord since 1926; spl. asst. atty. gen. N.Y. State, various rate cases since 1929; gen. counsel Corn Products Refining Co., Assn. Am. Shipowners, Asso. Latin Am. Steamship Confs.; dir. W.W. Norton & Co., Inc., Irving R. Boody & Co., Inc., Motor Haulage Co. Chief U.S. Econ. Mission to France, 1944; del. Internat. Conf. German External Debt, London, 1952-53; mem. Atty. Gen.'s adv. com. to study antitrust laws. Dir. Juilliard Sch. Music, N.Y.C.; dir., sec. N.Y. Philharmonic Symphony; trustee Barnard Coll., Columbia, Tufts Coll., Medford, Mass., Gramercy Park, N.Y., St. John's Guild, N.Y. Served as 1st lt. transportation corps., U.S. Army, 1917-19. Mem. Am., N.Y. State bar assns., Assn. Interstate Commerce Commn. Practitioners (pres.), N.Y. City Bar Assn., Am. Law Inst., Phi Beta Kappa, Zeta Psi. Clubs: Century, Downtown, Whitehall, Harvard (N.Y.C.); Met., Cosmos (Washington); Country (Fairfield). Co-author: Federal Motor Carrier Regulation, 1935. Author articles law. Home: 24 Gramercy Park, N.Y.C. 3; also Southport, Conn. Office: 25 Broadway, N.Y.C. 4. Died Jan. 11, 1954.

McCOMAS, O(liver) Parker, cigarette exec.; b. Balt., Sept. 1, 1895; s. Oliver Parker and Elizabeth (McClymont) McC.; Boys Latin Sch., 1908-12; A.B., Princeton, 1916, A.M., 1917; m. Rhoda Drew, Feb. 1, 1929; children—Oliver Parker, Rhonda Mary. Fgn. exchange trader Sutro Bros. & Co., 1919-26; bond trader Cowen & Co., 1926-28; Paris, London, N.Y. C., v.p. in charge comml. banking and fgn. depts. Bankers Trust Co., 1928-46; v.p., dir. Philip Morris & Co., Ltd., N.Y.C., 1946-47, exec. v.p., 1947-49, pres., chief adminstrv. officer 1949-54, chief executive officer, January 1955—. Chairman United Hosp. Fund drive, N.Y.C., 1950. Trustee Lenox Hill Hosp. Served as 1st lt., U.S. Army, maj. campaigns France, 1917-18. Recipient Silver Star. Club: University (N.Y.C.). Home: 888 Park Av., N.Y.C. 21. Office: 100 Park Av., N.Y.C. 17. Died Nov. 25, 1957.

McCOMB, Arthur James, retired, Otis Elevator Co.; b. Port Clinton, O., Apr. 2, 1880; s. Ezra J. and Rebecca (Moore) McC.; student U. of Calif., 2 yrs., 1902-03; m. Elizabeth Church, Dec. 12, 1906 (dec.); children—Marjorie (Mrs. Dorrance Sexton), Marian (Mrs. C. E. Hayward); married 2d, Lucille Dawes, Nov. 16, 1948; m. 3d, Ruth Roberts, Nov. 11, 1954. Asso. with Otis Elevator Co., 1904—, beginning as salesman, v.p., 1922—. Republican. Conglist. Club: Montclair Golf. Home: 10 Afterglow Av., Montclair, N.J. Died Aug. 27, 1958.

McCOMB, Edgar, lawyer; b. Wilmington, Del., Jan. 21, 1881; s. Thomas and Annie (Goodman) McC.; ed. Friends' (Quaker) Sch.; grad. Wilmington (Del.) High Sch., 1900; student U. of Pa. Law Sch., 1902-05; m. Anne V. Tederstrom, Jan. 2, 1939; 1 dau., Jane. Admitted to practice law, Colo., 1907; dep. dist. atty., Denver, 1909-13; engaged in pvt. practice since 1913. Mem. Denver Civil Service Commn., 1927-35; apptd. mem. Alien Enemy Hearing Bd., Dist. of Colo., 1941; apptd. by gov. to Colo. Council of Defense. Mem. Young Men's Republican League; hon. life member Republican Club of Colorado. Mem. Denver City Troop, 1st Squadron Cav., Colo. Mem. Am., Denver and Colo. bar assns., Internat. Assn. Ins. Counsel, Am. Judicature Soc., Denver Chamber of Commerce (dir. 1932-35; charter mem. members' council), Phi Sigma Kappa. Mason (K.T., Shriner). Clubs: Denver, Denver Press (life), Denver Athletic (life), City, Law (charter mem), Denver Country; Lawyers (N.Y.C.). Republican (hon. life). Home: 200 Gaylord St., Denver 6. Office: First National Bank Bldg., Denver 2. Died Aug. 19, 1956; buried Wilmington, Del.

McCOMB, William Randolph, engr. and govt. exec.; b. Dixon, Mo. Sept. 22, 1892; s. Charles Arthur and Betty Miller (Wilson) McC.; student Missouri Sch. of Mines, Rolla, 1914-16; B.S. in Mining Engring., Harvard, 1923; unmarried. Employed in Aztec mine, St. Louis, Rocky Mountain & Pacific Co., Raton, N.M., 1916-17; mining and metall. engr., Phelps-Dodge Co., Morencia, Ariz., 1917; engaged in mining exploration, Brazil and British Guiana, 1923; mng. dir. advertising and sales campaign of lead, zinc, oil and paint industry, New York, N.Y., 1924-27; vice pres. and dir. Craftex Co., New York, N.Y., 1927-28; vice pres. United Bldg. Materials Corp., Boston, 1928-30; vice pres. Flexwood Corp., Chicago, 1930-33; dep. adminstr. U.S. Nat. Recovery Adminstrn., Washington, D.C., 1933-36; dep. adminstr.

govt. contracts and wage and hour divs. of U.S. Govt., Washington, 1937-55, adminstr. Wage and Hour and Public Contracts Division, 1947-55; labor cons., Washington, 1955—. Officer, United States Army, 1917-18. Mem. Harvard Geol. Soc. (vice pres.), Am. Inst. Mining Engrs., Harvard Engring. Soc., Harvard Business School Soc., Newcomen Soc. (England). Clubs: Harvard (New York and Washington); Chevy Chase Country (Wash.). Home: 1516 33rd St. N.W., Washington. Died Dec. 21, 1957; buried Arlington Nat. Cemetery.

McCOMBS, Vernon Monroe; b. Parkers Prairie, Minn., July 7, 1875; s. Rev. George Nathan and Adaline B. (Warriner) McC.; grad. Minnesota Teachers Coll., St. Cloud, 1897; A.B., Hamline U., 1903, M.A., 1906, D.D., 1917; grad. Drew Theol. Sem., 1906; M.A., New York U., 1906; m. Eva M. White, Jan. 2, 1906; children—Frederick George, Anita Warriner, Kenneth Monroe. Licensed M.E. ministry, 1912, ordained, 1906; pastor Eden Prairie and Bloomington, Minn., 1902-03, Knickerbocker Av. Ch., Brooklyn, 1905-06; supt. N. Andes Mission, Peru, S.A., 1906-10; dist. supt. Southern Calif. Conf., 1913-19; supt. Latin-Am. Mission, Calif., Ariz., Nev. and Lower Calif. (Mexico), 1919-40; supt. Latin-Am. Prov. Annual Conf. since 1940; founded $300,000 Plaza Community Center, Los Angeles; $200,000 Spanish-Am. Inst., Gardena, Calif. Pres. Interdenom. Council on Spanish-Speaking Work; mem. Pi Gamma Mu fraternity. Republican. Mason. Author: From Over the Border, 1925. Lecturer: From Over the Border; Big Business and Brotherhood on the Border; Border Tales; Their Patria—Marvelous Mexico; etc. Home: 5202 Townsend Av., Eagle Rock, Los Angeles 41. Office: 125 E. Sunset Blvd., Los Angeles 12. Died Mar. 15, 1951; buried Forest Lawn Meml. Park, Glendale, Calif.

McCONN, Charles Maxwell, educator; b. Ironton, O., July 22, 1881; s. David Charles and Fanny (Lewis) McC.; B.A., U. of Minn., 1903, M.A., 1904; studied Harvard, 1921-22; Litt.D., Ursinus Coll., Collegeville, Pa., 1930; LL.D., Lehigh U., 1946; m. Prudence Emily Pratt, June 24, 1908; 1 dau., Margaret. Instructor in English, University of Illinois Acad., 1904-06, prin., 1906-10; registrar U. of Ill., 1910-20, also sec. bd. trustees, 1910-14, asst. to pres., 1920-21 and 1922-23; dean, Lehigh U., 1923-38; dean, Wash. Sq. Coll. of Arts and Sci., N.Y.U., 1938-46; emeritus since 1946. Mem. National Assn. Deans of Men, Eastern Assn. Coll. Deans (pres. 1930), Prog. Edn. Assn., Pa. State Edn. Assn. (pres. higher edn. dept. 1932), Sigma Alpha Epsilon, Omicron Delta Kappa, Phi Eta Sigma, Kappa Delta Pi. Democrat. Author: College or Kindergarten?, 1928; Studies Are Not Every Thing, 1931; Planning for College, 1937; also articles in North Am. Rev., New Republic, etc. Home: 628 Madison Av., York, Pa. Died Apr. 15, 1953.

McCONNEL, Mervin Gilbert, ret. army officer; b. Parma, Ida., Dec. 29, 1882; student U. Ida.; commd. 2d lt. Ida. N.G., 1909; 1st lt. F.A., Officers Res. Corps, 1917; maj. Cav., Ida. N.G., 1924, advanced to brig. gen. of the line, 1936; assigned to command 58th Cav. Brigade; inducted into Fed. Service as brig. gen., Adj. Gen. Dept. assigned as dir. Ida. SSS; ret., brig. gen., 1946. Address: 4614 Fairview Av., Boise, Ida. Died 1948.

McCONNELL, Charles Melvin, clergyman, educator; b. Indpls., Jan. 16, 1886; s. Israel and Nancy Jane (Chalfant) McC.; A.B., Ohio Wesleyan U., 1907; S.T.B., Boston U., 1910; D.D., Cornell Coll., 1941; m. Grace Dimmick, Apr. 20, 1911; children—Jane Chalfant, Louise Grace, Marguerite, Mildred Florence. Ordained to ministry M.E. Ch., 1907; minister successively in Galena, Middlefield, Berea, Lakeville, O., 1907-21; personnel sec. Bd. of Home Missions and Ch. Extension, 1921-26; prof. town and country ch. dept. Boston U. Sch. Theology, 1926—; prof. town and country ch. dept. Newton Theol. Sch. and Andover Newton Sch., 1929-35; mem. staff Interseminary Commn. for Tng. for Rural Ministry; mem. town and country ch. com. Home Missions Council and Fed. Council of Chs. of Christ in Am. Mem. Delta Tau Delta. Democrat. Author: Rural Billion, 1932. Contbr. chpt. to Solving the Country Church Problem by G. A. Bricker, 1912; also to religious jours. Home: 69 Walker St., Newtonville, Mass. Died Sept. 6, 1957.

McCONNELL, Francis John, bishop; b. Trinway, O., Aug. 18, 1871; s. I. H. and Nancy J. (Chalfant) McC.; A.B., Ohio Wesleyan, 1894, D.D., 1905; S.T.B., Boston U., 1897, Ph.D., 1899; D.D., Yale, 1930; LL.D., Wesleyan Univ., 1909, Boston Univ., 1929; m. Eva H. Thomas, Mar. 11, 1897. Entered M.E. ministry, 1894; pastor W. Chelmsford, Mass., 1894-97, Newton Upper Falls, Mass., 1897-99, Ipswich, Mass., 1899-1902, Harvard St., Cambridge, Mass., 1902-03, New York Av., Brooklyn, 1903-09; pres. De Pauw U., 1909-12; elected bishop M.E. Ch., May 1912; became senior bishop of Meth. Ch.; visiting prof., Columbia U., 1932-33; Drew U., 1934; Garrett Bibl. Inst., 1934; Yale, 1946; retired 1944; returned to active service Portland area, 1948. Pres. Religious Edn. Assn., 1916; pres. Fed. Council of Churches of Christ in America, 1929; Lyman Beecher lecturer, Yale, 1930; Barrows lecturer, India, 1931. Chairman City Affairs Committee of New York City. Trustee Chautauqua Institution. President American Association Social Security. Author: The Diviner Immanence, 1906; Religious Certainty, 1910; Christian Focus, 1911; The Increase of Faith, 1912; Personal Christianity, 1914; Understanding the Scriptures, 1917; Democratic Christianity, 1919; Public Opinion and Theology, 1920; The Preacher and the People, 1922; Is God Limited?, 1924; The Christlike God, 1927; Borden Parker Bowne, 1929; The Prophetic Ministry, 1930; The Christian Ideal and Social Control; Christianity and Coercion, 1933; John Wesley, 1939; Evangelicals, Revolutionists and Idealists, 1942; By the Way, An Autobiography, 1952. Home: Lucasville, O. Died Aug. 18, 1953; buried Lucasville, O.

McCONNELL, H(arold) S(loan), entomologist; b. Anderson, S.C., Dec. 30, 1893; s. James N. S. and Frances C. (Duckworth) McC.; B.S., Clemson Agrl. Coll., 1916; M.S., U. Md., 1931; m. Pearl Anderson, Aug. 22, 1926. Asst. prof. U. Md., 1916-18; asst. research entomologist Clemson Agrl. Coll., 1919-24; research entomologist U. Md., 1925—. Served in San. Corps., U.S. Army, 1918-19, 43-46. Mem. Am. Assn. Econ. Entomologists, Entomol. Soc. Am., Entomol. Soc. Washington, Sigma Xi. Home: 6812 Pineway, College Heights, Hyattsville, Md. Died May 11, 1958.

McCONNELL, W. Joseph, coll. pres.; b. Batesville, Ark., Apr. 12, 1883; s. James Perry and Patsy Ellen (Doughty) McC.; B.A., U. of Denver, 1915, M.A., 1918; Ph.D., Columbia, 1925; m. Clara Bradford, June 19, 1902. Supt. schs., Van Horn, 1908-11, Petrolia, 1911-16; asso. prof. mathematics, 1916-19, became prof. and dir. economics, 1919, dean, 1923, pres., 1934-51, pres. emeritus and counselor adminstrn. since 1951, N. Tex. State Teachers Coll. Mem. Commn. on Instns. of Higher Edn., Southern Assn. of Colleges and Secondary Schools (mem. executive committee 1942-46; president 1945). Member exec. com. Am. Assn. Teachers Colls., 1940-44. Del. to World Congress on Edn. for Democracy, N.Y., Aug. 1939. Fellow A.A.A.S., Tex. Acad. Science; mem. of the National Education Association, Phi Beta Kappa, also member Kappa Delta Pi, Pi Gamma Mu, Sigma Delta Pi, Alpha Phi Omega. Mem. Christian (Disciples) Ch. Democrat. Mason. (K.T.), Rotarian. Author: Social Cleavages in Texas, 1925. Co-author: Fundamentals of Citizenship (Tex. Supplement), 1940. Home: 1815 W. Oak St. Office: N.T. Sta., Denton, Tex. Died Nov. 24, 1955; buried Restland Meml. Park, Dallas.

McCORD, Alvin Carr, chmn. board McCord Corp.; b. Paris, Ill., Nov. 24, 1867; s. William B. and Mary Jane (Campbell) McC.; A.B., Princeton, 1889; student U. Minn. Law Sch., 1889-90; m. Emily Davis Rowe, Dec. 22, 1896 (dec.); 1 dau., Marjorie Carr (Mrs. Marjorie McCord Brigham); m. 2d, Phyllis I. Ellerton, Oct. 10, 1936; 1 dau., Phyllis E. Pres. McCord & Co., ry. equipment, Chgo., 1897-1920, McCord Mfg. Co., Inc., Detroit, 1908-35, McCord Radiator & Mfg. Co. (now McCord Corp.), 1923-48; v.p., gen. mgr. Ill. Car & Equipment Co., Chgo., 1900-02; pres. Western Steel Car & Foundry Co., Chgo., 1902-07. Mem. Engring. Soc. Detroit, Chgo. Hist. Soc. Clubs: Detroit, Princeton (Mich.); University (N.Y.C.); Cottage (Princeton). Home: 908 Trombley, Grosse Pointe Park, Mich. Office: 2587 E. Grand Blvd., Detroit. Died Aug. 7, 1956.

McCORD, Leon, judge; b. Conyers, Ga., June 21, 1878; s. William Henry and Ellen Grant (Davis) McC.; studied law in office of Captain Jesse E. Brown, Scottsboro, Alabama; m. Bobbie Tanner, February 20, 1906. Began practice of law, Scottsboro, 1900; sec. Supreme Court of Ala., 1903-09; in practice at Montgomery, Ala., 1901-16; railroad commissioner, Ala., 1911-15; judge Circuit Court, 15th Jud. Circuit, Ala., 1916-35, presiding judge, 1919-35; practiced under firm name McCord & Knabe, 1935-38; apptd. judge U.S. Circuit Court of Appeals, Fifth Circuit, 1938. Served as pvt. Tex. Vols., Spanish-Am. War; lt. col. Ala. Nat. Guard. Mem. Dem. Nat. Com., 1932-38. Presbyterian. Mem. United Spanish War Vets. (comdr. in chief, 1934-35). Sigma Delta Kappa. Mason, Elk. Author: I Believe in Man, 1929. Home: 800 S. Perry. Office: Federal Building, Montgomery 2, Ala. Died. Feb. 11, 1952.

McCORKLE, Thomas Smith, univ. dean; b Mexla, Tex., Apr. 9, 1898; s. Henry Thomas and Lemma Mae (Smith) McC.; Mus.B., Tex. Womans Coll. (now Tex. Wesleyan), Fort Worth, Tex., 1921, A.M., Southern Meth. U., 1936; Ph.D., U. of Tex., 1942; student Tex. Christian U., 1916-17, U. of Kan. (spl. student violin music), 1923-24, Am. Conservatory of Music, Chicago, Ill., summer 1928; violin pupil Carl Venth, Waldemar Geltsch, Jacques Gordon, Leon, Sammetini; m. Lilita Goodloe Wilson, Aug. 19, 1920. Teacher of violin, Westminster Coll., Tehuacana, Tex., 1914-15; student asst. in violin, Tex. Womans Coll., 1915-17; student dir. band and orchestra, Southern Meth. U., 1917-18; engaged in various work, 1918-22; prof. and dir. of music Kansas City (Kan.) U., 1922-25; mem. staff of music dept., U. of N.C., 1925-35, successively as instr., asst. prof., asso. prof. and acting head of dept.; asso. prof. of edn., Southern Meth. U., 1935-39, on leave until 1942; prof. of music and dean of sch. of fine arts, Tex. Christian U., 1942—; mem. staff Sch. of Edn., U. of Texas, summers 1939, 41, 47. Chairman Texas State Music Council, 1952-53. Has appeared as concert violinist, orchestra and choral dir. Mem. Tex. Assn. of Music Schs. (v.p. 1942-44, pres. 1944-47), Music Educators Nat. Conf. (Tex. State Chmn. for string instrn.), Southwest Music Education Conf. (chmn. string instrn. 1946-48), Music Tchrs. Nat. Assn., Tex. (pres. 1952-53), Ft. Worth (v.p. 1943-45) music tchrs. assns., Tex. Music Educators Assn. (chmn. coll. div. 1946-47, v.p., 1952-56, Phi Mu Alpha (province gov.), Sinfonia, Phi Delta Kappa, Alpha Tau Omega. Home: 3817 Winslow Dr. Office: Texas Christian Univ., Fort Worth, Tex. Died Dec. 1, 1955; buried Restland Meml. Park, Dallas.

McCORMACK, Alfred, lawyer; b. Brooklyn, N.Y., Jan. 13, 1901; s. Lawrence and Susan (Toal) McC.; A.B., Princeton, 1921; LL.B., Columbia, 1925; m. Winifred Byron Smith, May 31, 1930; children—Alfred, Walter B. S. (dec.), Robert C., Winthrop L. Teacher Thacher Sch., Ojai, Calif., 1921-22; law clerk to Mr. Justice Harlan F. Stone, Supreme Court of U.S., 1925-26; asso. law firm Cravath, de Gersdorff, Swaine and Wood, New York City, 1926-35, partner, 1935-42; partner Cravath, Swaine & Moore, N.Y. City, since 1947; spl. asst. to sec. of war, 1942; spl. asst. to sec. of state, 1945-46. Served 3 yr. enlistment, 101st Cav., N.Y. N.G., 1927-30; commd. col., Army of U.S., 1942; dep. chief, spl. br. Mil. Intelligence Div., War Dept. Gen. Staff, 1942-44; dir. intelligence Mil. Intelligence Service, 1944-45. Decorated Distinguished Service Medal (U.S.), Hon. Comdr. Order of British Empire. Chmn. bd. visitors Columbia Law Sch.; trustee Mannes Music School, Practicing Law Institute (both of N.Y. City), Brunswick School, Greenwich, Conn. Member American and N.Y. State bar assns., Assn. Bar of City N.Y., N.Y. Co. Lawyers Assn., Am. Geog. Soc., Am. Econ. Assn., Acad. Polit. Sci., Assn. of Ex-mems. of Squad. A (N.Y.), Phi Beta Kappa, Psi Upsilon. Clubs: Univ., Broad Street, Young Republican (N.Y.); Metropolitan (Washington); Casino (Chicago); Indian Harbor Yacht (Greenwich, Conn.). Contributor of articles to law and other periodicals. Home: 618 Lake Av., Greenwich, Conn. Office: 15 Broad St., N.Y.C. Died July 11, 1956; buried Putnam Cemetery, Greenwich, Conn.

McCORMICK, Anne O'Hare, writer; d. Thomas and Teresa Beatrice O'Hare; B.A., St. Mary's Coll., Columbus, O.; hon. LL.D., Smith Coll., U. of Dayton, Villanova Coll., Middlebury Coll.; hon. Litt.D., Elmira Coll., Columbia University, New York University, Wilson Coll., N.J. Coll. for Women, Lafayette Coll., Fordham University, Manhattan College; honorary L.H.D., Rollins Coll., Ohio State University; LL.D., Coll. Mount St. Vincent, Wellesley; m. Francis J. McCormick, Corr. and mem. editorial bd. N.Y. Times. Awarded N.Y. Evening Post medal, 1934, Pulitzer Prize for distinguished foreign corr., 1937, Medal for Eminent Achievement of the Am. Woman's Assn., 1939; medal Woman's Theodore Roosevelt Meml. Assn., 1941; Theodore Roosevelt D.S.M., 1950; Theta Phi Alpha Siena medal, 1941, Gold Medal of Nat. Inst. of Social Sciences, 1942, Laetare Medal, U. of Notre Dame, 1944, Distinguished Service Award of Internat. Altrusa, 1945. Women's Nat. Press Club Achievement Award 1945; Nat. Achievement Award of Chi Omega 1946; William the Silent award for journalism, 1952; U.S. delegate to UNESCO conf., 1946, 1948; adv. com., post-war fgn. policy Dept. State, 1942-43. Chevalier of Nat. Order of the Legion of Honor. Mem. Nat. Inst. of Arts and Letters. Author: The Hammer and Scythe, 1928. Address: The Times, N.Y. C. Died May 29, 1954.

McCORMICK, Bradley Thomas, mech. engr.; b. Marietta, O., May 28, 1880; s. Frank Ross and Maria Elizabeth (Thomas) M.; M.E., Cornell U., 1903. Apprentice in shops and later in charge induction motor design Bullock Electric Mfg. Co., Cin., 1903-05; chief elec. engr. charge elec. design Allis-Chalmers-Bullock, Ltd., Montreal, 1905-13; mem. firm Forbes & McCormick, cons. engrs., Montreal, 1913-15; chief engr. Miss. Valley Metal Products Co., St. Louis, 1915-17; apptd. engr. charge small motors Wagner Electric Mfg. Co., St. Louis, 1919; now engr. with Wagner Electric Corp. Civilian, later capt. and maj. U.S. Ordnance Dept., 1917-19, serving as chief of projectile and cartridge case br. of arty. ammunition and trench warfare div. Fellow Am. Inst. E.E. Home: 847 Belt Av. Address: Wagner Electric Corp., St. Louis. Died Mar. 14, 1945.

McCORMICK, Chauncey, business exec.; b. Chicago, Ill., Dec. 7, 1884; s. William Grigsby and Eleanor (Brooks) McC.; A.B., Yale, 1907; L.H.D., Northwestern U., 1934; Dr. Social Sci. (hon.), Cath. U. of America, 1952; m. Marion Deering, July 6, 1914; children—C. Deering, Brooks, Roger. Mfg. bus., 1907-22; v.p. Miami Corp., Chicago; dir. Internat. Harvester Co. since 1926. Served as lieut. to capt., in France and Poland with A.E.F., 1917-19; apptd. to Am. Relief Commn. by Herbert Hoover; in charge Eastern Poland, later in Roumania, 1918-19. Capt., 106th Cav., Ill. Nat. Guard, comdg. Chicago Black Horse Troop, 1930-1931. Awarded Purple Heart,

Victory Medal; citation from General Pershing; officer of the Legion of Honor, Croix de Guerre with bronze star (French); The King's Medal (British); Officer Etoil Noire de Benin, Merite Agricole; Officer Am. Field Service French, Order of Orange Nassau (The Netherlands); Commander Polonia Restituta, White Eagle of Llow, Officer Polish Red Cross (Polish). Apptd. by gov., mem. Child Welfare Commn. of Ill.; chmn. Citizens' Com. of United Home Finding Service; mem. Nat. Commn. on Children and Youth; chmn. bd. Ill. Children's Home and Aid Soc.; nat. pres. Commn. for Polish Relief, 1939; vice chmn. British War Relief Soc. of Ill.; Chairman Illinois Committee on Displaced Persons. Pres. Art Inst. of Chicago; founder, trustee and chmn. art exhibit, Chicago Century of Progress, 1933-34; trustee, Am. Foundation for the Blind, Chicago Foundlings' Home. Chmn. Alexander Hamilton Memorial Fund; dir. McCormick Theol. Seminary; dir. Chicago Council Social Agencies, Community Fund, Chicago; Ill. Soc. for Prevention of Blindness; adv. dir. Chicago Lighthouse for the Blind. Former pres. Northern Ill. Guernsey Breeders' Assn.; del. to Republican Nat. Convention, 1936. Mem. Nat. Inst. of Social Scis. (life), Soc. of the Cincinnati (N.C.), Alpha Delta Phi, Kappa Sigma. Clubs: Chicago, Casino, Racquet, Arts, Executives (Chicago); Chicago Golf (Wheaton); Bath (Miami Beach); Pot and Kettle (Bar Harbor, Me.); Harbor (president) (Seal Harbor, Me.). Republican. Presbyterian (elder). Address: 410 N. Michigan Av., Chgo. 11. Died Sept. 8, 1954.

McCORMICK, Frederick, journalist, war corrs.; b. Brookfield, Mo.; s. Isaac Newton and Sarah Elizabeth (Bryce) M.; m. Adelaide S. Gillis, Dec. 8, 1914. Art editor Woman's Home Companion, 4 yrs.; spl. corr. Harper's Weekly and London Graphic in Boxer War; spl. corr. N.Y. Sun and Laffan's Bur., Peking, China, 1901-03; corr. Reuter's Agy. and Asso. Press, with Russian Army in Manchuria 23 months, sole fgn. corr. reporting entire Russian-Japanese War from Russian side; accompanied Gen. Danieloff from Vladivostok on mission to evacuate Russian prisoners, 1st Russian ofcl. mission to Japan following peace and 1st arrival there of Russian war vessels; spl. corr. in Korea, 1905, on occasion Japanese assumption of Korean govtl. control, also 1907, reporting mutinies at Seoul and dethronement of Emperor; sole Western corr. reporting to European-Am. press the events of the deaths of Kwanghsu and the Empress-Dowager Tzu Hsi-An, 1908; promoted China Monuments Soc., for protection monuments and nat. art in China, 1908-09 (hon. sec.); corr. Asso. Press, Peking, 1907-10; spl. corr. Chinese revolutionary rebellion, 1911-12; promoted Asiatic Inst., conducting discussion Pacific area affairs, 1913-16; spl. corr. in European and Asiatic Russia—in Petrograd during bolshevik uprising, 1917; spl. corr. Asiatic Russia, contbg. East Siberian Travel Letters to Am. newspapers from Kamchatka, Saghalin, Maritime provinces and Russian Manchuria, 1921-22; spl. corr. in China, 1922. Secured annexation Wrangell Island, with all lands known and unknown in Russian Arctic to the Union of Socialist Soviet Republics, closing about half entire Arctic area against fgn. polit. and mil. encroachment adventure under existing flag-planting practices, also stimulating investigation and study of Arctic police patrol, residence, travel, and regulation of transpolar communication, 1924-26. Original mem. Am. Sch. Archaeology in China; mem. Peking Club, China. Contbr. monthly mags. and newspapers. Author: Tragedy of Russia in Pacific Asia (2 vols.); China's Monuments (pamphlet); The Flowery Republic; The Menace of Japan. Radio commentator on Pacific and Far Eastern affairs. Address: Pauma Valley, Cal. Died Aug. 8, 1951.

McCORMICK, George Wellesley, beet sugar mfr.; b. Napanee, Ont., Can., Sept. 12, 1871; s. James and Margaret (Sexsmith) McC.; grad. Collegiate Inst., Napanee, 1888; m. Anna Morrison, June 28, 1899; children—Morrison Ridgway, George Wellesley. Came to U.S., 1890, naturalized citizen, 1896. With publishing house, Kalamazoo, Mich., 1890-94; dist. mgr., Travelers Ins. Co. of Hartford, Conn., at Bay City, Mich., 1895-1901; organizer, with others, of Wallaceburg (Can.) Sugar Co., 1901, asst. mgr. and sec., 1901-03; v.p. Menominee River Sugar Co., 1903; v.p. Superior Sugar Refining Co.; dir. Flint Lumber Co., Flushing (Mich.) Lumber Co., Fed. Res. Bank of Mpls. Asst. state food adminstr., Mich., Wrld War I. Del. Rep. Nat. Conv., 1916. Farmers and Mfrs. Beet Sugar Assn., Eastern Beet Sugar Mfrs. Assn. (pres. 1917-25). Episcopalian. Mason (K.T.), K.P. Clubs: Rotary, Riverside Country; Union League (Chgo.); Milwaukee (Milw.). Home: 1522 1st St., Menominee, Mich. Died June 6, 1950.

McCORMICK, Gertrude Howard (Mrs. Vance C. McCormick), ret. newspaper exec., publisher; b. Richmond, Va., May 7, 1874; d. Conway Robinson and Jeannie (Colston) Howard; m. Marlin Edgar Olmsted, Oct. 26, 1899 (died July 12, 1913); children—Marlin Edgar (dec.), Gertrude Howard (Mrs. Spencer G. Nauman), Henry Cushing, Conway Howard, Jane (Mrs. Hugh McMillan); m. 2d, Vance Criswell McCormick, Jan. 5, 1925 (died June 16, 1946). Vice pres. Patriot Co., pub. Harrisburg (Pa.), Patriot and Evening News until 1948. Mem. Valley Forge Park Commn. Pa., 1935-39. Hon. v.p. Girl Scouts Am.; former mem. bd. nat. YMCA; hon. v.p. Civic Club, Harrisburg, Art Assn. Harrisburg; 1st v.p. Symphony Soc.; chmn. Dauphin County Com. of Pa. Soc. Colonial Dames Am. Episcopalian. Clubs: Colony (N.Y.); Sulgrave (Washington); Mt. Vernon (Balt.); Yeaman's Hall (Charleston, S.C.). Home: 105 N. Front St. and Cedarcliff Farms. Office: 242 N. 3d St., Harrisburg, Pa. Died Jan. 24, 1953.

McCORMICK, James Thomas, clergyman, educator; b. Taunton, Mass., Feb. 21, 1876; s. Thomas F. and Maria A. (Supple) McC.; student Boston Coll., 1892-96; entered Soc. of Jesus, at Frederick, Md., 1896; A.B., Woodstock (Md.) Coll., 1901, A.M., 1903. Ordained priest R.C. Ch., 1911; instr. mathematics, St. Francis Xavier Coll., N.Y. City, 1903-06, 1907-08, Holy Cross Coll., 1906-07; prof. mathematics, Boston Coll., 1912-13, Canisius Coll., Buffalo, N.Y., 1914-17; asst. to pres. of Boston Coll., 1918-24; rector Boston Coll. High Sch., 1925-31; pres. Weston Coll., 1931-32; provincial Soc. of Jesus of New England, 1932-37; prof. mathematics, Weston (Mass.) Coll., 1937-41; chaplain Holy Cross Coll., 1941—. Mem. Am. Math. Soc. Address: Holy Cross Coll., Worcester, Mass. Died Mar. 18, 1950.

McCORMICK, Langdon, playwright; b. Port Huron, Mich.; s. John and Ursula (Inman) McC.; ed. Albion (Mich.) Coll.; m. Sylvia Bidwell. On stage with Otis Skinner, 1897, 98, 99, later appearing in plays written by himself. Club: Green Room (N.Y.C.). Author (plays prod.) The Western Girl; Money and the Woman; How Hearts Are Broken; Wanted by the Police; The Convict and the Girl; When the World Sleeps; The Life of an Actress; The Pace; The Gulf; The Storm; The Burglar and the Lady; Toll Gate Inn; Shipwrecked, 1924; now playing in vaudeville, dramatic play Number 44. Home: Port Huron, Mich. Died June 1954.

McCORMICK, Lynde Dupuy, naval officer; b. Annapolis, Md., Aug. 12, 1895; s. Albert Montgomery Dupuy and Edith Lynde (Abbot) McC.; B.S., U.S. Naval Acad., 1915; m. Lillian Addison Sprigg, Oct. 2, 1920; children—Montrose Graham (dec.), Lynde Dupuy, James Jett, II. Commissioned ensign, U.S. Navy, 1915. Advanced through the grades to admiral. Comdr. in chief Atlantic Fleet, 1951; apptd. NATO supreme allied comdr. Atlantic, January, 1952; appointed president Naval War College, May 1954. Decorated Legion of Merit. Mem. U.S. Naval Inst. Clubs: Chevy Chase, Army and Navy, Army-Navy Country (Washington). Home: "Clermont," Berryville, Va. Office: Naval War Coll., Newport, R.I. Died Aug. 16, 1956; buried U.S. Naval Acad., Annapolis, Md.

McCORMICK, Patrick Joseph, prof. education; b. Norwich, Conn., Dec. 10, 1880; s. Daniel J. and Margaret Elizabeth (O'Donnell) McC.; St. Joseph's Sem., Dunwoodie, N.Y., 1899-1904; S.T.L., Catholic U. of America, 1906, Ph.D., 1911. Ordained priest R.C. Ch., 1904; supt. schs., Diocese of Hartford, Conn., 1906-10; instr. in edn., Catholic U. of America, 1910-14, asso. prof. edn., 1914-18, prof. since 1918, acting rector, 1935-36, vice rector, 1936-42; acting rector, 1942-43, rector since 1943; dean of Catholic Sisters College, 1921-36. Editor Catholic Educational Review, 1921-44; president Catholic Edn. Press since 1932. Made domestic prelate to Pope Pius XI, July 26, 1929; consecrated titular Bishop of Atenia, auxiliary to Archbishop of Washington, September 21, 1950. Author: History of Education, 1914. Contbr. to Catholic Ednl. Review, Thought, Catholic Encyclopedia, etc. Address: Catholic Univ. of America, Washington. Deceased.

McCORMICK, Robert Rutherford, editor, lawyer; b. Chicago, Ill., July 30, 1880; s. Robert Sanderson and Katherine Van Etta (Medill) M.; B.A., Yale, 1903; student Northwestern U. Law Sch.; LL.D., The Citadel, Charleston, S.C., 1932; married Amy Irwin Adams, Mar. 10, 1915 (died 1939); m. 2d, Mrs. Maryland Mathison Hooper, Dec. 21, 1944. Mem. Chicago City Council, 1904-06; mem. Chicago Charter Conv., 1907; pres. Sanitary Dist. of Chicago, 1905-10; mem. Chicago Plan Commn.; admitted to Ill. bar, 1908; mem. law firm McCormick, Kirkland, Patterson & Fleming, 1908-20; editor and publisher The Chicago Tribune. Maj. 1st Ill. Cav., on duty on Mexican border. 1916-17; attached to General Pershing's staff, A.E.F. in France, 1917, later assigned as major 5th F.A.; then adj. 57th Arty. Brig.; lt. col. 122d F.A, U.S.N.G.; col. 61st F.A., U.S. Army; served as commandant Ft. Sheridan, Ill. Awarded D.S.M. Republican. Presbyn. Mem. Chicago Bar Assn Clubs: Racquet and Tennis (New York); Chicago. Author: With the Russian Army, 1915; The Army of 1918, 1920; Ulysses S. Grant, the Great Soldier of America, 1934; Freedom of the Press, 1936; How We Acquired Our National Territory, 1942; The American Revolution and Its Effect on World Civilization, 1945; The War Without Grant, 1950; also shorter works on hist., mil., sci., legal and polit. subjects. Home: Du Page County, Ill. Office: Tribune Sq., Chgo. Died Apr. 1, 1955; buried Wheaton, Ill.

McCORMICK, Thomas Carson, educator; b. Tuscaloosa, Ala., Jan. 11, 1892; s. William Thomas and Virginia Marr (Carson) McC.; A.B., U. Ala., 1911; A.M., George Peabody Coll., 1918; Ph.D., U. Chgo., 1929; m. Lillie Anderson Griffith, Aug. 15, 1918; children—Virginia Marr (Mrs. Greggar P. Sletteland), Mary Luttrell (Mrs. Rolf N. Olsen), Lillie Griffith (Mrs. Roy G. Francis). High sch. tchr., 1912-21; prof. agr., East Central State Tchrs. Coll., Okla., 1921-27, prof. sociology, 1929-31; vis. prof. sociology U. Chgo., summer 1930; asst. prof. rural sociology U. Ark., 1931-34; research supr., acting coordinator of rural research WPA, Washington, 1934-35; prof. sociology U. Wis., 1935—, chmn. dept. sociology and anthropology, 1941-52; chmn. div. social studies, 1947-50. Chief statistician Wis. Citizens Com. on Public Welfare, 1936; research asso. Negro in America study, Carnegie Corp. of N.Y., 1939; mem. adv. com. population U.S. Census Bur. Am. Statis. Assn., Population Assn. Am., Phi Beta Kappa, Alpha Kappa Delta. Presbyn. Clubs: Professional Men's, West End (Madison, Wis.). Editor: (with A. S. Barr and H. L. Ewbank) Radio in the Classroom, 1942; Problems of the Postwar World, 1945. Author: Agriculture for Rural Teachers, 1929; Rural Relief and Non-Relief Households, 1935; Elementary Social Statistics, 1941; Sociology, 1952; Methods of Research in the Bahavioral Sciences, 1958. Contbr. to sociological and statis. jours. Home: 4202 Wanetah Trail, Madison, Wis. Died Nov. 9, 1954; buried Evergreen Cemetery, Tuscaloosa, Ala.

McCORMICK, William Laird, lumber exec.; b. Waseca, Minn., 1876; children—William D., Delinda Ann. Vice president and director Weyerhaeuser Timber Co.; dir. Gen. Ins. Co. of Am., Puget Sound Nat. Bank. Mason. Died Mar. 26, 1953; buried Tacoma (Wash.) Cemetery.

McCOSKER, Alfred Justin, radio exec.; b. New York, N.Y., Sept. 4, 1886; s. James and Catharine Angela (Hackett) McC.; student Manhattan Coll., N.Y. City, 1902-04; hon. LL.D., John Marshall Coll. of Law, Jersey City, 1937; m. Hazel Amelia Meeker, June 10, 1914; 1 dau., Angela Frances Sjöström. Began as newspaper man, 1902; reporter for various newspapers in N.Y. City, 1902-07; reporter for Denver Times, 1907-08, Denver Rocky Mountain News, 1909-13; originator and reporter Paint-up, Clean-up Movement, Boston, 1914-16; with Exhibitors' Trade Review (motion picture trade mag.), as writer and later editor, 1916-18; public relations counsel, A.F. of L., 1918-24; also press work for theatrical firms, 1918-24; dir. radio station WOR, Newark, N.J., 1924-33; dir. and gen. mgr. Bamberger Broadcasting Service, Inc., Sta. WOR, 1923-33, pres. since 1933. Elected chairman of Board of Bamberger Broadcasting Service, Inc., 1945, ret. 1947; chmn. bd. Mutual Broadcasting System, Inc., 1934-47; chairman Radio Committee, New York World's Fair, 1929; chairman radio div., New Jersey Crime Prevention League, 1933-34; mem. Sta. WOR, 1923-33, pres. since 1933; chmn. of bd. Mutual Broadcasting System, Inc., since 1934; chmn. Radio Com., N.Y. Worlds Fair, 1939; chmn. radio div. N.J. Crime Prevention League, 1933-34; mem. Radio Code Authority, 1934; mem. Mayor's Com. to Welcome Lindbergh, 1927; co-founder McCosker-Hershfield Cardiac Foundation; mem. N.Y. State Defense Bd. and Defense Communications Bd., Washington, 1941. Papal Knight of Malta, 1940. Awarded B'Nai B'Rith Meritorious Service medal, 1941. Mem. Nat. Association of Broadcasters (treas. 1928-32, president 1932-34). Named member of N.Y. City Mayor's Com. for Unity, 1944. Awarded "Distinguished Service Medal for War Entertainment," 1944. Roman Catholic. Clubs: Metropolitan, N.Y. Athletic, Lambs, Friendly Sons of St. Patrick, Economic, Advertising, Lotos (New York); Nat. Press (Washington, D.C.); Catholic Actors Guild. Contbr. articles on broadcasting to periodicals. Home: 5780 LaGorce Dr., Miami Beach, Fla. Died July 1, 1959; buried So. Meml. Cemetery, Miami.

McCOWEN, Edward Oscar (măk-kou'ĕn), ex-congressman; b. Scioto County, O.; s. William H. and Frances E. (McCammon) McC.; B.S., Ohio No. U., Ada, O., 1908; B.Edn., Ohio State U., 1917; Ed. M., U. Cin., 1939; m. Clara E. Smith, Aug. 19, 1902; children—Clara Frances (Mrs. Clarence W. Smith), Cecil Bernard (dec.), Eva Rosalie (Mrs. J. Lawrence Keller), Edward Reginald (lt. U.S.N.), John Donald Smith, Florence Kathryn (Mrs. William L. Carter, Jr.). Sch. tchr. then high sch. tchr., prin. and supt.; county supt., Scioto County, O., pub. schs., 1914-42; mem. 78th to 80th Congresses, 6th Ohio Dist., chmn. sub-com. edn. of Com. Edn. Labor. Trustee Rio Grande (O.) Coll. Mem. N.E.A. (life mem.), Ohio Edn. Assn. (pres. 1938), Phi Delta Kappa. Republican. Methodist. Mason, Kiwanian. Home: Wheelersburg, O. Died Nov. 4, 1953; buried South Webster, O.

McCOWN, Albert, physician; b. Lexington, Va., Aug. 11, 1890; s. James LaRue and Anna Calhoun (Smith) McC.; A.B., Washington and Lee U., 1910; M.D., Johns Hopkins, 1918, D.P.H., 1940. In pvt. practice of pediatrics, Tacoma, 1920-24, Seattle, 1924-34; dir. child health, Wash. Health Dept., Seattle, 1934-35; dir. Div. Maternal and Child Health,

U.S. Children's Bur., 1935-37; dep. commr. health, Mich. Health Dept., 1939; chief research and tng. unit, N.Y.C. Health Dept., 1940; dir. med. and health service A.R.C., 1941-43; dir. Bur. Communicable Disease Control, Va. Health Dept. Served at Base Hosp. No. 18, AEF, 1917-19; lt. col. to col., 1943-46; U.S. Army M.C., SHAEF, Mission to France. Mem. Am. Pub. Health Assn., A.M.A., Phi Beta Kappa, Nu Sigma Nu, Delta Omega. Democrat. Presbyn. Contbr. med. and pub. health jours. Home: 400 W. Franklin St. Office: State Office Bldg., Richmond, Va. Died Aug. 1953.

McCOY, Frank Ross, ret. army officer, diplomat; b. Lewistown, Pa., Oct. 29, 1874; s. Gen. Thomas Franklin and Margaret Eleanor (Ross) M.; grad. U.S. Mil. Acad., 1897; grad. Army War Coll., 1908; LL.D., Princeton, Yale, Columbia, Brown and Clark univs., Washington and Jefferson Coll.; m. Frances Field Judson, Jan. 26, 1924. Commd. 2d lt. Cavalry, 1897, advanced through grades to maj. gen.; aide to Pres. Roosevelt, 1906; mem. Gen. Staff Corps, 1910; gen. staff sec., A.E.F., 1917; chief of staff, Am. Mil. Mission Armenia, 1919; head Am. relief mission, Tokyo, 1923; mem. League Nations Commn. inquiry of Japanese seizure Manchuria, 1932; retired 1938. Dir. Equitable Life Assurance Soc., 1944—. Chmn. Far Eastern Commn., 1945-49. Clubs: Knickerbocker, Boone and Crockett (New York); Rittenhouse (Phila.); Metropolitan, Army and Navy, Chevy Chase (Washington). Home: Washington. Address: 1633 31st St., Washington, D.C. Died June 4, 1954; buried Arlington Cemetery.

McCOY, John Hall, banking; b. Harmar (now Marietta) O., Sept. 23, 1887; s. John Edwin and Rosa Estella (Hall) McC.; student pub. schs., Marietta; m. Florence Rebecca Buchanan, Nov. 10, 1909; children—Mary Carolyn (Mrs. William E. Mildren), John Gardner, Jane, Dorothy, Charles Wallace. Began as messenger Peoples Banking and Trust Co., Marietta, 1903; pres., dir. City Nat. Bank & Trust Co., Columbus, O.; chmn. bd. Buckeye Steel Castings Co., 1952—; dir. Capital City Products Co., Columbus; Pure Oil Co., Chgo. Trustee Marietta (O.) Coll. Republican. Presbyn. Mason (K.T., 32°, Shriner). Clubs: Columbus, Athletic, University, Faculty (Ohio State U.), Columbus Country (Columbus). Home: 2403 Canterbury Rd., Columbus 12. Office: 20 E. Broad St., Columbus, O. Died Nov. 18, 1958.

McCRACKEN, Charles Chester, educator; b. Bellefontaine, O., June 27, 1882; s. James Erskine and Mary Linda (Cooke) McC.; A.B., Monmouth (Ill.) Coll., 1908; A.M., Harvard, 1911, Austin fellow, 1914-15; Ph.D., 1916; m. Frances Cleo Fulton, Aug. 15, 1911; children—Janet May, Charles William, Mary Ruth, James Edward. Teacher country and village schs., Ohio, 1900-04; head science dept. high sch., Monmouth, Ill., 1906-07; head mathematics dept., high sch., Lancaster, O., 1908-10; dean Normal Coll., Ohio Northern U., 1911-14; prof. psychology and edn. Western Coll. for Women, 1915-17; prof. sch. adminstrn., Ohio State U., summers 1913, 14, 15, prof. sch. administration, 1917-30, sec. Coll. of Edn., 1917-20, asst. dean, 1920-22; research counselor, coll. dept. Bd. of Christian Edn., Presbyn. Ch. in U.S.A., 1928-29, 29-30 (half-time; on leave from Ohio State U.); pres. Conn. State Coll., Storrs, 1930-35; dir. college dept. Bd. of Christian Edn., Presbyn. Ch. in U.S.A., 1935-41; dir. (prof. rank) ednl. service bur., sch. edn. U. Pa., 1941-42; prin. specialist in higher edn. U.S. Office Edn., 1943; edn. counselor, Lake County (Fla.) schs., 1944-45; prof. ednl. adminstrn. Westminster Coll., summer 1945; pvt. ednl. counselor, 1945—; prof. edn. Duke, summer, 1948. Has made surveys of county school systems in Ohio and Fla.; mem. commmn. of 6, U.S. Bur. Edn., in survey of Negro colls. and univs. of U.S., 1926-27; spl. investigator for joint legislative com. on economy and taxation for Ohio Gen. Assembly, 1926-27; mem. exec. com. Am. Council on Edn., 1929-32; specialist, land grant college survey U.S. Bur. Edn., 1929-30. Mem. Phi Delta Kappa. Republican. Conglist. Author: Community Interests and School Consolidation of Logan County, Ohio, 1921-27; Survey of Logan County and Bellefontaine, Ohio, Schools, 1923; Local School District Boundaries Within the County School Districts of the State of Ohio, 1929; Survey of Student Personnel Services in Fifty Colleges (with Browne and McCracken); Graphs and Tabulations (an Analysis of Data from Selected Colleges, 1936-41). Contbr. articles on higher edn. to mags. Home: Tavares, Fla. Died Aug. 3, 1957.

McCRACKEN, Samuel, banker; b. Scranton, Pa., Nov. 12, 1876; s. Leroy and Charlotte (Little) McC.; student pub. sch., Scranton, 1886-93; m. Phebe Englert, June 4, 1902; children—George Englert, Elizabeth Jane. Clerk Traders Nat. Bank, Scranton, 1893-1903; treas. Union Savings & Trust Co., Pittstown, Pa., 1903-07; asst. cashier Peoples Bank of Wilkes-Barre, Pa., 1907-09, cashier, 1909-15; cashier Miners Nat. Bank of Wilkes-Barre, 1915-23, v.p., 1923-24, exec. v.p., 1924-41, pres., 1941-49, dir., 1921—; chmn. bd. Lehigh Valley Coal Co.; dir. Lehigh Valley Coal Sales Co., Lehigh Valley Coal Corp. Dir. Wilkes-Barre Y.M.C.A. Republican. Methodist. Home: 98 Academy St., Wilkes-Barre, Pa. Died Dec. 28, 1951.

McCRARY, John Raymond, lawyer; b. Lexington, N.C., Apr. 24, 1872; s. John Washington and Drusilla (Leonard) McC.; A.B., Trinity Coll. (now Duke U.), 1891; A.M., U. Mich., 1892; law study U. N.C., 1893-94; m. Mary Tatum, Sept. 20, 1904; children—Christine Tatum (Mrs. Louis Bowles), Virginia Rae (Mrs. Joe White), John Raymond (killed in the Battle of Belgium, Jan. 1945), Martha Penn. In practice of law in Lexington, Ky., 1894—; mem. McCrary & Ruark, 1904-08, McCrary & McCrary, 1908-20, McCrary & DeLapp, 1926—; U.S. atty., Middle Dist. N.C., 1932-34; v.p. Dixie Furniture Corp. Mem. N.C. Ho. of Reps., 1897-1917. Progressive candidate for atty. gen. of N.C., 1912, Rep. candiate, 1928; Rep. candidate elector at large, 1936. Mem. N.C., Davidson County (pres.) bar assns., 9019 Scholarship Assn., Duke U. Recipient Oratorical and Essayist medals Trinity Coll., 1891. Methodist. Rotarian (past pres.). Author: Thoughts About Things I Love, and other essays. Home: 300 N. Main St., Lexington, N.C. Died Oct. 4, 1951.*

McCRAW, William, judge; b. Arlington, Tex., Aug. 15, 1896; s. John ard Mollie (Cley) McC.; ed. pub. schs. and by pvt. study; m. Louise Carden Britton, July 22, 1931. Admitted to Tex. bar, 1915, at age of 19, and began practice at Dallas; criminal dist. atty. Dallas County 3 terms, 1926-32; atty. gen. of Tex., 1934-38; head consultant War Prodn. Bd., Sept., 1941-Feb., 1942; judge, Spl. Criminal Dist. Ct., Dallas Co., 1954—. Served as lt. U.S. Army, with A.E.F., World War I; capt. Air Corps Res.; in active service as capt. A.C., comdg. 85th Service Group, Air Service Command, Feb. 28-Nov. 2, 1942; promoted major; inspector gen. Mobile Air Depot Control Area Command, 1942-43; promoted lt. col., 1943; comdg. officer 2d Aircraft Repair Unit (floating), 1944-46; participated Saipan and Iwo Jima campaigns; promoted col., 1945. Mem. Tex. Bar Assn. Comdr. Am. Legion, dept. of Tex., 1948-49; exec. dir. Variety Clubs of Am. since 1946. Democrat. Baptist. Mason. Candidate for Dem. nomination for gov. 1938. Author: Professional Politicians. Home: 978 Hines Blvd. Office: Courthouse, Dallas. Died Nov. 8, 1955.

McCREA, Archie Elbert (mă-krā'), editor; b. Fremont, Mich., Dec. 15, 1880; s. Amos Stafford and Alma Aurelia (Stone) McC.; grad. Fremont (Mich.) High Sch., 1901; grad. student Muskegon High Sch., 1902-04; LL.D., Albion Coll., 1941; m. Eudora Hope Wells, Sept. 3, 1907; children—Olive Elberta (Mrs. Edward Elmer Cowles), Malcolm Roderick, Bruce Duncan. Rural school teacher, 1901-02; with Muskegon Chronicle, 1904—, as solicitor, collector and proofreader, 1904-05, reporter, 1905-08, city editor, 1908-11, mng. editor, 1911-36, editor, 1936—. Mem. Muskegon City Charter Commn., 1920; mem. Muskegon Bd. Edn., 1928-30; dir. Muskegon YMCA, 1916—, pres., 1918-28; mem. Nat. Council YMCA, 1926—, chmn. com. on public affairs, 1936-45, mem. internat. bd.; mem. editorial adv. bd., dept. of journalism U. Mich.; dir. West Mich. Tourist and Resort Assn., 1925-44; v.p., 1926-44; trustee Hackley Hosp. (pres.); trustee Meth. Found. of Mich., Detroit, Mich. (Meth.) Conf.; pres. Commn. on World Service and Finance. Mem. bd. publs. Meth. denomination. Award "Book of Golden Deeds," annual civic citation of Muskegon Exchange Club, 1938; Flowers for the Living annual citation of Muskegon Kiwanis, 1948. Mem. Am. Soc. Newspaper Editors. Methodist. Clubs: Kiwanis, Muskegon Country, Muskegon History; University Press. Contbr. to Mich. Christian Advocate. Home: 2471 Lake Shore Drive. Office: Muskegon Chronicle, Muskegon, Mich. Died May 1, 1950; buried Evergreen Cemetery, Muskegon.

McCREA, Roswell Cheney, economist; b. Norristown, Pa., July 30, 1876; s. William Henry Harrison and Fredericka (Frankfurter) M.; A.B., Harverford, 1897; A.M., Cornell, 1900; Ph.D., U. Pa., 1901; LL.D., Columbia, 1929; m. Marian I. Grater, June 19, 1901; children—Edith G., Winston, H. Thompson. Acting head dept. history and civics Eastern Ill. State Normal Sch., 1901-02; instr. econs. Trinity Coll., 1902-03; prof. econs. and sociology Bowdoin Coll., 1903-07; asso. dir. New York Sch. of Philanthropy, 1907-11; prof. econs. U. Pa., 1911-16, and dean Wharton Sch. of Finance and Commerce, 1912-16; prof. of economics Columbia, 1916-42, dean sch. of business, 1932-41, emeritus, Civilian commr. on conscientious objectors War Dept. 1918; dir. commercial examinations C. of C. State N.Y., 1919-43. Price adminstr. for Vt. under OPA, 1942. In joint charge of economic survey N.Y. Regional Plan, 1922-28. Fellow Am. Academy of Arts and Sciences; pres. Am. Assn. of College Schs. of Business, 1924-25; v.p. Acad. Polit. Science, 1930-42; mem. Phi Beta Kappa, Phi Gamma Delta, Beta Gamma Sigma (grand pres. 1925-30). Author: The Humane Movement, 1910. Writer on economic and social subjects, mainly in tech. publs. Home: Paulinskill Lake, R.D. 2, Newton, N.J. (winter) 400 W. 119th St., N.Y.C. Died July 2, 1951.

McCREERY, Elbert L., clergyman; b. Loveland, Colo., May 18, 1877; s. Rev. William H. and Martha (Marshall) M.; student Colo. Agrl. Coll., 1896; B.A., Monmouth (Ill.) Coll., 1901, D.D., 1926; grad. Xenia Theol. Sem. (now at St. Louis, Mo.), 1906; m. Hannah C. McLean, Aug. 20, 1909; children—John Kelly, William McLean, Samuel Wilson, Ruth Elberta, Martha Lucile, Anna Mary, Robert Elbert; m. 2d Mrs. Ruth Evans, Oct. 14, 1949. Tchr. Assiut (Egypt) Coll., 1901-03; teacher of Hebrew, Xenia Theol. Sem., 1904-06; ordained ministry U.P. Ch., 1906; missionary to Sudan, Africa, 1906-13, reducing to writing the Shulla and Nuer langs., and translating Gospel of John into Shulla; field sec. Laymen's Missionary Movement, 1914-18; synodical chmn., New World Movement, Neb. Synod U.P. Ch., 1919; pastor Mission Creek, Pawnee County, Neb., 1920-22; prof. N.T. Greek and phonetics and dir. pastors' course, Moody Bible Inst., Chicago, 1922-27; pastor Fort Morgan, Colo., 1927-29; dean faculty of Bible Inst. of Los Angeles, 1929-37; dean Bible-Missionary Inst., Western Bible Coll., Los Angeles, Calif., 1937-40; head dept. N. T. Greek, Westmont Coll., 1940-46; acting pres. Westmont Coll., Santa Barbara, Cal., 1946-47. retired 1948. Home: 1625 Cleveland Av., Loveland, Colo. Died Mar. 10, 1955; buried Lakeside Cemetery, Loveland, Colo.

McCROREY, Henry Lawrence, educator; b. Fairfield County, S.C., Mar. 2, 1863; s. James and Nancy McC.; A.B., Biddle University, Charlotte, North Carolina, 1892, B.D., 1895, D.D., 1902; graduate work University of Chicago, 1895-96 and 1930; LL.D., Lincoln U., 1925; m. Karie Novella Hughes, Dec. 27, 1897 (died May 6, 1911); children—Henry Lawrence, Novella Elizabeth, Madaline De Arona (dec.), Muriel Hughsine; m. 2d, Mary C. Jackson, Sept. 19, 1916. Ordained ministry Presbyn. Ch., U.S.A., 1895; teacher, Biddle U., 1895-1907, pres. Biddle U. (now Johnson C. Smith U.—colored), 1907-47, now emeritus. Commr. to Gen. Assembly of Presbyn. Ch., U.S.A., 6 times, and 5 times as del. to Alliance of Reformed Churches throughout the world holding the Presbyn. system; appointed by Governor W. W. Kitchin of N.C. del. to the Negro Nat. Ednl. Congress, St. Paul, Minn., 1912; appointed by Governor Locke Craig of N.C., del. to the Southern Sociol. Congress, Houston, Tex., 1915; pres. Nat. Assn. of Teachers in Colored Schs., 1923-24, now trustee; mem. N.C. State Interracial Commn.; mem. Bd. Christian Edn. of the Presbyterian Ch. in the U.S.A. Awarded certificate in 1931 by Bd. Nat. Missions of Presbyn. Ch. in the U.S.A. for distinguished service; received from Gen. Assembly of the Presbyn. Ch. of the U.S.A., Distinguished Service award for meritorious service in field of Christian edn., 1939. Mem. Southern Council on Internat. Relations; mem. exec. com. of Fraternal Council of Negro Churches of America; mem. Am. Acad. of Polit. Science. Mem. Pi Gamma Mu. Mason (33°). Editor Quarterly Review of Higher Education among Negroes, Africo-American. Has traveled extensively in Europe. Pres. Coll. Union of Presbyterian Church in U.S.A., 1940. Address: Johnson C. Smith University, Charlotte 2, N.C. Died 1951.

McCRORY, Samuel Henry, agrl. engr.; b. Iowa City, Ia., May 5, 1879; s. Charles Robert and Ruth Ann (Stevenson) M.; B.S. in Civil Engring., State U. Ia., 1904, C.E., 1908; A.E., Ia. State Coll., 1926; m. Blanche M. Severe, June 30, 1909 (died May 27, 1938); children—Dorothy Emogene, Ruth Roberta. In pvt. practice, Sioux City, 1904-06; drainage engr., drainage investigations Office Expt. Stas., U.S. Dept. Agr., 1907-12, engr. in charge, 1912-13, chief of drainage investigations, 1913-21, chief div. of agrl. engring., 1921-31, chief Bureau of Agrl. Engring., 1931-39, asst. chief Bureau of Agrl. Chemistry and Engring., 1939-42; dir. hemp div. CCC, 1942-46; cons. engr., 1946—; drainage adviser for the Near East, FAO of U.N., 1947-48; cons. drainage engr., Ministry of Agr., Cairo, Egypt, 1948. Mem. Am. Soc. C.E., Washington Acad. of Science, Washington Soc. Engrs., Am. Soc. Agrl. Engrs. (ex-pres.), First John Deer medalist Am. Soc. of Agrl. Engrs., 1938. Clubs: Engineers, Cosmos. Home: 6811 6th St., Washington 12. Died Feb. 18, 1949.

McCULLAGH, George C., newspaper pub.; b. London, Ont., Can., Mar. 16, 1905; s. George H. and Anne (Bates) McC.; ed. pub. schs.; m. Phyllis Laidlaw, Sept. 13, 1930; children—Robert, Ann, George. Asso. with Merchants Bank of Canada; with Globe Newspaper, 1921-28; mgr. Milner Ross & Co.; partner Barrett, McCullagh & Co., 1933-36; pres. and pub. The Globe and Mail newspapers, Toronto. since 1936; pres., pub. The Telegram, Toronto, 1948—. Director Mining Corp. of Can., Maple Leaf Gardens. Trustee Nat. Sanitarium Assn., Toronto Hosp. for Consumptives. Mem. bd. govs. U. of Toronto. Clubs: Empire of Canada; Toronto and North York Hunt; Boisclair Fish and Game; Engineers, Board of Trade (Toronto); York, National, Ontario Jockey, Mount Royal (Montreal). Home: Thornhill, Ontario. Office: 140 King St. W., Toronto, Ont., Can. Died Aug. 5, 1952; buried Mount Pleasant Cemetery, Toronto, Ont., Can.

McCULLEY, Johnston, novelist, dramatist; b. Ottawa, Ill., Feb. 2, 1883; s. Rolla Andrew and Belle (Raley) M.; ed. pub. schs. and under pvt. tutors;

m. Louris Munsey Powers, June 20, 1925; 1 d., Maurine. Formerly in newspaper work, spl. corr. U.S. and abroad. Mem. Authors' League, Authors' Guild, Screen Writers' Guild, Dramatists' Guild, Soc. Authors, Playwrights and Composers (London). Republican. Mason. Club: Authors' (London). Author: Land of Lost Hope, 1908; Daughter of the Idol, 1909; King of Chaos, 1910; Pennington's Choice, 1914; Captain Fly-by-Night, 1915; The Jungle Trail, 1917; Unclaimed Goods, 1918; Daughter of the Sun, 1918; The Brute Breaker, 1919; Broadway Bab, 1919; The Curse of Capistrano, 1920; The Mark of Zorro, 1920, reissue, 1958; The Masked Woman, 1920; The Black Star, 1921; The Further Adventures of Zorro, 1922; The Black Jarl, 1923; The Avenging Twins, 1923; The Rangers' Code, 1924; Black Star's Campaign, 1924; John Standon of Texas, 1924; The Brand of Silence, 1924; Who Killed William Drew?, 1925; The Spider's Den, 1925; The Demon, 1925; The Scarlet Scourge, 1925; Pancake Pete, 1926; The Broken Dollar, 1926; The Avenging Twins Return, 1927; The Crimson Clown, 1927; A White Man's Chance, 1927; The Crimson Clown Again, 1928; Alias the Thunderbolt, 1928; The Thunderbolt's Jest, 1928; Lawless Law, 1929; The Spider's Debt, 1930; The Spider's Fury, 1930; Who Killed the Caretaker?, 1930; Pest of the Rancho, 1930; Zorro Rides Again, 1931; The Flaming Stallion, 1932; The Blocked Trail, 1932; A Range Cavalier, 1933; Ten Radio Plays, 1933; The Trusted Outlaw, 1934; Rangeland Justice, 1934; Canyon of Peril, 1935; Riders Against the Moon, 1936; Reckless Range, 1937; Rose of the Rio Grande, 1937; Don Peon, 1937; Wench Caravan, 1938; Black Grandee, 1938; Guardian Devil, 1939; The Saga of Smoky Sarn, 1940; Saddle Mates, 1940; Cowboy Afoot, 1940; Holsters in Jeopardy, 1941; Range Lawyer, 1941; Rollicking Rogue, 1941; Gold of Smoky Mesa, 1942; South of the Pass, 1944; Ghost Bullet Range, 1945; The Cougar Kid, 1945; Senor Avalanche, 1946; The Caballero, 1947, 3d edit., 1959; Iron Horse Town, 1952; Showdown at Dawn, 1953; (also plays) The Heir Apparent, 1905; Wells of Wyoming, 1907; Love Ranch, 1909; Neutrality, 1941; The Little Fixer, 1934; Ripe Wheat, 1934; What Do You Like?, 1936, All Zorro T.V. series, 1957-59 for Walt Disney; also photplays. Contributor of fiction to mags. in U.S. and England, translated into French, Spanish, German, Hungarian, Portuguese and Scandinavian. Also writes under pseudonyms, Frederic Phelps, Rowena Raley and Raley Brien. Address: Twin Peaks, Cal.; also 6533 Hollywood Blvd., Hollywood, Cal. Died Nov. 23, 1958; buried Forest Lawn, Glendale, Cal.

McCULLOCH, Roscoe Conkling, ex-senator; b. Millersburg, Holmes County, Ohio, Nov. 27, 1880; s. John G. and Matilda (Harpster) M.; student University of Wooster; studied law Ohio State U. and Western Reserve U.; m. Helen Herbruck; children—Kathryn, Hugh H. Admitted to Ohio bar, 1903, and since practiced at Canton and Columbus; first asst. pros. atty. Stark County, 3 yrs. Rep. candidate for Congress in old 18th Ohio Dist., 1912; elected to 64th to 66th Congresses (1915-21), 16th Ohio Dist.; candidate for Rep. nomination for gov. of Ohio, 1920; spl. asst. atty. gen. of U.S., 1922-26; apptd. U.S. senator to succeed Theodore E. Burton, deceased, Nov. 12, 1929; Rep. nominee for U.S. Senate, 1930. Was chmn. Pub. Utilities Commission of Ohio. Methodist. Author: The Truth Will Keep Us Free, 1944. Home: 280 Queens Ct., West Palm Beach, Fla. Died Mar. 17, 1958; buried Hillcrest Cemetery, West Palm Beach.

McCULLOCH, William Alexander, army officer; b. Clinton Heights, N.Y., Feb. 10, 1889; s. Aiken and Lottie Lyon (Ham) McC.; B.S., U.S. Mil. Acad., 1913; Inf. Sch., 1922-23; Command and Gen. Staff Sch., 1927-28; m. Florence Alexander Sumner, June 18, 1921; children—Florence Turner, William Alexander. Commd. 2d lt., 1913; promoted through the grades to brig. gen. (temp.), Mar. 1943. Decorated Purple Heart (2 oak leaf clusters), Victory medal (4 battle clasps), Croix de Guejre (with bronze star), Chevalier (Black Star Order) Legion of Honor, Service medals for Army of Occupation, Defense, Asiatic-Pacific Campaign; hon. Citizen of Bourges (France); Gen. Hdqrs. citation (1918), Div. citation (1918); Legion of Merit "for meritorious conduct in the closing phases of the Guadalcanal Campaign," 1943. Home: 5504 Chevy Chase Parkway, Chevy Chase, Md. Died Dec. 2, 1959*

McCULLOCH, William Edward, clergyman; born Woodford County, Ill., June 5, 1869; s. Joseph McKee and Mary Jane (Phillips) McC.; A.B., Monmouth (Ill.) Coll., 1891; spl. course in history and polit. science, Johns Hopkins, 1 yr.; grad. Pittsburgh Theol. Sem., 1895; D.D., Maryville (Tenn.) Coll., 1909, Westminster Coll., Pa., 1909; m. M. Delphine Tyler, Sept. 10, 1896; children—Helen Tyler (dec.), Jean Delphine. Ordained United Presbyn. ministry, 1895; began in chg. Hamilton Av. mission, Pitts., which developed into the Homewood Ch. with membership of 900, resigned 1921; pastor 1st U.P. Ch., Los Angeles, Calif., 1921-39; supt. of missions of Synod of California, 1939-1949. In Y.M.C.A. work at Camp Lee, Va., Nov. 1917; made tour of United Presbyn. Ch. in war work confs., Feb. and March 1918; Y.M.C.A. service with 111th Machine Gun Battalion, 29th Div., July-Dec. 1918; served in Alsace sector and during Meuse-Argonne battle; speaking tour of 6 weeks, Nov.-Dec., to camps in France. Has served as sec. bd. dirs., Pittsburgh Theol. Sem., also as mem. Bd. Home Missions U.P. Ch., Nat. Evangelistic Commission of Federal Council of Chs. Moderator U.P. Gen. Assembly, 1917-18; pres. Ch. Fed., Los Angeles, 1925-27; pres. Christian Social Service Union, Pittsburgh, 3 years. Mem. Bd. Adminstrn. U.P. Church, 1933-39. Asso. editor United Presbyterian since 1913. Republican. Author: The United Presbyterian Ch., and Its Work in America; Who Is a Christian; Christianizing the Home: A Technique for the Quiet Hour; Prayers in the Lord's House on the Lord's Day; Sermon in The American Pulpit Series; pamphlets and sketches in religious publs. Contbr., as chmn. gen. assembly's com., to Manual of Worship, 1947. Home: 3901 Lime Av., Long Beach 7. Died July 26, 1952; buried Woodlawn, Pitts.

McCURDY, Fleming Blanchard, newspaper pub.; b. Old Barns, Nova Scotia, Feb. 17, 1875; s. James and Amelia Janet (Archibald) McC.; ed. Nova Scotia pub. schs.; m. Florence Bridgeman Pearson, Apr. 22, 1902; 1 son, Blanchard Pearson. Clerk, Halifax (N.S.) Banking Co., 1890-1901; established financial firm of F.B. McCurdy & Co., Halifax, 1901; elected to House of Commons (Can.) rep. constituency of Chelburne-Queens, 1911; rep. Colchester, 1917; apptd. parliamentary sec. Dept. of Militia and Defense, Can., 1916; sworn in as one of His Majesty's Privy Councillors, (Can.); apptd. minister of pub. works, 1920; retired from pub. life, 1921; pres. The (Halifax) Chronicle Company, since 1932, The Eastern Trust Co., since 1932, Halifax Ins. Co. since 1933, Eastern Utilities, Ltd., since 1940; vice pres. Bank of Nova Scotia since 1946; dir. Canadian Gen. Electric Co. Chmn. Nova Scotia div. Nat. War Finance Com. 1940-45. A gov. and hon. treas., Dalhousie College, Halifax, governor of Asbury Coll., Ottawa, since 1922. Past pres. Halifax Bd. of Trade. Decorated Jubilee (King George V) and Coronation (King George VI) medals. Conservative. Presbyterian. Home: Fernwood. Office: Bank of Nova Scotia Bldg., Halifax, Nova Scotia. Died Aug. 29, 1952; buried Fairview Cemetery, Halifax.

McCURDY, Laurence (Tatum), business exec.; b. Chicago, Aug. 15, 1897; s. Isaac and Elizabeth M. (Tatum) M.; student U. of Ill., 2 yrs.; m. Hilda M. Messinger, Mar. 1, 1922; children—Elmina E. (Mrs. Donald Moore, Jr.), Joanne, Laurence T., II. With Container Corp. of Am. since 1920, vice pres. since 1949. Served as sgt. 1st class U.S.A.A.S. World War I. Awarded Purple Heart. Republican. Presbyterian. Mem. Alpha Delta Phi. Clubs: Pine Valley Golf (Clementon, N.J.); Aronimink Golf (Newtown Sq., Pa.); Union League, Franklin Inst. (Phila.). Home: 255 Kent Rd., Wynnewood, Pa. Office: Nixon and Fountain Sts., Phila. 27. Died Aug. 1956.

McCUTCHAN, Robert Guy (măk-kŭch'ăn), hymnologist; b. Mt. Ayr, Ia., Sept. 13, 1877; s. Erastus G. and Margaret (Edie) McC.; student Park Coll., Parkville, Mo., 1893-94; Mus.B., Simpson Coll., 1904, Mus.D., 1927; D. Sacred Music, So. Meth. U., 1935; D.Litt., Southwestern U., 1943; Mus. Doctor, Depauw University, 1956; also studied in Berlin and Paris; m. Carrie Burns Sharp, Nov. 23, 1904 (died July 20, 1941); 1 son, Robert John; m. 2d, Helen L. Cowles, Dec. 11, 1944. With Baker U., 1904-10, first tchr. singing then organized Conservatory Music, of which dir., 1906-10; organizer, dir. Summer Sch. Music, Mt. Lake Park, Md., 1912-13; organizer community music activities for Ind. State Council Def., 1917-18; organizer, dir. Summer Sch. Music, Bay View, Mich., 1919-27; dir. Summer Sch. Music, Winona Lake, Ind., 1928-29; dean Sch., Music, De Pauw U. 1911-37, dean emeritus, 1937—; lectr. Summer Conf. Ch. Music, Northwestern, 1938-39, 41-42, 44-45, U. Mont., 1939; spl. lectr. religious music, Claremont Grad. Sch., 1939—; Earl lectr. Pacific Sch. Religion, 1942; Southwestern U. Found. lectures, 1943; vis. prof. ch. music Perkins Sch. Theology, So. Meth. U., Dallas, 1954-55; dir. choirs and festival orgns.; mem. Commn. Ch. Mus., M.E. Ch., 1924-28; member Joint Commn. Revision Meth. Hymnal and Psalter, 1928-35; mem. Gen. Conf. Music, M.E. Ch., 1937—; del. at large, Uniting Conf. Meth. Chs., Kansas City, 1939; mem. Gen. Conf. Commn. (Meth.) on Ritual and Orders of Service, 1940 (ed. com. 1942); mem. Gen. Conf. (Meth.) Ecumenical Commn., 1944, So. Calif.-Ariz. Conf. (Meth.) Com. Grad. Sch. of Religion, U. So. Cal., 1940. Mem. Music Tchrs. Nat. Assn. (ex-sec.), Ind. Music Tchrs. Assn. (ex-pres.), Hymn Soc., Am. Musicalogical Soc., Nat. Assn. Ch. Choir Dirs. (nat. ex-pres.) Com. Worship of Fed. Council Chs. Am., Phi Mu Alpha, Pi Kappa Lambda (ex-pres. gen.). Mason. Clubs: University (Claremont); Rotary (hon.). Author numerous books, 1937—; latest publ.: Hymns of the American Frontier, 1950; Hymn Tune Names, Their Sources and Significance, 1957. Home: 790 Mayflower Rd., Claremont, Cal. Died May 15, 1958; buried Greencastle, Ind.

McCUTCHEN, George, educator, economist; b. Church P.O., Williamsburg County, S.C., Apr. 16, 1876; s. Col. James and Mary Jane (Gilland) McC.; A.B., S.C. Coll., 1898, LL.B., 1903; summer student U. Wis., 1900, 08, U. Chgo., 1901, Harvard, 1902; m. Lilla Kennerly Johnstone, Dec. 22, 1904; children—Alan Johnstone, Hugh (dec.), George Thomas, James Malcolm, Wilmot Ruet. Instr. econs. U. S.C., 1900-06, adj. prof., 1900-09, asso. prof., 1909, prof. econs., 1910-48, ret. 1948, head dept., 1910-46. Served as specialist Census Bur. 1911; clerk to com. on agr. Ho. of Reps., U.S. Congress, 1917; spl. agt. meat packing investigation FTC, 1917-18; econ. adviser S.C. Land Settlement Commn., 1923; mem. price panel Richland County War Price and Rationing Bd. (past chmn.). Mem. Am. Econ. Assn., Pi Kappa Alpha, Phi Beta Kappa. Presbyn. Mason. Club: Kosmos (Columbia). Co-author: South Carolina, Economic and Social, 1945. Author of pamphlets, The Case for Cotton, 1915, The Torrens System, 1915, tax Reform in South Carolina, 1923. Home: 1517 Pendleton St., Columbia 1, S.C. Died Jan. 8, 1951; buried Elmwood Cemetery, Columbia.

McDANNALD, Alexander H., editor; b. Warm Springs, Va., Sept. 20, 1877; s. John P. and Sarah H. (McClintic) McD.; ed. pub. and private schs., Va. Poly. Inst.; B.L., U. of Va., 1898; student (spl. course) Columbia U., 1927; m. Mrs. Irene Elizabeth Drake, Aug. 14, 1929; stepson, Durling Drake. Manager J. P. McDannald estate, 1900-06; reporter Baltimore News, 1906-08; sec. Travelers and Merchants Assn., Baltimore, 1909; reporter, Baltimore Evening Sun, 1910-12, political editor, 1912-19, also acting political editor The Sun (morning), 1917-18; managing editor Encyclopedia Americana (30 volumes), 1919-20, editor-in-chief, 1920-48, editor emeritus, 1948—; editor Americana Annual, 1922-48; editor Hayward's Key to Knowledge (9 vols.), 1929-30; editor (for William H. Wise & Co.), Modern Ency. (1 vol.), 1933, Concise Ency. (8 vols.), 1937. Author: Across Germany, 1914; Costs of the World War, 1920; The Storied Hudson, 1927. Fellow Am. Geog. Soc. Mem. Acad. Polit. Science, Am. Acad. Polit. and Social Sci., Va. Hist. Soc., U. Va. Law Sch. Assn., Virginians (N.Y.C.), (hon.) Eugene Field Soc. Club: University (Winter Park). Address: 906 S.W. 27th Way, Forest Hills, Boynton Beach, Fla. Died Dec. 18, 1957; buried Warm Springs, Va.

McDERMOTT, Michael James, U.S. ambassador to El Salvador; born at Peabody, Mass., July 2, 1894; s. Michael and Delia (McHale) McD.; graduate Burdette College, Lynn, Mass., 1914; LL.B., National U. Law School, 1926, LL.M.; M.P.L., 1927; m. Rose Patricia Fuller, July 30, 1932; children—Michael James, Patricia Frances. With Massachusetts Fire & Marine Insurance Co., 1914-17; War Department, July-August 1917; executive office White House, July-December 1917; field clerk, United States Army, 1917-20; confidential clerk to Gen. Tasker H. Bliss, Am. sect. Supreme War Council, Versailles, France, 1918-20; sec. to Hon. Elihu Root, The Hague, May-Aug. 1920; spl. asst. Dept. State, 1920; pvt. sec. to under sec. of state, 1923; mem. President Harding's Alaskan trip, 1923; asst. chief Div. Current Information, Dept. State, 1924-27, chief, 1927—. Spl. asst. Am. delegation to Sixth Internat. Am. Conf., Havana, Cuba, 1928; Pact for Renunciation of War, Paris, 1938; Conf. Am. States on Conciliation and Arbitration, Washington, 1928-29; press liaison officer, Am. delegations, London Naval Conf., 1930; press officer 8th Internat. Conf. of Am. States, Lima, Peru, 1938; public relations dir. 8th Am. Scientific Congress, Washington, 1940; press officer, 2d meeting Ministers Foreign Affairs of American Republics, Habana, 1940; rep. secretary of State, Com. on War Information Policies, 1942—; member Committee on Political Planning, 1942-43; chief press relations officer, United Nations Conf. on Food and Agr., Hot Springs, Va., 1943; accompanied sec. of State to Moscow Conf., 1943; spl. asst. to sec. of State, 1944; mem. Dept. of State Com. on Postwar Programs, 1944; chief press officer, UN Monetary and Financial Conf., Bretton Woods, N.H., 1944; U.S. Group Dumbarton Oaks Conf., Washington, 1944; U.S. del. Inter-Am. Conf. on Problems of War and Peace, Mexico City, 1945; UN Conf. on Internat. Orgn., San Francisco, 1945; U.S. del., 1st session Gen. Assembly UN, London, 1945; Am. del. Conf. Fgn. Ministers, Paris, 1946; Paris Peace Conf. 1946 Am. del. Council Fgn. Ministers, New York, 1946, London, 1947; Conf. Fgn. Ministers, Mowcow, 1940; Inter-Am. Conf. for Maintenance of Peace and Security, Rio de Janeiro, 1947; Am. del. Interstate Conf. Am. States, Bogota, 1948 signing N. Atlantic Treaty, 1949; N. Atlantic Council, London and N.Y., 1950, Rome, 1951, Paris, 1952. Nominated U.S. ambassador to El Salvador, 1953. Home: 1855 Upshur St., N.W. Office: Dept. of State, Washington. Died Aug. 5, 1955; buried Arlington Nat. Cemetery.

McDERMOTT, William F., drama critic; b. Indpls., Feb. 17, 1891; s. John and Elizabeth (McCarthy) McD.; student Butler U., 1914; m. Georgia Richards, May 1910; 1 dau., Louise (Mrs. John Corcoran); m. 2d, Eva Pace, Feb. 1938. Drama critic, editorial writer Indpls. News, 1917-21; drama critic, columnist Cleve. Plain Dealer, 1921—, European corr. summers 1921-39, 43-44, 46, 48-50, 53, corr. South Am., 1940, around-the-world corr., 1930, 34, 39, Spanish Civil War, 1937, war corr., Eng., Africa, Italy, 1943-44; lectr. drama Western Res. U., 1934-38. Adv. panel ANTA. Club: Cleveland City. Home: 10311 Lake Shore Blvd, Cleve. 8. Died Nov. 16, 1958; buried Lakeview Cemetery, Cleve.

McDONALD, Ellice, bio-chemist, pathologist; b. Fort Ellice, Manitoba, Can., Oct. 27, 1876; s. Archibald and Ellen (Inkster) McD.; ed. St. John's Coll., Winnipeg, Can., McGill U. (M.D. 1901), Montreal, P.Q.; m. Ann Heebner, Oct. 15, 1907; children—Vicomtess Diane de Branges de Bourica, Ellice. Successively resident surgeon Kensington Hosp. and New York Lying-in Hosp., asst. in pathology, Albany Med. Sch., instr. Columbia U. Coll. of Pharmacy and Science, 1901-07; instr. surgery, N.Y. Post Grad. Med. Sch. and Hosp., 1907-16; asst. prof. of gynecology, Grad. Sch. of Medicine, U. of Pa., 1922-35; dir. Cancer Research Fund, 1928-35; dir. Biochemical Research Foundation of Franklin Inst. since 1935. Served with Canadian Army Med. Service, 1916-19. Awarded gold medal, Internat. Faculty of Sciences, London, 1937. Fellow Am. Coll. Surgeons; mem. Am. Inst. of City of New York, Biochem. Soc., Faraday Soc., Franklin Institute of Pa., Am. Assn. tion of Cancer Research, American Physical Soc., Am. Chem. Soc., A.A.A.S., Internat. Soc. Exptl. Cytology, N.Y. Pathol. Soc. (life), Gen. Alumni Soc. U. of Pa., Graduate Society of McGill University, Pa. Horticulural Society. Clubs: University; Wilmington Country. Author: Studies in Gynecology and Obstetrics, 1914; Ectopic Pregnancy, 1919. Editor: Reports of the Cancer Research Labratories of the University of Pa., Vol. 1, 1930-31, Vol. 2, 1932-33; Reports of the Biochemical Research Foundation of Franklin Inst., vol. 3, 1934-35, vol. 11, 1950-51, vol. 12, 1952-53; Neutron Effects on Animals, 1947. Contbr. author to biol. effects of external radiation, 1954. Home: Invercoe, Sedgely Farms, Wilmington, Del. Address: The Biochemical Research Found., Newark, Del. Died Jan. 31, 1955.

McDONALD, Eugene F., Jr., pres. Zenith Radio Corp.; b. Syracuse, N.Y., Mar. 11, 1890; s. Eugene F. and Mary McD.; ed. Syracuse U.; m. Inez Riddle, July 16, 1931; children—Jean Marianne, Eugene F. III. Southern rep. Franklin Automobile Co., Syracuse, N.Y.; in automobile comml. paper bus., Chicago, 1910-17; in radio business, 1920—; now pres. Zenith Radio Corp.; pres. Seneca Securities Corp.; pres. and dir. Wincharger Corp. (Sioux City, Ia.); dir. Hospital Service Corp. Served as lt. comdr., U.S. Navy, 1917-18; lt. comdr., U.S.N.R. Mem. MacMillan Arctic Expdn., 1923; 2d in command, MacMillan Nat. Geog. Expdn. to Arctic, comdr. S.S. Peary, 1925; comdr. Isle Royale Archaeol. Expdn., 1928, Cocos-Galapagos Islands Archaeol. Expdn., 1929, Georgian Bay Archaeol. Expnd., 1930, expdn. to find LaSalle's lost ship Griffin, 1937. Organizer, 1923, and 1st pres. Nat. Assn. of Broadcasters. Trustee Henrotin Hosp. Fellow Royal Geog. Soc.; mem. Outboard Motor Assn. (Am. nat. commodore). Clubs: Racquet, Chicago Athletic, Tavern, Macinac Island Yacht, Columbia Yacht (Chicago); McGregor Bay Yacht; Royal Canadian Yacht; Explorers (N.Y.C.). Author: Youth Must Fly, 1941; Television Will Cost Big Money, 1946. Home: 2430 Lake View Av. Office: 6001 Dickens Av., Chgo. Died May 15, 1958.

McDONALD, Harl, composer; b. near Boulder, Colo., July 27, 1899; s. Willis Burr and Floy (Taffemire) McD.; student Univ. of Redlands, 1917-18; Mus.B., Univ. of Southern California, 1921; University of Leipzig, 1922, hon. Mus.D.; Litt.D., Temple University, 1953; also studied in Berlin; m. Eleanor Gosling, 1925; children—Charlotte Burr, Frances Tabor. Composer since age of 7; teacher Acad. Tournefort, Paris, 1922, Philadelphia Musical Academy, 1924-26; with U. of Pa., 1926-39, successively as lecturer, asst. prof. and prof. of music, dir. music dept., 1935-39; research work in acoustics and sound measurement (Rockefeller Foundation grant), 1930-33; mgr. Philadelphia Orchestra since 1939; European debut with Berlin Philharmonic, 1922. Served in U.S. Army, 1918. Mem. Am. Musicol. Soc., Sigma Xi. Republican. Episcopalian. Clubs: Art Alliance (Phila.); Lotos (N.Y. City). Composer: 4 symphonies, 4 symphonic suites, 3 concertos, 2 string quartets, 2 trios; also tone poems and short works for symphony orchestra, chorus, violin, piano, voice, etc.; about 110 published musical compositions. Author of monograph (with O. H. Schuck); New Methods of Measuring Sound. Home: St. David's, Pa. Office: Phila. Orchestra Assn., Phila. Died Mar. 30, 1955; buried Valley Forge Meml. Cemetery.

McDONALD, James, engr., business exec.; b. nr. New Castle, Eng., May 15, 1875; s. James and Mary (Paterson) McD.; student Barnes Sch., 1882-88, St. John's Sci. and Art, 1888-1891 (both at So. Shields, Eng.); m. Mary Pass, Dec. 24, 1901 (died 1941). Came to U.S., 1908, naturalized, 1917. Apprentice engr. Middle Docks & Engring. Co., South Shields, 1891-96; marine engr. British-India Steam Nav. Co., R. Runciman & Co., 1896-1905; ship repair works supt. Middle Docks & Engring. Co., 1905-08; gen. mgr. Todd Combustion Equipment Corp. and predecessors, subsidiary Todd Shipyards Co., N.Y.C., 1908-19; v.p., 1919-41, pres., dir., 1946—; bd. dirs. and chmn. com. for cadet tng., Todd Shipyards Corp., N.Y.C., 1945—; dir. Thermo Products Corp. Obtained British Extra First Class Bd. of Trade Engrs. Certificate, 1901; licensed profl. engr., State N.Y., 1937. Mem. Soc. Naval Architects and Marine Engrs. Presbyn. Mason. Club: Doric 86. Home: Deeprocks, Campgaw Rd., Ramsey, N.J. Office: Todd Shipyards Corp., Columbia and Halleck Sts., Bklyn. Died Dec. 30, 1957.

McDONALD, James Walton, church official; b. Franklin, Tenn., Feb. 21, 1869; s. Rev. James Newton and Margaret (Gray) McD.; A.B., Cumberland U., Lebanon, Tenn., 1893, D.D., 1908; B.D., Lebanon Theol. Sem., 1896; grad. study, Union Theol. Sem., Columbia U., U. of Chicago; m. Nora Alice Gates, Mar. 9, 1899; 1 dau., Helen Gates. Ordained Presbyn. ministry, 1897; pastor West Side Ch., Logansport, Ind., 1897-1901, Westminster Ch., Decatur, Ill., 1901-23; exec. sec. Presbytery of Kansas City, 1923-39; gen. sec. Kansas City Council of Churches since 1935; counselor in adult education since Jan. 1, 1943; mem. exec. com. Radio Council of Kansas City. Mem. pub. relations and program coms. Internat. Council Christian Edn.; mem. field dept. of Fed. Council of Churches and Internat. Council Christian Edn. Mem. Kansas City Chamber of Commerce, Pi Kappa Alpha. Kiwanian. Edited Rethink Your Program Now, 1941; broadcasts weekly from 3 stations. Author: You and Your Mind, 1949; Cartoons From the Teachings of Jesus, 1950; What and How Are the People Thinking, 1951; contributed numerous articles on radio and adult education. Home: 4317 McGee St. Office: 200 Y.M.C.A. Bldg., Kansas City 6, Mo. Deceased.

McDONALD, John Daniel, ret. naval officer; b. Machias, Me., Nov. 1, 1863; grad. U.S. Naval Acad., 1884. Commd. ensign, 1886, promoted through grades to vice adm., 1930. Served on Monterey, Spanish-American War, 1898; at Naval Torpedo Station, Newport, R.I., 1904; navigator Ohio, 1904-07; in charge 1st Light House Dist., 1907-08, 10-11; comdr. Castine, 1908-09, Chattanooga, 1909-10, Hancock, 1911, Virginia, 1911-13; at Naval War Coll., 1913-15; chief of staff Atlantic Fleet, 1915-16; comdr. Arizona, 1916-18; apptd. comdt. Navy Yard, N.Y.C., 1918; became vice-adm., comdt. 14th Naval Dist., retired 1924. Address: Oakland Hotel Oakland, Cal. Died Sept. 2, 1952.*

McDONALD, Lloyd Davison, mfg. exec.; b. Dunkirk, N.Y., Jan. 7, 1894; s. Addison Maynard and Elizabeth Jessica (Davison) McD.; m. Winifred C. Morrell, Oct. 14, 1922; children—David, Janet (Mrs. Glenn Culp), Joan. Joined Warner & Swasey Co., Cleveland, 1918, dir. since 1936, v.p., 1939, exec. v.p. since 1950; v.p., dir. Sterling Foundry Co., Wellington, O.; dir., mem. exec. com. Osborn Mfg. Co.; dir. Rotor Tool Co. Past chmn., mem. Cleveland Met. Housing Authority. Mem. Controllers Inst. Am. (past. v.p.), Nat. Machine Tool Builders Assn. (past pres.). Republican. Episcopalian. Clubs: Union, Mid-Day, Country, Fifty (Cleveland). Home: 2720 Cranlyn Rd., Shaker Heights 22, O. Office: 5701 Carnegie Av., Cleve. 3. Died May 15, 1954.

McDONALD, Stewart, hon. chmn. Md. Casualty Co.; b. Owatonna, Minn.; s. John J. and Mary Elizabeth (Brown) McDonald; M.E., Cornell Univ. Was manufacturer of automobiles, farm implements and electrical apparatus, St. Louis; one time police commr. St. Louis; asst. federal housing adminstr., Washington, D.C., 1935, adminstr., 1935-40; dep. fed. loan adminstr., 1940-42; hon. chmn. bd. Md. Casualty Co.; director of the Savoy-Plaza Hotel, New York City. Mem. Inst. for Urban Land Use and Housing Studies; Columbia U. Member National Emergency Council, 1935-39; del. 14th Internat. Housing and Town Planning Congress, London, 1935; chmn. U.S. delegation 14th Internat. Congress of Architects, Paris, 1937, 6th Internat. Congress of Building Socs., Zurich, 1938. Pres. Army War Shows, 1942-43. Clubs: Turf and Field (Elmont, L.I.); Maryland (Balt.); Piping Rock (Locust Valley, N.Y.); Down Town Assn. (N.Y.C.). Home: 570 Park Av., N.Y.C. Office: 701 W. 40th St., Balt. 3. Died Jan. 3, 1957.

McDOUGALL, Alexander Miller, transportation and warehousing; b. Duluth, Minn., Sept. 10, 1884; s. Alexander and Emmeline (Ross) McD.; prep. edn., Phillips Acad., Andover, Mass.; student U. of Minn. 1 yr.; m. Kathryn Barclay Hoopes, June 23, 1906; children—Grant, Kathryn Barclay, Alexander Miller. Began in ship bldg. and transportation business at Duluth, 1904; organizer and former pres. Terminals & Transportation Corp. of America, and Minn. Atlantic Transit Co.; pres. Lake Railways, Inc. Builder of ships for U.S., World War. Mem. Psi Upsilon. Republican. Pioneered in hermetically sealing and subjecting food products to quick freezing; patents issued on ship designs. Address: 3260 Gough St., San Francisco, Cal. Died Aug. 14, 1951.

McDOUGALL, George Francis, coll. pres.; b. Plymouth County, Ia., Jan. 22, 1882; s. Alex and Kate E. (Noble) McD.; A.B., Hastings Coll., 1908, D.D., 1929; grad. McCormick Theol. Sem., 1911; m. Annie Phillips, July 1, 1911; children—Emily Jean, Lilian Frances (Mrs. Kieth Walker), George Francis, William Phillips. Ordained Presbyterian ministry, May 10, 1911; pastor Orleans, Nebraska, 1911-13, Bridgeport, Neb., 1913-18, Minden, Neb., 1918-20, Dodge City, Kan., 1920-26 (led in erection of $160,000 bldg.), Grand Junction, Colo., 1926-33 (led in erection of $100,000 bldg.), Trinidad, Colo. 1933-41; president of Huron (S.D.) College, 1941—; minister Bear Creek Community Presbyterian Church, Morrison, Colo., 1953-57, South Presbyterian Ch., Denver, Colo., 1957—. Chairman Synods Committee on National Missions, 1934-37 and 1940-41; organizer Grand Mesa Young People's Conf., 1927, Mountain Park Presbyn. Young Peoples Conf. in Pueblo Presbytery at Pueblo, Colo., 1938. Active in war work, World War I. Associated with Salvation Army and Boy Scout Council, Trinidad, Colo. Trustee Hastings (Neb.) Coll., 1912-20. Republican. Mason (Shriner); past patron Order Eastern Star. Club: Rotary (Huron). Contbr. to church papers. Pres. Church Related Colls., South Dakota Presidents Assn., 1947. Home: 2895 S. Forest St., Denver 22. Died Feb. 12, 1959; buried Memorial Park, Crown Hill Cemetery, Denver.

McDOUGLE, Ivan Eugene, coll. prof.; b. Huntington, Tenn., July 17, 1892; s. Ernest Clifton and Linna Alice (Caldwell) McD.; grad. Ky. State Normal Sch., 1910; A.B., Clark Coll., Worcester, Mass., 1915; A.M., Clark U., 1916, Ph.D., 1918; m. Hazel Agnes Montague, Dec. 28, 1918; 1 dau., Jean (Mrs. Edwin W. Bowen). Asst. in history, Clark Coll., 1915-18; prof. economics and sociology, Sweet Briar (Va.) College, 1919-24; asso. prof. economics and sociology, Goucher College, 1924-31, prof., 1931—; professor sociology, summer sessions, College of William and Mary, 1925-30, Johns Hopkins Univ., 1935—. Mem. Md. Commn. on Higher Edn. of Negroes, 1935-37; chmn. Md. Commn. on Scholarships, 1937—; chmn. Advisory Bd. Recreation, Baltimore, 1936-49; bd. trustees Morgan State Coll., 1939. Mem. bd. Prisoners' Aid Assn. (pres. 1949-52), Citizens Planning and Housing Assn., adv. bd. Child Study Assn. Mem. Am. Sociol. Soc., Am. Assn. of Univ. Profs., Population Assn. America. Mem. Disciples of Christ. Author: An Economic Study of Lexington, Ky. (1800-1820), 1916; Slavery in Kentucky (1792-1865), 1918; Mongrel Virginians (with Arthur H. Estabrook), 1926. Also articles in mags. Home: 1219 Roundhill Rd., Baltimore 18. Address: Goucher College, Towson 4, Md. Died Oct. 24, 1955.

McDOWELL, Clotilda Lyon; b. Galion, O., Mar. 14, 1858; d. Aaron J. and Olive W. Lyon; B.L., Ohio Wesleyan, 1880, A.M., 1911; m. William Fraser McDowell, Sept. 20, 1882. Pres. Woman's Foreign Missionary Soc. M.E. Ch., 1908—; del. World's Missionry Conf., Edinburgh, 1910 (mem. business com.); visited missions in Europe, India, China, P.I., Korea and Japan, 1910-11. Author: Our Work for the World. Home: 1936 Sheridan Rd., Evanston, Illinois. Died Dec. 27, 1930.

McDOWELL, John, ex-congressman; b. Pitcairn, Pa., Nov. 6, 1902; s. John Ralph and Eleanor (Allison) McD.; ed. Pitcairn grade and high sch.; grad. Randolph-Macon Mil. Acad., 1923; m. Virginia Cratty, Oct. 2, 1919; 1 dau., Patricia. Began as reporter on Pitcairn Express, 1912, worked on various newspapers to 1929; editor Wilkinsburg Gazette, 1929-33, pub., 1933—, also editor. Mem. 76th and 80th Congresses, 31st Pa. Dist. Served as magistrate, Pitcairn. Recipient distinguished service certificate Pa. Am. Legion. Mem. C. of C., Am. Geog. Soc., N.Y. Zool. Soc. Republican. Presbyn. Eagle, Rotarian. Home: 2120 Penn Hwy. Office: 771 Penn Av., Wilkinsburg, Pa. Died Dec. 11, 1957.

McDOWELL, John Anderson, ex-congressman; b. Killbuck, O., Sept. 25, 1853; s. James C. and Sarah (Anderson) McD.; grad. Mt. Union Coll., 1887; m. Esther E. Hole, Aug. 21, 879. Taught country school at 17; taught 7 winter terms; prin. Millersburg High Sch. 2 yrs.; supt. Millersburg schs. 17 yrs.; county sch. examiner 7 yrs.; has been instr. in tchrs.' insts. several counties in Ohio; also instr. in summer sch., Wooster U.; pres. Holmes Co. Agr'l. Soc. and Holmes County Farmers' Inst. Soc. for several yrs. Mem. Congress, 1897-1901, 17th Ohio dist. Democrat. Address: Millersburg, O. Deceased.

McDOWELL, (George) Tremaine, educator; b. Eagle Harbor, N.Y., Oct. 6, 1893; s. Howard Wilson and Eva Grace (Sweeten) McD.; A.B., U. Mich., 1915; A.M., Harvard, 1916; Ph.D., Yale, 1928; m. Mary Pearne Hubbard, Aug. 15, 1916 (died Oct. 1949); 1 dau., Dimmes Anne. Instr. English, De Pauw U., 1916-17; prof. English, Houghton (N.Y.) Coll., 1917-18, Miltonvale (Kan.) Coll., 1918-20, Marion (Ind.) Coll., 1920-22, Woman's Coll. of Ala. (Montgomery), 1922-24; asst., instr. and fellow in English, Yale, 1924-28; asst. prof. English, Univ. Minn., 1928-29, asso. prof., 1929-40, prof., 1940—, chmn. program in Am. studies, 1945—; prof. Bread Loaf (Vt.) Sch. of English, summer 1942. Guggenheim Memorial Foundation fellow, 1935-36. Mem. Modern Lang. Assn. (sec. Am. lit. group, 1937-42, chmn. 1943), Nat. Council of Teachers of English (chmn. coll. sect. and mem. exec. com., 1946-48), Am. Assn. Univ. Profs., Miss. Valley

Hist. Soc., Minn. Hist. Soc., The First Institute of Jazz Studies. Conglist. Author: American Studies, 1948. Editor: Washington Irving, A History of New York (with Stanley T. Williams), 1931; James Fenimore Cooper, The Spy, 1931; The Romantic Triumph, 1933; William Cullen Bryant; Representative Selections, 1935; American Sketchbook (with others), 1938; America in Literature, 1944; Study Guide to America in Literature (with Mary C. Turpie), 1945; America Through Literature (with others), 1948. Editorial bd. American Literature, 1932-33, 35-39, College English, 1945-49; asso. editor Am. Quarterly 1952-56. Officer: Univ. of Minn., Mpls. 14. Died Jan. 6, 1959.

McDUFFIE, Duncan, real estate developer; b. Jefferson, Ia., Sept. 24, 1877; s. Marshall Burnap and Sophie Bushnell (Warner) McD.; B.S., U. Cal, 1899; m. Jean Howard Schoonmaker, June 1, 1911. Engaged in development of residential subdivisions at Berkeley, Cal., 1905——. Chmn. Cal. Parks Council, 1925-30; pres. Save-the-Redwood League, 1944-—; chmn. Civic Arts Commn., Berkeley, 1913-17. Served with U.S. Food Adminstrn., Washington, 1917-18. Mem. adv. bd. Yosemite Nat. Park. Mem. Phi Delta Theta. Clubs: Faculty (U. Cal.); Sierra (pres. 1929-31, 43-45), Sierra Ski, Am. Alpine. Recipient Cornelius Amory Pugsley silver medal Am. Scenic and Hist. Preservation Soc., 1929. Home: 22 Roble Rd., Berkeley 5. Office: 2101 Shattuck Av., Berkeley 4, Cal. Died Apr. 23, 1951.

McDUFFIE, John, ex-congressman, U.S. judge; b. River Ridge, Ala., Sept. 25, 1883; s. John and Virginia Marion (Lett) M.; student So. U., Greensboro, Ala., 1 yr.; B.Sc., Ala. Poly. Inst., 1904; LL.B., U. Ala., 1908; m. Cornelia Hixon, Oct. 18, 1915 (died Mar. 2, 1935); 1 dau., Cornelia (Mrs. B. F. Turner); m. 2d, Mrs. Mary Clarke Maxon, Sept. 8, 1941. Mem. Ala. Ho. of Reps., 1907; admitted to Ala. bar, 1908; pros. atty., 1st Jud. Circuit of Ala., 1911-19; mem. 66th to 73d Congresses, 1st Ala. Dist.; resigned to become judge U.S. Dist. Ct., So. Dist. of Ala., 1935. Mem. Phi Beta Kappa. Home: 2007 Dauphine St., Mobile, Ala. Died Nov. 1, 1950; buried Pinecrest Cemetery, Mobile.

McEACHERN, John Newton, business exec.; b. Atlanta, Feb. 22, 1899; s. John Newton and Lula (Dobbs) McE.; student Ga. Sch. Tech., 1916-18; m. Sara Smith, June 10, 1924 (died 1943); 1 son, John Newton; m. 2d, Gladys Mewborn, Mar. 28, 1946. Agent, Life Ins. Co. of Ga., 1918, spl. agt., 1919, dist. mgr., 1921, v.p., supt. agencies, 1924, pres., 1927-—, chmn. bd., 1949-—. Dir. Ga. YMCA. Trustee Scottish Rite Hosp. for Crippled Children, Atlanta, John McEachern Sch., Cobb County, Ga. Mem. Atlanta, Ga. C.'s of C., Chi Phi. Methodist (trustee). Mason (Shriner). Clubs: Capital City, Atlanta Athletic, Piedmont Driving. Home: Route 1, Powder Springs, Ga. Office: 573 W. Peachtree St., Atlanta. Died Jan. 4, 1950; buried family cemetery Cobb County, Ga.

McEACHRON, Karl Boyer, research engr. Gen. Elec. Co.; b. Hoosick Falls, N.Y., Nov. 17, 1889; s. John Henry and Dora (Peters) McE.; O. Northern U., 1912, M.E., 1913, D. Engr., 1938; M.S. in E.E., Purdue U., 1920, D.Sc., 1941; m. Leila E. Honsinger, Aug. 28, 1914; children—Karl B., William D., Gertrude Louise (Mrs. Howard Babbitt), Robert E., Alice Clare (Mrs. Richard Smith). Test engineer General Electric Company and instructor electrical engring., O. Northern University, 1914-18; research work on nitrogen fixation, 1918-20; instructor elec. engring., Purdue U., 1918-22; head research and development sect. lightning-arrester dept., Gen. Elec. Co., 1922-33, head reasearch engr. high voltage engring. lab., 1933-45; asst. mgr. engring., 1945-49; mgr. engring., 1949-51; mgr. lab. engring. dept. 1952-53; cons. profl. employee relations, since 1953. Mem. bd. Mass. State Bd. Registration Professional Engrs. and Land Surveyors, 1941-51. Mem. panel, Research and Development Bd., Washington, 1947-49. Awarded Coffin prize for development of thyrite, 1931, Edward Longstreth medal by Franklin Inst., 1935; Edison medal of the American Institute E.E., 1949. Fellow Am. Inst. E.E. (dir. 1936-40, v.p. 1942-44); mem. Nat. Soc. Profl. Engrs., Am. Soc. Engring. Edn., Ind. Acad. Sci. Republican. Methodist. Clubs: Stanley, Rotary, Thursday Evening. Author: Magnetic Flux Distribution in Transformers, 1922; Lightning to the Empire State Building, I, 1939, II, 1941; Playing with Lightning (with K. Patrick), 1940. Author of many papers dealing with lightning and lightning protection problems. Home: 23 Waverly St. Office: General Electric Co., 100 Woodlawn Av., Pittsfield, Mass. Died Jan. 24, 1954; buried Pittsfield Cemetery.

McELDOWNEY, Charles Roy, banker; b. Chgo., Aug. 17, 1894; s. Charles and Laura (Bastable) Mc E.; student U. Ill., 1918; m. Ruth Kennicott, June 19, 1920; children—Jean (Mrs. Dave Fultz), John R. With Continental & Commercial Bank, Chgo., 1924-27, old Dearborn State Bank, Chgo., 1927-31; joined Chgo. Nat. Bank and predecessor, 1931, v.p., 1931-40, exec. v.p., 1940-53, vice chmn. bd., 1953-—. Served as lt. Inf., World War I. Episcopalian. Mason. Clubs: Mid-Day, Chicago Athletic Assn. Chgo. Farmers (pres. 1957). Home: Kennimac Farm, Route 1, Box 447, Chesterton, Ind. Office: Chgo. Nat. Bank, 120 S. La Salle St., Chgo. 90. Died May 16, 1959; buried Chesterton.

McELDUFF, John Vincent (măc-ĕl-dŭf), ret. naval officer; b. N.Y.C., Apr. 5, 1898; s. Patrick Edward and Sarah Ellen (Meenan) McE.; B.S., U.S. Naval Acad., 1919; grad. Army Chem. Warfare Sch., 1930, Naval War Coll., 1932; m. Mary Catherine Boyle, Jan. 26, 1921; children—Edward William, Mary Patricia. Commd. ensign, U.S. Navy, 1919, advanced through grades to rear adm., 1947; on combat duty, World Wars I and II; continuous naval service, 1916-47, ret. Mem. bd. dirs. Apollo Records, Inc. Dir. Civil Def., Delaware County, Pa. Awarded Combat Legion of Merit, 15 area campaign ribbons. Mem. Songwriters Protective Assn. Roman Catholic. Composer and lyricist: Eyes of the Fleet, 1938; The Navy Sweetheart Song, 1943; Men of Victory, The Airforce Song, 1948. Specialist in classical and popular mus. composition. Author: ABCs of Atomic Survival. Home: 152 Academy Lane, Highland Park, Upper Darby, Pa. Office: Court House, Media, Pa. Died Jan. 21, 1959; buried St. Peter and Paul Cemetery, Broomall, Pa.

McELHANY, J. L., pres. Gen. Conf. of Seventh Day Adventists Ch., 1936-50, now gen. sec. Former head various Cal. Adventists Confs. Address: Glendale, Cal. Died June 25, 1959.*

McELHINNEY, John H., business exec.; b. near Burlington, Ia., June 13, 1888; s. Frank Martin and Metta (Montgomery) McE.; student Geneva Coll., Beaver Falls, Pa., 1904-05; M.E., U. of Pittsburgh, 1909; m. Marian Vaughn, Mar. 1, 1922; children—John, Frank, Shirley Ann. Engr. United Engring. & Foundry Co., Pittsburgh, 1911-13, engr. Youngstown (O.) Sheet & Tube Co., 1913-20; asst. gen. mgr. Columbia Steel Co., Elyria, O., 1920-23, asst. and gen. supt., Lukens Steel Co., Coatesville, Pa., 1926-36; asst. vice pres. Wheeling (W. Va.) Steel Corp., 1936-43, v.p. since 1943, now also director and member of executive com.; dir. Wheeling Dollar Savings & Trust Co. Served as 1st lt. Ordnance Dept., U.S. Army, 1917-19. Mem. Am. Iron and Steel Inst., Assn. Iron and Steel Engrs., Am. Inst. Mining and Metall. Engrs., Am. Standards Assn. Republican. Presbyn. (elder). Clubs: Fort Henry, Wheeling Country. Home: Leatherwood Lane. Office: Wheeling Steel Corp., Wheeling, W.Va. Died Apr. 12, 1955; buried Wheeling.

McELREATH, Walter (măk-ĕl-rēth), lawyer; b. Lost Mountain, Cobb County, Ga., July 17, 1867; s. William Anderson and Matilda Jane (McEachern) McE.; student Washington and Lee U., 1890-92; m. Bessie Anderson, Nov. 26, 1896 (dec.); m. 2d, Mildred Dickey, Jan. 9, 1938. Admitted to Georgia bar, 1895, and practiced at Atlanta, Ga., since 1895; president Atlanta Federal Savings & Loan Association 1928-—; dir. and gen. counsel Industrial Life Ins. Co. of Ga. Mem. Gen. Assembly of Ga., 1909-12. Trustee Atlanta Art Assn.; mem. Am., Ga. State and Atlanta bar assns., Am. Law Inst., Atlanta Hist. Soc. (dir.). Democrat. Clubs: Civitan, Burns, Lawyers (Atlanta). Author: McElreath on the Constitution of Georgia, 1912; Methodist Union in the Courts, 1946. Home: 3512 Piedmont Rd. N.E. Office: Twenty-two Marietta Bldg., Atlanta. Died Dec. 6, 1951; buried Powder Springs, Ga.

McELROY, Benjamin Lincoln, educator; b. Racine, O., Mar. 22, 1860; s. Capt. Joseph Charles and Sarah Ann (Ward) M.; B.A., Ohio Wesleyan U., 1883, Ph. D., 1895; B.D., Drew Theol. Sem., 1897; studied U. Chgo. and Harvard; m. Lora Eleanore Cherington, Sept. 18, 1884; children—Enid, Mrs. Lora Jean Druhot, Mildred, Lillian. Ordained to M.E. ministry, 1888; pastor successively Granville, Delaware, Portsmouth, O., Ann Arbor, Mich., and Columbus, O., until 1905; prof. applied Christianity, Ohio Wesleyan U., 1905-30, now ret. Mem. Phi Gamma Delta, Phi Beta Kappa. Republican. Home: Delaware, O. Died Jan. 31, 1948; buried Oakgrove Cemetery, Delaware.

McELROY, Robert, historian; b. Perryville, Ky., Dec. 28, 1872; s. William Thomas and Eliza (Casseday) M.; B.A., Princeton, 1896, M.A., 1897, Ph.D., 1900; fellow Princeton, 1896-98; studied at univs. Leipzig and Berlin, and at Oxford U., 1900-01; LL. D., St. John's U., Shanghai, China, 1921; M.A., by decree of Convocation, Oxford, 1925; D.Litt., Oxon, 1934; m. Louise Robinson Booker, 1900; children—Elizabeth Hunt, Katharine Louise. Instr. history Princeton, 1898-1901, asst. prof. Am. history, 1901-09, Edwards prof. Am. history, 1909-25, head dept. history and politics, 1912-16. First Am. Exchange prof. to China, 1916-17; lectured upon govt. and edn. in leading univs. and cities of China, also Japan and Philippines (lectures pub. in Chinese and in English, 1917, with intro. of C. T. Wong, then v.p. Chinese Senate). Harold Vyvyan Harmsworth prof. Am. history, Oxford U., Eng., 1925-35, reelected, 1935 and 2d reelection, 1938, emeritus, 1939; Sir George Watson professorship, 1926, lecturing at Cambridge, Edinburgh, Bristol, Manchester and Leeds univs., and Royal Gallery of The House of Lords; Brooks-Bright lectr. 1928, 29, 30, to English pub. schs., Rugby, Winchester, Charterhouse, Stowe, etc.; lectr. Hellenic Traveller's Club, on cruise of 1930; series of lectures in the Royal Instn., 1932; the Centennial Address, N.Y.U., 1932. Mem. exec. com. Nat. Mil. Tng. Camps Assn. from its establishment until its work was taken over by govt. Granted leave of absence by Princeton, 1917-19, to act as ednl. dir. Nat. Security League. Organizer nat. campaign for celebration Constitution Day, 1919. Fellow Royal Hist. Soc.; fellow and mem. governing bd. Queen's Coll., Oxford, 1925-39. Mem. Nat. Publicity Com., Wood campaign for presdl. nomination, 1920; speaker Rep. Nat. Com., 1920, 24, 28; asso. adv. O.C.D., Region III, also historian for O.C.D. and for C.W.S., 1942-45. Author: Kentucky in the Nation's History, 1909; The Winning of the Far West, 1914; The Representative Idea in History, 1917; Grover Cleveland—the Man and the Statesman (2 vols.), 1923; The Pathway of Peace, 1927; The United States (Benn's Sixpenny Series), 1928. Editor: In the Name of Liberty (collection of speeches of William Bourke Cockran), 1925; Jefferson Davis—The Unreal and the Real (2 vols.), 1937. Co-editor Putnam's Historical Atlas, Phelps Historical Atlas, 1927. Asso. editor, Current History Mag. (in charge internat. topics), 1924-25. Contbr. Cyclo. of Am. Govt.; Harmsworth's Universal History, 1927; Social and Political Ideas of some Representative Thinkers of the Revolutionary Era. Editor (with Thomas Riggs): The Unfortified Boundary, A Diary of the First Survey of the Canadian American Boundary, 1943. Home: Nassau Club, Princeton, N.J. Died June 16, 1959.

McELWAIN, Frank Arthur (măk'el-wān), bishop; b. Warsaw, N.Y., Dec. 14, 1875; s. James Frank and Mary Stewart (Arthur) McE.; B.A., Trinity Coll., Conn., 1899, M.A., 1902, D.D., 1913; B.D., Seabury Div. Sch., Faribault, Minn., 1902; m. Helen Cantwell De Muth, Nov. 17, 1903; children—Dorothy De Muth (dec.), Frank Arthur, Mary McDonald; m. 2d, Mabel C. Lofstrom, July 28, 1920. Deacon, 1902, priest, 1903, P.E. Ch.; pastor chs. in Mo., 1902-05; instr. Seabury Div. Sch., 1905-07, warden, 1907-12; elected suffragan bishop, consecrated 1912; bishop of Minn., 1917, retired 1943; also prof. pastoral theology Seabury-Western Theol. Sem., Evanston, Ill., 1933-38, pres., dean, 1938-44, ret. Trustee Seabury-Western Theol. Sem. Mem. Alpha Chi Rho, Phi Beta Kappa. Mason. Home: Bellamy Apts., Lexington, N.C. Died Sept. 19, 1957; buried Faribault, Minn.

McELWAIN, J. Franklin (măk-ĕl'wān), shoe mfr.; b. Charlestown, Mass., Sept. 8, 1874; s. John Allen and Susan (Gilbert) McE.; ed. Boston Latin Sch., Mass. Inst. Tech.; m. Mary Barton Pratt, Nov. 9, 1898; children—Mary, Frances. Pres. W. H. McElwain Co., 1908-21; chmn. bd. J. F. McElwain Co.; hon. chmn. bd. Melville Shoe Corp. Mem. war service com. Shoe Industry; chairman shoe and leather supply com., Nat. Council of Defense; chief, Shoe, Leather and Rubber Div., Q.M. Dept., World War I; mem. Shoe and Leather Adv. Com., War Prodn. Bd., World War II. Vice pres. N.E. Shoe and Leather Assn.; hon. v.p. Nat. Shoe Mfrs. Assn. Clubs: Union, Country, Algonquin (Boston); Union League (New York). Home: (summer) Cohasset, Mass.; (winter) 21 Chestnut St., Boston. Office: 140 Federal St., Boston. Died July 3, 1958.

McENTIRE, Richard Brooke, lawyer; born Topeka, Kan., Feb. 19, 1911; s. George P. and Mabel (Brooke) McE.; student Washburn Coll, Topeka, Kan., 1928-31, LL.B., 1934; m. Esther M. Sharp, December 8, 1944; children—Linda Jo, James Ralph. Casualty insurance adjuster, 1931-34; entered gen. practice, Topeka, Kan., 1934; former law partnership of Claussen and McEntire, 1935; U.S. Commr., Dist. of Kansas, 1st Div., 1936-39; spl. atty., State Corp Commn. of Kan., 1939, sec. 1940-43, gen. counsel, 1943-44, chmn., 1944-46; mem. Securities and Exchange Commn., 1946-53. Mem. Am., Topeka, Kansas State, Fed. bar assns., Alpha Sigma Phi, Delta Theta Phi. Republican. Clubs: Topeka High Twelve, Topeka Knife and Fork; Capitol Hill. Mason (32°). Home: 704 Taylor St., Topeka, Kan., also 5416 Huntington Pkwy., Bethesda 14, Md. Office: Munsey Bldg., Washington 4. Died Feb. 18, 1958.

McEVOY, Joseph Patrick, writer: b. N.Y. City, Jan. 10 1895; s. Patrick Griffin and Mary A. (McCabe) M.; Notre Dame Univ., 1910-12; m. Mary B. Crotty, Apr. 15, 1914; children—Dorothy Mary, Dennis Griffin; married 2d, Eugenie Wehrle, February 15, 1923; married 3d, Margaret Santry, December 19, 1935; children—Patricia, Margaret. Roving editor for Reader's Digest magazine. Clubs: The Oversees Press, Dutch Treat. Author: Slams of Life (verse), 1919; The Bam Bam Clock, 1920; The Potters (comedy), 1924; The Comic Supplement (revue), 1925; Americana (revue); God Loves Us (drama), 1926; Allez Ooop (revue), 1927; New Americana (revue), 1928; Show Girl (novel), 1928; Hollywood Girl, 1929; Denny and the Dumb Cluck, 1930; Mister Noodle, 1931; Society, 1931; Are You Listening?, 1932; New Americana (revue), 1932; Father Meets Son, 1937; Stars In Your Eyes (musical comedy), 1939; Charlie

Would Have Loved This, 1956. Creator comic strip, Dixie Dugan, 1928. Address: care Readers Digest, Pleasantville, N.Y. Died Aug. 8, 1958.

McEWEN, Merrill Clyde, educator; b. Lawrenceville, N.Y., Sept. 7, 1900; s. Guy Carlton and Mary Aurelia (Reeve) McE.; student Clarkson Coll. Tech., 1918-19, Crane Sch. Music, 1919-21, U. Wis.; B.S., Columbia, 1925; M.A., Ohio State U., 1933; m. Marcella Marie Kammerer, Aug. 4, 1927 (dec. Dec. 1952); children—Douglas, Stephen, Michael, Carol, Ellen. Staff music dept. Bowling Green State U., 1921-25, 28—, successively instr., asst. prof., asso. prof., to 1945, prof. music, 1945—, chmn. music dept., 1941— ;supr. music Mansfield (O.) Pub. Schs., 1925-28. Mem. Ohio Music Edn. Assn. (pres. 1934-35), Music Educators Nat. Conf. Kiwanian. Home: 135 N. Grove St., Bowling Green, O. Died Nov. 2, 1957.

McFADDEN, James Augustine, clergyman; b. Cleveland, O., Dec. 24, 1880; s. Edward and Mary (Cavanaugh) McF.; St. Ignatius Coll., Cleveland, 1894-99; St. Mary's Sem., Cleveland, 1899-1905. Ordained priest R.C. Ch., 1905; asst. pastor St. Agnes Ch., Cleveland, O., 1905-14; pastor St. Agnes Ch., Elyria, O., 1914-17; rector St. Mary's Sem., Cleveland, 1917-23; made domestic prelate, Nov. 30, 1927; chancellor Diocese of Cleveland since Feb. 13, 1925; bishop-auxiliary of Cleveland, 1932-43; apptd. first bishop of Youngstown O., June 4. 1943. Home: 741 Bryson St., Youngstown 2, O. Died Nov. 16, 1952; buried Calvary Cemetery.

McFADDEN, John Francis, business exec. Pres. and dir. Am. Credit Indemnity Co. of N.Y., 1922-51, ret.; Am. Health Ins. Corp.; mem. exec. com., dir. Comml. Credit Co.; dir. Mfrs. Casualty Ins. Co., Mfrs., Fire Ins. Co. Home: 1901 Ruxton Rd., Ruxton, Md. Office: First Nat. Bank Bldg., Balt. Died May 4, 1957.

McFADDEN, Manus, editor, pub. relations counsel; b. Graceville, Minn., Sept. 2, 1888; s. David and Kathleen (O'Connor) McF.; student, U. Minn., 1909-10, m. Wanda Alexander, Nov. 9, 1920 (div. May 1945); children—Patricia Ann (Mrs. George Partridge), Margarethe Alice (Mrs. Margarethe Rottschaefer); m. 2d, Brenda Ueland, Nov. 10, 1945. Reporter Mpls. Tribune, 1909-13, Chgo. Tribune, 1914, Chgo. American, 1915-16, St. Louis Post Dispatch, 1920, N.Y. Sun, 1921-22; mng. editor Popular Sci., monthly mag., 1922-25; picture editor N.Y. Mirror, 1925-28; editor Elizabeth (N.J.) Times, 1929-30; asst. mng. editor Mpls. Jour., 1930-39; Sunday editor Mpls. Star-Journal and Times-Tribune, 1940-43; exec. editor Mpls. Times, 1943-48; pub. relations counsel, Mpls., 1948—. Served with USN, 1917-19. Mem. Soc. of Amateur Chefs of Am. Club: Minneapolis (Mpls.). Home: Pomerlau Lake, Hamel, Minn. Office: National Bldg., Mpls. 2. Died Feb. 16, 1955.

McFADDEN, William Hartman, oil business exec.; b. Moundsville, W.Va., June 11, 1869; s. Galbraith Stewart and Permelia Hill (Morton) McF.; student in pub. and pvt. schools; m. Helen Williams Levi, Apr. 21, 1920. Machine shop and drawing-room apprentice Mackintosh, Hemphill & Co., Ltd., Pitts., 1888, became gen. supt., 1894, asst. gen. mgr., 1896-1902, v.p., gen. mgr., 1902-10, pres. 1910; with E. W. Marland in oil and gas business, Tex., 1910—; sr. v.p. Marland Oil Co. of Delaware to 1928; pres., dir. Southland Royalty Co., 1930-39, chmn. bd., 1939—; exec. v.p. Louisiana Furs, Inc. Mem. Pitts. Mfrs. Assn. (pres. 1905), Am. Foundrymens Assn. (pres. 1906-07), Steel Founders Soc. Am. (v.p. 1909-10), Gen. Steel Casting Assn. U.S. and Can. (v.p., 1903-10). Republican. Methodist. Elk (hon. life mem.). Clubs: Ft. Worth Boat (hon. life), Rivercrest Country, Fort Worth, Colonial County (Ft. Worth); Broadmoor Golf (Colorado Springs). Recipient Luther Cullick award and was made life mem. Camp Fire Girls, Inc., for outstanding service, donation of time, money, and effort. Home: 4926 Crestline Rd. Office: Fort Worth Nat. Bank Bldg., Ft. Worth 2. Died Nov. 1, 1956; buried Brookville, Pa.

McFADYEN, Bernice Musgrove, army officer; born Portsmouth, Va., Oct. 21, 1896; s. Oscar Lee and Katherine R. (Musgrove) McF.; m. Courtenay Walthall Ross, Oct. 21, 1920; children—Courteney Walthall (Mrs. Leet), Ross M. Commd., U.S. Army; served with Old Hickory Div., World War I; wartime chief staff Yankee Div., World War II; dept. asst. chief staff, G-1, Dept. Army; presently comdg. gen. U.S. Troops, Free Territory, Trieste. Decorated Legion of Merit, Silver Star, Bronze Star Medal with oak leaf cluster, Army Commendation Ribbon with cluster. Protestant. Home: 6810 Wilson Lane, Bethesda, Md. Office: Dept. of the Army, Pentagon, Washington 25. Died July 23, 1954.

McFALL, John Monteith, lawyer, corp. exec.; b. Greenville, S.C., Sept. 3, 1885; s. Andrew Calhoun and Lillie Duncan (McCullough) McF.; A.B. Coll. Charleston, S.C., 1904; M.A., Columbia, 1906; LL.B., George Washington U. Law Sch., 1915; m. Eulalie McLeod, Aug. 31, 1929; 1 dau., Eulalie Swinton. Began as tchr., San Antonio, 1906; headmaster Peacock Mil. Acad., San Antonio, 1907-08; co-founder Donaldson Mil. Acad., Fayetteville, N.C., 1908-11; prof. law, George Washington U. Law Sch., 1918-20; admitted to Ga. bar, 1915, S.C. bar, 1950, practiced Atlanta, 1915-16; v.p., chief atty. U.S. Fidelity & Guaranty Co., Balt., 1928-50; now counsel, mem. firm Roberts and Jennings; pres. Allied Mortgage Cos., Inc. Asso. Mortgage Cos., Inc., Balt., 1935-50; pres. Finisterre, Inc., 1942-50. Lectr. ins. law, U. Md. Law Sch., Balt., 1926-50; spl. lectr. ins. U. S.C., 1950—. Admitted Md. bar, 1942. V.-chmn. Balt. County Planning Commn.; mem. Balt. County Schs. Council. Mem. Md. Commn. Higher Edn.; mem. Soc. Colonial Wars, The Benchers, Am., S.C., Richland Co. bar assns., Columbia Art Assn., Md. Hist. Soc., Phi Delta Phi, Phi Kappa Sigma. Episcopalian. Club: Bachelors Cotillon. Contbr. law jours. and legal periodicals. Home: 910 Henderson St. Office: Roberts & Jennings, Liberty Life Bldg., Columbia, S.C. Died July 2, 1958; buried Darlington, S.C.

McFARLAND, Archie J. steel corp. exec.; b. Pymatuning Twp., Mercer County, Pa., July 2, 1883; m. Lovina Thomas, Dec. 1, 1904; 1 dau., Martha Ann (Mrs. Donald Greider). With Wheeling Steel Corp., 1905-24, Follansbee Steel Corp., 1924-30; with Wheeling Steel Corp., 1930—, became exec. v.p., 1937, now pres.; dir. Wheeling Dollar Savings & Trust Co., Fed. Reserve Bank of Pitts., Peoples First Nat. Bank (Pitts.). Dir. Ohio Valley Gen. Hosp., Wheeling. Address: Wheeling, W.Va. Died Nov. 28, 1950; buried Greenwood Cemetery.

McFARLAND, David Ford, chemist, metallurgist; b. Mansfield, O., Aug. 1, 1878; s. Robert S. and Mary J. (McBride) McF.; A.B., U. of Kan., 1900, A.M., 1901; fellow Yale U., 1902-03, M.S., 1903, Ph.D., 1909; m. Martha Elizabeth Pittenger, June 23, 1909; children—George Robert, Mary Louise, Elizabeth Jean, David Ford. Instr. in chemistry, U. of Kan., 1900-02, asst. prof., 1903-10; asst. in chemistry, Yale U., 1908-09; asst. prof. applied chemistry, U. of Ill., 1910-14, asso. prof., 1914-20; prof. metallurgy and head of dept., Pennsylvania State Coll., 1920-45, acting dean School of Mine and Metallurgy, 1922 and 1927-28, professor emeritus, 1945; asst. chem. Kansas Geol. Survey, summers, 1899-1907; asst. chem. and metallographist, Engring. Experiment Station, University of Illinois, summers 1910-20. Discoverer, with H. P. Cady, of helium in natural gas and methods of extracting it on laboratory scale. Mem. Am. Soc. for Metals, Phi Beta Kappa, Sigma Xi, Phi Kappa Phi, Phi Lambda Upsilon, Alpha Chi Sigma, Sigma Gamma Epsilon, Phi Eta Sigma, Alpha Tau Omega; mem. Am. Chem. Soc., 1901-28 (chmn. U. of Ill. Sect. 1919, Central Pa. Sect. 1925). Republican. Presbyterian. Writer of papers and bulletins on organic and industrial chem. and metall. subjects. Home: 121 N. Atherton St., State College, Pa. Died Feb. 5, 1955; buried Centre County Meml. Park, Centre County, Pa.

McFARLAND, Eugene James, painter, univ. prof.; b. St. Louis, Sept. 10, 1908; s. Eugene Tennyson and Kate Jane (Curtis) McF.; B.F.A., U. of Kan., 1930; student, U. of So. Calif., 1940; M.F.A., Escuela U. de Bellas Artes, Mexico, 1941; grad. student Columbia, 1946; Ph.D., Ohio State U., 1947; m. Lydia May Catlin, July 18, 1931; children—David Eugene, Linda Kay. Traveled and painted in U.S., Eugope, S. Am., Mexico; one-man shows in museums of St. Joseph, Mo.; Tulsa, Okla.; Okla. City; Columbus, O.; U. of So. Calif.; U. of Kan.; U. of Okla.; Phillips U.; Okla. Coll. for Women; Christian Coll.; So. Ill. U.; Ohio Wesleyan U.; Internat. House, N.Y. City; Laurel Gallery, N.Y. City; awarded prizes in nat. and sectional shows; comml. artist, 1930-34; head art dept. Jr. Coll., St. Joseph, Mo., 1936-38; dir. Sch. of Art, Phillips U., 1938-42; dir. summer European art tours; head dept. fine arts, Ohio Wesleyan U., 1942-52; head dept. art, U. Wichita; dir. Wichita Art Mus., 1952—. U.S.O. artist, World War II. Dir. fine arts, Ohio State fair, 1948-51. Represented in exhbns.: American Federation of Arts; Corcoran Nat.; Butler Art Inst. New Years' shows; Midwestern, Kansas City, Mo.; Five States, Tulsa, Okla.; Art League, Columbus, O.; Okla. Artists, Okla. City; Ohio Valley, Athens; travelling exhbns., Kansas Painters; Ohio Watercolor Soc. Pres. Okla. Assn. Artists, 1940-42, Ohio Valley Art Conf., 1948-49, Columbus Art League, 1948-49; mem. Coll. Art Assn., Am. Fedn. Arts, Eastern Arts Assn., Midwest Coll. Art Confs., Ohio Watercolor Soc., Am. Assn. Univ. Profs., Delta Phi Delta, Alpha Kappa Lambda. Mem. Ch. Disciples of Christ. Author: Subject Matter in Painting, 1948. Address: Dept. Art, U. Wichita, Wichita, Kan. Died Oct. 21, 1955.

McFARLAND, Thomas C(lair), educator; b. Porterville, Cal., July 19, 1893; s. James Albert and Anne L. (Doggett) McF.; B.S., U. Cal., 1916, M.S., 1923; m. Esther A. Touraine, Feb. 21, 1923; children—Anna May, James Albert. Student engr. Gen. Electric Co., Schenectady, N.Y., 1916-18; instr. U. Cal. at Berkeley, 1920-25, asst. prof., 1925-31, asso. prof. elec. engring., 1931-48, chmn. div., 1943-53, prof. since 1948. Fellow Am. Inst. E.E. (chmn. San Francisco sect. 1949-50; v. chmn. 1948-49, sec.-treas. 1947-48); mem. A.A.A.S., Sigma Xi, Tau Beta Pi, Eta Kappa Nu, Scabbard and Blade. Mason. Author: D.C. Machinery, 1938; A.C. Machinery, 1948. Contbr. articles elec. engring. publs. Home: 1879 Catalina Av., Berkeley 7, Cal. Died Sept. 16, 1954.

McFEE, Henry Lee, artist; b. St. Louis, Mo., April 14, 1886; s. Theodore Ford and Harriet Potter (Mason) M.; grad. Kemper Mil. Sch., Boonville, Mo., 1905; studied Art Student League, 1909; m. Aileen Fletcher, Sept. 7, 1913 (dec.); m. 2d, Eleanor Fletcher Brown, Aug. 7, 1937. Associate prof., Scripps Coll. and Grad. Sch., Claremont, Cal. Represented Bklyn. Mus., Albright Art Gallery, Buffalo, Cleve. Mus. Arts, Detroit Inst. Arts, Corcoran Gallery, Washington; Whitney Mus. of Am. Art; Met. Mus. of Art; museums of St. Louis, Cin., Indpls., Toledo, San Antonio, Kansas City, Richmond, and others. Hon. mention Carnegie Inst., 1923; Clark prize, Corcoran Gallery, 1928; hon. mention and Garden Club prize, Carnegie Inst., 1930; Temple gold medal, Pa. Acad. of Fine Arts, 1937; gold medal Paris Internat. Exposition, 1937; Purchase prize, Pamona, 1940. Mem. Nat. Acad. Design, Nat. Inst. Arts and Letters. Address: 4239 Via Padova, Claremont, Cal. Deceased.

McGARVEY, Robert Neill, ex-congressman; born Philadelphia , Pennsylvania, August 14, 1888; son John W. and Mary (O'Neill) McGarvey; student Saint Paul's Acad.; married Marie Ryan, Sept. 15, 1920; children—Robert J., Mary (Mrs. Jean P. Turping), J. Neill, Anne (Mrs. William J. Mann). Ayleen M. (Mrs. Leonard G. Allen). With firm of Parrish & Co., Phila. since 1920; asso. with New York stock exchange houses. Mem. 80th Congress (1947-49), 2d Pa. Dist. Republican. Roman Catholic. Home: 2071 N. 63d St., Phila. 31. Office: 1421 Chestnut St., Phila. Died June 28. 1952.

McGAUGHY, James Ralph (māk-goi), author and lecturer; b. Chesterville, O., Sept. 4, 1888; s. Samuel and Anna Mary (McNay) McG.; A.B., Park Coll., Parkville, Mo., 1912; A.M., Columbia U., 1921, Ph. D., 1924; Ed.D., Ohio Wesleyan U., Delaware, O., 1937; m. Nellie Emerson, 1912; children—Howard Emerson, Eleanor Lucile (Mrs. George McGarrity), Alice Irene (Mrs. Raymond O'Connor), James Edward. Superintendent of schools, Sparta, Ohio, 1907-09; instructor mathematics and physics, Ohio Wesleyan University, 1912-15; supt. schs., Belle Center, O., 1915-20; dir. Nat. Com. for Chamber of Commerce Cooperation with Pub. Schs., N.Y. City, 1920-21; asso. in ednl. adminstrn., Teachers Coll., Columbia, 1921-23, asst. prof. edn., 1923-25, asso. prof., 1925-26, prof. edn., 1926-41; prof. emeritus of edn., 1941—. Mem. N.E.A., Am. Assn. Sch. Administrators, Am. Assn. Advancement Science, Dept. of Elementary Sch. Prins. of N.E.A., Am. Civil Liberties Union, Union for Democratic Action, League for Industrial Democracy, Phi Delta Kappa, Kappa Delta Pi. Presbyterian. Mason. Author: Know and Help Your Schools, 1921; the Fiscal Administration of City School Systems, 1924; Teachers' Salaries in New York City Schools, 1927; An Evaluation of the Elementary School, 1937. Editor of The New Wonder World (11 vols.), 1932; editorial adviser of Our America, 1937, Baker and Baker's Readers for Grades, 4, 5, 6, 1938. Contbr. articles to ednl. jours. Home: Chesterville, O. Died June 21, 1954; buried Maple Grove Cemetery, Chesterville.

McGEE, Clifford W., mfr.; b. Bklyn., 1873; ed. Sheffield Sci. Sch., Yale, 1893; chmn., dir. Chesebrough Mfg. Co. (now Chesebrough-Ponds Co.), N.Y. C., ret. 1953. Former gov. Meth. Hosp., Bklyn. Mem. Yale Engring. Soc. Club: University. Home: 1 Orchard Av., North Plainfield, N.J. Office: 17 State St., N.Y.C. 4. Died Aug. 12, 1958.

McGIFFIN, William J(unkin), newspaper pub.; b. Great Falls, Mont., July 8, 1893; s. Nathaniel and May (Junkin) McG.; ed. in pub. schs., Washington; m. Nell Florence Belz, Jan. 27, 1920; children—Mona (Mrs. W. J. Brehm), Thomas C. Began newspaper career with The Ledger, Fairfield, Ia., 1911, part owner and pub., 1916-19; pub. Ft. Madison (Ia.) Evening Democrat since 1919, pres. The Evening Democrat Co. since 1920; organized W. J. Mc Giffin Newspaper Co., Kansas City, Mo., 1924, pres. 1924—; pres. and pub. Industrial Post of Bell and Maywood, Cal. and affiliated newspapers; pres. The Arizona Daily Sun, Flagstaff, Bulletin Printing Co. Huntington Park, Cal., The Downey (Cal.) Shopping News, The Coconino Sun (weekly), Flagstaff, Ariz., The Press (weekly), The Hollydale Press, The Atlantic Avenue Press, (all in South Gate, Cal.), The Post-Star, Bell Gardens, Cal., Rivera Independent, Rivera, Cal. Served as sgt. U.S. Army, 1917-19. Mem. Am. Legion, Vets. Fgn. Wars. Republican. Methodist. Mason, Elk. Died Nov. 4, 1955; buried Inglewood (Cal.) Cemetery.

McGILL, William L(awrence), govt. ofcl., former educator; b. Corsicana, Tex., Aug. 19, 1899; s. James William and O'Neta (Kinsolving) McG.; A.B., U. Tex., 1922, M.J., 1923. Mng. editor Corsicana (Tex.) Daily Sun, 1917-18; bus. mgr. Tex. Student Publs., Inc., U. Tex., 1923-27, lectr. journalism, 1925-37, dir. Tex. Student Publs., Inc., 1927-40, chmn. U. pub. relations, 1928-40, prof. journalism,

1937-47 (on leave of absence, 1940 46); dir. U. Centennial Expn., 1935-36; acting exec. officer Tex. Meml. Mus., 1937; coordinator Tex. Industrialization Program, 1940-41; coordinator Tex. Development Program, state def. coordinator, office of gov., 1941-44; overseas service with A.R.C., 1944-46; exec. sec. to gov. of Tex., 1947-51; state coordinator of Def. and Disaster Relief, 1951—. Chmn. Tex. Meml. Stadium financial campaign; vice chmn. Tex. Meml. Union State campaign; chpt. chmn. A.R.C., Travis County, Tex., 1947; mem. bd. govs. Am. Nat. Red Cross, 1947-50; mem. Tex. Atomic Energy Com. Mem. Nat. Assn. State and Territorial Civil Def. Dirs. (pres. 1955-56), U. Tex. Ex-Students Assn. (past pres.), Sigma Delta Chi. Democrat. Methodist. Mason (K.T.; Shriner) Rotarian. Home: 2200 Stamford Lane. Office: Capitol Sta., Austin, Tex. Died Jan. 5, 1959; buried Oakwood Cemetery, Corsicana, Tex.

McGILVARY, Evander Bradley (măk-gĭl'vȧ-rĭ), emeritus prof.; b. Bangkok, Siam, July 19, 1864; son Rev. Daniel (D.D.) and Sophia Royce (Bradley) McG.; A.B., Davidson Coll., 1884; A.M., Princeton 1888; fellow Princeton Theol. Sem., 1889-90; Ph.D., U. Cal., 1897; m. Elizabeth Allen Paton, June 16, 1891 (died 1935); children—Margaret (Mrs. David Zimmerman), Paton (dec.). Translator, Presbyn. Bd. Fgn. Missions in Siam, 1891-94; grad. student, instr. and asst. prof., U. Cal., 1894-99; Sage prof. of ethics Cornell U., 1899-1905; prof. and chmn. dept. of philosophy U. Wis., 1905-34; Howison lectr., 1927, Mills lectr. in philosophy, 1928, U. Cal., Carus lectr., 1939. Mem. Am. Philos. Assn. (pres. 1912-13). Western Philos. Assn. (pres. 1910-11), A.A.A.S., Kappa Alpha (Southern), Phi Beta Kappa (hon.). Clubs: University, Dining, X-Club(Madison). Translated (with mother) Matthew, Luke, John, Acts of Apostles into Lao dialect, Siamese, 1892-94. Contbr. to New Internat. Ency., Internat. Year Book, Mind, Philos. Rev., Jour. of Philosophy, Hibbert Journal, Proc. of 6th Internat. Congress of Philosophy, U. Cal. Publs., Internat. Jour. of Ethics, etc. Address: 1920 Arlington Pl., Madison 5, Wis. Died Sept. 11, 1953; buried Forest Lawn Cemetery, Madison, Wis.

McGILVREY, John Edward, educator; b. Hollandsburg, Ind., Jan. 8, 1867; s. John and Mary Jane (Wimmer) McG.; diploma Ind. State Normal Sch., 1890; A.B., Ind. U., 1895; Pd.D., Miami, 1915; m. Mary Kelly, June 6, 1894. Tchr. rural schs., Ind., 3 yrs.; asst. Ind. State Normal Sch., 1890-91; prin. Paris (Ill.) High Sch., 1891-94, Freeport High Sch., 1895-96; asst. prof. pedagogy and high sch. visitor, U. Ill., 1896-99; prin. Cleve. City Normal Sch., 1899-1908; supt. City Farm Sch. for Boys, Hudson, O., 1908-09, head dept. edn., 1909-11, acting pres., 1911-12, Western Ill. State Normal Sch., Macomb, Ill.; pres. Kent (O.) State Normal Coll. (now Kent State U.), 1911-26, pres. emeritus, 1934—. Mem. N.E.A., Nat. Council Normal Sch. Pres.'s. Universalist. Club: City (Cleve.). Address: 956 Stow St., Kent, O. Died Oct. 3, 1945; buried Standing Rock Cemetery, Kent.

McGINTY, Francis Patrick, banker; b. Oneida, N.Y., Oct. 1, 1888; s. Patrick Francis and Mary Agnes (Dempsey) McG.; student Utica Cath. Acad. and Assumption Acad., Utica, N.Y.; m. Caroline F. Draschil, Aug. 27, 1913 (dec.); children—Francis, Robert, Caroline Jane; m. 2d, Kathleen T. Carney, July 16, 1924; children—Mary Therese, Kathleen, Peter, Terence. Was with (N.Y.) Utica City Nat. Bank, advancing to pres., 1903-25; v.p. Oneida County Trust Co., 1925-28; v.p. First Bank & Trust Co., Utica, 1928-30, pres., 1930-31; pres. First Citizens Bank and Trust Co. (merger of First Bank & Trust Co., Citizens Trust Co. and Utica Trust and Deposit Co.), 1931-40. First Bank & Trust Co. of Utica, 1940—. Republican. K.C. Clubs: Fort Schuyler, Yahnundasis Golf. City Club. Home: 121 Proctor Blvd. Office: First Bank and Trust Co., Utica, N.Y. Died June 5, 1949.

McGLYNN, Frank, actor; b. San Francisco, Oct. 26, 1866; s. Frank and Mary H. (Buckley) M.; ed. convent and pub. schs., Hastings Law Sch., and 7 yrs. in law office of Matthew I. Sullivan, San Francisco; m. Rose O'Byrne, Dec. 16, 1900; children—Mrs. Mary Rose O'Herron, Frank, Thomas, Grace, Helen, Virginia. Admitted to bar, 1894, and practiced in San Francisco. Began stage career in New York, 1896, playing minor parts, later important roles, on the road, in stock, and in motion pictures; toured world in charge of motion pictures of Giants and White Soc, 1913-14; scored success as Abraham Lincoln, in Drinkwater's play of same name, 1919-23; playing Rabbi Judah in Steadfast, 1923-24; played Andrew Jackson in That Awful Mrs. Eaton, 1924, Ephraim Cabot in Desire Under the Elm, 1925-26 in vaudeville, 1927-28; Massawinima in His Blossom Bride; Reb. Velvele in The Broken Chain; starred in revival of Drinkwater's Abraham Lincoln, 1929-30; playing in motion pictures, 1931—. Mem. Actors' Equity Assn., Soc. Cath. Pioneers, Young Men's Inst., Cath. Actors' Guild (pres.). Club: Friars. Died May 17, 1951.

McGOLDRICK, Thomas Aloysius, physician; b. Bklyn., Sept. 13, 1874; s. Lawrence and Mary (McGoldrick) McG.; A.B., Manhattan Coll., N.Y.C., 1893, A.M., 1895, LL.D., 1935; M.D., L.I. Coll. Medicine, Bklyn., 1896; m. Rita Connell, Nov. 26, 1912; children—Mrs. Mary M. McGee, Thomas A., Lawrence S., Joseph F., Mrs. Rita M. Cuddihy. Intern Bklyn. Hosp., 1898; engaged in practice as physician, Bklyn., 1898—; physician in chief St. Peter's Hosp., Bklyn., 1920; dir. Medicine St. Anthony's Hosp., Woodhaven, N.Y., 1925; med. dir. Welfare Hosp., open div., N.Y.C., 1938-45; chief med. officer N.Y. City Police, 1930-37. Vice pres. A.M.A., 1947-48. Decorated Knight of Saint Gregory by Pope Pius XII, 1944. Roman Catholic. Address: 294 Clinton Av., Bklyn. Died Mar. 8, 1956.

McGOORTY, John P(atrick) (mȧ-gōōr'tĭ). ex-judge; b. Conneaut, O.; s. Peter and Mary (Gaffney) McG.; grad. Chicago Coll. Law, 1892; LL.B., Lake Forest U., 1893; m. Mary E. Wiggins, Nov. 30, 1893 (died Feb. 11, 1920); children—John Patrick, Mary Francis (dec.), Margaret Theresa, Elizabeth Barbara, Robert Edward, Peter Joseph; m. 2d, Florence E. Carey, Sept. 7, 1921 (died Sept. 3, 1944). Admitted to Ill. bar, 1892, and began practice at Chicago, Ill.; was mem. McGoorty & Pollock. Mem. Ill. Ho. of Rep., 1896-1906 (minority leader of House 1899); formerly mem. Chicago Charter Conv.; judge, Circuit Court, Ill., 1911-21 (assigned to Appellate Court, 1915-16); judge, Superior Court, Cook County, 1923-47; read Chancery Division, 1945-47; chief justice Criminal Ct. Cook County, 1930-31; retired, Dec. 1947; Master in Chancery, Superior Ct., 1947. Maj., judge advocate Organized Reserves, U.S. Army (now retired). Mem. exec. com. Catholic Charities; regional Loyalty Bd., U.S.; chmn. Chicago Recreation Commn.; sec., John Howard Assn.; hon. chairman of Chicago Round Table Conf. of Christians and Jews; vice president Crime Prevention, Incorporated. Mem. Am., Ill. State and Chicago bar assns., Chicago Assn. Commerce (Ill. relations com.), Ohio Soc., Wis. Soc., Travelers Aid Society of Chicago. Mem. K.C., Catholic Order of Foresters, Royal Arcanum, Hibernians. Democrat. Clubs: Chicago Athletic, Iroquois, Irish Fellowship, Forty, White Lake Golf, Executives, Olympia Fields Country. Jewish War Veterans Americanization Award, 1948, Blind Service Assn. honorary citation. Home: 929 E. 45th St. Address: 105 S. La Salle St., Chgo. Died Aug. 23, 1953.

McGOVERN, James Lawrence, editor; b. Bridgeport, Conn., Nov. 13, 1869; s. Thomas and Anne (Coyne) McG.; ed. pub. and Cath. schs.; m. Cecilia Prendergast O'Hara, Sept. 23, 1896 (died Oct. 11, 1937); children—Cecelia, James L., Mary (Mrs. Fred J. Berger), Anne Hara (WAC), William L. (dec.), Virginia (Mrs. Thomas A. Mulligan), Roger (dec.), Martha (dec.), Julia (dec.). Learned trade of granite cutter; reporter Bridgeport Morning Union, 1891-92; reporter, city editor, mng. editor Bridgeport Evening Farmer, 1892-1914; collector of customs, Dist. No. 6, Conn., 1914-22; sec., dir. Bridgeport Times Pub. Co. during 2d term as collector; became editor Bridgeport Times-Star (formerly Bridgeport Farmer), 1923; now asso. editor Bridgeport Post and Bridgeport Telegram. Del. World Press Conf., Mexico City, Mex., 1933; pres. Asso. Press Group Newspapers of Conn., 1933-47; apptd. by Pres. Franklin D. Roosevelt mem. U.S. Assay Commn., 1938; apptd. by Gov. Cross chmn. Will Rogers Meml. Com. for Conn.; past chmn. Bridgeport chpt. interfaith orgn. Christians and Jews; chmn. Cath. Charitable Bur.; mem. exec. com. Bridgeport Community Chest; wartime chmn. Fairfield Co. Salvage Com.; dir. Newington (Conn.) Home for Crippled Children; dir. Conn. State C. of C. Mem. adv. bds. Conn. Cancer Soc. and Jr. Coll. of Conn., Bridgeport, Conn. Mem. Am. Soc. Newspaper Editors, Bridgeport Forum, Quill and Scroll (hon.), etc. Democrat. Mem. K.C., Elks (past chmn. Grand Lodge activities com.; chmn. War Vets. Commn. for Conn.). Clubs: Rotary, Algonquin, Laurel of Conn.; Catholic Club of New York; American-Irish Historical (N.Y.). Home: 865 Clinton Av. Office: 410 State St., Bridgeport, Conn. Died Feb. 3, 1952.

McGOVERN, Patrick Alphonsus, bishop; b. Omaha, Neb., Oct. 14, 1872; s. Patrick and Alice (McGearty) McG.; A.B., Creighton U., Omaha, 1891; completed theol. course, Mt. St. Mary's Sem., Cin. Ordained R.C. priest, 1895; pastor St. Philomena's Cathedral, Omaha (native parish), 1898-1907, St. Peter's Ch., Omaha, 1907-12; prominent in civic life during that time and mem. board of dirs. Associated Charities; apptd. by Pope Pius X, bishop of Cheyenne, Jan. 18, 1912, consecrated Apr. 11, 1912. Address: 3106 Carey Av., Cheyenne, Wyo. Died Nov. 8, 1951; buried Cheyenne.

McGOWAN, Arthur C., mfg. exec.; b. N.Y.C., Sept. 25, 1892; s. Thomas H. and Ida J. (Craft) McG.; student pub. schs.; m. Irene D. McCabe, Aug. 2, 1919; 1 son, Arthur C. With Wyandotte Worsted Co., 1912—, sec., dir., 1925—, treas., 1949—, pres., 1952—; pres. treas., dir. Gt. Eastern Fire Ins. Co.; v.p., dir. Stoney-Mueller Co., The Lyndhurst Chemical Corp.; chmn. bd., pres., dir. Peoples Nat. Bank and Trust Co., White Plains, N.Y., 1930-33. Hon. trustee White Plains Hosp.; former trustee St. Bernards Ch., White Plains. Served as 1st lt. Inf., U.S. Army, World War I. Clubs: Union League, National Republican (N.Y.C.); Westchester Country (Rye, N.Y.); Westchester Hills Golf (White Plains); Skyton (Pa.). Home: 180 Soundview Av., White Plains, N.Y. Office: 1071 Av. of Americas, N.Y.C. 18. Died Nov. 22, 1958.

McGOWAN, Edwin W., wool mfr.; b. N.Y.C., Dec. 28, 1894; s. Thomas H and Ida J. (Craft) McG; B.S., Dartmouth, 1917; m Irma K. Gilman, May 8, 1920; children—Edwin W., Thomas C. Woolen mill apprentice, 1919-22; asst. mgr. Wyandotte Worsted Co., 1923-33, v.p., gen. mgr., 1933-52, dir. since 1923, exec. v.p. since 1952. Served with A.E.F., U.S. Army, 1917-19. Awarded Purple Heart. Mem. Nat. Assn. Wool Mfrs., Beta Theta Pi. Republican. Roman Catholic. Clubs: Brae Burn Country; Algonquin (Boston). Home: Waterville. Office: Wyandotte Worsted Co., Waterville, Me. Died May 12, 1955.

McGRATH, John Joseph, surgeon; b. N.Y.C., Apr. 24, 1868; s. Hugh and Anne (Eary) M.; M.D., Coll. Phys. and Surg. (Columbia), 1889; m. Helene Bartenwerffer, 1900. Ex-pres. bd. of trustee Bellevue and Allied Hospitals; prof. on surgery and vis. surgeon Polyclinic Hosp.; cons. surgeon Fordham, Columbus, Unity, People's and Norwalk Gen. hosps.; formerly prof. surgery Fordham. Fellow A.C.S.; mem. A.M.A., Med. Soc. State of N.Y. Lt. col. Med. R.C. Author: McGrath's Textbook on Operative Surgery. Home: 22 Inlet Terrace, Belmar, N.J. Died May 18, 1953.

McGRATH, Joseph F., bishop; b. County Kilkenny Ireland; theol. edn. Grand Seminaire, Montreal, Can. Ordained priest, R.C. Ch., Dec. 21, 1895; consecrated bishop of Baker City, Ore., Mar. 25, 1919. Address: Box 879, Baker, Ore. Died Apr. 12, 1950; buried Mt. Hope Cemetery, Baker.

McGRATH, William H(enry), pub. utility executive; b. Quincy, Mass., July 26, 1879; s. Henry and Katherine (Hagen) McG.; grad. Adams Acad., Quincy, 1897; B.S., Harvard, 1901; m. Nan M. Turner, Oct. 4, 1906; children—Marian E. (Mrs. Wm. Pendleton Ford), Katherine T. (Mrs. F. B. Collins). Electrical engineer with Stone & Webster, Boston, Mass., 1901-02; elec. engr. Houghton County (Mich.) Electric Light Co., and Houghton County Street Ry. Co., 1902-05, mgr., 1905-09; asst. gen. mgr. Minneapolis Gen. Electric Co., 1909-12; mgr. for Stone & Webster in State of Wash., 1913; became executive vice president and director Puget Sound Power & Light Co., 1931, now retired. Director Diamond Ice & Storage Co., Pacific Nat. Bank. Mem. American Inst. E.E., Am. Econ. Assn., Am. Acad. Polit. and Social Science. Republican. Clubs: University (pres. 1931 and 1932), Rainier, Seattle Golf, Harvard (ex-pres.). Home: Yarrow Point, Bellavue, Wash. Died Mar. 1, 1954.

McGRAW, Curtis Whittlesey, publisher; b. Madison, N.J., Oct. 13, 1895; s. James H. and Mildred (Whittlesey) M.; grad. Lawrenceville Sch.; B.S., Princeton, 1920; m. Elizabeth Woodwell, May 7, 1921; 1 dau., Elizabeth Murtland (Mrs. George R. Webster). With McGraw-Hill Book Co., 1920—, asst. to treas., 1922-25, sec. and asst. treas., 1925-27, v.p., treas. and dir., 1927-50, chmn. bd. since 1950; pres., chmn. bd., dir. McGraw-Hill Pub. Co.; chmn. bd., McGraw-Hill Internat. Corp., McGraw-Hill Co. of Calif.; pres., dir. McGraw-Hill Bldg. Corp.; v.p., dir. Newton Falls Paper Mill; dir. First Nat. Bank of Princeton, Dragon Cement Co. Treas., dir. Princeton U. Press; pres., trustee Princeton Hosp. Trustee Nat. Soc. Crippled Children & Adults, Inc. Mem. Am. Book Pubs. Council (pres. 1948-50, dir. since 1946), Mag. Pubs. Assn., (dir.). Capt. and maj. 320th Inf., 80th Div., World War I. Republican. Presbyterian. Clubs: Union League, University, Players, Princeton (N.Y. City); Pine Valley Golf, Springdale Golf (Princeton); Fishers Island. Home: 130 Hodge Rd, Princeton, N.J. Office: 330 W. 42d St., N.Y.C. 36. Died Sept. 10, 1953; buried Princeton (N.J.) Cemetery.

McGREGOR, Alexander Grant (mȧ-grĕg'ôr), mech. engr.; b. Raymond, Kan., Mar. 1, 1880; s. Donald and Ada A. (Cole) McG.; B.S. in Mech. Engring., U. Mont., 1902; m. Beulah M. Morgan, June 15, 1905; children—Grant Morgan, Donald Thomas, John Porter, James Bennett; m. 2d, Harriet Rankin Sedman, July 11, 1935. Asst. supt. power plants and testing engr. Anaconda Copper Mining Co., 1902-08; mech. and elec. engr., design of Tooele plant, Internat. Smelting Co., 1909-10; as mem. firm Repath & McGregor, 1911-14, located and designed Ariz. Copper Co.'s smelting works, at Clifton, Ariz.; designed and directed constrn. Calumet and Ariz. Mining Co.'s smelting works, Douglas, Ariz.; located and made prelim. designs of Inspiration Consol. Copper Co.'s main hoisting shafts, etc., also its leaching plant; made general layout of United Verde Copper Co.'s smelting works. Practiced alone, 1915—, locating, designing and building many important mining and metallurgical plants, including Internat. Smelting Co.'s works, at Miami, Ariz., New Cornelia Copper Co.'s leaching plant and works at Ajo, Ariz.; United Verde Extension Mining Co.'s smelting works and mining plant, at Jerome, Ariz.; Cerro de Pasco Copper Corp.'s smelting works in Peru, S.A.;

Phelps-Dodge smelting units at Douglas. Cons. engr. in connection with new plants Internat. Nickel Co., Roan Antelope Copper Mines, Ltd., Mufulira Copper Mines, Ltd., Trepca Mines, Ltd. Asso. mem. Naval Cons. Bd. during World War I; in World War II cons. engr. to Brit. Ministry of Aircraft Prodn. and to Non-Ferrous Mineral Development Control. Mem. Am. Soc. M.E., Am. Inst. Mining and Metall. Engrs., Am. Soc. (London). Club: Royal Wimbledon Golf (Wimbledon, Surrey). Author: Right wages and Abundance; Collective Bargaining and Decadence; Britain's Way Out. Contbr. on econ. problems. Home: 89 Troy Court, Kensington, London W8. Address: Selection Trust Bldg., Mason's Av., Coleman St., London, E.C.2, Eng. Died Mar. 4, 1949.

McGREGOR, J. Harry, congressman; b. Unionport, O., Sept. 30, 1896; s. George and Elizabeth (Minnis) McG.; ed. West Lafayette Coll., 1915-16, Oberlin Coll., 1916-17; m. Twila Cox, May 29, 1918; children—Constance Louise (Mrs. Monroe Horst), Betty Jane (Mrs. Warde Butler), Harry Laird. Began as lumber dealer 1918; became contractor after World War. Mem. 76th, 77th, 78th, 79th to 85th Congresses, 17th Ohio Dist. Mem. West Lafayette School Board, 8 years, president Board of Trade, 8 years; mem. Ohio Ho. of Rep., 6 yrs. (majority floor leader 1939). Served with field artillery, U.S. Army, World War. Past commander American Legion. Republican. Member Methodist Protestant Ch. (trustee 10 years). Mason (33°, dist. dep. grand master 4 yrs.), Elk, Moose, Grange, Rotarian. Home: West Lafayette, O. Died Nov. 7, 1958; buried Fairfield Cemetery, West Lafayette.

McGREGOR, James Howard, zoölogist; b. Bellaire, O., July 23, 1872; s. Robert Alexander and Lucy (Watterson) McG.; B.S., Ohio State U., 1894; M.A., Columbia, 1896, Ph.D., 1899; Sc.D., 1954. Member zoöl. staff, Columbia U., 1897-—, professor zoölogy, 1924-42, prof. emeritus since 1942; mem. staff Marine Biological Laboratory, Woods Hole, Mass., 1899-1906; asso. in human anatomy, Am. Museum Natural History, since 1916. Fellow A.A.A.S., New York Zoöl. Society; mem. Am. Soc. Zoölogists, Am. Soc. Naturalists, Am. Society of Mammalogists, Am. Association of Physical Anthropologists, Soc. Vertebrate Paleontol., Soc. for Study of Evolution, American Philosophical Society, Sigma Xi, Phi Beta Kappa. Mem. Associé Étranger, Soc. d'Anthropologie de Paris. Specializes in study of primates and fossil races of man. Club: Explorers. Contributor various zoöl. papers, especially on reptilian and primate paleontology. Address: Columbia U., N.Y.C. 27. Died Nov. 14, 1954; buried Rose Hill Cemetery, Bellaire, O.

McGRIGOR, Sir Rhoderick, naval officer; b. York, Eng., Apr. 12, 1893; s. Maj. Gen. C.R.R. McGrigor and Ada (Bower) McG.; student Royal Naval Colls. Osborne, Dartmouth, 1906-09; LL.D., St. Andrews U., 1953, Aberdeen U., 1955; m. Gwendoline Glyn Greville, 1931; children—John, Andrew. Served European war, 1914-18; participated Dardanelles Campaign, Battle of Jutland; capt. 4th Destroyer Flotilla, 1936-38; chief staff, Comdr. in Chief China, 1939; comdr. His Majesty's Ship Renown, Malta convoys, Operations Mediterranean and Atlantic, 1941; Lord Commr. Admiralty, asst. chief naval staff, 1941-43; comdr. naval forces at capture Pantellaria, Invasion of Sicily, flag officer Sicily, Taranto, Adriatic, 1943; comdr. 1st Cruiser Sqdn. Home Fleet Aircraft Carriers, Norwegian Coast and Russian convoys, 1944-45; Lord Commr. Admiralty, vice chief naval staff, 1945-47; comdr. in chief Home Fleet, 1948-50, Plymouth, 1950-51; Lord Commr. Admiralty, First Sea Lord and Chief of Naval Staff, 1951-55; now Admiral of the Fleet; lord rector Aberdeen U., 1954-57. Decorated Knight Grand Cross of the Bath, Distinguished Service Order. Home: Hopewell Lodge, Tarland, Aberdeenshire, Scotland. Died Dec. 4, 1959.

McGUIGAN, F. H., ry. official; b. Cleveland, O. Entered ry. service as water boy on constrn. of Erie & Pittsburg (Pa.) R.R., 1863; held various positions until 1880; entered service of Wabash R.R. as foreman constrn. and div. roadmaster, 1880-5; gen. roadmaster lines west of Miss. River, 1885-8; supt. western div., 1888-95; apptd. gen. supt. Grand Trunk Ry., Feb. 15, 1896, mgr., Mar. 1, 1902, 4th v.p., Jan. 1, 1905; v.p. Great Northern Ry., 1907; resigned. Address: St. Paul, Minn. Deceased.

McGUINNESS, Eugene Joseph (mă-gĭn'ĕs), bishop; b. Hellertown, Pa., Sept. 6, 1889; s. Daniel and Mary Elizabeth (Flood) McG.; A.B. and A.M., St. Charles Sem., Overbrook, Pa.; Ph.D., Little Rock (Ark.) Coll.; LL.D., Villanova Coll.; J.U.D., Santo Tomas, Manila, P.I. Ordained priesthood R.C. Ch.; asst. priest, Phila., 1915-17; asst. dir. of Propagation of the Faith, Phila., 1917-19; field sec. Cath. Ch. Extension Soc., 1919-21, 2d v.p., 1921-25; became 1st v.p. and gen. sec., 1925; dir. Child Apostles and Order of Martha; became exec. sec. Am. Bd. Cath. Missions, 1923; created domestic prelate by Pope Pius XI, 1929; bishop of Raleigh, N.C., 1937-44; apptd. coadjutor bishop of Oklahoma City and Tulsa, with right of succession, Nov. 11, 1944; succeeded to the See, Feb. 1, 1948. Author of religious booklets; former asso editor Extension Magazine. Address: 1521 N. Hudson St., Oklahoma City, Okla. Died Dec. 27, 1957.

McGUIRE, James K., mayor of Syracuse, N.Y., 1895-1902; b. N.Y., July 12, 1868; ed. at Christian Brothers' School, Syracuse; is a hardware mcht. Elected mayor at 26; re-elected mayor, 1897, and again, 1899, chmn. Dem. State Exec. Com. of N.Y. Has lectured on political and social problems throughout U.S. Address: Syracuse, N.Y. Died June 1923.

McGUIRE, Louis David, surgeon; b. Wisner, Neb., Sept. 15, 1893; s. Richard Peter and Margaret Ellen (McMahon) McG.; M.D., Creighton U., 1917, B.S., 1919; M.S. in Surgery, U. Minn., 1924; m. Margaret Lucile Rau., Apr. 16, 1925; children—Richard George, Terence Francis, Laurence David, Michael Donald. Practiced in Omaha, 1924-—; with Creighton Med. Sch., 1924-—, prof. surgery, 1953-—; organizer surg. group McGuire, Johnson, McCarthy & Gatewood, 1946; attending surgeon St. Joseph's, St. Catherine's hosps.; surg. staff Children's Meml. Hosp. Regent Creighton U. Served as 1st lt. M.C., U.S. Army, 1918-19. Recipient first Award of Merit, Am. Med. Edn. Found., 1953. Diplomate Am. Bd. Surgery. Fellow A.C.S., Internat. Coll. Surgeons (regent for Neb., 1950-52); mem. A.M.A., Neb., Med. Assn., Douglas Co. Med. Soc. (pres. 1952), Creighton U. Alumni Assn. (pres. 1947-48), Phi Rho Sigma, Alpha Sigma Nu. Home: 3921 Nicholas St. Office: Medical Arts Bldg., Omaha 2. Died Apr. 20, 1955; buried Calvary Cemetery, Omaha.

McGUIRE, Michael Francis, surgeon; b. Dec. 7, 1886; M.B., B.Ch., B.A.O., U. Coll., Dublin, Ireland, 1911. Mater Misericordia Hosp., Dublin, 1913; prof. clin. surgery Loyola U., Chicago, since 1925; sr. attending surgeon Mercy Hosp., chief of staff 1943-47. Home: 4950 Chicago Beach Dr., Chicago. Office: 30 N. Michigan Av., Chgo. Died Sept. 1951.

McHALE, Kathryn, psychologist educator, adminstr.; b. Logansport, Ind.; d. Martin and Margaret (Farrell) McHale; B.S., Columbia, 1919, A.M., 1920, Ph.D., 1926; L.H.D. (hon.) Brown University, 1941, Russell Sage College, Troy, N.Y., 1942, MacMurray College, 1946. Instructor in edn. Goucher Coll., Baltimore, Md., 1920-22, asst. prof., 1922-26, asso. prof. 1926-27, prof. 1927-35, non-resident prof., 1935-—; prof. edn., summers Columbia, 1918-26, U. of Minn., 1928; gen. dir. Am. Assn. University Women, 1929-50 (dir.); apptd. mem. Subversive Activities Control Bd., 1950, reapptd., 1952. Trustee Purdue, 1936-46. Mem. Alfred I. du Pont Radio Awards com., 1944-46. Chairman citizen's federal committee on education U.S. Office of Education, 1947-50; member bd. educational advisers Nat. Found. for Education in American citizenship; member American Assn. for Adult Edn.; mem. U.S. Nat. Commn. for UNESCO, 1946-50, exec. com. mem., 1946-48; mem. adv. bd. Home Library Found.; mem. Jane Adams Achievement Award Committee. Mem. hon. committee, Am. Women's Hospitals. Fellow A.A.A.S.; mem. Am. Assn. Univ. Profs., American Psychol. Assn., Nat. Society for Scientific Study of Edn., National Society Coll. Tchrs. of Edn., Kappa Delta Pi, Delta Kappa Gamma (hon.). Author: Comparative Psychology and Hygiene of the Overweight Child, 1926; Current Changes and Experiments in Liberal Arts Education, 1932; Housing Coll. Students, 1934; also 43 brochures, pamphlets and articles on psychol. and ednl. subjects. Home: The Broadmoor 3601 Connecticut Av. Office: Lafayette Bldg., Washington. Died Oct. 8, 1956; buried Logansport, Ind.

McHANEY, Powell B., ins. exec.; b. White Oak, Mo., June 30, 1905; s. James Flake and Eva Ann (Moore) McH.; A.B., U. of Mo., 1925; LL.B., Harvard, 1928; LL.D., Washington University, St. Louis, 1955; m. Ida Ann Clark, Apr. 8, 1933; children—Ida Ann, Martha Moore, Powell Bassett. Admitted to Mo. Bar, 1928; asso. Igoe, Carroll, Higgs & Keefe, St. Louis, 1928-32; asst. atty. gen. of Mo., 1933; counsel Mo. Ins. Dept., Jefferson City, Mo., 1933-35; specializing in ins. law, St. Louis, 1935-42; v.p., gen. counsel Gen. Am. Life Ins. Co., St. Louis, 1942-49, exec. v.p., 1950-51, pres. 1951-—, mem. bd. dirs. and exec. com., 1936-—; dir. St. Louis Insurance Corp., Transit Casualty Company, Transit Ins. and Securities Corp., Mfrs. and Merchants Indemnity Co., Gen. Contract Corp., Securities Investment Co., Anheuser-Busch, Inc.; mem. bd. dirs., mem. exec. committee Southwestern Bell Telephone Co. Sec., St. Louis U.S.O. Council, 1942-47, chmn. Service Men's Center com., 1942-47; sec., mem. Citizens' Com. supervising $44,000,000 Post War Improvements and Employment Program, St. Louis, 1944-49, chmn., 1949-55; gen. chmn. Citizens' Com. for Home Rule on Earnings Tax, 1954; chmn. ednl. com. St. Louis Bond Issue Campaign, also mem. exec. campaign com. St. Louis County Bond Issue, 1955; mem. St. Louis Fgn. Relations Com.; pres. Civic Progress, Inc., 1953-55; mem. Met. bd. YMCA; exec. bd. St. Louis council Boy Scouts Am.; trustee Jefferson Nat. Expansion Meml. Assn.; dir. Urban Redevelopment Corp. of St. Louis, St. Louis Symphony Soc., City-Country Cavalcade, Inc., United Fund Greater St. Louis, St. Louis Crime Commn. Pres. bd. curators U. of Mo., 1951-55 (pres. 1955); dir. Lindenwood Female Coll. Recipient St. Louis award, 1953-54. Mem. Inst. Life Ins. (dir., mem. exec. com.), Nat. Com. for Edn. in Family Finance, C. of C. of U.S. (ins. com.), Harvard Law Sch. Assn., Mem. Am. Life Conv. (Mo. v.p., 1948, chmn. legal sect. 1950-51, mem. exec. com.), Am. Judicature Soc., Assn. Life Ins. Counsel, Am., Mo., St. Louis bar assns., C. of C. (dir.), Phi Beta Kappa, Pi Kappa Alpha (nat. pres. 1950-52), Phi Delta Phi, Alpha Kappa Psi. Democrat. Presbyn. (elder). Mason. Clubs: Noonday, Missouri Athletic, Bogey Golf, Bellerive Country, Harvard, Key, Old Warsaw Country (St. Louis). Author articles in profl. jours. Home: 14 Exmoor Dr., St. Louis 17, Mo. Office: 1501 Locust St., St. Louis 3. Died Dec. 4, 1957; buried, Kenett, Mo.

McILROY, Malcolm Strong (măk'il-roi), engring. educator; b. Rochester, N.Y., Aug. 28, 1902; s. Samuel Hugh and Mary Frances (Strong) McI.; E.E., Cornell, 1923; Sc.D., Mass. Inst. Tech., 1947; m. Dorothy Wellington, Aug. 26, 1929; children—M. Douglas, Nancy W. Test engr. Gen. Elec. Co., Schenectady, N.Y., 1923-25; equipment inspector Brooklyn-Manhattan Transit Corp., Brooklyn, 1925-26; elec. engr. and dist. supt. Central Hudson Gas & Elec. Corp., Poughkeepsie, N.Y., 1926-37; instr., later asst. prof., Mass. Inst. Tech., 1937-47, also asst. dir. Radar Sch., 1942-45; asso. prof. elec. engring., Cornell, 1947-48, prof. since 1948; cons. to Standard Electric Time Co., Springfield, Mass., since 1950. Recipient of the John M. Goodell prize of the Am. Water Works Assn., 1950. Mem. Am. Inst. E.E., Am. Water Works Assn., American Gas Association, American Society of Engineering Edn., Sigma Xi, Tau Beta Pi, Eta Kappa Nu. Mason. Inventor McIlroy pipeline-network analyzer, 1949. Home: 419 Triphammer Rd., Ithaca, N.Y. Died Mar. 4, 1956; buried Pleasant Grove Cemetery, Ithaca.

McILVAIN, Robert Wallace, oil co. exec.; b. Cassopolis, Mich., Feb. 26, 1875; s. William Wallace and Helen Jane (Read) McI.; student high sch.; m. Jennie Belle Ikard, Dec. 26, 1905; 1 son, Robert Wallace, Jr. Rancher in N.D. and Mont., 1894-99; miner Cripple Creek, Colo., 1899-1902; engaged in oil bus., 1902-—; charge Benedum & Trees interests, La., 1908-13; conducted own bus., Okla., 1913; div. mgr. Ohio Cities Gas Co., Charleston, W.Va., 1914; pres. Columbus Producing Co., 1914-17; v.p. Ohio Cities Gas Co. (now Pure Oil Co.), 1917; v.p. charge all producing divs. and properties, domestic and fgn. Pure Oil Co., hdqrs. Columbus, O., 1918-26, Chgo., 1926-—; pres., dir. Orinoco Oil Co., operating in Venezuela, S.A. Clubs: Skyline, Chicago, Lexington Country, Idle our Country, Iroquois Hunt and Polo. Home: 1448 Lake Shore Dr. Office: 35 E. Wacker Dr., Chgo. Died Feb. 16, 1959.

McINERNEY, Francis Xavier, naval officer; born Cheyenne, Wyo., Mar. 28, 1899; s. Thomas and Phyllis (O'Neill) McI.; student U. of Colo., 1916-17; B.S., U.S. Naval Acad., 1920; LL.B., George Washington U., 1935; m. Katharine Hammann, May 20, 1924; children—Joan, Robert. Commd. ensign, U.S. Navy, 1920, and advanced through grades to rear adm., 1947; comd. destroyer Smith, 1941, destroyer div. and squadron, 1942-43; comd. destroyers in Battle of Kula Gulf, 1943, Kolombangara and Solomons campaign, 1943; comd. battleship Washington, 1945-46, cruiser div., 1947-48. Admitted to bar U.S. Supreme Ct., D.C., 1935. Decorated Navy Cross, Silver Star Medal, Bronze Star Medal, Presidential Unit citation, Commendation ribbon with star, World War I and II medals, also various area ribbons and medals. Mem. Bar U.S. Supreme Ct. D.C., Delta Tau Delta. Clubs: Army-Navy Country (Arlington, Va.); Bohemian (San Francisco). Home: 306 E. 18th St., Cheyenne, Wyo. Died June 24, 1956; buried Ft. Rosecrans Cemetery, Point Loma, Cal.

McINNERNEY, Thomas H(enry); b. Dubuque, Ia., May 8, 1867; s. P. H. and Elizabeth (Williams) McI.; ed. U. of Ill.; LL.D., Lafayette Coll., 1935; m. Jessica Smith, Aug. 19, 1901 (died Jan. 25, 1940); married 2d Emma P. Adams, March 15, 1944. General manager Siegel Cooper Co., New York, 1906, Duffy-McInnerney Co., Rochester, N.Y., 1906-11; v.p. and treas. City Fuel Co., Consumers Co., 1912-14; pres. Hydrox Corp., 1914-23; pres. Nat. Dairy Products Corp., 1923-41, chmn. bd. 1941-52, elected chmn. Emeritus Apr. 17, 1952, now also dir. and mem. exec. com.; dir., chmn. exec. and finance com., Lehigh Valley Ry.; dir. and mem. executive com. McLellan Stores; dir. United Stores Corp., B. F. Goodrich Co., N.J., Ind. & Ill. R.R., Distillers Corp.-Seagrams, Ltd., Metropolitan Life Insurance Company (member welfare committee). Vice-president Northeastern Division, United States Chamber of Commerce, 1939-41, dir., 1938-41; v.p. and dir. Am. Lyric Theatre; president and director of Fifth & 63d St. Corp.; director N.Y. Osteopathic Clinic; former mem. Nat. Assn. Mfrs. cordinating com. and on agrl. cooperation; mem. com. on arbitration, N.Y. Stock Exchange; mem. Anti-Syphilis Com. of Am. Hygiene Assn.; chmn. Selected Gifts Com. of Greater New York Fund, 1938; chmn. Foods Div. N.Y. Emergency Unemployment Relief, 1932; served at various times as chairman of Foods and Dairies div. for fund raising drives of organizations such as Salvation Army,

N.Y. City Cancer Com., Am. Red Cross, Y.M.C.A., Y.W.C.A., U.S.O.; mem. com. for Study of Organization of N.Y. Stock Exchange (The Conway Com.), 1938. Mem. bd. dirs. Met. Opera Assn.; trustee and chmn. finance com., Lafayette Coll.; dir., mem. exec. and finance coms., gen. sponsor pre-Fair sale of tickets, N.Y. World's Fair. Mem. Soc. of Genesee, Pilgrims. Grad. member, Business Advisory Council for the Department of Commerce. Episcopalian. Clubs: Chicago, New York Athletic, Madison Square Garden, Bankers (board of governors), Metropolitan (board of governors), Turf and Field (New York); Round Hill (Port Chester, N.Y.); Blind Brook (Greenwich). Home: Greenwich, Conn. Office: 260 Madison Av., N.Y.C. 16. Died Sept. 30, 1952; buried, Putnam Cemetery, Greenwich, Conn.

McINTIRE, Paul Goodloe, philanthropist; b. Charlottesville, Va., May 28, 1860; s. George Malcolm and Catherine (Clarke) McI.; ed. U. Va.; m. Anna Deering Rhodes, 1921; 1 dau., Charlotte (by 1st wife). Brokerage bus., Chgo. and N.Y., many yrs. Donor U. Va., McIntire Amphitheatre, wing of Hosp., schs. of Music, Architecture, Commerce and Finance, also George Rogers Clark Monument; donor library to city, 2 city parks, statue of Robert E. Lee and Stonewall Jackson (both in City of Charlottesville), also monument to Lewis and Clark. Presbyn. Mem. Phi Beta Kappa. Home: Charlottesville, Va. Died July 1, 1952; buried Maplewood Cemetery, Charlottesville.

McINTIRE, Ross T., (măk'ĭn-tīr), former surgeon gen., U.S.N.; b. Salem, Ore., Aug. 11, 1889; s. Charles Thaddeus and Ada (Thompson) McI.; M.D., Willamette U., Salem, Ore., 1912; student U. Ore., 1907-12; post grad. student Washington U., St. Louis, 1921, U. Pa., 1928; m. Pauline Palmer, Jan. 18, 1923. Began practice of medicine, Oregon, 1912; commd. lt. (j.g.), Med. Corps, U.S. Navy, 1917, comdr., 1934, vice admiral, 1944; surgeon gen. of the Navy and chief Bureau Medicine and Surgery, 1938-46; specialist in ophthalmology and otolaryngology; instr. Naval Hosp., Washington, 1931-38; White House physician, 1933-45; chmn. president's com. Employment of Physically Handicapped, 1947-54; exec. dir. Internat. Coll. of Surgeons, 1955—. Fellow A.C.S.; mem. Am. Surg. Assn., A.M.A., Assn. Mil. Surgeons. Methodist. Mason (Shriner). Clubs: Army and Navy, Burning Tree (Washington). Home: 825 Adella Av., Coronado, Cal. Office: 1516 Lake Shore Dr., Chgo. Died Dec. 1959.

McINTOSH, Alexander Angus, ret. editor; b. Ontario, Can., 1874; s. Duncan C. and Margaret (Dougal) McI.; ed. pub. schs. of Ontario; m. Jean Thomson, 1902; 1 son, John. Reporter Syracuse (N.Y.) Post, 1895; mng. editor Syracuse Post-Standard, 1904-10; mem. editorial staff Toronto (Can.) Globe, 1910-13; asso. editor London, Ont. Advertiser, 1913-18; dir. indsl. relations men's clothing industry, Toronto, 1918-26; editorial writer, Toronto Globe, 1926-36; editor-in-chief, Toronto Globe and later Mail, 1936-48, retired, 1948. Presbyn. Home: Five Lauder Av., Toronto 10, Ont., Can. Died July 3, 1950; buried St. Mary's Cemetery.

McINTOSH, Arthur Tuttle, real estate; b. Clear Lake, Ia., Mar. 28, 1877; s. Gilbert Blodgett and Rose May (Tuttle) McI.; B.S., Northwestern U., 1900; m. Mabel Hannah, July 28, 1910 (died 1932); children—Arthur T., Jr., Alexander (died in infancy), Jane, Gilbert Blodgett, II, Mary; m. 2d, Genevieve Allen, Feb. 14, 1939. Engaged in real estate bus., Chicago, 1907—; pres. Arthur T. McIntosh & Co. Trustee Northwestern U. Mem. Chicago Real Estate Bd., Sigma Chi. Republican. Presbyterian. Mason (32°, Shriner). Clubs: University, Indian Hill, Barrington Hills Golf. Home: Inverness Farm, Palatine, Ill. Office: 105 W. Madison St., Chgo. Died Nov. 7, 1955; buried Evergreen Cemetery, Barrington, Ill.

McINTOSH, Charles Kenneth, banker; b. Connersville, Ind., July 23, 1867; s. James Cottingham and Elizabeth Whitley (Martindale) McI.; ed. De Pauw U., class of 1889 (non-grad.); m. Mary Aileen Goad, Apr. 7, 1897; children—Kenneth Goad (dec.), Mary Aileen, James Gordon. Began in First Nat. Bank, San Francisco, 1889; v.p. San Francisco Nat. Bank, 1905-10; elected v.p. Bank of Calif., 1910; pres. Bank of California N.A., 1925-38, chmn. bd., 1938-48; dir. California Packing Corporation, Pacific Gas & Electric Co., Russ Building Co., Pacific Telephone & Telegraph Co. Mem. Phi Kappa Psi. Republican. Clubs: Pacific Union, Burlingame Country. Home: 1925 Gough St., San Francisco. Died Dec. 22, 1950.

McINTOSH, Donald, veterinary surgeon; prof. veterinary sci. U. Ill. Address: Urbana, Ill. Died Sept. 5, 1915.

McINTOSH, Joseph Wallace, ex-comptroller of currency; b. Macomb, Ill., Dec. 23, 1873; s. Joseph Wallace and Frances Boone (Woodyard) McI.; m. Natalie Elise Jordan, July 10, 1907. Began with Farmers State Bank, Eustis, Neb., then with Citizens Bank, Macomb, Ill.; mgr. of dept. Armour & Co., Chgo., 1897-1905; receiver, later v.p. and treas. Western Stoneware Co., Monmouth, Ill., 1907-17; dir. finance U.S. Shipping Bd. Emergency Fleet Corp., 1920-24; comptroller of the currency, 1924-28; became partner W. J. Wollman & Co., stock brokers, New York, 1928; dir. Pure Oil Co. (Chgo.), 1st Nat. Bank (Miami, Fla.). Served from maj. to col. U.S. Army, 1917-20; chief of subsistence U.S. Army, 1st 6 mos. of 1918; served in France, Italy and the Balkans. Decorated Croix Merito di Guerra (Italian); Polonia Restituta (Polish); Order of Merit (Serbian); War Cross (Czechoslovakian). Republican. Episcopalian. Clubs: Monmouth Country; The Bath, Committee of 100 (Miami Beach, Fla.); Fauquire (Warrenton, Va.); Serpent and Committee of 100 Miami Beach; Rolling Rock (Laughlintown, Pa.). Home: (summer) Overlook Farm, The Plains, Va.; (winter) 6404 Allison Island, Miami Beach, Fla. Died Sept. 26, 1952.

McINTYRE, Augustine, ret. army officer; b. Chattanooga, Tenn., July 19, 1876; s. 2d lt. Augustine (U.S. Army) and Katherine (Donohue) McI.; grad. U.S. Mil. Acad., 1900; distinguished grad. Coast Arty. Sch., Ft. Monroe, Va., 1907; grad. Sch. of Fire for F.A., Ft. Sill, 1911, Army War Coll., 1921; m. Jane Clemens Swigerh, 1906 (died 1950). Commd. 2d lt. Cav., trans. to Arty., 1900, advanced through grades to col. Nat. Army, 1929; observer with Austro-Hungarian Army, 1914-15; comdg. gen. 63d F.A. Brigade, AEF, 1918-19; asst. comdt., dir. instrn. The Field Arty. Sch., 1919-20; with Office of Chief of Field Arty., 1921-25; gen. staff duty Hdqrs. Hawaiian Div., 11th F.A., 1928-29; comdr. 13th F.A., 1929-31; pres. Field Arty. Bd., Ft. Bragg, N.C., 1931-36; comdt. F.A. Sch., Fort Sill, 1936-40; retired as brig. gen. Home: San Antonio. Died Sept. 6, 1954; buried Fort Sam Houston Nat. Cemetery, Tex.

McINTYRE, John T(homas), dramatist, author; b. Phila., Nov. 26, 1871; s. Patrick and Sarah (Walker) McI. Author: The Ragged Edge, 1902; Blowing Weather, 1923; A Young Man's Fancy, 1925; Shot Towers, 1926; Slag, 1927; Stained Sails, 1928; Drums in the Dawn, 1932; Steps Going Down, 1936; Ferment, 1937; Signing Off, 1938. Home: 241 S. 42d St., Phila. Died May 21, 1951.

McISAAC, Archibald MacDonald, economist, educator; b. Beaver Falls, Pa., Jan. 21, 1903; s. Robert James and Hannah Jane (Howland) McI.; student Geneva Coll., 1919-22; A.B., U. Mich., 1923; M.A., Princeton, 1924, Ph.D., 1930; m. Lydia Lee Dickson, Apr. 17, 1927; children—Donald M., Robert W., Malcolm C. Instr. Princeton, 1926-30, asst. prof., 1930-39, asso. prof. dept. econs., 1939-47; prof. econs. Syracuse U., 1947—, chmn. dept., 1953—. Cons. OPA, 1942-43, OPS, 1951. Mem. Am. Econ. Assn., Am. Assn. U. Profs. Author: The Order of Railroad Telegrapher: A Study in Trade Unionism and Collective Bargaining, 1930; Elements of Economic Analysis, 1951; (with J. G. Smith) Introduction to Economic Analysis, 1937, Essential Economic Principles, 1941; (with G. M. Modlin) Social Control of Industry, 1938; (with J. G. Smith, J. W. Cadman) Postwar Prospects for American Textiles, 1946. Contbg. author: The Structure of American Industry, rev. edit. 1954. Home: 304 Farmer St., Syracuse 3, N.Y. Died Jan. 1960.

McIVER, George Willcox, ret. army officer; b. Carthage, N.C., Dec. 22, 1858; s. Alexander and Mary (Willcox) M.; grad. U.S. Mil. Acad., 1882; m. Helen Howard Smedberg, June 28, 1893. Commd. 2d lt. 7th Inf., 1882, advanced through grades to brig. gen. Nat. Army, 1917; duty with Cal. N.G., 1894; comd. Co. B, 7th Inf. at Battle of El Caney, Cuba, July 1, 1898, and throughout campaign in Cuba; Alaska, 1900-01, Philippines, 1903-04, 12-14; duty with refugees after San Francisco disaster, 1906; comdt. Sch. Musketry, 1907-11; duty with Militia Bur. War Dept., Washington, 1915-17; apptd. comdr. 161st Inf. Brigade, Camp Jackson, Columbia, S.C., Sept. 1917. Mem. Soc. Army of Santiago de Cuba. Presbyn. Club: Army and Navy (Washington). Address: War Dept., Washington. Died May 9, 1947.

McKAMY, David Knox, lawyer; b. Dalton, Ga., Mar. 30, 1893; s. David Knox and Laura Stanford (Wailes) McK.; grad. Ga. Mil. Acad., 1910; B.S., U. Ga., 1914, LL.B., 1915; grad. study Harvard, 1915-16. Admitted to Ga. bar, 1915, Ala., 1917, practiced in Birmingham, 1916—; mem. Percy, Benners & Burr, 1921-29, Benners, Burr, McKamy & Forman, 1929-43, Benners, Burr, Stokely & McKamy, 1943-50, Burr, McKamy, Moore & Tate, 1950-55, Burr, McKamy, Moore & Thomas, 1955—; apptd. spl. master in Miss. vs. La. by U.S. Supreme Ct., 1953; dir. Birmingham Soc. R.R., Title Guarantee & Trust Co., Walsh Ins. Agy., Bank for Savings & Trust, Realty Mortgage Co., Galloway Coal Mining Co., Nat. Birmingham Garage, Inc., Utopia Cleaners & Dyers, Inc. Served as 2d lt. inf. U.S. Army, 1918. Mem. Am., Ala., Birmingham (pres. 1944-45) bar assns., Am. Legion, Phi Beta Kappa. Democrat. Methodist. Elk. Clubs: Down Town, Rotary, Birmingham Country. Home: Ridgely Apartments. Office: Brown-Marx Bldg., Birmingham 3, Ala. Died Sept. 30, 1957; buried Dalton, Ga.

McKAY, Donald Cope, educator; b. Salt Lake City, Feb. 14, 1902; s. Ambrose Noble and Mary Eliza (Cope) McK.; A.B., Stanford, 1926; A.M., Harvard, 1927, Ph.D., 1932; m. Ruth Stephens Capers, June 16, 1930; children—Anne Capers, Ferguson, Donald Cope. Instr., tutor history, Harvard, 1927-38, asst. prof. history, 1938-41, asso. prof., 1941-46, prof., 1946-56, chmn. faculty com. internat. and regional studies, 1946-53; Anson D. Moorse Prof. history Amherst Coll., Mass., 1956—. Mem. bur., Internat. Com. Hist. Scis., 1947—. Chmn. com. press and writing, Am. Def., Harvard Group, 1940-41. On war service, Coordinator of Information, later OSS, Washington, and overseas, 1941-44. Fellow Royal History Soc.; mem. Am. Hist. Assn., World Peace Found., Société d'histoire moderne; Phi Beta Kappa. Clubs: Harvard Faculty (Cambridge); Harvard (N.Y.C.). Author: The National Workshops, 1933. Editor: Essays in the History of Modern Europe, 1936. Editor and translator: The Dreyfus Case, 1937. Editor: Makers of Modern Europe (biographical series), 1940 ff.; The American Foreign Policy Library (with Sumner Welles), 1945. Contbg. editor: Ency. of World History, 1940. Home: 100 Woodside Av., Amherst, Mass. Died Apr. 2, 1959.

McKAY, Douglas, ex-sec. of interior, ex-governor of Oregon; b. at Portland, Ore., June 24, 1893; s. E. D. and Minnie A. (Musgrove) McK.; B.S. agr., Oregon State College, 1917; LL.D., Williamette U., Dickinson Coll., U. Me., Ore. State Coll.; m. Mabel Hill, Mar. 31, 1917; children—Douglas (dec.), Shirley (Mrs. Wayne Hadley), Mary Lou (Mrs. Lester D. Green). Paper carrier, office boy, Union Pacific Railroad, 1909-13; automobile salesman, and sales mgr. Portland, 1920-27; established automobile business, dealer for Chevrolet and Cadillac, Salem (Ore.) 1927. Mayor of Salem, 1933-34; state senator, 1935-37; 39-41, 43-45, 47-49; gov. of Oregon, 1949-53; sec. of interior 1953-56; mem. Internat. Joint Commn. representing U.S. and Can., 1957—. Served as 1st lt. Infantry, 91st division, World War I; capt. and major, Service Command Unit, World War II. Mem. State Automobile Dealers Association (past president), Salem C. of C. (past pres.), Oregon State Coll. Alumni Assn. (past pres.), American Legion (past comdr.), Vets. of Fgn. Wars, S.A.R., Disabled Am. Vets., Phi Delta Theta. Decorated: Purple Heart. Republican. Presbyn. Mason (32°, K.T., Shriner), Elk. Home: 395 Jerris Av., Salem, Ore. Died July 22, 1959.

McKAY, Frederick Sumner, dentist; b. Lawrence, Mass., Apr. 13, 1874; s. Edward and Harriet Marilla (Wells) McK.; D.D.S., U. Pa., 1900, Sc.D. (hon), 1952; D.Sc., Western Reserve U., 1955, U. Colo., 1955, Colorado College, Colorado Springs, Colo., 1958; m. Gertrude Eleanor Ronaldson, Dec. 31, 1903; children—Helen Gertrude (Mrs. Bennett H. Horchler), Virginia Mary Neosho (dec.), Roberta Henrietta (widow of Robert Lusardi); m. 2d, Honora Bailey Fink, May 14, 1941. Practicing dentist, Colorado Springs, Colo., since 1901, N.Y.C., 1917-40; conducted research starting 1908, final determination, 1931, of fluorides in water as cause of mottling and reduction dent. decay; resulted in practice of adding fluorides to communal water systems. Awarded Sabin award, Colo. Pub. Health Assn.; Jarvie medal, N.Y. State Dental Soc.; Callahan medal, Ohio State Dental Soc., Spenadel medal, 1st Dist. Dental Soc. N.Y.; Illuninated Scroll, Am. Assn. Public Health Dentists; Lasker award, Am. Pub. Health Association; award for fifty years research on water fluoridation Colo. Dental Soc., 1958; Delta Sigma Delta award, 1959. Hon. fellow Am. Coll. Dentists; hon. mem. N.Y. Acad. Dentistry, Am. Assn. Orthodontists, Rocky Mountain Soc. Orthodontists, Colo., Colorado Springs dental socs., N.Y. chpt. Internat. Assn. Dental Research, Am. Dental Assn., Omicron Kappa Upsilon. Author treatises. Home: 17 E. Buena Ventura St. Office: Exchange Bank Bldg., Colorado Springs, Colo. Died Aug. 21, 1959; cremated.

McKAY, Neal H., army officer; b. Troupe, Tex., June 10, 1896; s. Coleman and Gertrude (Henry) McK.; grad. Taylor (Tex.) High Sch., 1914, Quartermaster Sch., 1939, Army Indsl. Coll., 1940; m. Dorothy Day, June 3, 1930; 1 dau., Eleanor Stuart. Commd. 2d lt., Q.M. Corps, U.S. Army, 1920, and advanced through the grades to brig. gen. Died June 11, 1951.

McKAY, William O., business exec.; b. Beverly, Mass., Dec. 8, 1889; s. William G. and Etta Osborne (Patch) McK.; m. Ivy Merle Lyons, July 21, 1915; children—Merle (Mrs. William G. Wood), Jean (Mrs. John F. Cleveland), Sally (Mrs. E. E. Libby). With Great Northern Paper Company, 1908—, assistant to the general manager, 1926-28, vice president and manager of manufacture, 1928-46, and president, 1946-51, dir. since 1936, mem. exec. com. since 1946, and chmn. exec. com. since 1946; pres. and director Millinocket Water Co., Northern Water Co.; vice pres. and director Knox Lime Company; director Champion Internat. Paper Co., 1937-46. Republican. Baptist. Home: Lake Shore Av., Beverly, Mass. Office: 201 Devonshire St., Boston 10. Deceased.

McKEAN, Frank Chalmers (măk-kān'), clergyman; b. Evans, Colo., July 7, 1874; s. Capt. Francis Crawford and Jane Eleanor (Dunlap) McK.; A.B., Lenox Coll., Hopkinton, Ia., 1894, D.D., 1907; grad. Princeton Theol. Sem., 1899; A.M., Princeton, 1902;

m. Ethel Vaughn Wallace, May 23, 1900; children—Frank Wallace, Donald Chalmers. Ordained Presbyn. ministry, 1899; pastor Holton, Kan., 1900-05, Salina, 1905-10, Winfield, 1910-13, Central Ch., Des Moines, Ia., 1913-24, 1st Ch., Spokane, 1924-30; pastor W. Hollywood Ch., Los Angeles, 1931-43, now pastor emeritus. Preacher Easter Sunrise Service, Hollywood Bowl, 1937. Chmn. Exemption Bd. No. 3, Des Moines, World War. Trustee Lenox Coll., Whitworth Coll. Chmn. ednl. commn. for Synod of Wash. Presbyn. Ch. U.S.A.; mem. Judicial Commn. Gen. Assembly Presbyn. Ch., 1925-29; chmn. Nat. Bd. Pensions for Los Angeles Presbytery, 1940-43. Mem. Pi Gamma Mu. Republican. Mason (32°, K.T.), Rotarian (pres. West Hollywood). Club: California Country. Author: The Magnetism of Mystery, 1922; The Legacy of Great Days, 1940; Abraham Lincoln, The First American 1953. Home: 1146 Hacienda Pl., Hollywood, Los Angeles. Died Mar. 18, 1958; buried Forest Lawn Meml. Park, Glendale, Cal.

McKEAN, Josiah Slutts, vice adm. USN, ret.; b. Mt. Hope, O., May 30, 1864; s. William and Rachel (Slutts) McKean; grad. U.S. Naval Acad., 1884; LL.B., U. Mich., 1888; m. Julie Hawxhurst, 1901. Promoted asst. engr., June 28, 1889; passed asst. engr., Nov. asst. engr., June 28, 1889; passed asst. engr., Nov. 5, 1895; transferred to line as lt., Mar. 3, 1899; lt. comdr., Feb. 12, 1905; comdr., June 18, 1909; capt., July 1, 1913; rear adm. (temp.), July 1, 1918; rear adm. (perm.), Apr. 14, 1920. Served on Charleston, Spanish-Am. War, 1898; on Ohio, 1904-07; ordnance officer, Navy Yard, League Island, Pa., 1907-09; exec. officer Conn., 1909-10; comd. Panther, 1910-11; at Naval War Coll., Newport, R.I., 1911-13; with Naval Dept., 1915-19; comd. Ariz., Feb.-Sept. 1918; asst. chief operations, Jan. 5, 1919, and actg. chief, Jan. 5-July 15, and Sept. 25-Nov. 1, 1919; comdg. Div. Six, Pacific Fleet, Flagship Wyoming, 1919-21; comdt. Navy Yard, Mare Island, Cal., 1921-24; vice-adm., comdr. Scouting Fleet, Dec. 22, 1924-Sept. 5, 1926; comdt. 11th Naval Dist. and Naval Operating Base, San Diego, Cal., Sept. 15, 1926-May 30, 1928, ret. Home: Homeport, Carmel Highland, Cal. Died Aug. 1951.

McKEE, Henry S(tewart), business exec.; b. Ft. Smith, Ark., Oct. 9, 1868; s. Henry E. and Jane (Richardson) McK.; E.M., Columbia, 1893; m. Ethel Rust Hay, Oct. 19, 1898; children—Stewart, Donald Hay. Partner McKee & Co., 1889—; treasurer of the La. and Salt Lake R.R., Los Angeles, Cal. 1894-1902; vice pres. Los Angeles Trust Co., 1902-07, pres. 1st. Nat. Bank, Long Beach, Calif., 1907-09; vice pres. Merchants Nat. Bank, Los Angeles, 1909-23; pres. Barker Bros., 1923-28; pres. Pacific Am. Investors since 1928; dir. Pacific Mutual Life Ins. Co., Pacific Nat. Fire Ins. Co., Barker Bros. Mem. dirs. adv. council Bank of Am., since 1930; mem. Federal Reserve Adv. Council, 1928-31. Served as pres. Calif. Bankers Assn., 1923-24, Los Angeles C. of C., 1903-04. Republican. Author: The A.B.C. of Business, 1921; Degenerate Democracy, 1932; Journeys in Understanding, 1948. Home: 538 S Flower St. Office: 530 W. 6th St., Los Angeles 14. Died Nov. 19, 1956.

McKEE, Joseph V., lawyer; b. Newark; s. John B. and Margaret (Catterson) McK.; A.B., Fordham, 1911, A.M., 1913, LL.B., 1918, LL.D., 1927; m. Cornelia Kraft, Nov. 27, 1918; children—Joseph V., Richard. Admitted to N.Y. bar, 1918; mem. N.Y. Assembly, 1918-24; justice of City Ct., N.Y.C., 1924-26; pres. Bd. of Aldermen, N.Y.C., 1926-33 (resigned); acting mayor of N.Y.C., 1932. Candidate for mayor of N.Y. on Recovery ticket, 1933, defeated. Trustee Title Guarantee & Trust Co. Mem. Hosp. Council; trustee St. Vincent's Hosp., N.Y. Foundling Hosp., A. E. Smith Found. Knight of Malta. Clubs: Metropolitan, New York Athletic, Recess. Home: 737 Park Av. Office: 14 Wall St., N.Y. C. Died Jan. 28, 1956.

McKEE, Ruth Karr (Mrs. James E. McKee), club woman; b. Hoquiam, Wash., Mar. 28, 1874; d. James A. and Abigail (Walker) Karr; B.Py., U. Wash., 1895, B.A., 1896, M.A., 1898; m. James S. McKee, May 6, 1902. Pres. Wash. State Fed. Women's Clubs, 1913-15; state vice regent D.A.R., 1915-17; woman mem. State Council Defense, 1917-19; first state councillor Minute Women, 1919-20; regent U. Wash., 1917-23, repptd. 1923 and elected pres. of bd. (1st woman in America to hold such a position). A residence hall at U. of Wash. named in her honor. Mem. (hon.) Internat. Mark Twain Soc., Phi Beta Kappa, Pi Lambda Theta. Republican. Author: Mary Richardson Walker; Her Book, 1945. Home: Yakima, Wash. Died Mar. 8, 1951.

McKEEHAN, Hobart Deitrich (măk-kē'ăn), clergyman; b. nr. Newport, Perry County, Pa., Apr. 26, 1897; s. Lincoln Scott and Eldorado (Mahaffy) McK.; student Valparaiso (Ind.) U., 1915-17; student 1 yr. under Prof. J. P. Mahaffy, of Dublin U.; grad. Ref. Theol. Sem., Lancaster, Pa., 1919; B.D. and S.T.M., Lincoln-Jefferson U., 1920; post-grad. work Oxford U.; D.D., Franklin and Marshall Coll., 1936; married Verna Marie Klinepeter, December 21, 1918; 1 son, Edward Mahaffy. Ordained ministry Reformed Church in U.S.A., 1919; spl. preacher, Bethel Church, High Point, N.C., summer 1918; pastor St. Paul's Ch., Dallastown, Pa., 1919-24, The Abbey Church, Huntingdon, 1924—. Spl. preacher at Oxford (England) in behalf of Anglo-American good will. Del. World Alliance Ref. Chs., Zürich, Switzerland, 1923, and to World Alliance of Reformed and Presbyterian Churches, Belfast, 1933; regent of Mercersburg Academy. Mem. Students' University Research Assn. (ex-pres.), Pi Gamma Mu. Member Maccabees, Sr. Order Am. Mech. Rotarian. Author: The Patrimony of Life, 1925; Anglo-American Preaching, 1928; What Men Need Most, 1940; Best Sermons, 1944. Contbr. Best Sermons, 1924, American Reformed Pulpit, 1928; For God and Country, 1942; Life's Golden Hours, 1947. Editor: Great Modern Sermons, 1923, The First Year, Home, 1945. Contbr. Christian World Pulpit, Minister's Annual (8 vols.), The Expository Times, The Speakers Bible, American Sermon Series, 1946; Preaching on the New Age, 1948; also literary revs. in Am. and British jours. Lecturer. Home: 607 Church St., Huntingdon, Pa. Died Mar. 14, 1953; buried Newport (Pa.) Cemetery.

McKEEHAN, Joseph Parker (măk-kē'ăn), lawyer, educator; b. nr. Carlisle, Pa., Nov. 20, 1876; s. Joseph Hamlin and Mary Graham (Parker) McK.; A.B., Dickinson Coll., 1897, A.M., 1899, LL.B., 1902; m. Helen Wile, June 6, 1917; 1 son, Joseph Parker. Instr. Latin, Dickinson Prep. Sch., 1897-99, vice prin., 1899-1900; prof. law Dickinson Sch. of Law, 1902—; spl. dep. atty. gen. Commonwealth of Pa., 1926-27. Pres. Carlisle Deposit Bank and Trust Co. Mem. Jury of Awards, Paris Expn., 1900; mem. jury and sec. deptl. jury for social economy St. Louis Expn., 1904; del. Universal Congress Lawyers and Jurists at St. Louis, 1904; mem. Bd. Appeals, Pa. Selective Service, 1940—. Mem. Am., Pa. bar assns., Pa. Scotch-Irish Soc., Phi Beta Kappa, Beta Theta Pi. Republican. Presbyn. Club: Carlisle Country. Contbr. numerous articles to Dickinson Law Rev. Home: 300 S. College St. Office: Public Square N.W., Carlisle, Pa. Died June 28, 1950.

McKELLAR, Kenneth Douglas, ex-senator; b. Richmond, Dallas County, Ala., Jan. 29, 1869; s. J. D. W. and Caroline (Howard) M.; B.A., M.A., U. Ala., 1891, LL.B., 1892. Removed to Memphis; Dem. presdl. elector, 1904; del. Dem. Nat. Conv., 1908; term of Gen. George W. Gordon; reelected to 63d and elected to Congress, Nov. 9, 1911, to fill unexpired 64th Congresses, 10th Tenn. Dist.; U.S. senator, 1916-53. Home: 1138 Peabody St., Memphis. Died Oct. 25, 1957.

McKELVIE, Samuel Roy, ex-gov. Neb.; b. Fairfield, Neb., Apr. 15, 1881; s. Samuel and Jennie (Glandon) McK.; student bus. coll. and U. Neb.; m. Flossie DeArnold, June 19, 1904. With Bee Pub. Co., Omaha, Neb., 1902-05; became editor Neb. Farmer, 1905, prin. owner and pub., 1908, now pres. Owns and operates By The Way Ranch, Valentine, Neb.; lt. gov. Neb., 1913-15, gov., 1919-23. Trustee Farm Found., Chgo., Cooper Found., Lincoln. Dir. Am. Hereford Assn., Kansas City. Mem. City Council, Lincoln, 1908-09; mem. Neb. Ho. of Reps., 1911-13; mem. Federal Farm Bd., 1929-31; pres. Sandhills Cattle Assn., 1938-50. Republican. Methodist. Mason, Odd Fellow, Elk. Clubs: Commercial University (Lincoln); Chicago Athletic. Address: 1420 P St., Lincoln 1, Neb. Died Jan. 6, 1956; buried Lincoln.

McKELVY, Francis Graham, pres. Alpha Portland Cement Co.; b. Pittsburgh, Pa., Aug. 9, 1883; s. William M. and Frances (Graham) McK.; student Shady Side Acad., Pittsburgh, 1894-99, Lawrenceville (N.J.) Acad., 1899-1900; A.B., Princeton U., 1904; m. Louise Corwin, Nov. 9, 1910; children—Louise Makepeace, William Graham. Clerk Alpha Portland Cement Co., Easton, Pa., 1906-07, asst. sec., 1907-08, purchasing agent, 1908-11, sec., 1911-14, 2d v.p., 1914-17, 1st v.p., 1917-34, exec. v.p., 1934-35, pres. 1935-49, and chairman of the board since 1949. Served as captain of Ordnance Department, Army, 1917. Trustee Lafayette College, Easton, Pennsylvania. Chmn. bd. dirs. Portland Cement Assn., Chicago, 1943. Mem. Am. Soc. Mech. Engrs., Am. Soc. for Testing Materials. Republican. Presbyterian. Clubs: Country of Northampton County (Easton); University, Princeton (New York, N.Y.); Nassau (Princeton, N.J.); Pine Valley Golf. Home: Oakhurst, High St. Office: 15 S. Third St., Easton, Pa. Died May 7, 1952; buried Hillside Cemetery, Middletown, N.Y.

McKENNA, Roy Carnegie, steel mfr.; b. Pittsburgh, Pa., Mar. 7, 1883; s. Thomas A. and Anna (Hogan) M.; E.E., U. of Pitts., 1903, LL.D., 1952; LL.D., honorary, St. Vincent Coll., Latrobe, Pa.; m. Mary Martin, Oct. 25, 1905; 1 dau., Jean Martin (Mrs. Jean McKenna Sorber). Partner McKenna Brass & Mfg. Co., Pitts., 1903-26, pres., 1926-37; pres. Vanadium-Alloys Steel Co., 1915-43, chmn. bd., 1943—; pres., dir. Anchor Drawn Steel Co., Latrobe, Pa.; v.p., dir. Colonial Steel Co., Monaca, Pa., Vanadium-Alloys Steel Societa Italiana p.A., Turin, Italy; dir. Pitts. Tool Steel Wire Co., Societe Commentryenne des Aciers Fins Vanadium—Alloys (Paris, France), Vanadium Alloys Steel Can., Ltd., London, Ontario, Can, Toyad Corp., Vulcan Mold & Iron Co. (Latrobe). Dir. Latrobe Hosp. Assn., Adams Meml. Library; trustee Westmoreland County Mus. Art, Council of Profit Sharing Industries; mem. nat. council Boy Scouts Am. (recipient Silver Beaver award). Trustee U. Pitts. Recipient Bronze medal Am. Cancer Soc., 1956. Mem. Pa. C. of C. (past pres., life dir.), Am. Iron and Steel Inst., Am. Soc. M.E., Am. Soc. for Metals, Newcomen Soc., Phi Gamma Delta. Clubs: Pittsburgh Athletic (charter mem.), Duquesne (Pitts.). Mason (33°, Shriner, K. T., Jester). Home: High Acres, P.O. Box 389, Latrobe. Office: Vanadium-Alloys Steel Co., Latrobe, Pa. Died July 11, 1958.

McKENNEY, A. Carlton, ins. exec.; b. Richmond, Va., Nov. 9, 1873; s. William Nicholas and Mary Augusta (Carlton) McK.; grad. Richmond High Sch., 1889; m. Helen Avery Morris, Dec. 28, 1921; children—Carlton Norris, Malcolm Stuart, Helen Nelson. Clerk in office of P. H. May & Bro., tobacco manufactory, Richmond, 1890-1904; with Life Ins. Co. of Va., Richmond, 1904—, became 1st v.p., resigned Dec. 1, 1943, but continues as dir. and mem. exec. com. Served with Richmond Light Inf. Blues, 1892-96. Trustee Va. Diocesan Center. Clubs: Country of Virginia, Richmond, Richmond German. Home: Westmoreland Pl., Richmond, Va. Died July 20, 1950.

McKENZIE, Fayette Avery, educator; b. Montrose, Pa., July 31, 1872; s. Edwin and Gertrude (Avery) M.; B.S., Lehigh U., 1895, LL.D., 1916; Ph.D., U. Pa., 1906; m. Nettie T. Tressel, Apr. 26, 1915. Instr. modern langs. and social sci., Juniata Coll., Huntingdon, Pa., 1897-1900; instr. modern langs., Blight Sch., Phila., 1900-03; tchr. Wind River Govt. Indian Sch., 1903-04; prof. econs. and sociology, Ohio State U., 1905-15; pres. Fisk U., Nashville, 1915-26, brough instn. to full recognition as a standard coll. and raised an endowment of a million dollars; prof. sociology, Juniata Coll., 1926-41, dean men, 1927-29, dir. extension, 1928—, developed in 1933 a complete freshman class, Altoona, Pa., as br. Juniata, prof. emeritus, 1941—. Spl. agt. Indian census and joint author Indian Census Report, U.S. Census Bur., 1910. Pres. univ. and social settlement sect. Ohio State Conf. Charities and Correction, 1909-15; pres. Pub. Recreation Commn., Columbus, 1910-12; mem. Indian Survey Staff of Inst. Govt. Research, 1926-27. Founder Soc. Am. Indians; mem. Am. Sociol. Soc., Phi Beta Kappa. Presbyn. Author: The American Indian in Relation to the White Population of the United States, 1908. Joint author Recreation Survey of Washington, 1915. Home: Huntingdon, Pa. Died Sept. 1, 1957.

McKEOWN, Tom D. (mă-kou'ăn), ex-congressman; b. nr. Blackstock, S.C., June 4, 1878; s. Theodore B. and Annie (Robinson) McK.; ed. pub. schs. and under pvt. tutor; attended spl. lectures Law Dept. Cornell U.; m. Anna Sanders, Jan. 9, 1902. Admitted to S.C. bar, 1899; moved to Malvern, Ark., 1899, to Ada, Ind. Ty., 1901; apptd. mem. State Bar Commn., Okla., 1907 (pres. 1909-10); judge 7th Jud. Dist. of Okla., 1910-16; presiding justice 5th Div. Supreme Court Commn., 1915-16; mem. 65th and 66th Congresses (1917-21) and 68th to 73d Congresses (1923-35), 4th Okla. Dist. Democrat. Address: Ada, Okla. Died Oct. 22, 1951; buried Ada.

McKINLAY, Arthur Patch, writer, educator; b. Osborn, Mo., Apr. 8, 1871; s. Rev. George Angus and Julia Brace (Patch) McK.; prep. edn., Sumner (Wash.) Acad.; A.B., U. of Ore., 1893; A.M., Harvard, 1904, Ph.D., 1906; m. Jessie Goddard, Feb. 21, 1914 (died Nov. 21, 1939). Instr. in English, Holmes Business Coll., Portland, 1893-94; instr. in Latin, high sch., Portland, 1894-1901; asst. prof. Latin, U. of Ore., 1902-03; asst. prof. Latin and Greek, U. of Ida., 1906-07; head dept. of Latin, Lincoln High Sch., Portland, 1907-12; instr. Greek and Latin, U. of Calif., 1912-13, in Latin, Lowell High Sch., San Francisco, 1913-14; chmn. dept. of langs., Lincoln High Sch., Portland, Ore., 1914-19; asst. prof. Latin, U. of Calif., Los Angeles, 1919-26, asso. prof., 1926-29, prof. 1929-41, emeritus; professor University of Texas, 1943-44. Mem. American Philol. Association, Philological Assn. Pacific Coast (president 1924), Classical Assn. Pacific States (president 1921), Medieval Acad. Am., Classical League, Phi Beta Kappa, Pi Gamma Mu. Rep. Presbyn. Author: Stylistic Tests and the Chronology of the Works of Boethius, 1907; HSCP, Studies in Arator I, the Manuscript Tradition of the Capitula and Tituli, HSCP, 1932; Studies in Arator II. The Classification of the Manuscripts of Arator, 1943; HSCP. The De Syllogismis Categoricis and Introductio ad Syllogismos Categoricos of Boethius, in Studied in Honor of Edward Kennard Rand, 1938; A Fragment of Juvenal in a Manuscript of Orléans (with E. K. Rand), 1938; Membra Disiecta of Manuscripts of Arator (Speculum), 1940; A New Fragment of Arator in the Bodleian (with Ker and Lowe), Spec., 1944; The Indulgent Dionysius, PAPC, 1939; How the Athenians Handled the Drink Problem Among Their Slaves, Cl. W., 1944; The Roman Attitude Towards Women's Drinking, Cl.B., 1945; The Wine Element in Horace, Classical Journal, 1946; Christian Appraisal of Pagan Temperance, Angl. Theol. Rev., 1947; Early Roman Sobriety, 1948; Ancient Experience with Intoxicating Drinks: Non-Classical Peoples, 1948; Non-Attic Greek States, 1949; Roman Sobriety in the Later Republic, 1949; In the Early Empire, 1950; Bacchus as a Health Giver, 1950; Attic Temperance, 1951; Latin Commentaries on Arator, 1952. Translator: Letters of a Roman Gentlemen (Cicero), 1926; Out of His Loveliness (sonnets), 1939; The Passing Show (sonnets), 1943. Editor: Arator; the Codices, Mediaeval Academy of America, 1943; Arator De Actibus Apostolorum, C.S.E.L. vol. 72, 1951; Latin Commentaries on Arator, 1952; also several translations. Home: 769 Glenmont Av., Los Angeles 24. Died Sept. 7, 1958.

McKINLAY, John, b. Greenock, Scotland, Aug. 31, 1874; s. James D. and Mary (Wilson) McK.; came to U.S. with parents, 1884; ed. pub. schs.; m. Helen Eddington, Nov. 1900; children—John, Dorothy (Mrs. John A. Middleton, Jr.). With Marshall Field & Co., 1888-1936, pres., 1930-36; with Nat. Tea Co., 1938-45, chmn.; director Bowes Industries, Incorporated; member and past pres. board of managers Presbyterian Hospital; president Washington and Jane Smith Home; director of First State Pawners Soc.; trustee John G. Shedd Aquarium; chmn. Land Clearance Commn., Chicago. Clubs: Union League, Mid-Day, Commercial, Beverly Country, South Shore Country, Big Foot Country. Home: 10400 Longwood Dr. Office: 1325 Harris Trust Bldg., 111 W. Monroe St., Chgo. Died Sept. 9, 1953.

McKINLEY, James Wilfred, lawyer; b. Los Angeles, Calif., July 8, 1891; s. James Wilfred and Lillian (Elder) McK.; A.B., U. of Calif., 1913; LL.B., Harvard U., 1916; m. Selena Pope Ingram, Jan. 27, 1940. Admitted to California bar, 1916; since in general practice of law; mem. California State Senate, 1927-34. Alternate Rep. National Convention, 1928, del., 1932. Served as 2d lt., F.A., 1917-19. with AEF, 1918-19. Vice pres. Los Angeles area U.S.O.; mem. bd. Seamen's Ch. Inst. of Los Angeles, 1920——, pres. 1920-51; mem. and sec. bd. govs. Ling Foundation since 1926; mem. advisory bd. Salvation Army, Los Angeles; mem. bd. dirs.; U.S.O., Los Angeles Area since 1943. Mem. Am., Calif. State and Los Angeles bar assns., Am. Legion, Phi Kappa Sigma. Republican. Episcopalian. Club: California (Los Angeles). Home: 5708 Lindenhurst Av., Los Angeles 36. Office: 609 S. Grand Av., Los Angeles 17. Died Aug. 3, 1957; buried Inglewood Park Cemetery, Los Angeles.

McKINLEY, J(ohn) Charnley, neuropsychiatrist; b. Duluth, Minn., Nov. 8, 1891; s. John and Alice Salome (Frizzell) McK.; B.S., U. Minn., 1915. A. M., 1917, M.D., 1919, Ph.D., 1921; grad. student in psychiatry, Psychiatric Inst., N.Y.C., 1919; m. Doris I. Swedien, Apr. 29, 1944; children—(1st marriage) Marian Louise (Mrs. Leland Phelps), Helen Alice (Mrs. George W. Miners), Ruth Elizabeth (Mrs. Roy Pistore), John Charnley. Instructor pathology, U. Minn., 1917-18, teaching fellow in nervous and mental diseases, 1918-21, asst. prof. of neuro-pathology, 1921-25, asso. prof. of neurology, 1925-29, prof. of neuropsychiatry, 1929-46, acting head dept. of medicine, 1932-34, head dept. of medicine, 1934-43, head dept. of neuropsychiatry, 1943-46, prof. emeritus 1946——. Sec.-treas. Minn. State Board of Examiners in Basic Sciences, 1931-45. Guggenheim Fellow (studies at univs. Breslau and Munich, Germany), 1928-29. Mem. bd. dirs. Am. Bd. of Psychiatry and Neurology. Fellow A.A.A.S., A.M.A.; mem. Minn. Acad. Medicine, Central Neuropsychiatric Assn., Am. Neurol. Assn., Nu Sigma Nu, Sigma Xi, Alpha Omega Alpha. Contbr. to met. jours. Editor: Outline of Neuropsychiatry. Co-author: Minnesota Multiphasic Personality Inventory. Home: 3501 E. 54th St., Mpls. 6. Died Jan. 3, 1950.

McKINNEY, Frank Cowen, lawyer, author; b. Pennsboro, W.Va., July 26, 1878; s. John Piatt and Lucy (Toothaker) McK.; A.B., Ohio State U., 1901, A.M., 1902; LL.B., Columbia. 1909. Instr. in English, U. Wis., 1903-04. Ohio State U., 1905-08; admitted to Ohio bar, 1906, N.Y. bar, 1909; editor Trust Cos. Mag., 1911-15; lectr. Bklyn. Law Sch., 1911-14; pres. North Am. Discount Corp.; dir. James M. Motley Co., Inc., Fiduciaries Pub. Co., Inc. Mem. Bd. of Edn., Montclair, N.J., 1922-26. First lt., gen. staff, U.S. Army, 1918. Mem. Ohio Soc. of N.Y. Republican. Clubs: Economic, New York Fraternity. Author: Argumentation and Debate (with J. V. Denney and C. S. Duncan), 1910; Trust Investments, 1914 (rev. edit., 1927); A Case Book in Discussion (with M. E. McKinney), 1930; Your Will and How to Write It, 1936. Editor: (with Frank White) Dill on Corporations, 1911. Contbr. to Encyclopedia of Corporation Law (1920), also to legal and business mags. Home: 27 Edgecliff Rd., Upper Montclair, N. J. Office: 135 Broadway, N.Y.C. Died Apr. 15, 1950.

McKINNEY, Luther Franklin, ex-congressman, ex-ambassador; b. nr. Newark, O., Apr. 25, 1841; s. Alexander and Elizabeth (Miller) M.; served in 1st Ohio Cav., 1861-3; A.B., St. Lawrence U., 1870; m. Sharlie Paine Webb, Aug. 1, 1870. Ordained Universalist ministry, 1870; pastor Bridgton, Me., 1870-3, Newfields, N.H., 1873-5, Manchester, N.H., 1875; in dry goods bus., Bridgton, Me., 2 yrs.; now pres. Bridgton Furniture Co. Preached 1 yr. in Kansas City, Mo. Mem. 50th and 52d Congresses, 1st N.H. Dist.; candidate for gov. N.H., 1892. E.E. and M.P. of U.S. to Colombia, 1893-97. Address: Bridgton, Me. Died 1922., buried Bridgton.

McKINNEY, Madge M., educator; b. Rome, O., Nov. 21, 1893; d. George and Bertha Maude (Hillier) McKinney; A.B., Western Reserve U., 1916, M.A., 1919; Ph.D., U. Chgo., 1927; 1 adopted dau., Bertha Joanne. Asst. in polit. science Western Reserve U., 1917-21; chmn. dept. hist. and social sciences Cedar Crest Coll., 1921-24; instr. Hunter Coll., 1926-29, asst. prof., 1929-45, asso. prof. 1945-53, prof., 1953-——, chmn. dept. polit. science, 1940-——. Mem. Am. Polit. Sci. Assn., Am. Soc. Pub. Adminstrn., Am. Assn. U. Profs. Author: (articles) Constitutional Amendment in New York State, 1939; The Personnel of the Seventy-Seventh Congress, 1942; Who Are the Men on Capitol Hill, 1942; Religion and Elections, 1944. Home: Home: Hudson View Gardens, 183d St. and Pinehurst Av., N.Y.C. Died July 29, 1956; buried Rome, O.

McKINNEY, Walter H., foreign service officer; b. Sault Ste. Marie, Mich., Sept. 6, 1889; s. Peter T. and Jessie (Bellows) McK.; student U. of Michigan, 1908-10; m. Julia Walker, Sept. 9, 1914; children—Joseph Steere, Walter Hastings, John Francis, Elizabeth (wife of William T. King, Jr.). Am. consul in Bordeaux, France, Vigo, Spain, Yarmouth, Nova Scotia, Canada, sec. Am. Legation, Guatemala City, Guatemala; Am. consul in Sheffield and London, England; with Dept. of State, Washington, D.C.; Am. consul, Barcelona, Spain; consul gen. Winnipeg, Canada; retired 1950. Mem. Sigma Nu. Mason, Elk, K.P. Home: Sault Ste. Marie, Mich. Died Apr. 13, 1952; buried Sault Ste Marie, Mich.

McKINNEY, William Mark, lawyer; b. Oquawka, Ill., Feb. 3, 1865; s. John and Elmira (Kendall) M.; A.M., LL D., Monmouth, Coll.; LL.B., Union Coll. of Law, Chicago, 1886; m Loretta Beebe, Oct. 20, 1891; children—Mira Frances, John. Mem. N.Y. Senate, 1901-02; del. N.Y. Constl. Conv., 1915; pres. Edw. Thompson Co., law publs., 1912-17. Maj. judge adv. U.S. Army, 1918. Editor: American and English Encyclopaedia of Law and Practice; Encyclopaedia of Pleading and Practice; Federal Statutes, Annotated; American and English Annotaetd Cases; Ruling Case Law; McKinney's Consolidated Laws of New York; California Jurisprudence; New California Digest; Texas Jurisprudence; McKinney's Digest. Author: A Treatise on the Law of Fellow Servants, 1889. Home: The Montecito, 6650 Franklin Av., Hollywood, Cal. Office: 200 McAllister St., San Francisco. Died Nov. 9, 1955; buried Cypress Lawn, San Francisco.

McKINNIS, George E., Sr., savings and loan banking; b. near Marbleden Hill, Mo.; s. J. A. and Drucilla (Donoho) McK.; moved to Tenn. with his parents in infancy, and to Kan. in 1884; honorary LL.D. Oklahoma Baptist University; m. Mary Dickson, Oct. 15, 1897 (dec.); 1 son, Lt. Comdr. Geo. E. McKinnis, Jr., U.S.N.R.; m. 2d, Mrs. Bess Ragland Chrisney, Sept. 1, 1945. Farmed in Kansas; moved to Tecumseh, Oklahoma, 1891 (at the opening to settlement of the Sac and Fox and Pottawatomie Indian reservations); manager McKinnis-Baird Lumber Company, 1891-93; principal public schools, Tecumseh, 1893-94, Shawnee, 1895, and superintendent of schs., 1896; in business in Shawnee, 1897-——; one of founders and organizers of State Nat. Bank, 1902, v.p., 1902-17, pres., 1917-19; founder, pres. Shawnee Realty & Investment Co., 1907; founder, 1912, pres.-mgr. 1st Fed. Sav. & Ln. Assn., Shawnee; founder, 1922, and pres. Southwestern States Savs. & Loan Conf. Pres. U.S. League of Savings and Loan Assn., 1926-27; director U.S. Savings & Loan League, 1926-35. Postmaster of Shawnee, 1903-07; pres. Chamber of Commerce, Shawnee, 1905-07. Chmn. Home Service Dept. Am. Red Cross during World War; chmn. Pottawatomie Chapter, 1938-39; director 4th District of American Red Cross; national rep. and pres. Canadian Valley Council of Boy Scouts of America, 1937. Gen. chmn. Shawnee's improvement, health and beautification ogn.; dir. Shawnee C. of C. and chmn. City Planning Com. Del. to Rep. Nat. Conv. Chicago, 1916. Baptist; one of the founders and pres. bd. trustees Okla. Bapt. U., 1914-26. Pres. Am. Savings, Building and Loan Inst., 1928-29; one of the organizers Federal Home Loan Bank of 10th Dist., Topeka, Kan., dir., 1932-41, chmn., 1938; mem. adv. council Fed. Home Loan Bank Bd., Washington, D.C., 1932-44; chairman F.H.A. Advisory Council; governor of National Savings and Loan League. Clubs: Shawnee Country, Rotary (charter mem., past pres.); gov. Rotary Internat., 1929-30; mem. Knife and Fork, Elks, Odd Fellow. Home: Shawnee, Okla. Office: 118 N. Broadway, Shawnee, Okla. Died Sept. 7, 1959; buried Shawnee, Okla.

McKINSEY, Folger, journalist; b. Elkton, Md., Aug. 29, 1866; s. James and Catherine N. (Nichol) M.; self-ed.; m. Fannie Holenrake Dungan, Jan. 4, 1886. Editor Shore Gazette, Ocean Beach, N.J., 1884, Cecil Whig, Elkton, Md., 1885, Daily News, Frederick, Md., 1886-98, Balt. News, 1898-05; on editorial staff Washington Post, 1906, Balt. Sun, 1906-——, as writer dept. of verse under pseudonym of Bentztown Bard. Independent Democrat. Episcopalian. Author: A Rose of the Old Regime, 1907. Home: Robinson, Md. Address: Sun Office, Balt. Died July 22, 1950.

McKINSEY, J(ohn) C(harles) C(henoweth), univ. prof.; b. Frankfort, Ind., Apr. 30, 1908; s. Arthur and Alma Julia (Winks) McK.; B.S., New York U., 1933, M.S., 1934; Ph.D., U. of Calif., 1936; m. May Berger, May 30, 1940; Blumenthal Research fellow New York U., 1936-37; instr. math., N.Y.U., 1937-42; Guggenheim fellow U. of Calif., 1942-43; asst. prof. Mont. State Coll., 1943-45, U. Nev., 1945-56; prof. math. Okla. A. and M. Coll., 1946-51; prof. of philosophy, Stanford Univ., since 1951; on leave as researcher for Rand Corp., Santa Monica, Calif., 1947-49. Mem. Am. Math. Soc., Math. Assn., Assn. for Symbolic Logic. Cons. editor, Journal of Symbolic Logic since 1941. Contbr. articles to math. and philos. jours. since 1934. Researcher in algebra and math. logic. Home: 4231 Suzanne Dr., Palo Alto. Office: Philosophy Dept., Stanford Univ., Stanford. Died Oct. 26, 1953.

McKNIGHT, Alexander G(alt), lawyer; b. Corwar, Ayrshire, Scotland, May 4, 1878; s. Charles and Marion (McCreath) McK.; came to U.S., 1893; ed. U. of Minn., 1898, U. of Chicago, 1899, U. of Mich. Law Sch., 1904; m. Grace May Wilson, Aug. 30, 1902; children—Malcolm Hugh, Isabella Marion (Mrs. Glen Weld), Paul Alexander, Donald Sinton (dec.), Kenneth Alan. Admitted to Minn. bar, 1904; referee in bankruptcy, 5th Div., Dist. Minn., 1928-33; dir. litigation NRA, Mar. 22, 1934-Dec. 1934; asst. gen. counsel, 1934-35; apptd. acting chmn. Indsl. Appeals Board NRA, May 1935. Atty. and dir. St. Louis County (Minn.), Federal Savings & Loan Assn.; alderman City of Duluth, 1908-10; mem. Charter Commn., Duluth, 1922-28; dir. Bd. of Trusts, Duluth, 1937-43; dir. Community Fund. Served as sec. YMCA, France, 1918-19. Del. Dem. Nat. Conv., 1936. Elected hon. pres. Burns Club World Fedn., Elgin, Scotland, Sept. 1936. Mem. Minn. State and 11th Dist. bar assns., Order of Scottish Clans (past nat. pres.); dir. Samaritan Life Assn. (past pres. and gen. counsel). Democrat. Mason (32°). Contbr. on works of Robert Burns; also to legal publs. Home: 431 N. 17th Av. E., Duluth, Minn. Died June 18, 1950.

McKNIGHT, James Rankin, banker; b. Junction City, Kan., July 31, 1878; s. George William and Mary Josephine (McClure) McK.; B.S., U. of Kan. Engring. Sch.; m. Mae Bach, Nov. 6, 1907. With engring. dept. Union Pacific R.R., 1902-03; with Pierre (S.D.) Nat. Bank since 1903, serving successively as clerk, asst. cashier and cashier until 1920, pres., 1920-49, chmn. bd. since 1949; dir. Federal Res. Bank of Minneapolis, 1939-51. Pres. S.D. Bankers Assn., 1937-38; apptd. mem. board govs. Smaller War Plants Corp., Region 12, Minneapolis, June 1943. Chmn. local Selective Service Board, 1940-45. Mason (K.T., Shriner). Club: Kiwanis International. Home: 218 W. Summit Av. Office: 358 S. Pierre St., Pierre, S..D. Died Aug. 14, 1951.

McKUSICK, Marshall Noah (măk-kōō'sĭk); b. Calais, Me., Dec. 24, 1879; s. Marshall Noah and Lucy Jane (Bassford) McK.; LL.B., Boston U., 1901, LL.D., 1935; LL.D., Yankton (S.D.) Coll., 1932; m. Alice Amelia Bates, Aug. 24, 1905; 1 dau., Frances Lucille. Connected with U. S.D., 1902-——, dean Coll. of Law, 1912-——. Chmn. Commn. of S.D. Bar Examiners, S.D. Judicial Council. Mem. S.D. Bar Assn. (past pres.), Delta Theta Phi. Republican. Conglist. Compiler: Case Pamphlet on Contracts, 1910. Contbr. to Marquette Law Rec. Prepared S.D. Annotations to Law of Contract Restatements by Am. Law Inst. Home: 208 Court St., Vermilion, S.D. Died Dec. 24, 1950; buried Vermilion, S.D.

McLAGLEN, Victor, actor; b. Tumbridge Wells, England, 1886; s. Rev. Andrew and Lillian (Burke) McL.; m. Enid Mary Lamont, 1919 (died 1942); children—Andrew Victor, Sheila Mary; m. 2d, Suzanna Maria Brueggemann, Nov. 20, 1943 (divorced 1948); m. 3d, Margaret Pumphrey, Dec. 19, 1948. Began as motion picture actor in England, 1920; came to Hollywood, 1924; played Captain Flagg in What Price Glory and Cockeyed World; has appeared in over 1935 pictures, including Sea Devils, Wee Willie Winkie, Battle of Broadway, Gunga Din, Laughing at Life, China Girl, Roger Touhy, Last of the Gangsters, Tampico. Won Academy award for role in The Informer, 1936. Latest pictures: Fort Apache, She Wore a Yellow Ribbon. Owns 1,000-acre ranch, Clovis, Calif. Served as provost marshal of Bagdad, Iraq, 1914-18. Author: Express to Hollywood (autobiography), 1934. Mason (32°). Address: Victor McLaglen Pure Bred Jersey Farms, Clovis, Calif. Died Nov. 7, 1959.

McLAIN, Chester Alden, lawyer; born Newton, Mass., June 22, 1891; s. Llewellyn Hilton and Harriet (McMahon) McL.; A.B., Harvard, 1913, LL.B., 1915, S.J.D., 1917; m. Sara Myers, June 23, 1917; children—Sally Ann, Hilton. Mem. war loan staff U.S. Treasury, 1919-20; asst. prof. Harvard Law Sch., 1920-23; lawyer Cravath, Henderson & de Gersdorff, N.Y., 1923-26, mem. of firm, 1926-46; gen. counsel Internat. Bank for Reconstruction and Development 1946-49; gen. counsel U.S. High Commissioner for Germany, 1949; partner Cravath, Swaine & Moore, 1950—. Enlisted, 14th Ry. Engrs., U.S. Army, 1917; 2d lt., 332d Inf., 1918-19. Home: Benedict Rd., Dongan Hills, S.I. 4, N.Y. Office: 15 Broad St., N.Y.C., 5. Died Sept. 25, 1953; buried Newton, Mass.

McLAIN, Raymond S., army officer; b. Washington County, Ky., April 4, 1890; s. Thomas A. and Lucetta (Stallings) McL.; student Hills Bus. Coll., Oklahoma City, 1909; grad. Sch. of Musketry, 1917, Command and Gen. Staff Sch., 1938; m. Norma Leeman, 1910; children—Raymond S., Dorothy V. (Mrs. Norman Rogers), Betty June, Norma Lee; m. 2d, Bertha Cunningham, Aug. 12, 1933; 1 son, Robert Duncan. Clerk in real estate office, 1907-11; abstractor, 1912-15; asst. county treas., 1916; pres. Central Title & Investment Co., 1919-23; v.p. Am. Nat. Co., 1923-28, Am.-First Nat. Co., 1928-33; pres. Am.-First Trust Co., Oklahoma City, 1933-53; chmn. bd. Am. First Title & Trust Co., 1953—; pres. Am. Mortgage & Investment Co., 1953—. Pvt. Nat. Guard, 1912; 2d lt. to 1st lt., serving on Mexican Border and in World War I, 1914-19; capt. O.R.C., 1920-21; capt. to brig. gen., Okla. Nat. Guard, 1921-37; brig. gen., U.S. Army, 1940, comdg. arty, of 45th Inf. Div., Sicily and Italy; transferred to England, Apr. 1944; comdg. general 30th Infantry Division Field Artillery, France, June 9, 1944 (D-3); comdg. 90th Inf. Div., July 1944; promoted to major gen., Aug. 31, 1944, corps comdr. XIX corps, Oct. 1944-45; lt. gen., June 6, 1945; in battles of France, Roer, Rhine, Elbe and Germany; permanent grade of brig. gen., U.S. Army, 1945; maj. gen. U.S. Army, 1948, ret. as lt. gen., 1952; asst. chief of information, War Department, 1946-47; appointed chief of information, Department of the Army, 1948; comptroller U.S. Army, 1949-53. Now member bd. commissioners Nat. Security Tng. Commn. Awarded Distinguished Service Cross with oak leaf cluster, Distinguished Service Medal with oak leaf cluster, Silver Star, Bronze Star with oak leaf cluster, Legion of Honor, Croix de Guerre with Palm (French); Order of Orange Nassau (Netherlands); medal by Belgian Patriots (not govt. honor); Order of Leopold (Belgian); Croix de Guerre (Belgian). Clubs: Oklahoma City Golf and Country; Lions, Men's Dinner (Oklahoma City); Chevy Chase, Army-Navy (Washington). Home: 1709 Pennington Way. Office: First Nat. Bank Bldg., Okla. City; also 811 Vermont St., N.W., Washington. Died Dec. 14, 1954; buried Oklahoma City.

McLAUGHLIN, Chester Bond (măk-lŏf' lĭn) lawyer; b. Port Henry, N.Y., Dec. 11, 1895; s. Chester Bentine and Lucy (Warner) McL.; A.B., Harvard, 1915, LL.B., 1919; m. Margaret F. Williston, June 1, 1918; children—Chester Bond, Margaret Fairlie (Mrs. Standrod Carmichael), Elizabeth Annesley. Admitted to N.Y. bar, 1919; lawyer Shearman & Sterling, N.Y. City, 1919-22; in charge uptown office Rounds, Hatch, Dillingham & Debevoise, 1922-24; formed McLaughlin & Royce, 1924; mem. McLaughlin, Knollenberg, Royce & Leisure, 1927-29, McLaughlin & Stickles, 1929-50, McLaughlin, Stickles & Hayden since 1950; asst. prof. law N.J. Law Sch., 1927-32; dir. Franco-Am. Aviation Corp., Rinehart & Co., Inc., Wainwright Realty Corp., A. S. Barnes & Co., Inc. Justice of Peace, Town of Eastchester, 1928-32, mem. town bd., 1928-47; acting police judge Village of Bronxville, 1928-32. Dir. Hermitage Found., Westchester Cancer com. Am. Cancer Soc., Inc. Served as 2d lt. to capt., Judge Adv. Gen. Dept., Selective Service Bur. Q.M.C., 1917-19. Mem. Am., N.Y. State, Westchester and City of N.Y. bar assns., Am. Legion (comdr. 1925-26). S.R. Presbyn. Mason (32°). Clubs: Harvard, University, New York Yacht, Bronxville Field, St. Andrews Golf. Author articles in legal jours. Home: 39 Forest Lane, Bronxville, N.Y. Office: 36 W. 44th St., N.Y.C. 18. Died Jan. 21, 1952; buried Bronxville, N.Y.

McLAUGHLIN, Henry Woods, church official; b. Marlinton, W.Va., June 13, 1869; s. Andrew Mathews and Mary Margaret (Price) McL.; A.B., Hampden-Sidney (Va.) Coll., 1893; student Union Theol. Sem., Richmond, Va., 2 yrs.; B.D., Presbyn. Theol. Sem., Louisville, 1896; D.D., Washington and Lee U.; certificate of merit, Va. Polytechnic, for contributions to the cause of agr., 1924; m. Nellie Brown, Aug. 31, 1897; children—Virginia Tompkins, Margaret Price (Mrs. W. F. Hogshead; dec.), John Calvin Brown, Andrew Mathews, Henry Woods, James Moore, Samuel Brown, Mary Moore (Mrs. Harry Temple), Lee Massey. Ordained in ministry of the Presbyterian Ch. in U.S., 1896; served at coal mines of West Virginia, 1896-98; pastor Hampton, Va., 1898-1900; spl. work among soldiers, Spanish-Am. War; pastor Liberty and Baxter chs., W.Va., 1900-03, Stuart Robinson Memorial Ch., Louisville, 1903-09, New Providence Ch., Valley of Va., 1909-25; dir. of country ch. dept., Presbyn. Ch. in U.S., Dec. 1925-Apr. 1947; former dir. Va. Summer Sch. for Rural Ministers; former pres. Va. Rural Ch. Conf. Board; moderator Presbyn. Synod Va., 1936. Conducted farm at Maxwelton, W.Va., 1925-36, for breeding registered Polled Shorthorn cattle and Hampshire sheep; winner of more than 1,000 first prizes and championships, including internat. grand champion. Dir. Hampden-Sidney Coll., Massanetta Springs Bible Conf.; former sec. Southern Rural Ministers Edn. Assn. Mem. Polled Shorthorn Breeders Society, Va. State Fair Assn. (v.p. since 1940); formerly first pres. Virginia Shorthorn Breeders Assn.; member Pi Kappa Alpha. Democrat. Mason. Author: The New Call, 1926; Christ and the Country People, 1928; Religious Education in the Rural Church; Agriculture and the Country Church; also contributor numerous mag. articles. Co-author: Youth and Sunday School Extension, 1939; Evangelism Through Sunday School Extension, 1942; The Gospel in Action, 1944. Editor: The Country Church and Public Affairs, 1930. Teacher courses on the country church in Presbyterian theological seminaries and Vanderbilt U.; dir. Round Table on "The Task of the Country Church." in Inst. of Pub. Affairs, U. of Va. Home: 1302 Avondale Av., Richmond, Va. Died Aug. 27, 1950; buried New Providence Ch., Raphine, Va.

McLEAN, James Stanley, packing exec.; b. Durham Co., Ont., May 1, 1876; s. William and Sarah (Jennings) McL.; B.A., U. Toronto, 1896; m. Edith Flavelle, June 20, 1912; children—Mary Flavelle (Mrs. Douglas Stewart), Amy Elizabeth (Mrs. Clair Stewart), William Flavelle. Clk. Harris Abattoir Co., Toronto, 1901-05, sec., treas., 1905-27; pres. Can. Packers, Ltd., Toronto, 1927—; dir. Canadian Bank of Commerce. Mem. United Ch. Clubs: York; Caledon Trout. Home: 1225 Bayview Av., Toronto 12. Office: 2200 St. Clair Av., Toronto 9, Can. Died Sept. 1955.

McLEAN, Milton Robbins, nat. guard officer; b. Clinton, Ill., Dec. 9, 1874; s. James Oldham and Emma Day (Robbins) McL.; ed. pvt. and pub. schs., Clinton, Ill., and high sch., Havana, Ill.; pvt. instrn. spl. course in elec. subjects, Northwestern U., 1893; grad. U.S. Army Signal Sch., Langre, France, 1918; m. Mary Dougherty Share, Oct. 19, 1898; 1 dau., Mildred Share. Cashier, dir. Farmers State, Wellington, Kan., 1894-1917. Commd. maj., 110th Field Signal Bn., 35th Div., AEF, 1917; promoted lt. col. Signal Corps, U.S. Army; assigned div. signal officer; served in Vosges (Alsace and Lorraine), St. Mihiel, Argonne, Sommedieu and Verdun; brig. gen., Adj. Gen. Dept., Kan. Nat. Guard, 1925—; adj. gen. Kan., 1925—; state dir. selective service for Kan., 1940-47. Dir. Kan. Safety Council. Mem. Mil. Order World Wars (past comdr. Topeka chpt.), Navy League Am., Am. Legion, Vets. Fgn. Wars, Adjutants Gen. Assn. U.S. (sec.-treas.), N.G. Assn. U.S. (treas., 1923—), Kan. Hist. Soc. (pres., dir.). Mason (32°, K.T., Shriner), Nat. Sojourner (comdr.). Office: State House, Topeka, Kan. Died Apr. 17, 1951.

McLEAN, Simon James, economist; b. Brooklyn, June 14, 1871; s. James and Mary M.; A.B., U. of Toronto, 1894, LL.B., 1895; A.M., Columbia U., 1896; Ph.D., U. Chgo., 1897; m. Helen Baillie MacDougall, Sept. 2, 1899. Prof. economics and sociology, U. Ark., 1897-1902; asso. prof. economics, Leland Stanford Jr. U., 1902-6; asso. prof. polit. economy, U. Toronto, 1906—; mem. Bd. of Ry. Commrs. for Can., Sept. 17, 1908—. Spl. commr. on "Ry. Rate Grievances" for Canadian Govt., 1901; expert spl. agt. in investigation made by the U.S. Bur. of the Census and Interstate Commerce Commn. in regard to ry. valuations in the U.S., 1904-5. Author: Tariff History of Canada, Toronto, 1885; also many articles, mostly on ry., econ. and financial topics, in various mags. Address: Board of Railway Commissioners, Ottawa, Can. Died Nov. 1946.

McLEAN, William L., Jr., newspaper exec.; b. Philadelphia, Pa., Oct. 23, 1895; s. William L. and Sarah Burd (Warden) McL.; A.B., Princeton, 1917; m. Eleanor Ray Bushnell, Nov. 24, 1926; children—William L. III, Ray. Vice pres. and treas., Bulletin Co., publisher Philadelphia Bulletin; dir. Phila. Nat. Bank. Pres. Pa. Newspaper Pub. Association, 1947. Treas. W.C.A.U., Inc., Pennsylvania Horticultural Society. Commd. 2d lt., F.A. Reserve Corps, 1917, promoted 1st lt., 1918; with A.E.F., 1917-19; served with 103 F.A. 26th Div., 316th F.A. 81st Div. and as instr. 2d Corps Arty. Sch. Home: Wynnewood, Pa. Office: Bulletin Bldg., Phila. 5. Died Mar. 10, 1954; buried West Laurel Hill Cemetery, Phila.

McLEOD, Clarence John (măk-kloud), ex-congressman; b. Detroit, July 3, 1895; s. Malcolm J. and Christina (Darvoux) M.; student U. Detroit; LL.B., Detroit Coll. Law, 1918; m. Marie C. Posselius (died Oct. 9, 1956), May 19, 1920; children— Clarence John, Rosemary, Malcolm, Eugenie; m. 2d, Mary Louise DeMarco, Feb. 9, 1959. Pvt. Aviation Sect., Ground Sch., Cornell U., 1918; trans. to Intelligence Div., U.S. Army; commd. 2d lt. U.S.R., 1919, capt., 1923, maj., 1928, lt. col., 1936. Began practice at Detroit, 1919; mem. law firm Clarence J. McLeod. Mem. 66th and 68th to 74th, also 76th Congresses, 13th Mich. Dist. Republican. Catholic. Mem. Am., Mich., Detroit bar assns., Am. Judicature Soc., Delta Theta Phi, K.C. (4°). Clubs: University, Detroit Golf, Detroit Athletic, Army and Navy. Address: 1440 Lincolnshire Rd., Detroit 3. Died May 15, 1959; buried Mt. Olivet Cemetery, Detroit.

McLEOD, Murdoch (măk-loud), church official; b. N.S., Can., Apr. 7, 1868; s. Donald Alexander and Ellen (Goodwin) McL.; brought by parents to U.S., 1872. Student Macalester Coll., St. Paul, Minn., 1888-91; A.B., Lake Forest (Ill.) Coll., 1892; grad. McCormick Theol. Sem., 1895; D.D., Coe Coll., 1906; m. Gratia Louise Clark, Jan. 21, 1895; children—Donald Clark, Margaret Virginia (Mrs. Ozni Carver Brown), Helen Elizabeth (Mrs. Robert Brooks Wasgatt), Robert Murdoch. Ordained ministry Presbyn. Ch., 1895; pastor Austin, Minn., 1895-1900, Merriam Park Ch., St. Paul, 1900-05, Central Ch., Des Moines, Ia., 1905-07, First Ch., Tacoma, Wash., 1907-15, Grace Ch., Minneapolis, 1915-23; mem. Bd. of Christian Edn., Presbyn. Ch. in U.S.A., 1923-26; asso. pastor Shadyside Ch., Pittsburgh, Pa., 1926-28; Pacific Coast sec. and dir. men's work, Bd. of Christian Edn., Presbyn. Ch. in U.S.A., 1928-32; field rep. Gen. Council Presbyn. Ch. in U.S.A., 1932-38; now asso. pastor First Presbyn. Ch., Monrovia, Calif. Nat. del. to Pan-Presbyn. Alliance, Aberdeen, Scotland, 1913. Republican. Mason. Home: 2889 San Pasqual St., Pasadena 10, Cal. Died Dec. 8, 1957; buried San Gabriel (Cal.) Cemetery.

McLESTER, James Somerville, physician; b. Tuscaloosa, Ala., Jan. 25, 1877; s. Joseph and Nannie (Somerville) M.; A.B., U. Ala., 1896, LL.D.; M.D., U. Va., 1899; post-grad. Göttingen, Freiburg, 1901-02, Berlin and Munich, 1907-08; m. Ada Bowron, 1903; children—Anna, James B., Jane. Prof. medicine U. Ala., 1919-50. Maj. Chief on Med., Base Hosp., Camp Sheridan, 1917; lt. col. AEF, comdg. officer Evacuation Hosp. 20, 1918; cons. AEF, 1918. Researches and scientific articles dealing chiefly with diseases of nutrition and metabolism; chmn. subcommittee on med. nutrition NRC. Fellow A.C.P.; mem. A.M.A. (chmn. sect. on practice of medicine, 1920; pres. 1935-36; chmn. council on foods and nutrition), Assn. Am. physicians, Am. Soc. Clin. Investigation, Am. Climatological and Clin. Assn., So., Ala. Med. Assn., (pres. 1920) med. assns. Democrat. Presbyn. Club: Mountain Brook. Author (textbooks): Nutrition and Diet in Health and Disease; The Diagnosis and Treatment of Disorder of Metabolism. Home: 3224 Country Club Rd. Office: 930 S. 20th St., Birmingham, Ala. Died Feb. 8, 1954.

McLOUTH, Donald B., business exec.; b. Cleve., 1901. Pres., dir. McLouth Steel Corp.; dir. Gaylord (Mich.) Mfg. Co. Home: Martel Dr., Bloomfield, Mich. Office: 300 S. Livernois, Detroit 17. Died July 10, 1954.

McLUCAS, Walter Scott, banker; b. Newcastle, Ind., July 28, 1875; s. John C. and Louisa Belle (Cooper) M.; ed. U. of Neb.; m. Grace Nichols, Oct. 12, 1898; children—Mrs. Marjorie McL. de Kuyper, John Nichols; m. 2d, Mrs. George B. (Ann Cole) Longan, Jan. 31, 1948. In live stock commn. and loan business, Omaha, Neb., 18 mos.; later official court reporter, 1st Jud. Dist. of Neb., 3½ yrs.; again in live stock commn. and loan business at St. Joseph, Mo., and Kansas City; v.p. and cashier Merchants Bank, St. Joseph, 1908-12, and upon consolidation, 1912, with First Nat. Bank, was made 1st v.p. First Nat. Bank; v.p. Commerce Trust Co. of Kansas City, 1915-17, pres., 1917-21, vice-pres. Nat. City Bank, New York, 1921-22, pres. Commerce Trust Co., Kansas City, Nov. 1922; chmn. bd., 1926-33; pres. Nat. Bank of Detroit, 1933-38, chmn. of bd. since 1938. Former mem. Nat. Credit Corp.; ex-chmn. for Kansas City, Reconstruction Finance Corp. Ex-pres. Chamber of Commerce of Kansas City, Trust Co. Div. of Am. Bankers Assn.; mem. Beta Theta Pi; former mem. Advisory Council Federal Reserve Bd. Republican. Mem. Christian (Disciples) Ch. Mason (K.T., 32°, Shriner), Elk. Clubs: Metropolitan (New York); Chicago (Chicago); Detroit, Detroit Athletic, Bankers, Recess, Country, Economic (Detroit); Grosse Pointe Club, Bloomfield Hills Country, Yondotega; River Kansas City Country (Kansas City, Mo.). Home: 415 Burns Drive, Detroit 14. Office: National Bank of Detroit, Detroit 32. Died Feb. 5, 1953.

McMAHON, Brien, U.S. sen.; b. Norwalk, Conn., Oct. 6, 1903; s. William H. and Eugenie J. (O'Brien) McM.; A.B., Fordham U., 1924; LL.D., 1946; LL.B., Yale, 1927; m. Rosemary Turner, Feb. 6, 1940; 1 dau., Patricia Rosemary. Admitted to Conn. bar, 1927 and practiced with Keogh and Candee of Norwalk, Conn.; judge City Court, Norwalk, 1933; special assistant to United States attorney general, 1933-35, acting asst., 1935-36, became asst. atty. general in charge Criminal Div., 1936; chairman attorney general's committee on Survey of Release Procedures, (published by Dept. of Justice 1939); elected U.S. Senator from Connecticut in November, 1944 for term expiring Jan., 1951, reelected Nov. 1950 for term expiring January 1957; had charge for government of prosecution of Harlan County Coal Operators Associations. Mem. Am. Bar Assn., Phi Alpha Delta. Democrat. Roman Catholic. Clubs:

Burning Tree, Metropolitan (Washington, D.C.); Shorehaven Golf (East Norwalk, Conn.). Author of McMahon Act for control of atomic energy. Chmn. Spl. Com. on atomic energy, U.S. Senate, 1945-47. Home: South Norwalk, Conn. Office: Senate Office Building, Washington. Deceased.

McMAHON, John Robert, author; b. British India, Sept. 1, 1875; s. Rev. John Todd and Sarah (Douglas) M.; mostly self-taught; m. Margherita Arlina Hamm (died 1907); 1 dau., Arlina Douglas (known on stage and in radio as Eileen Douglas; died 1939); m. 2d, Beatrice Lessey, June 17, 1913 (died 1942). Reporter and Sunday article writer for N.Y. newspapers from 1894; began writing fiction for mags., 1910; contributor Saturday Evening Post, etc.; traveled Europe widely after World War I, USSR in 1933. Private Co. D, 202d Regt. New York, Spanish-American War; 9 mos. service, including 3 mos. in Cuba. Mem. Authors' League America. Author: Toilers and Idlers, 1907; The House That Junk Built, 1915; Success in the Suburbs, 1917; Your House, 1927; The Wright Brothers—Fathers of Flight, 1930. Editor and part author of How These Farmers Succeeded, 1919. Home: Box 144, Little Falls, N.J. Died Jan. 13, 1956.

McMAHON, Stephen John, lawyer; b. Meeme, Manitowoc County, Wis., Jan. 13, 1881; s. Patrick J. and Margaret (Gray) McM.; grad. Milwaukee Normal Sch. (now State Teachers Coll.), 1900; Ph. B. U. of Wis., 1903 (sr class commencement orator), LL.B., 1906; studied Coll. of Law, U. of Chgo., 1903-04; m. Alice Mary Donohue, Feb. 1, 1916; children—Stephen John, Eugene Francis. Prin. pub. schs., Park Falls, Wis., 1900-01, Mt. Horeb High Sch., 1903-04; supt. schs., Black River Falls, 1906-07; admitted to Wis. bar, 1906, Supreme Court of U.S., 1914; practiced at Antigo, Wis., 1907-11, Milwaukee, 1911—; asst. U.S. atty., Eastern Dist. of Wis., 1911-12; mem. faculty Law Sch. of Marquette U., 1914-17; mem. firm Hoyt, Goff & McMahon, 1917-18; sr. mem. firm McMahon, McMahon & Hayes, 1921-25; govt. appeal agt., Div. 1, Milwaukee Draft Bd., World War; gen. counsel Northwestern Casualty & Surety Co., 1921-24; mem. bd. Nat. Aeronautic Assn., 1924-25; chmn. Wis. Hoover-Curtis Campaign Com., 1928; apptd. mem. U.S. Bd. Tax Appeals by President Hoover, 1929, term expiring June 2, 1938, resigned Nov. 1, 1936; legal specialist to commanding general U.S. Forces Pacific Ocean Area, Tokyo, Dec. 1945. Mem. Am., Wis. State and Milwaukee bar assns., Milwaukee Normal Sch. and U. of Wis. alumni assns., Civil Legion, Sigma Alpha Epsilon. Republican. Elk; mem. Knights of Columbus. Home: 830 N. 70th St., Wauwautosa 13, Wis. Office: First Wisconsin National Bank Bldg., Milwaukee, Wis. Died Feb. 14, 1960.

McMAHON, Thomas J. (măk-mă'hŭn), clergyman; b. Tuxedo Park, N.Y., Apr. 5, 1909; s. James and Elizabeth (Brennan) McM.; student Cathedral Coll., N.Y., 1928; A.B., St. Joseph's Sem., Yonkers, N.Y., 1930; S.T.B., Propaganda U., Rome, Italy, 1930-32; S.T.D., Gregorian U., Rome, 1932-36; cand. Ph.D., Fordham U., N.Y., 1938-40, LL.D., 1952; LL.D., Manhattan Coll., 1949; Ordained Roman Catholic priest, 1933; adminstr. Sacred Heart Ch., Newburgh, N.Y., 1936; prof. church history, St. Joseph's Sem., 1937-43 (staff lecturer, Catholic summer sch., 1938-41); nat. dir., Catholic Near East Welfare Assn., 1943, nat. sec., 1943-55; state advisor, K. of C. Radio Programs, 1941; moderator, Morgan Frat., 1939; mem. exec. council, Am. Cath. Hist. Soc., 1941-42. Spiritual dir. St. Paul's Guild, 1948-51; spl. rep. Am. hierarchy in work for Palestinian refugees, 1948; pres. Pontificial Mission for Palestine, 1949—. Rep. Vatican at ECOSOC, 1954, 55. Master of Cermonies to Archbishop Spellman, 1943; named Papal Chamberlain with title of Very Reverend Monsignor, 1945, Domestic Prelate, 1948, by His Holiness, Pope Pius XII Rt. Rev. Monsignor, 1948; Hon. Canon, Holy Sepulchre, Jerusalem, 1949; Knight comdr. with star Order Holy Sepulchre, 1950; Bernadotte medal League of Red Cross, 1950; named Prothonotary Apostolic by Pope Pius XII, 1953; awarded Grand Cross of Order of Holy Sepulchre, 1953; named consultor of Archdiocese by Francis Cardinal Spellman, 1955. Mem. Am. Hist. Assn., Am. Catholic Hist. Assn., Medieval Acad. of America, Am. Soc. of Church Hist., U.S. Cath. Hist. Soc., Fordham Conf. on Eastern Rites, Knights of Columbus. Medieval Club, Columbia U. Editor of publs. U.S. Cath. Hist. Soc., 1940; Historical Records and Studies. Home: 70 Park Av. Office: 480 Lexington Av., N.Y.C. 17. Died Dec. 6, 1956.

McMANAMON, James Emmett, lawyer; b. Indianapolis, May 1, 1905; s. Martin and Maria (Moran) Mc.; LL.B., Ind. U., 1931; m. Nancy Cordelia Pratt, Nov. 13, 1948; children—James Emmett, Patricia Louise. Admitted to Ind. bar, 1930; apptd. magistrate of Marion Co., Ind., 1945; atty. gen. of Ind., 1948-53; director, sec. Evansville (Ind.) Television, Inc.; sec., dir. Meadowbrook Corp. Member Nat. Assn. Attys. Gen. (mem. exec. com.), Am., Ind. State, Indianapolis bar assns., Sigma Delta Kappa. K.C. (grand knights, 1944-45). Clubs: Highland Golf and Country, Athletic, Columbia (Indianapolis); Dunham Woods Riding (Wayne, Ill.). Home: 3540 Watson Rd. Office: Suite 712, Electric Bldg., Indpls. Died Aug. 5, 1954; buried Holy Cross Cemetery, Indpls.

McMANUS, George, cartoonist; b. St. Louis, Mo., Jan. 23, 1884; s. George and Kathrine (Kenrick) McM.; hon. Dr. Humane Letters, Roanoke Coll., Va.; m. Florence Bergèr, Dec. 24, 1910. Began as cartoonist, St. Louis Republic, 1899; joined N.Y. World, 1905, N.Y. American, 1912. Creator of comic series: Let George Do It; Panhandle Pete; The Newly Weds and Their Baby; Rosie's Beau; Snookums; Bringing Up Father. Bringing Up Father appears in over 750 papers over the world and in 27 different languages; 7 Bringing Up Father shows have toured America for 11 years, and the comic strip has been running for more than 41 yrs.; radio programs have been based on the strip, also motion pictures made by Christie Bros., Vitagraph, Metro-Goldwyn-Mayer and Monogram; author appeared in 4 of most recent movies. "Jiggs" served as official insignia of 11th Bombardment Squadron in World War I and World War II; planes with Rosie's Beau, Snookums and Maggie insignia, in the Air Corps. Meritorious Service Award, by A.R.C.; Silver Lady award, Banshees, 1951. Mem. Beverly Hills C. of C. Mason (Shriner). Clubs: Beverly Hills; Silurians, The Jesters, Saints and Sinners, Metropolitan, Banshee (N.Y.); Bohemian (San Francisco); Los Angeles Country Club, National Cartoonists Soc. (N.Y.). Made Ky. col. by Gov. Flem Sampson, 1931. Hon. tribute in Senate Congl. Record, Jan. 26, 1932; Award of Honor, Nat. Father's Day Com., 1940; Awarded title Laff-Maker of 1944, by 1st Nat. Conv. of Laff-Makers. Has appeared on num. TV and radio programs. Author: Fun For All, 1948. Address: Beverly Hills Nat. Bank and Trust Co., 9600 Santa Monica Blvd., Beverly Hills, Cal. Died Oct. 22, 1954; buried McManus Mausoleum, Woodlawn Cemetery, N.Y.C.

McMARTIN, Charles, urologist; b. nr. Dunlap, Ia., May 11, 1880; s. Archibald I. and Harriet Amelia (Smith) McM.; Ph.B., Grinnel (Ia.) Coll., 1902; M.D., Rush Med. Sch., 1906; m. Mary Elizabeth O'Kelly (dec. Feb. 21, 1951); children—William Joseph, Harriet Margaret (Mrs. Dale Norman). Intern Alexian Hosp., Chicago, 1906-07; pvt. practice medicine, specialist urology, Omaha, since 1908; prof. urology Creighton U. Med. Sch. since 1910, prof. dermatology, urology, 1910-45, head dept. surgery, mem. bd. adminstrn. (also St. Joseph's Hosp.), 1936-50. Diplomate Am. Bd. Urology. Fellow A.C.S.; mem. A.M.A., Am. Urol. Assn. (pres. South Central sect. 1938, nat. pres. 1947), Neb. State (pres. 1945), Douglas Co. (pres. 1935), Omaha med. socs., Omaha Midwest Clin. Soc. (pres. 1941). Home: 1714 Douglas St., Omaha 2. Office: City Nat. Bank Bldg., Omaha 2, Neb. Died Sept. 14, 1954; buried Forest Lawn Cemetery, Omaha.

McMILLAN, Fred Orville, educator; b. Albia, Ia., May 12, 1890; s. William L. and Jennie R. (Donaldson) M.; B.S., Ore. State Coll., 1912; M.S., Union Coll., 1919; m. Elizabeth Denny, Oct. 18, 1914; children—Frederick Russell, Donald Denny, Kathleen Mae. With testing dept., Gen. Elec. Co., Schenectady, N.Y., 1912-14, designing engring., 1914-20; asst. prof. elec. engring., Ore. State Coll., 1920-23, asso. prof., 1923-30, research prof., 1930-37, prof. and dept. head 1937—; specialist in elec. engring. to Chinese Govt. in China, 1943-44. Mem. Corvallis Bd. Edn. (chmn. 1948-49). Fellow A.I.E.E. (v.p. 1934-36, dir. 48-51, pres. 51-52), A.A.A.S.; sr. mem. Inst. Radio Engrs.; mem. Am. Soc. Engring. Edn., Nat. Soc. Profl. Engrs., Profl. Engrs. of Ore. (pres. Mid-Willamette sect., 1948-49), Corvallis Engrs., Phi Kappa Phi, Eta Kappa Nu, Sigma Tau, Sigma Xi, Tau Beta Pi. Republican. Baptist. Contbr. numerous articles in various publs. Home: 2990 Harrison St., Corvallis, Ore. Died Apr. 28, 1956.

McMILLAN, Homer, ch. ofcl.; b. Cedarville, O., Dec. 20, 1873; s. James and Martha (Murdock) McM.; A.B., Cedarville Coll., 1897; B.D., New Brunswick (N.J.) Theol. Sem., 1900; D.D., Westminster (Mo.) Coll., 1911, LL.D., 1936; m. Mary Hannah Kitchen, June 12, 1900; children—Richard Hunt, Mary Ruth, Hugh Frederick, Luella Jane. Ordained ministry Ref. Ch. Am., 1900; pastor successively Bogota, N.J., Los Angeles, and Buford, Ga., until 1906; gen. sec. Exec. Com. Home Missions, Presbyn. Ch. U.S., 1906—. Mem. Alliance Presbyn. and Reform Chs.; rep. World Presbyn. Alliance, Pitts., 1920, Cardiff, Wales, 1925, Montreal, Can., 1937; mem. Home Mission Council (mem. adminstrv. com.); mem. World Conf. Faith and Order; mem. exec. com. World Council Chs.; mem. Assembly World Council Chs., Amsterdam, 1948. Pres. Interdenom. Home Mission Council, N.Y., 1939-40. Democrat. Author: Unfinished Tasks, 1922; Near Neighbors, 1930; Other Men Labored, 1937. Home: 74 Peachtree Way, Atlanta. Died Feb. 8, 1958.

McMILLEN, Fred Ewing, naval officer; b. Springfield, Wis., Apr. 11, 1882; s. Frederick Alonzo and Mary (Ewing) McM.; ed. Whitewater (Wis.) State Teachers Coll.; B.S., U.. Naval Academy, 1904; m. Ruth Burns, Dec. 4, 1907; children—Mary Thomas (Mrs. Robt. J. Schneider), Jean (Mrs. Hugh R. Jones), Alan Bourne. Instr., U.S. Naval Acad., 1904-07; commd. ensign (SC) Navy, 1907, advancing through the grades to rear adm., 1942. Home: 111 Paris Rd., New Hartford, N.Y. Died Sept. 17, 1959; buried Middleville, N.Y.

McMILLEN, James Adelbert, librarian; b. nr. Maryville, Mo., Jan. 23, 1889; s. Cyrus Grant and Mary Ann (Warner) McM.; student N.W. Mo. State Teachers Coll., 1906-07; A.B., with gen. honors, U. of Mo., 1913; B.L.S., N.Y. State Library Sch., 1915; m. Lillian Burk, July 3, 1930; 1 dau., Carol Jean. Asst. librarian Maryville Pub. Library, 1906-07, librarian, same, 1907-09; asst., U. of Mo. Library, 1910-13, N.Y. State Library, 1914-15, New York Pub. Library, summer 1914; librarian U. of Rochester, 1915-19; librarian Washington Univ., 1919-27; librarian La. State U. since Sept. 16, 1927, also dir. Sch. of Library Sciences, 1931-37, and dir. of libraries 1937-44, bibliographer since 1944, prof. library science, 1944-50; dir. Library Sch. since 1940; instr. Columbia U. Sch. of Library Service, summer, 1939. Chief Quartermaster (Aviation), U.S. Naval Aviation detachment, at Mass. Inst. Tech., summer and autumn, 1918. Mem. A.L.A. (sec. coll. and reference sect. 1923-29, chmn. 1931-32), Bibliog. Soc. America, La. Library Assn. (pres. 1937-38), N.Y. Library Assn., Southwestern Library Assn. (pres. 1928-30), Am. Assn. Univ. Profs., Am. Library Inst.; Phi Beta Kappa; president Missouri Library Association, 1923. Democrat. Member Disciples of Christ. Compiler: Inter-library Loans, 1928; The Works of James D. B. De Bow—A Bibliography, 1940. Contbr. to library periodicals. Home: 4641 Vanderbilt Dr., Baton Rouge. Died Apr. 29, 1953.

McMILLIN, Alvin Nugent (Bo), football coach; b. Prairie Hill, Tex., Jan. 12, 1899; s. Ruben Thomas and Matilda (Riley) McM.; A.B., Centre Coll., 1922; m. Marie Myers, Jan. 2, 1922 (died 1926); 1 dau., Fleurette Marie; m. 2d, Kathryn Gillihan, Oct. 6, 1930; children—Jere Robert, Kathryn Jane, Nugent Lewis, Michael. Football coach, Centenary Coll., 1922-24, Geneva Coll., 1925-27, Kansas State Coll., 1928-33, Indiana U., 1934—; asst. coach Chicago Tribune All-Star Football Team, 1936, head coach, 1938; gen. mgr. and head coach, Detroit Lions, Detroit Football Co., Mar. 1948-50; coach Philadelphia Eagles, 1951. President of National Football Coaches Assn., 1940. Mem. Am. Football Coaches Assn. (pres.; mem. rules com.), Beta Theta Pi. Democrat. Roman Catholic. Elk. K.C. Club: Bloomfield Hills Country. Addres: 812 S. Jordan Av., Bloomington, Ind. Died Mar. 31, 1952.

McMILLIN, John Milton, business exec.; b. Portsmouth, O., Nov. 19, 1883; s. Frank Emerson and Esther Allison (Black) McM.; B.S., Mass. Inst. Tech., 1907; m. Enid Nelle Shaw, Sept. 22, 1915; children—Leslie Shaw, John M. Engr. Veta Colo. and Palmilla mines, Minas Nuevas and Paral, Chihuahua, Mexico, 1907, Denver (Colo.) Gas & Electric Co., 1909-10; engaged principally in financial matters of Cities Service Co., New York, and subsidiaries and affiliates since 1910; dir., vice pres. and exec. com. Cities Service Co. since 1932. Dir. Ark.-La. Gas Co., Ark. Natural Gas Corp., Cities Service Oil Co., Ltd., Cities Service Oil (Pa.), Cities Service Refining Corp.; Sixty Wall Street, Sixty Wall Tower, Inc. Vice pres., dir. and exec. com. Empire Gas & Fuel Co. Home: 435 E. 52d St., New York 22. Office: 60 Wall Tower, N.Y. 5. Died Dec. 27, 1951; buried Ferncliff, N.Y.

McMILLIN, Stewart Earl, ret. consular officer; b. Arkansas City, Kan., Dec. 17, 1889; s. Frank R. and Emma May (Regal) McM.; A.B., U. Kan., 1914, LL.B., 1917; m. Laura May Miles, Sept. 15, 1913 (died Dec. 9, 1924); m. 2d Gwendolyne Olive Hill, July 2, 1926 (div. 1933); children—Patricia Joyce, Donald Hill; m. 3d, Olive Marjorie Roundy Lovell, Sept. 29, 1941; 1 step-dau., Joy Rosemary Lovell. Consul at Port Limon, Costa Rica, 1917-22, Antofagasta, Chile, 1922-25, La Paz, Bolivia, 1925-26, Belgrade, Yugoslavia, 1926-27; consul in charge, Zagreb, Yugoslavia, Oct.-Nov. 1927; consul Belgrade, 1927-31, Warsaw, 1931-33, Piedras Negras, Mexico, 1933-36, Caracas, Venezuela, 1936-41; Dept. State, 1941-43; consul at Mazatlán, Mexico, 1943-46, Winnipeg, Can., 1946-48, ret. Fellow Am. Geog. Soc. N.Y. Club: Explorers (N.Y.C.). Address: 1036 N B St., Arkansas City, Kan. Died Nov. 1, 1952; buried Riverview Cemetery.

McMORRAN, Henry, ex-congressman; b. Port Huron, Mich., June 11, 1841; s. Robert W. and Isabella M.; pub. sch. edn.; m. Emma C. Williams, Oct. 11, 1866. Engaged in wholesale grocery bus., 1865; one of original promoters (and constructors) Port Huron & Northwestern Ry., 218 miles, and mgr., 1878-89, until sold to P.M. Ry.; pres. Port Huron Light & Power Co., Port Huron Savs. Bank; v.p. Flint Pantaloon Co.; pres. McMorran Milling Co.; treas. Port Huron & Sarnia Ferry Co., Pawnee Boat Co.; mgr. Mills Transportation Co. Has held various local offices; mem. 58th to 62d Congresses, 7th Mich. Dist. Republican. Address: Port Huron, Mich. Died 1929.

McMORRIS, Charles H(oratio), naval officer; b. Wetumpka, Ala., Aug. 31, 1890; s. Spencer James and Annie Amanda (Robison) McM.; B.S., U.S. Naval Acad., 1912; grad. Naval War Coll., 1938; married, Dec. 27, 1916; 1 son, David Spencer. Entered USN, 1908, advanced through grades to vice adm., 1943; head war plans div., staff Comdr. in Chief, Pacific Area, 1941-42; comd. U.S.S. San Francisco during battle Lunga Point, 1942, Task Force in Aleutians during battle of Kormandorskis, 1943; chief of staff Pacific Fleet and Pacific Ocean Areas, 1943-45. Fourth Fleet, 1946. Chmn. Gen. Bd., 1947-48; comdt. 14th Naval Dist. and Hawaiian Sea Frontier, 1948. Decorated Navy Cross, D.S.M. (twice), Legion of Merit, Presdl. Unit Citation, Mexican Border, World War I, Second Nicaraguan, Pearl Harbor, Victory and Asiatic-Pacific ribbons. Home: Honolulu, Hawaii. Office: 14 Naval Dist., Pearl Harbor, Hawaii. Died Feb. 11, 1954; buried Arlngton Nat. Cemetery.

McMORROW, Thomas, writer, lawyer; b. N.Y.C., Oct. 29, 1886; s. Patrick and Catherine (Killeen) McM.; prep. edn. Clason Point Mil. Acad., N.Y.C., 1895-1901; B.A., Manhattan Coll., 1905; m. Hedwig Gertrude Evers, June 25, 1918; children—Thomas Evers, Frederick James. Admitted to N.Y. bar, 1908, began practice in N.Y.C. Served in Co. E, 53d Pioneer Inf., U.S. Army, participating in battles at St. Mihiel, Argonne and offensive on Meuse, World War; hon. discharged as sgt. Club: National Press (Washington). Real estate editor, New Brunswick Sun. Times Award. Author: The Sandalwood Fan; Tammany Boy; The Sinister History of Ambrose Hinkle. Contbr. about 350 stories to mags., mostly in Collier's and Sat. Eve. Post. Address: Ocean Beach, Fire Island, N.Y.; also 268 Livingston Av., New Brunswick, N.J. Died Nov. 18, 1957.

McMULLAN, Harry, lawyer; b. Hertford, N.C., July 23, 1884; s. John Henry (M.D.) and Carolina (Tucker) McM.; student Edenton Acad., 1891-1901; LL.B., University of North Carolina, 1905; LL.D., U. of North Carolina, 1946; m. Pattie Mary Baugham, Oct. 4, 1911; children—Pattie Mary (Mrs. W. T. Old, Jr.), Mildred Louise (Mrs. H. B. Rumley, Jr.), Harry, James Baugham. Admitted to N.C. bar, 1905, practiced at Edenton, 1905-07, Washington, N.C., 1907-33; mem. Small, MacLean & McMullan, 1908-13; chmn. Beaufort County Draft Bd., 1917-18; county atty. Beaufort County, 1926-33; elected mem. N.C. State Senate, 1st Dist., 1929; dir. Collections and Assessments, State Dept. of Revenue, 1933-34; chmn. N.C. Industrial Commn., 1934-36; asst. atty. gen. of N.C., 1936-38, atty. gen., May 1938—; dir. Bank of Washington, 1913—. Chmn. bd. trustees Washington Collegiate Inst., 1918-28. Mem. National Assn. Attorneys General (pres. 1951), Am. and N.C. bar assns., Delta Kappa Epsilon, Gimghoul; v.p. Nat. Assn. State Tax Adminstrs., 1933-34. Democrat. Episcopalian. Club: Carolina Country (Raleigh). Home: 107 E Lane St. Office: Justice Bldg., Raleigh, N.C.; also Washington, N.C. Died June 23, 1955; buried Washington, N.C.

McMULLEN, Chester Bartow, ex-congressman; b. Largo, Fla., Dec. 6, 1902; s. Eli Bartow and Emma (Cox) McM.; LL.B., U. Fla., 1924; m. Veda E. Ulmer, Dec. 25, 1923; children—Chester B., Elizabeth. Admitted to Fla. bar, 1924, since practiced in Clearwater; partner McMullen, McMullen & Pogue, 1925—; pros. atty. Pinellas County, 1927-28; states atty., 6th Judicial Circuit, Fla., 1931-50. Mem. 82d Congress, 1st Fla. Dist. Dir. The First Nat. Bank of Clearwater. Mem. Clearwater Bar Assn. (past pres.), Pi Kappa Alpha. Democrat. Methodist. Mason. (Shriner), Elk, Moose, Rotarian (past pres.). Home: 1008 Druid Rd., Clearwater, Fla. Died Nov. 3, 1953.

McMULLEN, Clements, ret. army ofcr.; b. Largo, Fla., Feb. 5, 1892; s. William and Rosa (Ramage) McM.; ed. Washington and Lee U., 1907-11; m. Adelaide Lewis; children—Edward L., Frank M., William C., Thomas H. Civil engr., 1911-17; entered USAAF, 1917; commd. 2d lt., 1918, promoted through grades to maj. gen., 1942; record flight to Buenos Aires from N.Y. in 5 days, Feb. 1930; chief Air Force Engring. Development Sect., 1931-33; operations officer, Gen. Hdqrs., 1936-37; comdg. officer 3d Air Force Area Service Command, Atlanta, 1942; assigned to Hdqrs. AS Command, Washington, chief maintenance div., 1942; comd. Far East AS Command, 1944-45; chief staff Pacific Air Command, 1946; dep. comdr. strat. air command; commd. San Antonio Air Materiel Area, 1949-54, ret.; chmn. indsl. com. San Antonio C. of C., 1955—. Vice pres. Community Chest; dir. United Fund, 1954-58; nat. comdr. Order of Daedalians, 1952-56. Rated command pilot, combat and tech. observer. Decorated Air Medal, D.S.M. with two oak-leaf clusters. Fellow Inst. Aero. Scis.; mem. Air Force Assn. (v.p. S.W. Region 1955-57). Address: San Antonio. Died Jan. 1959.

McMURRICH, J(ames) Playfair, educator; b. Toronto, Ont., Oct. 16, 1859; s. Hon. John and Janet (Dickson) M.; A.B., U. Toronto, 1879, A.M., 1881; Ph.D., Johns Hopkins, 1885; m. Katie Moodie, Sept. 20, 1882. Prof. biology Ont. Agrl. Coll., 1882-84; instr. mammalian anatomy Johns Hopkins, 1884-86; prof. biology Haverford Coll., 1886-89; docent, asst. prof. animal morphology Clark U., 1889-92; prof. biology U. Cin., 1892-94; prof. anatomy U. Mich., 1894-1907, dir. anat. lab., 1898-1907; prof. anatomy U. Toronto, 1907—, dean sch. grad. studies, 1922-30; instr. Woods Hole, Mass., 1887-91. Mem. adv. bd. Wistar Inst. Anatomy, Phila. Fellow Royal Micros. Soc., Royal Soc. Can. (pres. 1922), A.A.A.S. (pres. 1922); mem. Zool. Soc. London (corr.), Am. Philos. Soc., Am. Soc. Naturalists (pres. 1907), Assn. Am. Anatomists (pres. 1908-09), Am. Zool Soc. (sec. 1890-93). Author: Invertebrate Morphology, 1894; The Development of the Human Body, 1902, 7th edit. 1923; Leonardo de Vinci The Anatomist, 1930; also various papers on zool. and anat. subjects in Am. and European periodicals. Editor: Sobotta's Atlas of Anatomy, 1906; Morris' Human Anatomy, 4th edit., 1907. Home: Elgin St., Thornhill, Ont. Office: Dept. of Anatomy, U. Toronto, Toronto, Ont., Can. Died Feb. 9, 1939.

McMURTRY, James Gilmer (măk-mûr′trĭ), coll. dean and lecturer; b. Judson, Ind., Apr. 2, 1870; s. David William and Martha Elinor (Cooper) M.; A.B., Wabash Coll., 1893, A.M., 1895, Ph.D., 1898; fellow Am. Sch. of Archæology, Athéns, Greece, with travel and study in Europe, Palestine and Egypt, 1907; m. Mary Anice Bray, July 25, 1894; children—Mildred Oenone, James G. Prof. Greek and Latin, Carthage Coll., Mo., 1893-94; prof. Greek and philosophy, and v.p., Washington Coll., Tenn., 1895-97; prof. Greek and philosophy, Henry Kendall Coll., Okla., 1898-1902; prof. Greek, Parsons Coll., Ia., 1902-09; field sec. and banker, 1909-11; prof. Greek, 1911-13, pres., 1913-16, Drury Coll., Springfield, Mo.; dean and prof. Greek and Bible, Henry Kendall Coll., Tulsa, Okla., 1916, acting pres., 1917-18; prof. Bibl. lit. and applied religion, Colorado Coll., 1918-38, dean 1919-23, dean Shove Memorial Chapel, 1931-38; retired from teaching; pastor First Presbyn. Ch., Lufkin, Tex., 1938-47; interim minister Brazos Presbytery since 1947. Pres. Angelina County Ministerial Alliance 1939-47. Member Classical Association Middle West and South, Am. Philol. Assn., Phi Beta Kappa, Pi Gamma Mu, Eta Sigma Phi. Rotarian. Home: 3302 Plumb St., Houston. Died Mar. 3, 1954; buried Forest Park Cemetery, Houston.

McNAB, Alexander J., mining exec.; b. Ont., Can., 1877; student Queen's U., 1902, LL.D., 1952; m. Doris Elsa McNab; children—Norna B. Smith, Thomas Campbell. Chmn., dir. Copper Co., San Manuel Copper Corp.; v.p., dir. Hudson Bay Mining & Smelting Co., Ltd.; dir. O'Oklep Copper Co., Ltd., Tsumeb Corp., Ltd. Mem. Am. Inst. Mining and Metall. Engrs. Clubs: Canadian, Bankers (N.Y.C.); Siwanoy Country (Bronxville, N.Y.). Home: Mayfair House, Park Av. and 65th St., N.Y.C. Office: 14 Wall St., N.Y.C. 5. Died July 4, 1956.

McNALLY, Andrew, publisher; b. Chicago, Ill., July 31, 1886; s. Frederick G. and Lydia (Wyles) McN.; student Yale, 1909; m. Eleanor Vilas, 1908; children—Andrew III, Eleanor, Ward, Frederick George. Chmn. Bd. Rand McNally & Co. Clubs: Chicago, Glenview. Office: 124 W. Monroe St., Chgo. 3. Died May 20, 1954; buried Graceland Cemetery, Chgo.

McNALLY, Paul Aloysius, clergyman; b. Phila., Oct. 14, 1890; s. Charles S. and Martha Virginia (Tully) McN.; A.B., Woodstock Coll., Md., 1915, A.M., 1917; U. Innsbruck, Austria; Ph.D., Fordham U., 1921; student U. Calif., 1926-28; S.T.D., Gregorian U., Rome, Italy, 1925; D.Sc., St. Joseph's Coll., Phila., 1940; LL.D., U. San Francisco, 1943; D.Sc., Georgetown U., 1952. Mem. Soc. Jesus. Ordained priest Roman Catholic Ch., 1923; prof. mathematics Boston Coll., 1915-19; prof. higher mathematics and philosophy, Fordham U., 1919-21; asst. dir. Georgetown Coll. Observatory, 1925-28, dir., 1928-42; v.p. Georgetown U., 1942, regent and dean, Sch. of Medicine, 1946, regent Sch. of Dentistry, 1946-48, Sch. of Nursing, 1946-48, dir. Georgetown U. Med. Center, 1946, head physics dept., 1954; dir. Georgetown Eclipse Expdn., Fryeburg, Me., 1932; Georgetown-Nat. Geog. Eclipse Expdn., Kustanai U.S.S.R., 1936; mem. Nat. Geog. Soc. U.S.N. Eclipse Expdn. Canton Island, South Pacific, 1937, Nat. Geog. Soc. Nat. Bur. Standards Eclipse Expdn., Patos, Brazil, 1940. Trustee Hosp. Service Agency, Group Hosp., Inc.; hon. consultant Surgeon Gen. U.S. Navy and Army, Pub. Health Service. Fellow A.A.A.S., Royal Astron. Soc. of England; mem. Am. Astron. Soc., Astron. Soc. of Pacific, Washington Acad. of Sci. Club: Cosmos (Washington). Contbr. papers on eclipses, variable stars, occulations, Herschel areas. Office: Georgetown Med. Center, Washington 7. Died Mar. 4, 1955; buried The Jesuit Cemetery, Georgetown University.

McNAUGHT, James B(ernard), pathologist, educator; b. Girard, Kan., July 11, 1894; s. Joseph Ezra and Agnes Abbie (Johnson) McN.; A.B., U. of Kan., 1917, A.M., 1917; M.D., Stanford, 1931; unmarried. Instr. bacteriology U. Kan., 1919-21; dir. labs. Burnett Sanitarium, Fresno, Cal., 1923-27; asst. pathology Stanford, 1930-31, instr. pathol., 1931-35, asst. prof. pathol., 1935-40, asso. prof. pathol., 1940-45; exchange instr. pathol., U. Rochester, 1934-35; dir. and pathol. Palo Alto (Calif.) Hosp., 1937-45; prof. and head pathol. dept. U. Colo., 1945—. Served as 1st lt., Inf., U.S. Army, World War I. Cons. to A.E.C., Div. Biol. and Medicine, 1948—. Expert cons. to Surgeon Gen., U.S. Army, 1946—; cons. pathology to surgeon gen. U.S. Air Force, 1952—; area cons. in pathol. St. Louis Med. area, Vets. Admistrn., 1946—; mem. sci. adv. bd. consultants to Armed Forces Inst. of Pathology, 1955—. Trustee Belle Bonfils Memorial Blood Bank, Denver, 1945—. Diplomate Am. Bd. Pathology (trustee 1944-56, pres. 1953-55). Mem. A.M.A., Am. Soc. Clin. Pathol. (pres. 1949-50), Coll. Am. Pathol. (gov. 1947), Am. Assn. Pathol. and Bacteriol. (councilor 1949—, pres. 1953-54), Internat. Assn. Med. Mus. (councilor 1949-51, v.p. 1951-52, pres. 1952-53), Am. Phys. Art Assn. (charter mem.), Am. Soc. Exptl. Pathol., A.A.A.S., Am. Soc. Tropical Med., Am. Society Parasitol., Fedn. Am. Socs. for Exptl. Biol., Soc. for Exptl. Biol. and Med., Alpha Kappa Kappa (asso. editor, The Centaur of A.K.K., 1933-46, hon. grand v.p., 1938-40), Alpha Omega Alpha, Phi Delta Kappa, Sigma Xi. Research on various phases of trichinosis, 1936—. Contbr. sci. articles on bacteriol., pathol. and med. history to profl. pubs. Office: Univ. of Colo. Med. Center, 4200 E. Ninth Av., Denver 20. Died Aug. 7, 1959; buried Girard, Kan.

McNEAL, Edgar Holmes (măk-nēl′), educator; b. Almont, Mich., June 26, 1874; s. James Alexander and Margaret Elizabeth (Holmes) McN.; ed. Lake Forest Acad. and Lake Forest Coll.; A.B., U. Chgo., 1897, Ph.D., 1902; m. Caroline Clemence Norton, Jan. 2, 1915. Began teaching U. N.D., 1899; with Ohio State U. 1902—, prof. European history, 1913-25, prof. history, 1925—; vis. prof. history, U. Wis., 1926-27; prof. summer sessions, U. Wis., 1920, U. Mich., 1925, 28, 29, 32; Columbia, 1926. Fellow Royal Hist. Soc.; mem. Am. Hist. Assn., Medieval Acad. Am., Phi Beta Kappa. Author: Europe in the Middle Age (with O. J. Thatcher), 1921; Modern Europe and Its Beginnings, 1925. Compiler: A Source Book of Medieval History (with O. J. Thatcher), 1905. Translator: The Conquest of Constantinople from the Old French of Robert of Clari, 1936. Home: 721 Bryden Rd., Columbus, O. Died Mar. 13, 1955.

McNEALY, Raymond William (măk-nē′lĭ), surgeon; b. Chambersburg, Mo., Aug. 17, 1886; s. John Willard and Georgiana (Green) McN.; M.D., U. of Ill. Med. Sch., 1910; grad. study, Vienna, 1914; m. Mary Sarina Kinney, Sept. 4, 1926 (died Nov. 19, 1935); children—Raymond William, Richard Kinney, John Willard II, Thomas Warren; m. 2d, Dorothy Gallagher Frazier, Mar. 19, 1953; children—William Jay Frazier, Jr. (stepson), Douglas L., Roderick M. Intern Cook County Hosp., Chgo., 1910-12, since practice of medicine at Chicago; chief surgeon Wesley Memorial Hosp.; attending surgeon and pres. of staff Cook County Hosp.; cons. surgeon Ill. Masonic Hosp., Oak Forest Infirmary, Kenner Hosp.; associate prof. surgery, Northwestern Univ. Med. Sch.; prof. of surgery, Cook Co. Grad. Sch. of Medicine. Pres. United Research Found.; mem. Bd. of Pub. Health Advisors, Dept. of Pub. Health, State of Ill.; mem. adv. bd. Chgo. Health Dept.; mem. med. adv. bd. Cancer Research Found.; counsellor staff Dyslexia Memorial Inst. Wesley Hosp. Editorial bd. Ill. State Med. Journal, Internat Coll. of Surgeons. Sec. and treas. Hektoen Institute, Cook County Graduate School of Medicine; trustee Institute General Semantics; mem. board trustees Northwestern University (1941-42), Wesley Meml. Hosp. Served as lt. USN, World War I.; maj. Med. R.C., U.S. Army, 1931—. Decorated Comdr. Legion Merit-Juan Pablo Duarte, Dominican Republic. Fellow of International College of Surgeons, A.C.S.; mem. Western Surgical Assn., A.M.A., Ill. State Medical Soc., Chicago Med. Soc., Inst. of Medicine, U.S. Naval Inst., Chicago Surgical Soc., Alpha Omega Alpha, Alpha Kappa Kappa, Phi Kappa Epsilon. Clubs: Chicago Athletic, Bobolink Golf. Home: 2450 Lakeview Av., Chgo. 14. Office: 250 E. Superior St., Chgo. 11. Died July 29, 1958; buried Meml. Park Cemetery, Evanston, Ill.

McNEES, Sterling G(lenn), lawyer; b. Girty, Pa., Feb. 17, 1887; s. George Washington and Anna Rachel (George) McN.; student Kittanning (Pa.) Acad., 1900-05; A.B., Allegheny College, 1909, and LL.D. (honorary), 1954; LL.B., University of Pittsburgh, 1913; married Emily Louise Jackson, July 7, 1914; children—George Jackson, Marianna (Mrs. Norman S. Heaney), Sterling G., Jr. Admitted to Armstrong County (Pa.) bar, 1912; bar Pa. Supreme Court, 1913; Dauphin Co. bar, 1920; practiced law in Apollo, Pa., 1912-21, Harrisburg, Pa., since 1921; mem. firm of McNees, Wallace & Nurick; asst. to Pa. State supt. pub. instrn., 1920-21; dep. atty. gen. (Pa.), 1921-23; dir. Harrisburg Nat. Bank; Harrisburger Hotel Co.; lecturer corp. and constl. law, U. of Fla., 1947-48. Overseas service, Y.M.C.A. and Red Cross, World War I. Comdr. U.S. Coast Guard Auxiliary, Flotilla 53, U.S. C.G. Temp. Reserve. Govt. appeal agt. selective service, World War II; mem. Renegotiation Bd. Phila. Dist., World War II. Pres. and mem. bd. Harrisburg Polyclinic Hosp. since 1942; trustee and dir. Harrisburg Y.M.C.A.;

dir. Capital Hosp. Service. Chmn. (2 times) Community Welfare Campaign; pres. (3 times) Allegheny Coll. Alumni Assn. Fellow Am. Bar Found.; mem. Federal Bar Assn., Art Assn. of Harrisburg, Boy Scout Council, S.A.R., Pa. Soc. of New York, Pa. Chamber of Commerce, Harrisburg C. of C. (past dir.), Forestry Assn., Pub. Charities Assn. (past dir.), Am. Judicature Society, American Law Inst., Am., Pa. (pres. 1936-37), Armstrong and Dauphin Cos. (past pres.) bar assns., Interstate Commerce Practitioners' Assn., Phi Gamma Delta, Phi Delta Phi. Republican. Presbyterian (mem. session). Mason (Shrine). Clubs: Torch (past pres., dir.), Gibson Island Yacht, Travel. Home: 115 North St. Office: Commerce Bldg., Harrisburg, Pa. Died July 15, 1959.

McNEILL, Neal Edward, judge; b. nr. Onawa, Ia., Nov. 10, 1875; s. Edwin Ruthvens and Louisa (Younkin) McN.; LL.B., Drake U., 1899; m. Elizabeth Adams, June 1, 1911; children—Mary Elizabeth Conhaim, Martha Louisa, Neal Edward. Settled in Okla., 1904; practiced law, Jennings, 1904-07; mem. Orton & McNeill, Pawnee, 1911-14; asso. with brother as McNeill & McNeill, 1914-17. Mayor of Jennings, 1906-07; county atty. Pawnee County, 1909-11, county judge, 1909-10; Dem. nominee for Congress, 1st Dist. Okla., 1910; dist. judge, 21st Jud. Dist., 1917-19; justice Supreme Ct. Okla., 1919-25; vice chief justice, 1923, chief justice, 1924; practiced law, Tulsa, 1925—. Mem. Am., Okla. State bar assns., Phi Alpha Delta. Democrat. Presbyn. Mason. Club: Tulsa. Home: 1230 E. 17th Pl. Office: First National Bank Bldg., Tulsa. Died Sept. 11, 1958; buried Rose Hill Mausoleum.

McNEILL, Thomas W., corp. exec.; b. Brooklyn, May 24, 1900; s. Alexander James and Ellen (Nagle) McN.; B.C.S., N.Y.U., 1923; m. Helen Melvin, Oct. 3, 1928 (dec.); m. 2d, Mary Shiveley, Apr. 15, 1944. Sec. to pres. Am. Radiator & Standard Sanitary Corp., and predecessor, Pittsburgh, 1923-26, travelling auditor, 1926-27, purchasing dept., 1927-29, asst. to v.p., gen. mgr. mfg., 1929-35, gen. purchasing agt., 1935-51, became v.p. purchasing, 1951, pres. Air Conditioning div., 1953—. Mem. Psi Upsilon. Club: Engineers (N.Y.C.). Home: 12 Old Parish Rd., Darien, Conn. Office: 40 W. 40th St., N.Y.C. 18. Died Mar. 4, 1958; buried St. Johns Cemetery, Norwalk, Conn.

McNICHOLAS, John T., archbishop; b. Kiltimagh, Ireland, Dec. 15, 1877; s. Patrick J. and Mary Mullany) McN.; brought to U.S., 1881; student St. Joseph's Coll. (Phila.), St. Rose Priory (Springfield, Ky.), St. Joseph's House of Studies (Somerset, O.); Lector of Sacred Theology, Minerva U., Rome, 1904, S.T.M., 1917. Entered Dominican Order, 1894; ordained priest R.C. Ch., 1901; prof. and novice master Dominican Houses of Studies, Somerset, O., 1904-05, Washington, 1905-09; pastor St. Catherine of Siena, N.Y.C., 1913-16; nat. dir. Holy Name Society, and editor its publ. Holy Name Journal, 1909-17; asst. to Master General of Dominican Order, Rome, 1917-18; consecrated bishop of Duluth, 1918; trans. to Diocese of Indpls., 1925; apptd. asst. at Pontifical Throne, 1923; apptd. archbishop of Cin., 1925. Mem. episcopal com. on Confraternity of Christian Doctrine, 1934-45, 47—; chmn. dept. edn. Nat. Cath. Welfare Conf., 1929-35; 41-45; pres. gen. Nat. Cath. Ednl. Assn., 1947—; episcopal chmn. Nat. Legion of Decency (motion pictures), 1933-43; chmn. Pontifical Commn., Cath. U. Am., Washington, 1934—; chmn. adminstrv. bd. Nat. Cath. Welfare Conf., 1946—. Home: 5870 Belmont Av., College Hill, Cin. 24. Died Apr. 22, 1950; buried Gate of Heaven Cemetery, Cin.

McNINCH, Frank R(amsay), ret. govt. ofcl.; b. Charlotte, N.C., Apr. 27, 1873; s. Franklin A. and Sarah Virginia (Ramsay) McN.; student Barriers Inst., Charlotte; student Law Sch., U. N.C., 1899-1900; m. Mary Groome, June 21, 1905 (dec.); children—Frank Ramsay, Mrs. Mary Groome Hunter; Ariel (Mrs. L. E. Weit); m. 2d, Huldah Groome, Feb. 12, 1917; children—Huldah, Robert Groome. Began practice of law at Charlotte, 1900; mem. N.C. Ho. of Reps., 1905; mayor and commr. of finance, Charlotte, 1917-21 ; mem. FPC, 1930-37, chmn., 1933-37; chmn. FCC, 1937-39; spl. asst. to atty. general, 1939-46; now retired. President Roosevelt's rep. to Exec. Council, World Power Conf., The Hague, 1935. Democrat. Presbyn. Mason, K.P. Home: 3 Worthington Drive, Washington 16. Died Apr. 20, 1950.

McNULTY, C(hester) H(ugh), banker; b. Cochranton, Pa., Jan. 27, 1889; s. Michael and Flora Agnettie (Stainbrook) McN.; student Grove City Coll., Pa., 1907, Huron Coll., S.D., 1911-12, Dakota Wesleyan U., 1913; m. Frances J. De Hollander, Jan. 12, 1939; 7 sons by previous marriages—Walter R., Charles P., Warren E., Fred H., Clifford L., David L., Chester H. Schoolteacher, 1905-15; merchant, 1915-20; citrus grower, 1920-30; banker since 1934; pres. Bank of Melbourne, Okeechobee County Bank, Punta Gorda State Bank, Bank of Lake Alfred, Bank of Zephyrhills, Bank of Mulberry, State Bank of Haines City, First State Bank, Ft. Meade (all in Fla.); chmn. bd. Florida State Bank of Sanford. Served as lt., U.S. Coast Guard, 1942-45. Chairman Rep. State Com., 1936-42; served as Rep. Nat. Committeeman, 1942-48. Dir. Melbourne C. of C., Brevard Hosp. Assn. Mayor, Melbourne, 1936. Meth. Rep. Clubs: Eau Gallie Yacht, New Smyrna Yacht, Melbourne Country, Lions (dist. gov. Lions Internat., 1944-45; internat. counselor, 1946-47, pres. local, 1943; internat. dir., 1947-49). Home: 320 Avenue B, Indiana River Bluff, Melbourne. Office: 237 New Haven Av., Melbourne, Fla. Died May 3, 1957.

McNULTY, John Laurence, clergyman, educator; b. N.Y. City, Sept. 10, 1898; s. William and Mary (Bellew) McN.; A.B., Seton Hall Coll., 1921, M.A., 1922; student U. of Louvain, 1922-25; Ph.D., N.Y.U., 1935; diplome d'Etudes Superieures, U. de Lilles, 1937; LL.D., John Marshall Coll., 1950, Fairleigh Dickinson U., Rutherford, N.J., 1958. Ordained priest, Roman Cath. Ch., 1925; dir. recreation Essex Co. (N.J.) Playground Commn., 1917-21; instr. Latin Barringer High Sch., Newark, N.J., 1921-22; instr. French, religion Seton Hall Prep. Sch., 1926-28; instr. French, Seton Hall Coll., 1928-30, prof., 1930-35, head dept. modern langs., 1935-43, dean urban divs., 1943-49, pres. since 1949. Invested as Domestic Prelate of Pope Pius XII, 1950. Mem. Newark Civil Rights Commn.; chmn. Religious Adv. Com. for Civil Defense, N.J.; member Com. on Alcoholism, N.J. Dept. of Pub. Health, Commn. on Cultural Affairs, State Com. on Articulation of Colls. and Secondary Sch.; trustee Caldwell Coll. for Women, N.J.; trus. N.J. Heart Assn. Chmn. edn., pub. employees Community Chest, Orange and Maplewood. Mem. Gallery Living Cath. Authors, Am. Cath. Hist. Soc., Louvain Alumni Assn. (pres. U.S.). Author: La France Catholique, 1940; Ship Without Sails, 1938; Ecrivaines Modernes (with Benziger), 1946. Translation: Principles of Social Economy (with Benziger), 1935. Home: Seton Hall University, South Orange, N.J. Died May 27, 1959; buried Gate of Heaven Cemetery, Hanover, N.J.

McNUTT, Paul Vories, lawyer, diplomat; born Franklin, Indiana, July 19, 1891; son of John Crittenden and Ruth (Neely) McN; A.B., Ind. U., 1913; LL.B., Harvard, 1916; LL.D., U. of Notre Dame and Ind. Univ., 1933, Bethany Coll., 1936; Univ. of the Philippines, 1939, University of Maryland, American University, 1941; D. of Humanity, Florida Southern Coll., 1939; D.C.L., Boston U., 1942; m. Kathleen Timolat, Apr. 20, 1918; 1 dau., Louise. Admitted to Ind. bar, 1914, and began practice as mem. McNutt & McNutt, Martinsville; asst. prof. law., Ind. U., 1917, became prof. 1919, dean Ind. U. Sch. Law, 1925-33; gov. State of Ind., 1933-37; U.S. high commr. to P.I., 1937-39 and 1945-46; A.E. and P. to the Philippines, 1946-47; chmn. bd. Philippine-American Life Ins. Co. since 1948; gen. counsel, dir. U.S. Life Ins. Co., Am. Internat. Underwriters Corp., Am. Internat. Marine Agy. Fed. secur. adminstr., 1939-45; partner McNutt & Nash, N.Y.C., McNutt, Dudley & Easterwood, Washington; dir. Globe & Rutgers Fire Ins. Co., Am. Home Assurance Co., Am. Life Ins. Co., Am. Internat. Assurance Co. Member exec. com. Govs. Conf., 1933-36 (chmn. 1934-36); mem. nat. advisory bd. Works Progress Adminstrn.; pres. Council of State Govts., 1936-37; dir. Def. Health and Welfare Services 1941-43; chmn. War Manpower Commn., 1942-45; mem. WPB, Econ. Stblzn. Bd. Commd. capt. F.A. Res. 1917; Bd. 1917; major F.A., U.S. Army, 1918; lt. col. F.A. Reserve, 1919, col., 1923; instr. O.T.C., Camp Stanley, and comdg. officer successively 6th Regt., 5th Brig. and 2d Brig., F.A. Replacement Depot, World War; comdg. officer 326th F.A., 1924-37; mem. 5th Corps Area Adv. Bd., 1927-34; civilian aide to sec. of War for Ind., 1927-28. Chmn. sub-com. on survey and codification, Ind. Corp. Survey Commn.; chmn. faculty bd. editors Ind. Law Jour., 1926-33; pres. Harvard Legal Aid Bureau, 1915-16; mem. Alumni Council, Ind. U., 1924-30. Mem. Am. Bar Assn., Am. Law Inst., Ind. Bar Assn. (chmn. com. on legal edn. 1927), Assn. Am. Law Schs. (chmn. comml. law sect. 1927), Am. Assn. U. Profs., Reserve Officers Assn. U.S., Am. Peace Soc., Order of Coif, Phi Beta Kappa, Sigma Delta Chi, Beta Theta Pi, Phi Delta Phi, Acacia, Tau Kappa Alpha. Nat. Comdr. Am. Legion, 1928-29, mem. nat. exec. com., 1927-28; comdr. Dept. Ind., 1927; comdr. Burton Woolery Post, 1925-26; dir. Am. Legion Pub. Corp., 1928-31, pres., 1928-29. Decorated Medal for Merit (U.S.); Distinguished Service Star (P.I.), Comdr. Polonia Restituta (Poland); Comdr. Legion d'Honneur (France), Grand Cordon Order of Cambodia (Indo-China); Comdr. Legion of Honor (Philippines). Democrat. Methodist. Mason (32°), Elk. Clubs: University, Rotary, Kiwanis, Indianapolis Athletic (Indpls.); Army and Navy, Metropolitan, Burning Tree, Chevy Chase (Washington); Wall Street (N.Y.C.). Editor: Indiana General Corp. Act Annotated (with F. E. Schortmeier). Also author articles in law journals. Home: 1115 Fifth Av., N.Y.C. 28. Office: 84 William St., N.Y.C. 38; also Barr Bldg., Washington 6. Died Mar. 24, 1955.

McPHERSON, Harry Wright, clergyman, ednl. exec.; b. Neoga Twp., Cumberland County, Ill., Apr. 10, 1879; s. Elias and Mercy (Kelley) McP.; grad. Ill. Wesleyan Acad., 1902; B.S., Ill. Wesleyan U., 1906, D.D., 1921; S.T.B., Boston U., 1909, LL.D., 1935; m. Sadie E. Grisamore, June 20, 1905. Tchr. pub. schs., Cumberland County, Ill., 1898-1900; ordained ministry M.E. Ch., joined Ill. Conf., 1904; student pastor, 1903-09, pastor Arrowsmith, Ill., 1909-10, Ashland, Ill., 1910-13, Casey, Ill., 1914-15, First Ch., Paris, Ill., 1916-18, St. James Ch., Danville, Ill., 1919-22; supt. Springfield Dist., Ill. Conf. M.E. Ch., 1923-25; pastor First M.E. Ch., Springfield, Ill., 1926-31; pres. Ill. Wesleyan U., 1932-37; exec. sec. Bd. of Edn. of M.E. Ch., 1937-40; exec. sec. div. ednl. instns. Bd. of Edn. of Meth. Ch., 1940-48; exec sec. Univ. Senate, 1937-48; asso. exec. sec. Ill. Ch. Council, 1949—. Pres. Ill. Council Chs., 1931-34; v.p. Preachers Aid Soc. Ill. Conf., 1928-37; mem. Bd. Foreign Missions M.E. Ch., 1928-32, mem. book com., 1932-40, del. to Gen. Conf., 1928, 32, 36; del. to Uniting Conf. of Meth. Ch., 1939; del. to Gen. Conf. Meth. Ch., 1944, 48, Jurisdictional Conf., 1940, 44, 48; pres. Council of Church Bds. Edn., 1944; mem. bd. trustees Ill. Wesleyan U. Mem. Phi Kappa Phi, Tau Kappa Epsilon (Alpha chpt.). Mason (32°). Home: 817 S. Lincoln Av. Office: 100 W. Adams St., Springfield, Ill. Died Oct. 24, 1957; buried Oak Ridge Cemetery, Springfield.

McPHERSON, Hobart M., banker; b. Fairfield, Ia., July 5. 1896; s. C. D. and Adda C. (Chidester) M.; A.B., U. of Kan., 1920. With Nat. City Bank Coll. Tng. Class for Fgn. Service. 1920; asst. cashier. 1928, asst. v.p., 1931, v.p. in charge 5th Av. Branch, since 1945. Treas. Nat. Travelers Aid Assn., 1941-46, president, 1946-48, chmn. 1948-50. Treasurer Nat. Health and Welfare Retirement Assn., 1945, treas., 1948—. Treas., dir. U.S.O. Served as ensign, USN, 1918-19. Mem. U. Kan. Alumni Assn. N.Y. (dir.), Delta Tau Delta, Phi Beta Kappa. Republican. Presbyn. Clubs: University (N.Y.C.); Apawamis (Rye, N.Y.). Home: 200 E. 66th St., N.Y.C. 21. Office: 640 Fifth Av., N.Y.C. 19. Died Oct. 1, 1955.

McPHERSON, John Hanson Thomas, univ. prof.; b. Baltimore, Md., Oct. 30, 1865; s. John H. T. and Sallie J. (Cooke) M.; grad. first honors, Baltimore City Coll., 1884; hon. Hopkins Scholar, Johns Hopkins, 1884-86; A.B., Johns Hopkins, 1886, Ph.D., 1890; attended history courses univs. of Berlin, Sorbonne; m. at Geneva, Switzerland, Georgia Adams Rathbone, June 23, 1892 (died Nov. 13, 1893); m. 2d, Margaret Virginia Bonney, June 22, 1909; children—John Hanson Thomas, Robert Grier. Fellow in history, Johns Hopkins, 1889-90; instr. history, U. of Mich., 1890-91; head dept. of history and polit. science, University of Georgia, 1891-1945, lecturer Roman law, 1895-1914, head of social science div., 1933-45, prof. emeritus since 1945; chmn. social science group Univ. System, 1934-38. Lecturer Furman Institute of Politics, Georgia Institute of Politics, and other summer schs. Elector "Hall of Fame" since 1905; first appointee under Kahn Foundation to fellowship of foreign travel, 1911-12. Pres. Ga. Library Assn., 1910-13; mem. Am. Hist. Assn. (Ga. mem. Gen. Com. 1897-1900); corr. mem. Minn. Hist. Soc.; mem. Ga. Hist. Soc., Nat. Tax Assn., Southern Polit. Science Assn., N.E.A., Ga. Edn. Assn., Phi Beta Kappa (pres. Alpha Chapter of Ga. since 1914), Phi Kappa Phi, Beta Gamma Sigma, Alpha Delta Phi; hon. mem. Phi Eta Sigma. Author: A History of Liberia, 1892; The Civil Government of Georgia, 1895; The History and Civil Government of Georgia, 1908. Contbr. to various publs. including Dictionary of American Biography, Larned's History for Ready Reference and The South in Literature. Mem. Ga. Spl. Tax Commn., 1918-19, Ga. com. Woodrow Wilson Foundation, 1921, Nat. Budget Com., 1921, Ga. Special Tax Commn. of 1923, and 1928-29; mem. bd. dirs. Oconee Cemetery, Federal Savings & Loan Assn. of Athens, Ga. Mem. Emmanuel P.E. Ch. (former vestryman, treas., jr. and sr. warden; now warden emeritus). Home: 625 Milledge Av., Athens, Ga.; also Tallassee Farms, Clarke County, Ga. Died Sept. 17, 1953.

McPHERSON, Samuel Dace, physician; b. Liberty, N.C., Apr. 20, 1873; s. Samuel and Martha (Teague) McP.; grad. Liberty (N.C.) Acad., 1899; student U. N.C., 1899-1901; M.D., U. Md., 1903; post grad. N.Y. Polyclinic, 1910-11; in Vienna, 1929; m. Katie Lee Banks, Oct. 14, 1913; children—Samuel Dace, Mary Banks. Gen. practice medicine, Haw River, N.C., 1903-10; specialized in ophthalmology and otolaryngology, 1910—; practiced Durham, N.C., 1911—; McPherson Hosp., for eye, ear, nose and throat; mem. staff Watts Hosp., Lincoln Hosp.; mem. staff State Hosp. for Insane, 1925-29. Chmn. bds. of health City and County of Durham, 1928—; pres. Durham YMCA, 1926-28. Asso. mem. Nat. Bd. Med. Examiners. Fellow A.C.S.; mem. A.M.A., N.C., Durham-Orange Counties (pres. 1917-18), Tri State med. socs., So. Med. Assn., Acad. Ophthalmology and Otolaryngology. Democrat. Presbyn. (elder). Clubs: Rotary (Durham), Hope Valley Country. Home: 29 Oak Drive, Forest Hills. Office: McPherson Hosp., 1110 W. Main St., Durham, N.C. Died Sept. 12, 1953.

McPHERSON, William, chemist; b. Xenia, O., July 2, 1864; s. William and Mary (Rader) M.; B. Sc., Ohio State U., 1887, M.Sc., 1890, D.Sc., 1895, LL.D., 1940; Ph.D., U. Chgo., 1899; LL.D., Wittenberg Coll., 1927; m. Lucretia Heston, June 21, 1893; children—William Heston, Gertrude May; m. 2d, Mary B. Henderson, Apr. 18, 1925. Instr. chemistry and physics Toledo High Sch. and Manual Tng. Sch., 1887-89, chemistry and Latin, 1889-92; asst. in chemistry Ohio State University, 1892-93, assistant professor, 1893-95, associate professor general chemistry, 1895-97, professor chemistry, 1897-1937, gen. chemistry, 1895-97, prof. chemistry, 1897-1937, dean of grad. sch., 1911-37, emeritus dean and prof., 1937-—, acting pres., 1924, 38, pres. emeritus, 1938-—. Fellow A.A.A.S. (v.p. Sect. C, 1908-09, 15-16); mem. Am. Chem. Soc. (pres. 1929-30), Am. Inst. Chemists (hon.), Deutsche Chemische Gesellschaft, Phi Beta Kappa, Sigma Xi, Phi Delta Theta, Alpha Chi Sigma, Phi Lambda Upsilon. Commd. maj., N.A., 1918; chem. adviser to Trench Warfare Sect., Ordnance Dept.; lt. col. C.W.S., 1918-19. Coauthor (with William E. Henderson) of series of text books in chemistry; contbr. to chem. jours. Home: 198 16th Av. Address. Ohio State U., Columbus, O. Died Oct. 2, 1951.

McQUILKIN, Robert Crawford (măk-kwĭl'kĭn), college pres.; b. Philadelphia, Pa., Feb. 16, 1886; s. Robert Crawford and Lucy (Kirkpatrick) McQ.; B.A., Central High Sch.. Phila., 1902, U. of Pa., 1917; D.D., Wheaton (Ill.) Coll., 1935; H.H. D., Bob Jones Univ., 1948; m. Marguerite Lambie, Sept. 10, 1912; children—Agnes Virginia, Aimee Lambie, Robert Crawford (dec.), Marguerite Helen, Thomas Lambie (dec.), John Robertson, Lucy Anne. Clerk and estimator Wm. Steele & Sons Co., Phila., 1903-11; asso. editor Sunday Sch. Times, Phila., 1912-17; bible teacher and conf. dir., 1918-22; prof. and pres. Columbia Bible Coll. (S.C.) 1923-52; founder Ben Lippen School; director of the Ben Lippen Bible Conference Center, Asheville, North Carolina; director of Latin America Mission, Mexican Indian Mission. Presbyterian. Author: Victorious Life Studies, 1918; Studying Our Lord's Parables, 1925; The Lord Is My Shepherd, 1938; Victory in Christ, 1939; Message of Romans, 1947; Law and Grace, 1958; also author of brochures. Editorial and contributing writer for the Sunday School Times. Home: 1311 Cambridge Lane. Office: 1600 Hampton St., Columbia, S.C. Died July 15, 1952; buried Greenlawn Meml. Park, Columbia.

McRAE, George W., ret. telephone exec.; b. Malden, Mass., Oct. 5, 1888; s. Colin af Ella (Rankin) McR.; B.S., Mass. Inst. Tech., 1910; m. Harriet E. Bruning, Sept. 24, 1912; children—Colin W. With Am. Tel. & Tel. Co., 1910-22, toll traffic engr., 1920-22; chief engr. Ill. Bell Telephone Co., 1922-24; chief engr. N.Y. Telephone Co., 1924-25, gen. mgr. N.J. Area, 1925-27; v.p., gen. mgr. N.J. Bell Telephone Co., 1927-47, ret. 1947. Home: 18 Kenmore Rd., Belmont, Mass. Died July 14, 1950.

McRAE, James Wilson, elec. engieer; b. Vancouver, B.C., Oct. 25, 1910; s. James Hector and Isabel C. (Jamieson) McR.; B.S., U. B.C., 1933; M.S., Cal. Inst. Tech., 1934, Ph.D., 1937; D.Sc. (hon.), Hobart College, 1958. m. Marian Frances Wooldridge, July 20, 1937; children—Mary Caroline, Marion Elizabeth, James Dean, John Robert. Came to U.S., 1936, naturalized, 1940. Research transoceanic radio transmitters, microwave research Bell Telephone Labs., 1937-42, dir. radio projects, TV research, 1947, electronic, TV research, 1947-49, apparatus development, 1949-51, v.p. charge the systems orgn., 1951-53; v.p. Western Electric Co., 1953-58; pres. Sandia Corp., 1953-58; vice pres. Am. Tel. & Tel. Company 1958-—. Served as col. signal corps, U.S. Army, 1942-45. Awarded Legion of Merit. Fellow Inst. Radio Engrs. (pres. 1953, dir.); mem. Am. Inst. E.E., Phi Beta Kappa. Home: 10 West Lane, Madison, N.J. Office: 195 Broadway, N.Y.C. Died Feb. 1960.

McREYNOLDS, George Edgar, coll. dean; born Lynnville, Ind., Feb. 22, 1910; s. George Washington and Mabel (Powers) McR.; A.B., Ind. U., 1931, M. A., 1932; Ph.D., Clark U., 1937; m. Miriam Irene Lantis, Feb. 21, 1931. Instr. history Conn. State Coll., 1935, U. Me., 1935-39; asso. prof. govt. U. Conn., 1939-47, prof., head dept. govt. and internat. relations, 1947-50, dean coll. arts and sci. since 1950. Served with U.S.N.R., World War II. Mem. Far Eastern Assn., Am. Polit. Sci. Assn., Kappa Sigma. Democrat. Methodist. Author: Japan in American Public Opinion (with Eleanor Tupper), 1937; China, Japan, and the Powers (with M. Cameron, T.H.D. Mahoney), 1952. Editor: Inside Asia (by John Gunther), 1942; Essays in History and International Relations, 1949. Home: Storrs. Office: U. of Connecticut, Storrs, Conn. Died Mar. 28, 1954; buried Storrs, Conn.

McREYNOLDS, William Henry, ret. govt. ofcl.; b. Wilson County, Kan., Jan. 24, 1880; s. Chester C. and Mary (Adams) McR.; student pub. schools, Topeka, Kan.; LL.D., Am. U., 1939; m. Bernice Borst, June 3, 1907; children—Katherine (Mrs. Myron G. Britt), Margaret Helene (Mrs. John Holmead). Began as law clk. in office of Judge Jesse Arthur, Battle Creek, Mich., 1902-06; clk. inspective service P.O. Dept., Washington, 1906-13; investigator and asst. chief Bureau of Efficiency, Washington, 1913-29; dir. of Classification Bd., 1930-32; asst. to dir. Bureau of Budget, 1932, adminstrv. asst. to gov. FCA, 1933; adminstrv. asst. to sec. of treasury, 1933-39; mem. President's Com. on Civil Service Improvement, 1939-—; adminstrv. asst. to Pres. U.S., 1939-45; retired from govt. service; liaison officer for personnel mgmt., Exec. Office of the President, 1939-45; sec. Council of Nat. Defense and adv. commn. to Council of Nat. Defense, and liaison officer for Emergency Mgmt., 1940-41. Apptd. chmn. Mt. Rushmore Nat. Meml. Commn., 1939. Club: Congressional (Washington). Home: 4514 Connecticut Av. Washington. Died Jan. 17, 1951.

McRILL, Albert Leroy, lawyer; b. Richmond, Franklin County, Kan., Oct. 1, 1880; s. Calvin Whitefield and Amanda Viola (Tapley) McR.; A.B., Epworth U. (now Okla. City Univ.), 1909, M.A., 1910, LL.B.; m. 2d, Mary Swiczynski Horigan, Nov. 16, 1935; one son, James E. Horigan. Has served as editor successively Williamsburg Star, Quenemo Tribune, Ottawa (Kan.) Journal and Watonga (Okla.) Dispatch, 1898-1903; admitted to Okla. bar, 1905, and practiced at Watonga until 1910, at Oklahoma City 1911-—; mem. firm Scothorn, Caldwell & McRill, 1923-31; city atty. Watonga, 1907; mem. Okla. Code Commn., 1910-11; municipal counselor Oklahoma City, 1931-32; city mgr. Oklahoma City, 1932-33; practicing alone, 1933-—. Special justice Okla. Supreme Ct., 1936-37, asso. editor Card-Digest (Okla., Tex. and Calif. Law) 1935-—. Lecturer, Oklahoma City Coll. of Law, 1941-—. Trustee Oklahoma City U., 1911-— (pres. 1923); mem. C. of C. Oklahoma City. Mem. Am. and Okla. State bar assns. Democrat. Methodist. Mason (K.T., Shriner). Clubs: Men's Dinner; High Twelve; Compiler and Editor: Digest of Oklahoma Fire Insurance Law; Digest of Okla. Civil Law; Law of Oil and Gas; Okla. Community Property Law. Author: Okla. City Non-Partisan Sch. System; Off The Record. Author: My Silver Jubilee; In My Library; Summary of Okla. Law; Okla. Procedure; Inside Oklahoma City. Home: 1220 Sherwood Lane. Office: 804 Midwest Bldg., Oklahoma City. Died May 2, 1956; buried Rose Hill Cemetery, Oklahoma City.

McSOLEY, Raymond Joseph, hotel exec.; b. Woonsocket, R.I., July 16, 1897; s. James F. and L'Mina (Gilman) McS.; student public schools, Boston; married to Kathleen B. McAuley, September 30, 1931 (deceased September 1956); children—Kathleen Ann, Raymond Joseph. With Paine, Webber & Co., Boston, 1917-24; staff various resort hotels, 1924-29; clk. front office Hotels Statler, Boston, 1929-31, mgr. Chgo. office, 1931-34, sales mgr. Hotel Statler, Boston, 1935-38, exec. asst. mgr., 1938-43, gen. mgr. Hotel Statler, Cleve., since 1943. Adv. bd. Charity Hosp. Served with Flying Corps U.S.N.R., World War I. Mem. Am., Internat., Cleve. (past pres.) hotel assns., Ohio Hotels Assn. (past pres.), Cleve. C. of C., Cleve. Conv. and Trade Show Bur. (dir.), Euclid Av. Assn. (pres.). Clubs: Rotary, Advertising, Automobile (traffic panel), Athletic (Cleve.); Shaker Heights Country. Office: Hotel Statler-Hilton, Cleve. 1. Died Apr. 16, 1959.

McTARNAHAN, William Chamberlin, chmn. Petroleum Heat & Power Co.; b. Dogtown, Calif., Dec. 26, 1882; s. John Cowan and Adaline (Chamberlin) McT.; m. Grace Kaber, Apr. 18, 1925; children—William C. (dec.), Frederick Kaber. Engagd in bus. for himself in Calif. (contracting, building and gold mining); in 1907, financed company in San Francisco to mfr. oil burning equipment, and developed a large business on the Pacific coast; came East in 1915 and pioneered the use of fuel oil and oil burning equipment on the Atlantic Seaboard; organized Fess Rotary Oil Burner Co., Inc., which in 1920, was re-organized into the Petroleum Heat & Power Company, pres., 1925-45, and dir. since 1926, dir. Nat. Securities & Research Co., Taylor Petroleum Co., Boston Harbor Oil Co., East Coast Fuel Oil Co., Nat. Research Co., Taylor Petroleum Co., Boston Harbor Oil Co., East Coast Fuel Oil Co., Nat. Rsearch Distbn. Corp.; dir. Exercycle Corp. Pres. Fuel Oil Assn., N.Y. City. Clubs: Bankers, Uptown (New York), Sleepy Hollow Country. Home: 530 Park Av. Office: 511 Fifth Av., N.Y. City. Died Oct. 18, 1951.

McVEIGH, John Newburn, assn. exec.; b. Bklyn., Nov. 29, 1912; s. John Newburn and Josephine (Kopenkewich) McV.; B.S. in Health Edn., Columbia, 1936; m. Roberta N. Leber, Sept. 6, 1936; children —Janet, Judith, John Newburn, III. Various positions YMCA, 1935-37, 39-50; personnel and sales promotion, 1937-39; exec. sec. N.Y. Psychoanalytic Inst. and Soc., 1950-53, Am. Psychoanalytic Assn., N.Y. C., 1954-—. Trustee Friend's Sch. Mem. Phi Kappa Psi. Club: Lion's. Home: Leber Rd., Blauvelt, N.Y. Office: 36 W. 44th St., N.Y.C. 36. Died Jan. 14, 1959.

McVEY, Frank LeRond (măk-vā'), educator; b. Wilmington, O., Nov. 10, 1869; s. Alfred Henry and Anna (Holmes) McV.; A.B., Ohio Wesleyan U., 1893, LL.D., 1919; Ph.D., Yale, 1895; LL.D., U. of Ala., 1919, Transylvania Coll., 1929, Berea Coll., 1933; L.H.D., Rollins Coll., 1935, U. of Louisville, 1937, U. of Ky., 1940; m. Mabel Moore Sawyer, Sept. 21, 1898 (now dec.); children—Virginia. Frank LeRond, Janet; m. 2d. Frances Jewell, 1923. Editorial writer, New York, 1895; instr. in history, Teachers Coll. (Columbia), 1895-96; instr., asst. prof. and prof. economics, U. of Minn., 1896-1907; 1st chmn. Minn. Tax Commn., 1907-09; pres. U. of N.D., 1909-17; president State University of Kentucky, 1917-40, president emeritus, 1940-—; lecturer Univ. of Chicago, 1928-30. Pres. Minneapolis Associated Charities, 1898-1907; sec. Minn. Acad. Social Sciences, 1907-09 (editor Proceedings, 1907, 09); 1st v.p. Am. Econ. Assn., 1910, 28; mem. exec. com. Nat. Conf. Charities and Correction; mem. A.A.A.S., Am. Statis. Assn., N.E.A., Phi Gamma Delta, Phi Beta Kappa. Chmn. N.D. Temporary Ednl. Commn., 1912; chmn. 2d, 3d and 4th Nat. Conf. on Marketing and Farm Credits, 1914, 15, 16; mem. Nat. Ednl. Council, Commn. on Economy of Time in Edn.; sec. Nat. Assn. of State Univs., 1916-22, pres., 1923; state dir. Public Service Reserve, 1918-19; mem. ednl. surveys of Okla., 1922, Ind., 1926, Fla., 1930, N.C., 1932, Ky., 1933, La., 1940, Rhode Island, 1940, William and Mary Coll., 1940; ednl. advisor to Venezuelan Govt., 1943. Mem. Kentucky State Board Vocational Edn.; mem. com. of fifty Am. Hygiene Assn.; honorary vice-president National Consumers' League; director Ky. War Fund, 1943-45; member the Sixth Regional Civil Service Bd., 1948; mem. exec. com. Internat. S.S. Council of Religious Edn.; pres. S.E. Conf., 1933; pres. Nat. Assn. of State Univs., 1935; pres. Southern Assn. Schs. and Colleges, 1934; mem. State Planning Bd., 1934-45; pres. Assn. Land Grant Colleges, 1935; pres. Ky. Edn. Assn., 1937. State aide U.S. War Dept., 1922-26. Lecturer, Royal Frederick Univ., Christiania, Norway. Clubs: University (Washington); Arts (Louisville); Rotary, University (Lexington). Author: Populist Movement, 1896; History and Government of Minnesota, 1901; Modern Industrialism, 1904; Transportation, 1910; The Making of a Town, 1913; Economics of Business, 1917; Financial History of Great Britain, 1914-18; A University Is a Place—a Spirit, 1944; History of Edn. in Ky., 1948; Gates Open Slowly, 1949; and many reports, articles and revs. Editor Nat. Social Science Series. State chmn. United Service Orgns., 1942. Home: 249 Shady Lane. Lexington, Ky. Died Jan. 4, 1953; buried Lexington.

McVEY, William Estus, congressman; b. Lee's Creek, O., Dec. 13, 1885; s. Elkanah and Eliza Jane (McKay) McV.; B.S., Ohio U.; A.B., U. of Chicago, 1919, Ph.D., 1942; m. Elizabeth King, Mar. 3, 1910 (dec. 1923); children—Emerson King, Jeannette; m. 2d Katharine Johnson, June 20, 1928; 1 dau., Katharine Jane. Div. supt. P.I., 1908-14; dir. extension Ohio U., 1916-19; supt. Thornton Township High Sch., Jr. Coll., Harvey, Ill., 1919-47; lectr. U. of Pa., summer 1928, Emory U. summer 1929; prof. edn. DePaul U., 1948-50; mem. 82d to 85th Congresses, 4th Ill. Dist. Mem. bd. trustees Ingalls Meml. Hosp., Harvey, Ill. Recipient Efficiency award Am. Legion, 1923; citation by Amvets, 1947. Member Assn. Commerce, Ill. State Prins. Assn., N. Central Assn. Colls. and Secondary Schs., Phi Beta Kappa, Phi Delta Kappa, Tau Kappa Alpha, Phi Kappa Tau. Elk, Mason, Odd Fellow. Club: Rotary. Author: Minimum Essentials in Manners and Right Conduct, 1928; My Conduct and My Country, 1929; Find Yourself, 1929. Home: 15616 Lexington Av., Harvey, Ill. Office: House Office Bldg., Washington. Died Aug. 10, 1958; buried Linwood Cemetery, Galesburg, Ill.

McWHIRTER, Luella Frances Smith, club woman; b. Perrysville, Ind., Oct. 1, 1859; d. Rev. Hezekiah and Susan (Marsters) Smith; student E. Tenn. Wesleyan U., De Pauw U.; m. Felix T. McWhirter, banker, Nov. 18, 1878 (died June 5, 1915); children—Luella S. (Mrs. Frank F. Hutchins), Ethel T. (Mrs. Thomas B. Scoggins), Felix M., Susan McW. Ostrom. Dir. Peoples Bank & Trust Co. from orgn. to 1936 (1st woman bank dir. there). Trustee Ind. W.C.T.U. (past pres.; hon. pres. 1940-52); past pres. Legislative Council of Indiana Women; editor The Message, official paper Indiana WCTU, 1897-1913, 19-45; pres. Ind. Fedn. of Clubs, 1911-13, hon. pres., 1938-52, chmn. Am. home dept., 1924-27; Gen. Fedn. Women's Clubs, director, for Ind., 1916-20; transportation chmn. General Fedn. Women's Clubs, 1916-24, chmn. extension division 1925-27, trustee 1932-38; the founder who called first meeting for orgn. of Woman's Dept. Club Indpls., pres., 1922-26. Awarded G.F.W.C. Pioneer Club Woman's gold medal (1940), Ind. Fedn. Clubs in Golden Jubilee contest naming most outstanding (living) club women in each state, sponsored by Gen. Fedn. Women's Clubs; medal and certificate as regional mother, Am. Mothers Com. of Golden Rule Foundn., 1942. Ind. chairman Better Homes Am., 1927-37; pres. emeritus Ind. White Cross Guild for Meth. Hosps.; mem. edn. and service com. Pres. Herbert Hoover's Conf. Home Bldg. and

Home Ownership; mem. Jury of Award on Model Homes of Ind. FHA. Mem. League Am. Pen Women, Caroline Scott Harrison Chpt. D.A.R., Soc. Ind. Pioneers, Epsilon Sigma Omicron, Hermitage Assn. (Nashville); charter mem. Ind. Assn. Parliamentarians. Mem. Central Av. Meth. Ch. Permanent mem. bd. Auxiliary Marion County (Ind.) Juvenile Ct. Detention Home. Clubs: Woman's Press Ind. (charter mem.), Woman's Research, Woman's Department (organizer), Central WCTU. Home: 1512 N. Meridian St., Indpls. 2. Died Dec. 10, 1952.

McWILLIAMS, Roland Fairbairn, lt. gov. of Manitoba; b. Peterborough, Ont., Oct. 10, 1874; s. John Bannon and Isabella (Davidson) McW.; B.A., U. Toronto, 1896; LL.B., Osgoode Hall, 1899; m. Margaret Stovel, Sept. 3, 1903. Barrister, solicitor, Peterborough, Ont., 1899-1910; barrister, solicitor, McWilliams, Gunn and Lennox, Winnipeg, 1910—; apptd. King's counsel, 1919; lt. gov. Manitoba, 1940—. Mayor, Peterborough, Ont., 1907. Lt. col., comdg. U. Manitoba C.O.T.C., 1915-19. Pres. Nat. Council YMCA, Can., 1922-29. Mem. Liberal Party. Mem. United Ch. Author: Russia in 1926; If I Were King of Canada, 1931; Does History Repeat Itself, 1932, Italian translation, 1933. Home: Government House, Winnipeg. Address: 403 Avenue Bldg., Winnipeg, Man, Can. Died Dec. 9, 1957.

MEAD, D. Irving, pres. South Brooklyn Savings Bank; b. Brooklyn, N.Y., Feb. 9, 1875; s. George W. and Sarah Frances (Studwell) M.; A.B., Yale U., 1897; m. Elizabeth Young, 1920. Admitted to N.Y. bar, 1900, and practiced law in Brooklyn until 1911; v.p. Nat. City Bank of Brooklyn, 1911-19; v.p. Irving Trust Co., 1919-22; trustee South Brooklyn Savings Bank, since 1913, pres., 1922-49, now chmn. Pres., dir. Brooklyn Garden Apts., Inc., and pres. and dir. Mead Property, Inc., and the Studwell Foundation, Inc. Sec. Savings Banks Trust Co. and Instl. Securities Corp. Mem. exec. com. and dir. Brooklyn Chapter Am. Red Cross; trustee and asst. treas. Brooklyn Hosp.; Brooklyn Home for Aged Men. Trustee Long Island Historical Soc.; trustee Westchester County Historical Soc.; county historian of Westchester County. Mem. Chamber of Commerce, N.Y. Historical Soc., New York State Hist. Asso., St. Nicholas Soc. of Nassau Island, S.R. Clubs: University (New York); Graduate (New Haven); Waccabuc Country, Scarsdale Golf, Brooklyn. Home: Waccabuc, N.Y. Office: 130 Court St., Brooklyn. Died Nov. 30, 1951; buried Mead Family Cemetery, Waccabuc, N.Y.

MEADE, Francis Louis, univ. pres.; b. Phila., Pa., Sept. 8, 1894; s. Frank and Adrienne (Montbriand) M.; student St. Vincent's Coll., 1909-14, St. Vincent's Sem., 1914-20; M.A., St. Joseph's Coll., 1928; M.A., Niagara U., 1932, Ph.D., 1934; LL.D., St. John's University, Brooklyn, N.Y., 1947, Villanova Coll., 1950; Litt.D., LaSalle Coll., 1950. Ordained Roman Catholic priest (Vincentian Fathers), 1920; dir. discipline, St. Joseph's Coll., 1920-21; missionary, Kiangsi, China, 1921-23; asst. dir., Central Assn. Miraculous Medal, 1923-25; home missions, 1925-28; prof. edn. and philosophy, Niagara U., 1928-32, dean, college of arts and sciences, 1932-47, v.p., 1939-47, pres., 1947-57; instr. edn. Mary Immaculate Coll., 1957—; director Engineering Science, Management, War Tng., 1942-45; dir. Army Coll. Tng. Programs, 1943-45; ednl. adviser, 2d Service Command, Army Specialized Tng. Programs, 1943-45; mem. Niagara Falls Vets. Council, 1945-46. Recipient Papal Cross Pro Ecclesia et Pontifice, 1956; Emerito medal Niagara U., 1956. Mem. Nat. Cath. Edn. Assn (dir.), Middle States Assn. Colls. and Secondary Schs. (pres. 1950), Assn. Deans N.Y. State, Delta Epsilon Sigma (exec. com. 1944—), Delta Mu Delta, Zeta Sigma Pi, Sigma Alpha Sigma, Pi Delta Pi. K.C. (4°, Faithful Friar). Contbr. ednl. jours. Address: Mary Immaculate Seminary and College, Northampton, Pa. Died Feb. 13, 1958; buried St. Joseph's Coll. Cemetery, Princeton, N.J.

MEADE, James J., ret. Marine corps officer; b. Charlestown, Mass., Mar. 14, 1882; s. P. J. and Catherine (Doran) M.; LL.B., Georgetown U., 1917; student Army War Coll., 1928, Naval War Coll., 1938; m. Helen Parmelee, Aug. 27, 1908. Entered U.S. Marine Corps with rank of 2d lt., 1903, and advanced through grades to brig. gen., 1936; served various times in Nicaragua, P.I., Mexico, Cuba, Haiti, France; ret. from active service, 1939. Awarded various decorations and commendations including Navy Cross, 1927. Mem. Ancient and Honorable Artillery Company of Boston. Clubs: Rotary of Long Beach, Chevy Chase (Md.), Army-Navy of Washington, Pacific Coast. Home: 252 Ximeno Av., Long Beach 3, Cal. Died Dec. 26, 1949.

MEAGHER, Raymond (marr), clergyman; b. Boston, Dec. 24, 1872; s. William and Mary (Meagher) M.; prep. edn. Boston Latin Sch.; grad Dominican colls., Springfield, Ky., and Somerset, O.; S.T.L., U. Louvain, 1896; LL.D., Seton Hall (N.J.) Coll., 1917; LL.D., Manhattan Coll., N.Y.C., 1929. Joined Dominican Fathers, 1887; ordained priest R.C. Ch., 1895; prior St. Antoninun Ch., Newark, 1899-1907, St. Vincent Ferrer Ch., N.Y.C., 1907-10, St. Dominic Ch., Washington, 1910-13; vicar St. Peter's Vicarate and pastor St. Peter's Ch., Memphis; provincial of Dominicans 4 times. Erected priory at Newark; began Monumental Ch. of St. Vincent, Ferrer, N.Y.C.; founded and built Providence (R.I.) Coll., House of Studies, River Forest, Ill.; erected Aquinas Coll., Columbus, O., Dominican High Sch., Oak Park, Ill. Democrat. K.C. Home: 515 Sixth St., S.W., Washington. Died Oct. 19, 1954; buried Mt. Olivet Cemetery.

MEANS, Earl A., business exec.; born Brookfield, Ind., Oct. 15, 1877; s. Cornelius and Isabelle (Weaver) M.; B.S. in Pharmacy, Purdue U., 1899; m. Isabelle Callam, Aug. 15, 1909. Vice pres. and dir. Bristol-Myers Co., N.Y. City, retired. Member Kappa Sigma. Home: 570 Park Av. Office: 630 Fifth Av., N.Y.C. Died Jan. 5, 1952.

MEANS, Eldred Kurtz, clergyman, author; b. Taylor County, Ky., Mar. 11, 1878; s. George Hamilton and Virginia (Lively) M.; ed. Dodd's Univ. Sch., Cincinnati, O.; D.D., Centenary Coll. of La.; m. Ella Q. Crebbin, Jan. 11, 1905. Ordained ministry M.E. Ch., S., 1899; pastor Ghent, Ky., 1899-1900, Erlanger, 1901, Hodgenville, 1902, Louisiana Av. Ch., New Orleans, 1903-05, Baton Rouge, 1905-09, Minden, 1909-13, Shreveport, 1913-15, Arcadia, 1915-17, Monroe, 1917-21, Galloway Memorial Ch., Jackson, Miss., 1922-25, Court St. Church, Lynchburg, Va., 1925-29, Main Street Church, Danville, Va., 1929-33, Travis Street Ch., Sherman, Tex., 1933-37, First Ch., Helena, Ark., 1937-39, Central Methodist Ch., Rogers, Ark., 1939-44. Democrat. Author: The Squeeze Wheel, 1917; E. K. Means, 1918; More E. K. Means, 1919; The Ten Foot Chain (with Achmed Abdullah, Max Brand, and P. P. Sheehan), 1920; Further E. K. Means, 1921; Tarrapin Toes, 1924; Black Fortune, 1931. Home: 506 Hall St. Monroe, La. Died Feb. 19, 1957.

MEANS, Frank Wilson, business exec.; b. Davenport, Ia., July 30, 1879; s. Frank W. and Margaret (Skiles) M.; student Purdue U.; m. Cora Beard, Nov. 8, 1904 (died Nov. 7, 1933); m. 2d, Mrs. Ella A. Bowman, Nov. 21, 1935 (died Apr. 6, 1943). Chmn. bd. Chgo. Towel Co., clean towel service. Clubs: Chicago, Chicago Athletic Association, South Shore Country. Home: 222 E. Chestnut St., Chicago. Office: 2508 S. Wabash Av., Chgo. Deceased.*

MEANWELL, Walter E., physician orthopedics and physical medicine; b. Leeds, Eng., Jan. 26, 1884; s. Charles and Margaret (Cadman) M.; brought to U.S at age of 3; grad. Deichmann Coll. Preparatory Sch., Balt., 1905; M.D., cum laude, U. Md., 1909, B.M.C.; Dr. P.H., U. Wis., 1915; m. Helen Dorothy Gath, May 20, 1922; children—Margaret Carolyn, Helen Louise, Walter Alan. Supr. athletics, Pub. Athletic League, Balt., 1907-10; prof. physical edn. and med. supr. athletics, U. Wis., 1911-17; dir. phys. edn., U. Mo., 1917-20; prof. phys. edn. U. Wis., 1920-36, dir. dept. athletics, 1934-36, coach of basketball, 1912-34; co-dir. Rockne-Meanwell Sch. Coaches. Served as capt. M.C., U.S. Army, 1918-19. Mem. A.M.A., Am. Acad. Phys. Medicine, Am. Congress Phys. Therapy, Soc. Dirs. Phys. Edn. in Colls., Athletic Research Soc., Am. Phys. Edn. Assn., Nat. Basketball Rules Com., Olympic Games Basketball Com. (chmn.), Sigma Alpha Epsilon, Phi Chi, Square and Compass. Presbyn. Mason (32°). Author: Basket Ball, 1922; The Science of Basket Ball, 1924; Training and Care of Injuries (in collaboration), 1931. Home: 3202 Lake Mendota Dr., Madison 5, Wis. Died Dec. 2, 1953.

MEBANE, Daniel (mĕ'bĕn), publisher; b. New Albany, Ind., Feb. 2, 1894; s. Charles S. and Virginia E. (Bower) M.; A.B. cum laude, Ind. U., 1916; m. Daphne M. Hoffman, May 29, 1919; children—Alexander D., Anna Virginia. Asst. instr. English Ind. U., 1916-17; credit mgr. Robert H. Ingersoll & Bros., 1917-18; office mgr. Emergency Fleet Corp., Gloucester, N.J., 1918-19; pres., treas. Swiss Textile Co., N.Y. City, 1920-30; treas. New Republic, Inc., 1925-35, pub. New Republic since 1947; treas., dir. Editorial Publs., Inc., 1935-51; treas. Craft Horizons, Inc., 1951; treas. Westbury Publs., Inc., since 1951; v.p. Straight Enterprises, Inc., 1952—, dir., 1953—; formerly treasurer of Antiques Magazine, publisher, 1953—. Assistant treasurer New Sch. for Social Sci., 1923-26; treas. UN World, Inc., 1946-47. Mem. Grand Jury Assn. N.Y., Phi Beta Kappa. Democrat. Home: 138 W. 92d St., N.Y.C. 25. Office: 601 Fifth Av., N.Y.C. 17. Died Feb. 8, 1956.

MECHERLE, George Jacob, ins. exec.; b. Bloomington, Ill., June 7, 1877; s. Christian and Susan (Hull) M.; student Ill. State Normal U.; LL.D., Ill. Wesleyan U., 1943; m. Sylvia H. Caldwell, Jan. 8, 1944; children by previous marriage—Raymond P., G. Ermond, Mildred M. (Mrs. Kenneth H. Noll), Herbert L., Hubert C. (dec.). Founder and first pres. State Farm Mutual Automobile Ins. Co., 1922-37, chmn. bd. 1937; organizer and pres. State Farm Life Ins. Co., 1928-37, chmn. bd. 1937; organizer and pres., State Farm Fire Ins. Co., Bloomington, Ill., 1935. Chmn. Chinese Relief Com.; mem. exec. com. Republican Citizens Finance Com. of Ill. Mem. Community Chest, A.R.C. Republican. Presbyn. Mason (33°, Shriner), Odd Fellow, Elk, Moose. Clubs: Rotary, Young Men's, Bloomington Country (Bloomington, Ill.); Union League (Chgo.). Home: 1406 E. Washington St. Office: 112 E. Washington St., Bloomington, Ill. Died Mar. 10, 1951; buried Mausoleum, Park Hill Cemetery, Bloomington.

MECHERLE, Ramond Perry, insurance exec.; b. Bloomington, Ill., Feb. 19, 1904; s. George Jacob and May Edith (Perry) M.; student at Brown's Business Coll.; student Babson Inst., Boston, grad. cum laude, 1934; m. Mildred Elizabeth Murray, Oct. 9, 1926; children—Georgia Louanne, Ramond Perry. Began with State Farm Ins. Co.; vice pres., 1933-37, pres. since 1937; vice pres. State Farm Life Ins. Co.; v.p. State Farm Fire Ins. Co. Republican. Mason (Shriner). Home: 6 Country Club Pl. Office: State Farm Ins. Bldg., Bloomington, Ill. Died May 15, 1954.

MECKLIN, John Moffatt, educator; b. Poplar Creek, Miss., Jan. 21, 1871; s. Augustus Harvey and Judith Isabella (Naylor) M.; A.B., Southwestern Presbyn. U., 1890, instr., 1891, A.M., 1892; post-grad. Union Theol. Sem. of Va., 1892-94; B.D., Princeton Theol. Sem., 1896; grad. student Princeton, 1894-96; Ph.D., U. Leipzig, 1899; LL.D., Southwestern Coll., Memphis, 1925; mem. Am. Sch. of Classical Studies, Athens, 1899-1900; fellow Johns Hopkins, 1900-01; m. Mrs. Laurie Babcock, Apr. 27, 1897; m. 2d, Miss Hope Davis, Nov. 13, 1915; children—John Martin, Mary Hope. Ordained to Presbyn. ministry, 1896; pastor Dalton, Ga., 1896-97; instr. Lafayette Coll., 1901-02; prof. Greek, Washington and Jefferson Coll., 1902-05; prof. philosophy Lafayette Coll., 1905-13, U. Pitts., 1913-20; prof. sociology Dartmouth Coll., 1920-41, prof. emeritus, 1941—. Mem. Phi Beta Kappa. Author: Democracy and Race Fiction, 1914; Introduction to Social Ethics, 1920; The Ku Klux Klan—A Study in the American Mind, 1924 (new edit. in French 1934); The Survival Value of Christianity, 1926; The Story of American Dissent, 1934; The Passing of the Saint; A study of Cultural Type, 1941; My Quest for Freedom, 1945. Contbr. to profl. jours. Home: Hanover, N.H. Died Mar. 10, 1956.

MEDHURST, Sir Charles E(dward) H(astings), ret. Brit. air chief marshal; b. Yorkshire, Eng., Dec. 12, 1896; s. Rev. C. E. Medhurst; student St. Peters Sch., York, Royal Aif Force Staff Coll., Imperial Defence Coll.; m. Chistabel Elizabeth Guy, Feb. 1, 1919; children—Monica Elizabeth Hastings Fletcher, Rozanne Felicity Hastings Colchester, Richard Edward Hastings (killed in action 1944). Served with Royal Flying Corps, 1915-17, Royal Air Force, 1919—; service in France and Palestine, 1915-20, Iraq, 1920-28; dep. dir. intelligence, 1934-37; air attaché Rome, Berne and Athens, 1937-40; dir. plans Air Ministry, 1940-41; asst. chief Air Staff (intelligence), 1941-42, (pglicy), 1942-43; comdt. R.A.F. Staff Coll., 1943-44; air comdr. in chief Middle East, 1945-48; head Air Force staff Brit. Joint Services Mission, Washington, 1948-50. Decorated Knight Comdr. of Bath, Order British Empire, Mil. Cross (Gt. Britain); Polonia Restituta (Poland); Order White Lion (Czechoslovakia); Grand Cross King George of Greece (with swords); Legion of Merit (U.S.); Comdr. Order of King Leopold of Belgium. Mem. Ch. of England. Club: Army and Navy (London and Washington). Home: The White House, Bishopthorpe, York, Eng. Died Oct. 18, 1954.

MEEK, Charles Simpson, supt. schs.; b. Spencer, Ind., May 1, 1870; s. James S. and Mary (Joslin) M.; A.B., Ind. U., 1891; A.M., Columbia, 1908; m. Katherine S. Holmes, Dec. 1899; children—Dudley, Shirley. Prin. high sch., Elwood, Ind., 1891-94, Terre Haute, Ind., 1894-1901; supt. schs., Elwood, 1901-07, Boise, Ida., 1908-15, San Antonio, 1915-20, Madison, Wis., also prof. edn. U. Wis., 1920-21; supt. schs., Toledo, O., 1921—. Mem. N.E.A., Nat. Superintendence Assn., Cleve. Conf., Ind., Ida., Tex., Wis., Ohio state tchrs. assns.; Phi Delta Kappa. Co-author (with Estaline Wilson and M. J. Meek): English Today (3 vols. and teachers manual), 1930. Home: 2144 Robinwood Av., Toledo, O. Died Apr. 7, 1952.

MEEK, Robert Abner, clergyman, editor; b. Black Hawk, Miss., Dec. 7, 1867; s. Robert Drayton and Martha Anne (Johnson) M.; prep. edn., Meth. Dist. High Sch., Black Hawk, Miss.; Ph.B., U. Miss., 1888; D.D., Emory and Henry Coll., 1910; m. Cornelia Chew Crippen, Dec. 7, 1893; 1 son, Robert E. Ordained ministry M.E. Ch., S., 1890; pastor in Miss. at Carrollton, 1891-92, Vaiden, 1893, Coldwater, 1894, Clarksdale, 1896, Tupelo, 1897-98, Starkville, 1899-1901, West Point, 1902-03, Greenville, 1904-05; presiding elder Greenville Dist., 1906-09; editor New Orleans Christian Advocate, 1910-19; presiding elder Sardis Dist., 1919-22; editor The So. Meth., 1921-30, ret. 1930. Mem. Gen. Conf. M.E. Ch. S., 1910, 14, 18, 22, 26, 30; apptd. del. Ecumenical M.E. Conf., Toronto, 1911, London, 1921. Trustee Millsaps Coll., Jackson, Miss., 1904-19, Memphis Meth. Hosp., 1919-22. Mem. Delta Kappa Epsilon. Democrat. Mason, K.P., Woodman of

World. Home: Black Hawk, Miss. Died Feb. 4, 1949; buried Acona, Miss.

MEEKER, Royal, economist, statistician; b. Silver Lake, Pa., Feb. 23, 1873; s. William and Betsy (Hill) M.; B.Sc., Ia. State Coll., 1898; Columbia, 1899-1903, Ph.D., 1906; U. Leipzig, 1903-04; LL.D., Ursinus Coll., Collegeville, Pa., 1924; m. Dora A. Pierce, July 26, 1905. Prof. history, politics and econs. Ursinus Coll., 1904-05, preceptor Princeton, 1905-08, asst. prof. polit. economy, 1908-13; commr. of labor statistics by appmt. of President Wilson, 1913-20; chief scientific div. ILO of League of Nations, 1920-23; sec. of labor and industry Commonwealth of Pa., 1923-24; mem. Commn. on Social Research in China, 1924-25; prof. economics Carleton Coll., 1926-27; dir. of Survey of Aged Persons in Conn., 1932; pres. Index Number Inst., New Haven, 1930-36; spl. agt. Conn. Dept. of Labor, 1935, adminstrv. asst., 1941-46. Apptd. mem. meat commn., U.S. Govt., 1918. Sec.-treas. Internat. Assn. Indsl. Accident Bds. and Commns., 1916-20; mem. Fed. Electric Rys. Commn., 1919-20. Mem. Am. Econ. Assn., Am. Statis. Assn., Acad. Polit. Sci. Author: History and Theory of Shipping Subsidies, 1905; Directory of Conn. Manufacturing and Mechanical Establishments, 1939, 1942, 1943. Established the U.S. Bureau of Labor Statistics Monthly Labor Review, the Internat. Labor Review and other publs. of Internat. Labor Office. Contbr. to mags. Home: 625 Whitney Av., New Haven. Died Aug. 16, 1953.

MEEKS, Clarence Gardner, banker; b. Union Hill, N.J., 1880; s. Hamilton Victor and Euretta (Gardner) M.; student Columbia, 1898-1901; m. Eliza Bennett, Oct. 5, 1901; children—Hamilton B., Elizabeth M. (wife of Capt. Rufus C. Young, U.S.N.), Clarence Gardner; m. 2d Louise W. Furlong, Sept. 9, 1950. Various positions, lumber firm, 1902-20; mem. bd. mgrs. Hoboken (N.J.) Bank for Savs. since 1915, now mem. property appraisal, exec. coms.; dir. Hudson Trust Co. since 1918, mem. exec., real estate coms., 1918-29, v.p., 1929-41, pres. since 1941. Co-chmn. finance com., past pres. North Hudson council Boy Scouts; park commr. Hudson Co.; mem. N.J. State Bd. Geol. Survey. Mem. council Christ Hosp., Jersey City; pres. bd. trustees Stevens Hoboken Acad. Fed. food adminstr., North Hudson, World War I; co-chmn. war bond drives, World War II. Mem. N.J. Bankers Assn. (mem. exec., nominating, finance coms.; past treas., v.p., pres.), Am. Bankers Assn. (state v.p. since 1951), North Hudson C. of C. (dir., past pres.), Am. Inst. Management. Clubs: Alumni Assn. North Hudson, Gen. Alumni Assn. and Soc. Older Grads., Union League (gov.), Columbia U. (N.Y.C.); Seaview Country, Knickerbocker Country, Essex (Newark); Rotary (dist. gov. 1948-49, past pres. Union City). Home: 200 E. 66th St., N.Y.C. Office: 3100 Bergenline Av., Union City, N.J. Died Sept. 1954.

MEEKS, Everett Victor, architect, educator; b. Mt. Vernon, N.Y., May 16, 1879; s. Albert Victor and Sarah Anna (Diehl) M.; A.B., Yale, 1901, B.F.A., 1917, hon. M.A., 1919; Litt.D., Middlebury (Vt.) Coll., 1933; D.F.A., William and Mary College, 1940; student School of Architecture, Columbia, 2 yrs.; École des Beaux Arts, Paris, 4 yrs.; Diplômé par le Gouvernement, Paris, France, 1908; unmarried. Associated with Carrère & Hastings, architects, New York, 1908-14, practicing alone since 1914; actg. prof. architecture, Cornell, 1914-16; with Sch. of Fine Arts, Yale, since 1916, now dean and prof. emeritus architecture; pres. of Conn. State Archtl. Examining Bd. Member architectural advisory council, Cornell Univ., 1930-50; trustee emeritus American Academy in Rome, assistant director fine arts, Army Overseas Educational Commn., World War. Associate National Acad.; fellow A.I.A.; mem. Soc. Beaux Arts Architects, American Federation of Arts, Société des Architectes Diplômes par le Gouvernment Français, Zeta Psi. Decorated Officier de l'Instruction Publique and Officer Legion of Honor (France); elected academician Nat. Acad. of Design, 1949. Clubs: Century, Yale (New York); Graduate, Elihu, Elizabethan, Quinnipiack (New Haven); Ft. George (Fla.); Union Interalliée (Paris). Home: Quinnipiack Club, 221 Ch. St., New Haven, Conn. Office: 32 E. 57th St., N.Y. C. Died Oct. 27, 1954.

MEEKS, James A., ex-congressman; b. Washington County, O.; s. Moses and Susan (Hackathorn) M.; student Westfield (Ill.) Coll.; A.M., Ill. Coll.; m. Frances R. Pearson. In practice law, Danville, Ill.; master to chancery, 12 yrs.; mem. Meeks & Lowenstein; corp. counsel, Danville, 6 yrs.; v.p., counsel, dir. First Nat. Bank; dir., counsel Sugar Creek Creamery; dir. Am. Bldg. Assn.; mem. 73d-75th Congresses, 18th Ill. Dist. Chmn. county unit and exec. com. Council Def., World War. Del. Dem. Nat. Conv., 1920, 24, 28, 32. Trustee Ill. Coll. Mem. Am., Ill. State, Vermilion County bar assns., Sigma Pi. Elks, K.P. Home: Spring Glen, Danville. Office: First Nat. Bank Bldg., Danville, Ill. Died Nov. 10, 1946; buried Spring Hill Cemetery, Danville.

MEES, Otto (mās), educator; b. Columbus, O., Feb. 19, 1879; s. Theophilus K. Martin and Jennie (Brauer) M.; grad. Woodville (O.) Normal Sch., 1894; A.B., Capital U., Columbus, 1898; grad. magna cum laude, Evang. Luth. Theol. Sem. Columbus, 1901; studied Berlin and Leipzig, 1901-02; A.M., Wittenberg Coll., Springfield, O., 1916; D.D., Carthage (Ill.) Coll., 1920; LL.D., St. Olaf Coll., Northfield, Minn., 1929; m. Clara Alvina Christiansen, Aug. 26, 1903; children—Elsa Constance, Gertrude Joanna, Robert Theophilus, Ruth Elenore. Ordained Luth. ministry, 1902; pastor Zions Ch., Coraopolis, Pitts., 1902-12; pres. Capital U., Columbus, Dec. 26, 1912-46, pres. emeritus, 1946—. Sec. Eastern Dist. Joint (Luth.) Ohio, 1904-11; dir. Luth. Choral Soc., Pitts., 1910-12; organizer, dir. Luth. Choral Soc., Columbus, 1913—; v.p., dir. Luth. Brotherhood; pres. Nat. Luth. Ednl. Conf., 1925. Mem. exec. bd. Boy Scouts Am.; mem. nat. council Camp Fire Girls. Mem. Ohio Assn. Coll. Presidents (pres. 1930-31), Ohio Music Tchrs. Assn. (pres. 1925), Am. Luth. Conf. (pres. 1930-34). Republican. Clubs: Rotary (hon.), University, Kit Kat. Contbr. Luth. publs. Has traveled extensively in Europe and Near East. Lectr. Home: 2607 E. Main St. Address: Capital University, Columbus 9, O. Died Jan. 12, 1958; buried Forest Lawn, Columbus.

MEGARGEE, Edwin (mē-gär-gē), painter; born at Philadelphia, Penna.; son of Sylvester Edwin and Adelaide Conchetta (Picioli) M.; student Georgetown U., Washington, D.C., 1899-1900, Drexel Inst., Phila., 1900-04, Art Students League, N.Y. City, 1904-05; married Jean Inglee, Apr. 25, 1936 (divorced, 1950); 1 son, Edwin I. Megargee; m. 2d, Esther Kimball Hartshorne, Oct. 27, 1951. Has specialized as animal painter in domestic animals and sporting subjects painting many prize-winning horses, dogs and cattle, characterized by soundness in animal structure; they have appeared on mag. covers and have been exhibited in prominent galleries; also specialized in dry point and aquatint, especially cock fighting prints; portraits of thoroughbreds: Little Dan, Equipoise, Cavalcade, Flamenco, Quentin Durward, Marquerite and Gallant Fox; among equestrian portraits: Mr. and Mrs. Harvey Gibson of New York, Terrill Van Ingen, Mr. and Mrs. W. V. P. Ruxton, and T. W. Durant; painted portrait of Col. Clark Williams, in Faculty House, Williams College, Williamstown, Mass.; did 26 panels of dogs for The de Luxe Kennels of the new liner "America." An accredited judge of Am. Kennel Club. Republican. Catholic. Author and illustrator: Dogs, 1942; Horses, 1946; The Dog Dictionary, 1954. Painted series, Gun Dogs at Work, 1944. Home and studio: 159 E. 37th St., N.Y.C. Died Mar. 13, 1958.

MEGARO, Gaudens (mĕ'gâr-ō), historian; born Newark, N.J., Jan. 22, 1903; s. Frank and Mary M.; A.B., U. of Mich., 1924; student Yale Law Sch., 1924-25, 1926-27; Ph.D., Columbia, 1930, LL.B., 1931; hist. research Europe, 1925-26, 1932-33, 1946-47, summers, 1927, 1928 and 1938; m. Nancy Ainslie Molloy; children—Anne Ainslie, Mary Alice. Instr. history Coll. City N.Y., 1934-37, 38-39, Harvard, 1937-38; with Queens Coll., 1939—, successively instructor, assistant prof., associate prof., prof.; with OSS (formerly Coordinator of Information) as analyst and chief of Italian Section, 1941-1945; associate fellow in Contemporary Italy, Library of Congress, 1943-45; editorial adviser Am. Book Co.; contbg. editor Am. Hist. Rev. Fellow Royal Historical Soc. of Great Britain. Member Phi Beta Kappa, American Historical Association, Council on Foreign Relations. Author: Vittorio Alfieri, Forerunner of Italian Nationalism, 1930; Mussolini in the Making, 1938; Mussolini: Dal Mito alla Realta, Italy, 1947. Editor: Vol. II, The Cabinet Council of England in the 17th and 18th Centuries (by Edward Raymond Turner), 1932. Address: 308 Burns St., Forest Hills, L.I., N.Y.; (summer) South Sandisfield, Mass. Died Mar. 13, 1958.

MEGRAN, Herbert Brown, mfg. exec.; b. Harvard, Ill., Mar. 25, 1888; s. Hugh H. and Alice (Brown) M; A.B., U. Ill., 1909; m. Gladys Bell, Oct. 2, 1920; children—Elizabeth, Jeane, Joh. Pres., gen. mgr. Starline, Inc., Harvard, 1914-57, chmn. bd., 1957—; dir. Harvard State Bank. Former mem. nat. com. Boy Scouts Am., awarded Silver Beaver. Mem. farm equipment div. NPA, 1951, dir., 1952. Dir. U. Ill. Found.; trustee U. Ill., 1951-57, pres. bd., 1954-57. Mem. Am. Hardware Mfrs. Assn. (pres. 1953; mem. adv. bd.), Farm Equipment Inst. (pres. 1952; mem. exec. com.), Kappa Sigma. Methodist. Clubs: University, Executives (Chgo.); Big Foot Country (Lake Geneva, Wis.). Address: Harvard, Ill. Died Apr. 14, 1958.

MEGRAW, Herbert Ashton (mĕ-graw'), metallurgical engr.; b. Baltimore, Apr. 28, 1876; s. John Milton and Ellen Maria (Ryan) M.; grad. Baltimore Poly. Inst., 1894; B.S., in Chemistry, Cornell U., 1898; m. Mary Bollman French, Oct. 18, 1905. Assayer, 1899-1901, mill supt. and metallurgist, 1901-03, Guanajuato Consol. Mining & Milling Co.; staff engr. Charles Butters & Co., London, 1903; metall. engr., Iola Mining Co., 1904; mgr. Montgomery Mining Co., 1905-08; supt. Naval Milling Co., Guanajuato, Mex., 1908-12; consulting metall. engr., Mexico City, 1912; on editorial staff Engineering and Mining Journal, 1912-17, mgr. same, 1917-18; engr. Bur. of Aircraft Production, Air Service, U.S. Army, Dayton, O., and Washington, 1918-19; engr. Kennedy-Van Saun Mfg. & Engring. Corp., New York, 1919-22; v.p. and treas. Crown Oil & Wax Co. and N.C. Oil Co., Baltimore, 1922-26; v.p. and gen. mgr. Corchera Internacional, Seville, Spain, 1926-35, now practicing as cons. engr. Episcopalian. Mem. Am. Inst. Mining and Metall. Engrs., Phi Sigma Kappa. Clubs: Engineers, Tablada. Author: Practical Data for the Cyanide Plant, 1910; Details of Cyanide Practice, 1914; The Flotation Process, 1916. Extensive contbr. to leading mining and metall. jours. Home: 3902 Centerbury Road, Balt. Died Nov. 3, 1951; buried Druid Ridge Cemetery, Balt.

MEHORNAY, Robert Lee (mē-hôr'na), merchant; b. Kansas City, Mo., Feb. 25, 1888; s. Charles William and Nancy Eleanor (Crooks) M.; grad. high sch., Kansas City, 1907; student engring. U. of Mich., 1907-09; m. Mabelle Hanawalt, Oct. 17, 1911; children—Robert Lee, John William, Elizabeth. With Mehornay Furniture Co., retail home furnishers, since 1909, successively sec., treas., pres., chmn. board; deputy chmn. bd. Fed. Res. Bank, Kansas City, Mo.; formerly dir. First Nat. Bank Kansas City, Mo.; bureau chief, Office of Production Management, Washington, 1941; director Kansas City Power and Light Company. Member exec. com. bus. adv. council for Dept. of Commerce, Washington, D.C.; 1st chmn. Board of Govs. Midwest Research Institute, Kansas City, Mo. Served as captain A.S., U.S. Army, 1917-19, World War. Mem. advisory council for expenditure of city bond money, Kansas City, 1925; gen. chmn. Allied Charities, Kansas City, 1922; v.p. C. of C., 1924, pres. 1944; member Municipal Art Commn., 1926; pres. Kansas City Merchants Assn., 1937; trustee Liberty Memorial Assn. since 1926 (mem. bd. govs. since 1934); trustee U. of Kansas City; mem. Kansas City Sch. Dist., 1930-36, pres. 1935-36; mem. Nat. Retail Code Authority, 1933; director of American Heart Association since 1947. Mem. Nat. Retail Furniture Assn. (pres. 1926), Am. Legion (city central chmn. 1926), 40 and 8, Sigma Alpha Epsilon. Gen. Pershing's citation for meritorious and conspicuous service, Colomby les Belle, France, Apr. 19, 1919; Order Purple Heart (U.S. Army), 1932; honor award, Jackson County (Mo.) Medical Society. Democrat. Mem. Disciples of Christ Ch. Mason. Clubs: Cooperative (pres. 1915), Mission Hills Country; Furniture Club of America (Chicago). Home: 5049 Wornall Rd., Kansas City 2. Office: 1101 McGee St., K.C. 6. Mo. Died Nov. 19, 1951.

MEIGHEN, John Felix Dryden (mē'hĕn), lawyer; b. Spring Valley, Minn., Sept. 25, 1877; s. Joseph Peter and Mary Elizabeth (Smith) M.; B.Litt., Upper Ia. U., 1895, M.Litt., 1899, LL.D., 1945; LL. B., U. Mich., 1900; LL.D., Hamline U., 1935; m. Katherine Trusdell, Dec. 27, 1917. Admitted to Mich. bar, 1900, Minn. bar, 1901, began practice at Albert Lea; mem. Morgan & Meighen, 1901-13, Meighen & Knudson, 1913-20, Meighen, Knudson & Sturts, 1923-48, Meighan, Knudson, Sturtz & Peterson, 1948—; v.p. First Nat. Bank, 1931—; pres., dir. Empire Mut. Ins. Co.; dir. Minn. Trust Co., Jobs Bldg., Inc. Spl. asst. to U.S. atty. gen. as hearing officer conscientious objectors, 1942-53; judge Dist. Court, 10th Jud. Dist., Minn., 1920-23. Neutral arbitrator, G.N. Ry. vs. clerical and sta. forces, 1928; mem. Minn. Crime Commn., 1927; chmn. Minn. Advisory Bd. under Federal Emergency Adminstrn. of Pub. Works, 1933-34; mem. Minn. Planning Bd., 1934-37. Chmn. Freeborn County chpt. A.R.C., 1917-24; pres. Freeborn County War Chest, Inc., 1943; chmn. War Price and Ration Bd., Freeborn County, 1944. Del. to Dem. Nat. Conv., 1912, 32, 36, chmn. Dem. State Central Com., 1936-38; del. to Gen. Conf. M.E. Ch., Omaha, 1928. Vice-pres. trustees Hamline U. Mem. Am., Minn. (bd. govs.), 10th Jud. District bar assns., C. of C. (pres. 1931-32). Mason (Shriner), Elk, K.P. Clubs: Rotary, Albert Lea Country. Author: Today in the Holy Land, 1913. Home: 107 The Fairway. Office: 1st Nat. Bank Bldg., Albert Lea, Minn. Died Apr. 17, 1957; buried Graceland Cemetery, Albert Lea.

MEIGS, Arthur Ingersoll (mĕgs), architect; b. Phila., June 29, 1882; s. Arthur Vincent and Mary Roberts (Browning) M.; grad. William-Penn Charter Sch., Phila., 1899; A.B., Princeton, 1903; m. Harriet Geyelin, Sept. 13, 1935. Began practice Phila., 1906; mem. archtl. firm Mellor & Meigs, 1906-17, Mellor, Meigs & Howe, 1917-28, Mellor & Meigs, 1928-40; ret. from active practice, 1940. Works: Goodhart Hall, Bryn Mawr Coll.; Sci. Lab., Haverford Coll.; Princeton Charter Club; Phi Gamma Delta fraternity houses, Phila., State College, Pa., and Seattle; Gymnasium Bldg., Pa. Inst. for Deaf; aviary, Phila. Zool. Soc.; residences nr. Phila. for Arthur E. Newbold, Jr., F. S. McIlhenny, Robert T. McCracken, Caspar W. Morris, Melville G. Curtis, Morris E. Leeds, Christopher L. Ward, Col. Henry duPont, and Campbell Weir; residence for Radcliffe Cheston at Georgetown, S.C. Firm awarded gold medal by Archl. League N.Y. for residence of Arthur E. Newbold, Jr., 1925, and ann. medal in architecture, by Phila. Chpt. A.I.A., 1922, for residence of Robert T. McCracken. Fellow A.I.A. Served as capt. F.A., comdg. Co. B, Mil. Police, 4th Div.,

U.S. Army, 1917-19; in engagements at Aisne-Marne, St. Mihiel and Argonne. Episcopalian. Clubs: Philadelphia Club, Whitemarsh Valley Hunt, Historical Society. Author: A Monograph of the Work of Mellor, Meigs & Howe, 1923; An American Country House, 1924. Home: Radnor, Pa. Died June 9, 1956.

MEILINK, John Girard (mi'link), nwespaper publisher; b. Toledo, Mar. 11, 1889; s. John Girard and Katherine (Weisenburger) M.; ed. parochial and pub. sch.; m. Margaret Kirch, Sept. 21, 1920. Began as messenger boy, 1905; with Toledo News Bee, 1907-17, as advt. solicitor, classified advt. mgr. and advt. mgr.; bus. mgr. Des Moines (Ia.) News, 1919-21; advt. mgr. Cleve. Press, 1922-27, bus. mgr., 1927-36, gen. mgr., 1938-47; v.p. E. W. Scripps Co., pubs. Cleve. Press. Served as radio electrician in U.S. Navy, Feb. 1918-Mar. 1919, World War. Catholic. Club: Union. Home: 561 Camino Norte, Palm Springs, Cal. Died Sept. 2, 1957; buried Calvary Cemetery, Toledo.

MEINECKE, Emilio Pepe Michael, plant pathologist; b. Alameda, Cal., July 26, 1869; s. Charles and Angelita (Schleiden) M.; grad. high sch., Freiburg, Germany; studied univs. of Freiburg, Leipzig, Bonn and Heidelberg; Ph.D., Heidelberg, 1893; post grad. work in various European univs.; unmarried. Asst. Bot. Inst., U. Munich, 1893, U. Heidelberg, 1894; asst. Forestry Acad., U. Munich, 1898-1902; prof. botany U. La Plata, Argentine Republic, S.A., 1907-08; forest pathologist, 1910, pathologist, 1918, prin. pathologist, 1928—, U.S. Dept. Agr., in charge research planning and criticism, 1929—. Fellow A.A.A.S., Cal. Acad. Scis.; mem. Société Mycologique de France, Société de Pathologie Végétale et d'Entomologie Agricole de France, Bot. Soc. Am., Phytopathol. Soc. Am., Soc. Am. Foresters, Biol. Soc. Pacific Coast, Am. Acad. Polit. and Social Sci., Wash. Acad. Sci., Am. Mycol. Soc., Am. Soc. Naturalists, Am. Ecol. Soc., Cal. Bot. Soc., Société d'Études Océaniennes, Tahiti, Sigma Xi. Clubs: Faculty (U. Cal.); University, Commonwealth. Author: Die Hefe, 1898; Allgemeine Botanik, 1909; Forest Tree Diseases Common in California and Nevada, 1914; Forest Pathology in Forest Regulation. 1916; Les Vanillières de Tahiti et Moorea, 1916 (same in Tahitian transl., 1917); also papers on tree diseases. Home: 3157 Jackson St. Office: Forest Service, 446 Phelan Bldg., San Francisco. Died Feb. 1957.

MEINS, Carroll Leach, govt. ofcl.; b. Boston, Oct. 22, 1892; s. Walter R. and Grace Forster (Leach) M.; student pub. schs., Boston. Wholesaler of chocolate since 1919; mem. Mass. Ho. Reps., 1923-28; chief sec. Gov. Saltonstall, 1939-40; chmn. Mass. Dept. Pub. Utilities, 1941-47; collector U.S. customs Dist. of Mass. since 1953. Adminstrv. chmn. Met. Transit Recess Com., 1942-47; chmn. Met. Transit Authority, 1947-49. Lt., U.S. Army, World War I. Member Roxbury Charitable Soc. (exec. com.), Roxbury Hist. Soc. Republican (chmn. Rep. State Com. 1938). Conglist. Mason (32°, Shriner). Clubs: Union, Boothbay Harbor Yacht. Home: 171 Humboldt Av. Office: U.S. Customs House, Boston. Died Sept. 14, 1953; buried Cedar Grove Cemetery, Boston.

MEISENHELDER, Edmund W. (mīz'ĕn-hĕldĕr), surgeon; b. York, Pa., May 9, 1876; s. Edmund W. and Maria E. (Baughman) M.; A.B., Gettysburg Coll., Gettysburg, Pa., 1898, A.M., 1901, Sc.D., 1931; M.D., Johns Hopkins U., 1902; m. Frances Faust, May 9, 1914; children—Edmund W. III, Ruth L., Samuel F., Helen (dec.). Began practice at York, 1902; surgeon York (Pa.) Hosp., 1905-13, West Side Sanitarium, 1913-46, now pvt. surgical practice; cons. surgeon Gettysburg Hosp. Fellow Am. Coll. Surgeons; mem. A.M.A., Pa. State and York County med. socs. Republican. Lutheran. Mason (Shriner). Home: Box 266A, R.D. 4, Dover, Pa. Office: 1259 W. Market St., York, Pa. Died Apr. 25, 1952; buried Prospect Hill Cemetery, York.

MEISSNER, Edwin Benjamin, mfg. exec.; b. Milw., Dec. 5, 1884; s. Abraham and Fredericka (Katz) M.; student pub. schs.; m. Edna Rice, June 26, 1911. Messenger, Milw. Electric Ry. & Light Co., 1899, ccounting dept., 1900-05, chief clk. to pres., 1905-11; asst. to pres. St. Louis Car Co., 1911-15, v.p., 1915-22, pres., gen. mgr., 1922—; pres., treas. St. Louis Mining and Milling Corp., Joplin, 1941—; dir. Nat. Stock Yards, Ill., Nat. Bank of National City, St. Louis Malleable Casting Co., Wagner Electric Co., Consol. Retail Stores. Pres. St. Louis Crime Commn. Pres. Central Inst. for Deaf, St. Louis; pres., dir. New Mt. Sinai Cemetery Assn.; hon. pres., dir. Congregation Shaare Emeth, St. Louis; trustee Nat. Security Indsl. Assn. Served as lt. col. Ordnance Corps, U.S. Army, World War I. Mem. Mexico C. of C. in U.S., St. Louis Electric Bd. of Trade, Am. Inst. E.E., Mo. C. of C. (dir.). Mason (Shriner). Clubs: Mo. Athletic Assn., Westwood Country, Engineers (St. Louis). Home: 6244 Forsythe St., St. Louis. Office: 8000 N. Broadway, St. Louis 15. Died Sept. 10, 1956.

MEISSNER, K(arl) W(ilhelm), physicist; b. Reutlingen, Germany, Dec. 15, 1891; s. Karl Emil and Ottilie (Plankenhorn) M.; student Gymnasium Reutlingen, 1898-1910; Dr. rer. nat. U. Tuebingen, 1915; student U. Munich, 1912; m. Ita B. Kohn, Sept. 27, 1919 (died July 9, 1939); m. 2d Hanna Hellinger, May 22, 1942. Came to U.S., 1938, naturalized, 1943. Privat dozent, U. Zurich, 1919-25; prof. physics. U. Frankfurt Main, 1925-37; head dept. physics, 1931-37; asst. prof. physics, Worcester Poly. Inst., 1938-41; prof. physics, Purdue U., 1941—. Mem. Am. Phys. Soc., Optical Soc. Am., Sigma Xi. Researcher in spectroscopy and atomic physics. Home: 176 E. Stadium Av., West Lafayette, Ind. Died Apr. 13, 1959.

MELCHER, Carl A., business exec.; b. Burlington, Ia., Sept. 25, 1889; s. Joseph P. and Kate (Klopfenstein) M.; student Woodbury Bus. Coll., Los Angeles, 1906-07; m. Christine E. Cleghorn, Oct. 5, 1917. Rancher, land developer, 1910-31; v.p., mgr. ranch property Pacific States Savs. & Loan Co., 1931-39; v.p. Fontana Farms Co., 1939-40; gen. supt. Kern Co. Land Co., 1940-48, gen. mgr. since 1948, v.p., dir. since 1950. Mem. Cal. State C. of C. (dir.). Club: Rotary (Bakersfield). Home: 2300 Elm St. Office: 1712 19th St., Bakersfield, Cal. Died Jan. 3, 1954; buried Garden of Prayer Union Cemetery, Bakersfield.

MELDRUM, William Buell, educator; b. Hull, Que., Can., Dec. 18, 1887; B.A., McGill U., 1909, M.S., 1911; Ph.D., Harvard, 1914; m. Phillipa Ruth Coleman, Sept. 2, 1919; children—William Buell, Lestella, Thomas Wilson, Donald Nicol. Engaged in research in phys. and analytical chemistry and teaching McGill U., 1909-11, Montreal Tech. Inst., 1910-11, Harvard, 1911-12, Vassar, 1914-17; asso. Haverford Coll., 1917—, prof. chemistry, 1926—, now John Farnum prof. chemistry; research, geophys. lab., and War Industries Bd., 1919. Mem. Am. Chem. Soc. (chmn. Phila. sect. 1937-38, councillor 1938-44), Sci. Tchrs. Assn. (pres. 1926), A.A.A.S., Assn. Harvard Chemists, New Eng. Assn. Chem. Tchrs., Pa. Chem. Soc. (gov.), Franklin Inst., New Eng. Assn. Chemistry Tchrs. Author: Introduction to Theoretical Chemistry, 1936; Qualitative Analysis, 1938; Semimicro Qualitative Analysis, 1939; (with Frank T. Gucker, Jr.) Physical Chemistry, 1942; (with A. F. Daggett) A Textbook of Qualitative Analysis, 1946, Quantitative Analysis, 1955. Asso. editor Jour. Franklin Inst. Contbr. to sci. jours.; pub. many papers. Home: 747 College Av., Haverford, Pa. Died Dec. 31, 1956; buried Valley Forge (Pa.) Gardens.

MELEAR, James Melville (mê-lēr'), clergyman, editor; b. Sullivan County, Tenn.; s. Rev. John and Jennette (Bray) M.; A.B., U. of Chattanooga, 1891, A.M., 1894, B.D., 1895, D.D., 1904, hon. Litt.D., 1925; m. Grace Gertrude Stafford, Oct. 19, 1905 (dec. 1927); children—Gertrude Elizabeth, Mary Louise; m. 2d, Eda Selby. Joined Holston Conf. M.E. Ch., 1892; pastor Carnegie, 1892, Sherman Heights, 1893-95, Athens, 1895-97, Trinity Ch., Knoxville, 1897-1905, First Ch., Baraboo, Wis., 1905-07, First Ch., Frankfort, Ind., 1907-11, Centenary Ch., Lexington, Ky., 1911-16; editor Meth. Advocate-Journal (now Christian Advocate), Southern edition, Athens, Tenn., 1916-32; now treas. Endowment Fund Tenn. Wesleyan College. Trustee U. of Chattanooga, Tenn., Wesleyan Coll. Mason (K.T.), Odd Fellow. Club: Browning (Frankfort, Ind.). Author: Hopes That Perish, 1899. Home: Athens, Tenn. Died Dec. 28, 1955; buried Cedar Grove Cemetery, Athens.

MELENCIO, José P., Philippine consul gen.; b. Cabanatuan, P.I., Apr. 10, 1894; s. Emilio and Marcela (Payawal) M.; A.B. cum laude, U. of the Philippines, 1914, LL.B., 1917; LL.M., Georgetown U., Washington, 1918, M.Dip., 1919; m. Carmen R. Aquinaldo, Mar. 30, 1921; children—Ameurfina, Emilina. Dir. Philippine Publicity Bur., Washington, 1919-21; mem. Ho. of Reps., P.I., 1925-31; asst. solicitor gen., 1934; under-sec. of justice, 1936; asso. justice Ct. of Appeals, 1940; consul gen., New York, since 1946; mem. Philippine delegation to U.N. gen. assembly, Paris, 1948, rank of minister; chief Philippine mission in Japan, Ambasasador, 1951. Mem. Philippine C. of C., Philippine Columbian Assn. Clubs: Wack Wack Golf and Country (Manila); Athletic (New York). Home: 450 Lamayan, Manila, P.I. Office: Philippine Consulate General, 40 Exchange Pl., N.Y.C. Died Dec. 13, 1952.

MELLISH, Mary, operatic soprano; b. Albany, N.Y., 1890; d. Kyran and Margaret (Conboy) Flannery; grad. St. John's Acad., Albany; m. Jay A. Mellish, Apr. 1909 (died 1927); m. 2d, William Boyce Eakin, 1937 (died 1951). Joined Metropolitan Opera Co., 1918; soprana in Boris Godunov, Carmen, other operas, 1918-24. Author: Sometimes I Reminisce (autobiography), 1941. Home: 238 S. Manning Blvd., Albany, N.Y.

MELLOTT, Arthur J., judge; b. Wallula, Leavenworth County, Kan., Aug. 30, 1888; s. McClellan and Pauline Spence (Allen) M.; LL.B., Kansas City (Mo.) Sch. of Law, 1917; m. Florence M. Hiatt, Oct. 8, 1911; children—Margaret May, Arthur M., Howard A., Mary Nelle. Teacher county schs., 1907-14; supt. pub. instrn., Wyandotte County, Kan., 1914-17; asst. U.S. atty., 1917-18; practiced with Judge J. H. Brady, 1919-20, with W. E. Carson, 1921-22; judge City Court, Kansas City, Kan., 1923-24; county atty., 1927-29; apptd. dep. commr. internal revenue, Washington, D.C., May 1934; judge Tax Court of U.S. (formerly U.S. Bd. of Tax Appeals) July 1935-Nov. 1945. Nominated by President Truman as U.S. Dist. Judge for the Dist. of Kansas, Nov. 8, 1945; commd. Nov. 28, 1945. Democrat. Methodist. Mason (32°, Shriner), Odd Fellow, Woodman. Home: 921 Hillcrest Dr. Address: 910 S. 110th St., Edwardsville, Kan. Died Dec. 29, 1957; buried, Edwardsville Cemetery.

MELTON, Charles Lewis, educator; b. nr. Flint Hill, Va. Apr. 12, 1865; s. Wilson Nicholas and Sarah (McKay) M.; grad. Neosho (Mo.) Collegiate Inst., 1886; A.M., Randolph-Macon Coll., Ashland, Va., 1892; m. Gertrude Blackwell, June 24, 1896. Prin. Randolph-Macon Acad., 1899—. Dir. Winchester Meml. Hosp. Democrat. Methodist. Home: Front Royal, Va. Deceased.

MEMINGER, James Wilbert, clergyman; b. Ickesburg, Pa., Nov. 9, 1859; s. James Galbraith and Rebecca Ellen (Rice) M.; A.B., Ursinus Coll., Collegeville, Pa., 1884, B.D., 1886, D.D., 1905; B.O., Nat. School Oratory, Phila., 1886; m. Florence Hollinger, Nov. 4, 1891; children—Cyrus Hollinger, Elizabeth Hollinger. Ordained to ministry Ref. Ch. in U.S., 1886; pastor East Coventry, Pa., 1886-87, St. Paul's Ch., Lancaster, Pa., 1887-1920. Sec.-treas. bd. relief, Gen. Synod Ref. Ch. in U.S.A., 1920—; organizer, pres. Clergyman's Coop. Beneficial Assn.; pres. Tchrs.' Protective Union. Mem. bd. dirs. Central Theol. Sem. (Dayton, O.), Ursinus Coll.; trustee Shippen Sch. Girls. Republican. Knight of Malta. Home: Lancaster, Pa. Deceased.

MENCKEN, Henry Louis (mĕngk'ĕn), author, editor; b. Baltimore, Md., Sept. 12, 1880; s. August and Anna (Abhau) M.; ed. pvt. sch. and Baltimore Polytechnic; m. Sara Powell Haardt, Aug. 27, 1930 (died May 31, 1935). Reporter, Baltimore Morning Herald, 1899; city editor, 1903-05; editor Evening Herald, 1905-06; on staff Baltimore Sun, 1906-10; Evening Sun, 1910-17, 1920-35, both Sunpapers, 1936-41, since 1948; lit. critic Smart Set, 1908-23, co-editor, 1914-23; editor Am. Mercury, 1924-?3; contbg. editor The Nation, 1921-32. Dir. Alfred A. Knopf, Inc. Awarded gold medal for criticism and essays Nat. Inst. and Am. Acad. Arts and Letters. Mem. Modern Lang. Assn., Linguistic Soc., Am. Dialect Society. Club: Maryland. Author: Ventures Into Verse, 1903; George Bernard Shaw—His Plays, 1905; The Philosophy of Friedrich Nietzsche, 1908; The Artist (play), 1912; A Book of Burlesques, 1916; A Little Book in C Major, 1916; A Book of Prefaces, 1917; In Defense of Women, 1917; Damn—a Book of Calumny, 1917; The American Language, 1918, 4th revision, 1936, Supplement I, 1945, Supplement II, 1948; Prejudices —First Series, 1919, Second Series, 1920, Third Series, 1922, Fourth Series, 1924, Fifth Series, 1926, Sixth Series, 1927; Notes on Democracy, 1926, Treatise on the Gods, 1930; Making a President, 1932; Treatise on Right and Wrong, 1936; Happy Days, 1940; Newspaper Days, 1941; Heathen Days, 1943; Christmas Story, 1946; A Mencken Chrestomathy, 1949; Minority Report, 1956. Part Author: Men vs. the Man, 1910; Europe After 8:15, 1914; The Am. Credo, 1920; Heliogabalus (play), 1920; The Sunpapers of Baltimore, 1937. Editor: The Players' Ibsen, 1909; The Free Lance Books, 1919; The Charlatanry of the Learned, 1937; A New Dictionary of Quotations, 1942. Translator: The Antichrist, by F. W. Nietzsche, 1920. Home: 1524 Hollins St., Balt. 23. Died Jan. 29, 1956; buried Loudon Park Cemetery, Balt.

MENDENHALL, Walter Curran, director (retired) United States Geological Survey; b. Marlboro, Stark County, Ohio, February 20, 1871; s. William King and Emma Pierce (Garrigues) M.; B.S., Ohio Normal Univ., 1895; student Harvard, 1896-97, U. of Heidelberg, 1899-1900; hon. Sc.D., Colo. Sch. of Mines, 1928, U. of Wis., 1932; m. Alice May Boutell, Sept. 20, 1915; children—Margaret Boutell Smith, Alice Curran. Geologic aid, 1894-96, asst. geol., 1896-1901, geologist, 1901—, U.S. Geol. Survey. In charge ground water investigations of U.S., 1907-10; chief of Land Classification Board, 1910-22; chief geologist, 1922-31, dir., 1931-43. Fellow A.A.A.S. (v.p. sect. E. 1922), Geol. Soc. America (pres. 1936); mem. Nat. Acad. of Sciences, Am. Inst. Mining Engrs. (hon.), Am. Assn. Petroleum Geologists (hon.), Geol. Soc. Washington (pres. 1917), Washington Acad. Sciences. Clubs: Cosmos (Washington); Chevy Chase (Md.); Harvard (New York); Faculty (Cambridge, Mass.). Author of papers appearing mainly in the publs. of U.S. Geol. Survey. Home: 9 E. Lenox St., Chevy Chase 15. Md. Died June 2, 1957; buried Marlboro, Stark County, O.

MENDLESON, Alan N(orman), business exec.; b. Albany, N.Y., Feb. 18, 1904; s. Norman and Jane (Hyman) M.; student Albany Acad., 1908-19, Taft Sch., 1919, Yale, 1922-23; m. Babette Suzanne Kafka, Aug. 3, 1925; children—Jerry II, Alan Norman, Jane Irene. With B. T. Babbitt, Inc. (del.), 1923—. President, 1946-51, became chairman of the board, 1951, now retired; president of B. T. Babbitt Corp., N.Y.C., 1946—, B. T. Babbitt-Holly Products Corp., 1946—, Champion Chem. Works, Inc., 1946—, E. Meyers Lye Corp., 1946—; v.p. B. T. Babbitt, Ltd. Mem. Albany Soc. of N.Y. Mason. Clubs: Kiwanis; Country Tennis (Westchester, N.Y.); Yale (N.Y.C.); Officers Army and Navy; Sunningdale Country; Scarsdale Town; Harmonie. Home: 202 N. Washington Dr., St. Armond's Key, Sarasota, Fla.; also The Firs, Washington, Me. Died Aug. 14, 1956.

MENGE, Frederick (mĕn'jē), laryngologist; b. Chicago, Ill., Aug. 28, 1869; s. Frederick A. and Caroline Meyer (Zur Capellen) M.; grad. West Div. High Sch., Chicago, 1889; M.D., Northwestern U., 1892; post-grad. U. of Berlin, 1893; m. Alberta Richards, June 11, 1902. Practiced in Chgo., 1893-1930, ret.; prof. emeritus laryngology and rhinology, Northwestern U. Med. Sch. 1st lt. U.S. Army Med. Reserve Corps, Feb. 1911. Fellow Am. Coll. Surgeons; mem. Am. Laryngol., Rhinol. and Otol. Soc., A.M.A., Chicago Med. Soc., Laryngol. and Climatol. Soc. Chicago. Republican. Lutheran. Clubs: University, Chicago Athletic, Flossmoor Country. Commanding major, Medical R.C., April 1916; in active service as chief consultant in otolaryngology, Camp Zachary Taylor, Louisville, Ky., World War. Home and Office: 921 E. 42d Pl., Chicago. Died Jan. 8, 1951.

MENGES, Franklin, ex-congressman; b. Menges Mills, Pa.; m. May McIlhenny, Oct. 26, 1897. Instr. chemistry and physics, Gettysburg Col., 10 yrs.; later head sci. dept. York High Sch., lectr. before farmers' insts. until 1917; devoted attention largely to farming, 1917—; mem. 69th to 71st Congresses, 22d Pa. Dist. Republican. Home: York, Pa. Deceased.

MENKEN, S. Stanwood (mĕn'kĕn), lawyer; b. Memphis, Tenn., July 29, 1870; s. Capt. Nathan Davis and Sallie (Andrews) M.; student Coll. City of New York; B.L., Cornell U., 1890; post-grad. work same univ., 1890-91; M.A., LL.B., Columbia, 1894; m. Gretchen von Briesen, Nov. 29, 1899 (died 1939); 1 son, Arthur. Began practice of law as member Ogden & Beekman, N.Y. City. Active in Reform Club and reform city politics; organizer Hall or Records Assn., 1896, enrolled 10,000 members and had hall built at cost of $7,000,000 by N.Y. City; candidate for justice of City Court of N.Y. City, 1896; was organizer, 1908, and chmn. Dem. League, with 32,000 members; organizer, Dec. 1915, Nat. Security League; dir. Friends of Democracy. Mem. Assn. Bar City of N.Y., N.Y. Co. Lawyers' Assn., Pilgrims, S.A.R., Chi Phi Frat. Clubs: Cornell U., Cedar Creek (all N.Y.). Director Council of Democracy, New York. Home: E 3. 77th St., N.Y.C. Office: 44 Wall St., N.Y.C. 5. Died Jan. 7, 1954.

MENNER, Robert James, educator; b. Honesdale, Pa., Jan. 30, 1892; s. David Hornbeck and Barbara (Reif) M.; A.B., Yale, 1913, Ph.D., 1918; student U. of Clermont-Ferrand, 1919. Lectr. in English, U. Manitoba, 1913-15; instr. English, Yale, 1919-22, asst. prof., 1922-28, asso. prof., 1928-39, prof. English, 1940-47. Sterling prof. of English, 1947—. Served with 310th F.A., AEF, 1918-19. Mem. Modern Lang. Assn. Am., Mediaeval Acad. Am., Linguistic Soc. Am., Am. Dialect Soc., Phi Beta Kappa, Zeta Psi. Club: Elizabethan (New Haven). Editor: Purity, A Middle English Poem, 1920; Poetical Dialogues of Solomon and Saturn, 1941. Home: 531 Ellsworth Av., New Haven. Died Apr. 4, 1951; buried Honesdale, Pa.

MENOHER, Pearson, ret. army officer; b. Va., Nov. 14, 1892; B.S., U.S. Mil. Acad., 1915; grad. Cav. Sch., advanced course, 1927, Command and Gen. Staff Sch., 1928. Commd. 2d lt., U.S. Army, 1915, advanced through the grades to brig. gen., 1945, ret. 1952. Address: War Dept., Washington 25. Died Feb. 13, 1958; buried Arlington Nat. Cemetery.

MENTZ, George Francis Millen, naval officer; b. N.Y. City, Apr. 20, 1896; s. George William and Florence Livingstone (Millen) M.; student St. Luke's Sch., Wayne, Pa., 1905-08; Coll. Scientifique, Lausanne, Switzerland, 1912; B.S., U.S. Naval Acad., 1918; m. Erica Miller Pochon, Oct. 6, 1928; children—Susan Beverley, George F. M. Commd. ensign, U.S. Navy, June 6, 1918, and advanced through grades to capt., 1918, and ret. (physicial disability, wounded in action 1945) rank of rear admiral, 1947; served U.S.S. Cassin, 1918; commd. squadron subchasers, North Sea, 1918-19, U.S.S. Foote, 1921, U.S.S. Avocet, Asiaitc Fleet, 1929-31, flag. lt. and aide, U.S. High Commr. to Turkey, 1924-26; instr., U.S. Naval Acad., 1927-29; charge press relations Navy Dept., 1932-34; Gunnery officer, U.S.S. Richmond, and charge light cruiser gunnery sch., 1935-37; sr. staff officer, U.S. Mediterranean Squadron, 1938-40; exec. officer, Reserve Officers Training Sch., Fort Schuyler, N.Y., 1941-42; comdr. task group of heavy mine layers at Casablanca and invasion of Sicily, 1943; command Mine Force Atlantic Fleet, 1944, Diversionary Attrack Group connection invasion Linguayan Gulf, Philippine Islands, 1944; ret. active service 1947; with Internat. Refugee Orgn., June 1947—, as chief of Mission in Italy. Decorations: Navy cross, Legion of Merit (combat), Bronze Star, Purple Heart; Star of Solidarity, Knight Comdr. Order St. Gregory the Great, Mil. Class (Pope Pius XII), by Coronna d'Italia, Order of St. Mauritius and Lazarus (Italian). Catholic. Clubs: Army-Navy Country, Washington; Caccia, Rome. Home: "Mountain View," Front Royal Va. Offide: Palazzo Ruspoli, Rome, Italy. Died Nov. 29, 1957; buried U.S. Naval Acad. Cemetery, Annapolis, Md.

MENVILLE, Leon, radiologist; b. Napoleonville, La., Nov. 29, 1882; s. Charles M. and Arabella (Gouaux) M.; student La. State U.; M.D., Md. Med. Coll., Baltimore, 1904; m. Marie Marmande, Jan. 25, 1905; children—Muriel, John, Lucille. Began med. practice at Houma, La., 1904; prof. emeritus radiology, Tulane U.; dir. dept. of radiology, Charity Hospital, to 1950. Ex-pres. La. State Board Med. Examiners. Lt. comdr., U.S.N.R. (retired). Mem. La. State Med. Soc. (past pres.), American Coll. of Radiology (v.p. 1937), Cuban Radiol. Soc. (hon.), Alpha Omega Alpha, Sigma Xi. Democrat. Catholic. Club: Metairie Country. Mem. editorial staff Am. Jour. of Cancer. Awarded gold medal Radiol. Soc. of North America, 1932, for original work on the lymphatic system. Past pres. Radiol. Soc. of North America. Contbr. to Pillmore's Clinical Radiology. Home: 66 Fontainebleau Drive. Office: Maison Blanche Bldg., New Orleans. Died Jan. 24, 1955; buried Houma, La.

MERCER, Eugene LeRoy (mẽr'sẽr), educator; born Kennett Square, Pa., Oct. 30, 1888; s. Eugene P. and Mary Bernard (Hicks) M.; grad. George Sch., 1909; M.D., University of Pa. School of Medicine, 1913; Sc.D. (honorary) Gettysburg College; married Emily Atkinson, Jan. 7, 1914; children—Mary Ellen (Mrs. Ross G. Allen), Eugene LeRoy, David Hicks, Thomas Atkinson. Dir. of phys. edn. and athletics, Swarthmore (Pa.) Coll., 1914-31; dean and prof. dept. phys. edn. U. Pa., 1931-53, emeritus prof., 1953—. Mem. med. adv. bd. Glen George Sch. chmn. bd. Mills Sch. for Boys. Mem. Middle Atlantic States Colegiate Athletic Assn. (past pres.), Coll. Phys. Edn. Assn. (past pres.), Assn. Sigma Xi, Delta Upsilon, Alpha Mu Pi Omega. Clubs: Del. Valley Ornithoogical; Ozone; Varsity (U. Pa.). Home: 133 Ogden Av., Swarthmore, Pa. Died July 3, 1957.

MERCHANT, Frank Ivan, coll. prof.; b. N.Y. City, Dec. 23, 1855; s. Albert and Candace (Downs) M.; B.A., Shurtleff Coll., Upper Alton, Ill., 1880; M.A., Ph.D., U. of Berlin, 1890; studied U. of Rome, 1904; unmarried. Instr. Latin and Greek, Shurtleff Coll., 1880-85; instr. Sauveur Summer Sch. of Langs., 1884, 85; prof. Latin, U. of S.D., 1891-1903; prof. Latin and Greek, Ia. State Teachers Coll., 1907-34, and head of Dept. of Latin, Greek, and German, 1929-34, prof. emeritus since 1934. Mem. Am. Philol. Assn. Republican. Contbr. to philol. jours. Home: 1927 College St., Cedar Falls, Ia. Deceased.

MERCIER, Armand Theodore (mẽr'sĭ-ẽr), ret. ry. exec.; b. New Orleans, Dec. 11, 1881; s. Charles Sidney and Irene (Yenne) M.; prep. edn. Rugby Mil. Acad., New Orleans, 1896-99; C.E., Tulane U., 1903; m. Helen Ferris, Feb. 12, 1907; children—Sidney (dec.), Helen (Mrs. R. G. Polhamus), Theodora (Mrs. W. H. Paulman), Rodman S.P. Co., 1904-06, asst. engr., 1906-07, engr. and gen. foreman, 1907-08, asst. div. engr., 1908-11, asst. dist. engr. So. dist., Los Angeles, 1911-12, div. engr. San Joaquin div., Bakersfield, Cal., 1912-13, div. engr. Los Angeles div., 1913-17, asst. supt. Shasta div., Dunsmuir, Cal., 1917-18, supt. Portland div., 1918-21; pres., gen. mgr. San Diego & Ariz. Ry., San Diego, Cal., 1921-29; v.p., gen. mgr. Pacific Electric Ry., Los Angeles, 1929-33; gen. mgr. S.P. Co., Pacific Lines, 1933-38, v.p. 1938-41, pres., 1941-51. Mem. Cal. C. of C. (div.), Newcomen Soc., Kappa Alpha. Republican. Episcopalian. Clubs: Pacific Union, The Family (San Francisco); Menlo Country (Redwood City); California (Los Angeles). Home: 509 Coleridge Av., Palo Alto, Cal. Office: 65 Market St., San Francisco. Died Nov. 21, 1957.

MERCK, George Wilhelm, mfg. chemist; b. New York, N.Y., Mar. 29, 1894; s. George and Friedrike (Schenck) Merck; A.B., Harvard University, 1915; Phar.D. (honorary) Phila. Coll. of Pharmacy, 1938; D.Sc. (hon.), Temple U., 1948, Lafayette Coll., 1950, University Vt., 1952, Newark College of Engineering, 1954; LL.D., Middlebury Coll., 1951, Rutgers U., 1952; D. Eng. (hon.), Stevens Institute Tech., 1951; m. Serena Stevens, Nov. 24, 1926; children—George W., Jr., Albert W. (by prev. marr.); Serena M. (Mrs. Francis W. Hatch, Jr.), John H. C., Judith F. Associated with Merck & Co., Inc., mfg. chemists, Rahway, N.J., 1914—, pres., dir., 1925-50, chmn. bd., 1949—; chmn. bd. Merck & Co., Ltd., Merck (Pan Am.), Inc., Merck (North Am.), Inc.; dir. N.Y. & Long Branch R.R. Company, U.N.J.R.R. & Canal Co. Chmn. bd. trustees Merck Inst. for Therapeutic Research; mem. bd. Nat. Sci. Found., 1951—; mem. corp. Mass. Inst. Tech.; bd. trustees Nat. Fund for Med. Edn., Nutrition Found.; pres. and trustee Vt. Forest & Farmland Found.; member bd. Conservation Found. Mem. adv. com. Munitions Board, 1939-51, chmn. committee, 1949-51; member committee on drugs and medical supplies, National Research Council, 1942-45; director War Research Service (in charge biological warfare), 1942-44; special consultant to Secretary of War (biol. warfare), chmn. U.S. Biol. Warfare Com., 1944-45. Awarded Medal for Merit for wartime biol. services; Chem. Industry Medal by Am. sect. of Soc. of Chem. Industry, 1947. Fellow Am. Geog. Society. Mem. national executive council Am. Cancer Soc.; mem. National Conference of Christians and Jews; dir. Regional Plan Assn., New York City; Com. to Visit Dept. Biol. and Bussey Instn., Harvard U.; member exec. com. Mfg. Chemists' Assn., 1927-49, v.p., 1933-45, pres., 1949-52. Director American Forestry Assn.; past treas. N.J. State Rep. Com. Rep. Clubs: Essex County (West Orange); Metropolitan (Washington); University, Harvard, Chemists', Down Town, Railroad-Machinery, Links, Century (N.Y.); Essex (Newark); University (St. Louis); Jupiter Island (Hobe Sound, Fla.); Dorset Field (Dorset, Vt.). Home: Eagleridge Farm, Prospect Av., West Orange, N.J. Office: Lincoln Av., Rahway, N.J. Died Nov. 9, 1957.

MERICA, Paul Dyer (mẽr'ĭ-kȧ), metallurgist; b. Warsaw, Ind., Mar. 17, 1889; s. Charles Oliver and Alice (White) M.; student DePauw U., 1904-07; A.B., U. Wis., 1908; Ph.D., U. Berlin, 1914; D.Sc., De Pauw U., 1934, Lehigh U., 1938, Stevens Inst., 1942; m. Florence Young, Sept. 22, 1917. Research physicist U.S. Bureau of Standards, 1914-19; dir. research Internat. Nickel Co., 1919—; tech. asst. to pres. Internat. Nickel Co. of Can., 1929, successively asst. to pres., exec. v.p., pres., dir., now cons. research and development work on metals and alloys—their metallurgy and metallography; originator of the precipitation theory of hardening of alloys, developed in connection with rsch. on aluminum alloys. Fellow A.A.A.S.; mem. Am. Iron and Steel Inst., Am. Soc. for Testing Materials, Am. Phys. Soc., Am. Inst. Mining and Metall. Engrs., Am. Inst. C.E., Nat. Acad. Sciences, Inst. Metals and Iron and Steel Inst. (both Brit.), Canadian Inst. Mining and Metallurgy, Mining and Metall. Soc. Am., Am. Soc. for Metals, Beta Theta Pi, Phi Lambda Upsilon, Epsilon Chi. Republican. Presbyn. Clubs: Engineers, City Midday, University, Mining, Sleepy Hollow Country. Author articles and monographs in tech. publs. James Douglas medallist, 1929; John Fritz medalist, 1938; Institute Medals, Medallist, 1941; Franklin Institute medal, 1942; Gold medal, Am. Soc. for Metals, 1951. Home: P.O. Box 310, Ossining, N.Y. Office: 67 Wall St., N.Y.C. Died Oct. 20, 1957.

MERINGTON, Marguerite, playwright. Author: Daphne; Captain Letterblair (comedy), 1906; Love Finds the Way; Scarlet of the Mounted, 1906; Vicar of Wakefield, play, 1909; Holiday Plays, 5 one-act pieces, 1910; The Custer Story, others; also many poems in Scribner's Mag. Mem. Alliance Francaise. Club: Cosmopolitan. Home: 46 W. 97th St., N.Y.C. Died May 1951.

MERRELL, Irvin Seward, mech. engr., mfr.; b. Syracuse, N.Y., Oct. 12, 1875; s. Gauis Lewis and Mary Antoinette (Seward) M.; prep. edn., Cascadilla Sch., Ithaca, N.Y.; B.S. in Mech. Engring., Mass. Inst. Tech., 1896; m. Carolyn Louise Snow, Jan. 4, 1899; children—Seward Snow, Mary Antoinette (Mrs. John Parker Welch), Harriet Powers (Mrs. Jay E. Latimer, Jr.). Began, 1896, in employ of Merrell-Soule Co., Syracuse, and specialized in research in desiccation and evaporation of food products; patent issued, 1899, for double cylinder evaporator, for desiccating vegetable pulps, now used for making dried milk; asso. with others in investigations resulting in prodn. of Spray process milk powder and original development of vacuum pack can, for which many patents have been issued; ret. Jan. 1, 1928. Chmn. Draft Bd. No. 3, Syracuse, World War. Trustee Tuskegee (Ala.) Normal and Indsl. Inst.; mem. bd. govs. St. Petersburg Jr. Coll.; mem. exec. bd. Nat. Urban League, N.Y. Republican. Unitarian. Clubs: Pass-a-Grille Yacht, St. Petersburg Yacht. Address: 345 18th Av. N.E., St. Petersburg, Fla. Died May 9, 1959; buried Meml. Park, St. Petersburg.

MERRELL, John Hastings, asbestos and rubber mfr.; b. Detroit, Mich., Dec. 23, 1875; s. James Chandler and Julia (Wild) M.; student Prof. Ziwets Acad.; grad. Detroit High Sch.; U. of Mich., 1896; m. Lillian P. Nettleton, Oct. 28, 1903; one daughter, Honor (Mrs. Gordon Loud). Began with India Rubber Co., Akron, O., Aug. 1899; general Western mgr. Manhattan Rubber Mfg. Co., 1918-25; v.p. and dir. Raybestos-Manhattan, Inc., Reynolds Spring Co., The Cleveland Wire Spring Co., Cleveland, O.; vice pres. Manhattan Rubber Manufacturing Co. of Wis.; dir. Advance-Rumely Corp. Mem. Ill. Soc. Sons Am. Revolution, Art Inst. Chicago, Field Museum of Natural History, Soc. Mayflower Descendants. Treas. First Universalist Soc. of Chicago. Clubs: Chicago, Casino, Tavern (Chicago); Glen View; Old Elm Golf (Lake Forest, Ill.); Question (Detroit). Home: 229 Lake Shore Dr. Office: 6010 Northwest Hwy., Chgo. Died 1958.

MERRELL, William Dayton, biologist; b. Bklyn., Aug. 21, 1869; s. Jonathan Dayton and Clarissa Orcelia (Justus)M.; A.B., U. Rochester, 1891; Ph.D., U. Chgo., 1899; m. Winifred Boorman, Sept. 6, 1898. Began teaching, Beaver Dam, Wis., 1891; prof. biology U. Rochester, 1905-39, prof. emeritus of botany, 1939—, was dir. univ.'s first glee club. Fellow A.A.A.S.; mem. Rochester Acad. Science. Republican. Baptist. Home: Penfield Rd., Brighton, N.Y. Died Feb. 11, 1955.

MERRIAM, Charles Edward (mĕr'ĭ-ăm), univ. prof.; b. Hopkinton, Ia., Nov. 15, 1874; s. Charles Edward and Margaret Campbell (Kirkwood) M.; brother of John Campbell Merriam; A.B., Lenox College, 1893; A.B., State U. of Ia., 1895; A.M., Columbia, 1897, Ph.D., 1900; LL.D., Univ. of Colorado, 1920, Univ. of Mich., 1935, Washington Univ., 1946, Princeton University, 1946, Yale 1951; studied in Berlin and Paris from 1899-1900; m. Elizabeth Hilda Doyle, Aug. 3, 1901; children—Charles James, John Francis, Elizabeth, Robert Edward. Docent in polit. science, 1900-02, asso., 1902-03, instructor, 1903-05, asst. prof., 1905-07, asso. prof., 1907-11, prof. since 1911, U. of Chicago, also chmn. Dept. Polit. Science. Alderman, 7th Ward, Chicago, 1909-11 and 1913-17; was chmn. Commission on City Expenditures; Rep. candidate for mayor of Chicago, 1911; member U.S. Loyalty Review board, 1947-48. Mem. Social Science Research Council (pres. 1924-27), Am. Polit. Science Assn. (president 1924-25), Am. Philos. Soc., Hoover Commn. on Recent Social Trends; mem. Nat. Resources Bd., 1933-43; mem. President's Committee on Administrative Management. Author: The History of the Theory of Sovereignty Since Rousseau (in Columbia U. Studios in History, Economics and Public Law), 1900; A History of Am. Political Theories, 1903; Municipal Revenues of Chicago, 1906; Primary Elections, 1908; Am. Polit. Ideas, 1865-1917, 1921; The American Party System, 1922; Non-Voting (with H. F. Gosnell), 1924; New Aspects of Politics, 1925. Editor: History of Political Theories; Recent Times (with H. E. Barnes and others), 1924; Four American Party Leaders, 1926; Chicago, 1929; The Making of Citizens, 1931; The Written Constitution, 1931; Metropolitan Region of Chicago (with S. D. Parrott and A. Lepawsky), 1933; Civic Education in the U. S., 1934; Political Power, 1934; Role of Politics in Social Change, 1936; The New Democracy and the New Despotism, 1939; Prologue to Politics, 1939; What Is Democracy?, 1941; On the Agenda of Democracy, 1941; Public and Private Government, 1944; Systematic Politics, 1945; (with Robert E. Merriam) The American Government, 1954. Comdg. capt. Signal Reserve Corps, Aviation Sect., 1917; pres. Aviation Examining Bd.; apptd. commr. of Am. on Pub. Information, in Italy, 1918. Home: 6041 University Av., Chgo. 37. Died Jan. 8, 1953; buried Arlington Nat. Cemetery.

MERRIAM, Frank Finley, ex-gov. Cal.; b. Hopkinton, Ia., Dec. 22, 1865; ed. Lenox Coll., Hopkinton; m. Nellie E. Boronson-Day (died 1931); m. 2d, Mrs. Jessie Steward Lipsey (died 1948); 1 son, Howard (dec.). Served as prin. schs., Ia. and Neb.; mem. Ia. Ho. of Rep., 1896-98, and auditor State of Ia. 2 terms; engaged in newspaper business, Ia., Indian Ty., and with Long Beach (Cal.) Press; pres. Citizens State Bank, Long Beach, 1924-26; mem. Cal. Ho. of Reps., 6 terms, and elected to State Senate, 1928; lt. gov. of Cal., 1931-34, gov., 1934-39; in real estate bus. at Long Beach. Hon. pres. Cal. Real Estate Assn. Republican. Home: 20 Lindero Av., Long Beach 3, Cal.

MERRIAM, Henry M., ins. co. exec.; b. Tazewell County, Ill., Aug. 31, 1865; s. Col. Jonathan and Lucy (White) M.; student Shurtleff Coll., Alton, Ill. Began as clk. Ill. Nat. Bank of Springfield, 1886, cashier, 1906, later v.p.; mem. finance com. Franklin Life Ins. Co., 1902-14, chmn. v.p., chmn. finance com., 1914-23, pres., 1923-39, now chmn. bd. With A.R.C., France, 1918-19, attached to 1st Div. U.S. Army, div. rep., Nov. 1918-Mar. 1919. Republican. Elk. Clubs: Sangamo, Illini Country. Home: 1525 Willamore Av. Office: 812 S. 6th St., Springfield, Ill. Died Oct. 5, 1952; buried Atlanta, Ill.

MERRICK, J(ames) Hartley, b. Phila., Sept. 6, 1869; s. John Vaughan and Mary Sophia (Wagner) M.; A.B., U. Pa., 1890, A.M., 1921; m. Edith Lovering, Oct. 27, 1897 (died July 14, 1910). Asst. to dean of coll. U. Pa., 1892-94, asst. sec., univ., 1894-1904, sec., 1904-07, asst. to provost, 1920-22, acting vice provost, 1922-23, vice provost, 1923-25, dir. welfare, 1925-27. Dir. Bur. Camp Service, Pa.-Del. Div. A.R.C., World War; loaned 40-ton power yacht, Nirvana II, to Navy Dept. for duration of war. Mem. bd. mgrs. Meml. Hosp., Roxborough, Phila., Phila. Charity Ball. Mem. Pa. Acad. Fine Arts, Franklin Inst., Phila. Zoöl. Soc., Phila. Orchestra Assn., Phi Kappa Sigma. Republican. Episcopalian. Home: Forest Farm, Scarborough, Me.; (winter) Alden Park Manor, Germantown, Phila. Deceased.

MERRILL, Albert B., banker; b. Fabius, N.Y., Dec. 10, 1888; s. Edward S. and Mary C. (Ferris) M.; ed. Syracuse U.; m. Rena Wicks, Sept. 16, 1913; children—Jean E. (Mrs. John B. Hammeken), Hollis E. (Mrs. Richard W. Russell). In banking business as clk., 1913; pres. First Trust & Deposit Co., Syracuse, 1927-56, chmn. of bd. dirs. 1956—; dir. Syracuse Cold Storage Co., Netherland Dairy Co., Crouse-Hinds Co., Sealright-Oswego Falls Corp., A. E. Nettleton Co., The Syracuse Hotel, Syracuse Supply Co. Chmn. bd. trustees Syracuse U. Rep. Presbyn. Clubs: Century, Citizens, Skaneateles Golf and Country, Metropolitan (N.Y.C.); Onondago Golf and Country (Fayetteville, N.Y.). Home: Marvelle Rd., R.D., Fayetteville, N.Y. Office: 201 S. Warren St., Syracuse, N.Y. Died Feb. 25, 1960.

MERRILL, Barzille Winfred, director of music; b. Elgin, Ill., May 20, 1864; s. Asa and Jane (Spalding) M.; ed. high sch., East Aurora, Ill., and under pvt. tutors: studied violin with Joseph Joachim and Andreas Moser, theory with Bernhard Ziehn; m. Alma Shedd, 1889 (died 1891); 1 dau., Mrs. Elisabeth Frances Seely; m. 2d, Mary Ann Neely, of Phila., Pa., 1897; 1 dau., Winifred. Organized, directed first high sch. orchestra, East Aurora, Ill., 1880; dir. Tacoma (Wash.) Acad. Music, 1888-93, Merrill Sch. of Music, Atlanta, Ga., 1895-1900; head dept. orchestral music La. State Teachers' Coll., with rank of prof., 1903-19; dir. Dept. of Music with rank of prof., 1919-21, dean Sch. of Music, 1921-38, dean emeritus, 1938—, U. of Ind. Hon. mem. advisory bd. Nat. Bd. of Music. Mem. Delta Chi, Pi Gamma Mu. Republican. Conglist. Club: Nat. Arts (New York. Composer of "Dream Song"; of music of Centennial Pageant of Ind. Univ., 1920; etc. Home: 824 Sheridan Rd., Bloomington, Ind.: (summer) Blue Hill, Me. Died Oct. 17, 1954; buried Clear Creek Cemetery, Monroe County, Ind.

MERRILL, Charles Edward, investment banker; b. Green Cove Springs, Fla., Oct. 19, 1885; s. Charles Morton (M.D.) and Octavia (Wilson) M.; grad. Amherst, 1908, hon. M.A., 1933; LL.D. (hon.), John B. Stetson U., 1946, Amherst Coll., 1948, Kenyon Coll., 1949; D.C.S., N.Y.U., 1950; m. Eliza Ch., Apr., 1912; children—Doris M. (Magowan), Charles Edward; m. 2d, Hellen Ingram, Feb. 1925; 1 son, James Ingram; m. 3d, Kinta Des Mare, March 1939. Partner, Merrill, Lynch, Pierce, Fenner & Beane; founder Safeway Stores, Inc., 1926, and founder The Family Circle Magazine, 1932. President Chi Psi Fraternity, 1940-49. Member New York Stock Exchange, Sons of the Am. Revolution. Clubs: Everglades, Seminole, Palm Beach Yacht, Bath and Tennis (Palm Beach, Fla.); Shinnecock Hills, Meadow, National Golf Links, Southampton; Bankers', Downtown Assn., City, Amherst, River (N.Y.C.). Home: Merrill's Landing, Palm Beach, Fla. Office: 281 S. County Rd., Palm Beach, Fla. Died Oct. 6, 1956; buried Woodlawn Cemetery, West Palm Beach, Fla.

MERRILL, Charles Washington, metall. engr.; b. Concord, N.H., Dec. 21, 1869; s. Sylvester and Clara L. (French) M.; B.S., U. Cal. Coll. Mines, 1891; Met.E., U. Cal., 1922; m. Clara Scott Robinson, Feb. 9, 1898; children—Mrs. Beatrice Morse, John L., Gregor C., Bruce R.; m. 2d, Margaret Barker Cope, Sept. 14, 1938. Has designed, installed and operated many reduction works in U.S., Can., and Mex.; held over 25 patents in U.S. and fgn. countries for metall. processes and apparatus; pres., dir. The Merrill Co.; former chmn. bd., dir. Merco Centrifugal Co., San Francisco. Chief Div. Collateral Commodities, U.S. Food Administration, Washington, 1917-18; chmn. exec. com. San Francisco Community Chest, 1925-27; chmn. minerals com., Cal. State C. of C.; chmn. Cal. State Mining Bd., 1930. Regent U. Cal., 1924-25. Mem. Am. Inst. Mining and Metall. Engrs. (v.p. 1924), Alumni Assn. U. Cal. (pres. 1924-25), Sigma Xi, Mining and Metall. Soc. London, Australian Inst. Mining Engrs., Chem., Metall. and Mining Soc. S. Africa. Recipient James Douglas Internat. gold medal of Am. Inst. Mining and Metall. Engrs. for distinguished internat. metall. achievements, 1924; Nat. Modern Pioneer certificate of award N.A.M. in recognition of distinguished achievement in field sci. and invention which has advanced the Am. standard of living, 1940. Clubs: University, Engineers', Pacific Union, Commonwealth (San Francisco); Claremont (Oakland); Orinda Country (Orinda, Cal.). Home: 407 Camino Sobrante, Orinda, Cal. Office: Hobart Bldg., 582 Market St., San Francisco 4. Died Feb. 6, 1956.

MERRILL, Dana True, ret. army officer; b. East Auburn, Me., Oct. 15, 1876; s. Daniel C. and Mary (Noyes) M.; B.S., U. Me., 1898; distinguished grad. Army Sch. of the Line, 1908, Army Staff Coll., 1909; student Army War Coll., 1919-20; m. Edith Ferry, Oct. 21, 1903; children—Harwood Ferry, Dana Noyes, Virginia True. Commd. 2d lt. U.S. Army, 1898, promoted through grades to brig. gen., 1934; served in Spanish-Am. War, and Philippine Insurrection, 1898-1902; regt. duty, 1902-14; apptd. mem. Gen. Staff, 1917; chief of staff, 37th Div., AEF, 1917-18; gen. staff, 1920-24; insp. gens. dept., 1927-32; col. 10th inf., 1924-27, 33-34; comdg. 12th Brig. at Ft. Sheridan, Ill., 1935-37, Washington Provisional Brig., 1937-38, 10th Inf. Brig., Ft. Benjamin Harrison, 1938-40; retired. Decorated D.S.M. (U.S.); Officer Legion of Honor (France); Officer Order of Leopold, also Croix de Guerre (Belgium). Mem. Sigma Alpha Epsilon. Clubs: Army and Navy; Highland Golf (Ft. Thomas, Ky.). Address: 27 Tower Pl., Ft. Thomas, Ky. Died Aug. 3, 1957; buried Mt. Auburn Cemetery, Auburn, Me.

MERRILL, Elmer Drew, botanist, educator; b. East Auburn, Me., Oct. 15, 1876; s. Daniel C. and Mary A. (Noyes) M.; B.S., U. Me., 1898, M.S., 1904, Sc.D., 1925; student dept. medicine George Washington U., 1900-01; Sc.D., Harvard, 1936; LL.D., U. Cal., 1936; m. Mary Augusta Sperry, May 21, 1907; children—Lynne, Dudley Sperry, Wilmans Noyes (dec.), Ann. Asst. in natural sci. U. Me., 1898-99; asst. agrostologist U.S. Dept. Agr., Washington, 1899-1902; botanist Bur. of Agr., Manila, P.I., 1902, Bur. of Agr. and Bur. of Forestry, 1902-03, Bur. of Govt. Labs., 1903-05, Bur. of Science from 1906; asso. prof. botany and head of dept. U. Philippines, 1912-19, prof. 1916-19; dir. Bur. of Science, Manila, 1919-23; dean Coll. of Agr. and dir. Agrl. Expt. sta. U. Cal., 1923-29; prof. botany Columbia, 1930-35; dir. N.Y. Bot. Garden, 1930-35; prof. botany, dir. Arnold Arboretum, adminstr. bot. collections Harvard, 1935-46, Arnold prof. botany, 1946-48, emeritus. Specializes in taxonomy and phytogeography of Philippine, Polynesian and Indo-Malayan plants. Mem. Am. Acad. Arts and Scis., Nat. Acad. Sciences, Am. Philos. Soc., Royal Asiatic Soc. (Malayan branch); hon. mem. Deutsche Bot. Gesellschaft, Netherlands Bot. Soc., Royal Netherlands Geol. Soc., Acad. Sci., Inst. de France, Inst. Genevoise, Swedish Acad. Science; fgn. mem. Linnean Soc., London (medalist 1939). Clubs: Century, Harvard of Boston. Author over 500 papers on botany of North America, China, Philippines, Malaya and Polynesia. Home: 960 Centre St. Office: Arnold Arboretum, Jamaica Plain 30, Mass. Died Feb. 25, 1956; buried Maplewood Cemetery, West Upton, Mass.

MERRILL, Frank D., army officer; b. Woodville, Mass., Dec. 4, 1903; s. Charles W. and Katherine (Donovan) M.; B.S., U.S. Mil. Acad., 1929; B.S. in M.E., Mass. Inst. of Tech., 1932; m. Lucy Kelsall Wright, Nov. 4, 1930; children—Frank D. Jr., Thomas G. W. Commd. 2d lt. Cav., U.S. Army, 1929, and advanced through the grades to brig. gen., Nov. 1943, maj. gen. 1944; served as asst. mil. attaché to Japan, 1938-41; mem. Gen. Stilwell's staff 1943; dep. comdr. U.S. Forces in India—Burma theater, June-Dec. 1944; chief of staff 10th U.S. Army to Oct. 1945; chief of staff 6th U.S. Army, 1946-47, ret. 1947 for disability incurred World War II; commr. pub. works and hwys. for N.H., 1948—. Awarded Purple Heart, Distinguished Service Medal, Legion of Merit, Bronze Star, Cloud Banner (China); Companion, Order of Indian Empire (Great Britain); Comdr., Legion of Honor (Philippines). Home: Dimond Hill, Concord, N.H. Office: Dept. of Highways, State Capitol, Concord, N.H. Died Dec. 11, 1955; buried West Point, N.Y.

MERRILL, Hugh Davis, lawyer; b. Franklin, Ga., Dec. 20, 1877; s. James Benjamin and Mary Elizabeth (Faver) M.; A.B., Oxford (Ala.) Coll., 1896; LL.B., U. of Ala., 1897; m. Frances Abercrombie, Apr. 1899; 1 son, Ralph; m. 2d, Martha Chitwood, Dec. 27, 1906; children—Hugh Davis, Elizabeth, James William. Admitted to Ala. bar, 1897 and began practice with father at Edwardsville; practiced in Anniston since 1902; mem. firm Merrill, Merrill & Vardaman; now mem. firm Merrill, Merrill, Vardaman & Matthews; judge 7th Judicial Circuit of Ala., 1911-20; member Ala. State Leg., 1900-01, 1923-31 and 1939-43 (speaker); lt. gov. Ala. and presdg. ofcr. State Senate, 1931-35; chmn. com. to read and revise Code of Ala., 1923; mem. com. to read and revise Code of Ala., 1940. Dir. Commercial Nat. Bank, Anniston; mem. adv. com. Ala. Railroad Assn. Del. at large to Constl. Conv., 1933; del. Dem. Nat. Conv., Phila., 1936; trustee Ala. Poly. Inst. Trustee Ala. Polytechnic Inst. 1915-43. Mem. Am., Ala. State and Calhoun County bar assns. Democrat. Baptist. Mason (Shriner). Clubs: Kiwanis, Country (Anniston). Home: 710 Kirkwood Av. Office: Commercial National Bank Bldg., Anniston, Ala. Died Jan. 5, 1954; buried Highland Cemetery, Anniston, Ala.

MERRILL, John Buxton, electrical mfr.; b. Cumberland Center, Me., June 16, 1910; s. Wallace Lincoln and Harriet Melinda (Cutter) M.; student Northeastern U., 1 yr., B.S., Bowdoin Coll., 1933; M.S., Mass. Inst. Tech., 1936; m. Ann Killilea Tompkins, Sept. 2, 1950; children—Peter Gray, Martha Cutter. Asst. Mass. Institute of Technology, 1935-36; joined Patterson Screen Co., Towanda, Pa. as asst. of dir. of research, 1936; supt. fluorescent powder plant, 1940 until plant purchased by Sylvania Electric Co., 1941, and since asso. with latter firm, v.p. Sylvania Electric Products, Inc., also gen. mgr. Tungsten and Chem. Div., 1950, vice president operations Tungsten and Chemical, Atomic Energy and Electronics divisions, 1954—; partner Hotel David Wilmot, Towanda; dir. First Nat. Bank, Towanda. Mem. W.P.B., tungsten adv. com., 1943-45. Mem. Nat. Prodn. Authority Tungsten and Molybdenum Wire and Rod Industry Adv. Com. Trustee Robert Packer Hosp., Sayre, Pa.; dir. Salvation Army, Mills Community Hosp. Assn. Mem. Am. Soc. Metals, A.A.

A.S., Am. Phys. Soc., Optical Soc. Am., Alpha Tau Omega. Presbyn. Mason. Clubs: Rotary, Towanda Country. Home: 207 Pine St. Office: Towanda, Pa. Died Oct. 6, 1955; buried Oak Grove Cemetery, Towanda.

MERRILL, Joseph Francis, educator; b. Richmond, Utah, Aug. 24, 1868; s. Marriner Wood and Maria L. (Kingsbury) M.; grad. Normal Sch., U. of Utah, 1889; B.S., U. of Mich., 1893; Cornell, summers, 1893, 1902; U. of Chicago, summers, 1894, 96, 97; Ph.D., Johns Hopkins Univ., 1899; hon. D.Sc., U. of Utah, 1920; m. Annie Laura Hyde, June 9, 1898 (died Feb. 1917); m. 2d, Emily L. Traub, June 29, 1918. Asst. prof. chemistry, 1893-97, prof. physics and phys. chemistry, 1897-99, dir. Utah State Sch. Mines and Engring., 1897-1928, prof. physics and elec. engring., 1899-1928, dir. war training, 1918, U. of Utah; commr. of edn. Latter Day Saints Ch., 1928-33; mem. bd. trustees and of exec. com. Brigham Young U. and Church Board of Edn. since 1939. Mem. and sec. Utah State Conservation Commn., 1909-12. Advisory mem. Dem. State Central Com., campaigns, 1910, 12, 14, 16. Mem. Mormon Ch.; councilor Presidency Granite Stake, 1911-19; mem. Council of Twelve Apostles, Latter Day Saints Ch., since 1931; pres. European Missions, London, 1933-36. Fellow A.A.A S., Utah Acad. Science; mem. N.E.A., Utah Soc. Engrs. (pres. 1907-10), Utah Teachers' Assn. (pres. 1911). Mem. governing bd. Engring. Council of Utah, 1921-27, pres., 1923-24. Author: Manual of Physics, 1907, 3d edition, 1927; Descendants of Marriner W. Merrill, 1938; The Truth-Seeker and Mormonism, 1945. Home: 1324 East 1st South St., Salt Lake City 2, Utah. Address: 47 E. S. Temple St., Salt Lake City 1. Died Feb. 2, 1952; buried Salt Lake City Cemetery.

MERRILL, Oscar Charles, civil engr.; b. Manchester, Me., July 30, 1874; s. Josiah L. and Sarah Alexander (Chace) M.; B.A., Bates Coll., 1899. Sc. D., 1925; B.S., Mass. Inst. Tech., 1905; m. Elizabeth Watson, Oct. 17, 1906; 1 dau., Margaret (dec.); m. 2d, Marguerite Waters, Dec. 11, 1939. Instr. civil engring. U. Cal., 1905-06; dist. engr. U.S. Forest Service, 1909-13, chief engr., 1914-20; exec. sec. FPC, 1920-29. Chmn. Am. Com., World Power Conf., 1929-35, dir. 3d World Power Conf., 1935-38; engr.-economist U.S.-Mexico Oil Commn., 1942; prin. engr. Engr. Bd., U.S. Army, 1942; ret. 1943. Developed policy under which 85 per cent of water powers in the U.S. are under control of Fed. Govt. Life mem. Am. Soc. C.E.; mem. Washington Soc. Engrs. Universalist. Club: Cosmos (Washington). Author: Electric Power Development in the United States (Govt. Printing Office), 3 vols., 1916. Editor: Transactions Third World Power Conference; Second International Congress on Large Dams (Govt. Printing Office), 15 vols., 1938. Home: 9 W. Melrose St., Chevy Chase, Md. Died Jan. 15, 1951; buried Rock Creek Cemetery, Washington.

MERRILL, Robert V., educator; b. Middletown, Conn., Nov. 24, 1892; s. Elmer Truesdell and Edith (Valentine) M.; student U. Chgo., 1910-13, Ph. D., 1923; B.A., Oxford U., 1916; m. Mary Letitia Fyffe, June 17, 1922; children—Dania Valentine (Mrs. H. D. Brewster), John Fyffe (dec.), Colin Heslep (dec.). Tchr. dept. of French, U. Minn., 1919-20, U. Chgo., 1921-46; prof. French, chmn. French dept. U. Cal. at Los Angeles, 1947—. Served with U.S. Army, 1917-19. Mem. Modern Lang. Assn., Modern Humanities Research Assn., Medieval Acad. Am., Philol. Assn. Pacific Coast, Modern Lang. Assn. So. Cal. Author: The Platonism of Joachim du Bellay, 1925. Contbr. various articles to periodicals. Home: 216 S. Carmelina Av., Los Angeles 24. Died Jan. 1, 1951; buried Franklin, Me.

MERRILL, William Pierson, clergyman; b. Orange, N.J., Jan. 10, 1867; s. George and Emily Dodge (Abbot) M.; A.B., Rutgers, 1887, A.M., 1890, D.D., 1905; B.D., Union Theol. Sem., New York, 1890; D.D., New York U., 1923; S.T.D., Columbia, 1927; L.H.D., Rollins Coll., 1933; m. Clara Seymour Helmer, Sept. 15, 1896; children—Helmer (dec.), Ernest, William Pierson (dec.). Ordained Presbyn. ministry, 1890; pastor Trinity Ch., Chestnut Hill, Phila., 1890-95, Sixth Ch., Chicago, 1895-1911, Brick Ch., New York, Oct. 1, 1911-Oct. 1, 1938 (pastor emeritus since). Pres. trustees Church Peace Union, 1915—. Mem. Phi Beta Kappa. Independent. Author: Faith Building, 1885; Faith and Sight, 1900; Footings for Faith, 1915; Christian Internationalism, 1919; The Common Creed of Christians, 1920; The Freedom of the Preacher, 1922; Liberal Christianity, 1925; Prophets of the Dawn, 1927; The Way, 1933; We See Jesus, 1934; also hymns, "Rise Up, O Men of God"; "Not Alone for Mighty Empire," 1911. Club: Century. Home: 1 Lexington Av., N.Y.C. 10. Died June 19, 1954.

MERRIMAN, Harry Morton, former textile mfg. exec.; b. Waterbury, Conn., Apr. 16, 1874; s. Henry and Mary A. (Heminway) M.; ed. Sedgwick Inst., Great Barrington, Mass., and Mt. Pleasant Mil. Acad., Ossining, N.Y.; m. Maude A. Jackson, Jan. 9, 1900; children—Harry Morton, John A. Pres. Heminway Silk Co., 1912-27; chmn. bd. dirs. Belding-Heminway Co., 1927-33; dir. Belding Heminway Co., Ambassador Hotel Co., 115 East 53d St. Corp., Campobello Island Co., Yachting Pub. Co. Comdr. submarine patrol USN, World War I. Mem. bd. mgrs. Meml. Hosp., N.Y. Mem. Pilgrim Soc., Mil. Order Fgn. Wars. Formerly pres. Marine Mus. of City of N.Y.; formerly mem. Boy Scout Council of N.Y. Clubs: Century, Explorers, Army and Navy (Washington); Maryland (Balt.); Chesapeake Bay Yacht; Annapolis Yacht; Tred Avon Yacht, Royal Kennebacasis Yacht (Can.). Home: 204 S. Hanson St., Easton, Md. Died Dec. 30, 1954; buried Arlington Nat. Cemetery.

MERRIMAN, San Lorenzo, ret. educator; b. Pacific Ocean, Dec. 2, 1869; s. Walter and Lavinia A.M.; A.B., Bowdoin Coll., 1897; A.M., U. Me., 1936; m. Harriett F. Springer, July 3, 1901 (died May 2, 1929); m. 2d, Edith M. Peckham, Dec. 25, 1930. Prin. high sch., Island Falls, Me., 1897-1902; prin. Patten (Me.) Acad., 1902-04; prin. high sch., Presque Isle, Me., 1904-07; prin. Aroostook State Normal Sch., Presque Isle, 1907-40, ret. 1940. Republican. Conglist. Address: R.F.D., East Greenwich, R.I. Died Sept. 13, 1950; buried Harpswell, Me.

MERRITT, Hulett Clinton, financier, industrialist; b. Duluth, Minn., Aug. 17, 1872; s. Lewis J. and Eunice Annette (Wood) M.; ed. in rural schs., bus. coll., U. Iowa; m. Rosaline Calistine Ollivier, July 13, 1892 (died May, 1954). Began, 1887, selling real estate in Duluth when 16; asso. later with father and group building Duluth, Missabe & No. Ry.; connected with organization of, and dir. (1893), Lake Superior Consolidated Iron Mines (Merritt-Rockfeller syndicate); on selling mining (Missabe Mountain Iron Mines, Virginia, Minn.) and other iron mines and railroad interests to U.S. Steel Corp. became its principal stockholder. Obtained control, 1900, of United Electric Gas and Power Co., serving 17 cities in So. Cal. (sold, 1903, to Cal. Edison Co.). Invested, 1903, in 7,000 acres and developed as Tagus Ranch, which leads in growing of boysenberries; blackberries; apricots, nectarines, and canning, drying, and fresh shipping peaches; and resulted in acquiring important interests in other lines including alfalfa growing, honey production, and raising registered live stock. Developed leading enterprise in 31 lines, and has been or is (having been or being pres. or chmn. bds. 138 corps.) interested outstandingly in connection with 55 (actively with 83 additional); the lines, properties and products identified with these 138 businesses, including iron, gold, silver, coal and chromium mines and mining; charcoal burning; railroad bldg. and contracting; dredging; steam laundries; linen supply servs.; steamship lines; beet sugar; iron ore docks; gen. merchandising and women's ready-to-wear chains, and mercantile wholesaling; Great Lakes deep-water fisheries; pine and minl. lands; fruit orchards; real est.; bankg.; ins.; mfg.; public utilities cattle raising; publg.; hotels; restrnts. amusements, and building (built Wolvin Bldg., Duluth; Merritt Office Bldg., Los Angeles; largest pulp and paper mill in Minn.; 10,000-population water distilling and distributive piping facility; first U.S. super-heated steam power plant; art galleries; and day-and-night safety deposit vaults; and developing mile-and-quarter-street-frontage housing project in Pasadena). Executor, estate Lewis J. Merritt; life trustee, estate Annette W. Merritt; trustee, R. C. Merritt Trust. Formerly col. Gov.'s staff, Minn.; v.p. Am., English, French and Belgian Permanent Blind Relief War Fund; mem. council Los Angeles br. Boy Scouts Am.; nat. committeeman, Plymouth Tercentary Com.; mem. conf. com. on Nat. Preparedness; adv. dir. Cal. Liberty Fair Assn.; a founder of movement for monument establishing birthplace of Abraham Lincoln (Lincoln Farm Assn.); a founder and regent Henry W. Longfellow home. Fellow Am. Geog. Soc.; mem. U.S. Navy League, Nat. Aeroplane Defense Fund, League to Enforce Peace, Asiatic Assn. (asso.), Am. Civic Alliance (gov. for Cal.), Am. Acad. Polit. and Social Sci., Young Men's Republican Club, New Eng. Hist. and Geneal. Soc., Soc. for Preservation of New England Antiquities (v.p.), Save the Redwoods League, Am. Immigration and Distbn. League, Better Am. Fedn. Cal., United Americans (State N.Y.), Am. Defense Soc. (nat. committeeman), Nat. Economic League (nat. councilman), Luther Burbank Soc. (charter mem.). Republican. Methodist. Clubs: Army and Navy, Congressional Country (Washington) (life); California; Breakfast; California Yacht; Los Angeles Yacht; Automobile Club of Southern California; Annandale Golf; Bolsa Chica Gun; South Coast Yacht; Catalina Island Yacht. Home: Villa Merritt-Ollivier, Pasadena, Cal.; also The Oaks, Tulare, Cal. Office: Merritt Building, Los Angeles. Died Jan. 13, 1956.

MERRITT, Schuyler, ex-congressman; b. New York, N.Y., Dec. 16, 1853; s. Matthew F. and Maria (Shaw) M.; A.B., Yale, 1873, LL.D., from same, 1935; LL.B., Columbia, 1876; m. Frances, d. Joseph B. and Katharine (Krom) Hoyt, Oct. 21, 1879. Began with Yale & Towne Mfg. Co., 1877, former dir.; officer First Stamford Nat. Bank since 1902, now chmn. bd.; v.p. Stamford Gas & Electric Co. Elected to 65th Congress, 1917, 4th Conn. Dist. to fill unexpired term, and reëlected 66th to 71st and 73d and 74th Congresses (1921-31 and 1933-37), 4th Conn. Dist. Republican. Warden of St. John's P.E. Ch. Clubs: University, Yale (New York); Woodway Country, Wee Burn Golf (Stamford). Home: Stamford, Conn. Died Apr. 1, 1953.*

MERSHON, Ralph Davenport, elec. engr., inventor; b. Zanesville, O., July 14, 1868; s. Ralph Smith and Mary J. (Jones) M.; M.E., Ohio State U., 1890; asst. in electrical engineering, same, 1890-91; D.Sc., Tufts College, 1918; Dr. of Engring., Ohio State U., 1936. With Westinghouse Electric & Mfg. Co. at Pittsburgh and New York, 1891-1900; represented same at World's Industrial Expn., 1893; consulting practice since 1900. Designed transformers for which the Westinghouse Co. received an award at Chicago Expn., 1893; in charge investigations of phenomena which occur between conductors at high voltages for Telluride (Colo.) Power Transmission, and Westinghouse cos., 1896-97; chief engr. Colo. Electric Power Co., 1897-98; reconstructed the generating, transmitting and receiving equipment of Montreal & St. Lawrence Light & Power Co.; designed various plants in U.S., S. Africa and Japan; was chief engr. during design and constrn. of Niagara, Lockport and Ontario Power Co. Invented: 6-phase rotary converter; compounded rotary converter; system of lightning protection for elec. apparatus; compensating voltmeter (awarded John Scott medal by Franklin Inst.); etc. Mem. joint nat. com. on Reserve Corps of Engrs.; maj., Engr. O.R.C., 1917; maj. and lt. col., Engrs., U.S. Army; in active service, 1917-19, detailed to Naval Consulting Bd. Fellow A.A.A.S., Am. Inst. E.E. (pres. 1912-13); mem. Am. Soc. C.E., Am. Soc. Mech. Engrs., Franklin Inst., Inventors' Guild (ex-pres.), Engineering Inst. of Can., Instn. Elec. Engrs., Eng.; hon. life mem. Res. Officers Assn. of United States. Clubs: University, Engineers' (New York); Cosmos (Washington). Awarded Lamme engring. medal, by Ohio State U., 1932. For work in drafting legislation for R.O.T.C. and getting it included in Nat. Defense Act of 1916 was awarded citation by Ohio State U., 1942. Home: 2000 Tiger Tail Av., Miami, Fla. Died Feb. 14, 1952; buried Zaneville, O.

MERVIS, Meyer Bernard, corp. exec.; b. Connellsville, Pa., Mar. 23, 1893; s. Max and Minnie (Goodman) M.; student U. of Pittsburgh, 1907; m. Ruth Brenner, Dec. 2, 1915; children—Georgianna (wife of Judge J. J. Drucker), Jacob N., Esther Ruth (Mrs. Carl Dry), Pearl (Mrs. Norman Retchin), Natalie (Mrs. Marvin Nathan), Patricia Ann (Mrs. Milton Schwartz). Assistant sec. of Cudahy Packing Co., Braddock, Pa., 1911-13; livestock salesman, Chicago, 1913-16; exec. treas. Am. Insulated Wire & Cable Co., Chicago, 1916-18, sec. and gen. sales mgr., 1918, later v.p. and gen. mgr.; sec.-treas. Brenner-Moxley Mervis Co., 1918; sec. and gen. sales mgr. Brenner-Mervis Co., 1920-27; gen. mgr. western div. Gen. Cable Co., 1927; spl. rep. Inland Wire & Cable Co., 1928-30, Anaconda Wire & Cable Co., Chicago, 1930—; chmn. bd. Gen. Armature Corp., 1928—; v.p., dir. Copperweld Steel Co. Author: Copper Wire and Cable Ency., 1921; also articles on horse breeding. Breeder Arabian horses and show ponies; collector wooden horses and all types of miniature horse hitches. Home: The Oak Farm, Barrington, Ill. Office: 180 W. Washington St., Chicago 2. Died Sept. 23, 1959.

MESEROLE, Clinton Vanderbilt (mĕs'ĕr-ōl), chmn. bd. Pacific Fire Ins. Co.; b. Brooklyn, N.Y., 1876; s. Jeremiah V. and Anne S. (Richardson) M.; student Polytechnic Inst., Brooklyn; B.S., Princeton, 1898; m. Ida Lewis Brooke, May 2, 1905; children—Rhe B. (Mrs. Francis L. Van Dusen), Anne R. (Mrs. John E. Cookman), Clinton V., Jr., Jere S. Engaged in the fire insurance business since 1898; chairman of the board Pacific Fire Insurance Co., Bankers & Shippers Insurance Co. of New York, Jersey Ins. Co. of New York. Spl. representative of Ordnance Dept., U.S. Army, World War I. Rep. Presbyn. Clubs: University, Princeton, Down Town (New York); Knickerbocker Country, Ausable, Yeamans Hall. Home: 57 Lydecker St., Englewood, N.J. Office: 12 Gold St., N.Y. City. Died Jan. 8, 1951.

MESS, Otto (măs), univ. pres.; b. Columbus, O., Feb. 19, 1879; s. Theophilus K. Martin and Jennie (Brauer) M.; grad. Woodville (O.) Normal Sch. 1894; A.B., Capital U., Columbus, 1898; grad. magna cum laude, Evang. Luth. Theol. Sem., Columbus, 1901; studied Berlin and Leipzig, 1901-02; A.M., Wittenberg Coll., Springfield, O., 1916; D.D., Carthage (Ill.) Coll., 1920; LL.D., St. Olaf College, Northfield, Minn., 1929; m. Clara Alvina Christiansen, Aug. 26, 1903; children—Elsa Constance, Gertrude Joanna, Robert Theophilus, Ruth Elenore. Ordained Luth. ministry, 1902; pastor Zions Ch., Coraopolis, Pittsburgh, Pa., 1902-12; pres. Capital U., Columbus, December 26, 1912-46, president emeritus, 1946—. Secretary Eastern District Joint (Lutheran) Synod of Ohio, 1904-11; dir. Luth. Choral Soc., Pittsburgh, 1910-12; organizer and dir. Luth. Choral Soc., Columbus, 1913—; v.p. and dir. Lutheran Brotherhood; pres. Nat. Lutheran Ednl. Conf., 1925. Mem. exec. bd. Boy Scouts of America; mem. nat. council Camp Fire Girls. Mem. Ohio Assn. Coll. Presidents (pres. 1930-31), Ohio Music Teachers Assn. (pres. 1925), Am. Luth. Conf. (pres. 1930-

34). Republican. Clubs: Rotary (hon.), University, Kit Kat. Contbr. to Lutheran publications. Has traveled extensively in Europe and Near East. Lecturer. Home: 2607 E. Main St. Address: Capital University, Columbus 9, O. Died Jan. 12, 1958; buried Forest Lawn, Columbus.

MESSENGER, J(ames) Franklin, prof. edn.; b. Benton County, Ia., Jan. 30, 1872; s. James John and Mary Ann (Hamlin) M.; A.B., U. of Kan., 1895; A.M., Harvard, 1901; Ph.D., Columbia, 1903; m. Lora Estelle Olds, July 31, 1895 (dec. Feb. 26, 1952); children—Loren Eliot, Dorothy Elizabeth. Teacher Hutchinson (Kan.) High Sch., 1895-97, U. of N.M., 1899-1900; asst. in psychology, Harvard, 1901; fellow in psychology, Columbia, 1901-02; teacher psychology and edn., Va. State Normal Sch., 1905-09; prof. edn. and dir. Summer Sch., U. of Vt., 1909-20; dean Sch. of Edn. and dir. Summer Sch., U. of Ida., 1920-44, dean emeritus, Sept. 1944—. Fellow A.A.A.S.; mem. N.E.A., Nat. Assn. Coll. Teachers of Edn., Sigma Nu, Kappa Delta Pi, Phi Mu Alpha (hon.). Republican. Methodist. Author: An Interpretative History of Education, 1931; The Art of Going to College, 1937. Home: Address: Hawthorn, Fla. Died Apr. 29, 1952; buried Hawthorn.

MESSERSMITH, George S. (mĕs' ĕr-smĭth), exfgn. service officer; b. Fleetwood, Pa., Oct. 3, 1883; s. Charles A. and Sarah S. C. (Strausser) M.; grad. Keystone State Normal School, 1900; student Delaware Coll., Newark, Del.; m. Marion Lee Mustard, July 22, 1914. Supt. schs., various towns of Del., 1900-14; mem. and sec. State Bd. of Examiners for Teachers, Del., 1911-14; v.p. State Bd. of Edn., Del., 1912-14. Am. consul at Ft. Erie, Can., 1914-16, Curacao, Dutch W.I., 1916-19; apptd. consul on detail, Antwerp, February 1919; consul, Antwerp, 1919-23; consul gen. at Antwerp for Belgium and Luxembourg, 1923-28; Am. consul gen., Argentina, at Buenos Aires, 1928; foreign service insp., 1929—; consul gen., Berlin, 1930-34; apptd. E.E. and M.P. to Uruguay, 1934, to Austria, 1934; asst. Sec. of State, 1937-40; ambassador to Cuba, 1940-41, to Mexico, Nov. 1941-42, to Argentina, 1946, resigned June 1947; retired from fgn. service, Aug. 1947; hon. chmn. bd. Mexican Light & Power Co., Ltd. Presbyn. Clubs: Cercle de la Concorde, Antwerp Golf, Philotaxe Club, Royal Polo (Antwerp); Metropolitan (Washington). Author: The Government of Delaware, 1914. Home: 1285 Sierra Paralaima, Mexico City, Mex.; also 15 Calle Tetela, Cuernavaca, Mex. Died Jan. 1960.

MESTA, L. W., exec. vice pres. and dir. Mesta Machine Co. Home: Pittsburgh. Office: West Homestead, Pa. Died Dec. 30, 1953.*

METCALF, George P., pres. Providence Journal Company; director Rhode Island Hospital Trust Co. Trustee R.I. Hosp. Address: Hosp. Trust Bldg., Providence. Died July 27, 1957.

METCALF, Stephen Olney, mfr.; s. Jesse Metcalf; A.B., Brown U., 1878; m. Esther H. Pierce, Dec. 2, 1886. Treas. R.I. Sch. Design; dir. Providence Journal Co., Puritan Life Ins. Co. Trustee Brown U., 1899—, Butler Hosp. Mem. Delta Kappa Epsilon. Clubs: Hope, University, Agawam Hunt (Providence); Brown (N.Y.C.). Home: 132 Bowen St., Providence 6. Office: 15 Westminster St., Providence 3, R.I. Died Sept. 27, 1950; buried Swan Point Cemetery, Providence.

METCALF, Zeno Payne; zoölogist; b. Lakeville, O., May 1, 1885; s. Abel Crawford and Catherine (Fulmer) M.; A.B., Ohio State U., 1907; D.Sc., Harvard, 1925; m. Mary Luella Correll, Oct. 20, 1909; 1 dau., Katharine (Mrs. Micou F. Browne). Instr. entomology Mich. State Agrl. Coll., 1907-08; with N.C. Dept. Agr., 1908-12; prof. zoölogy N.C. State Coll. and entomologist expt. sta., 1912-50, also dir. instrn. sch. of agr., 1923-44, dir. graduate studies, 1940-50; asso. dean the graduate sch. U. N.C., 1943-50, research prof. of zoology and entomology, 1950—; instr. biol. lab. Ohio State U., 1916-18, U. Mich., 1920; vis. prof. zoölogy Duke, 1935-36. Fellow A.A. A.S., Micros. Soc. (v.p. 1922; pres. 1927), N.C. Acad. Science (v.p. 1914; pres. 1921); mem. entomol. Soc. Am., Assn. Econ. Entomologists (chmn. Cotton States br. 1940), Ornithol. Union, Ecological Soc., Nat. Assn. Biology Tchrs., Biol. Soc. Wash., Tenn. Acad. Sci., Kan. Entomol. Soc., Soc. Systematic Zoologists, Am. Soc. Limnology and Oceanology, Am. Assn. U. Profs., Entomol. Soc. Washington, Am. Museum of Natural History, Soc. Herpetologists, Liminol. Soc. Am., Ohio Acad. Sci., Wilson Ornithol. Club, Assn. S. Eastern Biologists, Am. Biol. Assn., Chgo. Acad. Sci., N.Y. Zoöl. Soc., Soc. for Study of Evolution, Sigma Xi, Alpha Gamma Rho, Alpha Zeta, Phi Kappa Phi. Dem. Presbyterian. Kiwanian. Clubs: Raleigh Kiwanis (pres. 1932), Raleigh Torch (pres. 1940). Author: Insect Pests in Rural Efficiency Guide, 1918; Key to Insects, 1918; Key to the Family Fulgoridae, 1923; General Zoölogy, —1927; Economic Zoölogy 1927; Text Book of Economic Zoölogy, 1930; Introduction to Zoölogy, 1932; General Catalgue of Hemiptera Tettigometridae, 1932; Cixiidae, 1936; Araeopidae, 1943; Derbidae, 1945; Achilixidae, 1945; Meenoplidae, 1945; Kinnaridae, 1945; Achilixidae, 1945; Meenoplidae, 1945; Kinnaridae, 1945; Dictyopharidae, 1946; Fulgoridae, 1947; Achilidae, 1948; The Fulgorina of Barro Colorado, 1938; Bibliography of the Homoptera of the World, 1943; Cercopidae of Cuba, 1944; Homoptera of Kartabo, 1945; Homoptera of Guam, 1946, Center of Origin Theorry, 1946; Cuban Flatidae (with S. C. Bruner), 1948; Catalog of the Hemiptera, Fulgoroidea Fascicle IV, 1957, Issidae, 1958 (both posthumous). Editor Homoptera, Biol. Abstracts; mem. editorial bd. Catalog of Hemiptera of World, editorial bd. ecology, 1935-37, and editorial bd. Ecological Monographs, 1940-42. Home: 315 Forest Rd. Address: State College Station, Raleigh, N.C. Died Jan. 5, 1956; buried Oakwood Cemetery, Raleigh.

METCALFE, Richard Lee, pres. Metcalfe Construction Co.; b. nr. Upper Alton, Ill., Oct. 11, 1861; s. Dr. Richard L. and Ellen T. (Edwards) M.; ed. in pub. schs.; LL.D., Creighton U., 1932; m. Bessie Buehler, April 30, 1885; children—Mrs. Harley Conant, Buehler, R. Lee, Theodore W., Kenneth. Began as printer's devil in country office, studying during leisure time; edited weekly paper at age of 19; reporter World-Herald, 1888; asst. to William J. Bryan, the editor, 1894; editor Omaha World-Herald, 1896-1905; asso. editor The Commoner, 1905-13; civ. gov. Panama Canal Zone, 1913-14; pres. Metcalfe Constrn. Co. Dem. nominee for U.S. Senate from Neb. 1928; mayor of Omaha, filling unexpired term of late James C. Dahlman, 1930, elected to same office for term, 1930-33. Author: Of Such Is the Kingdom, and Other Stories from Life, 1906; Bishop Sunbeams, 1909. Home: 5201 California St., Omaha, Neb. Died Mar. 31, 1954; buried Forest Lawn, Omaha.

METCALFE, Tristram Walker, university president and college dean; born at Brooklyn, New York, August 13, 1880; son of Alfred Tristram and Annie (Angevine) M.; grad. Boys High Sch., Brooklyn, 1897; student New York Univ., 1901; Litt.D., Long Island University, 1948; married Frances Taylor, October 24, 1907; 1 son, Tristram Walker. Reporter Brooklyn Daily Eagle, Commercial Advertiser; school editor Commercial Advertiser (New York Globe), Jan. 1903-June 1923; school editor, World (evening), 1923-31; school editor World-Telegram, 1931; consultant Translux Daylight Picture Screen Co., 1926-28, N.Y. State Teachers Assn.; asst. in edn., L.I. Univ., 1931-32, acting comptroller and asst. sec. bd. of trustees. 1932-33, dean and administrative head since 1933, member bd. of trustees and president since 1942; directing investigator New York School Survey, under N.Y. City Bd. of Edn., 1919. V.p. and dir. Crestchester Pub. Co., 1928, 29. Treas. Council of Yonkers Civic Assn., 1923-25, v.p., 1926; mem. Bd. of Education, Yonkers, 1926-31; mem. N.Y. City Commn. on Teachers' Salaries, 1926-27; pres. Colonial Heights Improvement Assn., 1935-38; mem. adv. bd. Yonkers Collegiate Center, 1936, 37; chmn. Eagle Scout Com., Brooklyn; com. mem. Y.M.C.A.; mem. bd. trustees Asso. Colls. of N.Y. State, 1945-50. Mem. N.E.A., Am. Assn. Sch. Adminstrs., N.Y. State Council of Supts., Horace Mann League, N.Y. Acad. of Public Edn., Am. Geographical Soc.; Soc. for Advancement of Edn., Am. Acad. Polit. and Social Sci., Zeta Psi. Democrat. Universalist. Clubs: Colonial Country (v.p. 1926). Press, Rotary. Home: 21 Puritan Av., Colonial Heights, Tuchahoe, N.Y. Office: 380 Pearl St., Bklyn. Died Feb. 1952.

METTLER, John Wyckoff, mfr.; b. East Millstone, N.J., Sept. 27, 1878; s. William E. and Gertrude Van Pelt (Howell) M.; B.Sc., Rutgers Coll., 1899, M.Sc., 1902, LL.D., 1930; LL.B., N.Y. Law Sch., 1901; m. Helen Fleischmann, June 5, 1909; children —Helen (dec.), Lt. Col. J. W., Jr. President Interwoven Stocking Company; dir. The Delaware & Hudson Co., Nat. Bank of N.J. (New Brunswick), Nat. Industrial Conf. Bd., Nat. Assn. Hosiery Mfrs. Trustee Rutgers U. Mem. Delta Phi. Republican. Mem. Ref. Dutch Ch. America. Clubs: University, Century, St. Nicholas Soc. Home: East Millstone, N.J. Office: 123 Church St., New Brunswick, N.J. Died Feb. 13, 1952; buried Cedar Hill Cemetery, East Millstone, N.J.

METZGER, Fraser, clergyman, ret. univ. dean; b. Gloversville, N.Y., Oct. 25, 1872; s. Albert Henry and Catherine (Lenz) M.; A.B., Union Coll., 1902; L.H.D., 1938; B.D., Defiance (O.) Coll., 1904; D.D., Middlebury (Vt.) Coll., 1921; D.D., Rutgers U., 1945; m. Jessie Lacy, June 12, 1902; children —Albert Lacy, Roscoe Fraser, Karl Edward. Ordained to ministry Congl. Ch., 1902; pastor Bethany Ch., Randolph, Vt., 1902-23; chaplain Pa. State Coll., 1923-25; dean of men Rutgers U., 1925-45, also acting chaplain, 1930-45, dean emeritus, 1945—; minister First Ch., South Windsor, Conn., 1945—. Served as chaplain U.S. Army Res. Corps, World War I. Mem. Vt. Legislature, two terms. Mem. Phi Beta Kappa, Tau Kappa Alpha, Delta Upsilon. Home: South Windsor, Conn. Died May 29, 1954; buried South Windsor, Conn.

METZGER, Frederick Elder, educator; b. Hanover, Pa., Oct. 26, 1868; s. Henry Clay and Cora (Myley) M.; B.A., Gettysburg (Pa.) Coll., 1888, M.A., 1890; grad. study, U. Leipzig, Germany, 1890-91, Am. Sch. Classical Studies, Athens, Greece, 1891-92; m. Martha Thomas, Sept. 9, 1896; 1 dau., Margaret Thomas (Mrs. Herbert Benjamin Williams). Began as high sch. prin., 1894; prof. Latin and Greek, Md. Coll. Women, Lutherville, 1895-1932, pres. 1932-41, pres. emeritus, 1941—. Mem. Phi Delta Theta. Republican. Lutheran. Home: Lutherville, Md. Died Jan. 7, 1952.

METZGER, Hutzel, agrl. economist, banker; b. Athens, Tenn., Dec. 12, 1894; s. Lynn J. and Mary Elizabeth (Hutsell) M.; student Mich. State Coll. Agr. and Applied Science, East Lansing, 1915-16; B.S., N.D. Agrl. Coll., 1920, M.S., 1923; Ph.D., U. of Minn., 1926; m. Emma E. Skeem, Aug. 14, 1922; children—Robert Lynn, Richard Bruce. Public sch. teacher, 1911-14; asst. agrl. economist N.D. Agrl. Coll., 1920-21, asso. agrl. economist and asst. farm management demonstrator, 1921-23; research asst. agrl. economics, Univ. of Minn., 1923-25; research fellow Social Science Research Council, 1925-26; sr. agrl. economist, div. coöp. marketing, U.S. Dept. of Agr., Washington, D.C., 1926-29; asst. chief, div. of coöp. marketing, Federal Farm Bd., 1929-32, regional rep., western states, 1932-33; pres. St. Paul Bank for Coöperatives since 1933. Served as pvt. 4th S.D. Inf., U.S. Army, 1916-17; 1st lt. A.S., 1917-19, World War. Mem. Am. Farm Econ. Assn., Am. Statis. Assn., Nat. Grange, Alpha Gamma Rho, Alpha Zeta, Phi Kappa Phi, Gamma Sigma Delta. Club: St. Paul Athletic. Home: 473 Woodlawn Av. Office: St., Paul Bank for Coöperatives, St. Paul. Died Dec. 7, 1951; buried Sunset Meml. Park, Mpls.

MEYER, Alfred, physician; b. N.Y.C., June 18, 1854; s. Isaac and Mathilda (Langenbach) M.; A.B., Columbia, 1874; M.D., Coll. Phys. and Surg. Columbia, 1877; m. Annie Florance Nathan, Feb. 15, 1887; 1 child (dec.). Began practice in N.Y.C., 1880; clin. prof. medicine N.Y.U.-Bellevue Med. Coll., 1910—; cons. physician, Mt. Sinai Hosp., Montefiore Hosp., Washington Heights Hosp. Hon. dir. Nat. Tb Assn. Fellow A.C.P.; mem. Am. Thoracic Soc., A.M.A., N.Y. State Med. Assn., N.Y. County Med. Soc., N.Y. Acad. Medicine, N.Y. Tb. and Health Assn. (dir.), Harvey Soc., Phi Kappa Psi, etc. Received citation of N.Y. Tb. and Health Assn., 1942. Home: 1225 Park Av., N.Y.C. Died July 14, 1950.

MEYER, Annie Nathan, author; b. N.Y. City, Feb. 19, 1867; d. Robert Weeks and Annie (Florance) Nathan; ed. privately at home; took exam. at Columbia (women not then permitted to attend as students); m. Dr. Alfred Meyer, Feb. 15, 1887. Known as founder of Barnard Coll. (women's dept. of Columbia), having first attained sanction of trustees of the university. Chmn. Emergency Com., Am. Home Economics Assn., World War I. Trustee Barnard Coll. Clubs: Women's Faculty of Columbia Univ., Barnard College Club (hon.), Woman's Republican Club of New York, English Speaking Union. Author: Woman's Work in America, 1891; Helen Brent, M.D., 1893; My Park Book, 1898; Robert Annys, 1901; The Dominant Sex, 1911; The Dreamer, 1912; also plays, A Dinner of Herbs; The Spur; P's & Q's, 1920; The District Attorney, prod. 1920; The Advertising of Kate, prod. 1921; The New Way, 1923; The Right to Dream; Black Souls, prod. 1932, pub. 1932; Barnard Beginnings, 1935. Contbr. articles and stories to mags. Home: 12 E. 86th St., N.Y. City 28. Died Sept. 23, 1951; buried Mt. Pleasant Cemetery, Pleasantville, N.Y.

MEYER, Arthur Simon (mī'ĕr), past chmn. N.Y. State Bd. of Mediation; b. N.Y.C., May 24, 1880; s. Simon and Carrie (Bernheim) M.; student N.Y. pub. and high schs., also pvt. study; m. Marion Wolff, June 11, 1912; children—Daniel, Leonard, Carolyn. Vice pres., dir. Schulte Retail Stores Corp., 1917-35; mem. City Indsl. Bd. of N.Y.C., 1936-37; mem. N.Y. State Bd. Mediation, 1937—, chmn., 1941-50, resigned; apptd. asso. mem. Nat. War Labor Bd., 1942; apptd. chmn. of panel investigating dispute between the 4 companies comprising "Little Steel" and the Steel Workers Organizing Com., 1942; apptd. chmn. of panel investigating dispute, known as Petrillo Case, between the recording companies and Am. Fedn. Musicians, 1943; joint chmn. Annual Wage Com., Office War Moblzn. and Reconversion, 1945; chmn. Mayor's Adv. Transit Com., N. Y.C., 1946; chmn. President's Emergency Bd., Ry. Express dispute, 1947. Clubs: Town (Scarsdale); Town Hall (N.Y.C.). Home: 31 Mamaroneck Rd., Scarsdale, N.Y. Died Aug. 6, 1955.

MEYER, Ben R., banker; b. San Francisco, Calif., 1879. Chairman board and president Union Bank and Trust Company, Los Angeles, California; dir. Southern Calif. Gas Co., Pacific Indemnity Co. Trustee Calif. Inst. Tech., U. of Southern Calif., Cedars of Lebanon Hosp. Home: Talmadge Apts. Office: 760 S. Hill St., Los Angeles. Died Mar. 6, 1957.

MEYER, Charles Garrison, real estate exec.; b. N.Y.C., Sept. 21, 1879; s. Cord and Cornelia Maria (Covert) M.; student Columbia U. Sch. of Arts, 1901; m. Sara Willets Leavitt, Oct. 8, 1902 (died 1939); children—Mrs. Margaret Meyer Lewis, Charles

Garrison, Gardiner Howland M., Samuel Willets M. Pres. The Cord Meyer Co., N.Y.C., 1910—; v.p., dir. Citizens Development, Inc., Citizens Water Supply Co. of Newton, Cord Meyer Development Co., Dick-Meyer Corp.; v.p., trustee Central Aguirre Assos.; mem. finance and exec. coms., dir. Franklin Fire Ins. of Phila., The Home Ins. Co., mem. exec. com., dir. Paul Revere Fire Ins. Co., Balt. Am. Ins. Co. of N.Y.C., of N.Y. Ins. Co., Ga. Home Ins. Co., Gibraltar Fire & Marine Ins. Co., Homestead Fire Ins. Co., The Home Indemnity Co., Nat. Liberty Ins. Co. of Am., New Brunswick Fire Ins. Co.; dir. many other cos. Dir., founder N.Y. World's Fair, 1939, Inc. Presdl. rep. to Internat. Housing Conf., London, 1935; rep. from Queens, Park Assn. Board. Clubs: Columbia University, Columbia Athletic Assn., Society of Older Graduates, Columbia Rowing, Columbia Varsity "C", The Links, The Links Golf, Madison Square Garden, New York Athletic, New York Yacht, Bayside Yacht, National Golf Links of America (founder), Oakland Golf, Racquet and Tennis, The New York Skating, Southside Sportsmen's (L.I.), Delta Phi. Home: Ritz-Calrton Hotel, N.Y.C. Office: 68 William St., N.Y. C. Died Apr. 9, 1950.

MEYER, Eugene, newspaper exec.; b. Los Angeles, Oct. 31, 1875; s. Eugene and Harriet (Newmark) M.; student U. Cal., 1892-93; A.B., Yale, 1895; studied banking and languages in Europe; Doctor of Laws, Yale, 1932, Syracuse University, 1934, Univ. Cal., 1942; married Agnes Elizabeth Ernst, Feb. 12, 1910; children—Mrs. Florence Homolka, Elizabeth (Mrs. Pare Lorentz), Eugene III, Katharine (Mrs. Philip L. Graham), Ruth (Mrs. William A. Epstein). Head of the firm Eugene Meyer, Jr. & Co., 1901-17, and dir. many corps. until resigned, 1917, to enter Government service; apptd. adviser non-ferrous metals, Advisory Commission of Council of National Defense, 1917; later in charge of the division of non-ferrous metals, War Industries Bd.; also mem. Nat. Com. War Savings, 1917 and special asst. to Sec. of War in connection with aircraft production, 1918; appointed by Pres. Wilson dir. War Finance Corp., April 29, 1918; elected managing director January 1919; resigned May 1920, when Corp.'s activities suspended; reapptd. by Pres. Harding, Mar. 1921, and elected mng. dir.; reapptd. by Pres. Coolidge, Mar. 1925, and again elected mng. dir.; apptd. mem. Fed. Farm Loan Bd., by President Coolidge, May 10, 1927, and designated farm loan commr., resigned, May 10, 1929. Apptd. by Pres. Hoover mem. and designated gov. of Federal Reserve Bd., Sept. 16, 1930, resigned May 10, 1933; also served as first chmn. bd. Reconstruction Finance Corp., Feb. 2-July 31, 1932; mem. Nat. Defense Mediation Bd., by appointment of Pres. Roosevelt, Mar. 19, 1941-Jan. 12, 1942; pub. The Washington Post, 1933-40; editor and pub., 1940-46, chmn. bd. 1947—. First president of Internat. Bank for Reconstruction and Development, June-December 1946, director, Allied Chemical Corp. Trustee Nat. Indsl. Conf. Bd., 1943-57, councillor 1954-59; trustee Com. Econ. Development, 1946-57, hon. trustee, 1957-59. Pres. Washington Criminal Justice Assn., 1936-45. Mem. Newspaper Industry Adv. Committee of War Prodn. Bd., 1943-45; vice chmn. Pres. Truman's Famine Emergency Com., 1946; Citizens' Food Com., 1947; pres. Nat. Com. Mental Hygiene, 1944-46; N.Y., Boys' Club of Washington; mem. Com. on Purchases of Blind-Made Products, 1953—. Recipient of Yale Gold Medal, 1954. Mem. Council on Fgn. Relations, Inc., Am. Soc. Newspaper Editors. Clubs: Players, Yale, Grolier, Recess (N.Y.C.); Metropolitan, Cosmos, Burning Tree, Nat. Press, Army and Navy Country, University, Yale (Washington). Home: Seven Springs Farm, Mt. Kisco, N.Y. Washington residence: 1624 Crescent Pl. N.W., Washington. Office: Washington Post, Washington 5. Died July 17, 1959.

MEYER, George William, composer; b. Boston, Mass., Jan. 1, 1884; s. Samuel Leopold and Johanna (Loewenberg) M.; ed. pub. schs.; m. Grayce Elizabeth Meyers, Dec. 9, 1909 (died 1936); m. 2d, Kathleen Howard, Dec. 23, 1942; 1 daughter Melody. Held various positions such as bookkeeper, office boy, carpenter and machinist; composer of popular songs, 1908—, among which are "Lonesome," "For Me and My Gal," "Tuck Me To Sleep in My Old 'Tucky Home," "My Mother's Rosary," "Brown Eyes, Why Are You Blue," "When You're a Long Long Way from Home," "I Believe in Miracles," "Ten, Ten Tennessee," "Sittin' in the Corner," "My Song of the Nile," "E'ry Thing Is Peaches Down in Georgia," "Hiawatha's Melody of Love," "That Mellow Melody," "Little Old Fashioned Music Box," etc. Sec. Am. Soc. Composers, Authors and Publishers. Address: 25 Central Park West, New York, N.Y. Died Aug. 28, 1959.*

MEYER, Henry Coddington, Jr., cons. engr.; b. Orange, N.J., Nov. 28, 1870; s. Henry Coddington and Charlotte English (Seaman) M.; M.E., Stevens Inst. Tech., 1892; m. Louise G. Underhill, Nov. 18, 1896; children—Henry Coddington, Emily Louise. Engring. practice, N.Y., 1893-1919; pres. Meyer, Strong & Jones, Inc., cons. mech. and elec. engrs., 1919-44; dir. Architects Offices, Inc. Mem. Am. Soc. M.E., Am. Soc. Heating and Ventilating Engrs., Loyal Legion. Club Union League. Author: Design of Steam Power Plants, 1902. Home: Montclair, N.J. Office: 101 Park Av., N.Y.C. Died June 17, 1957.

MEYER, Henry Herman, clergyman, ret. educator; b. Champaign, Ill., Nov. 21, 1874; s. Frederick William and Caroline (Frevert) M.; student Cal. State Normal Sch.; A.B., Baldwin-Wallace Coll., 1900, A.M., 1903, D.D., 1905; B.D., Drew Theol. Sem., 1903, Th.D., 1926; Ph.D., Yale, 1927; m. Minna McEuen, Aug. 4, 1898. Ordained to M.E. ministry, 1900; pastor Wilmington, Cal., 1895-96, Mt. Vernon, N.Y., 1906-08; prof. St. Paul's Coll., St. Paul Park, Minn., 1900-01; asst. editor church school publs. M.E. Ch., 1902-14, editor, 1914-29; editor Am. Standard Bible Readers; dean of Boston sch. religious and social work Boston U., 1929-42, emeritus dean, and emeritus dir. grad. div. of religion, sch. theology, 1942—; vis. instr. and lecturer in univs. and theol. seminaries in China, 1940-41; personnel adviser on adminstrv. staff Endicott Junior Coll., Prides Crossing, Mass., 1942-43; retired. Past mem. exec. council Religious Edn. Assn.; exec. com. Internat. Council of Religious Edn. and Worlds Sunday Sch. Assn. Mem. Am. Assn. Adult Edn., Mass. Council of Chs., Nat. Conf. of Social Work, Greater Boston Fedn. Chs. (mem. ednl. com.). Author: The Lesson Handbook (annual), 1904-27; The Graded Sunday School in Principle and Practice, 1910; Co-öperation in Christian Education, 1917; child Nature and Nurture According to Count Nicholas Ludwig von Zinzendorf, 1928. Editor: The International Graded Lessons (Berean and Graded Press series), until 1929. Contbr. to religious ednl. mags. and periodicals. Address: 21 Claremont Av., N.Y.C. Died Oct. 6, 1951; buried Woodlawn Cemetery.

MEYER, Herbert Alton, ex-congressman; b. Chillicothe, O., Aug. 30, 1886; s. John T. and Louise (Griesham) M.; student Stanton (Va.) Mil. Acad., 1900-04; LL.B., George Washington U. and Nat. U., 1909; m. Mary Davis Watts, Dec. 16, 1909; 1 son, Herbert A. Admitted to D.C. bar, 1909; asst. to sec. of Interior in charge of affairs Alaska R.R. and ty. affairs Alaska and Hawaii, 1915-17; asst. to chmn. Am.-Mexican Joint Commn., 1916; asst. to v.p. Prairie Oil & Gas Co., Independence, Kan., 1919-32; v.p. Sinclair Prairie Oil Marketing Co., Tulsa, 1932-37; mng. dir. Kan. Independent Oil & Gas Assn., Wichita, Kan., 1938-40, pub. Independence (Kan.) Daily Reporter, 1940—; mem. 80th, 81st Congresses, 3d dist. Kan. Served as capt. U.S. AAC, World War I. Mem. Kan. Press Assn. (past pres.), Am. Legion, Sigma Chi, Sigma Delta Chi. Republican. Presbyn. Elk. Clubs: Rotary, National Press. Home: 201 S. 6th St. Office: Reporter Bldg., Independence, Kan. Died Oct. 2, 1950.

MEYER, Maximilian Courtland, jewelry mfr.; b. Bklyn., Dec. 25, 1883; s. Heyman and Sarah (Meyer) M.; student pub. schs.; m. Lillian Greenfield, Feb. 4, 1914; children—Sara Maxine, Joseph H., Jeanne Lucile, Carol. Pres. Joseph H. Meyer Bros., N.Y.C., mfr. jewelry, artificial pearls, and plastic products. Referee N.Y. Bd. Arbitration, 1940. Mem. Assn.Profl. Baseball Players Am. Mason. Clubs: Unity (Bklyn.); Inwood (L.I.) Country. Home: 250 Underhill Av., Bklyn. 17. Office: 389 5th Av., N.Y.C. 1. Deceased.

MEYERHOF, Otto, university prof.; b. Hanover, Germany, Apr. 12, 1884; s. Felix and Bettina (May) M.; M.D., Heidelberg, 1909; LL.D. (hon.) U. of Edinburgh, Scotland, 1926; m. Hedwig Schallenberg, June 4, 1914; children—George Geoffrey, Bettina Ida (Mrs. Donald E. Emerson), Walter Ernst. Came to U.S. 1940, naturalized, 1946. Research worker, U. of Heidelberg and Zoological Station, Naples, Italy, 1909-11; lecturer, U. of Kiel, Germany, 1912-18, asso. prof., 1918-24; mem. Kaiser Wilhelm Inst. of Biologie, Berlin, 1924-29; dir. Kaiser Wilhelm Inst. of Physiology, Heidelberg, 1929-38; directeur de recherche, Centre Nationale, Paris, 1938-40; research prof., U. of Pa., since 1940. Received Nobel Prize for Medicine, 1923. Mem. Harvey Soc. (hon.), Royal Soc. of London, Sigma Xi. Author: Chemical Dynamics of Life Phenomena, 1924; Chemische Vorgange im Muskel Springer, 1930, French translation, 1932. Home: Hamilton Court Apts., Chestnut and 39th St., Phila. 4. Died Oct. 6, 1951.

MEYERS, Joseph, publisher; b. N.Y.C., July 19, 1898; s. Lewis and Ida (Wolinsky) M.; student pub. schs., N.Y.; m. Bessie Schwartz, 1925; children—Hope Murtha (Mrs. Henry Wayne Golding), Susan Lee. Co-partner Jefferson Myers & Co., 1924—, Illustrated Editions Co., 1930—; pres. Avon Publishing Co., Inc., Avon Book Sales Corp. Pres. Avon Books Charitable Found., Inc. Jewish. Club: Lotos (N.Y.C.). Home: 50 Sutton Pl., S. Office: 575 Madison Av., N.Y.C. Died Nov. 1957.

MEYLAN, George Louis (Julien), college prof.; b. Brassus, Switzerland, July 22, 1873; s. Louis Julien and Jenny Henriette (Capt) M.; elementary schs., Brassus; M.D., Univ. Med. Coll. (N.Y.U.), 1896; B.S., Harvard, 1902; diploma, Internat. Y.M.C.A. College, Springfield, Mass., 1903; A.M., Columbia, 1904; m. Marie Louise Mathot, July 28, 1897. Med. director Boston Y.M.C.A., 1896-1903; prof. physical edn. and med. dir., Columbia, U., 1903—. Lecturer, Harvard U. Summer School, 1899-1903; dir. White Mountain Camp for Boys, Sebago Lake, Me., 1907—. Trutee Internat. Y.M.C.A. Coll.; mem. com. management New York Y.M.C.A. Rep. Episcopalian. Fellow A.A.A.S.; mem. Am. Phys. Edn. Assn. (pres. 1907—), Am. Playground and Recreation Assn. (dir.), Am. Sch. Hygiene Assn. (nat. council), Soc. Dirs. Phys. Edn. in Colls. (pres. 1904-05), Boston Phys. Edn. Soc. (1901-03), etc. Address: Columbia Univ., New York, N.Y. Died Feb. 1960.

MICHAEL, Greek Orthodox archbishop of North and South America; b. Maroneia, W. Thrace, Greece, May 27, 1892; s. Michael and Filio (Constantinides) M.; D.D., Theol. Coll., Halki, Istanbul, 1907-14; Theol. Acads., Petrograd and Kiew, Russia, 1915-19; ordained priest, Greek Orthodox Ch., 1919; lecturer, Theol. Coll., Halki, 1914-15; Locum Tenens Metropolis of Maroneia in Western Thrace, 1919-23; vicar gen. of Archdiocese of Athens, 1923-27; dean. Greek Cathedral in London, England, 1927-39, Metropolitan of Corinth, Greece, 1939-49; archbishop of Americas, N.Y. City, since 1949. Author: Life and Work in the Archdiocese of Athens, 1928; The Orthodox Church, 1931; The Church of England, 1931; The Priest, 1931; Imitation of Christ (Gr. trans.), 1933; The Greek Orthodox Church in London, 1933; St. Antonios, 1933; My Life in Christ (trans. from Russian), 1934, 39; St. Athanasius, 1937; Relation between Anglican and Orthodox Churches, 1937; The Conference of Edinburgh, 1938; Treatise on Purgatory, 1939; Life in Christ, 1946; The Power of Prayer, 1949; A Guide for the Orthodox Christian, 1950; Faith, Hope, Love, and Prayer, 1950; A Manual for Orthodox Christians, 1950. Home: 10 E. 79th St., N.Y.C. Died July 13, 1954.

MICHAEL, Jerome, lawyer, educator; b. Athens, Ga., Jan. 1, 1890; s. Moses Gerson and Emma (Cohen) M.; A.B., U. Ga., 1909; LL.B., Columbia, 1912; m. Florence Meyer, Feb. 24, 1921. Admitted to Ga. bar, 1912, practiced at Athens until 1917, N.Y. C., 1917-24, 27—; dir. war trans. sect. U.S. Dept. Justice and spl. asst. to U.S. atty. gen., 1924-26, 42-44; prof. law Columbia, 1927—; city atty., Athens, 1913-16. Lt. inf., U.S. Army, in machine gun service, World War I. Mem. Am., N.Y. State bar assns., Assn. Bar City N.Y., Nat. Lawyers Guild. Author: (with M. J. Adler) The Nature of Judicial Proof, 1931; Crime, Law and Social Science, 1933; The Trial of an Issue of Fact, 1934; (with H. Wechsler) Criminal Law and Its Administration, 1940; The Elements of Legal Controversy, 1948. Home: 235 W. 76th St., N.Y.C. 23. Office: Columbia U., N.Y.C. 27. Died Jan. 11, 1953.

MICHAEL, Max, lawyer; b. Athens, Ga., May 28, 1884; s. Simon and Anna (Phillips) M.; A.B., U. Ga., 1904; A.M., Columbia, 1906, LL.B., 1907; m. Cecelia M. Solomons, Nov. 29, 1911; children—Cecilia (dec.), Max, Cecil, Simon (lt. U.S.A.; killed in action in Italy Jan. 22, 1944). Engaged in practice of law, 1907—; pres., dir. Nat. Bank of Athens, Bond Commn., Athens, Ga., 1932—. Trustee YWCA. Mem. Am., Athens bar assns., Phi Beta Kappa. Democrat. Jewish religion. Club: Athens Country. Home: 1260 S. Milledge Av. Office: Southern Mutual Bldg., Athens, Ga. Died June 10, 1949.

MICHAELS, Henry, pharm. mfg. exec.; b. San Francisco, Sept. 10, 1909; s. C. F. and Kathryn (Tuohy) M.; B.A., Stanford, 1930; m., 1932 (div.); m. 2d, Peggie Robbins, 1945. Held various positions with McKesson & Robbins, Inc., 1930-35, v.p., 1935—, sec., 1941—. Served with U.S. Army, World War II. Pres. bd. trustees Menlo Sch. and Jr. Coll., Menlo Park, Cal. Republican. Clubs: Pacific Union, Bohemian (San Francisco); Canadian (N.Y.C.); Greenwich Country, Indian Harbor Yacht (Greenwich, Conn.). Office: 155 E. 44th St., N.Y.C. Died Feb. 18, 1951.

MICHAL, Aristotle D(emetrius) (mī'käl), prof. mathematics; b. Smyrna, Asia Minor (Greek parents), May 1, 1899; s. Demetrius and Sophia (Chaousoglou) M., came to U.S., 1911, naturalized, 1924; A.B., Clark U., Worcester, Mass., 1920, A.M., 1921; Ph.D., Rice Inst., Houston, Tex., 1924; Nat. Research fellow in mathematics, univ. of Chicago, Harvard, Princeton, 1925-27; m. Luddye Charlotte Kennerly, June 9, 1924; 1 dau., Thalia Charlotte (dec.). Instr. in mathematics, Rice Inst., 1923-25, U. of Tex., summer, 1924; asst. prof. mathematics, Ohio State U., 1927-29; asso. prof. mathematics, Calif. Inst. Tech., 1929-38, prof. since 1938, dir. of research in math. analysis, geometry and applied mathematics, also dir. Engring., Sci. Mgt. War Training program in advanced training in math. and mechanics, World War II. Lecturer, Am. Math. Soc., 1938, U. of Ill., 1940, Stanford 50th anniversary symposium, 1941. Fellow A.A.A.S.; mem. Am. Math. Soc. (council 1938-40; sec. Far West 1942-44), Math. Assn. Am. (corr.) Acad. Nacional de Ciencias Exactas, Fisicas y Naturales de Lima, Assn. of Symbolic Logic, Am. Assn. Univ. Profs., Sigma Xi. Club: Athenaeum (Pasadena). Author: Matrix and Tensor Calculus with Applications to Mechanics, Elasticity and Aeronautics, 1947; Differential Equations in Abstract Spaces with Applications to Analysis; Geometry and Mechanics. Editor Mathematics Mag. since 1947. Contbr. numerous research papers to U.S. and fgn. tech. jours. Home: 2028 Amherst Drive, South Pasadena, Cal. Died June 14, 1953; buried Mountain View Cemetery, Altadena, Cal.

MICHELFELDER, Sylvester Clarence (mĭk'ĕl-fĕl-dēr), clergyman; b. New Washington, O., Oct. 27, 1889; s. Jacob C. and Caroline O. (Kline) M.; (student), Capital Univ., Columbus, O., Capital Sem., 1914, D.D. (hon.), 1944; m. Florence E. Kibler, June 24, 1914; children—Mary Elizabeth (Mrs. Howard E. Young), Theodore J. Ordained to ministry of Luth. Ch., 1914; pastor Willard, O., 1913-21, Pittsburgh, Pa., 1921-26; supt. Luth. Inner Mission Soc., Pittsburgh, 1926-31; pastor Toledo, O., 1931-45; Luth. rep. Am. sect. Luth. World Convention to World Council of Chs., Geneva, Switzerland, 1945-46; organizer and 1st dir. material aid div. World Council of Chs., 1945-46, mem. bd. mgrs. and adminstrv. com. Reconstrn. Dept., consultant to assembly and ecumenical com. Inst. Bossey; exec. sec. Luth. World Fedn. since 1947; sec. bd. of pubs., Am. Lutheran Church, 1940-45. Mem. bd. dirs. Toledo Community Chest, 1944, 45. Club: Torch (Toledo). Author: Life Adjustments, 1940; So You are Thinking, 1946. Republican. Home: 10 Route de Malagnou. Office: 17 Route de Malagnou, Geneva, Switzerland. Died Sept. 30, 1951; buried New Washington, O.

MICHENER, Earl Cory, ex-congressman; b. Attica, O., Nov. 30, 1876; s. Valentine A. and Sarah Adelia (Cory) M.; student law dept. U. Mich., 1900-02; LL.B., Columbia U., 1903; m. Belle Strandler, June 11, 1902; children—John Strandler, Elizabeth. Practiced at Adrian, 1903—; asst. pros. atty. Lenawee County, Mich., 1907-10, pros. atty., 1911-14; mem. 66th to 72d, and 74th to 81st Congresses, 2d Mich. Dist. Served as pvt. Co. B., 31st Mich. Vol. Inf., 1898-99, Spanish-Am. War. Mem. Phi Sigma Kappa, S.A.R. Republican. Presbyn. Mason. K.P., Elk. Clubs: Adrian, Lenawee Country, Rotary. Home: 340 S. Main St. Office: Adrian State Bank Bldg., Adrian, Mich. Died July 5, 1957; buried Oakwood Cemetery, Adrian.

MICHIE, A(ddinell) Hewson (mĭk'ĭ), law publisher; b. Northport, L.I., N.Y., Oct. 28, 1897; s. Thomas Johnson and Emily (Hewson) M.; prep. edn., Jefferson Prep Sch. for Boys, Charlottesville, Va.; LL.B., U. of Va., 1922; m. Katharine Barton Fishburne, Oct. 14, 1924; children—Katharine Hewson (Mrs. W. O. Lewis), Addinell Hewson, Jr. Admitted to Va. bar, 1921; with The Michie Co., law pubs., Charlottesville, Va., since June 1922, as contbg. editor, 1922-26, editor-in-chief, 1926-30, v.p., 1930-43, pres. since 1943; chmn. of bd. Michie City Publications Co. since 1945; pres. of Michie Casebook Company; reporter to Supreme Court of Appeals of Va. 1937-53; pres. M.B.G. Corporation, 1948—. Served with 116th Inf., U.S. Army, 1918-19, Argonne campaign. Mem. Phi Beta Kappa, Theta Delta Chi, Phi Delta Phi. Democrat. Episcopalian. Clubs: Red-Land (Charlottesville); Farmington Country (Albermarle Co., Va.). Editor: Digest of Fla. Reports, 1933; Colorado Statutes Annotated, 1935; Michie's Digest of Tenn. Reports, 1935; Virginia Code, 1936, 50; West Va. Code, 1937, 49; Michie's Va.-W. Va. Digest, 1929-31; Michie on Banks and Banking, 1931-33; also many others. Home: Meadowbrook Hills, Charlottesville, Va. Office: 7th and Market Sts., Charlottesville, Va. Died Dec. 9, 1957.

MICHIE, James Newton (mĭk'ē), mathematician; b. Charlottesville, Va., July 28, 1879; s. John Auggustus, M.D. and Susan (Jackson) M.; B.S., U. Va., 1908; A.M., U. Mich., 1919; m. Hazel Jacob, Dec. 29, 1909 (died Nov. 25, 1940); children—Sarah Jacob (Mrs. Victor Harris), Susan Jackson (Mrs. J. B. Johnson), Robert E. Lee, m. 2d, Johnnie McCrery, Aug. 14, 1943. Tchr., Miller's Sch., Va., 1899-1900, Eastern Coll., Front Royal, Va., 1902-93, Millersburg (Ky.) Mil. Acad. 1903-06; instr. mathematics, U. Va., 1906-09, asst. prof. summer sch., 1909-18, asso. prof., 1919-25; prof. 1925-29; asst. prof. mathematics Tex. A. and M. Coll., 1908-18, asso. prof., 1919-20; asst. prof. mathematics Mich., 1918-19; asso. prof. U. Tex., 1920-25; prof., head dept. mathematics Tex. Tech. Coll., 1925-50, now emeritus. Fellow Tex. Acad. Sci.; mem. A.A.A.S., Am. Math. Soc., Math. Assn. Am., Inc., Kappa Mu Epsilon. Democrat. Episcopalian. Clubs: Knife and Fork, Trailers Dancing. Author: Differential and Integral Calculus, 1947; Modifications of Graeffe's Method in the Colution of Numerical Equations of Higher Degree than Six, Proceedings of Texas Acad. of Science, Vol. XX; also articles in math. jours. Specialist in math. analysis particularly differential equations, differential geometry, vector analysis. Address: 5314 Swiss Av., Dallas 14. Died Nov. 24, 1958; buried Grove Hill Cemetery, Dallas.

MIDDLETON, Austin Ralph, prof. zoölogy; b. Baltimore, Md., Apr. 14, 1881; s. Christopher Byrne and George Anna (Belt) M.; grad. Baltimore City Coll., 1901; grad. Baltimore Teachers' Training Sch., 1902; A.B., Johns Hopkins, 1910, Ph.D., 1915; m. Margaret Mary Loughridge, July 3, 1917. Johns Hopkins scholar, 1912-14, fellow, 1914-15, and fellow by courtesy, 1915-16; prof. zoölogy, U. of Louisville, since 1916; organized biol. labs. of the university and dir. depts. of biology, 1916-28 prof. emeritus of biology since July 1952. Member Johns Hopkins Scientific Expedition, Jamaica, B.W.I., 1910. Capt. Sanitary Reserves, U.S. Army; colonel and comdg. ofcr., Medical Detachment, Kentucky Active Militia. Mem. committee of 100, 6th Internat. Congress Genetics. Fellow A.A.A.S. (member council and com. section F.), Conference on State Academies of Science (sec.), American Geog. Society, Royal Society Arts; member Am. Soc. Zoölogists, Ecol. Soc. America, Am. Soc. Mammalogists, Am. Soc. Parasitologists, Am. Acad. Polit. and Social Science, Am. Geneal. Soc., Kentucky Acad. Science (past pres.), Conf. of Acad. of Science (pres. 1952), Eugenics Society of America, Eugenics Research Assn., Ky. Cols. (chancellor), Pi Gamma Mu, Kappa Psi, Theta Kappa Psi, Kappa Alpha (Southern), Chi Beta Phi. Clubs: Quindecim, Torch (president 1929-31), University, Army and Navy, Kiwanis. Author College Biology, 1925-29; also numerous research articles. Editor for Ky. of The Naturalist's Guide to the Americas, biographies in American Men of Science, Index Biologorum and Menchen und Menchenwerke. Organized tropical biol. expdn. to jungles of Honduras, Central America, June-Aug. 1933 and 1934. Author (1938) of the plan for "The University of America." Home: 1329 S. Floyd St., Louisville 8. Died Apr. 11, 1956; Cave Hill Cemetery, Louisville.

MIDDLETON, Charles Gibson, lawyer; b. Louisville, Feb. 22, 1883; s. John and Elizabeth Harrison (Summers) M.; B.L., U. Va., 1905; m. Anita Gheens, June 6, 1912 (dec.); children—Charles Gibson, Edwin Gheens; m. 2d, Ann Wilhoyte, Mar. 4, 1946; 1 dau., Ann. Admitted to Ky. bar, 1905; asso. Humphrey, Hines & Humphrey, 1905-07; mem. Carroll & Middleton, 1907-10, Humphrey, Middleton & Humphrey, 1912-17, Humphrey, Crawford & Middleton, 1917-31, Crawford, Middleton, Milner & Seelbach, 1932-41, Bullitt & Middleton, 1942-48, Middleon, Seelbach, Wolford, Willis & Cochran, 1948—. Ensign, USNRF, World War I. Del. Rep. Nat. Conv., 1940. Pres. Louisville Grand Opera Assn.; dir. Louisville Park Theatrical Assn.; mem. Nat. Recreation Assn., Am., Ky. bar assns., Delta Psi. Republican. Clubs: Pendennis, Louisville Country, River Valley (Louisville); St. Anthony, Racquet and Tennis (N.Y.C.). Home: Harrods Creek, Ky. Address: 501 S. Second St., Louisville 2. Died Sept. 8, 1956; buried Cave Hill Cemetery, Louisville.

MIDDOUR, Emory J., educator; b. Quincy, Pa., July 4, 1890; s. George W. and Martha (Shockey) M.; grad. (1st in class), Shippensburg (Pa.) State Normal Sch., 1909; A.B., Princeton, 1916; postgrad. U. Pa., summers 1917, 18; m. Minnie Bell Henneberger, Aug. 20, 1917; 1 son, Emory J. Prin. Quincy Twp. High Sch., Franklin Co., Pa., 1909-12; sr. master, Nat. Cathedral Sch., Washington, 1916-20; head history dept., Mercersburg (Pa.) Acad., 1920-22, asst. to headmaster, 1922-28, asst. headmaster, 1928-35; supt. Staunton (Va.) Mil. Acad., 1935—. Democrat. Presbyn. Address: Staunton Military Academy, Staunton, Va. Deceased.

MIKESELL, Doyle (mĭk'sĕl), educator; b. Milo, Iowa, Mar. 2, 1915; s. Earl Jay and Lizzie (Schroeder) M.; B.S., Drake U., 1936, M.S., 1939; student summers, U. of Chicago, 1939, 40, 41; Ph.D., State U. of Iowa, 1949; m. Elaine Johnson, June 22, 1940; children—Mary, Kathryn, Kenneth. Teacher Washington Irving Jr. High Sch., Des Moines, 1937-38; instr. in edn., Drake U., 1938-41, asst. prof., 1941-42; head social science dept., Freeport (Ill.) High Sch., 1942-Mar. 1943; asst. prof. social science, Drake U., 1943-44, prof. of social sciences and head of basic studies div., 1949-57, head of social science department, 1957—; chairman dir. social relations Boston Univ. Jr. Coll., 1957-58; chief of training facilities sect., Iowa Regional Office, U.S. Vets. Adminstrn., Dec. 1944-Feb. 1948. Served with Air Force, U.S. Army, Mar.-Sept. 1943. Mem. social sciences com. of Am. Council on Education's study of evaluation in gen. edn. Mem. Nat. Soc. for Study of Edn., Assn. Higher Learning, Nat. Council for Social Studies, Phi Delta Kappa, Kappa Delta Pi. Methodist. Mason. Club: Frontier. Contbr. to ednl. publs. Home: 2618 35th St., Des Moines, Ia. Died Dec. 4, 1958.

MILAM, Arthur Yeager, lawyer; b. Leesburg, Fla., Oct. 26, 1889; s. Bob R. and Lulu (Yager) M.; B.S., Stetson U., 1912; m. Rhea Van Der Poel, Dec. 15, 1914; children—Lillian Taylor, Arden Yeager. Admitted to Fla. bar, 1912, and since practiced in Jacksonville, sr. partner Milam, McIlvaine, Carroll and Wattles since 1912; dir. Peninsular Life Ins. Co., Jacksonville, since 1937, Southeastern Greyhound Lines, Lexington, Ky., 1942-50; Lee Tidewater Cypress Co., Children's Home Society. Member, Fla. Ho. Reps., 1923, 25, speaker two sessions. Mem. C. of C. of U.S. (dir.), Fla. C. of C. (pres. 1946-48, dir.), Jacksonville C. of C. (pres. 1949). Mason (33°, Shriner). Home: Riverside Av. at Willow Branch. Office: Greenleaf Bldg., Jacksonville, Fla. Died Mar. 1956.

MILBANK, Dunlevy, estate mgr.; b. New York, N.Y., Oct. 8, 1878; s. Joseph and Ella (Dunlevy) M.; student Cutler Sch., N.Y. City, 1889-96; A.B., Yale, 1900; LL.B., N.Y. Law Sch., 1902; m. Katharine Sebring Fowler, June 1, 1910; children—Ella Dunlevy (Mrs. William Ward Foshay), Thomas Fowler. Admitted to N.Y. bar, 1902; practiced N.Y. City, 1902-04; estate mgr. since 1904; dir. Bank of N.Y. and Fifth Av. Bank. Mem. War Industries Bd., Washington, D.C., 1918. Trustee Children's Aid Society, Presbyterian Hosp., Ladies' Christian Union. Republican. Presbyn. Clubs: University, Century (N.Y.C.); Yeamans Hall of Charleston, S.C. Home: 39 E. 68th St., N.Y.C. 21. Died Oct. 16, 1959; buried Woodlawn Cemetery, N.Y.C.

MILES, Carlton Wright, writer; b. Fergus Falls, Minn., June 12, 1884; s. George Carlton and Harriet Ann (Richmond) M.; student U. Minn., 1902-04. With Mpls. Journal, 1907-28; active operation Lakewood summer theatre, Skowhegan, Me., 18yrs. Mem. Alpha Tau Omega. Club: Lambs (New York). Author: (plays) Portrait of Gilbert, Granite Lady; (with John Colton) Nine Pine Street, and The Flitting Lady; (with Eugene Courtwright) The Eldest. Co-Author: (talking picture) Ladies They Talk About. Contbr. to mags. Deceased.

MILES, Dudley (Howe), author, educator; b. Milwaukee, Wis., July 16, 1881; s. Edwin Chamberlain and Jane Anne (Estey) M.; A.B., with first honors, Southwestern U., Georgetown, Texas, 1902; A.M., University of Chicago, 1907; Ph.D., Columbia, 1910; married Matie Mitchell, December 25, 1913 (dec. 1915); married 2d, Florence W. Read, August 14, 1917. Professor of English and French, Hendrix College, Conway, Ark., 1902-03; instructor English and history, high sch., Cuero, Texas, 1903-05; instr. rhetoric, U. of Miss., 1905-07; asst. prof. English, Southwestern U., 1907-09; fellow comparative lit., Columbia, 1909-10; instr. English, extension teaching, Columbia, 1910-11, 1912-14; prof. English, U. of Ga. Summer School, 1917; teacher English, DeWitt Clinton High Sch., N.Y. City, 1911-14; chmn. English Dept., Evander Childs High Sch., New York City, 1914-47; asst. prin., 1924-30, director of Honor School since 1936, ret. Director prep. dept. of sch. maintained by New York Chapter of Am. Inst. Banking, 1917-32. With Friedsam Commission on Sch. Finance and Adminstrn., 1926. Member Nat. Society for Study of Education, Society for Advancement of Education, Nat. Council of Teachers of English (past pres.), New York Soc. for Experimental Study of Edn., Kappa Alpha (Southern), also many local organizations. Democrat. Clubs: Men's Faculty Club (Columbia University), English Graduate Union (Columbia University), Authors, Players; Western University, Shelter Island Yacht. Author: Influence of Molière on Restoration Comedy, 1910; English in Business, 1920, rev. edit., 1928; Teaching Literature, 1926, rev. edit., 1938, 44, 49. History of Eng. Literature, 1935, rev. edit., 1943, 48; Hist. of Am. Literature, 1936, rev. edit., 1943, 48. Editor: Photographic History of the Civil War (ten volumes), 1911; Poetry and Eloquence of the Civil War, 1911; Macaulay's Two Speeches on Copyright and Lincoln's Cooper Institute Address, 1915; Goldsmith's She Stoops to Conquer, 1917; Stories from the Spanish and Italian (eight volumes), 1920; Literature and Life, Books III and IV, 1923-24, and Book III, Special Edition, 1929. Editor-in-chief, Literature and Life Series, revised edition, Book I, 1933, 1940, 1947. Book IV, 1935. Book III, 1936. Book II, 1936, 1941, 1947; Literature and Life in America, 1943, 48; Literature and Life in England, 1943, 48. Contbr. to jours. and encys. Home: Box 173, Shelter Island Heights, N.Y. Died Sept. 5, 1954.

MILES, Edson Russell, educator; b. Mount Gilead, O., July 10, 1875; s. Warren S. and Maria B. (Russell) M.; A.B., St. Lawrence U., 1900; grad. study theol. dept., same univ., 2 yrs.; grad. Am. Acad. Dramatic Arts, N.Y.C., 1904; D.D., Tufts, 1930; m. Sarah Bowne Raymond, Sept. 4, 1900 (died Mar. 20, 1951); children—John Raymond, Richard Stoddard. Ordained to ministry Universalist Ch., 1900; pastor Binghamton, N.Y., 1900-03; actor and soloist, repertoire co. of E. H. Sothern and Julia Marlowe, 1904-07; in stock and repertoire, N.Y.C., 1907-12; pastor Grove Hall Universalist Ch., Boston, 1912-17; Ryder prof. homiletics and pastoral care St. Lawrence U. until 1945, asst. prof. speech, St. Lawrence Coll. until 1945, prof. emeritus, 1949—, also stage dir. St. Lawrence Dramatic Assn., 1917-44. Chmn. St. Lawrence County Bd. Child Welfare, 10 yrs. Mem. Nat. Assn. Tchrs. Speech, Boston Arts & Crafts Soc., N.Y. Soc. Craftsmen, Phi Beta Kappa, Alpha Tau Omega. Home: 49 Park St., Canton, N.Y. Died Feb. 13, 1958; buried Clinton, N.Y.

MILES, Lovick Pierce, lawyer; b. Marion, Va., May 17, 1871; s. Rev. George Washington and Rebecca (Austin) M.; A.B., Emory and Henry Coll., Emory, Va., 1891; law student U. Va., 1891-92; m. Kate Thompson Crawford, Nov. 14, 1906; children—Anne Crawford, Lovick P., Kate Crawford. Admitted Va. bar, 1893; reporter, asst. mng. editor and Washington corr. Memphis Comml. Appeal, 1894-99; began practice, Ft. Smith, Ark., 1899; asst. gen. atty. M.P. Ry., 1899-1908, gen. atty., 1908-12; since practicing in Memphis; pres., Comml. Pub. Co., Memphis; v.p. Rock Island, Memphis Terminal Ry. Co. Pres. Memphis Community Fund, 1940-44. Mem. Am. (chmn. pub. utility sec. 1933-34), Tenn. State (pres. 1924-25), Memphis, Shelby County bar assns., Phi Delta Theta. Democrat. Methodist. Elk. Clubs: Memphis Country, Oakdonic Outing, Horseshoe Lake. Home: 65 E. Parkway N. Office: Sterick Bldg., Memphis. Died Jan. 17, 1953.

MILES, Robert Whitfield, clergyman; b. Richmond, Va., Oct. 5, 1890; s. Robert Walton and Ida (Kates) M.; student Richmond Coll., 1907-08, A.B., Davidson Coll., 1911; Union Theol. Sem. of Va., 1914-17: B.D., Washington and Lee U., 1930 (hon. D.D.); m. Dorothy Ankeney Moomaw, Dec. 6, 1917; children—Robert Whitfield, Marian (Morris), Edward W., Matilda Cary (dec.). Instr. Highland Park High Sch., Richmond, Va., 1912-14; asst. pastor First Presbyn. Ch., Greensboro, N.C., 1920-21; pastor Presbyn. Ch., Auburn, Ala., 1921-25; univ. sec., Presbyn. Ch. of U.S., 1926; pastor Westminster Ch., Lynchburg, Va., 1927-33; pastor First Church, Lexington, Ky., since 1933. Moderator Synod of Ky. (U.S.), 1942. Served with Y.M.C.A., Camp Jackson and France, 1917-19. Trustee Centre Coll., Sayre Coll. Mem. Kappa Alpha, Omicron Delta Kappa. Democrat. Mason. Clubs: Lexington Country, Informal (Lexington). Author: That Frenchman, John Calvin, 1939; Christian Reconstruction, 1944. Contbr. articles to Union Seminary Review, Presbyterian of the South, Christian Observer and Presbyn. Survey. Home: 465 W. 3rd St. Office: 171 Market St., Lexington, Ky. Died Jan. 8, 1952; buried Lexington.

MILEY, Jess Wells, state supt. schs.; b. Crawford County Kan., Dec. 13, 1878; s. James and Serilda (Hammond) M.; student State Manual Tng. Normal Sch., Pittsburg, Kan.; m. Florence Montee, Aug. 7, 1917; children—Dorothy Jean, Frances Marion. Began teaching pub. schs., Kan., 1898; elected county supt. schs. Crawford County, 6 times; state supt. instrn., Kan., 1923-26. Pres. Kan. State Tchrs.' Assn., 1922, now dir. Republican. Presbyn. Odd Fellow, Elk, Woodman, Kiwanian. Home: 1100 Garfield St. Address: State House, Topeka, Kan. Died Jan. 14, 1952.

MILHAM, Willis Isbister, astronomer; b. Kinderhook, N.Y., Feb. 11, 1874; s. Edmund and Ellen Medora (Isbister) M.; B.A., Williams Coll., 1894, M.A., 1895, L.H.D., 1946; Ph.D., U. Strassburg, 1901, m. Betsey Morgan Fairweather, June 7, 1911. Instr. mathematics and physics Williams Coll., 3 yrs., asst., prof. math. sciences, 2 yrs., absent on leave 2 yrs. and Field Meml. prof. of astronomy, 1902-42, prof. emeritus, 1942—. Fellow A.A.A.S., Am. Phys. Soc., Am. Meteorol. Soc., Royal Astron. Soc.; mem. Am. Geog. Soc., Soc. Belge d'Astronomie, Soc. Astron. de France, Nat. Assn. Watch and Clock Collectors (v.p. 1946-49), Phi Beta Kappa. Author: How to Identify the Stars, 1909; Meteorology, 1912; Time and Timekeepers, 1923; Early American Observatories, 1938; The Columbus Clock, 1945. Contbr. to sci. mags. Home: 24 Hoxsey St., Williamstown, Mass. Died Mar. 23, 1957; buried Kinderhook, N.Y.

MILKS, Howard Jay, veterinarian; b. Candor, N.Y., June 25, 1879; s. William Jewett and Sarah Matilda (Smith) M.; student State Normal Sch., Cortland, N.Y., 1899-1901; D.V.M., N.Y. State Vet. Coll., Cornell U., 1904; m. Lena Mabel Vose, July 12, 1906; children—Clifford Howard, Raymond Claude, Richard Vose. Animal pathologist La. State Expt. Sta., 1906-08; asst. prof. materia medica and therapeutics N.Y. State Vet. Coll., Cornell U., 1909-14, prof. therapeutics and small animal diseases, dir. small animal clinic, 1914-47, now emeritus. Mem. Am., N.Y. State vet. med. assns., Sigma Xi, Phi Kappa Phi. Conglist. Mason. Author: A Laboratory Guide to Materia Medica and Pharmacy, 1916; Practical Veterinary Pharmacology and Therapeutics, 1917, 30, 36, 40, 43, 46. Home: 113 College Av., Ithaca, N.Y. Died Mar. 30, 1954; buried Candor, N.Y.

MILLAR, Robert Wyness (mĭl'lär), lawyer, educator; b. Falkirk, Scotland, Apr. 10, 1876; s. Walter Robert and Dolina (Wyness) M.; came to U.S., 1886; LL.B., Northwestern U., 1897, M.A., 1916; m. Anne Everett George, June 10, 1919. Admitted to Ill. bar, 1897; practiced with Johnson & Morrill, 1897-1901; in partnership with William Herbert Johnson, 1901-09; practiced independently, 1910-15; instr. John Marshall Law Sch., 1903-15; lectr. Northwestern U. Sch. Law, 1911-15; resident prof., 1915-42, prof. emeritus, 1942—. Commd. maj. judge advocate, U.S. Army, Mar. 18, 1918; lt. col., Oct. 29, 1918; col., July 10, 1919; on duty Office of Judge Advocate Gen., Washington, Mar. 18, 1918-Sept. 3, 1919. Cons. to Jud. Adv. Council of Cook County, Ill., 1929-47; sec. for U.S., Stair Soc. (Scotland). Spl. asst. to under-sec. also to asst. sec. of navy, May 1942-Sept. 1945. Received Distinguished Civilian Service Award, Navy Dept., 1945. Mem. Am., Ill. State, Chgo. bar assns., Chgo. Law Inst., Am. Judicature Soc., Delta Theta Phi (hon.); fgn. mem. Acad. Nazionale dei Lincei (Italy), 1947; hon. mem. Instituto Espanol de Derecho Procesal; corr. mem. Associazione Italiana fra gli Studiosi del Processo Civile. Republican. Presbyn. Clubs: University (Chgo. and Evanston), Arts (Chgo.). Author: Common Law Pleading in Library of American Law and Practice, 1912; Formative Principles of Civil Procedure, 1923 (Spanish version, 1945); Civil Procedures of the Trial Court in Historical Perspective, 1952. Translator: Garofalo's Criminology (Modern Criminal Science Series), 1912; portion of History of Continental Criminal Law (Continental Legal History Series), 1916. Translator and editor: History of Continental Civil Procedure by Engelmann and others (in Continental Legal History Series), 1927. Contbr. essays and articles to legal publs. Home: 1727 Wesley Av., Evanston, Ill. Office: 357 E. Chicago Av., Chgo. 11. Died Feb. 1959.

MILLARD, Floyd Hays, railway exec.; b. Central City, Neb., July 17, 1888; s. Howard Bruce and Elizabeth (Hays) M.; B.S., U. Colo., 1910, C.E., 1913; M.S., U. Ill., 1912; m. Marie Dopf Mar. 19, 1927. Connected with railroad work since 1911; with St. Louis Southwestern Ry. Lines since 1920, v.p. and comptroller since 1948. Mem. Sigma Chi, Tau Beta Pi. Office: care St. Louis Southwestern Railway Lines, 4th and Pine Sts., St. Louis 2. Died Feb. 3, 1955.*

MILLAY, Edna St. Vincent (mĭl-lā'), author; b. Rockland, Me., Feb. 22, 1892; d. Henry Tolman and Cora (Buzzell) Millay; A.B., Vassar Coll., 1917; Litt.D., Tufts, Russell Sage Foundation Coll., Colby Coll., U. of Wis.; L.H.D., New York U.; m. Eugen Jan Boissevain, 1923. Mem. Am. Acad. Arts and Letters, Am. Soc. Composers, Authors and Pubs. Author: Renascence and Other Poems, 1917; Figs from Thistles, 1920; Second April, 1921; Aria da Capo, 1921; The Lamp and the Bell, 1921; Two Slatterns and a King, 1921; The Harp-Weaver and Other Poems, 1923; The King's Henchman, 1927; The Buck in the Snow, 1928; Fatal Interview, 1931; Wine from These Grapes, 1934; Flowers of Evil (from the French of Charles Baudelaire, in collaboration with George Dillon), 1936; Conversation at Midnight, 1937; Huntsman, What Quarry?, 1939; Make Bright the Arrows, 1940; There Are No Islands Any More, 1940; Collected Sonnets, 1941; The Murder of Lidice, 1942; Letters of Edna St. Vincent Millay, 1952; Mine the Harvest, 1954. Collected Lyrics, 1943; Collected Poems, 1956. Winner Pulitzer prize, 1922. for best volume of verse. Address: Steepletop, Austerlitz, N.Y. Died Oct. 19, 1950; buried Steepletop, Austerlitz, N.Y.

MILLER, Adolph Caspar, economist; b. San Francisco, Calif., Jan. 7, 1866; s. Caspar and Fredericka M.; A.B., U. of Calif., 1887, hon. LL.D., 1940; A.M., Harvard, 1888; student univs. of Paris and Munich, 1895-96; m. Mary, d. O. S. A. Sprague, Oct. 7, 1895. Instr. economics, Harvard, 1889-90; asst. prof. history and politics, U. of Calif., 1890-91; asso. prof. polit. economy and finance, Cornell, 1891-92; prof. finance, U. of Chicago, 1892-1902; Flood prof. economics and commerce, U. of Calif., 1902-13; asst. to the sec. of the interior, Washington, 1913-14; mem. Federal Reserve Bd., Washington, 1914-36. Author of papers on finance, banking, etc., pub. in econ. and financial jours.; participated extensively in hearings before Banking and Currency Com., U.S. Senate, 1931, 32, 35, and of the House, 1926, 28. Clubs: Faculty (Berkeley); University, Delta Kappa Epsilon (New York); Metropolitan, Chevy Chase (Washington). Mem. Inter-American High Commn., 1921-33. Mem. Library of Congress Trust Fund Board, 1936—. 2230 S St., Washington. Died Feb. 11, 1953.

MILLER, Albert L., chmn. Federated Publs., Inc., pubs. of State Jour., Lansing, Mich.; Enquirer and News, Battle Creek, Mich.; Lafayette (Ind.) Jour. & Courier; The Chronicle, The Leader-Tribune, The Chronicle Tribune, Marion, Ind.; radio sta. WMRI AM-FM, Marion, Ind. Address: 19 Woodmer Lane, Battle Creek, Mich. Died Apr. 25, 1958.

MILLER, Andrew Jackson, Jr., paper co. exec.; b. Forrest City, Ark., Dec. 6, 1906; s. Andrew Jackson and Maggie M. (Holcomb) M.; B.S., U. Tenn., 1927; m. Maud Marcotte, June 3, 1936; (dec. Jan. 1955); children—Andrew Jackson III, Marcia M., Lisa K.; married 2d, Edwina L. McElfresh, February 4. 1958. From playgound instr. to dir. personnel, Memphis, 1929-41; indsl. relations dir. Concan Ordnance, Terre Haute, Ind., 1941-42; sec.-mgr. Lake States Pulp and Paper Assn., Appleton, Wis., 1942-44; with Mead Corp., Chillicothe, O., 1944—, v.p. indsl. relations, 1953—; guest lectr., speaker colls., univs., convs. Mem. Vets. Adv. Com. to Gen. Hershey, 1944-46; industry mem. WLS, 1943-46. Mem. Am. Pulp and Paper Assn. (indsl. relations com.), Am. Mgmt. Assn., Nat. Indsl. Conf. Bd., Order of Symposiarchs, Fibre Box Assn. (indsl. relations com.). Elk, Mason (Shriner, 32°, K.T.). Clubs: Rotary, Chillicothe Country; Athletic (Columbus, O.). Home: 128 Western Av. Office: Mead Corp., Chillicothe, O. Died Dec. 1959.

MILLER, Austin Vicente, physician; b. Salinas City, Calif., Feb. 7, 1877; s. Joseph and Sally (Rhodes) M.; M.D., Cooper Med. Coll., San Francisco, 1899; m. Katherine Gardner, June 29, 1906; children—Sally, Miriam, Marcia. Mem. Am. Med. Assn., Calif. Med. Assn., Tulare County Med. Soc., A.A.A.S. Republican. Home: Porterville, Cal. Died Dec. 25, 1955.

MILLER, Bina West, ex-pres. Woman's Benefit Assn.; b. Columbus, Mich.; d. Alfred and Elizabeth (Conant) West; grad. Normal Course for Tchrs.; A. M., U. Mich. 1924; m. George W. Miller, Mar. 28, 1929 (died 1932). Teacher pub. schs., 1888-90; mem. county bd. sch. examiners, St. Clair County, 1890-91; founder of Woman's Benefit Assn., pres., 1892-1948; rep. Nat. Council of Women at Geneva, 1908; elected 1st woman pres. of Nat. Fraternal Congress of Am., 1925. Mem. 1st woman's exec. com. of Rep. Nat. Com., 1919; 1st vice chmn. Mich. Rep. State Central Com., 1919; mem. Rep. Nat. Com. for Mich., 1923-32, mem. exec. com., 1924-32; mem. of com. on arrangements, Rep. Nat. Conv., Kansas City, 1928; mem. Com. on Program of 100 apptd. by Rep. Nat. Com., 1938. Mem. D.A.R., Woman's Relief Corps, Ladies Library Assn. Conglist. Mem. Order Eastern Star. Club: Congressional Country (Washington). Home: 2828 Military St., Port Huron, Mich. Died Apr. 18, 1954; buried Port Huron.

MILLER, Carl A(ugust), banker; born East Millstone, N.J., July 31, 1891; s. August Christian and Caroline Augusta (Porgess) M.; grad. Peekskill Mil. Acad., 1902-07; B.S. in Civil Engring., New York U., 1911, C.E., 1912; m. Charlotte Sanford Baker, Nov. 3, 1915; children—Carolyn Ten Eyck (Mrs. Joseph H. Holmes, Jr.), William Sanford, Jean Stewart (Mrs. Henry C. Williams). Instr. civil engring. New York U., 1913; with Am. Telephone and Telegraph Co., Commercial Engring. Dept., 1914-20 (except for service World War 1); asst. commercial engr. Irving Trust Co. (then Irving Nat. Bank), N.Y. City, 1920-26, asst. sec., 1926-28, asst. v.p., 1928, v.p. 1929-50, senior vice president since 1950; dir. Arkell & Smiths, Three States Realty Corp., Hudson House, Inc. Pilot, aviation section, Signal Corps, U.S. Army, 1917-19; disch. with rank of maj., Air Corps Res., 1919; commd. lt. col., U.S. Army, 1943; disch., 1945; with Mil. Govt. in North Africa, Sicily and So. Italy. Dir. and mem. exec. com. Tarrytown (N.Y.) Hosp., 1934-51; mem. vis. com. N.Y. U. Coll. Engring., 1948-51. Mem. Am. Inst. Banking, Pilgrims of U.S., Mil. Order World Wars, Vets. Fgn. Wars, Delta Phi, Ind. Rep. Episcopalian. Clubs: University, Racquet and Tennis (New York); Ardsley Country (Ardsley on Hudson, N.Y.); Blind Brook Golf (Port Chester, N.Y.); Adirondack League (Old Forge, N.Y.); U.S. Seniors Golf Assn. Home: Ardsley-on-Hudson, N.Y. Office: 1 Wall St., N.Y.C. Died Aug. 23, 1953.

MILLER, Charles Wilbur, business exec.; b. Winchester, Va., Feb. 17, 1879; s. Durbin G (D.D.) and Sara (Duffield) M.; student Johns Hopkins; grad. law sch., U. Md., 1899; m. Edith Davison, June 14, 1905; children—Edith (Mrs. Joseph Voss White), Grace (Mrs. T. Courtney J. Wedbee). Admitted to Md. bar. 1899; mem. firm Bond & Robinson, Balt. 1903-06; pres. Davison Chem. Co., 1906-35; dir. Jefferson Lake Sulphur Co., since 1946, chmn. bd. since 1952. Rep. candidate U.S. Senator, 1936. Served with Md. N.G., 1898-1905. Mem. The Pilgrims (N.Y.C.), Batchelor's Cotillon, Green Spring Hounds, Kappa Sigma. Episcopalian (vestryman). Club: Maryland. Home: Shawan House, Cockeysville, Md. Died Sept. 21, 1955.

MILLER, Christian Otto Gerberding, public utility official; b. San Francisco, Calif., Oct. 1, 1865; s. Albert and Mary A. (Kendall) M.; ed. U. of Calif., 1885; m. Miss E. Havemeyer Tucker, May 2, 1889 (died Mar. 28, 1896); m. 2d, Janet McAlpin Watt, Apr. 21, 1898. Began as cashier United Gas Improvement Co., San Francisco, Dec. 1, 1883; treas. Pacific Lighting Corp., San Francisco, 1886, pres. since 1898, chmn. since 1940; pres. Pacific Gas Improvement Co., 1900-03; pres. of San Francisco-Oakland Railroad Terminals, 1917-24; dir. and chmn. board dirs. American Trust Co.; dir. Kennedy Mine, Firemens Fund Ins. Co., Pacific Gas & Electric Co. and many other corps. In charge of San Francisco office of War Trade Bd. during war period. Trustee mem. investment com. Stanford U., 1923-50. Mem. Am. Gas Inst. (v.p. 1924), Pacific Coast Gas Assn. (pres. 1908), Am. Gas Assn. (v.p.). Rep. Conglist. Clubs: Pacific Union, Bohemian, Burlingame Country, McCloud River; California (Los Angeles). Home: 3001 Pacific Av. Office: 433 California St., San Francisco. Died Apr. 23, 1952; buried Mountain View Cemetery, Oakland, Cal.

MILLER, Clarence A(itha), lawyer, railroad exec.; b. nr. Fairchance, Pa., Feb. 11, 1890; s. Franklin Pierce and Anna Belle (Darby) M.; LL.B., George Washington U., 1919, M.L., 1921; m. Daisy M. Curstead, Sept. 7, 1910; children—Dorothy Agnes (Mrs. William F. McMahon), Reland Rita (Mrs. Samuel D. Amato). With U.S. Postal Service, 1908-20; admitted to D.C. bar, 1920; asst. to legislative counsel U.S. Ho. of Reps., 1921-22; asso. Baker & Baker, 1922-26; mem. Hitt, Miller & Munson, 1926-30; asst. gen.

counsel Am. Short Line R.R. Assn., Washington, 1931-33, gen. counsel, 1933-39, v.p., gen. counsel since 1939; specialist in practice before Interstate Commerce Commn. and other govt. agencies since 1926; lectr. law sch. Southeastern U., 1921-37, George Washington U., 1922-45. Mem. Assn. Practitioners before Interstate Commerce Commn. (past pres.), Am., D.C. bar assns., Am. Judicature Soc., Am. Arbitration Assn., Inst. Am. Genealogy, Am. Acad. Polit. and Social Sci., Assn. Traffic Clubs Am. (life). Mem. Ch. of the Pilgrims. Clubs: University, Cosmos, Cosmopolitan, Kenwood Golf and Country (Washington); Rowfant (Cleve.); Boswell (Chgo.). Author: Legislative Evolution of Interstate Commerce Act, 1930; I.C.C. Law and Procedure, 1939; Anecdotes of the Literary Club, 1948. Co-author genealogies of Miller and Darby families (awarded certificate of merit Inst. Am. Genealogy). Contbr. law jours. Home: 5710 Wilson Lane, Bethesda 14, Md. Office: 2000 Massachusetts Av., Washington 6. Died Nov. 1953.

MILLER, David Aaron, pub., business exec.; born Gilberts, Pa., Apr. 7, 1869; s. Dr. Edward Peter and Flora Anna M.; B.S., Keystone State Coll., Kutztown, Pa., 1891; A.B. and A.M., Muhlenberg Coll., Allentown, Pa., 1894; hon. LL.D. conferred by Muhlenberg, 1942, Litt.D. by Ursinus Coll., Collegeville Pa., 1937; m. Blanche A. Berkemeyer, Sept. 25, 1900; children—Edward L. (dec.), Robert K., Samuel W., Donald P., Paul B., Margaret B. (Mrs. John E. Phillips), Julia A. (Mrs. C. Ridgely Mering), Mary E. (deceased). Began as reporter Allentown Morning Call, Allentown, Pa., 1894, publisher, 1895-1920, retired 1920; part owner, mng. editor Call-Chronicle newspapers, 1934, president, pub.; director Merchants Nat. Bank, Allen Mut. Fire Ins. Co. Pres. emeritus Phoebe Home for Old Folks; past dir. Family Service; former mem. and past pres. Sch. Bd. of Allentown, State Sch. Dirs. Association; director Pennsylvania German Soc. Republican. Member Evangelical and Reformed Church. Mason, Odd Fellow, Elk. Club: Torch. Contbr. series of letters to Morning Call on world trip, 1933-34. Home: 2221 Chew St. Office: 6th and Linden Sts., Allentown, Pa. Died Jan. 22, 1958.

MILLER, Edgar Grim, Jr., univ. dean; b. Gettysburg, Pa., Feb. 22, 1893; s. Edgar Grim and Esther Amelia (Valentine) M.; B.S., Gettysburg Coll., 1911, Sc.D., 1955; Ph.D., Columbia, 1913; student Cambridge Univ., 1928-29, London Univ., 1929; m. Margaret Motter, Sept. 7, 1921; children—Margaret Esther (Mrs Ralph D. Junker), Edgar Grim (dec), Ledlie Sitgreaves (Mrs. L. Miller Graham). Asst. in biological chemistry, Columbia 1911-13, asso. in biochemistry, 1914-21, asst. prof. biochemistry, 1921-24, asso. prof., 1924-35, prof. of biochemistry, 1935-—; dean of the grad. faculties, 1953-—. Pathol. chemist, Bellevue Hospital, New York City, 1912-13; instr. in physiological chemistry, Coll. of Med., Univ. Ill., Chicago, 1913-14. Served as cadet, A.A. F., 1918. Fellow A.A.A.S., N.Y. Acad. Scis., N.Y. Acad. Med.; mem. Am. Soc. Biol. Chemists, Soc. Exptl. Biology and Medicine, Harvey Soc. (sec. 1945-47), Am. Chem. Soc., Internat. Assn. Dental Research, Phi Beta Kappa, Phi Gamma Delta, Phi Lambda Upsilon, Sigma Xi. Independent. Protestant. Club: Century Assn. Home: 4930 Goodridge Av., N. Y.C. 71. Died June 28, 1955; buried Oak Hill Cemetery, Washington.

MILLER, Edmund Thornton, prof. economics; b. Fort Worth, Tex., June 6, 1878; s. Henry and Eliza Elvira (Hollis) M.; A.B., Weatherford (Tex.) Coll., 1897; A.B., U. of Tex., 1900, A.M., 1901; A.M., Harvard, 1903, Ph.D., 1909; studied U. of Chicago, summer sessions, 1902, 04; m. Emily Maverick, June 7, 1913; children—Emily Maverick, Edmund Hollis, Mary Elizabeth. Teacher of English and history, Waxahachie (Tex.) High Sch., 1901-02; instr. economics, U. of Texas, 1904-07, 1909-13, adj. prof., 1913-17, prof. since 1917. Member Texas Tax Survey Committee, 1927, Governor's Tax Study Committee, 1949. Austin teaching fellow, Harvard Univ., 1907-08; Henry Lee memorial fellow, Harvard, 1908-09. Mem. Am. Econ. Assn., Am. Numismatic Assn., Phi Delta Theta, Phi Beta Kappa; fellow Tex. State Hist. Assn. Democrat. Episcopalian. K.P. Author: A Financial History of Texas, 1916. Home: 910 Poplar St., Austin, Tex. Died May 6, 1952; buried Austin.

MILLER, Ernest B., state ofcl.; b. Gloversville, N.Y., Sept. 15, 1898; s. George J. and Adelaide Rose (Brumaghim) M.; grad. Inf. Sch., Ft. Benning, Ga.; m. Anna Marie Hauber, Oct. 17, 1921; children—Marilynn Ann (Mrs. Paul A. Bender), Patricia Faith, James B. (died on Anzio beachhead 1944) Thomas H., Richard J. Civil engr., land surveyor, 1923-—, Park Rapids, Minn., 1923-30; chief engr. Camp Ripley Mil. Reservation, 1930-40; asst. commr. charge airport engring. Minn. Dept. Aeros., 1947-49; mem. state com. for topographic mapping state Minn., 1948-50, dir. Civil Def., 1950-55. Served as enlisted man 1st inf., Minn. N.G., Mexican Border campaign, 1916-17; with 135th inf. 34th Div., also 9th inf. 2d Div., U.S. Army, 1917-19; col., comdr. 194th tank bn., Bataan, 1941-47 (Japanese prisoner 3 yrs., 5 mos.). Mem. Internat. War Vets. Alliance (between U.S. and Can.), 2d v.p., 1950-51, 1st v.p., 1951-52, pres., 1952-53, mem. bd. dirs., 1953-55. Decorated 3 Presdl. Unit Citations, Medal of Valor, Silver Star, Purple Heart. Mem. Nat. Assn. State Civil Def. Dirs. U.S. (v.p.), Am. Legion (past adj., vice comdr., post comdr., dist. comdr., 1931-32, state dept. comdr. 1946-47, chmn. dept. nat. def. com.), 40 and 8, Minn. Soc. Profl. Engrs. (chmn. com. for study efficient procurement, assignment profl. engrs., allied professions for nat. emergency), Nat. Soc. Profl. Engrs. Author: Bataan Uncensored, 1949. Home: 124 Banning Av., White Bear Lake, St. Paul 10. Died Feb. 20, 1959; buried Ft. Snelling Nat. Cemetery, Mpls.

MILLER, Eugene Walter, lawyer; b. Ill., Aug. 28, 1877; s. Domonick Francis and Louise M. (Rosenbaum) M.; student No. Ind. Normal Sch., Washington U. Law Sch., 1901; m. Mercedes D. Snider, May 26, 1918 (dec. June 20, 1950). Admitted to Mo. bar, 1901, practiced in St. Louis, 1901-09, Globe, Ariz., 1910-26, San Diego, Cal., since 1926, now mem. Miller, Higgs, Fletcher & Mack. Admitted to state bars, Ariz., Cal. Mason (K.T., Shriner). Home: 2205 Bancroft St., San Diego. Died Nov. 1951.

MILLER, Francis Trevelyn, historian, author; b. Southington, Conn., Oct. 8, 1877; s. E. Hutchinson and Jane (Hull) M.; student in lit., Trinity Coll., Hartford, Conn., 1898; in law, Washington and Lee U., 1899; Litt.D., Washington Coll., Md., 1913; LL.D., U. of Ky., 1913; m. Clara E. Emerson-Bickford, Sept. 7, 1903; 1 dau., Virginia (Mrs. Seward E. Shaver); m. 2d, Ann Woodward, Jan. 25, 1941; 1 dau., Lanette Bradford. Editor, Connecticut Magazine, 1902-08, Journal American History, 1905-10, Success Magazine, 1923-26, Thinker Magazine, 1930. Engaged in hist. research throughout world, hdq. in London and Paris. Founder and pres. Hist. Foundations (for research); mem. editorial bd. Ednl. Foundations. Mem. Phi Beta Kappa and many learned socs. Organized Brady Secret Service negatives (authorized by President Lincoln) with bd. of 45 mil. authorities into Photographic History of the Civil War (10 vols.), 1910-11; with bd. of 50 authorities History of World War I (8 vols.), 1914-19; True Stories of Great War (6 vols.), 1914-18. Author: Martyrs on Altar of Civilization, 1907; American Hero Tales, 1909; Portrait Life of Lincoln, 1910; American Wonder Stories, 1913; Earth Study, 1913; America's Greatest Battleground—Gettysburg, 1913; World's Crisis, 1914; New Nativity, 1914; America—the Land We Love, 1915; International Geographical History of World (with Admiral Robert E. Peary); World Religions (6 vols.), 1927; Lindbergh—His Story in Pictures, 1928; The World's Great Adventure: History of 1000 Years of Polar Exploration, 1929; World in the Air: Documentary History of Aviation (2 vols.), 1930; Life of Thomas A. Edison, 1931; Biography General Douglas MacArthur—Fighter for Freedom (from family and War Dept. Records), 1942; Biography General Dwight D. Eisenhower, 1944; History of World War II, 1946 (with spl. messages from Pres. Roosevelt, Gen. Eisenhower, Gen. MacArthur and war leaders); Filius Nullus (novel) (cognomen St. Thomas Miller); collaborator (with Ann Woodward Miller) on People You Know, 1947; (with Connie Mack) My 66 Years in the Big League: Great Story of America's national game, 1950. Editor: Wonder Book of the Air, 1941. Dramatist Deliverance, with Helen Keller. Adapt.: (with Vera McCord) Booth Tarkington's Man on Horseback; Hamlet, with Asta Neilson; Macbeth; Christopher Columbus; Diana, from Grecian classics. Collaborated with Captain Rowan Thomas, on Born in Battle, 1943. Pres. Assn. Pub. Am. Records, Searchlight Orgn. for Economic Research; pres. Fine Arts of America; dir. National Survey. Now conducting research for History of the World, with bd. of eminent scientists. Home: 5 Old Kings Highway, Old Greenwich, Conn. Died Nov. 1, 1959.

MILLER, Frederic Magoun, lawyer; b. Des Moines, Ia., Feb. 18, 1896; s. Jesse A. and Emily Willston (Magoun) M.; B.A., Grinnell Coll., 1921 (as of 1918); J.D., State U. Ia., 1922; LL.D., Parsons Coll., 1946; m. Margaret Littleton, Sept. 8, 1922; children—Frederic L., Margaret Ann, Rosemary. Admitted to Ia. bar, Oct. 6, 1921, and since practiced at Des Moines; mem. Miller, Kelly, Shuttleworth & McManus, 1922-29, Miller, Miller & Miller, 1929-38; justice Supreme Ct. Ia., 1939-46; sr. mem. firm Miller, Davis, Hise & Howland, 1946-52; now mem. Brody, Parker, Miller, Roberts & Thoma. Served as 2d lt., 1st and 15th Cav., AEF, 1917-19. Mem. Am., Ia. State (pres. 1945-46) bar assns., Beta Theta Pi, Phi Delta Phi, Phi Beta Kappa, Order of Coif. Republican. Conglist. Mason (33°, Shriner). Club: Des Moines. Home: 7018 Del Matro St. Address: Empire Bldg., Des Moines 9, Ia. Died June 8, 1958.

MILLER, Frederick A., newspaper publisher; b. South Bend, Ind., Jan. 31, 1868; s. Alfred B. and Esther A. (Tarbell) M.; grad. high sch., South Bend, 1887; honorary LL.D., University of Notre Dame and Ind. U.; married Flora Dunn, June 8, 1892. With South Bend Tribune, 1887—, pres., 1924—. Delegate to Republican Nat. Conv., 1924. Mem. Am. Soc. Newspaper Editors, Ind. Republican Editorial Assn., South Bend Assn. of Commerce (1st pres.), Northern Ind. Hist. Soc., Ind. Hist. Soc., Royal Arcanum, South Bend Humane Soc., Citizens' Hist. Assn. Presbyn. Clubs: Rotary, Country; Nat. Press (Washington); South Bend Kiwanis (hon. mem.). Home: 1307 E. Jefferson Blvd. Address: 225 W. Colfax Av., South Bend, Ind. Died Nov. 29, 1954.

MILLER, Frederick A., shoe mfr.; b. Columbus, O., Oct. 14, 1879; s. William A. and Anne Marie (Halbedel) M.; Ph.B., Ohio State U., 1901; m. Roberta B. Miller, Apr. 28, 1909; children—Edward, William, Frances Anne. With H. C. Godman Co., mfrs. shoes, 1901-—, chmn. bd.; dir. Marble Cliff Quarries Co., Columbus-Coated Fabrics Co.; pres., dir. Berwick Corp., Leland Electric Co., The Skidoo Co. Vice chmn. Franklin County Community War Service, 1917-19; chmn. Colubus and Franklin County Community Fund, 1926-27; commd. lt. col. for services as chmn. relief and rehabilitation of Lorain after cyclone disaster, 1924; mem. War Service Com. and Code Authority of Boot and Shoe Industry, World War I; mem. Franklin County Public Housing Authority, 1934. Mem. Nat. Assn. Boot and Shoe Mfrs. (pres. 1935-36, chmn. bd. 1937-38, 39), Phi Beta Kappa, Sigma Alpha Epsilon. Clubs: Columbus, Columbus Athletic Athletic, Columbus Country, Rocky Fork Hunt and Country. Home: 2065 Barton Pl. Office: 46 E. Fulton St., and 2260 E. Main St., Columbus 9, O. Died 1948.

MILLER, George, shoe mfg. exec.; b. Paris, France, 1889; m. Lottie Rabinowitz, 1918; children—Richard Alan, Jacquelyn (Mrs. Katzenskin). Pres. I. Miller & Sons, Inc., and subsidiaries; dir. Nat. Shoe Mfrs. Assn., Compo Shoe Machinery Corp. Mem. shoe adv. bd. WPB, OPA, World War II. Home: 101 Central Park West, N.Y.C. Office: 43-10 23d St., Long Island City, N.Y. Died Oct. 3, 1950.

MILLER, Gerrit Smith, Jr., zoologist; b. Peterboro, N.Y., Dec. 6, 1869; s. Gerrit Smith and Susan (Dixwell) M.; A.B., Harvard U., 1894; m. Elizabeth Eleanor Page, 1897; m. 2d, Anne Chapin Gates, 1921. Asst. curator mammals, U.S. Nat. Mus., 1898-1909, curator, 1909-40, asso. in biology, 1941-—. Fellow A.A.A.S.; mem. Am. Acad. Arts and Scis., Am. Philos. Soc.; corr. mem. Acad. Natural Scis. (Phila.), Zool. Soc. London. Clubs: Cosmos, Arts (Washington). Wrote: The Families and Genera of Bats; Catalogue of the Land Mammals of Western Europe in the British Museum; List of North American Land Mammals in the United States National Museum, 1911; List of North American Recent Mammals, 1923; about 400 monographs and contbns. to sci. jours. Address: U.S. National Museum, Washington. Died Feb. 24, 1956.

MILLER, Harold C., govt. ofcl.; b. Saginaw, Mich., May 22, 1889; s. William H. and Bertha (Meyer) M.; B.S., E.M., Mich. Coll. Mines, 1911; m. Hazel Gunter Glarke, May 22, 1916; 1 dau., Barbara Jeanne. Engaged in engring. and contracting bus., Bishop, Cal., 1911-17; supt. Round Valley Tungsten Co., 1919-20; supt. Bishop Creek Mines, 1919-20; petroleum engr. Standard Oil Co. of Cal., 1920-23; petroleum engr. U.S. Bur. Mines, San Francisco, 1923-—, regional dir. Region III, 1949-—; inventor. Recipient Distinguished Service Award for outstanding contbns. to petroleum tech., Dept. of Interior, 1955. Mem. Am. Inst. Mining and Metall. Engrs., Am. Petroleum Inst. Club: Engineers (San Francisco). Author: Function of Natural Gas in the Production of Oil, 1929; other books and papers on petroleum engring. research. Home: 551 Florence Av., Oakland 18, Cal. Died Dec. 18, 1955.

MILLER, Harvey H., business exec.; b. Cin., O., 1883. Pres., dir. The American Laundry Machine Co.; v.p., dir. George Weidemann Brewing Co., Newport, Ky.; dir. Cin. Gas & Electric Co. Vice pres., dir. Mercantile Exchange; trustee Cin. Better Bus. Bur., Inc. Dir. Ohio C. of C., Campbell County Protestant Orphans Home. Mem. Newcomen Soc. of Eng. Clubs: Queen (gov.), Cincinnati Country, Commercial, Optimists. Home: 1102 Park Av., Newport, Ky. Office: 5050 Section Av., Norwood Station, Cin. 12. Died May 19, 1950.*

MILLER, Helen Topping, writer; b. Fenton, Mich., Dec. 8, 1884; d. Isaac Wallace and Maria Augusta (Chipman) Topping; grad. Mich. Agrl. Coll., 1905; m. F(rank) Roger Miller, June 16, 1910; children—John Wallace (dec.), F. Eugene. Episcopalian. Mem. Tenn. Press Writers Club. Author numerous books, 1931-—; latest publs.: Born Strangers, 1949; Cameo, 1950; The Proud Young Thing, 1951; Witch Water, 1952; Hollow Silver, 1953; Slow Dies the Thunder, 1954; Sing One Song, 1955; After the Glory, 1958. Home: Arrowhill Farm, Talbott, Tenn. Died Feb. 1960 .

MILLER, Henry Russell, author; b. Sidney, O., May 12, 1880; s. Robert Johnson and Anna Elizabeth (Shepherd) M.; A.B., Westminster Coll., New Wilmington, Pa., 1899; m. Jean Melrose Leitch, of New York, Apr. 8, 1809; 1 dau., Helen Jean. Admitted to bar, 1903, and since in practice at Pittsburgh; pres. The Crescent Press, Pittsburgh; dir. Pittsburgh Thrift Corp. Mem. United Presbyn. Ch. Author: The Man Higher Up, 1910; His Rise to Power, 1911; The

Ambition of Mark Truitt, 1913; The House of Toys, 1914; The First Division, 1920. Home: 6605 Virginia Av., Bn Avon, Pitts. 2. Office: 1414 Brighton Rd., Pitts. Died Dec. 16, 1955; buried Uniondale Cemetery, Pitts.

MILLER, Isaac Eugene, clergyman; b. Bloomingdale, O., Jan. 16, 1879; s. Thomas Johnson and Mary Ann (Munden) M.; A.B., Mt. Union-Scio Coll., Alliance, O., 1906; D.D., 1917; B.D., Drew Theol. Sem., 1909; m. Clara Palmer, Aug. 16, 1906; children—Kenneth Palmer, Clara Pauline (Mrs. Walter M. Koch). Ordained ministry M.E., Church, 1909; pastor Finley M.E. Ch., Steubenville, O., 1909-14, Salem, O., 1914-15, E. Liverpool, O., 1915-17; supt. Youngstown (O.) Dist., 1917-21, Cleve. Dist., 1921-25; pastor King Av. M.E. Ch., Columbus, O., 1925-38; became supt .Columbus Dist., 1930; pastor Hyde Park Meth. Ch., Cin., 1938-41; supt. Cin. Dist. Meth. Ch., 1941-1947, Urbana Meth. Ch., 1947-49. Chmn. O. Pastors Conv. 1932-33; mem. Gen. Conf. M.E. Ch., 1920, 28, 32, 36 (gen. chmn. entertainment com. at Columbus Conf., 1936). Pres. bd. trustees O. Ann. Conf. (chmn. Commn. World Service and Finance); dir. Ohio Council Chs. Home: 6837 Greismer Av., North Coll. Hill, Cin. 39. Died Jan. 3, 1955; buried Spring Grove, Cin.

MILLER, James Conelese, coll. pres.; b. Eugene, Mo., Nov. 14, 1891; s. James Perry and Emma (Curty) M.; B.S. in Edn., Central Mo. State Teachers Coll., 1925, M.A., U. of Mo., 1927, Ph.D., 1930; studied U. of Chicago, 1929; m. Ennell Harlan, Sept. 26, 1917; children—Jean Eleanor (Mrs. J. Greg Bartels), Carolyn Harlan (Mrs. Lawrence E. Stern, Jr.), Barbara Ann (Mrs. William F. Sikes). Teacher rural sch., 1909-11; supt. Otterville (Mo.) High Sch., 1913-15; cashier Bank of Fortuna, Fortuna, Mo., 1915-17; supt. Otterville (Mo.) pub. schs., 1922-26; prin. University Elementary Sch., U. of Mo., 1926-27; dean of faculty, Christian Coll., 1927-35; dean of faculty, Northwest Mo. State Teachers Coll., 1935-37; pres., Christian Coll., 1938-—. Served in U.S. Naval Res. Force, World War. Pres. Am. Assn. Jr. Colls., 1941; v.p. N. Central Assn. Colls. and Secondary Schs., 1946-47; mem. Am. Assn. Sch. Adminstrs., Phi Delta Kappa. Democrat. Mason. Clubs: Columbia Country, Columbia Rotary. Contbr. articles to Junior Coll. Jour. and U. of Mo. bull. Address: Christian Coll., Columbia, Mo. Died Nov. 16, 1956.

MILLER, Joseph Henry, railroad exec.; b. Hannibal, Mo., June 17, 1890; s. Henry and Margaret (Brady) M.; LL.B., St. Louis U., 1923, LL.M., 1924; m. Mary C. Reder, Feb. 11, 1915 (dec. 1950); 1 dau., Margaret Mary (Mrs. Courtney G. Pitkin). Admitted to Mo. bar, 1922; asst. atty. Wabash R.R., St. Louis, 1923-25, asst. gen. atty., 1925-40, gen. atty., 1940-45, gen. solicitor, 1945-50, gen. counsel, 1950-—; dir. Am. Refrigerator Transit Co. Mem. St. Louis C. of C. Clubs: Traffic, Glen Echo Country (St. Louis). Home: 7221 Northmoor Dr., University City 5, Mo. Office: Railway Exchange Bldg., St. Louis 1. Died Jan. 2, 1955; buried Calvary Cemetery Mausoleum, St. Louis.

MILLER, Joseph Hillis, educator; b. Reform, Va., Aug. 29, 1899; s. Joseph Walter and Millie Elizabeth (Brown) M.; student Randolph-Macon Academy; A.B., U. Richmond, 1924, LL.D., 1951, Alfred U., 1945; A.M., U. Va., 1925; Ph.D., Columbia, 1934; Litt.D., Keuka Coll., 1941; D.H.L., Yeshiva U., 1949; D.Sc., U. Tampa, 1951; m. Nellie M. Critzer, Sept. 11, 1925; children—Joseph Hillis, William Hopkins. Instr. psychology William and Mary Coll., 1926-28; dean freshmen, asst. prof. psychology Bucknell U., 1930-32, dean students, asst. prof. psychology, 1932-35; pres. Keuka Coll., 1935-41; asso. commr. edn. State of N.Y., 1941-47; pres. Univ. Fla. since 1947; lectr. tchrs. coll. Columbia, summer 1937. Dir. Jacksonville Br. Fed. Res. Bank Atlanta, since 1948, chmn., 1951. Mem. commn. development grad. studies So. Regional Council Edn. since 1949; mem. bd. control So. Regional Edn. since 1949; mem. com. coop. higher edn. So. U. Conf. since 1950; mem. exec. com. Southeastern Conf. since 1950. Mem. Nat. Commn. Citizens Com. Reorgn. Govt. since 1949; mem. Nat. Organizing Com. First Freedom Internat., 1951; chmn. March of Dimes Campaign, State of Fla., 1950, 51. Mem. bd. trustees Colgate-Rochester Sem.; mem. bd. dirs. Inst. Internat. Edn.; sponsor Found. Integrated Edn.; mem. adv. com. Yeshiva Med. Center, 1951; mem. bd. dirs. Gainesville (Fla.) Boys Club, 1951. Mem. Nat. Coll. Personnel Assn., Nat. Council Guidance and Personnel Assn., Am. Psychol. Assn., N.Y. State Examination Bd., Commn. Instns. Higher Edn. of Middle States Assn., Nat. Youth Adminstrn. (mem. nat., state adv. com.), Fgn. Policy Assn. (pres., Albany, N.Y. br.), N.E.A., Nat. Council Religion Higher Edn., Am. Council Edn. (mem. com. religion and edn., planning and policies com. since 1951), Newcomen Soc. Eng., Nat. Assn. State Univs. (mem. radio com.), Nat. Commn. Accrediting (mem. exec. com.), Nat. Selection Com. for Inst. Internat. Edn. (chmn. exec. com. 1951), Fla. State C. of C. (mem. bd. dirs. since 1947), Gainesville C. of C., Fla. Blue Key, Phi Beta Kappa, Phi Alpha Delta, Sigma Phi Epsilon, Phi Kappa Phi, Tau Kappa Alpha, Pi Gamma Mu, Omicron Delta Kappa. Baptist (mem. Gen. Council, No. Bapt. Conv.). Democrat. Mason. Clubs: University (N.Y.C.); Golf and Country, Rotary (Gainesville). Author: The Origin of Pragmatism; Radical Empiricism and Public Prayer, 1934; The Possible Blackout of Baptist Schools and Colleges, 1940; The Role of Higher Education in the War and After, 1944; The Higher Education of Veterans in New York State, 1947; The Veterans Challenge the Colleges, 1947. Contbr. to Student Personnel Services in Colleges and Universities; Religion in the State Universities; Religion and Public Education; The Teaching of Religion in American Higher Education; American Education and Religion; also more than 100 articles to leading jours. and mags. on same subjects. Home: 224 N.E. 10th Av., Gainesville, Fla. Died Nov. 14, 1953; buried Lebanon Cemetery, nr. Afton, Va.

MILLER, Kennth Hayes, painter, etcher; born Aneida Community, Oneida, N.Y., Mar. 11, 1876; s. George Noyes and Annie Elizabeth (Kelley) M.; ed. Horace Mann Sch., Art Students' League; studied at New York School of Art; in Europe, 1900; m. Irma Ferry, 1898; m. 2d, Helen Pendleton, 1911; 1 dau., Louise. Instructor drawing and painting, N.Y. Sch. of Art, 1899-1911, Art Students' League N.Y., 1911-36, 1943. Exhibited Luxembourg Galleries, Paris, Venice (Italy), Carnegie Internat., etc.; exclusive exhbn. Montross Galleries, New York, 1919, 22, 25, Rehn Galleries, 1929, 31, 33, 35, 38, 41. Rep. in collections Wadsworth Atheneum Hartford, Conn., Met. Museum, Pub. Library, and Whitney Museum of Am. Art, Museum of Modern Art (New York), Cleveland Museum of Art, Philadelphia Museum Art, Phillips Acad. (Andover, Mass.), Los Angeles Museum, Phillips Memorial Gallery (Washington, D.C.), Va. Museum of Fine Arts, Congressional Library (Washington), Art Institute of Chicago, Fine Art Gallery (San Diego, Calif.), Columbus (O.) Gallery of Fine Arts, Bibliothèque National (Paris), etc. Awarded gold medal for painting by Nat. Acad. Design, 1943; painting award, National Academy of Design, 1947. Awarded Ada S. Garrett prize, Art Institute of Chicago Annual, 1945. Mem. Nat. Inst. Arts and Letters, Am. Soc. Painters, Sculptors and Gravers, American Printmakers, Phila. Soc. Etchers, Soc. Am. Etchers; mem. Nat. Acad. of Design, Artists Equity, Audobon Artists. Home: 119 E. 10th St. Studio: 30 E. 14th St., N.Y.C. 3. Died Jan. 1, 1952; buried Oneida Community Cemetery, Kenwood, N.Y.

MILLER, Leo Edward, author, explorer; b. Huntingburg, Ind., May 11, 1887; s. Bernhardt and Maria (Herrndorf) M.; ed. high sch., business coll., Indianapolis Conservatory of Music, Sch. of Expression, Indianapolis, and under pvt. teachers; m. Clarissa Amelia Kelsey, of Clinton, Conn., and N.Y. City, Apr. 2, 1918; children—Leo Edward, Spencer Kelsey. With Oakley Chem. Co., New York. Student Plattsburg, O.T.C., 1917; commd. 1st lt. Aviation Service; instr. Camp Dix, Dallas, Tex., and Camp Jackson, Columbia, S.C. Chmn. of Board of Education, Stratford, Conn. Spent nearly 7 yrs. in S. America as leader of exploring parties; mem. Theodore Roosevelt's S. Am. expdn. Corr. mem. Zool. Soc. of Buenos Aires; mem. New Haven Co. Hort. Soc.; hon. mem. Dartmouth Alumni Assn. of Bridgeport. Clubs: Explorers' (New York); Towne Criers (Stratford). Author: In the Wilds of South America, 1918; The Hidden People, 1920; In the Tiger's Lair, 1921; The Black Phantom, 1922; Adrift on the Amazon, 1923; The Jungle Pirates, 1925. Home: Floral Park, Stratford, Conn. Died Oct. 6, 1952; buried Clinton (Conn.) Cemetery.

MILLER, Leslie Freeland, flour milling exec.; b. Valley City, N.D., Aug. 25, 1883; s. Arthur and Clara Adelle (Russell) M.; student U. Minn., 1902-05; m. Harriet Rowley, Nov. 24, 1914; children—Martha, Rowley, Arthur, Janet. Salesman with Russell-Miller Milling Co., 1905-07, mill mgr., 1907-21, western mgr., 1921-42, sec., 1928-39, v.p., treas., 1939-43, pres., 1943-53, chmn. bd. until 1954, ret. 1954; v.p. Sweetheart Bakeries Co., Minot, N.D., 1928, Bismarck Bakery Co., Bismarck, N.D., 1938, Sweetheart Bakery Co., Miles City, N.D., 1944, Sweetheart Bread Co., Billings, Mont., 1946-—; dir. N.P. Ry., 1946; v.p. Billings Investment Co., 1931-—. Conglist. Clubs: Woodhill; Minneapolis. Home: Route 3, Box 95, Wayzata, Minn. Office: 900 Midland Bank Bldg., Mpls. Died Nov. 29, 1958.

MILLER, Logan C., automotive exec.; b. Mattoon, Ill., Jan. 7, 1887; s. Charles Thomas and Martha Ann (Smith); student U. Ill., 1908-09; m. Blanche Grace Colby, Dec. 18, 1911; children—Richard C., Fredrick Allen. Various jobs tool and die and machinists trade, 1909-14; with Ford Motor Co., 1914-—, asst. mgr. Willow Run Bomber Plant, 1941-45, vice president of the basic products group. Mason (K.T.). Clubs: Detroit Athletic; Barton Hills Country. Home: 2107 Tuomy Rd., Ann Arbor, Mich. Office: Ford Motor Company, 3000 Schaefer Rd., Dearborn, Mich. Died Feb. 27, 1958; buried Washtenong Meml. Park.

MILLER, Loren Barker, govt. researcher; b. Menominee, Mich., June 20, 1906; s. Frederick F. and Florence E. (Barker) M.; A.B., U. Mich., 1924-28; student (intermittently), N.Y.U. 1934-39; married 1929; children—Loren Boyle, Paul Dirk. Staff asst. Detroit Bur. Govt. Research, 1928-29; asst. dir. Eric (Pa.) County Taxpayers Assn., 1929-30; spl. dir. study on local finance and procedure for Mich. Commn. Inquiry, Detroit Bur. Govt. Research, 1930-33; asst. dir., Citizens' Adv. Com., Newark, 1933-35; municipal credit analyst Dun & Bradstreet, 1935-36; asst. dir. Municipal Finance Officers Assn. U.S. and Can., 1936; Bur. Municipal Research, Newark, 1937-40; dir. Civic Research Inst., Kansas City, Mo., 1940-44, on leave in 1943 as dir. survey of field adminstrn. for Nat. Housing Agy.; dir. Citizens Research Council Mich., 1944-—; research dir. Joint Legislative Com. on Reorgn. Mich. Govt., 1949-53. Mem. Govt. Research Assn., Am. Soc. Pub. Adminstrn., Nat. Tex Assn., Phi Beta Kappa, Phi Kappa Phi. Office: 810 Farwell Bldg., Detroit 26. Died May 23, 1958.

MILLER, M. V., pres. Royal Typewriter Co., Inc. Address: 2 Park Av., N.Y.C. 16. Died Aug. 29, 1951.

MILLER, Nathan L., ex-gov. N.Y., lawyer; b. Solon, N.Y., Oct. 10, 1868; s. Samuel and Almera (Russell) M.; grad. Groton (N.Y.) Union Sch., 1883, Cortland Normal Sch., 1887; LL.D., Columbia, Syracuse, Colgate, Union; m. Elizabeth Davern, Nov. 23, 1896; children—Mrs. Mildred McCarthy, Mrs. Margaret Blakeley, Mrs. Marian Labourdette, Mrs. Elizabeth Adams, Mrs. Louise Robinson, Mrs. Eleanor Carmody, Mrs. Constance Phelps. Tchr. pub. schs., 1887-89; admitted to N.Y. bar, 1893; corp. counsel, Cortland, 1901-02; sch. commr. 1st dist. Cortland County, 1894-1900; state comptroller, 1902-03; justice Supreme Ct. of N.Y., 6th Jud. Dist., 1903-13; asso. justice Appellate Div., 2d Dept., 1905-10, 1st Dept., 1910-13; asso. judge Court of Appeals, 1913-15; resigned, and resumed practice of the law, 1915; gov. N.Y., 1921-23; gen. counsel, dir. and mem. finance com., U.S. Steel Corp. Republican. Home: Hotel Pierre, N.Y.C. Office: 71 Broadway, N.Y.C. Died June 26, 1953; buried Cortland, N.Y.

MILLER, Nellie Burget (Mrs. L. A.), author; b. Fayette, Ia., June 6, 1875; d. E. L. and Mary M. (Ashby) Burget; B.S., Upper Ia. U., 1894; hon. M. Litt., University of Colorado, 1925; Litt.D. (hon.) Upper Iowa Univ., 1945; m. L. A. Miller, M.D., 1894; children—Dorothy J. Benkelman, Arnold Hugh (lt. col. Med. Corps), Muriel Imogene Merritt. Pres. State Fedn. Women's Clubs, Colo., 1920-22; chmn. lit. for Gen. Fedn. Women's Clubs, 1922-26, chmn. fine arts, 1926-28; speaker at nat. and state convs.; poet laureate of Colorado by appointment of Governor Sweet, 1923. Member League of American Pen Women (president Colorado branch 3 years), P.E.O., Pi Gamma Mu (hon.), Delta Kappa Gamma (hon.). Club: Portia. Author: Garden Year Book, 1915; Land Where the Good Dreams Grow, 1921; The Fleece of Gold, 1921; The Flame of God, 1924; In Earthen Bowls, 1924; The Living Drama, 1924; The Blue Moon, Pictures from the Plains and Other Poems, 1936; The Sun Drops Red, 1947; In the Tents of the Shepherd Prince (folk-play), 1950. Organizer and pres. Colo. Springs Poetry Fellowship, 1943-47. Compiled anthology "Verses for Victory" for gratuitous distribution to service men 1944. Home: 20 W. Washington, Colorado Springs, Colo. Died June 4, 1952; buried Crown Hill Cemetery, Denver.

MILLER, Otto, investment banker; b. Cleve., July 3, 1874; s. James Hawkins and Sophie (Maxmilian) M.; prep. edn., University Sch., Cleve.; Ph.B., Yale, 1896; m. Elisabeth Clark Tyler, Dec. 4, 1901; children—Otto, Washington Samuel Tyler; m. 2d, Elsa Gertrude Woolworth, May 24, 1913; 1 dau., Barbara Woolworth. Began in investment banking business with Lamprecht Bros. & Co., Cleve., 1899; founded (with Warren S. Hayden) firm Hayden, Miller & Co., 1903; dir. of many corps. Mem. Ohio N.G. 13 yrs.; 2 mos., advancing to maj. Cav.; served as a.d.c. to Govs. Herrick, Pattison and Harmon; q.m. sgt. Ohio Cav., Span-Am. War, 1898; commd. maj. 37th Div., U.S. Army, 1917, later asst. chief of staff and lt. col.; in active service at Baccarat, Avocourt and Pannes sectors, also Mense-Argonne and Ypres-Lys offensives. Mem. S.A.R., Spanish War Vets., Loyal Legion, Am. Legion, Mil. Order Fgn. Wars. Decorated Croix de Guerre (Belgian and French). Republican. Clubs: Union, Mid-Day, Country (Cleve.). Home: 2700 Easton Rd., Shaker Heights, O. Office: 1840 Union Commerce Bldg., Cleve. 14. Died June 13, 1950; buried Lakeview Cemetery, Cleve.

MILLER, Paul E(mmert), banker; born Cedar Rapids, Ia., Oct. 30, 1888; s. Jacob Kurtz and Ida (Bluebaugh) M.; B.S., Ia. State Coll., 1911, M.S. in Agr., 1921; D.Econ. Sci. (hon.), Nat. U. Ireland, 1951; m. Margaret Jones, June 23, 1914; children—John, Edward, Paul. Instr. agronomy U. Minn. West Central Sch. Agr. and Expt. Sta., Morris, Minn., 1911-17; prof. and supt. W. Central Sch. of Agr. and Agrl. Expt. Sta., 1917-38; prof. and dir. U. Minn. Agrl. Extension Service, St. Paul, 1938-54; mem. bd. dirs. Mpls. Fed. Res. Bank, 1943-54, dep.

chmn. bd. dirs., 1953—; member board of governors Federal Reserve System, 1954—; member of board dirs. 7th district Farm Credit Adminstn., 1953-54. Federal Land Bank of St. Paul, 1946-49. Appointed drought relief dir. Minn., 1934; mem. Minn. State adv. com. Farmers Home Adminstrn., Minn. State Soil Conservation Commn. (chmn. 1941-49), Minn. State adv. com. U.S. Prodn., Marketing Adminstrn.; collaborator U.S. Dept. Agr., 1921; agrl. cons. Orgn. for European Econ. Coöp. to survey agrl. adv. services in Marshall Plan Countries, 1950; chief E.C.A. Spl. Mission to Ireland, 1950-51; apptd. to Pres.'s Commn. on Migratory Agrl. Labor, 1950; mem. nat. adv. com. on agrl. labor to Dir. U.S. Employment Service since 1948; chmn. nat. com. to survey 4-H Club work, 1947; mem. Nat. Com. of Extension Orgn. and Policy, 1946-48 (chmn. 1949). Mem. Am. Assn. Land Grant Colls. and Univs. (chmn. agrl. extension sect. 1946), Minn. Acad. Sci., Phi Sigma Kappa, Alpha Zeta, Gamma Sigma Delta, Delta Sigma Rho. Author numerous agrl. extension reports. Home: 5110 Marlyn Dr., Massachusetts Av. Hills, Washington 16. Office: Board of Governors, Federal Reserve System, Washington. Died Oct. 21, 1954.

MILLER, Paul Gerard, educator; b. Pickett, Winnebago County, Wis., Jan. 23, 1875; s. John Frederick and Julia Anne M.; grad. State Normal Sch., Oshkosh, Wis., 1896; B.A., U. of Wis., 1910, M.A., 1911, Ph.D., 1914; Doctor of Education, honoris causa. Univ. of Puerto Rico, 1940; m. Ella A. Rasmussen, Nov. 9, 1899; children—Virgil Rasmus, Horace Gerard, Edith Sarah (Mrs. Donald Macaulay). Began as teacher in the public schools of Wis., 1894; private Co. D, 2d Wis. Regt. Vol. Inf., Spanish-Am. War, Apr. 21-Nov. 14, 1898; participated in Puerto Rican expdn.; supervisor schs., San German, P.R., 1899-1902; supt. schs., San Juan, 1902; chief div. supervision, Dept. of Edn., P.R., 1902-03; prin. Insula Normal Sch., 1903-08; asst. in Romance langs., U. of Wis., 1908-10; prof. edn., Carleton Coll., Northfield, Minn., 1910-11; instr. Romance langs., 1911-14, asst. prof., 1914-15, U. of Wis.; commr. edn. Puerto Rico, 1915-21; with Rand McNally & Co., 1921-47, ret. Pres. trustees U. of P.R.; mem. Exec. Council of P.R., 1915-21; mem. Pub. Service Com. and pres. Teachers' Pension Fund Bd., 1917-21; del. from P.R. to 2d Pan-Am. Scientific Congress, Washington, 1915-16. Member Nat. Edn. Assn., Nat. Geog. Soc., United Spanish War Vets.; fellow Am. Geog. Society, honorary member, Comité Cultural Argentino. Editor: Sapnish-Am, edits. of Hale's A Man Without a Country, Shakespeare's Julius Caesar; Linares Rivas' El Abolengo y La Cizaña; Manual para Globos Terrestres. Author: Civil Government of Porto Rico; Spanish-American Readers; also 6 annual reports on Education in Porto Rico; Historia de Puerto Rico, 1922, 1939, 1946, 47, 48, 49. Contbr. to mags. Has traveled extensively in Spanish speaking countries. Address: Winneconne, Wis. Died May 21, 1952; buried Winneconne.

MILLER, R. T., Jr., educator, publisher; b. Scottsville, N.Y., Feb. 23, 1867; s. R. T. and Etta (Fraser) M.; Ph.B., Oberlin, 1891, A.M., 1898; LL.B., Harvard, 1896. Pres. Am. Sch., 1897-1936. Pres. Am. Tech. Soc. (pubs.), 1898-1940. Ret. 1936. Episcopalian. Clubs: Quadrangle, City, Harvard (Chgo.); University (Winter Park, Fla.). Home: Fraser Farm, Scottsville, N.Y. Died July 27, 1958; buried Scottsville.

MILLER, Ralph English, pathologist, educator; b. Tustin, Mich., Jan. 13, 1899; s. Ward Beecher and Agnes Philena (English) M.; B.S., Dartmouth, 1921-24, student medicine, 1924-25; M.D., Harvard, 1928; M.S., U. Minn., 1931; m. Elizabeth Skolfield, June 15, 1925; children—Ralph English, Elizabeth Giveen (Mrs. William Congdon), Barbara Jane (Mrs. Theodore Randell). Intern Mary Hitchcock Meml. Hosp., 1928-29; asst. instr. biology Dartmouth, 1925-26, asst. prof. pathology, 1931-41, prof., 1941—, asst. dean Med. Sch., 1936-44; pathologist Mary Hitchcock Meml. Hosp., 1931—, dir. labs., 1936—; sr. cons. VA Hosp., White River Junction, Vt., 1946—. Pres. N.H. Bd. Health, 1942-53. Recipient award Am. Cancer Soc., 1955. Mem. Am. Cancer Soc., Am. Assn. Pathologists and Bacteriologists, A.M.A., New Eng. Path. Soc., N.H. Med. Soc., New Eng. Cancer Soc., Coll. Am. Pathologists, A.A.A.S. Home: 9 Downing Rd. Hanover, N.H. Died Feb. 25, 1959.

MILLER, Richard Henry, surgeon; b. Fitchburg, Mass., Oct. 11, 1884; s. Ernest Parker and Myra Bolles (Richardson) M.; A.B., Harvard, 1905, M.D., 1910; m. Georgina Mary Jardine, Sept. 23, 1922; 1 son, Richard H., Jr. Began practice at Boston, 1910; mem. bd. consultation Massachusetts General Hosp.; cons. surgeon Boston Lying-in Hosp., Heywood, Leominster Hospital; consultant at Pawtucket Hospital, Pawtucket, R.I. Served as maj. Medical Corps, United States Army, regimental surg., 101st F.A., World War I. Awarded Purple Heart with oak-leaf cluster; Silver Star. Fellow American College Surgeons; mem. American Surgical Assn., Internat. Surg. Soc., N.E. Surg. Soc., Surg. Research Soc. Republican. Mason. Club: Harvard (Boston). Author: Tuberculosis of the Lymphatic System, 1934. Contbr. to med. and surg. jours. Home: 64 Myrtle St. (14). Office: 264 Beacon St., Boston 16. Died June 3, 1953.

MILLER, Robert Walter, oil exec.; b. Newark, N.J., May 5, 1896; s. William Henry and Emma (Hellriegel) M.; student N.Y.U., 1919-21, Columbia, 1917; m. Lillian J. Best, June 14, 1923; 1 dau., Lillian Jane (Mrs. Harry Ohde Bartlett). Accountant Diehl Mfg. Co., Elizabeth, N.J., 1914-16, W. A. Clark Wire Co., Elizabeth, 1916-17; timekeeper Standard Oil Co., Bayway Refinery, Elizabeth, 1919, transferred to Refinery Yield and Cost Div., 1919-20, mfg. dept. office N.Y. City, 1920-23, office dir. mfg., 1923-25, dept. coordinating worldwide operations, 1925-44, sales mgr. subsidiary N.J. Creole Petroleum Corp., N.Y. City, 1944-47, v.p., 1947—, dir., 1948—. Served in Naval Aviation U.S. N.R.F., active duty, 1917-18; mem. Caribbean Area Petroleum Com. of Petroleum Adminstr. for War, World War II. Mem. Fgn. Petroleum Supply Com. Mem. Am. Petroleum Inst., Venezuelan C. of C. Republican. Clubs: Shenorock Shore, Apawamis (Rye). Home: 52 Old Well Rd., White Plains. Office: 350 Fifth Av., N.Y.C. Died Dec. 10, 1954; buried Greenfield Cemetery, Hempstead, L.I., N.Y.

MILLER, Samuel Charles, dentist; b. New York, N.Y., Nov. 15, 1903; s. Abraham and Sarah (Miller) M.; student Coll. of City of N.Y., 1919-20; D.D.S., N.Y. Univ., 1925; m. Mae Rodgers, June 12, 1927; children—Barbara Marsak, Stphanie. Prof., chmn. Periodontia Dept.; honorary professor University Santo Domingo; cons. teacher U.S. Navy; consultant VA. Lt. USNR, ret. Chairman American Board of Oral Medicine. Fellow American College Dentists, Pierre Fanchard Acad., American Academy of Dental Medicine, A.A.A.S.; asso. fellow N.Y. Acad. Medicine; mem. Am. Dental Assn., N.Y. State Dental Society, Research Soc. Am., Am. Academy Periodontology, N.Y. Inst. Clinical Oral Pathology, Pan-Am. Odontological Soc. (v.p.), Harvey Soc., Assn. Advancement Oral Diagnosis, Omicron Kappa Upsilon (past pres.), Alumni Assn. New York U. College of Dentistry (past pres.); hon. mem. Bolivian Dental Assn. (Bolivia), El Primer Congreso Nacional de Odontologos (Colombia); president College Dental Soc. of New York U. College of Dentistry; councillor N.Y. Section, International Association for Dental Research. Author: Practical Periodontia (with Sidney Sorrin), 1928. Editor: Oral Diagnosis (with 28 contributors), 1936, 1946; Textbook of Periodontia, 1938, 43, 50. Editor: Spanish English Medical Dental Guide and Interpreter. Contbr. dental jours. Home: 101-05 72d Av., Forest Hills, N.Y. Office: 57 W. 57th St., N.Y.C. 19. Died Feb. 8, 1958; buried Mt. Hebron Cemetery.

MILLER, Sidney Lincoln, transportation economist; b. Ravanna, Kan., March 17, 1890; s. George Washington and Emma Victoria (Gettle) M.; A.B., Kan. State Teachers Coll., 1912; A.M., U. of Wis., 1916, Ph.D., 1920; m. Dorothy Agnes Cooper, March 14, 1936; children—Dorothy Rachael, Linda Karen, Sarah Ann; children by previous marriage—Margaret Emma (Mrs. Eliot Waples), Sidney Lincoln, George Andrew. Teacher in rural school, 1906-07; supt. pub. schs. in Kan., 1912-14; asst. in economics, U. of Wis., 1916-18, instr., 1918-20, asst., prof., 1920-25; prof. of transportation, U. of Ia., 1925-46; dir. bur. business research, 1926-46; prof. and head dept. of transportation and public utilities, U. of Pittsburgh, 1946—; research econ., United Light & Power Co., 1930; research economist, Assn. Am. Roads, 1936-37; consultant, Ia. Commerce Comm., 1941; on leave from U. of Ia., as adminstr. and transportation economist, War Prodn. Bd., Washington, D.C., 1941-43; asst. to dep. dir., Office of Defense Transportation, 1943-46. Consultant, office of Defense Transportation, 1946-47. Research economist W. Tex. C. of C., Tex. & Pacific Ry., 1947-55; transportation cons. Upper Ohio Valley Assn., 1948-49, 52, 54, FCDA, 1951, C.P. Ry., 1952-53; mem. transportation Council U.S. Dept. of Commerce, 1953—. Mem. American Econ. Assn., Am. Soc. Traffic and Transportation, Mid-West Econ. Soc. (pres., 1934-35), Order of Artus (pres.), Theta Chi, Alpha Kappa Psi, Beta Gamma Sigma. Clubs: Tri-City Traffic (Davenport-Rock Island-Moline); Faculty (U. of Pittsburgh), Traffic, Traffic and Transportation (Pittsburgh). Author: Railway Transportation, Principles and Point of View, 1924; Inland Transportation, 1933; (with Virgil D. Cover; Rates of Return, Class I Line-Haul Railways of the United States, 1921-48, 1951; West Texas Tomorrow, 1955. Contributor articles on econ. and transportation subjects to jours. Address: 1715 Ridgeway Dr., Iowa City, Ia. Died Nov. 9, 1957.

MILLER, Spencer, Sr., engineer (retired); b. Waukegan, Ill., Apr. 25, 1859; s. Samuel Fisher and Charlotte (Howe) M.; B.S. in Mech. Engring., Worcester Poly. Inst., 1879, E.Eng. (honorary), 1928; married Harriet M. Ruggles, Jan. 1, 1885; children—Marguerite (Mrs. P. E. Grannis), Spencer, Helen (Mrs. Aurelio Giorni) (deceased); married second, Mrs. L. MacD. Sleeth, 1931 (deceased). Began with Link Belt Company, Chgo., 1881; engr., later chief engr. Lidgerwood Mfg. Co., mfrs. hoisting engines, etc., N.Y.C., 1888-1926, retired. Perfected overhead cableway system used in constrn. of Gatun locks, Panama Canal, and extensively applied on construction of the Hoover Dam, and ther dams; invented an overhead log-skidding cableway now in use in lumber camps generally; a marine cableway for trans-shipping fuel under headway at sea; electric automatic tension towing engine; marine breeches buoy for transferring passengers from one ship to another at sea, used by USN. Mem. Naval Cons. Bd., 1915—. Mem. Am. Soc. M.E., Am. Soc. C.E., Am. Inst. Mining Engrs., Soc. Naval Architects and Marine Engrs., Sigma Xi. Republican. Episcopalian. Author of Joseph Miller of Newton, Mass. (a genealogy). Home: 217 Turrell Av., South Orange, N.J.; and Laguna Beach, Cal. Died June 16, 1953.

MILLER, Theodore Joseph, lawyer; b. N.Y.C., Apr. 15, 1901; s. Theodore D. and Katherine (Keating) M.; LL.B., Fordham U., 1922; m. Eleanor Cloonan, Dec. 10, 1935 (dec. 1942); children—Susan, Donna, Eleanor; m. 2d Gladys Ivie Bijou, May 15, 1948; 1 stepson, Anthony Bijou. Admitted to N.Y. bar, 1923, Conn. bar, 1928, Supreme Ct., 1934; pvt. practice, N.Y.C., 1923—; mem. firm Dunnington, Bartholow & Miller, 1936—. Mem. Assn. Bar N.Y. C., Gamma Eta Gamma. Clubs: Knickerbocker, Racquet and Tennis, Manhattan. Roman Catholic. Home: Starr Ridge Farm, Brewster, N.Y. Office: Chrysler Bldg. East, N.Y.C. Died Dec. 7, 1959.

MILLER, Troup, army officer (ret.); b. Perry, Ga., Feb. 10, 1879; s. Alexander Lawton and Katharine Elvira Flewellyn (Hurt) M.; B.S., U.S. Mil. Acad., 1902; grad. Mounted Service Sch., 1911, Army Staff Coll., Langres, France, 1918, Sch. of the Line, 1921, Army War Coll., 1925; m. Rosa Coffin, Nov. 4, 1903; children—Troup Jr. (Maj. Gen. USAF), Rosa Coffin (wife of Col. Frederic Wood Barnes, Air Force). Commissioned 2d lt., Cav., United States Army, June 12, 1902, and advanced through the grades to brig. gen., Feb. 2, 1943; served on Gen. Staff, 82d Div. I Army Corps, First Army, and Intermediate Sect., Services of Supply, World War I; inspector gen. Eastern Defense Command, Governors Island, N.Y., World War II; retired 1946. Decorated D.S.M., Legion of Merit, Army Commendation ribbon. Mem. Mil. Order World Wars, Assn. of Grads. U.S. Mil. Acad. Author: Supply Principles, 1920. Home: 2332 Dellwood Dr. N.W., Atlanta. Died Jan. 26, 1957; buried Arlington Nat. Cemetery.

MILLER, Walter, petroleum refining cons.; b. Canton Aargau, Switzerland, Mar. 4, 1881; s. John Rudolph and Lina (Hunziker) M.; brought to U.S., 1888, naturalized, 1893; ed. pub. schs., Flemington, Roselle and Elizabeth, N.J., also night schs. and corr. courses; Eng.D. (hon.), U. Tulsa, 1943; m. Katherine Mae McNair, Jan. 1, 1900; children—Katherine Mae (Mrs. Sherwood J. Lahman), Ruth Pitman, Walter (dec.). With Tide Water Oil Co. in refinery, Bayonne, N.J., 1909-17; gen. supt. U.S. refineries, Pierce Oil Corp., Tulsa, 1917; mfg. mgr. Cosden & Co., Tulsa, 1917-20; refinery cons., Tulsa, 1920-22; asso. with Marland Refining Co. (now Continental Oil Co.), Ponca City, Okla., 1922—, mgr., 1922-29, v.p. charge mfg., 1926-46; ret., 1946; petroleum refining cons., 1946—; dir. Gray Processes Corp. Mem. Am. Soc. M.E., Am. Inst. Mining and Metall. Engrs., Am. Soc. Testing Materials, Am. Chem. Soc., Inst. Petroleum (Brit.), Am. Petroleum Inst. Republican. Episcopalian. Clubs: Chemists (N. Y.C.); Conoco Golf (Ponca City). Hon. D. Eng. conferred by U. Tulsa, 1943. Home: 400 N. 4th St. Office: Continental Oil Co., Ponca City, Okla. Died June 8, 1949.

MILLER, William E., electrical mfg.; b. Parkers Landing, Pa., Mar. 26, 1889; s. Jonathan Walker and Mary Ellen (Evans) M.; student Amherst Coll., 1908-10; LL.B., Pittsburgh Law Sch., 1913; m. Elisabeth P. Looney, Oct. 23, 1916; children—Wesley A. L., William E. Mem. law dept. Westinghouse Electric Corporation, Pittsburgh, Pa., 1915-41, head law dept. Pittsburgh office, 1941-44, gen. atty. for co., 1944—. also vice pres. 1945-54, retired 1954. Awarded Westinghouse prize of merit, 1941. Mem. Delta Kappa Epsilon. Rep. Clubs: Duquesne (Pitts.); Seaview Country (Absecon, N.J.). Home: 5505 Atlantic Av., Ventnor, N.J. Died Dec. 28, 1956.

MILLER, William Jennings, ex-congressman; b. North Andover, Mass., Mar. 12, 1899; s. James Bruce and Katherine (Stewart) M.; ed. North Andover Pub. Schs.; m. Marguerite M. Parrish, Dec. 19, 1925. Served with Air Service, 80th and 1104th Aero Squadrons, U.S. Army, 1917; injured in airplane crash at Issodun, France, 1918, resulting in loss of both legs; patient in U.S. Vets. Hosp., 1919-31; underwriter N.Y. Life Ins. Co., 1931-38; mem. 76th and 78th Congresses (1939-41 and 1943-45), and 80th Congress (1947-49), 1st Conn. Dist. Mem. Am. Legion (past dept. comdr. Conn.; past nat. exec. committeeman; mem. nat. rehabilitation com.). Rep. Conglist. Clubs: Hartford City, Wethersfield Country, Rotary, Wethersfield Business Men's and Civic Assn. Home: 4 Fairmont St., Wethersfield, Conn. Died Nov. 22, 1950.

MILLES, Carl Wilhelm Emil (mil'lĕs), sculptor; b. Uppsala, Sweden, June 23, 1875; s. August Emil Anderson and Wahlborg Maria (Tisell) M.; came to U.S., 1929. Naturalized citizen, 1945; student Tech. Sch., Stockholm, Sweden 1895-97, Ecole des Beaux Arts, Paris, France, 1897-1904, also Munchen, 1904-06; Litt.D. (honorary), from universities in Europe and U.S.; m. Olga Louise Granner, 1905. Sculptor, 1896—. Decorated French Légion d'Honneur. Recipient honors, various awards, medals, etc., from European countries and the U.S.; awarded gold medal, Architectural League of New York; gold medal Archtl. Assn. of New York; medal of Am. Acad. of Arts and Letters, 1943. Member Royal Academy of London (hon.), Sculptors Soc. of N.Y.; life member American Academy Arts and Letters. Work represented in Stockholm, Göteborg, London, Brussels, Zurich, Hamburg, Lubeck, Berlin, Venice, New York, Chicago, St. Louis, Worcester, Phila., Detroit; monuments in Chicago, St. Paul, St. Louis, Wilmington (Del.), Harrisburg (Pa.), N.Y. City (at Rockefeller Center), Ann Arbor, Mich., and in Stockholm, Linköping, Göteburg, Uppsala, Vesterås, Halmstad (all Sweden), Met. Mus., Falls Ch., Washington, Va.; Malmo, Simrishamn, Rottneros, Millesgarden Mus'.; many works in England. Club: Century (New York). Author: Koper, 1916; Stanley Casson, 1918; Maurice P. Verneuil, 1918; Carl G. Laurin, 1930; Meyric Rogers, 1940; Sixteen Strömbom.' 1946; Alfred Westhalm, 1950; Henrik Cornell. Address: "Millesgården," Lindingo, Sweden. Died Sept. 19, 1955; buried Lindingo, Sweden.

MILLET, Clarence (mil lā'), artist; b. Hahnville, La., Mar. 25, 1897; s. Theophile and Matilda (Madere) M.; student Art Students League N.Y., 1922-24, cartography at Tulane, 1942; unmarried. Comml. artist, 1920; self taught painter; professional artist since 1928; exhibited N.Y. World's Fair, Pa. Acad., Art Inst. Chicago, Nat. Acad. Design, and over 50 cities in United States. Served in U.S. Army, 1918. Awarded gold medal, Mississippi Art Assn., 1928; Southern States Art League; Silver Medal, New Orleans Art Assn. Mem. bd. Isaac Delgado Museum of Art, New Orleans Art League (pres., 1941-43), A.N.A. Mem. Miss. Art Assn., New Orleans Art Assn. Home: 1231 N. Galvez St. Studio: 628 Toulouse St., New Orleans. Died Aug. 23, 1959; buried St. Louis No. 3 Cemetery, New Orleans.

MILLIGAN, Harold V., musician, author; born Astoria, Ore., Oct. 31, 1883; s. James Vincent and Alice (Criswell) M.; student Portland (Ore.) Acad., 1896-1901, Guilmant Organ Sch., N.Y. City, 1907-10; studied piano, organ, composition with private teachers; hon. Mus. Doc., Washington and Jefferson Coll.; m. Lucy Richardson, Oct. 15, 1912; children—Vincent, Robert Criswell. Began as organist Calvary Presbyn. Ch., Portland, Ore., 1901; organist Rutgers Presbyn. Ch., N.Y. City, 1908-13, Plymouth Ch., Brooklyn, 1913-15; organist Fifth Av. Bapt. Ch. (named changed to Park Av. Bapt. Ch., then to Riverside Ch.), 1915-40; taught music privately and in Centenary Collegiate Inst., Hackettstown, N.J., 1917-18; teacher Von Ende Conservatory, N.Y. City, 1918-20; toured as lecturer on early Am. music, 1920-25; exec. dir. Nat. Music League, 1925-35; lecturer on history of opera, Columbia U., 1948-49. Fellow Am. Guild Organists (gen. sec. 1914-16); pres. Nat. Assn. Organists, 1929-32. Hon. mem. Canadian Coll. of Organists; Chmn. of Music, Fed. Council of Churches; radio producer Metropolitan Opera Broadcasts, 1942-51. Author: Stephen Foster: A Biography, 1920; Music and You, 1940; Club Members Handbook, 1941; Best Loved Hymns and Prayers, 1942; Hymns of Fellowship, 1945; Hymns of the Rural Spirit, 1947; Opera on the Air, 1947; Opera Quiz Book, 1948; Opera Stories, 1948. Collector and editor (vols. on early Am. mus.) The First Am. Composer; Colonial Love Lyrics; Pioneer Am. Composers (vols. 1 and 2). Composer of anthems, operettas, songs, choruses and selections for organ and piano. Contbr. to music jours. Home: 853 Seventh Av., N.Y. City. Died Apr. 12, 1951; buried Kensico Cemetery, Valhalla, N.Y.

MILLIGAN, Jacob L., ex-congressman; b. Richmond, Mo., Mar. 9, 1889; s. Wm. M. and Mary (Rothrock) M.; U. Mo., 1910-14; married; 1 stepson, William Finley. Admitted to Mo. bar, 1913, and practiced at Richmond, as mem. Roberts, Milligan & Milligan, now Milligan, J. L. "Tuck". Kansas City, Missouri; member of the 66th Congress, 3d Missouri District February 1920, succeeding Joshua Alexander, term ending 1921; re-elected 68th to 72d Congresses (1923-33), 3d Mo. Dist. and 73d Congress (1933-35), Mo. at large. Capt., 6th Mo. Inf., June 2-Oct. 30, 1917; capt. 140th Inf., U.S. Army, Oct. 30, 1917-May 14, 1919; twice cited for bravery in Meuse-Argonne offensive. Decorated Silver Star, Purple Heart. Democrat. Mason. Home: 501 Knickerbocker Pl. Office: Nat. Fidelity Life Bldg., Kansas City, Mo. Died Mar. 9, 1951; buried, Liberty, Mo.

MILLIGAN, Orlando Howard, clergyman; b. East Brady, Pa., Sept. 11, 1873; s. William Minteer and Anna (Swan) M.; A.B., Muskingum Coll., New Concord, O., 1895; grad. Allegheny Theol. Sem., Pittsburgh, Pa., 1898; D.D., Muskingum Coll., 1916, LL.D., 1932; m. Ivy Pearl Moore, Sept. 7, 1898; 1 son, William Moore. Ordained to ministry of United Presbyn. Ch., 1898; pastor, Elderton and Shelocta, Pa., 1898-1903, Cedarville, O., 1903-09, Avalon United Presbyn. Ch., Pittsburgh, Pa., 1909-48; clerk Allegheny Presbytery, 1911-47; prin. clerk Gen. Assembly of United Presbyn. Ch. since 1931. Mem. bd. trustees Muskingum Coll. since 1910, pres., 1925-27. Mem. Western section Presbyn. Alliance. Mem. Alpha Tau Epsilon. Editor: The United Presbyterian Digest, 1942; also editor Minutes of General Assembly, United Presbyterian Church, annually, since 1931. Home: 108 S. Broadhead Rd., Aliquippa, Pa. Died Mar. 17, 1954; buried New Concord, O.

MILLIKAN, George Lee, govt., internat. affairs specialist, educator; b. Murphysboro, Ill., June 10, 1912; s. Elzie Clifton and Edith Leota (Rolens) M.; A.A. cum laude, Compton Jr. Coll., 1932; A.B. magna cum laude, U. So. Cal., 1934, grad. study, 1934-35, M.A., Yale (Cowles fellow govt.), 1938, Ph.D., 1942; grad. Naval Sch. Mil. Govt. and Adminstrn., Columbia, 1943; m. Gertrude Louise Mann, Aug. 23, 1941; children—Louise Cane, James Rolens. Instr. govt. Yale, 1938-39, polit. sci. U. Vt., 1939-45, asst. to dep. sec. U.S. Joint Chiefs Staff, 1945-1942-46; asst. prof. govt. La. State U., 1946-47; mem. Internat. Studies Group, Brookings Inst., Washington, 1947-49; staff cons., com. fgn. affairs U.S. Ho. Reps., 1949—. Served from lt. (j.g.) to lt. comdr. USNR., mem. staff, comdr. 12th Fleet and Naval Forces, Europe, 1943-44, aide, flag sec. to comdr. U.S. Naval Ports and Bases, France, 1944-45, asst. to dep. sed. U.S. Joint Chiefs Taff, 1945-46 Decorated Sec. Navy's Commendation medal and ribbon, E.T.O. Mem. Am., So. polit. sci. assns., Am. Soc. Internat. Law, Phi Beta Kappa, Phi Kappa Phi, Phi Theta Kappa, Phi Kappa Tau. Conglist. Author staff reports, com. fgn. affairs U.S .Ho. Reps. Editor, contbr. Major Problems of U.S. Fgn. Policy, 1947-48, 1948-49. Contbr. ednl. jours. Home: 2924 Cortland Pl. N.W. Office: Committee on Foreign Affairs, U.S. House of Representatives, Washington. Deceased.

MILLIKAN, Robert Andrews, physicist; b. Morrison, Ill., Mar. 22, 1868; s. Rev. Silas Franklin and Mary Jane (Andrews) M.; A.B., Oberlin, 1891, A.M., 1893; Ph.D., Columbia, 1895; univs. of Berlin and Göttingen, 1895-96; Sc.D., Oberlin, 1911, Northwestern, 1913, U. of Pa., 1915, Columbia, 1917, Amherst, 1917, U. of Dublin, 1924, Yale, 1925, Leeds U., 1927, Princeton, 1928, New York U., 1929, Harvard, 1932, U. of Rochester, 1934, U. of Melbourne, 1939; LL.D., U. of Calif., 1924, U. of Colo., 1927, Univ. of Mich., 1929, U. of Southern Calif., 1931, Mills Coll., 1935, Loyola University, 1938, University of Chicago, 1941, William Jewell College, Liberty, Missouri, 1944; hon. Ph.D., King John Casimer University, Poland, 1926, U. of Ghent, 1927; Docteur Honoris Causa University of Liege, 1930, U. of Paris, 1939; LL.D., Bradley University, 1952; married Greta Irvin Blanchard, April 10, 1902; children—Clark Blanchard, Glenn Allan (dec.), Max Franklin. Tutor physics, Oberlin, 1891-93; member physics staff U. of Chicago, 1896-1921; director Norman Bridge Lab. of Physics, and chmn. exec. council Calif. Inst. Tech., Pasadena, 1921-45; prof. emeritus, v.p. bd. trustees, since 1945. Served as lt. col. Signal Corps, U.S. Army, 1918, and chief of science and research div. of Signal Corps. Am. mem. Com. on Intellectual Coöperation of League of Nations, 1923. Fellow in Germany of Oberlaender Trust, 1931. Trustee Huntington Library. Awarded Comstock prize, National Academy of Sciences, 1913; Edison medalist Am. Inst. E.E., 1922; Hughes medalist Royal Soc. of Great Britain, 1923; Nobel prize in physics, 1923; Faraday medalist London Chem. Soc., 1924; Matteucci medalist Societa Italiana della Scienze, 1925; gold medalist Am. Soc. Mech. Engrs., 1926; Messel medalist Soc. of Chem. Industry (British), 1928; gold medal Holland Soc., 1928, Soc. Arts and Sciences, 1929, Radiol. Soc. of North America, 1930; gold medal from Roosevelt Memorial Assn., 1932; gold medal of Franklin Inst., 1937; Joy Kissen Mookerjee gold medal of the Indian Assn. for Cultivation Sci., 1939; Oersted medal of Am. Assn. of Physics Teachers, 1940. Decorated Chevalier de l'Ordre National de la Légion d' Honneur, 1931, comdr., 1936; Order of the Jade (China), 1940; Official of Order Al Merito (Chile), 1944; Medal for Merit (United States), 1947. Fellow of the American Academy Arts and Sciences, A.A.A.S. (pres. 1929); mem. Nat. Acad. Sciences, American Philosophical Society, Am. Physical Soc. (pres. 1916-18), and hon. member 21 foreign scientific societies; member Sigma Xi, Phi Beta Kappa; asso. Royal Acad. Belgium, 1935; hon. fellow Indian Acad. Sciences, Stanford U., 1941. Clubs: University Club (New York); Sunset (Los Angeles). Author: (or co-author) A Course of College Experiments in Physics, 1898; Theory of Optics (translated from the German), 1900; Mechanics, Molecular Physics and Heat, 1901; A First Course in Physics, 1906; A Laboratory Course in Physics for Secondary Schools, 1906; Electricity, Sound and Light, 1908; The Electron, 1917, 25; Science and Life, 1923; Elements of Physics, 1917; Evolution of Science and Religion, 1927; A First Course in Physics for Colleges, 1928; Science and the New Civilization, 1930; Time, Matter and Values, 1932; Electrons (+ and —), Protons, Photons, Neutrons, and Cosmic Rays, 1935, rev. edit., 1947; New Elementary Physics, 1936; Mechanics, Molecular Physics, Heat and Sound, 1937; Cosmic Rays, 1939; Autobiography, 1950. Contbr. to tech. jours. Home: 1640 Oak Grove Av., San Marino, Cal. Died Dec. 19, 1953; buried Forest Lawn Meml. Park, Glendale, Cal.

MILLIKIN, Eugene Donald, ex-U.S. Senator; b. Hamilton, O., Feb. 12, 1891; s. Dr. Samuel Hunter and Mary (Shelly) M.; LL.B., U. Colo., 1913; m. Delia Alsena Schuyler, Jan. 30, 1935. Admitted to Colo. bar, 1913, and began practice of law. Apptd. mem. U.S. Senate to fill unexpired term of Alva B. Adams, re-elected in 1950 for six year term. Served as pvt. U.S. Army, capt. and maj. Inf. and lt.-col. Engrs., World War. Awarded Pershing citation for meritorious services. Mem. Am., Colo., Denver bar assns. Republican. Home: 800 Washington St., Denver 3. Office: 818 17th St., Denver 2. Died July 27, 1958; buried Fairmount Mausoleum, Denver.

MILLINGTON, Ernest John Oldknow, lawyer; b. Derby, Eng., Apr. 5, 1871; s. Rev. William and Hannah (Oldknow) M.; brought to U.S., 1882; student U. Rochester, 1887-90; D.C.L., Hillsdale (Mich.) Coll., 1935; LL.D., Sioux Falls (S.D.) Coll., 1941; m. Bertha Seaman, Sept. 1, 1891; children—Ernest J. O., Bertha H. (Mrs. Fred W. Syers), Alfred E.; m. 2d, M. Maud Harris, July 6, 1925. Salesman and accountant, 1897-1908; ordained to ministry, Congl. Ch., 1908; pastor, Congl. Ch., Cadillac, Mich., 1908-12; admitted to Mich. bar, 1912; pvt. practice, Cadillac, 1912—; judge Recorder's Ct., Cadillac, 1918-38; city atty., Cadillac, 1940—. Pres. Mich. Bapt. Conv., 1936-39, No. Bapt. Conv., 1940-41; pres. Am. Bapt. Publ. Soc., 1938-40. Mem. Cadillac Bd. Edn., 1910-13. Trustee Hillsdale Coll., 1935-41. Mem. State Bar Mich., Am. Bar Assn. Mason. Lectr. ednl. subjects, 1927—. Address: 2373 Harrison Av., Cin. Died Mar. 9, 1958; buried Cadillac, Mich.

MILLIS, John, engineer officer U.S. Army; b. Wheatland, Mich., Dec. 31, 1858; s. Walter and Jane Clark (Carlow) M.; B.S., U.S. Mil. Acad., West Point, N.Y., 1881 (No. 1 graduate Class of 1881); m. Mary Raoul, Nov. 22, 1893; children—Ralph (dec.), Walter, Janet. Commd. 2d lt. engrs., June 11, 1881; 1st lt., 1882; capt., Sept. 20, 1892; major, Apr. 2, 1900; lt. col., June 7, 1907; col., June 13, 1910. Served Willets Point, N.Y., 1881-83; on lighthouse duty, 1883-90; devised and superintended the installation of electric light plant for illuminating the Statue of Liberty, New York Harbor, October 1886; in charge improvements New Orleans harbor and levees Miss. River, 1890-94; chief engineer U.S. Lighthouse Bd., Washington, 1894-98; on duty with engrs.' batt., Willets Point, N.Y., and in Cuba, 1898-1900; U.S. del. Internat. Congress of Navigation, Internat. Congress of Electricity and Internat. Congress of Physics, Paris Expn., 1900; inspected and reported upon the canal and reservoir system of the Nile—particularly the great reservoir dam at Assouan, nr. 1st cataract, Sept.-Oct. 1900; in charge of constructing fortifications on Puget Sound, of river and harbor improvements in Wash., Ida., Mont., of first road survey and constrn. in Mt. Rainier Nat. Park, of surveys and harbor improvements in Alaska, 1900-05, of all fortification constrn., P.I., 1905-07, including defensive works on Corregidor Island; on leave of absence, returning from P.I., visiting works, etc., in China, Burma, India, Egypt and Europe; in charge harbor and river improvement works, Lake Erie and in Ohio and Ind., and mem. spl. bds. on harbor works, etc., 1908-12, in charge of river and harbor improvement works and of sea coast defense works, Mass. and R.I.; sr. mem. spl. bd. on Lake Erie, Lake Mich. inland waterway, spl. duty under Bur. of Lighthouses for N.E. coast, 1912-16; div. engr. Southeast Div. for coast defenses, harbor improvements, and inland waterways, in S.C., Ga., Fla., western portion of N.C. and eastern portion of Ala., 1916-18; chief engr. Southeastern Dept., Savannah, Ga., 1917; dept. engr. Central Dept., Chicago, Ill., 1918-22; retired 1922. Mem. Am. Soc. C.E. (mem. spl. com. to investigate Japanese earthquake), Am. Inst. E.E., A.A.A.S., Am. Astron. Soc. Clubs: University, Century (New York); Cosmos (Washington). Author: Safety of Navigation on Great American Lakes (for 12th Internat. Congress Navigation, Phila., 1912); Commercial Waterways of the United States (for Atlantic Deeper Waterways Assn.); The Constructional History of the Solar System and of Our Earth (The Dualistic Theory), 1925; Unrealities of the Visible Skies, 1931; Evidences of a Planetoid Fall in East Central Africa, 1933; The Mystery of the Star-Chains, Endogenesis of the Earth 1940; also author of numerous papers on relativity, gravitation, glacial theory, cause of drumlins, cosmogony, navigation, etc. Originated, 1918, method of observing and photographing solar eclipses from aircraft, used by U.S. Naval Observatory for total eclipse of Jan. 1925. Devised plan for emergency flood relief of Lower Mississippi which saved city of New Orleans in flood of 1927. Devised polyhedral framing system for naval and merchant vessels, airships; earthquake and wind storm resisting buildings, bridges and other shore structures. Home: Fern Hall Hotel,

3250 Euclid Av., Cleve. Died Mar. 20, 1952; buried Wheatland, Mich.

MILLS, Augustus K(ing), III, business exec.; b. Boonville, Mo., Apr. 12, 1902; s. Augustus K. and Martha (Gibson) M.; student Central Coll., 1919-21, U. Mo., 1921-23; m. Louise Iselin, Feb. 11, 1942; children—Pauline Iselin, Peter Augustus. Publicity dir. Amelia Earhart flight, Europe, 1928, Byrd Antarctic Expdn., 1928-30; publicity dept. Batton, Barton & Durstine, 1931-34; dir. pub. relations March of Time, Inc., 1934-36; European rep. Life mag., London, Eng., 1936-38; asso., later partner Earl Newsom & Co., 1938-49; dir. pub. and employee relations Ford Internat., 1949-50; dir. Ford Motor Co. Archives, exec. dir. Henry Ford Mus. and Greenfield Village, 1950—; dir. Wayside Inn, South Sudbury, Mass., Dearborn (Mich.) Inn, Manhattan Storage Co., N.Y.C., Adlon Corp., N.Y.C. Served with Intelligence, A.A.C., Africa, Corsica, No. Italy, 1942-45, advancing from capt. to lt. col. Mem. Am. Assn. Museums, Sigma Nu. Clubs: Racquet and Tennis (N.Y.C.); Grosse Pointe (Mich.); Terratine Yacht (Dark Harbor, Me.). Home: 294 Lincoln Rd., Grosse Pointe. Office: 3000 Schaefer Rd., Dearborn, Mich. Died Sept. 12, 1954; buried Gate of Heaven, N.Y.C.

MILLS, Blake David; b. Port Blakeley, Wash., Nov. 9, 1867; s. David and Agnes (Smith) M.; student Central High Sch., Seattle, 1879-82; m. Gertrude R. Reitze, July 6, 1906; children—Eileen Elizabeth, Blake David. Clk. gen. store, Port Discovery, Wash., 1883-89; mgr. country store and postmaster, Clifton, Wash., 1889-97; joined Klondike gold rush and arrived in Dawson, Yukon Ty., 1898; mgr. Seattle Yukon Transportation Co. and N.A. Transportation & Trading Co., Eagle, Alaska, 1899-1903; mgr., owner Tanana Development Co., Fairbanks, Alaska, 1904-06, Seattle Coal & Fuel Co., and Cascade Coal Co., Seattle, 1908-27; pres. Marine State Bank, Seattle, 1926-32; now mng. own investments; dir. Nat. Bank Commerce, Marine Bancorporation, Marine Nat. Co., King County Bldg. Co. (all Seattle). Mayor of Eagle, Alaska, 1902-03, Fairbanks, 1906. Democrat. Mason (33°), K.T.; past comdr.). Club: University Commercial (Seattle). Home: 938 22d Av. N. Office: 4345 University Way, Seattle. Died June 20, 1949.

MILLS, Edwin Claude, counselor pub. relations, exec. dir. Song Writers Assn.; b. Denver, Oct. 5, 1881; s. Aaron Timothy and Ella Viola (Babcock) Mills; ed. San Antonio (Tex.) pub. schs.; m. Grace Marie Davis, June 2, 1908. Began as sch. tchr., 1900; traveling rep. Underwood Typewriter Co., 1901; employed operating dept. So. Pacific R.R., 1902-07; Examination of Accounts Div., Isthmian Canal, Panama, 1907-10; mgr. Interstate Amusement Co., Midwest Amusement Co. and various theatrical orgns., 1911-17; exec. Vaudeville Mgrs. Protective Assn., 1917-19; exec. mgmt. mus. trade assns., 1919—; chmn. bd. Music Pubs. Protective Assn., 1919-29; pres. Radio Music Co., 1929-32; became chmn. adminstrv. com. Am. Soc. Composers, Authors and pubs., 1932; exec. dir. Song Writers' Assn.; dir. United Artists' Corp.; adv. bd. Chem. Bank & T. Co.; pub. relations and copyright adv. counsel; now cons. Tv operations KFI-TV, Los Angeles; dir. Radio-Keith-Orpheum Corp., 1929-32. Served in 1st Tex. Vols., Spanish-Am. War. Decorated Officer Academie Francaise; Order of Merit (Rumania); Panama Canal Medal. Mason. Writer articles on theatrical and mus. orgn. and development. Home: 10794 Lindbrook Drive, Los Angeles 24. Office: 141 N. Vermont Av., Los Angeles 54. Died Mar. 13, 1959.

MILLS, Herbert Elmer, educator; b. Salem, N.H., Aug. 8, 1861; s. Edward and Esther (Butterworth) M.; A.B., U. Rochester, 1883, A.M., 1886; Ph.D., Cornell, 1890; m. Mary Louise Sansbury, July 30, 1890; 1 son, Harold Sansbury. Prin. Marion (N.Y.) Collegiate Inst., 1883-84, Union Sch., Palmyra, N.Y., 1884-86; acting instr., instr. history Cornell, 1887-90, asst. registrar, 1888-90; asso. prof. history and econs. Vassar, 1890-92, prof. econs., 1892-1931, now emeritus. Almshouse commr. Poughkeepsie, 1896-99; pres. bd. mgrs. State House Refuge for Women, Hudson, N.Y., 1899-1903; pres. Bd. Edn., Poughkeepsie, 1909-11. Mem. Am. Econ. Assn. Author: French Revolution in San Domingo, 1891; Practical Economic Problems, 1893; Labor Problem, 1895; Outlines of Economics, 1906; Socialism, 1918; Charities and Corrections, 1918; also articles and reviews mags. Dean Tng. Camp for Nurses, Vassar Coll., 1918. Home: 106 Academy St., Poughkeepsie, N.Y. Died Mar. 9, 1946; buried Poughkeepsie Rural Cemetery.

MILLS, James Edward, chemist; b. Winnsboro, S.C., Apr. 30, 1876; s. William Wilson and Sarah Edith Ann (Smith) M.; A.B., Davidson (N.C.) Coll., 1896, A.M., 1900; Ph.D., U. N.C., 1901; D.Sc., U. S.C., 1935; studied U. Berlin, 1904-05; m. Mary Gregory Hume, Oct. 15, 1921. Asst. in chem. N.C., 1900-01, instr., 1901-03, asso. prof., 1904-10; lectr. chemistry, 1911-13, prof., 1913-21, U. S.C.; tech. dir. research and development work, Chemical Warfare Serv., Edgewood Arsenal, 1921-24; chief chem. div., same, 1924-29; chmn. div. chemistry and chem. tech., Nat. Research Council, 1929-30; prof. chemistry U. S.C., 1930-34; chief chemist Sonoco Products Co., 1934-47, dir. chem. research, 1947-50. Recipient Herty Award, 1944. Commd. capt., Engr. O.R.C., Sept. 4, 1917; capt. Chem. Warfare Service; maj., Oct. 16, 1918; served as engr. officer, 1st Gas Regt. (30th Engrs.), A.E.F.; lt. col. C.W. Res., Mar. 14, 1925; ret. Apr. 1940. Fellow N.Y. Acad. Sci., A.A.A.S.; mem. Am. Inst. Chemists, S.C. Acad Sci., Am. Chem. Soc., Am. Electrochem. Soc., Kappa Sigma, Phi Beta Kappa, Sigma Xi. Presbyn. Contbr. sci. jours. Address: 1212 Home Av., Hartsville, S.C. Died Aug. 12, 1950; buried Camden, S.C.

MILLSPAUGH, Arthur Chester (mĭlz'paw), polit. scientist; b. Augusta, Mich., Mar. 1, 1883; s. Hiram E. and Lydia H. (Abbott) M.; A.B., Albion Coll., 1908; A.M., U. Ill.,, 1910; Ph.D., Johns Hopkins, 1916; m. Mary Helen MacConnell, Sept. 9, 1921; 1 son, Abbott. Prof. polit. sci. Whitman Coll., 1916-17; instr. polit. sci. Johns Hopkins, 1917-18; with drafting office Dept. State, 1918-21, petroleum specialist, 1920-22; apptd. consul class 4, assigned Dept. State, 1921; acting fgn. trade adviser, 1921-22; adminstr. gen. of finances, Persia, 1922-27; financial adviser, gen. receiver, Haiti, 1927-29; mem. staff Brookings Instn., 1929-42, 46-48; adminstr. gen. finances, Iran, 1943-45; cons. Teheran Conf. on Iran and underdeveloped nations, Iranian problems in wartime; editorial writer Kalamazoo Gazette. Dir. survey staff Miss. State Research Commn., 1931; participated state surveys, Ala., 1931-32, N.H., 1932; dir. survey Ia., 1933, asst. dir. Okla., 1935; mem. survey Montgomery County, Md., 1939. Mem. Phi Beta Kappa, Sigma Nu. Author: Party Organization and Machinery in Michigan, 1890—, 1917; The American Task in Persia, 1925; Haiti Under American Control, 1931; Public Welfare Organization, 1935; Local Democracy and Crime Control, 1936; Crime Control by the National Government, 1937; Democracy, Efficiency, Stability, 1942; Peace Plans and American Choices, 1942; Toward Efficient Democracy, 1949. Address: 1928 S. Westnedge, Kalamazoo, Mich. Died Sept. 24, 1955; buried Augusta, Mich.

MILLSPAUGH, Frank Crenshaw, ex-congressman; b. Shawneetown, Ill., Jan. 14, 1872; s. James Weeden and Sarah Sina (Hall) M.; ed. pub. schs.; m. Carrie Virginia Asbury, June 23, 1897; children—Nelle Elizabeth, Frances Victoria. Began as accountant with Goddard & Hall, grain commn., New Orleans, 1891; with Ft. Dearborn Nat. Bank, Chgo., 1893-94; mem. firm Goddard-Hall-Sheridan, commn. mchts., St. Louis, 1895-96; grain bus., Canton, Mo., 1897-99; cashier Citizens Bank, Canton, converted into Canton Trust Co., 1900-21; mem. 67th Congress, 1st Mo. Dist.; resigned, Dec. 5, 1922, to become commr. finance, State Mo. Mayor of Canton, 1911-15. Republican. Methodist. Mason. Odd Fellow. Clubs: Canton, Commercial (ex-pres.). Home: Canton, Mo. Deceased.

MILLSPAUGH, William Hulse, mfr.; b. Branchport, N.Y., Dec. 12, 1868; s. Levi and Sarah (White) M.; Keuk a(N.Y.) Coll., 1887-90; m. Carrie Sliger, April 17, 1900 (died Feb. 19, 1949); 1 dau., Elizabeth (Mrs. Thomas Darlington), (died Nov. 28, 1946). Mech. engr., Salem, O., 1895; organizer Sandusky Foundry & Machine Co., mfg. large bronze tubular products, pres. until sold co., 1929, retaining fgn. bus., organized Millspaugh, Ltd., Sheffield, Eng., until co. was sold by him, April 1946; pres., dir. Centrifugal Steel, Inc.; pres., dir. The Hulse Investment Co. (both Sandusky, O.). Patented, developed suction rolls and paper-making devices, establishing, new world records for speed and prodn. paper; also patented and developed centrifugal casting of metals, which processes are licensed to large firms and to U.S. Govt. Recipient 2d Edward Langstreth Medal, Franklin Inst., outstanding contributions, art paper making, 1949. Mem. Am. Soc. M.E., Tech. Assn. Am., Pulp and Paper Assn. (gold medalist), Cleve. Engring. Soc., U.S. Mil. Engrs., Instn. Mech. Engrs. (London, Eng.), Army Ordnance Assn. Mason. Clubs: Castalia (O.) Trout; Union (Cleve.); Engineers' of N.Y. Home: 519 Wayne St. Address: P.O. Box 547, Sandusky, O. Died Apr. 1959.

MILNE, Alan Alexander (mĭln), author and dramatist; b. Jan. 18, 1882; ed. Westminster and Trinity Coll., Cambridge; m. Dorothy de Selincourt, 1913; 1 son. Editor The Granta, 1902; journalist, London, 1903; asst. editor Punch, 1906-14. Author (plays) Mr. Pim Passes By; The Dover Road; The Truth About Blayds; The Ivory Door; Michael and Mary, etc.; (books) The Red House Mystery; When We Were Very Young; Winnie-the-Pooh; Two People; Peace with Honour; Chloe Marr; Birthday Party; A Table Near the Band; January to December; Year In, Year Out; Now We are Six; The House at Pooh Corners. Address: Cotchford Farm, Hartfield, Sussex, Eng. Died Jan. 31, 1956.

MILNE, J. Scott (miln), labor exec.; b. Vancouver, B.C., Can., Jan. 21, 1898; s. Robert and Martha (Steele) M.; m. Doris M. Ford, June 20, 1923; children—Robert E., J. Scott. Former bus. mgr., financial sec., local union 125 Internat. Brotherhood Elec. Workers, AFL, apptd. internat. rep., 1929, internat. v.p. 9th dist. West Coast, 1936-47, internat. sec., 1947-54, internat. pres., 1954—, also pres. AFL Labor Press. Served with Canadian Army, World War I. Editor Elec. Workers Jour. Home: 3811 Kanawha St., Washington 5. Died July 20, 1955; buried Shrine of Roses, Lincoln Meml. Park.

MILNE, John, educator; b. Scotland, Aug. 4, 1880; s. Thomas and Catherine (Beaton) M.; grad. State Normal Sch., Milwaukee, Wis., 1904; B.S., Univ. of N.M., 1929; Columbia U., summer, 1929, M.A., 1932; m. Jeannette A. Lawrence, May 7, 1907 (dec.); children—John Lawrence, James M.; m. 2d, Marie G. Balling, June 4, 1935. Teacher, country schools, 1899-1901; prin. schools, Milford, Wis., 1904-05; prin. high sch., Albuquerque, N.M., 1908-11, supt. schs. 1911-56, ret. Pres. N.M. State Bd. Edn., 1928-31. Mem. N.M. Ednl. Assn. (ex-pres.; founder and original pub. N.M. Sch. Rev.), N.M. Schoolmasters Club (ex-pres.), Am. Assn. Sch. Adminstrs. (adv. mem.), Phi Kappa Phi, Pi Gamma Mu, Phi Delta Kappa. Episcopalian. Mason. Clubs: Ninety-six, National; Albuquerque Country, Commercial, Rotary (ex-pres.). Home: 804 Park Av., Albuquerque, N.M. Died Sept. 5, 1956.

MILNOR, George Sparks; b. Litchfield, Ill., Dec. 11, 1880; s. Frank Richmond and Mary (Sparks) M.; ed. high sch., Litchfield, Culver (Ind.) Mil. Acad. and Metropolitan Bus. Coll.; m. Alice Ryrie, Oct. 1, 1913; children—George Bowman, Magnus Ryrie, Frank Richmond. With Sparks Milling Co., Alton, Ill., advancing from cashier to pres., 1900-30; vice pres. and gen. mgr. Farmers Nat. Grain Corp., 1930-34; new gen. partner Milnor & Sparks Grain Processors, Alton, Ill.; formerly pres. Grain Stabilizaton Corp., Nat. Corn Credit Corp.; chmn. bd. Millers Mutual Fire Ins. Assn. Chmn. 3d Liberty Loan com. 22d Congressional Dist., World War I; v.p. Alton dist. chapter Am. Red Cross. Past pres. Alton C. of C. Unitarian. Mason. Club: Tavern (Chicago). Home: 132 Abingdon Av., Kenilworth, Ill. Office: 75 E. Wacker Dr., Chgo. Died Aug. 11, 1959; buried Alton Cemetery, Alton, Ill.

MILTON, George Fort, editor, historian, economist; b. Chattanooga, Tenn., Nov. 19, 1894; s. George Fort and Caroline Weaver (McCall) M.; prep. edn., Baker-Himel Sch., Knoxville; student U. Tenn., 1912-13; A.B., U. Va., 1916; m. Helen I. Slentz, Sept. 18, 1944; 1 dau., Alice Fort (Mrs. Philip T. Dwight). Mng. editor Chattanooga News, 1919-24, pres. editor, 1924-39; pres., editor Evening Tribune, 1940. Served from 2d lt to 1st lt. F.A., 1917; Rainbow Div., A.E.F., 1918-19; a.d.c. to Brig. Gen. George C. Gatley, 1918-19. Nat. publicity dir. Wm. G. McAdoo's presdl. campaign, 1923-24. Chmn. So. Commn. on Study of Lynching, 1930-34; adv. U.S. delegation to Inter-Am. Conf. at Buenos Aires, 1936; spl. asst. to sec. state, 1937; mem. Industry Com. No. 1, under Fair Labor Standards Act; cons. Bur. of Budget and other U.S. Govt. agys., 1940-44. Editorial writer, St. Louis Post-Dispatch, 1944-45, Buffalo Evening News 1945-50. Mem. Phi Beta Kappa. Club: Cosmos (Washington). Author: The Age of Hate—Andrew Johnson and the Radicals, 1930; The Eve of Conflict—Stephen A. Douglas and the Needless War, 1934; Conflict: The American Civil War, 1941; Abraham Lincoln and the Fifth Column, 1942; Use of Presidential Power: 1789-1943, 1943. Contbr. various mags., etc. Address: 4920 Ft. Totten Dr., Washington 11. Died Nov. 12, 1955; buried Arlington Nat. Cemetery.

MIMS, Edwin, educator; b. Richmond, Ark., May 27, 1872; s. Andrew Jackson and Cornelia (Williamson) M.; A.B., Vanderbilt U., 1892, A.M., 1893; Ph.D., Cornell U., 1900; m. Clara Puryear, June 29, 1898; children—Edwin, Catherine Puryear, Thomas Puryear, Ella Puryear. Asst. in English, Vanderbilt U., 1892-94; prof. English, Trinity Coll., Durham, N.C., 1894-1909, U. N.C., 1909-12; head of English dept. Vanderbilt U., 1912-42, also chmn. div. of humanities, 1928-42, emeritus prof. since 1942. Prof. of English, summer schools Johns Hopkins, U. Va., U. So. Cal., Peabody Coll. Teachers, U. Tex. and Duke U.; Carnegie vis. prof. St. Andrews U., Trinity Coll. (Dublin), U. London, U. Wales, U. of Southwest (Exeter), 1935-36; vis. prof. Rollins Coll., 1945-46; spl. lectr. New Sch. for Social Research, N.Y.C., 1950-51; visiting professor Emory University, 1951-54. Member board of electors Hall of Fame since 1939. Mem. English-Speaking Union, Phi Beta Kappa, Delta Kappa Epsilon. Mem. Gen. Edn. Bd. (N.Y.), 1930-36. Joint editor South Atlantic Quarterly, 1905-09; adv. editor The Golden Book. Lectr., Chautauqua, N.Y., summers 1919-42, Cal. Inst. Tech., 1923, Northwestern U., 1943. Author: Life of Sidney Lanier, 1905; The Advancing South, 1926; Adventurous America, 1929; Chancellor Kirkland of Vanderbilt, 1940; History of Vanderbilt Univ., 1946, Great Writers as Interpreters of Religion, 1945; Christ of the Poets, 1948. Editor: Carlyle's Essay on Burns, 1903; Southern Prose and Poetry, 1910; volume on Southern Fiction, in "The South in the Building of the Nation," 1910; Stevenson's Inland Voyage and Travels with a Donkey, 1911; Carlyle's Past and Present, 1918. Contbr. to Dictionary of Am. Biography, Ency. Brit., Ency. Americana, Cambridge History of Am. Lit. Spl. lectr. Assn. of Am. Colls.

and Phi Beta Kappa, 1942-46. Address: Vanderbilt University, Nashville. Died Sept. 15, 1959; buried Woodlawn Memorial Park, Nashville.

MINAHAN, Victor Ivan (mĭn'ȧ-hăn), newspaper editor; b. Chilton, Wis., June 2, 1881; s. William Burke and Mary (Shaughnessey) M.; student Central Coll., Stevens Point, Wis., 1895-98; LL.B., University of Wisconsin, 1901, married to Bertha Bush Torinus, April 23, 1918 (died April 1959); children—John B. Torinus (stepson), Mary (Mrs. John M. Walter), Victor Ivan. Admitted to Wis. bar, 1901, and practiced in Green Bay, 1901-30; editor Green Bay Press-Gazette and Appleton (Wis.) Post-Crescent since 1930; pres. Green Bay Newspaper Co.; treas. Post Pub. Co.; dir. Kellogg-Citizens Nat. Bank. Capt. U.S. Army, 1917-19. Clubs: Tavern (Chicago); Elks (Green Bay). Home: 823 N. Broadway, De Pere, Wis. Office: Press-Gazette, Green Bay, Wis. Died Aug. 5, 1954; buried Greenwood Cemetery, DePere, Wis.

MINARD, Archibald Ellsworth (mĭn-ärd'), educator; b. King's County, N.S., 1878; s. David and Louisa (Chute) M.; brought to U.S., 1889, naturalized, 1899; ed. Boston Latin Sch., A.B., A.M., Harvard, 1901; student Rochester Theol. Sem., 1901-02; S.T.B., U. Chgo., 1904; student Oxford U., Eng., 1906-07, U. Wis., 1912; m. Gladys May Pease, Sept. 2, 1908; children—Edwin Lincoln, Lois Chute, David, Sara Doolittle; m. 2d, Elita Olson McArdle, Aug. 6, 1941. Instr. English and philosophy, N.D. Agrl. Coll., 1904-07, prof., head dept., 1907-20, head sch. sci. and lit., 1920-26, dean, 1926-35, dean sch. applied arts and scis., 1935—. Mem. A.A.A.S., N.D. Edn. Assn., Phi Beta Kappa, Phi Kappa Phi. Home: 1411 13th St., N., Fargo, N.D. Died May 9, 1950.

MINER, Edward Griffith, mfr.; b. Waverly, Morgan County, Ill., Dec. 19, 1863; s. Dr. James and Eleanor (Thomas) M.; m. Helen Branscombe Ranlet, Apr. 26, 1900. Chmn. exec. com. Rochester Gas & Electric Corp.; chmn. bd. The Pfaudler Co. of N.Y., The Pfaudler Co. of Can., Ltd., Pfaudler Werke Actien Gesellschaft, Enameled Metal Products Corp., Ltd. (1933), Internat. Pfaudler, Ltd.; pres. The Pfaudler Co. of Mich., The Pfaudler Sales Co. of Nev.; mem. bd. dirs. Lincoln Rochester Trust Co.; dir. all above named corps., also of Buffalo, Rochester & Pittsburgh R.R. Trustee, mem. finance com. The Reynolds Library; trustee U. Rochester, Rochester C. of C., Community Chest, Rochester Pub. Library, Rochester Hist. Soc., Rochester Mus. Arts and Scis., Strong Meml. Hosp., Sch. Medicine and Dentistry, Edward G. Miner Library (Sch. of Medicine and Dentistry); mem. bd. Rochester Civic Music Assn. Clubs: University, Fortnightly, The Club, Genesee Valley (Rochester). Home: 2 Argyle St. Office: 89 East Av., Rochester, N.Y. Died Oct. 10, 1955.

MINER, H. C., bus. exec. Chmn., dir. Century Circuit, Inc. of Del. Address: 100 W. Tenth St., Wilmington, Del. Died Aug. 11, 1950.*

MINER, Roy Waldo, curator, editor; b. North Adams, Mass., Feb. 24, 1875; s. Anson Dwight and Ella Eugenia (Wilbur) M.; A.B., Williams Coll., 1897, Sc.D., 1927; grad. Gen. Theol. Sem., 1900; Ph.D., Columbia, 1923; m. Anna Elizabeth Carroll, Sept. 15, 1903 (dec. Oct. 1924); children—Dwight Carroll, Dorothy Eugenia, Roy Waldo; m. 2d, Eunice Thomasina Thomas, June 23, 1926. Master Latin and biology Berkeley Sch., 1900-04; asso. headmaster Kelvin Sch., N.Y., 1904-05; asst. curator invertebrate zoology Am. Mus. Natural History, 1905-16, asso. curator, 1917-21, curator marine life, 1922-43, curator emeritus, 1943—, directed constrn. of marine invertebrate exhibits; now editor N.Y. Acad. Scis.; lectr. Mem. Nat. Research Council; mem. Internat. Fisheries Congress, Washington, 1909; mem. Am. Mus. expdn. to Lesser Antiles, 1911, Biol. Survey Passamaquoddy Bay, 1913, sci. expdn. to Danish W.I., 1914, Dominica, 1914, P.R., 1914-15; investigations coastal marine life, Mass. to N.B., 1916-29; submarine studies coral reefs, Bahamas, 1923, 24, 26, 30 33; with Templeton Crocker on South Pacific expdn. to Christmas Island, Tongareva, and Samoa for submarine sstudies of pearl beds and Pacific corals, 1936; studies of sponge reefs and fisheries, west coast of Fla., 1939-41, 42. Fellow N.Y. Acad. Sci. (past pres.), N.Y. Zool. Soc., A.A.A.S., Consular Law Soc.; mem. Am. Ecol. Soc., Am. Museums Assn., Am. Geophys Union, N.Y. Hist. Soc., Marine Hist. Soc., Mystic Art Assn., Phi Beta Kappa, Sigma Xi, Delta Tau Delta. Republican. Episcopalian. Clubs: Williams College Explorers Lotos (N.Y.C.). Author: Animals of the Wharf Piles, 1912; The Pectoral Limb Musculature of Eryops and other Primitive Vertebrates, 1925; Field Book of Sea Shore Life, 1950; Diving in Coral Gardens, 1933; A Transplanted Coral Reef, 1935; Exhibition Halls of the American Museum of Natural History, 1939; mag. articles on undersea life. Home: Chew Magna, Stonington, Conn. Address: 2 E. 63d St., N.Y.C. 21. Died Dec. 13, 1955; buried Elm Grove Cemetary, Mystic, Conn.

MINGOS, Howard L. (mĭng'ŭs), writer, artist; b. Athens, Pa., Apr. 24, 1891; s. George William and Lottie Ellen (Lynch) M.; grad. high sch., Athens, 1910; student Pa. Mus. Sch. Industrial Art, 1911-14; m. Kate Marjorie Hetrick, Aug. 7, 1923. Mem. staff Phila. Telegraph, 1914, Scranton Republican, 1915, New York Evening World, 1916, Evening Sun, 1919; spl. rep. Aeronautical Chamber Commerce of America, 1920-22; spl. writer, New York Times, 1922-30; contbr. about 1,000 articles to mags. and newspapers. Served as vol. Air Service, U.S. Army, July 1917-Dec. 1918, last 5 mos. in England. Republican. Protestant. Mason. Author: The Zeppelins (with E. A. Lehmann), 1927; The Birth of an Industry, 1929; The Air Is Our Concern (with others), 1935; American Heroes of the War in the Air, 1943. Editor of Aircraft Year Book, 1934-47. Editor, The American Swedish Monthly. Home: 299 W. 12th St., N.Y. C. 14. Office: 8 E. 69th St. N.Y.C. 21. Died Dec. 29, 1955; buried Tioga Point Cemetery, Athens, Pa.

MINICH, Verne Elwood, indsl. exec.; b. Bucyrus, O., Aug. 28, 1867; s. Luther and Mary Jane (Grubb) M.; student pub. schs., also pvt. tutor; m. Miriam Ruth Weisbord, Oct. 6, 1930. Gen. mgr. Haynes Automobile Co., 1903-04; asst. to gen. mgr. Nat. Cash Register Co., 1904-05, advt. mgr., 1905-06; comml. mgr. Franklin Automobile Co., 1906-08; Wheelabrator Corp. and predecessor cos., 1910—, pres., 1910-41, chmn. bd., 1941—. Rep. Presbyn. Clubs: Union League (N.Y.C.); Northhampton Country (Cape Charles, Va.); La Gorce Golf (Miami Beach, Fla.); Farmington (Va.) Country. Home: Vancluse Farm, Bridgetown, Northampton County, Va. Office: S. Brykit Av., Mishawaka, Ind. Died Dec. 13, 1958.

MINNICH, Harvey C., educator; b. Union, O., Mar. 10, 1861; s. Adam and Katherine (Ziegler) M.; B.S., O. Northern U., 1886, M.S., 1887; A.M., O. Wesleyan U., 1908; LL.D., U. of Vt., 1912; Ed.D., Miami U., 1928; m. Bertha Beatrice Minnich, Feb. 25, 1889; children—Dwight Elmer, Helen Marguerite (Mrs. Harold Keene). Supt. pub. schs., Hutchinson, Kan., 1889-92, Hillsboro, O., 1892-1902, Middletown, O., 1902-03; dean of School of Education and prof. school adminstrn., Miami University, 1903-29, professor school adminstrn., 1929-31, now prof. emeritus; lecturer on Am. edn., England, 1929. Del. M.E. Gen. Conf., Chicago, 1900, Los Angeles, 1904, Baltimore, 1908; mem. Bd. Edn. for Negroes, M.E. Ch., 1904-12. Member National Education Society (life), American Association Teachers Colleges (secretary-treas. 1922-26; pres. 1926-27), Ohio State Teachers' Association (president 1926-26), Federation of McGuffey Societies (sec.-treasurer), Phi Gamma Delta, Phi Beta Kappa, Kappa Delta Pi. Republican. Mason (K.T.). Author of Evolution of Public Education in Ohio—Certification; Evolution of Public Education in Ohio—Legislation; William Holmes McGuffey and the McGuffey Peerless Pioneer Readers; William Holmes McGuffey and His Readers; Old Favorites from the McGuffey Readers; Centeinnial History of Ohio Education Association. Lecturer; contbr. to mags. on ednl. subjects. Home: Oxford, O. Died May 12, 1952; buried Oxford (O.) Cemetery.

MINNIGERODE, C(uthbert) Powell (mĭn'ĭ-gĕ-rōd), art dir.; b. St. Louis, June 2, 1876; s. Charles, Jr. and Virginia Cuthbert (Powell) M.; ed. Episcopal High Sch. of Va., nr. Alexandria; m. Esther Gordon, Nov. 17, 1904. With Corcoran Gallery of Art, Washington, 1892—, becoming dir., sec., trustee, ret., 1947; now dir. emeritus and mem. bd. trustees. Mem. Internat. Jury Awards, San Francisco Expn., 1915. Dir. Riggs Nat. Bank. Hon. mem. Assn. of Arts Mus. Dirs. (pres. 1937-39). Episcopalian. Clubs: Chevy Chase (Md.); Metropolitan (Washington). Home: 1812 24th St. N.W., Washington 8, D.C. Died Mar. 1, 1951; buried Oakhill Cemetery, Washington.

MINOR, Robert, editor; b. San Antonio, July 15, 1884; s. Robert Berkeley and Routez (Houston) M.; student grammar schools, San Antonio, 1894-98; m. Lydia Gibson, Oct. 26, 1923. Began as a sign painter, 1898; later became a carpenter; became newspaper cartoonist, successively on San Antonio Gazette, St. Louis Post-Dispatch, N.Y. World, N.Y. Call; became war correspondent for Newspaper Enterprise Association, 1915; then became writer, organizer, lecturer on war subjects; headed committee of trade unionists to save Tom Mooney, 1916-18; associated with Communist movement, 1919— (one of the founders of movement of U.S.); Communist candidate for gov. of N.Y., 1932, for mayor of N.Y. City, 1933, for U.S. Senate, 1936; acting gen. sec. Communist party, Feb. 1941-May 1942; now political and theoretical writer for Communist Party and for Daily Worker (New York). Served as non-commissioned officer Nat. Guard, 1900. Home: Croton on Hudson, N.Y. Died Nov. 26, 1952; buried Ferncliffe Cemetery, Hartsdale, N.Y.

MINSCH, William J., investments; b. Hartford, Conn., June 25, 1884; s. Charles C. and Louise F. (Liefield) M.; B.A., Dartmouth Coll., 1907, M.A., 1937; M.C.S., Tuck Sch. Bus. Adminstrn., 1908; m. Neva N. Reynolds, 1910. Plantation mgr. in Guatemala, United Fruit Co., 1908-09; asso. with Lee, Higginson & Co., N.Y.C., 1909-20; pres. Minsch, Monell & Co., Inc., 1920-42; partner Minsch, Monell & Co., 1942-50, Robert Garrett & Sons, 1950—; gen. partner Aldred & Co., 1926-31; v.p. Aldred Investment Trust, 1928-39, trustee, 1930-41; dir. Gorham Inc. Commr., dir. of revenue Town and Montclair, N.J., 1942-46. Chmn. Dartmouth Alumni Fund Com., 1930-32; pres. Dartmouth Alumni Council, 1932-34; trustee Dartmouth Coll., 1937-48. Vice-chmn. Investment Banker Assn. Am. (N.Y. group), 1935-36; mem. dist. com. Nat. Assn. Securities Dealers, 1940-41. Clubs: Downtown Athletic, Bond (pres. 1927-28; gov. 1920-22, 1926-30), Dartmouth College, Broad Street, Lawyers, Tuxedo, New England Society of N.Y. (N.Y.). Home: 10 Crestmont Rd., Montclair, N.J. Office: 115 Broadway, N.Y.C. 6. Deceased.

MINSHALL, Robert J., corp. exec.; b. Sutherland, Neb., Aug. 25, 1898; s. Ralph Hudson and Fanny (Hawley) M.; B.S. magna cum laude, U. Wash., 1923; m. Margaret Gulick, Mar. 21, 1935; children—Carolyn Jean (Mrs. Harry D. Miles), Mary Otis, Dorothy Ellen. With Boeing Aircraft Co., 1918-41, v.p. in charge engring., dir., 1941; pres., gen. mgr. Pesco Products div., Borg-Warner Corp. since 1941. chmn. supervisory bd., dir. research and development. Cleve. commutator div. since 1951, Marvel-Schebler Products div. since 1951. Wooster div. since 1951. Awarded Wright Bros. Medal for outstanding contbn. to comml. aviation, 1937; Musick Meml. Trophy for contbn. to safety of air travel, 1940. Mem. Inst. Aero Scis., Soc. Automotive Engrs., Sigma Xi, Tau Beta Phi. Mason, Early Bird. Home: 20980 Brantley Rd., Shaker Heights 22, O. Died Sept. 7, 1954.

MINTON, Melville, publisher; b. Red Bank, N.J., July 5, 1885; s. Walter R. and Content (Sutphen) M.; educated public schools; m. Ida Harris, May 1, 1917; 1 son, Walter Joseph. With Charles Scribner's Sons over 20 years; founder with Earle H. Balch, 1924; Minton, Balch & Co., co. merged with G. P. Putnam's Sons in 1930; pres. of latter since 1932; pres. Minton, Balch & Co., Day-Putnam Corp.; dir. Coward-McCann, Inc., Remington-Putnam Co. Republican. Methodist. Clubs: Union League, Lotos (N.Y.C.). Office: 210 Madison Av., N.Y.C. Died Aug. 1, 1955; buried Fairview Cemetery, Red Bank, N.J.

MIRKINE-GUETZEVITCH, Boris, prof.; b. Kiev, Russia, Jan. 1, 1892; s. Serge and Therese (Frenkel) M.-G.; grad. (gold medal) Gymnasium, Kiev, 1909; LL.D., Univ. of Petersburg, 1914; magistrant of internat. law, Univ. of Petrograd, 1917; Doctor Honoris Causa, Univ. of Czernovitz, 1932; Doctor Honoris Causa, Univ. of Lima, 1938; m. Eugenie Poliakov, Dec. 15, 1913; 1 dau., Victoria (Mrs. Stephane Hessel). Came to U.S., Mar. 1941. Privat docent Faculty of Law, Univ. of Petrograd, 1917; left Russia for Paris, 1919, became French citizen, 1933; prof. Institut des Hautes Etudes Internationales, U. of Paris, since 1926; gen. sec. Institut de Droit Compare, Univ. of Paris, 1931-40, dir. Institut des Sciences de la Presse, 1937-40; asso. dir. Centre study of history of French Revolution, Sorbonne, 1932-37; prof. Acad. of Internat. Law, The Hague, 1928, 31, 33, 36, 53. Dean faculty law and polit. sci. Ecole Libre des Hautes Etudes, N.Y., since 1941; acting pres. French U. N.Y., 1947—; constl. cons. U.N. Secretariat, 1946-50, prof. Ecole Nationale d'Administration, Paris, 1948-53; vis. prof. Harvard, 1954—; dir. Inst. Advanced Internat. Studies, Ecole Libre des Hautes Etudes, N.Y.C., 1949—; v.p. Internat. Acad. Polit. Sci. and Constl. History since 1936; v.p. Coll. Social Scis. Paris; mem. bd. dirs. Soc. Comparative Legislation, Paris, since 1949; dir. a sect. Inst. Comparative Law, U. Paris since 1948. Decorated Chevalier Legion of Honor, 1932, Officer, 1948; Laureate Institut de France (7). V.p. Societe d'Histoire de la Revolution Francaise (pres. N.Y. chpt. since 1943), Institute Internat. de Droit Pub. (gen. sec. since Found., 1927), Institute International d'Histoire politique et constitutionelle (v.p. since foundation 1936), Institut Internat. des Etudes iberoamericaines (v.p.), Corr. mem. Spanish Acad. of Moral and Polit. Sci., Spanish Acad. of History, Rumanian Acad., Yugoslav Acad., Royal Soc. of Letters and Scis. of Bohemia, Nat. Acad. of History of Argentina; fgn. mem. acads. of Italy and Turin. Author: Les Constitutions de l'Europe nouvelle (2 vols.), 1938; Les Nouvelles tendances du droit constitutionnel (prize Acad. of Moral and Polit. Sciences); Droit constitutionnel international (prize of the Acad. of Moral and Polit. Scis.), 1933; Les Constitutions des nations americaines, 1932; Les Constitutions Européennes 2 vols. 1951. Editor (in Paris until 1940): Revue d'histoire politique et constitutionnelle, La Revolution Francaise, Cahiers de la Presse, Bibliotheque parlementaire et constitutionnelle contemporaine, Bibliotheque la Vie juridique des peuples, Annuaire de l'Institut internat. de droit public, Annuaire Interparlementaire, etc., La Republique Francaise, New York, 1943, Les Cahiers d'Histoire de la Revolution Francaise, New York, 1946. Home: 40 E. Tenth St., N.Y.C. 3. Died Apr. 1, 1955; buried Paris, France.

MISBACH, Lorenz (mĭz'bäk), psychologist; b. LeRoy, Kan., Mar. 13, 1901; s. Lawrence Ulysses and Ella Frances (Dill) M.; A.B., Baker U., 1929; A.M., Northwestern, 1930, Ph.D., 1933; fellow Nat. Research Council, Johns Hopkins U., 1934; m. Henrietta Louise Satterlee, June 27, 1928; children—Kathryn Louise, Henry Lorenz. Mem. faculty, U. Kansas City, 1935-47, prof. psychology, asso. dean Coll. Arts and Scis., 1957-—, acting vice chancellor, 1956-57. Fellow Am. Psychol. Assn.; mem. Phi Beta Kappa, Sigma Xi. Contbr. articles psychol. publs. Address: 11239 Hiway 71, Hickman Mills 34, Mo. Died May 3, 1958.

MISTRAL, Gabriela (Lucila Godoy Alcayaga), (mēs-trälʹ), writer, Chilean consul; b. Vicuña, Chile, Apr. 7, 1899; d. Jerónimo and Petronila (Alcayaga) Godoy; Dr. Honoris Causa, U. Guatemala, 1931, U. Florence (Italy), 1946, U. of Chile, 1954; U. Cal., Mills Coll., Oakland, Cal., 1947, D.H.C. Columbia University, 1954. Teacher in rural and secondary schools, Chile; dir. of schools, Liceó de Niñas, Santiago, Temuco, Los Andes, Punta Arenas; adviser to Ministry of Edn., Mexico, 1922-24; pensioned by Chilean govt. because of outstanding cultural work, 1925; made consul for life by special law of Chilean Congress, 1935; consul, Madrid, Lisbon, Nice, Petropolis (Brazil), Los Angeles (Cal.); consul Santa Barbara, Cal., 1947-54; counsel of Chile, United Nations, 1954-—. Vis. prof. Spanish-Am. lit., history and culture, Barnard Coll., N.Y.C., 1930, Vassar Coll., Poughkeepsie, N.Y., 1931, Middlebury (Vt.) Coll., summer session, 1931, U. Puerto Rico, 1933, U. Montevideo, 1935. Head of Com. of Letters at Internat. Inst. of Intellectual Coop., League of Nations, Paris, mem. permanent Com. of Arts and Letters, Geneva, Switzerland, 1926-39; adviser Inst. of Ednl. Cinema, League of Nations, Rome, 1930-36. On lecture tours was hon. guest of govts. of Brazil, Uruguay, Peru, Ecuador, Panama, Costa Rica, San Salvador, Guatemala; hon. guest Internat. Pen Club Congress, Paris, 1937, France, England, Italy, 1945-46. Awarded Nobel prize in lit., 1945. Decorated by Panama, Ecuador and Cuba. Hon. mem. cultural and ednl. societies in U.S., S.A., C.A., France and Italy. Roman Catholic. Author: Desolación, 1922; Antologia Lecturas para Mujeres, 1924; Tala, 1937; Antologia Gabriela Mistral, 1939; Ternura, 1946; Gabriela Mistral Dikter, 1946; Poems, 1946; Desolation, 1946; Lagar, 1955. Address: 15 Spruce St., Roslyn Harbor, L.I., N.Y. Died Jan. 1957.

MITCHELL, Albert (Carlyle), "The Answer Man"; b. Elsberry, Mo., May 31, 1893; s. Walter Addison and Charlotte (Grimes) M.; privately educated; m. Ann O'Neil, May 22, 1921 (divorced May 26, 1947); children—Jane Elizabeth, Dolly (Ann) O'Neil; m. 2d, Harriet Schweichler, Nov. 8, 1947. Began as pianist and organist; composer, condr. and arranger; concert tours, 1909-17; soldier and entertainer with A.E.F., France, and Army of Occupation, Germany, Apr. 1917-Sept. 1919; asso. with Paul Whiteman, 1920-27; master of ceremonies and condr. Paramount-Publix and Fox Theaters, 1927-32; musical dir. on various radio programs, 1933-36; widely known as "The Answer Man," answers all questions submitted by radio audience, Station WOR (New York) 1937-50, WNVC, 1950-—, also Don Lee network. In European countries for Marshall Plan, 1950-—. Mem. A.A.A.S., Soc. Stars and Bars. Office: 55 W. 42d St., N.Y. City; also rue de Grammont, Paris, France. Died Oct. 4, 1954.

MITCHELL, Arthur Evan, judge; b. Sidney, Ia., Sept. 10, 1883; s. Evan Howard and Mary (Evans) M.; A.B., Colo. Coll., 1907; J.D., U. Chgo., 1910; LL.D., Maryville (Tenn.) Coll., 1947; m. Joan McDougall, Oct. 15, 1912; 1 dau., Bessie McDougall (Mrs. Jerome Gregg Taylor). Admitted to Tenn. bar, 1911, practiced in Knoxville until 1934; judge Chancery Ct., Knox County, 1934-50; v.p. So. Indsl. Banking Corp. Mem. Knoxville Bd. Edn., 1929-34, chmn. 1931-34; dir. Maryville (Tenn.) Coll. Commr. Gen. Assembly Presbyn. Ch. U.S.A., 1928; mem. permanent jud. commn., class of 1947-53. Presbyn. Ch. U.S.A. Mem. nat. panel arbitrators, Am. Arbitration Assn. Mem. Am., Tenn. State bar assns., Phi Gamma Delta, Phi Alpha Delta. Republican. Presbyn. Clubs: Kiwanis, Cherokee Country (Knoxville). Home: 720 Scenic Dr. Address: Court House, Knoxville, Tenn. Died Jan. 9, 1956; buried Highland Meml. Cemetery.

MITCHELL, Charles Anderson, clergyman; b. Springfield, O., Jan. 18, 1864; s. John Forgy and Caroline Maria (Myers) M.; A.B., Bellevue Coll., 1892, A.M., 1895, Ph.D., 1902; D.D., 1906; grad. Princeton Theol. Sem., 1896; A.M., Princeton, 1896; m. Jennie B. Wallace, Apr. 12, 1898; children—William Wallace, Janet Bruce (dec.), Charles Ray. Prof. Greek and philosophy, Bellevue Coll., 1893-94, 1896-97, 1898-1902; ordained Presbyn. ministry, 1896; prof. N.T. lit., and exegesis, Presbyn. Theol. Sem., Omaha, 1902-37; prof. Bible and Greek, Buena Vista Coll., 1937-38; now ret. Author: The Model Prayer, 1918. Also various mag. articles. Home: 2965 Pacific St. Address: Presbyterian Theological Seminary, Omaha, Neb. Died July 13, 1948; buried Bellevue, Neb.

MITCHELL, Charles Edwin, banker; b. Chelsea, Mass., Oct. 6, 1877; s. George Edwin and Annie Maria (Knowlton) M.; A.B., Amherst, 1899; m. Elizabeth Rend, June 3, 1908; children—Rita, Craig, Began with Western Electric Co., Chicago, 1899, and became asst. mgr., 1904; asst. to pres. Trust Co. of America, New York, 1907-11; head of C. E. Mitchell & Co., investments, 1911-16; became pres. The Nat. City Co., 1916, chmn. bd., 1929-33; became pres. Nat. City Bank of New York, 1921, chmn. bd., 1929-33, chmn. bd. City Bank Farmers Trust Co., 1929-33; pres. C. E. Mitchell, Inc. (financial counsellors), 1935-41. Chmn. Blyth & Co., Inc. (investment bankers) since 1935; has been officer and dir. many cos. Mem. Chi Psi. Republican. Clubs: The Recess, Bond, River, Southampton, The Links, Nat. Golf Links, Piping Rock, Tuxedo. Home: 1 Sutton Pl. S. Office: 14 Wall St., N.Y.C. Died Dec. 14, 1955; buried Southampton, L.I., N.Y.

MITCHELL, David, psychologist; b. Aldershot, Can., Oct. 13, 1884; s. David and Mary (Henderson) M.; B.A., Toronto, 1910; M.A., U. Pa., 1911, Ph.D., 1913; married, 1913. Instr. psychology, U. Pa., 1913-17; dir. psychol. research, Bur. Edn. Experiments, 1917-19; asso. prof. psychology, Rutgers Coll., 1921-27; vis. psychologist, Kings Park State Hosp., 1921-26; lectr. psychology, Tchrs. Coll. (Columbia), 1923-24; vis. psychologist, Ohio State U., 1931, 32; cons. psychologist on problems edn., tng. and behavior; mem. Am. Psychol. Assn. Writer psychol. subjects, especially pertaining to children. Home: Stillson Hill, New Milford, Conn. Died July 14, 1956.

MITCHELL, Edwin Thomas, educator; b. Griersville, Ont., Sept. 28, 1886; s. William and Elizabeth Charlotte (Luton) M.; student Queen's U., Kingston, Ont., 1908-09; B.A., U. Alberta, 1912, M.A., 1913; Ph.D., U. Chgo., 1923; m. Decima Eveline Robinson, July 1, 1915; 1 dau., Joyce Margaret. Came to U.S., 1923, naturalized, 1936. Tchr. rural schs., Can., 1905-08; prin. high sch., 1913-18; insp. schs. Province of Alberta, 1918-20; adj. prof. philosophy U. Tex., 1923-27, asso. prof., 1927-33, prof., 1933-52, prof. emeritus, 1952-53; vis. prof. Beloit (Wis.) Coll., 1933-34, U. Cin., 1934-35, U. Minn., summer 1931, U. B.C., summer 1936, U. Alberta, summer 1941, 46. Mem. Am. Philos. Assn. (chmn. bd. 1936; sec. Western division 1931-34, pres. 1935-36), Southwestern Philos. Conf. (pres. 1938). Author: A System of Ethics, 1950; also numerous articles in philos. periodicals. Contbr.: Value, A Cooperative Inquiry, 1949. Home: 700 W. 32d St., Austin Texas., Died Apr. 2, 1953; buried Edmonton, Alberta, Can.

MITCHELL, George Franklin, pres. Peoples Gas Light & Coke Co.; b. Chicago, Ill., Mar. 20, 1888; grad. Armour Scientific Acad., Chicago; business and stenographic course 6 mos. Began working for Am. Steel Foundries at age of 14; later with various construction cos. as far west as Pacific Coast; became stenographer in contract dept. of Commonwealth Edison Co., Chicago, 1909, later stenographer and asst. to president's sec., then sec. to the pres.; asst. to chmn. bd. Peoples Gas Light & Coke Co., Jan.-Mar. 1919, asst. to pres., 1919-21, treas., 1921-24, v.p., 1924-30, pres. since 1930. Home: 425 Grove St., Evanston, Ill. Office: 122 S. Michigan Av., Chgo. Deceased.*

MITCHELL, Harold E(dgar), lawyer; b. Iron River, Wis., Nov. 28, 1901; s. William Henry and Ida Elizabeth (Mannel) M.; A.B., U. Wis., 1923; LL.B., Harvard, 1926; m. Elizabeth Church, June 23, 1928. Admitted to Conn. bar, 1927; law practice, Hartford, Conn., 1927-—; mem. firm, Alcorn Mitchell & Alcorn, 1928-39, Hewes & Awalt, 1939-—; asst. states atty., Hartford County, 1928-39; mem. adv. bd., Conn. Coll. Law; mem. Conn. House Reps., 1937-43, speaker 1943; chmn. Rep. State Central Com. (Conn.) 1944-48; com. from Conn. on Rep. Nat. Com., 1948-—, mem. exec. com., 1949-—; del.-at-large Rep. Nat. Conv. 1944, 1948. Mem. Am., Conn. bar assns., Sons of Union Vets. of Civil War, Sigma Alpha Epsilon. Republican. Conglist. Mason (32°, K.T., Shriner). Clubs: Hartford, Rotary (Hartford). Home: Cedar Lege Rd., West Hartford 7. Office: 93 Elm St., Hartford 6, Conn. Died June 19, 1950.

MITCHELL, Harry B., chmn. U.S. Civil Service Commn.; b. Scotland; s. David and Mary (Ferguson) M.; ed. schs., Fergus Falls, Minn.; m. Mary Greening, Aug. 8, 1895; children—Catherine (Mrs. A. W. Chapin), Fergus, Hugh. Came to U.S., 1880, father naturalized. Began as printer, 1887; published weekly newspapers at Barker and Neihart, 1892-96; mgr. Daily Leader, Great Falls, Mont., 1896-1900, editor Tribune, 1900-18; in livestock and dairying bus., 1918-—. Mayor Great Falls, 1923-29; pres. U.S. Civil Service Commn., 1933-49, chmn. 1949-51, ret. Democrat. Unitarian. Mason. Clubs: Rotary, National Press. Home: 117 Oxford St., Chevy Chase, Md. Office: U.S. Civil Service Commn., Washington. Died Sept. 30, 1955.*

MITCHELL, Henry Bedinger, educator, industrialist; b. Baylon, L.I., N.Y., Aug. 12, 1874; s. John Fulton Berrien and Mary (Bedinger) M.; E.E., Columbia, 1898, A.M. 1900; studied in Europe 1892-93. Asst. mathematics Columbia, 1898-1900, tutor, 1900-05, adj. prof. 1905-08, prof. 1908-25, editor Columbia U. Quarterly 1914; dir. Outer Court Inc. Chapel Farm Riverdale 1916-— Audiffren Refrigerating Co.; dir. Griscom-Russell Co. (formerly Griscom-Spencer Co.) 1912-—, mem. exec. com. chmn., bd. 1939-55. Co-founder Chapel of Comforter, N.Y., sr. warden, 1908-50; co-founder Open Door Mission, N.Y.C., 1913-23. Trustee Am. Def. Soc., 1917-18. Fellow A.A.A.S., Theosophical Soc. (treas. 1902-—, pres. N.Y. br., 1903-43, exec. com., 1906-—; editorial bd. Quar., 1903-38, Quar. book dept. 1905-—); mem. Order Living Christ. Episcopalian. Author: Meditation, 1906; Talks on Religion, 1908; The Theosophical Society and Theosophy, 1910; Letters to Friends (pseudonym John Gerard), 1925. Contbr. articles religious, philos., math. jours. Home: Chapel Farm, Riverdale, N.Y.C. 71. Office: 285 Madison Av., N.Y.C. 17. Died July 30, 1956.

MITCHELL, Henry Sewall, lawyer; b. Milw.; s. S. W. and Annie (Gee) M.; B.A., U. Minn., 1905, LL.B., 1909; Rhodes scholar, New Coll., Oxford, Eng., 1905-08, B.C.L., 1908; m. Caroline Smith, 1923. Instr. Law School, U. Minn., 1908-10; practiced at Mpls., 1910-14; spl. asst. to atty. gen., Washington, 1914-21; prosecuted cases under Act to Regulate Commerce, and anti-trust cases under Sherman Act; appeared as prosecutor in first "Open Competition Plan" cases, including the "hardwood lumber" case; gen. counsel M.,St.P.&S. Ste. Marie Ry., 1922-38; pvt. practice of law, 1938-—, also counsel C.P. Ry.; gen. counsel Wis. Central Ry.; pres. Duluth, South Shore and Atlantic R.R. Co., 1949-—. Mem. Phi Beta Kappa, Chi Psi. Clubs: Minneapolis, Minikahda. Home: 1776 Colfax Av. S. Office: 1734 First Nat. Soo Line Bldg., Mpls. Died Nov. 22, 1958.

MITCHELL, Homer Rawlins, ins. exec.; b. Lees Summitt, Mo., Oct. 22, 1871; s. David Thomas and Susan (Rawlins) M.; LL.B., U. Mo., 1895; m. Henrietta St. C. Price, Oct. 17, 1900; children—Ben H., James P. Admitted to Tex. bar, 1895; practice of law, Houston, 1895-1903; state agt. Travelers Ins. Co., 1903-08; gen. agt. Md. Casualty Co., 1910; v.p. Western Casualty & Guaranty Ins. Co., 1910-13; organized Tex. Employers Ins. Assn., 1913, Employers Casualty Co., Dallas, 1920, sec., gen. mgr., 1922-26, v.p., 1926-27, pres., chmn., 1937-—; chmn. Buckeye Tools Corp., Dayton, O. Pres., dir. Dallas Community Chest; regional chmn. Boy Scouts Am. Trustee David Graham Hall Found., Dallas Health Mus., Tex. Research Found., Am. Humanics Found. Mem. Dallas Hist. Soc. (v.p.). Home: 3500 Dartmouth St., Dallas 5. Office: 423 S. Akard St., Dallas 1. Died Aug. 7, 1956; buried Dallas.

MITCHELL, Hugh Chester, mathematician; b. Jackson County, Tex., Apr. 15, 1877; s. Isaac Newton and Callista (Stapp) M.; student St. Mary's Coll., San Antonio; C.E., U. Notre Dame, Ind., 1895, B.S., 1898; post-grad. study, Cath. U. Am.; m. Agnes V. Marr, Sept. 29, 1903 (died 1947); children—Mrs. Thomas Taylor Neill, Hugh Chester. Asso. with U.S. Coast and Geodetic Survey, 1898; duty, P.R., Chesapeake Bay, La.; astron. survey, Philippines, 1900-03; mathematician Gen. Office, Washington, 1903-11; presented Peary's North Pole data to Congress, 1911; in charge Hayford's 2d investigation of figure and size of earth, and of precise geodetic topog. survey of Cin.; pvt. engring. practice, 1913-16; ranching in Tex., 1916-20; reentered Coast and Geodetic Survey, 1921, becoming prin. mathematician; ret. from active service, Dec. 1, 1945; instr. in astronomy Cath. U. Am., 1927-35. Chmn. spl. coms. Fed. Bd. Surveys and Maps on Plane Coordinates and Definitions on Surveying and Mapping Terms. Club: Cosmos. Catholic. Author: Triangulation Along the East Coast of Florida, and on the Florida Keys, 1911; wrote (with C. R. Duvall) The Geographic Position of Camp Jesup, and the Reduction of the Observations of R. E. Peary in the Vicinity of the North Pole, X Congresso Internazionale Geografia, Rome, 1913; Topographic Survey of Cincinnati, 1914; California-Oregon Arc of Precise Triangulation, 1922; Geodetic Control for City Surveys, 1923; Triangulation in Maryland, 1925; Triangulation in Hawaii, 1929; First-order Triangulation in Texas, 1935; First and Second-order Triangulation in California, 1936; The State Coordinate Systems (a manual for surveyors), 1945; Definitions of Terms Used in Geodetic and Other Surveys, 1945; Economy of Controlled Survey, Military Engineer, 1954; Peary at the North Pole, 1959. Mem. Am. Geophys. Union, Am. Polar Soc. Mem. Nat. Geog. Soc. com. of experts which determined that Comdr. R. E. Byrd, U.S. Navy, reached the North Pole by airplane, 1926, and South Pole, 1930. Home: 3038 Newark St., Washington 8. Died Nov. 20, 1956; buried Mt. Olivet Cemetery, Washington.

MITCHELL, Humphrey, minister of labor, Can.; b. Old Shoreham, Sussex, Eng., Sept. 9, 1894; s. Fredfrick John and Eleanor Annie (Burgoyne) M.; ed. pub. and higher grade schs., Hove, Sussex Eng.; m. Violet Winnifred Webb, Oct. 20, 1919; children—Humphrey Frederick, John Burgoyne. Came to Can., 1912. Served with British Navy during World War 1. Electrical operator. Mem. Internat. Union Operating Engrs.; chmn. Ont. exec. bd. Trades and Labor Congress Can., 1929-32; sec. Hamilton Dist. Trades and Labor Council, 22 terms; alderman Hamilton, Ont., 1927-30, del. British Trade Union Congress Conv., Eng., 1933, Internat. Fedn. Trade Unions, Brussels, 1933; visited Russia as mem. trade union delegation, 1933. Mem. Hamilton Bd. Edn., 1935. Elected Ho. of Commons, Can., at by-election, Aug. 1931, defeated 1935, re-elected for Welland, Ont., at by-election, Feb. 1942, re-elected gen. election, June 11, 1945. Dir labor transference, Dept. Labor, 1936-39; sec. Interdept. Com. on Labor Coordination, 1940; sec. Nat. Labor Supply Council, 1940-41; chmn. Indsl. Disputes Inquiry Commn., 1941; chmn. Nat. Labor Bd., 1941-43; sworn to Privy Council and apptd. minister of labor Can., Dec. 1941. Home: 332 Island Park Dr. Address: Confederation Bldg., Ottawa, Ont., Can. Died Aug. 1, 1950.

MITCHELL, John Fulton Berrien, investment broker; b. N.Y.C., Jan. 26, 1878; s. John Fulton Berrien and Mary (Bedinger) M.; A.B., Columbia, 1898; m. Therese Hewitt, June 19, 1909; children—Mary McClintock, Agnes M. Forsyth, John Fulton Berrien, Henry B., II. With Redmond Kerr & Co., 1902, partner, 1909-25; partner Wood, Low & Co., 1926-41, Wood, Walker & Co., N.Y.C., 1941—; chmn. Ins. Co. Bondholders' Com. for reorgn. D., R.G.W. R.R., 1935-36; dir., chmn. exec. com. Investors Management Co., Inc., managing one of the larger mutual funds. Trustee Home for Old Men and Aged Couples. Served as 2d lt., 7th regiment U.S. Infantry, Regular Army, 1898, 1st lieutenant 12th regiment, 1899-1901; served in Philippine Insurrection. Member Phi Beta Kappa. Republican. Episcopalian. Clubs: Downtown Assn., University (N.Y.C.). Author: The War Debts: A Question Still Unanswered, 1928; Collegiate Education and Standards of Value, 1936; also articles. Home: Hamlet Hill, Salisbury, Conn. Office: 63 Wall St., N.Y.C. Died Feb. 13, 1956; buried Woodlawn Cemetery, N.Y.C.

MITCHELL, Leeds, investment broker; b. Chicago, Ill., Apr. 26, 1877; s. J. Sidney and Helen (Leeds) M.; student Phillips Acad. (Andover, Mass.), 1896; Ph.B., Yale Univ., 1899; m. Dorothy Day, July 10, 1910; children—Leeds Mitchell, Jr., Margaret M. (Mrs. Barrett Wendell, Jr.); m. 2d, Christel Tessa Brey, Oct. 24, 1935. Began with Otis, Wilson & Co., 1900; partner Pringle, Fitch & Rankin, 1909; partner Walter Fitch & Co. up to 1915, and of Harris, Winthrop & Co. until Dec. 1929; partner, Winthrop, Mitchell & Co., 1929-Dec. 29, 1941; parter Shearson, Hammill & Co., 1941—; president United Paperboard Company, 1943-45, director, 1912—. Director Board of Trade, Chicago, 1933-35; president Chicago Stock Exchange, 1922-23, dir., 1916—. Served as mem. of the Bd. of Education, Lake Forest, 1920. Mem. K.O.A. Soc., Soc. of the Mayflower. Clubs: Chicago, University, Casino, Racquet, Saddle and Cycle, Arts (all at Chicago); New York Yacht, Yale of New York; (Cloister) (Yale); Attic (Chicago); Nantucket Yacht, Sankaty Head Golf (Nantucket). Home: 1200 Lake Shore Dr., Chgo. 10. (summer) Polpis Rd., Nantucket, Mass. Died July 25, 1957; buried Nantucket.

MITCHELL, O(liver) W(endell) H(olmes), physician; b. Lancaster, Mo., Aug. 17, 1886; s. William Francis (M.D.) and Elizabeth (Marshall) M.; M.D., U. Mo., 1908; m. Preston Settle, May 15, 1913; 1 son, Phillip Marshall. Asso. prof. bacteriol. and path., U. Mo., 1913-14; prof. bacteriol. and pub. health, Syracuse U., 1914-40, prof. pub. health 1940—; dir. post-grad. med. edn., Med. Soc. State N.Y., 1938—. Mem. A.M.A., Assn. Am. Pathols. and Bacteriols., Exptl. Biology and Medicine, Sigma Xi, Phi Kappa Phi. Conglist. Home: 428 Greenwood Pl. Office: 428 Greenwood Pl., Syracuse, N.Y. Died Dec. 20, 1948.

MITCHELL, Philip Henry, physiol. chemist; b. Southbury, Conn., Dec. 13, 1883; s. Henry Painter and Phoebe (Stoddard) M.; Ph.B., Sheffield Sci. Sch. (Yale), 1904; Ph.D., Yale, 1907; m. Alice Hinman Friend, May 30, 1910; children—Margery Fuller, Edith Stoddard. Instr. physiology, Brown, 1907-11, asst. prof., 1911-20, asso. prof., 1920-26, prof., 1926-49; dir. Woods Hole Biol. Sta., U.S. Bur. Fisheries, summers, 1914-20; cons. chemist U.S. Dept. Agr., 1913-17, investigator Conn. State Bd. Fish and Game, 1923-24. Trustee Lincoln Sch., Providence, R.I.; mem. Woods Hole Marine Biol. Lab. Corp. Mem. A.A.A.S., Am. Soc. Biol. Chemists, Sigma Xi. Unitarian. Clubs: Faculty, Art, Sphinx. Author: Text book of General Physiology for Colleges, 1923, 4th edit., 1948; Text Book of Biochemistry, 1946; also many articles relative to purine metabolism, physiology of shellfish, especially oysters, permeability of cells and tissues, chemistry of sea water. Home: 33 Cushing St., Providence, R.I. Died Feb. 2, 1955.

MITCHELL, R. Verne, printing equipment manufacturing exec.; b. Rapids, N.Y., July 12, 1885; s. Almer W. and Alma (Utley) M.; LL.B., Cornell U., 1907; m. Helen Morris Weber, June 24, 1914; 1 son, Henry Weber. Law clk. Castle & Worthington, Hawaii, 1907-09; spl. agt. Travelers Ins. Co., Hartford, Conn., 1909-11; ins. broker, partner Leonard Agy. Co., Canton, O., 1911-14; investment Banker, 1914-43, head R. V. Mitchell & Co., 1914-29, Mitchell, Herrick & Co., 1930-39; chmn. exec. com. McDonald & Co., 1939-43; pres. Harris-Seybold & Co., 1922-44, chmn. bd., 1944-54, honorary chairman of the board, 1954—; director of Thompson Products, Inc., Dill Mfg. Co., Cleve., Union Metal Mfg. Co., Canton, Copperweld Steel Co., Glassport, Pa., Cornell-Dubilier Electric Mfg. Co., South Plainfield, N.J. Chmn. industry adv. com. Graphic Arts Industry OPA, 1944-46. Chmn. exec. com. or pres. Aultman Hosp., 1916-40; v.p., dir. Lithographic Tech. Found. over 20 yrs. Mem. N.A.M. (nat. v.p., dir.), Nat. Printing Equipment Assn. (dir.; pres. 1944-51), Asso. Industries of Cleve. (bd. govs.), Investment Bankers Assn. (past gov.). Episcopalian. Home: East Dr., Congress Lake, Hartville, O. Office: 4510 E. 71st St., Cleve. 5. Died Jan. 1, 1955; buried Westlawn Cemetery, Canton, O.

MITCHELL, Ruth Comfort (Mrs. Sanborn Young), writer; b. San Francisco, Calif.; d. John Samuel and Florence Standish (Mowatt) Mitchell; m. Sanborn Young, Oct. 3, 1914. Writer of verse. 1-act plays for vaudeville, novels, short stories. Mem. League Am. Penwomen, P.E.N., Colonial Dames, D.A.R., P.E.O. Sisterhood, So. Calif. Women's Press Club, Woman's Athletic Club; mem. and state chmn. internat. relations, Calif. Fed. of Bus. and Professional Women's Clubs, Soroptimist Club, hon. pres. Camp Fire Girls. Santa Clara County, delegate to International Congress, Vienna, 1931. Member Theta Sigma Phi (life mem.). Republican. Protestant. Author: The Night Court and Other Verse, 1916; Play the Game, 1921; Jane Journeys On, 1922; Corduroy, 1923; Narratives in Verse, 1923; A White Stone, 1924; The Wishing Carpet, 1926; Call of the House, 1927; Army with Banners, 1928; Water, 1930; The Legend of Susan Dane, 1933; Old San Francisco (in four novelettes), 1933; Strait Gate, 1935; Of Human Kindness, 1940; Dust of Mexico, 1941; They Shall Come Again, 1944; also contbr. short stories. State pres. Pro America, 3 yrs., nat. pres. 2 yrs. Home: P.O. Box 247, Los Gatos, Cal. Died Feb. 17, 1953.

MITCHELL, Samuel Alfred, astronomer; b. Kingston, Can., Apr. 29, 1874; s. John C. and Sarah (Chown) M.; M.A., Queen's U., Can., 1894, LL.D., 1924; Ph.D., Johns Hopkins, 1898; LL.D., U. of Western Ontario, 1940; m. Milly Gray Dumble, Dec. 28, 1899; 1 son, Allan Charles Gray. Instructor and adj. prof., Columbia U., 1899-1913; prof. astronomy and director McCormick Observatory, U. Va., 1913-45; dir. emeritus 1945—. Astronomer, Eclipse expeditions Georgia 1900, Sumatra, 1901, Spain, 1905, Oregon, 1918, Calif., 1923, Conn., 1925, Norway, 1927, Niuafoou Island, 1930, Quebec, 1932, Canton Island, 1937; research asso. Yerkes Observatory (U. Chgo.), summers, 1907, 09, 10, 11, asst. prof. astrophysics, 1912-13. Awarded Watson Medal, 1948. Penrose lecture, Am. Philos. Soc., 1938; Arthur lecture, Smithsonian, 1937. Mem. Nat. Acad. Sciences (council mem. 1940-44), chmn. astronomical sect., 1947-50). Am. Philosophical Society, Am. Academy Arts and Sciences, A.A.A.S. (v.p. 1921); fellow and foreign asso. Royal Astron. Soc.; hon. mem. Am. Assn. Variable Star Observers; mem. Am. Astronomical Society (v.p. 1925-27); research asso. Carnegie Institution, 1934-45, Internat. Astron. Union (chmn. com. on parallaxes, 1928-35, chmn. com. on eclipses, 1935-48), Astronomisches Gesellschraft, Société Astronomique de France, Am. Asso. U. Profs. (pres. 1934. 35), Royal Astronomical Society of Canada, Beta Theta Pi, Phi Beta Kappa, Sigma Xi, Tau Beta Pi, Pi Gamma Mu. Clubs: Colonnade, Farmington. Author: Parallaxes of 260 Stars, 1920; Eclipses of the Sun, 1923, 5th edit., 1950; Parallaxes of 440 Stars, 1927; Fundamentals of Astronomy (with C. G. Abbot), 1927; Solar Eclipses, 1929, 36; Variable Stars, 1935; Parallaxes of 650 Stars (with D. Reuyl), 1940. Address: P.O. Box 3466 University Sta., Charlottesville, Va. Died Feb. 22, 1960.

MITCHELL, Stewart, editor; b. Cincinnati, O., Nov. 25, 1892; s. Charles Lucius and Mary Piatt (Suter) M.; student Cincinnati pub. schs., 1899-1909, Franklin Sch., 1909-11; A.B., cum laude, Harvard, 1915, A.M., 1916, Ph.D., 1933; unmarried. Instr. English, U. of Wis., 1916-17; mng. editor, The Dial, N.Y. City, 1919-20; tutor in history, Harvard, 1927-1929; mng. editor the New England Quarterly, 1928-1937, member board of editors, 1942—; editor, Massachusetts Historical Society, 1929-39, director, 1947—. Served as private, Field Artillery, U.S. Army, 1917-19, with A.E.F. in France. Traveled and studied in France and England, U. of Montpellier, France, and Jesus College, Cambridge, 1921-1923, traveled in Italy and Spain, 1923. John Harvard fellow, 1926. Mem. Am. Acad. Arts and Sciences, Am. Antiquarian Soc., Colonial Soc. of Mass. (life), Essex Institute (life), Mass. Hist. Soc., Lincoln Group of Boston, New England Geneal. Society (life). Democrat. Episcopalian. Club: Odd Volumes, St. Botolph, Harvard (Boston). Author: Poems, 1921; Horatio Seymour of New York, 1938. Editor of various vols. of Proc. and Collections of Mass. Hist. Soc.; also New Letters of Abigail Adams, 1947. Home: 1 Chestnut St. Office: 1154 Boylston St., Boston 15. Died Nov. 3, 1957; buried Mount Auburn Cemetery, Cambridge, Mass.

MITCHELL, Sydney Bancroft, library science; b. Montreal, Can., June 24, 1878; s. James and Sarah (Cooper) M.; B.A., McGill U., 1901, M.A., 1904; student New York State Library School, Albany, N.Y., 1903-04; Litt.D., Occidental Coll., 1945; m. Rose Frances Michaels, Dec. 28, 1908. Came to U.S., 1908, naturalized, 1922. In charge reading room McGill U., 1902-03, cataloguer, 1904-08; chief of order dept., Stanford U., 1908-11; head of accessions dept., U. of Calif. Library, 1911-19, asso. librarian, 1919-26, also asso. prof. library sci., 1922-26; prof. library science Univ. of Mich., 1926-27; dir. School of Librarianship and prof. librarianship, U. of Calif., 1927-44, dean of school and prof. librarianship, 1944-46, emeritus since 1946. Mem. Am. Library Assn., Calif. Library Assn. (pres. 1938-39), Calif. Horticultural Soc. (pres. 1933-45). Awarded W. R. Dykes medal for best new American iris, 1927. Awards: American Iris Society Medal for Hybridizing, 1943, and (English) Iris Society Foster Memorial, 1944. Author: Gardening in California, 1923; Adventures in Flower Gardening, 1928; From a Sunset Garden, 1932; Your California Garden and Mine, 1947; Iris for Every Garden, 1949. Contbr. on librarianship to professional mags. and on gardening to Sunset and other periodicals. Home: 633 Woodmont Av., Berkeley, Cal. Died Sept. 21, 1951.

MITCHELL, Thomas Edward, clergyman; b. Staunton, Va., Sept. 4, 1901; s. Thomas Harnett and Margaret (Dore) M.; student St. Charles Coll., Catonsville, Md., 1915-21; A.B., St. Mary's Sem., Balt., 1922; S.T.D., Am. Coll., Rome, Italy, 1927; grad. study Cath. U., 1929-30. Ordained priest Roman Cath. Ch., 1927; asst. pastor at churches in the Diocese of Richmond, Va., 1927-29; dir. Cath. Charities, Richmond, 1930-38; dean Sch. Social Work, Cath. U., Washington, D.C., Nov. 1938-July 1947; now pastor St. Elizabeth's Ch., Richmond, Va. Mem. Am. Assn. Social Workers, Am. Sociol. Assn., Nat. Conf. Cath. Charities. Address: 925 Fourquen Lane, Richmond, Va. Died Mar. 4, 1950.

MITCHELL, Walter Jenifer, judge; b. Charles County, Md., Mar. 16, 1871; s. William Hebbard and Emily Ellen (Mitchell) M.; student Charlotte Hall Sch., 1886-88; LL.B., U. Md., 1894; m. Florence Campbell Jenifer, Jan. 18, 1899; children—Mary Emily, Hugh Maxwell, Walter Jenifer, James Craik, Florence Elizabeth. Admitted Md. bar, 1894; editor, pub. La Plata (Md.) Times Crescent, 1897-1934; mem. Md. State Senate from Charles County, 1918-34, pres., 1931-33, also pres. spl. session, 1933; apptd. chief judge 7th Jud. Circuit Ct. of Md., 1934, and elected to same for term 1935-50; also asso. judge Md. Ct. Appeals, 1934—. Trustee Charlotte Hall Sch. Mem. Soc. of Cin. Democrat. Episcopalian. Address: La Plata, Md. Now ret. Died Mar. 10, 1955.

MITCHELL, William DeWitt, lawyer; b. Winona, Minn., Sept. 9, 1874; s. William and Frances (Merritt) M.; father justice Supreme Court of Minn., 20 yrs.; prep. edn., Lawrenceville (N.J.) Sch.; student elec. engring., Sheffield Scientific Sch. (Yale) 2 yrs.; A.B., Univ. of Minn., 1895, LL.B., 1896; LL.D., Yale, 1929, Williams Coll., 1930, U. of Mich., 1931; m. Gertrude Bancroft, June 27, 1901; children—William, Bancroft. Admitted to Minn. bar, 1896, and began practice at St. Paul; sec. 1st Charter Commn., St. Paul, 1900; regional counsel U.S.R.R. Adminstrn., 1919; chmn. Citizens Charter Com., St. Paul, 1922; was mem. firm Mitchell, Doherty, Rumble, Bunn & Butler, St. Paul; solicitor gen. of U.S. by apptmt. of President Coolidge, 1925-29; atty. gen. of U.S., Mar. 4, 1929-Mar. 4, 1933; chairman Supreme Court of U.S. adv. com. on Fed. Rules of Civil Procedure since 1935; mem. law firm Mitchell, Capron, Marsh, Angulo and Cooney, N.Y. City, since Apr. 1, 1933; chief counsel, joint Congressional committee investgating Pearl Harbor disaster. Served as 2d lt. 15th Minnesota Volunteer Infantry, 1898-99, and as acting judge advocate 2d Army Corps, 1898; brigadier engr. officer, 3d Brig., 1st Div., 2d Corps, 1899; capt. and adj. 4th Regt., Nat. Guard Minn., 1899-1901; col. 6th Regt. (now 206th) Inf. Nat. Guard Minn., 1918; entered F.A., O.T.S., Camp Taylor, Ky., 1918. Mem. Central Com., also counselor Am. Red Cross, 1925-29. Mem. Am. Bar Assn., Assn. Bar of City of N.Y. (pres. 1941-43), Spanish War Vets., Am. Legion. Democrat. Presbyterian. Clubs: Somerset, University (hon.), White Bear Yacht (St. Paul); Metropolitan, Burning Tree (hon. life) (Washington); Garden City Golf, Century (N.Y.). Home: Syosset, Long Island, N.Y. Office: 20 Exchange Pl., N.Y.C. Died Aug. 24, 1955.

MITCHELL, William Henry, steel exec.; b. Cin., Feb. 15, 1891; s. Oliver Thomas and Lillian (Parker) M.; LL.B., Univ. Cin., 1914; graduate studies Harvard, 1913-15; Columbia; married Lucile Morris, Dec. 28, 1915 (dec., 1952); 1 son, William Morris; m. 2d, Margaret T. Duhme, 1955. With Hearst Publs., N.Y., Boston, Detroit and Cleve., 1913-17; organized The Steel Forgings Co., Cin., 1917, sold in 1922 and organized Mitchell Steel Co. of Cin., pres. since 1922; treas. Stuebing-Cowan Co., 1925-29; organizer, pres. Belmore Steel Products Co., 1940-45; organizer, pres. Ridgewood Steel Co., 1941-46; civilian chief Cin. Ordnance Dist., 1947-50; organizer, pres. Ridgewood Ordnance, Inc., 1950—; dir., mem. exec. com. Armco Steel Corp., Central Trust Co., Eagle-Picher Co., Lunkenheimer Co., Trailmobile Co., Wealdon Co., Union Central Life Ins. Co., Yale & Towne Mfg. Co. Trustee, vice president The Christ Hospital; trustee, Herman Schneider Found. Mem. Am. Ordnance Assn. (councillor at large, chmn. gun forging com. exec. bd. arty. div.), Newcomen Soc., Sigma Alpha Epsilon, Phi Delta Phi. Presbyn. Mason (32°, K.T., Shriner). Clubs: Cincinnati Country, Queen City (Cin.), Commercial, Optimists, Recess (Cin.). Home: 2383 Observatory Rd., Hyde Park, Cin. Office: care Mitchell Steel Co., Beckman and Fricke Sts., Cin. 25. Died Sept. 16, 1958; buried Cemetery of Spring Grove, Cin.

MITRE, Don Luis (mē'trā), Argentine newspaper publisher; b. Buenos Aires, Oct. 28, 1869; grad. law, Nat. Coll. Buenos Aires; m. Matilde Negrotto, 1 son, 1 dau. Prof., sec. Nat. Coll. Buenos Aires; comml. judge. Began as journalist (grandson of founder) on newspaper, La Nación, now dir., pres. bd. dirs.; has expanded its fgn. news and helped build it to one of foremost newspapers of S.A. Now lives on estate adjacent to Buenos Aires. Roman Catholic. Mem. Academis Nacional de la Historia of Buenos Aires, Comisión Nacional de Museos y de Momumentos y Lugares Históricos, Institución Mitre. Hon. dir., Mitre Mus. Decorated Comdr. of Order of Eagle of the Andes (Bolivia); gold medal of Ultramar (Spain). Address: San Martin 344, Buenos Aires, Argentina. Died Nov. 8, 1950.

MIX, Arthur Jackson, educator, mycologist; b. Bolivar, N.Y., Sept. 30, 1888; s. Charles Milford and Rose (Kenyon) M.; A.B., Hamilton Coll., 1910, D.Sc. (honorary), 1955; Ph.D., Cornell Univ. 1916; student Royal College of Science London, 1929-30, Botany Institute, Hamburg, 1930, Bot. Mus., Inst. Plant Protection, Stockholm, 1939; m. Katherine Lyon, Nov. 5, 1917. Asst. botanist N.Y. Agrl. Expt. Sta., Geneva, 1915-16; instr. U. Kan., 1916-17, asso. prof., 1919-24, prof. since 1924, chmn. dept. botany, 1931-53; asst. pathologist U.S.D.A., 1918-19, pathologist, 1944-45, collaborator plant disease survey since 1946; botanist Kan. State Bd. Agr. since 1935; asst. prof. plant pathology Cornell, 1940; physiologist Pa. State Coll., 1945-46; del. 7th Internat. Bot. Congress, Stockholm, 1950. Chmn. Save The Children Fedn. Jayhawk Nursery Com., 1941-43 (nursery for bombed-out English children). Fellow A.A.A.S.; mem. Mycol. Soc. Am. (councillor 1948, v.p. 1952), Bot. Soc. Am., Am. Phytopath. Society, Soc. Linneénne de Lyon, Kan. Acad. Sci., Am. Scandinavian Found., Phi Beta Kappa, Sigma Xi (pres. Kan. 1950-52), Phi Sigma, Alpha Delta Phi. Author: Manual of Medical Mycology, 1953. Home: 1311 Engel Rd., Lawrence, Kan. Died Sept. 9, 1956.

MIZE, Robert Herbert (miz), bishop; b. Chicago, Ill., Feb. 10, 1870; s. Edward A. and Caroline (Silliman) M.; A.B., St. Stephen's Coll., Annandale, N.Y., 1894, D.D., 1921; grad. Gen. Tehol. Sem., 1897, D.D., 1923; m. Margaret Talman Moore, June 10, 1904 (died 1923); children—Edward Moore, Robert H., Margaret. Deacon and priest, 1897, P.E. Ch.; rector, St. John's Ch., Hiawatha, Kan., 1897-98, St. John's Mil. Sch., Salina, Kan., 1898-1906, St. Andrew's Ch., Emporia, Kan., 1906-12, St. Paul's Ch., Kansas City, Kan., 1912-21; bishop of Salina, 1921-39, resigned Jan. 1, 1939. Del. Gen. Conv., 1910, 13, 16, 19. Home: 700 2d Av., Yuma, Ariz. Died Apr. 1, 1956; buried Gypsum Hill Cemetery, Salina, Kan.

MOCK, Harry Edgar, surgeon; b. Muncie, Ind., Oct. 27, 1880; s. John D. and Mary Minerva (Jackson) M.; prep. edn., Muncie High Sch.; student Franklin (Ind.) Coll., 1900-02, D.Sc., 1926; B.S., U. Chgo., 1904; M.D., Rush Med. Coll., 1906; m. Golda M. Taylor, Dec. 25, 1908; children—Harry Edgar (M.D.), William Byford Taylor, Marjorie (Mrs. Wayne L. Gregory), Charles Jackson (M.D.), John Edward (M.D.). Practiced in Chgo., 1906—. Interne Cook Co. Hosp., 1908; emeritus attending surgeon, St. Luke's Hosp.; emeritus asso. prof. surgery, Northwestern Med. Sch.; cons. Surgeon B.&O. R.R., Rock Island Railroad, I.C. R.R. Lt. M.C., U.S. Army, 1917; col. 1919; U.S. Army del. Interallied Conf. Disabled Soldiers, Rome, 1919. Trustee Franklin Coll., Chgo. Commons. Fellow A.C.S., Chgo. Inst. Medicine, Chgo. Surg. Soc.; hon. mem. Am. Assn. Indsl. Physicians and Surgeons; mem. Am. Bd. Surgery, Am. Assn. Surgery of Trauma, Am. R.R. Surgeons Assn., A.M.A., Ill. State, Chgo. med. socs. Ind. Soc., Am. Med. Golf Assn. (pres. 1941); mem. Am. Acad. Orthopedic Surgery. Republican. Episcopalian. Clubs: University, Press, Sunset Ridge Golf, Ill. Senior Golf Association, United States Senior Golf Association. Author: Industrial Medicine and Surgery, 1919; Skull Fractures and Brain Injuries; also many articles on surgery. Editor: Principles and Practices of Physical Therapy, 1932. Home: 1616 Forest Pl., Evanston, Ill.; (winter) Ormond Beach, Fla. Died 1959.

MOCKMORE, Charles Arthur, civil engineer; born Platte Center, Neb., Nov. 7, 1891; s. of George Washington and Della (Proctor) M.; B. Engring., State U. of Ia., 1920, C.E., 1926; M.S., State U. of Ia., 1932, Ph.D., 1935; married Adriana Mary Margaret Corso, June 1, 1921 (died December 20, 1942); children—Charlotte A. Spring, Regina Theresa; married 2d, Buena Margason-Maris, June 27, 1946, step dau., Marjorie Maris-Peterson. Assistant superintendent of grounds and buildings, University of Ia., 1920-21; instr. in civil engring., Ore. State Coll., 1921-31, asso. prof., 1932-34, prof. and head of dept. civil engring. since 1934; research asso., U. of Ia., 1931-32. Served in U.S. Army, 1918. Mem. City Council, Corvallis, Ore., 1935-40; mem. Ore. State Bd. of Engring. Examiners. Won Big Ten medal, U. of Ia., in dual field of scholarship and athletics, 1920; won Croes medal Am. Soc. Civil Engrs., article "Flow Characteristics in Elbow Draft Tubes," 1939. Mem. Am. Soc. Civil Engrs., Am. Soc. for Engring. Edn., Am. Legion, Theta Xi, Tau Beta Pi, Sigma Xi. Republican. Methodist. Mason. Club: Triad (Ore. State Coll.), Town Club. Author: Hydraulic Machinery, Estimating and Cost Analyses, 1935. Contbr. to professional jours. Home: R.F.D. 4, Corvallis, Ore. Died April 11, 1953.

MODARELLI, Alfred E., judge; b. Union City, N.J., Nov. 27, 1898; s. Michael and Rosa C. (Ricciulli) M.; A.B., Columbia, 1920, A.M., 1922, LL.B., 1922; m. Florence O. Koment, Aug. 3, 1927; children—Alfred E., Elaine, Marilyn. Admitted to N.J. bar, 1922, and practiced in N.J., 1922-48; judge Municipal Ct., Union City, N.J., 1925-34; asst. prosecutor Hudson Co., 1934-44, spl. asst. corp. counsel Union City, 1944-48; U.S. dist. atty. for N.J., 1948-51, U.S. dist. judge for N.J. since 1951. Mem. Am., N.J. State and Hudson Co. (past pres.) bar assns., Am. Legion (past comdr.), Am. Acad. Polit. Sci. Club: North Hudson Lawyers (past pres.). Home: 4508 Hudson Blvd., Union City, N.J. Office: U.S. Court House, Newark 1. Died Sept. 22, 1957.

MODDER, Montagu Frank (maud-der), educator, author, illustrator; b. Ceylon, Nov. 24, 1891; s. Frank Hudson and Edythe Blanche (Modder) M.; B.A., Royal Coll., 1912; M.A., Clarke U., 1920; grad. study Yale, 1923; Ph.D., U. Mich., 1935; m. Mary Work, Sept. 3, 1927; children—Anne and Lucy (twins). Came to U.S., 1913, naturalized, 1932. Journalist, illustrator, contbr. to periodicals in India, Ceylon, also on staff Shanghai (China) Times, 1911-13: asst. prof. English Miami U., Oxford, O., 1922-27; asso. prof. English W.Va. U., 1927-30; grad. instr. U. Mich., 1930-35; prof. English Beloit (Wis.) Coll., 1935-57; vis. prof. English literature Dickinson College, 1957—; former vis. prof. George Peabody Coll., Nashville, Northwestern U. Mem. Am. Assn. U. Profs. Author: The Jew in English Literature, 1939. Contbr., illustrator mags. and jours. Political Cartoonist of the Beloit Daily News. Home: 227 S. College St., Carlisle, Pa. Died May 31, 1958; buried Ashland Cemetery, Carlisle.

MODEL, Jean (mōdĕl'), business exec.; b. Brussels, Belgium, June 26, 1915; s. Richard and Irma Jeanne (Frank) M.; student pub. and pvt. schs.; m. Faith Rockefeller, May 7, 1941; children—Robert, Jeannette, Richard Avery. Came to U.S., 1940, naturalized, 1943. Pres. Sonrisa Mining Co., Colombia, S.A. since 1941; partner Colombian Mining & Development Co. since 1951; dir. Export Internat. Corp., N.Y.C., Popular Custodian Corp., N.Y.C. Presdl. elector, Conn., 1952; mem. Presdl. Assay Commn., 1952. Served with Belgian Army, 1939-40; civilian pilot Air Transport Command, 1942-45. Mem. Am. Inst. Mining and Metall. Engrs. Clubs: Racquet and Tennis, Lunch, Met. Opera (N.Y.C.); Round Hill, Field, Indian Harbor Yacht (Greenwich). Home: 555 Lake Av., Greenwich, Conn. Office: 135 E. 54th St., N.Y.C. Died May 29, 1955.

MODERWELL, Charles McClellan, coal operator; b. Geneseo, Ill., May 6, 1868; s. John B. and Maria Antoinette (McClellan) M.; grad. Geneseo Collegiate Inst., 1885; Ph.B., Coll. Wooster, O., 1889; m. Jennie L. Cadwallader, Oct. 6, 1897; 1 son, Horace McClellan. Began as bookkeeper Mont. Coal & Coke Co., Fairmont, W.Va., 1891; western mgr. same co., and its successor, the Fairmont Coal Co., 1895-1902; organizer Nat. Coal & Coke Co., succeeded in 1904 by C. M. Moderwell & Co., Inc., of which was pres. until 1928; associated with Chgo., Wilmington & Franklin Coal Co., 1928—; pres. United Coal Corp., 1905-28; pres. Mordue Colleries Co., 1918-27; mgr. for receivers O'Gara Coal Co., 1918-19, v.p., 1919-22; regional adviser U.S. Pub. Works Adminstrn., 1933-34; apptd. regional dir. Pub. Works Adminstrn. for Ill., Mich., Wis., Ia. and Minn., Mar. 1934. Pres. Chgo. Bd. Edn., 1923-25. Ex-pres. Ill. Coal Operators' Assn.; mem. Art Inst. Chgo., Field Mus. of Natural History, Chgo. Hist. Soc., Beta Theta Pi, Phi Beta Kappa (1931). Republican. Presbyn. Clubs: Union League (ex-chmn. polit. action com.; pres. 1929). Home: 1624 Judson Av., Evanston, Ill. Died Dec. 20, 1955.

MODZELEWSKI, Zymunt, govt. ofcl. Poland; b. Apr. 15, 1900, Sosnowiec, Poland; ed. Ecole des Sciences Politiques, Paris. Active in reorgn. Polish Army in U.S.S.R., resigning with rank capt., 1944; organizer Ofcl. Polish Telegraph Agy. "Pol-press;" 1st A.E. and P. to Moscow: served as vice minister fgn. affairs, now minister fgn. affairs, 1947-51; del. 1st Gen. Assembly, U.N., rep. Security Council and U.N. Prep. Commn., 1946; del. Paris Peace Conf., 1946. Mem. central com. Polish Community Party. Address: Ministry of Foreign Affairs, Warsaw, Poland. Deceased.*

MOEHLMAN, Arthur B. (māl'man), author and educator; b. Racine, Wisconsin, Aug. 10, 1889; son Reverend John Henry and Helen (Coords) Moehlman; B.A., University of Michigan, 1912, M.A., 1921, Ph.D., 1923; Cornell Univ. Grad. Sch., 1912-13; m. Grace Fletcher, June 30, 1919; children—John Henry, Jeanne Moehlman de Alzamora. Began as teacher, 1913; prin. high sch., evening high sch. and summer high sch. until 1918; dir. statistics, publs. and administrative research, Detroit pub. schs., 1918-25; p.of. of admin. and supervision, Sch. of Edn., U. of Mich., 1923-51; ed. The Nations Schs., 1932-48; chmn. Michigan State Com. on Child Accounting and Uniform Finance System, 1922-25; consultant, N.J. State Sch. Survey, 1928, Culver Mil. Acad., 1930-40, President's Advisory Com. on Edn., 1936-38, Mich. Pub. Edn. Study Commn., 1942-47; dir. finance, organization, personnel, plant surveys in Ann Arbor, Belleville, Birmingham, Hillsdale, Jackson, Pontiac, Port Huron, Saginaw (Mich.) schools and Glencoe, Rockford (Ill.) schools. Fellow A.A.A.S.; member American Education Fellowship, N.E.A., Am. Assn. Sch. Adminstrns., Am. Assn. Adult Edn., Am. Acad. Polit. and Social Science, Michigan Edn. Assn., Am. Ednl. Res. Assn. (pres. 1929), Coll. Teachers of Edn., Nat. Council on Schoolhouse Constrn. (pres. 1939), Mich. Acad. Science, Mich. Authors League. National Advisory Council on School Bldg. Problems (pres., 1935, 36), Phi Kappa Phi, Phi Delta Kappa and Sigma Delta Chi. Clubs: Detroit Players, University. Author: Survey of Michigan State Normal Schools, 1922; Child Accounting, 1923; Public Education in Detroit, 1925; Public School Relations, 1927; Public School Finance, 1927; Hamtramck School Code, 1927; Public School Plant Program, 1929; Finance Procedures for Hamtramck, 1929; Public School Budget Procedure, 1929; Public Elementary School Plant (with Spain and Frostic), 1930; Social Interpretation, 1938; School Administration, 1940. Improvement of Public Education in Michigan, 1945; School Administration, 1951. Address: Naples, Fla. Died May 2, 1952.

MOEKLE, Herman Liveright, business exec.; b. Pittsburgh, Pa., Oct. 11, 1885; s. Albert and Anna Christina Bruelheide M.; student Duffs Iron City Coll., Pittsburgh, Pa., 1907-08, U. of Pittsburgh, 1910-14; LL.B., Detroit Coll. of Law; m. Beatrice Cecilia Garinger, Aug. 3, 1914; children—John Albert, Herman Liveright. Gen. clerical work with Pittsburgh Coal Co., 1907-13; accounting, sales, legal and exec. work Ford Motor Co., Detroit, 1913-47; now handling own investments. Member of City Det. Street Ry. Commn., 1950-53. Mem. Mich. State and Detroit bar assns., Army Ordnance Assn. Mason. Clubs: Pittsburgh Athletic Assn.; Detroit, Detroit Athletic, Detroit Golf, Economic (Detroit). Home: 16731 Huntington Rd., Detroit 19. Died Nov. 23, 1957; buried Woodlawn Cemetery, Detroit.

MOELLER, Philip, playwright; b. N.Y.C., Aug. 26, 1880; s. Frederick and Rachel Kate (Phillips) M.; student Columbia, 1901-08, traveled in Europe studying the theatre; unmarried. One of the founders, 1914, and dir. Washington Sq. Players; also a founder N.Y. Theatre Guild and one of its dirs.; producer of many plays. Author: Madame Sand, prod., N.Y.C. (Mrs. Fiske in leading rôle), 1917; Five Somewhat Historical Plays, 1918; Molière (Henry Miller and Blanche Bates in leading rôles), 1919; Sophie, 1919; etc. Home: Navarro Hotel. Office: 245 W. 52d St., N.Y.C. Died Apr. 26, 1958.

MOFFAT, Donald, author; b. St. Hubert's, N.Y., July 18, 1894; s. George Barclay and Frances Hillard (White) M.; student St. Bernard's Sch., N.Y.C., 1907-08, Middlesex Sch., Concord, Mass., 1908-12; A.B., Harvard, 1916; m. Pauline Baker de Camp, Nov. 16, 1918; children—Edith de Camp, Harriet White, Pauline de Camp, Leonora. Began writing, 1925. Served in Am. Field Service, 1916-17; capt., U.S. Army, 1917-18; now serving as lt. comdr. USNR. Clubs: Tavern, Country, Harvard (Boston); Harvard (N.Y.C.). Author: A Villa in Brittany, 1931; The Mott Family in France, 1937; The Prejudices of Mr. Pennyfeather, 1938; France Will Live Again, 1941. Contbr. to leading mags. Home: 83 Leicester St. Brookline, Mass. Died May 4, 1958; buried Forest Hills Cemetery, Jamaica Plain, Mass.

MOFFAT, Douglas Maxwell, ambassador; b. Stanhope, N.J., Nov. 16, 1881; s. Edward S. and Anna (McCartney) M.; B.A., Yale, 1903, M.A., 1904; LL.B. cum laude, Harvard, 1907; m. Gertrude Mali, June 13, 1921; children—Keith M., Virginia (Mrs. E. Farrar Bateson, Jr.). Admitted to N.Y. bar, 1911; partner Cravath, Swaine & Moore and predecessor firms, N.Y.C., 1913-56; A.E. and P. to Australia, 1956—. Dep. alien property custodian, Manila, P.I., World War I; prin. rep. U.S. Govt. to Middle East Supply Center, 1943; mem. N.Y. Adv. Bd. on Rates of Pay and Hours of Employment of Pub. Works, 1950—; chmn. Temp. Comm. Use of TV for Ednl. Purposes N.Y. State,

1952-53; mem. N.Y.C. Transit Authority, 1953-55. Mem. Assn. Bar City N.Y., N.Y. County Lawyers Assn., Am. Bar Assn., Pilgrims U.S. (exec. com.). Episcopalian. Clubs: University, Century Assn., Yale, Harvard, Downtown Assn. (N.Y.C.); Piping Rock (Locust Valley, N.Y.). Home: 21 E. 79th St., N.Y.C. 21. Died 1956.

MOFFAT, James E(rnest), economist; b. Cambray, Ont., Can., Aug. 26, 1883; s. Robert J. and Margaret (Kelly) M.; A.B., McMaster Univ., Can., 1914; A.M., U. Chgo., 1916, Ph.D., 1924; student London Sch. Econs., 1923-24; m. Marion Gracie Janes, June 11, 1921; children—Jean Janes, Robert James Douglas. Came to U.S. 1914, naturalized 1934. Fellowship in econs., U. Chgo., 1915-16; instr. econ., Ind. U., 1916-19, asst. prof. 1919-20, asso. prof. 1920-21, prof., 1921—, head dept. econ. 1935-45, adminstrv. asst. to pres., 1938; Panel mem., Nat. War Labor Bd. Disputes Div., 1943. Mem. Royal., Am., Midwest econ. assns., Ind. Acad. Social Scis., Am. Assn. U. Profs., C. of C., Kiwanis, Phi Beta Kappa, Beta Gamma Sigma, Delta Sigma Pi, Sigma Nu. Baptist. Mason. Co-author: Economic Problems of War, 1942; editor and co-author: Economics, Principles and Problems, 1942 (4th edit. 1947); contbr. numerous articles and revs. prof. jours. Home: 925 E. Hunter Av. Office Indiana University, Bloomington, Ind. Died Jan. 9, 1957.

MOFFATT, James Hugh, educator; b. Cumberland, Md., Sept. 10, 1878; s. Rev. James E. and Mary Jane (Jamieson) M.; B.A., Princeton, 1900, M.A., 1907; m. Florence Hicks Pomeroy, June 3, 1908; children—James Hugh (dec.), Elizabeth Pomeroy Moffatt Drouillet. Instr. Central High Sch. Phila. 1900-03, asst. prof., 1903-05, prof. English lit., 1905—. Presbyn. Club: University. Editor: Burke's Letter to Sheriffs of Bristol, 1904; Burke's American Taxation, 1905; Bunyan's Pilgrim's Progress, 1905; (with others) History of Athletics at Princeton, 1901; Shakespeare's Richard the Second (in Macmillan's Pocket English Classics Series), 1908. Address: 104 W. Montgomery Av., Ardmore, Pa. Died Jan. 3, 1929.

MOFFETT, Charles Alexander (mŏf'fĕt); b. Tallahassee, Elmore County, Ala., April 4, 1864; s. William Manay and Lucy Carrie (Cox) M.; ed. high sch., Rome, Ga., and night schs.; m. Fannie Kirkland, Feb. 27, 1887; children—Charles William, Florence, Paul, Margaret, Grace, Harry (dec.), Frances, John Byron. Learned machinist's trade with Noble Bros. & Co., Rome, 1880-84; shop foreman Brierfield (Ala.) Coal & Iron Co., 1885, Williamson Iron Co., Birmingham, 1886-93; with Birmingham Machine & Foundry Co., 1894-1901; mem. Moffett & Bonholzer, founders, Birmingham, 1902-03; chief engr. Republic Iron & Steel Co., 1904-07; supt. Birmingham Coal & Iron Co., 1908-09; chief engr. Southern Iron & Steel Co., 1909-12; with Gulf States Steel Co., 1912, as works mgr. until 1916, v.p., gen. mgr., 1916-21, pres., 1921-26; pres. Ala. State Bd. of Administration, 1926-30; now retired. Democrat. Episcopalian. Mason (33° active, K.T., Shriner). Club: Rotary. Home: 1310 Old Altamount Rd. Office: Masonic Temple, Birmingham, Ala. Died Dec. 27, 1949; buried Elmwood Cemetery, Birmingham.

MOFFETT, George Monroe, food mfr.; b. Parkersburg, W.Va., 1883; A.B., Princeton, 1904; m. Countess Odette F. F. du Bourg. Chmn. bd. Corn Products Refining Co.; dir. Commercial Solvents Corp., S. Puerto Rico Sugar Co. Trustee Central Hanover Bank & Trust Co. Home: Queenstown, Md. Office: 17 Battery Pl., N.Y.C. 4. Died Dec. 22, 1951.

MOFFETT, James Andrew, chairman of board Calif. Tex. Oil Co.; b. Parkersburg, W.Va., June 30, 1886; s. James Andrew and Kate (Ingersoll) M.; prep. edn., Lawrenceville (N.J.) Sch.; student Princeton U.; m. Adelaide McMichael; children—Robert A., Margaret (Mrs. George J. Atwell, Jr.), Jackson, Adelaide, Ruth; m. 2d, Mrs. Adeline Kim Moran, Nov. 10, 1934; m. 3d, Irene C. Hutton. Began as clerk Vacuum Oil Co., 1906; appointed director of sales and assistant to president Standard Oil Company of La., 1909, dir. and mgr. sales, 1909-27; elected dir. Standard Oil Co. (N.J.), 1919, v.p., 1924, later sr. v.p., until 1933; mem. Industrial Advisory Bd. NRA, 1933; v.p. and eastern rep. Standard Oil Co. (Calif.), 1934-36; chmn. board California-Texas Oil Co., Ltd., since 1936; Federal Housing adminstr., 1934-35. In charge purchases fuel oil, gasoline, for armies and navies, Great Britain, France and Italy, 1917-18; as secretary Nat. Petroleum War Service Com. bought oil and gasoline supplies for U.S. and Allies; served as mem. Allocation Com. of U.S. Fuel Adminstrn. for Petroleum Products for oil and gasoline, U.S. and Allies, to close of war. Clubs: Deepdale Golf, Nat. Golf, Links, Turf and Field, Yacht, Racquet (New York); Pacific Union (San Francisco). Home: 4 E. 72d St. Office: 130 E. 43d St., N.Y.C. Died Mar. 25, 1953.

MOFFIT, S. P., exec. v.p., dir. The Ruberoid Co. Address: 500 Fifth Av., N.Y.C. 18. Died Mar. 14, 1950.*

MOFFITT, James Kennedy, banking; s. James and Delia (Kennedy) M.; B.S., U. of Calif., 1886, LL.D., 1941; m. Pauline Fore (dec. 1947), 1 dau., Genevieve (wife of Dr. Malcolm Watts). Pres. Blake, Moffitt & Towne; chmn. exec. com. Crocker 1st Nat. Bank of San Francisco; director California Insurance Co., Schmidt Lithograph Co. Club: University. Home: 86 Sea View Av., Piedmont, Calif. Office: 599 8th St., San Francisco 3, Cal. Died Aug. 16, 1955.

MOHLER, Daniel Nathan, banker; b. St. Albans, W.Va., Jan. 16, 1892; s. Wm. E. and Jennie A. (Reeves) M.; student Washington & Lee U., 1910-12; LL.B., W.Va. U., 1915; m. Barbara L. Byrne, Jan. 17, 1920; children—Barbara Reeves, William Edward, Daniel Nathan. Admitted to W.Va. bar, 1915; practiced at Charleston, W.Va., 1915-38; pres. Charleston Nat. Bank since 1938; dir. Pfaff & Smith Builders Supply Co., Capital City Supply Co., Mohler Lumber Co., Charleston Nat. Mortage Co. Mem. W. Va. State Bd. of Edn., 1933-40. Republican. Presbyterian. Home: 1504 Quarrier St. Office: 201 Capital St., Charleston, W.Va. Died Dec. 18, 1951.

MOHLER, Jacob Christian, sec. Kan. State Bd. Agr.; b. Osborne County, Kan., Apr. 7, 1875; s. Martin and Lucina (Hoover) M.; ed. pub. schs., Topeka, Kan., Dougherty's Business Coll. and Washburn Coll., Topeka; LL.D., Washburn, 1914; m. Ruth McClintock, Oct. 30, 1901; children—John McClintock, James Calhoun, Marcia. In office of Kan. Bd. Agr., 1893—, began as clerk, appointed asst. sec., 1901, elected sec. 1914; dir. Central Trust Co. Chmn. Kan. Entomol. Commn., Kan. Housing Bd., Kan. Poultry Industry Com. Former pres. Nat. Assn. Secs. and Commrs. of Agr.; sec. Kan. Council of Def., World War I; was chmn. state apportionment com., and mem. state adv. com. U.S. Fuel Adminstrn. Mem. Gamma Sigma Delta. Republican. Episcopalian, Mason. Club: Jayhawker. Editor and compiler reports Kan. State Bd. Agr. Contbr. numerous articles on agrl. topics to farm papers and mags. Home: 2501 Granthurst. Address: State House, Topeka, Kan. Died Jan. 18, 1953; buried Topeka.

MOINET, Edward Julien (moi-nĕt'), judge; b. Louisville, O., July 14, 1873; s. Julien J. and Adaline (Savageot) M.; LL.B., University of Michigan, 1895; m. Eda M. Steel, October 30, 1897 (died June 25, 1942); children—Margaret Steel (Mrs. Margaret M. Hathaway), Mrs. M. Ben Heftler, Alden Edward (deceased); married 2d, Virginia Lee Monteith, November 22, 1944. Admitted to Michigan bar, 1895, and began practice at Ithaca; prosecuting attorney, St. Johns, Michigan, 1909-15; judge Circuit Court, 29th Judicial Circuit, Michigan, 1918-27; judge U.S. District Court, Eastern Dist. Mich., 1927-46, ret. Republican. Episcopalian. Mason (K.T., Shriner). Clubs: Detroit Athletic, Women's City. Address: The Whittier, 415 Burns Drive, Detroit 14. Died Dec. 23, 1952.

MOISE, Harold A., jurist; b. Natchitoches, La., Aug. 23, 1879; s. Judge James Campbell and Marie Aline (Sompayrac) M.; B.A., Cote Brillient Coll., 1899; LL.B., Tulane U., 1902; m. Io Leigh Bres, Jan. 28, 1903 (dec. 1927); children—Alice, Marian, Harold, James, Ernestine; m. 2d Amelia Keyes O'Neal, Oct. 12, 1930. Admitted to La. bar, 1902; elected legislature New Orleans, 1908; practice New Orleans, 1902-37; gen. counsel bd. commrs. Port New Orleans, 1920-37; del. Constl. Conv., chmn. Com. Gen. Provisions, 1921; judge Civil Dist. Ct. Div. C. Parish Orleans, 1937-48; presiding judge, 1946-48; asso. justice Supreme Ct. La., 1948-52, 1952-66; mem. exec. dept. com. framing new constn. La., 1947. Home: 142 Bellaire Dr. Office: Supreme Court Bldg, New Orleans. Died Sept. 26, 1958.

MOLÉ, Harvey E. (mō-lā'), engr.; b. Phila., Apr. 16, 1869; s. Harvey E. and Amelia (Cartwright) M.; M.E., Cornell U., 1897; m. Vena Fenno, June 24, 1904; 1 son, Harvey E. With J. G. White & Co., engrs., 1897-1901; asst. mech. engr. Manhattan Ry. Co., 1901-02; in charge power station dept. British Westinghouse Co., London, Eng., 1902-06; chief engr. in charge bldg. St. Petersburg Electric Tramways, 32 miles double track power station, substations, car barns and cars, Russian Westinghouse Co., St. Petersburg, Russia, 1906-08; cons. engring., including gen. engring., design, installment and mgmt. pub. utilities properties, in N.Y.C., 1909-34. Mem. and twice pres. Bd. of Edn., Summit, N.J., 1933-43. Fellow Am. Soc. M.E., Am. Inst. E.E. Home: 17 Essex Rd., Summit, N.J. Died Apr. 9, 1957.

MOLLIN, Fernand E., assn. exec.; b. Genoa, Neb., Sept. 22, 1887; s. Gustave A. and Alta (Cook) M.; student Lincoln (Neb.) Bus. Coll.; m. Clara Matson, Oct. 13, 1906; children—Lawrence F., Edwin L., Betty Ann. With Kent & Burke Co., ranchers, Genoa and Omaha, Neb., 1907-29; exec. sec. Am. Nat. Live Stock Assn., Denver, 1929—. Mem. Denver C. of C. Republican. Conglist. Clubs: National Press; Denver Athletic (Denver). Author: If and When It Rains; Uncle Sam, World's Largest Landlord; contbr. articles to publs. Home: 1655 Leyden St., Denver 7. Office: Cooper Bldg., Denver 2. Deceased.

MOLLOY, Sister Mary Aloysius, educator, writer; b. Sandusky, O., 1880; d. Patrick John and Mary (Lamb) Molloy; Ohio State U., 1899-1905, Ph.B., 1903, M.A., 1905, teaching fellow in English, 1903-05; grad. fellow in English, Cornell U., 1905-07, Ph.D., 1907. Asst. prin. Winona (Minn.) Sem., 1907-11; co-founder, Coll. St. Teresa, dean, 1911-28, president, 1928-46, president emeritus same coll., 1946—. Roman Catholic. Entered the Novitiate of the Sisters of the Third Order Regular of Saint Francis of the Congregation of Our Lady of Lourdes, 1922. Mem. Concordance Soc., Authors League Am., Medieval Acad. Am., Am. Catholic Pilos. Assn., Phi Beta Kappa. Mem. Commn. on Instns. Higher Learning N. Central Assn., 1918-43; mem. exec. com. Coll. Sect. of Nat. Cath. Ednl. Assn., 1922— (1st women to be apptd.), v.p. exec. com., 1947 (1st woman to be apptd.), 1948; mem. spl. com. to draft New Standards for N. Central Colls. and Univs., 1923; co-founder, Conf. Cath. Colls. for Women, 1918; sec., 1918-33; mem. standardization com. Nat. Cath. Ednl. Assn., 1925—; mem. New Accreditation Com., 1933; mem. Nat. Problems and Plans Com., 1937—; mem. Nat. Library Com., 1938—; mem. joint commn. Nat. Cath. Ednl. Assn. and Nat. Cath. Hosp. Assn., 1933—; mem. council on edn., div, faculty tng., Nat. Cath. Hosp. Assn., 1934—. Awarded Cross Pro Ecclesia et Pontifice by Pope Benedict XV, Nov. 3, 1918, for "distinguished service in cause of Catholic higher edn."; granted Cross of Merit, Constantinian Order of St. George, for "distinguished scholarship," 1923. Author: A Concordance to the Anglo-Saxon Translation of Bede's Ecclesiastical History, 1907; The Celtic Rite in Britain (in Studies in Language and Literature), 1910; The Lay Apostolate, 1915; Catholic Colleges for Women, 1918; A Catholic Educational Directory, 1919; The Parochial Schools—A Study in School Organization and Teacher Training, 1919; A Teresan Ideal in Service and System, 1928; Training the Nursing School Faculty, 1930. Collaborator: Wordsworth Concordance, 1911; Horace Concordance, 1914. Address: College of Saint Teresa, Winona, Minn. Died Sept. 28, 1954.

MOLNAR, Ferenc (mōl'nār); author: The Devil, 1908; Liliom, 1921; Fashions for Men, 1922; Guardsman, 1924; Husbands and Lovers, 1924; Prisoners (translation), 1925; Eva and the Derelict Boat, 1926; Play's the Thing, 1927; Paul Street Boys, 1927; Olympia, 1928; Plays, 1929; Prisoners, 1929; Swan, 1929; Good Fairy, 1932; No Greater Glory, 1934; Angel Making Music (translation), 1935; All the Plays of Molnár, 1937; Blue Eyed Lady, 1942; The Captain of St. Margaret's, 1945; Farewell My Heart, 1945. Directed his new play, Miracle in the Mountains. Address: Hotel Plaza, N.Y.C. 19. Died Apr. 1, 1952; buried Linden Hill Cemetery, N.Y.

MOLONY, William Hayes, clergyman, physicist; b. Crawfordsville, Ind., Dec. 4, 1884; s. James Sullivan and Mary (Hayes) M.; Litt.B., U. Notre Dame, 1907; student Cath. U. Am., Washington, 1907-10; dir. studies St. Edward's Coll., Austin, Tex., 1912-19, dir. studies and registrar, 1934-43; prof. physics and math. U. Notre Dame, 1912-32, dir. studies and registrar, 1933-34, prof. physics, 1943—. Address: Corby Hall, U. Notre Dame, Notre Dame, Ind. Deceased.

MOLTER, Harold, Christian science lecturer; b. Brooklyn, N.Y.; s. William and Barbara (Schoening) M.; ed. Boys' High Sch., Brooklyn, N.Y., 1903-06; A.B., Adelphi Coll., 1910; grad. courses Teachers' Coll., N.Y., 1911-14; m. Isabel Marie Richardson, Nov. 24, 1921; 1 son, Harold. Instr. School for the Blind, Overbrook, Pa., 1911-14; principal boys' dept., Sch. for the Blind, Watertown, Mass., 1914-18; supervisor for blinded servicemen, Fed. Bd. for Vocational Edn., Baltimore, Md., and Washington, D.C., 1918-20; supt. Chicago Jr. Sch. for Boys, St. Joseph, Mich., 1920-22; concert pianist and accompanist, 1925-29; chmn. exec. com. Christian Science activities, A Century of Progress, Chicago, 1931-34; Christian Science practitioner, 1931—; C.S. Com. on Publ. for Ill., 1935-43, teacher of C.S., 1943—; mem. C.S. Bd. of Lectureship, 1946-53; asso. editor C.S. Jour., Sentinel & Herald, 1953-56, editor, 1956—. Club: Illinois Athletic (Chgo.). Home: 512 Beacon St. Office: 1 Norway St., Boston 15. Died Nov. 1, 1959.

MOMENT, John James (mō'mĕnt), clergyman; b. Orono, Ont., Can., Feb. 1, 1875; s. Robert and Sarah Wightman (Gairdner) M.; A.B., Princeton, 1896; B.D., Hartford Theol. Sem., 1906; D.D., Washington and Jefferson Coll., 1925; D.D., Princeton, 1947; m. Clara Louise Cross, May 21, 1908; children—Anne (Mrs. Reade H. Ryan), Jean Gairdner (Mrs. Walter S. Douglas), Robert (naval aviator, killed in war), John (paratrooper). Ordained Presbyn. ministry, 1906; asst. pastor 1st Presbyn. Ch., E. Orange, N.Y., 1906-08; asso. pastor Bergen Ref. Ch., Jersey City; later pastor High Street Presbyn. Ch., Newark, until 1918; pastor Crescent Avenue Ch., Plainfield, N.J., 1918-48. Mem. A.A.A.S., Phi Beta Kappa. Republican. Author: Faith in Christ, 1917; The Throne of David, 1929; We Believe, 1942; Words of Amos and Eucharist (cantatas). Author of many hymns and anthems. Home: 2 Crabapple Lane, Plainfield, N.J. Died May 11, 1959; buried Plainfield.

MONIZ, Egas (Antoine Caetano de Abren Freire), neurologist; b. Avanca, Portugal, Nov. 29, 1874; s. Fernando de Rezende and María de Rosario de Sousa; ed. univs. of Coimbra, Bordeaux and Paris; m. Elvira de Macedo Dias, 1902. Prof. U. of Coimbra until 1911; prof. neurology U. of Lisbon from 1911, now emeritus. Served as dir. Inst. of Neurology for Sci. Investigations, also physician Hosp. of Santa Marta (both Lisbon). Dep. Portuguese Liberal Parliament; minister to Madrid, 1918; minister fgn. affairs, 1918-19. Discoverer cerebral angiography and pre-frontal leucotomy. Recipient Nobel prize (joint) for physiology and medicine, 1949. Mem. Acad. des Ciencias (Lisbon), Acad. de Medecine (Paris), Acad. Brasileira de Letras, Acad. de Medecine (Madrid). Decorated Comdr. Legion of Honor, Grand Cross Isabella Catolica, Grand Cross Santiago de Espada. Author many books relating to field. Address: av. Cinco Outubro 73, Lisbon, Portugal. Died Dec. 1955.*

MONK, Wesley Elias (mŭngk), lawyer; b. Stoughton, Mass., Aug. 21, 1874; s. Hiram Alexander and Lucinda (Fuller) M.; A.B., Brown U., 1896; LL.B., Harvard, 1899; m. Clara L. Wilson, June 29, 1905; children—Alice (Mrs. Henry D. Locke), Marjorie (Mrs. O. Frank Burbank, Jr.). Admitted to Mass. bar, 1897; selectman town of Watertown, Mass., 1912-14, town counsel, 1915-20; mem. Mass. Ho. of Reps., 1915-20, Mass. Senate, 1921-22; State Commr. of Ins., 1923-28; gen. counsel Mass. Mut. Life Ins. Co., Springfield, 1929—. Mem. Am., Mass., Hampden County bar assns., Delta Phi. Republican. Unitarian. Mason. Club: Unitarian (Watertown, Mass.). Home: 118 Washington Av., Needham 92, Mass. Died Jan. 14, 1958.

MONNETT, Francis Sylvester, lawyer; b. Kenton, O.; s. Thomas J. and Henrietta (Johnston) M.; A.B. and M.A., Ohio Wesleyan U., 1880; LL.B., Nat. Law Sch., Washington, 1882; m. Ella K. Gormly, Feb. 17, 1887. Admitted to Ohio bar, 1883, began practice at Columbus; atty. gen. of Ohio, 1896-1900; anti-trust Republican until 1901, now Independent Republican. Prosecuted suits under Ohio anti-trust laws against Standard Oil Co.; spl. counsel in prosecution of oil trust cases under President Roosevelt; spl. counsel for State of Okla. in constitutional contest before President Roosevelt. Mem. Am., Ohio State bar assns., Phi Kappa Psi. Address: 44 E. Broad St., Columbus, O. Deceased.*

MONRO, Hugh Reginald (mŭn-rō'), mfr., banker; b. Orangeville, Ont., Can., June 18, 1871; s. Fisher and Agnes (Crawford) M.; LL.D., Cumberland University, 1932; married Florence Bean, Apr. 27, 1893; children—Hugh R. (dec.), Dorothy Adelle (Mrs. Wm. L. Dill, Jr.). Organized Kaumagraph Co., 1903, pres., chmn. bd., 1903-33; pres. and dir. Montclair (N.J.) Nat. Bank, 1928-36; pres. Montclair Clearing House, 1934-35; vice pres. and dir. Monro-King & Graemels Realty Co., 1929-39; pres., dir. Pennman Realty Corp.; pres. and dir. Montclair Printing Co.; vice pres. and dir. Niagara Lithograph Co.; director Guardian Life Ins. Co. of America, Montclair Trust Co.; v.p., dir. Watchung Title & Mortgage Guaranty Co., 1928-51. Chmn. Com. for Work Among War Prisoners, 1915-19; mem. Nat. Service Commn., 1917-18, Montclair Sinking Fund Commn., 1926-29; chmn. Town Planning Bd. (Montclair), 1930-33. Director Stony Brook Sch., Stony Brook Assembly (pres. 1924-49); past president Am. Tract Soc.; chmn. bd. Pocket Testament League; dir., treas., John Milton Soc. for the Blind; director New York Christian Home; dir. and sec. Presbyn. Pub. Company, 1926-48; director, member finance committee Society for Providing Religious Literature for the Blind: director and treasurer World Dominion Movement; trustee Water Street Mission, N.Y. City. Mem. Acad. Polit. Science, Pilgrims of U.S., Monro Clan (Scotland), Fgn. Policy Assn.; World's S.S. Assn. (chmn. N.A. 1928-40); Intl. Council Rel. Edn., (v.p., 1927-28), Met. Mus. Art, Am. Inst. Management, English Speaking Union U.S. Clubs: Clergy, Nat. Rep. Mem. Bd. Ch. Erection, Presbyn. Ch. U.S.A., 1922-40; Ch. Com., State of N.Y., 1926-42; West Side Assn. Comm., N.Y., v.p. 1928-32. Presbyterian. Ministers Fund (corporator). Elder First Presbyterian Church of Orange. Home: 5 Roosevelt Place, Montclair. Office: Montclair Center, Montclair, N.J.; and 386 4th Av., N.Y.C. Died Nov. 20, 1954.

MONROE, Pleasant Edgar, clergyman, ex-coll. pres.; b. Rowan County, N.C., Dec. 18, 1875; s. Thomas Burton and Victoria Cathrine (Cress) M.; A.B., N.C. Coll., A.M., 1898; grad. Chgo. Luth. Sem., 1901; D.D., Newberry (S.C.) Coll., 1919, LL. D., 1947; m. Julia Houseal Hentz, Apr. 2, 1902; 1 dau., Mary Kathryne (Mrs. Clyde Erson Gwin). Ordained to Luth. ministry, 1901; successively pastor Pulaski, Va., Ehrhardt and Johnston, S.C., Holy Trinity, Hickory, N.C., until 1930, St. James Ch., Concord, N.C., 1930-34; pres. Summerland, later Newberry (S.C.) Coll., 1913-24, pres. Lenoir Rhyne Coll., Hickory, N.C., 1925-26, 34-49. Pres. N.C. College Conf., 1945-46. Mem. Bd. Fgn. Missions United Luth. Ch.; pres. Luth. Synod, 2 terms. Democrat. Kiwanian. Home: 357 7th St. N.W., Hickory, N.C. Died July 31, 1954.

MONROE, Thomas, transportation exec.; b. Washington, July 19, 1899; s. Franklin and Margaret (Melton) M.; student Catholic U., 1919-20, C.F.S., Georgetown U., 1923; m. Helen Rosemary Schladt, July 26, 1923; children—Thomas Melton, Nancy Sue (Mrs. R. P. Briggs). With U.S. Lines, 1923—, v.p., European gen. mgr.; v.p., dir., European gen. mgr., U.S. Lines Operations, Inc; v.p. Roosevelt S.S. Co., Inc.; chmn. bd., dir. Atlantic Transport Co., Ltd. U.S. del. to and U.S. mem. standing com. Internat. Chamber of Shipping; mem. European com. Nat. Fedn. Am. Shipping. Pres. Service Consignation Atlantique, Paris, Societe Maritime Anversoise, Antwerp, Rossquai, G.m.b.H., Hamburg. Served as shipping advisor on Harriman Mission to Gt. Britain, 1941-42; dir. for United Kingdom and Continent, U.S. War Shipping Adminstrn. Served overseas, U.S. Navy, 1917-19; col. U.S. Army, asst. chief transportation, E.T.O., 1942-46. Decorated U.S. Legion of Merit, French Ordre Du Merite Maritime. Clubs: University, Army and Navy (U.S.); Verbersee (Hamburg); Royal Thames Yacht, Transportation, American (London). Home: 21 Dalecarlia Dr., Westmoreland Hills 16, Md.; also Highfields Farm, Frederick Co., Md.; also Dorset House, Gloucester Pl., London. Office: One Broadway, N.Y.C. 4.; also 50 Pall Mall, London, Eng. Died Dec. 9, 1959.

MONROE, William Stanton, mech. engr.; b. Chgo., Aug. 22, 1868; s. Henry Stanton and Martha (Mitchell) M.; M.E., Cornell U., 1890; m. Anna Hamill Clarke, Oct. 31, 1898 (died May 22, 1944); children—Ernest H. (dec.), Henry S. Engaged in constrn. work for elec. power prodn., 1891—; in 1900 entered office of Sargent & Lundy (founded in 1891); pres. Sargent & Lundy, Inc., cons. engrs. for large elec. power cos., 1919-38, now ret.; ex-dir. Western Light & Telephone Co.; dir. Central Cold Storage Co. Mem. bd. trustees, Ill. Inst. Technol. In 1922 state improvement in steam power stas. for electric power involving increased steam pressures and temperatures and reheating which led to great reductions in operation costs. Mem. Am. Soc. Mech. Engrs., Western Soc. Engrs. (pres. 1929-30), Am. Soc. Civil Engrs., Franklin Inst., Acad. Polit. Sci., A.A.A.S., Chgo. Geog. Soc. (dir.). Clubs: University, Tavern (Chgo.). Home: 64 E. Elm St. Office: 105 S. LaSalle St., Chgo. Deceased.

MONTAGUE, Robert Miller (mŏn'tȧ-gū), army officer; b. Portland, Ore., Aug. 7, 1899; s. Charles David and Effie (Miller) M.; student U. of Ore., 1916-17; B.S., U.S. Mil. Acad., 1919; grad. F.A. Basic Sch., 1920, F.A. Sch., Advanced Course, 1933, Command and Gen. Staff Sch., 1938; m. Mary Louise Moran, June 21, 1921; 1 son, Robert Miller. Commd. 2d lt., F.A., U.S. Army, Nov. 1, 1918, and advanced through the grades to lieutenant general, 1955; Operations and Training Div., G-3, July 1941; Artillery Comdr. 83d Inf. Div., June 1942-Mar. 1946; dir. of Antiaircraft and Guided Missiles Br. of the Artillery Sch., 1946-47; comdg. gen., Sandia Base, Albuquerque, N.M., July 1947-Feb. 1951; dir. OPOT Division, Hdqrs. EUCOM, 1951-52; dep. chief army Field Forces, 1952—; comdg. gen., I Corps, 1955-56; comdr. chief, Carribean Command, 1957—. Mem. Delta Tau Delta. Club: Army and Navy Country (Arlington, Va.). Home: 2120 Walnut Pl., Louisville 5. Address: Caribbean Command, Quarry Heights, Canal Zone. Died Feb. 20, 1958.

MONTAGUE, Wallace Tenney, business exec.; b. Worcester, Mass., July 2, 1889; s. George C. and Martha J. (Worth) M.; B.S., Worcester Poly. Inst., 1908-12; m. May W. Robbins, Sept. 27, 1913; children—Gordon R., Jane W. (Mrs. H.B. Wood, Jr.). Research lab. Norton Co., Worcester, 1912-13, sales dept., 1914-16, head sales engineering dept., 1916-19, asst. sales mgr. abrasive div., 1919-22, machine div., 1922-23, sales mgr. machine div., 1923-29, asst. gen. sales mgr., 1929-32, dir. sales abrasive products div., 1932-35, mgr. sales planning and development, 1935-39, asst. v.p., 1939-42, v.p., mgr. bus. planning and development since 1942, dir. since 1946; trustee Worcester Co. Instn. for Savs. Chmn. Worcester Municipal Airport Commn. since 1946; dir. Worcester Boys Club; dir. spl. gifts div. Community Chest, Worcester. Trustee Worcester Poly. Inst. since 1938. Mem. Worcester C. of C. (pres. 1940-41), Newcomen Soc. (chmn. indsl. development com.), Grinding Wheel Mfrs. Assn., Sigma Alpha Epsilon. Republican. Baptist. Mason. Clubs: Worcester, University, Worcester Country. Home: 14 Aylesbury Rd., Worcester. Office: New Bond St., Worcester 6, Mass. Died July 30, 1952.

MONTAGUE, William Pepperell, prof. philosophy; b. Chelsea, Mass., Nov. 24, 1873; s. William Pepperell and Helen (Cary) M.; A.B., Harvard, 1896, A.M., 1897, Ph.D., 1898; LL.D., U. Cal., 1945; m. Helen Weymouth Robinson, Aug. 5, 1896; children—William Pepperell, Robinson Prescott Cary. Instr. philosophy, Radcliffe Coll., and docent, Harvard, 1899; instr. philosophy, U. Cal., 1899-1903; instr. philosophy Barnard Coll., Columbia, 1903-07, adj. prof., 1907-20, prof., 1920-41, 1907-20, professor, 1920-41, Johnsonian prof., 1941-47; vis. prof. philosophy, Johns Hopkins, 1922; Mills lectr. in philosophy, U. Cal., 1928; vis. Carnegie prof. internat. relations, to Japan, Czechoslovakia and Italy, 1928; Terry lectr., Yale, 1930, Ingersoll lectr., Harvard, 1932, Carus lectr., Chgo., 1933; vis. Flint prof. of philosophy and Foerster lectr., U. Cal., 1943; vis. prof. philosophy, 1948; Johnsonian prof. emeritus, 1947—. Chmn. del. Am. Philos. Assn. to Internat. Congress of Philosophy, Oxford, Eng., 1920, Prague, 1934, Paris, 1937. Fellow A.A.A.S.; mem. Am. Philos. Assn. (pres. 1923), Aristotelian Soc. (London). Clubs: Harvard (New York); St. Andrews Golf. Author: (with others) The New Realism, 1912; The Ways of Knowing or the Methods of Philosophy, 1925; Belief Unbound, A Promethean Religion for the Modern World, 1930; The Chances of Surviving Death, 1934; The Way of Things—a Philosophy of Knowledge, Nature and Value, 1940. Co-editor Contemporary American Philosophy, 1930. Contbr. to Jour. of Philosophy, Ethics, Philos. Rev., etc. Home: 27 West 9th St., N.Y.C. Died Aug. 1, 1953.*

MONTELEONE, Frank Joseph, hotel exec.; b. New Orleans, Aug. 21, 1892; s. Antonio and Sophia (Jahraus) M.; student Jesuits Coll., Soule Bus. Coll.; m. Marie Elodie Attaway, June 20, 1927; 1 son, William A.; m. 2d, Isabelle Miller, May 31, 1952. Mng. dir., pres. Hotel Monteleone, New Orleans, 1935—. Served in USN, World War I. Mem. Am. Legion, C. of C., Internat. House, Am., Internat., La., New Orleans hotel assns., La. Travelers Assn., Hotel Greeters Am., Athenians, Rex Carnival Orgn. Clubs: New Orleans Country, Southern Yacht, Metairie Country, New Orleans Traffic, Opera (New Orleans); Pass Christian Country, Pass Christian Yacht (Miss.). Address: New Hotel Monteleone, 214 Royal St., New Orleans 12. Deceased.

MONTE-SANO, Vincent, fashion designer; b. San Mauro, Italy; s. Joseph and Catherine (Autera) M.; student pvt. Cath. sch., Italy; grad. Acad. Design, N.Y.C., 1903; m. Margaret Ugolini, June 28, 1911; 1 son, Vincent. Employed J. McCreery & Co., custom dept., 1903-12; own business, 634 Fifth Av., 1912-25; pres., designer Monte Sano & Pruzan, Ltd., N.Y. C., 1924—; creator Am. fashions, 1924—. Dir. Indsl. Council. Recipient Coty Am. Fashion Critics award, 1945; recognition Phila. Mus. Art, 1947; Neiman Marcus award, 1952. Mem. Italian C. of C. Roman Catholic. (mem. Cardinal's Com. of the Laity). Clubs: Shore, Men's, St. Augustine (Larchmont, N. Y.) Home: Chatsworth Gardens, Larchmont, N.Y. Office: 21 W. 46th St., N.Y.C. Died May 22, 1955; buried Gate of Heaven, Mt. Pleasant, N.Y.

MONTES DE OCA, Luis, chmn., exec. pres. Banco Internacional, S.A.; chmn. Banco de Fomento Urbano, S.A., Banco Internacional de Capitalizacion, S.A., Banco Internacional Immobiliario, S.A.; La Oceanica Casualty Ins. Co., Cementos Portland del Bajio, S.A., Cementos Guadalajara, S.A., Condominio, S.A. Formerly mem. Mex. consular service in Europe and U.S., also comptroller gen. minister of finance, chmn. Nat. Rys. of Mexico, and gov. Bank of Mexico (central bank of Mexican Reserve System). Commander of Legion of Honor (France). Address: Banco Internacional, S.A., Edificio Guardiola, Mexico City, Mexico. Died Dec. 4, 1958; buried Pantheón Francés, Mexico City.

MONTGOMERY, George Hugh Alexander, barrister; b. Philipsburg, P.Q., Can., Feb. 5, 1874; s. Rev. Hugh and Eliza Mary (Slack) M.; student Bishop's Coll. Sch., Lennoxville, 1886-98; B.A., U. Bishop's Coll., 1893; D.C.L. (hon.), 1924; B.C.L., McGill U., 1897; LL.D. (hon.), Dalhousie, Halifax, N.S., 1936; m. Gwendoline M. Baptist, June 18, 1909; children—George Hugh, Enid. Called to bar of Quebec, Jan. 1898; created K.C., 1909; partner Smith, Markey & Montgomery, Montreal, P.Q., 1898-1905; in charge legal dept., Montreal Light, Heat & Power Co., 1905-07; joined Brown, Montgomery & McMichael, 1907; appt. batonnier, Montreal bar, 1927; with firm Montgomery, McMichael, Common, Howard, Forsyth & Ker, 1938—; v.p. Can. Steamship Lines, Ltd. Dir. The Royal Bank of Canada, Montreal Trust Co., Dominion Engrng. Works, Ltd., Dominion Bridge Co., Ltd., Canadain Internat. Paper Co., Dominion Steel & Coal Corp., N. Am. Life Assurance Co., Canadian Spool Cotton Co., Bldg. Products, Ltd., United Corporations, Ltd., Investment Bond & Share Corp., Keystone Transports, Ltd. Chancellor, Bishop's U., Lennoxville, Que. Pres. Conf. Governing Bodies Legal Profession in Can., 1929-30. Hon. mem. Am. Bar Assn. Mem. Can. Bar Assn. (pres. 1935). Mem. Anglican Ch. Clubs: Mount Royal, St. James's, University, Forest & Steam, Montreal; Garrison (Quebec); Rideau (Ottawa). Home: 3940 Cote des Neiges Rd. Office: Messrs. Montgomery, McMichael, Common, Howard, Forsyth & Ker, Royal Bank Bldg., Montreal, Que. Died June 19, 1951.

MONTGOMERY, Guy, prof. English; b. Albion, Neb., June 9, 1886; s. George M. and Carrie (Letson) M.; A.B., U. of Neb., 1909; A.M., U. of Calif., 1917, Ph.D., 1921; hon. LL.D., St. Mary's (Calif.), 1937; m. Grace McGonagle, June 14, 1911. Instr., West High Sch., Salt Lake City, 1909-16; instr. in English, U. of Calif., 1917-20, asst. prof., 1921-24, asso. prof., 1925-29, prof. of English since 1929, chmn. of dept., 1930-42; asso. dean, Coll. of Letters and Science, 1930-39; exchange prof., U. of Heidelberg,

Ger., 1926. Mem. Cath. Commn. Intellectual and Cultural Affairs. Mem. Am. Assn. Univ. Profs., Phi Beta Kappa. Democrat. Roman Catholic. Clubs: Athenian-Nile (Oakland, Calif.); Faculty (Berkeley). Author: The New World, 1921; The Challenge of Restoration Comedy, 1928; Essays of Francis Bacon, 1930; Anthology of English Classics, 1936; John Dryden and the Battle of the Books, 1943. Home: 814 Oxford St., Berkeley 7, Cal. Died Sept. 23, 1951.

MONTGOMERY, Henry Arthur, lawyer; b. Topeka, Kan., Aug. 16, 1887; s. Hiram and Frances Matilda (Graves) M.; student U. Mich., lit. dept., 1904-07; LL.B., Detroit Coll. Law, 1921; m. Bessie E. Henderson, June 24, 1908; children—Harry Thomas, Lee Jay L., John Osborn. Pub. Clio (Mich.) Messenger, 1907-11; reporter, city editor, editorial writer, Detroit News, 1911-16; friend of the court (Social Service Dept., Wayne Circuit Court), 1916-19; publicity work, 1919-21; city editor, mng. editor, editor-in-chief Detroit Times, 1922-32; in practice law, 1921-22; clerk Wayne County, 1935-36; commr. Mich. Unemployment Compensation Commn., 1937-39; practice of law, 1932—, counsel Mich. Consol. Gas Co., 1941—. Mem. Am. Bar Assn., State Bar Mich., Detroit Bar Assn. (pres. 1953-54, dir. 1949-55), Detroit Hist. Soc., Adcraft Club Detroit, Detroit Mus. Art Founders Soc., Detroit Bd. Commerce, Pub. Relations Soc. Am., St. Andrews Soc., Detroit Philos. Soc., Baseball Writers Assn. Am. (hon.), Am., Mich. farm bureaus, Holstein-Friesian Assn. Am., Mich. Holstein-Friesian Assn. Mason (33°). Club: Detroit Athletic Republican. Home: 18695 Parkside Av. Office: Penobscot Bldg., Detroit 26. Died Mar., 1957.

MONTGOMERY, James Shera, clergyman; b. Mt. Carmel, Ind.; s. Rev. William M. and Anna (Newlove) M.; grad. Muncie (Ind.) Acad., 1881; collegiate edn., Northwestern, and Oxford, Eng.; B.D., Garrett Bibl. Inst., 1892, D.D., 1900; m. Emma Shortle, Oct. 21, 1885 (dec.); m. 2d, Elsie May Farnham, Apr. 21, 1924. Ordained M.E. ministry, 1893; pastor St. Paul's Ch., Toledo, O., Wesley Ch. and Fowler Ch., Mpls., to 1911, Met. Meml. M.E. Ch., Washington, D.C., 1911-16, Calvary M.E. Ch., 1916-26; Met. Ch., 1926-33; ret. 1933; chaplain U.S. House Reps., 1921-50, now emeritus. Chaplain Nat. House Reps., 1921—. Author: John Ruskin—The Voice of a New Age. Contbr. religious papers and revs. Lectr. sociologic and lit. subjects. Home: 100 Maryland Av. N.E., Washington, D.C. Died June 30, 1952.

MONTGOMERY, John Flournoy; b. Sedalia, Mo., Sept. 20, 1878; s. James Albert and Eudora Virginia (Meng) M.; ed. pub. schs. and Ramsdell Acad., Sedalia; m. Hedwig Wildi, Sept. 7, 1904 (died 1953); children—Marie, Jean. Advt. mgr. Helvetia Milk Condensing Co., 1902-07; sec., treas. The John Wildi Evaporated Milk Co., 1907-11, v.p., 1911-14, pres. 1914-25; managing dir. Nestle's Food Co., 1918-25; chmn. Internat. Milk Co., 1925-33, and since 1941. E.E. and M.P. to Hungary, 1933-41. Chmn. Berlin Chapman Co.; chmn. exec. com. Cloverdale Farms Co. Hon. pres. Am. Hungarian Federation. Was mem. Council Nat. Defense, chmn. army and navy com. for purchasing canned milk during World War. Democrat. Presbyterian. Mason (32d degree). Clubs: Metropolitan (N.Y.); Ekwanok Co., Equinox Links (Manchester, Vt.); Denham Golf, Walton Health (London). Author (book): Hungary, the Unwilling Satellite. Address: Manchester, Vt. Died Nov. 7, 1954.

MONTGOMERY, Richard D., oil exec.; b. Los Angeles, Dec. 31, 1889; s. George Arthur and Alice Jane (Richardson) M.; U. Calif., 1911; m. Mabel Phelps, May 7, 1917; children—Elizabeth (Mrs. Collier), Richard. Employee Standard Oil Co. of Calif., 1916-26; joined Richfield Oil Corp., Los Angeles, 1926, now v.p. in charge prdn. Mem. Phi Delta Theta. Clubs: Beach, California (Los Angeles). Home: 650 Muirfield Rd., Los Angeles 5. Office: 555 S. Flower St., Los Angeles 17. Died Dec. 10, 1952.*

MONTGOMERY, R(ichmond) Ames, clergyman, educator; b. Hendricks County, Ind., July 16, 1870; s. John Martin and Frances Caroline (Wright) M.; de Pauw U., 1886-87; Hanover (Ind.) Coll., 1888-91; A.B., Miami U., 1893; grad. McCormick Theol. Sem., 1896; D.D., Miami U., Oxford O., 1905; LL.D., Coe Coll., 1918; m. Mary Frances Allhands, May 1897 (died July 20, 1940); children—Mary Frances, Lillian Josephine, Elizabeth Ames, Kathleen O'Riley. Ordained Presbyn. ministry, 1896; pastor Edgerton, O., 1896-98, Glen Avon Ch., Duluth, Minn., 1899-1904, Xenia, O., 1904-09, Ottumwa, Ia., 1909-14, Tyler Pl. Ch., St. Louis, 1914-17; pres. Parsons Coll., Fairfield, Ia., 1917-22; pres. Centre Coll., Danville, Ky., 1922-26; pres. Ky. Coll. for Women, Danville, Ky., 1926; pres. Lane Theol. Sem., Cin., 1926-32; prof. missions and biography, Presbyn. Theol. Sem., Chgo., 1932-35; prof. homiletics, 1935-40, emeritus, 1940—, sec. Alumni, 1932-40. Mem. bd. trustees McCormick Theol. Sem., Omaha Theol. Sem. Del. Gen. Assembly Presbyn. Ch., U.S.A., 1901, 17, 22, 30, 40. Mem. Coll. Pres.'s Assn., etc. Republican. Clubs: Beta Theta Pi, Rotary (Fairfield, Ill.); Mercantile (St. Louis, Mo.); Anaconda (Danville, Ill.); Pendennis (Louisville, Ky.); International Torch (Cin.); Cleric Club (Chgo.). Author: Secret Place, 1901; The Triumphant Ministry, 1914; Thomas Dove Foster, A Biography, 1929; Preparing Preachers to Preach, 1939; Expository Preaching, 1939; Reality in Religion, 1941; Work-a-day Religion; also (brochures) The Open Door, The Challenge of the New Learning to the Church, The Function of the Christian Colleges, The Winning Team. Home: Manor School, Jonesville, Mich. Died 16, 1950.*

MONTGOMERY, Robert Hiester, lawyer, accountant; b. Mahanoy City, Pa., Sept. 21, 1872; s. Thomas and Annie (Kline) M.; ed. pub. and night schs.; LL.D., Dickinson Coll.; m. Elizabeth Adams Shaw, Nov. 5, 1904; children—Robert Shaw (dec.), Arthur, Elizabeth; m. 2d, Lois Cate Gibb, Jan. 6, 1928; m. 3d, Eleanor Foster, July 26, 1934. Partner in firm of Heins, Whelen, Lybrand & Co., accountants, 1896-97, Lybrand, Ross Bros. & Montgomery, 1898—; admitted to bar, Phila., 1900, New York, 1904; instr. economics, Sch. of Business, Columbia, 1912-14, asst. prof. accounting, 1914-19, prof. and mem. administrative bd., 1919-31. Served as pvt. Light Battery A, Phila. Light Arty., Pa. Vols., Spanish-Am. War, including Porto Rican campaign, 1898; mem. N.G. Pa., 1898-1902; commd. lt. col. N.A., Mar. 1918; chief of sect. on organization and methods, Office of Dir. of Purchases, Gen. Staff, Washington, Jan.-Apr. 1918; organizer and mem. War Dept. Bd. of Appraisers, Apr. 1918-Apr. 1919; War Dept. rep. on price fixing com., of War Industries Bd., May 1918-Feb. 1919; chief price fixing sect. of Purchase, Storage and Traffic Div. of Gen. Staff, Sept. 1918-Jan. 1919; hon. discharged Apr. 1919. Served as dir. research and planning under NRA. Founder and dir. Fairchild Tropical Garden, Coconut Grove, Fla. Mem. Assn. Bar City of New York, N.Y. State Bar Assn., Am. Bar Assn., Nat. Tax Assn., Am. Inst. Accountants (pres. 1935-37); pres. Am. Assn. Pub. Accountants, 1912-14, N.Y. State Soc. of C.P.A.'s (pres. 1922-24); exec. sec. War Policies Commn., Washington, 1931. Republican. Methodist. Mason. Clubs: Union League, Uptown, Round Hill, Greenwich Country. Author: Income Tax Procedure, 1917-27, 29; Federal Tax Practice, 1929, 39; Federal Tax Handbook, 1932-41; Excess Profts Tax Procedure, 1920-21; N.Y. State Income Tax Procedure, 1921; Auditing Theory and Practice, 1912-27, 1934, 1940; Auditing Principles, 1923; Financial Handbook, 1925, 1933; Federal Tax Handbook Supplement, 1941-42; Federal Taxes on Estates, Trusts and Gifts, 1941-51; Excess Profts and Other Federal Taxes on Corporations, 1941-42; Federal Taxes on Corporations, 1942-45; Federal Taxes—Corporations and Partnerships, 1946-52. Home: Coconut Grove, Fla. Office: 2 Broadway, N.Y.C. Died May 2, 1953.

MONTGOMERY, Valda Stewart (Mrs. Whitney Montgomery), author; b. Childress, Tex., Aug. 28, 1888; d. William R. and Butriss (Fowler) Stewart; educated public schools of Tex.; m. J. Arthur Boyd, Mar. 5, 1905; children—Thelma, Genevieve; m. 2d, Whitney Montgomery, June 9, 1927. Co-editor and co-pub. Kaleidograph (nat. mag. of poetry), 1929-59. Member Poetry Society America, Poetry Soc. of Texas (recording secretary, 1944-45), Texas Institute of Letters, Theta Sigma Phi. Democrat. Methodist. Author: (verse) Locoed and Other Poems, 1930; (handbooks) Signs and Markers, 1931; The Practical Rhymer, 1931; Verse Technique—Simplified, 1933; Verse Forms—Old and New, 1933; First Aid for Fictionists, 1933; (verse) Hail for Rain, 1948. Editor: Secrets of Selling Verse, 1934; A Century with Texas Poets and Poetry, 1934; anthologies with Whitney Montgomery—Bright Excalibur, 1933; Merry-Go-Round, 1935; Sparks Afar, 1936; Moon in the Steeple, 1937; Blood and Dust, 1939; 1st prize, Old South contest, Poetry Soc. of Tex., 1939 and 1944. Received Critic's award, Poetry Soc. of Tex., Dec. 1942 and Feb. 1944; Pioneer Prize, 1945; co-winner Prairie Narrative Prize, 1945; Lone Star Prize, 1946; Texas Inst. of Letters Poetry Book Award, 1948. Contbr. mags. and writers' jours. Home: 624 N. Vernon Av., Dallas 8, Tex. Died July 24, 1959; buried Laurel Land Memorial Park, Dallas.

MONTGOMERY, William, insurance exec.; b. Dungannon, Ireland, Dec. 26, 1869; s. Robert and Ellen (Heatherington) M.; ed. schs. of Donaghmore, Ireland; m. Maude M. Howlett, June 20, 1894 (died Feb. 1925); children—Howard H., William H., Robert (dec.), Maude (Mrs. Wm. Moffett, Jr.); m. 2d, Gizelle Goodwillig. Sec. Acacia Mutual Life Ins. Co. (then Masonic Mutual Relief Assn.), Washington, 1893-1919, pres., 1919—. Dir. YMCA, Pub. Library, Met. Police Boys' Club. Mem. Assn. Oldest Inhabitants of D.C., Friendly Sons of St. Patrick Soc. (dir.). Washington Bd. of Trade, Columbia Hist. Soc., Community Chest Fedn., Red Cross. Mem. Westmoreland Congl. Ch., Wash. Mason (past master, Shriner). Clubs: National Press, Metropolitan, Alfalfa, Advertising, Rotary, Burning Tree, Congressional Country. Home: 6200 Nebraska Av., Washington 15. Office: 51 Louisiana Av., Washington 1. Died Sept. 3, 1955; buried Rock Creek Cemetery, Washington.

MONTGOMERY, William Woodrow, Jr., lawyer; b. Radnor, Pa., Oct. 17, 1877; s. William Woodrow and Rebecca Waln (Leaming) M.; student U. Pa., 1894-95 (A.B. degree awarded 1930 as in course, Class of 1898); m. Fanny Brock, Nov. 29, 1913. Admitted to Pa. bar, 1899, and entered practice with father, Phila.; became asso. with Thomas Leaming, Phila., 1900; on latter's death formed, 1912, firm Roberts, Montgomery & McKeehan, Phila.; sr. partner Montgomery, McCracken, Walker & Rhoads, Phila.; 1930—; dir. Western Md. Ry. Co. Mem. Philomathean Soc., Phi Kappa Sigma. Episcopalian. Clubs: Philadelphia, University, Midday, University Barge, Merion Cricket (Phila.); University of Pennsylvania (N.Y.C.). Home: Radnor, Pa. Office: 1421 Chestnut St., Phila. Died Aug. 9, 1950.

MONTONNA, Ralph E(ugene), (mŏn-tŏn'nȧ), educator; b. Cape Vincent, N.Y., Oct. 13, 1894; s. William E. and Alberta (Van Vlack) M.; B.S., Syracuse U., 1916; Ph.D., Yale, 1924; m. Mary Louise Light, June 30, 1919; children—Margaret Ann (Mrs. William David Emmons), Mary Lou (Mrs. Dale Philip Williams). Research chemist Merrell-Soule Co., 1916-17; plant chemist Solvay Process Co., 1918-19; asst. dir. organic research Semet-Solvay Co., 1920-22 (all Syracuse, N.Y.); supt. U.S. Color & Chem. Co., Ashland, Mass., 1919-20; instr. chem. engring. Yale, 1922-24; dir. Inst. Indsl. Research Syracuse U., 1946-50; asst. prof. to prof., later asst. dean grad. sch. U. Minn., 1924-46, dir. Engring. Expt. Sta., 1950—; asso. dir. Northwest Research Inst., 1935-46; dir. Minn. Inst. Research, 1943-46; lectr. chem. econ. U. Birmingham (Eng.), 1937-38; dist. service lectr. Tex. A. and M. Coll., 1940. Mem. gov's. adv. com. Com. to War Industries (Minn.), 1943-45. Mem. Am. Chem. Soc., Am. Inst. Chem. Engrs., Am. Inst. Chemists, Am. Soc. Engring. Edn., A.A.A.S., Minn. Acad. Sci., Am. Assn. U. Profs. Clubs: Skylight, Campus (Minneapolis). Home: 1499 N. Cleveland Av., St. Paul 8. Died Jan. 7, 1952.

MOOD, Orlando Clarendon, army officer; b. South Carolina, Dec. 1, 1899; B.S., The Citadel, 1921; grad. Inf. Sch., company officers course, 1931, Tank Sch., 1932, Command and Gen. Staff Sch., 1937, Army Indsl. Coll., 1940. Commd. 2d lt., U.S. Army, 1921, and advanced through the grades to brig. gen., October 20, 1950; now chief of staff Second Army. Decorations: D.S.M., Legion of Merit with 2 Oak Leaf Clusters, Army Commendation Ribbon; Legion of Honor, Croix de Guerre with Palm (France); Order of Leopold II, Croix de Guerre with Palm (Belgium); Couronne de Chien, Croix de Guerre (Luxembourg). Address: care Adjutant General, Dept. of the Army, Washington. Died May 2, 1953.

MOODY, (Arthur Edson) Blair, ex-senator; born New Haven, Conn., Feb. 13, 1902; s. Arthur Edson Blair and Julia (Downey) M.; A.B., Brown U., 1922; m. Mary Williamson, June 6, 1925; 1 son, Arthur Edson Blair; m. 2d Ruth Curtis Amadon, Sept. 14, 1940; children—Christopher Sorenson, Robert Orton. Instr. and coach The Moses Brown Sch., Providence, 1922-23; with Detroit News, 1923-51, sports writer, 1923-24; reporter, 1924-33, Washington corr. and columnist, 1933-51; Washington corr. for Barren's Financial Weekly, 1934-48, North Am. Newspaper Alliance, 1936—; war corr. in North Africa, Italy, Iran, Britain, 1944, fgn. correspondent parts of 1947-50; director and moderator of the radio and television program, Meet Your Congress, 1946—. Apptd. United States senator from Mich., 1951 to fill unexpired term of late Senator Vandenberg. Economy consultant Com. Econ. Dev., 1944-45. Member Phi Beta Kappa, Psi Upsilon, Sigma Delta Chi. Clubs: Gridiron, National Press, Overseas Writers, University (Washington); Detroit; Cammarian (Providence). Author: Boom or Bust, 1941. Home: 5006 Tilden N.W., Washington; also 14575 Abington Rd., Detroit. Died July 20, 1954.

MOODY, H(oward) W(ilson), prof. civil engring.; b. Garrison, Ia., Oct. 24, 1877; s. James S. and Mary E. (Utley) M.; A.B., Cornell Coll., Mt. Vernon, Ia., 1902; Ph.D., U. Chgo., 1912; m. Lida Auld, Dec. 30, 1902; children—Hope Louise, Roger Lyle. Tchr. high sch., Ludington, Mich., 1902-05, Ft. Dodge, Ia., 1905-07; instr., Northwestern U. Acad., 1907-08; instr. physics Lafayette Coll., Easton, Pa., 1912-13; instr. physics, acting head, dept., Williams Coll., Williamstown, Mass., 1913-14; prof. physics head dept., Miss. A. and M. Coll., 1914-30, dean Sch. Engring., 1925-30; prof. C.E., Valparaiso (Ind.) U., 1930—, dean Coll. engring., 1930-40. Mem. Am. Phys. Soc., A.A.A.S., Soc. Promotion Engring. Edn., Am. Ry. Engring. Assn., Phi Beta Kappa, Sigma Xi. Republican. Methodist. Club: Rotary of Valparaiso; gov. Dist. 154, Rotary Internat., 1943-44. Home: 414 Elmhurst Av., Valparaiso, Ind. Died Mar. 25, 1949; buried Graceland Cemetery, Valparaiso, Ind.

MOODY, Lewis Ferry, hydraulic engr.; b. Philadelphia, Pa., Jan. 5, 1880; s. Carlton Montague and

Elizabeth Eddy (Lewis) M.; B.S., Towne Scientific School (U. of Pa.), 1901, M.S., 1902; m. Eleanor Carman Greene, June 22, 1909 (died 1937); children —Mary Elizabeth (dec.), Lewis Ferry, Arthur Maurice Greene, Eleanor Lowry (Mrs. Edw. M. Broadhurst). Instructor mechanical engineering Univ. of Pa., 1902-04; engineering staff hydraulic dept. of I. P. Morris Co., Phila., 1904-08; asst. prof. mech. engring., later prof. hydraulic engring., Rensselaer Poly. Inst., 1908-16, also independent practice; consulting engr. I. P. Morris Company (now Baldwin Lima Hamilton), 1911-46; consulting engr. Worthington Pump & Mchy. Corp. 1938-49; prof. emeritus hydraulic engring., Princeton. Fellow A.A.A.S.; Am. Soc. Mech. Engrs. (dir. at large, 1947-48; past chmn. Phila. sect.; past chmn. exec. com. hydraulic div.). Mem. Franklin Inst., Am. Soc. for Engring. Edn., Sigma Xi, Tau Beta Pi. Republican. Swedenborgian. Clubs: Nassau (Princeton). Inventor numerous improvements in hydraulic turbines, pumps and accessories; has been awarded many patents for inventions, including spiral draft tube, Moody spreading draft tube, Moody spiral pump, new high speed turbine, etc. Awarded Elliott Cresson medal by Franklin Inst., 1945. Author: Lectures on Machine Design, 1942; section on hydraulic machinery in Handbook of Applied Hydraulics, 1942-and various tech. papers read before engring. socs. and articles in tech. periodicals. Home: 930 Woodland Av., Plainfield, N.J. Died Apr. 18, 1953; buried Princeton (N.J.) Cemetery.

MOODY, Virginia Green, state librarian; b. Red Bank, S.C., Nov. 5, 1881; d. John and Mary (Jacobs) Green; student Presbyn. Coll. for Women, Columbia, S.C, 1896; m. R. Wells Moody, Oct. 25, 1899 (dec. 1905); children—Gladys Virginia (Mrs. N. P. Tafoya), Helen Wells (Mrs. John M. Brock). S.C. state librarian, 1914—. Mem. A.L.A., S.C. Library Assn., Nat. Assn. State Librarians, Soc. Mayflower Descs., D.A.R. Democrat. Presbyn. Home: 1508 Laurel St. Office: State House, Columbia, S.C. Died Dec. 10, 1955; buried Elmwood Cemetery, Columbia.

MOODY, William Lewis, Jr., business exec.; b. Freestone Co., Tex., Jan. 25, 1865; s. Col. William Lewis and Elizabeth (Bradley) M.; student Va. Mil. Inst., 1883-84, U. Tex., 1885; m. Libbie Rice Shearn, Aug. 26, 1890; children—Mary Elizabeth (Mrs. E. C. Northen), William Lewis III, Shearn (dec.), Libbie (Mrs. Clark W. Thompson). Began as cotton commn. mcht., 1885; pres. W. L. Moody & Co., bankers, Galveston, Tex., W. L. Moody Cotton Co., Galveston Cotton Compress & Warehouse Co.; organizer, pres., dir. Am. Nat. Life Ins. Co., City Nat. Bank, now Moody Nat. Bank; organizer, owner. Affiliated Nat. Hotel Chain, 30 hotels and courts, Silver Lake Ranches, Inc., of Tex., Okla., W.Va.; pres., dir. The News Pub. Co., pubs. Galveston News (Tex.' oldest newspaper), Galveston Tribune, Am. Printing Co. Treas. City of Galveston, 1921-23. Established (with wife) Moody Found. for Charitable, Ednl., Sci. and Religious purposes for Texans; donated the Moody State Sch. for Cerebral Palsied Children, to state Tex., 1950. Hon. col., Tex. Mem. Cotton Exchange, local clubs, Phi Delta Theta. Methodist. Home: 2618 Broadway. Office: Am. Nat. Ins. Co. Bldg., Galveston, Tex. Died July 21, 1954.

MOOG, Wilson Townsend, univ. prof.; b. Baltimore, Aug. 23, 1881; s. James Robert and Wilhelmina (Deibel) M.; A.B., St. Lawrence U., Canton, N.Y., 1902; student New Eng. Conservatory of Music, 1905; Mus. Bac., Yale Sch. of Music, 1916; studied in Paris under Louis Vierne, 1921; m. Helen Chapin Moodey, Mar. 25, 1916; children—Helen Antoinette (Mrs. John S. Cary), Barbara (Mrs. John P. Finlay). Dir. Smith Coll. Summer Sch. of Music, 1930-42; formerly prof. music, organist Smith Coll., ret. 1949; organist, dir. music First Congl. Ch., Northampton. Fellow Am. Guild Organists: mem. Phi Mu Alpha, Alpha Tau Omega. Home: 98 Bancroft Rd., Northampton, Mass. Died Jan. 6, 1953; buried Spring Grove Cemetery, Northampton.

MOON, Truman Jesse, author; b. Nicholville, N.Y., July 6, 1879; s. Asa and Lucinda M. (Smith) M.; student Potsdam State Normal Preliminary Sch. and Potsdam State Normal Tng. Sch. until 1899; A.B., Cornell U., 1903; m. Lena Crosby Jordan, June 29, 1904; 1 dau., Margaret Louise. Formerly student instr. Potsdam Normal sch. and Cornell U.; tchr. biology and chemistry Middletown High Sch., 1902—. Mem. N.Y.N.G., 1918-20. Mem. N.Y. State Tchrs.' Assn. Republican. Presbyn. Club: University. Author: Biology for Beginners, 1921; Laboratory Manual (for beginners), 1922; Biology for Beginners, 1926; Laboratory Manual, 1927; Modern Biology (with Otto and Towle), rev. edit. 1960; also articles in Scientific American, Bird Lore, etc. Home: Middletown, N.Y. Died July 13, 1946; buried Greensboro, Vt.

MOONEY, Edward, Cardinal (mōō'nē); born Mt. Savage, Md., May 9, 1882; s. Thomas and Sara (Heneghan) M.; student St. Charles Coll., Catonsville, Md., 1897-1903; A.B., St. Mary's Sem., 1905; D.D., North America Coll., Rome, Italy, 1909, Ph.D., 1907; LL.D., U. of Notre Dame, 1936. Ordained priest R.C. Ch., 1909; prof. St. Mary's Sem., Cleveland, O., 1909-16; prin. Cathedral Latin Sch., 1916-22; pastor St. Patrick's Ch., Youngstown, O., 1922-23; spiritual dir. North America Coll., Rome, 1923-26; apostolic del. India, 1926; titular archbishop of Irenopolis, Jan. 8, 1926; apostolic del. in Japan, 1931; became the bishop of Rochester, New York, Aug. 28, 1933; Archbishop of Detroit, May 26, 1937-46; proclaimed Cardinal, Feb. 18, 1946. Office: 1234 Washington Blvd., Detroit 26. Died Nov. 25, 1958.

MOONEY, James David; b. Cleve., Feb. 18, 1884; s. Hon. James David and Mary Elizabeth (Burns) M.; B.S., N.Y. U.; B.S. in Mining Engring., M.E., Dr. Engring., Case Inst. Tech.; m. Leonora Jane Watson, 1914; children—Martha Jane, James David, Patricia Avice; m. 2d, Ida May MacDonald, 1929; children—Michael MacDonald, John Burns, Alan Patrick. Formerly exec. v.p., dir. Gen. Motors Corp.; prin. J. D. Mooney Assos., indsl. cons., N.Y.C.; pres., dir. F. L. Jacobs Co., Detroit, 1953—. Served as capt., 309 Ammunition Reg., U.S. Army in France, World War I. Capt. U.S.N. (Res.) active duty, Bur. Aeros., Advanced Base Div., 11th Amphibious Force in Europe. Staff of Chief of Naval Operations, World War II. Mem. council N.Y. U.; gen. chmn. United Hosp. Fund Campaign, 1952. Mem. Vets. Fgn. Wars, Am. Legion, Am. Soc. Mech. Engrs., Am. Inst. Mining and Metall. Engrs., Soc. Automotive Engrs., Soc. Am. Mil. Engrs., Sigma Chi, Theta Nu Epsilon, Beta Gamma Sigma, Alpha Delta Sigma. Clubs: Univ., Union League (N.Y.); Creek, Piping Rock (Locust Valley, L.I.); Seawanhaka Yacht (Oyster Bay, N.Y.); Army and Navy (Washington). Author: Principles of Orgn. Home: Centre Island, Oyster Bay, N.Y. Died Sept., 1957.

MOORE, Albert Voorhis, pres. and dir. Moore McCormack Lines, Inc., Moore & McCormack, Inc., Am. Republics Line, Am. Scantic Line, Dir. Nat. Fgn. Trade Council; mem. Am. Com. Lloyd's Register of Shipping; mem. classification com. Am. Bur. Shipping. Mem. C. of C. State of N.Y., Argentine-Am. C. of C., Inc. (dir.). Am. Brazilian. Assn., Inc. (hon. v.p., dir.), Pan Am. Soc. of U.S., Inc. (hon. v.p.). Home: 65 Tennis Pl., Forest Hills, L.I. Office: care Moore McCormack Lines, 5 Broadway, N.Y.C. Died Jan. 8, 1953; buried Woodlawn Cemetery, Bronx, N.Y.C.

MOORE, Arthur Harry, ex-gov.; b. Jersey City, N.J., July 3, 1879; s. Robert White and Martha (McCoomb) M.; ed. Cooper Union and under pvt. tutors; LL.B., New Jersey Law Sch., 1924, LL.D., 1934; LL.D., Rutgers, 1927, Seton Hall Coll., 1928; M.A., Hahnemann Med. Coll., 1928; M.C.S., Rider Coll., Trenton, N.J., 1928; LL.D., John Marshall Coll. of Law, 1934, Princeton, 1938; m. Jennie Hastings Stevens, Mar. 1911. Began law practice at Jersey City, 1920; sec. to mayor of Jersey City, 1908-11; city collector, 1911-13; commr. Jersey City, under commn. form of govt., 1913-25; gov. of N.J., 1926-28, 1932-35, and 1938-41 (first gov. in history of state to be elected for 3d term); elected to U.S. Senate for term, 1935-41, resigned 1938; prof. of legal ethics, John Marshall Coll. of Law. A leader in civic drives; organizer boys' athletic league, and young men in industries; A. Harry Moore Sch. for Crippled Children built and named by Jersey City in recognition of his services for physically handicapped children; built Pershing Field; an authority on playgrounds; after dinner speaker. Awarded the annual medal by Ulster-Irish Soc. of N.Y. as American of Irish descent of greatest service during the year; Distinguished Service medal, N.J., for aiding in rescue of survivors, S.S. Morro Castle disaster off Sea Girt, N.J., Sept. 1934; Silver Beaver of Boy Scouts of Am., 1937; Silver Antelope, Boy Scouts of America, 1946. Member Hudson County Historical Society, St. Andrews Soc. of N.Y., Ulster Irish Soc. of N.Y., N.J. Hist. Soc., Ringoes Grange, Delta Theta Phi, Beta Sigma Pi. Democrat. Mason, Shriner, 33°), Elk, Moose, Forester, Eagle; mem. Scottish Clans (McLeod). Clubs: Carteret, Masonic, N.J. Rifle, N.J. Fish and Game, Circus Saints and Sinners; Riding and Hunt, University (Washington, D.C.); Lotos (New York). Home: 350 Arlington Av. Office: 921 Bergen Av., Jersey City. Died Nov. 18, 1952.

MOORE, Aubrey Shannon, clergyman; b. Hendrysburg, O., Oct. 13, 1883; s. Ellington Greenville and Sarah Jane (James) M.; A.B., Northwestern U., 1912; S.T.B., Garrett Bibl. Inst., 1913, D.D., 1933; m. Mary Elizabeth Wheldon, June 19, 1912; children —Audrie Mae (Mrs. H. R. Celley), Dorothy Kathryn (Mrs. Andie Deflandre), and Charles Ellington. Teacher in pub. schs. of Ohio 4 yrs., Wheeling Business Coll. 1 yr.; bookkeeper Bridgeport (O.) Nat. Bank, 1 yr.; ordained M.E. ministry, 1912; pastor Gage Park, Chicago, 1907-08, Congress Park, 1908-09, Melrose Park, 1909-11, Glen Ellyn, 1911-15, Washington Boulevard Church, Oak Park, 1915 to 1921, Dixon, Illinois, 1921-25, Evanston Covenant M.E. Church, 1925-29; district superintendent M.E. Ch., 1929-35; now supt. Chicago Home Missionary and Church Extension Soc. Del. Uniting Conf. of the Methodist Ch., 1939; del. Gen. and North Central Jurisdictional Confs., Meth. Ch., 1940, 44, 48, 52. Trustee Northwestern U., 1932-54, Garrett Biblical Inst. Republican. Mason. Home: 2315 Harrison St., Evanston, Ill. Office: 77 W. Washington St., Chgo. Died Dec. 12, 1955; buried Meml. Park.

MOORE, Ben Wheeler, judge; b. Salyersville, Ky., Jan. 1, 1891; s. John W. and Mary E. (Wheeler) M.; student Magoffin Inst., Salyersville, 1904-06; LL.D. (hon.), Marietta Coll., Marietta, O., 1954; children by previous marraige—Marian, Ben William; m. 2d, Cecile Bryant Colby, Aug. 7, 1941. Bank clerk Charleston, W.Va., 1907-11; auditor for st. ry., Charleston, 1911-13; auditor for land company, Dunbar, W.Va., 1913-14; studied law in offices of LeRoy Allebach and Braxton Miller, Charleston; admitted to W.Va. bar, 1915, and since engaged in gen. practice of law at Charleston; mem. firm Townsend, Bock, Moore & Townsend, 1929-40; commr. in chancery, Circuit Court Kanawha County, W.Va., 1918-40, judge Common Pleas Court, Kanawha County, 1941; judge U.S. Dist. Court, Southern Dist. of West Virginia, 1941—. Bd. directors, Laird Hospital Found., Goodwill Industries Charleston (first president). Organized Lions Club, Charleston, 1921, first pres.; first dist. gov. W.Va. Lions Clubs, 2 terms, life mem. Mem. W.Va. Bar Assn. Democrat. Baptist. Mason (32°). Clubs: Lions, Lotos, Anvil. Author: Heritage by Freedom, 1958. Recipient Humanities award W.Va. B'nai B'rith, 1958. Home: 1865 Louden Heights Road. Office: Fed. Ct. Bldg., Charleston, W.Va. Died Sept. 25, 1958.

MOORE, Bob, newspaper artist; b. N. Weymouth, Mass., Apr. 28, 1910; s. Bernard Joseph and Emma Frances (Shieble) M.; grad., Los Angeles Polytech. High Sch., 1928; m. Nadine Rose Sponenburgh, Mar. 1, 1938; 1 dau., Wendy. Editorial cartoonist, caricaturist, Los Angeles Daily News, 1935—; art dir., Los Angeles Press Club year book, 1948; caricaturist contracted to Universal-Internat. film studios, 1946—. Served with USCG; 1942, AUS, 1943-45. Mem. Am. Newspaper Guild. Club: Los Angles Press. Home: 1808 Strand St., Manhattan Beach, Cal. Office: Los Angeles Daily News, Los Angeles 54. Died June 9, 1950; buried Calvary Cemetery.

MOORE, Bryant Edward, army officer; b. Ellsworth, Me., June 6, 1894; grad. U.S. Mil. Acad.; commd. 2d lt. Inf., Aug. 1917, and advanced through grades to maj. gen., 1945; G-2 of expdn. to Caledonia, 1942; C.O. 164th Inf. on Guadalcanal, 1942; assigned 104th Inf. Div., Camp Adair, Ore., 1943; fought in Holland and Ger. with 104th div.; assigned Div. Comdr. 8th Inf. Div., 1945; assigned Div. Comdr. 88th Inf., Div., 1945. Awarded Distinguished Service Medal with 2 oak leaf clusters; Silver Star with cluster; Legion of Merit with cluster; Bronze Star with cluster; Distinguished Service Order (British); Legion of Honor, Croix de Guerre (French); Order of St. Lazarus (Italian). Address: care of The Adjutant General, War Dept., Washington 25. Died Feb. 24, 1951.

MOORE, Carl Richard, prof. zoölogy; b. Green County, Mo., Dec. 5, 1892; s. Johnathan Newton and Sarah Francis (Harris) M.; A.B., Drury Coll., Springfield, Missouri, 1913, M.S., 1914; Sc.D., 1948; Ph.D., University of Chicago, 1916; graduate study Marine Biological Laboratory, Woods Hole, Massachusetts, summers, 1914, 15, 16; m. Edith Naomi Abernethy, July 2, 1920; children—Howard Frederick (dec.), Harris Mason, Ellen Abernethy. Lab. instr., Drury Coll., 1911-14; asst., later asso. in zoölogy, U. of Chicago, 1914-18, instr. in zoölogy, 1918-22, asst. prof., 1922-25, asso. prof., 1925-28, prof. since 1928; mem. editorial bd. Biol. Bull. since 1926, mng. editor, 1926-29; mem. editorial bd. Physiological Zoölogy. Received First Francis Amory Award, 1941, medal from the Endocrine Society, 1955. Member American Society Zoölogists (vice pres. 1926), Am. Soc. Naturalists, A.A.A.S. (v.p. sect. F, 1943), Inst. Medicine, Marine Biol. Lab. Corp., Sigma Xi, Gamma Alpha, Assn. for Study Internal Secretions (pres. 1944-46), Soc. Exptl. Biology and Medicine, National Academy of Sciences. Republican. Club: Quadrangle. Home: 5702 Blackstone Av., Chgo. Died Oct. 16, 1955.

MOORE, Charles Arthur, corp. exec.; b. Lynn, Mass., June 23, 1880; s. Charles Arthur and Mary (Campbell) M.; student St. Paul's School, 1893-98; A.B., Yale, 1903; m. Annette Sperry, 1907; m. 2d, Elizabeth Hyde, June 5, 1920. Vice pres. Manning, Maxwell & Moore, Inc., until 1927, pres., 1927-31, chmn. bd., 1931—. Mem. Peary Expdn., 1897. Served with Montenegro Army, Balkan War; served as maj. 56th Arty. A.E.F., World War I. Life mem. Am. Mus. Natural History, N.Y. Zool. Soc. Clubs: Racquet and Tennis, Yale. Home: Round Hill, Greenwich, Conn. Office: Chrysler Bldg., N.Y.C. Died Aug. 23, 1949.

MOORE, Charles Calvin, ex-gov., commr. of General Land Office; b. Holt Co., Mo., Feb. 26, 1866; s. Socrates and Eliza (McCune) M.; ed. high sch., Mound City, Mo., also teachers' training schs., including Warrensburg (Mo.) Normal Sch.; children —Ira W. (deceased), George G., Mabel (deceased), Marion S.; married 2d, Clara E. Wallan, of Pendleton, Oregon, June 10, 1915. Auditor and recorder Holt Co., Mo., 1895-99; moved to St. Anthony, Ida., 1899; mem. Ida. Ho of Rep., 1903-04, 1905-06; lt. gov. of Ida., 1919-20, 1920-22; gov. of Ida., two terms, 1923-26 inclusive; commr. Gen. Land Office, 1929-33. Chmn. Fremont County War Bd., World War II. Republican. Mem. Christian Ch. Mason (Shriner), Odd Fellow, Woodman. Club: Elks. Home: St. Anthony, Ida. Died Mar. 19, 1958; buried Mt. Olivet Cemetery, Salt Lake City.

MOORE, David Richard, educator; b. Port Hope, Ont., Can., Oct. 26, 1877; s. David and Elizabeth (Morton) M.; grad. Port Hope Model Sch. for Tchrs., 1896; A.B., Victoria Coll. (U. Toronto), 1902; Ph.D., U. Chgo., 1910; traveled and studied in Europe, summers, 1912-14; m. Ethel May Hallam, July 7, 1910; children—Evelyn Elizabeth, Norman Hallam, Marian Louise. Instr. Washington and Jefferson Acad., Washington, Pa., 1902-04, Washington and Jefferson Coll., 1904-05; lectr. Central Inst., Chgo., 1907-09; prof. history Lawrence Coll., Appleton, Wis., 1910-13, Oberlin Coll., 1913-42. Pres. Bd. Edn., Oberlin, 1926-29; pres. Ohio Acad. of History, 1932-33. Mem. Am. Hist. Assn. Am. Acad. Polit and Social Sci., Phi Beta Kappa. Gold Medalist, Victoria Coll., 1902, for work in polit. science. Conglist. Author: Canada and the United States, 1815-1830, 1910; History of Latin America, 1938, rev. and enlarged edit., 1942; Historia de la America Latina, 1946. Home: 155 Elm St., Oberlin, O. Died Apr. 29, 1951; buried Oberlin.

MOORE, Edward (Small) Jr., business exec.; b. St. Louis, Mar. 18, 1906; s. Edward Small and Jean (McGinley) M.; student St. Paul's Sch., Concord, N.J., 1920-23; Hun Sch., Princeton, 1923-25; Princeton U., 1925-26; m. Jane C. Foster, Nov. 26, 1930; children—Edward S., Marion. Rancher Sheridan, Wyo., 1928-38; vice pres. Sheridan Press; daily newspaper, 1930-38; pres. Outsen-Gage-Moore Corp., Cheyenne, Wyo., 1939-42; state mgr. W.P.B., Cheyenne, 1942-45; exec. vice pres., dir. and mem. exec. com. Nat. Biscuit Co., N.Y. City, 1949; dir. First Nat. City Bank N.Y., Nabisco Foods, Ltd., Toronto, Shredded Wheat Co., Ltd., Eng., Republic Aviation Corp. Dir. Biscuit and Cracker Mfg. Assn., trustee U.S. council Internat. C. of C. Republican. Mason. Elk. Clubs: Racquet and Tennis, Links, N.Y. Yacht, Recess, Pinnacle. Home: 901 Lexington Av., N.Y.C. 21. Office: 425 Park Av., N.Y.C. 22. Died Oct. 23, 1959.

MOORE, Edward H., U.S. Senator; b. Nodaway County, Mo., Nov. 19, 1871; ed. Chillicothe (Mo.) Normal Sch.; grad. Kansas City Sch. Law, 1900; m. Cora McComb, 1905. Admitted to Okla. bar, 1901, practiced law until 1919; ind. oil producer, farmer, and cattle raiser, 1919-42; mem. U.S. Senate, 1943-49. Mem. Okla., Am. bar assns. Republican. Mem. Christian Ch. Mason (32°). Home: Tulsa. Died Sept. 2, 1950; buried Okmulgee, Okla.

MOORE, Edward Roberts, clergyman; b. N.Y. City, Jan. 9, 1894; s. Edward Aloysius and Mary (Roberts) M.; B.A., Fordham, 1915, M.A., 1921, Ph.D., 1923; studied St. Joseph's Sem., Yonkers, N.Y., 1915-19, N.Y. Sch. of Social Work, 1923-24. Ordained priest R.C. Ch., 1919; curate St. Peter's Ch., N.Y. City, 1919-23, St. Gregory's Ch., N.Y. City, 1923-29; curate St. Peter's Ch., N.Y. City, 1929-36; adminstr., 1936-37, pastor since 1937. Dir. Div. Social Action, Catholic Charities of the Archdiocese of New York, 1923-41; prof. Fordham U. Sch. of Social Service, 1924-38; mem. exec. com. Council on Adult En., 1924-32; City Conf. on Charities and Correction, 1927-28; mem. bd. of govs., Manhattan Council Boy Scouts of America; chmn. com. on social and economic activities, Nat. Conf. of Catholic Charities, 1927; chmn. com. on population decline and related problems, 1929-32, chmn. com. on neighborhood and community activities, 1935; mem. joint com. of the Welfare Council and United Neighborhood Houses for the Study of Settlement Houses in New York; mem. at large, Nat. Council Boy Scouts of America since 1930; mem. N.Y. City Housing Authority, 1934-44; mem. nat. advisory com., Nat. Youth Adminstrn. 1935-43; chmn. special com. on social aspects of public housing, Nat. Conf. of Social Work, 1936; chmn. N.Y. City-L.I. adv. com., Nat. Youth Adminstrn., 1935-43; mem. bd. of advisors Vocational Service for Juniors, 1937-38, sponsor since 1938; nat. dir. Cath. Com. on Scouting since 1938; archdiocesan dir. Catholic Youth Orgn. of Archdiocese of New York, 1936-40; mem. advisory bd. The Catholic Boy, Youth Leaders' Digest; mem. advisory com. Citizens' Housing Council of New York, 1937-42; mem. council Boy Scout Foundation since 1938; v.p. American Fed. Housing Authorities, 1938; chmn. Catholic groups division N.Y. State Committee of Nat. Pub. Housing Conf. since 1938; chmn. Com. on Youth Activities, Nat. Conf. of Catholic Charities, 1939; mem. Com. on Personnel Standards, Nat. Assn. of Housing Officials, 1939-43; mem. Nat. Com. Father Finn Medal Fund since 1939; mem. program com. community orgn. sect., N.Y. State Conference on Social Work, 1939; mem. adv. com. Mayor's Official World's Fair Housing Bur., Inc., 1939; mem. exec. com. Youth Div. of Civilian Defense Vol. office, 1942-43; v.p. and dir. joint Queensview Housing Enterprises, Inc., since 1948; mem. bd. editors, Cath. Book Club, since 1945. Received Order of Silver Star, Catholic Youth Organization, 1938, Club of Champions award, 1944; Silver Beaver, Boy Scouts of Am., 1936, Silver Buffalo, 1940; Ad Altari Dei Cross, 1941; Created Private Chamberlain of the Papal Household of His Holiness Pope XII, October 1941, created Domestic Prelate, Dec. 1949. Mem. Nat. Inst. of Social Sciences, Century Assn. Democrat. Clubs: Fordham, Malletts Bay Boat, Port Washington Yacht, Lake Champlain Yacht, Downtown Athletic. Author: The Case Against Birth Control, 1931; By His Bruises We Are Healed; Roman Collar, 1950; (with others) Heart in Pilgrimage, 1948. Home: 16 Barclay St., N.Y.C. Died June 2, 1952.

MOORE, Elon Howard, sociologist; b. Moscow, Mich., May 18, 1894; s. Newton I. and Belle (Sutfin) M.; A.B., Albion (Mich.) Coll., 1919; Ph.D., U. of Wis., 1927; m. Marjorie Kenney, Dec. 28, 1921; children—Martha Kenney, David Sutfin, Elon Howard, Patricia Marian. Master, Howe Boys' Sch., Howe, Ind., 1920-21; supt. of schs., Eaton Rapids, Mich., 1921-24; mem. staff, U. of Ill., 1926-28; prof. sociology, Ore. State Coll., 1928-35; prof. sociology, U. of Ore., 1935-53, chmn. grad. work in gen. studies, 1937-53, dept. head, 1943-53, ret.; vis. prof. Stanford U., of Ill., Wayne U. Served as pvt. 1st class, med. detachment, U.S. Army, Camp Custer, 1918-19. Dir. rural research studies for Ore., Federal Emergency Relief Adminstration, 1934-35; director in charge foreign area and language, Army Specialist Training Program, University of Oregon, 1943-44. Social Science Research Council grant, 1945-46, to study problems of retirement experience. Member American Sociology Society, Pacific Sociology Society (president, 1942), Population Society of America, Alpha Tau Omega, Delta Sigma Rho, Alpha Kappa Delta. Patron of husbandry. Club: Eugene (Ore.) Round Table. Contbr. chapters on sociology and on religion in Survey of Social Science (Breen); also numerous articles in professional jours. dealing with population mobility retirement and penology. Address: 876 E. 12th St., Eugene, Ore. Died Nov. 16, 1953.

MOORE, Ernest Carroll, univ. prof.; b. Youngstown, O., July 20, 1871; s. John A. and Martha Jane (Forsythe) M.; A.B., Ohio Normal U., 1892, LL.B., 1894; A.M., Columbia, 1896; fellow in edn., 1897-98, Ph.D., 1898, U. of Chicago; ad eundem A.M., Yale U., 1910; LL.D., U. of Southern Calif., 1916, U. of Arizona, 1923, Pomona College, 1931, University of California, 1942; m. Dr. Dorothea Lummis, Feb. 17, 1896 (died Mar. 4, 1942); 1 son, Kermit S. (adopted); m. 2d, Kate Gordon, Mar. 8, 1943. Instructor philosophy, 1898-1901, instr. edn., 1901-1902, asst. prof. edn., 1902-06, dean summer session, 1905-06, U. of Calif.; supt. schs., Los Angeles, 1906-10; prof. edn. Yale U., 1910-14, Harvard U., 1913-17; pres. State Normal Sch., Los Angeles, 1917-19; prof. edn. and dir. U. of Calif. at Los Angeles, 1919-29, dir. of univ. and v.p., 1929-31, prof. edn., v.p. and provost of univ., 1931-36, prof. of philosophy and edn., 1936-41, retired, 1941. Resident worker, University Settlement, New York, 1894-95, Hull House, Chicago, 1896-98; mem. Calif. State Bd. Charities and Corrections, 1903-10 (pres. 1903-06); pres. Calif. Teachers Assn., Southern section, 1909, 18; president New England Association Colleges and Secondary Schools, 1914; pres. Lincoln Club of Southern California, 1929-31; pres. Western Assn. of Colleges and Secondary Schs., 1930; dir. Los Angeles Chamber of Commerce, 1936; trustee Los Angeles Philharmonic Orchestra, 1936. Fellow A.A.A.S.; mem. Hellenic Soc. of Great Britain; hon. mem. Phi Beta Kappa (Stanford). Officer d'Académie (France), 1919; Chevalier Legion of Honor (France), 1932. Clubs: California, Sunset. Author: How New York City Administers Its Schools; What Is Education?; Fifty Years of Education in America; What the War Teaches about Education; The Story of Instruction, the Beginnings, 1936; The Story of Instruction—The Church, The Renaissances, The Reformations. Editor: Minimum Course of Study; Thomas Starr King's Socrates; Thomas Davidson's Education as World-building; The Story of the United States by Those Who Make It; California's Educator, 1950; I Helped Made a University, 1952. Home: 516 Woodruff Av., Los Angeles 24. Died Jan. 23, 1955; buried Forest Lawn Meml. Park, Glendale, Cal.

MOORE, Ethelbert Allen (mōr), retired mfr.; b. Kensington, Conn., Nov. 30, 1864; s. Nelson Augustus and Ann Maria (Pickett) M.; ed. high sch., Hartford, Conn.; m. Martha Elizabeth Hart, June 18, 1891; children—Allen, Roswell, Maxwell, Barbara (Mrs. Maurice H. Pease), Martha (Mrs. Allan McDowell). Began with The Stanley Works, mfrs. builders hardware, New Britain, Conn., 1889, pres. until 1923, chmn. bd., 1923-29, now a dir.; formerly dir. of many corporations and member of state commissions. Former mem. Conn. Ho. of Rep. Republican. Conglist. Author: Tenth Generation (autobiography); Four Decades (record of service with The Stanley Works); Life's Interlude (collection of 17 sonnets). Home: Sunnyledge, New Britain, Conn. Died Feb. 13, 1956; buried West Lane Cemetery, Kensington, Conn.

MOORE, Frank Gardner (mōr), educator; b. West Chester, Pa., Sept. 25, 1865; s. William Eves (D.D., LL.D.) and Harriet Francina (Foot) M.; B.A., Yale, 1886, Macy scholar, 1886-88, Ph.D., 1890; studied U. Berlin, 1890-91; L.H.D., Trinity Coll., Conn., 1921; Litt.D., Columbia, 1929; m. Anna Barnard White, Jan. 4, 1897 (died Sept. 22, 1943); children—Lawrence, Roger C., Janet G., Cynthia G. (Mrs. Henderson Mathews). Tutor in Latin, Yale, 1888-93; asst. prof. Latin, Dartmouth, 1893-1900, asso. prof. Latin and Roman archaeology, 1900-08; prof. Latin, Trinity Coll., Hartford, Conn., 1908-10; prof. classical philology Columbia, 1910-19, prof. Latin, 1919-37, prof. emeritus in residence, 1937-41, emeritus, 1941—. Sec. Am. Philol. Assn., 1904-16, pres., 1917. Chmn. Local Exemption Bd. 135, 1918. Editor: Cicero's Cato Major, 1904; Tacitus' Histories, I, II, 1910; Transactions and Proceedings Am. Philol. Assn., vols. 35-46 inc.; Orations of Cicero, 1925, revised edit. (with J. E. Barss), 1929. Translator: Pufendorf's De Officio Hominis et Civis, 1927; Livy, vol 6, in the Loeb Classical Library (books XXIII-XXV, text and translation), 1940, vol. 7 (books XXVI-XXVII), 1943, vol. 8 (books XXVIII-XXX), 1949. Author: Porta Latina, a Latin Reading Method (2d year), 1915; The Roman's World, 1936 (2d printing, revised, 1946). Address: 70 Hulda Hill Rd., Wilton, Conn. Died Nov. 18, 1955.

MOORE, Fred Atkins, educator; b. Concord, N.H., Oct. 26, 1882; s. Charles E. H. and Caroline (Atkins) M.; ed. pub. schs., Somerville, Mass.; A.B., Tufts Coll., 1904; S.T.B., Crane Theol. Sch. (Tufts), 1906, Brown U., 1911-12, U. of Chicago, 1916; m. Vivian E. Ross, July 30, 1907; 1 son, Lyman Sweet. Ordained Universalist ministry, 1906; pastor First Parish Ch., Saugus, Mass., 1906-09, Murray Ch., Attleboro, Mass., 1909-14. Ch. of Redeemer, Chicago, 1914-18; mem. bd. dirs. United Charities of Chicago, 1915-18; with War Camp Community Service and Community Service, Inc., 1918-21; pastor Beacon Universalist Ch., Brookline, Mass., 1922-25; exec. dir. Chicago Forum and Adult Edn. Council of Chicago, 1925-36; civic sec. City Club of Chicago, 1927-29; chmn. Oak Park (Ill.) Community lectures, 1931-36, 1938-39; a dir. Emergency Peace Campaign, 1936-37; exec. sec. A Movement for World Christianity, 1937-39; dir. Ch. Com. for China Relief, 1939-46; Church Com. for Relief in Asia, 1944-46; asso. exec. dir. Save the Children Fedn., Inc., since 1946; mem bd. dirs. CARE, Inc. Home: 450 W. 24th St. Office: 80 8th Av., N.Y.C. 11. Died Sept. 26, 1951.

MOORE, George Thomas, botanist; b. Indianapolis, Ind., Feb. 23, 1871; s. George T. and Margaret (Marshall) M.; B.S., Wabash Coll., 1894; A.B., Harvard Univ., 1895, A.M., 1896, Ph.D., 1900; m. Emma L. Hall, Dec. 30, 1896 (died Jan. 1934); children—Harriet Hall, Thomas Gaunt; m. 2d, Katherine H. Leigh, Feb. 20, 1937 (died Oct. 1945). Asst. in cryptogamic botany, Harvard; teacher Radcliffe Coll.; in charge botany, Dartmouth Coll., 1899-1901; became physiologist and algologist, Bur. Plant Industry, Dept. Agr., 1901; in charge Lab. of Plant Physiology, Dept. Agr., 1903-05; in charge of botany, Marine Biol. Lab., Mass., 1909-19; prof. applied botany and plant physiology, Shaw Sch. of Botany (Washington U.) and physiologist to Mo. Bot. Garden, Sept. 1909-May 1912; dir. Mo. Bot. Garden since May 1, 1912; pres. board of trustees Tower Grove Park. Pres. bd. trustees St. Louis Country Day School. Discoverer of a method for preventing pollution of water supplies by algæ and certain pathogenic bacteria; perfected method for inoculating the soil with bacteria which enable certain crops to use atmospheric nitrogen. Reviser for "algæ," Century Dictionary; contbr. to scientific jours. and Dept. Agr. bulls. upon Pollution of Water Supplies by Algæ, with recommendations for preventing these growths, and upon Fixation of Nitrogen by Bacteria, etc. Fellow A.A.A.S.; mem. Am. Philos. Soc., Washington Acad. Sciences, St. Louis Acad. Science, Botanical Society America, Bot. Soc. Washington, Soc. Am. Bacteriologists, English-Speaking Union (v.p.), Phi Gamma Delta, Sigma Xi, Phi Beta Kappa. Overseer, Harvard University. Clubs: University, Noonday, Round Table, Town and Gown, St. Louis Country; Cosmos (Washington); Harvard (St. Louis, New York and Boston). Address: Missouri Botanical Garden, St. Louis. Died Nov. 27, 1956; buried Bellefontaine Cemetery, St. Louis.

MOORE, Harry H., partner Hallgarten & Co.; dir. Anaconda Copper Mining Co., Chile Copper Co. Mem. bd. govs. N.Y. Stock Exchange, 1933-41. Home: 40 E. 54th St. Office: 44 Pine St., N.Y.C. Deceased.

MOORE, Hight C., clergyman, editor; b. Globe, Caldwell County, N.C., Jan. 28, 1871; s. Patterson and Nancy Ann (Moore) M.; A.B., Wake Forest (N.C.) Coll., 1890, D.D., 1915, student Rochester Theol. Sem., N.Y., 1893; Litt.D., Baylor U., 1920; m. Laura Miller Peterson, May 2, 1893; 1 son Joseph Peterson (dec.). Ordained Bapt. ministry, 1890; pastor Morehead City, N.C., 1890-93, Brown Memorial Ch., Winston-Salem, 1893-94, First Ch., Monroe, 1894-98, First Church, New Bern, 1898-1903, Chapel Hill Church, 1903-04; S.S. secretary Baptist

State Convention of North Carolina, 1904-07, statistical secretary, 1905-07, asst. recording sec., 1896-1907; field sec. S.S. Bd. Southern Bapt. Conv., Nashville, Tenn., 1907-08; editor Biblical Recorder, Raleigh, N.C., 1908-17; mng. editor Sunday School Bd. of Southern Bapt. Conv., Nashville, 1917-27, editorial sec. 1917-43; sec. Southern Bapt. Conv., 1914-46; also mem. exec. com., 1929-46, sec.-treas., 1929-33; dir. Am. Bapt. Theol. Sem., 1924-30. Sec.-treas. editorial sect. of Internat. Council of Religious Edn., 1924-26; mem. Internat. Sunday Sch. Lesson Com. (now Ednl. Commn. Internat. Council Religious Edn.) 1924-1943. Democrat. Author: Seaside Sermons, 1892; Select Poetry of North Carolina, 1894; The Books of the Bible, 1902, revised, 1925, 34; The Country Sunday School, 1905; North Carolina Baptist Hand-Book for 1912, 1911; The Man of Mark in the Church Tomorrow, 1912; Style Book for Writers and Printers, 1918, revised, 1927, 31; The Interwoven Testaments, 1931; Points for Emphasis in the Internat. Sunday Sch. Lessons (annual pocket commentary), 1918-52; From Bethlehem to Olivet and From Pentecost to Patmos, 1934—both pub. in one vol.; New Testament Biographies, 1935; The Better Christmas, 1948; Nuggets from Ridgecrest, 1950; Golden Texts, 1953; also various pamphlets. Home: "Moorehaven," Ridgecrest, N.C. Died May 24, 1957; buried Ridgecrest Meml. Park.

MOORE, Houston Burger, educator; b. Mingo, W.Va., Apr. 30, 1879; s. William John and Ida Ella (Burger) M.; A.B., Hampden-Sydney (Va.) College, 1902, A.M., 1903; m. Ida Virginia Jasper, Aug. 1, 1912; children—Caroline Nichols, William John, Ida Virginia (dec.), Jean Sitlington, Houston Burger. Fellow Latin and Greek, Hampden-Sydney Coll., 1902-03; instr. Latin and Greek, Mil. Acad., Blackstone, Va., 1903-04, Bingham Sch., Asheville, N.C., 1904-05; pres. Greenbrier Mil. Sch. since 1906. Past pres. Greenbrier County Nat. Farm Loan Assn.; sec. bd. Lewisburg & Ronceverte Electric Ry. Co., 1918-25; dir. Lewisburg Hotel Corp. Mem. State Soil Conservation Com. of West Virginia; appointed by governor. Dir. Union Theol. Sem. in Va., Davis Stuart Sch. for Dependent Children in W.Va.; mem. Home Mission Com. of Synod of W.Va. Presbyn. Ch., U.S.; Gen. Assembly's advisory com. on schs. and colls.; mem. gen. com. Layman's Missionary Movement, 1916-24; ex-moderator, Greenbrier Presbytery; v.p. Assn. Mil. Colls. and Schs., 1937-38; v.p., mem. bd. dirs. exec. com. President W.Va. State Dairymen's Association, 1944-45; regional chmn. War Bond Drives. Past pres. State Holstein Friesian Assn., 1943-44; pres. W.Va. Aberdeen-Angus Assn., 1942-44; mem. bd. dirs. W.Va. State Agrl. Fair; Atlantic Rural Expn., Richmond, Va.; dir. W.Va. A.F.B.E.; mem. W.Va. Congress of Agr.; v.p. W. Va. Farm Bur. Dir. Eastern Nat. Exposition. Democrat. Home: Lewisburg, W. Va. Died Oct. 5, 1953.

MOORE, Hoyt Augustus, lawyer; b. Ellsworth, Me., Sept. 15, 1870; s. Augustus Edwin and Susan (Tucker) M.; A.B., Bowdoin, 1895, LL.D., 1939; LL.B., Harvard, 1904; m. Lora Parsons, Oct. 10, 1906; children—Edward P., Dorothy Parsons (Mrs. James W. Tower). Began practice, 1904, in office predecessor of Cravath, Swaine & Moore, N.Y. City, mem. firm and predecessor firms, 1913-57, counsel to Cravath, Swaine & Moore, 1958—. Vice pres. bd. trustees Bowdoin Coll. Mem. Am. and N.Y. State bar assns., Acad. of Polit. Sci., Bowdoin Alumni Assn., N.Y. State C. of C., Delta Kappa Epsilon, Phi Beta Kappa Associates, Maine Soc. N.Y., Society of Colonial Wars, New York Geneal. and Historical Soc., New England Hist. Society. Republican. Mason. Clubs: University, Broad Street. Home: Hotel Westbury, 840 Madison Av., N.Y.C. 21. Office: 15 Broad St., N.Y.C. 5. Died Nov. 18, 1958.

MOORE, Jared Sparks, educator; b. Cambridge, Mass., Sept. 29, 1879; s. Benjamin P. and Florence (Sparks) M.; grad. Marston's U. Sch. for Boys, Balt., 1897; A.B., Johns Hopkins, 1900; A.M., Harvard, 1903, Ph.D., 1905; m. Elsie Linch, July 9, 1913. Asst. in philosophy, Harvard, 1905-07; instr. philosophy, Western Res. U., 1907-13, asst. prof., 1913-19, asso. prof., 1919-25, prof. 1925—. Trustee Holy Cross House for Crippled Children. Fellow A.A. A.S.; mem. Am. Philos. Assn. (v.p. 1925-27), Am. Soc. Aesthetics, Am. Assn. U. Profs., English-Speaking Union, United World Federalists, Federal Union, Beta Theta Pi. Republican. Episcopalian. Club: Novel. Author: The Foundations of Psychology, 1921, rev. edition (with Herbert Gurnee), 1933; Rifts in the Universe—A Study of the Historic Dichotomies and Modalities of Being, 1927. Home: 67 Pond St., Marblehead, Mass. Died Apr. 10, 1951; buried Mt. Auburn Cemetery, Cambridge, Mass.

MOORE, John Merrick, lawyer; b. Little Rock, Ark., Dec. 22, 1880; s. John M. and Annie C. (Turner) M.; ed. Va. Mil. Inst., 1897-99; student Vanderbilt Univ., 1899-1901; LL.B., Columbia, 1905; m. Rebecca Read, June 24, 1915. Began practice at Little Rock, 1905, mem. firm Moore & Smith, 1907-26; an organizer Moore, Gray and Burrow, 1927, now Moore, Burrow, Chowning & Mitchell; dir. Union Nat. Bank, Union Securities Co. Mem. Am. Bar Assn., Ark. Bar Assn. (pres. 1928), Little Rock Bar Assn. (pres. 1922), Kappa Alpha, Phi Delta Phi. Democrat. Presbyn. Club: Little Rock. Home: 2305 N. Spruce St. Office: Boyle Bldg., Little Rock, Ark. Died Mar. 22, 1954.

MOORE, Mrs. John Trotwood, librarian and archivist emeritus; b. Harrisonville, Mo., May 17, 1875; d. Henry Clay and Elizabeth Gillenwaters (Brown) Daniel; stud. Nashville Coll. for Young Ladies, 1893-94; corr. course library service, Columbia; m. John Trotwood Moore, June 13, 1900; children—Merrill, Helen Lane (Mrs. Whitefoord R. Cole, Jr.), Mary Daniel (Mrs. Joel M. Whitney). Tchr. pub. sch., Harrisonville, Mo., 1892-93, 94-97; music dept. Nashville Coll. for Young Ladies, 1897-99; pvt. classes, 1899-1900; sec. to John Trotwood Moore, 1903-19; engaged in hist. and geneal. research Tenn. State Library, 1919-29; Tenn. state librarian and archivist, 1929-49, state librarian and archivist emeritus, 1949—; editor weekly column Dropped Stitches on so. history in Memphis (Tenn.) Comml. Appeal, 1924-42. Mem. John Sevier Statue Commn., 1931; chmn. ednl. com. Women's Dept. Tenn. State Fair, 1931-32; mem. com. for Tenn., George Washington Bicentennial, 1931-32; mem. adv. com. Woman's Participation for N.Y. World's Fair, 1938-39; mem. nat. sponsoring com. Am. Women's Vol. Services, 1941; mem. commn. for new State Library and Archives Bldg., 1947. Mem. A.L.A., Nat. Assn. State Libraries (1st v.p. 1936-37), Am. Assn. Law Libraries, Soc. Am. Archivists (charter mem.), Am. Assn. State and Local Hist. Socs. (charter mem.), Tenn. Library Assn. (sec.-treas. 1930-31), Nat. Geneal. Soc., Tenn. Hist. Soc. (corr. sec. 1937-49), Tenn. Hist. Commn. (mem. bd. and com. on portraits and memorials, chmn. centennial celebration birth Pres. James K. Polk). Confed. Pension Bd. Tenn., Ft. Donelson House Hist. Assn., Tenn. Folklore Soc., Nat. Soc. Colonial Dames of Am. in Tenn. (mem. bd., rec. sec. 1943-45), Colonial Dames Am. in. Tenn. (v.p. 1947), Tenn. Soc. D.A.R. (state historian 1936-38, hon. historian for life), D.A.R. (nat. Soc. U.S.D., 1812, Sam Davis Meml. Assn. (trustee 1930-33), Nathan Bedford Forrest Meml. Assn. (trustee 1929-49), Tenn. Com. Conservation Cultural Resources (World War II), Nathan Bedford Forrest Cav. Corps (historian with rank col.), Ladies Hermitage Assn. (hon. mem. 1933-34), Womens Press and Authors Club (librarian 1949-50), Granny White Garden Club (historian, 1923—), Centennial Club (Nashville), D.A.R. Officers Club, Nashville Library Club. Methodist. Collaborator: The History of Homes and Gardens in Tenn., 1936. Compilor: Pictorial Map of Tenn., 1939. Transcriber: House and Senate Jours. of Second Gen. Assembly of State of Tenn., 1797-98, 1933; List Commd. Officers in the Tenn. Militia, 1796-1811, 1945. Contbr. profl. jours. Home: 3309 Fairmont Dr., Nashville 5. Died Aug. 2, 1957.

MOORE, John Walker, educator; b. McConnellsville, S.C., Jan. 29, 1884; s. James Oscar and Hattie (Walker) M.; B.S., Davidson (N.C.) Coll., 1906, hon. D.Sc., 1940; med. student Univ. of N.C., 1908-10; M.D., U. of Pa., 1912; m. Anna Stockett Kent, Aug. 19, 1920; children—Marjorie Kent, William Kent, John Walker. Interne Episcopal Hosp., Philadelphia, Pa., 1913-15; instr. in pathology and bacteriology, U. of Louisville, 1915-17, instr. in medicine, 1919-20, prof. research medicine, 1920-23, prof. medicine, 1923-49, dean of Sch. of Medicine, 1929-49, Alben W. Barkley prof. of medicine, since 1949; director division medicine and staff exec. Louisville City Hosp. 1923-49. Served as capt., Med. Corps, U.S. Army, later maj., lab. officer to hosp. center, Nantes, France, 1917-19. Received faculty award of merit, University of Louisville, 1936. Technical supervisor, American Red Cross Blood Donor Service, since 1942; consultant for Army Specialized Training Program. Member Association American Physicians, American Coll. Physicians, A.M.A., Central Soc. Clin. Research (pres. 1942-43), Am. Clin. and Clinatol. Assn., Southern Med. Assn. (chmn. sect. on med. edn. 1933), Assn. Am. Med. Colleges (v.p. 1942-43, pres. 1945-46), Alpha Omega Alpha, Kappa Sigma, Phi Chi, Phi Beta Kappa, Phi Kappa Phi, Gorgon's Head (U. of N.C.). Democrat. Presbyterian. Clubs: Pendennis, Pierian. Home: 623 Cochran Hill Rd. Office: Louisville General Hosp., Louisville. Died Nov. 10, 1952.

MOORE, Joseph Earle, physician; b. Phila., July 9, 1892; s. Joseph Howard and Adelaide Marie (Lovett) M.; A.B., U. of Kan., 1914; M.D., Johns Hopkins, 1916; m. Grace Douglas Barclay, May 24, 1917 (dec.); m. 2d Irene Mason Gieske, Dec. 23, 1954. Asst., instr., asso., asso. prof. medicine and adjunct prof. of pub. health adminstrn., Johns Hopkins, 1916-45, visiting physician Johns Hopkins Hospital 1923-45, physician in charge chronic disease div. Medical Clinic, Johns Hopkins Medical Sch. and Hosp., 1929—, prof. medicine, 1957—; spl. cons. USPHS; cons. Md. State Dept. of Health. Served as first lieutenant and as captain Marine Corps, U.S. Army, A.E.F., 1917-19; maj. M.C. Res., 1920-28. Awarded Medal for Merit. Mem. A. M.A., Assn. of Am. Phys., Am. Soc. for Clin. Investigation, Am. Clin. and Climatol. Soc., Med. and Chirurg. Faculty of Md., Phi Beta Kappa, Sigma Xi, Phi Chi. Author: The Modern Treatment of Syphilis, 1933, 2d edit., 1941; Penicillin in Syphilis, 1947. Co-editor, Jour. Chronic Diseases. Contbr. articles to med. jours. Home: Warrington Apts., 3908 N. Charles St., Balt. Office: Johns Hopkins Hosp., Balt. 5. Died Dec. 6, 1957; buried Greenmount Cemetery.

MOORE, Lyle Stickley, mfr.; b. Leadvale, Tenn., July 23, 1885; s. Thomas E. and Mattie E. (Houston) M.; student Maryville Coll., 1903-04; m. Margaret (Madge) Mims, Jan. 21, 1913; children—Lyle S., Myra Lucia (Mrs. Raymond D. Chamberlain). Pres. Newport Can Co., Inc., Moore Brothers Canning Co., Inc.; v.p. Stokely-Van Camp, Inc. Mem. bd. govs. Tenn. Mfrs. Assn. Methodist. Home: Newport, Tenn. Died Apr. 14, 1954; buried Union Cemetery, Newport.

MOORE, Lyman Sweet, city manager; born at Attleboro, Mass. August 15, 1910; son of Fred Atkins and Vivian Elizabeth (Ross) M.; B.A., University of Wis., 1931, M.A., 1933, Ph.D., Northwestern U., 1936; student Columbia U., 1933, U. of Chicago, 1934; m. Doris Abbott Sargent, Sept. 15, 1934; children—Fred Sargent, David Wells. Staff mem. Internat. City Mgrs. Assn., asst. dir. Inst. for Training in Municipal Adminstrn., asst. editor, Public Management, Municipal Yearbook, 1934-38; consultant Public Service Training, U.S. Office of Edn., 1938-40; administrative asst. to city mgr., City of Kansas City, 1940-42; consultant U.S. Bur. of the Budget, 1942; assistant administrator of National Housing Agency, 1942-46; city manager, Portland, Me., since 1946; cons. on adminstrv. procedures to the Nat. Govt. of Thailand in Bangkok, 1952. Cons. town management, Atomic Energy Commn. since 1947. Mem. Internat. City Mgrs. Assn. (cons. Pub. Employee Training), Am. Soc. for Pub. Adminstrn., Am. Polit. Sci. Assn., Municipal Finance Officers Assn., Civil Service Assembly, Theta Chi. Home: 30 Berkeley St. Office: City Hall, Portland, Me. Died Aug. 5, 1952; buried Gorham, N.H.

MOORE, Mary (Carr) (mōor), composer; b. Memphis, Tenn., Aug. 6, 1873; d. Byron O. and Sarah (Pratt) Carr; musical edn. under Emma Dewhurst, Louisville, Ky., John Haraden Pratt, San Francisco, Calif.; also voice under H. B. Pasmore, Mariner-Campbell; Mus.Doc., Chapman College, 1936; m. J. C. Moore, M.D., Feb. 15, 1898; children—Byron Carr, Marion (Mrs. C. M. Quinn), John Wesley, flight surg. (killed at Port Moresby, New Guinea, 1944). Concert and church singer until 1928, in charge theory dept., Olga Steeb Piano Sch., Los Angeles, 1926—; teacher at Chapman College; former prof. theory, Calif. Christian Coll. Mem. numerous orgns. Founder Mary Carr Moore Manuscript Club, having mems. Throughout U.S. and in foreign countries. Composer more than 300 songs, 10 operas, several orchestral scores, concertos, quartets, quintets, sonatas, choral works, instrumental solos. Conducted own orchestral scores, Intermezzo from opera David Rizzio with Ford Bowl Orchestra, Aug., 1936, and Indian Idyll with Federal Symphony Orchestra, May 1937; during the period 1938-40, Dr. Moore conducted programs of her works performed by the Bay Cities combined orchestras (90 member) at Oakland and San Francisco; also conducted own works performed by San Francisco Symphony Orchestra at Treasure Island, Golden Gate Internat. Expn., 1940. Awarded David Bispham memorial medal for "Narcissa," 1930, and 9 other prizes since 1927; 1st prize for chamber music from Nat. League Am. Penwomen 3 times in succession. Retired. Home: 5504 Village Green, Los Angeles 16. Died Jan. 9, 1957; buried Inglewood (Cal.) Park Cemetery Mausoleum.

MOORE, Merrill (mōr), psychiatrist; b. Columbia, Tenn., Sept. 11, 1903; s. John Trotwood and Mary Brown (Daniel) M.; student Montgomery Bell Acad., Nashville, 1916-20; B.A., Vanderbilt U., Nashville, 1924, M.D., Vanderbilt Med. Sch., 1928; married Ann Leslie Nichol, Aug. 14, 1930; children—Adam G. N. Moore, John Trotwood, Leslie and Hester. Interne, St. Thomas Hospital, Nashville, Tenn., 1928-29; teaching fellow neurology, Harvard Med. Sch., 1930-31, asst. in neuropathology, 1931-32, research fellow psychiatry, 1936-42; neurological house officer, Boston City Hosp., 1930-31, res. neurological physician, 1930-31; asst. physician, Boston Psychopathic Hosp., 1932-35; grad. asst., Psychiatric Clinic, Mass. General Hospital, 1933-34. Military service, S.W. Pacific, 1942-45; col. M.C., A.U.S.; surgeon, Nanking Hdqrs. Command, 1946. Vis. psychiat., Boston City Hosp.; clin. asso. psychiatry, Harvard Med. Sch.; research asso., Boston Psychopathic Hosp. Awarded Bronze Star (Bougainville), 1944; Army Commendation Ribbon (China), 1946. Fellow American Psychiat. Assn., Am. Neurol. Assn., Mass. Med. Soc., Am. Psychopathol. Assn., A.A.A.S.; mem. Am. Med. Assn., Sigma Chi, Phi Beta Kappa (hon. 1941). Author: The Noise That Time Makes, 1929; Six Sides to a Man, 1935; M: one thousand autobiog. sonnets; Clinical Sonnets, 1949; Illegitimate Sonnets, 1950; Case Record From a Sonnetorium, 1952; More Clinical Sonnets, 1952; A Doctor's Book of Hours, 1954; Dance of Death, 1957; The Phoenix & The Bees (poems), 1958; also other vols. of poetry, prose essays; contbr. articles on alcoholism, syphillis, suicide, psychiatry and conchology. Home: 10 Crabtree Rd., Squantum, Quincy 71, Mass. Died Sept. 20, 1957.

MOORE, Orval Floyd, corp. exec.; b. Duggar, Ind., Aug. 21, 1889; s. Elias and Susan Jane (Gabbard) M.; student pub. schs. and Brown Bus. Coll., Terre Haute, Ind.; m. Marjorie M. Neipling, Oct. 12, 1914; 1 son, Frederick John. Clk. Ohio Oil Co., 1909-15, asst. sec., 1943-44, asst. sec. and asst. mgr., 1944-46, now v.p., dir., also mgr. pipe line dept.; asst. sec. Ill. Pipe Line Co., 1915-17, dir., sec., 1917-38, dir., v.p., sec., 1938-42; dir., v.p., sec. Ill. Pipe Line of Tex., 1942-46, dir., pres., 1946-—. Pres. Findlay (O.) Hosp. Assn. Mem. Am. Petroleum Inst. (dir.). Republican. Lutheran. Elk. Clubs: Auto, Pipe Liners, Findlay County. Home: 1309 S. Main St. Office: 539 S. Main St., Findlay, O. Died Feb. 24, 1958.

MOORE, Paul, financier; b. Chgo., Nov. 30, 1885; s. William Henry and Ada Waterman (Small) M.; A.B., Yale, 1908; student Northwestern U. Law Sch.; LL.B., N.Y. Law Sch., 1911; m. Fanny Weber Hanna, Oct. 30, 1909. Dir. American Can Company, Del., Lackawanna & Western R.R., Nat. Biscuit Co., Republic Aviation Corp. Mem. S.A.R., Mayflower Soc., Soc. of Colonial Wars, St. Nicholas Soc. of N.Y.C. Clubs: Racquet and Tennis, The Links, Recess, Links Golf, Morris Country Golf, National Golf, Turf and Field, River, Myopia Hunt, Gulf Stream Golf. Home: Hollow Hill Farm, Convent, New Jersey. Office: 14 Wall St., N.Y.C. 5. Died Dec. 1959.

MOORE, Robert Martin, physician; b. Somerville, Ind., Nov. 18, 1884; s. Robert (M.D.) and Laura (Martin) M.; A.B., Ind. U., 1911, M.D., 1913; post grad work, Harvard Med Sch., summers 1920-21, 22; m. Eva Belle Van Dyke, Nov. 12, 1919; children—Robert (dec.), Philippe Van Dyke. Began practice, 1913; prof. clin. cardiology, Indiana University Sch. of Medicine, since 1931, and member of the board of councilors; chief of Cardiac Clinic, Indianapolis City Hospital; past pres. Ind. Heart Found.; chmn. bd. trustees, Ind. Heart Foundn.; member staff Indiana University Hosp.; mem. visiting staff St. Vincent's Hosp.; mem. staff and mem. adv. bd. Methodist Hosp. Capt. Med. Corps, U.S. Army, with A.E.F., World War I. Certified by American Board Internal Medicine and Cardiovascular Disease Fellow American Coll. Physicians (Ind. gov. 16 yrs.); mem. Am., Ind. State and Marion County med. assns., Indianapolis Med. Soc. (pres. 1938), Am. Heart Assn. (councilor), Indianapolis Acad. of Medicine and Surgery, Central Soc. for Clinical Research, Am. Assn. for Study of Goitre, Delta Tau Delta, Nu Sigma Nu, Sigma Xi. Republican. Presbyterian. Mason. Contbr. to med. jours. Home: 5617 N. Meridian St. Office: Home Mansur Bldg., Indpls. Died June 23, 1952; buried Crown Hill Cemetery, Indpls.

MOORE, Robert Thomas, zoölogist; b. Haddonfield, N.J., June 24, 1882; s. Henry Dyer and Mary J. (Smith) M.; A.B., U. Pa., 1903; A.M., Harvard, 1904; grad. study U. Munich; D.S. (hon.), Occidental Coll., Los Angeles, 1949; m. Selma Helena Muller, Dec. 22, 1903; children—Terris, Karlene; m. 2d, Margaret Forbes Cleaves, June 17, 1922; 1 dau., Marilynn; step-children—Waddell Austin, Paul Austin. Editor Cassinia, ofcl. publ. Del. Valley Ornithol. Club, 1911-16; breeder of silver black foxes; owner Borestone Mountain Fox Ranch, Onawa, Me., 1915-30, Western bus. inc., 1923, as Big Bear Fox Ranch of Cal.; asso. dept. vertebrate zoölogy Cal. Inst. Tech., 1929-50; asso. in vertebrate zoölogy and dir. zoölog. lab. Occidental Coll., Los Angeles 1950-55; formerly v.p. Moore Securities Co. (Phila.); pres. Big Bear Fox Ranching Co. until 1928; dir. Guanajuato Reduction & Mines Co., Empire Lumber Co., Cowichan Lake Lumber Co. Founder of World's 1st National Silver Fox Show, Boston, 1919. Leader of ornithol. expedition to Ecuador, 1927, zoölogical expedition to South Ecuador, 1929 (made first successful ascent of Mt. Sangai, active volcano, large zool. collection from hitherto unexplored regions; zoöl. species new to science), to Mexico for Calif. Inst. Tech., 1933, 34, 36, 37, 38, 42, 43, 45; (secured many birds new to science); lectured in Cultural Relations Mexico, 1942-45; chmn. Galapagos Com., 1934-38; instrumental in having a large part of Galapagos Archipelago set aside by Ecuador as sanctuary for zoölogical life. Trustee the Poetry Soc. Am. Fellow Royal Geog. Soc. (London), Am. Geog. Soc., Am. Ornithol. Union (mem. council); mem. Am. Com. for Internat. Wild Life Protection, Acad. Natural Sciences, Am. Nat. Fox Breeders Assn. (bd. govs. and first hon. pres.), Am. Fox Breeders Assn. (bd. govs.), Soc. Mayflower Descs., John Howland Descs., Phi Beta Kappa. Presbyn. (elder). Clubs: Twilight, Valley Hunt, (hon. mem.; gov.; past pres.) (Los Angeles); Orpheus (Phila.); Explorers (N.Y.C.); Cosmos (Washington). Author: Eileen, a Sonnet Sequence, 1946; chairman of authors: Check List of Mexican Birds, 1950; co-author: Biotic Provinces of Mexico (with A. E. Goldman). Editor in chief Poetry Awards, an annual anthology of mag. poetry. Contbr. more than 60 articles on zoology, breeding and exploration. Contbr. many poems to mags. Home: Zephyr Cove, Lake Tahoe, Nev.; (winter) Sunny Gables, Meadow Grove Place, Pasadena 3, Cal. Died Oct. 30, 1958.

MOORE, Roy (Donald), newspaper pub.; b. McArthur, O., Aug. 25, 1887; s. William Thomas and Elizabeth (Clark) M.; ed. pub. schs. of Middleport, O.; m. Lucile Dyke, Mar. 23, 1910; children—William (dec.), Esther Jane (Mrs. William I. Hershey). Ry. and comml. telegrapher, Middleport, Ohio, 1902-07; telegrapher Asso. Press, Cleveland, O., 1907-10, Cleveland Leader and Cleveland News, 1910-13; bur. mgr. Internat. News Service, Cleveland, Columbus, Chicago, 1913-17; gen. mgr. Fargo (N.D.) Courier News, 1918-19; salesman, asst. sales mgr. and asst. gen. mgr., King Features Syndicate, New York, N.Y., 1919-21, spl. assignment S.Am., 1922; gen. mgr. Portland (Me.) Press, 1921; purchased Marion (O.) Star, June 1923 with Louis H. Brush; with L. H. Brush and William H. Vodrey organized Brush-Moore Newspapers, Inc., Canton, (O.) Repository, Steubenville (O.) Herald Star, E. Liverpool (O.) Review, Salem (O.) News, Marion (O.) Star, Portsmouth (O.) Times, Ironton (O.) Tribune, Salisbury (Md.) Times, radio stas. WHBC (Canton) and WPAY (Portsmouth), 1927 (vice pres. and gen. mgr. to June 1946, pres. and pub. since 1946). Pre-conv. chmn. Ohio War Finance Com., 1941-43, campaign mgr. for John W. Bricker, Rep., 1943-44. Trustee Aultman Hosp. Assn., Canton, O. Trustee O. Development and Publicity Commn. Member Am. Newspaper Pubs. Assn. (chmn. governing bd. Bur. of Advt., 1944-47), O. Newspaper Assn. (pres. 1940, trustee). Presbyn. Mason (K.T.). Clubs: Ohio Soc. of New York, National Press, Union (Cleveland), Canton, Brookside and Congress Lake Country; Union League (New York). Home: Congress Lake, Hartville, O. Office: Brush-Moore Newspapers, Inc., Canton, O. Died May 1, 1954; buried Northlawn Cemetery, Canton.

MOORE, Thomas Justin, lawyer; b. Liberty Hill, La., Aug. 28, 1890; s. J. T. and Carrie L. (Preslar) M.; A.B., U. Richmond, 1908; LL.D., 1954; LL.B., Harvard Law Sch., 1913; LL.D., La. Coll., 1929; m. Caroline Willingham, Dec. 18, 1913; children—Carolyn H. (Mrs. Howard M. McCue), Cornelia B. (Mrs. James K. Hall, Jr.), T. Justin, Jr. Admitted to bar, June 1913; practice of law, Richmond, Virginia, since 1913, in own name until 1931, became partner firm Hunton, Williams, Gay, Moore and Powell; chmn. exec. com., gen. counsel, dir. Va. Electric and Power Co., 1925-—; prof. law, U. of Richmond, 1913-25; gen. counsel and dir. Virginia Transit Co.; dir. The Central National Bank of Richmond, Richmond Hotels, Inc. Elected rector U. Richmond, 1951. Mem. Am., Va. (p.p.), and Richmond (p.p.) bar assns., Phi Beta Kappa, Sigma Alpha Epsilon. Clubs: Country of Va., Commonwealth. Home: 16 Rio Vista Lane. Office: Electric Bldg., Richmond, Va. Died Mar. 10, 1958.

MOORHEAD, Frank Graham (mōr'hĕd), editor; b. Council Bluffs, Ia., Aug. 20, 1876; s. Samuel Wallace and Mary (Graham) M.; student Ia. State Coll. Agr. and Mechanic Arts, 1891-92, Grinnel Coll., 1893-94; m. Mildred Rhorer, Apr. 14, 1903; children—Graham Ellis (dec.), Robert Louis (dec.), Verlaine. With Keokuk Gate City and Keokuk Evening Press until 1895; free lance, St. Louis dailies, 1895-96; with Des Moines Daily Capital, 1898-1903; asso. editor Des Moines Register and Leader, 1903-08; Sunday editor Spokane, Spokesman-Review, 1908-09; asso. editor Pierce's Farm weeklies, Des Moines, 1910-20; editor The Farm Jour., Phila., 1920-22; editor in chief Pierce's Farm weeklies, 1922-29; western editor The Farm Jour., 1929-30; spl. agt. Ia. Dept. Justice, 1933-38; fature writer Ia. Ofcl. Register, 1939; 41; publicity dir. State Dem. Com., 1940; editor house mags. (Weekly Onward, Monthly Onward, Our Home Office), Bankers Life Co., Des Moines, Ia., 1942-45. Conglist. Club: Iowa Authors'. Author: Unknown Facts About Well Known People, 1893; Jazz History of the United States, 1925. Contbr. mags. Home: 2831 Ridge Rd., Des Moines, Ia. Deceased.

MOORHEAD, Louis David (mōōr'hĕd), surgeon; b. Chicago, Ill., Nov. 22, 1892; s. Edward Louis (M.D.) and Jeannette (Snell) M.; A.B., St. Ignatius Coll., Chicago, 1913; S.B., U. of Chicago, 1914, S.M., 1915; A.M., Loyola U., 1916; M.D., Rush Med. Coll., 1917; LL.D., Creighton U., 1931; m. Ann Patricia Dorsey, Aug. 25, 1932; children—Louis David, Edward Louis II, Patrick Henry. Practiced in Chicago since 1917; sr. house surgeon Cook County Hosp., 1917-19; became dean and asso. prof. surgery, Loyola U. Sch. of Medicine, 1918, dean, prof. and head of dept. of surgery, 1928-40; formerly chief of staff; sr. attending surgeon Mercy Hosp. since 1920; cons. surg. Rock Island R.R. System, C.&E.I. R.R., Belt R.R. of Chicago, Chief of med. bd. archdiocese of Chgo., Chgo. Bd. of Health, Chicago Fire Dept. Chmn. bd. trustees Lewis Memorial Maternity Hosp., Loretto Hosp., St. Georges Hosp., Holy Cross Hosp. Mem. bd. govs., Cath. Ch. Extension Soc. of U.S. and Can., since 1948; mem. bd. dirs. Cath. Charities, Chicago; adv. com., Institutem Divi Thomae. Fellow Am. Coll. Surgeons; mem. Founders Group, Am. Bd. of Surgery; mem. Internat. Coll. of Surgeons, A.M.A., Ill. State and Chicago med. socs., Phi Beta Pi, Kappa Pi Epsilon, Sigma Xi. Catholic. Decorated Knight of St. Gregory by the Pope, 1931; Knight of Order of Crown of Italy, 1932; Knight of Cap and Sword by Pope Pius XI, 1938, reknighted by Pope Pius XII, 1939; Knight Comdr. Order of Crown of Italy, 1946. Club: University. Home: 1101 N. Elmwood Av., Oak Park, Ill. Office: 31 N. State St., Chicago. Died Sept. 14, 1951; buried family mausoleum, Calvary Cemetery.

MOORHEAD, William Singer, lawyer; b. Greensburg, Pa., Aug. 2, 1883; s. James Sharpe and Elizabeth Williams (Singer) M.; grad. Lawrenceville (N.J.) Sch., 1902; A.B., Yale, 1906; LL.B., U. Pitts., 1909; m. Constance Barr, Feb. 10, 1915; 1 son, William Singer (USNR). Admitted to Pa. bar, 1909 and began practice at Pitts.; mem. firm Moorhead & Knox since 1917; lectr. U. Pitts. Sch. of Law, 1909-18. Chmn. U.S. Tax Simplification Board, 1922-24; chmn. orgn. com. Pitts. Community Fund, 1927. Trustee Carnegie Library, Carnegie Inst., Carnegie Inst. Tech.; Frick Art Reference Library; pres. Tuberculosis League of Pitts., 1940-50; pres. Law Club of Pitts.; chmn. Alumni Bd. of Yale U., 1935-37; mem. Am., Pa., Allegheny County bar assns., Am. Law Inst., Delta Kappa Epsilon. Presbyn. (trustee Shadyside Presbyn. Ch.). Clubs: Duquesne, Pittsburgh Golf, Fox Chapel Golf, Rolling Rock; Yale (N.Y.C.); Misquamicut (Watch Hill, R.I.). Home: 5725 Aylesboro Av. Office: Oliver Bldg., Pitts. 22. Died Feb. 12, 1952; buried Homewood Cemetery, Pitts.

MORAN, John Henry, transportation exec.; b. Brookline, Mass., Oct. 28, 1890; s. Edward and Mary (Kenney) M.; student Northeastern U., Boston U., Harvard. With Boston Elevated Ry. Co. since 1909, gen. auditor since 1920, v.p., comptroller, 1936-41, exec. v.p., treas. since 1941; pres. Eastern Mass. St. Ry. Co., Boston, since 1951; treas., dir. Transit Mut. Ins. Co.; dir. Union Freeport R.R. Co.; treas. Met. Transit Authority; trustee, mem. investment com. Union Savs. Bank. Mem. Am. Transit Assn. (exec. com.). Clubs: Engrs., Univ., Algonquin; Hatherly Country. Home: 3 Hilltop Rd., Chestnut Hill, Mass. Office: 161 Devonshire St., Boston 10. Died Nov. 8, 1954.

MORCOM, Clifford Bawden, ins. exec.; b. Cleveland, May 29, 1885; s. James and Mary A. (McKay) M.; student pub. schs. of Hartford, Conn.; m. Hazel Moore, June 18, 1912. With Aetna Life Ins. Co., Hartford, since 1902, asst. sec. accident and liability dept., 1913, sec., 1921, v.p. Aetna Life Ins. Co., Aetna Casualty & Surety Co. since 1923, v.p. Automobile Ins. Co., Standard Fire Ins. Co. since 1923; dir. Dime Savs. Bank of Hartford, Phoenix State Bank and Trust Co., Hartford, Aetna Life Ins. Co., Aetna Casualty & Surety Co., Automobile Ins. Co. Past pres. Assn. of Casualty and Surety Execs. Clubs: Hartford Golf, Wampanoag Country (Hartford). Home: Sunset Farm, West Hartford 7. Office: 151 Farmington Av., Hartford 15, Conn. Died Sept. 26, 1951.

MORDE, Theodore A. (môrd), writer; born at New Bedford, Massachusetts, Mar. 17, 1911; son of Albert and Louise (Ambrose) M.; graduate New Bedford High School, 1929; pvt. instruction, 1929-31; student Brown U., 1935-36; m. Gloria Elizabeth Gustafson, Aug. 7, 1948; children—Christine, Theodore A. Sports reporter New Bedford Times, 1929; news commentator, program dir., radio writer for broadcasting cos. in East and Calif., 1930-34; mem. Providence (R.I.) Jour.-Eve. Bull. news staff, 1935-37; freeland corr. and photographer, Europe, Spanish Civil War, 1938, covering both sides; cruise director and lecturer Raymond-Whitcomb, Inc., 1939; leader Third Honduran Expdn., 1940, under auspices Museum of the Am. Indian, in coop. with Am. Geog. Soc. and Nat. Museum of Honduras; conducted archeol. and ethnographical research in Mosquitia Terr., uncovered evidences of ancient Chorotegan civilization, explored and mapped unknown interior rivers. Spl. agent Mil. Intelligence Div., War Dept., Oct. 1940-Sept. 1941; later, chief, fgn. lang. sect., U.S. Coordinator of Information, assigned to Am. Legation, Cairo, Egypt, as asst. to Am. Minister, 1942; mem. Joint Anglo-Am. Relations Com. in Middle East; asst. dir. U.S. O.W.I. in Middle East, later dir. Egypt Div., 1942-43; accredited war corr., gen. mgr. Reader's Digest Middle East Br. (pub. Arabic and Am.-Brit. troop edits.), 1943-44; asst. chief of operations, Strategic Services Unit, War Dept., 1946; advisor to Prime Minister, Egypt, 1947, Royal Egyptian Embassy, Washington, 1948; owner, manager Theodore Morde, Inc., pub. orgn., 1949-—; pres. Spotnews Prodns., Inc., N.Y.; editor-in-chief AP-Spotnews TV daily newsreel, 1952. Commd. lt. (j.g.), U.S.N.R., 1944, serving with O.S.S. in European, S.E.A.C. and China theaters; promoted lt., 1945. Decorated Bronze Star Medal. Clubs: Brown Univ., Explorers (New York); Wamsutta (New Bedford); Nat. Press (Washington). Contbr. articles on travel, war and internat. politics to Am. and fgn. newspapers and mags. Address: South Dartmouth, Mass. Died June 26, 1954; buried Rural Cemetery, New Bedford, Mass.

MORDEN, William J(ames), explorer and field collector; b. Chicago, Jan. 3, 1886; s. William J. and Laura (Houston) M.; Ph.B., Sheffield Sci. School, Yale, 1908; m. Florence H. Rose, Apr. 24, 1920 (died Apr. 9, 1939); m. 2d, Irene Hambright, Apr. 27, 1940. Engr. and mfr., 1908-22; explorer and field collector, 1922—; dir. Union Bag & Paper Corp., mem. sci. staff Am. Museum of Natural History (field asso. dept. mammals), 1926-40, leader Morden-Clark Asiatic Expdn. of Am. Mus. Natural History, 1926-27, also various expdns. for mus., 1930-40; leader Morden-Graves North Asiatic Expdn., 1929-30, Morden African Expn., 1947. Served as 1st lt., Engrs., O.R.C., A.E.F., 1918-19, capt., 1919-20, 1924-36, major, 1936-40; major (inactive) A.U.S., 1940-42; major, Air Corps, A.U.S., 1942-44, lt. col., 1944-47; lt. col. hon. res., O.R.C., 1947-49, lt. colonel U.S. Air Force, retired; rated service pilot, 1943. Life fellow Royal Geog. Soc. (Eng.); hon. fellow Am. Museum Natural History; hon. mem. East African Professional Hunters Assn. Mason. Clubs: American Yacht, Union League, Yale, Explorers (past dir. and v.p.), Campfire, Wings (New York); Bohemian (San Francisco); Himalayan (India) (life mem.); Quiet Birdmen. Author: Across Asia's Snows and Deserts, 1927; articles in various mags. Home: Camp Fire Rd., Chappaqua, N.Y. Died Jan. 23, 1958.

MORE, Charles Church, engr., educator; b. Rock Island, Ill., Jan. 21, 1875; s. David Fellows and Sara Jane (Hubbell) M.; C.E., Lafayette Coll., 1898, M.S., 1901; M.C.E., Cornell, 1899; m. Myra Hadlock Ober, Aug. 24, 1904. Began with Pencoyd Iron Works, Phila., 1899; acting prof. civ. engring., U. Wash., 1900, asst. prof., 1904, asso. prof., 1907, prof., 1912, prof. and head dept., 1917-25, prof. structural engring., 1925-47, emeritus, 1947—; with Am. Bridge Co. (Phila.), D. H. Burnham & Co. (Chgo.), U.S. Engr. Dept. (Ft. Worden, Wash.), 1901-04; with C.,M.&St.P. Ry. Co., Seattle, 1906-07, Turner Constrn. Co., N.Y.C., 1911-12. Commd. capt. Engr. R.C., June 19, 1917; in training at Engr. O.T.C., Vancouver Barracks, Wash., Sept.-Oct. 1917; capt. O.R.C., Oct. 18, 1917; maj. ordnance, U.S. Army, July 25, 1918. On duty at Ordnance Office, Washington, Nov. 1917-Nov. 1918; instr. at Engr. Sch., Camp Humphreys, Va., Dec. 1918-Sept. 1919; hon. discharged Oct. 1, 1919. Mem. Soc. for Promotion Engring. Edn. (council, 1919-22), Am. Assn. Univ. Profs., Am. Soc. C.E., Am. Legion, Phi Beta Kappa, Sigma Xi, Tau Beta Pi, Phi Kappa Psi. Sec. John More Assn., 1900-25, asso. sec., 1925—. Conglist. Compiler: Genealogy of Descendants of John More, 1893. Home: 4545 Fifth Av. N.E., Seattle, Wash. Died Nov. 19, 1949.

MOREAU, Arthur Edmond (mô-ō), industrialist; b. Manchester, N.H., Mar. 5, 1885; s. Joseph Jean and Ella M. (Houde) M.; student Manchester High Sch., 1900-03, Hesser Bus. Coll., 1903-04; hon. M.A., Dartmouth Coll., 1937; m. Emilienne R. Tremblay, June 25, 1907; children—Lt. Arthur Joseph, Charlotte, Lily, Marjorie Andrea. Entered father's hardware bus., 1904; name changed to J. J. Moreau & Son, 1906, owner, mgr. J. J. Moreau & Son 1917-46; co. inc., 1946, now treas., dir.; organized Amoskeag Industries, Inc., to purchase closed mills of Amoskeag Mfg. Co. and provide industry for Manchester workers, 1936, also pres. same; pres. Manchester Coal & Ice Co.; dir. Manchester Nat. Bank, Pub. Service N.H., Acme Realty Co. Mayor City of Manchester, 1925-31; commr. Manchester Fire Dept., 1925-26; mem. Gov's. Council, 1925-26; commr. Manchester Police Dept., 1949-52; del.-at-large Rep. Nat. Conv., 1928; mem. Rep. Program Com., 1938; chmn. N.H. Post-War Planning and Rehabilitation Com.; vice chmn. Manchester Com. Econ. Development. Served as maj. on staff gov. of N.H., 1916-17, 32-33. Trustee N.H. State Indsl. Sch., U. N.H. Mem. adv. bd. Salvation Army; mem. N.E. Hardware Dealers Assn. (ex-pres.), Manchester C. of C. (ex-pres.), Canada-Am. Soc., Soc. of St. Jean Baptiste of Am., Newcomen Soc., Army Ordnance, Navy League U.S. Republican. Catholic. K.C., Elk. Clubs: Rotary (ex-pres.; dir.), Joliet, Derryfield, Manchester Country, N.H. Mayors (ex-pres., organizer), Execs., St. Petersburg Yacht. Home: 46 Bay St, Manchester, N.H.; and 146 14th Av. N., St. Petersburg, Fla. (summer) The Weirs, N.H. Office: 1127 Elm St., Manchester, N.H. Died July 4, 1951.

MOREHEAD, Charles Allen, lawyer; b. Port Gibson, Miss., Aug. 8, 1901; s. Benjamin Hughes and Emma (Allen) M.; B.S., U. Ala., 1922; B.S., LL. B., Cumberland U., 1925; m. Jean Shank, June 11, 1930; children—Jean (Mrs. Carroll P. Davis), Charles A. Admitted to Fla. bar, 1925; county solicitor Dade County, Fla., 1930-31; sr. partner Morehead, Forrest, Gotthardt & Orr, Miami, Fla., 1940—; dir. Central Bank & Trust Co., Am. Fire & Casualty Co. (Orlando, Fla.), Am. Ind. Reins. Co. (Orlando), State Fire and Casualty Co. Pres. Estate Planning Council S.E. Fla., 1950-51. Mem. Dade County Bar Assn. (past sec., dir.). Episcopalian. Mason (Shriner), Elk. Clubs: Kiwanis (past pres.), La Gorce Country, Surf (Miami Beach, Fla.). Author: (with J. K. Lasser; Handbook of Tax Techniques, 1950, Estate Planners' Handbook, 1952, Estate Tax Techniques, 1953, Encyclopedia of Tax Procedures, 1955; (with John Alan Appleman) Basic Estate Planning, 1956. Contbr. mags. and jours. Home: 5821 Pinetree Dr., Miami Beach, Fla. Office: 228 N.E. 2d Av., Miami 32, Fla. Died Aug. 27, 1957.

MOREHEAD, French Hugh, cons. engr.; b. Paris, Mo., Nov. 23, 1883; s. John Quarles and Mary Martha (Glascock) M.; B.S. in M.E., U. Mo., 1904; m. Clo Searcy, July 8, 1907 (died 1914); 1 son, T. Searcy (dec.); m. 2d, Frances Thornton, Aug. 10, 1925. Began as draftsman and surveyor, U.S. Geol. Survey, 1904; machine designer Am. Steel Wire Co., 1904-06; sales and office mgr. Kewanee Pvt. Utilities Co., 1906-18; successively works engr., chief engr. Walworth Co., 1918-29, v.p., cons. engr., 1929-46. Mem. Am. Soc. M.E., Am. Soc. Testing Materials. Republican. Contbr. tech. jours. Home: Sierre Madre, Cal. Died Nov. 27, 1949.

MOREHOUSE, Albert Kellogg, naval officer; b. Brooklyn, Apr. 29, 1900; s. Melvin Wilson and Alice (McHugh) M.; B.S., U.S. Naval Acad., 1922; student U.S.N. Flight Sch., Pensacola, Fla., 1924-25; m. Mrs. Sally B. Lanius, Sept. 8, 1925; children—Sue Gaylord, Sally (Mrs. John D. Price). Enlisted 1st N.Y. Cav., 1917 (later designated 105 MG bn. 27th Div.); commd. ensign U.S. Navy, 1922, and advanced through grades to rear adm., 1949; commanded U.S.N.R. Air Base, Miami, 1934-37; observer with Royal Navy and R.A.F. in Mediterranean, 1941; chief of staff to comdr. A.F., Atlantic Fleet, 1948-50, to comdr. Naval Force Far East, 1950-51; chief Naval Air Advanced Tng., Corpus Christi, Tex., 1951-54; comdr. naval forces of Continental air air def. command, 1954—. Decorated Navy Cross, Legion of Merit with gold star, Bronze Star, Silver Life Saving medal, Presdl. Unit citation. Mem. U.S. Naval Inst. Address: Colorado Springs, Colo. Died Dec. 18, 1955.

MORELAND, Edward Leyburn, cons. engr.; b. Lexington, Va., July 1, 1885; s. Sidney T. and Sally Preston (Leyburn) M.; A.B., Johns Hopkins U., 1905; M.S., Mass. Inst. Tech., 1908; m. Francina H. Campbell, Sept. 18, 1913. Asst. engr. D. C. and William B. Jackson, engrs., Boston, 1908-12, mgr. Boston office, 1912-16, mem. firm, 1916-18; mem. firm Jackson & Moreland, 1919—; head dept. elec. engring., Mass. Inst. Tech., 1935-38, dean engring., 1938-46, exec. v.p., 1946—. Regional adviser to the U.S. Office Edn. of Engring. Defense Training in Region I, 1940-42; mem. adv. com. for Coordinating Available Facilities for Def. Prodn., OPM, in Region I, 1941-42; also member Labor Supply Committee 1941-42; executive officer Nat. Def. Research Com., 1942-45; expert cons. to Sec. War, assigned G.H.Q.-Armed Forces in Pacific; chief, scientific survey in Japan, 1945. Served capt. and maj., E.C., U.S. Army Tech. Board and War Damage Bd., A.E.F., 1918-19. Fellow Am. Inst. E.E.; mem. Am. Soc. M.E., Am. Soc. C.E., Am. Acad. Arts and Sci., Am. Soc. for Engring. Edn., Engring. Socs. of N.E., Boston Soc. C.E., Phi Gamma Delta. Republican. Conglist. Clubs: Engineers (N.Y.C.); Engineers, Merchants, St. Botolph (Boston); Algonquin, Cosmos (Washington); Wellesley Country. Home: 4 Berkeley Court, Wellesley Hills 82, Mass. Office: Mass. Institute of Technology, Cambridge, Mass. Died June 17, 1951, buried Druid Ridge Cemetery, Pikesville, Balt.

MORENO, Arthur Alphonse (mō'rē-nō), lawyer; b. New Orleans, June 29, 1883; s. Arthur Bartholomew and Angele (Wells) M.; A.B., Tulane U., 1905; LL. B., 1909; grad. study U. Mich., 1906; m. Louise Gibbons Moore, Aug. 15, 1925. Tchr. English, high sch., New Orleans, 1906; instr. French, Tulane U., 1908; admitted to La. bar, 1909, and practiced since at New Orleans; dramatic editor New Orleans Daily Picayune, 1912-17; prof. practice, Law Sch., Tulane U., 1917-18; asso. gen. atty., Standard Oil Co. of La., 1914-31; judge ad hoc, La. Court of Appeals, Parish or Orleans. Chmn. New Orleans Tax Revision Commn. Mem. Am., La. State bar assns., New Orleans Bar Assn. (pres.), Assn. of Bar of City of N.Y. Clubs: Boston, Pickwick, New Orleans Country, Metairie Golf. Home: 4 Audubon Blvd. Office: Hibernia Bank Bldg., New Orleans. Died Oct. 16, 1950.

MOREY, Charles Rufus (môr'ē), educator, author; b. Hastings, Mich., Nov. 20, 1877; s. John and Addie C. (Stone) M.; A.B., U. Mich., 1899, A.M., 1900, Litt.D., 1938; L.H.D., Oberlin Coll., 1932; L.H.D., U. Chgo., 1941; D.F.A., N.Y.U., 1942; Litt.D., Yale U., 1951, Princeton U., 1954; m. Sara Tupper, May 29, 1915; 1 son, Jonathan Tupper. Fellow Am. Sch. at Rome, 1900-03; fellow Princeton, 1903-04; Marquand prof. art and archaeology Princeton, 1918, emeritus; prof. in charge Am. Sch. of Classical Studies in Rome, 1925-26; cultural attaché, U.S. Embassy, Rome, 1945-50; acting dir. Am. Acad. in Rome, 1945-47; pres. Internat. Union of Archaeol. and Hist. Inst. of Rome, 1945-50; trustee Am. Schs. of Oriental Research, 1936, Art News, 1941. Founder of the Index of Christian Art at Princeton University with copies at Dunbarton Oaks and at the Vatican Library, Rome, Italy. Decorated Ordre du Merite Syrien first Class, 1935; Chevalier, Order of Crown, Belgium, 1937; Silver Cross, Vatican, 1951; Stella d'Oro, Italy, 1952; recipient Silver medal Dante Alighieri Society. Fellow Mediaeval Acad., Am. Acad. Arts and Sciences, Pontifical Acad. of Archaeology, Rome, Academia dei Lincei, Rome, Virtuosi del Pantheon, Rome; mem. Archaeol. Inst. America, Am. Assn. U. Profs., Am. Philos. Soc., Soc. Antiq. de France (hon. corr.), Archaeol. Inst. Germany, Coll. Art Assn., Phi Beta Kappa, Theta Delta Chi. Democrat. Clubs: Princeton, Century (N.Y.C.). Author: East Christian Paintings in the Freer Collection, 1914; Lost Mosaics and Frescoes of Rome, 1915; Sardis, Vol. V, 1924; (with L. W. Jones) The Miniatures of the Terence MSS., 1931; Christian Art, 1935; The Mosaics of Antioch, 1938; Early Christian Art, 1941; Mediaeval Art, 1942; also various articles on art and archeology. Editor: Catalogue of Museo Sacro, Vatican Library. Decorated Ordre du Mérite Syrien, 1st class, 1935; Chevalier, Order of Crown of Beligum, 1937. Address: McCormick Hall, Princeton, N.J. Died Aug. 28, 1955; buried Greenmount Cemetery, Dansville, N.Y.

MOREY, Henry Martyn, clergyman; b. West Bloomfield, N.Y., Mar. 3, 1837; s. Handy J. and Sarah Ann (Hall) M.; A.B., Union Coll., N.Y., 1861, D.D., 1913; grad. Princeton Theol. Sem., 1865; m. Ellen Lemmex, June 21, 1866. Ordained to Presbyn. ministry, 1866; asst. pastor First Ch., Ft. Wayne, Ind., 1865-66; stated supply, Pittsford, N.Y., 1866-68; pastor Westminster Ch., Rochester, N.Y., 1868-74, First Ch., South Bend, Ind., 1874-79, Third Ch., Indpls., 1880-84; stated supply, Geneva, N.Y., 1884-86; pastor, Marshall, Mich., 1886-89, Ypsilanti, Mich., 1889-95; evangelist, 1895—. Mem. Gen. Assemblies, 1868, 72, 1911; moderator Synod of Mich., 1888; del. 1st World's Sunday Sch. Conv., London, 1889; trustee Western Coll. for Women, Oxford, O.; financial agt. Am. Inland Mission, 1907. Mem. Delta Kappa Epsilon, Phi Beta Kappa. Author of a reply to Ingersoll's Mistakes of Moses; also many sermons and articles. Address: Ypsilanti, Mich. Deceased.

MOREY, John William, wholesale grocer; b. Denver, Colo., Dec. 22, 1878; s. Chester S. and Anna L. (Clough) M.; grad. St. Paul's Sch., Concord, N.H., 1897; Sheffield Scientific Sch. (Yale), 1900; m. Mable Feldhauser, February 7, 1905; 1 daughter, Katherine Laura (Mrs. John A. Ferguson, Jr.). With Morey Mercantile Company since 1901, president since 1913; chairman board International Trust Company; director Denver, Rio Grande Western R.R., First National Bank, Denver Tramway Corp., Great Western Sugar Co. Div. mgr. Am. Red Cross, World War I; pres. Denver Community Chest, 1932. Pres. Nat. Wholesale Grocers Assn., 1924-25 and 1925-26. Republican. Episcopalian. Clubs: Denver, University, Athletic, Country, Cherry Hills Golf (Denver); Yale, University (N.Y.C.). Home: 1929 E. Alameda Av., Denver 9. Office: P.O. Box 5150, T.A., Denver 17. Died Nov. 3, 1956.

MOREY, Victor Pinkerton, coll. pres.; b. Narka, Kan., Jan. 18, 1905; s. Joseph Franklin and Viola (Wolff) M.; B.S., Ft. Hays Kan. State Coll., 1934; M.S., Kan. State Coll., 1937; Ph.D., U. Neb., 1944; m. Amy Livingston, Aug. 7, 1927; children—Lawrence, Barbara, Verl. Tchr., prin., elementary schs., Kan., 1923-30; prin., supt. high schs. 1930-40; univ. extension div., U. Neb., 1940-43, asst. dir. 1942-43; specialist ednl. services, U.S. Dept. Justice, 1943-46; pres., Neb. State Teachers Coll., Wayne, 1946—. Mem. N.E.A., Am. Assn. Sch. Adminstrs., Neb. Edn. Assn., Neb. Schoolmaters Assn., Phi Kappa Phi, Phi Delta Kappa, Delta Epsilon, Pi Gamma Mu, Psi Chi, Pi Mu Epsilon. Mason. Club: Kiwanis. Co-author: Elements of Pre-flight Aeronautics, 1942, Handbook for School Custodians, 1941. Contbr. articles ednl. jours. Home: 220 East 12th St., Wayne, Neb. Died May 18, 1951; buried Mahaska Cemetery, Mahaska, Kan.

MORFA, Raymond J., railroad exec.; b. Chicago, Ill., Jan. 1, 1894; s. John and Catherine Elizabeth (Cogan) M.; ed. pub. schs. With Pathe Film Co., Chicago, Ill., 1921-26, Piersons-Taft Co., 1926-32, Allegheny Corp., Cleveland, O., 1932-45; chmn. bd. M.-K.-T. R.R., also numerous subsidiary cos.; dir. Galveston, Houston & Henderson R.R., Tex. City Terminal Ry., Terminal R.R. Assn. of St. Louis, Dallas Union Terminal Co., Kansas City Terminal Ry., Airmaid Hosiery Mills, Dallas. Member of board of trustees Midwest Research Institute (Kansas City), Southwest Research Institute (San Antonio). Clubs: Noonday (St. Louis); Cloud, (New York); Chicago (Chicago); City, Downtown, Brookhollow Golf (Dallas); San Antonio (Texas) Country. Home: 5222 Park Lane. Office: Katy Bldg., Dallas. Died Oct. 19, 1952.

MORGAN, Angela, author; b. Washington, D.C., d. Alwyn (lawyer) and Carol Morgan (Baldwin) Morgan; ed. pub. schs. and under pvt. tutors, also spl. studies Columbia, and at Chautauqua, N.Y.; Litt.D., hon., Golden State U., Los Angeles, 1942. Began as writer newspapers, Chicago, New York and Boston; contbr. prose and verse to mags.; specialized writer and interpreter of verse; gives author's readings and interpretations. Read original poem, "The Unknown Soldier," over bier of unknown soldier in rotunda of Capitol, Washington, D.C.; first woman to occupy pulpit of Chapel Royal, Savoy, London, in author's reading, also appeared at Lyceum Club, London. Mem. Woman's Internat. League, Poetry Soc. America, Poetry Soc. London (a v.p.), League of Am. Pen Women (pres. Phila. br.), English-Speaking Union; chmn. Literary Arts Com. of Phila. Art Alliance; del. to Internat. Congress of Women, The Hague. Prize winner in contest for new Am. anthem. Clubs: MacDowell, Three Arts (hon.), both of New York. Author: The Hour Has Struck (verse), 1914; The Imprisoned Splendor (fiction), 1915; Utterance and Other Poems, 1916; God Prays (booklet), 1917; Forward March! (verse), 1918; Hail, Man! (verse), 1919; Because of Beauty (verse), 1922; Silver Clothes, 1926; Selected Poems, 1927; Creator Man, 1929; Angela Morgan's Recitals (verse); Heaven Is Happening, 1931; Awful Rainbow (novel), 1932; Crucify Me! (verse), 1933; Gold on Your Pillow, 1936 and 1941; Afterwhere, 1936; Drum Beats Out of Heaven, 1941; The Time for Love Has Come, 1942; Whirlwind Vision (poems), 1943; Behold the Angel!, 1945; Storm of Glory, 1945; My Spirit Sings, 1945; United Nations Hymn, 1947; (book) Rockets to the Sun, 1948. Nat. Fedn. of Women's Clubs at their meeting in Richmond, Va., 1933, voted to dedicate her poem, "When Nature Wants a Man," to Franklin D. Roosevelt; her poem, "Runway Gold" was voted best from Pa. in interstate competition for poems celebrating lighting of World's Fair, Chicago, 1933, by a beam from Arcturus; her poem to Will Rogers broadcast at dedication of Will Rogers Memorial Shrine. Elected honor poet, of Nat. Poetry Week, 1930, and awarded gold emblem; apptd. poet laureate of Gen. Fedn. of Women's Clubs. Gave lecture-recitals in Minnesota, Montana, Washington, Oregon, and Calif., 1940-41. Address: Home: Warren Myer Farm, Mount Marion, Vestu County, N.Y. Address: Ogontz Junior College, Ogontz School P.O., Pa. Died Jan. 24, 1957; buried Mountain View Cemetery, Saugerties, N.Y.

MORGAN, Anne; d. late J. Pierpont and Frances Louisa (Tracy) Morgan; educated private schs.; L.H.D., Russell Sage Coll., 1935. Mem. numerous philanthropic, civic orgns.; hon. pres. Am. Women's Assn.; mem. Les Amis du Musée de Blerancourt, Aisne, France. Founder and hon. pres. Am. Friends of France; hon. pres. Comité Am. Secours Civile, France. Clubs: Colony, Woman's National Republican. Recipient gold medal Nat. Inst. Social Scis., 1915; Anna W. Porter Meml. award Am. Woman's Assn., 1932, award for eminent achievement, 1943. Decorated Le Mérite Agricole, Croix de Guerre with palm (1918, 1940), Reconnaissance Française, Palme Académique, Médaille d'Epidemie, Comdr. Legion of Honor, Medal of Comdr. Ordre de la Santé Publique (France); plaque dedicated to her memory in Les Invalides, 1952. Home: 3 Sutton Pl., N.Y.C. Died Jan. 29, 1952.

MORGAN, Charles, novelist and critic; born Kent, England, Jan. 22, 1894; s. Sir Charles and Mary (Watkins) M.; cadet Royal Naval Coll., 1907-11; M.A., with honors, Brasenose Coll., Oxford U., England, 1921; M.A. (honorary), Oxford; LL.D., St. Andrews; m. Hilda Vaughan, June 6, 1923; children—Shirley Marchioness of Anglesey, Roger Hugh Vaughan Charles. Served with Atlantic and China fleets, Brit. Navy, 1911-13; with Royal Navy Div. in war serv. at Antwerp and as a prisoner of war, 1914-18. Asst. dramatic critic, The Times, London, 1921-26, prin. dramatic critic, 1926-39; London dramatic critic for the N.Y. Times, 1926-39. Fellow Royal Society Lit. Officier Legion of Honor (French); hon. Docteur univs. Caen and Toulouse; awarded Femina, Hawthornden and James Tait Black prizes for novels. Mem. l'Institute de France, English Assn. (pres. 1953-54), P.E.N. (internat. pres.). Club: Garrick (London). Author: The Gunroom, 1919; My Name Is Legion, 1925; Portrait in a Mirror, 1929; The Fountain, 1932; Epitaph on George Moore, 1935; Sparkenbroke, 1936; The Flashing Stream (play), 1938; The Voyage, 1940; The Empty Room, 1941; The House of Macmillan, 1943; Reflections in a Mirror, 1944; Reflections in a Mirror (2d series), 1946; The Judge's Story, 1947; The River Line, 1949; Liberties of the Mind, 1951; A Breeze of Morning, 1951; The River Line (play), 1952; The Burning Glass (play), 1953; Challenge to Venus, 1957; The Confession (play), 1958. Home: 16 Campden Hill Square, London W, 8, Eng. Died Feb. 6, 1958; buried West Kensington Cemetery, Gunnersbury, London.

MORGAN, Clifford Veryl, army medical officer; b. Elmwood, Neb., Dec. 18, 1901; s. Butler Garibaldi and Margaret Elizabeth (Murray) M.; A.B., Neb. Wesleyan U., 1922; B.S., U. Neb., 1925, M.D., 1927; grad. Army Med. Sch., 1929, Army Indsl. Coll., 1940, Command and Gen. Staff Sch., 1943, Indsl. Coll. Armed Forces and Nat. War Coll., E-1946; m. Anna Marie Herrmann, July 20, 1927; children—Monte Herrmann, Marvin Leon, Walter Albert. Commd. 1st lt. M.C., U.S. Army, 1927, advanced through grades to col., 1942; intern Walter Reed Gen. Hosp., Washington, 1927-28; internist William Beaumont Gen. Hosp., El Paso, Tex., 1929-30, Tripler Gen. Hosp., Honolulu, T.H., 1930-33, U.S. Army Hosp., Ft. Sill, Okla., 1933-36; specialist med. supply and adminstrn. N.Y. Gen. Depot and S.G.O., War Dept., 1936-39; army chief, commodities div. Army-Navy Munitions Bd., 1940-43; chief, commodities div., planning br. Office Under Sec. War, 1940-42; chief, raw materials br., resources div. Army Service Forces, 1942-43; dep. chief for materiel, supply div. S.G.O., 1943; dep. gen. purchasing agt., E.T.O., 1943-45; exec. officer Crile Gen. Hosp., 1945-46; dep. post comdr. Walter Reed Army Med. Center, Washington, 1946-48; dep. chief surgeon Hdqrs., European Command, 1948-52; insp. gen. Office Surgeon Gen., Washington, 1952-54; chairman Army Physical Review Council, 1954—. Decorated Legion of Merit with oak leaf cluster, Bronze Star Medal, Army Commendation with oak leaf cluster; Croix de Guerre with palm (France); Officer, Order of Oaken Wreath (Luxembourg). Fellow A.M.A., Assn. Mil. Surgeons, A.A.A.S.; mem. Am. Coll. Hosp. Adminstrs., Phi Kappa Tau, Phi Kappa Phi, Phi Chi, Alpha Omega Alpha. Editor of EUCOM Medical Bull., 1948-52. Home: 2945 Macomb St. N.W., Washington 8. Office: Army Physical Review Council, Pentagon Bldg., Washington 25. Died Oct. 3, 1954; buried Arlington Nat. Cemetery.

MORGAN, Clinton Emory, transportation cons.; b. Elizabethtown, Ind., Jan. 3, 1882; s. Sylvester A. and Sylviana (Showden) M.; ed. pub. schs.; m. Pauline Nellie George, Dec. 24, 1900. Auditor, purchasing agt. Indpls. & Greenfield Rapid Transit Co., 1899-1902; asst. gen. mgr., asst. to pres. Indpls. & Eastern Ry. Co., 1902-05; supt. Terre Haute, Indpls. & Eastern Traction Co., 1905-09; gen. mgr. Indpls., Crawfordsville & Western Traction Co., 1909-12; gen. supt. Mich. United Traction Co., and Mich. R.R. Co., 1912-19; v.p., gen. mgr. Bklyn. City R.R. Co., 1919-29; pres. The Cin. Car Corp., 1929-31, receiver for same, 1931-32; transportation cons., 1933-36; mgr. of operations, Los Angeles Transit Lines formerly Los Angeles Ry. Corp., 1936-46; transportation cons., 1946—. Republican. Methodist. Mason. Clubs: Pacific Railway (San Francisco); Electric (Los Angeles). Home and office: 4025 Degnan Blvd., Los Angeles 8. Died July 10, 1956.

MORGAN, Frank, motion picture actor; born N.Y. City, June 1, 1890; ed. Cornell U. Began on stage in vaudeville skits, juvenile lead in Mr. Wu, 1914; then entered motion pictures with Vitagraph; later became leading man with Anita Stewart's co., N.Y. City; now with Metro-Goldwyn-Mayer. Pictures include: The Great Ziegfeld, The Crowd Roars, Broadway Serenade, Wizard of Oz, The Mortal Storm, Boom Town, Hullabaloo, Washington Melodrama, Wild Man of Borneo, Honky Tonk, The Vanishing Virginian, Tortilla Flat, White Cargo, A Stranger in Town, Human Comedy, The White Cliffs of Dover, Casanova Brown, Dear Barbara, Miracles Can Happen, Green Dolphin Street. Address: Metro-Goldwyn-Mayer, 10202 Washington Blvd., Culver City, Calif. Died Sept. 18, 1949.

MORGAN, Fred Bogardus, physician, med. researcher; b. Belvidere, Ill., Apr. 17, 1874; s. Russell Williams and Sarah Amelia (Bogardus) M.; M.D., Chgo. Homeopathic Med. Coll., 1898; M.D. (hon.), Hahnemann Med. Coll., Chgo., 1904; numerous post-grad. courses; m. Louie Margaret Bucey, May 18, 1898; children—Russell Paul, Ruth Irene (Mrs. Arnold Rapp); m. 2d, Minnie Violet Smith, Sept. 18, 1926. In practice of internal medicine, Clinton, Ia., 1898—; mem. bd. med. examiners, State of Ia., 1942-44. Mem. Hahnemann Med. Assn. Ia. (pres. 1936, 1940), Am. Inst. Homeopathy (pres.-elect. 1943-44, 44-45, pres. 1945-47), Pan.-Am. Med. Congress, Internat. Homeopathic Med. Assn. Republican. Methodist. Contbr. many articles med. jours. Address: 716 S. 4th St., Clinton, Ia. Died Nov. 28, 1950.

MORGAN Geoffrey Francis, lecturer, educator; b. London, Eng., Aug. 8, 1882; s. Alfred William and Janet Wilson (Smiles) M.; diploma, Los Angeles State Normal Sch., 1903; A.B., Stanford, 1910; A.M., Columbia, 1914; unmarried. Teacher country schs., Calif., 1903-06; prin. schs., Riverside, Calif., 1910-13; prof. edn., Ohio U., 1914-16; supt. schs., Athens, O., 1916-20; platform lecturer since 1920; mgr. speakers bureau, Douglas Aircraft Co., Jan. 1941-47. Mem. Calif. legislature, 1934-38. Pres. Shoreline Planning Assn. of Calif., Inc., 1940-45, and since 1948. Mem. Actors Equity Assn., Dramatists Guild, Phi Alpha Tau, Tau Kappa Alpha. Episcopalian. Club: Rotary. Lecture subjects: Success with Ease; What's the Use?; The Blessings of Machinery; Sutter's Fort and Sutter's Gold; There Ought to be a Law. Author more than 20 plays and operettas for amateurs, including Sunbonnet Girl, Count and the Co-Ed, Tulip Time, Don Alonso's Treasure, Rose of the Danube, The Belle of Bagdad. Has filled more than 6,000 lecture engagements covering every state in the Union. Hoe: 533 23d St., Santa Monica, Cal. Died Mar. 2, 1952; buried Inglewood Park Cemetery, Inglewood, Cal.

MORGAN, George O(rlando), aluminum co. exec.; b. Pitts., Nov. 29, 1890; s. George O. and Harriet Murray (McKee) M.; A.B., Princeton, 1913; m. Sarah Edwards Schuyler Speir, Jan. 16, 1915; children—George Orlando, Sarah Edwards (Mrs. Charlesworth), Frances Speir (Mrs. Walters), Robert Forbes, Thomas McKee. With Am. Oil Refining Co., Okmulgee, Okla., 1913; apprentice Aluminum Co. Am., 1914-15, treas. Aluminum Co. S.A., 1916, treas., dir. all fgn. subsidiaries, 1917-28, treas. Aluminum, Ltd., 1928-33, v.p., dir., 1933—, financial cons., 1946—; former dir. Aluminum Co. of Can., Saguenay Power Co.; v.p. Stand Corp., N.Y.C. Home: 285 N. Ridgewood Rd., South Orange, N.J. Office: 620 Fifth Av., N.Y.C. 20. Died Nov. 7, 1958.

MORGAN, George Wagner, lawyer; b. Oshkosh, Wis., June 5, 1884; s. Frank B. and Clara (Wagner) M.; B.A., U. of Minn., 1905; LL.B., Harvard, 1908; m. Cornelia Hollinshead, Feb. 23, 1910 (died February 3, 1946); children—Samuel Huntington, Ann (Mrs. Edgar B. Ober, Jr.), Henry Hollinshead. Admitted to Minnesota bar, 1908; associated with firm of Davis, Kellogg & Severance, St. Paul, Minn., 1908-10; atty. subsidiaries of U.S. Steel Corp., Duluth, Minn., 1910-18; now mem. Morgan, Raudenbush, Morgan, Oehler & Davis (formerly Kellogg, Morgan, Chase, Carter & Headley); director Wisconsin Central Railroad Company. Past pres. Assn. Commerce, Community Chest, Children's Hosp.; trustee Hill Reference Library; pres. Amherst H. Wilder Found. Has served as chmn. or other exec. officer numerous civic and community projects, such as planning commns., improvement councils and charity orgns. Recipient U. Minn. Outstanding Achievement award, 1951. Mem. Am., Minn., Ramsey County bar assns., Beta Theta Pi. Clubs: Minnesota (St. Paul), Harvard, Century Assn. (N.Y.C.). Home: 710 Linwood Av., St. Paul 5. Office: First National Bank Bldg., St. Paul 1. Died Dec. 3, 1957.

MORGAN, (John) Harcourt Alexander, entomologist; b. Strathroy, Ont., Can., Aug. 31, 1867; s. John and Rebecca (Truman) M.; B.S.A., U. Toronto, 1889; grad. work, Cornell U., 1891-98, Marine Biol. Lab., Woods Hole, 1895; LL.D., Emory and Henry U., Southwestern U., 1920, U. Western Ont., 1939; Sc.D., Clemson Agrl. Coll., 1937; m. Sara Elizabeth Fay, June 25, 1895. Entomologist, horticulturist, La. State U. and Agrl. Expt. Stas., 1889-94; zoölogist, entomologist, same, 1894-1904; entomologist La. Expt. Sta. and crop pest commr., Feb. 1904-Jan. 1905; dir. U. Tenn. Agrl. Expt. Sta. and prof. zoölogy and entomology, 1905-19, dean Coll. Agr., 1913-19, pres., July 1, 1919-33, U. Tenn.; mem. TVA, 1933-48, chmn., 1938-41. Conductor farmers' insts. in La., 1895-1904; spl. field agt. Bur. Entomology, U.S. Dept. Agr., 1904. Food adminstr. Tenn., 1917. Asst. commr. La., Atlanta Expn., 1895; dir. Gulf Biol. Sta., 1900-05; Tenn. State entomologist, 1905-19; mem. Am. Commn. for Study of Rural Credits and Cooperation, 1913; chmn. Sec. of Agr.'s com. of scientists to investigate Mediterranean fruit fly situation in Fla. and advise concerning its control, 1929; mem. adv. council of Agr. Com. of Am. Bankers Assn., 1930-31; mem. com. on Capper Award for outstanding service to agr., 1930-31; mem. Nat. Land-Use Planning Com. Received Am. Farm Bur. Fed. award for distinguished service to agr., 1937, man of the year award, The Progressive Farmer, 1940. Trustee The Berry Schs.; mem. bd. advs., (V.P.I.) Inst. Rural Affairs. Mem. A.A.A.S., Soc. Promotion Agrl. Sci.; ex-pres. La. Soc. Naturalists; pres. Entomol. Sect. A.A.A.S., 1905; mem. Am. Fisheries Soc., Am. Assn. Econ. Entomologists (pres. 1907), Entomol. Soc. of Washington, Entomol. Soc. Am., Tenn. Acad. Sci., Assn. Land Grant Colls. and Univs. (pres. 1927), Am. Country Life Assn., Phi Kappa Phi, Gamma Alpha, Alpha Zeta. Mason. Rotarian. Home: Belfast, Tenn. Died Aug. 25, 1950; buried Knoxville, Tenn.

MORGAN, Harry Dale, lawyer; b. Leavenworth, Kan., Jan. 23, 1885; s. Albert Rufus and Mary Secelia (Gilbert) M.; student Bradley Poly. Inst., Peoria, Ill., 1902-04; A.B., U. of Chicago, 1906; student U. of Chicago Law Sch., 1906-09; m. Eleanor Ellis, July 9, 1911; children—Robert Dale, Donald Albert, David William, George Edward. Admitted to Ill. bar, 1909; partner Morgan & Galbraith, Peoria, 1910-12, McRoberts & Morgan, 1912-25, Todd, Morgan, Pendarvis & Arber, 1925-38. Morgan & Morgan, 1938-43, Morgan Pendarvis & Morgan since 1943; v.p., sec., dir. and gen. counsel, Peoria Newspapers, Inc. sec. and dir. Peoria Journal-Transcript, Inc., WDZ Broadcasting Co.; v.p., treas. and dir. Peoria Broadcasting Co. U.S. Commr. Southern Dist. Ill, 1913-17; U.S. Jury Commr., 1918-32; atty. Bd. Edn., Peoria, 1919-39. Dir. Peoria Y.M.C.A., Peoria Goodwill Industries; advisor Salvation Army; trustee Bradley Poly. Inst. Mem. Nat. Radio Personalities, Phi Beta Kappa, Delta Chi, Zeta Pi. Republican. Presbyterian. Mason (K.T., 33°, past potentate Mohammed Temple, Red Cross of Constantine. Clubs: Rotary, University, Creve Coeur, Mt. Hawley Country (Peoria). Home: 1020 N. Glenoak Av. Office: First National Bank Bldg., Peoria 2, Ill. Died July 25, 1956; buried Springdale Cemetery, Peoria, Ill.

MORGAN, Herbert Rollo, astronomer; b. Medford, Minn., Mar. 21, 1875; s. Henry D. and Olive Sabre (Smith) M.; B.A., U. Va., 1899, Ph.D., 1901; m. Fannie Evelyn Wallis, May 25, 1904; 1 dau., Amy Eleanor (Mrs. George Hoffman). Fellow in astronomy Leander McCormick Obs., 1896-1901; prof. mathematics Pantops Acad., Charlottesville, Va., 1900-01; computer Naval Obs., Washington, 1901-05; prof. astronomy and mathematics Pritchett Coll., also dir. Morrison Obs., 1905-07; asst. astronomer U.S. Naval Obs., 1907-24, astronomer, 1925-28, sr. astronomer, 1928-29, prin. astronomer, 1929-44; research asso., Yale, 1947—. Mem. Am. Astron. Soc. (v.p. 1940-42), Am. Geophys. Union, Internat. Astron. Union (pres. Com. Meridian Astronomy 1938-48), A.A. A.S. (v.p. 1935-36), Washington Acad. Sci. Methodist. Author publ. U.S. Naval Obs., Vol. XIII, and co-author of Vols. IX, XIV, XV. Contbr. to various sci. jours. Home: 2252 Hall Pl. N.W. Office: U.S. Naval Obs., Washington. Died June 11, 1957; buried Glenwood, Washington.

MORGAN, Isaac B., educator; b. S. Wales, Apr. 1862; s. Lewis and Sarah (Bowen) M.; student U. Kan., summer schs. Harvard, U. Colo.; M.A., Ottawa (Kan.) U.; m. Annie Byard Brewster, 1904; children—Brewster Bowen, William Wadsworth, Lloyd Eliot. Instr. history and civics Kansas City (Kan.) High School 1904-19, v.p., 1912-19; dir. Continuation Schs., Kansas City, Kan., 1909-32, instrn. given in the trades, home economics and elementary and high school studies; dir. Naturalization Kansas City and Wyandotte County, Kan., 1932—. Mem. Nat. Vocational Guidance Assn. (ex-treas.), Kan. State Tchrs. Assn. (ex-treas.), Northeast Kan. Tchrs. Assn. (ex-pres.), Kan. State Hist. Soc. (dir., life mem.), C. of C. (Kansas City, Kan.). Conglist. Mason (32°, Shriner). Clubs: Lions (ex-pres.), Kansas Authors (life; pres. 1935-36; mem. corporate bd.; ex-pres. 2d Dist.). Home: 706 N. 17th St. Office: Junior College Bldg., Kansas City, Kan. Died Feb. 1945.

MORGAN, James, journalist; b. Fleming County, Kentucky, December 18, 1861; s. William Franklin and Ann Threlkeld (Bruce) M.; A.M., Tufts College (Massachusetts), 1926; L.H.D., Williams Coll., 1938; m. Helen Dailey, Oct. 6, 1894. Began as telegrapher United Press Assn. at Washington, Albany and Boston; polit. reporter and Washington corr., and now on editorial staff Boston Globe. Reported all nat. convs. of both parties 1888-1940. Visited in 1913 all the principal backgrounds of Napoleon's active life in Europe, Asia and Africa, to gather impressions and material for a biog. work. Author: Theodore Roosevelt, The Boy and Man, 1907, new edit., 1919; Abraham Lincoln, The Boy and Man, 1908; The Life Work of Edward A. Moseley in the Service of Humanity, 1913; In the Footsteps of Napoleon, 1915; Charles H. Taylor, Builder of the Boston Globe, 1923; Our Presidents, 1924, 4th edit., 1950; The Birth of the American People, 1930. Home: 16 Prescott Rd., Lynn, Mass. Office: Boston Globe, Boston. Died May 12, 1955.

MORGAN, James W., coal co. exec.; b. Washington, Jan. 24, 1900; s. Charles H. and Ruth (Taylor) M.; E.M., Lehigh U., 1921; m. Olga Keifer, Aug. 22, 1925. Clk., foreman, supt. Lilly (Pa.) Coal Co., 1921-24; asst. gen. mgr. A. A. Hughes & Co., Cresson, Pa., 1924-32, v.p., treas., 1932-48; asst. to v.p. Truax-Traer Coal Co., Chicago, 1948-49; v.p., gen. mgr. Ayrshire Collieries Corp., Indianapolis, 1949-50, pres., dir. since 1950, Fairview Collieries Corp., Delta Collieries Corp., Meadowlark Farms, Incorporated, Gilbraltar Coal Corporation, Boonville Collieries Corporation, Ayrshire Oil Corp.; dir., chmn. bd. Frontenac Coal Corp.; dir. Republic Coal & Coke Co. Asst. dep. coal mines adminstr. Dept. of Interior, 1943-44, labor cons., 1945-47; mem. Nat. Bituminous Coal Adv. Council since 1948. Mem. Am. Inst. Mining Engrs., Kappa Sigma, Tau Beta Pi. Clubs: Chicago, Columbia, Meridian Hills Country, Athenaeum Turners (Indianapolis). Home: Marott Hotel, 2625 N. Meridian St. Office: 105 S. Meridian St., Indpls. Feb. 1, 1957.

MORGAN, Justin Colfax, dist. judge; b. Buffalo, July 8, 1900; s. Frank Howe and Luella Belle (Justin) M.; A.B., Colgate U., 1921; LL.B., U. Buffalo, 1924; m. Marion M. Moffat, Apr. 18, 1925; children—Marilyn Lois (Mrs. Albert L. Matthews Jr.), Justin Colfax. Admitted to N.Y. bar, 1925, practiced in Buffalo, 1925-56; asst. U.S. atty. Western Dist. N.Y., 1928-35, U.S. dist. judge, 1956—. Councilman Town of Tonawanda, 1934-40; rep. 7th Dist. N.Y. Assembly, 1941-43, 2d Dist. Erie County, 1944-56. Mem. Am. Legion, S.A.R. Mason (past master). Home: 143 Doncaster Rd., Kenmore 17, N.Y. Office: U.S. Court House, Niagara Sq., Buffalo 2. Died May 24, 1959.

MORGAN, Monta B., Sr., state ofcl.; b. Pendleton Tex., Apr. 7, 1890; s. J. Tom and Maggie (Gibson) M.; student Dallas Law Sch.; m. Katherine Cox, Aug. 1916; children—Helen (Mrs. Shelton), Monta B. Jr., Mary K. (Mrs. Goad). Various r.r. positions; telegrapher A., T. & S.F. Ry., Temple, Tex.; admitted to Tex. bar, 1932, practiced in Denison; mem. Tex. State Legislature, 3 terms, beginning in 1940; state labor commr. Tex. since 1947. Mem. Christian Ch. Mason. Home: 3111 Glenview. Office: Capitol Staton, Austin, Tex. Died June 19, 1958; buried Fort Worth.

MORGAN, Paul Beagary, mfr.; b. Worcester, Mass May 7, 1869; s. Charles Hill and Rebecca Ann (Beagary) M.; grad. Worcester Acad., 1887; B.S., Worcester Poly. Inst., 1890, Dr. Engring., 1929; student Royal Sch. of Mines, Stockholm, Sweden, 1891; m. Lessie L. Maynard, June 15, 1893 (died June 29, 1940); children—Philip M., Charles H., Paul B., Vincent, Elizabeth. With Morgan Constrn. Co., mfrs. rolling mill machinery, since 1891, now chmn. bd. dirs.; dir. Heald Machine Co.; vice president and trustee People's Savings Bank. Pres. trustees Worcester Acad., 1910-35; trustee Worcester Art Mus., Worcester Poly. Inst. Y.M.C.A., Archeol. Inst. Am., Public Reservations, Gore Place Soc. Republican. Episcopalian. Mem. American Antiquarian Soc. (v.p.), Am. Soc. of Mech. Engrs., Am. Iron and Steel Inst., Newcomen Soc. Clubs: Worcester, Tatmuck Country, Odd Volumes. Home: 21 Cedar St., Worcester 2. Office: 15 Belmont St., Worcester 5, Mass. Died Nov. 3, 1952.

MORGAN, Robert M(cIlwaine), business exec.; b. Petersburg, Va., June 5, 1877; s. Olive B. and Hope Alice (Davis) M.; B.S., Va. Mil. Inst., 1896; m. Grace L. Field, Oct. 25, 1904; children—Hope (Mrs. F. S. Johnston), Virginia (Mrs. R. J. Carpenter), Grace (Mrs. R. A. Young). Asst. sales mgr. Rucker & Witten Tobacco Co., Martinsville, Va., 1902-04, R. J. Reynolds Tobacco Co., Winston Salem, N.C., 1904-06; v.p., sec. Am. Furniture Co., Martinsville, 1906-08, Albert C. Field, Inc., N.Y.C., 1909-30, pres., dir., 1930—; pres., treas., dir. Robert M. Morgan, Inc., N.Y.C., 1932—. Pres., dir. N. Am. Export Grain Assn., 1932-39; former v.p. N.Y. Produce Exchange. Mem. Zoning Bd. Appeals (Pelham, N.Y.). Clubs: Union League (N.Y.C.); Country (Pelham, N.Y.). Home: 128 Monterey Av. Office: 87 Wolf's Lane, Pelham, N.Y. Died Oct. 29, 1959.

MORGAN, Russell Van Dyke, music educator; b. Burlington, Iowa, Mar. 1, 1893; s. Lee H. and Sade (Van Dyke) M.; Mus. G., Northwestern U., 1915, Mus. B. 1921, Mus. D. (hon.), 1936; m. Grace A. Wells, 1918 (died, 1942); 1 dau., Harriet; m. 2d Hazel Beckwith, Oct. 17, 1945. Supervisor of music, Highland Park, Ill., 1915-16; dir. of music State Teachers Coll., La Crosse, Wis., 1916-20; asst. supervisor of music Cleveland Pub. Schs., 1920-23; chmn. of music dept. Cleveland Sch. of Education, 1922-29; dir. of music Cleveland Pub. Schs. since 1923; asso. prof. of music Western Reserve Univ., 1929-36, prof. of music, 1936-50; organist and dir. Old Stone Church (First Presbyterian), Cleveland, 1923-50; dir. Am. Inst. of Normal Methods, Auburndale, Mass., since 1938 (summers); vis. prof. in summer sessions, Columbia U. Northwestern U., Stanford U., U. of Minn., U. of Wis., U. of Colo., U. of Hawaii; mem. adv. council on music, U. S. Dept. of State, Trustee Musical Arts Assn., operating The Cleveland Orchestra, Cleveland Music Sch. Settlement, Cleveland Philharmonic Orchestra, Cleveland Women's Symphony; past chmn. Music. Edn. Research Council. Mem. Music Educators Nat. Conf. (past pres.), Music Teacehers Nat. Assn. (past pres.; mem. exec. com.), Ohio Music Teachers Assn. (past pres.), Am. Guild of Organists (former dean, Northern Ohio chapter), Phi Mu Alpha Sinfonia. Presbyterian. Mason. Clubs: The Cleveland Singers (trustee), Cleveland Musicians (past pres.), City (past mem. bd. dirs. (Cleve.). Co-author: Music in the Junior High Sch. (with John W. Beattie, Osbourne McConathy, 1930, rev. edit., 1938; Fundamentals of Band Arranging (with William Skeath, Harry F. Clark), 1938, Thirty-fifth Yearbook Part II, Music Education, 1936. Mem. editorial bd. Music Educators Jour.; mem. adv. bd. Educational Music Magazine. Co-editor: New Music Horizons, 1944-49; Music of Many Lands and Peoples, 1932; Music Highways and Byways, 1936; Music, The Universal Language, 1941; School and Community Band Series, 1928; Instrumental Edition of the Golden Book of Songs, 1927. Home: 2949 Broxton Rd., Shaker Heights, Cleve. 20. Office: 1380 E. 6th St., Cleve. 14. Died June 12, 1952.

MORGAN, Walter Piety, educator; b. Prairie Creek, Vigo County, Ind., Dec. 30, 1871; s. William Riley and Nancy (Piety) M.; grad. Ind. State Normal Sch., Terre Haute, 1895; A.B., Ind. U., 1900; Ph.M., U. Chgo., 1909, post-grad. work, 1909-12; Ed.D. (hon.), Miami U., 1926; m. Effie J. Elliott, Mar. 11, 1893; children—Ralph Waldo, Mrs. Mildred Roth, William Ray, Mrs. Lucile Dyson. Tchr. dist. and town schs., Vigo County, Ind., 1888-94; head dept. mathematics Terre Haute High Sch., 1895-00; asst. dept. of mathematics Ind. State Normal Sch., 1900-06; supt. city schs., Terre Haute, 1906-08; tchr. U. High Sch. and Englewood High Sch., Chgo., 1908-12; pres. Western Ill. State Tchrs. Coll., 1912-42, pres. emeritus, 1942—. Mem. Nat. Adv. Com. on Edn., 1930-31; expert cons. on Nat. Survey Edn. Tchrs., 1930-31. Mem. Am. Assn. Tchrs. Colls. (pres. 1928-29), Ill. Tchrs. Assn. (pres. 1927), School Masters' Club Ill. (pres. 1919-20), N.E.A. (pres. normal sch. sect., 1921-22), North Central Assn. Colls. and Secondary Schs. (pres. 1929-30), Sons of Vets., Phi Delta Kappa. Progressive Republican. Mem. Christian Ch. Author: Manual of Arithmetic, 1905. Home: 314 Sherman Av., Macomb, Ill. Died Mar. 30, 1958; buried Macomb.

MORGAN, Walter Sydney; b. Whitman, Mass., Jan. 18, 1886; s. Sydney John and Ida (Shaw) M.; grad. Ricker Classical Inst., Houlton, Me., 1905; studied Colby Coll., 1905-06, Boston U., 1907-08; grad. Bryant & Stratton Comml. Sch., Boston, 1909; studied N.Y.U. Sch. Commerce, Accounts and Finance, 1910; m. Annie Urquhart, June 26, 1912; children—Balfour, Robert, Patricia. Tchr. Mitchell Mill Boys' Sch., Billerica, Mass., 1906-07, Rogers High Sch., Newport, R.I., 1909-10; pub. accounting, N.Y.C., 1910-11; resident mgr. Pace Inst., Boston, 1911-17, dean, 1917-21; pub. practice accountancy, as partner Morgan & Morgan, Boston, 1917—; dean Morgan Sch. of Accountancy and Finance, 1921-28; comptroller and mem. Commn. on Adminstrn. and Finance, Commonwealth of Mass., 1928-32, 40-44. Mem. Am. Inst. Accountants, Mass. Soc. C.P. A.'s, Delta Upsilon. Republican. Mason (33°, K.T.). Clubs: Boston City, Sharon Country. Author: Accounting—A Course in Theory and Practice, 1922. Home: 20 Maskwonicut St., Sharon, Mass. Office: 10 State St., Boston. Died Nov. 21, 1954.

MORISON, James Henderson Stuart, judge; b. Cumberland Gap, Tenn., Dec. 12, 1864; s. Dr. James Henderson Stuart and Amanda (Jones) M.; A.B., U. Tenn., 1887, A.M., 1889; LL.M., Nat. U., Washington, 1890; LL.D., Lincoln Meml. U., Cumberland Gap, 1930; m. Victoria Morgan, May 3, 1899; children—James Henderson Stuart (dec.), Edith Morgan (Mrs. William Brooke Powell). Admitted to Tenn. bar, 1890, began practice at Cumberland Gap; county judge Claiborne County, 1910-18; judge 19th Circuit, Tenn., 1928-34; apptd. U.S. Dist. judge, 2d Jud. Div., Alaska, 1934. Democrat. Mem. Disciples (Christian) Ch. Mason. Author: Morison's Pleadings and Forms, 1895. Home: Cumberland Gap, Tenn. Address: Nome, Alaska. Died Sept. 29, 1952.

MORITZ, John A., business exec.; b. Pekin, Ill., Feb. 1, 1890; s. August and Anna (Dissman) M.; student pub. schs. of Pekin; m. Sara Zimmerman, Nov. 16, 1910; children—Arlene (Mrs. L. J. Whitmarsh), John A. Supt. Mid-States Steel & Wire Co., 1928, v.p. in charge operations since 1934; supt. wire mills Keystone Steel & Wire Co. since 1936; inventor Moritz Fence Clip. Pres. Police Bd., Crawfordsville, Ind., 1934-36. Mem. Pekin and Peoria C. of C., Wire Assn. (dir. 1941, pres. since 1952). Mason. Club: Pekin (Ill.) Country. Home: 707 S. Fifth St., Pekin, Ill. Died Sept. 27, 1952; buried Lakeside Cemetery, Pekin.

MORK, P. Ralph, ret. mfg. exec.; b. St. Peter, Minn., Apr. 23, 1883; s. Christian P. and Helena (Pedersen) M.; grad. sch. commerce Gustavus Adolphus Coll., St. Peter, 1900; m. Anna Patricia Fitzgerald, Sept. 3, 1917; children—Ralph G., Jane (Mrs. David E. Carroll), Charlene (Mrs. Robert W. Liess). With Crane Co., 1901-51, warehouse and office clk., Mpls., 1901-11, mgr. Duluth br., 1911-24, Mpls. br., 1924-27, N.Y.C. br., 1927-31, v.p. charge N.Y. dist. branches, 1931-34, charge of sales and branches, hdqrs. Chgo., 1934-39, became dir., 1939, exec. v.p., 1945, ret. as bd. vice chmn., 1951; dir. Crane Co. of Minn., Crane Enamelware Co., Crane-O'Fallon Co., Trenton Potteries Co., Crane, Ltd. (Can.). Mem. Chgo. Athletic Assn. Club: Exmoor Country (Chgo.). Home: 1550 N. State Pkwy., Chgo. 10. Died Sept. 14, 1958; buried Queen of Heaven Cemetery, Chgo.*

MORLEY, Christopher (Darlington), author; b. Haverford, Pa., May 5, 1890; s. Frank and Lilian Janet (Bird) M.; A.B., Haverford Coll., 1910 (Phi Beta Kappa); Rhodes Scholar at New Coll., Oxford, Eng., 1910-13; hon. D. Litt. from Haverford (Pennsylvania) College, 1933; LL.D. (hon.), Adelphi Coll., 1944; m. Helen Booth Fairchild, June 3, 1914; children—Christopher, Louise (Mrs. James Cochrane), Helen (Mrs. Whitney Woodruf), Blythe (Mrs. James Brennan). Editorial staff, Doubleday, Page & Co., 1913-17, Ladies' Home Jour., 1917-18, Phila. Pub. Ledger, 1918-20, N.Y. Evening Post, 1920-24, Saturday Review of Lit., 1924-40. Clubs: The Three Hours for Lunch Club, Foundry Club, The Baker Street Irregulars. Author: The Eighth Sin, 1912; Parnassus on Wheels, 1917; Songs for a Little House, 1917; Shandygaff, 1918; The Rocking Horse, 1919; The Haunted Book Shop, 1919; In the Sweet Dry and Dry (with Bart Haley), 1919; Mince Pie, 1919; Travels in Philadelphia, 1920; Kathleen, 1920; Three's a Crowd (play, with Earl Derr Biggers); Pipefuls, 1920; Hide and Seek, 1920; Tales from a Rolltop Desk, 1921; Plum Pudding, 1921; Chimneysmoke, 1921; Where the Blue Begins, 1922; The Powder of Sympathy, 1923; Inward Ho! 1923; Parsons' Pleasure, 1923; Pandora Lifts the Lid (with Don Marquis), 1924; Religio Journalistici, 1924; One Act Plays, 1924; Thunder on the Left, 1925; The Romany Stain, 1926; The Arrow, 1927; Pleased to Meet You, 1927; I Know a Secret, 1927; Toulemonde, 1928; Off the Deep End, 1928; Seacoast of Bohemia, 1929; Rudolph and Amina, 1930; A Book of Days, 1930; John Mistletoe, 1931; Swiss Family Manhattan, 1932; Ex Libris Carissimis, 1932; Human Being, 1932; Mandarin in Manhattan, 1933; Shakespeare and Hawaii, 1933; Internal Revenue, 1933; Hasta la Vista, 1935; Streamlines, 1936;

The Trojan Horse, 1937; History of an Autumn, 1938; Letters of Askance, 1939; Kitty Foyle, 1939; The Trojan Horse (dramatized) produced at Roslyn, L.I., 1940; Thorofare, 1942; The Middle Kingdom (poems), 1944; Spirit Level (poems), 1946; The Old Mandarin, 1947; The Man Who Made Friends with Himself, 1949; The Ironing Board, 1949; The Ballad of New York, New York, 1950; Gentlemen's Relish, 1955. Editor-in-chief of revised edit. Bartlett's Familiar Quotations, 1937 and 1948. Honnold lecturer Knox Coll., 1938; visiting lecturer Adelphi Coll., 1939, 40. Fellow Am. Geog. Soc.; mem. Nat. Inst. Arts and Letters. Address: Roslyn Heights, N.Y. Died Mar. 28, 1957.

MORONEY, Carl J., bus. exec.; b. Greensburg, Ind., Apr. 6, 1886; s. John Henry and Agnes (Kessing) M.; A.B., Stanford, 1910; m. Nell Irene Dooley, Oct. 11, 1911; children—Thomas Carl, Helen Kessing (Mrs. John E. Lynch), Marian Josephine (Mrs. George R. Kane), Donald John. Engr., Western Sugar Refinery, San Francisco, 1911-15, supt., 1915-17, mgr., 1917-46, pres., 1946-48; v.p., gen. mgr. Spreckels Sugar Co., San Francisco, 1931-46, pres. 1946—. Roman Catholic. Clubs: California, Golf, Bohemian. Contbr. article, A Plan for Postwar Sugar Economy, to Sugar, Nov. 1944. Home: 249 W. Poplar Av., San Mateo, Calif. Office: 2 Pine St., San Francisco 11. Died Nov. 28, 1951.

MOROSO, John Antonio (mô-rō'sō), author; b. Charleston, S.C., Aug. 17, 1874; s. John Antonio and Sarah (Owens) M.; grad. S.C. Mil. Acad., 1894 (class poet); m. Virginia Osborne, June 24, 1900. Engaged in newspaper work, 1894-1907; contbr. verse to newspapers and mags., 1900-07. Mem. Authors' League Am., Poetry Soc. Am. Dickens Fellowship N.Y. Author: The Quarry, 1913; (play) Alias Santa Claus, production 1917; (play) Miracle Mary, prod., 1918; The People Against Nancy Preston, 1921; The Stumbling Herd, 1923; Cap Fallon, Firefighter, 1923; The City of Silent Men, 1923; Bread Eaten in Secret, 1931; Poor Passionate Fool, 1932; Marta Christiansen, 1933. Home: Cresskill, Bergen County, N.J. Died June 1957.

MORREY, Charles Bradfield, educator, bacteriologist; b. Chesterhill, O., Nov. 5, 1869; s. John Cheetham and Mary Jenkinson (Wright) M.; B.A., Ohio State U., 1890; M.D., Starling Med. Coll., Columbus, O., 1896; studied in Europe; m. Grace Hamilton Jones, 1898; children—Marion (Mrs. O. C. Richter), Jessie (Mrs. Michael Condoide), Charles Bradfield. Joined Faculty Ohio State U., 1899, founded dept. bacteriology, 1903, became prof. bacteriology, head dept., 1904, emeritus prof., 1935—; cons. in fields of medicine, agriculture, industry; pioneered in use of vaccine therapy. Mem. Soc. Am. Bacteriologists, Am. Chem. Soc., A.A.A.S., Ohio Acad. Sci., Sigma Xi. Club: University. Author: Laboratory Exercises in General Bacteriology, 1906, 10th edit. 1929; Fundamentals of Bacteriology, 4th edit. 1929; also various brochures. Home: 188 W. Tenth Av., Columbus 1, O. Died Apr. 21, 1954; buried Columbus, O.

MORRIS, Charles Shoemaker, junior coll. pres.; b. San Gabriel, Calif., Apr. 9, 1887; s. Brooks Samuel and Elizabeth Price (Shoemaker) M.; graduate Throop Polytechnic Institute (now California Institute of Technology), 1904; A.B., Stanford University, 1908; A.M., 1909; married Carlena Metcalf Cushing, Dec. 24, 1908; children—Charles Shoemaker, Jr., Elizabeth Cushing (Mrs. Lewis Bell Marquis). Asst. in biological science, Stanford U., 1909; instr., Palo Alto (Calif.) High Sch., 1909-15; vice prin., Modesto (Calif.) High Sch., 1915-22; asst. supt. of schs., Modesto, 1918-22; prin. Modesto (Calif.) Junior Coll., 1921-31; pres. San Mateo (Calif.) Junior Coll. since 1931; lecturer in education U. of Calif., summer session, 1933, Stanford U., spring quarter, 1938. Served as sergt., Calif. Nat. Guard, 1909-15; maj., Calif. High School Cadet Corps, 1918-21. Scoutmaster to council officer Boy Scouts of America, since 1913. Mem. budgets committee San Mateo County Community Chest. Mem. steering com. California Com. for Study of Edn. Mem. Calif. Jr. Coll. Assn. (chmn. legislative committee since 1922; mem. exec. com. 20 yrs.), San Mateo, Calif. State and Nat. edn. assns., Sigma Xi, Phi Delta Kappa. Mem. and past lt. gov. Kiwanis International. Contbr. articles to professional mags. Competitor 10 yrs. and coach 25 yrs. in amateur track athletics. Home: 31 Hayward Av., San Mateo, Cal. Died Feb. 24, 1952; buried St. John's Cemetery, San Mateo, Cal.

MORRIS, Constance Lily, writer; b. N.Y. City; d. V. Henry and Josephine (Wolf) Rothschild; ed. St. Mary's Sch., Wellesley Coll.; m. Ira Morris, 1898 (died 1942); children—Constance, Ia. Episcopalian. Clubs: Arts (Chicago); Woman's University, Nat. Penwomen's (New York); Woman's University (Boston); Essex Country (Manchester, Mass.); Ranelagh, Women's University (London); St. Cloud (Paris); National Country. Mem. Soc. Oxford Home Students of Oxford Univ. Author: On Tour with Queen Marie, 1926; Behind Moroccan Walls, 1931; Maria Theresa—The Last Conservative, 1937; Heritage From My Father, 1947. Home: 944 5th Av., N.Y.C. Died May 12, 1954.

MORRIS, Earl Halstead, archeologist; b. Chama, N.M., Oct. 24, 1889; s. Scott Neering and Juliette Amanda (Halstead) M.; A.B., U. Colo., 1914, A.M., 1916; postgrad. Columbia, 1916-17; D.Sc., U. Colo., 1942; m. Ann McCheane Axtell, Sept. 8, 1923; children—Elizabeth Ann, Sarah Lane; m. 2d, Lucile Bowman, June 4, 1946. Archaeologist for Am. Mus. Natural History 1917-24, Carnegie Instn., 1924—, leader of archeol. expdns. to Guatemala, 1914, 34; leader of expdns. to N.M. and Ariz. for U. Colo., 1913-16, 22, 24-28; explored Aztec Ruin in N.M. for Am. Mus. Natural History, 1916-24; dir. excavations in Yucatan for Carnegie Instn., 1924-29; research work in southwestern archaeology, 1929—. Recipient Norlin medal U. Colo., 1931. Mem. Am. Ethnol. Soc., Am. Anthrop. Assn., N.Y. Acad. Scis., Sigma Xi, Phi Beta Kappa. Republican. Episcopalian. Mason. Author: The Temple of the Warriors, 1931. Contbr. of anthrop. papers to scientific jours. Home: 626 14th St., Boulder, Colo. Died June 24, 1956.

MORRIS, Ernest Melvin, chmn. Associates Investment Co.; b. near Teegarden, Ind., Dec. 17, 1882; s. George and Maria (Thomas) M.; student Valparaiso U., 1901-05; LL.B., U. of Notre Dame, 1906; m. Ella Louise Keen, Jan. 24, 1914; children—Mary Louise (Mrs. Robert L. Oare), Ernestine (Mrs. O. C. Carmichael, Jr.). Pres. Associates Investment Co., 1918-46, chmn. bd. since 1946; president Emmco Insurance Company, 1936-50, chmn. bd. since 1950; pres. Emmco Casualty Insurance Company, 1939-50, chmn. bd. since 1950; pres. Associates Building Co. since 1923, First Bank and Trust Co. of South Bend, 1931-36 (chairman board since 1936); chairman board Durham Manufacturing Corp.; dir. Clark Equipment Co.; pres. Nat. Assn. Finance Cos., 1926-30, Bd. Public Works, 1914-18, Chamber of Commerce, South Bend, Ind., 1929-30; chmn. St. Joseph Co. Chapter Am. Red Cross, 1926-31; dir. Am. Finance Conf. (pres. 1944-45); pres. bd. lay trustees U. of Notre Dame, 1947-49, chairman finance committee Endowment Fund, 1943-47. Republican National Committeeman, 1940-46. Presbyn. Mason. Clubs: Country, Indiana, Knife and Fork, Izaak Walton (South Bend); Columbia (Indianapolis); Indiana Society (Chicago). Office: Associates Bldg., South Bend, Ind. Died May 3, 1951.

MORRIS, Evangeline Hall, educator; b. Quebec, Can., Sept. 24, 1899; d. Eli Landon and Evangeline Althea (Taber) Hall; A.B., Bishops U., 1921; B. Nursing, Yale, 1927; M.Edn., Harvard, 1949; m. Cecil R. Morris, Sept. 24, 1927; children—Grant Hall, Philip Rhodes. Came to U.S., 1924, naturalized, 1944. High sch. teacher, Province of Quebec, 1921-24; with Boston Visiting Nurse Assn., 1927-37; established courses in social hygiene at Syracuse, Western Reserve U., U. Minn., U. of N.C., U. Calif., 1935-45; dir. Sch. of Nursing, Simmons Coll., Boston, since 1950; consultant in social hygiene with several agencies and orgns. Mem. bd. of registration Commonwealth Mass., 1956—. Mem. Mass. Soc. Social Hygiene. Author: Public Health Nursing in Syphilis and Gonorrhea, 1946. Contbr. articles in med. jours. Home: 38 Riverdale Rd., Wellesley Farms, Mass. Office: 300 The Fenway, Boston 15. Died Jan. 12, 1958.

MORRIS, Frank R., educator; b. Pekin, Ind., June 18, 1885; s. Nelson and Mary Ellen (Murphy) M.; student pub. schs.; m. Lota E. Ray, July 3, 1913; 1 son, Bruce L. Tchr. Washington Co., Ind., 1903-06, Met. Bus. Coll., Chgo., 1908-09; prin. city schs., Santa Rosa, N.M., 1909-10; tchr. mathematics Glendale (Cal.) Union High Sch., 1913-18; mathematics instr. U. Cal., 1918-21; chmn. dept. mathematics Fresno State Coll., 1921-51, head phys. sci. div., 1951—. Chmn. Cal. State Com. Math. Edn., 1946-50. Mem. Am. Math. Soc., Mathematics Assn. Am. (regional gov. 1948-51), N.E.A., Am. Assn. U. Profs., Cal. Tchrs. Assn. Conglist. Clubs: Engineers (pres. 1938-39), Archers (sec.-treas. 1940-51) (Fresno). Home: 645 McKinley Av., Fresno, Cal. Died Jan. 6, 1956; buried Belmont Meml. Park, Fresno, Cal.

MORRIS, George Maurice, lawyer; b. Chicago, Ill., May 3, 1889; s. Frank Marion and Willa (Guffin) M.; grad. University High Sch., Chicago, 1907; A.B., Dartmouth, 1911; J.D., U. of Chicago, 1915; m. Miriam Warren Hubbard, Oct. 26, 1918; children—Miriam Patricia (Mrs. Kenneth T. Young, Jr.), Hillis Reid (Mrs. William L. Garlick), Hugh Ross. Admitted to Illinois bar, 1915, began practice at Chicago; moved to Washington, D.C., 1919; member of the law firm Morris, KixMiller & Baar, 1934-54; Morris, Pearce, Gardner & Pratt, 1954; Washington counsel before Federal agencies, dept. and courts; mem. bd. dirs. Potomac Poultry Food Co., Chesapeake Shell Co. Mem. bd. corporators Episcopal Ear, Eye & Throat Hosp. Chmn. U.N. Com. on Internat. Jurisdiction, Geneva, 1951. Pvt., 1st lt. U.S. Army, 1917-18. Decorated: Order El Sol del Peru; Commandor Order Carlos Manuel de Cespedes; Orden Launsa (Cuba); recipient gold medal, Am. Bar Assn., 1954. Mem. Am. Bar Assn. (sec. com. on fed. taxation, 1921-32, chmn. 1933-35, 1938-39; chmn. gen. council 1935-36; chmn. Ho. Dels., 1936-38; chmn. sect. of taxation, 1939-42; pres. of Assn. 1942-43), D.C. Bar Association, Inter-American Bar Association (chmn. exec. com.), International Bar Association (speaker of House of Deputies), Am. Judicature Soc., Washington Criminal Justice Assn. (charter mem.; dir.), Am. Law Inst., Am. Soc. Internat. Law, English Speaking Union (bd. govs. Washington br.), Am. Peace Soc. (bd. govs.), Inst. dos Advogados Brasileiros (hon.), Delta Kappa Epsilon (hon. pres. 1939), Phi Delta Phi, Delta Sigma Rho, Casque and Gauntlet. Chairman alumni advisory board Law School, University of Chicago, 1937-42; president Alumni Association, 1940-41; president General Alumni Assn., Dartmouth, 1940-41. Clubs: Chevy Chase, Metropolitan, University, Lawyers (Washington); Dartmouth (N.Y.). Author: Practice and Procedure Before United States Board of Tax Appeals, 1926; Hidden Taxes in Corporate Reorganizations, 1935. Contributor to Tax Mag., Trust Companies Mag., Advocate of Peace, law reviews, etc. Home: 2401 Kalorama Rd. Office: Am. Security Bldg., Washington. Died Aug. 21, 1954; buried St. Pauls Churchyard, Kent County, Md.

MORRIS, Gouverneur, author; b. N.Y.C., Feb. 7, 1876; s. Gouverneur and Henrietta (Baldwin) M.; father a grandson of Gouverneur Morris (revolutionary statesman and U.S. senator); B.A., Yale, 1898; m. Elsie Waterbury. Formerly pres. The Monterey (Cal.) Bank. Contbr. stories mags. Author: A Bunch of Grapes, 1897; Tom Beauling, 1901; Aladdin O'Brien, 1902; The Pagan's Progress, 1904; Ellen and Mr. Man, 1905; The Footprint, and Other Stories, 1908; Putting on the Screws, 1909; Spread Eagle, and Other Stories, 1910; The Voice in the Rice, 1910; It and Other Stories, 1912; If You Touch Them They Vanish, 1913; The Penalty; When My Ship Comes In, 1915; The Goddess; The Seven Darlings, 1915; We Three, 1916; His Daughter, 1918; The Wild Goose, 1919; Yellow Men and Gold, 1921; Keeping the Peace, 1924; Tiger Island, 1934; Diary of the French Revolution, 1939.* Died Aug. 14, 1953.

MORRIS, Homer Lawrence, economist; b. Dublin, Ind., July 1, 1886; s. Albert C. and Esther J. (Lawrence) M.; A.B., Earlham Coll., 1911; A.M., Columbia, 1918, Ph.D., 1921; m. Edna E. Wright, Sept. 19, 1916; 1 son, James Haisley. Instr. history and debating, Penn Coll., 1911-15; instr. economics, Hunter Coll., 1917-18; prof. economics, Earlham Coll., 1918-28; dir. child feeding relief, Berlin, Germany, under auspices of Am. Friends Service Com., 1921; field dir. famine relief, Buzuluk, Russia, 1922, and dir. child feeding relief in bituminous coal fields, 1931-32; dir. pub. relations, Reading (Pa.) Hosp., 1928-30; prof. economics, Fisk U., 1930-34; field supervisor Subsistence Homestead Div., U.S. Dept. Interior, 1933-35; sec. Social-Industrial sect. Am. Friends Service Com., 1935-46; sec. of Regional Offices since 1946. Commissioner to Europe for American Friends Service Com. on Refugee Problems, 1939. Trustee Earlham Coll.; mem. bd. of mgrs. Pendle Hill School. Mem. American Economics Association. Member Society of Friends. Author: Parliamentary Franchise Reform in England from 1885 to 1918, 1921; The Plight of the Bituminous Coal Miner, 1934. Home: Plush Mill Rd., Wallingford, Pa. Address: Am. Friends Service Com., 20 So. 12th St., Phila. 7. Died Nov. 26, 1951; buried Providence Meeting Burial Ground, Media, Pa.

MORRIS, John, philologist; b. Goochland County, Va., June 23, 1863; s. Charles and Mary (Minor) M.; A.B., A.M., Randolph-Macon Coll., Va., 1883; LL.B., U. Ga., 1885; John B. Minor's law lectures, U. Va.; U. Berlin, winter, 1891, summer, 1892, winter, 1900; Berlitz Sch., Copenhagen, Denmark; U. Freiburg, summer, 1901; m. Gretchen McCurdy Gallagher, June 23, 1904. Practiced law, Birmingham, Ala., 1886-90; instr. modern langs., U. Ga., 1893-97, prof. English lang. and Teutonic philology, 1897-1913, prof. Germanic langs., 1913—. Y.M.C.A. camp ednl. dir., Camp Gordon, Ga., June-Dec. 1918. Mem. adv. council Simplified Spelling Bd., Modern Lang. Assn. Am., Beta Theta Pi, Phi Beta Kappa. Author: Organic History of English Words, Part I, Old English, 1908; Bill Arp. in Library of Southern Literature; Minimum German Grammar, 1923. Contbr. English and German philol. jours. Home: Athens, Ga. Died Sept. 4, 1955.

MORRIS, Leland Burnette, b. Ft. Clark, Tex., Feb. 7, 1886; s. Louis Thompson (col. U.S. Army) and Susan Frances (Reece) M.; diploma Emerson Inst., Washington, D.C., 1904; student U. Pa., (part time) 1904-09; m. Marie Aimee de Zaba, Mar. 5, 1917; 1 son, Kenneth Archbell. Apptd. student interpreter, Am. embassy to Turkey, Apr. 1, 1910; dep. consul, Salonika, 1912-13; vice consul gen. Smyrna, 1913-17; detailed to Dept. of State, Washington, D.C., 1917-18; attached Brit. War Mission, Food Ministry Sec., N.Y.C., 1917; consul, Montreal, Can., 1918-19; detailed to Am. High Commn., Constantinople; consul, Salonika, 1919-24, Cologne, Germany, 1924-26, Athens, 1926; apptd. consul gen., Athens, Nov. 12, 1929, also 1st Sec. of legation, Feb. 20, 1932; chargé d'Affaires, Athens, Greece, 1932-33; consul gen., Jerusalem, Palestine, 1936; consul gen., Alexandria, Egypt, 1936-38; also counselor of legation, Cairo, 1937-38; consul gen. Vienna, 1938-40; counselor of Embassy and chargé d'affaires, Berlin, Germany, Sept. 1940-Dec. 11, 1941; E.E. and M.P. to Iceland, 1942-44. Ambassador E. and P. to Iran, 1944; detailed Fgn. Service Inspector to visit U.S. Diplomatic Missions in all Am. Republics, Jan.-June 1946; apptd. personal rep. of Pres., rank ambassador, to act as chief of Am. sect. of Allied Mission to observe revision of Greek Electoral Rolls and to observe the plebiscite on return to Greece of King George, June-Oct. 1946; designated a dep. Bd. of Examiners Fgn. Service, Nov. 1946. U.S. del. to 7th Internat. Congress for Unification of Penal Law, Cairo, 1938. Mem. Phi Gamma Delta. Mem. Am. Soc. Internat. Law. Fellow Am. Geog. Soc. Episcopalian. Address: 3009 45th St. N.W., Washington. Died July 2, 1950; buried Cedar Hills Cemetary, Washington.

MORRIS, Lloyd, author; b. N.Y. City, Sept. 23, 1893; s. Frederick and Eugenia (Mayer) M.; grad. Ethical Culture Sch. and High Sch.; A.B., Columbia, 1914. Instr. course current lit., extension dept. Columbia, 1923-32. Author: The Celtic Dawn, 1917; The Young Idea 1917; The New Carthage (trans. from French of Georges Eeckhoud), 1917; The Rebellious Puritan, 1927; Procession of Lovers, 1929; The Poetry of Edwin Arlington Robinson, 1923; This Circle of Flesh, 1932; A Threshold in the Sun (autiobiography), 1943; The Damask Cheek (play; with John van Druten), produced 1942, pub. 1943; Postscript to Yesterday, 1947; Not So Long Ago, 1949; William James, 1950; Incredible New York, 1951; (with Kendall Smith) Ceiling Unlimited; The Story of American Aviation from Kitty Hawk to Supersonics, 1953; Curtain Time: Story of the American Theatre, 1953. Book reviewer N.Y. Herald Tribune, N.Y. Eve. Post, etc. Contbr. nat. mags. Served as trade asst. censor U.S. Postal Censorship, N.Y. City, 1917-19, spl. asst. to dist. postal censor, 1941-44. Mem. fiction jury Nat. Book Award, 1951. Mem. Dramatists Guild. Address: 320 E. 53d St., N.Y.C. 22. Died Aug. 8, 1954.

MORRIS, Richard Lewis, investment banker; b. N.Y.C., Nov. 26, 1875; s. Stuyvesant Fish and Ellen (James) M.; ed. St. Mark's Sch., Columbia Coll. (1yr.); m. Carolyn Whitney Fellowes, June 9, 1908; 1 dau., Cornelia M. (Mrs. Malcolm G. Field). Began banking bus., N.Y.C.; ltd. partner Hayden, Stone & Co. since Jan. 1, 1949; dir. N.Y. Dock Co., U.S. Hoffman Machinery Co., H. L. Green Co., H. D. Kittinger Corp., Met. Stores, Ltd. Home: 132 E. 72d St. Office: 25 Broad St., N.Y.C. 4. Retired. Deceased.

MORRISON, A. Cressy; b. Wrentham, Mass., Dec. 6, 1884; s. Abram Batchelder and Mary Elizabeth (Pond) M.; ed. pub. schs.; m. Emma Webster Conway, June 18, 1900 (died Mar. 15, 1904); m. 2d, Marguerite Snow, May 14, 1908 (died May 6, 1946); 1 daughter, Valeria Elizabeth (Mrs. Dwight T. Bond); m. 3d, Mrs. Marion C. Jacobus, May 1947 (dec. June 30, 1949). Executive, Union Carbide & Carbon Corp., New York, and affiliated cos., 1906-30. Pres. of Am. Inst. City of New York, 1930-31; hon. mem., 1944 (Am. Inst., City of N.Y.); mem. exec. bd. Nat. Research Council, 1931-32; chmn. chemical advisory com. U.S. Dept. Commerce, 1925-32. Mem. council Amateur Astronomers' Assn.; fellow and chmn. Com. on Astronomy and Planetarium Am. Mus. Natural History; mem. vis. bd., dept. of atronomy, Harvard, since 1949. First v.p. League of Am. Wheelmen, 1896-98; fellow N.Y. Acad. Sciences (pres. 1938, 39); mem. A.A.A.S., Am. Chem. Soc., Electro-Chemical Soc., Am. Inst. Mining and Metall. Engrs., Internat. Fixed Calendar League (treas.), Nat. Assn. Mfrs. (tariff com.), Merchants Assn. of New York, Am. Mining Congress, Internat. Acetylene Assn. (sec.-treas. 1906-31; awarded Morehead medal for 1930; hon. mem.), Compressed Gas Mfrs.' Assn. (ex-pres.; hon. mem.), Am. Tariff League (chmn. exec. com. 1927-37), Synthetic Organic Chem. Assn. (bd. of govs., 1927-30), Mfg. Chemists Assn. of U.S., N.Y. Elec. Soc. (v.p. 1931), Royal Instn. of Great Britain, Am. Inst. of Chemists (hon.), U.S. Chamber Commerce, Home Market Club of Boston (dir.). Prepared for Ways and Means Com. of U.S. Ho. of Rep., exhaustive report on European wages and standards of living, 1921; unofficial observer for Am. Chem. Industry, World Econ. Conf., League of Nations, 1926; spokesman del. Internat. Chamber Commerce, League of Nations, 1931; chmn. finance com. Tercentenary Am. Chem. Industry, 1935, and of Unemployed Chemists, 1933-37; pres. R.O.T.C. Assn. of United States, 1937. Organized American Valuation Assn. (improved tariff administration for American Chemical Industry). Republican. Unitarian. Mason, K.P. Clubs: Union League, Chemists (N.Y. City); Cosmos, National Press, Congressional Country (Washington); The Authors' (London, Eng.). Author: Damon and Pythias—Lay Version, 1894; The Story of the Man Who Resembled Christ, 1897; The Baking Powder Controversy (2 vols.), 1902; Man in a Chemical World, 1937; Man Does not Stand Alone, 1944. Compiler: Encyclopedia of Superstition (3 volumes). Discovered method of separating oxygen and nitrogen in magnetic field; active in promotion of American policy of protection. Home: Spruce Harbor, Stonington, Me. Office: 30 E. 42d St., N.Y. City. Died Jan. 9, 1951; buried Wrentham, Mass.

MORRISON, Cameron, ex-congressman; b. Richmond County, N.C., Oct. 5, 1869; s. Daniel M. and Martha (Cameron) M.; privately ed.; read law in office of Robert P. Dick, of Greensboro, N.C.; m. Lottie May Tomlinson, Dec. 6, 1905 (died Nov. 12, 1915); 1 dau., Angelina; m. 2d, Mrs. Sarah Virginia Ecker Watts, Apr. 2, 1924. Admitted to N.C. bar, 1892, and began practice at Rockingham; chmn. Dem. Exec. Com. of Richmond County, 1898; presdl. elector at large, N.C., 1916; gov. of N.C., 1921-25; inaugurated constrn. of hard surface roads and rebuilding ednl. and charitable instns. of state; became mem. Dem. Nat. Com., 1928; apptd. mem. U.S. Senate, Dec. 13, 1930, to succeed Lee S. Overman, deceased, until election, Nov. 1932; mem. 78th Congress (1943-45), 10th N.C. Dist. Home: Charlotte, N.C. Died Aug. 20, 1953.

MORRISON, Donald Harvard, provost; b. Morgantown, W.Va., Oct. 10, 1914; s. Lewis French and Lilly (Hare) M.; A.B., W.Va. U., 1936; A.M., Princeton, 1939, Ph.D., 1940; m. Elizabeth Ann Gibson, Dec. 22, 1938; children—Donald Meigs, Elizabeth, William. Research, Princeton state and local govt. survey, 1937-40; instr., La. State U., 1940-41, dir., bureau of govt. research, asst. prof. of govt., 1941-42; budget examiner, adminstrv. analyst, U.S. Bur. of the Budget, 1942-45, cons., 1945-50; dir. Office of Def. History, 1950; asst. prof. govt. Dartmouth, 1945-47, prof. govt., 1947, dean of faculty, 1947-55, provost, 1955—. Chmn. com. on utilization of college teaching resources Fund for Advancement Education, 1956. Member Phi Beta Kappa, Kappa Alpha. Author: U.S. at War (with others), 1946; American Democracy in Theory and Practice (with others), 1951; Memo To A College Trustee (with others), 1959. Contbr. articles and reviews in pub. adminstrn. publs. Home: 4 Parkway, Hanover, N.H. Died Mar. 17, 1959.

MORRISON, Frank Barron, univ. prof.; b. Ft. Atkinson, Wis., May 19, 1887; s. Charles Irving and Harriet (Barron) M.; B.S., U. of Wis., 1911, post-grad. work, D.Sc., 1950; D.Sc., University of Vermont, 1947; married Elsie Rea Bullard, November 24, 1910; children—Roger Barron, Spencer Horton. Asst. agrl. chemistry, U. of Wis., 1911-12, instr., 1912-14, asst. prof. animal husbandry, 1914-17, asso. prof., 1917-19, prof., 1919-27; also asst. dir. Wis. Agrl. Expt. Sta., 1915-27, acting dean Wis. College of Agr., 1925-26; dir. N.Y. State Agrl. Expt. Sta. and Cornell U. Agrl. Expt. Sta., 1927-28; professor animal husbandry and animal nutrition, Cornell Univ., 1928-55, emeritus, 1955—. Member Am. Commn. to Study Live Stock Industry in Germany, 1928. Conducted survey of live stock industry of Philippine Islands for Philippine Gov., 1937; conducted survey of livestock prodn. in Argentina for Arlentina Livestock Producers Association, 1949, also for Venezuelan Ministry of Agr., 1953-54. Fellow A.A.A.S.; mem. Am. Chem. Soc., Am. Soc. Animal Production (ex-pres.), Am. Dairy Science Assn., Sigma Xi, Alpha Zeta, Phi Kappa Phi, Phi Lambda Upsilon, Phi Sigma Kappa. Republican. Presbyterian. Author: Feeds and Feeding (with W. A. Henry), 1915, 20th edit. (sole author), 1936, 22d edit. 1956; Feeds and Feeding Manual, 1915; Feeds and Feeding, Abridged (with W. A. Henry), 1917, 7th edit. (sole author), 1937, 8th edit., 1949, 9th edit., 1958. Home: 7769 Westmoreland Dr., Sarasota, Fla.; also Elsimore, Saranac Inn P.O., N.Y. Died Apr. 7, 1958.

MORRISON, Ivan (Gregg), educator; b. Fairbury, Ill., Aug. 11, 1893; s. Samuel Goodel and Rose (Gregg) M.; B.S.A., U. Ill., 1917; M.S., Cornell, 1936; m. Ruby Reynolds, Feb. 4, 1922; 1 dau., Becky Jane (Mrs. Donald G. Frier). Farmer, Fairbury, 1919-27; tchr. vocational agr. Argenta (Ill.) High Sch., 1928-35; asst. prof. agrl. edn., vocational agr. tchr. trainer in farm mechanics Purdue U., 1936-42, asso. prof., 1942-46, prof. agrl. edn., 1946—; spl. agt. Agrl. Edn., U.S. Office Edn., 1941. Served as master electrician AS, U.S. Army, 1917-19, French Theater. Mem. Am. Soc. Agrl. Engrs., Am. Vocational Assn., Am. Legion. Presbyn. Mason. Author: Repairing Farm Machinery, 1940; Farm Tractor Maintenance, 1946. Contbr. articles to prof. mags. Home: 900 Ravinia Rd., West Lafayette, Ind. Died June 28, 1957; buried Grand View Cemetery, West Lafayette.

MORRISON, James Dalton, clergyman; b. Hawkesbury, Ont., Can., Jan. 2, 1893; s. James Bolton and Mary Jane (Nichols) M.; B.A., McMaster U., Toronto, Can., 1914; B.D., Rochester (N.Y.) Theol. Sem., 1921; D.D., McMaster U., 1940; m. Marion Ruth Wilder, Oct. 5, 1921; children—Mary Elizabeth, George Robert, James Dalton, Marion Ruth, Patricia Ann. Ordained ministry Bapt. Ch., 1921; pastor North Ch., Camden, N.J., 1921-27, Immanuel Ch., Rochester, N.Y., 1927-31, Central Ch., Providence, R.I., 1931-40; Cornelius Woelfkin prof. preaching, Colgate-Rochester Div. Sch., 1940—. Served as lt. Canadian Army, 1916-19, officer in charge Mil. Y.M.C.A. activities, 1st Can. Inf. Brig., in France, 1918-19. Naturalized citizen of U.S., 1927. Trustee Colgate-Rochester Div. Sch., 1929-40; mem. Ministers and Missionaries Benefit Bd. of No. Bapt. Conv.; mem. Com. on Worship, Federal Council Chs. of Christ Am. Mem. Nat. Inst. Social Scis. Compiled, edited Minister's Service Book, for Pulpit and Parish Use, 1937; selected, arranged Aids to Worship and Responsive Readings in The New Church Hymnal, 1937; edited "Let Not Your Heart Be Troubled," 1938; Masterpieces of Religious Verse, 1948. Home: 383 Canterbury Rd. Office: Colgate-Rochester Divinity School, Rochester, N.Y. Died Apr. 5, 1950; buried Riverside, Rochester, N.Y.

MORRISON, Joseph Peter, clergyman; b. Chicago, Ill., Jan. 24, 1894; s. James Denis and Christina (Grant) M.; ed. coll. in France, St. Bernard Sem., Rochester, N.Y., 1912-15, St. Mary's Sem., Baltimore, Md., 1916-17, Catholic Univ. of America, Washington, D.C., 1917-18. Ordained priest R.C. Ch., 1918; asst. pastor St. Patrick's Ch., Joliet, Ill., 1918-23, St. Andrew's Ch., Chicago, Jan. 1-Sept. 29, 1923; asst., Holy Name Cathedral, Chicago, 1923, master of ceremonies to Cardinal Mundelein, 1924-28, adminstr. at Cathedral, 1928-32, rector of Cathedral, March 19, 1932; papal chamberlain with title Monsignor, 1934. Domestic Prelate with the title of Right Reverend Monsignor, 1938; pastor Immaculate Conception Ch., Highland Park, Ill., since Aug. 30, 1945. Gov. Catholic Church Extension Soc.; past pres. The Liturgical Conf.; bd. dirs. Nat. Cath. Rural Life Conf.; Chaplain Cath. Interracial Council Chgo. Mem. Cath. Lawyers' Guild Chgo. (bd. govs.), The Vernacular Soc. (past pres.), Knight Hospitaller Our Lady of Lourdes, also Chaplain of Honor. K.C. (4°). Club: Lake Shore. Address: 1590 Green Bay Rd., Highland Park, Ill. Died Aug. 14, 1957; buried All Saints Cemetery, Des Plains, Ill.

MORRISON, Roger Leroy, educator; b. Winnetka, Ill., Aug. 28, 1883; s. George H. (M.D.) and Della (Baker) M.; A.B., U. Ill., 1911, B.S., 1912, C.E., 1917; A.M., Columbia, 1914; m. Clare Weadock, Dec. 26, 1914; 1 dau., Isabel (Mrs. William P. Byrne). Engr. S.P. Co. and W.P. R.R. Co., 1905-09; instr. civil engring., U. Tenn., 1911-12; jr. engr. Ill. Hwy. Dept., 1912; supt. road constrn., then sales engr., United Gas Imp. Co., 1913-14; prof. hwy. engring., A. and M. Coll., Tex., 1914-19; engr. of tests, Pitts. Testing Lab., 1919-21; treas., gen. mgr. Concrete Products Co., Birmingham, Ala., 1921-24; dir. Mich. State Hwy. Lab., 1924-27; asso. prof., later prof. hwy. engring., hwy. transport, U. Mich., 1924—, also curator Transportation Library, 1945—; cons. engr., 1916—; mem. adv. bd. Mich. State Hwy. Dept.; mem. adv. com. Mich. State Safety Commn. Mem. Ann Arbor City Council, 1935-37. Capt. engrs. U.S. Reserves, 1918. Mem. Am. Soc. C.E. (p. chmn. hwy. div.), Army Transportation Assn., Assn. Asphalt Paving Technologists (past pres.), Inst. Traffic Engrs. (past pres.), Internat. Assn. Road Congresses, Am. Soc. Engring. Edn., Hwy. Research Bd. Nat. Research Council (past chmn.), Nat. Safety Council (past gen. chmn. traffic sect.), Eno Foundn. for Hwy. Traffic Control (mem. bd. cons.), Ann Arbor Engrs. Club, Engring. Soc. Detroit, S.A.R. (past pres. Washtenaw chapter), Sigma Xi, Sigma Rho Tau. Club: University (Ann Arbor). Author: (with A. H. Blanchard) Elements of Highway Engineering, 1928. Contbr. to tech. mags. and bulletins. Home: 1424 Kensington Dr., Ann Arbor, Mich. Died Mar. 23, 1952.

MORRISON, Wayland Augustus, surgeon; b. Los Angeles, Jan. 15, 1888; s. Norman Holt and Maria (Cobb) M.; A.B., Stanford U., 1910; M.D., Harvard Med. Sch., 1914; m. Lucile Gertrude Phillips, Dec. 27, 1917; children—Wayland Lee, Patricia Lee, Richard Holt, Lee Allen, Keith Norman. Surg. house officer, Mass. Gen. Hosp., 1914-16; in pvt. practice of surgery, Los Angeles, 1916, and, 1919—; med. dir. A.T.&S.F. Ry. System; pres. Los Angeles Med. Holding Corp.; dir. Pioneer Securities Corp., Pacific Indemnity Co., Grand Central Garage Co. Served as maj. Med. Corps, U.S. Army, AEF in France, Word War; comdr. Med. Corps, USNR, ret. Trustee U. So. Cal. Fellow Am. Coll. Surgeons; mem. Am., Cal. State med. assns., Pacific Coast Surgical Assn., Western Surg. Assn., Delta Tau Delta. Republican. Episcopalian. Mason (32°). Clubs: Bohemian (San Francisco); University, California, Beach, Wilshire Country, Westport Beach. Contbr. articles on surg. subjects. Home: 1916 Foothill Blvd., Duarte, Cal. Died Jan. 5, 1950.

MORRON, John Reynolds (mŏr'ŭn), mfr.; b. Peoria, Ill., Nov. 8, 1867; s. Rev. John H. and Eleanor (Reynolds) M.; student pub. schs.; m. Belle Goodridge Burch, Oct. 18, 1893. Resident of Chgo., 1887-1910, N.Y.C., 1910—; organized, 1888, and pres. until 1908, Diamond Glue Co.; also pres. Peter Cooper's Glue Co. until 1912; pres. Atlas Portland Cement Co., N.Y.C., 1910-29; dir. First Nat. Bank of New York, Pullman, Inc. Clubs: Chicago, The Links. Home: 6 Washington Sq. N. Office: 25 Broadway, N.Y.C. Died June 25, 1950; buried Gate of Heaven Cemetery, Hawthorne, N.Y.

MORROW, Mrs. Dwight Whitney (Elizabeth Reeve Cutter); b. Cleveland, O.; d. Charles Long and Annie E. (Spencer) Cutter; B.L., Smith Coll., 1896, L.H.D., 1937; grad. study, Sorbonne, Paris, 1896-97; L.H.D., Amherst College, 1933; LL.D., N.J. College for Women, 1935; Lit.D., Princeton University, 1940; LL.D., Lafayette Coll., 1940; L.H.D., New York U., 1940; Dr. the More Humane Letters, Colby College, 1942; m. Dwight Whitney Morrow, late ambassador to Mexico (died Oct. 5, 1931); children—Elisabeth Reeve (Mrs. Aubrey Niel Morgan, now dec.), Anne Spencer (Mrs. Charles A. Lindbergh), Dwight Whitney, Constance Cutter (Mrs. Aubrey Niel Morgan). Acting pres. Smith Coll., Sept. 1939-June 1940. Hon. trustee Smith Coll.; chmn. bd. The Elisabeth Morrow Sch., Englewood, N.J. Rep. Presbyn. Clubs: Cosmopolitan, Women's Univ., Colony, Smith College, Women's City (New York); Knickerbocker Country. Author: The Painted Pig, 1930; Quatrains for My Daughter, 1931; Beast, Bird and Fish, 1933; A Pint of Judgment, 1939; The Rabbit's Nest, 1940; Shannon, 1941; My Favorite Age, 1943. Contbr. articles and verse to magazines. Home: Next Day Hill, Englewood, N.J. Died Jan. 23, 1955.

MORROW, Frederick Keenan, chmn. bd. Wilsil, Ltd.; b. Essa Township, Ont., Can., 1886; s. Thomas and Mary (Keenan) Morrow; ed. Alliston High School; St. Michael's Coll., Toronto; m. Edna Lillian Mann, 1916. Pres. Essa Securities Co., Ltd.; chmn. of bd. Wilsil, Ltd., Montreal, Can., Loblaw Incorporated, Buffalo; v.p. Bank of Toronto; dir. Ogilvie Flour Mills Co., Ltd., Hiram Walker-Gooderham & Worts, Ltd., Reiss-Premeir Corp., Consumers Glass Co., Ltd., Consol. Bakeries of Can., Ltd., Ward Baking Co., Maple Leaf Gardens, Ltd., Remington Rand, Limited, Canadian International Paper Company. Governor Univ. of Toronto, St. Joseph's Hosp.; trustee Toronto Gen. Hosp., Stevenson Memorial Hosp., governor Connaught Med. Research Laboratories. Officer Order of British Empire; Knight of Grace, St. John Ambulance Assn.; member executive committee Royal Agrl. Winter Fair. Hon. life mem. Canadian Cancer Soc. Clubs: Rosedale Golf, Albany; York, Mt. Royal (Montreal). Home: Wychwood Park. Office: 67 Yonge St., Toronto, Ont., Can. Died May 29, 1953.

MORROW, Hubert T., lawyer; b. Waterbury, Conn., Mar. 29, 1881; s. John H. and Corinne R. (Thomas) M.; student pub. schs. of Cal.; m. May Langbein, June 12, 1907; children—John C., Marjorie (Mrs. Ashen), Barbara (Mrs. Weir). Admitted to practice Cal., Fed. Cts., U.S. Supreme Ct.; pvt. practice, 1902-26; partner Finlayson, Bennett & Morrow, 1927-48, Morrow & Trippet, Los Angeles, 1948-51, Morrow & Morrow, 1951——. Mem. Am., Los Angeles bar assns., State Bar Cal. Clubs: University, Los Angeles, Athletic. Home: 3913 27th St., Los Angeles 16. Office: 210 W. 7th St., Los Angeles 14. Died May 17, 1951.

MORSE, Charles Hosmer, mfr.; b. Chicago, Ill., Aug. 13, 1873; s. Charles Hosmer and Martha Jeannette (Owens) M.; grad. Chicago Manual Training sch., 1891; B.S., U. of Mich., 1895, M.E., 1897; m. Charlotte Ingersoll, Feb. 21, 1900. With Fairbanks, Morse & Company since beginning of active career, pres., 1915, chmn. bd., 1927——, chmn. officers com., 1931——; dir. Fairbanks, Morse & Co., Canadian Fairbanks-Morse Co., Harris Trust & Savs. Bank (Chgo.). Trustee Beloit Coll. Mem. A.S. M.E., Western Soc. Engrs., Soc. Colonial Wars, Phi Kappa Psi. Republican. Mem. Kenwood Evangelical Church. Clubs: Chicago, University, Onwentsia, Casino, Racquet, Coleman Lake. Mem. Royal Soc. St. George. Home: 45 Stone Gate Lane, Lake Forest, Ill. Died Aug. 4, 1959.

MORSE, Clark T., industrialist; b. Evanston, Ill., Dec. 31, 1888; s. Charles S. and Hattie (Tillinghast) M. Salesman Am. Blower Corp., Detroit, 1912, branch mgr.; sales mgr., 1923-33, pres. since 1933, dir. since 1933; pres. and dir. Canadian Sirocco Co., Ltd., Windsor, Ont., since 1933; chmn. and dir. Ross Heater & Mfg. Co., Inc., Buffalo, since 1935; dir. Am. Radiator and Standard Sanitary Corp., Detroit Lubricator Co. Mem. Am. Soc. Heating and Ventilating Engrs., Am. Soc. M.E. Clubs: Athletic, Recess (Detroit); Oakland Hills Country (Birmingham, Mich.); Engineers (N.Y. City). Home: Hillcrest Dr., Bloomfield Hills, Mich. Office: Am. Blower Corp., Detroit 32. Deceased.

MORSE, Glenn Tilley, clergyman; b. St. Louis, July 30, 1870; s. Thomas Perry and Mary Amelia (Glenn) M.; B.A., Harvard, 1898. B.D., Episcopal Theol. Sch., Cambridge, Mass., 1901. Deacon, 1901, priest, 1902, P.E. Ch.; asst. St. Anne's Ch., Lowell, Mass., 1901-02; asso. priest St. Stephen's Ch., Boston, 1902-04; rector St. James Ch., West Somerville, Mass., 1902-08; sr. curate Ch. of the Advent, Boston, 1908-09; founder, 1910, and rector All Saints Ch., West Newbury, 1910-38; retired 1938; founder and priest in charge All Saints Mission, Georgetown, 1916-38. Acting chaplain U.S. Mil. Acad., 1909. Trustee Governor Dummer Acad. Past pres. Chase Family Assn.; past pres. Fedn. of Religious Workers, Newburyport; past pres. Soc. for Prevention of Cruelty to Children. Trustee Soc. for Preservation of New Eng. Antiquities; past pres. Bay State Hist. League, Hist. Soc. Old Newbury (hon. pres.), Soc. Colonial Wars (chaplain), New England Historic-Geneal. Soc., Soc. of Gov. and Company of Mass. Bay in New Eng. (chaplain), Newburyport Garden Club (past pres.) (council), Cum Laude Soc., Poetry Soc., Soc. for Sanity in Art, Gloucester Soc. of Artists, Am. Antiquarian Soc., Mass. Hort. Soc., Essex Inst. (advisory bd.), Arts and Crafts Soc. of Boston, Bostonian Soc., Wedgwood Club (v.p.), English-Speaking Union, Palm Beach Art League, Clearwater Art Museum, Sarasota Art Assn. (past pres.) Art League of Manatee County (Fla.), Fla. Fedn. Art (v.p.). Republican. Clubs: Harvard, Boston Art, Business Men's Art (Boston); Rotary (past pres., also del. to internat.), Harvard (past pres.), Tuesday Night (Newburyport, Mass.). Author: Old Newbury Initiatives; Twenty-five Years of All Saints Church; etc. Lecturer on historic and antiquarian subjects and art. Has the largest collection of silhouettes in the world, also large collection of wax portraits, seals, medallions and Wedgwood. Painter of Landscapes and portraits. Author: The Ark and The Dove, Ancestral Ships of Maryland. Mem. Soc. Ark and Dove. Home: 186 High St., Newburyport, Mass. Died June 21, 1950; buried Episcopal Ch. Grounds, Newburyport.

MORSE, Leon Jeremiah, clergyman; b. Bethel, Vt., Dec. 24, 1880; s. Orlando and Ednah (Towne) M.; Randolph (Vt.) State Normal, 1897-1900; Montpelier (Vt.) Sem., 1902-05; A.B., Dartmouth, 1909; S.T.B., Boston U. Sch. of Theology, 1912; Litt.D. (honorary), Norwich University, 1952; m. Ethel Cambridge, Apr. 7, 1912. Teacher, pub. schs., Randolph, Vt., 1900-02; ordained ministry M.E. Ch., 1902; pastor Waits River and W. Topsham, Vt., 1902-03, W. Berlin, Vt., 1904, Wilder, Vt., 1905-08, Milford, N.H., 1909-11, Somersworth, N.H., 1912-13, Dover, N.H., 1913-39; now pastor churches in North Thetford, Vermont and Post Mills, Vt. Spl. lectr. on Am. home Norwich U., Northfield, Vt., 1940-41. Mem. N.H. Conf. to 1940. Hon. mem. Vets. of Foreign Wars. Republican. Mason. Author: Agamenticus the Purple Hill (with wife), 1917; He Came to Me, 1934. Editorial writer Foster's Daily Democrat, Dover, 1919-43. Writes column, "Your Friend," for Burlington (Vt.) Free Press; reader interest survey, topped all Free Press columns, 1948——, also "Your Friend" radio counsellor; columnist for the Newport (Vt.) Daily Express, Claremont (N.H.) Daily Eagle. Lecturer. Contbr. to other newspapers and mags. Home: Lyme, N.H. Address: North Thetford, Vt. Died Sept. 30, 1958; buried North Thetford Cemetery.

MORSE, Wilbur Jr., newspaper man; b. Phila., July 6, 1903; s. Wilbur and Katherine (Larnard) M.; student Harrisburg (Pa.) Acad., U.S. Naval Acad.; grad. Princeton 1926; m. Priscilla Christian Bullitt, Oct. 18, 1924; children—Priscilla Bullitt, Katherine Larnard; m. 2d, Elisabeth Schauffler, Dec. 1, 1931; 1 dau., Ann M.; m. 3d, Margaret Watson; 1 dau. Margaret Elizabeth. Served as pvt. Siberian Expdn.; successively with Harrisburg Patriot, Phila. Public Ledger and Camden Daily Courier, 1918-22; Washington corr. Phila. Evening Public Ledger, 1924-26; entered motion picture work 1926, acting as publicity writer and later scenario writer for Paramount, Fox and RKO-Radio Pictures; sometime prof. and head of Sch. of Journalism, Woodbury College; mem. staff Camden (N.J.) Courier-Post, 1947. Republican. Episcopalian. Clubs: Princeton (Phila.); National Press (Washington); AMPA (N.Y.). Author many magazine stories, motion picture scenarios and book of children's stories. "Let's Pretend." Home: 6317 Franklin Circle. Address: 18 Alexander Av., Merchantville, N.J. Died Mar. 1, 1955.

MORSE, Withrow, biochemist; b. at Dayton, O., May 7, 1880; s. David Appleton (M.D.) and Amanda (Withrow) M.; B.Sc., Ohio State U., 1903, A.M., 1904; Ph.D., Columbia, 1910; m. Winning Allan, 1934; children—John, Priscilla. Prof. biochemistry successively med. depts., U. of Neb., W.Va. Sch. of Medicine and Jefferson Med. Coll., 1916-29; served on staffs of U. of Wis., Cornell U. and Trinity Coll.; biochemist, N.Y. State Psychiatric Inst., Columbia U. Med. Center; also consultant to Lederle Labs., New York, Rohm & Haas Co., Inc., Phila., The Kalak Co. New York; vice pres. Vogelbach Associates, Ind. Mem. Am. Soc. Biol., Chemists (life mem.), British Biochemistry Soc., Sigma Xi, Phi Beta Kappa, Delta Upsilon. Author: Applied Biochemistry (2 edits.); Organizer of Biochemistry (a British-Am. coöperative treatise); Development of Biochemistry; Mineral Physiology; Flugel (blood transfusion substitute), 1940. Home: 32 Manchester Rd., Tuckahoe 7, N.Y. Offices: 30 Rockefeller Plaza, N.Y.C. 20. Died Feb. 10, 1951; buried London, O.

MORTIMER, Frank Cogswell, financier, author; b. Boston, April 10, 1876; son Harry W. and Lucy Cleveland (Smith) M.; acad. and pub. sch. edn. in Calif.; fellow Am. Inst. of Banking, 1911; m. Clara Mae Benton, Dec. 1917; children—Frances Charlotte Lucas, Elizabeth Jane Van Dyke, Ann Benton McGonigle; (by previous marriage) Wendell Reed. In banking bus. at San Francisco, 1896-1907; exec., First Nat. Bk., Berkeley 1907-16; treas. West-inghouse Pacific Coast Brake Co., 1914-16; exec. Nat. City Bank, New York, 1917-24; pres. Number Eight Realty Co., 1921-24; v.p. Citizens Nat. Bank, Los Angeles, 1925-31; federal receiver and trustee, 1931-41; financial advisor, W.P.B., 1942; commnr. State of Calif., 1943-51; chmn. adv. com., dir. Pioneer Savs. & Loan Assn., Los Angeles. Chmn. Liberty Loan Committee of American Inst. of Banking, 1917; regent Am. Inst. of Banking, 1918-21; trustee Nat. Soc. S.A.R., 1920-21; hon. mem. Fgn. Trade Club, Am. Inst. Banking, San Francisco. Clubs: Stock Exchange (Los Angeles); Bohemian (San Francisco). Author: Paragraphs on Thrift; The Investment of Trust Funds; School Savings Systems; The People and the Banks; War Bonds and the People's Purse; Put Dust Back (50 years in banking); etc. Home: Glendale, Cal. Office: 740 S. Broadway, Los Angeles 14. Deceased.

MORTIMER, James Daniel; b. Elmhurst, Ill., Nov. 23, 1879; s. Mathew and Rose Anna (McAuley) M.; Throop Poly. Inst., Pasadena, Cal.; B.S. in Mech. Engring., U. Cal., 1900, also post-grad. work; m. Esther May Woodward, Sept. 18, 1908. Asst. in elec. engring. U. Cal., 1900-02; supt. of power Puget Sound Electric Ry. Co., 1902-03; elec. engr. Puget Sound Power Co., 1903-05; engr., mgr., operating dept. and v.p. Electric Bond & Share Co., N.Y.C., 1905-09; v.p. North American Co., 1909-14, pres. co. and subsidiaries, 1914-20, resigned; pres. Western Power Co. of Can., 1917-20; chmn. reorgn. com. Winona Interurban Ry. Co., 1916-24; later specializing in investment securities. Mem. Am. Soc. C.E., Am. Soc. M.E., A.A.A.S., Am Inst. E.E. (asso.), Alpha Delta Phi, Phi Beta Kappa, Sigma Xi, Tau Beta Pi. Home: Northport Village, Me. Address: Belfast, Me. Died July 19, 1950; buried Belfast.

MORTON, David, writer; b. at Elkton, Ky., February 21, 1886; son of Thomas Beckwith and Mattie (Petrie) M.; B.Sc., Vanderbilt U., Nashville, Tenn., 1909; Litt.D. (hon.), U. of Kentucky, 1952; Litt.D. (hon.) U. of Mass., 1953; m. Elizabeth Kidder Merrick, 1943. Began as reporter Louisville Evening Post, 1909, later with Asso. Press, and editorial writer on Louisville Courier-Journal and Louisville Herald; teacher English and literature, Louisville Boys' High School, 1915-18, English and history Morristown (New Jersey) High School, 1918-24; asso. prof. English, Amherst, 1924-26, prof. 1926-1945; prof. English overseas br. Am. Internat. Coll., 1950-56. Mem. Poetry Society America, Lyric Society, The Poets, Delta Kappa Epsilon, Phi Beta Kappa. Episcopalian. Author: Ships in Harbour (verse), 1921; Harvest (verse), 1924; The Sonnet Today—and Yesterday (monograph), 1926; Nocturnes and Autumnals (verse), 1928; The Renaissance of Irish Poetry, 1929; A Man of Earth (verse), 1930; Six For Them (anthology in verse), 1931; Shorter Modern Poems (anthology in verse), 1932; Earth's Processional (verse), 1932; Spell Against Time (verse), 1936; This Is Their Acre (anthology in verse) 1936; All In One Breath (verse), 1939; Angle of Earth and Sky (verse), 1941; A Letter to Youth, 1942; This Is for You (verse), 1943; Poems; 1920-1945, 1945; New England Devotional, 1952; Like A Man In Love, 1953; Chimes at Lages (verse), 1955. Compiler: Amherst Undergraduate Verse, 1925-29. Home: care Mrs. Clyde P. Allen, 81 James St., Morristown, N.J. Retired. Died June 13, 1957; buried Restland Park Cemetery, Hanover, N.J.

MORTON, Ira Abbott, prof. religious edn.; b. Fairview, O., Nov. 21, 1876; s. Edward Cooper and Sarah Eleanor (Holtz) M.; A.B., Mt. Union Coll., Alliance, O., 1903; B.D., Drew Theol. Sem., 1905; M.A., Columbia, 1913; Ph.D., Northwestern U., 1923; m. Treva Diana Dewey, Jan. 8, 1908 (died May 5, 1943); children—Edward Wendell, Justin Dewey; m. 2d, Katherine Maran Troutman, June 29, 1944. Pastor M.E. Church at Cleveland, Canton and New Concord, Ohio, and N.Y. City, 1906-12; teacher Grand Prairie Seminary, Onarga, Ill., 1913-14; prof. psychology Willamette Univ., Salem, Ore., 1914-15; prof. edn. and psychology, Coll. of Puget Sound, Tacoma, Wash., 1915-17, dean and prof. religion, 1917-19; supervisor town and country survey of Western Washington, for Inter-Church Movement, 1919-20; instr. Northwestern U. 1920-21; prof. psychology and philosophy, Rockford (Ill.) Coll., 1922-23, prof. religion, 1923-25; prof. religious edn. and psychology, Iliff Sch. of Theology, Denver, 1925-47. Mem. Internat. Council Religious Edn., Nat. Assn. Bible instrs., Denver Council of Chs., Colo. Annual Conf. Meth. Ch., Phi Delta Kappa. Methodist. Author: A Laymen's Guide to Churchmanship, 1940. Contbr. chapter on administration of religious education to Studies in Religious Education, 1934. Co-author: Rethinking the Family, 1934. Contbr. to jours. on religious edn.; chapters on human relations and faith in The Quest for God Through Understanding, 1937; Making the Most of Church Membership, 1947. Home: 2135 S. Josephine St., Denver 10. Died Sept. 30, 1950; buried Fairmount Cemetery, Denver.

MORTON, Richard Albert Dunlap, lawyer; b. Paris, Tenn., Mar. 10, 1890; s. Albert Livingstone Eldridge and Darling Dunlap (Dawson) M.; A.B., U. of Tenn., 1910; LL.B., Cumberland U., Lebanon, Tenn., 1914;

m. Julianne More, June 20, 1929; children—Richard Albert Dunlap, Frederick Julian. Admitted to Ala. and Tenn. bars, 1914; practiced in Paris, 1914-19; admitted to Tex. bar, 1920 and since practiced in El Paso; counsel for numerous ins. cos. and corps. Mem. 1st O.T.C., Ft. Oglethorpe, Ga., 1917. Mem. Am. Bar Assn., Tex. State Bar Assn. (dir. 1932-33), El Paso Bar Assn. (pres. 1931), Internat. Assn. Ins. Counsel, Fedn. of Ins. Counsel (v.p. 1938-39; bd. govs. 1939-41), Kappa Alpha. Democrat. Presbyn. Author: I Am The Lawyer, 1922. Home: 1910 N. Stanton St. Office: Suite 711, Mills Bldg., El Paso, Tex. Died Sept. 10, 1954.

MOSELEY, Charles West, physician; b. Elkin, N.C., May 10, 1865; s. James Henry and Thersa Matilda (Hurt) M.; prep. edn. So. Normal Sch. and Bus. Coll., Bowling Green, Ky.; M.D., Balt. Med. Coll., 1893; post-grad. N.Y. and New Orleans polyclinics; m. Fannie Ogburn McKnight, Mar. 10, 1891; children—Thersa Lillian, Charles Andrew, Maude Ethel, Mary, Hugh Milner (dec.); m. 2d, Elizabeth Battle, Feb. 8, 1927. Began practice at Lewisville, N.C., 1893; moved to Greensboro, 1907; specializes in diseases of the stomach and in internal medicine; mem. staff St. Leo's Hosp., Clinic Hosp., Glenwood Park Sanitarium, Wesley Long Hosp. Mem. N.C. Med. Soc., Guilford County Med. Soc., Pi Gamma Mu. Democrat. Baptist. Home: 438 S. Mendenhall St. Office: Clinic Hosp., Greensboro, N.C. Died Mar. 1937.

MOSELEY, John Ohleyer, fraternity exec. b. Meridian, Miss., Oct. 21, 1893; s. Rev. John Watkins and Sophie (Ohleyer) M.; student Southwestern Presbyn. Univ. (Clarksville, Tenn.), 1908-10, Grad. Sch. Stanford, 1929-30, Columbia, summer 1920, Southern Br. U. of Calif., 1925; A.B., Austin Coll. (Sherman, Tex.), 1912, LL.D., 1936; grad. Southeastern Teachers Coll. (Durant, Okla.), 1913; A.M., U. of Okla., 1916; B.A., Oxford (England), 1922, M.A., 1928 (Rhodes Scholar); m. Marie V. Nichols, Dec. 19, 1923; children—John Nichols, Margaret Marie. Instr. Latin and English and athletic coach, high school, Durant, Okla., 1912-15; student asst. instr. Latin, U. of Okla., 1915-16, asst. prof. Latin and classical archeology, 1919-24, asso. prof., 1924-35, prof., 1935; prin. acad. and asso. prof. edn., Henry Kendall Coll. (now Tulsa U.), 1916-17; pres. Central State Teachers Coll., Edmond, Okla., 1935-39; dean students, U. of Tenn.. 1939-44; became pres. U. of Nev., 1944, now ret. Originator leadership-training schools for national social fraternities. Served as pvt. Nat. Guard (Durant, Okla.), 1912-15; O.T.C., Fort Logan Roots, 1917; 2d lt. Camp Pike (Ark.), 1917; 2d lt., 1st lt., capt. 32d div. A.E.F., 1917-19. Awarded Royal Victor fellowship, Stanford, 1930. Mem. Co-ordinating Bd., State of Okla.; mem. permanent com. Nat. Interfrat. Conf. Mem. Classical Assn. of the Middle West and South, Am. Philol. Assn., Am. Legion, Alumni Assn. of Durant State Teachers Coll. (pres. 1915), U. of Okla. Alumni Assn. (mem. advisory bd. 1920), Okla. State Council of Christian Edn. (pres. 1939), Sigma Alpha Epsilon (province recorder 1923-24; archon 1924-31; supreme herald 1931-32; supreme dep. archon 1932-34; supreme archon 1934-37; hon. supreme archon 1937-39; now executive secretary), Phi Delta Phi, Eta Sigma Phi, Sigma Tau Delta, Alpha Phi Sigma, Pi Kappa Delta, Kappa Delta Pi, Phi Delta Kappa, Phi Eta Sigma, Phi Kappa Phi. Presbyn. Mason. Club: Rotary (Evanston, Ill.). Author: articles on fraternal, classical, travel and mil. subjects. Home: P.O. Box 1856, Evanston, Ill. Died Oct. 10, 1955.

MOSENTHAL, Herman (Otto) (mō'zĕn-thăl), physician; b. N.Y. City, July 8, 1878; s. Joseph and Augusta Ernestine (Andreae) M.; student Williams Coll., 1895; A.B., Columbia, 1899; M.D., Coll. Phys. and Surg. (Columbia), 1903; m. Johanna Kroeber, Sept. 3, 1908; children—Barbara Andreae (Mrs. Winston T. Kellogg), Joseph, Joan Elizabeth (Mrs. Adrian William De Wind), Edward Kroeber. Served as interne at New York Hospital, 1904-06, N.Y. Foundling Hosp., 1906-07; asst. instr. and asso. in biol. chemistry and medicine, Columbia, 1908-14; attending physician in diseases of metabolism, Vanderbilt Clinic, 1910-14; asst. visiting physician Presbyn. Hosp., 1911-14; asst. prof. medicine and asst. physician, Johns Hopkins Med. Sch. and Hosp., Baltimore, Md., 1914-18; prof. of clinical medicine, New York Post-Grad. Med. Sch., Columbia U., and attending physician N.Y. Post-Grad. Hosp., 1922-48; consulting physician Bellevue Hosp., N.Y. City, Sea View Hosp., Staten Island; consultant in medicine N.Y.U.-Bellevue Medical Center; consultant St. Luke's Hospital, Newburgh, N.Y.; N.Y. Infirmary for Women and Children; Goshen Hosp., Goshen, N.Y.; dir. Dept. of Medicine N.Y. Post-Grad. Med. Sch. and Hosp., 1925-35. Associate clinic professor medical and assoc. attending physician, New York Medical College. Chairman New York Diabetes Association, 1935 (member board directors since 1936); president American Diabetes Association, 1941-42 (mem. Council since 1942). Served as captain Medical Officers Reserve Corps, 1918-19. Fellow American College Physicians; member A.M.A., Assn. Am. Physicians, N.Y. Acad. of Medicine, Internat. Soc. of Gastroenterology, Am. Soc. of Advancement Clin. Investigation, Soc. Exptl. Biology and Medicine, Nu Sigma Nu. Club: Century. Contributor on internal medicine to med. publs. Home: 210 E. 68 St. Office: 889 Lexington Av., N.Y.C. Died Apr. 24, 1954; buried Gaylordsville, Conn.

MOSES, Frederick Taft, ins. exec.; b. Ayer, Mass., Nov. 14, 1885; s. Frederick William and Anna S. (Taft) M.; B.S., Mass. Inst. Tech., 1907; m. Lillian M. Flood, May 7, 1908; 1 son, Harlan Taft; m. 2d, S. Ruth Lawton, Aug. 9, 1940. Asst. sec. Firemen's Mut. Ins. Co., Providence, R.I., 1911-15, vice-pres. and engr., 1915-26, pres., 1926-51, chmn. since 1951; pres. Union Mutual Fire Ins. Co., 1926-51, chmn. since 1951; pres. Appalachian Ins. Co. of Providence; dir. Providence Indsl. Nat. Bank, Protection Mut. Ins. Co., Textron, Inc. Pres. Nat. Fire Protection Assn., 1930, 31; mem. R.I. Aeros. Adv. Bd. Mem. Am. Soc. M.E., Providence Engring. Soc.. R.I. Soc. Protection Cruelty to Animals (pres.), R.I. Humane Edn. Soc. (pres.), Am. Humane Assn. (hon. v.p.), R.I. Hist. Soc., S.A.R., Soc. Colonial Wars, R.I. Police Chiefs' Assn., New Eng. Assn. Chiefs of Police, Navy League. Republican. Clubs: Turks Head, Providence Art, Rhode Island Country (Providence); Barrington Yacht. Home: Windholme, Warren, R.I. Office: 150 S. Main St., Providence. Died Apr. 6, 1959.

MOSES, Harry Morgan, assn. executive; b. Westville, Ill., Nov. 11, 1896; s. Thomas and Robena (Pringle) M.; student Wabash Coll., Ind., 1919; m. Ruth Cantrell, Jan. 9, 1918 (died Mar. 16, 1928); children—Thomas William, Marianne Morgan (Mrs. H.R.H. Smith), Richard Cantrell, Morgan Evan; m. 2d, Garnet Strawser, Aug. 7, 1929. Continuously engaged in bituminous coal industry since 1919; pres. H. C. Frick Coke Co., U.S. Coal & Coke Co., Connellsville & Monongahela Ry. Co. (U.S. Steel Corp. subsidiaries) to 1950; pres. Bituminous Coal Operators Assn. since 1950. Trustee Wabash Coll. Served as 2d lt., Field Arty., World War I. Mem. Am. Inst. Mining and Metall. Engrs., Am. Iron and Steel Inst., Am. Mining Congress, Engrs. Soc. Western Pa., Pittsburgh Athletic Assn., Sigma Gamma Epsilon, Lambda Chi Alpha. Republican. Episcopalian. Clubs: Pittsburgh Athletic, Duquesne, Cat Key, Longue Vue Country, Metropolitan (Washington); Surf (Miami Beach); 29 Club: Burning Tree, 1925 F Street (Washington). Home: 2101 Connecticut Av., N.W. Washington 8. Office: World Center Bldg., Washington 6. Died Apr. 1, 1956; buried Springhill Cemetery, Danville, Ill.

MOSES, Thomas, corp. official; b. Audenreid, Pa., Aug. 18, 1869; s. Morgan and Elizabeth (Stradling) M.; self-educated; m. Robena Hamilton, Feb. 13, 1906; children—Harry Morgan, Mabel Jean (Mrs. Harold T. Leverenz), George Thomas. Worked in coal mines, 1880-1905; sec. Ill. State Mining Bd., 1905-07, insp. 5th Mining Dist., 1907-10; supt. U.S. Fuel Co., 1910-15, gen. supt., 1915-27; pres. H. C. Frick Coke Co., 1927-—; also pres. Histetter-Connellsville Coke Co., Cumberland Coal Co., Sharon Coal & Limestone Co., Nat. Mining Co., U.S. Fuel Co., Mingo Coal Co., Republic-Connellsville Coke Co., U.S. Coal & Coke Co., Trotter Water Co., Standard Water Co., Connellsville & Monongahela Ry. Co., Youghiogheny Northern Ry. Co. Mem. Am. Iron and Steel Inst., Am. Inst. Mining and Metall. Engrs., Coal Mining Inst. of America, Mine Insps. Inst. of America, Ill. Mining Inst., Pittsburgh Coal Mining Inst. Republican. Mason. Elk. Clubs: Pittsburgh Athletic, Duquesne, Longue Vue Country. Home: 123 Franklin St., Danville, Ill. Office: Frick Bldg., Pittsburgh, Pa. Died Feb. 20, 1948; buried Spring Hill Cemetery, Danville, Ill.

MOSHER, Aaron Alexander Roland, assn. exec.; b. Can., May 10, 1881; s. Samuel I. and Mary Jane (Stevens) M.; student pub. schs. of Canada; LL.D., St. Francis Xavier University, 953; m. Leila Elnora Ernst, 1903; children—Cyril McKay, Leila Pearl, Alice Genevieve, Lloyd Arnold; m. 2d, Mary Pearl Hull, 1954. Became first grand pres. of Canadian Brotherhood of Ry. Employees and other transport workers, 1908, hon. life pres. 1952; pres. All Canadian Congress of Labour, 1927-40, pres. Canadian Congress Labour, 1940-—. Mem. Can. Labor Relations Bd. Decorated Comdr. Order Brit. Empire. Mem. Nat. Employment Com. Mason. Home: 722 Parkdale Av., Ottawa. Office: 230 Laurier Av. W., Ottawa, Can. Died Sept. 26, 1959.

MOSHER, Harris Peyton, surgeon; b. Woodfords, Me., Oct. 21, 1867; s. Andrew J. and Julia Harris (Woodford) M.; A.B., Harvard, 1892, M.D., 1896; Sc.D., U. Pa., 1925; Sc.D., Colby Coll., 1937; LL.D., Wayne U., 1939; m. Helen Augusta Clark, Mar. 22, 1913. Surg. house officer Mass. Gen. Hosp., 1896, Boston Lying-in Hosp., 1897; asst. surgeon U.S. Army, 1898; formerly instr. in anatomy, and prof. otolaryngology Harvard Med. Sch., now emeritus; 1st Am. Semon lectr. laryngol. sect. Royal Brit. Med. Soc. Mem. joint com. ophthalmology and otolaryngology, General Med. Bd., U.S. Army, 1918-19. Recipient Semon medal U. London. Fellow A.C.S.; mem. Am. Acad. Ophthalmology and Oto-Laryngology (past pres.), Am. Laryngol. Assn., Am. Laryngol. Rhinol. and Otol. Soc., Am. Otol. Soc., N.E. Otol. and Laryngol. Soc., laryngol. socs. of Paris, Vienna and Scotland, Am. Inst. of Arts and Sciences; corr. mem. Royal Medical Society, London; chmn. sub-com. on otolaryngology NRC, 1941. Republican. Conglist. Clubs: Harvard (Boston and New York). Address: 127 Front St., Marblehead, Mass.* Died Nov. 4, 1954.

MOSHER, Raymond Mylar, educator; b. Palo Alto, Calif., May 9, 1894; s. Charles A. and Minnie (Mylar) M.; A.B., Stanford, 1919, A.M., 1923; Ph.D., Columbia, 1926; m. Marie Aline Hall, June 17, 1922; children—John Francis, James Ross, Katharine Elizabeth, Raymond Mylar. Teacher psychology and edn., Santa Barbara State Coll., 1919-22; dir. of training sch., New Haven State Teachers Coll., 1924-28; lecturer, ednl. psychology, Yale, 1925-28; dir. student personnel, U. of Ida., also prof. ednl. psychology, 1928-31; head, dept. of psychology, San Jose State Coll., 1931-50, dean ednl. services and summer session, 1950-53; pres. Eastern Wash. Coll. of Education, 1953-54; administrative asst. San Jose State Coll., 1954-55; retired 1955. Served as pvt., 158th Field Hosp. Co., 115th Sanitary Train, U.S. Army, World War I. Mem. A.A. A.S., Am. Statis. Assn., Am. Psychol. Assn., Northwest Assn. Secondary and Higher Instns. (v.p., 1950-53, chmn. commn. on higher instns.), Kappa Delta Pi, Phi Delta Kappa, Phi Gamma Delta. Roman Catholic. Home: 505 S. 16th St., San Jose, Cal. Died Nov. 19, 1956; buried San Jose.

MOSLER, Edwin H., lock and safe mfr.; b. N.Y. C., July 14, 1875; s. Michael and Fanny (Trauer) M.; student N.Y.C. Coll., 1899; m. Irma Mosler, Jan. 16, 1916; children—Janet M. (Mrs. Martin S. Coleman), Edwin H., John. Pres. Mosler Safe Co., N.Y.C., 1922-—, Mosler Lock Co., Covington, Ky., 1922-—, Guardian Metals Co., Hamilton, O., 1925-—. Mem. Bank and Security Vault Mfrs. Assn. (v.p.), Safe Mfrs. Nat. Assn. (v.p.), Mexico C. of C., N.Y. State C. of C. Elk, Mason (Shriner). Home: 285 Central Park West. Office: 320 5th Av., N.Y.C. Died July 29, 1952.

MOSS, Herbert James, univ. dean; b. Elmira, N.Y., Feb. 27, 1910; s. Carl James and Helen Louise (Wright) M.; A.B., Wesleyan U., Middletown, Conn., 1931; A.M., Harvard, 1932, Ph.D., 1938; student Brown U., 1933-34; m. Elizabeth Bartlett Walton, Mar. 25, 1939; children—Helen Claybaugh, Virginia Bartlett, James Davidson. Head social sci. dept. Bennett Jr. Coll., 1938-40, Portland Jr. Coll., 1940-42, Bradford Jr. Coll., 1942-46; asst. prof. sociology U. N.H., 1946-48, asso. prof., 1948-—, sec. univ., 1950-52, dean grad. sch., dir. summer session and coordinator sponsored research, 1952-—; cons. edn. Sec. of the Army, 1953-—; research and study higher edn. in France, 1954-55. Mem. exec. council New Eng. Conf. Grad. Edn. Mem. Am. Sociol. Soc., Am. Assn. U. Profs., Phi Beta Kappa, Alpha Kappa Delta. Home: 29 Mill Rd., Durham, N.H. Died June 25, 1955.

MOSS, Joseph, lawyer; b. Dec. 7, 1886; s. Jacob and Nettie (Thoman) M.; LL.B., U. Pa., 1909; m. Ray L. Brod, Dec. 15, 1914; 1 dau., Natalie (Mrs. Philip H. Weinreich). Admitted to Pa. bar, 1909, since practiced in Phila.; sr. mem. Moss & Moss, 1920-—; spl. dep. atty. gen. State Pa., also chief counsel Dept. Banking, 1934-39; judge Family Ct. of Philadelphia County, 1937-38. Served with 1st Inf. Regt., U.S. Army, World War I; on staff Judge Adv. Gen. Corps, 1942-46, advancing to col.; comdr. 3d Inf. Regt. Vet. Guard, 1950-52. Mem. Am. Legion (life), Am., Pa., Phila. bar assns., Am. Numis. Assn. (pres. 1951-53; awarded Distinguished Service gold medal 1952), Nat. Sojourners (pres. Phila. chpt. 16, 1952). Author articles and legal and numis. publs. Home: 2601 Parkway, Phila. 30. Office: Commonwealth Bldg., 1201 Chestnut St., Phila. 7. Died Feb. 16, 1955.

MOSS, William Lorenzo, physician; b. Athens, Ga., Aug. 23, 1876; s. Rufus LaFayette and Elizabeth (Luckie) M.; B.S., U. Ga., 1901, D.Sc., 1928; M.D., Johns Hopkins, 1905; grad. student Berlin, 1907-08; m. Marguerite Eleanor Widle, June 1, 1925; children—Marguerite Eleanor, Elizabeth, William Lorenzo, II. Resident house officer Johns Hopkins Hosp., 1905-06, asst. resident physician, 1910-14; asst. physician Johns Hopkins Med. Sch., 1906-07, instr. medicine, 1908-10, asso., 1910-14; internist State Inst. Study Malignant Diseases, Buffalo, 1914-15; asst. prof. health dept. Yale, 1917; asst. prof., dept. preventive medicine and hygiene Harvard, 1919-21, bacteriology and immunology, 1924-29, acting dean, sch. pub. health, 1926; prof. preventive medicine and dean U. Ga. Sch. Medicine, 1931-34. Expeditions: Tropical Medicine, Central America, 1914; Harvard, Peru, 1916, Santo Domingo, 1920, 1925; Crane Pacific, Field Museum, 1928-29; Crane-Peabody Museum, New Guinea, 1937-38. Served from capt. to lt. col. M.C., AEF, 1917-19, col. Med. Res., 1924-—. Decorated Officer d'Acad., France, Order University Palms. Mem. A.A.A.S., Am. Assn. Pathologists and Bacteriologists, A.M.A., Am. Acad. Arts and Sciences, Med. Assn. Ga., Ga. Acad. Science, Am. Soc. Clin. Investigation, Assn. Am. Physicians, Am. Soc. Topical Medicine, Tb Assn.,

Phi Beta Kappa. Club: Cosmos. Contbr. sci. jours. on immunity, anaphylaxis, tuberculosis, hemorrhagic diseases, blood groups, transfusion, diptheria, influenza, etc. Home: 2815 Jefferson Rd. Address: P.O. Box 231, Athens, Ga. Died Aug. 12, 1957; buried Athens.

MOTEN, Roger Henwood (mŏt'ĕn); b. Erie, Pa., Aug. 31, 1879; s. Zacharias and Emily Jane (Henwood) M.; A.B., Allegheny Coll., 1901, A.M., 1915; post-grad. U. Denver, 1905, U. Colo., 1906-07; Litt.D., Colo. Coll., 1920; m. Jessie Caroline Barclay, Aug. 14, 1913; children—Roger Henwood, Clement Gile, Emily Jane. Tchr. St. John's Coll., Denver, 1901, Loveland (Colo.) High Sch., 1902-04; head of English dept. North Side High Sch., Denver, 1904-07; prof. English, Westminster U., Denver, 1907-09; asst. prof. English, Colo. Coll., 1909-13, prof., 1913-21, sec., 1916-21, also state high sch. insp. for coll.; chmn. com. on investigation of English teaching in Colo., 1912-20. Rep. of 8th dist. Nat. Collegiate Athletic Assn., 1912-20; gov. 21st dist. Internat. Assn. of Rotary Clubs, 1919-20, exec. sec., 1920-23, boys' work sec., 1922-25; exec. sec. Woodcraft League of Am., 1925-28; treas. of Trinity Coll., 1929-37; sch. dir. Wethersfield, 1934—; mgr. John Hancock Ins. Co., Hartford, Conn., 1939-42; dean, head dept. English, Hillyer Jr. Coll., 1942-45, dean emeritus, 1945—; chmn. dept. English, Hartford Branch, U. Conn., 1946—. Trustee Forman Sch., Litchfield, Conn. Mem. Selective Service Draft Board. Mem. exec. council of Episcopal Diocese of Conn. Mem. Colo. Tchrs. Assn., Coll. and Univ. Treas.' and Bus. Officers Assn. (exec. com. 1934-35), Conn. Assn. Boards of Edn. (pres), Phi Beta Kappa, Phi Delta Theta, Tau Kappa Alpha, Alpha Kappa Psi. Republican. Episcopalian. Clubs: Rotary, Winter Night (Colorado Springs). Author: Value of Poetry in the Schools. Has dramatized various works by standard authors. Home: 30 Center St., Wethersfield, Conn. Died Feb. 7, 1951.

MOTLEY, Emery Tyler, educator; b. Motley, Ala., June 20, 1889; s. Joseph Pinckney and Olive Ardecia (Middlebrooks) M.; B.S., Ala. Poly. Inst., 1913, M.S., 1916; grad. work Ia. State Coll., 1921-22, U. of Wis., 1922-24; m. Viola Bradley, Aug. 22, 1918. Grad. asst. Ala. Poly. Inst., 1914-16, instr. chemistry, 1916-17; head prof. chemistry Sch. Pharmacy Western Res. U., 1917-21; grad. asst. chemistry Ia. State Coll., 1921-22; instr. pharmacy U. of Wis., 1922-24; dean Sch. Pharmacy U. of S.C., 1924—. Mem. Am. and S.C. pharm. assns., S.C. Acad. Sci., Phi Pi Phi, Kappa Psi. Home: 802 Sumter, Columbia 1, S.C. Died June 24, 1952; buried Oak Hill Cemetery, Butler, Mo.

MOTRY, Hubert Louis, clergyman; degrees S.T.D., J.C.D.; prof. canon law and dean Sch. Canon Law, Cath. U. of Am., Washington. Died May 18, 1952.

MOTT, John R., Y.M.C.A. official; b. Livingston Manor, N.Y., May 25, 1865; s. John S. and Elmira (Dodge) M.; Ph.B., Cornell U., 1888; hon. A.M., Yale, 1899; LL.D., University of Edinburgh, 1910, Princeton University, 1911, Brown, 1931, Toronto University, 1944; married Leila Ada White, Nov. 26, 1891. Student sec. Internat. Com. Y.M.C.A.'s, 1888-1915, and gen. sec. same, 1915-31; also foreign sec. same, 1898-1915, and gen. sec. Nat. Council of Y.M.C.A.'s, U.S. of Am. to 1928; hon. life pres. World's Com. and World's Alliance of Y.M.C.A.'s, 1926—. Chmn. exec. com. Student Volunteer Movement, 1888-1920; gen. sec. World's Student Christian Fedn., 1895-1920; chmn. same, 1920-28; chmn. Continuation Com. World Missionary Conference, Edinburgh, 1910-20; chmn. Internat. Missionary Council, 1921, hon. chmn., Jan. 1942—. President (hon.) World Council of Chs., 1948—. Made repeated tours throughout world in interest World Mission to Christianity from 1900 to 1941. Member Mexican Comn. apptd. by President Wilson, 1916, and mem. Special Diplomatic Mission to Russia, 1917; during World War served as gen. sec. Nat. War Work Council Y.M.C.A. Extended assn. service to Allied armies and prisoner-of-war camps throughout Europe, Knight Legion of Honor (French); D.S.M. (U.S.), Order of the Sacred Treasure (Japan), Order of Jade (China), Commander, Order of White Lion (Czechoslovakia), Prince Carl Medal (Sweden), Nobel Peace Prize (Norway). Fellow Royal Geographical Society; member Phi Beta Kappa. Clubs: Yale, Princeton, Cornell. Author: Strategic Points in the World's Conquest, 1897; Evangelization of the World in This Generation, 1900; Christians of Reality, 1902; Pastor and Modern Missions, 1904; The Future Leadership of the Church, 1909; The Decisive Hour of Christian Missions, 1910; The Present World Situation, 1914; World Student Christian Federation, 1920; Confronting Young Men with the Living Christ, 1923; The Moslem World of Today, 1924; The Present Day Summons to the World Mission of Christianity, 1931; Liberating the Lay Forces of Christianity, 1932; Cooperation and the World Mission, 1935; Five Decades and a Forward View, 1939; Methodists United for Action, 1939; The Larger Evangelism, 1944; Addresses and Papers of John R. Mott, 6 vols. also many pamphlets and articles. Home: 528 E. Washington St., Orlando, Fla. Died Jan. 31, 1955; buried Washington Cathedral, Washington.

MOTT, T(homas) Bentley, army officer; b. Leesburgh, Va., May 16, 1865; s. Armistead Randolph and Virginia (Bentley) M.; grad. U.S. Mil. Acad., 1886; m. Georgette Saint Paul, May 1923. Commd. promoted through grades to lt.-col., 1911; retired, 1914; recalled to active service, 1917; col. Nat. Army, 1918; col. U.S. Army, 1918. Instr. in tactics U.S. Mil. Acad., 1890-94; a.d.c. to Maj.-Gen. Merritt, 1896-98, 1899-1900; commended in orders for gallantry and services in Manila campaign: mil. attaché Am. Embassy, Paris, 1900-05, 09-13; in banking business in Paris, France. With Root Mission to Russia, mission to Italy, 1917; attached to Gen. Pershing's staff, in France, 1918, Marshal Foch's staff as rep. of Gen. Pershing, mil. attaché to Am. Embassy, Paris, 1919-30. Decorated Silver Star, D.S.M., Legion of Merit (U.S.); Comdr. Legion of Honor (French); Officer de l'Ordre de Leopold (Belgian); Companion of St. Michael and St. George (British); Officer Order of St. Stanislas (Russian). Episcopalian. Clubs: Union (N.Y.C.); Metropolitan (Washington); Union (Paris). Author: Biography of Myron T. Herrick; Twenty Years as Military Attaché; also numerous articles on mil. service and travel; prize medal essayist, Mil. Service Instn. Address: American Battle Monuments Commission, 2 Ave. Gabriel, Paris, France. Died Dec. 1952.

MOTTER, Orton B., pub. relations counsel; born Riverside, Ill., Jan. 21, 1904; s. William Nelson and Grace (Williams) M.; A.B., Beloit (Wis.) College, 1925; student Washington and Lee U. Law Sch.; m. Helen Louise Wilcox, Feb. 26, 1932; children—Lucinda O., Victoria H. Began as correspondent for United Press, also reporter for Evanston (Ill.) News Index, Palm Beach (Fla.) Post; staff mem. Fairchild Publs., N.Y. City, 1925-27; dir. pub., B. Kuppenheimer & Co.; editor, Tomorrow's Merchant, Chicago, 1927-29; pres. Orton B. Motter & Associates, pub. relations, Chicago, 1929-32; lecturer and traveler, Spain and N. Africa, 1932-33; advt. mgr. Daily Palma Post, Palma, Majorca, Balearic Islands, 1933; asso. and vice pres. Carl Byoir & Associates, N.Y. City, 1934-45, v.p. since 1945; v.p. in charge pub. relations, Graham-Paige Motors Corp., Willow Run, Mich., since 1945, mem. board since 1946; president O. B. Motter and Associates, N.Y. City; formerly mem. board dirs. and v.p. in charge pub. relations, Kaiser-Frazer Corp., Willow Run, Mich.; formerly pub. relations account exec. for Merchandise Mart (Chicago), Marshall Field & Co., Libby-Owens-Ford Glass Co., Brown Paper Co., Freeport Sulphur Co., North American Co., Willys-Overland-Motors, nationally publicizing "jeep," Warren City Mfg. Co. Mem. Am. Acad. Polit. and Social Science, Beta Theta Pi, Sigma Delta Chi, Delta Sigma Rho. Episcopalian. Clubs: Press (Chicago); University, Metropolitan (N.Y.); Athletic (Detroit). Author: Advertising Our Way Back to Prosperity, 1932; Sytle: Our Newest Economic Dictator, 1933. Home: Great Oaks Farm, Rockrimmon Rd., R.F.D. 1, Stamford, Conn. Office: 500 5th Av., N.Y.C. Died Aug. 5, 1953.

MOULD, Elmer Wallace King (mōld), coll. prof.; b. Green Island, N.Y., Oct. 6, 1886; s. William C. and Lottie Agnes (King) M.; A.B., Union Coll., 1909; A.M., Yale U. Div. Sch., 1911, B.D., 1913; student U. of Jena, 1913-14, U. of Heidelberg, 1914, Am. Sch. Oriental Research, Jerusalem, 1914; Ph.D., U. of Chicago, 1930; m. Gertrude Van Auken Tyndall, October 14, 1915; children—Gertrude Tyndall (dec.), Jessie Charlotte Tyndall (Mrs. Rex Hanna Knowles). Instr. mathematics and Latin, Mercersburg Acad., 1909-10; asst. to pastor Center Church, New Haven, Conn., 1910-13; pastor First Reformed Ch., Little Falls, N.J., 1915-19; Alexander Cameron Mackenzie prof. Bibl. history and lit., Elmira Coll., since 1919; ordained minister Presbyn. Ch. U.S.A. George E. Day fgn. fellow of Yale U., 1913-14. Alumni lecturer, Yale U. Div. Sch., 1941. Lecturer, Chautauqua (N.Y.) Institution since 1947. Mem. Soc. Bibl. Lit. and Exegesis, Nat. Assn. Bibl. Instrs. (pres. 1934; treas. 1938-42, historian, 1949), Am. Assn. Univ. Profs., Phi Beta Kappa, Pi Gamma Mu, Theta Chi Beta. Author: Essentials of Bible History, 1939; The World-View of Jesus, 1941; Bible Tests, 1947; Bible History Digest, 1950. Home: 503 Fitch St., Elmira, N.Y. Died Nov. 15, 1950; buried Woodlawn Cemetery, Elmira.

MOULTON, Earl L., corp. exec.; b. LeRoy, Mich., Sept. 26, 1878; s. Belah G. and Mary C. (Smith) M.; student Albion (Mich.) Coll., U. of Chicago; honorary A.M., University of New Mexico, 1946; m. Louise Peirce, June 29, 1905; children—Ethel Louise Bond, Mary Easter Lovelace, Gertrude Earl Kinney. Teacher, public schs., Mich., 1897-98; private tutor, Chicago, 1899-1902; sheep herder, N.M., 1902-04; with partners in sheep business, 1904-07; real estate business, 1907-09; mercantile business, Lucy, N.M., 1909-12; mgr. and pres., Corona Trading Co., Corona, N.M., 1912-20; chmn. bd. Charles Ilfeld Co., and asso. wholesale gen. mdse. cos. (16 branches in New Mexico and Colo.). Chairman Tax Advisory Committee to New Mexico Legislature, 1947. United States Commr., New Mexico, 1907-10; postmaster; mem. Co. Sch. Bd.; chmn. Co. Commrs., 1907-20; dir. C. of C. U.S. 9th Dist., 1950-52; pres. Taxpayers Assn. N.M., N.M.; mem. Reclamation Assn.; chmn. Little Hoover Com. N.M., 1951-52, former pres. N.M. Council Boy Scouts of Am., mem. at large of Nat. Council. Clubs: Rotary (past pres.), Ten Dons, Albuquerque Country Club. Mason. Presbyterian. Author—Odyssey of a Flockmaster; New Mexico's Future; New Mexico in the War. Home: 1600 Los Alamos Dr. S.W., Albuquerque, N.M. Died June 25, 1958.

MOULTON, Forest Ray, astronomer; b. Le Roy, Mich., Apr. 29, 1872; s. Belah G. and Mary C. (Smith) M.; A.B., Albion Coll., 1894; Ph.D. summa cum laude, U. Chgo., 1899; Sc.D., Albion (Mich.) Coll., 1922; LL.D., Drake U., 1939; Sc.D., Case Sch. Applied Sci., 1940; m. Estelle Gillette, Mar. 25, 1897; 2 sons, 2 daus. Asso. in astronomy U. Chgo., 1898-1900, instr., 1900-03, asst. prof., 1903-08, asso. prof., 1908-12, prof., 1912-26; asso. editor Transactions Am. Math. Soc., 1907-12; adminstrv. sec. A.A.A.S., 1937-48. Research asso. Carnegie Instn., 1908-23; dir. Utilities Power & Light Corporation, 1920-38. Maj., Ordnance Dept. U.S. Army, in charge of ballistics of Am. arty., 1918-19; lt. col. Ordnance U.S.R. Fellow Royal Astron. Soc., A.A. A.S., Am. Philos. Soc., Am. Acad. Arts and Sciences; mem. Nat. Acad. Sciences, Am. Math. Soc., Am. Astron. Soc.; hon fgn. asso. Brit. Assn. Adv. Science. Author: Celestial Mechanics, 1902, 14; Introduction to Astronomy, 1905, 16; Descriptive Astronomy, 1911; Periodic Orbits, 1920; New Methods in Exterior Ballistics, 1926; Differential Equations, 1929; Astronomy, 1931; Consider the Heavens, 1935; Autobiography of Science (with J. J. Schifferes), 1945. Contbr. and editor of The World and Man, 1937. Editor of 25 A.A.A.S. sci. symposium vols. Contbr. to math. and astron. jours. Trustee and dir. of Concessions World's Fair, Chicago, 1933. Home: 1637 Orrington St., Evanston, Ill. Died Dec. 8, 1952.

MOULTON, Vern, insurance exec.; b. LeRoy, Mich., Feb. 14, 1880; s. Belah G. and Mary C. (Smith) M.; student U. of Chicago, Mich. State Coll., Lansing Business Univ.; Dr. Bus. Adminstrn., Albion College, 1955; m. Effie L. Campbell, August 24, 1910; 1 son, Donald C. Operated 480 acre farm, LeRoy, Mich., 1900-07; clerical position Mich. State Land Office and Mich. Dept. Ins., actuarial div., Lansing, Mich., 1909-12; mgr. Gold Reserve Life Assn., Mt. Pleasant, Mich., 1912-16; co-organizer Auto-Owners Ins. Co., 1916, treas., 1916-21, sec.-treasurer, 1921-28, president since 1928; president of the Michigan Refrigerating & Warehouse Company; pres. Peoples State Saving Bank, 1929-35; vice pres. Lansing Ice & Fuel Co., Dail Steel Products Co.; co-organizer and dir. Central Trust Co.; dir. Mich. Nat. Bank, Mich. Life Ins. Co.; bd. trustees Albion Coll. Mem. bd. govs. Meth. Childrens Village; mem. bd. trustees Lansing Central Meth. Ch. Mason. Clubs: Economic (Detroit); Union League (Chicago); Inter-City Wranglers, Lansing County. Home: 640 Kensington Rd., East Lansing. Office: 303 W. Kalamazoo St., Lansing 3, Mich. Died Jan. 28, 1959; buried Evergreen Cemetery, Lansing.

MOUNGER, W. M., banker; b. Collins, Miss., Oct. 8, 1901; s. M. U. and Alma (McKenzie) M.; student Miss. State Coll.; m. Veronica Robertson, Sept. 5, 1923; children—Marjorie, William, Libby, Henry, Veronica. Pres. Deposit Guaranty Bank & Trust Co., Jackson, Miss., until 1957, vice chmn. bd., chief exec. officer 1957—. Mem. Sigma Chi. Club: Kiwanis. Home: 3833 Old Canton Rd., Jackson. Office: 200 E. Capital St., Jackson, Miss. Died Oct. 26, 1957.

MOUNTIN, Joseph W., pub. health service officer; b. Hartford, Wis., Oct. 13, 1891; s. David W. and Margaret (Garvey) M.; M.D., Marquette U., 1914; m. Genevieve Bazan, June 30, 1923; children—David, Joan, Daniel. Intern, Milwaukee County Hosp., 1914-15, also Chgo. Lying-in Hosp.; dir. Marquette U. Clinic, 1916; with USPHS, 1917—, asst. surgeon gen., asso. chief, Bur. of States Services, 1947-51, chief of bur., 1951—. Mem. A.M.A. (chmn. preventive medicine sect. 1941-43), So. Med. Assn. (chmn. pub. health sect. 1935-36), Am. Pub. Health Assn. (sec. health officers sect. 1934-35; mem. com. on adminstrv. practice 1925—). Roman Catholic. Contbr. numerous articles on public health to tech. and professional publs. Home: 3637 Brandywine St., N.W. Office: USPHS, Federal Security Bldg., S., Washington. Died Apr. 26, 1952; buried Arlington Cemetery.

MOWBRAY-CLARKE, John (Frederick), sculptor; b. Annotta Bay, Jamaica, W.I., Aug. 4, 1869; s. Myrry and Margaret Ann (Hawkins) M-C.; student pvt. schs. and grammar sch., Eng.; apprenticed to chemist Chertsey, Surrey, 1885; later studied at Lambeth Art Sch., and with F. Pomeroy; winner in competition between all schs. in London; m. Mary Helena Bothwell Horgan, Feb. 1907; 1 son, John Bothwell. Came to U.S., 1897; with Massey Rhind's Studio, 1 yr.; dir. The Sunwise Turn, book and decorative bus. As v.p. Assn. Am. Painters and Sculptors, had charge sculpture Armory Exhbn. of Modern Internat.

Art, 1913; worked in Can., 1920-26, in Oxford, Eng., 1926-53, many sculptures in bronze in Common Rooms of Oxford Colls. Studio; Malt House, Oxford, Eng. Died Nov. 30, 1953.

MOWERY, William Byron (mou'ĕr-ĭ), author; b. Adelphia, O., Aug. 15, 1899; s. Byron and Anna (Straus) M.; student O. State U., 1919-20; A.B., U. of Ill., 1921, A.M., 1922; married; children—Margaret Ann, Billy Jean, Sue Allegra; married 2d, Dorothy Dunsing, 1935; 1 daughter, Leda Joyce. Member faculty University of Illinois, 1922, Univ. of Texas, 1924; fiction and screen writer, 1923-29; novelist since 1929. Founder (1944) and director, Professional Short-Story Writing, New York University. Served with Tank Corps during World War. Member Authors' League of America, Midland Soc. of Authors. Club: The Cliff Dwellers (Chicago). Author: The Silver Hawk, 1929; The Girl from God's Mercie, 1929; Heart of the North, 1931; Singer of the Wilderness, 1931; Forbidden Valley, 1933; Challenge of the North, 1933; Resurrection River, 1934; The Phantom Canoe, 1934; The Sword of Manitou, 1935; Paradise Trail, 1936; The Black Automatic, 1936; The Valley Beyond, 1937; Stukas Over the Jungle, 1941; The Smoke Tree, 1943; The Long Arm of the Mounties, 1948; Sagas of the Mounted Police, 1953; Professional Short Story Writing, 1953; Tales of the Ozarks, 1954; Swift in the Night, 1956. Contbr. various mags. Novels translated into all prin. fgn. langs. Home: Colonial Road, Warwick, N.Y. Died Apr. 2, 1957; buried Warwick.

MOWRY, Harold (mou'rĭ), agrl. research adminstr.; b. Valley Falls, Kan., Mar. 26, 1894; s. Lyman and Margaret Olive (Wilson) M.; B.S.A., University of Florida, 1929, M.S.A., 1934, Doctor of Science, 1950; married to Anne Stutz, September 11, 1915; 1 son, Ross Elbert. With Fla. State Plant Bd. engaged in citrus canker eradication, nursery inspection and plant quarantine work, 1916-22; asst. horticulturist Fla. Agrl. Expt. Sta., 1922-30, asso. horticulturist, 1930-32, horticulturist, 1932-33, asst. dir., 1933-42, asso. dir., 1942-43, dir. 1943-50; ret., emeritus; agriculturist, cons. dir. Office of Fgn. Agr. Relations, U.S. Dept. of Agriculture, 1950-54; cons. dir. U.S. Foreign Operations Adminstrn., 1954, cons. dir. Internat. Cooperation Adminstrn. also supr. U. Fla. Agrl. Mission to Costa Rica, 1954-58; mem. agr. survey missions to Surinam, British Guiana, area development mission Bolivia, 1954. Chmn. adv. com., agrl. div. Fla. State Defense Council, 1942-45. Received Distinguished Service award, Fla. Vegetable Com., 1947; Alpha Zeta Agricultural Fla. Entomological Society, Fla. State Florists Assn. award, 1950; Medal of Merit and scroll Govt. of Costa Rica, 1958. Fellow A.A.A.S.; mem. Bot. Soc. Am., Am. Soc. Hort. Sci., Fla. Acad. Sciences, (hon. life mem.), Fla. State Hort. Soc. (hon. life member) Phi Kappa Phi, Sigma Xi, Alpha Zeta, Phi Sigma, Pi Gamma Mu, Alpha Gamma Rho, Gamma Sigma Delta. Democrat. Conglist. Mason, Kiwanian (pres. Gainesville, 1942). Author numerous expt. sta. bulls., also tech. and popular articles on agrl. subjects. Home: 203 NW 15th Terrace, Gainesville, Fla. Died Nov. 12, 1958; buried Fort Lauderdale, Fla.

MOWRY, Ross Rutledge (mou'rĭ), lawyer; b. Baxter, Ia., Mar. 5, 1882; s. John E. and Louisa (Wilkins) M.; grad. high sch., Baxter; LL.B., State U. of Ia., 1903; m. Edith Mathews, Sept. 17, 1908; children—Virginia, Gertrude (Spaulding). Admitted to Ia. bar, 1903, and began practice at Newton; mem. firm Mowry & Cross, 1904-10; moved to Newton, 1904; pros. atty. Jasper County, Ia., 1911-15; asst. atty. gen. of Ia., 1916; U.S. dist. atty. for Southern Dist. of Ia., by apptmt. of President Coolidge, May 17, 1924-32; prosecuted Keith Collins and Fred Poffenbarger for $2,000,000 rail robbery, at Council Bluffs, Ia., and secured conviction, 1925; prosecuted case of U.S. vs. Ky. Distilleries & Warehouse Co. et al., in U.S. Court, at Des Moines—12 defendants convicted and sentenced to serve 16 mos. in Federal Prison at Leavenworth, and tax of $46,816 collected from the distillery; mem. Ia. State Senate, 29th Dist., 1939-47. Mem. Iowa State Bar Assn., Sons of the Am. Revolution, Iowa State Grange, Iowa Wittenberg Grange, Iowa Farm Bureau, Pi Gamma Mu. Republican. Methodist. Mason, K.P. Club: Kiwanis. Home: Miller Hotel. Office: 102½ N. 2d Av. E., Newton, Ia. Died Sept. 28, 1957; buried Newton.

MOYER, Andrew Jackson, microbiologist; b. Star City, Ind., Nov. 30, 1899; s. Edward R. and Minnie (McCloud) M.; A.B., Wabash Coll., 1922; student U. Wis., 1922-23; M.S., N.D. Agrl. Coll., 1925; Ph.D., U. Md., 1929; m. Dorothy Randall Phillips, Apr. 4, 1931. With Dept. Agr. 1929—, last assignment No. Utilization Research, and Development Div., Fermentation Sec., U.S. Dept. Agr., Peoria, Ill., research physiology of fungi; mold fermentations; gluconic, lactic, kojic, glauconic, citric and itaconic acids from glucose; penicillin. Devised methods for producing substantial increase in yields of penicillin, making large scale prodn. possible; discovered methanol process for submerged mold fermentation of crude carbohydrates to citric acid; improved fermentation of glucose and Molasses to fumanic acid. Lasker group award, 1946. Contbr. sci. jours. Mem. Bot. Soc. of Am., Ill. Acad. Sci Phi Kappa Phi, Sigma Xi. Presbyn. Patentee in field. Address: Montgomery County, Md. Died Feb. 17, 1959.

MOYER, Harvey Vernon, educator, chemist; b. Salina, Kan., Feb. 13, 1894; s. Milton O. and Amanda Jane (Kurtz) M.; student Baker U., 1915-16; A.B., Kan. U., 1923, A.M., 1925, Ph.D., 1937; NRC fellow, Yale, 1927-29; m. Blanche Mae Galutia, June 19, 1923; 1 son, John H.; m. 2d, Mary Elizabeth Winters, Sept. 12, 1953. Asst. prof. analytical chemistry Ohio State U., 1929-34, asso. prof., 1934-38, prof., 1938—, acting chmn. dept. chemistry, chmn., 1956—, asst. dean Grad. Sch., 1947-50. Served as pvt. U.S. Army, 1918-19. Mem. Am. Chem. Soc., A.A.A.S., Ohio Acad. Scis., Am. Legion, Phi Beta Kappa, Sigma Xi. Methodist. Author: Quantitative Chemical Analysis, 1952. Editor-in-chief Polonium, 1956. Home: 2993 Sudbury Rd., Columbus 21, O. Died Aug. 5, 1959.

MUDD, Harvey Seeley, mining engr.; b. Leadville, Colo., Aug. 30, 1888; s. Seeley Wintersmith and Della (Mulock) M.; student Stanford, 1906-08; E.M., Columbia, 1912, Sc.D., 1947; LL.D., U. of Calif., 1941, Loyola U., 1943; m. Mildred Hardy Esterbrook, Mar. 12, 1913; children—Henry Thomas, Caryll Esterbrook. Began as mining engineer, Bisbee, Ariz., 1912; chairman of the board dirs. Cyprus Mines Corporation; dir. So. Pacific Co., Texas Gulf Sulphur Co.; dir. Founders Inc., Co., Mesabi Iron Company, Marcona Mining Company; voting trustee Pacific Mutual Life Ins. Co. Trustee, Rand Corp. Engineer U.S. Bureau of Mines and asst. sec. War Minerals Committee, World War I. Awarded Egleston Medal. Trustee Southwest Museum, California Inst. Tech.; v. chmn. bd. of fellows Claremont College; mem. advisory com., Henry E. Huntington Library and Art Gallery. Mem. American Institute Mining and Metall. Engineers (mem., p.p.); mem. Mining and Metall. Soc. Am., Soc. Colonial Wars, S.R., Soc. Civil Engrs. (hon.), Sigma Xi, Delta Tau Delta, Tau Beta Pi. Republican. Conglist. Clubs: University, California. Bohemian, Los Angeles Country, Knickerbocker, Recess (N.Y.C.). Home: 1240 Benedict Canyon Drive, Beverly Hills, Cal. Office: Pacific Mutual Bldg., Los Angeles, Cal. Died Apr. 12, 1955.

MUDD, Mildred Esterbrook (Mrs. Harvey Seeley Mudd), hon. v.p. Girl Scouts; b. Jersey City, Feb. 21, 1891; d. Richard and Mary (Nichols) Esterbrook; student Louise Veltin Sch., N.Y.C., 1905-09; m. Harvey Seeley Mudd, Mar. 12, 1913; children—Henry Thomas, Caryll Esterbrook (Mrs. Norman F. Sprague, Jr.). Dir. Children's Hosp. of Los Angeles. Commr. Los Angeles Council, Girl Scouts, Inc., 1934-37, dep. commr., 1937-38, chmn. orgn. com., 1938-39, now 2d v.p. and chmn. membership nominating com.; mem. Nat. Bd., 1937—; nat. pres. Girl Scouts, Inc., 1939-41, 1st v.p., 1941-43, hon. v.p., 1943—. Viec pres. womens com. Los Angeles Philharmonic Orchestra; charter mem. Opera Guild of So. Cal. (bd. dirs.). Republican. Episcopalian. Clubs: Women's Athletic (Los Angeles); Women's National Republican (N.Y.C.); American Women's (London). Home: 1240 Benedict Canon Dr., Beverly Hills, Cal. Died Sept. 1958.

MUDGE, Isadore Gilbert, librarian; b. Bklyn., Mar. 14, 1875; d. Alfred Eugene and Mary Gilbert (Ten Brook) M.; grad. Adelphi Acad., Bklyn., 1893; Ph.B., Cornell U., 1897; B.L.S., N.Y. State Library Sch., Albany, 1900. Reference librarian and asst. prof. library sci. U. Ill., 1900-03, librarian Bryn Mawr Coll., 1903-08; instr. library sci. Simmons Coll., Boston, 1910-11; reference librarian Columbia, 1911-41, retired 1941, asso. prof. bibliography, 1927-38. Mem. A.L.A., N.Y. State Library Assn. (v.p.), N.Y. Library Club (pres.), Kappa Alpha Theta, Phi Beta Kappa. Author: (with M. E. Sears) Thackeray Dictionary, 1910; (with W. D. Johnston) Special Collections in Libraries in the United States (Govt. Printing Office), 1912; Bibliography, 1915; Guide to Reference Books, 6th edit., 1936; (with M. E. Sears) George Eliot Dictionary, 1924. Editor: Kroeger's Guide to the Study and Use of Reference Books (3d edit.); editor of Columbia Univ. Bibliography (ann.), 1911-30. Address: Yorktown Heights, N.Y. Died May 1957.

MUDGE, Verne Donald, army officer; b. Bangor, S.D., Sept. 5, 1898; ed. U. of Florida; B.S., U.S. Mil. Acad., 1920; grad. Cav. Sch., 1921, Command and Gen. Staff Sch., 1935, Army War Coll., 1940. Commd. 2d lt., U.S. Army, 1920, and advanced through the grades to maj. gen., 1944; on duty in personnel division, War Dept. Gen. Staff, Washington, D.C., 1940-42; chief of staff, 1st Cav. Div., 1942; comd. 5th Cav. Brigade, Fort Clark, Tex., 1942-43, 2d Cav. Brigade, Fort Bliss, Tex., Australia, New Guinea and Admiraltys, 1943-44; became commanding general, first Cav. Division, Southwest Pacific Area, Aug. 1944, and led the division in invasion of Leyte, Samar and Luzon, P.I. Wounded in action, Feb. 28, 1945. Apptd. to professional staff, Senate Com. on Armed Services, 1947-55. Awarded D.S.C., D.S.M., Legion of Merit, Silver Star, Bronze Star, Air Medal, Purple Heart. Address: 2674 Rosecrans St., San Diego 6, Cal. Died Jan. 29, 1957; buried Ft. Rosecrans Nat. Cemetery, San Diego.

MUDGE, William Leroy, clergyman; b. Yonkers, N.Y., Jan. 25, 1872; s. Rev. Lewis Ward and Elizabeth (Seymour) M.; A.B. cum laude, Princeton, 1892, A.M., 1893, grad. Princeton Theol. Sem., 1896; D.D., Ursinus Coll., Collegeville, Pa., 1934; m. Laura Maxwell Buck, July 25, 1901; children—William Leroy Mudge, Jr. (died Aug. 22, 1944 in service), Sidney Reeves, Mrs. Joseph Milliken Woods. Ordained to ministry of Presbyn. Ch., 1896; pastor Phoenixville, Pa., 1896-1904, Lewistown, Pa., 1904-15, Chambersburg, Pa., 1915-28; exec. sec. Mifflin County Inter-Ch. Fedn., 1908-15, of Franklin County Council of Chs., 1916-28; part-time exec. sec. Pa. Council of Chs., 1911-28, full time exec. sec., hdqrs. at Harrisburg, Pa., 1928-46, ret.; chmn. com. on ch. cooperation and union Presbyn. Synod Pa., 1910-46; commr. to gen. assembly Presbyn. Ch. in U.S.A., 1923. Mem. bd. trustees, Pa. Prison Soc. Chmn., Dept. Inter-ch. Relations, State Coll. Council of Churches. Mem. Fed. Council of Chs. of Christ in Am. (mem. dept. evangelism 1930-34), Nat. Assn. Exec. Secs. Councils and Fedns. Chs., Nat. Conf. Family Relations, Pa. Conf. on Family Relations, Pa. Anti-Saloon League, Pa. Welfare Conf., Pa. Country Life Assn. (one of organizers Ch. and Country Life movement, 1909), Pa. Soc. Christian Endeavor, Unified Staff of Pa. State Council of Christian Edn., others. Author numerous articles, leaflets, pamphlets on cooperative ch. movements, 1909—. Home: 306 E. Foster Av., State College, Pa. Died Aug. 8, 1956.

MUELLER, Edward, chemist; b. South Bend, Ind., Oct. 16, 1883; s. Frederick William and Anna Margaret (Sack) M.; B.S., Purdue, 1902; A.M., Harvard, 1905, Ph.D., 1907; studied Heidelberg U., Germany, 1908; m. Georgiana Crane, Aug. 21, 1913. Chemist Norfolk & Western Ry. Co., Roanoke, Va., 1902-04; asst. in chemistry, Harvard, 1905-07; instr. chemistry, Washington U. Med. Sch., 1907-10, Tufts Coll., 1910-11; instr. chemistry, Mass. Inst. Tech., 1911-13, asst. prof., 1913-20, asso. prof., 1920-29; chemical consultant since 1929; in charge of chemistry Franklin Tech. Inst., 1942-46. Fellow A.A.A.S., Am. Acad. Arts and Sciences; mem. Am. Chem. Soc., Tau Beta Pi. Translator: Holde's Hydro-carbon Oils and Saponifiable Fats and Waxes, 1915, 2d edit., 1922. Contbr. to publs. Carnegie Instn. Washington, also to Jour. Am. Chem. Soc., Chem. News, etc. Redetermined the atomic weights of potassium and chromium. Home: Burton Halls, 10 Dana St., Cambridge 38, Mass. Died Aug. 9, 1954.

MUELLER, John Howard, bacteriologist; b. Sheffield, Mass., June 13, 1891; s. John Henry and Sarah Eva (Pease) M.; B.S., Ill. Wesleyan U., 1912; M.S., U. of Louisville, 1914; Ph.D., Columbia U., 1916; m. Mary R. Gilbert, July 6, 1916. Instr. biol. chemistry, U. of Louisville, 1912-14; Alonzo Clark fellow, Columbia U., 1914-16; asst. in pathology, Columbia U., 1916-17, asst. in bacteriology, 1919-20, asst. prof. bacteriology, 1920-22, asso. prof., 1922-23; asst. prof. bacteriology and immunology, Harvard Med. Sch., 1923-30, asso. prof., 1930-42, prof. and head of dept. since 1942. Successively private, sergeant and 1st lt. Sanitary Corps, U.S. Army, May 1917-Mar. 1919. Consultant to Sec'y of War, 1941-45. Consultant to Fed. Sec. Agency, 1942-44, and to C.W.S., 1944-46. Mem. Nat. Acad. Sciences, Am. Acad. Arts and Sciences, N.Y. Acad. Sciences, Soc. Am. Bacteriologists, Soc. Biol. Chemistry, Assn. Pathology and Bacteriology, Soc. Immunology, Soc. Exptl. Biology and Medicine, Harvey Society. Fellow A.P.H.A. Author various articles on bacteriology and immunology. Club: Harvard of Boston. Home: 2176 Centre St., West Roxbury, Mass. Died Feb. 16, 1954.

MUELLER, Paul Albert, lawyer; b. Phila., Oct. 20, 1897; s. George P and Anna Catherine (Stump) M.; A.B., Franklin and Marshall Coll., 1921; LL.B., U. Pa., 1922, LL.M., 1923, LL.D., 1954; m. Alma C. Sprecher, Aug. 16, 1928; children—Paul A., John C. Admitted to Pa. bar, 1922, practiced in Lancaster, 1923—; dist. atty. Lancaster Co., Pa., 1932-36; dir. Animal Trap Co. Am., Consumers Ice Co. of Lancaster, Vulcan Machine Co., Mac-It Parts Co., William H. Nobble & Son, Inc., Buch Mfg. Co. Del. Rep. Nat. Conv., 1948. Pres. Lancaster Gen. Hosp., 1943-45; truastee Franklin and Marshall Coll., Law Sch. U. Pa. Am., Pa. (pres. 1955), Lancaster (pres. 1952-54) bar assns., Am. Judicature Soc., Am. Law Inst., Am. Legion, Phi Beta Kappa, Order of Coif. Republican. Lutheran. Elk. Clubs: Hamilton, Lancaster Country, Union League (Phila.). Home: 1412 Ridge Rd. Office: 45 N. Duke St., Lancaster, Pa. Died Nov. 7, 1956.

MUELLER, Theodore Edward, ret. chmn. Am. Radiator & Standard Sanitary Corp.; b. Louisville, Apr. 3, 1885; s. Adolph E. and Anna (Ahrens) M.; student pub. and pvt. schs.; m. Pattie C. Johnston, June 16, 1916. Asso. Am. Radiator & Standard Sanitary Corp., 1904-54, beginning as pattern maker, apptd. mgr. Louisville plant, 1913, v.p. 1929-46, pres., 1946-53, chmn. bd., 1953-54, ret. Republican. Clubs: Duquesne (Pitts.); Pendennis (Louisville); Metropolitan, Engineers (N.Y.C.). Home: Shady

Brook Farm, Upper River Rd., Louisville 7. Office: Bessemer Bldg., Pitts. Died Sept. 24, 1957.

MUELLER, Theodore Frederick, publisher; b. New York City, Jan. 24, 1899; s. Matthew and Anna Marie (Jensen) M.; ed. pub. and pvt. schs.; m. Joyce Nebeker, Aug. 24, 1940. With McGraw-Hill Pub. Co., Inc., 1917-37, asst. to pres., 1932-37; with Newsweek Mag. since 1937, bus. mgr., 1940-43, v.p., 1943-49, publisher since 1949; dir. Weekly Pubs., Inc. Mem. Mag. Pubs. Assn. (dir.), W. Side Assn. Commerce (dir.), American Arbitration Association. Clubs: Engineers', Salmagundi (New York); Winged Foot golf (Westchester). Home: One Fifth Av., N.Y.C. Office: Newsweek Bldg., N.Y.C. 36. Died Apr. 1, 1958; buried Ferncliff, Westchester County, N.Y.

MULDOON, Hugh Cornelius (mŭl-dōōn), educator; b. Truxton, N.Y.; s. Michael and Elizabeth (Warren) M.; Ph.G., Union U., Albany, N.Y., 1912; B.S., Valparaiso U., 1920, D.Sc., 1925; student Mass. Coll. of Pharmacy, and at Boston, Harvard, Ind., Duquesne univs.; D.Sc., St. Johns U. 1954; Pharm.D., Mass. Coll. Pharmacy, 1954. Instr. chemistry and Latin, Mass. Coll. of Pharmacy, 1912-18; prof. chemistry, Albany Coll. of Pharmacy, Union U., 1918-20, and acting dean, 1918-19; prof. chemistry and dean Sch. of Pharmacy, Valparaiso U., 1920-25; dean School of Pharmacy, Duquesne U., 1925-55, ret. Mem. revision com. U.S. Pharmacopoeia, 1930-50; pres. Am. Assn. Colls. Pharmacy, 1937-38. Fellow A.A.A.S., Royal Society of Arts of London; member American Chem. Soc., Am. Pharmacy Assn. (Remington honor medal 1953), Pa. Pharmacy Assn., Pa. Acad. Science, National Science Teachers Assn., Nat. Soc. Study of Edn., Phi Delta Chi, Phi Delta Psi, Rho Chi, Phi Sigma. Republican. Roman Catholic. Author: Lessons in Pharmaceutical Latin, 1946; Organic Chemistry for Students of the Medical Sciences, 1948; Laboratory Manual of Organic Chemistry, 1927. Editor of The Science Counselor since 1935. Contbr. to pharm. jours. Home: William Penn Hotel, Pittsburgh, Pa.; and "Lazy M," Dushore, Pa. Died May 4, 1956; buried St. James' Cemetery, Waverly, N.Y.

MULFORD, Clarence Edward, author; b. Streator, Ill., Feb. 3, 1883; s. Clarence C. and Minnie Grace (Kline) M.; ed. pub. and high schs., Streator, and Utica (N.Y.) Acad.; m. Eva E. Wilkinson, Jan. 5, 1920. Author: Bar-20, 1907; The Orphan, 1908, 24; Hopalong Cassidy, 1910; Bar-20 Days, 1911; Buck Peters, Ranchman, 1912; Coming of Cassidy, 1913; Man from Bar-20, 1918; Johnny Nelson, 1920; Bar-20 Three, 1921; Tex, 1922; Bring Me His Ears, 1922; Black Buttes, 1923; Rustlers' Valley, 1924; Hopalong Cassidy Returns, 1924; Cottonwood Gulch, 1925; Hopalong Cassidy's Protégé, 1926; Bar-20 Rides Again, 1926; Corson of the J. C., 1927; Mesquite Jenkins, 1928; Me an' Shorty, 1929; The Deputy Sheriff, 1930; Hopalong Cassidy and the Eagle's Brood, 1931; Mesquite Jenkins—Tumbleweed, 1932; The Round-Up, 1933; Trail Dust, 1934; On the Trail of the Tumbling T, 1935; Hopalong Cassidy Takes Cards, 1937; Hopalong Cassidy Serves a Writ, 1941. Died May 1956.

MULLEN, Thomas Richard, industrialist; b. Brooklyn, N.Y., Apr. 2, 1893; s. Thomas Richard and Elizabeth (Dellamore) M.; student St. Michael's Parochial Sch., Brooklyn, 1899-1908, Manual Training High Sch., Brooklyn, 1908-10, night high sch. classes, 1910-12; D.Sc (honorary), Lafayette College, 1951; LL.D. (honorary), Muhlenberg College, 1955; married Lillian Schetelig, February 22, 1919; children—Thomas R. (died Nov. 16, 1948), Ruth Elizabeth (Mrs. Thomas V. Sheehy), Richard Leslie. Entered structural steel fabricating industry as clerk, Levering & Garrigues, New York, New York, 1910-16; purchasing agent, Philadelphia office, The Austin Company, 1916-18; sales manager on formation Lehigh Structural Steel Co., Allentown, Pa., 1919-22, vice pres. in charge of sales, 1922-33, treas. and gen. mgr., 1933-44, pres. since 1944; pres. Lehigh Constrn. Co. since 1933, Utility Service Co. since 1933; dir. Lehigh Valley Trust Co. Trustee, Dr. Walter Kempner Found., Duke U. Development Campaign, Sacred Heart Hosp. Allentown, Pa. Nat. asso. Boys Club of America. Mem. Am. Inst. Steel Constrn. (dir. 1934—, treas., mem. bd. dirs. 1936-44, pres. 1946-48, mem. exec. com.), Iron League N.Y. (pres. 1944—), Acad. Polit. Sci., N.A.M. Republican. R.C. Clubs: Camp Fire of America (past treas. and mem. bd. govs.); Bergen Beach Yacht, Whitehall (N.Y.); Livingston (Allentown, Pa.). Author: (biography) Thomas R. Mullen, Jr., 1950. Home: 87 86th St., Brooklyn 9. Office: 17 Battery Pl., N.Y. City 4. Died Dec. 2, 1958; buried Holy Rood Cemetery, L.I., N.Y.

MULLENIX, Charles A. (mŭl'ĕn-iks), pres., treas. The Cuyahoga Estates Co.; b. Springfield, O., Jan. 21, 1887; s. Marcellus Q. and Mary (Klosterman) M.; student Wittenberg Coll., 1906-07; m. Grace L. Bailey, Mar. 26, 1908; one dau., Mary Jane (Mrs. Paul R. Abernathy); m. 2d Henrietta W. Hartwig, June 11, 1927, one dau., Gladys Emilie; m. 3d Alice R. Miller. Acct. P. P. Past & Co., 1908-10; chief-acct., Peoria (Ill.) Drill & Seeder Co., 1910-12; asst. sales mgr., New Idea Spreader Co., Coldwater, O., 1912-18; gen. mgr., Marion (O.) Tire & Rubber Co., 1920-21; asst. supt. of bldgs., Cleveland Bd. of Edn., 1922-26; pres., treas. The Cuyahoga Estates Co., Cleveland, O., since 1924; v.p., treas. Metropolitan Ohio Corp. since 1928. Mem. Mortgage Bankers Assn. (pres. 1943), Cleveland Assn. of Apartment House Owners (pres. 1932), Nat. Assn. Apartment House Owners (pres. 1933-34), Cleveland Mortgage Bankers Asso. (pres. 1938), Real Estate Board, Ohio and Nat. Real Estate Bds., Am. Inst. of Real Estate Appraisers. Republican. Mason. Club: Midday (Cleveland). Home: 21447 Avalon Dr., Rocky River, O. Office: 1220 Huron Rd., Room 510, Cleve. 15. Died Nov. 8, 1953; buried Lakewood Park Cemetery.

MULLER, Amelia A(nnie), newspaper woman, artist; b. Baltimore, Dec. 27, 1887; d. James Clay and Julia May (Keenright) Muller; early art training from father; art student, Md. Inst., Sch. of Art and Design. In newspaper work with Baltimore American, 1918-20; with Baltimore Sun, covering gen. assignments, ch. news, features and illustrating some stories, 1920-50; creator Calicolors (name, designating pictures in which media used includes pieces of calico, percale and other cotton materials), also workers in oils and crayons; had one-man show of calicolors at Maryland Institute School of Art and Design, Peale Museum (Baltimore), Baltimore Museum of Art, State Teachers College (Towson, Maryland), Washington Co. Museum of Fine Arts (Hagerstown, Md.), Arts Club (Washington) since 1938; represented in permanent pvt. collections. Home: Home for Incurables, 700 W. 40th St., Balt. 11. Died June 5, 1952.

MULLER, Margarethe (Magdalene Karoline Elisabeth), educator; b. Hanover, Germany, Sept. 25, 1862; d. Hermann Friedrich Christian and Emile Louise Elisabeth (Bauermeister) M.; grad. Hanover Normal Coll., 1884; student U. Göttingen, 1895-97; sem. work with Profs. Moritz Heyne and Lorenz Morsbach. Came to U.S., 1885. Tchr., Concord, N.H., 1885-89; instr. Wellesley Coll., 1889-95, asso. prof., 1897-1904, prof. dept. German, 1904-23, ret. Editor: Schiller's Maria Stuart, 1900; Keller's Legenden, 1901. Author: Gluck Auf, 1901; Carla Wenckebach, Pioneer, 1908; Elsbeth, a Story of German Home Life, 1914. Contbr. to Am. and German mags. Address: Munich, Germany. Died Jan. 5, 1934; buried Munich.

MULLIGAN, David B., ret. chmn. bd. Realty Hotels, Inc. Address: Hotel Barclay, 111 E. 48th St., N.Y.C. 17. Deceased.*

MULLINS, George Walker, educator; b. Fayetteville, Ark., Feb. 11, 1881; s. William Madison and Sophia (Freyschlag) M.; A.B., U. Ark., 1904, LL.D., 1935; A.M., Columbia, 1913, Ph.D., 1917; m. Hazel Provence, Dec. 24, 1908; children—Dorothy Provence (Mrs. E. Morton Holland), George Walker (dec.), John Madison. Instr. mathematics Mountain Home Coll. (Ark.), 1904-05, Simmons Coll. (Tex.), 1905-12; instr. math. Barnard Coll., Columbia, 1913-19, asst. prof., 1919-23, asso. prof., 1923-28, prof., 1928-48, prof. emeritus, 1948—, acting dean, 1929-31, chmn. exec. com., 1946—, Entrance Exam. Bd. Trustee Columbia U. Press, Woodstock (Vt.) Country Sch. Mem. bd. govs. Dunford House, London. Mem. Am. Math. Soc. (trustee 1929-48), Math. Assn. Am., Am. Assn. U. Profs., Phi Beta Kappa, Sigma Nu. Ind. Democrat. Baptist. Clubs: Century, Faculty. Author: Differential Invariants under Inversion Group; (with D. E. Smith) Freshman Mathematics, 1928; (with A. M. Harding) Analytic Geometry, 1924; Trigonometry, 1928; College Algebra, 1928. Editor: Geometry and Its Uses, 1930; Algebra and Its Uses, 1932. Home: Mountain Av., Woodstock, Vt. Died Mar. 11, 1956; buried Woodstock.

MULLOWNEY, John James (mŭl-lō-nē), med. educator; b. Seacombe, Eng., July 20, 1878; s. Michael and Hannah (Craven) M.; came to U.S. 1887, naturalized, 1902; student Phillips Exeter Acad., 1899-1902, Harvard, 1902-03; M.D., U. Pa., 1908; m. Emily Evans, June 30, 1908; children—John Evans, Penn Evans, William Thomas; m. 2d, Esther Garriss Thomas, Nov. 1, 1938 (died Apr. 19, 1942); m. Mrs. Mabel Mize, June 18, 1944 (died Oct. 11, 1952). Began as principal of high school, Bath, N.H., 1903-04; prof. nervous and mental diseases North China Union Medical Coll., Peking, 1908-12; insp. tenement and lodging houses, Phila., 1912-13; asst. chief Pa. Dept. Health, 1913-17; head dept. science and prof. chemistry and hygiene Girard Coll., Phila., 1917-21; prof. pub. health and pres. Meharry Medical Coll., Nashville, 1921-38, ret. Mem. Friends of Hist. Soc., Acacia, Kappa Delta, Pi Pi. Mem. Soc. of Friends. Author: Chinese Hospitals for Chinese; Revelation of Chinese Revolution; Epidemic of Pneumonic Type of Bubonic Plague; Hygiene of the Home; The Power of Thought; Effects of Depression on Internships; Development of Medical Education, Is State Medicine Coming?; The Crisis in Dentistry—What Can be Done About It? Medical History in Brief; A Doctor's Faith; America Gives a Chance; Asthma Is Not a Disease; Shall America Depend on the Way of Force or on Spiritual Power?; The Christ Religion as a Positive Dynamic Religion. I Believe, 1944, 2d edit. 1944 called a Gift Book on Christian Healing. Home: 630 E. Seminary St., Gainesville, Fla. Died Oct. 17, 1952.

MULLOY, William Theodore, bishop; b. Ardock, N.D., Nov. 9, 1892; s. William James and Margaret Ann (Doyle) M.; student St. Boniface Coll., Winnepeg, Can., St. Paul Sem., St. Paul, Minn. LL.D. (honorary), University of Kentucky, 1958. Ordained priest Roman Cath. Ch., 1916; asst. St. Michael procathedral, Grand Forks, N.D., 1916-20; pastor St. Boniface, Wimbledon, 1920-21, Sacred Heart Ch., Cando, 1921-25, St. Alphonsus Ch., Langdon, 1925-33; dean of Langdon Deanery, 1925-33; pastor St. John Evangelist Ch., Grafton, N.D., 1933-38, dean of Grafton Deanery; elevated to rank of Domestic Prelate, 1941; rector St. Mary Cathedral, Fargo, N.D., 1938-45; Bishop of Covington, Ky. since 1945; pres. Villa Madonna Coll., Covington, 1945-53, chancellor, 1953—. Diocesan consultor, Fargo, 1938-45, diocesan supt. of edn. 1938-45, diocesan director rural life, 1934-45; pres. National Catholic Rural Life Conf., 1935-37, and 1946-48, Episcopal adviser since 1948, mem. bd. dirs. since 1934, mem. exec. com., 1934-35, 37-41; member Episcopal Com., Confraternity of Christian Doctrine, since 1948; director Sisters of Service, 1939-45; dir. Lay Women's Retreat League, 1941-45; bd. dirs. N.Am. Coll., Rome, 1949-53. President Liturgical Conference of America, 1952-54. Mem. Catholic Biblical Assn. of Am., Am. Cath. Hist. Assn., Medieval Acad. of Am. K.C. Editor: Catholic Action News, 1937-45. Home: 1140 Madison Av., Covington, Ky. Died June 1, 1959; buried St. Mary Cemetery, Ft. Mitchell, Ky.

MULTER, Smith Lewis, lawyer; b. Worcester, N.Y., July 18, 1874; s. Madison Harmon and Hannah Mary (Smith) M.; Ph.B., Brown U., 1898; LL.B., New York Law Sch., 1900; m. Mary W. Wharton, June 30, 1922; 1 dau., Marjorie (Mrs. Joseph H. Bacheller, Jr.). Admitted to New York State bar, 1900; trial lawyer, New York City, 25 yrs.; asso. counsel Interborough Rapid Transit Co., in litigation and corporation work, 1912-39; retired from active practice since 1939, and engaged in care of estates, and as speaker on historical, patriotic, educational and civic occasions throughout U.S. Mem. Sons American Revolution (pres. N.J. Soc. 1941-43; chancellor Nat. Soc. 1934-39, pres. gen. 1943-46), Am. Friends of Lafayette, Bill of Rights Commemorative Soc., Revolutionary Memorial Soc., N.J. and N.Y. State hist. socs., N.J. Geneal. Soc. Presbyterian (past pres. bd. trustees and mem. Session, Presbyn. Ch., East Orange, N.J.). Mason. Club: Brown (N.Y.). Address: 219 3d Av. N., St. Petersburg, Fla. Died July 16, 1952; buried Worcester, N.Y.

MUMFORD, Frederick Blackmar, educator; b. Moscow, Mich., May 28, 1868; s. Elisha Charles Lindsley and Julia Ann (Camburn) M.; student Albion Coll., 3 yrs.; B.S., Mich. Agrl. Coll., 1891, M.S., 1893; student U. Leipzig, 1900, U. Zürich, 1901; Dr. Agr., U. Neb., 1927, Mich. State Coll., 1927; m. Jessamine Kennedy, Jan. 30, 1895; children—Margaret Kennedy (Mrs. M. G. Neale), Dorothy Jessamine (Mrs. D. B. Coleman), Catherine Adelia (Mrs. B. K. Hollyday), Ruth Elizabeth. Asst. Mich. Agrl. Expt. Station, 1891-93; asst. prof. agr. Mich. Agrl. Coll., 1893-95; prof. agr. U. Mo., 1895-1904, prof. animal husbandry, 1904—, acting dean Coll. of Agr. and acting dir. Agrl. Expt. Station, 1903-05, dean and dir., 1909-38, dean and dir. emeritus, 1938—. Mem. Mo. Bd. Agr. Chmn. Mo. Council of Defense, 1917-19; fed. food adminstr. for Mo., 1917-19. Apptd. mem. Mo. Commn. for Relief and Reconstruction, 1932; mem. Mo. Planning Bd., Mo. Agrl. Dept. Adjustment Commn. Fellow A.A.A.S.; mem. Land Grant Coll. Assn. (exec. com.), Mo. Acad. Sci., Am. Soc. Animal Prodn., Sigma Xi, Alpha Zeta; fellow A.A.A.S. Mem. Mission Américaine de Rapprochement to France, 1919; pres. Assn. of Land Grant Colleges and Universities, 1941. Methodist. Mason, Rotarian. Author: Animal Breeding; Land Grant College Movement; History Missouri College of Agriculture; also bulls. of Agrl. Expt. Sta. Home: Columbia, Mo. Died Nov. 12, 1946; buried Columbia Cemetery.

MUMFORD, Philip G., honorary chairman of the board and director American Machine & Metals, Inc.; director South Porto Rico Sugar Company, Peninsula Nat. Bank, Long Island. Home: Cedarhurst, L.I. Office: 233 Broadway, N.Y.C. Died Oct. 28, 1951; buried Rochester, N.Y.

MUMMART, Clarence Allen, clergyman, educator; b. Welsh Run, Franklin County, Pa., July 14, 1874; s. William L. and Catharine A. (Kerfoot) M.; ed. Cumberland Valley State Normal Sch., Shippensburg, Pa.; preachers' normal diploma, Huntington (Ind.) Coll., 1905, teachers' normal diploma, 1906, A.B., 1907, B.D., 1908, M.A., 1909, D.D., 1912; studied U. of Mich.; Ph.D., Oskaloosa (Ia.) Coll., 1913; S.T.M., Northwestern U., 1925; m. Lillie May Zimmerman, Mar. 10, 1896; children—Cletus Byron, Charles Otterbein (dec.), Ethel May (Mrs. Herschel Holmes Griffith), Mary Katharyn (Mrs. Russell Evans Griffith). Teacher public schools until 1903; ordained ministry U.B. Ch., 1901; pastor for 31 yrs., Pa., Ind., Ohio, Mich.; presiding elder, 1905-08,

1910-12; editor Christian Conservator, 1901-11, 1917-20; head dept. of Theology, Huntington Coll., 1911-17, 1919-20, pres. Huntington Coll., 1912-15 and 1925-32, prof. philosophy, history and practical theology, 1932-33; pastor Otterbein U.B. Ch., Greencastle, Pa., 1933——. Mem. Bd. of Edn. U.B. Church, 1913-17, 1921-32, and 1937-49; gen. sec. of edn., U.B. Ch., 1913-17 and 1925-32; pres. Bd. Christian Edn., U.B. Ch., 1921-25 and 1937-1941; mem. Exec. Com. Inter-Council Religious Edn., 1923-29; supt. sch. administrn., Franklin County Sunday Sch. Assn., 1934-41; supt. of schools, LaCenter, Ky., 1920-21; bishop U.B. Church, 1921-25 and 1937-41; mem. General Conference 6 times. Prohibition-Republican. Author of monographs on religious, Bibl. and ednl. subjects. Home: 236 S. Washington St. Church office: Corner E. Franklin and S. Washington Sts., Greencastle, Pa. Died 1959.

MUNCIE, J(esse) H(oward), plant pathologist; b. Middlebury, Ind., July 3, 1890; s. William Rasnic and Sarah (Varley) M.; A.B., Wabash Coll. Crawfordsville, Ind., 1912; M.A., Cornell U., 1916; Ph.D., Ia. State Coll., 1925; m. Helen Marie Baber, Sept. 20, 1913. Asst. botanist Ohio Agrl. Expt. Sta., 1913; asst. and research asst. in plant pathology Mich. Agrl. Expt. Sta., 1913-17; plant disease survey U.S. Dept. Agr., 1917-18; asst. prof. botany Pa. State Coll., 1918-21; agent U.S. Dept. Agr., 1922-29; research asso., research prof. Mich. State Coll., 1929——. Mem. Am. Phytopathol. Soc., Potato Assn. Am., Sigma Chi, Sigma Xi, Gamma Sigma Delta, Epsilon Sigma Phi. Author tech. bulls. and research papers in plant pathology. Research in diseases of potatoes, field crops, bacterial plant diseases. Home: 656 Sunset Lane, East Lansing, Mich. Died July 4, 1954.

MUNFORD, Walter F., steel exec.; b. Worcester, Mass., June 8, 1900; s. Ferdinand C. and Ida May (Michener) M.; student Worcester Poly. Institute, 1918-19; Certificate of graduation, Mass. Institute Tech., 1923; m. Camille Watson, Aug. 30, 1924; children—Robert W., Walter F. Open hearth helper South works, Worcester, 1923-24, supt., 1927-30, supt. open hearth Newburg works, Cleve., 1930-33, asst. supt. steel works Nat. Tub Co., 1933-34, asst. supt. Cuyahoga works Am. Steel & Wire Co., 1934-37, supt., 1937-39, asst. to v.p., 1939, asst. mgr. operations Pitts. dist., 1939-42, mgr. operations Worcester dist., 1942, asst. v.p. in charge operations, 1942-50, v.p. operations, 1950-53, Am. Steel & Wire div. U.S. Steel Corp., pres. div., 1953-56, asst. exec. v.p. operations U.S. Steel Corp., 1956-58, exec. v.p. engring. and research, 1958-59, president and chief administrative officer, 1959——. Seaman U.S. Mcht. Marine, 1918. Member American Iron and Steel Inst., Lambda Chi Alpha. Clubs: Worcester (Mass.); Cleveland Country, Pepper Pike Country, Union, 50 (Cleve.); Union League (Chgo.); M.I.T. (N.Y.C.); Oakmont Country, Duquesne, University (Pitts.). Home: 825 Morewood Av., Pitts. 13. Office: 525 William Penn Pl., Pitts. 30, Pa. Died Sept. 28, 1959.

MUNGER, Claude Worrell (mŭn-gẽr), hosp. adminstr. (ret.); b. Orleans, Ind., May 24, 1892; s. Charles Phelps and Mary Mitchell (Worrell) M.; B.S., U. Chgo., 1914; M.D., Rush Med. Coll., Chgo., 1916. Supt. Columbia Hosp., Milw., 1917-21; dir. Blodgett Meml. Hosp., Grand Rapids, Mich., 1921-24; dir. hosps. Westchester County, N.Y., 1924-37; dir. St. Luke's Hosp., N.Y.C., 1937——; prof. hosp. adminstrn. Columbia, 1945——; spl. lectr. Interam. Inst. Hosp. Adminstrs., Lima, Peru, 1944. N.Y. Inst. Hosp. Adminstrs., 1939-41, mem. editorial bd. Modern Hosp. Former chmn. Westchester County Council of Social Agencies. Chmn. Com. on Hosp. Exhibit, N.Y. World's Fair. Mem. and sec. subcom. on hospitals Council on Nat. Def., 1940——. Mem. White House Confs. Children in a Democracy, 1939-40. Cons. USPHS, Fed. Security Agy., N.R.C.; mem. adv. com. Fed. Hosp. Council; Comn. on Hosp. Care in Natl. Study, 1944-47, Joint Comm. on Edn. of Am. Hosp. Assn. and Am. Coll. of Hosp. Adminstrs., 1945. Fellow Am. Coll. Hosp. Adminstrs. (charter fellow 1933, pres. 1944-46), Hollywood (Cal.) Acad. Medicine (hon.); mem. N.Y. Acad. Medicine, A.M.A., Am. Hosp. Assn. (pres. 1936-37, chmn. council on govt. relations, 1937-45, co-organizer wartime service bur.), Am. Social Hygiene Assn., Am. Pub. Health Assn., N.Y. State (trustee; pres. 1929-30), Westchester (chmn.) hosp. assns., N.Y. County Med. Soc. Hosp. Assn. Greater N.Y. (pres. 1938-39), Nat. Com. for Mental Hygiene, Nat. Com. Moblzn. for Human Needs, Hosp. Council of Greater N.Y. (v.p. 1941——), Distbn. Com. of Greater New York Fund, Med. Supts. Club of N.A. (pres. 1946). Republican. Baptist. Clubs: University (N.Y.C.); Med. Supts. Club of U.S. Co-founder Wis. State Hosp. Assn. Research in cleaning, dietary and nursing methods in hosps. Contbr. articles to hosp. publs. Cons. various hosps. in admininstrn. and construction. Home: Gallows Hill Rd., West Redding, Conn. Died Feb. 3, 1950.

MUNN, Orson Desaix, lawyer; b. N.Y.C., July 26, 1883; s. Henry Norcross and Ann (Elder) M.; grad. Hill Sch., Pottstown, Pa., 1902, Litt.B., Princeton, 1906; LL.B., N.Y. Law Sch., 1911; Sc. D., Oglethorpe U., 1936; m. Margaret W. Lawrence, Dec. 14, 1911; children—Elizabeth Elder, Louisine Martin; m. 2d, Carolyn Nunder, Apr. 2, 1924; 1 son, Orson Desaix. Admitted to N.Y. bar, 1911; also sr. partner Munn, Liddy & Glaccum, handling suits or infringement of patents, trade marks and internat. law; formerly editor and pub. Scientific American. Mem. USNR, World War I. Home: Southampton, L.I., N.Y. Office: 24 W. 40th St., N.Y.C. Died Dec. 1958.

MUNNS, Mrs. Margaret Cairns, ex-treas. World's W.C.T.U.; b. Fairbury, Ill., Aug. 10, 1870; d. Rev. James and Sarah Spence (Ewart) Cairns; student Colfax (Wash.) Coll., 1887-90; A.B., Cal. Coll., Oakland, 1891, M.A., 1894; m. Horace G. Munns, Nov. 20, 1895 (dec.); 1 son, Harold G. (dec.). Began as tchr. Vancouver (Wash.) schs., 1891; corr. sec. W. Washington W.C.T.U., 1900-15; treas. nat. W.C. T.U., 1915-46 and World's WC.T.U., 1925-53; dir. Dept. Parliamentary Usage, Nat. W.C.T.U., 1946; parliamentarian Woman's Century Club, Seattle, 1910-15; Washington Fedn. of Women's Clubs, 1913-15; pres. Bus. and Profl. Woman's Club, Evanston, 1924-28, parliamentarian, 1929-46. Mem. Minimum Wage Commn., Seattle, 1913. Mem. Nat. Assn. Parliamentarians. Republican. Baptist. Home: 5602 42d Av. S.W., Seattle 6; (winter) 716 Newhall Av., Burlingame, Cal. Died Sept. 3, 1957.

MUNRO, Annette Gardner, educator; b. Bristol, R.I.; d. John Bennett and Abby Howland (Batt) Munro; grad. Wellesley Coll., 1886; A.M., U. Rochester, 1910, Litt.D., 1930. Tchr. Wheaton Sem., Norton, Mass., 1897-1905; cataloguer Portland (Ore.) Library Assn., 1907-09; dean for women U. Rochester, 1910-30, now emeritus. Mem. Am. Hist. Assn., Archaeol. Inst. Am. Home: 115 Butler Av., Providence, R.I. Died Oct. 2, 1955.

MUNRO, H(ector) G(ordon), lumberman; b. London, Eng., Sept. 27, 1905; s. Alexander Findlay and Elizabeth (Lutz) M.; B.A., U. B.C., 1927; m. Blanche Almond, Aug. 15, 1931; children—Gordon R., John H. Clk. Canadian Bank of Commerce, 1921-23; staff various depts., dept. mgr., dir. H. R. MacMillan Export Co., Ltd., 1927-53; gen. mgr. British Columbia Forest Products, Ltd., Vancouver, 1946, dir., 1947——, v.p., 1950-53, pres., 1953——; dir. Argus Corp., Ltd., 1943-46. Dep. timber controller Dept. Munitions and Supply, Canadian Govt. Clubs: Vancouver; Shaughnessy Golf. Home: 6337 Adera St., Vancouver 13. Office: 995 W. 6th Av., Vancouver, B.C., Can. Died Dec. 2, 1957.

MUNRO, Walter J., business exec.; b. St. Catharines, Ont., Can. Pres., dir. Schoellkopf, Hutton & Pomeroy, Inc., Buffalo, 1942——; dir. Barcalo Mfg. Co., Abstract Title Ins. Corp. Home: 42 Chapin Pkwy. Office: 70 Niagara St., Buffalo, N.Y. Died Oct. 7, 1958.

MUNRO, William Bennett, educator; b. Almonte, Ont., Jan. 5, 1875; s. John MacNab and Sarah (Bennett) M.; B.A., Queens U., 1895, M.A., 1896, LL. B., 1898; M.A., Harvard, 1899, Ph.D., 1900; studied at U. of Edinburgh and U. of Berlin; hon. M.A., Williams Coll., 1904; LL.D., Queens, 1912; Litt.D., U. of Southern Calif., 1930; LL.D., Mills Coll., 1931; m. Caroline Sanford Gorton, Feb. 19, 1913; 1 son. Instr. history and political science, Williams College, 1901-04; instructor in govt., Harvard, 1904-06, asst. prof., 1906-12, prof. municipal govt., 1912-25; Jonathan Trumbull prof. American history, 1925-29, Edward S. Harkness prof. of history and government, 1929-45, now treasurer, California Institute of Technology; dir. Security-First National Bank of Los Angeles, Southern Calif. Edison Co.; Jacob H. Schiff Foundation lecturer, Cornell U., 1926; Kirby Foundation lecturer, Lafayette Coll., 1928; Marfleet lecturer, U. of Toronto (Can.), 1929; dir. of the first special session, Harvard Grad. School of Pub. Adminstrn., 1936-37. Editorial writer on staff of Boston Herald, 1907-21, Commissioned major U.S. Army World War I, and assigned to duty with General Staff. Trustee Henry E. Huntington Library and Art Gallery; member board of overseers, Harvard (1940-46); trustee Scripps College, Huntington Memorial Hosp. Pres. American Political Science Assn., 1927, Am. Association of U. Profs., 1929-31. Fellow Am. Acad. Arts and Sci.; mem. Phi Beta Kappa. Clubs: Valley Hunt (Pasadena); California (Los Angeles). Author: The Government of European Cities, 1909; The Initiative, Referendum and Recall, 1911; The Government of American Cities, 1912; Selections from the Federalist, 1913; Bibliography of Municipal Government, 1915; Principles and Methods of Municipal Administration, 1916; Leading Cases on the Constitution, 1917; The Govt. of the U.S., 1919 (5th ed., 1946); Municipal Government and Administration (2 vols.), 1923; Personality in Politics, 1924; The Governments of Europe, 1936; The Invisible Government, 1927; American Influences on Canadian Government, 1929; Makers of the Unwritten Constitution, 1929; Municipal Administration, 1934; Social Civics (3d edit.), 1949. Frequent contbr. to literary and political reviews. Home: 268 Bellefontaine St., Pasadena, Cal. Died Sept. 4, 1957.

MUNROE, Charles Andrews (mŭn-rō'), public utilities exec.; b. Middlebury, Vt., Feb. 9, 1875; s. Merrick Adams and Henrietta Persis (Mason) M.; A.B Middlebury Coll., 1896; student Northwestern U. Law Sch.; m. Rhea Logan, Aug. 20, 1907; children—Josephine, Rhea, Logan. Practiced law at Chgo. until 1904; identified with development of water power on Des Plaines River, Ill., 1902; mgr. Economy Light & Power Co., Joliet, Ill., 1906, later connected with Ill. Valley Gas & Electric Co.; v.p. Pub. Service Co. of Northern Ill. until 1919; served as v.p. Peoples Gas Lught & Coke Co. until 1924; chmn. bd. Laclede Gas Light Co., 1924-27; pres. W. A. Harriman Securities Corp., No. Utilities Co., North Central Gas Co., Columbia Oil and Gasoline Co.; dir. I.C. R.R. Co., Yazoo & Miss. R.R. Co., Chgo., St. Louis & New Orleans, R.R. Co., Am. Nat. Bank, Winter Haven, Fla., Broadway Nat. Bank, Tampa, Fla. Retired from business, 1939. Trustee Middlebury College. Mem. Am. Gas Assn. (pres. 1920, 21), Chgo. Hist. Soc. (trustee). Republican. Conglist. Clubs: Casino, Chicago, Commercial, Old Elm, Racquet, Shoreacres, (Chgo.); Recess, Metropolitan, Creek, N.Y. Yacht (N.Y.C.); Greenwich Riding, Indian Harbor Yacht, Round Hill, Beach (Greenwich, Conn.); Middlebury Country (Vt.). Home: The Knowles Montague Fore Shore, Nassau, Bahamas. Died Dec. 1957; buried Middlebury, Vt.

MUNSN, John Maurice, educator; b. Kane, Pa., Feb. 19, 1878; s. Swan and Elma (Bengston) M.; grad. Ferris Inst., Big Rapids, Mich., 1901, State Normal Sch., Ypsilanti, Mich., 1903, Ed.M., 1913; Ph. B., U. Chgo., 1911; LL.D., Ashland Coll., 1939; Ed.D., Wayne U., 1942. Supt. schs., Harbor Springs, Mich., 1905-13; dep. state supt. pub. instrn. Mich., 1913-19; dir. tng. sch. Central Mich. Normal Sch., Mt. Pleasant, 1919-23; editor Moderator Topics, 1919-23; pres. No. State Tchrs. Coll., Marquette, 1923-33; pres. Mich. State Normal Coll., 1933-48, prof. emeritus, 1948——. Mem. Mich. State Bd. Library Commrs., 1913-17. Mem. N.E.A., Mich. Edn. Assn. (pres. 1926). Home: Ypsilanti, Mich. Died June 22, 1950; buried Kane, Pa.

MUNSON, John G(ephart), ret. v.p. U.S. Steel Corp.; b. Bellefonte, Pa., Jan. 6, 1885; s. Lorenzo T. and Sarah (Gephart) M.; B.S., Yale, 1905; m. Eliza Short, June 28, 1911; children—John Gephart, Alice Elizabeth. Rodman for N.Y. Continental Jewell Filtration Co., 1905, constrn. supt., 1906-08; constrn. supt. J. G. White Engr. Corp., 1909-19; operating mgr. Mich. Limestone & Chem. Co. and Bradley Transportation Co., Rogers City, Mich., 1919-25, v.p. 1925-28, pres., 1928-39; v.p. U.S. Steel Corp. of Del., 1939-50, ret. Mem. Am. Inst. Mining and Metall. Engrs., Am. Iron and Steel Inst., Am. Soc. C.E., Am. Soc. M.E. Republican. Episcopalian. Clubs: Engineers (N.Y.C.); University, Duquesne (Pitts.). Home: Schenley Apts., Fifth Av., Pitts. 13. Office: 436 7th Av., Pitts. 30. Died Mar. 29, 1952.*

MUNSTER, August W., ret. ry. exec.; b. Waltham, Mass., July 24, 1882; s. August and Mary (Singler) M.; M.E., Mass. Inst. Tech.; m. Ella Smith, Sept. 29, 1909. Machinist Northern Pacific R.R., 1904-09; engr. tests N.Y., N.H.&H. R.R., 1909-12; gen. storekeeper B.&M. R.R., 1912-17, purchasing agt., 1917-33, v.p., 1933-50, ret.; v.p. Maine Central R.R., 1933-50. Mason. Clubs: University, Engineers. Home: 12 Canterbury Road, Winchester, Mass. Died Jan. 14, 1958.

MURATORE, Lucien, opera singer; b. Marseilles, France; grad. Conservatoire, Marseilles, at age of 19, and studied later in Paris; m. 2d, Lina Cavalieri, 1914 (div. 1927). Sang with Calvé and Dufresne, in La Carmilite, at Opéra Comique Paris; later sang in Armide and appeared in rôles of Faust, Romeo, Walther, etc.; created leading parts in Bacchus, Le Miracle, Salome, Siberia, La Catalene, Francesca da Rimini, etc.; with Chgo. Grand Opera Assn., 1912-22. Home: Eze, France. Died July 16, 1954.

MURCHIE, Alexander, lawyer; b. Creetown, Scotland, March 1, 1887; s. William and Agnes Janet (Kellie) M.; student U. Mich. Law Sch., 1906-08; law study, office of Senator Henry F. Hollis, 1 yr.; m. Gladys Nelson Hammond, July 19, 1910; children—Jean, Alexander. Admitted to N.H. bar, 1909, began practice with Senator Henry F. Hollis at Concord; mem. firm Remick & Hollis, 1910-12, Hollis & Murchie, 1912-19, Murchie & Murchie, 1919-29, Murchie, Murchie & Blandin, 1929-41, Murchie & Murchie, 1941——; city solicitor, Concord, 1910-19; member N.H. Board Law Examiners, 1922-40, U.S. dist. atty. for N.H., 1934-44. Chmn. Dem. State Com., N.H., 1918-19 Mem. Am., N.H. bar assns. Club: Snow Shoe (Concord). Home: 7 Pine St. Office: 4 Park St., Concord, N.H. Died Oct. 20, 1949.

MURDOCK, Harris H., architect; b. Cambridge, Mass., June 2, 1879; s. Walter H. and Eleanor (Grigg) M.; A.B., Harvard, 1901; m. Marion Davidson, June 16, 1903; children—Robert and Richard (twins); m. 2d, Florence Walter, Apr. 19, 1919; children—Eleanor (Mrs. David Sloane), Josephine (Mrs.

William G. Donaldson). Vice pres. Library Bureau, 1901-10; partner firm Jardine, Hill & Murdock, later Jardine, Murdock & Wright, 1910-32; chmn. Bd. of Standards and Appeals of N.Y.C., 1932—. Former pres. N.Y. Bldg. Congress; former gov. N.Y. Real Estate Bd.; former trustee Citizens Budget Commn. Fellow A.I.A. Club: Harvard (N.Y.C.). Home: 60 W. 9th St., N.Y.C.; also Ridgefield, Conn. Office: 80 Lafayette St., N.Y.C. Died May 10, 1959.

MURDOCK, Thomas Patrick, physician; b. Meriden, Conn., Mar. 6, 1888; s. Patrick and Bridget (Callaghan) M.; M.D., U. of Md., 1910; m. Alice R. Keating, June 23, 1914; children—Francis (deceased), Thomas Keating, Brian Shane. Interne St. Francis Hosp., Hartford, Conn., 1910-11, Undercliffe Tuberculosis Sanatorium, Meriden, 1911; pvt. practice medicine Meriden, since 1911, attending physician, Meriden Hosp., 1914-49, chief med. services, 1925-49, when retired; consultant Bristol Hospital, 1945; Gaylord Farm Sanitarium, Wallinford, Conn., 1943 (bd. dirs.), Undercliffe Tuberculosis Hospital, Silver Hills Sanatorium. Chmn. bd. visitors Inst. of Living, Hartford, 1947. Mem. adv. bd., Hartford, Conn., Trust Co., 1926; bd. corporators Meriden Savings Bank, 1921; dir. Meriden Trust and Safe Deposit Co. Lt., M.C., U.S. Army, 1917-19. Mem. procurement and assignment com. for Conn., World War II. Diplomate Am. Bd. Internal Medicine, 1937; fellow A.M.A. (bd. trustees, 1950; mem. House of Dels., 1937-50), chmn. com. to study nursing problem in U.S., 1947, com. for the improvement of the care of the patient, 1948); mem. A.C.P. (governor for Conn. 1946-52, retired), Conn. Med. Examining Bd. (1931-49, sec. 1931-47, pres., 1947-49), Conn. State Med. Soc. (pres. 1935, mem. council, 1937-50, chmn. 1949-50), New Haven County Med. Soc. (pres. 1928), Meriden Med. Soc., Meriden Visiting Nurses Assn. (bd. dirs. 1922-47). Home: 19 Windsor Av. Office: 147 W. Main St., Meriden, Conn. Died Apr. 1, 1957.

MURFEE, Hopson Owen, educator; b. Marion, Ala., Dec. 11, 1874; s. James Thomas and Laura (Owen) M.; B.S., Marion Inst., 1892; B.A., M.A., U. Va., 1897, fellow in astronomy; LL.D., U. Ala., 1913; m. Mary McQueen Smith, June 26, 1901. Instr. mathematics, U. Va., 1896-97; fellow in physics, U. Chgo., and research asst. to Prof. A. A. Michelson, 1899-1900; prof. physics, 1900-6, pres. Marion (Ala.) Inst., 1906—. Mem. Bd. of Visitors U.S. Naval Acad., 1909 (chmn. com. on standards and scholarship and chmn. com. on annual report of visitors). Pres. Academic Class U. Va., 1895-96, YMCA U. Va., 1895-96, Tennis Assn. and holder tennis championship U. Va., 1895, 96, 97. Baptist. Address: Marion, Ala. Deceased.

MURFIN, Orin Gould, admiral; born at Ohio Furnace, O., Apr. 13, 1876; s. Henry C. and Margaret (Reilly) M.; prep. edn., pub. schs., Jackson, O., grad. U.S. Naval Acad., Annapolis, Md., 1897, Naval War Coll., Newport, R.I., 1926; m. Anna Williams, Jan. 1, 1903; 1 dau., Winifred Anne. Commd. ensign, U.S. Navy, July 1, 1899; advanced through grades to comdr., Aug. 29, 1916; capt., Feb. 1, 1918; rear admiral, Jan. 7, 1930. Organizer and comdr. mine bases north of Scotland, World War I; served as judge advocate general of the Navy, comdr. in chief Asiatic Fleet and comdt. Pearl Harbor Naval Station, Hawaii; retired from active service May 1, 1940. Recalled to active duty World War II to serve as pres., Pearl Harbor Naval Court of Inquiry. Awarded D.S.M. (U.S.); Companion Order of St. Michael and St. George (British). Presbyterian. Clubs: Army and Navy, Army Navy Country (Washington). Address: 825 Margarita Av., Coronado, Cal. Died Oct. 22, 1956; buried Rosecrans Nat. Cemetery, San Diego, Cal.

MURFREE, Walter Lee, educator; b. Marian, Ala., Feb. 14, 1880; s. James Thomas and Laura (Owen) M.; grad. Marion Inst. High Sch., 1893, Marion Inst. Jr. Coll., 1895; B.A., U. Va., 1899, M.A., 1900; m. Mary Turner Graves, June 4, 1902. Prof. mathematics and business mgr. Marion Inst., 1900-15, pres., 1915—; organized spl. college courses for appointees to U.S. Mil. Acad. and U.S. Naval Acad. Col. in comd. Sr. R.O.T.C. Unit, World War and since. Democrat. Baptist. Mason (K.T., Shriner). Club: Civitan. Home: Marion, Ala. Died May 22, 1954; buried Marion.

MURPH, Daniel Shuford, trade assn. exec.; b. St. Matthews, S.C., Dec. 31, 1879; s. Daniel J. W. and Euphrasia Ann (Wolfe) M.; A.B., Wofford Coll., Spartanburg, S.C., 1902; A.M., Trinity Coll., Duke Univ., Durham, N.C., 1903; LL.B., Georgetown Univ., 1916; married Annie E. Ketchin, Aug. 20, 1927; 1 son, Daniel Shuford. Instr. Trinity Park Sch., Durham, 1903-07; county supt. edn., Calhoun County, S.C., 1908-13; sec. Com. on Agr., U.S. Ho. of Rep., 1913-16; in charge cotton marketing and warehousing work, Bureau of Markets, U.S. Dept. Agr., 1917-20; practiced law at St. Matthews, S.C., 1920-33; apptd. chief of Cotton Processing and Marketing Sect., A.A.A., 1933; mem. staff Nat. Fertilizer Assn., 1934-50, secretary-treas., 1945-50, retired. Organizer and pres. Farmers Bank & Trust Co., St. Matthews, 1911-13; served under apptmt. as spl. judge Circuit courts of S.C. Mem. Kappa Sigma. Democrat. Presbyterian. Mason. Address: Newberry Rd., Winnsboro, S.C. Died July 5, 1958.

MURPHY, Arthur Alban, ry. exec.; b. Portland, Ore., Feb. 8, 1886; s. Daniel R. and Caroline (Kennedy) M.; A.B., Stanford, 1908; m. Saidee Lu Knapp, Nov. 5, 1913 (died Oct. 1, 1939); m. 2d, Mrs. Jeannette Tighe Kemp, Apr. 22, 1941. Admitted to Ore. bar, 1908, began practice at Portland; mem. Eastham and Murphy, 1910-13; dep. dist. atty. Multnomah County, 1913-17; atty. and gen. atty. O.-W. R.R. & N. Co., Portland, 1919-25, asst. gen. solicitor, 1925-26; asst. to pres. U.P. R.R., at Seattle, 1926-37, at Los Angeles, 1937-40, at Seattle, 1940—. Served as 1st lt. and capt. Co. C, 362 Inf., U.S. Army, 1917-19; in action Meuse-Argonne (France) and Lys-Scheldt (Belgium) offensives. Commander Dept. of Ore. Am. Legion, 1926-27; pres. Seattle C. of C., 1929-30, now trustee; pres. Wash. Athletic Club of Seattle, 1936-37. Mem. Am. Legion, Phi Delta Phi, Phi Beta Kappa. K.C. (4°). Clubs: Rainier, Seattle Golf, Washington Athletic (Seattle); Arlington (Portland); Bohemian (San Francisco); Tacoma (Tacoma). Home: The Gainsborough, 1017 Minor. Office: Union Station, Seattle. Deceased.

MURPHY, Daniel J., business exec. Dir. and mem. exec. com. Crocker First Nat. Bank, San Francisco; pres. and dir. Sierra R.R.; Santa Cruz Portland Cement Co.; dir. mem. adv. bd. Crocker Anglo Nat. Bank; v.p. dir. Bunker Hill Co., Union Sq. Garage Corp., Provident Securities Co., Pioneer Kettleman Co.; dir., treas. Thermo Materials, Inc.; director Fiberboard Paper Products Company, Healy Tibbitts Construction Company, Crocker Estate Co., Crocker Investment Co., Crocker-Huffman Land & Water Co., Pabco Products Co., Inc., Moore Securities Gladding McBean Co., Pacific Coast Aggregatos Co., Moore Dry Dock Co. Home: 2255 Octavia St. Office: Crocker First Nat. Bank, Post and Montgomery Sts., San Francisco. Died Jan. 12, 1957.

MURPHY, Edward Thomas, corp. exec.; b. N.Y. C., 1880; s. Timothy Edward and Sarah A. (Bangshardt) M.; M.E., Lehigh U., 1901; m. Doris Duncan, Oct. 2, 1929. Sales dept. Bethlehem Steel Co., 1901; constrn. work Buffalo Forge Co., 1902-04; sales engr. B.F. Sturtevant Co., 1904-06; mgr. Phila. office Buffalo Forge Co. and Carrier Air Conditioning Corp., 1907-15; v.p., Phila. mgr. Carrier Engring. Corp., 1915-27, v.p., sales mgr., Newark, 1927-32; pres. Carrier Corp., 1933, v.p., Chgo. dist. mgr., 1934-39, v.p. in charge marketing, 1939-42, sr. v.p. since 1942; v.p. Carrier Contracting Corp.; v.p., dir. Aerofin Corp.; dir. Carrier Corp., Iroquois China Co. Mem. Engrs. Air Conditioning and Refrigeration Machinery Assn., Theta Delta Chi, Sigma Chi (dir.). Clubs: Century, Onondaga Golf and Country (Syracuse, N.Y.). Home: 1055 James St., Syracuse, N.Y. Died Aug. 1951.

MURPHY, Ernest, ret. freight car mfr.; b. Lancashire, Eng.; student elec. engring.; m. Florence Murphy; 1 dau., Evelyn. Worked on London subway system before coming to Am. in 1909; with traction cos. in Pitts. and Albany, after supervising elect. installations of I. R. T. Subway in N.Y., until 1941; with Brit. Purchasing Commn. in N.Y., 1941; joined Pressed Steel Car Co., in charge tank prodn., named pres., 1945, ret. 1948. Served as civilian chmn. Tank Prodn. Integration Com. Recipient citation from Sec. of War for work Work. Home: Wilton, Conn. Deceased; buried St. Michael's Cemetery, Wilton, Conn.*

MURPHY, Francis Parnell, ex-gov.; b. Winchester, N.H., Aug. 16, 1877; s. Patrick E. and Ellen (Lambert) M.; LL.D., St. Anselm's Coll., 1935; U. of N.H., 1938; D.C.L., Boston Coll., 1944; A.B., Dartmouth Coll., 1938; married Mae B. Herrick, June 24, 1902; children—Madeleine Gertrude (Mrs. Edward F. O'Brien), Walter Wyman (deceased), Kathryn Herrick (Mrs. John W. Bryant), Eleanor Mae (Mrs. Donald Erion) and Francis Parnell. In charge of packing, Child Chamberlin Company, shoe mfrs., Newport, N.H., 1898-1902; in charge packing, McElwain Co., Manchester, 1902-06, supt. shoe mfg., Newport, N.H., 1908-14, gen. supt. and dir., 1915-19; gen. supt. Internat. Shoe Co., Newport, 1920-21; v.p. and dir. J. F. McElwain Co. since 1922; pres. and treas. Radio Voice of N.H., Inc.; v.p. and dir. Nashua Trust Co.; dir. Melville Shoe Corp., Boston and Maine Railroad; treas. Nashua-N.H. Found. Mem. N.H. legislature, 1931 (chairman ways and means com.); mem. Gov. Winant's staff, 1925, 26; mem. New Eng. Council, 1929, 30; del. Rep. Nat. Conv., 1932; mem. Gov.'s Exec. Council, N.H., 1933, 34; mem. Interstate Compact Commn.; gov. of N.H. for terms 1937-41. Trustee N.H. State Hosp. Mem. Ancient and Honorable Artillery Co. Republican. Member Knights of Malta, Knights of Columbus, Elks. Clubs: Rotary, Nashua Country, Boston City, Boston Madison Sq. Garden; Newport (N.H.) Country; Algonquin Club (Boston). Home: 88 Concord St., Nashua, N.H. Office: Elm St., Manchester, N.H. Died Dec. 19, 1958.

MURPHY, Frederick Vernon, architect; b. Fond du Lac, Wis., Feb. 16, 1879; s. John Vernon and Alice (McCue) M.; student Columbian (now George Washington) U., 1899-1901; Architecte Diplomé par le Gouvernement Français, École des Beaux Arts, Paris, 1923; LL.D., Canisius Coll., 1924; m. Marjorie Mary Cannon, Oct. 3, 1936; children—Frederick Vernon, Jr., John Christopher, Michael Vernon. Prof. architecture, head dept. (ret.), Cath. U. of Am. since 1910; mem. firm Murphy and Locraft, Architects; mem. bd. consultants Municipal Center, Washington; asso., cons. architect Nat. Shrine of Immaculate Conception, Washington; architect, with T. H. Locraft for St. Arnold War Monument, France. Dir. Allied Architects, Incorporated. Member design committee House of Representatives Office Building, New National Museum, New Naval Hospital. Prin. works: St. Charles Coll. Chapel, Catonsville, Md.; Martin Maloney Chem. Lab., Sacred Heart Ch., John Kerman Mullen Memorial Library, Papal Legation (all Washington); St. Francis de Sales Ch., Buffalo, N.Y.; St. Mary's Ch., Mobile, Ala.; etc. Associate National Academy of Design; fellow A.I.A. (ex-mem. bd. examiners, registration board); mem. Nat. Sculpture Soc., Commn. Fine Arts, Soc. Beaux Arts Inst. Disign, Soc. des Architectes Diplomés par le Gouvernement Française, Comité Permanent International des Architects. Registered architect with Nat. Council of Archtl. Registration Boards. Awarded gold medal for design of Sacred Heart Church and John Kenneth Mullen Memorial Library; decorated Chevalier Legion of Honor (France); Knight Comdr. Order of St. Gregory; Benemerenti Medal. Catholic. Clubs: Cosmos (Washington); Columbia Country (Chevey Chase, Md.); Union Interalliée (Paris). Contbr. to Universal Knowledge Found., 1927. Home: 3714 William's Lane, Chevy Chase, Md. Office: 1518 P St. N.W., Washington. Died May 4, 1958.

MURPHY, James A(loysius), govt. official; b. Woonsocket, R.I., July 3, 1895; s. John Francis and Margaret Ann (Garvey) M.; B.S., R.I. State Coll., 1919; Ed.M., Boston U. 1939; m. Veronica Anita Brennan, Aug. 20, 1927; children—John Thomas, Sheila Athnna. Chemist, Saylesville Finishing Co., Phillipsdale, R.I., 1919-21; teacher chemistry Woonsocket (R.I.) Senior High Sch., 1921-45; apptd. acting adj. gen. State of R.I., with rank brig. gen., 1945, chief of staff for Gov. of R.I. 1945—, acting dir. Civil Def. for R.I., 1952-53. Served with AUS, 1918-19; disch. 2d lt., inf.; mem. R.I. State Guard, 1940-45; retired with rank col. Mem. Adj.'s Gen. Assn., N.G. Assn., R.I. Inst. of Instrn., Delta Alpha Psi. Democrat. Roman Catholic. K.C. Home: 427 Harris Av., Woonsocket, R.I. Office: Office of Adj. Gen., 1051 N. Main St., Providence 4. Died Apr. 23, 1955; buried St. Charles Roman Catholic Cemetery, Woonsocket, R.I.

MURPHY, James B(umgardner), pathologist; b. Morganton, N.C., Aug. 4, 1884; s. Patrick Livingston and Bettie (Bumgardner) M.; B.S., U. N.C., 1905, D.Sc., 1927; M.D., Johns Hopkins, 1909; hon. Dr. U. Louvain, Belgium, 1927; D.Sc., Oglethorpe U., 1938; m. Ray Slater, 1919; children—James Slater, Ray Livingston. Med. intern. Pathol. Inst., N.Y.C., 1909-10; asst. in pathology and bacteriology Rockefeller Inst., 1910-13, asso., 1913-15, asso. mem., 1915-23, life mem., 1923—, in charge Lab. of Cancer Research; mem. Nat. Adv. Cancer Council 1938-44; mem. bd. visitors N.Y. State Institute for the Study of Malignant Diseases; bd. Sloan-Kettering Inst. for Cancer Research; com. on growth NRC. Thayer lecturer, 1934; Hatfield lecturer, 1936; Tufts College Harvey lecturer, 1937; Cancer ednl. lectr. U. Chgo., 1939; Cutter lecturer, Harvard, 1940; Phi Beta Pi lecturer, U. Va., 1940; Barnard Hosp. lectr., St. Louis, 1941. Commr. N.Y. Bd. Charities, 1922-30. Maj. M.C., staff of surgeon gen., 1917-19. Mem. bd. mgrs. Memorial Hosp. (New York), Mt. Desert Hosp. (pres. 1928, v.p. 1929—). Decorated Officer, Order of Leopold, 1939; Chinese medal of Honored Merit, 1940. Mem. Fedn. Am. Societies for Exptl. Biology, Am. Soc. for Exptl. Pathology, N.Y. Acad. of Medicine, A.A.A.S., Am. Soc. for Clinic Investigation, Assn. Am. Physicians, Am. Assn. for Cancer Research (council, v.p. 1921, pres. 1922), Assn. Française pur L'Étude du Cancer, Leewenhoek-Vereeniging, Am. Cancer Soc., Roscoe Jackson Meml. Lab. of Bar Harbor (mem. bd.), Nat. Acad. Sciences, Sigma Xi, Sigma Nu, Nu Sigma Nu. Clubs: Knickerbocker (gov.), Coffee House Club, Century (N.Y.C.); Seal Harbor Yacht (gov.), Pot and Kettle of Bar Harbor. Author of numerous articles in medical and sci. jours., dealing with tissue grafting, cancer immunity, also role of the lymphocyte in tuberculosis, and studies in X-ray effects, nature of malignant tumors of fowls, cancer inhibitor from normal tissues. Mem. advisory bd. and chmn. editorial com. of Cancer Research. Home: 177 E. 64th St., N.Y.C. Office: Rockefeller Inst., 66th St. and York Av., N.Y.C. 21. Died Aug. 24, 1950; buried Bethel Ch., Staunton, Va.

MURPHY, James William, ex-congressman; b. Platteville, Wis., Apr. 17, 1858; grad. State Normal Sch., 1873; taught sch. 5 yrs.; LL.B., U. Mich., 1880; married. Dist. atty., Grant Co., Wis., 4 yrs.; mayor of Platteville, 1907-7; mem. 60th Congress

3d Wis. Dist. Democrat. Address: Platteville, Wis. Died July 11, 1927.

MURPHY, John Vernon, ret. naval officer; b. Brownwood, Tex., June 12, 1893; s. John and Alice (Vernon) M.; A.B., U.S. Naval Acad., 1917, grad. student in elec. engring., 1920-22; M.S., Yale, 1924; m. Elizabeth Pearce, Nov. 1, 1928; children—John Vernon, Anne Pearce. Commd. ensign USN, 1917, advanced through grades to commodore, 1945; in charge research and design sect., radio div. Bur. of Engring., 1932-34; comdr. U.S.S. King, 1934-36; navigation officer U.S.S. Quincy, 1936-37; in charge radio and communication group, Post Grad. Sch., Naval Acad., 1937-40; exec. officer U.S.S. Honolulu, 1940-41; comdr. destroyer div. 10, U.S.S. Cushing, 1941-42; signal communication liaison officer War Dept. Gen. Staff, 1943; Joint Radio Bd., 1942; coordinator Joint Communications Bd. and Combined Communications Bd., Navy Dept., 1943; dep. dir. of Naval communications, 1943-46; alternate mem. War Communications Bd. and combined Communications Bd., 1943-46; ret. from active service, 1946. Mem. Acacia. Presbyn. Mason. Home: 3420 N. Lorcom Lane, Arlington, Va. Died July 31, 1949; buried Arlington Nat. Cemetery.

MURPHY, Joseph B., lawyer; b. Pompey, N.Y., Jan. 16, 1881; s. Michael C. and Jane (Carroll) M.; Coll. of Law, Syracuse U., 1905; m. Ruth M. Hawley, Jan. 24, 1912; children—Joseph Hawley, Warren B. Admitted to N.Y. bar, 1905, since practiced in Syracuse; with sons mem. partnership Murphy & Young; spl. attention to trial work; operates, maintains sheep and cattle farm nr. Syracuse. Mem. Am., N.Y. State, Onondaga Co. bar assns., Internat. Assn. Ins. Counsel, Syracuse C. of C. K.C. Home: 1827 James St., Syracuse 6. Office: State Tower Bldg., Syracuse 2, N.Y. Died Feb. 6, 1956.

MURPHY, Lambert, tenor; b. Springfield, Mass., Apr. 15, 1885; s. William Henry and Lida Coreille (Sibley) M.; A.B., Harvard, 1908; m. Jessie Stewart Rowe, Mar. 19, 1921. Début with Metropolitan Opera Co., New York, 1911; resigned, 1915, to devote entire time to concertizing; has appeared in prominent musical centres of U.S., and at musical festivals, including Worcester and Springfield, Mass., Cincinnati, Oberlin, Buffalo, Syracuse, Ithaca, North Shore, etc. Home: Hacock, N.H. Died July 24, 1954; buried Paucatuck Cemetery, West Springfield, Mass.

MURPHY, N. Barnard textile exec.; b. LaGrange, Ga., Oct. 26, 1898; s. George W. and Mollie (Newell) M.; student pub. schs., West Point, Ga.; student Georgia Sch. Tech., Atlanta, 1917-19; m. Susie Thomas, Dec. 25, 1920; 1 son, N. Barnard. Began as general textile employee, 1915; textile overseer Dixie Mills, LaGrange, Ga., 1919; asst. supt. West Point Mfg. Co., Shawmut div., Shawmut, Ala., 1920-24; supt. Lullwater Co., Thomson, Ga., 1924, Pelzer (S.C.) Mfg. Co., 1924-29; supt. The Trion (Ga.) Co., 1929-31, gen. mgr., 1931-32, v.p., 1932-41, exec. v.p., 1941-42, pres., gen. mgr., 1942—; v.p., dir. Riegel Textile Corp., N.Y., Farmers & Mchts. Bank, Summerville, Ga., Montgomery Knitting Mill; v.p., gen. mgr. Trion Div. of Reigel Textile Corp. Mayor, Town of Trion, 1931-46; trustee and pres. Trion Community Found., Inc.; mem. promotional com. So. Indsl. Relations Conf. Served with U.S. Marine Corps, 1918. Mem. Cotton Mfrs. Assn., Ga. (past dir., v.p. and pres.), Textile Edn. Found., Inc., Trion Y.M.C.A. (pres.), Kappa Sigma. Mason. Club: Capital City (Atlanta), Somerville-Trion Rotary (past pres.). Address: Trion, Ga. Died May 22, 1957; buried Trion.

MURPHY, Walter J., editor; b. Bklyn., Aug. 20, 1899; s. Richard and Ann (Heath) M.; B.S. in Chemistry, Polytechnic Inst. of Bklyn. 1921; student at Columbia, 1932; D.Sc. (hon.), Centre Coll., 1947; m. Gertrude B. McMahon, Feb. 22, 1927; children—Joan Ann, Walter J. Began as research chemist and chem. engr., 1921, in research and plant operation, Air Reduction Co., 1921-22; tech. service and development, Am. Cyanamid Co., 1922-25; market research, Naugatuck chem. div., U.S. Rubber Co., Feb.-Dec. 1926; v.p. of operations, George Chem. Co. and Seaboard Crystal Co., 1925-28; asst. to the pres. Mutual Chem. Co. of Am., 1928-30; mng. editor Chemical Industries, 1930-39, editor and gen. mgr., 1939-43; editor Industrial and Engineering Chemistry, Analytical Chemistry, Journal of Agricultural and Food Chemistry, also Chem. and Engineering News, Am. Chem. Soc. publs., 1943-56, editorial dir., 1956, also Advances in Chemistry Series; dir. Am. Chem. Soc. News Service; mem. AEC com. Reclassification Material for Industry; cons. Chem. Corps, AUS. Mem. research adv. bd. Fordham U.; adv. council on sci. and technology Notre Dame U. Served with U.S. Army, 1918. Mem. corporation Poly. Inst. of Bklyn. Mem. bd. trustees Midwest Research Institute, S.W. Research Inst. Fellow Am. Inst. Chemists (gold medalist 1950), A.A.A.S.; mem. of Washington Acad. of Sciences, Societe de Chemil Industrielle (Am. sect.); Soc. Bus. Mag. editors (pres. 1954), Armed Forces Chem. Association (vice pres., dir.), Tech. Indsl. Intelligence Com. Fgn. Econ. Administrn., Am. Inst. Chem. Engrs., Soc. Chem. Industry (Am. sect.); Salesmen's Assn. of Chem. Industry, Alpha Chi Sigma, Sigma Xi, Pi Kappa Phi. Republican. Clubs: Congressional Country, Chemists (N.Y.C.); Cosmos, National Press, University (Washington). Co-author: Strategic Materials in Hemisphere Defense, 1941. Published privately; I Did Leave Home; The Lagoon of Decision. Contbr. numerous articles to mags. Lecturer on sci. subjects. Home: 1825 Parkside Drive N.W. (12). Office: 1155 16th St. N.W., Washington 6. Died Nov. 1959.

MURPHY, William Gordon, lawyer; b. Brooklyn, Nov. 23, 1885; s. William Gordon and Mary Hett (Shepherd) M.; A.B., Wesleyan U., 1906; LL.B., N.Y. Law Sch., 1908; m. Mary Billings Stoddard, May 16, 1911; children—Gordon Stoddard, Martha Stoddard (Mrs. Henry Lee Ferguson, Jr.). Admitted to N.Y. State bar, 1908, and since practiced in N.Y. City; partner, 1916— firm now known as Olin, Murphy & Redmond; officer and dir. various real estate corps.; trustee Williamsburgh Savings Bank, 1943—; trustee numerous estates and trust funds. Mayor, Garden City, N.Y., 1947-49. Trustee Wesleyan University, 1933—, sec. of bd., 1943—; trustee Wesleyan University Press. Member New York State and New York City bar assns., Phi Beta Kappa, Delta Kappa Epsilon. Episcopalian (vestryman). Clubs: University, Down Town Association (N.Y. City), Fishers Island (N.Y.) Country; Cherry Valley (Garden City). Home: 56 Second St., Garden City, N.Y.; also Fishers Island, N.Y. Office: 120 Broadway, N.Y.C. 5. Died Oct. 25, 1954; buried Middleton, Conn.

MURPHY, William Larkin, lawyer; b. Phillipsburg, Mont., Jan. 4, 1877; s. Cornelius and Mary (Qualey) M.; student Gonzaga Coll., Spokane, Wash., U. of Mont., and Columbia; LL.B., Columbia, 1900; LL.D. (honorary), University of Montana, 1952; m. Edith Bickford, June 23, 1909. Practiced at Missoula since 1900. Mem. Western Mont., Mont. State and Am. bar assns. Clubs: Lawyers, Columbia U. (N.Y. City). Home: 414 Eddy Av. Office: Montana Bldg., Missoula, Mont. Died June 19, 1954; buried St. Mary's Cemetery.

MURRAY, Arthur T., mfr.; b. Norwalk, Conn., Jan. 23, 1890; s. Thomas and Pauline (Howard) M.; student pub. schs., Norwalk; m. Anna Louise Richards, June 21, 1912; 1 dau., Mrs. Alexander Davidson, Jr. Began as draughtsman Locomobile Co. of Am., Bridgeport, Conn.; later supt. N.Y. shops, Lozier Motor Car Co.; resigned (1910) to engage in business for self; later with Mack Bros. Motor Car Co., Allentown, Pa.; organized Brady-Murray Motors Co., 1912; became pres. Bethlehem Motors Corp., Allentown, Pa., 1916, United Am. Bosch Corp., 1918; active v.p. Moore Drop Forging Co., 1938—; dir. Third Nat. Bank & Trust Co. of Springfield. Republican. Mason. Clubs: Colony, Long Meadow Country (Springfield). Home: 184 Mill St. Office: 38 Walter St., Springfield, Mass. Died Apr. 24, 1949.*

MURRAY, Earle, business exec. Chmn. of bd. Northern Paper Mills; dir. Kellogg Citizens Nat. Bank. Home: 827 S. Quincy St. Office: Madison and Day Sts., Green Bay, Wis. Died June 15, 1951.

MURRAY, George Dominic, adm. USN, ret.; b. Boston, July 6, 1889; s. Michael Joseph and Mary Elizabeth (Sullivan) M.; grad. U.S. Naval Acad., 1911; Dr. Naval Sci., Boston Coll.; LL.D., Marquette U.; m. Corinne Montague Mustin, Oct. 10, 1925; children—Lloyd Montague Mustin, Henry Ashmead Mustin, Gordon Sinclair Mustin. Midshipman U.S. Naval Acad., 1907-11; 1st comdg. officer, Naval Air Sta., Anacostia, 1918; squadron comdr. 1st aviation unit ordered to Philippines, 1923-25; exec. officer, U.S.S. Wright, 1929; asst. naval attaché in London, Paris, Berlin, The Hague, 1930-33; air officer U.S.S. Saratoga, 1933-35; N.A.S. Pensacola, 1935-37; exec. officer U.S.S. Saratoga, 1937-38; comdg. officer U.S.S. Langley, 1938-39; Bur. Aeronautics, 1939-41; comdg. officer U.S.S. Enterprise, 1941-42; task force comdr. U.S.S. Hornet, Flagship, 1942; chief of Naval Air Intermediate Tng. and comdt. Naval Air Tng. Center, Pensacola, Fla., 1942-43; chief of Naval Air Tng. Comd., 1944; comdr. Air Force, Pacific Fleet, 1944-45; comdr. Mariannas, 1945-46; comdt. 9th Naval Dist., 1946-47; comdr. 1st Task Fleet, 1947-48; comdr. Western Sea Frontier and Pacific Res. Fleet, 1948-51, ret. Dir. Pacific Tel. & Tel. Co. Dir. Guide Dogs for Blind, Inc. Accepted formal capitulation of Japanese on Truk Atoll, Sept. 2, 1945. Decorated Navy Cross, D.S.M., Presdl. Unit Citation (U.S.S. Enterprise), Asiatic-Pacific Ribbon with stars, World War Victory medal, Vera Cruz Campaign medal (U.S.); Order of British Empire; 1915 qualified Naval Aviator No. 22. Clubs: English Speaking Union (pres. Cal. br.), Chevy Chase, Army and Navy (Washington); San Francisco Golf and Country, Bohemian, Pacific Union (San Francisco). Home: 2999 Pacific Av., San Francisco 15. Died June 18, 1956; buried Arlington Nat. Cemetery.

MURRAY, (George) Gilbert (Aimé), author; b. Sydney, New South Wales, Australia, Jan. 2, 1866; s. Sir. Terence Aubrey and Agnes (Edwards) M.; student Merchant Taylor's Sch., London, 1879-84; M.A. (fellow), Oxford, 1888, D.Litt., D.C.L.; LL. D., Glasgow U., also 1889; D.Litt., Birmingham U.; Litt.D., Cambridge U.; D. ès Lettres. Lyons; m. Lady Mary Henrietta Howard, 1889; children—Rosalind, Toynbee, Denis (deceased), Agnes (deceased), Basil (dec.), Stephen. Prof. Greek, Glasgow U., 1889-99; Regius Prof. Greek, Oxford U., 1908-36; Charles Eliot Norton Prof. Poetry, Harvard, 1926. Trustee Brit. Mus., 1914-18. Decorated Order of Merit, (Eng.), 1941, Ordre par le merite (Germany), 1957. Fellow Brit. Acad., Royal Soc. Lit.; mem. Soc. Australian Writers (pres. 1952), Internat. Com. Intellectual Cooperation (pres. 1928-40), League Nations Union (chmn. 1923-38, co-pres. 1938—). Author: Euripides, & His Age, 1910; Five Stages of Greek Religion, 1912; Faith War & Policy, 1917; Aristophanes, A Study, 1933 Aeschylus, Creator of Tragedy, 1940; Greek Studies, 1946; From the League to United Nations, 1947; Hellenism and the Modern World, 1953, (Greek) Euripidis fabulae (3 vols., and Aeschyli fabulae (1 vol.) in the Oxford Critical Texts; also others. Translator: Euripides and other Greek dramatists. Home: Yatscombe, Boars Hill, Oxford, Eng. Died May 20, 1957; buried Westminster Abbey, London, Eng.

MURRAY, Howell Worth, investment banker; b. Springfield, Mo., Dec. 1, 1890; s. Ben Alstrum and Melilla (Howell) M.; Ph.B., U. Chgo., 1914; m. Elisabeth Sherer, June 14, 1917; children—Howell Sherer (USN, killed service 1944), Virginia (dec.), Elizabeth Ann (Mrs. Heath Wakelee), Marjorie (Mrs. Grant Herman). Salesman Tobey Furniture Co., Chgo., 1914-16; with A. G. Becker & Co., Inc., 1916—, v.p., 1925—, dir., 1952—; dir. Gardner-Denver Co., Parker Pen Co., Gisholt Machine Co., Rhinelander Paper Co., Sherer-Gillett Co. Trustee U. Chgo., Carleton Coll., A.L.A. Endowment Fund; vice chmn. Chgo. Community and War Fund campaign, 1944; pres. bd. edn., sch. dist. 107, Highland Park, Ill., 1929-39; chmn. Ravinia Festival Assn. Mem. S.A.R., Chi Psi. Republican. Presbyn. Clubs: Chicago, Commercial, University, Midday, Exmoor, Quadrangle (Chgo.). Home: 1981 Linden Av., Highland Park, Ill. Office: 120 La Salle St., Chgo. 3. Died Nov. 27, 1958.

MURRAY, John Gregory, archbishop; b. Waterbury, Conn., Feb. 26, 1877; s. William and Mary E. (Connor) M.; A.B., Holy Cross Coll., 1897; studied Am. Coll., Louvain, Belgium, 1897-98; U. of Louvain, 1898-1900; Dr. Theology from same university, 1927. Ordained priest R.C. Church at Louvain, Apr. 14, 1900; apptd. prof. Greek and Latin, St. Thomas' Prep. Sem., Hartford, Sept. 1, 1900; chancellor Diocese of Hartford, Oct. 5, 1903; titular bishop of Flavias and auxiliary to the bishop of Hartford, Nov. 15, 1919; consecrated Apr. 28, 1920; transferred to the See of Portland, Me., May 29, 1925, installed as bishop of Portland at the Cathedral of the Immaculate Conception, Oct. 12, 1925; apptd. archbishop of St. Paul, Oct. 29, 1931, installed at Cathedral of St. Paul, Jan. 27, 1932. Member board of trustees Catholic Univ. of America, Washington, D.C.; chmn. bd. of trustees The Coll. of St. Thomas, St. Paul, Minn.; chmn. bd. of trustees The St. Paul Sem., St. Paul, Minn.; chmn. bd. of trustees Coll. of St. Catherine, St. Paul, Minn. Home: 239 Selby Av. (2). Office: 244 Dayton Av., St. Paul, Minn. Died Oct. 11, 1956; Resurrection Cemetery, Mendota, Minn.

MURRAY, Joseph Wilson, newspaper editor; b. Dillon, Kan., July 22, 1879; s. Albert Murray and Mary Jane (Sterling) M.; A.B., U. Kan., 1911; m. Agnes Anderson, Nov. 8, 1914; children—Ann, Jean, James, Andrew. Printer and newspaperman, 1900-06; instr. in journalism and supt. Dept. of Journalism Press, U. Kan., 1911-12; reporter Lawrence Gazette, 1912-15; mng. editor Lawrence Daily Journal-World, 1915-56; owner, pub. Winchester (Kan.) Star, 1957—. Served as sgt. 20th Kan. Inf., U.S.V., in P.I., 1898-99; with AEF, 1917-19. Mem. Phi Beta Kappa, Sigma Delta Chi. Republican. Mason. Clubs: University, Old and New, Kiwanis (Lawrence). Home: 504 Louisiana St. Office: 722 Massachusetts St., Lawrence, Kan. Died July 23, 1958; buried Lawrence.

MURRAY, Leo Tildon, biologist; b. Eastland County, Tex., May 4, 1902; s. Adrian Albert and Olivia May (Jones) M.; A.B., Sul Ross State Tchrs. Coll., Alpine, Tex., 1927; M.S., Cornell U., 1931, Ph.D., 1935; m. Zoe Ellen Jenne, June 18, 1921; children—Ellen, Leo Tildon, Jr. Tchr. Tex. pub. schs., 1922-30, night sch., Itaca, 1930-31, Doyle Academy, Ithaca, 1931-32; N.Y. State Biol. Survey, summers, 1932-35; asst. prof. biology Ball State Tchrs. Coll., Muncie, Ind., 1935-36; asso. prof. biology, and dir. of Museum, Baylor U., 1936-44; asso. prof. biology, A. and M. Coll. Tex., 1944-46; aquatic biologist U.S. Fish and Wild Life Service, 1946—; leader, project investigations Mo. River Basin Studies; asso. prof. zoology U. So. Cal., summer, 1947. Mem. A.A.A.S., Tex. Acad. Sci., Ecol. Soc. Am., Am. Soc. Ichthyologists and Herpetologists, Am. Soc. Mammalogy, Am. Fisheries Soc., Am. Ornithol. Union, Wilson Soc., Herpetologists Union, Ind. Acad. Sci., Tex. Herpetological Soc., Alpha Chi, Sigma Xi. Baptist. Home: 1227 Princeton, Billings, Mont. Died Mar. 2, 1958; buried Billings.

MURRAY, Sister M. Reparata, librarian; b. Stockton, Ill., Feb. 4, 1889; d. John and Ellen (Daly) Murray; A.B., U. of Wis., 1908-12; B.L.S., U. of Ill., 1924; student, U. of Chicago, 1932; Columbia U., 1936. Joined Order of St. Dominic, Sinsinawa, Wis., 1917. Asst. prin., Hurley (Wis.) High Sch., 1912-13; asst. U. of Wis. Library, 1914-17; instr. Latin and English, St. Clara Acad., Sinsinawa, Wis., 1917-18, 1919-21; instr. Cathedral High Sch., Sioux Falls, 1918-19; librarian Rosary Coll., 1922—, dir. department library sci., 1930-49, prof.; dir. Cardinal Stretch Parish Library Workshop at De Paul U., 1952; dir. dept. library sci., summer extension, University Portland, 1944-49; cataloger, Vatican Library, Vatican City, 1938-39. Member Catholic Edn. Assn. (vice chmn., library sect., 1929-31), Cath. Library Assn. (pres. 1949-51), Am. Library Assn., Illinois Library Association. Assistant editor, Catholic Periodical Index, 1930; editor, Catholic Library World, 1937-38. Address: Dept. of Library Science, Rosary College, River Forest, Ill. Died June 16, 1954; buried Sinsinawa, Wis.

MURRAY, Nathaniel Carleton, crop statistician; b. Cincinnati, O., Nov. 29, 1872; s. Charles Burleigh and Sallie (Powell) M.; B.Litt., U. of Cincinnati, 1898; m. Elsie Johnson, June 7, 1900; children—Donald P., Janet, Natalie. Market and financial reporter, 1892-94; asst. editor Cincinnati Price Current, 1898-1904; spl. agt. U.S. Dept. Agr., 1904-07; asst. statistician, 1907-10; statistician and asst. chief, 1910-21, chief statistician, 1921-23, Bur. of Crop Estimates; also permanent mem. crop reporting bd. same; initiated govt. monthly estimates of crop prodn., monthly farm prices, farm labor supply, demand and wages, and other agrl. investigations; crop statistician with Clement Curtis & Co., Chicago, 1923-38, making frequent trips to Argentina to investigate wheat crop; same with Jackson & Curtis, 1939-42. Am. del. to Internat. Inst. of Agr., Rome, 1922. Writer upon agrl. economics and statistics. Home: 4th and Chapman, Waynesville, O. Died Aug. 26, 1952; buried Waynesville.

MURRAY, Owen Meredith, mortgage banker; b. Crockett County, Tenn., Oct. 2, 1885; s. John Fulton and Emma (Hamil) M.; ed. country schs., 1893-1900; m. Lelia Marcum, Sept. 8, 1923. Was on farm from birth until 1904; clk. and part owner country store, Calvin, Indian Territory, 1904-08; in mortgage banking business since 1908; pres. Murray Investment Co., Dallas, 1920—; in oil producing and refining bus., 1934—; chmn. Paramount Fire Ins. Co.; dir. Occidental Life Ins. Co., Pacific Nat. Fire Ins. Co. Mem. Mortgage Bankers Assn. of America (pres. 1934-35), Tex. Mortgage Bankers Assn. (past pres.), Dallas Chamber of Commerce. Presbyterian. Mason. Club: Lakewood Country. Home: 3525 Turtle Creek Blvd., Dallas. Office: 1315 Pacific Av., Dallas 2. Died Oct. 20, 1958; buried Hillcrest Mausoleum, Dallas.

MURRAY, Philip, labor leader; b. Blantyre, Scotland, May 25, 1886; s. William and Rose Ann (Layden) M.; LL.D. (hon.), Howard U., Duquesne U., Boston College; m. Elizabeth Lavery, Sept. 7, 1910; 1 son, Joseph William. Came to U.S., 1902, naturalized citizen, 1911. Mem. Internat. Bd., United Mine Workers of America, 1912, pres. Dist. No. 5, 1916, Internat. v.p., 1926-42; pres. C.I.O. since Nov. 1940; pres. United Steelworkers of Am. since 1942 (chmn. of predecessor Steel Workers Organizing Com., 1936-42). Mem. Pa. Regional War Labor Bd., 1917-18; mem. Nat. Bituminous Coal Production Com., 1917-18, Nat. Industrial Recovery Bd. and NRA Advisory Council, 1935; co-chmn. United Labor Policy Com., 1950-51; mem. exec. bd. Internat. Confedn. of Free Trade Unions since 1941; mem. board of dirs. American Red Cross, 1951; mem. exec. com. Assn. for Advancement of Colored People; turstee Nat. Planning Assn.; dir. Nat. Cancer Found. Recipient Medal of Merit; Monsignor Ryan Award. Mem. Bd. of Edn., Pittsburgh, since 1918. Mem. Am. Acad. Polit. and Social Science. Democrat. Mem. K.C., A.O.H. Home: 752 Berkshire Av., Pittsburgh, Pa. Office: C.I.O., 718 Jackson Pl. N.W., Washington 6. Died Nov. 9, 1952; buried St. Anne Castle, Shannon, Pa.

MURRAY, Reid Fred, congressman; b. Ogdensburg, Wis., Oct. 16, 1887; s. George Chase and Kittie Sarah (Livermore) M.; B.S., U. of Wis. Coll. of Agr., 1916; m. Lyla Hermanson, May 1, 1929; children—Reid Fred, Hyde, Kittie Anne. Agrl. agent N.P. Ry. and G.N. Ry., St. Paul, 1914-17; county agrl. agt., Winnebago Co., 1917-19; dist. leader county agrl. agts., Madison, Wis., 1918-19; agrl. agt. First Nat. Bank, Oshkosh, Wis., 1919-22; prof. animal husbandry, Coll. of Agr., U. of Wis., 1922-27; owner and mgr. Waupaca Cattle Credit Co.; cow dealer and farmer, Waupaca, Wis., 1927-39. Mem. 76th to 82d Congresses 7th District, Wisconsin. Republican. Mason; mem. Acacia. Author of Agrl. bulletin pub. by U. of Wis. Home: Ogdensburg, Wis. Died Apr. 29, 1952.*

MURRAY, Roy Irving, educator; b. Brooklyn, Wis., July 25, 1882; s. Peter and Adelaide Antoinette (Rolfe) M.; student U. Wis., 1900-02; A.B., Hobart, 1904; grad. Gen. Theol. Sem., 1907. Deacon, 1907, priest, 1908, P.E. Ch.; asst. St. Luke's Ch., Scranton, Pa., 1908-11; curate Trinity Chapel, N.Y.C., 1911; rector Ch. of the Advent, Halboro, Pa., 1916-17; ednl. work, 1914—, now master in Latin and English, St. Mark's Sch., Southborough, Mass. Capt. A.R.C., 1917-18, in Eng., France and Italy. Mem. Kappa Alpha. Author: (with Mary Raymond Shipman Andrews) August First, 1915. Contbr. numerous short stories, articles and poems to mags. Home: St. Mark's School, Southborough, Mass. Deceased.

MURRAY, Sidney Charles, lawyer; b. Davenport, Ia., July 4, 1883; s. Thomas and Eva (Daniels) M.; grad. Yale, 1907, Northwestern U. Law School, 1910. Gen. counsel N.Y.C. R.R. Co. at Chicago, 1929-51, now ret., dir. 1944-49; mem. bd. of Affiliated cos. and other corps. many years. Mem. Am., Ill. State and Chicago bar assns. Presbyn. Clubs: Chicago, University of Chicago, Tavern, Yale of Chicago, Old Elm (Chicago); University, Yale (New York). Office: First National Bank Bldg., Chgo. 3. Died June 1, 1954.

MURRAY, William Henry ("Alfalfa Bill"), ex-gov.; b. Collinsville, Tex., Nov. 21, 1869; s. Uriah Dow Thomas and Bertha Elizabeth (Jones) M.; B.S., College Hill Inst., Springtown, Tex., 1889; m. Mary Alice Hearrell, July 19, 1899. Lost mother at two years of age; ran away from home at 12; picked cotton, chopped cordwood, worked in brick yard and on farm; taught sch. 5 yrs.; editor Farmer's World, Dallas, Tex., 1891; Daily News, Corsicana, 1894-95; admitted to bar, 1895; practiced at Ft. Worth, 1896-98; removed to Tishomingo, Ind. Ty., 1898; legal adviser of gov. of Chickasaw Nation, 1898-1901; mainly engaged in ranching, 1903—; mem. Choctaw-Chickasaw Coal Commn. in behalf of Chickasaws, 1903; v.p. Sequoyah Constl. Conv., Muskogee, Ind. Ty., 1905; pres. Okla. Constl. Conv., 1906; chmn. 1st Dem. State Conv. of Okla., under statehood, 1907; speaker Okla. Ho. of Reps., 1907-09 (unanimous choice); delegate-at-large Dem. Nat. Conv., 1908, 12, 16, 32; mem. 63d and 64th Congresses (1913-17), Okla.-at-large and 4th Okla. Dist.; governor of Oklahoma for term 1931-35; chmn. Okla. Code Commn., 1931-35; retired to his farm. Author: Essays on Pocahontas and Pushmataha; Rights of Americans Under Federal Constitution; The Presidency, Supreme Court, and Seven Senators; Uncle Sam Needs a Doctor; The Finished Scholar; Memoirs of Gov. Murray and True History of Oklahoma; Government from Theocracy to Foolacracy; Palestine: Should Jews or Arabs Control?; Negroes Place in the Call of Race. Home: Tishomingo, Okla. Died Oct. 15, 1956; buried Tishomingo Cemetery.

MURRAY, William Hilary, judge; b. Troy, N.Y., Jan. 13, 1883; s. Martin and Ellen (Frawley) M.; A.B., Williams Coll., 1905; LL.B., Albany Law Sch., 1907; m. Katherine Louise Irwin, Oct. 7, 1911; children—William Richard, Mary Frances, Jeanne Marie. Athletic instr. and coach of football Union Coll., Hobart Coll. and Rensselaer Poly. Inst., 1905-10; admitted to N.Y. bar, 1907, practiced in Troy, N.Y.; justice Supreme Court of N.Y., 1939—. Mem. Am., N.Y. State bar assns., Williams College Alumni Assn., Gargoyle Assn. (Williams Coll.), N.Y. State Hist. Assn. Democrat. Roman Catholic. Elk, Kiwanian. Home: 25 24th St. Address: Rensselaer County Court House, Troy, N.Y. Died Sept. 20, 1950.

MURRAY-JACOBY, H(erman), ret. economist, diplomat; b. Nov. 25, 1892; s. Surgeon General Eugene and Henriette (Jacquelin-Frank) Jacoby, of Germany; ed. U. of Berlin, 1913, Columbia, 1915-16, N.Y. U., 1916-17; m. Catherine Fairbanks Murray, Aug. 2, 1920; children—Elaine (Mrs. F. Courtney Stone), Beatrice (Dona Beatrice de Holguin). Bus. training with Hayden, Stone & Co. (N.Y.), Minerals Separation Syndicate (London); was at various times chairman of board Associated Public Utilities Corp., pres. N. Am. Water Works Corp. and dir. Southern Cities Utilities Co., W.Va. Utilities Co., Buffalo & Erie R.R., Metropolitan Fire Ins. Co., Guardian Fire Assurance Corp., Am. Equitable Assurance Corp., Merchants and Mfrs. Fire Ins. Co., New York Fire Ins. Co., Globe Ins. Co. of America, Knickerbocker Ins. Co. Apptd., 1930, head of diplomatic mission to Abyssinia, rank of ambassador extraordinary; econ. cons. Dominican Republic, 1934; elected pres. Dominican Chamber Commerce of U.S., dir. A.d.c. to Hon. Harry H. Woodring, rank of col., 1932; went to Puerto Rico to compile extensive report for Sec. of War Harry H. Wodring, 1936; appointed commercial adviser Dominican Republic, 1941; plenipotentiary del. Inter-Am. Conf. of Am. Republics on financial and economic control, 1942; one of signatories of final treaty Pan-Am. Union, Washington, D.C. United Nations Monetary and Financial Conference, technical advisor to chairman, U.S. Congressional Committee on Coinage, Weights & Measures. Appointed official delegate Ethiopian Red Cross in United States at outbreak of Italo-Ethiopian War; economic adviser to Egyptian finance minister, 1935. Appointed Aug. 1927, member National Housing Com., later vice-chmn. Comdr. Order of St. Sava (Yugoslavia); comdr. Order of Juan Pablo Duarte Dominican Republic); Grand Cordon Order of Menelik (Abyssinia); Comdr. Order of Al Mérito (Ecuador). Officer Order of Carlos Manuel de Céspedes (Cuba). Former trustee Friends Sem. and Friends Schools, Greater New York. Mem. Am. bd. of trustees Paris Theol. Sem. Mem. Soc. of Friends. Co-author Jacoby-Stillich Index Number of European Production, published annually by the Cambridge Assos. Mem. Brit. Schools and Universities Club. Home: 5 N.E. 4th St., Delray Beach, Fla. Died Jan. 27, 1955; buried Delray Beach Cemetery.

MURRIE, William F. R., former pres. Hershey Chocolate Corp., retired Mar. 1947; v.p. Hersey Nat. Bank. Address: Hershey, Pa. Died Sept. 8, 1950.

MURRILL, William Alphonso, botanist; b. Campbell County, Va., Oct. 13, 1869; s. Samuel Leroy and Virginia Daniel (Woodroof) M.; B.S., Va. Poly. Inst., 1887; B.S., Randolph-Macon Coll., Va., 1889, A.B., 1890, A.M., 1891; Ph.D., Cornell U., 1900; research student N.Y. Bot. Garden, 1900-04; m. Edna Lee Luttrell, Sept. 1, 1897. Prof. natural sci. Bowling Green Sem., Va., 1891-93, Wesleyan Female Inst., Va., 1893-97; scholar in botany Cornell U., 1897-98, asst. in botany, 1898-99, asst. cryptogamic botanist, 1899-1900; tchr. biology DeWitt Clinton High Sch., N.Y.C., 1900-04; asst. curator N.Y. Bot. Garden, 1904-05, 1st asst., 1906-07, asst. dir., 1908-22. Mem. Torrey Bot. Club, Bot. Soc. Am., N.Y. Acad. Sciences, Am. Phytopathol. Soc., Sigma Xi. Author: North American Flora, Vol. IX, parts 1-7, 1907, 08, 10, 15, 16, Vol. X, parts 1-3, 1914, 17; Northern Polypores, 1914; American Boletes, 1914; Southern Polypores, 1915; Western Polypores, 1915; Tropical Polypores, 1915; Edible and Poisonous Mushrooms, 1916; Billy, the Boy Naturalist, 1918; Three Young Crusoes, 1918; The Naturalist in a Boarding-school, 1919; The Natural History of Staunton, Virginia, 1919; also (pocket guides), Stars, Rocks, Trees, Reptiles, Autobiography, Florida Plants, Florida Animals, Historic Foundations of Botany in Florida (and America) and (illustrated guides), Ferns, Flowers, Pore Fungi, Familiar Trees; also many botany pamphlets and articles in scientific journals. Editor Mycologia, 1909-24; asso. editor North American Flora. Has named and described 1,700 species of fungi new to science. Has made extensive bot. explorations in Europe, tropical Am., S.A., and on the Pacific Coast, securing over 70,000 specimens and recently completed important studies of Florida fungi, Florida hawthorns and a botanic survey of Alachua County, Fla. Gold medal from Holland Soc. of New York, for mycological work, 1923. Address: Gainesville, Fla. Died Dec. 25, 1957.

MURRY, John Middleton, author; b. London, Eng., Aug. 6, 1889; s. John Murry; student Christ's Hosp. and Brasenose Coll., Oxford; m. Kathleen Beauchamp (Katherine Mansfield), 1912 (died 1923); m. 2d, Violet le Maistre, 1924 (died 1931); 2 children; m. 3d, Elizabeth Cockbayne (deceased 1954); 2 children; married 4th, Mary Gamble, 1954. Founded Rhythm (mag.) while in coll.; became lit. critic on Westminster Gazette, 1912; corr. London Times in Paris, 1913-14; writer for London Times Supplement, 1916-40; editor Peace News, 1940-46, edited Daily Review of the Foreign Press for Intelligence Dept., Brit. Army, 1916-19; editor Athenæum, 1919-21; founded The Adelphi (pacifist mag.), 1923, and editor 1923-30, 1936-48; lecture tour, 1934-35; founded Adelphi Sch. (school for Training in socialist-pacifist leadership; during war training conscientious objectors in land cultivation); radio talks on Europe in Travail, 1939-40. Mem. Ch. of Eng. Author of numerous books since 1916; latest publs.: The Mystery of Keats, 1950; The Conquest of Death, 1951; Community Farm, 1952; Jonathan Swift, 1953; Love, Freedom, and Society, 1957. Editor: Katherine Mansfield's Letters to John Middleton Murry, 1913-22, 1951. Home: Thelnetham, near Diss, Norfolk, Eng. Died Mar. 13, 1957; buried Thelnetham, Diss, Norfolk, Eng.

MUSCHENHEIM, Frederick Augustus (mŭsh'ĕn-hīm), hotelman; b. Braunfels, Germany, Feb. 27, 1871; s. Christian and Philippine (Schellenberg) M.; M.E., Stevens Inst. Tech., 1891; E.D., 1952; m. Elsa Unger, Aug. 21, 1901; children—William, Carl, Mrs. Linda M. Jaques; married 2d, Laura C. Jacobus, August 5, 1953. Came to U.S., 1887, naturalized, 1892. Draftsman New York Edison Co., 1891-93; engr. and factory supt. Western Electric Co., 1893-1903; president Hotel Association of New York City, Inc., 1921-30; vice president Hotel Astor, 1903-18, pres., treas., 1918-44, then chmn. bd., now retired. Hon. v.p. Broadway Assn. Trustee Stevens Inst. Tech., 1917—. Mem. A.S.M.E., Am. Inst. E.E., Hotel Association N.Y.C. (pres. 1921-28). Lutheran. Home: Hampton Bays, L.I. Died Dec. 18, 1956; buried Woodlawn Cemetery, N.Y.C.

MUSE, Vance (mūz), orgn. exec.; b. nr. Moran, Tex., Jan. 6, 1890; s. Henry Lawson and Henrietta (Harris) M.; student pub. schs. and Cullen Sch. of Business, Cleburne, Texas; m. Marie Buckingham, Nov. 6, 1912. Began as laborer Santa Fe R.R., successively bookkeeper-typist and publicity commr. Fort Worth C. of C., 1917-19, organizer, plans for West

Texas C. of C.; asso. with John Henry Kirby in tarriff matters affecting Tex. and southern products, 1919-25; dir. for nat. group sponsoring Mellon plan of taxation, 1926-32; with others formed So. Com. to Uphold the Constitution, 1934; an incorporator and pres. Christian American, Houston, 1936—. Sponsor Freedom to Work amendment to Ark. Const., also adopted by Fla., Ariz., Neb., S.D., others. Democrat. Address: 2708 Werlein St., Houston 5. Died Oct. 15, 1950.

MUSGRAVE, Walter Emmett (mŭs'grāv), bishop; b. Stockport, O., Sept. 7, 1880; s. Sidney Bartlett and Almyra (Coler) M.; student Huntington Coll., 1913-14, D.D., 1928; m. Anna Yarnell, Feb. 6, 1904; children—Wilford Paul, Leona Irene, Emmett Burton (dec.). Ordained ministry Ch. of United Brethren in Christ, 1902; pastor successively at Chesterhill, Pomeroy, Junction City, and Baltimore (all Ohio) until 1915; supt. Scioto Dist., Ch. of United Brethren in Christ, 1915-20; exec. sec. Otterbein Forward Movement, 1920-25; bishop of ch., 1925—. Pres. bd. edn. Huntington Coll.; pres. Domestic, Frontier and Fgn., Missionary Soc. of Ch. of United Brethren in Christ, 1933—, ofcl. historian, 1945. Republican. Author The Church of the United Brethren in Christ, Its Teachings and Progress, 1945. Contbr. to Christian Conservator. Home: 836 Hines St., Huntington, Ind. Died May 6, 1950; buried Pilgrims Rest, Huntington.

MUSSELWHITE, Harry Webster, ex-congressman; b. on farm, Branch County, Mich., May 23, 1868; s. Walter and Elida (Case) M.; ed. high sch., Coldwater, Mich.; m. Marcia Mahlke, Feb. 4, 1891; 1 dau., Gladys (Mrs. Clarence B. Goshorn); m. 2d, Nellie Austin, June 8, 1910 (dec Feb. 15, 1935); 1 dau., Helen (Mrs. A. Edward Colcord). Learned printer's trade; advt. salesman, reporter, news and feature writer, Detroit, Chicago, St. Louis, etc., 1887-1905; with Grand Rapids Herald, 1905-15; owner, editor and pub. Manistee (Mich.) Daily News-Advocate, 1915-28; now pres. and treas. News Pub. Co. Mem. 73d Congress (1933-35), 9th Mich. Dist. Supervisor Federal Census, 9th Mich. Dist., 1920, 4th Mich. Dist., 1930; vice chmn. Mich. State Hospital Commn., 1927-32; pres. Manistee Bd. of Commerce, 1930-31. Democrat. Mason (32°, K.T., Shriner), Eagle, Elk. Home: 214 Chesterton Pl., San Mateo, Cal. Died Dec. 14, 1955; buried Manistee, Mich.

MUSSER, Paul Howard, univ. provost; b. Bedford, Pa., Mar. 27, 1892; s. Cyrus John (D.D.) and Henrietta Edith (Mowry) M.; prep. edn., Mercersburg (Pa.) Acad.; student Franklin and Marshall Coll., 1912-13; A.B., University of Pennsylvania, 1916, Ph.D., 1928; LL.D., Gettysburg College, 1941; m. Mary Thaddeus Carr, Aug. 19, 1925; children—John Carr, Janet Anne, Virginia Ellen. With U. of Pa. since 1916, successively reader in English, asst. instr. English, instr., asst. prof., prof. since 1931, dean of coll. and dir. coll. collateral courses, 1929-39, administrative vice-pres., 1939-44, provost since 1944. Trustee U. of Pa. Moore Sch. Elec. Engring. Chmn. com. on adminstrn. Morris Arboretum; member board trustees Pa. School of Social Work; dir. Pa. Sch. for the Deaf; bd. regents Mercersburg Acad. Mem. Modern Lang. Assn. Am., Pa. Hort. Soc., Hist. Soc. of Pa., A.A.A.S., National Council of Teachers of English, Am. Assn. Univ. Profs., Eastern Assn. of Coll. Deans and Administrators of Men, Pa. Assn. Colls. and Univs. (pres. 1936), Alpha Psi, Alpha Phi Omega, Phi Beta Kappa, Phi Kappa Psi. Mem. Pa. Park Art Assn., Pa. Acad. of the Fine Arts, Community Chest of Phila. and vicinity. Clubs: Franklin Inn, Lenape, Philobiblon, Rittenhouse. Author: James Nelson Barker—Biography, 1929. Home: 730 S. Latches Lane, Merion, Pa. Office: College Hall, University of Pennsylvania, Phila. 4. Died Nov. 21, 1951.

MYER, Walter Evert (mī'ẽr), publisher; b. Winfield, Kan., Apr. 16, 1889; s. Zaccheus B. and Nancy (Miller) M.; A.B., Southwestern Coll., Winfield, Kan., 1910, hon. LL.D., 1934; A.M., U. of Chicago, 1913; m. Ruth Geeslin, July 3, 1912. Instr. history, high sch., Aurora, Ill., 1913-15; prof. history, Kan. State Teachers Coll., Emporia, 1915-18, head dept. of economics and sociology, 1920-25; mem. research staff, U.S. Tariff Commn., 1918-20. Owner and editor Civic Edn. Service, pubs. of Am. Observer, Weekly News Rev., Junior Rev., and The Young Citizen, Washington, D.C., since 1925. Mem. Am. Sociol. Soc. Clubs: National Press, Cosmos, University. Author: The Promise of Tomorrow (with Clay Coss), 1938; Education for Democratic Survival (wth Clay Coss), 1942; America's Greatest Challenge (with Clay Coss), 1952. Home: 3729 Fordham Rd. Office: 1733 K St. N.W., Washington. Died Oct. 25, 1955.

MYERS, Burton Dorr, anatomist; b. Attica, O., Mar. 30, 1870; s. John T. and Eliza E. (Meyers) M.; Ph.B., Buchtel Coll., 1893; A.M., Cornell U., 1900; M.D., U. of Leipzig, 1902; m. Maud A. Showers, Mar. 4, 1904; children—James Showers (dec.), Mary Isabel, Rudolf Burton, Margaret Ann. Supt. high sch., Grenwich, O., 1893-97; asst. in physiology, Cornell U., 1898-1900; asst. in anatomy, Johns Hopkins, 1902-03; prof. anatomy, Ind. U., 1903-40; also dean of the Indiana U. School of Medicine, at Bloomington, emeritus prof. and dean since July 1940. Mem. Am. Assn. Anatomists, A.M.A., Assn. Am. Med. Colleges (pres. 1928-29), Sigma Xi, Phi Beta Kappa, Alpha Omega Alpha. Methodist. Dist. gov. Ind. Kiwanis Dist., 1923; trustee Kiwanis Internat. Contbr. to med. mags. and revs. Vice chmn. Ind. State Planning Bd. Author: History of Medical Education in Indiana, History of Ind. Univ., 1902-37; Trustees and Officers of Indiana University, 1820 to 1950, 1951. Home: Bloomington, Ind. Died Fed. 28, 1951; buried Bloomington.

MYERS, Charles Augustus, mfr.; b. New York, N.Y., Jan. 26, 1889; s. Charles Augustus and Ella (Hays) M.; desc. (9th generation) Adolph Myer, who came from Westphalia, Germany, and settled in Harlem (New York), 1661; desc. (on mother's side) David Hays, one of soldiers serving under George Washington in Braddock's Defeat; student of spl. course in perfumes, extracts, and allied products, Columbia U. Coll. of Pharmacy, 1926-27; m. Harriet Horn, Apr. 5, 1913 (dec.); m. 2d, Ruth Glenn, June 17, 1933; children—Charles Augustus, Edith Hays. With Dodge and Olcott Company, manufacturer essential oils, aromatic chemicals, New York City and Bayonne, N.J., 1907-48, asst. to sec., 1911-19, asst. to vice pres., 1919-23, prodn. mgr. factory, 1923-26, gen. mgr. factory, 1926-38, became 1st v.p., 1938, member bd. dirs. 1928; vice pres. Dodge & Olcott, Inc., mem. bd. dir., 1945, exec. vice pres., 1946, pres. 1947-48. Served with U.S.N.R.F., 1917-19, chief petty ofcr. chem. service; in U.S.N.R.F., 1919-21. Contbd. a number of new devices to science of fuel analysis; holds navigator's license for vessels up to 15 gross tons. Awarded Victory Medal by U.S. and N.Y. State. Fellow Am. Geog. Soc.; mem. N.Y. Acad. Scis. (life), Am. Legion; Marine Mus. City N.Y. (life), Bayonne, N.J. C. of C. (dir.), Mus. of City of N.Y. Republican. Clubs: Railroad and Machinery (life). Chemists. Home: 99 Glenwood Rd., Englewood, N.J. Died July 29, 1955; buried Woodlawn Hays Mausoleum.

MYERS, Charles Franklin, clergyman; b. Lexington, Va., Jan. 11, 1876; s. Henry H. and Mary Ella (Nelson) M.; student Washington and Lee U., 1893-97, Union Theol. Sem., Richmond, Va., 1898-1901, Princeton Theol. Sem., 1902; m. Elsie Belle Smith, Sept. 9, 1903; children—Betty Lacy, Alexander Nelson, Charles Franklin. Ordained ministry Presbyn. Ch. in U.S., 1903; pastor First Ch., Williamson, later Bream Meml. Ch., Charleston, W.Va., until 1916. First Ch., Greensboro, N.C., 1916—. Trustee Hollins (Va.) Coll., Flora MacDonald Coll., Red Springs, N.C. Mem. Phi Gamma Delta. Rotarian. Home: Irving Park, Greensboro, N.C. Died July 20, 1948.

MYERS, Curtis Clark, mech. engr.; b. South Livonia, N.Y., July 9, 1879; s. James E. and Jennie (Eaton) M.; M.E., Cornell U., 1903, M.M.E., 1905; m. Florence MacClelland, July 22, 1908; 1 son, Curtis MacClelland (dec.). Instr. Cornell U., 1903; constrn. engr. Lackawanna Steel Co., 1906-07; mech. engr. Diamond Chain Co., Indpls., 1907-09; asst. prof. in charge coop. engring. courses, U. Cin., 1909-13, prof. indsl. engring., 1913-18; mech. engr. Aluminum Co. of America, 1919, chief mech. engr. Pitts., 1919-24; supt. Aluminum Co. of Can., Toronto, 1924-29; in charge fgn. bldg. program Aluminum, Ltd., Montreal, Can., 1929-32; chief prodn. engr. Ford Instrument Co., Long Island City, N.Y., 1934-35, factory mgr., 1935-37; N.Y. sales rep. Doyle Machine Tool Co., 1937-39, factory mgr., Syracuse, N.Y., 1939-40; asst. mgr. W.P.B., Syracuse, N.Y., 1940-41, spl. research engr., aluminum and magnesium br. Washington, 1941-43; resident dir. Daniel Guggenheim Airship Inst., Akron, O., 1943-49, ret. Served as capt. ordnance, U.S. Army, 1918-19. Life mem. Am. Soc. M.E. Clubs: Torch, Rotary (Akron); Engineers (N.Y.C.). Home: 211 Aurora St., Hudson, O. Died Dec. 3, 1954.

MYERS, David Albert, ex-justice, lawyer; b. Logansport, Ind., Aug. 5, 1859; s. Henry C. and Maria (Bright) M.; B.S., Danville (Ind.) Normal Coll., 1879; LL.B., Albany Law Sch. (Union U.), 1882; m. Margaret McNaught, Sept. 3, 1907. Began Rush counties, Ind., 1890-94; judge 8th Jud. Circuit of Ind., 1898; judge Appellate Court, 1904-13; asso. justice Supreme Court of Ind., 1917-35; vice chmn. Alcoholic Beverage Commn., 1935-37; now practicing law; pres. Corbett and Craig Hardware Co., Greensburg. Charter mem. of Ind. Bar Assn.; mem. Am. Bar Assn.; vice chmn. bd. dirs. and treas. bd. trustees YMCA, Greensburg, 1915-21. Mason (K.T., 32°), Odd Fellow; charter mem. K.P. and Elks. Republican. Clubs: Columbia (Indpls.); Sportsmen's (Greensburg). Home: Greensburg, Ind. Died July 2, 1955.

MYERS, David Moffat, cons. engr., specialist on indsl. power supply; b. Owasco, N.Y., Jan. 8, 1879; s. Rev. Alfred E. and Mary (Moffat) M.; M.E., Columbia, 1901; m. Emily N. Huyck, 1911 (dec.); m. 2d, Jennette Kennedy. Mech. engr. U.S. Leather Co., 1901-06; cons. engr. in pvt. practice, 1906-15; partner firm of Griggs & Myers, 1915-25; cons. engr., alone and later as mem. of firm Orrok, Myers & Shoudy, N.Y.C., later Myers & Addington; now cons. engr. with Seelye, Stevenson, Value & Knecht; consulting engr. Bur. of Yards and Docks, U.S. Navy, last 7 yrs. cons. engr. N.Y. Board of Water Supply. Served with U.S. Fuel Adminstrn. as volunteer during World War I, apptd. advisory engr. and chief of fuel engring. sect. which he organized. Dir. Gramercy Boys Club (N.Y. City), Larchmont (N.Y.) Civic Assn. Fellow Am. Soc. M.E., A.A.A.S.; mem. Am. Inst. C.E., Soc. Older Grads. of Columbia, Westchester Shore Humane Soc. (dir.). Mem. Dutch Reformed Ch. Clubs: Horseshoe Harbor Yacht (commodore 1939-40), Columbia U., Univ. (Larchmont); former mem. Cosmos (Wash., D.C.). Author: Factory Power Plants: The Power Plant; Cost Cutting for Industrial Power Plants Reducing Industrial Power Costs, 1935. Contbr. numerous articles and papers to tech. publs. and orgns. Inventor of furnaces for spl. fuels, sail slide guide and speed indicator for boats. Home: 3 Cliff Way, Larchmont, N.Y. Office: 101 Park Av., N.Y.C. 17. Died Jan. 20, 1954.

MYERS, Dean Wentworth, surgeon; b. Ionia County, Mich., Apr. 27, 1874; s. David Wallace and Rebecca Jane (Macomber) M.; grad. high sch., Muir, Mich., 1893; M.D., U. of Mich. Homeo. Med. Sch., 1899; post-grad. study same, 1899-1903; m. Cora Louise Owen, Aug. 29, 1900 (died May 4, 1904); 1 dau., Dorothy Louise; m. 2d, Eleanor Sheldon, Aug. 19, 1922. Asst. dept. ophthalmology and oto-laryngology, U. of Mich. Homeo. Med. Sch., 1899-1903; practiced in Grand Rapids, Mich., 1903-07; prof. otolaryngology, 1907-08, prof. ophthalmology and otolaryngology, 1908-22, U. of Mich. Homeo. Med. Sch. First lt. Med. Reserve Corps, U.S. Army, 1915. Fellow Am. College of Surgeons (gov. 1920-26); mem. Am. Med. Assn., Pan-American Assn. Ophthalmology, Am. Inst. Homeopathy, Am. Homeo. Ophthal., Otol. and Laryngol. Soc. (sec. 1910-14; pres. 1914-15), Mich. State Homeopathic Med. Soc. (pres. 1910-11), Michigan State Medical Society (house of delegates 1933-1943; councilor 14th District 1943-49), Washtenaw County Medical Society (president 1942), Alpha Sigma, Theta Kappa Psi, Ann Arbor Chamber of Commerce (pres. 1938), U.S. Chamber of Commerce (nat. councilor 1939). Pres. Ann Arbor City Council, 1929-31; mem. Ann Arbor School Bd., 1928-31. Pres. U. of Mich. Alumni Club of Ann Arbor, 1935-36. Mem. Internat. Rotary Clubs: pres. Ann Arbor Rotary Club, 1936-37. Democrat. Chmn. Washtenaw Co. Dem. Com., 1942-46. Presbyterian; elder since 1938. K.T. Contbr. numerous articles to med. jours.; widely recognized for successful surgery of the eye, and one of first surgeons in America to remove cataractous lens in its closed capsule; first to establish the exact center of rotation of the eye by a series of X-Ray photographs of a needle passed directly through eyeball. Home: 2220 Washtenaw Av., Ann Arbor, Mich. Died July 2, 1955; buried Forest Hill Cemetery, Ann Arbor.

MYERS, Francis John, ex-U.S. senator; b. Phila., Dec. 18, 1901; s. John Francis and Mary (Donnelly) M.; A.B., St. Joseph's Coll., Phila., 1923, LL.D., 1945; LL.B., Temple U., 1927, LL.D., 1946; LL.D., St. Vincent's Coll., Latrobe, Pa., 1946; m. Catherine M. Hall, Feb. 11, 1931; children—Francis John, Kathleen, Barbara. Admitted to Pa. bar, 1927, since practiced in Phila.; dep. atty. gen. for Pa., 1937-39; mem. 76th to 78th Congresses, 6th Pa.; mem. U.S. Senate, 1945-51. Dist. Sec. to Dist. Attys. of Phila., 1929-31. Democrat. Roman Catholic. K.C. Home: 6912 Greenhill Rd. Office: Land Title Bldg., Phila.; also Senate Office Bldg., Washington. Died July 5, 1956.

MYERS, Frank Clayton, lawyer, welfare promotion; b. York Springs, Pa., Feb. 1, 1883; s. Clayton Franklin and Sarah Elizabeth (Menges) M.; grad. Cumberland Valley State Tchrs. Coll., Shippensburg, Pa., 1902, Perkiomen School, Pennsburg, Pa., 1905; A.B., Princeton, 1909; LL.B., N.Y. Law Sch., 1918; m. Mary Leanora Harvey, June 3, 1914; children—Mary Lee (Mrs. A. P. Hornor, Jr.), Frank Clayton. Tchr. pub. schs. York County, Pa., 1902-04; state sec. YMCA, in charge student ednl. and immigration work, N.Y., also sec. N.Y. State Immigration Commn., 1909-10; editor College World, 1910-11; sec. N.Y. Child Welfare Com., 1912-32, pres., 1932—; also in practice of law, 1918—, now mem. firm Strange, Myers, Hinds & Wight, N.Y.C., and Williams, Myers & Quiggle, Washington; dir., counsel Gotham Advt. Co.; dir., v.p. Lee and Simmons, Inc., Simmons Lee Corp., Jarvis Shipping Corp.; v.p., counsel, dir. Home Playyards, Inc.; sec., dir. and counsel Thessalonica Agrl. and Industrial Inst. Dir. Nat. Motion Picture League; dir., chmn. exec. com. and counsel Children's Welfare Fedn. of N.Y.C.; trustee Mount Holyoke Coll.; hon. trustee West Essex Community Chest. Former mem. Com. on Pub. Relations, Motion Picture Producers and Distbrs. Am. Past pres. Princeton Alumni Assn. of Montclair; treas., dir. Nat. Child Welfare Assn.; mem. N.Y. County Lawyers Assn., N.Y. State C. of C. Republican. Presbyn. Clubs: Princeton (N.Y.C.); Princeton Terrace. Contbr. articles on govt., civic and social problems. Home: 38 Crane St., Caldwell, N.J. Office: 165 Broadway, N.Y.C. Died June 14, 1950; buried York Springs, Pa.

MYERS, George Hewitt; financier, art collector, authority on textiles; b. Cleveland, O., Sept. 10,

1875; s. John and Mary Ware (Hewitt) M.; grad. Hill Sch., Pottstown, Pa., 1894; B.A., Yale, 1898, M.F., 1902; studied at Harvard Univ., 1898-99; m. Louise Stoddard Chase, Apr. 21, 1908; children—Persis Chase (Mrs. Clair Rucker Batigne), Mary Hewitt (Mrs. Alexander Graham Stone), Louise Chase (Mrs. John Ramsey Pugh). With U.S. Forest Service, 1904-06, lectured Yale Forest Sch.; a founder Y. E. Booker & Co., investment banking firm which merged with Alexander-Brown & Sons, 1943; dir. Mergenthaler Linotype Co. Pres., trustee Textile Mus., D.C. Civilian mem. M.I., U.S. Army, 1918. Mem. Smithsonian Fine Arts Commn.; hon. curator of textiles Yale U. Art Gallery; mem. bd. Nat. Symphony Orchestra. Mem. adv. com. Boy Scouts Am.; active fund raising campaigns Community Chest. Mem. Soc. Am. Foresters, (asso.), S.R. Clubs: Cosmos, Metropolitan, Chevy Chase (Washington); Yale, Century Assn. (New York); Yeamans Hall (Charleston, S.C.). Home: 2310 S St. N.W., Washington 8. Office: 730 15th St. N.W., Washington 5. Died Dec. 23, 1957.

MYERS, Henry Alonzo, educator; b. Newburgh, N.Y., Apr. 9, 1906; s. James K. and Grace (Casey) M.; A.B., Niagara U., 1929; Ph.D., Cornell, 1933; m. Elsie E. Phillips, Aug. 2, 1935; children—James Phillips, Helen Priscilla. Mem. faculty, Cornell, 1935—, prof. English, 1947—, acting chmn. dept. English, 1952-53, chmn. com. Am. Studies, 1950—; vis. prof. dramatic literature, Stanford, 1945-46, in humanities, 1953-54, vis. prof. Am. literature and philosophy, Salzburg Seminar in Am. Studies, Salzburg, Austria, 1950; first vis. prof. Am. literature, U. London: King's Coll., 1951-52; research fellow Am. Council Learned Socs. and vis. scholar, Harvard, 1934-35. Mem. Am. Studies Assn., Am. National Theatre and Academy, Modern Language Association, College Conference of English, Phi Beta Kappa, Phi Kappa Phi. Clubs: Authors (London); Statler (Ithaca). Author: Short History English Literature 1938; The Spinoza-Hegel Paradox 1944; Are Men Equal: an inquiry into the meaning of Am. Democracy, 1945; 2d edit., 1955; Tragedy: A View of Life, 1956. Contbr. articles to nat. mags. Home: Ellis Hollow Rd. Ithaca, N.Y. Died May 2, 1955; buried East Lawn Cemetery, Ithaca.

MYERS, Howard Barton, economist; b. Knoxville, Ia., Feb. 13, 1901; s. Leonard Barton and Della Mae (Roberts) M.; A.B., Washburn Coll., 1923; fellow U. Chgo., 1923-27, Ph.D., 1929; m. Bernice Curry, Dec. 19, 1927; children—Ann Curry, Howard Barton, Robert Burris. Research asst. U. Chgo., 1923-27; asso. prof. econs., U. Fla., 1927-29; chief div. research and statistics Ill. State Dept. Labor, 1929-33; chief statistician Ill. State Emergency Relief Com., 1932-33; asst. dir. in charge research, statistics, finance Fed. Relief Adminstrn., 1933-36; dir. research Works Project Adminstrn., 1936-42; lectr. statistics Am. U., Washington, 1937-42; tech. adv. com. population, unemployment U.S. Bur. Census, 1940, 50; asso. chief munitions br. W.P.B., Washington, 1942-43; asso. dir. research Com. Econ. Development, 1943-49, exec. sec. research and policy com., 1944-49, dir. research since 1949; tech. cons. com. econ. policy, bus. adv. council Dept. Commerce; cons. econ. adv. com. Nat. Assn. Mfrs.; adv. com. econ. policy Econ. Stblzn. Agy., 1951-52. Adv. com. S.S.S., 1942-45. Fellow Am. Statis. Assn. (v.p. 1942); mem. Am. Econ. Assn., Am. Indsl. Relations Assn. Co-author: Jobs and Markets, 1946. Editor of The Labor Bull., 1929-33. Contbr. tech. articles econ., statis. jours. Home: 2940 Chain Bridge Rd., Washington 16. Office: 1729 H St., Washington 6. Died Mar. 9, 1956; buried Nat. Meml. Park, Falls Church, Va.

MYERS, Joseph Simmons, univ. prof.; b. Columbus, O., Feb. 3, 1867; s. Lorenzo D. and Harriet A. (Simmons) M.; A.B., Ohio State U., 1887; m. Amelia W. Spencer, Oct. 4, 1892; children—Edward S., Chester L. (dec.); m. 2d, Madelaine E. Davis, June 1, 1904 (died July 23, 1928). Newspaper work on the Columbus Times, 1887; on staff Cleveland Leader, 1888-89; telegraph editor, Pittsburgh Post, 1889-91, night editor, 1891-96, mng. editor, 1896-1914; also mng. editor Pittsburgh Sun, 1906-14; apptd. prof. journalism, Ohio State U., 1914, and dir. Sch. of Journalism; prof. emeritus since 1934; columnist Middletown (O.) Journal since 1935. Mem. Am. Assn. Teachers of Journalism, Assn. of Am. Schs. and Depts. of Journalism (pres. 1926), Am. Assn. Univ. Profs., Ohio State U. Alumni Assn. (nat. sec. 1914-16), Mil. Order Loyal Legion, Phi Gamma Delta, Phi Beta Kappa, Sigma Delta Chi, Pi Delta Epsilon (national president, 1927). Methodist. Mem. Internat. Assn. Torch Clubs. Compiler Vol. III, History of Ohio State University. Address: The Journal, Middletown, O. Died Oct. 17, 1953; buried Middletown, O.

MYERS, Louis Wescott, lawyer; b. Lake Mills, Wis., Sept. 6, 1872; s. Jesse Hall and Elizabeth Louise (Wescott) M.; B.Litt., U. Wis., 1893, LL.B., 1895; LL.D., U. So. Cal., 1925; LL.D., U. Cal., 1926; m. Blanche Brown, Nov. 27, 1901; children—Alice Elizabeth, John Wescott. Practiced with Spooner, Sanborn & Kerr, Madison, Wis., 1894-95, with Jesse A. and Henry Baldwin, Chgo., 1895-97; settled in Los Angeles, 1898; judge Superior Ct. Los Angeles County, 1913-23; apptd. asso. justice Supreme Court Cal., 1923, for term ending 1925 (chief justice, 1924-25); resumed practice at Los Angeles; mem. O'Melveny & Myers. Member Am., Cal. State, Los Angeles bar assns., Phi Beta Kappa, Sigma Chi, Phi Delta Phi. Republican. Protestant. Clubs: Cal., Los Angeles, Sunset, Tuna, Lincoln of Los Angeles (dir., pres.). Home: 269 S. Lorraine Blvd. Office: Title Insurance Bldg., Los Angeles, Cal. Died Feb. 15, 1960.

MYERS, William Kurtz, engr.; b. Millville, N.J. Dec. 17, 1883; s. Christian and Louisa (Kurtz) M.; B.S., Pa. State Coll., 1905; m. Margaret Steinbach, June 23, 1909; draftsman Pa. Steel Co., 1905-07; engr. Chicago Traction Co., 1908-19; valuation mgr. and engr. Phila. Rapid Transit Co., and Internat. Ry. Co. of Buffalo, 1919-23, v.p. Phila. Rapid Transit Co., 1923-26, pres., 1926-27; exec. v.p. Mitten Bank Securities Corp., 1927-29, pres., 1929-38; v.p. Mitten Management, Inc., 1927-43; chmn. exec. com. and vice chmn. bd. of dirs. Phila. Rapid Transit Co., 1928-31; mem. exec. com. Internat. Ry. Co., 1928-43; president Mitten Bank & Trust Co., 1928-40; chmn. bd. of dirs. Penn. Steel Castings Co., Chester, Pa., since 1933. Mem. Am. Soc. of M.E., Am. Soc. C.E. Club: Engrs. Home: Merion, Pa. Office: Penn Steel Castings Co., Chester, Pa. Died Sept. 7, 1953.

MYERS, William Starr, prof. politics; b. Baltimore, Md., June 17, 1877; s. John Norris and Laura Virginia (Starr) M.; B.A., U. of N.C., 1897; studied Johns Hopkins, 1897-1900, Ph.D., 1900; m. Margaret Barr, June 8, 1910; children—Virginia Starr, Margaret Barr. Master of history, Gilman Sch., Baltimore, Md., 1900-06; asst. prof. and preceptor in history and politics, 1906-18, professor of politics, 1918-43; emeritus, 1943—, Princeton University. Instr. history, University of Tennessee, summers 1911, 12; instructor history and politics, Johns Hopkins, summers 1913-16; lecturer Army War College, Washington, 1920-40, Naval War Coll., Newport, R.I., 1931-41; lectured and conducted Round Table Confs., Furman Inst. of Politics, Greenville, S.C., sessions 1924, 25, Inst. Pub. Affairs, U. of Va., session 1929. Mem. Small Loans Commn., N.J., 1931-32. Trustee Lake Placid Club Ednl. Foundation, 1929-31. Pres. bd. mgrs. Evang. Edn. Soc. of P.E. Ch., 1943-50, honorary president, 1950—; associate editor The Chronicle, Poughkeepsie, N.Y., 1939-48. Mem. Am. and Va. hist. socs., Am. Polit. Sci. Assn., Beta Theta Pi, Phi Beta Kappa. Episcopalian. Author: Socialism and American Ideals, 1919; American Democracy Today, 1924; Fifty Years of the Prudential, 1926; The Republican Party, a History, 1928; American Government of Today, 1931; General George B. McClellan, 1934; The Foreign Policies of Herbert Hoover, 1940; The Hoover Administration (with Walter H. Newton), 1936; Story of New Jersey, 1945. Editor, McClellan's Mexican War Diary, 1917; Stryker's Battle of Monmouth, 1927; Kitazawa's Government of Japan, 1929; Kraus' The Crisis of German Democracy, 1932; The State Papers of Herbert Hoover (2 volumes), 1934, Woodrow Wilson (joint author), 1946. On editorial staff of New York Journal of Commerce at various times. Contributor to newspapers and magazines. Lecturer on hist. and polit. subjects. Home: 104 Bayard Lane, Princeton, N.J. Died Jan. 28, 1956; buried Princeton Cemetery.

MYGATT, Gerald (mī-găt'), author, editor; born New York, N.Y.; s. Lemuel Carrington and Sophia Hartt (Weidemeyer) M.; ed. Collegiate Sch., N.Y.; A.B., Williams Coll.; m. Gertrude Hitz; children—Donald (lt. Army Air Corps), Judith, Antoinette, Peter. Successively reporter New York Sun; circulation mgr., The Outlook; sales-promotion mgr. Good Housekeeping Mag.; mng. editor and editor Cosmopolitan Mag.; mng. editor This Week Mag.; editor Our Navy Mag.; editor Liberty Mag.; copy chief, adv. dept., Columbia Broadcasting System. Mem. Alpha Delta Phi. Clubs: Williams (N.Y.); Dutch Treat (N.Y.). Author: Nightmare, a novel, 1928; Soldiers' and Sailors' Prayer Book, 1944. Contbr. short stories and serials to Sat. Eve. Post and other mags. Served as pvt., cpl., sgt., 1st sgt., 2d lt., 1st lt., F.A.; capt. 75th F.A., U.S. Army, 1917-19. Major, F.A., A.U.S., 1924-34. Address: Hotel Carteret, 208 W. 23d St., N.Y.C. 11. Died June 3, 1955; buried Rosedale Cemetery, Orange, N.J.

MYLES, Beverly Russell, lawyer; b. N.Y. City, June 2, 1895; s. Dr. Robert Cunningham and Edith G. R. (Platt) M.; student Hill Sch., Pottstown, Pa.; A.B. honoris causa (war service), Yale, 1918; LL.B., Columbia, 1924; m. Edith Harlan, Aug. 29, 1934; 1 dau., Edith B. Admitted to N.Y. bar, 1925 and since practiced in N.Y. City; partner Myles, Wormser & Koch; dir. Selective Issues, Inc.; mem. Bondholders Com. Cuba R.R. Mem. Republican Co. Com. (N.Y.). With Am. Field Service, 1917-18. Mem. Bar Assn. City of N.Y. Republican. Episcopalian. Clubs: Yale (N.Y. City); Bedford (N.Y.) Golf and Tennis. Home: 116 E. 63rd St., N.Y. City; (summer) Poundridge, N.Y. Office: 60 42nd St., N.Y.C. 17. Died Feb. 19, 1951.

N

NADAL, Thomas William (nādăl'), educator clergyman; b. Milroy, Ind., June 17, 1875; s. Benjamin Franklin and Jerusha (Richey) N.; A.B., DePauw U., 1898; student U. Chgo., summers, 1901-02; A.M., Harvard, 1903, Ph.D., 1909; M.Pd., Mich. State Normal Coll., 1917; LL.D., Olivet Coll., 1919, DePauw, 1924; Litt.D., Drury Coll., 1940; m. Kathryne Dillingham Wyckoff, June 2, 1909; children—Joseph Wyckoff, Robert Richey, Ruth Dillingham, Kathryne Louise. Instr. English and oratory Olivet Coll., 1898-1901, prof., 1901-16, dean, 1905-16, acting pres., 1915-16; pres. Drury Coll., Springfield, Mo., 1917-40, now pres. emeritus; minister Church-in-the-Gardens, Forest Hills, N.Y., 1941-42; minister First Congl. Ch., Olivet, Mich., 1942—; lectr. on lit., ednl., religious and popular subjects. Mem. Mich. Bd. Edn., 1911-17, pres. 1915-17. Republican. Conglist. Mem. Modern Lang. Assn. Am., Phi Beta Kappa, Delta Kappa Epsilon. Contbr. to philol. jours. Home: Olivet, Mich. Died June 28, 1958; buried Olivet.

NADLER, Carl S., sugar producer; b. Plaquemine, La., March 24, 1892; s. Henry and Jennie (Seepe) N.; B.S., La. State U., 1912, M.S. in engring., 1913; m. Genevieve Smitha, Aug. 7, 1916; children—Carl, William S. engr. South Porto Rico Sugar Co., Puerto Rico, 1913-18; engr. Cuba Cane Sugar Corp., Havana, Cuba, 1920; pres. Nadler Machine and Foundry Co., 1920-27; prof. sugar engring., La. State U., 1927-29; in charge sugar operations, Realty Operators, Inc., New Orleans, La., 1929-37; mng. partner Russell & Company, Ensenada, Puerto Rico, 1937-40; chairman of the board South Porto Rico Sugar Company. Mem. Sigma Nu. Episcopal. Clubs: India House (New York City). Home: Barton, La. Office: 99 Wall St., N.Y. C. Died Oct. 12, 1953; buried Plaquemine, La.

NAECKEL, Erwin George, advt. exec.; b. Davenport, Ia., May 17, 1897; s. Alexander and Fredericke (Tank) N.; student State U. Ia., 1916-19; m. Edna Wehling, June 16, 1926; 1 dau., Nancy Jill. With L. W. Ramsey Co., Chicago, since 1930, pres. since 1947, L. W. Ramsey Advt. Agy., Davenport, Ia., since 1924. Trustee Davenport Municipal Art Gallery, St. Luke's Hosp., St. Katharines (sch. for girls), Davenport. Served as ensign, U.S. Navy, 1918-19. Mem. Kappa Sigma. Episcopalian. Clubs: Tavern (Chicago); Davenport Country, Town, Davenport (Davenport). Home: 2026 Fernwood Av. Office: Union Arcade, Davenport, Ia. Died May 25, 1954; buried Oakdale Cemetery, Davenport.

NAGEL, Conrad F(rederick), Jr., metal co. exec.; b. N.Y.C., Aug. 19, 1891; s. Conrad Frederick and Paulina (Bahr) N.; A.B., Cornell, 1914, B. Chemistry, 1915; m. Mona Lois Crytzer, July 23, 1920; children—Lois Anne (Mrs. Ralph B. Martin), Eleanor (Mrs. Thos. I. Stephenson III), Conrad Frederick III. Asst. to chief chemist Aluminum Co., Am., 1915-17, in charge fabricating div. tech direction bur., 1919-28, chief metallurgist fabricating div. operating dept., 1928-44, chief metallurgist 1944-52, v.p., chief metallurgist, chmn. tech., and research policy coms., 1952-57, ret. Served in U.S. Army, O.T.C., 1917, 315th Inf., 79th Div., 1917-19. Mem. Inst. Aero. Scis., Brt. Inst. Metals, Am. Inst. Mining and Metall. Engrs., Am. Soc. Metals, Nat. Aeronautic Assn., Am. Ordnance Assn. Clubs: Hill Crest Country (New Kensington, Pa.); Duquesne, University, Longue Vue (Pitts.). Home: 712 St. James St., Pitts. 32. Died July 5, 1957.

NAGLE, Clarence Floyd, utility exec.; b. Mt. Cory, O., Aug. 3, 1882; s. John B. and Emma E. (Falk) N.; E.E., Lafayette Coll., 1904; m Elsie Smyser, Sept. 20, 1911; children—Smyser Floyd, John Carlyle. Engr. Westinghouse Electric Co., 1904-06; elec. engr. Pa. Coal Co., 1906-07; gen. supt. Citizens Electric Illuminating Co., Pittston, Pa., 1907-17; supt. distbn., transmission Scranton Electric Co., 1917-26, gen. supt., 1926-43, pres., dir., gen. mgr., 1943-56; pres., dir. West Pittston-Exeter R.R. Co., Scranton (until merger with Pa. Power & Light Company); dir. Pa. Power & Light, First Nat. Bank of Scranton, Scranton-Lackawanna Tr. Co., Scranton Indsl. Development Company, Lackawanna Industrial Fund Enterprise. Member of the American Institute E.E., Scranton C. of C. (dir.), Pa. Elec. Assn. (exec. com.), Phi Beta Kappa, Alpha Chi Rho, Tau Beta Pi. Mason (Shriner). Clubs: Scranton, Country, Kiwanis (Scranton). Home: 930 Clay Av., Scranton. Office: 507 Linden St., Scranton 3, Pa. Died Jan. 15, 1957; buried Abington Hills Cemetery, Clarks Summit, Pa.

NAGLE, Raymond Thomas, lawyer; b. Helena, Mont., June 2, 1897; s. Thomas Patrick and Mary Ann (Toole) N.; LL.B., U. Montana., 1922; m. Margaret Ann Walsh, Oct. 5, 1925; children—Thomas Gregory, Raymond Walsh (dec.), Richard Walsh, Patrick Walsh. Gen. office worker, Helena, 1915-19; began law practice at Helena, 1923; became mem. Walsh & Nagle, 1923; Mem. Mont. Ho. of Rep., 1925, 27, 29; city atty., Helena, 1930-33; atty. gen. Mont., 1933-37; dir. atty.-general's section, Council of State Govts., 1936-37; spl. asst.

Dept. of Justice, 1937-43; Commr. U.S. Ct. Dept. of Justice, 1937-43; Commr. U.S. Ct. of Claims 1943-—. Served as pvt., detached service, Provosk Marshal General's Dept., U.S. Army, World War. Mem. bd. corporators Carroll Coll., Helena. Mem. Am., Mont. bar assns., Phi Sigma Kappa, Phi Delta Phi. Catholic. Democrat. K.C. Address: Court of Claims, Washington. Died March 6, 1951.

NAGLER, Forrest (nâgler), mech. engr.; b. Freeport, Mich., Apr. 21, 1885; s. John G. and Helen (Moore) N.; B.S., U. Mich., 1906; m. Aletta Seefeld, Dec. 1911; children—John W., Mary (Mrs. Maynard Meyer). Hydro-electric power engring, hydraulic dept. Allis-Chalmers Mfg. Co., Milwaukee, 1908-30, chief mech. engr. engring. development div., 1942-48, mgr. chief engr. atomic power sect. since 1948; research engr. A. O. Smith Corp., Milwaukee, 1930-32; chief engr. Canadian Allis-Chalmers, Lt., Toronto, Ont., 1933-42; cons. mech. engr. since 1952; author, inventor. Served with 1st Wis. Cav. 1907-11. Mem. A.S.M.E. (life mem., past v.p.), Am. Soc. C.E., Wis. Soc. Profl. Engrs. Canadian amateur champion archer, 1935-39; Internat. Archery title since 1940; Wis. Archery champion, 1942. Home: 7428 Oakhill Ave., Wauwatosa 13, Wis. Office: Allis-Chalmers Mfg. Co., P.O. Box 512, Milw. 1. Died Apr. 1, 1952.

NAGY, Imre, Hungarian govt. ofcl.; b. Hungary, 1896; ed. comml. high sch. Joined Communist Party before World War II; radio broadcaster during war, Moscow; became minister of agr., Hungary, 1944; minister of interior, 1945; later minister of crop collection; prime minister, July 1953-56. Mem. Communist Workers Party. Executed July 1958.*

NAHM, Max Brunswick (năm), banking; b. Bowling Green, Ky.; s. Emanuel and Rosa (Brunswick) N.; A.B., Ogden College, Bowling Green, Ky., 1883; A.B., Princton Univ., 1885; m. Sunshine Friedman, Jan. 21, 1892; 1 dau., Emanie Nahm Arling. Mem. firm E. Nahm & Co., 1887-1924; vice-pres. Citizens Nat. Bank, Bowling Green, since 1901, and Bowling Green Trust Co. since 1911; sec. Hopkinsville (Ky.) Water Co.; dir. Fed. Reserve Bank of St. Louis, 1927-46; dir. Palmer Hotel (Paducah, Ky.), Turner, Day & Woolworth Handle Co., Paducah Traction and Light Co., Paducah Heating Co. Mem. city council, Bowling Green, 1901; chmn., 8 counties, Liberty Loan drives, World War; Ky. del. to Nat. Tax Congress, New Orleans, 1925; mem. Park Commn., Bowling Green, 1926; mem. Nat. and State Park Commn., Ky., 1929-—, chmn., 1934-41; chmn. Bowling Green, Warren Co. Hosp. Commn., 1946-52. Trustee Ogden Coll. (pres. bd.) chairman of the commnrs. of City and County Hosps. Dir. Branch Federal Reserve Bank of Louisville, Ky., 1926-27; mem. Am. Bankers Assn. (v.p. for Ky. 1917; mem. exec. council of the assn., 1922-25; chmn. federal legislative com., 1924-25, federal legislative council 1924-25; mem. econ. policy commn., 1926-27, 1931-33; del. to Internat. Chamber Commerce, Amsterdam, The Netherlands, 1929; mem. nominating com. from Ky., 1931; mem. com. on revision of Nat. Banking Act, 1933; apptd. mem. economic policy commn., 1934; mem. com. on banking studies, 1933-37); dir. Federal Housing Adminstrn. for Ky., 1934-35; mem. Ky. Bankers Assn. (pres. 1916, former chairman, now member resolutions committee, member 50 Year Club, member Agrl. Commn. 1947); apptd. mem. Ky. State Recovery Bd. of Nat. Recovery Adminstrn., 1933; chmn. Ky. Nat. Park Commn., 1932-41; mem. Mammoth Cave Nat. Park Assn. (pres., mem. exec. com., mem. operative com., 1931-42, still dir.); apptd. mem. Ky. State Planning Commn., 1935, and mem. Ky. Forestry Commission, 1935. Democrat. Clubs: Kiwanis (life), Lions (ex-pres.), Mo. Athletic, Calendar (pres.); Bowling Green Country (ex-pres.), Blue Grass; Pendennis (Louisville). Awarded Algernon Sidney Sullivan medallion by the U. of Ky. for being "most useful citizen" in Kentucky in yr. 1929. Dist. chmn. Victory Fund Com. for 7 counties in Ky., 1942, War Finance Com., 1943. Home: 1403 College St. Office: 422 Main St., Bowling Green, Ky. Died Mar. 1958.

NAIRN, Sir Michael, chmn. Michael Nairn & Co., Ltd. and Allied cos.; b. Feb. 19, 1874; s. 1st Bt. and Emily Frances (Spencer) Nairn; ed. Edinburgh Acad.; Sherbourne; Marburg Univ.; m. Mildred M. Neish, 1901; 1 son, 4 daughters. 2nd Bart., created 1904. Dir. Bank of Scotland. Address: Elie House, Fife, Scotland. Died Sept. 24, 1952.

NALLY, Edward Julian, communication exec.; b. Phila., Apr. 11, 1859; s. Patrick and Mary (Cullen) N.; common school edn.; m. Lee Warren Redd, June 10, 1897; children—Marylee (Mrs. Frederic H. Hahn), Edward Julian. Started as messenger boy in St. Louis, with Western Union Telegraph Co., Sept. 1, 1875, filling various positions in St. Louis and Mpls. until Oct. 1890; asst. gen. supt. and gen. supt. Western div. Postal Telegraph-Cable Co., hdqrs. at Chicago, 1890-1906, becoming v.p. and dir. at New York, Sept. 1906, and 1st v.p. and gen. mgr., Apr. 11, 1907-Oct. 1, 1913; v.p., gen. mgr., dir. Marconi Wireless Telegraph Co. of America, 1913-19; pres. RCA, which took over Marconi Co., 1919-23; mng. dir. internat. relations RCA, 1923-25; mng. dir. Commercial Radio Internat. Consortium (Paris), 1923-25; dir. RCA, RCA Communications, Inc., RCA Mfg. Co., Inc., NBC. Asso. with 1st Edison telephone exchange at St. Louis, 1878; supervised the accounting and prepared estimates for 1st telegraph lines to follow all Northwestern trans-continental ry. lines constructed during 1880-89; opened first commercial wireless circuit between U.S. and Hawaii, 1914, extended to Japan, 1916, and between U.S. and Great Britain, Norway, Germany and France, 1920, Italy, Sweden, Poland, Argentine, Brazil and Colombia, 1924-25. Retired Jan. 1, 1925, after 50 years' service; was a pioneer in telegraph, telephone and radio. Decorated Officer Polonia Restituta (Poland). Hon. mem. Wireless Veterans Assn., Nat. Geog. Soc., NBC 20-year Club, RCAC 25-year Club; mem. Friendly Sons of St. Patrick, Am. Irish Hist. Soc., Japan Soc., N.Y., Soc. for Japanese Studies. Roman Catholic. Clubs: Ends of the Earth, Century Assn. (N.Y.C.); Overseas Press (hon.). Home: 11 Northway, Bronxville, N.Y. Ofifice: 30 Rockefeller Plaza, N.Y.C. Died Sept. 22, 1953; buried Sleepy Hollow Cemetery, Tarrytown, N.Y.

NANZ, Robert Hamilton, distillery exec.; b. Louisville, Oct. 5, 1885; s. Henry J. and Mary E. (Holzheimer) N.; student pub. schs. of Ky.; m. Willie Virginia O'Brien, May 20, 1920; children—Dorothy Lawson, Robert Hamilton, Henry Geiger. Distillery operator Schenley Industries, Inc., Louisville, 1900-41, v.p., regional mgr., Lawrenceburg, Ind., since 1941; v.p. Schenley Products (Louisville), Schenley Distillers, Inc. Republican. Presbyn. Mason (K.T., Shriner). Home: 421 Ridge Av. Office: Foot of Mary St., Lawrenceburg, Ind. Died Nov. 23, 1957.

NARDIN, William Thompson (năr'dĭn), chmn. of the bd. Pet Milk Co.; b. Schuyler County, Ill., Oct. 2, 1874; s. James F. and Sarah Ellen (Thompson) N.; A.B., U. of Mo., 1903, A.M., 1904, LL.B., 1907; m. Mary Ellen Conway, Oct. 27, 1910. Practiced law in St. Louis, 1907-20; v.p. and gen. mgr. Pet Milk Co., 1920-50, now chmn. board; chmn. bd. and federal reserve agent Fed. Reserve Bank of St. Louis, 1937-45. Chmn. Mo. State Social Security Commn., 1941-44. Mem. Phi Beta Kappa. Club: Noonday. Home: 6253 Westminster Pl. Office: Arcade Bldg., St. Louis. Died Oct. 25, 1954; buried Vandalia, Mo.

NASH, Frank C. (Francis Carroll), lawyer, univ. prof.; b. Dannemora, N.Y., Aug. 19, 1910; s. George Erwin and Mabel Susan (White) N.; A.B., Holy Cross Coll., 1931; LL.B., Georgetown U., 1934, J.D., 1935; LL.D., St. Josephs Coll., Phila., 1952; LL.D. Georgetown U., 1953; LL.D. U. Scranton, 1954; unmarried. Admitted to D.C. bar, 1934; special asst. to gen. counsel Fed. Alcohol Control Adminstrn., Washington, 1934-35; asst. prof. law Georgetown U., 1935-37, prof. since 1937; spl. asst. to sec. navy, 1946, to sec. defense, 1948-49; partner law firm Nash, Ahern & Abell since 1946; dep. U.S. rep. to commn. on armaments, United Nations, 1949-52; asst. to sec. def. for internat. security affairs, 1951-53, asst. sec. def. 1953-54; mem. U.S. delegation to several internat. confs., 1951-53, 11th Gen. Assembly UN; mem. bd., exec. com. Gen. Dynamics Corp.; sec., mem. bd. Tri-Car, Inc., Tech. Products Corp.; spl. cons. to the President of the U.S., 1956-—. Mem. bd. dirs., exec. com. Am. council NATO. Active duty United States Naval Reserve, 1941, disch. to inactive duties as capt., 1946. Decorated Legion of Merit, Freedom Medal, Distinguished Civilian Service. Member Council on Foreign Relations, also Am. Bar Assn. (mem. tax council), D.C. Bar Assn. (chmn. com. on internat. adminstrn. agencies), Gamma Eta Gamma. Clubs: University, Congressional Country (gov.), Army-Navy Country (Washington); Lake Placid (N.Y.); Canadian (N.Y. City). Contbr. articles to legal periodicals. Home: 5035 Macomb St., Washington 16. Office: 1741 K St., Washington 6. Died Dec. 11, 1957.

NASH, J. Newton, lawyer; b. N.Y. City, Jan. 28, 1899; s. Joseph A. and Elisabeth (Switzer) N.; student Dartmouth, 1916-17, 17-18; A.B., Columbia, 1920, LL.B., 1922; m. Estelle Pengel, Dec. 12, 1924; children—Elizabeth (Mrs. Leander Gleynn Yeaton, Jr.), J. Newton, Suzanne (Mrs. André Pommellet). Admitted to N.Y. bar, 1923; asso. Loomis, Barrett & Jones, 1922-25, Hunt, Hill & Betts, 1925-28; partner Hill, Betts & Nash, and predecessors, N.Y.C., 1956-—; atty. village of Scarsdale (N.Y.), 1942-51, mem. zoning bd. appeals, 1952-—; justice of peace, acting police justice Town Scarsdale, 1941-42, police justice, 1959; counsel, dir. Belgian C. of C. in U.S., Inc.; dir., sec. Atlantic Overseas Corp., Transoceanic Terminal Corp., Seaborne Services, Inc., R. Maes Export & Import Corp., Mondial United Corp., Franklin Glass Corp., Ward-Garcia Corp., Belgian Line Inc. Trustee Village of Scarsdale (Westchester Co.), 1939-41. Mem. N.Y. State Bar Assn., N.Y. State Conf. Mayors, Nat. Inst. Municipal Law Officers, Assn. Bar City of N.Y., Maritime Law Assn. U.S. exec. com., chmn. spl. com.), Internat. Assn. Ins. Counsel, N.Y. Maritime Assn., Theta Delta Chi, Phi Delta Phi. Clubs: India House, Union League, Lawyers (N.Y.C.); Am. Yacht (Rye). Home: 314 Heathcote Rd., Scarsdale, N.Y. Office: 26 Broadway, N.Y.C. 4. Died July 12, 1959.

NATHAN, George Jean, editor, author, critic; b. Ft. Wayne, Ind., Feb. 14, 1882; s. Charles and Ella N.; A.B., Cornell, 1904; U. of Bologna, Italy, 1905; L.H.D., Ind. U., 1953, LL.D., 1953; m. Julie Haydon, 1955. Editorial staff N.Y. Herald, 1905-06; dramatic critic and asso. editor Bohemian Mag., and Outing, 1906-08; writer on theatre, Harper's Weekly, 1908-10, Associated Sunday Mags., 1909-14; dramatic critic Smart Set, 1908-23; dramatic critic nat. syndicate of newspapers, 1912-29; dramatic critic, Puck (with James Huneker), 1915-16; dramatic critic, Judge, 1922-35, dramatic critic, Life, 1935-36; editor of The Smart Set Magazine (with H. L. Mencken), 1914-23; founder and editor The American Mercury (with H. L. Mencken), 1924-25, contbg. editor, 1925-30 and dramatic critic, 1924-30; dramatic editor The New Freeman, 1930; cons. editor Arts and Decoration, 1924-34; editorial contbr. London Daily Express and guest-critic, 1930; dramatic critic, Vanity Fair, 1930-35; founder and editor Am. Spectator (with Theodore Dreiser, Eugene O'Neill, James Branch Cabell and Ernest Boyd), 1932; dramatic critic Saturday Review of Literature, 1937, Esquire, 1935-46; Scribner's, 1937-38; Newsweek, 1937-40; American Mercury, 1940-51, Liberty mag., 1940-42, N.Y. Journal-American and King Features national syndicate, since 1943. Dramatic critic Theatre Arts 1952-53. Contributor to Encyclopedia Britannica and to Britannica Book of the Year; editor The Theatre of Today dramatic library. Honorary member London Critics Circle. American member Maximilian Society (London, England); president New York Drama Critics Circle, 1937-39. Author: The Eternal Mystery, 1913; Europe after 8:15 (with H. L. Mencken), 1914; Another Book on the Theatre, 1916; Bottoms Up, 1917; Mr. George Jean Nathan Presents, 1917; A Book Without a Title, 1918; The Popular Theatre, 1918; Comedians All, 1919; Heliogabalus (with H. L. Mencken), 1920; The American Credo (with same), 1920; The Theatre, The Drama, The Girls, 1921; The Critic and the Drama, 1922; The World in Falseface, 1923; Materia Critica, 1924; The Autobiography of an Attitude, 1925. The House of Satan, 1926; The New American Credo, 1927; Land of the Pilgrims' Pride, 1927; Art of the Night, 1928; Monks Are Monks, 1929; Testament of a Critic, 1931; The Intimate Notebooks of George Jean Nathan, 1932; Since Ibsen, 1933; Passing Judgments, 1934; The Theatre of the Moment, 1936; The Avon Flows, 1937; The Morning After the First Night, 1938; Encyclopedia of the Theatre, 1940; The Bachelor Life, 1941; The Entertainment of a Nation, 1942; Beware of Parents, 1943; The Theatre Book of the Year, 1943-51; The World of George Jean Nathan, 1952; The Theatre in The Fifties, 1953. Contbr. to leading Am. and European mags. Address: 44 W. 44th St., N.Y.C. Died Apr. 8, 1958.

NATHANSON, Ira Theodore, surgeon, educator; b. Virginia, Minn., July 20, 1904; s. Herman Joseph and Rose Ella (Bloom) N.; B.S., Northwestern, 1926, M.D., 1930, M.S., 1934. Intern, resident Michael Reese Hosp., Chicago, 1929-33, asst. surg. pathology, 1933-34, resident tumor clinic, 1933-34; resident surgeon Pondville Hosp., Walpole, Mass., 1934-35, asst. surgeon, 1941-46, surgeon, 1946-—; asst. surgeon, research fellow Collis P. Huntington Meml. Hosp., Harvard, 1937-41; asst. surgey, med. sch., Harvard, 1939-40, instr., 1940-46, asso., 1946-47, asst. prof. surgery, 1947-51, assoc. clin. prof., 1951-—; asst. surgeon Beth Israel Hosp., Boston, 1940-44; asst. surgery Mass. Gen. Hosp., Boston, 1942-45, asst. surgeon, 1946-47, asso. vis. surgeon, 1947-—; cons. surgeon Mass. Eye and Ear Infirmary, 1946-—. Littauer Fellow cancer surgery, med. Sch., Harvard, 1935-37. Fellow A.C.S.; mem. Am. Cancer Soc., Am. Assn. Cancer Research (dir.), Nat. Research Council (chmn. com. cancer diagnosis and therapy, 1951-—), A.M.A. (chmn. com. steroids and hormones, Council on Pharmacy and Chemistry, 1952-—, chmn. com. steroids and cancer, 1947-—), Am. Acad. Arts and Scis., Am. Physiol. Soc., A.A.A.S., Soc. Clin. Investigation, N.E. Surg. Soc., N.E. Cancer Soc., Endocrine Soc., Soc. Exptly. Biology and Medicine, Sigma Xi, Alpha Omega Alpha. Club: Harvard. Author: Lymph Node Metastases, 1942; also numerous articles med., jours. Home: 16 Still St., Brookline 46, Mass. Office: Massachusetts General Hospital, Boston 14. Died May 3, 1954.

NAUMBURG, Walter Wehle, found. exec.; b. N. Y.C., Dec. 25, 1867; s. Elkan and Bertha (Wehle) N.; B.A., Harvard, 1889; L.H.D. (hon.), Rutgers U., 1951; m. Elsie Binger, Mar. 29, 1923. Retired banker. Mem. bd. The Group Health, Inc., a Blue Cross affiliate. Sponsor pub. orchestral concerts in the Mall, Central Park, originated by father, 1903; organized 1926, now pres. Walter W. Naumburg Found. (awards debut recital in Town Hall to worthy musicians, also recordings of their compositions to contemporary Am. composers). Mem. bd. Musicians Found. since inception, now pres.; trustee N. E. Conservatory of Music, Mt. Sinai Hosp., Frank M. Chapman Meml. at Am. Mus. Natural History, Greenwich Audubon Nature Center, Nature Centers for Young America, Inc. For many years member of overseers vis. com. to music dept. Harvard, now vice chmn.; mem. vis. com. to music dept. Princeton; adv. bd. Salvation Army. Mem. Pierian Sodality. Clubs: Harvard, Lotos, Westchester Country, Bankers, Lawyers, City Mid-Day, Bohemians. Home: 121 E. 64th St., N.Y.C. also Silvermine Rd., New Canaan, Conn. Died Oct. 17, 1959.

NAYLOR, James Ball, physician, author; b. Pennsville, O., Oct. 4, 1860; s. Robert W. and Nancy (Wells) N.; student prep. dept. Marietta (O.) Coll., 1879-80; M.D., Starling Med. Coll., Columbus, O., 1886; Litt.D., Marietta Coll., 1937; m. L. Villa Naylor, Aug. 6, 1888; children—Olive Nance, Nettie Lucile, Ann B., Lena E., James Robert, Bonnie Jean. Formerly editorial writer Marion (O.) Star and Chicago Jour. Commerce. Author: Current Coins, 1893; Goldenrod and Thistledown, 1896; Ralph Marlowe, 1901; The Sign of the Prophet, 1901; In the Days of St. Clair, 1902; Under Mad Anthony's Banner, 1903; The Cabin in the Big Woods, 1904; The Kentuckian, 1905; Old Home Week, 1906; The Witch-Crow and Barney Bylow, 1906; The Scalawags, 1907; Little Green Goblin, 1907; Songs from the Heart of Things, 1907; The Misadventures of Marjory, 1908; Dicky Delightful in Rainbow Land, 1909; A Book of Buckeye Verse, 1927; Vagrant Verse, 1935. Pub. speaker and entertainer. Home: Malta, O. Died Apr. 1, 1945; buried Malta.

NEAL, John Randolph, law educator; b. Rhea Springs, Tenn., Sept. 17, 1876; s. John Randolph and Mary Elizabeth Caroline (Brown) N.; A.B., U. of Tenn., 1893; A.M., Vanderbilt U., 1896, LL.B., 1896; Ph.D., Columbia, 1889; unmarried. Teacher of law, U. of Denver, Colo., 1899-1908; prof. of law, U. of Tenn., 1909-17 (lectured U. of Tenn. in spring, U. of Denver in fall); founder and since 1923 dean and trustee John Randolph Neal Coll. of Law, Knoxville, Tenn.; chief defense counsel for John T. Scopes in case to test anti-evolution act Tenn. Legislature, 1925. Mem. Kappa Sigma, Phi Kappa Phi, Phi Delta Phi, Scarabean Soc. (U. of Tenn.). Democrat. Mem. M.E. Ch., South. Mason. (Shriner), Elk. Author: Disunion and Restoration in Tennessee, 1899. Home: Rhea Springs, Tenn. Office: Fretz Bldg., Knoxville, Tenn. Died Nov. 23, 1959.

NEAL, Josephine Bicknell, physician; b. Belmont, Me., Oct. 10, 1880; d. Alton J. and Mary (Alexander) Neal; A.B. (1st honor, physics), Bates Coll., 1901, hon. D.Sc., 1926; M.D. (2d honor), Cornell U. Med. Coll., 1910; hon. D.Sc., Russell Sage Coll., 1937. Licensed to practice medicine, N.Y. State, 1913, practice limited to consultation in neurology, 1918—; asst. in meningitis div., research lab., Dept. of Health, N.Y. City, 1910-14, in charge of div., 1914—; instr. in medicine, Cornell U. Med. Coll., 1914-20; instr. in medicine, Coll. of Physicians and Surgeons, Columbia U., 1922-27, clin. prof. of neurology, 1929-44; attending physician Children's Tuberculosis Clinic and Vanderbilt Clinic, 1922-27; consultant in acute infections of central nervous system, N.Y. Infirmary for Women and Children, 1925—, Neurol. Inst. of N.Y., 1936-44, Vanderbilt Clinic, 1936-44; dir. dept. of infectious diseases, Neurol. Inst., 1937-39; visiting physician on neurol. service, Willard Parker Hosp., 1937—; asst. attending neurologist, Neurol. Inst. and Vanderbilt Clinic, 1939-—; consultant in pediatrics, St. Vincent's Hosp. Asso. dir. research lab., N.Y. Dept. of Health, 1937-44; dir. William J. Matheson Survey of Epidemic Encephalitis, 1927-29; exec. sec. Matheson Commn. for Encephalitis Research, 1929—; sec. Internat. Com. for Study of Infantile Paralysis, 1929-32. Certified in neurology by Am. Bd. of Psychiatry and Neurology, 1936. Awarded John Metcalfe Polk Prize, Cornell U. Fellow Am. Coll. Physicians; mem. N.Y. State, N.Y. County med. socs., A.M.A., Am. Pub. Health Assn., Assn. for Research in Nervous and Mental Diseases, N.Y. Acad. of Medicine, Phi Beta Kappa, Alpha Epsilon Iota, Alpha Omega Alpha. Author of chapters in Abt's System of Pediatrics; Tice's Practice of Medicine; Barr's Modern Medical Therapy in General Practice; 1st, 2d, and 3d Reports on Epidemic Encephalitis (Matheson commn.); Poliomyelitis (Internat. Commn. for Study of Infantile Paralysis); The Human Cerebral Spinal Fluid; Infections of the Central Nervous System; chapter on Viral Diseases of the Central Nervous System in Cyclopedia of Medicine, 1940; Encephalitis, A Clinical Study, 1942; also about 75 articles on acute infections of the central nervous system for med. jours. Home: 60 Gramercy Park. Office: William H. Park Laboratory, Foot of E. 15th St., N.Y.C. Died Mar. 19, 1955; buried Lewiston, Me.

NEAL, Paul Ardeen, officer U.S. Public Health Service; b. West Point, Tenn., June 25, 1901; s. Paul Ardeen and Madge May (Calloway) N.; M.D., Vanderbilt U., 1927; m. Lady Beatrice Munro, Sept. 29, 1932; children—Paul Whitaker, Robert Gordon. Commd. officer U.S.P.H.S., 1928, med. officer U.S. Marine Hosp., New Orleans, 1927-28, Mobile, Ala., 1928-29; attached to U.S. consulates, Germany, Italy, Denmark, Ireland and Poland, 1929-33; chief of Indsl. Hygiene Research Lab., Nat. Inst. of Health, Bethesda, Md., 1936-47; chief of Lab. of Physiol. Biology, National Inst. Health since 1947. Life fellow Am. Pub. Health Assn.; mem. Am. Med. Assn., A.A.A.S., Washington Academy of Science, Assn. Indsl. Phys., Am. Statis. Assn., Am. Genetic Assn., Sigma Xi, Alpha Tau Omega, Alpha Kappa Kappa. Clubs: Cosmos, Kenwood Golf and Country (Wash.). Author over 50 publs. on sci. subjects. Home: 6601 River Rd. Office: National Institute of Health, Bethesda 14, Md. Died Oct. 13, 1952.

NEAL, Will E., congressman; b. Lawrence County, O., Oct. 14, 1875; B.S., Nat. Normal U., Lebanon, O., 1900; M.D., U. Cin., 1906; married, three children. Practicing physician, Huntington, W. Va., 1907—; mem. W.Va. legislature, 1950; mem. 83d and 85th Congresses, 4th W.Va. Dist. Mem. W.Va. Pub. Health Council, 1936-40. Med. cons. FOA, Afghanistan and Nepal, 1955. Hon. mem. A. M.A. Republican. Methodist. Mason, Odd Fellow. Home: Huntington, W.Va. Office: House Office Bldg., Washington. Died Nov. 12, 1959.*

NEAL, William M(ills), steel co. exec.; b. S. Boston, Va., Dec. 10, 1900; s. John Louis and Virgie (Jennett) N.; A.B., Wake Forest Coll., 1921; LL.B., U. of Va., 1924; m. Flora Brown, Oct. 11, 1930 (div. Dec. 2, 1933); 1 son William Mills; m. 2d, Donie De Bardeleben, Oct. 14, 1937; children—Donie, Virginia, Henry. Admitted to Va. bar, 1924, practiced in Danville, 1924-26; admitted Ala. bar, 1926, practiced in Birmingham, 1926-40; sec. Sloss-Sheffield Steel & Iron Co., Birmingham, 1940-42, v.p., sec., 1942-55; v.p., sec. So. Electric Steel Co., 1955—. Mem. N.A.M. (dir. 1946—), Asso. Industries Ala. (dir. 1940—, pres. 1945-46), Am., Ala. and Birmingham bar assns., Sigma Nu, Phi Delta Phi, Phi Beta Kappa. Democrat. Episcopalian. Clubs: Mountain Brook, Redstone. Home: 909 Essex Rd., Birmingham 5. Office: 3300 First Av., Birmingham 2, Ala. Died Dec. 26, 1958.

NEAL, William Weaver, hosiery mfr.; b. Marion, N.C., Feb. 15, 1874; s. Joseph Grayson and Rowena (Weaver) N.; ed. Marion High Sch. and Davis Mil. Acad.; m. Addie Malone, Nov. 10, 1898; children—Joseph Grayson, William Weaver, Albert Malone. Clerk in War Dept., Washington, 1894; gen. agt. Knoxville, LaFollette & Jellico R.R. Co., 1903; traveling claim agt. L.&N. R.R. Co., 1904-09; traveling passenger agt. N.P. Ry., 1910-16; spl. agt. U.S. Fuel Adminstrn., 1917-18; with Marion Knitting Mills, Inc., 1908—, pres. and treas., 1917—. Apptd. mem. Review Advisory Bd., NRA, 1934; mem. N.C. Ho. of Reps., 1918—; mem. N.C. Hwy. Commn.; chmn. N.C. Park Commn. Dir. N.C. Sch. for the Deaf (pres. bd.), Carolina Motor Club. Democrat. Methodist. Clubs: Buck Creek Fishing, Marion Lake; Anglers (Sarasota, Fla.). Home: Marion, N.C.; also Sarasota, Fla. Died Apr. 6, 1952.

NEALE, Laurance Irving, clergyman; b. Boston, July 20, 1885; s. George F. and Mary Adelaide (Stetson) N.; A.B., Harvard, 1906, Union Theol. Seminary; D.D. (hon.), Tufts University, 1955; married Loretta G. Adamson, June 14, 1930. Asso. with George A. Fuller Co., 1906-08; with J. B. King & Co., jr. salesman to bd. of dirs., 1908-24; mgr. Architects Service Bur. and Insulation Dept., U.S. Gypsum Co., 1924-27; with Atlantic Gypsum Products Co., N.Y. Div., sales mgr., gen. sales mgr., v.p., 1927-36; acting minister Unitarian Ch. of All Souls, N.Y. City, 1940-41, asso. minister, 1941-42, minister, 1942-55, minister emeritus, 1955—. Served as 1st lieutenant, 168th Infantry, of 42d (Rainbow) Div., U.S. Army, 1917-19. Chmn. of com. to formulate code of practice for gypsum industry under N.R.A., 1933; mem. of N.R.A. Code Com. for Gypsum Industry and Insulation Bd. Industry, 1933-34; mem. bd. trustees, Meadville Theol. Sch., Chicago, 1926-32; mem. bd. dirs. Am. Unitarian Assn., Boston, 1940-43. Mem. Am. Inst. Mining and Metall. Engrs., Unitarian. Clubs: University, Harvard (N.Y.), Downtown, Century. Home: 8 E. 96th St., New York 28. Office: Unitarian Church of All Souls, 1157 Lexington Av., N.Y.C. 21. Died Mar. 31, 1956; buried Forest Hills Cemetery, Boston.

NEATH, Jasper Arthur, oil exec.; b. Red Rock, Pa., Nov. 17, 1896; s. Arthur W. and Elizabeth (Duffield) N.; m. Helen Wenning, 1919; children—Robert, John Arthur. With Texas Co., 1914, Gulf Pipe Line Co., 1915-18, So. Pipe Line Co., 1918-19; with Humble Pipe Line Co., 1919-42, gen. supt., 1924-28, bd. dirs., 1924-42, v.p., 1928-42; dir. Humble Oil & Refining Co. since 1942, v.p. since 1947, now v.p., dir. in charge transportation, crude oil marketing. Bd. dirs. St. Luke's Episcopal Hosp. Recipient Distinguished Service award Tex. Mid-Continent Oil and Gas Assn., 1951. Mem. Mid-Continent Oil and Gas Assn. (dir.), Houston C. of C. (dir., mem. exec. com.). Episcopalian (past vestryman). Clubs: Houston Petroleum, Houston, Ramada, Dallas Petroleum, River Oaks Country. Home: 2932 Chevy Chase Dr. Office: Humble Bldg., Houston. Died Nov. 16, 1957; buried Garden of Gethsemane, Houston.

NEEDHAM, Claude Ervin (nēd'ām), mineral economist, geologist; b. near Newton, Ill., Sept. 10, 1894; s. John Newton and Alice Amanda (Gibson) N.; ed. Central Normal Coll., Danville, Ind., 1915-16, Ia. State Coll., 1916-17, Miss. State Coll., 1922-25 (B.S., 1924, M.S., 1925), Northwestern U., 1927-31 (Ph.D.); m. Pauline Hyde Wesch, June 1927; children—John Wesch, Darrell Ervin. Chem. work, St. Louis, 1917-20; asst. in geol., Miss. State Coll., 1923-25; supt. of schools, Cortez, Colo., 1925-26; asst. prof. of geology, Miss. State Coll., 1926-27; instr. geology, Northwestern U., 1927-30, fellow, 1930-31; asst. prof. geology, N.M. Sch. of Mines, 1931-35, asso. prof., 1935-38, prof., 1938-39, pres., 1939-42; also dir. N.M. Bur. of Mines and Mineral Resources, 1939-42; economic analyst, editor Minerals Yearbook, U.S. Bur. of Mines, 1942-45; supervising engr., Salt Lake sect. Metal econ. div., U.S. Bur. Mines, since 1945; with Ill. Geol. Survey summers 1929, 30; visiting prof., U. of Miss., summers 1935, 36. Mem. Am. Assn. Petroleum Geologists, Am. Inst. Mining and Metall. Engrs., Geol. Soc. America, Utah Geol. Soc., Utah Acad. Sci., N.M. Miners and Prospectors Assn., Sigma Xi. Contbr. to professional jours. and Bur. of Mines publs. Home: 3303 Plains Blvd., Amarillo, Tex. Died Oct. 15, 1950; buried Cortez, Colo.

NEELY, Charles Gracchus; b. Benton, Ill., June 11, 1855; s. Dr. Isaac M. and Mary C. N.; B.L., U. of Ill., 1880; m. Lucia H. Fish, Sept. 9, 1880. Admitted to Ill. bar, 1884, and practiced in Chicago; mem. Ill. Ho. of Rep., 1887; 1st asst. state's atty., Cook Co., Ill., 1887-92; judge Circuit Court of Cook Co., 1895-1903; prof. constl. history and law, Pomona Coll., 1912—. Republican. Presbyn. Home: Claremont, Cal. Died Oct. 15, 1930.

NEELY, Matthew M., U.S. senator; born Grove, West Virginia; s. Alfred and Mary (Morris) N.; grad. mil. dept., W.Va. Univ.; A.B., W.Va. U. 1901, LL.B., 1902, LL.D., 1941; LL.D. Waynesburg College, 1938; Litt.D., Salem College, 1942; m. Alberta Claire Ramage, Oct. 21, 1903; children—Alfred, John, Corinne Neely Pettit. Engaged in practice of law, Fairmont, W.Va., 1902—. Mayor of Fairmont, 1908-10; clerk W.Va. Ho. of Dels., 1911-13; mem. 63d to 66th Congresses (1913-21), 1st W.Va. Dist.; U.S. senator from W.Va., 1923-29 and 1931-43; elected governor of West Virginia, Nov. 5, 1940 (4-yr. term), resigning from U.S. Senate to be inaugurated, Jan. 1941; mem. 79th Congress (1945-47), 1st W.Va., Dist.; U.S. senator from W.Va., 1949—; del.-at-large Dem. Nat. Conventions from 1932-52, chmn. W.Va. delegation Dem. Nat. Conv., 1956. Pvt. Co. D, 1st Infantry, W.Va. Vols. Spanish Am. War, 1898; served in W.Va. Nat. Guard, corporal to maj., 1900-11 (resigned). Mem. Sons Am. Revolution, United Spanish War Veterans, Phi Sigma Kappa, Delta Chi, Phi Beta Kappa. Democrat. Mason (32°), Odd Fellow, Elk, K. of P., Moose, Eagle. Home: Box 152, Fairmont, W. Va. Office: Senate Office Bldg., Washington. Died Jan. 18, 1958; buried Woodlawn Cemetery, Fairmont, W.Va.

NEET, George W., educator; b. Parke County, Ind., Mar. 15, 1863; s. Warren and Harriet Overpeck) N.; Ind. State Normal Sch., Terre Haute, 1888-93; Ind. U., 1893-94; Valparaiso U.; D.Pd., 1908; m. Callie Harlan, Aug. 14, 1894; children—Helen Harlan Kendall, Laura Neet Marimon. Tchr. pub. schs., Ind., 1885-92, high sch., Paris, Ill., 1893-94; supt. schs., Spiceland, Ind., 1894-98; became dean of edn. Valparaiso U., 1898; appointed receiver State Bank of Dana, 1931. Unitarian. Club: Fortnightly. Author: Studies in Pedagogy, 1899; Inductive Grammar, 1900; Practical Methodology, 1910; Studies in Psychology, 1912. Home: Thornapple Lane, Northbrook, Ill. Died Oct. 27, 1957; buried Newport, Ind.

NEFF, Charles Thompson, Jr., univ. administrator; b. Piedmont, W.Va., Feb. 4, 1899; s. Charles Thompson and Lena Drusella (Porter) N.; A.B., W.Va. U., 1921; LL.D., Waynesburg Coll., 1948; m. Inez Davis, Dec. 26, 1921. Employed as supt. schs., Piedmont, 1922-27; exec. sec. W.Va. U. Bd. Govs. since 1927; comptroller W.Va. U. since 1934, acting pres., 1945-46, v.p. since 1946. Private U.S. Army, 1918. Mem. Assn. Univ. and Coll. Bus. Officers, Controllers Inst. of Am., Am. Legion, Phi Kappa Sigma, Phi Lambda Upsilon, Mountain. Methodist. Mason. Home: 41 Euclid Av., Morgantown, W.Va. Died Oct. 27, 1953.

NEFF, Pat Morris, former gov. of Teaxas, coll. pres.; b. McGregor, Tex., Nov. 26, 1871; s. Noah and Isabella (Shepherd) N.; A.B., Baylor U., 1894, A.M., 1898; LL.B., U. Tex., 1897; LL.D., Howard Payne and Austin colls., 1921, Baylor U., 1923; m. Myrtle Mainer, May 31, 1899; children—Hallie Maude (Mrs. Frank Wilcox), Pat M. Practiced at Waco, 1897-1921; pros. atty. McLennan County, Tex., 1906-12; mem. Tex. Ho. of Reps., 1901-05 (speaker of House, 1903-05); gov. of Tex. 2 terms, 1921-25; mem. U.S. Bd. of Mediation, 1927-29; chmn. Tex. R.R. Commn., 1929-31; pres. Baylor U., 1932-47, retired, also chmn. bd. trustees, 1903-32. Mem. bd. dirs. Tex. Power & Light Co. since 1935. Mem. state draft appeal bd., 1942. Chmn. Conf. for Edn. in Tex., 1923-25; chmn. Tex. Ednl. Survey Commn., 1925-26. Originator Tex. State Parks System; chmn. State Parks Bd., 1932-36; created Tex. Hist. Bd.; pres. Tex. Watersheds Assn. since 1939. Pres. So. Bapt. Conv., 1942. State chmn. League to Enforce Peace.

Grand Chancellor K.P. of Tex., 1918-19. President Bapt. Gen. Conv. of Tex., 3 yrs., 1927-29; v.p. So. Bapt. Conv., Washington, 1933; v.p. Anti-Saloon League of America, 1934. Pres. So. Bapt. Conv. since 1942; chmn. of Draft Appeal Board since 1941. Democrat. Mason (32°, Shriner). Club: Rotary. Home: 2110 Austin St., Waco, Tex. Died Jan. 20, 1952.*

NEFF, Paul Joseph, ry. exec.; b. St. Louis, July 14, 1884; s. Will T. and Annie E. Neff; B.S. in Mining Engring. and C.E., Kansas U., 1906; m. Margaret Philbrook, Apr. 9, 1910; children—Helena (Mrs. Glenn Givens), Elizabeth (Mrs. R. B. Erckman), Margaret (Mrs. E. H. Bosse Jr.). Rodman, transitman, asst. engr., 1907-10, engr. of constrn., Memphis, St. Louis, Springfield, Mo., 1910-17, dist. engr., Springfield, Mo., 1917-18, St.L.-S.F. Ry., during fed. control of r.r. corporate chief engr. St.L.-S.F. Ry., St. Louis, 1918-20; gen. mgr. Wichita Falls, Ranger & Ft. Worth R.R. and Wichita Falls & Southern R.R., Ranger, Tex., 1920-21; chief engr. Tex. Lines, St.L.-S.F. Ry., Ft. Worth, 1921-22; asst. to pres., 1922-25, asst. exec. vice pres., 1925-26, I.G.N.R.R., Houston; gen. supt. M.P.R.R., St. Louis, 1926-28; asst. to pres. M.P.R.R. and vice. pres. and gen. mgr. M.P. Transportation Co., St. Louis, 1928-31; asst. vice pres. traffic M.P. lines, also v.p., gen. mgr. M.P. Transportation Co., St. Louis, 1931-43; sr. v.p. M.P. lines, Houston, 1943-46; chief exec. officer M.P. R.R., Gulf Coast lines, I.G.N. and subsidiary cos. since June, 1946. Mem. Am. Assn. Railroad Ticket Agts., Am. Ry. Engr. Assn., Am. Soc. C.E., Newcomen Soc. of Eng., Phi Delta Theta. Conglist. Clubs: Traffic, Racquet, Bellerive Country, Noonday, Bogey Country (St. Louis); City (Dallas); Houston, Riveroaks, Country (Houston); Bankers (N.Y.C.); Chicago. Office: Missouri Pacific Bldg., St. Louis 3. Died June 8, 1957.

NEFF, Ward Andrew, newspaper pub.; b. Kansas City, Mo., Feb. 11, 1891; s. Jay Holcomb and Ellen (Ward) N.; student Baker U., Baldwin, Kan., 1906-07 LL.D., 1958; Bach. of Journalism, U. of Mo., 1913; m. Lylian L. Bingham, Apr. 29, 1925 (dec. 1956); m. 2d, Adah W. Bauerle, Aug. 30, 1958. Began as reporter Daily Drovers Telegram, Kansas City, 1913, news and telegraph editor, 1914-15; moved to Chicago, 1917; pres., treas., dir. Corn Belt Pubs., Inc., pub. of Corn Belt Farm Dailies, comprising Chicago Daily Drovers Journal, Kansas City Daily Drovers Telegram, Omaha Daily Journal-Stockman, St. Louis Daily Live Stock Reporter, owner and operator radio sta. WAAF and Drovers Journal Press, Chicago; dir. Employers' Reinsurance Corp., Central Surety and Insurance Corp., (Kansas City). Served as private 164th Depot Brigade, 1918. Elected Hall of Fame, Sch. Journalism, U. Mo., 1959. Mem. Sigma Delta Chi (national pres. 1923, elected fellow 1956), Phi Gamma Delta. Republican. Methodist. Mason (32°, Shriner), Elk. Clubs: South Shore Country, Saddle and Sirloin. Home: 6740 Oglesby Av., 49. Office: 836 Exchange Av., Union Stock Yards, Chgo. Died July 11, 1959; buried Forest Hill Cemetery, Kansas City, Mo.

NEIDEG, William Jonathan (nīdĭg), writer; b. Western College, Ia.; s. Abram Hershey and Lucyna (Davis) N.; A.B., Stanford, 1896; postgrad. U. Cal., 1901, U. Chgo., 1904-05, fellow in English, 1905; m. Frieda Margaret Rychener, Nov. 28, 1925. Editor Railroad Gazetteer, San Francisco, 1897-98; sub-editor The Argonaut, 1898-99; book editor The Wave, 1899-1900; instr. English, Stanford, 1901-04, U. Wis., 1905-11. Author: The First Wardens, 1905; The Shakespeare Quartos of 1619, 1910; False Dates on Shakespeare Quartos, 1910 (containing proof now unanimously accepted that some of the Shakespeare quartos bear false imprint dates); The Fire Flingers, 1919; Wild Rice, 1932; Slug Seven, 1935; Water's Edge, 1941. Contbr. to Century, Harper's, Saturday Evening Post, Collier's, etc. Home: 612 W. Main St., Napoleon, O. Died Feb. 7, 1955; buried Locust Grove Cemetery, Ridgeville Corners, O.

NEIFERT, Ira Edward (nī'fert), educator; b. Galesburg, Ill., June 21, 1891; s. Edward and Caroline Catherine (Hechler) N.; B.S., Knox Coll., Galesburg, 1915, M.S., 1916; Ph.D., U. Ia., 1939; student U. Chgo., summers 1917, 31, Cornell, 1928, U. Colo., summers 1923, 25; m. Martha Gordon Campbell, June 15, 1917. Asst. in chemistry Knox Coll., 1916-17, prof. chemistry, 1920—, chmn. dept. chemistry, 1934—, Griffith prof. chemistry on Abbott Found., 1934—; chemistry and gas expert U.S. Dept. Agrl. Bur. Chem., Washington, 1919-20. Served as sgt. C.W.S., Am. U. Expt. Sta., U.S. Army, 1918-19. Fellow A.A.A.S.; mem. Am. Chem. Soc., Am. Assn. U. Profs., Ill. Acad. Sci., Sigma Xi, Alpha Chi Sigma, Omega Beta Pi, Phi Lambda Upsilon, Phi Gamma Delta. Conglist. Mason (32°). Club: Galesburg. Home: 755 N. Kellogg, Galesburg, Ill. Deceased.

NEIL, George M(ahon), newspaper exec.; b. Phila., Sept. 18, 1907; s. Dr. Thomas Franklin and Anne Guilbert (Mahon) N.; A.B., U. Pa., 1930, LL.B., 1933; m. Anna Frances Robinson, July 11, 1936; children—George Mahon, William Robinson. Admitted to Pa. bar, 1934; mag. editor Legal Intelligencer, Phila., 1934-35; instr. bus. law Wharton Sch., U. Pa., 1933-45; law clk. to chief justice Pa. Supreme Ct., 1936-40; librarian Pa. Supreme Ct., 1941-42; lectr. Phila. Coll. Pharmacy and Sci., 1942-45; asst. to gen. mgr. Triangle Publs., Inc., N.Y.C., 1945-47; bus. mgr. Phila. Inquirer, 1947-50, gen. mgr. since 1951. Mem. Phila. Better Bus. Bur. (dir.), Am. Judicature Soc., Pa. Soc. N.Y. Episcopalian. Clubs: Poor Richard (dir.), Union League, University (Phila.). Home: 107 Lodges Lane, Cynwyd, Lower Merion, Pa. Office: 400 N. Broad St., Phila. 1. Died Nov. 4, 1957; buried Cypress Hills Cemetery, Bklyn.

NEILD, Edward Fairfax, architect; b. Shreveport, La., Dec. 3, 1884; s. George Frederick and Elziabeth (Moss) N.; B.S., Tulane, 1906; m. Ethel Land, Dec. 17, 1907; children—Edward Fairfax, Elizabeth (Mrs. James A. Van Hook). Practicing architect, Shreveport, 1908—, including projects for U.S. Army Corps of Engrs., U.S. Treasury Dept., pub. and pvt. hosps., ct. houses, numerous coll. bldgs. for State La. Apptd. to Commn. of Fine Arts, Washington, 1951. Fellow A.I.A. Home: 1075 Erie St. Office: 960 Jordan St., Shreveport, La. Died July 6, 1955.

NEILSON, Charles Hugh (nēl'sŭn), univ. dean; b. Berkshire, O., July 19, 1871; s. Arthur Wright and Nellie Alice (Schanck) N.; A.B., Ohio Wesleyan U., 1894; A.M., 1897; Ph.D., Chicago U., 1903; M.D., Rush Med. Coll., 1905; post-grad. work in Germany, 1911; m. Ebba Amelia Anderson, June 11, 1903; children—Arthur Wright, Reka. Asso. prof. physiol. chemistry, St. Louis U., 1904-07, prof., 1907-11, dir. dept. medicine, 1911-24, asso. dean, sch. of medicine, 1928-49; asst. city pathol., 1906; staff, St. Mary's Infirmary, 1907-08, 1912, sec. exec. council, 1938—; chief of staff, Alexian Brothers Hosp., 1909-21; physician St. Louis City Hosp., 1912-35; dir. University staff, 1935—; physician in chief, St. John's Hospital, 1924-50, member council, 1924—; staff St. Mary's Group of Hosps., 1933—; pres. Mo. State Bd. of Health. Certified by Bd. of Internal Medicine. Mem. St. Louis Med. Soc. (past pres.), St. Louis Soc. for Internal Medicine (past pres.), Mo. State Med. Soc., A.M.A., Am. Coll. Physicians, Am. Soc. Biol. Chemists, Am. Therapeutics Soc., Southern Med. Assn., Assn. Am. Med. Colls., Nat. Bd. Med. Examiners, A.A.A.S., Alpha Tau Omega, Phi Rho Sigma, Phi Beta Kappa, Sigma Xi, Alpha Omega Alpha. Presbyterian. Mason. Club: University. Home: 6319 Alexander Dr., Clayton 5, Mo. Office: Humboldt Bldg., St. Louis. Died Aug. 13, 1958.

NEILSON, William LaCoste, mfg. exec.; b. Phila.; May 2, 1879; s. William George and Mary Louise (Cunningham) N.; Bachelor of Arts, Haverford (Pennsylvania) College, 1901; m. Dorothy Crawford, October 30, 1907 (deceased March 4, 1954); children—William LaCoste, Alan Crawford. Apprentice Standard Steel Works, Burnham, Pa., 1901-05; supt. Chester Steel Castings Co., Lamokin, Pa., 1905-07; asst. sales mgr. Norton Co., Worcester, 1907-10, foreign sales mgr., 1910-21, gen. sales mgr., 1921-34, v.p., 1919—; v.p. Norton Co., Ltd., Hamilton, Ont., 1907-50; mgr. Deutsche Norton Ges., Cologne, Germany, 1912-38; pres. Cie. des Meules Norton, Paris, France, 1922-39; pres. S. A. Mole Norton, Corsico, Milano, Italy, 1935-41; dir. Behr-Manning Corp., Norton Pike Co., Norton Grinding Wheel Co., Ltd., Herts, Eng., Australian Abrasives Pty., Ltd., Sydney, Australia. Cons. U.S. Treasury since 1941. Episcopalian. Clubs: Country, Worcester, Tatnuck Country (Worcester); Royal Automobile (London). Home: 254 Salisbury St. Office: 1 New Bond St., Worcester, Mass. Died Mar. 5, 1957.

NELLES, Percy W., Canadian naval officer; b. Brantford, Ont., Jan. 7, 1892; s. Brig. Gen. C. M. and Ida Maude Mary (Walker) N.; grad. Lakefield Prep. Sch.; student Trinity Coll., Port Hope, Ont.; Royal Naval Staff Coll., Eng., 1924, Imperial Defence Coll., Eng., 1933; m. Helen Schuyler Allen, May 17, 1915; children—Charles Macklem, William Allen. Commd. as cadet (2d to join) Royal Canadian Navy, 1908, advanced to vice admiral, 1941, chief naval staff, 1934-44. sr. flag officer (overseas) head Canadian Naval Mission, Eng., since 1944. Awarded war medals, 1914-18, Star, British War, Victory, King George V Coronation, King George V Jubilee, King George VI Coronation medals. Decorated Companion of the Bath, 1943. Home: Vine Lynne, 7 Rideau Gate. Office: Naval Service Hdqrs., Ottawa, Ont., Can. Died June 13, 1951.

NELLIGAN, Howard Paul, business exec.; born Ithaca, N.Y., Feb. 5, 1903; s. James A. and Mary M. (Brandon) N.; LL.B., Syracuse U.; m. Genevieve Katherine Derschug, May 13, 1933; children—John Derschug, Joan Bankes, James Edward. Lawyer with Hancock, Dorr, Kingsley & Shove, Syracuse, 1926-33, jr. partner, 1933-36; v.p., general counsel and dir. Easy Washing Machine Corp., Syracuse, N.Y., 1936-41, pres. since 1941; dir. Syracuse Trust Co., First Federal Savings and Loan Assn. Trustee St. Joseph's Hosp., Rheumatic Fever Foundation of Onondaga County; mem. bd. lay regents Le Moyne Coll.; mem. bd. govs. of Citizens' Found.; mem. adv. bd. Syracuse U. Inst. of Indsl. Research. Pres. and dir. Mfrs. Assn. of Syracuse; dir., mem. exec. com. Nat. Chests and Councils Am.; dir., pres. Syracuse Community Chest, Y.M.C.A., Syracuse C. of C. Mem. Am. Bar Assn., N.Y. State Bar Assn., Onondaga County Bar Assn., Am. Home Laundry Mfrs. Assn. (pres.). Clubs: Century, University, Rotary, Onondaga Golf and Country (Syracuse); Union League (N.Y. City); Cazenovia, Cazenovia Golf. Home: 1637 James St., Syracuse 6. Office: Spencer and Solar Sts., Syracuse 1, N.Y. Died May 17, 1952.

NELSON, Alfred Brierley, educator; b. nr. Gastonville, Pa., Mar. 14, 1844; s. James and Mary (Brierley) N.; grad. Centre Coll., Ky., 1864, A.M.; M.D., U. Pa., 1874; m. Mary Moore, Oct. 13, 1869. Ceased practice of medicine, 1876, became prof. mathematics Centre Coll. Fellow A.A.A.S.; mem. Am. Math. Soc. Address: Danville, Ky. Deceased.

NELSON, Arthur E., lawyer; b. Browns Valley, Minn., May 10, 1892; s. Nels Olaf and Emily Augusta (Barr) N.; student Macalester Coll., 1910-12, St. Paul Coll. of Law, 1912-15; m. Alice Blanche Carlson, Dec. 2, 1915; children—Arthur William, Albert Barr, James Louis, Roy Hugh, Alice Ann. Admitted to Minn. bar, 1915, Ill. bar, 1939; gen. practice until 1920; corp. counsel St. Paul, 1920-22; mayor St. Paul, 1922-26; mem. Nelson and Mohan, Chicago and St. Paul; U.S. senator from Minn., elected Nov. 3, 1942, for term ending Jan. 4, 1943. Enlisted as private Heavy Artillery, World War I; honorably discharged, Nov. 1918. Mem. American Legion. Episcopalian. York and Scottish Rite Mason. Clubs: Athletic, Town and Country (St. Paul); Union League, Chicago Athletic (Chgo.). Home: Commodore Hotel, St. Paul. Died Apr. 11, 1955.

NELSON C(arl) Ferdinand, educator; b. Morlunda, Sweden, May 25, 1882; s. Nels Aaron and Christina Maria N.; brought to U.S. in childhood; A.B., U. Wis., 1908, A.M., 1910, Ph.D., 1912; M.D., Rush Med. Coll., Chgo., 1917; m. Hearty Earl Brown, Aug. 18, 1919; children—Arthur Hunt, Carl Stanley. Instr. chemistry U. Ia., 1908-11; fellow in chemistry U. Wis., 1911-12; instr. chemistry U. Ill., 1912-13; asst. prof. chemistry U. Kan., 1913, asso. prof., 1914, prof. and head of dept. since 1948. Mem. Am. Soc. Biol. Chemists, Am. Chem. Soc., A.M.A., Kan. Acad. Science, Gamma Alpha, Sigma Xi. Conglist. Club: University. Contbr. numerous articles in Jour. Biol. Chemistry, Jour. of Pathology and Bacteriology, Jour. of Kan. Med. Assn., etc. Home: 625 W. 16th St., Lawrence, Kan. Died June 4, 1950; buried Lawrence.

NELSON, Clara Albertine, educator; b. Tiffin, O., Apr. 4, 1852; d. Alexander and Jane Zilpha (Morrison) N.; Baldwin U., Berea, O.; M.L.A., Ohio Wesleyan U., 1872, B.A., 1894; M.A., 1896; studied Friedricksdorf and Stuttgart, Germany, 1875, Paris, 1895-96, The Sorbonne and Collégé de France, 1902-03, diploma, Académie de Paris; unmarried. Prof. French and head of dept. Ohio Wesleyan U., 1896—; lecturer on art history in Ohio. Methodist. Mem. Modern Lang. Assn. America, Nat. Inst. Social Sciences, Y.W.C.A. (territorial com.), Phi Beta Kappa. Clubs: Shakespeare, Monday, Woman's Faculty. Editor: La Fille de Roland, Bornier, 1909. Chmn. Red Cross of Delaware Co. Home: Delaware, O. Died Sept. 7, 1931.

NELSON, Donald Marr, corporation executive; born in Hannibal, Missouri, on November 17, 1888; s. Quincy Marr and Mary Ann (MacDonald) N.; B.S., U. of Mo., 1911; LL.D., U. of Mo., Harvard, Northwestern U., 1942; Dr. Bus. Adminstrn., University So. Cal., 1947; m. Eleonore Erath (Lena M. Peters), Feb. 12, 1959. Chem. engr. Sears Roebuck & Co., 1912-21, mgr. men's and boys' clothing dept., 1921-26, asst. in gen. merchandise office, 1926-27, gen. merchandise mgr., 1927-30, v.p. in charge of merchandising, 1930-39, executive vice-pres. and chmn. executive com., 1939-42; resigned to become chmn. W.P.B., Jan. 1942; on leave as acting dir. procurement, U.S. Treasury, May-Sept. 1940; coordinator nat. defense purchases, Sept. 1940-Jan. 1941; dir. of purchases, Office Production Management, Jan.-July 1941, dir. of priorities, also exec. dir. Supply Priorities and Allocation Bd., July 1941-Jan. 1942; chmn. W.P.B., Jan. 1942-Oct. 1944; personal rep. of President to China, Russia, 1943-44. Chmn. of the board American Mollerizing Corporation; president Pressure Dispensers, Incorporated; director Molybdenum Corp. Am. Former pres. Soc. Ind. Motion Picture Producers. Mem. Alpha Chi Sigma, Phi Beta Kappa. Trustee Stephens Coll. Clubs: Commercial, Chicago, Tavern; Metropolitan (Washington). Author: Arsenal of Democracy, 1946. Home: 9033 Briar Crest Lane. Office: 9489 Dayton Way, Beverly Hills, Cal. Died Sept. 29, 1959; buried Forest Lawn, Hollywood Hills, Cal.

NELSON, Edgar Andrew, organist, teacher; b. Chicago, Ill., Mar. 14, 1882; s. Andrew P. and Mary Charlotte (Lundberg) N.; ed. pub. schs. Chicago, Bush Conservatory; m. Harriet Schuettler, Nov. 4, 1908; 1 son, Edgar Schuettler. Organist various chs., Chgo. and suburbs, 1895—; formerly condr. Apollo Mus. Club; condr. Sunday Evening Club; also president of the Chicago Conservatory of Music; teacher of piano and vocal coach. Mem. Chicago Artists' Assn. (ex-pres.) Soc. Am. Musicians. Republican. Presbyterian. Club: Swedish. Decorated Order of Vasa by King of Sweden, 1920. Home: 1510 Cullom Av. Office: 64 E. Van Buren St., Chgo. Died July 11, 1959; buried Rosehill Cemetery, Chgo.

NELSON, Elmer Martin, biochemist, govt. ofcl.; b. Clark, S.D., July 5, 1892; s. Eric and Adelina (Hanson) N.; B.S., U. Wis., 1918, M.S., 1919, Ph.D., 1923; m. Mariana Theresa Sell, June 19, 1923; children—Donald Sell, Edith Adeline (Mrs. Milton D. Clark). Faculty mem. dept. biochemistry U. Wis., 1920-25; dir. chemistry and nutrition Soft Wheat Millers Assn., Nashville, 1925-26; research nutrition Bur. Chemistry and Soils, Dept. Agr., 1928-35; chief vitamin div. Food and Drug Adminstrn., 1935-49, dir. div. nutrition since 1949. Del. Internat. Vitamin Conf. under League of Nations, 1934; mem. expert com. vitamin standardization WHO, 1949; mem. sci. adv. com. Nutrition Found., Inc.; mem. Nat. Research Council adv. com. on food for Q.M. Army. Served as pvt. M.C., U.S. Army, 1918. Recipient Am. Grocery Mfrs. award, 1949; Babcock-Hart award, 1957. Mem. Am. Chem. Soc., A.A.A.S., Am. Inst. Nutrition, Am. Soc. Biol. Chemists, Food and Nutrition Bd. NRC, A.M.A. (council on drugs), Vitamin Adv. Bd. U.S. Pharmacopeia, Sigma Xi, Alpha Zeta, Phi Lambda Upsilon, Sigma Phi Epsilon. Home: 300 N. Fillmore St., Arlington 1, Va. Office: Food and Drug Administration, Washington 25. Died Dec. 24, 1958; buried Fort Lincoln Cemetery, Washington.

NELSON, Godfrey Nicholas, lawyer, v.p., sec. N.Y. Times Co.; b. Sweden, Oct. 22, 1878; s. Peter and Anna (Swanson) N.; brought to U.S. in infancy; native born citizen U.S. by reason father's citizenship; student Adelphi Coll., Brooklyn, 1895-96; C.P.A., U. of State of N.Y., 1907; studied law pvtly.; m. Grace L. Remsen, 1899; children—Godfrey Nicholas, Arthur Remsen; m. 2d, Florence June Barning, 1927; children—Godfrey Nicholas II, Courtland Post. Admitted to N.Y. bar, 1904, and practiced law in N.Y. City until 1932; of counsel for N.Y. Times since 1920; sec. and vice-pres. N.Y. Times Co., succeeded late Adolph S. Ochs as dir. same, 1935; prepared cases for indictment and trial in office of Dist. Atty. William Travers Jerome, 1908; specialized in fed. and state taxation. Mem. taxation com. Commerce and Industry Assn. of N.Y. Mem. Bar Assn. of City of New York, Am. and N.Y. State bar assns., N.Y. County Lawyers Assn., U.S. Chamber Commerce. Republican. Baptist. Mason (Shriner). Clubs: Century Association, Nat. Republican. Author: Income Tax Law and Accounting, 1916, revised, 1918. Regular contbr. financial section N.Y. Times since 1932. Home: 10 Gracie Sq., N.Y.C. 28. Office: 229 W. 43d St., N.Y.C. 18. Died Nov. 4, 1954; buried Sleepy Hollow Cemetery.

NELSON, Harold Hayden, Egyptologist; b. New Orleans, Nov. 25, 1878; s. Aaron Hayden and Anna Louisa (Berry) N.; student Morgan Park (Ill.) Acad., 1893-97; A.B., U. Chgo., 1901, Ph.D., 1913; m. Lizzie Augusta Bull, Apr. 2, 1910; 1 dau. (adopted), Irene Louise. Instr., Syrian Protestant Coll., Beirut, Syria, 1904-08; prof. history Am. U. of Beirut, 1908-24; prof. of Egyptology and field dir. epigraphic and archtl. survey of Oriental Inst., U. Chgo., at Luxor, Egypt, 1924-47; acting dir. Oriental Institute, 1942-43; prof. emeritus, 1944—. Mem. Am. Oriental Soc., Delta Upsilon. Baptist. Author: The Battle of Megiddo, 1921; Epigraphic Survey of the Great Temple of Medinet Habu, 1929; The Calendar of Feasts and Offerings at Medinet Habu, 1934; Plans Locating Theban Temple Decorations, 1941. Joint author of Early Historical Records of Ramses III, Medinet Habu, Vol. I, 1930; Later Historical Records of Ramses III, Medinet Habu, Vol. II, 1932; The Calendar, the Slaughterhouse and Minor Records of Ramses III, Medinet Habu, Vol. III, 1934; Reliefs and Inscriptions at Karnak, Vols. I and II; Festival Scenes of Ramses III, Medinet Habu, 1940. Home: 1155 E. 58th St., Chgo. Died Jan. 24, 1954.

NELSON, Herbert Undeen, real estate exec.; b. Ellsworth, Wis., Oct. 20, 1886; s. Charles Gustaf and Hanna Elizabeth (Undeen) N.; A.B., U. Minn., 1910; m. Marion Randall Lawrence, June 7, 1913; children—Richard Lawrence, Abbott Lawrence, Lawrence Undeen. Fdr. Am. Real Property Fed., sec., 1954-56; fdr. Internat. Real Estate Fed., 1951, treas., 1951, joint sec., 1952-55, hon. treas., 1955-56; fdr., sec. Am. Inst. Real Estate Appraisers, 1932-55, The Inst. Real Estate Mgmt., 1935-55, Soc. Indsl. Realtors, 1941-55, Nat. Inst. Real Estate Brokers, 1942-55, Nat. Inst. of Farm Brokers, 1944-55; mem., sec. Urban Land Inst., 1939-51, trustee, 1939-56; cons. Defense Housing Coordinator, 1940-42, Office Decentralization of Service, 1941-42; exec. v.p. Nat. Assn. Real Estate Bds., 1922-55, cons., 1955-56. Mgr. News Boys Club of Mpls., 1910-13; sec. Juvenile Protective Assn. of Hennepin Co., Minn., 1913-16; mgr. Citizens Club of Mpls., 1913-16, Mpls. Real Estate Bd., 1917-22. Mpls. Planning Commn., 1919-20. Recipient Chevalier de l'Ordre du Merite Commercial, France, 1953; certificates of merit by Freedom's Foundation, Inc.; awards of honor by the Nat. Assn. of License Law Ofls., Am. Soc. Assn. Execs., Nat. Assn. Real Estate Editors and real estate orgns. Numerous scholarships for real estate education and research established as Herbert U. Nelson memorials. Made proposal which became Fed. Home Loan Bank System, 1931; mem. council to draft Nat. Housing Act creating Fed. Housing Adminstrn.; active in drafting law for Home Owners Loan Corp., Fed. Nat. Mortgage Assn. Republican. Lutheran. Clubs: Minneapolis Athletic; Union League (Chicago); Knollwood Country (Lake Bluff); The Capitol Hill and University (Washington, D.C.). Author: The Administration of Real Estate Boards, 1925; New Homes in Old Countries (with Marion L. Nelson), 1937. Editor National Real Estate Journal, 1925-27, Realtor's Headlines, 1942-55, mng. editor Freehold, 1937-42. Contbr. articles in field. Home: 373 Sunset Road, Winnetka, Ill. Died Nov. 19, 1956; buried Meml. Park Cemetery, Evanston, Ill.

NELSON, Jabez Curry, corp. exec.; b. Marion, Ala., Aug. 5, 1884; s. Jabez Curry and Mary (Jones) N.; student Ala. Poly. Inst., Auburn, 1902-03; C.E., U. Ala., 1905; student Cornell U., 1908; m. Elizabeth Pace, Dec. 22, 1913. Engr., Ford, Bacon & Davis, Inc., N.Y.C., 1905-07, 08-16, gen. mgr. Gary (Ind.) Interurban Railways, 1916-17; v.p., gen. mgr. Empire State Railways, Syracuse, N.Y., 1917-18, pres. and gen. mgr., 1918-20; v.p. Easy Washing Machine Corp., Syracuse, N.Y., 1920-36, pres. and gen. mgr., 1936-41, chmn. bd. since 1941, dir. since 1924; dir. First Trust and Deposit Co. (Syracuse), Garlock Packing Co. (Palmyra, N.Y.). Mem. Am. Soc. C.E., N.Y. Southern Soc., Phi Beta Kappa, Sigma Alpha Epsilon. Clubs: Century, Onondaga Golf and Country (Syracuse); Cornell (N.Y.C.). Home: 1072 James St., Syracuse 3, N.Y. Died Jan. 22, 1952; buried Birmingham, Ala.

NELSON, James Boyd, ins. exec.; b. Baltimore, Sept. 8, 1897; s. J. Arthur and Katie Leon (Triplett) N.; student Boys Latin School, Friends Sch., Baltimore; m. Ethel M. Kopf, June 23, 1921; 1 son, James Boyd. Joined New Amsterdam Casualty Co., Baltimore, 1915, v.p. since 1934, dir., mem. exec. and finance coms. since 1938; v.p., trustee, mem. exec. and finance com. U.S. Casualty Co., N.Y. City, since 1933; treas. Lenderking Metal Products, Inc. since 1946, Nelson & Co., Inc. since 1946. Home: 211 Goodwood Gardens, Baltimore 10. Office: 227 St. Paul St., Balt. 3. Died Oct. 1, 1956; buried Druid Ridge, Balt.

NELSON, John Edward, ex-congressman; b. China, Me., July 12, 1874; s. Edward White and Cassandra (Worthing) N.; A.B., Colby Coll., 1898, LL.D., 1931; LL.B., U. Me., 1904; m. Margaret Heath Crosby, July 17, 1900 (dec.); children—Margaret, John, Eleanor, Charles, Atwood, Edith, Jeanette, Faith. Began practice at Waterville with late Gov. W. T. Haines, 1904; moved to Augusta, and asso. with Charles L. Andrews, as Andrews & Nelson, 1913, title Andrews, Nelson & Gardiner until 1926; elected to 67th Congress, Mar. 1922, for unexpired term ending Mar. 3, 1923, and reëlected 68th to 72d Congresses, 3d Maine Dist. Republican. Mem. Phi Alpha Delta, Zeta Psi, Phi Beta Kappa. Rotarian. Mason (32°). Club: Abnaki (Augusta). Home: Augusta, Me. Died Apr. 11, 1955.

NELSON, John Evon, vice-pres. and dir. Gulf Oil Corp.; b. at Helensburg, Scotland, Aug. 30, 1879; s. Ambrose and Elizabeth (Forsythe) N.; came to U.S. with parents, 1880; prep. edn., Park Inst., Pittsburgh, 1894-97; A.B., Westminster Coll., Pa., 1900, L.H.D., 1948; m. Margaret N. Dodds, Sept. 6, 1905; children—Wenley Dodds, John Oliver, Douglas Evon, Margaret Elisabeth. Clerk Keystone Nat. Bank, Pittsburgh, 1900-02; sec. to Andrew W. Mellon, 1902-08; formerly exec. v.p., now dir. Gulf Oil Corp.; exec. v.p. and dir. Gulf Research and Development Co., Gulf Refining Co., Western Gulf Oil Co., Gulf Tire and Supply Co., Cuban Gulf Oil Co., Mexican Gulf Oil Co., Venezuela Gulf Oil Co., Gulf Exploration Co., Caribbean Gulf Oil Co., Colombian Gulf Oil Co., American Internat. Fuel and Petroleum Co., Canadian Altapenn Oil Co., Canadian Basin Oil Co., Canadian Gulf Oil Co., Canadian Northern Plains Oil Co., Canadian Peace River Oil Co., Canadian Plains Oil Co., Canadian Shield Oil Co., Coral Oil Co., Dominion Gulf Co., Great Northwestern Oil Co., Marine Oil Co., Mozambique Gulf Oil Co., Philippine Gulf Oil Co., Venezuela Gulf Refining Co., Western Canadian Oil Co., Western Gulf Oil Co.; dir. Lubricating & Fuel Oils, Ltd., London; dir. and vice pres. Pittsburgh Parking Garages, Inc. Dir. Pa. Chamber of Commerce, Pittsburgh Junior Achievement, Inc. Trustee Westminster Coll.; dir. and mem. exec. com. Children's Hosp. of Pittsburgh; mem. adv. bd. Indsl. Home for Crippled Children, Pittsburgh. Sec. and dir. The Art Soc. of Pittsburgh; mem. Pa. Soc. of N.Y., Pan Am. Soc. (New York), Kappa Phi Lambda. Presbyterian. Republican. Mason. Clubs: Pittsburgh, Duquesne, University, Longue Vue, Pittsburgh Athletic Assn., Fox Chapel (Pittsburgh); Nassau (Princeton); Rolling Rock (Ligonier, Pa.); Princeton, University (New York). Home: 201 N. Murtland Av. Office: Gulf Bldg., Pittsburgh. Died Oct. 6, 1951.

NELSON, Mack Barnabas, pres. Long-Bell Lumber Co., Kansas City, Mo., Adair Lumber Co., Longview, Portland and Northern Ry. Home: 5500 Ward Parkway. Office: R. A. Long Bldg., Kansas City, Mo. Died June 10, 1950.*

NELSON, Ole C., med. dir. Cook County Hosp.; b. Norway, Jan. 1, 1883; s. Lauritz and Sophie (Sorenson) N.; brought to U.S., 1883, naturalized by Act of Congress; M.D., Chicago Med. Sch., 1920; m. Myrtle Irene Kinsman, July 28, 1916; children—Jean Louise (Mrs. William Van Stone), William George. Engaged in practice as physician since 1920; now med. dir. Cook County Hosp. Mem. Am. and Ill. hosp. assns., Chicago and Ill. med. socs. Democrat. Lutheran. Mason. Club: Executive (Chicago). Home: 147 Le Moyne Parkway, Oak Park, Ill. Office: 1835 Harrison St., Chgo. Died Jan. 16, 1954.

NELSON, Oscar, carbon black mfr.; b. Hvena, Sweden, Mar. 2, 1879; s. Eric and Sophia (Carlsson) Nilsson; ed. pub. schs., Sweden; m. Harriet Engstrom, Dec. 4, 1918; children—John Oscar, Anna Marie, Thomas Arthur, Fredrik Eric. Pres. and gen. mgr. United Carbon Co. since 1925; pres. United Carbon Company, Incorporated, United Producing Company, Combined Carbon Company, Westoak Gasoline Co., United Gas Co. (of W.Va.); v.p. Texas Carbon Industries, Inc., Kosmos Carbon Co., Eastern Carbon Black Co., Nat. Gas Products Assn.; dir. Carbon Black Export, Inc. Mem. Newcomen Soc. Republican. Lutheran. Clubs: Edgewood Country, Charleston Boat. Home: 1557 Quarrier St., Charleston, W.Va.; and Morlunda, Lewisburg, W.Va. Office: United Carbon Bldg., Charleston, W.Va. Died Nov. 27, 1953.

NELSON, Reuben Emmanuel, clergyman; b. Lake Elizabeth, Minn., Apr. 12, 1905; s. Rev. Peter Gothard and Mary (Johnson) N.; A.B., Des Moines U., 1927; B.D., Bethel Theol. Sem., St. Paul, Minn., 1930; grad. student Yale Div. Sch., 1930-31; S.T.M., Andover Newton Theol. Sem., Newton Centre, Mass., 1933; m. Edith Catherine Peterson, Sept. 6, 1933. Ordained Baptist ministry, 1930; pastor, First Swedish Bapt. Ch., Brockton, Mass., 1931-34; promotional dir., Bethel Inst., St. Paul, 1934-37; prof., New Testament studies, Bethel Sem., 1937-39; exec. sec., Minn. Baptist Conv., Minneapolis, 1939-43; exec. sec. Detroit Bapt. Missionary Soc. and dir. Promotion for Detroit Area, American Bapt. Conv., 1943-45; exec. sec., Council on Finance and Promotion, Am. Bapt. Conv., 1945-50; gen. sec. Am. Bapt. Conv., 1950—; mem. Gen. Bd. of Nat. Council of Chs.; mem. Central Com. & del. of Am. Bapt. Conv. to World Council of Chs. Mem. Pi Kappa Delta. Office: 152 Madison Av., N.Y.C. 16. Died Jan. 1960.

NELSON, William Hamilton, clergyman, editor; b. New Orleans, Apr. 6, 1878; s. Henry and Mary (Castleraegh-Casserley) N.; student Centenary Coll., Jackson, La. (now at Shreveport), D.D., 1922; student Southwestern U., Georgetown, Tex., U. Chgo.; m. Emma Vandenbark, 1904 (died 1913); 1 dau., Esther Marian; m. 2d, Geraldine Mary Guill, June 26, 1916; children—William Hamilton, Fitzgerald C., Hollis Mary. Ordained minister M.E. Ch., S., 1902; pastor successively San Antonio, Palacios, Port Lavaca, Cuero, Angleton and Houston, Tex., Santa Rosa, Cal., Phoenix, Ariz., Chico and Yuba City, Cal. until 1918; editor Pacific Meth. Advocate, San Francisco, 1918-34; western corr. The Christian Advocate, Nashville, 1934-38; also pastor So. Meth. Ch., Woodland, Cal. Mem. Ecumenical Conf. Methodism, London, 1920; Gen. Conf. M.E. Ch., S., Hot Springs, Ark., 1922; spl. session Gen. conf., Chattanooga, Tenn., 1924; res. del. to Ecumenical Conf. of Methodism, Atlanta, 1931. Democrat. Mason. Author: Is Jesus Coming Soon?, 1918; Speaking with Tongues, 1918; Who Is Antichrist?, 1920; The Wisdom of Sufi the Scribe, 1925; Alluring Arizona, 1927; Tinker and Thinker—John Bunyan, 1928; Blood and Fire—General William Booth, 1929; A Burning Torch and a Flaming Fire; The Story of Centenary College of Louisiana, 1931; Twelve Wonders of the Western World, 1934. Address: 174 Ellis St., San Francisco. Deceased.

NELSON, William Lester, ex-congressman; b. nr. Bunceton, Mo., Aug. 4, 1875; s. Thomas Alpheus and Sarah Ann (Tucker) N.; student William Jewell Coll., Liberty, Mo., 1895-97, U. Mo. Coll. of Agr., 1908-10; m. Stella Corinne Boschert, June 9, 1909; 1 son, Will L. Agrl. journalist; asst. sec. of agr. for Mo., 1908-17; mem. Mo. Ho. of Reps., 1902-04, 06-08; mem. 66th Congress, and 69th to 77th Congresses, 2d Mo. Dist. Dir. War Bd. Services, War Food Adminstrn., 1943. Mem. Mo. Gov.'s staff 1945. Journalist. Democrat. Baptist. Farmer. Mem. Gamma Sigma Delta. Home: 813 Virginia Av., Columbia, Mo. Died Dec. 31, 1946.

NEPRASH, Jerry Alvin (nĕ'prăsh), educator; b. Cedar Rapids, Ia., July 1, 1904; s. Daniel Joseph and Frances (Fajman) N.; A.B., Coe Coll., Cedar Rapids, 1925; A.M., Columbia, 1926, fellow in sociology, 1925-28, Ph.D., 1932; m. Dorothy Ready, Sept. 7, 1929. Lecturer in sociology, Columbia U. Extension, 1927-28; asst. prof. sociology, Franklin and Marshall Coll., 1928-32, asso. prof., 1933-36, prof. since 1937; prof. of sociology, Coe Coll., summers 1929, 34. Chmn. Social Planning Com. of Lancaster Community Chest, 1935-40; vice chmn. Pa. Com. on Edn. for Public Social Welfare, 1950-51, chmn. since 1951. Mem. Am. Sociol. Soc., Am. Statis. Assn., Eastern Sociol. Soc., Am. Assn. Univ. Profs., Pa. Sociol Soc. (pres. 1950-51), Am. Acad. Polit. and Social Sci., Chi Phi, Phi Kappa Phi, Pi Gamma Mu, Sigma Pi Sigma. Club: Torch (Lancaster). Author: Brookhart Campaigns in Iowa, 1920-26, 1932. Contributor papers at annual meetings of profl. socs.; also articles on methods of research in psychol. aspects of society to jours. Home: 1323 Clayton Rd., Lancaster, Pa. Died Feb. 9, 1955; buried Bohemian Nat. Cemetery, Cedar Rapids, Ia.

NESBIT, William Marsiglia, clergyman, Orientalist; b. N.Y.C., Feb. 15, 1881; s. William Henry and Leonore Hermina (Cleveland) N.; A.B., Columbia, 1902, A.M., 1907, Ph.D., 1913; B.D., Drew Theol. Sem., 1905, fellow, 1905-07; post-grad. student in Hittite, Yale, 1928-29; m. Theodora Benedict Dennis, Oct. 5, 1917; 1 dau., Bessie Benedict (Mrs. Howard G. Nelsen). Entered the ministry of M.E. Ch., 1902; student pastor, East View, N.Y., 1902-06; asst. pastor Jersey City, 1906-08; minister Westwood, N.J., 1908, Basking Ridge, 1909-13, Ferry Ch., East Orange, 1913-17, Union Ch., Bklyn., 1917-19, First Ch., Bklyn., 1919-24, First Ch., New Rochelle, 1924-26, Glen Cove, 1926-28, Watertown, Conn., 1928-31, Union Ch., Wilmington, Del., 1931-33, Washington Ch., Hurlock, Md., 1933-35, Claymont, Del., 1935-36, Grace Ch., New Haven, 1936-38, Naugatuck, Conn., 1938-42, Meml. Meth. Ch., Unionville, Conn., 1942-46, Carpenter Meml. Ch., Glen Cove., N.Y., 1946-49, ret. 1949. Sec. N.Y. Area Council of Religious Edn., 1918-31, N.Y. East Conf. Bd. S.S., 1919-30. Mem. Soc. Bibl. Lit. and Exegesis, New Haven Philatelic Soc., Phi Beta Kappa; mem. stamp clubs, Waterbury, Conn., Wilmington, Del. Mason. Lectr. on religious edn., Bible, history of ancient Orient, Masonry, philately, etc. Author: Sumerian Records from Drehem, 1914; (with S. F. Davis) The Lesson Handbook for 1925; (with H. H. Meyer) The Lesson Handbook for 1926, 27, 28, 29. Contbr. Hastings' Single Volume Dictionary of the Bible, 1909; also to various religious and sci. publs. Home: 14 Tulane Rd., Glen Cove, N.Y. Died Aug. 13, 1950.

NESLAGE, Oliver J(ohn), business exec.; b. St. Louis, 1893; s. Otto W. and Emma (Hardt) N.; B.S. in Mech. Engring., U. Ill., 1916; m. Cleone Finck, Sept. 1, 1920 (dec. Apr. 1957), children —Oliver John, Nancy (Mrs. Melvin C. Wyler). Vice pres. comml. sales Joy Mfg. Co., Pitts., 1945-56, v.p. marketing, 1956—. Served as 1st lt. Engrs. Corps. 1918-19. Mem. Engring. Soc. Western Pa., Am. Inst. Mining, Metall. and Petroleum Engrs., The Moles. Republican. Mason. Club: Duquesne (Pitts.). Home: King Edward Apts., Pitts. 13. Office: Henry W. Oliver Bldg., Pitts. 22. Died June 19, 1957; buried St. Louis.

NESS, Eliot; b. Chgo., Apr. 19, 1903; s. Peter and Emma (King) N.; Ph.B., U. Chgo., 1925; m. Elisabeth Andersen Seaver, Jan. 31, 1945; 1 son, Robert Warren. Asst. spl. agt., headed investigation of Al Capone, Dept. Justice, Bur. Prohibition, Chgo., 1929-32; asst. investigator in charge F.B.I., Dept. Justice, alcohol beverage unit, O., Ky., Tenn., 1932-33; investigator in charge alcohol tax unit Treasury Dept., 1933-35; dir. pub. safety, investigated corruption police dept., Cleveland, 1935-41, re-organized police dept., 1938; established Cleveland Police Acad., 1936; reorganized Cleveland Traffice Bur., 1937-39; established Welfare Bur. in Cleveland Police Dept., 1936; founded Cleveland Boy's Towns, 1938; investigated, aided in indictment and conviction corrupt labor ofcls., Cleveland, 1938; dir. Div. Social Protection, Fed. Security Agy., Washington, 1941-45; advisor Dept. Pensions and Nat. Health, Dominion Can., 1944; consultant U.S. Children's Bur., Dept. Labor, 1943-44; sec. Nat. Adv. Police Com. Social Protection, 1943-45; chmn. bd. dirs. Diebold, Inc., Canton, Ohio, 1945-51; bus. consultant, 1951—; pres. Dorite Corp.; v.p. Methods Institute Inc. Chairman Ohio Traffic Safety Council, 1940-41; mem. exec. com. Nat. Safety Council, 1938-46, bd. dirs., 1938-46; mem. Nat. Veneral Disease Com., 1944. Rep. candidate for mayor, Cleveland, 1948. Awarded Vet's. Fgn. Wars Medal as Outstanding Citizen of Cuyahoga Co., 1936; Meritorious Service Citation (Navy), 1946. Member Boy Scouts America, (mem. national council), Internat. Assn. Police Chiefs, Sigma Alpha Epsilon. Clubs: Athletic, Mid Day (Cleveland); Canton (Canton). Author articles social def., traffic accidents, juvenile delinquency profl. jours. and fed. publs. Home: 1972 Ford Dr., Cleveland 6. Office: Union Commerce Bldg., Cleveland 14. Died May 7, 1957.

NETHERSOLE, Olga (Isabel), actress; b. London, Jan. 18, 1870; pvt. edn. in London, Holland and Germany. Made dédut in The Harvest, at Theatre Royal, Brighton, Eng., Mar., 1887, London, début, June, 1888; visited Australia, 1890; became mgr. Court Theatre, London, 1894, and later mgr. for various periods, of Her Majesty's Theatre, Shaftesbury Theatre and Adelphi Theatre; made first appearance in America at Palmer's Theatre, N.Y.C. 1894, and has frequently toured U.S. at head of own co. Début in Paris, June, 1907, under own mgmt. at Theatre Sarah Bernhardt in rôle of Paula Tanquary, subsequently playing in English language in other rôles. Prin. plays: The Second Mrs. Tanquary, La Dame aux Camelias, Adrienne Lecouvreur, Magda, Sapho, Carmen, Frou Frou, The Writing on the Wall, Mary Magdalene, Sister Beatrice, etc. Address: Heathland Lodge, East Heath, Hempstead, London, N.W., Eng. Died Jan. 9, 1951.

NETTLETON, George Henry, educator; b. Boston, July 16, 1874; s. Edward Payson and Mary Ellen (Tucker) N.; B.A., Yale, 1896, Ph.D., 1900; Litt. D., Baylor, 1920; m. Mary Clark Trat, Dec. 16, 1902; children—Edward Treat, Mary Treat (Mrs. Gordon S. Haight). Apptd. instr. English, Yale, 1898, asst. prof., 1906-16, prof., 1916-43, (leave of absence 1917-19), chmn. dept. English, 1921-31, fellow Branford Coll., 1933—, dean of coll., 1937-39, Lampson prof. English emeritus, 1943—; dir. Yale Bur. in Paris, 1917; dir. Am. U. Union in Europe, 1917-19; acting pres., Vassar, 1922-23; lectr. at the Sorbonne, 1919. Decorated Chevalier Legion of Honor, 1919. Trustee Am. U. Union in Europe, 1919—, Hill Sch., 1920-24; trustee Vassar Coll., 1919-39; chmn. Bd. of Control of Yale Athletics, 1925-30; clk. and treas. Ch. of Christ in Yale Univ., 1922-30; Harvard (Hyde) Foundation lecturer at French univs., 1930-31; chmn. Am. Univ. Union Com., 1933-47. Mem. Modern Lang. Assn. Am., Phi Beta Kappa, Psi Upsilon, Torch Honor Society. Republican. Clubs: Century (N.Y.C.); Graduate, Elizabethan (New Haven); Union Interalliée of Paris, France. Author: English Drama of the Restoration and Eighteenth Century, 1914; The Drama and the Stage (18th century) in Cambridge Hist. of Eng. Literature, Vol. X. Editor: Specimens of the Short Story, 1901; The Major Dramas of Richard Brinsley Sheridan, 1906; Old Testament Narratives, 1909; The Book of the Yale Pageant, 1916; Twelfth Night (Yale Shakespeare), 1921; Yale in the World War, 1925; British Dramatists from Dryden to Sheridan, 1939. Address: Peck Hill Rd., Woodbridge, Conn. Died Feb. 5, 1959; buried Grove St. Cemetery, New Haven.

NEUBERG, Carl Alexander, research prof.; b. Hanover, Germany, July 29, 1877; s. Julius Alexander and Alma (Niemann) N.; Ph.D., U. Berlin, 1900; student U. of Wurzburg, 1897-98; Dr. Medicine, U. Breslau, 1922; Dr. of Biology, U. Petersburg, 1925; Dr. of Engring., Danzig, 1929; Dr. Med. Chem., U. of Palermo, 1933; LL.D., St. Andrews U., Eng., 1934; Dr. Agr., U. of Milano, Italy, 1949; m. Hela Franzisca Lewinski, May 21, 1907; children—Irene Stephanie, Alma Marian. Began as asst. Path. Inst., U. Berlin, 1898, teacher, 1903-06, prof.-by-name 1906-16, prof., 1916-19, full prof., 1919-38; also full prof. Agrl. Acad. of Berlin, 1920; dir. Kaiser Wilhelm Inst. of Biochemistry and Exptl. Therapy, 1913-38; research prof. N.Y.U., 1941-50; vis. prof. Poly. Inst. Bklyn.; also research asso. prof. New York Med. College since 1951. Awarded Emil Fischer medal Assn. German Chemists; Scheele medal Soc. Swedish Chemists; Berzelius medal Swedish Med. Soc., Delbrück medal Agrl. Acad. of Berlin; Leblanc medal Société Chimique de France; Pasteur medal Société de Biochimie de France. Rep. of Germany at Institut International d'Agriculture à Rome, 1927-35; Neuberg Medal; v.p. or dept. pres. Internat. Congress for Bacteriology, Microbiology and Biochemistry, London, New York, Paris and Washington, 1937, 38, 39. Fellow N.Y. Acad. Sci.; mem. or hon. mem. acads. of sciences in Göttingen, Halle, Helsingfors, Copenhagen, Lisbon, Lund, Petersburg, Amsterdam, and Uppsala; Agrl. Acad. in Prague; mem. acads. in Barcelona and Rome; socs. of physicians in Budapest, Charkow, Moscow and Vienna. Home: 536 W. 113th St., N.Y.C. 25. Died June 1956.

NEUBURGER, Rudolf, pres. The Tuition Plan, Inc.; b. St. Gall, Switzerland, Dec. 15, 1889; s. Max and Anna Neuburger; B.A., Cornell U., 1911; m. Alice E. Scott, Sept. 28, 1940; 1 dau., Anne E. With Neuburger & Co., N.Y. City, 1911-29, v.p., 1918-20; mdsing. exec. Atlas Powder Co., 1929-36; v.p. United Wallpaper Factories, 1936-38; v.p. Tuition Plan, Inc., N.Y., originators installment plan financing sch. and coll. tuition fees, 1938-42, now pres. Mem. exec. com. Nat. Paint Recovery Bd., Inc., 1932-34; pres. Inst. of Leather Cloth Mfrs., 1933-36; member of com. on education of the Chamber of Commerce, State of N.Y., 1939. Served as asst. business mgr. Nat. Council of Defense, 1917-18; mem. local bd. SSS, 1951—. Dir. Hebrew Tech. Inst., N.Y.C., 1951—. Mem. Cornell University Club, N.Y. City. Contbr. articles on merchandising and distribution to mags. Home: 515 E. 89th St., N.Y.C. 28. Office: 347 5th Av., N.Y.C. 16. Died Feb. 15, 1958.

NEUMAN, Fred G., author; b. Paducah, Ky., Dec. 22, 1893; s. F. W. and Sophia (Hummel) N.; ed. public schools, Paducah; m. Catherine L. Graves, June 1, 1924; 1 dau., Catherine (Jones). Columnist and feature writer; with Sun-Democrat, Paducah, since 1917. Served in U.S. Army during World War I. Active in Boy Scout work for twenty-five years. Mem. Am. Legion, Internat. Mark Twain Society. Democrat. Baptist. Author: Paducahans in History, 1922; Youth and Other Things, 1923; The Story of Irvin S. Cobb, 1926; The Story of Paducah, 1927; Paducah's Super-Flood, 1937. Irvin S. Cobb, His Life and Letters, 1938. Dictionary of Humorous Similies, 1949. Contbr. to the Sun-Democrat and other publications. Home: 1621 Monroe St., Paducah, Ky. Died Mar. 31, 1953; buried Oak Grove Cemetery, Paducah.

NEUMANN, Ernest K(arl), lawyer; b. Delavan, Ill., Dec. 15, 1898; s. Ernest W. and Lina (Baessler) N.; LL.B., U. Kan., 1923; m. Elizabeth Ellen Hogue, Dec. 2, 1931. Admitted to N.M. bar, 1923, practiced at Carlsbad, until 1931; police judge, Carlsbad, 1924-25; city atty. of Carlsbad, 1926-31; atty. gen. of N.M., 1931-35; mem. N.M. Ho. of Reps. (Dem. floor leader), 1927; interstate river commr. of N.M., 1931-35; chmn. bd. supervisors N.M. Motor Patrol, 1934-35; mem. State Bd. Liquor Control, 1933-35; asst. gen. counsel in charge of litigation and asso. gen. counsel in charge legal dept. H.O.L.C., Washington; later asso. gen. counsel Fed. Home Loan Bank Bd.; gen. counsel, mem. bd. trustees Group Health Assn., Washington, 1935-42. Served with USN, 1917-19; c ommd. officer N.M. N.G., 1923, capt. cav., 1931-35; lt. comdr. USNR, 1935-41; to active duty USAF, 1942-47, assigned to mil. govt., 1943, separated as lt. col. and assigned exec. officer Mil. Govt. Hesse in civilian capacity; upon assumption of occupational duties by State Dept. assigned pub. affairs officer for Hesse-HICOG, resigned 1951; pvt. practice law Carlsbad, N.M., 1951; now mem. law firm Neal, Neuman & Neal. Mem. Am., N.M. bar assns., Am. Legion, Res. Officers Assn. U.S. (pres. Wiesbaden, Germany, chpt. 3d term; nat. v.p. for ETO), Phi Alpha Delta. Quaker. Mason (32°). Home: 712 Riverside. Office: 601 N. Canal St., Carlsbad, N.M. Died Apr. 3, 1959; buried Carlsbad Cemetery.

NEVILLE, Keith, ex-governor; b. N. Platte, Neb., Feb. 25, 1884; s. William and Mary Ann (Keith) N.; A.B., St. John's Coll., Annapolis, Md., 1905; m. Mary Virginia Neill, Oct. 21, 1908; children—Mary Nelson, Frances Elizabeth, Virginia Neill, Irene Morell. Engaged in banking, ranching and real estate business, N. Platte; chmn. bd. First Nat. Bank. Was mem. City Council and Bd. of Edn.; gov. of Neb., term 1917-19; formerly mem. Dem. Nat. Com. Chmn. Neb. State Advertising Commn., 1939-40; county chmn. Victory Fund Com. Democrat. Episcopalian. Member Phi Sigma Kappa. Hon. mem. Spanish-Am. War Vets. Mason, Elk, Odd Fellow. Awarded Rotary Club cup "for leadership in civic improvements," 1929. Home: 310 Circle Dr. E., North Platte, Neb. Died Dec. 4, 1959.

NEVILS, W(illiam) Coleman, clergyman, educator; b. Phila., May 29, 1878; s. Andrew Philip and Mary Cecilia (Coleman) N.; A.B., A.M., St. Joseph Coll., Phila.; Ph.D., Woodstock (Md.) Coll.; D.D., Georgetown U., LL.D., Loyola U., Los Angeles, 1934, St. Joseph's College, Phila., 1944. Joined Society of Jesus (Jesuits), 1896; ordained Roman Catholic priest, 1911; with instr. Latin and Greek, Boston Coll. and Loyola Sch., New York; served as prof. rhetoric, St. Andrew-on-Hudson, Poughkeepsie, N.Y., and as prof. philosophy Holy Cross Coll., and lectr. sociology Georgetown U., on psychology of edn. Boston Inst. of Archdiocese of Boston; dean Georgetown U., 1918-19, chancellor, 1919-24, regent, Sch. of Foreign Service, 1920-24; dean Shadowbrook Jesuit House of Studies, 1924-28; pres. Georgetown U., 1928-35; rector Loyola Sch., Regis High Sch. and St. Ignatius Ch., N.Y.C., 1935-40; pres. U. Scranton 1942-47; rector, Scranton Prep. Sch., 1944-47. Dir. International Textbook Co., Internat. Corr. Schools, I.C.S. Canadian, Ltd., Internat. Ednl. Pub. Co., Internat. Schools Co. of Latin Am. Dir. and v.p. Scranton Philharmonic Soc. Mem. Assn. Pa. Coll. Presidents. Member President's Unemployment Relief Orgn., U.S. Board Visitors, Naval Acad. (civilian mem.) nat. com. on Inter-Am. Intellectual Cooperation. Chmn. Cath. Students' Travel League. Mem. N.E.A., Nat Acad. of History (Venezuela), Pa. Soc. Decorated Grand Cordon of Order of San Sava (Jugoslavia); Comdr. and Grand Officer Order of Crown (Italy); 1930; Grand Officer, Order of Merit (Chile); Chapelain Ordre de Saint Lazare (Jerusalem); Comdr. Order of the Star (Rumania), 1931; Grand Officer Order of White Lion (Czechoslovakia); Chevalier Legion of Honor (France). Faithful Friar, K. of C. (4°). Clubs: Scranton, Scranton Country. Author: Miniatures of Georgetown, 1934; The Saving Sense, 1947. Contbr. to ch., endl. and sci. mags. Address: Campion House (America Press), 329 W. 108th St., N.Y.C. 25. Died Oct. 12, 1955; buried Georgetown U. Cemetery.

NEVIN, Robert Reasoner, judge; b. Dayton, O., Aug. 2, 1875; s. Robert Murphy and Emma Frances (Reasoner) N.; student Ohio State U. 2 yrs., Cincinati Law Sch. 2 yrs.; m. May Steely, Mar. 20, 1906; children—Robert Steely, Betty May (Mrs. Arthur L. Wadsworth). Admitted to O. bar, 1898; pros. atty., Montgomery County O., 1906-09; judge U.S. Dist. Court, Southern O. Dist., since 1929. Served as pvt., later 2d lt., U.S. Army, Spanish-Am. War. Del. Rep. Nat. Conv., 1924. Episcopalian (sr. warden emeritus Christ Ch.). Mason (33°), K.P., Odd Fellow. Clubs: Dayton City, Dayton Country. Home: 139 Wisteria Dr. Office: U.S. Government Bldg., Dayton, O. Died Dec. 31, 1952.

NEW, Gordon Balgarnie, physician, surgeon; b. Hamilton, Ont., Canada, Nov. 6, 1885; s. Henry and Marian (Balgarnie) N.; D.D.S., U. of Toronto (Canada), 1906, M.B., 1909, M.D., 1915; m. Ethel Bailey, June 27, 1914; children—Marian (dec.), Elizabeth (dec.), Gordon, Robert. Came to U.S., 1910, naturalized, 1924. Interne City Hosp., Hamilton, Ont., 1909-10; head sect. on laryngology, oral and plastic surgery Mayo Clinic, 1910-51, ret.; prof. Mayo Found. Grad. Sch., U. of Minn., 1921—. Pres. 1st Pan American Congress. Recipient spl. hon. citation Am. Soc. Plastic and Reconstructive Surgery, 1952. Fellow A.C.S. (2d v.p.); mem. Minn. Med. Assn., Olmsted County Medical Society, Minnesota Academy of Ophthalmology and Otolaryngology (past president), also American Laryngological, Rhinol. and Otol. Soc. (past pres.), Am. Laryngol. Assn., Am. Acad. Ophthalmology and Otolaryngology (past pres.), Am. Assn. Plastic Surgeons (past pres.), Am. Bd. Plastic Surgery, Am. Soc. Plastic and Reconstructive Surgery, Sigma Xi. Mason (thirty-second degree). Clubs: University, Country (Rochester, Minn.). Contbr. to various med. journals. Home: 822 9th Av. S.W., Rochester, Minn. Died Oct. 28, 1954; buried Rochester.

NEWBERRY, John Josiah, merchant; b. Sunbury, Pa., Sept. 26, 1877; s. Andrew T. and Mary H. (Walsmith) N.; ed. pub. schs. of Pa.; m. Myrtle Edith Homer, Feb. 20, 1901 (died May 9, 1944); children—John Josiah, Jr., Myrtle Virginia (Mrs. Philip F. Leach); m. 2d, Alice M. Malloy, Mar. 2, 1946. Messenger, Pa. R.R., Wilkes Barre, 1890-94; with Fowler Dick & Walker Dept. Store, 1894-99; with S.H. Kress & Co., chain variety stores, 1899-1911; started own business as J. J. Newberry & Co., Stroudsburg, Pa., 1911, chmn. bd. dirs. since 1923; chmn. bd. dirs. North Jersey Trust Co., Ridgewood, N.J. Trustee Princeton Theol. Sem. Republican. Presbyterian. Mason. Clubs: Union League, Rotary (N.Y.C.); Ridgewood Country, Knickerbocker Country, Englewood. Home: Englewood, N.J. Address: 245 Fifth Av., N.Y.C. Died Mar. 6, 1954.

NEWBERRY, Mary Wheeler (Mrs. Trusten Polk Newberry), educator; b. Waymart, Pa., June 14, 1861; d. Rev. Henry (D.D.) and Mary (Sparkes) Wheeler; grad. Wyoming Sem., Kingston, Pa., 1879; B.A., Ohio Wesleyan U., 1885, M.A., 1890; post-grad. Radcliffe Coll., 1903-04; m. Rev. Trusten Polk Newberry, July 29, 1886. Preceptress, Pennington (N.J.) Sem., 1900-03; prof. English and asso. dean of women Ohio Wesleyan U., 1904-15. Mem. Phi Beta Kappa, Delta Sigma Rho, Assn. Collegiate Alumnae, Woman's Club of Asbury Park, N.J. Methodist. Address: Ocean Grove, N.J. Deceased.

NEWBILL, Willard Douglas, ret. army officer; b. Tappahannock, Va., Aug. 28, 1874; s. William Jeffries and Annie Eliza (Cauthorn) N.; grad. U.S. Mil. Acad., 1897, Sch. Submarine Defense, 1905. Commd. add. 2d lt. 5th Inf., 1897, trans. to 7th Arty., 1898; capt. 34th Vol. Inf., 1899; hon. mustered out vols., Apr. 17, 1901; 1st lt. 6th Arty., Apr. 8, 1900; capt. Arty. Corps, Aug. 22, 1901; assigned to 3d Field Arty., Jan. 28, 1910; maj. 2d Field Arty., Dec. 27, 1912; trans. to 4th Field Arty., June 16, 1913; maj. q.m., Jan. 2, 1914; lt. col., July 26, 1916; col., May 15, 1917. Served in Spanish-Am. War in P.R., 1898-99, in P.I. 1899-1901; with Gen. Lawton in Northern Luzon campaign; served on Mexican border, 1911-13, 16-17; staff duty, 1906-10, 14-17; in charge reunion of Blue and Gray, Vicksburg Nat. Mil. Park, 1917; comd. 3d F.A., AEF, France, 1918-19; participated in last Meuse-Argonne offensive. Mem. S.A.R. Clubs: Army and Navy (Washington), University (Buffalo). Home: Irvington, Va. Deceased.

NEWBRANCH, Harvey Ellsworth, editor; b. Henry County, Ia., Apr. 11, 1875; s. Oliver Peter and Louisa A. (Rapp) N.; A.B., U. Neb., 1896; LL.D., Creighton U., 1929; m. Evalena Rolofson, 1896; children—Katharine Louise (Mrs. Harry B. Coffee), Margaret Evelyn Eleanor Isobel (Mrs. Lisle Reinhold). Reporter, and editorial writer Omaha World-Herald, 1899-1905, asso. editor, 1905-10, editor 1910, editor-in-chief, 1944; v.p. World Pub. Co. Recipient Pulitzer Prize (Columbia U. Sch. of Journalism) for best editorial The Law and The Jungle, written in 1919; Oberlaender Trust fellowship for study of conditions in Germany and Austria, 1933; gold medal Freedom's Found., 1949. Regent U. of Neb., 1909. Retired. Author editorial: God Hates a Coward! Home: Blackstone Hotel. Office: Daily World-Herald, Omaha, Neb. Died Jan. 27, 1959.

NEWBURY, Mollie Netcher (Mrs. S. Newbury), merchant; b. Chgo.; d. Morris and Ernestine Alpiner; m. Charles Netcher, 1891 (dec. 1905); m. 2d, S. Neuberger, 1913; (name changed to Newbury, 1918). Owner of the Boston (dept.) Store, of which has been pres. and treas. many years (business founded by Charles Netcher, 1873). Office: Boston Store, Chgo. Died Dec. 12, 1954.*

NEWBY, Nathan (nū'bē), lawyer; b. nr. Hertford, N.C., Sept. 30, 1868; s. Nathan and Frances Catherine (McMullan) N.; B.L., U. of Va., 1888; m. Pearl Putnam, Mar. 20, 1901; children—Nathan, John Herbert, Paul Duncan, Charles Ryland, Ellen Catherine, Perlita, Edith Evangelyn. Began practice at Bryson City, N.C., 1889; removed to Los Angeles, 1895; mem. Newby, Holder & Newby. Admitted to bars of Federal courts of Calif. and to U.S. Supreme Court, 1915. Mem. Am., Calif. and Los Angeles state bar associations. Delegate to Uniting Conference, Methodist Ch., Kansas City, Mo., 1939 (elected reserve mem. Judicial Council); lay del. Southern Calif. Ariz. Conf. to 1st gen. Conf. Method. Ch., 1940. Apptd. a dir. 6th Dist. Agrl. Assn. and mem. dist. bd. of agr., 6th Dist., 1940, pres. of the assn. 1942, 43. Mem. Acad. Polit. Science, S.R., United Nations Assn. Democrat. Methodist. Mason. Clubs: Wilshire Country (Los Angeles); Colonnade (U. of Va.). One of 15 freeholders to draft Charter of Los Angeles, adopted 1924. Dir. Los Angeles Co. Centennials Celebrations, Inc., to celebrate hundred years Calif. history, 1950. Home: 1657 S. Gramercy Place. Office: H. W. Hellman Bldg., L.A. Died Feb. 7, 1951; buried Forest Lawn Meml. Park, Glendale, Cal.

NEWCOMB, John Lloyd, univ. pres.; b. Sassafras, Va., Dec. 18, 1881; s. Benjamin Carey and Martha Jane (Coleman) N.; A.B., Coll. of William and Mary, 1900, LL.D., 1935; C.E., U. Va., 1903; D.Sc., Washington and Lee U., 1933; LL.D., George Washington U., 1934, Duke, 1935; m. Mrs. Grace Shields Russell, Oct. 24, 1924 (dec. Oct. 10, 1941). Began as computer in engineer's office Rapid Transit Subway Construction Co., N.Y.C., summer 1902; asst. engr. on location and constrn. Norfolk & Southern R.R. Co., 1903-04, div. engr. maintenance of way, 1904-05; adj. prof. civil engring. U. Va., 1905, asso. prof., 1907, prof., 1910-33, dean dept. of engring., 1925-33, asst. to pres., 1926-31, acting pres., 1931-33, pres., 1933-47, ret. Pres. Nat. Assn. State Univs., 1943-44. Mem. Spl. Com. on Aeronaut. Research in Ednl. instns.; mem. bd. trustees Carnegie Foundation for Advancement of Teaching; mem. bd. of visitors U.S. Naval Acad.; mem. wartime commn. Office of Edn.; mem. divisional com. on state and local sch. adminstrn., Office of Edn.; mem. bd. trustees Va. War Fund; pres. Nat. Assn. State Univs., 1934-44. Am. Asso. for United Nations, Inc., 1945-46. Supervisor Sect. B, S.A.T.C., U. Va., May-Dec. 1918. Mem. Soc. for Promotion Engring. Edn., Am. Assn. U. Profs., N.Y. Southern Soc., Soc. of Virginians, Newcomen Soc., Pi Kappa Alpha, Sigma Beta Pi, Phi Beta Kappa, Tau Beta Pi. Democrat. Episcopalian. Club: Colonnade. Home: 132 Bollingwood Rd., Charlottesville, Va. Died Feb. 22, 1954; buried U. Va. Cemetery, Charlottesville.

NEWCOMB, Kate Pelham, physician; b. Leoti, Kansas, July 26, 1885; dau. Thomas Walter and Kate (Callahan) Pelham; M.D., U. Buffalo, 1917; m. William Furman Newcomb, Sept. 22, 1922; children—William Thomas, Eldorah Kathleen. Intern Infirmary for Women and Children, N.Y.C., 1917; resident Womens Hosp. for Women and Children, Detroit, 1917-19; gen. practice of medicine, 1919—; practice in Detroit, 1919-24, Boulder Junction, Wis., 1930—, Woodruff, Wis., 1934—; founder, mem. staff Lakeland Meml. Hosp., Woodruff, 1954—, also St. Mary's Hosp., Rhinelander, Wis., Sacred Heart Hosp. Tomahawk, Wis. Recipient Career Woman outstanding achievement plaque Jr. Achievement, Inc., 1955. Mem. A.M.A., Gen. Practitioners Assn., N.Y. Acad. Sci. Home: Boulder Junction, Wis. Office: Woodruff, Wis. Died May 30, 1956; buried Boulder Junction Cemetery.

NEWELL, Herman Wilson, advt. exec.; b. Bellefontaine, O., Dec. 18, 1897; s. Oak M. and Mary Louise (Doty) N.; A.B., Dartmouth, 1920, M.C.S., 1921; m. Mary Elinor Emery, Dec. 1, 1921; children—Mary Elinor, John Philip. Sales promotion mgr. Eastern Mfg. Co., Boston and N.Y.C., 1921-24; mgr. Home Electric Light & Power Equipment Co., 1924-30, Frigidaire Sales Corp. of N.E., Boston, 1930-32; v.p. in charge sales Frigidaire Corp., Dayton, O., 1932-35; exec. v.p. Geyer, Newell & Ganger, Inc., 1935-52; pres. Lennen & Newell, N.Y.C., since 1952. Clubs: University (N.Y.C.); Greenwich (Conn.) Country. Home: Parsonage Lane, Greenwich, Conn. Office: 17 E. 45th St., N.Y.C. 17. Died Dec. 19, 1954.

NEWELL, Joseph Shipley, aero-structural engring.; b. Springfield, Mass., Aug. 10, 1897; s. Frederick William and Emma Freeman (Shipley) N.; B.S. in Civil Engring., Mass. Inst. Tech., 1918; m. Lena M. Dwelley, Aug. 29, 1922; children—Joseph Shipley, Naomi, Frederick Dwelley, Charles William. Employed as draftsman Frigorifico Armour, La Plata, Argentina, 1919-20; asst. dept. of civil engring., Mass. Inst. Tech., 1920-21; asst. engr. structures branch McCook Field, Dayton, O., 1922-26; instr. aero-structural engring., asst. prof., prof., exec. officer aero-engring. dept. and sec. of faculty, Mass. Inst. of Tech. since 1927. Mem. exec. com. Column Research Council. Fellow Inst. of Aeronautical Scis.; mem. Sigma Xi. Republican. Author: Airplane Struc-

tures (with A. S. Niles); papers in field of aeronautical structures. Home: Trapelo Rd., Lincoln, Mass. Died May 5, 1952; buried Lincoln, Mass.

NEWELL, Wilbur Charles, clergyman; b. Mansfield, Conn., Dec. 28, 1859; s. Frederick C. and Jane P. (Slater) N.; student Wesleyan U., Conn., 1878-80, Boston U. Sch. of Theology, 1881-82; m. Elizabeth F. Haynes, September 3, 1884 (deceased February 10, 1922); 1 daughter, Mrs. Elsie Jane Trull; married 2d, Mrs. Ida Lutz, 1936. Ordained to M.E. ministry, 1887; pastor, N.E. So. Conf., 1887-1901, Vt. Conf., 1901-07, Troy Conf., 1907-22, retired; supply preacher; speaker for prohibition, and on lit. social and religious subjects. Author: Truth About Hell, 1898; The Life Worth Living, 1902; Messages from God from the Life Story of George A. Buckman; Christmas Appraisal of Jesus Christ; Easter and the Life Immortal. Home: 20 Essex St., Amsterdam, N.Y.; (winter) Hickory, N.C. Died Jan. 2, 1947.

NEWELL, William Stark, chmn. Bath Iron Works Corp.; b. Albany, N.Y., May 31, 1878; s. William C. and Ellen A. (Doane) N.; B.S., Mass Inst. of Technology, 1899; M.A. (hon.), Bowdoin Coll.; LL.D. (hon.), Colby Coll.; D. Eng. (hon.), U. of Me., Stevens Inst. Tech.; m. Caroline E. Moulton, Feb. 2, 1907. Employed in machine shop, Sparrows Point, Md., 1899; instr. Mass. Inst. Tech., 1900-02; marine draftsman Bath (Me.) Iron Works, 1902-06, asst. supt. and engr., 1906-14, engring. works mgr., 1914-25; gen. mgr. New York Shipbuilding Co., Camden, N.J., 1926-27; pres. Bath (Me.) Iron Works Corp., 1927-50; pres. Bath Savings Instn., 1932-41; pres. United Seamen's Service, Inc., Kennebec Towage Co., Eastern Maine Towage Co.; dir. Bath Trust Co., Maine Central R.R., Union Mutual Life Ins. Co., Portland Port Authority Mack Trucks, Incorporated, Bates Manufacturing Co. Officer de Merite Maritime Marchande de France; Chevalier de la Legion d'Honneur of France. Pres. Bath Water District, 1916-41. Trustee Webb Institute, Colby Coll., Patten Library. Dir. National Council, Am. Shipbuilders; mem. Am. Newcomen Soc., Corp. Mass. Inst. of Tech., Am. Soc. Naval Architects and Marine Engrs. (past pres.); mem. Instutiton Naval Architects, Gt. Britain, Am. Soc. Naval Engrs., mem. North East Coast Inst. of Engineers & Shipbuilders; dir. Bath Y.M.C.A. Mason. Elk. Clubs: Engineers, India House, Union League (N.Y. City); University (Boston); Bath Country. Home: 1080 Washington St. Office: Bath Iron Works Corp., Bath, Me. Died Apr. 18, 1954; buried Bath, Me.

NEWHALL, Arthur Brock, dir. Hood Rubber Co.; b. Lynn, Mass., Aug. 17, 1884; s. Fred M. and Eva (Brock) N.; M.E., Tufts Coll., 1908; m. Charlotte A. Daniels, Aug. 19, 1910 (dec. 1951); children—Jane (dec.), Sally. Instr. sci., mechanic arts Salem (Mass.) Tech. High Sch., 1908-12; inst. mech. engring. Wentworth Inst., Boston, 1912-17; with Hood Rubber Co., Watertown, Mass., since Aug. 1917, successively office mgr., mdse. mgr., branch auditor, mgr. tire dept., gen. mgr., exec. v.p., pres. (1930), now dir. (Hood Co. merged with B. F. Goodrich Co., 1929); dir. and mem. exec. com. B. F. Goodrich Co., Akron, O., since Aug. 1937; dir. Arrow Mutual Liability Ins. Co., Watertown, Mass., Dennison Mfg. Co., Framingham, Mass., Second National Bank of Boston, Framingham National Bank; chairman board Cambridge Rubber Company, General Latex & Chemical Company; executive vice pres. Talon, Inc., Meadville, Pa., July 1939-Aug. 1941; since Aug. 1941 has served in various Dollar-a-Year positions, Washington, as dep. dir. purchasing War Prodn. Bd.; later coordinator of rubber, WPB; now executive dir. Combined Production and Resources Bd.; also treas. Dennison Mfg. Co., Framingham, Mass.; treas. and director Cambridge Rubber Co., Cambridge, Mass. Dir. Rubber Mfrs. Assn. (New York), Associated Industries of Mass. (Boston). Trustee Tufts Coll. Mem. Zeta Phi, Tau Beta Pi (hon.). Clubs: University (Boston); Meadville Country (Meadville, Pa). Home: 87 Edgell Rd., Framingham, Mass. Died Mar. 12, 1954; buried Mt. Auburn Cemetery, Cambridge, Mass.

NEWHALL, C. Stevenson, corp. ofcl.; b. Phila., Apr. 10, 1877; s. Gilbert H. and Elizabeth Stevenson (Smith) N.; student Germantown Acad., Phila.; unmarried. Associated with Pa. Co. for Ins. on Lives and Granting Annuities since 1896, exec. v.p., 1929-34, pres., 1934-38, chmn. bd. since 1938; officer or dir. other cos. Home: 217 W. Mt. Airy Av., Mt. Airy, Phila. 19. Office: 15th and Chestnut Sts., Phila. 1. Died Dec. 14, 1950.

NEWHALL, J. Lincoln, ex-congressman; b. of Am. parents, Can., Mar. 26, 1870; s. Wilbert and Emily V. (Sawtelle) N.; ed. Indiana University and University of Cincinnati; m. Nellie G. Kinsley, of Covington, Ky., Sept. 1, 1891; children—Lucy G. (Mrs. Stanley E. Wilson), Elwood L., Nell May (Mrs. Gail Duff). With internal revenue dept. 6th Ky. Dist., 1899-1905; musical work, 1905-13; dir. of music. pub. schs., Covington, 1913-29. Welfare service, France, World War. Mem. 71st Congress (1929-31), 6th Ky. Dist. Republican. Baptist. Mason (32°). Home: Dudley Rd., R. 1, Covington, Ky.

Died July 26, 1952; buried Forest Lawn Meml. Park, Erlanger, Ky.

NEWKIRK, Samuel Drake, lawyer; b. Tipton, Mo., Oct. 9, 1885; s. Francis M. and Ella J. (Rutherford) N.; LL.B., U. Mo., 1907. Admitted to Mo. bar, 1907, since practiced in Kansas City; partner Blackmar, Newkirk, Eager, Swanson & Midgley since 1923; dir. Mo. Bank & Trust Co., Mo. Safe Deposit Co., Mo.-Kan. Supply Co. Mem. Am., Mo., Kansas City bar assns., Lawyers Assn. Kansas City, Kansas City C. of C., Phi Delta Phi. Democrat. Clubs: Univ., Indian Hills Country (Kansas City, Mo.). Home: 4600 J.C. Nichols Rd., K.C. 2. Office: Commerce Bldg., Kansas City, 6, Mo. Died Nov. 14, 1953.

NEWLIN, Gurney Elwood (nū'lin), lawyer; b. Lawrence, Kan., Nov. 11, 1880; s. Thomas Elwood and Laurie (Hadley) N.; student Haverford (Pa.) Coll., 1898-1900; B.L., U. of Calif., 1902; LL.B., Harvard, 1905; LL.D., U. of Southern Calif., 1930; unmarried. Admitted to Calif. bar, 1905, and began practice at Los Angeles; mem. Newlin, Holley, Tackabury & Johnston (formerly Newlin & Ashburn); dir. and mem. exec. com. Security First Nat. Bank of Los Angeles; dir. Union Oil Co., of Calif. Mem. Nat. Conf. Commrs. on Uniform State Laws, 1914-31; chmn. Los Angeles chapter Am. Red Cross, 1917-18; mem. State Council Sect. Council Nat. Defense, 1917-18; federal wage examiner for Southern Calif., U.S. Shipping Bd., 1918; deputy commr. Am. Red Cross to France, 1918-19. Pres. Los Angeles Grand Opera Assn., 1926-29; v.p. and dir. Southern Calif. Symphony Assn. An incorporator, mem. Central Committee, 1940-46, and chmn. Los Angeles chapter Am. Red Cross, 1940-45; pres. (Calif.) Am. Cancer Soc. Mem. Am. Bar Assn. (exec. com. 1924-27; pres. 1928-29; mem. bd. editors Jour., 1935-40, State Bar of Calif.; hon. mem. Kan. State Bar Assn., Ia. State Bar Assn., Harvard Law Sch. Assn. of New York, W.Va. Bar Assn., Canadian Bar Assn., Bar. Assn. of City of N.Y., Delta Kappa Epsilon (hon. pres. 1932), Order of the Coif, Golden Bear (hon.). Decorated Medaille de la Reconnaisse Française. Republican. Clubs: California, Los Angeles Country (Los Angeles); Pacific-Union (San Francisco); The Links (New York). Home: 3 Berkeley Sq. Office: 601 W. 5th St., Los Angeles. Died May 4, 1955.

NEWLIN, William Jesse, educator; b. Port Carbon, Pa., Aug. 28, 1878; s. Jesse and Ellen Davis (McCool) N.; A.B., Amherst Coll., 1899, A.M., 1903; B.S., Mass. Inst. Tech., 1901; A.M. (Shattuck scholar in mathematics 1905-06), Harvard, 1906; studied Yale, summer, 1906, Oxford, Eng., 1912-13; m. Margaret Baird Randal, Sept. 4, 1907 (died Nov. 27, 1918); m. 2d, Marie Hibbard. Aug. 29, 1922 (dec.). Walker instr. mathematics Amherst Coll., 1902-05, asso. prof. math. and philosophy, 1906, asso. prof. philosophy, 1907, prof. from 1909, now emeritus, sec. student activities com., 1917-18, dir. admissions, 1922-37, sec. faculty, 1922-45; prof. philosophy Mass. State Coll., summer 1931, U. Cal., summer, 1938. Nat. ednl. recruiting sec. War Personnel Bd., YMCA, 1918; chief of govt. div., citizenship dept., Army Ednl. Corps, AEF, France, 1919; dir. of extension, Serbian Relief Commn., Tchatchak, Serbia, 1919-20. Decorated Cross of St. Sava (Serbian), 1920. Mem. Am. Philos. Soc., Am. Assn. U. Profs., Psi Upsilon, Phi Beta Kappa. Mason. Rotarian. Asso. editor Service with Fighting Men, 1921; editor Amherst Coll. Biog. Record, 1938. Home: Amherst, Mass. Died July 24, 1958.

NEWMAN, Albert Broadus, chem. engr.; b. Toronto, Canada, May 3, 1888 (parents U.S. citizens); son of Albert Henry and Mary (Ware) Newman; A.B., University of Michigan, 1910, B.Ch.E., 1911, M.S., 1926, Ph.D., 1928; grad. student U. of Mich., 1926-27; m. Esther Edwards, Sept. 2, 1911; children—Albert Henry II, Philip Edwards. Asst. chemist Corn Products Refining Co., Edgewater, N.J., 1911-12; instr. chemistry, Pa. State Coll., 1912-13; foreman charge production, Nat. Zinc Co., Kansas City, Mo., 1913-15; supt. chem. mfr., Am. Metal Co., Ltd. Langeloth, Pa. plant), 1915-17; works mgr., Monsanto Chem. Co., East St. Louis plant, 1918-19; gen. mgr. Thermo Chem. Co., St. Louis, Mo., 1920-25; chem. engr. research div., Gen. Chem. Co., N.Y. City, 1927-28; prof. chem. engr., and in charge dept., Cooper Union, N.Y. City, 1928-38; prof. chem. engring. and chmn. of dept., Coll. of City New York since 1938; dean of Sch. of Tech., Coll. of City New York, 1941-47; lecturer, chem. engring., New York U. Grad. Div., 1941-45; consultant in chem. engring., Northwestern Univ., 1939-41; consultant War Research, Columbia Univ., 1944; chmn. sect. on heat exchange, Chem. Engring. Congress of World Power Conf., London, June 1936; chmn. bd. dirs. Defense Training Inst. of Engring. Colls. of Greater New York, 1941-43; mem. com. on engring. schs. of Engrs. Council for Professional Development, and chmn. Region IV, com. on accrediting, 1938-41; dir. American Inst. of Chem. Engrs., 1936-38 and 1939-41, also chmn. com. chem. engring. edn., 1937-42; v.p., 1945, 47, pres. 1948; regional adv. Engring. War Training Program, U.S. Office of Edn. since 1941; regional representative Engrg. War Training Program to War Manpower Commission, 1943-45; chmn. advisory commn. to N.Y. City Hdqrs. Selective Service System, 1943; mem. Labor Supply Com., Office Production Management, for N.Y. State, 1941-42; heading chem. industries under Gen. Lucius D. Clay, U.S. Mil. Govt., Germany, 1945-46; U.S. rep. on quadripartite com. on liquidation of German war potential, Berlin, Mar.-June 1946; member Regional Loyalty Board (N.Y. and N.J.), U.S. Civil Service Commission since 1949. Member of Am. Soc. of Engring. Edn., Am. Inst. of Chem. Engrs., Am. Chem. Soc., Engrs. Council for Professional Development, Sigma Xi, Phi Lambda Upsilon, Iota Alpha, Tau Beta Pi, Sigma Chi. Club: Chemists (trustee 1940-43). Author numerous publs. on engring.; contbr. to engring. jours.; editor papers on engring. Home: 120 Cabrini Blvd., N.Y.C. 33. Died May 1952.

NEWMAN, E. M., travel lecturer; b. Cleve., Mar. 16, 1872; s. Frank and Irma (Zinner) N.; student Adelbert Coll. (Western Reserve U.), 1889-93; married. Lectured in 15 of the largest cities in the U.S.; has made eight trips around the world; in Africa with Theodore Roosevelt, 1908; completed 158 travel reels for Warner Bros., these translated into all principal languages and circulated all over world. Author: Seeing Italy, Seeing Russia; Seeing Egypt and the Holy Land; Seeing Germany; Seeing England and Scotland; Seeing France; Seeing Spain; Seeing Paris; Seeing London. Address: 569 N. Rossmore Av., Los Angeles. Deceased.

Coll., Thompson, Conn., since 1934. Painted portrait

NEWMAN, Ernest, music critic, writer; b. Nov. 30, 1868; ed. Liverpool Coll. and Liverpool U.; m. Kate Eleanor Woollett (died 1918); m. 2d, Vera Hands. Became music critic Manchester Guardian, 1905, Birmingham Post, 1906, later London Sunday Times. Author of numerous works, including: Hugo Wolf, 1907; Richard Strauss, 1908; Wagner as Man and Artist, 1913; A Musical Critic's Holiday, 1925; Stories of the Great Operas, 3 vols., 1930; Fact and Fiction About Wagner, 1931; Life of Richard Wagner, 1933 (Vol. 4, 1946); Man Liszt, A Study of the Tragi-comedy of a Soul Divided Against Itself, 1943; More Stories of Famous Operas, 1943. Recipient Order Knight 1st Class, White Rose Finland, Cross Order of Merit, Comdr. Class of Germany. Address: Sunday Times, London, Eng. Died July 7, 1959.

NEWMAN, Horatio Hackett, zoölogist; b. nr. Seale, Ala., Mar. 19, 1875; s. Albert Henry N. and Mary Augusta (Ware) N.; B.A., McMaster U., Toronto, 1896, D.Sc., 1933; spl. student, U. of Toronto, 1896-97; fellow in zoölogy U. Chgo., 1898-1900, 1904-05, Ph.D., 1905; m. Isobel Currie Marshall, 1907; children—Elizabeth Ware, Marshall Thornton; m. 2d, Marie E. Heald, June 5, 1954. Instr. biology and Latin, Des Moines (Ia.) Coll., 1897-98; instr. biology and chemistry Culver (Ind.) Mil. Acad., 1900-04; instr. zoölogy, 1905-08, asst. prof. elect, 1908, U. of Mich., prof. and head dept. zoölogy, U. of Tex., 1908-11; asso. prof. zoölogy and embryology U. Chgo., 1911-17, prof. zoölogy, 1917-40, emeritus since 1940, dean in the Colleges of Science, 1915-22. Head of instrn. force in physiology, Marine Biol. Lab., Woods Hole, Mass., 1909-12. Fellow A.A.A.S.; mem. Am. Soc. Zoölogists, Am. Soc. Naturalists, Sigma Xi, Sigma Chi, Phi Chi. Author: The Biology of Twins, 1917; Vertebrate Zoölogy, 1919; Readings in Evolution, Genetics. and Eugenics, 1921; The Physiology of Twinning, 1923; Outlines of General Zoölogy, 1924; The Gist of Evolution, 1926. Editor, contbr. to The Nature of the World and of Man, 1926; Evolution Yesterday and Today, 1932; Twins—A Study of Heredity and Environment (with F. N. Freeman and K. J. Holzinger), 1937; The Phylum Chordata, 1939; Multiple Human Births, 1940. Home: 173 Devon Dr., Clearwater, Fla. Died Aug. 29, 1957; buried Sylvan Abbey Meml. Park, Clearwater.

NEWMAN, John Grant, clergyman; b. nr. Dandridge, Tenn., Oct. 16, 1862; s. Samuel Blair and Nancy Elizabeth (Rankin) N.; A.B., Maryville Coll., 1888, M.A., 1894, D.D., 1908, LL.D., 1921; Litt. D., Coll. of Emporia, Kan., 1927; grad. Union Theol. Sem., 1893; m. Mary E. Minnis, June 28, 1893 (died 1901); m. 2d. Helen I. Minnis, Dec. 19, 1906 (died Dec. 23, 1939). Prin. New Market (Tenn.) Acad., 1888-90; prof. Latin, Maryville Coll., 1893-1903; ordained to ministry Presbyn. Ch., 1894; pastor Olivet Meml. Ch., N.Y.C., 1903-05, Wyoming Ch., Cin., 1905-08; pres. The Western Coll. for Women, 1908-12; pastor Chambers-Wylie Meml. Ch., Phila., 1912-37, since pastor emeritus. Republican. Clubs: Union League, City. Author: An Education for You. Mem. Jud. Commn. Presbyn. Ch. U.S.A., 1914-17 (chmn. 1916-17); exec. commn. Synod of Pa., 1915-18. Contbr. Internat. Sunday Sch. Lessons to Saturday Phila. Inquirer, 1925-40. Home: 4642 Hazel Av., Phila. Died Sept. 27, 1956; buried West Laurel Hill Cemetery, Phila.

NEWMYER, Arthur Grover, public relations counselor; b. Washington, D.C.; m. Edith Strasburger; children—Arthur Grover, James Morton, Secretary to pub. Washington Times, 1902; mem. editorial staff, 1904-05, advertising mgr., 1906-08; national advt. mgr. all Munsey newspapers, 1909-12; associate publisher New Orleans Item, 1912-34, as business mgr., 1912-27, asso. pub., 1927-34; pub. Washington Times, 1934-35; pub. New York Journal, 1936; asst. gen. mgr. Hearst newspapers, 1937-38; Arthur G. Newmyer & Associates since June 1941. Pres. Southern Newspaper Pubs. Assn., 1923-24; v.p. Asso. Advertising Clubs of World, 1918. Mason (33°, Shriner). Clubs: National Press, Alfalfa, Woodmont (Washington); Md. Yacht (Baltimore). Home: Mayflower Hotel. Office: Wire Bldg., Washington 5. Died Oct. 12, 1955; buried Washington.

NEWSHAM, Joseph Parkinson, mcht.; b. Preston, England, May 24, 1837; s. James and Nancy N.; ed. pub. schs.; clerked in store; studied law 2 yrs.; practiced Edwardsville, Ill., 1859-60. Was 1st lt. and adjt., 32d Mo. vol. inf., Blair's brigade, U.S.A., during Civil War. After war clerk on court, Ascension Parish, La.; practiced law, Donaldsonville, La.; taught school in La.; removed to St. Francisville, La., 1867; editor and propr. West Feliciana Republican. Mem. La. Constitutional Conv. under which State was readmitted to Union; was chmn. Rep. Parish Com., judge of parish court, parish att'y., dist. att'y., mem. of police jury, mem. Congress, 1868-71; Republican. Address: St. Francisville, La.

NEWSOM, Curtis Bishop, clergyman, educator; b. Elizabethtown, Ind.; s. Joel Stout and Edith M. (Armstrong) N.; Ph.B., Earlham Coll., 1896; studied U. Chgo.; grad. McCormick Theol. Sem., 1907; A.M., Northwestern U., 1908; S.T.B., Garrett Bibl. Inst., 1908; Ph.D.; Central U., 1916; B.D., McCormick Theol. Sem., 1928; m. Mattie Fitzallen Fisher, Dec. 29, 1901; children—Carroll Vincent, Rendel Harris, Arden Chalmers, Mardelle, Stuart Murray. Tchr. and supt. schs. until 1904; licensed to Presbyn. ministry, 1905, ordained, 1907; acting pastor Douglas Pk., Chgo., 1905-06; pastor Granville Av. Ch., Chgo., 1906-09, First Church, Sturgis, Mich., 1909-15; dean of the U., prof. philosophy and English Bible, Trinity U., Waxahachie, Tex., 1915-20; Bushnell prof. Bibl. history and lit. and edn. Coll. of Emporia, Kan., 1920-25; head prof. philosophy and psychology Whitworth Coll., Spokane, Wash., 1925-26; head prof. religious edn. dept. U. Tulsa, 1926-29; research scholar in religious edn. Northwestern U., 1929-30; pastor First Presbyn. Ch., Wheaton, Ill., 1930-38, First Ch., Goodland, Ind., 1938-47. Mem. Religious Edn. Assn., Internat. Council of Religious Edn., Pi Gamma Mu. Writer and lecturer on religious and ednl. topics. Club: Kansas Authors'. Home: 11417 E. Rincon Dr., Whittier, Cal. Died Dec. 23, 1954; buried Marion, Kan.

NEWSOME, Albert Ray, prof. history; b. Marshville, N.C., June 4, 1894; s. Richard Clyde and Julia (Ross) N.; A.B., U. of N.C., 1915; student, Columbia, summers, 1920-21; A.M., U. of Mich., 1922, Ph.D., 1929; m. Frances Vaughan, June 4, 1917; children—Jennie Wells, Julia Frances. Teacher high schs., Elizabeth City, N.C., 1915-16, Wilmington, N.C., 1916-18; prof. history, Bessie Tift Coll., Forsyth, Ga., 1919-21; instr. in history, U. of Mich., 1921-23; asst. prof. of history, U. of N.C., 1923-26; sec. N.C. Hist. Commn. and editor N.C. Hist. Rev., 1926-35; prof. history U. of N.C. since 1935, head dept., 1935-50; Duke U. summer sch., 1940, N.C. Coll. for Negroes, 1942-46, grad. school, same, 1940-46 (part time); U. of Ia. summer, 1949. Pres. Nat. Conf. of Hist. Socs., 1928-29. Served as ensign U.S.N.R.F., 1918-19. Mem. Am. Hist. Assn. (chmn. Pub. Archives Commn. 1932-34), Soc. of Am. Archivists (charter mem. and 1st pres. 1936-39), State Literary and Hist. Assn. of N.C. (sec. 1926-35; pres. 1938-39), Am. Legion (historian N.C. dept. 1931-41), Southern Hist. Assn., Lambda Chi Alpha, Phi Beta Kappa. Democrat. Episcopalian. Club: Chapel Hill Country. Compiler N.C. Manual, 1927, 1929; The Preservation of Local Archives: A Guide for Public Officials, 1932; editor N.C. Social Sci. Maps (10 wall maps), 1937; The Presidential Election of 1824 in North Carolina, 1939; The Growth of North Carolina, 1940 (with H. T. Lefler); Studies in History and Polit. Sci., 1947; contbr. to The American Archivist and hist. revs. Editor, The James Sprunt Studies in Hist. and Polit. Science since 1939. Address: Laurel Hill Rd., Chapel Hill, N.C. Died Aug. 5, 1951; buried Chapel Hill Cemetery.

NEWTON, Clarence Lucian, lawyer; b. Eden, Vt., July 31, 1877; s. Oliver E. and Anna H. (Cleveland) N.; student Montpelier Sem., 1894-97; Ph.B., Wesleyan U., Middletown, Conn., 1902; LL.B., Boston U., 1905, LL.M., 1905, J.M., 1905; m. Alice McLennan, June 8, 1909; 1 dau., Dorothy (Mrs. William B. Chace). Admitted to Mass. bar, 1905, since practiced in Boston, specialized in corporations, wills, estates and trusts; lectr. bankruptcy Boston U. Law Sch., 1906-10; prof. corps. and wills Northeastern U. Law Sch., 1906-18; lectr. comml. law Boston chpt. Am. Inst. Banking, 1907-12; pres., treas. and dir. L. W. Packard & Co., Inc., Ashland, N.H., 1950—; v.p., dir. Potter Press, Boston; clk., dir. A. Stowell & Co., Inc., C. B. Swift Co., Gentles Baking Co., Seamans & Cobb Co., White Bros. Milk Co., Davidson Rubber Co., Cohasset Hardware Co., Butts & Ordway Co.; dir. Tuells Hat Co., R. S. Brine Transportation Co., Wm. A. Meaffey Co., Mass. Bonding & Ins. Co., Warren Bros. Co., J. McKenna, Inc.; clerk Eliot Creamery, Inc.,

A. W. McAdam Co. Trustee Wesleyan U., Middletown, Conn. Mem. Am., Boston, Middlesex bar assns., Beta Theta Pi (nat. pres. 1937-40), Phi Delta Phi. Mason (32°, Shriner). Clubs: Union, Down Town, University (Boston); Brae Burn Country (West Newton). Home: 96 Lenox St., West Newton 65, Mass. Office: 60 State St., Boston 9. Died May 21, 1958.

NEWTON, Homer Curtis, educator, adminstr.; b. Adel, Ia., Feb. 5, 1879; s. Avery Cyrus and Martha Alice (Perkins) N.; A.B., U. Colo., 1899; A.M., 1900; Ph.D., Cornell U., 1902; student U. Berlin, summer 1903; m. Mabel Elvira Clinkscales, Aug. 23, 1905; 1 son, Avery Curtis. Tutor, Coll. City of N.Y., 1902, instr., 1903-14, asst. prof., 1914-19, asso. prof., 1919-37, prof., 1937-49, acting head-dept. of classical langs., 1936-38, chmn. dept., 1941-49, librarian of the college, 1917-30; librarian Fairleigh Dickinson Coll., 1949—. Clubs: Hudson River Country (Yonkers). Author: Epigraphical Evidence for Reigns of Vespasian and Titus, 1902. Home: 269 Broadway, Dobbs Ferry, N.Y. Office: Fairleigh Dickinson College, Rutherford, N.J. Died June 20, 1957.

NEYLAND, Harry (nē'lănd), artist; b. McKean Eric County, Pa., Aug. 9, 1877; s. George W. and Alletta F. (Wood) N.; ed. Pa. State Normal Coll., Edinboro; art edn., Zenerian Art Coll., Columbus, O., Art Students' League, New York, Pratt Inst., Brooklyn, Julian Acad. and Colarossi Acad., Paris; m. Jeanette Vermorel, Aug. 5, 1909 (died 1932); 1 son, Eugene. Painter and sculptor; dir. Swain Free Sch. of Design, 1911-30. Has exhibited at Nat. Acad. Design (New York), Pa. Acad. Fine Arts (Phila.), Royal Canadian Acad., Montreal Art Assn., Ontario Soc. of Artists, etc. Represented in collections of Pratt Inst., Boston Art Club, New Bedford (Mass.) Country Club, Marine Hist. Assn. (Mystic, Conn.), Mariners Museum, Newport News, Va., and in many private collections. Active in whaling; organized the Whalemen's Club, Inc., New Bedford, Mass.; purchased the "Charles W. Morgan" (oldest whaleship in the world) and interested others in forming "Whaling Enshrined, Ind.," located at Round Hill, South Dartmouth, Mass., where whaling relics and ship were on view until roads were destroyed and ship and dock damaged by hurricane, September 21, 1938; ship has been presented to Marine Hist. Assn., Mystic, Conn. Mem. Authors' League America, R.I. Ship Model Soc. Clubs: Providence Art, Boston Art, New Bedford Yacht, etc. collaborator and illustrator: Cap'n George Fred, 1928. Author: The Log of the Lina, 1928; The Isles of the Volcan, 1929; Padanaram Tales, 1952; The Village Church, 1952. Contbr. to Internat. Studio, Arts and Decoration, Am. Mag. of Art, Harpers, Scribner's, Sea Breeze, etc. Home: Padanaram, South Dartmouth, Mass. Studio: New Bedford, Mass. Died Oct. 23, 1958.

NEYMANN, Clarence Adolph (nā'măn), psychiatrist, neurologist; b. Chicago, Ill., Nov. 7, 1887; s. Adolph M. and Emma H. (Huscher) N.; A.B., Harvard, 1909, M.D., Heidelberg U., Germany, 1915; degree in medicine, honoris causa, U. of Ghent, 1946; m. Virginia Hall, May 7, 1927. Instr. psychiatry, Phipps Clinic, Johns Hopkins Hosp., 1915-18, also dir. lab. of Internal Med.; supt. of Cook County (Ill.) Psychopathic Hosp., 1919-22; asst. prof. psychiatry, Rush Med. Coll., 1919-21; asso. prof. psychiatry Northwestern U. Med. Sch., 1921-48, prof. since 1948, mem. University Senate, 1948; apptd. hon. prof. Med. Nat. U. of Mexico, 1933; exchange prof. Belgian-Am. Ednl. Foundation to univs. of Ghent, Louvain, Liege and Brussels, 1935; chief of staff Cook County Psychopathic Hospital; consultant in neuropsychiatry, Illinois Charitable Eye, Ear, Nose and Throat Infirmary, Veterans Rehabilitation Center, Chicago and Wesley Memorial Hospital, Chicago. Decorated officer Belgian Order de la Couronne; member Belgian League of Honor. Fellow A.M.A., Royal Society of Medicine, American Academy of Phys. Medicine, American Psychiatric Assn.; member Am. Psychopathol. Soc., Ill. Psychiatric Soc. (pres. 1943-44), Central Neuro-Psychiatric Soc., Chicago Neurol. Soc. (pres. 1946-47), Soc. de Medicine Mentale de Belgique (hon.), Indian Psychiatric Society (honorary), Chicago Inst. Med., Chicago Med. Soc., Chgo. Soc. of Med. Hist., Chicago Soc. for Personality Study, Chicago Acad. Criminology, Chicago Pathol. Soc., Ill. State Med. Soc., Soc. of Harvard Chemists, Johns Hopkins Med. Soc., Yucatan Med. Soc. (hon.), Phi Chi, Phi Kappa Epsilon. Contbr. to Rosanoff's Text Book of Psychiatry, Pemberton, Mock and Coulter's Principles and Practice of Physical Therapy; Goldberg's Clinical Tuberculosis. Author: Artificial Fever Produced by Physical Means, Its Development and Application, 1937. Contbr. articles to Journal A.M.A., Jour. of Nervous and Mental Disease, British Jour. of Physical Medicine, Proceedings of Royal Soc. of Medicine, Am. Jour. of Psychiatry, etc. Author under the pseudonyms of Clarence Sheraton and Jan Van Hoff, of a series of magazine stories. Home: 52 E. Elm St. Office: 104 S. Michigan Blvd., Chicago. Died Jan. 11, 1951.

NIAS, Henry, industrialist; b. N.Y.C., 1879. Entered bus. career with Elsas Paper Co., advancing to position as sales mgr. greater N.Y. div.; established own paper co., Bklyn., 1912; now chmn. bd. Lily-Tulip Cup Corp. Mem. bd. Brooklyn Hebrew Orphan Asylum. Home: Hotel Pierre, 795 Fifth Av., N.Y.C. 21. Office: Chanin Bldg., N.Y.C. Died Aug. 22, 1955.

NIBLO, Urban (nĭb'lō), army officer; b. Galveston, Tex., Nov. 20, 1897; s. Henry Grady and Anna (Fahner) N.; B.S., U.S. Mil. Acad., 1919; grad. F.A. Sch., basic course, 1920, Ordnance Sch., 1928; B.S. in Mech. Engring. and M.S., Mass. Inst., Tech., 1928; m. Katharine Louise Earle, June 8, 1921; children—Virginia Fahner (Mrs. Jewel Richard Browder), Katharine Elizabeth (Mrs. Kyle Watson Bowie). Commissioned second lt., Field Arty., U.S. Army, 1919, advanced through the grades to brig. gen., 1944; served with Army of Occupation in Germany, 1919; post ordnanace officer, Scofield Barracks, Hawaii, 1923-26; chief, experimental and research div., Springfield (Mass.) Armory, 1928-30, armory inspector, 1930-32; exec. officer, chief small arms div., Office Chief of Ordnance, 1932-35; exec. officer to ordnance officer, 8th Corps Area, Fort Sam Houston, Tex., 1936-39; chief of ordnance publications, Supt. Gen. Supply and Ammunition, Raritan (N.J.) Arsenal, 1939-41; ordnance officer, II Corps, 1942-43; participated in initial landing North Africa and advanced into Tunisia, 1942; army ordnance comdr., Fifth Army, 1943-45; participated in landing at Salerno, Italy, 1943, and then advanced northward in Italy; chief ordnance officer Medtierranean Theater, VE to VJ Day; ordnance officer, 4th Army, 1945-46; chief ordnance officer Far East Command, Tokyo, 1946-51; chief ordnance officer United Nations Command, 1950-51; ordnance officer Army Field Forces, 1952-54; dep. commandant Indsl. Coll. of Armed Forces, 1954—. Decorated D.S.M. With oak leaf cluster, Legion of Merit, W.W.I. Service Medal, Army of Occupation and Pre-Pearl Harbor ribbons, N. African Theater with 7 stars and arrowhead, World War II Service Medal; Silver Star (Korean Conflict, 1950); also decorated by Italy, France, England, Mexico, and Brazil and Korea. Mem. Am. Soc. M.E., Army Ordnance Assn., Heroes of '76. Mason, Sojourner. Address: 5016 Loughboro Rd., Washington 16. Died Aug. 12, 1957; buried Arlington Nat. Cemetery.

NICELY, Harold Elliott, clergyman; b. Beirut, Syria, Dec. 24, 1900; s. John Washington and Helen Nesbit (Mount) N. (parents U.S. citizens); A.B., U. Chgo., 1921; Th.B., Princeton Theol. Sem., 1924, A.M., Princeton, 1924; grad. student Westminster Coll., Cambridge, Eng., 1924-25; D.D., Washington and Jefferson Coll., 1941; m. Dorothy Russell Abbott, June 26, 1926; children—Patricia Elliott, William Abbott, John Washington. Ordained to ministry Presbyn. Ch., 1924; pastor Westminster Ch., Wilmington, Del., 1926-30, Central Brick Ch., East Orange, N.J., 1930-38, Brick Ch., Rochester, 1938—; lectr. homiletics Colgate-Rochester Div. Sch., 1942—. Mem. com. of direction Fed. Council Chs. Commn. on Just and Durable Peace; mem. Presbyn. permanent commn. on Interch. relations; mem. gen. bd. Nat. Council Chs. of Christ in U.S.A. Trustee Princeton Theol. Sem.; pres. Rochester Fedn. Chs., 1943-45; moderator N.Y. Synod, 1949-50; dir. Rochester Council Social Agencies, Rochester Sch. for Deaf. Recipient hon. citation U. Chgo. Alumni Assn., 1946; del. Conf. on Faith and Order of World Council Chs., Lund, Sweden, 1952. Mem. Rochester C. of C. (trustee), Psi Upsilon, Phi Beta Kappa. Clubs: Genesee Valley, Rochester Country, Rochester City (pres. 1945-46), Pundits (Rochester). Author: What Religion Does to Men, 1936. Home: 157 George St., Rochester 7, N.Y. Died June 1954; buried Greensboro, Vt.

NICHOL, Frederick William, business exec.; b. Ottawa, Can., Mar. 8, 1892; s. William Robert and Jemima (Davis) N.; ed. pub. and comml. schs., Ottawa; LL.D., Hartwick Coll., Oneonta, N.Y., 1944; m. 2d, Adair Stoughton Thayer, June 11, 1953. Came to U.S., 1907, naturalized, 1919. Began as clk. N.Y. & Ottawa Ry. Co., Ottawa, 1906, later sec. gen. passenger agt.; became successively stenographer tariff bur. N.Y. Central R.R., N.Y.C., later Nat. Rys. of Mexico; stenographer, corr., N.Y., and asst. sec. to gen. sales mgr. and sec. dist. mgr. Nat. Cash Register Co., Toronto, Can.; sec. sales mgr. Arbuckle Brothers, N.Y.C.; sec. pres. Internat. Bus. Machines Corp., 1914, later exec. sec., N.Y.C.; v.p., sales mgr. Turbine Air Tool Co., Cleve.; sales mgr. Internat. Bus. Machines Co., Ltd., Toronto, later asst. gen. mgr.; mgr. bus. service dept. Internat. Bus. Machines Corp., N.Y.C.; pres., dir. Dayton Scale Co. (subsidiary Internat. Bus. Machines Corp.); asst. to v.p. charge sales Internat. Bus. Machines Corp., asst. to pres., and in charge operations in fgn. countries; v.p.; v.p., gen. mgr., mem. bd. dirs., mem. exec. and finance com., directing head dept. of logistics; v.p., dir. Electromatic Typewriter Co., Rochester, N.Y., IBM of Del.; dir. IBM of Can., Maquinas, Commerciales Watson de México, S.A., Jugoslovensko Watson, A.D., Watson Belge, S.A. Dir. Holland House Corp. of The Netherlands, Maple Leaf Found., Inc.; governing mem., mem. bd. dirs. Nat. Fgn. Trade Council; asso. mem. staff faculty Babson Inst. Bus. Adminstrn., Boston; mem. bd. advisers Vocational Adv. Service for Jrs., Vocational Adv. Service; mem. governing council and exec. com. N.Y.U. (chmn. adv. com. Grad. Sch. Bus. Adminstrn. and Sch. Commerce, Accounts and Finance; mem. com. membership and honors; mem. exec. bd. soc. for libraries); dir., mem. exec. com. Inter-Am. Comml. Arbitration Commn. Served from pvt. to maj., U.S. Army, World War I; adminstrv. officer Ordnance Dept.; on spl. duty with sec. of war for 1 yr. after armistice; apptd. spl. adviser to sec. state on adminstrn., 1944. Mem. U.S. C. of C. (councilor representing Office Equipment Mfrs. Inst.), C. of C. State of N.Y., Internat. C. of C. (exec. com. U.S. Assos., Argentine-Am. Venezuelan and Mex. chambers commerce, Com. Internat. Econ. Reconstrn., Com. Internat. Econ. Policy (dir.), Nat. Fedn. Sales Execs. (chmn. adv. com.; mem. exec. com.; com. on coöp. schs. and colls.; com. ednl. coöp.; subcom. vocational guidance), Commerce and Industry Assn. N.Y. (mem. program com. of members council; spl. com. on priorities), N.A.M. (com. coöp. schs. and colls; com. ednl. coöp.; subcom. vocational guidance; exec. com. of nat. informaiton com.; com. world trade policy), Internat. Affiliation Sales and Advt. Clubs (life mem. at large), Am. Soc. Sales Execs. (chmn. exec. com.), Advt. Fdn. Am., Nat. Indsl. Advertisers Assn., Am. Arbitration Assn., Ry. Bus. Assn., Am. Marketing Soc. (charter mem.), N.Y. Bd. Trade (bd. dirs.), Maritime Assn. Port of N.Y., Travelers Aid Soc. N.Y., Pilgrims of U.S., Pan Am. Soc. (dir.), Canadian Soc. N.Y., Grand Central Art Galleries N.Y.; hon. mem. Beta Gamma Sigma. Presbyn. Clubs: Sales Executives (v.p., dir.), Advertising, Rotary, Export Managers, Metropolitan, India House, Bankers (N.Y.C.); Dallas Sales Managers; (hon. life mem.); Metropolitan, Army and Navy, University (Washington); Gulf Stream Golf (Delray Beach, Fla.); Rawdon (Que.) Golf and Country; Sewanee Harbor (Hewlett Harbor, (L.I.). Home: 167 E. 62d St., N.Y.C. 21. Office: Gallatin House, 6 Washington Sq. N., N.Y.C. 3. Died Oct. 27, 1955; buried Woodlawn Cemetery, N.Y.C.

NICHOLAS, Edwin August (nĭk'ô-lås), president Farnsworth Television & Radio Corp.; b. Cleve., O., Dec. 13, 1893; s. James and Louise (Ohm) N.; ed. pub. schs., Cleveland, Cleveland Sch. of Commerce; special student New York U.; m. Clara Edith Witt, June 13, 1921; 1 dau., Jeanne Clare. Messenger United Wireless, Cleveland, 1909-10; wireless operator, 1910-12; became mgr. Marconi Station, Cleveland, 1913; chief operator and inspector, Great Lakes Div., 1915, supt., 1917; became asst. to v.p. and gen. mgr. Radio Corp. America, N.Y. City, later sales mgr. Eastern Dist., 1925-26, mgr. Radiola div., 1926-29; v.p. Radiola div., RCA-Victor Corp., 1929-30; pres. E. A. Nicholas, Inc., Chicago, 1930-31; v.p. in charge of sales, RCA-Victor, 1931-34; mgr. licensing div. RCA and mem. advisory bd. RCA, 1934-38; pres. Farnsworth Television & Radio Corp. since 1938; dir. Thomasville (N.C.) Furniture Corp. Dir. Radio Mfrs. Assn.; mem. Radio Club of America; life mem. Vet. Wireless Operators Assn. Received Marconi Memorial Medal of Achievement, 1944. Mason. Clubs: Union League (Chicago); Indianapolis Athletic; Rockefeller Center Lunch, New York Athletic (New York); Ft. Wayne (Ind.) Country. Home: 1609 Forest Park Blvd. Office: 3240 N. Washington Rd., Ft. Wayne, Ind. Died Jan. 27, 1953; buried Lindenwood Cemetery.

NICHOLAS, Richard Ulysses, army officer; b. York, Pa., Nov. 16, 1890; s. Byrd Calvin and Annie Susan (Heiland) N.; B.S., U.S. Mil. Acad., 1913; grad. Engr. Sch., 1916, Command and Gen. Staff Sch., 1936, Army War Coll., 1940; m. Ethel R. Ballinger 1945. Commd. 2d lt. U.S. Army, 1913, and advanced through the grades to brig. gen., 1945; platoon comdr. 1st Engr. Regt., 1913-14, 16-17; served with 2d, 26th and 214th Engr. regts. and as instr. O.T.C., 1917-19; dist. engr. Chgo. U.S. Engr. Dist., 1940; engr. IX Corps, 1940-41; engr., 4th Army, 1941-43, 9th Army, 1943—. Decorated Legion of Merit, Bronze Star Medal (U.S.); Legion of Honor, Croix de Guerre with palm (France); Order of Wars for Fatherland, class 1 (U.S.S.R.). Mem. Soc. Am. Mil. Engrs. Home: 224 Primera Dr., San Antonio. Address: War Dept., Washington 25. Died May 7, 1953; buried Arlington Nat. Cemetery.

NICHOLLS, William Durrett (nĭk'ŭls), educator, agrl. economist, farm operator; b. Bloomfield, Ky., Feb. 6, 1885; s. Archibald Wilson and Elizabeth (Dougherty) N.; B.S., U. of Ky., 1907, M.S., 1915; Ph.D., Cornell, 1926; m. Elizabeth Hord, Sept. 1, 1913; children—William Hord, Mary Elizabeth, Louise. With U. of Kentucky since 1912, successively asst. prof. animal husbandry until 1915, prof. farm management, 1915-17, prof. farm economics and head of Dept. of Farm Economics, Coll. of Agr. and Agrl. Expt. Sta., same univ., since 1917. Contbg. editor Southern Agriculturist, Nashville, Tenn. Mem. Fayette County Bd. of Edn. Chief of farm labor mobilization for Kentucky, World War I. Mem. Am. Econ. Assn., Am. Farm Econ. Assn., Ky. Acad. Social Science, Kentucky School Boards Assn. (pres. 1937), Alpha Zeta, Sigma Xi. Presbyterian. Author of numerous bulls. and articles on economics and rural organization. Home: 126 University Av., Lexington, Ky. Died July 17, 1952; buried Lexington.

NICHOLS, Egbert Ray, educator; b. Mt. Ayr, Ind., May 6, 1884; s. John Frederick and Mary Ellen (Roberts) N.; Ph.B., Franklin Coll., 1907; M.A., Harvard, 1909; Litt.D., Franklin Coll., 1942; m. Elsie Grace Stubbe, June 16, 1911; 1 son, Egbert Ray. Asst. English dept. Ottawa (Kan.) U., 1909-11; head dept. English composition and pub. speaking Ripon (Wis.) Coll., 1911-13; head dept. English, U. Redlands, Cal., 1913-28, head dept. speech, 1928-52; research Sch. Drama. E. London Coll., U. London, 1925-26; Fulbright prof. Imperial U. Sendai, Japan, 1952-53; vis. prof. speech Bowdoin Coll., Brunswick, Me., 1955-56. Mem. Am. Assn. U. Profs., Western Assn. Tchrs. Speech (pres. 1934), Speecr Assn. Am. (2d v.p.), Nat. Assn. Tchrs. of Speech (nat. council 1934), Am. Legion, Redlands Fish and Game Conservation Assn. (sec. 1944-45), Pi Kappa Delta (founder, 1st pres., editor, bus. mgr. Forensic 1914-20) Theta Alpha Phi, Sigma Tau Delta, Sigma Alpha Epsilon. Baptist. Elk. Clubs: Fortnightly, Rotary. Co-author: Modern Debating, 1936. Editor: University Debaters Help Book series; also vols. in Reference Shelf series; editor, founder Debaters mag. (later Speech Activities), 1945. Compiler: Intercollegiate Debates (vols. 2-7), 1912-17, (vols. 8-22), 1927-58. Home: 814 Campus Av., Redlands, Cal. Died Apr. 5, 1958; buried Hillside Cemetery, Redlands.

NICHOLS, Frederick George, prof. education; b. Avon, Livingston County, N.Y., Mar. 18, 1878; s. George William and Ella (Fitzpatrick) N.; grad. Genesee Wesleyan Sem., Lima, N.Y., 1899; grad. Rochester (N.Y.) Business Inst., 1904; studied law 3 yrs. in offices of Reed & Shutt, Rochester, also at Univ. of Michigan; M.A., honorary, Harvard University, 1942; m. Bessie Louise Winans, Aug. 23, 1899 (dec. Nov. 1951); 1 dau., Catharine Freda (dec.); m. 2d, Mabel A. Evarts, Aug. 2, 1952. Head of commercial depts. Montpelier (Vt.) Sem., Martin Sch. (Pittsburgh, Pa.), high schs., Schenectady and Rochester, N.Y., Rochester Business Inst., until 1909; state supervisor commercial edn., N.Y. State Ednl. Dept., 1909-11; dir. business edn. pub. schs., Rochester, 1913-18; asst. dir. Federal Bd. for Vocational Edn., in charge dept. commercial edn., 1918-21; dir. commercial edn., Pa. Dept. of Pub. Instrn., 1921-22; asso. prof. edn., Harvard, 1922-44, emeritus, 1944—; lecturer Simmons Coll., 1922-35, Univ. of Denver summer 1944, Teachers College, Columbia U., 1944-45, N.Y.U., summer, 1947, 48, U. of Ky., summer, 1948; became editor McGraw-Hill Book Co., 1944, edited series of books on bus. edn.; research dir. Business Education Research Associates, Inc.; ednl. consultant Rochester Bus. Inst.; in practice as bus. edn. consultant. Investigated rehabilitation work in France for Federal Board, 1918. Pres. Nat. Com. Teacher-Training Assn.; pres. Eastern Bus. Tchrs. Assn., 1921; pres. Nat. Council of Bus. Edn., 1938-40; pres. Education Research Corp., 1938-44; pres. Henry O. Peabody School Corporation, 1944-46; agent Mass. Bd. of Collegiate Authority, 1944-45; educational consultant, 1945—. First recipient John Robert Gregg Award in Bus. Edn., 1953. Member National Education Assn. (pres. Business Edn. Sect., 1924), Nat. Commercial Teachers' Federation, American Vocational Association, National Office Management Assn., Phi Delta Kappa (Iota Chapter, Harvard), Pi Gamma Mu, Delta Pi Epsilon, Progressive Rep. Presbyterian. Author: Elementary Bookkeeping, 1918; Junior Business Training, 1923; New Junior Business Training, 1930; Commercial Education in the High School, 1933; The Personal Secretary—Duties and Traits, 1935; Training for Economic Living, 1936. Part Author: Principles of Bookkeeping and Farm Accounts, 1913; Brief Course in Commercial Law, 1913; First Lessons in Business, 1920; Secretarial Efficiency, 1938; How to Improve Your Personality, 2d edit., 1954. Writer of articles and bulls. on edn. Address: 196 Lafayette Parkway, Rochester, N.Y. Died June 1, 1954; buried Rochester.

NICHOLS, John Benjamin, physician and med. dir.; b. at Cazenovia, N.Y., Feb. 2, 1867; s. of George C. and Ellen Farr (Ingraham) N.; ed. Cazenovia Seminary; M.D., Columbian (now George Washington) Univ., 1891; m. Annie Gledhill, May 27, 1891; 1 son, Howard Gledhill. Asst. surgeon U.S. Soldiers' Home, D.C., 1894-99; pathologist Garfield Hospital, 1900-16, Episcopal Hosp., 1901-23; med. dir. Acacia Mutual Life Ins. Co., 1902-39, dir. since 1907, advisory med. dir. since 1939; lecturer on dietetics, George Washington Univ., 1908-19; attending physician Freedmen's Hospital, 1906-19. Member national and local medical societies; president Medical Society of D.C., 1912 (citation for meritorious service, 1943). Mason. Club: Cosmos. Author: Histology and Pathology (with Dr. F. P. Vale), 1899; Clinical Laboratory Methods, 1902; Numerical Proportions of Sexes at Birth (memoir Am. Anthrop. Assn.), 1907; Diet in Typhoid Fever (Fiske Fund prize essay), 1907; Medical Sectarianism, 1912. Compiler History of the Med. Soc. of D.C., Part II, 1833-1944. Contbr. to med. and other jours. Home: 4636 Hawthorne Lane, Washington 16. Office: 51 Louisiana Av., Washington 1. Died Feb. 22, 1954.

NICHOLS, Malcolm E., ex-mayor; b. Portland, Me., May 8, 1876; s. Edwin T. and Helen J. G. (Pingree) N.; A.B., Harvard, 1899; m. Edith M. Williams, Dec. 16, 1915 (dec. May 9, 1925); children—Clark Salisbury, Dexter Pingee, Marjorie Edith; m. 2d, Carrie M. Williams, Nov. 26, 1926. Newspaper reporter, polit. editor till 1908; mem. Boston Common Council, 1905-06; mem. Mass. Ho. of Reps., 1907-09, Senate, 1914, 17-19 (chmn. taxation com.); admitted to Mass. bar, 1908; served as school-house commr., Boston, and as chmn. Boston Transit Dept., and chmn. Rent and Housing Com.; fuel adminstr., Boston, 1920-21; U.S. collector internal revenue, Boston, 1921-25; mayor of Boston, 1926-29; practicing atty. for 33 yrs. Pres. Boston Industrial Home. Republican. Mem. Ch. of New Jerusalem. Mason. Home: 796 Centre St., Jamaica Plain, Mass. Died Feb. 7, 1950.

NICHOLS, Neil Ernest, naval officer; b. Mich., Sept. 16, 1879; entered U.S. Navy, May 1898; advanced to rear admiral, Feb. 1942; retired June 30, 1937; recalled to active duty. Deceased.

NICHOLS, Pierrepont Herrick, prof. English; b. Pataha, Wash., Jan. 27, 1893; s. John and Anna (Herrick) N.; diploma Williston Acad., 1911; B.A., Allegheny Coll., 1914; student Yale Grad. Sch., 1915; A.M., Harvard, 1921, Ph.D., 1924; m. Gladys Winslow, Sept. 9, 1921; 1 son, Thomas Gilbert. Instr. English, Pa. State Coll., 1916, Carnegie Inst. Tech., 1917; asst. prin. high sch., Pepperell, Mass., 1919; instr. English, high sch., Walpole, 1920, New York U., 1924-25; asso. prof. English, Evansville Coll., 1926-27, head of dept., 1928-30; head of English department, Lincoln Memorial University, 1931-35; professor English, Slippery Rock State Teachers Coll., since 1935. Seaman U.S.N.R.F., 1917-18. Mem. Am. Assn. Univ. Profs., Modern Lang. Assn., Phi Beta Kappa, Delta Sigma Rho, Delta Tau Delta. Conglist. Contbr. William Dunbar as a Scottish Lydgatian, 1931 and Lydgate's Influence on the Aureate Terms of the Scottish Chaucerians, 1932 (in publs. Modern Lang. Assn. America). Home: Slippery Rock, Pa. Died July 3, 1951; buried Assonet, Mass.

NICHOLS, Robert Hastings, prof. church history; b. Rochester, N.Y., Oct. 2, 1873; s. Gideon Parsons (D.D.) and Delia Briggs (Nichols) N.; B.A., Yale Univ., 1894, Eldridge fellow, 1894-96, Ph.D., 1896; studied Oxford U., Mansfield Coll., Oxford, Eng., 1899-1900; grad. Auburn (N.Y.) Theol. Sem., 1901; D.D., George Washington U., 1921; m. Marjorie Newton Wallace, June 9, 1910 (died Mar. 12, 1923); children—Ellen Shepard, Prof. James Hastings, Jane Hastings (Mrs. David E. Swift), Grace Wallace (Mrs. Douglas M. Knight); m. 2d, Winifred Hoyt, Aug. 8, 1925. Ordained Presbyn. ministry, 1901; pastor Unadilla, N.Y., 1901-02, Trinity Ch., South Orange, N.J., 1902-10; asst. prof. ch. history, 1910-13, prof., 1913-44, Auburn Theol. Sem. prof. emeritus, 1944—; professor of church history, Union Theological Seminary, 1939-44, prof. emeritus, 1944—, lecturer in church hist., 1944-48; in charge home study in church hist., Columbia, 1923-35; mem. faculty of political sci., 1941-44. Commr. to Gen. Assembly of Presbyn. Ch., 1907, 10, 24, 41; sec. Com. on Rveision of Presbyn. Book of Common Worship, 1928-32; mem. Permanent Judicial Commn. of Gen. Assembly, 1931-37; sec. of Presbyn. Colleagues, Inc., publishers of the Presbyterian Tribune; stated clerk Synod of N.Y, 1922-1951, emeritus, 1951—; associate Oxford Conference on Christian Life and Work, 1937. Mem. American Society Church History (president 1920, treasurer, 1922-1951), American Historical Association, N.Y. Hist. Assn., Presbyn. Hist. Soc., Phi Beta Kappa, Delta Kappa Epsilon, Quill Club, Chi Alpha. Author: The Growth of the Christian Church, 1914, rev. edit., 1941; Ancient Christianity (Columbia Univ. Home Study Courses), 1922; Mediaeval Christianity, 1925; Age of the Protestant Reformation, 1928. Contbr. to Dictionary of American Biography and to History of the State of New York (pub. by N.Y. Hist. Assn.); editor of Church History (quarterly); mem. editorial advisory council of Religion in Life and of Presbyn. Tribune. Home: 21 Claremont Av., N.Y.C. 27. Died July 18, 1955.

NICHOLS, Spencer Baird, artist; b. Washington, Feb. 13, 1875; s. Henry Hobart and Indiana (Jay) N.; pupil Corcoran Gallery Art Sch., Art Students' League, Washington, pupil of Howard Helmick; m. Helen Agnes Mather, Apr. 22, 1911. Taught illustrating at Art Students' League; dir. of art Marot Junior Coll., Thompson, Conn., 1934—. Painted portrait of Andrew Stephenson for U.S. Govt., in Ho. of Reps.; mural decorations Central Presbyn. Church, N.Y.C.; 2 murals for Kent (Conn.) High Sch.; mural for Litchfield (Conn.) High Sch.; 300 portraits of historical characters, Nat. Museum, Washington; book illustrator. Recipient 3d Corcoran prize Soc. Washington Artists, 1901, Altman prize N.A.D., 1931, Ranger purchase prize, 1928, 32. N.A. Mem. Archtl. League of New York. Progressive. Christian Scientist. Mem. Co. F, 3d Regt. Engrs., Spanish-Am. War. Clubs: Nat. Arts, Salmagundi, N.Y. Water Color, Am. Water Color (New York). Home: (summer) Kent, Conn. Died Aug. 27, 1950.*

NICHOLS, William LeRoy, business exec.; born Panama, Mo., Feb. 7, 1905; s. Eldred Taylor and Mary Virginia (Kidwell) N.; m. Mary Virginia Hawco, Apr. 15, 1933; children—Barbara, Mary Patricia. With B/G Foods, Inc., since 1923, mgr., St. Louis, Mo., 1923-24, Chicago and New York City, 1924-32, supt., Pittsburgh, Pa., 1932-36, New York City, 1936-43, vice pres. and dir. gen. mgr. Chicago, since 1943, pres., general manager since 1946; president Dinsmore & Co., Inc.; originator of Nichols plan for training discharged veterans for own business. Home: 226 Birchwood Rd., Hinsdale, Ill. Office: 174 W. Randolph St., Chgo. Died Dec. 22, 1958.

NICHOLSON, Frank Lee, civil engr.; b. Portsmouth, Va., Aug. 12, 1868; s. Francis James and Catharine Olevia (Culpepper) N.; ed. pub. and high schs. and Suffolk Mil. Acad. (2 yrs. civ. and railroad engring.); corr. courses in bridge engring., architecture, and elec. engring.; m. Ada Starr Parker, Dec. 4, 1890; children—Ethel (widow of Dr. Richard H. Peake), Clyde Parker. Rodman, chainman, levelman and office asst. to chief engr. on location surveys of Atlantic & Danville R.R. (now Danville div. of Southern Ry.), 1887-89; levelman, later resident engr. on construction, Wilmington, N.C., Terminal, and First Residency, Wilmington, Newbern & Norfolk R.R. (now Newbern branch of Atlantic Coast Line R.R.), 1889-90; private practice, Jan.-June, 1890; asst. engineer maintenance of way, Norfolk Southern R.R., 1890-92, acting engr. m. of w., 1892-98, engr. m. of w., 1898-1909, chief engr., 1909-47, ret. in charge of valuation of same ry. and allied properties, 1914-47; chief engineer Raleigh, Charlotte and Southern R.R. from 1912 until rd. was purchased by Norfolk Southern R.R.; cons. engr. Virginia Ry., July-Dec. 1918, and chief engr., 1918-19; served in Washington, D.C., as a representative of the Southern Region on a com. for drafting rules and working conditions for maintenance of way employees and shop labor during Federal administration of rys. Chmn. Com. XX on Uniform General Contract Forms of Am. Ry. Engring. Assn., 1932-37; chmn. City Planning Commission, Norfolk, Va. Mem. Am. Ry. Engring. Assn. (dir. 1937-40; chmn. com. Outline of Work, 1938-40; chmn. com. on standardization, 1939-42); member American Society Civil Engineers (director 1929-31; chairman com. on professional conduct 1931; pres. Va. sect. 1926-27; chairman Section Com. of Va. for Civilian Protection in War Time, chairman Transportation Div. of the Section Com. of Va.; chmn. local membership com. for Va., (1943-46), Assn. Am. Railroads (engring. sect.), Engrs. Club of Hampton Roads (pres. 1925-26), Norfolk Yacht and Country Club. Democrat. Baptist. Mason (K.T., Shriner), Odd Fellow. Home: 512 Graydon Park, Norfolk 7, Va. Died May 24, 1954; buried Elmwood Cemetery, Norfolk.

NICHOLSON, Leonard Kimball, publisher; b. New Orleans, La., Jan. 11, 1881; s. George and Eliza Jane (Poitevent) N.; grad. Va. Mil. Inst., 1901; m. Lois M. Poitevent, Dec. 17, 1915. Became pres. The Times-Picayune Publishing Co., New Orleans, 1918, later chmn. bd. Lt. comdr. USNR. Dir. Internat. House. Clubs: Boston, Louisiana, New Orleans Country, Southern Yacht, Pass Christian Yacht, Bay-Waveland Yacht. Home: 497 Audubon St. Office: The Times-Picayune, New Orleans. Died Oct. 19, 1952.

NICHOLSON, Paul Coe, file mfr.; b. Providence, R.I., Nov. 19, 1888; s. Samuel Mowry and Mary Jewett (Coe) N.; prep. edn., St. Paul's Sch., Concord, N.H.; A.B., Yale, 1911; m. Martha F. Sayles, June 23, 1917 (died 1947); children—Paul Coe Nicholson, Martha Sayles (Mrs. Stanley Livingston Jr.), William Sayles; married to second, Rosalind Shaw, September 28, 1948 (deceased 1955). Chairman bd. Nicholson File Co., Am. Screw Co.; dir. Indsl. Nat. Bank. Trustee Y.M.C.A. Mem. Soc. Colonial Wars, R.I. Hist. Soc, Newcomen Soc., Psi Upsilon. Republican. Episcopalian. Clubs: University, British Empire, Hope, Agawam Hunt, Turks Head, Squantum Assn. (Providence); Yale (Boston); Porcupine, (Nassau, N.P.); Cat Cay (Bahamas); Yale, New York Yacht, Ship Model Soc. (New York); Atlantic Tuna; East Greenwich Yacht, Rhode Island Yacht; Cruising Club of America; U.S. Power Squadrons, Bristol Yacht. Home: 288 Blackstone Blvd., Providence; (summer) "Wind Hill," Bristol, R.I. Address: Nicholson File Co., 23 Acorn St., Providence 1. Died June 28, 1956.

NICHOLSON, Soterios (name adopted), lawyer; b. Kalliani, Corinth, Greece, April 7, 1885; s. Nicolaos J. and Evdokia (Kerasiotis) Papasoteriou; came to U.S., 1903, naturalized, 1910; ed. pub. and pvt. schs. Athens and Tripolis; student Emerson Inst., Washington, D.C., 1906-08; LL.B., George Washington Univ., 1911; m. Anna Bresnahan, Sept. 21, 1916 (died 1918); m. 2d, Edith H. Tharp, Aug. 16, 1920 (died 1947); married 3d, Dora Papara, December 19, 1953. Washington correspondent Atlantis, Greek Daily, N.Y. since 1912. Admitted to bars: District of Columbia, 1911, Ct. of Claims, 1915, U.S. Supreme Court, 1917, District Court of U.S. for the District of Maryland, 1917, Supreme Court of Appeals, Va.,

1926, Court of Appeals of Md., 1928, Dist. Court of U.S. for 6th Circuit and Eastern Dist. of Mich., 1928; assisted in purchase by Greece from U.S. Govt. of U.S. ships Idaho and Mississippi, 1914, counsel for the Greek Embassy; asst. counsel, N.R.A. of U.S., Dec. 11, 1933-Nov. 5, 1934, asst. dep. adminstr., Nov. 6, 1934-June 16, 1935, tech. adviser June 17, 1935 to Oct. 15, 1935. Pres. and director Nicholson and Company, Incorporated Real Estate, Capital Features Syndicate. Campaign speaker for Rep. Nat. Com. 1916, 1920, 1924, for Dem. Nat. Com., 1936. Commd. capt. ordnance finance, U.S. Army, Dec. 11, 1917; served as disbursing office, summary Court officer, Motor Transport Corps Officer, Liberty Loan Officer, hon. disch. July 31, 1919. Decorated: Knight of the Royal Order of the Redeemer, Greece, 1922; Knight of the Order of the Holy Sepulcher, 1924, Greek Patriachate Jerusalem, comdr. same order, 1929; U.S.A. Service, 1920; selective service medal, 1946; gold cross of the Order of Phoenix Greece, 1949; gold cross of veterans of National Union of American and Greek W.W. Vets., 1950; gold cross of George A (Greece) 1953; Croix de Lorraine (France) 1954. Mem. D.C., Am., Fed. bar assns., Am. Soc. Internat. Law, Assn. Oldest Inhatitants of D.C., past comdr. Nat. Press Club No. 20 Am. Legion, Mid-City Citizens Association (president), Federation Citizens Assn. (del., interfederation council), Central Bus. Assn. (ex.-pres.), Fedn. Bus. Men's Assn. (general counsel), Washington Bd. of Trade. Member Greek Orthodox Church. Member Order of Ahepa. Club: National Press. Pub. Nation's Capital Mag., 1930-31. Author: War or A United World, 1916; A World City of Civilization (brochure), 1913. Home: Burlington Hotel, Washington 5. Office: 1120 Vermont Av. N.W., Washington. Deceased.

NICHOLSON, Watson, author; b. Pendleton, Ind., Sept. 23, 1866; s. Abraham and Maria (Davis) N.; student though jr. yr. at Ind. U.; A.B., Stanford, 1892; M.A., Harvard Grad. Sch., 1895; Ph.D., Yale, 1903; traveled and studied in Europe, 1905 and 1907; m. Florence Emily Beaver, Sept. 1, 1897. Teacher in schs. of Ind., 1884-87; Calif., 1892-94 and 1897-1901, Harvard, 1895-97; engaged in univ. extension teaching 1903-05; instr. English lit., Sheffield Scientific Sch. (Yale), 1905-08; worked in British Museum, 1910-15. Mem. Harvard Teachers' Assn., A.A. A.S., American Academy of Political and Social Science, Phi Beta Kappa, Sigma Chi. Honorary member the Mark Twain Society. Clubs: Authors' (London, Eng.); Stanford, Fortnightly, Harvard, Yale. Author: A Syllabus of Six Lectures on American Literature, with bibliography, 1903; The Struggle for a Free Stage in London, 1906; discovered all the sources of Defoe's famous Journal (1913), previously regarded as fiction, published as Historical Sources of Defoe's Journal of the Plague Year, 1919; Anthony Aston, Stroller and Adventurer, 1920. Address: 760 Phillips St., Deer Lodge, South Haven, Mich. Died Dec. 2, 1951; buried Lake View Cemetery.

NICKERSON, John, investment banker; b. St. Louis, Mo., July 22, 1882; s. John and Mary (King) N.; B.S., Princeton, 1905; m. Elizabeth Laird Smith, June 3, 1907; children—John III, Elizabeth Laird (Mrs. Charles Ingalls Morton), Mary Alicia (Mrs. Walton Campbell Ament), Clarke. Began in investment banking at St. Louis, Mo., 1905; settled in New York City, 1914; president John Nickerson & Co., New York City, since 1917; president and director Standard Utilities, Inc. Republican. Episcopalian. Clubs: Bankers, Bond, Racquet and Tennis, Downtown Athletic, Inc. (New York); University Cottage (Princeton); Noroton Yacht (Noroton, Conn.); Oxridge Hunt (Darien, Conn.). Home: Nearwater Lane, Noroton, Conn. Office: 1 E. 42d St., N.Y.C. 17. Died Oct. 26, 1956; buried Spring Grove Cemetery, Darien, Conn.

NICODEMUS, Frank Courtney, Jr., lawyer, r.r. ofcl.; b. Balt., Dec. 11, 1881; s. Frank Courtney and Mary Field (Weeks) N.; LL.B., U. Md., 1901; m. Dorothy Harcourt Townsend, Dec. 20, 1913; children—Anne H. T. (Mrs. Walter T. Carpenter), Jane M. (Mrs. Anthony Nicholas Brady Garvan), Margaret Fairlie, Frank Courtney III (dec.), Richard Townsend. Admitted to Md., bar, 1902, and began practice in N.Y.C., 1905; joined in purchase at foreclosure sale of the properties of the Western Md. Ry. Co., 1909, and in 1911 acted in similar capacity at foreclosure sale of the Internat. Great Northern R.R. Co.; identified in 1915 with reorganization of Wabash Ry. Co.; one of counsel, 1929, in readjustment of express operations of Am. railroads and creation of the Ry. Express Agency; co-receiver Wabash Ry. Co. and Ann Arbor R.R. Co., 1931-41; cons. counsel, dir., mem. finance com. Wabash R.R. Co.; mem. Pierce & Greer, counsel for Western Pacific Railroad Corp., also A.P.W. Products Co., Inc. Trustee, Soc. St. Johnland. Mem. Assn. Bar City of New York, Md. Hist. Soc. Ind. Democrat. Episcopalian. Clubs: Century, Down Town, Brook. Home: Smithtown, L.I., N.Y. Office: 44 Wall St., N.Y.C. 5. Died Nov. 17, 1957; buried St. James, L.I.

NICOLAI, Harry T., business exec.; b. Portland, Ore., 1881. Pres., dir. with Nicolai Door Mfg. Co., Portland, pres., dir. Ore.-Wash. Plywood Co., Garibaldi, Ore.; pres., mgr., dir. Nicolai Industries, Inc., Portland; dir. Gen. America Corp., Seattle, U.S. Nat. Bank, Portland. Home: 3011 N.W. Luray Circus, Portland 10. Office: 1014 U.S. National Bank Bldg., Portland 4, Ore. Died June 9, 1957.

NICOLAY, Helen (nĭk'ō-lā), author; b. Paris, France, Mar. 9, 1866; d. late John George (sec. to Abraham Lincoln) and Therena (Bates) Nicolay; ed. by father and pvt. teachers; hon. A.M., George Washington Univ., 1922; unmarried. Unitarian. Author: The Boys' Life of Abraham Lincoln, 1906; The Boys' Life of Ulysses S. Grant, 1909; Personal Traits of Abraham Lincoln, 1912; Our Nation in the Building, 1916; The Book of American Wars, 1918; The Boys' Life of Lafayette, 1920; Peter and Paul and Their Friends, 1922; Our Capital on the Potomac, 1924; The Boys' Life of Alexander Hamilton, 1927; Andrew Jackson, the Fighting President, 1929; Boys' Life of George Washington, 1931; Boys' Life of Thomas Jefferson, 1933; Boys' Life of Benjamin Franklin, 1935; Our Perennial Bible, 1937; Wizard of the Wires, 1938; The Bridge of Water, 1940; Decatur of the Old Navy, 1942; MacArthur of Bataan, 1942; China's First Lady, 1944; Born to Command, 1945; Lincoln's Secretary, 1949. Contbr. to mags. Address: 3133 Connecticut Av., Washington 8. Died Sept. 12, 1954.

NIEDERMEYER, Frederick David, clergyman; b. Decatur, Ill., Feb. 14, 1881; s. William and Annie Elizabeth (Jahn) N.; grad. Ill. State Normal U., 1900; A.B., U. of Ill., 1904; studied theology Princeton Sem., 1906-09; A.M., Princeton, 1908; D.D., Coll. of Ozarks, 1925; m. Maude Vernon Wilcox, Oct. 1, 1913; 1 son, Cedric Wilcox (dec.). Ordained ministry Presbyn. Ch., 1908; asst. minister Central Presbyn. Ch., pastor Mizpah Chapel, N.Y.C., 1909-12; pastor Adams Meml. Presbyn. Church, N.Y. C., 1912-19, First Presbyn. Church, Perth Amboy, N.J., 1919-46; pastor emeritus since 1946. Religious work sec. Army YMCA, Camp Gordon, Atlanta, 1917-18; speaker on Liberty Loan train, 3d Liberty Loan, Tenn., Ga., Ala., Fla., 1918. Moderator Presbytery of Elizabeth (N.J.), 1924-25; commr. Gen. Assembly Presbyn. Ch., U.S.A., 1933. Pres. Adelphia Ministers Assn., 1924-26; mem. Presbyn. and Ref. Ministers Assn. New York (pres. 1923-25); Chaplain Perth Amboy Fire Dept., 1937-46. Republican. Clubs: Rotary of Perth Amboy (pres. 1927-28); Illini, Clergy (New York); Benham (Princeton). Author: Palestine Pathways, 1928; The Ten Commandments Today, 1928; To Show the Mind of Christ (pageant), 1931; The Seven Words From the Cross, 1932; The Missing Cross (pageant), 1933; The Story of Our Lord (pageant), 1934; The Miracle of the Resurrection, 1937; A Vision of God, 1939. Home: Compo Mill Beach, Westport, Conn. Died Mar. 15, 1951; buried Milford, Conn.

NIERMAN, John L., chemist and coll. pres.; b. Howell, Mo., Feb. 11, 1887; s. John A. and Maria (Schierbaum) N.; B.Pd., Mo. State Tchrs. Coll., Kirksville, 1910; B.S., U. Mo., 1918, A.B., 1919, A.M., 1920, Ph.D., 1924; m. Augusta L. Mueller, Dec. 28, 1910; children—Florence, Anna May (Mrs. R. J. Tozer), Virginia (Mrs. William P. Stewart). Tchr. rural sch., St. Charles County, Mo., 1906-08; prin. village sch., Augusta, Mo., 1908-10, high sch., Wentzville, Mo., 1910-14; supt. schs., Hopkins, Mo., 1914-17; head dept. of chemistry Sweet Briar (Va.) Coll., 1919-22; head dept. chemistry Tex. Coll. Arts and Industries, Kingsville, since 1925, coll. dean, 1929-34, acting pres., 1932-33, 34-35, 41-42, dir. grad. studies since 1947. Mem. Tex. Acad. Sci., Am. Chem. Soc., Sigma Xi. Democrat. Presbyn. Home: 716 W. Richard Av., Kingsville, Tex. Died Oct. 9, 1950.

NIETO del RIO, Felix, Chilean diplomat; b. Cauquenes, Provine of Maule, Chile, Dec. 2, 1888; s. Felix Nieto and Elisa del Rio; LL.B., Univ. of Chile; B.S., Cath. Univ. of Santiago; Doctor Honoris Causa, Univ. of Southern Calif., 1943; m. Luz Perez de Castro, Feb. 27, 1943; children—(by previous marriage) Felix Nieto Sarratea, Teresita Nieto de Mussy. Attache spl. mission to Buenos Aires, 1915, to Chilean legation, Cuba, 1917, to embassy of Chile in U.S. 1918-20, sec. ad-interim, 1920-21; Chilean consul gen. Vienna, Aust., 1925; sec. Chilean Legation, Brussels, Belgium, 1926; minister resident, dir. diplomatic dept., Ministry Fgn. Affairs of Chile, 1927-30; minister on spl. mission to Peru, 1929; under-sec. of fgn. affairs, 1930-31; polit. advisor Ministry Fgn. Affairs (conf. ministers fgn. affairs of Chile and Argentina, 1933; negotiated polit. aspects Chilean-Argentinean Comml. Treaty, Buenos Aires, 1932-36; 3d consultative meeting ministers fgn. affairs of Am. States, Rio de Janeiro, 1942); mem. Inter-Am. Juridical Commn. of Rio de Janeiro, 1942-46; A.E. and M.P. to U.S. since 1946. Served as delegate: 1st Internat. Labor Conf., Washington, 1919; 5th Internat. Conf. Am. States, Santiago (sec. to pres.), 1923; League of Nations (sec. Chilean del.), 1926; 7th Internat. Conf. Am. States, 1933; Chaco Peace Conf. (mediation group), 1935-38; Inter-Am. Conf. for Consolidation of Peace, Buenos Aires, 1936; Inter-Am. Conf. on Problems of War and Peace, Mexico, 1945; pres. Chilean del. to 2d part 1st Assembly, 1946, permanent del. U.N. since 1946. Decorations: K.B.E., 1931; Officer of the French Legion of Honor, 1929; Grand Cross Sun of Peru, Liberator (Venezuela), Condor (Bolivia), Aztec Eagle (Mexico), Merit (Ecuador), Balboa (Panama), Boyaca (Colombia), Southern Cross (Brazil), Merit (Paraguay); Grand Officer of Isabel the Catholic (Spain), San Olaff (Norway), Leopold (Belgium), Nile (Egypt), Polar Star (Sweden); gold medal Pan. Am. Soc. Hon. mem. Argentine and Peruvian Socs. Internat. Law. Asso. mem. Chilean Acad. of History. Mem. Chilean Soc. History and Geog. (mem. bd. adminstrn.), Chilean Inst. Internat. Studies (pres.), Hispanic Soc. of New York, Am. Soc. Internat. Law. Author: Cronicas Literarias, 1912; The Independence of Brazil and the Republican Ideal, 1942. Contbg. editor on internat. affairs of El Mercurio, Santiago, since 1932; dir. Revista Chilena, 1927-30. Contbr. numerous articles in Chilean and fgn. pubs. Home: Embassy of Chile, Washington 6. Died Jan. 12, 1953.

NIHART, Benjamin Franklin, educator; b. Middlebury, Ind., Nov. 23, 1854; s. John and Elizabeth (Myers) N.; grad. high sch., Middlebury, 1871; B.S., Valparaiso U., 1878, A.B., 1879; Litt.D., Oklahoma City U., 1927; m. Henrietta Elizabeth Cummings, Sept. 1880 (died 1890); children—Pearl Elizabeth (Mrs. O. W. Jeffries, dec.), Myrtle May (Mrs. J. A. Myall, dec.), Mabel Corinne, Claude Eugene; m. 2d, Minnie A. Thorne, Dec. 1905 (died June 6, 1958). Tchr. country sch., Ind., 1871-74, graded sch., Middlebury, 1874-75; prin. high sch., Middlebury, 1875-76; tutor, Valparaiso U., 1877-79; prof. mathematics Monroe Inst., Atchison, Kan., 1880-83; prof. mathematics Kan. State Agrl. Coll., 1883-88; supt. schs., Herington, Kan., 1888-94; prof. mathematics Salina (Kan.) Wesleyan U., 1894-95; supt. schs. Council Grove, Kan., 1895-97, Oklahoma City, 1897-1900; prof. mathematics Central State Normal Coll., Edmond, Okla., 1900-08, 11-21, Epworth U., Oklahoma City, 1908-11; dean Oklahoma City U., 1921-31, now dean emeritus. Republican. Methodist. Modern Woodman. Author: New Century Arithmetics, 1916. Home: 1419 W. 28th St., Oklahoma City. Died Dec. 17, 1945; buried Fairlawn Cemetery, Oklahoma City.

NILES, Blair (Mrs. Robert Niles), author; b. Coles Ferry, Va.; d. Henry Crenshaw and Gordon (Pryor) Rice; m. William Beebee (div.); m. 2d, Robert Niles, 1913. Mem. of expdns. to Mexico, Venezuela, British Guiana, Ceylon, India, Burma, Java, Borneo, Malay States, China and Japan; visited Ecuador, Colombia, Haiti, French and Dutch Guianas, Guatemala, Peru, Mexico, Devil's Island Penal Colony. Contbd. series of articles describing conditions in the Penal Colony, to N.Y. Times. Fellow Soc. Am. Historians; mem. P.E.N.; a founder Soc. Woman Geographers. Author: Casual Wanderings in Ecuador, 1923; Colombia, Land of Miracles, 1924; Black Haiti, 1926; Condemned to Devil's Island (presented as a moving picture), 1928; Free (novel), 1930; Strange Brother (novel), 1931; Light Again (novel), 1933; Maria Paluna (novel), 1934; Day of Immense Sun (novel), 1936; Peruvian Pageant, 1937; The James, 1939; East by Day (novel), 1941; Passengers to Mexico: The Last Invasion of the Americas, 1943; The James: From Iron Gate to the Sea, 1945; Journeys in Time: From the Halls of Montezuma to Patagonia's Plains, 1946; Martha's Husband: An Informal Portrait of George Washington, 1951. Recipient gold medal by City of Lima on occasion of 117th anniversary of The Independence of Peru, 1938; Constance Lindsay Skinner medal of achievement, 1941; gold medal Soc. Woman Geographers, 1944. Mem. Internat. Jury in Latin American prize novel contest, 1941, 43. Address: 59 E. 54th St., N.Y.C. 22. Died Apr. 13, 1959.

NILES, Edward Hulbert, univ. dean; b. Oriskany, N.Y., Aug. 24, 1882; s. Andrew Julius and Susan (Owens) N.; Ph.C., Indpls. Coll. Pharmacy, 1912, Pharm. D., 1914, B.S., 1929; A.B., Butler U., 1936; student U. Chgo., 1923, Ind. U., 1937-38; m. Pearl Marguerite Coffin, Nov. 30, 1916; 1 son, Richard Hulbert. Instr. Indpls. Coll. Pharmacy, 1915-16, prof., 1917-20, dean, 1921-45; lectr. pharmacy Ind. Vet. Coll., 1920-23; lectr. in materia medica and pharm. Ind. U. Sch. Medicine, 1920—; dean Butler U., Coll. of Pharmacy, 1945—. Licensed chem. engr., Ind.; registered pharmacist, Ind.; cons. Mem. Am. Pharm. Assn., Am. Chem. Soc. (chmn. Ind. sect. 1939-40, councillor, 1940), Ind. Acad. Sci., Ind. Interprofessional Health Council, Ind. Pharm. Assn. (chmn. edn. and vets. program coms.), Phi Kappa Phi, Kappa Psi. Republican. Episcopalian. Mason (Shriner). Contbr. profl. jours. Home: 4071 College Av., Indpls. 5. Died Sept. 23, 1958; buried Washington Park.

NILES, Henry Carpenter, judge; b. Angelica, N.Y., June 17, 1858; s. Rev. Henry Edward and Jeannie Eliza (Marsh) N.; ed. York County Acad., 1868, York High Sch., 1870, York Collegiate Inst., 1874; LL.B., Columbia, 1880; LL.D., Franklin and Marshall Coll., 1935; m. Lillie Schall, Feb. 17, 1886. Began law practice at York, Pa., 1880; elected judge 19th Jud. Dist. Pa., 1925; Dem. nominee for judge of Superior Court of Pa., 1929, justice Supreme Ct. of Pa., 1930; reëlected pres. judge 19th Jud. Dist.

of Pa., 1935. Pres. Pa. Bar Assn., 1904-05; state chmn. Lincoln Party, 1905-06; mem. Am. Bar Assn., Civil Service Reform Assn., Am. Acad. Polit. and Social Science, Internat Law Assn., Nat. Assn. for Constl. Govt.; charter mem. Inst. of Law. Ind. Democrat. Presbyn. Club: University (Phila.). Occasional writer and speaker on legal and polit. subjects. Home: York, Pa. Deceased.*

NILES, Philip Bradford, mfg. exec.; b. N.Y.C., Dec. 10, 1901; s. Arthur L. and Clara Taylor (Hotchkiss) N.; student Collegiate Sch., N.Y.C., 1908-16, Hotchkiss Sch., Lakeville, Conn., 1917-18, Princeton, 1919-22; m. Mary E. Hambright, June 17, 1937. Financial reporter Wall Street Jour., 1922-24; pub. relations dir. Am. Water Works & Electric Co., 1924-47; asst. v.p., v.p. Water Works Service Co., 1947-48; v.p. Am. Water Works Co., 1947-48; pub. relations dir. Owens-Ill. Glass Co., 1948-49; v.p. Yale & Towne Mfg. Co., 1949—, dir., 1956—. Mem. nat. adv. council Jr. Achievement, Inc. Mem. French C. of C. of U.S.A. (councillor), N.Y. C. of C., Soc. of Silurians. Clubs: Union (N.Y.C.); Pocono Manor (Pa.); Pinnacle (N.Y.); Everglades (Palm Beach); Travelers (Paris). Home: 320 Park Av., N.Y.C. 22. Office: Chrysler Bldg., N.Y.C. 17. Died Sept. 24, 1958.

NIMS, Eugene Dutton, corp. ofcl.; b. Fond du Lac, Wis., Apr. 3, 1865; s. Alexander R. and Sarah (Dutton) N.; desc. Godfrey Nims, Northampton, Mass., abt. 1664; student pub. and pvt. schs. of Neb. and Kan.; m. Lotawana Flateau, July 9, 1914. Connected with lumber business at Humboldt, Neb., later Greenfield, Kan.; in charge liquidation of First Nat. Bank, Greenfield; moved to Kansas City, Mo., 1886, and entered employ of Lombard Investment Co.; made the "run," at opening of Cherokee strip, Okla., 1893, and settled at Perry; an organizer First Nat. Bank, Roff, Commercial Nat. Bank, Muskogee, and Security Nat. Bank, Oklahoma City; a founder, 1896, Ark. Valley Telephone Co., and the Pioneer Tel. & Tel. Co., merged with others, 1914, into the Southwestern Bell Telephone Co., of which was elected vice-pres. and treas., was pres., 1919-30, and chmn. bd., 1930-32, was dir.; dir. 1st Nat. Bank (St. Louis), St. Louis Union Trust Co. Mem. corp. bd. Washington U.; mem. adv. council U. of Mo. Mem. exec. bd. Boy Scouts Am. (nat.). Fuel administrn., St. Louis, World War, also mem. State Council of Defense; mem. bd. dirs. Park and Playground Assn. of St. Louis. Mason. Home: 56 Portland Pl. Office: Telephone Bldg., 1010 Pine St., St. Louis. Died Jan. 30, 1954; buried Bellefontaine Cemetery, St. Louis.

NISSEN, Harry Archibald (nĭs'sŭn), physician; b. Omaha, Neb., Mar. 6, 1891; s. George Christian and Louise Clare (Strenzke) N.; A.B., U. of S.D., 1911; M.D., Harvard, 1916; married Lillian Bruce, 1947. Interned at the Boston City Hospital, 1916-18, assistant and instr. in medicine Harvard Med. Sch., 1918-27; mem. staff New England Deaconess Hosp., 1932—. Mem. A.M.A., Mass. Med. Soc., Am. Rheumatism Assn., etc., Phi Beta Pi. Episcopalian. Mason (32°). Contbr. med. articles to jours. Developed continuous study life course of arthritics. Home: Leach-Holt, Sherborn, Mass. Died Dec. 14, 1956.

NISSEN, Henry W., psychologist; b. Chicago, Feb. 5, 1901; s. Adolf J. and Marie (Mendius) N.; B.A., U. Ill., 1923; M.A., Columbia, 1927, Ph.D., 1929; m. June 11, 1927; children—Dora Jane, Joanna Marie. Asst. in psychology Barnard Coll., Columbia, 1927-28; univ. fellow Columbia, 1928-29; research asso. Yale, 1929-33, asso. prof. psychobiology, 1933-39, asso. prof., 1939-44, research asso., 1944-56; asst. dir. Yerkes Labs. of Primate Biology, 1939-52, asso. dir., 1952-55, dir., 1955—; prof. psycholobiology, Emory U., 1956—; research associate Psychiatric Inst. and Hosp., N.Y. City, 1944, research cons., 1946-47. Mem. Am .(div. exptl. psychol.), Fla. (pres. 1954-55) psychol. assn., National Academy Sciences, Society Exptl. Psyhcologists, A.A.A.S., Am. Soc. Naturalists. Contbr. articles on primate psychology to profl. pubs. Home: Orange Park, Fla. Office: Yerkes Labs. of Primate Biology, Orange Park, Fla. Died Apr. 27, 1958.

NITZE, William Albert (nĭt'zĕ), univ. prof.; b. Baltimore, Mar. 20, 1876; s. Charles and Elizabeth (Bornemann) N.; A.B., Johns Hopkins, 1894, Ph.D., 1899; studied at European univs., 1896-98; L.H.D., Oberlin Coll., 1927, Northwestern, 1942, Chgo., 1951; LL.D., U. of Calif., 1949; m. Anina Sophie Hilken, June 8, 1901; children—Elizabeth Hilken (Mrs. Walter Paul Paepcke), Paul Henry. Lecturer in Romance langs., Columbia, 1899-1903; asso. prof. and prof. Romance langs., Amherst, 1903-08; prof. Romanic langs., U. of Calif., 1908-09; became prof. and head dept. Romance langs. and lits., U. of Chicago, 1909, Andrew MacLeish distinguished service prof., 1935, now emeritus; Pyne professor, Princeton University, 1932; professor of French, U. of California, Los Angeles, 1942-46. Trustee Newberry Library, 1935-42. Chevalier Legion of Honor (France), 1928. Mem. Modern Lang. Assn. (pres. 1929-30; trustee), Am. Council Learned Societies (chairmen Pacific Coast committee), Institut de France, Academie des Inscriptions et Belles Lettres, also member Phi Gamma Delta, Phi Beta Kappa Frat.; fellow Mediaeval Acad. Am., Am. Acad. Arts and Sciences; mem. Am. Philos. Soc.; del. Union Académique internationale. Editor: Corneille's Selected Works (with S. L. Galpin), 1907; Robert de Boron, Graal, 1927; Le Haut Livre du Graal, 2 vols. (with others), 1932-37. Author: The Grail Romance Perlesvaus, 1902; Glastonbury and Holy Grail, 1903; Handbook of French Phonetics (with E. H. Wilkins and C. E. Parmenter), 1918; A History of French Literature (with E. P. Dargan), 1922, Lancelot and Guenevere (with T. P. Cross), 1930; Arthurian Romance and Modern Poetry and Music, 1940; Perceval and the Holy Grail, 1949. Editor Modern Philology. Clubs: Cliff Dwellers, Tavern, Arts (Chicago); Century (New York). Address: 411 Lomond Av., Los Angeles 24. Died July 5, 1957; buried Balt.

NITZSCHE, Elsa Koenig (nĭtch'ĕ), portrait painter; b. Phila., Mar. 24, 1880; d. Prof. George A. and Wilhelmina Marquart Koenig; studied in Pa. Acad. and grad. Woman's Sch. of Design; in France, Germany, Switzerland and Italy, 8 yrs., under Bouveret and other eminent teachers; m. George E. Nitzsche, May 1, 1909. Has exhibited in prin. exhbns. in America and abroad; hon. mention, Paris Salon; represented in many Am. and several fgn. collections. Mem. of Longfellow Guild (pres., 1927-29). Dir. Priestley House for the Aged, 1927-29, v.p. since 1943; v.p. Les Chalets Francaise Camp Corp.; lectr. Served on a Pan Am. commn. (with Dr. Nitzsche) through South America, 1944-45. Clubs: Woman's, Art Alliance. Author: Dickel and the Penguin, other juvenile illus. stories. Awarded 1st prize in Germantown, Phila., Short Story competition. With Dr. Nitzsche gave Koenig Mineral Collection to U. of Pa. Home: "Inspiration," 1024 Westview Av., Germantown, Philadelphia; (summer) "Les Chalets Francais," Deer Isle, Me. Died Mar. 18, 1952; buried Westminster Cemetery, Phila.

NIVEN, John Ballantine, public accountant; b. Edinburgh, Scotland, Sept. 22, 1871; s. Alexander T. and Agnes H. (Ballantine) N.; ed. Aird House Sch., 1878-83, George Watson's Coll. for Boys, 1883-87; student Edinburg U., 1890-92; and extra-mural professional classes; m. Susan W. O. Gordon, June 1, 1905; 1 adopted son, William Seton Duys. Came to U.S., 1898, naturalized, 1905. Pub. accountant, Scotland, 1893-98; with firm of Price, Waterhouse & Co., Chicago, 1898-1900; established firm of Touche, Niven & Co., N.Y., 1900 (now Touche, Niven, Bailey and Smart). Trustee and mayor of the Village of Mill Neck, N.Y. Mem. Scottish Inst. Chartered Accountants, Am. Inst. Accountants (v.p. 1921-22, pres. 1924-25), N.Y. State, N.J., Calif., O., Minn., Mo., Conn. and Ill. Socs. of C.P.As, Nat. Assn. of Cost Accts., Inst. of Chartered Accountants of Ontario; St. Andrews Soc. of New York, British Schools and Universities Club, Pilgrims of U.S.A.; asso. mem. Am. Soc. Actuaries. Episcopalian. Mason. Clubs: Downtown Assn., New York Athletic, Seawanhaka Corinthian Yacht. Home Mill Hill Rd., Oyster Bay. Address: 233 Broadway, N.Y.C. 7. Died Nov. 17, 1954.

NIXON, George Felton, banker; b. Rome, Ga., Dec. 22, 1868; s. Robert Pleasant and Mary (Pennington) N.; ed. pub. schs. and 1 yr. under Prof. Neely; m. Eunice Adamson, 1906 (died 1930). In hardware business at Rome, with brother, Pennington M., as the Nixon Hardware Co., 25 yrs.; pres. First Nat. Bank, 1921-31; mem. bd. dirs. Home Building & Loan Co. Chmn. Civilian Relief Com., Rome, World War. Trustee Darlington Sch. Democrat. Presbyn. Club: Coosa Country. Home: Virginia Dr. Office: First National Bank, Rome, Ga. Died Jan. 27, 1947; buried Myrtle Hill Cemetery, Rome, Ga.

NIXON, Justin Wroe, clergyman, educator; b. Delphi, Ind., Feb. 23, 1886; s. Harmon Ausburn and Eva Arminta (Wroe) N.; grad. Doane Acad., Granville, O., 1901; A.B., Denison U., 1905; grad. Rochester Theol. Sem., 1908; post-grad. U. Chgo., Columbia; D.D., Coll. Ozarks and Denison U., 1925, Miami U., 1931, Oberlin Coll., 1937; m. Ida Elizabeth Wickenden, June 12, 1914; children—John Harmon, Charles Robert, Elizabeth, Alice Wroe, Justin Wroe. Ordained to Bapt. ministry, 1909; asso. pastor Calvary Ch., Mpls., 1908-09; pastor Judson Meml. Ch., Mpls., 1909-16; acting Hoyt prof. Hebrew lang. and lit. Rochester Theol. Sem., 1916-17, prof., 1917-19, Huntley prof. English Bible and Christian sociology, 1919-24; pastor Brick Presbyn. Ch., Rochester, 1924-37; William Newton Clarke prof. of Christian theology and ethics Colgate-Rochester Div. Sch., 1937-51; Cornelius Woelfkin prof., 1951-54, retired; lecturer summer terms, on Christian ethics Union Theol. Sem. 1924, 38, 44, Auburn Theol. Sem., 1931, 38, Chgo. Theol. Sem., 1932; Rauschenbusch lectr. Colgate-Rochester Div. Sch., 1931. Trustee Church Peace Union. Division sec. YMCA 90th div. AEF, 1918. Mem. Phi Beta Kappa. Author: An Emerging Christian Faith, 1930; The Moral Crisis in Christianity, 1931; Protestantism's Hour of Decision, 1940; Responsible Christianity, 1950; The United Nations and Our Religious Heritage, 1953; Man's New Hope, 1957. Editor: (with W. S. Hudson) Christian Leadership in a World Society, 1945. Home: 93 Beverly St., Rochester 10, N.Y. Died July 11, 1958; buried Granville, O.

NIXON, Paul, ex-coll. dean; b. Des Moines, Ia., May 23, 1882; s. William Goodin and Helen (Andrews) N.; A.B., Wesleyan Univ., Conn., 1904, A.M., 1905, L.H.D., 1927; LL.D., Colby College, 1938; L.H.D., Bowdoin College, 1943; Oxford University, 1904-07 (1st Rhodes scholar from Connecticut); m. Dorothea Margaret Thompson, July 30, 1907 (she died Oct. 3, 1917); m. 2d, Mathilde C. Spengler, July 7, 1919; children—Philip (adopted), Katrina. Instr. classics, Princeton U., 1907-08, at Dartmouth, 1908-09; assistant prof. Latin, 1909, prof., 1911-18, dean, 1918-47, resigned; now professor Latin, Bowdoin College. Professor Latin, University of Chicago, summer quarter, 1912. Mem. Am. Philol. Assn., N.E. Classical Assn. (exec. com., pres. 1924-25), Phi Beta Kappa. Assistant exec. sec. Me. Com. on Pub. Safety; state chairman "Four Minute Men," 1917. Director New England Council, 1942-46. First lieutenant Co. K, 3d Me. Nat. Guard, Apr.-Sept. 1918; 2d lt. inf., U.S. Army, Sept.-Dec. 1918. Democrat. Methodist. Author: A Roman Wit, 1911; Martial and the Modern Epigram, 1927. Translator: Plautus (Loeb Classical Library), Vol. I, 1916, Vol. II, 1917, Vol. III, 1923, Vol. IV, 1932, Vol. V, 1937. Contbr. to classical and other periodicals. Address: Brunswick, Me. Died Oct. 27, 1956; buried Brunswick.

NOAKES, Edward Bruce, advt. exec.; b. N.Y.C., Dec. 6, 1902; s. John Gordon and Louise (Goodall) N.; student Bordentown Mil. Inst., 1917-21; m. Anselma Borst, Mar. 10, 1932; children—John Gordon, Maragarete Jane, Carol Ann, Edward Bruce. Vice pres. McCann, Erickson Corp. Home: 46-41 243d St., Douglaston, L.I., N.Y. Office: 50 Rockefeller Plaza, N.Y.C. Died Dec. 23, 1958; buried Flushing Cemetery, Flushing, L.I., N.Y.

NOBACK, Gustave J(oseph) (nō'băk). prof. anatomy; b. New York, N.Y., May 29, 1890; s. Alfred and Marie (Mirejovsky) N.; prep. edn. Dwight Sch.; B.S., Cornell U., 1916; A.M., U. of Minn., 1920, Ph.D., 1923; m. Hazel Ogden Kilborn, June 17, 1917; 1 son, Richardson Kilborn. Asst. in histology and embryology, Cornell U., 1914-16; mgr. med. dept. Macmillan Co., Chicago, 1917-18; instr. in anatomy, U. of Minn., 1918-21; asso. prof. of anatomy. Med. Coll. of Va., 1921-22, prof., 1922-24; with New York U., 1924, asst. prof. anatomy, 1924-26, asso. prof., 1926-30, prof., 1930-45; chmn. biol. and geol. sciences, Grad. Sch.; dean, Essex Coll. Med., Newark, N.J., April 2, 1945; resigned July 21, 1945; asso. prof. Cornell Univ. Coll. Med., 1946-50; prof. of anatomy and head dept. U. of Puerto Rico Sch. Medicine, 1950-53, also chmn. board of anatomy; retired 1953. Fellow A.A.A.S., Am. Geo. Soc.; asso. fellow N.Y. Acad. Medicine; member American Assn. Anatomists, Am. Assn. Phys. Anthropologists, Harvey Soc., Soc. Med. Jurisprudence (pres.; sec. 1936-41), Gerontological Soc. Am. Artists Profl. League (national exec. com., pres.), Biol. Photographers Association, Society for Study of Arterio-Sclerosis, National Arts Club, Sigma Xi (v.p. Cornell U. Chapter, pres. New York Chapter 1938-39), Phi Alpha Sigma. Contbr. to scientific and professional jours. Research work in human growth and physical development; morphological and physiological changes incident to birth, especially respiratory and vascular systems; age changes in tissues and organs. Sculptor; exhibited 51st annual, 1st nat. exhbn., Archtl. League, N.Y. City, 1938; 135th annual, Pa. Acad. Fine Arts, Phila., 1940, 137th annual, 1942; 141st annual, 1946; 8th annual Metropolitan States (hon. mention), Washington, D.C., 1940; 28th annual, Allied Am. Artists, N.Y. City, 1941, 30th annual, 1943, 31st annual, 1944, 32d annual, 1945; 118th annual, Nat. Acad. Design, 1944, 120th annual, 1945. Home: 70-05 Groton St., Forest Hills 75, N.Y. Died Sept. 8, 1955; buried Quinnepiac Cemetery, Plantsville, Conn.

NOBLE, Edward John; b. Gouverneur, N.Y., Aug. 8, 1882; s. Harvey H. and Edna L. (Wood) N.; A.B., Yale, 1905; LL.D., St. Lawrence U., 1939; m. Ethel Louise Tinkham, Nov. 6, 1920; children—June, Sally. Chairman of the Civil Aeronautics Authority, Aug. 1938-May 1939; under-secretary of Commerce, June 1939-Aug. 1940; mem. Indsl. Advisory Com. of Fed. Res. Bank of N.Y.; was chmn. bd. Life Savers Corp., chmn. exec. com., 1955—; pres., dir. Heart Island Operating Co., Inc., Heart Island Transportation Corp., Inc.; mem. adv. com. Bankers Trust Co. of New York; chmn. bd. and dir., American Broadcasting Company, Inc., purchased controlling interest, Oct. 1943. Maj., Ordnance Dept., U.S.A., 1917-19. Founder and trustee Edward John Noble Foundation (a charitable orgn.). Pres. bd. trustees St. Lawrence Univ.; chmn. bd. trustees North Country Hosps. Gouverneur, N.Y. Mem. Beta Theta Pi. Rep. Unitarian. Clubs: Round Hill, Field, Greenwich Riding (Conn.); Chevy Chase (Md.); Cloud, Yale, Racquet and Tennis (New York); Thousand Islands Club, Inc. (pres. and dir.). Home: Round Hill Rd., Greenwich, Conn. Died Dec. 28, 1958; buried Greenwich, Conn.

NOBLE, Harold Joyce, historian; b. Pyeng Yang, Korea (of Am. parents), Jan. 19, 1903; s. William Arthur and Mattie (Wilcox) N.; A.B., Ohio Wesleyan U., 1924; M.A., Ohio State U., 1925; Ph.D., U. of

Calif., 1931; m. Myrtle Bell Rinehart, June 25, 1941; 1 dau., Joyce. Instr. Ewha Coll., Seoul, Korea, 1926-28; teaching fellow, U. of Calif., 1929-31; asst. prof. history, U. of Ore., 1931-34, asso. prof., 1934-45, prof. since 1945; prof., Third Coll., Kyoto, Japan, 1939-40; fgn. corr. Saturday Evening Post, Japan, Korea, China, Australia, 1946; Rockefeller fellow Chinese and Japanese studies, U.S., Japan and China, 1936-38, in humanities since 1946, chief publs. branch Civil Intelligence Sect., GHQ, Far East Command, Tokyo, Japan, 1947-48; chief of polit. liaison office, Hdqrs., Seoul, Korea, 1948; mem. U.S. delegation to U.N. Gen. Assembly, 1949-51; 1st sec. Am. Embassy, Korea, 1951-53; exec. with Com. for Free Asia, San Francisco. Served in U.S.N.G., 1920-23; US MC, 1942-44, maj., 1943, seeing service in New Zealand, New Caledonia, Solomon Islands, as combat intelligence and Japanese langs. officer and co-comdr.; now mem. USMC Res. Decorated Navy Commendation Ribbon (Bougainville campaign). Mem. Vets. Fgn. Wars, Marine Corps Res. Officers Assn. Author: What It Takes to Rule Japan, 1946; also articles in Am. Jour. Internat. Law, Pacific Hist. Rev., Far Eastern Quarterly, Nankai (Tientsin) Soc. and Econ. Quarterly, Transactions of Korea Branch of Royal Asiatic Soc., Ore. Law Rev., Amerasia, Saturday Evening Post, Current History. Mem. bd. editors, Pacific Hist. Rev.; contbg. editor, Far Eastern Quarterly. Specializes in history and current affairs of Japan, Korea, and China. Home: 5 El Patil, Orinda, Cal. Died Dec. 22, 1953.

NOBLE, Sir Percy Lockhart Harnam, Brit. naval officer; b. England, Jan. 16, 1880; m. Diamantina Campbell (dec. 1909); m. 2d, Celia Emily Hodgson, 1913. Joined Royal Navy, Great Britain, 1894, commd. lt., 1902, comdr., 1913, capt., 1918; served in Grand Fleet, World War I, 1914-19; has commanded (naval ships) Calliope, Calcutta, Barnham, and Shotley; served as capt. Naval Boys Tng. Establishment; dir. operations div., Admiralty Naval Staff, 1928-30; became rear admiral, 1929; naval aide-de-camp to the King, 1929; dir. naval equipment, 1931-32; served as rear admiral comdg. 2d Cruiser Squadron, 1932-34; became vice admiral, 1935; served as 4th sea lord and chief supplies and transport, 1935-37; comdr. in chief, China Station, 1938-40; became admiral 1939; apptd. comdr. in chief of the western approaches to Britain, 1941; apptd. head Brit. Admiralty delegation, Washington, 1942; ret. 1945 as rear adm. of United Kingdom. Decorated Knight Comdr. of the Bath, Companion of the Bath, Comdr. Royal Victorian Order. Address: 66 Ashley Gardens, London, S.W. 1, Eng. Died July 25, 1955.

NOBLE, Robert Ernest, army surgeon; b. Rome, Ga., Nov. 5, 1870; s. George and Lucy (Wadsworth) N.; M.S., Ala. Poly. Inst., 1891; M.D., Columbia, 1899; honor grad. Army Med. Sch., 1901; m. Ella L. Lupton, Nov. 23, 1905. Apptd. asst. surgeon, June 29, 1901; capt. asst. surgeon and capt. M.C., June 29, 1906; maj., Jan. 1, 1910; lt. col., May 15, 1917; col. N.A., Jan. 26, 1918; brig. gen. Med. Corps. N.A., May 9, 1918; maj. gen. (temp.) asst. surgeon gen. AEF, Oct. 30, 1918; brig. gen. asst. surg. gen. U.S. Army, Mar. 5, 1919. In Philippines, 1900-03; with dept. of sanitation, Isthmus Canal Commn., 1907-14; in charge anti-mosquito campaign, P.R., 8 mos., 1911-12; mem. san. commn. to Guayaquil, Eccuador, to study yellow fever, 1912-13; mem. commn. to Rand mines, Transvaal, South Africa, to study cause of pneumonia, 1913-14; at Vera Cruz, Mexico, May-Sept. 1914; duty War Dept., Washington, 1914-18; arrived in France, Oct. 25, 1918; returned to U.S., Aug. 3, 1919; retired as maj. gen., Feb. 8, 1925; mem. and later dir. Rockefeller Found. Yellow Fever Commn. to the West Coast of Africa, May 4-Dec. 3, 1920. Decorated D.S.M. (U.S.); Comdr. Legion of Honor (France). Mem. A. M.A., A.C.S., Soc. Colonial Wars. Soc. of the Cincinnati, Newcomen Soc. of England American (Ala.) Branch, Phi Delta Theta. Episcopalian. Club: Army and Navy (Washington). Address: Crowan Cottage, 1401 Woodstock Av., Anniston, Ala. Died Sept. 18, 1956; buried Anniston.

NOBLE, Thomas Tertius, organist; b. Bath, Eng., May 5, 1867; s. Thomas and Sarah (Jefferson) N.; grad. Royal Coll. of Music, London, 1889; M.A. (hon.), Columbia, 1917; Mus.D. (hon.), Trinity College, Hartford, 1926; also hon. degree of Mus. Doc., conferred by the Archbishop of Canterbury, 1931; m. Meriel Maud Stubbs, d. of late bishop of Truro, Eng., Decc. 29, 1897; 1 son, Philip Raymond. Organ positions at Colchester, London, and Trinity Coll., Cambridge, till 1892; at Ely Cathedral, 1892-98, York Minister, 1898-1913; organist and choir master St. Thomas's Ch., N.Y.C., since 1913. Was conductor York and Hovingham festivals. Hon. fellow Royal Coll. Organists; mem. Nat. Assn. Organists (pres. 1922-24). Mem. Ch. of England. Club: Columbia University. Composer of ch. music, organ music, songs, part songs, etc. Home: 121 West 55th St., N.Y.C. Died May 4, 1953.

NOBLITT, Quintin G. (nŏb'lĭt). mfg. exec.; b. Bartholomew Co., Ind., Oct. 11, 1882; s. John W. and Hannah (Barkes) N.; m. Grace M. Taylor, Oct. 7, 1906; childen—Aileen (Mrs. John C. Marshall), Ruth E. (Mrs. James M. Jewell). Co-founder, past pres., dir. and chmn. bd. Arvin Industries, Incorporated, formerly known as Noblitt-Sparks Industries, Inc., Columbus, Ind.; mem. bd. dirs. Am. Nat. Bank at Indianapolis, Irwin-Union Trust Co., Columbus, Ind. Member Nat. Assn. Mfrs. Methodist. Republican. Mason (Shriner). Clubs: Rotary, Indianapolis Athletic. Home: 1910 Washington St. Office: care Arvin Industries, Inc., Columbus, Ind. Died July 1st, 1954; buried Garland Brook Cemetery, Columbus.

NOBS, Ernest, pres. of Swiss Confederation; b. Funch, Switzerland, July 14, 1886; s. Jacob and Anna Nobs-Bernet; ed. sem. for schoolmasters, Hofwil near Berne; 1 dau., Erica. Schoolmaster, 1906-12; became journalist, 1912, joining Volksrecht (socialist paper), Zurich, as editor and chief editor; elected nat. councilor, 1919, mem. Swiss Parliament, 1919-43; mem. Govt. of Canton Zurich, 1935-42; mayor Town of Zurich, 1942-43; became mem. Fed. Council (1st socialist), 1943; head of finance custom dept. since 1944; pres. Swiss Confederation for 1949. Mem. Swiss Socialist Party. Author: Helvetische Erneuerung, 1943. Home: Bergshasse 73, Neileu, Zurich, Switzerland. Died Mar. 13, 1957; buried Friedhof Nauegg, Zurich.

NOEL, F(rancis) Regis (nō'ĕl), lawyer, author; b. Loretto, Pa., Apr. 12, 1891; s. John J. and Laura (Glass) N.; A.B., Mt. St. Mary's Coll., Emmitsburg, Md., 1912, A.M., 1914; LL.B., Nat. U., Washington, D.C., 1918; Ph.D., Catholic U. of America, 1918; post-grad. work Oxford U., Eng.; m. Renée Mouchel, Nov. 20, 1924. Associated in practice in Washington, D.C., with Joseph J. Darlington and Henry E. Davis; sometime mem. faculty of philosophy, Catholic U. of America; sometime prof. Roman jurisprudence, Georgetown U. Law Sch.; prof. mediaeval institutions, same, and prof. economics, Georgetown Coll. Mem. Attorney Generals' Nat. Crime Commn., 1934, D.C. Constitution Com. (chmn. essay com.); dir. Roger B. Taney Home, Good Samaritans. Mem. National Assn. for Constl. Govt. (exec. com.), Columbia Hist. Soc. (bd. mgrs.; pres. 1944-50), Isaac Walton League (Montgomery County, Md.), American Bar Association (chmn. committee on revision and codification of United States nationality and immigration laws, since 1938), Bar Assn. Dist. of Columbia (bd. dirs.; pres. 1934), Catholic Hist. Soc., Catholic Univ. Alumni (nat. sec.), Maryland Soc., Mt. St. Mary's Alumni (pres. Wash.-Baltimore Chapter), Am. Law Inst., Am. Soc. Internat. Law, Internat. Assn. Lawyers, American Judicature Society, The Thornton Society, Oxford Univ. Soc., New College Soc. of England (nat. sec. for D.C., Md. and Va.), Friends of U.S. Supreme Court Library (charter and life mem.); chmn. "The Old Woman in the Shoe." Chmn. Jury of Award U.S. Flag Assn., 1934; mem. bd. of advisors Am. Peace Soc.; del. Am. and D.C. bar assns., to 2d Internat. Conf. on Comparative Law, The Hague, 1937. Del. Inter-Am. Law Soc., Habana, 1940, 2d Conf. Inter-American Bar Assn., Rio de Janeiro, 1943, and 3d Conf., Mexico City, 1944. Mem. Isaac Walton League; organizer and 1st pres. Crime Commn., Dist. Columbia 1934; organizer 1st pres. Law Study Club of District Columbia, 1946. Clubs: Cosmos, Capital Yacht, Univ. (dir.), Barristers (chmn. legal aid com. 10 years), Circuit, Columbia Univ. (Wash., D.C.); Lex Club (Paris, France). Author: History of the Bankruptcy Law, 1919; History of the Courts of the District of Columbia, 1919; Biography of Joseph J. Darlington, 1920; Some Early Cases in the D.C. Courts; The Legal Setting of Radium & X-Ray; Some Observations on the American, English and French Legal Systems, 1933; Do Dead Men Tell Tales?, 1933; History of the Court House of the District of Columbia, 2d edit., 1939; also brochures and articles on professional topics. Editor in chief Cyclopedia of Practice for District of Columbia, 1923. Home: "Selsdon," Montgomery County, Md. Office: Evans Bldg.; 1420 New York Av. N.W., Washington. Died Mar. 29, 1952; buried Rockville, Md.

NOEL, Richard C(urtis), investment banker; b. Silver City, N.M., June 9, 1891; s. Harry W. and Lillian (Curtis) N.; grad. Inst. Law, St. Louis U., 1913; m. Marietta Thompson, Sept. 24, 1919; children—Richard Curtis, Martha (Mrs. Martha Baskowitz). Connected with investment banking since 1913; with William R. Compton & Co., St. Louis and N.Y. C., 1913-29; partner Van Alstyne, Noel & Co., N.Y. C.; v.p., dir. Hercules Steel Products Corp., Circle Wire & Cable Co.; dir. Consolidated Diesel Electric Corp., New Indria Mining & Chemical Co., Diana Stores Corp., Olympic Radio & Television Inc., Mem. C. of C. of U.S. Republican. Episcopalian. Clubs: Bankers, Bond, American Yacht (N.Y.C.); Town (Scarsdale, N.Y.). Home: 5 Carstenson Rd., Scarsdale, N.Y. Office: 52 Wall St., N.Y.C. 5. Died June 30, 1956.

NOEST, Jan Izaak, consul gen.; b. The Hague, The Netherlands, Aug. 2, 1895; s. Vriso and Johanna Judith (van Doorninck) N.; LL.B., U. of Leiden; m. Amalia von Schwanefluegel, Sept. 27, 1932; children —Jan Friso, Gerard Anton. Entered Netherlands consular service, 1924; vice consul London, Singapore, Calcutta, Shanghai, Capetown; consul N.Y.C., Ghent, San Francisco; charge d'affaires Bangkok, Rio de Janeiro, Caracas, Bogotá; conusl gen., Chicago, 1941, now Netherlands minister in Cuba. Reserve officer, Netherlands F.A., 1915-22. Home: 1349 N. Astor St. Office: 360 N. Michigan Av., Chgo. 1. Died Mar. 5, 1955.

NOFER, Edward John, pub.; b. Phila., Aug. 26, 1886; s. William Andrew and Emma (Burkert) N.; student pub. schs., Philadelphia; m. Elizabeth Alice Stull, July 3, 1912 (dec. Mar. 9, 1949); children—Edward John, Margaret Rosemary (Mrs. Herbert G. Reusch). Dir. Hubbell Pub. Co., N.Y. City, 1914-30, v.p., gen. mgr., 1929-30; v.p. Martindale-Hubbell, Inc., Summit, N.J., since 1934, gen. mgr., 1947-57, dir., 1944—, pres., treas., 1957—; dir. Bar Register Co., Inc.; cons. Survey of Legal Profession, 1949-52. Lutheran. Club: Lawyers. Died Mar. 5, 1958.‡

NOLAN, Dennis Edward, army officer; b. Akron, N.Y., Apr. 22, 1872; s. Martin N.; grad. U.S. Mil. Acad., 1896; m. Julia Grant Sharp, Aug. 21, 1901; children—Dennis Edward (dec.), Ellen Honora. Commd. add. 2d lt. 3d Inf., June 12, 1896; 2d lt. 1st Inf., Aug. 27, 1896; 1st lt. of inf., Dec. 14, 1898; assigned to 1st Inf., Jan. 1, 1899; trans. 13th Inf., Mar. 14, 1890; maj. 11th U.S. Cav., Aug. 10, 1899; hon. discharged vols., Mar. 13, 1901; capt. 30th inf., July 6, 1901; maj., July 1, 1916; lt. col. (temp.), Aug. 5, 1917; col. (temp.), Aug. 5, 1917; brig. gen. (temp.), Aug. 8, 1918; brig. gen. regular army, Mar. 6, 1921; maj. gen., Jan. 18, 1925. In Cuba, Spanish-Am. War; participted in Battle of El Caney, July 1, 1898; a.-d.-c. to Brig. Gen. Chambers McKibbin, at Santiago, Cuba, and Montauk Pt., N.Y.; duty at Camp Meade, Md., and Camp McKenzie, Ga.; in Philippines, 1901-02, 1906-11, in Alaska, 1912-13; duty Gen. Staff, 1903-06, 1915-19; arrived in France, June 9, 1917; with Gen. Staff Corps, AEF, 1917-19, chief of Intelligence Service, AEF, until demobilization; comd. 55th Brigade, 28th Div., in Argonne-Meuse offensive. Dep. Chief of Staff, U.S. Army, Sept. 14, 1924; chief of Army rep. with Prep. Commn. on Reduction and Limitation of Armaments, Geneva, 1926-27; comdr. 5th Corps Area, 1997-31, 2d Corps Area, 1931-36; retired. Dir. states participation N.Y. World's Fair, 1936-40; chmn. bd. trustees Citizens Budget Commn., N.Y.C., 1940-51. Recommended for bvts. of 1st lt. and capt., U.S. Army, for services in Spanish-Am. War; D.S.M., 1918, "for organizing and administering the Intelligence Service"; D.S.C., "for conduct in action" at Apremont; Croix de Guerre with Palm and Comdr. Legion of Honor (France); Comdr. of the Bath (Gt. Britain) Comdr. of the Crown (Italy); Comdr. of the Crown (Belgium); Medal of La Solidaridad (Panama). Roman Catholic. Clubs: Army and Navy (Washington); Chevy Chase (Md.). Home: 50 E. 58th St., N.Y.C. Died Feb. 24, 1953; buried Arlington Nat. Cemetery.

NOLAN, Edward James, oil operator; b. Rochester, N.Y., May 10, 1888; s. Peter and Margaret (Purcell) N.; LL.B., U. So. Cal., 1911; m. Grace Morse, July 12, 1928. Admitted to Cal. bar, 1911, and practiced at Los Angeles until 1924; v.p. Merchants Nat. Bank of Los Angeles, 1924-26; pres. Merchants Nat. Trust & Savings Bank, 1926-28; pres. Bank of America of Cal., 1928-30; chmn. Bank of America Nat. Trust & Savings Ass., 1930-19. Commd. as maj., A.C., 1942, promoted to lt. col., 1942, col., 1944; served on staff comdg. gen. 9th Air Force; later asst. to comdg. gen. First Allied Airborne Army; disch. Jan. 1946. Decorated Legion of Merit, Bronze Star, Purple Heart. Clubs: California, Los Angeles Country (Los Angeles); Tejas (Houston). Home: 7807 Meadow Lake Lane, Houston 27. Office: Gulf Bldg., Houston. Died Feb. 4, 1957.

NOLAN, John Henry, lawyer; b. Newport, R.I., Aug. 26, 1892; s. Frank F. and Mary A. (Carey) N.; A.B., Brown U., 1915; student Harvard Law Sch., 1915-17; m. Natalie D. Sheehan, Aug. 4, 1936. Admitted to R.I. bar, 1919, and since practiced in Newport and Providence; state senator, 1929-30; asst. atty. gen., 1923-24, 1933-39; atty. gen. 1941—. Served as ensign, U.S.N.R.F., World War. Mem. Am. Legion, Knights of Columbus, Elks, Ancient Order of Hibernians, Mil. Order of World War, Navy Club, Phi Kappa. Democrat. Roman Catholic. Home: 176 Eustis Av., Newport, R.I. Died Apr. 25, 1950.

NOLAN, John J., Jr., foundry exec.; b. Portsmouth, Va., Sept. 13, 1892; s. John J. and Martha (Pritchard) N.; grad. Andover Acad., 1911; B.S., Colgate U., 1915; m. Dorothy Tracy, Sept. 4, 1920. Asst. supt. Redington plant Bethlehem Shipbldg. Corp., then engr. Sanderson & Porter, N.Y.C., also Am. Brake Shoe Co.; with Central Foundry Co., N.Y.C., 1940—, pres., 1951—. Mem. Am. Soc. Naval Architects and Marine Engrs., Tau Beta Pi. Club: Union League (N.Y.C.). Home: 875 Park Av., N.Y.C. 21. Office: 932 Broadway, N.Y.C. 10. Died Oct. 1959.

NOLAND, William Churchill (nōland), architect; b. Hanover County, Va., June 4, 1865; s. Callender St. George and Mary Edmonia (Berkeley) N.; student pvt. schs. in Ashland, Va., Thos. H. Norwood's

Sch., Richmond, and Episcopal High Sch., nr. Alexandria; m. Mary Bleecker Miller, Sept. 30, 1914; children—Cynthia Berkeley (Mrs. Karl Young, Jr.), Ann Douglas (Mrs. Allan R. Spreen), Nelson Berkeley. In architects offices in Phila., N.Y.C., Roanoke, Va., and Richmond, Va., 1882-93; traveling and sketching in Europe, 1894-95; began practice of architecture in Richmond, 1896; mem. firm of Noland and Baskerville, 1897-1917; in individual practice, 1920-40. Mem. Va. State Art Commn., 1934-38, 1938-42. Fellow A.I.A. Home: 320 Oak Lane, Richmond 21, Va. Died Aug. 18, 1951; buried St. Martin's Ch., Hanover County, Va.

NOLL, Edward Angus August, file co. exec.; b. Cumberland, Md., May 19, 1867; s. Henry and Elizabeth (Sheermeeser) N.; student pub. schs.; m. Lulu Miller, Mar. 1893; 1 son, Edward Leonard. Pres., gen. mgr. The Nat. Tool Co., 1905-25; pres. The Nolvex File Co.; dir. The Lang Body Co. Joined Euclid Light Inf., 1888, Ohio N.G., 1889; promoted through grades to maj. Fifth Regt., 1900; capt. Ohio Vol. Inf., Spanish-Am. War. Mem. U.S., Cleve. C.'s of C., Nat. Aero. Assn. Mem. K.P. Clubs: Nat. Town and Country, Cleveland Aviation, Cleveland Athletic. Home: 570 Morewood Pkwy., Rocky River 16, O. Office: 10329 Detroit Av., Cleve. Died Oct. 19, 1939; buried Elmhurst Park, Avon, O.

NOLL, John Francis (nōl), bishop; b. Fort Wayne, Ind., Jan. 25, 1875; s. John G. and Anna (Ford) N.; ed. St. Lawrence Coll., Mt. Calvary, Wis.; grad. Mt. St. Mary's Sem., Cincinnati, O., 1898; LL.D., Notre Dame, 1917. Ordained priest R.C. Ch., 1898; pastor Kendallville, Ind., 1899-1902, Besancon, Ind., 1902-06, Hartford City, Ind., 1906-10, Huntington, 1910-25; consecrated bishop of Fort Wayne, 1925, named archbishop, bishop of Fort Wayne, Indiana, 1953. Built Mission Training Sch. at Huntington, costing $240,000, printing plant, $180,000, school, $120,000, orphanage, $500,000. Founder Our Sunday Visitor, weekly paper. Author: Kind Words from Your Pastor, 1904; Father Smith Instructs Jackson, 1913; The Fairest Argument, 1914; Catholic Facts, 1927; It Is Happening Here, 1936; The Decline of Nations, 1940; Our National Enemy Number One, 1942; Religion and Life, 1943; Christ Losing His World; Books of Meditation. Address: 1415 W. Washington Blvd., Fort Wayne 2, Ind. Died July 31, 1956; buried Victory-Noll, Huntington, Ind.

NOLLEN, John Scholte, educator, sec.; b. Pella, Ia., Jan. 15, 1869; s. John and Johanna Sara Susanna (Scholte) N.; A.B., Central Coll. of Iowa, 1885, Litt.D., 1943; A.B., State Univ. of Iowa, 1888, LL.D., 1910; Ph.D., Leipzig, 1893; L.H.D., Grinnell, 1940; graduate study, Zürich, 1890-91, Leipzig, 1891-92, Paris, 1892-93, Berlin, 1900-01; m. Emeline Barstow Bartlett, Sept. 11, 1906 (died Nov. 10, 1910); children—Anna Barstow (Mrs. John K. Eilert), Emeline Bartlett (Mrs. Parker Edwards); m. 2d, Louise Stevens Barlett, June 25, 1914. Instructor Central College of Iowa, 1885-87; tutor, Cham, Switzerland, 1888-90; prof. modern languages, Iowa (now Grinnell) College, 1893-1903; professor German, Iniana University, 1903-07; president Lake Forest (Ill.) U., 1907-18; served as gen. sec., work with the Italian Army, Internat. Com. Y.M.C.A., 1918-20; with Am. Red Cross Commn. to Europe, 1920; dean of Grinnell Coll., 1920-31, acting pres., 1931, pres. 1931-40, pres. emeritus since 1940. On leave of absence, at Pomona and Scripps colleges, Claremont, Calif., 1927-28; delegate to World Conf. on Faith and Order, Lausanne, Switzerland, 1927. Moderator, Congregational Christian Conf. of Iowa, 1935-36. Mem. Ia. State Bd. of Ednl. Examiners, 1933-40. Gov. Neb.-Ia. Dist. Kiwanis Internat., 1936; chmn. Ia.-Finnish Relief (under Herbert Hoover), 1939-40; state chmn. Defense War Savings Committee for Iowa since 1941. Member Phi Beta Kappa, Modern Language Association of America, Religious Educational Association, N.E.A., English-Speaking Union, Iowa Historical Soc., Goethe Gesellschaft, Newcomen Society; pres. Presbyn. Social Union, Chicago, 1910-11; pres. Assn. Am. Colls., 1917-18; pres. Ia. Assn. of Coll. Presidents, 1932-33. Decorated Italian War Cross and Comd. Order of Crown of Italy. Conglist. Clubs: Grinnell Country, Kiwanis (pres. 1925), Poweshiek. Author: Goethe's Götz von Berlichingen auf der Bühne, 1893; Chronology and Practical Bibliography of Modern German Literature, 1903; Outline History of Modern German Literature for Lake German Series, 1903; Two Addresses, 1907; What Is That in Thy Hand?, 1911; The Warfare of Peace, 1913; God and the Nations, 1914; Think on These Things, 1915. Ed.: Kleist's Prinz Friedrich von Homburg, 1899; Schiller's Poems, 1905; Schiller's Maria Stuart, 1909; German Poems, 1800-1850, 1912; Educational Pioneer: Centennial History of Grinnell Coll., 1946; The Way, The Truth, The Life, 1948. Contbr. to various philol. and lit. mags. and to The German Classics, 1913. Home: 916 7th Av., Grinnell, Ia. Died Mar. 13, 1952; buried Lake Forest, Ill.

NOOJIN, Balpha Lonnie (nōō'jin), Rep. Nat. committeeman; b. near Attalla, Ala., Aug. 10, 1885; s. Joshua Thompson and Margaret (Whitt) N.; student Birmingham-Southern Coll., 1903-07; B.S., U. of Ala., 1908; m. Willie McNaron, Dec. 26, 1916; 1 son, Balpha Lonnie. Prof. sciences and athletic dir., Ala. State Secondary Agrl. schs., Blountsville and Albertville, 1908-11; professional baseball player in N.C., S.C., Tex., S. Atlantic, Central, Southern and nat. leagues, 1908-13; prin Howard Coll Acad., 1912-15; athletic dir. Howard Coll., 1912-15; prof. Romance languages, sciences and athletic dir., U. of Ala., 1915-29; mgr. Noojin Hardware Co., Attalla, Ala., 1919-23; pres. Noojin Supply Co., Gadsden, Ala., 1923-26; owner since 1926. Dir. Asso. Industries of Alabama since 1939; director Alabama Power Company, 1946. Trustee, University of Alabama, 1945; member Gov's. Commn. to locate and build Alabama Med. Coll. Former pres. Civic Music Assn.; mem. Highway Users' Conf. of Ala. (chmn. since 1936), Southeastern Retail Hardware Assn. (former pres.), C. of C. (former pres.), U. of Ala. Alumni Assn. (pres. 1939-40), Northeastern Ala. Council Boy Scouts (former pres.), Phi Beta Kappa, Phi Kappa Sigma. Republican Nat. committeeman (since 1939). Methodist. Clubs: Kiwanis (former pres.; lt. gov. of Ala. state Kiwanis 1928), Rotary, Gadsden (Ala.), Country. Home: "Cliff Edge" Bellevue Highlands, Gadsden, Ala. Office: 119 N. 4th St., Gadsden, Ala. Died Sept. 7, 1950; buried Forrest Cemetery, Gadsden.

NOONAN, Herbert C., clergyman, educator; b. Oconto, Wis., Sept. 7, 1875; s. John and Mary (Moroney) N.; A.B., Marquette Coll. (now Univ.), 1896; normal work St. Louis U., 1897-99, science and philosophy, 1899-1902, Ph.D., 1902; divinity course Innsbruck U., Austria, 1906-10, D.D., 1910; Ph.D., Gregorian U., Rome, 1931. Joined Soc. of Jesus (Jesuits), 1896; prof. Creighton U., Omaha, Neb., 1902-03, St. Mary's (Kan.) Coll., 1903-06; prof. philosophy St. Louis U., 1911-12, ethics and pedagogy, 1912-15; pres. Marquette U., 1915-22; superior St. Ignatus High School, 1923-30; adminstrv. work St. Louis U., 1930; prof. philosophy Creighton U., Omaha, since 1931, head dept., 1936-47. Pres. Miss. Valley Jesuit Philos. Assn., 1937-40. Address: Creighton U., Omaha 2, Neb. Died July 6, 1956; buried Holy Sepulchre Cemetery, Omaha.

NOONAN, John A., dir. Swiss Corp. for Canadian Investments, Ltd. Address: 360 St. James St. W., Montreal 1, Quebec, Can. Died Mar. 10, 1955.

NOONAN, Joseph Michael, univ. pres.; b. Germantown, Phila., Pa., June 2, 1892; s. Michael Joseph and Elizabeth (O'Donnell) N.; La Salle Coll., Phila., 1905-08; St. Vincent's Apostolic Sch., Phila., 1908-11; St. Vincent's Sem., 1911-17; St. John's Coll., Brooklyn, N.Y., 1917-18; S.T.D. and Ph.L., Collegio Angelico, Rome, 1921. Joined Congregation of the Mission (Lazarist), 1911; ordained priest R.C. Ch., 1917; prof. fundamental theology and sacred scripture, St. John's Sem., 1921-32, dir. of seminarians, 1926-28, spiritual dir. of seminarians, 1928-32; pres. Niagara U., 1932—. Attended R.O.T.C., Plattsburg, N.Y., 1918. Address: Niagara University, N.Y. Died Sept. 29, 1959.

NOONAN, Thomas Hazard; b. Ferrisburgh, Vt., Dec. 17, 1865; s. Thomas Robert and Mary Esther (Anthony) N.; B.S., Middlebury (Vt.) Coll., 1891, LL.D., 1941; m. Eleanor L'Hommedieu, July 2, 1909; children—Thomas Robert, Donald James. Admitted to N.Y. bar, 1894, and practiced at Buffalo until 1912; dep. atty. gen. of N.Y., 1909-10; asso. judge City Ct., Buffalo, 1912-19; county judge Erie County N.Y., 1920-25; justice Supreme Court of N.Y., 1926-35; official referee of Supreme Court since Jan. 1936. Republican. Presbyn. Mason. Club: University. Home: 105 Norwood Av. Office: Erie County Hall, Buffalo. Died Aug. 31, 1957.

NOONAN, William T., ry. pres.; b. near Waverly, Minn., July 12, 1874, moving to Minneapolis at age of 6 yrs.; educated public schools and under private tutors at U. of Minn.; m. Harriette J. C. Duffy, Oct. 8, 1907; children—Loretto Douglass (Mrs. Francis P. Beattie), Jane Frances. Began in 1888 with Minneapolis & St. Louis R.R., serving in accounting, purchasing, operating, traffic and exec. depts.; made study of ry. conditions in Europe, 1900, and on return, 1902, was apptd. supt. in charge operating dept. Minneapolis & St. Louis R.R.; apptd. asst. to gen. mgr. Erie R.R., Jan. 1904; apptd. gen. supt. Buffalo, Rochester & Pittsburgh Ry. Co., Dec. 1904, promoted gen. mgr., 1906, v.p., 1909, pres. since 1910; also pres. Allegheny & Western Ry. Co., Clearfield & Mahoning Ry. Co.; v.p. Ontario Car Ferry Co.; elected v.p. B.&O. R.R. Co., 1932. Mem. Allegheny (N.Y.) State Park Commn., Memorial Art Gallery (Rochester), Monroe County (N.Y.) Tuberculosis Health Assn. Mem. Am. Ry. Guild, New York Chamber Commerce, Rochester Chamber Commerce, Nat. Recreation League, Soc. of the Genesee, Humane Soc., Am. Red Cross (life), Izaak Walton League of America, Navy League of U.S. Clubs: Automobile, Country, Genesee Valley (Rochester); Seigniory (Quebec, Can.). Home: 3435 East Av. Office: 155 W. Main St., Rochester 4, N.Y. Died July, 1952.

NORBERG, Carl F(olke), business exec.; born Klarrestrom, Sweden, Aug. 17, 1898; s. Carl Peter and Hilda Emma Charlotta (Brinck) N.; student Officer's Training Sch., Sweden, 1917-18; grad. Royal Inst. Tech., Stockholm, 1924; m. Audrey Irene Hagelin, June 21, 1927; children—Carl B., Audrey Joanne. Came to U.S. 1925, naturalized 1939. With Willard Storage Battery Co., 1925-43; president, director Electric Storage Battery Co., director of Ray-O-Vac Company, Atlas Mineral Products Co., Electric Storage Battery Co. (Can.) Ltd., president ESB Internat. Corp., N.Y.C., 1950—. Member U.S. C. of C., Am. Chem. Soc., Soc. Automotive Engineers, Society for Advancement Management, Franklin Inst., Am. Ordnance Assn., Phila. Chamber of Commerce. Republican. Episcopalian. Clubs: The Midday Union League, Philadelphia Country, Philadelphia Cricket. Research Center of ESB Co. dedicated in his memory The Carl F. Norberg Research Center. Home: 5740 Wissahickon Av., Phila. 44. Office: 2 Penn Center, Phila. 2. Died May 19, 1959.

NORBERG, Rudolph Carl, ret. battery mfg. exec.; b. Stockholm, Sweden, Mar. 18, 1881; s. Carl Martin and Elin Margareta (Nystrom) N.; E.E., Royal Tech. Inst., Stockholm, 1902; m. Ida Roberts, June 24, 1911; children—Charles Robert, James Franklin; m. 2d, Jean Levene, July 13, 1939; 1 dau., Mrs. Louis Halpern. Came to U.S., 1903, naturalized, 1920. Began as draftsman, 1903; sales mgr. Willard Storage Battery Co., 1917-19, v.p., gen. mgr., 1919-28, pres., 1928-41, now dir.; v.p. gen. mgr. The Electric Storage Battery Co., 1931-39, pres., 1940-49, chmn., 1950-52, ret., dir., 1928-51. Republican. Club: Midday (Phila.). Home: West Palm Beach, Fla. Office: The Electric Storage Battery Co., 19th and Allegheny Av., Phila. 32. Died Sept. 6, 1958.

NORDBY, Jorgen, clergyman; b. Hardanger, Norway, Dec. 9, 1852; s. Paul and Marie (Sponheim) N.; came to U.S., 1867; A.M., Luther Coll., Decorah, Ia., 1873; grad. Concordia Sem., St. Louis, 1876; m. Rosina Preus, Aug. 29, 1877. Ordained Norwegian Evang. Luth. ministry, 1876; pastor Northwood, Ia., 1876-80, Lee, Rochelle and Capron, Ill., 1880—; sec. Eastern Dist. Norwegian Luth. Ch. 1896-1907, pres., 1907—. Home: 602 Iowa Av., Decorah, Iowa. Died July 29, 1926; buried Lee, Ill.

NORDEN, N(orris) Lindsay, organist, condr.; b. Phila.; s. Norris Harkness and Helen Eugenia (Freas) N.; B.S., Columbia, 1909, Mus.B., 1910, A.M., 1911; m. Grace R. Vandiver, June 25, 1919 (dec.); children—Helen Virginia (dec.), Grace Elise, Warren Everett. Asst. organist St. Bartholomew's Ch., N.Y.C., and music dir. parish house, 1902-04; organist and choirmaster St. Mary's Episcopal Ch., Bklyn., 1906-15, All Saints Ch., Bklyn., 1915-17; organist Second Presbyn. Ch., Phila., 1917-27, Synagogue Rodelph Shalom, Phila., since 1922; organizer, 1912, condr., 1912-17, Aeolian Choir, Bklyn.; condr. Mendelssohn Club, Phila., 1916-26, Reading Choral Soc., 1920-39, Pottsville Choral Soc., 1923-25, Brahms Chorus of Phila., 1927-35; organizer, 1935, condr., 1935-41, Germantown Symphony Orchestra. Musical dir. First Presbyn. Ch., Germantown, 1927-40; organist and choirmaster Christ Ch. and St. Michael's, Germantown, 1941-44, Hanover Presbyn. Ch., Wilmington, Del., 1947-51, Prospect St. Presbyn. Church, Trenton, N.J., 1954—; instr. music High School of Commerce, N.Y.C., 1909-18, Episcopal Acad., Phila., 1918-21, Curtis Institute, Phila., 1924-26, Germantown Acad., 1929-33; guest condr. Fairmount Park Dell Concerts, 1931, 33; condr. Germantown "Pop" Concerts, 1932-33; instr. Cape Cod Inst. of Music, 1937. Composer of choral works, anthems, orchestral pieces, etc., also 125 arrangements of Russian choral music, 3 short operas. Editor of Linbar Musicological Records. Mem. Am., Phila. musicological socs., Am. Soc. for Physical Research, Am. Composers Alliance. Contbr. to Mus. Quarterly, Jour. of Musicology. Home: Churchville, Pa. Address: 615 N. Broad St., Phila. 23. Died Nov., 1956.

NORDFELDT, Bror Julius Olsson, (adopted mother's name), artist; b. Sweden, Apr. 13, 1878; s. Nels and Ingrid Sofia (Nordfeldt) Olsson; came to U.S., 1891; student Art Inst. Chgo., Academic Julian (Paris), Oxford Extension Coll. (Reading, Eng.); m. Margaret Doolittle, Dec. 29, 1909 (div.); m. 2d Emily Louise Abbott, 1944. Taught at Minneapolis School of Art 1933, 1944; painter, etcher and wood engraver; exhibited at Salon des Artistes Français and Salon d'Automne, Paris; Royal Acad. London, etc.; awarded silver medal Internat. Expn. Milan, Italy, 1906; silver medal, San Francisco Expn., 1915; bronze medal, Sesquicentennial Expn., Phila., 1926; Logan medal (for etching) Art Inst. Chgo., 1926; first prize Internat. Exhbn. of Etchings, Brooklyn Museums, 1928, Art Inst. Chgo., 1928; Yetter prize (for painting), Denver Art Museum, 1937; Purchase prize, Warchester, Mass., 1937; Bronze Medal, Corcoran Biennial, 1949. Work in the permanent collection of National Museum Sydney, N.S.W.; National Mus., Christiania, Norway; Bibliothèque d'Art et d'Archéologie, Paris; Toronto (Can.) Mus.; Art Inst. Chicago; Toledo Art Mus.; Detroit Mus. of Art; New York Pub. Library; Museum of N.M.; Corona Mundi Internat. Art Center, N.Y.C.; U. Okla.; Los Angeles Mus.; Mpls. Inst. Art.; U. of Minn.; Denver Art Museum; Art Museum of Wichita, Kan.; Met. Museum of Art, N.Y.C.; San Diego (Cal.) Museum; also Worcester (Mass.), Lincoln (Neb.) museums, U. of Ore., Rochester (N.Y.) Art Museum, Wilmington (Del.)

Art Assn. Prof. art U. Texas, 1941-42. Served as asst. dist. camoufleur, So. Pacific Dist., 1918. Represented in "Fifty Prints of the Year," 1926-27, 27-28. Address: Woodens Lane, Lambertville, N.J. Died Apr. 1955.

NORDSTROM, Sven Johan, engr.; b. Stockholm, Sweden, May 26, 1881; s. Martin Svenson and Hanna Gertrud (Askemstrom) N.; student tech. schs. of Stockholm, 1896-1901; Internat. Corr. Sch., 1901-04; manual training as machinist and carpenter, 1891-96; m. Lela Vandervort, Nov. 23, 1924. Came to U.S., 1901, naturalized, 1930. Mechanic and draftsman, Dr. De Laval, Stockholm, 1896-1901; draftsman and tool designer, 1901-10; designer and builder cyanide plants, 1910-18; invented Nordstrom valve, 1915, manufactured by Merrill Metall. Co., San Francisco, pres. mfg. since 1926; dir. Rockwell Mfg. Co. Clubs: Athens, Athletic (Oakland, Calif.); Tulsa (Okla.). Office: care of the Merrill Co., 582 Market St., S.F. 4. Died Dec. 11, 1951; buried Tulsa.

NORMAN, Bradford, Jr., banking exec.; b. Newport, R.I., Apr. 19, 1896; s. Bradford and Emma A. (Collins) N.; B.S., Harvard, 1918; m. Eleanor L. McKnight, Sept. 3, 1935; children—Bradford, III, Priscilla. Assistant vice president United States Shipping Board Emergency Fleet Corporation, 1921-23; partner Kimball & Co., 1923-26; with West & Co., 1926-28; v.p. The Comml. Nat. Bank & Trust Co. of N.Y., 1928-51; vice pres. Bankers Trust Co. since 1951; dir. Am. Sumatra Tobacco Corp., Eastern Steamship Lines, Hat Corp. of Am., Western Tablet and Stationery Corp. Trustee Staked Plains Trust, Ltd. Served as lieut., U.S. Navy, during World War I. Mem. Newport Hist. Soc. Mason. Clubs: Recess, Brook, Racquet and Tennis. Home: 435 E. 52d St., N.Y. City. Office: 16 Wall St., N.Y.C. Died Nov. 6, 1951.

NORMAN, Edward A(lbert), financier; b. Chgo., Mar. 9, 1900; s. Aaron Edward and Charlotte (Rosenfield) N.; A.B., Harvard, 1923; M.A., Columbia, 1944; m. Dorothy Stecker, June 10, 1925; children—Nancy, Andrew Edward; m. 2d, Elizabeth Blair, Nov. 8, 1953. Dir. Palestine Economic Corp., Trade Bank & Trust Co., N.Y.C. Dir. Health Ins. Plan of Greater N.Y., Play Schs. Assn. N.Y., Am. Friends of Hebrew U.; trustee Mt. Sinai Hosp.; gov. Hebrew U. in Jerusalem. Served from lt. to lt. comdr., USN, 1942-45. Mem. Group Farming Research Inst. (pres.), Am. Fund for Israel Instns. Clubs: Adirondack Mountain, Amateur Ski, Harvard, Goldens Bridge Hounds (N.Y.C.); Quissett Yacht (Falmouth, Mass.); Woods Hole (Mass.) Yacht; American (London, Eng.). Home: Pound Ridge, N.Y. Office: 654 Madison Av., N.Y.C. 21. Died June 20, 1954; buried Hickory Hill, Katonah, N.Y.

NORMAN, Jonathan Van Dyke, lawyer; b. Normandy, Spencer County, Ky., Aug. 13, 1877; s. Abner E. and Kate Linden (Barry) N.; B.A., Central U. (now Centre Coll.), Danville, Ky., 1898, B.L., 1899; m. Mary Robinson Cecil, Oct. 12, 1904; children—Jonathan Van Dyke, John Cecil, Mary Cecil. Admitted to Ky. bar, 1899, and began practice at Louisville; mem. Norman, Quirk & Webb, since 1923, offices in Louisville and Washington, D.C.; specializes in transportation law and practices largely before Interstate Commerce Commn. and federal courts; dir. Central Glass Co., Norman Lumber Co., Chief Am. Protective League, World War I. Pres. Louisville Fresh Air Home; trustee Neighborhood House. Chmn. Louisville and Jefferson Co. War Fund Campaign, years 1943, 1944 and 1945 Mem. American, Kentucky State and Louisville bar associations, Sigma Alpha Epsilon. Mason, Odd Fellow. Presbyterian. Clubs: Pendennis, Louisville Country (Louisville); Metropolitan (Washington). Author numerous pamphlets and papers on transportation law. Home: 648 Upland Road. Office: Kentucky Home Life Bldg., Louisville Ky.; also Continental Bldg., Washington 5. Died Nov. 18, 1952; buried Cave Hill Cemetery, Louisville.

NORMAN, Mark Wilber, lawyer; b. N.Y.C., June 28, 1878; s. Francis P. and Josephine F. (Hugart) N.; A.B., Columbia, 1900, LL.B., 1902; m. Florence R. Kendall, June 28, 1902; 1 son, Francis K. Admitted to N.Y. bar, 1902; practice largely abroad, 1916-32; mem. firm Cummings & Lockwood, Stamford, Conn.; dir., gen. counsel Gen. Ry. Signal Co., Ecuadorian Corp., Ltd.; chmn. bd., dir. Charter Oak Title Guarantee & Fidelity Co.; chmn. bd. Home Bank & Trust Co. (Darien, Conn.); dir. First Stamford Nat. Bank & Trust Co., Internat. Products Corp. Probate judge, Darien, 1925-31. Spl. asst. in Nat. Def. Adv. Commn. and OPM, 1940-41. Home: Darien, Conn. Office: 1 Atlantic St., Stamford, Conn.; and 29 Broadway, N.Y.C. Died July 4, 1951.

NORRIS, Edgar Hughes, educator; born La Grange, Ind., Oct. 19, 1893; s. Joseph Irving and Anna (Hughes) N.; student U. of Wooster (O.), 1911-12; B.S., U. of Minn., 1914, M.S., 1916, B.M., 1918, M.D., 1919; m. Loana M. Miller, 1919; children—Edgar Robert, Marguerite Loana, Helen Catherine; m. 2d, Lillian E. Elliott, 1932; children—Paul Elliott Hughes, Charles Irving, James Philip. Doctor of medicine, Oct. 1919—; asso. Dr. Arnold Schwyzer, St. Paul, Minn., 1919-22; partner of Dr. F. H. Neher, St. Paul, 1922-24; independent practice of surgery, 1924-31; inactive due to illness, 1931-35; retraining in pathology, 1935-38; prof. of pathology, Wayne U. Coll. of Med., 1938-46; dean, 1939-45; dir. med. sciences for Wayne Univ., 1943-45; visiting prof. anatomy, Washington University, 1945-46; research fellow, Massachusetts General Hospital, 1946-47; dir. edn. and research Lynn Clinic, Detroit. Member R.O.T.C., 1917-19. Founder of Am. Fedn. of Medical Centers, 1951. Fellow Am. Coll. of Surgeons; mem. A.M.A., Mich. State Med. Soc., Wayne County Med. Soc., Assn. Am. Med. Colls., Delta Tau Delta, Alpha Kappa Kappa, Sigma Psi, Alpha Omega Alpha. Presbyterian. Mason. Author: Medicine Rededicated, 1951. Home: 8106 E. Jefferson Av., Detroit 14. Office: 2900 S. Fort St., Detroit 17. Died Oct. 6, 1955; buried Mpls.

NORRIS, Ernest Eden, ry. official; b. Hoopeston, Ill., Jan. 21, 1882; s. Luther Calvin and Amanda (Lightner) N.; ed. pub. schs., Hoopeston; D.Sc., U. Tenn., 1951; LL.D., Davidson Coll., 1951; m. Kathryn Augusta Callan, Aug. 10, 1905; children—Frank Callan, Eden. Messenger boy Western Union, Hoopeston, 1892-95, mgr. Watseka (Ill.) office, 1895-96; asst. baggage master, telegrapher C. & N.W. R.R., Arlington Heights, Ill., 1896-97, clerk., telegrapher, Reedsburg, Wis., 1897-98, dispatcher at Chgo., 1898-99, trainmaster at Chgo., 1899-1901; became car service agent for the Southern Ry., at Washington, D.C., 1902; continued with same rd., trainmaster, Norfolk, Va., asst. supt., and supt. Knoxville, Tenn., supt., Atlanta, gen. supt., Knoxville, and asst. to pres., Washington, D.C., 1918-19; v.p. Mobile & Ohio R.R. Co., 1919-32, receiver, 1932-33; v.p. Southern Ry. System, 1933-37, pres., 1937-52, chmn. bd., 1952, dir., 1953—; dir. Riggs Nat. Bank, Washington, Met. Life Ins. Co. Comm. & col. transportation corps, U.S. Army, 1943, ordered to duty as regional dir. Southeastern Region 1943-44, 48, 50 during fed. seizures of railroads. Nat. asso. Boys Clubs Am. Mem. Nat. Geog. Soc. (life trustee), So. Research Inst. (adv. council), So. States Indsl. Council (dir.), Transportation Assn. Am. (dir.). Mason (Shriner). Clubs: Manhattan (N.Y.); Met. (Wash.). Voted one of America's 50 foremost bus. leaders, Forbes Mag. poll, 1947. Home: 2204 Wyoming Av. N.W. Office: Southern Ry. Bldg., McPherson Sq., Washington. Died Apr. 23, 1958; buried Hoopeston, Ill.

NORRIS, Herbert T(homas), music educator; b. N.Y. City, May 22, 1904; s. Thomas and Catherine (Froh) N.; A.B., Columbia, 1926, A.M., 1930; grad. study, Teachers Coll., 1949-50; m. Ruth Church, Jan. 1, 1930; children—Herbert Thomas, Donald Geoffrey. Vocal instr., Coatesville, Pa., 1926-27; dir. of music Kent (Conn.) Sch. for Boys, 1927-31; instr., Teachers Coll., Columbia, 1928-31; dir. of music, Tenn. State Coll., Johnson City, 1931-35; choral dir. and asst. prof. of music edn., State Coll. of Wash., Pullman, 1935-44, head dept. since 1937, prof. of music edn. since 1944. Mem. Music Educators Nat. Conf., Delta Chi, Phi Mu Alpha, Phi Delta Kappa, Phi Kappa Phi. Contbr. articles to profl. mags. Home: 402 High St., Pullman, Wash. Died Apr. 18, 1952; buried Pullman.

NORRIS, James, business exec.; b. Montreal, Canada, Dec. 10, 1878; s. James S. and Eleanor (Waud) N.; ed. McGill University, Montreal; came to U.S., 1898, naturalized, 1919; m. Ethel Carlisle Dougan, 1902 (dec. 1910); 1 son, James Dougan; m. 2d, Marguerite Loris, Feb. 20, 1919; children—Eleanor Waud (Mrs. Arthur R. Kneibler, Jr.), Bruce Arthur, Marguerite Ann. With Norris and Co. since 1906; pres. Norris Grain Co., Chicago, Ill., since 1908; dir. First Nat. Bank, Chicago, Rock Island & Pacific R.R. Co., West Indies Sugar Corp., St. Louis Arena Corp., Upper Lakes & St. Lawrence Trans. Co., Ltd., Indianapolis Coliseum Corp., Madison Square Garden Corp., New York, Toronto Elevators, Ltd., Toronto, Ont.; trustee Atlantic Mut. Ins. Co.; dir. Chicago Stadium Corp., Olympia Stadium Corp., Detroit. Mem. board dirs. Eastern L.I. Hosp., Greenport, Passavant Meml. Hosp., Chgo.; life mem. Art Inst. Chgo., Chgo. Hist. Soc., Chicago Zool. Society. Clubs: Chicago, Chicago Racquet, Chicago Athletic, Onwentsia; Racquet and Tennis (N.Y.); National Golf Links of America (Southampton, L.I., N.Y.); North Fork Country (Cutchogue, L.I., N.Y.); Seminole Golf, Bath and Tennis, Everglades (Palm Beach, Fla.); Seigniory (Que.). Home: 899 Deerpath, Lake Forest, Ill. Office: Bd. of Trade Bldg., Chgo. Died Dec. 4, 1952.

NORRIS, John Franklyn, clergyman; b. Dadeville, Ala., Sept. 18, 1877; s. James Warner and Mary (Davis) N.; A.B., Baylor U., 1903; Th.M., So. Bapt. Theol. Sem., Louisville, 1905; m. Lillian Gaddy, May 5, 1902; children—Lillian Gaddy (Mrs. Chas. B. Weaver), Jim Gaddy, J. Frank, George Louis. Ordained ministry Bapt. Ch., 1899; pastor Mt. Calm, Tex., 1899-1903, McKinney Av. Ch., Dallas, 1905-08, First Ch., Ft. Worth (membership 10,000), since 1909, also Temple Ch., Detroit (membership 8,000), 1935— (2 pastorates); editor Baptist Standard, 1906-09; also pres. Bible Baptist Sem. Fort Worth. Has made four world tours. Leader in fight for legislation against race track gambling, 1909, and for Sunday closing law, closing of pool halls, and prohibition. Radio pastor of stations KFJZ, WXYZ, WJDK, and Tex. network. Editor of The Fundamentalist. Home: Eagle Mountain Lake, Ft. Worth. Deceased.*

NORRIS, William Kibby, mfr.; b. Athens, O., 1875. Chmn. bd. dirs. McQuay-Norris Mfg. Co. Mason. Home: 12 Brentmoor Park, Clayton, Mo. Office: 2320 Marconi St., St. Louis 10. Died May 3, 1951.

NORTH, James Mortimer, newspaper editor; b. Jefferson, Tex., Aug. 29, 1886; s. James Mortimer and Anna Adele (Shaw) N.; student U. of Tex., 1905-06; m. Lottie Record, Aug. 18, 1914; 1 son, Philip Record. Began in newspaper business with Fort Worth Star, 1906; mng. editor Fort Worth Star-Telegram, 1909-23; editor Ft. Worth Star-Telegram; v.p. Carter Publications, Inc. Mem. Asso. Press (dir.), Southwestern Expn. and Fat Stock Show, Tex., Tex. Hereford Assn., Phi Kappa Psi. Clubs: Fort Worth, River Crest, Colonial. Home: 2136 Pembroke Dr. Office: Star-Telegram Bldg., Fort Worth. Died Oct. 16, 1956.

NORTH, Walter Harper, judge; b. Hillsdale County, Mich., Nov. 1, 1871; A.B., Hillsdale Coll., 1896, A.M., 1899; LL.B., U. of Mich., 1899. Practiced at Battle Creek, Mich., 1899-1906; judge 37th Judicial Circuit, Mich., 1906-27; apptd. justice Supreme Court of Mich., to fill vacancy, 1927, and elected for full term of 8 yrs., 1929, re-elected, 1937, for term, 1937-45, re-elected 1945, for term ending 1953. Home: Battle Creek, Mich. Address: State Capitol, Lansing, Mich. Died July 23, 1952.

NORTHCOTT, John A(ndrew), Jr., univ. prof.; b. Winton, N.C., Oct. 9, 1897; s. John A. and Maime (Lassiter) N., Sr.; B.S., N.C. State Coll., 1918; m. Virginia A. Williams, Jan. 5, 1924; 1 d., Virginia Wrenn. Mem. staff, dept. elec. engring., Notre Dame Univ., S. Bend, Ind., since 1922, prof. elec. engring. since 1932, head dept. since 1939. Mem. Am. Inst. E.E., Am. Soc. Engring. Edn.; Sigma Phi Epsilon. Home: 435 Parkovash Av., S. Bend, Ind. Died Apr. 4, 1956.

NORTHCOTT, William Newton, coll. adminstr.; b. Sugar Branch, Ind., Mar. 5, 1874; s. Thomas William and Mary L. (Newton) N.; grad. Moores Hill (Ind.) Coll., 1892; m. Lora Delle Gerkin, June 10, 1896; children—Mary Mildred (dec.), Roger Loraine. On internat. YMCA staff, r.r. dept., N.Y.C., 1911-13; metropolitan r.r. sec., YMCA, Chgo., 1912-19 (asst. exec., transportation dept., internat. YMCA, 1916-18); Ia. gen. state sec. YMCA, 1919-23; gen. sec. YMCA, Bridgeport, Conn., 1923-26; asst. to pres. Cornell Coll., Mt. Vernon, Ia., 1927-28; partner Howard T. Beaver and Asso., fund raising consultants, 1938-47; v.p. and dir. of expansion program and centennial Austin Coll., Sherman, Tex., 1947—. Originated plan for using stereopticon slides for daylight pictures to be used in safety program in r.r. shops and other indsl. centers, 1912, adapted same plan to teach English to immigrants, 1913. Pres., Chicago Parent-Teacher Orgn. for oral deaf, 1912-15, Ia. Parent-Teacher Orgn. for oral deaf, 1919-20. Presbyn. Mason. Home: Grayson Hotel, Sherman, Tex. Died June 21, 1950; buried Meml. Park Cemetery, Sherman.

NORTHEN, Edwin Clyde, business exec.; b. Lanier, Tex., Aug. 18, 1873; s. Edwin Coke and Mary Elizabeth (Walker) N.; student pub., pvt. schs., Pittsburg and Jefferson, Tex.; student med. coll. U. Tex., Galveston; m. Mary Elizabeth Moody, Dec. 1, 1915. Merchant, Jefferson, also Mt. Vernon, Tex.; apptd. receiver, operator irrigation and townsite project, lower Rio Grande Valley; staff Tremont Hotel, Galveston, 1908-13; staff USPHS, Galveston, 1908-13; organizer. propr. E. C. Northen & Co., 1913—; pres. Jack Tars Courts, McBride's, Inc.; vice president of the W. L. Moody & Company; organizer, director of the Bankers Home Building and Loan Assn., 1924—; v.p., dir. Fire Protection Co. Am., Southern Sprinkler Co., Aran Corp., Edgewater Cabanas, Falls Hotel Co., Gal.-Tex. Hotel Corp., Jean Lafitte Hotel Co., Hotel Wade Hampton, Inc.; dir. Am. Nat. Ins. Co., News Publishing Co., Galveston, Silver Lake Ranches, Inc., Beach Corp., Canal Street Hotel Corp., Texala Realty Corp.; owner, operator ranches, Tex., Okla., W.Va. Past member exec. bd. YMCA; past mem. Bay Area council Boy Scouts Am. Dir. Family Welfare Bur. Mem. Tex. Assn. Ins. Agts., Greater Galveston Beach Assn., Tex. Mardi Gras Assn., Friends Rosenberg Library, Galveston Hist. Soc., Civic Music Assn., Tex. Social Welfare Association, also member of Alpha Mu Pi Omega. Methodist. Clubs: Galveston Country, Galvez, Galveston Artillery, Rotary, Knife and Fork, Galveston Civic. Home: 2902 Broadway. Office: National Hotel Bldg., Galveston, Tex. Died May 30, 1954.

NORTHRUP, Elliott Judd, professor law; b. Syracuse, N.Y., Sept. 6, 1870; s. Ansel Judd and Eliza Sophia (Fitch) N.; Syracuse Univ., 1888-9 A.B., Amherst, 1892; LL.B., Cornell U., 1894; m. Ann Hero, June 27, 1914. Practiced in Syracuse in partnership with father, 1895-1902; assistant prof. law, 1902-6, asso. prof., 1906-10, U. of Ill.; prof. law,

1910-20, asst. dean College of Law, 1920—, Tulane University. Member Alpha Delta Phi, Phi Delta Phi. Wrote article on "Personal Property and Bailments," in American Law and Procedure, 1910; An Elementary Treatise on the Law of Real Property, 1919. Home: 1200 Pine St., New Orleans, La. Died 1950.

NORTON, Charles Hotchkiss, cons. engr. b. Plainville, Conn., Nov. 23, 1851; s. John C. and Harriet (Hotchkiss) N.; student pub. schs.; m. Julia E. Bishop, Jan. 1873; children—Ida (Mrs. William H. Munson), Fannie Norton; m. 2d, Mary E. Tomlinson, 1895 (died 1915); m. 3d, Mrs. Grace Harding, 1917 (died 1923). Began in employ of Seth Thomas Clock Co., Thomaston, and continued for 20 yrs., advancing to supt. machinery; asst. engr. Brown & Sharpe Mfg. Co., Providence, 1886-90; partner Leland, Faulconer & Norton Co. (now Cadillac Automobile Co.), Detroit, 1890-95; engr. Brown & Sharpe Co., 1895-1900; founder, 1900, Norton Grinding Co., Worcester, Mass., was originator of the modern methods of machine grinding; company merged, 1919, into the Norton Co., of which was chief engr. machinery div.; now retired. Recipient John Scott medal by Corp. of Phila. for invention of accurate grinding devices of high power, 1925. Mem. Am. Soc. M.E., Nat. Machine Tool Builders' Assn., Nat. Soc. for Constl. Govt., others. Republican. Conglist. Author: Principles of Cylindrical Grinding, 1917. Patentee in field. Home: Plainville, Conn. Deceased.

NORTON, Daniel Field, food mfr.; b. Evansville, Ind., Feb. 12, 1894; s. Daniel Field and Ella Belle (Hunter) N., Sr.; ed. pub. schs. of Evansville; m. Mary Helen Murray, Dec. 21, 1918; children—Daniel F., Jean (Mrs. Neil F. Campbell), Mary (Mrs. Robert E. Christie, III). Plant supt., sales rep. Carnation Milk Products Co., Oconomowoc, Wis., 1912-26; with The Nestle Co., Inc. (and predecessor, Nestle's Milk Products, Inc.), N.Y. City, since 1926, pres., mem. bd. dirs. since 1932, chmn., 1952; chmn. bd. dirs. Swiss-Am. Corp. since 1939, dir. Unilac, Inc. Presbyn. Clubs: Metropolitan (N.Y.C.); Scarsdale Golf; Blind Brook (Port Chester, N.Y.); El Paso, Broadmoor Golf, Cheyenne Mountain Country (Colorado Springs, Colo.); Denver (Denver). Home: Broadmoor Hotel. Office: 830 N. Tejon St., Colorado Springs, Colo. Died Jan. 14, 1956.

NORTON, J(ohn) Pease, financial writer; b. Suffield, Conn., July 28, 1877; s. John Hughes and Annie Lord (Lombard) N.; A.B., Yale, 1899, Ph.D., 1901; m. Nancy Jane Burwell Harris, July 29, 1940. Instr. economics and statistics, 1891-1904, asst. prof. ry. and trade statistics, 1905-10; Yale actuary and report writer for New York banking houses, 1905-14; ry. credit expert for 16 western states and western farmers' assns. in western rate advance case, 1915; editorial writer Wall Street Journal, 1916; railway credit expert for Western States, shippers' orgns. and Nat. Assn. Ry. Commrs., 1917. Oil statis. expert Fuel Adminstrn., 1918. Past mem. Acad. Polit. Science, Am. Mus. of Natural History, A.A.A.S. (sec. Sect. I, 1906-10, v.p. 1911-12), Econometric Society, Royal Economic Society of London, Sigma Chi, Phi Beta Kappa. Author: Statistical Studies in the New York Money Market, 1902; Theory of Loan Credit in Relation to Corporation Economics, 1904; Proposal for an Electric Dollar; Econometric Society; also Exhibits on Railway Credit in western rate advance case of 1915, and in fifteen per cent case of 1917. Home: 463 Ocean Av., West Haven, Conn.; also 140 Main St., Suffield, Conn., and 123 Arlington Way, Ormond Beach, Fla. Died July 16, 1952; buried Suffield, Conn.

NORTON, Laurence J., educator; b. Granville, N. Y., May 7, 1896; s. Isaac J. and Ada (Northrup) N.; B.S., Cornell U., 1917, Ph.D., 1921; m. Aurene Taubman, Oct. 13, 1922. Asst. Cornell U., 1918-22, asst. prof., 1922-23; asst. prof. econs. U. Ill., 1923-33, asso. prof. agrl. econs., 1934, prof., 1936—, head dept., 1955—; field organizer PCA, 1933-34; v.p., sec. Prodn. Credit Corp., St. Louis, 1935-36. Mem. Am. Farm Econ. Assn. (pres. 1945, sec.-treas. 1947-49), Internat. Conf. Agrl. Economists. Club: University (Urbana). Author text books on marketing farm products, farm financing. Home: 1108 S. Lincoln Av., Urbana, Ill. Died Feb. 3, 1956; buried Mount Hope Cemetery, Urbana.

NORTON, Mary Teresa, ex-congresswoman; b. Jersey City, N.J., Mar. 7, 1875; d. Thomas and Marie (Shea) Hopkins; ed. pub. schs. and business coll.; LL.D., St. Elizabeths Coll., 1930, Rider Coll., 1937; honorary LL.D., St. Bonaventure Univ., 1950; m. Robert Francis Norton (dec.); 1 son, Robert Francis (dec.). Apptd. to represent Hudson County on Dem. State Com., 1920; vice chmn. Dem. State Com., N.J., 1921-39, chmn., 1939-44; freeholder, Hudson County, 1923; del. at large Dem. Nat. Conv., N.Y., 1924, Houston, 1928, Chicago, 1932, 40, 44, Phila., 1936; mem. 69th to 72d Congresses (1925-33), 12th N.J. Dist., 73d to 80th Congresses (1933-49), 13th N.J. Dist.; chmn. Com. on Dist. of Columbia, Ho. of Reps., 1930-37, chmn. Com. on Labor, 1937-47; chmn. on House Adminstrn.; elected mem. Dem. Nat. Com., 1944; adviser to U.S. govt. dels. to Internat. Labor Orgns. Conf., Paris, 1945. Received Achievement Award as one of the 10 outstanding women of the yr., of Women's Nat. Press Club, 1946; 1947 Sienna Medal as outstanding Cath. woman of yr., particularly because of legislative service in conformity with Cath. doctrine, Phi Alpha (Cath. Univ. women). Pres. Queen's Daus. Day Nursery Assn., Jersey City, N.J., 12 yrs.; mem. Jersey City Woman's Club, Bus. and Profl. Women's Club, Zonta Club, Nat. Democratic Club (Washington), Cath. Daus. of America. Home: 2600 Boulevard, Jersey City, N.J. Died Aug. 2, 1959.

NORTON, Ralph Hubbard, corp. exec.; b. Chgo., Dec. 27, 1875; s. Oliver W. and Lucy (Fanning) N.; student Chicago Manual Training Sch., U. Chgo.; m. Elizabeth Calhoun, May 9, 1908; children—Beatrice N. Richards, Patricia N. Britton, Calhoun, Christopher; m. 2d, Ann Weaver, June 12, 1948. Entered employ Acme Steel Co., Chgo., 1904, pres., 1923-41, chairman board 1941—. Honorary president Chautauqua (N.Y.) Inst.; mem. bd. trustees and exec. com. Orchestral Assn. of Chicago; governing life mem. Art Inst. Chicago; mem. bd. dirs. Chicago Galleries. Dir. Asso. Employers of Ill. Mem. Mil. Order Loyal Legion, Alpha Delta Phi, Hon. pres. Norton Gallery and Sch. of art, West Palm Beach, Fla. Clubs: Union League, University, South Shore (Chgo.); Everglades, Bath and Tennis. Home: 4930 Woodlawn Av., Chgo. (summer); 253 Barcelona Rd., West Palm Beach, Fla. (winter). Office: 2840 Archer Av., Chgo. Died Dec. 14, 1953.

NORTON, Robert Castle, mining, shipping exec.; b. Cleve., Dec. 28, 1879; s. David Z. and Mary H. (Castle) N.; A.B., Yale, 1902. Chmn. bd. and dir. Oglebay, Norton & Co.; pres., dir. Fortune Lake Mining Co., D. Z. Norton, Inc., David Z. Norton Co.; vice president, director Lakeside & Marblehead R.R. Co.; director of the American Shipbuilding Co., Troop A. Armory Co., Union Commerce Bank. Trustee Church Home, Lakeview Cemetery Assn., Playhouse Found. Cleveland. Served from capt. to maj. U.S. Army, World War I. Mem. Am. Legion, S.A. R., Soc. Sons Colonial Wars, Western Res. Hist. Soc. (trustee), Yale Alumni Assn. (Cleveland past pres.), Cavalry Veterans Assn. (pres.), Alpha Delta Phi, Scroll and Key. Rep. Episcopalian. Clubs: Union, Tavern, Rowfant, Kirtland, Winous Point Shooting, Chagrin Valley Hunt (Cleve.); Yale (N.Y. C.). Home: 2215 Overlook Rd., Cleveland Heights 6, O.; also Woodnorton, Mentor, 9. Office: Hanna Bldg., Cleveland 15. Died Nov. 22, 1959.

NORWICH, Viscount (Alfred Duff Cooper), Brit. diplomat; b. London, Eng., Feb. 22, 1890; s. Sir Alfred and Lady Agnes (Duff) Cooper; student Eton Coll., 1903-97, New Coll., Oxford, 1908-11; m. Lady Diana Manners, June 2, 1919; 1 son, John Julius. Conservative mem. of Parliament for Oldham, 1924-29, for St. George's div. of Westminster, 1931-44; financial sec. War Office, London, 1928-29, 1931-34, treasury, 1934-35; privy councillor, 1935; sec. of state for war, 1935-37; first lord of the admiralty, 1937-38; minister of information, 1940-41; chancellor of the Duchy of Lancaster, 1941-43; spl. mission to the Far East, 1941-42; Brit. Ambassador in Paris, France, 1944-47. Rep. His Majesty's Government with the French com. of Nat. Liberation, Algiers, 1943. Served in the Grenadier Guards, 1917-19. Decorated D.S.O., mentioned in despatches, World War I; created 1st Viscount Norwich of Aldwick, 1952. Mem. Ch. of England. Clubs: Buck's, Beefsteak, St. James', Whites'. Author: Talleyrand, 1932; Haig, 1935; Volume II, 1936; The Second World War, 1939; David, 1943; Sergeant Shakespeare, 1949; Operation Heartbreak, 1950; Old Men Forget, 1952. Home: Chateau de St. Firmin Vineuil, Oise, France. Died Jan. 1, 1954.

NORWOOD, George, banking; b. Greenville, S.C., Sept. 9, 1892; s. John Wilkins and Lidie Cleveland (Goodlett) N.; Litt.B., Princeton U., 1916; student, Princeton Grad. Sch., 1916-17; m. Aimee Sloan, Feb. 14, 1923; children—Wilkins, Lillian Sloan. Cashier Norwood Nat. Bank, Greenville, S.C., 1920-25, pres., 1925-26; v.p. S.C. Nat. Bank, 1925-31; pvt. banker since 1931; pres. and treas., Convenience, Inc., Greenville. Staff officer with Adm. Dun, World War I, attached to Am. Peace Mission, Paris, 1919-20; lt. U.S.N.R.F., 1920-30; major, U.S. Army, 1942-45; served with B.E.F., Eritrea, Egypt, Tripolitania; with Am. Mil. Govt., Algeria; mgr. Allied Financial Agency, Sicily; with S.H.A.E.F., Eng., France, Germany; disch., 1945. Member S.C. Rep. Nat. Com. since 1940. Mem. Acad. of Polit. Science, Nat. Geographic Soc. Republican. Unitarian. Elks. Clubs: Poinsett (Greenville); Princeton, National Republican (New York). Home: 201 East Park Av. Office: 200-A W. McBee Av., Greenville, S.C. Died July 6, 1949; buried Springwood Cemetery, Greenville.

NOTNAGEL, Leland Hascall, lawyer; b. Saginaw, Mich., Mar. 8, 1903; s. F. William and Irene Hascall (Leland) N.; LL.B., U. Mich., 1925; m. Vera Schoenwald, Aug. 2, 1927; 1 dau., Nancy Ann (Mrs. James W. Garrett). Admitted to Mich. and Ohio bars, 1925, since practiced in Toledo; mem. Cobourn, Notnagel, Smith & Moran, 1950-52; mem. Cobourn, Yager, Notnagel, Smith & Moran, 1952-55, Cobourn, Yager, Notnagel, Smith, & Besh, 1955—; v.p., dir. Port Lawrence Title & Trust Co.; dir., sec. Charles R. Stevens, Inc. Member of the Am., Ohio and Toledo (exec. com.) bar assns., Internat. Assn. Ins. Council. Episcopalian (exec. com. Toledo City Mission). Elk (past trustee). Clubs: Toledo, Inverness (Toledo); Lions (Toledo); Lawyer's (Ann Arbor) Author: Check List, 1938, 1951. Home: 3339 Kingsgate Blvd., Toledo 6. Office: Toledo Trust Bldg., Toledo 4. Died Oct. 6, 1958.

NOTT, Stanley Charles, authority on Chinese jade; b. Wimbledon, Surrey, Eng., Aug. 4, 1902; s. Charles and Marian (Hughes) N.; ed. Westminster; Epsom; Oxford; m. Lucille Hardisty, Apr. 30, 1926; children—Graham Vaughan Charles, Ian Geoffrey, Stanlee Lucille. Came to U.S., 1940. Dir. Charles Nott, Ltd., London, 1936-39; pres. Stanley Charles Nott, Ltd., 1940-46, The House of Jade, Ltd. (president); consultant and adviser upon values and production dates for customs and ins. on jade jewels and ritual jades; assessor for customs on modern jade imports; founder, pres. The Chinese Culture Study Group of the Palm Beaches, Florida; dir. (and curator for life) Oriental Art, The Norton Gallery, West Palm Beach, Fla. Fellow Chinese Culture Study Group of America (nat. pres.); mem. Chinese Art Soc. of Am. (life mem.), A.A.A.S. (life mem.); College Art Assn. of America (life member); Am. Fedn. of Arts, Eugene Field Soc. (hon.), Internat. Mark Twain Soc. (hon.). Clubs: Sailfish (Fla.); The British (N.Y.); Royal Automobile (London); Thames Motor Cruising; Royal Motor Yacht; Old Epsomian; Old King's; St. Bartholomews Hospital Athletic; Westchester Country. Author: The Catalogue of Ch'ien Lung Jades, 1927; Chinese Hardstone Carvings, 1930; Imperial Jades in The Summer Palace Collection, 1931; Chinese Jade Throughout the Ages, 1937; Chinese Jade Carvings XVI-XIX Century (3 vols.), 1938-40; Catalogue of Rare Chinese Jade Carvings, 1940-41; The Symbolic Importance of Chinese Jade, 1941; The Geographical Locations of Chinese Jade, 1941; One Hundred and One Famous Chinese Jades, 1941; Chinese Jades in the Stanley Charles Nott collection, 1942; Chinese Art of World Renown, 1944; The Charm, 1944; Chinese Civilization, Past, Present and Future, 1945; Chinese Culture in the Arts, 1946; Voices From the Flowery Kingdom, 1947; Personalities in Chinese Art, 1948. Lecturer and educator on Chinese life and culture; appeared on radio programs and television programs; directed and produced technicolor motion pictures: Chinese Culture in the Arts, 1944; Historic Ritualistic Chinese Jades, 1948; World Famous Temple Animals in Jade, 1949; Rare Chinese Temple Jades, 1950; Chinese Jades Ritual or Commercial, 1951; Jade the Yu Stone of the Chinese, 1952; Ancestral Altar Jades, 1953; Chinese Temple Jades of World Renown, 1953; Jade Collecting, Ancient and Modern, 1954; Ancient Sacramental Chinese Jades, 1954. Home: (winter) Palm Beach, Fla.; also Highland, N.Y. Office: 955 Park Av., N.Y.C. 28. Died May 24, 1957; buried Lloyd Cemetery, Highland, N.Y.

NOTTER, Harley A(rthur), educator, govt. ofcl.; b. Sebewaing, Mich., Jan. 5, 1903; s. Arthur Henry and Wilhelmina Elizabeth (Armbruster) N.; A.B., Coll. of Puget Sound (Wash. State), 1925; A.M., Stanford, 1927, Ph.D. in Am. History, 1937; m. Margaret Olive Taylor, Sept. 8, 1926; children—Mary Margaret, Robert Harley, David Taylor. Asst. to head history dept. Stanford, 1926-27; prin. Roosevelt Jr. High Sch., Eugene, Ore., 1927-30; gen. supr. tchr. tng. U. of Ore., mem. State Com. on Jr. High Schs., 1928-30; instr. citizenship Stanford, 1931-35; writing asst. to Ray Stannard Baker, 1935-37; lectr. U.S. diplomacy Smith Coll., spring 1936; asst. prof. Am. history Western Reserve U. (O.) summer 1939; ofcl. U.S. State Dept., 1937, policy study officer div. Am., Republics, 1938, asst liaison officer with War and Navy depts., 1939-40, prin. polit. officer div. spl. research on postwar fgn. policy, 1941, asst. chief, 1942; exec. sec. President's adv. com. on postwar fgn. policy, 1942-43, chief div. polit. studies, 1943, mem. Internat. Orgn. Group, 1943-44, alternate mem. Policy Com. and of Postwar Program Com. under Sec. Hull, 1944; chief div. of internat. security and orgn., Jan. 1944, adviser Office Spl. Polit. Affairs and Office UN Affairs, 1944—; lecturer U.S. diplomacy, Sch. of Advanced Internat. Studies, Washington, 1947—. Gen. adviser U.S. delegation Dumbarton Oaks Conf. on Internat. Orgn., 1944; tech. officer U.S. delegation, Inter-Am. Conf. on Problems of War and Peace, Mexico City, 1945; adviser U.S. delegation UN Conf., San Francisco, 1945, UN Gen. Assembly London, 1946, New York, 1947. Mem. U.S. Civil Service Commn. of Expert Examiners for Dept. of State, 1948. Mem. Am. Hist. Assn., Am. Polit. Sci. Assn., Am. Soc. Internat. Law, Pi Kappa Delta. Author: The Origins of the Foreign Policy of Woodrow Wilson, 1937. Contbr. articles and reviews to mags. and profl. jours. Home: 6650 Barnaby St., Washington 15. Office: Dept. of State, Washington 25. Died June 18, 1950.

NOURSE, John Thomas, Jr., judge; b. Academia, Pa., Mar. 3, 1877; s. John Thomas and Eleanor Maclay (Pomeroy) N.; A.B., Stanford, 1901; m. Ruth Hoppin, June 11, 1908; children—John Lincoln, Elisabeth. Began practice of law at San Francisco, 1902; asst. city atty. San Francisco, 1904-11; dep. atty. gen. of Cal., 1911-17; judge Superior Court, San Francisco, 1917-19; asso. justice Dist. Court of Appeal, 1st Cal. Dist., 1919-30, became presiding justice, 1930. Republican. Mason. Club: Bohemian. Home: 666 Tennyson Av., Palo Alto, Cal. Died June 21, 1958.

NOURSE, Joseph Pomeroy, supt. schs., San Francisco, 1936-43. Home: 345 Arguello Blvd., San Francisco 18. Office: Board of Education, Civic Auditorium, Civic Center, San Francisco, Cal. Died Feb. 17, 1954; buried San Francisco. Meml. Columbarium.

NOVY, Frederick George (nō'vĭ), bacteriologist; b. Chicago, Ill., Dec. 9, 1864; B.S., U. of Mich., 1886, M.S., 1887, Sc.D., 1890, M.D., 1891; studied in Koch's lab., Berlin, 1888, Pasteur Inst., Paris, 1897, at Prague, 1894; LL.D. U. of Cincinnati, 1920, U. of Mich., 1936; m.; children—Robert L., Frank O., Marguerite F., Frederick G., Frances L. Asst., organic chemistry, 1886; instr. hygiene and physiol. chemistry, 1887-91, asst. prof., 1891-93, jr. prof., 1893-1902, prof. of bacteriology, 1902-35, and dir. Hygienic Lab., U. of Mich.; chmn. exec. com. and faculty of Med. Sch., U. of Mich., 1930-35, also dean Med. Sch.; dean emeritus and prof. emeritus since 1935. Russell lectr., 1927, Kober lecturer, 1931. Mem. U.S. Commn. to investigate plague 1901; mem. State Bd. of Health, 1897-99. Awarded gold medal, Am. Med. Assn., 1930; testimonial of Mich. Legislature, 1931; Bausch and Lomb's 250,000th microscope by A.A.A.S., 1936. Hon. pres. 3d Internat. Congress for Microbiology, 1939. Hon. fellow N.Y. Acad. Medicine, Internat. Coll. of Surgeons; mem. Nat. Acad. Scis., Am. Philos. Soc., A.M.A. (mem. council on pharmacy and chemistry, 1905-30), hon. mem. Assn. Am. Immunologists, Harvey Soc. (New York), Pathol. Soc. (Phila.), Am. Soc. Tropical Med., Soc. Am. Bacteriol. (Mich. branch), Am. Trudeau Soc., Wayne Co. Med. Soc., Detroit Acad. Med., Assn. Am. Physicians (emeritus), Am. Acad. Tropical Med. (emeritus), Am. Soc. Biological Chemists (emeritus), Société de pathologie exotique, Paris, Société royale des scis. médicales et naturelles, Bruxelles (asso. mem.); corr. mem. Société de Biologie Paris. Chevalier Legion of Honor (France); Order of White Lion (Czechoslovakia). Author: Cocaine and Its Derivatives, 1887; Laboratory Work in Bacteriology, 1899; Laboratory Work in Physiological Chemistry, 1898; Cellular Toxins (with Dr. V. C. Vaughan), 1902. Home: 721 Forest Av., Ann Arbor, Mich. Died Aug. 8, 1957; buried Forest Hill Cemetery, Ann Arbor.

NOWLIN, William Dudley, clergyman; b. Weakley County, Tenn., Mar. 10, 1864; s. William David and Caroline (Glass) N.; student Hickory Grove (Tenn.) Acad.; studied So. Bapt. Theol. Sem., 1895-98; two terms U. Chgo.; D.D., Georgetown (Ky.) Coll., 1904; LL.D., Union U., Jackson, Tenn., 1922; m. Mattie Wood, Nov. 10, 1887; children—Dudley Clinton, Bernice Elizabeth, William David, Annie Wood (dec.), James Wood, Bera Caroline, Martha Watson. Ordained to Bapt. ministry, 1892; pastor Calvary Ch., Lexington, Ky., 1899-1904, 3d Ch., Owensboro, 1904-09, 1st Ch., Mayfield, 1 yr., 1909-10, 1st Ch., Lakeland, Fla., 1911-14, Deaderick Av. Ch., Knoxville, Tenn., 1915-17, 22d and Walnut St. Ch., Louisville, 1917-19, 1st Ch., Greenville, 1919-24, 1st Ch., Arcadia, Fla., 1923-24. Pres. Ky. Bapt. Conv., 1907, 08; v.p. So. Bapt. Conv., 1922-23; pres. Fla. Bapt. Conv., 2 yrs.; moderator Peace River Bapt. Assn. 7 yrs.; formerly owner, editor Fla. Bapt. Witness, and asso. editor Western Recorder. Mem. Relief and Annuity Bd. of So. Bapt. Conv. Author: What Baptists Stand For, 1918; Fundamentals of the Faith, 1922; Kentucky Baptist History, 1922; Does Religion Pay?, 1923; Present Day Preaching, 1923; The Discovery of John Dumos, 1926. Now retired. Home: Delray Beach, Fla. Died July 30, 1950.

NOYES, Alfred, author; b. Staffordshire, Eng., Sept. 16, 1880; s. Alfred and Amelia Adams (Rowley) N.; student Oxford Univ., Eng., 1898-1902; Litt.D., Yale Univ., 1913; LL.D., Glasgow Univ., Scotland, 1927; L.H.D., Syracuse U., 1943; LL.D., U. of Calif., 1944; m. Garnett Daniels, 1907 (died 1926); m. 2d, Mary Weld-Blundell, 1927; children—Hugh, Veronica, Margaret. Made Comdr. Order of British Empire, 1918. Gave Lowell lectures, Boston, 1913; visiting prof., Princeton Univ., 1914-22. Mem. Phi Beta Kappa. Clubs: Athenaeum, Beefsteak (London). Author: Collected Poems (3 vols.); The Torch Bearers (3 vols.); (biography), Voltaire; Horace, 1947; (novel), No. Other Man); (prose and poetry), Orchard's Bay, (drama) Sherwood; Shadows on the Down (poems); Edge of the Abyss, 1942; Poems of the New World, 1942; The Secret of Pooduck Island, 1943; The Unknown God (philosophy); Two Worlds for Memory, (autobiography) 1953; The Devil Takes a Holiday (novel), 1955. Complete poems in one volume, 1947; A Letter to Lucian (poems) 1956; The Accusing Ghost or Justice for Casement, 1957. Home: Lisle Combe, St. Lawrence, Isle of Wight, Eng. Office: care Lippincott Co., Phila. 5. Died June 28, 1958.

NOYES, Carleton (Eldredge) (nois), author; b. Boston, Oct. 1, 1872; s. Increase Eldredge and Henrietta (Atwood) N.; A.B., Harvard, 1895, A.M., 1896; also univs. of Berlin and Paris; m. Charlotte Metcalfe, June 1, 1907. Asst. in English, Harvard, 1896-97, instr. 1899-1904; lectr. Am. Soc. for Extension U. Teaching, 1904-05; lecturer, summer Chautauqua, 1901. Formerly v.p., trustee North End Savings Bank. Republican. Conglist. Clubs: Harvard Faculty, Authors (Boston); Authors (N.Y.C.); Authors (London). Editor Coleridge's Ancient Mariner, 1900. Author: The Enjoyment of Art, 1903; The Gate of Appreciation, 1907; An Approach to Walt Whitman, 1910; Two Essays on Poetry in Harvard Classics, 1913; The Genius of Israel, 1924. Home: 30 Francis Av., Cambridge, Mass. Died 1950.

NOYES, C(harles) Reinold, economist; b. St. Paul, Minn., May 2, 1884; s. Charles Phelps and Emily Hoffman (Gilman) N.; student Barnard Sch., now St. Paul Acad., 1894-1901; A.B., Yale, 1905; spl. student Johns Hopkins, 1930-33; m. Dorothy Quincy Grinnell, Oct. 3, 1908 (divorced, 1931); children—Charlotte Irving (Mrs. William Raymond Driver, Jr.), Charles Phelps, Dorothy Quincy; m. 2d, Henriette Denney Turney McKnight, Jan. 14, 1933. Asso. Noyes Bros. & Cutler, Inc., St. Paul, Minn., 1905-29, vice pres., 1914-20, pres., 1920-29; economist, 1930—; dir. Nat. Bur. Econ. Research, New York, N.Y., 1940—, v.p. 1942-44, pres., 1946-48, chmn. 1948-50. Served as 1st lt., then capt., Chem. Warfare Service, A.E.F., 1918-19. Dir. Merchants, now 1st Nat. Bank, St. Paul, 1921-30, Empire Nat. Bank, St. Paul, 1926-30. Dir., trustee or officer numerous bus., civic, ednl. and charitable orgns., St. Paul, 1905-30. Fellow A.A.A.S.; mem. Am. Econ. Assn., Royal Econ. Soc., Am. Statis. Assn., Econometric Soc., Econ. Hist. Assn., Am. Polit. Sci. Assn., Acad. Polit. Sci., Council on Fgn. Relations. Clubs: Century (New York). Author: America's Destiny, 1935; The Institution of Property, 1936; Economic Man, 1948. Contbr. articles on economics to scientific jours., 1948—. Home: 12 Library Pl., Princeton, N.J. Died July 5, 1954; buried St. Paul.

NOYES, James Atkins, editor; b. Bklyn., Oct. 2, 1857; s. James Sullivan and Mary Ball (Edes) N.; Ph.B., Sch. Mines, Columbia, 1878; A.B., Harvard, 1883; m. Constance Winsor, Feb. 4, 1890 (died Jan. 1, 1895); 1 dau., Penelope Barker. Editor Quinquennial Catalogue, also mem. univ. council Harvard U., 1895-1905. Clubs: University, Harvard (N.Y.C.); Union (Boston). Hon. mem. Harvard Phi Beta Kappa, 1904. Home: 1 Highland St., Cambridge, Mass. Died Oct. 6, 1945; buried Cambridge.

NOYES, John Rutherford, army officer; b. Oneida, N.Y., Apr. 5, 1902; s. Charles Rutherford and Gertrude Hayes (Noyes) N.; B.S., U.S. Mil. Acad., 1923; C.E., Cornell, 1926; grad. Army Indsl. Coll., 1939; m. Eunice Gertrude Zimmerman, Mar. 6, 1928 (dec. 1952); children—John Zabriskie, Daniel Hayes; m. 2d, Lily Florence Ericson, Mar. 4, 1955; 1 son, Eric Rutherford. Commd. 2d lt., U.S. Army, 1923, advanced to col., 1942; served in C.E., 1923-50, in Alaska, 1926-28, 1931-32, 1948-51; asst. district engineer Juneau, 1926-28, Seattle, 1932-34, Conchas, 1935-37, Mobile Engr. Dist., 1939-42; instr. engrs., N.M.N.G., 1934-38; served as transportation officer, Services of Supply and Transportation Officer, Sixth Army Group, North Africa, Italy, France, and Germany, World War II; asst. to dir. gen. railways in Germany, 1945; transferred to Transportation Corps, 1950; commr. roads for Alaska, hdqrs. Juneau, 1948-51; transferred Corps Engineers, 1952, management officer, The Engr. Sch. U.S. Army, 1952, ret. 1953, brig. gen., N.G. U.S., adj. gen. Alaska, 1953. Lectr. hist. 1947, 48, 49. Awarded Bronze Star medal with Oak Leaf Cluster, Legion of Honor (French), Croix de Guerre (French). Fellow Am. Geog. Soc., Royal Geog. Soc. (British); mem. Am. Soc. C.E., Soc. Am. Mil. Engrs., Nat. Defense Transportation Assn., Permanent Internat. Assn. Navigation Congresses, A.A.A.S., N.G. Assn. U.S., Arctic Institute N. America (asso.), West Point Soc. N.Y. Elk. Author: Transportation in Alaska; the Influence of Geographical Environment Thereon (with Gen. James G. Steese), 1934; Transportation in Undeveloped Regions (with Gen. James G. Steese), 1938; Transportation in Alaska, 1952. Club: Army and Navy (Washington). Geographer-historian. Address: Kenwood Station, Oneida, N.Y. Died Jan. 30, 1956; buried Oneida.

NOYES, Pierrepont Burt, mfr.; b. Oneida, N.Y., Aug. 18, 1870; s. John Humphrey and Harriet (Worden) N.; student Colgate U., 1889, 90, Th.M., 1946, L.H.D.; Harvard; m. Corinna Ackley Kinsley, June 26, 1894; children—Mrs. Constance P. Robertson, Mrs. Barbara N. Smith, Pierrepoint Trowbridge. In charge depts. Oneida Community. Ltd. (now Oneida, Ltd.), 1895, gen. mgr., 1899-1926, pres., 1910-1950, hon. pres., 1950—; originated Community Plate, developed spl. system eliminating ordinary labor problems; dir. Syracuse Trust Co.; chmn. Saratoga Springs Commn., 1930-54, former pres. Saratoga Springs Authority using $5,000,000 to build the finest spa in the world. Asst. fuel adminstr. with H. A. Garfield, at Washington, 1917-18. Am. mem. Interallied Rhineland Commn., Coblenz, 1919-20. Decorated Officiale del Suo Ordine della Corona (Italian), 1921. Trustee Colgate U., 1926-49, trustee emeritus, 1949—. Mem. Delta Upsilon. Democrat. Author: While Europe Waits for Peace, 1921; The Pallid Giant (novel), 1927 (reprinted under title, Gentlemen: You Are Mad, 1946); (autobiography) My Father's House, 1937, A Goodly Heritage, 1958. Home: The Mansion House, Kenwood Sta., Oneida, N.Y. Died Apr. 15, 1959.

NUFER, Albert F. (nū'fĕr), foreign service; b. New York City, Oct. 21, 1894; s. Frank Xavier and Dorothy (Eypel) N.; ed. business schools, Bremen, Germany, 1907-10; m. Dolores Cabrera, Oct. 4, 1919; children—Hazel Vivian, Miriam Frances. English corr. in Germany, 1910; clerk in Am. consulates at Bremen and Barmen, 1910-16; vice consul at Erfurt, 1916-17; at Cienfuegos, 1917-19; partner and exec. in business firms in Cienfuegos, 1919-28; appointed trade commr. at Mexico City, July 11, 1928; asst. commercial attaché at Mexico City, Nov. 27, 1928; at Habana Feb. 4, 1930; commercial attaché at Habana, June 23, 1932; in Bureau of Foreign and Domestic Commerce 1934-35; commercial attaché, Madrid, Feb. 26, 1935; Habana, Sept. 23, 1937; consul and sec. in the Diplomatic Service, Nov. 16, 1939; counselor of Embassy for economic affairs, Habana, 1942-47; apptd. ambassador to El Salvador, Apr. 1947; dir. Office of Middle American Affairs, 1951; ambassador to Argentina, 1952-56, P.I., 1956—. Chmn. Am. delegation to Central Conf. of UNESCO, Montevideo, Uruguay, 1954. Promoted to class of career minister, 1947. Address: Dept. of State, Washington. Died Nov. 6, 1956; buried Colon Cemetery, Havana, Cuba.

NUGENT, Thomas Joseph, banker; b. Balt., June 30, 1884; s. Thomas Theobald and Mary (Kelly) N.; student St. Vincent's Coll., Chgo.; grad. St. Patrick's Comml. Acad., Chgo.; m. Loretta Catherine Cummings, Aug. 10, 1915; children—Thomas Andrew, Joseph Eugene, Mrs. Marie McKenzie, Mrs. Loretta Reynolds. Office boy Strauss, Eisendrath & Co., Chgo., 1901; with C. H. Baldwin & Co., 1901-02; filled various positionns First Nat. Bank, Chgo., 1902-20, asst. v.p., 1920-31, v.p., 1931—, ret. 1950. Mem. Am. Inst. Banking, Reserve City Bankers Assn., Robert Morris Assos., Serra Internat. Roman Catholic. K.C. Club: South Shore Country (Chgo.). Home: 7116 Coles Av. Office: 38 S. Dearborn St., Chgo. Deceased.

NULSEN, Charles Kilbourne, ret. army officer; b. Kilbourne, La., July 9, 1886; s. Augustus John and Minnie (Kilbourne) N.; student Georgetown (Ky.) Coll., 1901-02, Nat. Prep. Acad., Highland Falls, N.Y., 1903-04; B.S., U.S. Mil. Acad., 1908; grad. Inf. Sch. Advanced Course, 1926, Command and Gen. Staff Sch., 1927, Army War Coll., 1932, Chem. Warfare Sch., 1936; m. Marion Long, Sept. 15, 1914; children—Marion (Mrs. Jesse Duncan Elliott, Jr., dec.), Charles Kilbourne. Commd. 2d lt. Inf., U.S. Army, 1908, advanced through grades to brig. gen., 1943; served as capt. and maj., 15th and 13th Inf., 1917-18; with Army of Occupation of Germany, 1920-22; in command 23rd Inf., 1940-41; comdr. Ft. Sam Houston, 41-47; became comdg. gen. Ft. Sheridan, 1947; retired with permanent rank of brig. gen., 1947. Decorated Mexican Border, World War I, Army Occupation of Germany, and War Dept. Gen. Staff medals, World War II, Legion of Merit. Home: 332 Arcadia Place, San Antonio. Died Mar. 13, 1959.

NULTON, Louis McCoy, naval officer; b. Winchester, Va., Aug. 8, 1869; s. Joseph A. and Annie Virginia (Clark) N.; grad. U.S. Naval Acad., 1889; m. Minnie Clark Evans, Sept. 5, 1895; children—Virginia Adams, Dorothy Evans. Promoted asst. engr., July 1, 1891; passed asst. engr., July 4, 1896; transferred to the line as lt., Mar. 3, 1899; lt. comdr., July 1, 1905; comdr., July 1, 1910; capt., Nov. 26, 1915; rear admiral, Aug. 12, 1921; vice admiral, June 21, 1928; admiral, May 26, 1929. Served on Minneapolis, 1898, Texas, 1902-05; at U.S. Naval Acad., 1905-07; exec. officer Olympia, 1907; exec. officer and navigator Panther, 1907-08; ordnance officer Ohio, 1908; exec. officer Wisconsin, 1909-10; at U.S. Naval Acad., 1910-13, Naval War Coll., Newport, R.I., 1913; comd. Nashville, 1913, Montana, 1914-15; comdt. of midshipmen, U.S. Naval Acad., 1915-18; comdg. Pennsylvania, flagship of Atlantic Fleet, 1918-20; comdt. Phila. Naval Dist. until June 1923; comdg. Battleship Div. Three until Jan. 1925; supt. U.S. Naval Acad., 1925-28; vice admiral, in command battle divs., Battle Fleet, 1928-29; admiral, comdr. in chief U.S. Battle Fleet, 1929-30; apptd. comdt. 1st Naval Dist., Boston, May 1930; retired on account of age limit, Sept. 1, 1933. Participated in Cuban, Philippine and Boxer (China) campaigns, and in World War; was at Vera Cruz, 1914. Mem. U.S. Naval Inst., Mil. Order of the Dragon. Commendatory letters from Dept. of State for work done in diplomatic-naval service in Haiti and San Domingo; Grand Officer Order of the Crown of Rumania; awarded Navy Cross for services in World War I. Clubs: Army and Navy (Washington); New York Yacht.

Home: 321 N. Loudoun St., Winchester, Va. Died Nov. 10, 1954; buried U.S. Naval Acad., Annapolis.

NUNEMAKER, John Horace, educator; b. Harrisburg, Pa., Dec. 1, 1897; s. John and Agnes Gertrude (Willoughby) N.; A.B., Colgate U., 1920; A.M., Denison U., Granville, O., 1922; Ph.D., U. of Wis., 1928; grad. study, Ohio State U., 1923-26, in Madrid, Spain, 9 summers, 1921-30; m. Faythe Santway, Aug. 14, 1920; children—John Horace, Mary-Emma. Instr. Cazenovia (N.Y.) Sem., 1920-21; instr., asst. and asso. prof. modern langs. Denison U., 1921-26; prof. modern langs. Chautauqua (N.Y.) Instn., summers 1924, 25; instr. Spanish extramural div. N.Y.U., summer 1926; instr. Spanish, U. of Wis., 1926-28; prof. fgn. langs., chmn. div. humanities, curator Hispanic collection, State Coll. of Wash., 1928-—; dir. tours to Europe, summers 1921-23, 26-30. Served as sgt. Med. Dept., U.S. Army, Columbus Barracks, O., Camps Greenleaf and Hancock, Ga., 1918-19. Mem. Am. Assn. Teachers Spansih, Modern Lang. Assn. Am., Mediaeval Acad. Am., Am. Assn. U. Profs., Sigma Nu, Phi Beta Kappa, Sigma Kappa Phi. Presbyn. Mason. Editor foreign lang. publs. Contbr. to profl. mags. Home: 1909 B St., Pullman, Wash. Died June 24, 1949.

NUNN, Marshall (Elbert), educator; b. Anson, Kan., Aug. 4, 1902; s. Reuben Hannah and Mary Ellen (Heasty) N.; A.B., Stanford, 1924, A.M., 1925; Ph.D., U. Ill., 1939; m. Mildred Marie Resweber, June 17, 1926; children—Marshall Earl, Russell Anthony. Instr. Spanish, U. Tenn., 1925-26; instr. Spanish, U. Ala., 1927-30, asst. prof., 1930-39, asso. prof., 1939-46, prof. Spanish, 1946-—, head dept. Romance langs., 1947-—. Mem. Roosevelt Fellowship Com., 1941. Mem. Modern Lang. Assn., Am. Assn. Tchrs. Spanish and Portuguese, Instituto Ibero-Americano, S. Atlantic Modern Lang. Assn. (chmn. Spanish sect. 1941), Phi Beta Kappa, Sigma Delta Pi. Episcopalian. Author: A List of Related Spanish-English Words, 1944; Spanish-Am. ed., Dictionary of World Literature, 1942; editor: Sonata de Estio, 1946, scattered prose works of Julián del Casal Un Viaje a Cuba (with H. A. Van Scoy), 1942. Contbr. numerous articles to learned jours. in U.S., Cuba, Santo Domingo, Mexico, Panama, Costa Rica, Jamaica, England. Corr. mem. Ateneo of Santo Domingo, Asociación de Escritores y Artistas Americanos of Cuba. Home: 21 Hillcrest, Tuscaloosa, Ala. Died June 3, 1950.

NURI As-SAID, premier of Iraq; b. Baghdad, 1888; grad. Turkish Mil. Coll., Istanbul, 1906; married; 1 son, Sabah Nuri as-Said. Jr. officer Turkish Army, 1906-13; chief staff Arab partisan forces, promoted to rank of gen., World War I; Army chief of staff, Iraq, 1920; minister def., 1923-30, mem. for Baghdad Chamber Deputies, 1924-33, senator, 1933, pres. Senate, 1946-47; premier intermittently, 1930-—; minister fgn. affairs, 1933-36; minister interior, 1938-40, 46-47, 49; defense minister, 1953-—, also prime minister. Rep. Iraq to League Nations Assembly, 1930-32; chief del. UN Gen. Assembly, 1947. Address: House of Parliament, Baghdad, Iraq. Assassinated July 15, 1958.*

NUTT, Clifford Cameron, army officer; b. Kansas City, Mo., July 25, 1896; s. Alva V. and Blanche C. (Jett) N.; grad. Army Indsl. Coll., Washington, D.C., 1939, Air Corps Tactical Sch., 1938; m. Edna G. Morgan, Feb. 22, 1931. Commd. 2d lt., Jan. 1918, and advanced through ranks to brig. gen., U.S. Army, Oct. 25, 1945; rated command pilot, combat observer; served as dep. comdr. Fairfield Air Service Command, Patterson Field, Dayton, O., Feb. 1942-Mar. 1944; comdg. gen. Hawaiian Air Depot, Apr. 1944-July 1946; comdg. gen. Atlantic Overseas Air Materiel Dist., Port of Newark (N.J.) Aug. 1946-Apr. 1947; dep. comdr. 1st AF, Ft. Slocum, N.Y. since Apr. 1947. Decorated: Distinguished Flying Cross, Mackay Trophy award, 1920, Bronze Star medal, Commendation ribbon. Address: Hdqrs. First Air Force, Fort Slocum, N.Y. Deceased.*

NUTTER, Edmondson John Masters, clergyman, educator; b. Bradford, Yorkshire, Eng., Nov. 3, 1879; s. Samuel and Emma (Masters) N.; grad. U. Leeds, Eng., 1904; grad. Nashotah Theol. Sem., 1911, B.D., 1912, D.D., 1925, D.C.L., 1943. Came to U.S., 1905, naturalized, 1918. Deacon P.E. Ch., 1910, priest, 1911; curate Grace Ch., Chgo., 1911-14; rector St. John's Ch., Chgo., 1914-18, Ch. of the Messiah, Detroit, 1918-25; dean emeritus pastoral theology Nashotah Theol. Sem., 1948. Trustee Nashotah House. Mason. Clubs: University (Milw.); Detroit Athletic. Contbr. to Am. Church Monthly, The Living Church, Nat. Dictionary of Am. Biography. Home: Nashotah House, Nashotah, Wis. and 29 Perry St., N.Y.C. Died Apr. 6, 1953.

NUTTING, John Danforth, clergyman; b. Randolph, Vt., Mar. 8, 1854; s. Rufus and Sarah H. N.; A.B., Wheaton (Ill.) Coll., 1878, A.M., 1881; grad. Oberlin Theol. Sem., 1885; m. Nannie Keith Miller, June 23, 1885 (died 1886); 1 dau., Nannie Keith Miller; m. 2d, Lillis R. Morley, Jan. 1, 1890; children—John Morley, Lillis Ruth, Paul Thomas. Ordained to ministry in Congl. Ch., 1885; pastor Wauseon, O., 1885-88, Newport, Ky., 1888-90, St. Louis, 1890-92, Salt Lake City, 1892-98; sec. Utah Gospel Mission for spl. work in behalf of the Mormon people and against the Mormon system, 1898-—. Writer and lecturer on Mormonism and kindred subjects. Editor of Light on Mormonism, quar. Home: 9277 Amesbury Av. N.E., Cleve. 6. Died Oct. 4, 1949; buried Mentor (O.) Cemetery.

NUYTTENS, Pierre, artist; b. Antwerp, Belgium; s. Josef Cornelius and Anna (Caesar) N.; educated at Antwerp Academy, 1896-98; Antwerp Athenoeum, 1893-98; Ecole d'Industrie, Antwerp, 1893-95; Art Inst. Chgo., 1905-08. Portraitist, etcher and illustrator; specializes in etchings, portraits and stage presentations; has made portraits of many notable personages in U.S. and Europe; designed all costumes for Federal Theatre in Chgo. season 1938-39; designer of all costumes 1940 Lincoln Pageant, New Salem Park, Petersburg, Ill.; chmn. Nat. Arts Guild, Chgo. Decorated Chevalier Order of. Leopold for meritorious services during World War by King Albert of Belgium, 1918. Awarded 1st prize École d'Industrie, 1894. Exhibited at Art Inst. Chgo.; Anderson Art Galleries, Chgo.; Braun Art Galleries, N.Y.C.; Acad. of Fine Arts and Ecole d'Industrie, Antwerp. Works on exhbn. The White House, Washington; Congressional Library, Washington; New York Pub. Library; State House, Springfield, Ill.; War Museum, Brussels, Belgium, etc. Fellow Royal Soc. Arts, London, Eng. Home: 1819 Lincoln Park W., Chgo. Died Jan. 1960.

NYBURG, Sidney Lauer (ni-bûrg), lawyer, author; b. Balt., Dec. 8, 1880; s. Simon S. and Rebecca (Lauer) N.; student Balt. City Coll., 1895-98, completing coll. work under a tutor; LL.B., U. Md., 1901; m. Henrietta L. Nyburg, Jan. 9, 1907; 1 son, Robert S. Practiced in Balt., 1902-56; mem. Nyburg, Goldman & Walter. Mem. Bar Assn. Balt. City. Jewish religion. Mason. Club: University. Author: The Final Verdict, 1915; The Conquest, 1916; The Chosen People, 1917; The Gate of Ivory, 1920; The Buried Rose, 1932. Home: 2414 Linden Av. Office: First Nat. Bank Bldg., Balt. 2. Died June 19, 1957; buried Druid Ridge Cemetery.

NYCE, Benjamin Markley, clergyman; b. Cleve., Ded. 5, 1869; s. Rev. Benjamin Markley and Melissa (Hamilton) N.; student Oberlin Coll., 1885-87; A.B., Princeton, 1891; postgrad. U. Berlin, 1892, McCormick Theol. Sem., Chgo., 1892-94; D.D., Hanover Coll., 1909; m. Ursule Strong, Dec. 27, 1894. Ordained to ministry Presbyn. Ch., 1894; pastor, First Ch., Warsaw, Ind., 1894-96, First Ch., Lockport, N.Y., 1896-1904; pres. Talladega (Ala.) Coll., 1904-07; pastor First Ch., Muncie, Ind., 1907-20; later Lincoln, Neb., then Glendale, Cal. Address: Glendale, Cal. Died Dec. 28, 1934; buried Kingston Cemetery, Greensburg, Ind.

NYE, Reuben Lovell, educator; b. Dowagiac, Mich., Nov. 9, 1867; s. Benjamin F. and Arna A. (Lovell) N.; student U. Mich., 1896-98; B.S., Mich. State Agrl. Coll., 1912, M.Agr., 1921; m. Florence Helen Kinney, July 30, 1907; children—Franklin Kinney (dec.), Robert Lovell. Tchr. mathematics, high school, Battle Creek, Mich., 1898-1902; prin. high sch., Traverse City, Mich., 1902-08; tchr. mathematics Central High Sch., Detroit, 1908-10; asst. prof. agrl. edn. Mich. State Agrl. Coll., 1912-13; country agrl. agt. Porter County, Ind., 1913-14; dir. Agrl. Sch., Menominee, Mich., 1914-18; in U.S. service, promotion of sch. gardens, 1918-19; prof. agrl. teaching Syracuse U., 1919-20, dean Coll. of Agr., 1920-35; supt. Syracuse Univ. Farm, 1935-54, ret. Mem. Rural Life Assn. America, N.Y. State Agrl. Soc., Phi Kappa Phi, Theta Alpha. Republican. Methodist. Mason. Home: 2 Haven Ct., University Heights, Syracuse 10, N.Y. Died Aug. 30, 1956; buried Oakwood Cemetery, Syracuse.

NYQUIST, Carl, railway official; b. Chicago, Ill., Nov. 17, 1877; s. Carl Gustaf and Anna Matilda (Silfversvard) N.; ed. pub. schs., Chgo.; m. Nina E. Watts, June 12, 1906; 1 son, Eugene. Began as clk. treasury dept. C.,R.I.&P. Ry., Mar. 3, 1898, successively chief clk. to sec. of co., 1899-1910, asst. sec., asst. treas. and fed. treas. (during World War I.), 1910-18, sec. and treas., 1918-21, v.p., sec. and treas. since May 1, 1921, also dir., 1922-26 and 1934-—; pres. Consol. Ind. Coal Co.; v.p. and treas. Peoria Bur. Valley R.R.; ret. June 1, 1948. Mem. Art Inst. Chicago. Republican. Club: Union League. Home: 947 Lathrop Av., River Forest, Ill. Office: 139 W. Van Buren St., Chicago. Died Nov. 21 1959.

O

OAKLEY, Thornton, illustrator, mural painter; b. Pittsburgh, 1881; s. John M. and Imogen (Brashear) O.; grad. Shady Side Acad., Pittsburgh, 1897; B.S., U. of Pa., 1901, M.S., 1902 (both in architecture); studied art with Howard Pyle, Wilmington, Del., 1902-05; m. Amy Ewing, Mar., 1910; children—Amy (dec.), Lansdale. Illustrator and writer of articles in mags. since 1904. Mem. Phila. Water Color Club (sec. 1913-38, pres. since 1938); mem. jury of selection and of advisory com., dept. of fine arts, San Francisco Expn., 1915. Instr. drawing, U. of Pa., 1914-15; in charge dept. illustration, Phila. Museum Sch. of Industrial Art, Phila., 1914-19, and 1921-36; mem. jury of selection and award, Dept. of Fine Arts, Sesquicentennial Expn., Phila., 1926; spl. lecturer U. of Pa., Art Inst. Chicago, Metropolitan Museum of Art, Curtis Inst. (Phila.), Phila. Museum, etc. Chmn. of water color com. Phila. Art Alliance, 1917-36, sec., 1936-37, now dir.; mem. adv. council Art Assns. Phila., 1918. Represented in many pvt. and pub. collections in U.S. and in Phila. Museum, Pa. Acad. of Fine Arts, Wilmington Soc. of Fine Arts, Rehoboth Art League, Brooklyn Mus., Nat. Gallery, Library of Congress, Nat. Library of Brazil, British Mus. (London), Musée Pyrénéen (Lourdes, France), Musée de la Guerre, and Luxembourg Mus. (Paris). Chmn. com. of artists in charge of decoration of Phila. for Victory Loan campaign, 1919. Drawings of Hog Island Shipyard adopted by U.S. Govt. for foreign news service and reproductions sent to all parts of the world, 1918; industrial verse and drawings internationally distributed by Am. Fed. Labor. Designer and founder, 1935, of Oakley medal for achievement in creative art at Shady Side Acad., Pittsburgh, Phila. Museum School of Industrial Art, Phila., Sch. of Fine Arts of U. of Pa. Mem. William Penn Commemoration Com. (Phila.), 1932. Awarded Arthur Spayd Brooke memorial prize, U. of Pa., 1902; Beck prize water color, Phila. Water Color Exhbn. 1914; silver medal for water color, Panama Expn., 1915; 1st prize, Admiral Byrd Letter Contest by G. P. Putnam's Sons, 1931; decorated by the French Govt. with Palmes d'Officier d'Académie, 1931, and Chevalier of the Legion of Honor, 1949; cited by King Haakon VII of Norway for assistance to his country during fight for liberation, 1950; Philadelphia water color prize, Phila. Water Color Exhbn., 1935; awarded asso. membership for life in Franklin Inst., Phila., 1940; purchase prize for water color, Water Color Exhbn., Cape May, N.J., 1942. Mem. exec. com. Finnish Relief Fund Inc., 1940, and designer of Nat. Finnish Relief poster for Herbert Hoover; member exec. com. Norwegian Relief, Inc., 1940-46. Chairman Artists' War Relief Committee of Phila., 1941; pres. Art Council of Phila., 1942; mem. Mayor's com. for Victory, Phila., 1945; pres. Alliance Française, Groupe de Phila., since 1943; chmn. com. French societies, Phila., 1943-44. Chmn. exhbn. com. and trustee, Am. Swedish Hist. Museum, Phila., 1940-50. Philadelphia Water Color Club's Pennsylvania Week purchase prize, Harrisburg, 1950. Honorary member Pennsylvania Soc. of Miniature Painters, Internat. Mark Twain Soc., mem. Soc. of Illustrators, 1913-33, Wilmington Society Fine Arts, (emeritus) Sigma Xi. Clubs: Contemporary (president 1937-41), T-Square (prize membership, 1901), Alpin Français, Franklin Inn, University (Philadelphia, member board governors, 1944), Century Association (New York). Illustrator: Westward Ho!, 1920; Autobiography of Benjamin Franklin, 1926; Philadelphia (H. M. Lippincott), 1926; Folk Tales of Brittany (Elsie Masson), 1929; Awake America, 1934, and Six Historic Homesteads, 1935 (both by Imogen B. Oakley); and of following works by Amy Oakley: Hill Towns of the Pyrenees, 1923; Cloud-Lands of France, 1927; Enchanted Brittany, 1930; The Heart of Provence, 1936; Scandinavia Beckons, 1938; Behold the West Indies, 1941; Kaleidoscopic Quebec, 1947; Our Pennsylvania Keys to the Keystone State, 1950. Six mural panels in the Franklin Institute, Philadelphia, depicting epochs of science from alchemy to Franklin. With special permission of the secretary of war and secretary of the navy, visited war plants throughout U.S., and painted 16 pictures of Am. industries for war, for Dec. number, 1942, of Nat. Geographic Mag., also 16 paintings of Am. transportation vital to victory, for Dec. number, 1943; also 16 paintings of war-time science and research for Dec. number, 1945; engaged in indsl. paintings for Pa. R.R., Phila. Electric Co., Sun Oil Co., etc., since 1945. Author: Anthem, My Wondrous Land (music by Guy Marriner). Air raid warden, Radnor Twp., Pa., 1943-45. Home-studio: "Woodstock," Villa Nova, Delaware County, Pa. Died Apr. 4, 1953; buried Lower Merion Bapt. Churchyard, Bryn Mawr, Pa.

OATES, James Franklin, life insurance; b. Necedah, Wis., Dec. 22, 1870; s. James and Sarah (Froggatt) O.; Ph.B., Northwestern U., 1893; m. Henrietta M. Jennings, June 28, 1894; children—James F., Jr., Whitney J. Began active career as asst. sec. Central Dept. Y.M.C.A., Chicago, 1893, sec., 1895-1904; connected with Northwestern Mutual Life Insurance Co. since 1904; general agent for Chicago as member firm Hobart & Oates, Jan. 1911-May 1944. Trustee Northwestern Univ. since 1914, sec. board since 1918; awarded Alumni Achievement Medal by Alumni Assn. of Northwestern Univ., 1940; elected Life Trustee Northwestern Univ., 1946. Republican. Methodist. Clubs: University, Union League, Glenview; University (Evanston). Home: 2252 Orrington Av., Evanston, Ill. Office: 208 S. La Salle St., Chicago, Ill. Deceased.

OBERG, Erik, cons. editor Machinery; b. Vernamo, weden, Mar. 1, 1881; s. Andreas and Maria (Brostedt) O.; grad. Boras Tech. Coll., 1900; m. Emily A. Mitchell, Sept. 24, 1905 (dec. 1941); 1 son, Henry Valdemar; m. 2d, Helena E. Woodall, Aug.

25, 1941. Came to U.S., 1901, naturalized, 1908. Engr. with J. & C. G. Bolinders Co., Stockholm, 1900-01; in employ Pratt & Whitney Co., Hartford, Conn., 1901-03, Cincinnati Milling Machine Co., 1903; again with Pratt & Whitney until 1906; with Machinery since 1906, editor in chief, 1918-46, cons. editor, 1946—. Mem. bd. Industrial Press. Mem. Com. for Readjustment of Industries for War Work, 1918; War Industries Readjustment Com., 1919-20; John Ericsson Meml. Commn., 1915-25; chmn. editorial conf. N.Y. Business Publishers' Assn., 1924-25. Mem. Mfg. Engineering Com., WPB, 1943-45. Mem. Am. Soc. M.E. (treas. 1925-35). Soc. Automotive Engrs., Am. Soc. Swedish Engrs. Lutheran. Author: Handbook of Small Tools, 1908; Machinery's Handbook, 1914; Spur and Bevel Gearing, 1914; Spiral and Worm Gearing, 1914; Heat-treatment of Steel, 1914; Machinery's Encyclopedia (7 vols.), 1917; Developing a Gaging System, 1919; Shop Mathematics, 1920; Turret Lathe Practice, 1923; Elements of Mechanics and Machine Design, 1923. Home: 65 82d St., Bklyn. 9. Office: 90 Worth St., N.Y.C. Died Oct. 22, 1951.

OBERHARDT, William (o'ber-hard), portrait painter, illustrator, sculptor; b. Guttenberg, N.J., Sept. 22, 1882; s. William and Amalie (Waas) O.; student N.A.D., 1897-1900, Royal Acad. Fine Arts, Munich, Germany, 1900-03; m. Josephine Sonnleitner, Aug. 18, 1927; children—Rolland Bertram, Lorianne. Portrait painter, illustrator; represented in pvt. and pub. collections; spl. exhbn. portrait drawings Corcoran Gallery and Library of Congress, 2 yrs.; 4 portraits reproduced for permanent collection of Commn. of Fine Arts; executed portrait heads of numerous prominent people including Minnie Maddern Fiske, 1908; Emily Stevens, 1909; Hudson Maxim, 1910; Joseph Pennell, 1918; Charles Dana Gibson, 1919; Edwin H. Blashfield, 1919; Robert W. Chambers, 1920; President Harding, Henry Cabot Lodge, Joseph G. Cannon, Chief Justice Taft, 1921; Thomas A. Edison, 1923; Maj. Gen. James G. Harbord, 1924; Luther Burbank, 1925; Judge Elbert H. Gary, 1925; S. Parkes Cadman, 1926; also Professor Ludwig V. Herterich, 1927; Col. Edward M. House, 1926; Harry Emerson Fosdick, 1928; Walter Lippmann, 1931; Frank Weitenkampf, 1932; Henry Seidel Canby, 1934; William Green, 1935; Herbert Hoover, 1941; Henry J. Kaiser, 1945; Francis Joseph Cardinal Spellman, 1946; Clarence Birdseye, 1946; Gene Tunney, 1946; Paul de Kruif, 1946; Mayor William O'Dwyer, 1947; William C. Bullit, 1947; Bernard M. Baruch, 1949; Judge Harold Medina, 1949; Sir Willmott Lewis, 1949; Dr. Cornelius Packard Rhoads, 1949; Ezio Pinza, 1950; Ralph Bunche, 1950; Arthur Hays Sulzberger, 1950; A. J. Cronin, 1950; Edgar R. Murrow, 1950; John Foster Dulles, Herbert Hoover, Senator John J. Williams, Dr. Harry M. Archer, 1951; Senator Richard M. Nixon, 1952; Gen. Dwight D. Eisenhower, 1952; Henry Ford II, Harvey Firestone, Jr., 1953; Dr. Norman Vincent Peale, 1954; Atty. Gen. Herbert Brownell, Jr., 1957; John Gunther, 1958, many others. Commd. by U.S. Govt. to portray 25 mems. of Div. of Pictorial Publicity for records of archives of War Dept., Washington. Represented in N.Y. World's Fair Exhbn. Contemporary Art, 1939; by invitation, one man show Nat. Arts Club, N.Y.C., 1957, Soc. of Illustrators, 1958. Asso. N.A.D. Recipient award for sculpture N.A.D., 1956; distinguished career medal Soc. of Illustrators, 1956. Clubs: Art Directors (hon.), Society of Illustrators (life), Dutch Treat. Address: 538 2d Av., Pelham, N.Y. Died July 22, 1958; buried Ferncliff Cemetery, Hartsdale, N.Y.

OBERMANN, Julian J(oel), univ. prof., author; b. Warsaw, Poland, June 14, 1888; s. Judah Leo and Rachel (Weidenfeld) O.; Ph.D., U. of Vienna, 1915. Came to U.S., 1923, naturalized, 1931. Prof. Univ. of Hamburg, 1919-23; prof. Semitic philology, Jewish Inst. of Religion, N.Y. City, 1923-31; vis. prof., Hebrew Univ. of Jerusalem, 1929-30; prof. Semitic langs., Yale, since 1933; co-editor, Jour. of Biblical Lit., 1933-36; dir. Judaica research, Yale, since 1944; editor-in-chief Yale Judaica Series, since 1944, Sterling professor of Semitic Languages since 1950. Member Oriental Soc., Soc. Biblical Lit., Linguistic Soc., Archaeol. Inst. Am., Conn. Acad. Arts and Scis. Jewish religion. Author: Problem of Causality Among the Arabs, 1917; Philosophical and Religious Subjectivism of al-Ghazali, 1921; Studies in Islam and Judaism, 1932; Archaic Inscriptions from Lachish, 1938; Inscribed Tiles from the Synagogue of Dura, 1942; Islamic Origins, 1944; How Daniel Was Blessed with a Son, 1946; Ugaritic Mythology, 1948; Discoveries at Karatepe, 1948. Contbr. articles to professional jours.; research in Semitic philology, epigraphy, history and philos. of Islam. Home: 1217 Whitney Av., Hamden, Conn. Died Oct. 17, 1956.

OBERNDORF, Clarence Paul (ō'bērn-dôrf), psychiatrist; b. N.Y. City, Feb. 16, 1882; s. Joseph and Augusta (Hammerstein) O.; A.B., Cornell, 1904, M.D., 1906; grad. Bellevue Hosp., 1908; unmarried. Began practice at N.Y. City, 1908; instr. in neurology, Cornell U. Med. Sch., 1914-20; adj. neurologist, Bellevue Hosp., 1915-20; asso. psychiatrist, Mt. Sinai Hosp., 1925-39; editor Internat. Jour. Psycho-analysis since 1922; associate editor American Journal of Psychiatry, 1948; contbg. editor Psychoanalytic Review since 1937; clin. prof. psychiatry, Columbia U., 1936-49. Dir. Jewish Child Care Assn. of N.Y., Hillside Hosp. Recipient Samuel W. Hamilton Award, 1951. Mem. Am. Neurol. Assn., Am. Psycho-analytic Assn. (ex-pres.), N.Y. Psychoanalytic Soc. (ex-pres.), N. Y. Society Psychotherapy (ex-president), American Psychiatric Assn., Am. Psychopath. Assn. (president) New York Neurol. Society (ex-pres.), N.Y. Acad. of Med., N.Y. Psychiatric Soc., N.Y. Soc. for Clin. Psychiatry (ex-pres.), Bellevue Alumni Soc., Phi Kappa Tau. Club: Cornell. Author: The Psychiatric Novels of Oliver Wendell Holmes; Which Way Out; A History of Psychoanalysis in America. Contbr. on psychoanalytic and psychiatric subjects to technical jours. Address: 40 W. 59th St., N.Y.C. 19. Died May 30, 1954.

OBERTEUFFER, George (ō'bēr-toi-fēr), artist; b. Philadelphia, Pa., Oct. 31, 1878; s. George Herman and Sarah (Moulder) O.; student Lawrenceville Prep. Sch., 1890-96, Princeton, 1896-99; M.F.A., Art Inst. Chgo., 1933; m. Henriette Amiard, Dec. 1, 1905; children—Henriette Betty (Mrs. Paul Foley), Karl. Began as artist and painter, 1904; instr. painting, Art Inst. Chgo., Pa. Acad. Fine Arts. Served with Red Cross in France, 1917-18. Mem. Nat. Acad. Club: Nat. Arts (hon. life mem.). Represented at Brooklyn Museum, Duncan Phillips Gallery, New South Wales Nat. Gallery. Home: Gloucester, Mass. Died 1940.*

O'BRIEN, Denis Augustine, govt. ofcl.; b. Charlestown, Mass., Jan. 19, 1906; s. Dennis Edward and Elizabeth C. (Gill) O'B.; student High Sch. Commerce, Boston, 1919-23, Bentley Sch. of Accounting and Finance, Boston, 1929-30; corr. Am. U. Commerce, Chgo., 1926-28; m. Alice Margurite Levi, June 22, 1929; children—Hugh A., Alice Jane, Denise, Mark. Spl. delivery messenger Boston Post Office, 1923; warehouseman Western Electric Co., 1924; city letter carrier, Boston Post Office, 1925-38, post office insp., 1938-46, dep. 2d asst. postmaster gen., 1946-50; dir. budget and adminstrv. services Bureau of Transportation, Post Office Dept., 1950—. Democrat. Roman Catholic. Home: Ferry Mill, Marshfield, Mass. Office: Post Office Dept., Washington 25. Deceased.

O'BRIEN, Edward James, thoracic surgeon; b. Hatley, Wis., Apr. 28, 1887; s. James and Elizabeth (Hayes) O'B.; M.D., Detroit Coll. Medicine, 1909; m. Marion Robb, Nov. 11, 1911 (died 1946) m. 2d Marie Rasmussen, Aug. 18, 1958. Interne Harper Hosp., Detroit, and practiced medicine Detroit, 1911—, chief surgeon Herman Kiefer Hosp., 1922—, head div. chest surgery Harper Hosp., thoracic surgeon Detroit & Northville T.B Sanitarium; thoracic surgeon Am. Legion Hosp. (Battle Creek), Saginaw Co. Contagious Tuberculosis Hosp., 1926—, prof. surg. Wayne U., 1934—, cons. surgeon Mich. State T.B. Sanitarium 1938—, thoracic surgeon Lima Dist. T.B. Hosp., 1940—. Developed collapse therapy and other surg. methods for treatment t.b., also instigated Detroit program for early t.b. diagnosis and hospitalization; instrumental in obtaining state subsidies for tuberculosis patients. Pres. Mich. State Sanatorium Commn., 1930—. Mem. council Am. Assn. for Thoracic Surgery (pres.); fellow A.C.S., A.M.A.; mem. Am. Acad. Tuberculosis Phys. (pres.), Central Surg. Soc., Mich. and Am. Trudeau Soc., Detroit Acad. Surgeons, Wayne County Med. Assn., Mich. State Med. Assn. Contbr. numerous research papers to med. jours. Address: David Whitney Bldg., Detroit 26. Died Oct. 19, 1959.

O'BRIEN, George D., ex-congressman; b. Detroit, Jan. 1, 1900; s. John Patrick and Ellen (O'Donohue) O'B.; A.B., U. of Detroit, 1921, LL.B., 1924; m. Margaret Foley, Apr. 29, 1937; children—George D., Maureen, Joan, John P., Mary Ellen. Admitted to Mich. bar, 1924, and since practiced in Detroit; mem. 75th-79th and 81st-83d Congresses, 13th Mich. Dist. Del. Dem. Nat. Conv., 1944. Served in U.S. Army, Oct.-Dec. 1918. Democrat. Roman Catholic. Home: 1622 Lysander Av., Detroit. Died Oct. 25, 1957.

O'BRIEN, John P., lawyer; b. Worcester, Mass., Feb. 1, 1873; s. Patrick and Mary E. (Gibbons) O'B.; A.B., Holy Cross Coll., 1894, LL.D., 1920; M.A., Georgetown Univ., 1895, LL.B., 1897; LL.D., Fordham U., 1920; m. Helen E. C. Madigan, Oct. 6, 1908; children—Gerard J., James A., Lawrence J., John Gibbons, Helen E. (Betty). Practiced at N.Y. City, since 1897; asst. corp. counsel, N.Y. City, 1901-20, corp. counsel, 1920-22; surrogate of N.Y. County, 1922-32; elected Mayor of N.Y. City, Nov. 8, 1932; resumed law practice, 1934; dir. Starrett Corp.; pres. & dir. Western Hemisphere Corporation. Democrat. Delegate to Democratic National Conventions, Phila., 1936, Chicago, 1940, 1944. Trustee Ascension Ch.; chmn. Library Council, Holy Cross Coll.; member nat. com. Legion of Decency, Am. Bar Assn., N.Y. State Bar Assn. (jud. sect.), N.Y. County Lawyers Assn., Guild of Catholic Lawyers (cofounder and pres., 1928-39; mem. bd. govs. since 1928), Municipal Art Commn. Assos., Am. Irish Hist. Soc., Friendly Sons of St. Patrick, N.Y. (pres. 1927-28), Cath. Guardian Soc. (pres.), Catholic Charities Archdiocese of New York (dir.), Laymens League of Retreats (past pres.), Holy Name (exec. com. N.Y. Diocese), Cath. Big Brothers (cofounder) Tammany Society or Columbian Order (sachem). Knighted Equestrian Order of Holy Sepulchre by Patriarch of Jerusalem, 1931; commendatore Order of Crown of Italy, 1934. K.C. (ex-chmn. N.Y. Chapter; past dist. dept.; Internat. Mobilization Com., 1935), Elk. Clubs: City, Catholic, Manhattan, National Democratic, Wall Street, N.Y. Athletic. Home: 40 East 75th St., N.Y.C. 21. Died Sept. 22, 1951; buried Gate of Heaven, Hawthorne, N.Y.

O'BRIEN, Joseph John, ex-congressman; b. Rochester, N.Y., Oct. 9, 1897; s. John Joseph and Anna (Dolan) O'B.; student East Rochester pub. schs., S.S. Peter and Paul's Cath. Sch., St. Jerome's Coll., Kitchener, Ont., McGill U., Montreal; m. Mildred Marie Erway, Oct. 9, 1924. Chief constrn. insp. N.Y. Central R.R., 1919-38; mem. 76th to 78th Congresses, 38th N.Y. Dist. Professional heavyweight wrestler, 1919-26; professional football player to 1925. Served with USN, 1917-19. Mem. Am. Legion. Republican. Roman Catholic. K.C. Home: East Rochester, N.Y. Died Jan. 23, 1953; buried Holy Sepulchre Cemetery, Rochester, N.Y.

O'BRIEN, Kenneth, judge, b. N.Y.C., Mar. 15, 1895; s. Morgan J. and Rose (Crimmins) O'B.; student Newman School, Lakewood, N.J.; A.B., Yale, 1917; LL.B., Fordham U., 1922; m. Katherine Mackay, Sept. 21, 1922; children—Marie Louise, Katherine, Morgan J. Entered practice in New York, 1922; became mem. firm O'Brien, Boardman, Conboy, Memhard & Early, 1926; apptd. justice Supreme Court, N.Y., Feb. 1, 1934, elected, 1934, reelected for 14 yr. term, 1948. Del. Dem. Nat. Conv., 1928, 32. Served as capt. 306th F.A., 77th Div., AEF, 1917-19. Mem. Am., N.Y. State bar assns., Bar Assn. City N.Y., N.Y. County Lawyers Assn. Roman Catholic. Clubs: Yale, Catholic Club, Lawyers, Manhattan. Home: 28 E. 70th St. Address: 60 Centre St., N.Y.C. Died Jan., 1954.

O'BRIEN, Sister M. Raphael (Mary Elizabeth), a sister of St. Joseph; b. Monroe, Mich., 1857; d. Michael and Margaret O'Brien; student St. Mary's Acad., Monroe, Mich.; med. student U. Mich., 1890-92; M.D., Hahnemann Med. Coll., Chgo., 1893; student Polyclinic Sch., N.Y.C. The only Catholic nun in the world practicing medicine at this time; head of St. Camilus' Tng. Sch. for Nurses, in connection with Borgess Hosp., Kalamazoo, Mich. Address: Borgess Hosp., Kalamazoo, Mich. Died Jan. 13, 1923; buried Nazareth, Mich.

O'BRIEN, Patrick Henry, lawyer; b. Phoenix, Keweenaw County, Mich., Mar. 15, 1868; s. Patrck J. and Mary (Green) O'B.; grad. high sch., Calumet, Mich., 1887; LL.B., Northern Ind. Law Sch., 1891; m. Bessie Kelly, Jan. 23, 1897 (died Jan. 1921); children—Gerald K., (dec.), William D'Arcy (dec.), Mary L., Daniel P.; m. 2d, Florence E. Ingram, May 26, 1926 (dec. 1958). Admitted to Wis. bar, 1891, and began practice at Superior; moved to Calumet, 1899; village atty., Laurium, Mich., 1901-06; Dem. candidate for Congress. 12th Mich. Dist., 1908; judge Circuit Court, 1912-22; del. at large Dem. Nat. Conv., Balt., 1912, and seconded nomination of Woodrow Wilson for President; rendered opinion dissolving injunction in Mich. copper strike, 1913; settled in Detroit, 1922. Lecutrer on private corp., U. Detroit, 1923-32; as chief counsel of Am. Civil Liberties Union, Detroit branch, filed bill in Federal Court, attacking constitutionality of, and invalidating, Mich. Alien Registration Bill; candidate for gov. of Mich. at Dem. primaries, 1932, defeated for the nomination; elected attorney gen. of Mich. Nov. 1932, for term 1933-34; elected probate judge for Wayne County, 1939—, re-elected for term ending January 1, 1959; retired 1956. Mem. Jud. Council Mich., Am., Mich., Detroit bar assns.; hon. chmn. Detroit Chapter of Nat. Lawyers Guild. Catholic Lawyers Soc., Detroit Philos. Soc. Member K.C., Knights of Equity, Eagles. Clubs: Detroit Economic, Lecturer on legal, constitutional, social and economic subjects. Home: 7726 E. Jefferson Av. Office: Wayne County Bldg., Detroit. Died July 27, 1959.

O'BRIEN, Robert Lincoln, publisher; b. Abington, Mass., Sept. 14, 1865; s. Patrick and Lydia H. (Dunham) O.; A.B., Harvard, 1891; Litt.D., Dartmouth, 1922, Brown, 1924, Colby College, 1926, Boston U., 1927; m. Emily A. Young, Feb. 19, 1895. Personal sec. Grover Cleveland from his nomination in 1892 till Nov. 1895; Washington corr. Boston Transcript, 1895-1906, editor same 1906-10; pres., dir. Boston Pub. Co., also editor Herald until Dec. 31, 1928; chmn. U.S. Tariff Commn., Washington, 1931-37. Mem. adv. bd. Pulitzer Sch. of Journalism. Mem. Mass. Hist. Soc. Clubs: Gridiron, Cosmos, Metropolitan, Sulgrave (Washington); Merchants, Union, Middlesex (Boston). Home: Highlands, Washington. Died Nov. 1955.

O'BRIEN, Thomas Charles, lawyer; b. Brighton, Mass., June 19, 1887; s. Michael and Mary (O'Connor) O'B.; A.B., Harvard, 1908, student Harvard Law Sch., 1908-11; m. Julia M. Hartigan, Sept. 3, 1913;

children—Mary Joan, Katherine Margaret, Thomas Charles, Julia Mildred. Admitted to Mass. bar, 1911, and since practiced in Boston; mem. Bd. of Parole, Mass., 1913-16; dep. dir. of prisons, Mass. Commn. of Institutions, Boston, 1919-22; dist. atty. Suffolk Dist. of Mass., 1922-27; candidate, 1936, for v.p. of U.S., of "Union" Party (organized June 1936), 1941 and 1944. Adv. to U.S. Govt. Dels. to Internat. Labor Conf. Mem. Spl. Mass. R.R. Commn. since 1939; regional Counsel Brotherhood of R.R. Trainmen. Boylston prize orator, Harvard, 1908. Member Boston Bar Assn., Knights of Columbus, Mass. Catholic Order of Foresters, Ancient Order of Hibernians. Clubs: Boston City, Harvard (Boston); Hatherly Golf (Scituate, Mass.). Home: 76 Mapleton St., Brighton, Mass. Office: 11 Beacon St., Boston. Died Nov. 22, 1951; buried Holyhood Cemetery, Brookline, Mass.

O'BRIEN, Vincent, lawyer; b. Chicago, Dec. 12, 1897; s. John Edward and Agnes (Dwyer) O'B.; LL. B., Loyola U., 1920; m. Marion Purdy, Apr. 16, 1921. Admitted to Ill. bar, 1920, and since practiced in Chicago, Illinois; member of law firm Defrees, Fiske, O'Brien, Thomson & Simmons and predecessor firms, Chicago, 1928—; instructor law sch., Loyola U., 1925-27. Served ensign U.S. Navy, World War I. Mem. Am., Ill., Chgo. and Seventh Circuit bar assns., Am. Coll. of Trial Lawyers, Soc. of Trial Lawyers of Chicago (pres. 1946). Clubs: Law, Legal, The Attic, Ill. Athletic. Home: 1120 Lake Shore Dr. Office: 105 LaSalle St., Chgo. Died Dec. 1958.

O'BRIEN, William V(ollert) O., elec. mfg. exec.; b. Point Pleasant, W.Va., Nov. 18, 1900; s. William J. and Louise (Vollert) O'B.; grad. Va. Mil. Inst., 1922; m. Dorothy O. Taliaferro, Aug. 3, 1929; 1 son, William J., II. With Gen. Electric Co., 1922—, successively, test course, sales engr. S.E. dist., mgr. wire and cable dept., mgr. Central Sta. dept., asst. gen. mgr. apparatus sales, comml. v.p., 1950, gen. mgr. apparatus sales div., 1951, v.p., 1954, v.p., gen. mgr. apparatus sales div., 1954—. Mem. Am. Soc. Sales Execs., Newcomen Soc. Presbyn. Clubs: Mohawk (Schenectady); Engineers, Economic, Union League, Pinnacle (N.Y.C.); Scarsdale (N.Y.) Golf. Home: 50 Popham Rd., Scarsdale, N.Y. Office: 150 E. 42d St., N.Y.C. 17. Died June 21, 1958.

OCAMPOS, Bernardo, govt. ofcl. Paraguay; b. Villarrica, Paraguay, Aug. 20, 1898; s. José and Gregoria Ocampos; ed. Faculty of Law and Social Scis., Colegio Nacional, Villarrica; m. Maria L. Arbo; 2 children. Judge, Civil Ct. of First Instance, 1927-31; dep. Nat. Parliament, 1932; mil. judge with rank of major, Chaco War; prof. civil and comml. law procedure U. Asuncion since 1936; mem. governing body Faculty of Law and Social Scis. since 1945; now minister fgn. affairs. Pres. Coll. of Lawyers, 1945. Active in Nat. Republican Party. Address: Ministry of Foreign Affairs, Asuncion, Paraguay. Died July 17, 1953.*

OCHS, Milton Barlow (ŏx), b. Cin., Jan. 29, 1864; s. Julius and Bertha (Levy) O.; student Chickering Inst., Cin., U. Tenn.; m. Fannie Van Dyke, Apr. 26, 1893; children—William Van Dyke, Adolph Shelby, Margaret E. (Mrs. Theodore DeCue Palmer). Newsboy in Knoxville, Tenn., 1876; removed to Chattanooga, 1878, and entered service of elder brother (Adolph S.), then pub. Chattanooga Times, of which became v.p., mng. editor; gen. tourist agent passenger dept. Colo. Midland Ry., 1890, 91; again mng. editor Chattanooga Times, 1892-99, 1913-22; Sunday editor, later gen. mgr. Phila. Public Ledger, 1912-13; now v.p. Times Printing Co. Former exec. pub., controlling owner Nashville American, 1909-11; v.p. and chmn. exec. com. Chattanooga-Lookout Mountain Park (given to U.S. Govt. 1935); dir.Dixie Highway; former pres. Taft Meml. Hwy.; former pres. Lookout Mountain Scenic Hwy.; former chmn. Selective Service Bd. No. 3, Hamilton County, Tenn.; pres. Robert Burns Soc. of Chattanooga, Capt. 5th Tenn. Inf., Jan. 19, 1918; lt. col., Feb. 15, 1918; col. 4th Tenn. Inf., Nov. 23, 1918; resigned following Armistice. Elk. Comdr. N.B. Forest Camp Confederate Vets. (asso. mem.). Clubs: Mountain City Fairyland, Chattanooga, Half-Century (pres.); hon. mem. Kiwanis and Civitan. Home: Northcrest, Missionary Ridge. Office: Dome Bldg., Chattanooga, Tenn. Deceased.

OCHSNER, Edward H., surgeon; b. Honey Creek, Sauk County, Wis., Jan. 12, 1868; s. Henry and Judith (Hottiger) O.; B.S., U. of Wis., 1891; M.D., Rush Med. Coll., 1894; post-grad. study, Vienna, Leipzig, Hamburg, 1896-97; m. Julia I. Andersen, Sept. 2, 1899; children—Marion Louise (Mrs. Marion Pease), Herbert Edward, Alice Constance (Mrs. Homer Kieweg), Raymond Bertram. Intern Cook County Hosp., Chicago, 1894-95; attending surgeon St. Mary's of Nazareth Hosp., 1899-1903; attending surgeon Augustana Hosp., 1904-32, cons. surgeon since 1932. Adjunct prof. clin. surgery, Coll. of Physicians and Surgeons, Univ. of Illinois, 1900-16. Mem. Med. Advisory Bd. No. 3B, Selective Service, 1917-18. Pres. Ill. State Charities Commn., 1912-16. Fellow Am. Coll. Surgeons; mem. Chicago Med., Surg. and Pathol. socs., Ill. State Med. Soc. (pres. 1923-24), A.M.A., Southern Surg. Assn. Club: City. Author: Physical Exercises for Invalids and Convalescents; Chronic Fatigue Intoxication; Social Insurance and Economic Security; Social Security; Fundamentals of Personal Hygiene. Contbr. articles to med. and quasi-med. jours. Address: 3172 Sheridan Rd., Chgo. Died Jan. 22, 1956.

OCKERBLAD, Nelse Frederick (ŏk'ĕr-blăd), urologist; b. New York, N.Y., Nov. 27, 1881; s. Frederick Otto and Caroline (Olsen) O.; B.S., Hanover (Ind.) Coll., 1905; M.D., U. of Kan., 1916; m. Harriet Spencer McComb, June 10, 1907. Teacher phys. edn. in pub. schs. and colls., 1905-12; interne Phila. Gen. Hosp., 1916, Montreal Gen. Hosp., 1916-17; asst. prof. surgery, U. of Kan. Med. Sch., 1919-26, asso. prof., 1926-35, prof. clin. urology, 1935—; sr. attending urologist St. Luke's Hosp., Kansas City; cons. urologist U.S. Penitentiary, Leavenworth, Kan. Diplomate Am. Bd. Urology. Fellow Am. Coll. Surgeons, A.M.A.; mem. Southern Med. Soc., Am. Urol. Assn. (mem. exec. com. 1936-37), S.W. Branch Am. Urol. Assn. (past pres.), S.E. Branch Am. Urol. Assn., Kansas City Acad. of Medicine. Presbyterian. Rotarian. Author: Dispensary Urology, 1937; Urology for Nurses, 1938, Urology in General Practice, 1943; Surgical Urology, 1949. Contbr. many articles to professional jours. Home: 5559 Crestwood Dr., Kansas City 10. Office: Plaza Time Bldg., 411 Nichols Rd., Kansas City, Mo. Died May 23, 1954; buried Forrest Hill, Kansas City, Mo.

O'CONNELL, C(harles) Leonard, univ. prof., dean; b. Pittsburgh, Pa., Apr. 24, 1890; s. John H(enry) and Charlotte T(eresa) (Mullen) O'C.; Ph.G., Coll. Pharmacy, U. of Pittsburgh, 1912, A.B., Coll. Liberal Arts, 1916, Pharm.D., U. of Pittsburgh, 1929; Pharm. M., Philadelphia College of Pharmacy and Science, 1932; married Florence Sheridan, June 30, 1920 (died May 6, 1958); children—C(harles) Leonard, J(ohn) F(rancis) Regis, William S(heridan), Richard L(awrence). Apprentice in pharmacy (while attending high sch.), 1906; mdse. broker and mfrs. agent, 1916-22; instr. chemistry, U. of Pittsburgh, 1922-24, assistant prof. chemistry, 1924-26, prof. pharmacy since 1926, asso. dean, 1930-32, dean Sch. of Pharmacy 1932-46, now dean emeritus; pres., chmn. bd. O'Connell Pharmacy, Inc., 1952—. Mem. Com. on Revision of the U.S. Pharmacopoeia (1940-50). Chmn. bd. mgrs. Juvenile Detention Home, Allegheny Co., 1935-47; pres. Civic Club of Allegheny County, 1938-42. Mem. A.A.A.S., Am. and Pa. (pres. 1929-31), pharm. assns., Pa. Acad. Sci.; Fedn. Internat. Pharmaceutique, Kappa Psi (grand regent 1941-46), Omicron Delta Kappa, Phi Kappa, Phi Alpha Theta, Alpha Zeta Omega. Dem. Catholic. K.C. (4°). Clubs: Lions, Rotary Internat., Faculty (U. of Pittsburgh). Author: (with William Pettit) Manual on Pharmaceutical Law, 1938; (with Bernard F. Daubert) Manual on Pharmaceutical Technique, 1940. Manual on Pharmaceutical Latin (with Bernard F. Daubert), 1941. Home: 101 W. Steuben St., Crafton, Pitts. Died Sept. 1, 1958.

O'CONNELL, John Michael, Jr., editor; b. Bangor, Me., Sept. 2, 1895; s. John Michael and Sarah (Kavanaugh) O'C.; student U. Me., 1916-18; m. Esther Mary Kelly, Aug. 9, 1928; children—John Michael 3d, Sara Ann. Entered newspaper work, 1918; with Bangor Daily News, 1930—, beginning as city editor, mng. editor, 1933—, war corr., overseas, wrote daily Home Town column. Trustee U. Me., Orono, Bangor Pub. Library, Eastern Me. Gen. Hosp. Mem. journalism jury Pulitzer Awards. Served in U.S. Army, World War I. Recipient Medal of Honor, War Dept. Mem. N.E. Asso. Press Mng. Editors (pres., dir.). Roman Catholic. K.C. (4°), Rotarian. Home: 106 Congress St., Bangor. Office: Bangor Daily News, Bangor, Me. Died Nov. 19, 1955.

O'CONNELL, Michael John, clergyman; b. Chgo., Jan. 7, 1898; s. Patrick and Margaret (Mahoney) O'C.; student De Paul Acad., Chgo., 1912-16; M.A., St. Mary's Sem., Perryville, Mo., 1923; S.T.D., Collegio Angelico, Rome, Italy, 1925; LL.D., St. John's U., 1941. Ordained priest Roman Cath. Ch., 1923; dean of studies St. Mary's Sem., Perryville, 1925-26, pres., 1948—; dean of discipline Kenrick Sem., Webster Groves, Mo., 1926-31; head dept. of history Webster Coll., Webster Groves, 1926-31; v.p., prof. Am. history, also chmn. univ. council, dir. student activities De Paul U., Chgo., 1932-34, trustee, 1932—, dean of Coll. Liberal Arts and Sciences, 1934-35, pres., 1935-44; Superior of The Society of Priests of the Congregation of the Mission of Chgo., 1944-48. Democrat. K.C. Writes on religious subjects. Address: St. Mary's Seminary, Perryville, Mo. Died Dec. 29, 1958; buried St. Mary's Seminary.

O'CONNELL, Patrick Augustin, merchant; b. Lawrence, Mass., Feb. 13, 1871; s. Daniel P. and Catherine (Dolan) O.; ed. pub. schs.; LL.D. (hon.), Boston Coll.; m. Mary Frances O'Brien, Jan. 12, 1904; 1 son, Edmund Fabian (dec.). Connected with merc. business since 1890; president and owner E. T. Slattery Company, retail dry goods since 1907; director National Shawmut Bank, Union Savings Bank (bd. of investment), Boston Elevated Ry. (chmn. bd.), Boston Consol. Gas Company, Liberty Mut. Insurance Company; National Retail Dry Goods Association (advisory com.); past pres. Retail Trade Bd.; v.p., dir. Boston Chamber Commerce, Travelers' Aid Soc.; dir. Mass Med. Service Corp., Boston Municipal Research Bureau, Infants Hosp.; mem. bd. mgrs. Mass. Eye and Ear Infirmary; Charitable Irish Soc., Am. Irish Hist. Soc., mem. adv. council Boston College of Bus. Adminstrn. Trustee Boston U. Hon. mem. Beta Gamma Sigma (Alpha Chapter, Boston U.). Mem. Knights of Malta. Clubs: University, Algonquin, Clover. Home: Hotel Beaconsfield, Brookline, Mass. Office: 154 Tremont St., Boston. Died Mar. 6, 1958.

O'CONNOR, Frank Aloysius, lawyer; b. Independence, Ia., Aug. 2, 1875; s. Timothy and Ellen (Curran) O'C.; grad. Iowa City Acad., 1893; LL.B., State U. of Ia., 1898; special work in liberal arts dept., same univ.; m. May A. McNevin, Nov. 24, 1904 (dec.); children—Gerald F. (dec.), Charles E., Frank John; m. 2d, Mrs. Mabel Conover, Mar. 1939. Admitted to Ia. bar, 1898, practiced in New Hampton, Ia., until 1918 as mem. firm Smith & O'Connor; removed to Dubuque, 1918, mem. firm. Hurd, Lenehan, Smith & O'Connor, now O'Connor, Thomas, McDermott & Wright; co. atty. Chickasaw Co., 1902-06; U.S. dist. atty. No. Dist. of Ia., 1914-22; gen. counsel Farm Credit Adminstrn. (Omaha), 1934, gen. agent, Nov. 1934-June 1, 1937, also chmn. bd. dirs. 4 banks of Omaha unit of Farm Credit Adminstrn., resigned to resume law practice, 1937. Member Iowa Ho. of Rep., 1908-12; leader minority, 1911-12; mem. Gov.'s Council Nat. Def., 1917-18. Former president Dubuque Chamber of Commerce; member board of govs. Sch. of Religion, State U. of Ia.; dir. Archdiocese of Dubuque. Trustee Loras Coll., Dubuque, Ia. Mem. Am. Ia. State and Dubuque County bar assns. Decorated Knight Comdr. of St. Gregory, by Pope Pius XII, 1945. Catholic. Home: 300 N. Grandview Av. Address: 609 Bank and Insurance Bldg., Dubuque, Ia. Died June 24, 1954; buried Mt. Olivet Cemetery, Key West, Ia.

O'CONNOR, George Bligh, justice, Supreme Court of Alberta; b. Walkerton, Ont., Mar. 16, 1883; s. Frederic S. and Maria I. (Hamilton) O'C.; student Walkerton pub. and high schs., 1890-1900, Osgoode Hall, Toronto, 1903-05; LL.D. ex honoris causa, U. Alberta, 1952; married Hannah Margaret Fairlie, Oct. 28, 1913; 1 dau., Margaret Isabel Farnell. Called to bar, Ontario, 1905, Alberta bar, 1905, King's counsel, 1913; mem. firm, Griesbach, O'Connor & O'Connor, 1905-40; bencher Law Soc., Alberta, 1936-40; judge, Supreme Court of Alberta, since 1941, chief justice since 1950; chmn. Western Labor Bd., 1943; chmn. Industrial Disputes Inquiry Commn., Alberta and B. C. coal strike, 1943; chmn. Wartime Labor Relations Bd., Ottawa, 1943-47; chmn. Can. Labor Relations Bd., 1948-52. Mason, Forester. Home: 36 St. George's Crescent, Edmonton, Alberta, Can. Died Jan. 13, 1957.

O'CONNOR, John J., ex-congressman; b. Raynham, Mass.; s. Daniel B. and Elizabeth A. (Gorman) O'C.; A.B., Brown U.; LL.B., Harvard; m. Grace Brennan, Apr. 26, 1916 (dec.); children—John, Daniel, Robert, Harrison. Began practice at N.Y.C.; mem. N.Y. Assembly, 1921-23; mem. 68th to 75th Congresses, 16th N.Y. Dist.; pub. of Washington News Digest. Mem. Phi Kappa. Club: National Press. Office: 26 Broadway, N.Y.C.; also Washington Bldg., Washington. Died Jan. 26, 1960.

O'CONOR, Herbert Romulus, ex-senator; b. Baltimore, Md., Nov. 17, 1896; s. James P. A. and Mary A. (Galvin) O'C.; A.B., Loyola Coll., Baltimore, 1917, LL.D., 1924; LL.B., U. of Md., 1920, LL.D., 1939; LL.D., Villanova Coll., 1937, Georgetown, 1939, Washington Coll., Chestertown, 1939; m. M. Eugenia Byrnes, Nov. 24, 1920; children—Herbert Romulus, Mary Patricia, Eugene F., James P., Robert. Admitted to Md. bar, 1919, and since practiced in Baltimore; asst. state's atty. for Baltimore, 1921-22, state's atty., 1924-34; people's counsel to Pub. Service Commn., 1923-24; atty. gen. State of Md., 1935-39; gov. State of Md., 1939-47; U.S. senator from Md., 1947-53; labor adv. Balt. city govt., 1953-59; counsel Washington office, Am. Merchant Marine Inst., 1953—. Served in U.S. Naval Reserve. Chmn. Govs. Conf., Asheville, N.C., 1942 (mem. exec. com., chmn. govs. com. on law enforcement and adminstrn. of justice, 1941). Pres., Council of State Govts. in Chgo., 1943. Mem. Am. Bar Assn. (com. Communist tactics), Md. State Bar Assn. Nat. Pros. Attorneys Assn. (past pres.), Baltimore City Bar Assn., Am. Legion, Vets. Fgn. Wars, Phi Kappa Sigma. Democrat. Roman Catholic. K.C. Clubs: Metropolitan (Washington); Merchants, Baltimore Country. Home: 101 E. Highfield Rd., Balt. 18. Office: 10 Light St., Balt. 2. Died Mar. 1959.

O'CONOR, Norreys Jephson, author; b. New York, N.Y., Dec. 31, 1885; s. John Christopher and Maria Jephson (Post) O.; A.B., Harvard, 1907, A.M., 1911; m. Grace Corson, June 27, 1917 (dec.); children—Moira (dec.), Cathleen (Mrs. H. Epstein); m. 2d, Evangela Waller. With F. A. Stokes, pubs., later with John Lane Co., 1908-10; asst. English, Harvard, 1911-13; instr. English, Radcliffe Coll., 1918-19; asst. prof. English, Grinnell Coll., 1922-23; asso. prof.

English lit., Mt. Holyoke Coll., 1923-24; asso. prof. English composition, Bryn Mawr Coll., 1924-26. Lecturer at univs., including Harvard, Yale, Columbia, 1919-22. Mem. P.E.N. Republican. Episcopalian. Author: The Child's Hansel and Gretel, 1909; Celtic Memories and Other Poems, 1914; Beside the Blackwater, 1915; The Fairy Bride, 1916, rev. 1926; Songs of the Celtic Past, 1918; Battles and Enchantments, 1922; Changing Ireland, 1924; There Was Magic in Those Days, 1929; Memoir, prefacing Letters of Maarten Maartens; Godes Peace and the Queenes, 1934; A Servant of the Crown, 1938; Poems from the Handpress of Douglas Howell, 1947; Late Offering, 1952; also mag. articles. Contbr. weekly article Presenting Your Allies, to Los Angeles Times, 1942-44. Address: 512 Plaza Rubio, Santa Barbara, Cal. Died Oct. 24, 1958.

ODELL, Arthur Lee, clergyman; b. Excelsior Springs, Mo., Nov. 12, 1877; s. Joseph Titus and Lorena (Meyer) O.; A.B., Mo. Valley Coll., Marshall, 1904, D.D., 1914; B.D., Union Theol. Sem., 1907; m. Anne Elliott, July 9, 1908; children—Cary Elliott, Joseph Meyer (dec.). Ordained ministry Presbyn. Ch., U.S.A., 1905; pastor Madison Sq. Ch., San Antonio, 1907-10, First Ch., Frankfort, Ind., 1910-11, Kings Highway Ch., St. Louis, 1911-18; pres. Henry Kendall Coll., Tulsa, 1918-20; pastor First Ch., Phoenix, 1920-22, Westminster Ch., Detroit, 1922-26, Highland Park Ch., Los Angeles, 1926-28, Beverly Hills Community Ch., 1928-34, House of Hope Ch., St. Paul, 1934-42, Michillinda Ch., Pasadena, 1942-45; staff minister, Pasadena Presbyn. Ch., 1947—. Mem. bd. dirs. Monte Vista Groves Homes for Ministers and Missionaries. Clubs: Cleric (St. Louis); Rotary (Beverly Hills); Wranglers (Detroit); Chi Alpha (Los Angeles). Home: 443 S. Roosevelt Av., Pasadena, Cal. Died Apr. 25, 1956; buried Forest Lawn Cemetery, Los Angeles.

O'DELL, De Forest, univ. professor; b. Atlanta, Jan. 1, 1898; s. Thomas Allen and Ella Elizabeth (Haywood) O'D.; A.B., Butler University, 1921; A. M., Columbia University, 1922, Ph.D., 1935; married Margaret Caroline Godley, June 18, 1927; children—Mary (Mrs. John R. Adams), Natalie (Mrs. W. J. Peeler). On staff Indianapolis Star, 1916-17, Crawfordsville (Ind.) Review and Evansville (Ind.) Courier, Indianapolis Star, 1920-21; writer various N.Y. City newspapers, 1921-22; editorial staff Richmond (Ind.) Item, 1922-23; asst. prof. Lombard Coll., 1923-25; mem. editorial staff Indianapolis Star, 1925-26; instr., asst. prof. and prof. journalism, Butler U., 1925-31; staff mem. Asso. Press, N.Y. City, 1931-32; dean, Drake Sch. Journalism, N.Y. City, 1933-38; staff mem. Edgewood Park Jr. Coll., 1933-36; asso. prof. Western Ill. State Coll., 1938-44, Ill. State supervisor, Div. Vocational Rehabilitation, 1945-46; head dept. journalism, Butler U., 1946—; on leave from Butler U. to serve on fgn. staff World Literacy, Inc., as head dept. journalism, Osmania University, Hyderabad, India, 1954-56. Director of fund-raising campaigns for hospitals, schs., colls. and univs., 1944-45. Served with Ind. N.G., 1917, trans. to U.S. Field Arty., served U.S. and with A.E.F., 1917-19. Member American Association University Professors, Am. Legion, Sigma Delta Chi, Phi Delta Kappa, Sigma Chi, Sigma Tau Delta. Republican. Presbyterian. Mason (32°). Clubs: Indianapolis Literary, Torch, Indianapolis Press. Author: History of Journalism Education in the United States, 1935. Contributor articles in field to mags. Home: 4651 Rookwood St., Indpls. Died June 19, 1958; buried Crown Hill Cemetery, Indpls.

O'DONNELL, George Anthony, clergyman; b. Boston, Mass., Nov. 22, 1899; s. George Francis and Mary Anthony (Powers) O'D.; ed. Pub. Latin Sch., Boston, 1912-16, Boston Coll., 1916-17, St. Andrew on the Hudson, Poughkeepsie, 1917-21; A.B., Weston Coll., 1921-23; A.M., Woodstock Coll., 1923-24; Weston Coll., 1926-30, Ph.D., St. Louis U., 1931-35. Entered Society of Jesus, 1917; instr. math., Georgetown U., 1924-26; ordained to priesthood, 1929; dean of grad. sch., Boston Coll., since 1935; chmn. math. dept., Boston Coll., since 1935; dir. seismological observatory, Weston Coll., 1935-40. Mem. Math. Assn. of Am., Am. Math. Soc., London Math. Soc., Assn. of Math. Teachers in New England. Jesuit Science Assn. (chmn. math. sect., pres. 1937-38). Address: Boston College, Chestnut Hill 67, Mass. Died Jan. 1, 1952; buried Weston College Cemetery, Weston, Mass.

ODUM, Howard Washington (ŏd'ŭm); b. Bethlehem, Walton County, Ga., May 24, 1884; s. William Pleasants and Mary Ann (Thomas) O.; A.B., Emory Coll., 1904; A.M., U. of Miss., 1906; Ph.D., Clark U., 1909; Ph.D., Columbia U., 1910; Grant Squires Award, Columbia University, 1910; LL.D., Emory, U., 1931; Litt.D., Coll. of the Ozarks, 1935; LL.D., Harvard, 1939; L.H.D., Clark U., 1941; m. Anna Louise Kranz, Dec. 24, 1910; children—Eugene Pleasants, Mary Frances, Howard Thomas. Co-prin. Toccopola (Miss.) Sch., 1904-05; instr. U. of Miss., 1905-08; fellow Clark U., 1908-09; research expert, Phila. Bur. Municipal Research, 1910-12; asso. prof. ednl. sociology, 1912-15, prof., 1915-19, supt. Univ. Summer Sch. for Teachers, U. of Ga., 1916-19; dir. bur. of home service camps and camp cities, Southern Div. Am. Red Cross, 1918; dean Sch. Liberal Arts, Emory U., 1919-20; Kenan prof. sociology, U. of N.C. 1920-54, dir. Sch. Pub. Welfare, 1920-32; dir. Inst. for Research in Social Science, University of N.C., 1924-44; visiting professor, U. of Ill., winters, 1936, 1937. Walker-Ames prof., U. of Wash. 1942; visiting prof. and Silliman fellow, Yale U., 1946-47. Mem. and assistant director President's Research Committee on Social Trends, 1929-33; chief of social science div. Century of Progress Exposition, Chicago, 1933. Chairman N. C. Emergency Relief Adminstr., 1933-35; chmn. N.C. Civil Works Adminstr., 1933-34; chmn. N.C. Commn. on Interracial Co-operation, 1933-35.; mem. N.C. State Planning Board, 1935-54; pres. N.C. Conf. for Social Service, 1936-37; president Commission on Interracial Cooperation, 1937-44; pres. Southern Regional Council, 1944-46. Pres. Am. Sociol. Soc., 1930. Fellow A.A.A.S. (mem. exec. com. 1939-43); fellow, Soc of Am. Historians. Recipient Catholic Conf. of the South Award, 1943; Bernays Award, 1945; Am. Jersey Cattle Club Master Breeders Award, 1948; recipient of the O. Max Gardner award, 1953. Democrat. Methodist. Author: Social and Mental Traits of the Negro, 1910; Systems of Public Welfare, 1925; Southern Pioneers, 1925; Sociology and Social Problems; 1925; The Negro and His Songs, 1925; Public Welfare and Social Work, 1926; Negro Workaday Songs, 1926; Am. masters of Social Sci., 1927; Man's Quest for Social Guidance, 1927; Rainbow Round My Shoulder, 1928; Wings on My Feet, 1929; Introduction to Social Research, 1929; An American Epoch, 1930; Cold Blue Moon, 1931; Southern Regions of the United States, 1936; American Regionalism, 1938; American Social Problems, 1939; American Democracy Anew, 1940; Alabama Past and Future: The States at Work, 1941; Race and Rumors of Race, 1943; Understanding Society, 1947; The Way of the South, 1947; American Sociology, 1951. Editor: Social Forces; contbr. to learned and lit. jours. Home: 2 Brierbridge Lane, Chapel Hill, N.C. Died Nov. 8, 1954; buried Chapel Hill.

OENSLAGER, George, research chemist; b. Harrisburg, Pa., Sept. 25, 1873; s. John and Harriet (Freaner) O.; grad. Phillips Exeter Acad., 1890; A.B., Harvard, 1894; A.M., 1896; m. Ruth Alderfer, July 15, 1939. Chemist S. D. Warren & Co., Cumberland Mills., Me., 1896-1906; research chemist Diamond Rubber Co., 1906-12, B. F. Goodrich Co., 1912-20, 22-40; tech. adviser Yokohama Rubber Co., Japan, 1922. Trustee Akron Art Inst. Awarded Perkin medal for development in vulcanization, 1933; also Charles Goodyear Medal, 1948. Fellow Inst. Rubber Chemistry; mem. Am. Chem. Soc., Inst. Chem. Engrs., Instn. of Rubber Industry. Republican. Episcopalian. Clubs: Portage Country, University (Akron). Conducted experimental lab. 1940-56. Oenslager award, Japan, established, 1958. Home: 85 N. Wheaton Rd., Akron 13, O. Died Feb. 5, 1956; buried Glendale Cemetery, Akron, O.

OESTREICHER, John C(ahill) (ō'strīk-ẽr), journalist; b. Brooklyn, Sept. 22, 1905; s. Walter M. and Kathleen E. (Cahill) O.; grad. Erasmus Hall High Sch., Brooklyn; student Columbia, 1923-24; m. Zazelle Elizabeth Murphy, Nov. 4, 1927; children—Walter M. (dec.), David John, Anthony. Mem. staff Brooklyn Daily Times, 1923; joined Internat. News Service, 1924, London corr., 1927-29, news editor, 1930, fgn. editor, 1931-34, dir. fgn. service since 1934; writer daily news column, In View of the News. Mem. Assn. Am. Corrs., Fgn. Press Assn., Phi Delta Theta, Sigma Delta Chi. Roman Catholic. Clubs: Anglo-American Press (Paris and Rome); Bonnie Briar Country (Larchmont, N.Y.). Author: The World is Their Beat, 1945. Contbr. to numerous mags. and periodicals. Home: 60 Linwood Rd., New Rochelle, N.Y. Office: 235 East 45th St., N.Y.C. 17. Died Dec. 16, 1951; buried Woodlawn, N.Y.

OFFERMANN, Henry F., theologian; b. Hanover, Germany, July 11, 1866; s. John and Margaret (Ahlf) O.; ed. Gymnasium, Stade, Hanover, Germany; Theol. Sem., Kropp; came to U.S., 1889; post-grad. course in Semitics, U. Pa.; D.D., Muhlenberg Coll., 1908; m. Emily Saalmann, Feb. 13, 1890; children—Henry C., Magdalene, Emily, Irma. Ordained to Luth. ministry; German sec. Evang. Luth. Ministerium of Pa., 1900-08; prof. N.T. theology Luth. Theol. Sem., Phila., 1910-44, prof. emeritus, 1944—. Editor Lutherisches Kirchenblat, 1905-10; co-editor The Lutheran Church Review. Mem. bd. dirs. Mary J. Drexel Home, Phila. Author: Introduction To the Epistles and Gospels of the Church Year; Theological Studies; The Jesus of the New Testament; The Life and Work of Paul; Commentary on Matthew. Home: 355 East 19th St., N.Y.C. 3. Died May 21, 1953.

OFSTIE, Ralph Andrew, naval officer; b. Eau Claire, Wis., Nov. 16, 1897; grad. U.S. Naval Acad., 1918; m. Joy Bright Hancock, USN (ret.), former dir. of WAVES, Aug. 16, 1954. Commd. ensign, United States Navy, and advanced through the grades to vice admiral, 1952; served in U.S. ships Chattanooga and Whipple during World War I; asst. naval attaché, Am. Embassy, Tokyo, Japan, 1935-37; operations officer, staff of Adm. William F. Halsey, Jr. (on flagships Saratoga and Yorktown), 1939-41; naval attaché for air and asst. naval attaché, Am. Embassy, London, 1941-42; on staff comdr. in chief U.S. Fleet, 1942; aviation officer, staff of Adm. Chester W. Nimitz (Pacific Fleet), 1942-43; comd. U.S.S. Essex, 1943-44, participating in aerial attacks on Rabaul, invasion of Gilbert Islands, raid on Kwajalein (all 1943), operations against Truk, attacks on Tinian, Saipan and Guam, invasion of Marshall Islands, and First Battle of Philippine Sea (all 1944); comdr. carrier division, 1944-45, participating as comdr. carrier task group in amphibious assault on Anguar and Peleliu (Palau Group), and as 2d in command, under Rear Adm. C.A.F. Sprague, of escort force in Battle for Leyte Gulf; comdr. of another carrier div., Jan.-Apr. 1945; became chief of staff to Vice Adm. Patrick N. L. Bellinger, comdr. Air Force, Atlantic, Apr. 1945. Senior Naval Member, U.S. Strategic Bombing Survey, Japan, 1945-46. Member, Military Liaison Committee to the Atomic Energy Commission, 1946-50; comdr. carrier div. five, and Task Force 77 (Korea), 1950-51; chief of staff Naval Forces Far East, 1951-52; comdr. First Fleet, 1952-53; deputy chief Naval Operations (Air), 1953-54; became commander of Sixth Fleet, Dec. 1954. Decorated Navy Cross; D.S.M. and Gold Star; Silver Star Medal; Legion of Merit and three Gold Stars with Combat V; Gold Cross of Merit (Poland), White Cross of Naval Merit, 2d class (Spain). Home: 3516 N. Valley St., Arlington 7, Va. Address: Navy Dept., Washington 25. Died Nov. 18, 1956; buried Arlington Nat. Cemetery.

OGBURN, William Fielding, educator; b. Butler, Ga., June 29, 1886; s. Charlton Greenwood and Irene Florence (Wynn) O.; B.S., Mercer U., Ga., 1905, LL.D., 1932; A.M., Columbia, 1909, Ph.D., 1912, Stanford fellow, 1938; LL.D. U. N.C., 1946, U. Chgo., 1956; m. Rubyn Reynolds, 1910; children—Howard R. (dec.), Fielding. Teacher Morton Sch. for Boys, 1905-06; asst. prin. Darlington Sch., 1906-08; instr. economics, politics and history Princeton, 1911-12; prof. sociology and econs. Reed Coll., 1912-17; prof. sociology U. Wash., 1917-18; examiner and head of cost of living dept. Nat. War Labor Bd., 1918-19; spl. agt. U.S. Bur. Labor Statistics, 1919; prof. sociology Columbia, 1919-27; prof. sociology, U. Chgo., 1927-33, Sewell L. Avery distinguished service prof. sociology, 1933-51, emeritus prof., 1951—; vis. prof. sociology, Fla. State U., 1953-59; lectr. U. Calcutta, 1952; vis. prof. Nuffield College, Oxford, 1952-53; prof. Am. Hist. and Insts., Indian Sch. Internat. Studies, U. Delhi, India, 1956-57; dir. research President's Research Com. on Social Trends, 1930-33; dir., mem. Consumers Adv. Bd., NRA, 1933; spl. advisor Resettlement Adminstrn., 1936; research cons., mem. science com. Nat. Resources Com., 1935-43; chmn. Census Adv. Com. (chmn. 1940-53), Psychoanalytic Inst. (chmn. bd. 1938-53). Editor Journal Am. Statis. Assn., 1920-26. Recipient Centennary award Northwestern U., 1952. Fellow Am. Statis. Assn. (pres. 1931); mem. Internat. Statis. Inst., Population Assn., Am., Am. Sociol. Soc. (pres. 1929), Social Science Research Council (chmn. 1937-39), A.A.A.S. (v.p., 1932), Am. Philos. Soc., Am. Acad. of Arts and Science, Internat. Sociol. Inst., Society for History Technology (president, 1959), Sigma Alpha Epsilon. Clubs: Quadrangle; Cosmos (Washington). Editor: Recent Social Changes, 1933; Technological Trends and National Policy, 1937; Technology and International Relations, 1949. Author: Progress and Uniformity in Child Labor Legislation, 1912; Minimum Wage and the Increased Cost of Living, 1918; Social Change, 1922; The Social Sciences, 1927; American Marriage and Family Relationships, 1928; Economic Development of Post War France, 1929; You and Machines, 1935; Social Characteristics of Cities, 1937; co-author: Sociology, 1940; The Social Effects of Aviation, 1946; Technology and the Changing Family, 1953; also various articles on sociol., econ. and statis. subjects. Contbg. or asso. editor: Am. Jour. of Sociology, Social Forces, Metron, Sociologus. Home: 1661 Crescent Pl., Washington 9. Died Apr. 27, 1959; buried Rome, Ga.

OGDEN, Dunbar Hunt (ŏg'dĕn), clergyman; b. New Orleans, La., Apr. 12, 1878; s. William Frederick and Elizabeth (Hunt) O.; prep. edn., Chamberlain Hunt Acad. and Tulane High Sch.; A.B., Southwestern Presbyn. U. (now in Memphis, Tenn.), 1898; B.D., Presbyn. Div. Sch., Clarksville, Tenn., 1900; D.D., Davidson (N.C.) Coll., 1908; honorary LL.D., Southwestern (Memphis), 1948; honorary Litt.D., Maryville College, 1949; married Grace Augusta Cox, Oct. 10, 1901; children—Dunbar Hunt, Grace Augusta, Warren Cox, Elizabeth Hunt, Margaret Ten-Eyck, Frederick William, Esther Jonté. Ordained Presbyn. ministry, 1900; pastor First Ch., Columbus, Miss., 1900-05, First Ch., Knoxville, Tenn., 1905-09, Central Ch., Atlanta, Ga., 1909-18, Second Ch., Louisville, Ky., 1918-20, Government Street Ch., Mobile, Ala., 1920-30, Napoleon Avenue Ch., New Orleans, 1930-50; inaugurated, maintained weekly radio missionary sta. WSMB, New Orleans. Moderator of Synod of Georgia, 1916, Synod of Alabama,

1923; Synod of Louisiana, 1942; teacher of apologetics, Louisville Theological Seminary, 1919-20; lecturer Columbia (S.C.) Theol. Sem., 1924; preacher at Culver Mil. Acad. and at various colls. and univs., etc. Spl. teacher and lecturer Ft. McPherson, Camp Gordon and Camp Taylor, World War. Member Kappa Alpha. Democrat. Mason. Clubs: Round Table, Rotary. Author: The Heart of Mary; Wedding Bells; also articles pub. in ch. mags. Home: 4516 S. Debigny St., New Orleans 15. Died Apr. 12, 1952; buried Lafayette Cemetery No. 1, New Orleans.

OGG, Frederic Austin, polit. science; b. Solsberry, Ind., Feb. 8, 1878; s. William R. and Sarah S. O.; Ph.B., DePauw Univ., 1899, LL.D., 1928; A.M., Indiana Univ., 1900, Harvard, 1904, Ph.D., 1908; m. Emma Virginia Perry, Sept. 9, 1903. Instr. history, Indianapolis Manual Training High Sch., 1900-02, Ind. U., 1902-03; fellow and asst. in history, Harvard, 1903-08; instr. history, Boston Univ. and Simmons Coll., 1905-09; asst. prof. history, Simmons Coll., 1909-13, asso. prof., 1913-14; asso. prof. polit. science, 1914-17, prof. polit. science, 1917-48, emeritus since 1948; chmn. grad. div. of social studies, 1925-39, U. of Wis. Mem. Phi Beta Kappa, Phi Kappa Phi, American Historical Assn., American Political Science Assn., Am. Econ. Assn., American Sociol. Soc., Acad. Polit. Science, Am. Soc. Internat. Law, Wis. State Hist. Soc., Am. Assn. Univ. Profs., Am. Council of Learned Socs., Council on Foreign Relations, Am. Council on Public Affairs, Sociol. Soc. Czechoslovakia (hon.). Asso. editor Am. Polit. Science Rev., 1916-26, mng. editor since 1926; pres. Am. Polit. Science Assn., 1941. Republican. Author: The Opening of the Mississippi—A Struggle for Supremacy in the American Interior, 1904; Fordham's Personal Narrative of Travels in the West, 1906; A Source Book of Mediaeval History, 1908; Social Progress in Contemporary Europe, 1912; Governments of Europe, 1913, revised edit., 1920; Life of Daniel Webster, 1914; Economic Development of Modern Europe, 1917, revised edit., 1926; National Progress, 1907-17 (The Am. Nation, Vol. 27), 1917; The Old Northwest, and Reign of Andrew Jackson (Chronicles of America, Vols. 19, 20), 1919; National Governments and the World War (with C. A. Beard), 1919; Intro. to Am. Gov. (with P.O. Ray), 9th rev. edit., 1948; Essentials of Am. Gov. (with Ray), 1932, rev. edits., 1936, 40, 43, 47; Builders of the Republic (The Pageant of America), 1927; Research in Humanistic and Social Sciences, 1928; English Government and Politics, 1929, revised edits., 1936, 39; European Governments and Politics, 1934, revised edit., 1939; Modern Foreign Governments (with H. Zink), 1949. Editor Century Political Science Series. Clubs: University (Madison); Cosmos (Washington). Address: 1715 Kendall Av., Madison, Wis. Died Oct. 23, 1951; buried Madison.

OGILVIE, Clarence Cooper (ō'gil-vĭ), educator, lawyer, planter; b. Bellbuckle, Tenn., Mar. 20, 1874; s. Jasper and Josephine (Smith) O.; prep. edn., Webb School, Bellbuckle; student Vanderbilt U., 1892-93, U. Chgo., 1895-96; m. Jessie Clay Wright, July 26, 1899; 1 dau., Fay Ogilvie (Mrs. Alston Boyd Wade). Prof. English and Greek, high sch., Pine Bluff, Ark., 1896-99; admitted to Tenn. bar, 1901, since practiced at Memphis; mng. dir. Goodwyn Inst., ednl. instn., 1906-46, now dir. emeritus; dir. and atty. Memphis Bank & Trust Co. Mem. Bd. of Edn., Memphis, 1905-10, pres., 1908. Four-minute speaker, World War. Dir. Am. Platform Guild, Memphis Internat. and Inter-Am. Center. Mem. Memphis Bar Assn., A.L.A., Am. Lyceum and Chautauqua Assn., Tenn. Library Assn., Delta Kappa Epsilon. Democrat. Presbyn. Mason. Odd Fellow. Clubs: Rotary (gov. dist. 16, 1931-32, del. internat. convs. Ostend, Belgium, 1927, Vienna, 1931, Seattle, 1932, Boston, 1933, Detroit, 1934, Mexico City, 1935, St. Louis, 1943), Executives. Author: Guaranteed Success. Home: 2899 Iroquis Rd. Office: Goodwyn Inst. Bldg., Memphis 3. Died May 19, 1959.*

OGILVIE, Walter Ellsworth, railway pres.; b. Bklyn., June 15, 1864; s. Peter Egerton and Hannah J. (Post) O.; LL.B., Columbia, 1886; M.A. (hon.), Hamilton; m. Abby Leah Blood, 1889 (dec.); children—George Egerton (dec.), Walter Ellsworth, Geoffrey Airlie, John W. G., Mrs. Marianne Leah Rogers. In ry. business since 1907; dir. Internat. Tel. & Tel. phone & Telegraph Corp., Mexican Telephone & Co. Mem. New York C. of C. Republican. Baptist. Clubs: India House, Sleepy Hollow (New York); Royal Thames Yacht (London); Havana Yacht (Havana, Cuba). Home: Oscawana-on-Hudson, N.Y. Office: 89 Broad St., N.Y.C. Died Sept. 1, 1956.

OGLESBY, Nicholas Ewing (ō'g'lz-bĭ), chemical engineer, registered patent agent; b. in Wythe County, Va., May 25, 1892; s. John Thompson and Emma Montgomery (Painter) O.; student Emory and Henry Coll., Emory, Va., 1909-11; A.B., U. of Va., 1913; A.M., 1917, Ph.D., 1929; m. Mary Louise Sandidge, Nov. 4, 1920; children—Nicholas Ewing, John Thompson, 2d. High sch. teacher sci. and mathematics, 1913-15; asst. in chemistry, U. of Va., 1915-17; jr. chem. engr., Aluminum Co. of America, 1917; teaching fellow U. of Va., 1919-20; research chemist Glamorgan Pipe and Foundry Co., 1920; chief munitions dept., chem. div., Chem. Warfare Service, 1920-24, asst. chief chem. div., 1924-29; tech. dir. Behr-Manning Corp., mfrs. coated abrasives and spl. products, 1929-45; technical consultant, mgr. of Patent Dept. 1945—, bd. dirs., 1954—. Served Ordnance Dept., 2d lt. Chem. War Service, U.S. Army, 1918. Fellow A.A.A.S.; mem. Am. Chem. Soc., Am. Inst. Chem. Engrs. Mem. New York Acad. of Sciences, Eastern New York Section of Am. Chemical Soc. (Chmn.), 1943-45, S.R. in N.Y. State, Alpha Chi Sigma, Raven Soc. (U. Va.). Republican. Presbyn. Mason (32°, Shriner). Club: Country (Troy). Joint inventor of tear gas grenades used by police and airplane smoke curtain used by Army and Navy; inventor abrasive processes and products. Home: 181 Pinewoods Av., Troy, N.Y. Office: Behr-Manning Corp., Troy, N.Y. Died Mar. 8, 1957; buried Spring Hill Cemetery, Lynchburg, Va.

OGLESBY, Woodson Ratcliffe, ex-congressman; b. Shelby County, Ky., Feb. 9, 1867; student law Ill. Wesleyan U.; married; children—Frances Leewood, Woodson Ratcliffe, Kate. Practiced at Yonkers, N.Y.; mem. N.Y. Assembly, 1906; mem. 63d and N.Y. Vol. Inf., Spanish-Am. War, 1898. Democrat. 64th Congresses, 24th Dist. N.Y. Served as pvt. 71st Home: Mohegan Park, Yonkers, N.Y. Died Apr. 30, 1955.

O'HARA, Edwin Vincent, archbishop; b. Lanesboro, Minn., Sept. 6, 1881; s. Owen and Margaret (Nugent) O'H.; student St. Thomas Coll., St. Paul, Minn., 1898-1900; St. Paul Sem., 1900-05; Catholic University of America, 1910-11; Institut Catholique, Paris, 1918; LL.D., University of Notre Dame, 1917, St. Francis Xavier Univ., N.S., 1948. Ordained priest Roman Catholic Church, 1905; asst. pastor St. Mary's Cathedral, Portland, Ore., 1905-12, pastor, 1912-20; Supt. of Schools, Archdiocese of Portland, 1905-20; pastor Eugene, Ore., 1920-28; dir. rural life bur., Nat. Catholic Welfare Conf., 1920-30; bishop of Great Falls, Mont., 1930-39; bishop of Kansas City, Mo., 1939-56; 1st bishop Kansas City-St. Joseph Diocese, 1956—. Assistant at the Pontifical Throne, 1949; designated Archbishop "ad personam" by Pope Pius XII, 1954. Instr. Catholic U. of Am., 1929. Chaplain U.S. Army, 1918. Chairman Industrial Welfare Commn. of Ore., 1914-18; Episcopal chmn. social action dept. Nat. Catholic Welfare Conf., 1936-42; chairman Episcopal Committee on Confraternity of Christian Doctrine in charge revision of Baltimore Catechism, and Am. translation of Bible; 1934—. Established Nat. Catholic Rural Life Conf., 1923. Trustee Catholic U. of America. Author: Catholic Pioneer History of Oregon, 1911; Church and the Country Community, 1925. Contbr. to America, Commonweal, Jour. of Religious Instrn., Catholic World, Ecclesiastical Rev., Cath. Engy. Address: P.O. Box 1037, Kansas City 41, Mo. Died Sept. 11, 1956; buried Kansas City.

O'HARE, Thomas C(ourtney), business exec.; b. Boston; s. James and Alice (Courtney) O'H.; A.B., Boston Coll., 1914; M.B.A., Harvard, 1916; LL.B., Northeastern U., 1925; m. Deborah Marie O'Hare, June 8, 1952. Propr. O'Hare-Lewis, Boston, since 1935; v.p., dir. Araban Coffee Co., Inc., 1948—; treas., dir. N.E. Forestry Service, Inc., since 1939; dir. N.E. Electric System. Trustee several pvt. trusts. Served in Inf., U.S. Army, 1917-19, O.T.C., 1918. Mem. Boston and Mass. bar assns., Newcomen Soc. Eng., Boston Athenaeum. Republican. Roman Catholic. Clubs: Harvard, Algonquin (Boston). Home: Longwood Towers, Brookline, Mass. Office: 40 Central St., Boston 9. Deceased.

OHRSTROM, George Lewis, business exec.; b. Ford River, Mich., Aug. 16, 1894; s. John Richard and Christians (Boursche) O.; A.B., U. Mich., 1918; m. Elizabeth Jackson Burroughs; children—Ricard Riggs, George Lewis, Emma Magelen. Chmn. bd. Dover Corp., Carlisle Corp. Served as 2d lt. USAAF, World War I. Mem. Phi Delta Epsilon, Delta Chi. Republican. Lutheran. Clubs: Bond, University (N.Y. C.); Round Hill Golf (Greenwich); Racquet (Chgo.). Home: The Plains, Whitewood, Va. Office: 40 Wall St., N.Y.C. 5. Died Nov. 9, 1955.

OLD, Howard Norman, sanitary engr.; b. Phila., Pa., Aug. 17, 1890; s. Abner Howard and Kathryn Jeffries (Hunsicker) O.; grad. Germantown Acad., Phila., Pa., 1908; m. Mary Bennett, Apr. 11, 1918. Civil engr. with cons. firms, Phila., 1910-12; mining engr., Nevada, 1912-13; sanitary engr. Phila. City Health Dept., 1914-17; U.S. Pub. Health Service, Fort Riley-Camp Funston Zone, Kan., 1918-19; assigned to malaria control operations in various southern states, U.S.P.H.S., hdqrs. Memphis, Tenn., 1919-25; sanitary engr. in charge of shellfish sanitation activities in Middle Atlantic States, Baltimore, Md., 1925-28; dist. engr. of P.H.S. dist. No. 4, Memphis, Tenn., 1928-29, hdqrs. New Orleans, 1929-39; charge engring. activities incident to interstate travel, nation-wide, U.S.P.H.S., Washington, District of Columbia, 1939-48; liaison officer U.S. P.H.S. with various other federal agencies, 1948-50; sanitary engr. cons. branch of health, U.S. Indian Service since 1950; through grades from jr. asst. sanitary engr. (2d lt.), 1918, to sanitary engr. dir. (col.), 1944; commd. corps. of P.H.S. br. of Armed Forces since 1945. Mem. Am. Soc. of C.E., Fed. Sewage Works Assn., Am. Pub. Health Assn., Conf. of State Sanitary Engrs. (sec.-treas. 1940-48), Nat. Geog. Soc., Commd. Officers Assn. of U.S.P.H.S. Presbyterian. Author numerous papers prepared and presented before techn. groups engaged in sanitary engring. and pub. health work. Widely Known for improvements effected in living conditions of Am. Indians. Home: 6629 32d St. N.W., Washington 15. Office: 4130 Dept. of Interior, Washington 25. Died May 7, 1953; buried Germantown Ivy Hill Cemetery, Phila.

OLDS, Ransom Eli, automobile mfr.; b. Geneva, O., June 3, 1864; s. Pliny Fisk and Sarah (Whipple) O.; student high sch., Lansing; D. Eng. (hon.), Mich. State Coll., Mich. Coll. Mining and Tech.; D.Sc., Kalamazoo Coll.; m. Metta U. Woodward, June 5, 1889; children—Gladys Marguerite (Mrs. Gladys O. Anderson), Bernice E. (Mrs. C. S. Roe). A pioneer in automobile business; built the first 3-wheeled horseless carriage, 1886; brought out a practical 4-wheeled automobile, 1893, pres. Reo Motor Car Co., 1904-24, chmn. bd., 1924-36. Dir. Kalamazoo College, Hillsdale Coll. Donor Science Hall to Kalamazoo Coll., engring. bldg. to Mich. State Coll., club house to the affiliated women's clubs, civic social welfare house to City of Lansing, etc. Mason (33°, K.T., Shriner), Knight of Holy Sepulchre. Baptist. Clubs: Detroit, Detroit Athletic, Detroit Yacht, Detroit Boat; Congressional (Washington); City, Country (Lansing). Home: Lansing, Mich.; (winter) Daytona Beach, Fla. Died Aug. 26, 1950.

O'LEARY, Paul Arthur, dermatologist, syphilologist; b. Brooklyn, N.Y., Nov. 11, 1891; s. Jeremiah J. and Anna Belle (Coy) O'L.; student Dartmouth Coll., 1910-11; M.D., Long Island Coll., 1915; m. Ruth Youmans, June 18, 1921; children—Paul Arthur, Patricia. Interne Long Island Coll. Hosp., 1915-16; associate sect. on dermatology, Mayo Clinic, Rochester, Minn., 1917-24, head sect. on dermatology and syphilology since 1924; prof. of dermatology, Mayo Foundation Grad. Sch., U. of Minn., since 1924. Diplomate Am. Bd. Dermatology and Syphilology. Fellow Am. Coll. of Physicians; mem. Southern Minn. Med. Assn., Minn. Dermatol. Soc., Chicago Dermatol. Soc., Am. Dermatol. Assn. (pres. 1946), A.M.A. (chmn. sect. on dermatology, 1936-37), Pan-Am. Medical Association, A.A.A.S., Minnesota Academy Medicine, Minnesota Academy of Science, Minnesota State Medical Society, Soc. for Investigative Dermatology, Dermatol. Conf. Miss. Valley; former mem. National Advisory Health Council; mem. Cooperative Clin. Group, Am. Acad. of Dermatology and Syphilogy (pres. 1938-39), Am. Assn. Univ. Profs., Sigma Xi, Alpha Kappa Kappa, Beta Theta Pi; hon. mem. several foreign socs. Sec. gen., 10th Internat. Congress of Dermatology and Syphilology. Editor in Chief: Archives of Dermatol., 1947—. Home: 225 7th Av. S.W. Office: Mayo Clinic, Rochester, Minn. Died July 20, 1955; buried Oakwood Cemetery.

O'LEARY, William Doris, priest and educator; b. Augusta, Ga., Aug. 31, 1895; s. Thomas Joseph and Katherine (Doris) O'L.; student U. of Ga. (Athens), 1916-17; B.S., M.D., U. of Ga. Med. Sch., 1921; M.A., St. Louis U., 1931. Interne Cambridge (Mass.) City Hosp. and Boston City Hosp., 1921-23; in practice pediatrics, N.Y. City, 1923-25; ordained R.C. priest, 1934; president Spring Hill (Ala.) College, 1938-46; dean, Loyola U. Sch. of Dentistry 1948—, regent 1953—. Dir. radio station WWL, Loyola; dir. Mobile Red Cross Chapter; dir. Community Chest (Mobile); chmn. State (Ala.) Merit System Council of Department Public Welfare; member of Mobile County Personnel Board. Chmn. health com., Nat. Conf. of Catholic Charities, 1939, 44; pres. and mem. advisory com., Social Agencies, Mobile, Ala.; dir. C. of C. Mem. Alpha Omega Alpha. Democrat. Contbr. to Am. Jour. of Psychology, Am. Jour. of Pediatrics, Kan. State Med. Jour. Asso. editor, Thought, 1937-39. Address: Loyola University, New Orleans. Died Feb. 1, 1955.

OLESON, John Prince, banker; b. Bloomingdale, Ill., July 21, 1873; s. Charles Wilmot and Abbie (Bartlett) O.; ed. pub. schs., Lombard, Ill.; m. Annie Elizabeth Merrell, Sept. 6, 1906; children—Frances Cady, Marjorie Prince, Barbara Merrell. With First National Bank, Chicago, since Dec. 7, 1889, v.p., 1916-34, chmn. bd., 1934-39, dir. since Jan. 1920. Mem. Ill. Commandery Mil. Order Loyal Legion. Home: 2441 Marcy Av., Evanston, Ill. Died Nov. 4, 1952.

OLIN, Franklin W., business exec.; b. Woodford, Vt., Jan. 9, 1860; s. Truman and Sarah Ann Olin; C.E., Cornell U., 1886; m. Mary Mott Moulton, May 28, 1889; children—Franklin W. (dec.), John Merrill, Spencer Truman. Mechanic in designing knitting mill machinery, constrn. of black powder mill; dir. Olin Industries, Inc., First Nat. Bank & Trust Co., Alton, Ill., Ill. State Bank, East Alton, Ill.; pres. East Alton Pub. Service Co., Winchester Repeating Arms Co., Equitable Powder Mfg. Co. Trustee Cornell U. Mem. Am. Soc. M.E. Home: 1128 State St., Alton, Ill. Died May 21, 1951; buried Oak Grove Cemetery, St. Louis County.

OLIVER, Augustus Kountze; b. Pittsburgh, Pa., July 19, 1881; s. George Tener and Mary Dorothea

(Kountze) O.; prep. edn. Shady Side Acad., Pittsburgh, and St. Paul's School, Concord, N.H.; A.B., Yale, 1903; LL.D. hon., U. of Pittsburgh, 1946; m. Margaretta Wood, Nov. 12, 1907; children—Joseph Wood, Augustus K. (dec.), Margaretta Oliver Schroeder, Henry William, George S. II, John Bennett, Janet Oliver de Camp. Began as reporter Pittsburgh Chronicle Telegraph (owned by father), 1903; advt. mgr. same and Pittsburgh Gazette Times, 1906-09, secretary both, 1919-20, vice president, 1910-27; director Pittsburgh Consolidation Coal Co., Scholastic Corp., Dollar Savings Bank; dir. Insulmastic Corporation of America, Western Allegheny Railway Company. Mem. City Council, 1919-21. Trustee Shady Side Academy, Carnegie Institute of Tech. (secretary), Carnegie Inst. (sec.), Pittsburgh Chapter American Red Cross. Member Psi Upsilon, Wolf's Head Soc. (Yale). Republican. Episcopalian. Clubs: Duquesne, Pittsburgh Golf, Fox Chapel Golf (Pitts.); Yale (N.Y.C.). Home: Fox Chapel Rd., Pitts. 38. Office: Chamber of Commerce Bldg., Pitts. Died Oct. 15, 1954; buried Homewood Cemetery, Pitts.

OLIVER, Edward Allen, dermatologist; b. Crestline, O., Apr. 15, 1883; s. Ernest Allen and Carrie (Miller) O.; A.B., Kenyon Coll., Gambier, O., 1905; M.D., Rush Med. Coll., 1909; m. Bertha Montgomery, Dec. 30, 1911; children—Mrs. James B. Handy, Richard M. Began practice at Chicago, 1910; professor emeritus dept. of dermatology and Syphilology, Northwestern U. Med. Sch.; sr. dermatologist emeritus St. Luke's Hosp.; cons. dermatologist to Passavant, Vets., Wesley, Swedish Covenant and St. Francis Hosps.; cons. dermatologist U.S. Vets, Hines Hosp., Chicago; American Academy Dermatology and Syphilology (pres. 1946-47), Society for Investigative Dermatology; American Medical Assn., Chicago Medical Soc. Served as capt. Med. Corps, U.S. Army, 1918-19. Mem. Am. Dermatol. Assn. (pres. 1951-52), Chgo. Dermatol. Soc. pres., 1923-24, 1939-40. Inst. Medicine, Psi Upsilon, Nu Sigma Nu. Episcopalian. Club: University. Author numerous articles on dermatology. Home: 1161 Spruce St., Winnetka, Ill. Office: 55 E. Washington St., Chgo. Died Nov. 5, 1957.

OLIVER, Edwin Letts, mining engr.; b. San Francisco, Nov. 9, 1878; s. William Letts and Carrie (Brown) O.; student coll. of mines U. Cal., 1900, LL.D., 1945; m. Minnie Giffin Walker, Sept. 23, 1905; children—Roberta (Mrs. F. L. Greenlee), William, Mary (Mrs. A. F. Shannon), Edwin Letts. Various surveying jobs in several mines, 1900-03; surveyor, engr. North Star Mines Co., Grass Valley, Cal., 1903-06, research, designer builder two cyanide plants, 1906-10; operator Union Hill Mines, Grass Valley, 1914-17; pres. Idaho Maryland Mines Group, 1925-50; established Oliver Continuous Filter Co., San Francisco, 1910; pres. Oliver United Filters, Inc., 1928-54; merged with The Dorr Co. in 1954 to form Dorr-Oliver Inc., founder-chmn., 1954. Recipient James Douglas (gold) Medal for distinguished achievement in nonferrous metallurgy. Mem. Am. Inst. Mining and Metall. and Petroleum Engrs., Mining and Metall. Soc. Am., Chem. Metall. and Mining Co. of S. Africa, Soc. of Golden Bear, Sigma Xi, Delta Upsilon, Sigma Gamma Epsilon. Republican. Episcopalian. Clubs: Engineers, Bohemian (San Francisco); Claremont Country (Oakland); Tahoe Yacht. Home: 60 King Av., Piedmont, Cal. Office: 260 California St., San Francisco 11. Died 1955.

OLMSTEAD, Frank Robert, highway research engr.; b. Uniontown, Pa., Oct. 28, 1904; s. Harry R. and Bertha N. (Bowser) O.; B.S., Waynesburg Coll., 1928; M.S., U. Mich., 1930; m. Sarah Jenkins, Dec. 17, 1934. Research engr. Mich. State Highway Dept., 1929-34, engr. field testing in charge soil research, design and inspection secondary rds., design ednl. exhibits for engring. convs. and expns., spl. tng. programs field and lab. insps., 1934-43; sr. soils specialist, engr. soils U.S. Bur. Pub. Rds., 1943-51; supervising highway phys. research engr., asst. chief soil sect., 1951-54, chief soils branch, 1954-57, supervisory highway research engineer, 1957—; chmn. dept. of Soils, Geology and Found., Nat. Research Council, 1954—. Mem. sub-committee Standards for Basic Data of President's Water Resource Commn., 1950. Recipient Meritorious Service award Dept. Commerce, 1958. Registered profl. civil engr., Mich., Dist. Columbia. Mem. American Society of Photogrammetry, Assn. Asphalt Paving Technologists (past dir., pres., 1953), Nat. Research Council (chmn. com. surveying and mapping soils in-place for engring. purposes 1943-54), Am. Soc. C.E., Am. Soc. Testing Materials, Am. Assn. State Hwy. Ofcls., Sigma Xi, Sigma Gamma Epsilon. Mason. Contbr. tech. jours. Home: 3503 S. Wakefield St., Arlington 6, Va. Office: Bureau of Public Roads, Washington 25. Died Apr. 2, 1958; buried Uniontown, Pa.

OLMSTED, Frederick Law, landscape architect; b. Staten Island, N.Y., July 24, 1870; s. Frederick Law and Mary Cleveland (Perkins) O.; A.B., Harvard Univ., 1894; studied landscape architecture under his father; M.A., (hon.), Tufts Coll., 1926; m. Sarah Sharples, March 30, 1911; one daughter, Charlotte (Mrs. Robert Lee Gill, Jr.). Began as practicing landscape architect, 1895; mem. Olmsted Bros., Brookline, Mass., 1895-1950; landscape architect Met. Park System of Boston, 1898-1920, of Roland Park Company, Baltimore, Baltimore Park Commission, 1902-17. Sage Foundation Homes Company, Forest Hills, L.I., Palos Verdes Estates, Calif.; mem. commn. on improvement of Washington, 1902; mem. board supervising architects of the group plan, Cleveland, 1912; mem. com. on emergency constrn., War Industries Bd., May 1917-July 1918; mgr. town planning div. of U.S. Housing Corp., July 1918-May 1919; mem. Nat. Capital Park and Planning Commn., Washington, D.C., 1926-32; dir. of state park survey for Calif. Park Commn., 1929, and 1945-50; collaborator Nat. Park Services and Bur. of Reclamation Survey of Colo. River Basin, 1941—; member board of expert advisors to Nat. Park Service for Yosemite National Park, 1929-40, 51-56. An incorporator Am. Acad. in Rome, 1905, mem. council until 1949. Designed pub. parks, municipal improvements, subdivisions, pvt. and instnl. grounds in many cities. Instr. landscape architecture, 1901-03, prof., 1903-14, Harvard U. Mem. Nat. Commn. of Fine Arts, 1910-18; chmn. exec. com. Nat. Conf. on City Planning, 1910-19; gov. Am. City Planning Inst.; exec. bd. Am. Civic Assn.; fellow Am. Soc. Landscape Architects (past pres.); mem. Nat. Inst. Arts and Letters; N.A., 1929, A. I.A. (hon.), English Town Planning Inst. Awarded gold medal by Am. Acad. Arts and Letters and Nat. Inst. Arts and Letters, 1949, George Robert White medal, Mass. Hort. Soc., 1951, C. A. Pugsley gold medal, Am. Scenic Historic Preservation Society, 1954; Conservation Service award, United States Dept. Interior, 1956. Club: Sierra (hon. v.p.). Author report on restoration of scenery at Niagara Falls, 1907-08; prepared plan for conservation Redwoods; also reports and articles on parks, municipal improvements, city planning and landscape architecture. Home: 2303 Middlefield Rd., Palo Alto, Cal. Died Dec. 25, 1957.

OLMSTED, James Montrose Duncan, educator; b. Lake City, Ia., May 21, 1886; s. Jeptha Montrose and Ada Maria (Duncan) O.; A.B., Middlebury (Vt.) Coll., 1907, D.Sc., 1942; B.A., Oxford U., Eng. (Rhodes Scholar, 1908-11), 1911, M.A., 1914; A.M., Harvard, 1917, Ph.D., 1920; m. Evangeline Harris, June 30, 1927. Vice-prin. Spring Valley (N.Y.) High Sch., 1907-08; prof. natural sci. Shorter Coll., Rome, Ga., 1911-12; asst., later asso., prof. of biology Richmond (Va.) Coll., 1912-15; Austin teaching fellow Harvard, 1916-17, asst., 1919-20; asst. prof., later asso. prof. physiology U. Toronto, 1920-27; prof. physiology U. Cal., 1927-53, prof. emeritus, 1954-56. Served as pvt. Base Hosp. No. 7, U.S. Army, 1917-18; 2d lt. San Corps, 1918-19. Senior fellow Com. for Relief in Belgium, 1931. Fgn. corr. mem. Société Philomathique (Paris). Fellow A.A.A.S.; mem. Am. Physiol. Soc., Am. Assn. History Medicine, Soc. Exptl. Biology and Medicine, Delta Kappa Epsilon, Phi Beta Kappa, Sigma Xi. Author: Claude Bernard, Physiologist, 1938; Francois Magendie. Physician and Physiologist, 1945; Charles-Édouard Brown-Sequard, Nineteenth Century Neurologist and Endocrinologist, 1947; (with E. H. Olmsted) Claude Bernard and the Experimental Method in Medicine, 1952; (with others) Macleod's Physiology in Modern Medicine, 1924-47, Macleod's Laboratory Manual, 1924, Bard: Medical Physiology, 1956. Contbr. to sci. jours. Elected active artist mem. San Francisco Art Assn. (water-colors), 1939. Recipient French Acad. Scis. prix Binoux, 1949; French Acad. Medicine prix de Martignoni, 1953. Home: 2853 Buena Vista Way, Berkeley 8, Cal. Died May 26, 1956; buried Sunset View Cemetery, Berkeley.

OLNEY, Albert J(ackson), horticulturist; b. Fremont, Mich., Apr. 15, 1888; s. Bert John and Alice Maude (Beem) O.; B.S., Mich. State Coll., 1913, M.H., 1920; S.M., U. of Chicago, 1925; m. Lydia Marie Branstrom, July 8, 1914; children—Charles Bert, Robert Branstrom. Sci. and agrl. teacher, Greenville (Mich.) High Sch., 1913-14; horticulturist, Theodore N. Vail Agrl. Sch., Lyndon, Vt., 1914-16; horticulturist, U. of Ky., since 1916, asst. prof., 1916-26, asso. prof. 1926-28, prof. hoticulture since 1928, head dept. horticulture since 1930. Fellow A.A.A.S.; mem. Am. Soc. for Hort. Sci., Am. Pomol. Soc., Ky. Acad. Sci., Sigma Xi. Presbyterian. Home: 240 Tahoma Rd., Lexington 1, Ky. Died June 29, 1958.

OLSEN, Thomas Siegfried, business exec.; b. Brooklyn, N.Y., June 14, 1884; s. Thorvald and Sophie (Aletta) T.; student New York Prep. Sch., 1913-15, New York Univ., 1915-19; m. Gunhild S. Swenson, Feb. 27, 1914 (dec. May 1944); children—Thomas S., Albert Gierding, Norman Thorvald. Asst. auditor, General Baking Co., New York, N.Y., Oct. 1913, exec. vice pres. since 1945. Lutheran. Home: Undermountain Rd., Salisbury, Conn. Office: 420 Lexington Av., N.Y.C. 17. Died Dec. 12, 1956; buried Kensico Cemetery, Valhalla, N.Y.

OLSON, Axel Ragnar, prof. chemistry; b. Hälsingborg, Sweden, Feb. 6, 1889; s. Nels and Ingrid Sophia (Nordfeldt) O.; B.S., U. of Chicago, 1915; Ph.D., U. of Calif., 1917; m. Hanna Kinell, Aug. 22, 1919; children—William John, Peter Andrew; came to U.S., 1891, naturalized citizen, 1896. Fellow Nat. Research Council, 1919-22; asst. prof. of chemistry, U. of Calif., 1922-26, asso. prof., 1926-30, prof., 1930—. Served as lt., C.W.S., U.S. Army, A.E.F., 1918-19. Guggenheim fellow, 1929-30; mem. A.A.A.S., Am. Chem. Soc., Phi Beta Kappa, Sigma Xi, Alpha Chi Sigma, Alpha Sigma Phi. Club: Faculty (Berkeley). Home: 2696 Cedar St., Berkeley 8, Cal. Died Dec. 22, 1954; buried Sunset View Cemetery, Berkeley.

OLSON, Carl Walter, educator; b. N.Y.C., May 31, 1898; s. Gustaf and Augusta (Harstrom) O.; grad. Irving Sch., Tarrytown, N.Y., 1920; B.S., Wesleyan U., Middletown, Conn., 1924; m. Rae-Alcha Furman, Sept. 16, 1925; 1 son, William Furman. Tchr., registrar Irving Sch., 1924-25; mgr. paper dept. Union Selling Co., Cin., 1925-26; headmaster Irving School since Feb. 1, 1933. Chmn. Recreation Commn.; formerly chmn. Taxation Commn., North Tarrytown. Served with USN, 1917-19; duty at Newport (R.I.) Navy Yard and on U.S.S. Falcon (Seagoing Mine Sweeper No. 28) until hon. disch. Mem. com. on secondary schs., Wesleyan U., also mem. alumni council and ex-chmn. scholarship com. for New York and suburbs; mem. Wesleyan Westchester Assn.; mem. exec. com. North Tarrytown Civic and Business Men's Assn. Mem. Am. Legion, Delta Kappa Epsilon (ex-pres. Westchester Soc.). Republican. Episcopalian. Club: Delta Kappa Epsilon (New York); Young Men's Lyceum, Tarrytown Lions, Briar Hills Country. Address: Irving School, Tarrytown, N.Y. Died May 24, 1953.

OLSON, Ernst William, editor, author; b. Finja Parish, Sweden, Mar. 16, 1870; s. Johannes und Johanna (Gran) O.; brought to Am., 1878; B.A., Augustana Coll., Ill., 1891, L.H.D., 1926; M.A., Bethany Coll., Kan., 1899; m. Anna Elizabeth Strand, Dec. 20, 1899 (dec.); children—Irving E. W., Adele E. (Mrs. Clarence Hogberg), Eunice E., Herbert William Leroy, Alice Virginia; m. 2d, Mrs. Hannah Stock, June 10, 1930 (died 1937); m. 3d, Mrs. Hannah Morris Brown, Sept. 29, 1940. Editor Fostrelåndet, Chgo., 1897-1904, Observer, Rock-Island, 1892-94, Nya Pressen, Moline, 1893-96, Svenska Tribunen, Chgo., 1900-05; office editor with The Engberg-Holmberg Pub. Co., Chgo., 1906-11; office editor Augustana Book Concern, Rock Island, ofcl. pub. house Augustana Synod, 1911-49; editor The Lutheran Companion, 1913, monthly mag. Ungdomsvännen, 1914-18. Mem. exec. bd. Ill. Conf., 1926-32; mem. Bd. of Christian Edn., Augustana Synod, 1927-31; chosen historian Ill. Conf., 1928. Decorated Knight of Royal Swedish Order of Vasa, 1948; recipient 1st prize Swedish potery St. Eric Soc., N.Y., 1922. Charter mem. Swedish Hist. Soc. Am., Soc. for Advancement Scandinavian Study, Augustana Hist. Soc. Republican. Lutheran. Author: History of the Swedes of Illinois, 2 vols., 1908; En Bokhandelshistoria, 1910; Kantat för Jublesynoden (with music), 1910; Reformation Cantata (English and Swedish text, with music), 1917; The Swedish Element in Illinois, 1917; "Pilgrims of the Prairie," dedicatory cantata, rendered at Messiah Festival, Lindsborg, Kan., 1929 and 1931; The Augustana Book Concern —A History, 1934; Life and Work of Olof Olsson, 1941; poetic works, Swedish and English, in one vol., 1947. Collaborator in Svenskarna i Amerika, 2 vols., 1925; in 300th anniversary volume, Swedes in America, 1938. Editor Svensk Diktning, 2 vols., and other textbooks. Co-editor Hymnal of Augustana Synod, 1917-25. Awarded first prize in Swedish poetry, 1922, by St. Eric Soc., New York. Retired, 1949. Home: 7540 Stony Island Av., Chgo. 49. Died Oct. 6, 1958; buried Moline, Ill.

OLSON, Grant Franklin, business exec.; b. Two Harbors, Minn., Nov. 6, 1905; s. John Henry and Martina Elizabeth (Isackson) O.; B.A., U. Ill., 1928; m. Kathlyn Troja, May 16, 1931; children—Mary Elizabeth (dec.), John Henry. With Pitts. Steamship Co., 1920-23, 1925-27; sec. to supt. Augustana Hosp., Chgo., 1923-24; sales corr. W. A. Sheaffer Pen Co., Ft. Madison, Ia., 1928-30, asst. export mgr., 1930, export mgr., 1931, mgr. sales and service, export, 1931, mgr. advt., export, 1932-45, dir. advt., fgn. sales, 1945, v.p. charge advt., fgn. service, war contracts, mem. bd. dirs. since 1946, mem. merchandising com. since 1946, exec. com. since 1951; v.p. Sheaffer Realty (Ltd.) Can. since 1947; dir. W. A. Sheaffer Pen Co. of Can., Ltd. since 1945, W. A. Sheaffer Pen Co. (Australia) Pty., Ltd. since 1951, W. A. Sheaffer Pen Co. (Eng.) Ltd. since 1952. Spl. asst. to Sec. Commerce, 1953. Mem. Assn. Nat. Advertisers. Elk. Clubs: Nat. (Toronto, Ont.); Union League (Chgo.); Rotary; Ft. Madison Country; Keokuk, Country (Keokuk, Ia.); Nat. Republican (N.Y.C.). Home: 1334 Avenue B. Office: W. A. Sheaffer Pen Co., Ft. Madison, Ia. Died Mar. 13, 1954; buried Gethsemane Cemetery, Ft. Madison.

OLSON, Oscar Ludvig, educator; b. Chgo., Feb. 3, 1872; s. Andrew B. and Guroe Larson (Krogstad) O.; A.B., Luther Coll., Decorah, Ia., 1893; A.M., U. of Minn., 1903; Ph.D., U. Chgo., 1914; m. Clara

Elizabeth Gullixson, July 8, 1897; children—Walter Andrew, Paul Frederick. Became mem. faculty of Luther College, 1901, pres., 1921-32. Home: Decorah, Ia. Died Nov. 19, 1956; buried Decorah.

OLSON, Oscar William, corp. exec.; b. Chgo., May 11, 1889; s. Charles and Mary (Johnson) O.; student Lewis Inst., 1908-11; LL.B., Kent Coll. Law, Chgo., 1913; m. Eudora Landstrom, Sept 29, 1917; children—Mary, Eudora Ann (Mrs. B. E. Swanson), Oscar William. Broker butter and eggs, 1921-39; ednl. dir., asst. bus. mgr., Chgo. Merc. Exchange, 1939-43, exec. v.p., 1943-52, pres., 1952-53; ret. 1953. Treas. Poultry and Eggs Nat. Bd. Treas. Augustana Theol. Sem. Served with U.S. Army, 1918. Mem. Asso. Poultry and Egg Industries (treas.), Phi Delta Phi. Republican. Lutheran. Club: Union League (Chgo.). Home: 312 Wisconsin Av., Oak Park, Ill. Office: 110 N. Franklin St., Chgo. Died Nov. 28, 1959; buried Park Holm Cemetery, La Grange, Ill.

OLSON, Ralph O(liver), judge; b. Alden, Minn. Mar. 26, 1902; s. Ralph O. and Genevieve (Larson) O.; student Carleton Coll., 1918-19; LL.B., U. Minnesota, 1924; married Louise Moore, November 27, 1924; children—Phyllis Anne (Mrs. Robert S. Needy), Charles Ralph, Dan Ralph. Admitted to Wash. bar, 1924 and practiced in Bellingham, 1924-36; police and justice courts, Bellingham, 1926-36; superior ct. judge, Whatcom and San Juan cos., State Wash., 1936-51; supreme ct. judge State Wash. since 1951. Mem. Superior Ct. Judges Assn. (formerly pres. judge), Am. Bar Assn., Order of Coif, Phi Delta Phi (hon.), Beta Theta Pi. Presbyn. Club: University, M (U. Minn.). Home: Olympia, Wash. Office: Supreme Court of Washington, Temple of Justice, Olympia, Wash. Died Jan. 15, 1955.

OLSSON, Alexander, publisher; b. Onsala, Sweden, Feb. 27, 1868; s. Adolf Magnus and Augusta (Anderson) O.; received education in Sweden; m. Augusta Grahn, Sept. 9, 1897 (died Nov. 19, 1933); children —Martha Alexandra Elisabeth, Hugo Theodore Alexander. Came to America, 1889; printer by trade; propr. West Coast Pub. Co., publishers "Vestkusten" (The West Coast), oldest newspaper in Swedish lang. on Pacific Coast. Republican. Sec. Swedish-Am. Patriotic League of Calif. (an organizer, ex-pres. hon. mem.), a founder of Sveadal Recreation Home, Calif.; Swedish Society of S.F. (ex-president); hon. mem. Swedish Singing Society; mem. Scandinavian Civic League, Swedish Relief Soc. (hon.), Fylgia V.O. Secretary Swedish Expn. Com., 1913-15; hon. pres. Swedish Am. Com., Golden Gate Internat. Expn., 1939. Knight of Royal Swedish Order of Vasa, 1st class, 1915; Knight of Royal Swedish Order of the North Star, 1944; Gustav the Fifth Pioneer Medal, 1949. Mason. Odd Fellow, Druid. Clubs: Swedish (hon.), Swedish American of Alameda Co., U. of Calif. Scandinavian (hon.), Swedish Am. Authors Soc., New York (hon.), Swedish Journalists' Assn. of Am., Chicago. Author: Kallprat, 1893; Turistfärd, 1909. Home: 30 Sharon St. Office: 253 Church St., San Francisco 14. Died Sept. 21, 1952.

OLSSON, Elis, busines exec.; b. Karlskoga, Sweden, Apr. 2, 1880; s. I. and Anna O. (Olsson) O.; student Orebro Tech. Coll., 1895-99; m. Signe Maria Granberg, Dec. 12, 1911; children—Inga-Maja, Carl Arne, Sture Gordon. Pres. and dir. The Chesapeake Corp. of Va., West Point, Va., since 1929, chmn. bd. since 1945; dir. State Planters Bank and Trust Co., Richmond, Va., David Weber Co., Phila., Pa. Decorated Commander Royal Order of Vasa, 2nd class. Mem. Am. Soc. Swedish Engrs. (New York), Swedish Engrs. Soc (Chicago), Tech. Assn. Pulp and Paper Industry. Clubs: Country Club of Virginia, Commonwealth (Richmond); West Point (Va.) Country. Home: Romancoke Plantation. Office: The Chesapeake Corp. of Va., West Point, Va. Died May 24, 1959; buried West Point, Va.

OLT, George Russell, (ōlt), coll. dean; b. Dayton, O., Nov. 10, 1895; s. George Michael and Cora (Miller) O.; Ph.B., Lebanon U., 1916, A.B., 1917; A.B., Wilmington (O.) Coll., 1918; A.M., U. of Cincinnati, 1920; LL.D., Anderson (Ind.) Coll., 1933; student summer terms, Columbia, U. of Chicago, New York U.; m. Adeline Droscha, June 28, 1917; 1 dau., Dorothy Miriam. Prof. English and education, Lebanon U., 1916-17; prof. edn., Wilmington Coll., 1917-20, dir. summer school, also dir. extension dept. (organizer), 1918-25, prin., Queen City Coll. of Pharmacy (dept. Wilmington Coll.), 1918-19, dean of Wilmington Coll., 1921-25; grad. student and asst. dept. philosophy, U. of Cincinnati, 1924-25; dean and prof. philosophy and pschology, Anderson Coll. since 1925; on leave of absence making World Tour, 1950-51. Trustee Anderson College. Mem. Anderson Council Social Agencies (pres., 1935-37; chmn. social planning com., 1936-37, 1943-45; chmn. program com., 1937-39); Madison County Cancer Com., Mayor's Com. of Child Care (chmn., 1944-46), Madison County Tuberculosis Soc. (pres., 1944-45), Family Welfare Assn. (pres., 1933-39, 1944-45), Anderson Tuberculosis Soc. (1st vice pres., 1936-37), Anderson Community Chest (chmn. com. to revive and reorganize, also chmn. publicity committee, 1936),

A.A.A.S. Mem. interracial commn. Fed. Council of Church of Christ in America, 1945; chmn. interracial com. Church of God since 1940, chmn. peace commn. 1944—; chmn. Anderson Interracial Com., 1944; president Anderson Urban League, 1953-56; president Anderson Council Religious Education, 1933-34; chmn. Anderson Forum, 1934-37. Club: Anderson (Ind.) Rotary (pres., 1933-34). Author: William Carey, 1930; An Approach to the Psychology of Religion, 1956; The Efficient Young People's Society, 1932. Home: 827 High St., Anderson, Ind. Died June 28, 1958.

ONAN, David Warren, mfr.; b. Moorhead, Minn., July 4, 1886; s. Edward M. and Ellen M. (Morris) O.; student pub. schs.; m. Emily C. Roman, Aug. 28, 1907; children—Warren C., Geraldine (Mrs. Sherman Smith), Robert D. Supt. automotive div. Reinhard Bros., Mpls. 1909-18; mfr. testing devices and tools for the automotive industry David W. Onan, 1918-26; founder D. W. Onan & Sons, Mpls., 1926—, chmn. bd., 1946—. Treas., dir. Sister Elizabeth Kenny Found.; founder, treas., hon. chmn. bd. Mpls. Aquatennial. Mem. U.S., Mpls. (past pres.) C.'s of C. Club: Mpls. Optimist (past pres. internat.). Home: 1122 Tyrol Trail, Mpls. 5. Office: 2515 University Av. S.E., Mpls. 14. Died Feb. 1958.

O'NEAL, Charles Thomas, ry. exec.; b. Brandywine Springs, Del., Dec. 29, 1873; student pub. schs., Wilmington, Del., and Goldey Coll. Began as trainmaster's clerk Phila. & Reading Ry. (now Reading Co.), 1890; with Lehigh Valley R.R., in various capacities, 1891-1918, advancing to gen. supt.; furloughed to U.S. R.R. Adminstrn., 1919-20, and commd. maj. U.S. Army; v.p. Ft. Smith & Western Ry., 1921-29, Buffalo, Rochester & Pittsburgh Ry. Co., 1929-30; pres. Chicago & Eastern Ill. R.R. Co. 1931-44, chmn. bd. dirs. since 1944. Clubs: Chicago, Calumet Country, Old Elm. Home: 255 Genesee St., Avon, N.Y. Office: 332 S. Michigan Av., Chgo. Died Apr. 15, 1950; buried Allentown, Pa.

O'NEAL, Edward Asbury, III, ret. farm orgn.; exec.; b. nr. Florence, Ala., Oct. 26, 1875; s. Edward Asbury II and Mary (Coffee) O'N.; student State Normal Coll. and Paxton's Collegiate Acad. (both at Florence); A.B., Washington and Lee U., 1898; hon. Master of Farm Leadership, State Agrl. and Mech. Coll., Auburn, Ala., 1927; m. Julia Camper, Nov. 23, 1904; children—Edward Asbury IV, Moncure Camper, Amelia Brown. Engaged in farming nr. Florence, 1899—. Mem. President Harding's Agrl. Conf., 1921. Pres. Lauderdale Co. Farm Bur., 1921-22; v.p. Ala. Farm Bur. Fedn., 1922-23, pres. 1923-47, retired; pres. Ala. Farm Bur. Credit Corp., Ala. Farm Bur. Cotton Assn., Ala. Farm Bur. Mut. Supply Assn., Ala. Farm Bur. Poultry Assn.; v.p. Am. Farm Bur. Fedn., 1924-31, pres., 1931-47; mem. President's Com. to Direct Works Relief Expenditures, 1935; mem. Sec. Wallace's Agrl. Advisory Council, 1939; mem. Nat. Farm Orgn. Com. on Agrl. Prodn. for Def., 1940; mem. Fed. advisory council for employment security Social Security Bd., 1941—; mem. President's Econ. Stabilization Bd., 1942; mem. mgmt.-labor policy com. War Manpower Commn., 1942; mem. Nat. Agrl. Jefferson Bicentenary Com., 1943; mem. bd. dirs. Nat. War Fund, 1943; mem. at large, Nat. Council Boy Scouts of Am.; mem. bd. incorporators A.R.C.; mem. Agrl. Communities com., Com. for Economic Development; mem. President's Advisory Com., Office of War Moblzn. and Reconversion; mem. Citizens Fed. Com. on Edn. 1945. Mem. Phi Kappa Psi, Theta Nu Epsilon, Epsilon Sigma Phi. Omicron Delta Kappa. Democrat. Presbyn. Home: 221 W. Tuscaloosa St., Florence, Ala. Died Feb. 26, 1958.

O'NEAL, Samuel Amos, newspaperman; b. Blackwater, Mo., Sept. 23, 1899; s. Sanford Alonzo and Sarah Agnes (Reynolds) O'N.; B.J., U. Mo. 1922; m. Ethel Edith Maas, Aug. 23, 1932. Reporter St. Louis Post-Dispatch, 1922-27; asst. city editor Tulsa (Okla.) World, 1927-28; asst. city editor and polit. writer St. Louis Star-Times, 1928-36, Washington corr., 1936——, Chgo. Sun, Washington bur., 1943-45; dir. publicity for Dem. Nat. Com., 1945-47; pub. relations counselor, 1947——. Served with S.A.T.C., U. Mo.. World War I. Mem. Alpha Tau Omega, Kappa Tau Alpha, Sigma Delta Chi. Democrat. Catholic. Clubs: National Press, Kenwood Country, Burning Tree (Washington). Home: 4906 Brookeway Dr. N.W., Washington. Office: Nat. Press Bldg., Washington 4. Died June 17, 1956; buried family plot. Boonville, Mo.

O'NEILL, Albert T., ret. pub. utilities exec.; b. Manlius, N.Y., Jan. 15, 1885; s. James Adam and Margaret (Burns) O'N.; ed. Phillips Exeter Acad. and Colgate U., 1909; LL.D., Niagara U., 1952; m. Helen Frances Lynch, June 18, 1912; children—William D., Helen M. (Mrs. Joseph Brady), James A., John F., Thomas J., Robert C. Pres., dir. Canadian Niagara Power Co., Ltd.; dir. Niagara Mohawk Power Corp., Mfrs. and Traders Trust Co. Dir. Soc. for Protection Destitute Roman Catholic Children, N.Y. Catholic Welfare Committee; president Erie County Health Board; vice president, director Father Boland Foundation; member Erie County Laboratory Board;

mem. advisory bd. Buffalo Hosp. of Sisters of Charity; mem. gov. com. Buffalo Found., Buffalo Fine Arts Acad.; gov. D'Youville College; board of advisory regents, Canisius Coll.; advisory board, Kenmore Mercy Hospital. Decorated Knight of Order St. Gregory the Great, 1948; Knight of Sovereign Military Order of Malta (Am. chpt.), 1949. Mem nat. council and regional exec. com. Boy Scouts.Am. Mem. Newcomen Soc. Eng. (U.S. br.), Cath. Charities Buffalo, Inc. (dir.), Buffalo Redevelopment Com. Club: Buffalo. Home: 112 Leicester Rd., Kenmore, N.Y. Office: Electric Bldg., Buffalo 3. Died Aug. 23, 1959.

O'NEILL, Edward Emerson, business exec.; born Denver, Colo., Jan. 22, 1893; s. Patrick Frank and Mary Ellen (Lynch) O'N.; student pub. schs. of Denver, Colo.; m. Blanche Caroline Weldon, May 18, 1914 (dec.); children—Jean, Patricia, Barbara; m. 2d Mary Hinkley Stubbs, 1940. Salesman various concerns, 1913-17; Toledo (O.) branch mgr. Pyrene Mfg. Co., Toledo. O., 1917, Pittsburgh (Pa.) branch mgr., 1917-18, dist. mgr. Great Lakes div., 1918-19; est. Firefoam Co of O., Cleveland, O., v.p. and gen. mgr., 1919-22; v.p. and gen. mgr., Fire Equipment Co., Cleveland, O., 1922-26; Cleveland dist. mgr. Foamite-Childs Corporation, Utica, N.Y., 1926-27; Cleveland dist. mgr. Am.-LaFrance & Foamite Industries, Inc., Elmira, N.Y., 1927-31, sales mgr. fire protection equipment div., Elmira, 1931-35; gen. sales mgr. Am.-LaFrance-Foamite Corp., Elmira, 1935-36, v.p. and gen. sales mgr., 1936-39, exec. v.p. 1939, pres. and dir. since 1939; dir. LaFrance Fire Engine & Foamite, Ltd., Foamite, Ltd., Linn Mfg. Corp. Mason. Clubs: Rotary, City, Country (Elmira); Lotos (N.Y. City). Home: 405 Maple Av. Office: 100 E. LaFrance St., Elmira, N.Y. Died Nov. 11, 1951; buried Elmira, N.Y.

O'NEILL, Eugene Gladstone, playwright; b. N.Y. City, Oct. 16, 1888; s. James and Ella (Quinlan) O'N.; student Princeton Univ., 1906-07; Harvard, 1914-15; Litt.D., Yale, 1926; m. Kathleen Jenkins, 1909 (div. 1912); one son, Eugene (dec.); m. 2d, Agnes Boulton, April 12, 1918 (divorced 1929); children—Shane, Oona; m. 3d, Carlotta Monterey, July 22, 1929. Successively in various lines of business in United States, Central and South America, at sea 2 yrs., actor in vaudeville version of "Monte Cristo," and reporter on New London (Conn.) Telegraph; devoted attention to play-writing since 1914. Awarded gold medal for drama by Nat. Inst. of Arts and Letters, 1922; Pulitzer prize for drama, 1920, 22, 28; Nobel prize for literature, 1936. Member Authors' League America, Dramatists' Guild, Nat. Inst. Arts and Letters, Am. Acad. of Arts and Letters, Am. Philos. Soc., Irish Acad. of Letters. Author: (plays) The Moon of the Carribbees, and other plays of the sea, 1919; Beyond the Horizon, 1919; Emperor Jones, 1921; Diff'rent, 1921; The Straw, 1921; Gold, 1921; Anna Christie, 1922; The First Man, 1922; The Hairy Ape, 1922; Welded, 1923; The Fountain, 1923; Desire Under The Elms, 1924; Marco Millions, 1924; The Great God Brown, 1925; Lazarus Laughed, 1926; Strange Interlude, 1927; Dynamo, 1928; Mourning Becomes Electra (trilogy), 1931; Ah, Wilderness!, 1932; Days Without End, 1933, The Iceman Cometh, 1939; Long Day's Journey Into Night, 1940; A Touch of the Poet, 1942; A Moon for the Misbegotten, 1943; Beyond the Horizon, Hughie, 1943. Died Nov. 27, 1953.

O'NEILL, Harry P., congressman; b. Dunmore, Pa., Feb. 10, 1891; s. Thomas and Bridget O'N.; m. Margaret Shea, Aug. 1, 1916; children—Harry, Joseph D., Margaret A., William G., Paul D., Lois C., Marion T. Mem. 81st to 82d Congresses, 10th Pa. Dist. Democrat. K.C., Elks. Home: 1235 Clay Av., Dunmore, Pa. Office: House Office Bldg., Washington. Died June 24, 1953.

O'NEILL, John J(oseph), editor; b. New York, N.Y., June 21, 1889; s. James and Catherine (Kelleher) O'N.; ed. public schools and night school, New York, N.Y., and Internat. Corr. Schools; m. Marie Bock, July 7, 1912; children—Kenneth Horace, Peggy Theresa (Mrs. Clyde T. Grayson). Began as printer, 1903-04; electrician, 1905-06; with N.Y. (Astor) Public Library, 1906-07; with New York Herald library, 1907-08; reporter, 1908-15; reporter, Brooklyn (N.Y.) Daily Eagle, 1915-17, feature editor, 1918-22, radio editor, 1922-25, automobile and aviation editor, 1925-26, science editor, 1926-32, supervisor construction of new building and plant, 1929-30; science editor New York Herald Tribune since 1933. Organizer Suffolk County Home Defense Regt., 1917, Newspapermen's Officers Training Corps, 1917. Served as pvt., Machine Gun Co., 7th Regt., N.Y. Nat. Guard, 1917-19. Recipient of Pulitzer Award in Journalism, Columbia U., 1937; Best Science Story of Year, U. of Kan., 1938; Clement Cleveland Award (shared), N.Y. Cancer Soc., 1938; Westinghouse Distinguished Science Writing Medal from A.A.A.S., 1946. Revealed that atomic energy had been released, Mar. 1940. Mem. Arts and Science Conf., 1937. Fellow Am. Geog. Soc., Arctic Institute of North America; mem. Amateur Astronomers Association, A.A.A.S., Am. Genetic Assn., Am. Inst. City of N.Y. (chmn. bd. mgrs., 1933-37), Am. Soc. Psychical Research (chmn. research com. and trustee, 1933-37),

Am. Polar Soc., India-Am. Science Assn. (founding mem.), Am. Acad. Polit. and Social Science, Acad. Polit. Sci., Am.-Irish Hist. Soc., Am. Newspaper Guild (founding mem.), Am. Rocket Soc., Am. Oriental Soc., Am. Meteorol. Soc., Am. Geophys. Union, Nat. Assn. Science Writers (charter mem.; v.p., 1939, pres., 1940); Royal Astron. Soc. (Canada), Assn. Lunar and Obs., Astron. Society of Pacific, Am. Assn. Physics Teachers. Author: Enter Atomic Energy, 1940; Prodigal Genius, The Life of Nikola Tesla, 1944; Almighty Atom, The Real Story of Atomic Energy, 1945; You and the Universe, 1945; Engineering The New Age, 1949. Contbr. tech. articles to sci. publs. Home: 209 N. Long Beach Av., Freeport, L.I., N.Y. Office: 230 W. 41st St., New York, N.Y. Died Aug. 30, 1953.

O'NIELL, Charles Austin, judge; b. Franklin, La., Sept. 7, 1869; s. John A. and Isabella Margaret (Burnham) O'N.; student Tulane U., 1885-88, LL. B., 1893; A.B., LL.D., Christian Brothers Coll., Memphis, 1890; m. Bettie Singleton Gordy, Mar. 26, 1894; children—Erin (Mrs. J. Gibson Tucker), Kathleen Mavourneen (Mrs. G. T. McSween), Betty O'Niell Moore, Adrienne (Mrs. Charles R. Billeiter), Charles Austin, Nora Creina (Mrs. Henry F. Lewis), James, Margaret Isabel (wife of Judge Jack Lowe). Admitted to La. bar, 1893, practiced in La. until 1908; dist. judge, St. Mary Parish, 1908-12; justice of Supreme Court of La., 1912-22, chief justice, 1922—. Mem. Am. Bar Assn., Am. Law Inst., La. State Bar Assn., La. State Law Inst., Order of Coif. Democrat. Roman Catholic. K.C., Elk. Home: 307 Main St., Franklin, La. Address: Supreme Court Bldg., New Orleans. Deceased.*

OPDYCKE, John Baker ("Oliver Opdyke"), author; b. Doylestown, Pa.; s. John B. and Ann Conard (Shapland) O.; A.B., Franklin and Marshall Coll., 1898; A.M., New York University, 1903, D.Litt., 1950; A.M., Columbia University, 1904; diploma, Teachers College, 1906; student Oxford, 3 years, Boston Sch. of Expression; m. Theresa Helburn. Press rep. at Olympic meets in Athens, 1904, London, 1908, Stockholm, 1912; press traveler through Siberia, China, Japan, Straits Settlements, 1912-13. Mem. com. on pub. information Foreign Press Cable Serice, 1917-19. Professional staff, Friedsam State (N.Y.) Educational Commission, 1926. General editor and assistant dir., Vocational Survey Commission, New York City, 1931-33. Mem. Chi Phi. Author: The Lure of Life, 1910; The Unfathomable Sorrow, 1910; Amor Vitaque, 1912; Composition Planning, 1913; Elements of Composition (in collaboration), 1913; News, Ads, and Sales, 1914, part 2, 1915; Working Composition, 1917; Commercial Letters (in collaboration), 1918; Advertising and Selling Practice, 1918; English of Commerce, 1920, 28; Business Letter Practice, 1922; The Language of Advertising, 1925; The Literature of Letters, 1925; Good English (3 vols., in collaboration), 1925; In the Service of Youth, 1928; The High School Shakspere, 1930; Projects in Elementary English, 1931; Get it Right, 1935; Sentence, Paragraph, Theme, 1936; Take a Letter, Please!, 1937; Don't Say It, 1939; Telling Types in Literature, 1939; Harpers English Grammar, 1941; Handbook of English Usage (with Henry Seidel Canby), 1942; Say What You Mean, Residues, 1947; Part and Parcel, 1948; Mark My Words, 1949; Patterns for Pastime, The Opdycke Lexicon, 1950. Translator of Omar Sonnets, 1909. Contbr. newspaper and mag. articles. Formerly lecturer at New York U., Columbia Univ. Extension, and Johns Hopkins. Address: 153 E. 24th St., N.Y.C. 10. Died Nov. 3, 1956.

OPPENHEIM, Amy Schwartz (Mrs. Laurent Oppenheim) (ŏp'pĕn hīm); b. Louisville, Ky., July 10, 1878; d. Moses and Eugenie (Lehman) Schwartz; ed. public and private schs.; m. Laurent Oppenheim, June 6, 1900 (died Jan. 3, 1933); children—Laurent, Jean Paul (dec.). Promoter of lectures on art at Me. Museum Art for pub. sch. children; a founder and organizer School Art League and member board and chmn. scholarship committee, 1911-48, honorary president since 1949; active in campaign for woman suffrage in New York State, 1915-17; member women's committee, American Defense Society, 1918-19; formerly v.p. Woman's Municipal League; elected mem. Rep. County Com., N.Y. County, since 1925; exec. com. Citizens Union, 1924-38; hon. v.p. Woman's Theodore Roosevelt Meml. Assn.; mem. Adv. Com. on Women's Participation, New York World's Fair 1939, 40. Mem. governing bd. of auxiliary board Philharmonic Symphony Soc. of New York, 1929-30; mem. advisory com. New York Sch. Applied Design for Women; mem. Rep. advisory com. of New York County, 1930-33; mem. women's advisory com. of Regional Plan Assn., 1930-32; mem. women's com. N.Y. City for United China Relief, 1941; del. to Am. Federation of Art annual convention, 1951; member panel of hostesses Council Nat. Defense and Office Coordinator Commercial and Cultural Relations between Am. Republics, 1941. Del. to Am. Fedn. Arts Annual Conv., 1942, 44, 45. Asst. dir. Women Speakers Bur., Rep. Nat. Com. at Eastern Hdqrs., Hoover-Curtis Campaign, 1932, and Landon-Knox Campaign, 1936; mem. Rep. Mayoralty Com., N.Y. City 1933; mem. women's com. of 100, Nat. Pub. Housing Conference, 1936-39; mem. women's div. U.S. Sesquicentennial Commn.; mem. Stuyvesant Statute Com. of Netherland-America Foundation; mem. woman's com. Museum of City of N.Y., 1934. Dir. Am. Women's Voluntary Services, 1941-42; mem. nat. com. for Food for Small Democracies, 1941-45. Mem. Art Alliance of America (dir. 1922-23), Am. Fedn. of Arts (del. 22d annual conv. 1931), Associates in Fine Arts, Museum of Art, Yale, New York Chapter U.D.C., Am. Mus. Natural History, Nat. Inst. Social Sciences (life), School Art League (hon. pres.), Nat. Geog. Soc., French Inst. in U.S., Nat. Inst. Social Science (v.p.), English Speaking Union, Met. Museum of Art (life fellow, 1946). Episcopalian. Club: Woman's Nat. Republican (founder member); Women's City (charter mem.). Contbr. articles to Vols. I and II of The American Art Annual, 1898-99. Donor of J. Paul Oppenheim Memorial Collection of contemporary Am. prints to Yale Art Gallery. Home: Hotel La Salle, 30 E. 60th St., N.Y.C. Died May 4, 1955.

OPPENHEIMER, Sir Ernest, business exec.; b. Friedberg, Hesse, May 22, 1880; s. Edward and Nanette (Hirschhorn) O.; educated in private schs.; D.C.L. (hon.), Oxford U., 1952; LL.D., U. of Witwatersrand; m. Mary Lina Pollak, 1906 (dec. 1934); 1 son, Harry Frederick; m. 2d, Caroline Magdalen Harvey O., June 1, 1935. Mayor of Kimberley, 1912-15; represented Kimberley in Parliament of Union of South Africa, 1924-38; formed Anglo Am. Corp. of South Africa, Ltd., 1917, chmn. dir., since foundation; chmn. Anglo-Am. Corp. of S. Africa, Ltd., Anglo-Am. Prospecting Co. Ltd., Bancroft Mines, Ltd., Brenthurst Investment Trust (Pty.) Ltd., E. Oppenheimer and Son, Ltd., Spectrum Diamonds, Ltd., Boart Products S. Africa, Ltd., Cape Explosives Works, Ltd., Indsl. Distbrs., Ltd., Premier (TV) Diamond Mining Co., Ltd., Southwest Finance Corp., Ltd., Rhodesia Copper Refineries, Ltd., De Beers Consol. Mines, Ltd., 1929—; chmn. Rhokana Corp., Ltd., chmn. African Explosives and Chem. Industries, Ltd., Anglo Am. Investment Trust, Ltd., Consol. Diamond Mines of Southwest Africa, Ltd., De Beers Indsl. Corp., Ltd., Diamond Corp., Ltd., Diamond Trading Co., Ltd., Orange Free State Investment Trust, Ltd., Rhodesian Anglo Am., Ltd., De Beers Investment Trust, Ltd., Nchanga Consol. Copper Mines, Ltd., Rhodesia Broken Hill Development Co., Ltd., West Rand Investment Trust, Limited; dir. numerous investment, mining and development companies. Decorated Knight of Order of St. John of Jerusalem. Clubs: Rand (Johannesburg); Kimberley (Kimberley); City (Cape Town). Home: "Brenthurst", Federation Rd., Parktown. Office: 44 Main St., P.O. Box 4902, Johannesburg, South Africa. Died Nov. 25, 1957.

OPPENHEIMER, Sir Ernest, business exec.; b. Mar. 22, 1901; s. Harry F. and Mary (Gallup) R.; B.S. in Civil Engring., U. Ill., 1923; children—Judith Noyes, Alden Gallup, Jennifer Dean. While attending sch., worked in various capacities for Wabash, Alton & So., M.P. r.r.'s; with engring. dept. U.P. and M.P. r.r.'s, 1923-25; engr., supt. D. C. Bowman, engring. contractor and builder, St. Louis, 1925-27; joined Union Iron Works of Los Angeles, 1927, co. merged with Llewellyn Iron Works and Baker Iron Works to form Consolidated Steel Corp., 1929, became v.p. charge sales and engring. of new corp., 1934, dir., 1938, exec. v.p., 1938-41, pres., 1941-55 (name corp. changed to Consol. Western Steel Corp. upon acquisition properties of Western Pipe and Steel Co., 1948-55; pres. Columbia-Geneva Steel div. quired by U.S. Steel Corp., 1948; pres. Columbia Steel Co.. 1948-55; pres. Columbia-Geneva Steel div. U.S. Steel Corp., 1955—; cons. prof. bus. mgmt. Stanford Grad. Sch. Bus., 1955-56; dir. So. Cal. Edison Co., N. Am. Aviation, Inc., Indsl. Indemnity Co., 12th Dist. Fedn. Res. Bank in San Francisco. Mem. bus. adv. council to Sec. of Commerce, Cal. Traffic Safety Found. Trustee Com. for Econ. Development, Cal. Inst. Tech.; dir. Stanford Research Inst. Mem. Am. Mgmt. Assn. (v.p., dir.), Am. Soc. C.E.; asso. mem. Soc. Naval Architects and Marine Engrs. Clubs: Bohemian, California, Pacific Union, Family; Duquesne (Pitts.); Newport Yacht; Chicago; Cypress Point, Los Angeles Country; The River (N.Y.C.). Address: 1100 Sacramento St., San Francisco. Died Dec. 20, 1956.

ORCUTT, William Dana (ôr'kŭt), author, book designer; b. W. Lebanon, N.H., Apr. 18, 1870; s. of Hiram and Ellen (Dana) O.; A.B., Harvard, 1892; (hon.) 1894; m. Alice Wilson, 1893 (died 1894); 1 son, Reginald Wilson; m. 2d, Louie Thompson, 1896; 1 son, Philip Dana. Asso. with The Plimpton Press; designer Humanistic and Laurentian types. Decorated Knight Order of Cross of Crown of Italy, 1924. Clubs: Country, Authors (hon.), Harvard (Boston); Garrick (London, Eng.); Soc. of Printers (hon.). Author: Good Old Dorchester—A Narrative History of the Town, 1893; The Princess Kallisto, 1902, 1911; Robert Cavelier, 1904; The Flower of Destiny, 1905; The Spell, 1909; The Lever, 1911; Writer's Desk Book, 1912; The Moth, 1912; Madonna of Sacrifice, 1913; Authors' Desk Book, 1914; The Bachelors, 1915; Burrows of Michigan and the Republican Party, 2 vols., 1917; The Balance, 1922; Desk Reference Book, 1926; In Quest of the Perfect Book, 1926; The Kingdom of Books, 1927; The Book in Italy, 1928; Master Makers of the Book, 1928; The Magic of the Book, 1930; Dagger and Jewels—The Gorgeous Adventures of Benvenuto Cellini, 1931; Wallace Clement Sabine, a Biography, 1933; Changing Patterns, 1933; Celebrities off Parade, 1935; Escape to Laughter, 1942; From My Library Walls, 1945; Mary Baker Eddy and Her Books, 1950. Contbr. Encyclopedia Brittanica. Home: 512 Beacon St., Boston. Died Nov. 28, 1953.

ORDAL, Zakarias J., clergyman; educator; b. nr. Bergen, Norway, Mar. 11, 1875; s. Johannes Johanneson and Martha (Sandal) O.; brought to Am., 1880; A.B., Luther Coll., Decorah, Ia., 1898, postgrad., 1898-99; grad. Luther Sem., St. Paul, 1902; visiting leading schs. in U.S., 1911-12; studied Tchrs. Coll. (Columbia U.); m. Sina Carlovna Wulfsberg, June 25, 1902; children—Magnhild Esther, Dagny Christiane, Erling Joseph, Lillian Valborg, Selma Elizabeth, Zakarias Johan, Rolf Waldemar, Norman Jacob, Casper Reuben. Ordained to Luth. ministry, 1902; pastor Luverne, Minn., 1902-03; asst. to mgr. Luth. Pub. House, Decorah, Ia., 1903-05; pastor Paint Creek, Ia., 1905-08; pres. Luth. Normal Sch., Sioux Falls, S.D., 1908-17; pastor of Rush River Parish, River Falls, Wis., 1917—. Mem. Bd. of Edn. Synod for Norwegian Evang. Luth. Ch. Am., 1908-17; chmn. Parochial and Sunday Sch. Bd., 1910-17; chmn. joint Sunday Sch. Com. of Norwegian Synod, the United Ch., Houghes Synod and Free Ch., 1913-17. Trustee Luther Coll., Decorah, Ia., 1930-38. Republican. Editor Evangelisk Luthersk Folkekalder, 1906, 07, Skoleblad, 1911-14; The Resurrection of Jesus an Historical Fact, 1923, also pub. in Chinese, 1929. Address: R.F.D. 1, River Falls, Wis. Died Nov. 7, 1949; buried Rush River Cemetery, Pierce County, Wis.

ORDWAY, Thomas, physician; b. Dorchester (Boston), Mass., May 7, 1877; s. George Frank and Julia Maria (Gilbert) O.; A.B., Harvard, 1900, A.M., 1901, and M.D., 1905; hon. Sc.D., Union Coll., 1919; m. Mary Olive Baker, Apr. 6, 1906; 1 son, Thomas. Assistant in zoölogy, Harvard, and Radcliffe Coll., 1900-01; asst. in physiology, Harvard Med. Sch., 1902-03; asst. in pathol. dept. Boston City Hosp., 1905; house officer Boston City Hosp., 1905-07; asst. in pathology, Harvard Med. Sch., 1907-08; 1st asst. in pathology, Boston City Hosp., 1908-09; director Bender Hygienic Laboratory, Albany, N.Y., 1909-11, also Professor Pathology Albany Medical Coll.; physician in charge Huntington Hosp. Harvard Med. Sch., 1911-15 (resigned); was also lecturer in pathology, grad. dept. Harvard Med. Sch., instr. in medicine, Harvard Med. Sch. and asst. visiting physician, Boston City Hosp., 1911-15; prof. medicine, dean Albany Med. Coll., 1915-37; physician-in-chief, Albany Hosp., 1915-37; cons. physician Albany Hospital Member A.M.A., Assn. Am. Physicians, Am. Assn. Pathologists and Bacteriologists, Am. Assn. for Cancer Research, Soc. for Advancement Clin. Research, Mass. Med. Soc., Boston Soc. Med. Sciences (ex-sec.). etc. Club: Harvard (Boston and Eastern N.Y.). Contbr. to med. jours. Home: 297 S. Manning Blvd. Office: 161 S. Lake Av., Albany, N.Y. Died May 12, 1952; buried Rensselaerville Cemetery, Rensselaerville, Albany County, N.Y.

ORMSBY, Oliver Samuel (ôrmz'bĭ), dermatologist; b. Logan, Utah, Mar. 21, 1874; s. Oliver C. (M.D.) and Maretta S. O.; M.D., Rush Med. Coll., Chicago, 1895; m. Alice Etta Joscelyne, Dec. 14, 1896 (died 1936); 1 dau., Miriam; m. 2d, Mary Horton, Feb. 4, 1939. Practiced at Chicago since 1901; specialized in treatment of diseases of the skin; Rush professor emeritus dermatology, University of Illinois. Member Am. Med. Assn., American Dermatol. Association, Chicago Med. Soc., Chicago Dermatol. Soc., Chicago Pathol. Soc., Inst. of Medicine Chicago, Congress of Am. Physicians and Surgeons; hon. member Sect. Dermatology of Royal Soc. of Medicine, London; corr. mem. Société Française de Dermatologie et de Syphiligraphie, Paris; corr. mem. Dansk Dermatologisk Selskab, Copenhagen; hon. mem. Wiener Dermatologische Gesellschaft (Vienna), Japanese Dermatol. Soc., Greek Union of Dermatology and Venereology, Hellenic Antivenereal Soc. (pres. 10th Internat. Congress Dermatology), Asociación Argentina de Dermatologiá y Sifiologiá, German Dermatol. Soc., Dutch Soc. Dermatology. Club: Indian Hill Country. Author: Practice Treatise on Diseases of the Skin, 1915, 6th edit., 1943, 7th edit. 1948. Home: 651 Country Lane, Glencoe, Ill. Died Apr. 9, 1954; buried Rosehill Cemetery, Chgo.

ORNITZ, Samuel, author; b. N.Y.C., Nov. 15, 1890; s Morris and Deborah (Badisch) O.; student Coll. City of New York 2 yrs.; evening courses, N.Y. U., 1 yr.; m. Sadie Florence Lesser, Dec. 22, 1914; children—Arthur Jaques, Donald Ray. Asst. supt. Brooklyn Soc. for Prevention of Cruelty to Children, 1914-20; engaged in penol. research, probation and parole work, for Prison Assn. of N.Y. City, 1909-14; auly Pub. Co., 1925, 27, 28; photoplay Originator Paramount Studios 1928-29; with Metro-Goldwyn-editor Macfadden Publs., 1924-25; edit. dir. Mac-

Mayer Studio, 1929-31, RKO Studios, 1932-33, Universal Studios, 1934-35. Mem. Nat. Com. for Def. of Polit. Prisoners, Internat. Labor Defense Com., Hollywood Anti-Nazi League, Motion Picture Artists Com. Atheist. Clubs: Friday Luncheon, Bachman Loyal. Author: The Sock, 1919; Haunch, Paunch and Jowl, 1923; Round The World with Jocko The Great, 1925; A Yankee Passional, 1927; (motion picture plays) The Case of Lena Smity) Chinatown Nights; The Man Who Reclaimed His Head; Three Kids and a Queen; Portia on Trial; (also plays) One Year to Pay, In New Kentucky, Back to the Baboons, Mythical Kingdom. Known as a "freak fancier"; rescued many deformed young people who were being exploited by showmen. Home: 1632 N. Martel Av., Los Angeles. Died Mar. 1957.

O'ROURKE, William Thomas, librarian; b. Worcester, Mass., Oct. 13, 1903; s. Thomas J. and Brigid T. (Burke) O'R.; A.B., Holy Cross Coll., 1926; B.L.S., Columbia, 1927; m. Elizabeth C. Fallon, Sept. 1, 1928; children—William T., Jr., Elisabeth, Thomas, Marie. Reference librarian, asst. librarian, Holy Cross Coll., 1927-36; Librarian Brockton Pub. Library, 1936-41, New Bedford (Mass.) Pub. Library, 1941-48; asst. librarian Buffalo (N.Y.) Pub. Library, 1948-50, librarian, 1950, dir., 1950-54; dep. dir. in charge circulation Buffalo and Erie County Pub. Library, 1954—. Chmn. W. N.Y. Cath. Librarians Conf.; mem. Buffalo Youth Bd.'s Com. on Salacious Publs.; chief registration and inquiry div. Welfare Services of Consol. Erie County Office Civil Def. Mem. bd. W. N.Y. United Negro Coll. Fund, Inc., chmn. 1954 fund campaign, and pres. 1955; bd. trustees W. N.Y. Ednl. TV Assn., Inc. Mem. C. of C., A.L.A., N.Y. Library Assn., Am. Assn. Adult Edn., Institut Litteraire de la France. Clubs: Torch, Rotary. Author: Library Hand Book, 1937; Library Publicity, 1938. Roman Catholic. Home: 169 Hawthorne St., Buffalo 23. Office: Public Library, Lafayette Square, Buffalo 3. Died Aug. 21, 1957.

ORR, Flora Gracia, writer, splty. pub. relations; b. Mt. Hope, Wis.; d. Edward Dearth (M.D.) and Mary Jane (Holford) O.; B.S. in Home Economics and Journalism, U. of Wis., 1917. Writer for U.S. Food Adminstrn., 1917-18; asso. editor Delineator Mag., 1919-21; Washington corr. Omaha News and St. Paul News, 1922-26, St. Paul News, 1926-35; asst. regional information advisor U.S. Resettlement Adminstrn., 1935-37, inf. splst. War Manpower Com., W.P.B., 1942-46; contbr. Scripps-Howard Washington Newspaper Bur., Sci. Service and N.E.A. Sunday Feature Service. Mem. Theta Sigma Phi. Clubs: Women's Nat. Press, American Newspaper Women's. Co-author: Be Beautiful, 1932. Contbr. to mags. Home: 2028 Tunlaw Rd., Washington 7. Died Sept. 20, 1953; buried Hermitage Cemetery, Mount Hope, Wis.

ORR, H(iram) Winnett, surgeon; b. West Newton, Pa., Mar. 17, 1877; s. Andrew Wilson and Frances J. (Winnett) O.; U. of Neb., 1892-95; M.D., U. of Mich., 1899; m. Grace Douglass, Sept. 7, 1904; children—Douglass, Willard, Josephine, Dorothy, Gwenith. In practice at Lincoln, Neb., since 1899. Editor Western Medical Review, 1899-1906; lecturer on history of medicine, Coll. of Medicine, U. of Neb., since 1903; chief med. insp., Lincoln pub. schs., 1908; supt. Neb. Orthopedic Hosp., 1911-17, chief surgeon, 1919-47, cons. surgeon since 1947; cons. surgeon dept. orthopedic surgery Lincoln Gen. Hosp. Editor Jour. Orthopedic Surgery, 1919-21. Commd. capt., Med. R.C., May 18, 1917; on duty Welsh Met. War Hosp., Whitchurch, Cardiff, Wales, June 1917-Aug. 1918; with A.E.F., France, Aug. 1, 1918-Feb. 24, 1919; maj. M.C., Oct. 1, 1918; lt. col., Feb. 17, 1919; relieved, June 1, 1919; was col. M.C., U.S. Army Reserve, with spl. assignment as consultant orthopedic surgery. Librarian, Neb. State Med. Assn., 1900-12, sec., 1907, pres., 1919-20; sec. Am. Orthopedic Assn., 1915-17, editor, 1919-21, pres., 1936; sec. Central States Orthopedic Club, 1913-17. Recipient Distinguished Service award (posthumously) from the American College of Surgeons. Member A.M.A. (chmn. orthopedic sect., 1921-22), Miss. Valley and Mo. Valley med. assns., Elkhorn Valley Med. Soc., Lancaster County Med. Soc., Soc. Internat. de Chirurg Orthopedique (U.S.), Am. Med. Library Assn. (hon. mem.); Assoc. Bone and Joint Surgeons (hon.); member Chi Phi, Phi Rho Sigma, Sigma Xi, Alpha Omega Alpha (Nebraska). Clubs: Commercial, Country, Lincoln University; University (Chgo.). Author numerous books, 1903—; latest publ. Selected Pages from the History of Medicine in Nebraska, 1952; contbr. to Sajous Cyclo., 1931; speaker on osteomyelitis Brit. Med. Assn., Dublin, 1933, on surgery Ill. State Med. Soc., 1939, on compound fractures So. Med. Assn., 1940; lectr. Am. Acad. Orthopedic Surgeons, 1952. Home: 1601 Smith St., Lincoln 2. Office: 2300 S. 13th St., Lincoln, Neb. Died Oct. 11, 1956; buried Arlington Nat. Cemetery.

ORR, Isaac Henry, banker, lawyer; b. Louisiana, Mo., Feb. 14, 1862; s. William Campbell and Eliza (Jordan) O.; LL.B., Washington U., 1883; LL.D., Mo. Valley Coll., 1911; m. Virginia E. Pitman, July 9, 1893 (dec. Feb. 1915); m. 2d, Ann Marshall, Jan. 31, 1920; 1 son, Wm. Campbell. Began practice at St. Louis, 1883; mem. Orr, Christie, Bates & Bruce since 1896; chmn. bd. (hon.) St. Louis Union Trust Co.; dir. 1st Nat. Bank in St. Louis, American Auto Insurance Co., Securities Investments Co., Railway Exchange, Inc. Trustee St. Louis Community Fund, St. Louis Provident Assn., Mo. Valley Coll., St. Louis Community Sch., St. Louis YMCA. Mem. Am., St. Louis bar assns., Am. Bankers Assn., Phi Delta Phi. Republican. Presbyn. Mason. Clubs: University, Banker, Noonday, Contemporary, Round Table, Bogey Golf, St. Louis Country. Home: 57 Kingbury Pl. Office: 323 N. Broadway, St. Louis. Died Aug. 24, 1954; buried Bellefontaine Cemetery, St. Louis.

ORR, John Alvin, clergyman; b. Cedarville, O., Sept. 7, 1874; s. James Renwick and Josephine (Little) O.; student Wooster (O.) U.; A.B., Cedarville Coll., 1897; A.B., U. of Pa., 1898, A.M., 1900; grad. Pitts. Theol. Sem., 1901; m. Imo Jean Rodarmer, June 4, 1902 (dec. 1929); children—J. Alvin, James R., Lois Marjorie, Eleanor P.; m. 2d, Mary Wilson Edie, 1932. Ordained ministry United Presbyn. Ch., 1901; pastor Norris Sq. Ch., Phila., 1901-13; became pastor First Ch., Pitts. (North Side), Nov. 1913; built community house at cost of $465,000 and head of same; now prof. church history and pastoral theology Erskine Theol. Sem., and profl. English Bible, Erskine Coll., Due West, S.C. Moderator United Presbyn. Ch. of N.A., 1934-35, Asso. Ref. Presbyn. Ch. of N.A., 1947-48. Pres. bd. trustees Cedarville College; chmn. New World Movement. Pres. Citizens' League of Pittsburgh and Allegheny County; mem. Pittsburgh Council of Churches. Republican. Author: Saving the Home, 1908; How to Know Christ Is God, 1921; Chains We Wear, 1921; Things Missing in Heaven; What Comes After Death. Home: Due West, S.C. Died May 6, 1957; buried Cedarville, O.

ORR, Robert Williamson, advt. exec.; b. Phila., Jan. 20, 1897; s. John Barlow and Jane (Butterfield) O.; grad. Wharton Sch., U. Pa., 1924; m. Mildred Barock, Nov. 22, 1937; 1 dau., Ronnie Elizabeth. With Lennen & Mitchell, Inc., advt., N.Y.C., 1925-47; pres. Robert W. Orr & Assos., Inc., N.Y.C., Los Angeles, London, Paris, since 1947; dir. Parfums Schiaparelli, Inc. Clubs: Cloud, Metropolitan (N.Y.C.); Southampton. Home: 605 Park Av. Office: 4 W. 58th St., N.Y.C. Died Sept. 4, 1957.

ORR, Thomas E., engr.; b. Wheeling, W.Va., Apr. 9, 1894; s. Joseph Reid and Mary St. Clair (Hamilton) O.; **B.S., in C.E., Carnegie Inst. Tech., 1917, C.E., 1947; m. Kathryn Donald, Oct. 5, 1940; children—Thomas E., Janet B., Duncan H. Constrn.** work Am. Bridge Co., Panama Canal, Latin Am., 1911-12, U.S., 1912-13; **civil engring. bus., Pittsburgh, 1929-40, Cleveland since 1940. Pres. Plastray Corp., Detroit, since 1948; v.p., sec. Plastic Engring., Inc., Cleveland, since 1941; owner Lighthouse Service Co., Highway Lighthouse Service Co., Keystone Plastics Co. (all at Pittsburgh); pres. Plastray Ltd. (Canada), Port Credit, Ontario. Served in U.S. Army, 79th div., 2d French Colonials, 1917-19; maj. A.C., 1942-44. Awarded: Purple Heart with palm, service medals for combat. Mem. Engrs. Soc. Western Pa., Soc. Plastics Engrs. (hon. life, past pres.), Ohio Professional Engrs., Cleveland C. of C., Disabled Emergency Officers of the World Wars, Am. Legion, Vets. Fgn. Wars, 316th Inf. Assn. (past nat. pres.), Beta Theta Pi, Tau Beta Pi. Republican. Presbyterian. Mason. Club: Cleveland Athletic. Home: 12506 Edgewater Dr., Cleve. 7. Died Jan. 29, 1952; buried Knollwood Mausoleum, Cleve.**

ORR, Thomas Grover, surgeon; b. Carrollton, Mo., May 9, 1884; s. Thomas Albert and Mildred Jane (Cook) O.; grad. high sch., Carrollton, 1903; A.B., U. of Mo., 1907; M.D., Johns Hopkins, 1910; m. Irene Helen Harris, Dec. 22, 1913; 1 son, Dr. Thomas Grover. Instr. in surgery, U. of Kan., 1914-17, asso. prof. surgery, 1917-24, prof. surgery and head of dept., U. of Kan., and surgeon in chief to U. of Kan. Hosp., 1924-49; prof. of surgery and chief second surg. service University Kansas Med. Center, 1949-54, emeritus prof., 1954—; cons. surg. VA Hosp., Kansas City, U.S. Army Hosp., Leavenworth, Kan.; in spl. research in intestinal obstruction, 1922-31. Served as maj. Med. Corps, U.S. Army, 1918-19. Fellow American College Surgeons (gov.); mem. A.M.A., Amrican Surg. Assn. (former pres.), Southwestern Surg. Congress (former pres.), American Society of the History of Medicine, Southeastern Surgical Congress, Chicago Surgical Society (hon.), Western Surgical Association (former pres.), **Soc. Univ. Surgeons, Soc. Internationale de Chirurgie,** Central Surg. Assn., Am. Board Surgery (foundation mem.), Sigma Xi, Alpha Omega Alpha, Nu Sigma Nu, Beta Theta Pi. Republican. Episcopalian. Author: Modern Methods of Amputation, 1926; Operations of General Surgery, 1944, 49. Editor Am. Surgeon; Survey Surg. Technique; editorial board Surgery and Quarterly Rev. of Surgery. Contbr. articles to surg. publs. Home: 5930 Mission Dr., Kansas City, Mo. Office: University of Kansas Med. Center, Kansas City, Kan. Died Nov. 19, 1955.

ORR, William Anderson, public relations; b. Wingham, Ont., Can., Feb. 4, 1883; s. Robert and Christina (Anderson) O.; grad. Evanston (Ill.) High Sch., 1901; student Northwestern U., 1 year; m. Hazel Earhart, July 3, 1909; children—William E., Robert Doris (Mrs. William Spencer Doig), James Wendell. Reporter, Evanston Index, 1901; city editor South Bend (Ind.) Tribune, 1905; reporter Chicago Chronicle, 1906-07; reporter and editor New York News Assn., 1908; reporter and polit. corr. New York Tribune, 1909-12, city editor, 1913-14; sec. to Gov. Charles S. Whitman, Albany, N.Y., 1915-17; N.Y. State supt. of prisons, 1918; asst. to pres. B. Altman & Co., New York, 1919; gen. agt. Indemnity Ins. Co. of America, New York, 1920-23; pub. relations rep. Loew's, Inc., Metro-Goldwyn-Mayer Picture Co., since 1923; editor and pub. Peekskill (N.Y.) Daily Press Union, 1936-38. Dir. and sec. Yonkers Community Chest; chmn. publicity Yonkers Community and War Chest, 1942. Republican. Methodist. Past pres. Silurian Soc., New York, chmn. com. Silurian Annual Award to best newspaper achievement on New York newspapers. Clubs: Racquet of Park Hill (Yonkers) (gov.); City (dir.; N.Y.C.); Hudson River County. Contbr. to newspaper and mags. Home: Star Route Alcove, N.Y. Office: 1540 Broadway, N.Y.C. 19. Died Apr. 18, 1950.

ORTEGA y GASSET, Jose, Spanish writer; b. 1883. Former prof. philosophy and lit. Madrid U.; editor Revista de Occidente; critic and philosopher; deputy and leader group, In Service of Republic. Died Oct. 18, 1955.*

ORTHWEIN, Percy James, advt. exec.; b. St. Louis, Nov. 27, 1888; s. William D. and Emily (Thimler) O.; student Yale, 1908-12; m. Clara Busch, Nov. 1, 1916; children—Adolphus Busch, James Busch. Salesman D'Arcy Advt. Co., St. Louis, 1915-26, dir., 1926—, v.p., 1228-51, chmn. bd., 1951—, chmn. exec. com., 1953—; dir. Anheuser-Busch, St. Louis & O'Fallon Ry. Mem. Alpha Delta Phi. Republican. Clubs: Log Cabin, Racquet, Deer Creek, Noonday. Home: 2701 S. Lindbergh Blvd., St. Louis 22. Office: Missouri Pacific Bldg., St. Louis 3. Died July 2, 1957.

ORTON, Clayton Roberts, plant pathologist; b. East Hardwick, Vt., Apr. 1, 1885; s. Lyman Squire and Ellen Mandana (Stevens) O.; prep. edn., Essex Classical Inst., 1901-03, Hardwick Acad., 1904-05; B.S., U. Vt., 1909, Sc.D., 1942; M.S., Purdue, 1915; Ph.D., Columbia, 1924; m. Ethel M. Chapman, Sept. 22, 1911; children—Jan, Gardner Chapman, Patricia. Spl. agt. U.S. Dept. Agr. June 1909-Jan. 1910; asst. plant pathologist, U. of Wis., Feb.-Sept. 1910; asst. botanist, Ind. Agrl. Expt. Sta., 1910-12; asst. prof. botany, Pa. State Coll., 1913-16, asso. prof., 1916-19, also asso. prof. plant pathology, 1917-19, prof., 1919-27; plant pathologist, Pa. Agrl. Expt. Sta., 1913-27; also collaborator, Bureau Plant Industry of the U.S. Dept. of Agriculture, 1913-25 and 1930—; plant pathologist, in charge research and extension, agrl. dept. The Bayer Co., Inc., 1925-28, Bayer-Semesan Co., Inc., 1928-29; prof. plant pathology and head dept., W.Va. Univ., 1929-33; plant pathologist W.Va. Agrl. Expt. Sta. 1928-38; head dept. of biology, W.Va. Univ., 1933-36, head dept. plant pathology and forestry, 1936-38; dean, Coll. Agrl. Forestry and Home Economics, 1938—; dir. Agrl. Exptl. Sta., 1938—; on leave, 1950-53, spl. appointment as agrl. consultant to Liberia for OFAR, U.S. Dept. Agriculture. Sec. Advisory Bd. Am. Plant Pathologists, 1918-21; chmn., 1922-23; mem. Nat. Research Council (div. biology and agr., 1922-24; liaison mem. div. states relations, 1923-24); mem. bd. govs. Crop Protection Inst., 1920-25, 1935—; mem. W.Va. Planning Bd., 1935—, chmn., 1941—; chmn. Land-Use Com. of W.Va., 1934-38. Fellow American Assn. Advancement of Science (pres. State Coll. br., 1923); mem. Am. Phytopathological Soc. (pres. 1939), Mycological Soc. America, S. Appalachian Bot. Club, W.Va. Acad. Science, N.Y. Acad. Sci., Soil Conservation Soc. America. Sigma Xi, Kappa Sigma, Alpha Zeta, Gamma Sigma Delta. Episcopalian. Home: 369 Mulberry St., Morgantown, W. Va. Died June 16, 1955; buried East Grove Cemetery Morgantown.

ORTON, Helen Fuller (Mrs. Jesse F. Orton), author; b. Pekin, Niagara County, N.Y., Nov. 1, 1872; d. Merritt Bond and Lucy Ann (Taylor) Fuller; grad. high sch., Lockport, N.Y., 1893; m. Jesse F. Orton, 1895; children—Malcolm F., Lawrence M., Douglas T., Robert M., Philip H. (dec.). Baptist. Mem. D.A.R., Authors' League of America, New York State Hist. Assn., Schoharie County Hist. Soc., Newtown Hist. Soc. Author: Prince and Rover of Cloverfield Farm, 1921; Bobby of Cloverfield Farm, 1922; Summer at Cloverfield Farm, 1924; The Little Lost Pigs, 1925; Winter at Cloverfield Farm, 1926; Prancing Pat, 1927; Queenie, 1929; Good News Stories; The Philippines, 1929; Grandmother's Cooky Jar, 1930; The City Mrs. Winkle Built, 1931; The Twin Lambs, 1931; Snappy, the Puppy-Dog, 1931; The Treasure in the Little Trunk, 1932; Daddy's Adventure with the Animals, 1933; The Gold-Laced Coat—A Story of Old Niagara, 1934; Danny's Country Store, 1935; Hoofbeats of Freedom—A Story of the American Revolution, 1936; The Secret of the Rosewood Box,

1937; A Lad of Old Williamsburg, 1938; Knights of the Snowstorm, 1939; The Brave Frontier: A Story of Old Schoharie, 1940; Mystery at the Little Red Schoolhouse, 1941; The Little Lost Pigs in Town, 1942; Mystery at the Old Place, 1943; The Winding River: A Story of French Émigrés on the Susquehanna, 1944. Mystery of the Secret Drawer, 1945; Mystery of the Lost Letter, 1946; Mystery Up the Chimney, 1947; Mystery Up the Winding Stair, 1948; Mystery in the Pirate Oak, 1949; Mystery in the Old Cave, 1950; Mystery Over the Brick Wall, 1951; Mystery in the Old Red Barn, 1952; Mystery of the Hidden Book, 1953; Mystery of the Apple Orchard, 1954. Contbr. to children's mags. Talks on writing juvenile books. Home: 89-10 35th Av., Jackson Heights 72, N.Y.C. Died Feb. 16, 1955; buried Pekin, Niagara County, N.Y.

ORTON, William Aylott, prof. economics; b. Bromley, Kent, Eng., Feb. 9, 1889; s. William Amor and Emma (Aylott) O.; B.A., Cambridge, 1919, M.A., 1922; M.Sc., University of London, 1921, D.Sc., 1946; LL.D., 1947; married Olmen Marlais Moment, December 6, 1917; twins—Maurice Amor, Basil Evelyn (dec.). Came to United States, 1922. Lieutenant British Army, in Gallipoli, Egypt, France, 1914-17; on intelligence staff, War Office, London, 1917-19; wounded on Somme, 1916; staff officer indsl. relations dept., Ministry of Labor, 1919-22; prof. economics, Smith Coll., since 1922; lecturer, summer sessions, Bryn Mawr, 1925, U. of Calif., 1926, 29; visiting prof. economics, Amherst. 1929-30, Williams, 1939-40. Trustee U. of Mass. Member Am. Econ. Assn., American Cath. Hist. Assn., Am. Academy Polit. Science. Author: Labor in Transition, 1921; Prelude to Economics, 1932; America in Search of Culture, 1933; The Last Romantic, 1937; Twenty Years' Armistice, 1938; The Liberal Tradition, 1945; The Economic Role of the State, 1949. Home: Vernon St., Northampton, Mass. Died Aug. 13, 1952.

OSBORN, Alexander Perry, lawyer; b. Garrison-on-Hudson, N.Y., June 6, 1884; s. Henry Fairfield and Lucretia (Perry) O.; A.B., Princeton, 1905; LL.B., Harvard, 1909; student Trinity Coll., Cambridge Eng., 1905-06; m. Marie Cantrell, Aug. 22, 1933; children by previous marriage—Lucretia (Mrs. William H. McKleroy), Alexander Perry, Mary (Mrs. Duncan L. Marshall) and Anne (Mrs. Ezra P. Prentice, Jr.) (twins); adopted children—Lou Belew, Clyde Belew. Admitted to bar, 1909; with Winthrop & Stimson, 1909-11, Spooner & Cotton, 1911-15; partner in firm Beekman, Menken & Griscon, 1915-21, Redmond & Co., 1921-34; practicing alone since 1934. Dir. Western Pacific R.R. Corp., Denver & Rio Grande Western R.R. Co. Served as lt. col., U.S. Army, 1917-18. Decorated Chevalier of Legion of Honor (France). Commended by undersecretary of war for exceptional services in connection with reorgn. of gen. staff, 1918. Acting pres., 1st vice-pres. and trustee Am. Museum Natural History. Trustee Five Points House, Theodore Roosevelt Meml. Assn. Mgr. Hosp. of Special Surgery. Dir. Belgian War Relief Soc. Republican. Clubs: Ivy (Princeton); Down Town Assn., Racquet and Tennis, Century (N.Y.C.). Home: 990 Fifth Av., N.Y.C. 28. Office: 20 Exchange Pl., N.Y.C. 5. Died Mar. 6, 1951; buried Garrison, N.Y.

OSBORN, Herbert, biologist; b. Lafayette, Wis., Mar. 19, 1856; s. Charles Paine and Harriet Newell (Marsh) O.; B.S., Iowa State College, 1879, M.S., 1880, also D.Sc., 1916; LL.D. from U. of Pittsburgh, 1930; LL.D. from Ohio State Univ., 1936; m. Alice Isadore Sayles, Jan. 19, 1883; children—Morse Foster, Herbert Tirrill, Evelyn, Dorothy, Margaret Stanton. Asst. 1879-83, asst. prof., 1883-85, prof. zoology and entomology, 1885-98, Ia. State Coll.; entomologist, of expt. sta., 1890-98; state entomologist of Ia., 1898; prof. zoölogy and entomology, 1898-1916, research prof., 1916-33, emeritus prof. since 1933, Ohio State U.; also dir. of Lake Laboratory, 1898-1918. Dir. Ohio Biol. Survey since 1912. Spl. agt. div. entomology, U.S. Dept. Agr., 1885-94; cons. entomologist, Maine Experiment Sta. since 1913; cons. entomologist Tropical Plant Research Foundation, 1925, trustee of same, 1926-43; collaborator U.S. Bureau Entomology since 1930. Fellow A.A.A.S. (v.p. Sect. F, 1917); pres. Ia. Acad. Sciences, 1887 (sec. and editor Proc., 1890-98), Assn. Econ. Entomologists, 1898, Ohio Acad. Sciences, 1904-05, Am. Micros. Soc., 1907-09, Entomol. Soc. America, 1911 (mng. editor Annals, 1908-28), Soc. Promotion Agrl. Science, 1917-18; trustee Biological Abstracts, 1927-37; trustee Research Fund Ohio Acad. Science since 1917; fellow Calif. Acad. of Science, 1937; mem. Internat. Entomol. Congress, Am. Soc. Naturalists, Am. Entomol. Soc., Am. Soc. Zoölogists, Biol. Soc. Washington, Société Entomologique de France, Entomol. Soc. Washington, Sigma Xi (rec. sec. 1907-08), Phi Kappa Phi (hon.), Alpha Zeta (hon.), Gamma Alpha (hon.). Clubs: University, Faculty. Author: Pedicull and Mallophaga of Man and Lower Animals, 1891; Insects Affecting Domestic Animals, 1896; The Hessian Fly in the United States, 1898; The Genus Scaphoideus, 1900; Economic Zoölogy, 1908; Agrl. Entomology, 1916; Leafhopper of Ohio, 1928; Fragments of Entomol. History, 1937, part II, 1946; Meadow and Pasture Insects, 1939. Wrote articles Insects, Parasitic, and Insects, Poisonous, in Wood's Reference Handbook of the Med. Sciences (new edit.), 1903 and 1915; Neotropic Homoptera in the Carnegie Museum, 7 parts, 1923-39; also many papers in jours., proc., etc. Address: Ohio State U., Columbus, O. Died Sept. 20, 1954.

OSBORN, Loran David, clergyman, sociologist; b. Portland, Mich., Nov. 13, 1863; s. Rev. David and Eliza Maria (Faxon) O.; Kalamazoo Coll., 1887-89; A.B., U. Mich., 1891; student Newton Theol. Instn., 1891-92; Ph.D., U. Chgo., 1900; m. Rena Addie Richards, Aug. 13, 1896; children—Marian Lorena, Richards Clinton. Ordained to ministry Bapt. Ch., 1894; pastor Immanuel Ch., Elgin, Ill., 1894-98, 1st Ch., Centralia, Ill., 1898-1900, 1st Ch., Bloomington, Ill., 1900-05; pres. Des Moines Coll., 1905-11; asso. editor Home and School Reference Work, Chgo., 1911-12; organizer and dir. univ. extension div., prof. sociology U. Colo., 1912-20; chancellor Des Moines U., in charge ednl. and internal adminstrn., 1920-24, dean Coll. Arts and Sciences, 1924-26, also prof. sociology; prof. sociology U. of Redlands, 1926-31; dir. edn. dept. Am. Inst. of Family Relations Los Angeles, 1931-50. Pres. Colo. Conf. Social Work, 1918-20; chmn. Colo. Americanization Com., 1918-20; dir. ednl. dept. A.R.C., Mountain Div., 1919-20. Dir. Confs. on Family Relations, Div. Adult Edn., State Dept. Edn., emergency ednl. program, 1935-38. Mem. Pacific Sociol. Soc. Club: University. Author: Recovery and Restatement of the Gospel, 1903; The Community and Society—An Introduction to Sociology (with Martin H. Neumeyer), 1933. Home: 842 Wisconsin Av., Oak Park, Ill. Died May 17, 1954.

OSBORN, Marvin Griffing, journalism; b. nr. Winnsboro, La., Mar. 4, 1885; s. William Rapp and Nannie Eliza (Griffing) O.; B.A., La. State U., 1906, M.A., 1924; spl. work in journalism, summers, Ohio State U., 1919, Columbia, 1920, 23; m. Mamie Belle Hester, June 28, 1916; children—Hal Hester, William Griffing (dec.), Marvin Griffing, Marian Lynne. With La. State U., 1908—, sec.-registrar, 1908-10, editor Press Bulletin and editor Agrl. Extension Div., La. State U., 1913-22, Alumni News, 1924-28, asso. prof. journalism, 1921-23, prof. and head of dept., 1923-31, dir. Sch. of Journalism, 1931—; supervisor of Farm and Home Study Clubs of Agrl. Extension Div., La. State U., 1918-22; asst. to State food administrator, 1918; part time newspaper work, 1920-26. Mem. Nat. Council on Edn. for Journalism, 1931-36, and 1940-44. Mem. Am. Assn. Teachers of Journalism (pres. 1926; exec. com. 1927), Southwestern Journalism Congress (pres. 1934-35), Am. Assn. Agrl. Coll. Editors (pres. 1920-21), Am. Assn. Coll. News Bureaus (v.p. 1922-23), Am. Assn. of Univ. Profs., Press Congress of World, La. Press Assn., Kappa Sigma, Sigma Delta Chi, Kappa Tau Alpha (nat. pres. 1933-34), Phi Kappa Phi. Democrat. Methodist. Asso. editor of Headlining America. Contbr. to Book of Rural Life (Ency. of Agr.) and various publs. Home: 339 Stanford Av. Office: Journalism Bldg., La. State U., Baton Rouge. Died Jan. 23, 1958; buried Roselawn Cemetery, Baton Rouge.

OSBORN, Merritt J., chem. mfr.; b. Buchanan, Mich., Feb. 14, 1879; s. William and Charlotte B. (Armstrong) O.; student pub. schs.; m. Susan Bartley, Dec. 17, 1901; children—Stephen Armstrong, Edward Bartley. Sales rep. Parke Davis & Co., 1896-1903; v.p. Osborn-Colwell Co., mfg. chemists. N.Y.C., 1903-05; with Eli Lilly Co., Indpls., 1906-08; advt., sales mgr. medicinal malt extract dept. Hamm Brewing Co., St. Paul, 1908-11; pres. Merritt J. Osborn Co., 1911-17; receiver Neilson Tractor Co., Mpls., 1918-20; pres. M. J. Osborn, Inc., Ford dealer, St. Paul, 1921-23; founder, pres. Economics Lab., Inc., St. Paul, 1923-50, now chmn. Mem. Nat. Assn. Advt. Clubs (past dir.), St. Paul Town Criers Advt. (past pres.). Clubs: St. Paul Association, St. Paul Athletic, Minnesota (St. Paul); Union League (Chgo.). Home: 2233 Summit Av., St. Paul 5. Office: Guardian Bldg., 84 E. 4th St., St. Paul 1. Died Jan. 16, 1960.

OSBORN, William Church, lawyer; b. Chgo., Dec. 21, 1862; s. William Henry and Virginia Reed (Sturges) O.; B.A., Princeton, 1883, LL.D., 1942; LL.B., Harvard, 1889, LL.D., 1940; LL.D., U. Toronto, Can., 1915, Columbia, 1943; m. Alice Dodge, June 3, 1886. Practiced in New York, 1889—; mem. firm Osborn, Fleming & Whittlesey. Dir. Phelps Dodge Corp. Mem. N.Y. State Constl. Conv., 1894; legal mem. N.Y. State Commn. in Lunacy, 1899; legal adviser to Gov. Dix, 1911; chmn. markets com. N.Y. State Food Investigating Commn., 1912; mem. C. of C. com. on N.Y. City police problem, 1905; pres. Citizens Budget Commn. Trustee emeritus Princeton, (life), Met. Museum of Art (pres.; chmn. budget com.), Soc. Relief of Rputured and Crippled (pres. 1910-38); pres. Children's Aid Soc., Hudson River Conservation Society, Inc.; dir. New York World's Fair and president Temple of Religion, 1939; pres. Met. Mus. of Art, 1941-47, now pres. emeritus. Chmn. Dem. State Com., 1914-16. Decorated Officer Order of the Italian Crown, Sr. warden, St. Phillips Ch., Garrison, N.Y. Clubs: Down Town, Century Assn., University, City. Home: 40 E. 36th St., N.Y.C.; also Garrison, N.Y. Office: 20 Exchange Pl., N.Y.C. Died Jan. 3, 1951.

OSBORNE, James Insley, prof. English; b. Crawfordsville, Ind., Feb. 25, 1887; s. James Harvey and Grace (Insley) O.; A.B., Wabash Coll., 1906, A.M., 1907; Oxford U., 1911-14, A.B., 1913; Ph.D., Columbia, 1919; married to Elsie Alan Walkup, Apr. 21, 1921 (died Aug. 21, 1923); 1 son, James Insley, Jr.; married 2d, Frances Doane, July 6, 1927; 1 dau., Deborah. Instr. English, Columbia, 1914-17; prof. English, Wabash Coll., 1919-52. Matthew Arnold prize, Oxford, 1914. Served as 1st lt. Mil. Intelligence Div., U.S. Army, 1918-19, attached to Am. Peace Commn., Paris. Mem. Beta Theta Pi, Phi Beta Kappa. Presbyterian. Author: Arthur Hugh Clough; Wabash College, the First Hundred Years (with T. G. Gronert). Home: Crawfordsville, Ind. Died Jan. 27, 1952.

OSBORN-HANNAH, Jane, opera singer, soprano; b. Wilmington, O.; d. Parker B. and Rebecca A. (Randolph) Osborn; studied under Vitorio Carpi, Chgo. Cons. of Music; studied with William Shakespeare; Paris, with Marchesi and Sbriglia; later studied in Berlin and Bayreuth; m. Frank Sanford Hannah, Am. consul, Strassburg, Germany, Nov. 25, 1897. Sang in concerts in America previous to preparing for grand opera; made début as Elizabeth in "Tannhauser," Leipzig, Germany, Mar. 18, 1906-09; also sang in Berlin and leading German cities, Covent Garden, London; then came for 2 seasons to Met. Opera House, New York, with Chicago-Phila. Opera Co., 1912-13. Known as a Wagnerian soprano; greatest success has been as "Madame Butterfly." Died 1943.

OSBURN, Worth James, educator; b. Norborne, Mo., Nov. 9, 1882; s. Morris and Mary Virginia (Brown) O.; A.B., Central Coll., Fayette, Mo., 1903; A.M., Vanderbilt, 1905; B.S. in Edn., U. Mo., 1910; Ph.D., Columbia, 1920; m. Edmonia Mitchell, Sept. 2, 1914; 1 son, James Morris. Tchr. Central Coll. Acad., 1905-08; supt. pub. schs., Carterville, Mo., 1908-14; tchr. N.W. Mo. State Tchrs. Coll., Maryville, 1915-19; dir. research Wis. State Dept. Edn., 1920-28; prof. sch. adminstrn. Ohio State U., 1928-33, prof. edn., 1933-35; prof. edn. Buffalo State Tchrs. Coll., 1935-36; prof. edn. U. Wash., 1938-48, ret., part-time prof., 1948-54. Fellow A.A.A.S.; mem. N.E.A., Phi Delta Kappa. Democrat. Presbyn. Mason. Author: Foreign Criticism of American Education (U.S. Bur. Edn. bull.), 1921; Corrective Arithmetic, Vol. 1, 1924, Vol. 2, 1929; Corrective Exercises in the Fundamentals of Arithmetic, 1925; Are We Making Good in Teaching History?, 1926; Overlappings and Omissions in Our Courses of Study, 1928; Searchlight Arithmetic Series (with B. R. Buckingham), 1928; Enrichment of the Curriculum for Gifted Children (with B. F. Rohan), 1931; Dynamic Vocabulary Exercises (with W. T. Foster), 1939. Home: 5022 21st Av. N.E., Seattle. Died Mar. 16, 1956; buried Acacia Meml. Park, Seattle.

OSCAR, Stephen A., ins. exec.; b. Towerville, Wis., Sept. 26, 1875; s. Tobias Atley and Nellie (Christine (Kinney) O.; A.B., U. Wis., 1900; m. Mabel M. Smith, Nov. 22, 1901; children—Ruth Edna (Mrs. Charles E. McGinnis), Helen Grace (Mrs. Leo J. Federer). High school prin. and city supt. schs., Washburn, Wis., 1902-14; dir. Nat. Mutual Benefit Life Ins. Co., Madison, Wis., 1908—, sec., 1914-42, pres., 1942—. Mem. Wis. Tchrs. Retirement and Annuity Bd., 1939-42. Dir. Wis. C. of C. 1929, vice pres., 1942; pres. Presidents' Section of Nat. Fraternal Congress of America, 1944-45. Home: 1 Langdon St. Office: 119 Monona Av., Madison, Wis. Died Oct. 13, 1949.

OSGOOD, Alfred Townsend (ŏz'go͝od), surgeon; b. Upland, Pa., Oct. 14, 1872; s. Howard (D.D., LL.D.) and Caroline T. (Lawrence) O.; A.B., Yale, 1895; M.D., Coll. Phys. and Surg., Columbia, 1899; m. Ethna deL. Mackeye, Nov. 24, 1914. Practiced in N.Y.C., 1899-1947, ret.; prof. of urology U. and Bellevue Hosp. Med. Coll., 1912-36; cons. urol. surgeon Bellevue Hosp., N.Y.C. Cancer Inst., French Hosp., (N.Y.C.), Lawrence Hosp. (Bronxville), Muhlenberg Hosp. (Plainfield, N.J.), North Westchester Hosp. Fellow A.C.S.; mem. Am. Assn. Genito-Urinary Surgeons, Am. Urol. Assn., A.M.A., N.Y. Acad. Medicine, Soc. Internat. d'Urologie, Psi Upsilon, Elihu Club (Yale). Clubs: Century, Yale (N.Y.C.); Graduate (New Haven). Contbr. to Cabot's Modern Urology, Johnson's Operative Therapeutics, Dean Lewis Practice of Surgery, also articles in med. and surg. jours. Home: 225 E. 73d St., N.Y.C. 21. Died June 1959.

OSGOOD, Phillips Endecott, clergyman, author; b. North Attleboro, Mass., May 11, 1882; s. George Endecott and Helen Frances (Reed) O.; A.B., Harvard, 1904; B.D., Episcopal Theol. Sch., Mass., 1907; D.D., Seabury Div. Sch., 1923; L.H.D., Carleton Coll., 1933; m. Marion Stone, 1907; children—Marjorie, Catherine, Endecott; m. 2d, (Mrs.) Eunice Williams Simonds, 1945. Ordained deacon P.E. Ch., 1907, priest, 1908; curate Church of the Ascension, Boston, 1907-09; rector Ch. of Our Saviour, Roslindale, Mass., 1909-15; vicar Chapel of the Mediator,

West Phila., Pa., 1915-21; rector St. Mark's Ch., Mpls., 1921-33, Emmanuel Ch., Boston, 1933-45; summer rector Emmanuel Ch., Manchester-by-theSea, Mass., 1928-45. Pres. house of clerical and lay deputies Gen. Conv. Episcopal Ch., 1943-45; resigned Episcopal ministry, 1945 (for theol. reasons); asso. Protestant Film Commn., 1946-49; minister 1st Unitarian Ch. of Essex County, 1949—. Mem. Copley Soc., Delta Upsilon. Mason. Clubs: Attic (Mpls.); St. Botolph (Boston). Author: Soloman's Temple, 1908; Church Year Sermons for Children, 1917; Old Time Church Drama Adapted, 1928; A Sinner Beloved and Other Plays, 1929; Pulpit Dramas, 1929; Say I to Myself, 1944; also missionary and ednl. courses, and religious plays. Contbr. mag. articles. Lectr., cons. Address: 47 Cleveland St., Orange, N.J.; also St. Botolph Club, Boston 16. Died Nov. 1956.

OSGOOD, Robert Bayley, surgeon; b. Salem, Mass., July 6, 1873; s. John C. and Martha E. (Whipple) O.; A.B., Amherst Coll., 1895, Sc.D., 1935; M.D., Harvard, 1899; m. Margaret Chapin, Apr. 29, 1902; 1 dau., Ellen. Practiced at Boston, 1899—; former chief of staff of orthopedic dept. Mass. Gen. Hosp. and Children's Hosp., now cons. surgeon of both; John B. and Buckminster Brown prof. orthopedic surgery emeritus Harvard Med. Sch. Col. U.S. Army, Med. O.R.C. Chmn. adv. bd. orthopedic surgeons to the trustees of the Shriners' Hosps. for Crippled Children; mem. adv. com., services for crippled children Children's Bur., Department of Labor, Washington (chmn. 1938-40); mem. med. adv. bd. Armour Found. and Alfred I. Du Pont Inst., 1937-46. Trustee Mass. Hosp. Sch., Canton. Fellow A.C.S.; hon. fellow Royal College of Surgeons (Eng.); mem. A.M.A., Mass. Med. Soc., Am. Orthopedic Assn. (pres. 1920-21), Boston, N.E. (pres. 1928-29) surg. socs., Nat. Inst. Social Science, Am. Acad. Arts and Sciences; corr. mem. Belgian Orthopedic Assn., Internat. Soc. Orthopedic Surgery, Lique Internationale Contre le Rhumatisme; hon. mem. Brit., Italian, Scandinavian, Australian orthopedic assns., Royal Soc. of Medicine of England. Episcopalian. Clubs: Harvard, Union Boat. Author: Diseases of the Bones and Joints (with J. E. Goldthwait and C. F. Painter), 1909; Fundamentals of Orthopedic Surgery in General Medicine and Surgery (with Nathaniel Allison), 1931; The Medical and Orthopedic Management of Chronic Arthritis (with Ralph Pemberton), 1934). Home: 38 Chestnut St., Boston. Died Oct. 2, 1956; buried Harmony Grove Cemetery, Salem, Mass.

OSGOOD, Roy Clifton, banker; b. Springfield, Mass., Mar. 9, 1876; s. Alfred Gilbert and Sarah Ann (Sweeny) O.; grad. high sch., Athol, Mass., 1893; LL.B., George Washington U., 1903; m. Anna M. Hudson, Feb. 21, 1903; children—Gilbert Hudson, Robert Luey, Clifton Brooks, Alfred Morse. Bank clerk, Athol, 1893-1900; clerk Dept. of Commerce and Labor, Washington, D.C., 1900-05; practiced law at Milwaukee, Wis., 1905-06; connected with trust dept. First National Bank, Chicago, 1906, v.p., 1919-46; retired 1946; chmn. bd. Upper Avenue National Bank, 1929-40; re-elected director, 1946; director Mid-Am. National Bank, Chicago, 1956. Trustee Gads Hill Center, treasurer, 1910-54; treasurer of Behavior Research Fund, 1915-52. Member Investment Bankers Association of America (pres. 1920-21), Nat. Tax Assn., Am. Econ. Assn. (chmn. finance com.), Am. Bankers Assn. (chmn. inheritance tax com., 1925-27; chmn. fiduciary legislature committee, 1941-43), Am. Bar Assn.; life member of the Illinois Bar Association; mem. Chicago Bar Assn. (chmn. lecture com. 1926-27), Kappa Sigma (trustee endowment fund), Nat. Inheritance Tax Conf. Com., 1925-26; member Fed. Finance Com. of U.S. C. of C., 1924-52; treas. Chgo. Law Inst., 1926-48; Chgo. Tumor Inst. Repub. Unitarian. Clubs: University (pres. 1930-32), Chicago, Midday, Chicago Literary, Legal (pres. 1917-18), Law (pres. 1932), Indian Hill (Ill.); Meguntticook (pres. 1946-51), Camden Yacht (Camden, Me.). Home: 423 Essex Rd., Kenilworth, Ill. Office: 38 S. Dearborn St., Chgo. Died July 9, 1958; buried Meml. Park, Evanston, Ill.

O'SHAUGHNESSY, John K(ing), ex-govt. ofcl.; b. New Orleans, Sept. 24, 1887; s. Charles J. and Marguerite F. (Urban) O'S.; B.S., La. State U., 1909; m. Frances A. Hochette, Apr. 8, 1922; children—Marcelle (Mrs. Robert M. Rivello), Charles J. Design, constrn., operation, maintenance electric and communication systems, 1909-57; cons. engr., Bethesda, Md., 1935-37; with Rural Electrification Adminstrn., 1937-57, successively asso. engr., engr., sr. engr., asst. chief engr., chief engr., 1937-53, asst. adminstr., 1953-57. Trustee Suburban Hosp., Bethesda, Md. Served with Pa. N.G., Mexican Border campaign, 1916-17; 2d lt. 28th Div., A.E.F., France, 1917-19. Recipient Distinguished Service Award U.S. Dept. Agr., 1954. Mem. Washington Soc. Engrs., Sigma Nu. Home: 4816 Montgomery Lane, Bethesda 14, Md. Retired. Died July 28, 1958; buried Arlington (Va.) Cemetery.

O'SHEA, Benjamin (ô-shā), dir., mem. exec. com. Union Carbide and Carbon Corp. Home: Wilmot Rd., New Rochelle, N.Y. Office: 30 E. 42d St., New York, N.Y. Died May 2, 1952.

O'SHEA, William Joseph, lawyer; b. Bklyn., Jan. 27, 1899; s. William J. and Anna M. (Walsh) O'S.; A.B., Fordham U., 1919, LL.B., 1923, LL.D., 1951; m. Edwina Michel Shanley, Aug. 10, 1932; children—William Joseph, Michelle Marie, Edwina Ann. Admitted to N.Y. bar, 1923, U.S. Supreme Ct., 1932; faculty sch. law Fordham U., 1925-34; partner Saxe, Bacon & O'Shea, and predecessor law firms, N.Y.C., 1926—; spl. asst. U.S. atty. gen., 1953. Member of Board of Education of New York City. Mem. N.Y. State Constl. Conv. Com., 1937-38, del., 1938; presdl. elector 1944. Dir. Am. Relief to Austria, Inc. since 1945, Am. Overseas Aid, 1947-48, Cath. Youth Orgn., 1939-50; mgr. Lincoln Hall since 1931; adv. bd. War Relief Services-N.C.W.C. since 1943. Decorated Order of Dannebrog (Denmark), 1947, Sovereign Mil. Order St. John (Malta). 1949. Mem. N.Y. State Bar Assn. (exec. com., 1950—, chmn. 1956-57), Assn. Bar City N.Y. (exec. com 1940-44, v.p. 1945-46), N.Y. County Lawyers Assn. (dir. 1940-46, v.p. 1952, pres. 1954-55), Fordham U. Alumni Assn. (pres. 1942-43). Clubs: University, Manhattan, Athletic, Downtown Assn. (N.Y.C.); Ft. Orange (Albany, N.Y.) Home: 620 Park Av., N.Y. C. 21. Office: 20 Exchange Pl., N.Y.C. 5. Died Apr. 1, 1957.

OSK, Roselle H., artist; b. New York, N.Y., Feb. 27, 1884; d. Herman and Cornelia (Thalmessinger) Hellenberg; A.B., Hunter Coll., 1903; student Art Students League, 1903-06, Nat. Acad., 1912-15; m. Marcus L. Osk, Jan. 23, 1906; children—Richard, George, Virginia (Mrs. Kenneth Poli). Began as painter, 1920, and etcher, 1932; rep. in permanent collection, Met. Mus. Art, Hundred Selected Prints, 1937, 1938, 1941, 1947, Congl. Library, Fine Prints of the Year, 1938, N.Y. Pub. Library, Smithsonian Inst. Awarded prizes by Phila. Print Club, 1938; Nat. Assn. Women Artists, 1938, 46; Southern Printmakers, 1938; Mint Mus., Charlotte, N.C., 1945; Laguna (Calif.) Beach Art Assn., 1945. Mem. Soc. Am. Etchers, Nat. Assn. Women Artists, Conn. Acad. Fine Arts, Chicago Printmakers and Prairie Printmakers. Works included in American Prize Prints of the 20th Century. Address: 320 W. 87th St., N.Y.C. 24. Died May 4, 1954.

OSMUN, A(lbert) Vincent, botanist, educator; b. Danbury, Conn., Jan. 20, 1880; s. John Wilbur and Emma (Cook) O.; B. Agr., U. Conn., 1900; B.S., U. Mass., 1903, M.S., 1905; B.S., Boston U., 1903; m. Lena Latimer, June 27, 1907; children—Kenneth Latimer, John Vincent. Asst. Conn. Expt. Sta., 1900-02; mem. faculty U. Mass. and Mass. Expt. Sta., 1903-50, emeritus prof. botany, 1950—; botanist Mass. Dept. Agr., 1914-21. Mem. nat. com. on Dutch elem disease, 1934-50, chmn. Mass. com. Fellow A.A.A.S.; mem. Am. Fern Soc., Bot. Soc. Am., Phytopath. Soc., New Eng. Bot. Club, Sigma Xi, Phi Kappa Phi. Mason. Home: 78 Northampton Rd. Office: Shade Tree Labs., U. Mass., Amherst, Mass. Died Jan. 10, 1955.

OSMUN, Russell A. (ŏs'mŭn) ret. army officer; b. Detroit, May 19, 1887; s. Gilbert R. and Caroline (Conger) O.; grad. Central High Sch., Detroit, 1901-05; A.B., U.S. Naval Acad., 1910; student L'Ecole de l'Intendence, Paris, 1923-25; Comd. and Gen. Staff Sch., Ft. Leavenworth, 1928-30; Army Indsl. Coll., Washington, 1932-33; Army War Coll., Washington, 1933-34; m. Edith Moss, Dec. 30, 1914; children—William Gilbert, Helen Edith (Mrs. Pierce E. Parker). Commd. ensign USN, 1910, resigned because of physical disability, 1911; after 2½ yrs. convalescence on Colo. ranch was commd. in U.S. Army, CAC, 1914; asst. in organizing Plattsburg Tng. Camps, served as aide to Gen. Leonard Wood; served in various capacities in U.S. and Hawaii; observer in England at outbreak of World War II, later in India; with M.I. in Turkey, Syria, Palestine, Egypt and Persia; chief M.I. Service in U.S., 1943-44; brig. gen. comdg. Kansas City Q.M. Depot, ret. 1946. Decorated Legion of Merit (U.S.); Order of White Eagle of Yugoslavia; Comdr. Order of Brit. Empire. Mason (32°). Clubs: Army-Navy (Washington); Kansas City (Mo.). Home: 5305 Albemarle St., Washington 16. Died Aug. 9, 1954; buried Arlington Nat. Cemetery.

OSUNA, Juan José (ō'sōō'nä), educator; b. Caguas, P.R., June 24, 1884; s. Juan Jose and Cesárea (Rodriguez) O.; diploma State Normal Sch., Bloomsburg, Pa., 1906; A.B., Pa. State Coll., 1912; diploma Princeton Theol. Sem., 1915; A.M., Columbia, 1920, Ph.D., 1923, medallist, 1929; m. Laura Mae Gates, May 17, 1915 (died July 31, 1918); m. 2d, Margaret Logan Thompson, Aug. 22, 1923; children—Ann Thompson, James David. Came to U.S., 1901; citizen by spl. act of Congress for P.R., 1917. Tchr. pub. schs., Mayaguez, P.R., 1906-08; missionary at Añasco, P.R., under Presbyn. Bd. of Home Missions, 1915-17; prof. religious edn. Polytechnique Inst. of P.R., San Germán, 1917-18; research in Europe, 1920-21; prof. edn., dir. tng., dir. summer sch. U. P.R., 1922-28, dean Coll. Edn., 1928-44, dean emeritus, 1944, acting chancellor, 1935-36; exchange prof. edn. Pa. State Coll., 1932-33 (one semester); ednl. cons. for govt. Puerto Rico, Department Labor Employment and Migration Bureau, 1948-49. Travelled in Hispanic America on behalf World Fedn. Edn. Assns., 1938-39. Mem. Enemy Alien Bd. for P.R., U.S.O. Insular Council; chmn. Army and Navy com. YMCA (San Juan, P.R.). Fellow A.A.A.S; mem. N.E.A. and Dept. Sch. Adminstrs., Coll. Tchrs. of Edn., Puerto Rican Atheneum, Phi Delta Kappa, Phi Kappa Phi, Kappa Delta Pi, Kappa Phi Kappa, Scabbard and Blade. Presbyn. Author: Education in Porto Rico, 1923. Asst. editor World Education. Contbr. to Twenty-Five Years of American Education (symposium), 1924. Many articles on edn. in P.R. Address: 1300 24th St., S., Arlington, Va. Died June 18, 1950; buried Orangeville, Pa.

OTHMAN, Frederick C(ampbell), columnist; b. St. Louis, Mar. 19, 1905; s. John Frederick and Esther (Work) O.; A.B., Washington U., 1926; m. Hilda Roper, Oct. 30, 1931. Entered newspaper work with United Press as reporter, 1926; served as editor, feature writer, columnist in Chgo., Los Angeles, Washington; Hollywood columnist for United Press, 1937-44. Washington columnist for United Press, 1944-47, Washington columnist for United Feature Syndicate, 1947—. Member of the Sigma Delta Chi. Club: National Press (Washington). Author: Man on the Half Shell, 1947. Contbr. numerous mag. articles to Sat. Eve. Post, Colliers, Liberty, Readers Digest, Life; speaker for Forums, Convs., etc. Home: 2475 Virginia Av., Washington 7. Office: Daily News Bldg., Washington 5. Died Dec. 27, 1958; buried Memphis.

OTIS, Harold, lawyer; b. Bklyn., Aug. 23, 1883; s. Charles H. and Mary Isabel (Woods) O.; student Phillips Exeter Acad., 1897-1900; A.B., Harvard, 1904, LL.B., 1908; m. Alice Wardwell, 1914; children—Alice, Margaret, Mary. Began practice law, 1908; formerly mem. Miller, Owen, Otis & Bailly; now mem. Willkie, Owen, Farr, Gallagher & Walton. Dir. Allied Chem. & Dye Corp. Mem. Am. Bar Assn. Republican. Episcopalian. Clubs: Harvard, Recess (N.Y.C.). Home: 138 E. 65th St., N.Y.C. 21. Office: 15 Broad St., N.Y.C. Died Oct. 17, 1958.

OTIS, Joseph Edward, banker; b. Chgo., Mar. 5, 1867; s. Joseph Edward and Maria (Taylor) O.; ed. Harvard Sch., Chgo., Phillips Acad., Andover, Mass., and Sheffield Scientific Sch. (Yale); LL.D., Knox Coll., Galesburg, Ill., 1930; m. Emily Webster, Oct. 3, 1891; children—Joseph Edward, Jr., George Webster (of 17th Regt., U.S. Engrs.; died in France, 1918), Stuart Huntington, Raymond (deceased), Emily Huntington (Mrs. Nathaniel A. Owings). Began in real estate business, 1889; one of organizers and pres. of the Great Western Tin Plate Co., Joliet, Ill. (sold to Am. Tin Plate Co., 1897); mem. firm Otis, Wilcox & Co., stock brokers, 1897, business changed to pvt. banking and consolidated with Western State Bank, 1902, under title of Western Trust & Savings Bank, of which was pres. until 1911, when it consolidated with Central Trust Co. of Ill.; v.p. of latter and acting pres., 1917-22, pres., 1922-29, chmn. bd., 1929-31; chmn. bd. and dir. Industrial Nat. Bank of Chgo., 1921 until merger with Chgo. Terminal Nat. Bank under name Chgo. Nat. Bank of which is now hon. bd. chmn.; retired dir. A.,T.&S.F. Ry.; dir. Pure Oil Co., Chgo. Daily News. Pres. bd. trustees Little Traverse Hosp., Petoskey, Mich.; chmn. bd. Rosehill Cemetery Co. Governing life member Art Institute Chgo., Chgo. Zoöl. Soc.; life mem. Field Museum of Nat. History, Archeol. Soc. Am., Chgo. Hist. Soc., Geographic Soc. of Chgo. Republican. Episcopalian. Clubs: University, Commerical (Chicago). Home: 105 E. Delaware Pl. Office: 120 S. La Salle St., Chgo. Died Nov. 25, 1959; buried Rosehill Cemetery, Chgo.

OTTE, Louis Edward, educator; b. Marysville, O., Jan. 22, 1905; s. Louis Frank and Mary Catherine (Brown) O.; A.B., Ohio Wesleyan U., 1928; Ph.D., Ohio State U., 1945. Instr. history Ohio Wesleyan U., 1929-30; tchr. Marysville (O.) pub. schs., 1932-38; instr. Ohio Wesleyan U., 1944-45; dean coll. Kan. Wesleyan U., Salina, 1945-48; dean of univ. Ohio No. U., Ada, since 1948. Mem. N.E.A., Nat. Assn. Academic Deans, Phi Beta Kappa, Phi Delta Kappa, Pi Kappa Delta. Home: 407 S. Ream St., Ada, O. Died Aug. 23, 1951.

OTTERBEIN, H. C., pres. Provident Savings Bank & Trust Co., Cincinnati. Office: Seventh and Vine Sts., Cin. 2. Deceased.

OTTING, Bernard John, religious educator; b. Cin., Aug. 16, 1859; s. Frederic W. and Mary Bernardina (Kruse) O.; acad. and coll., St. Francis Xavier's Coll., Cin., 1877-81; normal course Florissant, Mo., 1881-84; philosophy science and mathematics Woodstock (Md.) Coll., 1886-89; theol. and Bibl. studies Oña, Spain, 1892-94, Cuenca, Spain, 1894-96. Entered the Soc. of Jesus, 1881; ordained priest, 1895; prof. English and classics Detroit Coll., 1884-86, 89-92; prof. English and classics St. Louis U., 1896-97, spl. metaphysics, 1898-99, theology, 1899-1913, dean schs. of divinity and philosophy, 1912-13, 1922-29, pres., 1913-20, prof. apologetics,

1920-31; prof. apologetics St. Mary's Coll., 1931—. Address: St. Marys, Kan. Deceased.

OTTING, Leonard Henry, clergyman, educator; b. Cincinnati, Jan. 28, 1890; s. John Gerard and Anna Marie Elizabeth (Herft) O.; A.B., St. Xavier Coll., Cincinnati, 1909; student Florissant (Mo.) Jesuit Normal Sch., 1911-13; A.M., St. Louis U. 1915, philos. and sci. studies, 1913-16; theol. studies St. Louis U., 1921-24, Ignitius Kolleg, Valkenburg, Holland, 1924-25, Parayle Monial, France, 1925-26; grad. work sociology Loyola U., Chgo., 1928-30, Fordham U., summers 1930, 31; Ph.D., Gregorian U., Rome, Italy, 1931. Entered Jesuit Novitiate, 1909, ordained priest Roman Cath. Ch., 1923; instr. St. Ignatius High Sch., Chgo., 1916-19, Rockhurst High Sch., Kansas City, Mo., 1919-21; dean John Carroll U., Cleveland, 1926, prof. philosophy and sociology, 1933—., dir. dept. philosophy, 1933-50; asso. prof. philosophy and psychology Marquette U., Milwaukee, 1927-28; asso. prof. philosophy and sociology Loyola U., Chgo., 1928-33; guest lectr. in philosophy Youngstown College, 1942-45. Mem. Am. Cath. Philos. Assn., Miss. Valley and Ohio philos. assns., Jesuit Ednl. Assn., Alpha Kappa Delta. Introduced and inaugurated the Cana Conf. Ohio (Cuyahoga Falls), 1944. Address: John Carroll University, Cleveland 18. Died Jan. 25, 1960.

OTTINGER, Lawrence (ŏt'tĭng-ẽr), corp. exec.; b. New York, N.Y., Mar. 25, 1884; student Columbia U.; m. Louise Lowenstein, Jan. 21, 1928; children—Richard, Patricia Louise. Became salesman Toch Bros. Paint Co., 1907; later founded U.S. Plywood Corp., of which is now pres. and dir.; dir. Algoma Plywood & Veneer Co., U.S. Plywood Corp. (S.C.). Organized Plywood Div., War Production Bd. Mem. Adv. Bd., Quartermaster Corps, U.S.A. Home: 55 Cushman Rd., Scarsdale, N.Y. Office: 55 W. 44th St., N.Y.C. Died Dec. 19, 1954.

OTTMANN, William, business exec.; chmn. bd., chmn. exec. com., dir. United States Printing and Lithographing Co.; exec. vice pres., mem. exec. com., dir. U.S. Playing Card Co.; chmn. bd., mem. exec. com., dir. C. G. Gunther's Sons; vice pres., dir. Window Advt., Inc., Consolidated-Dougherty Card Co.; dir. Consolidated Lithography Corp., Russell Playing Card Co. Home: 378 Madison Av., N.Y. City 17. Office: 103 Park Av., N.Y.C. Died Apr. 1954.

OUGHTERSON, Ashley W., surgeon; b. Geneva, N.Y., Sept. 28, 1895; s. Nathan and Mary Ann (Hatch) O.; student Syracuse U., 1918-20; M.D., Harvard Med. Sch., 1924; m. Dr. Marion Howard, March 21, 1942. Intern Peter Bent Brigham Hosp., Boston, Mass., 1924-25, New York Hosp., 1925-27, Bellevue Hosp., 1927-28, Peter Bent Brigham Hosp., 1928-29, William Harvey Cushing fellow in surgery, Yale Sch. of Medicine, 1929-30; postgrad. study, Europe, 1930. Surgeon, New Haven, Conn., 1930; asst. prof. surgery, Yale, 1930-34, asso. prof., 1934-42, now clinical prof. surgery. Served as cons. surgeon, Pacific Ocean areas; col. Med. Corps, World War II, 1942-46. Awarded Legion of Merit with oak leaf cluster. Chmn. Joint Commn. for Investigating Med. Effects of Atomic Bomb in Japan. Exec. v.p., med. and scientific dir. Am. Cancer Soc., Inc.; mem. Am. Med. Assn. A.C.S. (gov.), Am. Surg. Assn., Am. Cancer Soc., Am. Assn. Cancer Research, Am. Heart Assn., N.E. Surg. Soc. (pres.), New England Cancer Soc., Am. Radium Soc., Soc. Exptl. Biology and Medicine, Sigma Xi. Clubs: Lawn, Grad. (New Haven); Yale (New York). Contbr. numerous papers on Surgery and Cancer. Address: Rockefeller Found., 49 W. 49th St., N.Y.C. Died Nov. 17, 1956; buried Bellona Cemetery, Yates County, N.Y.

OURSLER, (Charles) Fulton (our'slẽr), author, editor; b. Baltimore, Md., Jan. 22, 1893; s. William Clarence and Lillian Phillips (Sappington) O.; Litt.D., Kalamazoo Coll., 1946; Loyola Coll., 1948, Loyola U. (New Orleans), 1950; m. 2d Grace Perkins, Sept. 7, 1925; children—(1st marriage) Helen, William; (2d. marriage) Grace April, Fulton. Reporter Baltimore American, 1910-12, music and dram. critic, 1912-18; began writing short stories for mags., 1918; mng. editor New York Music Trades, 1920-22; editor in chief Metropolitan Magazine, 1923; writer novels, plays and short stories since 1923; editor of Liberty Magazine, 1931-42; vice-president and editorial director Macfadden Publications 1941; senior editor, The Reader's Digest, 1944; editor and publisher of The Sandalwood Herald. Formerly trustee Andrew Carnegie Fund for Needy Authors; pres. The Cath. Inst. Press; dir. Alcoholics Anonymous Found. Mem. Dramatists Guild, Authors League Am. (mem. council), Am. Writers Assn. (vice pres.), Authors Guild, Magicians' Guild, Empire State S.A.R.; hon. mem. Internat. Assn. Police Chiefs, 5 yrs.; hon. dept. U.S. marshal for Dist. of Mass. Clubs: Players, Dutch Treat, New York Athletic, Baker Street Irregulars. Author: Behold This Dreamer!, 1924; Sandalwood, 1925; Step-child of the Moon, 1926; Poor Little Fool, 1928; The World's Delight, 1929; The Great Jasper, 1930; Joshua Todd, 1935; A Skeptic in the Holy Land, 1936; The Precious Secret, 1947; Cloven Hoof, 1947; Three Things We Can Believe In, 1942; There are Strange Tales, 1948; The Happy Grotto, 1948; The Greatest Story Ever Told, 1949; Father Flanagan of Boys Town (with Will Oursler), 1949; Modern Parables, 1950; Why I Know There Is A God, 1950; The Greatest Faith Ever Known (posthumous), 1953; (published under the pseudonym of Anthony Abbot) About the Murder of Geraldine Foster, About the Murder of the Choir Singer, About the Murder of the Night Club Lady, About the Murder of the Circus Queen; About the Murder of a Startled Lady, 1935; About the Murder of a Man Afraid of Women, 1937; The Creeps, 1941; The Shudders, 1943; (plays) Behold This Dreamer, The Spider, 1927; All The King's Men, 1929; The Walking Gentlemen (with Grace Perkins Oursler), 1941; The Bridge, 1946. Collaborator on The President's Mystery Story; (with Achmed Abdullah), Flower of the Gods, Emerald Annie, Paradise Kate, Shadow of the Master. Translated and edited: Das Wunderbuch der Zauberkunst, by Ottokar Fischer, Wrote many motion picture scenarios. Contributor to American Mercury, Atlantic Monthly, Cosmopolitan, Liberty, Readers Digest, and Good Housekeeping. Traveled and lectured through United States and in Palestine, Egypt, China, Japan, European and South American countries. Frequent broadcasts on national radio networks; created and supervises radio series "The Greatest Story Ever Told." Syndicated column "Modern Parables," A Child's Life of Jesus. Home: Sandalwood, W. Falmouth, Mass.; and 112 Central Park South, N.Y.C. Died May 24, 1952.

OURSLER, Grace Perkins, author, editor; b. Boston, Mass.; daughter James Lamont and Margaret (Judge) Perkins; student Columbia School of Journalism; married Fulton Oursler, 1925 (deceased 1952); children—April (Mrs. Martin F. Armstrong, Jr.), Fulton. Author: Music Al; Angel Child, 1927; Ex-Mistress, 1930; Night Nurse, 1930; Promiscuous, 1931; Personal Maid, 1931; Boy Crazy, 1931; No More Orchids, 1932; Modern Lady, 1935; Public Sweetheart No. 1, 1935; Riding High, 1937; Crazy Kid, 1938; The Unbreakable Mrs. Doll, 1938; Twilight Cheats, 1939; (with April Armstrong) When Sorrow Comes, 1950; also stories and articles in mags. Co-author with Fulton Oursler of play The Walking Gentleman, Produced in N.Y., 1942. Pennames: Grace Perkins and Dora Macy. Composer school songs and songs for children. Adv. editor Guideposts, Carmel, N.Y. Home: 112 Central Park S., N.Y.C. Died Dec. 16, 1955.

OVERSTREET, Lee-Carl, lawyer and prof. law; b. St. Louis, July 30, 1898; s. Lee and Anna M. (Schneider) O.; A.B., Westminster Coll., Fulton, Mo., 1922; LL.B., U. of Mo., 1925; LL.M., University of Michigan, 1941; married Mary Elizabeth Polk, September 11, 1926; children—Ann (Mrs. E. W. Kurtz, Jr.), Lynn Polk. Admitted to Missouri bar, 1925; investigator Mo. Crime Survey, 1925; asso. firm of Morrison, Nugent, Wylder & Berger, Kansas City, Mo., 1925-28; asst. prof. law, U. of Mo., 1928-29, asso. prof., 1929-31, prof. of law since 1931; University attorney, 1936-41, and since 1947; vis. law prof. U. of Mich., 2d semester, 1940-41; prof. law U. of So. Calif., summer 1948; teaching fellow in legal research, Michigan, 1940-41. Mem. The Missouri Bar, Boone County Bar Assn., Order of the Coif, Phi Delta Theta, Phi Delta Phi. Democrat. Contbr. to Missouri Law Review. Home: 16 Brandon Rd., Columbia, Mo. Died July 9, 1955; buried Oak Grove Cemetery, St. Louis.

OVERTON, Frank, physician; b. Bellport, N.Y., Dec. 29, 1867; s. Edward and Mary (Glover) O.; A.B., Lafayette Coll., 1890, D.Sc., 1919; M.D., Columbia, 1893; Dr. P.H., N.Y.U., 1917; m. Alena M. Conklin, Nov. 25, 1896; children—Mary C., David Edward. Began practice at Patchogue, N.Y., 1894; dist. state health officer for L.I., N.Y. Dept. Health, 1914-24; editor Jour. of Med. Soc. State N.Y., 1924-34, Jour. of Med. Soc. State N.J., 1934-43, retired 1944. Capt. Med. O. R.C., Camp Upton, World War. Republican. Conglist. Mason (K.T.). Author: Applied Hygiene, 1899; The Health Officer, 1919. Home: Patchogue, N.Y. Died Oct. 10, 1953; buried Bellport, N.Y.

OVERTON, Watkins, lawyer; b. Memphis, Tenn., June 5, 1894; s. Watkins and May (Hill) O.; A.B., Carroll Coll., Waukesha, Wis., 1916, LL.D., 1956; grad. Harvard, 1916-17; J.D., U. Chgo., 1921; LL.D., Southwestern U., Memphis, 1936; children by 1st marriage—May Hill, Nancy Lee, Watkins; m. 2d, Bessie Ganong, Jan. 18, 1937; married 3d, Helen Parker, Sept. 3, 1952; children—Helen Parker, Napoleon Hill. Admitted to the Tennessee bar, 1922, and began practice at Memphis with McKellar, Kyser & Allen, later mem. Kyser, Allen & Overton. Served as private, ambulance service, U.S. Army, 1918. Mem. Tenn. House of Rep., 1925, Tenn. State Senate, 1927; mayor of Memphis 3 terms, 1928-40; pres. bd. of edn. of Memphis City Schs., 1947-49; mayor of Memphis, Tennessee, 1949-1953; del. at large from Tennessee Nat. Democratic Convention 1956. Member Memphis and Shelby County bar assns., Phi Delta Phi, Tau Kappa Epsilon, Omicron Delta Kappa, Order of Coif, Memphis Chamber of Commerce, Vets. of Foreign Wars, Am. Legion. Democrat. Presbyterian. Mason (32°, Shriner). Club: Memphis Country. Home: 2250 Court Av. Office: Courthouse, Memphis. Died Dec. 2, 1958; buried Forest Hill Cemetery, Memphis.

OVINGTON, Mary White, social worker, author; b. Brooklyn, Apr. 11, 1865; d. Theodore Tweedy and Louise (Ketcham) Ovington; Radcliffe, 1891-93. Head worker at Greenpoint Settlement, Pratt Inst., Neighborship Assn., 1895-1903; fellow of Greenwich House Com. on Social Investigations, 1904-05. Treas. bd. N.A.A.C.P. Author: Half a Man, 1911; Hazel (juvenile), 1913; The Shadow (novel), 1920; Portraits in Color, 1927; Zeke (juvenile), 1931. Contbr. to mags. Home: 12 E. 97th St., N.Y.C. Died July 1951.

OWEN, Allison, architect and landscape architect; b. New Orleans, Dec. 29, 1869; s. Gen. William Miller and Caroline Amanda (Zacharie) O.; student Tulane U., 1885-88; Mass. Inst. Tech., 1892-94; course Sch. of Fire, U.S. Army, Ft. Sill, Okla., 1918; War Coll., Washington, 1924; m. Blanche Pothier, Sept. 16, 1896 (dec.); children—William Miller (dec.), Cecile Violet, Allison, Louis Benjamin (dec.). Began practice New Orleans, 1895; architect on $4,000,000 White Slum Clearance project, New Orleans. Prin. works: New Orleans Pub. Library, Municipal Office Bldg., La. Bank Bldg., Met. Bank Bldg. United Fruit Co. Bldg., Notre Dame Sem., Am. Sugar Refining Office, Pythian Temple Office Bldg., Mergenthaler Bldg., New Orleans Athletic Club Bldg., Criminal Court and Jail Bldg. (all New Orleans); Westminster Ch. (Kansas City): St. Joseph's Ch. (Mobile); Presbyn. Ch. (Yazoo City, Miss.); St. Landry Church, Opelousas, La.; and many schs., coll. bldgs., chs., etc. Pres. Judah P. Benjamin Meml. Assn.; past pres. Community Chest of New Orleans; pres. New Orleans Parkways Commn.; mem. City Planning and Zoning Commn.; mem. bd. St. Mary's Orphan Boys Asylum; past pres. Associated Catholic Charities; pres. Met. and Particular Council New Orleans Soc. St. Vincent de Paul. Served as maj. comdg. Washington Arty. (1st La. F.A.), on Mexican border, 1916; col. comdg. 141st F.A. (Washington Arty.), in France, 1918-19; brig. gen. comdg. 56th F.A. Brigade, 1924-33; maj. gen. retired, 1934. Decorated Chevalier Legion of Honor (France); Knight of St. Gregory the Great. Fellow A.I.A. (ex-pres. La. chpt.); mem. Mil. Order World War, Am. Legion, La. Hist. Assn. (pres.), New Orleans Assn. Commerce (pres. 1927, 32). K.C. (4°; past grand knight, Marquette Council). Democrat. Clubs: Round Table (past pres.), Army and Navy, Boston. Recipient of Annual Loving Cup, Times-Picayune, 1928. Home: 1237 State St. Office: Pere Marquette Bldg., New Orleans. Died Jan. 30, 1951; buried Metairie Cemetery, New Orleans.

OWEN, Carl Maynard, lawyer; b. Galena, O., Aug 17, 1879; s. William Bryant and Sarah Dorcas (Maynard) O.; student Ill. Coll., Jacksonville, 1896-97 A.B., Dartmouth, 1901; LL.B., Harvard, 1905; m. Shirley Barnes, June 15, 1907; children—Shirley Barnes (Mrs. John A. Sargent), David Barnes, Richard Barnes. Admitted to N.Y. bar, 1906, and since practiced in N.Y. City; associated with Henry M. Ward, 1905-06; with Hornblower, Byrne, Miller & Potter and successors since 1906, becoming mem. firm, 1910, now member Willkie, Owen, Farr, Gallagher & Walton; dir. General Reinsurance Corp., North Star Reinsurance Co., Purolator Products, Inc., Grand Central Galleries, International Minerals and Metals Corp., National Zinc Co., York Commercial Corp. Mem. Am., New York State bar assns., Bar Assn. of City of New York, National Health Council (director), National Multiple Sclerosis Society (dir.), Phi Delta Theta, Phi Beta Kappa, Phi Beta Kappa Associates, Sigma Pi. Republican. Presbyterian. Clubs: University, Recess, Blind Brook Golf, American Yacht, Metropolitan Opera, Shenorock Shore, Gulf Stream Golf. Home: 21 Claremont Av., N.Y.C.; also S. Ocean Blvd., Delray Beach, Fla. Office: 15 Broad St., N.Y.C. Died Apr. 12, 1954; buried Williamstown, Mass.

OWEN, Charles Archibald, educator; b. Winchester, Kan., Aug. 4, 1885; s. John Wesley and Eliza (Kirkpatrick) O.; B.A., Monmouth Coll., 1907; M.A., Yale, 1912, Ph.D., 1921, Sterling fellow, 1928-29; m. Margaret Jane Corette, July 31, 1913; children—John Corette, Charles Archibald, James Griffith, Richard Vincent, Margaret Jane. Instr. Assiut (Egypt) Coll., 1908-11, prof. English, 1913-37; prof. English, Monmouth Colll., 1937—; chmn. dept., 1938—. Mem. Am. Oriental Soc., Am. Assn. Univ. Profs. Republican. Presbyn. Author: (translation from Arabic) Arabian Wit and Wisdom, 1932. Home: 720 E. Archer Av., Monmouth, Ill. Died Apr. 1951.

OWEN, James, lawyer; b. Marshall County, Ia., June 7, 1872; s. William R. and Martha (Andrews) O.; A.B., U. of Kan., 1893, LL.B., 1895; m. Winifred Churchill, Nov. 5, 1896; children—Margaret (Mrs. Montgomery Dorsey), James Churchill, William Myron. Admitted to Colo. bar, 1895, and began practice at Pueblo; asst. dist. atty., 4th Dist. of Colo., 1898-99; mem. Colo. Senate, 1903-07; judge 4th Jud. Dist., Colo., 1907-13; settled in Denver, 1913; dir. U.S. Nat. Bank; officer or dir. various corps. Dir. Denver Community Chest. Mem. Phi Kappa Psi. Republican. Club: Denver. Home: 720 Emerson St., Denver. Died Sept. 23, 1949.

OWEN, John Paul, naval officer (ret.); b. Milford, Mo., Jan. 29, 1889; s. Walter Wilson and Mary Belle (Vick Roy) O.; M.D., St. Louis U., 1913; grad., U.S. Naval Med. Sch., 1917; m. Miss Coates, June 1, 1936. Interne, Kansas City (Mo.) General Hosp., 1914-15; commd. lt. j.g., U.S. Navy, 1915, and advanced through grades to rear adm., 1946; fleet surgeon, convoy task force, World War I; fleet surgeon, U.S. Asiatic Fleet, 1939-41; established and comd., U.S. Naval Amputation and Rehabilitation Center, Mare Island, Calif., 1942-44; fleet surgeon, U.S. 7th Fleet, World War II. Awarded Legion of Merit for rehabilitation of amputees; 2d Legion of Merit for work with 7th Fleet. Mem. Radiological Soc. of N. Am., A.M.A. Democrat. Mason. Club: Bohemian (San Francisco). Home: 1880 Pacific Av., San Francisco. Died June 14, 1954; buried Golden Gate Nat. Cemetery, San Francisco.

OWEN, L. F., business exec.; b. Randolph County, N.C., Dec. 23, 1871; s. Wesley Benton and Laura Ann (Bower) O.; student pvt. sch.; m. Mary Barrow, Apr. 21, 1896; 1 son, Allen K. Vice pres. Piedmont Constrn. Co., Inc., Winston-Salem, N.C.; asst. to pres. and dir. McLean Trucking Co., Inc., Winston-Salem; dir. Winston-Salem Terminal Corp.; with R. J. Reynolds Tobacco Co., 1899-1948, traffic mgr. and dir., 1928-48, retired 1948. Dir. Asso. Traffic Clubs of Am. Alderman City of Winston-Salem, 1915-25; chmn. Pub. Works Com., 1915-25; mayor pro tem, 1923-25. Trustee Salem Coll., Winston-Salem; mem. City Dem. Exec. Com. Mem. Office Def. Transportation coms., World War II. Received citation of Distinguished Service. Mem. Am. Soc. Traffic and Transportation. Democrat. Mem. Moravian Ch. K. of P. Clubs: Rotary (Winston-Salem), Forsyth Country. Home: 1087 Kent Rd., E. Office: P.O. Box 3172 Winston-Salem, N.C. Died May 23, 1954.

OWEN, Russell, newspaper corr.; b. Chicago, Ill., Jan. 8, 1889; s. William and Annie R. (Brown) O.; ed. pub. and pvt. schs., Providence, R.I.; married Ethel J. McGregor, April 12, 1913 (died January 15, 1948); 1 daughter, Jean (Mrs. L. A. Gibson). Began as stenographer, 1904; reporter N.Y. Sun, 1906-20, N.Y. Times since 1920; covered several famous trials including Scopes Trial, Dayton, Tenn., 1925; with Amundsen and Byrd at Spitzbergen, 1926; specialized in aviation, Lindbergh's Transantlantic flight and Pan-Am. tour at Mexico City and Havana; with Byrd's first Antarctic Expdn.; also on spl. assignments to Hawaii and Philippines. Awarded Pulitzer prize in journalism for articles covering the first Byrd Antarctic Expdn.. 1929-30; recipient of medal presented by Congress to members of expdn. Clubs: Century, Dutch Treat. Author: South of the Sun, 1934; The Antarctic Ocean, 1941. Co-author: We Saw It Happen, 1938. Contbr. articles to mags. Address: N.Y. Times, N.Y.C. Died Apr. 3, 1952.

OWENS, Grover Thomas, lawyer; b. Yellville, Ark., Nov. 26, 1887; s. James Spencer and Caroline (Durden) O.; student Springfield (Mo.) State Normal Sch., 1904-06; LL.B., U. of Ark., 1911; m. Ruby Johnson, Oct. 7, 1914; 1 dau., Olivia Owens Nisbet. Admitted to Ark. bar, 1911, since practiced Little Rock; sr. partner Owens, Ehrman & McHaney. Mem. Ark. State Senate, 1919-23; pres. Community Chest, 1931; chmn. bd. dirs. Ark. State Chamber of Commerce, 1939—. Mem. Little Rock Chamber of Commerce (pres. 1936). Mem. Delta Theta Phi. Democrat. Episcopalian. Mason (K.T., 32°). Clubs: Country, Little Rock (Little Rock); University (St. Louis). Home: 19 Edgehill Rd. Office: Pyramid Bldg., Little Rock, Ark. Died Apr. 3, 1954.

OWENS, Ray L., army officer; b. Chillicothe, Mo., April 7, 1891; s. David and Mary Margaret (Dryer) O.; student Moore's Normal Sch., Chillicothe, Mo., 1908-10, Northwestern State Normal, Alva, Okla., 1911; grad. Air Service Pilots Schs., 1921, Air Service Observation Sch., 1921, Air Corps Tactical Sch., 1935, Command and Gen. Staff Sch., 1938; rated command pilot, combat observer; m. Ada Louise Belt, Jan. 25, 1919; children—Ada Louise (wife of Capt. Leo Beldo, U.S. Army), Mary Margaret, Carolyn Ray. Teacher in pub. schs., 1912-17; served with U.S. Army, June 10, 1917 to Aug. 23, 1919; commd. 2d lt., Air Service, U.S. Army, Sept. 21, 1920, and advanced through the grades to brig. gen., Dec. 4, 1942. Decorated Victory Medal, Legion of Merit, Battle Honors (North Solomons). Club: Army and Navy (Manila, P.I.). Home: 1344 Ballou Rd., Spokane, Wash. Deceased.

OWENS, Walter D., ins. exec.; b. Jacksonville, Fla., May 16, 1903; student Fla. Mil. Acad., N. Ga. Agrl. Coll. With Aetna Casualty & Surety Co., Jacksonville, 1922-25, Bailey Owens & Co., Orlando, Fla., 1925-28; asst. so. mgr., So. Surety Co., Atlanta, 1928-30, Home Indemnity Co., Charlotte, N. C., 1930-32, U.S. Casualty Co., 1932-34, asst. to pres., 1934-35, v.p., 1935-36, v.p. and sec., 1936-40, exec. v.p. and sec., 1940-48, pres. since 1948; now v.p. and dir. New Amsterdam Casualty Co., N.Y. City. Mem. Pi Kappa Alpha. Mason. Clubs: Bankers of America, Casualty and Surety of New York. Home: 969 Park Av. Office: New Amsterdam Casualty Co., 60 John St., N.Y.C. 7. Died June 23, 1952; buried Waycross, Ga.

OWLETT, Gilbert Mason (ou'lĕt), Rep. Nat. committeeman; b. Wellsboro, Pa., June 13, 1892; s. Edward Howland and Ida (Wells) O.; B.S., Princeton, 1914; student U. of Pa. Law Sch., 1915-17; m. Sue Elizabeth Berkey, June 20, 1918; children—Ann Mary, Edward H. Admitted to Pa. bar, 1917, since practiced in Wellsboro, Pa.; mem. firm Crichton & Owlett, 1918-32; head Owlett, Webb & Cox, attys.; mem. Owlett, Cox, Wilcox & Owlett; director Commonwealth Telephone Company, Dallas, Pet Milk Co.; president, executive vice pres. and general counsel Pa. Mfrs. Assn. and its allied ins. companies; sec.-treas. Highland Milk Condensing Co.; pres. Tioga County Savings & Trust Co., Wellsboro Hotel Co., Wellsboro Elec. Co., Hubbell Realty Co. State senator, 1932-40; Rep. Nat. Committeeman since 1936. Mem. Am. and Pa. bar assns., Phi Delta Phi. Republican. Presbyterian. Mason, Odd Fellow. Clubs: Arch (Princeton); Ross (Williamsport); Tioga County Wellsboro), Union League (Phila.). Home: 14 West Av. Office: Owlett Bldg., Wellsboro, Pa. Died Jan. 24, 1957; buried Wellsboro Cemetery.

OWSLEY, Frank Lawrence, prof. history; b. Montgomery County, Ala., Jan. 20, 1890; s. Lawrence Monroe and Annie Scott (McGehee) O.; B.S., Ala. Poly. Inst., 1911, M.S., 1912; A.M., U. of Chicago, 1917, Ph.D., 1924; m. Harriet Fason Chappell, July 24, 1920; children—Frances Mildred (dec.), Frank Lawrence, Margaret Chappell. Member faculty Ala. Poly. Tech. Inst., 1912-19; prof. history, Birmingham-Southern Coll., 1919-20; asst. prof. history, Vanderbilt, 1920-24, asso. prof., 1924-27, prof., 1927-49; Friedman prof. So. history, U. of Alabama, 1949—, head dept. history, 1951-54; Fulbright lectr. history, St. John's Coll., Cambridge U., 1956; Guggenheim traveling fellow in Europe, 1927-28. Attended O.T.C., Ft. Oglethorpe, Ga., and Camp Sevier, S.C. Mem. Am. Hist. Asso., Mississippi Valley Historical Association, Southern Hist. Assn. (pres. 1940), Phi Beta Kappa, Omicron Delta Kappa. Methodist. Author: States Rights in the Confederacy, 1925; King Cotton Diplomacy, 1931, rev. 1959; Plain Folk of the Old South, 1949; A Short History of the American People, (with O. P. Chitwood and H. C. Nixon), Vol. I, 1945; Vol. II, 1948; The United States: from Colony to World Power, 1949. Contbr. numerous profl. jours. Address: 14 Hillcrest, Tuscaloosa, Ala. Died Oct. 21, 1956; buried Tuscaloosa, Ala.

P

PAASIKIVI, Juho Kusti (pä-sĕ'kē-ve), ex-pres. of Finland; b. Finland, Nov. 27, 1870; s. Johan August Hellsten and Karolina Wilhemina (Selin) P.; law student, Finland, 1890-97, Stockholm and Uppsala, 1898-1900, Leipsig, 1899; studied langs., Russia, 1891; LL.D., 1901; m. Anna Matilda Forsman, 1897 (died 1931); m. 2d, Alli Valve Hilden, 1934. Engaged in polit. activities since 1902; mem. Finnish Diet, 1907; senator and chief finance dep., 1908-09; prime minister of Finland, 1918; minister to Sweden, 1936-39; minister without portfolio, 1939-40; minister to Russia, 1940-41; became premier of Finland, 1944; pres. of Finland for terms 1946-56. Pres. Finnish delegation to Internat. Conf., Geneva, 1927; sec. Union of Pellervo, 1901-03, mem. bd. dirs., 1903-08; mem. and v.p. Helsingfors Exchange, 1916-30; v. pres. Industri-Hypoteksanken, Finland, 1924-28, pres. since 1928; mng. dir., bd. dirs., Kansallispankki, 1914-34, mem. adv. bd., 1934-46. Author of numerous articles in periodicals. Address: Helsinki, Finland. Died Dec. 1956.

PABST, Fred, brewery exec.; b. Milwaukee, Nov. 3, 1869; s. Fred and Maria (Best) P.; ed. Markham Acad., Milwaukee, Mich. Mil. Acad., Schwarz Brewing Sch., N.Y. City; student U. of Wis.; m. Ida C. Uihlein, Mar. 25, 1896; children—Pauline P. Wurlitzer, Fred, August U. (dec.), Rudolf, Robert E., David, Harald. Began as brewer and dir. Pabst Brewing Co., 1893, v.p., 1899-1905, chmn. bd., 1939-54, dir.; v.p. Pabst Farms, Inc.; pres. Pabst Corp., 1921-32; v.p. Premier Pabst Corp., 1932-39. Mem. Holstein-Friesian Assn. Am. Mason (life). Clubs: Milwaukee, Milwaukee Country, Milwaukee Athletic, Wisconsin, University, Milwaukee Yacht, Oconomowoc Lake, Old Settlers. Address: Oconomowoc, Wis. Died Feb. 21, 1958.

PACENT, Louis Gerard, electric and radio engr.; b. N.Y. City, June 23, 1893; s. Louis and Mary (Tomasino) P.; ed. Mt. Carmel Acad., spl. schs. abroad; grad. Pratt Inst.; m. Antoinette Marie Andriola, Sept. 10, 1917; children—Louis Gerard, Homer Cosmos. Employee Manhattan Electric Co., 1909-19; organizer, dir., Pacent Electric Co., 1919, Pacent Reproducer Corp., 1929, Pacent Engring. Corp. since 1933; engaged in development work on new throat microphone; cons. engr. Sonotone Corp., Elmsford, N.Y. Served as civilian engr., World War I. Recipient Engring. Key of Inst. Radio Engrs., 1946. Fellow Am. Inst. E.E., Inst. Radio Engrs., Soc. Motion Picture Engrs., Radio Club of Am., mem. Motion Picture Acad. (found mem.), V.W.O.A. (life mem.), A.S.A. Republican. Roman Catholic. Clubs: Norway Country, Pratt, North Hills, Engrs. (N.Y. City); Cosmos (Washington). Author: The Complete Radio Book; numerous tech. papers. Home: Little Neck, L.I.; (summer) Norway, Me. Office: 79 Madison Av., N.Y.C. Died Apr. 7, 1952.*

PACH, Walter (päk), artist, author; b. N.Y.C., July 11, 1883; s. Gotthelf and Frances (Wise) P.; B.S., Coll. City of N.Y., 1903; studied at N.Y. Sch. of Art, Académie Ranson, Paris; m. Magdalene Frohberg, Feb. 26, 1914; 1 son, Raymond. Exhibited at Pa. Acad. Fine Arts, 1905; Nat. Acad. Design N.Y., 1906; "Independents," Paris, 1908; Internat. Exhbn., N.Y. and Chgo., 1913; Independent Artists, N.Y.C., yearly 1917—; now prof. art City Coll.; 8 one-man shows in N.Y. Etchings in permanent collections Metropolitan Mus. N.Y. Pub. Library, etc.; paintings in Met. Mus., Phillips Meml. Gallery (Washington). Bklyn. Mus., and many pvt. collections. Dir. Masterpieces of Art, N.Y. World's Fair, 1940. Mem. Soc. Independent Artists (dir.). Author: Georges Seurat, 1923; The Masters of Modern Art, 1924; Raymond Duchamp-Villon, 1924; Ananias or the False Artist, 1928; Modern Art in America, 1928; An Hour of Art, 1930; Vincent van Gogh, 1936; Queer Thing, Painting, 1938; Ingres, 1939; The Art Museum in America, 1948; Ancient Fire in Modern Art. Translator: History of Art (by Elie Faure, 5 vols.), 1920-30; The Journal of Eugène Delacroix, 1937. Has lectured at Met. Mus., U. Cal., Nat. U. of Mexico, etc. Address: care The Fifth Av. Bank, 530 Fifth Av.; and 3 Washington Sq., N.Y.C. 3. Died Nov. 27, 1958.

PACK, Randolph Greene, business exec.; b. Cleveland, O., June 8, 1890; s. Charles Lathrop and Alice Gertrude (Hatch) P.; student Pa. State Sch. of Forestry, 1912; Williams Coll. (class 1913; D.Sc. (honorary), University Michigan, 1953; married Georgia Beatty Fuller, Apr. 18, 1914; children—Virginia Lathrop (Mrs. Edward H. Townsend, Jr.), Joan Beatty (Mrs. Richard H. Burns); m. 2d, Maxine Wells, Aug. 11, 1930; children—Polly Wells, Alice Gertrude. Vice pres. Tall Timber Lumber Co., Good Pine, La., 1913-15; prodn. mgr., sec., v.p. engring. dept., Am. Multigraph Co., Cleve., 1916-23; interested in oil developments, central Louisiana, 1940—; director Nebo Oil Co., Grant Oil Co., La-Salle Land Co., all of La. Trustee Conservation Found.; dir. Friends of the Land; dir. New Eng. Forestry Found.; mem. Am. Citizens Com. for United Nations Scientific Conf. on Conservation and Utilization of Resources. Mem.-at-large nat. council Boy Scouts Am.; chairman Am. Red Cross War Fund Drive, 1942; chmn. Darien (Conn.) chapter Am. Red Cross. Pres. Charles Lathrop Pack Forestry Foundation, 1937—; pres. Am. Tree Assn.; v.p. Am. Nature Assn.; exec. vice pres. and dir. Am. Forestry Assn., 1942; hon. mem. Soc. of Am. Foresters; mem. Soc. Colonial Wars State of N.J., Ohio Forestry Assn., La. Forestry Assn. Republican. Presbyterian. Clubs: Wee Burn; Tokeneke (gov.). Home: Darien, Conn. Office: 74 Trinity Pl., N.Y.C. Died Dec. 25, 1956.

PACKARD, Arthur Worthington; b. Boston, Mass., May 28, 1901; s. Charles Herbert and Charlotte R. (McKean) P.; Ph.B., Brown U., 1925; A.B., Oxford U. (Eng.), 1927, A.M., 1932 (Rhodes Scholar); m. Mary Whittle Moody, Nov. 24, 1928; children—David Bruce, William Moody. Teacher Mt. Hermon Boys' Sch., 1923; field sec. World Peace Foundation, 1928; asst. dir. Inst. Internat. Edn., 1929; asso. John D. Rockefeller, Jr., in matters of philanthropy since 1929; dir. and trustee of the Davison Fund, Inc., 1934-41; director Rockefeller Brothers Fund, Incorporated. Ex-mem. Budget Committee National War Fund. Trustee Institute International Education, Colonial Williamsburg, Inc.; bd. fellows Brown U. Chmn. Planning Commn., Rye, N.Y., 1943-45. Mem. Council on Foreign Relations, Phi Betta Kappa, Delta Upsilon. Protestant. Clubs: University, Am. Yacht, Brown, Coffee House, Century. Home: Old White Plains Rd., Mamaroneck, N.Y. Office: 30 Rockefeller Plaza, N.Y.C. Died Jan. 25, 1953.

PACKARD, Francis Randolph, physician; b. Phila., Mar. 23, 1870; s. John Hooker and Elisabeth (Wood) P.; grad. biol. dept., U. of Pa., 1889; M.D., U. of Pa., 1892, LL.D., hon., 1939; m. 1st, Christine B. Curwen (died 1901); m. 2d, Margaret Horstman, Feb. 10, 1906; children—Margaret, Ann, Elizabeth, Frances Randolph. Resident physician, Pennsylvania Hosp., 1893-95; ex-prof. otology, Post-Grad. Sch., Univ. of Pa.; chief otolaryngologist, Pa. Hosp. Served as 1st lt., asst. surgeon, 2d Pa. Vol. Inf., Spanish-Am. War; commd. 1st lt. M.C., U.S. Army, May 16, 1917; capt., Sept. 1, 1917; maj., Oct. 1, 1918; sailed for France, May 18, 1917; with Base Hosp. 10, chief centre consultant in oto-laryngology, Dist. of Paris, Oct. 1918-Jan. 1919. Pres. Am. Laryngol. Assn., 1930, Am. Otol. Soc., 1936; pres. Coll. of Physicians of Phila., 1931-34; pres. Library Company of Philadelphia, 1936-41; mem. Am. Philos. Soc., Delta Psi. Republican. Episcopalian. Clubs: Philadelphia, University Barge. Author: History of Medicine in the United States, 1901, 2d edit., 1919; Diseases of the Ear, Nose and Throat, 1909; The School of Salerno, 1920; The Life and Times of Ambrose Paré,

1921; Some Account of the Pennsylvania Hospital. Editor: The Gold-Headed Cane, 1915. Editor Annals of Medical History, 1917-42. Home: 304 S. 19th St., Philadelphia 3. Died Apr. 18, 1950.

PACKARD, Laurence Bradford, prof. history; b. Brockton, Mass., Jan. 20, 1887; s. William Forest and Mary Florence (Hyslop) P.; A.B., Harvard, 1909, Ph.D., 1921; studied in grad. sch., same univ., 1909-13, and as Rogers traveling fellow, 1911-12; A.M., Amherst (Mass.) Coll., 1934; m. Leonore Healey, May 6, 1927; 1 dau., Ann. Instr. in history, U. of Rochester, 1913-15, asst. prof. history, 1915-20, prof. history and head of dept., 1920-25; prof. history, Amherst Coll., since 1925; lecturer, U. of Mich., 1921, U. of Calif., 1923, Harvard, 1928; visiting prof. history, Yale, 1929-30, Wesleyan U., 1931, 32, New York U., 1933; visiting professor, Smith Coll., 1939, Mt. Holyoke Coll., 1940-43, 1947-48, Harvard Univ., 1942. Capt. Military Intelligence Div., Gen. Staff, U.S. Army, Siberia, 1918-19. Mem. Am. Hist. Assn., Société d'Histoire Moderne (France), Phi Beta Kappa, Delta Upsilon. Author: The Commercial Revolution, 1927; The Age of Louis XIV, 1929; also of monographs for U.S. War Dept. on Czecho-Slovaks in Siberia and on U.S. Expeditionary Force in Siberia. Asso. ed. Berkshire Studies in European History. Contbr. to Am. Hist. Rev. Quarterly Jour. Economics, Political Science Quarterly, Hist. Outlook, Jour. of Modern History, Jour. of Econ. History. Home: Amherst, Mass. Died Jan. 14, 1955; buried Mt. Vernon Cemetery, Abington, Mass.

PACKER, Francis Herman, sculptor; b. Feb. 13, 1873; student Cooper Inst., N.Y., pupil of Philip Martiny; m. Julia Bucher, June 30, 1896. Prin. works: Statue of Chief Justice Thomas Ruffin, and of Ensign Worth Bagley, USN, Raleigh, N.C.; statue of Atty. Gen. George Davis (under adminisdiers group in bronze, known as Monument to the Soldiers of the Confederacy, Wilmington; equestrian statue of Nathaniel Greene, Greensboro, N.C.; equestrian statue of Surgeon Gen. E. B. Wolcott, Milw.; Alfred Benjamin Meml. Fountain, Kansas City, Mo.; T. E. Sprunt Meml., Wilmington, N.C., etc. Awarded contract for design of medal commemorating Byrd Antarctic Expdn. Mem. Nat. Sculptors Soc. Mason. Home: 53 Lakeside Dr., Rockville Centre, L.I., N.Y. Died July 13, 1957.

PACKER, Fred Little, editorial cartoonist; b. Hollywood, Cal., Jan. 4, 1886; s. Jacob W. and Elizabeth (Little) P.; student pub. schs., Los Angeles, Los Angeles Sch. Art and Design, 1902-03, Chgo. Art Inst., 1904-05; m. Lillian Pabst Wilson, Feb. 14, 1941; 1 stepdau., Marjorie Wilson. Staff artist Los Angeles Examiner, 1906-07, San Francisco Morning Call, 1907-13; art dir. San Francisco Call Post, 1913-18; comml. artist for nat. advertisers, N.Y.C., 1919-32; cartoonist N.Y. Jour. and N.Y. American, 1932-33; editorial cartoonist N.Y. Daily Mirror, 1933—; book and mag. illustrator; v.p. Victory Builders, Inc. (creators posters to stimulate prodn. in war plants and industry), 1941-45. Recipient Pulitzer prize for editorial cartooning, 1952; citations by Treasury Dept., WPB, A.R.C., Am. Cancer Soc.; Page One award, for best cartoons Newspaper Guild, 1954, 56, 57; art award in watercolor Newspaper Guild, 1957; George Washington honor medal for cartoon Peaceful Security, Freedoms Found., 1957. Mem. South Shore Arts Assn. (founder, pres. 1950, honorary president); honorary member Joseph P. Carlin Chapter of the St. Charles Hospital Auxiliary, St. Charles Hosp. for Crippled Children. Presbyn. Club: Salmagundi. Cartoon collection requested by Library of Congress for permanent collection; Fred Packer Meml. Hall names in his honor. Home: 216 Lakeview Av. E., Brightwater, L.I., N.Y. Died Dec. 8, 1956.

PACKER, Horace Billings, lawyer; b. Wellsboro, Pa.; s. Dr. Nelson and Mary M. P.; ed. Wellsboro Acad. and Alfred, N.Y., Univ.; admitted to bar; unmarried. Was dist. att'y 4 yrs.; mem. Pa. ho. of reps., 1884-88; State senator, 1888; has presided over 2 State Rep. convs.; mem. Congress from 16th Pa. dist., 1897-1901; Republican. Has bought and sold timber and coal lands in Pa., W.Va. and Mich. Address: Wellsboro, Pa. Deceased.

PADDOCK, R(ichard) B(olles), mech. and elec. engr.; b. Ft. McKinney, Buffalo, Wyo., Apr. 16, 1891; s. Capt. Richard Bolles and Grace (Pershing) P.; student U. Neb., 1907-10; B.S., U.S. Mil. Acad., 1914; grad. Army War Coll. (war course), 1918; grad. U.S. F.A. Sch., Ft. Sill, Okla., 1921 and 1925; grad. U.S. Command and Gen. Staff Sch., 1926; m. 2d Kathryn Fowler Wilson, June 4, 1949; children by previous marriage—Richard Bolles, John Pershing. Commd. 2d lt., C.A.C., 1914; mil. instr., N.Y. City Police Dept., 1916; transferred to Signal Corps, 1916; promoted through grades to lt. col., 1918; transferred to Field Arty., 1920; chief engring. and research div., Signal Corps, 1919; instr. Signal Sch., 1919, 1920, Field Arty. Sch., 1921-25; served as maj. Gen. Staff Corps and chief of staff, Philippine Div., 1927-29; dep. adminstr. NRA, 1933-34; exec. dir. Cotton Garment Code Authority, 1934-36; v.p. Wilson-Jones Co., 1937-40; chief tech. service, engr. and gen. sales mgr., Western Plastics, Inc., 1943-45; pres. Bone Engring. Corp., 1945-46; internat. rep. Tech. Oil Tool Corp., 1949-50; mem. engring. staff Gilfillan Bros., Inc. since 1950. Mem., Gen. Pershing's original staff; tech. officer staff of chief signal officer, A.E.F.; signal officer 1st Div., A.E.F., World War I. Awarded Silver Star, Order of the Purple Heart, Oak Leaf Cluster (U.S.), Croix de Guerre (France) Fourragère, Croix de Guerre (France) as personal decoration (2d Field Signal Batn.). Mem. Inst. Radio Engrs., Phi Gamma Delta. Democrat. Episcopalian. Mason (32°, K.T., Shriner). Clubs: University (Washington); Baltic Society, University, Army and Navy (Manila); Jefferson Islands (Tilghman, Md.). Home: 156 S. Canyon View Dr., Brentwood, Los Angeles 49. Office: 1815 Venice Bldg., Los Angeles. Deceased.

PADDOCK, Wendell, educator; b. Three Oaks, Mich., July 1866; s. Stephen T. and Aurelia C. (Butler) P.; B.S., Mich. State Agrl. Coll., 1893, M.S., 1897; post-grad. work, Cornell U., 1895; m. Jessie G. Francis, of Laporte, Ind., Dec. 24, 1895; children—Francis Wendell, Elizabeth Gertrude, Evelyn Jessie. Asst. Hort. Expt. Sta., Geneva, N.Y., 1893-1900; prof. horticulture, Colo. State Agrl. Coll., Ft. Collins, Colo., 1900-09, Ohio State U. 1909. Fellow A.A.A.S.; mem. Soc. for Hort. Science, Am. Genetic Assn. Conglist. Author: Fruit Growing in Arid Regions, 1910. Home: 1085 Westwood Av., Columbus, O.

PADDOCK, Willard Dryden, sculptor; b. Brooklyn, N.Y., 1873; ed. pub. schs.; studied art, Pratt Inst., Brooklyn, and in France and Italy; married. Has exhibited Nat. Acad. Design, Nat. Sculpture Soc. and Archtl. League America—all N.Y.C.; Pa. Acad. Fine Arts, Phila.; Carnegie Inst., Pittsburgh; Corcoran Gallery, Washington; Boston, Providence, etc. A.N.A.; mem. Nat. Sculpture Soc., Artists Fellowship, Inc. Clubs: Century. Home: South Kent, Conn. Died 1956.

PAGE, Arthur Clinton, editor; b. Independence, Mo., July 21, 1888; s. Justin E. and Harriet J. (Nichols) P.; B.S. in Agr., U. of Mo., 1912; m. Inez Reeder, June 11, 1913; children—Thomas Justin, John Walter, David Arthur. Asst. editor Orange Judd Farmer, 1912-14, editor, 1914-27; asso. editor The Prairie Farmer, Chicago, since 1927; farm program dir. radio sta. WLS. Trustee Farm Found. Mem. food prodn. com. Ill. Counsel of Defense, World War, and agrl. com., Nat. Fire Waste Council. Mem. Agrl. Editors Assn., Ill. Rural Edn. Com., DuPage County Board of Health, Eckles Club. Methodist. Home: R.D. 1, Box 294, Wheaton, Ill. Died Apr. 4, 1953; buried Wheaton Cemetery.

PAGE, Frank Copeland, public utilities; b. Brooklyn, N.Y., Mar. 17, 1887; s. Walter Hines and Alice (Wilson) P.; Harvard, 1910; m. Anna Howard Harbison, Sept. 25, 1920; children—Shelby Harbison, Allison Francis, Cecily. Started as bond salesman White Weld & Co., N.Y. City, 1909-12; partner Page Bros., Aberdeen, N.C., 1912-15; edit. staff Doubleday Page & Co., Garden City, L.I., 1915-17; editor Country Life in America, Garden City, L.I., 1919-20; mng. editor Winston-Salem (N.C.) Journal, 1920; sec. Am. Relief Adminstrn., N.Y. City, 1920-23; dept. mgr. U.S. C. of C., Washington, D.C., 1923-28; v.p. Internat. Telephone & Telegraph Corp., N.Y. City, since 1928, former director; dir. Cuban-Am. Telephone & Telegraph Co., Am. Cable & Radio Corp. Served as capt., later maj. A.S., U.S. Army, 1917-18. Dir. Nat. Foreign Trade Council, Beekman-Downtown Hospital. Dir. Am. Children's Fund. Democrat. Episcopalian. Clubs: Metropolitan, Burning Tree (Washington, D.C.); Harvard (N.Y. City). Home: 1406 29th St. N.W., Washington. Office: 67 Broad St., N.Y. City. Died Dec. 18, 1950.

PAGE, John Chatfield, cons. engr.; b. Syracuse, Neb., Oct. 12, 1887; s. Walter Ernest and Emma Jerusha (Chatfield) P.; B.S., U. Neb., 1908; grad. work Cornell U., 1910-11; m. Mildred Rebecca Sloan, May 29, 1914; children—Jean Rebecca (Mrs. C. L. Killgore), Mildred (Mrs. P. Danielson). Topographer U.S. Bur. Reclamation, 1909; asst. city engr. Grand Junction, Colo., 1909-10; jr. engr. Bur. of Reclamation, 1911-25, supt. Grand Valley (Colo.) project, 1925-30, office engr. on constrn. of Boulder Dam, 1930-35, acting commr., 1936-37, commr. of reclamation, 1937-43; resigned as commr. Aug. 3, 1943, designated cons. engr. Mem. Am. Soc. C.E., Sigma Tau. Mason (32°, Shriner). Home: 5335 Montview Blvd. Office: Bureau of Reclamation, Dept. of the Interior, Denver. Died Mar. 23, 1955; buried Crown Hill Cemetery, Jefferson County, Colo.

PAGE, Kirby, author, social evangelist; b. Tyler County, Tex., Aug. 7, 1890; s. James Andrew Thomas and Isabella (Pounds) P.; B.A., Drake U., 1915, D.D., 1940; grad. work U. Chgo., Columbia, Union Theol. Sem.; m. Mary Alma Folse, Sept. 2, 1914; children—Kirby, Mary. Asst. sec. Y.M.C.A., Houston, 1908-11; student pastor Monteith, Ia., 1912-15; ordained ministry Disciples of Christ, 1915; pastor Morgan Park Ch., Chgo., 1915; Y.M.C.A. work in France and British Isles, 1916-17; traveled with Sherwood Eddy in evangelistic campaigns among students in Am., China, Japan, Korea, 1916-18; pastor Ridgewood Ch. of Christ, N.Y., 1918-21; social evangelist and author 1921—. Mem. Phi Beta Kappa. Author: Something More, 1920; The Sword or the Cross, 1921; Christianity and Economic Problems, 1922; War—Its Causes, Consequences and Cure, 1923; (with Sherwood Eddy) The Abolition of War, 1924; Imperialism and Nationalism, 1925; An American Peace Policy, 1925; (with Sherwood Eddy) Makers of Freedom, 1926; Dollars and World Peace, 1927; Jesus or Christianity, 1929; National Defense, 1931; Living Creatively, 1932; The Personality of Jesus, 1932; Individualism and Socialism, 1933; Living Triumphantly, 1934; Living Courageously, 1936; Must We Go to War?, 1937; (with Sherwood Eddy) Creative Pioneers, 1937; Religious Resources for Personal Living and Social Action, 1939; Living Prayerfully, 1941; Living Abundantly, 1944; The Will of God for These Days, 1945; Now Is the Time to Prevent a Third World War, 1946; The Light Is Still Shining in the Darkness, 1946. Editor: Recent Gains in American Civilization, 1928; A New Economic Order, 1930; also 22 pamphlets. Contbr. to mags. Made many trips to Europe and Asia to study internat. and econ. problems. Home: LaHabra, Cal. Died Dec. 16, 1957; buried Orange Grove Friends Meeting Cemetery, Pasadena, Cal.

PAGE, Leigh, physicist; b. South Orange, N.J., Oct. 13, 1884; s. Edward D. and Cornelia (Lee) P.; Ph.B., Sheffield Scientific Sch. (Yale), 1904; Ph.D., Yale, 1913; m. Mary Cholmondeley Thornton, June 27, 1910; children—Thornton Leigh, Barbara Helen, Marjory. Instr. physics, 1912-16, asst. prof., 1916-22, prof. math. physics since 1922, Yale. Apptd. judge Einstein contest by Scientific American, 1921; developed a new theory of electromagnetism. Fellow Am. Acad. of Arts and Sciences, Am. Phys. Soc., A.A.A.S.; mem. Am. Math. Soc., Nat. Research Council (1923), Sigma Xi, Phi Gamma Delta, Gamma Alpha. Republican. Conglist. Author: An Introduction to Electrodynamics, 1922; An Introduction to Theoretical Physics, 1928; Principles of Electricity, 1931; Electrodynamics, 1940; also numerous professional papers. Home: 244 Livingston St., New Haven, Conn. Died Sept. 14, 1952.

PAGE, Lewis Coues, publisher; b. Zürich, Switzerland (while father was U.S. consul there), Jan. 13, 1869; s. Charles Albert and Grace Darling (Coues) P.; A.B., Harvard, 1891. With Estes & Lauriat, pubs., 1891-92; treas. Joseph Knight Co., 1892-96, name changed to L. C. Page & Co., 1897, since pres. and gen. mgr., company acquired Dana Estes & Co. (formerly Estes & Lauriat), 1914; pub. Boston Evening Record, 1916-17; v.p. Boston Nat. League Baseball Co., 1911-12. Editor series of World Classics, 1892-93. Republican. Home: Page Court, Powell St., Brookline, Mass. Office: 53 Beacon St., Boston 8. Died May 9, 1956; buried Portsmouth, N.H.

PAGE, Richard Gregory, banker; b. Bklyn., Aug. 9, 1887; s. Richard Gregory and Ida (Williams) P.; student pub. schs. of Cranford, N.J.; m. Marjorie Adele Lyon, July 30, 1910. Messenger Bankers Trust Co., N.Y.C., 1903; v.p. Bankers Trust Co., N.Y.C. 1926—; pres., trustee The Provident Loan Soc. of New York; dir., voting trustee and mem. exec. com. Ohio Edison Co.; Unity Fire Ins. Corp.; dir., voting trustee Central of Ga. Ry. Co. Clubs: Union League, Downtown Assn., (N.Y.C.); Plainfield (N.J.) Country; Spring Lake (N.J.) Golf and Country. Author: Works of Corporate Trust Departments (with Payson G. Gates). Home: 744 Watchung Av., Plainfield, N.J. Office: 16 Wall St., N.Y.C. Died Dec. 1, 1951.

PAGE, William Herbert, prof. law; b. Mt. Union, O., Aug. 6, 1868; s. Robert Stuart and Mary Elizabeth (Guthrie) P.; B.A., Yale, 1889; LL.B., Ohio State U., 1892, LL.M., 1894; S.J.D., Harvard, 1914; m. Ruth Gray Brown, June 14, 1898; children—Robert Guthrie, Gilman Gray, Dorothy Brown, (died, Sept. 21, 1940) Ruth Torzier. Admitted to practice law in Ohio, 1894, Wis., 1917; prof. law Ohio State U., 1896-1917; prof. law, U. of Wis., since Feb. 8, 1917. Mayor of Grandview Heights, O., 1909-12. Mem. Am. Law Inst., Zeta Psi, Phi Beta Kappa, Phi Delta Phi, Order of Coif. Democrat. Conglist. Author: Page on Wills, 1901, 3d edit., 1941; Wills Pocket Parts, 1944-50; Page on Contracts, 1905, 2d. 1919, supplement, 1929; Page (and Jones) on Taxation by Assessment, 1909; Page's (and Adams) Annotated Ohio General Code, 1912, supplement, 1916, 2d edition, 1926, lifetime edition, 1938; Page's Ohio Digest, 1914, supplement, 1918; Compact Code, 1921; Annotations to General Code, 1922; Supplement to Digest, 2d edit., 1924, lifetime edit., 1932; Unannotated Code, 1930; also articles in law jours., addresses, book reviews, etc. Home: 515 N. Carroll St., Madison, Wis. Died July 22, 1952; buried Forest Hill Cemetery, Madison.

PAIGE, Clifford E., pub. utilities; b. Cleve., May 2, 1884; s. William H. and Laura Ann (Tubbs) P.; ed. Wesleyan Acad., Wilbraham, Mass.; m. Alice C. Perry, June 3, 1909; children—Marjorie (Mrs. Albert A. Teller), Lincoln, Stuart. Began with Springfield (Mass.) Gas Light Co., 1903, asst. supt., 1905-12, supt., mgr. Malden & Melrose Gas Light Co., 1912-

19; mgr. Worcester Gas Light Co., 1919-22; v.p. Charles W. Tenney & Co. (Boston), 1922-24; pres. Beverly Gas & Electric Co., 1922-24; v.p. Bklyn. (N.Y.) Union Gas Co., 1924-35, chief engr., 1927-39, dir. 1932-—, pres., 1935-52, chmn. of bd., 1940-52, ret. 1952. Trustee, vice chmn. exec. com. and trust investment com. Bklyn. Trust Co., 1927-50; vice chmn. exec. com., trustee So. Bklyn. Savs. Bank, Inst. of Gas Tech. (mem. finance com.); dir. Bklyn. City Safe Deposit Co., 1940-50, Greenwich (Conn.) Gas Co., Utilities Mutual Ins. Co. (mem. finance com.); mem. adv. bd. Mfrs. Trust Co. Mem. Nat. Govt. Finance Adv. Bd., Am. Standards Assn. Com. for Voluntary Standards. Dir. Downtown Bklyn. Assn., Bklyn. C. of C., 1938-47, Bklyn. Soc. for Prevention of Cruelty to Children, 1925-46; dir. Greater N.Y. Safety Council (chmn. exec. com., 1941-46, v.p. 1947); mem. Am. Gas Assn. (mem. adv. council; treas. 1926-29; v.p. 1929-30; pres. 1930-31; mem. exec. bd., 1924-34; dir. intermittently 1931-47; chmn. finance and control com., 1940; chmn. A.G.A. Munroe Award Com., 1946); chmn. com. Econ. Development of Bklyn., 1944-45; Kings Co. War Finance com., 1943-45, Bklyn. Salvation Army campaign, 1945, Bklyn. Cancer Com. Appeal, 1946. Mem. adv. bd. N.Y. and Bklyn. Salvation Army; mem. Guild of Gas Mgrs., Soc. Gas Lighting, N.Y. State, Borough of Queens C's of C., Mayor's Bus. Adv. com., adv. council, Boy Scouts of Am., Utilities Pub. com., 1940-48, Am. Mus. Nat. History, Victory Legion (charter mem.), Bklyn. Inst. Arts and Sci., L.I. Hist. Soc., Nat. Guard Assn. of Mass., N.E. Gas Assn. Vice pres. Internat. Gas Union, 1932-49. Club: Engineers (N.Y.C.). Home: 52 Lafayette Pl., Greenwich, Conn. Office: 176 Remsen St., Bklyn. 2. Died Nov. 2, 1958; buried Wilbraham, Mass.

PAINE, Bayard Henry, judge; b. nr. Painesville, O., Apr. 27, 1872; s. Ira Tuttle and Ella Myra (Huston) P.; grad. high sch., Grand Island, Neb., 1889; B.S., Northwestern U., 1894; law student U. of Mich., 1907; LL.D. from Nebraska Wesleyan University, 1934; m. Grace Bentley, Jan. 15, 1902 (dec. Feb. 1956); children—Alice Ella, Charles Bentley, Bayard H. Admitted to Neb. bar, 1904, and began practice at Grand Island, Neb.; admitted to practice before Supreme Court of U.S., 1908; U.S. referee in bankruptcy, 1906-17; judge, Dist. Court, 11th Dist., Neb., 1916-30; elected justice Supreme Court of Neb. for six-yr. term, 1930, reëlected, 1936, 1942, not a candidate for reëlection; pres, Grand Island Land Co. Trustee Southern Meth. U., Dallas, Neb. Wesleyan U. Member Episcopacy Com. of Gen. Conference Methodist Ch., 1904, 08. Mem. Am., Neb., Hall County (ex-pres.) bar assns., Am. Judicature Soc. (charter). Ind. Democrat. Mason (32°, K.T.), Elk, Eastern Star. Clubs: Rotary (ex-pres.), Interprofessional Institute (ex-president). Open Forum (ex-pres.), Lincoln University. Author: Pioneers, Indians and Buffaloes (a history of pioneer days in southwest Nebraska), 1935. Home: 819 W. 3d St., Grand Island, Neb. Died Apr. 19, 1955; buried City Cemetery, Grand Island.

PAINE, George Eustis, business exec.; b. Willsboro, N.Y., Sept. 14, 1893; s. Augustus G. and Maude Eustis (Potts) P.; ed. pvt. schs.; m. Helen Ellis, May 31, 1917 (dec. Apr. 27, 1948); children—Augustus Gibson, George Eustis; m. 2d Katryna Weed Dana, Jan. 23, 1950. Joined N.Y. & Pa. Co., 1914, successively asst. treas., treas., v.p., 1935, pres., mem. exec. com., dir. since 1935, chmn. bd. since 1945; chms. bd., mem. exec. com., dir. Nypen Corp.; mem. exec. com., dir. Gt. No. Paper Co., Fidelity-Phenix Fire Ins. Co.; mem. bd. trustees The Hanover Bank. Clubs: Brook, Turf and Field, St. Anthony, The River (N.Y. City); Clambake, Reading Room Spowhmg Rock Beach Assn. (Newport, R.I.); Travelers (Paris, France); Phila. Died Mar. 26, 1953.

PAINE, George H., army officer; b. Scranton, Pa., July 14, 1884; B.S., U.S. Mil. Acad., 1906; grad. Mounted Service Sch., 1911, Staff Sch., 1923, Army War Coll., 1924; distinguished grad. Sch. of the Line, 1922. Commd. 2d lt., Inf., June 12, 1906; advanced through grades to brig. gen., April 1941. Died May 11, 1949.†

PAINE, Howard Simmons, oculist; b. New Hartford, N.Y., July 14, 1856; s. Horace Marshfield and Charlotte (Mann) P.; B.A., Hamilton Coll., Clinton, N.Y., 1878, M.A., 1881 (prize essay, 1874, prize speaker, 1877, Underwood prize in chemistry, 1878); M.D., Albany Med. Coll., 1881; M.D., after exam., Regents U. of N.Y. (Gray prize); various eye clinics, U.S. and abroad; m. Sarah Maria Potter, Nov. 26, 1890. Asst. Swinburne Hosp. and Dispensary, Albany, N.Y., 1882-83; vis. phys. and surgeon, Albany House of Shelter, 1881-94; 1st asst., surg. staff, 1881, gen. and ophthalmic surgeon, 1883-85, Albany Homoeo. Hosp.; attending phys., Albany Open Door Mission and Home for Incurables, 1883-86; began as ophthalmic surgeon, 1897, pres. of staff, 1917-18, Glens Falls Hosp.; now retired from active practice; founder, 1915, and pres. Glens Falls Optical Co.; founder, 1882, pres. Paine's Tours Throughout the World. Fellow A.C.S.; mem. Med. Soc. State of N.Y., Homoeo. Med. Soc. No. N.Y., Tri-County Med. Soc. of No. N.Y., Albany Co. Homoeo. Med. Soc., Albany Co. Med. Soc., Albany Inst., Glens Falls Med. and Surg. Soc., Alpha Delta Phi, etc. Republican. Presbyn. Home: Glens Falls, N.Y. Deceased.

PAINE, Paul Mayo, librarian; b. Troy, Pa., Jan. 13, 1869; s. Charles Clement and Lucy (Bothwell) P.; C.E., Lehigh U., 1891, hon. M.A., Lehigh, 1913; Litt.D., Syracuse U., 1918; m. Maude E. Featherly, Sept. 15, 1903; children—David, Margaret Murray. Transitman, Pa. R.R., Phila., 1891-94; reporter Phila. Press, 1894; staff of Syracuse Post, 1894-98; asso. editor Syracuse Post Standard, 1899-1915; sec. to librarian, Syracuse Pub. Library, 1910-15, librarian, 1915-42. Ret. Tchr. Sch. Journalism, Syracuse U., 1920-—. Ret. Served as 1st sergt. Co. A, 203d N.Y. Vol. Inf., Spanish-Am. War. Pres. N.Y. Library Assn., 1918-19; founder and sec. Friends of Reading 1922-—. Mem. State Library Council, Delta Upsilon. Republican. Episcopalian (senior warden St. Paul's Church, Syracuse). Clubs: University, Faculty, Rotary. Editor: Bugle Calls of Liberty. Author: Map of Good Stories, 1924; Map of Adventures for Boys and Girls, 1925; Map of America's Making, 1926, revised 1939; Booklovers' Map of America, 1927, revised, 1939; Booklovers' Map of the British Isles, 1927; Map of History of New York State (with Alexander C. Flick), 1929; Story of Syracuse (brochure), 1933; The World of Good Stories (map), 1933. Home: 721 Lancaster Av. Office: Public Library, Syracuse 2, N.Y. Died July 3, 1955; buried Morningside Cemetery, Syracuse, N.Y.

PAINTER, Sidney, historian; b. N.Y.C., Sept. 23, 1902; s. Henry McMahon and Carrie (Stevens) P.; attended Taft Sch.; A.B., Yale, 1925, Ph.D., 1930; LL.D., Middlebury (Vermont) Coll., 1957; m. Nivea Forbes, Aug. 17, 1927; children—Mary Abigail (now Mrs. John H. Mathews), Ann Forbes, Julie Elizabeth, and Prudence Steel. Instr. history, Yale U. 1927-30. asst. prof., 1930-31; asso. history, Johns Hopkins U., 1931-36, asso. prof., 1936-45, prof. history, since 1945, chmn. dept. of history, 1945-—. Mem. adv. bd. of Speculum, 1943-45; mem. bd. of editors, Medievalia et Humanistica, since 1943; councilor of Medieval Acad. Am., 1944-46. Pres. bd. trustees Roland Park Country Sch., 1949-—; trustee Peabody Institute of Baltimore, 1957-—. Fellow Mediaeval Acad. Am.; mem. Am. Hist. Assn. (councilor 1951-55), Am. Council Learned Socs. (treas. 1952-55), (sec. 1957-—), Am. Acad. of Arts and Scis., Am. Philos. Soc. Clubs: Century, 14 W. Hamilton St., Johns Hopkins. Author: William Marshall, 1933; Scourge of the Clergy, Peter of Dreux, duke of Brittany, 1937; French Chivalry, 1940; History of the English Feudal Barony, 1943; Reign of King John, 1949; Rise of the Feudal Monarchies, 1951; Mediaeval Society, 1952; The Past That Lives Today (with Carl Beeker and Yu-Shan Han), 1952; A History of the Middle Ages, 1953. Home: 19 Elmwood Rd., Balt. 10. Died Jan. 12, 1960.

PALACHE, Charles, mineralogist; b. San Francisco, July 18, 1869; s. James and Helen M. (Whitney) P.; B.S., U. Cal., 1891, fellow, 1892-94. Ph. D., 1894, LL.D., 1941; m. Helen Harrington Markham, Aug. 15, 1899; children—Eliza Jeanette, Mary, Alice Helen. Instr. in mineralogy Harvard, 1896-1901, asst. prof., 1902-10. prof., 1910-40, prof. emeritus, 1940-—. Pres. Mineral. Soc. Am., 1921. Fellow A.A.A.S.; mem. Geol. Soc. America (pres. 1937), Nat. Acad. Sciences. Protestant. Home: 106 Appleton St., Cambridge, Mass. Died Dec. 5, 1954.

PALMER, Albert Wentworth, clergyman; b. Kansas City, Mo., May 18, 1879; s. Albert Wentworth and Deborah Anna (Brininstool) P.; B.L., U. Calif., 1901; B.D., Yale, 1904; D.D., Pacific Sch. Religion, Calif., 1922; LL.D., Olivet (Mich.) Coll., 1931; Litt.D., Boston U., 1939; m. Sara Antoinette Wedd, June 6, 1904; children—Helen M., Margaret W., Philip W. Ordained Congl. ministry, 1904; asst. pastor Redlands, Calif., 1904-07; pastor Plymouth Ch., Oakland, Calif., 1907-17, Central Union Ch., Honolulu, T.H., 1917-24, First Ch., Oak Park, Ill., 1924-30; prof. practical theology and pres. Chicago Theol. Sem., 1930-46, pres. emeritus since 1946; minister of radio First Congl. Ch., Los Angeles, 1946-49; instr. pastoral and social problems, Pacific Theol. Sem., 1911-17; lectr. religion U. So. Calif. since 1949. Moderator Gen. Conf. Congl. Christian Chs., 1946-48. Pres. Chicago Ch. Fedn., 1937-38. With Y.M.C.A., Calif. and Siberia, World War I. Mem. Alpha Tau Omega. Author: Drift Toward Religion, 1914; The Human Side of Hawaii, 1924; The New Christian Epic, 1927; Paths to the Presence of God, 1931; Orientals in American Life, 1934; The Minister's Job, 1937; The Art of Conducting Public Worship, 1939; Come, Let Us Worship, 1941; The Light of Faith, 1945; How Religion Helps, 1948. Home: 1587 Morada Pl., Altadena, Cal. Died Dec. 16, 1954; buried Evergreen Cemetery, Los Angeles.

PALMER, Arthur, physician; b. Oswego, N.Y., Aug. 30, 1889; s. William H. and Jennie (Roberts) P.; A.B., Brown U., 1911; M.D., Cornell U., 1915; student, U. of Pa., 1924-25, U. of Cincinnati, 1925, U. of Vienna, 1929; m. Lillis Oliver, Apr. 13, 1921; children—Arthur, Lillis Oliver; married 2d, Inga Wolford, January 1, 1950. Interne, Bellevue Hosp., New York City, 1916-17; consultant in laryngology and otology, Southside Hosp.; consultant laryngology, N.Y. Infirmary for Women and Children; consultant otolaryngology, Mather Memorial and State Reconstruction; prof. clin. surgery (otolaryngology), New York Hospital-Cornell Med. Assn.; attending surgeon, New York Hospital. Served as first lieutenant, Medical Corps Reserve, United States Army, 1917, captain, 1919, major, 1924-29. Certified by Am. Bd. Otolaryngology and Am. Bd. Plastic Surgery. Mem. Soc. Plastic and Reconstructive Surgery (pres. 1939-42), Am. Laryngol., Rhinol. and Otol. Soc., Am. Acad. Ophthalmology and Otolaryngology, N.Y. Acad. Medicine, Assn. Mil. Surgeons, Harvey Society, A.A.A.S., Nu Sigma Nu, Lambda Chi Alpha. Clubs: Carmel Country, North Hills Country. Contbr. med. articles to various publs. Home: 31 Greenway Terrace, Forest Hills, N.Y. Office: 667 Madison Av., N.Y. C. 21. Died Feb. 18, 1954; buried Spencerport, N.Y.

PALMER, Bertha Rachel, educator; b. Graham Lakes, Nobles County, Minn., Aug. 31, 1880; d. LaFayette and Eliza (Ludlow) Palmer; grad. State Teachers Coll., Mayville, N.D., 1903; grad. study U. Minn.; grad. Internat. Training Sch. for Sunday Sch. Leadership, Lake Geneva, Wis., 1922; unmarried. Teacher country schs. near Devils Lake, 1898-1903; teacher of primary work, later spl. teacher and supervisor pub. sch. music and art. Larimore, Dickinson, Rugby, Cando, Williston and Bismarck (N.D.), 1903-15; field deputy to supt. schs., Williams County, N.D., 1915-18; children's div. supt. and field workers. State S.S. Assn., 1918; asst. supt. pub. instrn., N.D., 1919-24; field worker N.D. Council Religious Edn., 1924-26; supt. pub. instrn., N.D., 1927-32; with Research Library of Scientific Temperence Fedn., Boston, Jan.-Nov. 1933; apptd. dir. dept. of scientific temperance instrn. of Nat. Woman's Christian Temperance Union, July 1933; apptd. head Bur. Scientific Research, Nat. W.C.T. U., Sept. 1944. Chmn. art div. N.D. Fedn. Women's Clubs, 1918-24; dir. religious edn.. First Presbyn. Ch., Bismarck, 1919-24, 1927-32.. Trustee State Teachers Ins. and Retirement Fund. Mem. D.A.R., P.E.O. Sisterhood, N.E.A., League of Am. Penwomen, Delta Kappa Gamma. Republican. Presbyterian. Daughter of Rebecca. Clubs: Current Events, Delphian Study Chapter, Business and Professional Women's Club of Evanston. Author: Beauty Spots in North Dakota, 1927; A Syllabus in Alcohol Education, 1933, revised edit., 1944; What Alcohol Is and What It Does, 1935. Home: 814 College Av., Wheaton, Ill. Office: 1730 Chicago Av., Evanston, Ill. Died Dec. 15, 1959.

PALMER, Clyde Eber, publisher; b. Spirit Lake, Ia., Aug. 24, 1876; s. Eber and Lydia (Denny) P.; ed. pub. schs., Spirit Lake, Ia., and Fremont (Neb.) Bus. Coll.; Litt.D. (hon.), Subiac oCollege, 1941; m. Bettie Maines, Feb. 2, 1910; children—(by 1st marriage) Alden Locke (Mrs. Alden Palmer Mooney), Wellington Denny; (by 2d marriage) Betty Maines (Mrs. Walter E. Hussmann). Successively stenographer, bookkeeper and office mgr. Texarkana Gazette and News, 1894-1909, publisher since 1909; published El Dorado News and Times, Hot Springs New Era and Sentinel Record since 1929; co-pub. Hope (Ark.) Star since 1929; pres. Texarkana Newspapers, Inc., El Dorado News-Times Pub. Co., Southern Newspapers, Inc., Hot Springs, Hope Star Pub. Co., Asso. Ark. Newspapers, Inc. (Hot Springs), KCMC, Inc. (Texarkana), Midwest Video Corp., Little Rock, Ark. Served as private, 2d Nebraska Regt., Spanish-Am. War; now col. on gov.'s staff, Ark. Chmn. Ark. Tenancy Commn., Ark. Centennial Commn. Established Palmer Foundation, Oct. 1944. Democrat. Mason. Clubs: Texarkana Country; National Press (Washington); Overseas Press (N.Y.C.). Home: 902 Olive St. Office: 315 Pine St., Texarkana, Tex. Died July 4, 1957.

PALMER, David J., soldier; b. Washington, Pa., Nov. 15, 1938; s. Samuel R. and Margaret (Munce) P.; ed. pub. schs.; m. Letitia Helen Young, Oct. 25, 1866. Enlisted as pvt. in Co. C, 8th Ia. Regt., Aug. 10, 1861; attached to Army of the West, later to Army of the Tenn.; severely wounded at Battle of Shiloh; organized Co. A, 25th Ia. Regt.; promoted capt., 1862; lt. col., 1863; participated in siege of Vicksburg, battles of Lookout Mountain and Mission Ridge, expdn. to relieve Knoxville, and Atlanta campaign; mustered out at Washington, 1865. Engaged in farming at Washington, Ia., since close of war; auditor Washington Co., 1876-80; mem. Ia. Senate, 1891-98; railroad commr. of Ia., 1898-1915; frequent del. to Rep. nat. convs.; elected comdr.-in-chief G.A.R., Sept. 1914; mem. Ia. Commandery Loyal Legion. Mem. State Council Def. Presbyn. Clubs: Commercial (Washington, Ia.), Grant (Des Moines). Home: Washington, Ia. Deceased.

PALMER, Edward L(ivingston), Jr., architect; b. Baltimore, May 27, 1877; s. Edward L. and Susan Catherine (Boyd) P.; A.B., Johns Hopkins, 1899, U. Pa., 1903; m. Jessie M. Loeffler, June 26, 1907; 1 dau., Anne Livingston (Mrs. Bruce Sinclair-Smith). Practicing architect since 1903; head archtl. dept. Roland Park Co., 1907-17; ind. practice as Edward

L. Palmer, Jr., 1917-25; partner Palmer & Landin, 1925-45; sr. partner Palmer, Fisher, Williams & Nes, Baltimore, since 1945. Fellow A.I.A. Home: Gibson Island, Anne Arundel County. Office: 1020 St. Paul St., Balt. 2. Died May 13, 1952.

PALMER, Elbridge Woodman, book mfr.; b. Meredith, N.H., Dec. 4, 1886; s. Francis Henry and Malina (Burtt) P.; ed. pub. schs., Norwood, Mass.; LL.D. (hon.), Tusculum Coll., U. of Chattanooga; m. Lillian Alice Weymouth, 1912; children—Weymouth Woodman, Elbridge William (killed Okinawa, 1945). With Plimpton Press, Norwood, Mass., 1905-09; J. F. Tapley Co., New York, 1909-25 (gen. mgr. 1920, pres. 1923); pres. Kingsport (Tenn.) Press since 1925. Pres. Nat. Soc. for Crippled Children, 1940-49, president emeritus since 1949; pres. Tenn. Taxpayers' Assn., Tennessee Soc. Crippled Children, 1935-52; chairman Kingsport Planning Welfare Commn., Sullivan Co. Planning Commn.; Tri-States Highlands Assn.; ex-chmn. Rotary Found. Campaign Co.; ex-dir. Rotary Internat.; chmn. interracial com., Nat. Council Boy Scouts of Am., mem. coms. on Boy's Life and Personnel, chmn. exec. com. Region 5, recipient Silver Beaver, Silver Antelope and Silver Buffalo Awards (ex-president of Sequoyah Council); director of Southern States Industrial Council; director Tenn. Manufacturers Assn. Trustee Peabody College (Nashville), Dep. dir. printing and publishing div., War Prodn. Bd., November 1941- May 1943; commd. col. Army U.S., A.G.O., July 1943; dep. dir. Publication Div., A.G.O., Washington, D.C. Chmn. bd. trustees Kingsport Pub. Library; dir. and mem. exec. com. Holston Valley Community Hosp.; sr. warden, St. Paul's Epis. Ch.; ex-mem. Tri-City Airport Commn., dir. Fed. Savings and Loan Assn., ex-pres. community chest; ex-pres. and chmn. textbook standards com., Book Mfrs. Inst.; ex-pres. Episcopal Laymen's League, Tenn. Mem. N.A.M. (dir., past nat. v.p.), Nat. Planning Assn. (chmn. committee south). Member Am. Society M.E., Society Advancement Management, Res. Officers Assn., Ben Franklin Soc., Nat. Aero. Assn., Tenn. Nat. Guard (hon. col.), Nashville Adv. Bd. R.F.C., Tenn. Adv. Com. Soc. Security; Research Corp., Tenn. U., Tenn. State Planning Commn. Republican. Mason (32°, K.T., Shrine), Eastern Star, Odd Fellow. Clubs: Country (Kingsport); Ridgefields Country (Kingsport); University (N.Y.C.); Cumberland (Nashville); East Tenn. Automobile (Knoxville). Associate editor Merriam Webster's Dictionary. Contbr. Ency. Brit., Collier's Ency., Richard's Cyclo., Quarrie's World Book, Lincoln Library of Essential Information, Production Year Book. Home: 1244 Watauga St., Kingsport, Tenn. Died Nov. 18, 1953.

PALMER, Frank Nelson, Bible tchr.; b. Danville, Ill., Oct. 12, 1859; s. Eben Hawkins and Frances Boyd (Nelson) P.; A.B., Wabash Coll., Crawfordsville, Ind., 1881, A.M., 1884, D.D., 1903; student Union Theol. Sem., 1883-84, McCormick Theol. Sem., 1884-85; m. Sarah Cynthia Hawkins, Dec. 8, 1892. Ordained Presbyn. ministry, 1887; pastor Monument, Colo., 1887, Alamosa, Colo., 1887-91, Mesa Ch., Pueblo, Colo., 1891-97, Dayton, Ind., 1897-1903. Instr. English Bible, Winona schs., Winona Lake, Ind., 1903-11; dir. Winona Bible Summer Sch., 1908-11; pastor 1st Ch., Warsaw, Ind., 1918—. Mem. World's Bible Conf., 1914-19. Prohibitionist. Author: A Bird's Eye View of the Bible, 1910; Old Testament Characters, 1912; David and the Psalms, 1913; The Mastery of Genesis, 1914; The Life of Christ, 1915. Home: Winona Lake, Ind. Deceased.

PALMER, Frederick, writer; b. Pleasantville, Pa., Jan. 29, 1873; s. Amos F. and Amy C. Palmer; grad. Allegheny Coll., 1893; LL.D., 1919; Litt.D., Princeton U., 1935; m. Mrs. Talmadge Runkle, Sept. 5, 1924; stepchildren—Helen, Harry. London corr., 1895-97, Greek war, 1897; Klondike and Philippines, 1897-98; retured around the world with Admiral Dewey, 1899; to Philippines and expdn. for relief of Peking, 1900; Central America and the Macedonian insurrection, 1903; with the first Japanese Army in the field for Collier's Weekly and London Times, 1904-05; with the around-the-world cruise of the Am. Battleship Fleet, 1907-08; investigation of Central Am. conditions, 1908-09, the Turkish revolution, 1909; the Balkan War, 1912; only accredited corr. Am. press with British army and fleet, 1914-16. Maj. and lt. col. Signal R.C., 1917-18, serving on staff duty at front with A.E.F. in France and as press censor; later traveled as corr. in Europe and Asia; with British Army in France, 1940, Am. forces Germany and Pacific, 1945. Decorated D.S.M. Mem. Phi Beta Kappa. Clubs: Century (N.Y. City); Cosmos (Washington). Mem. Soc. of Am. Historians. Author: Going to War in Greece, 1897; The Ways of the Service, 1901; The Vagabond (fiction), 1903; With Kuroki in Manchuria, 1904; Central America and Its Problems, 1910; Over the Pass (fiction), 1912; The Last Shot (fiction), 1914; My Year of the War, 1915; My Second Year of the War, 1917; American in France, 1918; Our Greatest Battle, 1919; The Folly of Nations, 1921; Clark of the Ohio, 1929; Newton D. Baker—America at War, 1931; With My Own Eyes, 1933; Bliss, Peacemaker, 1934; The Man With a Country, 1935; Our Gallant Madness, 1937; It Can Be Done, 1944; Life of John Pershing, 1948. Home: 1810 Edgewood Lane, Charlottesville, Va. Died Sept. 2, 1958; buried Grace Ch. Cemetery, Cismont, Va.

PALMER, George Louis, business exec.; b. Toledo, July 3, 1901; s. James C. and Mabel (Heilman) P.; student Toledo U., 1918-22; m. Dorothy M. Smith, Apr. 24, 1937. Cost accountant, 1922-27; chief accounting officer Pacific div., Willys-Overland Motors, Inc. (which is now named Willys Motors, Inc., 1927-42, comptroller, Toledo, 1942-47, treasurer, 1947—; v.p., controller Schemenauer Mfg. Co., 1955—; dir. Wilson Foundry & Machine Company, Pontiac, Mich. Mem. Controllers Inst. Am., Nat. Assn. Cost Accountants, C. of C. Club: Toledo. Home: 3614 Woodmont Rd., Toledo 13. Office: 940 N. Cove Blvd., Toledo 1. Died Feb. 9, 1956; buried Woodlawn Cemetery, Toledo.

PALMER, Gordon Davis, bank exec.; b. Joliet, Ill., July 7, 1896; s. Robert F. and Elinore (Davis) P.; B.S., U. Ala., 1920; m. Elizabeth Cade, Oct. 8, 1930; children—Elizabeth, Natalie. Foreman Sloss Sheffield Coke plant, 1920-21; bursar Birmingham So. Coll., 1921-23; exec. sec. U. Ala., 1923-26; asst. to pres., v.p., trust officer City Nat. Bank of Tuscaloosa, 1926-35; exec. v.p. First Nat. Bank of Tuscaloosa, 1935-41, pres., 1941-56, chmn. bd., 1956—; dir. So. Co., Atlanta, 1950—; dir. Ala. Gt. So. R.R., First Nat. Bank of Tuscaloosa, Ala. Power Co., Allen & Jemison Co., Birmingham Fire Ins. Co. Trustee, mem. exec. com., U. Ala., David Warner Found.; chmn. bd. trustees Stillman Inst., 1931-47; Synod of Ala., Ala. State Insane Hosp. Served as 2d lt. to capt., with 82d inf. div., U.S. Army, 1917-19, A.E.F. Mem. Tuscaloosa (past pres., dir.), Ala. State (past pres.) C.'s of C., Newcomen Soc., Am. (pres. nat. bank div., 1947-48), Ala. (past pres.) bankers assns., Phi Beta Kappa, Phi Gamma Delta, Omicron Delta Kappa, Beta Gamma Sigma. Presbyn. Kiwanian (past pres. Tuscaloosa br., lt. gov. Ala. Dist. of Internat. group). Home: 11 Druid Ct. Office: First National Bank Bldg., Tuscaloosa, Ala. Died July 11, 1956; buried Memorial Park, Tuscaloosa.

PALMER, Harold Gilbert, educator; b. Cedar Falls, Ia., Mar. 31, 1897; s. Gilbert E. and Ada Le (Valley) P.; A.B., Ia. State Tchrs. Coll., 1923; A.M., U. Ia., 1932; Ph.D., Ohio State U., 1950; m. Jean L. Lowrey, Aug. 26, 1923; children—Douglas, Phillip, Stephen. Instr. pub. schs., Hanlontown, Ia., 1917-21, Cedar Falls, 1921-23; supt. schs., Thornburg, Ia., 1923-24; instr. Ia. State Tchrs. Coll., Cedar Falls, 1924-40, head dept. indsl. arts, 1944-54, prof., 1948—. Mem. White House Conf. Children and Youth, 1950. Mem. C. of C., N.E.A., Am. Indsl. Arts Assn. (past pres.), Am. Assn. U. Profs., Am. Legion, Epsilon Pi Tau, Phi Delta Kappa. Republican. Methodist. Rotarian. Contbr. ednl. jours. Home: 912 W. 16th, Cedar Falls, Ia. Died Oct. 22, 1958.

PALMER, John McAuley, army officer; b. Carlinville, Ill., Apr. 23, 1870; s. John Mayo and Ellen (Robertson) P.; B.S., U.S. Mil. Acad., 1892; honor grad. Army Sch. of the Line, 1909; grad. Gen. Staff Coll., 1910; m. Maude Laning, June 14, 1893; children—John McAuley (dec.), Mary Laning (Mrs. George Helm Rockwell). Commd. 2d lt. inf., June 11, 1892; promoted through grades to brig. gen., Dec. 4, 1922; served in Cuba, 1899; Boxer Campaign, China, 1900; instr. chemistry U.S. Mil. Acad., 1901-06; gov. Dist. of Lanao, P.I., 1906-07; Gen. Staff Corps, 1911-12, 16-20; mem. com. apptd. by Sec. of War Stimson, 1912; to report on orgn. of land forces of United States; assistant chief of staff Author: Army of the People, 1916; Statesmanship of AEF, 1917-18; comdr. 58th Inf. Brig., Meuse-Argonne offensive, 1918; duty as mil. adviser to Senate Com. on Mil. Affairs, 1919-20; mem. tech. staff Conf. on Limitation of Armament, 1921-22; a.d.c. to Gen. Pershing, 1921-23; comd. 19th Inf. Brig., Canal Zone, 1923-25; retired, 1926; recalled to active duty, 1941-46. Decorated D.S.M. (U.S.), 1918, oak leaf cluster, 1946; Officer Legion of Honor, Croix de Guerre (French); Order of St. Maurice and St. Lazarus (Italian). Mem. U.S. Inf. Assn., Am. Legion. Episcopalian. Mason. Club: Army and Navy. Author: Army of the People, 1916; Statesmanship of War, 1927; Washington, Lincoln, Wilson—Three War Statesmen, 1930; General von Steuben, 1937; America in Arms, 1941, rev. edit., 1943. Contbr. to mags. Address: Washington. Died Oct. 26, 1955. Buried Arlington National Cemetery.

PALMER, John William, ex-congressman; b. Camden Co., Mo., Aug. 20, 1886; s. James M. and Temperance (Hix) P.; student Univ. Med. Coll., Kansas City, Mo.; LL.B., Lincoln-Jefferson U., Hammond, Ind.; m. Nannie J. Hutton, 1891; children—Burleigh (Mrs. W. S. Jeffries), Pearl (Mrs. George E. Crews), Hazel, John William. Admitted to Mo. bar, 1897, and began practice at Linn Creek, mem. firm Palmer & Palmer, Sedalia; served as mem. Mo. Ho. of Rep. and as pros. atty., Camden County; mem. 71st Congress (1929-31), 7th Mo. Dist. Mem. Mo. Bar Assn. Republican. Baptist. Mason, Odd Fellow. Home: 901 S. Vermont, Sedalia, Mo. Died Nov. 3, 1958; buried Crown Hill Cemetery, Sedalia, Mo.

PALMER, Leigh Carlyle, naval officer; b. St. Louis, Jan. 11, 1873; s. Enrique and Laura (Creighton) P.; grad. U.S. Naval Acad., 1896; LL.D., Wesleyan U., Conn., 1919; m. Bessie Draper McKeldin, June 10, 1911; 1 dau., Laura Creighton. Promoted lt. jr. grade, 1901; lt., 1903; lt. comdr., 1908; comdr., 1908; comdr., 1915; rear admiral, 1916. Participated in Battle of Santiago, 1898; Cuban Naval Campaign; Philippine Naval Campaign; duty in Atlantic, Pacific and Asiatic fleets; U.S. naval representative at wedding of King Alfonso of Spain, 1906; naval aide to Sec. of State Root, on S. Am. trip, 1906; gunnery officer of U.S.S. Vermont, battle efficiency pennant winner, 1908; dir. target practice and engring., 1909-12; naval aide to Pres. Taft, 1909-12; comdg. destroyers Aylwin and McDougal, and Seventh Destroyers Div., 1913-14; exec. officer, battleship New York, 1915-16; chief of staff, Battleship Fleet, 1916; chief Bur. of Navigation, 1916-18; chief of staff Am. Battleship Squadron in the North Sea, 1918-19; comdg. U.S.S. Georgia, 1919; pres. U.S. Shipping bd. Emergency Fleet Corpn., 1924-25. Decorated Order of Naval Merit (Spanish), 1906; D.S.M. (U.S.), 1918; Order of Leopold (Belgian), 1919. Clubs: Chevy Chase, Metropolitan, Army and Navy (Washington); Metropolitan (N.Y.C.). Home: 1709 Massachusetts Av. Address: Navy Dept., Washington. Deceased.

PALMER, Philip Mason, coll. dean; b. Westbrook, Me., May 8, 1880; s. Frederick Merrill and Clara (Parker) P.; A.B., Bowdoin, 1900, L.H.D., 1950; A.B., Harvard, 1902; grad. study U. of Heidelberg, 1906, 11, 13, U. Zurich, 1921-22; Doctor, honoris causa, U. of Padua, 1922; Litt.D., Moravian College, Bethlehem, Pa., 1941; m. Mary Frost Hodgdon, Aug. 4, 1903 (dec. 1911); 1 son, Philip Motley; m. 2d. Anne-Marie Bauer, June 16, 1914; children—Carl, Parker, Robert, Richard, John. Instr. in modern langs. Lehigh U., 1902-05, asst. prof., 1905-06, prof., 1906-10, prof. German, 1910—, dir. Coll. Arts and Sciences, 1921-36, dean, 1936-50, dean emeritus, 1950—, chmn. adminstrv. com., 1944-45. Mem. bd. pub. schs., Bethlehem, 1916-18, Pub. Library, 1918-21. Recipient Hillman award Lehigh U., 1946. Pres. Pa. German Folklore Soc., 1943. Mem. Modern Lang. Assn. America, Am. Assn. U. Profs., Kleistgesellschaft, Goethegesellschaft, Phi Beta Kappa, Theta Delta Chi, Omicron Delta Kappa. Republican. Mem. Evang. Ch. Author: (with R. P. More) Sources of the Faust Tradition. Contbr. articles on ednl. subjects. Home: 211 E. Arrow Hwy., Claremont, Cal. Died June 4, 1951; buried Meml. Cemetery, Buxton, Me.

PALMER, Robert (Conrad), chemist; born Rushville, Ill., Mar. 23, 1887; s. Samuel Cornelius and Annie Jane (Goodman) P.; B.S., U. of Mo., 1909, Chem. E., 1910; m. Myrtle L. Ogle, Feb. 23, 1911 (died 1921); 1 dau., Jane C. (Mrs. Alfred F. Wicke, Jr.); m. 2d, Florence V. Glass, June 5, 1923; children—Emma Glass, Robert C. Chemist, Forest Products Lab., U.S. Dept. Agr., Madison, Wis., 1910-16, Newport Turpentine & Rosin Co., Pensacola, Fla., 1916-21; chief chemist The Newport Co., Pensacola, 1921-31; chief chemist and dir. research Newport Industries, Inc., Pensacola, 1931-38, chem. dir., 1939—, v.p. and chem. dir. since 1944. Mem. Am. Chem. Soc., Am. Soc. Testing Materials, Fla. Soc. Colonial Wars, S.A.R. (p. state v.p.), Am. Camellia Soc., Order Founders and Patriots of America, General Society of Mayflower Descendants, also Sigma Xi, Alpha Chi Sigma. Democrat. Presbyn. Clubs: Kiwanis, Pensacola Country. Inventor. Home: 1380 N. Spring St. Office: Newport Industries, Inc., P.O. Drawer, 911, Pensacola, Fla. Died June 11, 1957; buried Bayview Meml. Cemetery, Pensacola, Fla.

PALMER, Theodore Sherman, naturalist; b. Oakland, Cal., Jan. 26, 1868; s. Henry A. and Jane (Day) P.; A.B., U. Cal., 1888, M.D., Georgetown U., 1895; m. Bertha M. Ellis, Nov. 21, 1911. First asst. ornithologist U.S. Biol. Survey, 1890-96, in charge Death Valley Expdn., 5 months in 1891, asst. chief, 1896-1902 and 1910-14, asst. in charge game preservation, 1902-10, 1914-16, expert in game conservation, 1916-24, biologist, 1924-28, sr. biologist, 1928-33; asso. in zoölogy, U.S. Nat. Museum from 1933; retired. Fellow A.A.A.S., Am. Ornithologists Union (sec. 1917-37), Cal. Acad. Sciences; mem. Am. Soc. Naturalists, Am. Bison Soc., Am. Fisheries Soc., Am. Forestry Assn., Am. Genetic Assn., Baird Ornithol. Club, Nat. Parks Assn., Save Redwoods League, Am. Game Protective Assn., Internat. Com. Bird Protection, Washington Acad. Sciences, Wilson Ornithol. Club, Sigma Xi; asso. mem. Soc. Am. Foresters, Am. Mus. Natural History, Boone and Crockett Soc.; corr. mem. Ornithol. Gesellschaft in Bayern, Royal Hungarian Inst. Ornithol.; hon. mem. Cooper Orrnithol. Club, Internat. Assn. Game Commrs., Soc. Preservation Fauna Empire (London); pres. Biol. Soc. Washington, 1909-10, Audubon Soc. D.C., 1924-41 (pres. emeritus, 1941—); v.p. Nat. Assn. Audubon Socs., 1905-35; v.p. Am. Soc. Mammalogists, 1928-34. Author: Jack Rabbits of United States (2d edit.), 1897; List of Generic and Family Names of Rodents, 1897; Legislation for the Protection of Birds Other than Game Birds (2d edit.).

1902; Review of Economic Ornithology in the United States, 1900; Index Generum Mammalium, 1904; Hunting Licenses, 1904; Chronology and Index American Game Protection, 1912; Game as a National Resource, 1922; Place Names of hte Death Valley Region, 1948; Chronology of the Death Valley Region, 1951; Biographies of members of the American Ornithologists Union, 1884-1954, 1954; also numerous shorter papers on game protection; (with Henry Oldys and others) Laws Regulating the Transportation and Sale of Game, 1900; Digest of Game Laws for 1901; Game Birds and Eggs for Propagation, 1904. Chmn. com. which prepared regulations under federal migratory bird law, 1913; prepared preliminary draft of treaty for protection of migratory birds in U.S. and Can., 1916, whaling treaty act, 1936. Club: Cosmos. Contbr. to ornithol. journals. Home: 1939 Biltmore St. N.W., Washington. Died July 23, 1955; buried Mountain View Cemetery, Oakland, Cal.

PALMER, Walter Walker, physician, educator; b. Southfield, Mass., Feb. 27, 1882; s. Henry Wellington and Almira Roxana (Walker) P.; B.S., Amherst, 1905, Sc.D., 1922; M.D., Harvard, 1910; Sc. D., Columbia, 1929; m. Francesca Gilder, Oct. 12, 1922; children—Helena Francesca Gilder, Gilder, Walter de Kay. H. P. Walcott fellow in medicine and instr. in physiol. chemistry Harvard, 1913, asst. in medicine, also resident physician Mass. Gen. Hosp., 1913-15; asst. in medicine Rockefeller Inst., N.Y. C., 1915-17; asso. prof. medicine Columbia, 1917-19, also acting dir. med. service Presbyn. Hosp.; asso. prof. medicine Johns Hopkins Med. Sch., 1919-21, also asso. vis. physician Johns Hopkins Hosp.; Bard prof. medicine Columbia, 1921-47; cons. Presbyn. Hosp., 1947—; dir. Pub. Health Research Inst. of N.Y., 1947—. Commd. 1st lt. Med. R.C., U.S. Army, 1917-19, maj., 1926-31. Mem. Nat. Bd. of Med. Examiners, 1921-43. Mem. A.M.A. (council pharmacy and chemistry), Soc. for Clin. Investigation, Assn. Am. Physicians, N.Y. Acad. Medicine, Harvey Society of N.Y.C. (pres. 1926-27), Theta Delta Chi, Phi Beta Kappa, Alpha Omega Alpha. Republican. Club: Century Assn. Specializes in research work in metabolic fields—diabetes, nephritis, etc. Contbr. to profl. jours. Home: 24 Gramercy Park. Address: Foot of E. 15th St., N.Y.C. 9. Died Oct. 28, 1950; buried Tyringham, Mass.

PALTSITS, Victor Hugo (pawl'sits), historian; b. New York, July 12, 1867; s. William Thomas and Sidonia Ida (Loose) P.; scientific course Cooper Inst., N.Y., 1882-86; German, Latin, Greek, Spanish and French at high schs. and pvt. tuition, Coptic and Egyptian hieroglyphics, Columbia; Litt. D., Brown University, 1936; Litt. D., Rutgers, 1938; m. Anne Mueller, July 21, 1891 (deceased June 29, 1944); children Florence (Mrs. Frederick W. Misch), Victor John. Worked for Thomas A. Edison in his first machine shop, N.Y. City, 1884-85; with Lenox Library, 1888-1907, asst. in reading room, 1890, sub-librarian, 1893, title later changed to asst. librarian (Lenox Library, now part of N.Y. Public Library—Astor, Lenox and Tilden Founds.); New York State historian, 1907-11; keeper of manuscripts, New York Pub. Library, Sept. 1914-1941, also in charge of exhbns., 1915-26, and chief of the Am. History Div., 1916-41; retired. Fellow A.A.A.S., N.Y. State Hist. Assn.; mem. Edison Pioneers, Nat. Soc. Autograph Collectors (founding mem., dir.), Am. Antiq. Soc., Am. Hist. Assn. (chmn. nat. pub. archives commn., 1913-22), A.L.A., Bibliog. Soc. Am. (hon. mem.; pres. 1938-39), Inter-Am. Bibliog. and Library Assn. (founding mem.), Bibliog. Soc. Eng. (hon. 1942), Am. Mil. History Foundation (founding mem.; name changed Am. Mil. Inst. 1939), History of Science Soc. (founding mem.), Soc. Am. Archivists (founding mem.; former councillor; hon. mem. 1942), N.Y. Library Club (ex-pres.), Me., Mass., N.J., N.Y., Minn. hist. socs. Hon. mem. New Brunswick Mus. of St. John, N.B., Can. Mem. exec. com. 250th Anniversary Transition Dutch to English Rule, N.Y. City, 1915. Presbyn. (elder). Editor: The Journal of Capt. William Pote, Jr., 1745-1747, 1896; Papers Relating to Siege of Charleston, 1780, Charleston, 1898; Rev. John Miller's New Yorke Considered and Improved, 1695, 1903; Narrative of the Captivity of Nehemiah How in 1745-1747, 1904; Across the Plains to California in 1852—Journal of Mrs. Lodisa Frizzell, 1915; Journal of Thomas Boylston Adams while Secretary to the United States Legation at Berlin in 1798, 1916; Cruise of the United States Brig Argus in 1813, 1917; Family Correspondence of Herman Melville, 1830-1904, 1929; Narrative of American Voyages and Travels of Capt. William Owen, R.N., 1766-1771, 1931, and 1942; Farewell Address of George Washington, 1935; Judge Augustus Porter, Pioneer of Niagara Falls, 1937; Facsimile of Daniel Denton's A Brief Description of New York, 1937; Herman Melville's Background, 1943. Served on editorial staff as bibliographical adv., Jesuit Relations and Allied Documents, 73 vols., 1896-1901; also mem. of advisory editorial boards of various historical publications. Revised volumes 3 and 5 Appleton's Cyclopædia of American Biography, edition 1898, and furnished 88 biog. sketches for same; contbr. to new Dictionary of American Biography. Critical adviser on hist. illustrations, etc., for Avery's History of the United States and other works. Contbr. to mags. and revs. on hist. and biblicg. subjects. As state historian edited: Minutes of the Commissioners for Detecting and Defeating Conspiracies, 1778-1781, 1909-10, 3 vols.; Minutes of the Executive Council of the Province of New York, 1668-1673, 1910, 2 vols. Author: Contbns. to Bibliography of the Lettres Edifiantes, Cleveland, O., 1900; Bibliography of Works of Philip Freneau, 1903; Bibliography of the Works of Father Louis Hennepin, 1903; Lewis and Clark Bibliography for Original Journals of Lewis and Clark, 1904; Bibliography of the Voyages of Baron de Lahontan, 1905; Scheme for Conquest of Canada in 1746, 1905; The Almanacs of Roger Sherman, 1750-1761, 1907; The Manuscript Division in the N.Y. Public Library, 1915; Inventory of Rensselaerswyck Manuscripts, 1924; Founding of New Amsterdam in 1626, 1925; Wilberforce Eames, 1925; The New York Tercentenary, 1524-1674, 1926. Associated, 1911-28, with I. N. Phelps Stokes, on The Iconography of Manhattan Island, 6 vols.; editor of American Book-Prices Current, 1915-16. Chmn. Mayor's Publ. Com. that issued N.Y. Common Council Minutes (1784-1831), 21 vols. Contbr. bibliographies of Chrêtien Leclercq, Nicolas Denys, Dièreville, Gabriel Sagard, etc., to Champlain Society of Canada publs.; Proposal of Henry Stevens for a Bibliographia Americana to 1850, 1942; Bio-Bibliographical Account of Two Rare Imprints, 1944; Hon. John Boyd Thacher, Man of Versatility, 1951; Henry Stevens's Recollections of James Lenox (1886) revised and elucidated with biog. of Stevens, 1951. Home: Hotel Whitman, 161 St. and 89th Av., Jamaica 2, L.I., N.Y. Died Oct. 3, 1952; buried Woodlawn Cemetery, N.Y.C.

PANCOST, E(rnest) Ellsworth, railroad exec.; b. Elkhart, Ind., July 13, 1895; s. Clarence E. and Elizabeth A. (Enos) P.; student Cleveland Coll., 1930-31; m. Alma H. Stenzel, July 22, 1916; children—Alma (Mrs. John J. Rucker), Carol (Mrs. Frank N. Kemmer). Various r.r. positions, 1911-15; agt., supervising agt., N.Y.C. R.R., 1915-29, head clk., asst. credit officer, 1929-37, credit officer, 1937-43, asst. to treas., asst. treas., 1943-52, treas. since Jan. 1952, also treas. N.Y. Central System; treasurer, director Linden Securities Corporation. Member Assn. Am. R.R.'s (adv. com. treas. div., vice chmn. Eastern sectional group), Newcomen Soc. N.Y. Episcopalian. Mason (32°; past master). Club: Ardsley Country. Home: Rosalind Gardens, Dobbs Ferry, N.Y. Office: 466 Lexington Av., N.Y. C. 17. Died Apr. 16, 1954; buried Fern Cliff Cemetery, Dobbs Ferry, N.Y.

PANETH, F. A., scientist; b. Vienna, Austria, Aug. 31, 1887; s. Dr. Joseph and Sophie (Schwab) P.; student U. Munich, U. Glasgow; Ph.D., U. Vienna, 1910; m. Else Hartmann, Dec. 6, 1913; children —Eva, Heinrich Rudolph. Asst., Inst. for Radium Research, Vienna, 1912-18; prof. Prague Inst. Tech., 1918, Hamburg U., 1919-22, U. Berlin, 1922-29; George Fisher Baker lectr. Cornell U., 1926-27; prof., dir. chem. labs. U. Koenigsberg, 1929-33; guest Imperial Coll. of Sci. and Tech., London, 1933-38; reader in atomic chemistry U. London, 1938; prof. chemistry Durham U., 1939-53; head chemistry div. Joint British-Canadian Atomic Energy Team, Montreal, 1943-45; dir. Max Planck Inst. for Chemistry, 1953—. Pres. Joint Commn. on Radioactivity, Internat. Council of Sci. Unions, 1949-55. Fellow Royal Soc. London; mem. Am. Acad. Arts and Scis. (hon.), Soc. Austrian Chemists (hon.), Austrian Acad. Scis. (corr.). Author: Radioelements as Indicators and Other Selected Topics in Inorganic Chemistry, 1928; Manual of Radioactivity (with G. Hevesy), 1938; The Origin of Meteorites, 1940; also articles in field. Home: Brentanostrasse 13, Wiesbaden, Germany. Office: Max-Planck-Institut für Chemie, Mainz/Rhein, Germany. Died Sept. 17, 1958; buried Vienna, Austria.

PANNILL, Charles Jackson (păn' nĭl), radio electronic cons.; b. Petersburg, Va., May 13, 1879; s. Capt. Thomas and Virginia Knox (Walthall) P.; m. Ethel M. Worrell, Dec. 10, 1910. Asso. with Prof. Reginald A. Fessenden, Old Point Comfort, Va., and elsewhere, in research and dev. wireless communication, 1902-07; transmitted pioneer wireless message across Atlantic Ocean, received at Machrehanish Bay (Scotland) Fessenden Wireless sta., 1906; sent and received pioneer wireless messages between Fessenden Wireless stas., Washington-Collinswood, N.J., and Jersey City, 1904; v.p., gen. mgr. pioneer wireless ship-shore communication co., Massie Wireless Telegraph Co., Providence, 1907-09; supt. So. Div. United Wireless Telegraph Co., Balt., 1909-12, Marconi Wireless Telegraph Co. of Am., 1912-14; v.p. Liberty Electric Co., Portchester, New York, 1919; organized Independent Wireless Telegraph Co., 1919; elected v.p., gen. mgr., dir., pres., 1927; merged radio div. RCA with Ind. Wireless Tel. Co. radio services, forming Radiomarine Corp. of Am., 1928, become v.p., gen. mgr., dir., 1928, exec. v.p., 1931, pres., 1935, also elected pres., dir. RCA Insts., Inc., 1932, retired from both corps., 1947; RCA cons. until 1950. Chmn. bd. editors RCA Rev., 1938-46; mem. Adv. com. RCA Lab., Princeton, 1941-45; mem. RCA President's Adv. Com., 1945-47; member RCA Internat. Committee, 1945-46; chmn. radiomarine adv. com. RCA Pension Bd., 1943-46. U.S. del. to internat. confs. on radio and telecommunications, Washington, 1927, Madrid, 1932, The Hague, 1937, Cairo, 1938, Atlantic City, N.J., 1947. Vice pres. Comité Internat. Radio-Maritime, Brussels, Belgium, 1928-39. Dir. bd. mgrs. Seamen's House, 1939-42. Served with U.S.N., 1898-1902, Spanish-Am. War; became expert radio aide Arlington Wireless Sta., 1914, later asst. to dir. naval communications Navy Dept., Washington. Recipient letter of commendation from sec. of navy for outstanding services to Navy, 1918, gold medal Vets. Wireless Operators Assn., 1942, for achievements during World War II. Decorated Chevalier Order King Leopold of Belgium, 1937. Fellow Inst. Radio Engrs. (hon. life mem. with fellowship); life mem. Vets. Wireless Operators Assn., Navy League of U.S.; mem. Soc. Naval Architects and Marine Engrs., Maritime Exchange of N.Y., Radio Pioneers Club (awarded scroll for outstanding pioneer work from 1902). Republican. Episcopalian. Gov. Propeller Club of U.S. (Port of N.Y.), 1943-55, mem. Pres's. adv. com., 1945-49, chmn. ways and means com., 1947-49. Clubs: Cosmos (Washington); Rockefeller Luncheon, Whitehall, India House (N.Y.C.); Lake Placid; Sleepy Hollow Country. Author: U.S. Naval Commercial Traffic Regulations, 1915. Received certificate of skill from U.S. Govt., 1911, No. 1 comml. wireless operators government license, 1912. Radiomarine Corp. received, during World War II, Army-Navy "E" with 4 gold stars, Victory Fleet Flag and Maritime "M" with four gold stars; RCA Inst. received letter of commendation from sec. of navy for training of naval personnel (under his direction). Home: Lawrence Park W., Bronxville, N.Y. Office: 30 Rockefeller Plaza, N.Y.C. 20. Died Feb. 7, 1955; buried Norfolk, Va.

PAPAGOS, Alexander, premier of Greece; comd. Greek armies in campaign against Italians in Albania, 1940-41; comdr. in chief Greek armed forces and mem. War Council, 1949-51; formed Greek Rally party, 1951; prime minister, 1952—. Home: Ekali, Athens. Office: Prime Minister's Office, Athens, Greece. Died Oct. 4, 1955.

PAPEZ, James Wenceslas (pāps), prof. anatomy; b. Glencoe, Minn., Aug. 18, 1883; s. Frank and Frances (Lhotka) P.; A.B., U. Minn., 1908, M.D., 1911; m. Bessie Pearl Sowden, June 5, 1912; children —James Pitney, Julia Francis and Loyd Sowden (twins). Asso. prof. anatomy, Atlanta (Ga.) Coll. of Physicians and Surgeons, 1911-14; prof. anatomy, histology and embryology, Atlanta Med. Coll., Emory U. Med. Sch., 1914-20; asst. prof. anatomy, Cornell U. Med. Coll., 1920-37, prof., 1937—. Mem. Selective Service Bd., N.Y., World War II. Awarded Congressional Medal of Selective Service. Mem. Am. Assn. of Anatomists, Am. Soc. of Phys. Anthropologists, A.A.A.S., Assn. for Research in Nervous and Mental Diseases, Am. Neurological Assn., Am. Ahthropol. Assn., Human Genetics Soc., Soc. Biol. Psychiatry, Alpha Epsilon Delta, Sigma Xi, Phi Kappa Phi. Author: Comparative Neurology, 1929; (with W. Haymaker) Hypothalamus, Anatomic, Functional and Clinical Aspects. Contbr. about 70 papers of neurological subjects to jours. Home: 101 Elmwood Av., Ithaca, N.Y. Died Apr. 13, 1958.

PAPPENHEIMER, Alwin M(ax), pathologist; b. N.Y.C., Dec. 4, 1878; s. Max and Henrietta (Loewenstein) P.; A.B., Harvard, 1898; M.D., Columbia, 1902; grad. study Vienna, Leipzig, Freiburg; m. Beatrice Leo, Nov. 12, 1907; children—Alwin M., Anne, John Richard. Intern Bellevue Hosp., N.Y.C., 1903-05, pathologist, 1905-11; demonstrator of pathology Columbia, 1909, asso., 1909-14, asst. prof., 1914-19, asso. prof., 1919-23, prof., 1923-45, prof. emeritus, 1945—; vis. pathologist, mem. med. bd. Presbyn. Hosp., N.Y.C. Mem. Com. on Pathology, NRC. Served from capt. to maj. M.C., U.S. Army, pathologist and dir. labs., 1917-18; mem. Trench Fever Commn., 1918. Fellow New York Acad. Sciences, New York Acad. Medicine; mem. Am. Soc. Exptl. Pathology, A.A.A.S., Soc. Exptl. Biology and Medicine, Am. Assn. Pathologists and Bacteriologists. Contbr. to med. jours. Home: 45 Holden St., Cambridge 38, Mass. Died Feb. 21, 1955.

PARIS, Auguste Jean, Jr., engr., inventor; b. N.Y.C., Jan. 31, 1874; s. Auguste Jean and Anne (Mercer) P. de Bourgogne; ed. under pvt. tutors; hon. Sc.D., St. John's Coll., Annapolis, 1921; m. Gertrude Eugenie van Ness deMore, 1900. Began as research chem. engr., at Bradford, Pa., 1900; has served as dir. and consulting engr. of many chem. and mfg. cos.; inventor of many processes, covered by patents. Upon entry of U.S. into the World War, offered his entire pvt. income and his services to War Dept., also the use of his inventions for the period of the war, to U.S., Great Britain, France and Italy; associated with brother, Capt. W. Francklyn Paris, in erection of plant at Charleston, W.Va., without govt. subsidy; work carried on under general direction of Nat. Advisory Com. for Aeronautics; assigned to War Dept. free use of invention relating to gaoline engines, contributed to govt. his services as research chem. engr. developing new methods of operating internal combustion engines; now operating research laboratories at Bradford and Charleston, mainly on processes relating to petroleum and chem. industries. Appt. by gov. of W.Va. del. to Yorktown (Va.) Sesquicentennial Expn., 1931. Mem. Soc. Am. Mil. Engrs.; hon. mem. Federation Ancien Combatants (French War Veterans), France. Office French Acad., 1930. Club: University (Washington). Home: Bradford, Pa. Died Mar. 1955.

PARIS, William Edward, automobile exec.; b. Toledo, Nov. 5, 1893; s. Morris and Lena (Kahn) P.; student Bus. Coll. Toledo, 1911; m. Ruth Kisseberth, Apr. 12, 1939; children—Arthur, Harvey, Robert. With Willys-Overland Motors, Inc. (now Willys Motors, Inc.), Toledo, 1939—, v.p., dir. operations, 1946—. Elk. Home: 2915 Pembrooke St., Toledo 12. Office: Toledo 1. Died Nov. 1, 1955; buried Toledo.

PARIS, W(illiam) Francklyn, architect-decorator; b. N.Y. City, 1871; s. Auguste Jean-Baptiste and Anne (Mercer) P.; ed. by pvt. tutors, at Art Students' League, N.Y.C., and in London, Paris, Rome; hon. L.H.D., St. John's Coll., 1917; hon. M.A., New York U., 1921; m. Margaret Wynne-Jones, Apr. 14, 1914; children—Francklyn Mercer (dec.), Francklyn Wynne. U.S. dir. of decorative art, Paris Expn., 1900; professional work in N.Y. since 1901; pres. Paris & Wiley Associates; archtl. decorative work in state capitols of Mo., Minn., and W.Va., also U. of Tex., Princeton, Yale, U. of Chicago, Fountain St. Bapt. Ch. (Grand Rapids), A.I.A., Elks Nat. Meml. (Chgo.), Detroit Pub. Library, supreme cts. of U.S., N.J., W.Va., N.Y. Life Ins. Co. new bldg. Exhibited at most of the important arch. exhbns. since 1901. Occasional lecturer on fine arts at Cornell, Vassar, St. John's, U. of Maryland, U. of Penn., U. of Wis., William and Mary Coll., Am. Inst. Architects. Inaugurated 1912 Museum French Art, French Inst. in U.S. (N.Y. City). Permanent expn. archtl. drawings, Columbia U. Sch. Architecture; an organizer of the Municipal Christmas Tree, Madison Square, New York City, 1912; organizer, 1919, and hon. dir. Hall of Am. Artists and Hall of Chancellors, N.Y.U. Mem. Louvain Library Com., Dec. 1921; inaugurated Cardinal Mercier Memorial at New York U., 1921; dir. Schola Cantorum 10 yrs.; chmn., 2d biennial art exhbn. of Americans at Venice, Italy, 1923. First sec., Art Alliance of Am.; hon. life mem. Met. Museum of Art; mem. Archtl. League, 1900-34, Beaux-Arts Inst. of Design, 1926-35; dir. Fountainbleau Sch., mem. National Sculpture Society, 1900-19; mem. Am. Fedn. Arts, Artists Fellowship, Bibliophile Soc. (Boston); corr. mem. Société des Gens de Lettres de France; mem. Soc. de l'Histoire de l'Art Francais, Spanish Acad., Acad. of Coimbra (Portugal); hon. mem. Comité Cultural Argentino (Buenos Aires); hon. mem. Inst. de Cultura Am. Republica Argentina (Tolosa); former v.p. and dir. Alliance Français; founded 1922, and v.p. Am. Soc. French Legion of Honor (pres. 1946). Hon. del. for United States at Antwerp Exposition, 1930; mem. orgn. com. 1935, dir., 1935-39, N.Y. World's Fair, 1939; chmn. Ambassador Jusserand Memorial, Rock Creek Park, Wash., D.C., 1936. Served in Naval Militia of N.Y., 1891-95; capt. 108th Regt. N.Y. Vols., May 1898. Volunteered as pvt., U.S. Army, 1917, commd. lt., June 23; 1st lt. acting adj. 102 Trains, 27th Div., U.S. Army, Aug. 5, 1917, capt., 1919. Represented 27th Division U.S. Army at unveiling of battle monument, Brest, France, August 1937. Member Union Fédérale Combattants (Veterans of France). Knight Crown of Belgium for services, World War I; Knight Crown of Italy, 1924; Knight St. John (honorary), Knight St. Michel (honorary); Officer Legion of Honor, for services to Art as "Architecte Décorateur"; Grand Officer Ordre du Nichan-Iftikhar, 1929; mem. d'hon. Ordre du St. Sepulchre, Province de France. Clubs: Century, Authors and Authors, Athenaeum (London); Cercle Interalliée (Paris, France). Author: Decorative Elements in Architecture, 1917; The House That Love Built, 1925; Napoleon's Legion, 1927; Personalities in American Art, 1930; French Arts and Letters and Other Essays, 1937; Personalities, Hall of American Artists, vol. II, 1942, vol. III, 1944, vol. IV, 1945-46, vol. V, 1948-49. Editor, French Legion of Honor mag., since 1930. Frequent contbr. lit. and art mags., U.S. and Europe. Home: Plaza Hotel, N.Y.C. Died June 5, 1954.

PARISH, Walter Alvis, lawyer; b. Huntsville, Tex., Oct. 5, 1887; s. John M. and Mary S. (Baker) P.; student A. and M. Coll. Tex., 1904-05; LL.B., U. Tex., 1910; m. Nettie Lee Underwood, Aug. 20, 1913 (dec. Nov. 7, 1951); children—Walter Alvis (dec.), Robert Underwood; m. 2d, Beth Boggess, June 4, 1955; children—June, Barbara. Admitted Tex. bar, 1910, since practiced in Houston, asso. Baker, Botts, Parker & Garwood, 1910-19, mem. firm Jones & Parish, 1919-20, Vinson, Elkins & Weems, 1920-22, Baker, Botts, Andrews & Parish (formerly Baker, Botts, Parker & Garwood), 1922-53, ret.; president Houston Lighting & Power Co., 1953—, dir., 1923—, chmn. bd., 1958—; dir. Southwestern Drug Corp. Dir. Edison Electric Inst.; v.p., dir. Tex. Atomic Energy Research Found., Inc. Mem. Am., Tex. State, Harris Co. bar assns., Phi Delta Theta. Presbyn. Clubs: Ramada, Houston, Houston Country, Petroleum (Houston). Home: 11 Courtlandt Pl., Houston. Office: Electric Bldg., Houston 2. Died Jan. 23, 1959; buried Forest Park Cemetery, Houston.

PARK, John Alsey, newspaper pub.; b. Raleigh, N.C., Nov. 19, 1885; s. Benjamin Franklin and Frances Carolina (Beavers) P.; B.E. in Mech. Engring., N.C. State Coll., 1905; post-grad. work and instr. in mathematics, same coll., 1905-09; extension courses in salesmanship and advertising, U. of N.C.; m. Lily Helen Pair, Dec. 23, 1909; children—John Alsey, Albert Pair, Elizabeth (Mrs. Marcus G. Lynch), Benjamin Franklin. Pres. Times Pub. Co., editor, pub. Raleigh Times, eve daily, 1911-55; owner, pub., 1920-25, of Daily Observer and Weekly Observer, Fayetteville, Daily Sun-Journal and Weekly Sun-Journal, New Bern, Daily News of Greenville and Turner's Almanac, Raleigh. Press Corr. U.S. Fleet Panama maneuvers, 1929, 30; air tour South America, 1935; War Dept. tour of Europe, 1947. Mem. N.C.N.G., 1902-08; chmn. War Savings, Wake County, N.C., 1917, also mem. Draft Com. and Intelligence Service. Past pres. Raleigh Community Chest; inaugurated U.S. Books for Peace program, 1948; leader U.S. college edn. fgn. youth. Past trustee North Carolina State Coll. (past pres. Alumni Assn.); past pres. Va.-Carolina Highway Association; past sec. Raleigh Auditorium Bldg. Com.; mem. Wake Co. Bd. of Edn. Past pres. N.C. Press Assn.; mem. Southern Newspaper Pubs. Assn. (ex-pres.), Raleigh Chamber Commerce (ex-pres.), Raleigh Merchants' Bureau, Raleigh Boy Scout Council, S.A.R., S.C.V., N.C. Lit. and Hist. Soc., N.C. Art Soc., Phi Kappa Phi, Pi Kappa Alpha. Ex-pres. Raleigh YMCA, ex-dir. YMCA. of N.C. State Coll. Ind. Democrat. Methodist (steward Hayes Barton Meth. Ch.). Clubs: Rotary (ex-pres.; gov. District 189, 1937-38), North Carolina Editors. Home: 2051 White Oak Rd. Office: Times Bldg., 211 W. Martin St., Raleigh, N.C. Died Mar. 15, 1956; buried Oakwood Cemetery, Raleigh.

PARK, J(ohn) Edgar, coll. pres.; b. Belfast, Ireland, Mar. 7, 1879; s. William and Susan (Edgar) P.; student New Coll., Edinburgh, Scotland, 1900-01, Royal U., Dublin, 1902, Princeton Theol. Sem., 1902-03; D.D., Tufts Coll., 1923; LL.D., Wesleyan U., 1927, Middlebury Coll., 1937; m. Grace Burtt, Apr. 28, 1906; children—Rosemary, William Edgar, Eileen Elizabeth, Beatrice Grace. Ordained ministry, 1903; stated supply, Stark and Sterling Pond, N.Y., 1903-04; pastor West Parish Ch., Andover, 1904-07, Second Ch. of Newton, West Newton, Mass., 1907-26; pres. Wheaton Coll. 1926-1944. Mem. faculty Boston U. Sch. of Theology, 1925; pres. Am. Congl. Assn.; Lyman Beecher lectr. Yale, 1936. Clubs: Winthrop, University, Authors (Boston). Author: The Keen Joy of Living, 1907; The Sermon on the Mount, 1908; The Wonder of His Gracious Words, 1908; The Man Who Missed Christmas, 1911; Parables of Life, 1912; The Dwarf's Spell, 1912; How I Spent My Million, 1913; The Rejuvenation of Father Christmas, 1914; Disadvantages of Being Good, 1915; Children's Bread, 1916; Bad Results of Good Habits, 1917; The Bad Results of Good Habits and Other Lapses, 1920; The Merrie Adventures of Robin Hood and Santa Claus, 1922; The Christmas Heretic, 1926; New Horizons, 1929; The Miracle of Preaching, 1936; Exodus (Interpreters Bible Series), 1949. Mem. Phi Beta Kappa. Home: Osterville, Mass. Died Mar. 4, 1956; burried Cotuit (Mass.) Meml. Cemetery.

PARK, J(oseph) A(ndrew), dean; b. Cleveland, O., Oct. 7, 1893; s. Robert H. and Mary (Greenwood) P.; B.A., Ohio State U., 1920, M.A., 1931; LL.D., Bowling Green State University (O.), 1949; m. Ruth Webb, June 26, 1920; children—Ruth Constance, Mary Esther. Exec. sec., Ohio State U. Y.M.C.A., 1920-27; dean of men, Ohio State U. since 1927. Served as 2d lt. Inf., 1917-19. Pres. Nat. Assn. Deans and Advisors of Men, 1942-43; treas. Ohio Coll. Assn., since 1943; treas. and mem. exec. com. Ohio-W.Va. Area Y.M.C.A. since 1934. Pres. Natl. Conf. on Coll. Frats. and Socs.; ednl. adviser Nat. Interfrat. Conf. Recipient gold medal award National Interfrat. Conf., 1951. Member Am. Legion, Sphinx Soc., Alpha Tau Omega, Phi Eta Sigma. Mason. Republican. Methodist. Clubs: Columbus Rotary, Faculty. Home: 1474 Doone Rd., Columbus 21, O. Office: Adminstrn. Bldg., Columbus 10, O. Died Apr. 19, 1952; buried Lakewood Park Cemetery, Rocky River, O.

PARK, Maud Wood, former pres. Nat. League Women Voters; b. Boston, Jan. 25, 1871; d. James Rodney and Mary Russell (Collins) Wood; A.B. summa cum laude, Radcliffe Coll., 1898; m. Charles Edward Park, 1898 (dec. 1904); m. 2d, Robert Hunter, 1908 (dec. 1928). A founder and pres. of 1st br. of Coll. Equal Suffrage League; traveled across continent speaking for women suffrage; actively identified with settlement work in Boston and in San Francisco; tour of world 2 yrs.; sec. Boston Equal Suffrage Assn. for Good Govt.; chmn. Congl. Com., Nat. Am. Woman Suffrage Assn., 1916-19, until after adoption suffrage amendment; first pres. Nat. League of Women Voters, 1920-24; mem. Am. Assn. U. Women, Phi Beta Kappa. Club: Radcliffe. Author: Front Door Lobby (story of the passage of Fed. Suffrage through U.S. Congress); (plays) Lucy Stone, Moonstruck. Home: 21 Ashmont St., Melrose 76, Mass. Died May 8, 1955; buried Forest Hills Cemetery, Boston.

PARKE, Francis Neal, judge; b. Westminster, Md., Jan. 6, 1871; s. George Motter and Mary White (Neal) P.; ed. private and parochial schs. and Western Md. Coll. (Westminster, Md.); student U.S. Mil. Acad., 1889-91. Admitted to Md. bar, 1893; practiced at Westminster and throughout State of Md.; div. counsel B.&O. R.R. Co.; apptd. asso. judge Ct. of Appeals of Md. (Supreme Ct.), 1924, elected for term, 1926-41. Pres. Md. State Bar Assn., 1924. Home: Westminster, Md. Died June 1, 1955; buried St. John's Cemetery, Westminster, Md.*

PARKE, John Shepard, hosp. adminstr.; b. Troy, Pa., Feb. 17, 1896; s. Albert T. and Della (Ballard) P.; B.Arch., Cornell U., 1923; m. Dorothy Simpson, Sept. 3, 1932; 1 son, John S. With Marc Eidlitz & Son, Inc., 1923-43, v.p., 1939-43; exec. v.p. Presbyn. Hosp., N.Y.C., 1944—. Vice chmn. N.Y.C. Housing Authority. Trustee Cornell U. Blood Transfusion Assn. Mem. Am. Coll. Hosp. Adminstrs. Am. Hosp. Assn., Am. Protestant Hosp. Assn., Sigma Alpha Epsilon. Clubs: Cornell, University, Gipsy Trail, Dutchess Valley Rod and Gun. Home: 165 Fort Washington Av., N.Y.C. Office: 622 W. 168th St., N.Y.C. 32. Died Aug. 13, 1954; buried Troy, Pa.

PARKER, Albert George, Jr., educator; b. Highland, Md., Sept. 6, 1892; s. Albert George and Jessie (Bewley) P.; A.B., Park Coll., Parkville, Mo., 1914; B.D., McCormick Theol. Sem., Chicago, 1917 fellow in Japan and China, 1917-19; Ph.D., University of Chicago, 1929; LL.D., Wabash College, 1930, D.D. (honorary), Park College, 1950; married Katharine McAfee, Aug. 10, 1920; children—Albert George, Harriet Anne, Jane McAfee, Susan Linnette. Ordained ministry Presbyn. Ch. in U.S.A., 1917; head of dept. social science, Shantung Christian U., Tsinan, China, 1920-28; pres. Hanover (Ind.) Coll. since 1929. In charge of grain distributing station, China, Internat. Famine Relief Commn., 1921. Author: Human Nature Becoming Christian Nature, 1927. Home: Hanover, Ind. Died Mar. 22, 1958.

PARKER, Arthur Caswell, museum director, author; b. Iroquois, N.Y., Apr. 5, 1881; s. Frederick Ely and Geneva H. (Griswold) P.; student Dickinson Sem., Williamsport, Pa., 1899-1903, archeology under Frederick Ward Putnam, Harvard, 1903-04; M.Sc., U. of Rochester, 1922; Sc.D. (hon.), Union Coll., 1940; L.H.D., Keuka Coll., Keuka Park, N.Y., 1943; m. Beatrice Tahamont, Apr. 23, 1904, (dec.); children—Melville A., Bertha A. (Mrs. Oscar Cody); m. 2d, Anna T. Cook, Sept. 17, 1914; 1 dau., Martha Anne. Archeol. at Harvard (Peabody Museum), 1903-04; ethnologist N.Y. State Library, 1904-05; archeologist N.Y. State Museum, 1905-25; dir. Rochester (N.Y.) Museum Arts and Scis., 1925-46, dir. emeritus since 1946; editor Parker Lit. Service, since 1904, Research. and Transactions, N.Y. State Archeol. Assn., since 1916, Museum Service, 1926-46, Research Records, 1926-46, The Galleon since 1949; associate editor of The Builder, 1922-24. Served as inspector draft boards and asst. to adjutant's officer, N.Y. State, World War I; chmn. speakers bur., Rochester War Council, 1943-45. Pres. Soc. Am. Indians, 1914-15, N.Y. State Archeol. Assn., since 1928; with Royal Danish Archeol. Survey, 1928, Soc. Am. Archeology, 1935, Genesee Country Hist. Fedn., since 1938, N.Y. State Hist. Assn., since 1945 (president, 1945-46); exec. vice pres., Rochester Museum Assn., 1945; history v.p. and councilor, Am. Assn. Museums, 1928-46; pres. Society of Colonial History, 1949-50; national council mem., Boy Scouts America, 1928-45; sec. N.Y. State Indian Commn., 1917-1919; rep. to State Council of Parks, 1922-23. Awarded Cornplanter Medal, Iroquoian Ethnology, 1916, Numismatic Medal, American Numismatic Assn., Rochester branch, 1929, Indian Achievement Medal, 1939; Civic Medal, City of Rochester (N.Y.), 1946; recipient of the Guggenheim award, Dec. 1954. Life fellow Rochester Acad. of Medicine, Philalethes Soc. Masonic Writers; member Nundawaga Society (founder, baord chmn.), Society of American Archeology, Rochester Engring. Soc., A.A.A.S., S.A.R. (past pres. Rochester chapter, 1933-36; awarded Good Citizen medal, 1947). Mason (K.T., 33°). Clubs: Torch (past pres.), Philosophers' (Rochester). Author: Erie Indian Village, 1907; Maize and Other Plant Foods, 1909; Code of Handsome Lake, 1913; Constitution of Five Nations, 1916; Life of General Ely S. Parker, 1919; Archeological History of New York, 1922; Seneca Myths and Folk Tales, 1923; The War of 1812, 1925; Skunny Wundy, 1926; Indian How Book, 1927; Rumbling Wings, 1928; Gustango Gold, 1930; Manual for History Museums, 1935; Red Streak of the Iroquois, 1950; Red Jacket, 1952; Last of the Seneca, 1952; also hist. dramas and pageants. Home: Parrish Hill Rd., Naples, N.Y. Office: 657 E. Av., Rochester 7, N.Y. Died Jan. 1, 1955.

PARKER, Charles A(mes), assn. exec.; b. Lynnfield Center, Mass., June 10, 1909; s. Bertram Munson and Mina Mary (Hoeffling) P.; diploma Tabor Acad., 1926; B. Indsl. Engring., Northeastern U., 1930; F.C.C. comml. radio license, F.C.C. amateur operators license, Gulf Radio Sch., 1931. Sales Curtiss-Wright Flying Service, 1929; treas., dir. Hyannis Airport Corp., 1933-37; v.p., dir. sales Inter-City Aviation, Inc., 1936-41, Eastern Aviation, Inc.,

1941-42; with Robinson Aviation, Inc., aircraft distbrs., 1946-48; exec. dir. Nat. Aviation Trades Assn. since 1949. Mem. air coordinating com. Aviation Industry Adv. Panel; air transportation adv. panel Fed. Civil Def. Adminstrn.; civil aviation air def. adv. com. Joint Civil Aeros. Adminstrn.-USAF Air Def. Planning Bd.; industry adv. com. Airport Use Panel of Air Coordinating Com. Served as maj. Air Transport Command, Hdqrs. USAAF, 1942-45. Recipient Certificate of Merit, 3rd Ann. Amvets., 1954. Mem. Nat. Aviation Trades Assn. (v.p., 1947-48), Amvets, National Air Taxi Conference (exec. vice president), Aviation Writers Assn., Am. Radio Relay League, Nat. Aeronautic Assn., Aircraft Owners and Pilots Assn. Editor of NATA-Operators Washington News Letter and the Aerial Applicators Washington Release (monthly) since 1949. Contbr. nat. aviation trade jours. Home: 327 Ocean St., Hyannis, Mass. Office: 1346 Connecticut Av., Washington 6. Died Apr. 21, 1959; buried Beechwood Cemetery, Centerville, Mass.

PARKER, Chauncey Goodrich, Jr., banker; b. New London, Conn., Sept. 4, 1897; s. Chauncey Goodrich and Dora Mason (Wright) P.; student St. Paul's Sch., Concord, N.H., 1911-14, Harvard, 1914-17; m. Cecilia Sherman McCallum, Jan. 2, 1923; children—Cecilia Sherman (Mrs. Philip L. Geyelin), Chauncey Goodrich. Gen. partner Auchincloss, Parker & Redpath, mem. N.Y. Stock Exchange, 1930—; dir. adminstrn. Internat. Bank Reconstrn. and Development, 1946-50; mem. Spl. Mission to Germany to set up Civilian High Commn. for Germany, 1950, asst. U.S. High Commr. for Germany, 1950-51; chief U.S. Spl. Econ. Mission to Italy, Mut. Security Agy., 1952—; treas., gov. Washington Stock Exchange, 1935-38; dir. Security Storage Co.; pres., dir Auchincloss, Parker & Redpath, Inc. Trustee St John's Orphanage, Northeast Boys Club. Served as 2d lt. F.A., U.S. Army, 1918-19; first chief div. finance and supply, exec. dep. dir. Selective Service System, 1939-43; col. U.S.M.C., 1942-45, chmn. Navy Price Adjustment Bd., 1944-45, Marine Corps rep. on world inspection tour with asst. sec. war, 1945. Decorated Legion of Merit with Star, Commendations Ribbons Army and Navy. Mem. Navy League U.S. (pres. Washington chpt.). Clubs: Bond (pres.), Ticker (pres.), Met. (pres.), Brook, Downtown Assn., Harvard (N.Y.C.); Alfalfa, Chevy Chase (Washington). Home: 3314 O St. N.W. Office: 729 15th St. N.W., Washington. Died Aug. 5, 1953; buried Arlington, Va.

PARKER, Cortlandt, army officer; b. Fort Apache, Ariz., Dec. 10, 1884; s. Major Gen. James and Charlotte (Condit) P.; student Newark (N.J.) Acad., 1897-1902; B.S., U.S. Mil. Acad., 1906; grad. Army Sch. of the Line, 1922, Army Staff Sch., 1923, Army War Coll., 1924; m. Elizabeth Gray, Nov. 11, 1918; children—Cortlandt, James. Commd. 2d lt., 5th Cav., U.S. Army, 1906, and advanced through the grades to maj. gen., 1942; retired 1946; with 6th F.A., 1907-13; other assignments in U.S. and Philippines, 1913-16; with 6th F.A. went to France with 1st Div., A.E.F., 1917; dir. training artillery, Camp Coëtquidan, 4 mos.; lt. col. and adj. F.A. Brigade, Feb.-Mar. 1918; comd. 6th F.A. Regt., Cantigny and Soissons, Apr.-July 1918; assigned 57th F.A., 19th Div., in U.S.; dir. gunnery dept. F.A. Sch., 1919-21; War Dept. Gen. Staff, 1924-28; mil. attaché Am. embassy, London, 1931-35; Hawaii, 1936-38; comd. 19th F.A., 5th Div., 1939-40; comd. div. arty. to May 1941, 5th Div. to June 1943 (last 15 mos. in Iceland); comdr. Southern Calif. sector, 1943-45. Decorated D.S.M., Silver Star, Legion of Merit. (U.S.), French Fourragère, Officer Legion of Honor (France). Mem. Soc. 1st Div., 5th Div., Cincinnati Club: Army-Navy Country (Washington). Address: Greenvale Farm, Newport, R.I.; also 51 Chestnut St., Boston. Died Jan. 19, 1960.

PARKER, Edward Burns, lawyer; b. Wedowee, Ala., June 21, 1895; s. Claude Lamar and Roxanna Elizabeth (Burns) P.; LL.B., Ala. U., 1921; m. Earle Bass, Sept. 28, 1921; 1 son, Earl Burns; m. 2d, Mary Oldham, Nov. 17. 1929; m. 3d, Opal Williams Murphy, Dec. 24, 1952. Began practice 1921; dep. solicitor, Randolph County, 1922-28; solicitor, Cleburne, County, 1929-35; U.S. atty. for Middle Dist., Ala., 1942-53. Mem. Legislature, 1931-35; mem. State Dem. Exec. Com., 1930-42; mem. State Bd. of Appeals No. 3, Selective Service. Served with Co. I, 167th Inf., U.S. Army, World War I; received regtl. citation. Awarded Selective Service medal, World War II. Mem. Ala. Bar Assn., Am. Legion, Vets. Fgn. Wars, Pi Kappa Phi. Democrat. Methodist. Mason. K.P., Lions. Home: Roanoke, Ala. Died Sept. 1, 1958; buried Roanoke, Ala. Died Sept. 1, 1958; buried Roanoke, Ala.

PARKER, George Howard, zoölogist; b. Phila., Dec. 23, 1864; s. George Washington and Martha (Taylor) P.; S.B., Harvard, 1887, S.D., 1891, Colby Coll., 1935; spl. student at univs. Leipzig, Berlin, Freiburg, 1891-93; m. Louise Merritt Stabler, June 15, 1894. Asst. and instr. zoölogy Harvard, 1888-91, Parker fellow in Europe, 1891-93, instr., 1893-99, asst. prof., 1899-1906, prof. zoölogy, 1906-35, prof. emeritus since 1935. William B. Clark lectr. Amherst Coll., 1914; sent by U.S. Govt. to investigate Pribilof seal herd, 1914. Exchange prof. to western colleges, 1921. Awarded Elliot medal Nat. Acad. Sciences, 1937, Lewis prize, Am. Philos. Soc., 1941. Fellow A.A.A.S. (v.p. 1916), Am. Acad. Arts and Sciences (pres. 1933); mem. Nat. Acad. Sciences, Am. Philos. Soc., Washington Acad. Sciences, Boston Soc. Natural History, Am. Zoöl. Soc. (pres. 1903), Mass. Med. Soc., Am. Soc. Naturalists (pres. 1929), Am. Physiol. Soc., Assn. Am. Anatomists, Soc. Exptl. Biology and Medicine, Ecol. Soc. America, Marine Biol. Lab., Soc. Vert. Paleontology, Phi Beta Kappa, Sigma Xi (nat. pres. 1934-35); hon. mem. Am. Otol. Soc., Cal. Acad. Sciences, Cambridge Philos. Soc., Buffalo Soc. Natural History; corr. mem. London Zoöl. Soc., Acad. Natural Sciences Phila., N.Y. Acad. Sciences, Soc. Biol. (Paris), Peking Soc. Nat. History; asso. mem. Soc. Belge de Biol.; foreign mem. Linnaean Soc., London. Club: Harvard (Boston). Author: Biology and Social Problems, 1914; The Elementary Nervous System, 1919; Smell, Taste and Allied Senses, 1922; The Evolution of Man (co-author), 1922; What Evolution Is, 1925; Creation by Evolution (co-author), 1928; Human Biology and Racial Welfare (co-author), 1930; Humoral Agents in Nervous Activity, 1932; The Problem of Mental Disorder (co-author), 1934; Color Changes in Animals in Relation to Nervous Activity, 1936; The World Expands, 1946; Animal Colour Changes and Their Neurohumours, 1948. Contbr. articles to zoöl. journals, dealing chiefly with anatomy and physiology of nervous organs and animal reactions. Home: 16 Berkeley St., Cambridge 38, Mass. Died Mar. 26, 1955.

PARKER, George Swinnerton, chmn. bd. Parker Brothers, Inc.; b. Salem, Mass., Dec. 12, 1866; s. George A. and Sarah M. (Hegeman) P.; m. Grace E. Mann, June 15, 1896. Founded firm of George S. Parker & Co., 1883, by publication of first game; changed firm name to Parker Brothers, 1888, as Parker Brothers, Inc., 1901, now chmn. bd.; dir. Naumkeag Steam Cotton Co., Naumkeag Trust Co., v.p. The Essex Inst. of Salem. Mem. budget com., Town of Petersboro, N.H.; vice president Salem Savings Bank. Clubs: Union (Boston), Cosmos (Washington, D.C.). Address: 365 Essex St., Salem, Mass. Summer home: "Brookwood", Peterborough, N.H. Died Sept. 26, 1952; buried Harmony Grove, Salem, Mass.

PARKER, Harry Lee, physician, educator; b. Limerick, Ireland, 1894; s. John Henry and Eleanor Margaret (Lee) P.; M.B., B.Ch., Trinity Coll. Dublin U., 1918, B.A., 1916, B.A.O., 1918, M.D., 1945; M.S., U. Minn., 1922; m. Florence Lampert, Aug. 4, 1923; children—Sheila Margaret, Thomas M. Came to U.S., 1919, naturalized, 1927. Practice of medicine, 1918—, specializing in neurology, 1921—; prof. neurology Trinity Coll. Dublin U., 1934-45, Mayo Found. U. Minn. Grad. Sch., 1945—; mem. Brit. Neurological Assn., Minn. Neuropsychiat. Soc., Central Neuropsychiat. Soc., Am. Neurologic Assn., A. M.A., Minn., Olmsted-Houston-Fillmore-Dodge County med. socs. Author: Clinical Studies in Neurology, 1955. Home: 903 Sixth Av. S.W. Office: 200 First St. S.W., Rochester, Minn. Died Mar. 1, 1959; buried Calvary Cemetery, Rochester, Minn.

PARKER, Henry Griffith, banker; b. New Brunswick, N.J., Sept. 2, 1866; s. William and Ann (Griffith) P.; hon. A.M., Rutgers Univ., 1920; m. Alice Florence Parker, 1896; 1 son, Henry Griffith. Chmn. bd. Nat. Bank of N.J., Interwoven Stocking Co.; chmn. bd., v.p. New Brunswick Savings Instn.; dir. Prudential Ins. Co. of America (finance com.), New Brunswick Fire Ins. Co. (exec. com.); pres. Middlesex County (N.J.) Sinking Fund Commn. Trustee Rutgers U. (finance com.), N.J. Bankers Assn. (past pres.); dir. and past pres. New Brunswick C. of C. Republican. Episcopalian. Home: 165 College Av. Office: 390 George St., New Brunswick, N.J. Died June 1953.

PARKER, H(ugh) E(verett), railroad exec.; b. White Plains, Ga., Jan. 6, 1887; s. Albert Sidney and Florence Lelia (Cofer) A.B., U. Ga., 1907; m. Eunie Leola Jones, Nov. 6, 1912; children—Eunie (Mrs. William R. Currie), Hugh Everett. With Southern Ry. Co., 1908-19, serving as clerk, asst. yardmaster, gen. yardmaster, trainmaster; with Tenn. Coal, Iron and R.R. Co., Birmingham, 1919-33, asst. supt., supt., gen. supt. of transportation; pres. Birmingham Southern R.R. Co., 1933—; pres. Warrior and Gulf Navigation Co., 1941—; pres. Ohio Barge Line, Inc., 1943—; v.p. Inland Waterways Corp., 1948—. Dir. Am. Short Line Rd. Assn. Mem. Am. Iron and Steel Inst. Democrat. Baptist. Clubs: Traffic and Transportation (Birmingham); Mountain Brook; Duquesne (Pitts.). Home: 3007 Canterbury Rd., Mountain Brook. Office: P.O. Box 579, Fairfield, Ala. Died July 1956.

PARKER, J. Heber, steel exec. Pres. and dir. Carpenter Steel Co. Home: 1154 Reading Blvd., Wyomissing, Pa. Office: 101 West Bern St., Reading, Pa. Died Dec. 28, 1956.

PARKER, J. Roy, publisher; b. Ahoskie, N.C., Jan. 11, 1895; s. Joseph T. and Julia (Newsome) P.; A.B., Wake Forest (N.C.) Coll., 1915; student U. of Mo., 1922; m. Louise Buffaloe, May 5, 1923; 1 son, J. Roy. Pub. Hertford County Herald, Ahoskie, Oct. 1, 1915—; editor, 1915-34; columnist for Hertford County Herald, Ledger-Advance, Windsor, N.C., The Jackson (N.C.) News, Gates County Index, Gatesville, N.C., 1935—; city editor, Logan (W.Va.) Democrat, 1922; sports editor Tribune Times, Hornell, N.Y., 1922; pres. Parker Bros., Inc., Ahoskie, pubs. and printers of Hertford County Herald, Bertie Ledger-Advance, Windsor, N.C., Jackson (N.C.) News, Gates County Index, 1940—; sec.-mgr. N.C. Weekly Newspaper Assn., Inc., Chapel Hill, 1941-49; prof. journalism, U. of N.C., 1941-49, emeritus; vis. lectr. journalism Chowan College. Mem. N.C. Gen. Assembly, 1956-57. Served as yeoman, U.S.N.R.F., 1918. Mem. N.C. Press Assn. (pres. 1934-35), Am. Legion, C. of C. Democrat. Baptist. Mason. Rotarian. Office: Parker Bros., Inc., Ahoskie, N.C. Died May 8, 1957; buried Ahoskie.

PARKER, James W., cons. engr.; b. Auburn, New York, Nov. 28, 1886; s. Charles A. and Sara (Cole) P.; M.E., Cornell U., 1908; M.S. in mech. engring. (hon.), Detroit Inst. Tech., 1935; E.D., Stevens Inst. Tech., 1942, Poly. Inst. Bklyn., 1948, Rensalaer Poly. Inst., 1950; LL.D., Wayne U., 1953; Dr. Engring., U. Mich., 1953; m. Dorothy Dow, 1913; children—Ann Cole (Mrs. R. E. Valk), Alan Breck; m. 2d, Verna Elmslie Dow, 1948; 1 stepson, Paul H. Dow. Plant operating engr. DeKalb (Ill.) Power & Light Co., 1908-09; chief plant engr. Vincennes (Ind.) Street Ry. Co., 1909; boiler room engr. The Detroit Edison Co., 1910-13, chief asst. engr. of power plants, 1913-14, supt. central heating, 1914-17, assistant to v.p., 1917-35, chief engr., 1924-43, v.p. and chief engr., 1935-42, v.p. and gen. mgr. 1943-1944; pres., dir., gen. mgr., 1944-51, cons., dir., 1952; dir. Air Preheater Corp. of N.Y., Liberty Life & Accident Insurance Company, Standard Accident Ins. Co., Mfrs. National Bank, Detroit Edison Co. President, trustee Rackham Engring. Found.; past pres. Assn. Edison Illuminating Cos., The Engring. Soc. of Detroit, Am. Soc. M.E.; mem. Tau Beta Pi, Sigma Xi. Clubs: Detroit, Detroit Athletic, Detroit Prismatic, University of Ann Arbor; Engineers (N. Y.C.). Address: 1125 Country Club Rd., Ann Arbor, Mich. Died Dec. 30, 1957; buried Moravia, N.Y.

PARKER, John, theatrical historian, journalist; b. N.Y. City, July 28, 1875; s. David and Florence (Joel) P.; ed. at London; m. Edith Maud Pizey, 1899 (died 1942); children—Doris Christine Maud, John David Douglas; m. 2d, Doris Mary Sinclair, 1944. Began as journalist, Illustrated London News, 1892; mem. staff The Era, Free Lance, 1900-06; London corr. New York Dramatic Mirror, 1903, critic and mgr. New York Dramatic News, 1903-20; rep. Great Britain, Internat. Congress of Critics, Paris, 1937; contbr. numerous theatrical biographies to each supplemental issue of Dictionary of Nat. Biography since 1910; compiler and editor, The Green Room Book, 1908-09; compiler and editor Who's Who in the Theatre since 1912; hon. editor The Critics' Circular, since 1923. Hon. sec., The Critics Circle since 1924 (pres. 1937-38); v.p. The Assn. of London Theatre Press Reps., 1950; mem. Inst. of Journalists. Clubs: The Savage, Green Room, Surrey County Cricket. Home: 9 Westbourne House, Richmond Rd., Twickenham, Middlesex. Office: Hall of Institute of Journalists, 2-4 Tudor St., London, E.C. 4, England. Died Nov. 18, 1952.

PARKER, John Bernard, biology; b. Danville, O., Sept. 24, 1870; s. Robert Selman and Rebecca Ann (McKenzie) P.; Danville (O.) Normal, 1886-88; A.B., Ohio State U., 1898, M.A., 1900, Ph.D., 1915; m. Lucy Sapp, Sept. 3, 1901; children—Agnes Hermene (dec.), Harold Leslie, Ruth Elizabeth, Edith Rita. Instr. biology, South High Sch., Cleve., 1900-06; asst. entomology, Kan. State Agrl. Coll., 1908-10; instr. biology, Catholic U. of Am. 1910-13, asso. prof., 1913-18, prof., 1918-40, ret. 1940; prof. biology, emeritus, 1940—. Mem. Entomol. Soc. Washington, Sigma Xi. Democrat. Roman Catholic. Author: A Revision of the Bembicini Wasps of North America, North of Mexico, 1917; A Generic Revision of the Fossorial Wasps of the Tribes Stizini and Bembicini, 1929; An Introduction to Animal Biology (with J. J. Clarke), 1939, and others. Contbr. to The Book of Popular Science, 1924. Home: 1217 Lawrence St. N.E., Washington 17. Died Sept. 2, 1951.

PARKER, John Gowans, insurance exec.; b. Hagersville, Ont., Sept. 6, 1883; s. William and Annie (Bethune) P.; B.A., U. Toronto, 1904, fellow, 1904-06; m. Edith Dunn, Oct. 20, 1914; 1 son, William George. Clk. actuarial dept. Imperial Life Assurance Co. Can., 1906-12, asst. actuary, 1912-14, asso. actuary, 1914-23, actuary, 1923-36, gen mgr., 1936-44, managing director 1944-47, president 1947-53, chairman board since 1953. Fellow Inst. Actuaries Great Britain; member American Institute Actuaries (pres. 1926-28), Actuarial Soc. Am. (pres. 1934-36), Life Ins. Inst. Can. (pres. 1937-38), Canadian Life Ins. Officers Assn. (pres. 1941-42). Mem. United Ch. of Can. Mason. Clubs: York, Nat., Toronto Hunt, Granite. Home: 45 Oriole Gardens, Toronto 12. Office: 20 Victoria St., Toronto 1, Ont., Can. Died Nov. 4, 1953.

PARKER, John Johnston, judge; b. Monroe, N.C., Nov. 20, 1885; s. John Daniel and Frances (Johnston) P.; A.B., U. of N.C., 1907, LL.B., 1908; LL.D., 1927; LL.D., Davidson Coll., 1940, U. of Mich., 1942, Tulane, 1948, U. Richmond, 1954, Northwestern U., 1956; m. Maria Burgwin Maffitt, Nov. 23, 1910; children—John Johnston (dec.), Sara Burgwin (Mrs. Rufus M. Ward), Francis Iredell. Admitted to N.C. bar, 1908, and began practice at Greensboro; moved to Monroe, 1909; mem. firm Stack & Parker, 1910-19, Stack, Parker & Craig, 1919-22; moved to Charlotte, 1922, becoming head of firm Parker, Stewart, McRae & Bobbitt. Rep. nominee for governor of North Carolina, 1920; special assistant to attorney general of United States, 1923-24; member Rep. Nat. Com., 1924; del. at large from N.C. to Rep. Nat. Conv., 1924; circuit judge U.S. Court, 4th Circuit, by apptmt. of President Coolidge, since Oct. 3, 1925; apptd. mem. Supreme Court of U.S. by President Hoover but apptmt. not confirmed by Senate; mem. commn. to draft revised constn. for N.C., 1931. Harlan Fisk Stone lectr. Amherst Coll., 1950; John Randolph Tucker lectr. Washington and Lee U., 1951; Tyrrell Williams Lecturer Washington Univ., 1954. Awarded Am. Bar Association medal for conspicuous service in cause of American Jurisprudence, 1943. Mem. adv. bd. on Just Compensation, to Way Shipping Adminstrn, 1943; alternate mem. Internat. Mil. Tribunal, 1945. Elected Hon. Master of Bench, Inner Temple, London (Eng.), 1946. Trustee University of North Carolina. Delegate to Gen. Conv. of Episcopal Ch., 1937. Delegate to Nat. Study Conference on a Just and Durable Peace, instituted by Federal Council of Churches, 1945. White lecturer, U. of Va., 1940. Mem. Am. Bar Assn. (v.p.; chmn. judicial sect. 1937; chmn. spl. com. on improving the administration of justice, 1940-47. N.C. Bar Assn., Am. Acad. Polit. and Social Science, Acad. Polit. Science, Am. Soc. Internat. Law, Am. Law Inst. (mem. council), Am. Judicature Soc. (v.p.), Phi Beta Kappa, Phi Delta Phi, Omicron Delta Kappa, Golden Fleece, Order of the Coif. Episcopalian. Mason. Author: Democracy in Government. Clubs: Kiwanis, Charlotte Country. Home: 135 Queens Rd., Charlotte, N.C. Died Mar. 17, 1958; buried Elmwood Cemetery, Charlotte, N.C.

PARKER, Laigh C(alhoun), airline exec.; b. Jackson, La., Nov. 25, 1902; s. Laigh C. and Mattie (Norsworthy P.; m. Kate Landreth, Oct. 11, 1929. Dist. sales mgr. Radio Corp. Am., Memphis, 1926-27, Crosley Radio Corp., Memphis, 1928; dir. broadcasting Lamar Life Ins. Co., Jackson, Miss., 1929; successively radio operator, sta. mgr., city traffic mgr., dist. sales mgr. Am. Airways, Inc., predecessor Am. Airlines, Inc., Jackson, 1930-34; gen. traffic mgr. Delta Air Lines, Monroe, La., 1934-35; v.p. traffic and sales, dir. Delta Air Lines, Inc., Atlanta, 1935-59, sr. vice pres., asst. to the pres., dir. 1959—; dir. Air Cargo, Inc. Pres. Air Traffic Conf. Am. 1941, 46, 48. Chmn. traffic conference, Internat. Air Transport Assn. Served as col. USAAF, 1942-45. Decorated Legion of Merit, Bronze Star, Army Commendation medal with oak leaf cluster. Clubs: Capital City, Athletic, Peachtree Racquet (Atlanta). Home: 2184 Peachtree Rd. N.W. Office: Delta Air Lines, Inc., Atlanta Airport, Atlanta. Died Dec. 23, 1959.

PARKER, Lawton S., portrait painter; b. Fairfield, Mich., Aug. 7, 1868; s. John W. and Sarah A. (Sawyer) P.; ed. Ecole des Beaux Arts, Paris; Dr. of Fine Arts, U. of Neb.; m. Beatrice Snow, Mar. 1927. Prof. St. Louis Sch. of Fine Arts, 1892; dir. of art, Beloit Coll., 1893; pres. N.Y. Sch. of Art, 1898-1899; dir. Parker Acad., Paris, 1900; non-resident prof. of painting, Art Inst. of Chicago, 1902; pres. Chgo. Acad. Fine Arts, 1903. Has painted portraits of Martin A. Ryerson, J. Ogden Armour, N. W. Harris, Harry P. Judson, Peter S. Grosscup. Hon. mention, Salon, Paris, 1900; 3d medal Salon, Paris, 1902; silver medal, St. Louis Expn., 1904; gold medal, Internat. Exhbn., Munich, 1905; hon. mention Carnegie Inst., 1907; 1st medal, Chicago Soc. of Artists, Art Inst. of Chicago, 1908; gold medal, Salon, Paris, 1913 (first American to receive this award); medal of honor, Panama P.I., Exposition, 1915; Altman prize, Nat. Acad. Desin, 1916. Represented in Luxembourg Gallery, Paris. Asso. of Nat. Acad. Home: 2475 Vista Laguna Terrace, Pasadena 2, Cal. Died Sept. 25, 1954. Buried Woodlawn Cemetery, Santa Monica, Cal.

PARKER, Maude (Mrs. Edmund W. Pavenstedt), writer; b. Galveston, Tex.; d. Daingerfield Leroy and Isabella Wysong (Johnston) Parker; ed. pvt. and pub. schs.; U. of Wis., 1914-15; m. Richard Washburn Child, Aug. 1916 (div. Nov. 1926); children—Anne, Constance; m. 2d, Edmund Wm. Pavenstedt, Mar. 30, 1931. Author: The Social Side of Diplomatic Life, 1926; Secret Envoy, 1920; Impersonation of a Lady, 1934. Contbr. of fiction and articles to various mags. Address: care Harold Ober, 40 E. 49th St., N.Y.C. Died Nov. 13, 1959.

PARKER, Robert, fgn. corr.; author; b. Newark, N.J., June 14, 1906; s. Robert Bogardus and Alice Marianne (Downing) P.; A.B., Union Coll., Schenectady, N.Y., 1930; m, Lorraine Wolcott Jackson;

children—Robert, Daphne Wolcott. Associated successively with Elizabeth (N.J.) Times, Newark (N.J.) Sunday Call, Schenectady (N.Y.) Gazette; reporter N.Y. Evening Journal, 1930-32; with Associated Press, 1933-41, as fgn. corr. (covering Spanish Civil War, League of Nations, etc.), Paris, France, 1934-39, dir. for Eastern Europe, Warsaw, Budapest, Bern, 1939-41; chief for Eastern Europe (hdqrs. Istanbul, Turkey, Office War Information, 1942-43; spl. asst. to Am. ambassadors to Turkey and Egypt, 1942-43; dir. pub. relations Atlantic City Conf. of United Nations Relief and Rehabilitation Adminstrn., Nov., Dec. 1943. Lecturer, orientation program U.S. Army Air Forces, under auspices of Writers War Board, 1944. Accredited war correspondent C.B.I. theater, 1945; chief UN bureau of New York Daily News, 1953—. Mem. Soc. of Cincinnati, Sigma Phi, Pi Gamma Mu. Clubs: National Press (Washington, D.C.); Anglo-American Press (Paris); Travelers (Budapest); Club d'Istanbul (Istanbul, Turkey). Author: Headquarters Budapest (Farrar and Rinehart), 1944; Ticket to Oblivion, 1950; Passport to Peril, 1951; Operation Birdcage, 1953. Address: 220 E. 42d St., N.Y.C. 17. Died Apr. 1955.

PARKER, Walter Robert, physician; b. Marine City, Mich., Oct. 10, 865; s. Leonard Brooks and Jane (Sparrow) P.; prep. edn. Mich. Mil. Acad.; B.S., U. Mich., 1888; M.D., U. Pa., 1891, Sc.D., City, Mich., Oct. 10, 1865; s. Leonard Brooks and 1927; Sc.D., U. Mich., 1934; m. Margaret W. Watson, Dec. 28, 1907. Practiced in Detroit 1894—; prof. ophthalmology, U. Mich., 1905-33 (emeritus); cons. ophthalmic surgeon Harper Hosp., Woman's Hosp. Served as ensign U.S. Navy, Spanish-Am. War; col. Med. Corps, U.S. Army, World War. Fellow Am. Coll. Surgeons; mem. A.M.A., Am. Acad. Ophthalmology and Oto-Laryngology, Am. Ophthal. Soc., Ophthal. Soc. of United Kingdom, Internat. Ophthal. Soc. (council). Republican. Presbyterian. Clubs: University, Detroit City, Detroit Country, Yondotega. Home: 1 Woodland Pl., Grosse Pointe, Mich. Office: David Whitney Bldg., Detroit, Mich. Died Apr. 1, 1955.

PARKER, Walter Winfield, college pres.; b. Howard County, Ark., Jan. 17, 1889; s. John Alexander and Susan Elizabeth (Pinkerton) P.; A.B., Hendrix Coll., 1912, LL.D., 1929; A.M., Columbia, 1915; LL.D. (hon.), Central College, Missouri, 1947; m. Martha Marion James, Sept. 4, 1912; children—Mary Elizabeth, John James, Walter Winfield, William Howard. Teacher English, Conway, Ark., 1909-10, Hendrix Acad., 1912-14, Teachers Coll., Warrensburg, Mo., 1915-23; dean of faculty, Teachers Coll., 1923-28; pres. State Teachers Coll., Alva, Okla., 1928-33; pres. S.E. Mo. State Teachers Coll., Cape Girardeau, Mo., 1933-56. Mem. bd. visitors U.S. Military Acad., 1950-53. Mem. N.E.A. (dept. of superintendence), Nat. Council Teachers of English, Kappa Delta Pi, Pi Kappa Delta. Methodist. Mason, Rotarian. Club: Country. Contbr. to jours. Home: 1746 Lacy St., Cape Girardeau, Mo. Died Feb. 9, 1957; buried Memorial Park, Cape Girardeau.

PARKHURST, Helen Huss, educator; b. N.Y. City, Jan. 3, 1887; d. Howard Elmore and Mary Sophie (Huss) Parkhurst; A.B., Bryn Mawr, 1911, A.M., 1913, traveling fellow, 1913-14, resident fellow, 1915-16, Ph.D., 1917; Cambridge U., Eng., 1913-14; hon. fellow, Johns Hopkins, 1915-16. Teacher, Dwight Sch., Englewood, N.J., 1911-12; lecturer on art, Bryn Mawr, 1916-17; asst. in philosophy, Barnard Coll., Columbia, 1917-18, instr. in philosophy, 1918-24, asst. professor, 1924-31, associate professor, 1931-44, professor, 1944-52, professor emeritus since 1952; John Simon Guggenheim Memorial fellow, 1931-32. Mem. Am. Philosophical Assn. Democrat. Author: Beauty—An Interpretation of Art and the Imaginative Life, 1930; Cathedral: A Gothic Pilgrimage, 1936. Home: 404 W. 20th St., N.Y.C. 11. Died Apr. 14, 1959.

PARKINSON, Thomas I., lawyer; b. Phila. Nov. 27, 1881; s. John Henry and Rose (Fleming) P.; m. Georgia C. Weed, June 4, 1912; children—Thomas I. C. V. Began practice of law in Philadelphia, 1902; admitted to N.Y. bar, 1909; dir. legislative drafting dept., Columbia U., since 1910; prof. legislation, Columbia, 1917-35; dean faculty of law, Columbia, 1923-24; pres., dir. Equitable Life Assurance Society, 1927-53; chmn. bd., director 1953-54; trustee Atlantic Mut. Ins. Company; director Niagara Fire Insurance Company, Centennial Insurance Co., Chase Nat. Bank, Pittsburgh Consolidation Coal Co., Continental Ins. Co., Westinghouse Electric Co., L.I. R.R. Co., Borden Co. Former trustee Gen. Edn. Bd., Rockefeller Found.; trustee Columbia U., U. Pa.; expres. N.Y. State Chamber Commerce. Maj., judge advocate U.S. Army, 1918-19. Spl. counsel, Bur. of War Risks Ins., 1919; legislative counsel, U.S. Senate Commns., 1919-20. Mem. Am. Bar Assn., N.Y. State Bar Assn., Phila. Bar Assn., Assn. Bar City of New York, Phi Delta Phi. Clubs: Century Assn., Lawyers, Cosmos, Pennsylvania, The Pennsylvania Society. Economic of New York. Home: 7 Park Av., N.Y.C. Died June 17, 1959.

PARKMAN, Henry, govt. ofcl.; born Boston, Apr. 26, 1894; s. Henry and Mary Frances (Parker)

P.; A.B., Harvard U., 1915, A.M., 1916; student Harvard Law Sch., 1915-17, Northeastern U. Law Sch., 1922-23; grad. School of Military Government, Charlottesville, Va., 1943; m. Doris Montague Leamy, June 26, 1936. Admitted to Mass. bar, 1924, and since in practice at Boston; now partner Parkman, Robbins & Russell, Boston. Member City Council of Boston, 1926-29, Mass. Senate, 1929-36; corporation counsel, Boston, 1938-40; Rep. candidate for U.S. senator (Mass.), 1940. Mass. dir. Office Price Adminstrn., May, 1942-Jan., 1943; Govt. affairs advisor, U.S. Mil. Govt., Germany, 1946-47; U.S. rep. Internat. Authority for Ruhr, Duesseldorf, 1949-50; chief E.C. A. Spl. Mission to France, 1950-51; assistant U.S. High Commr. Germany, 1953-55; dep. commr. Savs. Bank Life Ins. Co., Mass., 1956—. Capt. 320th Inf., U.S. Army, with A.E.F. 1918-19. Commd. lt. col., A.U.S., Jan. 13, 1943; col. Aug., 1944; brig. gen., Oct. 1945; served overseas as staff officer, Allied Hdqrs., and as A.C.S., G-5, Hdqrs. 6th Army Group; asst. U.S. High Commissioner for Germany, 1954. Awarded D.S.M., Legion of Merit; Comdrs. Cross Republic Germany, 1958; Commandeur French Legion of Honor, 1958. Former president American Legislators Assn.; pres. Rep. Club of Mass., 1928-30; v.p. Council of State Govts., 1936-38. Mem. Am. Bar Assn., Mass. Bar Assn., and Boston Bar Assn., Phi Beta Kappa. Republican. Unitarian. Mason. Clubs: Union Boat, Tavern (Boston). Home: 30 W. Cedar St., Boston. Office: 30 State St., Boston. Died May 27, 1958.

PARKS, Floyd Lavinius, army ofcr. ret.; b. Louisville, Feb. 9, 1896; s. Lyman L. and Lizzie Pratt (Manly) P.; student Cumberland Coll., Prep. Dept., 1912-13, Frazer Fitting Sch., Anderson, S.C., 1913-14; B.S., Clemson Coll., 1917, Doctor of Military Science, 1954; B.S. in Mech. Engring., Yale, 1924; grad. Tank Sch., 1924, Inf. Sch., 1933, Command and Gen. Staff Sch., 1935, Army War Coll., 1940; m. Mary M. Trowbridge, Nov. 26, 1924 (div. 1927); m. 2d, Harriet Marie Applebye-Robinson, Sept. 24, 1931; children—Edwyna Anne, William Robinson, Floyd Lavinius, Basil Manly. Private, 2d lt., 1st lt., and capt. Tank Corps, 1918; commd. 1st lt. regular army of U.S., July 1, 1920, and advanced through the grades to lieutenant general, 1953; became deputy chief of staff, Army Ground Forces, March 9, 1942, chief of staff, June 1942 to Feb. 1943; asst. div. comdr., 69th Inf. Div., Feb. 1943-July 1944; chief of staff, First Allied Airborne Army, Aug. 1944-May 26, 1945; comdg. First Airborne Army, U.S., May-Oct. 1945; comdg. U.S. sector and mil. govt., Berlin, from entry U.S. troops, July-Oct. 1945; chief, Pub. Information Division, Dept. of Army, 1945-48; deputy comdg. general U.S. Army, Pacific, 1948-49; chief of information Department of Army, 1949-53; comdg. gen. 2d Army, 1953-56, retired from active duty; exec. dir. Nat. Rifle Assn. Am., 1956—. Member exec. com. region 3, exec. bd. nat. capital area council, mem.-at-large nat. council Boy Scouts Am. Decorated D.S.M. with oak leaf cluster, Bronze Star Medal, Air Medal, Legion of Merit, Commendation Ribbon, Victory Medal (World War I); Nat. Defense Medal, Am. Theater Campaign Ribbon, European-African-Middle East Campaign Ribbon with 3 battle stars, Victory Medal (World War II), Occupation Medal (Germany); Abdon Calderon, 3d Class (Ecuador); Companion of Bath (Gt. Britain); Order Kutuzov, 1st Class (Russia); Polonia Restituta, Commander's Cross (Poland); Comdr. 1st Class, Order of Dannebrog (Denmark); Officer Legion of Honor (France); Grand Officer, Order Orange-Nassau (Netherlands); Croix de Guerre with Palm (Belgium). Mem. Washington Bd. Trade, Am. Legion, Vets. Fgn. Wars, Assn. U.S. Army, West Point Soc., Am. Ordnance Assn., Nat. Security Indsl. Assn. (hon. life), Nat. Rifle Assn. (endowment mem.), U.S., Am., So. srs. golf assns., Middle Atlantic Golf Assn. (v.p.), S.C. Soc. Washington, Nantucket Hist. Soc., Tau Beta Pi. Clubs: Chevy Chase, Columbia Country (Chevy Chase, Md.); Army-Navy Country, Army-Navy, University, Nat. Press (Washington). Home: 3650 Upton St., Washington 8. Office: 1600 Rhode Island Av., Washington 6. Died Mar. 10, 1959; buried Arlington Nat. Cemetery.

PARKS, Henry Martin, cons. geologist; b. Peoria, Ill., Nov. 29, 1872; s. Steen B. and Amanda (Yates) P.; B.S. in M.E., Ia. State Coll., 1902, E.M., 1909; studied Colo. Sch. of Mines 1 yr.; m. Alice Merritt, Dec. 31, 1903; children—Ruth Gwendolyn, Merritt Yates. Instr., mining engring. dept., Ia. State Coll., 1903-04; mining in Butte, Mont., Cripple Creek, Colo., and Tonopah, Nev., 1904-08; asst. prof. mining and metallurgy, Northwestern U., 1906-07; prof. mining engring., 1907-12, dean Ore. State Sch. of Mines, 1912-17; dir. Ore. Bur. of Mines and Geology, 1912-23; geologist and mining engr., 1923—; pres., mgr. Fort Rock Development Co. Capt., engr. O.R.C. 1917. Mem. Am. Inst. Mining Engrs., Am. Mining Congress, Am. Assn. State Geologists, Ore. Acad. Sci. Republican. Presbyn. Home: Fort Rock, Ore. Office: Spalding Bldg., Portland, Ore. Died Feb. 26, 1945.

PARKS, Robert Lee McAllister, newspaper editor; b. Savannah, Ga., Oct. 21, 1902; s. Robert L. M. and Frances (Morris) P.; ed. Richmond Acad., Augusta, Ga., and Washington and Lee U., Lexington, Va.; m. Margaret Stokes, Sept. 10, 1929; children—Jacquelyn, Robert Lee McAllister, III. Reporter Augusta (Ga.) Chronicle, 1923; free lance reporting, Europe, 1923-24; reporter Atlanta (Ga.) Constitution, 1925; with Augusta Chronicle continuously since 1926, successively reporter, sports editor, city editor to 1933, mng. editor and editorial writer, 1933-41, editor since 1941. Mem. Am. Soc. Newspaper Editors, Schs. of Journalism Com. of Southern Newspaper Publishers Assn.; chmn. Ga. Press Inst. Com. 1943-44; mem. bd. mgrs. Ga. Press Assn., 1947-48. Mem. Augusta Exchange Club, Sigma Delta Chi, Pi Kappa Phi. Episcopalian. Home: Pine Needle Rd., Forest Hills, Augusta, Ga. Office: Augusta Chronicle, Augusta, Ga. Deceased.

PARKS, Tilman Bacon, ex-congressman; b. Lewisville, Ark., May 14, 1872; s. William P. and Mattie (Douglass) P.; U. of Va., 1891-93; m. Fay Newton, Mar. 4, 1897. Admitted to Ark. bar, 1902, and began practice at Lewisville; removed to Hope, 1915; mem. Ark. Ho. of Reps., 1901-03, 1909; pros. atty. 8th Jud. Dist. of Ark., 1915-16, 17-18; mem. 67th to 74th Congresses, 7th Ark. Dist. Dem. presdl. elector at large, 1912, and messenger to carry electoral vote to Washington, 1913. Baptist. Mason, K.P., Woodman. Democrat. Home: Camden, Ark. Died Feb. 12, 1950.*

PARLIN, H(anson) T(ufts), univ. dean; b. Leadville, Colo., Nov. 7, 1879; s. Hanson Tufts and Mary Goodwin (Hall) P.; B.A., U. Colo., 1904, M.A., 1906; Ph.D., U. Pa., 1908; unmarried. With U. of Tex., 1908-—, as instr. in English, 1908-13, asst. prof. English also asst. dean Coll. of Arts and Sciences, 1913-19, asso. prof. English and asst. dean of the Coll., 1919-23, prof. of English and junior dean Coll. of Arts and Sciences, 1923-28, prof. English, also dean Coll. of Arts and Sciences, 1928-—. Mem. Phi Beta Kappa, Delta Tau Delta. Episcopalian. Democrat. Club: University. Home: Austin, Tex. Died Feb. 3, 1951.

PARMELEE, Cullen Warner, prof. ceramic engring.; b. Bklyn., June 27, 1874; s. Lauren Sylvester Everett and Mary Alida (Payne) P.; B.Sc., Rutgers Coll., New Brunswick, N.J., 1896, M.Sc., 1926, D. Sc., 1936; m. Julia Russell Davis, Oct. 3, 1901; children—Cullen Everett, Eleanor Paulding, Theodore Davis, Mary Payne (dec.). Chemist N.Y. & Boston Dyewood Co., 1896-1901; instr., asso. prof. chemistry, Rutgers Coll., 1901-08, organizer, dir. dept. ceramics; prof. ceramic engring., U. of Ill., 1916-42, head of dept., 1923-42, emeritus. Life mem. Am. Ceramic Soc. (pres. 1914-15; dean fellows, 1934-35). Fellow Soc. Glass Technology (Eng.), Mem. British Ceramic Soc., Deutsche Keramische Gesellschaft (hon.), Keramos, Inst. of Ceramic Engrs., Beta Theta Pi, Phi Beta Kappa, Sigma Xi, Gamma Pi Upsilon, Alpha Chi Sigma, Phi Kappa Phi. Episcopalian. Author: Clays and Some Other Ceramic Materials; Essentials of Glaze Composition. Home: 802 W. Florida St., Urbana, Ill. Died Aug. 1947.

PARMELEE, Howard Coon, editor; b. Omaha, Neb., Dec. 4, 1874; s. Edward Anson and Sarah Knox (Coon) P.; B.Sc., U. Neb., 1897, A.M., 1899; hon. Sc.D., Colorado Coll.; m. Eugenia E. McAusland, Apr. 10, 1922. Asst. chemist U.P. R.R., Omaha, 1899; chief chemist, Globe plant, Am. Smelting & Refining Co., Denver, 1900-02; cons. practice, Denver, 1902-05; editor Mining Reporter, Denver, 1905-06; editor Western Chemist and Metallurgist, 1907-10; western editor Metall. and Chem. Engring., 1910-16; pres. Colo. Sch. of Mines, 1916-17; acting editor Metall. and Chem. Engring. McGraw-Hill Pub. Co., 1917-19, and editor, 1919-28; editor Engring. and Mining Jour., 1933-51. Mem. Am. Inst. Chem. Engrs., Electrochem. Soc., Phi Delta Theta, Tau Beta Pi, Sigma Xi, Alpha Chi Sigma. Mason. Clubs: Mining (N.Y.C.); Teknik (Denver). Address: Bradenton, Fla. Died Nov. 17, 1959; buried Ferncliff Cemetery Mausoleum, Hartsdale, N.Y.

PARMELEE, Lewis Dwight, steamship exec.; b. Milton, Vt., Sept. 17, 1896; s. William and Harriet (Fairchild) P.; student St. Johnsbury Acad., 1914, Northwestern Univ., 1917-19; m. Marguerite Rabette, Apr. 29, 1923; 1 son, Truman Fairchild. Pub. accountant, 1920-21; with U.S. Shipping Bd. Merchant Fleet Corp., 1921-32; gen. comptroller Atlantic Gulf and West Indies Steamship Lines and subsidiary companies, 1932-40, exec. vice pres., 1940-46, pres., 1946-50. Member Am. Merchant Marine Inst. (dir.), Maritime Assn. of Port of New York (v.p.), Propeller Club of United States; member Am. Bur. Shipping, Controllers Inst. of Am. Republican. Mason. Clubs: Whitehall, India House, Downtown Athletic. Home: 460 W. 24th St. Office: Pier 34, North River, New York City 13. Deceased.

PARMENTER, Christine Whiting (Mrs. Kenneth R. Parmenter), author; b. Plainfield, N.J., Dec. 21, 1877; d. Frederic A. and Catherine Tracy (Allen) Whiting; m. Kenneth R. Parmenter, M.D., June 19, 1901 (deceased 1939); one daughter, Catherine (Mrs. Henry C. Newell). Former resident, Framingham Center, Massachusetts; moved Colorado, 1917; returned to New Eng., 1938. Member Authors League America. Unitarian. Republican. Author: Jean's Winter With the Warners, 1924; The Treasure At Shady Vale, 1925; The Unknown Port, 1927; The Real Reward, 1927; One Wide River to Cross, 1928; Silver Ribbons, 1929; The Dusty Highway, 1929; David's Star of Bethlehem, 1930; So Wise We Grow, 1930; Miss Aladdin, 1932; Shining Palace, 1933; The Long Quest, 1933; The Wind Blows West, 1934; The Kings of Beacon Hill, 1935; Swift Waters, 1937; I Was Christabel, 1938; Stories of Courage and Devotion, 1939; As the Seed Is Sown, 1940; Lights—And a Star, 1941; A Golden Age, 1942; Fair Were the Days, 1947; Stronger Than Law, (England), 1948. Contbr. short stories and serials to mags. since 1915. Address: 163 School St., Concord, N.H. Died Mar. 3, 1953; buried South Sudbury, Mass.

PARMENTER, George Freeman, chemist; b. Dover, Mass., Mar. 26, 1877; s. Freeman Artemus and Lucy (Goulding) P.; B.Sc., Mass. State Agrl. Coll., Boston U., 1900; M.A. and Ph.D., Brown, 1903; D.Sc., Colby Coll., 1916; m. Martha Elizabeth Ellis, Nov. 26, 1903 (dec. July 17, 1938); 1 son, Ellis Freeman; m. 2d, Lillian Esther Evans, Apr. 2, 1942. Instr. chemistry Mass. State Coll., 1900; asst. chemist R.I. Exptl. Sta., 1901; instr. chemistry Brown U., 1901-03; asso. prof. chemistry Colby Coll., 1903-04, prof., head of dept., 1904-47; emeritus prof., 1947-—. Fellow A.A.A.S.; mem. Am. Chem. Soc., Phi Sigma Kappa, Sigma Xi. Republican. Baptist. Author: Laboratory Experiments for Colby College. Home: No. 7 Sheldon Pl., Waterville, Me. Died Oct. 22, 1955; buried Pine Grove Cemetery, Waterville.

PARR, Jerome Henry, coll. dean; b. Balt., Sept. 30, 1909; s. George A. and Barbara (Mengel) P.; B.S., U. Dayton, 1932; B.M.E., Cath. U. Am., 1946; M.S., Carnegie Inst. Tech., 1947. Tchr. Chaminade High Sch., Dayton, 1928-30, Holy Trinity High Sch., Bklyn., 1930-38, Trinity Coll., Sioux City, Ia., 1938-41, Hamilton (O.) Cath. High Sch., 1941-45; prof. mech. engring. U. Dayton, 1947-—, head dept., 1948-—, dean coll. engring., 1953-—. Registered profl. engr. Ohio. Mem. A.S.M.E., A.I. M., Nat. Soc. Profl. Engrs., Am. Soc. E.E., Sigma Xi, Pi Tau Sigma, Phi Kappa Phi. Roman Catholic. Office: U. of Dayton, Dayton 9, O. Deceased.

PARR, Joseph Greer, banker; b. Jersey City, N.J., Dec. 11, 1881; s. James and Agnes (Greer) P.; ed. Jersey City High Sch., univ. extension courses, Am. Inst. of Banking; hon. LL.D., John Marshall College, 1941; m. Florence Vreeland, June 12, 1913; 1 daughter, Mrs. Dorothy Smith. With Liberty Nat. Bank of N.Y., 1900-09; pres. Claremont Bank of Jersey City, 1909-29; exec. v.p. Trust Co. of N.J., 1929-34, pres., 1934-48, chairman of the bd. to 1950, continue as consultant since 1950; former pres. Park Trust Co., Weehawken, N.J., Trust Co. of N.J. in W. New York (N.J.). Dir. Jersey City Chamber of Commerce (pres. 1931-34); former pres. Northern N.J. Clearing House Assn. and N.J. Bankers Assn. (past pres. Hudson Co. Group), 1943-44. Member Hudson Co. bd. elections, 1916; Rep. presdl. elector, 1932. Republican. Presbyterian. Mason (32°, Shriner), Elk. Clubs: Kiwanis of Jersey City (pres. 1931); Rumson Country (Rumson, New Jersey); Seabright Beach (Seabright, N.J.). Home: Holmdel, N.J. Office: 35 Journal Square, Jersey City, N.J. Died Aug. 21, 1952.

PARRETT, Arthur N., chemist; b. Marshalltown, Ia., July 7, 1896; s. Arthur N. and Margaret (Trotter) P.; B.S., Chem.E., U. Minn., 1922; Ph.D., U. Pittsburgh, 1924; m. Doreen Aldwell, Apr. 4, 1940. Research chemist E. I. duPont de Nemours & Co., 1925-30; asst. dir. chem. research A. O. Smith Corp., 1930-32; chem. dir. Rayonier, Inc. since 1932. v.p. since 1952. Mem. Am. Chem. Soc., Am. Inst. Chem. Engring., Tau Beta Pi, Alpha Chi Sigma, Phi Lambda Upsilon. Club: Rainier (Seattle). Holds U.S. and fgn. patents relating to cellulose mfg. and use. Home: 45 E. 62d St., N.Y.C. 21. Office: 122 E. 42d St., N.Y.C. 17. Died Dec. 27, 1956.

PARRIOTT, F(oster) B(rooks), oil exec.; b. near Moundsville, W.Va., March 15, 1878; s. Rev. George Wilson and Jane (Clark) P.; ed. county grade school; m. Kathleen Caldwell Tennyson, Sept. 1927; children—Van Caldwell, Jackson Clark; Robert Benedum (by former marriage). Began as worker in oil field, W.Va., 1900; later asso. with M. L. Benedum and moved to Pittsburgh, 1906; for exec. position with Benedum - Trees interest; started oil operations with W. E. Wrather and L. H. Cullum in Comanche County, Tex.; became pres. and dir. Trans-Continental Oil Co., Pittsburgh, later Tulsa, 1919; merged company with Ohio Oil Co., 1930; with W. I. Southern formed Leader Oil Co. for oil development Russell County, Kan., 1935-42; dir. Sunray Oil Corp., Tulsa, 1937-—, chmn. bd., 1943-52, chmn. exec. com., 1952-—; dir. First Nat. Bank & Trust Co., Tulsa. Mem. Tulsa Community Chest, YMCA. Mason (Shriner). Methodist. Clubs: Tulsa, Southern Hills Country. Home: Mayo Hotel, Tulsa. Office: Sunray Bldg., Tulsa. Died Feb. 5, 1957.

PARRISH, Albert Garrett, banker; b. at Greensboro, Ala., Oct. 13, 1850; s. John Henry (M.D.) and Clara (Peck) P.; student Southern U., Greensboro, 1867-88; m. Minna T. McColl, Aug. 10, 1875 (died 1878); m. 2d, Mary M. Baker, Sept. 20, 1882. With City Nat. Bank, Selma, Ala., 1869-—; pres. 1901-—; pres. Selma Compress Co.; dir. Selma Gas Light Co., Albert Hotel Co. Trustee Dallas Acad.; mem. Sch. Bd., Selma. Democrat. Presbyn. Home: 515 Selma Av. Office: 13 Broad St., Selma, Ala. Deceased.

PARRISH, Anne (Mrs. Josiah Titzell) (păr'ish), author; b. Colorado Springs, Colo., Nov. 12, 1888; d. Thomas Clarkson and Anne (Lodge) Parrish; educated The Misses Ferris' School, Colorado Springs, and The Misses Hebb's Sch., Wilmington, Del.; m. Charles Albert Corliss, December 29, 1915 (died 1936); married 2d, Josiah Titzell December 1, 1938 (died 1943). Author: Pocketful of Poses, 1923; Knee High to a Grasshopper (with Dillwyn Parrish), 1923; The Dream Coach (with same), 1924; Lustres (with same), 1924; Semi-Attached, 1924; The Perennial Bachelor (winner Harper prize), 1925; Tomorrow Morning, 1926; All Kneeling, 1928; The Methodist Faun, 1929; Floating Island, 1930; Loads of Love, 1932; Sea Level, 1934; Golden Wedding, 1936; Mr. Despondency's Daughter, 1938; Pray for a Tomorrow, 1941; Poor Child, 1945; A Clouded Star, 1948; The Story of Appleby Capple, 1950; And Have Not Love, 1954; The Lucky One (all under name of Anne Parrish). Home: Quantness, Peaceable St., Georgetown, Conn. Died Sept. 5, 1957.

PARRISH, Philip Hammon, editor; b. Constantine, Mich., Sept. 5, 1896; s. George Randall and Mary (Hammon) P.; student Oregon State Coll., 1913-16, U. of Wis., 1916-17; m. Irene Shope, 1918 (dec.); m. 2d, Margaret Sheridan, 1927; 1 dau., Pamela Ann. Reporter Morning Olympian, Olympia, Wash., 1917-18, Bellingham (Wash.) Herald, 1918, Oregon Journal, Portland, 1919-27; alumni editor Oregon State Coll., Corvallis, Ore., 1927-28; became reporter The Oregonian, Portland, 1928, successively asst. city editor, Sunday editor, editorial writer, asso. editor, editor editorial page, 1939-56, ret. Chmn. Old Ore. Trail Centennial Commn., 1942-43. Served in U.S. Army, Camp Lewis, Wash., 1918-19. Mem. Am. Legion, Portland Chamber of Commerce, Oregon Historical Soc. (dir.). Republican. Club: Multnomah Athletic. Author: Before the Covered Wagon, 1931; Historic Oregon, 1937. Home: 2725 Old Orchard Rd. Office: The Oregonian, Portland, Ore. Deceased.

PARROTT, Percival John, entomologist; b. Croydon, Eng., May 28, 1874; s. Joseph and Emma (Belgrove) P.; brought to America, 1882; A.B., Kan. State U., 1897, A.M., 1898; D.Sc., Kansas State College, 1943; m. Florence Mildred Hubbard, Sept. 5, 1906; children—Florence Margaret, John Percival. Asst. entomologist Kan. State Agrl. Coll., 1898-99, N.Y. Agrl. Expt. Sta., 1900-02; entomologist Ohio Agrl. Exptl. Sta., 1902-04; entomologist N.Y. Agr. Exptl. Sta., 1904-—, dir. 1938-42. Entomologist Kansas Agrl. Soc., 1898-99, Western N.Y. Hort. Soc., 1904-—. Mem. exec. com. Div. of Biology and Agr., NRC, 1920-21. Fellow A.A.A.S., Entomol. Soc. America; pres. Am. Assn. Econ. Entomologists, 1913-14 (v.p. 1909-10); mem. Sigma Xi, Phi Beta Kappa Republican. Presbyn. Mason. Contbr. articles on injurious insects, and systematic studies on Coccidae and Eriophyidae. Address: 386 Castle St., Geneva, N.Y. Died Aug. 10, 1953; buried Geneva, N.Y.

PARROTT, Thomas Marc, univ. prof.; b. Dayton, O., Dec. 22, 1866; s. Col. Edwin A. and Mary May (Thomas) P.; A.B., Princeton, 1888, A.M., 1891; Ph.D., Leipzig, 1893; m. Mary Adamson, July 18, 1895 (dec. Mar. 1958) children—D'Arcy, Lindesay Marc, Frances Mary. Prin. prep. dept. Miami U., Oxford, O., 1888-90; studied 3 yrs. in Germany; apptd. English fellow, Princeton, 1893-94; taught English and German, Lawrenceville (N.J.) Sch., 1894-96; asst. prof. English, 1896-1902, prof., 1902-35, Princeton, now emeritus; at Vanderbilt U., 1935-36. Mem. Phi Beta Kappa Fraternity. Presbyterian. Clubs: Princeton (N.Y.C. and Phila.), Nassau (Princeton). Editor: (with introductions and notes) Macaulay's Essays on Milton and Addison, 1901; English Poems, from Chaucer to Kipling (with A. W. Long), 1902; Shakespeare's Merchant of Venice, 1903; Shakespeare's Macbeth, 1904; Pope's Rape of the Lock and Other Poems, 1906; Chapman's All Fools and The Gentleman Usher, 1907; Chapman's Tragedies, 1910; Shakespeare's Othello, 1912; Chapman's Comedies, 1914; Poetry of the Transition (with Willard Thorp); William Shakespeare—A Handbook; Shakespeare—Twenty-three Plays and The Sonnets (with general introduction and notes); A Critical Edition of Hamlet, Quarto Two (with Hardin Craig). Author: Studies of a Book-Lover, 1904; A Short View of Elizabethan Drama (with R. H. Ball), 1943; Shakespearean Comedy, 1949. Address: Lawrenceville, N.J. Died Feb. 5, 1960, buried Lawrenceville Cemetery, Lawrenceville, N.J.

PARRY, Emma Louise, tchr., lectr.; b. Cin.; d. Brig. Gen. Augustus C. and Marie Louise (Haas) P.; B.L., U. Cin., 1887 (M.A., 1897); post-grad. work, U. Berlin, 1888-90; student of archaeology in Egypt and Greece, 1896-97. Asso. prin. H. Thane

Miller Sch., Cin., 1896—; lectr. on art, Art Acad. of Cin., 1896-97; lectr. on archaeology, univ. extension courses, 1897-98; lectr. on history on art before clubs, socs., etc. Mem. Phi Beta Kappa. Clubs: Woman's, Press. Author: Life Among the Germans, 1887; Women in the Reformation; The Two Great Art Epochs, 1914. Home: 655 June St., Walnut Hills, Cin. Deceased.

PARRY, John Jay, prof. English; b. Rome, N.Y., Sept. 30, 1889; s. Watkyn William and Augusta I. (Buek) P.; student Rome (N.Y.) Free Academy, 1903-07; Hotchkiss Sch., Lakeville, Conn., 1907-08; B.A., Yale, 1912, M.A., 1914, PH.D., 1915; m. Marion J. Austin, June 22, 1921; children—Anne Elizabeth, John Jay. Instr. U. of Calif., 1915-16; mem. faculty U. of Ill., 1916—, prof. English, 1939—. Served as 2d lt., A.E.F., 1917-19. Mem. Modern Lang. Assn., Mediaeval Acad. councillor, 1937-40. Linguistic Soc., A.A.A.S., Nat. Council Teachers of English, Soc. for Study Mediaeval Langs. and Lit., Modern Humanities Research Assn., Coll. English Assn., International Arthurian Society (advisory com.), Honourable Soc. of Cymmrodorion. Clubs: University (Urbana); Exchange (Champaign). Author: The Vita Merlini, 1925; A Bibliography of Critical Arthurian Literature (Vol. 1), 1930; Brut y Brenhinedd, Cotton Cleopatra Version, 1937; Andreas Capellanus,' the Art of Courtly Love, 1941. Co-author: A Bibliography of Critical Arthurian Literature (Vol. 2), 1936. Editor: The Poems and Amyntas of Thomas Randolph, 1917; adv. and editorial bds. of Speculum, 1931-37; editor, Jour. of English and Germanic Philology, 1942—. Contbr. to Dictionary of Am. Biography, Ency. Literature, 1946, and to Critical Bibliography of French Literature, 1947, and to mags. Home: 805 Iowa St. Office: 216 Gregory Hall, University of Illinois, Urbana, Ill. Died Oct. 8, 1954; buried Rome, N.Y.

PARSHALL, De Witt, painter; b. Buffalo, Aug. 2, 1864; s. William Henry and Lisette Celestine (Hotchkiss) P.; student De Veaux Coll., Niagara Falls, N.Y., 1877-81; B.S., Hobart Coll., 1885; Acad. Julian and Acad. Cormon, Paris, 1886-92; with T. Alexander Harrison; m. Carrie Ewell, Nov. 20, 1895; children—Douglass Ewell, Carol. Splty. landscapes; represented in Met. Mus., N.Y., Toledo, Detroit, Worcester, Syracuse, San Diego and Muskegon (Mich.) mus'., Los Angeles Mus. Sci., History and Art; Art Inst. of Seattle. Mem. jury awards, Pa. Acad. Fine Arts, Nat. Acad. of Design. Vice pres. Santa Barbara Mus. of Art; dir. Faulkner Art Gallery, Santa Barbara. Presbyn. Mem. Sigma Phi, A.N.A., 1909, N.A., 1917; mem. Soc. of Painters of the Far West, Internat. Soc. Arts and Letters, Allied Artists America, Painters of the West. Clubs: Century (trustee), Nat. Arts, Lotos, Sleepy Hollow Country, MacDowell (N.Y.C.); Santa Barbara, Santa Barbara Country, California Art, Valley. Awarded gold medal at Painters of the West Exhbn., 1929; $300 award at All Cal. Exhbn., 1934. Home: 288 Hot Springs Rd., Santa Barbara, Cal. Died July 7, 1956; buried Santa Barbara (Cal.) Cemetery.

PARSHLEY, Howard Madison (pärsh'lē), prof. zoölogy; b. Hallowell, Me., Aug. 7, 1884; s. John Howard and Julia Maria (Tuck) P.; student Boston Latin Sch., 1901-05; A.B., Harvard, 1909, A.M., 1910, Sc.D., 1917; student N.E. Conservatory of Music, 1906-09; m. Nancy Fredricson, June 28, 1910; children—Thomas Fredricson, Elsa Madison. Instr. zoölogy, U. of Me., 1911-14; research in zoölogy, Bussey Inst. (Harvard), 1914-17; asst. prof. zoölogy Smith Coll., Northampton, Mass., 1917-19, asso. prof., 1919-25, prof., 1925-52, emeritus since 1952; teacher summers Biol. Lab., Cold Spring Harbor, N.Y., and U. of Chicago. Mem. A.A.A.S., American Society Zoölogists, Entomological Society of America, Genetics Soc. of Am., Am. Soc. Naturalists, Sigma Xi. Author: Bibliography of North American Hemiptera Heteroptera, 1925; Science and Good Behavior, 1928; Science of Human Reproduction, 1933; Survey of Biology, 1940. Translator The Second Sex (Simone de Beauvoir's), Life and Habits of the Mammals (F. Bourliere's), 1953. Contbr. to books and jours. Home: 250 Elm St., Northampton, Mass. Died May 19, 1953.

PARSONS, Archibald Livingstone, retired rear admiral; b. Derry, N.H., Sept. 20, 1875; s. Benjamin Franklin and Mary Ann (Nesmith) P.; B.S., Mass. Inst. of Tech. 1897; m. Laura Reeves, July 1913. Commd. lieut. (j.g.) Navy Corps, Civil Eng., 1903; served as asst. and in charge of shore construction at various Navy yards and stations, 1903-12; Bureau of Yards and Docks, Washington, D.C., 1912-18, asst. chief of Bureau, 1916-18; Phila. Navy Yard 1919; engr. in chief, Republic of Haiti, 1920-24; Navy Yard, New York and Boston, 1924-29; chief of Bureau of Yards and Docks, Washington, D.C., 1929-33; New York Yard and District, 1934-38; retired own application, 1938; now cons. engr. with Frederic R. Harris, Inc., New York. Life mem. Am. Soc. of Civil Engrs. Awarded Navy Cross, World War. Clubs: Chevy Chase, Army and Navy (Washington, D.C.). Home: 160 Columbia Heights, Brooklyn, N.Y. Office: 27 William St., New York, N.Y. Died Sept. 24, 1953; buried Arlington Nat. Cemetery.

PARSONS, Arthur Hudson, Jr., librarian; b. Lynn, Mass., Sept. 30, 1910; s. Arthur Hudson and Mildred Roberts (Atkins) P.; A.B., Wesleyan U., 1932; student Harvard U. Grad. Sch., 1933; B.L.S., Columbia, 1938; m. Lucia Young Ranger, May 17, 1935; children—Lynn Hudson, Arthur Hudson III, Librarian, Swampscott (Mass.) Pub. Library, 1938-43; chief librarian Brockton (Mass.) Pub. Library, 1943-50, dir. Omaha (Neb.) Pub. Library, 1957—, now Enock Pratt Free Library. Member American Library Association (mem.-at-large council 1953—; mem. joint com. A.L.A.-N.E.A.), Mountain Plains (dir. 1950—, pres. 1953-54), Neb. (sec. 1952-54), Mass. (editor Bull. 1942-47), Public (pres. elect 1957-58) library associations, C. of C., Sigma Nu. Clubs: Rotary, Exchange. Author: The Horn that Stopped the Band, 1954. Home: 2905 N. Charles St. Office: 400 Cathedral St., Balt. Died Aug. 1959.

PARSONS, Charles Lathrop, chemist; b. New Marlboro, Mass., Mar. 23, 1867; s. Benjamin Franklin and Leonora (Bartlett) P.; B.S., Cornell U., 1888; D.Sc., U. Me., 1911; D. Chem., U. Pitts., 1914; D.Sc., U.N.H., 1944; m. Alice Douglas Robertson, Dec. 29, 1887 (dec.); children—Leonora Elizabeth, Charles Lathrop, Anna Guerard, Enith Alice, Priscilla Bartlett (dec.). Prof. chemistry N.H. Coll., 1890-1911; chief chemist Bur. of Mines, Washington, 1911; cons. practice since 1919. Mem. Nitrate Commn.; mem. Adv. Bd. on Gas Warfare. Vice pres. for America of Internat. Union Pure and Applied Chemistry, 1919-22. Awarded Nichol's medal for research on atomic weight of beryllium, 1904; Priestly medal for distinguished service, 1932, A.C.S. special gold medal of honor, 1946. Fellow A.A.A.S. (sec. Sect. C, 1904-08); mem. Am. Chem. Soc. (sec. 1907, sec. and bus. mgr. 1930), Am. Inst. Chemists (life), Sigma Xi, Kappa Sigma, Alpha Chi Sigma, Phi Lambda Upsilon, Soc. Colonial Wars, Mayflower Descendants, Colonial Govs.; hon. mem. Chem. Soc. of Rumania, Soc. of Chem. Industry; life mem. Soc. Chimique de France. Officer Legion of Honor (France), 1922; Officer Crown of Italy, 1926. Author: (with Prof. A.J. Moses) Mineralogy, Crystallography and Blow-pipe Analysis, 1895, 1901, 04, 09, 11, 16; Beryllium, Its Chemistry and Literature, 1908; also many sci. papers in chem. jours. and govt. bulletins. Address: Cosmos Club, Washington. Died Feb. 14, 1954.

PARSONS, Frederick Williams, physician; b. Buffalo, Nov. 13, 1875; s. Frederick John and Ann (Williams) P.; M.D., U. of Buffalo, 1901; unmarried. Began practice at Buffalo, 1901; in state hosp. service Hudson River State Hosp., Poughkeepsie, N.Y., advancing to 1st asst., 1902-19; supt. Buffalo State Hosp., 1919-26; med. commr. N.Y. State Hosp. Commn., 1926-27; commr. dept. mental hygiene, 1927-37. Mental hygiene cons. to US PHS. Mem. med. bd. U.S. Vets. Bur. Served from capt. to lt. col. M.C., U.S. Army, 1917-19; comdg. officer Base Hosp. 117, AEF. Diplomate Am. Bd. Psychiatry and Neurology. Mem. Am. Psychiatric Soc., Assn. Research Nervous and Mental Diseases, Buffalo Acad. Medicine, N.Y. State, Albany County med. socs., New York Psychiatric Soc., N.Y. Soc. for Clinical Psychiatry. Clubs: University (Albany); Amrita (Poughkeepsie). Home: 10 Park Av., Albany, N.Y. Died July 1957.

PARSONS, Geoffrey, newspaperman; b. Douglaston, N.Y., Sept. 5, 1879; s. Charles Chauncy and Julia Warth (Michael) Parsons; A.B., Columbia University, 1899, LL.B., 1903, Litt.D., 1941, L.H.D., Franklin and Marshall College, 1945; LL.D., Louisville U., 1947; married Carle Taylor, September 7, 1907; children—Geoffrey, David Taylor, Mary Catherine (Mrs. John Long), Carl Taylor. Asso. with New York Evening Sun, 1906-13, with New York Tribune, 1913-24; chief editorial writer New York Herald-Tribune, 1924-52; chief editorial adviser, 1952. Mem. Art Commn. N.Y. Republican. Clubs: Century, Players. Author: The Land of Fair Play, 1919; The Stream of History, 1928. Awarded Pulitzer prize for editorial writing, 1942. Home: 901 Lexington Av. Office: 230 W. 41st St., N.Y.C. Died Dec. 8, 1956; buried Dorset, Vt.

PARSONS, J(oseph) Lester, corp. official; hon. chmn. bd., dir. U.S. Fire Ins. Co., Crum & Forster, N. River Ins. Co., Westchester Fire Ins. Co.; chmn. bd., dir. Internat. Ins. Co. Office: 110 William St., N.Y.C. 38. Died Sept. 19, 1957.

PARSONS, Reginald Hascall, corp. official; b. Flushing, L.I., N.Y., Oct. 3, 1873; s. George Howland and Lorraine Fiske (Hascall) P.; prep. edn., Moses Brown Sch., Providence, R.I.; student Colo. Coll., Colorado Springs, and U. of Calif.; LL.D., Whitman Coll., 1934; m. Maude Bemis, Jan. 31, 1901; children—Alice Lorraine (dec.), Anne (Mrs. Howard A. Frame), Reginald Bemis, George Howland, Mary Bowne (Mrs. John Stewart Day). Auditor Colorado Springs Co., 1896-98; stock broker for W. P. Bonbright & Co., Colorado Springs Mining Exchange, 1898-1900; mgr. Bemis Bro. Bag Co., Seattle, Wash., 1904-09; pres. Parsons Investment Co., Parsons, Hart & Co., Pinnacle Packing Co.; chmn. bd. Seattle Title Trust Co., 1920-30; proprietor Hillcrest Orchard, Mountcrest Ranch; driector Northern Life Insurance Company. Chairman Seattle War Savings Com., 1918; pres. Seattle Community Fund, 1929-30, 1936-37; pres. Seattle Symphony Orch., 1931-32; dir. U. of Wash. Arboretum. Pres. Lakeside Sch. for Boys, 1926-31; pres. Seattle Council Boy Scouts of America, 1916-21, mem. nat. exec. bd. same. Mem. New England Hist. Soc., Social Welfare League (pres. 1919-23), Japan Soc. (pres. 1927), Am. Peace Soc. (director), Internat. Chamber Commerce (Am. sect.), U.S. Chamber of Commerce (dir. 1936-37), Seattle Chamber Commerce (pres. 1919), Family Soc. of Seattle (hon. pres.), S.R., Beta Theta Pi. Republican. Episcopalian. Clubs: University, Rainier, Washington Athletic (ex-chairman board of governors), Seattle Golf, Seattle Yacht (Seattle); Arlington (Portland, Ore.); Rogue River Valley University, (Medford, Ore.). Home: 618 W. Highland Drive, Seattle 99. Office: Northern Life Tower, Seattle 1. Died June 10, 1955.

PARSONS, Wallace Emery, mfg. exec.; b. North Anson, Me., s. Fred Stevens and Mae Richardson (Fletcher) P.; student Hebron Acad., 1905-07, U. Me., 1907-10; m. Lydia Skolfield, Aug. 25, 1915; 1 son, John Skolfield. Engr. U.S. Geol. Survey, 1910-11; asst. to supt. Orono (Me.) Pulp & Paper Co., 1911-13, constrn. engr., 1913-16; treas. Moulton Engring. Corp., 1916-17; purchasing agt. Cumberland Shipbldg. Co., 1917-18, asst. gen. mgr., 1918-20; treas. Fairfield Mfg. Co., 1920-25; asst. to pres. Keyes Fibre Co., 1926-28, gen. mgr., 1928-51, v.p., dir. 1942-51, pres., dir., 1951—. Trustee, pres. Thayer Hosp., Waterville, Me.; vice president, director U. Me. Pulp and Paper Found.; dir. New England Council. Mem. Nat. Assn. Mfrs. (dir.), Asso. Industries Me. (pres., dir.), Am. Soc. C.E., Beta Theta Pi. Mason. Clubs: Cumberland (Portland, Me.); Ekwanok Country (Manchester, Vt.); Waterville Country, Woodmar Country (Hammond, Ind.); Chgo. Home: 89 Silver St. Office: Keyes Fibre Co., Waterville, Me. Died Mar. 6, 1957; buried Pine Grove Cemetery, Waterville.

PARSONS, Wilfrid, clergyman, educator; b. Phila., Mar. 17, 1887; s. Paul J. and Alice (Avery) P.; M.A., Woodstock (Md.) Coll., 1908, Ph.D., 1910, S.T.D., 1919; grad. study, Gregorian U., Rome, 1919-21; Litt.D., St. Joseph's Coll., Phila., 1929, St. Francis Coll., Bklyn., 1934. Ordained priest R.C. Church, 1918; editor in chief America—a Catholic Rev. of the Week, 1925-36; prof. polit. sci. Georgetown U. Grad. Sch., 1936-1940, librarian and archivist, 1938, dean, 1939-40; became prof. polit. sci. Cath. U., 1940, now emeritus. Mem. Am. Polit. Sci. Assn., Acad. Polit. Sci., U.S. Cath. Hist. Soc., Am. Bibliog. Soc. K.C. Club: Columbus. Author: Mexican Martydom, 1936; Early Catholic Americana; Which Way Democracy?; The Pope and Italy; God and Governments; Church and State; The First Freedom, 1948. Address: 3303 10th St. N.E.; Washington 17. Died Oct. 28, 1958.

PARSONS, William Sterling, naval officer; b. Chicago, Ill., Nov. 26, 1901; s. Harry Robert and Clara Sterling (Doolittle) P.; B.S., U.S. Naval Acad., 1922; m. Martha Cluverius, Nov. 23, 1929; children—Hannah (deceased), Margaret Sampson, Clara Doolittle. Commd. ensign, U.S.N., 1922, and since advanced through grades to rear adm., 1946; assigned to exptl. ordnance development, Naval Proving Ground, Dahlgren, Va., 1939-42; special asst. to dir., O.S. R.D., for development of radio proximity fuse, 1942-43; ordnance div. leader, and later asso. dir., atomic bomb project, Los Alamos, N.M., 1943-45; flew with first atomic bomb to Hiroshima, Japan, Aug. 6, 1945; asst. chief Naval Operations (spl. weapons), 1945-46; dep. for tech. direction to Comdr. Joint Task Force One (Operation Crossroads, Bikini tests of atomic bomb), 1946; dir. Atomic Defense, Office Chief of Naval Operations; mem. Mil. Liaison Com. to the Atomic Energy Commn., 1946-49; dep. comdr. Joint Task Force 7 (atomic tests at Eniwetok Atoll), 1948; with Weapons Systems Evaluations Group of Joint Chiefs of Staff and Research and Development Bd., 1949-51; comdr. cruiser div. six Atlantic Fleet, 1951; dep. chief Bur. of Ordnance, Navy Dept., since 1952. Awarded Silver Star, Distinguished Service Medal. Mem. U.S. Naval Inst. Clubs: Army and Navy (Washington); Army and Navy Country (Arlington, Va.); Cosmos; Chevy Chase (Md.). Home: 6125 33d St. N.W., Washington. Office: Bur. of Ordnance, Navy Dept., Washington. Died Dec. 5, 1953; buried Arlington Nat. Cemetery.

PARTLOW, Ira Judson, lawyer; b. Rappahannock Co., Va., Feb. 20, 1876; s. Burrell T. and Ruth (Updike) P.; ed. Washington (Va.) Acad., Randolph-Macon Coll., Ashland, Va.; LL.B., Cumberland Univ., Lebanon, Tenn., 1904; m. Andrea Martin, May 23, 1905; children—Alice Ready (Mrs. Alden R. Billings), Helen Ruth (Mrs. Hector R. McLean), and Andrea Virginia (Mrs. Burchard P. Romain) (deceased), Martin Burrell (deceased). Engaged in practice of law, McDowell and Mingo Counties, 1904-33; city atty. of Welch, 1930-33; asst. atty. gen., of West Va., 1933-43, acting atty. gen., 1943-45, atty. gen., 1945-49, resigned to accept appointment as judge 8th Jud. Circuit of W.Va.; elected judge Eighth Jud. Circuit, 1950. Apptd. mem. Jud. Council of West Virginia. Mem. McDowell County, W.Va., Am. bar assns., Pi Kappa Alpha. Democrat. Presbyterian. Home: Welch, W.Va. Office: Office of Judge of the Circuit Court, Welch, W.Va. Died June 11, 1952.

PARTRIDGE, Albert Gerry, business exec.; born Jamestown, N.Y., Aug. 25, 1880; s. Elbridge Gerry and Althea (Merrill) P.; student pub. schs. of Jamestown, N.Y.; m. Edith Harpham, 1904 (dec.); children—Elspeth (Hall), Emily (Maier), David Gerry. Clerk Diamond Rubber Co., Akron, O. and mgr. N.Y. City, 1899-1905; dept. mgr. to vice pres. Firestone Tire & Rubber Co., Akron, O., 1905-21; mgr., Western Div. Goodyear Tire & Rubber Co., Akron, O., 1921-28; mng. dir. Goodyear Tire & Rubber Co. (Gt. Britain), Ltd., Wolverhampton, Eng., 1928-35; pres. Goodyear Tire & Rubber Co. of Can. Ltd., New Toronto, Ont., since 1935; pres. Goodyear Cotton Co., St. Hyacinthe, Que., since 1935; dir. North Am. Life Assurance Co.; chmn. planning bd. City of Toronto, 1941-45; pres. Ont. Safety League, 1937-47; dir. Canadian Mfrs. Assn. and Canadian C. of C., Rubber Assn. of Canada. Anglican. Mason. Clubs: Toronto, National, Canadian, Empire, Granite, Lambton Golf and Country (Toronto). Home: One Old Forest-Hill Rd., Toronto. Office: Goodyear Tire & Rubber Co. of Can., Ltd., Cor. Fleet and Bathurst Sts., Toronto, Can. Died Mar. 12, 1952; buried Akron, O.

PARTRIDGE, George Everett, psychologist; b. Worcester, Mass., May 31, 1870; s. George and Sarah Boyden (Capron) P.; student Harvard, 1889-90; Ph.D., Clark U., 1899; m. Emelyn Smythe Newcomb, Aug. 31, 1898; children—Elaine Newcomb (dec.), Miriam Newcomb (Mrs. John R. Speck), Philip Newcomb. Instr. psychology, State Normal School, Mankato, Minn., 1900-03; lecturer Clark U., 1904-06; psychologist, Pa. Hosp., Phila., 1923-26; for Phila. Com. for the Clinical Study of Opium Addiction, 1926; for Sing Sing Prison, Jan.-Sept. 1927; clin. research, The Sheppard & Enoch Pratt Hosp., Baltimore, Oct. 1927-30; psychopathologist Md. Training School for Boys, 1927-49; psychologist Md. Penitentiary, 1930-31; dir. Classification and Clin. Service, Dept. of Prisons, Md., 1931-35; research in psychopathic personality, delinquency, and in psychol. of internat. relations in the postwar world. Author: An Outline of Individual Study, 1910; The Nervous Life, 1911; Studies in the Psychology of Intemperance, 1912; Story-Telling in School and Home (with wife), 1912; Genetic Philosophy of Education (an epitome of ednl. writings of Pres. G. Stanley Hall), 1912 (Japanese translation); A Reading Book in Modern Philosophy, 1913; The Psychology of Nations, 1919. Contbr. to sci. jours. Address: Route 1, Box 163, Springfield, Va. Died Nov. 16, 1953; buried Hope Cemetery, Worcester, Mass.

PASCHALL, John, editor; b. Tullahoma, Tenn., June 3, 1879; s. Walter Goode and Mattie (Macpherson) P.; A.B., Vanderbilt U., 1901; LL.D., Atlanta Law School, 1939; m. Jesse Mai Aydelott, Dec. 27, 1906 (dec. Aug. 1911). Began as reporter Atlanta Journal, 1901, city editor, 1906-17, mng. editor, 1917-35, mng. and asso. editor, 1935-39, editor 1939-45, editor emeritus, 1945——. Mem. exec. bd. Ga. Press Assn., 1917-37; mem. Mng. Editors Assn. of Asso. Press, 1934-36; chmn. Ga. Press Inst., 1928, 34, 35, 36, 37; dir. Atlanta C. of C., 1938-39. Mem. Alpha Tau Omega. Clubs: Gridiron (U. Ga.), Civitan (pres. 1941-42). Democrat. Episcopalian. Elk. Home: 522 N. Highland Av. N.E. Address: The Atlanta Journal, Atlanta. Died May 8, 1953.

PASHKOVSKY, Theophilus Nicholas (päsh-kôf′skĭ), archbishop; b. Russia, Feb. 19, 1874; s. Nicholas and Natalie (Vlossov) P.; grad. Theol. Sem. of Kiev, 1894; hon. D.D. Nashotah Episcopal Sem., 1940; m. Helen A. Dabovich, Nov. 17, 1897 (died in Russia); children—Tikhon T., Boris T., Nina T. (dec.), Ljubov T. (Mrs. Alexis Gnesdiloff). Teacher Normal School, Kiev, 1894-95; mem. staff of cathedral, San Francisco, 1895-97; appointed sec. to North America Ecclesiastical Consistory, 1897; ordained priest Russian Orthodox Greek Catholic Ch. (Eastern Ch.), 1897; dean of cathedral, San Francisco, 1905; trans. to Warsaw, Poland, 1913; army chaplain, 1915-18. On account of war was affiliated with Y.M.C.A., in Moscow, 1918-22, later in charge parish in S. Russia; apptd. by the Patriarch, bishop of Chicago, and consecrated Dec. 10, 1922; apptd. bishop of Canada and Chicago, Aug. 4, 1923; relieved of charge in Canada, July 30, 1926, transferred to San Francisco, 1931; elected presiding bishop, 1934, later metropolitan archbishop of U.S. and Canada. Home: 1520 Green St., San Francisco. Office: 59 E. 2d St., N.Y. City. Died June 27, 1950; buried Serbian Cemetery, San Francisco.

PASSANNATE, Charles, paper merchant; b. Postiglione, Italy, May 14, 1887; s. Antonio and Carmella (Salvato) P.; student Army Coll. in Italy; m. Mildred Vianna, July, 1912; children—Anthony, Maurice, Marie, Anna, William, Josephine, Francis. Pres., dir. 80-82 Carmine St. Corp., N.Y.C., 1914——, Wilson Paper Stock Co., N.Y.C., 1915——; exec. v.p., dir. United Board & Carton Co., N.Y.C., 1951——; v.p., trustee, dir. Lafayette Finance, Inc., N.Y.C., 1923——; dir. Pa. Exchange Bank, N.Y.C., 1923——, Hudson & Manhattan R.R., N.Y.C., 1946——. Mason (32°). Elk. Home: 22 W. Eleventh St., N.Y.C. Office: 603 Greenwich St., N.Y.C. 14; also 2 Park Av., N.Y.C. Died Mar. 1956.

PASSARELLI, Luigi Alfonso (päs-sä-rĕl′lē), prof. Romance langs.; b. Isernis, Italy, Dec. 5, 1895; s. Antonio and Teresa (Fortini) P. Came with parents to U.S., 1907; B.A., Columbia, 1915; M.A., U. Toronto, 1917; U. Paris, 1918-19; m. Rosa Marinoni, Jan. 1, 1945. Tchr. of French and Spanish, Chief Sch., N.Y.C., 1914-16; instr. in Spanish and Italian, U. Toronto, 1916-17; instr. in Romance languages, U. Cin., 1917-21; asst. prof. same, U. Ark., 1921-27, asso. prof., 1927——. Served with A.E.F., World War. Mem. Modern Lang. Assn. Am., Am. Assn. Tchrs. Italian (sec.-treas. 1928-30; v.p. 1931-32); Am. Legion (past vice comdr. and comdr. local post; chmn. for Americanism Dept. of Ark., 1938-39), Am. Assn. U. Profs'., La Société des 40 et 8. Ind. Democrat. Clubs: Columbia Univ., Kiwanis. Author: Simple Spanish Lessons, 1926; Simple Italian Lessons (with A. Marinoni), 1927; Elementary French Grammar (with same), 1929; Contes Comiques (with Pierre Macy), 1930; Les Aventures de Renard (with André Pézard), 1930; Andiamo in Italia (with A. Marinoni), 1930. Contbr. reviews to Italica. Awarded gold medal and merit cross at Littoriale Fair and Expn., Bologna, 1933. Home: 617 Ida Av., Fayetteville, Ark. Died Dec. 24, 1953; buried Nat. Cemetery, Fayetteville, Ark.

PASVOLSKY, Leo (päs-vŏl′skĭ), author, economist; b. Pavlograd, Russia, Aug. 22, 1893; s. Michael and Maria P.; came with parents to U.S., 1905; A.B., Coll. City New York, 1916; grad. study, Columbia U., 1916-18, U. of Geneva (Switzerland), 1932-33; Ph.D., Brookings Instn., 1936; m. Christine McCormick, Nov. 6, 1926. Editor The Russian Review (monthly, in English), 1916-18, Russkoye Slovo (daily newspaper in Russian), 1917-20, Amerikansky Viestnik (monthly, in Russian), 1917-18; free lance writer, 1921-22; mem. research staff, Brookings Instn., Washington, D.C., since 1922; director international studies, Brookings Institution since 1946; economist United States Bureau Foreign and Domestic Commerce, 1934-35; economist Division of Trade Agreements, U.S. Dept. of State, 1935-36; spl. asst. to Secretary of State, 1936-38, and 1939-46, also chief division special research, 1941-42; supervisor division political and economic studies, 1943; executive director committee on Postwar Programs, 1944; in charge international orgn. and security affairs, supervisor, Office Special Polit. Affairs, 1945-46. With War Work Extension, U.S. Dept. of Interior, also mem. Mayor's Com. on Nat. Defense, N.Y. City, 1917-18. Am. mem. spl. com. of economists of the Internat. Chamber of Commerce to prepare documents for the World Monetary and Economic Conf., 1932-33; spl. observer at the Conf. for the Brookings Instn.; alternate Am. mem. League of Nations Econ. Com., 1936; adviser to Am. delegate, 2d meeting Ministers of Foreign Affairs Am. Republics, Havana, 1940; mem. Am. delegation, United Nations Monetary and Financial Conf., Bretton Woods, N.H., 1944; Dumbarton Oaks Conf. on Internat. Orgn., Washington, D.C., 1944; Inter-Am. Conf. on Problems of War and Peace, Mexico City, 1945; United Nations' Conf. on Internat. Orgn., San Francisco, 1945 (chmn. coordination committee); president first session of Preparatory Commn. United Nations, 1945; mem. Am. del. Gen. Assembly and Security Council, UN, London, 1946. Clubs: Cosmos (Washington, D.C.); Reform (London). Author: Economic Russia, 1917; The Economics of Communism, 1921; Russia in the Far East, 1922; Russian Debts and Russian Reconstruction (with H. G. Moulton), 1924; World War Debt Settlements (with same), 1926; Economic Nationalism of the Danubian States, 1928; Bulgaria's Economic Position, 1930; War Debts and World Prosperity (with H. G. Moulton), 1932; The Necessity for a Stable International Monetary Standard, 1933; Current Monetary Issues, 1933; Recovery Problem in the United States (co-author), 1936; Major Problems of U.S. Foreign Policy (co-author), 1947, 1948. Translator: The Bracelet of Garnets (from the Russian of A. Kuprin), 1917. Home: 3641 R St., Washington 7. Office: 722 Jackson Pl., Washington 6. Died May 5, 1953; buried Rock Creek Cemetery, Washington.

PATCH, Edith Marion, author, entomologist; b. Worcester, Mass., July 27, 1876; d. William Whipple and Salome (Jenks) Patch; B.S., U. of Minn., 1901; specializing in entomology, M.S., U. of Me., 1910; Ph.D., Cornell U., 1911; Sc.D., 1937. Teacher English and zoölogy Hastings (Minn.) High Sch., 1901-02; tchr., dept. English, Crookston (Minn.) High Sch., 1902-03; organized dept. entomology Me. Agrl. Exptl. Station, and entomologist, same, 1903-37, entomologist emeritus, 1937——. Research in entomology with problems concerning ecology and economic entomology; research guest Rothamsted Exptl. Sta, Harpenden, Eng., 1927. Fellow Entomol. Soc. America (pres. 1930), A.A.A.S.; mem. Am. Soc. Zoölogists, Assn. Econ. Entomologists, Am. Soc. Naturalists, Am. Nature Study Soc. (pres. 1937), Nat. Audubon Soc. (life), Fla. Audubon Soc. (life), Nat. Council on Elementary Science, Fla. Entomol. Soc. (hon.), Am. Sci. Tchrs. Assn., Sigma Xi, Phi Kappa Phi, Delta Delta Delta, Delta Kappa Gamma (hon.), Phi Sigma, Phi Beta Kappa, Pi Gamma Mu, Sigma Delta Epsilon (hon.). Club: Woman's. Author: Hexapod Stories (Little Gateways to Science Series), 1920; Bird Stories (same series), 1921; First Lessons in Nature Study, 1926; Holiday Pond, 1929; Holiday Meadow, 1930; Holiday Hill, 1931; Hunting; Outdoor Visits, 1932; Surprises; Through Four Seasons, 1933; Science at Home, 1934; The Work of Scientists, 1935 (last six in Nature and Science Readers series); Holiday Shore, 1935; Mountain Neighbors, 1936; Desert Neighbors, 1937; Forest Neighbors, 1938; Prairie Neighbors, 1940; also more then 80 entomol. publs. in bulls. and tech. periodicals. Address: P.O. Box 150, Orono, Me. died Sept. 28, 1954; buried Mt. Hope Cemetery, Worcester, Mass.

PATCH, Helen Elizabeth, prof. French lang., lit., Mt. Holyoke Coll.; b. Bangor, Me., Dec. 24, 1891; d. Willis Young and Frances (Foster) Patch; B.A., Mt. Holyoke, 1914; M.A., Ph.D., Bryn Mawr, 1921; attended Sorbonne, 1919-20; Ecole des Hautes Etudes, 1919-20, McGill U., 1941. Began career as tchr. in preparatory schs.; successively asst. prof., asso. prof., prof. Mt. Holyoke Coll., 1921, now prof. emeritus, chmn. French dept. 1935-1944. Has been vis. prof., 1935, head of dept. of French, 1937, U. of Me.; vis. lectr., Université de Grenoble. Dir. Juniors in France under U. of Del. plan; dir., v.p., Pontigny en Amérique, summers, 1942-44. Decorated by French govt. Officier d'Académie, 1938. Mem. Modern Lang. Assn., Am. Assn. Tchrs. of French, Am. Assn. of Univ. Profs., Phi Beta Kappa. Conglist. Author: Critique Dramatique de Théophile Gautier, 1921. Home: Grove St., Bangor, Me. Office: Mt. Holyoke Coll., S. Hadley, Mass. Died Jan. 15, 1959; buried Bangor, Me.

PATCH, Ralph Reginald, mfr.; b. Stoneham, Mass., May 9, 1882; s. Edgar Leonard and Matilda Smith (Ferguson) P.; S.B., Mass. Inst. of Tech., 1906; m. Christine Vaughn Johonnot, Sept. 4, 1907; children—Charlotte (Mrs. Earle L. Sims), Edgar Leonard, Alma Ferguson. Joined E. L. Patch Co., pharm. mfrs., 1906, gen. mgr., 1916-24, pres., treas., 1924-48, now chmn. bd. Served in Sanitary Corps Res., 1923-42; lieut. col., Sanitary Corps, U.S. Army, 1942-45. Vice pres., mem. exec. com. Am. Drug Mfrs. Assn.; pres., v.p., sec., treas., Am. Pharm. Mfrs. Assn.; trustee, Mass. Col. of Pharmacy, Charlestown Five Cents Savs. Bank, Student Loan Fund; dir., Stoneham Home for Aged; town moderator; mem. bd. of pub. works, planning bd. sch. com., organ com., town of Stoneham, Mass. Home: 28 Lincoln St., Stoneham, Mass. Office: 38 Montvale Av., Stoneham, Mass. Died Sept. 18, 1957.

PATCHIN, Philip Halsey, ret. bus. exec.; b. Des Moines, Ia., Sept. 11, 1884; s. Rober Azor and Calista (Halsey) P.; student pub. schs., Des Moines; m. Mary Wallace Mason, Dec. 29, 1909; children—Elizabeth Mason (Mrs. Thomas Gordon Greene), Mary Halsey (Mrs. Alfred Whittell, Jr.). Newspaper reporter Register Leader, Des Moines, 1902-04; corr. N.Y. Sun, Washington, 1904-06, 06-07, Brazil, 1906, China Press, China, 1911-13, N.Y. Tribune, Mexico, 1914, N.Y. Tribune and Curtis-Brown Syndicate, London, 1914-17; chief Div. of Information, U.S. Dept. of State, 1909-11, chief Div. Fgn. Intelligence, 1917-18, exec. sec. with rank of counsellor embassy Am. Peace Mission, Paris, 1918-19. sec. Am. delegation to Disarmament Conf., Washington, 1921-22; asst. sec. Standard Oil Co. of Cal., 1919, asst. to pres., 1921, dir., 1935, v.p. 1942, retired 1943. Mem. bd. mgmt. Golden Gate Internat. Expn., 1937-39. Decorated Comdr. Order of the Crown (Belgium). Clubs: Nat. Press, Metropolitan (Washington); Burlingame (Cal.) Country; Union Pacific (San Francisco). Home: 1410 Jasmine St., San Mateo, Cal. Died Nov. 29, 1954; buried Ivy Hill Cemetery, Va.

PATCHIN, Robert Halsey, ret. steamship exec.; b. Des Moines, Ia., Feb. 6, 1881; s. Robert Azor and Calista (Halsey) P.; student Ia. State Coll.; m. Mary Custis Lee Carter, 1904 (dec.); 1 dau., Phyllis Carter (Mrs. Soutter); m. 2d, Minga Pope Duryea, 1924. Reporter Des Moines Leader, 1899, Washington (D.C.) Times, 1900-02; mem. staff Washington Bur. New York Herald, 1902-09; spl. corr. New York Herald, world cruise of Atlantic Battleship Fleet, 1907-09; Canadian corr. same, 1909-11; chief of New York Herald Bur., Washington, 1911-13; sec. Nat. Fgn. Trade Council, 1914-17 (later served as dir. and treas.); mgr. W. R. Grace & Co., New York internat. trading and shipping firm, 1917-28, v.p., 1928-48; dir. Grace Line, Inc.; dir., v.p. Pan American-Grace Airways (Panagra), 1929-49. Hon. v.p., dir. Pan Am. Soc. of U.S. Episcopalian. Clubs: India House, Racquet and Tennis, Piping Rock, Coffee House (N.Y.C.); Metropolitan, Gridiron, Nat. Press (Washington). Home: Roslyn, L.I., N.Y. Office: 7 Hanover Sq., N.Y.C. 5. Died July, 1955.

PATERSON, Albert Barnett, utilities exec.; b. Blantyre. Ont., Can., Jan. 20, 1883; s. Albert Craig and Zillah (Sheperdson) P.; ed. Coll. of Commerce, Toronto; m. Annie Evans Brown, Jan. 22, 1908; children—Ann (Mrs. John A. Mills), Albert Brown, Margaret (Mrs. Eugene H. Countiss). Chmn. bd., pres. New Orleans Pub. Service, Inc.; chmn. bd. Hibernia Nat. Bank. Mem. bd. adminstrs. Tulane Ednl. Fund; mem. bd. liquidation City Debt, New Orleans. Clubs: Boston, Country, Audubon Golf, Southern Yacht (New Orleans). Home: 15 Audubon Pl., New Orleans. Died Aug., 1952.

PATIGIAN, Haig (pä-tǐg-yän'), sculptor; b. City of Van, Armenia, Jan. 22, 1876; s. Avedis and Marine (Hovsepian) Patigian; early edn. under father and mother (teachers in Am. Mission Sch., Van); self ed. in art; studied sculpture in Paris with occasional criticism from Alix Marquet, 1906-07; m. Blanche Hollister, Jan. 1, 1908 (dec. 1950); children—Hollis, Haig (dec.). Mem. Internat. Jury Awards Panama P.I. Exposition, 1915, hors concours; awarded commemorative medal for distinguished services, same expn.; mem. Internat. Jury of Awards for sculpture at 10th Olympiad, 1932 (hors concours), awarded diploma, same olympiad. Prin. works: McKinley Monument, Arcata, Calif., 1905; "Ancient History" (bronze), Salon des Artistes Français, 1907; "Guardian Angel," Dolbeer Mausoleum, San Francisco; Rowell Monument, Fresno, Calif.; allegoric figures of "Invention," "Imagination," "Steam Power," "Electrical Power," and other sculptural work for Machinery Palace, Panama P.I. Expn.; "Vanity" (marble) Apollo, Diana, etc., Palace of Fine Arts, same expn.; Alden J. Blethen Memorial, Seattle, Wash.; Lt. Gov. J. M. Eshleman, Univ. of Calif.; Gen. Funston, City Hall, San Francisco, 1917, pediment of Met. Life Bldg., San Francisco, Tympanum group and 10 figures, arts, sciences, Memorial Museum, San Francisco, 1919, Wm. Greer Harrison, Olympic Club; heroic statue of General Pershing, San Francisco, 1921; seated statue of Lincoln, Civic Center, San Francisco, 1926; "Friendship" group (original model in permanent gallery of Am. Acad. Arts and Letters, New York), 1926; Dr. Taylor memorial for Pub. Library, San Francisco, 1927; bust of President Hoover, White House, 1929; heroic statue of Thomas Starr King, Nat. Statuary Hall, Washington; "Aeronautics" pediment, Dept. of Commerce Bldg., Washington, 1931; heroic group of volunteer firemen, San Francisco, 1933; heroic busts of Gov. Rolph and Senator Phelan, City Hall, San Francisco; "Creation" (ultra heroic group), "The National Guard" (heroic group) and heroic figures of "Rain," "Sunshine," "Harvest" and "The Earth Dormant" for Golden Gate International Expdn., 1939-40; Henry Hadley medal for the Nat. Assn. for Am. Composers and Conductors; statue of Wm. H. Crocker, 1938; Wm. C. Ralston monument, 1941; St. Francis of the Crosbys, Woodside, Calif., 1942; also many busts, statuettes, bas-reliefs, fountain figures, etc. Awarded Josephine Hancock Logan 1st medal and cash prize for sculpture, 1939; medal and certificate of appreciation from the State of Calif. at the Golden Gate Internat. Expn., 1940. Mem. Calif. N.G. 5 yrs. Mem. Nat. Sculpture Soc., Nat. Inst. Arts and Letters; hon. life mem. Nat. Assn. for Am. Composers and Conductors, Calif. Hist. Soc. Clubs: Bohemian (hon. life mem.; pres. 1946-47); Press (hon.), Army and Navy (hon.). Home: 898 Francisco St. Studio: 3055 Webster St., San Francisco. Died Sept. 19, 1950.

PATON, William Kennell (pā't'n), banker; b. Paterson, N.J., Mar. 6, 1894; s. Dr. Thomas Lloyd and Kate (Kennell) P.; grad. Phillips Exeter Acad., 1911; A.B., Williams Coll., 1915; grad. U.S. Naval Acad. Reserve Officers Sch., 1918; m. Mary-Elizabeth Bendig, Apr. 25, 1925; children—William Kennell, Frederick Bendig. Messenger, Guaranty Trust Co. of N.Y., 1915, N.J. rep., 1916-17, asst. to gen. mgr., 1919-21, sales mgr. Philadelphia office, 1921-22; mgr. bond dept. Harrison, Smith & Co., Philadelphia, 1922-26; mgr. Newark office, Guaranty Co. of N.Y., 1926-30; v.p. and dir. Paterson Savings Instn., 1930-38; special rep. Baltimore & Ohio R.R., 1938-40; mgr. bond dept. Evans, Stillman & Co., New York, N.Y., 1940-41; pres. and dir. Farmers Bank, State of Delaware 1941—. Served as ensign in United States Navy during World War I; assigned Port guard detail officer, N.Y. Harbor; later overseas on U.S.S. Louisiana. Mem. tax survey commn. of Del., 1942-43; chmn. Kent County war finance com. U.S. Treasury Dept., 1942-45; mem. commn. on revision of banking laws, Del., 1943-45; mem. commn. on reorgn. of state govt., 1940-50; State chmn. for Del., U.S.O. (mem. national council 1942-46); v.p. Del. chpt. A.R.C.; mem. Gov.'s Adv. Bd. of Del., 1951—. Trustee Wesley Jr. College, 1955—; Dir. Del. Kent Gen. Hosp., 1949-52, Del. Episcopal Home for Aged, 1955—. Mem. Del. Soc. for Crippled Children and Adults, Inc. (director); Planned Parenthood (director), Theta Delta Chi. Mason, Sojourner. Mem. Episcopal Ch., Dover, Del. (vestryman). Clubs: Wilmington (Del.); Williams (New York). Author of privately printed pamphlets and studies on banking and finance. Contbr. to banking economic pubs. Home: 20 The Green. Office: care Farmers Bank of the State of Delaware, Dover, Del. Died Aug. 25, 1959.

PATRICK, Luther, ex-congressman; b. Morgan Co., Ala., Jan. 23, 1891; s. Francis Marion and Nancy Lucretia (Cobbs) P.; student Purdue U., 1916, La. State U., 1915; LL.B., U. of Ala., 1918; m. Pearl McPherson, Mar. 31, 1918; 1 dau., Patricia Pearl (Mrs. W. James Brasher). Admitted to Ala. bar, 1919, and began practice of law at Fairfield; city atty. Fairfield, 1919-21; asst. atty. gen. State of Ala., 1927-29; asst. United States attorney, Northern Alabama district, 1931-32; member, 75th to 77th Congresses (1937-43) and 79th (1945-47), 9th Alabama District; member law firm Patrick & Godwin; daily radio commentator WBRC and WAPI, 1925—. Served with inf., U.S. Army, World War. Mem. Birmingham Bar Assn., Ala. State Bar Assn. Democrat. Methodist. K. of P., Jr. Order United Am. Mechanics, Eagle. Club: Lions. Author: Hope You're Livin' an' Doin' Well, 1st edition, 1931; 2d edition, 1936; Friends, Nabors, Kinfolks, 1947; Goosepocket, 1955. Contbr. of verse. Home: 921 7th St. West, Birmingham, Ala. Died May 26, 1957; buried Elmwood Cemetery, Birmingham, Ala.

PATRICK, Roy Leonard, corp. ofcl.; b. Hinesburgh, Vt., Mar. 13, 1876; s. John Stephenson and Florence C. (Andrews) P.; grad. Burlington High Sch., 1894; Ph.B., U. Vt., 1898, LL.D., 1949; m. Harriet Stone, Oct. 10, 1900 (dec. Oct. 1936); children—John H., Robert F.; m. 2d, Gladys Baker, Feb. 7, 1942. Pres., dir. Rock of Ages Corp., 1925—, Blodgett Supply, Inc.; v.p., dir., chmn. bd. G. S. Blodgett Co., Inc., Eastern Magnesia Talc Co., Inc.; dir. Boston & Me. R.R., Fed. Res. Bank of Boston, Green Mountain Power Corp., Vt. Mut. Fire Ins. Co., E. B. & A. C. Whiting Co., Queen City Tulatex Co., Burlington Realty, O. C. Taylor, Inc., Majestic Theatre Co., Guarantee Co. of N.A. Pres. Mary Fletcher Hosp. Mem. Phi Delta Theta. Mason (Shriner). Clubs: Algonquin (Boston); Burlington Country, Rotary, Ethan Allen (Burlington); Tobique Salmon (N.B.); St. Bernard Fish and Game (Can.). Home: 275 S. Willard St. Office: 206 Bank St., Burlington, Vt. Died Jan. 14, 1953.

PATTEE, Fred Lewis, educator; b. Bristol, N.H., Mar. 22, 1853; s. Lewis F. and Mary P. (Ingalls) P.; A.B., Dartmouth, 1888, A.M., 1891, Litt.D., 1921, M.L., 1915; U. of Göttingen, 1902-03; U. of Marburg, 1910; Litt.D., Lebanon Valley, 1915; m. Anna L. Plumer, Mar. 9, 1889 (dec. Sept. 1927); 1 dau., Sarah L. (Mrs. John M. Stetson); m. 2d, Grace Garee, Nov. 25, 1928 (dec. Apr. 1946). Prof. Am. lit. Pa. State College, 1894-1928, now emeritus; prof. lit. Rollins Coll., Fla., 1928-41; vis. prof. Am. lit. U. of Ill., 1923-24; prof. Am. lit. Bread Loaf Summer School of English, Middlebury, Vt., 1924-36. Library at Pa. State Coll. named in his honor. Author: The Wine of May and Other Lyrics, 1893; Pasquaney, a Study, 1894; A History of American Literature, 1896; Reading Courses in American Literature, 1897; The Foundations of English Literature, 1900; Mary Garvin, 1902; The House of the Black Ring, 1905; Elements of Religious Pedagogy, 1909; The Breaking Point, 1911; Compelled Men, 1913; History of American Literature Since 1870, 1915; Sidelights on American Literature, 1922; The Development of the American Short Story, 1923; Tradition and Jazz, 1924; The New American Literature, 1930. Editor: Shakespeare's Macbeth, 1897; The Poems of Philip Freneau (3 vols.), 1902-07; Century Readings in the American Short Story, 1927; Beyond the Sunset (poems), 1934; The First Century of American Literature, 1935; also Mark Twain in American Writers series, 1935; Edition of American Writers by John Neal, 1937; The Feminine Fifties, 1940. Home: 188 New England Av., Winter Park, Fla. Died May 6, 1950; buried Bristol, N.H.

PATTEN, George Yager, lawyer; b. Virginia City, Mont., Apr. 14, 1876; s. Francis England Wall and Mary Amelia (Armstrong) P.; graduated high school, Butte, Montana, 1893; married Eleanor Eastman Ferris, July 10, 1901 (died July 24, 1943); children—Margaret, Mary Winter, Eleanor Hall; m. 2d, Sarah Frances Smith, Aug. 2, 1945. Court stenographer, Bozeman, Montana, 1895-1901; admitted to Montana bar, 1900; asst. attorney gen. of Mont., 1902-05; city atty., Bozeman, 1909-11 and 1913-15; asso. justice Supreme Court of Mont., Aug.-Nov. 1919; resigned to resume practice. Chmn. State Bd. Law Examiners. Mem. Mont. (pres. 1918-19), Gallatin County (pres. 3 terms) bar assns. Democrat. Elk. Rotarian. Author article in law review. Home: Bozeman, Mont. Died Feb. 27, 1951; buried Sunset Hills Cemetery, Bozeman.

PATTEN, Henry (Ayres), banker; b. Phila., Mar. 16, 1871; s. George D. and Louisa (Ayres) P.; student Allen's English Classical Sch., West Newton, Mass.; m. Frances Morse, Apr. 25, 1900; 1 dau., Frances M. (Mrs. E. Myron Bull). Began as office boy, Francis L. Hine, western mortgages, N.Y.C., 1889; since 1891 with Astor Place Bank, merged, 1899, with Corn Exchange Bank, now Corn Exchange Bank Trust Co., mgr. various branches until 1917, v.p., 1917-29, pres. 1929-32, v.p., 1932-—; dir. Corn Exchange Bank Trust Co., West Side Savings Bank, Standard Safe Deposit Co., Henri Bendel, Inc. Presbyn. Clubs: Union League, India House, Tuxedo. Home: 21 E. 82d St. Office: 13 William St., N.Y.C. Died July 31, 1955.

PATTERSON, Austin McDowell, chemist; born Damascus, Syria, May 31, 1876, of American parents; s. John Fulton Hutchison (M.D.) and Charlotte Isabella (McDowell) P.; A.B., Princeton, 1897; Ph.D., Johns Hopkins, 1900; honorary D.Sc., Antioch, 1944; m. Anne Elizabeth Bailey, May 31, 1911; children—John Fulton (dec.), Elizabeth (dec.), James Fulton, Nancy Elder. Instructor in chemistry, Centre College, Danville, Ky., 1900-01, Rose Poly. Inst., 1901-03; chemistry editor Webster's New Internat. Dictionary, 1903-53; associate editor Chemical Abstracts, 1908-09, editor, 1909-14; prof. chemistry, Antioch Coll., 1921-41, prof. emeritus, 1941—, also v.p., 1930-41, trustee 1941-45; principal specialist in chemical edn., Engineering, Science, and Management War Training, U.S. Office of Education, 1941-43. Chemist, United States Chemical Warfare Service, 1918-19. Received award in Documentation of Chemistry, sponsored by Dayton sect., Am. Chemical Soc., 1949. Mem. Internat. Com. organic chem. nomenclature, 1924-53; councillor Internat. Union Chemistry, 1925-31, 36-38; mem. National Research Council, 1932-41. Fellow American Association Advancement Science; member Am. Chemical Soc., Phi Beta Kappa, Sigma Xi and Phi Lambda Upsilon fraternities. United Presbyn. Clubs: Cosmos (Washington); Kiwanis. Author: A German-English Dictionary for Chemists, 1917; A French-English Dictionary for Chemists, 1921; A Guide to the Literature of Chemistry (with E. J. Crane), 1927; The Ring Index (with L. T. Capell), 1940. Home: Xenia, Ohio. Address: 221 N. King St., Xenia, O. Died Feb. 26, 1956.

PATTERSON, Grove Hiram, editor; b. Rochester, Minn., Nov. 5, 1881; s. Joseph Stephen and Nellie Maria (Sayles) P.; prep. edn., high sch., Carlyle, Ill., and Oberlin Acad.; student Syracuse U. 1901-02; A.B., Oberlin Coll., 1905, A.M. (honorary), 1925, L.H.D. (honorary), 1953; LL.D. (honorary), Lincoln Memorial University, 1931; Litt.D., Defiance College, 1932, Boston U., 1948; LL.D., U. Toledo, 1939; LL.D., Ohio Wesleyan U., 1940 LL.D., Ohio State U., 1951; m. Esther Argue, Apr. 17, 1919; stepson, Thomas Irving Belford. On staff, and asso. editor Lorain (O.) Times-Herald, 1905-08; copyreader and night city editor Cleveland Plain Dealer, 1908-09; mng. editor Toledo Times, 1909-10; news editor Toledo Blade, 1910-17, managing editor, 1917-19, executive editor, 1920-26, editor, 1926-46, editor in chief since 1946; editorial manager Newark (N.J.) Star Eagle, 1916-24, and Detroit (Mich.) Journal, 1919-22 (both under same management as the Blade). Trustee Oberlin Coll.; past pres. Toledo Y.M.C.A. (mem. internat. com.); ex-pres. Am. Soc. Newspaper Editors. Mem. Sigma Delta Chi, Sigma Alpha Epsilon. Member S.R. (Toledo), past pres. Ohio State Soc. S.R. Made mem. of Order of Isabella (Spain) in 1934. Received Gold Cross of Merit (Poland) in 1938. Republican. Methodist. Clubs: Toledo, Rotary; Rowfant (Cleveland); Nat. Press (Washington, D.C.). Lectr., pub. speaker. Author: I Like People. Home: 606 W. Woodruff. Office: The Toledo Blade, Toledo. Died Aug. 7, 1956.

PATTERSON, Harry Jacob, chemist; b. Yellow Springs, Pa., Dec. 17, 1866; s. William Calvin and Adaline (Mattern) P.; B.S., Pa. State Coll., 1886; post-grad. work in chemistry, same; D.Sc., Md. State Coll., 1912; m. Elizabeth Hayward Hutchinson, Oct. 25, 1895; children—Blanche Seely (Mrs. Francis T. Mack), William Calvin. Asst. chemist, Pa. State Agrl. Expt. Station, 1886-88; chemist and vice-dir., Md. Agrl. Expt. Sta., 1888-98, dir., chemist, 1898; pres. Md. Agr. Coll., 1913-17; dean Coll of Agr., U. of Md., 1925; emeritus, 1937—. Specialist in food, fertilizer and dairy chemistry and corn fodder products; author bulls. and articles on these subjects. Fellow A.A.A.S.; mem. Assn. Official Agrl. Chemists, Am. Chem. Soc., Soc. Chem. Industry, London, Master Md. State Grange, 1905-13; sec. Md. State Bd. of Agr., 1907-17. Home: College Park, Prince Georges County, Md. Died Sept. 11, 1948; buried St. Johns, Beltsville, Md.

PATTERSON, James Albert, clergyman, temperance reformer; b. Dayton, O., Oct. 19, 1864; s. William John and Anna (Ford) P.; A.B., Heidelberg U., 1891 (1st honors); grad. McCormick Theol. Sem., 1894; D.D., Miami U., 1900; m. Mildred T. Allen, July 18, 1904. Ordained Presbyn. ministry, 1894; pastor First Ch., Fostoria, O., 1894-98, First Ch., Sidney, O., 1898-1902, Central Ch., Columbus, O., 1902-09; pres. Ohio Anti-Saloon League, 1907-09; supt. N.Y. Anti-Saloon League, Jan. 1, 1909-13; pastor First Ch., Franklin, Pa., 1913—. Address: Franklin, Pa. Died July 18, 1923.

PATTERSON, Lillian Beatrice, univ. dean; b. Chgo., Nov. 20, 1900; d. William James and Mary Frances (Trace) Patterson; R.N., Presbyn. Hosp. Sch. Nursing, Chgo., 1923; C.P.H., U. Wash., 1940, B.A., 1941, M.A., 1943, grad. student, 1942-48; m. Claude William Patterson, Oct. 29, 1923; children—Joyce Marie (Mrs. Alexander Szoka), Larry Ray. Gen., pvt. duty nurse, 1926-30; sch. nurse, Sumner, Wash., 1930-40; staff nurse, supervisor nurses Pierce

Co. Health Dept., Tacoma, Wash., 1940-45; dir. pub. health nursing field work, sch. nursing U. Wash., 1945-50, dean sch. nursing, prof. since 1950. Tech. advisor Third World Health Assembly, Geneva, Switzerland, 1950. Mem. Wash. State (past pres., dir.), Am. (1st v.p.), nurses assn., Nat. League Nursing, Am. Pub. Health Assn., Am. Assn. U. Profs.. Home: 32915 102d S.E., Auburn, Wash. Office: U. of Washington, Seattle. Died Sept. 8, 1954; buried Mountain View Cemetery, Auburn.

PATTERSON, Paul, lawyer; b. West Newton, Pa., Aug. 25, 1888; s. John Gilfillan and Harriet (McCune) P.; A.B., Yale, 1911; LL.B., Harvard, 1914; unmarried. Admitted to Ohio bar, 1914, since practiced in Cleveland; mem. firm Baker, Hostetler & Patterson; controller and gen. counsel Scripps-Howard concern, 1936-50. Mem. Troop A. of Cleveland, and served on Mexican Border, 1916; entered First Officers Tng. Camp, 1917; served overseas with 42d Div., later detached as a balloon observer; comdg., officer, 4th Corps Balloon Group, 1918; mem. Third Army, Germany, 1918; disch. rank of capt. F.A. Mem. Am., Ohio, Cleve. bar assns., Psi Upsilon, Nisi Prius. Clubs: Union, Mid-Day, University, Kirtland Country, Pepper Pike Country (Cleve.); Yale (New York); Valley (Santa Barbara, Cal.); Duquesne (Pitts.). Home: University Club, Cleveland 15. Office: Union Commerce Bldg., Cleve. 14. Died Nov. 11, 1954.

PATTERSON, Paul Chenery, journalist; b. Jacksonville, Ill., Nov. 18, 1878; s. James March and Mary Abagail (Hamilton) P.; Rushville (Ill.) High Sch.; student U. Chicago 1 yr.; m. Elsie Jarvis McLean, Oct. 22, 1910; children—Walter Maclean, Donald Hamilton, Paul Jarvis, James March, Polly Chenery, Malcolm Maclean. Reporter Chicago Tribune, 1899-1900; reporter, copy reader, city editor, Chicago Journal, 1900-03; night city editor Chicago Inter Ocean, 1903-04; city editor Chicago Examiner, 1904-06, Washington Herald, 1906-07; city editor, mng. editor, gen. mgr. and treas. Washington Times, 1907-11; mng. editor Baltimore Evening Sun, 1911-13; business mgr., sec., treas. Sun and Evening Sun, 1913-19, pres., exec. editor, 1919-51; pres. The A. S. Abell Co., publishers The Sun papers; v.p. Associated Press, 1930, dir., 1932-50. Mem. Am. Newspaper Pubs. Assn. (pres. 1922-24), Am. Soc. Editors. Clubs: Maryland, Gibson Island, Elkridge Hunt. Home: 219 Northway, Guilford, Baltimore. Office: The Sun, Sun Square, Baltimore. Died Apr. 21, 1952; buried Druid Ridge Cemetery.

PATTERSON, Paul L., gov. of Ore.; b. Kent, O., July 18, 1900; s. George A. and Ada L. (Linton) P.; B.B.A., U. of Ore., 1923, J.D., 1926; m. Georgia S. Benson, May 16, 1927; children—Georgia S., Paul L., Virginia Lee. Admitted to Ore. State bar, and served as dept. dist. atty., Washington County, 1926-32; pvt. practice Hillsboro, 1932-52. Formerly state senator, State of Ore.; now gov. of Ore. Mem. Am. Legion, Ore. State Bar Assn., Chi Psi. Conglist. Mason (Shriner), Elk. Clubs: University, Rotary. Home: 326 E. Jackson. Office: Comml. Nat. Bank Bldg., Hillsboro, Ore.; and State Capitol, Salem, Ore. Died Jan. 31, 1956; buried Portland, Ore.

PATTERSON, Robert Porter, former secretary war; b. Glens Falls, N.Y., Feb. 12, 1891; s. Charles R. and Lodice E. (Porter) P.; A.B., Union College, 1912; LL.B., Harvard, 1915; m. Margaret T. Winchester, Jan. 3, 1920; children—Robert P., Aileen W. (Mrs. Timothy Seldes), Susan Hand (Mrs. Stephen R. Petschek), Virginia D. (Mrs. Robert L. Montgomery, II). Admitted to the N.Y. bar, 1915, and practiced at N.Y. City; apptd. judge U.S. Dist. Court, Southern N.Y. Dist., 1930; apptd. judge U.S. Circuit Court of Appeals, 1939; resigned, July 1940, to become asst. sec. of war; apptd. undersec. of war, Dec. 1940; apptd. sec. of war, U.S. War Dept., Sept. 1945; resigned, July 1947. Dir. Federal Reserve Bank of New York; pres. Practicing Law Inst. Trustee Union Coll., pres. Harvard Law Sch. Assn. 1937-49. Pvt. 7th Regiment Nat. Guard N.Y., Mex. Border, 1916; capt., maj. 306th Inf., U.S. Army, World War I. Pres. Freedom House. Mem. Am. Bar Assn. (chmn. commn. on organized Crime), N.Y. State Bar Assn., Association Bar City of New York (president), American Acad. Arts and Scis., Am. Legion, N.Y. Soc. Mil. and Naval Officers World Wars (pres.), Phi Beta Kappa, Phi Delta Theta. Awarded D.S.C. for "extraordinary heroism in action on Aug. 14, 1918." Awarded Silver Star and Purple Heart in World War I; awarded D.S.M. for service in World War II. Clubs: Harvard, Lawyers, Century Assn. Home: Cold Spring, N.Y., also 1 E. 84th St., N.Y.C. 23. Office: 1 Wall St., N.Y.C. Died at Elizabeth, N.J., Jan. 22, 1952; buried Arlington Cemetery, Arlington, Va.

PATTERSON, Robert Urie, physician, ret. army officer; b. Montreal, June 16, 1877 (parents Am. citizens); s. William James Ballantyne and Eleanor Haight (Lay) P.; prep. edn. San Antonio (Tex.) Acad., Bishop's College Sch., Lennoxville, Que., Berthier Grammar Sch., Berthier-en-haute, Que., Montreal Collegiate Inst., 1892-94; M.D. and C.M., McGill U. Montreal, 1898, LL.D., 1932; honor grad. Army Med. Sch., 1902; grad. Med. Field Service School, Fort Leavenworth, Kan., 1912, Army War Coll., 1921; m. Eda Beryl Lorraine Day, Mar. 28, 1905 (dec. Apr. 1918); children—Eleanor Lyman, Janet; m. 2d, Eleanor Reeve, Aug. 14, 1920; children—Margaret Baden, Robert Urie. House surgeon Montreal Gen. Hosp., 1898-99; resident accoucher Montreal Maternity Hosp., 1899-1900; in practice at Belt, Mont., 1900-01; commd. 1st lt. and asst. surgeon U.S. Army, June 29, 1901, and advanced through grades to col. M.C., 1927; served as temp. col. N.A., World War; surgeon gen. U.S. Army, rank of major gen., 1931-35; retired, Nov. 30, 1935; dean Med. Sch., U. Okla., 1935-42; dean Sch. of Medicine, U. Md., 1942—. Service in P.I., Cuba, Hawaii, Italy, France. Decorated D.S.M., 2 silver star citations for "gallantry in action," Philippine Campaign, Cuban Pacification and Victory medals (United States; British war Medal; mentioned in despatches by the British Commander-in-chief for gallantry on Western front, Dec. 1917; Fatiche di Guerra, Medale de Independencia, Officer Crown of Italy (Italy); Officer Order of White Lion (Czechoslovakia); Serbian Red Cross. Fellow A.C.S., A.C.P.; mem. A.M.A., Assn. Mil. Surgeons of U.S., Second Div. Vets Assn., Mil. Order of Carabao, Alpha Delta Phi, Phi Beta Kappa, Phi Beta Pi, Alpha Omega Alpha. Episcopalian. Mason (32°, K.T.). Clubs: Army Navy, Alfalfa (Washington); Army and Navy (Oklahoma City); Army and Navy (San Francisco); Chevy Chase (Md.); Hot Springs (Ark.) Golf and Country, Oklahoma City Golf and Country. Home: 5801 Roland Av., Balt. 10. Died Dec. 5, 1950.

PATTERSON, Roscoe Conkling, former U.S. senator; b. Springfield, Mo., Sept. 15, 1876; s. John A. and Mildred Lou (Bridwell) P.; student Drury Coll., Springfield, 1892-95, U. of Mo., 1895-96; LL.B., St. Louis Law Sch. (Washington U.), 1897; m. Ada Holman, Mar. 4, 1901; children—Paul (dec.), Hadley. Admitted to Mo. bar, 1897, and began practice at Springfield; pros. atty., Greene County, Mo., 1903-07; mem. 67th Congress, 7th Mo. Dist.; U.S. dist. atty. Western Dist. Mo., 1925-29; U.S. senator, term 1929-35. Mem. Rep. State Com., Mo., 1912-20; chmn. Rep. State Conv., 1920; Rep. elector at large, Mo., 1924. Republican. Mem. Sigma Nu. Mason. Home: 1657 S. Kimbrough Av., Springfield 4. Office: Landers Bldg., Springfield, Mo. Died Oct. 22, 1954; buried Maple Park Cemetery, Springfield.

PATTERSON, William J., transportation consultant; born at Neenah, Wisconsin, June 4, 1880; son of Amos and Mary (Bidwell) Patterson; graduate high school, Boyd, Wis., 1896; studied air brake and train operation with Internat. Corr. Sch. of Scranton, Pa.; m. Margaret M. Henderman, Apr. 29, 1912; children—Jane Bidwell (Mrs. George R. Kirk), William Amos. Started as call boy for Wis. Central Ry., at Stevens Point; later brakeman, fireman, switchman and conductor various roads; conductor N.P. Ry., 1906-14; insp. safety appliances, Interstate Commerce Commn., 1914-18, asst. dir. Bur. of Safety of same, 1918-34, dir., 1934-39; mem. mechanical advisory com. Fed. Coordinator of Transportation, 1934-36. Member Interstate Commerce Commission 1939-53, chmn., 1944; now transportation consultant. Formerly a member of several grand divisions of Order of Railway Conductors and represented employees in negotiations with employers. Member Newcomen Society (England). Mason (32°, Shriner, K.T.). B.P.O. Elks. Clubs: National Press (Washington, D.C.); Columbia Country (Chevy Chase, Md.); Union League (Chicago). Home: 3916 Legation St., Washington. Died Nov. 24, 1955.

PATTERSON, Wright A., editor; b. Kirksville, Mo., Aug. 4, 1870; s. William Evans and Susan (Beam) P.; ed. pub. schs.; m. Abbie E. Forquer, May 29, 1893; children—Wright F., Elizabeth E. Newspaper work, Ft. Madison and Keokuk, Ia., 1887-90; with A. N. Kellogg Newspaper Co. and its successor, the Western Newspaper Union, 1890—, editor-in-chief, 1905-36, editorial director, 1936-40; editor emeritus, 1940—. Member 1st Illinois Infantry, 1890-98; 1st lieutenant 1st Illinois Cavalry, Spanish-Am. War. Republican. Mason. Clubs: Nat. Press, Army and Navy (Washington, D.C.); Adventurers (Chicago). Made visit to Europe, 1918, with party of newspaper men as guests of British and French govts. Author: Ideas in Newspaper Making, 1915. Home: 1015 E. Chapman, Orange, Cal. Died May 17, 1954; buried Melrose Abbey, Orange.

PATTON, Fred (Frederick Henry), baritone; b. Manchester, Conn., Oct. 2, 1888; s. James and Charlotte Ann (Rogers) P.; student grammar sch. and high sch., Manchester, until 1903; m. Jessie David Woolley, Feb. 22, 1910; children—Mrs. Myrtle Evelyn Goll, Mrs. Jessie Norva Barkentin. Concert and opera singer since Jan. 18, 1919; singer with Cin. Opera Co., 1926-31, Phila. Civic Opera Co., 1925-30, Met. Opera Co., 1927-29; appearances with N.Y. Philharmonic-Symphony Orchestra, Phila., Boston, Chgo., Cin., Cleve., Detroit, Mpls., San Francisco and Manhattan symphony orchestras, as well as numerous festival and oratorio engagements throughout U.S.; broadcaster. Sang 8 yrs. at Broadway Tabernacle and 10 yrs. at Fifth Av. Presbyn. Ch., New York; prof. music Mich. State Coll., 1932-46; retired; dean Summer Music Sch., Bay View, Mich., 1934-44. Mem. Phi Kappa Tau. Republican. Methodist. Mason (32°), Rotarian. Home: East Lansing, Mich. Studios: 5300 John R St., Detroit; 530 Beech St., East Lansing, Mich. Died Oct. 26, 1951.

PATTON, Leroy Thompson, prof. geology; b. Fairpoint, O., Dec. 5, 1880; s. John and Lauretta Close (Thompson) P.; A.B., Muskingum Coll., New Concord, O., 1905; B.S., U. Chgo., 1913; M.S., State U. Ia., 1916, Ph.D., 1923; m. Bertha Eubank, Aug. 20, 1927; children—Joseph Thompson, Bruce Bransford. Prin. high sch. and supt. schs., 1905-12; prof. chemistry and geology, Geneva Coll., Beaver Falls, Pa., 1912-18; prof., head dept. chemistry and geology, Muskingum Coll., New Concord, O., 1918-21, prof. geology, head dept., 1921-22; asso. geologist, Bur. Econ. Geology, U. Tex., 1922-25; tech. adviser Tex. State Bd. of Water Engrs., 1923; prof. geology 1925—, head dept. geology, petroleum engring., Tex. Tech. Coll., Lubbock, 1925-48. Mem. water resources com. Tex. State Planning Bd., 1935-39; mem. council Ohio Athletic Conf., 1920-22. Fellow A.A.A.S., Geological Soc. Am., mem. Am. Assn. Petroleum Geologists, Soc. of Econ. Paleontologists and Mineralogists, Sigma Xi, Gamma Alpha. Presbyn. Author: Geology of Potter County, Texas, 1923; Geology of Stonewall County, Texas, 1930; also various papers on geol. topics. Home: 2415 19th St., Lubbock, Tex. Died June 22, 1957; buried Lubbock (Tex.) Meml. Park.

PATTON, Nat., ex-congressman; b. Tadmore, Tex., Feb. 26, 1883; s. Frank Marion and Bessie (Bland) P.; student Sam Houston State Tchrs. Coll., 1901-02; student Tex. State U.; m. Mattie Taylor, Jan. 1, 1907; children—Bessie Louise, Weldon Taylor, Nat, Bonnie Beatrice. Tchr. pub. schs. Tex., 1899-1912; mem. Tex. Legislature, 1912-13; taught sch. and farmed, 1913-18; judge Houston County, 1918-22; admitted to Tex. bar, 1922; in practice at Crockett, 1922—; mem. State Senate, 2 terms, 1929-34, resigned to accept place in Congress; mem. 74th-78th Congresses (1935-45), 7th Tex. Dist. Democrat. Mem. M.E. Ch., South. Mason. K.P. Club: Lions. Home: Crockett, Tex. Died July 1957.*

PATY, Raymond Ross (pā'tĭ), T.V.A. exec.; b. Bellbuckle, Tenn., Nov. 4, 1896; s. Robert Morris and Zula Matilda (Muse) P.; student U. of Tenn., 1914-16, 1919; A.B., Emory U., 1921, LL.D., 1938; A.M., Columbia U., 1927; student University of Chicago, summer 1930; LL.D., University of Alabama, 1942; L.H.D., Birmingham Southern College, 1943; married Adelaide Martha Pund, Sept. 10, 1921; children—Martha Anne, Mary Pund, Jane Muse. Teacher, Webb Sch., Bellbuckle, 1917, 1919-20; prin. Cumberland Mt. Sch., Crossville, Tenn., 1921-29; asso. prof. of Bible and religious edn., Emory U., 1929-37, dean of men, 1933-37; dir. of fellowships, Julius Rosenwald Fund, 1936-38; president Birmingham-Southern Coll., 1938-42; president University of Alabama, 1942-46; chancellor, Univ. System of Ga., 1947-48; dir. pub. relations, Rich's, Inc. since 1948, also dir. Rich Foundation; member board of directors T.V.A. since 1952. State dir. Nat. Youth Adminstrn., Ga., 1935-36. Grad. O.T.C., Camp Pike, 1918; served as 2d lt., brig. signal officer, 170th F.A., U.S. Army, Camp Knox, Ky., 1918. Mem. Phi Beta Kappa, Omicron Delta Kappa, Sigma Chi. Democrat. Methodist. Club: Kiwanis. Home: 6515 Orchard Rd. Office: 418 New Sprankle Bldg., Knoxville, Tenn. Died Aug. 7, 1957; buried Birmingham, Ala.

PAUL, A(nthony) J(oseph) Drexel; b. Phila., Feb. 10, 1884; s. James William and Frances (Drexel) P.; ed. Groton Sch.; A.B., Harvard, 1906; m. Isabel Biddle, Dec. 29, 1908; children—James William, Anthony Joseph Drexel, Anne (wife of Dr. Maitland Alexander), Isabel (Mrs. Jean Baltzell). Retired from active bus., 1920. Founder Pa. Economy League, 1935; mem. bd. supervisors, Tredyffin Twp., Chester Co., Pa., 1924-29; v.p. Seamen's Ch. Inst., Phila.; pres. Montgomery Sch., 1926-27; founder Sandlot Sports Assn., 1936; engaged in various civic and charitable works; chmn. Main Line Div. Salvation Army, 1940-41. Chmn. bd. trustees, Drexel Inst. Tech. 1932—, trustee for 5 estates; dir. numerous hosps. and charitable orgns. Served as lt., U.S.N.R.F., 1917-19. Republican. Protestant Episcopal. Clubs: Philadelphia, Corinthian Yacht, State-in-Schuylkill, Gulph Mills Golf, Officers (pres. World War II) (all Pa.). Home: Radnor, Pa. Office: Pub. Ledger Bldg., Phila. 6. Died July 7, 1958.

PAUL, Elliot Harold, author; b. Malden, Mass., Feb. 13, 1891; s. Howard Henry and Lucy Greenleaf (Douset) P.; high sch., Malden; student U. of Me., 1908-09; married to Barbara Mayock, 1945, married second to Nancy Dolan; one son Leslie. Sergeant in the 317th Field Signal Batallion, AEF, World War. Sec. Mass. Soldiers' and Sailors' Commn., 1919-21. Lit. editor Chicago Tribune, Paris Edit., 1925, 26; co-editor transition (international review), 1927, 28; lit. editor New York Herald, Paris Edit., 1930, Agnostic. Pianist, novacordist and folk music exponent. Author: Indelible (novel), 1922; Impromptu, 1923; Imperturbe (novel), 1925;

Lava Rock (novel); Low Run Tide 1928; The Amazon, 1929; The Governor of Massachusetts, 1930; Life and Death of a Spanish Town, 1937; Concert Pitch, 1938; Stars & Stripes Forever, 1939; All the Brave (with Luis Quintanilla), 1939; The Mysterious Mickey Finn, 1939; Hugger-Mugger in The Louvre, 1940; Mayhem in B-Flat; Fracas in the Foothills, 1941; The Death of Lord Haw Haw (pseud. Brett Rutledge), 1941; Intoxication Made Easy (with Luis Quintanilla), 1941; The Last Time I Saw Paris, 1942; With a Hays Nonny Nonny (with Luis Quintanilla) 1942; Our Russian Front (documentary film), 1942; I'll Hate Myself in the Morning, 1945; Summer in December, 1945; Rhapsody in Blue (screenplay) 1946; Linden on the Saugus Branch, 1947; Ghost Town on the Yellowstone, 1948; My Old Kentucky Home, 1949; Desperate Scenery, 1950; Springtime in Paris, 1950; Murder on the Left Bank, 1951; The Black Gardenia, 1952; Waylaid in Boston, 1953; Understanding the French, 1954; The Black and the Red, 1955; Desperate Scenery, 1955; That Crazy American Music, 1957. Co-author: A Women's Face (screenplay) 1941. Mem. Greek Orthodox Ch. Address: c/o Charles Scribner's Sons, 597 5th Av., N.Y.C. 17. Died Apr. 7, 1958.

PAUL, Randolph Evernghim, lawyer; b. Hackensack, N.J., Aug. 8, 1890; s. Charles and Martha (Evernghim) P.; A.B., Amherst Coll., 1911, LL.D., 1951; LL.B., N.Y. Law Sch., 1913; m. Muriel Shaver, Nov. 23, 1931; children—Martha Virginia, Richard H. Admitted to N.Y. bar, 1914, N.J. bar, 1915. D.C. bar, 1930, in practice in New York and District of Columbia; member law firm Paul, Weiss, Rifkind, Wharton & Garrison; ex-gen. counsel of Treasury, acting secretary of Treasury in charge of foreign funds control and tax advisor to Secretary of Treasury. Formerly special assistant to the President. Formerly Class C dir. Federal Reserve Bank of New York. Formerly Sterling lecturer on taxation, Yale University School of Law; visiting asso. professor of law and lecturer on taxation Harvard University School of Law. Awarded Ames Medal, 1946. Mem. Phi Gamma Delta. Clubs: India House, University (New York); Metropolitan (Washington); Tavern (Chicago). Author: Law of Federal Income Taxation (with Jacob Mertens), 1934; Studies in Federal Taxation, 1937; Selected Studies in Federal Taxation, 2d series, 1938; Studies in Federal Taxation, 3d series, 1940; Federal Estate and Gift Taxation, 1942 (supplement, 1946); Taxation for Prosperity, 1947; Taxation in the United States, 1954. Home: 3206 P St. N.W., Washington 7. Died Feb. 6, 1956.

PAUL, Ray Sherman, packing exec.; b. Waterloo, Ia., Sept. 10, 1896; s. Albert Daniel and Cora Ellen (Steely) P.; B.S. in animal husbandry, Ia. State Coll., 1918; m. Carol Cobb, Sept. 27, 1924; children—Patricia Lou (Mrs. Edward J. LaFave, Jr.), Julie Ann (wife of Dr. Thomas Harris Williams, Jr.), John Ray. Field man, Duroc Bulletin, 1919; with Rath Packing Co. since 1920, as mgr. beef, veal, lamb depts., dir. since 1934, v.p. since 1948. V.p., Family Service League, 1931-35; pres. Waterloo Community Fund, 1937-38; pres. Wapsipinicon area council Boy Scouts of Am., 1945-47, mem. region 8 exec. bd. since 1946, mem. nat. council, 1949; Silver Beaver Award, 1949; chmn. beef com. American Meat Inst. 1951-55. Member Ia. Heart Assn. (exec. committee, 1949), Theta Delta Chi, Alpha Zeta, Sigma Delta Chi. Republican. Methodist. Mason. Elk. Club: Kiwanis. Home: 521 Derbyshire Rd. Office: The Rath Packing Co., Elm and Sycamore, Waterloo, Ia. Died June 22, 1957; buried Fairview Cemetery.

PAULI, Wolfgang (pou'lē), physicist, b. Vienna, April 25, 1900; s. Wolfgang Joseph and Bertha (Schutz) P.; Ph.D., U. of Munich, 1921; m. Franciska Bertram, Apr. 4, 1934. Asst. at U. of Göttingen, 1921-22, U. of Copenhagen, 1922-23; dozent, U. of Hamburg, 1923-28; became prof. theoretical physics, Eidgenössische Technische Hochschule, Zürich, Switzerland, 1928—; visiting prof. theoretical physics, Inst. for Advanced Study, Princeton, N.J., 1935-36, 1940-45, 49-50, 54; lectr., U. Mich., summers 1931, 41, Purdue U., May-June, 1942. Awarded Lorentz Medaille, 1930; Nobel Physics Prize, 1945; also Franklin Medal, 1952; Max Planck medal, 1958. Member Royal Soc., London (foreign), Swiss Physics Society, American Physics Society, A.A.A.S. Contbr. to technical encyclopedias and other reference works in many countries. Address: care Physikal Institut E.T.H., Gloriastr. 35, Zurich, Switzerland. Died Dec. 15, 1958.

PAULLIN, James Edgar, physician; b. Fort Gaines, Ga., Nov. 3, 1881; s. James Edgar and Leola Elizabeth (Wiggins) P.; A.B., Mercer U., 1900, grad. study, same univ., 1901, LL.D., 1929; M.D., Johns Hopkins University, 1905; LL.D., Emory University, 1943; married Edna Frederick, December 17, 1908; children—Caroline, James Edgar (dec.). Resident pathologist R.I. Hosp., Providence, 1905-06; pathologist, Ga. State Bd. Health, 1906-11; asso. prof. pathology, Atlanta Coll. Phys. and Surg., 1907-11; asso. visiting physician Grady Hosp., 1909-13, now visiting physician; adj. prof. medicine Atlanta Med. Coll., 1913-15; prof. clin. medicine Emory U. and chief of medicine, Emory U. div., Grady Hospital, 1915-30; consultant internal medicine, central of Georgia Railway; consultant, Greenbrier Clinic. Served as maj. Med. Corps, U.S. Army, 1918-19. Member A.M.A. (chmn. med. sect. 1927; president 1943-44), Southern Medical Assn. (chmn. med. sect. 1920), Am. Clin. and Climatol. Soc. (pres. 1937), Assn. Am. Physicians, Am. Coll. Physicians (pres. 1942-43, master, 1947), Med. Assn. Ga. (ex-pres.), Fulton Co. Med. Soc. (ex-pres.), Med. Com. Nat. Research Council, Med. Bd. of Nat. Foundn. of Infantile Paralysis, Directing Bd. of Procurement and Assignment Agency for Physicians, Dentists and Veterinarians; mem. bd. trustees Nat. Foundation for Education; hon. consultant to the Surgeon General of U.S. Navy. Regent Am. Coll. Physicians, 1944; Corr. Mem. Soc. Internal Medicine, Buenos Aires, since Mar. 3, 1944; pres. Interstate Postgrad. Med. Assn., 1946-47. Mem. Order of Carlos Finley (Cuba), Sigma Nu, Phi Chi, Alpha Omega Alpha, Phi Beta Kappa. Presbyn. Clubs: Capital City, Piedmont Driving. Contbr. to Trans. Med. Assn. of Ga., So. Med. Jour., Jour. of A.M.A., etc. Home: 2834 Andrews Dr. Northwest. Office: Medical Arts Bldg., Atlanta, Ga. Died Aug. 13, 1951; buried Westview Cemetery, Atlanta.

PAULSEN, Howard C., Rep. nat. committeeman for Washington. Address: 805 Paulsen Bldg., Spokane, Wash. Died Mar. 4, 1959.

PAUNACK, August Oscar (paw'năk), banker; b. Madison, Wis., Apr. 3, 1879; s. August Oscar and Johanna (Fahrenbrook) P.; ed. high sch., Madison; m. Marion Leigh Reinhart, Nov. 11, 1914 (now dec.); children—Robert R., Jean Leigh. Began as messenger, Bank of Wis., Madison, 1897, asst. cashier, 1905-08; one of organizers, Commercial State Bank, Madison, 1908, cashier, 1908-18, pres. since 1927; organizer, 1911, since vice-pres. Cottage Grove (Wis.) State Bank; organizer, 1928, since pres. Madison Trust Co.; sec.-treas. Peoples Investment Co. Chmn. Wis. Banking Review Bd. Served as pvt. U.S. Army, World War; col., staff of gov. of Wis., 1920-23. Mem. Rep. State Central Com., Wis. Mem. exec. com. Wis. Bankers Assn. Lutheran. Mason (32°). Eagle. Club: Maple Bluff Golf. Home: 317 Norris Court. Office: 102 State St., Madison, Wis. Died June 24, 1954; buried Forest Hill Cemetery, Madison, Wis.

PAWLOWSKI, Felix Wladyslaw, prof. aeronautical engring.; b. nr. Warsaw, Poland, July 23, 1876; s. Joseph Korwin and Joanna (Wojciechowska) P.; M.E. and E.E., Tech. Coll., Mittweida, Saxony, 1896; Certificat d'Etude, U. of Paris, 1910; M.S., U. of Mich., 1914; married to Wladyslawa Buchwald (now dec.); children—George, Halina; married second to Emma Louise Minier, July 18, 1918. Came to the United States, 1910, naturalized, 1916. Designer, engr. and chief engr. with machine industries in Poland, 1896-1908; designer engines and cars with Am. automobile industries, 1910-12; teaching asst. to prof. aeronautical engring. in charge courses, U. of Mich., 1912-29, Guggenheim Prof. aeronautical engring., 1929-46; prof. emeritus since July 1946. Consultant Douglas Aircraft Co., Santa Monica, Calif., 1946-47. Aeronaut. engr., War Dept., World War I; chief div. aeronautics, Tech. Mil. Inst., Warsaw, Poland, 1919-20; lecturer Sch. Aeronautical Engring., U.S. A.A.F., Dayton, O., summer 1925. Fellow Royal Aeronautical Soc., Inst. Aeronautical Sciences. Hon. mem. Assn. Polish Engrs. in Am.; mem. Early Birds, Polish Inst. Arts and Sciences in Am., Union des Ingenieurs de France; hon. mem. Internat. Inst. Psychic Investigation; mem. Sigma Xi. Roman Catholic. Democrat. Author paper and articles in Am. and fgn. profl. jours. and tech. reports for various govts. and industries. Address: 3 rue de l'Ecole Normale Pau, Bassés-Pyrénees, France. Died Feb. 17, 1951.

PAXTON, James Dunlop, clergyman; b. Pittsburgh, July 26, 1860; s. Rev. Wiliam M. (D.D.) and Caroline S. (Denny) P.; grad. Princeton, 1880, A.M., 1883, Princeton Theol. Sem., 1883 (D. D. Wooster Univ., 1899); m. New York, May 22, 1883, Helen J. Paxton. Ordained to Presby'n ministry, 1883; pastor East Av. Ch., Schenectady, N.Y., 1884-89, Tenth Presby'n Ch., Phila., 1891-96; Students' Ch., Quartier Latin, Paris, 1897-98; House of Hope Ch., St. Paul, Minn., 1898-1902; 1st Presbyn's Ch., Lynchburg, Va., 1904-30, emeritus, 1930—. Address: Lynchburg, Va. Died Mar. 20, 1949; buried Spring Hill Cemetery, Lynchburg, Va.

PAXTON, J(ohn) Hall, fgn. service officer; b. Galesburg, Ill., July 28, 1899; s. John Wardlaw and Una Edith (Hall) P.; grad. Shanghai Am. Sch., 1917, Phillips Andover, 1918; A.B., Yale, 1922; student Magdalene Coll., Cambridge, 1922-23, L'Ecole Libre des Sciences Politiques, 1924; m. Vincoe Charity Mushrush, Jan. 9, 1943. Tutor and translator from French, 1924; entered fgn. service by exam., 1925; vice consul, Nanking, 1925-29, in charge, 1927-29; language attache, Embassy, Peiping, 1929-32; consul, Canton, 1932-34, Chefoo, 1934-36; 2nd sec., Embassy, Nanking, 1936-37; consul, Shanghai, 1938-41 (on detail Nanking, 1939-41); repatriated S.S. Gripsholm, 1942; 2nd sec. Legation, Tehran, 1943 (rep. on Middle East Supply Council); Embassy, Chungking, 1944-45; Embassy, Nanking, 1945-46; consul, Tihaw, 1946-49; chief, South and Southeast Asia sect., Internat. Broadcasting Div. (Voice of Am.), N.Y. City, 1950-51; consul, Isfahan, since 1951. Served as pvt., U.S. Army, 1918. Recipient Spl. Commendations by Sec. of State for action in Nanking Incident, 1927, and Panay Incident 1937; awarded Navy xpeditionary medal with commendation from Secretary of Navy for aid to survivors U.S.S. Panay; State Dept. Superior Service award for evacuating party from Tihwa to New Delhi over Karakorum Route, 1950. Presbyn. Mason (past mastor). Translator: Prehistoric Man (with V.C.C. Collum) by Jacques de Morgan, 1924, and other French sci. works. Contbr. mag. articles. Home: Danville, Va. Office: Care of Foreign Service Mail Room, Dept. of State, Washington 25. Died June 23, 1952; buried Isfahan, Iran.

PAXTON, William Percy, corp. official; b. Paducah, Ky., Aug. 2, 1879; s. William Francis and Frederica (Fisher) P.; ed. pub. sch.; m. Flora Dicke, Apr. 23, 1902; children—Barbaranelle (Mrs. James Rose Smith), William Francis, Tomas Adolph. Street car condr., 1895-98; accountant, 1898-1902; office mgr., 1902-14; with Southern Textile Machinery Co. since 1915; pres. since 1928; dir. Citizens Savings Bank; pres. Claussner Hosiery Co.; chmn. bd. Paducah Newspapers, Inc. Republican. Catholic. Elk. Club: Rotary. Home: Paxton Place, Paducah, Ky. Died Nov. 1, 1953; buried Mount Carmel, Paducah.

PAYNE, Byron Samuel, lawyer; b. Clay County, S.D., Feb. 2, 1876; s. Byron Spencer and Charlotte Elizabeth (Woodworth) P.; A.B., U. of S.D., 1897; LL.B., U. Minn., 1902-04; m. Blanche Mallery, Aug. 31, 1910; children—Elizabeth Blanche, Janice Nannette. Began practice at Pierre, 1906; city atty., Pierre, 1909-14; asst. atty. gen. S.D., 1915-19; atty. gen. S.D., 1919-23; resumed law practice; spl. counsel for State of S.D. in George W. Egan habeas corpus case and in tax litigation with C.&N.W. Ry. Co.; asst. U.S. atty., 1927-34; state's atty., Hughes County, S.D., 1941-45. Chmn. bd. Onida (S.D.) Bank. Mem. Am., S.D. bar assns., S.D. Council of Churches, Phi Beta Kappa. Republican. Conglist. Mason (K.T., Shriner), Woodman, Kiwanian. Home: 621 N. Euclid Av., Pierre, S.D. Died May 30, 1949; buried Riverside Cemetery, Pierre.

PAYNE, E(noch) George, dean emeritus; b. Barren Co., Ky., Dec. 25, 1877; s. Viscount Nelson and Jacyntha Antoinette (Wheeler) P.; Western Ky. State Normal Sch., Bowling Green, Ky.; Wesleyan Coll., Winchester; A.B., Lebanon (O) U., 1901; A. B., U. of Chicago, 1906; U. of Paris (Sorbonne and Coll. de France), univs. of Bonn and Berlin; Ph.D., Bonn, 1909; (hon.) L.H.D., Yeshiva College, 1943; married Anna Florence Smith, Aug. 4, 1910 (deceased May 19, 1956). Instructor at Alexander Academy, Burkesville, Kentucky, 1898-1900, Steinmann Coll., Dixon, Ill., 1902-03; prin. Paducah (Ky.) High Sch., 1903-07; dean dept. of edn. and prof. psychology, Eastern Ky. State Normal Sch., 1909-10; prof. sociology, 1910-16, pres., 1916-22, Harris Teachers' Coll., St. Louis; prof. ednl. sociology, U. of Chicago, summer 1922; prof. of ednl. sociology, N.Y.U., since 1922, acting dean, 1924, asst. dean Sch. of Edn., N.Y.U., 1927-28, acting dean, 1938-39, dean, 1939-45, dean emeritus since 1945; educational editor, Prentice-Hall, Inc., 1930-49; co-chmn. Woocheefee Inst. of Woocheefee Univ., N.Y.C., 1942-47; vice pres. Save The Children Fedn. Mem. commn. for establishment of the state normal schs. in Ky., 1903-04; chmn. commn. apptd. by gov. of Ky. to study and report on the German schs. Chmn. com. on Ednl. Reconstruction, 1943-45. Mem.-at-large Greater New York Council Boy Scouts of Am., 1943-45; mem. adv. bd. The Friends of Democracy, Inc.; mem. 25th anniversary com. The Jewish Forum. Mem. N.E.A., Am. Social. Assn., Nat. Assn. Coll. Teachers of Edn., Am. Assn. of Science, Nat. Assn. of Ednl. Sociologists, Internat. Narcotic Edn. Assn. (dir.). Chmn. ednl. sect. Nat. Safety Council, 1918-23. Mason (K.T.). Clubs: Scholia, Applied Sociology, New York University Faculty. Author; Einführung der Chinesenarbeit in Südafrica, 1909; System in German Schools, 1910; An Experiment in Alien Labor, 1912; An Experiment in Motivation; Education in Accident Prevention; Education in Accident Prevention with Methods and Results; Principles of Educational Sociology, 1928; We and Our Health (Books I and III); Menace of Narcotic Drugs, 1931. Joint author: Public School Methods, and Red Feather Reading Series; We and Our Health (Book IV); Health and Safety in the New Curriculum; Science Readers, Books I and II, 1927, Books III and IV, 1928; The Story of Aviation, 1930. Coauthor: Adolescent Court and Crime Prevention, 1938. Editor: Readings in Educational Sociology, Vol. I, 1932, Vol. II, 1934; Educational Series since 1932. Editor-in-chief of Jour. of Ednl. Sociology. Home: Pleasant Point, Me. Died June 28, 1953; buried Payne Family Cemetery, Tracy, Ky.

PAYNE, Frederick Huff, ex-asst. sec. war; b. Greenfield, Mass., Nov. 10, 1876; s. Samuel Brewer and Eva Caroline (Huff) P.; ed. pub. schs., Greenfield; m. Mary Blake, Nov. 8, 1900; children—Frederick Blake, Groverman Blake, Carolyn Huff (Mrs. Bernard Barnes). Bank examiner State of Massachusetts, 1906-09; pres. Mechanics Trust Co., Boston, 1910; v.p. Federal Trust Co., 1911; successively treasurer, v.p., pres. and chmn. bd. Greenfield Tap & Die Corp., 1912-40; assistant chief Springfield Ordnance District, Springfield, Mass., Sept. 1940-Jan. 1946; partner Tucker, Anthony & Co., investment bankers, New York and Boston, 1919-24; dir. Am. Mutual Liability Insurance Co., Boston. Trustee Franklin Savings Institution (v.p.). Asst. sec. of war, 1930-1933. Maj. ordnance U.S. Army and dist. procurement officer, 1918; mem. Bridgeport Dist. Claims Bd., 1919; asst. dist. chief Bridgeport Dist. Ordnance Dept., 1919-30 and 1933—; now colonel O.R.C. Rep. Unitarian. Clubs: Metropolitan (N.Y.); University (Boston); Colony (Springfield); Greenfield. Address: Colony Club, Springfield 5, Mass. Died Mar. 24, 1960.

PAYNE, Will, journalist; b. Whiteside Co., Ill., Jan. 9, 1865; s. William Augustus and Caroline (Ferriss) P.; student pub. sch., Morrison, Ill.; m. Katherine Whitney, June 24, 1886; children—Whitney, Donald Macvae. Reporter, editorial writer, city editor and financial editor, Chicago Daily News, 1890-96; financial editor Chicago Chronicle, 1896-97, The Economist, 1897-1904. Mem. Nat. Inst. Arts and Letters. Author: Jerry the Dreamer, 1896; The Money Captain, 1898; The Story of Eva, 1901; On Fortune's Road, 1902; Mr. Salt, 1903; When Love Speaks, 1906; The Automatic Capitalist, 1909; The Losing Game, 1909; The Scarred Chin, 1919; Overlook House, 1920. Contbr. short stories to mags. Home: 15340 Gulf Blvd., St. Petersburg, Fla. Died May 20, 1954.

PAZ, Ezéquiel P., Argentine publisher; b. San Fernando, Argentina, Apr., 21. 1871; ed. Buenos Aires and Paris; m. Celina Zaldarriaga. Co-dir. La Prensa, Argentina's and South America's largest newspaper, 1897-1900; sole dir. since retirement to Paris of father, its founder, in 1900. La Prensa seized by Argentine Govt., April 12, 1951. Assumed charge, 1912, of adminstrv. duties of La Prensa, an enterprise, including the Popular Lecure Inst., a separate instn. with its own mng. bd. and offering lectures by Argentine, European and North Am. scholars, without charge to public. Maintains original custom of filling first 7 to 9 pages with want ads, operates profitably and keeps it in Paz family as since founding, 1869; prints most fgn. news of all world's newspapers, uses the service of the United Press (which keeps Buenos Aires staff of 138), Reuters and special corrs. Hon. mem. of La Prensa of San Sebastian, Spain; pres. Nat. Press Club; founder and pres. Argentine Touring Club (to extend and develop nat. ry. system). Decorated Comdr. Order of Crown (Italy); Legion of Honor (France). Address: Avenida de Mayo 567, Buenos Aires, Argentina. Died 1953.*

PEABODY, Dean, Jr., prof.; b. Reading, Mass., July 3, 1888; s. Dean and Sarah H. (Pearson) P.; S.B., Mass. Inst. Tech., 1910, S.M., 1938; A.M. (hon.), Harvard, 1947; m. Marjorie Roberts, 1916; m. 2d, Florence E. Palmer, 1921; children—Elizabeth, Ruth, Constance, Dean III. Prof. architecture, Harvard, since 1947. Fellow A.A.A.S.; mem. Am. Soc. Civil Engrs., Boston Soc. Civil Engrs., Am. Concrete Inst. Clubs: Am. Alpine, Appalachian Mt. Author: Design of Reinforced Concrete Structure. Home: 362 Clyde St., Brookline; summer, Hubbardston. Office: Robinson Hall, Harvard U., Cambridge, Mass. Died Aug. 7, 1951.

PEABODY, Mrs. Henry Wayland (Mrs. Lucy Peabody), social welfare; b. Belmont, Kan., Mar. 2, 1861; d. John and Sarah Jane (Hart) McGill; ed. high sch., Rochester, N.Y., 1874-78, and various courses in coll.; m. Rev. Norman Mather Waterbury, Aug. 18, 1881 (died 1886); children—Norma Rose (wife of Rev. R. C. Thomas, M.D.), Howard Ernest; m. 2d, Henry Wayland Peabody, June 16, 1906 (died 1908). Tchr. of deaf, Rochester, N.Y., 1878-81, Madras, India, 1881-86; sec., editor Women's Bapt. Foreign Mission Soc., 1887-1906. Mem. Internat. Council for Missions, 1913-26; chmn. United Study Com., 1902-29; chmn. Oriental Coll. for Women Bldg. Fund, 1920-23; pres. Woman's Nat. Law Enforcement Com., 1922-34; dir. Women's Christian Coll., Madras, Women's Christian Med. Coll., Vellore, India, Shanghai (China) Med. Coll. (chmn. bd. 4 yrs.). Founder, 1908, later editor Everyland, Children's World Friendship Mag. Author of Everyland Series, booklets for children: Kidnaping the Constitution. Editor: Life of Henry Wayland Peabody, Merchant, 1907. Home: 31 North St., Georgetown, Mass. Died Feb. 25, 1949; buried Pittsford, N.Y.

PEACOCK, Joseph Leishman, clergyman; b. Paisley, Scotland, June 15, 1873; s. John and Mary (Leishman) P.; came to U.S., 1881; A.B., Brown U., 1900, D.D., 1925; A.M., Harvard U., 1902; grad. Newton Theol. Instn., 1903; D.D., Colby Coll., 1921; m. Edna Bigelow Arnold, June 26, 1901 (died June 10, 1927); children—Leishman Arnold, Arthur Bigelow, Carolyn Arnold (Mrs. W. Gordon Poole). Ordained Bapt. ministry, 1900; pastor Norwood, R. I., 1899-1901, 1st Church, Goffstown, N.H., 1901-03, Calvary Ch., Westerly, R.I., 1903-08; librarian Westerly Pub. Library, 1908-19; pres. Shaw U., Raleigh, N.C., 1920-31; pastor, Tarboro, N.C., 1932-40, Saxtons River, Vt., 1940-43, retired Interim pastor, Friends Church, Glens Falls, N.Y. Trustee Vt. Baptist State Conv. Mem. bd. mgrs. Am. Bapt. Publication Soc., 1914-20. Trustee United Dry Forces of N.C.; chmn. Edgecombe County Chapter Am. Nat. Red Cross; ex-chmn. N.C. Baptist Foundation; mem. Ednl. Commn. to Survey Bapt. Schs. and Colls. in State N.C., 1939; chmn. Com. on Biblical Recorder. Pres. R.I. Library Assn., 1910-12; mem. Phi Beta Kappa, Pi Gamma Mu. Mason (K.T.); elected Grand Comdr. Grand Comdry. of N.C., May 9, 1934; mem. Red Cross of Constantine, Priestly Order of the Temple; Grand Preceptor of Grand College of America, Holy Royal Arch Knight Templar Priests, 1940-41. Contbr. of articles on religion, edn. and social questions. Home: 1506 Scales St., Raleigh, N.C. Died Sept. 24, 1954; buried Westerly, R.I.

PEACOCK, M(artin) A(lfred), univ. prof., scientist; b. Edinburgh, Scotland, Jan. 15, 1898; s. Alfred Norman and Antonie Ida (Fuller) P.; B.Sc., Glasgow U., Scotland, 1922, Ph.D., 1925, D.Sc., 1932; A.M., Harvard, 1927; research asso. in crystallography, U. of Heidelberg, summers 1929, 33; m. Katharine Louisa West, Apr. 2, 1937; children—Barbara Clendon, Nancy Bligh. Lecturer geology and geography U. of B.C., Can., 1929-30, asst. prof., 1930-31; research asso. mineralogy Harvard, 1932-37; asso. prof. mineralogy and petrography U. of Toronto, Can., 1937-42, prof. mineralogy, 1942-46, prof. crystallography and mineralogy since 1946. Mem. Canadian Nat. Com. on Crystallography. Mem. Royal Soc. Canada, Walker Mineral. Club, Geol. Soc. Am. (v.p. 1948), Mineral. Soc. Am. (pres. 1948), Mineral. Soc. of Gt. Britain (abstractor since 1941), Crystallographic Soc. of Am. Author and editor of sci. papers on crystallography, mineralogy; study and recognition of minerals by X-ray diffraction. Home: 33 Fairlawn Av., Toronto 12, Ont., Can. Died Oct. 30, 1950; buried Toronto.

PEAKE, Alonzo William, corp. exec.; b. Kansas City, Mo., May 3, 1890; s. A. J. and Genette A. (Hawk) P.; A.B., Stanford, 1912; m. Meredith Elizabeth Knapp, Mar. 18, 1916. With Montebello Oil Co., Fillmore, Cal., 1912-16; with The Midwest Refining Co., Casper, Wyo., successively as field supt., supt. gas dept., chief engr. of field div., gen. supt. of producing dept., dir., 1916-28; with Dixie Oil Co., Inc., Shreveport, La., and Tulsa, Okla., 1928-30, v.p., and pres.; v.p in charge of production, Standard Oil Co. (Ind.), Chgo., 1930-44, pres., 1944-55, ret. 1955; dir. Pan Am. Petroleum & Transport Co., Continental Ill. Nat. Bank & Trust Co. of Chgo., Am. Petroleum Inst. Clubs: Chicago, Commercial (Chgo.), Glen View Golf. Bohemian (San Francisco). Home: 1426 Chgo. Av., Evanston, Ill. Office: 910 S. Michigan Av., Chgo. Died Aug. 1958.

PEALE, Charles Clifford (pēl), clergyman; b. Lynchburg, O., Aug. 4, 1870; s. Samuel and Laura Wingate (Fulton) P.; M.D., Med. Coll. of Ohio, 1892; grad. med. coll. phys. and surg., Cincinnati, Ohio; D.D., Ohio Northern U., 1915; LL.D., Lincoln Memorial U., 1934; m. Anna DeLaney, Oct. 20, 1895 (died 1939); children—Norman Vincent, Robert Clifford, Charles Nelson (dec.), Anna Grace (dec.), Leonard DeLaney; m. 2d, Mary M. Rines, Jan. 4, 1950. Practicing physician, also asso. prof. theory and practice of medicine and lecturer on physical diagnosis, Wisconsin Coll. of Physicians and Surgeons, 1892-95; ordained ministry M.E. Ch., 1895; pastor Sugar Tree Ridge (O.) Charge, 1895-96, Bowersville (O.) Ch., 1896-1900, Highland (O.) Ch., 1900-03, Asbury Ch., Cincinnati, 1903-05, Grace Ch., Norwood, O., 1905-10, Greenville (O.) Ch., 1910-13, Bellefontaine (O.) Ch., 1913-17, First Ch., Findlay, O., 1917-19; dist. supt. Findlay, O., 1919-24, Delaware, O., 1924-25; pastor Westwood Church, Westwood, Cincinnati, Ohio, 1925-31, First M.E. Church, Columbus, Ohio, 1931-36, First M.E. Church, Olean, N.Y., 1936-38; supt. Hornell (N.Y.) Dist., Meth. Ch., 1938-43, retired. Pres. Cincinnati Ministerial Assn., 1928-29; pres. Olean Protestant Ministerial Assn., 1937-38. Mem. Cincinnati Conf. of M.E. Ch., 1895-1912, West Ohio Conf., 1913-27, Ohio Conf., 1928-36; mem. Genesee (N.Y.) Conf., 1936—. Mem. Ohio Sons of Vets. (past grand chaplain). Republican. Mason (32°), Odd Fellows (past grand chaplain for Ohio). Clubs: Rotary, Kiwanis. Home: 40 Fifth Av., N.Y.C.; also Pawling, N.Y. and Harrison Valley, Pa. Address: 1 W. 29th St., N.Y.C. Died Sept. 21, 1955; buried Lynchburg, O.

PEARCE, John Musser, physician; b. N.Y. City, Oct. 23, 1908; s. Richard Mills and May (Musser) P.; Ph.B., Yale, 1930; M.D., Harvard, 1934; m. Moira Brady, Sept. 14, 1932; children—Mary, Jane. Intern Presbyn. Hosp., N.Y. City, 1934-36, resident pathology, 1937-38, Rockefeller Inst., 1938-39; asso. prof. pathology Long Island Coll. Medicine, 1939-48; prof. pathology and prof. pathology in surgery Cornell since 1948; surg. pathologist N.Y. Hosp., 1948—. Mem. Am. Assn. Pathologist and Bacteriologists, Soc. Exptl. Biology and Medicine, Am. Soc. Exptl. Pathology, Am. Pub. Health Assn., Am. Fedn. Clin. Research, A.A.A.S., N.Y. Pathol. Soc. (pres.), Sigma Xi. Contbr. articles dealing with the pathology of virus diseases and related conditions. Home: 156 E. 79th St. Office: 525 E. 68th St., N.Y.C. 21. Died Mar. 22, 1960.

PEARCE, Louise, med. research; b. Winchester, Mass., Mar. 5, 1885; d. Charles Ellis and Susan Elizabeth (Hoyt) Pearce; prep. edn., Girls' Collegiate Sch., Los Angeles, Calif., 1900-03; A.B., Stanford, 1907; M.D., Johns Hopkins, 1912; Sc.D. (hon.) Wilson College, 1947, Bucknell U., 1950; LL.D. (hon. Skidmore Coll., 1950; Litt.D. (honorary) Beaver College, 1948; D.M.S. (hon.), Women's Medical College, 1952. Medical house officer, Johns Hopkins, 1912-13; with Rockefeller Institute of Medical Research, 1913—, successively as fellow, assistant, associate, asso. mem., 1923-51; retired conducted African Sleeping Sickness Mission, Belgian Congo, 1920-21; visiting prof. medicine, Peiping Union Med. Coll., China, 1931-32; mem. bd. corporators Women's Med. Coll., Phila., 1941—, (pres., 1946-51); Gen. Advisory Council of Am. Social Hygiene Assn., 1925-44; Nat. Research Council, 1931-33; trustee New York Infirmary for Women and Children, 1921-28, Princeton Hosp. 1940-46. Awarded Order of the Lion; Elizabeth Blackwell Citation, 1951, Woman's Medical College Citation, 1952, Leopold II Award, 1953. Member of the executive board of Am. Med. Women's Assn., 1935-36. Mem. A.A.A.S., N.Y. Acad. Medicine, Harvey Soc., Am. Soc. Exptl. Pathology, Am. Assn. U. Women (dir. 1945-51), Am. Soc. Pharmacol. and Exptl. Therapeutics, Am. Assn. Pathologists and Bacteriologists, Soc. for Exptl. Biology and Medicine, Am. Assn. for Cancer Research, New York Soc. Tropical Medicine, Johns Hopkins Surgical and Medical Assn., American Society Tropical Medicine, College of Physicians of Philadelphia, Pathol. Soc. Gt. Britain and Ireland, Royal Soc. Tropical Medicine and Hygiene, British Soc. for Study of Venereal Disease (hon.), Société belge de Médicine tropicale, Peiping Soc. Natural History, Pi Beta Phi, Phi Beta Kappa, Sigma Xi, Alpha Omega Alpha. Awarded Order of the Crown (Belgium). Club: Cosmopolitan. Author: Treatment of Human Trypanosamiasis with Tryparsamide (monograph of Rockefeller Inst.), 1930; also author or co-author of many papers in med. jours. and procs. Home: Trevenna Farm, Orchard Rd., Belle Mead, N.J. Address: Rockefeller Institute for Medical Research, N.Y. City. Died Aug. 10, 1959.

PEARCE, William Greene, business exec.; b. Marietta, O., June 11, 1859; s. Frederick E. and Harriet L. (Greene) P.; ed. public schs. and Marietta Coll., Marietta, O.; m. Frances M. Cogswell, May 5, 1917. With Northern Pacific Ry., St. Paul, Minn., 1879-1902. beginning as clerk in auditor's office and advancing through positions of responsibility to gen. mgr.; 2d vice pres. Griffin Wheel Co., Chicago. Ill., 1902-10; became vice president American Brake Shoe Company, New York, N.Y., 1910, president 1916-19, chmn. exec. com., chmn. bd., 1939-50, dir. since 1910. Formerly pres. Yellowstone Park Assn. Clubs: Racquet and Tennis, Metropolitan (New York). Home: 580 Park Av., New York, N.Y.; also Mill Road, Falmouth, Mass. Died July 15, 1952.

PEARE, Robert S., business exec.; b. Bellmore, Ind., Jan. 11, 1901; s. Reeve Chipman and Addie Ellen (Swaim) P.; A.B., U. of Mich., 1922; m. Katharine Johns, May 12, 1924; children—Elizabeth Johns, Nancy Johns. Employed in accounting, statistics and advertising depts., General Electric Co., 1922-26; sec.-treas. and dir. Maqua Co. (an affiliate of Gen. Electric Co.), 1926-29, gen. mgr., 1929-34, pres., 1934-50; mgr. publicity dept. Gen. Electric Co. 1940-44, v.p. since 1944. Democrat. Methodist. Mason. Clubs: Mohawk, Edison, Mohawk Golf (Schenectady); University, Advertising (New York). Home: 1380 Van Antwerp Rd., Schenectady, N.Y. Office: 570 Lexington Av., N.Y. City. Died Mar. 18, 1951.

PEARSALL, Charles H. C., business exec.; b. Mauch Chunk, Pa., Dec. 26, 1887; s. David J. and Olive (Knight) P.; ed. Wharton Sch. Finance, U. of Pa.; m. Alice Smith, Jan. 14, 1914; children—David J., Olive Ann, Kathleen. Partner D. J. Van Dusen, produce exchange, 1911-15; sec. E. M. Raphel Co., Raporel Line, 1915-20; gen. mgr. fgn. services, Clyde Line, 1920-23; pres. Cia. de Navigation Santander, v.p. Atlantic Gulf and West Indies Steamship Lines; pres. N.Y. and Cuba Mail Steamship Co.; ret. 1954; v.p. Agwilines, Inc.; Hon. mem. Marine Soc. of N.Y.; past pres. Propeller Club of the U.S.; mem. Phi Delta Theta. Clubs: University of Pennsylvania, India House, University (N.Y.C.); University (Mexico City); Havana Country. Home: 40 E. 88th St., N.Y.C. Office: Pier 34, North River, N.Y.C. 13. Died May 6, 1958.

PEARSE, Arthur Sperry (pērs), zoölogist; b. Crete, Neb., Mar. 15, 1877; s. Sherman L. and Sarah Louise (Gardner) P.; B.S., U. Neb., 1900, A.M., 1904, LL.D., 1941; Ph.D., Harvard, 1908; m. Mary Oliver Lehmer, Dec. 22, 1902; children—Frederick Deweese (dec.), Richard Lehmer, Frank (dec.), Elizabeth (Mrs. William Henry Caufman). Tchr. Omaha High Sch., 1900-04; asst. in zoölogy Harvard, 1904-07, teaching fellow in zoölogy, 1908; tchr. Lake High Sch., Chgo., 1907; instr. in zoölogy

U. Mich., 1909-10, asst. prof., 1911; asst. prof. zoölogy U. Philippines, 3 mos., 1911; asso. prof. zoölogy St. Louis U. Sch. Medicine, 1911; asso. prof. zoölogy U. Wis., 1912; prof., 1919-26; mem. faculty grad. dept. Duke U., beginning 1927, now ret., dir. Marine Lab., 1938-45; editor of Ecology Monographs, 1931-51. Vis. prof. Keio U., Tokyo, Japan, 1929-30. Spl. investigator U.S. Bur. of Fisheries, 1913-25, 35-36, Internat. Health Bd., 1925-26, Carnegie Inst., 1928, 31, 32, 36. Cpl. 2d Neb. Vol. Inf., Spanish-Am. War. Fellow A.A.A.S. (v.p. sect. F, 1933); mem. Am. Soc. Zoölogists (pres. 1945), Am. Soc. Parasitologists, Am. Soc. Naturalists, Ecol. Soc. Am. (pres. 1925), S.E. Biol. Assn. (pres. 1942), N.C. Acad. Sci., Arts and Letters, Phi Kappa Psi, Phi Beta Pi, Phi Sigma, Phi Kappa Phi, Sigma Xi, Phi Beta Kappa. Contbr. books and papers on parasites, animal behavior, ecology, fisheries and crustacea; also articles on animals of U.S., P.I., Africa, Japan, Yucatan and S.A. Author: General Zoölogy; Animal Ecology; Homoiothermism; Environment and Life; Migration of Animals from Sea to Land; Cenotes of Yucatan; Fauna of Caves of Yucatan; Hell's Bells; Introduction to Parasitology; Fauna in Encyclopedia Yucateca. Home: 803 2d St., Durham, N.C. Died Dec. 11, 1956.

PEARSE, Langdon, engr.; b. Boston, Mass., Nov. 12, 1877; s. John Barnard and Mary Langdon (Williams) P.; A.B., Harvard, 1899; B.S., Mass. Inst. Tech., 1901, M.S., 1902; m. Eleanor Howard Dean, June 1, 1910. With Charles River Dam Commn.; Boston, 1902; commn. on additional water supply, N.Y. City, 1903; Augusta Water Dist.; also at Cleveland, O., and Jersey City, N.J., 1904; engr. for Columbus, O., 1904-07; engr. Peoples Water Co., Oakland, Calif., 1907-08; div. engr. San Dist. of Chicago, 1909-17, and san. engr. same 1918—; also cons. hydraulic and san. engr. Mem. Am. Soc. Civ. Engrs., Am. Inst. of Cons. Engrs., Inst. of Civ. Engrs., Inst. of San. Engrs., Western Soc. Engrs., Am. Pub. Health Assn., New Eng. Water Works Assn., Boston Soc. Civ. Engrs., Am. Chem. Soc., A.A.A.S., Engring. Inst. of Can., Phi Beta Kappa, etc. Clubs: University, Indian Hill. Contbr. various articles and papers on water and sewage purification, etc. Home: Winnetka, Ill. Office: 100 E. Erie St. Chgo.. Died July 20, 1956.

PEARSON, Herron Carney, ex-congressman; b. Taylor, Tex., July 31, 1890; s. John Lafayette and Annie (Herron) P.; A.B., Union U., 1910; LL.B., Cumberland U., 1912; m. Evelyn Pearcy, June 23, 1915. Admitted to Tenn. bar, 1912; in practice at Jackson, Tenn., 1912—; mem. 74th to 77th Congresses (1935-43), 7th Tenn. Dist. Trustee Union U. (Jackson, Tenn.). Mem. Am. and Tenn. bar assns., Kappa Sigma. Democrat. Presbyn. Mason, Elk. Club: Rotary. Home: Jackson, Tenn. Died Apr. 23, 1953.*

PEARSON, Joseph Thurman, Jr., artist; b. Germantown, Pa, Feb. 6, 1876; s. Joseph T. and Annie V. P.; pupil Pa. Acad. Fine Arts and under J. Alden Weir; m. Emily R. Fetter, Oct. 7, 1902; children—Ruth Elizabeth, Joseph Thurman, Emily, Julian Weir, Jane, Virginia, Justin. Fellowship prize, Pa. Acad., 1910; bronze medal, Buenos Aires Expn., 1910; Sesnan gold medal, Pa. Acad., 1911; 2d Hallgarten prize, Nat. Acad., 1911; hon. mention Carnegie Inst., Pittsburgh, 1911; Inness gold medal, Nat. Acad., 1915; gold medal, San Francisco Expn., 1915; Harris silver medal, Art Inst. Chicago, 1915; Temple gold medal and Stotesbury prize, 1916, and Beck gold medal, Pa. Acad., 1917; Palmer gold medal, Art Inst. Chicago, 1918; gold medal, Sesquicentennial, Phila., 1926; Joseph Pennell medal, Phila. Water Color Exhbn., 1933; 1st award Germantown Art Assn., 1934. A.N.A., 1917. Club: T Square of Phila. (hon.). Home: Huntingdon Valley, Pa. Died Feb. 21, 1951.

PEARSON, Lola Clark, editor; b. nr. Elwood, Ia., Nov. 29, 1871; d. Thomas Jefferson and Lydia (Burgin) Clark; student Cornell Coll., Ia., 1889, Morningside Coll., 1890-91; m. John C. Pearson, Sept. 6, 1899; children—Marion (Mrs. Dewey H. Neal), John Cannon, Clark William. Home editor Okla. Farmer, 1922-24; asso. editor The Farmer Stockman, 1925-46; editor dept. Women and the World's Work, Household Mag., 1926-28. Dir., chmn. dept. Am. citizenship, Gen. Fedn. Women's Clubs, 1928-32, chmn. div. Americanization 8 yrs., parliamentarian, 1935-38; pres. Okla. Fedn. Women's Clubs, 1919-21, state dir., 1921-23; state chmn. internat. relations, 1940-43. Del. Rep. Nat. Conv., Chgo., 1920; alternate del. Phila., 1940; vice chmn. Okla. Rep. Com., 1921-28; vice chmn. Red Cross, Logan County, Okla., World War; made hon. State mem. Okla. 4-H clubs, in recognition of service to rural boys and girls, 1942; made hon. mem. Okla. State Home Econs. Assn. in recognition of contbr. to better homemaking in the S.W., 1943. Mem. sub-com. on publicity Okla. Def. Com. 1941; mem. Okla. nutrition com. War Food Adminstrn.; mem. League of Women Voters, D.A.R., Indiana Acad. Science (v.p 1946), League Am. Pen Women, Athenaeum Lit. Soc. of Morningside Coll. Methodist. Mem. Order Eastern Star. Clubs: Woman's (Marshall); Cosmopolitan (Oklahoma City). Home: 2645 N.W. 24th St., Oklahoma City 8. Died Jan. 31, 1951; buried Meml. Park, Oklahoma City.

PEARSON, Matthew Edgar, supt. schs.; b. Plainfield, Ind., Mar. 8, 1862; s. Enoch S. and Edith (Stanley) P.; B.D., U. of Kan., 1885; M.A., Baker U., Baldwin, Kan., 1907; m. Carrie Davis, Dec. 31, 1885; children—E. DeWitt, M. Claudia, Myrle Loraine, Dorothy Gertrude. Connected with pub. schs. of Kansas City, Kan., 1887-1932, supt. city schs., 1902-32, ret. 1932. Trustee Bethany Hosp. Mem. Kan. State Tchrs'. Assn. Republican. Methodist. Club: Rotary. Author: Pearson's Kansas Speller, 1917. Home: 2214 N. 12th St. Address: Library Bldg., Kansas City, Kan. Died June 30, 1948.

PEARSON, Oscar William, transporation exec.; b. Halmstad, Sweden, July 25, 1895; s. Olof and Annette (Wahlquist) Pearson; student pub. schs. Sweden; m. Marion Hjordis Ekorenrud, Mar. 4, 1920; children—Oscar William, Jeannette, Victor Lloyd. Came to U.S., 1911, naturalized, 1918. Seaman, master mariner, 1908-22; supt. terminal operations Banning Co., Wilmington, Cal., 1922-31; supt., exec. v.p. Marine Terminal Corp., Long Beach, Cal., 1931-48; pres. Pacific Maritme Assn., San Francisco, 1949-50; asst. operations mgr., v.p. operations Am. Pres. Lines, 1950—; dir. Marine Terminals Corp. of Los Angeles, Nat. Cargo Bur., N.Y.C. Mem. adv. com. Munitions Bd. Mem. Nat. Acad. Sci. (adv. com.) Mason. Clubs: Rotary (Long Beach, Cal.); Merchs. Exchange, Commercial, Commonwealth (San Francisco). Home: 585 Pullman Rd., Hillsborough, Burlingame, Cal. Office: 311 California St., San Francisco. Died Dec. 22, 1957; buried Westminster Meml. Park, Garden Grove, Cal.

PEARSON, Ralph M., artist, author; b. Angus, Ia., May 27, 1883; s. Arthur T. and Kate M. P.; grad. Art Inst. Chicago, 1904; studied Modern Art Sch., New York; m. 2d, Louise Hayes, Oct. 9, 1923 (dec.); children—(1st m.) Pavla, Marion (dec.); (2d marriage) Ronald Hayes, Lorna. Exhibited etchings in cities of U.S. since 1915; awarded 1st prize, Internat. Expn., Chicago Soc. of Etchers, 1914; silver medal, San Francisco Expn., 1915; 1st award, Am. Bookplate Soc., 1916. Represented in permanent collections of City of Chicago and Art Inst., Chicago; Congressional Library, Washington, D.C.; Los Angeles Museum of Art; Rochester (N.Y.) Museum, New York Pub. Library; Newark (N.J.) Public Library; etc. Lecturer, New School for Social Research, New York, 1928-38; lecturer on modern art throughout country since 1925; inspector of wings, Avenger Torpedo Bomber, Eastern Aircraft, Tarrytown, N.Y., 1943-44. Mem. Chicago Society Etchers, Brooklyn Society Etchers, Am. Bookplate Soc., Am. Soc. Bookplate Designers and Collectors, Am. Inst. Graphic Arts, Am. Artists Congress, Am. Soc. Painters, Sculptors and Gravers, Internat. Assn. Art Critics. Author: Portfolio of Etched Bookplates, 1920; How to See Modern Pictures, 1925; Fifty Prints of the Year, 1925; Experiencing Pictures, 1932; The New Art Education, 1941; Experiencing American Pictures, 1943; Critical Appreciation Course II, 1951; The New Art Education, rev. edit., 1953; The Modern Renaissance in American Art, 1954; Forum Mag., 1937-40; also articles in art mags.; article on woodcuts and wood engraving in Ency. Britannica; columnist on The Art Digest, 1945-53. Founder of Design Workshop, school of creative art for adults. Address: 288 Piermont Av., Nyack, N.Y. Deceased.

PEARSON, Richard Metcalf, book pub.; b. Concord, N.H., Dec. 27, 1899; s. Harlan Colby and Laura Prucia (Metcalf) P.; A.B., Dartmouth, 1920; grad. study Columbia (Richard Crawford Campbell fellow), 1920-21; m. Robin Urquhart Macquire, Apr. 28, 1923. Salesman Lyons & Carnahan, textbook pubs., 1921-28; established, mgr. high sch. dept. Harper & Bros., 1928-48; mng. editor ednl. dept. Macmillan Co., 1948-49, head dept., 1949—, dir., v.p., 1949—; dir., v.p. Human Relations Studies, Inc., 1950—, president, 1952. Mem. N.Y. State Citizens Com. for Pub. Schs.; del. White House Conf. Edn., 1955. Member Am. Textbook Pubs. Institute (president, 1952), Dartmouth Alumni Council (v. p.), Phi Beta Kappa, Delta Tau Delta. Club: Dartmouth, Salmagundi (New York City); Apawamis (Rye, N.Y.). Home: Blind Brook Lodge, Rye. Office: 60 Fifth Av., N.Y.C. 11. Died Mar. 24, 1957; buried Blossom Hill Cemetery, Concord, N.H.

PEARSON, Robert Logan, ret. railroad exec.; b. Phila., Apr. 2, 1882; s. Robert and Amanda (Jones) P.; B.S. in Engring., Swarthmore Coll., 1902; m. Edna G. Bradley, June 3, 1911; children—Mary F. (Mrs. Clifford L. Porter), John (killed in action, France, Nov. 17, 1944); m. 2d, Kathryn H. Ferry, Jan. 29, 1930. With N.Y.,N.H.&H. R.R. Co., 1904-48, beginning in engring. dept., became v.p. in charge engring., maintenance and operation, 1933, v.p. exec. dept., 1946-48, ret. Clubs: Graduates, New Haven Country (New Haven); Algonquin (Boston). Home: Westport, Conn. Died 1952.*

PEARSON, William Alexander, educator; b. Van Wert, O., Apr. 6, 1879; s. Richard and Mary Elizabeth (Freshour) P.; Ph.C., U. of Mich., 1900; M.D., Hahnemann Med. Coll., 1915; Sc.D., La Salle Coll., 1928; Ph.D., Phila. Coll. of Pharmacy, 1935; m. Mary Longworth, Oct. 14, 1903; 1 dau., Mary Elizabeth. Research chemist, Parke, Davis & Co., Detroit, Mich., 1900-04; prof. chemistry, Ferris Inst., 1904-06, professor biochemistry, 1949-57; prof. chemistry, Hahnemann Med. Coll., 1906-49, prof. emeritus, 1949—; dean, 1914-44. Member of the American Inst. Homeopathy (pres. 1938-39), Am. Chem. Soc., Am. Pharm. Assn., Am. Assn. Clin. Research, Sigma Xi. Methodist. Mason (32°), Rotarian (past pres. Phila., dist. gov. Mich. union). Clubs: Penn, Union League, Hahnemann (Phila.); Merion Cricket) Cynwyd. Author: Medical Chemistry, 1911; Toxicology, 1931; Physiological and Clinical Chemistry, 1938. Home: 401 S. Narberth Av., Narberth, Pa. Died Feb. 16, 1959; buried Van Wert, O.

PEARSON, William Lazarus, theologian; b. Coonsboro, N.C., July 4, 1849; s. Lazarus and Sarah (Edgerton) P.; A.B., Earlham Coll., 1875; A.M., Princeton, 1880; grad. and awarded Hebrew fellowship, Princeton Theol. Sem., 1881; student theology and Semitic langs. and philology, U. Berlin, 1881-83, U. Leipzig, 1883-85, Ph.D., 1885; m. Nancy Greaves, Jan. 1, 1895 (died Nov. 1918); m. 2d, Alice G. Lewis, June 30, 1922. Prin. high sch., Fairmount, Ind., 1875-76, Southland Coll., Ark., 1876-77. Minister in Soc. of Friends 1882—; pastor Friends' Ch., Minneapolis, 1886-87; prof. modern langs., Penn Coll., 1887-91, prof. Bibl. lit. and prin. Bibl. dept., 1891-1906; prin. Bibl. Sch. and prof. Bibl. lit. and exegesis, Friends U., 1906-17; missionary in Tokyo, Japan, 1922-24. Organizer and 1st pres., 1916-20, sec. and treas. 1920-1922, Council of Ch. Coll. in Kan. Proposed establishing of Quinquennial Conf. of Am. Friends, and del. to same, 1892, 97; del. to Five Yrs. Meeting of Soc. of Friends in Am., 1912; del. and speaker, Am. All-Friends Peace Conf., Phila., 1901. Mem. Simplified Spelling Bd. (adv. council), Internat. Soc. of Apocrypha, Peace Assn. of Friends in Am., Fellowship of Reconciliation, Pasadena Commn. on Japanese Relations; mem. Soc. Bibl. Lit. and Exegesis 36 yrs.; former mem. Tokyo Pan-Pacific Assn., Japan League of Nations Assn. (foreign aux.), Asiatic Soc. of Japan. Author: The Prophecy of Joel—Its Unity, Its Aim, and the Age of Its Composition, 1885; Notes on the Sacraments, 1898; Studies in the Life of Christ. 1904; Syllabus of History of New Testament Times. 1909. Home: 2110 Navarro Av., Altadena, Cal. Died Oct. 26, 1935; buried Pasadena, Cal.

PEARY, Josephine Diebitsch, Arctic traveler; b. Washington, D.C.; d. Herman H. and Magdalena A. Diebitsch; ed. at Washington; m. Robert E. Peary, 1888 (died 1920). Accompanied him on his 1891-92 and 1893-94 expeditions as far as winter quarters in Greenland; was the 1st white woman to winter with an Arctic expn.; gave birth to a daughter (Marie Ahnighito), the most northerly born white child in the world; accompanied her husband on his Arctic trip in 1897; went north to meet her husband in 1900; ship caught in ice and she wintered with her little daughter at Cape Sabine, 78° 42' N. lat.; went north again in 1902, returning with her husband; a son, Robert E. Peary, Jr., born in 1903. Hon. mem. Phila. Geog. Soc., Am. Alpine Club; hon. v.p. Alaska Geog. Soc. Author: My Arctic Journal, 1894; The Snow Baby, 1901; Children of the Arctic, 1903. Address: 290 Baxter Blvd., Portland, Me. Died Dec. 19, 1955; buried Arlington Nat. Cemetery.

PEASE, Alan W., ret. banker; b. West Derby, Vt.; student Johns Hopkins; m. Ethel B. Shaifer; children—Mrs. McGowan, Mrs. Natalie Willis Preston. Formerly advt. rep. Curtis Pub. Co., with Guaranty Trust Co. of N.Y., 2 yrs.; joined staff Equitable Trust Co. of N.Y., 1921, after Equitable-Chase merger in 1930, became asso. Chase Securities Corp., until 1932; v.p. pub. utilities dept. Chase Nat. Bank of N.Y., 1932-52, ret. Home: 41 N. Fullerton Av., Montclair, N.J. Died May 12, 1955.

PEASLEE, Horace Whittier, cons. architect; b. Malden Bridge, N.Y., Nov. 9, 1884; s. John Nolan and Sarah (Rider) P.; B. Arch., Cornell U., 1910, Fellow, 1910-11; m. Frances Monroe Hopkins, Dec. 31, 1928; 1 son, John Rider. Public service and private practice (D.C.) since 1911. Lecturer, U. of Ill., 1912-13; served as capt. Engrs. Corps, U.S. Army, 1917-19. Architect, Office of Public Bldgs. and Grounds, 1911-22; sec. Allied Archts. of Washington, 1923-33, vice-pres., 1945; PWA Housing and USHA, 1933-38; consultant, Corps of Engrs., 1937-38; cons. archt., Pub. Bldgs. Adminstrn., 1938-42; sec. Central Housing Com. (U.S. agencies), 1935-42; sec. OCD Tech. Bd., 1942-44. Executed works include: Meridian Hill and other parks, gardens and cemeteries; resdntl. developments, motor courts, embassies of Peru and Korea, Cosmos Club, Marine Corps War Meml. setting; restorations, Belle Grave, Dumbarton, two Latrobe Churches; and private residences. Organized Architects Adv. Council; Dicesan Commn. on Architecture; A.I.A. com. on Nat. Capital (chmn., 1924-34); Joint Com. on Nat. Capital; Com. of 100 on Federal City. Fellow A.I.A.; Am. Planning and Civic Assn. Clubs: Cosmos, Cornell. Misc. writing on park architecture, controlled developments, national capital compilations. Home: 1234 19th St. N.W. Office:

1228 Connecticut Av. N.W., Washington. Died May 18, 1959; buried Prospect Hill Cemetery, Valatie, N.Y.

PEATTIE, Roderick, prof. geography; b. Omaha, Neb., Aug. 1, 1891; s. Robert Burns and Elia (Wilkinson) P.; B.S., U. Chgo., 1914; Ph.D., Harvard, 1920; m. Margaret Rhodes, June 11, 1917 (dec.); children—Roderick Elia, Anne, Michael Ransome; m. 2d, Ruth Cavett, Oct. 17, 1947. Asst. in physiography, U. Chgo., summers 1916, 19; asst. in physiography, Radcliffe Coll., 1915; Austin tchng. fellow, Harvard, 1916-17; topographic aid U.S. Geol. Survey, 1917; field geologist Cosden Oil & Gas Co., 1919, 20; asst. prof. geology, Williams Coll., 1919-20, Ohio State U., 1920-25; prof. geography, Ohio State U., 1925—; on leave of absence, chief of Office of War Information, Union of S. Africa, 1944-45. Lectr. U. Cal., summer 1921, Clark U., summer 1924; asso. prof. geography Northwestern U., summer 1925. Instr. Army Engring. Sch., A.E.F., 1918; lectr. U. of Wis., summer 1938. Mem. Assn. Am. Geographers, Ohio Acad. Sci., Sigma Xi, Aphal Delta Phi. Author: The Geography of Ohio, 1924; College Geography, 1926; Mountain Geography; Rambles in Europe; Exploring Geography; Geography in Human Destiny; The Incurable Romantic; How To Read Military Maps; Look to the Frontiers; Struggle on the Veld; The Teaching of Geography, published in 1950; Historical Geography of Commerce to 1800, 1955. Editor: American Mountain Series. Address: 1601 Perry St., Columbus, O. Died June 18, 1955; buried Vermont Farms, Wallingford, Vt.

PEAVY, George Wilcox (pē'vĭ), coll. pres.; b. Howell, Mich., Nov. 12, 1869; s. Adelbert F. and Rosette (Wilcox) P.; B.S., U. Mich., 1895, M.S. F., 1905, Sc.D., 1936; LL.D., Willamette, 1937; m. Leona Bradley, Aug. 31, 1894; children—Bradley A., George D., Norbert E. Prin. Jackson (Mich.) High Sch., 1895-96, Flint (Mich.) High Sch., 1896-1901; in U.S. Forest Service, 1905-10; dean Forest Sch., Ore. State Agrl. Coll., 1910-34, pres. of coll., 1934-40, pres. emeritus 1940—. Mayor of Corvallis 1947—. Mem. State Bd. of Forestry, 1911-41. Pres., League of Ore. Cities, 1949. Fellow Soc. Am. Foresters; mem. Phi Delta Theta. Xi Sigma Pi. Presbyn. Mason (32°, Shriner). Home: Corvallis, Ore. Died 1951.

PECK, Allen Steele, forestry; b. West Barre, N.Y., Apr. 17, 1880; s. Charles Bickford and Alice (Steele) P.; Ph.B., Union Coll., 1903, hon. M.S., 1933; B.S. in forestry, U. of Mich., 1905; m. Jessie Douglas Pearson, Nov. 11, 1908; children—Allen Steele, Alice Steele (wife of Rev. Arthur A. Vall-Spinosa), Kate Stott (Mrs. Arthur T. S. Kent). Student asst. Bur. of Forestry, Dept. of Agr., 1902; with U.S. Forest Service, 1905— (except for mil. service), regional forester in charge Rocky Mt. Region, including nat. forests of Colo., Eastern Wyo., S.D. and Neb., 1920-43, retired, 1944. Past pres. Colorado Engineering Council; member Denver Regional and National Councils Boy Scouts of America (ex-pres. Denver Council). Served as maj. and lt. col. Engrs. Corps, U.S. Army (1917-20), with A.E.F., 22 mos., asst. to dir. of constrn. and forestry G.H.Q., Chaumont. Decorated D.S.M. (U.S). Chevalier Legion of Honor (France). Fellow Soc. American Foresters, member Am. Forestry Assn., Colo. Forestry and Hort. Assn. (dir.), Soc. Am. Mil. Engrs., S.A.R., Am. Soc. French Legion of Honor, Am. Legion, Sigma Phi, Episcopalian. Clubs: Army and Navy (Washington, D.C.); University (Denver); Colorado Mountain; Mile High. Contbr. to jours. Home: 18 So. Ogden, Denver 9. Died Feb. 4, 1951.

PECK, Charles Horton, botanist; b. Sand Lake, N.Y., Mar. 30, 1833; s. Joel B. and Pamelia (Horton) P.; A.B., Union Coll., N.Y., 1859, later A.M. (D.Sc., 1908); m. Mary C. Sliter, Apr. 10, 1861. Taught in Sand Lake Collegiate Inst. and Albany Classical Inst., 1859-67; in charge bot. dept., N.Y. State Mus., and state botanist, 1883-1915. Republican. Presbyn. Author of annual reports giving results of bot. investigations, including Edible and Poisonous Fungi of N.Y.; Boleti of the United States. Fellow A.A.A.S.; mem. Bot. Soc. Am., N.E. Bot. Club, Am. Forestry Assn., Albany Inst., Hist. and Art Soc.; hon. mem. Dana Natural History Soc., Buffalo Soc. Natural Scis., and several mycol. clubs. Home: Menands. Office: Education Bldg., Albany, N.Y. Died July 11, 1917; buried Sand Lake, N.Y.

PECK, Willys Ruggles, ret. fgn. service officer; b. of Am. parents, Tientsin, China, Oct. 24, 1882; s. Albert Palmer (M.D.) and Celia (Flagg) P.; A. B., U. Cal., 1906; m. Alice Benton Jones, July 26, 1910 (dec.); 1 dau., Damaris Flagg. Apptd. student interpreter in China, 1906; asst. Chinese sec. to Legation, Peking, 1908-13, Chinese sec., 1913-14; consul at Tsingtau, 1914; vice consul gen. at Hankow, 1914-15; returned to Tsingtau; detailed to Shanghai, 1916; in charge at Tientsin, 1916; returned to Tsingtau, 1916; acting Chinese sec. Am. Legation, Peking, China, 1919-21, Chinese sec., 1921-26; detailed to Dept. of State, Washington, 1926; asst. chief Div. Far Eastern Affairs, 1928-30; apptd. consul gen., assigned to Nanking, designated counselor of Legation, 1931, counselor of embassy, 1935-40; apptd. minister to Thailand, 1941; interned at Bangkok, 1941-42; returned to U.S. through internat. exchange; apptd. spl. asst., div. of cultural relations, in charge of China sect. Dept. of State, 1942-44; asst. chief div. of cultural relations, in charge Far Eastern br., 1944-45; apptd. fgn. service 1st class, and consul gen. U.S., 1945, ret. Mem. Alpha Delta Phi. Home: Belmont, Cal. Died Sept. 2, 1952.

PEDERSEN, Victor Cox (pē' dĕr-sĕn), surgeon; b. N.Y.C., Nov. 15, 1867; s. Joseph Silvey and Victoria (Cox) P.; student Coll. City of N.Y., 1884-85, Trinity Coll., Conn., 1887-91; M.D., Coll. Physicians and Surgeons (Columbia), 1898; studied U. of Edinburgh; m. Winnifred Laura Hartley, Sept. 4, 1900. Practiced in N.Y.C., 1898-1948, ret.; cons. physician and surgeon to adj. gen. State of N.Y., Selective Service Hdqrs., City of N.Y., 1917-18; commd. maj. Med. Corps, U.S. Army, 1918; maj. Med. Corps (Res.), 1919; lieut. colonel Medical Reserves, 1926. Diplomate Am. Bd. of Urology; mem. A.M.A., N.Y. State and N.Y. County med. socs., Am. and N.Y. urol. assns. Am. Congress of Physical Therapy, N.Y. Physical Therapy Assn., N.Y. Acad. Medicine, Medico-Surg. Soc. of N.Y., Soc. Med. Jurisprudence, Alumni Assn. Coll. Physicians and Surgeons (Columbia), N.Y. Hosp. Soc. for Advancement Clin. Research, Delta Kappa Epsilon, Phi Beta Kappa, Nu Sigma Nu, Pi Gamma Mu, Mil. Order Foreign Wars, Mil. Order World War, Soc. Am. Wars, Am. Legion, Assn. Mil. Surgeons U.S. Mil. and Naval Officers World War, Old Guard of City of N.Y., Reserve Officers Assn. of U.S.; founder at St. Mark's Hosp., N.Y.C., 1st med. adv. bd. Episcopalian. Author: A Text-Book of Urology in Men, Women and Children, including Urinary and Sexual Infections, Urethroscopy and Cystoscopy, 1919; The Woman a Man Marries—An Analysis of Her Double Standard; The Man a Woman Marries—Problems in Consideration; Nature's Way—The Fertile and Sterile Periods of Marriage; also about 250 articles on med. subjects. Editor of Medical Epitome Series. Home: 45 W. 9th St., N.Y.C. Died Apr. 1958.

PEEBLES, James Clinton (pē'b'ls), dean emeritus of engring.; b. Dreghorn, Scotland, Nov. 28, 1879; s. George and Agnes (Armstrong) P.; brought to U.S., 1885, naturalized, 1890; student Lewis Inst., Chgo., 1900-02; B.S. in Elec. Engring., Armour Inst. Tech., Chgo., 1904; M.M.E., Cornell U., 1908; m. Lulu M. Lintner, Aug. 18, 1910; 1 son, James Clinton. High sch. tchr., Wabash, Ind., 1904-05; tchr. Howe Sch., Ind., 1905-06; instr. Cornell U., 1906-08; instr. and prof. Armour Inst. of Tech., 1908-40, acting chmn. dept. mech. engring., 1940-41, acting dean, 1941-42; dean of engring., Ill. Inst. Tech., 1942-48, ret.; chief engr. Ill. Commerce Commn., 1950-51. Mem. Am. Soc. M.E., Soc. for Promotion of Engring. Edn., Am. Soc. for Testing Materials, Am. Soc. Lubrication Engrs. (v.p.), Gamma Alpha, Sigma Xi, Tau Beta Pi, Pi Tau Sigma. Club: University (Chgo.). Author: Furnace Efficiency, 1915. Home: 9401 S. Bishop St., Chgo. Died Feb. 18, 1954.

PEELE, William Walter, bishop; b. Gibson, N.C., Nov. 26, 1881; s. Andrew and Nora Jane (Gibson) P.; A.B., Trinity Coll. (now Duke University) 1903, D.D., 1928; LL.D., Randolph-Macon Coll., 1941; m. Elizabeth Lytch, August 2, 1911. Professor mathematics, Rutherford Coll., Connelly Springs, N.C., 1903-06, pres., 1906-09; ordained ministry M.E. Ch., S., 1906; pastor St. Johns and Gibson, N.C., 1909. Aberdeen and Biscoe, N.C., 1910-11; headmaster Trinity Park Sch., Durham, N.C., 1911-15, prof. Bibl. lit., Trinity Coll., 1915-18; pastor Edenton St. Ch., Raleigh, 1918-23, Trinity Ch., Durham, 1924-28, First M.E. Ch., Charlotte, 1928-37; presiding elder Greensboro Dist., W.N.C. Conf., 1937-38; elected bishop Meth. Ch., 1938; assigned to Richmond Area Va. Conference and North Carolina Conference. Mem. Board of Missions and Ch. Extension (v.p. foreign div.), Bd. of Christian Edn., and Commn. on Army and Navy Chaplains (chmn.), Meth. Ch., Meth. Com. on Camp Activities (chmn.). Mem. Methodist Commission on Overseas Relief (chmn.). Mem. Gen. Conf. M.E. Ch., S., 1926, 34, 38. Trustee Duke U., Randolph-Macon Coll. Mem. Phi Beta Kappa, Theta Phi. Democrat. Address: Laurinburg, N.C. Died July 2, 1959.

PEEPLES, Thomas H. (pē'p'lz), lawyer; b. Beaufort, S.C., Aug. 4, 1882; s. Benjamin Franklin and Leila (Hay) P.; student U. of S.C.; m. Halie Armstrong, Jan. 8, 1921. Began practice in Blackville, S.C., 1908; mem. S.C. Ho. of Rep. from Barnwell County, 1911-12, from Richland County, 1925-26; mem. judiciary com. of House and chmn. spl. com. on investigation and consolidation of state offices; atty. general of S.C. 3 terms, 1913-18 inclusive. Commd. lt. col. governor's staff, 1913; maj. judge advocate U.S. Army, 1919, and assigned as chief counsel War Dept. Bd. of Appraisers; then maj. judge advocate; later lt. col. J.A.G. (Res.) Commd. by Gov., Apr. 17, 1944, as mem. Com. to Revise Code of Civic Procedure of S.C. Commissioner State and County Elections, 1948. President Nat. Assn. Attys. Gen., 1917. Hon. mem. Vets. Foreign Wars. Democrat. Presbyterian. Mason. Odd Fellow. Elk. Home: Blackville, S.C., Office: 1410 Main St., Columbia, S.C. Died July 31, 1954; buried Blackville (S.C.) Cemetery.

PEERY, George Campbell (pĕr'ĭ), ex-gov.; b. Cedar Bluff, Va., Oct. 28, 1873; s. James (M.D.) and Mary Letitia (Spotts) P.; B.S., Emory and Henry Coll., Va., 1894, LL.D., 1934; B.L., Washington and Lee U., 1897; LL.D., Coll. of William and Mary, 1934; m. Nancy Bane Gillespie, June 19, 1907; children—Albert Gillespie, George Campbell, Nancy Letitia. Prin. high sch., Tazewell, 1894-96; began practice at Tazewell, 1897; moved to Wise, Va., 1899; mem. firm Vicars & Peery, 1904-15; returned to Tazewell, 1915; formerly mem. law firm of Chapman, Peery and Buchanan; dir. Coeburn Home Co., Inc., Buckhorn Coal Co., Richmond, Fredericksburg & Potomac R.R. Co.; dir. Hazard Coal Corp.; sec. Banner Raven Coal Corp. Democratic elector at large for Va., 1916; del. Democratic Nat. Conv., 1920; mem. 68th to 70th Congresses (1923-29), 9th Va. Dist.; mem. Va. State Corp. Commn., 1929-33; gov. of Va., 1934-38. Food adminstr. Tazewell County, World War. Trustee Washington and Lee U. Mem. Va. State Bar Assn., Kappa Sigma, Phi Beta Kappa. Methodist. Home: Tazewell, Va. Died Oct. 14, 1952; buried Maplewood Cemetery, Tazewell, Va.

PEET, Albert W., soap mfr.; b. Cleve., Nov. 21, 1871; s. William and Jeannette (Zueter) P.; student Woodland School, Kansas City, Mo., St. James Mil. Acad., Macon, Mo.; m. Orelle Smith, July 15, 1890; children—Jeannette, Mildred, Herbert. Began as office boy Peet Bros. & Co., 1886, sec., treas., 1901-07, pres., gen. mgr., 1907-27; chmn. bd. Palmolive-Peet Co., 1927-31, became chmn. Colgate-Palmolive-Peet Co., 1931, now hon. chmn. Republican. Episcopalian. Mason. Clubs: Kansas City, Kansas City Country. Home: The Walnuts, 5049 Wornall Rd. Office: 17th St. and Kansas Av., Kansas City, Kan. Died July 22, 1952; buried The Pantheon, Forest Hills Cemetery, Kansas City, Mo.

PEFFER, Henry Ira (pĕf'fĕr), retired mfr.; b. N.Y.C., Aug. 5, 1879; s. William N. and Regina (Fish) P.; student Coll. City N.Y.; m. Clara Elizabeth Ziegler; 1 dau., Virginia Jane. Salesman, sales mgr., gen. mgr., v.p. F. W. Thurston Co., Chgo., 1901-07; v.p. U.S. Indsl. Alcohol Co.; pres. U.S. Indsl. Alcohol Sales Co. and its subsidiary, Agni Motor Fuel Co., 1917-25; organized in 1925 and became pres. and chmn. Am. Solvents and Chem. Corp., which consol. with Rossville Alcohol and Chem. Corp., elected pres. and chmn.; elected chmn. Joseph E. Seagram & Sons, 1933; pres. Seagram Distillers Corp. and subsidiaries; dir. and chmn. exec. com. Sylvania Indsl. Corp.; pres., dir. Laurel Club Beverage Corp. of Boston; dir. W. A. Taylor Co., Cellulose Holding Corp., Sylvanic Co., Inc., Filatex Corp., Alden-Cowdery Corp., Cornell-Caten Co., Guardian Safe Deposit Co., White Rock Bottling Co. of Los Angeles; dir., pres. White Rock Corp., 1944, chmn., 1949, now ret. Mason (K.T., Shriner). Clubs: Cloud, Uptown, Lotos, (N.Y.C.); Westchester Country (Rye, N.Y.). Home: Westchester Country Club, Rye, N.Y. Died Apr. 1952.

PEGRAM, George Braxton (pē'grăm), physicist; b. Trinity, N.C., Oct. 24, 1876; s. William Howell and Emma Lenore (Craven) P.; A.B., Trinity Coll., Durham, N.C., 1895, Ph.D., Columbia, 1903; studied U. of Berlin, 1907, Cambridge U., 1908; D.Sc., Trinity (Duke), 1918, Columbia, 1929, George Washington, 1937, U. of N.C., 1946, Northwestern U., 1946, Case Inst. Tech., 1951; LL.D., U. of Denver, 1950; married Florence Bement, June 3, 1909; children—William Braxton, John Bement. With Columbia U. since 1901 as asst. in physics, 1901-03, tutor, 1903-05, instr., 1905-07, Tyndall fellow, 1907, asst. prof. physics, 1909-12, asso. prof., 1912-18, prof. since 1918, acting dean Sch. of Mines, Engring. and Chemistry, 1917-18, dean, 1918-30, dean, Grad. Faculties, 1937-49, v.p., 1949-50, spl. adviser to the pres. since 1950; chmn. Columbia com. on War Research, 1941-45; sci., also ednl. consultant Oak Ridge Institute Nuclear Studies. Fellow A.A.A.S., Am. Phys. Soc. (treas. 1917-57), Am. Soc. M.E., Inst. Aero. Scis.; mem. Am. Inst. Physics (treas., 1939-55), Nat. Acad. Scis., Am. Philos. Soc., Inst. Radio Engrs., Sigma Xi (pres. 1949-51). Contbr. research papers in physics. Clubs: Columbia University, Century. Home: 220 Kings Rd., Madison, N.J. Office: Columbia U., N.Y.C. 27. Died Aug. 12, 1958.

PEIK, Wesley Earnest (pīk), univ. dean; b. Clearwater, Minn., Oct. 5, 1886; s. Rev. Anton and Maria (Bublitz) P.; A.B., U. of Minn., 1911, Ph.D., 1928; A.M., Columbia, 1924; m. Katherine Elizabeth Laurie, July 23, 1914; 1 dau., Helen Peik Dahl. Rural teacher, Scott County Minnesota, 1905-07; supt. of schs. in Minnesota, Blackduck, 1911-17, Tracy, 1917-21, Faribault, 1921-24; lecturer, University of Minnesota, 1924-28, asst. prof., 1928-31, asso. prof., 1931-34, prof. since 1934, acting dean, Coll. of Edn., U. of Minn., 1937-38, dean since 1938. Chmn. Minnesota Ednl. Policies Commn. since 1943. Chairman, N.E.A. Commission on Teacher Preparation and Professional Standards, 1946-48. President, National Soc. of College Teachers of Education, 1946-47. Mem. N.E.A., Minn. Edn. Assn., Am. Ednl. Research Assn., Nat. Soc. for Study of Edn., Am. Assn. University Professors, American Education Fellowship, College Teachers of Education, Department of Superintendents, Horace Mann League, Minnesota Society for Study of Education, Phi Delta Kappa. Protestant. Clubs: Automobile, Scholia (Minneapolis and St. Paul); Riley, Gown in Town. Author: The Professional Education of Secondary Teachers, 1930; The Training of Teachers (in N.D. Survey Report), 1930; Instructional Problems in the University (Vol. IV, U. of Chicago Survey), 1933; Teacher Education Curricula (Vol. III, Nat. Survey Education of Teachers), 1935. Contributor to jours. Home: 2225 Hoyt Av., W. St. Paul 8. Died Dec. 6, 1951.

PEIRCE, George James (pûrs), botanist; b. Manila, P.I., Mar. 13, 1868; s. George Henry and Lydia Ellen (Eaton) P.; S.B., Lawrence Scientific Sch. (Harvard), 1890, fellow, 1892-94; univs. of Bonn, Leipzig, Munich, 1892-94; A.M., Ph.D., Leipzig, 1894; m. Anna Hobart, June 14, 1897; children—Elizabeth, Carolyn, Rosamond Hobart. Asst. prof. botany, Ind. U., 1895-97; asst. prof. botany, Stanford, 1897-1900, asso. prof., 1900-10, prof., 1910-33, now emeritus. Collaborator U.S. Forest Service, 1909-10; spl. agt. Dept. of Justice, studying effect of smoke on vegetation, 1910-11; studied effect of cement dust on vegetation, 1911. Mem., later chmn., Palo Alto Cal. Bd. Health; chmn. Palo Alto Chpt. Red Cross, 1914-41; mem. wood fuel adv. com., Fuel Adminstrn. for Cal., 1917-18. Fellow Am. Acad. Arts and Scis., A.A.A.S., Bot. Soc. Am. (pres. 1932); mem. Brit. Assn. for Advancement of Sc., Deutsche Botanische Gesellschaft; charter mem. Am. Assn. Univ. Profs. Clubs: Commonwealth, Harvard (San Francisco). Author: Textbook of Plant Physiology, 1903; The Physiology of Plants—The Principles of Food-Production, 1925; Experimental Plant Physiology, 1931. Joint Author: General Biology. Contbr. articles to Dictionary of Am. Biographies, Sci. Monthly, Botanical Gazette, etc. Home: 281 Embarcadero Rd., Palo Alto, Cal. Died Oct. 15, 1954.

PEIRCE, Harry H., actuary; b. Taunton, Mass., Mar. 26, 1891; A.B., Amherst Coll., 1912. Began as teacher of mathematics, Hill School, Pottstown, Pa.; now director and v.p. Mass. Mutual Life Ins. Co. Fellow Actuary Soc. of America. Home: 59 Maple St. Address: Mass. Mutual Life Insurance Co., Springfield, Mass. Died Nov. 1, 1954.

PEIRCE, Paul Skeels, prof. economics; b. Niagara County, N.Y., Oct. 25, 1874; s. Andrew McDowell and Clara Louisa (Skeels) P.; Ph.B., Cornell U., 1897; Ph.D., Yale, 1900; student U. of Chicago and London Sch. of Economics; m. Hattie M. Wasmuth, Aug. 22, 1906; 1 dau., Faith. Prof. history, Hedding Coll., Abingdon, Ill., 1900-02; instr. history, State U. of Ia., 1902-04; asst. prof. history, Ia. State Coll., Ames, 1904-06; asst. prof. history and economics, 1906-11, prof. of economics, 1911-19, State U. of Ia.; prof. economics, Oberlin Coll., 1921-40, emeritus since 1940, Northwestern U., 1919-20, U. of Minn., summer 1931, Rollins Coll., 1942. Dir. ednl. service, Central Div., Am. Red Cross, 1919-21. Mem. Am. Econ. Assn., Fgn. Policy Assn., Acad. Political and Social Science. Sec.-treas., 1912-16, pres., 1917, Iowa Conf. Charities and Correction; chmn. Ia. State Child Labor Com., 1913-19. Conglist. Club: University (Winter Park). Author: The Freedmen's Bureau, 1904; Social Surveys of Rural Townships in Iowa, 1917; International Commercial Policies (joint author), 1923. Contbr. to scientific, hist., polit., econ. and ednl. publs. Home: Winter Park, Fla. Died Mar. 31, 1951.

PEISER, Solomon, pres. Consolidated Chem. Industries, Inc. Address: 111 Sutter St., San Francisco 4. Died Dec. 5, 1951.*

PELL, Stephen H(yatt) P(elham), museum dir.; b. Flushing, N.Y., Feb. 3, 1874; s. John Howland and Caroline Townsend (Hyatt) P.; student Flushing (N.Y.) Inst.; L.H.D., Union Coll., Schenectady, Middlebury (Vt.) Coll.; LL.D., Norwich U.; m. Sarah Gibbs Thompson, Apr. 17, 1901; children—Robert Thompson, John Howland Gibbs. Dir. Fort Ticonderoga (N.Y.) Museum. Vice pres. Huntington Library, N.Y. Served on U.S.S. Yankee, Spanish-Am. War; received Sampson Medal (Santiago), West Indian Campaign medal. Served in French Army, 1916-17, brigadier (corpl.) S.S.U. 5. Decorated Officer Legion d'Honneur, Croix de Guerre with Star and Palm (France). Combatant, Reconnaissance medals; U.S. Army, Oct. 1917, Ambulance Service; received American Service Medal, Purple Heart, N.Y. State Conspicuous Service Cross, Order of Merit, San Domingo, others. Mem. N.Y. Hist. Soc. (v.p.), Am. Numis. Soc. (past pres.), Soc. War 1812 (mem. council), Colonial Order Acorn, Soc. Colonial Wars, Colonial Lords of Manors. Republican. Episcopalian. Mason. Club: Union (N.Y.C.). Home: Fort Ticonderoga, N.Y. Died June 22, 1950; buried Fort Ticonderoga.

PELLETT, Frank Chapman, naturalist; b. Atlantic, Ia., July 12, 1879; s. Ambrose and Ellen (Chapman) P.; student pub. schs.; m. Ada E. Neff, Apr. 8, 1902; children—Kent Louis, Frank Melvin, Fred Gustin, Ruth Mona. Admitted to Mo. bar, 1905, practiced at Salem 2 yrs.; returned to farm, 1907; state apiarist of Ia., by apptmt. of gov., 1912-17. Fellow A.A.A.S., Am. Assn. Econ. Entomologists, Ia. Acad. Sci. (life), Royal Hort. Soc. (London); mem. Beta Beta Beta (hon.). Republican. Methodist. Odd Fellow. Author: Productive Bee-keeping, 1915; Practical Queen Rearing, 1917; Our Backdoor Neighbors, 1916; Beginner's Bee Book, 1919; American Honey Plants, 1920; Birds of the Wild, 1928; Practical Tomato Culture (with Melvin Pellett), 1930; Romance of the Hive, 1931; Flowers of the Wild, 1931; History of American Beekeeping, 1938; A Living from Bees, 1943; How to Attract Birds, 1947; Success with Wild Flowers, 1947. Field editor Am. Bee Jour. Home: Hamilton, Ill.; (summer) Pellett Gardens, Atlantic, Ia. Died Apr. 28, 1951; buried Atlantic, Ia.

PENBERTHY, Grover Cleveland, surgeon; b. Houghton, Mich., Mar. 1, 1886; s. Edward Rawlings and Ellen Martha (McKernan) P.; M.D., U. Mich., 1910, M.S. (hon.), 1942; U. Pa., 1918 (Army assignment); m. Elizabeth Wardner, July 16, 1921 (div. 1939); children—Philip Edward, Grover Wardner, John McKernan. House officer, N.Y.C. Hosp., 1910-12, dep. med. supt., 1912-13; began genl. practice, Detroit, 1913; instr. anatomy, Detroit Coll. Medicine (now Med. Coll., Wayne U.), 1913-14; asst. to Harry N. Torrey, surgeon, 1915-17; in gen. practice of surgery, 1919-42; in military service, 1942-46; surgeon, out-patient clinic, Harper Hosp., Detroit, 1915, junior surgeon Harper Hospital, 1919, surgeon, 1934-48, chief, general surgery, 1948-49, and sr. surgeon, cons. staff since 1950; asso. surgeon Childrens Hospital of Mich., 1919, dir. dept. of surgery, 1920, cons., 1953; asso. surgeon Herman Kiefer Hosp., 1926, also chief of staff; non-resident lecturer, dept. surgery U. Mich., 1920-55, prof. emeritus, 1955—, prof. clin. surgery, Wayne U., 1935; now clin. surgeon at Wayne State U.; extramural lecturer, Post Graduate School, U. Mich. cons. surgeon, Detroit Receiving Hospital, Jennings Memorial Hospital, Detroit Orthopedic Clinic, Sinai Hosp., Detroit Meml. Hosp. and Blain Hospital, surg. dir., Mich. Mutual Liability Co., 1946, Cons. Surgeon, Herman Kiefer Hospital, 1946; cons. surgeon Vets. Adminstrn. Hosp., 1946. Mem. adv. bd. to Surgeon Gen. AUS, 1951-52. Member Detroit City Plan commn., 1957—. Served as seaman Michigan Naval Brigade, 1908, hospital steward, 1909; lieut., Med. Corps, U.S. Army, 1917, advancing through grades to maj, 1918; lt. colonel, Med. Reserve Corps, 1919, col., 1925; called to active duty as col., Med. Corps, U.S. Army, 1942; serving as surg. cons., 7th S.C. Hdqrs., Omaha, Neb., discharged as col. June 1946. Hon. Reserve Med. Corps, U.S. Army, 1948. Dir. Cranbrook Sch., 1950-55, chmn. bd. dirs., 1954-55. Legion of Merit, Res., 1946. Diplomate Am. Bd. of Surgery, 1928. Fellow A.C.S. (gov., regent); mem. Soc. Med. Consultants to Armed Forces (pres. 1951-52), Wayne Co. Med. Soc., Mich. State (pres. 1935-36), Medical Society, Detroit Academy Surgery (past pres.), Detroit Academy of Medicine (past pres.) Mich. Soc. Mental Hygiene (past pres.), Detroit Med. Club (hon.), Flint (Michigan) Academy Surgery (hon.), Terre Haute (Ind.) Acad. Med. (hon.), A.M.A. (rep. surg. sect., sci. exhibit 1938-44; del. sect. abdominal and gen. surgery 1942-45), Royal Soc. Medicine (London), Am., So., Western surg. assns., Am. Assn. Surgery Trauma (pres. 1944-45), Central Surg. Assn. (pres. 1941-42), Am., Mich. (past pres.) indsl. med. assns., Detroit Bd. Commerce, Assn. Mil. Surgeons, Société Internationale de Chirurgie, Detroit Bd. of Commerce, A.A.A.S., Phi Rho Sigma, Alpha Omega Alpha. Republican. Episcopalian. Mason (Shriner). Clubs: Detroit, University, Athletic, University Mich. (gov. 1957), Economic, Torch (Detroit). Home: 1130 Parker Av. Office: 1553 Woodward Av., Detroit 26. Died Sept. 2, 1959.

PENCE, Arthur W(illiam), army officer; b. Ft. Monroe, Va., July 18, 1898; s. William Perry and Alice (Dunbar) P.; grad. Poly. Prep. Sch., Bklyn., 1915, Columbia Prep. Sch., Washington, 1916; B.S., U.S. Mil. Acad., 1918; m. Elizabeth E. Fuller, Sept. 5, 1923; children—Arthur William, William Fuller, Betty Sue. Commd. 2d lt., U.S. Army, 1918, advanced through grades to maj. gen., 1948. jr. officer U.S., P.I., 1918-28; in charge R.O.T.C. unit U. Ala., 1928-32; assigned U.S. area engr., Greenville, Miss., 1932-33; in charge tunnel constrn. Ft. Peck Dam, Mont., 1933-37; grad. Command and Gen. Staff Sch., Ft. Leavenworth, Kan., 1937-38; instr. Engr. Sch., Ft. Belvoir, Va., 1938-41; exec. officer constrn. Atlantic bases, N.Y., 1941-42; dep. engr. S.O.S., E.T.O., 1942; engr. Mediterranean Base sect., 1942; comdg. gen. Eastern Base sect., Tunisia, 1943, Peninsular Base sect., Italy, 1943-44; comdt. Sch. Logistics, Ft. Leavenworth, 1944-48; chief of staff Engr. Center, Ft. Belvoir, 1948-49; U.S. dist. engr., Nashville, 1949-50; U.S. div. engr., Cin., 1950-51; asst. chief C.E., Washington, 1951-53; comdg. gen. 6th Armored Div., Ft. Leonard Wood, 1953-54, comdg. gen. Engr. Center, Ft. Belvoir, Va., 1954—. Decorated D.S.M., Legion of Merit with oak leaf cluster, Bronze Star medal, Typhus Commn. medal. Mem. Soc. Am. Mil. Engrs. Office: Hdqrs. TEC, Ft. Belvoir, Va. Deceased.

PENCE, John Wesley, coll. pres.; b. Hamilton, Ill., Jan. 16, 1896; s. Owen Eli and Ella (Miller) P.; A.B., Oberlin Coll., 1917, A.M., 1923; grad. study W.Va. U.; LL.D., Davis and Elkins College, 1953; m. Helen Jones, Nov. 16, 1917; children—Edward Arthur, Robert E. Instr. polit. sci. and econs. Yankton (S.D.) Coll., 1921-23, Kansas City (Mo.) Jr. Coll., 1923-26; instr. Central Mo. State Tchrs. Coll., Warrensburg, summers 1923-26; lectr. W.Va. U., 1940-46; instr., dean men Fairmont (W.Va.) State Coll., 1926-46, dean, 1946-52, pres. Fairmont State Coll. since 1952. Chmn. W.Va. State adv. com. Nat. Youth Adminstrn., 1939-42; chief adminstrv. officer O.P.A., W.Va., 1942; member 4th Civil Service Regional Loyalty Bd., Washington since 1948. Served in U.S. Army, 1917-19. Decorated Croce de Guerra (Italy). Mem. Am. Polit. Sci. Assn., N.E.A., W.Va. Edn. Assn., Phi Beta Kappa, Am. Legion. Presbyn. Club: Rotarian. Mason. Home: Fairmont State Coll., Fairmont, W.Va. Died Nov. 25, 1959.

PENDER, Harold, elec. engr.; b. Tarboro, N.C., Jan. 13, 1879; s. Robert H. and Martha Wallace (Hanks) P.; A.B., Johns Hopkins, 1898, Ph.D., 1901; Sc.D., U. of Pa., 1923; m. Alice Matthews, June 28, 1905; m. 2d, Ailsa Craig MacColl, December 22, 1934; 1 son, Peter Alexander. Teacher McDonogh School, Maryland, 1901-02; instr. Syracuse U., 1902-03; spent winter of 1903 La Sorbonne, Paris, France, upon special invitation of univ. authorities where established beyond question the existence of a magnetic field around a moving electrically charged body; elec. engr. Westinghouse Electric & Mfg. Co., 1903-04, N.Y.C. R.R., 1904-05; associated with Cary T. Hutchinson, elec. engr., New York, 1905-09; sec.-treas. McCall Ferry Power Co., 1905-09; prof. elec. engring., Mass. Inst. Tech., 1909-13; dir. research div., dept. of elec. engring., Mass. Inst. Tech., 1913-14; dir. dept. elec. engring., U. of Pa., 1914-23, dean Moore Sch. Elec. Engring., 1923-49; cons., July 1949—. Mem. Internat. Electrotechnical Com. Fellow Am. Academy Arts and Sciences, Am. Inst. E.E.; mem. Am. Philos. Soc., Franklin Inst. Author: Principles of Electrical Engineering, 1911; Electricity and Magnetism for Engineers, 1918; Direct-current Machinery, 1921; Electric Circuits and Fields (with S. R. Warren, Jr.), 1943. Editor-in-chief Electrical Engineering Handbook (new edit.). Has written numerous scientific and technical papers. Unitarian. Clubs: Merion Golf, Merion Cricket. Home: 313 Hathaway Lane, Wynnewood, Pa. Office: 200 S. 33d St., Philadelphia 4. Died Sept. 5, 1959.

PENDLETON, Moses, pres. Am. Woolen Co.; b. Stonington, Conn., May 6, 1884; s. Nelson A. and Ida (Levy) P.; ed. Stonington High Sch. and business coll., Providence, R.I.; m. Marguerite Claflin, July 19, 1907 (died December 10, 1949); one son, Nelson A. With the American Woolen Co. since 1905, beginning as clerk in yarn dept., 1905, became mgr. yarn dept., 1923, mgr. waste dept., 1925, mgr. wool dept., 1928, gen. mgr., 1930, v.p. and gen. mgr., 1930, pres., 1936. Home: The Plaza, Fifth Av. Office: 225 4th Av., N.Y. City. Died Apr. 23, 1950; buried Stonington, Conn.

PENDLETON, Robert L(arimore), soil scientist; b. Minneapolis, June 25, 1890; s. John Louis and Jessie (Larimore) P.; B.S., U. of Calif., 1914, Ph.D., 1917; student N. India Hindustani Lang. Sch., 1918, N. China Lang. Sch., 1931-33; m. Anne Laurel Miltimore, June 10, 1917. Asst. in soil survey, Calif. Soil Survey, 1914-15; asst. dir. Dept. Agrl., Gwalior State, India, 1918-20, dir., 1920-23; prof. soil technology Coll. Agrl. U. of Philippines, Los Baños, Laguna, 1923-35, head, dept. soils, 1930-35; chief soil technologists Nat. Geol. Survey of China, 1931-33; soil scientist and agriculturist, dept. agr. Siamese Govt., Bangkok, 1935-42; soil scientist Office Fgn. Agrl. Relations, United States Department Agriculture, 1942-52; soil scientist S.T.E.M. to Siam, Mut. Security Agency, 1952-53; and prof. topical soils and agrl. Isaiah Bowman Sch. Geography, Johns Hopkins University, 1946-55, emeritus, 1955; soil technologist to Ministry Agriculture, Thailand Government, 1956—; field work in soils and land use in Central and S. Am., Philippines, Siam, China, India, Central and Brit. W. Africa. Mem. Mindanao Exploration Commn., Philippines, 1939. Adviser FAO Misssion to Siam, 1948. Fellow Belgian Am. Ednl. Found., Belgian Congo, 1948-49. Cons. War Dept., 1942-44, E.C.A., 1949-50. Decorated Knight Comdr., Order Crown Thailand, 1946; The David Livingstone Centenary medal, Am. Geog. Soc., 1950. Hon. mem. Am. Geog. Soc.; mem. Assn. Am. Geographers, Am. Chem. Soc., Am. Soc. Agronomy, Soil Sci. Society Am., Am. Geophys. Union, A.A.A.S.; Siam Society, Bangkok, Sigma Xi, Alpha Zeta. Clubs: Cosmos (Washington), Army and Navy (Manila); Royal Bangkok Sports (Bangkok). Author: Lateritte and Lateritic Soils (with J. A. Prescott), 1952. Translator (from Dutch); Soils of Equatorial Regions, 1944. Editor of Natural History Bull. of the Siam Soc., Bangkok. Address: Kasetsart University, Bangkhen, Bangkok, Thailand; also Box 3519 Terminal Annex, Los Angeles 54. Died June 23, 1957.

PENDLETON, Thomas P., ret. chief topographic engr. U.S. Geol. Survey; b. Nicolaus, Cal., Sept. 25, 1885; s. Samuel Alvah and Carrie (Arens) P.; U. Cal., 1911; m. Florence H. Beel, April 14, 1925; 1 son, Thomas Arens. Topographic mapping U.S. Geol. Survey western U.S., 1905-17, Alaska, 1919, Palestine and Balkan states, 1920-22, chief sect. photo-mapping, 1923-26; chief engr. Brock & Weymouth, Inc., Phila., 1926-30; chief engr. Aerotopograph Corp., Washington, 1931; chief photo compiler U.S. Coast & Geodetic Survey, 1932-33; asst. sect. chief in charge Chattanooga, Tenn. office U.S. Geol. Survey, 1934-41, chief sect. photo-mapping, Washington, 1942, chief topographic engr., Washington, 1943-47. Del. second Consultative Pan-Am. Conf. on Geography and Cartography, Rio de Janeiro, 1944. Received Award for Distinguished Service, Dept of Interior. Past pres. Am. Soc. Photogrammetry (hon. mem.). Served as 2d lt., E.O.R.C., U.S. Army, 1918. Mem. Tau Beta Pi. Club: Cosmos. Author: Map Compilation from Aerial Photographs, U.S.G.S. Bulletin 788. Contbr. numerous articles on photogrammetry to tech. jours. Home: 6005 Dellwood Pl., Bethesda, Md. Died May 28, 1954.

PENFIELD, Clarence Miller, exec. sec., Am. Defense Soc.; b. Elyria, O., Feb. 4, 1882; s. Myron F. and Minnie (Miller) P.; unmarried. Exec. sec. Am. Defense Soc.; sec. and dir. Bill of Rights Commemorative Soc., New York City; editor American Defense; Major S.R., retired. Former treas. and member council. Reserve Officers Assn. (Manhattan Chapter); officer Foch Nat. Memorial. Former Comptroller, American Arbitration Association. Home: 210 Riverside Dr., N.Y.C. 25. Office: 225 5th Av., N.Y.C. 10. Died Nov. 1951.

PENFIELD, Thornton B., clergyman; b. Madura, S. India, Nov. 13, 1867; s. Thornton B. and Charlotte E. (Hubbard) P.; grad. St. Johnsbury (Vt.) Acad., 1886; B.A., Columbia, 1890; M.A., New York U., 1893; grad. Union Theol. Sem., 1893; Ph.D., Taylor Univ., Upland, Ind., 1903; D.D., Central University, Denver, Colo., 1922; m. Martha Mee Martin, Sept. 12, 1894; children—Charlotte Martin (wife of Dr. Reginald M. Atwater), Rev. Thornton Bancroft, Paul Livingstone. Ordained Presbyn. ministry, 1893; asst. sec. Presbyn. Bd. Home Missions, 1893-98; sec. Brooklyn Central Y.M.C.A., 1898-1900; sec. Internat. Com. Y.M.C.A.'s, 1900-14; personnel sec. Dept. of East, War Work Council Y.M.C.A., 1914-18; same Inter-ch. World Movement, 1918-20; metropolitan sec. Gen. Council Presbyn. Ch. U.S.A., 1922-24; pastor Teaneck Church, 1915-22, Norwood (N.J.) Ch., 1922-31; supt. Nat. Missions, Presbyn. Ch. Northern N.J., 1928-48; pres. Silver Bay Assn. for Christian Confs. and Training, N.Y., 1948—, pres. Bergen Co. Council of Chs.; moderator Presbytery of Jersey City, 1938-39; pres. bd. of trustees Synod of N.J. Exec. sec. Camp Merritt Religious Activities Com. and sec. Food Conservation Commn., Northern N.J., World War; sec. 6 Student Volunteer convs. and of Latin-Am. Conv., Panama. Mem. bd. dirs. Eastern Assn. Training Sch. for Y.M.C.A. Secs. Mem. Hymn Soc., Delta Upsilon. Mason. Republican. Clubs: Clergy, Town Hall, Columbia Univ. Club, Union Theol. Sem. Club, Delta Upsilon. Home: 156 Maple St., Englewood, N.J. Office: 347 Madison Av., N.Y.C. Died Feb. 4, 1958.

PENHALE, Clayton Archbold, ret. pub.; b. Albuquerque, N.M., Dec. 23, 1883; s. George Francis and Alice (Thornberry) P.; ed. by pvt. tutors; student Peddie Inst., Hightstown, N.J., 1900-04; m. Frances McEutee, Nov. 9, 1916 (div. 1930); children—Garet Osmund, Jeanne (Mrs. Wm. C. Bryan; m. 2d, Gertrude Atmore Fellows, Sept. 23, 1930). Engaged in real estate bus., N.Y.C., 1908-12; mem. editorial staff The Annalist (econ. weekly), N.Y.C., 1912-17; financial and bus. editor N.Y. Tribune, 1917-20; mem. editorial staff Standard Statistics Co., v.p., 1920-40, pres. 1940, pres. successor corp. Standard-Poor's Corp., 1940-46, retired, 1946. Republican. Methodist. Club: New York Stock Exchange Luncheon. Home: 180 Summit Av., Summit, N.J. Died Sept. 26, 1950; buried Hanover (N.J.) Cemetery.

PENICK, Edwin Anderson, bishop; b. Frankfort, Ky., Apr. 4, 1887; s. Edwin Anderson and Mary Atchinson (Shipman) P.; A.B., U. of the South, 1908, D.D., 1922; A.M., Harvard, 1909; grad. Theol. Sem. of Va., 1912, D.D., 1922; honorary LL.D., U. of North Carolina, 1948; married Caroline Inglesby Dial, June 20, 1917; children—Edwin Anderson, George Dial, Charles Inglesby. Deacon, 1912, priest, 1913, P.E. Ch.; rector St. Paul's Ch., Bennettsville, S.C., 1912-14, Ch. of the Good Shepherd, Columbia, S.C., 1914-17, St. Peter's Ch., Charlotte, N.C., 1919-22; consecrated bishop coadjutor Diocese of N.C., Oct. 15, 1922, bishop Diocese of N.C., Dec. 27, 1932. Ex-chmn. N.C. Commn. on Interracial Cooperation; ex-pres N.C. Council of Chs. Civilian chaplain Episcopal Ch. War Commn., Camp Jackson, S.C., Feb.-Sept. 1918; 1st lt. chaplain U.S. Army; hon. discharged, Jan. 1919. Trustee U. of the South, St. Augustine's Coll., Raleigh (pres. bd.); pres. bd. trustees St. Mary's Sch. (Raleigh); pres. bd. mgrs., Thompson Orphanage, Charlotte; vice pres. House of Bishops, 1946. Mem. Alpha Tau Omega, Phi Beta Kappa. Democrat. Club: Rotary (hon.). Home: Raleigh, N.C. Died Apr. 6, 1959.

PENMAN, John Simpson, clergyman, author; b. Glasgow, Scotland, Mar. 10, 1864; s. Robert Hedderwick and Janet Russell (Swan) P.; brought to U.S. at age of 5; B.A., Coll. City N.Y., 1884; grad. Union Theol. Sem., 1887; M.A., Columbia, 1912; m. Georgie Ransom Law, June 3, 1890 (died Mar. 4, 1941); children—Janet Russell (Mrs. T. Evans Baxter), Edith Law (Mrs. Walter Bogner), Margaret E. (Mrs. David D. Jacobus, dec.), Mrs. Martha P. Robinson. Ordained to Presbyn. ministry, 1887; asst. pastor, Yonkers, 1887-88; pastor Irvington-on-Hudson, 1888-93; left Presbyn Ch., 1893, on account of Briggs controversy and trial; pastor Central Congl. Ch., Bangor, Me., 1894-1905, Poughkeepsie, N.Y., 1905-10; student, Oxford, Eng., 1911; devoted attention during later yrs. to writing and study of polit. history. Mem. Cambridge (Mass.) Hist. Soc. Republican. Clubs: Columbia University (N.Y. C.); Authors' (London, Eng.); Authors' (Boston). Author: Poverty the Challenge of the Church, 1915; The Irresistible Movement of Democracy, 1923; Lafayette and Three Revolutions, 1929. Home: Jefferson, N.H. Died Aug. 30, 1949.

PENN, John Roby, business exec.; b. Reno, Pa., Aug. 11, 1875; s. John R. and Clara (Darnell) P.; student Amherst Coll., Amherst, Mass., 1896-97; m. Olive Yerian, Dec. 31, 1918; 1 son, John R., III. Pres. Ill. Pipe Line Co., 1914-17; v.p. Mid-West Refining Co., 1917-19; pres. Tex. Pacific Coal and Oil Co., 1920-26, since 1933, chmn. exec. com. since 1950; dir., mem. exec. com. Fort Worth Nat. Bank; mem. city council, Ft. Worth, 1926-33. Mem. Am. Petrol. Inst., Independent Petrol. Assn. of Am. Dem. Methodist. Mason (Shriner). Clubs: Fort Worth, Rivercrest Country. Home: 4936 Crestline Road. Office: 2300 Fort Worth National Bank Bldg., Fort Worth. Died Feb. 8, 1958; buried Greenwood Cemetery, Fort Worth.

PENNINGS, B. H., college pres.; b. Gemert, Holland, June 9, 1861; s. John and Mary (Hoeveners) P.; student Gemert Coll., 1873-79, Abbey Berne (Holland), 1879-86; LL.D. (hon.), Marquette-Univ., 1937. Founder, pres. St. Norbert College, West De Pere, Wis., 1898—. Address: 103 Grant St., West De Pere, Wis. Died Mar. 17, 1955; buried St. Norbert Abbey, DePere, Wis.

PENNINGTON, Mary Engle, chemist; b. Nashville, Oct. 8, 1872; d. Henry and Sarah B. (Molony) Pennington; Ph.D., U. Pa., 1895, U. fellow in botany, 1895-97; fellow physiol. chemistry Yale, 1897-98. Research worker dept. hygiene U. Pa., 1898-1901; pres. Phila. Clin. Lab., 1900-08; bacteriologist Municipal Lab., Phila., 1904-07; bacteriol. chemistry, bur. of chemistry U.S. Dept. Agr., 1905-08, chief of food research lab., 1908-19; in charge of dept. of research and development Am. Balsa Co., N.Y., 1919-22; consultation and research, 1922—; mem. adv. bd. Subsistence Research and Development Br., Mil. Planning Div. Office Q.M. Gen.; cons. Food Control Div., War Shipping Administrn. Fellow A.A.A.S., Am. Soc. Refrigerating Engrs. (dir.); mem. Am. Chem. Soc., Soc. Biol. Chemists, Am. Inst. Refrigeration, Inst. Food Technol., Inst. Am. Poultry Industries, Poultry Sci. Assn., Sigma Xi, Kappa Kappa Gamma, Iota Sigma Pi. Awarded Francis P. Garvan gold medal by the Am. Chem. Soc., 1940. Home: 100 Riverside Drive. Address: 233 Broadway, N.Y.C. 7. Died Dec. 27, 1952.

PENNOYER, Albert Sheldon (pĕn-noi'ĕr), artist; b. Oakland, Calif., Apr. 5, 1888; s. Albert Adams and Virginia (Edmands) P.; prep. edn., Chateau de Lancy, Geneva, Switzerland, and Lawrenceville (N.J.) Sch.; student U. of Calif., 1908-09; art edn., École des Beaux Arts, in architecture, 1912, in painting at Acad. de la Grande Chaumiére, 1913 (both of Paris), Pa. Acad. Fine Arts, Phila.; pupil of Casciaro, Naples, of Los, Rome, of Harold Speed, London. Represented Met. Mus. Art, N.Y.C., deYoung Mus. and Cal. Palace Legion of Honor, San Francisco. Served as sergeant Camouflage C.E., United States Army, 1917-20; 2d lt. O.R.C., 1922-28. Capt. U.S. Air Forces (camouflage), 1942; capt. Corps of Engrs. (camouflage), 1943. Member American Water Color Club; Monuments, Fine Arts and Archives Subcommission, Italy, 1944-45; Psi Upsilon. Republican. Episcopalian. Clubs: Century Association (New York); Sanctum (Litchfield, Conn.) Studio: 8 E. 62d St., N.Y.C. 21. Died Aug. 17, 1957; buried Britsih Cemetery, Madrid, Spain.

PENNYPACKER, Bevan Aubrey, lawyer; b. Phila., July 29, 1881; s. Samuel Whitaker and Virginia Earl (Broomall) P.; grad. Willam Penn Carter Sch., 1898; B.S., U. Pa., 1902, LL.B., 1905; m. Katharine Roberts Stackhouse, Oct. 19, 1907 (dec. 1933); 1 son, Samuel W., II; m. 2d Mary R. Ferguson, Nov. 21, 1935. Admitted to Pa. bar, 1905, practiced with firm of Morgan, Lewis & Bockius, 1905—, mem. firm, 1922—. Mem. Am., Pa. and Phila. bar assns., Phi Delta Phi. Clubs: Union League, Phila. Cricket, The Midday (Phila.); University of Pennsylvania (N.Y. City). Home: 6636 McCallum St., Phila. 19. Office: Fidelity-Philadelphia Trust Bldg., Phila. 9. Died July 27, 1954; buried Phoenixville, Pa.

PENROSE, Charles, cons. engineer; b. Philadelphia, Pa., Jan. 24, 1886; s. Walter Elliot and Emily (Thompson) P.; student Prep. Sch., Dresden, Germany, 1896-97; grad. Episcopal Acad., Phila., 1903; B.S., Princeton, 1907, E.E., 1910; LL.D., Cumberland University, Lebanon, Tenn., 1940; D.Eng., South Dakota School Mines and Technology, 1944; Litt.D., Ursinus Coll., Pa., 1951; L.H.D., Whitman Coll., Walla Walla, Washington, 1951; m. Beatrice de'Este, June 4, 1910 (deceased); children—Beatrice (Mrs. John Cadwalader, Jr.) (deceased), John Rowan, Julian d'Este, Charles; m. 2d, Virginia Carlisle, June 11, 1930; 1 daughter, Barbara (Mrs. Edmund Charles Tarbell, II). Began as assistant to elec. engr. of Phila. Electric Co., 1910; engr. in charge erection Schuykill No. 2 Sta. for same co., 1914-15, later other power constrn. work; with Day & Zimmermann, Inc., cons. engr., Philadelphia, New York and Chicago, 1917—, asst. gen. mgr., 1920-32, v.p., 1932-56, cons., 1956—; pres. Newcomen Publs. in N.A., Kittery, Me., 1947—. Progress engr. A.U.S. Supply Base, Phila., 1918-19. Special consultant to U.S. Govt. in Federal Housing Adminstrn., 1934. Cyrus Fogg Brackett lecturer Princeton Univ.; Henry J. Fuller lecturer, Worcester Poly. Institute; served as mem. Bartol Research Foundation Com. (administering Henry C. Bartol Found., Phila. Fellow Royal Soc. Arts (London). Mem. Am. Soc. Mech. Engrs., Am. Inst. Elec. Engrs., Franklin Inst. (bd. mgrs.), Pa. Electric Assn., Nat. Assn. Cotton Mfrs. (Boston), Am. Cotton Mfrs.' Assn. (Charlotte, N.C.), Pa. State Chamber of Commerce (industrial relations Com.), Princeton Engring. Assn. of N.Y. (past pres.), Md. Acad. of Sciences, Hist. Soc. of Pa., N.H. Hist. Soc., Hist. Soc. of N.M., R.I. Hist. Soc.; Old Dartmouth Hist. Soc. (Mass.); English Speaking Union, St. George Soc. of N.Y., Engrs. Soc. Winston-Salem, N.C. (hon.); Constrn. Div. Assn. (U.S. Army), Newcomen Soc. of England (council, London; Am. sr. v.p.); The Guild of Brackett Lecturers of Princeton Univ. (exec. com.); The Pilgrims of the U.S.; Pa. Soc. of New York; assoc. mem. Am. Soc. Civil Engrs., Econ. Hist. Assn., Portsmouth Athenaeum (Proprietership), Piscataqua Pioneers, Pi Tau Sigma (hon.). Mem. adminstrative bd., Am. Engring. Council. Republican. Episcopalian. Clubs: Princeton, Midday (Phila.); Princeton (New York); Hope (Providence, R.I.); Charter (Princeton, N.J.). Author: New England's Power Resources, 1922; Power in Pennsylvania, 1925; American Colonial Transportation (1629-1783), (1933); Industrial Surveys, 1935; New England—Today! (Boston), 1937; Industry and The State (Alabama), 1937; 1838 April Fourth 1938, (Atlantic Centenary Address, New York), 1938; Initiative for Americans, 1938: . . . That This Nation 1940; Retrospect of Mountain Pilgrimage, 1940; They Faced to the East: 1784, 1941; To The Sea for Whales: 1846; . . . Whether in New Hampshire or South Dakota, 1944; Brackett of Maine: A Fragment of Northern New England in the 1850's, 1945; Look Towards the Sea—There is England (1946); Samuel Vaughan Merrick (1801-1870)—Merchant, Engineer, Industrialist, First President of The Pennsylvania Railroad (1946); Old Kittery, 1647—Land of Adventure, 1947; British Royalty in North America, 1860; vice Admiral James Pine, U.S.C.G., 1947; John P. Benson; American Artist (1865-1947), 1948; William Carter Dickerman, (1874-1946), Locomotive Builder, Scholar, Good Citizen, 1951; William C. Dickerman (1874-1946) Never his Courage Faltered!, 1951; Two Men—and their Contributions in Two Countries, 1951; The Sands of Times, 1953; George B. Cortelyou (1862-1940), 1954; L. F. Loree, 1955; Newcomb Carlton, 1956. First Newcomen lecturer before U.S. Coast Guard Acad., New London, Conn. Home: Hilltop Cottage, R.F.D. 2, West Chester, Pa. and Bayberry House, Kittery Point, Me. Office: 500 Fifth Av., N.Y.C. 36; 1700 Samsom St., Phila. 3; P.O. Box 113, Downington, Pa. Died May 16, 1958; buried West Chester, Pa.

PENROSE, Stephen B(easley) L(innard), Jr., coll. pres.; b. Walla Walla, Wash., Mar. 19, 1908; s. Stephen B.L. and Mary Deming (Shipman) P.; A.B. Whitman Coll., 1928; Ph.D., Columbia, 1934; LL.D. (honorary), Whitman College, 1953; married Margaret Pressly Dale, June 29, 1934; children—Margaret Dale, Mary Shipman, Stephen B.L. III. Instr. in physics Am. Univ. of Beirut, 1928-31; instr. in philosophy and psychology Whitman Coll., 1934-37, dean of men, 1936-37; asst. prof. philosophy and psychology Rockford (Ill.) Coll., 1937-38; asst. dir. Near East Coll. Assn., N.Y. City, 1938-42; pres. Am. Univ. of Beirut and Internat. Coll. since 1948. Served as spl. asst. Office Strategic Services, 1942-45; asst. to sec. of defense, Washington, 1947-48. Adviser U.S. delegation to 3d Gen. Conf. of UNESCO,

1948; pres. UNESCO Internat. Com. for Translation of the Classics. Corporate mem.-at-large Am. Bd. Commrs. of Foreign Missions. Comdr., Order of Polonia Restituta (Free Poland), 1950. Recipient Bronze Star Medal (U.S.), Comdr. Order of Orange Nassau, Netherlands for wartime services, 1948. Mem. Am. Philos. Assn., Royal Central Asian Soc. London, Phi Beta Kappa, Beta Theta Pi. Republican. Cong'ist. Clubs: St. George (Beirut); Wagon Wheelers (Walla Walla); Century Association (New York City, New York). Author: Reputation and Influence of Francis Bacon in the 17th Century, 1934; That They May Have Life, History of American University of Beirut, 1941; The Palestine Problem: Retrospect and Prospect, 1954. Contbr. to The Asian Legacy and American Life, 1945. Address: American University of Beirut, Beirut, Lebanon. Died Dec. 9, 1954.

PEPPER, Charles Hovey, painter; b. Waterville, Me., Aug. 27, 1864; s. George Dana Boardman and Annie (Grassie) P.; A.B., Colby Coll., 1889, A.M., 1891, L.H.D., 1912; studied Art Students' League, 1890-93, at Paris in Aman-Jean Atelier and Julian Acad., under Jean Paul Laurens and Benjamin Constant, 1893-95; m. Frances Coburn, July 16, 1889; children—Stephen C., Eunice P. (Mrs. Langenbach). Resided at Paris, France, 1893-99, at Concord, Mass., 1899-1933, Brookline, Mass., 1933—. Exhibited 30 works at L'Art Nouveau Gallery, Paris, 1898; 40 at Rembrandt Gallery, London, 1899; 57 at Doll-Richards Gallery, Boston, 1903; 39 painted in Japan, at Kimball Gallery, Boston; 26 works of North Country Guides, Doll-Richards Gallery, Boston, Mass., 1921-22; also in Salon Champs Elysée, Paris France, and at Berlin, Vienna, Phila., Chgo., N.Y. C.; annual exhibitor 15 Gallery, N.Y.C. Went to Japan, 1903, painting and studying the old art of xylographs; traveled in Java, Burmah, India-Ceylon, 1904. Represented in Museum Fine Arts, Boston; Fogg Art Museum, Cambridge; Worcester Art Museum; R.I. Sch. of Design; Mills Coll., Cal.; Colby Coll., Me.; J. T. Spaulding Collection, Boston, other pvt. collections. Mem. N.Y. Water Color Clubs, Copley Soc., Phi Beta Kappa, Delta Kappa Epsilon. Clubs: City, Sr. Bololph; Concord Social Circle, Middlesex, Republican. Home: 66 Griggs Rd., Brookline, Mass. Died Aug. 25, 1950; buried Concord, Mass.

PEPPERDAY, Thomas M., newspaper pub.; b. Brooklyn, N.Y., Sept. 16, 1886; s. Joseph A. and Mary (Fox) P.; mother's name Mary P. Thompson (dec.); ed. pub. schs., N.Y. Prep. Sch.; m. Helen Merrell, 1927. Pub. Albuquerque (N.M.) Herald since 1922, consolidated with Albuquerque Journal under name of latter, 1926; chmn. bd. Journal Pub. Co.; pres. Albuquerque Publishing Company. Served as capt. arty., U.S. Army in France 2 years, World War I. Mem. Associated Press. Republican. Presbyterian. Mason. Home: 1625 Los Alamos Dr. Office: 703 Silver Av. S.W., Albuquerque, N.M. Died May 16, 1956; buried Albuquerque.

PÉRARD, Victor Semon (pā-rär), artist; b. Paris, France, Jan. 16, 1870; s. Victor A. and Theresa (Pardessus) P.; studied art at École des Beaux Arts, Paris, under Gérôme; also Art Students' League, New York; m. at New York, Ernestine Fezandié. Illustrator for Harper's, Scribner's; instr. Traphagen Art Sch.; formerly instr. Cooper Inst. Represented in the Museum of the City of New York, New York Pub. Library Metropolitan Museum of Art (New York City), The Mariners' Museum (Newport-News, Va.), Library of Congress, National Museum (Washington, D.C.), John H. Vanderpoel Art Assn. Gallery, Rochester (N.Y.) Atheneum. Mem. Art Students League (life), Illustrators Society. Clubs: Salmagundi, and Kit Kat. Author: Anatomy and Drawing; Hands and Their Construction; How to Draw—Dogs, Horses, Trees, Heads and Faces, The Human Figure, Children; Blackboard Fun. Address: Bellport, L.I., N.Y. Died July 9, 1957; buried Mt. Bethel, Plainfield, N.J.

PERCY, Nelson Mortimer, surgeon; b. Dexter, Ia., Nov. 7, 1875; s. Mortimer and Mary F. (Amidon) P.; prep. edn. Dexter Normal Sch.; M.D., Rush Med. Coll., Chgo., 1899; m. Alfie Hokland, Feb. 5, 1927. Practiced in Chgo., 1901—; surgeon in chief Augustana Hospital, 1925-35, chief of staff, 1935-57, emeritus chief of staff, 1957—; senior attending surgeon St. Mary's of Nazareth Hospital; professor emeritus clinical surgery University Illinois. Served as lt. col. U.S. Army in France, 1918-19, organized Base Hosp. 11. Founder mem. Am. Bd. Surgery. Fellow Am. Surg. Assn., A.C.S..; mem. Chgo. Surg. Soc., A.M.A., Ill. State, Chgo. med. socs., Am. Assn. for Study of Goiter, Mil. Order World Wars, Assn. Commerce and Industry, Art. Inst., Chgo. Natural Mus.,, Phi Rho Sigma. Republican. Methodist. Clubs: University; Lake Shore. Author (with Albert J. Ochsner) Clinical Surgery, 1912. Contbr.; Ochsner's Surgical Diagnosis and Treatment, 1920. Home: 2130 Lincoln Park W. Office: 2051 Sedgwick St., Chgo. Died Oct. 10, 1958; buried Meml. Park, Evanston, Ill.

PERGLER, Charles (pĕrg'lĕr); b. Liblin, Bohemia, Mar. 6, 1882; s. Francis and Josephine (Zpevacek) P.; brought to U.S., 1890; grad. business coll., Prague, Bohemia; LL.B., Chicago Kent Coll. of Law, 1908; LL.M., American U., 1924, D.C.L., 1927; LL.D., Nat. U., Washington, 1928; m. Ella Strunc, Mar. 25, 1905; children—Ella, Carl, Vera. Newspaper work, Chicago, 1903-05; practiced law in Howard County, Ia., 1908-17; active in movement for freeing oppressed people under rule of Austria-Hungary, during World War; represented the Czechoslovaks at Congress of Small Nations, Washington, D.C., 1917; accredited as diplomatic rep. of Czechoslovaks in U.S., Nov. 1918; Czechoslovak minister to Japan, 1920-21; Washington rep. Czechoslovak Nat. Council of America, 1924-27; rep. in Czechoslovak parliament, 1929-31; elected mem. Prague City Council, 1931. Dean Sch. of Economics and Govt., Nat. U., and dir. Sch. Grad. Studies, 1933-36; dean National University School of Law and prof. constitutional law and jurisprudence, 1936-46, also lecturer on government, Catholic University of America, School of Social Science, 1944-46, lecturer on constitutional law, Grad. Sch., American U., 1932-34; Chief, Legal Opinions Bur. Pres. Prop. Claims Commn., Special Adviser to Military Gov., Korea, 1946-48. Mem. Am., Ia. State, D.C. bar assns., Nat. Panel of Arbitrators, Am. Arbitration Assn., Sigma Nu Phi (hon.). Unitarian. Mason. Club: Cosmos (Washington) Author: The Czechoslovak State, 1919; also (in Prague) Towards the National State; American Essays; America in the Struggle for Czechoslovak Independence, 1926 (also pub. Prague); Judicial Interpretation of International Law in the United States; The American Constitutional System (Prague), 1929; Delivered addresses on problems of internat. politics and internat. law before So. Polit. Inst., 1925-27, U. Md., summer 1937; speaker under auspicies Fgn. Policy Assn., 1929-30. Contbr. various law jours. and reviews. Home: 1661 Crescent Pl. N.W. Office: 1225 New York Av., Washington 5. Died Aug. 14, 1954.

PERIGORD, Paul (pā-rē-gôr'), univ. prof.; b. Toulouse, France, Oct. 25, 1882; s. Jean and Marie (Isalier) P.; came to U.S. 1902; grad. U. of Toulouse, France, 1902; A.M., U. of Chicago, 1912, Columbia, 1913; grad. study, Harvard, 1914, U. of Paris, 1923; Ph.D., U. of Minn., 1924; m. Emily McBride, Feb. 22, 1920; children—Lorraine McBride, James McBride. Prof. ethics, St. Paul (Minn.) Sem., 1907-14; prof. European hist., Cal. Inst. Tech., Pasadena, 1919-24; prof. French civilization, 1924—, acting dean Coll. of Letters and Science, 1931-32, U. of Cal. at Los Angeles; visiting prof. Santa Barbara College, 1947-49. Commanding captain inf., French Army, 1914-17; mil. instr. N.E. Div., Camp Devens, Mass. 1917; mem. French High Commn., Washington, D.C., 1918-19; Am. rep. Com. o Intellectual Cooperation, League of Nations, Geneva, 1923; mem. advisory bd. Internat. Labor Office, Washington Br. Ex-pres. Pasadena Community Guild and Pasadena Community Playhouse; mem. advisory bd. Nat. Acad. of Am. Lit. Chevalier, Legion of Honor, 1919, Officer, 1937. Nat. Advisor of Girl Scouts, 1940—; pres. of "Free France" for Southern Cal., 1940—; chmn. United Nations Com. Southern Cal. 1942-43. Corr. member Université de la Mediterranée (Nice); member A.A.A.S., Am. Philological Association, Am. Association University Profs., Soc. Comparative Legislation (Paris), Alliance Française of Pasadena (hon. pres.), Salon Français of Hollywood (hon. pres.), Alliance Française of Los Angeles (v.p.), Scabbard and Blade, Phi Beta Kappa, Phi Delta Phi, Sigma Delta Pi, Theta Xi, Lambda Sigma Pi (nat. ednl. dir.). Decorated Chevalier Legion of Honor, Cross of War, Officier d'Académie (French), Officer Polish Order Polonia Restituta. Clubs: University, Kiwanis (Pasadena); Sunset (Los Angeles, California). Author: The International Labor Organization, 1926; Great American Personalities (3 vols.); Our Intellectual and Spiritual Heritage—Emerson, Whittier and Lowell; Foreign Policies of France, 1939; Politics—The Old Order and the New, 1941; The Outlook for European Civilization, 1944. Asso. editor Calif. Southland, 1920-23. Home: 2129 Ridge Lane, Santa Barbara, Cal. Died Nov. 1959.

PERITZ, Ismar John (pĕ'rīts), educator; b. Breslau, Germany, Jan. 8, 1863; s. Adolph and Sarah (Wieluner) P.; student Friederichs and Elisabeth gymnasia, Breslau; came to America, 1883; student Drew Theol. Sem., Madison, N.J., 1884-87; A.M., Harvard, 1893, Ph.D., 1898; Litt.D., Syracuse U., 1922, S.T.D., 1933; m. Caroline Louisa Irwin Cooper, Nov. 27, 1885. Changed faith from Judaism to Christianity at age of 17; pastor of chs. in N.Y. Conf. M.E. Ch., 1887-93; prof. Semitic langs. and lit. Syracuse U., 1896—, Willard Ives prof. English Bible, 1904-33, now prof. emeritus; resident lectr. Newman Bibl. Inst., Jerusalem, Syria, 1913. Del. Ecumenical Meth. Conf., London, 1921. Mem. Phi Beta Kappa, Am. Oriental Soc., Soc. Bibl. Lit. and Exegesis. Club: Syracuse Harvard. Author articles in Ency. Biblica, 1899-1903; also articles in sci. and popular mags., Sunday Sch. notes. Author: Old Testament History, 1915. Editor emeritus, Journal of Bible and Religion. Contbr. to Abington Bible Commentary. Home: Lake Bluff, Wolcott, N.Y.; and 1121 Washington Av., Winter Park, Fla.* Died July 16, 1950.

PERKINS, Carroll N., lawyer; b. South Penobscot, Me., Sept. 9, 1880; s. Horace D. and Augusta (Norton) P.; A.B., Colby Coll., Waterville, Me., 1904, LL.D., 1950; LL.B., Harvard, 1907; m. Emily F. Fales, June 18, 1907; children—Priscilla (Mrs. Gordon W. Schumacher), Frances N., Carroll N., Horace D., Roger W. Admitted to Me. bar, 1907, since practiced Waterville; partner Johnson & Perkins, 1911-17, Perkins & Weeks, 1921-39, Perkins, Weeks & Hutchins, 1940—; v.p., dir. Central Me. Power Co.; dir. N.E. Pub. Service Co. Mem. Me. State Bd. Legal Examiners, 1914-31. Trustee Colby Coll. Mem. Am. Me. State (pres., 1937-39) bar assns., Am. Law Inst. Home: 11 Park St. Office: Depositors Trust Bldg., Waterville, Me. Died June 29, 1954; buried Waterville.

PERKINS, Edwin Ruthven, Jr., former railway exec.; b. Cleveland, O., Apr. 23, 1879; s. Edwin Ruthven and Harriet (Pelton) P.; ed. Western Reserve Acad.; m. Emma M. Hunt, Nov. 28, 1900; 1 son, Edwin R, III. Office The Cleveland & Mahoning Valley Ry. Co., 1910-34, pres., 1915-34; retired, 1934. Republican. Presbyterian. Club: Union. Home: 2517 Guilford Rd., Cleveland Heights, O. Died Jan. 1960.

PERKINS, George Walbridge, exec., adminster.; b. Riverdale-on-Hudson, N.Y., May 2, 1895; s. George Walbridge and Eveline (Ball) P.; student Hill Sch., 1910-13; Litt.B., Princeton U., 1917, LL.D., 1957; M.A., Columbia, 1921; m. Katharine Trowbridge, June 19, 1917 (died 1918); m. 2d, Linn Merck, Dec. 17, 1921; children—Penelope, George Walbridge, Jr., Linn Marie-Anne. Sec. Princeton Endowment Fund Com., 1919-20; executor George Walbridge Perkins Estate since 1920; exec. sec. to Postmaster Gen. Hays, Washington, 1921-22; asst. treas. Rep. State Com., 1922; exec. vice-pres., dir. Merck & Co., Inc., 1927-48, treas., 1927-June 1947, now mem. bd. of directors; chief industries div. E.C.A., Paris, July 1948-Aug. 1949; asst. sec. of state for European affairs, 1949-53; U.S. permanent rep. N. Atlantic Council and Orgn. European Econ. Cooperation, rank of ambassador, 1955-57; dir. various corps. Dir. of American Council on NATO, 1957. Served as pvt., regimental supply sergeant, 2d lt., F.A., 1st Div., U.S. Army, A.E.F., Army of Occupation, 1917-19. Col., Chem. Warfare Service, U.S. Army, 1942-45; service in European, Pacific Theatres, and Washington. Awarded Legion of Merit. Mem. Palisades Interstate Park Commn., 1922—, pres., 1945—; pres. bd. edn. Cold-Spring-on-Hudson, N.Y., 1933-42; dir., treas. N.Y.C. YMCA, 1935-40; trustee Hill School, Pottstown, Pa., pres., 1946-48, 53-54; trustee of Robert College, Istanbul, pres., 1954; alumni trustee Princeton, 1935-39; adv. bd. Inst. Nutrition Scis., Columbia. Republican. Presbyterian. Clubs: University, Union League, Princeton, City, National Republican, Down Town Assn., Century Assn., Knickerbocker (N.Y.C.); Chevy Chase, Metropolitan (Washington). Home: Glynwood Farm, Cold Spring-on-Hudson, N.Y. Office: 342 Madison Av., N.Y.C. Died Jan. 1960.

PERKINS, Harold E(verett), newspaper exec.; b. Rushvlle, Ind., Aug. 20, 1900; s. Walter and Margaret (Tharp) P.; A.B., Wabash Coll., 1922; m. Kathrine Wyatt, June 6, 1924. Nat. advt. mgr., Indianapolis (Ind.) News, 1923-28, Indianapolis Star, 1928; advt. dir. Pittsburgh (Pa.) Press, 1929-40; bus. mgr. Minneapolis (Minn.) Star and Tribune, 1940-47, v.p. and dir. since 1947. sec. Mem. Beta Theta Pi, Phi Beta Kappa. Republican. Methodist (mem. ofcl. bd. Hennepin Av. Ch.). Mason (Shriner). Clubs: Rotary, Minneapolis, Minnekahda. Home: 1273 W. Minnehaha Parkway, Minneapolis 19. Office: 427 Portland Av., Mpls. 15. Died Apr. 28, 1952; buried Rushville, Ind.

PERKINS, Henry Augustus, physicist; b. Hartford, Connecticut, November 14, 1873; s. Edward H. and Mary E. (Dwight) P.; A.B., Yale, 1896; M.A., E.E., Columbia, 1899; graduate student Yale, 1900-02; University of Paris, 1908-09; College de France, 1921-22; Sc.D., Trinity, 1920; L.H.D., Gallaudet, 1944; m. Olga Flinch, April 8, 1903; children—Henry Augustus, Evelyn Ingeborg (Mrs. Amyas Ames). Prof. physics, Trinity Coll., Hartford, 1902-42, ret. 1942, recalled 1943, ret. 1946; acting pres. 1915-16 and 1919-20. Dir. Phoenix Mutual Life Ins. Co. Pres. bd. Am. School for Deaf, 1913—; president Hartford Park Board, 1919-20; president Hartford Public Library, 1945—. Chmn. of Bd. of Avon Old Farms Sch., 1946—. Mem. Am Inst. Elec. Engrs., Am. Physical Soc., Société Française de Physique, Am. Alpine Club, Explorers' Club, Alpha Delta Phi (pres., 1949—), Phi Beta Kappa, Sigma Xi, Elihu (Yale). Clubs: Hartford, Hartford Golf, Century (N.Y.); Graduate (New Haven). Contbr. to Am. Jour. of Science, Le Radium, Science, Am. Journal of Physics, Physical Review, Journal de Physique. Author: Thermodynamics, 1912; College Physics, 1938; College Physics, Abridged, 1941; Basic College Physics, 1949; also articles in Educational Review, Yale Review, North American Review, Am. Mercury, Physical Review. Research in velocity of magnetism, discontinuous discharges, metallic conductivity, residual magnetism, etc. Address: 55 Forest St., Hartford, Conn. Died July, 1959.

PERKINS, John Carroll, clergyman; b. Auburn, Me., June 6, 1862; s. John William and Martha (McKenney) P.; A.B., Bates Coll., 1882. A.M., 1885; studied univs. of Berlin and Marburg, 1886-87; A.M., S.T.B., Harvard, 1891; D.D., Bowdoin, 1904, Bates Coll., 1932; m. Edith Burnside Milliken, June 28, 1892. Prin. of West Lebanon (Maine) Acad., 1882-83; tchr. Roxbury Latin Sch., 1883-86; ordained unitarian ministry, 1891; pastor First Parish, Portland, Me., 1890-1913, University Ch., Seattle, 1914-26; minister in charge, later minister King's Chapel, Boston, 1927-33, now minister emeritus. Mem. Colonial Soc. of Mass., Soc. Colonial Wars, Mayflower Soc. (Me.), Phi Beta Kappa. Hon. mem. Portland Rossini Club, Saturday Evening Club Portland. Hon. naval chaplain, Seattle; ch. extension rep. N. Pacific (Unit.) Conf.; 1st v.p. Pacific Unitarian Conf. Clubs: Fraternity (Portland); Cosmos, Clerical Study (Seattle); Union (Boston). Author: Annals of King's Chapel, Vol. III, 1940. Home: 90 Commonwealth Av. Office: 27 Marlborough St., Boston 16. Deceased.*

PERKINS, S. Albert, publisher; b. Boston, Mass., May 6, 1865; s. George Goodwin and Emily (Cleveland) P.; pub. sch. edn.; m. Ottilie, d. Dr. Edward Walther, Dec. 17, 1896; children—Sydney Albert (dec.), Virginia Thorne, Ottilie Walther (dec.), Eleanor Cleveland. Asst. sec. Rep. Nat. Com., 1896; sec. Hon. Mark A. Hanna, 1896-1901; now owns and operates Bellingham Daily Herald (morning and evening) and Daily Olympian of Olympia (morning and evening); pres. Perkins Invest. Co.; Mexican Occidental Co.; pres. and mem. bd. dirs. Standard Gypsum Co. (chmn. finance com.). Mem. Rep. Nat. Com., 1912-20; ex-mem. Rep. State Central Com. Mem. bd. Navy League of U.S. Pres. Wash. Good Roads Assn., 1911-12; ex-commodore Internat. Yachting Assn. Pres. Wash. State Hist. Soc. Hon. mem. Wash. State Senate. Clubs: Tacoma Yacht (exec. commodore), Chamber of Commerce, Country and Golf (Tacoma); Bohemian, Press (San Francisco); Rainier (Seattle); Santa Barbara (Santa Barbara); Tacoma (ex-pres.). Home: 501 N. D St. Office: Perkins Bldg., Tacoma, Wash. Died Oct. 31, 1955.

PERKINS, Thomas Jefferson, lawyer; b. Phila., Aug. 6, 1873; s. Abraham Robinson and Louise M. (Fiske) P.; student Germantown Acad., 1883-90; A.B., Princeton, 1894; LL.B., N.Y. Law Sch., 1896; m. Isabella McWhorter, Oct. 15, 1901; children—Louise Mary (Mrs. Wm. Cecil McHenry, dec.), Isabel McWhorter (Mrs. E. Walter Fischer). Admitted to N.Y. bar, 1896, Pa. bar, 1918; legal dept. Am. Tel. & Tel., 1898-1917; gen. counsel of Pa. Power & Light Co. and predecessor cos., 1917-49, ret. as v.p., gen. counsel, 1949, now dir., legal cons. Home: R.F.D. 4, Easton, Md. Office: 901 Hamilton St., Allentown, Pa. Died Feb. 1, 1952; buried West Laurel Hill Cemetery, Phila.

PERLMAN, Nathan D., judge; b. Poland, August 2, 1887; s. Victor and Rachel P.; College City of N.Y., 1901-05; Universitiy Law Sch., New York, 1907; m. Florence Sylvia Bierman, 1917; 1 son, Jack Marvin. Began practice of law at N.Y. City, 1909; spl. dep. atty. gen. State of N.Y., 1911-14; mem. N.Y. Assembly, 1915-17; elected to fill vacancy in 66th Congress, and to 67th to 69th Congresses (1920-27), 14th N.Y. Dist.; city magistrate of City of N.Y., 1935-36; justice Court of Special Sessions of City of N.Y. since 1936. Mem. New York City Mayor's Committee on Unity. Member New York Bar Association, Bar Association City of New York, N.Y. County Lawyers Assn.; past grand master Independent Order B'rith Abraham. V.p. Beth Israel Hospital; trustee Fedn. for Support of Jewish Philanthropic Socs. of N.Y. City. Home: 25 E. 9th St. Address: 100 Centre St., N.Y.C. Died June 29, 1952.

PERLMAN, Selig, economist, educator; b. Bialystok, Poland, Dec. 9, 1888; s. Mark and Paulina (Blankstein) P.; Candidate of Commerce, Sch. Commerce, Bialystok, 1900-06; student U. Naples, Italy, 1906-07; A.B., U. Wis., 1910, Ph.D., 1915; m. Eva Shaber, June 23, 1918 (dec. 1930); children—David, Mark; m. 2d, Fannie Shaber, Aug. 22, 1930; children—Eva (Mrs. Ernst Silversmith), Rachel. Came to U.S., 1908, naturalized, 1913. Research asst. U. Wis., 1909-13; spl. investigator U.S. Commn. on Indsl. Relations, 1913-15; research in econs. U. Wis., 1916-18, instr. econs., 1919-21, asst. prof., 1921-25, asso. prof., 1925-27, prof., 1927-59, John R. Commons research prof., 1957-59, prof. emeritus U. Wis., 1959—; Culp vis. prof., U. Pa., 1959; lectr., cons. Hebrew U., Jerusalem, summer 1957; vis. prof. indsl. relations Univ. Coll. of South Wales, 1938-39. Mem. gov.'s commn. on human rights, Wis., 1946—. Mem. Am. Econ. Assn., Am. Jewish Com., Jewish Publ. Soc. Jewish religion. Club: University. Author: History of Labor in the U.S. (with J. R. Commons and others), 1918; A History of Trade Unionism in the U.S., 1922. A Theory of the Labor Movement, 1928; Labor Movements, 1896-1932 (with P. Taft), 1935. Co-Author: Organized Labour in Four Continents, 1939, Postwar Problems, 1945. Home: 2737 Lynn Terrace, Madison 5, Wis. Died Aug. 14, 1959.

PERRET, Auguste, architect; b. Ixelles, Belgium, Feb. 12, 1874 (French parentage); s. Claude Marie and Pauline Lucie (Lorimey) P.; diploma Fine Arts Sch. (Alsacienne), 1891; Dr. honoris causa, U. Helsinki, Princeton U.; m. Jeanne Cordeau, Jan. 30, 1902. Prof. Ecole Speciale d'Architecture; prof. Ecole Nationale Superieure des Beaux-Arts. Pres. Salon des Tuileries (painting); mem. Institut de France. Decorated Grand Officer Legion of Honor; recipient Royal Gold Medal (Gt. Britain), gold medal A.I.A ; meml. plate at birthplace from Soc. Belge des Urbanistes et Architects modernistes; also numerous other honors. Pres. Superior Council of Order of Architects. Author: Contribution a une Theorie de l'Architecture. Pioneered an architectural style in use of reinforced concrete. Home: 51 rue Raynouard, Paris 16e, France. Died Feb. 28, 1954.

PERRIGO, James, prohibitionist; b. of U.S. parentage, Salisbury, N.B., Can., Oct. 25, 1859; s. Robert and Annie (Crandall) P.; came to U.S. with parents, 1869; ed. pub. schs. Began working for Prohibition Party, 1884; chmn. of State Com., Me., for 12 yrs.; Prohibition candidate for gov. of Me., 1902, polling largest vote ever cast for any candidate of that party in the State; editor Prohibition papers; printer and publisher; pub. speaker. Mem. Am. Inst. Phrenology. Protestant. Author: (brochures) The Sheriff, 1912; The Forest Tavern, 1914; Bits of Maine Verse, 1914; also many tracts, short stories and newspaper articles. Address: Sebago Lake, Me. Deceased.

PERRIN, Dwight Stanley, ret. newspaper editor; b. River Falls, Wis., Feb. 26, 1888; s. Frank and Fannie Warfield (Ball) P.; student The Principia, St. Louis, Mo., 1898-1907; Peddie Inst., Hightstown, N.J., 1908-09; m. Miriam Devore Gilmore, Oct. 15, 1914; children—Suzanne Warfield (Mrs. Sam. W. Reyburn), Barbara Devore (Mrs. Charles J. Warner); m. 2d, Julie Mechling Kerby, July 12, 1946. Reporter, St. Louis Times, 1909-13; city editor Reno Evening Gazette, 1913-14; with New York Evening World, 1914-15; New York Morning Telegraph, Evening Telegram, New York Tribune, 1915-17; head of publicity, Goldwyn Pictures Corporation, 1918-19; night city editor, New York Tribune, 1919-20; v.p. and gen. mgr., F. B. Warren Corp., 1920-21, city editor, N.Y. Tribune, 1923-24, N.Y. He ald, 1924. N.Y. Herald Tribune, 1924-26; asst. mng. editor, St. Louis Post-Dispatch, 1926-39; mng. editor, Phila. Evening Bulletin, 1939-47; exec. editor Syracuse (N.Y.) Herald-Journal, 1948-50. Mem. Am. Soc. Newspaper Editors, Sigma Delta Chi. Republican. Clubs: National Press; Silurians. Home: 4126 E. Haynes Av., Tucson. Died Oct. 20, 1952.

PERRINE, Henry Pratt (pĕr rin'), army officer; b. Trenton, N.J., July 22, 1891; s. Henry Pratt and Louisa (Scudder) P.; B.S., U.S. Mil. Acad., 1913; M.B.A., Harvard, 1931; m. Anita Allen, Nov. 4, 1917; m. 2d, Florence Bradley, June 18, 1924; children—Henry Pratt, David Perry. Commd. 2d lt., Inf., U.S. Army, June 12, 1913, and advanced through the grades to brig. gen., 1943; became exec. officer Inf. Sch., Ft. Benning, Ga., 1941; comdg. Inf. Sch., Ft. Benning, Ga., 1943, comdg. IRTC., Camp Jos. T. Robinson, Ark., Feb. 1945. Died Dec. 30, 1954†.

PERRINE, Van Dearing, artist; b. Garnett, Kan., 1869. Silver medal, Charleston Expn., 1902, Panama P.I. Expn., 1915; hon. mention. Carnegie Inst., 1903. Conducting a research into abstract mobile design and instrumental color orchestration. Recipient Altman prize, 1930. Represented in many American collections, N.A., 1931. Lectures on Art in Child-Development. Mem. Prometheans, Soc. Am. Painters Sculptors and Gravers, Grand Central Art Assn., Milburn and Shorthills Art Center. Club: National Arts (life). Author: Let the Child Draw. Home: Maplewood, N.J. Died Dec. 10, 1955.

PERRY, Bliss, univ. prof., author; b. Williamstown, Mass., Nov. 25, 1860; s. Arthur Latham and Mary (Smedley) P.; A.B., Williams, 1881, A.M., 1883; at univs. of Berlin and Strassburg; hon. A.M., Princeton, 1896; L.H.D., Princeton, 1900, Williams, 1902, U. of Vt., 1912; Litt.D., Bowdoin Coll., 1904, Harvard Univ., 1925, Brown Univ., 1930; LL.D., Wake Forest (N.C.) College, 1906, U. of Pa., 1916; married Annie L. Bliss, 1888; children—Constance Goodnough (Mrs. Thomas M. Woodward), Margaret Smedley, Arthur Bliss. Professor English, Williams, 1886-93, Princeton, 1893-1900; editor Atlantic Monthly, 1899-1909; prof. English lit. Harvard, 1907-30. Harvard lecturer U. of Paris, 1909-10. Decorated Chevalier Legion of Honor (France). Mem. Am. Acad. Arts and Letters, Mass. Hist. Soc.; fellow Royal Society of Literature. Trustee emeritus of Williams Coll.; overseer of Harvard College, 1935-41. Editor: Selections from Burke; Scott's Woodstock and Ivanhoe, and Little Masterpieces (18 vols.); gen. editor Cambridge editions of the Poets, 1905-09; The Heart of Emerson's Journal, 1926; Selections from Emerson's Prose, 1926; The Heart of Emerson's Essays, 1933. Author: The Broughton House, 1890; Salem Kittredge, and Other Stories, 1894; The Plated City, 1895; The Powers at Play, 1899; chpt. on poetry in Counsel Upon the Reading of Books, 1900; A Study of Prose Fiction, 1902; The Amateur Spirit, 1904; Walt Whitman, 1906; Whittier, 1907; Park Street Papers, 1909; The American Mind, 1912; Carlyle, 1915; The American Spirit in Literature, 1918; A Study of Poetry, 1920; Life and Letters of Henry Lee Higginson, 1921; The Praise of Folly, 1923; Pools and Ripples, 1927; Emerson Today, 1931; Richard Henry Dana (1885-1931), 1933; And Gladley Teach (reminiscences), 1935. Home: Exeter, N.H. Died Feb. 13, 1954; buried Eventually, Williamstown, Mass.

PERRY, George Sessions, writer; b. Rockdale, Tex., May 5, 1910; s. Andrew Preston and Laura (Van de Venter) P.; ed. Allen Acad. (Bryan, Tex.), Southwestern U. (Georgetown, Tex.), Purdue U., and Houston (Tex.) U.; m. Claire E. Hodges, Feb. 20, 1933. War correspondent, New Yorker and Saturday Evening Post since 1942. Editor: Roundup Time, a collection of southwestern writing, 1943. Author: (movie) The Arkansas Traveler (with Viola Brothers Shore), 1938; Walls Rise Up, 1939; Hold Autumn In Your Hand (chosen best Tex. book of yr. by Tex. Inst. of Letters; received Nat. Book Sellers Assn. Award, 1941; later filmed with title The Southerner), 1941; Thirty Days Hath September (with Dorothy Cameron Disney), 1942; Texas: A World in Itself, 1942; Hackberry Cavalier, 1944; Where Away (with Isabel Leighton), 1944; Cities of America, 1947; Families of America, 1949; My Granny Van, 1949; Tale of a Foolish Farmer, 1951; The Story of Texas A & M, 1951; The Story of Texas (for children), 1956. Home: Rockdale, Tex. Address: Curtis Brown, Ltd., 575 Madison Av., N.Y.C. 22. Died Dec. 13. 1956; buried Rockdale, Tex.

PERRY, John Holliday, publisher; b. Port Royal, Ky., Mar. 3, 1881; s. William M. and Mattie (Atterbury) P.; B.A., Hanover (Ind.) Coll., 1902; LL.B., U. of Va., 1904; hon. LL.D., Hanover (Ind.) College, 1945; married Dorothy Lilly, 1914; children—John, Jr., Farwell Wilmot. Formerly nat. counsel United Press Assns., The Scripps' Newspapers, Newspaper Enterprise Assn., and part owner James G. Scripps' western newspapers until 1918; owner and chairman of the board Palm Beach Post-Times, West Palm Beach, Fla., Palm Beach Daily News Palm Beach Life; owner and publisher John H. Perry Publications, Publishers Autocaster Service, Jacksonville (Fla.) Journal, Pensacola (Fla.) News, Pensacola (Fla.) Journal, Panama City (Fla.) News-Herald, Ocala (Fla.) Star-Banner, DeLand (Fla.) Sun-News, The Lake City Reporter and Columbia Gazette (Fla.), New Smyrna Beach (Fla.) News, Avon Park Sun; Delray Beach News; Playground News, Ft. Walton; Ocean Beach Reporter, Jacksonville Beach; Kissimmee Gazette; Leesburg Commercial Ledger; Melbourne Times; Public Record, Pensacola; Highlands County News, Sebring; Fernandina News-Leader; Jackson Co. Floridan, Marianna, (all Fla.); Frankfort (Ky.) State-Journal, Owenton (Ky.) News-Herald; owner, radio stations WJHP (Jacksonville, Fla.), WCOA (Pensacola, Fla.), WDLP (Panama City, Fla.), WTMC (Ocala, Fla.); chmn. of the bd. Western Newspaper Union, Harry W. Brintnall Co., Inc., E. C. Palmer & Co., Ltd., Jonperry Realty Co., Perry Mercantile Co., Glenwood Farms Hatcheries. President American Riviera Association. Mem. Beta Theta Pi, Phi Delta Phi. Presbyterian. Clubs: Metropolitan, Racquet and Tennis (New York); Everglades, Bath and Tennis, Palm Beach Country, Gulf Stream Golf (Palm Beach, Fla.); Timoquana Club (Jacksonville). Author; Newspaper Law; Who Runs the Country. Coauthor: Florida in the Making; So This Is Florida. Home: Palm Beach, Fla. Office: Post-Times, West Palm Beach, Fla. Died Dec. 4, 1952.

PERRY, John Lester, ex-pres. Carnegie-Ill. Steel Corp.; b. Worcester, Mass., Mar. 11, 1881; s. Fred George and Ella Matilda (Bailey) P.; grad. Worcester (Mass.) English High Sch., 1899; m. Kathryn Thayer, Aug. 31, 1904; children—Elizabeth (Mrs. James E. Walter), John Lester, Jr. With Am. Steel & Wire Co., 1899-1935, clerical and supervisory work, 1899-1917, supt. South Works, Worcester, Mass., 1917-18, North Works, 1918-25, asst. mgr. Worcester Dist., 1925-28, mgr. Worcester Dist., 1928-32, v.p. Am. Steel & Wire Co., 1933-35; pres. Tenn. Coal, Iron & R R. Co., Birmingham, Ala., 1935-38; pres. Carnegie-Illinois Steel Corp., 1938-46; president Columbia Steel Co., 1947-49; adviser U.S. Steel Corp., since 1949. Member American Iron and Steel Institute, Newcomen Society (Philadelphia), Pa. Soc., Engrs. Soc. of Western Pa. Republican. Unitarian. Clubs: Worcester (Worcester); Pittsburgh Athletic Assn., Duquesne, Fox Chapel Golf (Pittsburgh); Mountain Brook (Birmingham, Ala.); Rolling Rock Country. Home: Schenley Apts., Pittsburgh 13. Office: 434 Fifth Av., Pitts. Died May 27, 1952.

PERRY, John Morris, lawyer; b. Brooklyn, N.Y.; s. John Morris and Catherine (Evans) P.; LL.B., Columbia, 1887; m. Amy V. Marder, Sept. 12, 1894; children—Frances Catherine (Mrs. Donald B. Knight), John Marder (dec.). Practiced at N.Y. City since 1887; member firm Rathbone, Perry, Kelley & Drye; assistant district attorney Kings County, 1912-13. Vice-pres. Juilliard Sch. of Music. Mem. Met. Opera Association, Member American, New York State bar associations, Association Bar City of New York. Republican. Presbyterian. Clubs: Down Town, Rockland County, Rembrandt. Home: Palisades, N.Y. Office: 70 Broadway, N.Y.C. Died Mar. 1, 1951.

PERRY, John Richard, naval officer; b. May 24, 1899. Commd. Civil Engrs. Corps USN, 1923, advanced through grades to rear adm., 1953; now chief of Civil Engrs., USN. Address: 4220 43d St. N.W., Washington. Died Sept. 25, 1955.*

PERRY, Lawrence, journalist, author; b. Newark, N.J.; s. William Aurelius and Mary (Hayes) P.; g.s. on Hon. Nehemiah Perry; m. Larry Louise Crossman, November 1, 1902; 1 son, Glen. With N.Y. Sun, 1901, New York Evening Sun, 1904, Evening Journal, 1904-05, Evening Post, 1906; editor Yachting, 1906-10, New York Evening Post, 1910-20, Consolidated Press Assn., 1920-33, North Am. Newspaper Alliance, 1933——. Mem. New York Soc. Sons of Revolution. Episcopalian. Clubs: Dutch Treat, Princeton (New York); Cap and Gown (hon.), Nassau (Princeton, New Jersey). Author: Dan Merrithew, 1910; Prince or Chauffeur, 1911; Holton, 1913; The Fullback, 1916; The Big Game, 1918; Our Navy in the War, 1918; The Romantic Liar, 1919; For the Game's Sake, 1921; Touchdowns, 1924; Old First, 1931; Beyond the Terrace (play). Writer of syndicated columns "For the Game's Sake and "New York Skylines." Dramatic critic, North Am. Newspaper Alliance. Supervisor sports arts, Encyclopedia Britannica. Home: 12 Rudd Ct., Glen Ridge, N.J. Office: 229 W. 43d St., N.Y.C. Died Sept. 5, 1954.

PERRY, Ralph Barton, univ. prof.; b. Poultney, Vt., July 3, 1876; s. George Adelbert and Susannah Chase (Barton) P.; A.B., Princeton Univ., 1896; A.M., Harvard Univ., 1897, Ph.D., 1899; Litt.D., Princeton, 1936; Doctor of Humane Letters, Clark Univ., 1939; LL.D., Colby College, Waterville, Me., 1942; LL.D., U. of Penn. 1944; Litt.D., Harvard Univ. 1944; m. Rachel Berenson, Aug. 15, 1905 (died Oct. 23, 1933); children—Ralph Barton, Bernard Berenson. Instr. philosophy, Williams Coll., 1899-1900, Smith Coll., 1900-02; instr. philosophy, Harvard Univ., 1902-05, asst. prof., 1905-13, prof., 1913-46, prof. emeritus, 1946——. Gifford lecturer at the University, Glasgow, Scotland, 1946-47, 1947-48. Maj. U.S. Army and secretary War Dept. Com. on Education and Spl. Training, 1918-19; Hyde lecturer in French univs., 1921-22. Chmn. Am. Defense-Harvard Group, 1940-45; chmn. Univs. Com. on Postwar Internat. Problems, 1942-45. Decorated Chevalier Legion of Honor (France), 1936. Mem. of National Institute of Arts and Letters. Mem. Am. Philos. Soc. Author: The Approach to Philosophy, 1905; The Moral Economy, 1909; Present Philosophical Tendencies, 1912; The New Realism, 1912; The Free Man and the Soldier, 1916; The Present Conflict of Ideals, 1918; Annotated Bibliography of the Writings of William James, 1920; The Plattsburg Movement, 1921. Editor: William James's Essays in Radical Empiricism, 1912; William James's Collected Essays and Reviews, 1920; Revision of Weber's History of Philosophy, 1925; Philosophy of the Recent Past, 1926; General Theory of Value, 1926; A Defense of Philosophy, 1931; The Thought and Character of William James (Pulitzer prize biography), 1935 (briefer edit. 1948); In the Spirit of William James, 1938; (with others) The Meaning of the Humanities, 1938; Shall Not Perish from the Earth, 1940; On All Fronts, 1941; Plea for an Age Movement, 1942; Our Side Is Right, 1942. Puritanism and Democracy, 1944; Hope for Immortality, 1945; One World in the Making, 1945; Characteristically American, 1949; General Theory of Value, 1950; The Citizen Decides, 1951; Realms of Value, 1953; The Humanity of Man, 1956. Home: 985 Memorial Dr., Cambridge 38, Mass. Died Jan. 22, 1957.

PERRY, Stella George Stern, author; b. New Orleans, La.; d. George and Carolyn (Silverstein) Stern; grad. Southern Academic Inst., New Orleans, 1893; student Newcomb Coll., New Orleans, 1893-94; A.B., Barnard Coll., 1898; m. George Hough Perry, Sept. 19, 1906 (dec. 1945); 1 son, Ralph R. Corr. sec. Consumers' League of N.J.; chmn. publicity com., N.J. State Child Labor Com.; spl. insp. of labor, N.J., 1912-13. Sec. joint com. of San Francisco Child Labor Com. and Juvenile Protective Assn., 1914-15; asso. dir. Woman's Bd. Panama P.I. Expn., 1913-15. Lecturer and organizer for Nat. and Calif. councils of defense, 1917-18. Mem. Alpha Omicron Pi Fraternity (was a founder). Clubs: Barnard College, Pan-Hellenic, Woman Pays (N.Y. City); Studio Club (Hollywood, Calif.). Author: Go-To-Sleep, 1911; Melindy, 1912; When Mother Lets Us Act, 1913; The Kind Adventure, 1914; The Sculpture and Murals of the Panama-Pacific International Exposition (official handbook), 1915; The Sculpture of the Exposition (with A. Sterling Calder), 1915; All the Children (child labor pageant performed at Panama P.I. Expn.), 1915; Little Bronze Playfellows, 1915; Clever Mouse, 1916; Angel of Christmas, 1917; The Girls' Nest, 1918; Palmetto, 1920; Come Home, 1923; Barbara of Telegraph Hill, 1925; The Defenders, 1927; Extra Girl, 1929; Richardson: General Server, 1940; also scenarios, stories, poems, and articles, History of Alpha Omicron Pi, 1953. Edited for Martha Vivian, Down the Avenue of Ninety Years, 1924. Address: 37 Willow St., Bklyn. 1. Deceased.

PERRY, Stuart Hoffman, editor, pub.; b. Pontiac, Mich., Oct. 13, 1874; s. Aaron and Sallie (Hoffman) P.; A.B., U. of Mich., 1894, LL.B., 1896, hon. A. M., 1919; LL.D., Adrian Coll., 1921; m. Maude E. Caldwell, Oct. 14, 1895; children—Elizabeth R. (Mrs. C. Kenneth Wesley), Lydia (dec.). Practiced law at Pontiac and Detroit, 1896-1900; mng. editor Pontiac Press, 1901; pub. St. Johns (Mich.) News, 1902-06, Adrian Daily Telegram, 1907——. V.p. Monroe (Mich.) Evening News, 1927——. Dir. Mich. State Bur. Mil. Relief at N.Y. City, 1918; chmn. Mich. Reconstruction Com., 1919; mem. Mich. Community Council Commn., Industrial Relations Commn., 1919-29; second vice president Associated Press, 1921-22; director, 1923-51; member of the Michigan Judicial Council, 1929——, Mich. Advisory Council on State Finance, 1931-32, Mich. Civil Service Commn., 1937-38. Mem. advisory com. Columbia U. Sch. of Journalism, 1926——. Asso. mineralogist U.S. Nat. Museum, Lawrence Smith Medal, Nat. Acad. Sciences, 1945; Minn. Award for Distinguished Service in Journalism, 1947. Fellow A.A.A.S., Cranbrook Institute of Science, Meteoritical Soc., Am. Geog. Society; mem. Am. Judicature Soc., Am. Soc. Newspaper Editors, Am. Acad. Polit. and Social Science, Acad. Polit. Sci., Inland Daily Press Assn. Republican. Episcopalian. Clubs: Lotos (N.Y.C.); Nat. Press (Washington); University of Michigan Press (an organizer). Author: The Metallography of Meteoric Iron, 1944. Home: 225 Front St. Office: Adrian Telgram, Adrian, Mich. Died Feb. 14, 1957; buried Adrian.

PERRY, (John) Wallace, editor, publisher; b. Neosho, Mo., Feb. 3, 1883; s. Rev. John Wesley and Margaret Ann (Poage) P.; A.B., U. Okla., 1907; m. Lena Alice Stubblefield, June 15, 1907. City editor of the Lawton (Okla.) News-Republican and Lawton Constitution, 1907-13, McAlester (Okla.) News-Capital, 1913-17; state editor Daily Oklahoman, Oklahoma City, 1917-19; adv. mgr. and editor house organ, Seamans Magazine, Seamans Oil Co. and Continental Asphalt & Petroleum Co., N.Y. City, 1919-20; editor publs. of Okla. Agrl. and Mech. Coll., Stillwater, 1921-23; mng. editor El Paso Post, 1923-27, editor, 1927-31; editor El Paso Herald-Post, 1931-37; editor and owner Las Cruces Sun-News 1939-47; bus. mgr. N.M. Farm and Ranch 1952-54; editor, gen. mgr., 1954——. Pres. Las Cruces C. of C., 1942-43; pres. N.M. Press Assn., 1942-44. Member board gents, Univ. of Oklahoma, 1908-10; mem. Commission of Control for Texas Centennial Celebrations; mem. N.M. Hist. Soc., El Paso Hist. Soc. (life mem.), Beta Theta Pi, Sigma Delta Chi. Democrat. Presbyn. Clubs: Country, Kiwanis. Author: Each Purple Curtain, 1954. Home: 530 W. Court Av. Office: Farm Bureau Bldg., 114 E. Griggs Av., Las Cruces, N.M. Died Feb. 29, 1956; buried Las Cruces.

PERSKIE, Joseph B. (pûr'skē), judge; b. Alliance, N.J., July 20, 1885; s. Harris and Minne (Levit) P.; student U. Pa. Law Sch., 1904-07; m. Beatrice Maslansky, Nov. 27, 1910; children—David M., Marvin, Lawrence. Admitted to N.J. bar, 1907; counsellor at law, 1910——; asst. city solicitor, Atlantic City, 1916-26, city solicitor, 1926-33, solicitor Bd. of Edn., 1916-26; asso. justice Supreme Ct. of N.J., also mem. Ct. of Errors and Appeals, 1933-47; now partner Perskie and Perskie, Atlantic City. Mem. Commn. for Uniform Legislation in U.S., 1930-33. Dir. Fed. of Jewish Charities, Atlantic City. Mem. N.J., Atlantic County bar assns. Republican. Jewish religion. Mem. B'nai B'rith (past pres.), Elk, Eagles, Moose. Club: Country (Linwood, N.J.). Home: 5 N. Plaza Place. Office: Guarantee Trust Bldg., Atlantic City, N.J. Died May 29, 1957.*

PERSON, Harlow Stafford, economist; b. Republican City, Neb., Feb. 16, 1875; s. Rollin Harlow and Ida M. (Madden) P.; Ph.B., U. Mich., 1899, A.M., 1901, Ph.D., 1902; m. Mary Trowbridge Carson, Oct. 29, 1902; children—Eleanor Madden, Harlow Stafford (dec.), Miriam Frances. Instr. in commerce and industry Amos Tuck Sch. of Adminstrn. and Finance, Dartmouth, 1902-04, sec. and asst. prof., 1904-08, dir. and prof. of business orgn. and mgmt., 1908-22; mng. dir. Taylor Society, N.Y., 1919-33; cons. bus. orgn. and mgmt., 1933——; mem. Miss. Valley Com., 1934; acting chmn. water planning com., actind dir. water resources sect. Nat. Resources Bd. and Nat. Resources Com., 1934-35; econ. cons. Nat. Resources Com., 1935, Rural Electrification Adminstrn., 1935——; mem. President's Great Plains Com. 1936; cons. economist and chief of staff, U.S.-Mexico Oil Commn., 1942. Major Ordnance R.C. and maj., Insp., Gen's Dept., 1918. Mem. Am. Econ. Assn., Taylor Soc., Am. Statis. Assn., Am. Soc. for Pub. Adminstrn., Am. Assn. U. Profs., Nat. Planning Assn., Masaryk Acad. (Prague, hon.), Phi Beta Kappa, Artus. Recipient Taylor Key of Soc. for Advancement Mgmt.; gold medal Comite Internat. de L'Orgn. Sci., 1947. Decorated Knight Order of White Lion (Czechoslovakia). Clubs: Faculty (Columbia U.), City. Author: Industrial Education, 1907; Little Waters, 1935; Mexican Oil, 1942; also articles on indsl. and comml. edn., sci. mgmt. Editor and part author of Scientific Management in American Industry, 1929; many govt. reports. Home: 94 Southlawn Av., Dobbs Ferry, N.Y. Office: 420 Lexington Av., N.Y.C. Died Nov. 7, 1955; buried Lansing, Mich.

PERSON, Seymour Howe, ex-congressman; b. Howell Tp., Livingston County, Mich., Feb. 2, 1879; s. Ozro S. and Martha A. (Howe) P.; LL.B., U. of Mich., 1901; m. Mabelle Pierson, Sept. 22, 1909. In practice of law at Lansing, Mich., 1901-57; v.p. Ingham Abstract & Title Co.; dir. Knollwood Cemetery Co. (Cleve.); mem. 72d Congress, 6th Mich. Dist. Mem. Mich. Ho. of Reps., 1914-18, Mich. Senate, 1927-29. Mem. Am., Mich. State and Ingham County bar assns., Am. Judicature Soc., Mich. State Hist. Soc. (trustee), State Grange. Republican. Universalist. Mason, Odd Fellow, Modern Woodman, Elk, Eagle. Clubs: Kiwanis, Lansing City, Wranglers, Hiawatha Sportsmen, Economic, Lawyers (U. of Mich.). Home: 210 N. Pine St. Office: Mutual Bldg., Lansing, Mich. Died Apr. 7, 1957; buried Deepdale Cemetery, Lansing, Mich.

PERSONS, William Frank, social worker; b. Brandon, Ia., Aug. 31, 1876; s. William and Mary E. (Stainbrook) P.; Ph.B., Cornell Coll., Mt. Vernon, Ia., 1900; LL.B., from Harvard University, 1905; m. Eugenia M. Bray, October 6, 1909 (she died August 2, 1941); children—William Frank, Edward Bray. Admitted to Ia. bar, 1905; practiced at Sioux City, 1905-06; dir. Dept. Gen. Work, Charity Orgn. Soc., New York, 1906-17; industrial relations work, North Am. Co., 1922-24; asst. to pres. Milwaukee Electric Ry. and Light Co., 1925-29; exec. v.p. Am. Assn. Personal Finance Cos., 1929-32; field rep., Am. Pub. Welfare Assn., 1932-33; dir. enrollment Civilian Conservation Corps, 1933-42; dir. U.S. Employment Service, 1933-39; spl. asst. to dir. Civilian Conservation Corps from May 1939-April 1942; director industrial relations Consolidated Aircraft Corporation, Apr. 1942-May 1943; dir. indsl. relations Ryan Aeronaut. Co., May 1943-Sept. 1945; dir. personnel, Civil Serv. Department, San Diego County, California, 1948-50. With American Red Cross in United States and abroad, World War; director general Department Civilian Relief, 1917-18; dir. Dept. of Adminstrn., League Red Cross Socs., Geneva, 1919-20; v. chmn. Am. Red Cross, 1921-22. Mem. Nat. Council Boy Scouts America, Am. Assn. Social Workers, Nat. Conf. Social Workers, Phi Beta Kappa. Clubs: Harvard (New York); Cosmos (Washington). Received Citation of Merit from Instl. Assn. of Pub. Employment Services, 1950. Address: 410 Orchard St., Cranford, N.J. Died May 27, 1955.

PETEGORSKY, David W., (pĕtĕgórsky), polit. scientist; b. Ottawa, Can., May 31, 1915; s. Leon and Beckie (Wolinsky) P.; student Lisgar Collegiate, Ottawa, 1927-30; A.B., Yeshiva Coll., N.Y. City, 1935 Rabbi, 1936; Ph.D., London (Eng.) School Economics, 1940; married Carol Coan, 1951; children—Stephen, Dan. Instructor in the department govt. Antioch College, O., 1940-41; dir. indsl. div. Canadian Wartime Information Bd., Ottawa, 1942-45; nat. exec. dir. Am. Jewish Congress, N.Y. City, since 1945, mem. exec. com., World Jewish Congress since 1948. Came to U.S., 1945. Jewish religion. Author: Left-Wing Democracy in the English Civil War, 1940; Strategy for Democracy (with J. Donald Kingsley), 1942. Lecturer. Contbr. to academic and popular publs. Home: 139 E. 94th St. Office: 15 E. 84th St., N.Y.C. 28. Died July 15, 1956; buried Beth El Cemetery, Paramus, N.J.

PETER, William Frederick, lawyer; b. Seymour, Ind., Oct. 26, 1888; s. William Frederick and Minna (Frey) P.; grad. Lake Forest Acad., 1901; A.B., Yale Univ., 1905; LL.B., Columbia Law Sch., New York, 1908; m. Marion Mason, Jan. 1, 1917; children—Sylvia (Mrs. Charles Preston), Phyllis (Mrs. Robert Matthews), Marion (Mrs. James McMahon). Began practice in Indpls., 1908; moved to Chgo., 1911; engaged in r.r. law practice, 1911——; asst. gen. counsel C.R.I.&P. Ry. Co., 1919-40. now dir., v.p., ret. gen. counsel; dir. Chgo., Terre Haute & Southeastern Ry. Co., 1911——; dir. Peoria & Bur. Valley Ry. Co.; director The Freeman Magazine, N.Y. City. Mem. Psi Upsilon. Republican. Clubs: University (Chgo.); Onwentsia Country (Lake Forest, Ill.). Home: 990 E. Illinois Rd., Lake Forest, Ill. Office: 1025 La Salle Station, Chgo. Died Jan. 15, 1956.

PETERS, David Wilbur, coll. pres.; b. Rocky Mount, Va., Nov. 21, 1889; s. Stephen Benjamin and Susan (Bowman) P.; B.S., Roanoke Coll., Salem, Va., 1913; M.A., Teachers Coll., Columbia U., 1928, Ph.D., 1934; m. Anne Bruce, June 16, 1916; children—Barbara Anne (Mrs. James Wilborn, Jr.), Mary Bruce (Mrs. C. C. Cunningham, Jr.). Susan Bowman. Teacher and high school principal, Rustburg, Virginia, 1913-15; teacher and assistant principal, elementary schs., Richmond, Va., 1915-16; prin., Cape Charles (Va.) High Sch., 1916-20; supt. schs., Northhampton (Va.) County, 1921-27, Henrico County, 1928-29; state high sch. supervisor, 1929-31; state director. Instrn., 1934-38; president Radford College Woman's Division of Virginia Poly. Institute, Radford, Va., since 1938; chmn. City Planning Bd., Radford. Mem. Va. Acad. Science, Nat. Soc. for

Curriculum Study, Nat. Edn. Assn., Phi Delta Kappa. Democrat. Baptist. Clubs: Rotary, Pulaski Country (Pulaski, Va.). Author: Teachers' Plan Book (with W. C. McGinnis), 1929; The Status of the Married Woman Teacher, 1934. Home: Radford, Va. Died Aug. 2, 1951; buried Evergreen Cemetery, Roanoke, Va.

PETERS, James L(ee), ornithologist; b. Boston, Mass., Aug. 13, 1889; s. Austin and Frances Howie (Lee) P.; student Roxbury Latin Sch., 1902-08; A.B., Harvard, 1912; m. Eleanor K. Sweet, May 28, 1932. Expeditions to Mexico, West Indies, Central and South America, 1911-30; asst. curator of birds, Museum of Comparative Zoölogy, Harvard Coll., 1927-32, curator since 1932. Served as 2d lt. U.S. Army, in France and Germany, World War I, 1917-19. Fellow Am. Orintholog'sts Union, Am. Acad. of Arts and Sciences; mem. Washington Acad. of Sciences, Am. Soc. of Mammologists, Internat. Commn. Zoölogical Nomenclature, Deutsche Ornithologische Gessellschaft (corr.), Ornithologische Gesellschaft Bayern (corr.), Sociedad Ornithologica del Plata (corr.), Nuttall Ornithological, Cooper Ornithological, Biol. Soc. of Wash. Clubs: Harvard of Boston, Faculty. Author: Check-List of Birds of the World. Vols. I-VII, 1931-48; contbr. numerous articles to professional jours. Home: Harvard, Mass. Office: Museum Comparative Zoölogy, Cambridge 38, Mass. Died Apr. 19, 1952.

PETERS, John Punnett, physician; b. Phila., Pa., Dec. 4, 1887; s. John Punnett and Gabriella Brooke (Forman) P.; A.B., Yale, 1908; M.D., Coll. of Phys. and Surg. (Columbia), 1913; m. Charlotte Morse Hodge, 1915; children—John Hodge (M.D.), Alice Richmond (Mrs. David B. Irwin), Richard Morse (M.D.), Charles Hodge. House physician Presbyn. Hospital, New York, 1913-15, asst. physician, 1916-17; instructor in clinical medicine, Coll. of Phys. and Surg., 1916-17; fellow Russell Sage Inst. Pathology, 1917-20; adj. asst. visiting phys., Bellevue Hosp., 1919-20; asso. prof. medicine, Vanderbilt U., 1920-21, Yale, 1921-27; John Slade Ely prof. medicine, Yale, and asso. phys. New Haven Hosp. and New Haven Dispensary, 1927—; cons. physician Norwalk and Stamford hosps., 1947—. Served as capt. Med. Res. Corps., U.S. Army, World War. Mem. Nat. Acad. Sci., Royal Soc. Medicine, A.A.A.S., Am. Soc. Biol. Chemists, Assn. Am. Physicians, Am. Soc. for Clin. Investigation, Harvey Soc., Soc. for Exptl. Biology and Med. Clubs: Interurban Clinical, Century. Author: Quantitative Clinical Chemistry (2 vols.), 1931 and 1946; Body Water, 1935. Home: 123 Marvel Rd. Office: New Haven Hosp., New Haven. Died Dec. 29, 1955.

PETERS, R. Earl, lawyer; b. Bingen, Ind., Apr. 25, 1886; s. Isaac and Elizabeth (Nelson) P.; LL.B., Georgetown (D.C.) U., 1916; m. Estella Leas; 1 dau., Leah. Admitted to Ind. bar, 1917; formerly mem. firm of Peters & Fleming, Ft. Wayne; dir. Federal Housing Adminstrn. in Ind., 1934-52. Mem. Am. and Ind. bar assns. Democrat. Presbyterian. Mason (32°, Shriner, Royal Jesters), Elk, K.P. Clubs: Athletic (Indianapolis); University, Optimists, Quest (Ft. Wayne); Highland Country (Indpls.). Home: 1520 Forest Park Blvd., Ft. Wayne, Ind. Died Feb. 18, 1952; buried Lindenwood Cemetery, Ft. Wayne.

PETERS, Ralph, Jr., banker, ret.; b. Cin.; grad. civil engring. Princeton, 1908; m. Helen Frew; children—Ralph Frew, Mrs. Helen Peters Victor. With L.I. R.R., 1908-25; with Corn Exchange Bank Trust Co., which later became The Chem. Corn Exchange Bank, 1925—, pres., 1941-51, ret.; mem. bd. Franklin Savs. Bank, Woodlawn Cemetery. Dir. Community Hosp., Glen Cove, L.I. Mem. S.R. Clubs: Creek, Piping Rock, India House. Home: Cedar Swamp Rd., Glen Head, L.I., N.Y. Died Feb. 28, 1957; buried Woodlawn Cemetery.*

PETERS, Walter Harvest, animal husbandryman; b. Keokuk, Ia., July 9, 1885; s. Henry C. and Katherine (Wende) P.; B.S.A., Ia. State Coll., 1908, hon. M.Agr., 1920; m. Millie Gillette, Aug. 7, 1912; children—Robert Gillette, Eunice Margaret. Instr. animal husbandry Ia. State Coll., 1908-09; prof. animal husbandry Manitoba Agrl. Coll., Winnipeg, Can., 1909-14; head of animal husbandry sect. N.D. Expt. Sta., 1914-18, U. Minn., 1918—. Mem. Am. Soc. Animal Prodn. (pres.). Methodist. Author: Livestock Production (coll. textbook), 1942; (with Geo. P. Deyoe) Raising Livestock, 1946. Contbr. to The Farmer, Farm Stock and Home. Peters Hall, St. Paul campus U. Minn. named in his honor. Home: 1452 Hythe St., St. Paul. Died Aug. 8, 1949; buried Keokuk, Ia.

PETERSEN, Martin, etcher; b. Viele, Denmark, Nov. 23, 1866; student Nat. Acad., Cooper Union; wife Anna Petersen; children—Mrs. Sadie Horter, Mrs. Anna Zabriskie, Marguerite. Art anatomist Columbia Med. Sch., 50 yr. A.N.A. mem. Mem. Am. Water Color Soc., Soc. Am. Etchers, Audubon Artists. Address: 725 Riverside Dr., N.Y.C. 31. Died Nov. 21, 1956.*

PETERSEN, William Ferdinand, physician; b. Chicago, Mar. 25, 1887; s. Eduard and Wilhelmina Joanna (Klockziem) P.; student Armour Inst., 1904-06; B.S., U. of Chicago, 1910; M.D., Rush Med. Coll. (U. of Chicago), 1912; m. Alma Catherine Schmidt, Sept. 16, 1919; children—Eduard Schmidt, Conrad William, William Otto. Instr. pathology, Vanderbilt U., 1913, asst. prof. exptl. medicine and pathology, 1914-17; asso. in pathology and bacteriology, U. of Ill. Coll. of Medicine, 1919-24, prof., 1924-42; pres. Petersen Oven Co. Served as pvt. and 1st lt. with M.C., U.S. Army, 1917-19. Mem. A.M.A., Inst. of Medicine, Soc. Exptl. Pathology, Am. Soc. Pathology and Bacteriology, Chicago Pathol. Soc., Chicago Soc. Internal Medicine, Am. Assn. Physical Anthropology. Clubs: University, Chicago Literary (Chicago). Author: Protein Therapy and Non-Specific Reactions, 1922; Skin Reactions, Blood Chemistry and Physical Status of Normal Men and Clinical Patients (with S. A. Levinson), 1930; The Patient and the Weather (monographs with Margaret E. Milliken), 1934-38; Destiny—Lincoln-Douglas, 1943; Hippocratic Wisdom, 1945; Man-Weather-Sun, 1947. Home: 1322 Astor St., Chicago. Died Aug. 20, 1950.

PETERSON, Elmer George, coll. pres.; b. Plain City, Utah, Aug. 26, 1882; s. Augustus and Agnes (Geddes) P.; B.S., Utah Agrl. Coll., 1904; U. of Chicago, 1906; A.M., Cornell U., 1909, Ph.D., 1911; LL.D., Utah State Agricultural College, 1945; married Phebe Nebeker, September 3, 1913; children—Phebe Marian Thomas, Elmer George, Martha Almira Peterson, Chase Nebeker. Instructor and assistant professor bacteriology, Cornell Univ., 1909-10; prof. bacteriology, Ore. Agr. Coll., 1910-11, also bacteriologist Oregon Expt. Sta.; prof. bacteriology, 1911-12, dir. Extension Div., 1912-16, pres., Sept. 1, 1916-July 1, 1945; pres. emeritus, since July 1945; dir. Utah Sci. Research Foundation, 1945—, Utah State Agrl. Coll. Fellow A.A.A.S., Am. Geog. Soc.; member Society of American Bacteriologists, Am. Genetic Assn., Nat. Agrl. Society, Nat. Economics League, Newcomen Soc. Eng., Nat. Econ. Council, Nat. Council on Rural Scouting, Am. Forestry Assn. (mem. bd. dirs.); mem. executive committee Assn. Land Grant Colls. and Univs., 1940-44. Member Church of Jesus Christ of Latter-day Saints (Mormons). Home: 156 E. 1st St. N., Logan, Utah. Died May 16, 1958; buried Logan (Utah) City Cemetery.

PETERSON, Henry John, prof. polit. sci.; b. Story City, Ia., Sept. 3, 1877; s. Christian and Malinda (Burke) P.; A.B., St. Olaf Coll., Northfield, Minn., 1905; A.M., State U. Ia., 1907, Ph.D., 1914; studied U. Chgo., 1909-10; m. Katharine W. Constant, Dec. 26, 1914; 1 son, Robert Constant. Began as instr. polit. sci., Ia. State Tchrs. Coll., Cedar Falls, Ia., 1910, prof., 1913-20; prof. polit. sci., chmn. dept., U. Wyo., 1920-47, emeritus prof. polit. sci., 1947—. Mem. 9th Regional War Labor Bd. Served with Y.M.C.A., World War I. Mem. Am. Polit. Sci. Assn., State Hist. Soc. of Ia., Colo.-Wyo. Social Sci. Assn. (pres. 1935-36), Phi Delta Theta. Republican. Presbyn. Author: Corrupt Practices Legislation, 1912; Selection of Public Officers, 1914; Teaching of Citizenship, 1922; wrote "County Government," in Kaplan's Proc., Citizens Conf. on Govt. Management, 1939; "Wyoming—a Cattle Kingdom," in Donnelly's Rocky Mt. Politics, 1940; contbr. proc. Constl. Convention of Wyo., 1940; contbr. to Dictionary Am. Biography, and to profl. jours. Home: 1308 S. Vine, Denver 10. Died Mar. 30, 1957; buried Oak Ridge Cemetery, Springfield, Ill.

PETERSON, J. Marvin, banker; born Randall, Ia., May 7, 1902; s. John and Anna (Christianson) P.; A.B., St. Olaf Coll., Northfield, Minn., 1923; A.M., U. of Wis., 1926, Ph.D., 1931; student (summer), U. of Ia., 1926, U. of Chicago, 1927, U. of Minn., 1929; m. Eunice Eleanore Rossing, June 25, 1926; children—James Marvin, Borgny Ann. Prin. of high sch. and supt. of schools, Colton, S.D., 1923-25; graduate asst., University of Wis., 1929-31; assistant prof. economics, Miami University, 1926-29 and 1931-34, asso. prof. and acting head of dept., 1934-37, prof. and head of dept., 1937-48; visiting prof. Coll. of City of N.Y., summers 1938, 1939, Humboldt State Coll., Arcata, Calif., summer 1941; School of Banking, U. of Wis., summers since 1945; lecturer in econ., U. of Cincinnati Evening Coll., 1931-48; dir. research, Fed. Reserve Bank of Minneapolis, 1948-53, vice pres. since 1953. Mem. Am. Econ. Assn., Delta Sigma Pi, Beta Gamma Sigma. Author: (with Delmas Richard Cawthorne) Money and Banking, 1941 (revised 1949). Contributor to economics journals and business reviews. Home: 3740 48th Av. S. Office: Federal Reserve Bank of Minneapolis, Mpls. Died Mar. 28, 1954.

PETERSON, J. Whitney, president U.S. Tobacco Co.; b. Brooklyn, N.Y., Apr. 30, 1898; s. Jonathan and Henrietta Jacques (Bissett) P.; student Choate Sch.; m. Clementine L. Lockwood, Oct. 15, 1925; 1 son, Jonathan. With U.S. Tobacco Co., N.Y. City, since 1921, v.p., 1929-37, exec. v.p., 1937-46; pres. since 1946, also dir.; dir. Nat. Tobacco Co. of Can., Irving Trust Co. Club: Union League. Home: Zaccheus Mead Lane, Greenwich, Conn. Office: 630 5th Av., N.Y.C. 20. Died Oct. 6, 1959.

PETERSON, Lawrence John, pub. health ofcl.; b. Nampa, Ida., Mar. 23, 1903; s. Iver and Isabelle (White) P.; B.S., U. Ida., 1926; M.S.P.H., U. Mich., 1940; m. Irene McBirney, Oct. 1, 1927; children—Betty Louise, Kenneth. Dir. of labs., Dept. of Pub. Health, State of Ida., Boise, 1926-57, dir., 1943-57; asst. chief Bur. Crippled Children Service, Cal. Dept. Pub. Health, 1957—. Mem. Am. Pub. Health Assn. (mem. governing council, mem. regional bd. western br., past sec., past pres. lab. sect., western br.), State Pub. Health Labs. Dirs. Conf., Ida. State Cancer Soc. (exec. bd.), Ida. Anti-Tuberculosis Assn. (exec. bd.). Mem. exec. bd. Girl Scouts of Boise Area, Boy Scouts of Am. (health and safety chmn.). Mem. com. of consultants, Nat. Sanitation Found., Ann Arbor, Mich. Mem. Sigma Xi, Delta Omega, Physanden. Roman Catholic. Elk (past exalted ruler, trustee, 1945—). Club: Boise Kiwanis. Address: Berkeley 4, Cal. Died Oct. 27, 1957; buried Morris Hill Cemetery, Boise, Ida.

PETERSON, May (Mrs. Ernest O. Thompson), operatic soprano; b. Oshkosh, Wis., Oct. 7, 1889; d. Niels and Mary (Jensen) P.; studied with William Dale, Mpls., William Nelson Burritt, N.Y.C., Mary Peck Thompson, Chgo., Madame Barrachia, Florence, Italy, George Ferguson, Berlin and Jean De Reszke Paris; m. Col. Ernest O. Thompson, June 9, 1924. Debut, Vichy, France, as Manon in opera Manon, 1911; sang in Opera Comique and Theatre Lyrique, Paris, 1912-14, in principal cities of Europe; with Met. Opera Co., N.Y.C., 1918-23; has appeared as soloist with the symphony orchestras of U.S.; widely known as concert singer. Hon. col. 142d Inf., U.S.A., and of 90th Div. Mem. Phi Epsilon. Shriner (hon.). Home: Amarillo, Tex. Address: Care Haensel & Jones, Aeolian Hall, N.Y.C. Died Oct. 8, 1952.

PETERSON, Virgil Lee, ret. army officer; b. Campbellsville, Ky., Sept. 22, 1882; B.S., Centre Coll. (Ky.), 1902, U.S. Mil. Acad., 1908; grad. Engring. Sch., 1910, Army War Coll., 1933; hon. grad. Command and Gen. Staff Corps Sch., 1925. Commd. 2d lt., 1908, advanced through grades to maj. gen., 1939; insp. gen. War Dept., 1940-46, ret. Decorated D.S.M. Address: Office of Inspector General. War Dept., Washington. Died Feb. 15, 1956; buried Arlington Nat. Cemetery.*

PETRIKIN, William Lloyd, sugar mfr.; b. Muncy, Pa., Feb. 17, 1871; s. Henry William and Sarah Brown (Lloyd) P.; ed. high sch., Muncy; m. Eloise Neilson Delbridge, May 24, 1900; children—Barbara Lloyd (Mrs. Leo Francis Welch), Charlotte Delbridge (Mrs. E. Sanford Gregory), John Delbridge, Mary Evelyn (Mrs. Henry A. Kugeler). Began as clk., 1893; entered employ Great Western Sugar Co., Denver, 1902, and advanced as cashier, auditor, sec., gen. mgr., v.p., pres. 1931—, chmn. bd. dirs.; dir. Federal Reserve Bank, Kansas City, Mo., 1924-32. Chmn. Sugar Distribution Com., World War. Mem. adv. com. R.F.C., Denver br.; dir. St. Luke's Hosp. Republican. Mason. Clubs: Denver, Denver Country, Cactus, Mile High (Denver); Congressional Country (Washington). Home: 2109 E. Ninth Av. Office: Sugar Bldg., Denver. Died 1951.

PETTEE, Charles Holmes, educator; b. Manchester, N.H., Feb. 2, 1853; s. Horace and Elizabeth Fairbanks (Wilson) P.; grad. high sch., Manchester, 1870; A.B., Dartmouth, 1874, A.M., 1877; C.E., Thayer Sch. of Civ. Engring. (Dartmouth), 1876; LL.D., N.H. Coll. Agr. and Mechanic Arts, 1913; m. Luella Elizabeth Swett, July 24, 1877; children—Alvena (Mrs. Edward E. Nelson), Horace James, Sarah Elizabeth, Charles Swett. Instr. civ. engring. Thayer Sch., 1876-77; with N.H. Coll. Agr. and Mechanic Arts, 1876—, successively instr. mathematics, 1876-78, prof. mathematics and civ. engring., 1878-1916, instr. meteorology, 1876—, dean, 1888-1937, dean emeritus and univ. historian, 1937—. Mem. Constl. Conv. N.H., 1917 and 1930; chmn. Pub. Safety Com., Durham, 1917-18; trustee Trust Funds, Durham, 1920—. Mem. N.H. Tb. Assn. (exec. com.). Mem. A.A.A.S., Soc. for Promotion Engring. Edn., Phi Beta Kappa, Phi Kappa Phi. Conglist. Republican. Home: Univ. of New Hampshire, Durham, N.H. Died Mar. 23, 1938.

PETTEE, Lemuel Gardner, tchr.; b. Sharon, Mass., Apr. 10, 1875; s. Daniel Webster and Emily Frances (Allen) P.; grad. Phillips Acad., Andover, Mass., 1894; A.B., Yale, 1898 (Phi Beta Kappa), A.M., 1903; m. Mabel O. Barnes, June 29, 1903; children—Lemuel Gardner, Emily Barnes. With Westminster Sch., 1899-1922; tchr. mathematics and coach athletic teams; headmaster sch., 1920-22. Dir. Simsbury Bank & Trust Co. Conglist. Address: Westminster School, Simsbury, Conn. Deceased.

PETTENGILL, George (Tilford), naval officer (ret.); b. Boise, Ida., Oct. 25, 1877; s. George and Anne (Worden) P.; grad. U.S. Naval Acad., 1898; m. Leila Marion Price, Jan. 16, 1909; children—George Tilford, III (lost on U.S.S. Liscome Bay, 1943), William Van Horne. Commd. ensign U.S Navy, 1898, and advanced through grades to rear adm., 1930; served on U.S.S. New York and U.S.S. Puritan, Spanish-Am. War, participating in Battle of Mantanzas; served in Samoan trouble, 1899, and Boxer Rebellion in China; with British Grand

Fleet, 1917-19, U.S.S. Wyoming; insp. Midvale Steel Co., Phila., 1919-22; comd. U.S.S. Destroyers, Asiatic Fleet, 1922-24, with Bur. Navigation, 1924-25; naval attaché Peking, China, 1925-28; capt. U.S.S. Tenn., 1928-29; student War Coll., 1929-30; comd. submarine force, Battle Fleet, 1930-31, mine force, U.S. Fleet, 1931-32, submarine base, New London, Conn., 1932-34, base force, U.S.S. Fleet, 1934-35, Battleship Div. 2, battle force, 1935-1936; comdt. Washington Navy Yard and supt. Naval Gun Factory, 1936-42; comdt. Potomac River Naval Command, 1941-42; comd. U.S. Naval Ordnance Plant, Charleston, W.Va., 1942-45; ret., 1946. Awarded Sampson Medal (Spanish-Am. War), Navy Cross, Legion of Merit, Order of Striped Tiger (Chinese), 1928. Mem. Mil. Order of Caraboa, Mil. Order of Dragon. Clubs: Chevy Chase (Md.); Old Lyme Beach (Conn.), Old Lyme Country. Home: Old Lyme, Conn. Died Jan. 11, 1959; buried at sea from U.S.S. Tringa.

PETTINGILL, William LeRoy (pĕt'in-gĭl), clergyman; b. Central Square, N.Y., Aug. 27, 1866; s. John Benjamin and Sarah Melissa (Yerton) P.; student pub. schs.; D.D., Potomac U., 1923, Wheaton (Ill.) Coll., 1927; m. Harriet Brock Lockhart, 1890; 1 dau., Ruth; m. 2d, Mrs. Etta Turner Dodge, 1936. Ordained to ministry Bapt. Ch., 1899; pastor North Church, Wilmington, Del., 1903-23; dean Phila. Sch. of the Bible, 1914-28; pastor First Ch., N.Y.C., 1948—. Author: Israel, Jehovah's Covenant People; Simple Studies in Daniel; Simple Studies in Matthew; Simple Studies in Romans; Simple Studies in The Revelation; God's Prophecies for Plain People; Bible Questions Answered; Christ in the Psalms; By Grace, Through Faith. Plus Northing: Simple Studies in Galatians; Into the Holiest: Simple Studies in Hebrews; Bible Doctrine Primer; Simple Studies in I and II Corinthians; Simple Studies in I and II Thessalonians, I and II Timothy, Titus and Philemon; Simple Studies in James, I and II, Peter, I, II and III; John and Jude; Christian Fundamentals; Bible Doctrine Primer; Believe and Live; Light in Darkness, Loving His Appearing; The Family of God; Nearing the End; The Truth About Hell. Founder and editor Serving-and-Waiting (monthly mag.), 1911-28. Consulting editor Scofield Reference Bible. Home: 104 S. Douglas Av., Margate City, N.J. Died Sept. 15, 1950; buried Silver Brook Cemetery, Wilmington, Del.

PETTUS, Maia, author; b. at Elkmont, Ala., 1875; d. Dr. J. A. and Musie (Cartwright) P.; grad. Cox Coll., Atlanta, spl. studies in music. Mem. United Daus. of the Confederacy. Regular contbr. to Uncle Remus, Golden Age; Am. corr. Cosmos, Amsterdam, Holland; contbr. to various mags. Author: Princess of Glenndale, 1902; Meda's Heritage, 1906. Address: 202 N. Beaty, Athens, Ala. Died Aug. 20, 1956; buried Athens (Ala.) Cemetery.

PETTUS, Willaim Bacon, coll. pres.; b. Mobile, Ala., Aug. 28, 1880; s. Willie Tinsley and Emma Jeter (Pettus) P.; student U. Mo., 1898-1901; B.A., Columbia U., 1904; grad. student U. Nanking (China), 1908-10, Hamburg and in Oriental Seminar, Berlin U. (Germany), 1912; D.Ped., U. So.Cal., 1930; Columbia U. Medal of Excellence, 1941; m. Sarah Lydia De Forest, June 13, 1905; children—Rev. John De Forest, Dr. William Winston. With Coll. of Chinese Studies, Peiping, China, 1916-45; pres. 1916-45, now emeritus; pres. of Cal. Coll. in China since 1930; responsible for development both colls. and lib. of Coll. of Chinese Studies which largest on China in China; sometime lecturer in oriental dept. U. Cal., Claremnt Coll., U. Nanking, Stanford U., U.So. Cal., and Mills Coll. Sec. internat. com. Y.M.C.A. of N. Am., 1906-42; national committee Y.M.C.A. of China, 1906-42; mem., dir. Inst. of Fine Arts, Peiping. Life mem. Internat. Phonetic Assn., N. China branch and Korean branch of Royal Asiatic Soc.; life fellow Royal Geog. Soc.; mem. Phi Tau Phi (Yenching U.), Phi Theta (U. Cal.). Baptist. Mason (33°). Clubs: University (Los Angeles); Shanghai American (Shanghai, China); Peking, Western Returned Students (Peiping); Bohemian (San Francisco); Faculty Club Berkeley, Cal. Writer and lecturer on Chinese phonetics, Chinese jades, painting and gardens, Chinese porcelains, Mohammedanism in China, Masonic symbols and Masonry in China. Address: College of Chinese Studies, Peiping, China; and also California College in China, 1700 Spruce St., Berkeley 9, Cal. Died Dec. 8, 1959; buried Chapel of the Chimes, Oakland, Cal.

PEURIFOY, John E(mil), ambassador; born Walterboro, S.C., Aug. 9, 1907; s. John H. and Emily (Wright) P.; student U.S. Mil. Acad.,1926-28, bus. adminstrn., Am. Univ., 1935, internat. law, George Washington Univ., 1939-40; m. Betty Jane Cox, Oct. 2, 1936; children—John Clinton, Daniel Byrd. Asst. to ins. head, Kansas City Land Bank, 1928-29; ins. underwriter, New York, 1929-31; asst. mgr. and cashier The Childs Co., N.Y. City, 1931-34; acting chief of sect. procurement div. Treasury Dept., Washington, D.C., 1935-37; clerk U.S. Capitol, Jan.-Aug. 1938; econ. analyst, Labor Dept., Aug.-Sept., 1938, State Dept., 1938-39, divisional asst., 1939-42; mem. policy commn., reviews and appeals commn. on export applications Bd. of Econ. Warfare, 1942-43; detailed to Embassy, Rio de Janeiro, Oct.-Dec. 1942; mem. program adjustment commn. and alt. mem. requirements commn. War Prodn. Bd., 1942-44; exec. officer, Office Pub. Information, State Dept., 1944-45; spl. asst. to sec. gen. U.N. Conf. on Internat. Orgn., San Francisco, 1945; acting dep. dir. Office of Internat. Information and Cultural Affairs, and spl. asst. Office of Pub. Affairs, 1945-46; spl. asst. to under sec. of State, Mar. 24, 1946-47; acting asst. sec. of State, Jan. 23-Mar. 17, 1947, apptd. asst. sec. of state, 1947, dep. under sec., 1949-50; ambassador to Greece, 1950-53, to Guatemala, 1953-54, to Thailand, 1954—. Decorated D.S.M. of Dept. of State, 1950. Episcopalian. K.P. Address: care Dept. State, Washington. Died Aug. 12, 1955; buried Arlington Nat. Cemetery.

PEW, John G., pres. Sun Shipbldg. & Dry Dock Co., ret. 1950; dir. Sun Oil Co., Del. County Nat. Bank, Chester. Home: Moylan, Pa. Office: Chester, Pa., also 25 Broadway, N.Y.C. Died July 1, 1954.

PEYSER, Ethan Allen, lawyer; b. Poughkeepsie, N.Y., Nov. 21, 1897; s. David M. and Ida Mary (Purdy) P.; LL.B., U. of Wash., 1922; George Washington U., 1943; m. Marie Delvendahl, Dec. 20, 1923; children—Barbara Marie, Ethan Allen. Criminal deputy prosecuting attorney, King County, Wash., 1923-29; sr. mem. law firm Peyser, Cartano, Botzer & Chapman, Seattle, 1929—; chmn. Bd. Triplex Corp. of Am., 1936—; pres. Washington Gas & Electric Co., 1950-55; v.p., Lake Washington Shipyards, Seattle, 1939-46; mem. bd. dir. U.S. Finishing Co., 1951; consultant Board of Economic Warfare, mem. Censorship Operating Bd., 1941-42; dir. fgn. div. War Production Bd.; alternate mem. President's Soviet Protocol Com.; mem. non-military Supplies Com. of combined production and resources bd. (British, Can. and Am.); mem. Chinese Petroleum Com., Foreign Petroleum Requiremets Com., W.P.B. Requirements Com., 1942-43; exec. dir. Combined Production and Resources Bd. (British, Can. and Am.) 1944; cons. to chmn. Nat. Security Resources Bd., 1948-53, dir. office of spl. security program, 1951—; chairman N.W. Seminar of International Law, 1947-48. Commd. 2d lt. Inf., Machine Gun Sect., World War I. Mem. Seattle Chamber of Commerce, Am. Bar Assn., S.A.R., (pres. Washington State Chapter 1935-36). Home: 2855 Magnolia Blvd. Office: 1415 Vance Bldg., Seattle, Wash. Died Feb. 1, 1958; buried Acacia Meml. Park, Seattle.

PEYSER, Julius I., lawyer, banker; b. Washington, D.C. son of Philip and Natalie (Goodman) P.; LL.B., Georgetown University Law Sch., 1899; LL.M., Columbian (now George Washington U.), 1900; D.C.L., George Washington School of Diplomacy and Comparative Jurisprudence, 1901; married Miriam I. Prince, October 2, 1906; children—Philip Prince, Victoria Prince (Mrs. Aaron W. Jacobson). Admitted to D.C. bar, 1899, and began practice at Washington; member Darr, Peyser, Whiteford & Darr, 1899-1917, Peyser, Edelin & Peyser, 1917-26; now associated with Aaron W. Jacobson; chairman of bd. Security Bank, 1915—; pres. R. Harris & Co.; treasurer Judd & Detweiler, Inc.; prof. equity practice George Washington U. (formerly Nat. U. Law Sch.); formerly v.p. Traders Nat. Bank and Mchts. & Mechanics Bank. Capt. U.S. Army, chief of Housing and Health Div., Office Sec. of War, 1918-19; maj., Specialist R.C., now lt. col., U.S. Army Res. (Specialist). Decorated Memorial Medal Union of Gladiators of Macedonia; Cross of Order of Compassionate Heart; Fundacion Internacional, Eloy Alfaro (Ecuador), American Legion decoration for meritorious services. Member Bd. of Edn., D.C., 1924-25; gen. counsel Parent-Teachers Assn., 1925-26. Pres. D.C. Pub. Sch. Assn.; elected pres. Bar Assn. of D.C., 1929; v.p. for D.C. of Am. Bar Assn., 1920 (comm. on current banking decisions and legislation, 1946-47); charter mem. U.N. League of Lawyers; treas. United Nations War Relief Inc., Washington, D.C.; financial advisor Children's Art Center; dir. Am. Youth Hostels. Former v.p. Federation Interallié des Anciens Combattants, elected Belgrade, 1929; Commrs. Planning Com., D.C.; v.p. Citizens Council for Community Planning. Member Board of Trade, Merchants and Manufacturers Assn., Am. Legion (dept. commander D.C., 1925-26), Mil. Order World War, 40 Hommes et 8 Chevaux, El Toro, Pi Gamma Mu. Clubs: Sojourners, Commanders, First Last Man, Officers, Post Mortem, University, Woodmont Country; Fossils (New York); Heroes of '76. Address: Sheraton Park Hotel, Washington. Died June 7, 1953.

PEYTON, Bernard Robertson (pā'tŭn), army officer; b. Raymond, Miss., Sept. 24, 1886; s. John William and Lucretia (Moseley) P.; B.S., U.S. Naval Acad., 1910; grad. Mounted Service Sch., 1914, Field Arty. Sch., 1923, Command and Gen. Staff Sch., 1925, Army War Coll., 1933; m. Evelyn Haile, June 20, 1917; 1 dau., Evelyn Haile (wife of Capt. Richard Watson, U.S.A.). Commd. 2d lt., F.A., U.S. Army, 1910; advanced through the grades to col. 1939. Served as capt. with 6th F.A., 1st Div., France, 1917-19; prof. mil. sci. and tactics, Stanford, 1936-39; mil. attaché Berlin, Germany, Sept. 1939-July 1941. Democrat. Episcopalian. Club: Rotary (pres. 1939), Palo Alto, Calif. Died Mar 2, 1959†.

PEYTON, Ephraim Goeffrey, army officer; b. Gallatin, Miss., Jan. 19, 1876; s. Judge Ephraim Geoffrey and Annie (Coleman) P.; B.S., U.S. Mil. Acad., 1899; m. Bertha Augusta Moore, Oct. 15, 1919; 2 step-daus., Helen Van Rensselaer Stillman (wife of Gen. George Honnen, U.S. Army), Charlotte Aleta Crawford Stillman (wife of Col. Norman A. Matthias, U.S. Army). Commd. 2d lt. U.S. Army, 1899, advanced through grades to brig. gen., 1938; assigned to 6th U.S. Inf. and participated in The Philippines Insurrection, Spanish-Am. War, 1899-1901, with 18th U.S. Inf., 1901-10, with Philippine Scouts, 1910-12; served under Gen. Pershing in his Moro disarmament campaigns, 1910, 11, 12; with 18th Inf., Mexican Border, 1913-15; tactical officer, U.S. M.A., 1915-17; trained emergency officers, Fort Meyer, Va., 1917; with 320th inf., 80th div., Camp Lee, Va. and in France, 1917-19, served on British front, July-Sept. 1918; comd. 320th Inf., 80th Div. in St. Mihiel offensive, and in Meuse Argonne offensive, 1918; assigned to command of Mil. Personnel assisting Am. Commn. to negotiate peace in Paris, 1919; ret. for disability in line of duty, 1940; organized Atlanta Ga. Civilian Defense Corps, 1941, and served as comdr., 1941-42. Decorated D.S.M., Purple Heart, Silver Star citation. Presbyn. Mason (Shriner). Elk. Home: 147 17th St. N.E., Atlanta 5. Died Jan. 1, 1950; buried Arlington Nat. Cemetery.

PEYTON, Harlan Ide, Rep. nat. committeeman; b. Spokane, Wash., Jan. 22, 1894; s. Isaac Newton and Victor Anne B. (Ide) P.; student Harvard Mil. Sch., Los Angeles Chauncy Hall, U. of So. Calif.; m. Ruth Avery, Jan. 22, 1914; children—Harlan Avery, David Wakefield; m. 2d, Ruth Cherrier Burke, July 23, 1935. Pres. Peyton Investment Co., Spokane, Wash., also Calif. and Ida., 1931—; Composite Bond and Stock Fund (Spokane). Served as civilian instructor Untied States Sch. Mil. Aeronautics, U. Calif., World War I; ineligible for service with Air Corps by reason of faulty vision. Pres. Spokane C. of C., 1924-25, 44-45; past pres. Asso. C. of C. of Wash.; past pres. Spokane Phliharmonic Orchestra; dir. Community Concert Assn.; past v.p. U.S. C. of C.; v.p. Spokane Red Cross; mem. adv. com. Inst. Tech., Wash. State Coll. Rep. nat. committeeman for Wash.; past vice chmn. Rep. Nat. Com. Episcopalian. Mason. Clubs: Shadow Mountain (Palm Desert, Cal.); Chevy Chase (Md.); Metropolitan (Washington); Rainier (Seattle); Spokane, Spokane Country (past pres.), Northwest Golf Assn. (past pres.). Home: E. 1522 Woodcliff Rd. Office: Peyton Bldg., Spokane, Wash. Died May 23, 1958; buried Spokane, Wash.

PFAHLER, George Edward (fä'lẽr), radiologist; b. Numidia, Pa., Jan. 29, 1874; s. William H. and Sarah A. (Stine) P.; B.E., Bloomsburg State Normal Sch. (now Tchrs. Coll.), 1894; M.D., Medico Chirurg. Coll., Phila., 1898; Sc.D., Ursinus Coll., also LL.D., 1942; D.M. R.E., Cambridge U., Eng., 1926; m. Frances Simpson, Nov. 8, 1908 (died Mar. 15, 1910); m. 2d, Muriel Bennett July 10, 1918. Intern Phila. Gen. Hosp., 1898-99, asst. chief resident physician, 1899-1902; clin. prof. roentgenology Medico-Chirurg. Coll., 1909-12, prof., 1912-16; prof. radiology U. Pa., 1916—; dir. radiological dept. Misericordia Hosp., Phila. Trustee Ursinus Coll. Hon. fellowship Faculty Radiologists, London, 1950. Mem. Am. Roentgen Ray Soc. (pres. 1910), Am. Electrotherapeutic Assn. (pres. 1912), Am. Radium Soc. (pres. 1922), Am. Coll. Radiology (pres. 1923), A.M.A., Pa. Med. Soc., Phila. Dermathol. Soc. (pres. 1956-57), Phila. County Med. Soc. (pres. aid assn. 1953—); hon. mem. Brit., French, German, Austrian, Scandinavian and Russian, Panama, Cuba, Peru radiol socs., Radiol. sect. Royal Soc. Medicine London, England, and Mexico. Episcopalian. Clubs: Medical, Medical Literature (Phila.). Pioneered in radium and X-ray treatment of cancer. Contbr. to med. jours. Home: 6463 Drexel Rd. Office: 1930 Chestnut St., Phila. Died Jan. 29, 1957; buried Valley Forge Cemetery.

PFEFFER, Edward Charles, business exec.; b. New Orleans, Feb. 20, 1884; s. Emile and Margaret (Rische) P.; student pub. schs.; m. Rose Skilnik, June 30, 1933; children—Edward Charles, Elizabeth Louise (dec.). Stock clerk Cluett, Peabody & Co., Inc., New Orleans; successively salesman for Tex., office mgr. Dallas, office mgr., Phila., office mgr., Chgo., mgr. and dir. Chgo., became v.p. sales, N.Y.C., 1938, v.p. sales and merchandising, 1940-49. Mem. adv. coms. OPA and WPA, during World War II. Former dir. Nat. Shirt and Pajama Assn. Roman Catholic. Home: 20 Church St., Greenwich, Conn. Office: 10 E. 40th St., N.Y.C. Died Nov. 26, 1954.

PFEIFFER, Robert Henry, univ. prof., curator; b. Bologna, Italy, Feb. 14, 1892; s. George Washington and Adelia (Rodenbach) P.; parents U.S. citizens; student Lycée, Bologna, 1908-11, Theol. Sch., Geneva,

Switzerland, 1911-13, 1914-15 (B.D.), U. of Geneva, 1914-15 (B.D.), U. of Berlin and Tübingen, 1913-14; A.M., Harvard, 1920, Ph.D., 1922, S.T.M., 1923; LL. D., Bennett College, 1949; D.D. (hon.), Cal. Western U., 1954; D.H.L. (hon.), Ill. Wesleyan U., 1956; m. Matilde Valenti, Mar. 29, 1916; children—Paul Henry, Louise Anna. Ordained to ministry of Meth. Ch., Oct. 8, 1916; pastor, Sanborn, N.Y., 1916-19; instr., Harvard, 1922-28, lectr., 1929-30, asst. prof., Semitic langs. and hist., 1930-36, lecturer 1936-53; Hancock prof. of Hebrew and other oriental langs. since 1953, curator of Semitic Museum since 1931; instructor, Boston University, 1924-25, assistant professor, 1925-27, asso. professor, 1927-29, professor, 1929-30, and since 1947; director Harvard-Baghdad School excavations, Nuzi, Iraq, 1928-28. Vis. prof., U. of Rome (Italy), Fulbright grant, 1951. Lebanese Order of Merit, 1st class, gold medal, 1949. Corp. member Am. Schs. of Oriental Research. Mem. Am. Acad. Arts and Sciences, Archæol. Inst., Soc. Bibl. Lit., Am. Oriental Soc., Nat. Assn., Bibl. Instr., Am. Assn. Univ. Profs. Republican. Methodist. Club: Harvard Faculty. Author: The Archives of Shilwateshub, 1932; State Letters of Assyria, 1935; One Hundred New Selected Nuzi Texts (with A. E. Speiser), 1937; Introduction to the Old Testament, 1941; History of New Testament Times, 1949. Collaborator: Dictionnaire Encyclopédique de la Bible, I, 1932, II, 1935. Editor of Jour. of Bibl. Lit., 1943-47. Author of numerous papers and monographs. Home: 57 Francis Av., Cambridge, Mass. Died Mar. 16, 1958; buried Mount Auburn Cemetery, Cambridge, Mass.

PFLAGER, Harry Miller (flā'gẽr), director Gen. Steel Castings Corp.; b. St. Louis, Mo., Nov. 29, 1866; s. Henry Wilt and Jessie (Miller) P.; ed. St. Louis Manual Training Sch. and Washington U.; m. Alyce Louise Barber, Apr. 5, 1893; 1 son, Henry Barber. Mech. supt. Pullman Co. until 1901; v.p. Am. Clock Co., 1901-03; asst. v.p. Am. Steel Foundries, 1903; v.p. and sr. v.p. Commonwealth Steel Co., 1904-29; senior vice president successor of same, Gen. Steel Castings Corp., 1929-46; dir. First Nat. Bank, Gen. Steel Castings Corp., St. Louis, Metropolitan Y.M.C.A., St. Louis. Fellow Am. Soc. M.E. (hon. mem.); mem. St. Louis C. of C., Congl. City Missionary Soc. St.L., Franklin Inst. (recipient of Henderson medal). Republican. Congregationalist. Clubs: Noonday, Bogey Golf, St. Louis Country, Racquet (St. Louis). Developed manufacture of large steel castings, notably trucks used under passenger cars, etc., locomotive beds, etc. Home: 19 Kingsbury Pl., St. Louis, Mo., and Sulphur Springs, Mo. Office: Boatmen's Bank Bldg., St. Louis. Died Oct. 28, 1951; buried Bellefontaine Cemetery, St. Louis.

PFORZHEIMER, Carl Howard, investment banker; b. New York City, Jan. 29, 1879; s. Isaac and Mina (Heyman) P.; ed. schs. of N.Y. City; m. Lily M. Oppenheimer, Jan. 16, 1906; children—Carl H., Jane P. Long. Est. Carl H. Pforzheimer & Co. (formerly Carl H. Pforzheimer), N.Y. City, 1902; pres. Petroleum & Trading Corp., N.Y. City, 1928—; treas. The Purchase Community, Inc., Westchester Co., 1919-43. Pres. Carl and Lily Pforzheimer Foundation, Inc.; chmn. Westchester Co. Planning Commn., 1939-42, Emergency Work Bur., 1931-34, Commn. on Govt., 1934-36. Trustee United Hosp. of Port Chester, N.Y., Institute of Pub. Adminstrn.; chmn. bd. Horace Mann School; mem. board governors White Plains (New York) Hospital; treas. Westchester County Assn.; director Westchester Cancer Committee; dir. Westchester County Council of Social Agencies, Inc. (treasurer of The New York Public Library, N.Y. C. Member National Municipal League (treasurer), Newcomen Soc. of Eng., Modern Language Assn. of Am., Bibliographical Soc. of Eng., Bibliographical Soc. of Am. Clubs: Elizabethan of Yale (hon. mem.); Bankers, City Midday, Grolier (N.Y. City); Westchester Country (Rye, N.Y.); Century Country, Quaker Ridge Golf. Pub. The Carl H. Pforzheimer Library English Literature 1475-1700 (3 vols.), 1940. Home: Hidden Brook Farm, Purchase, N.Y. Office: 25 Broad St., N.Y.C. Died Apr. 4, 1957.

PHALEN, Harold Romaine (fā'lĕn), mathematics; b. Acton, Mass., Apr. 21, 1889; s. Edwin Anthony and Harriet Davis (Reed) P.; B.S., Tufts, 1912; M.S., U. Chgo., 1923, Ph.D., 1926; m. Lucie Hortense Snyder, Dec. 20, 1914 (died Aug. 1933); children—Carolyn Annette, Edward Snyder (dec.); m. 2d, Elizabeth Nagle Kinder, July 2, 1938. Draftsman with Improved Paper Machine Co., Nashua, N.H., 1912, Am. Locomotive Co., Providence, R.I., 1913; instr. in mathematics, James Millikin U., 1913-15, Berea Coll., 1915-18, Armour Inst. Tech., 1918-26; prof. mathematics, St. Stephen's Coll. (now Bard Coll.), Columbia, 1926—, provost, 1929-33; (on leave) prof., Brown U., 1939-40; asso. prof. mathematics, Coll. William and Mary, 1941-46, prof. 1946-54, head dept., 1954—. Mem. Am. Math. Soc., Math. Assn. Am., A.A.A.S., Sigma Xi, Sigma Tau Alpha, Triangle. Episcopalian. Mason. Club: Exchange of Red Hook, N.Y. (ex-pres.). Author: History of Action, 1954. Translator: Lezioni de Geometria Proviettiva (by Enriques). Home: 130 Chandler Court, Williamsburg, Va. Died May 30, 1955; buried Action, Mass.

PHALEN, James Matthew (fā'lĕn), editor; b. Harvard, Ill., Nov. 26, 1872; s. John Dennis and Anastasia (Lawless) P.; Ph.G., Northwestern U., 1892; M.D., Univ. of Ill., 1900; hon. grad. Army Medical Sch., 1902, London Sch. Tropical Medicine, 1907; distinguished grad., Army Sch. of the Line, 1920; grad. Gen. Staff Sch., 1921, Army War Coll., 1922; m. Gertrude Sibley, Apr. 14, 1904. Interne Cook County Hosp., Chicago, 1900-01; commd. 1st. lt. Med. Corps, U.S. Army, 1901, and advanced to col. 1927; pres. Army Bd. for Investigation of Tropical Diseases, Manila, 1907-10; lecturer on tropical medicine, N.Y. Post-Grad. Med. Sch., 1911-13; chief hosp. div., Surgeon Gen. Office, 1922-24; librarian, Army Med. Library, 1924-27; surgeon, Panama Dept., 1927-30; editor, The Military Surgeon, since 1940. Served as div. surgeon, 86th (Blackhawk) Div., Med. inspector First Army A.E.F.; surgeon, Port of Bordeau; surgeon 6th Div., in Army of Occupation in Germany, World War I. Sec. Asso. Military Surgeons. Fellow Am. Coll. of Surgeons; mem. Am. Med. Assn., Am. Legion, Mil. Order Carabao. Awarded Hoff medal, 1902. Clubs: Army and Navy, Army and Navy Country. Author: Chiefs of Med. Dept. U.S. Army, 1940; Sinnissippi, 1942; I Follow Thackeray, 1945; In the Path of Stones, 1950; also 150 jour. articles on military and medical history and biography. Contributed to Dictionary of American Biography. Home: 3000 Tilden St. N.W. Office: Armed Forces Inst. of Pathology, Washington. Died Oct. 5, 1954; buried Arlington Nat. Cemetery.

PHANEUF, Louis Eusébe, physician; b. St. Helaire, P.Q., Can., Feb. 27, 1884; s. Wilbrod E. and Laura (L'Heureux) P.; Pharm.D., Mass. Coll. Pharmacy, 1905, Ph.C., 1905; M.D. summa cum laude, Tufts Coll., 1913, D.Sc., 1933; M.D. (hon.), Laval University, 1952; married Florence Alles, September 24, 1921. In practice as gynecologist and obstetrician 1915—; prof. gynecology, Tufts Coll. Med. Sch., 1927; surgeon-in-chief, dept. obstetrics and gynecology, Carney Hospital, South Boston, Massachusetts; consultant, department of gynecology, New England Medical Center and Malden (Mass.) Hospital; surgeon-in-chief dept. of gynecology, Boston Dispensary (unit of N.E. Med. Center); consulting gynecologist, Beth Israel, Leonard Morse, Henrietta D. Goodall, Noble and Attleboro hosps.; cons. gynecol. and obstetrician, Fall River Gen. and St. Anne's hosps. (both Fall River), Burbank Hosp. (Fitchburg, Mass.); cons. specialist in gynecology, U.S. Marine Hosp., Boston. Served as 1st lt., Med. Corps, U.S. Army, World War I. Decorated Officer of Order of Crown (Belgium). Fellow Am. Coll. Surgns.; mem. A.M.A., Am. Gynecol. Soc., Am. Assn. Obstet., Gynecol. and Abdominal Surgeons, Mass. Med. Soc., Am. Bd. Obstetrics and Gynecology (dir. 1938-47), Internat. Soc. of Surgery, Am. Radium Soc., Boston Surg. Soc., Boston Obstet. Soc., New Eng. Obstet. and Gynecol. Soc., Am. Assn. History of Medicine; hon. mem. Société Royale de Gynécologie et d'Obstétrique (Belgium), Gynecol., Obstet. Soc. of Bucharest (Roumania), Los Angeles Surg. Soc., Los Angeles Obstet. Soc.; corr. mem. Société d'Obstétrique et de Gynécologie de Paris, Assn. des Gynécologues et Obstétriciens de Langue Francaise (both France); mem. Alpha Omega Alpha, Sigura K. Club: Algonquin (Boston). Author of over 120 monographs, also numerous articles in French and Belgian med. jours. Home: 84 Hammondswood Rd., Chestnut Hill, Mass. Office: 270 Commonwealth Av., Boston 16. Died Sept. 20, 1953.

PHELAN, John, coll. prof.; b. Homer, Mich., Sept. 19, 1879; s. John and Alice Mary (Walshe) P.; grad. Western State Teachers Coll., Kalamazoo, Mich., 1908; A.B., U. of Mich., 1910, A.M., 1912; m. Ida May Densmore, Jan. 1, 1913; 1 son, John Densmore. Teacher, later prin. rural schs., Calhoun County, Mich., 1896-1902; prin. pub. schs. Hoopeston, Ill., 1904-06; acting dir. rural sch. dept., Western State Teachers Coll., 1910-12; dir. rural sch. dept., State Normal Sch., Stevens Point, Wis., 1912-15; prof. rural sociology, and head of dept., Mass. Agrl. Coll., Amherst, 1915-24, dir. short courses, 1918-24, and summer sessions, 1920-24; instructor summer sessions, University of Minn., 1917, Teachers College (Columbia), 1919; Ohio University 1946-50; lecturer Simmons Coll., Boston, 1923-24; professor of edn. and head of department, Mich. State Coll., East Lansing, 1924-27, also dean of coll., 1925-28; prof. edn., Carleton College, 1928-1932, prof. sociology and anthropology, 1932-50, chmn. dept., 1932-47; prof. sociology Hanover Coll., 1950-51, ret. On leave, research in anthropology and sociol., Am. U. at Cairo, Egypt, 1937-38. YMCA work, Camp Devens, Ayer, Mass., 1918. Mem. Minn. Ednl. Assn., Minn. Inst. of Governmental Research, Nat. Assn. Schs. Social Adminstrn. (v.p., mem. exec. com.), Am. Sociol. Soc., Nat. Country Life Assn. Minn. Acad. Science, Phi Kappa Phi, Kappa Epsilon. Conglist. Club: Quadrangle (U. of Mich.). Author: Elements of Rural Economics and Rural Sociology, 1914; Readings in Rural Sociology, 1919. Co-author: Society Under Analysis, 1942. Home: 4068 Graceland Av., Indpls. Died Mar. 15, 1952; buried Oaklawn Cemetery, Northfield, Minn.

PHELAN, Sidney M., Jr., business exec.; b. Vicksburg, Miss., Mar. 8, 1886; s. Sidney Marcellus and Emma Harrison (Balfour) P.; grad. St. Paul's Sch., Garden City, L.I.; A.B., Yale, 1909; m. Lois Baylor Perley, Oct. 20, 1923; children—William Balfour, Anne Baylor. Clerk Garnett & Allen Paper Co., St. Louis, 1909-11, dept. head Graham Paper Co., St. Louis, 1911-17; sales mgr. Eddy Paper Co., Three Rivers, Mich., 1917-21; asst. mgr. Mac Sim Bar Paper Co., Otsego, Mich., 1922-24; v.p., gen. mgr. Foster Paper Co., Utica, N.Y., 1925-27; v.p. W.Va. Pulp & Paper Co., N.Y.C., 1940, dir., 1945—, 1st v.p., 1948—. Mem. adv. coms., kraft paper industry for WPB and OPA in 1942. Vice-pres. Nat. Paperboard Assn., 1936-39. Served in U.S. Army as pfc. F.A., Central Officers Tng. Sch., Camp Zachary Taylor, Ky., 1918. Mem. S.A.R., Phi Beta Kappa, Alpha Delta Phi. Republican. Episcopalian. Clubs: Elihu, Yale (N.Y.C.); Tavern (Chgo.); Stamford Rural Republican. Home: Old Wire Mill Rd., Stamford, Conn. Office: 230 Park Av., N.Y.C. Died Nov. 8, 1950; buried Bellefontaine Cemetery, St. Louis.

PHELPS, Earle Bernard, sanitarian; b. Galesburg, Ill., July 10, 1876; s. Lucius Joshua and Ida May (Taylor) P.; desc. of William Phelps, the immigrant, Dorchester, Mass., 1630; B.S. in Chemistry, Mass. Inst. of Tech., 1899; m. Helen May Ellis, Oct. 29, 1902; children—Ellis K., Eleanor Frances, Winston, Barbara Ruth, Natalee Helen. Asst. bacteriologist, Mass. St. Bd. of Health, Lawrence Expt. Sta., 1899-1903; chemist and bacteriologist, Sanitary Research Lab., Mass. Inst. Tech., 1903-13; asst. prof. chem. biology, Mass. Inst. Tech., 1908-13; asst. hydrographer, U.S. Geol. Survey, 1906-11; consulting sanitary expert, 1906-13; prof. chemistry and chief div. of chemistry, Hygienic Lab., U.S. Pub. Health Service, 1913-19; prof. sanitary science, Coll. Physicians and Surgeons (Columbia), 1925-43; prof. emeritus since 1943; prof. sanitary sci., University of Fla., since 1944. Recipient Lasker award Am. Public Health Assn., 1953. Mem. Am. Public Health Association A.A.A.S., Member medical section, Advisory Commission of Council National Defense, 1917. Author: Principles of Public Health Engineering, 1925; Stream Sanitation, 1944; Public Health Engineering, 1948, Vol. II, 1949; also papers on sewage disposal and pub. health subjects in proceedings of socs. and tech. journals. Address: University of Florida, Gainesville, Fla.; (summer) South Harwich, Mass. Died May 29, 1953; buried Gainesville, Fla.

PHELPS, Esmond, lawyer; b. New Orleans, May 21, 1888; s. Ashton and Blanche (Moulton) P.; A.B., Tulane, 1907, LL.B., 1909; m. Harriott Kinloch Barnwell, Apr. 9, 1912; children—Ashton, Joseph Barnwell, Harriott Kinloch (Mrs. Charles F. Gay). Practiced at New Orleans, 1909—; mem. Spencer, Phelps, Dunbar & Marks. Mem. New Orleans Exec. Com. Good Govt. League, 1911, 12. Del. Progressive Party Nat. Conv., Chgo., 1916. Mem. La. Constl. Conv., 1921. Pres. bd. adminstrn. Tulane Ednl. Fund. Pres. bd. trustees Howard Meml. Library. Mem. Am., La. State bar assns., Sigma Chi, Phi Beta Kappa. Episcopalian. Clubs: Boston, New Orleans Country, Louisiana. Home: 384 Walnut St. Office: United Fruit Bldg., New Orleans. Died Oct. 18, 1950.

PHEMISTER, Dallas B(urton) (fĕm'ĭs-tẽr), surgeon; b. Carbondale, Ill., July 15, 1882; s. John T. and Elizabeth (Fox) P.; M.D., Rush Med. College, 1904; m. Katherine Gannon, Dec. 10, 1914; children—Katharine, Dean Bevan, Bruce, Mary (Mrs. John Beal). Practiced in Chicago since 1904; attending surg. and professor emeritus of surgery, University of Chicago Sch. Medicine. Major Med. Corps, A.E.F., 1917-19. Fellow and pres. American Coll. Surgeons, 1948-49; American Surgical Association (past pres.); hon. fellow Royal College Surgeons (England). Mem. Soc. Clinical Surgery, Chicago Surg. Soc., Interurban Surg. Club. Clubs: University, Quadrangle, Commercial, Wayfarers (Chicago). Home: 5755 Kenwood Av. Office: 950 E. 59th St., Chgo. Died Dec. 28, 1951; buried Crypt of First Unitarian Ch., Chgo.

PHILIP, Hoffman, ret. ambassador; b. Washington, July 13, 1872; s. Col. William Henry and Eliza Phillips (Worthington) P.; prep. edn. Lawrenceville (N.J.) Sch. and by pvt. tutors; studied Magdalene Coll. (U. Cambridge), and Columbian U. Law Sch., Washington; m. Josephine Roberts, Nov. 7, 1925. Served in Santiago Campaign, Spanish-Am. War, 1898, 1st Vol. Cav., "Rough Riders"; vice consul gen. consul gen. and sec. of Legation at Tangier, Morocco, 1901-08; mem. Mixed Claims Commn. at Casa Blanca, 1908; apptd. minister resident and consul gen. to Abyssinia, 1908; sec. of Embassy, Rio de Janeiro, 1909-10, Constantinople, 1910-12; apptd. chief Div. of Near Eastern Affairs, Dept. of State, 1912; re-appointed sec. of Embassy at Constantinople, 1912; received from President of U.S. the Red Cross Balkan War medal for services at San Stefano and Constantinople, 1912-13; vol. aid to ambassador to France, at Paris, 1914; apptd. sec. of Embassy of Class One, 1915, and counselor of Embassy at Constantinople, 1916, also charge d'affaires with representation of interests of allied powers at the Sublime Porte, 1916; instructed by sec. of state, Jan. 1917, to attempt to deliver by sea, Am. relief supplies to starving population of Syria; apptd. E.E. and M.P. to Colombia, 1917, and empowered by President to exchange treaty ratifications between U.S. and Colombia, relative to the Panama question; apptd. E.E. and M.P. to Uruguay, 1922; spl. ambassador for Uruguayan presdl. inauguration, 1923; E.E. and M.P. to Persia, 1925; E.E. and spl. rep. of the President for coronation of Shah of Persia, 1926; E.E. and M.P. to Norway, 1930-35; A.E. and P. to Chile, 1935-37. Chmn. delegation of U.S. to meeting of Am. states mems. ILO, Santiago, 1935; mem. delegation for Haiti to Pan-Am. Conf. for arbitration of claims against Santo Domingo, 1938. Mem. Soc. of Army of Santiago, 1898. Clubs: Alibi, Metropolitan (Washington,); Ends of the Earth (N.Y.C.). Home: 2228 Massachusetts Av., Washington. Died Oct. 31, 1951.

PHILIPP, Richard, architect; b. Mayville, Wis., Aug. 2, 1874; s. Julius Henry and Anne Sophia (Melcher) P.; ed. Wis. pub. schs., studied under Dr. Gerhard Balg; m. Ella Smith, Aug. 23, 1923. Draftsman, 1892-1906; practice architecture in partnership with Peter Brust, 1906-27; in independent practice, 1927—, architect for Lawrence Coll., Appleton, Wis. 1932-50, Kohler Village and Kohler Co., Wis. Fellow Am. Inst. Architects (past pres. Wis. chpt.). Clubs: University (Milw.); Cliff Dwellers (Chgo.). Traveled extensively in Europe in connection with the study of architecture. Home: Route 1, Waukesha, Wis. Address: 756 N. Milwaukee St., Milw. Died Mar. 18, 1959.

PHILIPS, William Pyle, lawyer; b. West Chester, Pa., June 29, 1882; s. George Morris and Elizabeth M. (Pyle) P.; grad. West Chester State Normal Sch., 1898; studied Germany, 1898-99; A.B., Haverford (Pa.) Coll., 1902; A.M. Harvard, 1903, LL.B., 1907. Admitted to N.Y. bar, 1908; mem. Byrne & Cutcheon, 1912; mem. banking firm of J.&W. Seligman & Co., 1912-28; dir. Sinclair Oil Corp., Helena Rubinstein, Inc., Twentieth Century Fox Film Corp., United Artists Theatre Circuit, Inc. Mem. bd. mgrs. Haverford Coll. (alumni rep.). Fellow in perpetuity Met. Mus. of Art; founder in perpetuity N.Y. Zool. Soc. Mem. Phi Beta Kappa. Clubs: University, Piping Rock, Turf and Field, Harvard. Office: 200 W. 56th St., N.Y.C. 19. Died Dec. 18, 1950; buried Oakland Cemetery, West Chester, Pa.

PHILLIPS, Alexander Van Cleve, mfr.; b. Dubuque, Ia., Feb. 24, 1868; s. John Van Cleve and Mary (Byles) P.; ed. pub. schs.; m. Anna Davis Mills, Mar. 7, 1894; children—John Mills, Alice Elvira Weeks, Dr. Robert Titus, Dr. Richard Betts, Alexander Van Cleve, Juliet P. Miller, Barbara Wilson. With Bemis Bro. Bag Co., Boston, 1891—, v.p. 1911—, principal duty, buying burlaps from Calcutta. Made 11 trips to Calcutta, 1895-1932, including one around the world, 1919. Lived in Calcutta, 1923-32; was dir. and chmn. of The Angus Co., Ltd., Calcutta, owning and operating a jute mill for making jute cloth and bags, and an engring. works for making jute mill machinery, with over 7,000 employees. Charter mem. Boston C. of C. (42 yrs.) Owns 270 acre farm West Peabody and Lynnfield Centre, Mass. Home: 9 Commonwealth Av. Office: 40 Central St., Boston 5. Died Nov. 15, 1956.

PHILLIPS, Carl Chrisler, history; b. Bloomfield, Ind., Nov. 15, 1883; s. Joseph A. and Lily F. (Chrisler) P.; A.B., Ind. U., 1906, A.M., 1910; Ph.D., U. of Ill., 1911; m. Alice M. Martin, Aug. 27, 1911. Prof. history, U. of Mont., 1911-54; became emeritus, 1955; exec. v.p., 1936-37; dir. Student's Army Training Corps, 1918, and Summer School, 1919. Chmn. Missoula and Regional planning boards, 1935-39; state dir. Hist. Records Survey for W.P.A., 1936-39; regional dir. Federal Archives Survey for W.P.A., 1936-38; special rep. U.S. Employment Service, 1937. Historian, War Dept., Transportation Corps, 1944-46. Consultant, Federal Power Commission, 1946. Dir. museum and northwest history collections. Member American Historical Assn., Miss. Valley Hist. Assn., Sigma Pi, Phi Kappa Phi. Democrat. Mem. Disciples of Christ. Author: The West in the Diplomacy of the American Revolution, 1913; (with N.J. Lennes) The Story of Columbus, 1919. Editor: (with W. S. Lewis) The Journal of John Work, 1923; Forty Years on the Frontier, 1925; (with Seymour Dunbar) The Fort Owen Journals, 1927; Scenery of the Plains, Mountains and Mines (by Franklin Langworthy), 1932; Life in the Rocky Mountains, 1939. Asso. editor Pacific Northwest Quarterly, 1932-54; editorial bd. Montana Magazine of History; historical Editor Frontier and Midland, 1930-39. Author: Fur Trade in Montana, 1955; Fur Trade and the March of Empire, posthumously. Contbr. to hist. periodicals, Ency. Britannica, Britannica Year Book, 1938-39, Dictionary of Am. Biography, Dictionary of Am. History, 1938, Ency. Americana, Americana Annual, 1950, etc. Home: 419 Ford, Missoula, Mont. Died Dec. 23, 1956; buried Missoula Cemetery.

PHILLIPS, Charles Henry, bishop; b. Milledgeville, Ga., Jan. 17, 1958; s. George Washington and Nancy P.; student Atlanta (Ga.) U., 1874-78; A.B., Walden U., 1880, A.M., 1885; M.D., Meharry Med. Coll., 1882; theol. course, Walden U.; D.D., Wiley U., 1890, Philander Smith Coll., 1890; LL.D., Wilberforce, 1916; m. Lucy Ellis Tappan, Dec. 16, 1880 (died 1913); children—Charles Henry, Jasper Tappan, Mrs. Lady Emma Conway, Mrs. Lucy Shaw Stewart, Mrs. Lottie Beatrice James; m. 2d, Ella Checks, Aug. 1918; 1 dau., Laura Nancie. Ordained Colored M.E. ministry; pres. Lane Coll., Jackson, Tenn., 1883-84; pastor, Memphis, 1885-87, Washington, 1887-91, Louisville, 1891-93; presiding elder Mt. Sterling (Ky.)Dist., 1894; editor Christian Index, 1894-1902; elected bishop, May 1902. Mem. each Ecumenical Conf. 1891— (one of secs., Toronto, 1911). Founder chs. N.M., Ariz., Cal., Ind., also developed ch. in Ohio from 2 preaching points, Cleve. and Ripley, Ohio, to two presiding elders' dists. Has made three trips to Europe where he represented his church. Author: History of the Colored M.E. Church, 1898, 1925. Home: 10828 Drexel Av., Cleve. Died Apr. 12, 1951.

PHILLIPS, Coles, editor and writer; b. New Rochelle, N.Y., July 3, 1912; s. Coles and Teresa Kimball (Hyde) P.; ed. Capt. Mocatta's Sch., Glion, Switzerland, New Hampton Inst., U. of Va.; m. Isabelle Georgianne Schirer, Oct. 1, 1943 (div. Sept. 1947). Advertising space salesman, The Elks Mag., 1931, advancing through various positions to editor, 1936-49; Pacific war corr. (acctd. both Army and Navy), 1945. Mem. Sigma Nu. Elk. Contbr. to Elks Mag. Died Feb. 17, 1959.

PHILLIPS, Edward Charles, educator; b. Germantown, Philadelphia, Pa., Nov. 4, 1877; s. Charles Lacey and Mary (Steward) P.; A.B., Coll. of St. Francis Xavier (New York, N.Y.), 1898; student Woodstock (Md.) Coll., 1901-04 and 1909-13; Johns Hopkins U., 1904-06 and 1907-08; Ph.D., Johns Hopkins, 1908. Mem. Soc. of Jesus; ordained priest, Roman Catholic Ch., 1912; instr. in Classics, Coll. of St. Francis Xavier, 1906-07; lecturer on Apologetics, Woodstock Coll., 1913-14, Dogmatic Theology, 1915-19, prof. Mathematics and Astronomy, 1919-25, and dean, 1922-25; dir. Georgetown Coll. Obs., 1925-28; Provincial Superior, Md.-N.Y. Province of Jesuit Order, 1928-35; dean, Sch. of Philosophy, Woodstock Coll., 1935-40; asso. dean, Grad. Sch., Georgetown U., 1937-40, dean 1940-43; treas. N.Y. Province of Jesuit Order, 1943-46; spiritual director St. Andrew-on-Hudson since 1946. Member Am. Astron. Society, American Math. Assn., Philos. Soc. of Washington, D.C., Am. Assn. Jesuit Scientists (pres., 1941-46), Soc. Astronomique de France, The Royal Astron. Soc., Société Scientifique de Bruxelles. Contbr. articles to scientific jours. Address: St. Andrew-on-Hudson, Poughkeepsie, N.Y. Died May 9, 1952; buried St. Andrew-on-Hudson, Poughkeepsie.

PHILLIPS, Ellis Laurimore, corp. ofcl.; b. Naples, N.Y., Mar. 1, 1873; s. Richard Covel and Rhoda Jane (McConnell) P.; M.E., Cornell U., 1895, E.E., 1895; LL.D., Ohio Wesleyan, 1942, Fla. Southern, 1942; m. Kathryn Sisson McLean, Sept. 21, 1919; children—Ellis Laurimore and Jean McLean Phillips (Mrs. John E. Burri). Engaged as engr. in charge design and construction for Westinghouse, Church, Kerr & Co., 1895-1904; cons. engr., 1904—; pres. Long Island Lighting Co., 1912-37, chmn. bd., 1937-45; pres. Eastern Seaboard Securities Corp., 1930-50; pres., dir., E. L. Phillips & Co. Fellow Am. Soc. M.E., mem. Am. Inst. E.E., Am. Soc. Refrigerating Engrs., S.A.R. Republican. Methodist Mason (32°). Clubs: Union League, Metropolitan, Cornell, Downtown, Athletic, Railroad-Machinery (N.Y.C.); North Hempstead Country (L.I.). Home: 820 Fifth Av., N.Y.C. Office: 50 Church St., N.Y.C. Died Jan. 29, 1959; buried Woodlawn, N.Y.C.

PHILLIPS, Frank, banker, oil producer; b. Greeley County, Neb., Nov. 28, 1873; s. Lewis F. and Lucinda J. (Faucett) P.; student country schs., Ia.; m. Jane Gibson, Feb. 18, 1897; 1 son, John Gibson. In various lines of business until 1898; engaged in banking, Creston, Ia., 1898-1903; removed to Bartlesville, Okla., 1903, organized and pres. of Citizens Bank & Trust Co., now First Nat. Bank, of which is chmn. bd.; in oil business (with L. E. and Waite), 1903-17; hon. dir. and hon. chmn. bd. Phillips Petroleum Co.; rancher in Okla.; dir. First Nat. Bank (St. Louis), First Nat. Bank (Bartlesville). Former chmn. Gen. Dist. Com. No. 2 for petroleum industry, apptd. by Harold L. Ickes, petroleum coordinator; hon. dir. First American Assn. (Albuquerque, N.M.). Financial backer of Col. Arthur C. Goebel who won the Dole prize ($25,000) for first successful flight from Pacific Coast to Hawaii, 1927. Trustee The John and Mary R. Markle Found. (N.Y. C.), Kan. Wesleyan U. (Salina, Kan.); life mem. bd. trustees Lafayette Coll. (Easton, Pa.); patron Am. Museum Natural History (N.Y.C.); chmn. The Frank Phillips Found., Inc.; nat. councillor research inst. U. Okla. Mem. exec. com. Petroleum Industry War Council, Washington. Recipient Silver Buffalo for distinguished service to boyhood, also Silver Beaver award, Boy Scouts of America; adopted mem. Osage Tribe of Indians, 1930, and named Wah-Shah - She - Hlu-Ah-Ki-He-Kah (Eagle Chief); admitted to Okla. Hall of Fame, 1930. Decorated Chevalier Legion of Honor (France). Pres. Culver Fathers Assn., 1930; pres. 25 Year Club of Petroleum Industry, 1943. Mem. nat. council Nat. Econ. League, Nat. Audubon Soc., U.S. Air Force Assn., Am. Geog. Soc., Am. Soc. French Legion Honor, Nat. Inst. Social Sciences, Neb., Ia., Miss. Valley hist. socs., Native Sons and Daus. Neb., Am. Assn. Museums, Okla. State Archeol. Soc., Isaak Walton League, Ind. Petroleum Assn. Am., Am. Petroleum Inst. (dir.), Columbia U. Acad. of Polit. Science, Nat. Aero. Assn., Office Pub. Opinion Research (Princeton U.), Phi Beta Kappa (hon., Okla. chapter). Mason (33°, K.T., Shriner). Clubs: Lotos (art com.), Bankers, Metropolitan, Recess (N.Y. C.); Hillcrest (Bartlesville). Address: Bartlesville, Okla. Died Aug. 23, 1950; buried Family Mausoleum, Woolaroc Ranch, Bartlesville.

PHILLIPS, Henry A., business exec.; b. Allegheny, Pa.; s. Ormsby and Anne Stevenson (Bakewell) P.; student U. Pitts. Cashier and asst. business mgr. Pitts. Dispatch, 1885-95; junior bookkeeper A. W. and R. B. Mellon, Pitts., 1896-1904, confidential man to their children, 1913—; trustee Dollar Savings Bank (Pitts.); dir. Mellon Nat. Bank & Trust Co., Union Fire Ins. Co., Pa.-Pittsburgh Corp. (Mellon real estate); v.p., sec. and dir. Rockwell Mfg. Co.; 1st v.p., dir. Union Storage Co. (all Pitts.); pres., dir. Indian Creek Coal & Coke Co.; treas., dir. Indian Creek Valley Mine Drainage Co.; dir. Carborundum Co. (Niagara Falls, N.Y.). Trustee Mellon Inst. Indsl. Research; treas., mem. bd. mgrs. Kingsley Assn. Episcopalian. Clubs: Duquesne, Faculty Rolling Rock, University. Home: 5823 Kentucky Av., Pitts. 6. Office: 525 William Penn Way, Pitts. 22.* Died Jan. 14, 1950.

PHILLIPS, Henry Albert, author, editor; b. Brooklyn, Jan. 28, 1880; s. Henry Albert and Addie A. (Stanhope) P.; ed. Nashotah (Wis.) House, Gen. Theol. Sem., 1901-02; m. Margaret Wheeler Shepard, May 30, 1908; 1 son, Robert Henry Shepard. Asso. editor Metropolitan Mag., 1909, 10, Motion Picture Mag., 1910-11; lecturer and instr. Brooklyn Inst. Arts and Sciences, 1916-18, and Y.M.C. Assns. of New York. Sent abroad by Success Magazine and others to interview celebrities of foreign countries, 1925; spent 1926-27 in Central Europe and 1928-29 in Spain, gathering information for book; 1930, studying conditions in Japan, China, Manchuria and Korea, at invitation of Japanese Govt.; 1934, in Germany making survey of nat. socialism and polit. studies in Scandinavia, Austria and Italy; 1935-36, studying economics and social conditions in Caribbean and West Indies, also visiting all countries of South America via Straits of Magellan; 1937, completely covering Mexico on assignments for articles and books. Dramatic feature writer N.Y. Sunday Herald-Tribune, 1928-33; wrote "Traveling With News," dept. in New Outlook, 1932-33; wrote story of rum in West Indies for Lit. Digest, 1933, also made exploration in Hayti, and visited S. America; following beginning of World War II, covered Jugoslavia, Rumania, Transylvania, Bukowina, Hungary, and Italy; article "Europe Faces Famine (Am. Mercury, Reader's Digest); survey address of Europeana, findings before special group in Washington; mag. and news corr., S. America, study of conditions in relation to U.S., 1941; contbr. articles relating to tour of S.A., to Nat. Geog. Mag., This Week, Christian Herald, Country Gentleman, Outdoor Life, 1942; also gathered material in southern and southwestern states for article "Raw Materials and People of Home Front in the War"; contributor to symposium in Reader's Digest, 1943. Mem. honorary board Baypath Coll., Worcester, Mass. Fellow Am. Geographic Soc.; corporate mem. of Gunn Memorial Library. Republican. Episcopalian. Clubs: Players, Explorers, Lambs, Playwrights (founder 1910). Author: Plot of the Short Story, 1912; Art in Short Story Narration, 1913; The Photodrama, 1914; The Universal Plot Catalog, 1916; The Feature Photoplay, 1921; Other People's Lives (novel), 1924; Meet the Germans, 1929; Meet the Spaniards, 1931; Meet the Japanese, 1932; Germany To-day and Tomorrow, 1935; White Eelephants in the Caribbean, 1936; New Designs for Old Mexico, 1938; Argentina—Pivot of Pan-American Peace, 1944; Brazil—Bulwark of Inter-American Relations, 1945; Venezuela—Oil for the Bombers of Democracy; also 25 photoplays, and plays, "House of Yesterday." Contributor to mags. including Cosmopolitan Journal of Living; Material on drama to Encyclopedia Americana. Lecturer and speaker over radio. Visited 9 republics of S.A., also 26 islands of Mexico and West Indies, 1935-36; studying conditions in Mexico and Yucatan, 1937, Germany, Italy, Hungary, Turkey, the Balkans, 1939; spl. expdn. studying oil fields of Venezuela via air, motor car and water, concluding 25,000 mile air journey through interior of all S. America, 1941; tour of South and Mexico, studying econ. and social problems; airlane survey in S. America; articles pub. in mags., 1946, 1947; corr. Newsweek and N. Am. Newspaper Alliance; covered S. African tour of Brit. royal family, 1947; fact-finding tour S. and S.W. Africa, N. and S. Rhodesia, Zululand, Basutoland, Belgian Congo etc.; addresses on S. African radio; articles in Am. and S. African newspapers and magazines; author (book) Cape of Good Hope to the Mountains of the Moon, 1949. Home: "Hasta Luego," Washington, Conn Address: Washington,

Conn. Died Jan. 28, 1951; buried East Morichas, L.I., N.Y.

PHILLIPS, Henry Disbrow, bishop; b. Phila., Jan. 16, 1882; s. Henry Desborough and Nancy (Phillips) P.; B.A., U. of the South, 1904, B.D., 1906; D. D., Oglethorpe U., 1920, U. of Ga., 1923, U. of South, 1938, Va. Sem., 1939; m. Ella d. Bishop and Mrs. Frederick Focke Reese, Sept. 25, 1907; children—Ella Parr (Mrs. Sam J. Slate), Nancy (Mrs. O. B. Mayer), Henrietta (Mrs. G. Simms McDowell, Jr.). Ordained deacon Protestant Episcopal Ch., 1906, priest, 1907; minister in charge St. Mark's Ch., LaGrange, Ga., and warden LaGrange Settlement, 1906-15; chaplain, U. of South, 1915-22; prof. English Bible, U. of the South and rector Otey Meml. Parish, Sewanee, Tenn., 1916-22; rector Trinity Ch., Columbia, S.C., 1922-38; bishop Diocese of Southwestern Va., Roanoke, 1938-54. Pres. bd. trustees Va. Episcopal Sch. (Lynchburg, Va.), Stuart Hall (Staunton, Va.), Boys' Home (Covington, Va.); trustee Theol. Sem. in Va., Episcopal High Sch. (Alexandria, Va.). Deputy to Gen. Conv. of Episcopal Ch., 1916, 25, 28, 31, 34, 37, associate sec. Nat. Field Dept., 1925-37; pres. Province of Washington, 1947-50. Founder LaGrange Settlement and Training Sch. for Ch. workers, 1906. Pres. Southern Intercollegiate Athletic Assn., 1919-22. Received citation for community service from Nat. Community Chest, 1938. Served in S.A.T.C., World War I. Mem. Delta Tau Delta, Omicron Delta Kappa, Phi Beta Kappa. Democrat. Mason (32°). Author of a number of pamphlets. Address: 1523 Devonshire Dr., Columbia, S.C. Died June 29, 1955; buried Trinity Episcopal Church Yard, Columbia.

PHILLIPS, Jesse Snyder, insurance official, lawyer; b. Allegany County, N.Y., May 4, 1871; s. Peter and Elizabeth (Snyder) P.; LL.B., U. of Mich., 1893; Doctor of Laws, Alfred University, 1939; married Mary T. Cannon, Sept. 3, 1902 (died 1939); children—Francis William, Mary Elizabeth; m. Emily M. Rosebery, July 1, 1944. Admitted to N.Y. bar, 1894; general practice, 1894-1921; general manager and counsel, Nat. Bur. of Casualty & Surety Underwriters, 1921-26; pres. Great Am. Indemnity Co., 1926-32, chairman board, 1933-50; director Great Am. Ins. Co., Am. Alliance Ins. Co., Rochester-Am. Ins. Co.; and all affiliate ins. companies in Great Am. Group; dir. Andover Nat. Bank. Supervisor Town of Andover, N.Y.; also village atty.; member N.Y. Assembly, 1901-11; mem. N.Y. Constl. Conv., 1915; state supt. of ins. N.Y., 1915-21; pres. Nat. Conv. Ins. Commrs., 1917; member State Ins. Bd., 1933—. Fellow Casualty Actuarial Soc.; mem. Am. Bar Assn., N.Y. Bar Assn., Chamber Commerce State of N.Y. Medal 50 yrs. a Mason, Grand Lodge Masons, N.Y., 1948. Republican. Presbyn. Clubs: Bankers of America, Downtown Athletic, University of Mich., Nat. Republican (N.Y.C.). Siwanoy (Bronxville); Westchester Country (Rye, N.Y.). Home: 25 Dellwood Rd., Bronxville, N.Y. Died Nov. 6, 1954.

PHILLIPS, John Marshall, museum dir.; born Kennett Square, Pa., Jan. 2, 1905; s. Marshall and Isabel Smith (Walter) P.; A.B., U. of Pa., 1927, A.M., 1929; M.L.A. (hon.), Trinity Coll., 1941. Curator silver, Mabel Brady Garvan Collections, Yale U., 1930-35; curator Americana, Garvan Collections, 1935-42; asst. dir. Yale Art Gallery, 1945-46; acting dir. gallery, 1946-47, dir., 1948—; prof. history art, 1948—; fellow Timothy Dwight Coll., Yale; dir. Textile Museum, Dist. Columbia; Liveryman and Freeman, Worshipful Co. of Goldsmiths, City of London (serving on Antique Plate Com., London 1945). Specialist in Am. silver and exposing forgeries in silver. Served with U.S. Army Intelligence, 1942-44; Monuments, Fine Arts and Archives, S.H.E.A.F., Apr.-Dec. 1944; Office Strategic Services, Looted Art Investigating Unit, London, 1944-46. Mem. Am. Numismatic Soc., Philomathean Soc., Walpole Soc., American Antiquarian Society, Colonial Soc. of Mass., Phi Beta Kappa. Republican. Quaker. Author: Early Connecticut Silver 1700-1830 (1935); Masterpieces of New England Silver 1650-1800 (1938); American Silver (1949). Home: Timothy Dwight College, Yale University. Office: Yale University Art Gallery, New Haven. Died May 7, 1953; buried Kennett Square, Pa.

PHILLIPS, John McFarlane, mfg., conservationist; b. Feb. 15, 1861; s. James and Anna (Provost) P.; grad. Pitts. High Sch., 1878, continued studies under private tutors; m. Harriet T. Duff, Feb. 1906; children—Anna Jane Shuman, Mary T. Henry, Margaret Chalfant, John M., James M. Began as asst. mgr. and in 1885 was made mgr. mine and mill supply dept. of Lewis, Oliver & Phillips; associated, 1889, with his uncle, John Phillips, of Lewis, Oliver & Phillips, in organizing the Phillips Mine Supply Co., pres., 1900—. dir. Fourteenth Street Bank (Pitts.). Mem. and pres. Bd. of Game Commrs. of Pa., 1905-24; dir. South Side Hosp. Trustee Am. Wildlife Inst. Mem. nat. exec. bd. Boy Scouts of Am.; hon. pres. Pitts. Zool. Soc. Mem. Engrs. Soc. Western Pa., N.Y. Zool. Soc., Campfire Club Am. (hon.), Lewis and Clark Big Game Club, Boone and Crockett Club, Pitts. C. of C. (past dir.). Republican. Presyn. Mason (32°, K.T., Jester). Clubs: Duquesne, South Hills Country. Collaborator (with Dr. William Temple Hornaday): Campfires in the Canadian Rockies, 1906; Campfires on Desert and Lava, 1908. Awarded medal and citation as leading conservationist in U.S., 1923; citation by Pa. Legislature, 1941. Home: 2336 Brownsville Road. Office: 2227 Jane St., Pitts. Died Sept. 8, 1953; buried South Side Cemetery, Pitts.

PHILLIPS, Lena Madesin, lawyer; b. Nicholasville, Jessamine County, Ky.; d. William Henry and Alice (Shook) Phillips; grad. Jessamine Inst., Nicholasville, 1899; student Goucher Coll., 1899-1900 and 1901-02, Peabody Conservatory of Music, 1901-03; LL.B., University of Ky., 1917, LL.D., 1939; LL.M., New York U., 1923. Teacher of music, organizer and dir. of music sch., Nicholasville, until 1916; admitted to Ky. bar, 1917, N.J. bar, U.S. Dist. Ct. (N.J.), 1922, N.Y. bar, 1924; sec. nat. bd. Y.W.C.A., N.Y. City, 1918-19; exec. sec., 1919-22, Nat. Fedn. of Business and Professional Women's Clubs. Pres., 1926-29, now hon. pres.; founder Internat. Fedn. of Business and Professional Women and its president 1930-47, now founder-president; practice law, New York City, 1924-35; associate editor Pictorial Review, 1935-39. Pres. National Council of Women, 1931-35, now honorary president; vice pres. National Kindergarten Assn.; vice pres. Internat. Council of Women, 1938-47; consulting member Consumer's Advisory Board under NRA. Member Fed. Council of Churches (adv. com. on a just and durable peace). Sent O.W.I. special mission to Sweden, 1943-44. Member of American Bar Association, New York League of Business and Professional Women (hon. pres.), Southern Women's Ednl. Alliance, Kentucky Soc., Consumers' Cooperative Assn., Saturday's Children of N.Y. City, Soroptimist Club, Chi Omega, Phi Delta Delta, Order of Coif. Episcopalian. Home: Stonybrook Road, Westport, Conn. Died May 20, 1955; buried Nicholasville, Ky.

PHILLIPS, Leon C., ex-governor of Okla.; b. on farm, Worth County, Mo., Dec. 9, 1890; s. Rufus and Bertha (Bressler) P.; student Epworth U., Oklahoma City, 1909-11; LL.B., U. of Okla., 1916; m. Myrtle Ellenberger, June 19, 1916 (div. 1951); children—Robert, Lois Ann; m. 2d, Helen Conklin, 1953. Admitted to State bar, 1916, later to bar U.S. Supreme Court; practiced at Okemah, Oklahoma, as firm Rowe & Phillips, Phillips & Long, 1916-38. Member Oklahoma State Legislature, 1933-38, speaker of House of Representatives, 1935, Dem. minority leader, 1937; gov. of Okla., 1939-43. Served as pvt., Arty., U.S. Army, during World War. Mem. Okla. State Bar Assn. Democrat. Presbyn. Mason (33°), Elk, K.P. Club: Kiwanis. Home: Pitchfork Ranch, Weleetka, Okla. Died Mar. 27, 1958; buried Weleetka Cemetery.

PHILLIPS, Louis, lawyer; b. nr. Neustadt, Poland, Mar. 31, 1893; s. Jacob and Sarah (Danziger) P.; brought to U.S., 1901, naturalized (father's citizenship), 1908; LL.B., N.Y.U., 1915; m. Helen Klein, June 20, 1920; children—Gerald F., Howard W. Admitted to N.Y. State bar, 1916; sr. mem. Phillips, Nizer, Benjamin & Krim, N.Y. City, since 1926, now Phillips, Nizer, Benjamin, Krim & Ballon; asst. gen. counsel Paramount Pictures Corporation, 1945-55, general counsel, 1955—, v.p., 1955—. Member American and City of N.Y. bar assns., Co. Lawyers Assn. Club: Lawyers (Brooklyn). Home: 35 E. 84th St., N.Y. City 28. Office: 1501 Broadway, N.Y.C. 18. Died Aug. 29, 1959.

PHILLIPS, Merton Ogden, economist; b. Fremont, O., Mar. 24, 1900; s. Merton Ogden and Marguerite (Dickinson) P.; student U.S. Naval Acad., 1919-20; A.B., Miami U., Oxford, O., 1924; A.M., U. of N.C., 1926, Ph.D., 1937; grad. student U. of Chicago, Columbia U., Nat. U. of Mexico, at intervals, 1926-32; m. Jane Agnor, Jan. 23, 1942; children—Barbara Jane, Merton Ogden III. With Goodyear Tire & Rubber Export Co., Akron, O., 1924-25; instr. in econ. resources and fgn. trade, U. of Fla., 1926-27, asst. prof., 1927-28; asst. prof. economics and commerce, Washington and Lee U., 1929-38, asso. prof., 1938-41, prof., 1941-49, Wilson prof. econ., head of dept. econ. since 1949; econ. adviser to U.S. Maritime Commn., summer 1937; vis. prof. of econ. geography, Columbia U., summers 1942, 43, 46. Mem. Am. Econ. Assn., Southern Econ. Assn., Am. Geographical Society, Assn. of Am. Geographers, Va. Geographical Society, Phi Beta Kappa, Beta Gamma Sigma, Delta Kappa Epsilon. Author: Report of U.S. Maritime Commn. on Tramp Shipping Service, 1938; (with J. Russell Smith) North America, 1940; (with J. Russell Smith) Industrial and Commercial Geography, 1946. Contbr. articles to econ. and geog. jours. Home: 15 University Place, Lexington, Va. Died Mar. 25, 1958; buried Stonewall Jackson Cemetery, Lexington, Va.

PHILLIPS, Paul Chrisler, history; b. Bloomfield, Ind., Nov. 15, 1883; s. Joseph A. and Lily F. (Chrisler) P.; A.B., Ind. U., 1906, A.M., 1910; Ph.D., U. of Ill., 1911; m. Alice M. Martin, Aug. 27, 1911. Prof. history, U. of Mont., 1911-54; became emeritus, 1955; exec. v.p., 1936-37; dir. Student's Army Training Corps, 1918, and Summer School, 1919. Chmn. Missoula and Regional planning boards, 1935-39; state dir. Hist. Records Survey for W.P.A., 1936-39; regional dir. Federal Archives Survey for W.P.A., 1936-38; special rep. U.S. Employment Service, 1937. Historian, War Dept., Transportation Corps, 1944-46. Consultant, Federal Power Commission, 1946. Dir. museum and northwest history collections. Member American Historical Assn., Miss. Valley Hist. Assn., Sigma Pi, Phi Kappa Phi. Democrat. Member Disciples of Christ. Author: The West in the Diplomacy of the American Revolution, 1913; (with N. J. Lennes) The Story of Columbus, 1919. Editor: (with W. S. Lewis) The Journal of John Work, 1923; Forty Years on the Frontier, 1925; (with Seymour Dunbar) The Fort Owen Journals, 1927; Scenery of the Plains, Mountains and Mines (by Franklin Langworthy), 1932; Life in the Rocky Mountains, 1939. Asso. editor Pacific Northwest Quarterly, 1932-54; editorial bd. Montana Magazine of History; historical Editor Frontier and Midland, 1930-39. Author: Fur Trade in Montana, 1955; Fur Trade and the March of Empire, posthumously. Contbr. to hist. periodicals. Ency. Brit., Brit. Year Book, 1938-39, Dictionary Am. Biography, Dictionary Am. History, 1938, Ency. Americana, Americana Annual, 1950, etc. Home: 419 Ford, Missoula, Mont. Died Dec. 23, 1956; buried Missoula Cemetery.

PHILLIPS, Samuel Edgar, newspaper pub.; b. Charlestown, W.Va., Apr. 2, 1892; s. Marcellus Edgar and Mary Elizabeth P.; ed. high sch., Greencastle, Pa.; m. Isabel Snyder, July 28, 1917; children—Samuel Edgar, Richard Snyder, Jack Marcellus. With transportation dept. Pa. R.R. and N.&W. Ry., 1912-19; pub. Hagerstown (Md.) Herald, 1919—; gen. mgr. and treas. Herald-Mail Co. Served as 1st sergt. U.S. Army, 1917-19; lt. cav., U.S.R. Mem. Am. Legion. Decorated D.S.C. (U.S.), Croix de Guerre (France). Republican. Presbyterian. Kiwanian. Home: Hagerstown, Md. Died Dec. 1, 1951.

PHILLIPS, Thomas Ashley, ins. exec.; b. Arthur, Ont., Can., Dec. 23, 1881; s. Thomas J. and Maria J. (Buschler) P.; B.A., Toronto U., 1905; m. Lorena Harrison, Apr. 2, 1921; children—Ellen Jane (Mrs. Harold C. Fleming), Lorena Lucille (Mrs. Paul N. Coates, Jr.). Came to U.S., 1905, naturalized, 1917. Mem. actuarial dept., N.Y. Life Ins. Co., 1905-09; with Minn. Mutual Life Ins. Co., St. Paul, since 1909, as sec. and actuary, 1908-18, v.p., 1918-29 (on mil. leave, 1918), pres., 1929-47, chairman board, since 1947; director Am. Nat. Bank, First Trust Co., St. Paul Fire & Marine Ins. Co., Northern States Power Co.; past dir. Inst. of Life Ins.; dir. Life Ins. Med. Research Fund. Fellow Society of Actuaries; past pres. Am. Inst. Actuaries; mem. Inst. Actuaries of Gr. Brit. (asso.), Am. Life Conv. (past pres., past mem. exec. com.), Life Ins. Assn. of Am. (past mem. bd.), U.S. C. of C. (past mem. ins. com.), St. Paul Assn. of Commerce (past director and treas.). Clubs: Minnesota, Athletic, Somerset, Rotary (past pres. and treas.) (St. Paul); Union League (Chicago). Home: 684 Lincoln Av., St. Paul 5. Office: 345 Cedar St., St. Paul 1. Died Jan. 6, 1957.

PHILLIPS, Thomas I., elec. mfg. exec.; b. London, Eng., July 25, 1887; s. Thomas and Isabel (Sinclair) P.; m. Grace Graham, Jan. 13, 1913. With Westinghouse Electric Co. (Westinghouse Elec. & Mfg. Co.), 1915—, v.p., 1941—, charge East Pitts. div., 1943—. Mem. Nat. Elec. Mfrs. Assn., Nat. Assn. Mfrs., Pitts. C. or C. Clubs: University, Duquesne. Home: 6922 Thomas Blvd., East Pittsburgh, Pa. Died Sept. 1956.

PHILLIPS, Thomas Wharton, Jr., ex-congressman; b. New Castle, Pa., Nov. 21, 1874; s. Thomas W. and Pamphila (Hardman) P.; Ph.B., Phillips Andover, 1894, Sheffield Sci. Sch. (Yale), 1897; m. Alma Sherman, May 28, 1908 (died Jan. 4, 1945); children—Janet (Mrs. Leander McCormick-Goodheart, dec.), Katharine (Mrs. Frederick L. Rutgers), Alma (dec.), Margaret (Mrs. Augustus Craig Succop), Thomas Wharton, Roger Sherman; m. 2d, Gerta M. Schoenwald, Feb. 28, 1946. In the petroleum and natural gas business since 1897; president T. W. Phillips Gas & Oil Co. Dir. Butler Consolidated Coal Company, Pennsylvania Investment & Real Estate Corporation, Butler. Member 68th and 69th Congresses (1923-27) 26th Pa. Dist. Trustee Bethany (W.Va.) Coll., Y.W.C.A. (Butler). Republican. Mem. Ch. of Christ. Mason. Clubs: Butler Country (Butler); Duquesne, University (Pittsburgh); Woodmont Rod and Gun (Md.). Home: Phillips Hall. Office: 205 N. Main St., Butler, Pa. Died Jan. 2, 1956; buried North Cemetery, Butler.

PHILLIPS, T(imothy) Redfield, banker, business exec.; b. Montpelier, Vt., Aug. 12, 1879; s. Andrew Jackson and Alice M. (Redfield) P.; student St. Albans Coll., Knoxville, Ill., 1895-98; student Boston Univ. Law Sch., 1902-03; m. Cora K. Johonott, June 30, 1903; children—Alice Redfield, Mary Johonott (Mrs. W. G. Ricker), Arthur R. Admitted to Vt. bar, 1903, and practiced in Montpelier, 1903-13; breeder of pure-bred Guernsey cattle, Montpelier, 1913-43; dir. and mem. exec. com. Vt. Mutual Fire Ins. Co. of Montpelier since 1930; dir. Montpelier Savings Bank & Trust Co since 1931, pres. since 1944; vice pres. Montpelier Tavern, Inc., since 1932. Mem. Montpelier C. of C., Vt. Guernsey Breeders

Assn. (past pres.; dir. since 1917), Gamma Eta Gamma. Democrat. Episcopalian. Clubs: Apollo, Rotary (past pres.). Home: Towne Hill. Office: 90 main St. Montpelier, Vt. Died Nov. 18, 1953.

PHILLIPS, Wallace Banta, mfg. exec.; b. N.Y. C., Mar. 30, 1886; m. Ann Lewis, 1915. Dir. Pyrene Mfg. Co., Newark, 1915—, pres., 1950—; pres.; chmn., mng. dir. Pyrene Co. Ltd., London, 1913-51; dir. Avon India Rubber Co., Ltd., 1931-51. Founder, 1st dir.-gen. Am. Ambulance Gt. Britain, 1940; mem. London adv. com. A.R.C., 1940. Trustee Am. Mus. Safety, 1950—; dir. Nat. Indsl. Conf. Bd. and Nat. Safety Council, 1951—. Served as chief circulation, G-2, AEF, France, 1917-19; spl. asst. to dir. Naval Intelligence, USN, Washington, 1940-41; dir. Spl. Information Services, OSS, Washington, London, 1941-43. Decorated King's Medal; Hon. Comdr. Brit. Empire. Mem. Royal Soc. Prevention Accidents (founder mem. 1923, v.p., hon. treas., chmn. exec. com. 1945-51), Am. C. of C. in London (pres. 1943-51), Internat. C. of C. (treas., vice chmn. budget commn., 1944—, mem. exec. com. U.S. Council 1951—), Nat. Union Mfrs. (mem. exec. council 1936-51), Pilgrims of Gt. Britain (mem. exec. com. 1946-51), English-Speaking Union (council mem. 1941-51), Am. Soc. in London (pres. 1950-51). Clubs: Bath, American (gov. 1919-51), Royal Automobile (London); Links, Monday Luncheon (chmn. 1937-51), Metropolitan, Recess, River (N.Y.C.); Metropolitan, F. Street (Washington); St. Cloud Country, Travellers (Paris). Home: 465 Park Av., N.Y.C. 22. Office: 10 Empire St., Newark. Died Apr. 14, 1952.

PHILLIPSON, Irving Joseph, ret. army ofcr.; b. Dowagiac, Mich., Apr. 3, 1882; s. Emanuel and Barbara (Guggenheim) P.; B.S., U.S. Mil Acad., 1904; attended Sch. of the Line, 1921-22, Gen. Staff Sch., 1922-23, Army War Coll., 1923-24; m. Florence Morrison, Sept. 1, 1909 (dec.); m. Elsie Salvadori, April 27, 1954. Commd. 2d lt. Inf., U.S. Army, 1904, advanced through ranks to maj. gen., 1941; chief, Budget and Legislative Planning Branch, War Dept. Gen. Staff, 1930-35; comd. 30th Inf., Presidio, San Francisco, 1935-38, 2d Brigade, 1st Div., 2d Corps Area, 1938-40; chief of staff, Governor's Island, N.Y., 1940, comdg. gen., 2d Corps Area, Governor's Island, 1940-42; exec. dir. Army Emergency Relief, 1942-44; member War Department Dependency Bd., Jan. 11, 1944 to Dec. 31, 1944; retired as maj. general, U.S. Army, Dec. 31, 1944; dir. of indsl. relations, Botany Mills, Inc., Passaic, N.J., 1944-52. Chmn. Civil Defense Council, Passaic, N.J. 1950-53. Trustee Disabled Am. Vets. Service Found. and chmn. budget and finance com. Comd. bn. regt. and brigade, 142d and 143d Inf., 36th Div., in Meuse-Argonne, France, 1918. Awarded Distinguished Service medal, Victory medal (2 bronze stars), Croix de Guerre (Gold Star). Mem. Scabbard and Blade, Newcomen Soc. of Eng., New York Society, Military and Naval Officers, World Wars; New York Chapter, M.O.W.W. (comdr., 1945-46), Honorary vice pres. Am. Hygiene Soc. Clubs: Army and Navy (Washington) Address: 240 Central Park South, N.Y.C. Died April 4, 1955.

PHIPPS, John Shaffer, corp. ofcl.; b. Allegheny, Pa., Aug. 11, 1874; Ph.B., Sheffield Scientific Sch. (Yale), 1896; LL.B., Harvard, 1899; m. Margarita Celia Grace, of Sussex, Eng., Nov. 4, 1903; children—John Henry, Hubert Beaumont, Margaret Helen, Michael Grace. Former dir. U.S. Steel Corp., Internat. Paper Co, Grace (Steamship) Line, Guaranty Trust Co. Commd. maj. U.S.A., and served as liaison officer at aviation hdqrs., Ft. Worth, Tex., World War. Clubs: Links, Orange County Hunt, Meadow Brook, Racquet and Tennis. Home: Palm Beach, Fla. Office: 800 2d Av., N.Y.C. 17. Died Apr. 27, 1958.

PHIPPS, Lawrence Cowle, ex-senator; b. Washington County, Pa., Aug. 30, 1862; s. Rev. William Henry and Agnes (McCall) P.; grad. high sch., Pittsburgh, at 16; hon. M.A., U. of Denver, 1916; married; children—(by 1st marriage) Lawrence C., Emma (Mrs. William White); (by 2d marriage) Dorothy (Mrs. Van Holt Garrett), Helen (Mrs. Donald Bromfield); (by 3d marriage) Allan R., Gerald H. Began in iron mills owned by Carnegie Co., 1879; resigned as v.p. and treas. Carnegie Co. when it was acquired by U.S. Steel Corp., 1901; settled in Denver, Colo.; founded and endowed, 1904, at Denver, the Agnes Meml. Sanatorium for treatment of Tb.; mem. U.S. Senate, 2 terms, 1919-31. Republican. Episcopalian. Clubs: University, Denver, Cactus, Mile High, Denver Athletic, Denver Country (Denver). Home: 3400 Belcaro Drive. Office: Denver Nat. Bldg., Denver. Died Mar. 1, 1958.

PICARD, Ralph Alan, former govt. official; b. Decatur, Ill., Oct. 17, 1898; s. Alexander A. and Katherine Elizabeth (Betzold) P.; m. Nancy Bean, June 2, 1934. Reporter, editorial writer, advt. salesman Enterprise-Am., Bogalusa, La., 1920-22; reporter, asst. sports editor Pioneer Press, St. Paul, 1922; feature writer, farm-page editor Duluth (Minn.) Herald, 1922-25; city editor New Scimitar, Memphis, 1925-28, acting mng. editor, 1926-28; exec. sec. to mayor Memphis, 1928-32; dir. personnel and efficiency for city of Memphis, 1932-33, exec. asst. to bd. commrs., 1933-36, mem. bd. commrs. and commr. pub. service, 1936-39, commr. finance and instns., 1939-40; pub. relations cons., Memphis, 1940; feature writer, reporter Columbus (O.) Citizen, 1940-41; regional information chief Farm Security Adminstrn., Indpls., 1941-44, dir. information, 1944-45, spl. asst. to adminstr., 1945-46; asst. adminstr. Farmers Home Adminstrn., 1946-52. Nat. Committeeman from Tenn., Young Democratic Clubs, 1936-41; chmn. finance com. Shelby County (Tenn.) Dem. com., 1936. Served with U.S.M.C., 1918-19. Mem. Am. Pub. Relations Assn., Pub. Relations Soc. Am., Am. Legion. Democrat. Methodist. Odd Fellow. Author and editor of Why Pay Taxes?, A Story of Progress Made Possible by Taxes, Memphis, 1935-36. Home: 3902 Southern Av. S.E., Washington 20. Died Oct. 15, 1952; buried Arlington Nat. Cemetery.

PICCIRILLI, Furio, sculptor; b. Massa, Italy; s. Joseph and Barbera (Giorgi) P.; pupil Accademia San Luca, Rome. Came to U.S., 1888. Awarded hon. mention Pan-Am. Expn., Buffalo, 1901; silver medal St. Louis Expn., 1904; silver medal Panama-Pacific Expn., San Francisco, 1915. N.A., 1936. Address: 467 E. 142d St., New York, N.Y. Died 1949.*

PICHEL, Irving (pĭch'ĕl), motion picture dir.; b. Pittsburgh, Pa., June 24, 1891; s. Julius and Rachel (Stadtfeld) P.; A.B., Harvard, 1914; m. Violette Stitt Wilson, Dec. 31, 1916; children—Pichel Wilson, Julian Irving, Marlow Agnew. Began as stage dir. Shubert Theatrical Co., N.Y. City, 1919; dir. of little theaters in Detroit, St. Paul, St. Louis, Berkeley, Santa Barbara, 1915-30; lecturer at U. of Calif., Stanford U., U. of Calif. at Los Angeles, U. of Wis., Mills Coll.; featured actor Paramount Pictures, 1930-33; dir. R.K.O., 1933-34; dir. 20th Century-Fox Film Corp., 1939-44; pictures directed include The Man I Married, Hudson's Bay, Life Begins at 8:30, The Pied Piper (1942), A Medal for Benny, Tomorrow is Forever, The Miracle of the Bells, They Won't Believe Me, Mr. Peabody and the Mermaid; Without Honor UA, Quicksand UA, The Great Rupert E-L, Destination Moon E-L, 1949; Santa Fe, Columbia, 1950; Martin Luther, De-Rochemont, 1952. Stage dir. world premier The Dybbuk, N.Y.C. Opera Co. 1951. Faculty, Theater Arts Dept., U. of California, 1953—. Mem. Screen Dirs. Guild. Democrat. Clubs: Harvard of Southern Calif. Author: Modern Theaters, 1926; St., Francis of Assisi, 1927. Editorial bd. Radio and TV, U. of Cal. Home: 5317 Harter Lane, La Canada, Cal. Died July 13, 1954.

PICK, Albert, chmn. Pick Hotels Corp.; b. Chicago, Ill., May 17, 1869; s. Charles and Jeanette (Chladek) P.; ed. Chicago Pub. Schools and Notre Dame University; LL.D., U. Miami, Coral Gables, Fla., 1955; married Gertrude Frank, December 27, 1892 (dec.), children—Pauline (Mrs. Charles L. Staiger, (dec.), Albert, Laurence Mercer (dec.), Dorothy Gertrude (deceased), Gertrude Pauline (adopted); married Mrs. Rafael (Florence) Torrico, Aug. 16, 1949; stepson, Rafael R. Began as merchant, 1893; pres. Albert Pick & Co., Chgo., to Jan. 5, 1929, Albert Pick Hotels, Inc., Miami Beach, Fla., Ft. Hayes Hotel Co., Columbus, O.; pres. Pick Hotels Corp. to 1930, chmn. bd., Dec. 4, 1930—. Member Chicago Hist. Soc., Arts Inst. Chicago. Clubs: Illinois Athletic (Chicago); Committee of One Hundred. Home: 4609 Pine Tree Dr., Miami Beach, Fla. Office: 20 N. Wacker Dr., Chgo. Died July 9, 1955; buried Rosehill Cemetery, Chgo.

PICK, Lewis Andrew, army officer; b. Brookneal, Va., Nov. 18, 1890; s. George and Annie (Crouch) P.; B.S. Va. Poly. Inst., Blacksburg, Va., 1914; grad. Engrs. Sch. Ft. Belvoir, Va., 1924, Command and Gen. Staff Sch., Ft. Leavenworth, Kan., 1934, Army War Coll., Ft. Humphries, D.C., 1939; m. Alice Cary, Dec. 15, 1925; 1 son, Lewis Andrew, Jr. Civil engr. with Southern Ry., 1914-16; commd. 1st lt., Corps of Engrs., U.S. Army, 1917, advancing to lt. gen., 1951; comd. Co. E, 23d Engrs., A.E.F., France, 1917; on duty in Philippines, 1920-23; U.S. dist. engr., New Orleans, La., 1925-28; instr. Command and Gen. Staff Sch., Ft. Leavenworth, Kan., 1934-38; exec. officer to div. engr., Ohio River Div., Cincinnati, Ohio, 1939-41; division engineer, Missouri River Division, Omaha, Nebraska, 1942-Sept. 1943; comd. Advance Sect. 3, China-Burma-India, in charge constrn. Ledo Rd., 1943-45; assigned Missouri River Div. engrs., 1945; comdr. 5th army emergency relief in midwest, Operation Snowbound, Feb. 1949; chief of engrs., Dept. of Army, March 1949. Vice chmn. Georgia-Pacific Plywood Co., 1953—. Decorated Distinguished Service Medal with Oak Leaf Cluster; Cloud and Banner (China); Royal Order of Bath (Britain). Mem. Am. Society C.E., Soc. Am. Mil. Engrs., Theta Chi, Chi Epsilon. Author of the Pick Plan for development of Mo. River Basin. Address: 360 N. College St., Auburn, Ala. Died Dec. 2, 1956; buried Old Cemetery, Auburn.

PICKARD, Frederick William (pĭk'ärd), dir. E. I. duPont de Nemours & Co.; b. Portland, Me., Sept. 2, 1871; s. Charles Weston and Henrietta Maria (Groth) P.; A.B., Bowdoin Coll., Brunswick, Me., 1894, LL.D., 1933; m. Jane Alice Coleman, Oct. 4, 1899; 1 son, John Coleman. Mng. editor Portland Transcript, 1895-1900; sec. King Mercantile Co. and Oriental Powder Co., Cincinnati, 1900-03; asst. mgr. E. I. duPont de Nemours & Co., Cincinnati, 1903-05, mgr., 1905-07, asst. mgr., Denver, Colo., 1908-09, mgr., Pittsburgh, Pa., 1909-17, dir. sales, Wilmington, Del., 1917-18, v.p. 1918-46, mem. exec. com., 1918-35, mgr. dyestuffs dept., 1922-24; pres. Brookdale Land Co. Mem. borough council, Thornburg, Pa., 1915-17. Trustee Bowdoin Coll. Mem. Synthetic Organic Chem. Mfrs. Assn. (dir. 1922-24), Nat. Foreign Trade Council, Am. Chem. Soc., Phi Beta Kappa, Theta Delta Chi. Republican. Clubs: Wilmington, Wilmington Country, DuPont Country (Wilmington); Bankers, University, Theta Delta Chi (New York); Kedgwick Salmon (New Brunswick, Can.). Author: Sixteen British Trout Rivers, 1936; Monaco and the French Riviera, 1937; Trout and Salmon Fishing in Ireland, 1938, Trout Fishing in New Zealand, 1940. Donor Pickard Field to Bowdoin Coll. Home: Greenville, Del.; summer res. Keene Valley, N.Y. Office: Nemours Bldg., Wilmington, Del. Died Mar. 7, 1952; buried Keene Valley, N.Y.

PICKARD, Greenleaf Whittier, electrical engr., inventor; b. Portland, Me., Feb. 14, 1877; s. Samuel Thomas and Elizabeth Hussey (Whittier) P.; grandnephew John Greenleaf Whittier; ed. Westbrook Sem., Lawrence Scientific Sch., Harvard, and Mass. Inst. Tech.; m. Miriam Watson Oliver, Apr. 5, 1902 (died Dec. 17, 1912); m. 2d, Helen Liston, Apr. 27, 1914; children—Helen Liston, Elizabeth Whittier, Geraldine, Greenleaf Whittier, Mary Katherine, John. Specialized in radio communication, receiving many U.S. and foreign patents for inventions. One of the first to obtain successful transmission of speech by electrical waves; inventor of the crystal detector, the radio compass and the static eliminator. Engr. Am. Telephone & Telegraph Co., 1902-06; consulting engineer Wireless Specialty Apparatus Co., 1907-30, R.C.A. Victor Co. of Mass., 1930-31; consultant, 1932-42; dir. of Research Am. Jewels Corp., Attleboro, Mass., 1942-45; president Pickard & Burns, Inc., 1945-52, chairman of board, 1952—. Past president and fellow Institution Radio Engineers (medal of honor 1926); fellow Radio Club of America (Armstrong medal 1941); Am. Inst. E.E., A.A.A.S., Am. Acad. Arts and Sciences; mem. Am. Meteorol. Soc. Home: 59 Dalton Rd., Newton Centre 59, Mass. Office: 240 Highland Av., Needham, Mass. Died Jan. 8, 1956; buried Newton Cemetery.

PICKEL, Margaret Barnard, univ. dean; b. Sweetsburg, P.Q., Can., May 26, 1897; d. Thomas Reid and Louisa W. (Baker) Pickel; A.B., McGill U., 1919, A.M., 1923; Ph.D., Columbia, 1936. Came to U.S., 1923, naturalized, 1940. Adviser, women grad. students Columbia, 1940-45, dean univ. women since 1945. Trustee Am. Coll. for Girls, Istanbul, Turkey. Mem. American Association University Women. Author: Charles I as Patron of Poetry and the Drama, 1936; Century Readings in Victorian Prose (with J. W. Cunliffe), 1936; contbr. articles on women's work and edn. to N.Y. Times. Am. Assn. U. Women designated ann. internat. fellowship grant as the Margaret Pickel Grant for 1954-55. Home: 501 W. 113th St., N.Y.C. 25. Died Jan. 7, 1955.

PICKENS, William, govt. official; b. Anderson Co., S.C., Jan. 15, 1881; s. Jacob and Fannie (Porter) P.; A.B., Talladega (Ala.) Coll., 1902; A.B., Yale, 1904; diploma from Brit. Esperanto Assn., 1906; A.M., Fisk U., Tenn., 1908; Litt.D., Selma U., Ala., 1915; LL.D., Wiley U., Tex., 1918; m. Minnie Cooper McAlpine (A.B., Tougaloo U.), Aug. 10, 1905; children—William, Harriet Ida, Ruby Annie. Instr. Latin and German, 1904-09, prof. Greek, Latin and German, 1909-14, Talledega Coll.; prof. Greek and sociology, Wiley U., Marshall Tex., 1914-15; dean, 1915-18, v.p., 1918-20, Morgan Coll.; field sec. Nat. Assn. for Advancement of Colored People, 1920, also dir. of branches of the Assn., 1935-42; asst., defense savings staff, U.S. Treasury Dept., 1941-42; chief of interracial sect., nat. orgns. subdivision, war savings staff, U.S. Treasury Dept., since Aug. 1942; dir. interracial sect., savings bond div., since Feb. 1946. Mem. Am. Negro Acad., Phi Beta Kappa (Yale), Phi Beta Kappa Associates, Omega Psi Phi; ex-pres. Alabama State Teachers' Association. Mason, K.P., Odd Fellow. Author: Abraham Lincoln, Man and Statesman, 1909; The Heir of Slaves, 1910; Frederick Douglass and the Spirit of Freedom, 1912; Fifty Years of Emancipation, 1913; The Ultimate Effects of Segregation and Discrimination, 1915; The New Negro, 1916; The Negro in the Light of the Great War, 3 edits 1919; The Vengeance of the Gods, 1921; Bursting Bonds, 1923; American Aesop, 1926, Visited Europe, 1913, 1926-27, 1929, 1932, 1938, and lectured in England, Scotland, Germany, Poland and Russia, 1926-27; lectured in Geneva, Vienna, Germany, etc., 1932; forum leader United States Govt. Forums, under U.S. Commn. of Edn., 1937-38. Club: Civic. Contbg. editor Associated Negro Press of U.S. Home: 260 W. 139th St., New York, N.Y.; and 400 T St. N.W., Washington. Office: Savings Bonds

Div., U.S. Treasury Dept., Washington. Died Apr. 6, 1954; buried at sea in the Caribbean.

PICKERING, Loring, editor; b. San Francisco, Aug. 31, 1888; s. Loring and Rose (Crothers) P.; student Stanford, Oxford U., Sorbonne, U. Chgo. Law Sch.; m. Harriett Alexander, June 17, 1916 (div. 1938); children—Loring, Alexander; m. 2d, Chouteau Scott Walker, 1940. Organizer, 1922, and since gen. mgr. N. Am. Newspaper Alliance, N.Y.; asso. editor The Bulletin, San Francisco. Commd. capt. Air Service, U.S. Army, 1917; maj. (pilot) 1918; comdr. A.S., Panama Canal Zone, 1918-19. Lt. col. A.C., U.S.A., 1942-43, col. Air Staff, 1943-45; organized Army Courier Service. Organizer of Capt. Wilkins Expedition to North Pole. Charter mem. Am. Soc. of Newspaper Editors, Am. Soc. Colonial Wars, NE. Historic-Geneal. Soc.; fellow Am. Geog. Soc., Royal Geog. Soc.; mem. gen. com. Pan-Am. Congress of Journalists, Washington, 1926. Clubs: Players, Dutch Treat (N.Y.C.); Army and Navy (Washington); Burlingame (Burlingame, Cal.); Pacific-Union (San Francisco); Savile (London); Travellers (Paris); Peking (Peiping, China). Address: Todos Bancos, Woodside, via Redwood City, Cal. Died Mar. 11, 1959.

PICKETT, Hugh Dale, clergyman; b. Moundsville, W.Va., Dec. 14, 1900; s. Edwin Courtland and Adaline Belle (MacCarriher) P.; student Broaddus Jr. Coll., Philippi, W.Va., 1919-21; A.B., Denison Univ., 1923; Th.M. Southern Baptist Theol. Sem., Louisville, Ky., 1927; D.D., Alderson-Broaddus Coll., 1942; m. Edna Thelma Petit, June 30, 1927; children—Hugh Dale, Rachel Ann. Ordained to ministry of the Baptist Ch., May 8, 1925; dir. youth work, West Va. Baptist Conv., hdqrs., Parkersburg, W.Va., 1923-27; prof. religious edn., dean of men, Broaddus Coll., Philippi, W. Va., 1927-29, pres. Alderson-Broaddus Coll., 1933-36, chmn. exec. com., since 1938, also trustee; minister 1st Baptist Ch., Fairmont, W.Va., 1929-40; exec. sec., dir. of promotion, W. Va. Baptist Conv., Parkersburg, since 1940; editor The West Virginia Baptist since 1940. Trustee Storer Coll., Harpers Ferry, W.Va.; dean of State Boys' Camping Program since 1930. Mem. Baptist Young People's Union of America (vice president 1926-27), American Baptist Convention (member of ministers council, mem. Council on Missionary Cooperation, administrative com.), Council of Chs. and Christian Edn. for W. Va. (mem. exec. com.), Central Council of Social Agencies (pres.). Rep. W.Va. Baptist Convention at Baptist World Congress, London, 1955. Mem. Lambda Chi Alpha. Democrat. Contbr. religious mags. New library bldg. at Alderson-Broaddus named Hugh D. Pickett Library. Home: 1706 Nineteenth St. Office: 1019 Juliana St., Parkersburg, W.Va. Died Aug. 23, 1957; buried Arlington Meml. Gardens, Parkersburg.

PICKETT, John Erasmus, editor; b. Jasper County, Mo., June 23, 1885; s. Henry Dixon and Elizabeth (Thomas) P.; student Agrl. Coll., U. of Mo., 1905-07; m. Margie Jane Roberson, Feb. 2, 1913; children—John Thomas, (twins) Robert Roberson and Elizabeth Jane (Mrs. C. H. Francee). Began business career as editor of Carthage (Mo.) Democrat, 1907-08; reporter Carthage Press, 1909; editor Daily News, Richmond, Mo., 1911-12; reporter Daily and Sunday Kansas City Star, 1913-15; editor Weekly Kansas City Star, 1916; asso. editor Country Gentleman, Phila., 1917-19; mng. editor Ladies Home Jour., 1920; editor Country Gentleman, 1921-24; editor Pacific Rural Press, San Francisco, 1924-48; editor Cal. Farmer, 1948—. A founder, pres. Cal. Water, Transit and Defense Project. Mem. San Francisco C. of C. (dir. 1944-46, 2d v.p. 1946, chmn. agrl. com. 1944-46), Sigma Delta Chi, Pi Delta Epsilon. Club: Commonwealth (San Francisco). Home: 1942 Los Angeles Av., Berkeley, Cal. Office: 83 Stevenson St., San Francisco. Died Dec. 25, 1952; buried Berkeley.

PICKETT, Warren Wheeler, clergyman; b. Bridgeport, Conn., July 24, 1895; s. Frederick Buell and Jennie Elizabeth (Wheeler) P.; B.A., Yale, 1917, B.D., 1920; D.D., Olivet (Mich.) Coll., 1935; Litt.D., Marietta Coll., 1940; m. Christine Hubbard, Aug. 2, 1921; children—Christine Winifred (Mrs. Gordon L. Corbett), Barbara Elizabeth (Mrs. Charles C. Stewart), Warren Wheeler, Patricia Louise. Ordained Congl. ministry, 1920; pastor 1st Ch., Bethel, Conn., 1920-21, 1st Ch., Ft. Dodge, Ia., 1921-26, Ch.-in-the-Gardens, Forest Hills, N.Y. City, 1926-32, 1st Ch. Detroit, 1932-44; Plymouth Congl. Church, New Haven, Conn., 1944-49. Served with Battery E, 341st F.A., World War. Pres. bd. of dirs. New York Congl. Conf., 1929-31; Moderator N.Y. City Congl. Assn., 1930-31; dir. Bd. Home Missions of Congl. Christian Chs., 1936-1944; mem. exec. com., 1937-44; president Protestant Pastors' Union of Detroit, 1938-39; moderator Detroit Congl. Assn., 1938, 39; mem. ad interim com. Missions' Council of Congl. Christian Chs., 1939-44, chmn., 1940-44; moderator Mich. Congl. and Christian Conf., 1940-41. V.p. Bd. of Home Missions of Congl. Christian Churches, 1942-44. Trustee Olivet Coll., 1933-48. Mem. Alpha Chi Rho, Delta Sigma Rho. Author: Worship Services for Young People (brochure), 1931. Contbr. articles and sermons. Home: 123 Broadway, Milford, Conn. Died Apr. 18, 1952.

PIEPER, Ezra H(enry), educator; b. Telbasta, Neb., Dec. 5, 1902; s. Herman and Louise (Bohlmeier) P.; A.B., North Central Coll., Naperville, Ill., 1925; A.M., U. Ill., 1926, Ph.D., 1931; m. Donna Ruth Johnson, Dec. 25, 1931; 1 dau., Elaine Louise. Asst. in history U. Ill., 1927-30; instr. social studies Duluth State Tchrs. Coll., 1930-38, chmn. social studies div., 1938-47, acting pres., Mar.-July 1946, academic dean, 1946-47; prof. history and chmn. social studies div. U. Minn., Duluth br., 1947—. Mem. Am. Hist. Assn., Am. Assn. U. Profs., N.E.A., Minn. Edn. Assn., Phi Alpha Theta, Pi Gamma Mu, Kappa Delta Pi. Conglist. Contbr. articles and abstracts on The Fenian Movement in Dictionary of American History pubs. Address: U. Minn., Duluth, Minn. Died Dec. 21, 1950.

PIERCE, Anna Eloise (pērs), educator; b. Worcester, N.Y.; d. Edmund and Susan (Sloan) Pierce; grad. N.Y. State Normal Sch. (now N.Y. State Coll. for Tchrs.), 1884, hon. Pd.M., 1920. Preceptress Lisle (N.Y.) Acad., 1885-86; sec. N.Y. State Normal Sch. (now N.Y. State Coll. for Tchrs.), 1886-87, instr., 1887-91, prin. primary dept. (Model Sch.), 1891-1909, asst. prof. edn., 1909-14, dean of women, 1914-33, ret.; dean Albany Sch. of Religious Edn., 1917, 19-30. An organizer, 1919, mem. Albany Council Girl Scouts; former mem. bd. dirs. Women's Found. for Health; dir. survey of student health service in secondary schs. and instns. of higher edn. in Am., 1925-27. Mem. N.E.A., Nat. Assn. Deans Women, N.Y. Assn. of Deans, Alumni Assn. N.Y. State Coll. for Tchrs. (dir.); hon. mem. Delta Kappa Gamma (chpt. Albany, N.Y., 1945). Republican. Presbyn. Author: Handbook for Deans and Advisers; The Dean's Responsbility to Secure Better Health for Her Students; The Problem of Social Health in Schools; also various published addresses. Compiler: Catalog of Literature for Advisers of Young Women and Girls; Catalog of Student Health Literature. Address: 225 Ontario St., Albany 3, N.Y. Died Nov. 6, 1956.

PIERCE, Charles Sumner, lawyer; b. Milton, Mass., Sept. 5, 1874; s. Edward L. and Elisabeth H. (Kingsbury) P.; A.B., Harvard, 1895, LL.B., 1900; m. Caroline W. Merriam, Mar. 7, 1908; children—Henry Lillie, Caroline Merriam. Admitted to Mass. bar, 1900, since practiced in Boston; formerly v.p., gen. counsel New Eng. Tel. & Tel. Co., retired 1939; dir. New Eng. Telephone Co., Blue Hill Bank and Trust Co. (Milton). Chmn. Local Draft Bd. Pres. Peter Bent Brigham Hosp.; trustee Public Reservations. Moderator of Milton, 1919—. Home: Milton, Mass. Died March 25, 1949.

PIERCE, Dante Melville, publisher; b. Bedford, Ia., Aug. 29, 1880; s. James Melville and Kate L. (Southard) P.; student Ia. State Agrl. and Mech. Coll., 1899; m. 3d, Grace O. Doane, Sept. 10, 1936. Pub. Wallaces' Farmer and Iowa Homestead, and Wisconsin Agriculturist and Farmer; writer on economic, agricultural and political subjects. Mem. Co. I, 5th Mo. Regt., Spanish-Am. War. Republican. Clubs: Des Moines, Wakonda. Home: 4140 Grand Av., Des Moines 12. Office: 1912 Grand Av., Des Moines 5, Ia. Died July 27, 1955.

PIERCE, Edward Lillie, ret. corp. exec.; b. Milton, Mass., Mar. 28, 1866; s. Edward Lillie and Elizabeth Helen (Kingsbury) P.; S.B., Mass. Inst. Tech., 1886; A.M., Princeton; m. Mary Nelson, July 3, 1901; children—Henry Nelson (dec.), Mrs. Margaret Hortense Millholland, Elizabeth Kingsbury (dec.). Began in paper mfg. business, 1886; connected with Solvay Process Co., Syracuse, 1895-1922, pres. 1917-22, ret., v.p. Allied Chem. & Dye Corp., 1921-22. Served in P.R. as 1st lt., 1st U.S. Vol. Engrs., Spanish-Am. War Clubs: Nassau (Princeton); University (N.Y.C.); Union (Boston). Home: 15 Hibben Rd., Princeton, N.J. Died Dec. 1, 1954; buried Milton, Mass.

PIERCE, Frank Reynolds, exec. Dearborn Motors Corp.; b. Monticello, Ark., Mar. 29, 1901; s. Benjamin R. and Custis (Welsh) P.; m. Christine Smith, Apr. 21, 1924; children—Frank R., Nancy Joel. Salesman, Frigidaire div. Gen. Motors, 1920, advancing through sales forces to sales mgr., 1932, Kelvinator, 1939, v.p. charge sales for Nash-Kelvinator to 1943; mgr. Detroit office public relations Gen. Motors Corp., 1943; dir. of exec. and employee relations, 1944, v.p. charge employe cooperation staff, 1945; pres. Dearborn Motors Corp., 1946—; Wood Bros. Inc., Des Moines, Ia.; v.p. Farm Equipment Inst. Episcopalian. Mason. Clubs: Bloomfield Hills Country, Detroit Athletic. Home: 421 Arlington Dr., Birmingham, Mich. Office: 15050 Woodward Av., Detroit 3. Deceased.

PIERCE, George Edwin, banker; b. Brattleboro, Vt., Aug. 7, 1887; s. George W. and Ida M. (Weed) P.; B.A., Amherst, 1909; studied law, Boston U., 1911-13; m. Vashti Bitler, Sept. 22, 1915; children—Helen C. (Mrs. George A. Nagle, Jr.), Sylvia B. (Mrs. Robert L. Edwards), George G., Willard W. Teacher Cushman School, Bernardston, Mass., 1909-11; legal and credit investigator, Bradstreet's, 1911-16; banking business since 1916; asst. cashier National Shawmut Bank, 1919-26, v.p., 1926-37, 1st v.p. since 1937, sr. v.p., since 1948; trustee Shawmut Bank Investment Trust, Shawmut Assn.; dir. Shawmut Corp., Caribbean Sugar Co., General Mortgage & Credits Corp., Lord Jeffrey Inn, Amherst, Mass., Nevada-Mass. Co. Mem. adv. bd. R.F.C.; mem. N.E. com. National Credit Corp.; mem. N.E. com. Deposit Liquidation Bd.; mem. Nat. Com. for Development of Use of Acceptances. Permanent trustee Amherst Coll.; incorporator Northeastern U.; dir. Boston C. of C. Mem. Theta Delta Chi. Republican. Conglist. Clubs: Algonquin and Bass Rocks Golf Club. Contbr. to newspapers on internat. finance. Home: Eastern Point, Gloucester, Mass. Office: 40 Water St., Boston. Died Oct. 7, 1951; buried Brattleboro, Vt.

PIERCE, George Washington, educator; b. Webberville, Tex., Jan. 11, 1872; s. George W. and Mary Elizabeth (Gill) P.; B.Sc., U. Tex., 1893, M.A., 1894; Harvard, 1898-1900, A.M., 1899, Ph.D., 1900; U. Leipzig, 1900-01; m. Florence H. Goodwin, Aug. 12, 1904 (died 1945); m. 2d, Helen Russell, Nov. 2, 1946. Asst. prof. physics Harvard, 1907-17, prof., 1917-21, Rumford prof., 1921-40, emeritus since 1940, Gordon McKay prof. communication engring., 1935-40, chmn. div. phys. sciences, 1927-40, emeritus since 1940; dir. Cruft High Tension Elec. Lab., 1914-40. Fellow Am. Acad. Arts and Sciences; mem. Nat. Acad. Sciences, Am. Physical Soc., Am. Inst. E.E., Inventors Guild, Philos. Soc. of Texas. Pres. Radio Inst., 1918. Awarded medal of Inst. of Radio Engrs. for distinguished services in radio communication, 1928; Franklin medal of Franklin Inst. for inventions, theoretical and expreimental. Contbr. in field of electric communication, and teaching, 1943. Clubs: Harvard (Boston); Faculty (Harvard U.). Author: The Principles of Wireless Telegraphy, 1910; Electric Oscillations and Electric Waves, 1920; The Songs of Insects, 1948. Home: 7 Berkeley Pl. Office: Cruft High Tension Elec. Lab., Harvard Univ., Cambridge, Mass. Died Aug. 25, 1956.

PIERCE, Shelly, financial editor, columnist; born Pendleton, Ore., Aug. 11, 1898; s. Henry F. and Dora (Auerbach) P.; A.B in economics, Stanford Univ., 1922; m. Helen Zagat, Oct. 23, 1925. Reporter San Francisco Examiner, 1922, staff corr. San Jose, Calif., 1923-24; reporter San Francisco Bulletin, 1925, San Francisco Daily News, 1926; with United Press, New York, 1926; editor Asso. Press, N.Y. City, 1927-31; with N.Y. Jour. of Commerce, 1931—, financial editor, 1942—; instr. journalism Drake Bus. Sch., 1939-45; financial columnist Newark (N.J.) Evening News, 1945-48; radio, TV speaker on financial subjects. Member Aviation Writers Association. Society of the Silurians, N.Y. Soc. Security Analysts, N.Y. Financial Writers Assn., Sigma Delta Chi. Club: Nat. Press (Washington). Contbg. editor to Financial Handbook, 3d edit., 1948. Contbr. articles on railroad subjects and others to mags. Office: 80 Varick St., N.Y.C. 13. Died Apr. 17, 1956.

PIERCE, Walter Marcus, ex-congressman, ex-gov. Ore.; b. Morris, Ill., May 30, 1861; s. Charles M. and Charlotte L. (Clapp) P.; LL.B., Northwestern U., 1896; m. Clara Rudio, June 15, 1887 (died Dec. 3, 1890); m. 2d, Laura M. Rudio, Sept. 3, 1893 (died Mar. 1925); children—Clara R. (dec.), Lloyd B. (dec.), Mrs. Lucile Hall, Mrs. Helen Wilson, Mrs. Edith S. Whitten, Mrs. Lorraine Stadelman; m. 3d, Cornelia Marvin, 1928. Settled in Oregon, 1883; supt. schs. Umatilla County, 1886-90, county clk., 1890-94; practiced law 10 yrs., later banking, power and light utilities, operated stock and wheat farms, 1907-39; gov. of Ore., 1923-27; mem. 73d to 77th Congresses, 2d Ore. Dist. Mem. Ore. Senate, 1902-06, 16-20. Mem. Dem. Nat. Com., 1932-36; chmn. U.S. Dem. Presdl. Electors for Oregon, 1944. Regent Ore. Agrl. Coll., 1905-26. Home: 4561 Dallas Rd., Salem, Ore. Died Mar. 27, 1954; buried Mt. Crest Abbey, Salem.

PIERSON, Lewis Eugene, banker; b. Metuchen, N.J., Mar. 12, 1870; s. Edgar L. and Anna B. (Southard) P.; pub. schs., Metuchen, N.J., and Brooklyn; Doctor of Commercial Science, New York University; m. Blanche Thorne, June 10, 1891; children—Anna R., Alene S., Grace T., Lewis Eugene. Clerk, Hanover Nat. Bk., New York, 1885-98; cashier and v.p., 1898-1904; pres. N.Y. Nat. Exch. Bk., 1904-06; pres. Irving Nat. Exchange Bank (consolidation of New York Nat. Exchange and Irving Nat. banks), 1906-12, chairman executive committee, 1912-16; president Austin, Nicholas & Company, Inc., 1912-16; chmn. bd. Irving Trust Co., 1916-35, hon. chmn., 1939-41; chmn. and acting pres. M.K.&T. Ry. Co., 1945; dir., chmn. exec. com. Mchts. Refrigerating Co.; dir. Shell Oil Co., L.I. Duck Packing Co., Am. Smelting & Refining Co., Cruikshank Co., Heelbarp Corp., Westhampton Agy. N.Y. state chmn. U.S. Savs. Bond Div. and downstate chmn. N.Y. War Finance Com., 1941-52; chmn. adv. com. of state chairmen Savs. Bonds Dir., U.S. Treasury, 1950-52. Chmn. Washington Pan Am. Financial Conf., 1927. Vice pres. N.Y. State Chamber of Commerce, 1939-43. Chmn. financial sect., Iternational Chamber of Commerce, 1919; pres. U.S. Chamber of Commerce, 1927-28,

Merchants Assn. of New York, 1922-23, Nat. Foreign Trade Council; pres. Am. Acceptance Council, 1919-20; chmn. Nation's Business, 1923-37; first chmn. bd. regents Grad. Sch. of Banking, Rutgers U., 1935-42; v.p., N.Y. City Citizens Budget Commn., 1945-49; mem. Am. Bankers Assn. (pres. 1909-10), S.A.R., New Eng. Soc. Awarded Legion of Honor (France); Krzyz Walicznych, and Restituti Polski (Poland); Officer, Order of Orange-Nassau (Netherlands). Mason. Clubs: Metropolitan; Quantuck Beach, Westhampton Country, Swordfish, Yardarm, Oneck Gun, Recess, Labrador Retriever. Home: Westhampton Beach, L.I., N.Y. Office: 1 Wall St., N.Y.C. Died Nov. 10, 1954.

PIKE, F(rank) H(enry), coll. prof.; b. Aurora, Ill.; A.B., Ind. U., Bloomington, Ind., 1903; Ph.D., U. of Chicago, 1907; married; 1 son, Eugene Wilmoth. Instr. physiology, U. of Chicago, 1907-11; asst. prof. of physiology, Columbia U., 1911-16, asso. prof., 1916-42; retired 1942; special lecturer in physiology, 1942. Fellow A.A.A.S., N.Y. Acad. of Sciences (v.p., and chmn. sect. biology, 1918-20); mem. Am. Physiol. Soc., Am. Soc. Zoölogists, Ecol. Soc. America, Sigma Xi. Cons. physiologist U.S. Air Service, 1917. Mem. subcom. on physiology of shock, Nat. Research Council, 1917-19, subcom. on vestibular research, 1921—; mem. Commn. of Assn. for Research in Nervous and Mental Diseases, 1929. Origin of nervous System of vertebrates. Awarded A. Cressy Morrison prize, N. Y. Acad. Science, 1937. Contbr. articles on physiol. and biol. subjects; mem. editorial bd. of Ecology, 1923-24. Home: 510 Audubon Av. Office: 437 W. 59th St., N.Y.C. 19. Died Nov. 13, 1953.

PILLEMER, Louis (pill' em-er), biochemist; b. Johannesburg, South Africa, July 4, 1908; s. Jacob and Rebecca Alice (Faivus) P.; came to U.S., 1909, naturalized, 1916; B.S., Duke, 1932; Ph.D. in Biochemistry, Western Res. U., 1938; m. Jean Burrell, June 30, 1948; children—Stephen Jacob, David Burrell, Eric Anthony, Karl Andrew. Demonstrator immunology Western Res. U., 1938-39, instr. immunology, 1939-41, sr. instr. immunology, 1941-44, asst. prof. immunochemistry, 1945-46, asso. prof. immunochemistry, 1946-50, prof. biochemistry, 1950—. Asso. commn. immunization Armed Forces Epidemiological Bd., 1954. Recipient R. E. Dyer lectureship award, 1956. Fellow N.Y. Academy Science, A.A.A.S., Internat. Soc. Hematology; mem. Am. Chem. Soc., Soc. Exptl. Biology and Medicine, Am. Assn. Immunologists, Am. Soc. Biol. Chemists, Inc., Sigma Xi. Contbr. profl. jours. Home: 2634 Dartmoor Rd., Cleveland Heights 18, O. Office: 2085 Adelbert Rd., Cleve. 6. Died Aug. 31, 1957.

PILLSBURY, Alfred Fiske, flour mfr.; b. Mpls., Oct. 20, 1869; s. John Sargent and Mahala (Fiske) P.; prep. edn. Mpls. High Sch., U. Minn.; LL.B., U. Minn. Coll. of Law, 1894; m. Eleanor L. Field, May 15, 1899. With the Pillsbury-Washburn Flour Mills Co., Ltd., from 1895, until death of father, 1901; devoted attention to family estate until 1908; dir. Pillsbury Mills, Inc. (treas. to 1939); dir., exec. com. First Nat. Bank; dir. First Bank Stock Corp.; trustee Farmers and Mechanics Savings Bank; dir. Northwestern Nat. Life Ins. Co. Pres. Mpls. Inst. Arts; trustee Mpls. Symphony Orchestra. Mem. Chi Psi. Republican. Universalist. Clubs: Minneapolis, Skylight, Woodhill Country. Home: 116 E. 22d St. Office: Pillsbury Bldg., Mpls. 2. Died Mar. 12, 1950.

PILLSBURY, Harriette Brown, educator; b. Ironton, Mo., July 1, 1871; d. Walker Livingston and Sarah Joyce (Doty) Brown; ed. Belleview Collegiate Inst. and Rubicam Coll., St. Louis, m. Edwin Stanton Pillsbury, June 17th, 1907; children—Frederick Hobart, Joyce Sanborn, William Edwin. Sch. tchr., Ironton and Pilot Knob, Mo., 1889-1904. Trustee Stephens Coll., Columbia, Mo. Trustee Woman's Found. (offices in N.Y.C. and Columbia, Mo.). Clubs: University Literary, S.T.D., Stephens College Patrons (St. Louis, Mo.). Home: 680 McKnight Rd., St. Louis 5. Died Dec. 8, 1957.

PILLSBURY, Henry Church, ret. army officer; b. Lowell, Mass., May 27, 1881; s. George Harlan and Mary (Boyden) P.; A.B., Dartmouth, 1902; M.D., Harvard, 1906; attended Army Med. Sch., 1906-07; m. Janet Wood, June 5, 1912 (dec.). Commd. 1st lt. M.C., U.S. Army, 1907, advanced through grades to brig. gen., 1941; div. surgeon, 11th Div., 1918-19; prof. roentgenology Army Med. Sch., 1919-25; chief health officer Panama Canal, 1936-39; surgeon 3d Corp Area, 1940; comdg. officer Lovell Gen. Hosp., Ft. Devens, Mass., 1941; comdg. officer Thayer Gen. Hosp., Nashville, 1943-45, retired. Fellow A.C.S., A.C.P.; mem. A.M.A., Soc. Tropical Medicine Episcopalian. Mason. Club: Army and Navy (Washington, D.C.). Author: U.S. Army X-Ray Manual, 1933. Home: Ross, Cal. Died July 18, 1955.

PILLSBURY, William Howard, ednl. cons.; born Haverhill, Mass., Jan. 3, 1880; s. William Edward and Emma Jane (Marshall) P.; A.B., Carleton Coll., Northfield, Minnesota, 1906; L.H.D., Union College, 1939, LL.D. (honorary) 1952; m. Palma H. Hansen, November 1, 1905 (deceased December 23, 1930); m. 2d, Welthie Buker, June 28, 1934. Teacher rural schs., Minn., 1899-1902, Carleton Acad., Northfield, 1902-04; supt. schs., Dodge Center, Minn., 1914-17; prin. Van Buren Sch., St. Paul, 1917-18; dep. supt. schs., Buffalo; mem. faculty Buffalo U., editor Buffalo School Magazine, 1918-27; supt. schs., Pelham, N.Y., 1927-29; supt. schs., Schenectady 1929-46; teacher, summers, State Teachers College, St. Cloud, Minn., 1916-18, State Teachers Coll., Buffalo, 1918-27, N.Y. Univ., 1929, U. of Rochester, 1930-31, Cornell, 1933-35; ednl. adviser Coll. Dentistry, U. Buffalo, 1923-27; dir. study of adminstrv. and supervisory orgn. of edn. in Conn. Pres. N.Y. State Teachers Assn., 1931-33, treas., 1934-48; mem. N.Y. State Examinations Bd., 1931-46; expert examiner for U.S. Office of Edn., 1946-49; president Internat. Assn. Torch Clubs, 1936-37; pres. N.Y. State Council City and Village Supts., 1938-39; pres. Am. Assn. of Sch. Adminstrs., 1941-42. Mem. Nat. Edn. Assn. (life), Phi Delta Kappa, Pi Gamma Nu. Republican. Episcopalian. Co-author of New York State edit. of Champion Arithmetics, 6 grades, 1934. Asso. dir. New Haven (Connecticut) School Survey. Address: 194 Central Av., New Haven 15. Died Apr. 11, 1953; buried New Haven.

PILSBRY, Henry Augustus (pĭlz'brĭ), zoologist; b. Iowa City, Ia., Dec. 7, 1862; s. Dexter Robert and Elizabeth (Anderson) P.; student State U. Ia., Sc.D. (hon.), 1899; Sc.D., U. Pa. 1940, Temple U., 1941; m. Adeline Bullock Avery, 1890 (died 1924); children—Elizabeth, Grace P. Barcroft. Leading authority on mollusks, especially land shells; curator of molluske and other invertebrates Acad. Natural Scis., Phila., 1888-1957. Author: The Manual of Conchology, 31 vols. 1888-31; Marine Mollusks of Japan, 1895; Guide to the Study of Helices; Barnacles of the United States, 1916; Mollusks of the Belgian Congo, 1927; Land Mollusca of North America, 2 vols. 1939-47; other books and articles on conchology, paleontology, zoology. His sci. contbns. pub. by Am. Malacological Union, lists 986 titles, 1882-39, The Nautilus, lists 154 titles, 1940-57. Pub. and editor The Nautilus, 1889-1957. Recipient Leidy Medal, 1928. Fellow Am. Acad. Arts and Scis. (Boston); mem. Malacological Soc. London, Am. Soc. Naturalists, A.A.A.S., Am. Conchological Soc. (1st pres. 1907), Am. Malacological Union (1st pres. 1931), Phila. Shell Club (hon. life pres.), Sigma Xi; corr. mem. Academia De Ciencias de Madrid, Zool. Soc. London; hon. fgn. corr. Zoöl. Survey of India; hon. mem. Conchological Soc. Gt. Britain and Irland, Birmingham Natural History and Philos. Soc., Société Royale zoologique de Belgique, Senckenbergische naturforschende Gesellschaft, Cal. Acad. Scis., Sociedad de historia natural Felipe Poey, Sociedad Malacológica Carlos de la Torre, Sociedad Geológica del Peru. Address: Acad. Natural Scis., Phila. 3. Died Oct. 26, 1957; buried St. Asahp's Church Yard, Bala, Pa.

PILZER, Maximilian, violinist; b. N.Y.C., Feb. 26, 1890; Jacob and Hulda (Cohen) P.; m. Ilona G. Liptak, June 22, 1915; 1 dau., Doris Marie. Has concertized extensively in U.S. Address: 230 West End Av., N.Y.C. Died 1958.*

PIM, W(illiam) Paul, cartoonist; b. nr. Freeport, Pa., Dec. 1, 1885; s. Ira Lester and Mary Ella (Dougherty) P.; grad. Cabot (Pa.) Inst., 1903; student Bissell Coll. Photo-Engraving, Effingham, Ill., 1906; life class of John Huntington, Poly. Inst., Cleve., 1917-18; m. Lenna Hales, July 14, 1917. Studio, Cleve., until 1914; cartoonist Birmingham News, 1915-17, Cleve. Plain Dealer, 1917-18, Birmingham Ledger, 1919-20; started W. Paul Pim Advt. Art Studio, Birmingham, 1921, drawing Baby Mine, syndicated newspaper comic; studio closed; now drawing syndicated newspaper strip, Telling Tommy; instr. art Birmingham So. Coll., 1922-31. Republican. Methodist. Mason. Author Telling Tommy About Mother Nature's Curious Children, 1939; Telling Tommy About Famous People in Their Youth, 1940; Telling Tommy About Days We Celebrate, 1941; Telling Tommy about Famous Inventors, 1942; Telling Tommy about Our Good Neighbors, 1943; Telling Tommy About Things We Use, 1946. Writer and lecturer. Home: 4300 10th Av. S., Birmingham 5, Ala. Died July 26, 1950; buried Forest Hill Cemetery, Birmingham.

PINCHBECK, Raymond Bennett (pĭnch'bĕk), coll dean; b. Amelia County, Va., Aug. 31, 1900; s. William Thomas and Mary Jane (Walthall) P.; B.S., U. of Va., 1922, M.S., 1923, Ph.D., 1925; m. Charlotte Edith Holt, Dec. 27, 1924. Instr. in economics, U. of Va., 1922-25; prof. and head dept. of business adminstrn., Roanoke Coll., Salem, Va., 1925-29, dean of students, 1927-29; instr. of accounting, U. of Va., Extension Dept., 1927-29; lecturer in investments, Roanoke (Va.) Am. Inst. Banking, 1928-29; prof. applied economics, U. of Richmond, Va., 1929—, dean Richmond Coll., U. of Richmond, 1932—; prof. econ. Coll. of William and Mary, summer 1930, U. of Va., summer 1931-32; lecturer on credit, Richmond Credit Men's Assn., 1929-31; displaced persons adminstr., U.N.R.R.A., Jan.-June 1945. Commd. lt., U.S.N.R., active duty, May 1943-Jan. 1945, now lt. comdr. Labor compliance officer, N.R.A., 1934-35; mem. Gov's. Commn. on Unemployment Res., 1933-34; research adviser Va. State C. of C. Com. on Taxation, 1935-36; chmn. Henrico County Sch. Bd., 1934-42; pres. Va. Assn. of Colls., 1936-37; chmn. Va. Commn. on County Govt., 1938-40; mem. Va. Council on Public Adminstrn., 1938-42; special rep. United States Employment Merit Examination Program, 1937, 39; mem. Va. State Dept. Pub. Welfare Merit System Council, 1940-42; mem. Va. Pub. Service Tax Study Com., 1947-48, Va. Tax Commn., 1948—, Va. State Legislature Commn. on State and Local Finance, 1948-49, Va. adv. legislative council com. on Indsl. Loan Assns., 1949, research com. on pub. finance of Adv. Council on Va. Economy, 1948—; mem. Richmond Salvation Army Bd., 1936-40, Va. State price officer, U.S. Office Price Adminstrn., 1942-43. Trustee Virginia Intermont Junior College for Women, Bristol. Virginia, 1935—; trustee Collegiate Preparatory School for Girls, Richmond, 1939-42. Mem. Va. Social Science Association (pres. 1933-34), Am. Econ. Assn., Southern Econ. Assn., Va. Soc. Pub. Accountants, Va. Assn. of Sch. Trustees, Southern Conf. of Coll. Deans, Richmond First Club (pres. 1935-36), Sons of American Revolution, American Legion, Richmond C. of C., Raven Soc., Lambda Chi Alpha, Phi Beta Kappa, Phi Delta Kappa, Alpha Kappa Psi, Tau Kappa Alpha, Pi Gamma Mu, Omicron Delta Kappa. Democrat. Baptist. Mason. Author of monograph "Virginia Negro, Artisan and Tradesman," 1926. Editor of "A Study of Richmond, Va., City Government," 1934. Contbr. to ednl. and professional jours.; author of several govt. reports. Address: University of Richmond, Va. Died Feb. 4, 1957; buried Arlington Nat. Cemetery.

PINCKNEY, Josephine Lyons Scott (pĭnk'nē), writer; b. Charleston, S.C., Jan. 25, 1895; d. Thomas and Camilla (Scott) Pinckney; prep. edn. Ashley Hall, Charleston; studied Coll. of Charleston, Columbia U., Radcliffe Coll.; hon. LL.D., Coll. of Charleston. Author, writer. A founder Poetry Society of South Carolina; trustee Charleston Museum. Hon. mem. Phi Beta Kappa; mem. Carolina Art Assn., Soc. for the Preservation of Spirituals. Independent Democrat. Author: (poems) Sea-drinking Cities, 1927; Hilton Head (novel), 1941; Three O'Clock Dinner (novel), 1945; Great Mischief (novel), 1948; My Son and Foe (novel), published, 1952. Contributor verse and articles to Virginia Quarterly Rev., Yale Rev., Saturday Rev. of Lit., etc. Home: 36 Chalmers St., Charleston 1, S.C. Died Oct. 4, 1957.

PINE, James, ret. Coast Guard officer; b. Cin., O., Oct. 19, 1885; s. James Arthur Washington and Mary (Hattersley) P.; grad. U.S. Coast Guard Acad., Dr. Eng. (hon.), Rensselaer P.I., 1946; m. Ysabel Cooper, 1911; children—Barbara Alice (wife of Comdr. Lawson P. Ramage, U.S.N.), James Francis (dec.), Robert Beekman, Joan. Commd. ensign, 1908; advanced through grades; retired as vice adm. 1947, after 41 years service on Atlantic, Pacific, Great Lakes and Arctic ocean; in command U.S.S. May and U.S.S. Zeelandia during first World War; in command Div. III, destroyer force, and as force gunnery officer; chief ordnance and gunnery section, Hdqrs., member general board and special asst. to The Commandant, Coast Guard; supt. Academy, 1940-47. Decorated: Victory medal (patrol clasp), Congressional gold life saving medal of honor, Legion of Merit, Danish Order of Danneborg, 1st cl., American Defense (sea clasp), American Theatre, Victory, World War II. Mem. Naval Inst., Newcomen Soc. of England. Clubs: University (New York) (hon.); Ariston (New London). Author: The Place of the Coast Guard in the Government; Procurement and Education of Coast Guard Officers, The Sea and Its Lore; and service pamphlets. Home: South Harwich, Mass. Address: care U.S. Coast Guard Hdqrs., Washington. Died Feb. 21, 1953; buried Arlington Nat. Cemetery.

PINERO, Jesús T. (pē-nyā'rō), ex-gov. P.R.; b. Carolina, P.R., Apr. 16, 1897; s. Emilio and Josefa (Jiménez) P.; student schs. of P.R., and Colegio Janer, Balt., U. P.R., 1914-16, U. Pa., 1916-18; m. Aurelia Bou, June 8, 1931; children—Haydée, José E. Engaged in farming in P.R.; chmn. Municipal Assembly, Carolina, P.R., 1928; candidate, Senate of P.R., 1936; elected mem. Ho. of Reps., P.R., 1940; resident commr. from P.R. to U.S. Congress, Washington, 1944-46; gov. P.R., 1946-48. Co-founder of Popular Democratic Party (P.R.), 1938. Mem. exec. bd. P.R. council Boy Scouts Am. Pres. Sugar Cane Farmers Assn., 1933; mem. bd. dirs., P.R. Rehabilitation Assn., 1935. Home: Canovansas, P.R. Address: San Juan, P.R. Died Nov. 19, 1952.

PINK, Louis Heaton; b. Wausau, Wis., Dec. 4, 1882; s. Bernhard J. and Evelyn (Heaton) P.; A.B., St. Lawrence U., Canton, N.Y., 1904, LL.D., 1941; LL.B., N.Y. Law Sch., 1906; L.H.D., Lincoln Memorial U., 1941; m. Hazel Kelley, June 1907; children—George Bernhard (dec.), Lucia Anna (Mrs. Newton Millham), Austin Kelley. Admitted to N.Y. bar, 1906, and since practiced in N.Y. City; resident University Settlement, 1905-06; head worker United Neighborhood Guild (settlement), 1910-12; gen. counsel Liquidation Bur., State Ins. Dept., 1932-34, head Title and Mortgage Bur., 1934-35; supt. of insurance

State of N.Y., 1935-43; pres., chmn. bd. Asso. Hosp. Service, 1943-50, chmn. bd., 1950-53; pres. United Housing Foundation; chmn. N.Y. State Board of Housing, 1937-39. President Upanin Hotels, Inc. (model lodging house) since 1925; pres. Brooklyn Garden Apts., Inc. (model tenements under State Housing Bd.), 1928-32, v.p. since 1932; mem. N.Y. City Bd. of Edn., 1913-14, N.Y. State Housing Bd., 1926-34 (chmn. 1933-34), N.Y. City Municipal Housing Authority, 1934-35. Trustee St. Lawrence U., Ga. Warm Springs Foundn., Nat. Foundn. Infantile Paralysis, Mutual Life Ins. Co. of N.Y., Nat. Pub. Housing Conf. Special adviser to President Osmena of Philippines, 1945. Chairman Citizens Conference on International Economic Union. Member National Assn. Ins. Commrs. (chmn. exec. com., 1935-39), Nat. Public Housing Conf. (chmn. of board), Beta Theta Pi. Democrat. Author: Life of Mayor Gaynor, 1931; The New Day in Housing, 1928; Freedom from Fear, 1944. Home: 200 E. 66th St., N.Y. City. Office: 345 E. 46th St., N.Y.C. Died May 18, 1955.

PINKERTON, Lowell Call, U.S. ambassador; born Medora, Ill., Oct. 24, 1894; s. James Van and Lura (Call) P.; A.B., William Jewell Coll., Liberty, Mo., 1915; U. of Mo., 1915; m. Marian Elizabeth McKay, Dec. 1, 1919. High sch. teacher, 1915; prin., Salisbury (Mo.) High; supt., Clarksville, 1916-17; consular asst., 1917-19, consul, 1919, detailed Dept. State until 1923; consul, London, 1923-29; foreign service insp., 1929-33; director Fgn. Service Officers Training Sch., 1933-37; consul gen., Wellington, N.Z., 1937-41, Jerusalem, 1941-46; minister to Lebanon, 1947-51; fgn. service insp., 1951-56; A.E. and P. to the Sudan, 1956-58, career minister, 1958—. Mem. Kappa Sigma. Mason. Home: 4000 Cathedral Av. Office: Dept. of State, Washington. Died Feb. 19, 1959; buried Fort Lincoln Cemetery, Washington.

PINZA, Ezio (pĕn'tzä), basso singer; b. Rome, Italy; s Cesare and Clelia (Bulgarelli) P.; studied voice with Ruzza and Vezzani; m. Doris Leak; children—Celia, Ezio Pietro, Gloria, Claudia. Opera début in Soncino in Norma, 1914; drafted to Italian Army served until disch. as capt., 1919; début Rome Opera, 1919, La Scala, Milan, 1921; has appeared with San Francisco, Chgo., St. Louis Municipal, Metropolitan Opera Cos., also all important ones in many countries; has sung 82 different operatic roles, including: Don Giovanni, Boris Godunoff, Figaro, Mephisto, Don Basilio and Father in Louise. Co-starred in South Pacific (play), N.Y.C., 1949, in Fanny (play) N.Y.C.; motion pictures under contract to MGM: Mr. Imperium; Strictly Dishonorable; Carnegie Hall, Tonight We Sing; starred in TV programs Bonino, The Ezio Pinza Show. Records for RCA and Columbia in U.S., H.M.V., Eng., La Voce Del Padrone, Italy. Home: Stamford, Conn. Died May 9, 1957; buried Putnam Cemetery, Greenwich, Conn.

PIPER, Alexander Ross, railroad exec.; b. Fort Wadsworth, S.I., N.Y., Mar. 1, 1865; s. Capt. James Wilson and Sarah Van Dyke (Ross) P.; B.S., U.S. Mil. Acad., 1889; m. Marie Susan Cozzens, June 24, 1890 (dec.); children—Marie Adelaide (Mrs. Frank Richardson Oates), Alexander Stanley (dec.), Marjorie Wheaton (widow of Herman Siefke), Anne Alexandra (wife of Rev. Hollis Samuel Smith) (dec.), Emily Cozzens (Mrs. Philip Keep Reynolds), Alexander; m. 2d, Ruth Evelyn Fitch. Began as 2d lt., inf., U.S. Army, 1889; participated in Sioux campaign, 1890-91 capt. C.S. of V. in Porto Rican expedition, 1898, ret. as capt., 1899; recalled to active service, 1917; lt. col., later col., Q.M.C.N.A.; depot Q.M. N.Y.C. and port supply officer N.Y.C. and Newport News, Va.; utilities officer, Port of Embarkation, N.Y., 1918-19, World War; relieved active duty, 1919; col. Q.M. Res. 1922, now ret. Dep. police commr. N.Y., 1902-03, established Block Control System of Traffic; gen. supt. Am. Ry. Traffic Co., 1904-08; gen. freight agt. S. Bklyn. Ry. Co., 1908-16, pres., 1916-40, ret., 1940; asst. gen. mgr. Bklyn. Rapid Transit Co., 1919-24; in charge Med. and Welfare Bur., Bklyn.-Manhattan Transit Corp., 1923-40, ret. 1940; dir. Technicolor, Inc., 1932-34. Pres. Assn. of Grads. U.S. Mil. Acad., 1934-36; trustee Eno Foundation. Awarded Silver Star Citation (U.S.), 1898. Mem. West Point Soc. of N.Y., Order of Indian Wars, S.R., Soc. of Colonial Wars. Republican. Episcopalian. Clubs: University (New York), Farmington Country (Va.). Home: South Salem, N.Y. Died Nov. 22, 1952; buried West Point (N.Y.) Cemetery.

PIPER, Fred LeRoy, author, clergyman; b. Melvin Village, N.H., Feb. 1, 1858; s. Thatcher W. and Nancy M. (Allen) P.; ed. pvt. acad.; D.D., Aurora (Ill.) Coll., 1921; m. Anna L. Remick, Dec. 25, 1883. Ordained Advent Christian ministry, 1881; pastor chs. at St. Johnsbury (Vt.), Rochester (N.Y.), East Norwalk (Conn.) until 1934; now retired. Sec. Am. Advent Mission Soc., 1891-1900; editor World's Crisis (denom. organ), Boston, 1900-22. Pres. N.E. Sch. of Theology, Boston. Author: Conditionalism, 1904; Lights of Home, 1912; Life of Miles Grant, 1915; The Second Advent in Poetry and Song, 1917; The Return of Christ, 1922. Home: Melvin Village, N.H. Died July 7, 1940; buried Milton Mills, N.H.

PIRIE, Emma Elizabeth, home econs.; b. San Antonio; d. John Marshall and Bennie (Grayson) Pirie; spl. courses Coll. Industrial Arts, Denton, Tex.; U. of Tenn.; Miss Farmers' Cooking Sch., 1910; Columbia, 1916. Began as tchr. pub. schs., San Antonio, 1893; asst. dept. of home econs., same schs., 1904-06, supervisor, 1906—. Editor household dept. Daily Express, San Antonio, and Houston Daily Post, 1907-12; mem. Tex. State Bd. of Health. Chmn. pure food com. Mothers' Congress; mem. Tex. State Tchrs. Assn. (chmn. home econs. sect. 1915-16), Tex. Home Econs. Assn. (pres. 1914-15, 1915-16), Am. Home Econs. Assn., Equal Franchise Assn., League of Women Voters, D.A.R. Episcopalian. Clubs: San Antonio History, Woman's, Altrusa. Author: A Sewing Course, 1906; Science of Home Making, 1915. Contbr. to Hygeia. Home: Sulphur Springs Rd. Address: R. 6, Box 279, San Antonio. Died Jan. 17, 1951; buried Mission Burial Park, San Antonio.

PIRIE, Frederick W., Canadian senator, bus. exec.; b. Red Rapids, Victoria, Can., Feb. 1, 1893; s. William and Phoebe Jane (Roberts) P.; student Allison Comml. Coll., 1907-09; LL.D., Mt. Allison U., 1943; m. Adeline Clarke Limestone, June 12, 1917; children—Frederick William, Betty Adeline, Dawn Jean, Judith Ann. Pres. F. W. Pirie Co. Ltd. since 1920, Atlantic Chems. Co. Ltd. since 1946; dir. Maritime Trust Co. since 1948, Maritime Life Ins. Co. since 1943, Can. Cement Co. Ltd. since 1951; developed new variety seed potatoes White Bliss, 1929. Mayor Grand Falls, N.B., City Council, 1928-30; elected to N.B. Legislature, 1930, re-elected, 1935, 1939, 1944; minister Lands and Mines, 1935-45; apptd. Can. Senate, 1945. Awarded King George V Medal, 1935, King George VI Medal, 1937. Presbyn. Mason (Shriner). Home: Grand Falls. N.B. Office: Senate, Ottawa, Can. Died Oct. 3, 1956.

PISAR, Charles Juneau (pē'sär), consular service; b. Sheboygan, Wis., June 8, 1890; s. Charles and Elizabeth P.; ed. pub. schs., pvt. tutors and business coll.; m. Mrs. Eileen Hart Davies, Sept. 12, 1921; children—Patrick Hope, Valerie Anne. In newspaper and magazine business, 1905-09; sec. to auditor of Deering Works, Internat. Harvester Co., Chicago, Ill., 1909-10; sec. to pres. Carleton Coll., Northfield, Minn., 1910-11; with R. G. Dun & Co., Buenos Aires, Argentina, 1913-14; clerk in Am. Consulate Gen., Buenos Aires, 1914-15; apptd. vice-counsul, same city 1915; retired, 1917; apptd. vice-consul at Cape Town, Cape of Good Hope, 1917, vince-consul de carriere, 1919, consul, 1922; consul, Rangoon, India, 1924-26, Calcutta, India, 1926, Salonika, Greece, 1927-32, Ghent, Belgium, 1932-33, Lyon, France, 1933-37, Liverpool, Eng., 1937-43; in Bristol (temp.), Jan. 1941. Apptd. sec. in the Diplomatic Service, Aug. 12, 1937; apptd. Am. consul gen., Liverpool, June 30, 1942; retired, 1943. Congregationalist. Mason. Address: 1232 Birch St., Boonton, N.J. Died Oct. 16, 1955; buried Rosedale Crematory, Orange, N.J.

PITKIN, Walter Boughton, psychologist, writer; b. Ypsilanti, Mich., Feb. 6, 1878; s. Caleb S. and Lucy T. (Boughton) P.; A.B., U. of Mich., 1900; grad. study Sorbonne, Paris, U. of Berlin, U. of Munich, Hartford (Conn.) Treol. Sem., 1900-05; m. Mary B. Gray, 1903; children—Richard Gray, John Gray, David Bartholomew, Robert Bolter, Walter Boughton; married 2d, Katharine B. Johnson. Lecturer in psychology, Columbia University, 1905-09, professor journalism, 1912—; mem. editorial staff N.Y. Tribune, 1907-08, Evening Post, 1909-10, Parents' Mag., 1927-30; American managing editor Encyclopedia Britannica, 1927-28; story supervisor Universal Pictures Company 1929; editorial director Farm Journal 1935-38; cons. psychologist, adviser on teaching methods. Author: The Art and Business of the Short Story, 1913; Must We Fight Japan?, 1920; How to Write Stories, 1922; Seeing America—Farm and Field (with Harold Hughes), 1924; Seeing America—Mill and Factory (with Harold Hughes), 1926; The Twilight of the American Mind, 1928; The Art of Rapid Reading, 1929; The Psychology of Happiness, 1929; The Young Citizen, 1929; The Art of Sound Picturs (with William M. Marston), 1930; The Psychology of Achievement, 1930; Vocational Studies in Journalism, 1931; The Art of Learning, 1931; How We Learn, 1931; Short Introduction to History of Human Stupidity, 1932; Life Begins At Forty, 1932; The Consumer—His Nature and His Changing Habits, 1932; More Power To You, 1933; The Chance of a Lifetime, 1934; Take It Easy!, 1935; Let's Get What We Want, 1935; Capitalism Carries On, 1935; Careers After Forty, 1937; Making Good Before Forty, 1939; Seeing Our Country (with Harold F. Hughes), 1939; The Art of Useful Writing, 1940; Escape from Fear, 1940; On My Own, 1944; The Best Years, 1946; Road to a Richer Life, 1949. Editor and contbr.: The New Realism, 1913; As We Are, 1923. Home: Los Altos, Cal. Died Jan. 25, 1953.

PITKIN, Wolcott H., lawyer; b. Albany, N.Y., Dec. 6, 1881; son Wolcott H. and Mary Wool (Southwick) P.; A.B., Harvard, 1902, LL.B., 1906; m. Felicie M. Riehl, 1932. Asst. U.S. atty., So. Dist. of N.Y., 1909-12; atty.-gen. P.R., Apr. 1912-Dec. 1914; acting gen. adviser and adviser in foreign relations to the Siamese Govt., 1915-17; now v.p., gen. attorney and dir. Internat. Telephone and Telegraph Corp.; also exec. affiliated cos. Mem. various bar assns. Clubs: Harvard, Century Association, City Midday, Downtown Athletic (N.Y.C.); Jefferson Islands (Washington). Home: 318 Wearimus Rd., Ho-Ho-Kus, N.J. Address: 67 Broad St., N.Y.C. 4. Died Aug. 18, 1954.*

PITMAN, J(oseph) Asbury, educator; b. Appleton, Me., June 30, 1867; s. William Henry and Ruth Anne (Richardson) P.; grad. State Normal Sch., Castine, Me.; spl. student, Clark U., 1895-96, Harvard, 1896-97, Columbia, 1917-21; hon. Ed.D., R.I. Coll. of Edn., 1929; m. Flora Etta Carver, July 23, 1890; children—Earle Carver, Arthur Loring. Tchr., prin., high schs., Me., 1884-90; prin. grammar schs., Mass., 1891-92; dist. supt. of schs., Mass., 1892-97; city supt. schs., Marlboro, Mass., 1897-1906; pres. State Tchrs. Coll., Salem, Mass., 1906-37, pres. emeritus, 1937—. Mem. Salem City Planning Bd., 1911-39, chmn., 1929-39. Mem. N.E.A., Am. Assn. of Tchrs. Coll., Nat. Econ. League, Salem C. of C. (ex-pres.) Nat. Council of Normal Schs. Pres. and Prins. (ex-pres.), Mass. Soc. S.A.R., Phi Delta Kappa, Pi Gamma Mu.; ex-pres. Mass. Schoolmasters Club, Mass. Supts. Assn., Mass. Normal Sch. Tchrs. Assn., Am. Inst. Instrn. Republican. Congregationalist. Mason. Rotarian. Home: 45 Northport Av., Belfast, Me. Died Aug. 27, 1952; buried Maplewood Cemetery, Lincolnville, Me.

PITT, David Alexander, clergyman; b. Tamlaght, Ireland, Mar. 14, 1877; s. David and Margaret (Hamilton) P.; student Bucknell U., 1898-1900; A.B., U. Pa., 1902; B.D., Rochester Theol. Sem., 1905; D.D., Berkeley (Cal.) Bapt. Div. Sch., 1921; m. Maud Elizabeth Hanna, Sept. 1, 1904 (died June 19, 1945); children—Carson Hanna, Courtnay Hamilton, Ledlie Carson, Hamilton, Gavin Alexander; m. 2d, Harriet Sampson, Apr. 1946. Ordained to Baptist ministry, 1905; pastor successively Cuba, N.Y., Lockport, N.Y. and Berkeley, Cal., until 1921, Central Ch., Norwich, Conn., 1921-42, First Congl. Ch., Woodstock, 1942-45. Mem. bd. dirs. Conn. Bapt. Conv. (pres. 5 yrs.); pres. No. Cal. Bapt. Conv., 1916-17; alumni orator Rochester Theol. Sem., 1925, 35; first v.p. Am. Bapt. Fgn. Mission Soc., 1929-30, Conn. rep. on Nat. Bd. of Missionary Cooperation, 1931, 32; mem. President's Cabinet No. Bapt. Conv., 1933, mem. survey com.; mem. exec. com. Ministers and Missionaries Benefit Bd. Progressive Republican. Home: 50 E. 67th St., N.Y.C. 21; also Woodstock, Conn. Died Nov. 7, 1949; buried Maplewood Cemetery, Norwich, Conn.

PITT, Louis Wetherbee, clergyman; b. Middletown, Conn., Mar. 7, 1893; s. George Stuart and Cornelia (Risk) P.; A.B., Wesleyan U, 1915, D. D. (hon), 1940; S.T.D (hon.), Berkeley Divinity Sch., 1941; honorary S.T.D., New York University, 1951; married Blanche Parmelee, June 22, 1918; children—George Selden, Elizabeth Bulkley, Louis Wetherbee. Ordained to Episcopalian ministry, 1918; rector Christ Ch., Newark, 1918-20; minister-in-charge St. Mary Magdalene's Ch., 1918-20; asst. St. Luke's Ch., Montclair, 1920-22; rector St. Mark's Ch., Newark, 1922-29, St. Mary's Ch., Ardmore, Pa., 1929-40, Grace Ch., N.Y. City, since 1940. Trustee Cathedral of St. John the Divine, N.Y. City, 1945-56; mem. standing com. Diocese of N.Y., 1947-50; Dean Convocation of Manhattan, Episcopal Ch., 1950-52; vis. chaplain, Columbia, 1948-49; dep., gen. conv. Episcopal Ch., San Francisco, 1949; exec. com. Fed. Council Chs. of Christ in Am., 1944-49. Trustee Wesleyan U., 1956—, Berkeley Div. Sch., 1956—; mem. exec. com. N.Y. Billy Graham Crusade, 1957. Mem. Alpha Delta Phi. Club: The Century (N.Y.C.). Home: 804 Broadway, N.Y.C. 3. Died Apr. 2, 1959.

PITTENGER, Lemuel Arthur, educator; b. De Soto, Ind., Sept. 27, 1873; s. Isaiah Sheller and Sarah Josephine (Swander) P.; student Lebanon (O.) Normal U., 1894; A.B., Ind. U., 1907, A.M., 1908; hon. Litt.D., Taylor U., Upland, Ind., 1932; LL.D., Franklin Coll., 1936; LL.D., DePauw U., 1937; m. Bertha Orr, Aug. 2, 1900; children—Arthur Orr, Mary Josephine. Tchr. rural schs., 1893-95, 96-97; tchr. English, high sch., Muncie, Ind., 1900-06; critic in English, Ind. U., 1908-13; prof. English, head of dept., Kent (O.) State Normal Sch., 1913-19; prof. rural edn., Ball State Tchrs. Coll., Muncie, 1922-27, pres., 1927-1942; emeritus, 1942—. Mem. Ind. Ho. of Rep., 1923-27 (budget com., 1923-26; majority floor leader, 1925, 27; author Ind. budget laws). Mem. Ind. State Bd. of Edn., 1927-32 and 1937-41; pres. Am. Assn. of Tchrs. Colls., 1937-38; mem. of exec. com. North Central Assn. of Colls. and Secondary Schs., 1937-41; dir. Ball Meml. Hosp., Muncie Fed. and Loan Assn. Mem. N.E.A. (life), Am. Country Life Assn., Ind. Soc. Mental Hygiene, Ind. Acad. Sci. Ind. State Tchrs. Assn., Ind. Schoolmen's Club, Ind. Hist. Assn., Muncie C. of C., Phi Beta Kappa, Phi Gamma Delta, Phi Delta Kappa. Republican. Presbyn. Mason (32°). Clubs: Kiwanis, Rotary (Muncie); Columbia (Indpls.). Home: Selma, Ind. Died July 12, 1955.

PITTENGER, William Alvin (pĭt'ĕn-jĕr), attorney at law, former congressman; b. Crawfordsville, Ind., Dec. 29, 1885; s. Frank and Elizabeth (Harshbarger) P.; A.B., Wabash Coll., 1909; LL.B., Harvard, 1912; m. Phoebe Bell, Aug. 1918; children—Richard William, Dorothy Elizabeth. Admitted to Minn. bar 1912; began practice at Duluth; mem. Minn. Ho. of Rep. 1917, 19; mem. 71st, 72d, 74th, 76th to 79th Congresses (1929-33, 1935-37, 1939-47), 8th Minn. Dist. Republican. Unitarian. Grand Sire Independent Order of Oddfellows, 1935-36; elected Supreme Councilman, Loyal Order of Moose, Aug. 30, 1939, Phila. Home: 2826 E. 2d St. Office: 404 First National Bank Bldg., Duluth. Died Nov. 26, 1951; buried Forest Hill Cemetery, Duluth.

PITTMAN, Marvin Summers, ednl. cons.; b. Eupora, Miss., Apr. 12, 1882; s. John Wesley and Ellen (Bradford) P.; ed. Bellefontaine Acad. and Millsaps Acad., Miss.; A.B., Millsaps Coll., 1905; A.M., U. of Ore., 1917; Ph.D., Columbia, 1921; m. Anna Terrell, February 13, 1915; children—Catherine Ellen (Mrs. Harry Watkins), and Marvin (deceased). Began teaching at Monroe, Louisiana, 1905; served as teacher of high schs., prin. high sch., county supt. schs., and prof. of history in the State Normal Coll. in La.; became dir. of rural edn., State Normal Sch., Ore., 1912; dir. rural edn., Mich. State Normal Coll., 1921-29; organizer, 1923, Lincoln Consolidated Sch., a demonstration and training sch. for Mich. State Normal Coll., Ypsilanti, dir. teacher training of the college, 1929-34; pres. Ga. State Teachers Coll., Statesboro, 1934-41, and 1943-47; dir. of instruction, Louisiana State Normal Coll., 1942-43; taught summers, U. of Mich., 1923-26, U. of Manitoba, 1927, Pa. State Coll., 1928, U. of Neb., 1929. Dir. ednl. program, Korea, assignment by U.S. Army, working with Korean teachers colls., and depts. edn., 1948 (6 mos.); ednl. cons. Inst. Internat. Education, 1951; head spl. mission of tech. assistance, Costa Rica, 1952-53. Member National Dept. Rural Edn. (dir.), Kappa Delta Pi, Phi Delta Kappa, Kappa Alpha (Southern); pres. La. State Teachers Assn., 1911-12; pres. Ypsilante Board of Commerce, 1929-30. Dir. Am. Assn. of Teachers Colls. Pres. Ga. Assn. of Colls., 1938. Democrat. Methodist. Mason, Odd Fellow. Rotarian. Author: Value of School Supervision, 1921; A Guide to the Teaching of Spelling, 1921; Successful Teaching in Rural Schools, 1922; Problems of Rural Teacher, 1924; The Practical Plan Book, 1931; Profitable Farming, 1932. Studied operation of rural schools in France, Spain, Germany, Denmark and England, 1928; invited to Mexico by the U. of Mexico and the Mexican Govt. to study the Nat. Rural Edn. Program and to hold a series of conferences with federal directors and inspectors of schools, summer of 1929; made study of primary and secondary edn. and of teacher training for Dept. of Edn., Cuban Govt., autumn of 1932; served as mem. of spl. commn. dealing with rural edn. and organization sent to Germany by War Dept., 1947. Home: Statesboro, Ga. Died Feb. 27, 1954.

PIUS XII (Eugenio Pacelli), Pope; b. Rome, Italy, Mar. 2, 1876; s. Filippo and Virginia (Graziosi) P.; student, Capranica Coll., Gregorian U., Roman Sem. Ordained priest Roman Catholic Church, Apr. 2, 1899. Called to service of the Secretariat of State; sec. of Pontifical Commn. for the Codification of Canon Law; sec. Extraordinary Ecclesiastical Affairs; Apostolic Nuncio to Bavaria; Titular Archbishop of Sardi, May 1917; Apostolic Nuncio to Berlin (negotiated and signed a new concordat with Bavaria, March 1924, with Prussia, August 1929); created cardinal, December 1929; secretary of State, February 7, 1930-Feb. 10, 1939; Pope since March 2, 1939. Cardinal Legate to Internat. Eucharistic Congress, Buenos Aires, 1934, Lourdes, 1935, at Lisieux for the dedication of the Basilica of Sainte Therese de l'Enfant Jesus, 1937, at Paris (delivered address on Church in France), 1937, and to Internat. Eucharistic Congress, Budapest, 1938; elected Pope, assuming name of Pius XII, Mar. 1939. Held Solemn Consistory in which 32 new cardinals belonging to 18 nations were created, Feb. 18, 1946. Delivers radio-messages to persons of every continent and social order. Primarily interested in world peace and the relief of suffering peoples. Home: The Vatican, Vatican City, Rome, Italy. Died Oct. 8, 1958; buried St. Peter's Basilica.

PIZITZ, Louis, mcht., philanthropist; b. Poland, Apr. 3, 1868; s. Samuel and Bertha P.; student Hebrew Coll., Poland, 1885; m. Minnie Smolian, Nov. 14, 1893 (dec.); children—Bertha (Mrs. Joseph Smolian), Isadore, Silvia; m. 2d Mrs. Bessie Jaffee, Mar. 31, 1938. Came to U.S., 1892, naturalized, 1893. House-to-house salesman, Swainsboro, Ga., 1892; chmn. bd. Louis Pizitz Dry Goods Co., Birmingham, Ala., 1936-—. Chmn. Liberty Bond drive Jefferson Co. Ala., 1917-18, Four Minute Men finance com., 1917-18; mem. Ala. State Council Def., 1917-18; city chmn. Asso. Charities drive, 1918; mem. bd. commrs. Swainsboro. Founder Ensley Negro Hosp.; founder, past pres. Y.M.H.A., Birmingham. Mem. bd. dirs. United Jewish Fund; dir. Tuggle Inst.; Ala. State chmn. Hillel Fund. Exec. Ala. State Archives; fund chmn. Tuskegee Inst.; patron Smithsonian Inst. Recipient Silver Cup award for services as city chmn. K.C. drive, 1941; Good Will award by Nat. Conf. Christians and Jews, 1948. Mem. U.S. C. of C., Birmingham C. of C., B'nai B'rith. Mem. Temple Beth-El (founder, hon. life pres.). Elk, Mason, Lion, K.C. (hon. knight comdr.). Clubs: Hillcrest Country, Fairmont Country (Birmingham). Nominated Man of the South, 1951. Home: 2980 Mountain Brook Parkway. Office: Pizitz, Birmingham, Ala. Died June 1959.

PLANK, William Bertolette, mining engr.; b. Morgantown, Pa., June 24, 1886; s. David Heber (M.D.) and Ida Eugenie (Bertolet) P.; prep. edn., Keystone State Normal Sch.; B.S. in Mining Engring., Pa. State Coll., 1908, E.M., 1909; m. Helen Josephine Beck, Apr. 8, 1912; 1 dau., Adaline Jane. Instr. Sch. of Mines, Pa. State Coll., 1908-09; mining engr. with Phila. & Reading Coal & Iron Co., Shamokin, Pa., 1909-12, Pitts. Coal Co., 1912-16; with U.S. Bur. Mines, 1916-20, successively as jr. mining engr. (Pitts.), asst. mining engr. (Pitts.), mining engr. (Urbana, Ill.), dist. mining engr. (Birmingham, Ala.); head dept. mining and metall. engring. and John Markle prof., Lafayette Coll., 1920-52, emeritus prof., 1952-—; now cons. mining engr., dir. Boys Engring. Conf. of Coll., 1934-36; dir. A.S. T.P. engring. studies, 1943-44; coordinator, U.S. Army Ordnance Research Project, Lafayette Coll., 1941-45. Mem. mine safety com. U.S. Coal Commn., 1923, pres. Civil Service Bd. of Easton, 1926-52; chmn. Emergency Fuel Commn. of Easton during anthracite strike, 1925-26; chmn. Smoke Abatement Commn. of Easton, 1929; mem. engr. div., Pres'. Com. on Civil Service Improvement, 1939. Pres. Northampton County Pa. Hist. Soc., 1941-42; London rep., Metals and Minerals Sect. Tech. Indsl. Intelligence Com. of F.E.A., summer 1945. Mem. Am. Inst. Mining and Metall. Engrs. (mgr. Lehigh Valley sect.; chmn. div. of mineral industries edn., 1936-38; sec. 1938-47), director 1945-48, mem. Mining and Metall. Soc. of Am. Coal Mining Inst. Am., Engrs. Council for Profl. Development (one of 3 reps. of Am. Inst. Mining and Metall. Engrs.), Am. Soc. for Testing Materials (chmn. com. D-16 on slate, 1928), Am. Soc. for Engring. Edn. (chmn. mining and metall. com., 1936; Council, 1938-46; chmn. Lafayette Chpt., 1940-41), Am. Mine Rescue Assn., Am. Soc. for Metals, Pa. Acad. Sci., Am. Coll. Personnel Assn., Am. Assn. U. Profs., Civic Assn. (pres.), Engrs. Club of Lehigh Valley, Newcomen Soc. of England, Phi Kappa Phi, Tau Beta Pi, Delta Tau Delta, Sigma Gamma Epsilon. Episcopalian. Mason. Clubs: Faculty of Lafayette Coll. (pres., 1926-27, 1939-40), Rotary (pres., 1926-27, 1953-54). Contbr. articles on mineral technology field pub. principally by Am. Inst. Mining and Metall. Engrs. Address: Morgantown, Pa. Died June 19, 1956; buried Coernarvon Cemetery, Morgantown, Pa.

PLASSMANN, Thomas (plăs'măn), clergyman, educator; b. Avenwedde, Westphalia, Germany, Mar. 19, 1879; s. Otto and Elisabeth (Paschedag) P.; came to U.S., 1894; A.M., St. Francis Solanus Coll., Quincy, Ill., 1898; joined Franciscan order, 1898; ordained priest R.C. Ch., 1906; studied philosophy and theology, Holy Name Province, Paterson, N.J., 1898-1902; Ph.D., Catholic U., 1907; S.T.D., Appollinaris Coll., Rome, 1909; studied Louvain and Bonn; hon. degree Lector Generalis S. Scripturae, 1932; Litt.D., 1929; LL.D., 1945; LL.D., Canisius College, Buffalo, N.Y., 1934, St. Francis Coll., Brooklyn, 1939, Niagara U., 1945. With St. Bonaventure's Coll., Alleghany, N.Y., 1910-—; pres. St. Bonaventure's High Sch., Coll., and Ecclesiastical Sem., 1920-49; appointed provincial Holy Name Province, N.Y.C., 1949. Specialized in Oriental langs., lits., Bibl. studies and theology. Author: The Signification of Beraka, 1913; Baronius, 1922; The Book Called Holy, 1932; The Priest's Way to God, 1937 (rev. edit., 1945); From Sunday to Sunday, 1948. Contbr. to Catholic Ency., Ecclesiastical Review, N.C.E.A. Bull. and Archivum Franciscanum Historicum. Home: 135 W. 31 St., N.Y.C. 1. Died Feb. 1959.

PLASTIRAS, Nicholas, Former Premier of Greece; b. Karditza, a small town in Thessaly, 1833; profl. soldier since youth; admitted to the Officers Tng. Sch., from which he was grad., 1912 with a 2d lts. comms. Address: Athens, Greece. Died July 26, 1953.

PLATT, Frederick Joseph, business exec.; b. Franklin Furnace, N.J., July 21, 1871; s. Joseph Curtis and Katharine Judd (Jones) P.; A.B. in Elec. and Mech. Engring., Cornell U., 1892; m. Jessie Blair, Jan. 24, 1895 (dec.); children—Joseph C., Austin Blair, Frederick J.; m. 2d, Anna S. Williams, Sept. 6, 1952. With Wightman Co., mfrs. st. railway motors, Scranton, Pa., 1892-93; engr. for coal cos., Scranton, 1893-94; organizer and pres. Scranton Elec. Constrn. Co., elec. equipment in coal mines; dir. 1st Nat. Bank & Trust (Scranton); v.p. Scranton Lackawanna Trust Co. Pres. bd. trustees Y.M. C.A., Y.W.C.A. Trustee Keystone Jr. Coll., La-Plume, Pa. Clubs: Rotary (hon.), Kiwanis (hon.), Scranton (Scranton); Waverly (Pa.) Country; Madison Beach (Madison, Conn.). Republican. Presbyterian. Home: 610 N. Webster Av. Office: Connell Bldg., Scranton, Pa. Died Nov. 27, 1959.

PLATTEN, John Wesley, financier; b. Port Perry, Ont., Can.; student pub. schs.; m. Anne Bender; children—John Homer, Mrs. Charles F. Hurd, Jr. Began work in Bank in Toronto, 1883; in office of asst. gen. passenger agt. N.Y., P.&O. R.R., Cleve., 1888; with Erie R.R., New York, 1888, in office of 2d v.p. and gen. mgr., as chief clk. ins. dept., chief clk. operating dept. and asst. purchasing agt., 1889-1901, treas. rd. and subsidiary lines, 1901-03; asst. to president Lehigh Valley R.R., financial accounting and purchasing depts., 1903-04, 2d v.p., 1904-05; v.p. U.S. Mortgage & Trust Co., N.Y.C., 1905-10, pres., 1910 until merger with Chem. Bank & Trust Co., 1929, chmn. bd., 1929-31; was also chmn. bd. G.,M.&N. R.R., ret. 1931; dir. Chem. Bank & Trust Co. Mem. commn. apptd. to make report on Canadian Northern Ry. System. Home: 325 West End Av., N.Y.C. 23. Died Nov. 1954.

PLAYER, William Oscar, Jr., newspaperman; b. Greensboro, N.C., Aug. 27, 1906; s. William Oscar and Elizabeth (Ferrell) P.; student Presbyterian Coll., S.C., 1922-25, A.B., U. of N.C., 1926, grad. sch. of English, U. of S.C., 1926-27; m. Nell M. Caudill; 1 son, William Oscar III. Began as reporter, The Columbia (S.C.) Record, 1926-27; reporter, asst. city editor, telegraph editor, Birmingham (Ala.) Post, 1927-29; copy reader, reporter, utility desk man, Baltimore (Md.) Sun, 1929-35; re-write man, spl. assignment and feature writer, The N.Y. Post, 1935-42. Washington corr. and columnist, 1942-49, specializing in fgn. affairs; covered various internat. confs., etc., U.S., Can., Mexico, England, France, Germany; apptd. spl. asst. to asst. Sec. State, 1949-—. Collaborates on daily column, Washington Memo. Mem. R.O.T.C. Presbyterian Coll. of South Carolina, 1922-24. Mem. White House Corr. Assn., Overseas Writers, Senate and House Press Galleries, Am. Newspaper Guild, Kappa Alpha (Southern). Club: National Press (Washington). Contbr. articles, fiction, verse, to Sat. Evening Post, Country Gentleman, Coronet, McClure Syndicate, etc. Home: 207 S. Fairfax St., Alexandria, Va. Office: 1370 Nat. Press Bldg., Washington 4. Died Mar. 30, 1951; buried Cedar Hill Cemetery, Washington.

PLEADWELL, Frank Lester (pleed-'wĕl), medical officer U.S. Navy, ret.; b. Taunton, Mass., Aug. 9, 1872; s. Wm. Henry and Kate Sophia (Bradley) P. M.D., cum laude, Harvard, 1896; grad. Naval War Coll., 1920; m. 2d, Laura Mell Stith, 1931; 1 dau., Theodora Hunt (by first marriage). Asst. surgeon U.S. Navy, 1896; promoted through grades to capt., Feb. 1, 1918. Served on "Nashville," Spanish-Am. War; spl. observer, British services, 1916-17; asst. naval attaché Am. Embassy, London, and aide on staff comdr. in chief U.S. Naval Forces in European waters; fleet surgeon and aide on staff of comdr. in chief Atlantic Fleet, 1920-21; asst. Bureau Medicine and Surgery, Washington, D.C., 1921-24; comdg. naval hosp., Pearl Harbor, Hawaii, 1925-28; comdg. naval hospital, Boston, 1928-29 (retired). Awarded bronze medal for services at Cienfuegos, Spanish-Am. War; recommended by Adm. Sims for Navy Cross, World War; received certificate of commendation; Comdr. British Empire. Del. of U.S. Navy at internat. congresses on Nomenclature of Diseases, Paris, and Alcoholism, London, 1909; tech. adviser to Am. delegation at Geneva, July 1929; del. of U.S. Govt. and chmn., Am. delegation, XI Internat. Congress, History of Medicine at Zagreb, Belgrade, Sarajevo and Dubrovnik, Yugoslavia, 1938. Fellow Am. Coll. Surgeons, Am. Coll. Physicians, A.M.A.; Assn. of Mil. Surgeons (pres. 1921-22). Clubs: New York Yacht; Authors' (London); Pacific (Honolulu). Editor: (with Prof. T. O. Mabbott) Life and Works of Edward Coote Pinkney, 1925; Life and Works of Joseph Rodman Drake, 1935. Contbr. professional and biog. articles to Mil. Surgeon, Navy Med. Bull. and Annals of Med. History. Address: 1522-C Alewa Drive, Honolulu 17, Hawaii. Died Jan. 30, 1957 buried Arlington Nat. Cemetery.

PLEASANTS, J(acob) Hall, physician; b. Baltimore Co., Md., Sept. 12, 1873; s. Richard Hall and Elizabeth Moale (Poultney) P.; ed. private tutors, 1885-91; A.B., Johns Hopkins, 1895; M.D., 1899; m. Delia Tudor Wilmer, Jan. 30, 1902; children—Skipwith Wilmer (dec.), Elizabeth Poultney (Mrs. Francis Haynes Jencks), Delia Tudor. Intern, Johns Hopkins Hosp., 1899-00; engaged in gen. practice med. Baltimore, 1901-10; instr. and asso. med., Johns Hopkins U., 1902-34; served as pres., Municipal Dept. Charities and Corrections of City of Baltimore, 1907-21. Trustee, Johns Hopkins U. since 1920; trustee Peabody Inst. since 1922 (pres. bd. trustees, 1937-49); trustee Municipal Museum of Baltimore since 1931, Baltimore Museum of Art since 1914, St. Timothy's Sch., Stevenson, Md. (pres. bd. trustees, 1937-49), Md. Historical Soc. (vice pres. 1934-57). Mem. A.M.A., Medical and Chirurgical Faculty Maryland since 1902, Am. Art Research Council since 1942, Am. Antiquarian Soc. since 1937, Walpole Soc. Ind. Democrat. Episcopalian. Clubs: Alpha Delta Phi, Johns Hopkins (Baltimore). Editor, Archives of Maryland, 1929-45. Author: Maryland Silversmiths, 1715-1830 (with Howard Sill), 1930; Four Late Eighteenth Century Anglo-American Landscape Painters,

1943; George William West, a Baltimore Student of Benjamin West, 1949. Contbr. articles to med. jours., art and hist. jours. on early American painters. Address: 201 Longwood Rd., Balt. 10. Died Aug. 24, 1957.

PLEASANTS, James Jay, Jr., mayor of Memphis; b. Clarksdale, Miss., July 16, 1907; s. James Jay and Julia (Smith) P.; student U. Va., 1925-27; LL.B., U. Miss., 1930; m. Virginia Francis, Nov. 1, 1933; children—James Jay III, Michael Francis. Admitted to Tenn. bar, 1930, practiced in Memphis, 1930-42; asso. firms Metcalf, Metcalf and Apperson, 1930-35, Pleasants and Hickox, 1935-39, Livingston and Henderson, 1939-42; asst. city atty., Memphis, 1939-42; apptd. judge Memphis Criminal Ct., Jan. 1942, elected for term 1942-50 (on leave of absence for mil. service, 1943-46); resigned from Criminal Ct. bench and apptd. city atty., 1946; mayor of Memphis., 1948—. Mgr. Memphis and Shelby County Dem. hdqrs., 1946, co-chmn. Memphis and Shelby County Com., 1948; del. to 1948 Dem. Nat. Conv. Served from lt. (j.g.) to lt. USN, 1943-46. Mem. Am., Tenn., Memphis and Shelby County bar assns., Sigma Chi, Phi Delta Phi. Democrat. Episcopalian. Home: 1142 Peabody Av., Memphis 4. Office: 203 Courthouse, Memphis 3. Died June 2, 1950.

PLIMPTON, George Lincoln, educator; b. Sturbridge, Mass., July 8, 1865; s. James Hervey and Elizabeth (Fairbanks) P.; grad. Hitchcock Free Acad., Brimfield, Mass., 1887; A.B., Wesleyan U., Conn., 1891, hon. A.M., 1899; honorary A.M., Dartmouth, 1929; m. Etta Ione Ferry, Aug. 10, 1892; children—Esther Elizabeth, Theodore Ferry, George Lincoln. Instr. 1891-96, headmaster, 1896-1929, Tilton (N.H.) Boys' Sch. Twice elected men. Gen. Conf. M.E. Ch. Mem. N.E. Classical Assn., N.E. Assn. Colls. and Secondary Schs., Nat. Assn. Secondary Sch. Principals, N.H. Assn. Classical Teachers (pres.), Head Masters' Assn., Delta Kappa Epsilon, Phi Beta Kappa. Methodist. Mason. Clubs: University, Twentieth Century (Boston). Home: Madison, N.H. Died 1946.

PLUM, Harry Grant; b. Johnson County, Ia., Nov. 3, 1868; s. Martin and Elizabeth (Morgan) P.; descendant of Revolutionary Va. Morgans; Ph.B., State U. of Ia., 1894, M.A., 1896; studied Sorbonne, Paris, 1907; Ph.D., Columbia, 1906; m. Margaret Budington, Nov. 30, 1905; 1 dau., Alice Katharine (dec.). With State U. of Ia., 1894—, prof. European history, 1900—. Rep. of U.S. Com. of Pub. Information at Camp Dodge, Ia., 1918; mem. Com. on S.A.T.C., State U. of Ia.; speaker for League to Enforce Peace, and in advocacy of League of Nations, 1919. Mem. Am. Hist. Assn., Miss. Valley Hist. Assn., Ia. Social Sci. Assn. Republican. Presbyterian. Author: The Teutonic Order, 1906; also (monographs) The Monroe Doctrine and the War; The Economic Interpretation of the Protestant Revolution; English History in The American High School; A Modern and Contemporary History of Europe (with G. G. Benjamin); Restoration Puritanism. Home: 248 Black Spring Circle, Iowa City, Ia. Died Sept. 29, 1956; buried Viltwyck Cemetery, Kingston, N.Y.

PLUME, Stephen Kellogg (plū-mē'), brass mfr.; b. Waterbury, Conn., May 16, 1881; s. Frank Cameron and Sarah Andrews (Kellogg) P.; ed. Taft Sch. and Holbrooks Mil. Acad.; m. Pauline Brooke Parke, Oct. 20, 1917; 1 son, Stephen Kellogg (U.S. Army). Began in brass mfg. bus. with Plume & Atwood Mfg. Co., Waterbury, now chmn. bd. dirs.; dir. Thomaston Nat. Bank. Served as capt., U.S. Army, World War I; lt. col., U.S.R.C.; served as exec. officer, Aberdeen (Md.) Proving Ground, with grade of col., U.S. Army, World War II; ret. Republican. Episcopalian. Mason. Clubs: Waterbury, Watertown Golf; Army and Navy (Washington); American Legion, Thomaston Rod and Gun. Address: Watertown, Conn. Died May 6, 1950.

PLUMMER, Daniel Clarence, corp. exec.; b. Chicago, Oct. 7, 1896; s. Daniel Clarence and Jessie (Turnbull) P.; student U. Chgo., 1915-17; m. Ida May Hayden, May 19, 1921; children—Martha (dec.), Daniel Clarence, Robert Hayden, Nancy Carroll (Mrs. Raymond Santi). Began career as pub. accountant; asst. gen. mgr., treas. Earnshaw Knitting Co., 1919-22; asst. to v.p. in charge merchandising Montgomery Ward & Co., 1922-26; pres., treas. The H.P.W. Stores, Inc. (3 outlying dept. stores), 1926-29; mdse. mgr., comptroller Harvey, Inc. (Fred Harvey), 1929-35; with Sanderson & Porter, management engrs., 1935-44; pres., dir. Franklin-McAllister Corp., 1940-52; dir. Globe Am. Corp., 1935-45; joined Nu Enamel Corp., 1947, chmn. bd., 1948-51; with Lee Higginson Corp. since 1952; dir. Young Radiator Co., Controls Corp. Am., Allison Steel Corp. Served as lt., flying instr. U.S. A.S., 14 mos., World War I. Mem. Am. Legion, Psi Upsilon. Republican. Clubs: Univ. (Chgo). Home: 818 Ingleside Pl., Evanston, Ill. Office: 231 S. LaSalle St., Chgo. Died June 30, 1956; buried Oak Woods Cemetery, Chgo.

PLUMMER, James Kemp, chemist; b. Middleburg, N.C., Sept. 20, 1886; s. James Kemp and Mary Boyd (Henderson) P.; B.S., N.C. State Agrl. and Engring. Coll., 1907, M.S., 1909; M.A., Cornell, 1911, Ph.D., 1915; m. Lucy Williams Haywood, June 12, 1912; 1 dau., Emily Haywood (Mrs. Baker). Chemist Rockdale Iron Co., Rockdale, Tenn., 1907; asst. chemist, N.C. Expt. Station, 1909, soil chemist, 1911; explosive chemist Hercules Powder Co., Kenvil, N.J., 1917; cons. chemist Tenn. Copper and Chem. Corp., N.Y. City, 1918; state chemist of N.C., 1919-20; gen. mgr. Tenn. Corp., Atlanta (bd. dirs.); chmn. research com., dir. Products Div. Mem. A.A.A.S., American Institute of Chemical Engineers, American Society Agronomy, Am. Chem. Soc., Civil Legion, Sigma Xi, Pi Gamma Mu. Episcopalian. Club: Capitol City. Author various research articles in professional jours. and bulletins. Home: 2492 Habersham Road. Office: Grant Bldg., Atlanta, Ga. Deceased.

POEBEL, Arno (pû'bĕl), univ. prof.; b. Eisenach, Germany, Jan. 26, 1881; s. Philipp and Barbara (Burkhardt) P.; student univs. of Heidelberg, 1900-01, Marburg, 1901, Jena, 1901-04, Zurich, 1902; Ph.D., U. of Pa., 1906; m. Friederike Martienssen, Mar. 9, 1925; 1 son, Rudolf. Came to U.S., 1930. Research fellow in Assyriology, U. of Pa., 1905-07; Privatdozent der semitischen Sprachen, U. of Breslau, 1910-19; lecturer history of ancient Orient, Johns Hopkins U., 1911-13; with Univ. Museum, Phila., for publication of cuneform tablets, 1913-14; ausserordentlicher Professor der semitisehen Sprachen, U. of Rostock, 1919-25, ordentlicher, 1925-30; prof. Sumerology, Oriental Inst., Univ. of Chicago, 1930-33, became professor Assyriology and Sumerology and editor of Assyrian dictionary project, 1933, professor emeritus, 1946—; editor of Persepolis Elamite tablets project. Served in German army in Poland and Turkey, 1915-19. Mem. Altorientalische Gesellschaft (Berlin), Am. Oriental Soc. Lutheran. Author: Babylonian Lega and Business Documents, 1909; Historical Texts, 1914; Historical and Grammatical Texts, 1914; Grammatical Texts, 1914; Grundzuege der sumerischen Grammatik, 1923; Sumerian Prefix Forms e- and i- in the Time of the Earlier Princes of Lagas, 1931; Das appositionell bestimmte Pronomen der 1. Pers. Sing. in den westsemitischen Inschriften und im Alten Testament, 1932; Chronology of Darius' First Year of Reign (Am. Jour. Semitic Lang.), 1938; The Duration of the Reign of Smerdis, the Magian (same), 1939; Studies in Akkadian Grammar, 1939. Author of other ancient Orient publications published in U.S., Germany, France, Sweden, Finland. Home: 5132 Ellis Av., Chgo. 15. Died Mar. 3, 1958.

POGANY, Willy (William Andrew) (pō-gä'-nē), artist; b. Szeged, Hungary, Aug. 24, 1882; s. Joseph Stephen and Helena Paula (Kolis) Pogany; educated U. of Budapest, 1 year; Art Sch., Budapest, short time; studied Munich and Paris; m. Lilian Rose Doris, Dec. 9, 1908 (div.); children—John, Peter; m. 2d, Elaine Cox, 1934. Gold medals, Budapest, Leipzig, Panama P.I. Expn., 1915; medal of honor N.Y. Soc. Architects. Fellow Royal Society Arts (London, Eng.); mem. Archtl. League N.Y. Illus. more than 150 books. Stage decoration and costume designer, mural painter and art dir. of motion pictures, sculptor, architectural designer, portrait painter. Lect. Author: Willy Pogany's Drawing Lessons; Water-Color Lessons; Oil Painting Lessons. Address: 1 W. 67 St., N.Y.C. 23. Died July 30, 1955.

POHLERS, Richard Camillo, textile exec.; b. N.Y. C., July 30, 1901; s. Camillo Arno and Rudolphine (Lehmann) P.; grad. Phila. Textile Inst., 1921; m. Elizabeth Widmaier, Oct. 19, 1946. Vice pres. Simmons Co., 1943—, gen. mgr. Simtex Mills div., 1943—; dir. Roanoke Mills Co., Rosemary Mfg. Co., Patterson Mills Co., Gen. Garment Mfg. Co., George F. Brasfield & Co. Mem. Phi Psi. Clubs: Canoe Brook Country (Summit, N.J.); Merchants, Union League (N.Y.C.). Home: 18 Warwick Rd., Summit, N.J. Office: Empire State Bldg., N.Y.C. 1. Died Apr. 21, 1959; buried Fairmont Cemetery, Chatham, N.J.

POHLMAN, Augustus Grote (pōl'mån), anatomist, otologist; b. Buffalo, Feb. 21, 1879; s. Julius and Louise (Grosser) P.; M.D., U. Buffalo, 1900; U. Freiburg, 1901-03; m. Kathleen Black, Sept. 12, 1904 (died Feb. 10, 1933); children—Kathleen (dec.), Dorothea, David, Max, Margaret; m. 2d, Heln Bridge Shartle, Nov. 21, 1933. Asst. in anatomy Cornell U., 1900-01, instr., 1901-03; asst. in anatomy Johns Hopkins, 1903-04; asst. prof. Ind. U., 1904-06, asso. prof., 1906-07, jr. prof., 1907-08, prof., 1908-13; prof. anatomy St. Louis U., 1913-32; dean and prof. anatomy U. S.D., 1932-33; prof. anatomy Creighton U., 1933-38; asso. prof. dept. otolaryngology U. So. Cal. Asso. Riverbank Labs., Geneva, Ill., 1922-28. Fellow A.A.A.S., Acoustical Soc. Am.; mem. Am. Physiol. Soc., Assn. Am. Anatomists. Collegium oto-rhino-laryngologicum, Sigma Xi, Nu Sigma Nu, Alpha Omega Alpha. Contbr. to med. lit. on embryology of urolonital system, circulatory system, hearing mechanism in vertebrates, middle ear prostheses, etc. Address: 1306 Seal Way, Seal Beach, Cal. Died Apr. 31, 1950.

POILLON, Howard Andrews (poi-lŏn), former mining engr., ret. research corp. exec.; b. N.Y.C., July 22, 1879; s. Cornelius and Clara Louise (Andrews) P.; student Columbia Sch. Mines; m. Frances Hanford Wright, Sept. 22, 1914; children—Cornelius III, Jeanne, Peter. Engaged in mining in Alaska, B.C., Western U.S. and Mexico, 1900-12; pres. Research Corp., 1927-45; Thatcher Furnace Co., Concrete Plank Co. Vice chmn. div. engring. and indsl. research NRC. Mem. Am. Inst. Mining and Metall. Engrs., Mining and Metall. Soc. Am., Met. Mus. Art. Episcopalian. Mason. Clubs: Union, Columbia University. Home: 20 E. 74th St., N.Y.C.; also Westhampton Beach, L.I. Office: 405 Lexington Av., N.Y.C. Died Jan. 20, 1954.*

POINDEXTER, Joseph Boyd (poin'dĕks-tẽr), governor; b. Canyon City, Ore., Apr. 14, 1869; s. Thomas W. and Margaret (Pipkin) P.; student Ohio Wesleyan U., Delaware, O.; LL.B., Washington U., St. Louis, Mo., 1892; m. Margaret Conger, Apr. 22, 1897. Admitted to Mont. bar, 1892, and practiced at Dillon; county atty., Beaverhead County, Mont., 1897-1903; dist. judge, 5th Judicial Dist. of Mont., 1909-15; atty. gen. of Mont., 1915-17; U.S. dist. judge, Dist. of Hawaii, by appmt. of President Wilson, Mar. 16, 1917; retired from bench and resumed law practice; gov. Territory of Hawaii (apptd. by Pres. Roosevelt), Mar. 1, 1934-Aug. 24, 1942. Democrat. Episcopalian. Mem. Am. and Hawaii bar assns. Mason (32°, Shriner). Home: Honolulu, T.H. Died Dec. 3, 1951; buried Dillon, Mont.

POLACK, William Gustave (pōl'äk), religious educator; b. Wausau, Wis., Dec. 7, 1890; s. Herman A. and Wilhelmina (Stohs) P.; student Concordia Coll., Ft. Wayne, Ind., 1906-10, Concordia Sem., St. Louis, 1910-14; m. Iona Gick, Aug. 9, 1914; children—William Gustave, Paula Polack Wolk, James, Robert, Charles William, Shirley. Ordained to ministry Luth. Ch., 1914; pastor Evansville, Ind., 1914-25; prof. church history Concordia Sem., 1925—; also head dept.; pres. Concordia Hist. Inst., 1945—. Minister at Clear Lake Lutheran Chapel, summers, 1938—. Chmn. Inter-synodical Com. on Hymnology and Liturgics. Sec. Lutheran Editors Assn.; mem. Lutheran Academy for Scholarship. Author: John Eliot, 1926; David Livingstone, 1929; Into All the World, 1930; Story of Luther, 1931, 3d edit., 1947; Day by Day with Jesus, 1933, 7th edit., 1939; The Story of C. F. Walther, 1935; Beauty for Ashes, 1935; The Lord Is My Shepherd, 1937; Fathers and Founders, 1938; Martin Luther. In English Poetry, 1938; Story of Our Favorite Hymns, 1939; Hymns from the Harps of God, 1940; The Building of a Great Church, 1941, 2d edit., 1947; Handbook to the Lutheran Hymnal, 1942, 2d edit., 1947; Rainbow Over Calvary, 1943. Co-author: The Seven Ways of Sorrow, 1949. Editor in chief of Concordia Historical Inst. Quarterly, The Lutheran Hymnal, 1941; chmn. editorial staff Lutheran Witness; assoc. editor The Cresset. Contbr. to church papers. Recieved hon. degree, doctor of letters, Valparaiso Univ., 1942. Address: 7 Seminary Terrace N., St. Louis 5. Died June 5, 1950; buried Clear Lake (Ind.) Luth. Cemetery.

POLE, John William, ex-comptroller of currency; b. Kings Lynn, Eng.; ed. pvt. schs., and Instn. of Civ. Engrs., London; m. Harriet Vincent Booker, Oct. 3, 1900; 1 son, John Henry. Served as asst. engr. City of Mansfield, Eng.; came to U.S., 1893, and engaged in exportation of lumber, later in banking bus., Decatur, Ala.; apptd. nat. bank examiner, 5th Federal Res. Dist., 1915, trans. to 4th Dist., Cleve.; apptd. chief nat. bank examiner 6th Dist., 1919, chief nat. bank examiner for U.S., 1923; comptroller of the Currency, 1928-32 (resigned); mem. Fed. Reserve Bd.; spl. adviser to Fed. Reserve Bd., 1933-34; dept. of credits, Export Import Bank of Washington until 1935. Home: Franklin, Ky. Died May 1958.

POLIVKA, Jaroslav Joseph, cons. engr., educator; b. Prague, Bohemia, Apr. 20, 1886; s. Joseph and Francisca (Urbanova) P.; Master deg., Tech. U., Prague, 1909, Dr. Tech. Sci., 1917; grad. study Conf. Tech. U., Zurich; m. Maria I. Polakova, Sept. 16, 1913; children—Belca, Jan, Milos. Came to U.S., 1938, naturalized 1945. Asst. constrn. navigation locks, Bohemia, 1907-09, concrete arch bridge over Ohre River, 1910; chief engr. Sander & Co., Soc. Cemento Armato, Zurich, Florence, 1911-13; cons. engr., Zurich, research asst. Inst. Testing Materials, Zurich, 1914-15; chief engr., partner Dr. E. von Emperger, Vienna, 1916-17; chief engr. design and constrn., Ruse, Austria, 1918; Czechoslovak govt. expert charge study pub. works program, France 1919; research with Prof. Mesnager, Ecole des Ponts de Chaussées, 1920, cons. engr., architect, Prague, research engr. Material Lab., 1921-38; research photoelastic stress analysis, Podolsko Bridge, Bohemia, 1937; research asso. civil engring. U. Cal., 1939-45; research Bethlehem Alameda (Cal.) Shipyard, Kaiser Shipyards on various heavy constrn. projects, 1943-45; cons. engr., Berkeley, San Francisco, 1946—; pres. Soil Solidification Engrs., Inc., San Francisco, Los Angeles; structural design of bridges, factories, dams, theaters, apartment houses, hotels, industrial buildings, churches, using special types and materials; cons. engr. F. L. Wright, on Guggenheim's

Modern Gallery, N.Y.C., Johnson's Research Tower, Racine, Wis., Toiga Bldg., Berkeley, Cal., and other structures in precast and prestressed concrete; lecturer on contemporary structures Stanford U., 1951-—; organized Internat. Assos.-Engrs. and Architects, 1958. Winter internat. competition Belvedere Tunnel, Prague, 1909; Colombet award, French Soc. Civil Engrs., for best structural achievements in past 4 yrs., 1936; gold medal and two diplomas of honor, Paris Internat. Expn., 1937; Officer Legion of Honor, French Etoile Noire de Benin, 1951. Mem. Masaryk Acad., Com. Research and Testing Structural Material, Am. Soc. C.E., Am. Concrete Inst., Am. Soc. Profl. Engrs., Soc. Am. Mil. Engrs., Inst. Aero. Scis., A.S.M.E, Am. Welding Soc., Soc. Seismology, Am. Soc. Ceramics, Am., Swiss socs. testing materials, Mexican Soc. Engrs. and Architects, French Soc. Civil Engrs., Sigma Xi. Author books and articles in the field. Inventor hyperbolic-paraboloid-structures (with Victor di Suvero). Patentee in field. Home: 1150 Arch St., Berkeley 8, Cal. Died Feb. 9, 1960.

POLK, James G., congressman; b. Highland Co., O., Oct. 6, 1896; s. William Alexander and Amy Isyphena (Ockerman) P.; M.A., Wittenberg Coll., 1923; m. Mary Smith; children—Martha Jean, William A., Helen R., Lois Mae. Farmer; mem. 72d to 76th, 81st to 86th U.S. Congresses, 6th Ohio Dist. Spl. asst. Dept. of Agr., 1942-46. Mem. Kappa Phi Kappa. Democrat. Methodist. Elk, Mason. Home: R.F.D. 1, Highland, O. Died Apr. 28, 1959.

POLLAN, Arthur Adair, fruit co. exec., dir. of cos.; g. Cold Springs, Tex., Jan. 1, 1885; s. Alonzo Vernon and Clara A. (Ellisor) P.; ed. pub. schs. of S.E. Tex.; m. Rebekah Means, Nov. 18, 1914; children—Arthur Means, William Morris, Elizabeth Pollan Wetterhall. Vice chmn. bd. United Fruit Co., ret. 1952, dir. Caribbean Enterprises, Inc., Chiriqui Land Co., Cia. Frutera de Sevilla, Cia. Agricola de Guatemala, Cia. Agricola del Guayas, Cia. Bananera de Costa Rica, Cia. Bananera del Ecuador, Cukra Development Co., Darien Shipping Co., Food Concentrates, Inc., Grenada Co., Magdalena Fruit Co., Tela R.R. Co., Tonosi Fruit Co., Tropic Foods, Inc., United Fruit Steamship Corp., United Fruit Tanker Corp., United Mail Steamship Co., Venezuela Fruit Co., Banana Selling Corp., Canadian Banana Co., Ltd., Fruit Dispatch Co., Jacksonville Precooling Co., Meloripe Fruit Co., Boston, Munargo Line Co., Refrigerated Steamship Line, Inc., Revere Sugar Refinery, Unifruit Bldg. Co., Elders & Fyffes, Ltd., United Fruit Sugar Co. Clubs: Downtown Athletic, Whitehall (N.Y.C.). Home: 97 Lake Av., Newton Center, Mass. Office: 80 Federal St., Boston. Died June 1958.

POLLARD, Cash Blair (pŏl'ärd), chemist, toxicologist; b. Hannibal, Mo., Feb. 22, 1900; s. William Braxton and Nannie Elizabeth (Robinson) P.; A.B., William Jewell Coll., 1921; M.S., Purdue U., 1923, Ph.D., 1930; D.Sc., Purdue U., 1954; student U. Wis., 1924; m. Ailene Atherton; 1 son, Thomas David. Grad. asst. chemistry, Purdue U., 1921-23; with Graver Corp., 1923; instr. chemistry, Purdue U., 1923-30; asst. prof. chemistry, U. of Fla., 1930-35, asso. prof., 1935-37, prof., 1937-—, chmn. organic div.; cons. chemist, toxicologist, 1927-—; cons. chemist Fla. states attys. sci. crime detection, 1930-—; expert witness Fla. and Fed. cts., on toxicology, blood stains and powder marks. Research engr., Office of Production Research and Development, W.P.B., 1944; mem. faculty Alachua Gen. Hosp. Nurses Tng. Sch.; lectr. physiol. and pathol. chemistry, 1945-—. Cons. toxicologist Alachua Gen. Hosp., Morton Plant Hosp., Clearwater, Fla., Munroe, Meml. Hosp., Ocala, Fla. Served as pvt., W.W.I. Recipient Fla. Acad. Scis. Achievement Award (with John H. Pomeroy), 1945, for a study of the Sensitivity of Aldehyde Reagents; recipient U.S. Pub. Health Service Research Grant, 1948, 49, research grants, Navy Department, Office Naval Research 1948, 49, 50, Parke, Davis and Co., 1950-— ; Fla. award of Am. Chem. Soc., 1954; research grant from Dow Chem. Co., 1956. Fellow A.A.A.S., Am. Inst. Chemists (chmn. S.E. Regional com. on membership, 1942); mem. Am. Chem. Soc. (chmn. Fla. sect., 1935), Fla. Acad. Sci.; life mem. (hon.) Fla. Peace Officers Assn., Eugene Field Soc., Am. Legion, Am. Assn. Clin. Chemists, Nat. Rifle Assn., Sigma Xi, Phi Lambda Upsilon, Gamma Sigma Epsilon, Phi Kappa Phi, Alpha Epsilon Delta, Kappa Sigma. Democrat. Baptist. Mason. Clubs: Kiwanis, Fla. West Coast Pistol League, Gainesville Pistol, Alachua County Riding Horse Assn. Author: Laboratory Manual and Study Outline of General Chemistry (with L. A. Test), 1928, rev. 1937; Bibliography of Animal Venoms (with Ralph W. Harmon), 1947; Problems in Organic Chemistry (with E. G. Rietz), 1951; asst. editor: Outline of Organic Chemistry, 1937; asso. editor: Quadri-Service Manual of Organic Chemistry, 1938. Collaborator on Fundamental Organic Chemistry, 1940; The Work Book of Fundamental Organic Chemistry, 1941. Contbr. research articles to sci. jours. Home: "Holly Brook," Newberry Rd. Address: Leigh Hall, University Station, Gainesville, Fla. Died May 31, 1959.

POLLARD, Harold Stanley, journalist; b. Hyde Park, Mass., May 28, 1878; s. George Fisher and Katherine Louise (Sykes) P.; A.B., Harvard, 1902, grad. study, 1902-03; married Chrystal Herne, August 31, 1914 (deceased September 19, 1950). Began as special article writer Boston Transcript, 1904; reporter and assistant dramatic critic, New York Times, 1905-06; literary sec. to Joseph Pulitzer pub. New York World, 1906-11; chief editorial writer, New York Eve. World, 1911-18, editor, 1918-31; editorial writer N.Y. World-Telegram since 1931. Mem. adv. board, School of Journalism, Columbia, 1937-51. Mem. Empire State Soc., S.A.R., Phi Beta Kappa, Phi Beta Kappa Alumni in New York, Delta Upsilon. Democrat. Club: Harvard (New York). Writer of editorials and articles on law reform, prisons, parole, etc.; wrote biog. sketch of Joseph Pulitzer for 50th anniversary edition of St. Louis Post Dispatch, 1928. Home: Harvard Club, 27 W. 44th St., N.Y. City 18. Office: World-Telegram and Sun Building, N.Y.C. 18. Died Sept. 21, 1953.

POLLARD, William B., Sr., banker; b. Chester, Miss., July 23, 1896; s. Henry Austin and Emma (Fancher) P.; student Miss. State Coll., 1915-17; m. Vera Cochran, July 30, 1919; 1 son, William B., Jr. With First Nat. Bank, Hattiesburg, Miss., 1917; office mgr. lumber firm, Orvisburg, Miss., 1919-20; owner mercantile bus., Ackerman, Miss., 1920-26; state bank examiner, Miss., 1926-33; asst. examiner, examiner and asst. dir. div. examinations, Fed. Res. Bd., Washington, 1933-46; v.p. Fed. Res. Bank of St. Louis; mgr. Memphis br. Fed. Res. Bank of St. Louis, 1946-48; pres. Nat. Bank of Commerce, Memphis, since June 1948. Past president Memphis Community Chest. Served with United States Army, 1918. Mem. C. of C. (treas.), A.R.C. (dir.), Mem. Kappa Alpha Order. Democrat. Methodist. Clubs: Memphis Country, University, Rotary. Home: 693 E. Parkway South. Office: 45 2d St., Memphis 1. Died July 11, 1957; buried Ackerman, Miss.

POLLIA, Joseph P(asqual), sculptor; b. Italy, 1894; s. Pasqual and Santa (Murlino) P.; student Boston Mus. Fine Arts. Works include Equestrian Statue of Gen. Stonewall Jackson, Manasses Battlefield, Commonwealth of Va.; Meml. to Babe Ruth, Gate of Heaven Cemetery, Pleasantville, N.Y.; Christ, the Good Shepherd, Cardinal Hayes Meml., N.Y.C.; Nine Figure Panels in stone, Ind. U.; Gen. Phillip H. Sheridan, portrait statue, Sheridan Sq., N.Y.C.; Spanish Am. War Meml., San Juan Hill, Santiago, Cuba, State of N.Y.; Cuban Meml., Membi Victoriese, San Juan Hill, Cuban govt.; The Indian on the Trail, Mohawk Indian statue for Order of Red Men; World War I Meml. statue, Uniontown, Pa., Pa. State Art Commn.; World War I Meml., statue, Ia. Soldier's Home, Marshalltown, Ia.; also others. Mem. Nat. Sculptor Soc., N.A.D. Office: 1947 Broadway, N.Y.C. 23. Died Dec. 12, 1954.

POLLOCK, Horatio Milo, statistician, editor; b. Patria, N.Y., Sept. 2, 1868; s. Jesse W. and Mary Malvina (Daggett) P.; B.S., Union Coll., N.Y., 1895, M.S., 1897, LL.D., 1946; M.A., Ph.D., U. Leipzig, 1897; m. Georgiana Shafer, Sept. 18, 1895; children—Katherine Esther (dec.). Robert Shafer (dec.), Dorothy Affiah, Carolyn Mary; m. 2d, Mary Culver, Feb. 1, 1939. Tchr. sci. and German, Albany High Sch., 1897-1900; sr. examiner N.Y. State Civil Service Commn., 1900-07; sec. Civic League of Albany, 1907-11; tchr. econs. State Normal Coll., Albany, 1907-08; tchr. sociology and econs. Union Coll., 1908-10; dir. statis. bur. N.Y. Dept. Mental Hygiene, 1911-44, ret. Asso. editor Am. Education (monthly), 1905-25; editor Psychiatric Quarterly and predecessor The State Hospital Quarterly, 1915-35, Mental Hygiene News, 1935-43. Pres. N.Y. Edn. Co., pub. Am. Edn., 1912-23; organizer, 1908, and pres. N.Y. State Tchrs.' Bur. Fellow Am. Statis. Assn. (v.p. 1933); mgr. Am. Occupational Therapy Assn., 1927-36; mem. Nat. Com. for Mental Hygiene, Internat. Com. on Mental Hygiene, Am. Assn. on Mental Deficiency (pres. 1942-43), Medical Council U.S. Vet. Bur., Philos. Soc. of Albany, Phi Gamma Delta, A.A.A.S., Am. Acad. of Social and Polit. Sci., Sigma Xi.; hon. mem. Am. Psychiatric Assn. Cons. statistician with rank of 1st lt. Office Surgeon Gen. of the Army, 1917. Adv. statistician Nat. Com. for Mental Hygiene, 1916-—; organized statistical work in instns. of Ill., 1920; spl. adviser Federal Census Bureau, 1921-26; statis. adviser Joint Com. on Methods of Preventing Delinquency, 1924-25; chmn. com. on statistics, Internat. Congress on Mental Hygiene, 1930. Del. of U.S. to Pan-Am. Neuropsychiatric Conf., Lima, Peru, 1939. Unitarian. Author: Modern Cities (with W. S. Morgan); U.S. Census Report on Patients in Instns. for Mental Disease, 1923; Expectation of Mental Disease; Family Care of Mental Patients; Hereditary and Environmental Factors in the Causation of Manic-Depressive Psychoses and Dementia Praecox (with Benjamin Malzberg); Mental Disease and Social Welfare; The Story of Old Bill Marshall, 1948; also numerous educational and statistical monographs. Edited 4-vol. History of Care of the Mentally Ill in the State of New York, 1946. Clubs: Torch, University. Home: 447 Manning Blvd., Albany, N.Y.; summer home: Middleburgh, N.Y. Died May 8, 1950; buried Schenectady.

POLYAK, Stephen, scientist; b. Gjurgjevac, Yugoslavia, Dec. 13, 1889; Emilian and Anna (Shostarets) P.; student Classical Gymnasium at Zagreb, Croatia, 1901-09, med. sch. at Graz, Austria, 1909-14, Zagreb, Yugoslavia, 1920; spl. studies London, Madrid, Chicago; m. Donna Irene Bibler, Apr. 11, 1931; 1 son, Stephen Francis. Came to U.S., 1928, naturalized, 1936. Asst. prof. neuroanatomy U. Calif., 1928-30; asst. prof. neurol. U. of Chicago, 1930-32, asso. prof., 1932-42, prof. anatomy since 1942. Mem. Am. Assn. Anatomists, Am. Neurol. Assn. Investigator nervous system, especially of visual organs and centers, including their structure and function; history of optics and of the investigations of brain, and of the sense organs, particularly the eye. Interested in natural history, history of civilization, and allied subjects. Home: 5801 Harper Av., Chgo. Died Mar. 9, 1955; buried Oakwood Cemetery, Mt. Morris, Ill.

PONCHER, Henry George, pediatrician; born Odell, Ill., Feb. 15, 1902; s. Harry and Rose (Fine) P.; student Valparaiso (Ind.) U., 1920-22; M.D., U. of Mich., 1927; m. Gretchen Cliff Marquart, July 19, 1928; 1 son, John Robert. Resident in pediatrics U. of Ill. Research and Ednl. Hosps., 1928-29, instr. pediatrics, 1929-31, asst. prof., 1931-38, asso. prof.; 1938-41, prof. dept. of pediatrics, 1941-44, head dept., 1945-53; prof., head dept. biology, dir. student health Valparaiso U., 1952; dept. pediatrics U. Mich., 1924-27. Former chief of staff LaRabida Jackson Park Sanitarium. Former v.-chmn. Rheumatic Fever Council Chgo. Fellow A.M.A.; diplomate Am. Bd. Pediatrics (past sec.-treas.); mem. Am. Pediatric Soc. (mem. council), Soc. Pediatric Research, Am. Acad. Pediatrics (formerly state chmn.; chmn. com. drug dosage), Chgo. Pediatric Soc., Chicago Med. Society, Illinois State Medical Society, Society for Research in Child Development, Central Soc. for Clin. Investigation, Am. Heart Assn., Chicago Heart Assn. (bd. govs.), Inst. Med. of Chicago, Sigma Xi, Alpha Omega Alpha. Former editor, Yearbook of Pediatrics; mem. editorial bd. Jour. Pediatrics. Contbr. chapters to pediatric textbooks and profl. articles to med. publs. Home: R.F.D. 2, Valparaiso, Ind. Died May 31, 1955; buried Graceland Cemetery, Valparaiso.

POND, Alonzo Smith, educator; b. Salt Lake City, Apr. 6, 1905; s. Moses A. and Sarah (Smith) P.; A.B., U. of Utah, 1926; Ph.D., Northwestern U., 1942; m. Bernice Fagg, Aug. 17, 1933; children—Douglas W., Virginia, Donna Rae. Research associate, Ill. Tax Commn., 1936-37; instr. economics Brigham Young U., 1937-38, asst. prof., 1938-43, asso. prof., 1943-48, prof. since 1948, chairman department agrl. econs., 1938-55, department econs., 1952-55, acting dean Coll. Humanities and Social Sciences, 1955-57, dean graduate school, 1957-59; assistant regional price economist, U.S. Bureau Labor Statistics, Denver, 1942; executive officer, Price Division for Colorado, O.P.A., 1942-43, regional econ. analyst, 1943-44, regional educational director, 1944-45, asst. to regional adminstrn., Rocky Mountain Area, 1945-46; acting regional economist, acting regional price exec., acting dep. dir. OPS, 1951. Mem. Am., Pacific Coast econ. assns., Utah Conf. on Higher Edn. (pres. 1955-56). Mem. Ch. of Jesus Christ of Latter-Day Saints. Author: Essential Economics, 1956; Essential Economics, 1956. Home: 1292 Apple Av., Provo, Utah. Died Apr. 1, 1959; buried Provo, Utah.

POND, Bremer Whidden, coll. prof.; b. Boston, 1884; s. Charles Choate and Annie Louise (Whidden) P.; S.B., Dartmouth Coll., 1906; M.L.A., Harvard, 1911. Practicing landscape architect, 1914-—; chmn. dept. landscape architecture, grad. sch. design, Harvard, 1928-50. Served as capt., U.S. Army, 1917-18, major, Q.M. corps, 1918-19. Fellow Am. Soc. Landscape Architects, 1921-— (sec. 1921-35); mem. Chi Phi, Phi Beta Kappa (hon.). Home: Pittsburg, N.H. Died Sept. 2, 1959.

POOLE, DeWitt Clinton, diplomat, educator; b. Vancouver Barracks, Wash., Oct. 28, 1885; s. DeWitt Clinton and Maria Woodward (Pettes) P.; A. B., U. of Wis., 1906; M. Dip., George Washington U., 1910; LL.D., U. of Del., 1934; m. Mrs. Rachel Simmons Blanding, Sept. 1, 1920; stepson, Alan Cornell. Entered consular service, Dec. 20, 1910; vice-consul at Berlin, Germany, 1911-14, vice-consul, Paris, 1914-15; duty Dept. of State, 1915-17; promoted consul, July 1916, and assigned to Moscow, July 1917; apptd. spl. asst. to Am. ambassador in Russia, Oct. 1918; Am. charge d'affaires in Russia, Nov. 1918-June 1919; apptd. chief Div. of Russian Affairs, State Dept., Oct. 1, 1919; promoted consul gen. Nov. 23, 1921. Mem. tech. staff Conf. on Limitation of Armament, 1921-22. Apptd. consul gen. at Cape Town, Oct. 1, 1923; apptd. counselor embassy, Berlin, Jan. 1926, resigned, 1930; chmn. advisory bd., dir. Sch. of Pub. Affairs, Princeton, 1930-48, dir. 1933-39; member Inst. for Advanced Study, Princeton, 1941; dir. Foreign Nationalities Branch, Office of Strategic Services, 1941-45; spl. rep. Sec. of State on mission to Germany, 1945; visiting lecturer on internat. politics, Harvard, 1946-47; pres. Nat. Com. for Free Europe, 1949-51, vice chmn. since 1951; pres.

Free Europe U. in Exile, since 1951. Fellow Am. Geog. Soc. Mem. Council on Foreign Relations, Inst. of Pacific Relations, Academie Diplomatique Internationale, Chi Psi, etc. Clubs: Century (New York); Metropolitan (Wash., D.C.); Nassau (Princeton). Author: Democracy and the Conduct of Foreign Relations. Mem. editorial bd. of The Public Opinion Quarterly. Home: 6 Edgehill St., Princeton, N.J. Office: 730 5th Av., N.Y.C. 21. Died Sept. 3, 1952; buried Madison, Wis.

POOLE, Fenn E., physician; b. Coldwater, Mich., June 10, 1906; s. Nathan H. and Nora E. (Stone) P.; B.S., Emmanuel Missionary Coll., Berrien Springs, Mich., 1929; M.D., Coll. of Med. Evangelists, Los Angeles, 1932; m. Maybelle Hansen, July 3, 1930; children—Loren W., Lynda Sue. Interne, Los Angeles Gen. Hosp., 1931-33, surgical resident, 1933-36, attending surgeon since 1937; pvt. practice gen. surgery, Glendale, Calif., since 1936; chief of staff, St. Joseph Hosp., Burbank, 1944; med. dir., Lockheed Aircraft Corp. Burbank, since 1938, Rexall Drug Co., Los Angeles, since 1946; asst. prof. surgery, Coll. of Med. Evangelists, since 1937. Trustee Chapman Coll., Los Angeles, 1946-50. Mem. med. adv. group, Nat. Assn Mfrs.; mem. research com., President's Conf. on Indsl. Safety, 1949. Fellow A.M.A., Aero Med. Assn., Am. (past dir.) and Western (dir., 1945-50) assns. indsl. physicians and surgeons. Mem. Calif. State and Los Angeles County med. assns., Airline Med. Dirs. Assn., Los Angeles Heart Assn. (chmn. com. of cardiacs in industry). Associate editor: Archives of Industrial Hygiene and Occupational Med. since 1949, Annals of Western Medicine and Surgery since 1948. Contbr. articles on indsl. medicine. Home: 1535 Ridge View Dr., Glendale 7. Office: 600 Broadway, Glendale 4, Cal. Died Sept. 21, 1952.

POOLE, Robert Franklin, college pres.; b. Gray Court, S.C., Dec. 2, 1893; s. Ula Barto and Lila (Yeargin) P.; B.S., Clemson (S.C.) Agrl. Coll., 1916, M.S., Rutgers U., 1917, Ph.D., 1921; D.Sc., Clemson (S.C.) Agrl. Coll., 1937; LL.D., U. of S.C., 1942; Litt.D., Furman U., 1950; m. Sara Margaret Bradley, Feb. 28, 1922; children—Robert Franklin, Thomas Bradley, Margaret Lillian, Mary Marcia, and William James. Student asst. in botany, Clemson Agrl. Coll., 1916-17; research asst. in plant pathology, Rutgers U., 1917, 1919-20; asst. plant pathologist, N.J. Agrl. Expt. Sta., 1920-22, asso. 1922-26; asso. prof. and asso. plant pathologist, N.C. State Coll., 1926-28, prof. and plant pathologist, 1928-40; pres. Clemson Coll. since 1940. Attended U.S. War Sch., Hampton, Va., studying aerial photography, Nov. 1917-Feb. 1918; sergt. 1st class, A.E.F., Mar. 1918-July 1919. Fellow A.A.A.S.; mem. Am. Phytopathol. Soc., Southern Phytopathol. Soc. (pres. 1928), Am. Mycology Soc., Am. Assn. Univ. Profs., Am. Hort. Soc., N.C. Acad. Science, Southern Assn. Colls. and Secondary Schs. (pres. 1948), Assn. Southern Agrl. Workers (pres. 1948); Assn. Southern Colls. (pres. 1948), Assn. Land-Grant Colleges and Universities (president, 1951), Patrons of Husbandry, Am. Legion, Phi Kappa Phi, Alpha Zeta, Sigma Xi, Phi Pi Phi. Presbyn. Club: Rotary. Discovered and perfected econ. control measures for diseases of the sweet potato. Author of various bulls. on pathology and contbr. to scientific jours. Lecturer. Address: Clemson Coll., Clemson, S.C. Died June 6, 1958; buried Clemson College, S.C.

POOLE, Sidman Parmelee, geographer; b. Syracuse, N.Y., Oct. 19, 1893; s. Theodore Lewis and Carrie (Law) P.; B.S., Syracuse Univ., 1921, M.S., 1925; Ph.D., Univ. of Chicago, 1932; student Cambridge (Eng.) Univ., 1925; m. Rachel Sumner, August 31, 1922. Instr. Syracuse Univ., 1921-25, asst. prof. of geography, 1925-32, asso. prof., 1932-39, prof., 1939-40; summer lecturer Cornell Univ., 1932; prof. and chmn. Dept. of Geography, Univ. of Va., since Sept., 1946; dir. Virginia Geographical Institute since 1947. Geographer to Syracuse Andean Expdn., 1930-31, Syracuse Gaspe Expdn., 1933, dir. and geographer to Syracuse Yucatan Expdn., 1937-38; detailed field work in New York State, Vermont (with Vt. geol. survey), upper Great Lakes region, Chicago area, England, Brittany, Venezuela, Gaspe and Yucatan. Geographic advisor Air Command and Staff Sch., Air Univ., Maxwell Field, Ala. since Oct. 1946. Served as 1st lt., F.A., A.E.F., World War I; capt. and maj. F.A., O.R.C., 1920-40; col. chief topographic br., War Dept., Washington, D.C., U.K., N. Africa, 1940-46. Decorated Hon. Comdr. Order British Empire, Am. Legion of Merit. Mem. U.S. Bd. on Geog. Names, 1943-46. Fellow Am. Geog. Soc., Royal Geog. Soc.; mem. Nat. Council Geography Teachers (contbg. mem. and chmn. com. on geographic edn. for world understanding), Assn. Am. Geographers (mem. com. on Atlas of U.S., inter-soc. com. on sci. foundation legislation), Am. Soc. for Profl. Geographers (v.p. 1947), Am. Unitarian Assn. (nat. dir.), Phi Beta Kappa, Sigma Xi, Phi Gamma Delta. Clubs: Cosmos (Washington); Farmington Country (Charlottesville, Va.); Colonnade; Rotary International; Explorers (New York). Author: Manual for College Geography, 1933; chapter on Geography of Central New York (An Inland Empire by W. Freeman Galpin), 1941; chapter on Geography in America's Life (Twentieth Century America), 1947-51; History of Virginia (junior author). Contbg. editor: Econ. Geography. Contbr. articles to geog. pubs., mags. and newspapers. Consultant editor Bobbs-Merrill Co. series of geog. texts and readers 1945—. Home: Rio Rd., Box 83, R. 5, Charlottesville, Va. Died Oct. 28, 1955; buried U. Va. Cemetery, Charlottesville.

POOR, Charles Lane, astronomer; b. Hackensack, N.J., Jan. 18, 1866; s. Edward Eri and Mary Wellington (Lane) P.; B.S., Coll. City N.Y., 1886, M.S., 1890; Ph.D., Johns Hopkins, 1892; m. Anna Louise Easton, Apr. 19, 1892; children—Charles Lane, Alfred Easton, Edmund Ward. Asso. in astronomy Johns Hopkins, 1892-96, asso. prof., 1895-99; prof. astronomy Columbia, 1903-10, prof. celestial mechanics, 1910-44, prof. emeritus, 1944—. Inventor of various navigational devices. Fellow Am. Acad. Arts and Sciences (asso.), Royal Astron. Soc. Club: New York Yacht. Author: Simplified Navigation, 1918; Gravitation versus Relativity, 1922; Relativity and the Motion of Mercury, 1925; The Relativity Deflection of Light, 1926; Rules and Regulations for the Construction of Racing Yachts, 1928; Men Against the Rule, 1937. Home: Dering Harbor, N.Y. Address: 35 E. 69th St., N.Y.C. Died Sept. 27, 1951.

POOR, Frank A., elec. mfg. exec.; b. Salem, Mass., 1880; s. Joseph H. Poor; student pub. schs., comml. sch.; m. Margaret E. Linehan, 1908; children—Joseph F., Robert H., William F., Mrs. J. Franklin Millea, Mrs. Edmund E. Fahey. Formerly with Vaughan Machine Co., Peabody, Mass., later bookkeeper Abbott & Reynolds Co., Salem, then owner Bay State Lamp Co.; organized Hygrade Incandescent Lamp Co., 1909, become gen. mgr., treas., entered radio tube mfg. field, 1928, merged with Nilco Lamp Works, Inc., subsidiary Sylvania Products Co., 1931, became treas. combined co. known as Hygrade-Sylvania Corp., until 1942, when it became Sylvania Electric Products, Inc., then served as chief operating officer, became vice chmn. bd. dirs., 1950; dir. Naumkeag Trust Co., A. & G. J. Caldwell, Inc., Newburyport, Mass. Home: 202 Atlantic Av., Swampscott, Mass. Office: 60 Boston St., Salem, Mass. Died June 17, 1956; buried Harmony Grove Cemetery, Salem.

POOR, Fred Arthur, ry. supplies, exec.; b. Andover, Me., Apr. 16, 1870; s. William C. and Hattie (Smith) P.; grad. high sch., Port Chester, N.Y., 1887; m. Nettie Baylies, June 20, 1894 (died June 3, 1938); 1 dau., Betty; m. 2d, Martha Buehring Dalton, Aug. 5, 1944. Began with Adams Express Co., with which held various positions until 1892; with engring. dept. Hall Signal Co., 1892-93; with engring. dept. I.C. R.R., 1893-1900; western rep. Weber Rail Joint Mfg. Co., 1900-07; European rep. The Rail Joint Co., 1907-09, western rep. 1909-14; pres. The P. & M. Co., 1914-29; former pres. Poor & Co., now chmn. bd. Republican. Presbyn. Clubs: Chicago, Chicago Athletic Association, Tavern, Racquet, Electric, Knollwood, Old Elm, Onwentsia (Chgo.); Cloud, Metropolitan, River, New York Yacht (N.Y.C.); Bath, Indian Creek (Miami Beach); Bohemian (San Francisco). Home: 1448 Lake Shore Dr. Office: 224 S. Michigan Av., Chgo. Died Aug. 26, 1953.

POOR, Walter Everett, mfg. exec.; b. Peabody, Mass., Nov. 23, 1885; s. Joseph H. and Margaret J. (Linehan) P.; grad. Salem High Sch., 1904, B.S., Mass. Inst. Tech., 1908; m. Elizabeth Russell Phippen, Oct. 9, 1912; children—George Russell, Arthur Phippen; m. 2d, Mary Bradshaw, June 1943. Elec. engr. Boston Elevated Ry., 1908-09, Hugh Naron Contracting Co., 1909-11; became asso. with Hygrade Lamp Co., 1911; company reorganized as Hygrade Sylvania Corp., 1931, later as Sylvania Electric Products, Inc., of which is chmn. bd. and dir. Mem. Am. Inst. E.E., Inst. Radio Engrs. Conglist. Clubs: Union League, Economic (N.Y.C.); Siwahoy (Bronxville, N.Y.); Salem Country (Peabody, Mass.). Home: 1150 Fifth Av., N.Y.C. 28. Office: Sylvania Electric Products, Inc., N.Y.C. 18. Died Apr. 4, 1950.

POORMAN, Alfred Peter, prof. engring. mechanics; b. Altamont, Ill., Feb. 13, 1877; s. George Warner and Eliza Jane (Watson) P.; B.S. in C.E., U. of Ill., 1907; A.B. and C.E., U. of Colo., 1909; m. Sarah Elizabeth Ellmaker, June 22, 1910 (died Jan. 30, 1935); children—Mary Esther, George Ellmaker; married 2d, Genevieve Louise Lippoldt, June 29, 1936. Engineer, Weber Concrete Chimney Company, June-Aug. 1907; instructor in civil engineering, Univ. of Colo., 1907-09; hydrographer, Wind River Indian Reservation, July-Nov. 1909; asst. prof. applied mechanics, Purdue, 1909-17, 1919-20, asso. prof., 1920-22, prof. since 1922, head dept. applied mechanics, 1942-44, professor emeritus, 1947. Capt. Engr. Corps U.S. Army, 1917-18; supply officer, Gen. Hdqrs., A. E.F., June 1918-June 1919. Mem. Am. Soc. Civil Engrs., Am. Soc. for Testing Materials, American Soc. of Engring. Edn., Am. Concrete Inst., A.A.A.S., Am. Assn. Univ. Profs., Tau Beta Pi, Sigma Xi, Chi Epsilon, Scabbard and Blade. Methodist. Club: University. Author: Applied Mechanics, 1917 (5 edits.); Strength of Materials, 1925 (4 edits.); Sect. on theoretical mechanics O'Rourke's Engineering Handbook, 1940. Home: 329 Russell St., West Lafayette, Ind. Died Feb. 12, 1952; buried Grand View Cemetery, West Lafayette.

POPE, Gustavus Debrille, born in Humboldt, Tennessee, June 4, 1873; son of Benjamin F. (colonel U.S. Army) and Sarah Lee (Poston) P.; ed. pub. schs., Army posts and old Central High Sch., Detroit, Mich.; m. Mary Theresa Soper, Oct. 12, 1904 (died 1940); children—John A., Elizabeth Lee, Gustavus D, Jr.; m. 2d, Edna Page Austin, 1941. Railroad work in South, 1894, later field engr. in Southwest and with Canadian Bridge Co., Walkerville, Can.; with Digestive Ferments Co., mfg. chemists, Detroit, 1904-17, pres. of corp., 1914-17; resigned and entered Red Cross work, 1917; dir. Difco Laboratories, Inc., of Detroit, Safety Car Heating & Lighting Co. of New York. Commissioner Detroit Dept. of Health, 1917-39; mem. Board of Supervisors, Wayne County, Mich., 1921 and 1925-29. Pres. Detroit Community Fund, 1919-26. Chmn. Detroit Chapter Am. Red Cross, 1917-41; mem. Central Com. Am. Nat. Red Cross, 1921-42, now hon. mem., also mem. Bd. Incorporators; del. Internat. Red Cross Conf., Tokyo, 1926, 34; chmn. U.S. delegation to Pan-Am. Red Cross Conf., Rio de Janeiro, 1935. Trustee Cranbrook Foundation; v.p. Cranbrook Inst. of Science. Past pres. Nat. Rifle Assn. Episcopalian. Clubs: Detroit, Country, Witenagemote, Turtle Lake, Boone & Crockett. Home: Apple Lane Farm, Bloomfield Township, Mich., R.D. 3, Pontiac, Mich. Office: 1818 Ford Bldg., Detroit 26. Died Mar. 2, 1952.*

POPE, Henry Francis, mfr.; b. Cleveland, O., Sept. 10, 1867; s. John Lang and Frances Emily (Whipple) P.; grad. Cleveland High Sch., 1884; m. Sarah Rogers Collins, Apr. 18, 1900; children—Harriette Frances (Mrs. Erdman Harris), John Collins, Sarah (Mrs. William Steele Stewart). Began as office boy with Cleveland Malleable Iron Co., 1884, and since with it and its successors, Nat. Malleable Castings Co. (1891), Nat. Malleable & Steel Castings Co. (1923); became asst. treas. for Cleveland Works, 1891, dir., 1899, v.p. of the company, 1909, pres., 1913; became chmn., 1934; resigned as chmn. and dir., 1945. Trustee Western Reserve University. Republican. Presbyterian. Clubs: Union, Rowfant (Cleveland); Mayfield Country (South Euclid, O.). Home: 1686 Magnolia Dr. Office: 10600 Quincy Av., Cleveland. Died July 28, 1950.

POPE, Herbert, lawyer; b. Cleveland, O., Dec. 16, 1870; s. John L. and Frances (Whipple) P.; ed. pub. schs.; LL.B., Harvard, 1898; married; children—Isabel, Lydia. Admitted to Ohio bar, 1898, Ill. bar, 1900; mem. Pope and Ballard, ret. Mem. Am. Ill. State, Chgo. bar assns. Clubs: University, Indian Hill. Home: 41 Indian Hill Rd., Winnetka, Ill. Office: 33 N. LaSalle St., Chgo. 2. Died July 20, 1958; buried Cleve.

POPE, Ralph Elton, ret. naval officer; b. Waupaca, Wis., Jan. 28, 1875; s. George Freeborn and Jennie Maria (Fisher) P.; M.A., U.S. Naval Acad., 1899; student Naval War Coll., 1926-27, Georgetown U., 1931; m. Nellie Belle Drum, June 4, 1904; 1 son, Earl Hallet. Commd. ensign U.S. Navy, 1901, and advanced through grades to rear adm., 1934; ret., 1934; served in West Indies Campaign, 1898, and on U.S.S. Texas; served in Cuban Pacification, 1908, in Mexico, 1911-17, Nicaraguan Pacification, 1912, with U.S. Naval escort, 1918, in Europe, 1918-19. Awarded Santiago Medal, 1898; U.S. Navy Cross (for disablement of German submarine off coast of Africa), 1918; Merito di Guerra, Italy (for rescue of Italian Seaplane and compilation of war instructions for Italy), 1918. Mem. Ancient and Hon. Sons of Gunboats (Philippine order, 1899-1905), Hi-Hatters (Cal.). Republican. Clubs: Coronado (Cal.) Country, Coronado Beach. Author articles for U.S. Naval Inst. Home: 475 A Av., Coronado, Cal. Died May 13, 1959.

PORTER, Earle S(ellers), business exec.; born Triumph, Ill., Sept. 23, 1888; s. Albert Erwin and Henrietta (Sellers) P.; A.B., Okla. Univ., 1911, A. M., 1912; grad. student U. of Chicago, 1913, Columbia, 1915; m. Pearl Goodrich, Dec. 17, 1913; children—Phil, Helen (Mrs. A. J. Viehoever), Mary Margaret (Mrs. John G. Burke). Instr. U. of Okla., 1912-15, asst. prof. chemistry, 1916-17; chem. E.I. duPont de Nemours & Co., Arlington, N.J., 1918-20, asst. dir. research lab., 1918-19; asst. chem. supt. plant, 1920; with Amerada Petroleum Corp., New York, 1921-27; Tulsa, Okla., since 1927; research chemist, 1921-22, asst. to vice pres., 1923-26, prodn. mgr., 1927, asst. gen mgr., 1928-37, vice pres., 1938, dir. since 1948. An incorporator, dir. and past pres. (1947), U. of Okla. Research Inst. Trustee Okla. Expenditure Council. Mem. Am. Inst. Mining and Metall. Engrs., Am. Petroleum Inst. (gen. prodn. com.), Phi Beta Kappa, Phi Delta Chi, Sigma Nu. Methodist. Clubs: Southern Hills Country, The Tulsa. Home: 1225 25St., Tulsa 5. Office: Amerada Petroleum Corp., Tulsa 2, Okla. Died Aug. 14, 1951; buried Memorial Park, Tulsa.

PORTER, James Pertice, psychologist; b. Hillsboro, Ind., Sept. 23, 1873; s. Alfred and Elizabeth (Marksbury) P.; student Normal Sch., Terre Haute, 1890-91, 1892-93; A.B., Ind. U., 1898, A.M., 1901; hon. fellow Clark U., 1903-07, Ph.D., 1906; Sc.D., Waynesburg Coll., 1917; m. Myrta Wayne Brown, Dec. 24, 1895; children—Ernest C. (dec.), Helen, Marjorie. Instr. psychology Ind. U., 1900-03; asst. prof. psychology Clark Coll., 1907-12, prof. psychology, 1912-22, dean of faculty, 1909-22; prof. psychology Ohio U., 1922-43, prof. emeritus, 1943; instr. psychol. U. Ill. Extension, Danville, Ill., 1948. With Adj. Gen.'s Office, N.Y. 1944. Has made spl. studies of the English sparrow, of spiders, and of intelligence and imitation in birds, human intelligence and personality. Lecturer ednl., psychology, Columbia, 1913-14. Capt., Sanitary Corps U.S. Army, 1918; maj. R.C. Mem. Am., Midwestern (pres. 1941-42) psychol. assns., N.E.A., Internat. Congress of Zoology, Am. Assn. Applied Psychologists, Sigma Chi, Phi Beta Kappa. Editor Journal of Applied Psychology, 1920-43. Mem. Internat. Congress of Psychology and Psycho-technique, Paris, 1927. Home: 1124 Grant St., Danville, Ill. Died Sept. 1956.

PORTER, James W(inters), judge; b. Humeston, Ia., June 16, 1887; s. Harvey and Nevada (Ulm) P.; LL.B., Drake U., 1910; m. Birdie Gwinn, Sept. 25, 1910; 1 son, Gwinn Ulm. Admitted to Ida. bar, 1910, practiced in Twin Falls, 11910-37; dist. judge 11th Jud. Dist., 1937-48; justice Supreme Court of Ida., 1949-—, chief justice, 1953-54, 54-59, 59-—. Served with the Mexican Border Service, 1916-17; capt. F.A., U.S. Army, A.E.F., France and Germany, 1917-19. Decorated Campaign medal with five stars. Mem. Am. Legion (past post comdr.), Ida. State Bar Assn. Democrat (past co. chmn., state committeeman). Elk. Clubs: Kiwanis, Nat. "D." Home: 1603 E. Jefferson. Office: Statehouse, Boise. Died Dec. 9, 1959.

PORTER, Joe Frank; b. on farm nr. Williamsport, Tenn., June 11, 1880; s. William Todd and Mary Jane (Russell) P.; ed. community schls.; m. Lillie Pearle Stallings, June 5, 1902; children—Joe Frank, William Todd, Otey James, Dorothy Pearle (Mrs. John L. McLean). Began farming early age, purchasing home place and later enlarging farm; dealt in livestock, 1909-20 pres. (active) Tenn. Farm Bureau, 1921-46; Tenn. Cooperative Supplies Assn., 1923-46, Tenn. Farm Mutual Fire Ins. Co., 1944-46. Vice pres. Tenn. Livestock Marketing Assn. since 1932. Mem. exec. com. Tenn. Burley Tobacco Growers Assn., 1941-47, president, Jan. 1947-Nov. 1948, Tennessee Taxpayers Assn. since 1936, Tenn. War Service Council since 1941, Maury County Farmers Mutual Fire Insurance Co., since 1944; mem. bd. and dep. chmn. Fed. Reserve Bk. of Atlanta, 1937-48; pres. Farmers & Merchants Bank (Columbia) since 1950. Dir., mem. exec. and legislative com. Am. Farm Bureau Fedn., Chgo., 1928-46; chmn. Southern Regional Group, Amer. Farm Bureau Fedn., Tenn. Rural Electrification Com.; mem. Tenn. Tax Commn., 1947-48. Received award from Progressive Farmer, 1938, as outstanding farm leader; as man of the year, 1941, from Southern Agriculturist; Am. Farm Bur. Fedn. Gold Medal Award, 1946. Chmn. bd. stewards, Sunday Sch. teacher Methodist Ch., 1905-45. Home: Williamsport, Tenn. Died Feb. 2, 1951.

PORTER, John Clinton, ex-mayor; b. Leon, Ia., Apr. 4, 1872; s. Josephus Clinton and Matilda (Gardiner) P.; ed. Whittier Acad. and Bus. Coll., Los Angeles; m. Mattie Lee, Jan. 10, 1892; children—Lee Clinton, Helen Catherine. Began as telegraph operator, S.P. R.R. Co., 1891; automobile sales bus., Los Angeles, 1906-29; dir. Suburban Hosps., Inc., South Gate, Cal. Mayor of Los Angeles, 1929-33. Republican. Mason, Moose. Home: 815 Lorraine Boul., Los Angeles, Cal. Died May 27, 1959.*

PORTER, Lucius Chapin, missionary ed.; b. Tientsin, China, Oct. 31, 1880; s. Henry Dwight and Elizabeth Colton (Chapin) P. (missionaries); B.A., Beloit (Wis.) Coll., 1901, hon. D.D., 1924; B.D., Yale, 1906; Yale U. traveling fellow, 1906-07, Berlin, Am. Sch. Archaeology (Jerusalem), and Marburg U.; student Union Theol. Sem., 1907-08; A.M., Columbia, 1916; L.H.D., N.Y. U., 1924; m. Lillian Lee Dudley, May 16, 1908 (dec., 1956); children—Marion Elizabeth, Henry Dudley, James W. (dec.). Missionary of A.B.C.F.M. in China, 1908-—; tchr. N. China Union Coll. until 1918; prof. philosophy, dean Yenching U., 1918-22; prof. Chinese, Columbia, U., 1924-—. Vis. lectr. in Chinese philosophy, Harvard 1928-29, 1931-32; spl. lectr. in Chinese philosophy, W. China Union U., Chengtu, Szechwan, 1935; vis prof. Chinese philosophy, The Claremont (Cal.) Colleges, 1938; on leave of absence to assist guarding Am. Bd. Mission property at Fenchow, Shansi, and to guard Oberlin-Shansi Meml. Acad. property at Taiku, Shansi, during occupation by Japanese militarists, 1938-39; apptd. Brewer lectr. in Chinese philosophy and religion, Beloit (Wis.) Coll., 1940-41 (in U.S. on furlough), 1946; returned to Yenching U., China, 1941, interned by Japanese, 1941 until end of World War II, returned to U.S., 1945; resumed duties at Yenching U., 1947; ret. 1949; lectr. on present situation in China and U.S. Fgn. policy toward China; lectr. Beloit Coll. 10 weeks, 1950. Mem. Am. Oriental Soc., China Soc. Am., Psychol. Assn. China, Anthropol. and Anat. Assn. China, Phi Beta Kappa, Sigma Chi (life mem.), Delta Sigma Rho, Phi Tau Phi. Clubs: Peking American College of North China, Wen Yu Hui, Andiron. Author: China's Challenge to Christianity, 1924; Aids to the Study of Chinese Philosophy, 1934. Writer and lecturer on Chinese topics. Home: 735 College St., Beloit, Wis. Died Sept. 7, 1958.

PORTER, Roland Guyer, electrical engr.; b. South Norwalk, Conn., June 9, 1894; s. William Lovett and Ella Cook (Guyer) P.; B.E.E., Northeastern Univ., 1918; M.S., Harvard Grad. Sch. of Engring., 1932; m. Mildred Claire Plummer, June 18, 1921; 1 son, Robert Guyer. Comml. radio operator Marconi Co. of Am. at Sea, 1913-14; student apprentice standardizing and testing dept., Boston Edison Co., 1914-16; instr. mathematics and physics, Northeastern Univ., 1919-20, instr. elec. engring., 1920-23, asst. prof., 1923-29, asso. prof., 1929-37; prof. and head elec. engring. dept., 1937-—. Mem. sch. com., Beverly, Mass., 1937-41. Served as ensign U.S.N.R.F., 1st class radio electrician, chief radio electrician, radio gunner, June 1917-Apr. 1919. Registered professional engr. (elec.), Mass., 1942-—. Fellow Am. Inst. Elec. Engrs. (past chmn. Boston sect., mem. nat. sect. com. and nat. ednl. com., 1943-48; member national student branch committee, 1948-—; national summer convention committee 1948-49); mem. Inst. Radio Engrs. (past sec.-treas. Boston sect., member national educational committee 1947-49), Illuminating Engr. Soc. (past mem. bd. mgrs., Boston), Am. Soc. Engring. Edn., Harvard Engring. Soc., Engring. Soc. of New England, Tau Beta Phi, Eta Kappa Nu. Republican. Episcopalian. Club: North Shore Harvard. Home: 19 Woodbury St., Beverly, Mass. Office: 360 Huntington Av., Boston 15. Died Sept. 2, 1953; buried North Beverly (Mass.) Cemetery.

PORTER, Seton, corp. exec.; b. N.Y.C., July 8, 1882; s. Henry Hobart and Annie (Dwight) P.; ed. Fay Sch., St. Mark's Sch., Southboro, Mass.; A.B., Yale, 1905; m. Frederica V. Berwind, Aug. 4, 1936. Asst. engr. and asst. gen. mgr. in Calif., Union Constrn. Co., 1906-09; with Sanderson & Porter, engrs., since 1909, mem. firm since 1913; chmn. and dir. Am. Sumatra Tobacco Corp., Nat. Distillers Products Corp., John de Kuyper & Son, W. & A. Gilbey, Ltd.; dir. Republic Aviation Co., 20th Century Fox Film Corp., Gen. Precision Equipment Corporation, Illinois Zinc Company, Tobacco & Allied Stocks, Inc., General Aniline and Film Corporation; trustee New York Trust Company. Mem. American Institute Electric Engineers; asso. member Society Naval Architects and Marine Engrs. Clubs: Union, Yale, City Midday, Bankers, Racquet and Tennis (New York); Turf and Field, Piping Rock, Tuxedo. Home: 834 5th Av., N.Y. City 21. Office: 120 Broadway, N.Y.C. 5. Died Feb. 6, 1953.

PORTERFIELD, Allen Wilson, coll. prof.; b. Bedington, W.Va., Aug. 30, 1878; s. Alexander Robinson and Susan Virginia (Small) P.; A.B., W.Va. U., 1900, A.M., 1901; studied Berlin, Munich and Copenhagen; Ph.D., Columbia, 1911; m. Elsie de Valois Chesley, Sept. 7, 1915; children—Allen Wilson, 2d lt., (A.A.F.), Joseph Arthur (killed in action, Dec. 8, 1943), Erik Adolph. Instr. Germanic langs. and lits., U. of W.Va., 1901-05; Carl Schurz fellow in German, Columbia, 1905-06; instr. in German, Columbia, 1907-17; 1st lt., A.S.S.C., U.S. Army, Sept. 10, 1917-July 1, 1919; editorial staff N.Y. Evening Post, 1919-22; prof. German, Randolph-Macon Woman's Coll., 1922-24; prof. German, W.Va. U., 1924-40; mil. intelligence ofcl., 1942-43. corr. for Ebasco Internat. Corp., 1944-—. Mem. Modern Lang. Assn. Am., Linguistic Soc., Am., Soc. for Advancement of Scandinavian Studies, Delta Phi Alpha, Phi Beta Kappa, Phi Kappa Psi, Scabbard and Blade. Dem. Meth. Author: Karl Lebrecht Immermann, 1911; Outline of German Romanticism, 1914. Translator: The Goose Man, 1922; Power of a Lie, 1923; Wolfgang Goethe, 1924; The Soul of the Moving Picture, 1924; Oberlin's Three Stages and Other Stories, 1926. Editor: Modern German Stories, 1927; Arthur Schnitzler—Stories and Plays, 1929. Contbr. to numerous mags. Home: 41 Winnebago Rd., Yonkers, N.Y. Office: Ebasco Internat. Corp., 2 Rector St., N.Y.C. Died May 10, 1952; buried Kensico Cemetery, N.Y.C.

PORTERIE, Gaston Louis (pŏr'tĕr-ē), lawyer; b. Mansura, La., Jan. 22, 1885; s. Louis and Felicie (Monnin) P.; B.S., La. State U., 1904, LL.B., 1915; LL.D. honoris causa, U. of Montreal, 1937; m. Viola Joffrion, Oct. 15, 1919; children—Gaston Louis, Louis Bennett. Prin. high sch., Mansura, La., 1905-09; supt. schs. Avoyelles Parish, La., 1909-13; began law practice at Marksville, La., 1915; dist. atty., 14th La. Dist., 1916-20; atty. gen. of La., 1932-39; U.S. dist. judge, Western District of La., since 1939; presiding judge Southern District Court of New York, 1946-47. President National Association of Attorneys-General, 1938-39; v.p. Interstate Commission on Crime, 1938-39. Member-at-large La. Dem. Exec. Com., 1928-40. Capt. Am. Red Cross, A.E.F., France, Sept. 1918-Feb. 1919. Decorated Chevalier Legion of Honor, 1940. Mem. State Bar of La. (pres. 1935-36; gov.), La. State U. Alumni Council, Kappa Sigma, Phi Kappa Phi, Omicron Delta Kappa, Gamma Gamma Nu. Democrat. Address: 2050 Marye St., Alexandria, La. Died Mar. 24, 1953; buried Cushman Cemetery, Marksville, La.

PORTOR, Laura Spencer (Mrs. Francis Pope), author; b. Covington, Ky.; d. William Hamilton and Mary Louise (Halsted) Portor; m. Francis Pope. Editorial staff Woman's Home Companion. Author: The Greatest Books in the World, 1913; Genevieve, 1914; Story of the Little Angels, 1917; Adventures in Indigence, 1918; The Larger Vision (under pen name, Anne Bryan McCall), 1919; The Little Long Ago, 1927; New York, the Giant City, 1939; You Yourself, An Introduction to General Psychology also Psychology Work Book and Note Book (under pen name, Anne Bryan McCall), 1937; Shakespeare, Is Yours, 1947; Music Shakespeare Loved, Twelve Shakespearean Songs, If Angels Could, 1947; Shakespeare Himself, 1947; Shakespeare Teacher Manual, 1947; Craftsmanship of Shakespeare, 1947; Story of New York The Giant City, Enlarged America edition, 1953; America-Map of New York City, 1955. Conducted under name of Ann Bryan McCall, human relations dept. of Woman's Home Companion. Contributor to Atlantic Monthly, Harper's, Scribner's, Century, North Am. Rev. and others. Lecturer on Shakespeare and other subjects. Home: Brookwood, Garrison-on-Hudson, N.Y. Died Aug. 15, 1957.

POSEGATE, Mabel (pōz-gāt), poet; b. Cin., O.; d. Oliver Franklin and Gertrude (Knighton) Bear; ed. Walnut Hills High Sch., Cin., bus. coll., and U. Cin.; m. Charles Sargent Posegate, Dec. 5, 1905; children—Mabel Victoria (Mrs. Gendall H. Brownlee), Aaron Knighton, Elinor Knighton (Mrs. Urban A. Krogmann), Charles Knighton. Mem. adv. com. on women's participation, New York World's Fair, 1939. Apptd. poet laureate of Ohio, 1936. Ohio rep. of League to Support Poetry, N.Y. City 1940-—. Received an award in Nat. Book Contest by Nat. League Am. Pen Women, 1936, 1st prize in nat. poetry contest, 1941, 50; pink dogwood tree planted in her honor in Authors' Grove, Eden Park, Cincinnati, 1937. Rec. sec. Nat. Fedn. Poetry Clubs. Mem. Poetry Soc. Am. (active), Poetry Soc. Ohio, Nat. League Am. Pen Women (chmn. lectures for Eastern Central Div. 1937-38; nat. 3d v.p. 1940-41), Composers and Authors Assn. Am., Verse Writers Guild Ohio, D.A. R.; patroness Alpha Gamma Delta of U. of Cincinnati, Omega Chapter of Phi Beta Music and Speech Frat. Clubs: Cincinnati Eastern Hills Literary (past pres.), Cincinnati Woman's, Hist. and Philos. Soc. of Ohio, Hyde Park Literary (hon.), Cincinnati Woman's Press, Republican Women's. Author: (verse) Silver 'Scutcheon, 1928; Once When Arcturus Shone, 1935; White Moment, 1938; Burning Gold, 1947. Wrote Ohio's flower poem, "Carnation," 1939. Edited Ohio Sect., wrote foreword to N. American Book of Verse, 1939. Contbr. to Christian Century, Lit. Digest, Sat. Review of Literature, New York Times, Chicago Tribune, Washington Post, Washington Evening Star, Voices, and Poetry Review (London). Poems have appeared in Braithwaite's, Louis Untermeyer's, and in other anthologies, and many have been set to music. Hon. editor (with Ted Malone) The Dream Shop, 1943. Home: 3637 Ault Park Av., Cin. 8. Died Apr. 28, 1957; buried Spring Grove Cemetery, Cin.

POST, Chandler Rathfon, prof. fine arts; b. Detroit, Mich., Dec. 14, 1881; s. William R. and Anne M. (Rathfon) P.; A.B., Harvard, 1904, A.M., 1905, Ph.D., 1909; student American School at Athens, 1904-05; L.H.D. (honorary), University of Michigan, 1953. With Harvard, 1905-—, various positions, including asst. in English, 1905-06, instr. in English, French, Italian, Greek, Romance langs., fine arts, until 1912, asst. prof. Greek and fine arts, 1912-20, asso. prof., 1920-23, prof., 1922-34, Boardman prof. fine arts, 1934-50. Capt. inf., World War, serving as asst. to mil. attaché, Rome, 1917-18. Chevalier Order of St. Maurice and St. Lazarus (Italy), 1918; Real Academia de Bellas Artes De San Jorge (Barcelona), 1957; Real Academie de la Historia, 1958; Commendador Encomienda De Isabel La Catolica (Spain), 1959. Mem. Am. Acad. Arts and Scis., Coll. Art Assn. Hispanic Soc. of Am., Am. Philos. Soc., Academia de San Luis (Saragossa, Spain), Acad. de Bellas Artes de Santa Isabel de Hungrid (Seville). Phi Beta Kappa. Democrat. Episcopalian. Club: Faculty (Cambridge). Author: Mediaeval Spain, Allegory, 1915; A History of European and American Sculpture, 1921; A History of Sculpture (with George H. Chase), 1924; A History of Spanish Painting (12 vols.), 1930-47. Contbr. to periodicals. Home: 11 Hilliard St., Cambridge, Mass. Died Nov. 2, 1959; buried Foxboro Cemetery, Foxboro, Mass.

POST, Charles Johnson, artist journalist; b. N.Y. City, Aug. 27, 1873; s. Louis Freeland and Anna (Johnson) P.; ed. Coll. City of N.Y., and Penn Charter School, Phila.; m. Alice Litta Craft, April 29, 1909; 1 dau., Phyllis Bradford. Since 1893 engaged as artist-journalist and editorial writer with the Asso. Press, N.Y. Daily News, Recorder, World, Jour., Herald, Globe, Illustrated American, N.Y. Times, Phila. Inquirer, the Century Mag., Parson's, Cosmopolitan, Harper's Weekly, and Harper's Mag.,

Everybody's, and Outing. Explored interior of S.A. for Harper's Mag., 1903-04. Served as private Co. F, 71st N.Y.V., Spanish War, 1898, later 1st lt. and battalion q.-m. in same; participated in battles of Las Guasimas and San Juan, skirmishes in trenches and siege of Santiago; later 1st lt. 22d Co., 9th Regt. Coast Artillery, Nat. Guard, N.Y. Organized publicity dept. Triangle Film Corp., Los Angeles; dir. film, "The Making of a Sailor," made for Navy Dept., 1917; dir. and organized Publishers' Advisory Bd., 1917—. Mem. exec. campaign com. and chmn. publicity com. Woodrow Wilson Ind. League of So. Calif., 1916. Organizer and pres. Am. Assn. for Scientific Taxation; dir. and trustee Schalkenbach Found.; pres. Tax Protective League. Apptd. by Pres. Truman as commr. conciliation, U.S. Dept. of Labor spl. adviser Internat. Labor Orgn. Conf. of All Americas, Mexico City, 1946 (retired). Now active as artist, one-man exhibit, Smithsonian and National Museum, Washington, D.C., 1952-53, 71st Reg't Armory, N.Y.C., 1952. Loan exhibition of Spanish American War paintings to Cuban Govt. Mem. Authors League America, Soc. of Santiago. Democrat. Club: Bayside Chess. Author: Jimmy's Infant Industry; Across the Andes; Manual of Pack Transportation; The Rock Island Scandal; Some Postal Economics; Motion Picture Madness; The Mrs. Hogan on Bachelors, Matrimony, San Juan, etc.; Private Enterprise Did This; The Little War of Private Post, pub. 1960. Demonstrated first successful talking motion pictures. Inventor of Post process of subtractive color photographs. V.P. Am. Journal Economics and Sociology. Painter famous Spanish War Collection of Spanish Am. War in Cuba, 1898; represented in permanent collections Naval Mus. at Annapolis, Roosevelt Found.; also 10 pages in Color Life Mag., July 7, 1958. Home: 38-39 214 Pl., Bayside, L.I., N.Y. Died Sept. 25, 1956; buried Arlington Nat. Cemetery.

POST, Chester Leroy, consulting engr.; b. Gordon, O., Aug. 2. 1880; s. Ezra and Mary Frances (Berry) P.; B.S., Rose Poly. Inst., 1903, M.S., 1905, C.E., 1934; m. Jennie Marie Jensen, May 6, 1908. Asst. engr. C.,C., C.&St.L. Ry., 1902; assistant engineer and masonry insp. same rd., 1903-04; supt. with A. J. Yawger Co., 1905-06, and R. M. Shankland, 1907-08; with Unit Constrn. Co. and Chicago Unit Constrn. Co. in charge of all work in Chicago territory, 1908-10; with T. L. Condron, and v.p. and mgr. Condron Co., 1910-18, v.p. and sec., 1919-24, designing and superintending constrn. large number bldgs for Sears, Roebuck Co., Ford Motor Co., Wagner Electric Corp., etc.; mem. Condron & Post, 1924-42, engaged in the design and construction of South Park Boulevard Viaduct, Western Electric Co., American Colortype Co., etc. Supervising designing engr. Q.M. Corps, U.S. Army, Army Supply Base Brooklyn, N.Y., etc., 1918-19. Cons. engr. and chmn. engrng. advisory com. Federal Works Agency. Pub. Bldgs. Adminstrn., Washington, D.C., 1935—. Cons. to Division 2, National Defense Research Com., Washington, D.C., 1943. Mem. Am. Concrete Inst. (chmn. bldg. code com.; mem. award com.). Mem. Am. Soc. Civ. Engrs., Western Soc. Engrs., Republican. Methodist. Mason (K.T.), Shriner. Club: Chicago Engineers. Author: Building Superintendence for Reinforced Concrete, 1916. Home: 1 Scott Circle, Washington 6, D.C. Office: 19th & F, Washington 25. Died Aug. 21, 1950; buried Chgo.

POST, Hoyt Garrod, lawyer; b. Holland, Mich., Sept. 22, 1884; s. John Coatsworth and Harriet Kate (Garrod) P.; A.B., U. Mich., 1905, LL.B., 1907; m. Ruth Norris, June 14, 1919; 1 son, Norris (lt., A.A.F.). Admitted to Mich. bar, 1907; now engaged in practice with offices, N.Y.C. and Washington. Sec. Gen. Soc., Sons Revolution, 1931-52, hon. gen. sec., 1952—; mem. council Boy Scouts Am. Republican. Conglist. Home: 4 Linwood Pl., White Plains, N.Y. Office: Rm. 1305, 450 7th Av., N.Y.C. 1. Died May 15, 1958; buried Ann Arbor, Mich.

POST, James Otis, architect; b. Bernardsville, N.J.; s. George B. Post; student, class of 1897, Columbia U., Ecole des Beaux Arts, Paris. Began as draftsman and designer with Geo. B. Post, 1901; engaged in individual practice of architecture, 1902; mem. firm Geo. B. Post & Sons, architect-engineers 1904—; has carried on practice of Geo. B. Post & Sons, individually,1938—; joined by son, E. Everett Post (who later became partner), 1934. Partnership consisted of J. Otis Post and Lessing W. Williams, 1944-47; son Edward Everett Post became partner, 1947. Practice established 1860, now aggregating over $170,000,000; projects include; New York Stock Exchange; Wis. State Capitol; Olympic Hotel (Seattle); Mutual Benefit Life Ins. Co. (Newark); Hotels Statler in Cleveland, Boston, Detroit, etc.; Stamford (Conn.) Hosp. (introducing pavilion type of hosp.); Cleveland Trust Co.; Prudential Ins. Co. (Newark) and numerous other buildings. Cons. to War Dept., 1917, on cantonments; assisted in orgn. U.S. Housing Bur. Fellow Am. Inst. Architects; sec. Am. Sect., Internat. Congress of Architects; past pres. Beaux Arts Inst. Design and Soc. Beaux Arts Architects; mem. Archtl. League (mem. former adv. com. to instns. and agencies, State of N.J.); mem. Squadron A Ex-Members Assn., Delta Psi. Clubs: Union League, National Arts. Contbr. to professional jours. Home: Cold Spring Harbor, L.I., N.Y. Office: 101 Park Av., N.Y.C. 17. Died Apr. 20, 1951.

POST, Kenneth, educator; b. Lake Odessa, Mich., Nov. 24, 1904; s. C. Walter and Blanche (Howlett) P.; B.S., Mich. State Coll., 1927; M.S., Ia. State Coll., 1928; Ph.D., Cornell, 1936; m. Elaine Ainsworth, June 1930; children—Larry Walter, Linda Louise, Kenneth Howard. Extension specialist floriculture Mich. State Coll., 1928-30; instr. floriculture Cornell, 1930-36, asst. prof., 1936-40, asso. prof., 1940-46, prof. floriculture, 1946-55, head dept., 1955—. Mem. Soc. Am. Florists, N.Y. State Flower Growers, Am. Soc. for Horticulture Sci. (pres. 1952), Am. Carnation Soc. (hon.), Chrysanthemum Soc. Am. (hon.), Sigma Xi, Pi Alpha Xi, Alpha Zeta, Pi Kappa Pi. Republican. Presbyn. Author: Florist Crop Production and Marketing, 1949; Plants and Flowers in the Home, 1944; also articles sci. and comml. publs. Home: Ellis Hollow Rd., Ithaca, N.Y. Died Oct. 25, 1955.

POST, Lawrence T., physician; b. St. Louis, Dec. 25, 1887; s. Martin Hayward and Mary Lawrence (Tyler) P.; A.B., Yale, 1909; M.D., Johns Hopkins, 1913; m. Bernice Lightner, Mar. 15, 1924; children—Lawrence Tyler, Jr., Stephen Lightner, Robert Henshaw. Surg. interneship, Johns Hopkins Hosp., 1913-14; asso. surgeon, S. Balt. Eye, Ear, Nose and Throat Hosp., 1914-15; pvt. practice in St. Louis, 1915—; editor Am. Jour. Opthalmology, 1924—, editor-in-chief, 1931-40, acting editor-in-chief, 1942-45; prof. clin. ophthalmology and head of dept., Washington U., 1933-53; opthalmologist-in-chief to Barnes Hosp., St. Louis Children's Hosp., McMillan Hosp. Capt. Med. Res. Corps, U.S. Army, 1917, maj., 1919; surg. dir. Am. Mobile Hosp. No. 4, A.E.F.; lt. col. Reserve Corps, 1927-32; mem. Ophthal. Com. of Nat. Def. Surg. Adv. Com., 1941. Pres. Ophthalmic Pub. Co. Recipient of Howe Medal, 1947; of Dana Medal, 1949. Fellow Am. Coll. Surgeons; mem. Am. Acad. of Ophthalmology and Otolaryngology (v.p., 1928, pres. 1944); mem. So. Med. Soc. (past chmn. Ophthalmic Sect.), St. Louis Med. Soc. (past chmn. Ophthal. Sect.); Am. Med. Assn. (past-chmn. Ophthal. Sect.); Am. Ophthal. Soc., Mo. State Med. Assn., St. Louis Ophthal. Soc. (past pres.), Sigma Psi, Zeta Psi, Phi Beta Pi. Clubs: University, St. Louis Country, Round Table (St. Louis); Pithotomy (Balt.). Co-author: Ophthalmological and Otolaryngological Military Surgical Manuals. Contbr. to profl. jours. Home: 8030 Rosiline Dr., St. Louis 5. Office: 508 N. Grand Blvd., St. Louis 3. Died May 13, 1959.

POST, Waldron Kintzing, lawyer; b. N.Y.C., July 7, 1868; s. Albert Kintzing and Marie Caroline (de Trobriand) P.; A.B., Harvard, 1890; LL.B., Columbia, 1894; m. Mary Lawrence Perkins, Oct. 27, 1894. Admitted to bar, 1895. Author: Harvard Stories, 1893; Smith Brunt, 1899. Home: Bayport, N.Y. Office: 120 Broadway, N.Y.C. Died Feb. 6, 1955.

POTEAT, Edwin McNeill (pō-tēt'), clergyman; b. New Haven, Conn., Nov. 20, 1892; s. Edwin McNeill and Harriet Hale (Gordon) P.; student Furman Fitting Sch., 1908, A.B., Furman U., 1912, A.M., 1913; Th.M., Southern Baptist Theol. Sem., 1916; D.D. (hon.), Wake Forest Coll., 1934, Duke U., 1936, Hillsdale Coll., 1940; m. Wilda Hardman, June 27, 1917; children—William Hardman, Harriet Alden (deceased), Elizabeth McNeill, Haley Gordon. Traveling sec., Student Volunteer Movement, N.Y., 1916-17; missionary, Southern Baptist Conv., Kaifeng, Honan, China, 1917-26; asso. prof. philosophy and ethics. U. of Shanghai, China, 1926-29; ordained to ministry of Baptist Ch.; minister Pullen Memorial Ch., Raleigh, N.C., 1929-37, Euclid Av. Ch., Cleveland, O., 1937-44; pres. Colgate-Rochester Divinity Sch., 1944-48; minister Pullen Memorial Bapt. Ch., Raleigh, N.C., since 1948. Mem. N.C. State Bd. charities and pub. welfare, 1930-37, Governor's commn. State Hospitals, N. C., 1936-37; pres. commn. Interacial Coop. (Atlanta, Ga.), 1933-37, Cleveland Ministers' Assn., 1942-43, Cleveland Bapt. Assn.; on commn. on worship, etc., Nat. Council of Chs. of Christ of Am. since 1941; nat. pres. Protestants and Others United for Separation of Church and State. Religion and Labor Center, Cleveland, O. Clubs: Quaternion (Furman U. 1910-12), Watauga (Raleigh, N.C., 1936-37). Composer of hymns; anthems: In the End of the Sabbath, 1938; Jesus Thou Joy of Living Hearts, 1950; Indifference, 1942. Author: Coming to Terms With the Universe, 1931; Jesus and the Liberal Mind, 1933; The Rev. John Doe, D.D., 1934; Thunder Over Sinai, 1936; The Social Manifesto of Jesus, 1937; Centurion (dramatic poem), 1938; These Shared His Passion, 1938; These Shared His Cross, 1939; These Shared His Power, 1941; Four Freedoms and God, 1943; Over the Sea, The Sky (poetry), 1945; Last Reprieve?, 1945; Parables of Crisis, 1950; God Makes the Difference, 1951; Mandate to Humanity, 1953. Contbr. articles and verse, various mags. Lyman Beecher lecturer on preaching, Yale, 1940. Home: 2802 Exeter Circle, Raleigh, N.C. Died Dec. 17, 1955; buried Montlawn Meml. Park, Raleigh.

POTEAT, Hubert McNeil (pō-tēt), coll. prof.; b. Wake Forest, N.C., Dec. 12, 1886; s. William Louis and Emma James (Purefoy) P.; A.B., Wake Forest Coll., 1906, A.M., 1908; Ph.D., Columbia, 1912; m. Essie Moore Morgan, June 26, 1912; children—Hubert McNeill, William Morgan. Prof. of Latin, Wake Forest Coll., 1912—; Columbia (summer sessions), 1924-42. Mem. Classical Assn. of the Middle West and South (pres. 1937-38), Brit. Classical Assn., Am. Philol. Assn., Kappa Alpha (past exec. councilor), Omicron Delta Kappa, Phi Beta Kappa; pres. N.C. Litry. and Hist. Assn., 1944. Democrat. Baptist (organist 40 yrs., choir dir. Wake Forest Ch.). Mason (33°, K.T.), Past Grand Master of the Grand Lodge of N.C.; Shriner (Past Potentate; Imperial Potentate, Shrine of N. Am., 1950-51). Author: Repetition in Latin Poetry, 1912; Selected Letters of Cicero, 1916, 2d edition, 1931; Practical Hymnology, 1921; Selected Epigrams of Martial, 1931; Selected Letters of Pliny, 1937; T. Livius Narrator, 1938; trans. Cicero's Brutus, Nature of the Gods, Divination, Duties, 1950; numerous articles. Home: Wake Forest, N.C. Died Jan. 29, 1958; buried Wake Forest, N.C.

POTTER, Chester Magee, newspaper reporter; b. Pitts., Jan. 23, 1899; s. Chester D. and Jeanne I. (Oldfield) P.; student pub. schs.; m. Hazel Camp, June 16, 1955; 1 adopted dau., Kathryn Jeanne Potter. Stenographer Reliance Life Ins. Co., Pitts., 1915-18; clk. Carnegie Steel Co., 1919-24; reporter Vineyard Gazette, Martha's Vineyard, Mass., 1924, Boston Post, 1924-28, Providence Jour. and Evening Bull., 1928-39, Phila. Record, 1939-42, Pitts. Post-Gazette, 1942-45; reporter Pitts. Press, 1945-56, Washington corr., 1951-56. Served with AEF, 1918-19. Club: Nat. Press (Washington). Home: 3763 Gunston Rd., Alexandria, Va. Office: 1013 13th St. N.W., Washington. Died Oct. 16, 1956.

POTTER, Ellen Culver, ret. state med. officer; b. New London, Conn., Aug. 5, 1871; d. Thomas Wells and Ellen (Culver) Potter; M.D., Woman's Med. Coll. Pa., 1903, Dr. of Social Science, 1950; LL.D., Rutgers U., 1936. In gen. practice of medicine, 1903-18; med. dir. woman's Coll. Hosp. (Phila.), 1918-20; chief of div. of child health, Pa. Health Dept., 1920-21; dir. bur. of children, Pa. Welfare Dept., 1921-23, sec. of welfare, Pa., 1923-27; supt. N.J. Woman's Reformatory, and State Home for Girls, 1928-30; dir. of medicine N.J. State Dept. Instns. and Agencies, 1930-49, ret. 1949; dep. commr. for Welfare, N.J., 1946-49. Former pres. Woman's Med. Coll. of Pa. Pres. Nat. Conf. of Social Work, 1944-45. Mem. adv. commn. on children in war time, and chmn. day care of children of working mothers adv. com., Fed. Children's Bur.; state chmn. child care com. N.J. State Def. Council; mem. adv. council on chronic sick N.J. State Dept. Health. Recipient: Elizabeth Blackwell Award, 1953; Medical Woman of the Year, 1954, by Am. Med. Women's Assn. Fellow Am. Pub. Health Assn.; mem. Am. Med. Assn., Am. Coll. of Physicians, Am. Psychiatric Assn., Am. Assn. of Social Workers, Am. Assn. Univ. Women, Am. Med. Women's Assn. (ex-pres.), Am. Sociol. Assn., Am. Pub. Welfare Assn. (bd. dirs.), Nat. Organization of Pub. Health Nurses, Nat. Assn. Mental Health, Nat. Com. on Care Transients and Homeless (ex-chmn.), N.J. Welfare Council (ex-pres.), League of Women Voters, Am. Geriatrics Assn., Zonta Internat. Ind. Republican. Baptist. Clubs: College (Trenton), Business and Professional (N.J.). Contbr. of articles on pub. welfare adminstrn., sociology, penology, and care chronically ill. Terry Award A.P.W.A. Home: 301 W. State St., Trenton, N.J. Died Feb. 8, 1958.

POTTER, George W., writer; b. Fall River, Mass., Sept. 20, 1899; s. Joseph H., Jr., and Ellen (McKenny) P.; Ph.B., Brown U., 1921; Litt.D. (hon.), 1946; M.S. (hon.), Bradford Durfee Tech. Inst., 1955; m. Erna C. Dingwell, Feb. 17, 1927. Reporter, Rall River (Mass.) Herald, summers, 1914-16, New Bedford (Mass.) Times, summer 1919; asst. in English, Brown U., 1921-23; asst. editor, Providence (R.I.) Tribune, 1922-23, editor, 1923-29; editorial writer, Providence (R.I.) Journal, 1929-39; chief editorial writer Providence Journal Bulletin, 1939-46; instr. in journalism Brown U. Extension Dept., 1927-39. Served with S.A.T.C., Brown U., 1918. Recipient Pulitzer Award for editorial writing, 1945; Guggenheim fellow, 1956-57. Mem. Am. Soc. Newspaper Editors, Phi Beta Kappa, Phi Kappa. Author: An Irish Pilgrimage, 1950; The Golden Door-History of Irish in America from 1820-1860. Home: 30 Mount Av. Office: 75 Fountain St., Providence 2. Died Aug. 10, 1959; buried New Bedford, Mass.

POTTER, Marion E., editor, cataloguer; b. St. Louis, Dec. 6, 1869; d. John William and Josephine (Ryan) Potter; B.A., U. Minn., 1897. Dir. H. W. Wilson Co., pubs. Mem. Phi Beta Kappa. Episcopalian. Editor: The Cumulative Book Index, 1898-1918; Readers' Guide to Periodical Literature, 1901-02; U.S. Catalog, 1900, 02, 12; Children's Catalog, 1909. Editor The Industrial Arts Index, 1913-52, editor emeritus, 1952—. Home: 900 Summit Av., N.Y.C. Died June 3, 1953.

POTTER, William Chapman, banker, formerly engr. (ret.); b. Chgo., Oct. 16, 1874; s. Edwin Augustus and Harriet (Berry) P.; B.S. in Mining Engring., Mass. Inst. Tech., 1897; m. Caroline Morton, 1902; children—Jean, Charlotte; m. 2d, Rose Lee Saltonstall, 1923. Formerly engr. various mining cos., also for A.,T.&S.F. Ry.; mgr. Guggenheim Exploration Co.; gen. mgr. Am. Smelting & Refining Co.; pres., chmn. bd. Guaranty Trust Co. of N.Y.; dir. Anaconda Copper Co., others. Mem. Am. Inst. Mining and Metall. Engrs., Delta Kappa Epsilon. Republican. Episcopalian. Clubs: The Links, Nat. Golf Links, Links Golf. Home: Old Westbury, N.Y.; also Blue Springs Plantation, Albany, Ga. Office: 140 Broadway, N.Y.C. 15. Died Jan. 2, 1957.

POTTS, Charles Edwin, business man; b. Brooklyn, N.Y., July 3, 1873; s. Thomas and Emeline (Wright) P.; Brooklyn Collegiate Polytechnic Institute, 1885-88; Bachelor of Science, Polytechnic Institute Brooklyn, 1892, E.E., 1893, LL.D., 1954; married Mary Louise Dubernell, Apr. 27, 1899 (died Oct. 8, 1904); children—Thomas Jackson, John Wright, David Valentine; m. 2d, Fanny Louise Ruprecht, June 1, 1909; children—Dorothy Louise, Walter Buel. Engaged in engring., 1893-96; importer, converter and distributor of textiles, 1896-1926; sec. J. B. Locke & Potts, 1906-15, pres., 1916-26; pres. Linen Fabrics Importing Corp., 1918-23; mfr. and distributor of food products since 1919; pres. Jacquard, Inc.; treas. Korbro Oil Corp.; vice pres. Polytechnic Research and Development Co., Inc. Mem. Nat. Guard N.Y., 1894-1909, maj. ordnance dept., 1918-22; comdr. mounted div. Home Defense League, 1917. Chmn. Corporation (chairman, 1924-54) of Poly. Inst. Brooklyn. Mem. Bd. of Edn., Westhampton Sch. Dist.; chmn. Zoning Commn., Westhampton Beach. Sigma Phi Sigma. Democrat. Episcopalian. Clubs: Rembrandt, University (Brooklyn); Union League, Lawyers, University (New York). Home: (legal) Westhampton Beach, L.I., N.Y.; also 885 Park Avenue, New York 21, N.Y. Office: 15 William St., N.Y.C. 5. Died Aug. 28, 1956; buried Greenwood Cemetery, Bklyn.

POTZGER, John E., educator; b. Presque Isle County, Mich., July 31, 1886; s. Bruno and Augusta (Glaess) P.; certificate Concordia Tchrs. Coll., River Forest, Ill., 1906; student Ithaca Conservatory Music, summer, 1914-15; A.B., Butler U., 1927, M.A., 1931; Ph.D., Ind. U., 1932; m. Margaret Esther Whitney, June 9, 1947. Tchr. Luth. Day Schs., 1906-30; instr. botany Butler U., 1932-37, asst. prof., 1937-40, asso. prof., 1940-48, prof., 1948—, head dept. botany, also editor Butler Botanical Studies, 1953—; field botanist biol. survey group U. Wis., summer 1940; vis. lectr. ecology Purdue Conservation Camp, 1946-52; guest mem. sci. team, dir. research, Mont Tremblant Biol. Sta., P.Q., summers 1952-54. Recipient Eli Lilly Research Labs. grant, 1954,55. Fellow A.A.A.S. (mem. council, 1955), Ind. Acad. Sci. (research grants, 1945, 46, 54); mem. Am. Philos Soc. (research grants 1941, 48, 53), Wis. Acad. Sci., Arts and Letters, Ohio Acad. Sci., Ecol. Soc. Am. (pres. 1953-54), Bot. Soc. Am., Nature Conservancy, Central Assn. Sci. and Mathematics Tchrs. (pres. 1948), Am. Soc. Limnology and Oceanography, Am. Bryological Soc. Lutheran. Editor biology sect. School Science and Mathematics, 1952-54. Conducted pioneer research in palynology (pollen analysis) dealing with post-Pleistocene forest history and climatic changes in eastern N.A., plant sociology studies, forest surveys; research and spl. bull. for President's Com. on Quetico-Superior Internat. Peace Meml. Forest, 1950-53; studies of primeval forests in Ind., based on records of witness trees in original U.S. land survey, 1949-55; bog expdns. by plane to wilderness areas about James Bay and into tundra of No. Quebec, summers 1953-55 (sponsored by Service de Biogeographie of U. Montreal, Dept. of Fish and Game, Biol. Bur. of P.Q.). Author numerous contbns. to Am. and Canadian sci. and ednl. jours. Home: 2814 N. Park Av., Indpls. 5. Died Sept. 18, 1955; buried Concordia Cemetery, Indpls.

POUCH, William Henry, business exec.; b. Brooklyn, N.Y., Jan. 1, 1875; s. Alfred J. and Harriet (Hascy) P.; student Adelphia Acad., Brooklyn, 1883-93; Sheffield Sci. Sch., Yale Univ., 1893-96; m. Helena R. Hellwig, Nov. 7, 1897; 1 dau., Helen. Started as clerk and advanced to pres. and treas., Newburgh Electric Ry. Co., Newburgh, N.Y., 1896-1907; formed Concrete Steel Co., New York, N.Y., 1907, served as pres. and treas., 1907-47, pres. since 1923; pres. and dir. Delawan Co. since 1942. Mem. indsl. adv. com. Fed. Reserve Bank, Chemical Nat. Bank. Mem. New York Credit Men's Assn. (pres. 1924-26), Nat. Assn. Credit Men (pres. 1926), Boy Scouts of Am. (pres. Greater New York Council, 1941, 46), Y.M.C.A. New York City Assn. (vice pres. 1936-46). S.A.R. vice pres. Empire State Soc. 1940-46). Presbyterian. Home: 1 E. 66th St. Office: 2 Park Av., N.Y.C. Died Feb. 1959.

POUND, Louise, educator; b. Lincoln, Neb., June 30, 1872; d. Judge Stephen Bosworth and Laura (Biddlecombe) Pound; B.L., U. Neb., 1892, diploma in music, 1892, A.M., 1895; student U. Chgo., summers, 1897, 98; Ph.D., U. Heidelberg, 1900; Litt.D. (hon.), Smith Coll., 1928. Fellow in English lit. U. Neb., 1894-97, instr., 1897-99, adj. prof., 1900-06, asst. prof., 1906-08, asso. prof., 1908-12, prof., 1912-45; instr. English subjects, summer session, U. Cal., 1923, Yale Linguistic Inst., 1928, U. Chgo. 1929, Columbia, 1930, Stanford, 1931. Recipient Kiwanis Medal, 1947; Neb. Alumni Medal, 1948. Mem. Modern Lang. Assn. Am. (v.p. 1916, 25; exec. council, 1921-23, 25; pres. (first woman pres. 1954-55) Humanistic Research Assn. of Eng. (mem. exec. com. Am. branch 1925), Am. Assn. U. Profs. (v.p. 1936-37), Am. Dialect Soc. (western v.p. 1921-25; nat. v.p. 1928-37; nat. pres. 1938-41), Nat. Council English Tchrs. (dir. 1915-19; nat. treas. 1917), Am. Folk-Lore Soc. (pres. 1925-27; nat. councillor 1928-—), Spelling Reform Assn. (v.p. 1927), Medieval Acad. Am. Linguistic Soc. Am. (v.p. 1939), Neb. Writers' Guild; actg. state head and chmn. over-seas relief com. Nat. League for Woman's Service, 1918; mem. woman's com. State Council Defense, 1918; head lit. sect. State Teachers' Assn., 1915; head folk-lore and ethnology sect. Neb. Acad. Sciences, 1917-22; mem. D.A.R., Assn. of Collegiate Alumnae (Neb. dir. 1906-08; nat. council 1913), Am. Assn. Univ. Women (mem. com. on fellowship awards 1935-37; nat. v.p., 1937-45), Kappa Kappa Gamma (province pres. 1915-17), Phi Beta Kappa, Sigma Tau Delta, Theta Sigma Phi, Delta Omicron, Chi Delta Phi Pi Gamma Mu, Delta Kappa Gamma, Alpha Lambda Delta, Mortar Board; mem. advisory council Guggenheim Foundation, 1928-32; mem. exec. com. National Folk Festival, 1935— ,v.p. 1954. Clubs: Country, University (Lincoln). Holder of women's western lawn tennis championship, 1897; central western (Kansas City) and western championships, women's doubles, 1915; holder local women's golf championship, 1906-23, 1925-27; city golf champion, 1926; state tennis champion, Neb., 1891, 1892; state golf champion, 1916; first woman elected Neb. Sports Hall of Fame, 1955. Author, editor books, studies, and contributor various periodicals on lit., linguistic, folk-lore, and educational subjects including: Poetic Origins and the Ballad, 1921; American Ballads and Songs, 1922; Selected Writings of Louise Pound, 1949. Editor of University of Nebraska Studies in Language, Literature and Criticism, 1917-40; senior ed. Am. Speech, 1925-33, asso. and dept. editor, 1933-38; adv. bd. New England Quarterly, 1928-30, Am. Literature, 1929-45, Folk-Say, 1929, Southern Folklore Quarterly, 1937-—, College English, 1939-46, Bull. Am. Assn. of U. Profs. 1941-—. Home: 1632 L St. Lincoln 8 Neb. Died June 27, 1958.

POWEL, Harford, writer, editor; born Phila., Aug. 20, 1887; s. Harford W. Hare and Marion C. (Howard) P.; St. George's Sch., Newport, R.I.; A.B., Harvard, 1909 (pres. Lampoon, 1909); m. Harriet S. Motley, February 17, 1952; 1 son, Harford, by previous marriage. With the Vogue Company of New York, 1909-14, also International Mag. Co., 1914-17; editor Harper's Bazaar, 1917; editor Collier's, 1919-22, The Youth's Companion, 1925-28; v.p. Kimball, Hubbard & Powel, Inc., 1932-38; exec. and vice-pres. Inst. of Pub. Relations, 1938-41; information dir. Defense and War Bonds, Treasury Dept., 1941-42. Publicity dir. Selective Service, N.Y. City, 1948. Capt. Air Service, 1918. Publicity director, Block-Aid Campaign, N.Y. City, 1931; lt. col., Air Corps, 1945. Club: Harvard. Author: Walter Camp, 1926; What About Advertising? (with Kenneth M. Goode), 1927; The Virgin Queene, 1928; Married Money, 1929; The Invincible Jew, 1930; Oh Glory! 1931; Widow's Mite, 1935; Good Jobs for Good Girls, 1949. Editor (with Grantland Rice): Omnibus of Sport, 1933. Address: 65 Main St., Concord, Mass. Died Aug. 17, 1956; buried Newport, R.I.

POWELL, Alden L(eslie), educator; b. Rockton, Ill., Nov. 27, 1902; s. Dwight Ephraim and May Agnes (Pollock) P.; A.B., U. Ill., 1929, M.A., 1930, Ph.D., 1934; m. Vera Claudia Mace, Aug. 16, 1930; 1 son, William Mace. Asst., U. Ill., 1931-34, instr., 1934-35, vis. prof., summer 1946; asst. prof., La. State U., 1935-38, asso. prof., 1938-42, prof. 1942-—; vis. prof., U. Ariz., summer 1939; mem. com. on adminstrv. personnel 10th region, U.S. Civil Service Commn. 1945-—. Mem. Southwestern Social Sci. Assn. (chmn. govt. sect. 1937-38), So. Polit. Sci. Assn. (v.p. 1938-39, exec. council 1948-51), Am. Legion (asso. dir. boys and girls states, for La., 1940-44), Am. Arbitration Assn. (vol. panel of arbitrators 1948-—), Am. Polit. Sci. Assn. (com. on election statis. 1946-48), Am. Assn. U. Profs., Phi Beta Kappa, Omicron Delta Kappa, Pi Gamma Mu, Pi Sigma Alpha. Democrat. Methodist. Author: National Taxation of State Instrumentalities, 1936; State and Local Government in Louisiana, 1941; Government in Louisiana, 1943; A Primer on Government in Louisiana, 1946; also numerous articles, principally on econ. and hist. subjects. Home: 2105 Ferndale Av., Baton Rouge 15. Died June 9, 1950.

POWELL, Arthur Gray (pou'ĕl), lawyer; b. Blakely Ga., Sept. 2, 1873; s. Richard Holmes and Keturah (Perry) P.; student Mercer U., Macon, Ga., 1889-90; LL.D., 1917; m. Annie Wilkin, Dec. 31, 1896; children—Arthur Wilkin, Frances (Mrs. Clarence Laws), Grace (Mrs. Edward H. Hammond). Admitted to Ga. bar, 1891, and began practice at Blakely; moved to Atlanta, Ga., 1912; judge Court of Appelas of Ga., 1907-12; mem. Powell, Goldstein, Frazer & Murphy, formerly Little, Powell, Reid & Goldstein, since 1912; div. counsel Central of Ga. Ry. Co.; gen. counsel Atlanta St. Andrews Bay R.R. Mem. Am. Bar Assn. (v.p. 1934-35; mem. house of delegates, 1937-40; state del. since 1940), Am. Law Inst., Am. Judicature Soc., Ga. Bar Assn. (pres. 1921-22), Internat. Assn. of Insurance Counsel (v.p. and mem. exec. com. 1933-35), Atlanta Bar Assn. (pres. 1917-18), Kappa Alpha. Baptist. Clubs: Capital City, Piedmont Driving, Ten Club of Atlanta, Atlanta Lawyers. Author: Powell on Actions for Land, 1911; revised edit., 1945; Powell on Land Registration, 1918; I Can Go Home Again, 1943. Home: 1338 Peachtree St. N.E. Office: Citizens and Southern Nat. Bank Bldg., Atlanta 3. Died Aug. 5, 1951.

POWELL, Arthur James Emery, artist; b. Vanwert, O., Dec. 11, 1864; s. Curtis W. and Martha (Stockett) P.; student pub. schs.; art edn., San Francisco Sch. of Design, St. Louis Sch. of Fine Arts, Julian Acad., Paris. Represented in Milw. Art Inst., Nat. Arts Club, N.Y.C., Chgo. Theatre. Winner of Vezan Thumb Box sketch prize, 1913; Salmagundi sketch prize, 1928; Isidor prize, Allied Artists of America, 1930; Hanson prize, New Rochelle, 1930; Nat. Arts sketch prize, 1930; Salmagundi lay members prize, 1931; Salmagundi annual oil purchase prize, 1931. Mem. Ore. N.G., 1886-88, Nat. Academician, 1937; mem. N.Y. Water Color Soc., Allied Artists Am., Artists Fund Soc., Kent Art Assn., Dutchess County Art Assn. Methodist. Clubs: Salmagundi, Nat. Arts, N.Y. Water Color. Home: Dover Plains, N.Y. Died July 15, 1956.

POWELL, Charles Underhill, civil engr., city planner; b. Glen Head, L.I., July 16, 1896; s. George S. and Hannah (Jackson) P.; desc. Thomas Powell, of Bethpage, 1641; C.E., Cornell University, 1898; m. Harriet L. Van Nostrand, October 15, 1902; children—Fred Jackson, Eleanor Frost (Mrs. Paul E. Case), Louise Underhill (Mrs. John F. Burke). Engineer Brooklyn Bridge and Jersey Central Railroad, 1898-99; engineer subway construction, N.Y. City, 1901-02, and for City of New York, 1902-42; planned Borough of Queens, 75,000 acres, 2,500 miles of streets; as chief engr. of Topog. Bureau, 1915-42; introduced Phila. system of house-numbers and street names for the Borough; was in charge of title surveys for acquiring property for streets costing $180,000.000; planned and laid out public ocean beach at Rockaway, 6 miles long, and 1,100 acres of Queens Parks; promoted 30 public improvement laws including Rockaway boardwalk, Conduit Boulevard, Cross-Bay Rd. and street-closing laws; cons. engr. Queen's Planning Commn., 1929-42, planning layout of State Parkway System through Borough of Queens costing over $18,000,000; a founder, 1910, Flushing Nat. Bank, dir., 1910-28. Chmn. New York World's Fair Zoning Com.; mem. com. on basis improvements, New York World's Fair 1939, planned and mapped land acquisitions for improvements costing 80 million dollars in and leading to the Fair. Mem. Com. of 5, 1909-20, promoting N.Y. State licensing of civil engrs. and surveyors. Chmn. Highway and Traffic Com. of Queens until 1942. Trustee Queens Company Savings Bank; vice president Flushing Cemetery Assn. Mem. Board of Examiners for City Surveyors, New York. Mem. Flushing Hist. Soc.; former pres. Upper Flushing Assn., Municipal Engineers City of N.Y.; mem. Am. Soc. C.E., Farmers' and Taxpayers' Assn. of Boro of Queens (secretary); member Municipal Engineers of New York City. Trustee Flushing Meeting Society of Friends. Club: Fireside (Flushing, N.Y.). Wrote: Private and Family Cemeteries of Borough of Queens, Paving Primer, Erosion of Rockaway, Graphic History of Queens Borough, City N.Y., The Quakers in Flushing, 1657-1937. American and Canadian high jump champion, 1896, and Intercollegiate champion, 1898. Home: 43-23 165th St., Flushing, N.Y.; Stony Creek, Warren Co., N.Y. and Delray Beach, Fla. Died May 26, 1956; buried Flushing (N.Y.) Cemetery.

POWELL, Doane, portrait masks; b. Omaha, Neb., Mar. 4, 1881; s. Archibald Campbell and Minnie (Ketchum) P.; student U. of Neb., 1901-02, Sch. of Art Inst. Chicago, 1904; m. Edna Rudersdorf, June 1, 1914; children—Jane Katherine, Jocelyn. Studied in Paris, France, under Jean Paul Laurens Academie Julien, Academie de la Grand Chaumiere and Colorossi, 1908; became cartoonist Omaha (Neb.) Bee and News, 1909; art directing and layout work, advertising agencies in Chicago and Milwaukee, 1923-32; instr. Chicago Acad. Fine Arts, 1924-28; developer of portrait masks. Mem. Soc. Illustrators, Phi Kappa Psi. Author: Masks and How to Make Them, 1947. Address: 1 Sheridan Sq., N.Y.C. Died Aug. 27, 1951.

POWELL, E. Alexander, author, traveler; b. Syracuse, N.Y., Aug. 16, 1879; s. Edward Alexander and Lucy Caroline (Smith) P.; m. Jessie Northrup; children—Edward A., III, Lady Monson; m. 2d, Florence Josephine Taylor. With Am. Foreign Service, Syria and Egypt, 1906-08; sent by various magazines to Near East, Africa, Central Asia, Mexico; war corr., N.Y. World, London Daily Mail, and Scirbner's Mag. with Belgian, British, French, Italian and German armies, 1914-17. Served from capt. to lt. col. AEF, 1917-19. Sent by Italian Govt. on spl. mission to Balkans, 1919; chief Goldwyn-Bray-Powell Malaysian Motion Pictures Expdn., 1929. Traveled overland from Paris to Persia, 1922; sent by Century Mag. to Abyssinia, Madagascar and across Africa, 1924, to Morocco and Sahara, 1925-26, to Nepal, 1928; traveled 15,000 miles by air in Latin America, 1933; flew across Pacific Ocean, Asia, Europe, 1937; sr. polit. analyst Office of Naval Intelligence, Feb. 1, 1942; transferred to Office of Censorship as polit. editor; apptd. prin. adminstrv. officer Venezuela and Caribbean area, Fgn. Econ. Adminstrn., resigned for health, 1944. Lectr. in U.S. and Can. Commentator on foreign affairs CBS. Decorated Chevalier Order Leopold (Belgian); Chevalier Legion of Honor (French); Comdr. Order of Merit (Hungarian); Officer Order of Crown of Italy; Comdr. Order of the Crown (Roumanian); Comdr. Order of Danilo (Montenegrin); Comdr. Order of Gand Duke Gedeminas (Lithuania); Fattiche de Guerra medal (Italian); Grand Officer Order of Lion and Sun (Persian); Gold Shield of Ethiopia, by Emperor Haile Selassie; recipient silver medal for lit. Commonwealth Club of Cal. Author: The Last Frontier, 1912; Gentlemen Rovers, 1913; The End of the Trail, 1914; Fighting in Flanders, 1914; The Road to Glory, 1915; Vive la France, 1915; Italy at War, 1917; Brothers in Arms, 1917; The Army Behind the Army, 1919; The New Frontiers of Freedom, 1920; Where the Strange Trails Go down, 1921; Forgotten Heroes, 1921; Asia at the Crossroads, 1922; By Camel and Car to the Peacock Throne, 1923; The Struggle for Power in Moslem Asia, 1923; Beyond the Utmost Purple Rim, 1925; The Map That Is Half Unrolled, 1925; In Barbary, 1926; Embattled Borders, 1928; The Last Home of Mystery, 1929; The Danger on the Danube, 1929; Thunder Over Europe, 1931; Marches of the North, 1931; Undiscovered, Europe, 1932; Yonder Lies Adventure, 1932; Slanting Lines of Steel, 1933; The Long Roll on the Rhine, 1934; Red Drums, 1935; Aerial Odyssey, 1936; Free Lance, 1937; Gone Are the Days, 1938; Ever the World So Wide, 1954. Adventure Road, 1954. Home: Riverain, Falls Village, Conn. Died Nov. 12, 1957; buried Falls Village.

POWELL, Joseph Wright, shipbuilder; b. Oswego, N.Y., Feb. 15, 1877; s. Elisha Barclay and Addie Gay (Wright) P.; grad. U.S. Naval Acad., 1897; 2 yrs. spl. post-grad. course in naval architecture at same; grad. U. of Glasgow, 1900; m. Bertha Allen Osterhout, Sept. 7, 1899. Asst. naval constr. U.S. Navy until 1906; asst. to pres. Cramp's Shipbuilding Corp., Phila., 1906-14; pres. Fore River Shipbuilding Corp., Quincy, Mass., 1914-21; v.p. Bethlehem Shipbuilding Corp., Ltd., 1917-21; pres. U.S. Shipping Bd. Emergency Fleet Corp., 1921-22; pres. United Shipyards, 1930-39. Dir., mem. exec. com. Republic Aviation Corp., Am. Shipbuilding Co., Cleveland, O., Eastern Steamship Lines, Inc., Boston; director International Telephone & Telegraph Corporation, New York, Gen. Capital Corp., Boston; mem. Progressive Trust, Boston; engaged in engineering projects relating to shipbuilding and shipping, since 1944; bd. mgrs. American Bureau Shipping, N.Y. Pres. emeritus, trustee Webb Inst. of Naval Architecture; mem. Corp. Mass. Inst. Tech. Served on flagship New York, Spanish-American War. Spl. asst. to sec. of Navy, deputy chief procurement and material, Navy Dept., Washington, 1940-44. Past pres. Naval Architects and Marine Engineers; member Institute Naval Architects. Republican. Clubs: Country, Somerset (Boston), India House, University (New York); Metropolitan, (Washington); Glen Arven Country (Thomasville, Ga.). Home: 79 President's Lane, Quincy, Mass. Office: 200 Berkeley St., Boston. Died Jan. 26, 1954.

POWELL, Lula E., Rep. Nat. committeewoman; b. Balt., May 21, 1879; d. William H. and Ann R. (LeBrun) Lilly; ed. pub. schs. and Eastern High Sch., Balt.; m. David T. Powell, Nov. 28, 1899; children—John W., Evelyn Lilly (Mrs. Keller). Sec., Rep. State Com., Md., 1934-42; sec., Rep. City Com., Balt., 1929-42; Rep. Nat. committeewoman for Md., 1940-48; magistrate, 1935-39. Home: 1530 Ralworth Rd., Northwood, Balt. Died Nov. 13, 1953; buried Oak Lawn Cemetery.

POWELL, Thomas Reed, prof. law; b. Richford, Vt., Apr. 29, 1880; s. E. Henry and Georgiana (Reed) P.; A.B., U. of Vt., 1900, LL.D., 1925; LL.B., Harvard, 1904; Ph.D., Columbia, 1913, LL.D. 1955; D.C.L., U. N.M., 1930; m. Mary Lee Hale, July 27, 1915; children—Mary Lee (Mrs. Neil G. Melone), Georgiana Reed (Mrs. Brent Maxwell Abel), Thomas Reed, Jr. Was admitted to Vermont bar, 1904, and practiced at Burlington, 1904-06; asst. treas. U. of Vt., and State Agrl. College, 1904-06; lecturer in public law, Columbia, 1907-08, 1911-12; asso. in polit. science, U. of Ill., 1908-10; hon. fellow administrative law, Columbia U., 1910-11, asso. in law, 1912-13, asso. prof. constl. law, 1913-20, prof., 1920-23, Ruggles prof. constl. law, 1923-25; prof. law, Harvard Law Sch., 1925-28, Langdell prof. law, 1928-38, Stroy prof. law, 1938-39, emeritus, 1949—; professor constitutional law Suffolk University, 1950—; lecturer New School Social Research, 1951. Admitted to Mass. bar, 1942; U.S. Supreme Ct. Bar, 1945. Visiting professor, U. of Calif., 1923-24, Columbia, 1929; Carpentier Lectr. Columbia, 1955. Special assistant to Atty. Gen. of U.S., 1936, 41. Mem. Pres.'s Emergency Bd. on Nat. Ry. Strike, 1941. Mem. Am. Bar Assn., Am. Polit. Science Assn. (exec. council, 1918-20; 3d v.p. 1921; pres. 1937), Acad. Polit. Science (trustee, 1913-16), Soc. Colonial Wars, Loyal Legion, Associé de l'Institut International de Droit Public, Delta Psi, Phi Beta Kappa, Phi Delta Phi. Clubs: Harvard, St. Botolph (Boston); Signet (Cambridge); Harvard, Century (New York). Author: Separation of Powers, 1913; Indirect Encroachment on Federal Authority by the Taxing Powers of the States, 1919; The Supreme Court and State Police Power (1922-1930), 1932. Managing editor Political Science Quarterly, 1913-16. Contbr. to legal periodicals. Home: 246 Brattle St. Address: Harvard Law School, Cambridge 38, Mass. Died Aug. 16, 1955; buried Burlington, Vt.

POWELL, Warren Thomson, student counselor; b. Delaware, O., Nov. 28, 1884; s. Thomas Edward and Eliza (Thomson) P.; A.B., Ohio State U., 1907, A.M., 1911; B.D., Garrett Bibl. Inst., Evanston, Ill., 1917; post grad. study, Harvard, 1932; m. Helen Hays, June 15, 1913 (died Dec. 1918); m. 2d, Marie Cole, Feb. 4, 1922. Tchr. in Japanese govt. sch., 1908; instr. in English, U. of Minn., 1911-14; asso. dir., later dir. young people's work for Bd. of Edn., M.E. Ch., 1920-28; dir. student counseling and religious activities, Boston U., 1929—. Served as chaplain U.S. Army, 1918-19, World War I. Mem. exec. com. for Fgn. Students of Greater Boston; mem. Coll. Profs. of Internat. Council of Religious Edn., Am. Assn. Univ. Profs., Nat. Vocational Guidance Assn., Am. Coll. Personnel Assn., Delta Tau Delta. Author: Recreational Leadership in Church and Community, 1923; also brochures on work among young people. Editor: Recreation in Church and Community, 1938. Home: Independence Road, Concord, Mass. Address: Boston University, Boston. Died Dec. 28, 1946.

POWER, Frank W., newspaperman; b. Halifax, N.S., Can., Mar. 26, 1886; s. William Joseph and Mary E. (McCormack) P.; student pub. schs.; m. Fanny D. Woodill, Sept. 30, 1913; 1 dau., Mary Frances. Engaged in newspaper promotion work to 1922; with Times Pub. Co., Tacoma, 1922—, pres., 1938-48. Catholic. K.C. Clubs: Tacoma, Serra, Washington States Press (Seattle). Home: 1231 N. Prospect St. Office: Times Pub. Co., Tacoma. Deceased.

POWER, Howard Anderson, obstetrician, gynecologist; b. Pittsburgh, Aug. 10, 1893; s. Howard S. and Nancy (Anderson) P.; B.S., U. of Pittsburgh, 1918, M.D., 1920; m. Monna Elms, Aug. 29, 1922. Interne Mercy Hosp., Pittsburgh, 1920-21; instr. obstetrics, U. Pittsburgh, 1921-30, asst. prof., 1920-33, prof. of obstetrics, 1948—, chmn. dept. of obstet. and gynecol., 1950—; sr. staff obstetrician, Magee Hosp.; mem. cons. staff Montefiore Hosp., South Side Hosp., Alleghany Valley Hosp. Diplomate Am. Bd. Obstetrics and Gynecology. Fellow Am. Coll. Surgeons, A.M.A.; mem. Allegheny County Med. Soc., Pittsburgh Obstet. and Gynecol. Soc. (pres.), Pittsburgh Acad. Med. Clubs: Oakmont Country, Farmington Country, Pinehurst Country. Contbg. editor Pa. Med. Jour. Contbr. numerous articles to med. jours. Home: 6847 Juniata Pl., Pitts. 8. Office: 3400 Forbes St., Pitts. 13. Died Sept. 3, 1957.

POWER, Tyrone (Edmund), actor; b. Cincinnati, O., May 5, 1914; s. Frederick Tyrone and Helen Emma (Reaume) P.; ed. Prep. Sch., U. of Dayton, O., 1928-29, St. Xavier and Purcell High Sch., Cincinnati, 1929-31; m. Ann Carpentier, Apr. 23, 1939 (divorced); m. 2d, Linda Christian Jan. 27, 1949 (div.). Extra on tour Shakespearean Repertoire Co., 1931-32; extra in motion pictures, 1932-34; appeared with Leontovitch in "Romance," Blackstone Theatre, Chicago, 1935, with Katherine Cornell in Romeo and Juliet and St. Joan, New York, 1935-36; played in summer stock company, West Falmouth, Mass., 1935; radio artist since 1935; in motion pictures since 1936; played in Lloyd's of London, Thin Ice, Cafe Metropole, Second Fiddle, Second Honeymoon, In Old Chicago, Alexander's Ragtime Band, Suez, Jesse James, Marie Antoinette, Rose of Washington Square, The Rains Came, Daytime Wife, Blood and Sand, A Yank in the R.A.F., The Razor's Edge, Captain from Castile, Prince of Foxes, Rawhide, Diplomatic Courier, Mississippi Gambler, Dark Is Light Enough, Long Gray Line, Eddy Duchin Story, The Sun Also Rises; also appears on TV; and on stage in reading John Brown's Body, 1953. Member of Screen Actors Guild, Actors Equity Assn., American Fed. Radio Artists. Awards: Old Gold Popularity Award, 1937, 38; King of the Movies award, 1938. Catholic. Club: Players (New York). Served in U.S. Marine Corps World War II. Home: 407 N. Rockingham, Los Angeles 24. Office: 20th Century-Fox Pictures, Los Angeles. Died Nov. 15, 1958.

POWERS, John Craig, banker; b. Rochseter, N.Y., July 18, 1869; s. Daniel William and Helen Maria Powers; grad. St. Paul's Sch., 1888; A.B., Harvard, 1892; married, Apr. 4, 1894. Began with Powers Bank, 1892-98; with Fidelity Trust Co., 1898-1919; Rochester (N.Y.) Trust & Safe Deposit Co., 1919-45; Lincoln Rochester Trust Co., 1945—; dir. Rochester Gas & Electric Corp., Rochester Telephone Co., Rochester Savings Bank, Rochester Gen. Hosp. Treas. Church House, Rochester Childrens Nursery. Republican. Episcopalian. Clubs: Genesee Valley, Rochester Country; Harvard (New York). Home: 700 East Av., Rochester 7. Office: Lincoln Rochester Trust Co., 5 Main St. W., Rochester, N.Y. Died Sept. 12, 1955; buried Mt. Hope Cemetery, Rochester.

POWERS, Leon Walter, lawyer; b. Webster County, Ia., June 12, 1888; s. Walter and Katherine (McIntire) P.; A.B., State U. Ia., 1912; J.D., U. Chgo., 1914; m. Blanid Lally, June 28, 1916 (dec. 1954); children—Mary, Genevieve, James, Walter (dec. 1947). Admitted to Ia. bar, 1914, and practiced in Denison; mem. Conner & Powers, 1914-24, Powers & Gilchrist, 1928-34; mem. Ia. Legislature, 1919-22; judge Supreme Court of Iowa, 1934-36; gen. counsel Farm Credit Adminstrn. of Omaha; 1936-43; chmn. bd. dirs. Fed. Land Bank, Fed. Intermediate Credit Bank, Bank of Co-op. Production Credit Corp. all of Omaha, 1936-43; now practicing law with law firm Powers & Reimer, Dennison, Iowa. Mem. mil. tribunal, Nurnberg, Germany, 1947-48. Del. to Dem. nat. conv., 1924-32, 44. Mem. Am. and Ia. State bar assns. Democrat. Catholic. Address: Denison, Ia. Died Jan. 7, 1959.

POWERS, Tom (Thomas McCreery), actor; b. Owensboro, Ky., July 7, 1890; s. Joshua Devere and Clara (Hawes) P.; student pub. schs.; m. Meta Janney, Sept. 7, 1929. First stage appearance at Lancaster, Pa., 1910; has appeared in more than 150 plays in U.S. and London; mem. Theatre Guild Co., 1926-37; starred in Mile a Minute Kendall, Ole Boy, First Fifty Years, Apple Cart, He, Julius Caesar; appeared in When We Are Married, 1940; Fledgling, 1941; has conducted Life Studies program over NBC network, 1935—. Wrote and broadcast That's Not New York, 1940-41; played in Three Sisters, 1942-43; came to Hollywood, 1943, appeared in pictures for various companies; still acts in pictures. Served as flight lt. British R.A.F., 1916-18. Club: Players (N.Y.C.). Author: Need, 1930; Scotch Circus, 1933; Life Studies, 1939; Virgin with Butterflies, 1945; Sheba on Trampled Grass, 1946; The Flood Is Spent, He Knew Them All (in press). Home: Manhattan Beach, Cal. Died Nov. 9, 1955.*

POWLEY, N(ed) R(ansom) (pow'lē), ex-chmn. dirs. Pacific Telephone and Telegraph Co.; b. Clarkson, N.Y., Oct. 19, 1885; s. William and Mary Catherine (Ransom) P.; A.B., Amherst Coll., 1908; m. Hazel E. Bone, July 12, 1919; children—June Frances (Mrs. Andrew David Thomas) (dec.), Ned Ransom II. With American T. & T. Co., Boston and N.Y.C., 1908-12; Pacific Q. & Q. Co., 1912—, rate engr. San Francisco, 1912-19; comml. supt. Southern Calif. Telephone Co., Los Angeles (subsidiary of Pacific Telephone & Telegraph Co.), 1919-25, v.p. and gen. mgr., 1925-28, dir., 1924-47; v.p. in charge operations, Pacific Telephone and Telegraph Co., San Francisco, 1928-30, dir., 1928-—, 1st v.p., 1930-35; pres., 1935-47, chmn. bd., 1947-50; pres. So. Calif. Telephone Co., Bell Tele. Co. of Nevada, 1935-47; chmn. bd. dirs. Southern Calif. Tele. Co. Jan.-Mar. 1947 (company ceased business); chmn. board Bell Telephone Company of Nevada, 1947-50. Mem. bd. trustees, Mills Coll., 1944—; dir. San Francisco C. of C., 1929-30, 1932-38; president Telephone Pioneers of America, 1941. Mem. California Historical Soc., Psi Chi. Republican. Baptist. Clubs: Pacific Union (San Francisco); University, Amherst (N.Y.); Burlingame Country (Burlingame, Calif.). Home: 315 Arden Rd., Hillsborough, Cal. Died Dec. 18, 1956.

POYNTER, Charles William McCorkle (point'ẽr), anatomist, anthropologist; b. Eureka, Ill., July 16, 1875; s. William Amos and Maria Josephine (McCorkle) P.; B.S., U. Neb., 1898, M.D., 1902; grad. study Vienna, Austria, 1907-08, Harvard, 1912, 14; m. Clara Eliza Axtell, Sept. 3, 1907; 1 dau., Helen Josephine. Instr. in anatomy U. Neb., 1903-10, prof., 1910—, charge dept., 1912-14, head prof., 1914—, apptd. acting dean Coll. of Medicine, 1929, dean, 1930-46, dean emeritus, 1946—. Trustee Omaha Child Savings Inst.; mem. exec. com., bd. Trustees Children's Meml. Hosp., Omaha. Fellow A.A.A.S. (sec. med. sect. 1930-33); mem. Am. Assn. Med. Colls. (v.p. 1934, exec. com. 1935, pres. 1941-44, Am. Assn. Anatomists, Am. Assn. Anthropologists, British Assn. Anatomists, Sigma Xi, Alpha Omega Alpha, Phi Rho Sigma. Republican. Episcopalian. Mason. Writer of papers on growth phenomenon, blood vessels and lymphatics. Home: 625 S. 37th St., Omaha, Neb. Died Oct. 25, 1950.

POYNTER, Paul, newspaper pub.; b. Eminence, Ind., Mar. 29, 1875; s. Jesse A. and Letitia (Bennett) P.; A.B., DePauw U., 1897; m. Alice Wilkey, Apr. 11, 1900; children—Eleanor Allen, Nelson Paul.

Began as pub. Sullivan (Ind.) Democrat, 1897; pub. Sullivan Daily Times; publisher St. Petersburg (Fla.) Daily Times; pres. Times Pub. Co. (St. Petersburg). Mem. Delta Upsilon. Democrat. Christian Scientist. Mason, Elk. Home: 200 Brightwater Blvd. Address: The Times, St. Petersburg, Fla. Died Nov. 21, 1950; buried Sullivan, Ind.

PRATT, Agnes Edwards Rothery (Mrs. Harry Rogers Pratt), author; b. Brookline, Mass.; d. John Jay Elmendorf and Rosamond Dale (Pentecost) Rothery; B A., Wellesley, 1909; spl. course in English, Radcliffe, 1912; m. Harry Rogers Pratt, Sept. 24, 1917. Began in editorial work on Ladies' Home Journal, 1909; became editor woman's page, Boston Herald, later lit. editor same paper, contbg. many popular essays under title "Agnes Edwards' Morning Talks"; contbg. editor Youth's Companion and the House Beautiful. Lecturer on lit. subjects. Author: Our Common Road, 1913; The House of Friendship, 1915; The Romantic Shore, 1915; A Garden Rosary, 1917; Cape Cod, New and Old, 1918; The Old Coast Road from Boston to Plymouth, 1921; Miss Coolidge—A Play, 1922; The House by the Windmill, 1923; The High Altar, 1924; New Roads in Old Virginia, 1929; Central America and the Spanish Main, 1929; South America, West Coast and East, 1930; Into What Port?, 1931; Sweden, the Land and the People, 1934; Images of Earth, Guatemala, 1934; Finland—The New Nation; Denmark—Kingdom of Reason; Norway: Changing and Changleless; The New Dominion of Virginia, 1940; South American Round-about 1940; Washington Round about 1942; Family Album, 1942; A Fitting Habitation, 1944; Ports of British Columbia, 1943; Central American Round-about, 1945; Scandinavian Round-about, 1946; Balm of Gilead, 1946; Round-about Maryland and Virginia, 1947; Iceland, New World Outpost, 1948; Iceland Round-about, 1948; The Joyful Gardener, 1949; Houses Virginians Have Loved, 1954. Writes under the name of Agnes Rothery. Contbr. to mags. and newspapers. Home: Rothery Rd., Charlottesville, Va. Died Aug. 11, 1954; buried U. Va. Cemetery.

PRATT, Charles, ex-chmn. Pratt Inst.; b. Bklyn., N.Y., Oct. 13, 1892; s. Frederic Bayley and Caroline Ames (Ladd) P.; grad. Westminster Sch., Simsbury, Conn., 1912; A.B., Yale, 1916; LL.D., Pratt Institute, 1955; married to Catharine Mumford, January 20, 1917; children—Caroline, Anne Mumford, Charles. Asst. to sec., Pratt Inst., Brooklyn, 1919-23, sec. bd. trustees, 1923-37, exec. dir., pres., 1937-53, chmn. bd., 1953-55, pres. emeritus; partner Charles Pratt & Company, private bankers; trustee Bklyn. Savs. Bank. Trustee N.Y. Pub. Library. With War Trade Intelligence Bur., Wash., D.C., 1917-19. Trustee Brooklyn Inst. Arts and Sciences. Mem. Delta Kappa Epsilon. Republican. Presbyterian. Clubs: Racquet and Tennis, Brook, Century Association (N.Y. City); Piping Rock (Locust Valley, N.Y.). Home: Glen Cove, N.Y. Died Jan. 7, 1956.

PRATT, Charles C., ex-congressman; b. New Milford, Pa., Apr. 23, 1854; s. Ezra A. and Mary (Fink) P.; ed. Sedgwick Inst. Great Barrington, Mass., State Normal Sch., Bloomsburg, Pa.; m. Lillie B. Goff, July 15, 1878; children—Harriette Louise, Ezra Goff, Grace Isabelle, Helen Lee. Pres. Susquehanna Oil Co.; v.-p. Cayuga Lake Cement Co.; treas. Ensign Lumber Co.; dir. First Nat. Bank (Binghamton, N.Y.), Electric Light & Power Co. (New Milford). Mem. 61st Congress (1909-11), 14th Pa. Dist.; Republican. Mem. staffs of Gov's. Stone and Pennypacker, of Pa. Address: New Milford, Pa. Died Jan. 27, 1916.

PRATT, Charles Henry, clergyman, educator; b. Saltville, Va., Jan. 20, 1881; s. Capt. John Marion and Hettie Virginia (McCready) P.; A.B., King Coll., Bristol, Tenn., 1902, D.D., 1918, LL.D., 1922; B.D., Union Theol. Sem., Richmond, Va., 1905; M.A., Princeton, 1907; Ph.D., So. Bapt. Theol. Sem., 1933; m. Pattie Foster Ward, June 7, 1905; children—Charles McCready, Lanier Ward, Pattie Virginia, Ellen, Mary Elizabeth. Ordained ministry Presbyn. Ch. in U.S., 1905; various pastorates until 1920, Trinity Presbyn. Ch., Montgomery, Ala., 1920-24; prof. mission, Presbyn. Theol. Sem., Louisville, 1924. Sec. Foreign Mission Bd., Presbyn. Ch. in U.S., 1918-21; orginator of Inter-Ch. World movement, 1918. Author various published addresses before missionary convs. and articles in Union Sem. Rev., etc. Home: 1576 Parsons Pl. Address: 109 E. Broadway, Louisville. Died Jan. 26, 1950.

PRATT, Fletcher, author; b. Buffalo, N.Y., Apr. 25, 1897; s. Robert Murray and Alice (Horton) P.; student Hobart Coll., 1915-16, U. of Paris (France), 1931-33; m. Inga Stephens. Librarian, 1916-20; newspaper reporter, 1920-23; free lance magazine writer and author since 1923. Served with War Library Service during World War I. Republican. Christian Scientist. Clubs: Authors (pres. 1941), Trap Door Spiders (N.Y.C.). Author: The Heroic Years, 1934; Ordeal by Fire, 1935; The Cunning Mulatto, 1935; Hail, Caesar, 1936; The Navy—a History, 1938; Secret and Urgent, 1939; Road to Empire, 1939; Sea Power and Today's War, 1939; America and Total War, 1941; Fletcher Pratt's Naval War Game, 1940; What the Citizen Should Know About Modern War, 1943; The Navy's War, 1944; Short History of the Army and Navy, 1944; Empire and the Sea, 1945; Night Work, 1946; Fleet Against Japan, 1946; The Marines' War, 1947; The Empire and the Glory, 1949; Eleven Generals, 1949; The Third King, 1950; War for the World, 1950; Preble's Boys, 1950; Double in Space, 1951; Double Jeopardy, 1952; E. M. Stanton, 1953; Undying Fire, 1953; The Blue Star, 1953; (with Thomas M. Johnson) The Lost Battalion, 1938; (with L. Sprague de Camp) The Incomplete Enchanter, 1941, Land of Unreason, 1942, The Carnelian Cube, 1948, Castle of Iron, 1950; (with L. A. Abercrombie) My Life to the Destroyers, 1945; (with Robeson Bailey) A Man and His Meals, 1946. Home: 110 Portland Rd., Highlands, N.J. Died June 10, 1956.

PRATT, Frank Randall, ret. educator; b. Warsaw, N.Y., Apr. 19, 1876; s. Addison Warren and Lucy Arlett (Lathrop) P.; grad. high sch., Warsaw, 1895, Tchrs. Tng. Class, 1897; B.Sc. with first honor, Rutgers, 1906, M.Sc., 1908; Ph.D., Princeton, 1917; m. Lottie Emeline Morey, July 6, 1911. Tchr. pub. schs. until 1903; with Rutgers Coll., 1903-46, instr. physics, 1910-12, asst. prof., 1912-17, asso. prof., 1917-21, prof., 1921-46; head dept. of physics N.J. Coll. for Women (Rutgers U.), 1927-46. Tchr. physics S.A.T.C., Rutgers Coll., World War I; apptd. coöperating expert by NRC, 1923. Fellow A.A.A.S.; mem. Am. Physical Soc., New Brunswick Sci. Soc., Alumni Assn. Rutgers U., Phi Beta Kappa, Sigma Xi, Pi Kappa Alpha; charter mem. Am. Assn. Physics Teachers. Republican. Baptist (deacon). Mason. Contbr. exptl. articles to mags. Home: 41 N. 7th Av., Highland Park, N.J. Died Feb. 25, 1954; buried Warsaw, N.Y.

PRATT, Frederick Haven, physiologist; b. Worcester, Mass., July 19, 1873; s. Frederick Sumner and Sarah M. (Hilliard) P.; student Fish and Dalzell Prep. schools, 1887-92; A.B., Harvard, 1896, A.M., 1898, M.D., 1906; student U. of Göttingen, 1899; m. Margery Wilerd Davis, June 12, 1912; children—Frederick Sumner, Margery Willard (Mrs. James C. Koren), Roger Conant, Elisabeth Haven (Mrs. George Cheely), Stephen Davis. Instructor in physiology, Wellesley Coll., 1909-12; prof. of physiology, Univ. of Buffalo, 1912-19; hon. fellow in biology, Clark U., 1919-20; teaching fellow in physiolgy, Harvard, 1920-21; prof. of physiology, Boston U., 1921-42, emeritus prof. since 1942. Hon. mem. Mass. Med. Soc. Fellow Am. Acad. Arts and Sciences (librarian 1941-48); mem. Am. Physiol. Soc., Soc. Exptl. Biology and Medicine, Am. Antiquarian Soc., Marine Biol. Lab., Woods Hole, Bermuda Biol. Sta. Author technical papers on muscle and heart physiology; biographical studies. Home: 105 Hundreds Rd., Wellesley Hills, Mass. Died July 11, 1958; buried Worcester, Mass.

PRATT, George K., psychiatrist; b. Detroit, Mich., Dec. 17, 1891; s. George Oscar (M.D.) and Alice Elizabeth (Beedzler) P.; M.D., Detroit Coll. Medicine and Surgery, 1915; grad. study, State Psychopathic Hosp., U. of Mich., 1917; m. Neva Emma MacArthur, Dec. 30, 1916; children—Shirley Jane (Mrs. Carleton W. Clark), Rodney George, Douglas MacArthur. Asst. physician Oak Grove Hosp., Flint, Mich., 1915-20; capt. U.S. Army Medical Corps, Neuro-Psychiatric Div., 1917-19; in private practice and asst. health officer, Flint, 1920-21; med. dir. Mass. Soc. for Mental Hygiene, 1921-25; also in out-patient dept. Boston Psychopathic Hosp., 1921-25; lecturer in mental hygiene, Smith Coll., 1923-25; asst. med. dir. Nat. Com. for Mental Hygiene, New York, 1925-33; med. dir. Mental Hygiene Com. N.Y., State Charities Aid Assn., 1930-35, and Conn. Society for Mental Hygiene, 1936-42; consultant mental hygiene, U. of Vt., 1925-29; grad. study psychoanalytic therapy, Europe, 1926; mem. faculty New Sch. for Social Research, N.Y. City, 1930-33, and Brooklyn Inst. Arts and Sciences; consultant in psychiatry, St. Christopher's School, Dobbs Ferry, N.Y., 1932-36 and since 1942; assistant clinical professor of psychiatry and mental hygiene, School of Medicine, Yale, 1936-43; psychiatric director Stamford Child Guidance Service, also Bridgeport Mental Hygiene Clinic, 1936-1947; instr. Mental Hygiene, New Haven State Teachers Coll., 1939-42. Nat. chmn. mental hygiene, Congress of Parents and Teachers, 1926-34; chmn. tech. advisory com. Emergency Work Bur., N.Y. City, 1933. Consultant in psychiatry Med. Adv. Bd. No. 5, Fairfield County, Selective Service System; psychiatric examiner, Induction Center, New Haven, 1943-46; associate neuro-psychiatrist, Bridgeport Hospital; medical director Hall-Brooke Sanitarium, 1948-54. Diplomate Am. Board of Psychiatry and Neurology. Fellow American Psychiatric Association, also Royal Medico-Psychological Assn. Great Britain, Connecticut State and Fairfield County med. socs. Nu Sigma Nu. Author: Your Mind and You, 1924; Why Men Fail (with others), 1928; Our Neurotic Age (with others), 1932; Morale; the Mental Hygiene of Unemployment, 1933; Three Family Narratives, 1935; Soldier to Civilian, 1944. Contbr. tech. articles. Home: Woods Grove, Westport, Conn. Office: 881 Lafayette St., Bridgeport 4, Conn. Died Dec. 11, 1957; buried Westport, Conn.

PRATT, Harry Edward, historian; b. Cambridge, Ill., Dec. 16, 1901; s. Edward and Katie (Hall) P.; B.S., U. of Ill., 1923, M.S., 1927, Ph.D., 1930; Lincoln Diploma of Honor, Lincoln Memorial University; Litt.D., Lincoln College, 1954; married Yordie Lind, July 3, 1927 (died Sept. 3, 1949); 1 dau., Patty Ellen (Mrs. Devere R. Boyd); m. 2d Marion D. Bonzi, Oct. 1, 1950. Teacher high sch., Athens, O., 1923-24; dir. student enterprises Moraine Park Sch., Dayton, 1924-26; sr. master Valley Ranch Sch., Cody, Wyo., 1926-28; dean Blackburn Coll., Carlinville, Ill., 1930-34; prof. history Ill. Wesleyan U., 1934-36; exec. sec. Abraham Lincoln Assn., Springfield, 1936-43; prof. history Ball State Teachers Coll., Muncie, Ind., 1943-44; with Sears, Roebuck & Co., Beloit, Wis., 1944-45, Muskegon, Mich., 1946-50; state historian Ill. State Hist. Library since 1950. Mem. Miss. Valley, Am. Hist. associations, Ill. State Historical Society (secretary-treasurer, 1950—; editor of Journal), American Association State and Local History, Illinois Library Association, The Manuscript Society, and Sigma Pi. Methodist. Author: The Personal Finances of Abraham Lincoln, 1943; Lincoln, 1809-1839, 1939; Lincoln, 1840-1846, 1941; Concerning Mr. Lincoln, 1944. Author articles on Lincoln & history of Ill. in hist. publs. Address: Ill. State Hist. Library, Centennial bldg. Home: 1821 S. 7th St., Springfield, Ill. Died Feb. 12, 1956; buried Oak Ridge, Cemetery, Springfield.

PRATT, Harry Emerson, ret. U.S. dist. judge; b. Norton, Kan., Jan. 26, 1884; s. Louis K. and Lyde (Donaldson) P.; A.B., U. of Colo., 1907. LL.B., 1909; m. Helen B. Baker Aug. 17, 1927; children—Octavia Theron, (Mrs. Edmund O. Hansen), Andrea (Mrs. David L. West). Admitted to Alaska bar, 1909; and practiced in Fairbanks, 1909, 1912-19, and since 1923; practiced in Pueblo, Colo., 1910-11, Eastland, Tex., 1919-22; asst. U.S. atty., 4th Div., Alaska, 1915-18; territorial senator, 1925-29; U.S. dist. judge, Ter. of Alaska, 1935-56. Democrat. Home: 7007 Katchina Circle, Tucson, Ariz. Died Dec. 14, 1957. Cremated.

PRATT, Harry Rogers, teacher; b. Wellesley Hills, Mass., Jan. 7, 1884; s. Daniel Sharp Pratt and Annie Fearing (Brigham) P.; spl. student Harvard, 1902-05; studied composition with Percy Goetschius and George W. Chadwick; m. Agnes Rothery, Sept. 24, 1917. Actor (as Henry Fearing) with Richard Mansfield, Sir Philip Ben Greet, Charles Coburn, David Belasco; asst. prof. music, U. Va., 1923-27, organized sch. of dramatic art, 1927 (now sch. of speech and drama), asso. prof. since 1927; instr. in air navigation and Am. history, Naval Units, U. Va., 1943-45; lecturer in theory and history of music, U. Cal., summers 1926, 28, U. Ore., summer 1937; dir. U. Va. Glee Club, 1932-43; former dir. (now chmn.) The Virginia Players. Democrat. Roman Cath. Contbr. to mags. and newspapers. Home: University Station, Charlottesville, Va. Died May 1956.

PRATT, Orville Clyde, educator; b. Marion, Ind., Jan. 19, 1873; s. Joseph and Dora A. (Hawley) P.; Ph.B., DePauw U., 1895, LL.D., 1937; studied summers at Columbia, Ind. U., U. Chgo.; m. Martha A. Riley, July 1, 1899 (dec.); 1 son, Reginald John; m. 2d, Laura L. Smith, Dec. 29, 1934. Prin. high sch., Danville, Ind., 1895-97; supt. schs., Danville, 1897-1907, Clinton, Ind., 1907-11, Wabash, Ind., 1911-15; head dept. of edn., DePauw U., 1915-16; supt. schs., Spokane, Wash., 1916-43. Cons. Nat. Survey of Sch. Finance. Mem. N.E.A. (pres., 1936-37, v.p., mem. exec. com., 1937-38, com. investigating adminstrv. practices N.Y.C. 1944, Chgo. 1945, Wash. State dir., 1933), Inland Empire Edn. Assn., (pres. 1920-21), Wash. Edn. Assn. (pres. 1930-31). Author: The Story of Spokane. Contbr. to ednl. mags. Home: S. 1303 Grand Blvd., Spokane 10. Deceased.

PRATT, Richardson, business exec.; born Glen Cove, N.Y., June 16, 1894; s. Charles M. and Mary Seymour (Morris) P.; B.A., Amherst Coll., 1915, m. Laura Parsons, Nov. 9, 1917; children—Mary (Mrs. C. M. Barringer), Richardson. Began with Standard Oil Co., N.J., 1919-45; dir. U.S. Trust Co. since 1951; partner Charles Pratt & Co. since 1925; trustee Bklyn. Savs. Bank. Trustee and chmn. bd. Pratt Inst.; trustee and sec. Am. Acad. in Rome; trustee St. Luke's Hosp., N.Y.C., Amherst Coll.; chmn. bd. trustees YWCA of N.Y. Home: Glen Cove, N.Y. Office: 26 Broadway, N.Y.C. Died Aug. 16, 1959.

PRATT, Stewart Camden, banker; b. Washington, D.C., Sept. 30, 1885; s. James Calcott and Margaret Stewart (Johnston) P.; student Trinity Coll., 1904; LL.B., U. of Pa., 1907; m. Geraldine Fleshman Graham, June 20, 1936; 1 dau., Ann Leigh Graham. Admitted to N.Y. Bar, 1908; asso. with law firm, Winthrop & Stimson, New York, N.Y., 1907-09; asst. gen. counsel, Lehigh Valley R.R. Co., 1910-17; partner, Cobe & Pratt, investments, 1920-24; asst. to pres., Farmers Loan & Trust Co., 1925-29; v.p., The Nat. City Bank of N.Y. and City Bank Farmers Trust Co., N.Y. City, 1929-50. Chmn., rep. N.Y. banks to negotiate with German govt. settlement of payments due on German dollar bonds outstanding in U.S., exclusive of Young and Dawes loans, 1935-39.

Served as maj., U.S. Army, on duty with storage officer for Port of New York, 1918-19. Mem. Delta Kappa Epsilon, Phi Delta Phi. Clubs: Union (N.Y. City). Home: Bleak Hill Farm, Culpepper, Va. Died June 14, 1951.

PRATT, William Veazie, naval officer; b. Belfast, Me., Feb. 28, 1869; s. Nichols and Abigail Jane (Veazie) P.; grad. U.S. Naval Acad., 1889; m. Louise Johnson, Apr. 15, 1902; 1 son, William Veazie. Ensign, July 1, 1891; promoted through grades to rear adm., June 3, 1921; served on Atlanta and Chicago in White Squadron, 1889-91; on U.S.S. Petrel, 1891-95; at U.S. Naval Acad., 1895-97; on Mayflower, Spanish-Am. War 1898; on U.S.S. Newark, Bennington, Monterey, 1898-1900; at Naval Acad., 1900-02; navigator Kearsarge, flagship Atlantic Fleet, 1902-05; at U.S. Naval Acad., 1905-06, 1906-08; navigator Newark, 1906; exec. officer St. Louis, 1908-10, California, 1910; at Naval War Coll., Newport, R.I., 1911-13; on staff of comdr. Torpedo Flotilla, Atlantic Fleet, and comdg. U.S.S. Birmingham, 1913-15; duty Panama, Canal Zone, 1915-16; at Army War Coll., Washington, D.C., 1916-17; duty Office Chief of Naval Operations, Navy Dept., May 1917; asst. chief of naval operations, Aug. 1917-Jan. 1919; accompanied President Wilson on trip to France, Dec. 1918; comdg. U.S.S. New York, 1919-20; commanding destroyer force, Pacific Fleet, 1920-21; duty with General Board U.S. Navy, 1921-23; naval expert asst. to Am. Commn. at Washington Conf. on Limitation of Armaments, 1921-22; comdg. Battleship Div. 4, Battle Fleet, 1923-25; spl. duty with Gen. Bd. U.S. Navy, June-Sept. 1925; pres. Naval War Coll., 1925-27; apptd. comdr. Battleship Divisions, Battle Fleet, with rank of vice admiral, Sept. 1927; comdr. in chief Battle Fleet, 1928-29; comdr. in chief U.S. Fleet, 1929-30, with rank of admiral; naval advisor to Am. delegation at London Conf., 1930; chief of naval operations, Sept. 17, 1930-July 1, 1933; became adm. on retired list Aug. 14, 1938; recalled to active duty, Jan. 6, 1941, and returned to inactive status July 1941. Associate editor Newsweek, 1940. Decorations: service medals of Spanish-Am. War, Philippine Insurrection, Boxer Insurrection; D.S.M. (Navy and Army); Grand Officer Legion of Honor (France); Order of El Merito (Chile). Home: Belfast, Me. Died Nov. 25, 1957; buried Family Mausoleum, Grove Cemetery, Belfast.

PREBLE, Edward A., naturalist; b. Somerville, Mass., June 11, 1871; s. Edward Perkins and Marcia (Alexander) P.; ed. high sch., Woburn, Mass., 1886-89; m. Eva A. Lynham, Dec. 29, 1896; children—Dorothy Marcia (dec.), Marjorie Elizabeth, Evelyn Morgan. With Biol. Survey, U.S. Dept. Agr., 1892-1935. Has specialized in geog. distbn., life habits, and ecology of birds, mammals and plants. Established wild life sanctuary and library, Ossipee, N.H. Member Am. Ornithologists Union, Biological Soc. Washington, Am. Soc. Mammalogist, Am. Soc. Ichthyologists and Herpetologists, etc. Associate editor Nature Mag., Washington. Republican. Author: A Biological Investigation of the Hudson Bay Region (U. S. Govt. publ.), 1902, A Biological Investigation of the Athabaska-Mackenzie Region, 1908; The Fur Seals and other life of the Pribilof Islands, Alaska, in 1914 (in collaboration), 1915. Birds and Mammals of the Pribilof Islands, Alaska (in collaboration), 1923. Contbr. many sci. and popular articles. Home: 3027 Newark St., Washington. Died Oct. 4, 1957; buried Ossipee, N.H.

PRENDERGAST, William A. (prĕn'dĕr-găst); b. New York, May 25, 1867; s. Laurence and Josephine (Keating) P.; LL.D., New York U., 1917; m. Mary Agnes Hull, Oct. 18, 1894; children—Thomas Hull, Eleanor, William A., Jr. Commercial experience until 1899; pres., dir. of New York & Honduras Rosario Mining Co. Active in Republican party; made speech nominating Theodore Roosevelt for President at Progressive National Convention, Chicago, 1912; issued call in New York State for formation of Progressive party. Elected register of Kings County, Nov. 1907; comptroller City of N.Y., 1910-17; chmn. Pub. Service Commn., N.Y., 1921-30. An active supporter of Gov. Hughes in behalf of his administrative and polit. reform measures. Dir. Mont., Wyo. & Southern R.R. Co. Catholic. Pres. (hon.) Pan-Am. Soc. of U.S., Inc. Mem. Am.-Irish Hist. Soc. Clubs: Union League, Bankers, Nat. Republican, Catholic (New York). Author: Credit and Its Uses, 1906 (co-author rev. edit. 1931); Financing the City of New York, 1916. The Extension of Municipal Activities, 1917; Public Utilities and The People, 1933. Home: 1100 Park Av., N.Y.C.; also Lakeville, Conn. Office: 120 Broadway, N.Y.C. 5. Died June 20, 1954; buried Gate of Heaven Cemetery, Hawthorn, N.Y.

PRENTICE, E(zra) Parmalee, lawyer; b. Davenport, Ia., July 29, 1863; s. Sartell and Mary Adeline (Isham) P.; B.A., Amherst, 1885, M.A., 1888, L.H.D., 1940; attended Harvard Law School, 1887-88; LL.D., Olivet (Mich.) Coll., 1911; D.Agr., U. of Neb., 1935; Sc.D., Williams Coll., 1940; m. Alta, d. John D. Rockefeller, 1901. Admitted to Ill. bar, 1886; practiced law, Chicago, 1888-1900, and was gen. counsel Ill. Steel Co., L.S.&Eastern Ry.; mem. Murray, Prentice & Aldrich, N.Y., 1900-24, Maj. U.S. Army, 1918; col. Inf., 1927. Owner of Mount Hope Farm, Williamstown, Mass., to which Dept. Agr. of Mass. awarded a gold medal for agrl. research, 1924. Decorated Comdr. Order of Crown of Italy (for services to Italian agr.), 1934; Order of Civil Merit of Bulgaria (for services to Bulgarian agriculture), 1936. Member of Phi Beta Kappa. Clubs: Chgo. (Chicago); University, Century (New York City); Metropolitan (Washington). Author: The Commerce Clause of the Federal Constitution (with John G. Egan), 1898; Federal Power over Carriers and Corporations, 1907; Breeding Profitable Dairy Cattle, 1935, trans. into Japanese, 1936; Farming for Famine, 1936; Hunger and History, 1939, trans. into Spanish, Argentina, 1946, Mexico, 1947; Am. Dairy Cattle, Their Past and Future, 1942; Food, War and the Future, 1944. Publisher of The Mount Hope Classics, 7 vols., modern stories translated into Latin, by Dr. Arcadius Avellanus. Contbr. to jours. Home: 5 W. 53d St. Office: 15 Broad St., N.Y.C. Died Dec. 16, 1955; buried Manchester, Vt.

PRENTIS, Henning Webb, Jr. (prĕn'tĭs), chmn. bd. Armstrong Cork Co.; b. St. Louis, July 11, 1884; s. Henning Webb and Mary Morton (McNutt) P.; A.B., U. of Mo., 1903; A.M., U. of Cincinnati, 1907; LL.D., Hampden-Sydney Coll., 1932, Grove City Coll., 1939, Franklin and Marshall Coll., 1940, Univ. of Pa., 1943, University of Cincinnati, 1943, Jefferson Medical College (Phila.), 1945; U. of Rochester, 1946, Middlebury (Vt.) Coll., 1946, Temple U., 1949; D.Eng., Lehigh U., 1949; D.C.S., N.Y.U., 1950, LL.D., U. Missouri, 1950, U. Akron, 1952; L.H.D. (hon.), Ursinus Coll., 1951; m. Ida Bernice Cole, Sept. 2, 1909. Sec. to pres. U. of Mo., 1903-05; sec. U. of Cincinnati, 1905-07; with the Armstrong Cork Co., 1907—, asst. mgr. insulation div., Pittsburgh, Pa. 1907-11, organizer, and mgr. advertising dept. of the co., 1911-20, gen. sales mgr. of floor div., 1920-28, elected v.p. and mem. bd. dirs., 1926, 1st v.p., 1929, pres., 1934-50, chmn. bd., 1950—; dir. Mellon Nat. Bank & Trust Co., Pitts., Borden Co., N.Y., Alco Products, Inc., N.Y. Atlantic Refining Company, Philadelphia. Chmn. Pa. Postwar Planning Com.; dep. dir. War Prodn. Bd. (Phila.), 1942; v.p. Pa. War Fund; mem. bus. adv. council U.S. Dept. Commerce; mem. governing body Nat. Indsl. conf. Bd. Mem. Personnel Security Review Bd. A.E.C., 1948-49; mem. Pa. Planning Bd., Commn. on Financing Higher Edn., 1949-52; chmn. Overseas Econ. Operations Task Force, Hoover Commn. Trustee Buchanan Found. Preservation Wheatland (p. pres.), Carnegie Instn. (Wash.), Teachers Ins. and Annuity Assn. Stock, New York, Franklin and Marshall College, also Wilson College, 1937-57, vice pres., 1939-49, president, 1949-57. Decorated Officer Legion of Honor (France), 1954; recipient Henry Lawrence Gantt gold medal American Management Assn. and Am. Society M.E. Nat. Assn. Mfrs. (dir., 1936—, pres. 1940, elected Hon. Vice-President for life 1946), U.S. Chamber of Commerce (former dir.), Am. Soc. Sales Executives, Am. Academy Political and Social Science, Pennsylvania Society of S. R., Donegal Soc., Scotch Irish Soc., Phi Beta Kappa, Sigma Alpha Epsilon, Omicron Delta Kappa, Alpha Delta Sigma, Phi Beta Kappa Assos. Republican. Presbyn. Mason (32°). Clubs: Hamilton, Country (Lancaster); University (N.Y.); Union League (Philadelphia); Cosmos (Washington, D.C.); Ross Mountain Club (New Florence, Pennsylvania); Rolling Rock Club (Ligonier, Pa.); Duquesne (Pitts.). Home: "Yeardley," 151 School Lane. Office: Armstrong Cork Co., Lancaster, Pa. Died Oct. 29, 1959; buried Lancaster, Pa.

PRENTISS, Theodore, retired lawyer; b. Montpelier, Vt., Sept. 10, 1818; s. Samuel and Lucretia P.; academic ed'n; admitted to Vt. bar, 1844; removed, 1845, to Watertown, Wis.; m. Martha J. Perry, Dec. 4, 1855. Mem. 1st Wis. Constitutional Conv., 1846, and the 2d, 1847-8; served in legislature; 1st mayor Watertown and twice mayor later; regent State Univ. Address: Watertown, Wis. Died Aug. 3, 1906.

PRESCOTT, Frederick Clarke, prof. English; b. Salina, Kan., Sept. 29, 1871; s. John H. and Mary (Lee) P.; A.B., Harvard, 1894; grad. student same univ., 1895-97; L.H.D., U. Vt., 1932; m. Katharine Eddy, June 16, 1904 (died Aug. 1947). Asst. in English, Harvard, 1895-97, instr. English, Radcliffe Coll. during same period; asst. prof. English, Cornell U., 1897-1919, prof., 1919-40, prof. emeritus, 1940—. Mem. Kappa Alpha. Author: Poetry and Dreams, 1912; The Poetic Mind, 1922; Poetry and Myth, 1927. Editor: Selections from Jonathan Swift, 1901; Critical Writing of E. A. Poe, 1909; Prose and Poetry of the Revolution, 1923; Introduction to American Prose, 1931; Introduction to American Poetry, 1932; Hamilton and Jefferson, 1934. Home: 2 Grove Pl., Ithaca, N.Y. Died July 26, 1957; buried Geneva, N.Y.

PRESCOTT, John S., vice pres., gen. counsel, sec. and dir. Gen. Foods Corp. Home: 156 Calton Rd., New Rochelle, N.Y. Office: 250 Park Av., N.Y.C. 17. Died May 19, 1949.

PRESTON, Austin Roe, ret. fgn. service officer; b. Buffalo, N.Y., Aug. 9, 1894; s. Austin Roe and Alice Elizabeth (Lewis) P.; student Taft Sch., Watertown, Conn., 1911-14; A.B., Yale, 1918; post grad. U. Edinburgh, Scotland, 1919-20; m. Marjorie Grace Powell, Dec. 17, 1923; children—Austin Roe, Shirley Ann. Began in ins. business N.Y.C., 1920; Am. vice consul Melbourne, Auckland, New Zealand, Tokyo, Japan, 1922-28; consul at Nagoya, Japan, Brisbane, Australia, Kingston, Jamaica, Oslo, Norway; then consul gen. at Lourenco Marques, Mozambique, Antwerp, Belgium, Lahore, Pakistan, Curaçao, N.W. I. Served as sgt. U.S. Army, base hosp. unit 1, Vichy, France, 1917-19. Mem. Zeta Psi. Presbyn. Mason. Address: 294 Bedford Av., Buffalo 16. Died Oct. 10, 1956; buried Buffalo.

PRESTON, Elwyn Greeley, corp. official; b. Burlingame, Kan., Aug. 11, 1866; s. Hiram D. and Emily F. (Greeley) P.; ed. pub. schs. of Nashua, N.H.; m. Emily H. Brown, Oct. 6, 1897; children—Richard G., Jerome, Roger, Elwyn G. With B.&M. R.R., 1883-92; sec. Boston Chamber Commerce, 1892-1905; treas. R. H. White Co., 1905-11; v.p. and director S.S. Pierce Co. since 1911; director John Hancock Life Insurance Co., Boston Safe Deposit & Trust Co., S.S. Pierce Realty Co., West Point Manufacturing Co., Bay State Milling Co., Dixie Cotton Mills. Republican. Congregationalist. Clubs: Union, Algonquin. Home: 4 Bennington Rd., Lexington, Mass. Office: 133 Brookline Av., Boston. Died Dec. 18, 1951.

PRESTON, Guy Henry, army officer; b. in Mass., May 29, 1864; grad. U.S. Mil. Acad., 1888. Commd. add. 2d lt. 1st Cav., June 11, 1888; 2d lt. 9th Cav., July 16, 1888; 1st lt. 4th Cav., Feb. 25, 1896; trans. to 9th Cav., Mar. 14, 1896; maj. 41st Vol. Inf, Aug. 17, 1899; hon. mustered out vols., June 30, 1901; capt. U.S.A., Feb. 2, 1901; trans. to 13th Cav., Aug. 28, 1901; to 8th Cav., Dec. 27, 1911; maj. 4th Cav., Feb. 29, 1912; later trans. to 2d Cav.; lt. col., July 1, 1916; col., May 15, 1917; brig. gen. N.A., Apr. 16, 1918. Organized 4th F.A. Brigade, Camp Greene, N.C., comd. 160th F.A. Brig., Camp Custer, Mich.; sailed with brigade July 31, 1918, to training center, Coetquidan, Brittany; with brigade at front, operations 2d Army, 6th Corps, as corps arty., Oct. 30-Nov. 11, 1918; attached to Provost Marshal Gen.'s Office, Advance G.H.Q., Treves, Germany, Mar. 9-June 12, 1919; hon. discharged as brig. gen., July 15, 1919; col. comdg. 1st Cav., Douglas, Ariz., 1919-20; now comdg. Gen. Intermediate Depot, San Francisco. Address: War Dept., Washington, D.C. Died Dec. 12, 1952.

PRESTON, Howard Hall, educator; born Battle Creek, Ia., May 13, 1885; s. Andrew and Anna Janet (Ferguson) P.; B.S., Coe Coll., 1911, hon. LL.D., 1938; M.A., State U. of Ia., 1914, Ph.D., 1920; m. Lucy Helen Steele, June 12, 1916; children—Frank Steele, Mary Belle (Mrs. Robert H. Wells), Anna Ferguson, Genevieve Howard (dec.), Jean Cora. Instructor economics and sociology, State University of Iowa, 1915-16, University of Tex., 1916-17; asst. prof. econ., Oberlin Coll., 1917-20; asso. prof. econ., U. of Wash., 1920-22, prof., 1922-38, prof. and dean, Coll. of Econ. and Bus., 1938-48, prof. since 1948; lecturer, University of California, 1922; acting professor, Dartmouth College, 1928-29; summer appointments at University of Iowa, 1921, 1923, University of Chicago, 1924, U. of Tex., 1925, U. of Mich., 1928, Stanford U., 1931. Mem. exec. com. Washington State World Commerce Commn., 1944; public panel member War Labor Board, 12th Region, 1943-45. Educational dir. Pacific Coast Banking School. Trustee University Presbyterian Ch.; trustee, treas., Westminster Foundation; mem. board management, Seattle Y.M.C.A. Mem. Pacific Coast Economics Association (v.p., 1929-30; trustee, 1947-49), State Historical Society of Iowa, American Economics Assn., Washington Hist. Soc., Am. Assn. Univ. Prof., Beta Gamma Sigma (nat. exec. com. 1939-42), Beta Alpha Psi. Clubs: Faculty (U. of Wash.), Lion's, China of Seattle (pres.). Author: History of Banking in Iowa. Contbr. professional jours. Mem. editorial bd. Am. Econ. Review, 1934-36. Home: 5026 15th N.E. Office: Univ. of Washington, Seattle 5. Died Sept. 30, 1952; buried Seattle.

PRESTON, Josephine Corliss, educator; b. in Minn., May 26, 1873; d. John Wesley and Josephine (Kinney) Corliss; student Carleton Coll., Northfield, Minn., L.H.D., 1925; Whitman Coll., Walla Walla, Wash., hon. M.A., 1914, life diploma as tchr. by examination, 1904. Began teaching in Minn., 1887; county supt. schs., Walla Walla Co., Wash., 3 terms; apptd. by Gov. M. E. Hay, mem. State Bd. of Edn., 1911; served as state supt. pub. instruction, Wash., 1913-29. Mem. N.E.A. (pres. 1919-20; life mem. and life dir.), Inland Empire Tchrs. Assn., State Federation of Women's Clubs, Am. Assn. Univ. Women, D.A.R.; chmn. rural sect. World Conf. on Edn., San Francisco, 1923; pres. Council of State Supts. and Commrs. of Edn., 1925-26; mem. Nat. Rural Com. of N.E.A. Mem. Rep. Exec. Women's Com., 1918-20. Conglist. Clubs: Art, Educational (Walla Walla). Lectr., 1929—; teaching remedial education, 1937-38. Contbr. series of articles to The

Instructor, 1931-32; School Board Journal, 1934-36. Home: Burton, Vashon Island, Wash. Died Dec. 10, 1958.

PRESTON, Ord, business exec.; b. St. Helena, Cal., Aug. 15, 1874; s. Albert Wm. (col. U.S. Army) and Mary Elizabeth (Ord) P.; grad. Phillips Andover Acad., 1894; A.B., Yale, 1899; m. Frances Jane Converse, June 7, 1902 (died 1911); children—Mary Ord, Eleanor Converse; m. 2d, Carolyn Merritt Murray, Dec. 4, 1912 (died Apr. 30, 1941); children—Arthur Murray, Ord; m. 3d, Margaret Helen Coe, Oct. 14, 1946. Clk. with W. H. Goadby & Co., brokers, N.Y.C., 1900-02; with Neale & Thorne, coal operators, Minerville, Pa., 1903-05; mem. N.Y. Stock Exchange and mem. C. E. Welles & Co., 1905-12; elected dir. Washington Gas Light Co., 1910, pres., 1923-30; dir. Union Trust Co., 1912—, pres., 1932-45, chmn. bd. dirs., 1945-46. Served as maj. AS, U.S. Army, World War I. Republican. Episcopalian. Clubs: Metropolitan, Chevy Chase (Washington); University (N.Y.C.); Tennis and Beach (La Jolla). Home: 7910 Prospect Pl., La Jolla, Cal. Died Feb. 4, 1949.

PRESTON, Roger, merchant; b. Woburn, Mass., June 21, 1900; s. Elwyn G. and Emily H. (Brown) P.; student Phillips Andover Acad., 1917; A.B., Williams Coll., 1922; m. Anita L. Bowditch, Feb. 26, 1927; children—Frederic B., David, Philip. With S.S. Pierce Co., importers and grocers, Boston, since 1922, treas., dir. since 1941, pres. since 1947; v.p., dir. S.S. Pierce Realty Co.; dir. New Eng. Tel. and Tel. Co., Boston Safe Deposit & Trust Co., Plymouth Cordage Co., Nat. Food Products Corp., Colonial Stores, Inc., New Eng. Mutual Life Ins. Co., Gorham Mfg. Co.; trustee Suffolk Savs. Bank. President com. of Permanent Charity Fund. Trustee Northeastern U., South End House. Mem. Gargoyle Soc., Kappa Alpha. Republican. Episcopalian. Clubs: Union (Boston); Williams (N.Y. City); Country (Brookline); University (N.Y.); Commercial Merchants (Boston). Home: 15 Circuit Rd., Chestnut Hill 67, Mass. Office: 133 Brookline Av., Boston 17. Died Nov. 28, 1954; buried Westview Cemetery, Lexington, Mass.

PRESTON, Thomas L., lawyer; b. Richmond, Oct. 25, 1897; s. William Carruthers and Eliza Kennon (Myers) P.; student Episcopal High Sch., 1912-15; B.S., U. Va., 1918, LL.B., 1922; student Harvard Med. Sch., 1919; m. Anne Gordon Brockenbrough, Jan. 6, 1930; children—Mercer B., Edmund R. Admitted to Va. bar, 1922, practiced as asso. W. R. Perkins, N.Y.C., 1923-24; asso. firm of Leake & Buford, Richmond, 1924-28; atty., law dept. C.&O. Ry., Richmond, 1928-33, asst. gen. solicitor, 1933-38, gen. solicitor, 1938-43; gen. solicitor S.A.L. R.R., Norfolk, 1943-45; asst. gen. counsel Assn. Am. R.R.'s, Washington, 1945-46, gen. solicitor, 1947—, now v.p. Commd. 2d lt., F.A., R.O.T.C., 1918. Mem. Am., Va. bar assns., Assn. I.C.C. Practitioners, Phi Beta Kappa, Delta Psi, Raven Soc. Episcopalian. Home: 1522 31st St., Washington 7. Office: Transportation Bldg., Washington 6. Died May 21, 1957.

PRESTON, Thomas Ross, banker; b. Woodbury, Tenn., Nov. 29, 1868; s. Hugh L. and Thankful C. (Doak) P.; grad. Woodbury Acad., 1888; m. Roberta C. Clift, June 5, 1895; children—Mrs. Arwin Preston Lawson, Thomas Ross. Began in employ of Traders Nat. Bank, Tullahoma, Tenn., 1889; removed to Chattanooga, 1889, became clk. in South Chattanooga Savings Bank; an organizer, 1905, chmn. bd., dir. Hamilton Nat. Bank, Chattanooga; pres., dir. Hamilton Nat. Assos., Inc.; dir. Hamilton Nat. Bank (Knoxville), Penn-Dixie Cement Corp., Standard-Coosa-Thatcher Co., N.C.&St.L. R.R., Volunteer State Life Ins. Co., Provident Life & Accident Ins. Co., O. B. Andrews Co., Ross-Meehan Foundries, Crown Cotton Mills (Dalton, Ga.). Candidate for Dem. nomination for gov., 1914. Mem. Am., (pres. 1927-28), Tenn. (past pres.) bankers assns., Dixie Highway Assn. (dir.), Chattanooga, U.S. (past dir.) C.'s of C. Presbyn. Mason. Clubs: Golf and Country, Mountain City. Home: 122 N. Crest Rd., Missionary Ridge. Office: Hamilton Nat. Bank, Chattanooga, Tenn. Died Oct. 30, 1953.

PREUS, Ove J. H., clergyman, educator; b. Spring Prairie, Wis., Jan. 21, 1880; s. Christian K. and Louise A. (Hjort) P.; A.B., Luther Coll., Decorah, Ia., 1901; C.T., Luther Theol. Sem., St. Paul, 1904; studied Johns Hopkins, 1904-05; J.D., Southwestern U., Los Angeles, 1917; D.D. honoris causa, Augustana Coll., Sioux Falls, S.D., 1948; m. Magdalene Forde, June 30, 1908; children—Christian, Nora, Paul G., Nelson F., David W., Ove J. H. Ordained ministry Lutheran Ch., 1905; pastor Tacoma, 1905-11, Los Angeles, 1911-17, Beloit, Wis., 1917-18, De Forest, Wis., 1918-28; dist. pres., 1926-29; pres. Augustana Coll., 1929-32; pres. Luther Coll., 1932-48, pres. emeritus, also prof. of Bible and Norse culture, since 1948. Republican. Home: 408 High St., Decorah, Ia. Died Feb. 13, 1951; buried, Decorah, Ia.

PREUSS, Lawrence (prois), polit. scientist; b. Utica, Ill., May 19, 1905; s. Anton E. and Hermine (Nielsen) P.; A.B., U. Mich., 1927, A.M., 1928, Ph.D., 1932; Faculte de Droit, U. Paris, 1930-31; m. Pauline H. Reinsch, July 11, 1944. Successively instr., asst. prof., asso. prof. polit. sci. U. Mich., 1928-46, prof. polit. sci., 1946—; research asso. Harvard Research in Internat. Law, 1929-40; fellow Carnegie Endowment for Internat. Peace, 1931-32, Social Sci. Research Council, 1933-34; lectr. Acad. de Droit Internat. a la Haye, 1949; officer Dept. of State, 1942-45, asst. chief div. internat. orgn. affairs, 1943-44, asso. chief, 1945. Dep. U.S. rep. U.N. War Crimes Commn., London, 1943-44; asst. sec. Dumbarton Oaks Conversations, 1944; tech. expert U.S. delegation San Francisco Conf. Internat. Orgn., 1945; also prin. sec. UN Com. Jurists. Mem. Am. Polit. Science Assn., Am. Soc. Internat. Law (exec. council 1937-40, 43-46), Phi Beta Kappa. Author: Article 2 (7) of the U.N. Charter and Matters of Domestic Jurisdiction; internat. law, law orgn., polit. theory articles Am. and European profl. jours. Mem. bd. editors Am. Jour. Internat. Law, 1946—. Home: 1709 Ferndale Pl., Ann Arbor. Died July 7, 1956.

PRICE, Andrew, banker; b. Denver, Colo., Feb. 18, 1890; son of John Ewing and Mary D. (Hickman) P.; Yale, 1908-10; married Virginia Wiley, February 2, 1922; children—Andrew IV, Mary Barbara, Virginia (Mrs. Virginia Price Kitchell). Began in investment banking business with father at Seattle, 1910; organizer, with father, John E. Price & Company, 1918, Marine Nat. Bank, 1919, v.p., 1919-25, pres. 1926-28 (consol. with Nat. Bank of Commerce); v.p. and dir. Nat. Bank of Commerce, 1928-32, dir., pres., 1932-48, chmn. since 1948. Organizer Nat. Credit Co., 1925, Marine Central Bank (now Central Branch of National Bank Commerce), 1926; organizer, 1927, since president, director Marine Bancorporation; director Seattle Branch Federal Reserve Bank of San Francisco, 1939-45. Served as lt. Motor Transport Corps. U.S. Army, 1917-18. Trustee, Whitman Coll., Walla Walla, Wash. Mem. National coun., Boy Scouts of America. Mem. Victory Fund Com., 12th Fed. Res. Dist.; chmn. 7th War Loan, King Co. Exec. bd. Boy Scouts America. Member Washington Bankers Assn. (president 1933-34), Am. Bankers Assn. (v.p., Nat. Bank Div., 1939-40, pres. 1940-41; mem. research council 1937-40; mem. adminstrv. com. 1940-41), Assn. of Reserve City Bankers (dir. 1940-43), Clearing House Assn. of Seattle (v.p. 1937-38, pres. 1939-40), Alpha Delta Phi, Phi Delta Phi. Republican. Clubs: Rainier; Country Club of Bainbridge Island. Home: 1815 10th Av. N. Office: Nat. Bank of Commerce, Seattle, Wash. Died July 7, 1955.

PRICE, Burr, editor; b. St. Louis, Mo., July 17, 1888; s. late William Marmaduke and Margaret (McQuillan) P.; ed. pub. and pvt. schs., St. Louis; m. Madeleine Coffee, Nov. 27, 1926; children—Margaret Jane Therese, Thomas Coffee, Catherine Madeleine Hughes, Eleanor Gorsuch. Reporter and sub-editor St. Louis Republic and Globe-Democrat, 1904-10; asst. telegraph editor and asst. night editor New York Herald, 1910-17; editor in charge European edition of the Herald, May 1917-Oct. 1918; corr. at front with Am. armies, in Argonne and on Meuse, Oct.-Dec. 1918; with army on march to and across the Rhine; spl. corr. for Herald at Peace Conf., Paris, Dec. 1918-May 1919; dir. Belgian Economic Press Bur., May-Dec. 1919, in which capacity accompanied King Albert on his Am. tour; spl. corr. in Poland for English papers, 1920; spl. corr. Washinbton Conf. on Limitation of Armament, Agence Telegraphique Belge, 1921-22, dir. of advertising and publicity for Distinctive Pictures Corp., 1923-25; now v.p. Schnell Publishing Co., Inc., and editor National Painters Mag. Author: The World Talks It Over (history of the League of Nations), 1927. Contbr. tech. and practical painting articles to mags. Home: Scarsdale, N.Y. Office: 30 Church St., N.Y.C. 7. Died Mar. 18, 1952.

PRICE, David James, research engr.; b. Ashland, Pa., Mar. 27, 1884; s. James and Anna Jane (Vaughan) P.; B.S. in mining engr., Pa. State Coll., 1925, E.M., 1927; M.S. in engring., George Washington U., 1927; Ph.D., Am. U., 1931; m. Esther Bevan Leib, Sept. 30, 1908; children—David George, Frank Leib. Chainman engring. corps, Lehigh Valley Coal Co., Lost Creek, Pa., 1900-02; mining engr. with H. J. Hinterleitner, Spangler, Pa., 1902-05; resident mining engr. Clearfield Bituminous Coal Corp., Clymer, Pa., 1905-12; asst. mining engr. U.S. Bureau of Mines, Pittsburgh, 1912-14; engr. in charge of dust explosion investigations and development work, Bureau of Chemistry, U.S. Dept. of Agr., Washington, 1914-27; principal engr. in charge chem. engring. research div. Bureau of Chemistry and Soils, 1927-39, and principal chemical engineer in Bureau of Agricultural Chemistry and Engineering and Bureau of Agricultural and Industrial Chemistry since 1939. Dept. Agr. Superior Service Award from Sec. of Agr. Brannan, 1949; hon. life mem. National Fire Waste Council, 1951. Mem. Nat. Fire Protection Assn. (pres. 1942-44; hon. life mem., 1950; mem. dust explosion hazards com., chmn. 1922-42; chmn. farm fire protection com. 1927-45), U.S. Chamber of Commerce (mem. nat. fire waste council), Am. Standards Assn. (as rep. of U.S. Dept. Agr.). Tau Beta Pi, Sigma Gamma Epsilon, Sigma Phi Sigma; hon. mem. Internat. Assn. Fire Chiefs, Internat. Assn. Fire Fighters, Grain Elevator Supts. Assn. of N. America, also firemen's orgns. of several states. Methodist. Mason (32°, Shriner). Author: Dust Explosions, Theory and Nature of Phenomena, Causes and Methods of Prevention (with H. H. Brown and others), 1922; also many bulletins on dust explosions in industrial plants and on farm fires. Contbr. to Nat. Fire Protection Assn. Quarterly and other jours. Nat. authority on dust explosion prevention, farm and rural community fire prevention and indsl. utilization of agrl. products. Home: 701 Whittier St. N.W. Office: U.S. Dept. of Agriculture, Washington. Died May 28, 1951; buried Cedar Hill Cemetery, Suitland, Md.

PRICE, Franklin Haines, librarian; b. Phila., July 3, 1882; s. Dr. Ferris Thomas and Mary Pine (Haines) P.; student Palms Bus. Coll., Phila., 1898, Pa. Sch. of Indstl. Arts, 1906-07, 1912; Master of Letters, U. Pa., 1952; m. Alice H. Howe, Apr. 28, 1906; children—Franklin Haines, Jr., Alison Howe, Lewis Hall. Began as asst. Free Library of Phila., 1899, head of dept., 1906-10, in charge of spl. collections, 1911-25, asst. librarian, 1926-34, librarian, 1934—; librarian, Jefferson Med. Coll., 1901; supervisor A.L.A. War Service, Phila. dist., 1918-19, Am. Merchant Marine Library Assn., Port Phila., 1919-20. Received The Phila. Award, bronze medal and $10,000, 1951. Mem. Am., Pa. library assns., Booksellers' Assn. of Phila., Pa. Library Club. Spl. Libraries Council of Phila., Mus. Coun. of Phila. Rep. Epis. Clubs: Philobiblon, Rotary. Home: Earle's Lane and Sawmill Rd., Newtown Sq., Pa. Died Jan. 7, 1958; buried Woodland Cemetery, Phila.

PRICE, George Merriman, surgeon, educator; b. Liverpool, N.Y., Mar. 3, 1865; s. George Tayler and Emily H. (Merriman) P.; M.D., Syracuse U., 1886; post-grad. study, London and Vienna hosps., 1887; m. Nettie Belle Reese, Jan. 19, 1888 (died Apr., 1938) children—James Reese, Emily Henrietta (Mrs. H. Clifford Fulmer, M.D.), Letitia Elizabeth (Mrs. Dana Reed Bellows), Willis Henry, George Tayler; m. 2d, Minnie Elizabeth Coble, Nov. 11, 1938. Began practice at Syracuse, 1886; mem. faculty Syracuse U. Med. Coll., 1890-93, prof. anatomy, 1899-1906, prof. clin. surgery, 1906-33, now emeritus; cons. surgeon Univ. Hosp., formerly Hosp. of The Good Shepherd (former pres. of staff); surgeon to Syracuse Free Dispensary; cons. surgeon Onondaga Gen. Hosp. Formerly dir. Syracuse Y.M.C.A. and exec. dir. Tumor Clinic of the Univ. Hosp.; dir. Rescue Mission Alliance. Fellow Am. Coll. Surg.; mem. A.M.A., N.Y. State Med. Soc., Central N.Y. Med. Assn. (ex-pres.), Onondaga County Med. Soc. (ex-pres.), Syracuse Acad. Medicine (ex-pres.), Onondaga County S.S. Assn. (ex-v.p.), Alpha Omega Alpha, Alpha Kappa Kappa, Pi Gamma Mu. Republican. Presbyn. Mason (32°, K.T.). Clubs: Faculty. Home-Office: Brewerton, N.Y. Died Mar. 20, 1956; buried Central Sq., N.Y.

PRICE, Harvey Lee, horticulturist; b. Price's Fork, Va., Mar. 18, 1874; s. William Taylor and Margaret Ellen (Hawley) P.; B.S., Va. Poly. Inst., 1898, M.S., 1900; m. Daisy Conway, Sept. 21, 1904; children—Wm. Conway, Harvey L., Margaret Hawley (dec.), Mary Luster, Jule. Instr. horticulture, Va. Poly. Inst., 1900-03, prof., 1903-45, also dean of agr. Fellow A.A.A.S.; mem. Soc. for Horticultural Science, Am. Pomol. Soc., Am. Genetic Assn. Mem. Ch. of the Disciples. Mason (K.T., Shriner). Home: Blacksburg, Va. Died Feb. 18, 1951; buried Blacksburg.

PRICE, Homer Charles, fruit grower; b. nr. Newark, O., February 13, 1875; s. Thomas Davis and Sarah Jane (Jones) P.; B.Sc. in agr., Ohio State U., 1897; M.Sc. in agr. Cornell U., 1899; U. of Halle, Germany, 1911-12; m. Gertrude Harlan, June 18, 1903; children—Thomas Harlan, Mary Elizabeth. Fellow in agr., Cornell U., 1898-99; asst. in horticulture and forestry, Ohio State U., 1899-1901; prof. horticulture and forestry, Ia. State Coll., 1901-03; dean Coll. of Agr., and prof. rural economics, Ohio State U., 1903-15. Mem. Ohio Agrl. Commn., 1913-15, Ohio State Bd. Agr., 1917-21; now engaged in farming and apple growing. Mem. Sigma Xi, Alpha Zeta. Republican. Baptist. Home: Newark, O. Died Mar. 25, 1943; buried Welsh Hills Cemetery, Granville, O.

PRICE, Howard Campbell, army officer (ret.); b. Chester, Pa., Apr. 15, 1872; s. William Gray and Jane Eliza (Campbell) P.; student pub. and pvt. schs., Pa.; grad. Army Sch. of the Line, 1921, Command and Gen. Staff Sch., 1924, Army War Coll., 1928; m. Alice Blakeley Gilroy, June 16, 1908; children—Howard Campbell, Jane Blakeley (wife of Capt. Walter Coulter Winn). Commd. 2d lt. U.S. Army, 1899, advanced through grades to brig. gen. (ret.), 1940; served in Spanish-Am. war; with Army of Cuban Occupation, 1899-1900, Philippine Insurrection, 1900-03; comd. 360 Inf., 90th Div., France and Germany, 1917-18, 38th Inf., Fort Douglas, Utah, 1928-31, 57th Inf. (Philippine Scouts), P.I., 1931-34; ret., 1936. Decorated D.S.M., 3 Silver

Star citations (U.S.); Croix de Guerre (France). Mem. Mil. Order World Wars, Pa. S.R. Republican. Episcopalian. Mason. Club: Army and Navy (Manila, P.I.). Home: 1218 Prospect St., La Jolla, Cal. Died Feb. 1, 1950.

PRICE, James Woods, physician; b. Albemarle County, Va., Jan. 30, 1877; s. Charles Harper and Sarah Jane (Woods) P.; M.D., U. Va., 1901; grad. study Phila. Polyclinic Hosp., 1901-03, in Europe, 1903-04; m. Sophie Mary Hoerner, Sept. 3, 1919. With Stony Wold Sanatorium, Lake Kushaqua, N.Y., and Saranac Lab., Saranac Lake, N.Y., 1904-08; specialist in Tb, Saranac Lake, 1908—; pres. bd. trustees and med. dir. Reception Hosp. of Saranac Lake; cons. physician Stony Wold Sanatorium; attending physician Gen. Hosp. of Saranac Lake; instr. Trudeau Sch. Tb. Maj. Med. R.C., U.S. Army, 1917-19. Mem. adv. com. Saranac Lab. Mem. A.M.A., N.Y. State, Franklin County and Saranac Lake med. socs., Nat. Tb Assn. (v.p., dir.), Sanatorium Assn., Climatol. and Clin. Assn. (ex-pres., mem. council), Alpha Omega Alpha, Phi Delta Theta, Phi Beta Kappa. Democrat. Episcopalian. Clubs: Saranac Lake Golf; Colonnade (U. of Va.). Home: Saranac Lake, N.Y. Died Feb. 24, 1951.*

PRICE, John D., ret. naval officer; b. Augusta, Ark., May 18, 1892; s. David Flournoy and Anna Frances (Corley) P.; B.S., U.S. Naval Acad., 1916; grad. Naval Aviation Sch., Pensacola, Fla., 1920; m. Miriam Johnston, May 17, 1924; children—Dale (Mrs. A. B. Conner), John. Commd. ensign, 1916, and advanced through the grades to adm.; gunnery and mining officer U.S.S. Quinnebang, World War I; commended by sec. of navy for experimental flying on aircraft carriers; comd. U.S.S. Jason, U.S.S. Pocomoke (aircraft tenders), 1931, 1939, Naval Air Sta., Seattle, 1928-30, Anacostia, D.C., 1937-39, Jacksonville, Fla., 1942-43, Patrol Wings 3 and 8; comdr. A. F. Pacific; nominated chief Naval Air Operations, Washington; ret. 1954. Awarded W.W. I medal, Mexican, Yangtse medals; Navy Cross, Distinguished Flying Cross, Legion of Merit. Club: Army-Navy Country (Washington). Home: 1801 S. Taylor St., Little Rock, Ark. Address: care Naval Operations (Air), Navy Dept., Washington 25. Died Dec. 19, 1957.*

PRICE, P. Frank (Philip Francis), foreign missionary; b. Richmond, Va., July 2, 1864; s. Rev. Philip Barbour and Mary Snowden (Pleasants) P.; ed. Hampden-Sydney (Va.) Coll., 1882-84, Union Theol. Sem., Va., 1886-89; D.D., Davidson Coll., N.C., 1908; m. Esther Eckard Wilson, Apr. 6, 1892; children—Frank Wilson (D.D.), Philip Barbour (M.D.), John Leighton (dec.), Julian Pleasants (M.D.), Harry Bayard (A.M.). Began as foreign missionary, 1890; pioneer evangelist, Chekiang Province, China, 1892-1912; prof. of systematic theology, Nanking Theol. Sem., 1912-35, acting pres., 1914-16, 1933-35, prof. emeritus, 1938—. Moderator Ch. of Christ in China (1st meeting), 1922; moderator Gen. Assembly Presbyn. Ch. in U.S. (Southern), 1936-37; co-chmn. Nanking Internat. Relief Assn. (in Shanghai). 1937—; pres. China Christian Endeavor Union, 1908—; chaplain McLeod Infirmary, Florence, S.C., 1948. Decorated 4th Order of the Flowering Harvest (China), 1913. Mem. Phi Gamma Delta. Author of books and booklets printed in Chinese: "Short Steps to Great Truths" (5 vols. used in teaching Chinese written lang.), Catechism Series (3 vols.), Wayside Series (all pub. by China Religious Tract Soc.); also in English, "Our China Investment," pub. by Exec. Com. of Foreign Missions, 1928. Home: Florence, S.C. Address: care Bd. Foreign Missions, Box 330, Nashville, Tenn., or Florence, S.C. Died May 10, 1954; buried Stonewall Jackson Cemetery, Lexington, Va.

PRICE, William Jennings, lawyer, diplomat, univ. prof.; b. Lancaster, Ky., Dec. 15, 1873; s. William Cicero and Martha Elizabeth (Graham) P.; A.B., Centre Coll., Danville, Ky., 1892 (class honors); A.M., LL.B., 1895, LL.D., 1917; LL.D. and Dr. Polit. Sci., Nat. Inst., Panama, 1917; m. Beatrice Detwiler, Aug. 15, 1931. Practiced law, Ky., and other states; county atty. Boyle County, Ky., 1901-09; master commr. Boyle Circuit Court, Ky., 1910-13; mem. law faculty Central U., Danville, 7 yrs., E.E. and M.P. to Panama, Aug. 20, 1913-Dec. 28, 1921; prof. law Georgetown U., 1922-31; counsel Fed. Deposit Ins. Corp., 1933-44, Dem. presidential elector, Ky., 1900; alternate del. at large, Ky., to Dem. Nat. Conv., Denver, 1908. Negotiated and executed Lefevre-Price Conv., delimiting Panama Canal Zone and exchanging important lands and waters between the U.S. and Panama; also formal vesting in U.S. of complete control of all radio communications in Rep. of Panama, passage of legislation and apptmt. of an Am. fiscal adviser for Panama, and of an Am. police adviser for Panama. Made spl. reports for State Dept. upon presdl. elections of 1916 and 1920, in Panama. Chmn. Liberty Loan and War Chest drives in Panama, World War; conducted negotiations resulting in Panama being first nation to declare allegiance with U.S. and her Allies after entrance of U.S. into World War, and in declaration by Panama of war on Germany. Apptd. by Pres. Coolidge one of two delegates representing U.S. at Pan-Am. Congress in Panama, 1926, Centennial Anniversary Congress, commemorating 1st Pan-Am. Congress held in western hemisphere, also apptd. by gov. to represent Ky. at same Congress on account of intimate connection of Henry Clay with 1st Congress; designated by legislature of Ky. as del. to represent state at unveiling and presentation of statue of Henry Clay to Rep. of Venezuela at Caracas, 1930; aide-de-camp on staff of gov. of Ky. with rank of col. Mem. Am. Bar Assn., D.C. Bar Assn., Am. Soc. Internat. Law (exec. council 1931-34), Sigma Chi (former Grand Praetor, 3d Province). Phi Beta Gamma (hon).; mem. bar of Supreme Court of U.S. Pres. Ky. Soc., Washington, 1924-27. Clubs: Cosmos (Washington); Filson (Louisville, Ky.). Democrat. Baptist. Contbr. articles to legal and other mags. Attended sessions of Assembly of League of Nations, Geneva, 1931, followed by visits to leading countries around world, 1931-32. Home: Danville, Ky. Address: 2101 Connecticut Av., Washington 8. Died May 20, 1952; buried Danville, Ky.

PRICKETT, Joe Milroy, railway exec.; b. Ligonier, Ind., Jan. 21, 1887; s. Thomas and Martha Matilda (Darr) P.; student Vories Bus. Coll., Indianapolis, 1903-04; m. Emma White, Dec. 12, 1908. Stenographer Cincinnati, Hamilton & Dayton Ry., Indianapolis, 1904-06; sec. to gen. mgr. Kan. City Southern Ry., 1906-13; sec. to gen. supt. transportation B.&O. R.R., Baltimore, 1913-14; sec. to pres. K.C.S. Ry., 1914-17, chief clerk to gen. mgr. 1917-19, chief clerk to pres., 1919-23, supt. of personnel, 1923-36, asst. to pres., 1936-44, vice pres. in charge of labor and pub. relations since 1944; vice pres La. & Ark. Ry. Co. since 1944. Dir. Kan. City Terminal Ry. Co., Southern Development Company. Dir. Indsl. Council of Kan. City; gov. Kan. City Safety Council. Mason. Republican. Clubs: Kansas City, Advertising and Sales Executives, Western Railway. Home: 4828 Liberty St. Office: 114 W. 11th St., Kansas City 6, Mo. Died Dec. 8, 1952.

PRIEST, James Percy, congressman; b. Carter's Creek, Tenn., Apr. 1, 1900; s. George Matison and Harriet Axie (Hastings) P.; student Teachers Coll., Murfreesboro, Tenn., 1921-22, University of Tenn., 1923, George Peabody College, Tenn., 1925-26; m. Mildred Webster Noland, Feb. 14, 1947; 1 daughter, Harriet Frances. Teacher rural schs., Maury County, 1919-21; tchr. Hist. and Eng. Culleoka (Tenn.) High Sch., 1921-26; on editorial staff, Nashville, 1926-40; mem. 78th to 82d Congresses, 6th Tenn. Dist., 83d-84th Congresses, 5th Dist. Democrat. Baptist. Clubs: Civitan (Nashville); National Press (Washington). Home: 417 Fairfax Av., Nashville, Tenn. Address: House of Representatives, Washington. Died Oct. 12, 1956; buried Woodlawn Meml. Cemetery, Nashville.

PRIEST, Wells Blodgett, ret. lawyer, ex-judge; b. Webster Groves, Mo., July 13, 1888; s. Henry Samuel and Henrietta (King) P.; student Westminster Coll., Washington U., and St. Louis Law Sch.; m. Marjorie Everts; children—Marjorie Jean (dec.), Wells Blodgett, Jr.; m. 2d, Asenath Cox, 1923. Began practice of law, with firm Boyle and Priest, St. Louis, 1910; asso. counsel United Ry. Co., St. Louis; judge Ct. of Criminal Correction, St. Louis; mgr. Depository Bur., Alien Property Custodian, U.S. Govt.; asso. counsel, U.S. Dept. of Justice, Bur. of Investigation. Served as pvt. U.S. Army, World War I. Pres. Lawyers Assn., 8th Judicial Circuit, St. Louis. Apptd. by Supreme Court of Mo. to the Mo. State Bar Com., 8th Jud. Circuit of Mo. Received Bench and Bar Award for distinguished service, 1935-36. Mem. Selective Service Bd., Warren County, N.J. Mem. Am. Bar Assn. Am. Judicature Soc., Kappa Alpha, Phi Delta Phi. Home: Deer Crossing Farm, Hackettstown, N.J. Deceased.

PRIMROSE, John, corp. exec.; b. Pictou, N.S., Can., May 27, 1873; s. Howard and Olivia (Campbell) P.; student Pictou Acad., Upper Can. Coll., Toronto, and McGill U., Montreal; m. Eleanor Baskerville Girouard, Apr. 29, 1937; children by 1st marriage—Charity, Elizabeth. Engr. Henry R. Worthington, 1895-1901; chief engr., later v.p. Power Specialty Co., 1901-27; v.p. Foster Wheeler Corp., N.Y.C. 1927, vice chmn. bd., retired from active bus., 1947, cons., 1947—. Mem. Am. Soc. M.E., Zeta Psi. Republican. Episcopalian. Clubs: Richmond Country; Bankers of America (N.Y.C.). Home: Roadside Cottage, Dongan Hills, S.I., N.Y. Office: 165 Broadway, N.Y.C. Died Aug. 1955*

PRINCE, Arthur Warren, educator; b. Ironton, Mo., Nov. 4, 1879; s. Arthur Samuel and Lucy Jane (Brown) P.; A.B., William Jewell Coll., 1904, A.M., 1905; Sc.D. (hon.), Union U., 1932; postgrad. U. Chgo., summers 1907, 11, 14, 20, 21, 23, Columbia, summer 1930; m. Mayme Frey, Aug. 19, 1908. Prin. pub. schs., Annapolis, Mo., 1901-02, asso. instr. in physics, William Jewell Coll., 1904-05; head of science dept. Western Mil. Acad., Alton, Ill., 1905-08; prof. chemistry and head of science dept. Union U., Jackson, Tenn., 1908-18, prof. chemistry and dean, 1918-37, dean and acting pres., 1931-32, head of chemistry dept., 1937-48. Capt. Chem. Warfare Reserve, U.S. Army, 1926-36. Fellow Am. Inst. Chemistry; mem. Am. Chem. Soc., A.A.A.S., Tenn. Acad. Sci., Am. Geog. Soc., Phi Gamma Delta. Baptist. Mason. Rotarian. Author: Laboratory Outlines of Physiological Chemistry, 1927; The World Beyond Our Senses, 1927; Science and Religion, 1930. Home: 321 Edgar Rd., Webster Groves, Mo. Died Jan. 26, 1951; buried Jackson, Tenn.

PRINCE, Frederick Henry, banker; b. Winchester, Mass., Nov. 24, 1859; s. Frederick O. and Helen S. (Henry) P.; Harvard U., class 1882; m. Abby K. Norman, Mar. 1884; children—Frederick Henry, Norman. Owner Frederick H. Prince & Co., chmn. board Union Stock Yard & Transit Co.; pres. Chgo. Stock Yards Co.; dir. Armour & Co., Live Stock National Bank, Union Stock Yard & Transit Co., Chgo. Stock Yards Co.; also officer or dir. various other cos. Home: Bellevue Av., Newport, R.I. Office: Hospital Trust Bldg., Providence. Died Feb. 2nd 1953; buried Washington Cathedral, Washington.

PRINGEY, Joseph Colburn, ex-congressman; b. Somerset, Pa., May 22, 1858; s. George and Effie (Colburn) P.; ed. country schs.; m. Josephine Young, Oct. 1905. Farmer; settled in Okla., 1891; mem. Senate, Okla. Ty., 1893; del. Rep. Nat. Conv., 1900; mem. bd. regents U. of Okla. 4 yrs.; co. clk., Lincoln Co., Okla., 1912-20; mem. 67th Congress (1921-23), 4th Okla. Dist. Mem. Christian (Disciples) Ch. Mason (32°), Odd Fellow, K.P. Home: Chandler, Okla. Died Feb. 11, 1935; buried Oak Park, Chandler, Okla.

PRINGLE, Ernest Henry, investment banker; born in Charleston, South Carolina, July 16, 1881; son of Ernest Henry and Mary (Ford) Pringle; A.B., College of Charleston, 1900; married Nell McColl, Mar. 20, 1906; children—Mary Ford (Mrs. George Corner Fenhagen), Dorothy Duncan McColl, Eleanor Evans Thomas (Mrs. Walter Tilghman Hart, Jr.), Clara Margaretta, Ernest Henry, McColl. Mem. Pringle Bros., wholesale dry goods, Charleston, 1901-06, gen. accountant, 1906-07; asst. cashier Bank of Charleston, 1907-11, v.p., 1911-22, pres., 1922-23, chmn. bd., 1923-25, was also chmn. bd. Charleston Security Co., Charleston Trust Co., resigned from banking, 1925; with Merchants Fertilizer & Phosphate Co., 1925-30; formed E. H. Pringle & Co., investment bankers, 1930, which he headed until 1955; v.p. Charleston Import and Forwarding Co.; treas. Midland Timber Co. Chmn. Liberty and Victory loans Charleston County, 1917-19. Trusete Coll. of Charleston. Democrat. Episcopalian. Home: 20 S. Battery St., Charleston, S.C. Died Oct. 14, 1955; buried St. Philips Church, Charleston.

PRINGLE, Henry Fowles (pring'ĕl), author; b. New York, N.Y., Aug. 23, 1897; s. James Maxwell and Marie (Juergens) P.; A.B., Cornell U., 1920; m. Helena Huntington Smith, Sept. 14, 1926 (div.); children—Margot (Mrs. Forrest J. Liberty), Robert Maxwell; m. 2d, Katharine Douglas, May 23, 1944. Reporter New York Sun, 1920-22, New York Globe, 1922-24, New York World, 1924-27; free lance writer, since 1927; asso. editor of The Outlook, 1929-31; asso. in journalism, Columbia, 1932-36, prof. journalism, 1936-43; chief, Div. of Publs., Office of War Information, Feb. 1942-Apr. 1943; cons. A.A.F., 1945, Sec. War, 1945-46. Democrat. Presbyn. Club: Century (N.Y.). Author: Alfred E. Smith, a Critical Study, 1927; Big Frogs, 1928; Industrial Explorers (with Maurice Holland), 1928; Theodore Roosevelt, a Biography, 1931; The Life and Times of William Howard Taft, 1939; Pioneers in Philanthropy: a History of the General Education Board (with his wife) (in preparation). Contbr. to Saturday Evening Post, to Harpers', etc. Winner Pulitzer prize for biography, 1931; Guggenheim fellow, 1944-45. Address: 3319 N St. N.W., Washington 7. Died Apr. 7, 1958.

PRINGLE, Ralph W., author; b. Potsdam, N.Y., Oct. 5, 1865; s. Ralph and Nancy (Blain) P.; B.S., St. Lawrence U., Canton, N.Y., M.S., 1892; A.B., Harvard, 1892; m. Lillian Smith, Mar. 20, 1891; children—Helen Smith, Kenneth Ralph. Successively prin. St. Regis Falls Acad. 2 yrs., high schs., Oregon City, Ore., 2 yrs., Brodhead, Wis., 3 yrs., Appleton, Wis., 12 yrs., Lyons Twp., La Grange, Ill., 4 yrs.; prin. Univ. High Sch., prof. secondary edn., Ill. State Normal U., 1912-35, now prof. emeritus. Taught grad. courses U. Pa. summer 1925; lectured and taught advanced courses in Boston U., summer 1930. Mem. N.E.A., Ill. State Tchrs. Assn., Nat. High Sch. Principals' Assn., Ill. Acad. Sci. (psychology-education sect.), Alpha Tau Omega, Pi Gamma Mu, Kappa Phi Kappa. Republican. Presbyn. Royal Arch Mason. Clubs: Consistory, College Alumni, Longfellow. Author: Adolescence and High-School Problems, 1922; Methods with Adolescents, 1927; The Psychology of High School Discipline, 1931; The Junior High School, A Psychological Approach, 1937. Speaker on ednl. subjects. Home: Normal, Ill. Died 1948.

PRINZ, Hermann (prints), prof. dental Materia medica; b. Schwittersdorf, Saxony, Germany, June 13, 1868; s. August and Friederika P.; ed progymnasium, Leipzig, Germany; student University of Michigan, 1893-96, D.D.S., 1896, hon. A.M., 1912; student U. of Halle, Germany, 1895-96; St. Louis University 1897-1900; M.D., Barnes Med. Coll., 1901; graduate study Univ. of Berlin, 1913-14; Sc.D., U. of Pa., 1926; D.M.D., U. of Cologne, Germany, 1929; Sc.D., Washington U., 1941; m. Lily Koop, July 5, 1905 (died Jan. 22, 1939); m. 2d, Helen Bryant, Aug. 10, 1940. Apprentice to apothecary, Germany, 1884-87; came to U.S., 1889, naturalized citizen, 1896; prof. materia medica and therapeutics, Washington U., 1899-1913; same, Evans Dental Inst., U. of Pa., 1913-38, prof. emeritus, 1938—. Served as lieut. comdr. U.S. Navy Reserve Corps. Member A.M.A., American Dental Association, American Academy American Acad. Arts and Sciences, Sigma Xi; fellow Kaiserlich Leopold-Carolin. Akademie der Naturforscher, Halle, Germany, 1933. Awarded gold medal, Dental Soc. State N.Y., 1923; Callahan memorial award (gold medal), Ohio State Dental Soc., 1933; Jenkins memorial medal, Conn. State Dental Assn., 1934; Alumni award, U. of Pa., 1939. Author: Dental Formulary, 1907; Dental Materia Medica and Therapeutics, 1910; Diseases of the Soft Structures of the Teeth, 1928; Diseases of the Mouth and their Treatment (with Dr. S. S. Greenbaum), 1935; Dental Chronology, 1945. Contbr. to Dental Cosmos; chpts. in text books also articles. Editor Dental Era, 1900-07. Home: 400 S. Lansdowne Av., Lansdowne, Pa. Died Nov. 24, 1957.

PRIOR, Herbert M., banker; b. Stamford, Conn., May 7, 1904; s. Edward M. and Alice L. (Miller) P.; student U. Pa., 1926; m. Anne C. Perterick, June 14, 1930; 1 son, Roger M. With home comml. office Western Union, 1926-27, Bank Am., N.Y.C., 1928-29; credit dept. Internat. Trust Co., 1930; credit dept. Continental Bank & Trust Co., 1933-39, asst. treas., 1939-41, v.p., 1940-48; v.p. Chem. Bank & Trust Co., 1938-49; v.p. Merc. Nat. Bank, Dallas, 1949-50, sr. v.p. since 1950; dir. Lewis Supply Co., Warren-Balderston, Southland Company. Mem. Community Chest, Boy Scouts. Presbyn. Clubs: Northwood, Athletic. Home: 6512 Belmead, Dallas. Office: 1704 Main St., Dallas 1. Died Aug. 12, 1957; buried Dallas.

PRITCHETT, Clifton Augustine, army officer; b. Baltimore, Dec. 6, 1888; s. Capt. Thomas A. and Cora Elizabeth (Marlatt) P.; attended U. of Md., 1907-10; grad. Inf. Sch. Co. Officers, 1922, Field Officers, 1927, Command and Gen. Staff Coll., 1930; Field Officers Chemical Warfare School, 1930; m. Elsie May Freedenburg; children—Jacqueline Anne (Mrs. Vernon L. Smith), Patricia Eileen, Clifton Augustine. Commd. 2d lieut., 1st lt. (1950) Md. N.G., 1912-17; capt., U.S. Army, 1918, advancing through grades to col., 1941; assigned Gen. Pershing's Staff, GHQ, A.E.F., 1918-19; chief of staff, G.S.C. Mil. Dist. of Washington, 1942-47; v.p. U.S. Inf. Jour., Inc., 1946-50. Awarded Legion of Merit, Army Commendation Ribbon, Mexican Border, Victory Ribbon (with 3 stars), Occupation of Ger. Ribbon, Am. Defense Ribbon (with 1 star), North American Theatre Ribbon, Victory Ribbon World War II, French Croix de Guerre (World War I), French Commemorative Ribbon, Verdun Medal. Dir. U.S. Inf. Assn., 1941-50; mem. Mil. Order World Wars, Am. Legion, 40 et 8. Episcopalian. Mason (32°, K.T., Shriner). Clubs: Army and Navy, U.S. Naval Gun Factory, Carabao, Officers (Washington); Officers (Ft. Meyer, Va.); Army and Navy (Manila), Mil. and Naval, Camp Fire of Am. (N.Y. City). Home: "Stack Arms," 2316 N. Stafford St., Lee Heights, Arlington 7. Office: 2173 N. Glebe Rd., Arlington 7, Va. Deceased.

PROCOPÉ, Hjalmar Johan Fredrik (prō'kō-pē), Finish diplomat; b. Helsinki, Finland, Aug. 8, 1889; s. C. A. F. and Elin Hedvig Vendla (von Torne) P.; ed. Nya Svenska Laroverket, U. Helsinki (grad. in law); hon. LL.D., U. Rochester; m. Margaret Shaw, Mar. 30, 1940. Practicing lawyer, 1915-22; various positions in fgn. office, Finland, 1918; mem. Municipal Council of Helsinki, 1918-19; mem. Finnish Parliament, 1919-22, 24-26; mem. Trade Treaty Com., 1921-39; chmn. supervisory bd. of forwarding firm of Victor Ek, 1922-24; minister commerce and industry, 1920-21, 1924; Finnish minister at Warsaw, 1926-27; minister foreign affairs, 1924-25, 27-31; gen. mgr. Finnish Paper Mill Assn., 1931-39; E.E. and M.P. from Finland to U.S., 1939—; concluded or took part in the concluding of trade treaties with France, Denmark, Iceland, Poland, Japan, Lithuania, etc.; Finnish del. Internat. Hague Conf., 1922; World Economic Conf., 1933; Finnish rep. Assembly of League of Nations, 1924, 28, 29, 30; meetings of League of Nations Council, 1928-30 (chmn. 51st and 52d meetings, 1928, rapporteur for financial questions, 1928, and for mandate questions, 1928-30, and mem. various council coms.); mem. Chamber of Commerce at Helsinki, 1932-39; chmn. Am. Egyptian Comm. of Conciliation, 1933—. Decorated Finland's Liberty Cross I and IV classes; Grand Crosses of Finland's White Rose; Italian St. Mauritius and Lazarus Order; Royal Swedish North Star Order; Norwegian Order of St. Olaf; Danish Dannebrog Order; Icelandic White Hawk Order; Eagle Cross of the Esthonian National Guard; Latvian Three Stars Order; Polish Restoration Order; Serbian St. Sava Order; Spanish Order of Isabel the Catholic; Belgian Crown Order; Brazilian South Star Order; Grand Officer French Legion of Honor; Japanese Rising Sun Order, etc. Clubs: Academie Diplomatique Internationale, Club de la Bourse, Helsinki, Metropolitan, Chevy Chase (Washington), etc. Author: Independence or Continued Oppression, 1917; Customs Tariffs and Treaty Policy, 1923; Our Customs Tariff System from the Point of View of Trade Treaty Policy, 1926; Finland and the International Situation in Northern Europe, 1932 (in French); Some Comments on the Trade Treaty Policy of Finland, 1933; Trends in International and Scandinavian Trade Policy, 1935; The Most Favored Nations Clause in the Present Trade Policy, 1938; Economic Co-operation between the Northern Countries and the Joint Delegations for its Promotion, 1938. Address: 2144 Wyoming Av., Washington. Died Mar. 8, 1954.

PROCTER, William, scientist; b. Cincinnati, O., Sept. 8, 1872; s. Harley Thomas and Mary Elizabeth (Sanford) P.; grad. Phillips Exeter Acad., 1891; Ph.B., Yale, 1894; grad. student Sorbonne (Paris), 1896-97, Columbia, 1917-20; D.Sc., U. of Montreal, 1936; m. Emily Pearson Bodstein, Feb. 3, 1910. During early career specialized in railroad organization and securities; organized firm of Procter & Borden, 1902, retired, 1929; established lab. on Mt. Desert Island (Me.), 1921; established Biol. Survey of Mt. Desert Region, 1936; has contributed to curricula of univs. and state biol. depts. Trustee Am. Mus. Natural History, N.Y. City. Mem. bd. of mgrs. Wistar Inst. of Anatomy and Biology (Phila.), 1928-40. Director Procter & Gamble Co. Mem. advisory bd., dept. of zoölogy, Columbia U. Fellow Entomol. Soc. America, A.A.A.S.; mem. Acad. Natural Sciences, Boston Soc. of Natural History, Entomological Soc. of Am. (mem. edit. bd., 1940-47), Am. Microscopical Soc., Acad. Natural Sciences of Phila., Ornithologists Union, Santa Barbara Natural History Soc., Brooklyn Entomol. Soc., Genetic Soc., Ray Soc. of London (England), Plymouth Marine Assn. (England), Southern Calif. Acad. Sciences, New York Entomol. Soc., Entomol. Soc. of Washington, Ecologists Union, Ecol. Soc. of America, Royal Canadian Institute, Am., Pacific Coast and Cambridge entomol. socs., Sci. Research Soc. Am. (co-founder and a gov.), Sigma Xi. Episcopalian (warden). Clubs: Century, University (New York); Graduate (New Haven, Conn.). Author of publs. on the marine life and the insect life of the Mount Desert Region. Home: Bar Harbor, Me. Died Apr. 19, 1951.

PROCTOR, A(lexander) Phimister, sculptor, painter; b. Ontario, Can., Sept. 27, 1862; s. Alexander and Tirza (Smith) P.; pupil Puech and Ingallbert, Paris; m. Margaret Gerow, Sept. 1893; children—Hester, Alden Phimister, Nona, Jean, William, Gifford, Joanne. Awarded Rinehart Paris scholarship; designer's medal, Chicago Exposition, 1893, where exhibited sculptural groups; exhibited Paris Expn., 1900 (mem. sculpture jury), received gold medal; furnished quadriga for U.S. Pavilion, Paris Expn., 1900; groups for Buffalo Expn., 1901 (mem. sculpture jury of selection and awards); gold medal, St. Louis Expn., 1904 (mem. jury); gold medal, San Francisco Expn., 1915; gold-medal of honor, Archtl. League, N.Y., 1911. Represented in public parks, New York and Denver, in Zoöl. Park, New York, in Pittsburgh; also lions, McKinley Monument, Buffalo; permanent works at St. Louis Art Gallery, Met. Museum of Art, Corcoran Art Gallery; heroic bison and tigers, Washington; 2 equestrian statues at Denver; monument of Oregon pioneer mother, Campus of U. of Ore.; Princeton tigers, Princeton U.; heroic equestrian statue of circuit rider, Salem, Ore.; equestrian statue of Col. Roosevelt as Rough Rider, Portland, Ore., and Minot, N.D; "Pioneer Mother," equestrian group, Kansas City, Mo.; equestrian statue, "Western Sheriff," Pendleton, Ore.; fountain group, trapper and Indian, Wichita, Kan.; double equestrian statue, Gen. R. E. Lee and Young Soldier, Dallas, Tex.; heroic group Mustangs, seven wild Mustangs for Campus of U. of Tex.; "Oregon Pioneer," U. of Oregon; (with son) statues of Dr. John McLaughlin and Rev. Jason Lee for Hall of Fame, Washington. Mem. Art Commn., City of New York, 1903-06; N.A., 1904; mem. Nat. Inst. Arts and Letters, Nat. Sculpture Soc, Am. Water Color Soc., Roosevelt Pilgrimage, Nat. Council Boy Scouts of America, Soc. Colonial Wars, S.R. Clubs: hon. mem., Adventurers' (Los Angeles), hon. mem. Bohemian, 1944 (San Francisco), Nat. Arts, Century, Camp Fire Club of America, Boone and Crockett (New York). Address: 3615 42d Av. N.E., Seattle. Died Sept. 4, 1950; buried Seattle.

PROCTOR, Bernard Emerson, educator, food technologist; b. Malden, Mass., May 5, 1901; s. Arthur L. and Vina (Dolloff) P.; B.S., Mass. Inst. Tech., 1923, Ph.D., 1927; m. Miriam H. Patten, Oct. 18, 1924. Instr. biochemistry sch. medicine, Boston U., 1923-27; instr., later prof. food tech., Mass. Inst. Technology, 1926; head dept. food tech., 1952—; cons. to U.S. Pub. Health service, 1951—; cons. food development research and prof. dir. food research Office Q.M., Gen. U.S. Army. Recipient of the Nicholas Appert medal, 1957. Fellow American Public Health Assn.; mem. A.A.A.S., Am. Chem. Soc., Soc. Am. Bacteriologists, Inst. Food Technologist (pres. 1952-53), Am. Soc. Refrigeration Engrs., Sigma Xi. Club: Cosmos (Washington, D.C.) Baptist. Author: Food Technology (with S. C. Prescott), 1937; over 100 papers on food tech. in science periodicals. Home: 100 Memorial Drive, Cambridge 42, Mass. Died Sept. 24, 1959.

PROCTOR, James McPherson, judge; b. Washington, D.C., Sept. 4, 1882; s. Alexander M. and Annie Elizabeth (Ashford) P.; LL.B., George Washington U., 1904, LL.D.; married Mary S. Harrington, September 20, 1902 (died September 1946); children—Edward A., James M.; m. 2d, Elizabeth Barry Coleman, Sept. 30, 1947. Admitted to District of Columbia bar, 1903; asst. U.S. atty. for D.C., 1905-09, chief asst., 1909-13; private practice until 1931; spl. asst. atty. gen., 1929-31, in charge suits of U.S. to clear titles to river front properties in D.C.; asso. justice Dist. Court of U.S. for the Dist. of Columbia, 1931-48; circuit judge, U.S. Court of Appeals, since Mar. 9, 1948. Served as capt. inf., A.E.F., World War. Mem. American Bar Association, Gen. Alumni Assn. George Washington University (past pres.). Mason. Clubs: Chevy Chase, Civitan (ex-pres.), Lawyers. Home: Kennedy-Warren Apts. Address: U.S. Court of Appeals, Washington 1. Died Sept. 17, 1953; buried Arlington Nat. Cemetery.

PROCTOR, Redfield, ex-gov. Vt., marble co. exec.; b. Proctor, Vt., Apr. 13, 1879; s. Redfield and Emily J. (Dutton) P.; Mass. Inst. Tech., 1902; M.S., U. Vt., 1916, LL.D., 1924; LL.D., Middlebury Coll., 1923; m. Mary Sherwood Hedrick, Oct. 24, 1905; children—Margaret (Mrs. Jos. P. Kelly), Robert Dutton, Katharine (Mrs. Rowland Douglas). Began practice as mech. engr., 1902; chmn. bd. dirs. Vt. Marble Co., Yule Colo. Marble Co. Mem. Vt. Ho. of Rep., 1912, 15, Senate, 1917-19; del. Rep. Nat Conv., 1920; gov. of Vt., 1923-25; pres. N.E. Council, 1929-31. Trustee Middlebury Coll.; mem. corp. Mass. Inst. Tech. Served as capt. Engr. Corps, 1917-19. Mem. bd. dirs. U.S. C. of C., 1932-38; mem. N.A.M. (dir. 1942-47), Am. Soc. M.E., Vt. Soc. Engrs., S.A.R., Loyal Legion, Mil. Order World War, Am. Legion, Newcomen Soc., Delta Upsilon. Republican. Clubs: University (N.Y.C.); Union (Boston). Home: Proctor, Vt. Died Feb. 5, 1957; buried Proctor.

PROKOFIEFF, Serge (prō-kō'fyĕf), composer; b. Ekaterinoslav, South Russia, Apr. 23, 1891; studied music with mother; student under Glière, 1901; grad. (3 diplomas) Moscow Conservatory, 1914. Toured world several times as pianist presenting his own work, 1918-38; lived in U.S., 1918-22, Paris, until 1935, now in Russia. Wrote opera, "The Love of Three Oranges." (played by Chicago Opera Co.), 1921. Awarded Rubinstein prize, Russia, 1910. Prin. works: 4 symphonies, 5 piano concertos, 1 violin concerto; Chant, Le Pas d'Acier, Le Fils Prodigue and Sur le Borysthène (ballets); They Are Seven (choral); Overture on Hebrew Themes, Quartet for Oboe, Clarinet, Viola and Double-bass and Scherzo for 4 Bassoons; also many songs and piano pieces. Address: Moscow, Russia. Died Mar. 8, 1953.

PROUT, G(eorge) R(ussell), indsl. mfg. exec.; b. Quincy, Mass., Nov. 13, 1899; s. George and Ellen (Rundle) P.; S.B., Mass. Inst. Tech., 1923, M.S., 1923; m. Marion Snow, Jan. 29, 1921; children—George Russell, Nancy L. (Mrs. W. A. Ganther). Student engr. Gen. Electric Co., 1923-24, motor and control specialist and petroleum industry specialist, 1924-39, dist. indsl. dept. mgr., 1939-40, sales mgr., control div., 1940-41, mgr., indsl. control div., 1941-44, mgr. comml. refrigeration and air conditioning div., 1944-45, gen. mgr., air conditioning dept., 1945-48, v.p. since 1945, gen. mgr. nucleonics div., Richland, Wash., since 1949. Mason. Club: Kiwanis. Author numerous articles in engring. trade mags. Office: General Electric Co., Richland, Wash. Died Mar. 8, 1953.

PRUITT, Raymond S. (prōō'ĭt), lawyer, corp. exec., ret.; b. Gettysburg, S.D., July 31, 1887; s. Andrew J. and Laura G. (Kelly) P.; A.B., DePauw U.; LL.B., Northwestern U.; m. Florence Hemingway, Feb. 24, 1927; children—Barbara, Joan, Andrew. Vice pres., sec., dir. Avco Mfg. Corp.; sec., dir. Avco of Canada, Ltd., Crosley Broadcasting Corp., WLW Promotions, Inc.; dir. U.S. Freight Co.; gen. counsel Griswold & Bateman, Inc.; mem. firms Pruitt, Coursen, Oechler & McLaughlin, N.Y. C., and Pruitt & Grealis, Chgo., now ret. Clubs: Chicago Athletic Assn.; Berrien Hills Country; Saddle and Cycle (Chgo.); University, Cloud, Wings (N.Y.C.). Home: 85 Lake Shore Drive, St. Joseph, Mich.; also 2006 deLeon Av., Vero Beach, Fla. Died Sept. 1, 1957; buried Meml. Park Cemetery, Evanston, Ill.

PRYOR, Thomas Brady, lawyer; b. Jackson, La., July 25, 1869; s. William Kernan and Elizabeth Jane (Brady) P.; student Centenary Coll. of La.; m. Lena Harper, Jan. 29, 1902; children—Thomas Brady, Frances, Grace. Admitted to Ark. bar, 1893; practiced in Greenwood until 1908, in Ft. Smith since 1908; asst. gen. atty. Mo. P. Ry., 1908-12, gen. atty. for Okla. and West Ark., 1912-47; partner with son, firm Pryor & Pryor; v.p. Ft. Smith Suburban Ry. Co., 1908-47. Dir. Ft. Smith pub. schs. 3 yrs. Dem. presdl. elector, 1904, 1940; chairman Ark. delegation, Dem. Nat. Conv., 1928; mem. Ft. Smith Chamber of Commerce. Mem. Am., Ark. State and Ft. Smith bar assns. Mem. Christian (Disciples) Ch. Mason, Woodman, Elk. Club: Hardscrabble Country. Home: 123 N. 17th St. Office: Merchants Nat. Bank Bldg., Ft. Smith, Ark. Died May 20, 1952; buried Forest Park Cemetery, Fort Smith.

PUBLICKER, Harry, business exec. Chmn. bd. and dir. Publicker Industries Inc. Address: 1429 Walnut St., Phila. 2. Died Mar. 15, 1951.

PUCKETT, Erastus Paul, coll. dean; b. Summit, Ala., Apr. 11, 1882; s. Erastus Peru and Susan (Henry) P.; A.B., Howard Coll., Birmingham, Ala., 1903; M.A., Tulane U., 1907; student Harvard, 1912-13, Columbia U., summer, 1929, U. of Mo., 1930-31; LL.D., Kentucky Wesleyan, 1930, Howard Coll., 1931, Central Coll., 1933, U. Mo., 1952; m. Anna Pryor, Sept. 7, 1910; children—Anna Sue, Florence Jean, Helen Gertrude. Prin., Scottsboro Baptist Inst., 1903-05; teaching fellow, Tulane U., 1906-07, instructor, 1907-08; prin., Acad. of Central Coll., 1908-10; prof., Economics and History, Central College since 1910, dean, 1913-52, dean emeritus since 1952; acting president 1924, 1940-41, and 1947-50. In S.T.C., 1918. Democrat. Methodist. Rotarian. Lectr. on coll. adminstr., hist. topics; author hist. and ednl. articles. Home: 303 Spring St., Fayette, Mo. Died Apr. 6, 1959; buried Glasgow, Mo.

PUCKETTE, Charles McDonald, newspaper exec.; b. Sewanee, Tenn., July 28, 1887; s. Charles McDonald and Charlotte Barnwell (Elliott) P.; A.B., Univ. of the South, Sewanee, Tenn., 1907, A.M., 1908; m. Elizabeth Argyle Gettys, Nov. 8, 1913; children—Charles McDonald, Isabelle McKeldin (Mrs. Raymond R. Howe), Stephen Elliott. Reporter New York Evening Post, 1908-16, city editor, 1916-17, mng. editor, 1917-24; asst. to bus. mgr., New York Times, 1924-32, asst. to pub., 1932-42; gen. mgr. Chattanooga (Tenn.) Times, 1942—; v.p., dir. Chattanooga Pub. Co., 1942—. Regent U. of the South. Mem. Phi Beta Kappa. Independent Democrat. Episcopalian. Contbr. various encys. and mags. on journalism. Home: 216 Fairy Trail, Lookout Mountain, Tenn. Office: 117 E. Tenth, Chattanooga, Tenn. Died Jan. 15, 1957; buried Sewanee, Tenn.

PUFFER, J(oseph) Adams, writer, lecturer; b. Harrington, Me., Feb. 13, 1872; s. William Henry and Susannah Wood (Coffin) P.; A.B., Wesleyan U., Conn., 1896; S.T.B., Boston U., 1900; student reform and industrial schs. of Eng., 1904; hon. fellow in psychology and pedagogy, Clark U., 1905-07; grad. student of edn., U. of Ill., 1913-14; student vocational edn., Harvard, 1925; m. Emily Hope Rice, Oct. 1, 1903; children—Evelyn Hope, Ruth Rice, Stanwood Adams, Marjorie. Teacher, Harrington, Me., 1888-89; pastor M.E. Ch., Biddeford Pool, Me., 1900-1901; prin. high sch., Richmond, Me., 1902; prin. Mass. Industrial Sch. for Boys, Westboro, Mass., 1902-05; pastor First Unitarian Ch., Gardner, Mass., 1905-08, First Parish Ch., Needham, Mass., 1908-11; probation officer Boston Juvenile Court, 1907-10; dir. Beacon Vocation Bur., Boston, 1910-18; instr. teachers' inst., 1910-13; lecturer in farmers' inst., U. of Ill., 1913-14; lecturer on vocational problems, normal schs. and colls., 1914-18; field sec., Nat. Pub. Welfare League, Kansas City, Mo., 1918-20; asso. editor of Public Welfare, 1918-20; lecturer and vocational sec. Army Y.M.C.A., Eastern, Central and Southern depts., 1918-19; field sec. Nat. Child Welfare Assn., N.Y., 1920-21, of Nat. Pub. Welfare League, Kansas City, Mo., 1921-23; field dir. Co-operative Club International, Kansas City, Mo. Dir Beacon Boys' Bur., Boston. Author: The Boy and His Gang, 1912; Vocational Guidance, 1914. Editor of Vocational Guidance Series, 1915. Home: Berlin, Mass. Died July 29, 1958.

PUGH, William Barrow, church ofcl.; b. Utica, N.Y., Jan. 20, 1889; s. William Barrow and Mary Jane (Albro) P.; A.B., Central High Sch., Phila., 1907, A.B., U. Pa., 1910; M.A., Princeton, 1912; student Princeton Theol. Sem., 1910-13; D.D., Coll. of the Ozarks, 1933; LL.D., Tusculum Coll., 1939; Litt.D., Waynesburg Coll., 1941; m. Emma Marie Schaperkotter; children—William Barrow, Donald Henry. Ordained to ministry Presbyn. Ch., 1915; pastor Beacon Ch., Phila., 1915-28, First Ch., Chester, Pa., 1929-38; asst. to stated clerk of Gen. Assembly, Presbyn. Ch., U.S.A., 1922-38, stated clerk, 1938—; mem. spl. com. on revised Book of Discipline, 1932-38; mem. spl. com. on conservation of property; mem. com. on book of Common Worship; sec. Gen. Council, Presbyn. Gen. Assembly, U.S.A., 1938—; sec. Dept. Ch. Cooperation and Union of Presbyn. Ch., U.S.A.; sec. Joint Com. on Ch. Union of P.E. and Presbyn. Chs.; sec. Presbyterian United World Emergency Fund (now Restoration Fund Presbyn. Ch. in U.S.A.) and Presbyterian Emergency Service Commn. (now Presbyn. Com. on Camp and Ch. Activities); Sec. Pres. Com. on Army and Navy Chaplains; mem. National Commission on Evangelism of Presbyterian Church; member American Committee for World Council of Churches. Del. World Council of Chs., Amsterdam, Holland, 1948; mem. Central Committee, World Council Chs. Delegate to Federal Council of Churches of Christ in America, 1932-34, 36, 38, 41, 42, 44, 46, 47; executive com., 1932—, chmn. advisory com., 1940-42, mem. coms. on Conscientious Objectors of Federal Council; Am. sec. of Alliance of the Reformed Chs. throughout the world holding the Presbyn. system; del. to World Alliance of Presbyn. and Reformed Chs., 1937-48; del. to N. American Ecumenical conf., Toronto, 1941; vice chmn. elected chmn. in 1943. Gen. Commn. on Army and Navy Chaplains; visited American troops throughout the world at invitation of President as representative of Protestant churches, 1943, and visited Am. troops in Pacific Ocean Area, 1945; member of Christian Commission on Camp Communities; member of Army and Navy Dept. Com. of Nat. Council of YMCA; mem. Joint Army and Navy Com. on Welfare and Recreation; chmn. Nat. Council Service Men's Christian League. Served as chaplain 28th Div., U.S. Army, participating in Oise-Aisne, Meuse-Argonne, Ypres-Lys offensives, World War I; chaplain Pa. N.G., 111th Inf., 1919-41. Awarded Citation of Merit, Navy Dept., 1946; Medal for Merit, 1947. Trustee Princeton Theol. Sem. (sec. of board, 1929-44). Trustee Lincoln U., Pa. Lecturer, ecclesias. theol., Princeton Theol. Sem. Gen. Assembly Presbyn. Ch. U.S.A.; trustee Maryville (Tenn.) Coll.; mem. exec. council Presbyn. Hist. Soc. Mem. Am. Legion (chaplain Dept. of Pa. 1925), Mil. Order World War. Republican. Clubs: Union League (Phila.); Springhaven Country. Editor of The Constitution, The Digest, and The Manual of Presbyn. Church, U.S.A. Contbr. articles on ch. law to mags. Home: Providence Rd., Wallingford, Pa. Office: Witherspoon Bldg., Phila. Died Sept. 14, 1950; buried Arlington Nat. Cemetery.

PUGH, William Samuel, mining engr.; b. Pottsville, Pa., June 27, 1871; s. John and Rosanna (Beidelman) P.; grad. high sch., Pottsville, 1888; grad. corr. course Internat. Corr. Schs., Scranton, Pa., 1896; m. Jennie June Edwards, Oct. 27, 1896. Pvt. practice as civil and mining engr., 1892—; now cons. mining engr. for Schuylkill County, Pa.; frequently called to testify before cts. of anthracite region and Pub. Service Commn. of Pa.; employers' rep. Fed. Labor Bd., Schuylkill County, Pa., 1917-18. Mem. Pa. Engrs. Soc. Am. Inst. of Mining and Metall. Engrs. Republican. Presbyn. Mason (33°, K.T Shriner). Home: 1816 Mahantango St., Pottsville, Pa. Office: Mortimer Bldg., Pottsville, Pa. Died Jan. 19, 1954; buried Chas-Barber Cemetery, Pottsville, Pa.

PUGMIRE, Ernest Ivison, exec. in religious and charitable organization; b. Kansas City, Mo., Mar. 4, 1888; s. Joseph Smith and Marian (Ivison) P.; student Salvation Army Training Coll., Toronto, Ontario, Can., 1906; m. Grace Mary Vickers, Sept. 14, 1911; children—Arthur Wroughton, Eileen (Mrs. Aubrey Malphurs), Meriel (Mrs. F. Richmond Chadwick, Jr.), Josephine (Mrs. Herbert Gearing), John McLeod. With finance dept. Salvation Army, Toronto, Can., 1907-15, financial sec., Winnipeg, Can., 1915-19, Pekin, China, 1919-20, Tokyo, Japan, 1920-25, chief sec., 1925-31, financial sec., Chicago, 1931-33; chief sec., 1933-35; territorial comdr., embracing 15 southern states, Atlanta, Ga., 1935-39; territorial comdr., embracing 11 central states, Chicago, Ill., 1939-42; territorial comdr., embracing 11 eastern states, New York, 1942-44; nat. comdr., since Jan., 1944. Decorated: Officer Order Orange-Nassau, Netherlands; King's Medal for Services in Cause of Freedom, Gt. Britain. Survivor of Empress of Ireland disaster, 1914; Salvation Army relief worker in great earthquake, Japan, 1923. Dir. Nat. U.S.O. Club: Rotary (New York). Home: 64 Shadyside Dr., Wyckoff, N.J. Office: 122 W. 14th St., N.Y.C. 11. Died June 24, 1953; buried West View Cemetery, Atlanta.

PULITZER, Joseph (pŭll'it-sur), editor; b. N.Y. City, Mar. 21, 1885; s. Joseph and Kate (Davis) P.; prep. edn. St. Mark's Sch., Southboro, Mass.; student Harvard, 1904-06; LL.D. (hon.), Columbia University, 1952; married Elinor Wickham, June 1, 1910 (died Mar. 13, 1925); m. 2d, Elizabeth Edgar, Apr. 7, 1926. Entered journalism in New York, 1906; pres. Pulitzer Pub. Co., pubs. St. Louis Post-Dispatch, 1912—. Chmn. Pulitzer Prize advisory board, 1921—. Episcopalian. Commn. ensign U.S. Navy, Nov. 1918. Home: Clayton, Mo. Office: Post-Dispatch, St. Louis. Died March 31, 1955.

PULLEN, Roscoe LeRoy, physician, med. educator; b. Princeville, Ill., Jan. 6, 1915; s. Ensley Flavo and Mabel Mae (Stotler) P.; A.B., Knox Coll., Galesburg, Ill., 1935; B. of Medicine, Northwestern, 1939, M.D., 1940; m. Gwendolen Sophia Ellen Williams, Dec. 12, 1942; children—Richard Owen, Douglas Roscoe. Fellow clin. endocrinology Duke U. Sch. Medicine and Duke Hosp., 1940-41; rotating intern Charity Hosp. La., New Orleans, 1939-40, resident internal medicine Tulane U. unit, 1941-44, asst. clin. dir., 1943-44, asst. dir., 1944-46, sr. vis. physician, 1949-52; instr. medicine Tulane U., 1943-46, prof. grad. medicine, dir. Div. Grad. Medicine, vice dean Tulane U. Sch. Medicine, 1949-52; asso. prof. medicine U. Wash., 1947-49; med. dir. King County Hosp. System, Seattle, 1947-49; cons. to surgeon gen., Dept. Army, Washington, 1947—; cons. medicine V.A. Hosp., New Orleans, 1949-52; lectr. medicine V.A. Hosp., Gulfport, Miss., 1949-52; dean and prof. of medicine, U. of Tex. Postgrad. Sch. of Medicine, Houston, 1952-53; prof. of clin. medicine, Baylor U. Coll. of Medicine, 1952-53; dean and prof. of medicine, U. of Mo. Sch. of Medicine 1953-59; dir. Univ. Hosp.; past med. cons. Mo. State Crippled Children's Service; med. adv. com. Charity Hosp. Sch. Nursing; mem. med. adv. bd. Flint-Goodridge Hosp. of Dillard U. Recipient Knox Coll. Alumni Achievement award, 1945, Northwestern U. Alumni Achievement award, 1955. Diplomate Am. Bd. Internal Medicine. Fellow A.M.A., A.C.P., Mo. Heart Assn., Am. Heart Assn.; member Mo. State Med. Assn., Boone Co. Med. Soc., Mo. Trudeau Soc., So. Medical Association, American Medical Writer Association, mem. Phi Beta Kappa. Alpha Omega Alpha, Sigma Nu, Phi Beta Pi, Delta Omega Soc. Editor: Med. Diagnosis: Applied Phys. Diagnosis, 1944-50; Communicable Diseases, 1950; The Internship, 1952; Pulmonary Diseases, 1955. Editor: Bull. Tulane Med. Faculty, 1949-52; Am. Lectures in Internal Medicine since 1950. Home: E. 1715 39th St., Spokane 34. Office: Paulsen Med. & Dental Bldg., Spokane 1, Wash. Died Mar. 2, 1960.

PULLIAM, William Ellis, ret. treaty ofcl.; b. Louisville, Ky., Dec. 25, 1871; s. Henry Clay and Mary Thomas (Page) P.; LL.B., U. Ore., 1895; m. Muriel Helm Cartwright, July 1, 1896; children—Ellis Page, Phyllis (wife of Major Wm. Wesson Jervey). Apptd. dep. collector of customs, Portland, 1893; spl. agt. Treasury Dept., 1898-1901; customs expert, Manila, 1901-03; spl. dep. collector of customs, P.I., 1903-07; receiver gen. of Dominican customs, 1907-39, ret. from customs service, 1939, having served under 6 pres'. Originated project of a Pan-Am. Columbus Meml. in Santo Domingo, 1914; idea adopted by Fifth Internat. Conf. at Santiago de Chile, 1923, Am. Senate, 1927, adopted House Concurrent Resolution No. 41, approving project and expressed "desire of people of U.S. to participate in this movement to honor the memory of the great navigator and discoverer," made subject of spl. message of Pres. Coolidge to Congress, 1928; action affirmed by Pan-Am. Conf., 1933. With Guggenheim mining interests Chile, 1916, 19. Commd. col., Staff of Gov. of Ky., 1935. Decorated Order of Juan Pablo Duarte (Dominican Republic), 1935; Order of the Crown (Italy), 1938. Episcopalian. Home: Carmel-by-the-Sea, Cal. Died Aug. 9, 1949.

PURCELL, Charles Henry (pûr-sĕl'), civil engr.; b. North Bend, Neb., Jan. 27, 1883; s. John and Mary (Gillis) P.; student Stanford U., 1903; C.E., U. of Neb., 1906; E.D., 1936; LL.D., U. of Calif., 1937; m. Minnie Pullen, Feb. 24, 1914. Resident engr. on railroad constrn. in Wyo., 1906-07; asst. chief engr. smelting and power development, Peru, 1909-10; highway and bridge engr. in Northwest on state and pvt. projects, 1910-17; bridge engr. for U.S. Bur. Pub. Roads, Ore., 1917-27; highway engr. State of Calif., Division Highways, 1928-42; appointed dir. public works, Calif.; ex-officio chmn. Calif. Highway commn.; ex-officio chmn. State Reconstruction and Reemployment Commn., 1943; apptd. sec. Hoover-Young San Francisco-Oakland Bay Bridge Commn., 1929; made traffic survey and design for San Francisco-Oakland Bay Bridge in 1931; apptd. chief engr. San Francisco-Oakland Bay Bridge. Rep. of U.S. on the Permanent Internat. Commn. of the Permanent Internat. Assn. of Road Congresses; mem. Interregional Highway Committee since 1941. Mem. Am. Soc. Civil Engineers (hon.), Am. Assn. of State Highway Officials (past president; mem. executive committee), Chi Phi. Clubs: Family, Press, Commonwealth (San Francisco); Sutter and Del Paso Country Club (Sacramento). Home: 2231 N. St. Office: P.O. Box 1079, Sacramento. Died Sept. 7, 1951.

PURCELL, George William, newspaper pub.; b. Vincennes, Ind., Dec. 6, 1888; s. Royal Ellis and Georgie (Wise) P.; Vincennes U., 1906-07; A.B., Ind. U., 1909, A.M., 1910; m. Ella R. Rosenbaum, Oct. 7, 1914; children—George W., Royal E., Robert A. Teaching fellow Ind. U., 1909-10; began newspaper work as reporter Vincennes Sun, 1910, became partner, 1910, pub., 1918-26; purchased Evening World, Bloomington, Ind., 1926; sec.-treas. Purcell Pub. Co.; apptd. postmaster, Bloomington, 1933; reappointed 1938; 1st v.p. nat. Assn. of Postmasters, 1937-38; pres. 1938-39. Former trustee Purdue, Vincennes U. Mem. Associated Press, Inland Daily Press Assn., Am. Philatelic Soc., Phi Gamma Delta, Sigma Delta Chi, Phi Delta Kappa. Democrat. Elder, Presbyn. Ch. Home: 217 S. Dunn. Office: 113 W. 4th St., Bloomington, Ind. Died Oct. 25, 1952; buried Vincennes, Ind.

PURCELL, Richard J., prof. history; b. Minneapolis, Dec. 19, 1887; s. Richard Dwyer and Mary (Reedy) P.; A.B., U. of Minn., 1910, M.A., 1911; Ph.D., Yale, 1916; LL.B., Georgetown U., 1939; m. Clara A. Fick (A.B., M.A.), June 23, 1923; children

—Capt. Richard Fick, Mary Magdalen, Patricia Eileen. Asst. in history, U. Minn., 1911-12; fellow and asst. in history, Yale, 1912-16 (Addison Porter prize); head of dept. history and govt., St. Thomas Coll., St. Paul, 1916-20; instr. in history, Catholic U. of America, 1920-22, asso. prof. history and sec. Sch. of Philosophy, 1922-29, prof. history since 1929, head of dept., 1931-42, gen. sec. of univ., 1930-35; lecturer Grad. Sch., Georgetown Univ., 1940-43; with W.P.B. since 1944; at George Washington U., since 1945. Guggenheim Memorial fellow to study Irish immigration, 1927-28. Mem. Bar of D.C., Am. History Assn., Am.-Irish Hist. Soc. (historiographer), Nat. Council for Social Studies, Soc. Am. Archivists, Am. Assn. Univ. Profs. (pres. local chapter); Middle States Assn. of History and Social Science Teachers (pres. 1941), Pi Gamma Mu, Yale Club. Editorial adviser, Young America, Catholic Messenger. Author: Connecticut in Transition (awarded Justin Windsor prize), 1918; American Nation, 1929, and 1937; Labor Policies of the N.P.A.C. and O.P.M., 1946. Contributor to America, Studies, Irish Ecclesiastical Record (Dublin), Thought, Commonweal, London Tablet, Catholic World, Catholic Ednl. Review, Catholic Historical Review, Georgetown Law Journal, Social Studies, Social Education, World Book, Grolier and Catholic Encys.; also chapters in several volumes, and 175 sketches in Dictionary of Am. Biography. Home: 1233 Lawrence St. N.E., Washington 17; and Lake City, Minn. Died Jan. 3, 1950; buried Washington.

PURCELL, Theodore Vincent, former public utility co. official; b. New York, N.Y., Mar. 11, 1866; s. John and Louisa (O'Toole) P.; B.S. and M.E., Cooper Inst., New York, 1894; m. Anna Loretta Wallace, Feb. 3, 1892 (dec.); children—Dorothy, Kathryn (Mrs. Donald S. Johnson), Theodore (dec.), John Wallace, Natalia (Mrs. Carl J. Weber), Theodore V. Began with Equitable Gas Light Co. of New York, 1883, gen. supt., 1895, until consolidation with New Amsterdam Co., of which was asst. engr., 1899-1901; gen. mgr. and sec. Ogden Gas Co., 1901-07; sec. Peoples Gas Light & Coke Co., 1907-24, v.p., 1924-36; lectr. on ratemaking. Received C. A. Munroe Award, 1931. Pres. Chicago Plant Flower & Fruit Guild, 1926—. Mem. Western Soc. Engrs. Club: Westmoreland Country (charter). Home: 1126 Judson Av., Evanston, Ill. Office: 122 S. Michigan Av., Chgo. Died Oct. 6, 1957; buried Calvary Cemetery, N.Y.C.

PURDY, Lawson, trustee; b. Hyde Park, New York, Sept. 13, 1863; s. James S. (D.D.) and Frances H. (Carter) P.; A.B., Trinity Coll., Conn., 1884, A.M., 1887, LL.D., 1908; m. Mary J. McCrackan, 1885; m. 2d, Mrs. Helene Wexelsen, 1940. Admitted to bar, 1898; sec. New York Tax Reform Assn., 1896-1906; pres. Dept. Taxes and Assessments, New York, 1906-17; vice chmn. Commn. on Bldg. Districts and Restrictions, New York, 1914-16; gen. dir. Charity Orgn. Soc. City of N.Y., 1918-33; comptroller Trinity Ch., 1933-37; dir. Seamen's Bank for Savings, 1930-45, sec., 1934-45; trustee Provident Loan Soc. Trustee Trinity Coll.; pres. Robert Schalkenbach Foundation. Pres. Nat. Conf. on City Planning, 1920, 21; pres. Nat. Municipal League, 1916; sec. Commn. to Revise Tenement House Law, 1927; chmn. Emergency Work and Relief Adminstrn., 1932-33; acting pres. and pres. Russell Sage Foundation, 1931-44. Recipient Am. Soc. Planning officials award, 1952, Am. Inst. Planning award, 1952; Regional Planning Assn., 1954. Home: 76 Murray Av., Port Washington, N.Y. Died Aug. 30, 1959; buried Rye, N.Y.

PURDY, Ross Coffin, ceramic engr.; b. Jasper, N.Y., Mar. 3, 1875; s. Andrew and Mary Elizabeth (Coffin) P.; student Syracuse U., 1894-96; Ceramic Engr., Ohio State U., 1908; D.Sc., Alfred U., 1936; m. Myra J. Watts, June 27, 1901; children—Reliance S., Constance H., Lois B. Chemist and asst. supt., Mosaic Tile Co., Zanesville, 1899-1901; chemist Roseville Pottery Co., Zanesville, 1901-02; asst. in ceramics, Ohio State U., 1902-04; 1st instr. in ceramics, U. of Ill., 1904-06; asst. prof. ceramics Ohio State U., 1906-08, prof., 1908-12; dir. research, Norton Co., Worcester, Mass., 1912-18. Gen. sec. and editor Jour. Am. Ceramic Soc., 1921-46; author forty tech. papers. Formerly mem. Ohio Nat. Guard; four-minute man, World War, also chmn. N.E. Fuel Conservation and active in Liberty Loan drives. Fellow A.A.A.S., Am. Soc. for Testing Materials; hon. fellow. Am. Ceramic Soc., Soc. of Glass Technology (Eng.); hon. life mem. Ohio Ceramic Industries Assn., Canadian Ceramic Soc., Czechoslovak Ceramic Soc., Indian Ceramic Soc.; mem. Psi Upsilon, Sigma Xi, Keramos. Republican. Presbyterian. Mason (Shriner). Club: Internat. Rotary. Home: 59 E. Longview Av., Columbus 2, O. Died Jan. 6, 1949.

PURINGTON, Florence (pûr'ing-tŭn), educator; b. Burnt Hills, N.Y., Aug. 12, 1862; d. Rev. Lewis Madison and Emily (Sherman) Purington; grad. Mt. Holyoke Sem. (now Coll.), 1886, B.S., 1896, Litt. D., 1912; summer schs., Harvard and U. Mich. Instr. mathematics Mt. Holyoke Coll., 1887-1905, dean, 1907-1929, elected trustee, 1925. Mem. Nat. Assn. Deans of Women (pres. 1925-26; 2d v.p. 1926-27), Am. Assn. U. Women; Am. Assn. for UN, Phi Beta Kappa. Mem. Am. sect. of governing bd. Women's Christian Coll., Madras, India. Conglist. Home: South Hadley, Mass. Died May 22, 1950.

PURINTON, Edward Earle, author; b. Morgantown, W.Va., Apr. 24, 1878; s. Daniel Boardman and Florence Abbey (Lyon) P.; grad. Doane Acad., Granville, O., 1895; A.B., Denison U., 1899; unmarried. Instr. Doane Acad., 1900, later editorial counsel or dir. various publs., lecturer on health, psychology and efficiency, etc.; now research specialist, efficiency analyst and counsel; dean Am. Efficiency Foundation, dir. Reconstruction Ednl. Alliance, dir. National Prosperity Survey, pres. National Efficiency League, all of N.Y. City. Mem. Nat. Inst. Social Sciences, Am. Acad. Polit. and Social Science. Sigma Chi. Republican. Author: Efficient Living, 1915; The Triumph of the Man Who Acts, 1916; Pétain, the Prepared, 1917; Practical Course in Personal Efficiency, 1917; Personal Efficiency in Business, 1919; also many brochures, pamphlets, and numerous articles to mags. Home: 76 Grandview Av., Morgantown, W.Va. Office: 475 Fifth Av., N.Y.C. Died 1945; buried Oak Grove Cemetery, Morgantown, W.Va.

PURNELL, Frank, steel company exec.; b. Youngstown, O., October 11, 1886; s. Edward and Ann (Hanson) P.; ed. pub. schs.; m. Anne Watkins, May 12, 1911. Began as office boy with Youngstown (O.) Sheet & Tube Co., serving in various positions until 1919; became v.p. Consol. Steel Co. in charge sales, later v.p. Bethlehem Steel Co. in charge export sales; returned to Youngstown Sheet & Tube Co. as v.p., president, 1930-50, chmn. of bd. since 1950; director Youngstown Steel Door Co., Youngstown Foundry & Machine Company, Interlake Steamship Company, National City Bank of Cleveland, Emsco Derrick & Equipment Company, Los Angeles. Member board govs. Youngstown Coll.; trustee Y.M.C.A. of Youngstown; dir. Community Corp., Youngstown Chapter Am. Red Cross, Am. Iron & Steel Inst., Ohio Soc. Conglist. Mason. Clubs: Youngstown, Youngstown Country; Duquesne (Pittsburgh); Union (Cleveland); Chicago. Home: 280 Tod Lane, Youngstown 3. Office: Stambaugh Bldg., Youngstown 1, O. Died Apr. 18, 1953.

PURNELL, William Reynolds, naval officer; b. Sept. 6, 1886; entered U.S. Navy, 1904, and advanced through the grades to rear adm., 1941; serving as member munitions assignment board of U.S. and Great Britain. Address: 31 Tevis Pl., Palo Alto, Cal. Died Mar. 5, 1955; buried Golden Gate Nat. Cemetery.

PURYEAR, Charles, educator; b. nr. Boydton, Va., Oct. 21, 1860; s. Bennet and Virginia Catherine (Ragland) P.; M.A., Richmond Coll., Va., 1881; C.E., B.S., U. Va., 1885; LL.D., Daniel Baker, 1914. Tchr. Bellevue (Va.) High Sch., 1882, McGuire's Sch., Richmond, Va. 1883, Cleve. High Sch., Markham, Va., 1886; instr. mathematics, U. of Mich., 1888; asso. prof. civ. engring. and physics, 1889, prof. mathematics, 1890-1932, dean of the coll., 1907-32, dean of grad. sch., 1924-32, now emeritus, Agrl. and Mech. Coll. of Tex. Mem. Phi Beta Kappa; past pres. Assn. Tex. Colls. Baptist. Democrat. Author: (with Prof. T. U. Taylor) Elements of Plane and Spherical Trigonometry, 1902. Home: College Station, Tex. Deceased.

PUSEY, Brown (pū'zē), ophthalmologist, ret.; b. Elizabethtown, Ky., Dec. 14, 1869; s. Robert B. and Bell (Brown) P.; student Vanderbilt U., class of 1889; M.D., U. Pa., 1892; grad. student 15 mos. in Germany and Vienna, 1898-99, in Freiburg and Vienna, 1904. Asst. surgeon USN, 1893-96; house surgeon N.Y. Eye and Ear Infirmary, 1896-97; began practice at Chgo., 1899; instr. pathology of the eye U. Chgo., 1902-08; prof. ophthalmology and head dept. Northwestern U., 1908-27, now prof. emeritus; ophthalmologist to Cook County Hosp., 1905-10. Fellow Inst. of Medicine Chgo.; mem. Am. Ophthal. Society, A.M.A., Ill., Chgo. med. socs. Clubs: University, Glenview Golf. Contbr. on ophthalmology. Home: (summer) Glen View Club, Golf, Ill.; (winter) 76 E. Monroe St., Chgo. 3. Died July 4, 1953.

PUTNAM, Albert William, lawyer, corp. exec.; b. Spuyten Duyvil, N.Y., Sept. 22, 1877; s. Albert Edward and Margaret Elizabeth (Morrison) P.; A.B., Columbia, 1897, LL.B., 1900; grad. Gen. Staff Coll., U.S. Army, 1918; m. Grace Witherbee Tucker, May 23, 1908; children—Mary Elizabeth (Mrs. Jonathan Fairchild Butler), Betty Waters (Mrs. Challen R. Parker, Jr.), Nancy Tucker (Mrs. Walter K. Howard), Grace Mitchell (Mrs. Augustus B. Wadsworth, Jr.). Engaged in practice of law, N.Y.C., 1900—; with Winthrop & Stimson, 1904-08, mem. firm, 1908—, now Winthrop, Stimson, Putnam & Roberts; dir. Rye Trust Co., Tingue Brown & Co. Mem. Troop B, Squadron A, N.Y. Cav., 1898-1917; capt. of troop, Mexican Border, 1916; capt. Machine Gun Bn., later major cav. and maj. F.A., U.S. Army, 1918. Trustee Columbia U., United Hosp., Port Chester, N.Y.; pres. N.Y. Law Inst. Mem. Phi Beta Kappa, Alpha Delta Phi, Phi Delta Phi. Republican. Clubs: Century, University, Down Town, Columbia University (N.Y.C.); Ekwanok Country (Manchester, Vt.); Manursing Island, Apawamis. Home: Highland Rd. Rye, N.Y. Office: 40 Wall St., N.Y.C. 5. Died Mar. 31, 1955.

PUTNAM, Eben Fiske Appleton, corp. official; b. Danvers, Mass., Apr. 23, 1891; s. Eben and Florence M. (Tucker) P.; grad. Staunton (Va.) Mil. Acad., 1909; M.E., Norwick U.; spl. engring. courses, Harvard; m. Frenelia L. Uhle, Oct. 30, 1915; 1 dau., Muriel Putnam Smith. Began career in employ of Commercial Engring. Dept., Gen. Electric Co.; with Conn. Light and Power Co., 1913-25, dist. mgr. Greenwich, 1917-18, Norwalk, 1919-24, New Britain, 1925; President, Pickwick Arms Hotel, Greenwich, Conn.; pres. Greenwich Water and Gas System, Inc., 1926-36; pres. Greenwich Gas Co., New Canaan Water Co., New Rochelle Water Co.; v.p. Bristol Co. Water Co., Dedham Water Co., New Rochelle (N.Y.) Water Co.; director Alcoma Packing Co. (Lake Wales, Fla.), Cohasset (Mass.) Water Co., Hingham Water Co., all 1928-36. Now pres. Greenwich Gas Co.; former trustee South Shore Utilities Assns. (Mass.); director First National Bank in Greenwich. Treas. Greenwich Y.M.C.A. (utility adminstr. war council). Chmn. Greenwich Selective Service Board. Sergt. Greenwich Mil. Police, 1918, disqualified for active war service by injuries; insp. U.S. Fuel Administration, 1918-19. Pres. Greenwich Social Service League; v.p. Greenwich Community Chest, trustee Norwich U. and various charitable, ednl. or pub. instns.; mem. Greenwich Chamber of Commerce (ex-pres.), Conn. Chamber Commerce, Guild of Gas Mgrs., Hist. Soc. Town of Greenwich (dir. and treas.), Greenwich Y.M.C.A. (v.p.), Soc. of Gas Lighting, Saints and Sinners (N.Y.). Republican. Conglist. Mason. Clubs: Masonic, Greenwich Country, Indian Harbor Yacht, Riverside Yacht, Milbrook Country, Rotary (Greenwich); University, Down Town (Boston); Norwich, Union League (New York). Home: 35 West Brother Drive. Office: 33 Greenwich Av., Greenwich, Conn. Died Feb. 14, 1953; buried Putnam Cemetery, Greenwich.

PUTNAM, George, trustee; b. Boston, June 4, 1889; s. William Lowell and Elizabeth (Lowell) P.; student Noble and Greenough Sch., 1898-1906; A.B., Harvard, 1910, LL.B., 1913; m. Katherine Harte, June 15, 1915; children—Barbara, Katharine, Elizabeth Lowell, George, Helen Harte. Admitted to Mass. bar, 1913, practiced law in Boston, 1913-16; with Richardson Hill & Co., 1916-24; chmn., dir. Gorton Pew Fisheries Co., Ltd., 1924—; pres. Inc. Investors, 1925-33; mem. Townsend, Anthony & Tyson, 1936-37; chmn. bd. trustees George Putnam Fund of Boston 1937—; dir. Package Machinery Co., Am. Mut. Liability Ins. Co., Spray Engring. Co. Pres., dir. Mass. Hosp. Service Corp. (Blue Cross). Served Plattsburg O.T.C., 1917; 1st lt. C.A.C., U.S. Army, 1917-18; disch. as capt. Clubs: Somerset (Boston); Essex Country (Manchester, Mass.). Home: Manchester, Mass. Office: 60 Congress St., Boston 9. Died Jan. 24, 1960.

PUTNAM, George Martin, farmer; b. Hopkinton, N.H., Jan. 18, 1864; s. Charles and Almira (Eastman) P.; ed. pub. schs., Hopkinton and Contoocook (N.H.) Acad.; hon. A.M., U. N.H., 1929; m. Flora Etta Clough, Jan. 19, 1899 (died Feb. 1, 1929). Engaged in farming, stock raising and dairying since boyhood; winner of 1st 2 gold medals in N.H. from Am. Jersey Cattle Club; pres. and mng. dir. N.H. Farm Bur. Fedn., 1917—; pres. Merrimack Farmers Exchange, Concord Dairy Co., chmn. N.H. Agrl. Conf., 1945-46. Farm Bureau Mutual Automobile Ins. Co.; treas. Merrimack County Mutual Fire Ins. Co., Farm Bur. Mut. Fire Ins. Co.; dir. United Dairy Credit Corp., Hopkinton Telephone Co., Grange Mutual Fire Ins. Co. of N.H.; clk. United Dairy Co. Mem. N.H. Ho. of Rep., 1899; mem. N.H. Constl. Conv., 1902; mem. advisory bd. N.H. State Dept. Agr.; mem. N.E. R.R. Com. by apptmt. of Gov. Tobey; mem. Nat. Civil Def. Com.; mem. State Bd. of Appeal, SSS; mem. State War Finance Agrl. Com.; pres. Agrl. Service Inc.; rep. American Farm Bureau Fed. at 3d World Power Conf., Washington, 1936; mem. coordinating com. Northeastern Dairy Conf.; mem. com. on govt. credit, Twentieth Century Fund, Inc. Dir. Am. Farm Bureau Fedn., N.E. Milk Producers Assn., Hopkinton Fair Assn. Central Wool Marketing Corp., Forest Products Assn., Inc.; treas. Granite State Dairymen's Assn. Recipient gold sheaf for 50 years' mem. Nat. Grange; gold medal for distinguished service to organized agriculture Am. Farm Bur. Fedn., 1928; Charles Holmes Pettee medal U. N.H. Alumni, 1943; citation N.H. Extension Service for service to 4H Clubs, 1946; hon. life mem. N.H. Young Farmers Assn. Mem. Grange. Democrat. Conglist. Established Putnam Agrl. Foundation in memory of wife, 1931. Home: Contoocook, N.H. Office: 28 S. Main St., Concord, N.H. Died Feb. 9, 1951; buried Contoocook, N.H.

PUTNAM, George Rockwell, engr., author; born Davenport, Ia., May 24, 1865; s. Charles E. and Mary L. (Duncan) P.; B.S., Rose Poly. Inst., 1890, M.S., 1895, Dr. Engring., 1933; D.Sc., Stevens Inst. of Technology, 1922; married Marta, d. Thomas P. Wick, September 11, 1913; children—Elizabeth Duncan (Mrs. C. L. Barber), Kristi Aresvik (Mrs. John Hay). Entered field service, United States Coast and Geodetic Survey, 1890; was on Mexican and Alaskan boundary surveys; in 1895 made series of gravity measurements, and developed reduction, results of which were the first consistent confirmation of isostatic condition of earth's crust; accompanied scientific expedition to Greenland, 1896; engaged on survey of Pribilof Islands, 1897, and of the delta of the Yukon River, 1898-99; made observations connecting Am. and European gravity stas., 1900; 1st dir. coast surveys in the P.I., 1900-06; developed plan of Philippine coast surveys; prepared plan for revision of charts of coasts of U.S.; commr. of lighthouses, 1910-35; carried out reorganization of U.S. Lighthouse Service; del. Internat. Lighthouse Conference, London, 1929. Mem. Am. Soc. C.E., Washington Soc. Engrs. (pres. 1915), Washington Acad. Sciences. Author: Sentinel of the Coasts; Lighthouses and Lightships of the United States; Nautical Charts; Radiobeacons and Radiobeacon Navigation; also tech. papers and reports. Clubs: Cosmos (pres. 1920), Chevy Chase. Home: 2126 Bancroft Pl., Washington, D.C.; also Dorset, Vt. Died July 2, 1953; buried Dorset.

PUTNAM, Helen Cordelia, M.D.; b. Sept. 14, 1857; d. Herbert Asa and Celintha T. (Gates) P.; A.B., Vassar, 1878; M.D., Woman's Med. Coll. of Pa., 1889; grad. Harvard (Sargent) Sch. of Physical Training; grad. N.E. Hosp. for Women and Children, Boston, 1891; LL.D., Western Reserve U., 1912; unmarried. Dir. Gymnasium, Vassar Coll., 1883-90; on bds. of mgrs. of R.I. Woman Suffrage Assn., summer playgrounds and vacation schs. com., etc. Sec. conf. on R.I. reformatory work for women. Fellow Am. Acad. Medicine (v.p. 1894, 1897, pres. 1908-09; chmn. exec. com. of Conf. on Prevention of Infant Mortality, 1909); mem. American Assn. for the Study and Prevention of Infant Mortality; mem. A.A.A.S.; hon. fellow Lehigh Valley Med. Assn.; v.p. Am. Assn. for Adv. Physical Edn., 1885-88; fellow Am. Pub. Health Assn. and A.M.A.; chmn. Com. Racial Well-Being, Nat. Council Edn. of N.E.A.; mem. Nat. Assn. for Study and Prevention of Tuberculosis, International Congress on Tuberculosis; del. Internat. Congress on School Hygiene, London and Buffalo, N.Y.; mem. Nat. Council of Playground Assn. of America; mem. Council Bureau permanent de l'Union Internationale pour la protection de l'enfance du premier âge; mem. council Am. Sch. Hygiene Assn.; delegate 2d Internat. Cong. Eugenics; mem. Mass. Soc. of Mental Hygiene. Lecturer on ednl. topics. Address: 312 Laurel Av., Providence, R.I. Died Feb. 3, 1951.

PUTNAM, Herbert, librarian; b. N.Y.C., Sept. 20, 1861; s. George Palmer and Victorine (Haven) P.; A.B., Harvard, 1883; law student Columbia, 1883-84; admitted to bar, 1886; Litt.D., Bowdoin Coll., 1898, Brown U., 1914, Princeton, 1933, Cath. U. of America, 1939; LL.D., Columbian (now George Washington) U., 1903, U. Ill., 1903, U. Wis., 1904, Yale, 1907, Williams Coll., 1911, Harvard, 1928, N.Y. U., 1930; m. Charlotte Elizabeth Munroe, October 5, 1886 (died October 26, 1928); children—Brenda, Mrs. Elliott O'Hara. Librarian Mpls. Athenaeum, 1884-87, Mpls. Pub. Library, 1887-91; practiced law, Boston, 1892-95; librarian Boston Pub. Library, 1895-99; librarian of Congress, 1899-1939, librarian emeritus since 1939. Mem. bd. Congress Arts and Sciences, La. Purchase Expn., 1904. U.S. del. to Internat. Library Conf., London, 1897, Congres Internat. de Bibliographie, Paris, 1900, Internat. Library and Bibliog. Congress, Rome, 1929. U.S. rep. at 500th anniversary of birth of Johann Gutenberg, Mainz, 1900. Overseer, Harvard, 1902-06. Fellow Am. Acad. Arts and Sciences, Nat. Inst. Arts and Letters; mem. Am. Acad. Arts and Letters, Am. Antiquarian Soc., Am. Philos. Soc., Hispanic Soc. America, Mass. Hist. Soc., Colonial Soc. of Mass.; hon. mem. Royal Asiatic Soc. (N. China br.). Pres. A.L.A., 1898, 1904; gen. dir. A.L.A. Library War Service, Oct. 1917-Oct. 1919. Decorated Knight Royal Order of Pole Star, Sweden, 1928. Awarded Roosevelt D.S.M., 1929. Clubs: Cosmos (Washington); Grolier (hon.), Century (N.Y.C.); Tavern (Boston). Contbr. to reviews and profl. jours. Home: Hotel Breakwater, Woods Hole, Mass. Died Aug. 14, 1955; created Forest Hill Cemetery, Boston.

PUTNAM, Russell Benjamin, Marine Corps officer; b. Abbeville Vermillion Parish, La., Jan. 7, 1878; s. James Henry and Mary Pauline (Johnson) P.; B.S., Centenary Coll., Jackson (now at Shreveport) ,La., 1894; M.E., Cornell U., 1901; m. Mabel Henry Triplett, Apr. 5, 1909; children—Edwina Triplett (wife of William Vincent Deutermann, U.S. Navy), Mary Russell (Mrs. Charles M. Bounds), Russell Henry. With Buffalo (New York) Forge Company, 1901-02, Am. Blower Company, New York, 1902-04; commd. 2d lt. U.S. Marine Corps, 1904, and advanced through the grades to brig. gen., Marine Corps May 1, 1938; served in the Philippines, 1909-12, Nicaraguan campaign, Sept.-Dec. 1912, occupation of Vera Cruz, 1914, Haitian campaign, 1915-16, Dominican campaign, 1916-17, Hdqrs. U.S. Marine Corps, 1917-19, duty in Haiti, 1919-21, Hdqrs. and stations of Paymaster Dept., 1921-38; retired, Feb. 1942. Wounded in action Guayacannes, San Domingo, July 3, 1916; awarded Purple Heart, Legion of Merit; also medals of Nicaraguan Campaign, 1912, Vera Cruz Campaign (with star), 1915, Dominican Campaign, 1916, Victory medal, 1919 (U.S.); Medaille Militaire (Haiti), 1921. Mem. Kappa Sigma. Mason, Sojourner, Heroes of '76. Clubs: Army and Navy, Army and Navy Country (Washington, D.C.); Huntington Valley Country (Ridal, Pa.). Home: 801 Russel Rd., Alexandria, Va. Office: Hdqrs., U.S. Marine Corps, Washington, D.C. Died May 29, 1959.

PUTNAM, William Hutchinson, investment banker; b. Brooklyn, Conn., Feb. 1, 1878; s. Albert Day and Harriet Eliza (Dorrance) P.; ed. pub. schs.; hon. M.A., Trinity Coll., 1942; L.H.D., Hillyer College, Hartford, Conn., 1955; m. Adabelle C. Lyon, Mar. 8, 1899 (died Apr. 17, 1944); children—Lyonel Hutchinson, Marcella Rockwell, Albert Day. Clerk in Windham County Nat. Bank, Danielson, Conn.; with New England Mutual Life Ins. Co., William A. Read & Co., N.Y.; partner Richter & Co., Hartford predecessor of Putnam & Co.; sr. partner Putnam & Co., 1921—; dir. Hartford Spl. Machinery Co. Mem. N.Y. Stock Exchange. Chmn. Greater Hartford Bridge Authority, Redevelopment Commn.; dir. YMCA; mem. Hartford Park Commn., 1931-48; past pres. Hartford Community Chest; mem. Hartford Finance Commn., 1916-22; treas. Conn. State Tercentary Commn., 1935-36; chairman, member bd. directors Hartford Hosp.; dir. St. Francis Hospital, Children's Museum. Mem. of Conn. River Valley Flood Control Commn. Chmn. bd. trustees Conn. Coll. for Women, New London, Suffield Acad., trustee Horace Bushnell Memorial, Conn. chmn. Liberty Loans, 1917-19, Conn. Hist. Soc. (finance com.), Soc. of Cincinnati of Conn., Soc. of Colonial Wars, Mayflower Soc., Soc. of Founders and Patriots, Walpole Society, Laurel Garden Club, Royal Horticulture Society of England. Episcopalian. Republican. Mason (32°, Shriner, K.T.). Clubs: Hartford; Union League, Century Assn. (N.Y.C.); Tobique Salmon, (New Brunswick, Can.). Home: 1010 Prospect Av. Office: 6 Central Row, Hartford, Conn. Died Mar. 10, 1953; buried Old Trinity Church Yard, Brooklyn, Conn.

PUTNAM, William Rowell, public utility exec.; b. Red Wing, Minn., Aug. 17, 1876; s. William Herrick and Adeline M. (Rowell) P.; A.B., U. Minn., 1897; m. Jessie Gale Eaton, July 2, 1901; children—William H., Charlotte A., Alice E. Mgr. Red Wing (Minn.) Gas & Elec. Co., 1899-1909; gen. supt. Menominee & Marionette Light & Traction Co., Menominee, Mich., 1909-11; gen. mgr. Dakota Power Co., Rapid City, 1911-14; comml. mgr. Utah Power & Light Co., Salt Lake City, 1914-19; now v.p., gen. mgr. Ida. Power Co., Nev. Power Co., Electric Investment Co.; v.p. Boise Valley Traction Co., Phoenix Utility Co. Republican. Presbyn. Mason. Club: Sleepy Hollow Country. Home: Alger Ct. Apts., Bronxville, N.Y. Died Nov. 14, 1957.

PUTNEY, Elmore M., business exec.; b. Port Sanilac, Mich., Oct. 16, 1895; s. Charles G. and Jessie A. (Moore) P.; student Okla. Agr. and Mining Coll., 1914-18; m. Lela Marie Bunte, May 14, 1926; children—Marie, Elmore, Philip, Charles, Mary Marjorie. With Sprankle Constrn. Co., Ft. Smith, Ark., 1919; oil field work in Okla. and Tex., 1921; stock chow demonstrator, Ralston Purina Co., 1922, asst. div. sales mgr., 1922-27, div. sales mgr., 1927-40, vice pres. and gen. sales mgr. since 1940. Mem. bd. dirs., St. Luke's Hosp., St. Louis; mem. bd. edn., City of St. Louis, 1944-49, pres., 1947-48. Served as 2d lt., U.S. Army, 1917-19. Mem. St. Louis C. of C., Am. Soc. Sales Execs., Am. Legion, Sigma Chi. Presbyterian. Mason. Clubs: Missouri Athletic, Normandy Country (St. Louis). Home: 15 Washington Terrace, St. Louis 12. Office: Ralston Purina Co., 835 S. 8th St., St. Louis 2. Died Oct. 2, 1951; buried Oak Grove Cemetery.

PYLE, Robert, rose grower, nurseryman; b. London Grove, Pa., Mar. 7, 1877; s. Robert Lewis and Elizabeth David (Walton) P.; ed. London Grove Friends Sch., 1884-93; A.B., Swarthmore Coll., 1897; grad. work, Internat Sch. for Social and Religious Study, Woodbrooke, Eng., 1907; m. Hannah Warner Cadbury, Mar. 15, 1910. Acting supt. Swarthmore Coll., Pa., 1897-98; sec., 1899-1906. Pres. The Conard-Pyle Co., Star Rose Growers, West Grove, Pa. (formerly The Conard & Jones Co.), since 1906; v. pres. Nat. Bank & Trust Co., 1917-30, dir. since 1930. Lecturer on roses and rose gardens, since 1912; Am. rep. Am. Rose Soc., serving as judge, Internat. Rose Contest at Bagatelle, Paris, France, 1911, 1925, 30, 35, 38, 46, 48, 50; trustee Am. Rose Soc., 1913-40, v.p., 1913-14, pres., 1919-23, sec., 1923-32. Awarded Am. Rose Soc. Gold Medal "for his untiring effort and invaluable service to the rose"; Officer Grand Ducal Order of Crown of Oak, Luxembourg, 1947. Nat. councillor U.S. Chamber of Commerce, representing Am. Assn. Nurserymen; chmn com. on arboretums and bot. gardens, Am. Assn. Nurserymen. Trustee, Swarthmore Coll., 1910-50. Co-founder and charter member Am. Assn. Bot. Gardens and Arboretums; mem. Nat. Arboretum Adv. Council (exec. com.), Am. Hort. Soc., Washington, D.C. (pres. 1932-35), Nat. Assn. Plant Patent Owners (pres. 1940-43), All-Am. Rose Selections, Inc. (v.p. 1940-48), Am. Hort. Council, Inc. (pres. 1943-48; founding com. for United Horticulture), Royal Horticultural Soc., Delta Upsilon, Sigma Xi, Phi Alpha Xi. Republican. Religious Soc. of Friends. Clubs: Cosmos (Washington); University (New York); University (Phila.). Author: 1st 16 edits of, How to Grow Roses (joint editor last 3 edits), 1930-48. Home: Rose Hill House. Office: The Conard-Pyle Co., West Grove, Pa. Died Sept. 28, 1951.

PYNE, Percy Rivington II (pin), banker; b. N.Y. C., June 23, 1882; s. Moses Taylor and Margaretta (Stockton) P.; A.B., Princeton, 1903. With Farmers Loan & Trust Co., N.Y.C., 1904-07, with Estate of Moses Taylor, 1907-09; founded firm of Pyne, Kendall & Hollister, 1909; retired, 1927; now executor and trustee. Formerly trustee or dir. many corps., among them Nat. City Bank, Del. and Hudson Railroad Co., Empire Trust Co., Farmers Loan & Trust Co., Princeton Bank & Trust Co., etc. Served as asst. dir. and business mgr. Council of Nat. Defense and War Industries Bd., 1917-19. Now or formerly trustee Princeton U., St. Luke's Hosp., Children's Aid Soc., YMCA of N.Y.C. (chmn. E. Side br.), Perkiomen Sch., Kipp's Bay Boys Club, Diocesan Conv. of Chs. N.Y.; vice chmn. Nat. Americanization Com.; treas. Patterson Sch. of N.C.; mem. standing com. St. Paul's Sch., N.H.; exec. com. Boy Scouts Am. of Nassau County. Mem. Am. Acad. Polit. and Social Science, Princeton Engring. Assn., N.J. Hist. Soc., N.Y. Zoöl. Soc., Pan Am. Soc., St. Nichols Soc., Motor Car Touring Soc. (v.p., gov.), U.S. Golf Assn. (treas., mem. exec. com.). Episcopalian. Republican. Clubs: The Brook (pres. gov.), Union (gov.), Knickerbocker, Racquet and Tennis (gov.), Princeton (gov.), Church, Links, Turf and Field (v.p., gov.), Westminster Kennel (gov.), Southside Sportsman (gov., sec.), New York Yacht (N.Y.C.); Ivy of Princeton (gov.); Piping Rock, Meadowbrook, Garden City Golf, Nat. Golf Links (L.I.); Metropolitan (Washington); Philadelphia, Racquet and Tennis (Phila.); Tennis and Racquet (Boston); White's Club (London); Travelers (Paris); Metamajaw, (gov.), Alamance Quail (gov.). Decorated Chevalier Order of the Crown and Officer Order of Leopold II (Belgium); La Crux, 3d Class, Order del Merito Naval (Spain). Was intercollegiate golf champion, 1900. Home: 111 E. 54th St., N.Y.C.; also Roslyn, L.I., and Princeton, N.J. Died Aug. 15, 1950 (Vol. 1 erroneously listed as deceased in 1929).

PYRON, Walter Braxton, army officer; b. Matthews, N.C., April 10, 1882; married Gertrude Magdalena Drach, May 19, 1946. Commd. 1st, lt. Cav. Tex. N.G., 1921, advanced to brig. gen. of the line, 1938; on active duty with 56th Cav. Brigade, Ft. McIntosh, Tex., 1940-41; in office of under sec. of war, Washington, 1941-42; became liaison officer, for petroleum in the resources div. at hdqrs. Services of Supply (Production Div., Army Service Forces), 1942-43; on duty in the Office Q.M.G., Washington, 1943; duty with Army-Navy Petroleum Bd.; mem. Joint Chiefs of Staff; lived in Europe, 1946-50. Home: 4909 Fairview Dr., Austin 3, Tex. Died Jan. 8, 1951.

Q

QUAIFE, Milo Milton (kwāf), author, historian; born in Nashua, Iowa, October 6, 1880; s. Albert E. and Barbara S. (Hine) Quaife; Ph.B., Iowa College, Grinnell, 1903; A.M., U. Missouri, 1905; Ph.D., U. Chicago, 1908; Litt.D., Wayne University, 1951, Eastern Michigan University; married Letitia Goslin, June 1909; children—Helen Elizabeth, Donald Lincoln, Dorothy Barbara, Mary Louise. Instr. history, 1908-09, asst. prof., 1909-12, prof., 1912-13, Lewis Inst., Chicago; supt. Wis. State Hist. Soc., 1914-20, editor, 1920-22; grad lecturer Wayne U., 1931-42, Univ. of Detroit, 1932-35. Pres. Anthony Wayne Memorial Assn., 1941-47. Member American Antiquarian Soc., Miss. Valley Hist. Assn. (pres. 1919-20), etc.; co-founder of Algonquin Club, Detroit, 1935 (pres. 1935-47). Author: The Doctrine of Non-Intervention with Slavery in the Territories, 1910; Chicago and the Old Northwest, 1913; The Development of Chicago, 1674-1914, 1916; Chicago's Highways, Old and New, 1923; Wisconsin—Its History and Its People, 1924; The Kingdom of Saint James, 1930; Chegagou—From Indian Wigwam to Modern City, 1933; Condensed Historical Sketches for Each of Michigan's Counties, 1940; The Flag of the United States, 1942; Lake Michigan, 1944; The Life of John Wendell Anderson, 1950; also various publications, relating to the West and to American history in general; author (with Sidney Glazer), Michigan from Primitive Wilderness to Industrial Commonwealth, 1948; (with John C. Lodge) I Remember Detroit, 1949; Here is Detroit, a pictorial history of 250 years, 1951; (with Joseph E. and Estelle L. Bayliss) River of Destiny: the Saint Marys, 1955; (with Joe L. Norris) Forty-six Years: The Published Writings of Milo M. Quaife, 1915-1955. Editor: When Detroit Was Young, 1951; mng. editor Miss. Valley Hist. Rev., 1924-30. Editor ann. vols. Lakeside Classics Series, 1916—; secretary and editor Burton Historical Collection, Detroit Public Library, 1924-47; advisory editor Dictionary of American History, 1937-39; advisory editor Atlas of American History, 1941-43; editor American Lakes Series, 1941-49. Organizer and chmn. Mich.-Ontario Hist. Conv., 1938, Maumee Valley Hist. Conv., 1940. Editor: From the Cannon's Mouth: The Civil War Letters of General Alpheus S. Williams. Home: 56 Louise Av., Highland Park 3, Mich. Died Sept. 1, 1959; buried White Chapel Cemetery.

QUARLES, Donald A(ubrey), dep. sec. of def.; b. Van Buren, Ark., July 30, 1894; s. Robert W. and Minnie (Hynes) Q.; B.A., Yale, 1916; grad. study Columbia, 1920-24; D.E., U. Ark., 1953, N.Y.U., 1956; D.Sc., Grinell Coll., Stevens Inst., 1956; LL.D., Yale, 1957; m. Rosina Cotton, Oct. 27, 1939; children (by former marriage)—Carolyn Anne, Donald Aubrey, Elizabeth Whittemore (Mrs. Stanley C. Lewis). Engineer with the Bell Telephone Labs. (formerly engineering department Western Electric Co.), 1919-53, v.p., 1948-52; v.p. Western Electric Co., pres. Sandia Corp., 1952-53; asst. secretary of defense (research and development), Washington, 1953-55, sec. Air Force, 1955-57; dep. sec. of defense, 1957—. Former mayor of Englewood N.J. Recipient award of merit American Inst. Cons. Engrs., Exceptional Service award, Dept. Air Force, 1957; Cruz Peruana Al Merito Aeronautico, 1956; Brazilian Ordem Do Merito Aeronautic 1957; Capo dell Ordine Al Merito della Republica Italiana; Spanish Grand Cross, Order of Mil. Merit (posthumous), Medal of Freedom United States (posthumous). Served as captain, FA, U.S. Army, 1917-19. Fellow Am. Inst. E.E. (pres. 1952-53), Am. Phys. Soc., Am. Inst. Radio Engrs.; mem. A.A.A.S., Yale Engineering Society, Telephone Pioneers of America, Sigma Xi., Phi Beta Kappa, also Eta Kappa Nu (honorary). Republican. Clubs: Englewood; Knickerbocker Country (Tenafly, N.J.); Cosmos (Washington); Engineers (N.Y.C.). Address: 3041 Porter St., Washington 8. Office: The Pentagon, Washington. Died May 8, 1959; buried Arlington Nat. Cemetery.

QUARLES, James (kwôrlz), lawyer; b. Lexington, Mo.; s. Rev. James Addison (D.D., LL.D.) and Caroline Wallace (Field) Q.; prep. edn. Wentworth Mil. Acad., Lexington, Mo.; LL.B., Washington and Lee U., 1889; m. Fanny Kent, dau. Judge George M. Harrison, Oct. 26, 1898; children—Caroline Field, Frances (Mrs. Alex F. Robertson, Jr.). Admitted to Ky. bar, 1889, began practice at Louisville; practiced with John Roberts, later with Col. Thomas W. Bullitt, and as partner with Maj. A. E. Richards, title of Richards & Quarles; chancellor Jefferson Circuit Court, 1911-15; prof. law Washington and Lee U., 1917-19; mem. bd. referees to fix compensation for use of railways under Fed. control, 1920; asst. chief counsel ICC, 1920-21; resigned, and settled in Milw., as mem. Lines, Spooner & Quarles, until 1931; returned to Washington and opened office for general practice. Mem. Am. Bar Assn., Am. Law Inst., Acad. Polit. Science (New York), Phi Kappa Psi, Phi Delta Phi; pres. Louisville Bar Assn., 1916-17. Democrat. Presbyn. Club: Cosmos (Washington). Author: Powers of the President as Commander-in-Chief, 1943; Union Labor in Peace and War, 1943; How the Constitution Fared During the Last Decade, 1943; Predestination and Election: A Lawyer's View, 1944; Body and Mind—A Layman's Thoughts and Gleanings, 1948; also numerous articles in profl. publs. and newspapers. Home: Staunton, Va. Died Sept. 9, 1950.

QUAY, Arthur Hayes, banker; b. Geneva, N.Y., June 28, 1895; s. Joseph Fearon and Mabel (Willoughby) Q.; student Wayzata High Sch., 1915; m. Marion Swaggert, June 17, 1922; children—Elizabeth, Jean, Carolyn, Nancy. Started in credit dept., First Nat. Bank of Minneapolis, 1917, asst. cashier, 1927, v.p., 1938-50, pres. since 1950, dir. since 1949; v.p., dir., First Bank Stock Corp.; dir. First Service Corp., Northwestern Fire & Marine Ins. Co.; pres., dir., First Bloomington-Lake Nat. Bank; dir. Fed. Res. Bank of Minneapolis, First Bancredit Corp., Northwestern Nat. Life Ins. Co., St. Paul & Sault Ste. Marie R.R. Trustee Minneapolis Found. Served with F.A., U.S. Army, 1917-19. Mem. Assn. Res. City Bankers, Assn. Credit Men, Am. Inst. of Banking, Am. Legion, Newcomen Soc. Conglist. Clubs: Minikahda, Minneapolis, Ahtletic, Interlachen Country, Chicago. Home: Wayzata, Minn. Office: First National-Soo Line Bldg., Mpls. 2. Died Sept. 26, 1951.

QUAYLE, Oliver A., Jr., pres. Oliver A. Quayle, Jr.; b. Albany, N.Y., Mar. 6, 1894; s. Oliver A. and Belle K. (Blampied) Q.; m. Signa Norstrand, June 20, 1915; children—Oliver A., 3d, Susannah N. Pres. Quayle & Son Corp., bank note engravers, N.Y. City; pres. Oliver A. Quayle, Jr., Inc., operating The Gilbert Hall of Science, Washington, D.C. Executive assistant to sec. Dem. Nat. Conv., 1936; treas. Dem. Nat. Com., 1937-40, gen. mgr., 1941-42; asso. dir. expansion dept. Miami U., 1953—; sales representative Miami Citrus Packing House, 1954—. Served in Ordnance Dept., Bur. of Printing and Engraving, World War. Mem. Albany Soc. of N.Y. ceedings of the Democratic National Convention, 1936. Democrat. Clubs: Washington Golf and Country; Arlington (Va.); Dartmouth (New York). Author: Pro-Home: 4000 Cathedral Av., Washington 16. Died July 3, 1956.

QUAYLE, Osborne R(obinson), univ. prof.; born Cleveland, O., Dec. 15, 1898; s. William Osborne and Lucy Ellen (Robinson) Q.; A.B., Swarthmore Coll., 1919; M.A., Harvard, 1921; Ph.D., Johns Hopkins U., 1924; m. Zaidee T. Miller, June 22, 1922; children—Nancy Elizabeth (Mrs. Benjamin H. Smith, Jr.), Louise Tevis (Mrs. W. W. Kling). Asst. prof. chemistry, Emory U., Atlanta, Ga., 1924-27, asso. prof., 1927-31, prof. chemistry, since 1931, chairman dept. since 1950, adminstrv. council since 1929, chmn. research com. since 1941, exec. com. grad. sch. since 1944, Univ. senate since 1950, exec. com. since 1950. Recipient Herty Medal, 1949. Mem. Ga. Acad. Sci. (past president), American Chem. Society (councilor and past chmn. Ga. sect.), A.A.A.S., Delta Upsilon, Alpha Chi Sigma, Sigma Xi, Phi Beta Kappa. Episcopalian. Home: 1307 Emory Circle, N.E., Atlanta, Ga. Office: Emory University, Emory University, Ga. Died Dec. 7, 1954.

QUEALY, Susan Jane (Mrs. Patrick J. Quealy), Dem. Nat. committeewoman; b. Omaha, Neb., Jan. 17, 1870; m. Patrick J. Quealy, Oct. 21, 1890; children—Jay A., Patrick J., Thomas A., John, Mahlon K. Came to Wyoming with her husband who opened the coal fields at Kemmerer (also founded the town), 1890. Vice president 1st Nat. Bank of Kemmerer, Wyo.; operator 21,000 acre livestock ranch, Carbon County, Wyo.; pres. Medicine Bow Oil Co., LaBarge Oil Co. Dir. Western Oil Refining Co. Mem. Wyo. State Bd. Edn. Served as Dem. state woman's chmn., 1932-45, Nat. committeewoman from Wyo. since 1945; presidential elector, 1932-36, 40. Roman Catholic. Home: 821 Cedar Av., Kemmerer, Wyo. Died July 26, 1956; buried Kemmerer.

QUIGLEY, Samuel, educator; b. Princeton, Minn., Jan. 26, 1873; s. William Merwin and Sarah Jane (Crawford) Q.; grad. Ia. State Teachers Coll., 1895; A.B., U. Ia., 1906; studied Harvard, 1905-6; M.A., U. Chgo., 1911; Litt.D., U. Denver; m. Marie Christine Dunn, Jan. 25, 1923. Prin. of high sch. New Sharon, Ia., 1895-8; supt. schs., Brighton, Ia., 1898-1902; head of English dept. Okla. Inst. Tech., Tonkawa, Okla., 1902-11; asst. prof. edn., U. Minn., 1911-15, also dir. extension; dean and prof. edn., Western State Coll., Gunnison, Colo., 1915-18; welfare work with A.E.F. in France, 1918-19; pres. Western State Coll. of Colo., July 1919—. Mem. N.E. A., Phi Delta Kappa. Methodist. Home: Gunnison, Colo. Died Nov. 1946.

QUIGLEY, William Middleton, ret. naval officer; b. Bklyn., July 9, 1890; grad. U.S. Naval Acad., 1911; m. Jeannette Orr; children—Stephen M., Jane Orr. Commd. ensign USN, 1912, advanced through grades to commodore, 1943; served in U.S. ships Michigan, Monterey, Wilmington, Mohican, 1911-15; comd. submarine A-7, 1915-16, U.S.S. F-3, 1917-18, O-16, 1918-19, U.S.S. Delaware, 1919, S-2, 1920-21; chief of U.S. Naval Mission to Peru, 1940-42; on duty with amphibious force, Atlantic Fleet, 1942, assigned landing craft group, Dec. 1942; comdr. naval bases, Solomon Islands, naval bases, Forward Area, and comdr. South Solomons, sub. area, 1943-44; comd. Forward Area, Central Pacific, 1944-45; became comdr. Naval Base, Port Heune, Calif., 1945, retired with rank of commodore, 1946. Decorated Legion of Merit, Victory Medal with submarine clasp, Am. Def. Service Medal with fleet clasp, Am. Area Campaign and Asiatic-Pacific Area Campaign medals; Legion of Merit; Comdr. Order British Empire; Comdr. Order of Sun (Peru). Home: 9 E. 96th St., N.Y.C. 28. Address: Navy Dept., Washington 25. Died Apr. 1957.*

QUIN, Clinton Simon, bishop; b. Louisville, Ky., Sept. 28, 1883; s. J. B. and Nettie J. Q.; LL.B., U. of Louisville, 1904; grad. Va. Theol. Sem., 1908; D.D., U. of the South; S.T.D., Gen. Theol. Sem.; m. Hortense Pilcher, June 1909. Engaged in business, 1897-1905; deacon and priest, 1908, P.E. Ch.; rector St. James Ch., Pewee Valley, Ky., 1908-11, Grace Ch., Paducah, 1911-17, Trinity Ch., Houston, Tex., 1917-18; elected bishop coadjutor, May 16, 1918, consecrated, Oct. 31, 1918; bishop of Tex., 1928-55, ret. Rotarian. Home: 417 Hillcrest Dr., Richmond, Tex. Office: 520 San Jacinto St., Houston 2. Died Nov. 29, 1956; buried Houston.

QUINLAN, Joseph A., business exec.; b. St. Remi, Quebec, Can., Oct. 30, 1889; s. Michael and Mary L. (O'Gleman) Q.; ed. grade and high schools, Can.; m. Colleen V. Payne, Aug. 5, 1914; children—Mary Catherine (Mrs. A. H. Brown), Virginia Ann, Robert Paul. With traffic dept., N.Y. Central R.R., 1906-20; gen. traffic mgr. St. Regis Paper Co., N.Y. City, 1920-43, v.p. since 1944, dir. since 1941; exec. vice pres. and dir., St. Regis Sales Corp.; director of the St. Regis Timber Corporation; vice pres., dir. Ogdensburg Terminal Corporation, New York, also St. Regis Paper Co. (Can.) Ltd., New York; pres. and dir. Norwood & St. Lawrence R.R. Co., New York; director Lehigh & New England Railroad Company, Rutland Railway Corporation. President Atlantic States Shippers Adv. Bd., 1945, 1946, mem. exec. com., 1947; dir. Nat. Shippers Adv. Bd., 1945-46; mem. adv. com. Paper Transportation Industry, W.P.B., 1942. Mem. Transportation Assn. of Am. (dir.), Pulp and Paper Traffic League (dir.), Am. Paper and Pulp Assn., Nat. Indsl. Traffic League. Republican. Roman Catholic. Clubs: Traffic of New York (pres. 1939), Black River Valley (Watertown, N.Y.). Home: 201 Soundview Av., White Plains; (summer) Henderson Harbor. Office: 150 E. 42d St., N.Y.C. 1. Died Jan. 17, 1959; buried Ferncliff Mausoleum, Hartsdale, N.Y.

QUINN, Patrick Henry, lawyer; b. Phoenix, R.I., Dec. 16, 1869; s. Peter and Margaret (Callaghan) Q.; ed. pub. schs.; studied law in office of Hon. W. B. Tanner, Providence, R.I.; m. Margaret M. Conners, July 22, 1909; 1 son, Thomas Henry. Admitted to R.I. bar, 1895; active practice with Thomas H. Quinn, as Quinn & Quinn; treas. Warwick Lace Works, Bancroft Lace Co.; pres. Phenix Lace Mills; dir. Phenix Branch, Indsl. Trust Co. First probate judge of Warwick (now West Warwick), R.I.; former solicitor for W. Warwick; pres. 1st town council of W. Warwick; del. Dem. nat. convs., 1900-36; Dem. candidate for gov. of R.I., 1914; mem. Dem. Nat. Com., 1916-32. Chief of staff of Gov. Garvin, with rank of colonel, 1903-04. 1st v.p., trustee Kent Co. Memorial Hospital. Former pres. Kent County Bar Association, American Lace Mfrs. Assn., West Warwick Chamber of Commerce, Rhode Island Bar Association, Pawtuxket Valley Library; member American Judicature Soc., Am. Bar Assn. Clubs: Turks Head, Columbus, West Warwick Country. Home: 75 Woodside Av., West Warwick, R.I. Office: Industrial Trust Bldg., Providence, R.I. Deceased.

QUIRINO, Elpidio (kē-rē-nō), former pres. Philippines; b. Vigan, Ilocos Sur, P.I., Nov. 16, 1890; s. Mariano and Gregoria (Rivera) Q.; LL.B., U. of Philippines, 1915, LL.D., 1949; hon. LL.D., Univ. of Manila, Adamson Univ., 1948; m. Doña Alicia Syquia, Jan. 16, 1921 (killed by Japanese together with 3 of her children, 1945); children—Tomas, Armando (dec.), Norma (dec.), Victoria, Fe (dec.). Admitted to Philippine bar, 1915; sec. to Manuel Quezon, 1917; rep. of 1st dist. of Ilocos Sur., 1919; senator, 1925-35 (majority floor leader); mem. Philippine Constl. Conv., 1934-35; sec. of finance under last Am. gov.-gen., 1934-35, under Commonwealth, 1935-36; sec. of interior under Commonwealth, 1936-38; senator-at-large, 1941-45; pres. pro-tem. of Philippine Senate, 1945; v.p. and sec. of finance, 1946; v.p. and 1st sec. of fgn. affairs under Republic, 1946-48; pres. Republic of the Philippines, 1948-53. Rep. Philippines House of Reps., Internat. Bar Conf., Peking, China, 1921; ranking mem. of last Philippine Independence Mission to U.S., which obtained Tydings-McDuffie Independence Act, 1934; chmn., Nat. Relief Bd., Nat. Information Bd. and Nat. Radio Bd.; dean, Adamson Law Coll.; led in Philippine negotiations for gen. relations, conciliation, friendship and mil. agreements with U.S., China, France, Italy, Spain, 1946-47. Vice chmn. bd. dirs., Agrl. and Indsl. Bank; mem. bd. dirs. Nat. Development Co. Decorated Grand Officer, Legion of Honor (France); Grand Cordon of Order of Propitious Clouds (China); Grand Officer, Royal Order of Cambodia (Indo-China); Orden de Isabela Catolica (Spain). Mem. Phi Kappa Phi. Mem. Liberal Party. Roman Catholic. Author: Philippine Economic Problems, 1935. Drafted and sponsored Commonwealth Settlement Act, 1935 and Nat. Defense Act, 1935. Died Feb. 1956.

QUONIAM de SCHOMPRE, Guy Emile Marie Joseph, French diplomat; b. St. Servan, France, May 27, 1905; s. Emile and Alice (Martialis) Quoniam de S.; B.A. in Latin Langs., Philo Sorbonne, Faculte or Droit, Sciences Politiques, 1932; m. Evelyn Middleton, Feb. 20, 1941; children—Dominique, Philippe, Anne, Emmanuelle, Bertrand. Entered French diplomatic service, 1936; vice consul, Glasgow, Scotland, 1934-35; dep. consul, Shanghai, 1936-37, Oporto, 1937-38, Kharbin, 1938-39; sec. of embassy, Peking, 1939; supt. consul, Tientsin, 1939-40; French minister, Liberia, 1945-49; consul gen., Belgian Congo, 1949-51, New Orleans, 1952—. Volunteer Free French Forces, 1940-45; rep. Gen. de Gaulle in Far East, 1940-41. Mem. Nouveau Circle, Paris. Clubs: Pickwick, Boston (New Orleans). Home: Chateau de Kerjegu, Rostrenen, France; also 2406 Prytania St., New Orleans. Office: Consulate of France, Whitney Bank Bldg., New Orleans. Died Feb. 28, 1958.

R

RACE, John H.; b. Paupack, Pike County, Pa., Mar. 10, 1862; s. Rev. James Lee and Jane (Humble) R.; A.B., Princeton U., 1890, A.M., 1894; D.D., Syracuse U., 1899; LL.D., U. of Chattanooga, 1915; m. Alice Bannister, June 25, 1890 (died Apr. 22, 1940). Ordained M.E. ministry, 1890; teacher Greek and rhetoric, Wyoming Sem., Kingston, Pa., 1890-94; pastor Centenary Ch., Binghamton, N.Y., 1894-98; pres. Grant U., 1898-1906, and its successor, U. of Chattanooga, 1906-13; one of publishing agts. Meth.

Episcopal Ch., 1913-36, emeritus, 1936—. Mem. Gen. Conf. 7 times, 1908-32, del. emeritus, 1936-44; mem. Ecumenical Meth. Conf., 1911; mem. Bd. Edn., 1908-36, Bd. of Foreign Missions, M.E. Ch., 1924-41 (mem. exec., finance and investment coms.). Trustee Wyoming Sem., U. of Chattanooga, Syracuse U., Bennett Coll., Greensboro, N.C.; mem. bd. of mgrs. Methodist Hosp., Brooklyn., N.Y., also chmn. exec. com. Mem. Phi Beta Kappa. Home: 316 W. 79th St., N.Y.C. 24. Died Oct. 14, 1954; buried Floral Park Cemetery, Binghamton, N.Y.

RADBILL, Samuel, petroleum products mfr.; b. Norristown, Pa., Apr. 20, 1894; s. Charles and Eva (Tompkins) R.; student pub. schs., pvt. studies; m. Florence Kaplan, Oct. 28, 1924; 1 dau., Ruth Gloria (wife of Dr. Earl Scott). Pres. Radbill Oil Co., Phila., 1918—, Renuzit Home Products Co., 1936—; partner Radbill Assos., 1936—. Pres. Phila. Psychiatric Hosp., 1939-53, now hon. pres.; dir. Phila. Community Chest, Phila. Fedn. Jewish Charities; hon. dir. Palm Beach (Fla.) County Guidance Center. Mem. Nat., Phila. C.'s of C., Better Bus. Bur., N.A.M., Soc. Automotive Engrs. Clubs: Philmont Country, Locust (Phila.); Palm Beach (Fla.) Country. Home: 229 W. Uppal St., Phila. 19; also 150 Dunbar Rd., Palm Beach, Fla. Office: 1724 Chestnut St., Phila. 3. Died Nov. 28, 1956.

RADCLIFFE, Amos H., ex-congressman; b. Paterson, N.J., Jan. 16, 1870; grad. high sch., Paterson, and evening course N.Y. Trade Sch. Sec. James Radcliffe & Sons Co., structural steel mfrs.; v.p. bd. trustees, treas. Franklin Trust Co.; mem. N.J. Assembly 5 terms, 1908-12; sheriff Passaic Co., N.J., 1912-15; mayor Paterson, 1916-19; mem. 66th and 67th Congresses (1919-23), 7th N.J. Dist. Pres. Benlin Securities Co., Frankham Realty Co. Mem. Fish and Game Commn. N.J., term 1917-22; mem. Paterson Bldg. Code Commn. Mem. N.J. N.G. 6 yrs. Mem. Iron League of N.J. Republican. Methodist. Mason Elk. Home: 35 18th Av. Office: 96 Prospect St., Paterson, N.J. Died Dec. 29, 1950.

RADFORD, Cyrus S(ugg), retired brig. gen.; b. Hopkinsville, Ky., June 3, 1868; s. William Tandy and Mary Elizabeth (Sugg) R.; student U. of the South, Sewanee, Tenn., 1884-85; grad. U.S. Naval Acad., 1890; m. Catherine Thomas Manson, June 12, 1907; children—Francis Manson, Margaret Lewis, Catherine Manson, Cyrus S. Commd. 2d lt. USMC, 1892, advanced through grades to q.m. gen. 1929; retired with rank of brig. gen., 1929; v.p. Bankers Tust Co., Phila., until 1930. Served in U.S.S. Texas, Battle of Santiago, Spanish-Am. War; with USMC, Guantanamo expdn. to Cuba and Panama; in Philippines, 1901-03; built, equipped and developed USMC mfg. and supply base, Phila., 1903-29; tech. adviser on mil. supplies and equipment for Cuba, Haiti, San Domingo and Nicaragua. Assisted in developing Adm. Farragut Acad., Pine Beach, N.J., 1933—, now pres. bd. trustees. Democrat. Episcopalian. Clubs: University, Corinthian Yacht (Phila.). Home: 501 Main St., Toms River, N.J. Died Jan. 19, 1951; buried Arlington Nat. Cemetery.

RADIN, Max (rā'dĭn), law educator; b. Kempen, Poland, Mar. 29, 1880; s. Adolph Moses and Johanna (Theodor) R.; brought to U.S., 1884; A.B., Coll. City N.Y., 1899; LL.B., N.Y.U., 1902; Ph.D., Columbia, 1909; LL.D., Whitman Coll., 1948; m. Rose Jaffe, July 2, 1909 (died Oct. 11, 1918); 1 dau., Rhea; m. 2d, Dorothea Prall, June 30, 1922 (died Oct. 15, 1948). Tchr. pub. schs., New Sch., 1901-07; admitted to N.Y. bar, 1902, Cal. bar, 1920, 1st asst. Newtown High Sch., 1907-19; instr. Columbia, 1918-19; lectr. in Roman and civil law Coll. City N.Y., 1917-19; prof. law U. Cal., 1919-40, John Henry Boalt prof. law, 1940-48, emeritus, 1948—; mem. Inst. for Advanced Study, Princeton, Jan. 1949. Stanford Univ. Law Sch., summer 1930; Northwestern U. Law Sch., summer 1936, Columbia U., summer 1946; Storrs lectr. Yale Law Sch., 1940; Hillman lectr. Pacific U., Ore., 1946; vis. prof. law Columbia, 1947. Chmn. Commn. for Uniform Laws; mem. Social Science Research Council of Pacific Coast, Am. Council Inst. Pacific Relations, Soc. Legal History, Phi Beta Kappa, Société d'Histoire du Droit (Paris), Stair Soc. (Edinburgh), Am. Bar Assn. Recipient Townsend Harris medal Alumni Assn. Coll. City N.Y., 1940. Author: The Legislation of the Greeks and Romans on Corporations, 1909; The Jews Among the Greeks and Romans, 1916; Handbook of Roman Law, 1927; Life of the People in Biblical Times, 1929; The Lawful Pursuit of Gain, 1931; The Trial of Jesus of Nazareth, 1931; Handbook of Anglo-American Legal History, 1936; The Law and Mr. Smith, 1938; Marcus Brutus, 1939; Manners and Morals of Business, 1939; Law as Logic and Experience, 1940; The Day of Reckoning, 1943; The Law and You, 1947; Epicurus My Master, 1948; also numerous articles in philol., historical, and legal periodicals. Home: 2683 Buena Vista Way, Berkeley, Cal. Died June 22, 1950.

RADIN, Paul, ethnologist; b. Lodz, Russian Poland, Apr. 2, 1883; s. Dr. Adolph M. and Johanna Theodor R.; brought to America in infancy; B.A., Coll. City of New York, 1902; studied univs. of Berlin and Munich and worked on material culture of S. Am. Indians at Berlin Mus. of Völkerkunde; studied biology, history and anthropology at Columbia, Ph. D., 1911; m. Rose Robinson, May 26, 1910. Ethnologist, Bur. Am. Ethnology, June 1, 1910-12; field ethnologist, Geol. Survey of Can., 1912—. Has specialized on Winnebago Indians in particular, and Woodland Indians and Sioux in gen., 1908-12; specialized on the Ojibwa, 1912—, for Geol. Survey of Can. Harvard and Columbia fellow to Internat. Sch. Am. Ethnology and Archaeology in Mexico, 1912-13, and while there studied the Zapotecan and Huave Indians. Author: Zur Netztechnik der Suedamerikanischen Indianer, 1909; Contributions to the Study of the Bororo, 1909; Description and Significance of the Winnebago Medicine Dance, 1909; Winnebago Tales, 1910; The Peyote Cult of the Winnebago, 1913; Some Myths and Tales of the Ojibwa of S. E. Ontario, 1913; The Religion of the North American Indians, 1914; The Social Organization of the Winnebago Indians, 1915; Literary Aspects of North American Mythology, 1915; also various articles relating to Winnebagos, and articles on the Ojibwa, Zapotecan and Huave, etc. Mem. Am. Anthropol. Assn., Am. Folk-Lore Soc., Nat. Inst. Social Sciences; organizer and sec. Southwestern Anthropol. Soc. Address: Geological Survey, Ottawa, Can. Died Feb. 21, 1959.

RADINSKY, Ellis, social worker; b. N.Y.C., Feb. 13, 1904; s. Harris and Rose (Latice) R.; B.S., N.Y.U., 1930, A.M., 1935; M.S., N.Y. sch. social work Columbia U., 1941; m. Elizabeth Kaplan, Sept. 27, 1930; 1 dau., Naomi. Casework supervisor Dept. Welfare, N.Y.C., 1934-41; nat. exec. dir. League for Labor Palestine, 1941-42; field rep. Council Jewish Fedns. and Welfare Funds, 1942-45; nat. exec. dir. United Israel Appeal, 1945—; asst. exec. vice chmn. Nat. United Jewish Appeal, 1955—. Mem. Internat., Nat. confs. Jewish social work. Home: 258 Riverside Dr., N.Y.C. 25. Office: 41 E. 42d St., N.Y.C. 17. Died Mar. 27, 1955.

RADNER, William (răd'ner), lawyer; b. New York, N.Y., Feb. 14, 1908; s. Barnet and Annie (Russell) R.; A.B., Columbia Coll., 1929; LL.B., Columbia U., 1931; m. Irene McCauley, Feb. 4, 1938; children—John Barnet, Mary Anne, Kathleen, Barbara. Admitted to New York bar, 1931; private law practice, New York City, 1931-34; counsel Reconstruction Finance Corporation, Washington, D.C., 1934-36, U.S. Maritime Commn., 1936-38; sec. Matson Navigation Co., San Francisco, 1938-42; gen. counsel War Shipping Adminstrn., Washington, 1942-46; practice of law since 1946. Home: 6511 Meadow Ln., Chevy Chase, Md. Office: Tower Bldg., 1401 K St. N.W., Washington. Died Oct. 22, 1951; buried George Washington Meml. Cemetery.

RADOSAVLJEVICH, Paul Rankov, univ. prof.; b. Obrez, Serbia, Jan. 11, 1879; s. Ranko A. and Bosiljka (Gajich) R.; Studied at Vienna, Jena, Stanford Univ.; Ph.D., U. of Zürich, Switzerland, 1905; Pd. D., N.Y.U., 1908; m. Ljubica R. Krulj, July 12, 1902; children—Zarko (dec.), Milenko. Came to U.S., 1905, naturalized citizen, 1914. With N.Y.U., 1908—, prof. exptl. pedagogy, 1913—. Mem. Am. Psychol. Assn., A.A.A.S., Acad. Polit. and Social Sci., Am. Eugenics Soc., Am. Soc. Advancement of Slavic Study, Croatian Pedagog.-Lit. Acad., Serbian Soc. for Child Study. Republican. Mem. Greek Ch. Author. Who are the Slavs°, 1919 Das Behalten und Vergessen, 1907; also various works in Serbian, Russian and other European langs. Home: 25 Stuyvesant Av., Brooklyn, N.Y. Address: N.Y. University, Washington Sq., N.Y.C. Died Apr. 1958.

RAEMAEKERS, Louis (ra'mä-kers), cartoonist; b. Roermond, Holland, Apr. 6, 1869; s. Josephus Christianus Hubertus and Margaretha Amalia (Michels) R.; ed. lower and middle schs., Roermond, Holland, 1879-89; states diploma, Art Sch. of Amsterdam, Holland, 1891; hon. LL.D., Univ. of Glasgow, 1924; m. Petronella Johanna van Mansvelt, July 10, 1902; children—Frederique Louise (Mrs. Louis Heribert Sandberg), Margarete Mathilde (Mrs. Jean de Sturler), Robert Louis. Came to U.S., 1940. Dir. Art and Craft Sch., Holland, 1895; prof. Hort. High Sch. (1896), Agrl. High Sch. (1898), Ryks Hoogere Burger Sch. (1899), Wageningen, Holland; gave up teaching to become a cartoonist, 1913. Decorated Officier Legion d'Honneur (France); Chevalier Ordre de Leopold, Comdr. Order of the Crown (Belgium); Officer Order of Orange Nassau (Holland); Comdr. Polona Restituta (Poland), Comdr. Order of the Crown (Italy), Comdr. Order of Grand Duke Gediminas (Lithuania), Comdr. Order of St. Sava (Yugoslavia), Comdr. Order of Three Stars of Lethonia. Hon. mem. several internat. instns. Author: Another Peace Conference, 1912; The Great War, 3 edits., 1916, 17, 18; La Grand Guerre, 1916; Raemaekers and the War (cartoons; popular edits. in 18 languages). Address: Orienta Point Apts., Mamaroneck, N. Y. Deceased.

RAFFERTY, James A., vice pres., mem. exec. com., dir. Union Carbide & Carbon Crop. N.Y.C.; chmn., dir. Bakelite Co. (Can.), Ltd.; chmn. bd. Carbide & Carbon Chems., Ltd.; dir. Oxweld R.R. Service Co., Union Carbide & Carbon Research Labs., Inc. Home: Rye. Office: 30 E. 42d St., N.Y.C. 17. Died Dec. 19, 1951.

RAGIR, Benjamin A., mfg. exec.; b. Chicago, Oct. 16, 1913; s. Alex and Sophia (Zirlin) R.; A. B., U. Chicago, 1934, J.D., 1936; m. Julia Nathan, Sept. 21, 1936; children—Sonia Ruth, John Arthur. Admitted to Ill. bar, 1936 and practiced with Mayer, Meyer, Austrian & Platt, Chicago, 1936-42; asso. solicitor and tax counsel, U.S. Alien Property Custodian, Washington, 1942-45; exec. v. p. and sec. Ekco Products Co., Chicago, 1946-50, pres., 1950-58, ret. pres., dir. Aluminio-Ekco, Mexico City, Mexico; dir. Platers and Stampers, Ltd., London, Eng. Mem. Am. and Chicago bar assns. Club: Standard. Home: 720 Greenleaf Av., Glencoe, Ill. Office: 1949 N. Cicero Av., Chgo. Died July 29, 1958.

RAGLAND, George, clergyman; b. Richmond, Va., Aug. 4, 1876; s. John Fendall and Alice Taylor (Walden) R.; A.B., Richmond (Va.) Coll., 1896; Ph.D., Johns Hopkins, 1921; m. Elizabeth Margaret Rawlings, Aug. 20, 1902 (died Oct. 10, 1939); children—George, Alice Taylor, Rawlings, Elizabeth Margaret, Benjamin, David Walden. Fellow Johns Hopkins, 1901, by courtesy, 1904; prof. Greek, Baylor U., Waco, Tex., 1901-10; prof. ancient langs., Georgetown (Ky.) Coll., 1910-22, acting dean, 1920; ordained Baptist ministry, 1922; pastor First Bapt. Ch., Lexington, Ky., 1922—. Moderator Elkhorn Bapt. Assn. of Ky., 1922-27; trustee Southwestern Bapt. Theol. Sem., 1924-26; former mem. exec. bd. and exec. com. Gen. Assn. of Bapts. in Ky.; former dir. and mem. exec. com. Bapt. Edn. Soc. of Ky.; moderator Gen. Assn. of Bapts. in Ky., 1946-48; chmn. dept. Christian edn.; mem. exec. and adminstrv. coms. So. Bapt. Conv., 1942-48, com. on relations with other religious bodies, 1948-50. Trustee So. Bapt. Hosp., New Orleans. Democrat. Editor: The Sling and Stone, monthly ch. publ., 1926—. Home: 340 Irvine Rd., Lexington, Ky. Died May 19, 1957; buried Lexington.

RAGLAND, Samuel Evan, banker; b. Lafayette County, Miss., Aug. 1, 1874; s. Samuel Evan and Margaret Elizabeth (Pearson) R.; student U. Miss., 1892-93; m. Elinor Marion Cary, June 14, 1905; children—Elinor Marion, Margaret Elizabeth, Fairfax Cary. Began as bookkeeper, 1893, and became mgr. Oxford (Miss.) Hardware Co., 1895; moved to Memphis and entered real estate business, 1899; organizer, 1912, and pres. So. Trust Co.; made active v.p. Central State Nat. Bank, Jan. 1913, pres. Jan. 1914, and since consolidation with the First Nat. Bank, 1926, has been pres. of latter. Mem. Fed Adv. Council, Washington, Mem. Am. Bankers Assn. (exec. com. nat. bank div.), Memphis C. of C. Trustee, pres. Goodwin Inst. Ch. Home. Democrat. Presbyn. Clubs: Memphis Country, Menasha Outing (dir.). Home: Memphis Country Club. Office: First National Bank, Memphis. Died Nov. 1949.

RAGSDALE, Tallulah (Lulah Ragsdale), writer; b. Cedar Hall, Lawrence Co., Miss.; d. James Lafayette and Martha Louise (Hooker) R.; grad. Whitworth (Miss.) Coll.; studied dramatic art with Fanny Hunt (actress), N.Y. Taught expression and dramatic art in Whitworth Coll., Brookhaven, Miss., and Belhaven Coll., Jackson, Miss. Appeared as reader of poems, negro stories, etc., Miss. and La. Presbyn. Club: Peripatetics of Brookhaven, Miss. (ex-pres.). Author: A Shadow's Shadow; Miss Dulcie from Dixie, 1917 (screen adaptation, 1919); Next-Besters, 1920; If I See Green (verse), 1930; author's readings. Poems have appeared in Anthologies. Won prizes for short story and poem, offered by Miss. Federation Women's Clubs, 1916, 17. Contbr. stories and poems to mags. Home: Brookhaven, Miss. Deceased.

RAGSDALE, Van Hubert, naval officer; b. Aug. 9, 1892; entered U.S. Navy, 1912, and advanced through the grades to rear adm., 1942. Decorated Navy Cross. Address: Navy Dept., Washington 25, D.C. Deceased.*

RAHMAN, Tunku (or Prince) Abdul, prime minister, minister fgn. affairs Malaya; b. Alor Star, Kedah, Malaya, Feb. 8, 1903; s. Sultan of Kedah; B.A., St. Catherine's Coll., Cambridge, U.; student law in Eng., 1938 and 1947; m. Roziah Barakbah; children—1 son, 1 dau.; 2 adopted children. Called to bar, 1949; practiced in Malaya, becoming dep. pub. prosecutor Fed. Legal Dept.; active as a leader of Alliance Party; chief minister and minister home affairs, 1955-57; prime minister and minister external affairs Fedn. of Malaya (became ind. nation within Brit. Commonwealth 1957), 1957—. Address: Govt. Offices, Kuala Lumpur, Fedn. of Malaya. Died Apr. 1, 1960.*

RAHN, Otto (rän), prof. bacteriology; b. Tiegenhof, West Prussia, Apr. 9, 1881; s. Isbrand and Marie (Claassen) R.; Real-Gymnasium, Elbing, Germany, 1891-99; Ph.D., Göttingen U., 1902; m. Bell S. Farrand, Sept. 4, 1911; children—Hermann, Marie, Margarete, Otto. Asst. in dairy science, Göttingen U., 1902-06; asst. in soil bacteriology, Halle Expt. Sta., 1906-07; asst. prof. bacteriology, Mich. State Coll. Agr. and Applied Science, East Lansing, 1907-

12; asst. prof. bacteriology, U. of Ill., 1912-14; served in Germany army, 1916-18; asst. in soil bacteriology, Agrl. Coll., Berlin, 1919; prof. dairy physics, Research Inst., Kiel, Germany, 1920-26; prof. bacteriology, Cornell U., 1927-49, Ida. State Coll., 1949-54; retired 1949. Dir. Physikalischen Institut (Prusz-Versuchs) and Forschungsanstalt für Milchwirtschaft (Kiel), 1922; first to establish lab. for colloidal and physical chemistry of milk. Co-Author: Physik der Milchwirtschaft (with P. F. Sharp), 1928; Handbuch der Milchwirtschaft (with others), 1931; Physiology of Bacteria, 1932; Invisible Radiation of Organisms, 1935; Mathematics in Bacteriology, 1939, Microbes of Merit, 1945; Injury and Death of Bacteria by Chemical Agents, 1945. Contbr. to Jour. of Bacteriology, Jour. of Gen. Physiology, Centralblatt für Bakteriologie, etc. Home: Millsboro, Del. Died Sept. 26, 1957.

RAILEY, Thomas Tarlton, r.r. atty.; b. Harrisonville, Mo., Feb. 4, 1885; s. Judge Robert T. and Martha Stuart (Beattie) R.; A.B., U. of Mo., 1907; law edn. U. of Mo. and in law office; m. Emma Meyer, Sept. 7, 1920. Admitted to Mo. bar, 1909; with law firm Jeffries & Corum, St. Louis, 1911-15; mem. law dept., gen. office, M.P. R.R., St. Louis, 1915—, now gen. solicitor; gen. counsel Am. Refrigeration Transit Co. Mem. Phi Beta Kappa, Delta Tau Delta. Home: 69 Willmore Rd., St. Louis 9. Office: Mo. Pacific Bldg., St. Louis 3. Died Dec. 3, 1956; buried Oak Grove Mausoleum, St. Louis.

RAINE, William MacLeod, author; b. London, Eng., June 22, 1871; s. William and Jessie Watt (Muir) R.; came to U.S., Oct. 1881; prep. edn., Searcy (Ark.) Coll.; A.B., Oberlin (O.) Coll., 1894; M.L. from U. of Colo., 1920; m. Jennie P. Langley, Mar. 25, 1905 (died Dec. 8, 1922); m. 2d, Florence A. Hollingsworth, June 30, 1924 (died Oct. 21, 1942); 1 dau., Patricia; m. 3d, Claire Parmeley, Nov. 17, 1945. Prin. South Seattle (Wash.) Sch., 1897-98; reporter for Seattle and Denver newspapers, 1905; edit. writer for Rocky Mountain News, Denver, Colo., 1910, Denver Rep., 1913. Clubs: University, Denver Country, Press. Author: A Daughter of Raasay, 1902; Wyoming, 1908; Ridgway of Montana, 1909; Bucky O'Connor, 1910; A Texas Ranger, 1911; Mavericks, 1911; Brand Blotters, 1912; Crooked Trails and Straight, 1913; The Vision Splendid, 193; The Pirate of Panama, 1914; A Daughter of the Dons, 1914; The Highgrader, 1915; Steve Yeager, 1915; The Yukon Trail, 1917; The Sheriff's Son, 1918; A Man Four Square, 1919; Oh You Tex, 1920; The Big Town Round Up, 1920; Gunsight Pass, 1921; Tangled Trails, 1921; Man Size, 1922; The Fighting Edge, 1922; Ironheart, 1923; The Desert's Price, 1924; Roads of Doubt, 1925; Troubled Waters, 1925; Bonanza, a Story of the Gold Trail, 1926; The Last Shot, 1926; Moran Beats Back, 1927; Judge Colt, 1927; Colorado, 1928; Texas Man, 1928; Famous Sheriffs and Western Outlaws, 1929; The Fighting Tenderfoot, 1929; The Valiant, 1930; Cattle (with Will Barnes), 1930; Rutledge Trails the Ace of Spades, 1930; Beyond the Rio Grande, 1931; The Black Tolts, 1932; Under Northern Stars, 1932; The Broad Arrow, 1933; For Honor and Life, 1933; Roaring River, 1934; The Trail of Danger, 1934; Square Shooter, 1935; Border Breed, 1935; Run of the Brush, 1936; To Ride the River With, 1936; Bucky Follows a Cold Trail, 1937; King of the Bush, 1937; On the Dodge, 1938; Sons of the Saddle, 1938; Moran Beats Back, 1939; The River Bend Feud, 1939; Riders of the Rim Rocks, 1940; The Way of Life of a Frontier Peace Officer, 1940; Guns of the Frontier, 1940; They Called Him Blue Blazes, 1941; Justice Deferred, 1942; The Damn Yank, 1942; Hell and High Water, 1943; Courage Stout, 1943; Cry Murder, 1944; Who Wants To Live Forever, 1945; Clattering Hoofs, 1946; This Nettle Danger, 1947; The Bandit Trail, 1949; Ranger's Luck, 1950; Jingling Spurs, 1951; Glory Hole, Dry Bones in the Valley, 1953. Lecturer on journalism, University of Colo., 1911-16. Dir. div. syndicate features, Com. on Public Information, 1918. Home: 601 Franklin St., Denver 18. Died July 25, 1954.

RAINES, George Neely, psychiatrist, neurologist; b. Jackson, Miss., Apr. 2, 1908; s. William Giles and Bessie Whitworth (Hoskins) R.; B.S., U. of Miss., 1928; M.D., Northwestern U., 1930; m. Kate Oliver St. Clair, July 12, 1932; children—Mary Anne, George Neely. Intern U.S. Naval Hosp., Mare Island, Calif., 1930-31, U.S. Naval Med. Sch., Washington, 1934-35, St. Elizabeths Hospital, 1935-36 Washington-Baltimore Psychoanalytic Institute, 1946-53; entered M.C., U.S. Navy, 1930, commd. June, 1930, advanced through grades to capt., 1945; served aboard U.S.S. Idaho and in spl. service squadron, 1931-34, U.S.S. Saratoga and U.S.S. Lexington, 1938-40; med. officer in psychiatry and neurol. U.S. Naval Hosp., Washington, 1934, 1941-42, U.S. Naval Hosp., Phila., 1935-38, 1940-41, Bethesda, Md., 1942-43, chief neuropsychiatry U.S. Naval Hosp., Portsmouth, Va., 1943-45, U.S. Naval Hosp., Nat. Naval Med. Center, Bethesda, 1945-50; med. officer charge Naval med. unit, St. Elizabeths Hosp., head dept. neurology and psychiatry Naval Med. Sch., 1945-50; head, neuropsychiatry br., Bur. Medicine and Surgery, Navy Dept., 1950-53, 1955-58, retired; exec. officer U.S. Naval Hosp., Portsmouth, Va., 1953-55. Prof., dir. dept. psychiatry, Georgetown U. Med. Center since 1948; asso. Wash. Sch. Psych., since 1950; instr. clin. neurol. Temple U. Sch. Med., 1937-41; clin. prof. psychiatry, Georgetown U. Sch. Med., 1947-48. Cons. neurol., psychiatry to profl. div., Bur. Med. and Surgery Navy Dept., 1949-50; cons. Naval Dispensary, 1949-50; spl. cons. to Nat. Inst. Mental Health, U.S. Pub. Health Service, Bethesda, since 1949. Diplomate Am. Bd. Psychiatry and Neurol. (dir.); fellow A.M.A., Am. Psychiatric Assn. (chmn. committee on nomenclature and statistics 1948-54; councillor, 1954-57), A.C.P.; mem. Am. Neurol. Association, Washington Psychoanalytic Society, Assn. Research Nervous and Mental Diseases, Am. Psychopathol. Assn., Wash. Psychiatric Soc. (councillor 1950-51), Sigma Chi, Phi Chi. Contbr. to profl., med. jours. Office: 3800 Reservoir Rd., N.W., Washington 7. Died Sept. 16, 1959.

RAINS, Léon, opera singer; b. N.Y.C., Oct. 1, 1870; ed. pub. schs.; won scholarship and studied in Nat. Conservatory, N.Y.C., under Oscar Saenger, finishing under Mons. Jacques Bouhy, Paris; m. Elizabeth Schimmel. Sang as a boy with Lawrence Barrett, in Francesca de Rimini, 1882; became ch. and opera singer in New York; appeared in prin. European cities and at Beyreuth Festival; royal chamber singer, Dresden Opera House; has established a wide reputation as singer of German songs; sang at Met. Opera House, N.Y.C., 1908. Address: Dresden, Germany. Died June 11, 1954.

RAK, Mary Kidder (răk), author; b. Boone, Ia., Aug. 4, 1879; d. Ichabod Norton and Eliza Allen (Luce) Kidder; ed. Troop Poly. Inst. at Pasadena, Calif., 1893-96; A.B., Leland Stanford U., 1901; m. Charles Rak, Mar. 30, 1917 (dec.). Teacher pub. schs., San Francisco, 1902-05; social worker San Francisco, 1905-17, becoming supt. of Asso. Charities; lecturer, U. of Ariz., 1918-19; cattle raiser, 1919—; owns ranch adjoining that of husband, using separate brands, but operating as a unit. Mem. Daus. Am. Revolution. Republican. Episcopalian. Author: Social Survey of Arizona, 1921; A Cowman's Wife, 1934; Mountain Cattle, 1936; Border Patrol, 1938; They Guard the Gates, 1941. Contbr. to mags. Home: Hell's Hip Pocket Ranch, Cochise County, Ariz. Address: Hell's Hip Pocket Ranch, P.O. Box 632, Douglas, Ariz. Died Jan. 25, 1958.

RAKE, Geoffrey William, med. scientist; b. Fordingbridge, Eng., Oct. 18, 1904; s. Herbert Vaughan and Rosemary (Satchell) R.; student Cliff House, Bournemouth, Eng., 1910-11, Christ Ch., Choir Sch., Oxford, Eng., 1911-19, King's Sch., Canterbury, Eng., 1919-21; Guy's Hosp. Medical School, London, Eng., 1922-28, M.B., B.S., 1928; came to U.S., 1928; became naturalized U.S. citizen, Dec. 14, 1942; m. Orpha May McNutt, July 1, 1932; 1 son, Adrian Vaughan; m. 2d, Helen Jones, March 23, 1946; children—Geoffrey, Juliet, James, Jane, Neave. House officer Guy's Hosp., London, 1926-28; asst., pathol., Johns Hopkins U., 1928-29, instr., 1929-30; asst. pathol., and bacteriol., Rockefeller Inst., New York, 1930-32, asso., 1932-36; research asso. Connaught Labs., U. of Toronto, Canada, 1936-37; head division of microbiology, member of the Squibb Inst. for Med. Research, New Brunswick, N.J., 1937-49; med. director E. R. Squibb & Sons, 1949-53; Consultant to pres., 1953-56; scientific director Internat. div. Olin Mathieson Chem. Corp., 1956—; director Squibb Institute of Medical Research, 1949-53; research prof. Sch. Medicine, U. Pa.; member Wistar Inst. Anatomy and Biology, Phila., 1953—. Fellow Royal Society Medicine (London), New York Academy of Medicine, American College of Physicians; licentiate Royal College Physicians (London); mem. Royal Coll. Surg. (Eng.), Harvey Soc., Am. Epidemiol. Soc. Awarded Hiltonprize in anatomy, 1923, Stokes prize in pathology, 1924, Beaney prize in pathology, 1927, gold medal in medicine, 1927—all Guy's Hosp.; Rettlinger prize, London, 1928, Stokes traveling scholarship in pathology, London, 1930. Episcopalian. Clubs: New York Bacteriological; Guy's '28 (London, Eng.); Charaka, University (N.Y.). Home: Great Rd., Princeton, N.J. Office: 745 5th Av., N.Y.C. Died Apr. 20, 1958.

RALPH, Stuart Harrison, business exec.; b. Oil City, Pa., May 27, 1893; s. William Bates and Roscena Catherine (Bockmire) R.; ed. specialized business schs., and Boston U.; m. Elizabeth Spotswood Dodge, Feb. 16, 1918; children—Elizabeth Spotswood (Mrs. V. P. Bevelacqua), Virginia Bates Washington (Mrs. V. Ralph Merurie). Sec. Builders Exchange, Memphis, 1912; asso. McKnight & Merz, gen. contractors, Memphis and Jackson, Tenn., 1914; sales mgr. John A. Denie's Sons Co., Memphis, 1918; eastern mgr. The Flintkote Co., Boston, 1920, gen. sales mgr., 1928, v.p., 1933—; dir. The Flintkote Co., Beckman Dawson Roofing Co., The Flintkote Co. (Nfld.); past pres., dir. Insulation Board Inst.; past pres., dir. and mem. exec. com. Asbestos Cement Products Assn.; past pres., dir. and member of executive committee. Insulating Siding Association. Clubs: Saugatuck Rod and Gun, Fairfield Country. Home: Over-Rock Lane, Westport, Conn. Office: R.C.A. Bldg., 30 Rockefeller Plaza, N.Y.C. Died Sept. 6, 1956; buried Willowbrook, Westport, Conn.

RALSTON, Mrs. Samuel M., Dem. nat. committeewoman; b. Center Valley, Hendricks County, Ind., Nov. 15, 1861; d. Reece and Sarah (Bray) Craven; A.B., Central Normal Coll., Danville, Ind., 1881; m. Samuel Moffett Ralston (ex-gov. Ind.; former U.S. Senator), Dec. 26, 1889 (dec. Oct. 1925); children—Emmet, Julian, Ruth LaRue. Tchr., Hendricks Co.; supt. Ellettsville schs.; prin. Bloomington High Sch. Dem. nat. committeewoman for Ind., 1932-53. Mem. bd. trustees Ind. Girls Sch., 1919-22. Club: Indiana Woman's Press. Address: 99 Highland Manor Ct., Indpls. Died June 25, 1954; buried Lebanon, Ind.

RAMAGE, James Savage (răm'āj), pres. Continental Coal Co.; b. Lake Megantic, Que., Can., Dec. 17, 1868; s. James Douglas and Helen M. (Savage) R.; ed. high sch., Worthington, Minn.; m. Jessie A. Forbes, Mar. 5, 1888; children—Muriel (Mrs. Zola Olds Brooks), Jerrine (dec.). Came to U.S., 1884, naturalized citizen, 1892. In retail fuel and lumber business, operating line of lumber yards at Worthington, 1890-1905; moved to Spokane, Wash., 1907, and engaged in retail fuel business until 1911; organizer, 1911, and since pres. and general manager Continental Coal Company; president Columbia Lumber Company. With Am. Expeditionary Forces, S.O.S. for Army and Am. Red Cross, 1 year; in charge Liberty Loan campaigns, Spokane, World War. Trustee Spokane C. of C. (exec. bd.; pres. 1914). Republican. Mason (43°). Clubs: Rotary, Spokane City, Spokane Athletic, Spokane Country, Spokane Gun, Calispel Duck. Home: Spokane City and University Club. Office: The Continental Coal Co., North 705 Washington, Spokane, Wash. Died Oct. 23, 1956.

RAMEY, Frank Marion, congressman; b. Hillsboro, Ill., Sept. 23, 1881; s. James Thomas and Mary Ann (Ammerman) R.; grad. high sch., Hillsboro; student Eastern Ill. Normal Sch.; m. Lena M. Laws, Nov. 28, 1918. Admitted to Ill. bar, 1907, and began practice at Hillsboro; city atty. Hillsboro 6 yrs.; state's atty. Montgomery County, Ill., 2 terms, 1921-29; mem. 71st Congress (1929-31), 21st Ill. Dist. Republican. Methodist. Mason (32°), Odd Fellow, K.P., Elk, Moose; mem. Security Benefit Assn. Club: Hillsboro Country. Home: Hillsboro, Ill. Died Mar. 27, 1942; buried Oak Grove Cemetery, Hillsboro.

RAMSAY, David Marshall, coll. pres.; b. Greenville, S.C., Oct. 10, 1857; s. Andrew and Martha (Gaines) R.; Richmond (Va.) Coll. (now U. of Richmond), 1884; Th.M., Southern Bapt. Theol. Sem., Ky., 1887 (D.D., 1893); m. Mary Robertson Woolfolk, Feb. 9, 1888; children—Mrs. Eudora Richardson, David Marshall, Allan Brodie. Ordained Bapt. ministry, 1887; pastor Tuscaloosa (Ala.) Ch., 1888-92, Citadel Sq. Ch., Charleston, S.C., 1892-1907, Grace St. Ch., Richmond, Va., 1907-11; pres. and prof. Bibl. lit., Greenville (S.C.) Woman's Coll., June 1911—. Trustee Furman Univ., Richmond Coll., Greenville Woman's Coll. Clubs: "The Club" (Richmond), The Club of 39, Rotary (Greenville). Author mag. articles and chapters in books. Home: Greenville, S.C. Deceased.

RAMSAY, Erskine (răm'zĭ), corp. ofcl.; b. Pitts., Sept. 24, 1864; s. Robert and Janet (Erskine) R.; grad. commercial tech. course, St. Vincent's Coll., Westmoreland County, Pa., 1883. Trained in mining under father; made supt. H. C. Frick Coke Co.'s Monastery Mines at age of 19; supt. Morewood Coke Co. and South West Coal & Coke Co. at 20, later asst. engr. H. C. Frick Coke Co.; in 1887 went with the Tenn. Coal, Iron & R.R. Co. as supt. and engr. Pratt Mines, later became chief engr. and asst. gen. mgr. same co., 1894-1901; in 1901 became v.p. and chief engr. Pratt Consol. Coal Co. (now part of Ala. By-Products Corp.); chmn. bd. and gen. cons. engr. Ala. By-Products Corp.; pres. Ramsay-McCormack Land Co.; v.p. Goodall-Brown Dry Goods Co., Avondale Mills; dir. and cons. engr. Newcastle Coal Co.; chmn. bd. Ala. Mineral Land Co.; dir. Protective Life Ins. Co.; Birmingham Fire Ins. Co., First Nat. Bank of Birmingham (exec com.), Buffalo Rock Co. (chmn. bd.). Dollar-a-year man and mem. Peabody Com., World War. Pres bd. edn., Birmingham, 1922-41; mem. bd. dirs Boys' Club (all of Birmingham). Awarded the William Lawrence Saunders gold medal by Am. Inst Mining and Metall. Engrs., 1937, for bituminous coal mining inventions; for improvement in coke making that resulted in the establishment of the steel industry in Ala.; for administering large enterprises and for benefactions to ednl. instns. Mem. Am. Soc Mech. Engrs., Am. Soc. C.E., Am. Inst. Mining and Metall. Engrs., Coal Mining Inst. of Am., Mine Inspectors' Inst. of Am. Republican. Presbyn. Mason. Clubs: Birmingham, Country (ex-pres.), Mountain Brook Club (ex-pres.). Kiwanis (ex-pres., dist gov. of Ala.). Patented about 40 inventions in coal mining. Home: 3720 Redmont Rd. Office: First Nat Bldg., Birmingham, Ala. Died 1953.*

RAMSAY, Robert Lincoln, lawyer; ex-congressman; b. New Castle, Eng., Mar. 24, 1877; s. John and Elizabeth (Lumsdon) R.; LL.B., W.Va. U.

1901; m. Edna Brindley, Feb. 12, 1908; 1 dau., Charlotte (Mrs. Phillips). Came to U.S., 1882, derivative citizen. Admitted to W.Va. bar, 1901; practice of law, Wellsburg, W.Va., 1905—; asst. atty. gen. W.Va., 1943-45, 45-58; dir. Bank of Follansbee; mem. Congress, 1st dist. W.Va., 1933-39, 42-44, 48-53. Democrat. Mem. Disciples of Christ Ch. Odd Fellow. Address: Wellsburg, W.Va. Died Nov. 15, 1956; buried Oak Grove Cemetery, Follansbee, W.Va.

RAMSAYE, Terry (răm'sā); motion picture writer; b. Tonganoxie, Kan., Nov. 2, 1885; s. Lee M. and Georgia (Yates) R.; student U. of Kan., 1903-05; m. Helene Thompson, Sept. 18, 1931. In engring. depts. of Am. Bell Telephone Co. and Western Electric Co., 1905-06; reporter for Kansas City (Mo.) Star and Kansas City Times, 1906; spl. writer Leavenworth Times, Omaha Bee, St. Paul Pioneer Press, Chicago American, Chicago Tribune, 1907-14; with motion pictures as editor, producer, 1914-20; prod. and edited screen material for Treasury Dept. World War I period, including "Price of Peace," editor in chief Pathé News and Pathé Review, 1928-30; editor Motion Picture Herald, Fame and Motion Picture Almanac, N.Y. City, 1931-50; cons. editor Quigley Publication 1950—. Lectr. Columbia, New York and Princeton universities. Fellow Soc. of Motion Picture Engrs.; mem. Silvermine Guild of Artists (Norwalk, Conn.). Club: Nat. Press (Washington, D.C.). Author: A Million and One Nights (2 vols.)—history of the motion picture, 1926. Contbr. to Ency. Britannica etc. Home: Tinker's Green, New Canaan, Conn. Died Aug. 19, 1954.

RAMSBURG, C(harles) J(oseph), sr. Koppers Co., retired; b. Washington, May 31, 1877; s. Cornelius Stille and Sarah Hassler (Nourse) R.; student Cornell U., 1895-98; studied coal gas production in Europe, 1910; m. Jane Heath, June 1, 1904; children—Margaret Heath (Mrs. H. G. C. Williams), Harriet Nourse (Mrs. R. Putnam Goldsbury), Charles Joseph. Began as cadet engr. United Gas Improvement Co., Phila., 1898, in various capacities from works chemist to engr. of mfr., 1898-1913; became v.p. H. Koppers Co., Chgo., 1913; v.p. Koppers Co., Pitts., 1915-46; v.p. Phila. Coke Co.; mem. Internat. Nitrogen Conference, Adriatic Sea, 1928; mem. Guild of Brackett Lecturers, Princeton U., 1938. Recipient Beal medal Am. Gas Assn. Del. 1st Internat. Coal Conf., Pitts., 1926, 2d World Power Conf., Berlin, 1930. Fellow Royal Soc. Arts and Commerce, London, Eng.; mem. Franklin Inst., Am. Gas Assn., Soc. Gas Lighting, Delta Upsilon; hon. mem. Princeton Engring. Soc. Republican. Episcopalian. Clubs: Duquesne (Pitts.); Allegheny Country (Sewickley, Pa.). Contbr. tech. articles to profl. socs. and confs. Home: Sewickley, Pa. Office: Koppers Bldg., Pitts. Died Jan. 17, 1954.

RAMSEN, Halsey Edmund, educator; b. Newark, N.J., Dec. 22, 1885; s. Henry Calvin and Charlotte Augusta (Coeyman) R.; A.B., Miami U., 1910; student U. Md., evening sch., 1924-25; Johns Hopkins Evening Coll., 1925-26; U. Chgo., summer 1940; M.B.A., Ohio State U., 1943; LL.D., Hanover Coll., 1950; m. Ruth Jane Cameron, May 1, 1914; children—John Cameron, Jane (Mrs. James M. Lehman). Field rep. Middletown (O.) Machine Co., 1910-11; salesman The Whitaker Paper Co., Balt., 1911-18 (winner 1st prize co. nat. sales contest 1918), asst. mgr. Indpls., 1918-21, mgr. Phila., 1921-22, asst. mgr. Balt., 1922-39; instr. Johns Hopkins U., 1927-39; asst. prof. indsl. mgmt. Miami U., Oxford, O., 1939-41, asso. prof., 1941-48, prof. and head dept., 1948—; instr. E.S.M.W.T., Dayton, O., 1942-45; lectr. in marketing U. Cin. Evening Coll., 1945—; sales cons. Dayton Power & Light Co., 1941. Mem. Am. Mgmt. Assn., Soc. Advancement Mgmt., Am. Marketing Assn., Am. Assn. U. Profs., Miami U. Alumni Assn., Delta Sigma Pi, Delta Kappa Epsilon. Presbyn. Mason (32°, Shriner). Club: Kiwanis. Author: Case Problems in Supervisory Management, 1952. Contbr. articles in numerous publs. Home: 101 Oberlin Court, Oxford, O. Died July 18, 1957; buried Oxford (O.) Cemetery.

RAMSEY, Rolla Roy, prof. physics; b. Morning Sun, O., Apr. 11, 1872; s. Joseph Steele and Sarah (McQuiston) R.; grad. high sch., Oxford, O., 1891; student Miami U., 1891-92; A.B., Ind. U., 1895, A.M., 1898; studied Clark U., 1898-99; Ph.D., Cornell U., 1901; studied in Europe, 1912-13; m. Clara Ethel Smith, of Bloomington, Ind., Dec. 29, 1897; 1 son, Hugh Smith. Teacher high sch., Decatur, Ind., 1895-96; lab. asst. Ind. U., 1896-97; prof. physics, Westminster Coll., New Wilmington, Pa., 1897-98; asst. in physics, Cornell U., 1899; instr. in physics, Ind. U., 1900; instr. physics, U. of Mo., 1901-03; asst. prof. physics Indiana University, 1903-05, asso. prof., 1905-19, became professor, 1919, now retired; acting head of physics department Indiana University, 1937-38; radioactivitiy specialist for Bur. of Standards, Washington, D.C. Chief instr. U.S. Radio Sch., Ind. U., 1918. Fellow A.A.A.S., Ind. Acad. Science, Am. Physical Soc.; mem. Inst. Radio Engrs., Phi Beta Kappa, Sigma Xi. Republican. United Presbyn. Kiwanian. Author: Experimental Radio, 1923, 4th edit., 1937; The Fundamentals of Radio, 1929, 2d edit., 1935; also about 98 papers in scientific mags. **Inventor of model of the atom. Home: 420 E. 1st St., Bloomington, Ind. Died June 11, 1955; buried Covenanter Cemetery.**

RANCK, Samuel H(averstick), librarian; b. nr. Lancaster, Pa., Oct. 23, 1866; s. Jacob Eby and Martha Bausman (Haverstick) R.; studied First Pa. Normal Sch. (now Millersville State Tchrs. Coll.), 2 yrs.; A.B., Franklin and Marshall Coll., 1892, A.M., 1895, Litt.D., 1942; m. Judith A. Blackburn (Wellesley Coll., 1897), Oct. 15, 1901 (died Dec. 1936); children—Elizabeth Powell (Mrs. Charles E. Hodgman), Theodore Valentine, Wilson Marcy. Tchr. in rural sch. of Lancaster Country, Pa., winters 1885-86 and 1886-87; engaged in library work during freshman year in coll.; librarian Goethean Soc. Library (about 6,000 volumes), 2 yrs., and re-catalogued it; librarian's asst., Enoch Pratt Free Library, 1892, asst. librarian, 1898-1904; librarian Pub. Library, Grand Rapids, Mich., 1904-41, retired; now librarian emeritus; chmn. ofcl. city com. to finance and develop the Garfield Meml. Gardens; chmn. citizens' com. which secured adoption of the block system of house numbering for the City of Grand Rapids. Editor: Franklin and Marshall Coll. Catalogue of Officers and Students, 1787-1903, with the addresses of those living, etc., 1903. Contbr. to Library Jour, 1896—. Editor-in-chief of Franklin and Marshall Coll. Alumni Assn. publs. (almost 10 yrs.). Fellow Am. Library Inst.; life mem. A.L.A. (exec. bd., 1915-18; 1st v.p., 1921-22; chmn. of the com. which drafted the resolution and secured its adoption by the A.L.A. that one dollar per capita of the population served is the minimum annual financial income required for reasonably adequate library service which resulted in the addition of millions of dollars to the support of pub. libraries; mem. council and chmn. various coms. for many years); life mem. Mich. State Hort. Soc.; mem. Nat. Geographic Soc., Am. Hist. Assn., Md. Hist. Soc., Lancaster Co. Hist. Soc., Mich. Pioneer and Hist. Soc. (hon. life mem.), Hist. Soc. of Grand Rapids (sec., 1905—), Bibliog. Society of Am., Mich. Library Assn. (pres. 1905-07; hon. life mem. 1942), Pa. Library Club, Phi Beta Kappa (pres. Grand Rapids br.), Izaak Walton League of Am. Mem. adv. council of alumni Franklin and Marshall Coll., 1903-38 (pres. 1903-28). Mem. Mich. State Bd. Library Commrs., 1919-21; A.L.A. librarian, Camp Custer, 1918; rep. of A.L.A. in Base Sect. No. 1, France, at St. Nazaire, in charge over 300 libraries, Jan.-Aug. 1919. Awarded alumni gold medal for distinguished service to his Alma Mater, 1937. Co-dir. to compile records of soldiers and sailors of Kent County, Mich.; mem., sec.-treas. bd. of trustees David Wolcott Kendall Meml. Sch. of Art (since founding, 1928); pres. Grand Rapids Anti-Tb Soc., 2 yrs., now hon. life v.p., mem. bd. dir. Elected by regents and hon. alumnus U. Mich., 1934; mem. Alumni Adv. Council, U. Mich. Clubs: Camera (hon. life), Grand Rapids Tchrs. Club (hon. life), C. of C. (hon. life), U. (a founder; hon. life mem. 1942), U. Mich. Alumni of Grand Rapids, Schubert. As library expert has made surveys of libraries and submitted recommendations as to reorganization or more efficient service, of pub. libraries Balt., Montclair, N.J., Muskegon, Mich., Mich. State Prison, etc. Served as sec. exec. com. Campau Centennial Celebration, commemorating 100th anniversary of arrival of Louis Campau, the founder of the city of Grand Rapids. Contbr. many articles on library finance, library ventilation and lighting, library architecture and planning, etc. Has canoed some 60 rivers in U.S. and Canada from source to mouth; now using vacations, with son Wilson, to canoe route of Père Marquette (about 4,000 miles). Home: Woodbrooke Farm, Comstock Park, Mich. Died Dec. 19, 1952.

RAND, Edgar Eugene, shoe mfr.; b. St. Louis, Sept. 26, 1905; s. Frank C. and Nettie Lumpkin (Hale) R.; student Webb Sch., 1922; A.B., Vanderbilt U., 1927; m. Frances Moore, Dec. 1, 1928; children—Jeanette Hale, Mary Frances, Helen Octavia. With Internat. Shoe Co. since 1927, v.p., 1947-50. pres. since 1950; mem. bd. Merc. Trust Co. since 1949; dir. Am. Investment Co. of Ill., Columbia Terminals Co. Savage Shoes, Ltd., Can., Scruggs Vandervoort Barney, Inc., St. Louis San-Francisco Ry. Co., Am. Investment Trust Co., Columbia Terminals. Mem. Civic Progress, Inc. Dir. Community Chest, St. Louis, 1952—. Trustee Webb Sch., Barnes Hosp., Vanderbilt U. Mem. C. of C. (exec. com., dir.), St. Louis Symphony Soc. (bd. mem.), Big Brother Orgn. St. Louis. Methodist. Clubs: Racquet, Noonday, St. Louis Country, Log Cabin; Links (N.Y.C.). Home: 50 Overhills, Clayton 17, Mo. Office: 1509 Washington Av., St. Louis 3. Died Oct. 26, 1955.

RANDALL, Alexander, urologist; b. Annapolis, Md., Apr. 18, 1883; s. John Wirt and Hannah Parker (Parrott) R.; B.A., St. Johns Coll., Annapolis, 1902, M.A., 1907; studied Johns Hopkins, 1902-03. Johns Hopkins Med. Sch., 1903-07, M.D., 1907; m. Edith T. Kneedler, June 2, 1915; children—Alexander, Peter, Virginia. Resident German Hosp., Phila., 1907-09; pvt. asst. to Dr. H. H. Young, Balt., 1910; resident urologist Johns Hopkins Hosp., 1911; asst. prof. surgery U. Pa., 1923-26, asso. prof., 1926-29, prof. urology, 1929-46; retired. Served from lt. to maj. M.C., U.S. Army, 1917-19; with AEF, 1918-19. Fellow A.C.S.; mem. A.M.A., Phila. Acad. Surgery, Coll. Physicians Phila., Am. Surg. Assn., Am. Urol Assn (pres. 1932), Am. Assn. Genito-Urinary Surgeons (pres. 1938), Société Internationale d'Urologie. Republican. Episcopalian. Clubs: Rittenhouse, Corinthian Yacht (Phila.). Author: Surgical Pathology of Prostatic Obstructions, 1931; also articles giving results of med. research. Home: 20 Laughlin Lane, Phila. Office: Medical Arts Bldg., Phila. Died Nov. 18, 1951; buried St. Thomas Cemetery, White Marsh, Pa.

RANDALL, Frank Alfred, structural engr.; b. Cambridge, Ill., Nov. 1, 1883; s. Samuel Benjamin and Anna Louise (Carlson) R.; B.S. in Civil Engring., U. Ill., 1905, C.E., 1909; m. Mabel Madeline Morris, Feb. 1, 1908; children—Ruth Louise, Helen Anna, Frank Alfred, John Deacon. Draftsman Am. Bridge Co., 1905; bridge designer and insp. C., M.&St.P. Ry., 1906; cons. engr. Morey, Newgard & Co., Chgo., 1907, 11-14; bridge designer Sanitary Dist. Chgo., 1908-11; structural engr. Randall & Warner, 1914-17; N.Y. rep. for Seattle, North Pacific Shipbuilding Co. and Patterson MacDonald Shipbuilding Co., 1918; mem. Berlin, Swern & Randall, Chgo., 1919-23; practicing alone, 1923-47, partner Frank A. Randall & Sons, 1947—; cons. bridge engr. Chgo. Park Dist., 1935—; cons. structural engr. Dept. of Subways and Superhighways, City of Chgo., 1938—; structural engr. for 1400 Lake Shore Drive, Chgo. (21 stories, concrete) Medinah Athletic Club bldg. (42 stories), Foshay Tower, Mpls. Ramsey Tower, Oklahoma City, Victor Lawson YMCA, Dearborn Homes, 27th to 30th sts. on S. State St.; building commr. Century of Progress Expn., 1933-34; charge constrn. Outer Drive Improvement, 1936-37. Mem. bd. edn., Wilmette, Ill., 1940-45, Wilmette Planning Bd., 1945—. Mem. Am. Soc. C.E., Western Soc. Engrs., Chgo. Bldg. Congress (dir.), Am. Concrete Inst., Am. Soc. for Testing Materials, Soc. Naval Architects and Marine Engrs., N.E. Historic Geneal. Society, Order of the Founders and Patriots Am., S.A.R., Newcomen Soc. Alpha Delta Phi, Tau Beta Pi, Sigma Xi, Phi Kappa Phi. Republican. Mason (K.T., Shriner). Clubs: Union League, Chicago Engineers', Illini. Author and pub.: William Randall of Scituate and his descendants with ancestral families of Frank A. Randall; History of Building Construction in Chicago, 1949. Home: 912 12th St., Wilmette, Ill. Office: 205 W. Wacker Dr., Chgo. 6. Died Dec. 2, 1950; buried Meml. Park, Evanston, Ill.

RANDALL, J(ames) G(arfield), author, educator; **b. Indianapolis, Ind., June 24, 1881; s. Horace and Ellen Amanda (Kregelo) R.; A.B., Butler Coll., 1903; A.M., U. of Chicago, 1904, Ph.D., 1911; Litt.D., Washington and Lee U., 1948; LL.D., Butler U., 1948; m. Edith Laura Abbott, July 18, 1911 (died 1913); m. 2d, Ruth Elaine Painter, Aug. 21, 1917. Teacher history and polit. sci. at Ill. Coll., Jacksonville, 1907-08, U. of Mich., 1908-09, Syracuse U., 1910-11, Butler College, 1911-12, Roanoke College, 1912-18; Harrison research fellow, U. of Pa., 1916-17; prof. history, Richmond (Va.) Coll., 1919-20; asst. prof. history, U. of Ill., 1920-24, asso. prof., 1924-30, prof. since 1930; teacher summers, Duke U., University of Chicago, U. of Pa., Columbia, Harvard, University of California, Los Angeles. Special expert with U.S. Shipping Bd., 1918-19; mem. Va. War History Commn., 1919 20, Pub. Archives Commn., 1926-31. Mem. Am. Hist. Assn. (pres. 1951-52), Miss. Valley Hist. Assn. (pres. 1939-40), Ill. State Hist. Soc. (pres. 1945-46), Abraham Lincoln Assn., Southern Hist. Assn., American Polit. Science Assn., Phi Beta Kappa. Club: University. Author: Confiscation of Property During the Civil War, 1913; Constitutional Problems Under Lincoln, 1926; The Civil War and Reconstruction, 1937; Lincoln the President: Springfield to Gettysburg, 2 vols., 1945; Lincoln and the South, 1946; Lincoln the Liberal Statesman, 1947; Midstream, vol. III of Lincoln The President, 1952** (awarded Loubat First Prize by Columbia, 1953, Vol. IV, 1955 (recipient Bancroft prize Columbia, 1956); **also articles on Lincoln, etc., in Dictionary of Am. Biography. Contbr. to North Am. Rev., American Hist. Rev., Am. Polit. Science Rev., Yale Rev., Cyclo. of Am. Govt., New York Times mag., etc. Joint editor of The Diary of Orville H. Browning, 2 vols., 1927-33. Joint editor of Democracy in the Middle West, 1941. Home: 1101 W. Oregon St., Urbana, Ill. Died Feb. 20, 1953; buried Mount Hope Cemetery, Urbana.**

RANDALL, R. C., vice pres. Erie Railroad, Cleveland. Office: Midland Bldg., Cleve. 15. Died Apr. 1951.*

RANDAU, Clem J., newspaper and radio exec.; b. Ames, Ia., Jan. 7, 1895; s. Fred and Bertha (Eymann) R.; A.B., Stanford U., 1920; student Sorbonne U., 1919; m. Beatrice M. Lyons, Jan. 30, 1926; children—John Alan, Paul Clemens. With United Press, 1919-42, reporter, San Francisco, 1919, successively reporter, bureau mgr., salesman, sales mgr., bus. mgr., N.Y. City, 1921-42, vice pres., 1936-42; with Marshall Field, 1942-46, bus. mgr. Chicago

Sun, 1942-46, vice-pres. and dir. Field Enterprises, Inc., WJJD, Inc., Chicago, Buckeye Broadcasting Co. (WSAI), Cincinnati, Ohio, KOIN, Inc. Portland, Ore., Totem Broadcasters, Inc. (KJR), Seattle, Wash., 1944-46; dir. New Rochelle Fuel & Lumber Co., New Rochelle, N.Y.; pres., dir. KFBI, Inc., Wichita, Kan., 1948-49; pres., dir. Ill.-Wyoming Co., Chgo., 1947-49; co-publisher New Milford (Conn.) Times, since 1948; dir. Story-A-Day, Inc., Charlotte, N.C., WNEW, N.Y.; pres., gen. mgr. Radio Station KXOB, Stockton, Cal. Executive dir. Civil Defense Administration, 1951-52. Served as 1st lieutenant, Air Service, 1917-19; with 22nd Squadron, 2d Pursuit Group, Meuse-Argonne offensive, France, 1918. Member of the American Legion, Sigma Chi, Sigma Delta Chi. Clubs: Stanford (New York), National Press (Washington), Stockton Golf and Country, Yosemite (Stockton). Home: 1200 Paloma Av. Office: KXOB, Hotel Stockton, Stockton, Cal. Died Sept. 21, 1954.

RANDLE, Thurman, small arms expert; b. Glen Rose, Tex., Oct. 24, 1890; s. George D. and Emma (Thurman) R.; grad. Carlisle Mil. Acad., U. Tex.; m. Betty Polvozt, Dec. 25, 1927. Dir. Nat. Rifle Assn., 1928-—, mem. exec. com., 1931-—, pres. 1944-45; officer-in-charge Navy Small Arms Program, 192-45; pres. Texas State Rifle Assn., 1933-36; coach, Pershing trophy U.S. Internat. Team, Bisley, Eng., 1937; rifle championships, Texas, 1927-31-36-42, Oklahoma, 1931-33-37-39, California, 1933, nat. midwinter, 1933-34, eastern small bore, 1934, eastern all around, 1942; partner, gen. mgr. Thurman Randle & Co., 1934-—; commd. to organize, standardize and put into operation entire small arms tng. program USN, 1942. Dir. Small Arms Firing Sch. Nat. Matches, Camp Perry, O., 1941. Commd. lt. comdr. USN, 1942, comdr., 1944. Recipient Distinguished Marksman Medal, 1937. Mem. U.S. Dewar Internat. Rifle Team, 1926-34, capt. 1931 and 1939; R.W.S. Internat. Rifle Team, 1933; F.I.D.A.C., U.S. Internat. Rifle Team, 1929-30-31-32-34, capt., 1933; U.S. Internat. Rifle Team to British Nat. Matches, 1931, 37; mem. Am. Legion. Home: 6930 Lakewood Blvd. Office: 208 N. Akard St., Dallas. Died Feb. 1957.

RANDOLPH, Harrison, coll. pres.; b. New Orleans, La., Dec. 8, 1871; s. John Feild (of Petersburg, Va.) and Virginia Dashiell (Bayard) R.; A.M., U. of Va., 1892; LL.D., Washington and Lee, 1899, University of South Carolina, 1905, The Citadel, Military College of S.C., 1943, College of Charleston, 1945; married Louise Wagener, June 27, 1911. Instructor mathematics, U. of Va., 1890-95; prof. same, U. of Ark., 1895-97; pres. Coll. of Charleston, 1897-1942, pres. emeritus, 1942-—. Leave of absence for special duty in Dept. of State to aid in drafting work in connection with foreign relations, 1919-20. Democrat. Episcopalian. Mem. S.C. Hist. Soc., Va. Hist. Soc., Huguenot Soc., Alpha Tau Omega, Phi Beta Kappa. Home: 179 Rutledge Av., Charleston, S.C. Died Dec. 27, 1954; buried Magnolia Cemetery, Charleston.

RANDOLPH, Robert Isham, cons. engr.; b. Chicago, Ill., Apr. 14, 1883; s. Isham and Mary Henry (Taylor) R.; student Cornell U., 1903-04; m. Martha A. Maclean, Oct. 17, 1912. Asst. engr. Sanitary Dist. of Chicago, 1904-07, sec. Internal Improvement Commn. of Ill., 1908-11, Rivers and Lakes Commn. of Ill., 1911-13; sec. Isham Randolph & Co., 1913-21, Randolph-Perkins Co. since 1921; dir. of operations, Century of Progress Exposition, Chicago, 1932-34; chief engr. Construction Div., Office of Quartermaster General, Zone 6, Chicago, 1941. Served on Mexican border with Battery C, 1st Ill. F.A., 1916; maj. comdg. 535th Engrs., A.E.F., 1918; lt. col. comdg. 381st Engrs., O.R.C., 1923-24; colonel Gen. Staff Corps, Asst. Chief of Staff, G-4, Seattle Port of Embarkation, 1942-43. Deputy chief Chicago ordnance district, 1943-46; associate director War Assets Adminstrn., Chicago, 1946-47. Mem. Am. Soc. C.E., Western Soc. Engrs., Psi Upsilon, Citizens' Assn. (dir.), Mississippi Valley Assn. (pres., 1932-35), Chicago Assn. Commerce (pres. 1930-31). Republican. Episcopalian. Clubs: University, Engineers'. Home: 1731 Santa Barbara St., Santa Barbara, Cal. Died Oct. 18, 1951.

RANKIN, Carroll Watson, author; b. Marquette, Mich., May 11, 1864; d. Jonas William and Emily (Wood) Watson; ed. pub. schs., Marquette, Taylor's Acad., Greenock, Scotland, 1 yr., Kemper Hall, Kenosha, Wis., 2 yrs., Chgo. Female Coll. (Morgan Park) 1 yr., Bridgeport, O., pub. schs., 1 yr.; m. Marquette, Ernest Rankin, Jan. 28, 1886; children—Florence Imogene,, Ernest Harvey, Eleanor Wood, Phyllis Spencer. Episcopalian. Contbr. of many short stories and humorous skits to Century, Harper's Monthly, Youth's Companion, etc. Author: Dandelion Cottage, 1904; The Girls of Gardenville, 1906; The Adopting of Rosa Marie, 1908; The Castaways of Pete's Patch, 1911; The Cinder Pond, 1915; Girls of Highland Hall, 1921; Gipsy Man, 1926; Finders Keepers, 1930; Wolf Rock, 1933; Stump Village, 1935. Home: Marquette, Mich. Died Aug. 13, 1945; buried Park Cemetery, Marquette, Mich.

RANKIN, Emmet Woollen, clergyman; b. Paola, Kan., s. Rev. John N. (D.D.) and Cordelia (Woollen) R.; A.B., A.M., Park Coll., Parkville, Mo., 1888; grad. McCormick Theol. Sem., 1891; hon. fellow philosophy, U. Chgo., 1892; post-grad. work, Princeton, Princeton Theol. Sem.; m. Alberta Lott, 1892 (dec.); 1 son, Karl Lott. Ordained Presbyn. ministry, 1892; pastor Marshall, Mich., 1892-94, Manitowoc, Wis., 1896-99; moderator Lansing Presbytery, 1893, Milwaukee, 1897; engaged in journalism in Minn. and Kan., later a sec. of Federal Council of Chs., N.Y.; Y.M.C.A. dir. at Gibraltar and in Paris, during World War I; dir. Y.M.C.A. at Smyrna, 1920-21; business mgr. and dir. of Orphanages of the Near East Relief in the Caucasus area 1921-26; pastor First Presbyn. Ch., Baldwin, L.I., N.Y., 1926-28, Congl. Ch., New Gloucester, Me., 1928-30, South Bridgton, Me., 1930-40. Del. Nat. Congl. Council, Oberlin, O., 1934. Member Maine State legislature, 1941-49. Republican. Mason. Member Grange, Lions Club. Home: South Bridgton, Me. Died Sept. 3, 1954; buried South Bridgton, Me.

RANKIN, Fred Wharton, surgeon; b. Mooresville, N.C., Dec. 20, 1886; s. Watson Wharton and Margaret (Houston) R.; A.B., Davidson Coll., 1905; M.D., U. of Md., 1909; A.M., St. John's Coll., 1913; hon. Sc.D., Davidson Coll., 1937, U. of Md., 1939, U. of Ky., 1942; LL.D., Temple U., 1943, Northwestern U., 1943; Sc.D., U. of Louisville, 1947; m. Edith Mayo, June 12, 1923; children—Fred Wharton, Edith Graham, Charles Mayo, Thomas Alexander. Resident surgeon Univ. Hosp., Baltimore, 1909-12; asst. demonstrator anatomy and asso. in surgery, Univ. of Md. Med. Sch., 1913-16; asst. surgeon St. Mary's Hosp., Mayo Clinic, Rochester, 1916-22; prof. surgery, U. of Louisville, 1922-23; served as asso. prof. surgery, U. of Minn. Med. Sch., Mayo Foundation; surgeon to Mayo Clinic, 1926-33; surgeon to St. Joseph Hospital, Lexington, Ky., since Jan. 1, 1934; clinical prof. of surg., U. of Louisville, since 1941. Pres. Interstate Postgrad. Assembly, 1943. Served as maj. Medical Corps, U.S. Army, 17 mos., World War; attached to 1st A.C., 4th and 26th divisions, in France; commanding officer Base Hospital No. 26; col. Med. Reserve, U.S. Army; chief cons. surg. U.S. Army, rank brig. gen. Awarded Victory Ribbon, World War I; Distinguished Service Medal, Victory Ribbon, E.T.O. Ribbon, Asiatic-Pacific Ribbon, Am. Defense and Am. Theatre Ribbons; Cross, Chevalier Legion of Honor, World War II. Fellow Am. Coll. Surgeons, Am. Surg. Assn. (pres. 1948-49), A.M.A. (pres. 1942), Am. Proctologic Soc. (hon.), Southern Surg. Assn. (last pres.); fellow Internat. Société Chirurgie; mem. Eastern Surg. Assn., Western Surg. Assn., Southern Med. Assn., Southeastern Surg. Congress (past pres.), Minn. and Ky. medical societies, Southern Minnesota Medical Society, Society of Clinical Surgery, Visiting Surgeons Club, Beta Theta Pi, Phi Chi, Phi Beta Kappa, Sigma Xi, Alpha Omega Alpha; founder mem. Am. Bd. Surgery. Democrat. Episcopalian. Clubs: Army-Navy, Idle Hour Country, Filson. Author: (monograph) Surgery of the Colon. Co-Author: (with J. A. Bargen and L. A. Buie) The Colon, Rectum and Anus, 1932; (with A. S. Graham) Cancer of the Colon and Rectum, 1939. Contbr. chapter in Lewis' Surgery entitled "Malformations of the Colon"; chapter Sajous Med. Cyclo. "Surgery of the Colon"; chapters "Carcinoma of the Rectum," "Carcinoma of the Colon" in Christopher's A Textbook of Surgery; also numerous papers on operative and clin. surgery. Home: Cave Hill Farm. Office: Security Trust Bldg., Lexington, Ky. Died May 22, 1954.

RANKIN, John Hall, architect; b. Lock Haven, Pa., Sept. 23, 1868; s. William Washington and Maria Amelia (Jefferies) R.; grad. Lock Haven High Sch., 1885; spl. course in architecture, Mass. Inst. Tech., 1886-88; m. Mrs. Anne Frisbie Shepard, Aug. 20, 1907. In practice at Phila., 1891-1941; mem. Rankin & Kellogg, 1891-1903, Rankin, Kellogg & Crane, 1903-25, Rankin & Kellogg since 1925, Rankin, Kellogg & Doe, since 1943; consultant architects Pa. Turnpike Commn., 1938; designers State Asylum for Chronic Insane; Free Pub. Library, Newark, N.J.; U.S. P.O. bldgs., at Camden, N.J., and Indianapolis; Philadelphia (new); administration bldg., U.S. Dept. Agr., Washington; Mechanic Arts High Sch., St. Paul; U.S. Army Supply Depot, Fort Mason, Cal.; Hamilton County Court House, Cin.; Provident Trust Bldg., Phila.; Montgomery County Court House Annex, Norristown, Pa.; Haddon Hall Hotel, Atlantic City; Camden (N.J.) Safe Deposit & Trust Bldg.; Camden County Court House, Camden; Thomas M. England Gen. Hosp., U.S. Army Atlantic City, N.J. Served as 2d lt., bn. adj. 2d Pa. Vols. Inf., Spanish-Am. War; capt. and regtl. adj. 6th Inf., Pa. N.G., 1900-01. Apptd. by Pres. Roosevelt, 1909, mem. Nat. Advisory Bd. on Fuels and Structural Materials; apptd., 1912, mem. Permanent Com. on Comprehensive Plans, City of Phila.; mem. and 1st pres. Pa. State Bd. Examiners of Architects, 1919-40; former mgr. Fourth Area, Pa. Works Progress Adminstrn. Democrat. Episcopalian. Fellow A.I.A. (past pres. Phila. chpt.; past pres., hon. mem. So. Pa. chpt.); mem. S.R., Soc. War of 1812, Colonial Society of Pa., Naval and Mil. Order of Spanish-Am. War. Clubs: T-Square (Phila.); Cosmos (Washington); Rittenhouse (Phila.). Home: Mayfair House, Phila. 44. Office: 1717 Sansom St., Phila. 3. Died June 19, 1952.

RANKIN, Milledge Theron, missionary executive; b. Newberry, S.C., July 28, 1894; s. Milledge Whitfield and Emma (Croxton) R.; A.B., Wake Forest (N.C.) Coll., 1918; Th.M., Southern Baptist Theological Sem., Louisville, Ky., 1921, Ph.D., 1928; D.D. (hon.), Union U., Jackson, Tenn., 1936, William Jewell Coll., Liberty, Mo., 1944; Wake Forest Coll., N.C., 1946; LL.D. (hon.), Baylor U., Waco Texas, 1946, Okla. Bapt. U., 1948; m. Valleria Dora Greene, March 7, 1922; children—Valleria Page, Mary Lee. Ordained to ministry of Baptist Church, 1921; missionary of Foreign Mission Board of Southern Baptist Conv., 1921-35; pres. Graves Theol. Sem., Canton, China, 1925-32; sec. for orient, Foreign Mission Bd. of Southern Baptist Conv., 1935-44, exec. sec., since 1945. Mem. bd. founders, U. of Shanghai. Mem. Joint Conf. Com. on Pub. Relations, Baptist World Alliance (mem. exec. com.), Pi Kappa Phi. Mason, Kiwanian. Home: 111 Tuckahoe Blvd., Richmond 21. Office: Box 5148, Richmond 20, Va. Died June 27, 1953; buried Hollywood Cemetery, Richmond, Va.

RANKIN, Thomas Ernest, coll. prof.; b. Edgerton, Kan., Apr. 10, 1872; s. John Newton and Cordelia (Woollen) R.; student Princeton, 1897-98; A.B., U. Mich., 1898, A.M., 1905; student San Francisco Theol. Sem., 1900-01; m. Jennie Morgan Woods, June 19, 1902; children—Ruth Aileen, Bertha Woods, Helen Cordelia, Marian; m. 2d. Esther E. Ransom, July 15, 1937; children—Katherine Ann, Thomas Ernest. Instr. in English and history, Ann Arbor (Mich.) High Sch., 1901-02; prof. English and history, Coll. of Emporia, Kan., 1902-05; instr. in rhetoric, U. Mich., 1905-07, asst. prof., 1907-13, asso. prof., 1913-16, prof., 1916-28; sec. summer session U. of Mich., 1912-28; prof. English and chmn. dept., Carleton Coll., 1929-46; ret. Fellow Am. Geog. Soc., A.A.A.S.; mem. Modern Lang. Assn. of Am., Mich. Authors Assn. (exec. council), Phi Beta Kappa, Alpha Sigma Phi. Clubs: University, Adelphic; Authors' (London). Author: Materials for the Study of Rhetoric and Composition (with J. R. Brumm), 1912; The Method and Practice of Exposition, 1917; English Literature (with W. M. Aikin), 1917; American Authorship of the Present Day, 1st edit., 1918, 2d edit., 1920; History of Am. Literature (with W. M. Aikin), 1921. Editor: Adventures in Essay Reading, 1924; The Way of Composition, 1925; Further Adventures in Essay Reading, 1928; College Composition (with Thorpe and Solve), 1929. Contbr. to lit. and critical mags. Home: Northfield, Minn. Died Jan. 20, 1953; buried Northfield, Minn.

RANNEY, Leo, engineer; b. New Hartford, Ia., Aug. 26, 1884; s. Wallace Austin and Adelaide (Clayton) R.; B.Di., Iowa State Teachers Coll., 1905; B.S., Northwestern Univ., 1911; m. Claire Sussex Fairbank, July 2, 1927; stepsons—Charles O., Henry, Robert Fairbank. Began as consulting engineer, 1914, in Texas and Okla., 1920-25; pres. Ranney Oil Mining Co. (subsidiary of Standard Oil Co. N.J.), 1926-30; vice chmn. Industrial Water Commn. of Ohio, 1940; appointed director of oil production by Australian government, 1941; in charge Ranneywells oil installations for Australian govt. and prodn. natural gas from coal seams; dir. Seerley Foundation. Spl. asst. to chief of ordnance, U.S. Army, 1918-19; mem. O.R.C. Designer and builder of largest water well; driller of first horizontal oil well. Inventor of Ranney processes of mining water, oil from exhausted fields, charging flood and waste water into the ground; protecting city water supplies against atom bombs; converting coal to gas without mining; of forming underground gas storage reservoirs; of degasification of unmined coal; of excavating and earth moving processes and machinery. Mem. A.A.A.S., Am. Petroleum Inst., Am. Inst. Mining and Metallic Engrs., Am. Soc. Mech. Engrs., Phi Beta Kappa, Sigma Chi, Deru, Sigma Gamma Epsilon. Contbr. to Am. and European tech. jours. Club: Santa Barbara. Home: Petrolia, Ont., Can.; Morro Bay, Calif. Died Sept. 15, 1950; buried Morro Cayucos Cemetery.

RANNEY, Winthrop Rodgers, educator; b. Tewksbury, Mass., Mar. 21, 1900; s. Archibald Joel and Mabel Florence (Howard) R.; A.B., Dartmouth, 1922; M.A., Harvard, 1927. Mem. faculty N.Y.U., since 1923, prof. English since 1947, sec. faculty U. Coll. since 1933. Mem. Phi Beta Kappa. Home: Pittsfield, Vt. Died Sept. 20, 1951*

RANOW, George R(abenovish) (rānō), editor; b. Kamenetz-Podolsk, Russia, Jan. 19, 1893; s. Moishe and Esther (Altman) R.; A.B., Valparaiso (Ind.) U., 1916; student U. London, Eng., 1919, U. Chgo., summers 1921, 22; A.M., Columbia, 1924; m. Natalie Milber, Jan. 15, 1934; 1 dau., Maxine Estaire. Asst. prin. Eagle (Ida.) High Sch., 1916-17; prin. Genesee (Ida.) High Sch., 1917-18; supt. schs., Edgerton, Minn., 1919-20, Holcombe, Wis., 1920-23; editor Holcombe Tribune, 1922; editor U.S.P.H.S., 1925; editor U.S. Govt. Printing Office, 1925-—, chmn. Style Bd., 1950-—; chmn. U.S. Bd. on Geog. Names, 1953-—. Mem. Internat. Typog. Union Am. Legion. Home: 1110 Aspen St., Washington 12.

Office: Govt. Printing Office, Washington 25. Died Jan. 17, 1954; buried Arlington Nat. Cemetery.

RANSDELL, Joseph Eugene, ex-senator; b. Alexandria, La., Oct. 7, 1858; s. John H. and Amanda (Terrell) R.; A.B., Union Coll., N.Y., 1882; LL.D., Union Coll., 1907, St. Charles Coll., Grand Coteau, La., 1914, and Notre Dame U., 1914; m. Olive Irene Powell, Nov. 15, 1885 (dec.). Admitted to bar, 1883; practiced at Lake Providence, 1883-99; interested in cotton planting, 1899—. Owner of Olivedell Pecan Grove, Lake Providence. Dist. atty. 8th Jud. Dist., La., 1884-96; mem. levee bd., 5th La. Levee Dist., 1896-99; mem. La. Constl. Conv., 1898; elected 56th Congress, 1899, for unexpired term (1899-1901) of S. T. Baird, deceased; reëlected to 57th to 62d Congresses (1901-13) 5th La. Dist.; candidate for U.S. senator, 1911; elected to U.S. Senate, 3 terms, 1913-31. Democrat. Former pres. and one of organizers, Nat. Merchant Marine Assn., 1919; hon. Chancellor Union Coll., 1907—. Past pres. Nat. Rivers and Harbors Congress. Author of bill creating Nat. Inst. of Health, U.S. Pub. Service. Home: Lake Providence, La. Died July 27, 1954.

RANSOM, Elmer (Inglesby) author; b. Augusta, Ga., Feb. 25, 1892; s. George Mortimer and Susie (Harker) R.; B.S., U. Ga., 1913; m. Lillian Van Dyke, Aug. 30, 1916; children—Caroline (Mrs. T. Paul Freeland), Sue (Mrs. M. Eugene Flater). Teacher of physics, Acad. of Richmond County, 1913-15, 1919. Served as 1st O.T.C., Ft. McPherson, Ga., 1917; commd. 1st lt. Ordnance Dept., U.S. Army, with A.E.F., 6 months; hon. disch., 1919. Guest lectr. on short story, Sch. of Journalism, U. Ga., 1937, 38, 39 and 40. Began writing short stories, 1928; contbr. short stories and articles to Cosmopolitan, Good Housekeeping, Country Gentleman, Am. Mag., Field and Stream, Sports Afield, Liberty, etc. Mem. Am. Legion, Forty and Eight, Phi Beta Kappa (hon.). Mason. Club: Authors' (Augusta) (past pres.). Author: The Last Trumpeters, 1941; Fishing's Just Luck, Woodland Brevities (nature sketches), 1945; Your Hobbies Keep You Sane, 1947. Home: 2670 Henry St., Augusta, Ga. Died Oct. 28, 1942; buried Westover Cemetery, Augusta, Ga.

RANSOM, William Lynn, lawyer; b. Harmony Twp., Chautauqua County, N.Y., June 24, 1883; s. Nelson Fullam and Rose (Wiltsie) R.; grad. Jamestown (N.Y.) High Sch., 1899; LL.B., Cornell University, 1905; m. Mary Crawford Hope, Sept. 14, 1909 (died Apr. 3, 1941); children—Dorothy Hope (Mrs. Laurence W. Fairfax), William Lynn, Jr., Robert Crawford, Mary Louise; m. 2d, Elizabeth Brennan Erikson, May 20, 1944. Exec. sec. to mayor of Jamestown, N.Y., 1901; mem. Ransom & Cawcroft, Jamestown, 1905-07; chmn. citizens' com. on charter revision, 1906-07; removed to N.Y. City and asso. with William M. Ivins, 1907-11; asst. sec. Public Service Commn., 1st Dist. State of N.Y., 1911-13; justice City Court of New York, 1914-17; chief counsel Pub. Service Commn., 1st Dist., 1917-18; mem. Whitman, Ransom, Coulson & Goetz. Republican state presdl. elector, N.Y., 1916; Rep. and fusion candidate for dist. atty. N.Y. County, 1917; mem. Council on Foreign Relations, Am. Soc. Internat. Law, Internat. Law Assn., Internat. Bar Assn. (patron); chmn. Town of Pelham Council of Defense, 1940-42. Adviser to rep. Permanent Court of International Justice, at San Francisco Conf., 1945. Mem. Am. bar assn. (exec. com. 1932-35, pres. 1935-36; bd. govs. 1936-37; mem. house of dels. since 1936; chmn. com. on labor employment and soc. security, 1938-42, chairman committee on United Nations, since 1944); member N.Y. State, Westchester County bar assns., Association Bar City of New York, N.Y. County Lawyers Association, Cornell Law Assn. (pres. 1924-27), Am. Law Inst., N.Y. Law Inst., Nat. Municipal League, Am. Assn. for Labor Legislation, Am. Acad. Polit. and Social Science, Am. Econ. Assn., Acad. Polit. Science (trustee), Canadian bar assn. (hon.), Pilgrims in U.S. Clubs: Union League, Manhattan, Downtown Assn., Cornell (New York); Gatineau Fish and Game (Quebec); Blind Brook Golf, Pelham Country, Westchester Seniors Golf Assn. Editor-in-chief Am. Bar Assn. Journal. Contbr. to law reviews and economic periodicals. Home: 65 Rockledge Dr., Pelham Manor, N.Y. Office: 40 Wall St., New York, N.Y. Died Feb. 19, 1949.

RANTOUL, Neal (ran tool'), bus. exec.; b. Beverly Farms, Mass., Sept. 17, 1870; s. Robert Samuel and Harriet Charlotte (Neal) R.; ed. pvt. schs. Mass. and abroad; A.B., Harvard, 1892; m. Lucy Saltonstall, June 24, 1893; children—Josephine Lee (Mrs. Henry A. Murray), Lucy (Mrs. Richard K. Thorndike) (deceased). With Am. Telephone & Telegraph Company; F. S. Moseley, 1893—, partner 1897—; director American Felt Co., Daniel Green Co., Bigelow Sanford Carpet Co., Boston Gas Co., Pepperell Mfg. Co. Clubs: University, Harvard (N. Y. City); Harvard (Boston); Eastern Yacht (Marblehead); Essex County Somerset. Home: Beverly Farms, Mass; (winter) 30 Fairfield St., Boston Office; 50 Congress St., Boston. Died Aug. 26, 1956; buried Harmony Grove Cemetery, Salem, Mass.

RAPER, Charles L., univ. prof.; b. High Point, N.C., Mar. 10, 1870; s. Solomon Andrew and Luzena (Hitchcock) R.; A.B., Trinity Coll., 1892; Ph. D., Columbia, 1902; LL.D., Lenoir-Rhyne College, 1917; LL.D., Duke Univ., 1939; LL.D., Syracuse U., 1944; m. Henrietta Frost Williams, 1904; 1 dau., Mary Lee. Instr. Greek and Latin, Trinity Coll., N.C., 1892-93; prof. Latin, Greensboro (North Carolina) Female Coll., 1894-98; lecturer in history, Barnard Coll. and Columbia, 1900-01; asso. prof. and head dept. of economics, and asso. prof. history, Univ. of N.C., 1901-06, prof. economics, 1906-20, dean Grad. Sch., 1909-20; prof. transportation, Syracuse Univ., 1920-43, dean College of Business Adminstrn., 1921-43, vice chancellor 1936-42. Mem. Syracuse and Onondaga Co. Council, N.Y. State Commn. Against Discrimination in Employment, 1946—. Author: The Church and Private Schools of North Carolina 1898; North Carolina—A Study in English Colonial Government, 1904; Principles of Wealth and Welfare, 1906; Railway Transportation, 1912; also papers on taxation, state and local, and on transportation. Connected with traffic bur. of Chamber of Commerce of Syracuse, 1920-43. Mem. N.Y. State Planning Council, 1934-41. Administrator War Transp. Com. of Syracuse and Onon. County, 1942-45. Home: 700 Ackerman Av., Syracuse, N.Y. Died Dec. 27, 1957; buried Rosedale Cemetery, Orange, N.J.

RAPPARD, William Emmanuel, educator; b. N.Y. C., Apr. 22, 1883; s. Auguste and Julie (Hoffmann) R.; student University of Geneva, Switzerland 1901-04, U. Berlin, 1904-05, University Munich, 1905, U. Vienna, 1906-07, U. Paris, 1907-08; LL.D., U. Geneva, 1908; Ph. D. (hon.), Harvard, 1936; LL.D., U. Pa., 1940, U. Algiers, 1942, U. Lyons, 1946, Princeton, 1947, U. Cal., 1948; m. Alice Gautier, Sept. 18, 1907; children—Max, Charles, Liliane (Mrs. Pierre de Claparede), Alfred. Sec. Internat. Labor Office, Basle, Switzreland, 1909-10, mem. com. experts Internat. Labor Orgn., 1927—; asst. prof. Harvard, 1911-12; prof. U. Geneva, 1913—, rector, 1926-28, 36-38; dir. mandates sect. League of Nations, 1920-25; mem. Swiss del. assembly, 1928-39; dir. Grad. Inst. Internat. Studies, Geneva, 1928-55; pres. Internat. Conf. Econ. Statistics, 1928; Swiss govt. del. to ann. Internat. Labor Conf., 1945—, pres., 1951, diplomatic missions, Washington, Paris, France, London, Eng., 1917-19, 45-46. Mem. Inst. of France (corr. mem.). Author books and articles on foreign affairs. Home: Valavran nr. Geneva. Office: 132 rue de Lausanne, Geneva, Switzerland. Died Apr. 29, 1958.

RAPPOLD, Marie (Mrs. Rudolf Berger): maiden name Winteroth; soprano; b. Bklyn., 1880; studied voice with Oscar Saenger, N.Y.C.; m. Dr. Julius Rappold (div. 1918); m. 2d, Rudolf Berger, tenor, 1913. Began as concert singer; début in opera at Met. Opera House, 1905, and has almost ever since been identified with Met. Opera Co.; principal rôles: Desdemona, Aïda, Leonora, Eurydice, etc.; voice tchr. North Hollywood, Cal., 1942—. Address: North Hollywood, Cal. Died May 1957.

RASCHEN, John Frederick Louis (rā'shŭn), univ. prof.; b. Bremen, Germany, Feb. 19, 1875; s. John Henry and Caroline (Schrader) R.; came to U.S., 1889; A.B., Baldwin-Wallace Coll., 1895; S.T.B., Nast Theol. Sem., 1898; post-grad. work Lafayette Coll., Columbia, U. of Heidelberg, 1905-07; A.M., Lafayette Coll., 1905; Litt.D., Dickinson Coll., 1912; Dr. Humanities, Baldwin-Wallace Coll., 1949; m. Jennie Louise Schmidt, July 2, 1902 (died June 1929); children—Harriet F. Carolyn (Mrs. S. J. Wolff), Edith Louise (Mrs. J. C. Tibbetts); m. 2d, Leonie E. L. Zeyen-Zeller, June 14, 1933. Pastor M.E. chs., Akron, N.Y., 1898-1900, Despatch, N.Y., 1900-01; head master Greek and Latin Dickinson Sem., Pa., 1901-02; instr. modern langs., Lafayette Coll., 1902-05, asst. prof., 1905-06, prof., 1906-14; prof. Germanic lang. and lit., U. Pitts., 1914-21, prof. modern langs., 1921-45; ret., 1945; vis. lectr. U. Mich., 1946—; exec. officer grad. council, 1917-24; sec. univ. senate. On leave of absence at U. Miami, 1926-27. Personnel officer U.S. Army, 1918-19. Mem. A.A.A.S., Modern Lang. Assn. Am., Nat. Inst. Social Sci., Am. Dialect Soc., Pa. Modern Lang. Assn. (pres. 1920-21), Linguistic Soc. Am., Verse Writers Guild of Am., Goethe Soc. Am., Schiller Akademie, Munich, Franklin Soc. (Zurich), Otto Ludwig Soc., Scabbard and Blade, Sigma Kappa Phi, Phi Gamma Delta, Pi Gamma Mu. Clubs: Authors, Polygon, Faculty. Contributor to German secular and religious press and scientific jours.; on review staff of Social Sci. Abstracts. Translator Goethe's Faust, I and II, 1949. Author of Modern Language texts of International Modern Language Series, 1907, 10, 32, 33, 34. Home: 191 Sunset Terrace, Orchard Park, N.Y. 912 State Tower Bldg., Syracuse, N.Y. Died June 1, 1958; buried Mt. Hope Cemetery, Rochester, N.Y.

RASCHIG, Frank Elmer, lodge exec.; b. Indianapolis, May 15, 1887; s. Frank H. and Jean (Mull) R.; A.B., Ind. U., 1910; m. Marie Schoener, June 17, 1919. Reporter Indianapolis News, 1910-12; Indianapolis Times, 1912-14; Indianapolis Star, 1914-47; editorial writer and columnist, 1919-47; grand sec. gen. Supreme Council 33° Scottish Rite, Northern Masonic Jurisdiction of U.S.A., Boston, 1947—. Mem. Alpha Chi Sigma, Alpha Tau Omega, Sigma Delta Chi. Episcopalian. Mason (33°). Clubs: Algonquin (Boston); Indianapolis Literary. Home: 381 Newtonville Av., Newtonville, Mass. Office: Statler Bldg., Boston 16. Died Jan. 1960.

RASCOE, Burton, author, editor, critic; b. Fulton, Ky., Oct. 22, 1892; s. Matthew Lafayette and Elizabeth (Burton) R.; University of Chicago, 1911-13; married Hazel Luke, July 5, 1913; children—Burton (deceased), Ruth Helen. With Shawnee (Oklahoma) Herald, 1908-11, Chicago Tribune, 1912-20, lit. and dramatic editor; mgr. Chicago Bur. Newspaper Enterprise Assn., 1920-21; asso. editor McCall's Mag., 1921-22; lit. editor New York Tribune, 1922-24; editor Johnson Features, Inc., 1924-27; editor The Bookman, 1927-28; writer syndicated column "The Daybook of a New Yorker," appearing in over 400 daily papers, 1924-28; mem. editorial bd. Lit. Guild of America, 1928-37; also lit. critic Arts and Decorations Magazine, 1922-28, of D.A.C. News, 1922-30, of Vanity Fair, 1923-24; asso. editor of Plain Talk, 1929-30; lit. critic New York Sun, 1930-32; lit. critic Esquire (mag.), 1932-38; lit. critic Newsweek, 1938-39; critic American Mercury, 1939-41; gen. editorial adviser of Doubleday, Doran & Co., 1934-37; drama critic and editorial writer, New York World-Telegram, 1942-46. Teacher playwriting, supervisor Playwrights' Ednl. Theater, Adelphi Coll. Enrolled in Okla. Hall of Fame, 1944. Mem. Soc. Am. Historians, Am. Classical Assn., Sigma Nu. Clubs: Dutch Treat (N.Y.). Editor and co-author of Morrow's Almanack for 1928, 29, co-author, 1930. Author: The Case of Jaroslav (pamphlet), 1914; Theodore Dreiser, 1925; A Bookman's Daybook, 1929; Titans of Literature, 1932; Prometheans, 1933; Before I Forget, 1936; The Joys of Reading, 1937; Belle Starr; "The Bandit Queen," 1941; We Were Interrupted, 1947. Collaborator: H. L. Mencken, 1930; The Bookman Anthology of Essays, 1923; The Literary Spotlight, 1924; These United States, 1924; The American Caravan, 1928; The Critique of Humanism, 1930; A High Wind in Jamaica (by Richard Hughes), 1930; Floyd Gibbons (by Douglas Gilbert), 1930; Boom in Paradise (by T. H. Weigall), 1932; Essay Annual, 1933; Spoofs, 1933; Modern American Prose (edited by C. Van Doren), 1934; The New Republic Anthology (edited by G. Conklin, 1936); The Patriotic Anthology, 1941. Edited and wrote introduction to Madame Bovary (by Gustave Flaubert), 1919; Manon Lescaut (by Abbé Prévost), 1919; Mademoiselle de Maupin (by Théophile Gautier), 1920; Nana (by Emile Zola), 1922; Chivalry (by James Branch Cabell), 1922; The Triumph of Death (by Gabriele D'Annunzio), 1923; Eric Dorn, by Ben Hecht, 1924; Tricks of Women and Other Armenian Tales (tr. P. F. Cooper), 1928; Decameron (by Boccaccio), 1930; The Natural Philosophy of Love (by Remy de Gourmont), 1932; The Smart Set Anthology (with G. Conklin), 1934; Extra! Extra! (by H. J. Smith), 1934; Memoirs of Vincent Nolte, 1934; The Great Trek (by Max Miller), 1935; The Ballad of Reading Gaol (by Oscar Wilde), 1938; Sister Carrie, by Theodore Dreiser, 1939; compiled, edited and wrote 50,000 words for An American Reader, 1938. Contributor to Ency. Brit., Ency. Americana, etc., and articles, stories, etc., to mags. Address: 525 E. 89th St., N.Y.C. 28. Died Mar. 19, 1957.

RASELY, Hiram Newton (rāz'lē), educator; b. Phila., Pa., Dec. 23, 1887; s. Sylvanus Oscar and Sarah Ann (Miller) R.; A.B., Clark U., 1912, A.M. (hon.), 1942; student Burdett Coll., 1913-14; m. Myrtie Eleanor Pettigrew, Oct. 10, 1916; children—(twins) Eleanor Louise (Mrs. Robert L. Eldredge), Mrs. Barbara Randall Belmont. Office mgr. Norton Company, Worcester, Mass., 1915-20; cons. on management and sales problems, 1920-22; staff sec. Burdett Coll., Boston, 1922-28, exec. vice pres. since 1928; treas. Lynn (Mass.) Burdett Coll. since 1936. Alumni trustee Clark U., 1948-52; pres. Nat. Fedn. Pvt. Sch. Assns., 1948-50. Cons. adv. committee to Gen. Carl E. Gray, Jr., Vets. Adminstr., education and training benefits to vets., since 1948. Fellow National Office Management Association (exec. sec. 1918-21; founder, 1917, and for 3 years exec. sec. Better Letters Assn. (now affiliated with Direct Mail Advertising Assn.); member National Office Management Assn. (pres. Boston chapter, 1931-33); Boston Chamber of Commerce, Nat. Assn. of Accredited Comml. Schs. (pres. 1944), Nat. Council of Bus. Schs. (pres. 1943, 45), Clark University Alumni Association (pres. 1935-37), Kapa Phi. Republican. Methodist. Mason. Clubs: Boston City, Republican of Mass., Mass. Schoolmasters, Boston Clark (past pres.), Executives (Boston). Author: Finding Yourself, 1937; Better Letters, 1944. Home: 227 Common St., Belmont, Mass. Office: Burdett College, 160 Beacon St., Boston. Died June 7, 1955; buried Mt. Auburn Cemetery, Cambridge, Mass.

RASKOB, John J. (răs'kŏb), capitalist; b. Lockport, N.Y., Mar. 19, 1879; s. John and Anna Frances (Moran) R.; ed. pub. schs. and bus. coll.; m. Helena Springer Green, June 18, 1906; 12 children. Resigned as chmn. finance com. Gen. Motors Corp., 1928, to become chmn. Democratic Nat. Com.; now vice pres. and director Empire State, Inc. Member

President Wilson's Industrial Conf., Washington, D.C., Oct. 1919. K.C. Clubs: Catholic, Metropolitan. Home: Centreville, Md. Office: Empire State Bldg., 350 5th Av., N.Y.C. Died Oct. 15, 1950.

RASMUSSEN, Otho Mills, educator; b. Irving, Kan., May 3, 1913; s. Ernest Otho and Hazel Susan (Mills) R.; B.S., A.B., Kan. State Tchrs. Coll., 1938, M.S., 1940; Ph.D., U. Kan., 1952; m. Charlotte Louise Emmingham, June 25, 1939; children—Sandra Ann; Laura Louise. Tchr. rural schs. Marshall County, Kan., 1931-35; research asst. bur. ednl. measurements Kan. State Tchrs. Coll., 1938-41; prin. Hoyt (Kan.) High Sch., 1941-42; instr. mathematics U. Kan., 1945-52; asst. prof. mathematics U. Denver, 1952—, chmn. dept., 1953—; asso. Denver Research Inst., 1955—. Chmn. bd. Meth. Student Found., Denver, 1955—. Lt. comdr. USNR. Mem. Am. Math. Soc., Math. Assn. Am., Nat., Colo. councils tchrs. mathematics, Am. Assn. U. Profs., Kan. Assn. Tchrs. Mathematics, Kappa Mu Epsilon, Pi Mu Epsilon, Phi Delta Kappa, Lambda Delta Lambda. Author ednl. and mathematics tests. Home: 2476 S. Madison St., Denver 10. Died June 20, 1958.

RASOR, Samuel Eugene, prof. mathematics; b. Clayton, O., Feb. 21, 1873; s. Henry and Malinda (Baker) R.; B.Sc., Ohio State U., 1898, M.A., 1902; M.S., U. of Chicago, 1906; studied U. of Berlin, 1910-11; m. Vinnie Adams, 1903; children—Alice Elizabeth, Eugene Adams, Lana Harriet. Fellow in mathematics, Ohio State U., 1898-99; prof. mathematics, Amity (Ia.) Coll., 1899-1900; mem. faculty Ohio State U., 1900—, prof. mathematics, 1913—. Fellow A.A.A.S.; mem. Am. Math. Soc., Math. Assn. America, Sigma Xi, Alpha Tau Omega. Republican. Conglist. Author: Theory of Functions of a Complex Variable, 1913; Farm Arithmetic, 1917; Mathematics for Students of Agriculture, 1920. Home: 1594 Neil Av., Columbus, O. Died Oct. 20, 1950.

RATCLIFF, John Moses, clergyman, coll. dean; b. Greenup, Ill., June 6, 1892; s. Thomas and Sarah (Reed) R.; Ph.B., Univ. of Chicago, 1916, A.M., Univ. of Chicago Divinity Sch., 1919; Ed.M., Harvard, 1928; student Boston Univ., 1924-25, Columbia, 1925-26; Ed.D., Harvard, 1934; m. Lucille Smith, Sept. 15, 1918; children—Nadine (Mrs. William J. Robbins), Roselyn. Ordained to ministry Universalist Ch. of Am., 1915; pastor McHenry, Ill., 1915-17, Ch. of Redeemer, Chicago, 1917-18, Halifax, N.S., Can., 1919-21, Rockland, Maine, 1921-24, Beverly-Essex, Mass., 1924-27; instr. in religious edn., Tufts Coll., Medford, Mass., 1927-29, asst. prof., 1929-39, asso. prof., 1939-46, prof. since 1946, chmn. dept. of religion since 1939, dean sch. of religion since 1946. Served with War Camp Community Service, World War I. Member exec. bd. Gen. Sunday Sch. Assn., Universalist Ch., 1928-31, prs., 1931-35, sec. Universalist Ch. of Am., 1939-42; supt. Mass. Univ. Conv., 1942-46. Mem. Am. Assn. Univ. Profs., Nat. Assn. Biblical Instrs., Religious Edn. Assn., New England Assn. Coll. Teachers of Edn. (pres. 1938), Phi Delta Kappa, Acacia. Author: A Case Study in Discovering the Resources of a Church, 1937; The Wakefield Plan, 1938; What the Church Means to Me, 1939; Lifting Life to a Religious Level, 1941; Equating Measures of Mental Growth (chapter in Predicting the Child's Development by W. F. Dearborn, W. F. and J. W. Rothney) 1941; The Opportunities and Obligations of Theological Education, 1945. Contbr. to religious jours. Home: 20 Professors Row, Tufts Coll., Medford, Mass. Died. Feb. 23, 1953.

RATH, Ruben A., meat packer; b. Waterloo, Ia., Sept. 16, 1892; s. Edward Frederick and Anna (Kudobe) R.; grad. Ia. State Coll., 1915; m. Neva Walker, June 29, 1918; children—Richard W., Rebecca (wife Dr. R. L. Miller), Jean (Mrs. R. L. Hall, Jr.). With Rath Packing Co., Waterloo, 1914—, beginning as salesman, successively sales mgr., sec., v.p., pres., now chmn. bd., chief exec. officer; trustee Equitable Life Ins. Co. of Ia.; dir. Northwestern Bell Telephone Co., Waterloo Baseball Club. Chmn. Waterloo Airport Commn. Mem. Am. Meat Inst. (dir., vice-chmn. bd.), Ia. Mfrs. Assn. (dir.). Home: 214 Highland Blvd. Office: Sycamore and Elm St., Waterloo, Ia. Died Feb. 14, 1956.

RATH, W. John, packer; b. Ackley, Ia., Feb. 26, 1872; s. John and Elizabeth (Moser) R.; student pub. schs., Ackley, Iowa; m. Maude Harbin, Aug. 21, 1895; children—Anita Louise (Mrs. Allan D. Donnell), Howard Harbin. Bookkeeper, shipping clerk, salesman, asst. mgr. Rath Packing Co., Waterloo, Ia., 1891-98, president 1898-1943, chmn. bd., 1943-50, chairman of the finance committee since 1950; dir. Nat. Bank in Waterloo, I.C. R.R. Co. Mem. Waterloo C. of C. (exec. com.), Inst. Am. Meat Packers (dir and mem. exec. com.), Nat. Live Stock & Meat Bd. (pres. 1945). Republican. Presbyterian. Mason. Clubs: Union League, Commercial, Sunnyside Country, Rotary, Elks (Waterloo). Home: 225 Highland Blvd. Office: Elm & Sycamore Sts., Waterloo, Ia. Died Dec. 22, 1951.

RATHBORNE, J(oseph) Cornelius, business exec.; b. Harvey, La., June 17, 1909; s. Joseph Cornelius and Georgie (Winship) R.; student Aiken (S.C.) Prep. Sch., 1919-23; St. Pauls Sch., Concord, N. H., 1923-27; A.B., Yale, 1931; m. Nancy Nelson Huidekoper, Nov. 23, 1935 (dec. 1953); children—Joseph Cornelius, Prescott Huidekoper, Nancy Ernestine; m. 2d, Beatrice Trostel Weicker, Feb. 20, 1954. Head expdn. on Yale U. Peabody Mus. to Kenya, East Africa, 1931; clerk in credits and security analysis, N.Y. Trust Co., 1933-37; asst. to partners in pvt. banking firm of H. E. Talbott & Co., 1937-40; pres. Joseph Rathborne Land Co., Harvey, La., 1938—; dir. Nat. Bank of Commerce in New Orleans, Oil Royalties Asso., Times Picayune Pub. Co. Dir. Fair Ground Corp., New Orleans, 1947, C. of C. New Orleans Area, 1951, New Orleans Community Chest, 1951, La. Forestry Association, 1952-53. Served as 1st lt. to maj., A.A.F., 1942-45; overseas E.T.O., with 8th Fighter Comd. Hdqrs. 16 mos. Awarded Bronze star medal. Mem. squad U.S. Polo Team vs. England, 1930, Internat. games vs. Argentina, 1932. Mem. Nat. Small Bus. Mens Assn., Yale Alumni Assn. of La. (vice pres.; regional mem. for La. and Ark. Yale Univ. development com.), Delta Kappa Epsilon. Roman Catholic. Clubs: Boston (New Orleans); Links, Racquet and Tennis, Yale, Meadowbrook (New York). Home: Harvey, Jefferson Parish, La. Died July 21, 1954.

RATHBUN, Elmer Jeremiah, judge; b. Coventry, R.I., Apr. 16, 1870; s. James and Melissa D. (Capwell) R.; A.B., Brown U., 1896; LL.B., Boston U., 1898, LL.D., 1930; m. Virginia Stratton Pollock, Aug. 9, 1914, married 2d, Martha M. Macomber, July 26, 1944. Mem. R.I. Ho. of Rep., 1897-1909; admitted to bar, 1898; clerk Dist. Court, 1900; justice 4th R.I. Jud. Dist., 1900-09; asso. justice Superior Court of R.I., 1909-19; asso. justice Supreme Ct. of R.I., 1919-35. Home: 54 Barnes St., Providence, R.I. Died Dec. 21, 1952.

RATHBUN, John Charles, educator, civil engr.; b. Mondovi, Wis., Mar. 14, 1882; s. John Chauncey and Elizabeth (Goldenberger) R.; A.B., U. Wash., 1903, A.M., 1904, B.S., 1908, C.E., 1909; Ph.D., Columbia, 1934; m. Dora Frances Breece, June 29, 1910; children—Elizabeth (dec.), John Charles (dec.), Mary Charlotte. Asst. prin. Tung Wen Inst., Amoy, China, 1904-06; engr. Seattle (Wash.) Park Bd., 1908-09; chief draftsman Wash. State Highway Commn., 1909-11; designing engr. City Water Dept., Tacoma, Wash., 1911-12; engr. Bur. Pub. Works, Philippine Govt., Manila, 1912-15; engr. Weymouth Constrn. Co., Seattle, Wash., 1915; supt. bridge constrn. City of Seattle, 1915-18; supervising draftsman, bridge and bldg. dept., C.,M. & St.P. Ry., Seattle, 1918; asst. prof. civ. engring., U. Wash., 1919-25; hydraulic investigator City of Seattle, 1920; Peters fellow research lab., Columbia, 1923-24; head dept., prof. civ. engring. S.D. Sch. Mines, Rapid City, 1925-29; also consultant Westchester County (N.Y.) Park Commn., 1926; State Highway Dept., Conn. 1927-28; prof., chmn. dept. engring., Antioch Coll., 1929-30; asso. prof. civ. engring., College City of N.Y., 1930-41, prof., 1941-49, prof. emeritus, 1949—. Investigated wind stresses in tall buildings for Am. Inst. Steel Constrn. Mem. Am. Soc. C.E., Soc. Promotion Engring. Edn., Internat. Assn. for Bridge & Structural Engring. Circumnavigators Club, Kappa Sigma, Acacia, Phi Beta Kappa, Sigma Xi, Tau Beta Pi. Republican. Methodist. Mason (Shriner). Originator and developer of the elastic skew arch theory. Contbr. tech. articles, etc., trans. and proc. Am. Soc. C.E. Home: 706 Riverside Dr. N.Y.C. 31. Office: College of City of N.Y., N.Y.C. Died Nov. 12, 1958; buried Kensico Cemetery, Valhalla, N.Y.

RATHER, Howard C(hristian) (rā'thĕr), coll. dean, agronomist; b. Bay Port, Mich., Sept. 17, 1895; s. Henry Robert and Mary Ann (Bueschlen) R.; B.S., Mich. State Coll., 1917; m. Emilie McKnight, June 1922 (died Aug. 1923); m. 2d, Hazel Cobb, Oct. 23, 1926; 1 son, Henry Lee. Agrl. extension agt., Marquette, Mich., 1917; salesman R. H. Jones Advt. Co., Cin., 1919; extension specialist farm crops Mich. State Coll., 1920-28 (including dir. European corn borer control campaign in Mich. for U.S. Dept. Agr., 1926-28), prof. farm crops and head dept., 1928-44, dean Basic Coll., 1944—. Served as 2d lt. F.A., U.S. Army, 1917-19; with AEF, France, 26th and 80 Divs., St. Mihiel and Meuse-Argonne campaigns. Fellow Am. Soc. Agronomy; mem. Soc. Advancement Edn., A.A.A.S. Kiwanian (pres. 1943, dist. lt. gov. 1946). Author: Field Crops, 1942. Contbr. sci. and popular articles on agrl. topics and gen. edn. in various pubs. Home: 823 Oak St., East Lansing, Mich. Died Dec. 28, 1950; buried Deepdale Cemetery, Lansing, Mich.

RATHMANN, Walter Lincoln (răth'măn), architect; b. St. Louis, Mo., Sept. 16, 1880; s. Carl Gustav George and Anna Elizabeth (Crecelius) R.; ed. Ednl. Inst., Kansas City, Mo., St. Louis Manual Training Sch., St. Louis, Mo.; Certificate of Proficiency in Architecture, U. of Pa., 1907; m. Nellie Katherine Niekamp, June 18, 1908; 1 dau., Betty (Mrs. Clarence H. Howard, Jr.). Began as archtl. draftsman, 1899; partner Klipstein & Rathmann, Architects, 1908-31; continued practice under firm name to 1945; partnership with Rathmann, Koelle & Carroll, 1945—. Dir. St. Louis Screw & Bolt Co., Beck & Corbitt Co. (chmn. bd.). Awarded Bronze medal, Louisiana Purchase Exposition, St. Louis, 1904. Fellow A.I.A.; mem. Mo. State Bd of Registration for Architects and Professional Engrs., St. Louis C. of C. Prin. works: U.S. post office, St. Louis; South Side Y.M.C.A., St. Louis; post office, court house, Jefferson City, Mo.; indsl. plants. Clubs: Missouri Athletic; Noonday. Home: 6424 Cecil Av., Clayton, Mo. Office: 316 N. 8th St., St. Louis. Died July 13, 1954.

RATNER, Bret, physician; b. Brooklyn, N.Y., Apr. 28, 1893; s. Dr. Leo and Sonia (Maazel) R.; student New York U.; M.D., New York U. Sch. of Medicine, 1918; m. Jeanne Schulman, June 5, 1917; 1 dau., Barbara (Mrs. Murray Dworetzky). Served internships in pathology, N.Y. City Hosp., in pediatrics, N.Y. Nursery and Child's Hosp., for 3 yrs.; pediatric research, Cornell Med. Coll., 1920-22; immunology research (under Prof. Zinsser), Physicians and Surgeons Coll., 1922-23, dept. of physiology and immunology, New York U., Coll. of Medicine, 1923-36; asst. visiting pediatrician Manhattan Maternity Hosp., Harlem Hosp., City Hosp., 1922-27; lecturer in immunology, N.Y. Coll. of Medicine, 1928-36; clin. prof. of pediatrics, N.Y. U., 1928-49; professor clinical pediatrics (allergy) and associate prof. immunology N.Y. Med. Coll.; attending pediatrician, Flower and Fifth Avenue Hosp. and director Pediatric Allergy; director of pediatrics and visiting pediatrician Sea View Hospital for Tuberculosis; associate attending physician children's medical div. Bellevue Hosp., 1928-49; cons. pediatrician French Hosp. Mem. bd. govs. Playtex Park Research Institute; mem. Child Welfare Com. County Med. Soc. of N.Y.; chmn. sect. of allergy, Am. Acad. of Pediatrics; member board of allergy, Board of Pediatrics; member board of trustees Am. Found. Allergic Diseases; Cons. on med. information, N.Y. Acad. of Medicine. Served in Med. Reserve Corps, World War I. Invited to address 3d Internat. Congress of Pediatrics, London, Eng., 1933; appointed Nobel Prize com. on medicine, 1935; pres. Metropolitan Med. Soc., 1943. Fellow Am. Acad. Pediatrics, Am. Acad. Allergy, Internat. Assn. Allergists (hon.), A.A.A.S., N.Y. Acad. of Medicine, N.Y. Acad. of Sci.; mem. Am. Immunologists, Am. Soc. for Exptl. Pathologists, Am. Pathologists and Bacteriologists, Am. Coll. Chest Physicians, Am. Coll. of Allergists (board of regents), Society of Exptl. Biology and Medicine, American Public Health Assn., Harvey Soc., N.Y. County Med. Soc., N.Y. Acad. of Science, Am. Tuberculosis Assn., Alpha Omega Alpha, Sigma Xi, Phi Delta Epsilon. Licentiate, Am. Board of Pediatrics. Pediatric Board of Allergy. Democrat. Clubs: N.Y. Andiron; The Bohemians. Author: Allergy, Anaphylaxis and Immunotherapy, 1943; Allergy in Relation to Pediatrics, 1950. Contbr. articles to med. jours. on problems of allergy in childhood; asso. editor, Annals of Allergy. Laid basis for placental permeability in various animal species, reproduced experimental asthma in the guinea pig, etc. Home: 22 E. 88th St. Office: 50 E. 78th St., N.Y.C. Died Oct. 11, 1957.

RATTELMAN, William Adam, ins. exec.; b. Pitts., Sept. 17, 1893; s. William Henry and Mathilda (Weidman) R.; student Columbia (nights), U. Pitts. (nights); m. Ann O'Brien, Oct. 20, 1919; 1 dau., Caroline (Mrs. David H. Esperson); m. 2d Rita Kastner, Oct. 20, 1939. Pres. Nat. Union Fire Ins. Co. since 1951, dir. since 1949; pres. Birmingham Insurance Company, 1951—, National Union Indemnity Company, 1951—. Served with the infantry, A.E.F., France, Army of Occupation, Germany, Mexican Border, 1916-19; disch. as maj. Clubs: Duquesne, Oakmont Country, Athletic Assn. (Pitts.). Home: 724 S. Negley Av. Office: 139 University Pl., Pitts. Died July 3, 1956.

RATZLAFF, Carl Johann, educator; b. Valley City, N.D., Oct. 19, 1895; s. Herman and Georgina (Pedersen) R.; student U. N.D., 1916-17; B.S., U. Minn., 1922, M.A., 1924; grad. study U. Chgo., 1925; M.A., Harvard, 1928, Ph.D., 1930 (Henry Lee fellow); European scholar Bur. of Internat. Research, Rockefeller Found., Harvard, in Geneva, Berlin, Stockholm and London, 1930-31; m. Lydia Nelson, June 15, 1921. Instr. econs. Hamline U., St. Paul, 1922-24, asst. prof., 1924-26; instr. U. Minn., 1925-26; instr. and tutor Harvard, 1928-31; asso. prof. econs. Lafayette Coll., Easton, Pa., 1932-33, prof., head dept., 1933-42; prin. econ. analyst Bd. Econ. Warfare, Washington, 1942; regional specialist Office Fgn. Relief and Rehabilitation Operation, Dept. of State, Washington, 1943; prin. econ. analyst Fgn. Econ. Adminstrn.; chief Area Problems Branch Dept. of State, Washington, 1944; prin. economist, U.S. Tariff Commn., Washington, 1946; vis. lectr. George Washington U., 1945-47, Georgetown U., 1945; prof. internat. econs. U. Md., 1946—, head dept. econs., 1947—. Mem. Intelligence Service 1st Div., U.S. Army, France, 1917-19. Mem. Am. Internatl. Labor Orgn. Com. of League of Nations; mem. Pa. Com. on Pub. Assistance and Social Security Legislation; mem. Pa. Conf. on

Social Work. Mem. Am. Econ. Assn., Am. Assn. U. Profs., Found. Econ. Edn. (affiliate), Acad. World Economics (dir.), Pi Gamma Mu, Alpha Kappa Psi. Republican. Author: The Scandinavian Unemployment Relief Program, 1934; Economics, Sociology and the Modern World (co-author), 1935; The Theory of Free Competition, 1936; Planned Society—Yesterday, Today, Tomorrow (co-author), 1937. Contbr. to econ. jours. Home: 2245 N. Quincy St., Arlington, Va. Died Mar. 22, 1951.

RAU, Sir Benegal Rama, diplomat; b. 1889; ed. Presidency Coll., Madras, India, and Kings Coll., Cambridge, Eng. Entered Indian Civil Service, 1913, held various positions, 1922-31; sec. Round Table confs. and Joint Parliamentary com., 1931-34; dep. high commr. for India, London, 1934-38; agt. gen. South Africa, 1938-40, high commr., 1941; chmn. Bombay Port Trust, 1942-47; ambassador Indian Liaison Mission, Tokyo, 1947-48; A. E. and P. to U.S., Washington, 1948; judge World Court, 1952—; prime minister Kashmir, 1944-45; former permanent rep. UN. Office: Reserve Bank of India, Bombay, India. Died Nov. 30, 1953.

RAUB, Edward B(enjamin) (rŏb), insurance; b. Chalmers, Ind., Dec. 23, 1871; s. Jacob and Sallie Cole (Reynolds) R.; Ph.B., DePauw U., 1894; DL.B., Ind. Law Sch., 1895; m. Martha Drapier, Dec. 28, 1898; children—Edward B., Eleanor. Began practice of law, Indpls., 1895; chmn. Indpls. Life Ins. Co.; dir. Security Trust Co. City atty., Indpls., 1903-05; county atty., Marion County, 1910-11, 1915; pres. City Council, Indpls., 1928-29 and 1935-38; chmn. Dem. City Com., Indpls., 1905-07. Mem. exec. com. of last 3 Liberty Loan campaigns, Indpls. Trustee Cornelia Cole Fairbanks Found. Pres. Indpls. Bd. of Trade, 1919-20. Mem. Delta Upsilon. Presbyn. Mason (33°). Clubs: Indianapolis Country, Indianapolis Athletic. Home: 60 W. 43d St. Office: 2960 N. Meridian St., Indpls. Died July 29, 1955; buried Crown Hill Cemetery, Indpls.

RAUCH, Harry Lee, business exec. Pres., gen. mgr. and dir. Consolidated Paper Co.; pres. First Nat. Bank of Monroe. Home: 306 S. Macomb St. Office: Monroe, Mich. Deceased.*

RAUDENBUSH, George King (rou'dĕn-bŭsh), conductor and composer; b. Jersey Shore, Pa., Mar. 13, 1899; s. Henry William and Creacie Cordelia (Bower) R.; student Detroit Conservatory of Music, 1908-09, New Eng. Conservatory of Music, 1912-13, Am. Inst. of Applied Music, N.Y.C., 1914-17; studied violin with Arnold Volpe, Henry Schradedick, Theodore Spiering, Eugene Ysaye; studied composition with R. Huntingdon Woodman, Mortimer Wilson, etc.; fellow in composition MacDowell Colony, 1934; m. Marguerite Wernimont (stage name, Marion Wells). Began as concert violinist at age 11, N.Y.C., 1910; asst. tchr. violin to Henry Schraedick, Am. Inst. Applied Music, 1915-17, to Theodore Spiering, 1919-21; concert tour, West Coast, 1921; made debut recital Aeolian Hall, N.Y.C., 1922; on concert tour and studying, Germany, 1922-23; mem. City Symphony Orchestra, N.Y.C., 1923; asst. concertmaster, German Opera, N.Y.C., 1923; 1st violinist N.Y. Symphony, 1923-29; asst. music dir. with Elliott Schenck, Theatre Guild, and Walter Hampden Repertoire Co., N.Y.C., 1922-29; asst. condr. Fairbanks-Pickford Studios, Special Features, N.Y.C. and Boston, 1928-29; asst. concertmaster NBC Orchestra with Walter Damrosch on Gen. Motors Hour, Packard Hour, Music Appreciation Hour, 1929-34; concertmaster Barrere Little Symphony, 1929-31, Chatauqua (N.Y.) Opera Co., 1930-31, Worcester Festival, Spartenburg Festival, Harrisburg Mozart Festival and others, 1928-31, founder, 1929, and condr., 1929-50 of Harrisburg (Pa.) Symphony Orchestra; founder York (Pa.) Symphony Orchestra, 1933-34; founder and musical dir. Harrisburg Symphony Choir, 1938; founder, 1939, and conductor, 1939-43 of Toledo Symphony Orchestra; condr. N.Y. Philharmonic Symphony Orchestra, Lewisohn Stadium, N.Y.C., 1937, guest condr. Phila. Orchestra, 1938, 39, 44; musical dir. Piedmont Music Festival, Winston Salem, N.C., 1943-47; musical dir. Music Festival Assn. of Central Pa., 1945-47; guest condr. Nat. Symphony Orchestra, Washington, 1946; engaged in research and musical composition, 1950-53. Served as regtl. sgt. maj. 16th, 57th and 80th Inf., U.S. Army, 1917-19. Mem. MacDowell Colony Assn., Am. Fedn. of Musicians, Am. League of Composers and Conductors. Composer many unpub. orchestral, choral and chamber music works. Died May 26, 1956.‡

RAUL, Minnie Louise, (rawl) etcher; b. Temple Hills, Md., daughter William Dennis and Anne Mary (Minnix) Pyles; educated by private tutors, and Corcoran School of Art and Hill School of Art, Washington, D.C.; m. Edson W. Briggs, 1906 (divorced 1938); 1 son, Vernon Mason; m. 2d, Harry Lewis Raul, 1943. Etcher of wild flowers and trees. Exhibited: Soc. of Washington Etchers, 1935; Washington Water Color Club, 1936; Miniature Painters, Gravers and Sculptors Soc., 1937; Corcoran Art Gallery, Washington, Nat. Museum Arts Club, Washington, D.C.; has had one-man shows in Baltimore, New York City, Chicago, San Francisco, Newark, New Jersey, and Alexandria, Va. Awarded 1st prize Nat. League of Am., 1934; Hill School of Art, 1939; Washington Water Color Club, 1948; Nat. League of Am. Pen Women, 1948. Works: "West Wind," "Old Fence Line Cedars," "Old Blacksmith Shop," "Iris in the Rain," "Moccasin Flower," "Rugged Oak," Rep. in Wentworth Ho. (London) and Johns Hopkins Univ. (Baltimore). Forty prints exhibited in Memorial Pier Gallery (Dec. 1940). Sponsored by Art League of Manatie County, Bradenton, Fla. Mem. Soc. Washington Etchers (organizer past officer), League American Pen Women American Fedn. of Arts, Miniature Painters, Sculptors and Gravers Society. Methodist. Club: Water Color. Contbr. article and illustrations, Wild Flowers of the Holy Land in Cathedral Age, 1947; article and etchings, "Famous Trees of District of Columbia" to Washington Star, 2d trees series, Trees, Great Comrades of the Road, 1951; lectr., writer articles on nature, old houses, trees, illustrated by own drawings. Has made over 500 plates of wild flowers and trees, old houses and nature moods; Wild Flowers of the Holy Land (Vol. I of Go, Lovely Road Series). Home and studio: 2115 Huidekoper Pl., Washington 7. Died Feb. 9, 1955.

RAUTENSTRAUCH, Walter (rou'tĕn-strouk), indsl. engr., educator; b. Sedalia, Mo., Sept. 7, 1880; s. Julius and Anna (Nichter) R.; B.S., U. of Mo., 1902; LL.D., 1932; M.S., U. Me., 1903; studied Cornell, 1903-04; m. Minerva Babb, Sept. 7, 1904. Instr. U. Me., 1902-03; asst. prof. Cornell, 1904-06; prof. indsl. engring., Columbia, 1906-46, emeritus prof., 1946—; cons. indsl. econs. Bank of Mex., Mexico City. Cons. engr. to mfg. industry. Mem. NRC. Fellow N.Y. Acad. Sciences, A.A.A.S.; mem. Am. Soc. Refrigerating Engrs., Am. Soc. M.E., Franklin Inst., Am. Acad. Polit. and Social Science, Tau Beta Pi, Sigma Xi. Author: Syllabus of Lectures on Machine Design, 1906; Machine Drafting, 1908. The Economics of Business Enterprise, 1939; Who Gets the Money?, 1939. Co-Author: Mechanical Engineers Handbook, 1916; The Successful Control of Profits, 1930; Tomorrow in the Making, 1939; Industrial Surveys and Reports, 1940; The Design of Manufacturing Enterprises, 1941; Principals of Modern Industrial Organization, 1944; Economics of Industrial Management, 1949. Contbr. mags. Home: 235 Dorin Court Rd., Palisade, N.J. Died Jan. 3, 1951.

RAVEN, Anton Adolph, educator; b. Metuchen, N.J., Oct. 26, 1895; s. John Howard and Elizabeth Grier (Strong) R.; A.B., Rutgers Coll. (now Rutgers U.), 1916; A.M., Harvard, 1920; A.M. (hon.), Dartmouth Coll., 1937; m. Winifred Storrs Perkins, Aug. 10, 1918 (died May 1946). Instr. in English, U. of Maine, 1916-17; instr., Dartmouth Coll., 1919-23, asst. prof., 1923-37, prof. of English since 1937, and chmn., dept. of English, 1947-51. Ordinary seaman, U.S. Coast Guard, 1917-18; cadet, pilot training, U.S. Naval Res. Flying Corps, 1918. Trustee Howe Library (pub.), Hanover; formerly trustee Mary Hitchcock Meml. Hosp., Hanover. Mem. Am. Assn. Univ. Profs., Modern Lang. Assn., Zeta Psi. Author: A Hamlet Bibliography and Reference Guide, 1877-1935, 1936. Home: Four Parkway, Hanover, N.H. Died Mar. 7, 1955.

RAVENEL, Beatrice Witte (Mrs. S. Prioleau Ravenel), writer; b. Charleston, S.C., Aug. 24, 1870; d. Charles O. and Charlotte S. (Reeves) Witte; spl. student Radcliffe Coll. 5 yrs., until 1897; m. Francis Gualdo Ravenel, Nov. 21, 1900 (died 1920); 1 dau., Beatrice de St. Julien; m. 2d, S. Prioleau Ravenel, Nov. 27, 1926. Democrat. Episcopalian. Author: The Arrow of Lightning (poems), 1926. Contbr. short stories to mags. Home: 126 Tradd St., Charleston, S.C. Died Mar. 15, 1956; buried Magnolia Cemetery, Charleston.

RAVENSCROFT, Edward Hawks, former emeritus chmn. Abbott Labs.; b. Edinburgh, Scotland, Sept. 8, 1871; s. Percy and Mary Jane (Hawks) R.; B.S., U. Mich., 1898; m. Lucy May Abbott, Mar. 1896; children—Darthea (Mrs. Charles Tuttle), Edward Abbott, Verna (Mrs. Arno Myers), Violet (Mrs. Hinson Thomas). Came to U.S., 1887, naturalized, 1900. Began as civil and structural engr., 1898; with Ralph Modjeski, Chgo., until 1908, in charge of office last 3 years; with Abbott Labs., Chgo., 1908-49, first as contracting engr., then prodn. engr., later v.p., became chmn. bd. dirs., 1933, chmn. emeritus and dir., 1946-49. Home: 677 Valley Rd., Glencoe, Ill. Died Mar. 23, 1951; buried North Shore Garden of Memories, North Chicago, Ill.

RAVLIN, Grace, artist; b. Kaneville, Ill.; d. Hon. Needham N. and Frances A. (West) Ravlin; studied at Art Inst., Chgo., Pa. Acad. Fine Arts, Phila., and Simon-Ménard Cour., Paris. Exhibited at the Salon (Nationlale), Paris; Orientalist's exhbn., Paris, and in prin. exhibits in U.S. Recipient 3d medal, Ams des Arts, Toulon, France, 1911; silver medal, Amis des Arts, Toulon, France, 1911; silver prize and Butler purchase prize, Art Inst. Chgo., 1918, and Peterson prize, 1922. Represented in Luxembourg Museum, Paris, and by 3 other pictures in collection of French Govt.; in collection Friends of Am. Art.; etc. Asso. Société Nationale des Beaux Arts, Paris, 1912. Home: Kaneville, Ill. Died Sept. 25, 1956.

RAWIDOWICZ, Simon, educator; b. Grajevo, Poland, Feb. 22, 1897; s. Chajim Isaack and Hannah Batja (Eubelinker) R.; Ph.D., U. Berlin, 1926; m. Esther Eugenie Klee, Oct. 10, 1926; 1 son, Ben Chajim Isaac Ravid. Came to U.S., 1948. Faculty Brandeis U., Waltham, Mass., 1951—, prof. Hebrew lit. and Jewish philosophy, 1951—, chmn. grad. com. Near Eastern and Judaic studies, 1953—; chmn. dept. Near Eastern and Judaic Studies, 1956—; writer in Hebrew, English, Yiddish, German. Fellow Am. Acad. Arts and Sci.; mem. World League for Hebrew Culture (founder, 1st pres.). Author: Moses Mendelssohn the Philosopher of Enlightenment, 1930; Ludwig Fuerbach's Philosophy, 1934; Saadya Gaon's Purification of the Idea of God, 1937; Maimonides Studies, 1935-43; Unconditional Survival, 1944; Extinction or Survival, 1948; Babylon and Jerusalem, 1952; Maimonides' Sepher Ha-Madda, (rev. edit.), 1953, others. Editor: N. Krochmal's Works, 1924; N. Sokolov Memorial Book, 1943; Simon Dubnow Memorial Volume, 1953; Metsudah, seven volumes, 1943-55, others. Home: 112 Virginia Rd., Waltham 54, Mass. Died July 20, 1957.

RAWLINGS, Marjorie Kinnan, author; b. Washington, D.C., Aug. 8, 1896; d. Arthur Frank and Ida May (Traphagen) Kinnan; A.B., U. of Wis., 1918; hon. LL.D., Rollins Coll., 1939; hon. L.H.D., U. of Fla., 1941; m. Charles Rawlings, 1919 (divorced 1933); m. 2d, Norton Sanford Baskin, Oct. 1941. Writer since 1907; with Y.W.C.A., war work publicity, Nat. Headquarters, 1918-19; asst. service editor mag., Home Sector, 1919; adv. and newspaper writing, Louisville Courier-Jour., Rochester (N.Y.) Jour., 1919-23; syndicated verse writer, United Features, 1925-27; writer of fiction since 1931. Awarded O. Henry Memorial award for short story, 1933; Pulitzer prize, 1939. Mem. Kappa Alpha Theta, Phi Beta Kappa. Author: South Moon Under, 1933; Golden Apples, 1935; The Yearling, 1938; When the Whippoorwill, 1940; Cross Creek, 1942; Cross Creek Cookery, 1942; Jacob's Ladder; The Sojourner, 1953. Contributor to Scribner's magazine. Short story, "Benny and the Bird Dogs" in anthologies, Dashiell's "Editors Choice," Uzell's "Short Story Hits, 1933." "College Omnibus." Elected to Nat. Inst. of Arts and Letters, 1938. Owns and manages 72-acre orange grove. Home: Cross Creek, Hawthorn, Fla. Died Dec. 14, 1953.

RAY, Arthur Benning, chemist; b. Leaksville, N.C., Sept. 12, 1889; s. Bryant Wesley and Helen (Betts) R.; A.B., Wake Forest (N.C.) Coll., 1910, M.A., 1911; Ph.D., Cornell U., 1916; m. Deolice Hickman, June 21, 1919; children—Margaret Benning, Joan Rutledge. Asso. prof. Industrial Chemistry, Texas A. & M. Coll., 1916-17; chemist, Nat. Carbon Co., Inc., New York, N.Y., 1919-34; sales engr. and exec., Carbide and Carbon Chem. Corp., New York, N.Y., since 1934. Capt., C.W.S., U.S. Army, 1917-19; member National Technol. Advisory Com. Mem. Am. Chem. Soc., Am. Inst. Chem. Engrs. Club: Chemists. Author technol. monographs. Home: 104 Summit Rd., Port Washington, N.Y. Office: 30 E. 42d St., N.Y.C. Died Dec. 24, 1951.

RAY, E. Lansing, newspaper editor, pub.; b. St. Louis, Mo., Aug. 30, 1884; s. Simeon and Jessie (Lansing) R.; ed. Smith Acad.; hon. LL.D., Washington U., 1925; m. Mary Hayes Burkham, Jan. 25, 1910; 1 son, E. Lansing (dec.). With Globe-Democrat since Jan. 1903; advt. mgr., dir., sec., v.p., elected pres., editor, gen. mgr. Globe-Democrat Pub. Company, 1919, elected chairman of the board and editor, 1950. Director Associated Press; member bd. curators and chmn. exec. bd. Univ. of Mo., 1921-27; dir. Nat. Better Business Bur., 1926; pres. St. Louis Newspaper Publishers' Assn.; chmn. spl. newspaper com. Audit Bur. of Circulations, 1925-26; v.p. Mo. Press Assn., 1922-23; dir. St. Louis Municipal Opera Assn., St. Louis Symphony Soc. (v.p.) Republican. Presbyterian. Clubs: University, Commercial (pres. 1925-26), Noonday, Log Cabin, Racquet, Round Table, St. Louis Country, Missouri Athletic, St. Louis Chamber Commerce, St. Louis Advertising; Advertising (New York); Nat. Press (Washington, D.C.). Home: 22 Westmoreland Pl., St. Louis 8. Office: Globe-Democrat, St. Louis 1. Died Aug. 30, 1955; buried Chapel Hill Garden West.

RAY, Guy W., fgn. service officer; b. Wilsonville, Ala.; Oct. 17, 1897; s. Robert J. and Frances Caroline R.; A.B., Howard Coll., Birmingham, Ala., 1917; m. Emily Dolores Ables, Nov. 12, 1931; 1 son, Walter Alan. Newspaper reporter, Birmingham, Ala., summers 1916-17; sec. to pres., Kaul Lumber Co., Birmingham, Ala., 1917-18; clk. Am. Embassy, Paris, France, 1918-33, Reparations Commn., 1923-26; press attaché, Paris, 1926-30; vice consul, London, Eng., 1930-33, Guaymas, Mexico, 1934-35; diplomatic sec., Mangua, Nicaragua, 1935-37; consul Porto Alegre, Brazil, 1937-40; in charge Central Am. desk, Dept. of State, Washington, 1940-41; 2d sec. Am. Embassy, Mexico City, 1941, 1st sec. and consul in charge publicity and pub. relations; press officer UN Conf. on Internat. Orgn., San Francisco, 1945; chief Div. of Mexican Affairs, 1946, counselor of embassy, 1947; minister of U.S. to Buenos Aires, Argentina, 1948—. Mem. Sigma Nu. Club: Army and Navy (Washington). Home: Wilsonville, Ala. Office: Dept. of State, Washington 25. Died Sept. 23, 1950.

RAY, Jefferson Davis, clergyman, educator; b. Victoria, Tex., Nov. 24, 1860; s. William L. and Ava (Dollahite) R.; diploma Nat. Sch. of Oratory, Phila., 1879; A.B., Baylor U., 1882, D.D., 1903; student Southern Bapt. Theol. Sem., Louisville, 1895-97, U. of Chicago, 2 summers; m. Josephine Wood, Oct. 21, 1884 (died 1918); m. 2d, Lillian Spight, Jan. 4, 1922 (died July 22, 1937); m. 3d, Georgia Miller, July 23, 1938. Ordained Bapt. ministry, 1882; pastor Huntsville, Tex., 1882-85 and 1889-95; dir. Bapt. S.S. and colportage work in Tex., 1886-89; pastor, Eminence, Ky., 1895-97, Caldwell, Tex., 1897-1901, Corsicana, 1901-03, Waco, 1903-07; prof. homiletics Southwestern Bapt. Theol. Sem., Ft. Worth, Tex., since 1907. Bapt. camp pastor, Camp Bowie, Tex., World War I. Democrat. Author: The Highest Office, 1923; The Country Preacher; B. H. Carroll; Trouble, 1929; Expository Preaching, 1939; Meant for Men, 1939; The Scarlet Sin, 1942. Home: Ft. Worth, Tex. Died June 18, 1951; buried Greenwood Cemetery, Fort Worth.

RAY, Louise Crenshaw (Mrs. Benjamin Franklin Ray), poet; b. near Greenville, Ala., May 17, 1890; d. Thaddeus Henry and Anne Hadden (Calvin) Crenshaw; B.S., Woman's Coll. of Ala. (now Huntingdon Coll., Montgomery); student U. Ala., summer 1916; m. Benjamin Franklin Ray, Jan. 23, 1918; children—Anne Innes (Mrs. Richard W. Massey, Jr.), Mary Crenshaw (Mrs. Thomas M. Lacey). Author (poetry vols.): Color of Steel, 1932; Secret Shoes, 1939; Strangers on the Stairs, 1944; Autumn Token (published after her death, 1957); contbr. verse papers and mags. U.S. and Eng. Recipient Alumnae Assn. first achievement award, Huntingdon Coll., 1937; awards for poetry: Ala. Fedn. Women's Clubs (seven, 1926-37), Gammadion, best poem for 1926; first nat. Poetry Exhbn., 1928; Poetry Soc. Ala., 27 (1929-45); Poetry Soc. S.C.—best poem by mem., 1930; Versecraft popular, 1932; Poetry Soc. Ga.—"Ga. award," 1933, Lynnhaven award, 1936; John Clare Meml. award, 1944; Thomas Gamble award, 1945, popular award, 1946; Chattanooga Writers' Club, nature poem by so. writers, 1933; Stardust, Popular, 1929, Portrait, 1931; Bozart A. T. Merrill, 1934; Westminster Mag., 1939; certificate of merit for geneal. research Inst. Am. Genealogy, 1939; Kaleidograph Book Publ. award, 1944. Mem. Poetry Soc. Am., Poetry Soc. Ala. (pres. 1933-35, treas. 1944-45), Nat. Soc. Colonial Dames Am. (chmn. Batre scholarship com. 1934-56), Birmingham Writers Club (corr. sec. 1928-29), Poetry Soc. Ga., Poetry Soc. London, D.A.R., Beta Tau Sigma. Democrat. Episcopalian. Editor: Alabama Anthology, 1945. Home: 920 S. 31st St., Birmingham, Ala. Died Oct. 23, 1956.

RAYCORFT, Joseph Edward, prof. hygiene; b. Williamstown, Vt., Nov. 15, 1867; s. William and Eliza (Kelty) R.; grad. Worcester (Mass.) Acad., 1892; A.B., U. of Chicago, 1896; Northwestern Med. Coll., 1896-98; M.D., Rush Med. Coll., Chicago, 1899; m. Sarah Elizabeth Butler, June 14, 1899. Inst., Worcester Acad., 1888-92; instr. hygiene, U. of Chicago, 1892-99, asst. prof., 1899-1904, asso. prof., 1904-11; prof. hygiene, Princeton, 1911-36, retired; med. consultant N.J. Dept. Instns. and Agencies, 1936—. Pres. bd. mgrs. N.J. State Hosp. for Insane; mem. N.J. Commn. on Mental Hygiene; v.p. Camp Fire Girls America, Am. Olympic Assn. Fellow Am. Physical Edn. Assn.; mem. Nat. Inst. Social Sciences, Am. Sch. Hygiene Assn., N.J. State Med. Soc. (hon.), Alpha Delta Phi, Nu Sigma Nu, Phi Beta Kappa. Clubs: Alpha Delta Phi, Princeton (New York); Nassau (Princeton). Mem. War Dept. Commn. on Training Camp Activities, 1917-19. Address: 37 Palmer Sq. Wes,t Princeton, N.J. Died Sept. 30, 1955; buried Princeton Cemetery.

RAYMOND, Alexander Gillespie, cartoonist-illustrator; b. New Rochelle, N.Y., Oct. 2, 1909; s. Alexander Gillespie and Beatrice Wallaz (Crossley) R.; student Iona Prep. Sch., New Rochelle, 1925-28, Grand Central Sch. of Art, 1928-29; m. Helen Frances Williams, Dec. 31, 1930; children—Alexander Gillespie III, Lynne Clark (wife of Doctor William Arthur Ryan), Duncan Laurens, Judith, Helen Frances. Began as clerk Chisholm & Chapman, stock brokers, N.Y. City, 1928-29; solicitor James Boyd, mortgage broker, 1929-30; artist's apprentice King Features Syndicate, 1930-32; originated cartoon strips, Flash Gordon and Jungle Jim, 1934, co-creator with Dashiell Hammett, cartoon strip, Secret Agent X-9, 1935; creator newspaper feature, Rip Kirby, since 1946; spare-time illustrator nat. mags. since 1935. Commd. capt., U.S.M.C. Reserve, 1944; served as art dir., publicity bur., U.S.M.C., Phila., June-Nov. 1944; combat duty as pub. information officer and combat artist with U.S. Navy, aboard aircraft carrier U.S.S. Gilbert Islands, off Okinawa, Balikpapan, Borneo, Southern Japan; permanent rank major, U.S.M.C.R., 1946; inactive since 1946. Recipient DeBeck award outstanding cartoonist of year, 1949. Mem. Soc. Illustrators, Nat. Cartoonists Soc. (pres. 1950-52), Artists & Writers, The Lambs, Banshees, Marine Public Relations Assn., Marine Corps League, Marine Corps Reserve Officers Assn., Seventh Co. Vets. Assn. (Co. G, 7th Regt., N.Y.N.G.), Arts for Youth Council, Gamma Eta Kappa. Republican. Roman Catholic. Clubs: Kiwanis Internat., Woodway Country (Stamford, Conn.). Home: Mayapple Rd., Stamford, Conn. Office: King Features Syndicate, N.Y. City 17. Studio: 55 Ridgeway Professional Bldg., Stamford, Conn. Died Sept. 6, 1956.

RAYMOND, C(larence) Rexford, clergyman; born Angola, N.Y., Feb. 29, 1872; s. Lyman Rexford (M.D.) and Rosella Elizabeth (Ryneck) R.; grad. Angola Acad., 1889, Oberlin Prep. Dept., 1891; B.A., Oberlin Coll., 1895; student Andover Theol. Sem., 1897-98; B.D., Oberlin Theol. Sem., 1900; studied Columbia, 1918; D.D., Berea (Ky.) Coll., 1914; m. Estella Rose Landon, June 28, 1900 (dec. June 18, 1948); children—Dorothy (wife of Rev. O. D. Ullom), Ruth (Mrs. Thomas E. Bailey); m. 2d Mrs. Lillian B. Miles, Sept. 28, 1949. Instr. Greek and English, Berea Coll., 1896-97; supt. extension work, same, 1900-03; ordained Congl. ministry, 1900; pastor First Ch., Bellevue, O., 1903-06, First Ch., Flushing, N.Y., 1906-10, South Ch., Brooklyn, 1910-18; dean religious edn. and prof. Bibl. lit., Berea Coll., 1918-23, v.p., 1919-20; pastor Park Ch., Greeley, Colo., 1923-27, Pilgrim Ch., Chattanooga, 1927-33; exec. v.p. and prof. ch. adminstrn., Atlanta Theol. Sem. Foundation, Vanderbilt U., 1933-34; pastor Ch. of Wide Fellowship, Southern Pines, N.C., 1934-37, pastor emeritus since 1937; acting pastor Congl. and Christian churches, Gates County, N.C., 1938-41; pastor Circular Congl. Ch., Charleston, S.C., 1941-50. Republican. Author: (book of sonnets) Immortal Love, 1949. Home: 43 Brooks St., Maynard, Mass. Died Jan. 15, 1958; buried Forest Av. Cemetery, Angola, N.Y.

RAYMOND, Clifford Samuel, writer; b. Franklin, Pa., Nov. 11, 1875; s. Harvey and Harriet (Rhodes) R.; A.B., Wittenberg Coll., Ohio, 1895; A.B., Harvard, 1896; m. Louise Streed, Dec. 29, 1903. Became editorial writer Chicago Tribune, 1907, now ret. Author: The Honorable John Hale, 1946; Sad Azrall, 1947. Home: 1122 Wade St., Highland Park, Ill. Office: Chicago Tribune, Chgo. Died Oct. 21, 1950.*

RAYMOND, Mary Elizabeth, educator; b. Royalston, Mass., Dec. 13, 1867; d. Alfred Dwight and Martha Genette (Willis) R.; grad. Wheaton Sem., Norton, Mass., 1886; B.S., Smith Coll., Northampton, Mass., 1891, M.A., 1897, L.H.D., 1934; A.B., Radcliffe Coll., 1896; grad. study U. Berlin, Germany, 1897-98. Tchr. pvt. sch., Portland, Me., 1894-96; tchr. of English, Hathaway-Brown Sch., Cleve., 1898-1911, prin. and trustee of sch., 1911-38, prin. emeritus, 1938—. Trustee Goodrich House Social Settlement (resident 10 yrs.). Mem. adv. council of Coll. for Women, Western Reserve U.; pres. Nat. Assn. of Headmistresses of Schs. for Girls, 1932-34. Mem. Am. Assn. Univ. Women, Nat. Assn. Prins. of Schs. for Girls (mem. council and exec. com.). Winner of several prizes in internat. photographic exhbns. Address: Royalston, Mass. Deceased.

RAZMARA, Ali, former Prime Minister of Iran; b. Apr. 1, 1901; s. Hadj Mohamad and Qamar Razmara; Diploma, Tehran Alliance French College, 1918; diploma, Saint Cyr Mil. Coll., France; m. Anvar-ul-Muluk Hedait, June 15, 1929; children—Seemeen, Now zar, Hormoz, Kambiz, Parviz. Adj. of regt. Pahlavi, 1922-26; comdr. regt. Mansor in Western Iran, 1927-32. Khorramabad Brigade, 1932-35; prof. geography Mil. U., 1930-40; chief comdr. 1st Div. in Tehran, 1941-43; chief of staff, Army of Iran, 1944-50; gen. adj. to the Shah, 1946; Prime Minister of Iran, 1950, until date of assassination, Mar. 1951. Awarded: Decoration of Coronation, Decoration of Sepeh, 3d and 2d degrees, Decoration of Merit, 3d and 1st degrees, Royal Decoration, 1st degree, Order of Knowledge, 1st and 2d degrees, Decoration of Honor, Decoration of Azar Abadagan, Decoration of Crown. Author: Military Geography of Iran, 19 vols.; Military Geography of Neighbouring Countries Surrounding Iran, 5 vols., 1936-45. Home: 58 Djam St., Tehran, Iran. Died Mar. 1951.

READ, Conyers, univ. prof.; b. Phila., Pa., Apr. 25, 1881; s. William Franklin and Victoria Eliza (Conyers) R.; A.B., Harvard, 1903, A.M., 1904, Ph.D., 1908; B.Litt., Oxford U., 1909; Litt.D., Ursinus Coll., 1938, Temple U., 1955; D.C.L., U. Pa., 1951; m. Edith Coulson Kirk, June 14, 1910; children—Elizabeth, William Franklin III, Edward C. Kirk; m. 2d, Evelyn Plummer Braun, Mar. 25, 1939. Instr. in history, Princeton, 1909-10; instr. history, U. Chgo., 1910-12, asst. prof., 1912-15, asso. prof., 1915-19, prof., 1919-20, non-resident prof. since 1920; treas. Wm. F. Read & Sons Co., mfrs. textiles, Phila., 1920-27, v.p. and gen. mgr., 1927-30, pres., 1930-33; exec. sec. Am. Hist. Assn., 1933-41, pres., 1949; prof. Eng. hist. U. Pa., 1934-51; Guggenheim fellow, 1951-53; O.S.S., Washington, 1941-45. Served with A.R.C. overseas, 1918. Mem. Royal Hist. Soc. (London, corr. mem.) Am. Philos. Soc., Council on Fgn. Relations, Am. Acad. of Arts and Scis. Historical Society of Pa. (v.p.), and Phi Beta Kappa. Clubs: Merion Golf (Phila.). Author: Mr. Secretary Walsingham and the Policy of Queen Elizabeth (3 vols.), 1925; The Tudors, 1936; Social and Political Forces in the English Reformation, 1953. Editor: The Bardon Papers, 1909; Bibliography of British History (1485-1603), 1933; The Constitution Reconsidered, 1938; Clapham's Elizabeth (with E. P. Read), 1951; Mr. Secretary Cecil and Queen Elizabeth, 1955. American Historical Review, English Hist. Rev., Jour. Modern History, etc. Home: Wiston Rd., Villanova, Pa. Died Dec. 23, 1959.

READ, William Thackara (III), insurance exec.; b. Camden, N.J., Nov. 22, 1878; s. William Thackara II and Lucretia Swindell (McCormack) R.; grad. William Penn Charter Sch., Philadelphia, Pa., 1896; B.S., U. of Pa., 1900; m. Florence Atmore, Nov. 12, 1903; children—Edith (wife of Col. George B. German), Dr. William Thackara IV, Walter N. (officer U.S.N.R.). Served as mem. N.J. Senate, 1911-16 (pres. 1916); treas. State of N.J., 1916-28; pres. Camden Fire Ins. Assn., 1929-43, chmn. bd., 1944; dir. First Camden Nat. Bank and Trust Co., West Jersey and Seashore R.R. Co., West Jersey Title and Guaranty Co. Mem. N.J. State Bd. of Institutions and Agencies, 1936—. Delegate New Jersey Constitution Convention, 1947. Club: Union League (Philadelphia). Home: 103 Greenleigh Court, Merchantville, N.J. Office: Fifth and Federal Sts., Camden, N.J. Died Aug. 7, 1954.

READING, Richard William, ex-mayor Detroit; b. Detroit, Feb. 7, 1882; s. Richard William and Louise (Harrington) R.; student U. Detroit; m. Blanche White, Aug. 27, 1901; children—Richard William, Clarence Samuel, Ralph Edward, Marion Blanche (Mrs. Ernest Fontaine). Printer on Detroit News; later with Detroit Times, succesively as foreman, mgr. job dept., circulation mgr., business mgr., sec.-treas.; then sales mgr. City and Suburban Homes Corp.; later city assessor, Detroit, city comptroller, 1924-25, then city clerk, and chmn. City Election Commn., mayor for term ending Jan. 1940. Mem. Detroit Bd. Commerce, U.S. Conf. Mayors, Turnverein. Republican. Mason (K.T., 32, Shriner), Eagle, Elk, Odd Fellow. Conglist. Clubs: Detroit Athletic, Detroit Golf, Detroit Boat, Detroit Yacht, Variety, Bay View Yacht. Home: White Lake, nr. Milford, Mich. Died Dec. 9. 1952.

READY, Joseph Louis, army officer; b. Brighton, Mass., Nov. 17, 1895; s. Patrick and Annie Elizabeth (Keenan) R.; grad. Inf. Sch., 1923, Command and Gen. Staff Sch., 1936, Army War Coll., 1939; m. Inez Eliza Stevens, Aug. 2, 1927; children—Joseph Leo, Helen Elizabeth, Barbara. Promoted through grades to brig. gen., 1942; asst. div. comdr. 7th Inf. Div.; comdr. forward echelon inf. attack on Marshall Islands, Feb. 1944; asst. comdr. 7th Div. in Leyte campaign and battle of Okinawa; 1st mil. occupational comdr. Seoul, Korea, 1944-45; sr. comdr. N.G. Me., 1946-49; ret. Camp Keyes, Augusta, Me., 1949; asst. civil defense dir. Me., 1951-52. Awarded Silver Star, Bronze Star, Legion of Merit (Oak-Leaf Cluster), American Defense Service Medal, American Campaign Medal, Victory Medal, Army of Occupation Medal (Japan clasp), Asiatic Pacific Campaign Medal (four Bronze Service Stars), Philippine Liberation Ribbon (two Bronze Stars). Address: 641 49th St. N., St. Petersburg, Fla. Died Feb. 14, 1955; buried Arlington Nat. Cemetery.

READY, Michael Joseph (rē'dē), churchman; b. New Haven, Apr. 9, 1893; s. Michael Thomas and Mary Ann (Ellis) R.; B.A., St. Vincent Coll., Latrobe, Pa., 1913; M.A., St. Bernard's Sem., Rochester, N.Y., 1915; LL.D., Notre Dame U., Duquesne U., Villanova Coll.; grad. work St. Mary's Sem., Cleve. Ordained priest, R.C. Church, 1918; curate St. Mary's Ch., Painesville, O., 1918-23; prof. Cath. Latin Sch., Cleve., 1923-27; diocesan dir. Propagation of the Faith, Cleve., 1927-31; asst. gen. sec., Nat. Cath. Welfare Conf., Washington, 1931-36, gen. sec., 1936-44; bishop of Columbus, O., 1944—; pres. bd. trustees, Nat. Cath. Sch. Social Service. Papal Chamberlain, 1934; Domestic Prelate (by His Holiness, Pius XI), 1937. Address: 198 Broad St., Columbus 15, O. Died May 2, 1957; buried St. Joseph Cemetery, Columbus.

REAGAN, Frank J(oseph), communications exec.; b. Natick, Mass., Nov. 24, 1883; s. William and Mary C. (Coveney) R.; student Phillips Andover Acad.; grad. Dartmouth, 1909; m. Marguerite M. Shipman, July 12, 1925. Gen. traffic supervisor Pacific Tel. & Tel. Co., 1913-20, div. traffic mgr., 1920-25, gen. comml. mgr., San Francisco, 1926-28, asst. to pres., 1928, v.p. since 1929, dir. since 1948; gen. traffic mgr. Up-State N.Y., N.Y. Telephone Co., 1925-26; pres., dir. Hobart Estate Co., San Francisco; dir. Californians, Inc. Clubs: Son Francisco Golf, Pacific Union (San Francisco). Home: 25 Oakvale Av., Berkeley, Cal. Office: 582 Market St., San Francisco. Died Apr. 24, 1955.

REAVES, Samuel Watson (rēvz), mathematician; b. Dillon County, S.C., July 27, 1875; s. James Robert and Sarah Frances (McMillan) R.; grad. S.C. Mil. Acad., 1895; B.S., U. N.C., 1899; A.B., Cornell U., 1900; A.M., U. Chgo., 1912, Ph.D, 1915; m. Ella Betha, Aug. 28, 1901 (died Apr. 8, 1945); 1 son, Henry Wilson (adopted); m. 2d, Ima James, June 6, 1946. Tchr. high sch., Marion, 1895-98; tchr. mathematics Mich. Mil. Acad., Orchard Lake, 1900-

01; asst. prof. mathematics Clemson (S.C.) Coll., 1901-05; prof. mathematics U. Okla., 1905-48, prof. emeritus, 1948—, head dept., 1905-40, acting dean Coll. Arts and Sciences, 1923-25, dean, 1925-40, dean emeritus, 1949—. Mem. exec. com. Okla. State Bldg. and Loan Assn.; dir. Norman Building & Loan Assn., 1908—. Studied arty. at Ft. Sill, Okla., summer 1918, and later gave instrn. in same to 150 univ. students. Chmn. Cleveland County (Okla.) chpt. A.R.C., 1918-19. Mem. Am. Math. Soc., Math. Assn. Am., Sigma Xi, Phi Beta Kappa, Delta Chi. Democrat. Episcopalian. Mason. Club: Lions (pres. 1924). Home: 527 Chautauqua Av., Norman, Okla. Died Aug. 2, 1950.

REAVIS, William Claude (rĕv'ĭs), educator; b. Francisco, Ind., Aug. 18, 1881; s. Franklin Sherman and Sarah L. (Wood) R.; A.B., Oakland City (Ind.) Coll., 1905; Ph.B., U. of Chicago, 1908, A.M., 1911, Ph.D., 1925; m. Anna Lanphar, June 14, 1907. Teacher Ind. rural schs., 1899-1905; prin. Ind. high schs., Francisco, 1905-07, Hazleton, 1907-08; supt. schs., Oakland City, Ind., 1908-12; prin. Pierre Laclede Sch., St. Louis, 1912-17; prof. ednl. sociology, Harris Teachers Coll., St. Louis, 1917-18; supt. schs., Alton, Ill., 1918-21; prin. U. of Chicago High Sch., 1921-27; prof. edn., U. of Chicago, 1927-47, emeritus, 1947. Chmn. com. on appointments and field services, Dept. Education. Member Illinois State Teachers College Board. Mem. Nat. Soc. Study of Edn., Am. Ednl. Research Assn., Nat. Soc. Coll. Teachers of Edn., Am. Association School Adminstrs., Am. Association Univ. Profs., Nat. Assn. of Secondary Sch. Prins., Phi Delta Kappa. Baptist. Mason. Club: Quadrangle. Author: Pupil Adjustment, 1926; Office Practices in Secondary Schools, 1930; The Elementary School, 1931, rev., 1938; Guidance Programs, 1932; Non-Athletic Extracurriculum Activities, 1934; Relations of School Principals to Central Administrative Office in Large Cities, 1937; Administering the Secondary School, 1940; Duties of School Principals, 1941, rev. 1950; The Teacher and Ednl. Adminstrn., 1942; Evaluation of Teacher Merit in City Sch. Systems, 1945; Administrating The Elementary School, 1953; A Cooperative Educational Enterprise, 1953; The Effective School Principal, 1954. Editor: Critical Issues in Educational Adminstr., 1938; Democratic Practices in School Administration, 1939; Evaluating the Work of the School, 1940; Administrative Adjustments Required by Socio-Economic Change, 1941; The School and the Urban Community, 1942; War and Post-War Responsibilities of American Schools, 1943; Significant Aspects of American Life and Postwar Education, 1944; Forthcoming Developments in American Education, 1945; Educational Administration: A Survey of Progress, Problems and Needs, 1946. Contbr. articles to sch. ednl. jours. Home: 5819 Blackstone Av., Chgo. 37. Died June 2, 1955; buried Francisco, Ind.

REBER, John, ex-congressman; b. Schuylkill Co., Pa., Feb. 1, 1858; grad. Eastman Bus. Coll., Poughkeepsie, N.Y., 1875; married. Tchr. later bookkeeper, dep. county treas.; mfr. of hosiery, 1885-1917; mem. 66th and 67th Congresses 1919-23, 12th Pa. Dist. Republican. Home: Pottsville, Pa. Deceased.

REBER, John U(hrich), advt. exec.; b. Reading, Pa., Oct. 6, 1893; s. James Calvin and Mary Jane (Uhrich) R.; student Philips Exeter Acad., 1910-12; A.B., Amherst Coll., 1912-16; m. Helen C. Hutchins, Dec. 30, 1916; children—John Hutchins, Ann Chadwick; m. 2d, Milena Miller, Mar. 19, 1948; children—Richard John, Christopher John. Joined J. Walter Thompson Co., advt., N.Y.C., 1917, London office mgr. charge internat. operations, 1923-26, v.p., 1929—, dir., 1933—. Served with USNRF, World War I. Mem. Pa. Soc. Mem. Reformed Ch. Club: Berkshire Country. Home: 800 Park Av., N.Y.C. 21. Died July 2, 1955; buried Charles Evans Cemetery, Reading, Pa.

RECTOR, Lizzie E., ret. educator; b. N.Y.C., Nov. 11, 1866; d. George and Sarah (Roome) Rector; grad. Jersey City High Sch., 1883, Chgo. Normal Coll., 1886; Pd.D., N.Y.U., 1895. Tchr., 1886-1900; prin. pub. sch. No. 4, N.Y.C., 1900-18; dist. supt., dists. 36 and 37, Bklyn., 1918-36, ret.; lectr. on edn. and sociological subjects. Mem. Nat. Soc. for Study of Edn. Contbr. to mags., newspapers and ednl. jours. Selected, translated and annotated Montaigne's The Education of Children (in Internat. Edn. Series), 1899. Home: 37 Madison Av., N.Y.C. 10. Died Jan. 5, 1955.*

RECTOR, Thomas M., chemist; b. Warrenton, Va., Feb. 26, 1894; s. Jacquelin and Elizabeth Frances (Rector) R.; grad. Western High Sch., Washington, 1911; m. Elizabeth Hall Schoenly, Feb. 22, 1919; children—Jacqueline Lee (Mrs. Robert A. Stringer), Virginia Phoebe (Mrs. Norbert Osterland). Lab. asst., later asst. chemist Inst. of Indsl. Research, Washington, 1911-15, chief chemist, founder div. food technology, 1919-20; chief chemist Pompeian Olive Oil Co., Balt., 1915-17, 19; mgr. mfg. dept. Franklin Baker Co., N.Y.C. and Phila., 1922-27; dir. chem. dept. Pease Labs., 1920-22; dir. engring. research v.p. in charge research and development Gen. Foods Corp., 1927—. Served as 1st lt. C.W.S., U.S. Army, 1917-19. Mem. Am. Chem. Soc., Inst. Food Technologists, Franklin Inst., Indsl. Adv. Com. of Nutrition Found., Sci. Council of Refrigeration Found. Recipient Nicholas Appert Medal for contbns. field food technology (posthumously), 1950. Author: Scientific Preservation of Food, 1925; also numerous articles in scientific jours. on lab. management food preservation and processing. Holder approximately 30 U.S. and fgn. paetnts covering mech., phys. and chem. processes, principally in the food industry. Introduced cashew nuts into U.S. from India. Home: 100 Burnham Parkway, Morristown, N.J. Office: 250 Park Av., Died Mar. 31, 1950.

RECTOR, Walter Whiting, corp. exec.; b. Fennimore, Wis., Aug. 18, 1887; s. Fred Ernest and Emma (Osborne) R.; A.B., U. Wis., 1909; m. Lillian Post, Sept. 18, 1913; 1 son, William George. With Marshall Wells Co., Duluth, Minn., 1909-32; with Montgomery Ward Co., Chicago, 1932-38; with True Temper Corp., Cleveland, since 1938, now pres.; dir. Welland Vale Mfg. Co., Ltd. Clubs: Shaker Heights (O.) Country; Union, Mid-Day, (Cleveland); Nat. Golf (Dunedin, Fla.). Home: 13415 Shaker Blvd., Cleve. 20. Office: 1623 Euclid Av., Cleve. 15. Died Apr. 1953.

REDDICK, Donald, plant pathologist; b. Sheridan, Mo., Mar. 1, 1883; s. Elias Albert and Ruth Anna (Boone) R.; A.B., Wabash Coll., 1905; Ph.D., Cornell, 1909; m. Emma Brill, Oct. 19, 1909; children—Robert Brill, Emma Louise, Anna Elizabeth; m. 2d, Adeline Newman, Oct. 30, 1946. Asst. in botany, Cornell U., 1905-07, instr. plant pathology, 1907-09, asst. prof., 1909-11, prof., 1911—; botanist N.Y. Agrl. Expt. Sta., 1920-24; bus. mgr., later editor, "Phytopathology," 1911-17; editor for pathology of Bot. Abstracts, 1918-19, chmn. bd. control, 1918-20, bus. mgr., 1922-24. Fellow A.A.A.S.; Soc. Am. Naturalists, Am. Phytopathol. Soc. (pres. 1921), Am. Assn. Univ. Profs., Gamma Alpha, Sigma Xi.; corr. mem. Nederlandsche Botanische Vereeniging; lime mem. Société Linnéenne de Lyon; v.p. Internat. Union of Biol. Scis., pres. sect. for pathology, 1935-47. Researches in grape diseases and methods of control; mosaic diseases of plants; breeding for disease resistance, potato blight. Home: 18 N.W. 27th St., Gainsville, Fla. Died Apr. 2, 1955; buried East Lawn Cemetery, Ithaca, N.Y.

REDDING, Charles Summerfield, business exec.; b. Phila., Pa., Nov. 20, 1883; s. Thomas A. and Elizabeth Lois (Kennedy) R.; ed. North East Manual Training Sch., Phila., Pa., 1898-1901; B.S. in E.E., University of Pa., 1906; honorary Doctor Science, 1947; married Luella May MacDermond, October 24, 1911; children—Charles Thompson, Janet Luella, James Karcher, Andrew Compton. Began career as instrument maker for Morris E. Leeds & Co., Phila., Pa., 1901-02; instr. mech. engring., U. Pa., 1906-08; asso. Leeds & Northrup Co., mfrs. elec. instruments, 1909—, v.p., dir., 1928-39, pres., 1939-53, chmn. bd., 1953—; dir. Phila. Mfrs. Mutual Fire Ins. Co., Electric Storage Battery Co., Phila. Electric Co. Served in the Pennsylvania Nat. Guards, 1909-11. Trustee Drexel Inst.; dir. Asso. Hosp. Service of Phila.; mem. bd. mgrs., Savings Fund Soc. of Germantown and Vicinity, Franklin Inst. (pres. 1941-46); mem. borough council, Jenkintown, Pa., 1921-30. Mem. A.A.A.S., Am. Inst. Elec. Engrs., Am. Phys. Soc., Kappa Sigma. Rep. Methodist. Mason. Clubs: Union League, Rittenhouse, Engineers (Phila.). Home: Baederwood, Jenkintown, Pa. Office: 4901 Stenton Av., Phila. 44. Died Jan. 2, 1959.

REDFERN, Merrill F(rank), business exec.; b. Maple Rapids, Mich., Dec. 1, 1901; s. Frank W. and Bertha May (Westbrook) R.; student Albion (Mich.) Coll., 1919-21; A.B., Univ. of Mich., 1924; m. Louise Shriver, Oct. 7, 1929; children—William C., Robert F. Dist. traffic mgr. United Airlines and predecessor cos., Kansas City, Phila. and New York, 1927-36, asst. personnel dir., Chicago, 1937-38; exec. sec. Air Traffic Conf. of Am., Washington, D.C., since 1939, v.p. traffic and sec. Air Transport Assn. of Am. since 1942; past president Army Transportation Assn. Dir. Eastern Timetable Distributing Co. Home: 5640 Audubon Rd., Bethesda. Office: 1107 16th St. N.W., Washington. Died June 23, 1952.

REDFIELD, Robert, anthropologist; b. Chicago, Ill., Dec. 4, 1897; s. Robert and Bertha (Dreier) R.; Ph.B., U. of Chicago, 1920, J.D., 1921, Ph.D., 1928; L.H.D. (hon.), Fisk University, 1947; m. Margaret Park, June 17, 1920; children—Lisa Redfield Peattie, Robert (dec.), Joanna (Mrs. David Gutmann), James Michael. Instructor sociology, University of Colorado, 1925-26; fellow Social Science Research Council, 1926-27; instructor in anthropology, University of Chicago, 1927-28, asst. prof., 1928-30, asso. prof., 1930-34, prof. and dean of Div. of Social Sciences, 1934-46, chmn. dept. of anthropology, 1947-49, Robert Maynard Hutchins Distinguished Service prof. since 1953; Messenger lectr. Cornell University, 1952; Gottesman lecturer at Upsala University, 1954; research associate Carnegie Institution of Washington, in charge of ethnol. and sociol. fieldwork, 1930-46; research in Yucatan and Guatemala, 1930-48. Ambulance driver, American Field Service, 1917. Member Social Science Research Council, 1935-43; dir. Am. Council Race Relations, 1947-50; dir. Social Sci. Found. Recipient Viking medal, 1954; Huxley Meml. medal, 1955. Fellow A.A.A.S., Am. Philos. Society; member American Anthrop. Association (pres. 1944), Phi Beta Kappa, Phi Gamma Delta, Sigma Xi. Author: Tepoztlan, A Mexican Village, 1930; (with Alfonso Villa) Chan Kom, A Maya Village, 1934; The Folk Culture of Yucatan, 1941; A Village That Chose Progress, 1950; The Primitive World and its Transformations, 1953; The Little Community, 1955; Peasant Society and Culture, 1956. Home: Windy Pines, 4335 W. Lake Av., Glenview, Ill. Office: 1126 E. 59th St., Chgo. Died 1958.

REDMOND, Daniel George, editor; b. Philadelphia, Pa., Nov. 13, 1896; s. Daniel Henry and Margaret (Tinney) R.; grad. William Penn Charter Sch., Phila., 1914; student Amherst Coll., 1914-16; special student Columbia, 1916-17; m. Claire Patterson, Sept. 6, 1919; children—Daniel George, Mary Ellen (dec.). Social worker Hudson Guild, New York, N.Y., 1917-18; asst. to treas. Fairmount Foundry Co., Phila., Pa., 1919-22; editor and treas. Milo Pub. Co., 1922-35; editor Column Review, 1936-43. Current History (Phila.), 1943—. Mem. Am. Acad. Polit. and Social Science, Am. Hist. Soc., Phi Delta Theta. Home: 247 S. 46th St., Philadelphia 39. Office: 108 Walnut St., Phila. 6. Died Feb. 21, 1955.

REDSTONE, Edward H., librarian; b. St. Johns, Newfoundland, June 22, 1882; s. George and Lucy (Fleet) R.; student Meth. Coll., St. Johns; grad. high sch., Cambridge, Mass.; student Boston YMCA; m. Alice Eaton Hitchcock, Jan. 15, 1908; children—Barbara, Edward H. (dec.), Constance. Came to U.S., 1897, naturalized, 1911. Asst. in Harvard Law Sch. Library, 1900-06; asst. librarian Social Law Library, Boston, 1908-13, librarian, 1913-19; librarian Mass. State Library, 1919-36; supr. reference div. Boston Pub. Library, 1936—; dir. Commonwealth Co-operative Bank. Mem. A.L.A., Nat. Spl. Libraries Assn. (ex-pres.), Mass. Library Club (ex-pres.), New Eng. Deaconess Hosp., New Eng. Edn. Soc. (treas.). Republican. Author: Massachusetts Citations Table of English Cases, 1916. Home: 31 Linnaean St., Cambridge 38, Mass. Office: Public Library, Boston. Died Jan. 10, 1950; buried Mt. Auburn Cemetery, Cambridge.

REECE, Richard H., educator; b. Springfield, O., Mar. 29, 1879; B.S. in Elec. Engring., Kan. State Coll., 1906; A.M., U. Colo., 1921; student U. Mich., summers 1908-09, U. Wis. summers 1911-12, U. So. Cal., summer 1928; m. A. Louise Miller, Sept. 2, 1913; children—Kathleen M., Robert H. Tchr. Champion (Mich.) High Sch., 1908; instr. mathematics and physics, N.M. Sch. of Mines, Socorro, N.M., 1917-42, pres., 1942-46, ret. 1946. Home: 322 McCutcheon Av., Socorro, N.M. Died 1954; buried Socorro, N.M.

REED, Carroll Roscoe, supt. schools; b. Malden, Mass., Nov. 4, 1884; s. Will R. and Flora (Merrill) R.; B.A., Harvard, 1906; M.A., 1914; L.H.D., Carleton Coll., 1935; m. Marian Gould, June 1906; 1 son, Robert Gould. Teacher, Rumford (Me.), Marlboro (Mass.), East Providence (R.I.) until 1910; supt. schs., East Providence, 1910-11; supervising prin. Newton, Mass., 1911-15; supt. schs. Amherst, Mass., 1915-17, Rockford, Ill., 1917-20, Akron, O., 1920-25 (rebuilt sch. system of Akron); supt. schs. Bridgeport, Conn., 1925-29, Minneapolis, Minn., 1929-41; 1st asst. supt. schs., Washington, D.C., 1941-47, retired. Pres. Am. Assn. of Sch. Adminstrs. Club: Rotary. Home: Orleans, Mass. Died Jan. 1959.

REED, Cass Arthur, educator, clergyman; b. Port Huron, Mich., Nov. 25, 1884; s. Arthur Lucius and Anna Virginia (Kelley) R.; B.S., Pomona Coll., Claremont, Cal., 1906, D.D., 1928; B.D., Union Theol. Sem., N.Y.C., 1911; M.A., Columbia, 1911; M.A., Harvard, 1912, Ed.D., 1921; m. Rosalind C. MacLachlan, May 13, 1916; children—Arthur Lachlan, Howard Alexander, Joan Anna. Instr. Yamaguchi (Japan) Middle Sch., 1906-08; ordained ministry Congl. Ch., 1911; prof. edn. Internat. Coll., Smyrna, Turkey, 1912-14, dean, 1914-26, pres., 1926-36; vis. prof. religion Am. U. Beirut, Syria, 1934-35; pastor Pilgrim Congl. Ch., Pomona, 1936-44; with UNRRA, 1944-46, Finance Officer Greece Mission; co-pastor Plymouth Congl. Ch., Whittier, 1947—; asso. prof. philosophy Chaffey Coll., Ontario, 1947—. In relief work, Turkey, World War I; dir. Smyrna Unit, Near East Relief, 1919-20; mem. Smyrna Disaster Relief Com., 1922-23. Dir. Whittier Nat. Trust and Savs. Bank. Mem. Phi Beta Kappa, Phi Delta Kappa, Pi Gamma Mu. Mason. Clubs: Kiwanis (Pomona); Clergy (Los Angeles). Home: 580 E. Columbia Av., Pomona, Cal. Died Aug. 22, 1949; buried Claremont, Cal.

REED, Chauncey William, congressman; b. West Chicago, Ill., June 2, 1890; s. William Thomas and Margaret (Campbell) R.; student Northwestern U., 1908-10; LL.B., Webster Coll. of Law, 1915; m. Ella D. Stegen, Oct. 3, 1929; children—Barbara Ann, James William, Thomas Henry. Admitted to Ill. bar, 1915; in practice at Wheaton, Ill.; state's atty. Du Page County, 1920-35; chairman Rep. County Central Com. Du Page County, 1926-34; mem. 74th to 84th

Congresses, 14th Ill. District. Served as sergeant U.S. Army, World War. Member Ill. State Bar Assn. (mem. com. to revise criminal laws of Ill. 1933), Ill. State's attys. Assn. (past pres.), Du Page County Bar Assn. (sec. 4 terms), Am. Bar Assn., Delta Upsilon, Delta Theta Phi, Am. Legion (past comdr.), 40 and 8 Soc. Republican. Mason, Odd Fellow, Moose, Elk. Home: 241 E. Washington St., West Chicago, Ill. Office: 447 House Office Bldg., Washington 25. Died Feb. 9, 1956; buried Glen Oak Cemetery, West Chicago, Ill.

REED, Daniel Alden, congressman; born Sheridan, Chautauqua County, N.Y., Sept. 15, 1875; s. Anson William and Alfreda R.; student Cornell U., 1896-99, LL.B., 1898; m. Georgia E. Ticknor; children—William Ticknor, Ruth Alden. Began practice of law at Dunkirk, N.Y.; atty. for excise dept., State of N.Y., 5 yrs.; spl. mission to France for U.S. Govt., 1918-19; mem. 66th-80th, 83d-86th Congresses, 43d N.Y. Dist.; chairman House of Reps. Ways and Means Com. Del. to Interparliamentary Union, 1939, 48, 49, 50, 52; member Republican National Committee Post-War Planning Group; chmn. Rep. Conf. Com. on Internat. Econ. Problems. Mem. Cornelian Council, Cornell University. Member Society Am. Arts and Letters, Delta Chi, Quill and Dagger. Mem. bar State of N.Y., Federal Dist. Court, U.S. Ct. of Appeals, Supreme Court of U.S. Republican. Mason (32°), K.P., Kiwanian. Lecturer on commercial and civic subjects. Home: 761 Central Av., Dunkirk, N.Y. Died Feb. 1959.

REED, David Aiken, lawyer; b. Pittsburgh, Pa., Dec. 21, 1880; s. James H. and Kate J. (Aiken) R.; grad. Shadyside Acad., Pittsburgh, 1896; B.A., Princeton, 1900, LL.D., 1925; LL.B., U. of Pittsburgh, 1903; m. Adele Wilcox, November 12, 1902; children—David Aiken, Rosamond; married 2d, Edna French, December 15, 1948. Began practice of law at Pittsburgh, 1903; apptd. mem. U.S. Senate, by gov. of Pa., Aug. 8, 1922, to succeed William E. Crow, deceased, and elected to same office following Nov., term 1923-29; reelected, term 1929-35; now mem. Reed, Smith, Shaw & McClay, Pittsburgh. Del. to London Naval Conf., 1930. Major 311th F.A., A.E.F., World War. Trustee of Princeton University. Member American Battle Monuments Commission, 1923-47. Awarded D.S.M. (U.S.); Chevalier Legion of Honor (French). Republican. Protestant. Home: 5611 Aylesboro Av. Office: 747 Union Trust Bldg., Pitts. Died Feb. 10, 1953; buried Arlington Nat. Cemetery.

REED, Frank Hynes, chemist; b. Carroll County, Ind., Jan. 12, 1890; s. Jacob A. and Effie Alice (Hynes) R.; A.B., Wabash Coll., Crawfordsville, Ind., 1911; Ph.D., U. of Chicago, 1917; m. Helen Louise Kennedy, Oct. 27, 1917 (died Apr. 22, 1945); children—Sherman Kennedy, Mary-Alice (Mrs. Robert L. Sutherland); m. 2d, Frances Elizabeth Brown, August 24, 1946. Instr. in chemistry, Wabash Coll., 1913-14, Mich. State Coll., 1914-15, chemist Sherwin-Williams Co., Chicago, 1917-19, Butterworth-Judson Corp., Newark, N.J., 1919-22; supt. chem. plant Tower Mfg. Co., Newark, N.J., 1922-27; chemist Chem. Dye & Mfg. Co., Springfield, N.J., 1927-28; plant supervisor Nat. Aniline & Chem. Co., Buffalo, N.Y., 1928-30; chemist Roessler & Hoslacher Chem. Co., Niagara Falls, N.Y., 1930-31; chief chemist in mineral industries research, coal chemistry, etc., Ill. Geol. Survey, Urbana, Ill., since 1931; consultant, National Defense Research Com., 1942-43, War Production Board, 1943-45, sci. cons., Fed. Econ. Adminstrn., Northwest Europe, 1945; vis. expert to Gen. MacArthur's hdqrs., Tokyo, Dec. 1948-Feb. 1949. Fellow A.A.A.S.; mem. Am. Chem. Soc. (chmn. gas and fuel div. 1939, chmn. U. of Ill. sect. 1946-47), Am. Inst. Mining and Metal. Engineers (sec.-treas. industrial minerals div. 1939-40; chmn. chem. raw materials com. 1937-38; mem. sectional com. on classification of N. Am. Coals since 1933), Nat. Research Council (mem. com. on chem. utilization of coal since 1938), Sigma Xi, Phi Lambda Upsilon, Alpha Chi Sigma, Kappa Sigma. Club: Urbana Golf and Country. Home: 1207 S. Busey. Office: Natural Resources Bldg., Urbana, Ill. Died Apr. 27, 1957; buried Roselawn Cemetery, Urbana, Ill.

REED, George William, coal mining; b. Dubuque, Ia., Sept. 3, 1878; s. Fred A. and Frances M. (Ash) R.; grad. high sch., Amboy, Ill., Coll. Commerce, Freeport, Ill., 1896; m. Evalou Robinson, Aug. 7, 1920; children—George William, Mary Frances, Reed Deveney. Sec. Lincoln-Springfield Coal Co., 1904-11, pres., 1911-16; sales mgr. Peabody Coal Co., Chgo., 1916-17, v.p., 1917-49, ret.; v.p. Superior Smokeless Coal & Mining Co., Hawthorne Coal Co., The Black Mountain Corp., Am. Eagle Colliery, Crerar Clinch Coal Co., Hawthorne Fuel Co. Served as fed. coal adminstr. World War I. Former chmn. bd. Washington and Jane Smith Home. Mem. Ill. Mfrs. Assn., Southern Ill. Coals, Inc., Ill. Coal Traffic Bur., Ill. C. of C. Republican. Methodist. Mason (32°, Shriner). Clubs: Union League, Chicago, South Shore Country, Midlothian Country (Chgo.); Burning Tree (Washington). Home: 2122 Hopkins Pl. Office: 231 S. La Salle St., Chgo. Died Sept. 9, 1957.*

REED, Guy Euclid, ret. banker; b. Holdrege, Neb., July 11, 1890; s. Jeremiah M. and Nettie G. (Koontz) R.; B.A., U. of Neb., 1911; L.H.D., Neb. Wesleyan U., 1956; m. Florence Angle, Nov. 11, 1916; children—Robert A., Barbara A. In banking bus., Lincoln, Neb., 1917-23; exec. v.p., dir. Harris Trust & Savs. Bank, Chgo., 1923-55; ret. 1955; dir. Am. Steel. Foundries, Universal Oil Products, Sci. Research Assos., G. D. Searle Co., Kawneer Company, Northern Natural Gas Co. Chmn. Am. Library Assn. Endowment Trustees. Pres. Chgo. Crime Commn., 1942-47, chmn., 1947-50; dir. Chgo. Assn. Commerce; pres. Chgo. Assn. Commerce and Industry, 1951-52; pres. Citizens of Greater Chgo., 1953-54. Trustee South West Research Inst. Mem. Art Inst., Neb. Foundn., Alpha Tau Omega. Distinguished Service Award, U. of Neb., 1941; Chgo. Merit Award for distinguished service, 1949; Northwestern U. Centennial award, 1951. Mason. Clubs: University, Commercial, Chicago, Midday, Bankers. Home: Prairie View, Ill. Retired. Died Jan. 2, 1959.

REED, Howard Sprague, plant physiologist; b. North East, Pa., Aug. 6, 1876; s. Joseph Harlan and Emma Gertrude (Sprague) R.; A.B., U. Mich., 1903; Ph.D., U. Mo., 1907; m. Mary Hannah Dewey, Aug. 17, 1904 (died July 5, 1939). Asst. in plant physiology U. Mich., 1899-1903; instr. botany U. Mo., 1903-06; soil expert Bur. of Soils, U.S. Dept. Agr., 1906-08; prof. mycology and bacteriology Va. Poly. Inst., and plant pathologist Va. Agrl. Expt. Sta., 1908-15; prof. plant physiology U. Cal. Citrus Expt. Sta., Riverside, 1915-35; prof. plant physiology U. Cal., 1935-46, emeritus, 1946—; guest prof. Inst. de Botanique, Geneva, 1930. Fellow A.A.A.S. (exec. com. Pacific div. 1938-45); mem. Am. Soc. Biol. Chemists, Bot. Soc. Am. (chmn. physiol. section 1938), Cal. Bot. Soc. (pres. 1943), Western Society Naturalists (pres. 1923), Phytopathol. Soc. (pres. Pacific div. 1921-22), Western Soc. Soil Science (sec. 1926-28), Am. Soc. Naturalists, Washington Acad. Sci., Cal. Hist. Soc., Soc. Linnéenne de Lyon, Inst. Sieroterapico Milanese, Sigma Xi; mem. 9th Internat. Hort. Congress, London, 1930, 3d Internat. Congress of Comparative Pathology, Athens, 1936; Bronze medal Société Nationale d'Acclimation de France, 1935; corr. Museum National d'Histoire Naturelle de France. Presbyn. Club: Faculty (Berkely). Asso. editor U. Cal. Publs. in Agrl. Science, 1922-35; mem. council of editorial bd. of Growth, 1936—. Author: Manual of Bacteriology, 1914; What Can Biology Contribute to the World of Today?, 1923; La Nature de la Croissance, 1933; A Short History of the Plant Sciences, 1942; Ingenhausz' Experiment upon Vegetables, 1948, also about 180 papers on plant physiology and pathology. Home: 3044½ Telegraph Av., Berkeley 5, Cal. Died May 12, 1950.

REED, James Calvin, educator; b. Tuscola, Ill., Feb. 20, 1869; s. John Taylor and Anna (Walter) R.; student U. Ill., 1886-87; B.Litt., U. Mich., 1895; LL.B., U. Kansas City, 1898; post-grad. work U. Chgo.; m. Effie Anna Howe, Sept. 13, 1893; 1 dau., Mildred (Mrs. W. A. Buck). Tchr. high sch. Riverside, Cal., 1895-16, 98-1900; practiced law Kansas City, Mo.; tchr. McKinley High Sch., Chgo., 1902-13; dir. State Normal Commercial Sch., Whitewater, Wis., 1913-19; prof. and head dept. of business law U. Pitts., 1919-39, prof. emeritus, 1939—. Founder and editor Comml. Tchrs.' Mag., 1917-21. Pres. Nat. Assn. of Tchrs. of Law in Collegiate Schs. of Bus., 1924-29. Mem. Nat. Comml. Tchrs. Fedn. (pres. 1919-21), Beta Gamma Sigma, Lambda Chi Alpha. Republican. Presbyn. Mason. Club: Faculty. Author: Rowe's Commercial Law, 1915; A Selection of Cases on Commercial Law, 1917. Home: 192 N. Lansdowne Av., Lansdowne, Pa. Died Mar. 27, 1949.

REED, John C., engr.; b. Glenfield, Pa., May 20, 1902; s. William F. and Emma Jane (Royston) R.; E.M., Pa. State Coll.; m. Elizabeth Jane Moorman, July 3, 1935. Vice pres. research Am. Radiator & Standard San. Corp., Pittsburgh, since 1951. Mem. Am. Soc. San. Engrs., Am. Chem. Soc., Am. Soc. M.E., Am. Soc. Heating and Ventilating Engrs., Am. Soc. Mining and Metall. Engrs. Clubs: Duquesne (Pittsburgh); Engineers, Metropolitan (N.Y. City). Home: Harrods Creek, Ky. Office: American Radiator & Standard Sanitary Corp., Pitts. Died June 14, 1952.

REED, Walter Lawrence, army officer; b. Ft. Apache, Ariz., Dec. 4, 1877; s. Maj. Walter and Emily Blackwell (Lawrence) R.; ed. in high schs. and Randolph-Macon Acad., Bedford City, Va.; grad. Army Sch. of Line, 1921, Army Gen. Staff Coll., 1922, Army War Coll., 1923, Navy War Coll., 1924; m. Lucy Landon Carter Blackford, Oct. 28, 1901; children—Mary Berkeley (Mrs. Charles H. Royce), Landon Carter (wife Dr. John K. Monro). Enlisted in 2d U.S. Arty., June 1898, and served in Cuba, 1898-1901; commd. 2d lt. 10th Inf., 1900, and advanced through grades to maj. gen., 1935; was insp.-gen. of the army, Washington; served in Philippines, 1902-03, in Panama, 1911-14, in France, as div. insp., asst. army insp., later insp.-gen. of Am. forces in France, 1918-20; ret., 1940. Awarded D.S.M. for service in France. Home: 2810 36th Pl., N.W., Washington. Died May 1, 1956; buried Arlington Nat. Cemetery.

REED, Washington, utility exec.; b. Smithfield, Va., Nov. 23, 1891; s. James Washington and Imogen (Loyall) R.; E.E., Va. Mil. Inst., 1912; m. Katherine Mitchell, Apr. 26, 1922. Began as electrician's helper with Lexington Utilities Co., 1914, and advanced through grades to office of pres., 1935 (company consol. with Ky. Utilities Co., 1940); became v.p. Ky. Utilities Co.; v.p. Old Dominion Power Co. Served with 60th Inf. A.E.F., U.S. Army, World War. Awarded D.S.C., Purple Heart (U.S.); Chevalier of Legion of Honor, Croix de Guerre (France). Republican. Episcopalian. Mason. Clubs: Lexington, Rotary, Idle Hour. Home: 315 Holliday Rd. Office: 120 S. Limestone St., Lexington, Ky. Died Nov. 30, 1951.

REED, William Hale, newspaper pub.; b. Taunton, Mass., Feb. 17, 1874; s. William and Katherine Tracy (Hale) R.; A.B., Harvard, 1895; m. Emma Belle Robinson, Oct. 8, 1903; children—William Robinson, Thomas Hale, Milton, Sarah, George Hall, Edward Waldo. Reporter Taunton Daily Gazette, 1895, editor, 1900, pub., 1900—. Mem. code authority for daily newspaper NRA, mem. old common council, bd. of aldermen, sch. com., Taunton. Trustee Taunton Savings Bank. Trustee Bristol Acad. Mem. N.E. Daily Newspaper Assn. (former pres.), Am. Daily Newspaper Pubs. Assn. (com. on fed. laws), Taunton Assn. Commerce, Old Colony Hist. Soc. Republican. Unitarian. Clubs: Harvard, Rotary (Taunton). Home: 209 S. Walker St. Office: Taunton Daily Gazette, Taunton, Mass. Died Oct. 5, 1950.

REED, William M., company exec.; b. Louisville, Mar. 3, 1892; s. J.D. and Ella (Ferguson) R.; student public schs., Louisville; m. Grace Pilcher, Sept. 20, 1924; children—Ellen Bateman, Joan F. Boone. Pres. Reed Air Filter Co., 1922-29, Am. Air Filter Co., Inc.; 1929-56, now chmn.; director Louisville Trust Co., Consider H. Willett, Inc., Robertson Co.; v.p., dir. Reliance Varnish Co. Episcopalian. Clubs: Country, Pendennis (Louisville). Home: Mocking Bird Valley. Office: 215 Central Av., Louisville 8. Died Feb. 2, 1956.

REEDER, Edwin Hewett, educator; b. Normal, Ill., Dec. 30, 1892; s. Rudolph Rex and May (Hewett) R.; student Brown U., 1909-10; A.B., Columbia, 1913, A.M., 1924, Ph.D., 1926; m. Constance Fox, July 9, 1915; 1 son, Edwin Hewett. Prin. Springdale Sch., Stamford, Conn., 1913-15; supt. Sweetser Orphanage, Saco, Me., 1915-17; acting supt. N.Y. Orphanage, Hastings-on-Hudson, 1917-18; ednl. editor Community Motion Picture Bur., N.Y.C., 1918-21; supr. visual edn. Detroit Pub. Schs., 1921-23; part-time instr. edn., Tchr. Coll. Columbia, 1923-26, asst. prof., 1926-28, asso. prof., 1928-33; asso. prof. edn. U. Vt., 1933-37; prof. edn. U. Ill., 1937—; faculty woman's coll. U. N.C., summers 1933, 37, U. Ia., summer 1937. Mem. N.E.A. (life), Am. Assn. Sch. Adminstrs., Nat. Council Geography Tchrs. (pres. 1938-39), Am. Assn. U. Profs., Nat. Soc. for Study Edn., Progressive Edn. Assn., Phi Delta Kappa, Kappa Delta Pi, Kappa Phi Kappa. Republican. Mem. Soc. of Friends. Club: University (Urbana, Ill.). Author: Directing Children's Study of Geography, 1926; Simplifying Teaching, 1929; Geography for School Administrators, 1931; Geography in the Elementary School (with Zoe A. Thralls), 1931; Home Geography (with George T. Renner), 1944; Supervision in Elementary Schools, 1953. Contbr. ednl. jours. and yearbooks of Nat. Soc. for Study Edn. and Nat. Council Social Studies. Home: 803 Fairway Dr., Campaign, Ill. Died May 6, 1957.

REEDY, J(oel) Martin, supt. schs.; b. Letcher Co., Ky., Mar. 19, 1889; s. Hezekiah and Lovada (McFall) R.; grad. Hiwassee Jr. Coll., Madisonville, Tenn., 1915; A.B., Emory (Va.) and Henry Coll., 1918; grad. study U. of W.Va., summer 1922; M.S. in Edn., U. of Tenn., 1930; studied Peabody Coll. for Teachers, summers 1931-35; m. Ruth Overby, Dec. 5, 1918; children—Edward Overby, Betty Jean. Began as coal miner at age of 10, losing right leg at age of 16; teacher rural schools, Dickenson County, Va., 1908-14; Y.M.C.A. sec. Camp Lee, Va., 1918-19; prin. high sch., Beckley, W.Va., 1919-23; instructor mining extension, U. of W.Va., 1923-24; pres. Hiwassee Coll., 1924-31; supt. schs., Copperhill, Tenn., 1931-48. Retired. Mem. Tenn. State Teachers' Assn., E. Tenn. Ednl. Assn., Kappa Phi Kappa, Phi Delta Kappa. Democrat. Methodist. Mason, Odd Fellow. Rotarian. Home: Umatilla, Fla. Died Feb. 22, 1955.

REEMAN, Edmund Henry, clergyman; b. Barking, Essex, Eng., July 5, 1881; s. George and Jane (Whiting) R.; ed. chiefly under pvt. tutors; took spl. exams. Bapt. Union of Great Britain, for entrance Bapt. ministry; m. Winifred Augusta Siddons, Mar. 17, 1910; children—Joan, Muriel Siddons. Entered ministry Bapt. Ch., 1905, but left the ch. for theol. reasons; came to U.S., Feb. 1913; pastor 1st Unitarian Ch., Trenton, N.J., 1916-19, 1st Unit. Ch., Des Moines, Ia., 1919-24. Author: Do We Need a New Idea of God?, 1917. Lecturer on modern drama. Contbr. to and reviewer of books for religious periodicals. Home: Vineland, N.J. Died Jan. 9, 1950.

REES, William Henry, judge; b. Maysville, Ky., Aug. 30, 1882; son Daniel James and Margaret (Bramel) R.; B.S., Ky. Wesleyan Coll., Winchester, 1901, LL.D., 1930; Vanderbilt Univ., 1901-03; LL.B., University of Va., 1908; LL.D., University of Kentucky, 1946; m. Elizabeth Foster Barbour, Dec. 22, 1914 (died Aug. 1, 1927); m. 2d Henrietta Spragins Mastin, June 29, 1935. Admitted to Ky. bar, 1908, and began practice, Maysville, Ky.; mem. Slattery & Rees, Maysville, 1909-26; apptd. judge Court of Appeals, Ky., June 1, 1926, and elected to same office, Nov. 1926, 1934 and 1942, present term expiring 1951; chief justice Apr. 1933-Jan. 1935, Jan. 1941-Jan. 1942, and 1945-47, ret. as judge, 1951; v.p. State Nat. Bank and State Trust Co. (both Maysville). Mem. Delta Phi. Dem. Presbyterian. Mason. Clubs: Frankfort Country; Maysville Country. Home: 102 E. 4th St., Frankfort, Ky. Died Aug. 2, 1952; buried Frankfort (Ky.) Cemetery.

REESE, Dale F(leming), ins. exec.; b. Harrisburg, Pa., May 25, 1883; s. Thomas and Annie E. (Weldon) R., Jr.; student Newark Acad., 1895-1901; M.E., Cornell, 1905; 1 son, Dale F., Jr. Supt. engring dept. Ocean Accident & Guarantee Corp., N.Y.C., 1906-27; v.p. Hartford (Conn.) Steam Boiler Inspection & Ins. Co., 1927—. Clubs: Drug and Chemical (N.Y.C.); Hartford (Conn.). Home: 37 Hughes St., Hartford 6. Office: 56 Prospect St., Hartford 2, Conn. Died Feb. 24, 1957; buried Mt. Pleasant Cemetery, Newark, N.J.

REESE, Herbert Meredith, prof. physics; b. Balt., Dec. 1, 1873; s. John Evan and Alice Virginia (Gibbs) R.; A.B., Johns Hopkins, 1897, Ph.D., 1900; studied U. of Berlin, U. of Leyden; m. Anna Willis Pape, June 4, 1921; children—Jane Willis (Mrs. Alfred Walter Schultz), Ann Meredith (dec.). Fellow and asst., Lick Observatory, 1900-03; asst. Yerkes Obs., 1903-04; successively instr., asst. prof., asso. prof., prof. physics, U. Mo., 1904-43, prof. emeritus, 1944—. Fellow Am. Physical Soc.; mem. Optical Soc. Am., Phi Beta Kappa, Sigma Xi, Gamma Alpha, Sinfonia. Methodist. Author: Laboratory Instruction in General Physics, 1914; Light, 1921. Contbr. to Bull. of Lick Obs., Sci., Astrophys. Jour., Physical Rev., etc. Home: Georgetown, Colo. Died May 10, 1954; buried Columbia, Mo.

REESE, Lowell Otus, writer; b. Linden, Ind., Dec. 31, 1866; s. David Archer and Amanda (Weaver) R.; ed. pub. schs.; m. Sadie Lenore Older, June 24, 1915. Began as farmer in Ind.; moved to Cal., 1894; tchr. of brass band and mining prospector, 1894-1900; feature writer, Los Angeles Times, 1900, San Francisco Bull., 1901-06; went East, 1906; magazine writer, 1916—. Home: 3249 Crane Way, Oakland, Cal. Died Sept. 21, 1948.

REESE, Millard, lawyer; b. Eatonton, Ga., Apr. 6, 1880; s. Joseph Benjamin and Lou Emma (Sparks) R.; LL.B., Mercer U., 1903; m. Emma Leila Callaway, Jan. 23, 1907. Ga. bar 1903; mem. Twitty & Reese, Brunswick, Ga., 1904-10, Bennet, Twitty & Reese, 1910-27, Reese, Bennet & Gilbert, 1929—; v.p. and dir. Am. Nat. Bank of Brunswick; member board directors Filtered Rosin Products, Inc. Mem. Ga. Ho. Reps., 1909-10, Ga. Senate, 1927-28. Former trustee Mercer U.; former dir. Ga. State Coll. for Women. Mem. Ga. Bar Assn. (pres. 1927-28), Am. Bar Assn., Sigma Alpha Epsilon. Democrat. Baptist. Clubs: Sea Island Golf (St. Simon's Island, Ga.); Oglethorpe, Brunswick. Address: Brunswick, Ga. Died July 3, 1955.

REESE, T. T., banker; b. Elizabethton, Tenn., Nov. 29, 1867; s. D. N. and Anna M. (Johnson) R.; educated in country public schools. Pres. Farmers Bank & Trust Co., West Palm Beach, Fla. Home: 230 Brazillian Av., Palm Beach. Office: West Palm Beach, Fla. Died Sept. 23, 1957.

REESIDE, John Bernard, Jr. (rē'sīd), geologist; b. Baltimore, Md., June 24, 1889; s. John Bernard and Florence May (Feathers) R.; A.B., Johns Hopkins U., 1911, Ph.D., 1915; m. Adelaide C. Quisenberry, May 3, 1918; children—John Bernard III, Corinna. Geologist U.S. Geol. Survey since 1915, charge Sect. of Paleontology and Stratigraphy, 1932-49. Served as 1st lt. field arty., United States Army, 1918. Awarded Mary Clark Thompson Medal, 1946. Fellow A.A.A.S.; Geol. Soc. of America, Nat. Acad. of Sciences, Paleontological Soc. (pres. 1943); mem. Am. Assn. Petroleum Geologists, Washington Acad. Science, Washington Geol. Soc. (pres. 1941), Biol. Soc., Soc. Geol. Perú, Phi Beta Kappa, Sigma Xi. Episcopalian. Club: Cosmos (Washington, D.C.). Contributor to geol. jours. Home: 5104 41st Av., Hyattsville, Md. Office: U.S. Nat. Museum, Washington. Died July 2, 1958.

REEVES, John Ruel, lawyer; b. Washington, July 7, 1906; s. Frederick Wells and Alice A. (Alderman) R.; LL.B., Nat. U., 1929; m. Lucille Mabel Brown, Aug. 30, 1930; children—Margaret (wife of Lt. (j.g.) Robert K. Leopold), John Ruel. Clerk, clk. of claims com. U.S. Ho. of Reps., 1925, Fed. Am. Nat. Bank, 1926, Chesapeake and Potomac Telephone Co., 1926-29; admitted to D.C. bar, 1930; atty. examiner FTC, 1929-31, asso. atty., 1934-35; pvt. practice, Washington, 1931-34; atty. Associates Investment Co., 1935-36; pvt. practice, 1936-38, in Bethesda, 1938-44, 46-56, 58—; judge 6th Judicial Circuit of Md., 1956-58; pres. Met. Fed. Savings & Loan Assn., Bethesda, 1951-56, now chmn. bd.; v.p. Abstract and Title Co. of Md., Hyattsville, 1947-56; sec. Grady Motors Corp., Bethesda, 1946-56. Delegate Maryland General Assembly, 1947-51; sec. of state Md., 1951-55. Chmn. citizens adv. com. to advise and consult with Md. Bd. on Integration in Pub. Schs., 1955; dir. Montgomery County (Md.) Youth Opportunity Camp, Inc. Served as lt. USNR, 1944-46. Mem. Md., D.C., Montgomery County (pres. 1956-57) bar assns., Bethesda C. of C., Edgemoor Citizens Assn., Montgomery County Hist. Soc. (pres. 1956—). Presbyn. Clubs: Lions (pres.) (Bethesda-Chevy Chase, Md.); Elks (Silver Spring, Md.). Home: 5860 Marbury Rd., Bethesda. Office: 110 Commerce Lane, Rockeville, Md. Died June 1, 1959.

REEVES, Thomas Rosser, clergyman; b. Front Royal, Warren County, Va., Sept. 21, 1876; s. James Thomas Zacharias and Charlotte Anne (Balthis) R.; grad. Randolph-Macon Acad., Front Royal, Va., 1897; B.A., Vanderbilt U., 1901; D.D., Randolph-Macon Coll., 1920; m. Mary Scott Watkins, June 6, 1906 (died 1912); children—Rosalie (Mrs. W. H. Fore), Thomas Rosser, Mary Watkins (Mrs. Jesse W. Mahoney); m. 2d, Annie Mabel Kennedy, Oct. 27, 1914. Ordained to ministry M.E. Ch., South, 1897; prof. Latin, Central Female Coll., Lexington, Mo., 1901-02; professor, Randolph-Macon Academy, Bedford City, Va., 1902-03; pastor Clarksville, Va., 1903-05, Franklin (Va.), 1905-07, Mt. Vernon Ch., Danville, Va., 1907-09, Washington St. Ch., Petersburg, Va., 1909-10; pres. Blackstone (Va.) Coll. for Girls, 1910-14; pastor McKendree Ch., Norfolk, Va., 1914-18, Trinity Ch., Salisbury, Md., 1918-21, Monumental Ch., Portsmouth, Va., 1921-25, Union Station, Richmond, 1925-28, Central Ch., Richmond, 1928-32, Boulevard Ch., Richmond, 1932-33; district supt. Lynchburg Dist. M.E. Ch., S., 1933-37; pastor First Ch., Martinsville, Va., 1937-46, retired, Oct. 1946; pastor pro tempore Fort Hill Meth. Ch., Lynchburg, Va., 1st Meth. Chs., Clermont, Fla., Hampton, Va. Mem. Am. Hist. Assn. Democrat. Mason (Royal Arch). Speaker and writer on religious, ednl. and social welfare subjects. Home: 1609 Rivermont Av., Lynchburg, Va. Died Apr. 29, 1951; buried Forest Hill Burial Park, Lynchburg, Va.

REEVES, Walter Perkins, r.r. exec.; b. Portland, Me., Mar. 12, 1884; s. John F. and Caroline G. (Perkins) R.; grad. high sch.; m. Gertrude E. Morse, Oct. 10, 1919; children—John F., Warren M. With Me. Central R.R. Co., 1901—, v.p., 1953—; v.p., dir. Me. Central Transportation Co.; v.p. Portland Terminal Co. Mem. Am. Assn. Variable Star Observers, Astron. Soc. Me., Portland Soc. Natural History (treas.). Republican. Conglist. Club: Portland. Home: 64 Carleton St. Office: 222 St. John St., Portland, Me. Died Dec. 22, 1957.

REGAN, Louis John, physician, lawyer; b. East Bloomfield, N.Y., Feb. 20, 1892; s. John and Anna Mary (Brown- R.; M.C., George Washington U., 1913; grad. Army Med. Sch., 1917; LL.B., LaSalle Extension U., 1938; grad. med. courses Am. and European univs.; m. Isabelle Williamson Price, Apr. 13, 1914; children—Jean (Mrs. Eugene Robert Purpus), Louis John. Intern, asst. phys. George Washington U. Hosp., Utica State Hosp., 1913-16; specialist in legal medicine, Los Angeles, 1939—; cons. staff Hollywood Presbyn. Hosp., Meth. Hosp. So. Cal., Phys. and Surg. Hosp., Glendale, Cal., prof. legal medicine Coll. Med. Evangelists, 1942—, sch. medicine U. So. Cal., 1952—; instr. extension div. U. Cal. at Los Angeles, 1950, 52. Served with M.C., U.S. Army, ret. as maj. Fellow Am. Pub. Health Assn.; mem. Am. Acad. Forensic Scis. (dir., pres.-elect), A.M.A., Cal. State, Los Angeles bar assns., Hollywood Acad. Medicine (past pres.), Cal. (former councillor), Los Angeles Co. (legal counsel, past pres.) med. assns., Cancer Prevention Soc. Cal. (dir.), Los Angeles Co. Med. Assn. Research Found. (dir., past pres.), Phi Chi. Author: Medical Malpractice, 1943; Doctor and Patient and the Law, 1949; also articles legal medicine. Home: 122 N. Carmelina Av., L.A. 49. Office: 1925 Wilshire Blvd., Los Angeles 5. Died Dec. 3, 1955; buried Forest Lawn Meml. Park, Glendale 5, Cal.

REGAR, Robert Smith (rē'gär) ret. postal ofcl. b. Swartzville, Pa., Jan. 15, 1882; s. Richard V. and Sarah (Smith) R.; ed. pub. sch., bus. coll.; LL.B., Georgetown U., 1912; m. Estella I. Burky, Oct. 21, 1913; 1 dau., Sarah Harriet. Admitted to D.C. bar.; mem. bar, Supreme Court of U.S.; personnel officer Post Office Dept., 1918-23, chief clerk, 1923-25, 3d asst. postmaster gen., 1925-29, adminstrv. asst. to postmaster gen., 1929-33, supt. office procedure, 1933-49, ret. 1949. Mem. S.A.R., Masonic Vets. Assn. Supt. S.S. 1st Evangel. and Ref. Ch., D.C. 1916-46. Mason (K.T. Shriner, 33°, Potentate 1930, Grand Master, D.C., 1935, Red Cross of Constantine, Grotto). Odd Fellow: mem. M.W.A., P.O.S. of A., P.O. of A. Home: 1329 Jefferson St., N.W., Washington 11. Died Oct. 21, 1955; buried Muddy Creek Church Cemetery, Swartzville, Pa.

REGENSBURGER, Richard William, business exec.; b. Chicago, Apr. 3, 1899; s. Henry and Marie (Hutter) R.; B.S., Armour Inst. Tech., 1920; m. Betty Dee, Dec. 22, 1934. Engineer Swift & Co., Chicago, 1920-28, asst. to v.p. charge operations and constrn., 1928-41, supt. meat packing plant, Nashville, Tenn., 1941-42, asst. to v.p. in charge operations and constrn., Chicago, 1942-48, v.p. since Nov. 1948. Mem. Tau Beta Pi, Theta Xi. Club: Economic (Chicago). Home: Flossmoor, Ill. Office: 4115 Packers Av., Chgo. 9. Died Oct. 11, 1957.

REGER, David Bright (rē'ger), cons. geologist; b. Rural Dale, W.Va., Apr. 11, 1882; s. Joseph Socrates and Sirene (Bunten) R.; prep. edn., W.Va. Conf. Sem. (now W.Va. Wesleyan Coll.; A.B., West Virginia University, 1909, B.S. in Civil Engring., 1911; m. Ella Gertrude Mattingly, Nov. 24, 1914; children—Helen E. (Mrs. M. K. Armentrout), Jane (Mrs. D. Cruise), Joseph E. Field asst. U.S. Geol. Survey, 1903-06; hydrographic surveyor U.S. Naval Sta., Guantanamo Bay, Cuba, 1906-07; with W.Va. Geol. Survey, 1909-30, as field asst., 1909-13, asst. geologist, 1913-27, acting state geologist, 1927-29, asso. geologist, 1929-30; cons. geologist for oil, gas and coal, water supply, etc., 1919—, office in Morgantown, W.Va., 1930—; pres. Pringle Run Coal Co., 1918-38; v.p. Columbia Coal & Coke Co., 1918-22; sec.-treas., mgr. Reger Oil Co., 1920-29. Member Am. Assn. of Petroleum Geologists, Am. Inst. Mining and Metall. Engrs., Geol. Soc. America, Soc. Econ. Geologists, A.A.A.S., W.Va. Acad. Science (v.p. 1932-33; pres. 1933-34), W.Va. Coal Mining Inst., Appalachian Geol. Soc., Phi Kappa Psi (dir. James Cochran House Assn.), Phi Beta Kappa, Sigma Xi. Rep. Methodist. Author: (Geologic Reports of the W.Va. Geol. Survey) Preston County (with R. V. Hennen), 1914; Logan and Mingo Counties (with R. V. Hennen), 1914; Lewis and Gilmer Counties, 1916; Barbour and Upshur Counties and Western Portion of Randolph County, 1918; Webster County, 1920; Nicholas County, 1921; Tucker County, 1923; Mineral and Grant Counties, 1924; Mercer, Monroe and Summers Counties, 1926; Randolph County, 1931; also contbg. author to other reports. Contbr. numerous articles to scientific jours. Home: 112 Wilson Av. Office: 68 High St., Morgantown, W.Va. Died Sept. 10, 1958; buried Beverly Hills Meml. Gardens, Morgantown.

REGISTER, Henry Bartol, architect; s. Dr. Henry Carney and Terasita (Bartol) R.; grad. William Penn Charter Sch., 1905; student Sch. of Architecture, 1909-12; married; children—Henry Bartol (dec.), Philippe deM. Employed in various offices, 1912-14; with Tilden & Register, 1914-20, Tilden, Register & Pepper, 1920-36; asso. Davis & Dunlap, 1936—. Served 1st lt. to capt., World War I, 1917-19; A.E.F. Fellow A.I.A.; mem. Art Alliance of Phila., Sigma Xi, Psi Upsilon. Clubs: University (Phila.); Merion Cricket (Haverford, Pa. Office: 1717 Sansom St., Phila. Died Dec. 10, 1956.

REHERD, Herbert Ware (rērd), educator; b. Geneseo, Ill., Aug. 23, 1869; s. Jacob K. and Lucy Louise (Ware) R.; A.B., Parsons Coll., Ia., 1893, M.A., 1897; Princeton Theological Sem. 1894-95; grad. McCormick Theol. Sem., Chgo., 1897; D.D., Buena Vista Coll., Ia., 1910, Parsons, 1911; LL.D., Westminster Coll., Salt Lake City, 1945; LL.D., Maryville Coll., Tenn., 1946; m. Margaret Louise McClure, June 15, 1898; children—Elizabeth Louise (Mrs. R. D. Steele), Harold McClure. Ordained Presbyn. ministry, 1897; pastor 1st Ch., Milan, Ill., 1897-1901, Bethany Ch., Detroit, 1901-06, 1st Ch., Waterloo, Ia., 1906-13; pres. Westminster Coll., Salt Lake City, 1913-39, chmn. bd. and pres. emeritus, 1939—. Made trip around the world, studying missions, 1911-12, under a commn. from Presbyn. Bd. Foreign Missions. Moderator Synod of Utah, 1933; mem. Presbyn. Coll. Union, pres., 1930-31. Recipient of award of Presbyn. Bd. of Christian Edn. for distinguished service in field of Christian Edn., 1938. Mem. Phi Kappa Phi. Clubs: Rotary (Salt Lake City); Bonneville Knife and Fork. Joint Author: Around the World Studies and Stories of Presbyterian Foreign Missions, 1912. Editor: History of Protestant Churches in Utah. Contbr. to mags. Home: Westminster Coll., Salt Lake City 5. Died July 28, 1952; buried Mt. Olivet, Salt Lake City.

REICHARD, Gladys Amanda (rī'kärd), anthropologist; b. Bangor, Pa., July 17, 1893; d. Noah W. and Minerva Anna (Jordan) Reichard; A.B., Swarthmore (Pa.) Coll., 1919; Ph.D., Columbia, 1925; post grad. study, U. of Hamburg, Germany (Guggenheim Memorial fellowship), 1926-27; unmarried. Teacher rural schs. Northampton County, Pa., 1909-11, grade schs. Bangor, 1911-15, Robert Louis Stevenson Sch., N.Y. City, 1920-21; asst. in anthropology, Barnard Coll., N.Y. City, 1921-22; research fellow U. of Calif., 1922-23; instr. in anthropology, Barnard Coll., 1923-28, asst. prof., 1928-41, professor since 1951. Member American Folk-Lore Soc. (sec., editor, pres.), Am. Ethnological Soc. (sec.), Am. Assn. for Advancement of Science (sec. Sect. H 1944-45); mem. Phi Beta Kappa, Sigma Xi. Awarded Morrison prize in natural sciences by New York Acad. Sciences, 1932; Prize, Chgo. Folklore Society, 1948. Author: Wiyot Grammar and Texts, 1925; Social Life of the Navajo Indians, 1928; Melanesian Design, 1933; Spider Woman, a Story of Navajo Weavers and Chanters, 1934; Navajo Shepherd and Weaver, 1936; Sandpaintings of the Navajo Shooting Chant, 1937; Grammar of Coeur d'Alene Language, 1938; Dezba Woman of the Desert, 1939; Navajo Medicine Man, 1939; Prayer: The Compulsive Word, 1944; The Story of the Navajo Hail Chant, 1944; An Analysis of Coeur d'Alene Indian Myths, Memoir American Folklore Society, Vol. 41, 1947; Navaho Religion, 2 vols., 1950; Navaho Grammar, 1951. Address: Barnard College, N.Y.C. 27. Died July 25, 1955.

REID, Albert Turner, publisher, writer, artist; b. Concordia, Kan., Aug. 12, 1873; s. William Emery and Jean Margaret (Turner) R.; ed. Clyde (Kan.) High Sch., Lawrence (Kan.) Business Coll., U. of Kansas; studied at the New York Sch. of Art and at Art Students' League; honorary M.A., Kansas Wesleyan U., Salina, 1935; m. Vera Low; 1 dau., Marianne (Mrs. Robert S. Wild); m. 2d, Dorothy Chisholm; 1 dau., Constance. Artist on Kansas City Star, 1897-99; with Chicago Record, 1899, the New York Herald, 1899-1900, Judge, 1900, McClure's, Saturday Evening Post, American and other mags., 1901-15; founded and pub. Leavenworth Post (daily), 1905-23; pres. Standard Farm Papers Assn., 1914-15; pres. and pub. Kansas Farmer, Topeka, 1908-16; vice-pres. Kansas Life Insurance Co., 1912-18; owner of the Albert T. Reid Syndicate, 1919-—. Designed and directed Kansas Semi-Centennial, Topeka, 1911; pres. Kan. Commn. to Panama Pacific and San Diego expns., 1915; dir. pictorial publicity, Rep. at Com., 1919-20. Awarded San Francisco Expn. and George Washington bi-centennial medals; cited by Kan. State Hist. Soc. for services to Kan.; received grand prize for mural at San Francisco Exposition; awarded Gold Medal of Honor, Am. Artists Professional League; received award of Kappa Pi. Painted murals, Romance of the Mail, for post offices at Sabetha and Olathe, Kan., and Sulphur, Okla. Mem. Author's League America, Am. Artists' Professional League (nat. v. pres., 1928-—; listed on Honor Roll), Artists' Guild (ex-pres., hon. life member), Soc. Am. Illustrators, Cartoonists Club (chmn.). Mason (32°). Clubs: Downtown Athletic (New York); Nat. Press (Washington). Did hist. painting "Coronado Entrada," for Coronado Quarto-Centennial, 1941, Meeting of the Two Great Emancipators, for Vincennes (Ind.) Meml. Painting Main Street, Concordia, Kan., Birthplace, 1873. Equestrian picture Coronado for Lyons, Kan.; Custer Rides out from Ft. Hays; Pawnee Rock-Indian Attack. Vice pres. Eisenhower Meml. Found. Office-studio: 208 W. 23d St., N.Y.C. Died Nov. 26, 1955; buried Clyde, Kan.

REID, E(dward) C., paper co. exec.; b. N.Y.C., Nov. 12, 1900; s. Albert and E. Hortense (Fargo) R.; B.A., N.Y.U., 1923; m. Florence Lewis, Apr. 18, 1931. With purchasing dept. Am. Chicle Co., 1924-28; dir. purchases Snider Packing Corp., 1928-37; with Am. Writing Paper Corp., Holyoke, Mass., 1937-—, pres., dir., 1952-—; trustee Mechanic Savings Bank, 1948-—. Mem. Tech. Assn. Pulp and Paper Industry, Writing Paper Assn. Mason. Clubs: Lions, Rotary. Home: Ferry Hill Rd., Granby, Mass. Office: 10 Eagle A Av., Holyoke, Mass. Died Nov. 11, 1958; buried Springfield (Mass.) Cemetery.

REID, Kenneth, editor; b. Norwich, Conn., Aug. 23, 1893; s. James and Martha Florence (Rodgers) R.; grad. Mechanic Arts High Sch., Boston, 1911; M.E., Lowell Inst., Boston, 1914; B.S. in Architecture, Mass. Inst. of Tech., 1918; m. Rose E. Lawson, Apr. 24, 1925; children—Kenneth, Rosalind. Sales engr. The Angus Co., Ltd., Calcutta, India, 1920-22; personnel mgr., div. of indsl. corp. and research, Mass. Inst. of Tech., 1922-26; asso. editor Pencil Points, archtl. mag., New York, N.Y., Mar. 1926-Dec. 1931, mng. editor, 1932-35, editor-in-chief, 1936-46; cons. editor book div. Reinhold Pub. Corp., N.Y.C., Jan. 1947-May 1948; editor book dept., Agricultural Record, 1948-—. Served as lt. (j.g.) Construction Corps, U.S. Navy, 1918-20. Mem. Am. Inst. Architects, Archtl. League of N.Y., N.Y. Bldg. Congress (bd. of govs., 1940-42), Citizens' Housing Council of N.Y., Lambda Chi Alpha. Clubs: Century Association, National Press (Washington). Contributor miscellaneous articles on archtl. subjects to professional pubs. Home: East Dorset, Vt. Office: 119 W. 40th St., New York. Died Mar. 17, 1960.

REID, Kenneth Alexander, league exec.; b. Connellsville, Pa., Apr. 14, 1895; s. James Madison and Nannie Blackstone (Johnston) R.; student Phillips Andover, 1912-14; Ph.B., Yale, 1917; m. Henry Ruth Lassiter, Oct. 1, 1920; children—Nancy Lassiter, Betty Jane. Sales mgr., gen. mgr., pres. Equipment Co., Ft. Worth, Tex., 1919-28; sales mgr. Boyts Portco & Co., Connellsville, Pa., 1928-38; exec. sec. Izaak Walton League of America, 1938-49, now conservation cons.; dir., co-founder Izaac Walton League of America Endowment; superintendent natural resources Whitney Park, Adirondack Mountains, New York, 1949-55. Mem. Pa. Bd. Fish Commrs., 1932-38. Served as lt. Air Service, 1917-19. Mem. Soc. Am. Foresters, Natural Resources Council Am. (co-founder), Am. Fisheries Soc., Wildlife Society, Phi Gamma Delta. Republican. Presbyterian. Clubs: University (Chicago); Cosmos (Washington); Yale, Anglers (New York). Former editor dept. fishing, Nat. Sportsman Mag. Contbr. articles on fishing and conservation to numerous outdoor mags. Editor Outdoor America, 1938-49. Mount Reid, Grand Teton Nat. Park named in his honor. Address: Reidmore, Connellsville, Box 833, Pa. Died May 21, 1956.

REID, Silas Hinkle, judge; b. at Du Quoin, Ill., Sept. 27, 1870; s. William and Artemisia (Estes) R.; ed. high sch., Du Quoin, and Northern Ill. Normal Sch., 1887-90; LL.B., Wesleyan Law Coll., Bloomington, Ill., 1891; m. Florence E. Goodwin, of Decatur, Ill., Jan. 2, 1901. Practiced Du Quoin, Ill., 1891-1901, El Reno, Okla., 1901-7; was city atty., Du Quoin; pres. bd. edn., El Reno; co. atty., Canadian Co., Okla.; candidate for atty.-gen. of Okla., 1907; U.S. dist. judge Dist. of Alaska, 1907-9; Republican. Address: Fairbanks, Alaska. Deceased.

REID, Thorburn, electrical engr.; b. London, Eng., May 1, 1864; s. Charles Henry and Mary Helen (Cochran) R.; A.B., Hampden-Sidney Coll., 1882; U. of Va., 1882-85; M.E., Stevens Inst. Tech., 1888; m. Bertha Van Kleeck, Jan. 9, 1900; children—Thorburn, Graeme. Instr. mech. engring., U. of S.C., 1888-89; head of testing dept. U.S. Elec. Illuminating Co., Newark, N.J., 1889-90; in charge alternating current design, Edison Gen. Electric Co., N.Y.C. and Schenectady, N.Y., 1890-91; with Gen. Elec. Co., Schenectady, and Lynn, Mass., 1891-97; consulting engr. N.Y.C., 1897-1912; head of cost dept. Simms Magneto Co., East Orange, N.J., 1912-25. Retired. Mem. Am. Inst. E.E., Phi Gamma Delta. Presbyn. Discovered cause and effect of sparking, at the commutators, of direct current dynamos and motors. Home: Essex Fells, N.J. Died Nov. 22, 1933.

REID, Walter Williamson, confectionery mfr.; b. Balt., Aug. 12, 1881; s. Walter Williamson and Emma Virginia (Legair) R.; student pub. schs.; m. Louise Bernice Burgermaster, June 6, 1912; children —Walter Williamson III, Phyllis Jane (Mrs. Ross B. Cameron). Founder, Charms Co., Asbury Park, 1912, became pres., 1917, chmn. bd., 1946-—; v.p. Allenhurst Nat. Bank & Trust Co. 1926-40, pres., 1940-—. Commr. Borough of Allenhurst. Pres. Monmouth County chpt. Cancer Soc.; pres. Monmouth Meml. Hosp., Long Branch, N.J. Mayor, Borough of Allenhurst. Home: 10 Cedar Av., Allenhurst, N.J. Office: 611 Heck St., Asbury Park, N.J. Died Mar. 4, 1960.

REID, Will J., oil executive; b. St. Thomas, N.D., May 6, 1889; s. Alexander and Mary (Bates) R.; student Alberta Coll., Edmonton, Can., 1905-06, Strathcona Collegiate Inst., Edmonton, Can., 1906-09, U. of Alberta, Edmonton, 1909-11; m. Ella Tyler Hancock, June 19, 1913; 1 dau., Virginia Hancock. Mgr. ins. dept., Long Beach (Calif.) Improvement Co., 1912-17; organizer Inter-Insurance Exchange Tuna Fishermen of Southern Calif., 1917, mgr., 1917-24; organized Calif. Funding Corp. of Calif., 1919, exec. v.p., 1919-40; pres. Hancock Oil Co., 1922-53, chmn. bd., 1953-—; pres. Long Beach Oil Development Co., 1939-—; dir. Hancock Chem. Co., Southwest Exploration Co. Mem. nat. council Boy Scouts Am., regional dir. and commodore; trustee Ducks Unlimited, Inc.; dir. Ducks Unlimited of Can.; mem. and ex-chief Cal. Indians. Elk. Clubs: Virginia Country, Pacific Coast, Long Beach Yacht, Dominguez Gun and Fly Casting (Long Beach); California, Athletic (Los Angeles); Bear River (Utah); Fin 'n Feather (Chgo.). Author: History of the Cerritos, 1940. Home: 2801 E. Ocean Blvd. Office: Security Bldg., Long Beach, Cal. Died Apr. 8, 1956.

REID, William R., business exec. Pres. and dir. Torrington Co.; dir. Torrington (Conn.) Nat. Bank & Trust Co., Union Hardware Co., Hendley Machine Co., Westfield Mfg. Co. Home: 210 Migeon Av. Office: Torrington, Conn. Died Sept. 16, 1950.

REIFF, Cecil K. (rīf), educator; b. North Manchester, Ind., Oct. 23, 1888; s. Jacob and Catherine (Baer) R.; Manchester Coll., 1906-07; A.B., Ind. U., 1915, A.M., 1917; grad. study, Columbia and Univ. of Chicago; Ed.D., Oklahoma City University, 1932; m. Dorothy Ellen McCloud, Aug. 27, 1915; children —William Henry, John Cecil, Margaret Ann. Teacher rural schs., Wabash County, Ind., 1907-09; prin. Consol. High Sch., North Manchester, 1909-13; asst. to bursar Ind. U., 1913-15; dir. dept. commerce, Central High Sch., Muskogee, Okla., 1915-19, prin., 1919-25; supt. city schs., Muskogee, 1925-31; same, Oklahoma City, Okla., 1931-40, supt. emeritus since 1940; Okla. State supervisor, Distributive Edn., 1941-42; prof. dept. bus. edn., Okla. A. & M. Coll., since 1942; teacher and lecturer in univs. and colls. of Okla. Mem. Am. Arbitration Assn. (motion picture panel). Mem. exec. com. North Central Assn. Secondary Schs. and Colls., 1924-25; pres. Conf. of Supts. for Okla., 1928-29, 1932-33. Mem. N.E.A. (dir. Okla. 1926-27, v.p. 1934-35), Dept. Superintendence and Dept. Elementary Prins. same, Okla. Edn. Assn. (pres. 1930-31), Horace Mann League, Am. Acad. of Polit. and Social Sciences, Okla. Soc. for Crippled Children; member Phi Delta Kappa, Delta Pi Epsilon, Iota Lambda Sigma and Phi Delta Theta fraternities. Democrat. Member of the Disciples of Christ Church (Christian), Member Lions International (pres. Muskogee Chapter 1923-24), K. of P. Club: Men's Dinner (Oklahoma City). Author: Curriculum in Arithmetic for the State of Oklahoma, Grades 1-8, 1930; Oklahoma Distributive Education, 1941; effective Business Education (with others), 1944. Contbr. articles to sch. publs. Mem. writing com. 9th Yearbook, Nat. Bus. Teachers' Assn., 1943. Editor, The Distributor. Home: 1521 W. 4th St., Stillwater, Okla. Died Apr. 28, 1952; buried Fairview Cemetery, North Manchester, Ind.

REIFSNIDER, Charles Shriver (rif'snī-dēr), missionary bishop; b. Frederick, Md., Nov. 27, 1875; s. Charles David and Elizabeth Sarah (Shriver) R.; student Heidelberg U., 1894-96; B.A., Kenyon Coll., Gambier, O., 1898, M.A., 1904, L.H.D., 1912; D.D., Bexley Hall Div. Sch., Gambier, 1924; m. Mary Duke Gordon, June 15, 1904; children—Charles Shriver, Mary Louise, Alice Donald, John Gordon. Deacon, 1900, priest, 1901, P.E. Ch.; missionary to Japan, 1901-41; pres. St. Paul's U., Tokyo, 1912-40 (built and established acad. and univ.); suffragan bishop of North Tokyo, 1924-35, bishop, 1935-47; ret., 1947. Mem. Asiatic Soc., Delta Tau Delta. Decorated Fourth Order of the Sacred Treasure, Japan, 1928, and Third Order, 1941. Clubs: Tokyo, Yokohama United, etc. Home: 2333 Paloma St., Pasadena 7, Cal. Died Mar. 16, 1958.

REIFSNIDER, Lawrence Fairfax, (rĕf'snī-dēr, naval officer; b. Westminster, Md., Nov. 26, 1887; s. John Milton and Eleanor Fisher (Reese) R.; student Western Md. Coll., Westminster; grad. Naval Acad., 1910; grad. Submarine School, New London, Conn., 1917, and qualified to command submarines; grad. senior course Naval War College, Newport, R.I., 1936; m. Louise Munroe, 1912; 1 dau., Mary Louise (wife of Glover T. Ferguson, USN). Commd. ensign 1912, advanced through grades to rear adm., 1943; served in varoius types of ships and on shore in Navy Dept.; chief 1st USN Mission to Colombia, 1939-41; comd. 8th Naval Dist. and comdr. Gulf Sea Frontier, 1947-—. Participated in amphibious operations World War II: in command Transport Group, Guadalcanal, 1942; tactical comd. transports Bougainville landing, 1943; attack group comdr. seizure of Emirau, 1944; comdr. of an attack group during assault and capture of Guam, 1944; comdr. of an attack force during assault on Okinawa, 1945; attack group comdr. for capture of Ie Shima, 1945; attack group comdr. for seizure of Iheya Shima and Aguni Shima, 1945; task group and subsequently task force comdr. for occupation of Southern and Western Japan, 1945. Decorated Navy Cross (submarine service World War I); D.S.M. with two gold stars for services at Bougainville, Guam, and Okinawa Gunto operations; Legion of Merit with combat distinguishing device for Guadalcanal operations; Mexican Service medal; World War I Victory medal with Submarine clasp; Am. Def. Service medal with bronze star; Am. Theatre Service Medal; European-African-Middle Eastern Service Medal; Asiatic-Pacific Area Service Medal with six engagement stars; World War II Victory medal; Navy Occupation Service Medal (Japan). Address: 839 Adella Av., Coronada 18, Cal. Died May 14, 1956; buried Ft. Rosecrans Nat. Cemetery, San Diego, Cal.

REILLY, James Aloysius, exec. v.p. Colgate-Palmolive-Peet Co.; b. Jersey City, N.J., Jan. 26, 1904; s. Martin and Mary Elizabeth (Condron) R.; ed. Watchung Sch., North Plainfield, N.J.; student Mercer Sch., Pittsfield, Mass., 1915-19, Pittsfield (Mass.) High Sch., 1920-23; m. Ethel M. Bohan, Nov. 29, 1930; 1 dau., Judith Ann. With Colgate-Palmolive-Peet Co. since 1925, as asst. salesman, 1925-28, salesman, 1928-29, sales supervisor, 1929-31, dist. mgr., 1931-34, divisional mgr., 1934-35, asst. to mgr., 1935-36, asst. mgr., 1936-37, sales mgr., 1937-44, vice pres. also mgr. soap sales dept., 1944-52, exec. v.p. in charge of soap dept. since 1952, dir. since 1953. Trustee, 1st v.p. The Beard Sch., Orange, N.J. Trustee Catholic Extension Soc. Member Grocery Manufacturers of America (director). Clubs: Baltusrol (Springfield, N.J.); Advertising (N.Y. City). Home: 75 Propspect St., East Orange, N.J. Office: 105 Hudson St., Jersey City 2, N.J. Died July 24, 1953.

REILLY, Joseph John, educator; b. Springfield, Mass., Jan. 16, 1881; s. James Henry and Catherine Frances (Monroe) R.; A.B., Holy Cross Coll., Worcester, Mass., 1904, hon. A.M., 1906, Litt.D., 1940; A.M., Columbia, 1909, Ph.D., Yale, 1912; Litt.D., Fordham U., 1932; m. Anna May Walsh, Oct. 17, 1922; 1 son, Joseph John. Instr. English Fordham, 1904-07, Coll. City of N.Y., 1907-10; University fellow Yale, 1911-12; chief examiner Mass. Civil Service Commn., 1912-21; supt. schools Ware, Mass., 1921-26; asso. prof. English, Hunter Coll., 1926, prof., 1927-—; librarian Hunter Coll., 1928-48; prof. English, Fordham Summer Sch., 1927-31. Vice pres. Nat. Assn. Civil Service Commrs., 1919-20, pres. 1920-21. Mem. Am. Assn. U. Profs., Modern Lang. Assn. Am., Sigma Tau Delta, Phi Beta Kappa. Club: Holy Cross of N.Y. Author: Lowell as a Critic, 1915; Newman as a Man of Letters, 1925; Dear Prue's Husband and ther People, 1932; Of Books and Men, 1942. Editor:

Masters of Nineteenth Century Prose, 1930; Fine Gold of Newman, 1931. Co-editor (with Katherine Crofton) of Gillis: This Our Day, 1933. Contbr. to America, Commonweal, Catholic World, Thought. Died Jan. 25, 1951; buried St. John's Cemetery, Middletown, Conn.

REILLY, Peter C., corp. exec.; b. Providence, R.I., Jan. 12, 1869; s. John and Bridget R.; student LaSalle Acad.-Christian Brothers; LL.D., U. Notre Dame, 1939. With Mica Roofing Co., N.Y.C., 1886; established own firm, Western Co., 1898; organized Republic Chem. and Creosoting Co., 1899, Republic Creosoting Co., 1905, creosoted wood materials; purchased Internat. Combustion Tar & Chem. Corp., 1932, later Reilly Tar & Chem. Corp., 1933; dir. Real Silk Hosier Mills, Ind. Nat. Bank, Union Trust Co. Mem. bd. lay trustees Notre Dame U.; dir. Butler U.; mem. state adv. council Ind. U. Med. Center; mem. adv. bd. St. Joseph Coll.; mem. Hoosier Salon Assn. Mem. Am. Chem. Soc., Citizens Hist. Soc. K.C. Clubs: Indpls. Athletic, Highland Golf & Country, University, Chemists. Office: Merchants Bank Bldg., Indpls. Died Jan. 5, 1952.

REILY, E. Mont., ex.-gov. P.R.; b. Sedalia, Mo.; s. John Gamble and Sarah Ann (Guy) R.; student Ft. Worth U., 4 yrs.; Minnie Mountfortt; children—Gillie-Ann (Mrs. A. J. English), Virginia Lee (dec.), Hortense Montgomery (dec.). Mortgage loan business 1910—; v.p., treas. Met. Bank and Trust Co., 2 yrs. Student Civil War history and lectr. on and Warren G. Harding; originated movement to nominate Theodore Roosevelt for President of U.S., while McKinley was living, 1901; v.p., treas. upon invitation accompanied Roosevelt home from Africa; organized and elected colonel of regiment to accompany Theodore Roosevelt to World War (orgn. was not accepted by President Wilson); began orgn. of movement for Warren G. Harding for President, Jan. 1918, immediately after death of Roosevelt, was Western campaign mgr. for Harding; gov. of Puerto Rico, by apptmt. of Pres. Harding, 1921-23, resigned on account of injuries received in an automobile accident; organized, 1937, club number one to nominate Senator Vandenburg for President in 1940. Re-engaged in brokerage investment business, but has devoted much time in making public addresses on P.R. and the insular possessions of the U.S., defending Gen. Woods' administration in the Philippine Islands; now mem. Nat. Com. to Erect Bronze Statue to Gen. Pershing in Washington. Mem. S.A.R., Am. Irish Hist. Soc., Clean Amusement Assn. (mem. nat. com.). Republican. Presbyterian. K.P. Author: Truth About President Harding; also writer of history of many Civil War battles. Lecturer on Eminent American Statesmen, also on fulfillment of prophecies concerning Christ. Contbr. articles on Am. polit. history and events. Home: 3516 Wabash Av. Office: 12th and Oak Bldg., Kansas City, Mo. Died Nov. 4, 1954; buried Kansas City, Mo.

REILY, George W., banker; b. Harrisburg, Pa., Nov. 21, 1870; s. George W. and Elizabeth (Hummel) R.; Ph.B., Yale, 1892; m. Louise Haxall Harrison, Apr. 29, 1903 (now dec.); 1 son, George W., 3d. Clerk, Harrisburg Nat. Bank, 1892-93; asst. treas. Harrisburg Trust Co., 1893-97; nat. bank examiner, 1897-1903; treas. Harrisburg Trust Co., 1903-10, v.p., treas., 1910-18, pres., 1918—; pres. Harrisburg Nat. Bank, 1927—; pres. Harrisburg Bridge Co.; chmn. Harrisburg Clearing House Assn.; dir. Fed. Res. Bank of Phila., Harisburg Rys. Co., Chestnut Street Market Co., Magee Carpet Co., No. Central R.R., Penn Harris Hotel. Mem. Pa. State Banking Bd., mem. Pa. State Planning Board, chmn. Capitol Park Extension Commn.; mem. Pa. Postwar Conservation Com.; former dir. Harrisburg School Dist.; ex-pres. Harrisburg Welfare Fed.; trustee Wilson Coll., Harrisburg State Hosp. Mem. Pa. Bankers Assn. (ex-pres.), Pa. Soc. Colonial Wars, Pa. Soc. S.R., Book and Snake Soc. (Yale). Presbyn. Clubs: Country (Harrisburg); University Philadelphia, Racquet (Phila.); University (N.Y.C.); Graduate (New Haven). Home: 1501 N. Front St. Office: 16 S. Market Sq., Harrisburg, Pa. Died June 5, 1954.*

REIMERS, Frederick W., lumber co. exec.; b. Rock Island, Ill., Oct. 7, 1877; s. John J. and Marietta (Denkmann) R.; B.S., U. Ill., 1900; m. Fay Warren, Sept. 20, 1905; children—Warren D., Marietta (Mrs. Schneider), Frederick Fay (killed in action). President of the Reimers-Schneider Lumber Co., Hammond, La., R. & K. Creosote Co., Hammond; chmn. bd. Citizens Nat. Bank Hammond; dir. Weyerhaeuser Timber Co. Named Citizen of the Year, Hammond, 1950. Mem. So. Pine Assn. (pres. 1927-28), Tau Beta Pi. Mason (32°). Clubs: Internat. House (New Orleans); Oak Knoll Country (Hammond). Home: 708 W. Thomas St. Office: 211 W. Thomas St., Hammond, La. Died July 31, 1958.

REINHART, Earl F., business exec.; b. Houghton, Mich., Jan. 31, 1898; s. Charles J. and Mary B. (Kull) R.; ed. high sch. and business coll.; m. Vivian Norris. Asst. purchasing agent Haskell & Barker Car Co., 1918-22, Pullman-Standard Car Mfg. Co., 1922-30; asst. to pres. Latrobe (Pa.) Tool Co., 1930-31, v.p., 1931-33; v.p. United Drill & Tool Corp., Detroit, Mich., 1933-40; pres., dir. Republic Drill & Tool Co., Chgo., 1940—. Apptd. mem. drill and reamer industry advisory com., WPB, 1942. Republican. Presbyn. Clubs: Chicago Athletic, Westchester Country (N.Y.), Pottowattomie Country (Mich. City, Ind.); Engineers (N.Y.C.). Home: 32 W. 40th St. Office: 386 4th Av., N.Y.C. Died Oct., 1949.

REINHAUS, Stanley Marx, lawyer; b. Santa Ana, Cal., Dec. 14, 1889; s. Max and Martha (Straus) R.; B.L., U. Cal., 1911, M.L., 1913; m. Selma M. Haas, Mar. 14, 1923; children—Margaret, Stanley M. Admitted to Cal. bar, 1912, since practiced in Santa Ana; mem. Forgy, Reinhaus, Miller & Kogler, and predecessor firms, 1919—. Gov. State Bar Cal., 1933-36, v.p., 1935-36. Fellow Am. Coll. Trial Lawyers; mem. Am., Cal., Orange County (pres. 1930) bar assns., Am. Legion. Republican. Mason, Elk. Clubs: Balboa Bay, Santa Ana Country. Home: 2406 Oakmont Av. Office: First Western Bank Bldg., Santa Ana, Cal. Died May 21, 1956; buried Fairhaven Cemetery, Santa Ana.

REISNER, Edward Hartman, (ris'nĕr), prof. edn.; b. Fredericksburg, Va., Apr. 27, 1885; s. Jacob G. and Henrietta (Hartman) R.; student Cumberland Valley State Normal Sch., Shippensburg, Pa., 1899-1901, Ursinus Coll., Collegeville, Pa., 1903-06; A.B., Yale, 1908, A.M., 1909; grad. study Columbia, 1909-11, Ph.D., 1915; m. Elizabeth Johnson, Aug. 28, 1913 (dec. 1951); children—Edward Hartman, David Johnson; m. 2d, Louie Jamieson Divoll, 1952. Tchr. country schs., 1901-03; sec. Nat. Soc. Promotion of Indsl. Edn., 1910-11; acting prof. philosophy and edn., Washburn Coll., Topeka, Kan., 1911-13; asst. prof. edn., Kan. State Agrl. Coll., 1913-15, asso. prof., 1915-17; lectr. Tchr. Coll., Columbia, 1917-19, asst. prof. edn., 1919-21, asso. prof., 1921-24, prof. 1924-50, prof. emeritus, exec. officer Advanced Sch. of Edn., 1943-47. Mem. Draft Exemption Bd., N.Y.C., 1918. Mem. Nat. Edn. Assn., Nat. Soc. Coll. Tchrs. of Edn. (pres. 1929-30), Am. Assn. Univ. Prof., Phi Beta Kappa, Phi Delta Kappa, Sigma Nu. Democrat. Baptist. Author: Religious Values and Intellectual Consistency, 1915; Nationalism and Education Since 1789, 1922; Historical Foundations of Modern Education, 1926; The Evolution of the Common School, 1930; Faith in an Age of Fact, 1937. Gen. editor McGraw-Hill Edn. Classics. Home: Bellows Falls, Vt. Died May 30, 1958.

REISS, Jacob L. (rīs); Sheboygan, Wis., Mar. 20, 1873; s. Clemens and Mary (Mallman) R.; ed. Cath. parochial sch., Sheboygan, St. Lawrence Coll., Mount Calvary, Wis. 1888. Mitchell Cutting Acad., New York, 1890, and business coll.; m. Mary Detmer, Aug. 5, 1896; children—Raymond H., Marion (Mrs. Emil D. Tietje), Julian J. Organized, also president Internat. Tailoring Co., New York, 1896; president Rway Furniture Company, Sheboygan, 1916—; pres. Reiss Mfg. Co.; dir. Irving Trust Co. of New York, Reiss S.S. Co., C. Reiss Coal Co., Sheboygan, Wis. Republican. Roman Catholic. Clubs: Manhattan, Union League, New York Athletic, Metropolitan (New York); Deal Golf (Deal, N.J.). Home: 59 Deal Esplanade, Deal, N.J. Office: 111 4th Av., N.Y.C. Died Jan. 11, 1955; buried Immaculate Conception Cemetery, Montclair, N.J.

REITZ, Walter R(aleigh), (rītes), oil exec.; b. Barnesville, O., Dec. 8, 1885; s. George Frederick and Annie (Richter) R.; student pub. schs. Marion, Ind. and Sistersville, W. Va.; student U. W. Va., 1905-08; m. Annie Elder Stanbery, Sept. 29, 1919 (dec. Jan. 15, 1929); m. 2d Dorothy Anne Brown, June 30, 1934. Asst. cashier Farmers & Producers Nat. Bank, Sistersville, 1908-10, cashier, 1910-22; pres. Union Nat. Bank, 1922-31; sec., treas. Reno Oil Co., 1919-40, pres., 1940; sec., treas. Ohio Valley Refining Co., 1919-31; v.p., sec., dir. Quaker State Oil Refining Corp., 1931-52, pres., 1952-55, chairman bd., 1955-57, now director; chairman of board Oil City National Bank; dir. Enterprise Oil Co., Curtis Pub. Co. Mem. W. Va. State Senate, 1927-31. Served as 1st lt. Ordnance Dept., U.S. Army. World War I. Mem. Pa. Grade Crude Oil Assn. (dir), Nat. Petroleum Council, Delta Tau Delta. Republican. Presbyn. Mason. Clubs: Wanango Country, Oil City (Oil City, Pa.); Bradford, Pennhills (Bradford, Pa.); Everglades, Bath and Tennis (Palm Beach, Fla.). Home: 501 W. Sixth St. Office: 10 Center St., Oil City, Pa. Died May 25, 1957; buried Oil City, Pa.

REMBAUGH, Bertha, lawyer; b. Phila., Pa., June 5, 1876; d. Alonzo C. and Martha B. (Crum) R.; A.B., Bryn Mawr, 1897, A.M., 1898; LL.B., N.Y. Law Sch., 1904. Practiced at N.Y. City 1904—; mem. Prog. Party Com. of N.Y. Co., 1912-13; Rep. candidate for justice Municipal Court, 1st Dist. of Manhattan, 1919. Mem. N.Y. Co. Lawyers' Assn., Women Lawyer's Assn., Alpha Omicron Pi. Clubs: Women's City, Gamut, Hill, Bryn Mawr. Author: Political Status of Women in United States, 1911. Home: 30 Charlton St. Office: 165 Broadway, New York, N.Y. Died Jan. 31, 1950.

REMENYI, Joseph, educator, writer; b. Pozsony, Hungary, Dec. 1, 1892; s. Frank and Johanna (Sanderffy) R.; Ph.D., Francis Joseph Royal U., Szeged, Hungary, 1934; m. Margaret Papolczy, Aug. 23, 1918. Came to U.S., 1914, naturalized, 1920. Lectr. Western Res. U., Cleve., 1929, instr., 1935, asst. prof., 1939-45, asso. prof., 1945-49, prof. comparative lit., 1949—. Trustee Cleve. Music Sch. Settlement. Mem. Am. Aesthetic Soc. (past chmn. Ohio chpt.), Am. Assn. Tchrs. Slavic and Eastern European Langs. (vice chmn. Ohio chpt.), Modern Lang. Assn., Am. Assn. U. Profs., Council World Affairs. Author books in Hungarian, also translator publs. from English into Hungarian; American Decameron, 1934; American Writers, 1938; Hungarian Literature, 1947; Sixty Poems by Alexander Petofi (introduction), 1949. Co-editor: A World of Great Stories, 1948; collaborator: Columbia Dictionary of Modern European Literature, 1947; contbr. to scholarly publs. Home: 1517 East Blvd., Cleve. 6. Died Sept. 26, 1956.

REMINGTON, Franklin, contractor; b. Utica, N.Y., Nov. 16, 1865; s. Samuel and Flora (Carver) R.; A.B., Harvard, 1887; m. Maude Howard Willets, May 8, 1902. Engaged in farming, 1889-92; constrn. work (water works, r.rs. etc.); organizer 1902, later pres. and chmn. bd. The Found. Co. of N.Y., builder of founds. for Woolworth, Municipal and Singer bldgs., New York; Canadian Pacific Railroad bridge, over St. Lawrence River, at Montreal, Canada; C.&N.W. R.R. bridge over Mississippi River at Clinton, Iowa; locks and dams for U.S. Govt. over Ohio River at Wheeling, W.Va., etc.; about 148 ships for U.S., British and French govts. during World War I; besides the U.S. carried on constrn. work in 16 foreign countries; etc. Retired from active business, 1929. Chairman Prat-Daniel Corp., Thermix Corp., Aerotec Corp. Trustee Seaman's Ch. Inst. Republican. Episcopalian. Clubs: Harvard, Seawanhaka, Pilgrims, Piping Rock. Home: Oyster Bay, N.Y. Died Oct. 20, 1955.

REMINGTON, Preston, museum ofcl., curator; b. New Bedford, Mass., July 17, 1897; s. Frank Logan and Alice (Preston) R.; student Mass. Inst. Tech., 1917-18; A.B., Harvard, 1920. Instr. Mass. Inst. Tech., 1920-23; asst. dept. decorative arts Met. Mus. Art, N.Y.C., 1923-25, asst. curator, 1925-30, asso. curator, 1930-34, curator Renaissance and Modern art 1934-55, vice director, 1949-55, curator of decorative art, 1955—. Author of books: Catalogue of Exhibition of French Painting and Sculpture of the XVIII Century (with H.B. Wehle), 1935; Catalogue of Exhibition of French Domestic Silver, 1938; Catalogue of Exhibition of Victorian and Edwardian Dresses, 1939; Picture Book of Sculpture by Barye in the Metropolitan Museum of Art Collection, 1940; Picture Book of English Domestic Needlework, 1945; also articles. Home: 3 E. 77th St., N.Y.C. 21. Office: Metropolitan Museum of Art, Fifth Av. and 82d St., N.Y.C. 28. Died Apr. 5, 1958.

REMÓN CANTERA, Jose Antonio, pres. Republic of Panamá: b. Panamá, June 1, 1908; s. Alejandro and Maria (Cantera) Remón C.; B.S. and Humanities, Instituto Nacional, 1927; Cav. Officer, Colegio Militer México, 1931; m. Cecilia Pinel, Feb. 11, 1942. Nominated candidate for presidency Republic of Panama Reform Party, Ofcl. Revolutionary Party, Nat. Revolutionary Party, Liberal Party, Popular Union Party, 1952; elected pres. Republic of Panama, May 1952, term beginning Oct. 1952. Pres. publ. La Nacion. Commd. capt., Armed Forces of the Republic (Nat. Police), 1931, advanced through grades to col., 1947; named comdr. in chief Nat. Police Body, 1947. Mem. Nat. Revolutionary Party. Roman Catholic. Decorated GranOficial Orden de Vasco Nuñez de Balboa, Comendador Orden de Vasco Nuñez de Balboa (Republic of Panama); Orden del Libertador, Orden Francisco de Miranda (Venezuela); Legion of Merit (U.S.); Mérito Militar (Mexico); Comendador de la Orden de Ayacucho, Orden del Nérito de la Guardia Civil y Policía, Gran Cruz con Brilliantes de la Orden (Peru); Cruz de la Fundación Internacional Eloy Alfaro, Abdón Calderón (Republic of Ecuador). Clubs: Union, Panamá Golf. Address: Apartado Postal 1428 Panama Republic of Panama. Assassinated Jan. 2, 1955.

RENISON, Robert John, clergyman; b. Cashel, Co. Tipperaray, Ireland, Sept. 8, 1875; s. Robert and Mary (Kennedy) R.; A.B. with honours, U. Toronto, 1896, A.M., 1897; student Sycliffe Coll., 1892-97, D.D., 1932; D.D., St. John's Coll., Winnipeg, 1909, Emmanuel Coll., Saskatchewan, 1932, U. Trinity Coll., Toronto, 1952; m. Elizabeth Maude Bristol, Jan. 3, 1914; children—Robert John, George Everett Bristol. Ordained as deacon Toronto Ch., 1897, priest, Moosonee, 1899; curate Ch. of Messiah, Toronto, 1897; missionary-in-charge of Moose Fort, 1899-1901, Albany, 1901-06; rector Ch. of the Ascension, Hamilton, Ont., 1912-27; archdeacon of Moosonee, Can., 1907-12, bishop, 1944-52, archbishop, 1952-54, ret.; archdeacon of Wellington, 1920-25, Hamilton, 1925-27; rector Christ Ch. Cathedral, Vancouver, 1927-31; bishop of Athabasea, 1931-32; rector St. Paul's Toronto, 1932-44; Metropolitan of Ont., 1952-54, ret. Chaplain 86th batn., 1915, capt., 1917; recruited Co. Indians for forestry batn.; served as hon. Wing Comdr., Royal Canadian Air Force, 1940-45. Recipient George VI Jubilee Medal, Queen

Elizabeth II Coronation Medal. Mason (33°). Clubs: York, Rotary, Royal Canadian Military Inst. (L. M.), Imperial Vets. Assn. (L M.), Canadian Legion (hon. chaplain). Author: Hymn Book in Cree Lang.; Canada at War (with Fermany), 1914-18; A Summer Odyssey, 1937. Co-author (with McClelland and Stewart): Wednesday Morning, 1944; Varia, 1946; For Such a Time as This. Editorial writer for Globe and Mail. Address: 106 St. Leonard's Av., Toronto, Ont., Can. Died Oct. 1957.

RENNER, George Thomas, Jr., geographer; b. Winfield, Kan., July 11, 1900; s. Rev. George Thomas and Mildred May (Dodd) R.; B.A., Cornell College, Mount Vernon, Ia., 1922, LL.D., 1943; M.A. Columbia Univ., 1924, Ph.D., 1927; grad. study, U. of Chicago, summers, 12922, 23, 24, 25; m. Mayme Margaret Pratt, June 12, 1924; 1 son, George Thomas, 3d. Athletic dir. high sch., Anita, Ia., 1920-21; lecturer in econ. geography, Columbia, 1922-26, instr. in geography, 1926-27, visiting asso. prof., summer 1929; asso. prof. geography and chmn. dept., U. of Wash., 1927-33; visiting asso. prof. geography, U. of Minn., summer 1932; geographer Ia. Forest Survey, 1933-34; professorial lecturer in economics, George Washington U., 1934-35; asst. agrl. economist, land policy sect., U.S. Nat. Resources Bd., 1934-36; senior economist and mem. tech. com. regional planning, U.S. Nat. Resources Com., 1935-36; geographic consultant, U.S. National Resources Planning Bd. 1936-43; visiting asso. prof. of edn. Teachers College, Columbia, 1936-37, asso. prof. geography, 1937-39, prof., 1939—; vis. prof. geography Stanford U., 1947-48, Fresno State Coll., 1948, 49, San Jose State College, 1951, U. So. Cal., summer, 1952; geographical editor T. V. Crowell, N.Y., 1944—. Spl. educational consultant to the Air Force, 1951; edn. consultant on Air Force Academy affairs, to U.S. Air Force, 1952. Mem. aviation edn. research com. U.S. Civil Aeronautics Adminstrn., 1942. Am. Geographers, Am. Geophys. Union (meteorology, oceanography), Nat. Council of Geography Teachers, Am. Inst. of Planners, American Legion, Sigma Xi, Pi Gamma Mu, Beta Gamma Sigma, Phi Delta Kappa, Alpha Kappa Psi. Unitarian. Mason. Author: Primitive Religion in the Tropical Forests, 1927; Geography of Washington (with A. L. Seeman), 1928; World Climatic Regions, 1930; Regional Factors in National Planning and Development (with J. Crane, M. Dimock and J. Gaus), 1935; Maladjustments in Land Use (with C. P. Barnes and C. I. Hendrickson), 1936; Geography—An Introduction to Human Ecology (with C. L. White), 1936; Conservation and Citizenship (with W. H. Hartley), 1940; Conservation of National Resources—An Educational Approach to the Problem, 1942; Human Geography in the Air Age, 1942; The Air We Live In, 1942; Geographical Education for the Air Age, 1942; World Map for the Air Age, 1942; Global Geography (with others), 1944; Home Geography (with E. H. Reeder), 1944; Human Geography (with C. L. White), 1948; World Economic Geography (with Durand, White, Gibson), 1951. Contbr. to Econ. Geography, Geog. Review, Jour. of Geog. (asso. ed.), Annals of Assn. Am. Geographers, Social Forces, Frontiers of Democracy, Social Edn., Collier's, The Saturday Evening Post, Harpers, American Magazine, Aero Digest, geographical editor The Kings English Dictionary, 1930; edn. map editor Denoyer-Geppert Co., 1933—. Home: 128 Lakeview Av., Leonia, N.J. Address: Teachers College. Columbia University, N.Y.C. 27. Died Oct. 14, 1955; buried Anita, Ia.

RENNER, Karl, fed. pres. of Austria; b. Unter-Tannowitz, Dec. 14, 1870; s. Matthias and Maria (Habiger); student Vienna Univ.; m. Luise Stoisits, Nov. 5, 1890; 1 dau., Leopoldine. Dep., 1907; mem. Nat. Assemblies, 1918-20; head Austrian Peace Delegation, St. Germain, 1919; chancellor, 1919-20; minister fgn. affairs, 1920; mem. Nationalrat, 1920-34 (pres., 1921); pres. Internat. Assn. for Social Progress Basle, 1926-34; exec. and pres. Wholesale Buying Soc. of Austrian Co-operatives. 1909-34; imprisoned, 1934; founder and pres. Workers Bank, 1922-34; prime minister, 1945; pres. of Republic since 1945. Mem. Social-Democratic party. Author: Das Selbstbestimmungs-recht der Nationen, 1917; Die Wirtschaftals Gesamtprozess und die Sozialisierung, 1925; Die Rechtsinstitute des Privatrechts und ihre soziale Funktion, 1930 (Eng. edition Routledge); Denkschrift uber die Geschichte der Unabhangigkeitserklarung Osterreichs, 1945; Die heue Welt und der Sozialismus, 1946. Address: Vienna I, Hofburg, Austria. Died Dec. 31, 1950; buried Vienna, Zentralfriedhof.

RENNIE, Thomas A. C., physician, psychiatrist; b. Motherwell, Scotland, Feb. 28, 1904; s. David and Elizabeth (Cumming) R.; brought to U.S., 1911, naturalized, 1916; B.S., U. of Pittsburgh, 1924; M.D., Harvard, 1928. Interne Peter Bent Brigham Hospital, Boston, 1928-29; resident in medicine and instr., U. of Mich., 1929-30; house officer in psychiatry, Henry Phipps Psychiatric Clinic, Johns Hopkins, 1930-31, asst. resident in psychiatry, 1931-32, resident psychiatrist, 1932-36, instr. in psychiatry, 1933-36; asso. psychiatrist, 1936-41; visiting psychiatrist, Baltimore City Hosp., 1937-41; asso. prof. psychiatry, Cornell Med. Sch., 1941-50; prof. psychiatry (social psychiatry) since 1950; attending psychiatrist N.Y. Hosp.; cons. in psychiatry F.D.R. VA Hosp., Montrose, N.Y. Dir. Nat. Assn. for Mental Health; chmn. N.Y.C. Community Mental Health Bd.; mem. tech. adv. com. on research N.Y.C. Youth Bd.; mem. Army advisory com. of Greater N.Y.; trustee American Found. Mental Hygiene. Fellow Am. Psychiat. Assn., N.Y. Acad. Medicine; mem. New York Soc. for Clinical Psychiatry, A.M.A., Med. Soc. of State N.Y., Am. Psychopathol. Assn., A.A.A.S. Clubs: Century (N.Y.C.); Hamilton Street (Balt.). Author: (with L. E. Woodward) Jobs and the Man, 1945; (with L. E. Woodward) Mental Health in Mod. Society, 1945; (with others) Tchng. Psychotherapeutic Med., 1948; Vocational Rehabilitation of Psychiatric Patients: A Study of Post-Hospital Vocational Work (with others); Vocational Services for Psychiatric Clinic Patients (with Bozeman). Co-editor Internat. Jour. of Social Psychiatry. Contbr. articles to profl. jours. Home: 34 Gramercy Park. Office: 525 E. 68th St., N.Y.C. 21. Died May 21, 1956; buried Washington, Conn.

RENTSCHLER, Frederick B(rant) (rĕnt'shlẽr), aircraft mfr.; b. Hamilton, O., Nov. 8, 1887; s. George Adam and Phoebe (Schwab) R.; B.S., Princeton, 1909; LL.D., Trinity Coll., 1955; m. Faye Belden, July 25, 1921; children—Helen R. Patch, Ann B. Cassady. Associated with family plants, Hamilton, Ohio, 1910-17; served as captain Air Service. U.S. Army, in charge aircraft production, New York District, 1917-18; a founder and pres. Wright Aeronautical Corp., 1919-24; founder, 1925. pres. until 1930. Pratt & Whitney Aircraft Corp.; an organizer, 1928, United Aircraft & Transport Corp., and pres. until 1933; now chmn. United Aircraft Corp.; director Nat. City Bank of N.Y., Hamilton Foundry & Machinery Company; trustee Hartford Nat. Bank & Trust Company. Dir. Hartford Hosp. Officer French Legion of Honor; recipient U.S. Air Force Civilian Service Award; Guggenheim award, 1957; spl. gold medal, State of Conn., 1953. Clubs: Hartford, Hartford Golf; Links (New York City); Everglades Bath and Tennis (Palm Beach, Fla.); Gulf Stream (Delray Beach, Fla.). Home: "Renbrook," W. Hartford, Conn. Office: E. Hartford, Conn. Died Apr. 25, 1956; buried Fairview Cemetery, West Hartford, Conn.

RENYX, Guy Worden, business exec.; b. Moscow, Mich., Apr. 28, 1868; s. John Henry and Selina Cordelia (Worden) R.; student Detroit Bus. Coll.; m. Flora May Rice, Oct. 4, 1904. Officer, dir. various corps., 1888—; v.p. Renyx, Field Co., Inc., N.Y.C., 1945—; pres. Corporate Leaders of Am., Inc., 1934—, Am. Trusteed Funds, Inc., 1945—; trustee Lexington Trust Fund, 1948—. Home: 1215 5th Av., N.Y.C. 29. Office: 250 Park Av., N.Y.C. 17. Died Aug. 4, 1956.

REPPLIER, Agnes (rĕp'lẽr), author; b. (of French parentage) Phila., Pa., Apr. 1, 1855; d. John George and Agnes (Mathias) R.; ed. Sacred Heart Convent, Torresdale, Pa.; Litt.D., U. Pa., 1902, Yale, 1925, Columbia, 1927, Princeton, 1935. Prominent as essayist; spends much time in Europe. Roman Catholic. Recipient Laetare medal, U. Notre Dame, 1911; gold medal Acad. Arts and Letters. Mem. Nat. Inst. Arts and Letters. Author: Books and Men, 1888; Points of View, 1891; Essays in Miniature, 1892; Essays in Idleness, 1893; In the Dozy Hours, 1894; Varia, 1897; Philadelphia—The Place and the People; The Fireside Sphinx, 1901; Compromises, 1904; In Our Convent Days, 1905; A Happy Half Century, 1908; Americans and Others, 1912; The Cat, 1912; Counter Currents, 1915; Points of Friction, 1920; Under Dispute, 1924; Life of Pere Marquette, 1929; Mere Marie, of the Ursulines; 1931; To Think of Tea, 1932; Junipero Serro, 1933, 1947; In Pursuit of Laughter, 1936; Eight Decades, 1937; Fireside Sphinx, 1939. Compiler: Book of Famous Verse. Clubs: The Acorn, College, Cosmopolitan. Home: Lincoln Court Apts., Overbrook, Phila. Died Dec. 15, 1950; buried St. John's Ch., Phila.

REPPY, Alison, law sch. dean; b. Hillsboro, Mo., May 11, 1893; s. John H. and Martha (Butcher) R.; Ph.B., Mo. Normal Sch., 1914; A.B., Mo. State U., 1916; J.D., U. Chgo., 1922; m. Virginia Lee, June 15, 1935; children—John David, Virginia Lee. Admitted to Mo. bar, 1922, mem. Buder & Buder, St. Louis; prof. law Okla. State U., 1922-24, N.J. Law Sch., 1924-26, N.Y.U., 1926-50; dean N.Y. Law Sch., 1950—. Mem. Am. Bar Assn. Author: Rainbow Memories, 1920; Civil Rights in the United States, 1950; (case books): New Jersey Law of Wills (2 vols.), 1926; Common Law Pleading, 1927; Historical and Statutory Background of Wills, 1928; Cases on the Law of Succession, 1930; Introduction to Civil Procedure, 1953; also articles profl. jours. Editor: Law: A Century of Progress, 1937; David Dudley Field Centenary Essays, 1949; Annual Survey of American Law, 1942-48. Edtior of Air Law Rev., 1930-42, N.Y.U. Law Quarterly Rev., 1926-50. Home: 15 Relay Pl., Stamford, Conn. Office: N.Y. Law Sch., N.Y.C. Died Aug. 20, 1958.

REVERE, Edward H. R., business exec.; b. Boston, 1867; s. John and Susan (Torrey) R.; student pvt. schs. Trustee, dir. Am. Mut. Liability Ins. Co., Canton Instn. for Savs.; dir. Norfolk & Dedham Mut. Fire Ins. Co., Revere Copper & Brass, Inc. Republican. Unitarian. Club: Somerset (Boston). Address: 74 Neponset St., Canton, Mass. Died May 3, 1957.

REVILL, Milton Kirtley (revel), banker; b. Covington, Ky., Jan. 8, 1900; s. Rankin R. and Elizabeth (Kirtley) R.; A.B., U. Ky., 1921; student Harvard Sch. Bus. Adminstrn., 1921-22; m. Elizabeth Reeves, Mar. 15, 1934. With Harris Forbes & Co., N.Y.C., 1922-23, Harris Trust & Savs. Bank, Chgo., 1923-27; v.p. Union Planters Nat. Bank, Memphis, 1927-50, bd. dirs. since 1947, exec. v.p. since 1950; dir. Bluff City Abstract Co., Union Planters Title Guaranty Co., Goodman Bldg. Co., Loeb's Laundry. Apprentice seaman to ensign, USN World War I; U.S.N., World War II, chief staff officer Naval advanced bases Italy, So. France, Palermo, comdg. officer bases Toulon, Marseille, chief staff officer operating base Oran, comdg. officer bases Algeria; commodore U.S.N.R., 1946. Decorated Bronze Star medal (2); Comdr. Order of Crown (Italy). Mem. Am. Bankers Assn., Assn. Res. City Bankers, Sigma Alpha Epsilon, Phi Alpha Delta, Tau Kappa Alpha. Democrat. Baptist. Clubs: Memphis Hunt and Polo, Tennessee. Home: 471 Yates Rd., Memphis. Office: Union Planters Nat. Bank, Memphis 1. Died Feb. 8, 1955.

REW, Irwin; b. Buffalo, N.Y., Mar. 11, 1868; s. Henry C. and Theresa M. (Irwin) R.; Ph.B., Yale, 1889; m. Katharine Jones, June 4, 1902; children—Theresa, Ada K. Elinor. Began as clerk for A. O. Slaughter & Co., Chgo., 1890; identified with the Nat. Gas & Water Co. as treas., 1892-96, pres., 1896-1915. Mem. bd. trustees Northwestern Univ. Home: 217 Dempster St., Evanston, Ill. Died Jan. 28, 1958.

REYES, Alfonso (rā'yās), Mexican writer and diplomat; b. Monterrey, Nuevo Leon, 1889; ed. U. Mexico (law degree), 1913; LL.D., U. Cal., 1941; LL.D. (hon.) Tulane U., 1942; Litt.D. Harvard, Princeton, Universidad de la Habana, Sec., Sec. Sch. of Higher Studies, Mexico City, 1912-13, hon. prof. history of Spanish lang. and lit.; 2d sec. to legation in Paris, 1913-14; commr. (ad honorem) to study pub. edn. in France, 1913; sec. to Mexican Hist. Commn., Spain, 1919-20; 2d sec. of legation, Madrid, 1920; 1st sec. of legation, Madrid, 1921; minister plenipotentiary to Argentina, 1924; France, 1924; pres. commn. to examine Mexican consular personnel, France, 1925; ambassador, special mission, to France, 1925; minister plenipotentiary to Spain, 1926; Argentina, 1927; ambassador to Argentina, 1927; to Brazil, 1930-36; substitute del. of Mexico to League of Nations, 1931; pres. of Mexican delegation to Inaugural Assembly of Pan-Am. Inst. of Geography and History, Rio de Janeiro, 1932-33; Mexican del. to 7th Pan-Am. Conf. of Montevideo, 1933; ambassador to Argentina, 1936-37; del. to U. Mexico to 2d Congress of Am. History at Buenos Aires, 1937; ambassador, special mission, to Brazil, 1938-39. Pres. Colegio de Mexico; prof. Colegio Nacional. Member Junta de Historia y Numismática Americana (Buenos Aires), Academie Diplomatique Internationale (Paris), Club Internacional de Escritores (Mexican branch), International Inst. of Intellectual Co-operation (Paris). Hon. mem. Club Internacional de Escritores (Buenos Aires), Graça Aranha Foundation (Brazil), Instituto Mexicano de Investigaciones Lingüísticas. Director Academia Mexicana de la Lengua correspondiente de la Española, 1957—. Mem. of the fifteen Governors Com. U. Mexico; Am. del. plenipotentiary to peace conf., Chapultepec, 1945. Awarded the Grand Cross of the Order of Isabella the Catholic of Spain; Grand Cross Order of Southern Cross of Brazil; Comdr. de la Legion d'Honneur, France; Great Cross of Boyaca (Columbia); doctor, honoris causa, U. Nuevo León. Author several books, poems, short stories and other prose, since 1911; latest publs.: La Vega y el Soto, 1946; Las Visperas de España. Editor and dir. lit. rev., Monterey. Address: Av. Gral. Benjamin Hill, 122, Mexico 11, D.F. Died Dec. 1959.

REYMERT, Martin (Luther) (rī'mẽrt), psychologist; b. Holmestrand, Norway, Nov. 10, 1883; s. Jens and Inga (Mathiesen) R.; grad. Gymnasium, Oslo, 1903; grad. Army Officers Sch., Oslo, 1904; grad. State Normal Sch., 1905; Examen Philosophicum, U. of Oslo, 1906, grad. study, 1906-16 (with intervals of teaching and mil. service); grad. study and research, Clark U., Worcester, Mass. (as fellow Am. Scandinavian Foundation, New York), 1916-17, Ph.D., 1917; m. Dorothy Dix Markley, Aug. 3, 1931; children—Randi Dix, Karen Jenine, Martin Luther Harvey. Hon. fellow Am. Scandinavian Foundation and fellow in psychology, State U. of Iowa, 1918-19; research asso. Ia. Child Welfare Research Station, 1919-20; est. Scandinavian Scientific Review (quarterly, in English lang.) 1921, editor-in-chief until 1926; asst. prof. exptl. psychology, U. of Oslo, and lecturer on ednl. psychology, State Agrl. Coll. of Norway, 1920-25; standardized group and individual intelligence tests for Norway, at U. of Oslo, 1920-25; est. psychol. lab., Wittenberg Coll., Springfield, O., and head dept. psychology and dir. of lab., 1925-30; est. The Mooseheart Lab. for Child Research, Mooseheart, Ill., since

1930 (dir.). Fellow Ohio Acad. Science (v.p. in charge psychology, 1929-30). Mem. A.A.A.S., Am. Psychol. Assn. (chmn. Clin. Sect., 1935-36), Midwest. Psychol. Assn., Ill. Society Cons. Psychologists (pres. 1939-42). Deutsche Gesellschaft für Psychologie; founder and pres. Springfield (O.) Chapter, Am. Scandinavian Foundation, 1925-30; mem. com. for intelligence research, 1922-23; mem. Am. Ednl. Research Assn., Child Development Committee of the Univ. of Chicago, Ill. Acad. of Science, Ill. Div. for Delinquency Prevention (president advisory council, 1939-45; mem. adv. bd., St. Chrarles (Ill.) Sch. for Boys; mem. Illinois Board Public Welfare Commrs., Psychometric Society; mem. bd. govs. Dyslexia Institute, Chicago; mem. adv. council, Ill. Conf. Family Relations. Originator and chairman Wittenberg Symposium on Feelings and Emotions, in which 35 scientists from 11 countries participated, and editor "Feeling and Emotions," 1928; chmn. Symposium on Mental Tests of the 9th Internat. Congress of Psychology, Yale University, Sept. 1929. Originator and chmn. 2d International Symposium on Feelings and Emotions, Mooseheart Symposium in cooperation with University of Chicago, 1948. Co-editor: Character and Personality, an international jour.; Psychological Abstracts, Psychological Records; The Nervous Child. Author of numerous brochures and articles on psychology and child development. Clubs: Rotary International, Pi Kappa Alpha, Psi Chi, Chicago Psychological, Loyal Order of Moose, Chicago Norske. Consultant in radio programs for children and children's lit. Home: 231 N. Batavia Av., Batavia, Ill. Died June 1953.

REYNOLDS, Bruce D(odson), univ. prof.; b. Gretna, Va., June 28, 1894; s. Keene Johnson and Mary Susan (Brumfield) R.; grad. Fork Union (Va.) Mil. Acad., 1914; B.S., U. of Va. (Miller scholar, 1916-17, 1919-20), 1920; student U. of Ia., 1920-21; D.Sc., Johns Hopkins (research fellow Sch. Hygiene and Pub. Health, 1921-23), 1923; m. Katharine Brown Grason, Oct. 7, 1922; children—Bruce Dodson, Katharine Grason (Mrs. Carl E. Stark), May Hollingsworth (Mrs. James P. Elkins). Instr. in biology U. of Va., 1919-20; instr. animal biol. U. of Ia., 1920-21; asst. prof. zoölogy U. of Ark., 1923-24; asst. prof. biol. U. of V.A, 1924-27, asso. prof., 1927-38, prof. biol., 1938—, chmn. dept., 1957—. Chmn. organizing com. Blandy Exptl. Farm, Boyce, Va., 1927—; dir. Mountain Lake (Va.) Biol. Sta., 1930-32, and, 1946—. Served as 2d lt., A.S. Signal Corps, U.S. Army, 1917-18; 1st lt., A.S., Aircraft Production, 1918-19. Fellow A.A.A.S.; member Assn. of Southeastern Biologists (pres., 1953), Society Protozoologists, A.I.B.S., Am. Society Parasitologists, Am. Soc. Zoologists, Va. Acad. Sci., Sigma Xi. Democrat. Clubs: Colonnade, Farmington Country. Editor: William Allison Kepner, 1946. Contbr. numerous sci. articles dealing with protozaa and treatodes to sci. publs. in U.S. and abroad. Home: 1505 Dairy Rd., Charlottesville, Va. Died Apr. 26, 1957; buried University of Virginia Cemetery.

REYNOLDS, Chester A(rthur) (rĕn'olds), business exec.; b. Fostoria, O., Aug. 7, 1887; s. Rev. James T. and Eunice A. (Slusher) R.; student pub. schs.; m. Cora Hicks, Jan. 1, 1915. Retail clk., 1905-10, propr. gen. store, 1910-15; salesman H. D. Lee Co., 1915-21, successively sales mgr., br. mgr., general sales mgr., asst. treas., asst. sec., v.p., 1942-52, chmn. bd., 1952-56, dir., 1930-56, ret.; pres., dir. Eloessor-Heynemann Co.; v.p., dir. Bruce Co., Chetopa Mfg. Co., Sun Garment Co. Founder Cowboy Hall of Fame and Museum, Chmn. bd. 1955—. Republican. Conglist. Mason (32°, Shriner). Clubs: Ambassador's, Sales Executives, Advertising, Tower. Headed nat. sales orgn. voted one of ten most aggressive sales orgns. in all lines of bus. in U.S.A., 1934. Home: Riviera Apt., 229 Ward Parkway, Kansas City, Mo. Retired. Died Dec. 11, 1958; buried Mt. Moriah Cemetery, Kansas City, Mo.

REYNOLDS, Frank James, advt.; b. N.Y.C., Feb. 19, 1890; s. James and Vera (Frank) R.; grad. N.Y. Mil. Acad., Cornwall-on-Hudson, N.Y., 1908; m. Lillian Heidelbach, Feb. 19, 1909; children—Marguerite Vera (Mrs. Lawrence T. Rassmussen, now deceased), Vivian Gunther (Mrs. Jon Williams); m. 2d, Margaret G. Madar, Sept. 10, 1927; 1 dau., Hope Valerie. Began as file clerk with advt. agy., 1908; v.p. Albert Frank Co., 1911-17, pres., 1917-32; v.p. Hamilton Press, 1912-17, pres. 1917-50, v.p., 1951; pres. Albert Frank-Guenther Law, Inc., advt., 1932-50, vice chmn. bd., 1951. Served as 1st lt. Air Corps, U.S. Army, 1917-19; now capt. U.S. Air Corps; ret. Trustee N.Y. Mil. Acad., Cornwall-on-Hudson. Roman Catholic. Clubs: Lawyers', Advertising (N.Y.C.); Westchester Country (Rye, N.Y.). Home: 180 E. 79th St. Office: 131 Cedar St., N.Y.C. Died Feb. 1958.

REYNOLDS, Grace Morrison, lecturer; b. Wakefield, Mass., May 24, 1880; d. William Harrison and Alice Webb (Beckford) Morrison; grad. Salem (Mass.) Normal School, 1900; L.H.D., Boston U., H.H.D., 1931; m. J. Harry Poole, 1904 (died 1919); m. 2d, Dr. H. Gilbert Reynolds, Sept. 29, 1937. Lecturer on world affairs, 1913—. Pres. Gen. Fedn. Women's Clubs, 1932-35. Dean Stoneleigh College, Rye, N.H., 1935-37. Mem. Consumers' Adv. Bd., NRA. Mem. Nat. Inst. Social Sciences, Am. Geog. Soc. Republican. Universalist. Clubs: Nat. Travel, Women's Republican of Mass., and many others. Contbr. articles on civicl problems and travel. Home: Paducah, Ky. Deceased.

REYNOLDS, John Whitcome; b. Jacksonport, Wis., Oct. 1, 1875; s. Thomas and Jennie (Foley) R.; spl. student U. Mich., 1897-99; LL.B., U. Wis., 1902; m. Madge Flatley, July 17, 1906; children—Florence, Thomas, Ruth, John; m. 2d, Florence C. Stehn, Jan. 30, 1939. Admitted to Wis. bar, 1902, and began practice at Green Bay; mem. firm Kaftan & Reynolds, 1903-21; atty. gen. of Wis., 1927-33; formerly asst. atty. gen. in charge of Indian claims. Republican. Home: 1025 Cherry St. Office: 301 Minahan Bldg., Green Bay, Wis. Died Feb. 4, 1958.

REYNOLDS, Richard Samuel, corp. official; b. Bristol, Tenn., Aug. 15, 1881; s. Abram D. and Senah (Hoge) R.; student King Coll., Bristol, Tenn., U. of Va., 1900-02, also Columbia U.; m. Julia L. Parham, Dec. 1905; children—Richard S., J. Louis, William G., David Parham. Began with R. J. Reynolds Tobacco Co., 1903, resigned, 1912; organized own business; pres. and dir. U.S. Foil Co., Reynolds Alloys Co., Reynolds Research Inst., Inc.; chairman bd. Reynolds Sales Co., Reynolds Metal Company, Reynolds Research Corp., Reynolds Corp., Reynolds Mining Corporation, Eskimo Pie Corp., Robertshaw Fulton Controls Company; Richmond Radiator Company, Reynolds Internacional de Mexico, Reynolds Reduction Co.; director Mutual Trading Corporation, Reynolds Jamaica Mines, Ltd. Plantation Yacht Harbor Inc., Reynolds Aluminum Co., U.S. Sanitary Mfg. Co. Presbyn. Clubs: New York Yacht, Metropolitan, Nassau Country (New York); Pendennis, Pendennis (Louisville); Country Club of Va., Commonwealth (Richmond); Surf, Indian Creek Country, Hialeah (Miami Beach). Home: 300 Old Lock Lane. Office: Reynolds Metals Bldg., Richmond 18, Va. Died July, 1955.

REYNOLDS, William Neal, tobacco mfr.; b. Patrick County, Va., Mar. 22, 1863; s. Hardin W. and Nancy (Cox) R.; ed. Trinity Coll. (now Duke U.), 1882-83; m. Kate G. Bitting, Mar. 6, 1889. With R. J. Reynolds Tobacco Co. since 1881; admitted as partner, 1886, and placed in charge of leaf purchasing dept.; has served continously as dir. since company was inc., 1889, made v.p., 1889, pres. 1918, chmn. bd., 1924, chmn. executive committee, 1931-42 (retired); president Piedmont Park Company, partner Down Town Garage. Mem. bd. trustees Duke U., Duke Endowment. Democrat. Presbyn. K.P., Elk. Clubs: Twin City, Forsyth Country, Oldtown (Winston-Salem); Trotting Horse Club of America (Goshen, N.Y.). Home: Winston-Salem, N.C. Died Sept. 10, 1951.

RHÉAUME, Louis (ray-home), bishop; born Levis, Quebec. Can., Nov. 17, 1873; s. Jérémie and Philomen (Nadeau) R.; ed. Ottawa and Rome; Ph.D., Gregorian U., 1902. Ordained priest (Order of O.M.I.) Roman Catholic Ch., 1904; prof. mathematics, U. of Ottawa, 1905; dir. Grand Seminary of Ottowa, 1913-15, 1921-23; rector U. of Ottawa, 1915-21; consecrated bishop, 1923; bishop of Haileybury, Ont., 1923-38; bishop of Timmins, Ont., since 1938. Asst. at Pontifical Throne and Roman Court, since Mar. 24, 1940. Address: Bishop of Timmins, Haileybury, Ont., Can. Died May 8, 1955; buried Holy Cross Cemetery, Haileybury, Ont., Can.

RHOADES, Edward Henry, Jr. (rōdz), lawyer; b. Toledo, Aug. 9, 1872; s. Edward Henry and Hannah Sophia (Rhoades) R.; prep. edn., Toledo Central High Sch.; A.B., Oberlin, 1896; LL.D., Denison U., 1926; m. Maude Hosler, Nov. 21, 1899; children—Wm. Hosler, Edward Henry III. Admitted to Ohio bar, 1899, now in adv. capacity firm Rhoades & Rhoades, with brother and son Wm. H.; specializes in corporate banking, real estate, probate law; v.p. Franklin Creamery Co. (O.); sec.-treas. Hosler Realty Co. Former trustee, mem. prudential com. Hillsdale Coll. Pres. Ohio Baptist Conv., 1916-25; pres. Northern Bapt. Conv., 1925-26; pres. Francis Wayland Found. (for Christian work among students, Ohio State U.), 1920-27; supt. Ashland Av. Bapt. Ch., Toledo, 1904-29; budget adviser Northern Bapt. Conv. 1935—. Mem. Phi Beta Kappa. Republican. Home: 2136 Glenwood Av. Office: Security Bldg., Toledo. Died July 16, 1949; buried Meml. Park Cemetery, Toledo.

RHOADS, Charles James (rōdz); b. Germantown, Philadelphia, Oct. 4, 1872; s. James E. (1st pres. of Bryn Mawr Coll.) and Margaret Wilson (Ely) R.; grad. William Penn Charter Sch., Phila., 1889; A.B., Haverford Coll., 1893 (Phi Beta Kappa); m. Lillie Frishmuth, November 9, 1912 (deceased, May 17, 1951). Began career as a clerk for Girard Trust Co., Phila., 1893; asst. treas. same, 1898-1900, treas., 1900-04, v.p., 1904-14 (resigned); gov. Federal Reserve Bank of Phila., Oct. 8, 1914-Feb. 1918; pres. Central Nat. Bank, Phila., 1920; dir. Girard Trust Co., Provident Mutual Life Insurance Co. (Phila.); Phila. Saving Fund Soc.; Phila. Contributionship for the Insurance of Houses from Fire; partner Brown Bros. & Co., bankers, 1921-29; commr. of Indian Affairs, 1929-Apr. 21, 1933. Chmn. Phila. County Relief Bd., Apr. 1934-July 1935. Acting treas. Y.M.C.A, Feb.-May 1918; chmn. Y.M.C.A. War Prisoners Aid, and chief Friends Bur., Am. Red Cross (France) for relief and reconstruction work in devastated France, May 1918-Sept. 1919. Mem. bd. mgrs., Haverford Coll.; pres. bd. of trustees Bryn Mawr Coll. Mem. Am. Acad. Polit. and Social Sci. (treas.), Hist. Soc. Pa., Am. Philos. Soc., Council Fgn. Relations. Orthodox Quaker. Clubs: Phila., University, University Barge, Merion Golf (Phila.); Metropolitan (Washington); Century Association (N.Y. City). Home: Ithan Mill Farm, Bryn Mawr, Pa. Died Jan. 2, 1954.

RHOADS, Cornelius Packard, dir. hosp. research; b. Springfield, Mass., June 20, 1898; s. George Holmes and Harriet (Barney) R.; A.B., Bowdoin Coll., 1920, D.Sc. (hon.), 1944; M.D. cum laude, Harvard, 1924; D.Sc. (honorary), Williams College, 1952; married Katherine S. Bolman, Sept. 9, 1936. Interne, dept. of surgery, Peter Bent Brigham Hosp., Boston, 1924-25, Trudeau fellow, Trudeau Sanatorium, N.Y.C., 1925-26; instr. in pathology Harvard Med. Sch., and asst. pathologist Boston City Hosp., 1926-28; asso. Rockefeller Inst. for Med. Research, 1928-33; asso. mem. in charge service for study hematologic disorders, 1933-39; pathologist Hosp. of Rockefeller Inst. for Med. Research, 1931-39, dir. Memorial Center for Cancer and Allied Diseases, N.Y.C., 1940-52, scientific dir., 1953—; dir. of The Sloan-Kettering Inst. for Cancer Research, 1945—, James Ewing Hosp., N.Y.C., 1950—; prof. pathology, dept. pathology, Cornell U. Med. Coll. 1940-52; prof. pathology, dept. biology and growth, Sloan Kettering Div., Cornell U. Med. Coll., 1952—. spl. cons. U.S. Public Health Service, Nat. Adv. Cancer Council, 1947—; cons., med. div., Chem. Corps, Army Chem. Center, Md., 1948-50. Col., M.C., A.U. S.; chief med. div., Chem. Warfare Service, 1943-45. Awarded Legion of Merit. Mem. com. to visit dept. of chemistry, Harvard. Trustee Kettering Foundation. Member National Research Council (member sub. com. on blood substitutes 1940-42; chmn. blood procurement 1941-42; mem. com. for treatment of war gas casualties 1941-43; mem. com. on veterans med. problems 1945-47; chmn. com. on growth 1945-48; mem. com. on atomic bomb casualties, 1946; chmn. exec. com. of com. on growth, 1946-47; mem. adv. com. of chem.-biol. coordinator center 1946-47; mem. at large, div. of med. sciences 1946-49), Office of Sci. Research and Dev. (mem. com. on insect and rodent control 1945-46). Fellow A.C.P., N.Y. Acad. Medicine (mem. com. on public health relations 1942-43; v.p. 1943-45), A.A.A.S. (v.p. 1953, chmn. sect. med. sci. 1953), Am. Geriatrics Soc.; mem. Am. Pub. Health Assn., Am. Soc. Control Cancer, Am. Cancer Soc. (bd. dirs. 1941-46; exec. com. 1944-46; mem. N.Y.C. cancer com. 1943-51) Blood Transfusion Assn. (bd. 1940-51), Harvey Soc., Soc. Exptl. Biology and Medicine, Soc. of Med. Jurisprudence, Am. Assn. Pathologists and Bacteriologists, Am. Assn. for Cancer Research, Am. Indsl. Hygiene Assn., A.M.A., Am. Radium Soc., Am. Soc. for Clin. Investigation, Am. Soc. Exptl. Pathology, Am. Soc. Tropical Med., Armed Forces Chem. Assn., Assn. Am. Physicians, Med. Soc. of State of N.Y., Med. Soc. of County of N.Y. (mem. spl. com. on cancer control, spl. com. on illegal practice of medicine), N.Y. Soc. Tropical Medicine, N.Y. Acad. Scis., N.Y. Zool. Soc., N.Y. City Welfare Council (mem. com. on chronic illness), Harvard Med. Alumni Assn., Interurban Pathol. Club, Interurban Clin. Club, Halsted Club. Clubs: University, Century Assn. (N.Y.C.); Harvard (Boston). Contbr. med. articles in profl. jours. Address: Sloan-Kettering Institute for Cancer Research, 410 E. 68th St., N.Y.C. 21. Died Aug. 13, 1959.

RHOADS, Joseph J., coll. pres.; b. Marshall, Tex., Oct. 30, 1890; s. Dennis Collins and Mary J. Rhoads; B.S., Bishop College, 1910, LL.D. (honorary), 1951; student at Yale University, 1922-23; M. A., U. of Mich., 1935; m. Lucile O. Bridge, May 30, 1918. Asst. prin., Pemberton High Sch., Marshall, Tex., 1910-18; teacher, Tuskegee Inst., 1919-22; prin. Booker T. Washington High Sch., Dallas, Tex., 1923-29; President of Bishop College, 1929-51, retired as president. President of the Texas Council of Negro Orgns.; chmn. Texas Commn. on Democracy in Edn. since 1941. Author: Democracy's Debt of Honor. America's Ideals of Brotherhood, Thirty-Three Proposals. Address: Bishop College, Marshall, Tex. Died Oct. 9, 1951.

RHODE, Clarence J., govt. ofcl.; b. Sultan, Wash., Apr. 15, 1913; s. Charles J. and Cora Grace (Sanders) R.; student pub. schs. Colville, Wash., bus. coll. Seattle; m. Gazil E. Burcham, Sept. 8, 1935; children—Jack, James, Sally. Alaska game warden, later wildlife agt., 1935-43; airline pilot, 1943-46; aircraft supervisor Fish and Wildlife Service, Alaska, Dept. of Interior, 1947, regional dir. since 1948. Mem. Wildlife Soc., Northwest Peace Officers Assn. Elk. Home: 546 Hemlock St. Office: Box 2021, Federal Bldg., Juneau, Alaska. Disappeared on flight Aug. 21, 1958.

RHODES, Charles Dudley (rōdz), army officer; b. Delaware, O., Feb. 10, 1865; s. Maj. Dudley Woodbridge and Marcia (Parrish) R.; A.B., Columbian (now George Washington) U., 1885; grad. U.S. Mil. Acad., 1889; honor grad. Inf. and Cav. Sch., 1907; grad. Army Staff Coll., 1908; Army War Coll., 1920; m. Mary F. Counselman, Dec. 2, 1890. Apptd. add. 2d lt. 7th Cav., 1889; advanced through grades to brig. gen. N.A., 1918, maj. gen. U.S. Army (temp.), 1918, brig gen. regular army, 1925, maj. gen., 1928; ret. from active service, 1929. In Sioux Indian Campaign, 1890-91; prof. mil. sci. and tactics, Ohio Wesleyan U., 1893-95; in Santiago Campaign as a.d.c. to insp. gen. of Army, and adj. gen. 2d Brigade, 2d Div., 5th Army Corps, 1898; recommended bvt. maj. "for gallant and meritorious services," at Santiago de Cuba, 1898; comd. Troop C, 6th Cav., on China Relief Expdn., 1900, later adj. gen. 1st Brigade in China and adj. gen. combined Anglo-Am. Expdn.; in numerous engagements with insurgents in Philippine Islands, 1900-03; published in Division orders "for distinguished conduct in action," P.I., 1901; received surrender insurgent battalion of Tiradores, at Binan, 1902; participated in Gen. Bell's campaigns in Philippine Islands; twice commended for services; commended for killing Moro outlaw, Jammang, Island of Jolo, 1910; duty Gen. Staff Corps, 1903-06, 1909-12; comdt. Mounted Service Schs., 1914-17 (awarded silver medal, San Francisco Expn., 1915, for excellence of exhibit of Mounted Service Schools); mem. Cav. Equipment Bd., 1915-17; comd. 21st Cav. (79th F.A.), 1917; brig. gen. comdg. 157 F.A. Brig., 1917-18, in Aisne-Marne, St. Mihiel, and Meuse-Argonne offensives, France; maj. gen. 42d and 34th divs., France; chief Am. sect., Permanent Interallied Armistice Commission, Spa, Belgium, 1918-19; maj. gen. comdg. Base Sect. 2 (Bordeaux), 1919. Awarded D.S.M. and D.S.C. (U.S.), also the Distinguished Service Star (U.S.); Knight Comdr. of the Bath (British); Comdr. Legion of Honor (French); Comdr. Order of the Crown (Belgium). Editor Jour. U.S. Cav. Assn., 1899-1900; prize essayist, same, 1898; Seaman prize essayist, Mil. Service Instn., 1901; gold medalist same, 1904. Asso. editor Upton's Military Policy of U.S., 1903. Lectr. before Army War Coll., 1906, Nat. Guard Assn. Pa., 1907, Nat. Guard Cal., 1908, Va. Mil. Inst., 1912. Trustee Assn. Graduates, U.S. Mil. Acad., 1935. Mem. Mil. Order of the Dragon, Mil. Order World War, Vets. Fgn. Wars, Army and Navy Union, Order of Shrine, Soc. of Army of Santiago de Cuba (pres. 1934-35), Phi Kappa Psi. Episcopalian. Clubs: Army and Navy (Washington and Manila). Author: The Cavalry, 1911; Robert E. Lee—The West Pointer, 1932. Address: War Dept., Washington. Died Jan. 24, 1948.*

RHODES, Edward Everett, actuary; b. Newark, N.J., Feb. 21, 1868; s. Wesley and Frances H. (Broadhead) R.; ed. pub. schs. of Newark; m. Clara S. Littell, Apr. 22, 1896; children—Marion Littell (Mrs. Marion Rhodes Steuart), Helen B. (Mrs. Bertrand L. Gulick, Jr.), Robert D. Rhodes. Began as actuarial student with The Mutual Benefit Life Ins. Co. of Newark, 1886, since remained in the service of that co.; was asst. mathematician (actuary), 1902-05, mathematician (chief actuary), 1905-19, v.p., 1908-45, hon. chmn. bd., 1946-51, now hon. chmn. emeritus, dir. 1912-51. Served as expert adviser to the N.Y. (Armstrong) legislative com. investigating life ins. cos. under leadership of Hon. Charles E. Hughes and assisted in drafting remedial legislation; mem. of com. (1909-31) of 4 actuaries and 4 med. dirs. of mortality investigation, 1909—, pub. first findings in 5 vols., 1912-14; served as chmn. of com. on taxation of Assn. of Life Ins. Pres'. in early period of fed. income taxation, participating in congressional hearings and the framing of tax laws. Fellow of Actuarial Soc. Am. (pres., 1926-27), Am. Inst. of Actuaries, Inst. of Actuaries of Gt. Britain, and Ins. Inst. Am.; mem. Am. Math. Soc., Internat. Congresses of Actuaries; hon. mem. Assn. of Life Ins. Counsel, Assn. of Life Ins. Med. Dirs. Mem. of various charitable and social service orgns. in Newark. Author of various papers pub. by actuarial socs. Presbyn. Clubs: Essex (Newark). Home: 233 Elwood Av., Newark, N.J. Died Jan. 19, 1959.

RHODES, Henry Abraham, ret. merchant; b. Trempealeau, Wis., Apr. 14, 1863; s. Joshua and Susan E. (Stevens) R.; student Galesville (Wis.) U., 1878-82; m. Birdella Victoria Booher, Jan. 20, 1886; children—Vera Lucille (Mrs. Audsley M. Fraser), Edward Byron (dec.). Tchr. country schs. of Trempealeau, Wis., 1882-84; began as merchant in small store with brother Albert; pres. Rhodes Investment Co., Henry A. Rhodes, Inc.; dir. Rainier Nat. Park Co. Republican. Conglist. Clubs: Union, Tacoma Country and Golf. Home: Ansonia Apts. Office: Broadway Theatre Bldg., Tacoma. Died Oct. 1954.

RICE, Alexander Hamilton, geographer, explorer; b. Boston, Aug. 29, 1875; s. John Hamilton and Cora Lee (Clark) R.; A.B., Harvard, 1898, M.D., 1904, A.M. (hon.), 1915; D.Sc. (hon.), Hamilton, 1951; surgical intern Mass. Gen. Hosp., 1903-05; certificate Royal Geog. Soc. Sch. of Geog. Surveying and Field Astronomy, 1908-10; m. Mrs. Eleanor Elkins Widener, Oct. 6, 1915 (died July, 1937); m. 2d, Mrs. Dorothy Farrington Upham, Nov. 5, 1949. Surgeon, dir. Hosp. No. 72, Société de Secours aux Blessés Militaires, Paris, France, 1914-15; surgeon Am. Ambulance, Neuilly, 1914-15; commd. lt. U.S. N.R., 1917; instr. navigation and nautical astronomy, 2d Naval Dist. Training Sch., Newport, R.I., 1917; dir. same sch., 1917-19; lectr. Lowell Inst., 1922; instrumental in establishing Indian Sch., hosp. and créche at São Gabriel, Brazil; established Inst. of Geog. Exploration, Harvard, dir., prof. same; hon. curator S.A. sect. Peabody Mus. Archaeology and Ethnology; lectr. diseases of tropical S. America, Dept. Tropical Medicine, Harvard Med. Sch. Has devoted much time to exploration, research and sci. investigations of tropical S.A.; organized and conducted 7 expdns. into the Colombian Caqueta, Brazilian Amazonas and Venezuelan Guayana, exploring, surveying and mapping an area of 500,000 sq. miles, carrying out at the same time investigations of geol., biol., anthropol., ethnol., character; expdn., 1924-25, to Rio Branco-Uraricuera-Parima, hydroplane successfully employed in reconnaissance and air photography, efficiency of short wave, low power wireless in such work first conclusively demonstrated. Fellow Royal Astron., Soc., Royal Meteorol. Soc., Royal Anthrop. Inst., Geol. Soc., Am. Assn. Advancement of Sci. N.Y. Acad. Medicine; mem. Royal Geog. Society, London (hon. corr. fellow, former v.p.), Am. Geog. Soc., Reale Società Georgrafica Italiana, Société des Américanistes (Paris), La Sociedad Geogràfica (Madrid) (hon. fellow all three), Instituto Hispano Americano de Relaciones Culturales, Madrid (hon. councillor), Hispanic Soc. of America (corr. mem.), Newport County Med. Soc., Am. Museum of Health (dir.); Socio Honorario Touring Club do Brasil, Rio de Janeiro; chmn. Spanish National Relief Committee; mem. Geol. Soc. Am., Société de Geographie de Paris, Société de Geographie d'Anvers, Phila. Geog. Soc., Royal Institution of Great Britain, Am. Anthrop. Soc., Council on Fgn. Relations, Nat. Inst. Social Scis., Soc. of Cin., Mass. Soc. Mayflower Descendants, Soc. Colonial Gov's., Soc. Colonial Wars, The Pilgrims, Mass. Hist. and Geneal. Soc., N.Y. Hist. Soc., N.Y. Geneal. and Biog. Soc., Soc. N.Y. Hosp., Soc. Descs. of Knights of Most Noble Order of the Garter, Hereditary Order Descs. Colonial Gov's. (hon. v. gov. gen.); Newport Hist. Soc., R.I. Hist. Soc.; patron Phila. Mus. of Art; trustee Am. Mus. Natural History, Lycée Français de N.Y., Mus. of City, N.Y., Am. Soc. French Legion of Honor, Cathedral St. John the Divine. N.Y. Dispensary; Institut Français aux Etats-Unis, N.Y. Awarded Patron's gold medal, Royal Geog. Soc., 1914; David Livingstone centenary medal, Am. Geog. Soc., 1920; Elisha Kent Kane medal, Phila. Geog. Soc., 1920; gold medal Harvard Travellers Club, 1914; Resolution and Testimonial for geog. exploration and sci. research carried out in S.A. tendered by the City of Newport, 1925; gold medal Société Royale de Geographie d'Anvers, 1931; gold medal Soc. Mayflower Descs. State of N.Y.; Chevalier de la Legion d'Honneur, 1934; Cross of Commander, 1938; gold medal, Soc. de Geog., Paris, 1939; Gran Cruz Ordem de Isabel la Catolica by decree of Gen. Franco, 1940. Republican. Episcopalian (vestryman Emmanuel Ch., Boston). Clubs: Tavern, Tennis and Racquet, Harvard, Harvard Travelers of Cambridge (ex-pres.), Somerset (Boston); Knickerbocker, Union, Brook, River, Turf and Field, Harvard, Explorers, New York Yacht, Racquet and Tennis, Ends of the Earth, Boone and Crockett, Automobile (New York); Philadelphia (Phila.); Hope (Providence); Geographical, Hurlingham, Internat. Sportmen's, Boodle's, Royal Automobile (London); Travellers, Union Interalliée (Paris). Contbr. numerous articles to Geog. Jour. Quito to Iquitos via River Napo, Apr. 1903; The River Uaúpes, with Map, June 1910; Further Explorations in Northwestern Amazon Valley, Map, Aug. 1914; Notes on the Rio Negro (Amazonas), Map, Oct. 1912; The Rio Negro, the Casiquiare Canal and the Upper Orinoco (map), Nov. 1921; Rio Branco-Uraricuera-Parima (maps), 1928; El rio Negro (Amazonas) y sus grandes afluentes de la Guayana Brasileña, 1934; Exploration en Guyane Brésilienne, Paris, 1937. Address: Miramar, Newport, R.I. Died July 23, 1956; buried St. Columbia's Berkeley Meml. Cemetery, Middletown, Newport, R.I.

RICE, Charles M., lawyer; b. St. Louis, Apr. 8, 1882; s. Jonathan and Aurelia (Stix) R.; student Smith Acad., St. Louis; A.B., Washington U., 1904; LL.B., St. Louis Law Sch., 1907; m. May Goldman, Sept. 23, 1908; children—Erna (Mrs. Wm. N. Eisendrath, Jr.), Jay, Jonathan. Admitted to Mo. bar, 1906, since practiced in St. Louis; co-founder firm of Lewis, Rice, Tucker, Allen & Chubb since establishment, Mar. 1909; pres. N. America Elec., Lamp Co. since 1928, Crawford County Caverns Co. since 1944; vice pres. Berland Shoe Stores, Inc., since 1940; dir. May Dept. Stores Co. Dir. St. Louis Acad. Sci. Mem. Temple Israel. Mem. Am., Mo. bar assns., Phi Delta Phi. Clubs: St. Louis Bird, Garden. Home: One Oak Knoll. Office: 408 Olive St., St. Louis 2. Died June 18, 1950; buried New Mt. Sinai Cemetery.

RICE, Craig, author; born at Chicago, Ill., June 5, 1908; daughter Harry M. and Mary Walker (Randolph) Craig; educated privately; m. Lawrence Lipton, Mar. 31, 1939 (div. Apr. 23, 1948); children by previous marriages—David Ferguson, Nancy, Iris; married H. W. DeMott, Jr. In newspaper work, 1925-30; radio writing and producing, 1931-38; writer of mystery novels, 1938—; pen names, Michael Venning and Daphne Sanders. Author: 8 Faces at 3, 1939; Corpse Steps Out, 1940; Wrong Murder, 1940; Right Murder, 1941; Trail by Fury, 1941; Telefair: the house on the island, 1942; Big Midget Murders, 1942; Man Who Slept All Day, 1942; Sunday Pigeon Murders, 1942; Having Wonderful Crime, 1943; Thursday Turkey Murders, 1943; Murder Through the Looking Glass (Michael Venning), 1943; To Catch a Thief (Daphne Sanders), 1943; Jethro Hammer (Michael Venning), 1944; Home Sweet Homicide, 1944; The Fourth Postman, 1948; The Innocent Bystander, 1949; Sunday Pigeon Murders, 1948; Trial by Fury, 1941; 45 Murders: a collection of True Crime Stories, 1952; My Kingdom for a Hearse, 1956; Knocked for a Loop, 1957; The April Robin Murders (with Ed McBain), 1958. Address: care Scott Meredith, Inc., 580 Fifth Av., N.Y.C. 36. Died Aug. 28, 1957.

RICE, Edward Loranus, zoölogist; b. Middletown, Conn., Mar. 18, 1871; s. William North and Elizabeth Wing (Crowell) R.; A.B., Wesleyan U., Conn., 1892; U. Berlin, 1892-93; U. Munich, 1893-95, Ph.D., 1895; U. of Chicago, summer 1898; Columbia, 1st semester, 1906-07; U. Freiburg, 2d semester, 1906-07; Harvard, 2d semester, 1916-17; Sc.D., Wesleyan U., 1927; Johns Hopkins, 2d semester, 1927-28; m. Sarah Langdon Abbott, Mar. 20, 1901; children Charlotte, William Abbott. Asst. in zoölogy, Wesleyan U., 1896; prof. biology and geology, Allegheny (Pa.) Coll., 1896-98; prof. zoölogy, Ohio Wesleyan U., 1898-1941, emeritus since 1941, acting pres., 1938-39, prof. zoölogy, (war emergency), 1942-45. Inst. zoölogy, Lake Lab. (Ohio State U.), Sandusky, O., summers, 1905, 06, 08, 09, 12; instr. biology, Bay View (Mich.) Summer College, 1943. Fellow A.A.A.S. (v.p. and chmn. Sect. F, 1923), Ohio Acad. Science (pres. 1906-07; sec. 1912-23); mem. Am. Soc. Naturalists, Assn. Am. Anatomists, Am. Soc. Zoölogists, Am. Genetic Assn., Phi Beta Kappa, Sigma Xi, Phi Nu Theta. Methodist. Author: An Introduction to Biology, 1935. Home: 2241 S. Seneca Av., Alliance, O. Died Feb. 4, 1960.

RICE, Ernest, pres. Federal Land Bank of Louisville; b. Orysa, Tenn., Aug. 31, 1872; s. Charles Stephen Olin and Lucie Quarles (Estes) R.; prep. edn., Big Hatchie Acad., Orysa, Tenn.; LL.B., Cumberland U., Lebanon, Tenn., 1893; m. Katherine Klyce, Dec. 30, 1902; children—Katherine Estes (Mrs. Harold Gladstone Lowe), Ernest, Henry Klyce. Admitted to Tenn. bar, 1893, and practiced at Dyersburg until 1913, was city attorney and county attorney there; v.p. Chicago, Memphis & Gulf R.R., 1907-13; pres. Lake County Mfg. Co., 1907-21, Cottonseed Products Co., 1912-25, Covington Cotton Oil Co., 1918-22, Nat. Cottonseed Products Corp., 1926-33; pres. Fed. Land Bank of Louisville (retired, Sept. 1947); gen. agent Farm Credit Adminstrn., 4th Dist.; pres. West Tenn. Soya Mill, Inc.; regional dir. Surplus Property Disposal; director, Union Compress & Warehouse Co.; president Lake County Oil Mill, English Plantation Co., Campbell Brown Farms. Mem. Tenn. State Senate, 1903-07 (speaker of Senate and lt. gov., 1905-07). Chmn. State Dem. Judicial Conv., 1916, State Dem. Conv., Nashville, 1924; chmn. Liberty Loan drives, Dyersburg, World War I; dist. v.p. Regional Agrl. Credit Corp., Washington, D.C.; mem. Kentucky State, U.S. Department Agriculture War Board; mem. Kentucky State War Bond Com., Tenn. State Tax Commn., Tenn. State Dem. Exec. Com. Former trustee Lambuth Coll., Jackson, Tenn. Mem. Beta Theta Pi, Sigma Delta Kappa. Del. Gen. Conf. M.E. Ch., S. Club: Pendennis. Home: 2106 Harding Pl., Nashville, Tenn. Office: 224 E. Broadway, Louisville 1, Ky. Died 1956.

RICE, Frederick Adolph, pub.; b. Matawan, N.J., Apr. 13, 1888; s. Joseph L. M. and Clara Evelyn (Anderson) R.; A.B., Cornell U., 1908; m. Mattie Louise Van Siclen, July 16, 1912; children—Marjorie Cornelia (Mrs. Edward D. Gray), Frederick Adolph, Jr. Fellow Am. history, Cornell U., 1908-09; head history dept., vice prin. Everett (Wash.) High Sch., 1909-11; asso. with Ginn and Co., 1912-58, beginning as sales rep. in San Francisco office, elected to partnership, 1937, Pacific Coast mgr., 1939-42, dir., 1940-58, pres., 1942-47; chmn. bd., pres., 1947-58; ret. 1958; dir. Ginn and Co., Ltd. (London), 1945-54. Trustee Mills Coll., 1937-42; dir. Oakland Forum, 1935-40, pres., 1935-37; mem. Cornell U. Council. Mem. Am. Textbook Pubs. Inst. (dir. and 1st v.p. 1951-54), Am. Hist. Assn., Phi Beta Kappa, Alpha Chi Rho. Republican. Conglist. Clubs: Algonquin (Boston); Commonwealth (San Francisco); Cornell (N.Y.C.). Co-author: Workbook in Geography of California, 1921. Editor: America's Message, 1924. Home: 28 Sunset Dr., Berkeley 7, Cal. Died June 8, 1959; buried Sunset View Cemetery, Berkeley, Cal.

RICE, Grantland, author; b. Murfreesboro, Tenn., Nov. 1, 1880; s. Bolling H. and Beulah (Grantland) R.; prep. edn., Nashville Mil. Acad. and Wallace U.

Sch., Nashville, Tenn.; B.A., Vanderbilt U., 1901; m. Katharine Hollis, Apr. 11, 1906; 1 dau., Florence Davenport. Successively with Nashville News, 1901, Forester Magazine, 1901, Atlanta Journal, 1902-04, Cleveland News, 1905, Nashville Tennesseean, 1906-10, New York Mail, 1911-14, New York Tribune (now Herald-Tribune), 1914-30; "The Sportlight" (column) syndicated since March 1930; pres. Grantland Rice Sportlights, Inc. (moving pictures). Served as 1st lt. 115th Regt. F.A., 30th Div., U.S. Army, with A.E.F., in France, 1918-19. Mem. Phi Beta Kappa, Phi Delta Theta, Berzilius. Democrat. Presbyterian. Clubs: Players, Coffee House, Dutch Treat, National Golf Links, Maidstone Golf. Author: Songs of the Stalwart, 1917; Sportlights of 1923, 1924; Songs of the Open, 1924; Only the Brave, 1941. Home: 1158 Fifth Av., N.Y.C. Died July 13, 1954; buried Woodlawn Cemetery, N.Y.

RICE, Greek Lent, lawyer; b. Cascilla, Miss., May 18, 1886; s. Lent Irvin and Ann (Pressgrove) R.; B.S., Miss. Coll., Clinton, 1908; law study Cumberland U., 1910-11. Admitted to Miss. bar, 1911, began practice at Charleston; atty. in office of alien property custodian, Washington, 1918-19; mem. Miss. Ho. of Reps., 1920; judge circuit Ct., 17th Miss. Dist., 1921-31; atty. gen. of Miss., 1932-—. Mem. Sigma Alpha Epsilon. Democrat. Baptist. Mason, Odd Fellow. Home: 728 Pinehurst St. Office: State Capitol, Jackson, Miss. Died Feb. 21, 1950; buried Masonic Cemetery, Charleston, Miss.

RICE, Harry Lee, shoe mfr.; b. Hudson, Mass., July 28, 1862; s. William Ball and Emma Louise (Cunningham) R.; grad. English High Sch., Boston, 1881; m. Fannie Austin Manson, June 2, 1900; children—William Ball, Benjamin Manson, Edmund. Began in shoe mfg. business with Rice & Hutchins, 1881, became pres., 1909; director Pantex Mfg. Corp., Universal Winding Co., Liberty Mut. Ins. Co. Unitarian. Clubs: Algonquin, Mergantic Fish and Game, Neighborhood (Quincy, Mass.). Home: Farm St., Dover, Mass. Address: 10 High St., Boston. Died Mar. 4, 1951.

RICE, Heber Holbrook, lawyer; b. Paintsville, Ky., Dec. 21, 1882; s. Harvey Burns and Mary Louisa (Hurt) R.; B.S. U. Ky., 1904, LL.D., 1956; LL.B., Harvard, 1907; LL.D., Athens Coll., 1944; m. Ruth Straughan, Sept. 6, 1917; children—Heber H., Jr., Craig Shelby. Admitted to Ky. State bar 1907, W. Va., 1908, Tenn., 1919, D.C. 1922, Ct. of Claims, 1923, U.S. Supreme Ct., 1928; practiced law Huntington, W.Va., 1908-16; asst. pros. attorney, Cabell County, 1909-11; counsel for gov. in martial law litigation, 1914-15; atty. Old Hickory Powder Plant, Nashville, 1919-21; atty., later spl. asst. to U.S. Atty. Gen., Washington, D.C., 1921-34; also spl. asst. to U.S. atty., D.C., 1922-23; atty., later head atty. H.O.L.C., Washington, 1934-44, supervising 150,000 land law suits and proceedings in all 48 states; on gen. counsel staff, comptroller gen. Office, Washington, D.C., 1944-52; exec. director Federal Bar Assn., 1952-53; pvt. practice law 1952-—; director various organizations. Served as maj. comdg. bn., U.S. Army, Mex. Border Service, World War I, 1916-18; lt. col., judge advocate gen. Dept. Reserve, War Dept., World War II, 1940-43; asst. chief legal div., Office Chief Chem. Warfare, Washington, D.C., 1942; staff judge advocate and chief of legal div., Huntsville (Ala.) Arsenal, 1942-43; inactive status since Dec. 1943, promoted to col. Inactive Res., 1945. Mem. Am. Bar Assn. (former chmn. com. on pvt. claims, and of com. on comparative land laws, mem. ho. dels., rep. Fed. Bar Assn. 1948), Columbia and Montgomery historical societies, Inter-American Bar Association (delegate to Havana conf., 1941), Fed. Bar Assn. (chmn. of admissions com., member nat. council, pres. 1940-41, former chmn. membership, speakers, keymen, reception Coms., recipient meritorious service award, 1952), Am. Trade Assn. Execs., U.N. League of Lawyers (hon. pres. original sec. gen., 1946, del. to Paris Conf., 1948), U. of Ky. Alumni Assn., W. Va. Soc. of D.C. (pres. 1938-40). Judge Advocates Assn. (chmn. Harvard Law Class Reunion, 1947, 57), Conference of State Societies (pres. 1953-54), Ky. and Md. State Societies, Am. Legion (past comdr.), Mil. Order World Wars, Res. Officers Assn., Sigma Alpha Epsilon. Meth. Mason (Shriner). Clubs: Post Mortem, Sertoma, Harvard. Author: Collected Speeches, 1947; U.S. Land Law Procedural Map; Thirty Years in the Nations Capital, 1957; articles: Behind the Iron Curtain, etc. Contbr. to law jours. Home: 3807 Taylor St., Chevy Chase, Washington 15. Deceased.

RICE, Lloyd Preston, economist; born at Granby, Conn., Feb. 3, 1889; s. Edward Preston and Lilian Vesta (Colton) R.; student Mount Hermon Sch., 1905-09; A.B., Wesleyan U., 1913; A.M., Harvard, 1914, Ph.D., 1920; (hon.) A.M., Dartmouth, 1934; m. Gertrude Brown Judd, Aug. 27, 1921; children—Stanley Lloyd, and Marjorie Bird (now Mrs. Alden E. Fallows). Engaged as an instructor of economics, Tufts Coll., 1916-17; instr. economics, Wesleyan U., 1917-19, asso. prof., 1919-20; asst. prof. economics, Dartmouth, 1920-34, prof. economics 1934-—, emeritus, 1956; mem. economics div. Federal Farm Bd. summers 1930-31; chief economic analyst U.S. Tariff Commn., 1934-35; chmn. of fats and oils com. under Trade Agreements Program, 1935; chief economic analyst U.S. Dept. State, Office of Philippine Affairs, 1937; financial adviser to Joint Prep. Com. on Philippine Affairs, 1937; financial adviser to Philippine Govt., 1938-40. Member Finance Committee, Hanover, N.H., 1932-37, and 1941-47 (chmn. 1941-47). Mem. Am. Econ. Assn., Am. Acad. Polit. and Social Science, Nat. Tax Assn., Tax Institute, Delta Tau Delta, Delta Sigma Rho, Phi Beta Kappa. Republican. Congregationalist. Co-author: Report of the Tax Commission of the Philippines on National Internal Revenue Laws, 1939; author of Financing Social Security by Means of Payroll Taxes, in Tax Policy League Symposium "How Shall Business Be Taxed," 1937; also other articles on taxation. Home: 4 Webster Terrace, Wilmot Center, N.H. Died May 10, 1958; buried Granby, Conn.

RICE, Paul Harper, mfg. exec.; b. Delphi, Ind., Oct. 23, 1893; s. Harris G. and Rilla (Hays) R.; A.B., Coll. of Wooster, 1916; LL.B., Western Res. U., 1921; m. Marion E. Downer, Sept. 30, 1927; children—Jean E. (Mrs. J. L. D. Hilton), Margaret D. With White Motor Co., Cleve., 1921-—, charge legal dept., 1949-—, asst. sec., 1923-49, sec., 1949-—, dir., 1956-—; dir. White Motor Co. Can., Ltd.; dir., sec. Autocar Sales & Service Co. Trustee, clk., treas. East Cleveland Pub. Library. Served with air force, U.S. Army, 1917-18. Mem. Ohio, Cleve. chambers commerce, Phi Alpha Delta. Presbyn. Mason (Shriner, K.T.), Rotarian. Home: 16157 Glynn Rd., East Cleveland 12, O. Office: 842 E. 79th St., Cleve. 1. Died Mar. 23, 1958.

RICE, Philip Blair, philosopher, editor; b. Martinsville, Ind., May 8, 1904; s. Franklin Aleston and Jean (Blair) R.; student U. Ill., 1921-22; A.B., Ind. U. 1925; B.A., Oxford (Rhodes Scholar, Balliol Coll., 1925-28), 1928, M.A., 1945; m. Kathryn Clark, Aug. 27, 1932; children—Elise, Evan. Instr., research fellow philosophy U. Cincinnati, 1930-37, asst. prof., 1937-38; asso. prof. Kenyon College, Gambier, O., 1938-44, prof. philosophy since 1944, chmn. dept. since 1938; spl. lectr. Columbia, 1944, 45. Fellow Kenyon Sch. English, 1948-50; fellow Ind. U. Sch. Letters since 1951; Guggenheim fellow, 1943-44; Rockefeller Found. grant for study in France, 1947; visiting prof. Sage Sch. philosophy Cornell University, spring 1952; Bollingen Found. grant, 1952-53. Newspaper man, Paris (France) Times, 1928-29, Cincinnati Times-Star, 1929-30. Mem. Am. Philosophical Association (president 1952-53), American Society for Aesthetics, Phi Beta Kappa, Phi Gamma Delta. Author: Value: A Co-operative Inquiry (editor R. Lepley), 1949; On the Knowledge of Good and Evil, 1955. Editor: Classic American Philosophers (with M. H. Fisch and others), 1951. Contbr. Literary Opinion in America, 1937; The Philosophy of George Santayana, 1940; The Reorganization of Congress (U.S. Govt. Pub.), 1945; The Stature of Thomas Mann, 1947; The Kenyon Critics, 1951. Mng. editor Kenyon Rev., 1938-44, asso. editor since 1944, acting editor, 1949-50. Home: Amity Rd., Gambier, O. Died Jan. 25, 1956.

RICE, Richard Ashley, educator, author; b. Burlington, Vt., Jan. 29, 1878; s. Richard Austin and Marion Ashley (Foster) R.; grad. Lawrenceville (N.J.) Sch., 1896; B.A., Williams, 1899; M.A., Harvard, 1903; studied Sorbonne, Paris, 1906; m. Anne Mary Dye, June 22, 1916; children—Richard Ashley, Marianne; m. 2d, Jean D. Macdonald, Sept. 21, 1933; m. 3d, Frona Brooks Hughes, July 11, 1951. Asst. master at Lawrenceville Sch., 1899-1900; instr. in English and law, U.S. Naval Acad., 1903-06; asst. in English, Harvard, 1907-09; asst. prof. English, Ind. U., 1909-14, asso. prof., 1914-16; prof. English lit. Smith Coll., 1916-46, prof. emeritus, 1946-—; vis. prof. English Wesleyan U., 1946-47. Mem. English Assn., Kappa Alpha, Phi Beta Kappa (hon.). Conglist. Author: College and the Future, 1915; Robert Louis Stevenson—How to Know Him, 1916; A Book of Narratives, 1917; Studies of Wordsworth and Byron, 1924; Rousseau and the Poetry of Nature, 1925; The Best of Byron, 1933, new edit., 1941. Home: 47 Dryads Green, Northampton, Mass. Died Aug. 6, 1955.

RICE, Stephen Ewing, judge; b. Apalachicola, Fla., July 23, 1905; s. Stephen Ewing and Carolyn (Floyd) R.; B.S., U.S. Naval Acad., 1922-26; LL.B., Columbia U., 1931; m. Lida Carolyn Johns, Dec. 26, 1936; children—Stephen Ewing, Jeffrey Bourke. Admitted to N.Y. bar, 1932; asst. legislative counsel United States Senate, 1933-42, legislative counsel 1945-50; judge U.S. Tax Court, Washington, since October 1950. Served as ensign, U.S. Navy, 1926-28; asst. air officer, U.S.S. Lexington, Pacific, wounded in action off Manila, 1944, ret. as capt. USNR. Mem. bar U.S. Supreme Ct. and Dist. of Columbia. Awarded Bronze star, Purple Heart, Presidential Unit Citation with bronze star, Am. Theatre and Asiatic Pacific Campaign medals with 9 combat stars, Philippine Liberation and Victory medals. Club: Army-Navy Country, (Arlington, Va.). Home: Holly Ridge, R.F. D. 1, Oakton, Va. Office: 12th and Constitution Av. N.W., Washington. Died Feb. 1958.

RICE, Thurman Brooks, bacteriology, public health; b. Landess, Ind., Aug. 17, 1888; s. Robert Tilton and Ruth (Porter) R.; B.S., Marion (Ind.) Normal Coll., 1909; B.Pd., Valparaiso U., 1912; A.B., Muncie (Ind.) Normal Inst., 1913; A.B., Ind. U., 1914, A.M., 1917, M.D., 1921; m. Ada Charles, Sept. 1, 1910 (died Feb. 13, 1922); 1 dau., Aïda Louise; m. 2d, Ruby Orene Caster, Mar. 29, 1923; children—Robert Caster, Thurman Brooks, James Abel, Reed Porter. Teacher pub. schs., Huntington County, Ind., 1906-08; teacher high sch., Wheeler, Ind., 1910-12; instr. in biology, Winona Coll., 1914-16; instr. in pathology, Ind. U., 1921-24; dir. lab., Ind. State Bd. of Health, 1924-26; prof. bacteriology and pub. health, Ind. U., 1926-46, prof. public health, chmn. Dept. Pub. Health, since 1946; asst. dir. Ind. Div. of Pub. Health, 1933-36; chief div. of health and phys. edn., Ind. State Bd. of Health and Ind. State Bd. of Edn., 1936-42; State Health Commn. and sec. Indiana State Bd. of Health, 1942-45; cons. on Pub. Health, Ind. State Bd. Health, since 1945. Served as pvt., S.A.T.C., World War I. Recipient of Gold Medal award, Am. Cancer Soc., 1949. Fellow Am. Med. Assn.; mem. Am. Public Health Assn., Ind. Assn. Clin. Pathologists, Ind. State Med. Assn., Ind. Assn. of the History of Medicine, Ind. Hist. Soc., Ind. Cancer Soc. (pres.), Phi Beta Kappa, Nu Sigma Nu, Alpha Omega Alpha, Sigma Xi. Awarded Ravdin medal, Ind. University Sch. of Medicine, 1921; member White House Conf. on Rural Edn., Oct. 1944. Democrat. Presbyn. Clubs: Professional Men's Forum, Ind. University Club, Indianapolis Literary, Schoolmasters. Author: The Conquest of Disease, 1927; Racial Hygiene, 1929; Applied Bacteriology, 1932; Sex Education, 1933; Textbook of Bacteriology (medical), 1935, 4th edit., 1947; The Human Body, 1936; The Hoosier Health Officer (a biography of John N. Hurty; Serial), 1939-46; Living, 1940. Co-author: Adventures in Health Series for Common Schools, 1936; Public Safety, 1937; Microbiology and Pathology, 1942; Sex, Marriage and Family, 1946; March Against Cancer, 1946; Effects of Alcohol, Tobacco and Habitforming Drugs, 1949; "The Salt Free" or Low Sodium Diet, 1951; The Story of the Medical Campus, Ind. Univ. Sch. of Med., 1949. Editor, Indiana State Bd. of Health Bulletin. Contributor to Hygeia, Jour. Outdoor Life, etc. Lecturer on sex edn. preparation for marriage and public and personal health. Research on vital statistics, therapeutic bacteriology, etc. Home: 3167 N. Delaware St., Indianapolis, Ind. Died Dec. 27, 1952; buried Crown Hill Cemetery, Indpls.

RICH, John Lyon, educator; born at Hobart, Delaware County, N.Y., Dec. 1, 1884; s. Thomas and Marion Augusta (Lyon) R.; A.B., Cornell U., 1906, A.M., 1907, Ph.D., 1911; m. Genevieve Cynthia Potts, June 28, 1912 (dec.); children—Ralph Albert, Catherine Louise (Mrs. Donald Salisbury Getchell); m. 2d, Nellie Okla Barrett, Apr. 22, 1922. Instr. in geology, Cornell U., 1908-09; instr. and asso. in geography, U. of Ill., 1911-18; petroleum geologist with oil cos., 1919-22; cons. petroleum geologist, 1922-31; successively asst. prof., asso. prof. and prof. of economic geology, U. Cincinnati, from 1931, later research prof. of geology, now emeritus professor; geologic aid, U.S. Geol. Survey, part time, 1907-10, 1917; asst. geologist, Ill. Geol. Survey, part time, 1914-17, N.Y. Geol. Survey, part time, 1916, 17, 19, technical cons., Petroleum Adminstrn. for War; mem. Am. War Prodn. Mission to China, Apr.-June 1945. Member Ohio Natural Resources Commn., 1952-—. Vice pres., chmn. Sect. E (geol. and geog.), Am. Assn. Advancement Sci., 1946. Editor Bull. of Am. Assn. Petroleum Geologists, 1926-29. Capt. Mil. Intelligence Div., U.S. Army, 1918-19. Mem. Geol. Soc. Am. (mem. publ. com.). Am. Inst. of Mining and Metall. Engrs., Soc. Economic Geologists, Assn. Am. Geographers, Geophys. Union, Am. Geog. Soc., American Association of Petroleum Geologists, Ohio Acad. Sci., Gamma Alpha, Sigma Xi, Sigma Gamma Epsilon. Author: Glacial Geology of the Catskill Mountains, 1935; The Face of South America; an Aerial Traverse, 1942; and numerous papers in scientific jours. Home: 848 Dunore Rd., Cin. 20. Died May 21, 1956; buried Hobart, N.Y.

RICH, Raymond Thomas, public relations consultant; b. Hyde Park, Mass., May 13, 1899; s. Willis Doane and Mary Louise (Babb) R.; grad. Phillips Acad., Andover, Mass., 1917; Amherst, 1917-19; A.B., Brown U., 1922; m. September 4, 1929 (div. 1928); 1 daughter, Eleanor; m. 2d, Wilmer Shields, May 19, 1944. Sec. German student dept. of European Student Relief, 1922-23, acting exec. sec. at Geneva hdqrs., 1923; eastern dir., Am. Student Friendship Fund, 1923-24; instr. in contemporary history, Canton (China) Christian Coll. (now Lingnan U.), 1924-25; nat. field sec. Foreign Policy Assn. (also Far Eastern specialist, 1925-26), 1925-27; dir. World Peace Found. 1927-36; chmn. Raymond Rich Associates, counselors on pub. relations, mgmt. and financial promotion for pub. interest organizations and foundations since 1936 (direction transferred to wartime trustees, 1942, activities temporarily suspended, 1943, resumed 1946); chief Div. Organized Groups, Office Facts and Figures 1942; prin. civilian mobilization adviser, U.S. Office Civilian Defense, 1942-43; with Office Coordinator Inter-Am. Affairs, 1942-44; as dir. Inter-Am. Centers in

U.S.; asso. dir. dept. U.S. activities and spl. services; director Council for Inter-Am. Cooperation, Inc., 1944-46; pub. affairs asso. for Twentieth Century Fund, 1936-40; spl. cons. to Am. Council on Education, Am. Law Inst., Am. Youth Commn. of Am. Council on Edn., Lab. of Anthropology, Nat. Conf. of Christians and Jews, Colonial Williamsburg, Common Council for Am. Unity, Nat. Information Bur., Westchester County Dept. Health, Chgo. Inst. for Psychoanalysis, Am. Med. Assn., Joint Structure Com. of Am. Nurses Assn., Assn. Collegiate Schs. of Nursing, Am. Assn. Indsl. Nurses, Nat. Assn. Colored Grad. Nurses, Nat. League Nursing Edn., Nat. Orgn. for Pub. Health Nursing; cons. to Med. Soc. State of Pa., Colo. State Med. Soc., Am. Diabetes Assn., Colo. Sch. of Mines, Nat. Health Council, Council for Survey of the Legal Profession, Menninger Found., Urban League, Permanente Hosps., Lingnan U. (China), St. Francis Xavier U. (N.S.), Am. Pub. Health Assn., Alton Ochsner Found., Am. Pub. Welfare Assn., Am. Acad. Orthopedic Surgeons, Antioch Coll., English Speaking Union. Mem. Pub. Relations Soc. Am., U.S. Children's Bur. (adv. com. maternal and child health and crippled children's services). Mem. Council on Fgn. Relations, Am. Legion, Phi Beta Kappa, Delta Upsilon. Conglist. Clubs: Cosmos (Washington). Author: Extra-territoriality and Tariff Autonomy in China, 1925 (with Denys P. Myers) Syllabus for Study of Implementation of the Pact of Paris, 1931. Editor World Affairs Books, 1936-37. Pub. periodic editions of American Foundations and Their Fields, since 1938 and American Found. News 1949—; sponsor Am. Foundations Information Service, 1952-56, dir. 1956-59. Author: Am. Foundation's Activities for United States Information Agency. 1959. Address: 510 E. 58th St., N.Y.C. 25. Died July 15, 1959; buried Woodlawn Cemetery, Everett, Mass.

RICH, Ronald Emil, univ. prof.; b. Mishawaka, Ind., Jan. 4, 1907; s. Daniel Mario and Inez (Ferrettie) R.; B.S., U. of Notre Dame, 1928, M.S., 1936; student, U. of Wis., 1935; m. Lucille Cecilia Bickel, Sept. 30, 1930; children—Daniel Thomas, Mary Virginia, Joseph Ronald. Chem. engr. Gen. Chem. Co., 1928-29, asst. foreman, sulphuric acid mfg., 1929-30, plant engr., 1930-31; instr. chem. engring., U. of Notre Dame, 1931-36, asst. prof., 1936-39, asso. prof., 1939-44, prof. 1944—, asst. head dept. chem. engring., 1939-42, head 1942—; mem. faculty bd. in control athletics, 1942-51; consultant in heat transfer and distillation processes 1940—, process and equipment design 1950—. Registered profl. engr. Mem. Am. Inst. Chem. Engrs., Am. Chem. Soc., Am. Soc. Engring. Edn., Am. Assn. Univ. Profs., Ind. Chem. Soc., Ind. Acad. Sci. Kappa Phi. Club: Engineers of the St. Joseph Valley. Home: 1146 East South St., South Bend 15. Office: P.O. Box 1374, Notre Dame, Ind. Died Nov. 25, 1959.

RICH, Williston C., business exec.; b. Red Wing, Minn., Feb. 9, 1882; s. John H. and Julia Wilder (Williston) R.; grad. Shattuck Sch., Faribault, Minn., 1901; student Mass. Inst. Tech., 1905; m. Sophia H. Rich, Dec. 29, 1906; children—Williston C., Barbara R. (Mrs. L. W. Dietrick), Julianne R. (Mrs. R. H. White. With Minneapolis Steel & Machinery Co. and its successor, Minneapolis-Moline Co. since 1905, sec. since 1940. Mem. Delta Tau Delta. Mason (K.T.). Club: Minneapolis Athletic. Home: 1921 James Av. S., Minneapolis 5. Office: P.O. Box 1050, Minneapolis 1. Died July 16, 1952.

RICHARD, Harold Charles, banker; b. New York, N.Y., Oct. 13, 1884; s. Oscar L. and Alice (Littauer) R.; A.B., Princeton, 1906; m. Vera Lanman Van Buren, Jan. 21, 1914; children—Harold Van Buren, Trumbull, Phyllis (Mrs. Joe W. Gerrity, Jr.), Vera (Mrs. Valentine Wood). In banking business, N.Y. City, 1907—; pres. and chmn. bd., State Bank & Trust Co., 1919-29; chmn. bd. General Bronze Corporation, 1936-45; dir. and mem. trust committee Manufacturers Trust Co.; chmn. bd. Hartford Electric Steel Corp., Walter P. Jacob Industries, Inc.; dir. The Murray Corp. Am. (Detroit), Midland Steel Products Co. (Cleveland), Pell, Ltd., United States Vitamin Corporation, U.S. Vitamin Exports Corp., Fidel. Assn. of N.Y., Inc., Vorac Co., 1060 Fifth Av. Corp. Pres., director Richard Found.; trustee Clinton Hall Assos., York (Maine) Hospital, Mercantile Library Association. Clubs: Manhattan, Princeton, Bankers', New York Athletic, Whist., Church, Metropolitan Opera, Madison Square Garden, Pine Valley Golf, Creek, Turf and Field, Regency, Agamenticus Yacht Club, York Country Club; Metropolitan (Washington); Travelers', St. Cloud Country (Paris). Home: York Harbor, Me.; and 1060 Fifth Av., N.Y.C, Office: 681 8th Av., N.Y.C. 18. Died July 28, 1958; buried York, Me.

RICHARDS, Cyril Fuller, college dean; b. Dunedin, New Zealand, Nov. 15, 1894; s. Edward and Mary (Pannett) R.; came to U.S., 1905, naturalized 1920; B.S., Linfield Coll., McMinnville, Ore., 1918; B.D., Colgate-Rochester (N.Y.) Theol. Sem., 1924; A.M., Univ. of Manitoba, 1935; honorary L.H.D., Linfield College, 1947; married Alice Louise Wood, May 23, 1920; 1 dau., Margaret (dec.). Instr. of biology, Linfield Coll., 1918-21; prof. of philosophy, Brandon Coll., Manitoba, Can., 1924-37, coll. dean, 1935-37; dean of men Denison Univ., Granville, O., 1937-43. Dean coll., 1943—, acting pres., 1950-51. V.p., dean, 1951—. Mem. A.A.A.S., Am. Conf. Academic Deans, Am. Psychol. Assn., Omicron Delta Kappa. Bapt. Mason. Author: Denison—A Small College Studies Its Program. Contbr. to ednl. periodicals. Home: 4 Sheppard Pl., Granville, O. Died Sept. 7, 1954; buried College Cemetery Denison U.

RICHARDS, Donald, singer, actor; b. New York, N.Y., March 24, 1919; s. Samuel and Mamie (Goldstein) Kornreich; pre-medical student Columbia, 1936-38; m. Skippy Kolby, Jan. 12, 1946. Radio singer, 1936-40; played juvenile singing lead, Why Not New?, Cherry Lane Theatre, 1937; sang leading roles in Pagliacci, Faust, with St. Louis Grand Opera Co., 1939, at Chase Hotel, St. Louis, 1940; toured with Streets of Paris, 1939; appeared in Folies Bergere, 1940, Count Me In, 1942, in night clubs, hotels, 1945-1946, Finian's Rainbow, 1947; baritone with New York City Center Opera Co., season 1947-48; singing star N.B.C.-TV "Sat. nite" Jack Carter Show. Served in U.S. Army Special Services, 1941-45, appeared as soloist with Winged Victory, Army Air Corps show. 1942-43. Office: care Actors' Equity, N.Y. City. Died Sept. 26, 1953.

RICHARDS, Edward A., banker; b. Bklyn.; LL. B., N.Y.U.; m. Rosina Jane Smith; children—Roger E., Mrs. Caryl E. Kiendl. Admitted N.Y. bar, 1900; judge Municipal Court, 1907-19; pres. East N.Y. Savs. Bank, 1919—; pres. Concord Freeholders, Inc. Dir. Bklyn.-Queens YMCA, 40 yrs.; mem. bd. Highland Park br. YMCA, 1909—, chmn. bd. 1914—; active Boy Scouts Am. Recipient gold medal Downtown Bklyn. Assn., 1956. Mem. Nat. Assn. Mutual Savs. Banks (pres. 1925-26), Savs. Bank Assn. N.Y. (chmn. housing com.), Bklyn. C. of C. (dir. 25 yrs.). Protestant Episcopalian. Address: 50 Bow St., Forest Hills, Queens, N.Y. Died Oct. 14, 1956.

RICHARDS, George Franklin, church exec.; b. Farmington, Utah, Feb. 23, 1861; s. Franklin Dewey and Nanny (Longstroth) R.; grad. in English lang. and lit., U. Deseret (now U. Utah), 1881 (first degrees issued by U. Utah in 1886); m. Alice Almira Robinson, Mar. 9, 1882 (died Apr. 21, 1946); children—George Franklin, Jr., Alice Minerva (Mrs. George L. Tate), LeGrand, Joe, Sarah Ellen (Mrs. Hugh J. Cannon), Amy May (dec.), Ruby (Mrs. Gerald S. Brown, dec.), Lucena (Mrs. Orson Rega Card), Mamie (Mrs. Clarence W. Silver), Alverda (dec.), Nina (Mrs. F. Orin Woodbury), Edna Moselle (Mrs. Lewis J. Wallace), Oliver L., Estella (Mrs. Spencer C. Taylor), Ray L.; m. 2d, Betsy Hollings, July 20, 1947. Farmer near Tooele, Utah, 1883-1906; merchant under name of Richards Implement and Machinery Co., Tooele, 1890-1906; dir. Heber J. Grant & Co., Ins. Apostle, Ch. of Jesus Christ of Latter-day Saints, Salt Lake City, 1906—. Pres. European mission, Liverpool, Eng., 1916-19; pres. Salt Lake Latter-day Saints Temple, 1921-37; pres. Council of Twelve Apostles, 1945—, supr. of Temples 1937—. Mem. Utah State Legislature, 1898-99; treas. Tooele County about 1897; chmn. Tooele sch. bd., 1893. Home: 29 S. State St. Office: L.D.S. Church Offices, 47 E. So. Temple St., Salt Lake City 1. Died Aug. 8, 1950.

RICHARDS, George Gill, physician; b. Mendon, Utah, Sept. 5, 1883; s. Dr. Stephen L. and Emma Louise (Stayner) R.; student U. of Utah, 1898-1902, U. of Chgo., 1903-04; M.D., N.Y. U., Bellevue Hosp. Med. Sch., 1906; grad. work, Vienna, 1910-13; engaged in practice as physician, 1906—; clin. prof. internal medicine U. of Utah, 1942—. Served as capt. M.C., U.S. Army Reserve, 1918-34. Mem. med. adv. bd. Selective Service 1940—. Lt. col. USPHS. Mem. Am. Bd. Internal Medicine, 1936-46. Fellow Am. Coll. Physicians (gov. 1924-34; regent 1934-37; v.p. 1937-38); mem. A.M.A. (chmn. med. sect. 1932), Salt Lake County, Utah State med. assns., Salt Lake Clinic, Interurban Club of Pacific Coast. Clubs: Salt Lake Country, Rotary, Alta (Salt Lake City). Home: 360 A St., Salt Lake 3. Office: 115 East South Temple, Salt Lake City. Died Apr. 20, 1950; buried Salt Lake City Cemetery.

RICHARDS, George Handyside, corp. exec.; born Edinburgh, Scotland, Mar. 10, 1901; s. Charles and Margaret Pollock (Handyside) R.; student Edinburgh Univ.; m. Marjorie Beaumont, Apr. 8, 1933; children—Jean Marjorie, Margaret Elizabeth, Barbara Ann Chartered accountant, Great Britain; pub. accountant, New York; v.p. Celluloid Corp., Newark, N.J.; v.p., dir. Celanese Corp. of Am. to 1956, senior vice pres., dir., 1956—; v.p., dir. Petrocel Corp., Celatino, S.A.; director Celanese Columbiana, S.A., Celanese Venezolana, S.A.; dir. Canadian Chem. Co., Ltd., Celgar Company, Limited, Columbia Cellulose Company, Limited, Celanese Mexicana, S.A., Can. Chem. & Cellulose Co., Ltd. Rep. Presbyn. Clubs: Union League (N.Y.C.); Upper Montclair Country, American (Mexico); Mount Royal, St. James (Montreal); Pinnacle (N.Y.C.). Home: 206 Upper Mountain Av., Montclair, N.J. Office: 180 Madison Av., N.Y.C. Died Oct. 26, 1958; buried Emily F. French Meml. Cemetery, Shelter Island, N.Y.

RICHARDS, George Warren, clergyman; b. Farmington, Berks County, Pa., Apr. 26, 1869; s. Milton S. and Louisa (Fritch) R.; A.B., Franklin and Marshall Coll., 1887, A.M., 1890, D.D., 1902; studied at univs. of Berlin and Erlangen; D.Th., Heidelberg U., Germany, 1925; D.D., Edinburgh U., 1933; m. Mary A. Mosser, Nov. 19, 1890. Ordained ministry Ref. Ch. in U.S., 1890; pastor Salem Ref. Ch., Allentown, Pa., 1890-99; prof. ch. history, 1899—, pres. Theol. Sem. of Ref. Ch. in U.S., Lancaster, Pa.; travel and study in Europe, 1890, 99, 1904, 09; lecturer Bibl. Sem., New York, 1932-33; visiting prof. theology, Temple U., Phila., 1935-37. Pres., mem. exec. com. Alliance Ref. Chs. holding Presbyn. System (Western sect.); formerly pres. Alliance of Ref. Chs. holding Presbyn. Systems throughout the World; former sec. of Com. of Conf. of Theol. Schs. of U.S. and Can.; vice-president of American section of Continuation Committee of World Conference on Faith and Order; ex-pres. Am. Soc. Ch. History, Gen. Synod of Ref. Ch. in U.S.; pres. Gen. Synod Evang. and Reformed Church; v.p. and pres. Evangelical and Reformed Church, now president emeritus; vice-pres. Federal Council Chs. of Christ in America, 1934-36. Mem. Am. Theol. Soc. (ex-pres.), Cliosophic Soc. of Lancaster; vice-pres. continuation com., Edinburgh Conf. on Faith and Order, 1937; chmn. Am. Theol. Com. on Faith and Order; Sprunt lecturer, Union Theol. Sem., Richmond, Va., 1938; lecturer Internat. Theol. Sem., Geneva, Switzerland, 1938; lecturer, Temple School of Theology, 1944-48, Union Theol. Sem., N.Y., 1946, Ursinus College, 1946; vice chairman World Conference on Faith and Order (continuation com.), United States and Can.; chmn. theol. com. Faith and Order, U.S. and Can.; mem. Nat. Preaching Mission Fed. Council, 1942-47. Del. Evangelical Reformed Church to World Council of Chs., Amsterdam, 1948. Clubs: University (Phila.); City (New York). Author: Historical and Doctrinal Studies on the Heidelberg Catechism; Christian Ways of Salvation; Reformed, What?; Beyond Fundamentalism and Modernism?; Creative Controversies in Christianity, 1938; also various pamphlets on ch. history. Translator of sermons from the German into English, under title of "Come, Creator Spirit," and "God's Search for Man." Home: Lancaster, Pa. Died June 11, 1955; buried Greenwood Cemetery, Lancaster.

RICHARDS, James L., financier; b. E. Longmeadow, Mass., Jan. 8, 1858; s. R. P. and Sarah E. R.; educated public schools, Longmeadow and Springfield, Mass.; married to Cora E. Towne, Feb. 7, 1882 (deceased, 1951). Chairman of the board, director and mem. exec. com., Boston Consol. Gas Co.; dir. and chmn. bd., Middlesex & Boston St. Ry. Co.; pres. and trustee, Suburban Electric Securities Co.; dir. and chmn. exec. and finance coms., Mass. Bonding & Ins. Co.; dir. and mem. exec. com., Am. Sugar Refining Co., Mchts. Nat. Bank, United-Rexall Drug Co.; dir. Boston Wharf Co., Newton Hosp.; trustee Northeastern University, Boston; trustee Wesleyan U., Middletown, Conn. Unitarian. Clubs: Union (Boston); Pocassett Golf. Eastern Yacht. Home: 47 Kirkstall Rd., Newtonville, Mass. Office: 250 Stuart St., Boston. Died Jan. 2, 1955.

RICHARDS, Paul William, lawyer; b. Red Oak, Ia., Mar. 16, 1874; s. Charles Emery and Mary Louise (Mills) R.; A.B., Grinnell, 1894; LL.D., 1939; m. Stella E. Powell, Nov. 19, 1906; children—Paul William (dec.), Jonathan Barlow. Admitted to Ia. bar, practicing atty., 1896—; county atty. Montgomery County, 1919, and referee in bankruptcy Western Div., Southern Dist. of Ia., 1923; justice of the Supreme Ct. of Ia., 1935-41; referee on Nat. R.R. Adjustment Bd., 1941, 43; now in practice of law. Hon. sergeant of Coif, 1937. Democrat. Elk. Home: Red Oak, Ia. Died Dec. 27, 1956; buried Red Oak, Ia.

RICHARDS, Preston, govt. ofcl.; b. Chariton Co., Mo., Nov. 23, 1905; s. William D. and Lula Belle (Hampton) R.; B.S. in agr., U. Mo., 1927, A.M., 1929. Livestock economist Bur. Agrl. Economics, U.S. Dept. Agr., 1930-41, livestock br., 1941-42, dep. dir., 1946-50, dir. dairy br. Prodn. Marketing Adminstrn. 1950-53, asst. adminstr. commodity operations, 1953; now dep. adminstr. Commodity Stablzn. Service. Served as maj., Q.M.C., U.S. Army, 1942-45. Home: 3130 Wisconsin Av. N.W., Washington 16. Office: Adminstration Bldg. Agr., Washington 25. Died Aug. 26, 1957.

RICHARDS, Ray, newspaperman; b. Minot, N.D., May 18, 1894; son Frederick Edward and Sarah (Young) R.; ed. pub. schools, Wentworth Military Academy, Lexington, Missouri, and Okla. Agriculture and Mechanical College, Stillwater, Oklahoma; married 2d Frances Spatz, June 17, 1948; 1 daughter (by previous marriage), Dejon Jean. Reporter, Tulsa (Oklahoma) Daily World, 1910; later became reporter, feature writer and editor on various newspapers until 1926; with Honolulu Star-Bulletin, 1926-30; with Tokyo (Japan) Advertiser, Shanghai (China) Sunday Post-Mercury, Shanghai (China) Press, also correspondent for London Daily Express and various Am. newspapers, covering successive stages of Japanese occupation of Manchuria and China, 1930-40;

with Los Angeles (Calif.) Examiner, 1941-42; became Washington (D.C.) corr. for Hearst Newspapers, 1942; returned to Far East, 1947-48, covering Communist polit. and mil. conflicts of China, Manchuria and Korea. Club: National Press (Washington). Address: 607 Times-Herald Bldg., Washington. Died July 10, 1950.

RICHARDS, Robert Haven, lawyer; b. Georgetown, Del., Nov. 15, 1873; s. Charles Fleming and Mary Catherine (Sudler) R.; prep. edn., Dickinson Prep. School; B.A., Dickinson College, Carlisle, Pa., 1895, LL.D., 1923; LL.D., University of Delaware, 1947; married Lydia Newsham Haddock, June 26, 1901; children—Jane Rebecca (Mrs. William A. Worth), Charles Fleming, Robert Henry. Admitted to Delaware bar, 1897, and began practice of law at Georgetown; deputy attorney general of Delaware, 1901-05, atty. gen., 1905-09. Counsel State of Del. in original suit brought in Supreme Court of U.S., by State of N.J. vs. State of Del., 1905, to determine boundary between the two states, and mem. of commn. representing Del. to negotiate compact; dir. Wilmington Trust Co., Continental Am. Life Ins. Co., Electric Hose & Rubber Co. Trustee Dickinson Coll., U. of Del. Mem. Am., Del. and New Castle bar assns., Am. Soc. Polit. and Social Science, Am. and Del. hist. assns., Soc. Colonial Wars, S.A.R. (ex-pres. Del. Chapter), Phi Beta Kappa, Phi Kappa Sigma. Republican. Presbyterian. Clubs: Wilmington, Wilmington Country; Union League (Phila). Home: 2102 Park Drive. Office: du Pont Bldg., Wilmington 41, Del. Died Aug. 27, 1951; buried Wilmington Brandywine Cemetery, Wilmington.

RICHARDS, Samuel H., lawyer; b. Bridgeport, N.J.; s. Samuel and Sarah A. (Cheesman) R.; LL.B., Columbia U. Law Sch.; m. Harriet Torbert; children—Ruth (Mrs. J. Everett Magin), H. Jerome. Admitted to practice courts of N.J., Supreme Court of U.S. and other fed. courts; engaged in gen. practice of law, Camden, N.J.; mem. firm Richards, Capehart, & Wood. Served as member of New Jersey Commn. to Commemorate 300th Anniversary of Settlement by Swedes and Finns on the Delaware. As mem. Am. Bar Assn. attended meeting in Montreal and London; also various places in U.S.; served as v.p. for N.J. and regional v.p. for Pa., N.J., Del. Mem. N.J. and Camden bar assns., Selden Soc. Home: Haddonfield. Office: 217 N. 6th St., Camden, N.J. Died May 11, 1957; buried Harleigh Cemetery, Camden.

RICHARDS, Stephen L., church official; b. Mendon, Utah, June 18, 1879; s. Stephen Longstroth and Emma Louise (Stayner) R.; student U. of Utah, 1895-98, U. of Mich. Law Sch., 1902-03; LL.B., U. of Chicago, 1904; m. Irene Merrill, Feb. 21, 1900; children—Lynn Stephen, Irene Louise (Mrs. Stephen G. Covey), Lois Bathsheba (Mrs. Frederick R. Hinckley), Alice Leila (Mrs. J. Knight Allen), Helen Merle (dec.), Georgia Gill (Mrs. Ralph Harvard Olsen), Joseph Albert (dec.), Philip Longstroth, Richard Merrill. Admitted to Utah bar, 1904, and began practice at Salt Lake City; city atty. Murray, Utah, 1905-06; pres., gen. mgr. Wasatch Land & Improvement Co.; v.p., dir., exec. com. Granite Furniture Co.; v.p., dir., Zion's Securities Corp.; vice chairman, dir. Zions First Nat. Bank Zions Cooperative Mercantile Instn., Utah Idaho Sugar Co., Beneficial Life Ins. Co., Hotel Utah Co., Radio Service Corp. of Utah; dir., exec. com. Utah Power & Light Co.; member board of directors Utah Oil Refining Co. Trustee Brigham Young Univ. Member Council of 12 Apostles of Ch. of Jesus Christ of Latter-day Saints 1917-51; sustained as first counselor in the First Presidency of the Ch.; mem. Ch. Bd. of Edn. Former mem. Utah State Bd. Corrections; formerly sec. Utah State Bar Assn., and v.p. for Utah of Am. Bar Assn. Home: 105 E. South Temple. Office: 47 E. South Temple, Salt Lake City. Died May 19, 1959.

RICHARDSON, Clarence H., prof. mathematics; b. West Plains, Mo., July 21, 1890; s. Elias F. and Nannie H. (Hudson) R.; B.S., U. of Kentucky, 1913; M.S., U. of Illinois, 1918; Ph.D., U. of Michigan, 1927; m. Agnes Brownfield, Nov. 7, 1913; children—Lucile (dec.), C H, Robert Byron. Teacher, Marion (Ky.) High Sch., 1911-12 and 1913-14; instr. mathematics, U. of Ky., 1912-13; prof. mathematics, Columbia Coll. (Fla.), 1914-16; asst. in mathematics, U. of Ill., 1916-18; prof. mathematics, Georgetown Coll. (Ky.), 1918-28; prof. mathematics, Bucknell U., 1928—, chmn. dept. mathematics, 1928—. Mem. Math. Assn. of Am., Institute of Math. Statistics, Phi Beta Kappa, Phi Delta Kappa, Pi Mu Epsilon. Baptist. Democrat. Author: Statisical Analysis, 1934, rev. edit., 1944; Commercial Algebra (with Isaiah L. Miller), 1935; Financial Mathematics (with Isaiah L. Miller), 1935; Elementary Algebra, 1950; Intermediate Algebra, 1951; The Calculus of Finite Differences, 1954. Home: 401 South 6th St., Lewisburg, Pa. Died Mar. 13, 1955; buried Buffalo, Ky.

RICHARDSON, Dorothy, author; b. Prospect, Pa.; d. Dr. Newton M. and Ianthe Elmira (Sullivan) Richardson; unmarried. Began journalistic career Pitts. Dispatch, 1896; engaged in work on local newspapers and socialist propaganda, connected successively with The Social Democrat, Eugene V. Debs' organ of socialism, and The New Time Mag., Chgo., 1897-99; mem. staff N.Y. Herald, 1899-1909; gen. press representative for David Belasco, 1909—. Author: The Long Day, 1905; The Book of Blanche, 1924. Home: 148 Pymouth St., New Haven, Conn. Died Mar. 27, 1955.

RICHARDSON, Edward Elliott, educator; b. Rockingham, Vt., Feb. 19, 1873; s. Marshall Clark and Sarah Augusta (Stowell) R.; grad. Vt. Acad., Saxtons River, Vt., 1892 (1st honors mil. dept.); M.D., Columbia, 1895; B.S., George Washington U., 1904, M.Sc., 1905, Ph.D., 1907; corr. course Crozer Theol. Sem.; m. Grace Dell Potter, Oct. 6, 1896; children—Elizabeth Laura, Edward Marshall. Prosecutor to chair of anatomy, George Washington U., 1897-99, asst. demonstrator anatomy, 1898-1908, instr. philosophy, 1908-09, acting prof., 1912-14, prof. philosophy, 1914-38, prof. emeritus 1938—. Licensed ministry Bapt. Ch., 1911, ordained, 1913; pastor Congress Heights Ch., Washington, 1913—. Pres. Luther Rice Christian Coll., 1943—. Mem. Soc. for Philos. Inquiry (sec. 1905-10, pres. 1910—), Med. Soc. D.C., Am. Assn. U. Profs. Club: Graduate of George Washington U. (ex-pres.). Author: Problem of the Imperfect, 1908; Philosophy of Religion, 1928; Organic Idealism, 1932; Way of the Orient, 1935, numerous papers read before philos. socs. and articles in mags. and revs. Editor of Memoirs of Soc. for Philos. Inquiry, 1909; joint editor Memoirs of Soc. for Philos. Inquiry, series 1927; editor for 5th Series, 1939. Pres. of Bapt. Ministers Conf., Washington, 1922. Congress Hts. Citizens Assn., 1920; trustee Bapt. Bible Inst. of New Orleans, 1921-24; pres. Central Union Mission, Washington, 1911-24; world trip vis. mission stas. in the Orient, 1932-33. Mem. Citizens' Adv. Council (Washington), British Inst. of Philosophy, Southern Soc. of Philosophy and Psychology. Author: First Principles of Religion, 1941; Metaphysics of Evolution. Home: 3214 10th St., S.E., Washington 20. Died July 17, 1950; buried Cedar Hill Cemetery, Washington.

RICHARDSON, Edwin Sanders, educator; b. Minden, La., Aug. 31, 1875; s. James Sanders and Sally C. (Havis) R.; B.S., Peabody Coll., 1900; LL.D., Centenary Coll., 1936; m. Zenobia Longino, May 10, 1903; children—Leland, Ruth, Don L., Evelyn (Mrs. J. E. Mulhearn), Edwin Sanders. Began as tchr. 1898; tchr. La. State U., 1911-20; supt. schs., Webster Parish, La., 1921-36; pres. La. Poly. Inst., 1936—. Mem. exec. com. Ruston C. of C. Exec. sec. Webster Council, Minden, La., 1941-42; area rent dir. Office Price Adminstrn. 1942—. Mem. N.E.A., La. Teachers Assn. (pres. 1926), Nat. Assn. Sch. Adminstrn., Minden C. of C. Democrat. Baptist. Club: Lions. Home: Minden, La. Died Oct. 11, 1950.

RICHARDSON, George Adams, business exec.; b. Auburn, N.Y., Nov. 23, 1887; s. Frank Wood and Charlotte Letchworth (Adams) R.; grad. Groton Sch., 1906; A.B., Yale, 1910; m. Mrs. Anne Thompson Morse, Oct. 19, 1918; stepchildren—Samuel F.B. Morse, Jr., John B. Morse, Mrs. Kenneth S. Walker. Ranch hand, Durango, Mexico, 1911-14; with Armour & Co., Chgo., 1914-21, No. Trust Co., 1921, Estate of Marshall Field, 1921-27, trustee, 1927-43. asst. to Marshall Field, 1943—; v.p., dir. Field Enterprises, Inc.; owner The Inn at Rancho Santa Fe, Cal. Alderman, Lake Forest, 1923-27. Asst. dir. aviation div. Surplus War Property Adminstrn., 1944-45. Trustee Chgo. Mus. Natural History; pres. Chgo. Council Fgn. Relations, 2 terms. Served as capt. Battery C, 149th F.A.; maj. adj., 171st F.A. Brigade, World War I, subsequently lt col. 865th F.A., O.R.C.; lt. col. Air Transport Command, A.A.F., 1943-44. Mem. Alpha Delta Phi. Republican. Episcopalian. Clubs: Chicago, Attic (Chgo.); Old Elm (Lake Forest, Ill.); Kona Kai (San Diego, Cal.). Home: Rancho Santa Fe, Cal. Office: 135 S. La Salle St., Chgo. Died Apr. 15, 1958; buried Fort Rosecran Nat. Cemetery, San Diego, Cal.

RICHARDSON, Ira, educator; b. Three Springs, Hart County, Ky., Sept. 2, 1871; s. Sinclair Valentine and Narcissa Francis (Minton) R.; student Mo. State U., 1893-94; Ph.B., Central Coll., Fayette, Mo., 1897; A.M., Columbia, 1908; Master's Diploma in Edn., Teachers Coll. (Columbia), 1908; grad. student, Stanford; Dr. of Humanities, University of Colo., 1942; m. Mayme Perry, Nov. 29, 1899 (died 1926; m. 2d, Tessie M. Degan, Dec. 20, 1928 (died 1951). Tchr., rural schs., Mo., 1891-93; supt. schs., Shelbyville, Mo., 1897-1901, Shelbina, Mo., 1901-07; commr. pub. schs., Shelby County, Mo., 1898-1903; prof. edn., State Teachers Coll., Springfield Mo., 1908-11, also dir. practice teaching, 1910-11; head dept. of edn. and training, State Teachers Coll., Maryville, Mo., 1911-13, pres. Apr. 15, 1913-Sept. 1, 1921; prof. edn., U. of Wyo., summer 1922; asst. dir., extension div. and asso. prof. of edn., U. of Ore., 1922-23, summer 1923; prof. edn., State Teachers Coll., Greeley, Colo., 1924, and U. of Ore., summer 1924; prof. edn., Reed Coll., Portland, Ore., 1924-25; president Adams State College, Alamosa, Colo., 1925-50, now president emeritus, professor of philosophy since 1950. Mem. N.E.A., Mo. State Teachers' Assn. (pres. 1917), Colo. Edn. Assn., Soc. for Scientific Study of Edn., Sigma Nu, Phi Delta Kappa. Democrat. Mason (Shriner). Clubs: Rotary (gov. 7th Dist., 1932-33), Colo. Schoolmasters, Agora. Home: 103 Blanca Av., Alamosa, Colo. Died Oct. 6, 1958; buried Crown Hill Cemetery, Denver.

RICHARDSON, Lunsford, corp. exec.; b. Greensboro, N.C., Nov. 26, 1891; s. Lunsford and Mary Lynn (Smith) R.; ed. public schools and Davidson Coll. (N.C.); m. Margaret Blakeney, May 17, 1923; children—Lunsford, Mollie Smith, Bess Martin, Margaret Ball, Dora Laurinda. With Vick Chemical Co. since 1913, as salesman, sales promotion mgr., sales and advertising mgr., v.p. and asst. gen. mgr., pres., 1929-38, now chmn. bd.; dir. Nat. Reinsurance Corp. and Piedmont Financial Co. Served in Naval Aviation during World War. Presbyterian. Ind. Democrat. Former trustee Davidson Coll.; co-donor (with H. S. Richardson) of Richardson Field, Davidson Coll.; trustee and donor (with family) of the L. Richardson Memorial Hosp. (Greensboro, N.C.); trustee Round Hill Community Church (Conn.). Mem. Kappa Sigma, Omicron Delta Kappa. Clubs: Round Hill, Field (Greenwich, Conn.); Greensboro (N.C.) Country, Clouds, River Hills, Camp Fire. Home: Round Hill Rd., Greenwich, Conn. Office: 122 E. 42d St., N.Y. City. Died Aug. 9, 1953.

RICHARDSON, Sir Owen Willans, physicist; b. Dewsbury, Eng., Apr. 26, 1879; s. Joshua and Charlotte Maria (Willans) R.; B.A., U. of Cambridge, Eng., 1900, M.A., 1904; B.Sc., U. of London, 1900, D.Sc., 1903. Fellow of Trinity Coll., Cambridge, 1902-8; m. Lilian Maud Wilson, June 12, 1906. Prof. physics, Princeton, 1906-13; dir. research physics Kings Coll., 1924-44. Has made exptl. discoveries fundamental to electronic and kinetic theories of matter. Created Knight, 1939. Recipient of Nobel Prize, 1928. Author of numerous papers in Philos. Mag., Trans. Royal Soc., London, Phys. Review, etc. Fellow Royal Soc. London, Cambridge Philos. Soc., Phys. Soc. London; mem. Am. Philos. Soc., Am. Phys. Soc., Soc. Francaise de Physique (council). Author: The Electron Theory of Matter, 1914. Died Feb. 15, 1959.

RICHARDSON, Robert Charlwood, Jr., ret. army officer; b. Charleston, S.C., Oct. 27, 1882; s. Robert Charlwood and Julia Anna (Driscoll) R.; student Coll. of Charleston, S.C., 1898-1900; B.S., U.S. Mil. Acad., 1904; student U. of Grenoble, France, 1908; grad. Command and Gen. Staff Sch., 1924, Ecole Superieure de Guerre, Paris, 1926, Army War Coll., 1934; m. Lois Elbertine Farman, Nov. 18, 1916; 1 son, Robert Charlwood, 3d. Commd. 2d lt., U.S. Army, 1904, advanced through grades to general, 1954; served with 14th Cavalry, P.I., 1904-06; asst. instr. of modern langs., U.S. Mil. Acad., 1906-11; with 23d Inf., Tex., 1913-14; asst. prof. of English, Mil. Acad., 1914-16; maj. and lt. col., with A.E.F., as liaison officer, 1918; with Army of Occupation, Germany, and Peace Commn., Paris; Philippine Dept., Manila, 1921-23; mil. attaché, Am. Embassy, Rome, 1926-28; comdt. of cadets, U.S. Mil. Acad., 1929-33; comd. 5th Cav., Ft. Clark, Tex., 1935-38, Cavalry Sch., Ft. Riley, Kan., 1939-40; comd. 1st Cav. Div., 1940-41; dir. War Dept. Bur. of Pub. Relations, 1941; apptd. comdg. gen. 7th Army Corps, 1941; apptd. comdr. Hawaiian Dept. and mil. gov. of Hawaii, 1943; ret. 1946. Named comdg. gen. U.S. Army Forces in the Central Pacific area, 1943. Became comdg. gen. U.S. Army Forces in the Pacific Ocean Areas, 1944. Decorated D.S.M., Legion of Merit (1944), Allies Victory medal with 3 stars, Purple Heart, Silver Star (U.S.); Navy Distinguished Service Medal, Air Medal; Croix de Guerre with Palm, Officer Legion of Honor (France); Order of Leopold (Belgium); Officer Order of St. Maurizio and St. Lazarus (Italy); Officer La Solidaridad (Panama). Episcopalian. Clubs: Ends of the Earth (N.Y.); Army and Navy (Washington, Manila). Author: West Point—An Intimate Picture of the National Military Academy, 1917. Home: Upper Village, Bath, N.H. Died Mar. 2, 1954; buried West Point, N.Y.

RICHARDSON, Robert Kimball, prof. history; b. Hartford, Conn., June 6, 1876; s. Elias Huntington and Jane Maria (Stevens) R.; B.A., Yale, 1898, Ph.D., 1902; M.A., Columbia, 1899; LL.D., Beloit Coll., 1947; studied in France and England; m. Bessie Clarke Perkins, 1903 (died 1936); m. 2d, Helen Louisa Drew, July 1940. Instr. hist. Beloit Coll., 1901-02, asst. prof., 1902-05, prof., 1905-47; ret. Fellow Royal Hist. Soc. Mem. Am. Hist. Assn., Wis. Acad. Scis., Arts and Letters (pres.), Wis. State Hist. Soc. (pres. 1946-49), Phi Beta Kappa. Republican. Conglist. Author: The Bishopric of Durham under Anthony Bek, 1283-1311. Contributor Internat. Jour. Ethics. Home: 829 Church St., Beloit, Wis. Died Aug. 8, 1952.

RICHARDSON, Robert Newton, lawyer, pres. Citizens' Bank and Trust Co., Franklin, Tenn.; b. Franklin, Tenn., Aug. 5, 1841; attended Franklin Acad.; studies interrupted by war; m. Marienne Sims. Dec. 13, 1871. Served C.S.A., 1861-5; wounded battle Missionary Ridge; admitted bar, 1868; judge county court to complete unexpired term of W. O. N. Perkins; nominated for gov., People's Party, 1898. Address: Franklin, Tenn. Deceased.

RICHARDSON, Seth Whitley, lawyer; b. Otterville, Ia., Feb. 4, 1880; s. Rev. Ira H. and Electa (Whitley) R.; desc. Amos Richardson, Boston, 1639; student Hamline U., 1899, 1900; LL.B., U. of Wis., 1903; m. Nina C. Baker, Aug. 30, 1919; 1 dau., Martha. Admitted to Wis. and N.D. bars, 1903, and began practice at Kenmare; mem. Barnett & Richardson, Fargo, N.D., 1905-25, Richardson, Green & Wattam, 1925-28, later Richardson, Thorp & Wattam; mem. law firm of Davies, Richberg, Beebe, Busick and Richardson, Washington, D.C., since July 1, 1933. Was asst. state's atty., Cass County, N.D., 1904-08; spl. asst. atty. gen. N.D., 1919-20; U.S. dist. atty., by apptmt. of President Harding, 1923, President Coolidge, 1924; apptd. asst. atty. gen. of U.S. by President Hoover, May 1, 1929, and assigned by Atty. Gen. Mitchell to head of pub. lands and Indian affairs div. Appeared for State vs. Standard Oil Co., 1919, vs. lignite coal operators, 1920; also before Supreme Court of U.S., in grain grading litigation since 1922; conducted for Dept. of Justice, an investigation of Salt Creek Oil frauds, 1929, also investigation of Dept. of Interior in readministration of U.S. oil shale lands, 1930; rep. U.S. in an investigation, under Senate resolution, of law enforcement conditions in T.H., 1932. Council for Am. Med. Assn. and Pullman, Inc., and other corps., in pending govt. antitrust suits; counsel for various airlines before Civil Aeronautics Board; attorney, becoming chief counsel, for Congressional Committee investigating Pearl Harbor bombing, 1946. Nominated February 1933, by President Hoover, as judge Circuit Court of Appeals, 8th Circuit, but Senate did not act on nomination; apptd. by Pres. Truman chmn. Loyalty Review Bd., 1947, chmn. Subversive Activities Control Bd., 1950. Served as pvt., later capt. inf., Camp Pike, Ark., 1918. Mem. Am. Legion. Republican. Elk. Clubs: Metropolitan, Burning Tree, Chevy Chase, Yeaman's Hall (Washington, D.C.). Home: 3115 Chain Bridge Rd. Office: R & G Bldg., Washington. Died Mar. 17, 1953; buried Ortonville, Minn.

RICHARDSON, Sid Williams, oil producer; b. Athens, Tex., Apr. 25, 1891; s. John Isidore and Nannie (Bradley) R.; student Baylor U., 1911-12. Oil well supply co. salesman, scout and leaseman, 1913-17; ind. oil producer, Ft. Worth, 1919—; chmn. bd., dir. Sid Richardson Refining Co., Texas City, Tex.; pres. Sid Richardson Gasoline Co., Kermit, Sid Richardson Carbon Co., Odessa, Sid W. Richardson, Inc., Ft. Worth; partner Richardson & Bass, oil producers, Ft. Worth; chmn. bd. Hotel Texas, Ft. Worth; owns and operates cattle ranches on St. Joseph Island, Gulf of Mexico, Tarrant, Armstrong, and Donley counties Tex.; vice chmn. bd. Ft. Worth Air Terminal, operating Greater Ft. Worth Internat. Airport; dir. Tex. State Network (Ft. Worth), Carbisulphoil Co., Tex. Pacific Coal & Oil Co., New York Central Railroad, Atlas Corporation. Councilor Tex. A. and M. Coll. Research Found. Mem. Am. Petroleum Inst. (dir.), Ind. Petroleum Assn. Am. (dir.), Nat. Petroleum Council, Tex and Southwestern Cattle Raisers Assn. Club: Ft. Worth (bd. govs., v.p.). Home: Ft. Worth Club. Office: Ft. Worth Nat. Bank Bldg., Ft. Worth. Died Sept. 29, 1959.

RICHARDSON, Willard Samuel; b. Woburn, Mass., July 30, 1866; s. Jesse and Mary M. (Pearson) R.; student Denison U., Granville, O., Internat. Y.M.C.A. Coll., Springfield, Mass., U. of Rochester; A.B., Brown U., 1894; B.D., Union Theol. Sem., New York, 1897; D.C.L., Acadia U., 1932; Master of Humanics, Springfield Coll., 1935; m. Laura Alexander, October 26, 1900; children—Alice Mary, Ruth Alexander, Elisabeth. Ordained Bapt. ministry, 1897; asst. and asso. minister 5th Av. Ch., N.Y. City, 1894-1909; head master Neighborhood House, New York, 1906-09; dir. religious activities, U. of Minn., 1909-12; staff of J. D. Rockefeller, Sept. 1912-Jan. 1941. Trustee Internat. Sem., East Orange, N.J., since 1924, Internat. Y.M.C.A. College, Springfield, Mass., since 1925, Am. Inst. of Christian Philosophy since 1926, Colgate-Rochester Divinity Sch. since 1933. Mem. 7th Regt. N.Y. N.G. 2 yrs. Mem. Mil. Order Loyal Legion, Alpha Delta Phi. Author: David, 1907. Home: 350 Ridgewood Av., Glen Ridge, N.J. Retired. Died Nov. 21, 1952.

RICHART, Duncan Grant, army officer; b. Ludys, Ky., Nov. 10, 1887; B.S., U.S. Mil. Acad., 1910; grad. Cav. Sch., advanced course, 1925, Command and Gen. Staff Sch., 1926, Army War Coll., 1938. Commd. 2d lt., U.S. Army, 1910; resigned from army, 1914; in fed. service as 1st lt., Utah Nat. Guard, 1916; commd. 2d lt., U.S. Army, 1916, and advanced through the grades to brig. gen., 1944; on border duty, 1916-18; comd. Fort Oglethorpe, Ga., 1941-43; assumed command Fort Jackson, S.C., 1943. Address: War Dept., Washington 25. Died June 11, 1950.

RICHART, Frank Erwin (rĭch'ărt), educator; b. Lena, Ill., May 11, 1892; s. Carrolen K. and Ida Florence (Gamber) R.; B.S., U. Ill., 1914, M.S., 1915, C.E., 1922; m. Mary Fern Johnson, Sept. 11, 1917; children—Frank Edwin, Kathryn Mary. Employed in various engring. work, 1913-16; with U. Ill. in theoretical and applied mechanics 1916—, research prof. engring. materials 1931—; pres. Am. Concrete Inst., 1939-40. Ill. faculty rep. Intercollegiate Conf. (Big Ten); dir. U. Ill. Athletic Assn., 1936-41. Awarded Wason medal, Am. Concrete Inst., 1938, Alfred E. Lindau award, 1950. Mem. Am. Soc., C.E., Am. Soc. Testing Materials (hon. mem., 1st v.p.), Am. Concrete Inst. (hon.), Western Soc. of Engrs., Tau Beta Pi, Sigma Xi, Phi Kappa Phi. Republican. Methodist. Club: Urgana Golf and Country, Kiwanis. Author or co-author of many bulls. on strengths of materials pub. by U. of Ill. and U.S. Bureau of Standards. Home: 604 Pennsylvania Av., Urbana, Ill. Died July 16, 1951.

RICHEY, Frederick David (rĭch'ē), geneticist; b. St. Louis, Mo., Sept. 3, 1884; s. Frank Evans and Fannie (Lippman) R.; B.S.A., U. of Mo., 1909; D. Sc. (honorary), University of Missouri, 1949; married Hazel Grace Clough, Dec. 11, 1912; children—Frances, Guida. Began as mgr. of farm, 1909; with Food and Drug Commn. of Mo., 1910-11; with U.S. Dept. Agr., engaged in corn investigations, 1911-33, in charge, 1922-33, collected maize in S.A., 1923, asso. chief Bur. of Plant Industry, Dept. of Agr., Washington, D.C., 1934, chief, 1934-38, professional corn breeding, 1938-42, prin. agronomist in charge Southern corn breeding, U.S. Department Agriculture 1943-54; pvt. cons. & corn breeder, 1954—. Dept. Agrl. Award. Fellow A.A.A.S. Am. Soc. Agronomy (v.p. 1936, pres. 1937); mem. Am. Genetic Assn., Genetics Soc. of America (v.p. 1932), Am. Soc. of Naturalists, Am. Soc. of Plant Physiologists, Gamma Sigma Delta, Sigma Xi. Club: Cosmos. Writer numerous publs. on corn growing, breeding and statis. methods. Address: 11 Century Ct., Knoxville, Tenn. Died Sept. 11, 1955.

RICHEY, Lawrence, former sec. to ex-Pres. Hoover; b. Harrisburg, Pa., Dec. 21, 1885; ed. pub. schs., Phila.; m. Mabel Hunter (died Feb. 28, 1930). Agent U.S. Secret Service, Treasury Department, 1901-09; editorial staff Everybody's Magazine, 1909-12; special magazine and newspaper work, 1912-17; asst. office mgr. U.S. Food Adminstrn., 1917-19; spl. asst. to Herbert Hoover, 1919-29; sec. to the President, Mar. 4, 1929-Mar. 4, 1933; asst. curator Hoover War Library, Stanford U. and spl. agt, Stanford, 1933-41; asst. to the chairman of the Hoover Commission, 1947-49; spl. asst. to Herbert Hoover, Commn. on Govt., 1953-55. Past pres. Brotherhood of Jungle Cock; life member Outdoor Writers of America. Republican. Clubs: National Republican (New York); Chicago Rod and Gun, Adventurers (Chicago); Corinthian Yacht (hon.), Nat. Press (Washington). Home: 1801 16th St., Washington 9. Died Dec. 27, 1959; buried Rock Creek Cemetery, Washington.

RICHMOND, Adam, army officer; b. Council Bluffs, Ia., Sept. 24, 1889; s. William and Anna (Fulton) R.; A.B., U. of Wis., 1912, LL.B., 1914; m. Anna Pagenstecher, Aug. 22, 1917; children—Virginia (Mrs. John Bernard Wagoner, Jr.), Ruth May (Mrs. James Kenneth Chenault), Frances Anna (Mrs. Vitaly Kovalevsky). Practiced law at Milw., 1914-17; Inf. capt. in World War I; commd. capt. Inf., U.S. Army, 1920; transferred to Judge Advocate, General's Dept., 1924, and promoted through grades to brig. gen., Mar. 1943. Went overseas 1942. Served in England, Africa and Italy; retired, Feb. 1947. Awarded Legion of Merit in 1948; Oak Leaf Cluster, 1946; Hon. Comdr. Order Crown of Italy, 1945; Order of British Empire, 1946. Mem. Phi Delta Phi. Home: 7816 Glenbrook Rd. Bethesda Md. Died Dec. 1, 1959. Buried Arlington National Cemetery.

RICHMOND, Grace S., author; b. Pawtucket, R.I.; d. Charles Edward and Catherine A. (Kimball) Smith; ed. Syracuse (N.Y.) High Sch., and coll. course under pvt. tutors; Litt.D., Colby, 1924; m. Dr. Nelson Guernsey Richmond, Oct. 29, 1887; children—Joyce Kimball (dec.), Marjorie Guernsey (Mrs. John Stewart Sickels), Edward Guernsey, Jean Kimball. Mem. League Am. Pen Women, Authors League America, Authors Guild, Soc. Authors, Playwrights and Composers (Brit.). Contbr. stories mags. Presbyn. Author: The Indifference of Juliet, 1905; The Second Violin, 1906; With Juliet in England, 1907; Around the Corner in Gay Street, 1908; On Christmas Day in the Morning, 1908; A Court of Inquiry, 1909; On Christmas Day in the Evening, 1910; Red Pepper Burns, 1910; Strawberry Acres, 1911; Mrs. Red Pepper, 1913; The Twenty-fourth of June, 1914; Under the Country Sky, 1916; Red Pepper's Patients, 1917; The Brown Study, 1917; Red and Black, 1919; Foursquare, 1922; Rufus, 1923; Red of the Redfields, 1925; Cherry Square, 1926; Lights Up, 1927; At The South Gate, 1928; The Listening Post, 1929; High Fences, 1930; Red Pepper Returns, 1931; Bachelor's Bounty, 1931. Home: Fredonia, N.Y. Died Nov. 28, 1959; buried Forest Hill Cemetery, Fredonia.

RICHTER, John Frederick, govt. ofcl.; b. Washington, Dec. 11, 1897; s. John Frederick and Lottie M. (Keefer) R.; LL.B., Georgetown U., 1921, LL.M., 1922; m. Laurette M. Martin, Feb. 18, 1939. Newspaper reporter, mag. writer, pub. relations advisor, Washington, N.Y. Jour. Commerce, Central News London and N.Y.C., 1914-21; admitted to D.C. bar; practiced in Washington; U.S. legal advisor Tacna-Arica Plebiscitary Boundary Commn., Chile-Peru; N.R.A. legal code advisor, 1921-33; sr. atty. Fed. Trade Commn., 1933-40, sr. atty., legal advisor since 1948. Dir. Big Brothers of Washington. Served as col. judge adv. gen. dept., U.S. Army, World War II; staff Judge Adv. U.S. Armed Forces South Atlantic; acting dir. war crimes office Judge Adv. Gen. Office, 1940-46. Mem. Inter-Am., D.C., Fed. (1st v.p.), bar assns., Barristers (gov.) Club: Nat. Press (Washington). Home: 19 W. Underwood St., Chevy Chase 15, Md. Office: Tower Bldg., Washington. Died Jan. 25, 1954; buried Arlington Nat. Cemetery.

RICKARD, Brent Neville (rĭ-kärd'), metallurgist; b. Anaconda, Mont., June 28, 1885; s. Stephen and Constance (Neville) R.; ed. Manual Training High Sch., Denver, Colo., and University of Michigan; m. Edith Cutter, Apr. 7, 1916; children—Constance Neville (Mrs. Wyndham Kemp White), Brent Neville. Began as chemist for Am. Smelting & Refining Co., Monterey, N.L., Mexico, 1905; chief chemist Cia. Minera de Peñoles, Mapimi, Durango, Mexico, 1907-10; with Am. Smelting & Refining Co. since 1910, successively as metallurgist and asst. supt. Murray, Utah, 1910-14, Monterey and Chihuahua, Mexico, and Garfield, Utah, 1915-16, Tacoma, Wash., 1916-18, Murray, Utah, 1919-21, asst. mgr. Utah Dept., Salt Lake City, 1922-25, mgr. E. Helena, Mont., 1926-27, mgr. El Paso, Tex., 1928-39, mgr. Southwestern Ore. Purchasing Dept., Tucson, Ariz., 1939-50, ret. Mem. Am. Inst. Mining and Metall. Engrs. (past dir.), Sigma Chi. Republican. Episcopalian. Address: 2211 East Speedway, Tucson, Ariz. Died Mar. 8, 1951; buried Evergreen Cemetery, El Paso, Tex.

RICKARD, Edgar (rĭk'ärd), mining engr.; b. Pontgibaud, France, Jan. 17, 1874; s. Reuben and Mary Elizabeth (Humphreys) R.; brought to U.S., 1875; B.S. in Mechanics, U. Cal., 1895, post-grad. course in mining, 1896; Dr. Applied Sci. U. Louvain, 1928; LL.D., U. Brussels, 1930, U. Cal., 1936; m. Abigal Church, Oct. 24, 1906 (did Feb. 8, 1938); children—Mary Elizabeth, Marguerite Abigal. Mining engr. in U.S., Mexico, Australia, 1896-1905; pub. of tech. mining publs., San Francisco, London, Eng., 1906-16. Adminstrv. asst. to Herbert Hoover in all war and postwar orgns. including Commn. for Relief in Belgium, U.S. Food Adminstrn., 1914-24. Chmn. Hazeltine Corp., Hazeltine Electronics Corp. Dir. Pitney-Bowes, Inc., chmn. Belgian Am. Ednl. Found., Inc.; pres. Am. Children's Fund, Inc.; dir. Hoover Library on War, Revolution and Peace, Stanford U., 1941—. Mem. Am. Inst. Mining and Metall. Engrs. (life). Treas. White House Conf. on Child Health and Protection. Decorated Chevalier Legion d'Honneur (French), 1919; Officer Order of the Crown (Belgium), 1919; Gold Medal of Honor (U. Vienna), 1922; Comdr. Order Polonia Restituta (Polish), 1923. Comdr. The Golden Grand Cross of Honor (Austrian), 1925; Comdr. Order of Leopold (Belgian), 1930; medals of honor, U. Liege, 1938, U. Ghent, 1938; Comdr. First Class, Order of White Rose (Finland), 1941; Silver Buffalo, Boy Scouts of Am., 1941; Thanks Badge, Girl Scouts, Inc., 1941. Clubs: University, Nat. Republican, The Pilgrims (N.Y.); Bohemian (San Francisco). Home: 277 Park Av. Office: 420 Lexington Av., N.Y.C. Died Jan. 21, 1951.

RIDDELL, Robert Gerald, U. N. rep.; b. Edmonton, Alberta, Can., May 4, 1908; s. Dr. John H. and Florence M. (Armstrong) R.; B.A., with honours, U. Manitoba, 1930; M.A., U. Toronto, 1931; B.A., Oxford U., 1933, B. Litt. (Beit sr. scholar in Colonial history), 1934, M.A., 1937; m. Katherine P. Dobson, June 13, 1936; children—John P., Susan. Lectr. history U. Toronto, also sr. tutor Victoria U., 1934-42; research officer Nat. Research Council, Ottawa, 1942-43; asst. to Under-Sec. of State, Dept. External Affairs, 1943; chief First Polit. Div. (U.N. affairs), 1946; attended numerous internat. confs. connected with U.N., 1946-49, spl. asst. to Sec. of State for External Affairs, 1949; permanent rep. of Can. to U.N., since 1950. Mem. United Ch. of Can. Editor, Proc. of the Canadian Historical Association, 1940-42. Contbr. articles on history and internat. affairs pubs. Home: 58 Nassau Dr., Kensington, Great Neck, L.I., N.Y. Office: Canadian Delegation to United Nations, 620 Fifth Av., N.Y. City 20. Died Mar. 16, 1951.

RIDDELL, William Hugh, univ. prof.; b. Fort Langley, B.C., Can., June 19, 1897; s. Robert William and Hester (McKee) R.; B.S.A., Univ. Brit. Columbia, 1922; M.S., Univ. of Minn., 1924, Ph.D., 1932; m. Wilhelmina Bates, Aug. 16, 1926; children—William H., Martha G.; naturalized U.S. citizen, 1940. Instr. Kansas State Coll., 1923-26; grad. fellow and instr. U. of Minn., 1926-29; asst. and asso. prof., Kan. State Coll., 1929-39; prof. and head dairy dept. U. of Ariz., 1939-43; med. officers field service sch., Carlisle, Pa., nutrition officer sch., Walter Reed Hosp., Washington, 1944; fgn. service sch., Dept. of State, Washington; agrl. attaché, Am. Embassy, The Hague, 1945; chmn. animal and dairy husbandry dept., U. of Vt., since Sept. 1948. Mem. 4-Party Supply Com. for the Netherlands, Brussels, Apr. 1945; mem. Conf. Agrl. Attachés on European Food Situa-

tion, Paris, Sept. 1945; U.S. rep., Internat. Seed Conf., The Hague, 1946; advisor to Hoover Party on food problems of the Netherlands, May 1946; advisor, Special Cereals Conf., I.E.F.C., Paris, July 1947; U.S. rep. Internat. Livestock Prodn. Conf., Zurich, Oct. 1947. Served with Canadian Expeditionary Forces, 1917-18. Decorated Comdr. Order Orange-Nassau (Netherlands). Mem. A.A.A.S., Am. Dairy Science Assn., Am. Soc. Animal Prodn., Sigma Xi. Address: U. of Vermont, Burlington, Vt. Died June 27, 1958.

RIDDICK, Walter Garrett (rĭd'ĭk), judge, U.S. Circuit Court of Appeals; b. Gainesville, Ark., Sept. 13, 1883; s. James Edward and Emma Wade (Mack) R.; student Wash. and Lee U. 1901-04; LL.D., 1944; LL.B. U. of Ark., 1908, LL.D., 1943; m. Hebe Gower Fry, Oct. 17, 1925; children—Walter Garrett, Hebe Fry. Practice of Law, Little Rock; judge U.S. Circuit Court of Appeals, 8th Circuit, since 1941. Mem. Little Rock, Ark. State, Am. bar assns., Am. Law Inst., Am. Judicature Soc., Pi Kappa Alpha, Phi Beta Kappa (hon.). Home: 2416 Wolfe St. Office: Federal Bldg., Little Rock, Ark. Died July 31, 1953.

RIDENOUR, Louis N(icot), Jr., physicist; b. Montclair, N.J., Nov. 1, 1911; s. Louis Nicot and Clare (Wintersteen) **R.; B.S., U. of Chicago, 1932; Ph.D., Calif. Inst. Tech., 1936; m. Gretchen Hinckley Kraemer, June 18, 1934; 2 daus., Eleanor, Nancy Page. With Inst. for Advanced Study, Princeton, N.J., 1935-36; instr. Princeton U., 1936-38; asst. prof., U. of Pa., 1938-41, asso. prof., 1941-46, prof. 1946-47; prof. physics, dean Grad. Coll., U. of Ill.,** 1947-51, on leave as spl. asst. to Sec. of Air Force, 1950-51; dir. of research for Missile Systems div. Lockheed Aircraft Corp., 1956-59, v.p. in charge electronics and avionics div., 1959—; v.p. Internat. Telemeter Corp. Cons., Sec. of War, 1942-46, radar adviser U.S. Strategic War Forces in Europe, 1944, member radar committee, Combined Chiefs Staff, **1943-45; mem. div. 5, div. 15, Nat. Defense Research Com. Awarded Bronze Star; President's Medal for** Merit. Fellow Am. Phys. Soc., A.A.A.S. (councillor), Institute of Radio Engrs.; mem. Phi Beta Kappa, **Sigma Xi. Clubs: Cosmos (Washington); University (Chgo.). Contbr. articles on mil. and sci. subjects to various publs. Editor-in-chief Radiation Lab. Series of 27 tech. vols. Editor Radar System Engineering,** 1947, Modern Physics for the Engineer, 1954. Home: 1425 University Av., Palo Alto, Cal. Office: Missile Systems div. Lockheed Aircraft Corp., Sunnyvale, Cal. Died May 21, 1959.

RIDGLEY, Douglas Clay (rĭj'lē), geographer; b. Wabash County, Ind., Mar. 18, 1868; s. George Washington and Catherine (Yohe) R.; diploma, Ind. State Normal Sch., Terre Haute, 1891; A.B., Ind. U., 1893; studied 2 summers at Ind. Biol. Sta., Lake Maxinkuckee; M.S., U. of Chgo. 1922; Ph.D., Clark U., 1925; m. Bessie Cushing, Aug. 26, 1891 (dec.); 1 dau., Winifred (Mrs. Cecil L. Rew); m. 2d, Florence Johnson, July 25, 1920. Began as tchr. rural sch., 1884; tchr. grammar sch., North Manchester, Ind., 1888-89; prin. high sch., North Manchester, 1891-92, Delphi, 1893-95; tchr. biology and physical geography, West Div. High Sch., Chgo., 1895-1900; prin. Victor F. Lawson Grammar Sch., Chgo., 1900-03; prof. and head geography dept., Ill. State Normal U., 1903-22; spl. lectr. geography and hon. fellow, Clark U., 1922-24, asso. prof. geography in edn., 1924-27, prof., 1927-37, prof. emeritus 1937—. Prof. geography, Army Air Crew Program Jefferson Coll. St. Louis, 1943-44. Dir. of geography AEFU, in France, 1919; prof. geography First Coll. Cruise around the World, 1926-27; vis. prof. The Principia Coll., 1935-36. Mem. Nat. Council Geography Tchrs. (pres. 1931; received distinguished service award 1935), Am. Meteorol. Soc., Army Ednl. Corps, Gamma Theta Upsilon (nat. pres. 1928-35), Phi Beta Kappa, Sigma Xi. Republican. Christian Scientist. Author: Geography of Illinois, 1921; Geographic Principles—Their Application to the Elementary School, 1925; A Study of Children's Learning about Places, 1928; many workbooks in geography and mag. articles. Co-author: Influence of Geography on Our Economic Life, 1938; Problems in Economic Geography, 1938. Editor series of pamphlets on Important Topics in Geography; asso. editor Journal of Geography, Education (mag.); geography editor Bus. Edn. World. Home: Bloomington, Ill. Died Oct. 10, 1952.

RIDGWAY, Arthur Osbourne (rĭj'wā), engineer; b. Lawrence, Kan., Feb. 23, 1870; s. Robert M. and Sarah (Schimmel) R.; B.Sc., U. of Kan., 1892; m. Mary Rayhawk, May 18, 1905; children—Louise, Dorothy. Draftsman D.&R.G. R.R. Co., 1892-93; with Bellefontaine (O.) Bridge & Iron Co., 1893-94; again with D.&R.G. Ry. Co. successively as instrumentman, 1895; asst. div. engr., 1895-98, acting div. engr. and div. engr., 1898-1902, in charge design and constrn. steel bridges; locating engr. in charge constrn. R.G.& Southwestern R.R., 1903-04; gen. supt. maintenance and operation Silverton Ry. and Silverton Northern Ry. (branches of D.&R.G.), 1904-05; office engr. and acting engr. bridges and buildings, D.&R.G. R.R. Co., 1905-08, asst. chief engr., 1909-23, also chmn. valuation com., 1913-23, and safety officer, 1918-23, D.&R.G. and associate cos.; chief engr. D.&R.G. Western Ry. System, 1923-1941, also Denver Union Terminal Railway Co., Salt Lake Union Depot & Railway Co. and Denver & Salt Lake Western R.R. Co., engring. consultant same companies, 1941-48. Awarded Colo. Engring. Councils' gold medal, 1940. Mem. Am. Soc. C.E. (life), Am. Ry. Bridge and Bldg. Assn. (ex-pres.), Colo. Engring. Council (ex-pres.), Am. Ry. Engring. Assn. (life), Colo. Sci. Soc. (hon. life), Sigma Xi, Tau Beta Pi, Chi Epsilon; fellow A.A.A.S. Republican. Presbyterian. Author of History of Transportation in Colorado, Effects of Route Characteristics on Cost of Rail Transportation; The Figure of the Earth; Arkansas River Flood of 1921; The Mission of Colorado Toll Roads; Engineering in Colorado (inc. in History of Colorado), 1947. Home: Olin Hotel, Denver 3. Died Jan. 18, 1953.

RIDPATH, Robert Ferguson, physician; b. Jenkintown, Pa., Apr. 3, 1876; s. John Waddell and Rachel Ann (Ferguson) R.; M.D., Medico-Chirurg, Coll., 1899; Sc.D., Ursinus Coll., 1935; m. Johanne Ogrodowski, Nov. 22, 1922; 1 son, Robert Ferguson. Asso. prof. of rhino-laryngology, Medic-Chirurg. Coll., Sept. 1913-24; asst. prof. U. of Pa. Post Grad. Sch., 1924-30; prof., Temple U. Sch. of Medicine, 1930—; practicing physician 1900—. Cons. in rhinology at Phila. Skin & Cancer Hosp.; cons. otology and rhinology, Seashore Home (Atlantic City). Served as capt. in Med. Corps, U.S. Army, World War. Fellow A.C.S., Coll. Physicians (Phila.), Am. Laryngol., Rhinol. and Otol. Soc., Am. Laryngol. Soc.; mem. A.M.A. (chmn. rhinolaryngol. sect.), Am. Acad. Ophthalmology, Otology and Laryngol., Phila. Laryngol. Soc., Pa., Montgomery County med. socs. Republican. Mason. Clubs: University. Medical (Phila.). Contbr. to sci. and profl. jours. Home: 1117 New Jersey Av., Cape May, N.J. Office: 1720 Spruce St., Phila. 3. Died Aug. 10, 1950; buried Hillside Cemetery, Jenkintown, Pa.

RIDSDALE, Percival Sheldon (rĭdz'dāl), editor; b. Bradford, Eng., July 5, 1872; s. Charles and Jean Gordon (Thompson) R.; ed. Wyo. Sem. and pub. sch., Wilkes-Barre, Pa.; m. Gertrude Marie Cassidy, January 1, 1903 (died Nov. 1, 1946); children—John Gordon (lt. col. U.S. Army), Betty (Mrs. Donald F. McCall), Patricia (Mrs. Patricia R. Somers); married 2d, Mrs. Vivian H. Bailey, June 8, 1948. Editor Wilkes-Barre News, 1890-1900, Wilkes-Barre Evening Leader, 1900-04; mag. writer, corr. N.Y., Phila., Boston, Chgo. newspapers, 1904-12; editor Am. Forestry Mag., sec. Am. Forestry Assn., Washington, 1912-22; mng. editor Nature Mag., dir. Am. Nature Assn., Am. Tree Assn., Washington, 1923-37; dir. Charles Lathrop Pack Forestry Found., 1931. Sec., treas. Nat. War Garden Commn., Washington, 1917 until dissolution, 1919 (awarded "Great Medal" by the Commn.); mng. dir. Lumber and Forest Regts., Relief Fund. Decorated Officer des Merité Agricole and Medal of Honor, France; mem. Société Nationale d'Acclimation de France. Fellow Royal Geog. Soc.; mem. A.A.A.S., Am. Nature Assn., U.S. Sr. Golf Assn.; Royal British Arboricultural Soc. (hon.). Republican. Clubs: Chevy Chase, University, Sunnehanna. Home: Chevy Chase Club, Chevy Chase, Md. and 639 Luzerne St., Johnstown, Pa. Died Dec. 23, 1953; buried Grandview Cemetery, Johnstown, Pa.

RIECKEN, William Emil (rē'kĕn), dean; b. Mt. Vernon, Ind., Jan. 23, 1892; s. Henry Christian and Elizabeth (Gebhardt) R.; student Oakland City (Ind.) Coll., 1911, Ind. State Tchrs. Coll., Terre Haute (part) 1912, 14, 16; B.A., Ind. U., 1923, M.A., 1925, Ph.D. 1928; m. Alma Ellanora Gollner, June 28, 1928; children—William Emil, Ellnora Alma. Rural sch. tchr., 1911-17, jr. high sch. tchr., 1917-21; prin., jr. high sch., 1923; instr. botany, Ind. U., 1925-28; asst. prof. botany, Ohio Wesleyan U., 1928-34; head dept. biology, Millsaps Coll., Jackson, Miss., 1939—, dean, 1939—; taught botany summers, Ind. State Tchrs. Coll., Evansville Coll., 1929; asst. prof. Texas A. and M., summer 1925. Served F.A., World War I. Mem. A.A.A.S., Ind. Acad. Sci., Miss. Acad. Sci., Phi Beta Kappa, Sigma Xi, Phi Delta Kappa, Omicron Delta Kappa, Alpha Epsilon Delta. Methodist. Mason. Home: 625 Broadway, Jackson, Miss. Died Jan. 21, 1958; buried Jackson, Miss.

RIEMENSCHNEIDER Albert (rē'mĕm-schnī-dĕr), organist, conductor; b. Berea, O., Aug. 31, 1878; s. Carl H. and Emelia (Smith) R.; A.B., Baldwin Wallace Coll., Berea, O., 1899; studied music with father until 15, piano, pipe organ, harmony and theory with James H. Rogers, Cleve., organ with Charles E. Clemens, Cleve., piano with Hugo Reinhold, of Vienna, counterpoint and composition with Robert Fuchs, of Vienna, pipe organ with Guilmant, pipe organ and orchestration with Widor, both of Paris; hon. Mus. D., Sherwood Music School, Chgo. m. Selma Marting, July 21, 1904; children—Edwin Albert, Lois (dec.), Wilma, Paul Arthur. Dir. emeritus Baldwin Wallace Conservatory of Music, acting pres. Baldwin-Wallace Coll., 1948—; dir. Annual Bach Festivals, 1931-47. Dedicated many organs throughout the country; series of 70 recitals at Baldwin Wallace Coll. without repetition of a single composition; presented entire 10 organ symphonies of Widor in 5 programs, Cleve. Mus. of Art, 1925; soloist with Cleve. Symphony Orchestra, 1928; gave recitals for nat. conv., Nat. Assn. National Association Organists, Phila. and Am. Guild of Organists, Chgo. Conducted master class for organist Balboa Park open air organ, San Diego, 4 summers to 1931; played at Sesquicentennial, Phila., 1926. Mem. Ohio Music Tchrs. Assn. (pres. 1930-31); Music Tchrs. Nat. Assn. (pres. 1933); Nat. Assn. Schs. of Music, (treas. 1937-47). Mem. Hymnal Commn. of Meth. Ch. Apptd. to conduct a survey of music edn. in the North Central Assn. of Colls., 1939, 40. Contbr. articles: "Widor Symphonies" and "Bach's Liturgical Year," in Am. Organist, N.Y.; "The Organ Works of Leo Sowerby" (5 installments) and "The Development of Organ Music" in the Diapason, Chgo.; "Review of the Biographies of J. S. Bach" in Diapason; "Rise and Fall of the Appreciation of Bach," Am. Organist and M.T.N.A. Year Book, "The Heart of Bach" (3 installments), in Etude. Editor "The Liturgical Year," J. S. Bach, 120 Bach Chorales for Score Reading (with C. H. Boyd), 2 vols. Edited 371 chorales and 69 chorale melodies by J. S. Bach for G. Schirmer; Bach 6 Schübler Chorales, Theo. Presser, 1942. Home: 67 Harnagy St., Berea, O. Died July 20, 1950.

RIES, Heinrich (rēs), geologist; b. Bklyn., Apr. 30, 1871; s. Heinrich and Caroline Bowman (Atkins) R.; Ph.B., Columbia, 1892, A.M., 1894, Ph D., 1896; Sc.D. (hon.) Alfred U., 1945; m. Millie Timmerman, July 1, 1893; (dec.); children—Victor H., Donald T.; m. 2d, Adelyn Halsey Gregg, June 7, 1948. On N.Y. geol. survey, 1891-92; asst. geologist summer of 1895; lectr. pub. schs. N.Y., 1895-97; asst. in mineralogy, Columbia, 1896-97; instr. econ. geology, Cornell U., 1898-1902, asst. prof., 1902-05, prof., 1905-39, head dept., 1914-37, emeritus prof. 1939—. Asst. dir. N.Y. sci. exhibits, Chgo. Expn., 1893; mem. jury of awards, Cotton States and Internat. Expn., 1896, Buffalo Expn., 1901, St. Louis Expn. 1904. Del. Geol. Congress, St. Petersburg, 1897, Internat. Geol. Congress, Paris, 1900, Mexico, 1906, Toronto, 1913, Washington, 1933; Fellow. Am. Geog. Soc., Am. Mineral. Soc., A.A.A.S., Seismol. Soc., British Ceramic Soc., Soc. Econ. Geologists; mem. Am. Ceramic Soc. (hon., pres. 1910-11); Am. Foundrymens Assn., (tech. dir., hon.), Rochester Acad. Sci.; Ky. Acad. Sci.; Geol. Soc. Am. (1st v.p. 1925-26, pres. 1928-29); Am. Inst. Mining Engrs. (life mem.); Can. Mining Inst. (life mem.). Author: Economic Geology; Clay, Occurrence, Properties and Uses; History of Clay Working Industry of United States (with H. Leighton); Building Stones and Clay Products; Engineering Geology (with T. L. Watson); Elements of Engineering Geology (with same); Elementary Economic Geology; Conservation in United States (with others). Has published reports on clays of N.Y., Ala., La., Fla., N.C., Mich., Md., Colo., N.J., Va., Tex., Wis., Can., in state geologists' and govt. reports. Contbr. articles on geology and mining, Internat. Year-book, 1898-1901, articles on geology, New International Encyclopaedia. Address: 401 Thurston Av., Ithaca, N.Y. Died Apr. 11, 1951.

RIESER, Leonard Moos (rē̄'ser), lawyer; b. Chicago, Jan. 8, 1893; s. Herman and Minnie (Moos) **R.; A.B., U. Mich., 1914; LL.B., Harvard, 1917; m. Margaret Wallerstein, Sept. 6, 1920; children—Leonard Moos, Jr., William Herman, Lawrence, Catherine. Practiced in Chicago since 1917; asso. with Mayer, Meyer, Austrian & Platt until 1919; with Sonnenschein, Berkson, Lautmann, Levinson & Morse, 1919-**25; admitted to firm 1925, name changed to Sonnenschein, Lautmann, Levinson, Rieser, Carlin and Nath. Chairman of the Zoning Committee of Highland Park, 1926-40; member Ill. State Housing Com., 1931-33; dir. Jewish Fedn., Chgo., **1943-52; trustee Julius Rosenwald Fund, 1933-48, Am. Council on Race Relations, 1944-54; member Com. to Draft Mental Health Code of Ill., 1950-51. Treas. trustee Industrial Areas Found.; chmn. board of trustees Fisk U.; v.p., trustee Emil Schwarzhaupt Found.; mem. bd. govs. Metropolitan Planning and Housing Council Chicago. Mem. Am. Inst. Planners, Am. Law Inst. (tax adv. group), Am., Ill. State Chgo. bar assns. Clubs: Tavern, Cliffdwellers, Standard. Home: 877 Dean Av., Highland Park, Ill. Office: 77 W. Washington St., Chgo. 2. Died Mar. 10,** 1959.

RIGBY, William Otto, ex-mayor; b. Fairfield, Ia., Nov. 7, 1872; s. Millard Fillmore and Martha Ann (Simmons) R.; ed. pub. schs. and Pond's Bus. Coll., Topeka, Kan.; m. Grace M. Hopkins, June 25, 1919; children—Millard Frederick, William Warren. Began as confectioner, Topeka; in wholesale candy bus., 1922-25; in real estate and ins. bus., 1925—. Postmaster, Topeka, 1914-22; mayor of Topeka, 1927-32; proprietor Rigby Pub. Co. Mem. Topeka C. of C. Democrat. Presbyn. Mason (K.T., Shriner), Elk. Clubs: Co-Op, Hi-Twelve, Lakeview Hunting and Fishing. Author: Rigby Reliable Candy Teacher, 1907. Home: 907 W. 10th St., Topeka, Kan. Died May 6, 1943; buried Topeka (Kan.) Cemetery.

RIGGS, Ernest Wilson; b. Merzifoun, Turkey, July **3, 1881; s. Edward (D.D.) and Sarah Hinsdale (Dwight) R.; A.B.,** Princeton University, 1904; grad.

Auburn Theol. Sem., 1910; m. Alice Claudia Shepard, Aug. 31, 1910; children—Lorrin Andrews, Douglas Shepard, Margaret Mary. U.S. vice-consul at Harpoot, Turkey, 1904-07; ordained Presbyn. ministry, 1910; pres. Euphrates Coll., Harpoot, Turkey, 1910-21. Child welfare dir., Near East Relief, 1920-21; asso. sec. A.B.C.F.M., 1921-27, corr. sec., 1927-32; elected pres. Anatolia College, Thessaloniki, Greece, 1933, pres. emeritus since 1950. Cooperated establishing Greek mil. hosp. in college buildings, campaign against Italy; directed office Greek War Relief, Thessaloniki, 1940-41; escaped with wife 24 hours before Germans made college hdqrs. for operations in southern Balkans; lectured in 31 states on Greece, 1941-44; returned and reopened Anatolia Coll., 1945. Mem. Nat. Inst. of Social Sciences. Home: 55 Walnut St., Needham, Mass. Office: 14 Beacon St., Boston 8. Died Mar. 25, 1952.

RIGGS, Henry Harrison, missionary; b. Sivas, Turkey, Mar. 2, 1875; s. Edward and Sarah Hinsdale (Dwight) R.; A.B., Carleton Coll., Northfield, Minn., 1896; grad. Auburn Theol. Sem., N.Y., 1902; m. Annie C. Tracy, July 13, 1904 (died July 23, 1905); m. 2d, Emma H. Barnum, May 2, 1907 (died Apr. 27, 1917); 1 dau., Annie B. (dec.); m. 3d, Annie M. Denison, at Harpoot, May 6, 1920; children—Ruth Elizabeth, Helen Sarah. Teacher in Anatolia Coll., Marsovan, Turkey, 1896-99; missionary, Cesarea, Turkey, under A.B.C.F.M., 1902; pres. Euphrates Coll., Harpoot, Turkey, 1903-10; evangelistic missionary work, Harpoot, Turkey, 1912-15; relief and rescue work in Armenia, 1915-17; lecturing in U.S. in interests of Armenian Relief, 1917-18; relief, reconstruction and missionary work in Turkey, 1919-20; missionary work, Constantinople and Beirut, 1920—; chmn. Near East Christian Council. Presbyn. Republican. Address: American Mission, Beirut, Syria. Died Aug. 17, 1943.

RIGHTMIRE, George Washington (rīt-mīr), univ. pres.; b. Center Furnace, Lawrence County, O., Nov. 15, 1868; s. William Henry and Louisa (Miller) R.; Ph.B., Ohio State U., 1895, M.A., 1898; student law dept., same univ., 1898-1902 (part of time); m. Edna Garner, Sept. 10, 1902 (dec. Dec. 1942); 1 son, Brandon Garner. Tchr. North High Sch., Columbus, 1895-1902; practiced patent law, trademark and copyright law, 1904-19; instr. in law, Ohio State U. 1902-06, prof., 1906, acting dean, 1908-09, acting pres. 1925-26, pres., 1926-38, pres. emeritus, 1938—. Pres. City Council, Columbus, 1906-10. Mem. Am., Ohio State bar assns., Am. Assn. Univ. Profs., Alpha Tau Omega, Delta Chi, Phi Beta Kappa, Order of the Coif. Episcopalian. Clubs: Faculty, Columbus. Author: Case Book—Jurisdiction and Procedure in Federal Courts, 1917; Democracy—What Is It? 1943; Federal Aid and Regulation of Agriculture and Industry, 1943. Contributor to legal periodicals and articles on preparatory edn. for admission to the bar. Compiler and editor 2d edit. Loveland's Forms of Federal Practice (3 vols.), 1920; editor of The Law of England at the Norman Conquest, 1932. Address: 1445 E. Broad St., Columbus 5, O. Died Dec. 23, 1952; buried Greenlawn Cemetery, Columbus, O.

RIGNEY, Hugh M., congressman; b. Arthur, Ill., July 31, 1873; s. Dr. John D. and Orra F. (McDonald) R.; ed. pub. schs., Arthur; m. Lena E. Hawkins, Dec. 25, 1923; children—Hugh P., Harold W. Printer, 188?-1905; pub. Arthur Graphic-Clarion 1900-25; city treas., 1910-11; mem. Ill. Ho. of Rep., 1935-37; mem. 75th Congress (1937-39), 19th Ill. Dist. Pres. Arthur Assn. of Commerce, 1930; mem. sch. bd. ten years; chmn. Moultrie Co. Dem. Com., 1930-34; mem. exec. com. Ill. Dem. Editorial Assn., 1934-36. Democrat. Mem. Christian Ch. Home: Arthur, Ill. Died Oct. 1950.

RIIS, Roger William (rēs), writer, publicist; b. Richmond Hill, N.Y., Mar. 15, 1894; s. Jacob A. and Elisabeth (Nielsen) R.; grad The Hill Sch., Pottstown, Pa., 1913; A.B., Williams Coll., 1917, hon. M.A., 1943; m. Elizabeth Hipple, June 5, 1941. Began as reporter, N.Y. Sun, 1917; asso. editor, Am. Legion Weekly, 1920; asso. editor, Collier's Weekly, 1921-22; free lance public relations and publicity work connected with many leading corporations and movements, 1922-42; roving editor, Reader's Digest, 1943. Served with U.S. Naval Intelligence, 1917-18; civilian adviser to Bureau of Aeronautics, U.S. Navy, 1941-45. Dir. Cancer Com. of N.Y.; dir. Am. Civil Liberties Union; dir. Urban League; mem. Free Denmark; v.p. Williams Alumni, 1940-42. Contbr. numerous articles to mags. Home: Wilton, Conn. Died Jan. 23, 1953.

RIKER, Franklin Wing, singer, teacher; b. Burlington, Vt., Mar. 12, 1876; s. George Peters and Ella Jeanette (Wing) R.; pub. sch. edn.; m. Henrietta A. Scheibe, Feb. 22, 1908. Tenor soloist leading New York chs., 1897-1903; conductor Vt. Festival Chorus, supervisor music pub. schs., Burlington, Vt., etc., 1903-6; mem. Conried Met. Opera Co., 1907; solo tenor Christ Ch. (Episcopal), New York. Teacher of singing; pupil of Arthur Edward Stahlschmidt, New York. Composer of several songs, anthems and piano pieces. Christian Scientist. Died July 1958.

RIKER, Thad Weed (ri-ker), prof. modern European history; b. Stamford, Conn., Nov. 2, 1880; s. Thaddeus Weed and Louise Draper (Nesbitt) R.; B.A., Princeton, 1903, M.A., 1904; B.Litt., Oxford U., Eng., 1908; D.Litt., Oxon, 1935; m. Fannie Rhea Preston, June 2, 1923; children—Malcolm Preston, Janet Louise. Spl. fellow in Latin, Princeton, 1903-04; instr. English history, Cornell U., 1908-09; instr. modern European history, U. Tex., 1909-13, adj. prof., 1913-17, asso. prof., 1917-23, prof., 1923—; vis. prof. modern history, U. Chgo., 1931-32; spl. research prof., U. Tex., 1941. Mem. org. com. on edn. tng., War Plans Div., Gen. Staff, war period. Mem. Am. Hist. Assn., Société d'histoire moderne, Royal Hist. Soc., Delta Upsilon, Phi Beta Kappa; corr. mem. Academia Romana (Bucharest). Episcopalian. Author: Henry Fox, First Lord Holland (2 vols.), 1911; The Making of Roumania—A Study of an International Problem, 1856-66, 1931; Roumanian translation as Cum S'a Infaptuit Romania); Michael of Serbia and the Turkish Occupation (serial), 1933-34; A Short History of Modern Europe, 1935; The Story of Modern Europe, 1942; A History of Modern Europe, 1949. Contbr. revs. and mags. Mem. bd. editors, Jour. of Modern History, 1928-32, acting editor, 1931-32; mem. bd. editors, Am. Hist. Rev., 1943-48, Home: 2300 Leon. Office: University of Texas, Austin, Tex. Died Feb. 17, 1952; buried Stanford, Conn.

RILEA, Thomas Edward (rī-lē'ä), adj. gen. Ore.; b. Chicago, Ill., May 5, 1895; s. George Washington and Mary Eve (Minnick) R.; E.E., Ore. Inst. Tech., 1916; m. Helen Coe Webster, 1946. Began as elec. engr., 1916. Served as bugler and corporal of inf. on Mexican Border, 1916; in World War served in U.S. and with A.E.F., France; successively sergt. maj., 2d and 1st lt., capt.; following World War I, became exec. officer Ore. Nat. Guard, and advanced through grades to brig. gen. comdg. 82d Brigade, 1931, maj. gen. 1948; Fed. service, 1940-46; asst. comdr. 41st Div. S.W. Pacific; participated New Guinea, Papuan campaigns; comd. large supply base, Australia. Now adj. gen. of Ore. Decorated D.S.M., Bronze Star Medal, Purple Heart, Commendation Ribbon, Presidential Unit Citation, Mexican Border, World War I, German Occupation, Defense, Am. Theater, Asiatic-Pacific and Victory (World War II) ribbons, Legion of Merit. Cited outstanding service, Ore. legislatiure, 1931. Mem. Nat. Guard Assn. U.S. (v.p., 1934-35, pres., 1935-36), exec. council 6th Army Area. Mem. Am. Legion, Vets. Fgn. Wars. Mason (32°, Shriner). Clubs: Portland Army-Navy, Columbia Athletic. Home: Box 145, Clackamas, Ore. Office: Military Dept., State Office Bldg., Salem, Ore. Died Feb. 3, 1959.

RILEY, George Washington, osteopathic physician; b. Lerna, Ill., Dec. 7, 1866; s. Nimrod and Martha (Sexson) R.; prep. edn. Lee's Acad. Loxa, Ill.; grad. Ill. State Normal U., 1892; Ph.B., U. of Pa., 1895; studied Ill. Wesleyan Law Sch.; D.O., Am. Sch. Osteopathy, Kirksville, Mo., 1904; LL.D., Phila. Coll. of Osteopathy, 1942; D.Sc., Kirksville Coll. Osteopathy and Surgery, 1944; m. Chloe Canterbury Carlock, June 29, 1904 (died Sept. 7, 1929); one stepson, Major John Bruce Carlock, Pittsburgh. Tchr., prin., superintendent schools, Illinois, until 1893; practiced, N.Y.C., 1904-53, ret. Ex-trustee A. T. Research Inst., Chicago. Member American Osteopathic Association (trustee 1913-17; pres., 1917-18; chmn. program com., convention 1936); chmn. entertainment com. 50th annual convention, 1946; Osteopathic Soc. City of N.Y. (pres. 1909-10), N.Y. State Osteopathic Soc. (sec. 1905-07, pres. 1907-08, and dir. 1908-09), Eastern Osteopathic Assn.; mem. professional staff New York Osteopathic Clinic (chmn. Clinic library com.); trustee Osteopathic Research Trust (Chicago); dir. Kirksville Osteopathic Alumni Assn. Chmn. committee of American Osteopathic Assn. to propose plan for celebration of 50th anniversary of osteopathic edn., Oct. 3, 1942; gave dedication address of the Anna R. Still Memorial Osteopathic Convalescent Home, Kirksville, Mo., Oct. 1946. Member American Museum of Art, Am. Acad. Polit. and Social Science, Am. Museum Natural History, Drama League of N.Y., Nat. Travel Club, Soc. Friendly Sons of St. Patrick, Am. Irish Hist. Soc., Rep. County Com., Beta Theta Pi, Sigma Sigma Phi. Awarded Distinguished Service Certificate by Am. Osteopathic Assn., 1929. Republican. Baptist. Mason (K.T., Shriner), Elk. Clubs: New York Athletic, Masonic, Elks, Republican; Atlas Club (Kirksville, Mo.). Author: Chapter in The Lengthening Shadow of Dr. A. T. Still, by Dr. A. G. Hildreth, 1938. Contbr. article on osteopathy to Ency. Britannica and various articles to professional mags. Address: D'Arlington Apts., Pitts. 13. Died Sept. 25, 1954; buried Gibson City, Ill.

RILEY, Henry Ware, banker; born in Greenville, S.C., Apr. 13, 1902; s. Harry Lee and Margaret Louise (Ware) R.; A.B., U. Richmond, 1923; grad. student in economics, commerce and adminstn., U. Chgo., 1923-24; m. Ruth Walton Wood, July 10, 1923 (died Apr. 2, 1945); children—Nancy Ware (wife of Lt. Gordon Robinson), Henry Wood; m. 2d, Lillian M. Smith, July 15, 1947. Pub. accountant practicing in South Carolina, 1924-30; licensed C.P.A., S.C., since 1927; instr. Furman U., Greenville, S.C., 1924-28; mem. staff Ernst & Ernst, accountants and auditors, Richmond, Va., 1930-33; acting chief auditor, conservatorship div., Office Comptroller of the Currency, Treasury Dept., 1933-34; asst. to special asst. to sec. of treasury, 1934-35; with Fed. Deposit Ins. Corp., Washington, 1935-46, controller, 1935-41, exec. officer, 1941; exec. officer Office of Alien Property Custodian, 1942-44; dep. adminstr. Fgn. Econ. Adminstrn., 1943-45; dir., sec. and treas. U.S. Commerical Co.; treas. Petroleum Reserves Corp., International Finance Corporation, 1956—; became assistant treasurer Internat. Bank for Reconstrn. and Development, 1946, treas. since 1953. Mem. Omicron Delta Kappa, Phi Kappa Sigma. Democrat. Moderator, 1943-44, and chmn. bd. deacons, First Baptist Ch., 1945-47; Washington. Home: 5601 Potomac Av., N.W. Office: 1818 H St., Washington 18. Died Sept. 16, 1959; buried Hollywood Cemetery, Richmond, Va.

RILEY, James Breinig, judge; b. Wheeling, W.Va., July 26, 1894; s. Thomas Sylvester and Minnie (Breinig) R.; A.B., W.Va. U., 1916; student Georgetown U., 1916-17; LL.B., Columbia, 1921, A.M., 1921; m. Frances Wood, Oct. 25, 1925; children—Frances Wood, James Breinig. Admitted to W.Va. bar, 1921; mem. Riley and Riley, Wheeling, 1921-37; judge W.Va. Supreme Court of Appeals since 1937. Served as 2d lt., 1st lt. and capt. U.S.M.C., 1917-19. Mem. Am., W.Va. State, and Ohio County bar assns., Am. Law Inst. Democrat. Roman Catholic. Elk. Club: Fort Henry (Wheeling). Home: Wheeling, W.Va. Address: Capitol Bldg., Charleston, W.Va. Died June 29, 1958.

RILEY, John Alexander, business exec.; b. North Canton, O., May 23, 1888; s. Jason Elsworth and Ida (Shook) R.; student pub. schs. Elyria, O.; studied law and accountancy Ohio night schs.; m. Lucia Manning, July 22, 1911; children—Lucia Iris (Mrs. Robert Rybolt), Nancy Helen (Mrs. Albert Heavilin), Jack Thomas. Sec., treas. Timken Roller Bearing Co., Canton, also subsidiaries. Treas. Stark Co. Tax League (Canton). Mem. Christian Ch. Mason. Club: Brookside Country (Canton, O.). Author illustrated article interpreting Beagle Standard of Am. Kennel Club. Home: 3145 Tuscarawas St. W., Canton 8. Office: 1835 Dueber Av. S.W., Canton 8, O. Died Oct. 15, 1955; buried North Lawn Cemetery, Canton, O.

RILEY, Philip Henry, educator; b. Portland, Me., Sept. 11, 1898; s. James H. and Mary Ellen (Burke) R.; B.B.A., Boston U., 1922; Ph.B., U. of Chgo., 1932; A.M., Columbia, 1936; m. Rose Frances Monagle, Sept. 5, 1927; children—Rose Marie, Kathryn Ann, Muareen Susan, Philip Ferdinand. Tchr. high sch., continuation sch., Aibonito, P.R., 1922-23; instr. English, Acad de San Agustin, Rio Piedras, P.R., 1923-24; prof. Spanish, U. Notre Dame (Ind.) 1924. Mem. Am. Assn. Tchrs. of Spanish and Portuguese, Am. Assn. U. Profs. Co-translator: The Scandal, by Pedro A. de Alarcon (with Hubert James Tunney), 1945; The Wisdom of Sorrow (with Hurbert J. Tunney), 1950. Reviewer books for pub., Books on Trial. Home: 428 E. Angela Blvd., South Bend 17, Ind. Died Nov. 5, 1950.

RILEY, William F., judge; b. 1884; A.B., State U. Ia. Admitted to Ia. bar, 1909; practiced in Des Moines; U.S. dist. judge So. Dist. Ia., 1950-56. Mem. Ia. State Bar Assn. (pres., 1949-50). Address: Federal Court House, Des Moines, Ia. Died Dec. 29, 1956; buried Des Moines, Ia.

RILEY, William G., business exec., investment banker; b. Brooklyn, N.Y., Sept. 23, 1897; s. Nicholas S. and Elizabeth M. (Fletcher) R.; ed. pub. schs., State of New York; m. Ellen E. Bryne, May 29, 1919; children—Frances Ellen, William G. Investment banker since 1929; chmn. bd. and pres. Ind. Limestone Co., Inc., Bedford, Ind. since 1946; asso. F. H. Koller & Co., Inc., New York, N.Y., 1943-48; pres., dir. Bedford Heights Realty Co. since 1947. Mem. The Security Trades Assn. of N.Y., Inc., Nat. Security Traders Assn., Inc., Am. Legion, 40 and 8. Roman Catholic. Elk. Home: Bedford Heights, Ind. Office: 405 I St., Bedford, Ind. Died Mar. 23, 1953.

RIMINI, Giacomo, baritone; b. Verona, Italy; m. Rosa Raisa, operatic soprano, 1920; 1 dau., Rose Giulietta Segala; dau. by previous marriage, Raffaelle Bettei. Debut at Verona; scored success in "Falstaff," at Milan and sang in Venice, Palermo, Naples and Rome; was invited to Buenos Aires; became a mem. Chgo. Opera Co. in 1917; now ret. from stage; operated voice and opera tutoring sch., Chgo. Address: Chgo. Died Mar. 1952.

RIMMER, Harry, clergyman; b. San Francisco, Calif., Sept. 9, 1890; s. William Henry and Katherine (Duncan) R.; student Hahneman Med. Coll., San Francisco, 1912, Whittier Coll. (Calif.), 1915-16, Bible Inst., Los Angeles, 1917-18; hon. D.D., Colquith College, 1926; honorary Sc.D., Wheaton College, 1936; LL.D., John Brown University, 1942; married Mignon Brandon, February 13, 1915; children—Charles Brandon, Duncan Ray, Kathryn Elizabeth. Ordained to ministry of Friends Church, 1915; pastor First

Friends Ch., Los Angeles, 1916-19; on leave for war work, 1918-19; phys. dir. Nat. War Work Council, Ross Field, Pacific Fleet at San Diego; transferred to Presbytery of Los Angeles, 1919; conf. speaker Internat. Com. Y.M.C.A., 1920-25; pastor 1st Presbyn. Ch., Duluth, Minn., 1934-40; lecturer on science and the Bible; pres. Research Science Bureau, Inc., since 1920; dir. Winona Lake (Ind.) Conf.; mem. board of directors, John Brown University; dir. Voice of the Andes Radio Station (HCJB) Quito, Ecuador, S.A.; trustee John Laurence Frost Fund, Wheaton Coll.; conducted 6 field expdns. in archeology. Served in Coast Arty., U.S. Army, 1908-11. Received Eugene Field Soc. award for best contribution to English religious literature, 1937. Member A.A.A.S., Alpha Gamma Omega; fellow Am. Geog. Soc. Republican. Author: The John Laurence Frost Memorial Library of Apologetics, 6 vols.; Harmony of Science and Scripture; Modern Science and the Genesis Record, 1938; Internal Evidence of Inspiration; Dead Men Tell Tales, 1939; Voices From Calvary, 1935; Crucible of Calvary; Voices from the Silent Centuries, 1935; Evidences for Immortality, 1935; Purposes of Calvary, 1939; New Testament and the Laws of Evidence, 1939; The Prayer Perfect, 1940; From Cana to Calvary, 1940; The Theories of Evolution and the Facts of Science, 1938; Palestine: The Coming Storm Center, 1940; The Coming War and the Rise of Russia, 1940; The Lawsuit Against the Bible, 1940; Crying Stones, 1941; The Coming League and the Roman Dream, 1941; The Coming King, 1941; Flying Worms, 1942; Christology: The Magnificence of Jesus, 1943; Lot's Wife and the Science of Physics; Seven Wonders of the Wonderful Word; Straight Ahead Lies Yesterday; Re-thinking Prophecy; Inspiration by Revelation, 1943; Calvary; According to the Scriptures, 1944; The Golden Chain, 1944; Christianity and Modern Crises, 1944; The Last of The Giants, 1948; The Ways of God and Man, 1949; We Surely Believe, 1949; Golden Text (2 vols.), 1950; Nuts for Monkey-Men to Crack, 1950. Also editor Christian Faith and Life; contbg. editor Religious Digest, The Northwestern Pilot; Moody Monthly. Home: 1244 Rimmer Av., Pacific Palisades, Cal. Office: 423 E. 6th St., Duluth 5. Died Mar. 19, 1952; buried Inglewood (Cal.), Cemetery.

RINEHART, James Fleece, pathologist; b. Oakland, Cal., May 7, 1901; s. James Fleece and Malvina (Raybourne) R.; student Centre Coll., 1920; A.B., U. Cal., 1923, M.D., 1927; m. Marie McCord, Jan. 20, 1930; children—James Fleece, Robert McCord. Intern Alameda Co. Hosp., 1926-27; asst. dept. pathology U. Cal. Med. Sch., 1927-28, instr. pathology, 1929-30, asst. prof., 1931-36, asso. prof. 1936-39 asso. prof. pathology and medicine, 1939-42, prof. pathology, chmn. dept., 1942—; research fellow Thorndike Meml. Lab., Boston, 1930-31. Vice pres. Cal. State Bd. Pub. Health, 1945—. Diplomate Am. Bd. Pathology. Mem. Am. Soc. Exptl. Pathology (pres. 1950), A.A.A.S., A.M.A., Am. Rheumatism Assn., Am. Soc. Clin. Investigation, Am. Assn. Pathologists and Bacteriologists, Soc. Exptl. Biology and Medicine, Alpha Tau Omega, Phi Beta Pi, Alpha Omega Alpha. Club: Bohemian. Home: 259 Bridge Rd., San Mateo, Cal. Office: University of California School of Medicine, San Francisco. Died Nov. 30, 1955.

RINEHART, Mary Roberts (rin'härt), author and playwright; b. Pittsburgh, Pa.; d. Thomas Beveridge and Cornelia (Gilleland) Roberts; educated Pittsburgh pub. and high schs., Pittsburgh Training Sch. for Nurses; Litt.D., George Washington U., 1923; m Stanley Marshall Rinehart (M.D.), Apr. 21, 1896 (died Oct. 28, 1932, children—Stanley M., Jr., Alan G., and Frederick R. Republican. Episcopalian. Author: The Circular Staircase, 1908; The Man in Lower Ten, 1909; When a Man Marries, 1909; Window at the White Cat, 1910; Amazing Adventures of Letitia Carberry, 1911; Case of Jennie Brice; Where There's a Will; The After House; The Street of Seven Stars, 1914; "K," 1915; Kings, Queens and Pawns, 1915; Tish, 1916; Bab—A Sub-Deb, 1917; Long Live the King, 1917; Tenting Tonight, 1917; The Amazing Interlude, 1917; The Altar of Freedom, 1917; Love Stories: Dangerous Days; A Poor Wise Man, 1921; Isn't That Just Like a Man? (with Irvin S. Cobb), 1921; Twenty-three and One-Half Hours' Leave; Sight Unseen and The Confession, 1922; Affinites, 1922; More Tish, 1922; The Breaking Point; The Truce of God, 1922; The Out Trail, 1923; Temperamental People, 1924; The Red Lamp, 1925; Nomad's Land, 1926; Tish Plays the Game, 1926; Lost Ecstasy, 1927; Two Flights Up, 1928; This Strange Adventure, 1929; The Romantics, 1929; The Door, 1930; Mary Roberts Rinehart's Mystery Book, 1930; My Story, 1931 (revised 1948); Rinehart's Romance Book, 1931; Book of Tish, 1931; Miss Pinkerton, 1932; The Album, 1933; Crime Book, 1933; The State Versus Elinor Norton, 1934; The Doctor, 1936; Married People, 1937; Tish Marches On, 1937; The Wall, 1938; Writing is Work, 1939; The Great Mistake, 1940; Familiar Faces, 1941; Haunted Lady, 1942; Alibi for Isabel, 1944; The Yellow Room, 1945; A Light in the Window, 1948; Episode of the Wandering Knife, 1950; The Swimming Pool, 1952; The Frightened Wife, 1953; The Best of Tish, 1955; The Mary Roberts Rinehart Crime Book, pub., 1957; author (plays) Double Life, N.Y.C., 1908; (with husband) The Avenger (1-act play), 1908; (with Avery Hopwood) Seven Days (farce), produced at Astor Theatre, N.Y., 1909; Cheer Up (farce), prod. Harris Theatre, 1913; Tish, prod. Chicago, Apr. 1919; Bab, prod. Park Theatre, New York, 1920; Spanish Love (with Avery Hopwood); The Bat (with same), prod. Morosco Theatre, 1920; The Breaking Point, prod. Klaw Theatre, 1923. Home: 635 Park Av., N.Y.C. Died Sept. 22, 1958; buried Arlington Nat. Cemetery.

RINEHART, Roy James, dean; b. nr. Deland, Ill., Oct. 24, 1880; s. Joel and Mary (Miles) R.; student Marion (Ind.) Coll.; D.D.S., Western Dental Coll., Kansas City, Mo., 1902; m. Myrtle Harmision, Sept. 24, 1903. Practiced denstistry, Canton, Ill., 1902-07, Peoria, Ill., 1907-10, Kansas City, 1911; lectr. dentistry Western Dental Coll., 1912-16, sec.-treas. and supr., 1916-17, dean, sec.-treas., trustee and chmn. exec. com. Kansas City-Western Dental Coll., 1919-27, exec. dean, 1922-27, dean, 1927—. Merged Kansas City-Western Dental Coll. with U. of Kansas City as Sch. of Dentistry, 1941, dean and mem. adv. council of u., interim acting pres., 1953. Examiner of dentists for commns. in U.S. Army, 1918; mem. Med. Adv. Bd., Kansas City, 1917-19; major Dental Corps, U.S. Army, 1925-City, 1917-19; major Dental Corps, U.S. Army, 1925-45; profl. counselor Office of Surgeon Gen., 7th Corps Area; chmn. defense com., State of Mo., 1940-42. Established Lowry Dental Clinic. Del. to Am. Dental Assn., 1916-45. Pres. legislative sect. Internat. Dental Congress, 1926; Mo. del. to Internat. Dental Congress, Vienna, 1936. Mem. Am. Coll. Dentists, Am. Assn. History Medicine, Am. Social Hygiene Assn., Spl. Libraries Assn., A.A.A.S., Central Hist. Com. of Mo., Am. Assn. Dental Editors, Am. Assn. Dental Schs. (pres. 1948), Pan-Am. Odontol. Assn., Mo. State Dental Assn. (pres. 1928), Kansas City Dist. Dental Soc. (pres. 1912), Alumni Assn. Western Dental Coll. (pres. 1915), Kansas City C. of C., Xi Psi Phi, Omicron Kappa Upsilon. Republican. Mason (Shriner). Clubs: University, Professional Men's (Kansas City); Mission Hills Country. Contbr. to profl. jours. Home: 850 W. 55th St., Kansas City, Mo. Died Mar. 22, 1957.

RINER, William A. (rī'nẽr), judge; b. Greene, Ia., June 26, 1878; s. William Wesley and Anna L. (Thompson) R.; A.B., U. of Southern Calif., 1899; LL.B., U. of Mich., 1902; m. Fanny Borst, Oct. 16, 1907; children—Frances (dec.), William, Mary (Mrs. Richard Yoder). Admitted to Michigan bar, 1902, and began practice at Lansing; moved to Cheyenne, Wyo., 1902; city atty. Cheyenne, 1908-11; asst. U.S. dist. atty., Dist. of Wyo., 1911-12; apptd. judge Dist. Ct., Wyo., 1922, later elected to same office for term 1922-28; apptd. justice Supreme Ct., Wyo., by gov., 1928, later elected to same office for term 1928-34, reëlected for term, 1935-42; chief justice, Jan. 1939-Jan. 1943; reelected to same court for terms 1943-51, 1951-59; chief justice, 1947-51, 55-—. Mem. Phi Beta Kappa. Republican. Conglist. Mason (33°, Shriner). Home: 114 W. 27th St. Office: Supreme Court and Library Bldg., Cheyenne, Wyo. Died Nov. 20, 1955; buried Lakeview Cemetery, Cheyenne, Wyo.

RINES, George Edwin, editor; b. Maitland, N.S. Can., Dec. 28, 1858; s. William and Margaret (Miller) R.; Colgate U., 1887-90; grad. Hamilton Theol. Sem., 1893. Ordained Bapt. ministry, 1893; pastor Binghamton, N.Y., 1893-95, Ridgewood, N.J., 1896-99; engaged in literary work 1899—; was mng. editor first edition Encyclopaedia Americana, 1902-05; mng. editor United Editors' Encyclopaedia and Dictionary, 1906, The South in The Building of the Nation, 1907-08; gen. editor The Foundation Library for Young People, 1910-11. Mng. editor of The German Classics, 1913-15; co-editor Encyclopaedia of Latin-America, 1917; editor in chief Encyclopaedia Americana, 2d edit., 1917. Author: Getting the Most Out of Life; As the Wind Blows, 1946. Address: Bklyn. Died Nov. 30, 1951.

RINEY, Earl Alvin, clergyman; b. Vandalia, Mo., May 3, 1885; s. John Alexander and Frances Eldora (Music) R.; A.B., William Jewell Coll., Liberty, Mo., 1908, A.M., 1910; B.D., U. of Chicago, 1914; Th.D., Central Baptist Theological Sem., 1937; m. Elizabeth Lyman Rowland, June 2, 1907; children—Frances (dec.), Lyman Hassler. Ordained to ministry of Baptist Church, 1903; served as pastor at St. Joseph, Missouri, 1914-20, Norman, Oklahoma, 1920-22, Coffeyville, Kan., 1922-30, First Bapt. Ch., Waterloo, Ia., 1930-34, Roanoke Ch., Kansas City, Mo., 1934-46; now retired and engaged in writing. Member of the faculty of the Kansas Baptist Assembly; chmn. evangelism com. Cedar Valley Assn.; trustee Ottawa (Kan.) U., 1926-32; mem. exec. com. Kansas City Council Churches 1936-45; chairman program com. Pastors Conference Greater Kansas City, 1943-44; pres. Kansas City Bapt. Ministerial Alliance, 1941. Member Kansas City Bapt. Assn. (mem. bd. 1935-45), S.E. Kan. Bapt. Assn. (chmn. Associational Board, Executive Board), Kansas Baptist State Board, Kansas State S.S. Board, Iowa S.S. and State Board, 1928-32, Iowa Bapt. Assembly (faculty), Kansas City Associational Bd., Philomathian Lit. Soc. Mason (Shriner). Clubs: Lions (Coffeyville); Lions (Waterloo). Author: Lines for Living, 1951; Family Life in Focus, 1953. Contbr. religious mags. Writer newspaper column "Selected Short Sermons," 1936—. Home: 29 W. 58th Terrace, Kansas City 13, Mo. Died Oct. 20, 1955; buried Floral Hills Meml. Gardens, Kansas City.

RING, Richard Warner, accountant; b. Savannah, Ga., Sept. 27, 1901; s. John R. and Agnes (Meskel) R.; grad. Eastman Coll., Poughkeepsie, N.Y., 1923; m. Ethel Marshall, Aug. 5, 1930; children—John M., Michael W. Partner firm Ring, Mahony & Arner, C.P.A.'s, Miami, Fla., 1926—. Mem. Fla. Bd. Accountancy, 1955—; pres. So. States Accountants Conf., 1955-56. Pres. Dade County Citizens Safety Council, 1955—; v.p. Dade County Community Chest, 1954—. Served as comdr. USNR, 1942-45. Mem. Am. Inst. Accountants (v.p. 1956-57; com. on awards, 1954—; trial bd. 1955—). Catholic. Clubs: Kiwania (pres. 1957), Miami (Miami); Bath La Gorce country (Miami Beach, Fla.). Home: 672 N.E. 98th St., Miami Shores, Fla. Office: duPont Bldg., Miami 32, Fla. Died June 7, 1958.

RINGER, Paul Henry, physician; b. New York, N.Y., Nov. 6, 1881; s. Severin and Elisa (Minot) R.; A.B., Columbia, 1901, M.D., 1904; m. Eleanor Varick Morrison, May 1, 1915 (died September 1942); children—Paul Henry, Eleanor Morrison; married 2d, Mary Averell Brown, April 27, 1946. Engaged in practice as physician in Ashville, N.C., 1906-50; mem. Asheville Mission Hosp. staff, 1909-35; cons. physician 1935-50. Pres. N.C. Med. Soc., 1935-36; pres. Southern Tuberculosis Conf., 1937-38, Southern Med. Assn., 1940-41; Pres. Asheville Community Chest, 1936, Asheville Civic Music Assn., 1937-47; dir. Y.M.C.A. Captain Med. Corps, U.S. Army, with A.E.F., 1918-19. Presbyterian. Clubs: Columbia University (New York); Asheville Civitian (pres. 1929), Pen and Plate, Biltmore Forest Country (Asheville). Author: Clinical Medicine for Nurses, 1918. Contbr. to med. jours. Retired. Home: 423 Park Av., N.Y.C. 22. Died May 8, 1952; buried Riverside Cemetery, Asheville, N.C.

RINGLAND, Joseph Ford, banker; b. Wayne, Neb., July 22, 1901; s. Harvey S. and Myrtle (Ford) R.; B.S., Iowa State Coll., 1924; m. Rebecca Moore, Oct. 25, 1930; children—Joseph Ford, James M. Began with U.S. Nat. Bank, Omaha, Neb., 1924, became asst. cashier, 1929; v.p. Great Falls Nat. Bank, Great Falls, Mont., 1933-36; pres. Stock Yards Nat. Bank, South St. Paul, 1936-42, Empire Nat. Bank & Trust Co., St. Paul, 1943; v.p. Guaranty Trust Co., N.Y.C., 1943-44; v.p. Northwestern Nat. Bank of Mpls., 1944, pres., dir. 1945—; dir. Northwest Bancorporation, Northwestern Nat. Life Ins. Co., Northwestern Fire & Marine Ins. Co., (all Mpls.) Red Owl Stores, Inc., Hopkins, Minn., Western Air Lines, (Los Angeles). Dir. Community Chest & Council Mpls., Mpls. Area council Boy Scouts Am. Trustee Shattuck Sch., Faribault, Minn. Mem. Assn. Reserve City Bankers, Fed. Res. Bd. Adv. Council. Clubs: Minneapolis, Minikada (Mpls.); Woodhill Country (Wayzata, Minn.); Minnesota (St. Paul); Chicago. Home: 1625 W. 25th St. Office: 620 Marquette Av., Mpls. Died Nov. 8, 1957.

RINGLING, Henry E(llsworth), mem. Rep. Nat. Com.; b. Chgo., Sept. 13, 1906; s. Henry and Ida Belle (Palmer) R.; student Culver Mil. Acad., 1920-23; B.C.S., U. Fla., 1929; student London Sch. Econs., 1930; B.S.A., U. Wis., 1935; m. Jean Cathrine Fowler, Sept. 6, 1936; children—Salome Juliar, Henry Ellsworth. Vice pres., dir. Baraboo Nat. Bank since 1947. Mem. Rep. Nat. Com. since 1952. Served as lt. U.S.C.G., 1941-45. Mem. Am. Legion, Sigma Chi. Episcopalian (jr. warden). Elk, Mason. Clubs: Adventurers, University (Chgo.). Home: 201 Eighth St. Office: Al. Ringling Theater, Baraboo, Wis. Died Dec. 9, 1955; buried Baraboo, Wis.

RINGO, Helen (Colburn), pianist, teacher; b. Topeka, Kan.; d. Ira Delos and Lottie Eleanor (Martin) Colburn; B.M., Kan. State Coll., 1922; student Chicago Music Coll., 1922, Am. Conservatory, Chicago, 1922, Cincinnati Conservatory of Music, 1924-25, Juilliard Grad. Sch. of Music, 1935-36; piano student Sturkow-Ryder, Leo Paalz, Heniot Levy, Joseph Lhevinne, Guy Maier; m. Boyd Ringo, July 3, 1923; 1 son, Boyd Colburn. Professional accompanist, Chicago, 1921-22; teacher, piano, Kan. State Coll., 1922-24; prof. piano, U. of Tulsa, since 1924; nat. tours with Boyd Ringo as duo-pianists, since 1924; concert, Nat. Music Teachers Assn., Minneapolis, 1941; Nat. Fedn. Women's Clubs, Ft. Worth, Tex., 1942, 1st 50-piano festival U.S. on radio, 1934; 1st 100-piano festival, on radio, Tulsa, 1935; 4 state confs. for pianists and teachers, U. of Tulsa, 1943; organized, directed Chopin piano festival, U. of Tulsa, 1947; directed Schumann Festival, 1948; French Music Festival, 1949; dir. Southwestern Music Camp, Hollister, Mo., 1937-39; coaching, teaching, training teachers of piano, judging competitions. Author: complete outlines and procedures for teachers of piano, 1930. Presbyterian. Home: 2446 E. 18th St., Tulsa 4. Died May 12, 1952; buried Rose Hill Mausoleum, Tulsa.

RIORDAN, William O., merchant; b. Boston, 1890. Pres., dir. Stern Bros. Home: 63 Melrose Drive, New Rochelle. Office: 41 West 42d St., N.Y.C. Died Dec. 1950.*

RIPLEY, Clements, writer; b. Tacoma, Aug. 26, 1892; s. Thomas Emerson and Charlotte Howard (Clement) R.; prep. edn., Taft Sch., Watertown, Conn.; A.B., Yale, 1916; m. Katharine Ball, June 7, 1919 (dec. July 1955); 1 son, William Young Warren. Commd. 2d lt. F.A., U.S. Army, 1916, and advanced to capt., leaving service 1920; engaged in peach growing and writing, 1920-28. Episcopalian. Author: Dust and Sun, 1929; Devil Drums, 1931; Black Moon, 1933; Murder Walks Alone, 1935; Gold Is Where You Find It, 1936; Clear for Action, 1940; Mississippi Belle, 1942. Contbr. fiction and articles mags. Short story, "Cities of Fear," included in World's Best Short Stories of 1929. Author of motion pictures, Jezebel; Love, Honor and Behave; Buffalo Bill; In Old Los Angeles. Home: 1922 S. Bentley Av., Los Angeles 25, (winter) 18 Lamboll St., Charleston, S.C. Died July 22, 1954.

RIPLEY, Edward Lafayette, treas. The Mother Ch., The 1st Ch. of Christ, Scientist, Boston; b. Montaque, Mich., Jan. 1, 1876; s. Lafayette Gilbert and May Edith (Brackney) R.; student Montague, later Grand Rapids (Mich.) High Schs., 1889-94; m. Hilda Johnstone, Nov. 20, 1920. Clerk U.S. Post Office, Kansas City, Mo., 1894-96; accounting, sales, r.r. and mercantile activities, 1896-1916; asst. to treas. The 1st Ch. of Christ, Scientist, Boston, 1916-18, treas., 1918-41; ret., 1941. Republican. Home: 143 Beaconsfield Rd., Brookline, Mass. Died Feb. 18, 1944.

RIPLEY, Katharine Ball (Mrs. Clements Ripley), author; b. Charleston, S.C., Mar. 20, 1899; d. William Watts and Fay (Witte) Ball; ed. pvt. schs.; m. Clements Ripley, June 7, 1919 (dec. July, 1954); 1 son, William Young Warren. Mem. Jr. League Club. Author: Sand in My Shoes, 1931; Sand Dollars, 1933; Crowded House, 1935. Contbr. short stories to Atlantic Monthly. Home: 8 Orange St., Charleston, S.C. Died July 24, 1955; buried Charleston.

RIPPEL, Julius S., investment securities; b. Newark, Sept. 21, 1868; s. Godfred C. and Susan Seivert) Rippel: ed. pub. sch., Coleman's Bus. Coll., Newark; m. Fannie Estelle Traphagen, 1898 (dec.). With Graham & Co., stock brokers and steamship agts., 1887-91; organizer J. S. Rippel & Co., investment securities, 1891; chmn. bd., pres. Merchants & Newark Trust Co.; pres. Guaranty Co., N.J., Securities Co., N.J., Stock and Bond Corp., N.J.; chmn. exec. com. Nat. State Bank, Newark. dir. N.J. Realty Title Ins. Co., Newark Provident Loan Assn. Mem. Reconstrn. Finance Corp. adv. bd. Fed. Res. Dist. Mem. Reformed Ch. Clubs: Essex, Down Town. Home: 67 Johnson Av. Office: 18 Clinton St., Newark. Died Dec. 9, 1950; buried Newark.

RIPPIN, Jane Deeter (Mrs. James Yardley Rippin), editor for women; b. Harrisburg, Pa., May 30, 1882; d. Jasper Newton and Sarah Emely (Mather) Deeter; B.S., Irving Coll., Mechanicsburg, Pa., 1902, M.A., 1914; post-grad. work, U. of Pa., 1909-10; m. James Yardley Rippin, Oct. 11, 1913. Asst. to prin. high sch., Mechanicsburg, Pa., 1902-08; asst. supt. Children's Village, Meadowbrook, Pa., 1908-10; supervisor case work, Soc. Prevention of Cruelty to Children, Phila., 1910-14; chief probation officer, Phila., 1914-17. Organized probation work of Municipal Court of Phila.; in charge of orgn. first Woman's Court Bldg., Phila., where social, mental and physical diagnoses are presented before presiding judge at time of hearing; dir. sect. of women and girls of Commn. on Training Camp Activities of War and Navy depts., 1917-19; made spl. study of women camp followers, World War; nat. dir. Girl Scouts, Inc., 1919-31 (developing Girl Scout movement into nation-wide organization); woman's editor Westchester County Publishers. Mem. bd. dirs. Nat. Information Bureau, National Institute for Social Sciences; Adirondack Mountain Club. Member National Council Social Agencies, National Conference Social Work, National Conference of Out Door Activities, National Institute of Social Sciences. Republican. Episcopalian. Clubs: Cosmopolitan, Women's Republican (New York); Civic (Phila.). Home: 45 Tappan Landing Road, Tarrytown, N.Y. Office: Westchester County Publishers, 8 Church St., White Plains, N.Y. Died June 2, 1953.

RISTER, Carl Coke, historian; b. Hayrick, Tex., June 30, 1889; s. Craton and Sarah (Parker) R.; A.B., Simmons U., Abilene, Tex., 1915; M.A., Geo. Washington U., 1919; summer terms, U. of Calif., 1921, 1922; Ph.D., Geroge Washington U., Washington, 1925; hon. Litt.D., Hardin-Simmons U., 1941; m. Mattie May, June 11, 1916. Supt. of schs., Hutto, Tex., 1915-16, O'Brien, Tex., 1916-17, McCauley, Tex., 1917-18; asst. prof. of history, asso. prof. and prof. Simmons U., Abilene, Tex., 1920-29; editor of West Texas History Yearbook, 1925-29; mem. bd. of editors since 1929; asso. prof. history U. of Okla., 1929-35, prof., 1935-45, chmn. dept. of history, 1944-45, research prof., 1945-51; distinguished prof. Texas Technol. Coll. since 1951; summer teaching assignments U. of Okla., 1928, U. of Tex., 1929, George Washington U., 1931, Denver U., 1939, U. of Colo., 1940, U. of Mo., 1941, New Mexico Highlands U., 1942, U. of Colo., 1947; on leave for research, Library of Congress and Nat. Archives, Washington, 1937, history of Southwestern Oil, 1946-47, 1947-48. Awarded grant by Social Science Research Council of New York for study on Southern Plains Social History, 1933, study of mil. history of Great Plains Frontier, 1936; awarded grant Standard Oil Co., (N.J.) for compilation of materials and writing history of Southwestern oil. Mem. Am. Hist. Assn. (Pacific Coast Br.), Miss. Valley Hist. Assn. (mem. exec. com., pres. 1949-50), Texas Institute of Letters, Society of American Historians, Texas Hist. Soc., Okla. Hist. Soc., West Texas Hist., Assn., Westerners (Chicago), Phi Beta Kappa (hon.). Democrat. Baptist. Author: The Southwestern Frontier, 1865-1881, 1928; The Greater Southwest (with R. N. Richardson), 1934; The Southern Plainsmen, 1938; Border Captives, 1940; Western America (with L. R. Hafen), 1941; Land Hunger, 1942; Baptist Missions Among The American Indians, 1944; Border Command, 1944; Robert E. Lee In Texas, 1946; No Man's Land, 1948; Oil! Titan of the Southwest, 1949. Contributor of chapters and articles to Dictionary of American History, 1940; Scribner's Atlas of American History, 1943; and Harold Williamson's Growth of the American Economy, 1943. Contbr. numerous articles to various profl. periodicals. Home: 2216 14th St., Lubbock, Tex. Died Apr. 16, 1955.

RISTINE, Frank Humphrey, educator; b. Crawfordsville, Ind., Apr. 11, 1884; s. Theodore H. and Katherine Williams (Thomson) R.; student Wabash Prep. Sch., 1898-1901; A.B., Wabash Coll., 1905, L.H.D., 1933; A.M., Columbia, 1907, Ph.D., 1910; m. Katherine C. Longwell, June 4, 1918; children—Thomas H., Anne L. (Mrs. Robert T. Eckfeldt). Acting prof. of English, Wabash Coll., 1909-10; instr. in English, Columbia, 1911-12; prof. of English lit. Hamilton Coll., Clinton, N.Y., 1912-52; ret. 1952, dean 1932-42. Served as 1st lt. 327th F.A. (84th div.), 1917-19. Trustee Wabash Coll., 1940—. Mem. Modern Lang. Assn., Shakespeare Assn., Am. Legion, Phi Beta Kappa, Beta Theta Pi. Republican. Presbyn. Author: English Tragicomedy, 1910; Bibliography of John G. Whittier, 1918, in Cambridge History of American Literature, vol. 2. Editor: (with H. R. Steeves) Representative Essays in Modern Thought, 1913, and Byron's Don Juan, 1927. Home: College Hill Rd., Clinton, N.Y. Died July 28, 1958; buried Hamilton Coll. Cemetery, Clinton, N.Y.

RITCHIE, William (ritchiē), lawyer; b. Ravenswood, Ill., July 28, 1886; s. Wiliam and Charlotte (Congdon) R.; LL.B., U. Neb., 1915; m. Eunice Arthur, Apr. 26, 1916. Admitted to Neb. bar, 1915, U.S. Supreme Ct., 1926; engaged in practice of law 1915-53; dir. Kennedy & Parsons Co., C. B. Brown Co., Omaha. Trustee U. Neb. Found. Served as capt. 69th Inf., U.S. Army, 1917-19. Mem. Am., Neb. and Omaha bar assns., Am. Legion (dept. comdr. 1921-22), S.A.R., Beta Theta Pi, Phi Delta Phi. Democrat (state chmn.; nominee for Senate 1952, for gov. 1954). Catholic. Home: 5822 Western Av., Omaha 3, Neb. Died Feb., 1956.

RITER, Henry G., III, corp. exec.; b. Phila., Pa., Oct. 6, 1892; s. Henry G. and Mary L. (Cram) R.; student Germantown Acad., 1901-08; m. Margaret A. Chase, Oct. 9, 1913; children—Margaret R. (Mrs. David T. Agens), Henry G., IV, Maryl R. (Mrs. John Y. G. Walker, Jr.). With Dillon, Read & Co., 1919-33, mem. of firm, 1927-33; sr. partner Riter & Co., 1933-51, became ltd. partner 1952, now spl. partner; former pres., dir. Thomas A. Edison, Industries of McGraw-Edison Company, 1957, director corporate relations McGraw-Edison Co., 1958—. dir. McGraw-Edison Co.; became chmn. bd. Copperweld Steel Co., 1942, now hon. chmn. bd., chmn. finance com. Pres., mem. bd. trustees Montclair (N.J.) Y.M.C.A., N.J. C. of C. (v.p. dir.); chmn. exec. com. N.A.M.; mem. Newcomen Society of N. Am., Pilgrims of U.S. Rep. Conglist. Clubs: Bond, Montclair Golf, Union League, Bay Head Yacht. Home: 36 Stonebridge Rd., Montclair, N.J. Office: 51 Lakeside Av., West Orange, N.J. Died June 30, 1958.

RITSCHEL, Wilhelm (rĭt'shĕl), painter; b. Nuernberg, Bavaria, July 11, 1864; s. Josef and Elise (Duenkel) R.; ed. Latin and technical sch., Germany; student at the Royal Acad., Munich; m. 2d, Nora Havel, of Tacoma, Wash., 1929. Came to America, 1895; splty. marines; exhibited at all important exhbns. in U.S. and abroad. N.A., 1914; mem. New York Water Color Club, Am. Water Color Soc., Am. Federation Arts, Union Internationale des Beaux Arts et des Lettres, Paris. Clubs: Salmagundi, Nat. Arts of New York (life); hon. mem. Bohemian (San Francisco). Address: Carmel Highlands, Carmel, Calif. Died 1949.

RITT, Joseph Fels, mathematician; b. New York, N.Y., Aug. 23, 1893; son of Morris and Eva (Steinberg) R.; student Coll. of City of N.Y., 1908-10; A.B., George Washington U., 1913. D.Sc., 1932; Ph.D., Columbia, 1917; m. Estelle Fine, June 29, 1928. Instr. in mathematics, Columbia, 1910-21, asst. prof., 1921-27, asso. prof., 1927-31, prof. since 1931, executive officer, department of mathematics, 1942-45, Davies Prof. Mathematics since July 1, 1945. Master computer ordnance dept., 1918-19. Mem. Nat. Acad. Sciences, Nat. Research Council, 1938-41, Am. Math. Soc. (v.p. 1938-40). Author; Differential Equations from the Algebraic Standpoint, 1932; Theory of Functions, 1947; Integration in Finite Terms, 1948; Differential Algebra, 1950. Contbr. to math. jours. Address: Columbia U., N.Y. City. Died Jan. 5, 1951; buried Mt. Zion Cemetery, Maspeth, L.I., N.Y.

RITTER, Claude Dowd, lawyer; b. Carthage, N.C., Aug. 2, 1880; s. William Lewis and Harriett (Dowd) R. Student pub. schs. of N.C.; legal edn. Wake Forest (N.C.) Coll.; m. Bessie Gunter, Dec. 21, 1911; children—Claude Dowd, Mary Elizabeth. Admitted to N.C. bar, 1903, Ala. bar, 1904, bar of U.S. Supreme Court, 1919; practiced in Birmingham 1904—; sr. partner Ritter, Wynn & Carmichael. Mem. Am., Ala. State Birmingham bar assns., Loyal Knights of Round Table (internat. pres. 1928-29; local pres. 1925-26), comml. Law League Am. (pres. 1923-24) Democrat. Baptist. Mason (Shriner). Home: 726 Euclid Av. Office: Frank Nelson Bldg., Birmingham, Ala. Died Aug. 30, 1948.

RITTER, Halsted Lockwood, judge; b. Indpls., July 14, 1868; s. Eli Foster and Narcissa (Lockwood) R.; Ph.D., DePauw U., Greencastle, Indiana, 1891, LL.B., 1892, A.M., 1893, LL.D., 1930; m. Grace Lurline May, July 14, 1897; children—Elinor May (Mrs. Merle R. Walker), Thurston. Admitted to Ind. bar, 1892, and practiced at Indpls. until 1895; practiced at Denver, Colo., 1895-1925, West Palm Beach, Fla., Dec. 1925-Feb. 1929; judge U.S. Dist. Court, Southern Dist. of Fla., since Feb. 25, 1929. Mem. Colo. R.R. Commn., 1907-08; mem. Colo. Food Commn., World War. Prof. law Denver Law Sch., 1898-1902; pres. Denver Bar Assn., 1908-09; pres. Social Service Bur. of Denver, 1915-24; mem. Colo. Child Welfare Bur., 1919; pres. Denver Community Chest, 1924; pres. Am. Assn. for Community Organization, 1924-25; founder Denver Legal Aid Soc., 1925. Mem. Phi Beta Kappa, Delta Kappa Epsilon. Republican. Conglist. Mason (32°, K.T.). Author: George Washington the Business Man, 1931. Address: U.S. Dist. Court, Federal Bldg., Miami, Fla. Deceased.

RITTMAN, Walter Frank, consulting engineer; born at Sandusky, Ohio, December 2, 1883; s. Christian A. and Louisa A. (Scheel) R.; C.E., Ohio Northern U., 1905; A.B., Swarthmore Coll., 1908, M.A., 1909, M.E., 1911, Chem. E. 1917; Ph.D. Columbia, 1914; m. Anna Frances Campbell, Sept. 11, 1913; children—Frank Sears, William Campbell, Eleanor Anne. Chemist with United Gas Improvement Co., Phila., 1908-09; consulting engr., Phila., 1909-12; chem. engr. U.S. Bur. of Mines, 1914-21; prof., head engring. dept., Carnegie Inst. Tech., 1921-33; cons. engr. to State of Pa., 1923-24; cons. engr. U.S. Dept. Agr., 1925-37; lecturer on industrial chemistry, Swarthmore Coll., 1909-12, at Columbia U. 1913. Trustee Ohio Northern Univ., 1928-41. Fellow A.A.A.S.; mem. Am. Chem. Soc., Am. Inst. Chemical Engrs., Franklin Inst., Am. Soc. M.E., Am. Inst. Mining and Metall. Engrs., Soc. Industrial Engrs. (nat. pres. 1925-30), Administrative Bd. Am. Engring. Council, 1925-30, Sigma Psi, Phi Lambda Upsilon, Tau Beta Pi, Sigma Phi Epsilon, etc. Clubs: Chemists, University (New York); Union League (Chicago); Duquesne (Pittsburgh). Contbr. numerous articles dealing with application of physical chemistry to industrial processes, especially those dealing with fuel, oil and gas. Address: 6112 Alder St., Pitts. 6. Died Sept. 26, 1954; buried Chautauqua, N.Y.

RITZMAN, Ernest George, animal nutrition; b. Switzerland, May 20, 1875; s. John George and Maria Ursula (Gisel) R.; brought to U.S., 1883; B.S., Ia. State Coll. Agr. and Mech. Arts, 1903; M.S. (hon.), New Hampshire U., 1928; m. Lois Alexander, Nov. 25, 1909; children—Thomas Alexander, Barbara Bicknell Asst. animal husbandman Bur. Animal Industry, Washington, 1903-08; animal husbandman, Expt. Sta., Puerto Rico (Fed. sta.), 1908-13; prof. animal husbandry, U. of Puerto Rico, 1913-15; research prof. in animal nutrition and genetics, U. New Hampshire, 1915-47, now emeritus; research asso. Carnegie Instn. Washington, 1934-40. Served as vol. in Spanish-Am. War, 1898-99; vol. Plattsburg Camp, 1918. Pres. Central Wool Marketing Corp. (eastern br. Nat. Wool Marketing Corp.); mem. com. animal nutrition Nat. Research Council. Mem. Am. Soc. Animal Prodn., Genetic Soc. Am., Am. Inst. of Nutrition, Am. Dairy Sci. Assn., Phi Kappa Phi. Co-author of monographs 324, 377 and 494 (Carnegie Instn.) issued 1923, 1927 and 1937. Contbr. 50 tech. articles, ann. reports or bulls. and popular articles. Home: Durham, N.H. Died May 15, 1955; buried Durham (N.H.) Cemetery.

RIVERA, Diego (rē-vĕr'ä), **(Diego Maria Concepción Juan Nepomuceno Estanislao de la Rivera y**

Barrientos Acosta y Rodríguez), Mexican painter; b. Andrés Ríos; Felix Para, Santiago Rebull, José María Velasco, 1889-1907; worked in atelier of Éduardo Guanajuato, 1886; ed. Nat. Acad. Art; pupil of Holland, Eng., Spain, Portugal; on govt. scholarship in Paris, Italy; m. 4th, Emma Hurtado, Aug. 1955; children by previous marriage—Ruth, Guadalupe. Prin. works include: Decoration of auditorium of Nat. Prep. Sch., Mexico City, 1922; murals in Secretariat of Edn., Mexico City; in Nat. Sch. Agr., Chapingo, 1923-26; frescos in Stock Exchange Luncheon Club, San Francisco, 1930; in San Francisco Sch. Fine Arts, 1930; murals, Detroit Inst. of Fine Arts, 1932. Awarded First Prize at Pan-Am. Exhibition, San Francisco, 1926; medal of Am. Inst. of Architects. Author: Portrait of America, 1934. Address: Londres 127, Coyacan, Mexico. Died Nov. 25, 1957.*

RIVES, Edwin Earle (rēvz), judge; b. Winston Salem, N.C., Nov. 19, 1898; s. Edward Andrew and Florence (Goldston) R.; LL.B., U. N.C., 1922; m. Mary Tankersley, Nov. 15, 1922 (dec.); children—Frances Adele, Edwin Earle, Mary Roselia; married 2d, Margaret Hunter Stout, Aug. 15, 1953. Admitted to N.C. bar, 1922 and practiced in Greensboro, 1922-29; judge Municipal Ct. apptd. by Greensboro City Council, 1929-33; apptd. judge Municipal-Co. Ct. by Gov. of N.C. since 1933; spl. assignment as personal rep. Sec. of Army, Berlin, 1947-48; cons. Sec. Army since 1948, apptd. Civilian Aide, 1952; apptd. dir. Fed. Prison Industries, Inc. by Pres., 1949. Dem. candidate for nomination U.S. Congress, 1946. Served as sgt., A.U.S., World War I; lt. col., Judge Adv. Gen. Dept., World War II. Mem. Am., N.C. (chmn. exec. com., 1937, v.p., 1941), Greensboro (v.p., 1942) bar assns., N.C. Bar, Inc., Gen. Alumni Assn. U. N.C. (pres., 1951-52), Phi Delta Theta, Phi Delta Phi. Club: Kiwanis. Home: 207 N. Ridgeway Dr. Office: Post Office Box 2759, Greensboro, N.C. Died Dec. 12, 1953; buried Greenhill Cemetery, Greensboro, N.C.

RIVINUS, Francis Markoe (rĭ-vīn'ŭs), lawyer; b. Germantown, Phila., Pa., Oct. 6, 1882; s. David Caldwell Florens and Emilie (Markoe) R.; prep. edn. DeLancey Sch. (now merged with Episcopal Acad.), Phila., Pa.; A.B., Harvard, 1904; m. Lillian Megary Welsh, Sept. 8, 1914 (divorced 1942); children—Francis Markoe, David Caldwell, Martha; m. 2d, Isabel Phelps Wootton, 1943; 1 son, Randolph Phelps; stepchildren—Diane Phelps Wootton, Jeannette Elmo Wootton. Admitted to Pa. bar, 1906, and began practice in Phila.; legal dept. of N.&W. Ry. Co. since 1910, gen. counsel since 1935. Home: 2516 Longview Av. Office: N.&W. Ry. Co., Roanoke, Va. Died Aug. 30, 1951.

RIVITZ, Hiram S., chmn. Indsl. Rayon Corp. Address: Union Commerce Bldg., Cleve. Died June 4, 1951.

RIXFORD, Elizabeth M. Leach (Mrs. Oscar H.), genealogist; b. Bakersfield, Vt., Jan. 7, 1866; d. Horace B. and Caroline A. (Phelps) Leach; ed. Fairfield Sch., Brigham Bakersfield Acad.; m. Oscar H. Rixford, Sept. 8, 1889; 1 son, Oscar A.; m. 2d, Rev. A. A. Bailey; 1 son, Charles. Vice pres., sec., Rixford Mfg. Co., 1926-47. Mem. Washington Bi-Centennial Com. (apptd. by gov. of state), Vt. Huguenot Soc. (life), Gen. Soc. Mayflower Descendants (sec. 5 yrs.), Soc. for Vt. (dep. gov. gen.), Daughters of Founders and Patriots of Am. (pres. 3 yrs., historian 3 yrs.), Magna Charta Dames (nat. regent, life mem.), Vt. Soc. U.S. Daus. of 1812, Colonial Daus. of the 17th Century, Daus. of the Union, Order of the First Crusade (state regent for Vt. and N. H., nat. life mem.), Daus. Am. Colonists (state regent, chmn. colonial and gen. records com. for Atlantic Coast sect.), Assn. for Preservation of Va. Antiquities (Richmond). Awarded Certificate of Merit, in Geneaology, Am. Inst. Geneaology, Compiler and pub.; 300 Colonial Ancestors, and Supplements I, II, III, IV; Families Directly Descended from All the Royal Families in Europe, Mayflower Descendants. Address: Eight Highgate, Vt. Died May 1, 1956.

ROACH, Alden G., steel co. exec.; b. St. Louis, Mar. 22, 1901; s. Harry F. and Mary (Gallup) R.; B. S. in Civil Engring., U. Ill., 1923; children—Judith Noyes, Alden Gallup, Jennifer Dean. While attending sch., worked in various capacities for Wabash, Alton, So., M.P. R.R.'s; with engring. dept. U.P. and M.P. R.R.'s, 1923-25; engr., supt. D. C. Bowman, engring. contractor and builder, St. Louis, 1925-27; joined Union Iron Works of Los Angeles, 1927, co. merged with Llewellyn Iron Works and Baker Iron Works to form Consolidated Steel Corp., 1929, became v.p. charge sales and engring. of new corp., 1934, dir., 1938, exec. v.p., 1938-41, pres., 1941-55 (name corp. changed to Consol. Western Steel Corp. upon acquisition properties of Western Pipe and Steel of Los Angeles and San Francisco), co. acquired by U.S. Steel Corp., 1948; pres. Columbia Steel Co., 1948-55; pres. Columbia-Geneva Steel div. U.S. Steel Corp., 1955—; cons. prof. bus. mgmt. Stanford Grad. Sch. Bus., 1955-56; dir. So. Cal. Edison Co., N. Am. Aviation, Inc., Indsl. Indemnity Co., 12th Dist. Fedn. Res. Bank in San Francisco. Mem. bus. adv. council to Sec. of Commerce, Cal. Traffic Safety Found. Trustee Com. for Econ. Development, Cal. Inst. Tech.; dir. Stanford Research Inst. Mem. Am. Mgmt. Assn. (v.p., dir.), Am. Soc. C.E.; asso. mem. Soc. Naval Architects and Marine Engrs. Clubs: Bohemian, California, Pacific Union, Family; Duquesne (Pitts.); Newport Yacht; Chicago; Cypress Point, Los Angeles Country; The River (N.Y.C.). Address: 1100 Sacramento St., San Francisco. Died Dec. 20, 1956.

ROACH, David James, business exec.; b. Sedalia, Colo., Apr. 12, 1887; s. Phillip and Louisa (Cook) R.; B.S., Colo. State Coll., 1908; m. Katherine B. Higgins, June 14, 1911; children—Mary Louise (Mrs. John D. Edmiston), Elizabeth Ann (Mrs. Robert F. Hemphill). Chief chemist and traveling chem. Great Western Sugar Co., 1908-17, asst. to gen. supt., 1917-20, plant mgr., Ft. Collins and Windsor, 1920-29, Scottsbluff and Gering, 1929-35; dist. mgr., Neb. Dist., 1935-39, asst. gen. mgr., Denver, 1939, v.p., 1940-47, exec. v.p., 1947—. Republican. Presbyn. Mason. Clubs: Denver Rotary, Denver. Writer on economics, agr. and technol. of beet sugar industry. Home: 2222 E. Seventh Av. Office: 1530 Sixteenth St., Denver. Died Oct. 1953.

ROBB, Russell, director and trustee; born in Concord, Mass., Nov. 13, 1900; son of Russell and Edith Owen (Morse) R.; A.B., Harvard Coll., 1923; married Katharine Moxley Armstrong, Jan. 3, 1933; children—Gale Armstrong, Russell Jr. With Stone and Webster, Inc. (except for war leave with the Armed Services), 1923-49, v.p. and dir., 1929-41, 1946-49, still dir.; dir. Stone and Webster Engring. Corp., Stone and Webster Service Corp., N.Y., Colonial Fund Inc., Stone and Webster Realty Corp., Boston; trustee, Franklin Savings Bank City of Boston. Joined Army Air Forces, 1941, with rank of capt., released 1946, with rank of col. Awarded Legion of Merit. Trustee Concord (Mass.) Acad., Concord, trustee Museum of Science, Boston. Member Delta Psi. Unitarian. Clubs: Fly (Cambridge); Somerset, Harvard (Boston); Social Circle (Concord); Brook (N.Y.). Home: Concord, Mass. Office: 75 Federal St., Boston 10. Died June 3, 1957.

ROBBINS, Burnett W., advt. exec.; b. Paw Paw, Mich., Dec. 14, 1876; s. Burr and Nett (Webster) R.; m. Louise L. Lamberton, Sept. 30, 1896; 1 son —Burr L. Robbins. Treas. American Posting Service, 1902-04, v.p. and gen. mgr., 1906-08, pres., 1908-18; dir. Outdoor Advt. Assn. of America, Inc., since 1912; dir. and sec. Outdoor Advt. Assn. of Ill. since 1908; pres. and dir. Chicago Poster Advt. Co., 1919-25; v.p. and dir. General Outdoor Advt. Co., Inc., 1925-31, pres., dir., 1931-51, chmn. bd., 1951—; dir., mem. exec. com. Outdoor Advt. Inc., N.Y.; pres. and dir. Old Colony Advt. Co., Providence, R.I.; dir. Traffic Audit Bureau, Inc., N.Y.; dir. Loveridge Poster Advt. Co., Lexington, Ky.; dir. Pittsburgh Outdoor Advt. Co.; pres. O. J. Gude Co., N.Y., since Sept. 11, 1931. Mason (32°). Clubs: Chicago Athletic, Edgewater Golf, Lake Shore, Glen View, Delavan Country. Home: 3500 Lake Shore Drive, Chicago. Office: Harrison and Loomis Sts., Chgo. Died Apr. 10, 1952; buried Graceland Cemetery, Chgo.

ROBBINS, Charles F., business exec.; b. Indianapolis, Ind., July 6, 1886; s. Charles F. and Venora E. (Hammond) R.; ed. St. Paul's Sch. (Concord, N.H.); B.A., Yale, 1907; m. Elizabeth Brown, Nov. 1, 1919. Engaged in stock brokerage business in Wall St., 1907-12; small mfg. business, 1912-15; with A. G. Spalding & Bros. since 1915, successively as credit mgr., store mgr., asst. treas., v.p., and pres. 1933-52, chairman of board of directors since 1952; director National Blank Book Co., Mass. Mutual Life Ins. Co. Mem. Board of Directors Y.M.C.A. (Orange). Clubs: Yale (New York); Rock Spring (West Orange, N.J.); Orange Lawn Tennis (South Orange, N.J.); Colony Club (Springfield, Mass.). Home: Llewellyn Park, West Orange, N.J. Office: 161 Sixth Av., N.Y.C. Died Sept. 9, 1957.

ROBBINS, Harry Wolcott, educator; b. Vershire, Vt., Jan. 31, 1883; s. Henry Clarke and Caroline Abagail (Wolcott) R.; A.B., Brown U., 1908, A.M., 1908; student U. of Chgo., summer 1912, U. of Wis., summer 1914, U. of Grenoble, 1919; Ph.D., U. of Minn., 1923; m. Florence Bliss Lyon, Aug. 30, 1910. Asst. in English, Brown U., 1908-09; instr. in English, Marblehead (Mass.) High Sch., 1909-11, Calumet (Mich.) High Sch., 1911-14, North High Sch., Mpls., 1914-17; instr. in English, U. of Minn., 1919-23; prof. English, Bucknell U., 1923-54, ret. prof. Enlisted in 1st O.T.C., Ft. Snelling, Minn., 1917; commd. 2d lt. and advanced to capt.; served as adj. 804th Pioneer Inf., with A.E.F., 1918-19; capt. Inf. O.R.C., 1920-39; 2d lt. Cav., Pa. Nat. Guard, 1925. Mem. Modern Lang. Assn. Am., Am. Assn. Univ. Profs., Phi Beta Kappa, Sigma Tau Delta, Lambda Chi Alpha. Republican. Baptist. Author: Advanced Exposition (with R. E. Parker), 1933; Developing Ideas for Essays and Speeches (with R. T. Oliver), 1943. Editor: Le Merure de Seinte Eglise, 1925; Western World Literature (with W. H. Coleman), 1938. Translator: Le Roman de la Rose. Contributor to journals. Home: 124 S. George Street, Lewisburg, Pa.; (summer) Colchester, Vt. Died June 19, 1954.

ROBBINS, Howard Chandler, clergyman; b. Phila., Dec. 11, 1876; s. Rev. Francis L. and Lucy Morton (Hartpence) R.; B.A., Yale, 1899; student Princeton Theol. Sem.; B.D., Episcopal Theol. Sch., 1903; D.D. Williams Coll., 1916, Middlebury Coll., 1927, Yale, 1928, Trinity Coll., Episcopal Theol. Sch., 1931; S.T.D., Theol. Sem. of Va., 1933; D.D., U. Vt., 1938, Kenyon Coll., 1939; m. Mary Louise Baylis, Apr. 30, 1907. Deacon, 1903, priest, 1904, P.E. Ch.; curate, St. Peter's Ch., Morristown, N.J., 1903-05; rector, St. Paul's Ch., Englewood, 1905-11, Ch. of the Incarnation, N.Y., 1911-17; dean Cathedral of St. John the Divine, N.Y., 1917-29; prof. pastoral theology, Gen. Theol. Sem., 1929-1941; vis. preacher St. John's Ch., Washington, 1942-44; Dep. to Gen. Conv. P.E. Ch., 1928, 31, 34, 37; del. to World Conf. on Faith and Order, 1937; del. to N.A. Ecumenical Conf., 1941. Mem. Soc. Mayflower Descs. Soc. Colonial Wars, S.R., Nat. Inst. Social Scis., Phi Beta Kappa. Club: Century. Co-Author: The Eternal Word in the Modern World, 1937. Author: Family Devotions, 1927; Sursum Corda, 1927; Cathedral Sermons, 1927; Simplicity Toward Christ, 1927; Dana Malone of Greenfield, 1928; Vita Nova, 1929; Charles Lewis Slattery, 1931; The Way of Light, 1932; Treasure in Earthen Vessels, 1933; Paul Revere Frothingham, 1935; Bond of Honor (with B. S. Easton), 1938; Preaching the Gospel, 1939; Dr. Rudolf Bolling Teunsler, 1942. Home: 2712 36th St. N.W., Washington. Died Mar. 20, 1952.

ROBBINS, Reginald Chauncey, author, composer; b. Boston Mass.. November 10, 1871; s. Royal E. and Mary Elizabeth (Horton) Robbins; A.B., summa cum laude, Harvard University, 1892 (with highest honors in political science); studied philosophy in Graduate School, 1896-1900; married Jane Ruthven Hall, May 17, 1907; 1 son, Reginald Chauncey. V. treas. Waltham Watch Co. several yrs.; partner Robbins & Appleton; also dir. various corps.; retired, 1909. Social service work, 1894-1900. Founder Robbins Library of Philosophy and Psychology, Harvard, 1905. Delegate to International Congress of Philosophy, Bologna, 1908, Paris, 1921 Was chairman board trustees Public Library and chairman finance committee, Hamilton, Mass., also chairman visiting com. on philosophy and psychology, Harvard, and pres. Cecilia Soc., Boston. Curator of botany, Museum of Natural History, Santa Barbara, Calif., 1926-33, also curator of ornithology, 1932-33; radio speaker for Conservation. In active service, lieut. (j.g.) Naval Reserve, U.S. coast and overseas, 1917-19; Commanding various patrol boats and serving on staff of Vice Adm. Wilson at Brest, France. Republican. Clubs: Valley (Montecito); Northeast Harbor Fleet (hon.); Century (New York). At various times commodore Beverly Yacht Club, Manchester Yacht Club; Rear-commodore North East Harbor Fleet; member Eastern Yacht Club, Corinthian Yacht Club; Myopia Hunt Club, Norfolk Hunt, Middlesex Hunt, New Riding Club, Union, St. Botolph, Harvard (Boston), Faculty (Cambridge). Mem. Am. Philos. Assn., Mass. Audubon Soc., Am. Legion, Vets. Foreign Wars, Mil. Order World War, Delta Kappa Epsilon, Phi Beta Kappa. Author: Bird-Killing as a Method in Ornithology, 1900; Love Poems, 4 vols., 1903-12; Poems of Personality, 3 vols., 1904-19; Earlier Poems, 1913; Poems Domestic, 1919; Vegetation (essay), 1930; also various essays and criticisms in philosophy; also unpublished mss. volume on outline of a Gen. Aesthetics. Composer of more than 150 songs, published 1922 and since. Home: North East Harbor, Me.; also Valley Club, Montecito, Santa Barbara, Cal. Died Nov. 19, 1955; buried Cambridge, Mass.

ROBBINS, Walter, ret. mfg. exec.; b. Marquette, Mich., Mar. 8, 1875; s. Byron Philander and Ellen M. (Everett) R.; B.S. in E.E., U. of Mich., 1896; m. Emma S. Edwards, Feb. 3, 1911; 1 dau., Jane. With Western Electric Co., Chgo., 1896-1906, Wagner Electric Mfg. Co., St. Louis 1906-17, 1919-21, Marlin Rockwell Corp., 1922-23; Kissel Kinnicutt & Co., investment bankers, N.Y.C., 1923-31, partner, 1927-31; pres. Gen. Cable Corp., 1927-29, chmn. bd., 1929-38, cons., 1939—; joined Brit. Purchasing Commn. as purchasing agent for metals and chems., 1940 (service was discontinued 1941, following the passage of the Lend Lease Act); served as asst. to Baruch Rubber com. investigation 1942; now ret. Mem. War Industries Bd., Washington, 1917-19. Former pres. Central Inst. for Deaf, St. Louis. Mem. Am. Inst. E.E., Soc. Automotive Engrs., Psi Upsilon. Republican. Presbyn. Mason. Clubs: Union League (N.Y.C.); Edgartown (Mass.) Yacht, Edgartown Golf. Home: Hotel Weylin, Madison Av. at 54th St., N.Y.C. 22. Died July 21, 1956.

ROBBINS, Wilfred William, prof. botany; b. Mendon, O., May 11, 1884; s. Isham B. and Jennie Marie (Hussey) R.; B.A., U. of Colo., 1906, M.A., 1909; Ph.D., U. of Chicago, 1917; m. Louise Falk, June 15, 1911; children—Wilfred Theodor, Hertha Marie; m. 2d, Barbara Richards, Apr. 21, 1939. Instructor in biology, high sch., Pueblo, Colo., 1907-08; same, U. of Colorado, 1908-11; instr. in botany and forestry, Colo. Agrl. Coll., 1911-13, asst. prof.,

1913-14, prof. same and botanist Colo. Expt. Sta., 1914-19; plant physiologist and pathologist, Great Western Sugar Co., 1919-21; botanist Office of Cereal Investigations, U.S. Dept. Agr., 1921-22; asso. prof. botany, U. of Calif., 1922-29, prof. and botanist Calif. Expt. Sta., since 1929. Mem. Botany Soc. America, Am. Soc. Naturalists, A.A.A.S., Sigma Xi, Alpha Zeta, Phi Sigma, Sigma Phi Epsilon. Republican. Unitarian. Mason. Club: Faculty (Berkeley). Author: Botany of Crop Plants, 1914; Textbook of General Botany (with R. M. Holman), 1924; Principles of Plant Growth, 1927; Elements of Botany (with R. M. Holman), 1928; Plants Useful to Man (with Francis Ramaley), 1933; Sex in the Plant World (with Helen Pearson), 1933; Practical Problems in Botany (with Jerome Isenbarger), 1935; Weeds of California (with Margaret K. Bellue and Walter S. Ball), 1941; Weed Control—A Textbook and Manual (with Alden S. Crafts and Richard N. Raynor), 1942. Contbr. to tech. publs. Home: Carmel-by-the-Sea, Carmel, Cal. Died Mar. 4, 1952; buried Monterey, Cal.

ROBERTS, Benjamin Franklin, lawyer; b. Franklin, Tenn., July 23, 1880; s. Benjamin Franklin and Sallie White (Frierson) R.; ed. pub. schs., Mooney Sch., Franklin; studied law, 1904-07; m. Rookh Atkins, Dec. 23, 1907; children—Frances, Mary (Mrs. Rene James Brock). Tchr. 1900-06; admitted to La. bar, 1907, since practiced in Arcadia and Shreveport; city atty., Shreveport, 1918-30, 1946—; U.S. atty. Western Dist. La., 1935-37. Trustee Centenary Coll., Shreveport; mem. bd. La. Orphanage, Ruston, La. Democrat. Methodist. Mason (32°, Shriner). Home: 248 Gladstone Blvd. Office: Comml. Bank Bldg., Shreveport, La. Died July 17, 1949.

ROBERTS, Benjamin H., business exec.; b. Eureka Springs, Ark., June 14, 1897; s. William Sherman and Anna E. (McGuire) R.; B.S. in Elec. Engring., Washington U., St. Louis, Mo., 1917; m. Edith S. Keener, Oct. 9, 1922. Engr., Alexander Engring. Co., 1919-21; supt. Bird & Son, Inc., Chicago, Ill., 1921-30, staff engr., East Walpole, Mass., 1930-34, pres., 1935-46, vice chmn. bd. dirs., 1946-47; pres. Berry Asphalt Co., Chicago, 1935-47. Served as 1st lt., Air Force, U.S. Army, 1917-19. Mem. Sigma Xi, Theta Xi. Rep. Home: 820 South St., Walpole, Mass. Died May 26, 1955; buried Rosehill Cemetery, Harrison, Ark.

ROBERTS, Charles Burleson, business exec.; b. Dallas, June 25, 1892; s. Sterling Griffin and Lila Elizabeth (Oliver) R.; grad. high sch.; night and extension work, Southern Meth. U.; m. Helen Hazel Jarvis, Mar. 26, 1919; 1 dau., Helen Elizabeth (Mrs. Dick Leonard Chick, Jr.). Vice pres. Sears, Roebuck & Co., since 1948, dir. since 1936; dir. Republic Nat. Bank, Dallas; pres., dir. So. Provident Life Ins. Co. Trustee Baylor Coll.; dir. Freeman Memorial Children's Hosp.; v.p. Dallas Civic Fedn.; dir. Dallas Community Chest; chmn. bd. Better Bus. Bur. of Tex.; pres., chmn. bd. Tex. Chain Store Assn.; Regional dir. Nat. Bus. Bur. Brig. Gen. United Confederate Veterans. Mem. Reserve Officers Assn. Baptist (deacon First Ch., Dallas). Democrat. Home: 7270 Turtle Creek Blvd., Dallas. Died Sept. 17, 1953.

ROBERTS, Charles George Douglas, author; b. Douglas, N. B., Can., Jan. 10, 1860; grad. U. New Brunswick, 1879 (A.M., 1880); m. 1880, Mary I. Fenety. Head Chatham Grammar School, 1879-81; York St. School, Fredericton, 1881-3; editor Week, Toronto, 1883-4; prof. English and French literature, Kings Coll., Windsor, N.S., 1885-8; prof. English and economics, same, 1888-95; asso. editor Illustrated American and resided in New York, 1897-98. Author: (verse) Orion and Other Poems; In Divers Tones; Ave—An Ode for the Shelley Centenary; Songs of the Common Day; The Book of the Native; New York Nocturnes; The Book of the Rose; (prose) The Canadians of Old; Earth's Enigmas; The Raid from Beauséjour; A History of Canada; The Forge in the Forest; Around the Campfire; Reube Dare's Shad Boat; A Sister to Evangeline, 1898; Appleton's Canadian Guidebook, 1889; By the Marshes of Minas, 1900; The Heart of the Ancient Wood, 1900; Poems (collective edit.), 1901; The Kindred of the Wild, 1902; Barbara Ladd, 1902; The Prisoner of Mademoiselle, The Little People of the Sycamore, 1905; The Return to the Trails, 1905; Red Fox, 1905; The Heart that Knows, 1906; In the Deep of the Snow, 1907; The Young Acadian, 1907; Editor: The Alastor and Adonais of Shelley (with intro. and notes), 1902. Address: 226 5th Av., New York, and Fredericton, N.B., Can. Died 1943.

ROBERTS, Clifford, mfg. exec.; b. Burnley, Lancashire Eng., Nov. 1, 1896; s. Tom Hartley and Bertha (Baron) R.; ed. Mill Hill Sch., Eng., and Trinity Coll., Cambridge, Eng.; m. Olga Muriel Purchase, Mar. 17, 1921; children—Jean Mary, Elizabeth Joyce, Clifford Peter, John Baron. With United Shoe Machinery Corp., Boston, 1928—, vice president and director, 1944—; director of Turner Tanning Machinery Co., Peabody, Mass. Epis. Club: Union. Home: 264 Sagamore St., Hamilton, Mass. Office: 140 Federal St., Boston. Died Sept. 1959.

ROBERTS, Edward Howell, theol. sem. dean; born Middle Granville, N.Y., Aug. 1, 1895; s. Edward and Mary (Davies) R.; student Ripon (Wis.) College, 1915-17; A.B., U. of Wis., 1919, M.A., 1920; Th.B., Princeton Theol. Sem., 1923, Th.M., 1923; student University of Southern California, 1925-26; University of California, 1925-26; Doctor Divinity, Grove City Coll. and Waynesburg Coll., 1939; m. Esther Davison Hill, Dec. 22, 1928; 1 son, John Howell. Asst. pastor First Presbyn. Ch., New Rochelle, N.Y., 1923; ednl. work, Los Angeles, 1926-30; instr. in systematic theology, Princeton Theol. Sem., 1930-37, registrar, 1932-37, asso. prof. homiletics 1937-53, professor 1953—, dean students, 1937-45; dean 1945—. Mem. American Association of Theological Schools (president, 1952-54); member of board of Christian Edn., Presbyn. Ch., U.S.A., 1939-47; mem. Council on Theol. Education. Address: 74 Mercer St., Princeton, N.J. Died Dec. 13, 1954; buried Princeton, N.J.

ROBERTS, Harold DeWitt, lawyer; b. Denver, Mar. 4, 1887; s. DeWitt Clinton and Fannie Belle (Pace) R.; A.B., Colo. Coll., 1908; student Harvard, 1908-10, Denver U., 1910; E.D. (hon.), Colo. Sch. Mines, 1946; m. Rhoda Norton Haynes, Aug. 22, 1911; children—Neil Fletcher, Esther Adair (Mrs. Stuart Lancefield), Jane Norton (Mrs. Richard Knight). Admitted to Ore. bar, 1912, Colo. bar, 1916; law practice, Salem, Ore., 1913-15, Greeley, Colo., 1916-17, Denver, since 1917; mem. Dines, Dines & Holme, 1921-49, Holme, Roberts, More, Owen & Keegan since 1950; gen. counsel Frontier Refining Co. since 1945; dir. U.S. Nat. Bank of Denver; lectr. oil and gas law U. Denver, 1928-31. Trustee Denver Mus. Natural History, Colo. Coll. (chmn. bd. 1949-54). Mem. Am. and Colo. State bar assns., Bar U.S. Supreme Ct., Phi Beta Kappa, Delta Epsilon. Republican. Conglist. Clubs: Mile High, Denver (Denver) Author: Salt Creek, Wyoming-The Story of a Great Oil Field, 1956. Co-author: Some Common Colorado Wild Flowers, 1953. Color photographs used as illustrations in Am. Wild Flowers, 1949. Home: 4025 E. 18th Av., Denver 20. Office: Mile High Center., Denver 2. Died July 24, 1956.

ROBERTS, Herbert Rufus, coll. prof.; b. Brooksville, Me., Jan. 21, 1865; s. Darius Lawrence and Lydia Maria (Tibbetts) R.; A.B., Boston U., 1892; A.M., Norwich U., 1896, D.C.L., 1908; student Alliance Francaise, Paris, 1898; m. Martha Louise Sargent, Aug. 20, 1902; 1 dau., Alethe Maud (Mrs. John W. Davis). Instr. Norwich U., 1892-93, prof. Latin and French, 1893-1932, dean of undergrads., 1907-1932, acting pres., 1915, 1917-20, dean emeritus, 1933—; pres. Northfield Trust Co. Has served as trustee Brown Pub. Library; supt., dir. pub. schs., Northfield, Vt. Mem. Vt. Ho. of Rep., 1931-32, 1937-38; justice of peace, 1933. Incorporator Northfield Savs. Bk.; trustee, pres. Northfield Trust Co. Mem. Vt. Hist. Assn., Pi Gamma Mu. Methodist. Mason (K.T.). Clubs: Conversational, Norwich Outing. Address: Northfield, Vt. Died Dec. 26, 1950.

ROBERTS, John S., ret. naval officer; b. Danville, Ky., Oct. 30, 1892; s. John Summerfield and Susan Eleanor (Gilmore) R.; B.S., U.S. Naval Acad., 1916; m. Margaret Vail Jenkins, July 13, 1918; 1 son, John S. Jr. Commd. ensign U.S. Navy, 1916, and advanced through grades to rear adm., 1945; convoy duty, U.S.S. De Kalb, 1917-19; destroyer duty, Aisatic sta., 1925-28; comdr. destroyer div., later destroyer squadron in cooperation with Brit. fleet, North Atlantic and Iceland waters, 1941-42; comdg. officer U.S.S. Boise, Mediterranean, 1943, S.W. Pacific, 1944; ret. from active duty, 1945. Awarded Navy Cross and Legion of Merit. Home: 728 Glorietta Blvd., Coronado, Cal. Died Apr. 9, 1953; buried Arlington Nat. Cemetery.

ROBERTS, Joseph Harry Newton, cons. engr.; b. Naugatuck, Conn., Oct. 30, 1892; s. Joseph William Pfaff and Clara Rebecca (Leas) R.; ed. pub. schs. in Conn. and by pvt. tuition. Began as apprentice, 1907; successively draftsman, checker, designer, chief draftsman, sales engr., supt. of Hallden Machine Co.; cons. engr. (Conn., Mass., and N.Y. state registration), specializing on machinery design, tools, buildings, indsl. problems and patent matters in cooperation with Edward Thomas (successor to late Philip Farnsworth, of New York) since 1926; also asso. with architect Joseph T. Smith, 1936-43; with Louis Alexander, architect asso. until 1946; member of the Joseph H. Roberts & Associates, Milford, Conn., 1949—, now president. Engineer, Colts Patent Fire Arms Manufacturing Company, planning fabrication of The Browning Machine Guns, 1917. Mem. Am. Soc. M.E., Conn. Soc. Professional Engrs., Conn. Soc. C.E. Republican. Christian Scientist. Mason. Address: P.O. Box 389, Milford, Conn. Died Apr. 5, 1959; buried King's Highway Cemetery.

ROBERTS, Kenneth (Lewis), author; b. Kennebunk, Me., Dec. 8, 1885; s. Frank Lewis and Grace Mary (Tibbetts) R.; A.B., Cornell, 1908; Litt.D., Dartmouth, 1934, Colby Coll., 1935, Bowdoin Coll., 1937, Middlebury Coll., 1938, Northeastern U., 1945; m. Anna Seiberling Mosser, Feb. 14, 1911. Reporter, columnist Boston Post, 1909-17; staff Life (N.Y.), 1915-18, Puck, 1916-17; European corr. Sat. Eve. Post, 1919-29, Washington corr., 1921-26; retired from journalism, Porto Santo Stefano, 1929-37. Served as capt., Intelligence Sect., Siberian Expeditionary Force, 1918-19. Recipient of a Special Pulitzer Prize, 1957. Mem. Nat. Inst. Arts and Letters, Order of Cincinnati of State of N.J., Phi Beta Kappa, Chi Psi, Kappa Beta Phi, Ends of the Earth Club. Club: Royal Bermuda Yacht. Author: (nonfiction) Trending Into Maine, 1938; March to Quebec, 1939; Good Maine Food (with Marjorie Mosser) 1939; The Kenneth Roberts Reader, 1945; I Wanted to Write, 1949; Don't Say That About Maine, 1950; Henry Gross and His Dowsing Rod (also pub. in Germany), 1951; The Seventh Sense, 1953; Foods of New England (with Marjorie Mosser), 1957; Water Unlimited, 1957; (novels) (also pub. in Braille and Talking Books) Arundel, 1930; The Lively Lady, 1931; Rabble in Arms, 1933; Captain Caution (filmed by Hal Roach), 1934; Northwest Passage (filmed by MGM), 1937; Oliver Wiswell, 1940; Lydia Bailey (filmed by 20th Century-Fox), 1947. Translator: (with Anna M. Roberts) Moreau St. Méry's American Journey, 1793-1798, 1947. With Henry Gross, pioneered in locating fesh water springs, Bermuda, 1949; cooperated in successful drilling of springs at Royal Barracks. Home: Kennebunkport, Me. Died July 21, 1957; buried Arlington Nat. Cemetery.

ROBERTS, Mary Fanton, editor; b. N.Y.C.; d. W. H. and Isabel Agnes Annable Fanton; ed. Albany Female Acad.; m. W. Carman Roberts, Dec. 14, 1906. Was staff writer on Herald, Tribune, Journal, Sun, N.Y.C., 4 yrs.; editor Demorest Mag.; editor-in-chief New Idea Woman's Mag.; on editorial staff Woman's Home Companion; mng. editor The Craftsman; creator, editor The Touchstone Mag., Decorative Arts Mag.; editor Arts and decoration, 17 yrs., now ret. Clubs: MacDowell, Pen and Brush, Women's City, Town Hall. Home: Hotel Chelsea, 222 W. 23d St., N.Y.C. Died Feb. 14, 1956.

ROBERTS, Mary M(ay), editor, nurse; b. Cheboygan, Mich., Jan. 31, 1877; d. Henry W. and Elizabeth Scott (Elliot) Roberts; R.N., Jewish Hosp. Sch. of Nursing, Cin., 1899; B.S., Tchr. Coll., Columbia, 1921. Supt. of nurses Savannah (Ga.) Hosp. (now Warren A. Chandler Hosp.), 1900-02; asst. supt. Jewish Hosp., Cin., 1902-04; supt. C. R. Holmes Hosp.; Cin., 1908-17; dir. nursing service, Lake div., A.R.C., Cleve., 1917-18, chief nurse and dir. Unit of Army Sch. of Nursing, Camp Sherman, O., 1918-19; editor Am. Jour. of Nursing, N.Y., 1921-48, emeritus. Decorated Bronze medal of Ministry of Social Welfare of France, July 1933. Certificate of Appreciation from Dept. of Army; Florence Nightingale Medal, Internat. Red Cross. Formerly trustee Tchrs. Coll., Columbia. Mem. Am. Nurses Assn., Nat. League for Nursing. Republican. Episcopalian. Club: Cosmopolitan. Author: American Nursing: History & Interpretation, 1954. Contbr. articles ency., publs. Home: 8309 94th St., Woodhaven, L.I., N.Y. Died Jan. 1959.

ROBERTS, Owen Josephus, former justice, U.S. Supreme Court; born at Philadelphia, Pa., May 2, 1875; s. Josephus R.; A.B., University of Pa., 1895, LL.B., 1898; LL.D., Beaver Coll., 1925, Ursinus Coll., 1926, University of Pa., 1929, Lafayette Coll., 1930, Pa. Mil. Coll., 1931, Dickinson Coll., 1931, Trinity Coll., 1931, Williams Coll., 1933, Princeton U., 1934, Temple U., 1946; D.C.L., Oxford Univ., 1951; m. Elizabeth Caldwell Rogers, 1904; 1 dau. Elizabeth (Mrs. Roger Hamilton). Began practice in Philadelphia, 1898; 1st asst. dist. atty., Phila. Co., 1901-04; instr., asst. prof., prof. law, U. Pa., 1898-1918; apptd. spl. dep. atty. gen. to represent U.S. Govt. in prosecution of cases arising under Espionage Act in Eastern Dist. of Pa., World War I; chmn. War Dept. Adv. Board on Clemency, 1945-47, Board for Award of Medals for Merit, Am. Commn. for Monuments in War Areas, 1943-46; President's Amnesty Board, 1946-47; director City Trusts, Phila., 1920-29, Bell Telephone Co. of Pa., 1920-29, Am. Telephone & Telegraph Co., 1927-29, Real Estate Title & Trust Co., 1920-27, Franklin Fire Ins. Co., 1923-29; apptd. by President Coolidge one of two attys. to prosecute "oil cases," Feb. 1924; asso. justice Supreme Ct. U.S., 1930-45, justice, resigned. Dean Law Sch., U. Pa., 1948-51. Trustee Jefferson Med. Coll., 1921-24, U. Pa. (life), 1943—, Lincoln Coll. Chmn. bd. trustees Chester County (Pa.) Boy Scouts of America, 1930—, ex-member National Exec. Bd.; chmn. bd. The Fund for the Advancement of Edn.; chmn. Pa. com. of selection for the Rhodes Scholarships. Mem. Pa. Bar Assn. (pres., 1947), American Philosophical Society (president 1952), Psi Upsilon, Phi Beta Kappa. Republican. Episcopalian (pres. House of Deps., 1946 gen. conv.). Home: R.D., Chester Springs, Pa. Address: 1421 Chestnut St., Phila. 2. Died May 17, 1955.

ROBERTS, T(homas) Scott, cotton mfr.; b. Nashville, Tenn., Sept. 26, 1878; s. Albert and Edith Mary (Scott) R.; grad. pub. schs., Nashville, Tenn., 1895; student business coll., 1895; m. Mary Adelaide Robinson, June 24, 1905; children—Leonard Huxley, Thomas Peyton, Katherine Lorraine (Mrs. Horace Frierson III). With Southern Lumberman (publ.),

1895-99; mining business in Ala., 1899-1902; cotton seed oil mfg., Ala., 1903-06; with Adelaide Mills, Anniston, Ala., mfrs. cotton yarns, since 1906, pres. 1919-48, now chmn.; v.p. and dir. Classe Ribbon Works; pres. Ala. Cotton Mfrs. Assn., 1906-38, of bd., 1937-38; former mem. U.S. Chamber of Commerce (com. on state compacts); mem. Ala. State Chamber of Commerce, Anniston Chamber of Commerce (ex-pres.; chmn. industries com.); former dir. Am. Cotton Mfrs. Assn.; dir. Cotton Textile Inst. until 1947; member camp and hosp. service council Am. Red Cross; mem. Ga.-Ala. Textile Traffic Assn., Asso. Industries of Ala. Episcopalian. Clubs: Rotary (ex-pres.), Anniston Country. Address: Sunset Drive, Anniston, Ala. Died May 14, 1956; buried Anniston, Ala.

ROBERTS, W. Frank, trustee; b. Pennsylvania, Jan. 25, 1879; s. Albert W. and Eliza R.; M.E., Lehigh U., 1902; m. Laura H. Hackman, 1904. Pres. bd. trustees Johns Hopkins Hosp.; trustee Johns Hopkins U. Home: 4007 Greenway. Office: Keyser Bldg., Baltimore. Died July 11, 1957.

ROBERTS, William Alva, business exec.; b. Osceola, Mo., Aug. 25, 1897; s. Charles Wilson and Valeria Alma (Embry) R.; student of Springfield, Mo. Business Coll., 1915; m. Alma Embrey, Sept. 28, 1919. president Allis-Chalmers Mfg. Co., Milwaukee since 1951; dir., First Wis. Nat. Bank, Milwaukee. Past pres. Farm Equipment Inst.; past regional v.p., Am. Road Builders Assn.; mem. Am. Soc. Automotive Engrs., Am. Soc. of Agrl. Engrs. Clubs: University, Westmoor Country, Milwaukee, Electrical Mfrs. Home: 6536 Hillcrest Drive, Wauwatosa 13, Wis. Office: Allis-Chalmers Mfg. Co., Box 512, Milw. 1. Died Apr. 12, 1955; buried Fort Scott, Kan.

ROBERTSON, Charles Raymond, ex-congressman; b. Arlington, Wis., Sept. 5, 1889; s. William and Janet (Mais) R.; ed. high sch.; grad. Parker Coll., Winnebago, Minn.; m. Mary A. Armstrong, Feb. 14, 1914. Began with Wyman-Partridge Co., wholesale dry goods, Mpls.; buyer for Olwin Angell Co., Aberdeen, S.D., 1910-12; mem. firm Robertson-Schwartz Co., Redfield, S.D., 1912-17, Cummins-Robertson Co., Mandan, N.D., 1917-21; organized Robertson's Inc., women's wear, Valley City, N.D., 1921, opened branches at Jamestown, N.D., 1925, Wahpeton, N.D., 1926, Bismarck, N.D., 1928; mem. 77th, 79th and 80th Congresses, N.D. at large, mem. appropriations com. Chmn. N.D. State Russian Relief, Inc.; Com. for Econ. Development, 1943-44. Republican. Presbyn. Mason. Clubs: Rotary, Eagles, Elks. Home: 500 Fifth Av., Bismarck, N.D. Died Feb. 18, 1951.

ROBERTSON, George Lawrence, lawyer; b. Roanoke, Mo., July 14, 1902; s. William and Helen (Hunker) R.; LL.B., University of Mo., 1923; married Delores Stover, Dec. 10, 1926; 1 dau., Susan (Mrs. George Gerard); married 2d, to Nadine Kramer, Mar. 11, 1949. Admitted to N.M. bar, 1923, Cal., 1929, Mo., 1931; asst. dist. atty. 4th Jud. Dist. N.M., Las Vegas, 1924-28; pvt. practice, Pasadena, Cal., 1929-31, Salisbury, Mo., 1931-41, Randolph Co., Mo., 1946-51; U.S. Atty. Eastern Dist. Missouri, St. Louis, 1951-53; private practice, in Moberly, Missouri, 1954-56. Mayor of Salisbury, 1936-38; pros. atty. Chariton Co., Mo., 1938-41; dist. enforcement atty. O.P.A., St. Louis, 1941-46. Mem. State Bar Cal. (inactive), Randolph Co., St. Louis, Mo. bar assns., Alpha Tau Omega, Phi Delta Phi. Mason. Home: Roanoke Farms, Roanoke, Mo. Office: Moberly, Mo. Died May 8, 1956.

ROBERTSON, Harold Hansard, business exec.; b. St. John, N.B., Apr. 21, 1878; s. James Charles and Calista C. (Harris) R.; ed. private, pub. schs., Upper Can. Coll.; m. Jebba Dixon Moorhouse, Dec. 20, 1938; children—Sylvia (Mrs. Alexander M. Brooks), James Burnett. Mfr. bldg. materials and steel specialties, 1904—; organized H. H. Robertson Co., Pitts., 1919, formerly pres., chmn. bd.; pres. H. H. Robertson Co., Ltd., Can.; dir. Robertson-Irwin, Ltd., Can. Mem. Am. Iron and Steel Inst., Am. Soc. for Testing Materials, Am. Soc. C.E., Engrs. Soc. Western Pa., Nat. Safety Council. Episcopalian. Clubs: Duquesne, Pittsburgh, Allegheny Country, Fox Chapel Golf, Pittsburgh Golf, Rolling Rock, Edgeworth. Home: Park Mansions. Office: Farmers Bank Bldg., Pitts. Died Sept. 19, 1950; buried Sewickley (Pa.) Cemetery.

ROBERTSON, Harrison M(arshall), lawyer; b. Albemarle County, Va., Dec. 8, 1892; s. Harrison and Mary Longley (Vawter) R.; grad. Episcopal High Sch., Alexandria, Va., 1911; A.B., Univ. of Va., 1914, LL.B., 1916; m. Mary Mackenzie, Jan. 18, 1918; children—Harrison Marshall, Colin Mackenzie, Mary Bowie (Mrs. Chapin Carpenter, Jr.); married to 2d, Lorena G. Maxwell, Oct. 18, 1941. Admitted to N.Y. bar, 1916; asso. Stetson, Jennings & Russell, lawyers, N.Y.C., 1916-23; gen. counsel in U.S., British-Am. Tobacco Co., Ltd., Louisville, Ky., 1923-55, ret., 1955; mem. firm Robertson & Ardery; retired general counsel Brown & Williamson Tobacco Corp. Trustee Village of Scarsdale, N.Y., 1928-31. Spl. tax com., City of Louisville, Ky., 1939-40; mem. board of water commissioners, Louisville, 1942—; commr. industrial relations State Kentucky. State and nat. chmn. for Ky., finance com., Democratic Nat. Campaign, 1944; chmn. adv. com. of Dem. Party, Jefferson County, Ky., 1946; Dem. candidate U.S. Congress, 3d Dist. Ky., 1952. Served as officer U.S. Army F.A., 1917-19. Mem. Am. Econ. Assn., Tax Inst., Inc. (mem. bd. dirs.), Am. Bar Assn., Louisville Philharmonic Soc. (dir.), Louisville Conf. Christians and Jews (dir.), U.S. Trade Mark Assn. (dir.), Assn. of Bar City of N.Y., Phi Beta Kappa, Delta Kappa Epsilon, Phi Delta Phi. Democrat. Protestant Episcopalian. Clubs: Louisville Country, Pendennis (Louisville); University (N.Y., Va); Colonnade, Farmington Country. Home: Belvedere Farm, Charlottesville, Va. Office: 310 W. Liberty, Louisville. Died Oct. 26, 1958.

ROBERTSON, J. Breathitt, insurance exec.; b. Marshall, Mo., Feb. 28, 1892; s. D. H. and Minnie G. (Smiser) R.; A.B., Kansas Univ., 1914; LL.B., Northwestern U., 1917; m. G. Elizabeth Gillam, Sept. 19, 1925. With Charles M. Howell, ins. counsel, 1917-18; partner Cowgill & Robertson, 1919-21; atty. for Employers Reins. Corp., 1921-27, v.p., 1926, gen. counsel since 1927, exec. v.p., 1939-43, pres. since 1943. Mem. Am. and Missouri bar assns., Internat. Assn. of Ins. Counsel. Clubs: Kansas City, Mission Hills Country, University. Home: 1020 W. 59th St. Office: 21 W. 10th St., Kansas City, Mo. Died Dec. 8, 1952.

ROBERTSON, Marion Clinton, ret. naval officer; b. Calvert, Tex., Sept. 30, 1885; s. Julian and Mary (Taylor) R.; student U. of Tex., 1903-05; B.S., U.S. Naval Acad., 1909. Commd. ensign U.S. Navy, 1911, and advanced through grades to rear adm.; ret. from active service, 1947. Served as sea, World Wars I and II. Awarded Legion of Merit with 2 gold stars, combat insignia. Mem. Mil. Order of Carabao. Sigma Nu. Presbyn. Clubs: Yacht (N.Y.C.); Army-Navy (Washington); Army-Navy Country (Arlington, Va.). Address: Army-Navy Club, Washington.* Died Nov. 19, 1953.

ROBERTSON, Reuben B., Jr., corp. exec.; b. Asheville, N.C., June 27, 1908; s. Reuben B. and Hope (Thomson) R.; Chem.E., Sheffield Scientific Sch., Yale, 1930; m. Margaret Watkins, Dec. 17, 1938; children—Reuben B., III, Daniel Huger, Peter T., Margaret, Louise Hope, George. With Champion Paper & Fibre Co., 1930—, successively asst. mgr. Canton div., prodn. mgr. and v.p., 1938, gen. prodn. mgr. all divs., dir. personnel, 1940, pres. 1950—; dep. sec. of def., 1955-57; dir. B. F. Goodrich & Co., Procter & Gamble Co. Served from capt. to lt. col. Army of U.S., Mem. Tech. Assn. Pulp and Paper Industry, Am. Inst. Chem. Engrs., Employers Labor Relations Information Com. N.Y.C. (pres.). Episcopalian. Mason. Home: 9974 McKelvey Road, Cin. 15. Office: 601 N. B St., Hamilton, O. Died Mar. 13, 1960.

ROBERTSON, Thomas Aaron, writer, editor; b. Battle Creek, Mich.; s. George Anthony and Mary Eliza (Durand) R.; prep. edn., high sch., Battle Creek; student U. of Mich.; m. Isobel Julia Knight. Reporter Battle Creek Journal; with St. Louis Republic, Asso. Press, St. Louis, Houston (Tex.) Post; mng. editor Cleve. Daily Leader, Sunday Leader, Daily and Sunday News-Leader, Boston Am., editor Saturday Home Mag., King Features Syndicate, N.Y.C. 1935—. Author of various mag. articles, etc. Home: 290 Park Av., N.Y.C.; also Cavalry Rd., Westport, Conn. Died Feb. 18, 1950.

ROBERTSON, W. Spencer, mfr.; b. Bklyn., Jan. 10, 1885; s. William and Minnie Louise (Higgins) R.; ed. pub. schs., Bklyn.; m. Mabel Brooks, Oct. 16, 1906; children—Whitney Spencer, Rodney Taylor, Malcolm Brooks, Enid. With Simpson, Thacher & Bartlett, attys., N.Y.C., 1900-08; asst. to v.p. Am. Locomotive Co., 1908-15, sec., 1915-30, dir., 1919-30; pres. The Permutit Co., mfrs. water conditioning equipment, N.Y.C., 1930-1944, chmn. 1944-54; chmn. Zeolite Corp., Ionac Co., Limited, Permutit Co. of Canada, Ltd., Gen. Water Treatment Service Corp., Simplex Valve & Meter Co., Simplex Valve & Meter Co. Can., Ltd., all 1944-54. Pres. Natl. Council YMCA of U.S., 1928-29, treas. 1933-37, mem. Nat. Bd., 1927-48, chmn. 1940-44, mem. exec. com. Internat. Com., 1937-48; dir. U.S.O. 1941-48, chmn. exec. com. 1941-45, v.p. 1945-48; trustee Drew U. Rep. Methodist. Clubs: Union League (N.Y.C.); Morris County Golf (Morristown, N.J.). Home: 6 Dogwood Dr., Madison, N.J. Died Nov. 26, 1958.

ROBERTSON, Walter Melville, ret. army officer; b. Nelson Co., Va., June 15, 1888; s. William Walter and Mary Fannie (Pettit) R.; grad. Central State Normal Sch., Okla., 1907; student U. of Okla., 1907; B.S., U.S. Mil. Acad., 1912; grad. Infantry Sch. (advanced course), 1925; hon. grad. Command and Gen. Staff Sch., 1926; grad. Army War Coll., 1930; m. Lorene Powell Crebs, Aug. 10, 1916. Commd. 2d lt., June 12, 1912; promoted through grades to major general, January 24, 1948; served in Hawaii, 1912-15, with A.E.F., May 1918-Feb. 1920, in P.I., 1933-36; inspector Gen. Dept., 1920-24; instr. Command and Gen. Staff Sch., 1926-29, Army War Coll., 1930-33; mem. War Dept. Gen. Staff, 1936-40; comdg. officer, 9th Inf., Nov. 8, 1940-Dec. 15, 1941; asst. div. comdr. 2d Inf. Div., Dec. 15, 1941-May 11, 1942; div. comdr., 2d Inf. Div., May 1942-June 1945; comdg. gen. XV Corps (occupational forces in Austria), June-July 1945; occupation Germany, Aug. 1945-Mar. 1946; head U.S. delegation A.C.C., Bulgaria, Mar. 1946-Sept. 1947; deputy comdr. 6th Army, 1947; Cal. state dir. Civil Defense, Sacramento, Cal., since 1950. Decorated Distinguished Service Cross, Distinguished Service Medal, Legion of Merit, Silver Star, Bronze Star Medal, E.T.O. Service Medal with five campaign stars (U.S.); Companion of the Bath (British); Legion of Honor, Croix de Guerre with Palm (French); Military Cross, Order of White Lion, 3rd Class (Czechoslovakia); Order of Wars of Fatherland (Russian). Mem. Newcomen Soc., Kappa Alpha. Democrat. Methodist. Clubs: Army and Navy, Army and Navy Country (Washington); Columbia Country, Chevy Chase Country (Chevy Chase, Md.). Address: 1960 10th Av., Sacramento, Cal.; also 311 W. Main St., Carmi, Ill. Died Nov. 22, 1954; buried Arlington Nat. Cemetery.

ROBERTSON, William Joseph, editor; b. Fincastle, Botetourt County, Va., Sept. 19, 1888; s. William Gordon and Anne Anthony (Breckinridge) R.; ed. high sch. and 1 yr. at Virginia Mil. Inst., Lexington, Va.; m. Susan Radford Preston, of "Greenfield," Nov. 14, 1918; children—Preston Breckinridge, William Joseph, Mason Gordon, Susannah Preston. With engring. dept. Louisville & Nashville Ry. at Louisville, Ky., 1905-09; civ. engr. in mountains of Ky., Tenn., Va. and Ala., 1909-12; began newspaper work with Roanoke (Va.) Times, 1912; later with newspapers and Associated Press in South and dailies in Del. and Phila.; then editor Easton (Pa.) Express; asso. editor, Savannah Morning News, 1944-48, editor since 1948. Commd. capt. inf. U.S. Army, O.T.C., Ft. McPherson, Ga., 1917; later served at Camp Gordon (Ga.), Kelly Field (Tex.) and Camp McClellan, Anniston, Ala.; hon. discharged, Feb. 1919. Mem. Society of Colonial Wars. Democrat. Episcopalian. Clubs: Rotary, Cosmos. Author: The Changing South, 1927; A History of du Pont Company's Relations with the American Government, 1927; contbr. to mags. Office: Savannah News, Savannah, Ga. Died July 19, 1955.

ROBERTSON, William Spence, prof. history; b. Glasgow, Scotland, Oct. 7, 1872; s. John and Anne (Spence) R.; came to U.S., 1880; B.Litt., U. of Wis., 1899, M.Litt., 1900; Ph.D., Yale, 1903; m. Gertrude Mueller, June 30, 1913; children—Jean, James M. Instr. history, 1903-06, asst. prof., 1906-09, Coll. for Women (Western Reserve U.); absent on leave and acting prof. Am. history, Ind. U., 1909; asst. prof. history, U. of Ill., 1909-18, asso. prof., 1918-20, prof., 1920—; head of dept. of history, 1937—; prof. emeritus, 1941—; recalled for active service, 1943-45. Albert Shaw lectr. on diplomatic history, Johns Hopkins U., 1939. Awarded Herbert Baxter Adams prize in European history by Am. Hist. Assn., 1907. Travel and study in Spain, Portugal, Eng., France, Austria, Mexico and S.A. Corr. mem. Nat. Acad. History of Venezuela; hon. mem. Nat. Acad. History of Colombia, Nat. Acad. History of Argentina; mem. Am. Hist. Assn., Hispanic Soc. Am., Phi Beta Kappa, Sigma Delta Pi, Phi Kappa Phi. Decorated with the Order of Liberators of Venezuela. Awarded Mitre medal by the Hispanic Soc. Am. Author: Francisco de Miranda and the Revolutionizing of Spanish America, 1909 (transl. into Spanish by Sr. Diego Mendoza Bogotá, 1918), Rise of Spanish-American Republics, 1918-42); History of Latin-American Nations, 1922, 23, 25, 32, 43; Hispanic-American Relations with the United States, 1923; The Life of Miranda (2 vols.), 1929; (transl. into Spanish at Buenos Aires in Proc. of 2d Internat. Congress of History); France and Latin-Am. Independence, 1939; Iturbide of Mexico, 1952; author of the sects. on History of United States and Canada, in "Historia de America," by R. Levene, edited 1940, 41, 43, 47; contbr. on the Monroe Doctrine, the diplomatic relations between the U.S. and Latin America, etc. Editor: The Diary of Francisco de Miranda. Translator and editor: Levene's Historia Argentina, 1937. Contbr. articles on S.A. countries to vols. supplementary to the 11th ed. of Ency. Britannica, also to Ency. of Social Scis. and to Dictionary of American History. Advisory editor Hispanic Am. Hist. Review; contbr. to Handbook of Latin-American Studies, 1935-39; and to Levene, Historia de la Nación Argentina. Home: 103 E. Florida Av., Urbana, Ill. Died Oct. 24, 1955.

ROBEY, William Henry, physician; b. Boston, Mass., July 3, 1870; s. William H. and Mary V. (Smith) R.; M.D., Harvard, 1895; m. Isabelle T. Alexander, Apr. 22, 1897; 1 son, Andrew Alexander. House physician Boston City Hosp., 1894-96, Boston Lying-In Hosp., 1896; practiced at Boston since 1897; asst. in bacteriology, Harvard, 1900-04; with med. dept. Harvard since 1904, asst. prof. medicine, 1919-27, now clin. prof. medicine, emeritus; George W. Gay lecturer Harvard Med. Sch., 1930; cons. physician to Boston City, Milton, Marlborough and Norwood hosps. Mem. exec. com. Permanent Charity Fund, Boston. Maj. Med. Corp, U.S. Army and chief of med. service Camp McClellan, 1917-18; lt. col. and consultant in medicine, Advance Sect., A.E.F.,

World War; col. Med. O.R.C., U.S. Army. Diplomate American Board of Internal Medicine; fellow A.M.A., A.A.A.S., Mass. Med. Soc. (Shattuck lecturer, 1929; pres. 1933-35), Am. Coll. Physicians; mem. Am. Assn. Pathologists and Bacteriologists, 1901-38; mem. Am. Clin. and Climatol. Assn., Am. Heart Assn. (pres. 1929-31, hon. life mem. since 1948, mem. Founders Group for Sci. Research) (Silver Medallion Distinguished Service Award), Suffolk Dist. Med. Soc. (pres.), Northeast Heart Association (pres. 1927-30), Delta Upsilon, Phi Beta Pi (hon.), Æsculapian Club (hon.). Republican. Conglist. Clubs: St. Botolph, Harvard (Boston). Author: Causes of Heart Failure, 1922; Headache, 1930; also of various articles on medicine, especially the heart and circulation. Editor: Health at Fifty, 1939. Office: 202 Commonwealth Av., Boston. Died Feb. 23, 1954; buried Stonington (Conn.) Cemetery.

ROBINEAU, Simon Pierre (ro-bī-no), lawyer; b. Versailles, France, Apr. 8, 1882; s. Jean and Helene (Copelin) R.; A.B., Lake Forest Coll., 1908; A.M., U. of South, 1909; post grad. Sorbonne and U. Freiburg, 1908-09; LL.B., Harvard, 1912; m. Frances Oliver, May 19, 1917 (died July 5, 1942); children—Jeanne Jacqueline (Mrs. F.W. Ludington, Jr.), Frances Patricia (Mrs. Robineau Van Devere). Tchr. modern langs. Sewanee Mil. Acad., U. of South, 1908-09; social service worker West Edn. House, Boston, 1910-13; practice of law, Boston, 1912-15, Miami, Fla., since 1915; sr. mem. firm. Robineau, Budd & Levenson; city atty. Miami, 1919-21; v.p. Zonite Products Co., 1924-25; regent and lectr. coml. law U. Miami, 1934-35. Mem. Fla. State Legislature, 1929-37. Served as capt. M.I., A.E.F., 1917-19; col., U.S. A.A.F., 1942-46. Decorated 5 battle stars, Bronze star, Purple Heart, Legion of Merit, Citation by Gen. Pershing, 1918. Mem. Am., Fla. and Dade Co. bar assns., Am. Legion, Mil. Order World Wars, Alpha Tau Omega. Democrat. Episcoplian. Mason (33°). Clubs: Harvard, Bankers, Lawyers (N.Y. City); Army-Navy, National Press (Washington); Surf, Comittee of 100 (Miami Beach). Author various mags. and newspaper articles. Home: 454 N.E. 23rd St., Miami 37. Office: Alfred I. DuPont Bldg., Miami 32, Fla. Died Dec. 6, 1952.

ROBINS, John Aloysius, business exec.; b. Cin., July 15, 1911; s. Samuel J. and Mary Elizabeth (Best) R.; hon. grad., Arsenal Tech. Schs., Indpls.; student prep. sch. U.S. Mil. Acad., 1929-32; student Cleve. Coll. of Western Res. U., 1935-36; m. Thelma Mae Hackler, June 4, 1934; 1 dau., Daphne Ann. Various exec. positions Gen. Baking Co., 1932-44; orgn. planning supr. Nat. Tube div. U.S. Steel Corp., 1944-48; asso. mem. Robert Heller & Assos., 1948-51; adminstrv. v.p. Stokely-Van Camp, Inc., 1951-55; pres., dir. Fairmont Foods Co., Omaha, Neb., 1955, chmn. bd. 1959-—. Cons. Hoover Commn. on Orgn. Exec. Br. of Govt. Mem. A.I.M., N.A.M., Nat. Assn. Cost Accountants. Home: 1421 S. 87th St., Omaha 24. Office: 3201 Farnam St., Omaha, Neb. Died July 10, 1959; buried Forest Lawn Cemetery, Omaha.

ROBINS, Raymond, social economist, lecturer and writer; b. Staten Island, New York, Sept. 17, 1873; s. Charles Ephraim and Hannah M. (Crow) R.; educated at home and in country schs., Ohio, Ky., and Fla.; LL.B., Columbian (now George Washington) U., 1896; LL.D., Hillsdale College (Mich.), 1923 and U. of Florida, 1941; m. Margaret Dreier, June 21, 1905. Superintendent Chicago Municipal Lodging House, 1902-05; head worker Northwestern Univ. Settlement, 1903-05; mem. Chicago Bd. of Edn., 1906-09; mem. Chicago Charter Conv.; social service expert The Men and Religion Forward Movement campaign, 1911-12, and world tour, 1913; chmn. State Central Com. Prog. Party in Ill.; Prog. party candidate for U.S. senator, 1914; temporary and permanent chmn. Prog. Nat. Conv., 1916. Leader in Nat. Christian Evangelistic Social campaign in Am. univs. and colls., 1915-16, under Internat. Y.M.C.A. and Y.W.C.A. Dep. commr. and maj. U.S. Army, in Am. Red Cross mission to Russia, June 1917; promoted commr. and lt. col. U.S. Army, comdg. Am. Red Cross mission in Russia, Nov. 1917-May 1918. Mem. exec. com. Rep. Nat. Com., campaigns, 1920-24; trustee and charter mem. Roosevelt Memorial Assn.; v.p. William Jennings Bryan Memorial Assn. Advocate of organized labor and land value taxation. Transcontinental and European tour advocating the outlawry of war, 1923; v. chmn. Am. Com. for Outlawry of War, 1925-27; v.p. Citizens Com. of 1000 for Law Observance & Enforcement; campaigned Fla. citrus belt for growers' coöp. control in marketing citrus crop, 1931. Deeded with wife, Apr. 9, 1932, as donation to Federal Dept. of Agr., their Chinsegut Hill Plantation Groves and Forest Winter Home, 2080 acres, now U.S. wild life refuge forest conservation agrl. and hort. expt. station, known as Chinsegut Hill Sanctuary, Hernando County, Fla.; traveled 8,000 miles in April, May and June, 1933, in Soviet Union, studying mass production on farms, in mines and factories, and primary education under Soviet system of social control. Conglist. Clubs: City (Chicago. Home: Chinsegut Hill, Hernando County (P.O.) Brooksville, Fla. Died Sept. 26, 1954; buried Chinsegut Hill.

ROBINS, Thomas, inventor, mfr.; b. Highland Falls, N.Y., Sept. 1, 1868; s. Thomas and Emma (Davis) R.; student Princeton Prep. Sch., N.J., 1886-87; Princeton, 1887-89; m. Winifred Howard Tucker, Apr. 26, 1894; children—Thomas, Samuel Davis. Began series of inventions, 1892, leading to the "belt conveyor," now largely used for carrying ores, coal, etc.; awarded Grand Prize, Paris Expn., 1900, and highest in its class at Buffalo and St. Louis expositions; chmn. bd. Hewitt-Robins, Inc., ret., 1955. Mem., sec. Naval Cons. Bd., U.S., 1915-—. Mem. Princeton Engrng. Assn. (ex-pres.), Inventors' Guild (sec.), Am. Inst. Mining and Metall. Engrs., Nat. Research Council. Episcopalian. Mason. Clubs: Century, Down Town, Pilgrims (N.Y.C.); Royal Thames Yacht. Home: Saybrook Point and 40 E. 66th St. Office: 370 Lexington Av., N.Y.C. Died Nov. 4, 1957.

ROBINSON, A(braham) L., univ. prof., librarian; b. Chicago, Ill., Oct. 17, 1902; s. Harris and Celia (Saperstein) R.; B.S. in Ch.E., U. of Pa., 1923, M.S., 1924; Ph.D., U. of Pittsburgh, 1926; student Univ. of Munich, Germany, 1929-30. Instr. chemistry, U. of Pittsburgh, 1926-28, asst. prof. 1928-40, asso. prof. 1940-42, prof. since 1942, acting librarian, 1944-49, univ. librarian since 1949. Mem. A.L.A., Assn. Am. Univ. Profs., Sigma Xi. Author: (with Alexander Silverman) Selective Experiments in General Chemistry, 1939. Home: 549 Neville St., Pittsburgh 13. Office: University of Pittsburgh, Pitts. 13. Died Aug. 4, 1952; buried Phila.

ROBINSON, Alexander Cochrane, banker; b. Ripley, N.Y., Oct. 19, 1864; s. Alexander Cochrane and Catherine Mather (Ely) R.; B.S., U. Pitts., 1882, M.A. (hon.), 1916; m. Emma Payne Jones, Oct. 2, 1890 (died 1909); children—Alexander Cochrane. John Noel (dec.), David (dec.). Began as clerk Robinson Bros., bankers, Pitts., 1882, partner, 1891; firm dissolved 1910; v.p. Commonwealth Trust Co., Pitts., 1910-16; pres. Peoples-Pitts. Trust Co., 1916-33, chmn. bd., 1933-40, ret., 1940; dir. Peoples First Nat. Bank & Trust Co., Pitts.; dir. Western Allegheny R.R. Co., Pa. Bankshares, Nat. Union Fire Ins., Nat. Union Indemnity Co., dir. Sewickley Pub. Schs., 1925-43; trustee Sewickley Pub. Library; chmn. Sewickley Valley Br. A.R.C., 1917-41; mem. exec. com. Pa. Council Nat. Def., 1917-19; trustee Western Theol. Sem.; trustee Pa. Coll. for Women, Valley Hosp. Mem. Hist. Soc. of Western Pa., Am. Bankers Assn. (ex-pres. savs. bank div.). Republican. Presbyn. Clubs: Duquesne, Rolling Rock, Allegheny Country, Edgeworth. Speaker and writer on financial subjects. Home: Manada, Sewickley, Pa. Office: Peoples Bank Building, Pitts. Died Apr. 17, 1957.

ROBINSON, Beverley Randolph, lawyer; b. New York, N.Y., June 24, 1876; s. Dr. Beverley and Anna Eliza (Foster) R.; prep. edn. Cutler Sch., New York, 1885-94; A.B., Harvard, 1898; LL.B., Columbia, 1901; m. Gladys Endicott, June 6, 1917. Admitted to N.Y. bar, 1900; clerk law Strong & Cadwalader, New York, 1901-02; clerk Masten & Nichols, New York, 1902-09, mem. of firm, 1909-31; mem. of successors, Milbank, Tweed, Hope & Webb, now Milbank, Tweed, Hope & Hadley; dir. Borden Co., Borden's Farm Products Co., Drake Bakeries, Incorporated. Mem. Bd. of Aldermen, New York, 1904-06; mem. Assembly, N.Y. Legislature, 1907-09; former pres. 27th Assembly Dist. Rep. Club; del. Rep. Nat. Conv. and asst. treas. Rep. Nat. Com., 1916; Rep. nominee presdl. elector, 1912; mem. exec. com. 27th Assembly Dist. of N.Y. Rep. Co. Com., 1911-12. Trustee Museum of City of New York; trustee Five Points House, Am. Museum of Natural History, N.Y. Geneal. and Biog. Soc.; chmn. Nassau County (N.Y.) Bridge Authority; trustee Lawrence Beach Club, Inc., Member Association of Bar of City of New York, N.Y. County Lawyers Assn., N.Y. State Bar Assn., American Bar Association, New York State Chamber of Commerce, Pilgrims, St. George's Society, St. Nicholas Soc. (former mgr.), S.R., Soc. of Colonial Wars, Phi Beta Kappa, Phi Beta Kappa Assos., Phi Delta Phi. Episcopalian. Clubs: Knickerbocker, Brook, Union (pres.), University, Century, Down Town (trustee), Grolier, Harvard (all N.Y. City); Rockaway Hunting of Cedarhurst, L.I. (gov.); Boone and Crockett. Pres. Winterthur Corp., 1930-51. Trustee Henry F. duPont Mus. Home: 4 E. 66th St. Office: 15 Broad St., N.Y.C. Died Sept. 21, 1951.

ROBINSON, Boardman, cartoonist, painter; b. Somerset, N.S., Sept. 6, 1876; s. John Henry and Lydia Jane (Parker) R.; ed. in Can. and Eng.; Mass. Normal Art Sch.; Académie Colarossi and École des Beaux Arts, Paris; m. Sally Senter Whitney, Nov. 1903; children—Barbara (dec.), John Whitney, Bartlett Whitney. After painting for 6 yrs. in Paris and San Francisco located in New York and illustrated for various mags. and newspapers; staff of Morning Telegraph, 1907-10, New York Tribune, 1910-14; went with John Reed to the Balkans and Russia to make drawings for Metropolitan Magazine, 1915; staff of The Masses, Liberator and Harper's Weekly, 1915-22; cartoonist for Outlook, London, 1922-23; served as instr. Art Students' League, New York, 1918-29; resident art instr. Fountain Valley Sch. and dir. Colorado Springs Fine Arts Center 1930-47. Awarded gold medal, Architectural League of New York, 1930, for murals, Kaufmann's Store, Pittsburgh, also for mural in RKO Bldg., Rockefeller Center, New York, 1932, Dept. of Justice, Washington, D.C., 1937. Co-author: (with John Reed) The War in Eastern Europe, 1916; Cartoons of the War, 1916; illustrated, The Brothers Karamazov, 1933; The Idiot, 1935; King Lear Limited Editions Club, 1939; Spoon River Anthology, 1941; Moby Dick, 1942. Represented in collections: Metropolitan Museum N.Y., Whitney Museum, Los Angeles, Minneapolis, Denver, Wichita museums and others. Address: Colorado Springs, Colo. Died Sept. 5, 1952.*

ROBINSON, David Moore, univ. prof.; b. Auburn, N.Y., Sept. 21, 1880; s. Willard Haskell and Ella (Moore) R.; student Polytechnic Inst., Brooklyn, 1890-94; A.B., U. of Chicago, 1898, fellow in Greek, 1898-1901, Ph.D., 1904; student Am. School of Classical Studies, Athens, Greece, 1901-03, fellow, 1902-03; student Halle, 1902, Berlin, 1903-04, Bonn, 1909; mem. excavating staff, Corinth, 1902-03, Sardis, 1910; LL.D., Jamestown Coll., 1915; L.H.D., Trinity Coll., 1925; Litt.D., Syracuse U., 1933; Ph.D., U. Thessalonica, Greece, 1951; married Helen Haskell, Aug. 31, 1910; 1 dau., Alice Bradford (dec.). Asst. prof. Greek, and head of the Classical Dept. Illinois College, 1904-05; asso. in classical archeology, 1905-08, asso. prof., 1908-12, prof. Greek archeology and epigraphy, 1912-13, prof. classical archeology and epigraphy, 1913-20, W. H. Collins Vickers prof. archeology and epigraphy, 1920-47, member academic council, 1931, 32, 1935-40, 1943-47, lecturer in Greek lit., 1915-47, chmn. Latin dept. 1944-45, Johns Hopkins, prof. emeritus art and archaeology, 1947-—; professor classics and archaeology, University of Miss., 1948-—. Acting director and prof. Greek language and literature, Am. Sch. Classical Studies in Athens, 1909-10 (now mem. mng. and executive coms.); Professor of Greek and Archaeology and Librarian, 1946-47; lecturer Bryn Mawr College, 1911-1912; professor of classical philology, summer session, Columbia University, 1919; lecturer Bur. Univ. Travel, 1922; prof. Greek, Notre Dame Coll., Md., 1921-35. Dir. of excavations at Pisidian Antioch and Sizma for U. of Mich., 1924; Charles Eliot Norton lecturer, Archaeol. Inst. of America, 1924, 25, 28, 29, Harry Wilson lecturer, 1935-36; dir. excavations, Olynthus, 1928-38; C. L. Moore lecturer, Trinity Coll., Conn., 1925. Lecturer in fine arts, New York U., 1926-31; summer session, U. of Calif., 1927; on leave of absence for research in Rome and Greece, 1927-28, 1937-38; prof. Latin, Syracuse U., summers, 1929, 1931-33; visiting prof. U. of Chicago, summer, 1930, U. of Calif. at Los Angeles (courses in anthropology and sociology), summer, 1941; McBride lecturer, Western Reserve U., 1930; Larwill lecturer Kenyon Coll., 1932; Berlin U. and Deutsches Archeol. Inst. lecturer, 1934; leader of Augustan Pilgrimage, 1937; mem. faculty Sch. of Fine and Practical Arts, Md. Art Inst., 1930-43. Member Internat. Epigraphical Congress, Amsterdam, 1938, Internat. Congress Fine Arts, London, 1939; prof. Latin Inst. William and Mary, 1941; lecturer for Association American Colleges, 1944-46. Received citation, as useful citizen, University of Chicago, 1941. Served in Military Intelligence Div., United States Army, 1916. Asso. editor Classical Weekly, 1913-36, American Jour. Philology, 1920-— (hon. editor, 1943-—), Internat. Humanistic Review Litteris, Supplementum Epigraphicum Graecum, 1923-38; editor-in-chief Art and Archaeology, 1914-18, asso. editor 1918-34; editor Johns Hopkins Studies in Archaeology (40 vols.); chmn. publ. com. Art Bulletin, 1921-38 (editor-in-chief, 1919-21, mem. ed. bd., 1938-—); editor, with Hadzsits, of series Our Debt to Greece and Rome (45 vols.); publ. com. Am. Sch. at Athens, 1931-38. Trustee Baltimore Art Museum; dir. Johns Hopkins Museum; hon. pres. Baltimore Sch. Arts League; hon. pres. Baltimore Archaeol. Soc.; sec. Johns Hopkins Philol. Association, 1915-20, president, 1921-22, 1935-36, 1945-46, v.p., 1944-45; president Baltimore Classical Club, 1914-15, 1939-46; recorder Archaeol. Institute Am., 1913-14, gen. sec. 1921-23, vice p., 1914-30, 1st v.p., 1930-35; bus. mgr. Am. Jour. of Archaeol., 1921-23, ed. news discussions and bibliography, 1932-38, asso. editor, editor bibliography, etc., 1938-—. Fellow Am. Acad. Arts and Sciences, Am. Geog. Soc., Inst. Am. Genealogy, Royal Numismatic Soc. of England; mem. Am. Classical League (v.p. 1945), Am. Philol. Assn., Coll. Art Assn. (president 1919-23, dir. 1923-43, hon. dir., 1943-—), N.E.A., Am. Association Univ. Profs., Am. Hist. Soc., Am. Linguistic Soc., Am. Sch. Classical Studies at Rome (chmn. advisory council, 1920-21), Am. Numismatic and Antiquarian Soc., Am. Oriental Soc., Am. Fedn. of Arts, Classical Association Atlantic States (pres. 1920-21), Archaeology Club, Am. Philosophical Soc., Am. Soc. Archtl. Historians, Am. Assn. Museums, A.A.A.S., Palamas Soc., Am. Polit. Science Assn., Am. Acad. Polit. and Social Science, Am. Soc. Colonial Wars, Maryland Hist. Soc., Art Forum S.A.R., Sons Revolution, Université Internationale, Am. Research Center in Egypt, Am. Schs. of Oriental Research, Soc. for Advancement of Edn., Am. and Brit. Commonwealth Assn. (mem. council), Classical Assn. of Can., Founders and Patriots of America, Institut International de Recherches Hellenistiques, Phi Beta Kappa (pres. Johns Hopkins chpt. 1941-42), Eta Sigma Phi; hon. mem. Archaeol. Soc. Greece, German Archaeol. Inst.; hon. pres. Helleno-Am. Soc. of Northern Greece. Pan-Macedonian Assn., Reese Meml. Assn., Baltimore, 1939-—; pres. U. of Chicago Alumni of Md., 1940-48; pres. Md. br. Greek War Relief Assn., 1940-—; mem. council Nat. Soc. for Restoration of Greece, Friends of Greece, Dodecanesian Nat. Council; mem. bd. of advisers, pres. Soc. of Byzantine and Modern Greek Studies; executive committee Am. Council Learned Societies. Air raid warden, 1942-45. Member Presbyterian and Greek Orthodox Churches. Clubs: Johns Hopkins, Roland Park Country, Bachelors Cotillon, University (vice-president, 1941, president, 1942-47), Coin. Author: Ancient Sinope, 1906; Inscriptions from the Cyrenaica, 1913; The Songs of Sappho (with M. M. Miller) 1925; Sappho and Her Influence, 1924; The Greek Idyls, Theocritus, Bion, Moschus (with M. M. Miller), 1926; The Deeds of Augustus, 1926; Roman Sculptures from Pisidian Antioch, 1926; Greek and Latin Inscriptions from Asia Minor, 1926; Greek and Latin Inscriptions of Sardis (with W. H. Buckler), 1932; A Catalogue of the Greek Vases in the Royal Ontario Museum of Archaeology, Toronto (2 vols.), 1930; Excavations at Olynthus (Vol. II), Architecture and Sculpture, 1930; (Vol. III) Coins of Olynthus, 1931; (Vol. IV) Terra Cottas of Olynthus, found in 1928, 1931; (Vol. V) Mosaics, Vases and Lamps of Olynthus, 1933; (Vol. VI) The Coins found at Olynthus in 1931, 1933; (Vol. VII) The Terra Cottas found at Olynthus in 1931, 1933; (Vol. VIII with J. W. Graham) The Hellenic House, 1938; (Vol. IX with P. Clement), The Chalcidic Mint and the Excavation Coins, 1938; (Vol. X) Metal and Miscellaneous Minor Funds, 1941; (Vol. XI) Necrolynthia, a Study of Greek Burial Customs, 1942; (Vol. XII) Domestic and Public Architecture, 1946; (Vol. XIII) Vases Found at Olynthus, 1934, 38, 50; (Vol. XIV) Terracottas, Lamps, Coins, 1952; A Hoard of Silver Coins of Carystus, 1952; New Greek Jewelry, 1953; A Study of Greek Love-Names, including a discussion of Paederasty and a Prosopographia (with E. J. Fluck), 1937; The Robinson Collection, Corpus Vasorum, Baltimore, Vol. I, 1933, Vol. II, 1937, Vol. III, 1938; A Short History of Greece, 1936; Pindar—A Poet of Eternal Ideas, 1936; Inscriptions from Macedonia, 1938. Prahistorische und Griechische Hauser, 1939; The Great Glory and Glamor of the Dodecanese, 1944; Baalbek-Palmyra, 1946; America in Greece, 1948; The Greek View of Life, 1953; also some 400 philological and archeol. articles. Republican. Member Greek Orthodox Church. Address: U. of Miss., Oxford, Miss. Died Jan. 2, 1958; buried Greenwood Cemetery, Bklyn.

ROBINSON, Doane, author; b. Sparta, Wis., Oct. 19, 1856; s. George McCook and Rhozina (Grow) R.; christened Jonah Leroy, but is only known by pen-name. Doane; ed. country schs.; admitted to bar, 1882; senior yr. at law sch., U. Wis., 1883; M.A., S.D. Univ., 1911; Litt.D., Yankton, 1922; m. Jennie Austin, Dec. 4, 1884 (died Jan. 24, 1902); children—Harry A., Will Grow. Sec. Territorial R. R. Commn. of Dak., 1889, and of 1st R.R. Commn. of S.D., 1890-91. Established the Monthly South Dakotan, 1898, mag. devoted to state history and literature; sec. and supt. Dept. of History, S.D., and ex-officio state librarian, 1901-1926; librarian Supreme Court of South Dakota, 1926-33; trustee Yankton Coll., 1908-—, president S.D. Acad. of Science, 1921; pres. State History Teachers' Assn., 1921. Originated nat. memorial on Rushmore Mountain (Black Hills), and sec. commn. constructing it, 1926-1932. Author: Coteaus of Dakota (verse), 1899; A History of South Dakota from the Earliest Times, 1900; History of Dakota (2 vols.), 1903; History of Sioux Indians, 1904; History of Leavenworth's Expedition and Conquest of Ree Indians, 1902; Brief History South Dakota, 1906; The Green Butte (verse), 1920; Doane Robinson's Encyclopedia of South Dakota, 1925; South Dakota Sui Generis, 1927; Life of Gen. Henry Leavenworth, 1931. Editor vols. I to XII, South Dakota Hist. Collections. Operating a large ranch, 1933-—. Republican. Congregationalist. Home: Pierre, S.D. Died Nov. 27, 1946; buried Riverside Cemetery, Pierre, S.D.

ROBINSON, Dwight Parker, engineer; b. Boston, Mass., May 1, 1869; s. Edgar and Susannah (Powell) Robinson; A.B., Harvard, 1890; S.B., Mass. Inst. Tech., 1892; m. Mary Elizabeth Stearns, May 20, 1897 (died Nov. 20, 1907); m. 2d, Mary Elizabeth Dahlgren, July 25, 1912 (deceased). With Stone & Webster, constrn. engrs., etc., Boston, 1893, admitted to partnership, 1911, and served as pres. Stone & Webster Engring. Corp., Stone & Webster Constrn. Co., etc.; organized Dwight P. Robinson & Co., Inc., 1919, with headquarters in New York, and engaged in engineering and construction work in U.S. and abroad; merged, Jan. 1, 1928, with three other orgns. to form the United Engrs. & Constructors, Inc.; now retired. Fellow Am. Inst. E.E. Home: Pocasset, Cape Cod, Mass. Died Mar. 17, 1955.

ROBINSON, Erdis; b. Champaign, Ill., Jan. 24, 1872; s. Stillman Williams and Mary Elizabeth (Holden) R.; C.E., Ohio State U., 1893; m. Flora Louise Stalter, Aug. 29, 1905. Surveyor for Kan. City, Watkins & Gulf Ry., 1894-97; div. engr., later asst. chief engr., Mexican Central Ry., 1897-1904; with Robinson-Houchin Optical Co. (formerly Robinson Optical Co.) since 1904, pres. since 1910. Mem. Columbus C. of C. (dir.), U.S. C. of C. Mem. Columbus Bd. of Edn., 1926-32, and 1943. Pres. and trustee Columbus Gallery of Fine Arts; mem. Columbus Art Commn.; pres. Ohio State Student Loan Found.; pres. School of Social Adminstrn. Associates, Ohio State U.; chmn. Ohio Pub. Instnl. Bldg. Authority; pres. and trustee Godman Guild Assn.; v.p. Columbus English Speaking Union; trustee Children's Hosp., Sinking Fund Columbus Public Schs.; dir. Columbus Community Fund; chmn. Columbus Found. Mem. S.A.R. (pres. Ohio Soc.), Ohio Council of Chs. (v.p. 1926-31), Am. Soc. C.E. (life), Ohio Soc. of N.Y., Soc. of Colonial Wars (Gentleman of Council). Republican. Conglist. Clubs: Torch, Faculty, Rotary, Columbus Athletic, Columbus Country. Home: 355 W. 9th Av. Office: 79 Thurman Av., Columbus, Ohio. Died Oct. 13, 1953.

ROBINSON, George Livingstone, theologian, archaeologist; b. W. Hebron, N.Y., Aug. 19, 1864; s. William and Mary Elizabeth (Archibald) R.; A.B., Princeton, 1887, A.M., 1890; student Princeton Theol. Sem., 1890-93, U. Berlin, 1893-94; Ph.D., Leipzig, 1895; D.D., Grove City, 1906; S.T.D., Toronto, 1915; LL.D., Macalester, 1912, Wooster, 1916; m. Jessie Patton Lee Harvey, Mar. 27, 1894 (dec.); m. 2d, Lillian V. Mueller, Jan. 1, 1920. Traveled and taught in Syrian Protestant Coll. (Am. Univ.). 1887-90; prof. O.T. lit. and exegesis, Knox Coll., Toronto, 1896-98, and McCormick Theol. Sem., Chgo., 1898-—; lectr. L. P. Stone Found., Princeton Sem., 1939; prof. emeritus, 1939-—. Explorer of Sinai Peninsula and Kadesh-Barnea; discoverer of the original "High Place" at Petra, Edom. Dir. Am. Sch. of Oriental Research, 1913-14. Interchange preacher; lectr., Great Brit., 1930, 34. Mem. Am. Oriental Soc., Soc. Bibl. Lit. and Exegesis, Irving Club (Chgo.). Author: Leaders of Israel, 1906; The Book of Isaiah, 1910; The Abiding Value of the Old Treatment, 1911; The Twelve Minor Prophets, 1926; Where Did We Get Our Bible?, 1928; The Sarcophagus of an Ancient Civilization, 1930; The Bearing of Archaeology on the Old Testament, 1941; Live Out Your Years, 1951; The Short Story of A Long Life, 1957. Contbr. to theol. jours. Address: 2424 Orchard St., Chgo. Died Dec. 17, 1958.

ROBINSON, George Wilse, neuro-psychiatrist; b. St. Clair County, Mo., Aug. 1, 1871; s. George Woodford and Cornelia (Beckwith) R.; grad. Appleton City Acad., 1892, M D., Beaumont Hosp. Med. Coll., St. Louis, 1896; grad. study in nervous and mental diseases, England, Switzerland and Germany; m. Olive Bradley, Dec. 28, 1898; children—Dr. George Wilse, Jr. (U.S. Navy), Paul Edward (U.S. Army). Began practice at Appleton City, 1896; became professor of physiology, University Medical College, Kansas City, Mo.; supt. State Hospital No. 3, Nevada, Mo., 1907-09, Kansas City Gen. Hosp., 1909-10; supt. Punton Sanitarium, 1910-23, G. Wilse Robinson Sanitarium, 1923-35; med. director The Neurological Hospital of Kansas City. Served as neuro-psychiatrist, Base Hosp. 28, Limoges, France, capt. and maj. Med. Corps, U.S. Army, World War; lt. col. Med. R.C. Fellow A.M.A.; mem. Am. Psychiatric Assn., Central Neuro-Psychiatric Assn., Mo. State Med. Assn. (pres. 1923), Kansas City Acad. Medicine (pres. 1920), Jackson County Med. Soc. (pres. 1917), Kansas City Chamber Commerce, Phi Beta Pi. Democrat. Presbyterian. Clubs: Rotary, Mission Hills Country. Contbr. papers on neuroolgy and psychiatry. Home and Office: 2625 Paseo, Kansas City, Mo. Died Jan. 22, 1958.

ROBINSON, G(erard) B(riscoe), physician; b. Indpls., Sept. 6, 1898; s. Will B. and Florence (Hoyt) R.; A.B., Yale, 1920, M.D., 1924; m. Cleo V. Peck, Sept. 12, 1923; children—Jeanne P., G. B., John D. Practicing physician, Mt. Gilead, O., 1925-—; mgr., partner Dr. Nathan Tucker Lab., 1925-—; chmn., dir. Peoples Savings Bank Co., 1928-—; cons., dir. The Koehring Co., Milw.; dir. Northern Union Realty Co. of Columbus, O. President staff Morrow Co. Hosp.; chmn. Morrow County Found. Methodist. Mason. Clubs: Westbrook Country (Mansfield); Columbus (O.) Athletic, Kiwanis. Home: 165 N. Main St. Office: 72 S. Main St., Mt. Gilead, O. Died Sept. 1, 1959.

ROBINSON, Ira Ellsworth, lawyer; b. near Grafton, W.Va., Sept. 16, 1869; s. William and Mary (Sayre) R.; grad. Fairmont State Normal Sch., 1889; studied law U. Va., 1890; m. Ada Sinsel, Oct. 25, 1892 (dec.); children—William Arthur (dec.), Ada May (dec.); m. 2d, Loretta Malone, 1951. Began practice at Grafton, 1891; pros. atty., Taylor County, W.Va., 1896-1900; mem. W.Va. Senate, 1902-04; apptd. by gov. judge Supreme Ct. of Appeals, to fill vacancy, 1907, elected, 1908; resigned 1915; pres. (chief justice) of that ct. 1910, 15; Rep. nominee for gov. of W.Va., 1916; regent state Normal Schs., 1901-07; apptd. to adjudicate War Minerals Claims, Washington, 1921; spl. asst. to Atty. General of U.S. on purchase by the Govt. of the Cape Cod Canal; 1926-28; mem. Fed. Radio Commn., 1928-32, chmn., 1928-30. Lecturer W.Va. U. Coll. of Law, Northwestern U., 1920. Mem. Am. Bar Assn., Am. Law Inst., W.Va. Bar Assn., Harrison County Bar Assn. Mem. Gen. Conf. M.E. Ch., 1912, 16. Chmn. Draft Appeals Bd., 1917-18. Contbr. to legal periodicals. Home: 108 N. Walnut St., Philippi, W.Va. Office: Goff Bldg., Clarksburg, W.Va. Died Oct. 28, 1951; buried Bluemont Cemetery, Grafton, W.Va.

ROBINSON, Jesse Mathews, entomologist; b. Higginsport, O., Jan. 30, 1889; s. George Foster and Mary Etta (Mathews) R.; A.B., Miami U., Oxford, O., 1911; A.M., Ohio State U., 1916; student Ia. State Coll., summer 1923; m. Lena May Shinkle, Aug. 21, 1919. Asst. prof. of zoology-entomology, Coll. of Agr., and asst. entomologist, Ala. Agr. Expt. Sta., Ala. Poly. Inst., Auburn, 1919-21, asso. prof. and asso. entomologist, 1921-24, acting entomologist and head prof., 1924-29, chief entomologist and head prof. since 1929. Fellow A.A.A.S.; mem. Assn. Econ. Entomology, Entomol. Soc. America, Am. Genetics Assn., Eugenics Research Assn., Ala. Acad. Science, Ohio Acad., Phi Kappa Phi, Gamma Sigma Delta, Alpha Epsilon Delta, Alpha Gamma Rho, Phi Kappa Tau. Democrat. Presbyterian (elder). Mason. Club: Rotary. Home: 337 Armstrong St., Auburn, Ala. Died Aug. 27, 1949; buried Felicity, O.

ROBINSON, John S., ex-congressman; b. Wheeling, W.Va., May 4, 1856; ed. pub. schs.; admitted to bar 1880. Removed to Madison, Neb., 1884; co. att'y., Madison Co., Neb., 1886-92; judge 9th jud. dist. Neb., 1893-9; mem. Congress, 1899-1903, 3d Neb. dist.; Democrat. Home: Madison, Neb. Deceased.

ROBINSON, John Sherman, judge; b. Mansfield, O., Dec. 17, 1880; s. Samuel and Caroline (Mattayaw) R.; A.B., U. of Mich., 1903; LL.B., Columbia, 1910; m. Edith J. Lind, June 22, 1916; children—John Sherman, Samuel Williard, Irving Lind. Instr. Mich. Mil. Acad., 1903-04; prin. high sch., Bessemer, Mich., 1904-06, supt. schs., 1906-07; admitted to Wash. bar, 1910, practiced in Seattle, 1910-36; judge Wash. Supreme Court, 1937-51, chief justice, 1941, 1942. Member executive com. National Conference of Judicial Councils, 1941. Chairman State Board Bar Examiners, 1933-36; pres. Seattle Bar Association, 1935-36. Member Alpha Delta Phi, Phi Delta Phi. Republican. Conglist. Club: College (Seattle). Home: 101 N. Sherman, Olympia, Wash. Died Oct. 8, 1951.

ROBINSON, Joseph E(vans), lawyer, newspaper editor; b. Lancaster, Ky., June 10, 1873; s. James and Sallie (McDonald) R.; grad. Garrard Coll., Lancaster, 1891; student Transylvania Coll., Lexington, 1892; LL.B., Centre Coll., Danville, Ky., 1896; m. Frances Collier, June 10, 1903. Admitted to Ky. bar, 1896, and practiced since at Lancaster; mem. firm Robinson & Kauffman, 1924-—; owner and editor Central Record, weekly newspaper, Lancaster, 1910-—; pres. Garrard County Canning Co., Lancaster Bldg. & Loan Assn.; dir. and atty. Garrard Bank & Trust Co. County atty. Garrard Co., 1904-12; city atty. Lancaster, 1912; chmn. Bd. of Control of Pub. Instns. of Ky., 1925-27; mem. Dem. Nat. Com., 1928-32. Mem. Christian (Disciples) Ch. Mason. Clubs: Pendennis, Rotary. Home: Lancaster, Ky. Deceased.*

ROBINSON, Lennox, playwright, author; b. Douglas County, Cork, Ireland, Oct. 4, 1886; student Bandon Grammar Sch.; m. Dorothy Travers Smith, 1931. Managed Abbey Theatre, Dublin, various periods. Plays: The Clancy Name, 1908; The Cross Roads, 1908; Harvest, 1910; Patriots, 1912; The Dreamers, 1915; The White Headed Boy, 1916; The Lost Leader, 1918; The Round Table, 1922; Never the Time and the Place, 1924; Crabbed Youth and Age, 1924; The Portrait, 1925; The White Blackbird, 1925; The Big House, 1926; 'Give a Dog—,' 1927; The Faroff Hills, 1928; Ever the Twain, 1929; All's Over Then?, 1932; Is Life Worth Living?, 1933; Church Street, 1934; Killycregs in Twilight, 1937, Birds' Nest, 1938; Pictures in a Theatre, 1947; The Lucky Finger, 1948; Fathers and Sons. Author (books) A Young Man from the South, 1917; Bryan Cooper; W. B. Yeats, a study, 1939; Three Homes (with Tom Robinson and Nora Dorman), 1938. Curtain Up, 1939. Editor: Letters of J. B. Yeats, 1920; Golden Treasury of Irish Verse, 1929; Lady Gregory's Journals, 1946; An Appreciation of the Theatre, 1946; The Irish Book of Oxford Verse (with Donagh MacDonagh), 1958. Address: 20 Longford Terrace, Monkstorm, County, Dublin, Ireland. Died Oct. 14, 1958; buried St. Patricks Cathedral, Dublin, Ireland.

ROBINSON, Louis Newton, economist; b. Tunkhannock, Pa., Nov. 3, 1880; s. John Marklin and Annie Elizabeth (Thacher) R.; A.B., Swarthmore Coll., 1905; studied Cornell U., 1905-06, Ph.D., 1911; Universities of Halle and Berlin, 1906-07; married

Caroline Hadley, June 18, 1908; children—Walter Hadley, Miles Hadley, Alice, Christine, John Mark, T. Thacher; m. 2d, Marylyn C. Wyse, Aug. 30, 1947. Instr. economics, Swarthmore Coll., 1908-09, asst. prof., 1909-13, prof., 1913-18; chief probation ofcr., Municipal Ct. Phila., 1918-21; directed survey small loan bus. under auspices of Russel Sage Foundation, 1922-24; mem. and sec. Pa. State Penal Commn. of 1913; mem. Pa. Commn. to Investigate Prison System of 1917; mem. Pa. Parole Commn., 1925-27; mem. Pa. Crime Commn., 1927-29; sec. com. of Nat. Crime Commn on Pardons, Parole, Probation, Penal Laws and Institutional Correction, 1926-28; chmn. Pa. Com. on Penal Affairs; chmn., Pennsylvania Bd. Parole, 1942-43; mem. and later chmn. bd. Prison Industries Reorganization Adminstrn., 1935-38; dir. Household Finance Corp., Swarthore National Bank and Trust Company. President of Home for Aged and Infirm Colored Persons. Mem. Am. Inst. Criminal Law and Criminology, Am. Statistical Assn., Delta Upsilon, Phi Beta Kappa. Quaker. Author: History and Organization of Criminal Statistics (Hart Schaffner & Marx prize essay series), 1911; Penology in the United States, 1921; Should Prisoners Work?, 1931; (with Maude E. Stearns) Ten Thousand Small Loans, 1930; (with Rolf Nugent) Regulation of the Small Loan Business, 1935; Jails—The Care and Treatment of Misdemeanant Prisoners, 1944; also numerous articles and pamphlets on criminology and finance. Home: 411 College Av., Swarthmore, Pa. Died Nov. 25, 1952.

ROBINSON, Luther Emerson, educator, author; b. Columbus, Miss., Apr. 10, 1867; s. Zenas and Margaret Love (Murphy) R.; A.B., Drury Coll., Springfield, Mo., 1894, A.M., 1897, D.Litt., 1927; studied U. of Chgo. U. of Bonn; research student Oxford U., 1906-07; research student in English in British Museum 6 weeks, 1907; research student, Library of Congress, 1924-25; hon. L.H.D., Monmouth (Illinois) College, 1938; m. Anna Elizabeth Dysart, July 28, 1897; children—Ina Lenore, Edgar Emerson, Harriet Dysart. Formerly reporter and city editor Springfield (Mo.) Republican; prof. English, Monmouth Coll., 1900—. Dir., trustee and sec. Warren Co. (Ill.) Library. Republican: United Presbyn. Author: History of Illinois, 1909; Abraham Lincoln as a Man of Letters, 1918; Life and Letters of Elmer Ephriam Ellsworth (for Ill. State Hist. Soc.), 1923; History of Warren County, Ill., 1927. Selected Poems of Robert Browning, 1930. Home: Monmouth, Ill. Died July 25, 1945.

ROBINSON, Orin Pomeroy, Jr., mfg. exec.; b. Corning, N.Y., July 17, 1891; s. Orin Pomeroy and Mary Louise (Clark) R.; student Amherst College, 1910-11, Cornell, 1915; m. Estella Ann Scroggie, Sept. 4, 1926; children—Orin Pomeroy, III, Ann. Chaser New London Ship & Engine Co., 1915-18; with Electric Boat Co., N.Y.C. since 1918, gen. mgr. Groton plant since 1938, sr. v.p. since Dec., 1951; with Pacific Bank, 1921; diesel engr. designer Sperry Gyro Co., 1921-22; dir. New London Bldg. Loan Assn., Hartford Nat. Bank & Trust Co.; corporator Savs. Bank of New London. Dir. Lawrence Hosp., Mystic Marine Mus.; active Y.M.C.A., Boy Scouts Am.; director Connecticut State Chamber of Commerce. Member Shipbuilders Council Am., Am. Arbitration Assn. (panel mem.), Soc. Naval Architects and Marine Engrs., Newcomen Soc. Home: Sea Meadows, Goshen Point, Waterford. Office: General Dynamics Corp., Groton, Conn. Died Feb. 26, 1956.

ROBINSON, Richard Hallett Meredith, naval architect; b. Ravenna, O., Apr. 2, 1875; s. George Foreman and Mary A. (Gillis) R.; grad. U.S. Naval Acad. (first honors), 1896; grad. in naval architecture and engring., U. of Glasgow, 1898; m. Rosalind Wood Smith, Jan. 2, 1899; children—Rosalind (Mrs. Henry L. Chisholm), George Foreman. In service of U.S. as naval constructor at Cramp's Shipyard, Phila., 1898-1902; in charge battleship Connecticut, New York Navy Yard, 1902-05; naval constructor (lt.-comdr.) and asst. to chief constructor, in charge of design and constrn. of all ships, 1905-13; resigned, with rank of naval constructor, Feb. 1913; chmn. bd., Minn. & Ont. Paper Co., dir. subsidiaries; dir. Merchant Sterling Corp. Decorated Commander Order of White Rose of Finland. Member Society Naval Architects and Marine Engineers (honorary vice president), Military Order Fgn. Wars (past comdr. Conn. Commandery), U.S. Naval Inst., Loyal Legion. Republican. Episcopalian. Clubs: University, Tuxedo (New York); Army and Navy (Washington); Chicago (Chicago); Minneapolis Club. Office: Baker Arcade Bldg., Minneapolis. Died Apr. 23, 1951.

ROBINSON, Rodney Potter, philologist; b. Council Bluffs, Ia., Mar. 15, 1890; s. Lyman Bartlet and Lucy Ann (Lamb) R.; A.B., U. of Mo., 1910, M.A., 1911; Ph.D., U. of Ill., 1920; m. Rachel L. Sargent, June 20, 1931. Tchr. Latin, Lexington (Mo.) High Sch., 1911-13, Anaconda (Mont.) High Sch., 1913-14; faculty U. of Cin. 1920—, prof. classics, 1927—, fellow Grad. Sch. of Arts and Scis., 1931—, dean Grad. Sch. 1940-45; prof., charge of classical studies, Am. Acad., Rome, Italy, 1935-37. In Ambulance Service, U.S. Army with French Army, 1917-19. Decorated Croix de Guerre. Guggenheim fellow, 1928-29. Mem. Am. Philol. Assn., Classical

Assn. of Middle West and South, Classical League, Soc. for Promotion of Roman Studies, Phi Beta Kappa. Protestant. Author of philological monographs; editor of classical texts. Home: 338 Probasco St., Cin. Died Apr. 1, 1950; buried Spring Grove Cemetery, Cin.

ROBINSON, Thomas John Bright, ex-congressman; b. New Diggings, Wis., Aug. 12, 1868; s. Isaac and Eliza (Graham) R.; ed. pub. and high schs.; m. Belle Clinton; children—Mrs. Jessie Thornton, Walter Thomas, Mrs. Marguerite French, Mrs. Dorothy Clinton, Lee Clinton. Banker and farmer; pres. Citizens Nat. Bank, Hampton, 1907-23; now in real estate and mortgage investments bus. Mem. State Senate, Iowa. 1912-16; mem. 68th to 72d Congresses 1923-33, 3d Ia. Dist. Chmn. Franklin County war activities during World War. Pres. Hampton Pub. Library, Hampton Bd. Edn. Del. M.E. Ch. to Ecumenical Conf., Toronto, 1911, London, 1921; mem. Gen. Conf. M.E. Ch., 1908, 12, 16. Mason (K.T.). Rotarian. Home: 120 1st Av. S.W., Hampton, Ia. Died Jan. 27, 1958; buried Hampton (Ia.) Cemetery.

ROBINSON, Wilfred Henry, dentist; b. Oakville, Cal., Jan. 14, 1882; s. James Henry and Frona Sarah (Root) R.; student Coll. of Physicians and Surgeons, San Francisco, 1905-08; m. Lillian Adele Anderson, June 23, 1910; children—Wilfred Henry, Adele Marie. Attendant in office of Dr. W. P. English, Vacaville, Cal., 1897-1901; asst. operator in office of Dr. R. P. Chandler, Reno, Nev., 1901-05; practice of dentistry, Reno, 1908-09, Oakland, Cal., 1909—, retired, 1945. Chmn. Am. Dental Assn. exhibit, Treasure Island, 1938-39. Mem. Cal. State Bd. Dental Examiners, 1930-39, pres. bd., 1932-36; mem. Nat. Assn. Dental Examiners (pres. 1935); fellow Am. Coll. Dentists; mem. Am. Dental Assn. (trustee 1932-39, pres. elect 1939-40, pres. 1940-41; chmn. Jour. com. 1935-38, mem. research com. 1941-46), Cal. State Dental Assn. (pres. 1929; del. to Am. Dental Assn., 1928-45; mem. council State Assn., 1927-35; gen. chmn. 1931 meeting), Alameda County Dist. Dental Soc. (pres. 1928), Psi Omega (pres. state chapter 1927), Tau Kappa Omega, Omicron Kappa Upsilon, Alumni Assn. Coll. of Physicians and Surgeons. Republican. Clubs: Athens Athletic, Lake Merritt Breakfast (v.p. 1940-41), Nat. Exchange, Oakland Exchange (pres. 1938-39), Oakland Forum (Oakland). Mem. Alameda County Apt. House Assn. (chmn. bd. dirs. 1944-45, pres. 1945-47). Mem. Alameda Co. Taxpayers Assn. Bd. of Dirs., 1945-46, pres., 1946. Member Crippled Children Soc. of Alameda Co. Bd. of Dirs. 1936-—, pres., 1945-1946-1947. Home: 859 Santa Ray Av., Oakland, Cal. Died Sept. 12, 1948.

ROBINSON, William Alexander, educator; b. New Haven, Sept. 5, 1884; s. James and Elizabeth (Graham) R.; B.A., Bowdoin, 1907; M.A., U. of Wis., 1910; Ph.D., Yale, 1913; M.A., Dartmouth, 1919; m. Ruth Barbara Rule, Dec. 20, 1931. Asst. in Am. history, U. of Wis., 1909-11; asst. polit. sci., Yale, 1911-13; asso. prof. polit. sci., U. of Ida., 1913-14; asst. prof. polit. sci., Washington, 1914-17, asso. prof., 1917-19; prof. polit sci., Dartmouth, 1919—. Mem. Am. Polit. Sci. Assn., Hist. Soc., Kappa Sigma, Phi Beta Kappa. Author: Jeffersonian Democracy in New England 1916. Joint editor (with Allen Johnson), Readings in Recent American Constitutional History, 1927; (with Thomas B. Reed), Parliamentarian, 1930. Contbr. to Dictionary of Am. Biography, Dictionary of Am. History, mags. Home: Hanover, N.H. Died June 10, 1950; buried Hanover, N.H.

ROBINSON, William Dean, mfr.; b. Detroit, 1898; Yale, 1921; married; five children. Chmn. board and dir. Briggs Mfg. Co., dir. Fred J. Robinson Lumber Co.; dir. Nat. Bank of Detroit. Dir. Detroit Baseball Co. Home: 41 Provincial Rd., Grosse Pointe 36, Mich. Office: Bull Bldg., Detroit 26. Died July 20, 1957.

ROBINSON, William Henry, lumberman; b. Chgo. Oct. 21, 1848; ed. pub. schs. m. M. Edith Anderson. Established in lumber business at Portland, N. Dak. 1882; State senator, 1889; pres. bd. trustees State Penitentiary in Bismarck, 1892; pres. bd. trustees Agr'l. Coll. of N. Dak., 1894. Delegate Rep. Nat. Conv., Minneapolis, 1892; chmn. Rep. State Central Com., 1892; mem. Nat. Rep. Com. 1896-1900; chmn. Rep. State Central Com. 1898. Address: Mayville, N.D. Died Dec. 24, 1910; buried Fargo, N.D.

ROBINSON, William Theodore, educator; b. Unitia, Tenn., Feb. 26, 1877; s. William Alexander and Nancy Estalyn (Donaldson) R.; B.A., U. Tenn., 1903; M.A., Peabody Coll. for Tchrs., 1917; m. Julia Gray Hamlin, Dec. 27, 1907; children—Mary Estalyn, William Theodore. Tchr., prin. in rural and pvt. schs., 1896-1910; prin. elementary schs., Paris, Tenn., 1910-11, secondary schs., 1911-17; prin. Chattanooga High Sch., 1917-27; supt. Chattanooga Schs., 1927-42; prin. Clara Carpenter Sch. and dir. instr. in elementary edn. U. of Chattanooga, 1942-47; prin. Highland Park Sch., 1947—. Mem. N.E.A., Tenn. Edn. Assn., State Pub. Sch. Officers Assn. Methodist. Home: 317 Crestway Dr., Chattanooga, Tenn. Died Nov. 13, 1953.

ROBINSON, Wm. Henry, univ. prof., clergyman; b. LaFayette, Ind., July 22, 1897; s. Wm. Henry and Clementine (Gruber) R.; ed. parochial and pub. schs., Ind.; grad. Notre Dame Prep Sch., 1916; A.B., U. of Notre Dame, 1920; Ph.D., Gregorian U., Rome, 1923, S.T.D., 1927. Final vows as Religious of Congregation of Holy Cross, 1924; ordained priest, of Roman Cath. Ch., Rome, Italy, Apr. 16, 1927; prof. dogmatic theology, Holy Cross Coll., Catholic U., Washington, 1927-39; Master of Novices, St. Joseph's Novitiate, Rolling Prairie, Ind., 1939-42; prof. philos., Univ. Notre Dame, 1942-43, asst. religious superior, 1946-52, prof. theol. since 1946; pres. St. Edward's U., Austin, Tex., 1943-46. Served as auxiliary chaplain to U.S. Army and Air Corps Camps in central Tex., World War II. Mem. Am. Cath. Philos. Assn. K.C. (4°). Republican. Collector periodical articles on theology, Christian practice, religious life; writer for Cath. periodicals. Home: Univ. Notre Dame, Notre Dame, Ind. Died Jan. 30, 1955; buried Notre Dame, Ind.

ROBISON, Henry Barton, educator; b. Auburn, Ga., Jan. 2, 1866; s. William Thomas and Elizabeth (Elder) R.; A.B., Transylvania Coll., Lexington, Ky., 1893, A.M., 1894; classical diploma, Coll. of The Bible, Lexington, 1893; Ph.D., U. Chgo., 1907; m. Dora Sledd, July 2, 1895; children—Amy Jean (Mrs. H. C. Sarvis), Georgia (Mrs. Howard K. Beale). Instr. classics, Transylvania Coll., 1893-1900; ordained ministry Disciples of Christ, 1890; pastor Wilmore, Ky., 1897-1900; instr. U. of Chgo. extension dept., Apostolic Fathers, 1907-12; pastor El Paso, Tex., 1907-09, Mobile, Ala., 1910; prof. N.T. lang. and lit., philosophy of Christian religion, Culver-Stockton Coll., Canton, Mo., 1910-—, dean Sch. of Religion. Mem. Bd. of Higher Edn. of Disciples of Christ, 1935-46; mem. adv. bd. Revision Com. Am. Revised Bible 1940—. Democrat. Author: (brochures) Syntax to the Participle in the Apostolic Fathers, 1913; Achieving the Ideal of Our Fathers, 1924; The Undergraduate Curriculum of Biblical Studies, 1928; The Origin and Nature of the Bible, 1929. Compiler: (with others) Index to the Apostolic Fathers, 1907. Writer of S.S. lessons for Christian Bd. of Publ., St. Louis, 1924, and David C. Cook Co., Elgin, Ill., 1925. Contbg. editor The Christian, Kansas City, 1926. Home: 2816 Columbia Rd., Madison 5, Wis. Died Oct. 11, 1953; buried Forest Grove Cemetery, Canton, Mo.

ROBISON, Samuel Shelburn (rŏb'i-sŭn), ret. naval officer; b. Juanita County, Pa., May 10, 1867; grad. U.S. Naval Acad., 1888; m. Mary Louise Clark, 1893. Commd. ensign, 1890 advanced through the grades to rear admiral, 1918. Served in U.S.S. Boston during Spanish-Am. War, 1898; with Bur. of Equipment, Navy Dept., 1904-06; navigator Tennessee, 1906-08; exec. officer U.S.S. Pennsylvania, 1908-09; with Bur. Equipment, 1909-10, Bur. of Steam Engring., 1910-11; comd. U.S.S. Cincinnati, 1911-13; asst. to Bur. Steam Engring., Navy Dept., 1913-14, 1914-15; comd. in U.S.S. Jupiter, 1914; comd. U.S.S. South Carolina, 1915-17; comdr. Submarine Force, Atlantic Fleet, 1917-18; mem. Naval Armistice Commn., 1918-19; comdt. Navy Yard, Boston, 1919-21; mil. gov. Santo Domingo, 1921-22; mem. Gen. Bd., Navy Dept. 6 mos., 1923; adm. in command Battle Fleet, 1923-25, U.S. Fleet, 1925-26; comdr. 13th Naval Dist., 1926-28; apptd. supt. U.S. Naval Acad., 1928; ret. 1931; now supt. Adm. Farragut Acad., Tom's River, N.J. Author: History of Naval Tactics, 1942. Home: Tom's River, N.J.; (summer) Academia, Juniata County, Pa. Deceased; buried Arlington Nat. Cemetery.

ROBNETT, Ronald Herbert (rŏb'nĕtt), educator; b. Salem, Ore., Oct. 15, 1905; s. James Herbert and Myra Eugenia (Murphy) R.; B.S., U. of Ore., 1928; M.B.A., Harvard, 1934; m. Roberta Bernice Wilcox, June 17, 1930; 1 son, Richard Alan. Research asso. Bur. Business Research, U. of Ore., 1928-30, asst. grad. mgr., 1928-32; instr. accounting Mass. Inst. Tech., 1934-37, asst. prof., 1937-42, asso. prof., 1942-47, prof. accounting 1947—, fiscal officer (sponsored research div.) 1943-52, asso. dean, sch. indsl. management, 1952—; visiting lecturer Harvard Grad. Sch. Bus. Adminstrn. 1942. Member adv. bd. relationships of A.E.C. with its contractors, 1947; mem. adv. com. research and development contracts for Dept. of the Army, 1948; cons. to chmn. Research and Development Bd., Nat. Mil. Establishment, 1949. Mem. Am. Accounting Assn., Nat. Assn. Cost Accountants (pres., Boston chpt. 1944-45), Cambridge C. of C. (dir. 1942-44), Phi Beta Kappa, Phi Sigma Kappa, Beta Gamma Sigma, Alpha Kappa Psi, Phi Mu Alpha. Mason. Author: Accounting—a Management Approach (with T. M. Hill and J. A. Beckett), 1951. Contributor Cost Accountants Handbook, 1945. Home: 15 Cambridge St., Winchester, Mass. Office: Mass. Inst. Tech., Cambridge, Mass. Died Feb. 16, 1954.

ROCHE, John Pierre, advt. exec.; b. Aberdeen, S.D., May 11, 1889; s. Edmund Henry and Anna (Dwyer) R.; A.B., Columbia, 1911; m. Frances Ambler, Apr. 26, 1923; children—John Kirby, Pierre Dwyer, David Kerry. Copywriter McJunkin Advt. Co.,

Chgo., 1911-21, v.p., 1921-26; established, 1926. Roche Advt. Co., pres., 1926-32; pres. Roche, Rickerd & Cleary, Inc., advt., Chgo., 1932—. Served as lt., Hdqrs. 87th Div., U.S. Army, 1917-19. Mem. Art Inst., Phi Beta Kappa, Theta Delta Chi. Roman Catholic. Clubs: Chicago, Union League (Chgo.). Author: Rimes in Olive Drab, 1928; Rimes from France, 1928. Home: 1316 Lake St., Evanston, Ill. Office: 135 S. LaSalle St., Chgo. 3. Died Jan. 1960.

ROCK, George Frederick, banker, lawyer; b. Telluride, Colo., Apr. 26, 1907; s. George Frederick and Lena (Pollack) R.; LL.B., Westminster Law Sch., 1937; grad. Sch. of Banking, Rutgers U.; m. Marie Kathleen Duddy, June 1, 1935; children—George F. III, Eugene, Linda. Pres. Nat. Finance Co., Denver, 1934-41; pres. Bank of Denver, 1941—. County clerk and recorder, pub. trustee, election commr. for city and co. Denver, 1938-41; regional rent exec. OPA, 1942-46; regional dir. OPS, 1951-52. Advisory bd. Salvation Army, chmn. bd., 1958; dir. Colo. Tb Soc., Colo. Mental Health Assn., United Funds. Chmn. Colo. Advt. and Publicity Commn., 1956-57; mem. Colo. Banking Bd.; mem. bd. trustees Nat. Foundation for Consumer Credit, 1958—. Dem. Nat. committeeman, Colo., since 1952; pres. Denver Dem. Club: mem. Am. Bankers Assn., Denver Jr. C. of C. (pres. 1940-41), Am. Indsl. Bankers Assn. (pres. 1949-50), Denver, Colo., Am. bar assns. Mason (Shriner). Clubs: Kiwanis, Athletic (Denver). Home: 1515 E. 12th Av., Denver 18. Office: 1534 California St., Denver, Colo. Died Dec. 1959.

ROCKENBACH, Samuel Dickerson (rŏk'ĕn-băk), army officer; b. Lynchburg, Va., Jan. 27, 1869; s. Frank J. R. (lt. C.S.A.); C.E., Va. Mil. Inst., 1890; Army War Coll., 1912; m. Emma Baldwin, Oct. 19, 1898. Commd. 2d lt. 10th Cav., 1891; promoted through grades to brig. gen. regular army, 1924. Served as brig. gen. N.A., 1918-20; comdt. Va. Mil. Inst., 1894-95; participated in Santiago Campaign, 1898, Porto Rican Expdn., 1898; engr. officer Dept. of Santiago, Cuba, 1900-02; civ. gov., Cottabato Dist., Mindanao, P.I., 1908; arrived in France, 1917; chief q.-m. Base Sect. No. 1, 1917; chief of Tank Corps, A.E.F., 1917-19; comdr. Base Sect. No. 1, 1919; chief Tank Corps, U.S. Army, 1918-20; ret., 1933. Awarded D.S.M.; Officer Legion of Honor and Croix de Guerre with palm (French); hon. Companion of the Bath (British); campaign badges—Cuba, Porto Rico, Mexican border, Victory Medal with four stars. Mem. D.C. Chpt. Soc. Colonial Wars, Va. Soc. S.A.R., Pa. Soc. War of 1812, Soc. Army Santiago de Cuba. Episcopalian. Clubs: Army and Navy, and Chevy Chase. Home: Brownsville, Tex. Deceased.

ROCKWELL, Robert Fay, ex-congressman; b. Cortland, N.Y., Feb. 11, 1886; s. Lemuel Wilson and Elizabeth (Smith) R.; ed. The Hill School, Pottstown, Pa., 1902-05, Princeton U, 1905-06; m. Aileen Miller, June 24, 1908 (died 1938); children—Wilson Miller, Robert Fay; married second, to Elizabeth Armstrong, 1948. In cattle raising and ranching, Colorado, since 1907. Mem. Colorado House of Representatives, 1916-20, Colorado Senate, 1920-24, 1938-40, 1940-44; lieut. governor of Colorado, 1922-24; Republican candidate for governor, 1930; mem. 77th, 78th, 79th and 80th Congresses (1941-49), 4th Colo. Dist. Mem. State Bd. of Agr., 1932-40, 1940-48. Mason (K.T., 32°). Republican. Episcopalian. Club: Rotary. Address: Maher, Colo. Died Sept. 28, 1950; buried Hornell, N.Y.

ROCKWELL, William Walker, librarian; b. Pittsfield, Mass., Oct. 4, 1874; s. Francis Williams (M.C., 1884-1891) and Mary Gilbert (Davis) R.; A.B., Harvard, 1895; S.T.B., Andover Theol. Sem., 1900; univs. of Berlin and Marburg, 1900-04, S.T.L., Marburg, 1903; A.M., Ph.D., Göttingen, 1914; Doctor of Theology, U. of Marburg, 1930; m. Ethel Dean Converse (A.B., Radcliffe), Sept. 19, 1906 (deceased August 19, 1933); 1 daughter, Dorothy Converse (Mrs. Drexell C. Clark); married second, Katharine Lambert Richards (B.A., Smith; M.A., Ph.D., Columbia), Nov. 8, 1934. Foreign fellow Andover Theol. Sem., 1900-02, and instr. in history, same, 1904-05; ordained Congl. ministry, 1905; with Union Theol. Sem. since 1905, respectively asst. prof. ch. history, 1905-17, asso. prof., 1917-25, acting librarian, 1908-13, librarian ranking as prof., 1925-42; librarian emeritus since 1942; assigned a seat in faculty of polit. science, Columbia Univ., 1912-42; also in faculty of philosophy, 1935-37; visiting professor Divinity School of University of Chicago, or at Chicago Theol. Sem., 4 summers, 1925-31. Studied and traveled in Europe 6 yrs. since 1900. Chmn. Nat. Council Congl. Chs. Commn. on Internat. Relations, 1929-31. Mem. adv. panel Com. on Free Ch. Policy ond Unity, apptd. by Gen. Council Congl. Christian Chs., 1950. Mem. Am. Com. for Armenian and Syrian Relief, 1915-19. Mem. Am. Soc. Church History (pres. 1926), Mediaeval Acad. of America, N.Y. Mediaeval Club, Spl. Libraries Assn., Bibliog. Soc. America, Bibliog. Soc. (London), Oxford Bibliog. Soc., Soc. of Genealogists (London), New England Hist. Geneal. Soc., Hymn Soc. America (librarian and fellow), N.Y. Geneal. and Biog. Soc., N.Y. and Conn. hist. socs. Republican (mem. N.Y. Co. com. since 1934, co-leader 7th assembly dist. north, Manhattan Island 1951-56). President board of deacons Broadway Tabernacle Church, 1947. Clubs: Century, Grolier, Quill, Columbia University Faculty, Chi Alpha (president 1924), Archons of Colophon. Author: Die Doppelehe des Landgrafen Philipp von Hessen, 1904; Liber miraculorum Ninivensium Sancti Cornelii Papæ, 1925 (preliminary edit., 1914); Rival Presuppositions in the Writing of Church History, 1935. Edited Papers of Am. Soc. of Ch. History, 3 vols., 1912, 14, 17; The Pitiful Plight of the Assyrian Christians (Am. Com. for Armenian and Syrian Relief), 1916. Contbr. to Ency. Brit. (on popes and on councils, 1910-11), Die Religion in Geschichte und Gegenwart, Dictionary of Religion and Ethics. Sec. bd. editors Am. Ency. of Christianity, 1920-26. Had general oversight of transl. of Latin works of Huldreich Zwingli. Home: 39 Claremont Av., N.Y.C. 27. Died May 30, 1958; buried Pittsfield, Mass.

ROCKWOOD, Robert Everett, educator; b. Worcester, Mass., Mar. 1, 1887; s. John and Harriet Eldora (Butterfield) R.; A.B., Clark U., 1908; A.M., Harvard, 1915, Ph.D., 1924; student Université de Grenoble, 1908, La Sorbonne, France, 1908-09; m. Helen Louise Miller, June 14, 1921; 1 son, Albert Miller. Instr. Romance langs., Harvard, 1915-16, Columbia, 1916-17, Ohio State U., 1911-13, asst. prof., 1919-24, professor, 1924-57, professor emeritus, 1957—, chairman of the department, 1948-57. Served with U.S.N.R.F., 1917-19; disch. rank lt.; lt. comdr., U.S.N.R., 1942-44, inactive since 1944. Officier d'Academie. Mem. Modern Lang. Assn. Am., Am. Assn. Teachers French, Phi Beta Kappa (hon.). Home: 173 Parkview Av., Bexley 9, O. Office: Derby Hall, Ohio State University, Columbus 10. Died Aug. 3, 1958.

RODDIS, Hamilton, mfg. exec.; b. Milw., June 26, 1875; s. William Henry and Sara Louise (Denton) R.; m. Catherine Prindle, July 7, 1908; children—Sara, Mary, Catherine, Augusta, William, Ellen. With Roddis Plywood Corp., formerly Roddis Lumber and Veneer Company, 1899—, pres. 1920-58, chmn., 1958—; pres. Roddis Lumber & Veneer Co. of Can., Ltd., 1947-55, chmn. bd., 1955—; pres. Roddiscraft, Inc., 1948-54, dir. 1954—. Mem. S.A.R. Republican. Episcopalian. Mason. Rotarian (hon.). Office: Marshfield, Wis. Died Mar. 27, 1960.

RODE, Ralph Becker (rō'dē), oral surgeon; born Brownstorn, Ill., Sept. 5, 1893; s. Samuel William and Antonette Claire (Becker) R.; student McKendree Coll., Lebanon, Ill.; D.D.S., St. Louis U., 1916; m. Bernice Brown, Feb. 6, 1912 (dec.); 1 daughter, Georgia Ann (Mrs. Lee Anthony Waldbart); married second, Ethel Flury, August 21, 1948. Supt. clin. dental surgery St. Louis Univ., 1916-17, vice dean and supt. operating clinic, 1917-19, lecturer exodontia and oral surgery, 1919-24; in practice of oral surgery, St. Louis, Mo. since 1919; prof. clin. oral surgery Washington U., St. Louis, Mo., since 1943; mem. staff Jewish, Deaconess, St. Luke's and St. Anthony's hosps. Served as 1st lt., U.S. Army, World War I. Recipient St. Appallonia award par excellence in field of dental arts, science and research from St. Louis U. Diplomate Am. Bd. Oral Surgery. Fellow Internat. Coll. of Surgeons; mem. St. Louis Dental Soc., Mo. State Dental Assn., Am. Dental Assn. (past pres. St. Louis Dental Soc.), Am. Soc. Exodontic Oral Surgeons, Acad. Internat. Dentistry, Delta Sigma Delta. Mem. Christian Ch. Mason. Home: 11 Ladue Hills, Clayton 24, Mo. Office: Frisco Bldg., 906 Olive St., St. Louis 1. Died Nov. 5, 1953.

RODEHEAVER, Homer Alvan (rō-dē-hā-vĕr), music dir.; b. Union Furnace, O., Oct. 4, 1880; s. Thurman Hall and Fanny (Armstrong) R.; student Ohio Wesleyan U. (non-grad.); Dr. of Sacred Music, Bob Jones Coll., Tenn., 1942; unmarried. Musical dir., with William A. Sunday in his evangelistic campaigns, 1909-31; has directed choruses in nearly all leading cities in U.S.; pres. The Rodeheaver Hall-Mack Co., gospel music pubs., Winona Lake, Ind. Founder Rodeheaver's Boys Ranch, Inc. Trombone player with 4th Tenn. Regtl. Band, 4 mos. in Cuba, Spanish-Am. War, 1898; with Y.M.C.A. in France, Aug.-Dec. 1918. Methodist. Mason (K.T., Shriner), K.P. Author: Song Stories of the Sawdust Trail, 1917; 20 Years With Billy Sunday; Singing Black; also various gospel songs, compilations, etc. Tour of the world with Evangelist W. E. Biederwolf, 1923-24; tour of African mission field, Belgian Congo, 1936. Founder and promoter of Summer Sch. of Sacred Music, Winona Lake, Ind. Platform mgr. for large assemblies. Community song programs on N.B.C. and C.B.S. networks; producer of religious transcriptions. Owner, Rainbow Ranch, Palatka, Fla., also farm and Westminster Hotel in Winona Lake and farm near Vincennes and Oaktown, Ind. Home and Office: Winona Lake, Ind. Died Dec. 18, 1955; buried Oakwood Cemetery, Warsaw, Ind.

RODEN, Carl Bismarck (rō'dĕn), ret. librarian; b. Kansas City, Mo., June 7, 1870; s. Charles Ernest Ludwig and Louisa Henrietta (Strack) von R.; LL.B., Chgo. Coll. of Law (Lake Forest U.), 1891; hon. M.A., Northwestern U., 1928; admitted to bar but never practiced; m. Harriette Amy Johnson, June 2, 1909 (dec.); 1 dau., Marion Louise; m. 2d, Lora A. Rich, 1921. Entered Chgo. Pub. Library as page, 1886; progressed through various positions, to supt. of cataloguing dept., 1908; actg. librarian, May 1-Oct. 10, 1909; asst. librarian, 1909-18, librarian, 1918-50, ret. Republican. Episcopalian. Mem. A.L.A. (pres. 1927-28; treas., exec. board, council), Am. Library Inst., Bibliog. Soc. Am. (ex-pres.), Ill. Library Assn. (ex-pres.). Clubs: University, Caxton, Tavern, Cliff Dwellers, Chicago Literary (pres. 1926-27), Chicago Library (twice pres.), City. Author of numerous articles on profl. topics in library mags. Home: 5838 Newark Av. Address: Public Library, Chgo. Died Oct. 25, 1956; buried Graceland Cemetery, Chgo.

RODEY, Pearce Coddington (rō'dē), lawyer; b. Albuquerque, N.M., Nov. 8, 1889; s. Bernard Shandon and Minnie (Coddington) R.; prep. edn., Mercersburg (Pa.) Acad., 1903-07; A.B., Harvard, 1912, LL.B., 1915; m. Dorothy McMillen, July 1, 1918 (dec. March 1932); children—Sheila (Faust), Lon McMillen (dec.); m. 2d, Maria-Elise Johnson, Dec. 19, 1934 (dec. Jan. 1955). Admitted N.M. bar, 1915, began practice at Albuquerque; mem. Rodey & Rodey, 1915-27, Rodey & Dailey, 1927-34, Rodey & Dickason, 1934-41, Rodey, Dickason & Sloan, 1941—; sr. partner Rodey, Dickason, Sloan, 1941—; sr. partner Rodey, Dickason, Sloan, Mins & Akin, 1951—; atty. Middle Rio Grande Conservancy Dist., 1925-36; asso. counsel for N.M. Rio Grande Compact; of counsel for N.M. Conf. of Upper Basin States for div. of waters of Colo. River; state rep. to Nat. Conf. on Uniform Aero. Regulatory Laws, 1930; del. Comparative Law Conf. The Hague, 1937. Rep. nominee for Cong., 1938; counsel First Nat. Bank; v.p., dir. Occidental Life Ins. Co., Raleigh, N.C.; dir. Peninsular Life Ins. Co., Jacksonville, Fla. Del. Internat. Bar Assn., 1954; confrere Comparative Law, Paris, 1954. Lt. U.S.N.R. Mem. Am., N.M. State and Bernalillo County, N.Y. County bar assns., Am. Legion, Sigma Chi. Republican. Episcopalian. Mason (32°, Shriner). Clubs: Kiwanis (ex-pres.), Country (Albuquerque); University, Army and Navy (Washington), Harvard, Lawyers (N.Y.C.). Home: 501 N. 11th St. Office: First Nat. Bank Bldg., Albuquerque, N.M. Died May 3, 1958.

RODGERS, Cleveland, editor; b. Greenville, S.C., Mar. 3, 1885; s. Collier Augustus and Fannie (Leach) R.; educated in public schools; married Antoinette Sylvia Durland, September 18, 1911; 1 daughter Isabel Durland (Mrs. A. K. MacRury). With Brooklyn Eagle, 1906-37, as spl. writer, dramatic critic, editorial writer, asso. editor, and editor. Lecturer Bd. of Edn., 1919-23. Mem. N.Y.C. Planning Commn., 1938-51; cons. Bklyn. Civic Center, 1952. Pres. Walt Whitman Birthplace Assn. Vice pres. Am. Soc. Planning Ofcls., 1942. Club: Century (N.Y.C.). Author: (play) The Legend of the Hills, 1911; (with Theodore B. Sayre) Ransomed, prod. 1912. Co-Ed.: The Gathering of the Forces (Walt Whitman's writings), 2 volumes, 1920; The Roosevelt Program, 1933; New York Plans for the Future, 1943; American Planning, 1947; (with Rebecca B. Rankin) The World's Capital City, 1948; Robert Moses: Builder for Democracy, 1952. Editor: Working for the People, 1956 (Robert Moses). Contributor short stories and articles to mags. Home: 80-32 Grenfell St., Kew Gardens 15, N.Y.C. Died May 21, 1956.

RODKEY, Robert Gordon (rŏd'kē), prof. banking; b. Mahaffey, Pa., July 18, 1885; s. Robert Lipton and Margaret Emily (Olp) R.; A.B., University of Mich., 1914, A.M., 1915, Ph.D., 1928; unmarried. Instr. in accounting, U. of Mich., 1914-17; asso. prof. accounting, Washington U., St. Louis, 1917-18; dir. of personnel, Chase Nat. Bank, N.Y. City, 1918-21; prof. economics, Tulane U., New Orleans, 1922; lecturer in economics, U. of Mich., 1923-25; asso. prof. banking and investments, U. of Mich., 1925-28, prof. since 1928; visiting prof., Stanford U., summer 1941; dir. State Savings Bank, Ann Arbor. Served as capt. statistics br. Gen. Staff, U.S. Army, 1918. Mem. Am. Econ. Assn., Financial Analysts Soc., Economists Nat. Com. Monetary Policy, Acacia, Delta Sigma Pi, Beta Gamma Sigma. Mason (32°). Clubs: University (Ann Arbor); Bankers (Detroit). Author The Banking Process, 1928; Legal Reserves in American Banking, 1934; Sound Policies for Bank Management, 1944; also monographs: Preferred Stocks as Long-Term Investment, 1932; State Bank Failures in Michigan, 1935; Readings in Banking, 1951. Home: 303 Michigan Union, Ann Arbor, Mich. Died Sept. 20, 1956; buried Mahaffey, Pa.

RODMAN, John Stewart, surgeon; b. Abilene, Tex., July 21, 1883; s. William L. and Bettie Crawford (Stewart) R.; m. Eunice B. Hinman, Apr. 10, 1915; children—Eunice Russell, William Louis. Interne, Pa. Hosp., Phila., and Mayo Clinic, Rochester, Minn., 1906-08; in practice of surgery at Phila., 1908—; prof. emeritus surgery Womens Med. Coll.; cons. surgeon to Womens Coll., Bryn Mawr and Presbyn Hosps. Mem. med. sec. Nat. Bd. Med. Examiners. Mem. Am. Bd. Surgery (sec.), Phila. Acad. Surgery (past pres.), Am. Surg. Assn. (past v.p.), Delta Psi. Clubs: Philadelphia, St. Anthony. Home:

6 Matsonford Rd., Radnor, Pa. Office: 1726 Spruce St., Phila. Died Apr. 26, 1958; buried Washington Meml. Cemetery, Valley Forge, Pa.

RODZINSKI, Artur (rō-jĭn'skē), conductor; b. Spalato, Dalmatia (of Polish parents), January 2, 1892; grad. U. of Vienna, LL.D.; musical edn., Vienna Acad. Music; Mus.D., Oberlin Coll., 1938; married 2d, Halina Wieniawska Lilpop, July 19, 1934; 2 sons, Witold (1st marriage), Richard. Came to U.S., 1925, naturalized, 1933. Began as condr. of chorus in Lwow; condr. opera and Philharmonic Orchestra concerts in Warsaw 4 yrs.; invited by Leopold Stokowski to join Philadelphia Orchestra as asst. condr., 1926-29; dir. orchestra and operatic dept. Curtis Inst. Music, Phila.; condr. Los Angeles Philharmonic Orchestra, 1929-33, Cleveland Orchestra 1933-43, and introduced production of opera into the orchestra's regular schedule; on leave for 8 weeks, 1937, was condr. N.Y. Philharmonic-Symphony; selected personnel, trained orchestra and co-condr. with Arturo Toscanini of NBC Symphony Orchestra, 1937; condr. Salzburg Music Festival, 1936-37, first condr. Am. symphony orchestra to conduct this festival and first condr. to introduce there an Am. symphonic composition; conductor and musical dir. N.Y. Philharmonic Symphony Orchestra, 1943-47; dir. Chicago Symphony Orchestra, 1947-48; guest condr. Europe, S.A., U.S., 1948—; world premier Prokofieff's War and Peace, May Festival, Florence, Italy, 1953; guest condr. Italy and other European countries, 1955—. Awarded medal Polonia Restituta, Poland, 1938; Diploma d'Honneur, France, 1937. Brought from Russia and presented Lady Macbeth from Mzensk; identified primarily with Wagnerian operas, particularly with Tristan, 1948—. Home: P.O. Box 707, Lake Placid, N.Y. Died Nov. 27, 1958; buried St. Agnes Cemetery, Lake Placid, N.Y.

ROE, Vingie Eve (Mrs. Raymond C. Lawton), author; b. Oxford, Kan., Dec. 7, 1879; d. Maurice Pool and Clarissa Caroline (Castanien) Roe; ed. at home; m. Raymond C. Lawton, Apr. 12, 1907. Republican. Author: The Maid of the Whispering Hills, 1912; Heart of Night Wind, 1913; The Primal Lure, 1914; A Divine Egotist, 1916; Tharon of Lost Valley, 1919; Val, of Paradise, 1921; Nameless River, 1923; The Splendid Road, 1925; Monsieur of the Rainbows, 1926; Bitter Laurel, 1928; Wild Hearts, 1932; Flame of the Border, 1933; Sons to Fortune, 1934; Black Belle Rides the Uplands, 1935; Glory in the Gum Woods, 1937; Guns of the Round Stone Valley, 1938; The Golden Tide, 1940; Wild Harvest, 1941; Dust Above the Sage, 1942; Yukon Danger, The Teamstress; The Great Trace, 1948, Golden Tide to be filmed; Beyond The Chisholm Trail. Contbr. short stories to Ladies' Home Journal, McCall's, Collier's, Hearst's, Cosmopolitan, Good Housekeepkng, Liberty, This Week, etc. Mem. Authors' League Am., League of Am. Pen Women, Cal. Writer's Club, P.E.N. Home: Cloverdale, Sonoma County, Cal. Died Aug. 13, 1958; buried Tulocay Mausoleum, Napa, Cal.

ROELKER, William Greene (rōl'kĕr). hist. soc. dir.; b. Providence, Apr. 9, 1886; s. William Greene and Eleanor (Jenckes) R.; grad. Groton Sch., 1905; A.B., Harvard, 1909, A.M. (postgrad. 1937-40), 1939; m. Anna Rossiter Koues, Aug. 22, 1912; children—Nancy Lyman, Helen Koues (Mrs. John Alexander Kessler). Advt. mgr. Providence Journal, 1912-18; with A.R.C., Nat. Hdqrs., Washington, 1918-19; asst. sec., v.p. Industrial Trust Co., 1920-29; connected with brokerage offices, 1930-32; receiver, Middlesex Nat. Bank of Lowell (Mass.), and Leominster (Mass.) Nat. Bank, 1932-35; with Harvard Tercentenary Fund, 1936; librarian, R.I. Hist. Soc., 1940-41, dir. and director, 1941—. Chmn. Providence chpt. A.R.C., 1920-25. Chmn. war records subdivision State Council of Defense, 1942—. Pres. East Greenwich Free Library. Mem. Council, The Am. Assn. for State and Local History, Am. Antiquarian Soc., Colonial Soc. of Mass. (corr.), Soc. of Cincinnati (hon.), Mass. Hist. Soc. (corr.), Am. Philos. Soc. (library research associate), Mayflower Descs., Phi Beta Kappa. Republican. Episcopalian. Mason. Author: Benjamin Franklin and Catherine Ray Greene: Their Correspondence, 1949; Francis Wayland; A Century of Butler Hospital; One Hundred Years of the Providence. Contbr. numerous articles chiefly historical and biographical. Lecturer Brown Univ. Home: Greene Farm, 777 Love Lane, East Greenwich, R.I. Office: John Brown House, 52 Power St., Providence 6. Died May 29, 1953.

ROEMER, Joseph, ret. coll. dean; b. Sugar Grove, Ky., Sept. 25, 1884; s. Adolph and Sallie Trice (Tuck) R.; student So. Normal Sch., Bowling Green, Ky., 1902-06, Western Ky. State Normal Sch., 1906-07, Bowling Green Bus. U., 1907; A.B., U. Ky., 1914; A.M., Peabody Coll. for Tchrs., 1915, Ph.D., 1919; grad. study Columbia, 1924-25; LL.D., Tampa U., 1938; m. Louise Beasley, June 15, 1911; 1 dau., Mary Jo (Mrs. E. N. Higgins). Prin. Peabody Demonstration School, 1914-16; head of dept. edn. Sam Houston State Tchrs. Coll., Huntsville, Tex., 1916-20; prof. secondary edn. and high sch. visitor U. Fla., 1920-31; prof. secondary edn. and dir. instr. Peabody Jr. Coll. and Demonstration Sch., 1931-36; dean Peabody Jr. Coll., 1936-41, dean of the college, 1941-52; helped organize grad. dept. McMurray Coll., Abilene, Tex., 1952-55; mem. faculty, summer schs. Peabody Coll. for Tchrs. 1920, 26, U. Wyo., 1927, 29, U. Mich., 1928, 29, U. Pa., 1930; chief tchr. tng. br., sect. edn. and cultural relations br. OMGUS, Germany, 1948. Dist. supr. S.A. T.C. personnel, World War; maj. O.R.C. Sec. Com. on Secondary Schools, So. Assn. Colls. and Secondary Schools, 1921-36. (pres. 1932)); mem. cons. com. Nat. Survey of Secondary Edn.; pres. Officers of Regional Standardizing Agencies. Pres. Fla. YMCA, 1921-31. Mem. N.E.A., Fla. Edn. Assn. (pres. 1926), Phi Beta Kappa, Phi Delta Kappa, Kappa Delta Pi, Phi Kappa Phi, Tau Kappa Alpha, Alpha Phi Epilon, Kappa Phi Kappa (nat. pres., 1933-36), Kappa Sigma, Blue Key (nat. v.p.). Democrat. Presbyn. Mason (K.T.). Kiwanian. Co-author: Extra Curricular Activities, 1926; Readings in Extra Curricular Activities, 1929; Syllabus of a Course in Extra Curricular Activities, 1929; Secondary School Administration, 1932; Basic Student Activities, 1935; Gentleman Commander, 1936; My Activity Book, 1937; Dean of Boys in High School, 1939; The Administration of the Modern Secondary School, 1941. Contbr. to High Sch. Quarterly, Junior-Senior High Sch. Clearing House, Sch. Review, etc. Home: Leesburg, Fla. Died July 1, 1955.

ROEVER, William Henry (rō'vĕr), mathematician; b. St. Louis, Mo., May 26, 1874; s. William and Sophie (Deppe) R.; grad. St. Louis Manual Training Sch., 1893; B.S., Washington U., 1897; A.M., Harvard U., 1904, Ph.D., 1906; m. Minnie D. Hamilton, June 23, 1906; children—William Alexander, Frederick Hamilton. Instr. astronomy, Washington Univ., 1899-1901; instr. mathematics, Mass. Inst. Tech., 1905-08; asst. prof. mathematics, 1908-16, asso. prof., 1916-17, prof. since 1917, Washington U., head dept. mathematics and astronomy since 1932; leave of absence for study and travel in Europe, 1931-32; professor emeritus teaching veterans since 1947. Taught nautical astronomy, U.S. Naval Auxiliary Reserve Sch., Municipal Pier, Chicago, and mathematics, U. of Chicago, summer, 1918; master computer Aberdeen (Md.) Proving Ground, fall of 1918; taught mathematics, U. of Tex., summer 1920. Fellow A.A. A.S. (sec. sect. A, 1921-25, chmn. 1926); mem. Am. Math. Soc., Math. Assn. America, Am. Forestry Assn.; v.p. and trustee Acad. of Science of St. Louis. Represents Am. Math. Soc. on Sectional Com. on Standards for Graphical Presentation sponsored by Am. Soc. M.E. Episcopalian. Contbr. book and papers in fields of geometry and mechanics. Home: 6802 Waterman Av., St. Louis. Died Jan. 31, 1951; buried St. Louis.

ROGAN, Fred Leon (rō'găn), publisher; b. Bristol, Va., Nov. 21, 1880; s. John Webb and Isabel (Smith) R.; prep. edn., Hotchkiss Sch., Lakeville, Conn., and Louisville Training Sch., Belmont, Ky.; student King Coll., Bristol, 1896-98, Vanderbilt, 1899-1900; m. Clara Taylor, Oct. 4, 1913; 1 dau., Elizabeth (Mrs. R. Cocks). With Harper & Bros., 1900-06; Chgo. mgr. Good Housekeeping Mag., 1905-11; mgr. in N.Y. City for Curtis Pub. Co., 1911-21; engaged in business research, 1921-27; publisher of Judge, 1927-37; business, ednl. and welfare agency research since 1937. Mem. legal advisory bd. N.Y. State Selective Service Draft, World War. Mem. Phi Delta Theta. Home: Mantoloking Rd., Adamston, N.J. Deceased.

ROGAN, James S., business exec.; b. Brownwood, Tex., 1888. Pres., dir. Am. Nat. Bank, Indpls; dir. Indpls. Water Co., Lynch Corp., Anderson, Ind. Address: 1321 N. Meridian St., Indpls 2. Died June 12, 1954; buried Austin, Tex.

ROGAN, Ralph Frederic, business exec.; b. Chicago, Ill., Feb. 4, 1875; s. John Bell and Mary Josephine (Kemper) R.; M.E., Cornell, 1897; m. Bessie E. Procter, Nov. 14, 1900; children—Elizabeth (Mrs. Thomas H. Carruthers), Mary (Mrs. William Burchenal). Vice pres. The Procter & Gamble Co., Cincinnati, O., 1940—, director 1932—. President Bd. Park Commrs., Hamilton Co.; chmn. board Hosp. and Home for Friendless, Glendale, O.; treas. Little Traverse Hosp., Petoskey, Mich., since 1937. Mem. bd. trustees Children's Hosp., Cincinnati. Home: Glendale, O. Office: Gwynne Bldg., Cin. Died Apr. 1, 1955.

ROGERS, Austin Flint, (rŏj-ĕrz), univ. prof.; b. Lathrop, Mo., Aug. 15, 1877; s. Benjamin Franklin and Julietta (Leabo) R.; ed. Mo. Sch. Mines; A.B., Kan. U., 1899, A.M., 1900; Ph.D., Columbia, 1902; m. Carolyn Howe, Sept. 10, 1902; children—Genevieve, Ronald Howe. Asst. in mineralogy, Kans. U., 1898; asst. Univ. Geol. Survey, Kans., 1899, 1900, 1908; tutor in mineralogy, Columbia, 1902-05; asst. prof., Stanford, 1905-10, assoc. prof., 1910-19, prof., 1919-42, emeritus, 1942—. Served with Nat. Research Council, 1918. Named minerals: Kempite, sanbornite, cornuite, (with A. S. Eakle) wilkenite. Fellow Mineral. Soc. Am. (pres. 1927), Geol. Soc. Am. (v.p. 1926, 1935); mem. A.A.A.S., Am. Acad. Arts and Scis., Mineral. Soc. of Great Britain, Société Français de Mineralogie, Sigma Xi. Methodist. Author: Introduction to the Study of Minerals, 1912, 1921, 1937; Optical Mineralogy (with P. F. Kerr), 1933, 1942. Asso. editor Am. Mineralogist, 1919—. Contbr. many articles on mineralogy and crystallography. Home: 549 Salvatierra St., Stanford University, Cal. Died Mar. 10, 1957; buried Alta Mesa Meml. Park, Los Altos, Cal.

ROGERS, Bruce, designer of books; b. Lafayette, Ind., May 14, 1870; s. George and Ann E. (Gish) R.; B.S., Purdue U., 1890, hon. L.H.D., 1932; hon. M.A., Yale, 1928, Harvard, 1939; m. Anne Baker, June 20, 1900 (dec.). Mem. art staff Indpls. News, 1891-92; designer for Ind. Illustrating Co., Indianapolis, 1893-94, L. Prange & Co., Boston, 1894-95; with Riverside Press, Cambridge, Mass., as designer of fine printing and limited editions, 1895-1912; in bus. on own account, 1912-17; went to London, Eng., 1917, to join firm of Emery Walker, Ltd.; printing adviser to the Univ. Press, Cambridge, Eng., 1917-19; same to Harvard U. Press, 1920-34; asso. of William Edwin Rudge, printer, Mt. Vernon, N.Y., 1920-28, Emery Walker, Ltd., London, 1928-31. Recipient first Aldus Award, Limited Editions Club. Hon. life mem. Am. Inst. of Graphic Arts. Clubs: Book Club of Calif. (San Francisco); Odd Volumes, Society of Printers (Boston); John Barnard Asso. (Cambridge, Mass.); Caxton (Chicago); Quarto (New York); Double Crown (London); Grolier of New York (hon. mem. of all). Author: Paragraphs on Printing, The Centaur Types. Home: New Fairfield, Conn. Died May 18, 1957.

ROGERS, Charles Gardner, zoölogist, physiologist; b. Perry, N.Y., Mar. 4, 1875; s. James Harvey and Cornelia M. (Gardner) R.; A.B., Syracuse U., 1897, A.M., 1899, hon. Sc.D., 1920; studied U. Chgo., Ph.D., U. Cal., 1904; m. Rose Humann, July 3, 1906; children—Mary Cornelia, Martin Humann. Instructor physiology Syracuse U., 1899-1902, asst. prof., 1905-07, asso. prof., 1907-10, prof. 1910-13; asst. in physiology U. Chgo., autumn quarter, 1902, U. Cal., 1903-04, U. Kan., 1904; prof. zoölogy Oberlin Coll., 1913-15, prof. comparative physiology, 1915-41, acting dean, Coll. Arts and Sciences, 1924-25, head zool. dept., 1936-41, prof. emeritus, 1941—; vis. prof. zoology Duke, prof. 1942-43. Mem. embryological staff Marine Biol. Lab., Woods Hole, Mass., 1914-30. Fellow A.A.A.S., Ohio Acad. Science; mem. Am. Physiol. Soc., Am. Soc. Zoölogists, Soc. Naturalists, Sigma Xi, Phi Beta Kappa, Phi Kappa Phi, Delta Upsilon. Conglist. Author: Textbook of Comparative Physiology, 1927, 2d edition, 1938; Laboratory Outlines in Comparative Physiology, 1929, 2d edition, 1938; also numerous papers on physiological subjects. Home: 378 Reamer Pl., Oberlin, O. Died Oct. 12, 1950; buried Oberlin.

ROGERS, Daisy Fiske, worker for the blind; b. New York, N.Y.; d. Alexander C. and Margaret Rogers; ed. pub. schs. and under pvt. tutors. Asso. with N.Y. Assn. for Blind since its orgn.; pvt. sec. to Mrs. J. Pierpont Morgan, 1907-22, to Anne Morgan 1907-52; asst. sec. New York Assn. for Blind (mem. woman's exec. comm.). Active in establishment of Lighthouse Music Sch., Camp Lighthouse for Blind Youth. Sec. American Friends of France. Reconnaissance Francaise, 1950 (France). Member Town Hall Club Roll of Honor, 1930; awarded 1952 Medal, American Foundation for the Blind. Mem. Nat. Inst. Social Sciences. Episcopalian. Club: Cosmopolitan. Member advisory committee General Services Recreation and Lighthouse Press. Founder Lighthouse Gleams (Braille Publ. for blind). Home: 1 Sutton Place South, N.Y.C. 22. Died Jan. 22, 1954.

ROGERS, Donald G(raydon), chemical mfg. exec.; b. Worcester, Mass., Oct. 14, 1892; s. William T. and Ada M. (White) R.; B.S., Worcester Poly Inst., 1915; m. Marie B. Yahraes, Apr. 27, 1918; children—William D., David W., C. Graydon. Research chemist General Chem. Co., N.Y. City and Easton, Pa., 1915-17; research chemist Nat. Aniline & Chem. Co., Buffalo, 1917-29, asst. research, development dir., 1929-32, asst. to gen. mgr., N.Y.C., 1932-45, gen. mgr. div. Allied Chem. & Dye Corp., N.Y. City, 1945-48, v.p., 1948-50, exec. v.p., 1950-51, pres. Nat. Alline division 1951-57, ret., 1957. Mem. Am. Chem. Soc., A.A.A.S. Presbyn. Clubs: The Chemists', Downtown Athletic (N.Y. City). Home: 725 Belmont Rd., Ridgewood, N.J. Office: 40 Rector St., N.Y.C. 6. Died Dec. 30, 1958; buried Easton Heights Cemetery, Easton, Pa.

ROGERS, Dwight L., congressman; b. Reidsville, Ga., Aug. 17, 1886; s. William Millard and Augusta (Laing) R.; B.S., U. of Ga., 1909; LL.B., Mercer U., Macon, Ga., 1910; m. Florence Roberts, Nov. 15, 1916; children—Dwight L. (officer U.S.N.R.), Paul G. (officer U.S. Army), Doyle. Admitted to Ga. bar, 1910, and practiced law, Ocilla, Ga., 1910-25; practiced with John E. Morris, Fort Lauderdale, Fla. 1925-30; representative to Florida legislature from Broward County, 1930-38; mem. 79th to 83d Congresses, 6th Fla. Dist. Mem. Phi Delta Theta, Sphinx. Kiwanian. Home: Fort Lauderdale, Fla. Died Dec. 1, 1954; buried Lauderdale Meml. Park.

ROGERS, Ernest Andrew, educator; b. St. Peter, Minn., July 31, 1881; s. Charles Butters and Dorothe

Christine (Cohrs) R.; A.B., Gustavus Adolphus Coll., St. Peter, Minn., 1904; student in edn., Stanford U., 1910; m. Caroline Hawley, June 10, 1922. Vice-prin. high sch., Minneota, Minn., 1904-06, high school, Lakefield, 1906-08; principal pub. schs., Ceylon, fall of 1908; dir. and originator of "Knights of Brawn" Boys' Club, Lakefield, Minn., 1907-08, Ceylon, 1908, St. Peter, 1909, Denver, and Fort Collins, Colo., and Berkeley, Cal., 1909; instr. Latin, Mt. Tamalpais Mil. Acad., San Rafael, Cal., 1909-10; instr. Hoitt Sch. for Boys, Mayfield, 1910; pres. Montezuma Mountain School, Los Gatos, Cal., 1910-—. Founder and gen. organizer World's Federation of Boys, Junior World Democracy, and Junior Statesmen of America. Mem. Pi Gamma Mu. Address: Los Gatos, Cal. Died Oct. 16, 1957.

ROGERS, Francis, musician; b. Roxbury, Mass., Apr. 14, 1870; s. Henry Bromfield and Frances (Stetson) R.; A.B., Harvard, 1891; m. Cornelia Barnes, of New York, May 17, 1911. Singer and teacher of music since 1898, formerly instr. singing, Yale U.; now instr. in singing at Juilliard Grad. Sch. of Music, New York. In France with Y.M.C.A., Oct. 1917-Apr. 1918; chmn. Am. Com. Fontainebleau (France) Sch. of Music. Chevalier Legion of Honor (France), 1927. Clubs: Harvard, Century. Author: Some Famous Singers of the 19th Century, 1914. Address: 144 E. 62d St., N.Y. City. Died May 15, 1951.

ROGERS, Frazier, engr.; b. Ora, Miss., Feb. 7, 1893; s. Joel Cooper and Mary (Duckworth) R.; B.S.A., Miss. State Coll., 1915; student Kan. State Coll., 1929; M.S.A., U. of Fla., 1930; m. Gladys Tanner, May 26, 1917; children—Frazier Vernon, Mildred R. Brown, Marion R. Kennard, Thomas, Betty Ann. Insp. Fla. State Plant Bd., 1916-17; county agt. Perquimans Co., N.C., 1917-18; asst. prof. agrl. engring U. of Fla., 1918-22, prof. since 1923; head agrl. engr. Fla. Agr. Extension Service, since 1946, head research agr. engr., Fla. Agr. Expt. Sta., since 1947. Mem. Fla engring. com., Soil Conservation Service; mem. state adv. com., Nat. Defense Training; mem. bd. dirs. Univ. Athletic Assn., Inc. Mem. Kiwanis, Phi Kappa Phi, Alpha Zeta, Sigma Delta Psi, Alpha Gamma Rho. Democrat. Baptist. Mason. Home: 211 NE 6th St., Gainesville, Fla. Died July 22, 1959.

ROGERS, Fred A., engring.; b. nr. Grand Rapids, Mich., Sept. 26, 1869; s. Chauncey Langdon and Emma Jane (Currier) R.; B.S. in E.E., U. Mich., 1894; m. Jennie Irene Birdsall, Dec. 18, 1899 (dec.); children—Dorothy Jean (dec.), Frederick Andrew. Instr. physics and elec. engring., Lewis Inst., Chgo., 1896-1902, asst. prof., 1902-07, prof. 1907-—, dean engring., 1933-40; dir. engring. defense courses, Ill. Inst. Tech., 1941-45. Tech. adviser Isko Co., 1919-20; cons. engr., tech. expert for various concerns; ret. Fellow A.A.A.S.; member Am. Inst. Elec. Engrs., Western Soc. Engrs., Illuminating Engring. Soc., Order of Founders and Patriots of America. Club: Physics (Chgo.). Republican. Home: 320 Wisconsin Av., Oak Park, Ill. Died Mar. 18, 1949.

ROGERS, George McIntosh, business man; b. Ashtabula, O., December 4, 1879; s. Judson Artemus and Florence Elizabeth (Bates) R.; grad. high sch., Willoughby, O., 1897; student Adelbert Coll. (Western Reserve U.), 1897; m. Florence Fontaine Stone, Apr. 23, 1903 (dec. 1931); children—Martha Stone, Joan VanDusen, Herbert Stone; m. 2d, Selma Hortense Darmstader, Sept. 16, 1933. With Cleveland Plain Dealer, 1898-1934, last 15 yrs. as v.p. and gen. mgr.; now v.p. and gen. mgr. G. H. Mead Co. of Dayton, O., and N.Y.C. U.S. reps. of Abitibi Power & Paper Co., newsprint mfrs. of Toronto, Ont., Can. Home: Mill Rock Road, Saybrook, Conn. Died Sept. 1949.

ROGERS, Harry H., b. Wheatland, Mo., May 24, 1877; s. Pleasant Jasper and Nancy Frances (Dent) R.; ed. Weaubleau (Mo.) Christian Coll. and Warrensburg (Mo.) State Tchrs. Coll.; m. Anna Holmes Johnston, June 26, 1901. Admitted to Indian Ty. bar, 1903, and practiced at Wewoka and Tulsa, also engaged in oil production; pres. Exchange Nat. Bank of Tulsa, 1928-31. Pres. Internat. Conv. Disciples of Christ, 1929; pres. Welfare Council, San Antonio, 1945-46; pres. Fifth District Conv., Christian Chs., 1946-47. Mem. Okla. (pres. 1917-18), Am. and Tex. bar assns. Republican. Mem. Christian (Disciples) Ch. Mason, Woodman. Rotarian (pres. 1926-27). Home: 2103 San Pedro Av., San Antonio, Tex. Died Dec. 3, 1957.

ROGERS, Harry Stanley, college pres.; b. Detroit, Mich., Aug. 7, 1890; s. Samuel Hartshorne and Martha Eliza (Hall) R.; B.S., Univ. of Wyoming, 1914, C.E., 1926, LL.D., 1942; grad. work, U. of Ia., 1914, U. of Wash., 1916; Sc.D., Northeastern U., 1935; D.Eng., Rensselaer Polytechnic Institute, 1950; married Grace F. Larsen, Aug. 29, 1916; 1 son, Robert Hall. Instr. civ. engring., U. of Ia., 1914-15, U. of Wyo., 1915-16, U. of Wash., 1916-18; asst. prof., Lafayette Coll., 1918-19; designing engring. and spl. rep. Truscon Steel Co., 1919-20; prof. hydraulic engring., Oregon State Coll., 1920-27, dean engring., 1927-33, also dir. Engring. Expt. Sta., 1928-33; pres. Polytechnic Inst. of Brooklyn since 1933; dir. N.Y. Telephone Company, Namm Loeser's, Incorporated, McGraw-Hill Publishing Company, Brooklyn Savings Bank, Intertype Corp.; mem. adv. board Brooklyn br. Chem. Corn Exchange Bank; chairman Polytechnic Research & Development Co., Inc. Cons. engr. water supply and power, 1921-33; chmn. exec. com. on correction indsl. pollution, Willamette River, 1933; mem. Ore. State Reconstr. Advisory Bd., 1933, chmn. gen. products, Priorities Div., O.P.M., Apr.-Sept. 1941; chief, Rubber Branch, WPB, Apr.-Oct. 1942. Trustee Bklyn. Hosp.; director Downtown Bklyn. Assn. (pres. 1948-53), Bklyn. C. of C. (pres., 1944-46), Bklyn. chpt. A.R.C. Mem. N.Y. State Chamber of Commerce, American Society of C.E., Am. Soc. Mech. Engrs., Am. Inst. Cons. Engrs., Am. Soc. for Engineering Edn. (pres. 1944-46); Professional Engrs. of Ore. (pres. 1932), A.A.A.S., Newcomen Soc., Alpha Tau Omega (Chairman of High Council), National Interfraternity Conf. (chairman 1939), Tau Beta Pi, Sigma Tau, Phi Kappa Phi, Sigma Xi. Republican. Episcopalian. Clubs: University (Manhattan), Rembrandt, Brooklyn, Rotary (pres. 1940-41), Gypsy Trail, Municipal (Bklyn.); The Century. Contbr. articles to journals and tech. books. Home: 160 Columbia Heights, Bklyn. Died June 6, 1957.

ROGERS, Howard J., banker; with Bank of Manhattan Co., N.Y.C., 32 yrs., head fgn. dept., v.p., ret.; spl. cons. The World Bank; pres. Weylin Corp.; former dir. Banco Nacional de Nicaragua; dir. Mark Cross, States Marine Shipping, Drake Am. Former officer The Greater N.Y. Fund. Mem. Bankers Assn. for Fgn. Trade. Clubs: Metropolitan (Washington); Metropolitan, India House (N.Y.C.); Seawanee Harbor (Hewlett, L.I.); Laurence (L.I.) Beech. Home: 21 E. 52d St., N.Y.C. Died Feb. 12, 1957.

ROGERS, Hubert E., lawyer; b. Milw.; student U. Wis., N.Y. Law Sch.; m. Anne Endicott Martin; 1 son Alexander. Admitted N.Y. bar, 1894; dir. Hammermill Paper Co., United Shipyards, Inc., Goldschmidt Chem. Corp., several other cos.; mem. adv. com. Chem. Corn Exchange Bank. Mem. firm Rogers & Condon. Clubs: Union League, Cloud, University, Sleepy Hollow Country. Home: Scarborough-on-Hudson, N.Y.; also Savoy-Plaza, 5th Av. and 59th St., N.Y.C. Office: 51 E. 42d St., N.Y.C. Died Dec. 31, 1958.

ROGERS, J(ames) Speed, biologist; b. Dayton, Ind., Nov. 4, 1891; s. Henry Martin and Alma Goodloe (Smith) R.; A.B., U. of Mich., 1915, A.M., 1916, Ph.D., 1930; m. Irene Russell, Apr. 18, 1918; children—James Speed, Irene Russell (Mrs. J. N. Howard). Asst. prof. zoology, Grinnell (Ia.) Coll., 1920-22; prof. biology, U. of Fla., 1922-46; prof. zoology and dir. Mus. of Zoology, U. of Mich., since 1947. Served with A.E.F., 1918-19. Mem. Am. Soc. Naturalists, Am. Entomol. Soc. (fellow), Soc. for Study Evolution, Soc. for Study of Systematics. Home: 240 Oakway, Ann Arbor, Mich. Died May 17, 1955; buried Hanover, Ind.

ROGERS, Joseph Egerton, corporation exec.; b. Barrie, Ont., Can., Aug. 28, 1880; s. Richard Robert and Edith Cameron (Perry) R.; educated in pub. schs. of Canada; m. L. Margaret Floyd, Sept. 1902 (dec.); children—Ailene Margaret (Mrs. Fauquier) (dec.), Virginia Edith (Mrs. J. Douglas Davis); m. 2d, Grace Marian Brownell, Sept. 25, 1922; m. 3d, Virginia Rogers Johnson, July 14, 1934; one dau., Jane Egerton. Salesman, Kalamazoo (Mich.) Cycle Co., 1897; Toronto mgr., Gould Bicycle Co., 1898-1902; asst. gen. sales manager, Nat. Cash Register Co., 1902-13; v.p. Internat. Business Machines Co., 1915-26; pres. Addressograph-Multigraph Corp., 1926-45, now dir.; dir. Addressograph-Multigraph Co. of Can., Ltd., Addressograph-Multigraph Ltd., London. Episcopalian. Clubs: New York Yacht (New York); Union, Mayfield Country (Cleveland); Royal Canadian Yacht (Toronto, Can.). Home: 17901 Shaker Blvd. Office: 2509-10 Terminal Tower, Cleve. 13. Died Aug. 27, 1951; buried Union Cemetery, Barrie Ont., Can.

ROGERS, McLain, surgeon; b. Clyde, N.C., June 5, 1874; s. James Jackson and Amanda (Stillwell) R.; student Weaverville (N.C.) Coll. 1 yr.; M.D., Atlanta Coll. Physicians and Surgeons, 1902; m. Bessie E. Alexander, Apr. 27, 1907. Practiced at Geary, Okla., 1903-09, Clinton, 1909-—. Fellow Am. Coll. Surgeons; mem. A.M.A., Southern Surgical Congress, Clinical Congress of Surgeons of N.A., Okla. State Med. Assn. (pres. 1922-23). Served as capt. M.C., U.S. Army, June 7-Dec. 16, 1918. Democrat. Methodist. Mason (Shriner). Home: Clinton, Okla. Died Jan. 29, 1960.

ROHDE, Ruth Bryan (Ruth Bryan Owen: Mrs. Borge Rohde) (rō'dă); b. Jacksonville, Ill., Oct. 2, 1885; d. William Jennings and Mary Elizabeth (Baird) Bryan; student Monticello Sem., Godfrey, Ill., 1899-1901, University of Neb., 1901-03; LL.D., Rollins College, Fla., 1927, Woman's College of Fla., 1935; L.H.D., Russell Sage Coll., 1931, also L.H.D., Temple University; LL.D., Denison University, 1946; married 2d, Reginald Owen (major Royal Engineers, Brit. Army), May 3, 1910 (died Dec. 1927); children—Ruth (Mrs. Jonas Reiner), John, Reginald, Helen (Mrs. Harrison Brown); m. 3d, Capt. Borge Rohde, July 11, 1936 (mem. Danish Royal Guards, also Gentleman-in-waiting to King Christian X of Denmark). Lyceum and Chautauqua lecturer, 1919-28; mem. 71st and 72d Congresses (1929-33), 4th Fla. Dist.; E.E. and M.P. to Denmark, Apr. 1933-36; alternate U.S. rep. to 4th Gen. Assembly of U.N., Oct. 1949. Served as nurse, vol. aid detachment, Brit Army, Egypt-Palestine campaign, World War. V.p. bd. of regents U. Miami (Fla.), 1925-28, mem. faculty, 1926-28. Member Beta Sigma Phi, Business & Professional Woman's Club, D.A.R., Women's Overseas League, Delta Gamma, Chi Delta Phi. Democrat. Episcopalian. Author: Elements of Public Speaking, 1931; Leaves from a Greenland Diary, 1935; Denmark Caravan, 1936; The Castle in the Silver Wood, 1939; Picture Tales from Scandinavia, 1939; Look Forward Warrior, 1943; Caribbean Caravel, 1949. Home: Wolden Rd., Ossinning, N.Y. Died July 27, 1954; buried St. Albans Ch., Copenhagen, Denmark.

ROHLFING, Charles Carroll, educator; b. Baltimore, Jan. 29, 1902; s. Charles F. and Emma L. (Tieman) R.; B.S., U. of Pa., 1923, A.M., 1925, Ph.D., 1930; LL.B., Temple U., 1934; m. Ethel O. Runk, Apr. 15, 1932; children—Charles Carroll, James Herbert. Instr., U. of Pa., 1923-30, asst. prof., 1930-34, asso. prof., 1934-40, prof. of polit. sci., 1940-— chmn. polit. sci. dept., 1934-40, 1952-—. Mem. bd. supervisors Middletown Twp., 1943—; v.p. Assn. Twp. Supervisors and Auditors of Del County, 1948-—. Co. chmn. exec. com. Nat. Found. for Edn. in Am. citizenship, 1940—; mem. exec. com. Pa. Pub. Charities Assn., 1939—; arbitrator comml. and labor cases Am. Arbitration Assn., 1941—; mem. Motion Picture Panel Arbitration, 1941—; chmn. com. adminstrv. personnel, U.S. Civil Service Commn., 3d region, 1945-—. Mem. Govs. Com. Investigation of Alleged Disfranchisement of Voters in Phila., 1938; mem. Govs. Com. to Investigate Phila. Registration Commn., 1940-41; mem. exec. com. and chmn. legal affairs com., Greater Phila. Movement, 1949-—; mem. exec. bd. and consultant Inst. Local and State govt., U. of Pa., 1937-49. Mem. Pa. Polit. Sci. and Pub. Adminstrn. Assn. (pres., 1941-43; exec. council, 1943-46), Am. Polit. Sci. Assn. (member exec. council 1944-47), Am. Assn. Univ. Profs., Am. Acad. Polit. and Social Scis., Nat. Municipal League, Pi Gamma Mu. Clubs: Lambda Chi Alpha, Lenape. Author: National Regulation of Aeronautics, 1931; Business and Government (with others), 1953; The American Government, 1952. Member board of editors Am. Polit. Sci. Review, 1946-49; chmn. publs. com. Pa. Township News, 1948-50. Home: R. 2, Media, Pa. Office: University of Pennsylvania, Phila. 4. Died Apr. 3, 1954; buried Media, Pa.

ROHLMAN, Henry P. (rōl'măn), ret. bishop; b. Germany, Mar. 17, 1876; s. Bernard and Bernardine (Husman) R.; brought by parents to U.S., 1879; student St. Lawrence Coll., Mt. Calvary, Wis., 1890-96; A.B., Columbia Coll., Dubuque, Ia., 1898; S.T.B. and J.C.B., Grand Sem. Montreal Can., 1901; M.A., Cath. U. Am., 1907; D.D., Am. U. of Rome, 1927. Ordained priest R.C. Ch., 1901; asst. pastor St. Mary's Ch. Dubuque, 1901-05; missionary at Dubuque, 1907-11; pastor St. Mary's Ch., Waterloo, Ia., 1911-17; business mgr. Columbia Coll., 1917-22; pastor Ch. of Nativity, Dubuque, 1922-27; bishop of Davenport, 1927-44; Archbishop of Dubuque, 1944-54, ret. Address: Mt. St. Bernard Sem., Dubuque, Ia. Died Sept. 13, 1957; buried Mortuary Chapel, St. Rafael Cathedral, Dubuque.

ROHNSTOCK, J. Henry (rōn'stŏk), stained glass artist; b. Ribe, Denmark, Sept. 20, 1879; s. August and Lucia (Christopherson) R.; came to U.S., 1887; naturalized, 1901; ed. pub. schs., art student Boston Latin Sch., 1897-1901; m. Alice Dadmun, Mar. 15, 1902 (died 1919); children—Barbara (Mrs. Walter C. Stone), Henry Dadmum. Apprentice, later cutter and worker in stained glass, 1897-1920; organized, and mem., firm Reynolds, Francis & Rohnstock since 1921. Represented by windows in Cathedral of St. John the Divine (N.Y.C.), East Liberty Presbyterian Ch. (Pitts.), Princeton U. Chapel. Houghton Memorial Chapel (Wellesley, Mass.), Shove Memorial Chapel (Colorado Springs), Am. Memorial Chapel (Belleau Wood, France), St. Joseph's Ch. (Laconia, N.H.), Riverside Bapt. Ch. (N.Y.C.), Nat. Episcopal Cathedral (Washington), St. George's Sch. Chapel (Newport, R.I.), St. Luke's Ch. (Schenectady, N.Y.), St. Mary's Ch. (Hudson Falls, N. Y.), Ch. of the Ascension (Lakewood, O.), Brick Presbyn. Ch. (N. Y.C.), Providence Hosp. Chapel (Oakland, Cal.), All Saints Ch. (Beverly Hills, Cal.). Awarded City of Boston Tercentenary Fine Arts Exhbn. gold medal, 1930. Mem. Ancient and Hon. Arty. Co. of Mass., Boston Soc. of Arts and Crafts. Home: 44 Richfield Rd., Scituate, Mass. Office: 1 Washington St., Boston. Died Nov. 24, 1956; buried Bellevue Cemetery, Harvard, Mass.

ROHR, Elizabeth, assn. exec. sec.; b. Baltimore, Md., Apr. 12, 1908; d. J. Winton and Anna M. (Gemmill) Getzendanner; student Goucher Coll.; m. Charles J. Rohr, Feb. 3, 1930; 1 son, David B. Vice pres. Mass. League of Women Voters, 1941-42; chmn. consumer div., Mass. Com. on Pub. Safety, 1942-43; price panel coordinator, Office of Price Adminstrn.,

1944-45; Washington rep., Consumers Union of U.S.; treas. Nat. Emergency Com. for Price Control, 1945-46; asst. consumer relations advisor, O.P.A., 1946; exec. sec., Nat. Assn. of Consumers, Washington, D.C., since 1947. Mem. Consumer Adv. Com., O.P.A., 1945-46; mem. Consumer Adv. Com., Council of Econ. Advisors to Pres. of U.S., since 1946; mem. League of Women Voters (pres. Montgomery Co. league 1955—, exec. dir. charter com. 1954-55), Americans for Democratic Action, Alpha Phi. Home: 4404 Fairfield Dr., Bethesda 14. Md. Died Apr. 5, 1958; buried Old St. Pauls, Kent County, Md.

ROHRBACH, John J., business exec.; b. Allentown, Pa., 1896. Pres., dir. Gen. Optical Co., Mt. Vernon, N.Y., Shuron Optical Co. Home: 1780 Culver Rd., Rochester, N.Y. Office: Lyceum St., Geneva, N.Y. Died July 29, 1953; buried Irondequoit Cemetery, Rochester, N.Y.

ROHRBOUGH, Edward G. (ror bow), ex-congressman; born Buckhannon, W.Va., s. William Harrison and Ann (Conley) R.; W.Va. Wesleyan Coll., Buckhannon, 1893-95; A.B., Allegheny Coll., 1900; A.M., Harvard, 1906; grad. study U. of Chicago, 1914-15; Pd.D., Salem Coll., 1936; LL.D., W.Va. Wesleyan Coll., 1939; m. Lilian M. Hartman, Aug. 28, 1907; 1 son, Edward G. Teacher high school, Brookville, Pa., 1900-01, Glenville (W.Va.) State Normal Sch., 1901-05, 1906-07; asst. to pres. Fairmont (W.Va.) State Normal Sch., 1907-08; pres. Glenville State Coll., 1908-42, pres. emeritus since 1942. Chmn. Gilmer Co. Council of Defense, 1917-18. Mem. 78th Congress (1943-45) and 80th Congress (1947-49), 3d W.Va. Dist. Trustee Deaconess Hosp. Mem. W.Va. Athletic Assn. (past pres.), Sigma Alpha Epsilon. Republican. Methodist. Mason. Rotarian. Home: Glenville, W.Va. Died Dec. 12, 1956; buried Glenville, W.Va.

ROHRER, Albert Lawrence (rôr'ẽr), engr.; b. Farmersville, O., Feb. 29, 1856; s. Aaron and Elizabeth (Ozias) R.; ed. common schs., followed by spl. course in physics and mechanics, Ohio State University; m. Carrie L. Gould, Apr. 8, 1891; 1 dau., Miriam (Mrs. Joseph Bryan Shelby). Entered employ of the Thomson-Houston Electric Co., June 1884; has been with that Co. and its successor, The Gen. Electric Co., since; recruited the engineering personnel and supervised training, 1894-1914. Had 70 U.S. colls. and univs. on the visiting list and maintained corrs. in England, France, Germany, Sweden, China, Japan and South American countries. In that period 3,000 coll. graduates were brought to the General Electric Co.; elec. supt. Schenectady works, Gen. Elec. Co., 1892-1923, advisory engr., 1923-26, retired. Ex-pres. Bd. Edn.; ex-treas. Free Pub. Library, Schenectady. Mem. Am. Inst. E.E., Am. Soc. M.E., Ohio Soc. New York, Phi Gamma Delta. Unitarian. Fifth class Order of Chia Ho (China). Author: History and Genealogy of the Ozias Family. Home: 307 Wyoming Av., Maplewood, N.J. Died Oct. 18, 1951.

ROIG, Antonio A(gripino), banker, sugar mfr.; b. Humacao, P.R., June 23, 1888; s. Antonio and Eulogia (Guzman) R.; student pvt. schs., U.S.; m. Angelina O. Dalmau, Apr. 14, 1912; children—Antonio, Gladys (Mrs. Agustin Cabrer). Field timekeeper Antonio Roig Suc, 1906-10, gen. supervisor field dept., 1911-33, mng. partner since 1933; pres. Roig Comml. Bank, Humacao, since 1933; vice chmn. bd. Govt. Development Bank of P.R.; dir., owner Fellsmere (Fla.) Sugar Producers Assn. since 1942; dir. Stirling Sugars, Inc., Franklin, La., Minford & Co., Inc., N.Y.C., Textron, Inc., U.S. and P.R., P.R. Telephone Co. Address: Humacao, P.R. Died June 10, 1956.

ROLLEFSON, Gerhard Krohn, chemist; b. Grand Forks, N.D., Jan. 12, 1900; s. Carl Jacob and Marie (Krohn) R.; A.B., U. of Wis., 1920, A.M., 1921; Ph.D., U. of Calif. (DuPont fellow, 1922-23), 1923; fellow John Simon Guggenheim Foundation, Gottingen, Germany, 1925-26; m. Nellie Marie Fogerty, Aug. 10, 1928; 1 son, Gerhard Carl. Prin. Minong (Wis.) High Sch., 1917-18; teaching asst. U. of Wis., 1919-21; teaching fellow, U. of Calif., 1921-22, instr. in chem., 1923-27, asst. prof., 1927-31, asso. prof., 1931-40, prof., 1940—, dir. of labs., 1945-47; cons. Los Alamos Scientific Lab., 1947—. Member Am. Chem. Soc., A.A.A.S.; Phi Beta Kappa, Sigma Xi, Phi Lambda Upsilon, Alpha Chi Sigma. Club: Faculty. Author: Photochemistry of the Halogens, 1938; (with M. Burton) Photochemistry and the Mechanism of Chemical Reactions, 1939; (with E. D. Eastman) Physical Chemistry, 1947. Editor of Annual Review of Physical Chemistry, 1948—. Contbr. articles in various sci. jours. Home: 920 Regal Rd., Berkeley 8, Cal. Died Nov. 15, 1955.

ROLLER, Thomas J., educator; b. Ft. Defiance, Va., Dec. 19, 1878; s. Charles S. and Rosabelle J. (Moorman) R.; grad. Augusta Mil. Acad., Ft. Defiance, 1896; student U. of Va., 1896-97, 1900-01; m. Virginia Hilton Greider, June 8, 1910; children—Virginia Hilton, Thomas Antrim. Supt. Augusta Mil. Acad., 1905—; pres. Roller Uniform Mfg. Co.; v.p. Staunton Nat. Bank; dir. Mt. Sidney Bank. Mem. County Sch. Bd.; v.p. Community Welfare League. Mem. Classical Assn. of Va., Va. Hort. Assn., Kappa Alpha, Omicron Delta Kappa. Maj. U.S. Reserve Corps. Republican. Presbyn. Mason. Clubs Beverley, Staunton Golf. Home: Ft. Defiance, Va. Died Mar. 10, 1946.

ROLLINS, Charles E., Jr., ins. exec. Formerly pres., partner Rollins & Burdick Co.; dir. Rollins Burdick Hunter Co., Chgo., 1912—, hon. chmn., 1944—. Office: 231 S. LaSalle St., Chgo. 4. Died Nov. 24, 1957.*

ROLLINS, Hyder Edward, univ. prof.; b. Abilene, Tex., Nov. 8, 1889; s. Nathaniel G. and Elva (Hyder) R.; B.A., Southwestern U., 1910, LL.D., 1933; M.A., U. of Tex., 1912; grad. student Johns Hopkins, 1914-15; M.A., Harvard, 1916, Ph.D., 1917; L.H.D., U. Vt., 1954; Fellow in Eng. U. Tex., 1911-12, instr., 1912-14; Sheldon traveling fellow, Harvard, in Eng. and France, 1919-20; asst. prof. English, New York U., 1920-21, asso. prof., 1921-24, prof., 1924-26; prof. of English, Harvard University, 1926-39, Gurney professor, 1939-1956, professor emeritus, 1956—; J. S. Guggenheim memorial fellow, England and France, 1926-27. Fellow Am. Acad. of Arts and Sciences. Clubs: Harvard (New York); Harvard (Boston); Elizabethan (New Haven). Enlisted as private Signal Corps, U.S. Army, Sept. 16, 1917; 2d lt., Aug. 1918; with A.E.F., 1918-1919. Mem. Phi Kappa Psi, Phi Beta Kappa. Editor or author: Old English Ballads, 1920; A Pepysian Garland, 1922; Cavalier and Puritan, 1923; A Handful of Pleasant Delights, 1924; A Gorgeous Gallery of Gallant Inventions, 1926; The Pack of Autolycus, 1927; The Paradise of Dainty Devies, 1927; Tottel's Miscellany (2 vols.), 1928, 29; The Pepys Ballads (8 vols.), 1929-32; The Phoenix Nest, 1931; A Poetical Rhapsody (2 vols.), 1931-32; Breton's Bowre of Delights, 1933; Charles Dickens' Letters to Charles Lever (with F. V. Livingston), 1933; England's Helicon (2 vols.), 1935; Arbor of Amorous Devices, 1936; Shakespeare's Poems (New Variorum Shakespeare), 1938; Addie Frances Rowe, 1939; The Golden Aphroditis, 1939; The Passionate Pilgrim by Shakespeare, 1940; Shakespeare's Sonnets (2 vols. New Variorum Shakespeare), 1944; Keats' Reputation in America to 1848, 1946; The Keats Circle (2 vols.), 1948; Keats and the Bostonians (with S. M. Parrish), 1951; The Renaissance in England (with Herschel Baker), 1954; The Keats Circle Letters, 1955. Compiler: An Analytical Index to the Ballad-Entries in the Stationers' Registers, 1924. General editor Harvard Studies in English, 1933—; editor, A New Variorum Shakespeare, 1947—. Contbr. to mags. Address: 1 Waterhouse St., Cambridge, Mass. Died July 25, 1958.

ROLLINS, Wallace Eugene, clergyman, educator; b. Marshall, N.C., Jan. 26, 1870; s. Maj. W. W. and Eliza J. (Gudger) R.; A.B., U. of N.C., 1892; B.D., Yale Div. Sch., 1895; D.D., Va. Theol. Sem., 1915, U. of North Carolina, 1935; m. Helen Collins, Oct. 14, 1903; m. 2d, Marion J. Benedict, Sept. 3, 1946. Deacon, 1897; priest, 1898, P.E. Ch.; rector Emanuel Ch., Covington, Va., 1897-1904, St. Thomas Ch., Christiansburg, Va., 1906-08; chaplain Sweet Briar Coll., 1908-13; prof. eccles. history P.E. Theol. Sem. in Va., 1913—, dean, 1931-40. dean emeritus 1940—; Reinicker lecturer, The Virginia Theol. Sem., 1942; lectr. Coll. of Preachers, Washington, 1944. Received Sullivan award, Sweet Briar Coll., 1943; Wallace E. Rollins Professorship of Religion, Sweet Briar Coll., established in his honor, 1957. Author: Jesus and His Ministry (with Mrs. Marion Benedict Rollins), 1954. Address: Sweet Briar, Va. Died Dec. 14, 1959.

ROLPH, John Gladwyn, economist; b. Markham, Ont., Can., July 23, 1889; s. William and Frances A. (Reesor) R.; student sch. bus. adminstrn., Harvard, 1924-25; m. Dorothy F. Levy, Aug. 15, 1927. With Bank of Nova Scotia, Can., 1906-24; br. mgr., 1920-24; sr. v.p., Amalgamated Bank of N.Y., 1925-42; exec. dir., Amalgamated Ins. Fund, 1942-44; ret., 1946; vice pres. H. L. Green Pension Holding Corporation; director H. L. Green Co., Met. Stores, Ltd.; past dir, MP RR, Bellanca Aircraft Co., Habirshaw Wire & Cable Co. Consultant to N.R.A. and O.P.A. 1st lt. Royal Flying Corps., 1916-19. Member of the American Economic Soc., Am. Statis. Assn. Club: Harvard of N.Y. Contbr. articles on banking and reviews of tech. books in econ. jours. Home: 227 East 57th St., N.Y.C. 22. Died Nov. 2, 1958; buried Grace Ch. Cemetery, Markham, Ont., Can.

ROMAN, Victor M. Reyes Y, pres. of Nicaragua; b. Jinotepe, Depto. de Carazo, Nicaragua, Oct. 3, 1872; s. Desiderio and Carmen (Reyes) R.; B.A., Instituto Nacional De Oriente, 1888; M.D., Hanneman Med. Coll., Phila., 1895; m. Mamie Keim, 1895; children—Desiderio Roman Keim, Jaime Roman Keim (dec.), Laura Roman vda. de Arana; m. 2d, Mercedes Arevalo, 1923. Interne, San Lucas Hosp., Phila., 1896-97; appt. consul gen. of Nicaragua, San Francisco, 1901-02; mayor of Jinotepe, 1909-10; appt. 1st sec., Nicaraguan Legation, 1909; senator of Nicaragua, 1923, vice pres. of the Republic, 1923; appt. Minister of Pub. Health, 1931; gov., State of Carazo, 1938-46; sec. of state, Dept. of Fgn. Affairs, 1946-47; pres. of Nicaragua, 1947—; owner, coffee plantation near Jinotepe, 1905—. Awarded The Order of San Martin, Argentina, 1947; The Medal of Gold, Pub. Health Dept. for distinguished services rendered during earthquake, 1931. Mem. Liberal Party. Roman Catholic. Home: Jinotepe, Departamento de Carazo. Office: Presidential Palace, Managua, Nicaragua. Died May 6, 1950.

ROMBERG, Sigmund, composer; b. Hungary, 1887; s. Adam and Clara R.; ed. elementary and high schs., Zeged, Hungary, and Univ. of Vienna; m. Lillian Harris, Mar. 1925. Mem. Am. Soc. Composers, Authors and Publishers. Democrat. Mason. Clubs: Lambs, Rotary (New York); Uplifters Country Home, Hillcrest Country (Los Angeles). Composer of musical productions: Maytime, 1917; Student Prince, 1924; Blossom Time, 1926; Desert Song, 1926; New Moon, 1927; Nina Rosa, 1929; East Wind, 1931; Melody, 1933; May Wine, 1935; also The Night is Young, Rosalie, My Golden Girl, My Maryland, Maytime, Ruggles of Red Gap. Address: Lambs Club, 130 W. 44th St., N.Y.C. Died Nov., 1951.*

ROME, Charles A., judge; b. Boston, Mass., Dec. 22, 1896; s. Bernard and Anna (Herzberg) R.; A.B., Harvard Coll., 1913-17; LL.B., Boston University School of Law, 1923-26; hon. LL.D., Boston University, 1946; m. Esther Edythe Rome, June 19, 1923; children—Bernard, Joel. Asso. Tyler, Eames, Wright & Hooper, 1926-27; pvt. practice, 1927-33; asst. U.S. Atty. for Massachusetts, 1934-37; engaged in private practice, 1938-49; faculty of Boston Univ. School of Law, 1926-49; apptd. justice Superior Court of Massachusetts 1949. Trustee Boston U. since 1938; sec. Frances Stern Nursery Sch., Brookline, Mass., 1932-47; trustee, Hebrew Teachers Coll., Boston, since 1945; sec. bd. trustees, 1947-49; mem. S.S.S. bd. 114, Newton, Mass., 1940-47; chmn. Boston Area Univ. War Bond Com., 1942-43; chmn., Roosevelt Campaign Com. Mass., 1932. Enlisted as pvt., A.U.S., 1917, disch. 2d lt. res. after 14 months service. Mem. Boston U. Alumni Assn. (pres. 1938-41), Am. Mass., and Boston bar assns., Woolsack, Sigma Alpha Mu (achievement medal 1952), Zionist Orgn. Am. Mason (32°), B'nai B'rith. Clubs: Harvard (Boston and New York), University (Boston). Office: Superior Court Lobby, Boston 8. Died Sept. 17, 1959.

RONDTHALER, Howard Edward (rŏn'tăl-ẽr), ret. col pres., bishop; b. Bklyn., June 17, 1871; s. Edward and Mary E. (Jacobson) R.; Moravian Male Acad., N.C., 1882-89; Ph.B., U. N.C., 1893, LL. D., 1931; B.D., Moravian Theol. Sem., 1896, D.D., 1913; A.M., Moravian Coll., Pa., 1907; m. Katharine G. Boring, Sept. 29, 1898; 1 son, Theodore. Ordained Moravian ministry, 1896; asst. pastor Salem, N.C., 1896-1903; resident prof. Moravian Coll., 1903-09; pres. Salem Acad. and Coll., 1909-49, ret.; consecrated bishop So. Province Moravian Ch., 1948. Chmn. personnel com. N.C. YMCA. Mem. Draft Board World War II. Mem. N.C. Geol. Survey, Elisha Mitchell Science Soc., Soc. for Propagation of Gospel, Sigma Alpha Epsilon. Clubs: Fossils, Torch, Cosmos, Newcomen Soc. of Great Britain and Am., Ginghoul; pres. N.C. State Lit. and Hist. Assn., 1915, N.C. Conf. for Social Service, 1917. Dist. gov. Rotary, 1918. Dir. State Sch. for Deaf, 1926. Home: Winston-Salem, N.C. Died Oct. 22, 1956; buried Salem Moravian Graveyard.

ROOD, Paul William, clergyman; b. Barnum, Minn., Aug. 1, 1899; s. Peter and Emma (Christenson) R.; student North Park Coll., Chicago, 1908-11; D.D., Wheaton (Ill.) Coll., 1932; LL.D., John Brown U., Siloam Springs, Ark., 1941; m. Neva Nystrom, June 25, 1913; children—Paul Woodrow Lyman, Rodney Wilbur Stanley, Bonevieve Florence, Donald Bryan, Pauline Beulah. Ordained ministry Mission Convenant Ch., 1914; pastor South Chicago Mission Ch. 1911-13, Broadway Temple, Minneapolis, 1913-15, Swedish Tabernacle, Seattle, 1915-22, Beulah Tabernacle, Turlock, Cal., 1922-33, Lake View Mission Ch., Chicago, 1933-35; pres. Bible Inst. of Los Angeles, 1935-38; editor King's Business, 1935-38. Pres. World Christian Fundamentals Assn., 1929-51; pres. Russian Gospel Assn.; pres. emeritus Child Evangelism Fellowship (both Chgo.), pres. National Fellowship for Spiritual Awakening. Member Mission Covenant Ch. Author: Russia in the Light of Prophecy; The Heavenly Home; Give God a Chance; Let The Fire Fall; Can We Expect a World Wide Revival? The Future is in Your Hands; The Midnight Cry. Home: 4405 El Camino Corto, La Canada, Cal. Died Feb. 22, 1956.

ROOP, Hervin Ulysses, ret. univ. pres., clergyman; b. Highspire, Pa., Nov. 16, 1869; s. Henry J. and Justina M. (Backenstoe) R.; grad. Lebanon Valley Coll., 1892; post-grad. U. Wooster, Chgo. Theol. Sem., Clark, Cornell, U. Pa., Yale, U. Chgo. A.M., B.D., Ph.D., LL.D., L.H.D.; m. E. May Kephart, Aug. 26, 1897; 1 dau., Margaret Kephart Roop Sagars. Ordained to ministry, 1890; teacher in pub. schs., State Normal Sch. and Rittenhouse Acad., Phila.; state supt. normal dept. of Pa. State S.S. Assn., 1895-97, during which time organized tng. work for S.S. teachers throughout the state; pres. Lebanon Valley Coll., 1897-1909. Eastern Coll., 1909-19, York Coll., 1919-22; head dept. of philosophy, psychology and edn. Wheaton Coll., and univ. extension lecturer in edn., 1922-28; pres.

and prof. philosophy, psychology and edn., Lincoln Meml. U., 1928—, now ret. Visited the univs. and pub. schs. in England and continental Europe. Mem. N.E.A., Am. Acad. Polit. and Social Science, A.A.A.S., Phi Beta Kappa; pres. Am. Assn. Conservative Colleges, 1926-28. Author: (text-books) Christian Ethics, or The Science of Christian Living, 1926; General Psychology, 1927; Educational Psychology, 1928; Logic, 1929; also extensive writer on psychol. and philos. subjects. Address: 1205 E. 60th St., Chgo. Died Sept. 1955; buried Annville, Pa.

ROOS, Charles Frederick (rōōs), statistician, economist; b. New Orleans, La., May 18, 1901; s. Charles Eschbach and Mary Isabelle (Holdsworth) R.; B.A., Rice Inst., Houston, Tex., 1921, M.A., 1924, Ph.D., 1926; studied U. of Chicago, 1926-27, Princeton, 1927-28; m. Mary Mae Barkuloo, Mar. 24, 1925; 1 son, Charles Edwin; married second, Marguerite Elizabeth Miller. Began as teaching assistant in mathematics, Rice Inst., 1920; civ. engring. contractor, 1921-23; teaching fellow Rice Inst., 1924-26; Nat. Research Council fellow in mathematics, 1926-28; asst. prof. mathematics, Cornell U., 1928-31; sec. sect. K (economics, sociology and statistics), A.A.A.S., 1928-31, permanent sec. and mem. exec. com. A.A.A.S., Feb. 1931-33; fellow John Simon Guggenheim Memorial Foundation, Apr. 1933-July 1933; prin. economist and dir. of research NRA, 1933-34; prof. econometrics Colorado College, 1934-37; now president Econometric Inst., Concord Fund, a mutual investment trust. V.p. and fellow Econometric Soc. (joint-founder), secretary-treasurer 1931-32, secretary and member council, pres. (1948); mem. International Statistical Institute, American Math. Soc., Math. Assn. America, Am. Statis. Assn. (fellow); Inst. of Mathematical Statistics (fellow); member Committee on Applied Mathematical Statistics, National Resarch Council; mem. Sigma Xi, Delta Kappa Epsilon, Ind. Democrat. Presbyterian. Clubs: Union League, Cosmos, Metropolitan. Author: Dynamic Economics, 1934; NRA Economic Planning, 1937; Charting the Course of Your Business, 1948; The General Outlook for the American Economy, 1954-1974. Joint Author: Economic Measures, 1938; Dynamics of Automobile Demand, 1939; Money, Men & Machines, 1953; also Dynamics of American Economy, 1957. Editor and contbr.: Stabilization of Employment, 1933. Contbr. to scientific jours. Research concerned chiefly with statis. technique and analysis and development of math. theories of dynamic econs. Home: 60 Sutton Place S. Office: 230 Park Av., N.Y. Died Jan. 6, 1958.

ROOS, Delmar Gerle, mech. and elec. engr.; b. N.Y.C., Oct. 11, 1887; s. Christian Philip and Alexandra A. (Gerle) R.; grad. Cornell U., 1911, degree in mech. and elec. engring.; m. Chrsitine H. Flagler, June 11, 1914 (div.); children—Katherine Harloe, Robert Barnard; m. 2d, Frances Homer; 1 dau., Delmar Alexandria. Engr. turbine research, Gen. Elec. Co., 1911-12; with Locomobile Co. of Am., 1912-20, as research engr. and chief engr., then v.p. in charge of engring. and production; chief engr. Pierce-Arrow Motor Car Co., 1920-21; v.p. Locomobile Co. Am., 1921-25; chief engr. Marmon Motor Car Co., 1925-26; chief engr. and then v.p. in charge of engring. Studebaker Corp., South Bend, Ind., 1926-37; then tech. adviser to Studebaker Corp. of America and cons. engr. to Humber, Hillman, Talbot and Sunbeam motor cos., hdqrs. Coventry, Eng.; now dir., cons. engr. Willys-Overland Co.; dir. Gear Grinding Co., Form Spray Co., Baker Bros. Machine Tool Co. Councilor St. Joseph Co., 1935. Fellow Nat. Geog. Soc.; mem. Soc. of Automotive Engrs. (past pres.), Army Ordnance Assn., British Inst. Mech. Engrs., French Societé des Ingeneurs Automobile. Mason (32°, K.T.). Clubs: Country, Answer, Toledo. Home: 2234 Meadowood Av. Office: Willys-Overland Co., Toledo. Died Feb. 13, 1960.

ROOS, Robert Achille, corporation official; b. San Francisco, Calif., June 7, 1883; s. Adolphe and Ernestine (Mahler) R.; B.S., Univ. of Calif., 1904; m. Louise Swabaker, Apr. 26, 1915; 1 son, Robert A. With Roos Bros., Inc., since 1904, pres. and gen. mgr. since 1927. Govt. industrial adviser for NRA; asst. coordinator of Nat. Defense Purchases, 1940-41; mem. advisory commn. to Council of Nat. Defense, 1940. Organizer and pres. San Francisco Fair Play League; organizer and chmn. Labor Relations Com., San Francisco-Oakland Met. area; ex-v.p. Nat. Retail Dry Goods Assn., re-elected vice-president, January 1944; (originator of economic committee to prevent unwarranted price increases); mem. Boston Retail Conf. on Distribution; former pres. Civic League of Improvement Clubs of San Francisco; dir. Chamber of Commerce, panel mem. 10th Regional Labor Bd. Chief of Sect., Staff of Comdg. Gen., 9th Corps Area, July 1, 1941-Dec. 29, 1941, Chief of Sect., Staff of Comdg. Gen., Western Defense Command and 4th Army, Dec. 30, 1941-Apr. 14, 1942. Chief of Branch, Staff of Comdg. Gen. 9th Service Command, Apr. 14, 1942-Nov. 16, 1943; retired with rank of col. Inf.. Recipient Legion of Merit. Hon. mem. Beta Gamma Sigma. Author of Roos Plan (1940) adopted by many municipalities and industries, to pay full month's wage to men volunteering for Army training and to return them to their jobs without impairment of service; also many pub. addresses, broadcasts, articles, relating to business and to distributive and econ. problems. Home: 615 Brewer Dr., Burlingame. Office: 798 Market St., S.F. Died June 30, 1951.

ROOT, Jesse L., judge; b. Tazewell Co., Ill., Nov. 27, 1860; s. Charles M. and Miranda B. (Burnidge) R.; ed. pub. schs. and bus. coll.; studied law in office of Hon. Samuel M. Chapman, of Plattsmouth, Neb.; admitted to bar, 1889; m. Evelyn A. Wise, June 8, 1888. Practiced at Plattsmouth; co. atty. and pub. prosecutor Cass Co., Neb., 1899-1905; mem. Neb. Senate, 1906-7; commr., Jan.-Dec., 1908, asso. justice, 1908-11, Supreme Ct. of Neb.; now in practice at Omaha; asst. solicitor for Neb., C.,B.&Q. R.R. Co. Republican. Congregationalist. Address: 1307 S. 34th St., Omaha, Neb. Died Sept. 8, 1947.

ROOT, Robert Kilburn, ex-univ. dean; b. Brooklyn, N.Y., Apr. 7, 1877; s. William Judson and Mary Louisa (Kilburn) R.; A.B., Yale, 1898, Douglas fellow, 1899-1900, Ph.D., 1902, hon. Litt.D., 1937; hon. LL.D., Brown Univ., 1940; unmarried. Tutor in English, Yale, 1900-03, instr., 1903-05; asst. prof. of English, Princeton, 1905-16, prof. 1916-46, dean of faculty 1933-46, dean and prof. emeritus since 1946, Acting prof. Eng., Stanford U., summer 1921. Lecturer on Eng., Harvard U., Feb.-June, 1927; vis. prof. of Eng., Yale U., 1927-28. Mem. Mod. Lang. Assn. Am., Am. Assn. Univ. Profs.; fellow Mediæval Acad. America, Am. Acad. Arts and Sciences. Episcopalian. Democrat. Clubs: Century, Princeton (New York). Author: Classical Mythology in Shakespeare, 1903; The Poetry of Chaucer, 1906, 22; Manuscripts of Chaucer's Troilus, 1914; The Textual Tradition of Chaucer's Troilus, 1916; The Poetical Career of Alexander Pope, 1938; The Princeton Campus in World War II, pub. 1951. Translator: The Legend of St. Andrew, 1899. Editor: Ruskin's Sesame and Lilies, 1901; Specimen Extracts from the Unprinted Manuscripts of Chaucer's Troilus (with Sir William S. McCormick), 1914; Chaucer's Troilus and Criseyde, 1926; (with P. R. Lieder and R. M. Lovett) British Poetry and Prose (2 vols.), 1928, rev. 50; British Drama (with same), 1929; Letters of Lord Chesterfield to His Son, 1929; Pope's Dunciad Variorum, 1929; (with L. I. Bredvold and G. Sherburn) Eighteenth Century Prose, 1932. Contbr. to philol. journals and various magazines. Commd. capt. Ordnance Dept., U.S. Army, Dec. 15, 1917; aircraft armament officer, 1st Army A.E.F.; maj., Feb. 17, 1919; discharged, Mar. 17, 1919; service in France, Feb. 1918-Mar. 1919; maj. Ordnance Dept. U.S.R., 1919-29. Address: 25 Mercer St., Princeton, N.J. Died Nov. 20, 1950.

ROOT, Walter Harold, state ofcl., civil engr.; b. Bradford, Ill., Dec. 8, 1888; s. Edwin Simonson and Maria Miriam (Stephenson) R.; B.S. in civil engring., Ia. State Coll., 1911, C.E., 1920; m. Gladys Ura Mauller, Sept. 2, 1913; children—Robert Walter, Marguerite Gladys (Mrs. Earl W. Cryer), Dorothy May (Mrs. Paul D. Metzler). Insp. Des Moines Union Ry., 1911-12; insp. Ia. State Highway Commn., 1912-13, dist. engr., 1913-19, maintenance engr. 1919-54, dep. chief engineer 1954—. Mem. American Society of Civil Engineers, Ia. Engring. Soc., Nat. Research Council (chairman exec. com., highway research bd.), Am. Assn. State Highway Ofcls., Ia. Highway Research Bd., Theta Xi, Tau Beta Pi (hon.). Methodist. Mason (Shriner). Club: Rotary (Ames, Ia.). Contbr. profl. publs. Home: 904 Brookridge. Office: Iowa State Highway Commission, Ames, Ia. Died Apr. 27, 1954; buried Ames Municipal Cemetery, Ames, Ia.

ROPER, Denney Warren, ret. elec. engr.; b. Grafton, Ill., Oct. 18, 1869; s. John Sylvester and Adelaide Thompson (Benner) R.; M.E., Cornell U., 1893; m. Anne Bartlett Newell, Apr. 15, 1903; children—Helen Jessie (Mrs. V. M. Marquis), John Newell; m. 2d, Sarah M. Farley, Sept. 16, 1924. With Gen. Electric Co., Schenectady, 1894, Niagara Falls Power Co., 1894-95, Mo. Edison Electric Co., 1897-1901; cons. engring. work, 1901-03; with Chgo. Edison Co., and its successor Commonwealth Edison Co., 1903—, as asst. to chief operating engr., 1905-15, supt. street dept., 1915-33, asst. elec. engr., 1933-35; retired. Past chmn. com. Nat. Elec. Light Assn. and Assn. Edison Illuminating Cos.; supervising cable insulation research at Harvard, Mass. Inst. Tech., Johns Hopkins, U. Ill.; mem. U.S. Nat. Com. of Internat. Electrotech. Commn., 1924-30; mem. conf. on elec. insulation NRC. Mem. Am. Inst. E.E. (past chmn. Chgo. sect.), Western Soc. engrs. (ex-v.p.). Unitarian. Recipient Chanute medal by Western Soc. Engrs., 1907; best paper prize by Am. Inst. E.E., 1927. Home: Carmel-by-the-Sea, Cal. Died Oct. 5, 1949.

ROPER, John Caswell, clergyman; b. Marlboro County, S.C., Nov. 4, 1873; s. John Thomas and Martha Angeline (Heustess) R.; A.B., Wofford Coll., Spartanburg, 1896, A.M., 1904; B.S., Coll. of Charleston, 1904; Ph.D., U. S.C., 1929; m. Edith Bull Moseley, June 14, 1898; children—John Caswell (dec.), Sheldon Moseley, Olin Watson (dec.), Rufus Child, Julian Westfield, Dr. Charles Pinkney, Margaret Frances. Ordained ministry Methodist Episcopal Ch. South, 1896; pastor Union, S.C., 1896-98, Greer, 1898-1901, Charleston, 1901-04, Darlington, 1904-06, Abbeville, 1907; presiding elder Cokesbury dist., 1907-11; pastor Chester, 1911-15; Rock Hill, 1915-17, Main Street Ch., Columbia, 1918; sec. mission, M.E. Ch., S. 1918-20, sec. edn., 1921-27; pastor Green Street M.E. Ch., Columbia, 1928-29; St. Paul Ch., Greenville, S.C., 1929-33, Union, S.C., 1933-34, Clinton, S.C., 1934-38, Buford St. Ch., Gaffney, S.C., 1938-42, York, S.C., 1942-46; First Ch., Clover, S.C., 1946-52, Sharon, S.C., 1952—. Acting prof. edn., Presbyn. Coll., Clinton, 1936, 38. Chmn. bd. of edn., Upper S.C. Conf., 1926-30, chmn. Bd. of Temperance and Social Service of same, 1930-34, chmn. of Bible cause and Sabbath Observance, 1934-38; del. to Gen. Conf. M.E. Ch., S., 1930; chaplain S.C. State Senate, 1929; chmn. Prohibition Promotion Movement in S.C., 1928; founder and first pres. Fedn. of Orgn. for Temperance and Prohibition, S.C., 1931-33; mem., v.p. S.C. State Constl. Conv., 1933; mem. bd. mgrs. Southern Christian Advocate 1930-1944; pres. Inter-Ch. Movement in S.C. in Interest of Temperance, Social Service, Civic Righteousness, Prohibition and Ch. Co-op., 1931-48, pres. emeritus, 1948—; del. at large M.E. Ch., S., to Fed. Council of Chs., 1930-34; mem. Internat. Relations Com., 1932—; pres. of Legal Conf., The Inc. Body of Upper S.C. Conv., 1916-45; (now chmn. bd. of trustees, Upper S.C. Conf.); pres. S.C. Epworth League, 1903-05. Mem. Kappa Sigma. Democrat. Mason, Odd Fellow, K.P., Woodmen of World. Clubs: Kiwanis, Rotary. Author: Religious Aspects of Education, 1926; The Supreme Law, and The Historical Basis for a Methodist Theodicy, 1932; The New Theodicy, 1948; The Reality of the Invisible, 1949. Contbr. So. Christian Advocate, Christian Advocate, etc. Radio preacher over station WSPA, 1930. Home: Sharon, S.C. Died Oct. 18, 1958.

ROSANOFF, Martin André (rō'sä-nōf), chemist; b. Nicolaeff, Russia, Dec. 28, 1874; s. Abraham H. and Clara (Bertinskaya) R.; Imperial Classical Gymnasium, Nicolaeff, 1883-91; Ph.B., New York U., 1895; studied U. of Berlin, 1895-96, U. of Paris, 1896-98; research fellow, New York U., 1899-1900, Sc.D., 1908; m. Louise Place, Feb. 2, 1901 (died Aug. 30, 1918); children—Boris Place, Elizabeth Place, Marian Place (dec.), James Keyes Place; m. 2d, Charlotte Adèle Walker, Nov. 17, 1932. Editor for exact sciences, New Internat. Ency., 1900-03; research asst. to Thomas A. Edison, Orange, N.J., 1903-04; instr. theoretical chemistry, 1904-05, asst. prof., 1905-07, New York U.; head dept. of chemistry, and dir. chem. labs., Clark U., 1907-14; also prof. organic chemistry, Clark Coll., 1910-12; prof. chem. research, Mellon Inst., U. of Pittsburgh, 1914-15, head dept. of research in pure chemistry, 1915-19; prof. chem. research, Duquesne U., 1933-40, dean of the grad. school, 1934-40; local research adminstr. office of edn., U.S. Dept. of Interior, 1936-37; Public Panel Chmn. War Labor Bd., 1943-46. Received United States Certificate of Merit, 1943. Fellow Am. Acad. Arts and Sciences, A.A.A.S.; mem. Am. Chem. Soc. (Nichols medalist), Royal Soc. of Arts, Nat. Inst. Social Sciences, Am. Arbitration Assn. Hon. Mem. Internat. Mark Twain Soc. Phi Beta Kappa. Clubs: Chemists (New York); Royal Societies (London). Contbr. to Jour. Am. Chem. Soc., Chem. News (London), Zeitschrift für physikalische Chemie (Leipzig). Administrative dir. of "Guide to the School Laws of Pennsylvania," 1938; Supplement, 1940; Edison in his Laboratory, 1932, repub. 1942; Select Topics of Plane Analytic Geometry, 1944. Home: 124 Longuevue Drive, Mt. Lebanon, Pa. Died July 30, 1951; buried Homewood Mausoleum, Pitts.

ROSE, Flora, home economist; b. Denver, Colo., Oct. 13, 1874; d. Samuel Patrick and Mildred Lewis (Boyd) Rose; B.S., Kan. State Agrl. Coll., 1904; M.A., Columbia, 1909; Pd.D., Albany State Teachers Coll., 1931; D.Sc., Kansas State Coll., 1937. Began as teacher, 1903; instr. home economics, Cornell U., 1907-11, prof. and head of dept., 1911—, dir. Coll. of Home Economics, 1932-40, emeritus dir., 1940—; asst. home making editor of Delineator Mag., 1920-26; mem. Weight Control Conf. called by N.Y. Acad. of Medicine and Am. Med. Assn., 1924; former mem. N.Y. State Agr. Com. Made survey of nutrition of Belgian sch. children at request of King of Belgium, 1923. Dir food conservation program, N.Y., 1917-19. Decorated Chevalier Order of Crown (Belgium). Former member board National Council of Parent Educatoin. Fellow A.A.A.S.; American Home Econ. Association, Phi Kappa Phi, Omicron Nu, Pi Lambda Theta, Kappa Delta Phi, Phi Upsilon Omicron, Epsilon Sigma Phi, Mortarboard. Democrat. Collaborator on Home Making Manual; contbr. to Your Weight and How to Control It; author of articles and pamphlets on nutrition and home making. Home: 900 Euclid Avenue, Berkeley 8, Calif. Address: New York State Coll. of Home Economics, Ithaca, N.Y. Died July 25, 1959; buried Sunset View, Berkeley, Cal.

ROSE, Floyd, mfr.; b. Pittsburgh, Sept. 23, 1875; s. Cyrus L. and Anna Jackson (Ritz) R.; Metall. Engr., Univ. Pittsburgh, 1896, Sc.D., 1950; m. Gertrude A. Stedman, Nov. 18, 1903; 1 son, Robert Stedman. Employed in chem. lab., Carbon Steel Co., 1896-1905, asst. supt. of mill, 1905-07; gen. supt.

Portsmouth Steel Co., 1907-09; pres. Floyd Rose Engring. Co., 1909-17; v.p. Heppenstall Co., 1917-26; v.p. Vandium Alloys Steel Co., 1926-40, pres., 1940-45; chmn. bd. dirs. Firth Sterling Steel & Carbide Corp., 1945-50; v.p. Colonial Steel Co., Anchor Drawn Steel Co., Vascoloy-Ramet Co. Served with U.S. Ordnance, 1917-18, in charge Pittsburgh div. gun forging prodn. in Western Pa. Mem. exec. com. bd. trustees U. Pittsburgh. Pres. U. Pittsburgh Alumni Assn. Mem. Am. Soc. Metals, Phi Gamma Delta. Mem. Third Presbyterian Ch., Pittsburgh. Clubs: Duquesne, Pittsburgh Athletic, University (Pittsburgh). Home: King Edward Apts. Office: Grant Bldg., Pitts. Died July 29, 1950; buried Allegheny Cemetery, Pitts.

ROSE, Henry Reuben, clergyman; b. Philadelphia, Oct. 22, 1866; s. David Henry and Emma Frances (Longaker) R.; student Tufts Coll. and Harvard; B.D., Tufts Div. Sch., 1891, S.T.D., 1935; D.D., St. Lawrence U., 1916; m Ida Louise Jones, Apr. 4, 1893; children—Dorothy (dec.), Edith Lydia (Mrs. Andrew Wilson, Jr.), Henry Brooks, David Kenneth. Ordained ministry Universalist Ch., 1891; pastor Portsmouth, N.H., and Auburn, Me., until 1898, Newark, N.J., 1898-1929, pastor emeritus since 1929. V.p. Newark Bur. Asso. Charities 25 yrs. Trustee U. of Newark. Mem Pa. Soc. of N.J., Delta Tau Delta. Republican. Mason; Past Grand Chaplain Grand Lodge of Masons of N.J., Odd Fellow. Clubs: Wednesday (Newark); Essex Country (East Orange, N.J.); City History Club (New York); Colony Club (Harpswell Harbor, Me.). Author: Good Sense in Religion, 1897; The Outside of the Cup, 1914; If I Were 21, 1918; Hungerings of the Human Soul, 1919; The Road to Happiness, 1920. Widely known as lecturer on psychology, the drama, travel, biography and history. Address: 334 Grove St., Montclair, N.J. Died Jan. 24, 1950; buried Evergreen Cemetery, Elizabeth, N.J.

ROSE, Josiah Tryon, lawyer; b. McLean County, Ill., Feb. 13, 1869; s. Albert H. and Mary Ann (Cameron) R.; B.A., Ohio Northern U., Ada, O., 1894, M.A., 1896; law course, same univ.; m. Cora V. McKinniss, 1898 (died 1905); children—Ydoine (Mrs. Ralph W. Cornelisen), Charles A.; m. 2d, Anna Crisman, 1910 (died 1912); m. 3d, Mrs. Jessie Setzer Marks, 1935. Began with Toledo Bridge Co., 1896; contract mgr. Am. Bridge Co., 1901-07; v.p. Atlanta Steel Co., 1907-14; v.p. J.B. McCrary Co., 1914-21; collector of Internal Revenue for Ga., 1921-33. Pres. Universal Distributors, Inc. Pres. Washington Memo Bible Assos.; vice pres. Atlanta Humane Soc.; dir. and attorney, Burns Club of Atlanta; trustee Atlanta Hist. Society; dir. Churches Homes for Girls, Atlanta. Mem. Ga. and Atlanta bar assns. Republican. Methodist. Mason (K.T., 32°). Clubs: Atlanta Athletic, East Lake, Masonic, Civitan. Home: 2640 Peachtree Rd., N.W. Office: William-Oliver Bldg., Atlanta, Ga. Died Oct. 19, 1951.

ROSE, Lisle A(bbott), editor; b. Chicago, Feb. 6, 1904; s. Frank Lisle and Jessie May (Allen) R.; Ph.B., U. of Chicago, 1925, M.A., 1928, Ph.D., 1935, fellow 1926-28; m. Mildred Elizabeth Maddux, Sept. 25, 1926; children—David Allen, Lisle Abbott, Jr. Instr. Culver Mil. Acad., 1925-26; on staff Mich Coll. of Mining and Technol., successively instr. to prof., head dept. of languages, 1928-47, dir. public relations, adminstrv. officer, 1945-47; prof. and editor engring. expt. station, dir. engring. information and publications, U. of Ill., 1947—, professor general engineering 1954—, secretary and member exec. com. of coll. of engring., sec., mem. executive staff of engring. expt. station; consultant on tech. reports since 1932; active in establishing Upper Mich. Adult Edn. Program and Sault St. Marie Br., Mich. Coll. Mining and Tech., 1944-46. Served as civilian pub. relations rep., 3656th and 3650th Units of Army Service Forces, 1943-46. Fellow Royal Soc. Arts; mem. Am. Soc. for Engring. Edn. (co-founder Mich. Coll. Mining and Tech. br., and chmn.; mem. bd. mgrs. North-Midwest Sect., 1941-46, chmn.-elect, 1946-47, mem. nat. coms., 1944 and since 1951, chmn. 1954 ann. convention; public relations dir., also editor 1955—), Academy of Political Science; Am. Acad. Political and Social Science, Assn. U.S. Army, National Council Teachers of English (member editorial board Good Reading), Am. Assn. Univ. Profs., Hist. Science Soc. Member Delta Sigma Phi, Blue Key, Quadrangle, Sigma Rho Tau. Clubs: University, Rotary (Urbana). Author: The Modern American Novel: A Synopsis, 1930; sr. author Engring. Reports, 1950; editor and sr. author Preparing Technical Material for Publication, 1951; Am. Soc. Elec. Engrs. Convention Manual, 1955; editor and one of authors Mathematical Needs of Prospective Students, 1952; Careers in Engineering, 1952; numerous articles and reviews in scholarly and tech. jours. Home: 112 Flora Dr., Champaign, Ill. Died May 23, 1955; buried Sharpsburg, Md.

ROSE, William Ganson, advertising executive, public relations counsel; b. Cleveland, O., Oct. 29, 1878; s. William Russell and Eliza E. (Ganson) R.; A.B., Western Reserve U., 1901; m. Julia Miller, July 1, 1927; 1 dau., Nancy. Dramatic editor Cleveland Plain Dealer, 1902-07; exec. sec. Cleveland Conv., N.E.A., 1908; exec. sec. joint tax com. Ohio State Bd. of Commerce and Cleveland Chamber of Commerce, 1908; mgr. Cleveland Industrial Expn., 1909, Detroit Industrial Expn., 1910, Newark (N.J.) Industrial Expn., 1912, Cleveland Art Loan Expn., 1913, Cleveland Elec. Expn., 1914. Organizer Cleveland Better Business Bur., 1913. V.p. Alumni Assn. Western Reserve U. Lecturer Western Reserve U., 1913. Pres. Advertising Affiliation of Buffalo, Cleveland, Detroit and Rochester, 1915; adv. mgr. First Nat. Bank and First Trust and Savings Co., Cleveland, 1915-19. Chmn. com. 100 orgns. which secured Cleveland pub. hall; exec. sec. City Plan Commn., 1917; pres. William Ganson Rose, Inc., 1918—. Vice pres. Financial Advertisers' Assn. of Associated Advertising Clubs of World, 1918-19; dir. Am. Red Cross campaign, Ohio, Ind., Ky., 1917; dir. Bur. of Expns., U.S. Govt., 1918; trustee Welfare Federation of Cleveland, 1918, Cleveland Community Fund, 1920, The Hiram House, 1920—. Program chmn. Cleveland Chamber of Commerce, 1927—; chmn. dedicatory com. Cleveland Union Terminal, 1929; dir. Gordon-Bennett Internat. Balloon Race, 1930; chmn. County Emergency Relief Com., 1931. Speaker before business and civic groups and national associations; promotional counsel Great Lakes Exposition, 1936, and originator and developer of "The Making of a Nation," keynote exhibit of Exposition, 1937, chmn. Cleveland World's Fair Commn., 1939; dir. special events, B. F. Goodrich Co. at New York World's Fair, 1939 and 1940; Ohio representative of Fair, 1940; dir. Cleveland Sesquicentennial celebration, 1946. Mem. Am. Press Humorists, Cleveland Chamber Commerce, Delta Tau Delta, Asso. Advertising Clubs of the World (dir. 1916-17), New England Soc. of Cleveland and the Western Reserve (pres. 1929-30); Early Settlers Assn. Western Reserve (v.p.), The Associated Charities (life mem.), Sight Saving Council of Cleveland (charter mem.); hon. mem. Elec. League of Cleveland, 1912—. Republican. Presbyn. Clubs: Cleveland Advertising (pres. 1914-16), Shaker Heights Country, Mid-day. Author: Comic History of Cleveland, 1901; Cleveland Industries, 1910; The Ginger Cure, 1911; Putting Marshville on the Map, 1912; Success in Business; Waking Up Bolton, 1913; The Rousing of Parkside, 1914; Cleveland, the Making of a City, 1949. Co-author: Cut Down That Score. Home: 3224 Warrington Rd., Shaker Heights, Cleve. Office: Williamson Bldg., Cleve. Died Aug. 15, 1957; buried Lake View Cemetery, Cleve.

ROSELAND, Harry, artist; b. Bklyn., 1866; s. Henry H. and Mary F. (Hartigan) R.; student pub. schs.; studied Adelphi Acad., Bklyn. Art Guild; m. Lillian May Whitney, Oct. 1898; m. 2d, May Olive Sands, June 24, 1904. Recipient gold medal Bklyn. Art Club, 1887; 2d Hallgarten prize N.A.D., 1898; silver medal, Boston, 1901; bronze medal, Charleston, 1902; silver medal, Phila., 1902; gold medal, Boston, 1904; gold medal, Phila., 1907. Has pictures in many pvt. collections. Large painting, Lincoln, at Sparks Mus., Jackson, Mich.; George Washington on Horse, Borough Hall, Bklyn.; others. Mem. Soc. Bklyn. Artists, Soc. Painters and Sculptors. Clubs: Brooklyn Art, Salmagundi. Home: 389 Bergen St. Studio: Ovington Bldg., 246 Fulton St., Bklyn. Died Dec. 20, 1950; buried Greenwood Cemetery, Bklyn.

ROSEN, Charles (rōz'ĕn), landscape painter; b. Westmoreland County, Pa., Apr. 28, 1878; s. David Franklin and Lorain (McClain) R.; ed. high schs., Pa.; studied art, Nat. Acad. Design, and New York Sch. of Art; m. Mildred Holden, Dec. 3, 1904; children—Katharine, Polly; m. 2d, Jean Inglis, Dec. 29, 1934. Awarded 3d Hallgarten prize, 1910; 1st Hallgarten prize, 1912; Shaw purchase prize, Salmagundi Club, 1914; hon. mention, Carnegie Inst., Pittsburgh, 1914; silver medal, San Francisco Expn., 1915; Inness gold medal and 1st Altman prize ($1000), N.A.D., 1916; 1st prize, Columbus (O.) Art League, 1926; Jennie Sesnan medal, for best landscape, Pa. Acad. Fine Arts, Phila., 1926. Represented in permanent collections, Duluth Art Assn., Minneapolis Soc. Fine Arts, Delgado Museum, New Orleans, Butler Art Inst., Youngstown, O., Witte Museum, San Antonio, Tex., Toledo Museum, City Art Museum, St. Louis, Whitney Museum, Am. Art, N.Y. City, Pa. State Coll., Dartmouth Coll., Univ. of Mich. and many pvt. collections. Actg. dir. Art Sch., Columbus Gallery Fine Art, 1925-26; dir. Witte Museum Sch. of Art, San Antonio, Tex., 1940-42; dir. San Antonio Art Inst., San Antonio, Tex., 1942-43. Instr. landscape painting Woodstock Sch. Painting. A.N.A., 1913; N.A., 1917. Clubs: Salmagundi, National Arts (New York). Home: Woodstock, Ulster County, N.Y. Died June 21, 1950; buried Woodstock (N.Y.) Meml. Cemetery.

ROSEN, Max, violinist; b. Rumania, Apr. 11, 1900; brought to U.S. in infancy; began study of violin under father, later under Willy Hess at Berlin, Germany, and Leopold Auer; grad. Berlin Conservatory, 1915; m. Nanette Guilford, 1928 (div. 1930); m. 2d, Gertrude Buchbinder; 1 dau., Carol. Debut at Royal Opera House in Dresden, 1915, N.Y. debut Carnegie Hall with the Philharmonic Orchestra, 1918; toured U.S., 1918-20, Europe, 1921-25, U.S., 1925—. Home: 177 E. 77th St., N.Y.C. Died Dec. 16, 1956.*

ROSEN, Peter, clergyman, author; b. Orsfeld, nr. Kylburg, Rhineprovince, Prussia, Dec. 15, 1850; served with distinction in German army at Diedenhofen, Lorrain, 1872-5; came to U.S., 1876, to visit Centennial Exp'n, and entered U.; of Notre Dame, Ind. finished ed'n Am. Coll., Louvain, Belgium; ordained priest, Mar. 30, 1882, at Simpelveld, Holland. Pastor Deadwood, S. Dak., 1882-9, Fairfax, Minn., 1889-95; after trips to Cal. and Europe took his present parish of St. Patrick's, Hollandale, Wis. Supporter of Catholic ed'n and Catholic socs.; took active part against so-called Faribault plan of ed'n in Minn.; took stand against secret socs. and was instrumental in settlement of question at Rome, 1894. Author: Pa-ha-sap-pah, or History of the Black Hills of South Dakota, 1895; 100 Tage in Europa (German), 1895; History of Fort Ridgeley, Minn., and Its Siege, August, 1862, 1895; The Catholic Church and Secret Societies, 1902; Reply to My Critics, 1903. Address: Hollandale, Wis. Died Oct. 1906.

ROSENBACH, Abraham S. Wolf (rō'zĕn-bäk), writer, bibliographer; b. Phila., Pa., July 22, 1876; s. Morris and Isabella (Polock) R.; B.S., University of Pa., 1898, Ph.D., 1901, honorary D.A.E., 1927, hon. D.H.L., 1945, D.H.L., 1947, LL.D., 1947; m. Sec. The Rosenbach Co., dealers in rare books and manuscripts. Pres. Gratz Coll.; mem. bd. govs. Dropsie Coll.; trustee Free Library, Phila.; hon. pres. Am. Jewish Hist. Soc., Philobiblon Club, Am. Friends of Hebrew Univ. of Palestine, Pa. Library Club; asso. trustee and mem. of Board of Grad. Edn. and Research, University of Pa.; trustee Philadelphia Museum of Art. Mem. Historical Society of Pa. (corr. sec.), N.Y. Hist. Soc., Grolier Club, Am. Antiquarian Soc., Am. Philos. Soc., Bibliog. Soc. London, Shakespeare Assn. Am. (hon. pres.); Am. Shore and Beach Preservation Soc. (dir.). Founder fellowship in bibliography at U. of Pa., 1930. Editor: (with Austin Dobson) Dr. Johnson's Prologue, 1902. Compiler: Catalogue of the Books and Manuscripts of Robert Louis Stevenson in the Library of the Late Harry Elkins Widener, 1913; Catalogue of the Widener Memorial Library in Harvard College, 1918, etc. Contbr. various articles on lit. topics. Author: The Unpublishable Memoirs, 1917; An American Jewish Bibliography, 1926; Books and Bidders, 1927; The All-Embracing Doctor Franklin, 1932; Early American Children's Book, 1933; The Libraries of the Presidents of the U.S., 1934; A Book Hunter's Holiday, 1936; The First Theatrical Company in America, 1939; Description of Widener Four Folios of Shakespeare, 1945; Tribute volume "To Dr. R. Essays collected and published in honor of seventieth birthday" with bibliography of writings, 1946. Home: 2010 De Lancey St., Philadelphia, 322 E. 57th St., New York 22, and Strathmere, Corson's Inlet, N.J. Office: 1618 Locust St., Phila. Died July 1, 1952.

ROSENBACH, Joseph Bernhardt (rōz'ĕn-bäk), educator; b. N.Y. City, Oct. 5, 1897; s. Louis and Anne (Wohlgemuth) R.; student Brooklyn Poly. Inst., 1914-15; A.B., U. of N.M., 1915-17; student U. of Colo., 1917; M.S., U. of Ill., 1919; m. Florence Roberta Simon, June 3, 1924; children—Loren Marshall, Ronald Neil. Intr. mathematics, U. of N.M., 1917-18, U. of Ill., 1918-20; instr., Carnegie Inst. of Tech., 1920-23, asst. prof., 1923-28, asso. prof., 1928-35, prof. since 1935, sec., div. of humanistic and social studies, 1943-45, acting head dept. of math., 1945-46, asst. head 1946-50, head since 1950. Engr. of maintenance, A.T. & S.F. Ry., summers 1915-16, 1921; in charge of evening courses in mathematics, Coll. of Engring. and Science, 1933-45. Fellow A.A.A.S.; mem. Am. Soc. for Engring. Edn. (sec., Allegheny Sect., 1939-40), Am. Math. Soc., Math. Assn. Am. (chmn. Allegheny Mt. sect. 1946-49), Circolo Matematico di Palermo, Am. Assn. Univ. Profs., adv. com. council of Teachers of Math., Zeta Beta Tau, Beta Sigma Rho (hon.), Phi Kappa Phi, Tau Beta Pi, Pi Mu Epsilon, Sigma Xi. Democrat. Jewish religion. Clubs: Illini, Westmoreland Country. Author: College Algebra, 1933, 3d edit., 1949; Plane Trigonometry and Plane and Spherical Trigonometry with and without Four-place and Five-place Tables, 1943; Mathematical Tables, 1943; Essentials of Plane Trigonometry with and without Tables, 1950; Essentials of College Algebra, 1951; Intermediate Algebra for Colleges, 1951; also Math. Sect. of Pre-Engineering Inventory and Achievement Tests in Mathematics, 1947-48. Home: 2550 Beechwood Blvd., Squirrel Hill, Pitts. 17. Died Nov. 5, 1951.

ROSENBAUM, Lewis Newman (rō'zĕn-boum), business organizer; b. Homak, Hungary, Mar. 29, 1881; s. David and Fani (Newman) Rosenbaum; m. Bella Weternikove Mar 19, 1905; children—Adrian Weternikove, Joseph Hirsch, Francis Newman, Ruth Beatrice, Doris Frima. Came to U.S., 1888, naturalized, 1892. Admitted to Tenn. State bar, 1901, Wash. State bar, 1905. Organized in 1924, chain of office bldgs. in U.S., including Flatiron and Internat. Combustion bldgs. (New York), Coca Cola in N.Y. Life bldgs. (Kansas City, Mo.), Metropolitan Life Bldg., Transportation Bldg. and Annex (Minneapolis), Auditorium Bldg. (Spokane), Railway Exchange (Seattle); chmn. finance com. Continental Motors

Corp. of Detroit, 1933; now financial and bus. cons. to numerous bankers, indsl. corps., etc.; organizer Spokane Bldg. Corp.; organizer and pres. Downtown Corp., Terminal Corp. (Jersey City, N.J.); Capitol Vehicle Corp. (N.Y.); pres. Rodibell Corp. (Seattle), Newman Corp. (Washington), Rosenbaum Properties, Inc. (N.Y.), Downtown Corp. (Phila.), Terminal Realty Corp. of N.J.; organizer and dir. Paramount Theatre and Studios, Uptown Corp., Gen. Pershing Hotel Corp., United Bldgs. Corp. of Seattle, Fox West Coast Theatre (Spokane), Spokane Bldg. Corp.; reorganized and financed Brooklyn (N.Y.) Daily Eagle; reorganized Donahoes, Inc. (Pittsburgh); organizer, president, director of the Greater Jersey City Industrial Terminal, Incorporated; negotiated financing and recapitalization of Triumph Explosives, Inc., and other firms; director Investment Assos. of N.J., Inc. (N.J.); pres. and dir. Rose-Gran Corporation of New York, Railroad Properties, Inc., Newman-Mamaroneck Corp., Downtown Corp. of Jersey City, L. N. Rosenbaum, Inc., Tube Concourse Bldg., Jersey City. Apptd. commnr. Soo Locks Centennial Celebration Commn., 1950; honorary trustee Columbia Basin Irrigation League. Sponsor, Universal Jewish Encyclopedia. Member American Jewish Hist. Soc. Mem. Ref. Hebrew Ch.; hon. life mem. Herzl Congregation, Seattle, Wash.; mem. Community Synagogue, Rye, N.Y. Home: 25 Mendota Av., Ry., N.Y. Office: 565 Fifth Av., N.Y.C. Died Jan. 9, 1956.

ROSENBERG, Henry A., oil industrialist, civic leader; b. 1898; m. Ruth Blaustein; children—Henry A., Mrs. Martin J. Davidson, Mrs. Stanley A. Hoffberger. Pres. Crown Central Petroleum Corp. Mem. bd. Asso. Jewish Charities of Balt.; past pres. Sinai Hosp.; mem. mgmt. com., past treas. Balt. Symphohy Ircg Orachestra. Served in USN, World War I. Home: Rainbow Hill, Eccleston, Md. Office: American Bldg., Balt. Died Feb. 23, 1955.*

ROSENBERG, Israel, rabbi; b. Lomzo, Poland, Mar. 1875; s. Gershon and Zipporah (Rachmilevitch) R.; ed. Rabbinical Sem., Lomzo, Rabbinical Sem., Slobodko, Kollel Navaredok; m. Sarah Greenberg, 1895; children—Sadie (Mrs. Abraham A. Redelheim), Leah (Mrs. Israel Jacobs), Beatrice (Mrs. Joseph Pekelner), J. Mitchell. Came to U.S., 1902, naturalized, 1914. Ordained orthodox rabbi, 1899; rabbi, Poughkeepsie, N.Y., 1902-03, Bayonne, N.J., 1903-10, Burlington, Vt., 1910-12, Paterson, N.J., 1912-19, Jersey City, 1919-20, 1st v.p., rabbi Isaac Elchanan Theol. Coll. of Am. (Yeshiva) 1910-12; acting dean Rabbi Isaac Elchanon Theol. Coll. of Am., 1923-24; pres. Union of Orthodox Rabbis of U.S. and Can., 1940—; president Central Relief Committee, Ezras Torah Fund for Relief of European and Palestinian Rabbis, American Committee Kenesseth Israel of Palestine (Ramban), Am. Com. United Charity Instns. of Jerusalem, Am. Com. for Yeshivah Meah Shearim, Jerusalem, Am. Com. for Lomza Yeshiva, Kollel Navaredok, Kollel Kovno; hon. pres., treas. Yeshiva of Telz; past presiding officer presidium, Vood Ha-Zolah (Emergency Com. for War-torn Yeshivoth); presiding judge Rabbinical Tribunal of Supreme Court, Province of Ontario, 1926; treasurer American Com. Grodno, Yeshiva; hon. pres. American Committee Kamynetz Yeshiva; president Central Orthodox Committee. Del. World Zionist Congress, London, 1920, Zurich, 1929; chmn. del. Central Relief Com. to Europe, 1920. Mem. Union of Orthodox Rabbis of U.S. and Can. (pres. 1928-30 and 1940—; chmn. presidium, 1926-28; 1st honorary president, 1930-39); director Joint Distribution Committee. Member com. of 5 representing leading Jewish nat. orgns. received by Pres. Roosevelt Dec. 9, 1942, leaving memorandum relative to Nazi persecuted Jewry. Contbr. to rabbinical publs. Home: 901 Av. H, Bklyn. Died Jan. 26, 1956; buried Lebanon Cemetery, Queens, N.Y.

ROSENBERGER, Carl, jewelry mfr.; b. Germany, Feb. 28, 1872; s. Gotlieb and Rosa (Stern) R.; student pub. schs., Germany and U.S.; m. Ninette Eichberg, May 1902; 1 son, Gerald; m. 2d, Eva Rosenfield, Mar. 1942. Came to U.S., 1886, naturalized, 1894. Founder Coro, Inc., 1901, became pres., now chmn. bd. Jewish religion. Clubs: Harmonie (N.Y.C.); Metropolis Country. Home: Waldorf Astoria Towers. Office: 47 W. 34th St., N.Y.C. Died Oct. 8, 1957.

ROSENBERRY, Marvin Bristol, judge; b. River Styx, Medina County, O., Feb. 12, 1868; s. Samuel C. and Mary (Hitchcock) R.; student Mich. State Normal Sch., Ypsilanti, 3 yrs.; LL.B., U. of Mich., 1893, LL.D., 1926; LL.D., Univ. of Wis., 1930, Marquette U., 1938, Nashotah House, Wis., 1942; M.Ed., Mich. State Normal Sch., 1941; D.H.L., Beloit Coll., 1946; m. Katherine Landlair, Sept. 2, 1897 (died Jan. 26, 1917); children—Florence (dec.), Katherine (dec.), Samuel Landfair; married 2d, Lois Kimball Mathews, June 24, 1918. Began practice at Wausau, Wis., 1893; mem. Bump, Kreutzer & Rosenberry, 1895-1901, Kreutzer, Bird & Rosenberry, 1901-16; city atty., Wausau, 1902-08; apptd. justice Supreme Court of Wisconsin. February 12, 1916; reelected for fourth time April 1939, for term ending January 1, 1950; chief justice 1929-50, ret. 1950. Awarded silver antelope, Boy Scouts of Am., 1944. Mem. American Bar Assn., Wis. Bar Assn., American Law Institute. Republican. Episcopalian. Mason (33°), Elk. Clubs: Madison, Maple Bluff Golf, University. Home: 81 Cambridge Rd., Madison 4. Address: 1 S. Pinckney St., Madison, Wis. Died Feb. 15, 1958.

ROSENBERRY, M(orris) Claude, dir. music edn.; b. Lower Mt. Bethel Twp., Northampton County, Pa., Jan. 7, 1889; s. Edward Shimer (M.D.) and Gertrude (McDonald) R.; student State Normal Sch., E. Stroudsburg, Pa., 1908-10; Cornell U., summers 1912-15; B.S., N.Y. U., 1926; Mus.D. (hon.), Temple U., 1937; Pd.D. (hon.), Lebanon Valley Coll., 1939; m. Mary E. Hoffman, June 12, 1915; 1 son, Edward Hoffman. Rural sch. tchr., 1906-08; head dept. of English, Westerleigh Collegiate Inst., New Brighton, N.Y., 1910-11; supr. music, East Stroudsburg, Pa., 1911-15, Easton, Pa., 1915-19; dir. music, Girard Coll., Phila., summers 1915-19; dir. music, Reading, Pa., 1919-26; state dir. music edn., Dept. Pub. Instrn., Harrisburg, Pa., 1926—; mil. leave of absence as capt. A.U.S. (music officer, Army Service Forces), 1943-44. Music Educators Nat. Conf., Eastern Music Educators Conf. (pres. 1929-31), N.E.A., Pa. State Edn. Assn., Pa. Music Educators Assn. (sec.-treas.), Nat. Assn. of State Dirs. Music Edn. (founder; pres. 1950-52), Civic Music Assn. of Harrisburg (hon. pres.), Harrisburg Symphony Soc., Phi Mu Alpha, Sinfonia. Lutheran. Mason (32°, Shriner). Clubs: Wednesday Music Club, Torch, West Shore Country. Contbr. to mags. Home: 219 N. 23d St., Camp Hill, Pa. Address: State Dept. of Public Instruction, Harrisburg, Pa. Died Mar. 2, 1957; buried East Stroudsburg, Pa.

ROSENGARTEN, Frederic, ret. pharm. co. exec.; b. Phila., 1877; grad. Princeton, 1899; student U. Jena, Germany, 2 yrs.; m. Marion Sims; children—Frederic, Mrs. Morris Stroud. Mem. bd. and dir. Merck & Co., Inc., Rahway, N.J., chmn. bd., 1927-50, ret. Home: Chestnut Hill, Phila. Office: Western Savings Fund Bldg., Phila. 7. Died Oct. 1955.*

ROSENKAMPFF, Arthur H., univ. prof.; b. New York, N.Y., Nov. 3, 1884; s. Emil and Alma (Schultz) R.; B.C.S., New York U. Sch. of Commerce, Accounting and Finance, 1910; m. Emma Ott, June 26, 1916. Bookkeeper, N.Y. Insulated Wire Co., 1905-12, office mgr., 1912-16; part time instr. in accounting, New York U., 1912-16, full time instr., 1916-20, asst. prof., 1920-22, prof. and chmn. dept. since 1922; dir., co-op. C.P.A. exams., coaching course since 1921. Mem. Am. Accounting Assn. (past pres.), N.Y. State Soc. C.P.A. (past dir.), Am. Inst. of Accountants, Beta Gamma Sigma, Alpha Kappa Psi, Delta Nu Epsilon, Sigma Eta Phi. Clubs: Lawyers, New York U. Faculty, Accountants of Am. (all New York). Author: Bookkeeping, Theory and Practice, 1918; A Detailed Audit, 1927. Co-author: (Madden and Wider) Principles of Accounting, 1918; Elementary Accounting Problems and Advanced Accounting Problems, 1938 (Wallace); Bookkeeping Principles and Practice, Introductory and Advanced, Bookkeeping and Accounting Courses, 1929; Theory of Accounts, 1940; Auditing Procedure, 1942. Home: 153 Washington St., Mt. Vernon, N.Y. Office: 100 Washington Sq. E., N.Y.C. 3. Died Nov. 1952.*

ROSENSTENGEL, W(illiam) E(verett), educator; b. Perry, Mo., Dec. 4, 1896; s. Joshua and Sarah Jane (Howald) R.; B.S., N.E. Mo. State Tchrs. Coll., 1923; student A.E.F. U., Beaune, France, summer 1919; A.M., U. Mo., 1927, Ph.D., 1931; m. Freda Brainerd Woodruff, Aug. 4, 1923; children—William Everett. Rural sch. tchr. near Perry, Mo., 1915-17; prin. high sch., Center, Mo., 1919-20; supt. sch., Maywood, Mo., 1920-24, LaGrange, Mo., 1924-25; Memphis, Mo., 1925-26; state high sch. insp., State Dept. Edn., Jefferson City, 1926-29; prof. edn. N.E. Mo. State Tchrs. Coll., 1929-32; supt. city schs. Columbia, Mo., 1932-41; prof. edn. U. N.C., 1941—; vis. prof. edn., U. of Mo., summers 1935, 36, 37, 38, 39. Served as sgt., 1st class, U.S. Army, 1917-19; A.E.F., 1918-19. Boy Scout lay worker, Columbia, Mo., 1932-41. Mem. Am. Assn. Sch. Adminstrs., Am. Assn. Univ. Profs., N.E.A., Nat. Congress Parents and Tchrs. (bd. mgrs.), Mo. Congress Parents and Tchrs. (life mem.), Mo. State Tchrs. Assn., N.C. Edn. Assn., Am. Legion, Vets. Fgn. Wars, Phi Delta Kappa. Democrat. Presbyn. Mason (K.T., Shriner). Vice pres. Mo. P.T. Assn., 1939-41, pres. dept. supts., Mo. Tchrs. Assn., 1939-40. Dist. rep. No. VII Phi Delta Kappa. Contbr. research articles in ednl. publs. Author: Criteria for Selecting Curricula For Public Jr. Colleges, 1931. Co-author: Public School Administration (with Calvin Grieder), 1954; School Finance (with Jefferson Eastmond, 1957. Worked out financial accounting records for Mo. sch.; conducted several sch. surveys in N.C. Kiwanian. Home: 128 North St., Chapel Hill, N.C. Died Apr. 23, 1958; buried Chapel Hill, N.C.

ROSENTHAL, Benjamin, chmn. of board The U.S. Playing Card Co.; b. East Brady, Pa., 1881; s. Arnold and Henrietta R.; ed. pub. schs. With The U.S. Playing Card Co., exec. v.p., dir., 1929, now chmn.; pres. Russell Playing Card Co.; v.p. Consol. Card Co.; mem. advisory Bd. and dir. Chem. Bank & Trust Co.; officer and dir. The Rosenthal Co. Treas. Montefiore Hosp. Mem. N.Y. State C. of C., Arbitration Soc., Nat. Assn. Mfrs., Mchts. Assn. Clubs: Harmonie, City Athletic, Hollywood Golf, Quaker Ridge Golf National Republican, Advertising, Economic. Address: 190 Ocean Av., Deal, N.J. Died Oct. 6, 1950; buried Mt. Sinai Cemetery, Phila.

ROSENTHAL, David S., business exec.; b. N.Y. City, July 10, 1900; s. Sol. D. and Lena (Roemer) R.; student Townsend Harris Hall, N.Y. City, 1913-17; m. Blanche A. Davis, Apr. 22, 1926; children—David E., Ann D. Salesman, Cohn-Hall Marx Co., N.Y. City, 1922-26, mgr. curtain fabrics dept., 1926-30; sales and merchandise mgr. United Merchants & Mfrs., Inc., 1930-35; organized Sudamtex S. A. Textil Sudamericana, Buenos Aires, Argentina, 1935, and served as gen. mgr., 1935-38, pres., 1938-1948; pres. United Internat. Corp. since 1946; pres. Sudamtex de Uruguay S.A.; dir. Sudamtek de Venezuela, S.A., affiliated activities in S. Am. since 1946; vp. and dir. United Merchants & Mfrs., Inc., since 1945; v.p. Cohn-Hall-Marx Co., Inc., N.Y. City, since 1949. Dir. Sudamtex de Venezuela, C.A., Telares de Cumana C.A. Served with U.S. Army, 1917-19. Clubs: Harmonie, Metropolis Country (New York); American, Belgrano, San Andres Golf, Sudeste Yacht (Buenos Aires); Cantegril Country, Punta Del Esie Yacht (Uruguay). Home: Moldes 1882 Office: Girardot 1560, Buenos Aires, Argentina. Died Aug. 17, 1954.

ROSENTHAL, Morris Sigmund, fgn. trade cons.; b. N.Y. City, Sept. 8, 1897; s. Max and Henrietta (Oppenheimer) R.; B.A., Columbia, 1917; m. Mary Elizabeth Ralph, Sept. 12, 1923; children—Alan, Ann; m. 2d, Helen Rose Cohen, Mar. 29, 1936; children—Jon, David. Mgr. export dept., Stein, Hall & Co., Inc., 1917-26, asst. sec., 1926-34, v.p. and dir., 1934-48, pres., 1948-53; lectr. on fgn. trade, Columbia, 1925-41, 1944-48, Coll. City N.Y., 1929-36; formerly dir. Hall Trading Corp., Stein-Hall Ltd., U.S. Comml. Corp. Trustee U.S. Council Internat. C. of C. (chmn. com. internat. comml. arbitration, chmn. fgn. trade terms com.); vice chmn. commn. on trade and contracts, commn. on internat. comml. arbitration, Internat. C. of C.; hon. dir., past pres. American-Indonesian C. of C.; mem. import adv. com., Dept. of Commerce, 1945—; pres. Nat. Council of Am. Importers, Inc., 1948-51, sr. councillor 1951-55, 57—, pres., 1955-57. Trustee William Alanson White Inst. of Psychiatry, N.Y. Served as student cadet, U.S. Naval Aviation, World War I; asst. dir. Bd. Econ. Warfare in charge Office of Imports, 1941-43. Decorated Officer de l'Ordre du Merite Comml. (French Republic). Award of National Am. Importers, 1953. Mem. Am. Arbitration Assn. (dir. mem. exec. com., mem. adv. editorial bd.), Nat. Planning Assn., Nat. Consumers League (dir., chmn. bd.), Ams. Democratic Action (nat. bd., exec. vice chmn. nat. business men's council), Beta Gamma Sigma. Clubs: Chemists (N.Y. City); Cosmos (Washington). Author: Technical Procedure in Exporting and Importing, 1922; Techniques of International Trade, 1950; Where Does the Money Come From, 1950. Contbr. articles on internat. trade to jours. Address: 1185 Park Av., N.Y.C. 28. Died Feb. 13, 1958.

ROSEWATER, Stanley Meinrath, lawyer; b. Omaha, June 24, 1885; s. Andrew and Frances (Meinrath) R.; B.S., U. Mich., 1906, LL.B., 1908; m. Barbara McAlvay, Oct. 19, 1912; children—Stanley McAlvay (dec. Jan. 1946), Barbara (Mrs. William W. Brady). Admitted to Neb. bar, 19—; practiced, Omaha, 1908-49; mem. Rosewater, Mecham, Stoehr & Mecham, 1946-49. Mem. Omaha C. of C. (dir., mem. exec. com., 1915), Am. Counsel Assn. (dir., 1931-32), Neb. State, Am., Omaha bar assns., Internat. Assn. Ins. Counsel, Mich. Law Sch. Alumni Assn. (pres., 1939-49). Mason (32°). Club: Omaha. Author legal, ins. articles. Home: 105 Happy Hollow Blvd. Office: City Nat. Bank Bldg., Omaha 2. Died Jan. 27, 1951.

ROSIER, Joseph (rōz-ēr'), educator, ex-senator; b. Wilsonburg, W.Va., Jan. 24, 1870; s. John Wesley and Rebecca (Miller) R.; B.Pd., Salem (W.Va.) Coll., 1895, A.M., 1915; LL.D., Marshall Coll., 1933; m. Iva Randolph, Aug. 14, 1895; children—Nellie (Mrs. Hugh Simpson), Robert, Mary Josephine (Mrs. Herndon Smith). Tchr. village sch., 1890; prin. pub. schs., Salem, 1891-92; supt. schs., Harrison County, W.Va., 1893, 94; mem. faculty, Salem Coll., 1894-96; tchr. State Normal Sch., Glenville, 1896-97; with State Normal Sch., Fairmont, 1897-1900; supt. schs., Fairmont, 1900-15; pres. State Tchrs. Coll., Fairmont, 1915-43. Apptd. mem. U.S. Senate, 1941. Resumed presidency at Fairmont, 1943, pres. emeritus, 1945—. Elected to legislature, W. Va., 1946. Appt. mem. State Bd. Edn., 1947. County food adminstr., World War. Con. on edn., Works Progress Adminstrn. Life mem. N.E.A. (pres. 1932-33), Am. Assn. Teachers Colls., Nat. Soc. for Study of Edn. Democrat. Methodist. K.P.; mem. A.O.U.W. Rotarian. Lectr. before tchrs. insts. Home: 730 Benoni Av., Fairmont, W.Va. Died Oct. 7, 1951; buried I.O.O.F. Cemetery, Salem, W.Va.

ROSS, Albert Randolph (raws), architect; b. Westfield, Mass., Oct. 26, 1869, s. John Wesley and Clara Louise (Scarlett) R.; office of McKim, Mead & White, N.Y.C., 1890-97, studied architecture in Greece, Italy, France; m. Susan Chadwick Husted, Oct. 30, 1901 (dec. 1931); m. 2d, Theadores Winlack, 1933. Architect, Carnegie Library, Washington; Union County Ct. House, Elizabeth, N.J.; pub. libraries, Columbus, O., Denver; N.Y. State Normal Coll.; Central Police Sta., County Ct. House, Milw.; many other pub. bldgs. and monuments. Address: Boothbay Harbor, Me.; and 4858 Pine Tree Dr., Miami Beach 40, Fla. Deceased.

ROSS, Austin C., mfg. exec.; b. Ont., Can., July 25, 1893; s. Roderick and Mary (Climie) R.; B.Sc., U. Toronto, 1915; m. Anna M. Rice, Nov. 17, 1917; children—Alexander R., Robert C. Purchasing agt. Rolls-Royce of Am., Inc., Springfield, Mass., 1919-30, v.p., 1930-31; asst. gen. purchasing agt. Worthington Corp., Harrison, 1932-35, asst. works mgr., 1935-40, works mgr., Buffalo, 1940-50, v.p. Mem. Buffalo C. of C., Profl. Engrs. Assn. Episcopalian (vestryman). Mason. Clubs: Buffalo, Buffalo Athletic. Home: 824 Oakland Av., East Aurora, N.Y. Office: Roberts Av., Buffalo. Died Jan. 28, 1960.

ROSS, Charles Griffith, press secretary; b. Independence, Mo., Nov. 9, 1885; s. James Bruce and Ella (Thomas) R.; A.B., U. of Mo., 1905, LL.D., 1936; LL.D., George Washington U., 1935; m. Florence Griffin, Aug. 20, 1913; children—John Bruce, Walter Williams. With Columbia (Mo.) Herald, 1904-06, Victor (Colo.) Record, 1906, St. Louis Post-Dispatch, 1906-07, St. Louis Republic, 1907-08; mem. faculty Sch. of Journalism, U. of Mo., 1908-18; on sabbatical leave, 1916-17, and served as sub-editor Melbourne (Australia) Herald; chief Washington corr. St. Louis Post-Dispatch, 1918-34; editor of editorial page, St. Louis Post-Dispatch, 1934-39, contributing editor, 1939-45. Appointed secretary to President Truman, in charge press relations, May 15, 1945. Member Phi Beta Kappa, Sigma Chi, Sigma Delta Chi (honorary nat. pres. 1935). Clubs: Gridiron (pres. 1933), Overseas Writers (chmn. 1927), Nat. Press (Washington). Author: The Writing of News, 1911. Awarded Pulitzer prize for newspaper correspondence, 1932, awarded medal for work in journalism, U. of Mo., 1933. Home: 117 Kennedy Drive, Chevy Chase, Md. Office: The White House, Washington. Died Dec. 5, 1950; buried Washington.

ROSS, Frederick Jeffery, advertising; b. Toronto, Can., Jan. 30, 1879; s. William Wilson and Kate (McLeod) R.; ed. pub. schs. of Can. and Jarvis St. Collegiate, Toronto; m. Marion Clark, 1913 (now dec.); 1 dau., Elizabeth (Mrs. John S. Crocker); m. 2d, Gladys Kennedy, 1916; children—Patricia Kennedy, Muriel Nasmith, McLeod Adams, Lawrence Frederick James. Came to U.S., 1898, naturalized, 1903. Clk. Western Assurance Co., Toronto, 1894-98; salesman J. E. Bates, N.Y., 1898-1902; mgr. Westchester Hat Mfg. Co., 1902-04; advertising writer Frank Presbrey Co., 1904-08; v.p. Blackman-Ross Co., 1908-20; pres. F. J. Ross Co., 1920-30; chmn. bd. Fuller and Smith and Ross, Inc., 1930-38; retired. Served on boards of St. Johns Hospital, Y.M.C.A., Charity Organization Society; formerly pres. Yonkers Council Boy Scouts America, N.Y. Tuberculosis and Health Assn.; chmn. Yonkers Community Chest. Republican. Clubs: Canadian (New York); Granite, Chattan (Toronto). Home: 26 Old Forest Hill Rd., Toronto, Canada. Died Dec. 1957.

ROSS, Harold Wallace, mag. editor; b. Aspen, Colo., Nov. 6, 1892; s. George and Ida (Martin) R.; educated high school, Salt Lake City, Utah; m. 3d, Ariane Allen, 1940. Reporter for the Salt Lake City Tribune, 1906, Marysville (Calif.) Appeal, 1910, Sacramento (Calif.) Union, 1911, Panama (Republic) Star and Herald, 1912, New Orleans Item, Atlanta Journal, San Francisco Call, 1915-17; Butterick Pub. Co., 1919-21; editor American Legion Weekly, 1921-23, Judge, 1924, The New Yorker since 1925. Served with Railway Engineer Corps, U.S. Army; one of editors Stars and Stripes, official service newspapers, 1917-19. Home: Wire Mill Road, Stamford, Conn. Office: 25 W. 43d St., N.Y.C. Died Dec. 6, 1951.

ROSS, John Jacob, clergyman; b. Lochaber, Quebec, Can., June 1871; s. Jacob and Julia (Pelette) R.; ed. pub. and high schs., Can., and under tutelage of Lord Cecil; gen. course, Woodstock Bapt. Coll.; select course, McMaster U.; studied Bible archaeology, British Mus., in Bible lands, and 3 summer readings and lecture courses, U. of Chgo.; D.D., Northern Bapt. Theol. Sem., Chgo., 1918; m. Georgina May Graham, May 1902. Ordained Bapt. ministry, 1898; pastor successively, Chatham, London (Ont.), Toronto, Hamilton, 2d Ch., Chgo. now pastor 1st Ch., Vancouver, B.C. Bible teacher; lecturer on bible lands; was made defendant in libel case, at Hamilton, Ont., 1912, brought by late "Pastor" Charles T. Russell, resulting in Russell being found guilty of charges made against him. Lectured on new Testament Introduction and Analysis at Northern Bapt. Theol. Sem., Chgo., 4 yrs. Author of various books on religious subjects. Address: First Baptist Church, Vancouver, B.C. Died Oct. 10, 1935.

ROSS, Lester J., business exec.; b. Avon, Ill., Aug. 8, 1890; s. Joseph H. and Mary L. (Woods) R.; student Lombard Coll., Galesburg, Ill., 1908, 09, 10; m. Alice Cropper, May 7, 1913; children—Virginia M. (Mrs. Albert H. Way), Jean Ann. Adv. dept. Waterloo (Ia.) Times-Tribune, 1910-12; with Dart Mfg. Co., Waterloo, Iowa, 1912; The Torrington (Conn.) Co. since 1913, pres. since 1946, dir. since 1942; dir. First Federal Savings and Loan Assn., Turner & Seymour Mfg. Co., Torrington Nat. Bank & Trust Co., Scovill Mfg. Co. Dir. Charlotte Hungerford Hospital. Dir. Naugatuck Valley Indsl. Council, Inc. Home: Old South Rd., Litchfield, Conn. Office: 59 Field St., Torrington, Conn. Died Nov. 14, 1953.

ROSS, Letitia Roano Dowdell (Mrs. Bennett Battle Ross); b. Chambers Co., Ala.; d. William Crawford and Elizabeth Caroline (Thomas) Dowdell; grad. Lucy Cobb Inst., Athens, Ga.; student U. of Ga., Ala. Poly. Inst., Auburn, 1890-91, U. of Berlin, 1901; m. Prof. Bennett Battle Ross, Aug. 18, 1897. Formerly teacher in State Normal Coll., Jacksonville, Ala., Martin Female Coll., Pulaski, Tenn., North Tex. Female Coll., Sherman. Pres. Ala. Federation Women's Clubs, 1900; pres. Ala. Div., U.D.C., 1909-11, and as such managed semi-centennial celebration of inauguration of Confed. Govt. at Montgomery in 1861; participated in celebration of 75th anniversary of inauguration of Jefferson Davis, 1936; honorary life president of Ala. U.D.C., 1931—; 1st v.p. gen. U.D.C. (hon. pres., 1939—; mem. edn. com. chmn. memorials, historic places and events com., Ala.); former dir. from Ala. of Jefferson Davis Highway; mem. com. of 100, Woman's Titanic Memorial, 1913. V.p. Woman's Foreign Missionary Soc. of Ala. Conf. M.E. Ch., S., 1904-06 (mem. com. Spiritual Life Group). Mem. Com. on Internat. Relations and Com. on Scholarships and Com. of Approved Schools for Alabama of D.A.R. Home: Auburn, Ala. Died Dec. 18, 1952.

ROSS, Lewis T., army officer (ret.); b. D.C., March 16, 1896; B.S., U.S. Mil. Acad., 1918; grad. Engr. Sch., civil engr. course and basic course, 1921; m. Marian E. Kutz, 1920; children—Marian, Tenney K., Katharine R. Commd. 2d lt., U.S. Army, 1918, and advanced through grades to brig. gen., 1944; ret. 1946; civil engr. with Sverdrup & Parcel, St. Louis, 1946. Home: 419 Belleview Av., Webster Groves 19. Office: 1118 Syndicate Trust Co., St. Louis 1. Died Sept. 3, 1958; buried Arlington Nat. Cemetery.

ROSS, Philip James, lawyer; b. Vergennes, Vt., Jan. 18, 1875; s. Frank A. and Anna (Tucker) R.; prep. edn., Vt. Episcopal Inst., Burlington; A.B., U. of Vt., 1895; LL.B., New York Law Sch., 1900; m. Mrs. Adah Price Vernam, June 10, 1915 (died 1936); m. 2d, Mrs. Gertrude B. Gardner, 1936. Admitted to N.Y. bar, 1900, and began practice at N.Y. City; formerly mem. Ross, Dodge & Miller; dir. and gen. counsel Manhattan Life Ins. Co.; trustee and counsel Manhattan Savings Bank. Trustee Univ. of Vt., 1919-23. Mem. Am. N.Y. State and Westchester County bar assns., Assn. Bar City N.Y., Assn. Life Ins. Counsel, Vt. Soc., N.E. Soc. of N.Y., N.Y. Alumni Assn. U. of Vt. (pres. 1929), Sigma Phi (nat. sec. 1911-29). Republican. Episcopalian. Mason. Club: University. Home: 1 Sage Terrace, Scarsdale, N.Y. Address: 120 W. 57 St., N.Y.C. 19. Died Sept. 25, 1952.

ROSSBACH, Edgar Hilary, lawyer; b. Newark, N.J., Aug. 20, 1903; s. Adam J. and Rhoda (Krais) R.; student Colgate U., 1922-25, South Jersey Law Sch., Camden, N.J., 1930-32; m. Ann J. O'Connell, Aug. 31, 1936; 1 dau., Joanne Eileen. Admitted to N.J. bar, 1935, and since practiced in Newark; junior mem. firm Rossbach and Crummy, 1935-36; partner firm Rossbach and Rossbach, since 1936; asst. U.S. attorney, 1942-45, U.S. attorney, 1945-48. Vice chairman of the Democratic County Committee, Morris County, N.J., 1940-42; mem. Morris County election bd., 1940-42. Mem. Am., Fed., N.J. State, Essex County bar assns., Catholic Lawyers Guild, Holy Name Soc., Pi Kappa Alpha. K.C., Moose. Home: 157 S. Harrison St., East Orange, N.J. Died Nov. 11, 1952.*

ROSSBY, Carl-Gustaf Arvid (rŏs'bĭ), meteorologist; b. Stockholm, Sweden, Dec. 28, 1898; s. Arvid and Alma Charlotta (Marelius) R.; studied U. of Stockholm, 1917-18, 1922-25; student Geophysical Inst., Bergen, Norway, 1918-19, U. of Leipzig, 1920; hon. D.Sc., Kenyon Coll., 1939; m. Harriet Marshall Alexander, Sept. 2, 1929; children—Stig Arvid, Hans Thomas, Carin. Came to U.S., as fellow Swedish-Am. Found., 1926. Research asso. in meteorology Daniel Guggenheim Fund for Promotion of Aeronautics, and chmn. com. on aero meteorology, 1927-28; prof. meteorology Mass. Inst. Tech., 1931-39; research asso. Woods Hole Oceanographic Inst. since 1931; asst. chief for research and edn. U.S. Weather Bureau, 1931-41; distinguished service prof. meteorology U. of Chicago since 1943, on leave to serve as prof. meteorology U. of Stockholm, 1947-48. Expert cons. to Office of Sec. of War, and cons. on weather problems to comdg. gen. of A.A.F., during World War II. Hon. fellow Royal Meteorol. Soc., London; mem. Inst. Aero. Sciences, Am. Meteorol. Soc. (pres. 1944-45), Am. Philos. Soc., Nat. Acad. Sciences, Det Noske Videnokaps-Akademi (Oslo). Received (with H. C. Willett) the Sylvanus Albert Reed award from Inst. Aero. Scis., 1934; received the Robert Losey award, 1947. Club: Quadrangle (Chicago). Organizer model aero-weather service for Guggenheim Fund, 1928. Contbr. articles to sci. jours. in U.S. and abroad. Home: Stockholm, Sweden. Died Aug. 19, 1957.

ROSSETTER, George W. (rŏs-ĕ-tẽr), C.P.A.; s. George W., Sr., and Mary A. (Flood) R.; m. Marjorie Aylesworth Mihills; children—George M., William A., Thomas B. Pres. Rossetter Industries, Inc., Peoria, Ill.; chmn. bd. Rossetter Motor Co., Dealers Equipment Co., both Peoria, Ill. Former pres. Chgo. Assn. of Commerce; former mem. price adjustment sect. bd., Chgo. Ordnance District War Dept.; mem. Northwestern U. Associates. Served as machine gun officer, with A.E.F., World War I. Lt. Colonel Illinois Reserves Militia, World War II. Mem. Illinois and Minnesota socs. C.P.A.'s, Am. Instn. Accountants, S.A.R., Am. Legion, Beta Alpha Psi, Beta Gamma Sigma. Republican. Episcopalian. Clubs: Chicago, Economic (ex-pres.), Knollwood (ex-pres.) Forty, Commercial, Mid-way, Chicago Farmers (ex-pres.); Peoria (Ill.) Country; Creve Coeur (Peoria), Illinois Seniors Golf Assn. (past pres.). Home: Wadsworth, Ill. Office: 621 Franklin St., Peoria, Ill. Died Sept. **1959.**

ROSTOVTZEFF, Michael Ivanovich (rŏs-tŏv'-tsĕf), prof. history; b. Kieff, Russia, Nov. 10, 1870; s. John J. and Maria I. (Monachova) R.; grad. Classical Gymnasium, Kieff, 1888; student U. Kieff and U. Petersburg, 1888-92; Ph.D., U. Petersburg, 1903; studied in the classical lands; LL.D., U. Leipzig, Oxford U., Cambridge U., U. Wis., Harvard U. Athens, U. Chgo.; m. Sophie M. Kulczycki, May 8, 1901. Began teaching in Russia, 1898; prof. ancient history, U. Wis., 1920-25, ancient history and archeology, Yale, 1925-44, prof. emeritus, 1944—. Dir. Yale Expedition at Dura-Europos (Euphrates, Syria), 1928-38. Pres. Am. Hist. Assn.; mem. Am. Philos. Soc., Am. Philol. Assn., Archeol. Inst. Am., Am. Acad. Arts and Scis., Conn. Acad., hon. mem. Mass. Hist. Soc., Am. Numis. Soc.; mem. or corr. mem. numerous European acads. and socs. Mem. Greek Orthodox Ch. Author: A Large Estate in Egypt in the Third Century, B.C., 1922; Iranians and Greeks in South Russia, 1922; Social and Economic History of the Roman Empire, 1926; A History of the Ancient World (2 volumes), 1926-27; Inlaid Bronzes of the Han Period, 1927; Mystic Italy, 1928; Animal Style in South Russia and China, 1929; Caravan Cities, 1932; Out of the Past of Greece and Rome, 1932; Dura and the Problem of Parthian Art, 1935; Dura-Europos and Its Art, 1938; Social and Economic History of the Hellenistic World (3 vols.), 1941; also numerous books and articles in foreign langs. Home: 470 Whitney Av., New Haven, Conn. Died Oct. 20, 1952; buried Grove St. Cemetery, New Haven, Conn.

ROTH, Ben, cartoonist; b. Seletyn, Austria, Oct. 28, 1909; s. Rubin and Mollie (Baer) R.; came to U.S., 1922, naturalized, 1927; student Art Students League, N.Y.C., 1929-40; m. Ruth E. Siff, Aug. 8, 1937; children—Alan D. and Peter M. (twins). Cartoonist nat. mags. and newspapers, 1934—; owner Ben Roth Agy., syndicating Am. cartoons in fgn. countries, Scarsdale, N.Y., 1945—. Served with AUS, 1944-45; art dir. psychol. warfare br., Australia. Recipient Prefect Cup, Internat. Cartoon Exhbn., Bordighera, Italy, 1958. Mem. Nat. Cartoonists Soc. (treas. 1957—), Art Students League (life). Author: (annual) Best Cartoons From Abroad (with Lawrence Lariar). Address: 8 Longview Dr., Scarsdale, N.Y. Died Jan. 22, 1960.

ROTHENBERG, Morris, judge; b. Dorpat, Esthonia, June 15, 1884; s. Joel and Anna R.; came with parents to U.S., 1893; LL.B., N.Y.U., 1905; m. Anna Shomer, of New York, Dec. 19, 1909; children—Nathaniel, Ruth; m. 2d, Dr. Mona Williams, July 30, 1947. Began law practice at N.Y. City, 1905; apptd. by Mayor LaGuardia a city magistrate, July 19, 1937 for full term; apptd. for 10 yr. term in Magistrate's Ct. by Mayor William O'Dwyer, July 1947. Mem. Federal Price Fixing Commn. and Jewish Welfare Bd. for Army and Navy, World War. Former pres. Zionist Orgn. Am. (mem. actions com.); co-chmn. council Jewish Agency for Palestine (mem. the Executive); co-chmn. United Jewish Appeal; nat. chmn. United Palestine Appeal; pres. Jewish Nat. Fund; chmn. bd. dirs. Palestine Found. Fund; mem. exec. com. Joint Distbn. Com. Vice pres. Weizman Inst.; mem. bd. trustees Am. Com. of the Hebrew U. Mem. N.Y. County Lawyers Assn. Ind. Democrat. Home: 110 W. 55th St., N.Y. City. Died Sept. 17, 1950; buried Westchester Hills, Hastings-on-Hudson, N.Y.

ROTHSCHILD, Louis F(rank), business exec.; b. N.Y. City, Sept. 4, 1869; s. Frank and Amanda (Blum) R.; B.S., Coll. City N.Y., 1889; Ph.B., Columbia, 1890, LL.B., 1891; married to Cora Guggenheim, January 3, 1899 (deceased, 1956). Law practice, 1891-93; manufacturing business,

1893-1902; partner L.F. Rothschild & Co., bankers, N.Y. City, since 1902. Club: Westchester Country (Rye, N.Y.). Home: Carlton House, N.Y.C., Office: 120 Broadway, N.Y.C. Died June 15, 1957; buried Salem Field Cemetery, Bklyn.

ROUAULT, Georges (rwō), artist, painter; b. Paris, France, Mar. 27, 1871; s. Alexander and Marie-Louise (Champdavoine) R.; student Ecole des Beaux Arts, Atelier Gustave Moreau; m. Marthe LeSidaner, 1908; children—Genevieve, Isabelle, Michel, Agnes. Painter, engraver, writer; curator Musée Gustave Moreau, 1908—. Paintings have been exhibited in U.S.; altra-modern school. Roman Catholic. Author: Passion, Cirque de l'Etoile Filante, 1939; Stella Vespertina, 1947; Miserere. Address: Musée Gustave Moreau, 14 rue LaRochesfoucauld, Paris (IX°), France. Died Feb. 14, 1958.

ROUSH, Gar A. (roush), mineral economist; b. Harrisburg (now Gas City), Ind., Oct. 21, 1883; s. Isaac N. and Clementine H. (McCarty) R.; A.B., Ind. U., 1905; M.S., U. Wis., 1910; m. Lillian Belle Coleman, July 16, 1911. Asst. prof. metallurgy, 1912-20, asso. prof., 1920-26, Lehigh U.; acting prof. metallurgy, Mont. Sch. Mines, 1926-27; spl. adviser Mus. Peaceful Arts, N.Y., 1927-30; editor, 1913-43, Mineral Industry, ann. devoted to world mineral interests; mineral technologist, U.S. Bur. of Mines, 1943-46; became metals engr., Strategic and Critical Materials Div., bur. Fed. Supply (formerly U.S. Treasury Dept.) 1946, with planning br. procurement div., Gen. Service Adminstrn. until 1955, ret. 1955. Appointed supr. tng. of inspection div. Ordnance Dept., AUS, 1918; commd. capt. Ordnance Dept., 1918, and appointed head of ednl. br., inspection div., and later chief of tests, metall. br.; hon. discharged, 1919, commd. maj., Staff Specialist Reserve, U.S. Army, 1924, and for several years served as spl. lectr. on strategic mineral supplies, Army Industrial Coll.; later assigned to Commodities Div., Planning Branch Office of Asst. Sec. of War; mem. Inactive Reserve, 1941—. Mem. Electrochem. Soc. (asst. sec. 1912-18), Am. Inst. Mining and Metall. Engrs. (mng. editor 1917), Soc. of Am. Mil. Engrs. (Toulmin medalist, 1939). Presbyn. Contbr. numerous articles on electrochem. and metall. and mineral econs. in the tech. press, various standard encyclos. and other works of reference. Author of the sect. on Mineral Industries in rev. edit. Van Hise's Conservation of Natural Resources; sect. on Electrochemistry and Electrometallurgy in 6th edit. and on Electrochemistry in 7th edit. Standard Handbook for Electrical Engineers; Strategic Mineral Supplies; articles on strategic mineral supplies in foreign countries in Mil. Engr. Home: 4416 Seventeenth St. North, Arlington, Va. Address: Planning Branch, Procurement Div., General Service Administration, Washington 25. Died Aug. 17, 1955.

ROUTZOHN, Harry Nelson, ex-congressman; b. Dayton, O., Nov. 4, 1881; student pub. schs.; LL.B (hon.), U. Dayton; wife Leona; children—Norman, Mrs. Jesse MacMillan, Mrs. Ronald Harsha; 1 stepson, C. Palmer Boyle. Asst. county prosecutor, 1906-09; probate judge, 1917-29; asst. U.S. dist. atty., 1930-32; mem. 76th Congress, 3d Dist. Ohio; now chief legal officer Dept. Labor. Home: Dayton, O. Office: Dept. Labor, Washington 25. Died Apr. 14, 1953.

ROVENSKY, Joseph Charles, banker; b. Pittsburgh, Pa., June 15, 1886; s. John and Agnes (Benes) R.; Ph.G., U. of Pittsburgh, 1909; hon. LL.D., Washington and Jefferson Coll.; m. Josephine Walthour, Sept. 20, 1912. Vice-pres. Chase Nat. Bank, 1928-45; dir. The Chase Bank; chmn. Patino Mines & Enterprises Consol., Inc., Luria Steel & Trading Corp.; v.chmn. Morris Plan Corp.; dir. N.Y. Hanseatic Corp., Foundation Co., North Am. Philips Co., Inc., Am. & Fgn. Power Co., Inc., Indsl. Bank of Commerce, Drake-Am. Co., Bankers Security Life Ins. Soc., Lone Star Cement Corp. (all of N.Y.), Massey Concrete Products Co., Chicago, Anglo-Huronian, Ltd., Toronto; pres. Patican Co., Toronto; asst., coordinator Inter-Am. Affairs, Washington, 1941-43. Financial expert to Am. Mems. Internat. Conf., Basle, 1931; mem. Am. Com. German Credit Agreement, Berlin, 1931-39; dir. Foreign Trade Council; pres. Bankers Assn. for Foreign Trade, 1940-41; arbitrator Am. Arbitration Association. Decorated Knight Comdr. of the Crown (Italy); Order of Al Merito (Ecuador); Fgn. Service Medal; Order of the Phoenix (Greece). Life trustee Washington and Jefferson Coll. Chmn. and dir. Huguenot Y.M.C.A., New Rochelle, N.Y.; v.p. and dir. New Rochelle Hospital. Member Phi Delta Chi. Lutheran (trustee Holy Trinity Lutheran Church, New Rochelle, N.Y.). Mason. Clubs: Bankers, Recess (New York); Country (Greensburg, Pa.); Country (Pelham, N.Y.); the Everglades, Bath and Tennis (Palm Beach, Fla.). Author of articles on foreign trade and finance. Home: Witherbee Court, Pelham Manor, N.Y. Office: 103 Park Av., N.Y.C. 17. Died Dec. 17, 1952.

ROWE, Walter Ellsworth, civil engr.; b. Bristol, Ind., Sept. 18, 1875; s. Perry and Lydia Louisa (Weed) R.; student U. of Ore., 1891-92; B.S. in C.E., U. of Neb., 1896; post-grad. work, U. of Chicago, summers, 1899, 1900; m. Adaline Meech Hume, Aug. 27, 1903; children—Gilbert Hume, Gertrude Hume, Helen Hume, Ann Ellsworth (dec.). County supt. schs., Greeley County, Neb., 1897-98; prof. mathematics and comdt. Cadets, Trinity Hall Sch., Louisville, Ky., 1898; supt. schs., White Sulphur Springs, Mont., 1898-1901; prof. science, high schs., Butte, Mont., 1902-03; prin. high sch., Anaconda, Mont., 1903-04; prof. mathematics and physics, U. of N.M., 1904-05; prof. civ. engring., Okla. Agrl. and Mech. Coll., 1905-06; dean Coll. Civ. Engring., U. of Ky., 1906-17; dean of engring., U. of S.C., 1917-18; head prof. civil engring., Drexel Inst., Phila., 1918-19; exec. evening sch. Drexel Inst., 1919-20; engr., and mgr. John E. Hand & Sons Co., New Orleans and Baltimore, 1920-22; dean Sch. of Engring. and dir. engring. expt. sta., U. of S.C., 1922; now dean emeritus; partner Rowe & Chapman, design & cons. engrs., 1950—; consulting engineer S.C. Pub. Service Authority; mem. Archtl. Exam. Bd. for S.C. Organizer, and pres. Ky. Civ. and Sanitary Engring. Assn., 1916-17; mem. Am. Soc. C.E., Am. Assn. Engrs., Soc. Promotion Engring. Edn., Le Conte Scientific Soc. (pres.), Tau Beta Pi. Promoter state highway laws for Ky.; chief of Road Material Survey for S.C. Appointed May 16, 1931, by S.C. Supreme Court, a member of Bd. of Rehabilitation Engrs. for Columbia St. Ry. System. Episcopalian. Home: Williston, S.C. Died Sept. 5, 1952; buried Williston, S.C.

ROWELL, James G(arfield) (rou-ll); b. Gallitan, Mo., Nov. 16, 1883; s. Loren Godfrey and Jane (Ballinger) R.; LL.B., Kan. City Sch. of Law, 1905; C.S.B., Mass. Metaphysical Coll., 1934; m. Caroline Stoner, Sept. 2, 1911. Entered pub. practice of Christian Science, Oct. 1, 1913; mem., Christian Sci. Bd. of Lectureship, 1927-43; mem. bd. of trustees, Christian Sci. Pub. Soc., Boston, Mass., since June 14, 1943. Home: 114 Fenway, Boston. Office: 1 Norway St., Boston 15. Died July 16, 1956.

ROWELL, Wilfrid Asa, clergyman; b. Chichester, N.H., Mar. 5, 1877; s. Rev. John A. and Alma (Holmes) R.; grad. Beloit Coll. Acad., 1895; B.A., Beloit Coll., 1899; B.D., Yale Div. Sch., 1906; D.D., Beloit Coll., 1926, Olivet Coll., 1926; married Teresina Peck, June 5, 1907 (deceased 1945); 1 dau., Teresina (Mrs. Joseph D. Havens). Instr. Greek and English, high sch., Janesville, Wis., 1899-1900; instr. English, Beloit Coll., 1901-03; ordained ministry Congl. Ch., 1906; asst. pastor United Ch., New Haven, Conn., 1904-07; pastor 1st Ch., Beloit, 1907-18, Union Ch., Hinsdale, Ill., 1918-42; chaplain Beloit (Wis.) Coll., 1942-46; acting dean of the chapel, 1948-49; asso. pastor 2d Congl. Ch., Beloit, since 1950. Sec. bd. dirs., mem. exec. com. Chgo. Theol. Sem.; trustee Beloit Coll.; exec. com. Am. Missionary Assn., 1916-23; exec. com. Nat. Council Congl. and Christian Chs., 1942-48. Mem. Phi Beta Kappa, Sigma Chi, Delta Sigma Rho. Clubs: University, Apollos, Emerson, Faculty and Alumni of Beloit, Rotary. Awarded Beloit Distinguished Service Citation, 1946. Author: Patriotism and the Christian Life, 1918; Practical Benefits of Religion; The Story of the Old Mission. Home: 918 Chapin St., Beloit, Wis. Died Nov. 26, 1956; buried Oaklawn Cemetery, Beloit, Wis.

ROWLAND, Harry T., aviation exec.; b. Henderson, N.C., May 11, 1899; s. Thomas V. and Hattie (Parham) R.; ed. N.C. State Coll., 1915-18, U.S. Mil. Acad., 1919-23; grad. Brooks and Kelly Fields, 1924; m. Marjorie Crume; children—Harry M., Barbara, Tatem. Instr., Kelly Field, also Brooks Field; with combat squadron as engr. officer and test pilot in Army Air Corps overhaul and repair depots; resigned from service, 1931; comml. airline pilot; aviation advisor to Generalissimo Chiang Kai-shek, Chinese govt., 3 yrs.; asso. with Glenn L. Martin Co., Baltimore, from 1935, test pilot. export rep. travelling in various fgn. countries, sales mgr., 1939, v.p. in charge of sales, 1942, became dir., exec. v.p. and gen. mgr., 1945; pres. and dir. The Glenn L. Martin-Nebraska Co.; pres., dir. Skyline Corp., Wichita, Kan.; pres. Aircraft Armaments, Inc., Balt. 15; pres., gen. mgr. Hayes Aircraft Corp., Birmingham, Ala. Clubs: Advertising; Baltimore Country Club; Downtown (Birmingham). Home: 301 Windsor Dr., Birmingham 9, Ala. Office: Hayes Aircraft Corp., P.O. Box 2287, Birmingham. Died Aug. 28, 1955.

ROWLAND, James Marshall Hanna, obstetrician; b. Liberty Grove, Cecil County, Md., Feb. 14, 1867; s. William Hopkins and Sarah Margery (Hanna) R.; prep. edn., West Nottingham Acad., Colora, Md.; M.D., Balt. Med. Coll., 1892; m. Mary Virginia Zollikofer, Dec. 28, 1898; children—Mary Z., William M., Marjorie J. Began practice at Balt., 1892; prof. obstetrics, Balt. Med. Coll., 1900-13; prof. obstetrics, U. of Md., 1920-37, dean Sch. of Medicine, 1916-39; med. dir., sec. Balt. Life Ins. Co. Mem. bd. dirs. Md. Gen. Hosp. Fellow Am. Coll. Surgeons; mem. A.M.A., Med. and Chirurg. Soc. of Md. (ex-pres.), Southern Med. Assn., Balt. City Med. Soc., Balt. County Med. Soc. Democrat. Methodist. Clubs: University, Gibson Island. Home: 1118 St. Paul St. Office: Baltimore Life Ins. Co., Balt. Died July 24, 1954; buried West Nottingham, Colora, Md.

ROWLEY, Francis Harold (rou'lē), humanitarian; b. Hilton, N.Y., July 25, 1854; s. John R. (M.D.) and Mary Jane (Smith) R.; A.B., U. of Rochester, 1875; B.D., Rochester Theol. Sem., 1878 (D.D., U. of Rochester, 1897); m. Ida A. Babcock, June 11, 1878 (dec. 1940); children—John, Charles, Alice L., Henry Esmond. Minister, Titusville, Pa., 1879-84, N. Adams, Mass., 1884-92, Oak Park, Ill., 1892-96, Fall River, Mass., 1896-1900, First Baptist Ch., Boston, 1900-10; preacher at Univ. of Chicago and Harvard; pres. Mass. Soc. for Prevention of Cruelty to Animals; president Am. Humane Edn. Society, 1910-45, chairman of the board since 1945; chmn, animal protection com., Mass. Com. on Pub. Safety; v.p. Boston Children's Friend Soc.; v.p. and trustee New Eng. Bapt. Hosp., Mass. Bible Soc.; councillor Willard Settlement; mem. advisory council Yenching U., China; mem. alumni com. U. of Rochester. Member Alpha Delta Phi, Phi Beta Kappa. Author: The Humane Idea; The Horses of Homer; The Relation of the Home to Character Formation; The Need of the Hour; and numerous pamphlets and addresses on humane subjects. Home: 20 Dean Road, Brookline, Mass. Office: 180 Longwood Av., Boston. Died Feb. 14, 1952.

ROWLEY, Frank S., prof. of law; b. Chicago, Ill., Dec. 16, 1896; s. John Arthur and Florence Mary (Smithies) R.; A.B., George Washington Univ., 1923, LL.B., 1923, LL.M., 1924; m. Lorel Bowling, Apr. 2, 1919. Asst. prof. law, Univ. of N.D., 1923-24; asso. prof. of law, Univ of N.C., 1924-26; prof. of law, Univ. of Cincinnati, since 1926, dean, Coll. of Law since 1946; vis. prof. of law, summer, Univ. of Ia., 1929, Cornell, 1930, Chicago, 1931, Ohio State, 1936, Stanford, 1942. Served in U.S. Navy, 1918-20; U.S. Army, Jan. 1943-Feb. 1946; chief, legal br., hdqrs. A.S.F., War Dept., 1944-46; major, 1943, lt. col., 1944, col., 1945; released from active duty, rank of colonel, Feb. 1946. Awarded Legion of Merit and Army Commendation Ribbon. Pres., League of Ohio State Law Schools, 1948. Mem. bd. dir. Legal Aid Soc., Cincinnati. Mem. Cincinnati Bar Assn., Am. Assn. Univ. Profs., Order of the Coif, Phi Sigma Kappa, Phi Delta Phi, Omicron Delta Kappa. Club: Army and Navy (Washington, D.C.). Republican. Contbr. numerous articles to legal periodicals. Home: Hill Top Lane, Wyoming 15, O. Office: College of Law, Univ. of Cincinnati, Cin. Died July 26, 1952; buried Resthaven Meml. Park, Cin.

ROYALL, Ralph, lawyer; b. N.Y.C., 1881; s. Nathaniel B. and Elizabeth (Davidge) R.; student Williams Coll., 1899-1900; LL.B., Columbia, 1903; m. Jean Richards, Sept. 20, 1921. Admitted to N.Y. bar, 1903, since practiced in N.Y.C.; partner Ehrich, Royall, Wheeler & Holland since 1928; dir. Godchaux Sugars, Inc., Republic Investors Fund, Inc., Sovereigh Investors, Inc., Bridgeport Rolling Mills Co. Dir. Beekman-Downtown Hosp., Alice Mandeleck Flagler Found., Accountants Found. Mem. Theta Delta Chi, Chi Phi. Republican. Episcopalian. Home: Davis Wharf, Va. Office: 20 Exchange Pl., N.Y.C. 5. Died Mar. 3, 1954.

ROYER, J. E. E., public utilities; b. Gettysburg, O., Feb. 17, 1885; s. John S. and Melinda (Wenrich) R.; ed. Ohio State U.; m. Eva Baxter, Nov. 28, 1910; children—Richard B., Bernadine Kelsey. Asst. gen. mgr. The Washington Water Power Co., 1924-30, gen. mgr. since 1930, v.p. since 1932; dir. The Washington Water Power Co. Mem. gov. bd. local unit Shriners' Hosp. for Crippled Children; mem. bd. Pacific Northwest Power Company, 1954—. Clubs: Kiwanis, City, Spokane Country. Home: Culmstock Arms Apt. Hotel, W. 328 Eighth Av., Spokane 4. Office: The Washington Water Power Co., P.O. Drawer 1445, Spokane 10, Wash. Died May 22, 1957.

RUBEN, Barney, chmn. and pres. Bond Stores, Inc. Address: 380 Fifth Av., N.Y. City 18. Died Oct. 27, 1959.*

RUBENDALL, Clarence (rū-bĕn'dawl), physician; b. Orangeville, Ill., Aug. 21, 1883; s. Peter and Anna (Matter) R.; B.Sc., U. of Neb., 1906, M.D., 1908; m. Elizabeth Shortliff, Oct. 14, 1912; children—Elizabeth, Claire (Mrs. John L. Hoppe). Chmn. dept. otorhinolaryngology, U. Neb. Coll. of Medicine, prof. emeritus. Mem. A.M.A., Am. Acad. of Ophthalmology and Otolaryngology, Sigma Xi, Phi Rho Sigma, Chi Phi. Republican. Presbyn. Mason. Club: Omaha Concord (past pres.). Home: 721 Hackberry Rd. Office: Medical Arts Bldg., Omaha 2, Neb. Died June 6, 1950; buried Forest Lawn, Omaha, Neb.

RUBIN, J. Robert, lawyer; b. Syracuse, N.Y., Mar. 4, 1882; s. Marcus and Frances (Epstein) R.; Ph.B., LL.B., LL.D., Syracuse U.; LL.D., Oglethorpe University; married to Reba Lillian Hitchcock, December 26, 1910; one son, Robert Hitchcock. Practiced law with Hornblower, Miller & Potter, 1906-10; asst. dist. atty. N.Y. County, 1910-14; dep. police commr., N.Y. City, 1914; resumed practice of law, New York City; vice president, and general counsel of Loew's, Incorporated, until 1954; also v.p., sec., dir. Moredall Realty Corp.; dir. MGM Pictures, Ltd., The New Empire, Ltd., Hearst Metrotone News, Robbins Music Corp., until 1954, Coty, Inc., Coty Internat., Am. Theater Wing, Inc. Dir. Nat. Football Found., and Hall of Fame, Inc.; trustee Syracuse U., Actors Fund Am.; gen. chmn.

amusement div. Nat. Conf. Christians and Jews; v.p., trustee Walter Kempner Found., Inc.; mem. visitors com. N.Y. Pub. Library; film adv. com. Mus. Modern Art. Mem. OSS during World War II. Mem. Nat. Inst. Social Scis., Am., N.Y. State bar assns., Assn. Bar City N.Y., N.Y. County Lawyers Assn., Phi Delta Phi, Phi Delta Theta. Clubs: Syracuse University, Phi Delta Theta (N.Y.); Varsity, Nat. Republican, Westchester Country, Turf and Field, United Hunts. Home: 993 Fifth Av., N.Y.C. 28. Office: 620 Fifth Av., N.Y.C. 20. Died Sept. 10, 1958; buried Woodlawn Cemetery, N.Y.C.

RUBINSTEIN, Beryl (rōō'bin-stīn), pianist, composer; b. Athens, Ga., Oct. 26, 1898; s. Isaac and Matilda (Abrahams) R.; studied under father and Alexander Lambert, in Europe with José Vianna da Motta and Ferrucio Busoni, 1913-14; hon. Mus.D., West. Reserve University, 1931; m. Elsa Landesman, Dec. 29, 1925; children—Ellen (Mrs. Edric A. Weld, Jr.), Beryl David. Toured America as child pianist, 1905-11; made debut with Metropolitan Opera Orchestra, 1911; professional debut, N.Y. City, 1916; joined faculty Cleveland Institute of Music, 1921, head piano department, 1925-29, dean of faculty, 1929-32, director since 1932; director Singers Club of Cleveland, 1930-36; soloist with major orchestras; premiere of second Piano Concerto with Dr. Rodzinski and Cleveland Orchestra, 1936. Hon. mem. Phi Mu Alpha; national patron Delta Omicron. Served in U.S. Army, 1942-44; capt. in recreational work in Africa, and Sicily. Composer: (for orchestra) Scherzo, Suite; (opera) The Sleeping Beauty; (for piano) Sonatina in C Sharp Minor; Two Studies, Four Fantastic Pieces, Suite Romantique, Musical Fancies, Twelve Definitions for Piano, Thirty-two piano studies, A Day in the Country (5 impromptus), Gavotte, Sarabande, Gigue, Arabesque, Nocturne, Caprice, (piano) Scenes from Carrolls Alice in Wonderland, Concerto in C for piano and orchestra, Suite for Two Pianos; (for violin) Scherzo Serenade, Plainte de Pierrot; (for string quartet) Passepied; (for voice) Three Songs, Prayer of Praise for male chorus); (orchestra with male chorus) Letter From the Front, Dedication; arrangements for piano solo of four songs from Gershwin's Porgy and Bess. Latest compositions: The Pied Piper, 1951; Fantasy for Violin and Piano, 1951; Partita for Piano, 1952. Author: Outline of Piano Pedagogy; Pianist's Approach to Sight-reading and memorizing. Has made several recordings. Home: 2195 St. James Parkway, Cleveland Heights, O. Address: 3411 Euclid Av., Cleve. Died Dec. 29, 1952; buried Mayfield Cemetery, Cleve.

RUBIO, Antonio, educator; b. Havana, Cuba, Mar. 3, 1888; s. Antonio and Carmen (Gonzalez) R.; grad. Escuela de Artes, Havana, 1907 (awarded fellowship for U.S. study); D.V.M., Cornell U., 1911; D.V.M., Universidad Nacional, Havana, 1912; Ph.B., A.M., Brown U., 1928; attended Centro de Estudios Historicos, Madrid, Spain, summer 1928; Diplôme, Université de Poitiers, France, 1929; Ph.D., U. of Chgo., 1934; m. Anna Peña Hass, Aug. 25, 1915; children—Nestor (dec.), Alfredo Martin, Carlos Manuel, Jeanne-Marie (Mrs. David G. Coffing), Ann Elvira. Came to U.S., 1919, naturalized, 1936. Instr. Spanish, Brown U., 1921-28; asso. prof. Romance langs. De Paul U., 1931-35, prof., modern langs., 1935—, became chmn. dept., 1935, now ret. lectr. Latin Am. Workshop, U. of Chgo., 1943, cultural programs sponsored by Coordinator of Inter-Am. Affairs. Mem. Instituto de las Españas (past v.p. Chgo. chpt.), Pan Am. Council (pres. Chgo., 1951—), Am. Ethical Union, Chgo. Ethical Soc. (trustee), Henry Booth Community House, Chgo. Mem. Am. Assn. Univ. Profs., Am. Assn. Tchrs. of Spanish and Portuguese (past pres. Chgo. chpt.; co-chmn. local com. for annual meeting, Chgo., 1945), Nat. Fedn. Modern Lang. Tchrs., Chgo. Soc. Romance Lang. Tchrs., Am. Assn. Tchrs. of French. Author: Comments on 18th Century Purismo, 1935; La Critica del Galicismo en España, 1937. Contbr. to Hispanic Revue, Modern Lang. Jour., Hispania, and others. Home: 4324 Ellis Av., Chgo. 15. Office: 64 E. Lake St., Chgo. 1. Died 1955.

RUBLEE, George (rōōb'lē), lawyer; b. Madison, Wis., July 7, 1868; s. Horace and Kate (Hopkins) R.; grad. Groton (Mass.) Sch., 1886; A.B., Harvard, 1890, LL.B., 1895; LL.D., Dartmouth, 1931; LL.D., Amherst Coll., 1940; m. Juliet Barrett, Jan. 12, 1899. Instr., Harvard Law Sch., 1896. With Rublee & Burling, Chgo., 1897-98; Victor Morawetz, N.Y.C., 1898, later mem. Spooner & Cotton; apptd. mem. Federal Trade Commn., by Pres. Wilson, 1915-16; mem. of Eight-Hour Commn., apptd. by Pres. Wilson to report on operation of Adamson 8-hour law, 1916; mem. Comml. Economy Bd., Council of Nat. Defense, 1917; spl. counsel Treasury Dept., 1917; apptd. to rep. U.S. Shipping Bd. and Emergency Fleet Corp. on priorities com. of War Industries Bd., 1917; Am. del. to Allied Maritime Transport Council, London, 1918-19; former mem. Covington, Burling, Rublee, Acheson & Shorb; retired. Legal adviser to Am. Embassy, Mexico City, 1928-30; adviser to Am. delegation London Naval Conf., 1930; adviser to Govt. of Colombia, S.A., 1930-33. Decorated Chevalier Legion of Honor (France); Comdr. Order of the Crown (Italy). Mem. bd. of overseers Harvard, 1938-44; dir. Inter-governmental Com., 1938-39; pres. Harvard Alumni Assn., 1947-48; trustee Roosevelt Meml. Assn. Clubs: Century, Harvard (N.Y.C.); Metropolitan, Chevy Chase (Washington). Died Apr. 1957.

RUDD, Thomas Brown, lawyer, ednl. adminstr.; b. Utica, N.Y., Nov. 27, 1898; s. Joseph and Daisy (Brown) R.; A.M. (hon.) Hamilton Coll., 1934; LL.D. (hon.), 1946; LL.B., Cornell, 1921; LL.D. (hon.) Union Coll., 1948; m. Helen Neilson, Apr. 28, 1928; children—Neilson, Joseph. Admitted to N.Y. State bar, 1921, practiced in N.Y. City with Root, Clark, Buckner & Howland, 1921-22, in Utica, 1922—, sr. mem. firm of Rudd, Penberthy & Nelson, 1935—; asst. U.S. atty., Northern Dist. of N.Y., 1929-30; dist. atty., Oneida County, 1932-35; v.p., treas. Munston-Williams-Proctor Inst., 1939—, now pres.; controller Hamilton Coll., 1940—, pres., June 1947-Feb. 1949; dir. Hayes Nat. Bank of Clinton, N.Y., Indsl. Bank of Utica, Niagara Mohawk Power Corp., Utica Radiator Corp., N.Y. Abstract Corp. Broad Street Warehouse Corp.; trustee Savings Bank of Utica. Trustee House of Good Shepherd, American Federation of Art (president, 1952-54). Member American, New York State and Oneida County bar assns., Scout Masters' Assn. of Utica (past pres.), Family Welfare Soc. of Utica (past pres.), Oneida County Tuberculosis Assn. (vice pres.), Phi Delta Phi, Alpha Delta Phi. Republican. Clubs: Skenandoa, Clinton, Ft. Schuyler, Utica, Cornell, N.Y. City. Home: Bristol Rd. Office: Hamilton College, Clinton, N.Y. Died Apr. 11, 1955.

RUDDIMAN, Edsel Alexander (rŭd'ĭ-măn), chemist; b. Dearborn, Mich., Dec. 27, 1864; s. William and Catherine (Noble) R.; grad. Detroit High Sch., 1884; Pharm. Chemist, U. Mich., 1886; M.Pharm., 1887; M.D., Vanderbilt U., 1893; m. Jennie Evelyn Perry, July 29, 1889; children—Stanley Perry, Edith Helen. Chemist in charge mfg. lab. of Milburn & Williamson, 1887-90; chemist to Tenn. Bd. Pharmacy, 1897-1920; food and drug inspection chemist, 1907-14; prof. pharmacy and materia medica, in dept. of pharmacy, 1890-1920, dean Sch. of Pharmacy, 1919-20, Vanderbilt U.; chief chemist John T. Milliken & Co., pharm. chemists, 1921-26; research chemist with Ford Motor Co., 1926-42. Author: Incompatibilities in Prescriptions, 1897; Whys in Pharmacy, 1906; Manual of Materia Medica, 1907; Theoretical and Practical Pharmacy, 1917. Home: 22179 Long Blvd., Dearborn, Mich. Died Mar. 21, 1954; buried Evergreen Cemetery, Dearborn, Mich.

RUDOLPH, Herbert Blaine, judge; b. Canton, S.D., May 22, 1894; s. Martin Ernest and Claudia (Shedd) R.; A.B., U. of S.D., 1916; LL.B., Univ. of Mich., 1918; m. Neva Streator, June 5, 1923; children—Blaine O., Henrietta. Began practice at Canton, 1919; judge of Circuit Court, S.D., 1924-29; apptd. judge Supreme Court of S.D., Apr. 1, 1931, for term ending Dec. 31, 1934, then elected 4 terms, present term ending Dec 31, 1958. Served as 2d lt. field arty., World War. Mem. Am. Arbitration Assn. (commn. on uniform legislation), Am., S.D. (pres. 1956-57) bar assns., Phi Delta Theta, Phi Delta Phi. Republican. Conglist. Mason. Home: 304 N. Highland Av., Pierre, S.D. Died Sept. 2, 1957; buried Canton, S.D.

RUDOLPH, Jacob H., army officer; b. Mar. 25, 1886. Commd. 2d lt. inf., Sept. 25, 1908; promoted through grades to col., Feb. 1, 1938; temporary rank of brig. gen., Oct. 1, 1940; apptd. comdg. gen. Spokane Air Depot Control Area, Jan. 1943; retired July 1944. Address: War Dept., Washington. Died Mar. 19, 1960.*

RUEBUSH, James Hott, educator; b. Singers Glen, Va., Oct. 19, 1865; s. Ephraim and Lucilla Virginia (Kieffer) R.; ed. Shenandoah Collegiate Inst. (Dayton, Va.), Otterbein U. (Westerville, O.), 1884-85, Grand Conservatory of Music (New York), 1885-87; pupil of Bartlette, Root, Palmer and others in music; (hon. M. Mus., Lebanon Valley Coll., Pa., 1914); m. Ella V. Funkhouser, Aug. 7, 1889; children—Jenny Lind (Mrs. Garland Shirley), James Lowell. Teacher and dir. music Shenandoah Collegiate Inst., 1887-93; dir. music, Kee Mar Coll., Hagerstown, Md., 1898-1909; head of music dept., Shenandoah Collegiate Inst., 1908—, also v.p. of the inst.; dir. The Ruebush-Kieffer Co., pubs. Trustee Rockingham Memorial Hosp. (Harrisonburg, Va.), Quincy (Pa.) Orphanage. Mem. Fgn. Missionary Bd. U.B. Ch. Author: Practical Harmony and Composition, 1897; Family Prayer Book, 1900; Practical Music Reader, 1904; Choir and Concert, 1912; Glory Songs, 1916; Tribute of Praise, 1918; Gospel Message in Song; Music Reader No. 2; Revival Echoes; Salvation Songs; The Harvester. Home: Dayton, Va. Died Apr. 4, 1948.

RUEDEMANN, Rudolf, curator; b. Georgenthal, Germany, Oct. 16, 1864; Ph.D., U. Jena, 1887, Strassburg U., 1889. Asst. geology Strassburg U., 1887-92; tchr. high schs., N.Y., 1892-99; asst. state paleontologist, N.Y., 1899-1926, state paleontologist, 1926-27; curator paleontology N.Y. State Mus., 1913-37. Recipient Walker prize Boston Soc. Natural History, 1901. Mem. Nat. Acad. Sci., Am. Geol. Soc. (v.p. 1916), Paleontological Soc. (pres. 1916). Address: 161 Dana Av., Albany 3, N.Y. Died July 19, 1956.

RUEHE, Harrison August (rōō'hē), dairy husbandman; b. Gilman, Ill., June 26, 1888; s. August Henry and Sarah (Williams) R.; B.S., Univ. of Ill., 1911, M.S., 1916; Ph.D., Cornell U., 1921; m. Phoebe Olive Barnicoat, Sept. 7, 1918; children—Harrison Barnicoat, Richard Williams. Instr. in dairy manufactures, U. of Calif., 1911-12, U. of Ill., 1912-14; asso., dairy mfrs. U. of Ill., 1914-18, asst. prof., 1918-21, actg. head dept. dairy husbandry, 1919-20 (leave of absence, 1920-21), prof. dairy mfrs. and head of dept. dairy husbandry, 1921-45 (leave of absence 1943-45); sec. Am. Butter Inst., Chicago, 1943-45; prof. dairy sci., Coll. of Agr. and Chief Dairy Sci. Ill. Agrl. Experimental Station, 1945—. Member American Dairy Science Assn. (pres. 1935-36), Sigma Pi, Alpha Zeta, Phi Kappa Phi, Gamma Sigma Delta, Sigma Xi, Alpha Tau Alpha, Phi Sigma. Episcopalian. Author of many bulletins on dairying and articles in trade papers; devised method of inverting sugar for ice-cream making widely used during the war. Developed method for standardizing intensity of flavor in butter. Apptd. official state del. to World's Dairy Congress, Washington, 1923; official state del. to Internat. Dairy Congress, Copenhagen, 1931; chmn. Commn. to Study Milk Markets, 1939. Republican. Mason. Contbr. to dairy journals, World Book Ency. and Ency. Britannica. Home: 908 S. Lincoln Av., Urbana, Ill. Died Oct. 8, 1953; buried Roselawn Cemetery, Urbana.

RUGGLES, Clyde Orval, educator; b. Jefferson County, Ia., Dec. 7, 1878; s. John Henry and Theodosia (Doggett) R.; A.B., Ia. State Teachers Coll., 1906; A.M., U. of Ia., 1907; Ph., Harvard, 1913; Litt.D., Suffolk Univ., 1938; m. Maud Vittetoe, 1898 (she died 1900); m. 2d, Frances Holmes, August 30, 1906; children—John Holmes, Catherine Grace, Rebecca Dorothy, Richard Francis. Spl. research on federal reserve banking law for Nat. Monetary Commission, Jan.-Sept. 1909; head dept. history and social science, Winona (Minn.) State Teachers Coll., 1909-13; asst. prof. economics, Ohio State U., 1913-14, prof., 1914-20; instructor U. of Chicago, summer session 1916, 20. Head, Sch. of Commerce and of dept. of economics, State U. of Ia., 1920-21; head dept. business administration, Ohio State U., 1921-26, dean Coll. of Commerce and Administration, 1926-28; prof. pub. utility management and regulation, Harvard, 1928-48, prof. emeritus, 1948—; visiting prof., business orgn. and econ., Ohio State University, 1948-49; graduate center Ohio State University, Wright-Patterson Air Force Base, Dayton, Ohio, 1949-53. Special expert on investigation of terminal charges at United States ports, for U.S. Shipping Bd., 1918-19. Dir. of Survey for the Electrical Industry of the Extent of College instruction in Pub. Utilities, and of the Industry's Demand for College Graduate, 1927-28. Spl. cons. service, Civil Aeronaut. Bd., Mar.-May 1942. Mem. Am. Acad. Arts and Scis., Am. Econ. Assn., Am. Soc. Pub. Adminstrn., Alpha Kappa Psi, Beta Gamma Sigma, Pi Gamma Mu. Baptist. Author: (rept.) Terimnal Charges at U.S. Ports, 1919; Problems in Public Utility Economics and Managemet, 1933, 2d edit., 1938; Aspects of the Organization, Functions and Financing of State Public Utility Commissions, 1937. Home: 321 Mt. Auburn St., Cambridge, Mass. Died Apr. 6, 1958; buried Mt. Auburn Cemetery, Cambridge.

RUHL, James Brough (rūl), judge; b. on farm near Lisbon, O., May 21, 1864; s. John Conser and Eliza (Barrick) R.; B.S., Ohio Northern U., 1888, M.S., 1891, LL.B., 1891, LL.M., 1903, LL.D., 1923; LL.D., Mount Union Coll., Alliance, O., 1926; m. Mary Williams, Apr. 2, 1894 (died Feb. 23, 1925); m. 2d, Edna L. Sturgis, Jan. 26, 1927. Supt. pub. schs., McComb, O., 1888-89; instr. in mathematics, Ohio Northern U., 1889-91; began law practice at Cleveland, 1891; tax commr., Cuyahoga County, O., 1915; pres. John Marshall Sch. of Law and prof. pleading and procedure since 1916; judge Court of Common Pleas, 1923-33; mem. firm Ruhl & Graham. Served as pvt., 1st lt., capt. and regtl. adj., Ohio Nat. Guard, 1892-97. Alumni trustee Ohio Northern U. Mem. S.A.R., Alpha Tau Omega, Delta Theta Phi. Republican. Presbyterian. Mason (33°; Grand Master F. and A.M. of Ohio 1924), K.P. Home: 17455 Lake Av., Lakewood, O. Office: Society for Savings Bldg., Cleveland, O. Deceased.*

RULAND, Lloyd Stanton (rōōl'ănd), church exec.; b. Russell, Pa., Nov. 10, 1889; s. Claude E. and Anna (Stanton) R.; A.B., Westminster Coll., New Wilmington, Pa., 1911, D.D., 1932; B.D., McCormick Theol. Sem., 1916; m. Margaret Sylvia Hayward, June 18, 1918; children—Sylvia Eleanor, Margaret Anne, Virginia Louise, Lloyd Stanton. Teacher and athletic dir. Elgin (Ill.) Acad., 1911-12, prin., 1912-13; ordained to ministry Presbyn. Ch., May 1916; missionary, Shantung, China, 1916-18; pastor Presbyn. Ch., Gibson City, Ill., 1918-21; student work, Nanking, China, 1921-26; pastor West Presbyn. Ch., Binghamton, N.Y., 1927-38; sec. for China, Bd. Foreign Missions, Presbyn. Ch., U.S.A., 1938-

52; Pacific Coast Rep. Presbyn. Bd. Fgn. Missions, 1952-53. Chmn. Com. on United Promotion, Presbyn. Synod of N.Y., 1935-38; chmn. Binghamton Civic Ednl. Forum, 1936-38. Travel seminar, Europe, summer 1928, Palestine and Near East, summer 1935; adminstrative visit to Japan, Chosen, China and Thailand, 1939-40, to Mexico, 1943, to Indonesia at invitation of Internat. Missionary Council, 1950. Vice pres. Church World Service 1948-51. Pres. Bd. Deputation to China, 1946; v.p. United Bd. Christian Colls. in China; chmn., N.A. Council, Coll. of Chinese Studies; mem. bd. dirs. Assn. for Chinese Blind; founder, pres. China Stamp Soc.; mem. Am. Philatelic Soc. Clubs: Quill, Shanghai Tiffin (N.Y. C.). Contbr. to religious jours. and philatelic publs. Home: 39 Wayne Av., White Plains, N.Y. Office: 156 5th Av., N.Y.C. 10. Died May 16, 1953; buried Ferncliff, Hartsdale, N.Y.

RULE, Arthur Richards, community builder; b. Goshen, Ky., Dec. 6, 1876; s. Rev. John and Mary W. R.; student dist., pvt. schs. and acad.; m. Elizabeth Bacon Wright, Mar. 21, 1903; children—Patricia K. (wife of Albert Kellogg Stebbins, U.S. Army), Arthur R. (USN), Walter W., Mary W. (wife of George B. Coale, USN), Elizabeth W. (wife of D. B. Johnson, U.S. Army). With Crutchfield & Woolfolk, fruit distbrs., Pitts., 1898-1911; orgnr. Fla. Citrus Exchange, 1908; orgnr. No. Am. Fruit Exchange, N.Y., 1911; organizer Gen. Sales Agy. Am., 1915; an organizer, 1922, gen. mgr., 1923-30, Federated Fruit and Vegetable Growers; chmn. orgn. com. United Growers, Am., 1929—; pres. Mutual Service Corp.; owner, developer of Wychwood, Westfield, N.J. (home community, awarded 1st place by Am. Inst. Architects for archtl. standard, 1936); v.p., dir. Deerfield Groves Co.; pres. Sixteen Jane Street, Inc., 37 East 67th St. Corp., 26 East 83d Street Corp.; mem. gen. organizing com. 2d Pan Am. Standardization Conf., Washington, 1927; mem. exec. com. Nat. Council of Farmers' Coop. Marketing Assn. Mem. Home Builders Inst. of Am. (charter), Am. Inst. of Coöperation (charter, dir.), Am. Friends of Lafayette, Acad. Polit. Sci., Am. Com. Inst. of Agr. at Rome. Presbyn. Clubs: Economic, Southern Society; Filson (Louisville). Contbr. on coop. marketing of fruits and vegetables. Home: 1011 Wychwood Rd., Westfield, N.J. Office: 580 Fifth Av., N.Y.C. Died June 27, 1950; buried Goshen, Ky.

RUMELY, William Nicholas, capitalist; b. LaPorte, Ind., Mar. 20, 1858; s. Meinrad and Theresia R.; ed. Notre Dame U., 1872-5, Stevens Inst. Tech.; m. Anna Long, Oct. 3, 1888. Ex-pres. M. Rumely Co., mfrs. agrl. implements, LaPorte; now president Ill. Thresher Co., Sycamore; dir. Colonial Trust & Savings Bank, North Av. State Bank, Chgo. Mem. Am. Soc. Mech. Engrs., Franklin Inst. Address: Sycamore, Ill. Died Nov. 24, 1936.

RUNDALL, Charles O., lawyer; b. Ridgeway, Wis., July 5, 1885; s. John C. and Ida V. (Roberts) R.; LL.B., Northwestern U., 1906; m. Mary Josephine Worster, June 20, 1911; children—Charles Worster, Georganne Worster (Mrs. John Alden Sears), John Albert. Admitted to Ill. bar, 1906, and since in practice of law at Chicago. Mem. Am., Ill. State (pres.1939-40) and Chicago bar assns., Northwestern Univ. Asso., Law Club, Legal Club (pres. 1936-37), Sigma Chi, Alpha Omega. Mem. Ill. Nat. Guard, 1909-11. Republican. Conglist. Clubs: Literary Club of Chicago, University, Skokie Country, Glenview. Home: 1239 Asbury Av., Evanston, Ill. Office: 135 S. LaSalle St., Chicago, Ill. Deceased.

RUNDELL, Oliver Samuel (rŭn'dĕl), law prof.; b. Rewey, Wis., Oct. 6, 1881; s. Hiram Augustus and Angeline (Livingston) R.; grad. Platteville (Wis.) State Normal Sch., 1905; LL.B., U. of Wis., 1910; m. Abigail Erna Parmley, June 24, 1916; children—Ruth Eleanor Rowley, John Philip (killed in action, Germany, Nov. 29, 1944), Hugh Augustus, Barbara Jean, Janet Evelyn. Prin. graded school, Osseo, Wis., 1905-06, Lyons, Wis., 1906-08; admitted to Wis. bar, 1910; practiced law, Monroe, Wis., 1912-14; city atty., Monroe, 1913-14; instr. in law, U. of Wis., 1910-12, asst. prof., 1914-16, asso. prof., 1916-18, prof. since 1918, acting dean of law school, 1929-33 and 1943-45, dean, 1945-53, dean emeritus, Jackson prof. law, 1953-55, dean and prof. law emeritus, 1955—; prof. law U. Kansas City, 1956—; acting prof. law, U. Chgo., 1924-25, U. Mich., 2d semester, 1940-41; adviser to reporter for subject of Property, American Law Institute, 1926-39 and 1940-44, associate reporter for Property, 1936-39 and 1941-44, adviser to associate reporter for Torts, 1934-39. Mem. Am., Wis., Dane County bar assns., Am. Assn. U. Profs., Phi Delta Phi, Phi Kappa Phi, Phi Beta Kappa, Order of Coif. Clubs: University, Blackhawk Country (Madison). Author: Cases and Materials on Rights in Land. Home: 432 Toepfer Av., Madison 5, Wis.; (schoolyear) 5100 Brookside Blvd., Kansas City, Mo. Died Dec. 12, 1957.

RUNGIUS, Carl (Clemens Moritz) (run'gĭ-ŭs), artist; b. Berlin, Germany, Aug. 18, 1869; s. Rev. H. and Magdalene (Fulda) R.; ed. Gymnasium, Burg bei Magdeburg und Giessen; studied painting at Berlin Art Sch., Sch. of Applied Arts and Acad. of Fine Arts; m. Louise M. Fulda, June 15, 1907. Began painting, Berlin, 1889; came to U.S., 1894, and has since been engaged in painting, making specialty of Am. big game; has exhibited at Soc. Am. Artists, Nat. Acad. Design, Pa. Acad. Fine Arts, etc. A.N.A., 1913; N.A., 1920. Life mem. Zoöl. Soc. N.Y.; mem. Painters of the Far West, Soc. Animal Painters and Sculptors; elected hon. scout Boy Scouts of America, 1927. Clubs: Salmagundi, Nat. Arts (life), Boone and Crockett, Century, Camp-Fire Club of America. Home: (summer) Banff, Alberta, Can. Address: 27 W. 67th St., N.Y.C. Died Oct. 1959.

RUNYAN, William B., iron mfg. exec.; b. Mansfield, O, 1877; ed. schools in Mansfield; grad. pharmacist Ohio Northern U., Ada., O.; m. Ethel Ditwiler, 1911. With Dayton Maleable Iron Co. since 1912, advancing through positions of responsibility to that of pres., 1936, chmn. bd. since 1942. Presbyn. Address: Dayton Malleable Iron Co., 1307 W. 3d St., Dayton 1, O. Died May 9, 1953.*

RUPPEL, Louis (rŭp'el), publisher; b. N.Y.C., N.Y., June 11, 1903; s. Frederick and Lillian (Schultz) R.; m. Margit Gabrielsen, Dec. 5, 1926; children—Philip, Joseph. Reporter, N.Y. Am., 1924-27, N.Y. Jour., 1928-29; polit. writer, N.Y. News, 1929-33; U.S. dep. commr. of narcotics, Washington, 1933-34; mng. editor, Chgo. Times, 1935-38; publicity dir. Columbia Broadcasting System, 1939-41; asst. to pres. Crowell-Collier Pub. Co., 1942; exec. editor Chgo. Herald-Am., 1945, resigned, Sept. 1945; editor of Collier's Weekly, 1949-52; owner, pub. Mill Valley (Cal.) Record, 1953-54; news editor Phila. Daily News, 1954-56; asso. editor Am. Weekly, 1956—. Served as capt. U.S.M.C., 1943-44; South Pacific Medal with 1 star. Member Mill Valley Post 284 American Legion, Sigma Delta Chi. Clubs: Nat. Press (Washington); Tough (N.Y.C.). Address: 25-29 120th St., College Point, Queens, N.Y.C. Died Jan. 1958.

RUPPRECHT, Frederick Kelsey (rōōp'rĕkt), corp. ofcl.; b. Bklyn., July 30, 1872; s. Adam C. and Julia (Kelsey) R.; ed. pub. schs.; adopted children—Marta, Douglas Hamilton, Alison; m. 2d, Elsie B. Storm, Oct. 21, 1926. Formerly pres. Consol. Selling Co., Inc., Consol. Textile Corp., B.B. and R. Knight, Converse & Co. Decorated Knight of Order of Crown, Italy. Mem. Am. Soc. Royal Italian Orders, United Hunts Racing Assn., Am. Mus. Natural History, New Eng. Hist. Geneal. Soc. Clubs: Bankers, Madison Square Garden, Metropolitan, Boys' Clubs of America, Inc. (N.Y.C.); Riomar (Vero Beach, Fla.); Katahdin Country. Home: 51 High St., Rye, N.Y. Office: 320 Broadway, N.Y.C. Died Nov. 29, 1954.

RUSK, Henry Perly, cattle husbandry; b. Rantoul, Ill., July 19, 1884; s. William Humphrey and Anna L. (Renner) R.; B.S., Valparaiso U., 1904; B.S. in Agr., U. of Mo., 1908, M.S., 1911, D.Sc., 1950; D. Sc., Purdue University, 1949; LL.D., Illinois Wesleyan University, 1951; married Edith Elizabeth Hartley, June 28, 1911; children—Elizabeth Hartley, Martha Hartley (Mrs. George A. Huff, Jr.). Assistant in animal husbandry, University of Missouri, 1908-09, Purdue Expt. Station, 1909-10; with U. of Ill. since 1910, beginning as asso. in beef cattle husbandry and 1st asst. in Expt. Sta., later asst. prof. and prof. beef cattle husbandry, and asst. chief and chief in Expt. Sta. until 1922; head of animal husbandry dept., same univ., 1922-39, dean College of Agr., dir. Agrl. Expt. Station, and dir. Extension Service in Agr. and Home Economics, same univ., 1939-52; dean, dir. emeritus, 1952—. Mem. bd. gov. U. of Ill. Found. Trustee of Farm Foundation; mem. Agrl. board, National Research Council, 1944-46. Mem. Ill. State Fair adv. bd., 1940-52; member Agr.-Industry Com., Ill. Chamber of Commerce, since 1944; adv. bd., Livestock Commrs., since 1945; chmn. Agr. Task Force, Commn. on Orgn. Exec. Br. of Govt., 1948; mem. joint U.S. Dept. Agr. and Assn. Land-Grant Colls. and Univs. on Study of Coop. Extension Work, 1948, on Agrl. Services to Fgn. Areas since 1950; chmn. Nat. Farm Electrification Conf., 1949; chmn. div. of agr., mem. exec. com. Assn. of Land-Grant Colleges and Universities 1949-51. Secretary Indiana Cattle Feeder's Assn., 1909-10, Illinois Cattle Feeders' Assn., 1911-18, Ill. Hereford Cattle Breeders' Assn. Mem. Ill. State Council of Defense. Member American Society Animal Production (vice-pres. 1924-25; president 1925-26), Sigma Xi, Alpha Zeta, Gamma Sigma Delta, Alpha Gamma Rho, Farm House; mem. div. of biology and agr. Nat. Research Council, 1926-29. Judge of beef cattle at many nat., state and dist. shows. Methodist. Home: 508 Florida Av., Urbana, Ill. Died Jan. 9, 1954; buried Roselawn Cemetery, Champaign, Ill.

RUSS, John T(aylor), pub., radio exec.; b. Haverhill, Mass., May 31, 1904; s. Wilfred Wesley and Addie Frances (Wright) R.; ed. Mercersburg Acad. (Pa.), 1921-24, Bryant and Stratton Business Coll., Boston, 1924-26; m. Muriel Jennings, July 27, 1927; children—Jacquelyn (Mrs. Ronald Natalino), Joan (Mrs. Richard Wholley). Manager of the Merrimack Wood Heel Company, Salem Depot, New Hampshire, 1926-30; executive F. W. Mears Heel Co., Lawrence, Mass., 1930-39; partner, Merrimack Valley Airways, Haverhill, Mass. and Manchester, N.H., 1933-39; pres., treas., Haverhill (Mass.) Gazette Co., 1939—; pres. and treas. radio stations WHAV and WHAV-FM, 1947—; dir. Merrimack Nat. Bank, Haverhill. Mem. C. of C. (dir.), Am. Newspaper Pubs. Assn., Bureau Advt., N.E. Daily Newspaper Assn., Nat. Assn. Broadcasters, U.S. Power Squadrons. Club: American Yacht. Home: Maple Av., Atkinson, N.H. Office: 179 Merrimack St., Haverhill, Mass. Died Dec. 30, 1954; buried Linwood Cemetery, Haverhill.

RUSSELL, (George) Alexander, musician; b. Franklin, Tenn., Oct. 2, 1880; s. George Alexander and Felicia Aiken (Putnam) R.; Mus.Bach., Syracuse Univ., 1901, Mus.Dr., 1921; studied in Berlin with Leopold Godowsky and Edgar S. Kelley, in Paris with Charles Marie Widor and Harold Bauer; Pd.D., Cincinnati U., 1929; m. Eloise Holden, Oct. 16, 1915. Asso. prof. piano and organ, Syracuse U., 1902-06; concert pianist, Paris, 1908; general music dir. Wanamaker Stores, New York and Phila., 1910-52; dir. music, Princeton U., 1917-35. Brought to America Marcel Dupré, organist at Notre Dame, Paris, Courboin, Hollins, Germani, Bossi, Cunningham. Decorated Order of Crown of Belgium, 1932. Mem. Singing Teachers Assn., Am. Guild of Organists, Am. Soc. Composers, Authors and Publishers. Republican. Presbyterian. Clubs: Bohemian, University, Dutch Treat. Composer songs, also for piano and organ. Home: 405 Park Av., New York 22, N.Y. and Onondaga Country Club, Fayetteville, N.Y. Died Nov. 24, 1953.

RUSSELL, Charles, educator; b. Ithaca, N.Y., Apr. 24, 1893; s. James Earl and Agnes (Fletcher) R.; student Haverford (Pa.) Coll., 1910-12; B.S.A., Macdonald Coll. (McGill U.), St. Anne de Bellevue, Quebec, Can., 1915; Ph.D., Columbia, 1922; m. Kathleen Brinley Lawson, Apr. 25, 1916; children—Charles Brinley, David Lawson. Asso. prof. agrl. edn. U. Toledo, 1919-22, prof. elementary edn., dir. div. elementary edn., 1922-25; pres. State Tchrs. Coll., Westfield, Mass., 1925-38, chmn. edn. 1933-48; asso., 1946—, department of forestry and gen. botany Am. Mus. Natural History, N.Y.C., 1946-53, ret.; instr. Audult Edn. Seminar, Kreutstein, Austria for UNESCO, 1950. Instr. Columbia summers, 1923-39, Colo. Coll. of Edn., 1935; peripatetic prof. Assn. of Am. Colleges, 1942-44. Mem. com. on Vol. Tng. Nat. Council Boy Scouts Am.; mem. Com. on Medicine and Pub. Health, N.Y. World's Fair; dir. Am. Assn. for Indian Affairs (treas., 1946-48); pres. Truro Neighborhood Assn., 1941-45. Dir. Navy Terrain Model Workshops, 1943-45. Mem. Com. on Edn., chmn., 1950-53, adv. mem. Com. on Children, Internat. Council Mus'.; mem. nat. adv. com. on Indian Rights, Am. Civil Liberties Union. Fellow A.A.A.S.; mem. Phi Delta Kappa, Kappa Delta Pi, Pi Gamma Mu; Am. Assn. Univ. Profs. (hon.). Mem. White House Conf. on Child Health and Protection, 1930. Republican. Congregational. Author: The Improvement of the City School Teacher in Service, 1922; Classroom Tests, 1926; Standard Tests, 1930; Classroom Grader and Scaler, 1931; Rating School Pupils, 1932; Teaching for Tomorrow, 1937. Adv. editor Compton's pictorial Ency.; mem. cons. staff Compton's Pictorial Teaching Unit Materials. Address: Depot Rd., Truro, Mass. Died Nov. 3, 1957; buried Bethel-Gilead, Vt.

RUSSELL, Charles Tier, lawyer; b. of Am. parents, Liverpool, Eng., Dec. 11, 1877; s. Charles Tweed and Mary Elizabeth (Tyler) R.; prep. edn. in pvt. schs. and under tutors; LL.B., Yale, 1899; m. Florence Sprague Shailer, May 26, 1903 (died June 1948). Admitted to Conn. bar, 1899, N.Y. bar, 1900, practicing at N.Y.C.; mem. Atwater & Cruikshank, 1903-06; in law dept. N.Y. Telephone Co., 1906-43, v.p., gen. counsel, dir.; v.p., gen. counsel and dir. Empire City Subway Co., Ltd., Holmes Electric Protective Co.; trustee Union Dime Savings Bank; ret., 1943. Mem. Am. Bar Assn., N.Y. State Bar Assn., Assn. Bar City N.Y., Yale Law Sch. Assn. Phi Delta Phi. Democrat. Clubs: Yale, Racquet and Tennis (N.Y.). Home: Hillsboro Beach, Pompano, Fla. Died Jan. 1958.

RUSSELL, Elbert, educator; b. Friendsville, Tenn., Aug. 29, 1871; s. William and Eliza (Sanders) R.; A.B., Earlham Coll., Richmond, Ind., 1894, A.M., 1895; U. Chgo., 1901-03, fellow in N.T., 1902-03, Ph.D., 1919; m. Lieuetta Lilian Cox, Aug. 14, 1895; children—Josiah Cox, Marcia Rachel. Prof. Bibl. studies, 1895-1901, Bibl. lit. and ch. history, 1903-15, Earlham Coll., coll. pastor; instr. in Oriental Sem. and fellow by courtesy, Johns Hopkins, 1915-17; dir. Woolman Sch., Swarthmore, Pa., 1917-24; spl. lectr. for Am. Friends Service Com., in Germany and Austria, 1924-25. Prof. Biblical interpretation, Sch. of Religion, Duke U., 1926-45, dean 1928-41, dean emeritus, 1941—; prof. of religion, Guilford Coll., 1945-46. Progressive Party candidate for Congress, 1914. Mem. Soc. Bibl. Lit. and Exegesis, Am. Orient. Soc., Phi Beta Kappa. Lectr. Ch. history, Grad. Sch. of Haverford Coll., 1921-26, on Bible, Swarthmore, 1922-26; also at chautauquas, summer schs., etc. Del. of the Five Years Meeting of Friends, Stockholm Conf., 1925, Oxford and Edinburgh Ch. Confs., 1937, Utrecht Conf., 1938. Author: The Parables of Jesus, 1909; Jesus of Nazareth in the Light of Today, 1909; As Each Day Comes, 1923;

The Beatitudes, 1929; The Message of the Fourth Gospel, 1932; A Book of Chapel Talks, 1935; More Chapel Talks, 1938; The History of Quakerism, 1942. Contbr. on religious and peace topics. Home: 2619 Bayside Dr. So., St. Petersburg 5, Fla. Deceased.

RUSSELL, Ernest John, architect; b. London, Eng., Mar. 5, 1870; s. John Stokes and Mary J. (Mayhew) R.; brought to U.S. in childhood; ed. pub. schs., Colo.; m. Elizabeth Dunlap, 1896; children—Mary Dunlap, Elizabeth Bacon. Began study of architecture, 1887; mem. Mauran, Russell & Garden, St. Louis, Mo., 1900-09, Mauran & Russell, 1909-11, Mauran, Russell & Crowell, 1911-37, Mauran, Russell, Crowell & Mullgardt, 1937-48; Russell, Crowell, Mullgardt & Schwarz, 1948-50, Russell, Mullgardt & Schwarz, 1950-55; Russell, Mullgardt, Schwarz & Van Hoeten, 1955—. Architect Railway Exchange Building, Laclede Gas Light Building, Second Baptist Church, First Church of Christ Scientist, Federal Reserve Bank Building (St. Louis), Rice Hotel and Municipal Auditorium (Houston, Tex.), Galvez Hotel (Galveston), Gunter Hotel (San Antonio), Lee Huckins Hotel (Oklahoma City, Okla.), Southwestern Bell Telephone Co. (St. Louis), etc.; architect (asso. with A. B. M. Corrubia) U.S. Housing Administrn. Project MO-1-2; architect with Giffels & Vallet, Inc., engrs. on small arms plant in St. Louis. Mem. St. Louis Pub. Recreation Comm., 1908-09, 1911, St. Louis House of Dels., 1909-1911; mem. Bd. of Appeals, 1911, 12; chmn. St. Louis City Plan Commn., 1917-37, 1944; chairman St. Louis Transportation Survey Commission, 1928-30; first vice president Construction League of the United States, 1934. Fellow A.I.A. (v.p. 1923, 1930-32; pres. 1932-35; pres. St. Louis chapter, 1916, 17); mem. Am. Soc. Testing Materials, Nat. Housing Conf., Nat. City Planning Conf.; hon. cor. mem. Royal Inst. British Architects. Decorated Knight 1st Class, Order of Vasa (Sweden). Clubs: University, Noonday (St. Louis), Bellerive. Dep. chief prodn., housing div. U.S. Shipping Bd., 1918; chmn. Nat. Bd. Awards for Jurisdictional Disputes in the Bldg. Industry, 1919-23. President Mercantile Library Association, 1938-39. Home: 5814 Cabanne Av. Office: 1620 Chemical Bldg., St. Louis 1. Died July 11, 1956.

RUSSELL, Francis Thayer, clergyman; b. Boston, June 10, 1828; s. William and Ursula (Wood) R.; grad. theol. dept., Trinity Coll., Conn., 1854 (hon. A.M., 1956; S.T.D., Hobart, 1894); m. Mary Huntley Sigourney, Oct. 25, 1855. Deacon, 1855, priest, 1856, P.E. Ch.; rector St. Mark's, New Britain, Conn., 1855-64; prof. Hobart Coll., 1864-6; rector St. Stephen's, Ridgefield, Conn., 1866-8; asso. rector St. John's, Waterbury, Conn., 1868-75; rector St. Margaret's Diocesan Sch. for Girls, Waterbury, 1875-1903, rector emeritus, 1909—; also prof. elocution, Berkeley Divinity Sch. and Gen. Theol. Sem. until 1903, when retired and removed to Grand Rapids, Mich. For 20 yrs. prof. oratory Trinity Coll. Author: Juvenile Speaker, 1845; Practical Reader, 1852; Vocal Culture (reëdited), 1875; Use of the Voice, 1882 Address: Grand Rapids, Mich. Died Oct. 8, 1910; buried Fulton St. Cemetery, Grand Rapids, Mich.

RUSSELL, George Edmond, prof. hydraulics; b. Boston, Mass., Dec. 25, 1877; s. George Reed and Emma Adelaide (Edmond) R.; S.B., Mass. Inst. Tech., 1900; m. Mary E. Emerson, July 17, 1901; 1 son, Edmond Emerson; m. 2d, Jean K. Parker, July 8, 1933; 1 son, Richard Evans. Began as asst. instr. civil engring., Mass. Inst. Tech., 1900, instr., 1905-07, asst. prof., 1907-13, asso. prof. hydraulic engring., 1913-21, prof. 1921-43; prof. emeritus and hon. lectr. in civil engring., 1943-48; instr. Cornell U., 1904-05; designing engr. Am. Car & Foundry Co., N.Y., 1901-05; developed the all-steel freight car and designed the first non-combustible steel passenger car for use in subways, N.Y.; designing engr. Charles River Basin Commn., State of Mass., 1906; employed by Transit Commn. to study vehicular traffic in city of Boston, 1907-08; made a survey for the Mass. Met. Dist. Commn. of passenger traffic in Met. dist., 1908-09; state civil service examiner in civ. engring., Mass., 1912-25; served various municipalities in Mass. as advisor on water supply. Mem. Arlington (Mass.) Sch. Bd., 1922-28. Mem. Adv. com. U.S. Coast Guard Acad., New London, Conn. Cooperated with U.S. Navy Dept. in design of new type of submarine, World War. Fellow Am. Acad. Arts and Sciences; mem. Am. Soc. C.E. Boston Soc. C.E., New England Waterworks Assn., Alpha Tau Omega, Chi Epsilon, Tau Beta Pi. Author: Text Book on Hydraulics, 1909 (5th edit., 1942). Home: 6 Audubon Road, Lexington, Mass. Died Dec. 11, 1953.

RUSSELL, Henry Norris, astronomer; b. Oyster Bay, N.Y., Oct. 25, 1877; s. Alexander Gatherer and Eliza Hoxie (Norris) R.; A.B., Princeton, 1897, A.M., 1898, Ph.D., 1899; research student, King's Coll., Cambridge U., Eng., 1902-03; Docteur, Lauvain, 1927; D.Sc. (hon.), Dartmouth, 1923, Harvard, 1929, U. Chgo., 1941, Michoacau, Mexico, 1942, Yale, 1951, Princeton, 1954; married Lucy May Cole, Nov. 24, 1908; children—Lucy May, Elizabeth Hoxie, Henry Norris, Emma Margaret. Research asst. Carnegie Instn., Washington, stationed at Cambridge, Eng., 1903-05; instr. astronomy Princeton, 1905-08, asst. prof., 1908-11, prof. 1911-27, dir. of obs. 1912-47, research prof. 1927-47, emeritus 1947; research associate Harvard College Observatory, 1947-52, Mt. Wilson Observatory, 1922-42. Engineer Aircraft Service U.S. Army, 1918. Fellow A.A.A.S. (pres. 1933); mem. Nat. Acad. Sciences, Am. Philos. Soc. (pres. 1931-32), Am. Acad. Arts and Sciences, Am. Astron. Soc. (pres. 1934-37), Am. Phys. Soc.; fgn. asso. Royal Astron. Soc., London (gold medalist 1921); fgn. mem. Royal Soc., 1937; hon. fellow Royal Soc. of Edinburgh; asso. Belgian Royal Acad.; corr. French Acad. of Sciences; fgn. asso. Academia dei Lincei, Rome, 1948. Awarded Henry Draper medal Nat. Acad. Sciences, 1922; Lalande medal, French Acad., 1922; Bruce medal Astron. Soc. Pacific, 1925; Rumford medal, Am. Acad. Arts and Sciences, 1925; Franklin medal, 1934; Janssen medal French Acad., 1936. Presbyn. Author: Determinations of Stellar Parallax, 1911; Astronomy, 1926; Fate and Freedom, 1927; The Solar System and Its Origin, 1935; The Masses of the Stars, 1940. Contbr. on astron. topics to sci. jours. Address: 79 Alexander St., Princeton, N.J. Died Feb. 18, 1957; buried Princeton (N.J.) Cemetery.

RUSSELL, Herman, utility exec.; b. Manistee, Mich., Sept. 21, 1878; s. Edwin and Fanny Lincoln (Hopkins) R.; B.Sc. and M.S., U. of Mich. Chmn. bd., pres. Rochester (N.Y.) Gas & Electric Corp. Mem. Edison Electric Inst., Am. Gas Assn. (psst pres.). Home: 101 Brookside Drive. Office: Rochester Gas & Electric Corp., Rochester, N.Y. Died Mar. 14, 1956; buried Mt. Hope Cemetery, Rochester, N.Y.

RUSSELL, J. J., corp. exec.; b. Rome, N.Y. Formerly pres. Revere Copper & Brass, Inc., chmn. bd., 1951—, dir. Address: 230 Park Av., N.Y.C. 17. Died Aug. 1953; buried St. Peter's Ch. Cemetery, Rome, N.Y.*

RUSSELL, John, author; b. Davenport, Ia., Apr. 22, 1885; s. Charles Edward (publicist) and Abby Osborn (Rust) R.; Northwestern University, Evanston, Ill., 1903-05; m. Grace Nye Bolster, June 7, 1905; 1 daughter, Lydia Rutledge; m. 2d, Lili Hilson, Nov. 14, 1932. Traveled widely in early yrs.; spl. corr. New York Herald in Panama and Peru, 1908, later staff writer fiction, features, verse and interviews for N.Y. Herald; began writing for magazines, 1912, notably on South Sea, Oriental, adventure and seafaring themes. Has explored widely in South America, Asia and Oceania; consulting specialist and adapter many film cos.; now chiefly employed in magazine fiction writing. In charge U.S. Govt. propaganda for Gt. Britain and Ireland, World War. Mem. Authors' League America, Sigma Alpha Epsilon. Mason. Author: The Society Wolf, 1910; The Red Mark, 1919; Where the Pavement Ends, 1921; In Dark Places, 1922; Far Wandering Men, 1928; Cops 'n Robbers, 1930; Color of the East, 1930; Ambra (Copenhagen), 1930; Fjerne Horisonter (Copenhagen), 1930; Klippen Im Korallenmeer (Hanover), 1931; Die Dochte von Macassar (Leipzig), 1931; Vagabonds du Pacifique (Paris), 1932; Policias y Ladrones (Madrid), 1932; Mirages des Iles (Paris), 1933; Adventuriers des Tropiques (Paris), 1936; The Lost God, and Other Adventure Stories, 1947: and some 1,000 published short stories. Adopted chief among the Samoans, 1920, with title of "Tole a foa Tusitala." Named "master of short story" by Club Littéraire, 1936. Address: 442 Mesa Rd., Santa Monica, Cal. Died Mar. 6, 1956.

RUSSELL, Joshua Edward, ex-congressman; b. nr. Sidney, O., Aug. 9, 1866; s. William A. and Laura A. (Beck) R.; grad. Sidney High Sch.; m. Jennie C. Laughlin, May 9, 1894 (deceased). Admitted to Ohio bar, 1893, and practiced in Sidney; dir. 1st Nat. Exchange Bank, Peoples Saving & Loan Assn.; served as city solicitor and as mem. Ohio Senate; mem. 64th Congress 4th Ohio Dist. Republican. Sec. and mgr. Shelby County Agrl. Soc. since 1897. Presbyn. Mason. Home: Sidney, O. Deceased.

RUSSELL, Nelson Vance, coll. pres.; b. Birmingham, Mich., Apr. 15, 1895; s. Harry Montford and Ada Jane (Young) R.; student Coll. of Wooster, 1914-17; A.B., U. of Mich., 1918, M.A., 1921, Ph.D., 1925; mem. Am. Seminar to Russia, 1931; Lloyd traveling fellow in England and France, 1931-32; spl. student, American University, 1938; LL.D., College of Wooster, 1951; married Alvaretta Rosella Pottinger, June 30, 1923; children—Richard Morling, Bryce Wellington, Morley Egerton. Teacher Am. history, Wyandotte (Mich.) High Sch., 1919-20; asst. in history, U. of Mich., 1920-22, instr., 1922-25; instr. in history, U. of Calif. at Los Angeles, 1925-26, asst. prof., 1926-29; prof. Am. History and chmn. dept., Coe Coll., 1929-35; organized and established, 1935, Div. of Reference in Nat. Archives, served as first chief of div., 1935-38; prof. Am. History and chmn. dept. history and polit. science, Carleton Coll., 1938-46; pres. Carroll Coll., Waukesha, Wis., since 1946; editor-in-chief hist. br., Chemical Warfare Service, U.S. Army, 1944; member faculty, summer schs., U. of Calif., 1927, U. of Neb., 1941. Chmn. Rice Co. Republican Party, 1942-44; chmn. Rice Co. U.S.O. Committee, 1942. Mem. bd. trustees McCormick Theol. Sem.; mem. permanent jud. commn. Presbyn. Ch. U.S.A. since 1950. Served in Aviation section, U.S. Army, World War I. Mem. American Historical Assn., Miss. Valley Hist. Assn., Wis. Historical Society, Quadrangle Society, American Legion, Phi Kappa Phi, Tau Kappa Epsilon, Phi Mu Alpha. Republican. Kiwanian. Mason (32°). Presbyn. (elder). Club: University (Milwaukee, Wis.). Author: The British Regime in Michigan and the Old Northwest, 1760-1796 (1939). Contributor articles to Dictionary of American History, British Education, Year Book, 1932; articles and reviews to Canadian History Review, Hispanic Am. Hist. Review, Miss. Valley Hist. Review, U. of Mich. Hist. Studies, I, and several local hist. jours. Home: 115 S. East Av., Waukesha, Wis. Died Oct. 12, 1951.

RUSSELL, Norman Felt Shelton, chmn. bd. U.S. Pipe & Foundry Co.; b. Jersey City, Sept. 29, 1880; s. William Jay and Francelia (Felt) R.; A.B., Colgate U., 1901, LL.D., 1940; m. Ella Dewees Eisenbrey, May 15, 1920; children—Norman Felt, Louis (dec. 1944), Ella King, Grace Felt. With Colgate. Hoyt & Co., bankers and brokers, N.Y., 1902-09; with U.S. Pipe and Foundry Co. since 1910, pres., 1923-48, chairman board since 1948; dir. Pa. Co. for Banking & Trusts, Colgate-Palmolive-Peet Co. (Jersey City, N.J.), U.S. Sugar Corporation (Clewiston, Florida), West Jersey & Seashore R.R., Sloss-Sheffield Steel & Iron Co., Cramp Shipbuilding Co., Cotton & Woolen Mfrs. Mutual Ins. Co. of New England, Penna. & Atlantic R.R. Co., United Concrete Pipe Corporation, Am. Mut. Liability Ins. Co., Trustee Colgate U., Jefferson Medical College. Member and medalist (1938) Franklin Institute; member Am. Water Works Assn., Am. Gas Assn, Am. Inst. of Mining and Metall. Engrs., Am. Iron and Steel Inst., Army Ordnance Assn., Gen. Soc. Colonial Wars, Delta Kappa Epsilon. Mason. Republican. Baptist. Clubs: City Midday, (N.Y.); Mountain Brook (Birmingham, Ala.); Pine Valley Golf, Seaview Country. Racquet, Union League (Phila.). Home: Neshaminy Hall, Edgewater Park, N.J. Office: Burlington, N.J. Died Feb. 24, 1954; buried Hamilton, N.Y.

RUSSELL, Robert Lee, judge; b. Winder, Ga., Aug. 19, 1900; s. Richard Brevard and Ina (Dillard) R.; student, Fifth Dist. A. and M. Sch., Monroe, Ga., 1913-16, Gordon Inst., Barnesville, Ga., 1916-18, Univ. Ga., 1918-19, studied law in office of father (afterwards Chief Justice Supreme Ct. of Ga.) and admitted to bar on examination, 1920; married Sybil Millsaps, June 27, 1923; children—Robert Lee, Betty (Mrs. S. Ernest Vandiver, Jr.), Richard Brevard, III, Mary Ina. Private practice of law in Atlanta, Ga., 1920-23; sec., Chief Justice Supreme Court of Ga., 1923-29; private practice, Winder, Ga., 1929-40; U.S. district judge, Northern Dist. of Georgia, 1940-49; judge U.S. Court of Appeals 5th Circuit, 1949—. Mem. Am. Law Inst., Ga. Bar Assn. (mem. first bd. of govs.), Am. Judicature Soc., Am. Bar Assn., Am. Legion (past post comdr.), Sigma Alpha Epsilon. Presbyterian. Clubs: Kiwanis, Athletic, Capital City (Atlanta); Boston (New Orleans). Home: "Russell," Winder, Ga. Died Jan. 18, 1955; buried Russel Meml. Park, Winder.

RUSSELL, Scott, broadcasting exec.; b. Atlanta, May 21, 1895; s. James Simeon and Mary (Scott) R.; student Randolph-Macon Acad., Bedford, Va.; student Mercer U., Macon, Ga., 1924-26; m. Emma Sutherland, Nov. 26, 1919 (died May 1943); children—James Sutherland, Benjamin Scott; m. 2d, Christie Kennedy, Nov. 2, 1944. In wholesale lumber bus., 1912-16, admitted to Ga. bar, 1926; lawyer, 1926-38; U.S. dist. atty., 1928; cotton textile mfg., 1938-43; pres. Bibb Mfg. Co., 1941-43; resigned 1943; counsel Senate Postwar Planning Com., 1943-44; pres. Greenville Broadcasting Co. (S.C.). Served as lt. US AAF, World War I. Home: Poinsett Hotel. Address: 1 College St., Greenville, S.C. Died Apr. 21, 1950; buried Macon, Ga.

RUSSELL, Stanley Addison, bus. exec.; b. Des Moines, Ia., Nov. 20, 1889; s. Samuel A. and Mary D. (Davidson) R.; M.E., Cornell, 1912; m. Eleanor Harriet Agar, Sept. 26, 1913 (dec.); m. 2d, Helene B. Norris, Oct. 22, 1952. With Harris Trust & Savs. Bank, Chgo., 1912-18; with Nat. City Co., N.Y.C., 1918, asst. v.p., 1921, v.p., 1922-34; pres. Lazard, Fereres & Co., Inc., 1934-38, partner, 1938-41; pres., dir. Comml. Investing Corp. Club: Recess, Bankers, Cornell, University (N.Y.C.); Baltusrol Golf, Montclair (N.J.) Golf; Chicago (Chgo.); Pine Valley (N.J.). Home: 24 Crestmont Rd. Office: Box T, Montclair, N.J. Died Dec. 31, 1958; buried Mt. Hebron Cemetery, Montclair, N.J.

RUSSELL, Walter C(harles), biochemist; b. Bellaire, O., Oct. 1, 1892; s. Charles C. and Eliza Jane (Kneff) R.; B.S., Ohio Wesleyan, 1914, Sc. D. (hon.), 1947; student Sorbonne, 1919, Harvard (grad. fellow in biochem.), 1919-20; M.S., Syracuse U., 1923; Ph.D., U. of Chicago (Swift fellow in chem., 1923-25), 1927; m. Mildred Irene Stephens, Aug. 25, 1923; 1 dau., Ruth Elizabeth. Teacher Chillicothe (O.) high sch., 1914-15; instr. chem., Ohio Wesleyan, 1915-17, Syracuse U., 1920-23; asst. prof. agrl. biochem., Rutgers, 1925-29, asso. prof. agrl. biochem., 1929-31; prof. and chmn. dept.

agrl. biochem.; research splst. in agrl. biochem., N.J. Agrl. Expt. Sta., Rutgers, since 1925; exec. sec. grad. faculty, Rutgers U., 1935-52, dean of the graduate school since July 1952. Member adv. scientific council Com. on Foods of Am. Vet. Med. Assn. and Am. Animal Hosp. Assn. since 1937; mem. Nat. Research Council since 1943. Served as pvt. to capt., San. Corps, U.S. Army, 1917-19; overseas. Mem. Am. Chem. Soc., Am. Soc. Biol. Chemists, Am. Inst. Nutrition (mem. council 1950-53), Assn. Land-Grant Colls. and Univs. (chairman council on instrn. 1952), A.A.A.S., Society Exptl. Biol. and Medicine, Delta Tau Delta, Sigma Xi, Phi Lambda Upsilon, Alpha Chi Sigma, Phi Kappa Phi, Phi Beta Kappa (hon.). Presbyn. Author: Grass Silage and Dairying (with Ray Ingham, Willis A. King and Carl B. Bender), 1949. Mem. editorial bd. Journal of Nutrition, 1945-49. Contbr. articles on nutrition and biochemistry to various professional jours. Home: 27 Oak Hills Rd., Metuchen. Office: Rutgers Univ., New Brunswick, N.J. Died Mar. 10, 1954.

RUSSELL, William Fletcher, govt. ofcl.; b. Delhi, Delaware County, N.Y., May 18, 1890; s. James Earl and Agnes (Fletcher) R.; A.B., Cornell U., 1910; Ph.D., Columbia, 1914; LL.D., George Washington U., 1928, U. of Pittsburgh, 1928, Colby Coll., 1929, Columbia, 1929; Ed.D., Colo. Coll. of Edn., 1935; Ed.D., Sofia, Bulgaria, 1939; fellow E.I.S., Univ. of Edinburgh, 1947; married Clotilde Desjardins, June 17, 1913; children—William Fletcher, Jr., James E. II, Robert. Assistant professor of history and sociology, State Teachers College of Colo., 1911-12; grad. scholar, 1912-13, hon. fellow and assistant in philosophy of edn., Teachers College, Columbia, 1913-14; asso. prof. secondary education, 1914-15, prof., 1915-17, George Peabody Coll. for Teachers, Nashville, Tenn.; dean Coll. of Edn., State U. of Ia., 1917-23; prof. edn. since 1923, asso. dir. internat. inst., 1923-27; dean, 1927-49, pres., 1949-54, Teachers Coll. (Columbia Univ.), prof. emeritus 1954; dep. dir. tech. services, Fgn. Operations Adminstrn., 1954-—. Dir. ednl. section, Russian Division, Com. on Pub. Information, July 1918-Feb. 1919; mem. China Ednl. Commn., 1921-22; chmn. Am. delegation World Federation of Edn. Assn., 1925-27; ednl. adviser A. L.A., 1924-30; chmn. Am. Council on Edn., 1933-35; mem. Nat. Advisory Com. on Edn., 1928-31; mem. of The Am. Youth Commn. (Am. Council on Edn.), 1935-42; dir. Nat. Citizenship Education Program, Department of Justice 1941-45; expert, War Dept., during World War II. Chmn. Adv. Com. on Human Relations of Bd. of Education of the city of New York, N.Y., 1945-47; president of the World Organization of the Teaching Profession 1947-52; hon. v.p. of the Ulster Teachers Union, 1952. Member Phi Beta Kappa (Cornell), Phi Delta Kappa (Laureate chpt.). Commander the Order of St. Sava (Jugoslavia); Officer of the Legion of Honor (France); Commander Order of St. Alexander (Bulgaria). Awarded Butler medal, silver, 1928. Awarded medal for distinguished achievement by Alumni Association of Horace Mann School. Mason (K.T., 32°). Episcopalian. Clubs: Columbia University, Century Association, Union Club (New York); Pequot Yacht; Cosmos (Washington); Country Club (Fairfield Conn.); Union Interalliée (Paris), Atheneum (London). Author: Economy in Secondary Education, 1916; Education in the United States (in Sandiford's Comparative Education), 1917; Education in a Democracy (in Russian), Vladivostok, 1918; Schools in Siberia, 1919; The Short Constitution (with M. J. Wade), 1921; School Finance in Iowa Cities, 1921; The Financing of Education in Iowa (with others), 1925. Contbr. to Christian Education in China, 1922; Schools in Bulgaria, 1923; Liberty vs. Equality, 1936; The New "Common Sense," 1941; The Meaning of Democracy (with T. H. Briggs), 1941. Editor: The Rise of a University, Vol. I, 1937. Address: Executive Office Bldg., Washington. Died Mar. 26, 1956.

RUSSELL, William Logie, psychiatrist; b. New Brunswick, Can., July 24, 1863; s. William and Jane (Logie) R.; student U. of N.B., 1879-81; M.D., U. Med. Coll. (N.Y.U.), 1885; m. Addie Lena Lewis, Feb. 15, 1888. Hosp. work, N.J., 1885-87; pvt. practice, N.Y.C., 1888-97; 1st asst. physician Willard State Hosp., N.Y., 1897-1903; med. insp. N.Y. State Hosp. Commn., 1903-10; med. supt. L.I. State Hosp., 1910-11; med. dir. Bloomingdale Hosp., 1911-26; psychiatric dir. Soc. N.Y. Hosp., 1926-36; cons. psychiatrist N.Y. Hospital, Grasslands Hospital; emeritus prof. psychiatry, Cornell U. Med. Sch. Mem. A.M.A., Am. Psychiatric Assn. (ex-pres.), Nat. Com. for Mental Hygiene (v.p.), N.Y. Psychiatric Soc. (ex-pres.), N.Y. Soc. Clin. Psychiatry, Med. Soc. State of N.Y., Westchester County Med. Soc. (ex-pres.), Assn. for Research Nervous and Mental Diseases, N.Y. Acad. Medicine, A.A.A.S. Republican. Episcopalian. Club: National Arts (N.Y. C.). Home: Mountain Laurel Farm, Cheshire, Conn. Office: 525 E. 68th St., N.Y.C. Died Mar. 30, 1951; buried Plainfield, N.J.

RUSSUM, B(enjamin) C(arl), physician; b. Topeka, Kan., Jan. 6, 1892; s. William Benjamin and Louisa May (Gunn) R.; A.B., Creighton U., 1912, M.D., 1916; m. Harriett May Jarrett, Aug. 14, 1922; children—Dorothy May (Mrs. Walter Gerhard Nelson), William John, Paul Eugene. Intern, Kings Co. Hosp., Brooklyn, 1916-17; postgrad. study pathology Rush Med. Coll., Chicago, 1920; resident pathology St. Joseph Hosp., Omaha Neb., 1921-22; mem. faculty Creighton U. Sch. Medicine since 1922, prof. pathology, head dept. since 1947; attending pathologist St. Joseph's, Douglas Co. hosps.; cons. pathologist St. Catherine's Hosp., Veterans Administration Hospital, Omaha; pathologist U.P. Ry. Co. since 1943. Served as 1st lt. to capt. Med. Res. Corps. U.S. Army, France, 1917-19; maj. Med. Res. Corps, 1925-35. Fellow A.M.A., Coll. Am. Pathologists; mem . Internat. Assn. Med. Mus., American Association for Advancement Sci., Am. Soc. Clin. Pathologists, Physicians Health Assn. (pres. dir.). Editor of Jour. Omaha Mid-West Clin. Soc. 1950-53. Home: 2524 N. 55th St., Omaha 4. Office: 306 N. 14th St., Omaha 2, Neb. Died May 25, 1956; buried Hillcrest Meml. Park, Omaha, Neb.

RUST, Charles Herbert, clergyman; b. Winchester, Mass., Dec. 18, 1869; s. Charles M. and Mary Louise R.; ed. pub. schs. and Gordon Sch. (now Gordon Coll. and Divinity Sch.), Boston, and Rochester (N.Y.) Theol. Sem.; m. Bertha W. Smart, Dec. 18, 1893. Ordained Bapt. ministry, 1898; home missionary work, 1894-1906; pastor Second Ch., Rochester, N.Y., 1906, then Immanuel Ch., Scranton, Pa., Plymouth Congl. Ch., Worcester, Mass., 1925. Dist. sec. Am. Bapt. Publ. Soc., N.Y., 1905-06. Retired. Author: A Church on Wheels, 1905; Personal Religion, 1915; The Church a Field for Service, 1914; The World I Love (verse), 1925; The Christmas Birth, 1927; The Christmas Bells, 1928; The Educated Layman, 1930; I Wish It Were True, 1942; It Will Be Different This Time, 1943; Both Feet on the Earth, 1946. Home: 2107 University Dr. Orlando, Fla. Died Jan. 2, 1953; buried Holden, Mass.

RUST, John Daniel, inventor, executive, cons. engr., student of world affairs; b. Stephens County, Tex., Sept. 6, 1892; son of Benjamin Daniel and Susan Minerva (Burnett) R.; ed. public schools of Texas and private study; married Thelma Ford, December 1, 1933. Assisted in development of better farm machinery 1922-27; inventor of Rust cotton picker, discovered its basic principles, 1927, and since engaged in perfecting and promoting it; also inventor of Rust cotton cleaner, 1940, attachment for lawn mowers, 1945; cons. engr. Allis-Chalmers Mfg. Co., 1944-47; cons. engr. Ben Pearson, Inc.; founder and pres. John Rust Found., Inc., and The John Rust Co., 1951. Mem. Internat. Auxiliary Lang. Assn., World Calendar Assn., Am. Acad. Polit. and Social Science, Nat. Geographic Soc., West Tenn. Hist. Soc. Home: 3520 Cherry St. Office: 1416 Poplar St., Pine Bluff, Ark. Died Jan. 20, 1954.

RUST, Walter L., president of the Chippewa Trust Company; b. Randolph, Ill., June 7, 1892; s. Lee and Mattie Elizabeth (McFarland) R.; student in law Ill. Wesleyan U., 1913-15; m. Ethel Deloras Wiley, Dec. 24, 1913; 1 dau., Suzanne Elizabeth. Began as messenger, resigned as pres., McLean County Bank, Bloomington, Ill.; dir.; pres. Federal Land Bank of St. Louis, 1933-42, resigned Sept. 1942); pres. Chippewa Trust Co., since Mar. 1949. Chmn. Price Adjustment Bd., St. Louis Ordnance Dist. (St. Louis). Mem. Modern Woodmen, Moose, Phi Delta Phi. Mason (Consistory). Clubs: Rotary, Missouri Athletic (St. Louis). Home: 329 Belt Av., St. Louis 12. Address: 3803 S. Broadway, St. Louis. Died Nov. 5, 1958.

RUTAN, Harold Duane, banker; Newark, Dec. 1, 1898; s. David Dodd and Mary (Starkweather) R.; LL.B., N.Y.U., 1921; m. Silva Downs, Apr. 15, 1925; children—Harold Duane, William David. Admitted to N.J. bar, 1922; mem. law dept. Prudential Ins. Co. Am., 1924-25, mgr. Montreal mortgage office, 1925-27, regional appraiser charge city mortgages in Ill., Ind. and Ia., 1927-28, asst. supr. charge city mortgage loans, 1928-29, supr., 1929-39; exec. v.p. The Bank for Savs., N.Y.C., 1939-53, sr. exec. v.p., 1953-56, vice chmn. bd., 1956-—; mem. adv. bd. Met. br. Chase Manhattan Bank. Vice pres. bd. trustees Savs. Banks Retirement System, 1946-56; mem. gen. development com. Savs. Bank Life Ins. Council, 1955-56; pres. Mortgage Conf. City N.Y., 1944-47. Served with USNRF, World War I. Mem. N.Y. State Savs. Bank Assn., Phi Delta Phi. Club: Union League (N.Y.C.). Home: 36 E. 36th St., N.Y.C. 16. Office: 280 4th Av., N.Y.C. 10. Died Nov. 13, 1956.

RUTH, Henry Swartley, physician, anesthesiologist; b. Phila., Pa., Aug. 12, 1899; s. Henry Laban Swartley and Carrie Anders (Kindig) R.; student Swarthmore Coll., 1917-18; student Hahnemann Sch. of Science, 1918-19, B.S., 1921; M.D., Hahnemann Med. 1923; m. Lola Althouse Zendt, July 16, 1924; children—Patricia Anne (Mrs. James C. Straus, 3d), Henry Swartley, Jr. Anesthetist Hahnemann Hosp., 1924-—, St Luke's and Children's Hosp., Phila., 1927-41; clin. prof. anesthesia, Hahnemann Med. Coll. and Hosp., 1933-40, prof. and head dept. Anesthesiology since 1942; chief, div. of anesthesia Phila. Gen. Hospital, 1933-40, consulting anesthetist since 1940; chief, anesthetic service, West Jersey Homeo. Hosp., Camden, 1941-42. Civilian cons. U.S. Naval Hospital, Phila., 1948-52. Served in S.A.T.C., 1918. Director courses in anesthesiology, U.S. Army and Navy, World War II. On Am. Bd. of Anesthesiology, 1937-52 (pres. 1943-44). Fellow Internat. College of Surgeons, Am. Med. Writers Assn.; mem. Soc. of Anesthetists, Inc. (pres. 1938); Phila. County Med. Soc. (chmn. anesthesia study commn.), A.M.A., (rep. sect. on anesthesiology in Ho. Dels., 1941-54), Internat. Anesthesia Research Soc., Homeo. Med. Soc. of Pa., Germantown Homeo. Med. Soc. of Phila. (pres. 1936), Am. Inst. Homeop., Montgomery Co. Med. Society, Phila. Soc. Anesthesiol. (pres. 1947-48), Pa. Soc. Anesthesiol. (pres. 1943-49), World Med. Assn. Episcopalian. Mason. Clubs: Union League, Rotary, Penn, Merion Golf, Bachelor's Barge, Merion Cricket (Phila.). Author: Sect. on "Anesthetics," Revision Service Vol. of Cyclopedia of Medicine, 1944; sect. on "Regional Anesthesia," Bancroft's Operative Surgery, 1941. Asso. editor: Anesthesia Subjects in Cyclopedia of Medicine, Surgery and Specialties, 1939-52; articles on anesthesia, scientific and medical subjects in med. jours. Editor: Anesthesiology (organ of Am. Soc. Anesthetists, Inc.) since 1940. Mem. editorial bd., Am. Journal of Surgery. Home: 225 Cheswold Lane, Haverford, Pa. Office: Hahnemann Med. Coll. and Hosp., 230 N. Broad St., Phila. 2. Died 1956.

RUTHERFORD, Alexander H., business exec.; b. San Francisco, Aug. 31, 1876; s. Alexander H. and Emma M. (Hanchett) R.; student Belmont (Cal.) Sch., 1889-93; Phillips Andover Acad., 1893-96; Yale, 1899; m. Helen D. Smyth, Oct. 1911 (div. 1924); m. 2d, Lucy (Stevens) Kingsley, June 2, 1934. Mem. N.Y. Stock Exchange, 1900-12; rancher, Pleyto ranch, Cal., 1912-25; asso. Hanchett Oil Co., Santa Rosa, N.M., 1925-30; ret. active bus., 1932; dir. Revere Copper & Brass, Inc. Mem. Delta Phi. Republican. Episcopalian. Elk. Clubs: Rome (N.Y.C.); Blind Brook Golf (Port Chester, N.Y.); Racquet and Tennis, Links (N.Y.C.); Bath and Tennis, Everglades, Gulf Stream Golf (Palm Beach, Fla.). Office: 137 N. James St., Rome, N.Y. (P.O. Box 271). Died July 22, 1955; buried Rome (N.Y.) Cemetery.

RUTLEDGE, Carl P., ins. exec.; b. Early, Ia., July 6, 1894; s. Walter A. and Jessie M. (Soper) R.; student pub. schs. Des Moines; m. G. Naomi Huntoon, Oct. 12, 1915; children—George F., Phyllis A. (Mrs. Alan P. Vierheller), David A., Nancy J. Ins. writer Farmers Mutual Hail Ins. Co. Ia., Des Moines, 1913-15, agy. supervisor, adjustor, 1915-33, dir. since 1933, pres. since 1937. Dir. Farmers Mutual Hail Ins. Co. Mo. since 1935, Farmers Mutual Windstorm Ins. Co. Mo. since 1939, Am. Mutual Reins. Chicago since 1946. Mem. Nat., Ia. assns. mutual ins. assns. (dir. Nat. 1944-47, pres. Ia. 1950-51). Mason (Shriner). Clubs: Rotary, Golf and Country. Home: 6124 Harwood Dr., Des Moines 12. Office: 1019 High St., Des Moines 9, Ia. Died Jan. 28, 1952.

RUTTER, Josiah Baldwin, business exec.; b. Waltham, Mass., March 30, 1892; s. Nathaniel and Elizabeth M. (Lang) R.; B.S., Civil Engring., Tufts Coll., Medford, Mass., 1914; student law, N.Y. U., 1915-16; m. Miriam Goss, May 18, 1918; children—Nathaniel P., Miriam G. (Mrs. E. T. Otis, Jr.). Dir. Rutland R.R., 1942-47; chief engr. Merrimac Chem. Co., 1922; dir. engring. Monsanto Chem. Co., 1936, vice president, gen. mgr. Merrimac div., 1947-49; industrial consultant since 1949; director Merritt-Monsanto Corp., Nat. Shawmut Bank, New England Alcohol Co.; pres. and dir. Merrimac Chem. Transportation Corp.; cons. engr. J. R. Worcester, 1914-15; industrial mgr. Russell Co., Boston, 1919-20; trustee New England Alcohol Co. Served as capt. engrs., U.S. Army, World War I. Mem. Am. Soc. C.E. Clubs: Algonquin (Boston); Detroit (Detroit); Tuscarora (Lockport, N.Y.); Metropolitan (N.Y. City); Mo. Athletic (St. Louis). Home: 90 Commonwealth Av., Boston. Office: 90 Commonwealth Av., Boston 16. Died Jan. 28, 1951.

RUUTZ-REES, Caroline (rōōtz'rēs), educator; b. London, Eng.; d. Louis Emile and Janet (Meugens) Ruutz-Rees; came to U.S., 1883; LL.A., St. Andrew's (Scotland), 1904; Élève Tit. École des Hautes Études, U. of Paris, 1906; M.A., Columbia. 1907, Ph.D., 1909; children (adopted)—Roland, Elizabeth (Mrs. James Brickell). Taught in various pvt. schs., 1885-90; founded Rosemary Hall, Wallingford, Conn., 1890, now at Greenwich, Conn., ret. Chmn. Conn. Div. Woman's Com. Council Nat. Def., 1917; chmn. for Conn. of Women's Overseas Canteen Sect., Y.M. C.A., 1918; mem. Conn. State Council Def., 1918; mem. Dem. Nat. Com., Dem. State Central Com. until 1926; mem. edn. com. English-Spearking Union; trustee Fairfield State Hosp. to 1948; state chmn., NRA, 1933; hon. chmn. Greenwich Chpt. Brit. War Relief; former chmn. Greenwich Br. Brit-Am. Ambulance Corps. Mem. price and rationing bd. OPA. Mem. Greenwich Bd. Edn. Mem. Archaeol. Inst. Am., Classical Assn. of N.E., Am. Assn. Univ. Women, Modern Lang. Assn., Soc. des Études Rabelaisiennes, Mus. of French Art, Nat. Inst. of Social Sci. Episcopalian. Clubs: Field (Greenwich); Cosmopolitan (N.Y.C.); Albemarle, Women's University (London); Union Interallié (Paris). Author: Charles de Sainte Marthe, a study in the French Renaissance; Places and Other Poems, 1947. Contbr. Modern Lang. Assn. Publ., Modern Lang. Notes, Romanic Rev., etc. Home: Greenwich, Conn. Died Feb. 15, 1954.

RUYLE, John Bryan (rōōl), archeologist, dentist; b. Athensville, Ill., Oct. 5, 1896; s. John and Celia Pricilla (Biggs) R.; ed. U.S. Mil. Acad., 1915-16; Valparaiso (Ind.) U., 1916; Chicago Coll. of Dental Surgery, 1916-18; St. Louis (Mo.) Dental Coll., 1918-19; U. of Ill., 1934-36; m. Mary Esther Gaul, Aug. 7, 1918; children—Jo Ann Virginia, John Bryan, Joyce Elaine. Served in U.S. Army, 1918. Mem. American Dental Society, Champaign-Danville District Dental Society, Illinois State Dental Society, Miss. Valley Fedn. Archeol. Socs. (pres.), Ill. State Archeol. Soc. (pres. emeritus and dir.), Champaign County Archeol. Soc. (pres.), Soc. Am. Archeology, Mo. and Wis. archeol. socs., Ill. State Acad. Science, Ill. State Hist. Soc., McLean Co. Hist. Soc., Sons of the Revolution (Ill. chap.), S. Ill. Historical Soc., Psi Omega, Sigma Xi, Phi Sigma. Awarded gold medal and citation from Ill. State Archeol. Soc., Northwestern University, 1941, for outstanding research in the field of Am. archeology and notable contributions to the advancement of archaeology. Merit badge, counselor Indian lore, Arrowhead Council (Champaign). Democrat. Mem. Christian Ch. Clubs: Exchange, Audubon, Champaign Country. Contbr. to archeol. and sci. publs. Dir. Animal Ecology, Inc., Vivarium Bldg., U. of Ill. Home: 1411 W. Church St. Office: 133 W. Park St., Champaign, Ill. Died May 7, 1952.

RUZICKA, Charles (roo zik - kå), lawyer; b. Baltimore, June 1, 1896; s. Dr. Charles and Marie (Brohmann) R.; Johns Hopkins U., 1920; LL.B., U. Md., 1918; Charles U., Prague, 1922; m. Phyllis Tutein, Oct. 20, 1923. Admitted Md. bar, 1918, practiced law Baltimore, since 1918; mem. firm Cook, Ruzicka, Veazey & Gans since 1949. Commr. of The Interstate Commn. on Crime, 1935-44. Served U.S. Navy, 1917-19. Chmn. com. on co-operation with International Bar and Inter Am. Bar Assns. Mem. Am. Bar Assn. (mem. bd. govs., 1947-50; mem. gen. council, 1935-38, mem. House Dels., 1938-49; chmn. dels. to Internat. Bar Conf., London, 1950; del. to Inter-Am. Bar Conf., Mexico City, 1944, Montevideo, 1951), Am. Law Inst., Am. Judicature Soc., Md. Bar Assn., Bar Assn. of Baltimore City, Am. Legion, Gamma Eta Gamma. Republican. Clubs: Baltimore Country, Merchants, Candem Yacht. Home: 5803 Roland Av., Baltimore 10. Office: First Nat. Bank Bldg., Balt. 2. Died Nov. 17, 1952; buried Druid Ridge Cemetery, Pikesville, Md.

RYAN, Clendenin J(ames), business exec.; b. Suffern, N.Y., July 16, 1905; s. Clendenin James and Caroline (O'Neil) R.; student St. Georges' School, 1918-24; Princeton, 1924-28; m. Jean Harder, Nov. 18, 1937; children—Clendenin James, Caryn, Cyr Annan, Jean. With Guaranty Trust Co. of N.Y., 1929-32; vice pres., 15th Assembly Dist. Republican Club, N.Y., 1932-33; asst. to Mayor La Guardia, 1933-38; asst. commr. dept. of sanitation, N.Y. City, 1938-40; commr. of commerce, N.Y. City, 1940; director Companhia de Diamantes de Angola (Portugal); owner Panther Ledge Farms, New Jersey. Delegate from New Jersey to Republican Nat. Conv., 1948. Served as lt., U.S.N.R., active duty, 1941, flag sec. to comdr. of Carrier Task Force, So. Pacific, 1942-43, and on staff of comdr. air, Solomon Islands, Feb.-March 1943; Guadalcanal; comdr. U.S. N.R., inactive duty, 1945. Received citation and Naval Commendation Ribbon. Fellow Pierpont Morgan Library. Mem. Am. Legion, Reserve Officers Assn., Am. Irish Hist. Soc., Nat. Urban League (dir.). Republican. Roman Catholic. Clubs: Ivy of Princeton, Brook, Racquet and Tennis, Knickerbocker (N.Y.). Home: Allamuchy, N.J. Office: 515 Madison Av., N.Y. C. 22. Died Sept. 1957.

RYAN, Edward Francis, bishop; b. Lynn, Mass., Mar. 10, 1878; student Boston Coll., North Am. Coll., Rome. Ordained priest, Roman Cath. Ch., 1905; pastor Holy Name Ch., West Roxbury, Mass.; bishop of Burlington, 1944—. Address: 52 Williams St., Burlington, Vt. Died Nov. 3, 1956.*

RYAN, Elmer James, ex-congressman; b. Rosemount, Minn., May 26, 1907; s. John Owen and Agnes Teresa (Hyland) R.; LL.B., U. of Minn. Law Sch., 1929; m. Elenore Ann Moravec, June 21, 1932 (died Feb. 1938); children—Elmer James, Jacqueline Marie; m. 2d, Marjorie Fuller, July 31, 1939; children—John Fuller, Geoffrey Fuller, Jeremy de March, Joseph de March. Admitted to Minn. bar, 1929; in practice at South St. Paul, asso. with Harold E. Stassen, atty. of City of South St. Paul, 1933-34; mem. 74th to 76th Congresses (1934-41), 2d Minn. Dist. Ordered to active duty as 1st lt. Officers Res. Corps, U.S. Army 1942, capt., 1942, maj., 1945, discharged 1945. Democrat. Catholic. K.C. Home: 89 Virginia St., St. Paul, Minn. Office: Grand Bldg., South St. Paul, Minn. Died Feb. 1, 1958.

RYAN, Evelyn Althea Murphy (Mrs. Charles Gaston Ryan), Dem. nat. committeewoman; b. Maquoketa, Ia., July 28, 1869; d. Michael and Eliza (Humphrey) Murphy; student pub. schs. and Brownell Hall; m. Charles Gaston Ryan, Dec. 24, 1896; 1 dau., Evelyn. Pub. sch. tchr., 1889-96. Del. Dem. Nat. Conv., 1928 mem. Bd. Clarkson Hosp., Omaha. Mem. League of Women Voters. Episcopalian (del. to Gen. Conv. of Episcopal Ch., 1937). Clubs: Business and Professional Women's, Grand Island Woman's. Home: 206 S. Lincoln Av., Grand Island, Neb. Died Feb. 12, 1951; buried Grand Island, Neb.

RYAN, Franklin Winton, economist; b. Meadville, Pa.; s. Augustus Eddy and Femma Jane (Marley) R.; M.B.A. cum laude, Harvard, 1921, M.A., 1923; Ph. D., 1925; m. Katherine Ann MacMillan, July 5, 1925; 1 dau., Sara Grace. Teaching asst. U. Chgo., 1920; instr. bank mgmt. Harvard, 1922-25; asst. chief finance div. U.S. Dept. of Commerce, 1925-26; v.p. Gilbert Badger's investment banking enterprises, N.Y. and N.J., 1927-32; asst. dir. div. research and statistics Fed. Home Loan Bank System, D.C. charge statistics HOLC, 1935-40; research adviser WPB, 1941-42; economist in depts., Army and Navy, 1943—. Commd. maj. finance dept. res. AUS, 1926; mem. staff Indsl. Coll. Armed Forces, Office Sec. War, 1944-47. Recipient Jesse Isidor Straus prize scholarship, Harvard, 1922, Hart, Schaffner & Marx $1000 prize, 1923, Rockefeller Found. grant for municipal research at Harvard, 1933-35. Mem. Am. Econ. Assn., Pi Gamma Mu. Episcopalian. Club: Harvard. Author: Usury and Usury Laws, 1924; Municipal Control of Retail Trade, (with Miller McClintock), 1935. Home: 2437 N. Taylor St., Arlington 7, Va. Died Mar. 13, 1957; buried Arlington Nat. Cemetery.

RYAN, Frederick Behrens, advertising; b. New York, N.Y., Aug. 21, 1883; s. Charles Edgar and Florence (Behrens) R.; prep. edn. Cheshire (Conn.) Acad.; Ph.B., Sheffield Scientific Sch., Yale, 1904; m. Elizabeth Cady, Oct. 8, 1904; children—Frederick Behrens, Quincy G., Bruce E. (dec.). In engring. until 1912; in advertising bus. with W. B. Ruthrauff 1912—; former chmn. bd. Ruthrauff & Ryan, Inc. Mem. Chi Phi. Republican. Episcopalian. Clubs: University, Yale, New York Yacht, Larchmont Yacht, Devon Yacht, (New York); National Golf Links (Southampton, L.I.); Cloud; Short Hills, Maidstone. Home: Appoquoque Rd., East Hampton, L.I., N.Y. Office: 405 Lexington Av., N.Y.C. Died Nov. 29, 1955.

RYAN, James, bishop; b. Thurles, Co. Tipperary, Ireland, 1848; came to U.S. in childhood; studied for priesthood in sems. of St. Thomas and St. Joseph, Bardstown, Ky. Ordained R.C. ministry; prof. in St. Joseph's Sem.; pastor in Ky., Wataga, Danville, and Ottawa, Ill., to 1888; consecrated bishop of Alton, Ill., 1888. Address: Alton, Ill. Deceased.

RYAN, James Augustine, army officer; b. Danbury, Conn., Oct. 22, 1867; s. James Ryan and Hanna (Doran) R.; grad. U.S. Mil. Acad., 1890; honor grad. Inf. and Cav. Sch., 1906; m. Rosemary Tarleton, Feb. 16, 1911. Commd. 2d lt. 10th Cav., June 12, 1890; 1st lt., Feb. 3, 1897; capt. 15th Cav., Feb. 2, 1901; maj. 5th Cav., Sept. 15, 1912; assigned to 13th Cav., Sept. 1, 1914; lt. col., Oct. 1, 1916; col., July 22, 1917; brig. gen. N.A., Dec. 17, 1917. Apptd. comdr. 1st Cav. Brigade, 15th Cav. Div. Roman Catholic. Clubs: Army and Navy (Washington), Catholic (N.Y.C.). Home: 14 Bellevue Pl., Chgo. Died Jan. 14, 1956.

RYAN, Stanley Martin, lawyer; b. Janesville, Wis., June 1, 1898; s. Patrick William and Maria (Murphy) R.; student Columbia Coll., Dubuque, Ia., 1916-19; LL.B., U. Wis., 1922; m. Edith Irene McCarthy, Nov. 3, 1925; children—Ellen Anne, Paul Murray. Admitted to Wis. bar, 1922, practicing at Janesville; mem. Dougherty, Ryan & Campbell; asst. U.S. dist. atty., Western Dist. Wis., 1922-26, U.S. dist. atty., 1926-35; dir. Rock County Nat. Bank, Rock Co. Savs. and Trust Co., Janesville Citizens Loan & Investment Co., Schleuter Co., J. J. Smith's Jewelry Inc., Midwest Markets, Desens, Inc. Chmn. Janesville Police and Fire Commn., 1936—. Served with U.S. Army, Oct.-Dec. 1918. Mem. Am., Rock County (pres. 1944-45) bar assns., Wis. Bar Assn. (bd. govs., 1940), Phi Delta Theta, Phi Delta Phi, Am. Legion. Republican. K.C. Clubs: Wisconsin, Janesville Country (Janesville), Madison (Madison). Home: 420 Oak Rd. Office: Jackman Bldg., Janesville, Wis. Died Mar. 9, 1957; buried Mount Olive Cemetery, Janesville, Wis.

RYAN, Vincent J., bishop; b. Arlington, Wis., July 1, 1884; s. Thomas Francis and Ann R. (Welch) R.; student St. Francis Sem., Wis., 1902-06, St. Paul (Minn.) Sem., 1906-12; S.T.B., Catholic U. of America, 1906; LL.D., U. of N.D.,1938. Ordained priest, 1912; chancellor Diocese of Fargo, N.D., 1912-34, adminstr., 1935, officialis, 1936-39, vicar gen., 1939-40, diocesan dir. of charities, 1936-40; pastor St. Anthony's Ch., Fargo, 1918-40; bishop of Bismarck, N.D., since 1940. Pres. N.D. State Conf. of Social Work, 1933-34; mem. exec. bd. Conf. of Catholic Charities, 1935-40; pres. Nat. Catholic Rural Life Conf., 1939-41; dir. Fargo Catholic Welfare Bureau, 1926-40. Co-author and editor: Manifesto on Rural Life (with A. J. Muench, William T. Mulloy), 1939; also author occasional religious and sociol. articles in Catholic Rural Life Bulletin and Catholic Charities Rev. Address: 420 Raymond, Bismarck, N.D. Died Nov. 10, 1951; buried St. Mary's Cemetery, Bismarck.

RYCKMANS, Pierre, U.N. del.; b. Antwerp, Belgium, Nov. 26, 1891; s. Alphonse and Clémence van Ryn; LL.D., U. of Louvain, 1913; m. Madeleine Neve, February 3, 1920; children—Elisabeth, Jeannine, Jacques, Hélène, Jeane-Pierre, André, Claire, Etienne. Practiced law, Antwerp, 1913; civil servant in Belgian Congo, 1919-28; prof. Louvain Univ., 1929; gov. gen. of Belgian Congo, 1934-46; Belgian del., U.N. Gen. Assembly, 1946—; Belgium rep. trusteeship council, U.N. since 1947. Served with Belgian Army, World War I, 1914-19. Mem. Royal Colonial Inst. (Belgium), Internat. Colonial Inst., Internat. African Inst. Author: Dominer pour Servir, 1931; La Politique Coloniale, 1934; Allo Congo, 1935; Messages de Guerre, 1945; Etapes et Jalons, 1946; Barabara, 1946; A l'autre bout du Monde, 1948. Home: Uccle, Belgium. Office: Ministere des Affaires Estrangéres, Brussels, Belgium. Died Feb. 18, 1959.

RYGEL, John, fire ins. exec.; b. Independence, Mo., June 25, 1888; s. Leon and Anna (Morris) R.; m. Alma M. Corbin, Oct. 1, 1923; 1 dau., Nancy A. (Mrs. Richard Cavnar). Vice pres., dir. Hanover Fire Ins. Co., N.Y., Fulton Fire Ins. Co., N.Y. Clubs: Union League (Chgo); Drug and Chemical (N.Y.C.); Wykagyl Country (New Rochelle, N.Y.). Home: 1 Sutton Pl. S. Office: 111 John St., N.Y.C. Died Oct. 19, 1955.

RYGG, Andrew Nilsen (rĭg), ret. editor; b. Stavanger, Norway, Aug. 15, 1868; s. Ole Nilsen Rygh and Severine N. (Larsen) R.; came to U.S., 1888, naturalized, 1910; ed. Norwegian schs.; LL.D., St. Olaf College, Northfield, Minn.; m. Andrea Carlsen, 1895; children—Agnes, Einar. Editor Norwegian News, Bklyn., 1912-29. Mem. bd. dirs. various Norwegian-Am. instns. Decorated Comdr. of St. Olaf with star (Norway). Lutheran. Author, Norwegians in New York, 1825-1925; American Relief For Norway. Home: 974 52d St., Bklyn. Died Sept. 21, 1951; buried Greenwood Cemetery, Bklyn.

RYLAND, Robert Knight (ri-lănd), artist; b. Grenada, Miss., Feb. 10, 1873; s. William Semple and Mary Elizabeth (Morton) R.; B.A., Bethel Coll., Ky., 1892; studied Nat. Acad. Design and Art Students League, N.Y., 1894-1900; Lazarus scholarship for mural painting, at Rome, 1903-05; unmarried. Instr. drawing, Cooper Union, 1908-19; instr. N.Y. Evening Sch. of Industrial Art, 1923-26. Awarded Altman prize, Nat. Acad. Exhbn., 1924; hon. mention Art Inst. Chgo., 1926. Associate mem. Nat. Acad., 1940. Mem. Am. Soc. Mural Painters, Sigma Alpha Epsilon. Club: Salmagundi. Home: 51 West 10th St., N.Y.C. 11. Died 1951.

S

SAALFIELD, Albert George, publisher; born New York City, July 24, 1886; s. Arthur James and Ada L. (Sutton) S.; grad. Culver (Ind.) Mil. Acad., 1905; m. Elizabeth Myers Robinson, June 7, 1911; children—Henry Robinson, James Albert, Mary Robinson, Elizabeth Robinson. Began with Saalfield Publishing Co., Akron, 1905, sec., 1910-19, pres. and manager, 1919-52, chairman of the board of directors, 1952—; director Saalfield Pub. Co., Robinson Clay Products Co., First National Bank. Republican. Presbyterian. Clubs: Rotary, Akron City, Portage Country. Publisher and developer of one of the largest lines of books for children in America, also inventor of games and originator of activity books for children. Home: 3591 Granger Rd. Akron 13. Office: care Saalfield Publishing Co., Saalfield Square, Akron 1, O. Died Feb. 7, 1959; buried Akron, O.

SAARINEN, Eliel, architect; b. Helsingfors, Finland, 1873; grad. Inst. Poly., Helsingfors, 1897; hon. degreees: Ph.D., U. Helsingfors, U. Helsinki; Dr. Architecture, Tech. U. Finland; D.Eng., Tech. U. Karlsruhe, U. Karlsruhe, Germany; Dr. Architecture and City Planning, U. Mich.; ArtsD., Harvard; LL.D., Drake U.; Hon. Dr., Bethany Coll., Lindsborg, Kan. Asso. with Herman Gesellius and Armas Lindgren, architects, Finland, 1896-1907; most important work of firm, Nat. Museum, Helsingfors; built Finnish Pavilion at Paris Expn., 1900, railroad station, Helsingfors; practicing alone, 1907—; has erected for Cranbrook Found. (Bloomfield Hills, Mich.), 1925—, Acad. of Art (of which is pres.), Boys' Sch., Girls' Sch., Inst. of Science; other works in U.S. include Kleinhans Music Hall, Buffalo, N.Y. (with asso. architects), 1939; Tabernacle Christian Ch., Columbus, Ind., 1940-41; opera, concert shed, chamber music hall and studios, Berkshire Music Center, Stockbridge, Mass., 1941. Awarded 1st prize for city planning, Reval, Estonia; 2d prize city planning, Yas Canberra, Australia; 1st prize Gewerbeverein-Haus, Riga, Latvia; 2d prize Chgo. Tribune Tower; 1st prize in nat. competition Smithsonian Gallery of Art (with asso. architects); gold medal Archtl. League N.Y., A.I.A., Royal Inst. Brit. Architects; hon. medal Acad. Architects Soc. Denmark; apptd. hon. prof. Finnish Govt.;

Comdr. 1st Class Order of White Rose, Finland. Vice pres. Internat. City Planning Confs. Academicion Nat. Acad. Design, 1946. Mem. Finnish Acad. Art, Imperial Acad. Art (St. Petersburg, Russia), Royal Swedish Acad. Art; hon. mem. or corr. mem. numerous Am. and fgn. insts. socs. Author: The City; Search for Form. Home: Cranbrook Academy of Art, Bloomfield Hills, Mich. Died July 1, 1950; cremated.

SABATH, Adolph J., former dean U.S. Ho. of Reps.; b. Czechoslovakia, Apr. 4, 1866; came to U.S., 1881; student Bryant and Stratton's Bus. Coll., Chgo.; grad. Chgo. Coll. Law, 1891; LL.B., Lake Forest U., 1892; m. Mae Ruth Fuerst, Dec. 31, 1917. Admitted to Ill. bar, 1891, practiced law, Chgo., 1891-95; municipal judge and police magistrate, Chgo., 1895-1907; in 1906 had distinction of being nominated for two offices, municipal ct. judge and U.S. congressman, choosing the latter; re-elected 23 times; served under eight presidents and nine speakers; was a member of historic Com. on Fgn. Affairs of World War I period; attended joint conf. at White House of the Senate and House coms. on fgn. affairs on first return of Pres. Wilson from Europe; aided in bringing about the independence of Czechoslovakia, Poland and other small nations; mem. Com. on Immigration and Naturalization, 24 yrs., also served as mem. Com. on Interstate and Fgn. Commerce; chmn. Select Com. to Investigate Real Estate Bondholders' Reorgns.; chmn. Com. on Rules, 1938-45; ranking minority mem. 80th Congress, reapptd. chmn. 81st and 82d Congresses; introduced the first workmen's compensation bill; introduced the first RFC bill, 1931. Mem. Cook County (Ill.) Dem. Central Com., 49 yrs., mem. exec. com., 36 yrs., chmn. exec. com., 10 yrs.; del. Dem. Nat. Conv., 1896——. Mem. various social and civic orgns. Mason, Elk, K.P. Died Nov. 6, 1952; buried Forest Home Cemetery, Ill.

SABEN, Mowry, writer; b. Uxbridge, Mass., Mar. 24, 1870; s. Israel and Lydia Jane (Albee) S.; student Harvard, Oxford, Heidelberg univs. Began as lecturer, doing editorial writing most of career on Tacoma News, Portland (Ore.) Telegram, Denver Republican, Detroit Free Press, Chicago Journal, Rochester (N.Y.) Herald; contbd. editorials to Boston Transcript, New York Times, Baltimore American; asso. editor Washington Challenge; weekly econ. contbr. to Nat. Republican and The Argonaut; formerly U.S. commr. of conciliation and asst. to Sec. of Labor James J. Davis; became editor of The Argonaut, San Francisco, 1934. Author: The Twilight of the Gods, 1903; The Spirit of Life, 1914; Broken Lights (in Neal's Monthly); articles in The Forum. Home: Washington Hotel, San Francisco. Died Oct. 7, 1950; buried San Francisco.

SABIN, Florence Rena, anatomist; b. Central City, Colo., Nov. 9, 1871; d. George Kimball and Rena (Miner) Sabin; B.S., Smith Coll., 1893, Sc.D., 1910; M.D., Johns Hopkins, 1900; Sc.D., U. of Mich., 1926, Mt. Holyoke, 1929, New York U., 1933, Wilson Coll., 1933, Syracuse U., 1934, Oglethorpe, 1935, U. of Colo., 1935, U. of Pa., 1937, Oberlin Coll., 1937, Russell Sage College, 1938, U. of Denver, 1939, Woman's Medical Coll. of Pa., Phila., 1950; LL.D., Goucher Coll., 1931. Teacher mathematics, Wolfe Hall, Denver, Colo., 1893-94; asst. in zoölogy, Smith Coll., 1895; interne, Johns Hopkins, 1900-01; fellow Baltimore Assn. for Advancement of Univ. Edn. of Women, 1901; asst. in anatomy, Johns Hopkins, 1902, asso., 1903-05, asso. prof., 1905-17, prof. histology, 1917-25; mem. Rockefeller Inst. for Med. Research, 1925-38; mem. emeritus since 1938. Pres. board Finney-Howell Res. Foundn. Mem. Am. Assn. Anatomist (v.p. 1908-09; president 1924-26), Am. Assn. Physiologists, Soc. Exptl. Biology and Medicine (councilor 1932), Nat. Tb Assn., Nat. Acad. Scis.; hon. life member N.Y. Acad. Scis., Harvey Society, A.A.A.S., Am. Assn. Univ. Women, Nat. Achievement award, 1932; M. Carey Thomas prize, 1935; Lasker award, 1951. Clubs: Cosmopolitan, Am. Woman's Assn., Soc. Colonial Dames. Author: An Atlas of the Medulla and Mid-Brain, 1901; Biography of Franklin Paine Mall, 1934; also articles on the lymphatic system in Am. Jour. of Anatomy and Anatomical Record; on the blood vessels and origin of blood cells in the Contributions to Embryology pub. by the Carnegie Inst. of Washington and Johns Hopkins Hosp. Bull.; on blood and bone marrow in Physiol. Rev. and Proc. Soc. Exptl. Biology and Medicine; and on tuberculosis in the Jour. of Exptl. Medicine, Trans. of Nat. Tuberculosis Assn. and Am. Rev. of Tuberculosis. Bronze statue of her placed in Statuary Hall, Washington. Address: 1333 E. 10th Av., Denver. 18. Died Oct. 3, 1953; buried Fairmount Mausoleum, Denver.

SABIN, Louis Carlton, civil engr.; b. Memphis, Mich., June 25, 1867; s. Carlton and Cordelia (Bristol) S.; B.S., U. of Mich., 1890; C.E., 1894, hon. M.E., 1916; m. Nellie Blanchard, June 22, 1890 (dec.); children—Hope (Mrs. F. E. Bagger), Carlton Richard; m. 2d, Ruth E. Doucette, Sept. 1945. Insp. with Morison & Corthell, engrs., 1887-88; insp., engr. U.S. Engring. Dept., 1890-1905; sec. Am. sect. Internat. Waterways Commn., 1905-06, study regulation of Lake Erie and other waterway problems of Great Lakes; asso. engr. U.S. Engr. Dept. and gen. supt. St. Marys Falls Canal, 1906-25, design and constrn. Davis and Sabin locks, channel improvements, emergency dams, etc.; v.p. Lake Carriers' Assn., 1925-48; ret. Hon. mem. Am. Soc. C.E., Cleve. Engring. Soc.; mem. Ohio C. of C. (hon. mem. bd. dirs.), Mich. Engring. Soc., Internat. Assn. Navigation Congresses, Tau Beta Pi. Clubs: University of Michigan, Mid-day. Author: Cement and Concrete, 1894. Home: 2160 St. James Pkwy., Cleveland Heights 6, O. Died Dec. 30, 1950; buried Lakeview Cemetery, Cleve.

SACHS, Curt, music historian, author; born Berlin, Germany, June 29, 1881; s. Louis Eduard and Anna (Fröhlich) S.; B.A., Königliches Französisches Gymnasium, Berlin, Germany, 1900; Ph.D., Berlin University, 1904; L.H.D. honoris causa, 1950; Ph. D. honoris causa, West Berlin, 1956; married to Irene Julia Lewin, Apr. 2, 1908; children—George (dec.), Judith, Gabrielle, Ernest. Prof., Berlin U., 1919-33; curator Museum of Musical Instruments, Berlin, 1919-33; prof., Nat. Acad. of Music, Berlin, 1920-33, Nat. Acad. of Sch. Music, Berlin, until 1933; mem. advisory bd., Nat. Museums, Berlin, 1917-33, Nat. Radio until 1933; chargé de mission, Paris Ethnographic Museum, 1933-37; visiting prof., New York U., 1937-57; consultant to N.Y. Public Library 1937-52; adjunct professor, Columbia Univ. 1953——. Appointed by Egyptian government adviser on preservation and orgn. of oriental music, 1930; commr. to various music and theater exhbns. Hon. fellow several learned socs.; hon. citizen father's birth place, Juliusburg, Germany. Mem. Am. Musicol. Soc. (pres. 1948-50), Am. Ethnomusicological Soc. (honorary pres.). Author: Reallexikon der Musikinstrumente, 1913; Geist und Werden der Musikinstrumente, 1929; World History of the Dance, 1937; The History of Musical Instruments, 1940; The Rise of Music in the Ancient World, 1943; Commonwealth of Art, 1946; Our Musical Heritage, 1948; Rhythm and Tempo, 1953; also the author of two series of phonograph records: Two Thousand Years of Music, Berlin, 1930, and L'Anthologie Sonore, Paris, 1934-38 (won Grand Prix of the French Record each year). Has lectured in Germany, Denmark, Belgium, England, France, Spain, Switzerland, Czechoslovakia and U.S. Address: 1781 Riverside Dr., N.Y.C. 34. Died Feb. 5, 1959.

SACHS, Ernest, surgeon; b. N.Y. City, Jan. 25, 1879; s. Julius and Rosa (Goldman) S.; prep. edn. Dr. J. Sachs' Collegiate Inst. for Boys, N.Y. City; A.B., Harvard, 1900; M.D., Johns Hopkins, 1904; interne Mt. Sinai Hosp., New York, 1904-07; grad. work, Berlin and Vienna, 1907-08, and Queen Square Hosp., London Lab. of Sir Victor Horsley 1908-09; m. Mary Parmly Koues, Oct. 28, 1913; children—Mary Parmly (dec.), Ernest, Jr. (M.D.), Thomas Dudley. Attending neurol. surgeon, Montefiore Home and Beth Israel Hosp., New York, 1909-11; adj. surgeon Bellevue Hosp., 1910-11; asso. in surgery, 1911, asso. prof. surgery, 1914, acting prof. surgery, 1917-19, prof. clin. neurol. surgery, 1919-46, emeritus prof. since 1946, Washington U. Sch. Medicine; research asso. in physiology and prof. Yale since 1949; pioneer prof. neurol. surgery in Am. univs.; in charge of teaching (1917-18) Sch. of Neurol. Surgery, estab. at St. Louis by order of surgeon general of U.S.; asso. surgeon Barnes and St. Louis Children's hosps.; cons. surgeon St. Louis Maternity Hosp.; cons. neurol. surgeon, St. Louis City Sanitarium; consultant in Neuro-Surgery Ellis Fischel State Cancer Hospital. Pres. Am. Neurological Assn., 1942-43. Mem A.M.A., Soc. Neurol. Surgeons, Am. Physiol. Soc. Am. Neurol. Assn., So. Surg. Assn., Southern Med. Assn., Mo. State Med. Assn., St. Louis Med. Soc., St. Louis Surg. Soc.; hon. mem. Cushing Soc., Royal Soc. of Medicine, Section of Neurology (London), Deutsche Akademie der Naturforscher; mem. Sigma Xi, Phi Beta Pi; fellow Am. Coll. Surgeons; mem. Founders' Group, Am. Bd. of Surgery; Am. Bd. of Neurol. Surgery. Clubs: University, Harvard. Author: Diagnosis and Treatment of Brain Tumors, 1931; The Care of The Neurosurgical Patient, 1945; The History and Development of Neurological Surgey, 1952; The Prerequisite of Good Teaching and Other Essays, 1954; Fifty Years of Neurosurgery, 1958; also articles in various profl. jours. Home: 28 Marlborough Rd., North Haven, Conn. Office: Historical Library, 333 Cedar St., New Haven, Conn. Died Dec. 2, 1958; buried Keene Valley, Essex County, N.Y.

SACHS, Morris Bernard, (saks), retail clothing mcht., city ofcl.; b. Lithuania, Mar. 23, 1896; s. Benjmain and Rhoda (Chananau) S.; student pub. schs.; came to U.S., 1910, naturalized, 1924; m. Anna Shirley Baker, Sept. 2, 1916; children—Rhoda (Mrs. Morris Mendelson), Zenia (Mrs. Lawrence Goodman), Morris B. Engaged in retailing wearing apparel, as Morris B. Sachs, Chicago, 1923——, operator Morris B. Sachs, Inc., retail apparel stores, 1945——. City treas., Chgo., 1955——. Founder Amateur Hour on radio, 1934. Dir. Chgo. Med. Sch. Research Found. Recipient awards of merit from Chgo. unit Ladies Auxiliary Voluntary Workers, Vets. Fgn. Wars U.S., Chgo. Police post of Am. Legion, Elks Club, Nat. Found. Infantile Paralysis, Chgo. Heart Assn., A.R.C., Cerebral Palsy Assn., and others. Mem. Chgo. Retail Mchts. Assn. Mason, Elk, Moose. Clubs: Lions, Variety, Garment, Chgo. Merchants. Home: 4950 Chicago Beach Dr., Chgo. 15. Office: 6638 Halsted St., Chgo. 21. Died Sept. 23, 1957.

SACHS, Teviah, watch exec.; b. N.Y.C., Sept. 6, 1902; s. Kolman and Bessie (Feinberg) S.; student pub. schs. N.Y.C.; m. Lea Klein, May 11, 1944; 1 son, Coleman Joseph. Buyer Walter & Co., N.Y. City, 1919-29; gen. mgr. Wholesale Am. Watch House, N.Y.C., 1929-31; self-employed Am. Watch Distributors, Rochester, N.Y., 1931-35; v.p., asst. treas., dir. Gruen Watch Co., Cin., 1935-41; pres. H. S. Chandler Co., N.Y.C., 1945; exec. v.p., gen. mgr. Multi-Facet Diamond Co., N.Y.C., 1946; v.p. Waltham Watch Co., Waltham, Mass., 1949-50, pres., treas., dir., 1950-55; pres., treas. Pearls by Deltah, Inc., Pawtucket, R.I., 1958——; sec., treas. La. Tausca Sperry Corp. Dir. Waltham Hosp., Boys' Club. Clubs: Twenty Four Karat, Brandeis U. Men's. Home: 24 Winthrop Dr., Barrington, R.I. Office: 560 Mineral Spring Av., Pawtucket, R.I. Died July 21, 1959.

SACHSE, Richard, consulting engineer; b. Saxony, Germany, 1881; s. Robert and Augusta (Heide) S.; grad. Inst. Tech., Dresden and Hanover, Germany; m. Katherine A. Golden, 1906; children—Franz R., Mary Elizabeth (Mrs. R. Wyman). Engring. work in Europe and Africa, 1901-03, Chicago and Milwaukee, 1903-06; with U.S. Reclamation Service in Wash. and Nev., 1906-07; construction Western Pacific R.R., San Francisco to Salt Lake City, 1907-11; chief engr., Calif. Railroad Commn., 1912-23; const. engr., 1923-39; chmn. Calif. Employment Commn., 1939-41; dir. Dept. Natural Resources of Calif., 1940-41; commr. Calif. Railroad Commn., 1941-43; pres., 1944-45; mem. Fed. Power Commn., 1945-46, vice chmn. since 1947. Vice chmn. Calif. State Planning Bd., 1940-41; mem. Governor's Council, Calif. State Council for Defense, Calif. State Conservation Commn., 1940-41. Deceased.*

SACK, Alexander Naoum (săk), univ. prof.; b. Moscow, Russia, Oct. 18, 1890; s. Naoum Basil (M.D.) and Elisabeth (Shoub) S.; B.A., magna cum laude, Moscow Gymnasium, 1907; student Imperial Poly. Inst., Sch. of Economics, Petrograd, 1907-08; J.D., summa cum laude, Moscow U., 1911; Magistr. of Financial Law, Petrograd U., 1917; also studied in Berlin, Munich, Paris, London; m. Nina George Douguin, Jan. 14, 1923. Came to U.S., 1930, naturalized, 1936. Became mem. Russian bar, 1911; counsel All-Russian Central Bank of Mutual Credit Societies, Petrograd, 1912-14; mem. council Ministry of Finance, Petrograd, 1917; counsel All-Russian Com. of Commercial Banks, Petrograd, 1917-18; asst. prof. law, Petrograd U., 1917-19, asso. prof., 1919-21, prof. Sch. of Commerce, Petrograd, 1918-21; legal and financial adviser to Esthonian Govt., 1921-24; prof. Institut des Sciences Sociales et Politiques, Paris, 1927-30, Institut des Hautes Etudes Internationales, U. of Paris, 1927-28, Acad. Internat. Law, The Hague, 1928; visiting prof. internat. law, Northwestern Univ., 1930-32; visiting prof. of law, New York Univ., 1932-35, prof. law, 1935-43; spl. asst. to attorney general U.S., 1943-45; spl. atty. Dept. of Justice, 1945-47; admitted to New York bar, 1937. Engaged in research for Harvard University, 1953——. Mem. com. on peace problems, Am. Jewish Com., 1945——. Fellow John Simon Guggenheim Foundation, summer 1936; grant-in-aid Social Science Research Council, 1936. Mem. Assn. Bar City of New York (mem. com. on fgn. law), Am. Bar Assn., New York County Lawyers Assn., Internat. Law Assn. (U.S. and England), Société de Legislation Comparée, Assn. pour la Culture Juridique Française, Vereinigung fuer Rechts-und Wirtschaftsphilosophie. Author: The Peasants' Land Bank, 1883-1910, 1911; Germans and German Capital in Russian Industry, 1914; Central Banks—Unions of Banks, 1914; Financing the Land Reform, 1917; Russian and Foreign Law on Debentures of Railway Companies, 1917; Russian Currency in 1914-17, 1918; State Bankruptcy, Theory and Practice, 1918; Apportionment of Public Debts in Case of Dismemberment of the Debtor State, 1923; Fixing the Gold Value of Money, 1925; Les Effets des Transformations des Etats sur Leurs Dettes Publiques et Autres Obligations Financieres, 1927; La Succession aux Dettes d'Etat Publiques, 1928; Conflicts of Laws in the History of the English Law, 1938; also of papers on law of war crimes, 1943-45, on U.N. and on Israel, 1946-48; report to Internat. Law Assn. on outlawry of atomic warfare, 1950; History of Privative International Law in England since 13th Century, 1953. Contbr. numerous articles to law jours. and other periodicals. Home: 1125 Grand Concourse, N.Y.C. 52. Died May 30, 1955.

SACK, Leo R., pub. relations; b. Tupelo, Miss., July 9, 1889; s. Isaac and Sarah Lee (Romansky) S.; high sch., Greenville, Miss., 1907; student U. Mo., 1907-09 (one of student founders of U. of Mo. Sch. of Journalism, 1st of its kind in U.S.); m. Regina Rogers, Nov. 12, 1913; 1 dau., Sarita (Mrs. Joseph Lester Jones). Began as reporter with Natchez (Miss.) News, 1909, and continued with Springfield (Mo.) Rep., city and night editor Texarkana Four State Press until 1911; with San Antonio Express, 1911-15; Washington corr. San Antonio Light, Ft.

Worth Star-Telegram, Houston Chronicle, 1915-17, Scripps-Howard group of newspapers, 1919-33; apptd. E.E. and M.P. to Costa Rica, 1933-37; v.p. in charge pub. relations Schenley Products Co., 1937-39; pub. relations cons. Washington, 1939——. Negotiated and signed Reciprocal Trade Agreement between Costa Rica and U.S., 1936. Spl. asst. to James A. Farley. Chmn. Dem. Nat. Com. during 1936 Presidential Campaign. Author of newspaper articles which led to investigation of Pa. and Ill. senatorial elections resulting in refusal of Senate to seat William S. Vare and Frank L. Smith; dir. Washington bur. Am. Zionist Emergency Council, Washington, 1943-48. Capt. and maj. Air Service, U.S. Army, A.E.F., 1917-19; maj. Res. Hon. mem. Boy Scouts; benefactor mem. Costa Rica Red Cross; hon. col. on staff gov. of Miss.; lt. col. on staff Gov. of Tex. Independent Democrat. Mason. Clubs: National Press (Washington); Union (San José); Overseas Press (N.Y.C.). Speaker at Latin Am. Seminar, Panama and U. of Mo. Sch. of Journalism, 1935, and Washington Seminar for Better Understanding Between Christians and Jews, 1940. Mem. and former dir. Nat. Assn. of Accredited Publicity Dirs., Inc. Home: 841 South Serrano Av., Los Angeles 5. Office: National Press Club, Washington. Died Apr. 15, 1956; buried Mausoleum, Hollywood (Cal.) Cemetery.

SACKS, Emanuel, broadcasting executive; born Phila., Jan. 30, 1904; s. Harry and Ida (Rose) S.; grad. Pa. Mil. Coll. Began as mdse. mgr., chain women's apparel stores; then. v.p. Universal Artists Bur., subsidiary WCAU radio sta. in Phila.; later talent agt. Music Corp. of Am., v.p. charge artists and repertoire, also dir. Columbia Records; now staff v.p. RCA, also v.p. charge TV network programs NBC., also dir. NBC. Home: Germantown, Phila. Office: 30 Rockefeller Plaza, N.Y.C. Died Feb. 9, 1958.

SADLEIR, Michael, author and publisher; b. Oxford, Eng., Dec. 25, 1888; s. Michael Ernest and Mary Ann (Harvey) S.; student Rugby, 1903-07; B.A., Balliol Coll., Oxford, 1912, M.A., 1913; Sanders Reader in Bibliography, Cambridge Univ., 1937; m. Edith Tupper-Carey, June 4, 1914; children—Ann Penelope (Mrs. Miles Hornby), Michael Thomas Carey (killed in action at sea), 1943), Richard Ferribee. Entered office of Constable & Co., Ltd., pubs., London, 1912; with Houghton Mifflin Co., Boston, Mass., 1913-14; dir. Constable Co., Ltd., since 1921. With War Trade Intelligence Dept. (Blockade), London, 1915-18. British del. to Paris Peace Conf., 1919, head publs. service League of Nations, Brussels and Geneva, 1920. Awarded Stanhope Essay prize, Oxford, for Political Career of Richard Brinsley Sheridan, 1912. Council member Friends of Nat. Libraries; mem. Bibliog. Soc. (past pres.), Friends of Bodleian. Clubs: Garrick, Roxburghe (London); Grolier (N.Y.C.). Author: (novels) Privilege, 1921; Desolate Splendour (new edit. 1948); The Noblest Frailty (pub. in U.S. with title "Obedience"), 1925; These Foolish Things, 1937; Fanny by Gaslight, 1940; Forlorn Sunset, 1946; (non-fiction): Excursions in Victorian Bibliography, 1922; Daumier, 1924; Trollope: a Commentary, 1927; Trollope, a Bibliography, 1928; Evolution of Publishers Binding Styles, 1930; Bulwer and his Wife, 1931; Blessington-d'Orsay: a Masquerade, 1933; Things Past, 1944; Michael Ernest Sadler: A Memoir by his Son, 1949. Bibliographical Catalog of Nineteenth Century Fiction (in preparation), 2 vols., 1951; also numerous introductions, articles, revs., etc. Interested in collecting and using as literary material 19th century fiction and books relating to 19th Century London. Home: Willow Farm, Oakley Green, Windsor. Office: 10 Orange St., London W.C. 2. Deceased.

SAFAY, Fred A. (sā-fâ), army officer; b. Jacksonville, Fla., June 15, 1898; s. Abraham and Jasmine (Dumont) S.; student Fla. Mil. Acad., Jacksonville, Fla., 1916-17, spl. student, U. of Fla., 1930-38; m. Iva McKendree, Apr. 25, 1921; children—Dorothy Louise (Mrs. Paul E. Hall). Sanitation officer, Fla. Health Dept., 1923-38, dir. sanitation dept., 1938-40; mil. service, 1940-46, sanitation cons. Fla. State Bd. of Health, 1946——. Served with A.E.F., 1917-18, Army of Occupation, 1919; commd. 1st lt., inf., Fla. Nat. Guard, and advanced through the grades to col., comdr., 124th Inf., 1940; inducted into Fed. service, 1940; brig. gen., Sept. 1942; ret. as brig. gen. Mem. Fla. and Am. Pub. Health Assn., Forty and Eight, Am. Legion. Home: 2751 Post St., Jacksonville, Fla. Died Jan. 4, 1952; buried Evergreen, Cemetery, Jacksonville, Fla.

SAGENDORPH, Kent (sā'gĕn-dôrf), author, publicist; b. Jackson, Mich., Apr. 23, 1902; s. William Kent and Ethel (Abbott) S.; grad. Jackson High Sch., 1920; student U. of Mich. and U.S. Army Tech. Sch., 1922; m. Ruth D. Howard, Nov. 11, 1933; children—Mary Lou, Wallace Kent. Aerial photographer, U.S. Army Air Service, Clark Field and Nichols Field, Philippine Islands, 1922-24; travel in China, Siberia, Japan, summer and fall, 1924; commercial aerial photographer, Los Angeles, 1925, Mexico, 1926; mem. staff Fairchild Aerial Surveys, preparing tech. manuals and trade magazine summaries to 1929; contbr. editor Aero Digest, 1929-31; author of 800 magazine articles on aviation and current history; lecturing on aviation since 1939. Lt. col., U.S. Air Force Reserve; on active duty May 1942-Nov. 1945. Pres. Veterans' Flying Assn. of America. Grad., Air Command & Staff Sch. USAF, 1950. Club: Aero. (Omaha). Author: Radium Island, 1937; Beyond the Amazon, 1937; Sin Kiang Castle, 1938; Thunder Aloft, 1942; Stevens Thomson Mason, 1947; Michigan, the Story of the University, 1948; Charles Edward Wilson, American Industrialist, 1949; How to Solve a Problem, 1952. Home: 333 W. Mason St., Jackson, Mich. Died Feb. 5, 1958; buried Woodland Cemetery, Jackson, Mich.

SAHLER, Helen, sculptor, painter; b. Carmel, N.Y.; d. Rev. D. DuBois and Adeliza F. (Merriam) Sahler; student pvt. schs., N.Y.C.; studied Art Students' League (New York), and under Hermon MacNeil and Enid Yandell. Exhibitor at N.A.D., Archtl. League, Pa. Acad. Fine Arts, Panama P.I. Expn., Phila. Sesquicentennial. Principal works: relief, Dr. G. E. Brewer, Medical Centre, New York; relief, Dr. Percy S. Grant, St. Mark's Church, Fall River, Mass.; Playfellows, fountain, Scarborough, N.Y.; The Spirit of Revolt, College Library, Macon, Ga.; Angel of Light Sundial; The Happy Farmer; Gov. Charles S. Whitman; Norman Thomas; Marshal Viscount Montgomery; Frederick S. Dellenbaugh; Mus. of Am. Indian; Dean John Wyckoff; N.Y.U. Med. Sch. Represented in Numismatic Museum and private collections. Recipient Proctor prize N.A.D., 1945. Mem. Nat. Assn. Women Artists, Municipal Art Soc. of New York, Conn. Acad. Fine Arts, North Shore Art Assn., Allied Artists of America. Clubs: Cosmopolitan, Huguenot Society of America. Address: 535 Park Av., N.Y.C. Died Dec. 3, 1950.

SAINSBURY, William Charles, clergyman; b. London, Eng., Jan. 11, 1882; s. Charles Augustus and Mary Annie (Aylett) S.; full course, Hartley Theol. Coll., Manchester, 1905-07; B.A., Ripon (Wis.) Coll., 1917; D.D., Hamline, 1925; m. Euphemia W. Scott, Dec. 20, 1909; children—Euphemia Steele Scott, Augustus William, Leonard Robert. Came to U.S., 1911, naturalized, 1917. Ordained ministry M.E. Ch., 1908; pastor Orfordville, Wis., 1911-14, Ripon, Wis., 1914-17, Green Bay, Wis., 1917-19, St. Paul, Minn., 1919-29, First Church, Fargo, N.D., 1929-32, University M.E. Church, Brooklyn, N.Y., 1936-46; pastor Fenimore Street Methodist Church, Bklyn., 1946-51; retired 1951. Member Dickens Fellowship, New York City. Dir. Brooklyn Tuberculosis and Health Assn., Brooklyn Bible Society. Member Brooklyn Clerical Union. Republican. Mason (32°, Shriner). Contbr. health articles in "Everybody's Health"; radio speaker under title "The Gist of Things" (weekly); lecturer and dramatic impersonator many seasons in Chautauqua and Lyceum courses; reader of Dickens' works. Contbr. devotional articles to mags. Home: 18 Scotland Rd., Canandaigua, N.Y. Died Feb. 8, 1956; buried Woodlawn Cemetery, Canandaigua.

SAINT-GAUDENS, Homer Schiff (sānt-gaw'dĕnz), dir. fine arts; b. Roxbury, Mass., Sept. 28, 1880; s. Augustus and Augusta F. (Homer) S.; A.B., Harvard, 1903; m. Carlota Dolley, June 3, 1905 (died Oct. 24, 1927); children—Augustus, Carlota; m. 2d, Mary Louise McBride, Feb. 27, 1929. Asst. editor The Critic, N.Y., 1904; mng. editor Met. Mag., 1905; stage dir. for Maude Adams in "Legend of Leonora," "Kiss for Cinderella," etc., 1908-17; dir. production of "Beyond the Horizon," "The Red Robe," etc., 1919-21; asst. dir. Fine Arts, Carnegie Inst., Pitts., 1921, dir., 1922-50, dir. emeritus, 1950——. Capt. Co. A, 40th Engrs. (1st Camouflage Unit), A.E.F. in charge camouflage work on front; completed various temporary duties in Engrs. Res. Corps to Jan. 4, 1941; active service 1941-45; col., Corps of Engrs., Chief of Camouflage Sect., Office of Chief of Engrs., Washington, 1941-43; chief, Camouflage Sect., for Chief Engr., E.T.O., 1943-45; thereafter with Office of Chief of Engrs., Washington. Decorations: Legion of Merit, Bronze Star Medal, Purple Heart, Victory Medal, six stars, Am. Def. Medal, one star, Am. Theatre Medal, European Theatre Medal, five stars; Meritorious Medal, State of Pa.; Officer Legion of Honor, Croix de Guerre with palm (France); Officer Crown of Italy; Chevalier, Order of Leopold (Belgium); Comdr. Hungarian Order of Merit. Hon. corr. mem. Royal Acad., London. Clubs: Century, Harvard (N.Y.C.). Author: Reminiscences of Augustus Saint-Gaudens, 1909; The American Artist and His Times, 1941; also short stories and spl. articles in mags. Lectr. on art subjects. Home: Box 246, Route 2, Miami, Fla. Died Dec. 8, 1958; buried Cornish, N.H.

SAKEL, Manfred Joshua (sā'kĕl), physician; born Nadvorna, Austria, June 6, 1900; s. Mayer and Judith Golde (Friedman) S.; student First State College of Brno, Czechoslovakia, to 1920; U. of Vienna Med. Sch., 1920-25 (med. degree, 1925); hon. D.Sc. Colgate U., 1938; unmarried. Asso. physician Vienna (Austria) Hosp., 1925-27; research fellow Urban Hosp., Berlin, 1927; psychiatrist in chief Lichterfelde Hosp., Berlin, 1927-33; asso. in Neuro-psychiatric Univ. Clinic, Vienna, 1933-36; on the invitation of Commr. Frederick Parsons, of New York, taught his method of treatment for nervous and mental diseases (shock with insulin and metrazol) to various doctors of U.S., 1936; came to U.S., 1936, and has since practiced privately in N.Y. City; med. director Manfred Sakel Research Foundation. Fellow Am. Psychiatric Assn.; life member New York Academy of Sciences. Author: Theory of Addiction; New Treatment of Addiction (Morphinism, Alkoholism); New Method of Treating Nervous and Mental Ailments; The Pharmacological Shock Treatment of Mental Diseases; The Results of Shock Therapy; The History of the Origin of Shock Therapy; Medical Psychiatry and Psycological Medicine; An Approach to the Causative Treatment of Idiopaaic Epilepsy; Schizophrenia; Epilepsy. Home: 4 E. 64th St. Office: 4 E. 64th St., N.Y.C. 21. Died Dec. 2, 1957; buried Ferncliff Cemetery.

SAKOLSKI, Aaron M., economist, editor; b. Balt., May 12, 1880; s. David I. and Ida (Morton) S.; Ph.B., Syracuse U., 1902; Ph.D., Johns Hopkins, 1905; unmarried. Financial statistician, 1905——; instr. finance N.Y.U., 1910-24; served as valuation expert D. & H. Co., 1914-17; examiner FTC, 1917-19; statistician Paine, Webber & Co., N.Y.C., 1922-31; asso. prof. Coll. of City of New York. Asst. editor Comml. and Financial Chronicle, 1944. Mem. Plattsburg O.T.C., 1916. Mem. Am. Econ. Assn., Nat. Tax Assn., Am. Museum of Natural History, Am. Jewish Hist. Soc., Econ. Hist. Assn., Phi Beta Delta. Jewish religion. Clubs: Civic (N.Y.C.); Judeauns. Author: Finances of American Trade Unions, 1906; Conditions of Entrance to Principal Trades (with Walter E. Weyl), 1906; American Railroad Economics, 1913; Railroad Securities, 1921; Elements of Bond Investment, 1921; The Analysis of Financial Statements, 1923; Principles of Investment, 1925; (with Myron L. Hoch) The Evolution of American Economic Life, 1935. Contbr. to American Business Practice, 1931; The Great American Land Bubble, 1932; (with Myron L. Hoch) American Economic Development, 1936; Land Tenure and Land Taxation in America, 1957. Office: 25 Park Pl., N.Y.C. 8. Died Dec. 29, 1955; buried Syracuse, N.Y.

SALES, Murray W., business exec.; b. Detroit, Nov. 21, 1865; s. William and Agnes (Adam) S.; student Detroit High Sch.; m. Jessie Carter, Dec. 26, 1892; children—Carter, Frances (dec.), Murray William (dec.), Leonard (dec.). Began as clk. wholesale dry goods store; Chgo. mgr. for Detroit Copper & Brass Rolling Mills branch; returned to Detroit joining brother, Chas. V. Sales in wholesale plumbing and heating supplies; purchased brothers interest, 1901; organized Murray W. Sales & Co., 1908, now dir. and pres. Murray W. Sales Investment Co., Sales Realty Co., Detroit; dir. Mfrs. Nat. Bank of Detroit, Detroit Steel Products Co. Mich. Bell Telephone Co., Nat. Steel Corp., Michigan Consol Gas Co., Detroit. Dir. Elmwood Cemetery, Grace Hosp. (both at Detroit). Cllbs: Detroit (past pres.), Recess, Yondotega, Detroit Country (past pres.), Grosse Pointe (past pres.). Home: 17743 E. Jefferson Av., Grosse Pointe, Mich. Office: 801 W. Baltimore Av., Detroit. Died Jan. 27, 1951.

SALIERS, Earl Adolphus (săl'yĕrz), prof. accounting; b. Attica, O., Apr. 25, 1884; s. Henry Adelbert and Amanda (Cole) S.; B.S., Heidelberg Coll., Tiffin, O., 1908; M.A., Ohio State U., 1910; studied U. of Wis., summer 1910; Ph.D., U. of Pa., 1911; m. Lillian DeVore McGinnis, June 15, 1908; children—Earl Adolphus (dec.), Lillian Jean (dec.), Marceline DeVore (Mrs. D. C. Cline). Instr. accounting, Lehigh U., 1911-15; instr. accounting, Yale U., 1915-16, asst. prof., 1916-22; editorial staff Ronald Press Co., 1922-23; asso. prof. accounting, Northwestern U., 1923-24, prof., 1924-27; asso. editor book div. A. W. Shaw Co., Chicago, 1927-28; writing and research, 1928-29; prof. accounting and head of accounting dept., La. State U., since 1929; cons. practice. Expert Bur. Aircraft Production, U.S. Army, Mar.-Sept. 1918; dist. accountant S.A.T.C., Oct. 1918-June 1919. Hon. mem. La. Soc. Certified Public Accountants; mem. Am. Accounting Assn., Southern Econ. Assn., National Association of Cost Accountants, American Inst. Accountants, American Assn. Univ. Profs., Nat. Comml. Teachers Fedn., Southern Business Educators Assn., Southwestern Social Science Assn., Civil Legion, Nat. Rifle Assn., Beta Gamma Sigma, Beta Alpha Psi, Delta Sigma Pi, Phi Kappa Phi, Pi Gamma Mu; foreign corr. mem. Société de Compatibilite de France. Conglist. Author: Principles of Depreciation, 1915; Financial Statements Made Plain, 1917; Accounts in Theory and Practice, 1919; Depreciation Principles and Applications, 1922; 3d edit., 1939. Intermediate Accounting, 1925; Handbook of Corporate Management and Procedure, 1929; Fundamentals of Accounting, 1933; Intermediate Accounting, 1935; Basic Accounting Principles (with A. W. Holmes), 1937; How to Keep Accounts and Prepare Statements, 1938; Modern Practical Accounting, Elementary, 1946; Modern Practical Accounting, Advanced, 1946. Contributor to scientific jours. Editor: Accountants Handbooks (1st edit.). Home: Baton Rouge, La. Died Dec. 23, 1952.

SALINAS, Pedro, educator, author; born Madrid, Spain, Nov. 27, 1891; s. Pedro and Soledad (Serrano) S.; B.A., Instituto de San Isidro, Madrid, 1909; Licenciado in philosophy, U. of Madrid, 1913,

Ph.D., 1916; Doctor Honoris Causa, Middlebury Coll., 1937; professor honoris causa, Colegio Mayor, Guanajuato, Mexico, 1940; Universidad de San Marcos, Lima, Peru, 1947; m. Margarita Bonmati, Dec. 29, 1915; children—Soledad (Mrs. Juan A. Marichal), Jaime. Came to U.S., 1936. Lecturer, U. of Paris, 1914-17, prof. of U. of Seville, 1918-30; dir. of the summer schs. for fgn. students, Centro de Estudios Historicos, Madrid, 1928, head div. of contemporary Spanish literature, 1930; gen. sec., summer Internat. U. of Santander, 1933; prof. of Spanish literature. Wellesley Coll., 1936-40; prof. of Spanish literature Johns Hopkins U. since 1940; vis. prof. Middlebury Coll., U. of So. Calif., U. of Calif., Duke U., Bryn Mawr, U. Perto Rico; guest lecturer in European, American and Latin American univs., Chevalier de la Legion d'Honneur, 1933. Mem. Ateneo de Madrid, Hispanic Soc. of Am., Ateneo Americano, Modern Lang. Assn. of Am. Club: The Johns Hopkins (Baltimore). Author: Poetry: Presagios, 1923, Seguro Azar, 1929; Fabula y Signo, 1931; La voz a ti debida, 1933; Razon e Amor, 1936; Error de Calculo, 1938; Poesia Junta, 1942; El Contemplado, 1946; Todo mas Claro, 1949; Literary Criticism: Literatura espanola, Siglo XX, 1939, Joge Manrique, 1948; LaPoesia de Ruben Dario, 1948; El Defensor, 1948; Fiction; Vispera del Gozo, 1926; La Bomba Increible, 1950; El Desnudo Impecable, 1951; Teatro, 1952; Poesias Completas, 1955. Translations into English: Reality and the Poet, 1940; Lost Angel, 1938; Zero, 1947; Truth of Two, 1940; Sea of San Juan, 1950. Chief editor Indice Literario, 1932. Home: care Prof. J. Marichal, Harvard U., Cambridge 38, Mass. Died Dec. 4, 1951; buried Old Cemetery, San Juan, Puerto Rico.

SALINGER, Harry, banker; b. Chgo., Mar. 7, 1883; s. Simon A. and Henriette (Lebrecht) S.; M.D., Jenner Med. Coll., Chgo., 1912; m. Rae Davis, June 30, 1909 (dec.); children—Bernice, Shirley Jacqueline, Alan Harry; m. 2d, Ciel Grunewald, Mar. 15, 1941. With First Nat. Bank of Chicago successively as messenger, general man, traveling auditor, asst. mgr. fgn. dept., mgr. fgn. dept. 1901-24, v.p. fgn. banking, 1924—. Vice-pres. Bankers Assn. Fgn. Trade, 1939-41, pres., 1941, 42, dir., 1943-46; v.p., dir. Chicago Assn. Commerce; chmn. Chicago World Trade Conf., 1944, 45, 46, 47, 48, 49; also chmn. Fgn. Commerce Com. and mem. ednl. com.; mem. Fgn. Adv. Com., U. Ill.; mem. exec. com. Foreign Reconstruction Com. of Nat. Fgn. Trade Council, also mem. stabilization of currency com. and fgn. trade reconstruction com., mem. potential post war problems com. and reestablishment of banking relations with reoccupied territories com. of Bankers Assn. Fgn. Trade; mem. Latin American Arbitration Com.; dir. Bd. of Pan American Council, Chgo.; mem. Ill., Chgo. med. socs. Nat. dir. Far East-America Council of Commerce and Industry, Inc., 1945—. Mem. com. on fgn. investments U.S. Assos. Dir. Internat. House, New Orleans, 1945-46. Mason. Club: Standard (Chgo.). Address: 1100 N. Dearborn, Chgo. 10. Died Apr. 8, 1951; buried Rosehill.

SALISBURY, Stuart McFarland, lawyer; b. Washington Court House, O., Sept. 14, 1885; s. Samuel Scott and Anna (Brown) S.; student Occidental Coll., Los Angeles, and Pomona Coll., Claremont, Calif.; A.B., Stanford, 1907; law study Harvard, 1907-09; married Lois Chamberlain, February 21, 1912; children—Robert, Susanne, Eleanor; married second, Nilwon Nowlin. Admitted to the California bar, 1910, and began practice at Los Angeles; partner firm of McClean, Salisbury, Petty and McClean; chmn. bd. dirs. Los Angeles By-Products Co.; dir., v.p. Warman Steel Casting Co., Los Angeles Steel Casting Co., Los Angeles Foundry Co.; local counsel Celotex Corp., Am. Brake Shoe Co. Mem. Am., Cal., Los Angeles bar assns., Los Angeles C. of C. (past dir.; past chmn. water and power resources com., also air pollution com.), Delta Upsilon, Psi Delta Phi. Republican. Presbyn. Clubs: University (pres. 1928-29). Chaparral, Jonathan. Home: 45 Kewen Place, San Marino, Cal. Office: 2975 Wilshire Blvd., Los Angeles 5.

SALOMON, Herbert, investment banker; b. N.Y. City, Aug. 28, 1883; s. Ferdinand and Sophie (Heilbron) S.; m. Nellie Franck, Dec. 8, 1908; children—Marion S. (Mrs. Clarke), Jane H. (Mrs. Bernheim). In financial field since 1897; partner (sr.) Salomon Bros. & Hutzler since 1910. Mem. C. of C. of State of N.Y. Club: Harmonie (N.Y. City). Home: Three E. 69th St., N.Y. City. Office: 60 Wall St., N.Y.C. 5. Died Mar. 1951.

SALSGIVER, Paul L(oughry), educator; b. Indiana, Pa., Dec. 1, 1907; s. Fulton S. and Sara (Sell) S.; B.S., State Teachers Coll., Indiana, Pa., 1928; A.M., U. Pittsburgh, 1930; m. Ethel H. Fredericks, Oct. 20, 1928; 1 son, John Paul. Supervisor comml. student teaching, pub. schs., Indiana, Pa., 1929-36; prof. comml. edn., Boston U., 1936-46 (on mil. leave, 1942-45); dir. Sch. of Business, Simmons Coll., Boston, 1946—; vis. prof. U. N.C., summer, 1942, U. Cin., 1942, U. Pitts., 1948, Boston University, 1949. Consultant on business tng. programs for vets., Bd. of Collegiate Authority, Mass. State Dept. Edn., 1946. Lt. col., Res. Officers Corps. Mem. bd. trustees Henry A. Peabody Sch. for Girls. Mem. Milton (Mass.) Sch. Com., 1949-50. Vice chmn. joint publs. commn. Nat. Bus. Tchrs. Assn. and Eastern Bus. Tchrs. Assn., 1946-50. Mem. Nat. Assn. Bus. Tchrs. Tng. Instns. (v.p. 1939-40, pres. 1940-41), Nat. Bus. Tchrs. Assn., N.E.A., Nat. Office Mgrs. Assn., Am. Management Assn., Soc. Advancement of Management, Eastern Bus. Teachers Assn., C. of C., Phi Delta Kappa, Gamma Rho Tau, Kappa Delta Pi, Phi Sigma Pi. Author: General Business Workbook for General Business, Manual for General Business (with Ernest H. Crabbe). Editor Am. Business Education Yearbook, 1949, Yearbook of Eastern Business Teachers Assn., 1942. Contbr. to various ednl. and bus. publs. Home: Cornet Stetson Road, Scituate, Mass. Office: 300 The Fenway, Boston 15. Died July 11, 1954; buried Forest Hills, Boston.

SALSICH, LeRoy, mining engr.; b. Hartland, Wis., Dec. 20, 1879; s. Hamilton Enos and Jane Withington (Atwater) S.; B.S.C.E., Univ. of Wis., 1901; m. Elizabeth Frazer, Aug. 15, 1904 (dec. Dec. 28, 1943); m. 2d, Margaret Culkin Banning, Nov. 15, 1944. With Oliver Mining Co., Duluth, Minn., 1901-46, pres., 1930-46, ret.; cons. engr., 1946—. Recipient William Lawrence Saunders Gold Medal awarded by Am. Inst. Mining and Metall. Engrs. for achievement in mining and for significant contbn., as operating head of World's largest mining enterprise, to nation's prodn. of steel during World War II. Mem. Am. Inst. Mining and Metall. Engrs. (vice pres., 1941-44, dir., 1938-44). Republican. Episcopalian. Clubs: Kitchi Gammi, Northland Country (Duluth); Minneapolis (Minneapolis); Chicago (Chicago). Home: 60 E. Kent Rd., Duluth 5, Minn. and Tryon, N.C. Office: Alworth Bldg., Duluth 2, Minn. Died Oct. 26, 1957; buried Polk Meml. Gardens, Tryon, N.C.

SALTER, Robert Mundhenk, agronomist; b. Huntington, Ind., Mar. 31, 1892; s. William Anderson and Minnie Elta (Mundhenk) S.; B.S., M.S., Ohio State U., grad. student, 1924-25; hon. D.Sc., Rutgers University, 1944; m. Sarah Godfrey, August 14, 1917; children—Elizabeth Ann, Robert Mundhenk, Barbara Jane, Richard Godfrey. Instr. agrl. chemistry, Ohio State U., 1914-15; asst. soil chemist, W. Va. Agrl. Expt. Sta., 1915-16; soil chemist and asst. prof. of soils, W.Va. U., 1916-19, agronomist and prof. agronomy, 1919-2; prof. soils, Ohio State U., 1921-25; chief in agronomy, Ohio Agrl. Expt. Sta., 1925-40; also chairman dept. agronomy, Ohio State U., 1929-40; asso. dir. Ohio Agrl. Expt. Sta., 1940; dir. N.C. Agrl. Expt. Sta., 1940-41; chief Div. of Soil and Fertilizer Investigations, Bur. of Plant Industry, U.S. Dept. of Agr., 1941-42, chief, Bureau Plant Industry, Soils and Agrl. Engring., 1942-51; chief of Soil Conservation Service, 1951—. Fellow American Society Agronomy (pres. 1936), A.A.A.S. (v.p.; chmn. Sect. O, 1938); mem. Sigma Xi, Phi Lambda Upsilon, Gamma Sigma Delta. Presbyterian. Contbr. to scientific jours., bulls. and farm papers. Home: 154C Colony Rd., Silver Springs, Md. Died Sept. 13, 1955; buried Zanesville, Ind.

SALTER, William Thomas, pharmacologist; b. Boston, Mass., Dec. 19, 1901; s. William Thomas Hall and Frances B. F. (Patten) S.; student Roxbury Latin Sch. grad. 1918, A.B., Harvard Univ., 1922, M.D., Harvard U. Med. Sch., 1925; m. Eleanor Vallandigham, June 27, 1935; children—Frances V., Eleanor C., Katharine C. Medical interne, Mass. Gen Hospital, 1925-27, resident, 1927-28; Moseley traveling fellow, Harvard Univ., 1928-29, research fellow in medicine, 1929-32; instr. biochem. sciences, Medical Sch., 1928-39; asst. prof., 1934-41; asso. physician Huntington Memorial Hosp., 1929-39; jr. asso. in medicine, Peter Bent Brigham Hosp., 1937-39; research fellow in biochemistry, Harvard Univ. Cancer Commn., 1929-39; faculty instr. medicine, Harvard U., 1932-34; prof. pharmacology, Yale U. Sch. of Medicine, since 1941; asso. physician, Thorndike Memorial Laboratory, 1939-41. Received Iodine Ednl. Bur. Inc. award for research in pharmaceutical chemistry of iodine. Mem. American College Physicians, Am. Assn. for the History of Medicine, Am. Assn. for Cancer Research, Am. Inst. of Nutrition, Am. Soc. Clin. Investigation, Assn. for Study of Internal Secretions, Biochem. Soc. (Eng.), Am. Chem. Soc., Alpha Chi Sigma, Sigma Xi, Phi Beta Kappa, Alpha Omega Alpha. Episcopalian. Home: 178 Cold Spring St. Office: 333 Cedar St., New Haven 11. Died July 30, 1952.

SALVANT, Robert Milton, pub. utility exec.; b. New Orleans, Oct. 5, 1889; s. James M. and Katherin M. (Glaser) S.; m. Isabel Schaumburg, Apr. 30, 1913; children—R. Muriel, Robert J., Thomas H. Pres. Continental Bldg. & Loan Assn., New Orleans, 1932—; v.p., sec., dir. La. Power Light Co., New Orleans, 1928—. Pres. New Orleans City Park Improvement Assn., 1957—, also dir.; adminstr. Isaac Delgado Museum, New Orleans, 1957—; dir. Hosp. Assn. New Orleans (Blue Cross); mem. adv. bd. Coll. Bus. Adminstrn., Loyola U. of South. Mem. New Orleans Retail Bur. (dir.), 5th Dist. Homestead Soc. (dir.). K.C. Home: 3201 Ursuline Av., New Orleans 19. Office: 142 Delaronde St., New Orleans 14. Died Feb. 15, 1958.

SALVEMINI, Gaetano, educator; b. Molfetta, Italy, Sept. 8, 1873; s. Ilarione and Emanuela (Turtur) S.; Ph.D., U. of Florence, Italy, 1894; m. Fernande Dauriac, July 14, 1916. Came to U.S., 1932, naturalized, 1940. Tchr., Gymnasium, Palermo, Italy, 1895-96, Lyceum of Faenza, 1896-98, Lyceum of Lodi, 1898-1900, Lyceum of Florence, 1900-01; prof. medieval and modern history U. of Messina, Italy, 1901-08, U. of Pisa, 1910-16, U. of Florence, 1916-25; mem. Italian Parliament, 1919-21; vis. prof., Harvard, 1930, Yale, 1932; Lauro de Bosis lectr. in history of Italian civilization, Harvard, 1933-48, emeritus 1948. Fellow Medieval Acad. Am. Acad. Arts and Scis. Author: Dignitá Cavalleresca, 1896; Magnati e Popolani, 1899; Studi Storici, 1900; Mazzini, 1905; Rivoluzione Francese, 1906; La Riforma della Scuola Media (with A. Galletti), 1908; Come siamo Andati in Libia, 1913; La Questione dell' Adriatico (with C. Maranelli), 1918; Partito Popolare e Questione Romana, 1922; Dal Patto di Londra alla Pace di Roma, 1925; L'Italia politica nel secolo XIX, 1925; The Fascist Dictatorship in Italy, 1927; Mussolini Diplomat, 1932; Under the Ax of Fascism, 1936; Historian and Scientist, 1939. Contbr. articles and hist. studies to periodicals. Home: 30 Via San Gallo, Florence, Italy. Died Sept. 6, 1957.

SAMALMAN, Alexander (săm' ălmăn), editor, writer; b. N.Y.C., Jan. 11, 1904; s. Hersh and Rose (Manowicz) S.; student Coll. City N.Y.; m. Bella Maria Messer, Mar. 28, 1931 (deceased 1950); children—Herbert Manual, Robert Elias, Bella May. Contbr. short stories Pearson's mag., 1921—, staff, 1923; editor Fourth Estate, journalist trade paper, 1924-27; drama critic N.Y. Morning Telegraph, 1927; writer syndicated features Publishers Autocaster Service, 1927-29; editor Barber's Jour., 1927-28, Long Island Sunrise Trailer, 1927; asso. editor Standard Mag., Inc., N.Y.C., 1930-53, sr. editor 1953—; writer verse under name of Helen Ardsley. Mem. Men's Ort of Manhattan. Home: 225 W. End Av., N.Y.C. 23. Died Jan. 21, 1956.

SAMES, Albert Morris (sāmz), judge; b. Rockford, Ill., Feb. 9, 1873; s. Peter and Ellen M. (Griffith) S.; LL.B., U. of Wis. Law School, 1894; LL.M., Columbian (now George Washington) U., 1895; m. Nancy Elizabeth Crail, Aug. 28, 1923; 1 son (by 1st marriage), Albert Ayres. Admitted to Wis. bar, 1894, to Ariz. bar, 1900; rep. of claimants for injuries during Mexican revolutions. Asst. dist. atty., Cochise Co., Ariz., 1904; city clk. and treas., Douglas, 1905; U.S. commr., 1906-14; chmn. Rep. Territorial Central Com., 1911-12; city atty., 1914-16; chmn. Rep. State Com., 1918-20; chmn. Ariz. delegation Rep. Nat. Conv., 1920; judge Superior Court, Cochise County, 1921-31; judge U.S. Dist. Court, Ariz., 1931-45; ret. 1945. Conglist. Mem. Am. Bar Assn., Ariz. Pioneers Hist. Soc., Delta Upsilon, Phi Delta Phi. Mason (32°, K.T., Shriner), Elk. (P.E. R.). Club: Los Angeles Athletic. Home: 1349 Toberman St., Los Angeles 15. Died Mar. 16, 1958.

SAMINSKY, Lazare (sā-mĭn'skĭ), composer; b. Odessa, Russia, Oct. 27, 1882; s. Joseph and Marie (Grieber) S.; student U. of St. Petersburg (Russia) and Imperial Conservatory of Music, M.A.; m. Lillian Morgan Buck, Apr. 22, 1923; married 2d, Jennifer Gandar, February 1, 1948. Made debut as composer-orchestra condr., Moscow, 1913; condr. of his 1st symphony, Imperial Opera House, Petrograd, 1917; lectured at British univs., 1919-20; music dir., Duke of York, London, 1919-20; came to U.S., 1920, naturalized, 1926; made U.S. debut as guest composer and condr., Detroit, 1921; condr. Friends of Music, N.Y. City, 1922, N.Y. Philharmonic, 1923, New York Symphony, 1923 and 1924; dir. Three Choir Festivals of New York since 1936; lecturer and condr. U.S. Music in South America, 1940; condr. Festivals of Am. Music, Paris, France, 1923, 25, 26. Founder and director League of Composers; lectured and conducted in Canada, 1941-42; directed concerts in honor of France, England and Russia, New York, Spring 1944; conducted his 3 shadows, lectured in France and over State radio, 1949; Premiere 5th Symphony N.Y.C., 1958; directed his works in Jerusalem. Member Am. Society of Composers, Authors and Publishers; allied mem. MacDowell Assn., Peterborough (N.H.) Colony, Jewish religion. Club: P.E.N. (N.Y.C.). Composer: Defeat of Julian, the Apostate Caesar (opera); The Daughter of Jephtha (opera-ballet); also other operas, ballets and 5 symphonies. Author: Music of the Ghetto and the Bible, 1934; Music of Our Day, 1939; Living Music of the Americas, 1949; Essentials of Conducting, Physics and Metaphysics of Music, Essays on Philosophy of Mathematics, all 1957; autobiography Third Leonardo, 1958. Home: Locust Av., Rye, N.Y. Office: 1 E. 65th St., N.Y.C. Died June 30, 1959.

SAMMET, G. Victor, chem. co. exec.; b. Boston, May 5, 1880; s. George W. and Victoria (King) S.; S.B., Mass. Inst. Tech., 1901; Ph.D., U. of Leipzig, Germany, 1905; m. Viola White, Apr. 14, 1926; 1 son, George V. Chemist Merrimac Chem. Co., Woburn, Mass., 1905-07; pres. No. Indsl. Chem. Co., Boston, 1908-56, ret.; dir. Mass. Mutual Life Ins. Co. Mem. Soc. Plastics Industry. Home: 24

Vineyard Rd., Newton Centre 59, Mass. Office: Seven Elkins St., South Boston 27, Mass. Died Apr. 13, 1958.

SAMMONS, F. Elmer, ins. exec.; b. Brooklyn, N.Y., Mar. 13, 1888; s. Charles H. and Annie E. (Bond) S.; ed. public school; m. Hazel Jane Smith, Nov. 1939. With Hanover Fire Ins. Co., New York, N.Y., since 1902, beginning as office boy and advancing through positions of responsibility to pres., Jan. 1945, dir. since 1938; pres. and dir. Fulton Fire Ins. Co.; dir. Mt. Beacon Ins. Co., Bankers Commercial Corp., New York; dir. First National Bank of Mount Vernon. Clubs: Drug and Chemical, New York Athletic (New York), Pelham (N.Y.) Country; Larchmont (N.Y.) Shore. Home: 221 Corlies Av., Pelham 65, N.Y. Office: 111 John St., N.Y.C. 38. Died Mar. 25, 1959.

SAMMONS, Wheeler, publisher Who's Who in Am.; b. Tacoma, Wash., Dec. 1, 1889; s. Thomas and Elizabeth (Wheeler) S.; grad. Canajoharie (N.Y.) High Sch.; B.S. cum laude, Harvard Coll., 1912; m. Dorothy Webbe, June 28, 1913; children—Wheeler, Elizabeth (Mrs. E. J. Connor). With William Filene's Sons Co., Boston, 1912-13; with A. W. Shaw Co., publishers, Chgo., 1913-28, pres., 1925-28; publishing independently from 1928; v.p., treas. The A. N. Marquis Co., pub. Who's Who in America and similar biographical reference books, Chgo., 1937-38, pres., 1938-53, pres. of successor organization Marquis —Who's Who, Inc. (a non-profit foundation), from 1953. Served as mng. dir. Inst. of Distbn., Inc., treas., dir. Utah Radio Products Co.; dir. Lake Shore Trust & Savs. Bank, Nestle Le Mur Co. Fellow Royal Econ. Soc. (Eng.); mem. S.A.R., Am. Econ. Assn., Nat. Council of Nat. Econ. League, A.I.M. (bd. dirs.), Acad. Polit. Sci., Am. Acad. Polit. and Social Sci., Authors League of Am., Chgo. Hist. Soc. Republican. Methodist. Clubs: Lake Shore, Executives, Chicago, Midday, University (Chgo.); Harvard, Bankers (N.Y.C.); Jefferson Island. Author: Keeping Up With Rising Costs, 1914; How to Run a Retail Business at Greater Profit, 1915 (4th edit. 1919); Making More Out of Advertising, 1919; Attracting and Holding Customers, 1919; Rising Tide of Hidden Taxes, 1936. Home: 536 Deming Pl., Chgo. Office: 210 E. Ohio St., Chgo. 11. Died Feb. 21, 1956.

SAMPLE, Paul Lindsay, merchant; b. Manteo, N.C., Sept. 17, 1897; s. Augustus Gambrel and Ida Mae (Shaw) S.; student Elizabeth City (N.C.) High Sch., 1910-14; A.B., Trinity College (now Duke U.), Durham, N.C., 1918; m. Helen Henrietta Heinz, Oct. 31, 1929; children—Miriam Elizabeth, Dorothy Jean, Becky Ann and Mathilda Mae (twins). With G. C. Murphy Co., chain variety stores, McKeesport, Pa., since 1918, as floorman, 1918-19, asst. store mgr., 1919-20, store mgr., 1921-23, supt. of stores, 1924-27, dir. of personnel, 1926-29, asst. sales mgr., 1928-30, sales mgr., 1931-37, v.p. in charge sales, 1938-46, dir. since 1929, exec. v.p., 1946, pres. since 1947; pres. Mack Realty Co. since 1946; chmn. Morris Stores, Bluffton, Ind. since 1951. Trustee, chmn. bd. Chautauqua (N.Y.) Instn.; nat. councillor U.S. Chamber of Commerce; trustee Duke U.; dir. A.R.C. Mem. Am. Management Assn., Nat. Assn. of Mfrs., Boston Econ. Conf., (mem. adv. bd.), Limited Price Variety Stores Assn. (chmn.), Acad. Polit. Sci. (life), Am. Legion, Omicron Delta Kappa (hon.). Republican. Methodist (trustee). Mason (Shriner). Clubs: Youghiogheny Country (McKeesport); Duquesne, Pitts. Athletic Association, University (Pittsburgh); Union League (New York City); Chautauqua Yacht, Chautauqua Golf. Home: Park Plaza Apts., Pitts. 13; (summer) 14 Emerson Av., Chautauqua, N.Y. Office: 531 5th Av., McKeesport, Pa. Died Dec. 8, 1953; buried Mt. Royal Mausoleum.

SAMS, Earl Corder, merchant; b. Simpson, Kan., Apr. 3, 1884; s. Green Lee and Amanda (Day) S.; student high sch., Beloit; m. Lula Ammerman, Aug. 4, 1904; children—Gladys (Mrs. Dean R. Porter), Camille (Mrs. Larry F. Lightner). With J. C. Penney Co. (over 1600 stores), 1907—, pres., 1917-46, chmn. bd., 1946—. Pres. Earl C. Sams Found., Inc. Mem. nat. council YMCA; mem. Bd. of Nat. Missions, Presbyn. Ch. in U.S.A.; chmn. bd. mgrs. William Sloane House (YMCA), N.Y.C.; mem. nat. exec. bd. Boy Scouts of Am. Trustee Kan. Wesleyan U., Salina (donor of Sams Auditorium in memory of father and mother). Mem. U.S. C. of C., Com. of One Hundred (Miami Beach, Fla.). Republican. Presbyn. Clubs: Union League, Kiwanis (pres. 1925) (N.Y.C.); Wykagyl Country, Bonnie Briar Country; Indian Creek Country (Miami Beach); Bald Peak Colony (Melvin Village, N.H.); Surf (dir.) (Miami Beach, Fla.). Home: 460 Beechmont Dr., New Rochelle, N.Y.; (winter) Miami Beach, Fla.; (summer) Luearlann Pines, Mirror Lake, N.H. Office: 330 W. 34th St., N.Y.C. Died July 23, 1950.

SAMUEL, Bernard, former mayor of Phila.; b. Phila., Mar. 9, 1880; s. Samuel and Christina (Streeton) S.; student Central High Sch., Phila.; m Eleanor Hamm, June 3, 1903; 1 son, Richard Russell. Began as office boy in investment house; elected to City Council, 1923, pres., 1939; became acting mayor or Phila., 1941, mayor, 1944-51. Trustee Free Library of Phila., Phila. Comml. Mus., Phila. Museum of Art, Temple U.; dir. Phila. Transportation Co.; mem. bd. dirs. of City Trusts; mem. Commrs. of Fairmount Park, Delaware River Joint Commn. of Pa. and N.J. Home: 1342 Shunk St. Address: City Hall, Phila. Died Jan. 12, 1954.

SANBORN, Charles Henry, physician; b. Hampton Falls, N. H., Oct. 9, 1821; academic edn.; grad. Harvard Med. Coll., 1856; ever since engaged in practice. Was 2 years member N. H. legislature; has been asst. sec. of state and State librarian; and for 30 years justice of peace and quorum throughout the State of N.H. Author: The North and the South. Address: Hampton Falls, N.H. Deceased.

SANBORN, Mary Farley, author; b. Manchester, N.H., May 8, 1953; d. Alden W. and Elizabeth Haseltine (Abbott) Sanborn; ed. in Dr. Gannett's Sch., Boston; afterward studied for concert stage (vocal music) with Mme. Erminie Rudersdorff; m. Fred C. Sanborn, Oct. 18, 1876; children—Robert Aldin, Bertha Elizabeth (dec.), Hilda Winslow. Has done book reviewing, short articles, etc. Author: Sweet-and-Twenty, 1890; It Came to Pass, 1891; Paula Ferris, 1892; The Revelation of Herself, 1904; Lynette and the Congressman, 1905; The Canvas Door, 1909; The First Valley, 1920. Home: 30 Williston Rd., Brookline, Mass. Died Nov. 25, 1941.

SANDERS, Charles Finley, clergyman, educator; b. Mifflinburg, Pa., Feb. 11, 1869; s. Joseph and Eva Catharine (Miller) S.; B.A., Pa. Coll., Gettysburg, Pa., 1892; grad. Luth. Theol. Sem., Gettysburg, 1895, B.D., 1899; studied U. Leipzig, Germany, 3 semesters, 1905-06; D. D. Lafayette, 1913; m. Harriet E. Hesson, Dec. 27, 1894 (died Sept. 1944); m. 2d, Sarah E. Saxton, Oct. 20, 1945. Ordained to ministry of Lutheran Ch., 1895; pastor Avonmore, Pa., 1895-98, Blairsville, 1898-1905; tchr. Blairsville Coll. for Women 1901-05; acting prof. mental sci., 1906, prof. philosophy 1907—, Pa. Coll. lectr. in war camps, 1919. Mem. Am. Sociol. Soc. Progressive Republican. Translator: (from the German) Introduction to Philosophy (by Prof. Jerusalem), 1910, revised edit., 1932; Brief History of Modern Philosophy (Hoffding), 1912; Problems of the Secondary Teacher (Jerusalem), 1918. Author: The Taproot of Religion and Its Fruitage, 1931; Freshman Orientation, 1936. Mem. Phi Beta Kappa, Kappa Phi Kappa, Pi Gamma Mu. World tour, 1928-29, studying conditions in Japan, China and India; lectures on polit. and social conditions in the Orient. Wrote The Challenge of the Trinitarian to the Neopagan, 1937, The Clergyman as a Teacher, Pastor, and interim St. John's Luth. Ch., Lewistown, Pa., 1943. Address: 251 15th Av. N.E., St. Petersburg, Fla. Died Apr. 18, 1959; buried Gettysburg, Pa.

SANDERS, Everett, lawyer; b. Clay County, Ind., Mar. 8, 1882; s. James and Melissa Everal (Stark) S.; student Ind. State Normal Sch., 1900-02; LL.B., Ind. U., 1907; m. Ella Neal, Dec. 13, 1903 (dec.); m. 2d, Hilda Sims, July 11, 1936. Taught sch. 3 yrs.; began practice at Terre Haute, Ind., 1907; mem. 65th to 68th Congresses, 5th Ind. Dist.; sec. to President Coolidge, 1925-29; now mem. law firm Sanders, Gravelle, Whitlock & Howrey. Chmn. Rep. Nat. Com., 1932-34. Republican. Missionary Baptist. Author: Coolidge Character; and other mag. articles. Home: 3601 Connecticut Av., Washington 8. Office: Shoreham Bldg., Washington 5. Died May 12, 1950; buried Terre Haute, Ind.

SANDERS, Harold Frederick, utilities exec.; b. Bklyn., Jan. 5, 1906; s. Louis C. and Anna (Schenzel) S.; student pub. schs. of Bklyn.; m. Florence Frances Adams, June 6, 1931; children—Harold F., Judith Carol. Has been secretary-treasurer Middle South Utilities, Inc., N.Y.C., 1949-58, vice president, secretary, and director, 1958—. Member Controllers Inst. Am., Am. Soc. Corporate Secs., Am. Gas Assn., Acad. Polit. Sci., Am. Mgmt. Assn. Republican. Presbyn. Mason. Club: Wall Street (N.Y. C.). Home: 15 Gerard Av., Malverne, N.Y. Office: 2 Broadway, N.Y.C. Died Apr. 14, 1959; buried Greenfield Cemetery.

SANDERS, Henry Arthur, philologist; b. Livermore, Me., Oct. 22, 1868; s. John and Luretta (Gibbs) S.; student Farmington (Me.) State Normal Sch., 1883-86; Coburn Classical Inst., Waterville, Me., 1886-87; A.B., U. of Mich., 1890, A.M., 1894; U. Berlin, 1895-96, U. Munich, 1896-97, Ph.D., Munich, 1897; L.H.D., Colby Coll., 1940; m. Charlotte Ione Poynor, Feb. 12, 1913; 1 dau., Catherine Abigail. Instr. in Latin, U. of Mich., 1893-95, U. Minn., 1897-99; instr. in Latin, U. Mich., 1899-1902, asst. prof., 1902-08, jr. prof., 1908-11, prof., 1911-39, chmn. dept. speech and gen. linguistics, 1932-39, prof. emeritus, 1939—; acting prof. of Latin, U. Ill., 1942, lectr. Latin Dept., 1943. Member Archaeological Institute American, American Philol. Assn. (pres. 1936-37), Am. Oriental Soc., Soc. Bibl. Lit. and Exegesis, Classical Assn. of Middle West and South, Bezan Club, Mediaeval Acad. Am., Am. Philos. Soc., Am. Acad. Arts and Sciences, Research Soc. of U. Mich., Phi Delta Theta, Phi Beta Kappa. Author: The Old Testament Manuscripts in the Freer Collection, Part I, 1910, Part II, 1917; The New Testament Manuscripts in the Freer Collection, Part I, 1912, Part II, 1917; The Papyrus of the Minor Prophets in the Freer Collection, 1927; The Berlin Papyrus of Genesis (with Carl Schmidt), 1927; Beati in Apocalipsin Libri Duodecim, Papers and Monographs of the American Academy in Rome, Vol. VII, Rome, 1930; A Third-Century Papyrus Codex of the Epistles of Paul, U. Mich. Studies, Vol. XXXVIII, 1935; Latin Papyri in the Michigan Collection, U. Mich. Studies, Vol. XLVIII (Papyri, Vol. VII), 1947. Editor: U. of Michigan Studies (Humanistic Series). Contbr. numerous articles to philol., archaeol. and ednl. jours. Acting dir. Sch. of Classical Studies of Am. Acad. in Rome, 1915-16; prof. in charge, 1928-31 (on leave of absence from U. of Mich.). Home: 2037 Geddes Av., Ann Arbor, Mich. Died Nov. 16, 1956.

SANDERS, Morgan Gurley, ex-congressman; b. Van Zandt Co., Tex., July 14, 1878; s. L. Lindsey and Sarah F. S.; ed. pub. schs. Admitted Tex. bar, 1901, and began practice at Canton; elected to Tex. Ho. of Rep., 1902, 04; county atty. Van Zandt County, 1911-14; dist. atty. 7th Jud. Dist. of Tex., 1915, 16; mem. 67th to 75th Congresses (1921-39), 3d Tex. Dist. Democrat. Baptist. Home: Canton, Tex. Died Jan. 7, 1956; buried Hillcrest Cemetery, Canton, Tex.

SANDERS, Robert David, textile exec.; b. Tuscaloosa, Ala., Sept. 28, 1898; s. James William and Julia (Lockett) S.; student U. of South, 1915, Mercer U., 1916; A.M., Coll. of Miss., 1917; m. Catherine Williams, Sept. 1940; children—James William, Julia Sheila, June Kelley, Robert David. Began as mill and office employee, Aponaug Mfg. Co., Kosciusko, Miss., 1920; office mgr. and gen. supt. cotton mills operated by father, Kosciusko, Starkville, Natchez, Winona, and Yazoo City, Miss., and Mobile, Ala., 1920-27; purchasing agt. for all mills and asst. to pres., Jackson, Miss., 1927-37; pres. and treas. since 1937 various corps. Sanders Industries including Aponaug Mfg. Co., Kosciusko, J. W. Sanders Cotton Mill, Inc., Starkville, Miss., Magnolia Textiles, Inc., Magnolia, Miss., Delta Chenille Co., Inc., Summit, Winona and Durant, Miss., Kay Ruth Dress Co., Inc., Jackson, Miss., Jackson Opera House Co., The Sanders Co., Jackson, Miss., Sanders Motors, Inc., Jackson, Miss., Deep South Motor Co., Jackson, Miss., Indsl. Suppliers, Inc., Jackson, Miss. Dir. Century Aviation Co., M.-K.-T. R.R. Lt. col., Govs. Staff, State Ga., since 1948; col. Govs. Staff, State Miss. since 1948. Served as capt., Tank Corps, U.S. Army, 1918-20, overseas, 1918-20. Pres. Robert D. Sanders Foundation. Mem. Internat. Trade Mart, Nat. Assn. Mfrs., Am. Cotton Mfrs. Inst., Nat. Cotton Mfrs. Inst., Nat. Cotton Council Am. (del. mem.), Nat. Football Hall of Fame (charter mem.), Miss. Economic Council, Jackson C. of C., Kappa Alpha (life mem. scholarship fund, exec. council), Omega Delta Kappa, Beta Gamma Sigma. Raises pheasants and turkeys and registered cattle, Kaywood Plantations; interested in reforestation. Home: Kaywood Plantations, Hazlehurst, Miss. Office: Century Bldg., Jackson, Miss. Died Sept. 24, 1954; buried Lakewood Meml. Park, Jackson.

SANDERS, Thomas Henry, accounting; b. Brierley Hill, Staffordshire, Eng., Apr. 7, 1885; s. Thomas and Catherine (Nock) S.; B. Commerce, Birmingham University, 1905, M. Commerce, 1914; Ph.D., Harvard, 1921; married Gertrude Schulz, Mar. 25, 1914; children—Catherine Anna (Mrs. Frank E. Plumley, Junior), Mary Elizabeth, Thomas Charles, John Robert, William Huston (killed in action Dec. 5, 1944). Came to United States 1917, naturalized, 1926. With Rudge-Whitworth, Ltd., Coventry, Eng., 1905-10; instructor in commercial practice, Yamaguchi, Japan, 1911-17; asst. prof. accounting, U. of Minn., 1918-20; asst. prof. accounting, Harvard, 1921-24, asso. prof., 1924-27, prof. Harvard Grad. Sch. of Bus. Adminstrn. since 1927. Mem. Am. Acad. Arts and Sciences, Nat. Assn. Cost Accountants (pres. 1931-32), Am. Econ. Assn., Am. Accounting Assn. Decorated Order of the Rising Sun, 5th Class (Japan). Episcopalian. Mason. Club: Harvard (New York). Author: My Japanese Year, 1915; Problems in Industrial Accounting, 1923; Bookkeeping and Business Knowledge (with J. H. Jackson and A. H. Sproul), 2 vols., 1926; Cost Accounting for Control, 1934; A Statement of Accounting Principles (with H. R. Hatfield and U. Moore), 1933; Accounting Principles and Practice (with H. R. Hatfield and N. L. Burton), 1940; Company Annual Reports, 1949. Contbr. to profl. publs. Home: 95 Avon Hill St., Cambridge 40, Mass. Deceased.

SANDERSON, Charles Rupert, librarian; b. Bury, Eng., May 19, 1887; s. Charles and Ellen (Oates) S.; B.Sc., U. London, Eng., 1925; M.A., U. Toronto, Can., 1940, LL.D., 1951; m. Ethel Marshall, May 2, 1915; 1 son, Capt. Charles Graham Sanderson, R.C.A.M.C. (killed in action, France, Aug. 14, 1944). Asst. librarian, John Rylands Library, Manchester, Eng., 1909-14; librarian, Gladstone Library, London, 1914-29; lectr. U. London Sch. of Librarianship, and summer schs. at Brussels, Florence, Paris, Heidelberg, 1919-29; lecturer, U. of Wales, Aberystwyth, summer, 1927; William Warner Bishop lecturer, U. of Mich., 1942; dep. chief librarian, Public Libraries, Toronto, Ont., 1929-37, chief librarian, since 1937; member exec. bd., Am. Library Assn., 1942-45. Chairman Toronto civic historical committee. Served with British Army, France and Africa, 1915-19; maj. Canadian Reserve Officers, U. of Toronto, Canadian Officers Training Corps. Member (Ontario) Royal Commission on Education. Member A.L.A.; chairman Canadian Library Council, 1941-43; fellow Am. Library Inst.; pres. Empire Club of Can., 1942; Methodist. Mason, Rotarian (pres. Toronto 1938). Home: 117 St. George Apts. Office: Toronto Public Libraries, College and St. George Sts., Toronto, Ont., Can. Died July 24, 1956; buried Caledon East, Ont.

SANDERSON, John, corporation exec.; b. Philadelphia, Pa., Feb. 23, 1891; s. James C. and Rose E. (Mayer) S.; graduate Girard Coll.; Pace & Pace Inst.; m. Marion O. Hornibrook, Nov. 6, 1918. Began with Haskins & Sells, C.P.A.'s, 1912-17; served as lieut. in U.S. Navy, 1917-19; comptroller, Gaston Williams & Wigmore, Inc., 1919-21; treas. and dir. Gaston & Co., Inc., 1921-28; treas. and dir. North Am. Aviation, Inc., 1929-33; treas. and dir. Sperry Corp., 1933-55, v.p., 1933-52, sr. v.p., 1952-55, co. merged with Remington Rand to form Sperry Rand Corp., of which is v.p. for finance, secretary, dir.; v.p., dir. Vickers, Inc., Wright Machinery Company, Wheeler Insulated Wire Co., Inc.; dir. Sperry Gyroscope Co. of Can., Ltd., Sperry Gyroscope Ottawa, Ltd. Clubs: Sleepy Hollow Country, Scarborough-on-Hudson (N.Y.); Girard, Rockefeller Center Luncheon (N.Y.); Clayton (N.Y.) Yacht. Home: 930 Fifth Av. Office: 30 Rockefeller Plaza, N.Y.C. Died Dec. 1958.

SANDIFER, Joseph Randolph (săn'dĭ-fẽr), educator; b. Mecklenburg County, N.C., July 28, 1878; s. Thomas Thorne (M.D.) and Elizabeth (Graham) S.; A.B., Erskine Coll., Due West, S.C., 1902; studied U. of Tenn., summer 1904, Piedmont Summer Sch., Davidson Coll., N.C., 1902; m. Mittie Doris Moore, Dec. 20, 1928. Teacher in boys' schs. 10 yrs.; Founded, 1913, and pres. Blue Ridge Sch. for Boys, Hendersonville, N.C. Democrat. Presbyterian. Mason (K.T., Shriner). Clubs: Shriners', Commercial, Rotary (former dist. gov. and past dir., R.I.), Executive. Mem. N.C. Soc. S.A.R. Home: Hendersonville, N.C. Died Apr. 11, 1956; buried Shepherd Meml. Park, Hendersonville.

SANDS, Frank (Elbert), newspaper pub.; b. New Fairfield, Conn., July 17, 1863; s. Jesse and Mary M. (Turner) S.; Ph.B., Yale, 1885; m. Alice Louise Brasee, Apr. 26, 1888; 1 dau., Anna Brasee. Founder, 1886, since pub. Meriden (Conn.) Daily Journal; chmn. bd. Journal Publishing Co.; former v.p. Meriden Savings Bank. Maj., Conn. State Guard, 1917-21. Former v.p. Meriden Hosp.; former pres. Curtis Meml. Library. Past pres. Conn. Soc. S.A.R. Republican. Episcopalian. Mason (32°, K.T.) Clubs: Rotary, Home. Home: 64 Lincoln St. Office: Journal Bldg., Meriden, Conn. Died June 8, 1951; buried Meriden.

SANDS, Merrill Burr, business exec.; b. Portland, Me., 1884; grad. Yale, 1906. Pres. and dir. Dictaphone Corp. Home: 70 Undercliff St., Yonkers 5, N.Y. Office: Graybar Bldg., N.Y.C. Died Mar. 26, 1951.

SANDZÉN, Sven Birger (sănd-săn'), painter; b. Blidsberg, Sweden, Feb. 5, 1871; s. Rev. John Peter and Clara Elizabeth (Sylven) S.; grad. Coll. of Skara, Sweden, 1890; studied U. of Lund; studied painting at Art Sch. of Artists' League, Stockholm, under A. Zorn and R. Bergh, and at sch. of Aman-Jean, Paris; also at principal art museums of the world; received hon. degrees of Litt.D., LL.D., D.F.A.; came to Am., 1894; m. Alfrida Leksell, Nov. 28, 1900; 1 dau., Margaret Elizabeth. Prof. aesthetics and painting, Bethany Coll., Kan., 1894-1945, emeritus, 1945-—. Has exhibited in Stockholm and Gothenburg, Sweden, Paris, Chicago, St. Louis; has collection of 500 paintings and drawings of the West; represented in British Mus., Bibliotheque Nationale Dec. Knight Royal Order of North Star (Sweden). Lutheran. Author: With Brush and Pencil, 1905; also many articles for mags. and newspapers on art subjects and travel. Represented in Library of Congress, Washington; Art Inst. of Chicago; Nat. Mus., Stockholm, Sweden; etc. Lecturer, lithographer, and wood engraver. Home: Lindsborg, Kan. Died June 19, 1954; buried Lindsborg.

SANFORD, Albert Hart, author; b. Platteville, Wis., June 21, 1866; s. Henry C. and Mary (Greene) S.; Litt.B., U. of Wis., 1891; A.M., Harvard, 1894; m. Luella M. Roberts, Aug. 14, 1895; children—Marian, Eleanor. Engaged in teaching 1886-1936; instr. history and civics, State Normal Sch., La Crosse, Wis., 1909-36, ret. 1936. Mem. North Central History Tchrs.' Assn. (pres. 1901-02). Author: (with ames Alton James, q.v.) Government in State and Nation, 1901; Our Government, 1903; American History, 1909; A History of LaCrosse 1841-1900 (with Harry Hirschheimer). Address: LaCrosse, Wis. Died Aug. 27, 1956; Oak Grove Cemetery, LaCrosse, Wis.

SANFORD, Arthur Hawley, physician; b. New Albin, Ia., Jan. 12, 1882; s. Alcimore Mead and Amanda Elizabeth (Gilbert) S.; A.B., Northwestern U., 1904, A.M., 1907, M.D., 1907; m. Margaret Loretta Seager, Aug. 23, 1906; children—Hawley Seager, Raymond Arthur, Gertrude Loretta Elizabeth. Asst. prof. physiology, Med. Sch., Marquette U., 1907-08, asso. prof., 1908-09, prof. 1910-11; bacteriologist, Mayo Clinic, 1911; head div. of clin. pathology, 1915; now emeritus; apptd. asso. prof. pathology, 1915, prof. pathology, Mayo Found., U. of Minn., 1921-50; dir. lab. Rochester State Hosp., 1950-—. Served as maj., Med. Corps, U.S. Army, with inactive reserves. Hon. Cons. Army Med. Library. Mem. Rochester (Minn.) Pub. Library Bd., 1914-24; pres. Bd. of Edn., 1924-40. Spl. cons. U.S.P.H.S. Ex-pres. Am. Bd. Pathology. Fellow Am. Coll. Physicians; mem. A.M.A., Am. Soc. Clin. Pathology (pres. 1927-28; recipient Ward Burdick medal, 1933), A.A.A.S., Am. Soc. Immunologists, Soc. Exptl. Biology and Medicine, Sigma Nu, Alpha Kappa Kappa, Phi Beta Kappa, Sigma Xi, Alpha Omega Alpha. Mason (32°, K.T.). Author: Clinical Diagnosis by Laboratory Methods (with Dr. J. C. Todd), 11th edit., 1948. Home: 506 10th Av. S.W. Office: 102-110 2d Av. S.W., Rochester, Minn. Died Apr. 28, 1959.

SANFORD, Conley Hall, physician; b. Yorkville, Tenn., Sept. 12, 1893; s. Allan Hansford and Frances Lee (Hall) S.; student Freed-Hardeman Coll., 1910-13, Valparaiso U., 1913-14; M.D., U. of Tenn., 1918; post-grad. work, Harvard, summer 1922, U. of Vienna, Austria, 1928; m. Mary Elizabeth Henderson, Dec. 16, 1929; children—Joseph Sledge, Sara Frances. Began as physician, 1918; intern Phila. Gen. Hosp., 1919-20; in practice internal medicine, Memphis, Tenn., since 1920; prof. medicine, U. of Tenn., since 1939, chief Div. of Medicine since 1939; chief of staff John Gaston Hosp., Memphis, since 1939. Served as lt. (j.g.), Med. Corps, U.S. Navy, stationed at Naval Hosp., Charleston, S.C., 1918-19. Fellow Am. Coll. Physicians; licentiate Am. Bd. Internal Medicine; mem. Phi Chi, Alpha Omega Alpha. Democrat. Contbr. to med. jours. Home: Whitehaven, Tenn. Office: 899 Madison Av., Memphis. Died Nov. 16, 1953.

SANFORD, Edward Field, Jr., sculptor; b. N.Y. City, Apr. 6, 1886; s. Edward F. and Anna M. (Hopkins) S.; student Art Students' League (New York), Nat. Acad. Design, Paris and Munich. Exhibited at Salon (Paris), Nat. Acad. of Design, Pa. Acad. Fine Arst, etc. Prin. works include Core Mausoleum, Norfolk, Va.; two heroic pediments and four colossal figures, Sacramento, Calif.; two colossal bronze statues for State Library, Sacramento; bronze finial figure for building of Ala. Power Co., Birmingham, Ala.; Francis P. Garvan Mausoleum; Marble statue estate of Col. H. H. Rogers; colossal stone statue, Payne Whitney memorial, Yale University; two groups, Bronx County Court House; animal frieze, N.Y. State Roosevelt Memorial; memorial portrait of Dr. W. A. R. Goodwin, Bruton Parish Church, Williamsburg, Va.; colossal bronze "Inspiration," Va. Museum Fine Arts, Richmond; bronze statue, Inspiration, Brookgreen Gardens, Georgetown, S.C. Mem. Nat. Sculpture Soc., Beaux Arts Inst. of Design (former dir. of its dept. of sculpture). Home: St. Augustine, Fla. Died Oct. 12, 1951.

SANFORD, Harold Williams, editor; b. Silver Creek, N.Y., Feb. 15, 1890; s. George Beardsley and Essa May (Ball) S.; A.B., U. Rochester (N.Y.), 1912; m. Rena Etta Cole, Sept. 1, 1913; children—Peter Cole, Ann Cole (Mrs. William C. Gamble). Reporter Rochester Democrat and Chronicle, 1911-15, asst. city editor, 1915-22, city editor, 1922, news editor, 1922-25, mng. editor, 1925-35, asso. editor, 1935-37, editor, 1937-—, author of column The International Scene. Sec. Rochester World Court Com., 1929; mem. Monroe County Charter Commn., 1934-35. Chmn. Family and Child div. Council Social Agys. Mem. bd. visitors Brockport State Tchrs. Coll.; co-founder and trustee, State, Town and County Officers Tng. Sch. Mem. Rochester C. of C. (trustee), Am. Soc. Newspaper Editors, N.Y. State Soc. Newspaper Editors (pres. 1938-40), Nat. Municipal League, Am. Soc. Planning Ofcls., Legal Aid Soc. (dir.), Tuberculosis and Pub. Health Assn., Phi Beta Kappa. Republican. Unitarian. Clubs: Rochester Torch (ex-pres.), Philosophers', Twenty, Fortnightly. On editorial bd. The Torch (internat. organ). Home: 219 Culver Rd. Office: 61 Main St., E. Rochester 4, N.Y. Died Apr. 5, 1950.

SANFORD, Joseph William, penologist, warden; b. Washington, D.C., Jan. 14, 1889; s. Andrew Joseph and Annie Margaret (Tupper) S.; prep. edn. pub. schs., Washington, D.C.; student U. of Md., 1903-06; m. Nellie Gertrude Cowsill, Nov. 30, 1907; children—Joseph Nathan, Margaret Tupper, Evelyn. Business, 1906-11; probation officer Juvenile Court, Dist. of Columbia, 1911-15, chief probation officer, dir. of probation, 1915-27; chief investigator U.S. Bureau of Efficiency, 1927-31; warden U.S. Bureau of Prisons, Dept. of Justice, since 1931, at Federal Reformatory, Chillicothe, O., 1933-38, U.S. Penitentiary, Atlanta, Ga., 1938-48; commr. of corrections, Mich., Feb.-Dec. 1948; U.S. Bureau of Prisons, 1949; penologist Department of the Air Force since 1949. Mem. Council for the Clin. Training of Theol. Students, New York; member advisory bd., The Osborne Assn., New York. Past pres. Am. Prison Assn., Wardens Assn.; mem. Alumni Assn. of U. of Md., Civ. Episcopalian. Home: 4220 Reno Rd. N.W., Washington 8. Office: Pentagon Bldg., Washington. Died Feb. 6, 1952; buried Fort Lincoln Cemetery.

SANFORD, Roscoe Frank, astronomer; b. Faribault, Minn., Oct. 6, 1883; s. Frank William and Alberta Arilla (Nichols) S.; B.A., U. Minn., 1905; Ph.D., U. Cal., 1917; m. Mabel Aline Dyer, Dec. 12, 1917; children—Jane Dyer, Eleanor Nichols, Wallace Gordon, Allan Robert, Marguerite Anne. Tchr. mathematics, Marshall (Minn.) High Sch., 1905-06; Carnegie asst., Lick Obs., Mt. Hamilton, Cal., 1906-08, So. Obs. of Carnegie Inst., San Luis, Argentina, 1908-11; with D. O. Mills Expdn., Lick Obs., Santiago, Chile, 1911-15; on staff Dudley Obs., Albany, N.Y., 1917-18, Mt. Wilson Obs., Pasadena, Cal., 1918-50, Naval Ordnance Test Sta., Pasadena br., 1950-—. Mem. Am. Astron. Soc., Astron. Soc. of Pacific, Internat. Astron. Union (Commn. No. 30), A.A.A.S. Presbyn. Contbr. to pubs. of astron. socs. Home: 1521 E. Mountain St. Office: Mt. Wilson Observatory, 813 Santa Barbara St., Pasadena, Cal. Died Apr. 7, 1958.

SANGER, Henry H., banker; b. Detroit, Mich., Sept. 21, 1866; s. Henry Prentice and Frances Allen (Hulbert) S.; B.L., Cornell Univ., 1891; m. Margaret Snow, June 1, 1909; children—Henry Snow, Frances Margaret (Mrs. Philbrook Cushing), Cornelia (Mrs. John Linch), Marie (Mrs. Harold Sack). Past pres. Nat. Bank Commerce, Detroit; chmn. bd. Manufacturers Nat. Bank, ret. 1948. Member Kappa Alpha. Republican. Episcopalian. Clubs: Detroit, Yondotega, Bankers, Detroit Boat, Detroit Country. Home: 333 University Place, Grosse Pointe 30, Mich. Died Jan. 3, 1956; buried Elmwood Cemetery, Detroit.

SANGER, John Pomeroy, business exec.; b. Evansville, Ind., Apr. 4, 1900; s. Andrew Lewis and Louise (Pomeroy) S.; B.S. in Mech. Engring., Armour Inst. Tech. (now Ill. Inst. Tech.), Chgo., 1921; m. Dora L. Schumacher, June 12, 1926; children—Nancy Jane, Richard Hastings. Vice pres. U.S. Gypsum Co., 1936-—. Trustee Ill. Inst. Tech., Armour Research Found.; mem. Adv. com. to Hoover Commn. on Fed. Supply Project. Pres. Chicago Purchasing Agents Assn. (pres. 1935-36), Tau Beta Pi. Republican. Presbyn. Mason. Clubs: Union League, Economic (Chgo.); Skokie Country (Glencoe, Ill.). Home: 2714 Grant St., Evanston, Ill. Office: 300 W. Adams St., Chgo. Died Feb. 10, 1951.

SANTAYANA, George, poet and philosopher; b. Madrid, Spain, Dec. 16, 1863; s. Augustin Ruiz and Josefina (Borrás) de Santayana; grad. Harvard, 1886; studied in Berlin, Germany, 2 yrs.; student King's Coll., Cambridge (Eng.), 1896-97; degrees, M.A., Ph.D., Litt. D. Came to U.S., 1872; now living abroad. Teacher, later prof., philosophy, Harvard, 1889-1911; Hyde lecturer, Sorbonne, Paris, 1905-06; Spencer lecturer, Oxford U. (Eng.), 1923. Writings include: (verse) Sonnets and Other Verses, 1894; Lucifer, a Theological Tragedy, 1898; The Hermit of Carmel and Other Poems, 1901; Poems, Selected by the author and revised, 1923; (philosophical) The Sense of Beauty, 1896; Interpretations of Poetry and Religion, 1900; The Life of Reason, or The Phases of Human Progress (5 vols.; Reason in Common Sense, Reason in Society, Reason in Religion, Reason in Art, Reason in Science), 1905-06; Three Philosophical Poets—Lucretius, Dante and Goethe, 1910; Winds of Doctrine, 1913; Egotism in German Philosophy, 1916; Little Essays, 1920; Character and Opinion in the United States, 1920; Soliloquies in England and Later Soliloquies, 1922; Scepticism and Animal Faith, Introduction to a System of Philosophy, 1923; Dialogues in Limbo, 1925; Platonism and the Spiritual Life, 1927; Realms of Being (4 vols.: The Realm of Essence, The Realm of Matter, The Realm of Truth, The Realm of Spirit), 1920-40; The Genteel Tradition at Bay, 1931; Some Turns of Thought in Modern Philosophy, 1933; The Last Puritan, a Memoir in the Form of a Novel, 1935; Obiter Scripta, 1935; The Philosophy of Santayana, Selections, 1936; Realms of Being, 1 vol. edition, 1942; Persons and Places, the Background of My Life, 1944; The Middle Span, vol. 2 of Persons and Places, 1945; The Idea of Christ in the Gospels, or God in Man, 1946; Dominations and Powers, Reflections on Liberty, Society and Government, 1951. Address: via Stefano Rotondo 6, Rome, Italy; also care Charles Scribner's Sons, 597-599 Fifth Av., N.Y.C. 17. Died Sept. 26, 1952; buried Tomba Degli Spagnuoli, La Verano Cemetery, Rome, Italy.

SAPIRO, Aaron, lawyer; b. San Francisco, Calif., Feb. 5, 1884; s. Jacob and Selina (Wascerwitz) S.; grad. Lowell High Sch., San Francisco, 1900; B.A., U. of Cincinnati, 1904, M.A., 1905; studied Hebrew Union Coll., Cincinnati; B.L., Hastings Law Coll. (U. of Calif.), 1911; m. Janet Arndt, of Stockton, Calif., Nov. 17, 1913; children—Jean Louise, Andree, Stanley, Leland. Admitted to Calif. bar, 1911; served as 1st sec. and counsel Calif. Industrial Accident Bd.; moved to Chicago, Ill., 1923, N.Y. City, 1927; specializes in combinations, coöperative transactions and rural credits; with co-author, Standard Coöperative Marketing Act, adopted in whole or in part in 41 states; assisted in organizing the Canadian wheat pools, Burley Tobacco Assn., Tex. and other cotton assns. Enlisted in F.A., U.S.A., 1918; batt. sergt.-maj. 38th F.A.; at F.A. Officers' Training Sch. at Armistice. Mem. Phi Beta Kappa. Republican. Jewish religion. Clubs: Concordia (San Francisco); Covenant, Standard (Chicago). Home: Scarsdale, N.Y. Office: 11 W. 42d St., New York, N.Y. Died Nov. 1959.

SAPPINGTON, Samuel Watkins, pathologist; b. Phila., 1874; prep. edn. Friends Central High School, Phila.; M.D., Hahnemann Coll. and Hosp., Phila., 1897, Sc.D., 1941. Intern Hahnemann Med. Hosp.; apptd. demonstrator of pathology Hahnemann Coll., 1900, asso. prof., 1905, prof., 1907, served for many yrs. as prof. pathology and bacteriology (emeritus, 1947—) and as pathologist Hahnemann Hosp. Mem. A.M.A., A.C.P., Am. Inst. Homeopathy, Soc. of Immunologists, Soc. Am. Bacteriologists, etc. Address: Box 528, Bryn Mawr, Pa. Died May, 1951.

SARDESON, Frederick William (sär'dē-sŭn), geologist, paleontologist; b. Owego Mills, town of Wiota, Wis., Feb. 22, 1866; s. Joseph and Petra (Rossing) S.; B.L., U. of Minn., 1891, M.S., 1892; Ph.D., U. of Freiburg, 1895; m. Edna A. Mitchell, June 16, 1903; 1 dau., Marion Petra. Instr. of palaeontology, 1892-94, 1898-1905, asst. prof., 1905-14, Univ. of Minn. Geologist, U.S. Geol. Survey, 1911-24; geologist examiner for Minn. State Securities Commn., 1917-34, now cons. geologist. Mem. Internat. Geol. Congress, 1894. Fellow A.A.A.S., Geol. Soc. America, Phi Beta Kappa, Sigma Xi, etc. Writer geology reports and contbr. on geol., paleontol., philos. and ednl. subjects. Address: 2434 S. 158 St., Seattle 88. Died Aug. 28, 1958; buried Forest Lawn Mausoleum, Seattle.

SARETT, Lew (sär-et'), author, lecturer, prof. speech; b. Chicago, Ill., May 16, 1888; s. Rudolph and Jeanette (Block) S.; student Univ. of Mich., 1907-08; A.B., Beloit (Wis.) Coll., 1911; Harvard, 1911-12; LL.B., University of Illinois, 1916; hon. Litt.D., Baylor University, 1926; L.H.D. (honorary), Beloit College, Wisconsin, 1945; married Margaret Elizabeth Husted, June 17, 1914 (died February 27, 1941); children—Lewis H., Helen (Mrs. John Stockdale); married second, Juliet Barker, March 19, 1943 (deceased Nov. 7, 1945); married third, Alma Johnson, Apr. 19, 1946. Woodsman, guide and U.S. ranger in the Northwest several months each year for 16 years; instructor in English and pub. speaking, 1912-16, head of div. pub. speaking, 1916-18, asso. in English, 1918-20, Univ. of Ill.; asso. prof. oratory, Northwestern Univ., 1920-21; prof. of persuasion and professional speech, Northwestern Univ. School of Speech, 1921-53, professor emeritus, 1953—; vis. professor of speech University of Fla., 1951-54 (on leave). Lecturer on Canadian North, Indians and wild life, literature, etc. Honored by Northwestern U. through establishment of Lew Sarett Chair of Speech, 1953. Mem. Soc. Midland Authors, Speech Association of Am., Poetry Soc. Am. (regional vice pres. for south), Delta Sigma Rho, Phi Delta Phi, Zeta Psi, Phi Beta Kappa, Sigma Tau Delta, Authors' Club (London, England), Michigan Authors' Association. Presbyn. Author: Many Many Moons (verse), 1920; The Box of God (verse), 1922; Ode to Illinois (read at the dedication of the War Memorial Stadium at the Univ. of Ill.), 1924; Slow Smoke (verse), 1925; Wings Against the Moon (verse), 1931; Basic Principles of Speech (with W. T. Foster), 1936; Modern Speeches on Basic Issues (with W. T. Foster), 1939; Collected Poems of Lew Sarett, 1941; Speech: A High School Course (with W. T. Foster and J. H. McBurney), 1943; Basic Principles of Speech (revised edit.) (with W. T. Foster), 1946; Covenant with Earth (edited by Alma Johnson Sarett), 1956; Basic Principles of Speech (third edition revised by Alma Johnson Sarett), 1958. Winner of the Helen Haire Levinson prize for poetry, 1921; Poetry Soc. of America prize for best vol. of poetry pub. in America, 1925; Chicago Foundn. for Lit. award, 1934. Contbr. verse and articles to mags. Home: 1025 N.W. 13th Av., Gainesville, Fla. Died Aug. 17, 1954; buried Evergreen Cemetery, Gainesville, Fla.

SARGENT, Fitzwilliam, business exec.; b. Bridgewater, Mass., Oct. 10, 1892; s. Winthrop and Emma Harvard, 1914; m. Bernice Wellington, Sept. 9, 1914; children—Fitzwilliam, Compton (dec.), With Standard Supply and Equipment Co., Phila., since 1914, sales mgr., 1914-25, v.p., 1925-29, pres. 1929-30; v.p. Budd Co., Phila., since 1940; dir. Avonmore Coal & Coke Co., 1930-40. Served as lt. (j.g.) U.S.N.R. F. Aviation, 1917-19. Mem. U.S. Srs. Golf Assn., Soc. War of 1812. Republican. Clubs: Essex County (Manchester, Mass.); Harvard (Phila.); Harvard, New York Railroad (N.Y.C.); Merion Cricket (Haverford, Pa.); Merion Golf (Ardmore, Pa.); New England Railroad (Boston); Owl (Cambridge, Mass.). Home: 1918 Rittenhouse Sq., Phila. 3. Office: 2450 Hunting Park Av., Phila. 32. Died Mar. 13, 1955.

SARGENT, James Clyde, physician and surgeon; b. Piqua, O., Oct. 3, 1892; s. Charles Roger and Emma G. (Bishop) S.; student Denison U., 1909-10; M.D., Ohio State U., 1915; m. Mary Genevieve Cook, Jan. 3, 1917; children—James Wellington, Mary Genevieve (Mrs. Andrew Galbraith Miller), Suzanne (Mrs. Robert Llewellyn Warnock). Intern, Minneapolis City Hosp., 1915-16; post grad. study James Buchanan Brady Urologic Inst., Johns Hopkins Hosp., 1916-17; pvt. practice medicine limited to urology, Milwaukee, 1917—; mem. faculty Marquette U. Sch. Medicine, 1917—, clin. prof. and dir. dept. urology, 1919—; staff St. Joseph's, Evang. Deaconess, Milwaukee Co. Gen., Milwaukee Co. Emergency and Johnston Emergency hosps.; urology consultant U.S. Naval Hosp., Great Lakes, Ill., 1947—, to Surgeon Gen., U.S. Navy, 1949—; sr. consultant urology U.S. V.A. Hosp., Wood, Wis., 1946—. Served as capt., med. corps U.S.N.R., active duty, 1942-45. Mem. med. adv. com. to med. services div. Nat. Security Resources Bd., 1949-50, health resources adv. com., 1950, trans. to ODM, 1951—. Presidential apptmnt. to Nat. Adv. Com. on the selection of doctors, dentists and allied specialists advisory to the Selective Service System, 1950—. Recipient Carnegie Hero Bronze medal and award, 1915; Alumni Achievement award, Ohio State U. Coll. Medicine, 1951. Diplomate Am. Bd. Urology. Fellow A.C.S., A.M.A. (Wis. mem. ho. dels. 1938-50; chmn. council Nat. Emergency Med. Service, 1947-—), Acad. Internat. of Medicine, Am. Urol. Assn. (pres. N. Central sect. 1947), Assn. Genito-Urinary Surgeons, Wis. State (pres. 1937-38) and Milwaukee Co. (pres. 1933) med. socs., Phi Gama, Delta, Alpha Kappa Kappa, Mason (Shriner). Club: Rotary. Contbr. chpt. on Injuries of the Genital Tract in Urology (edited by Dr. M. F. Campbel), 1952. Home: 2138 E. LaFayette Pl., Milw. 2. Office: 324 Wisconsin Av., Milw. Died Oct. 7, 1954.

SARGENT, Porter E., publisher; b. Bklyn., June 6, 1872; s. Francis Porter and Roselyn (Hitchcock) S.; A.B., Harvard, 1896, A.M., 1897; m. Margaret Upham, Mar. 9, 1907; children—Upham (dec.), F. Porter. Dist. sch. tchr., Cal., 1890-92; prin. grammar school, San Bernardino, Cal., 1892-93; asst. in botany, later in zoölogy Harvard, 1897-99; master of science Browne and Nichols Sch., Cambridge, Mass., 1896-1904; engaged in research in comparative neurology, Harvard, 1897-1901, and independently with grants from carnegie Inst., 1902-04; dir. of science Nautical Prep. Sch., 1903-04; founder, 1904, and for 10 yrs. dir. Sargent's Travel Sch. for Boys (5 times round the world); organizer and dir. Sargent Sch. Service, 1920-40. Organizer, with W. P. Everts, of Boston, Harvard Liberal Club, Club: Harvard (Boston). Editor and pub. Sargent's Handbooks, 1914—; Handbook of New England, 3 edits.; Private Schools, 32 edits.; Summer Camps, 12 edits.; Handbook for Private School Teachers; Summer Camp Guide, 6 edits.; Private School News, 1925-1944. Editor Elihu Vedder's Poems, Edgar Waterman Anthony's A History of Mosaics, etc. Author: Spoils: Poems From a Crowded Life, 1935; The New Immoralities: Clearing the Way for a New Ethics, 1935; Human Affairs, 1938; Education: A Realistic Appraisal, 1939; What Makes Lives, 1940; Getting US Into War, 1941; Education in Wartime, 1942; War and Education, 1943; The Future of Education, 1944; Between Two Wars; The Failure of Education, 1920-1940, 1945; The Continuing Battle for Control of the Mind of Youth, 1945; Mad or Muddled, 1947; Dangerous Trends, 1948; Extending Horizons, 1951; also numerous mag. articles, manuscripts. Home: 26 Weybridge Rd., Brookline, Mass. Office: 11 Beacon St., Boston 8. Died Mar. 27, 1951.

SARTHER, John M(artin), corp. exec.; b. Chicago, Feb. 26, 1889; s. Frederick and Mary (Bode) S.; student pub. and night schs. Chgo.; m. Madalyn Scearce, May 22, 1919. Sales mgr. Anglo Am. Provision Co., Chgo., 1903-12; owner Gt. Am. Stores Co., 1912-48; pres. Certified Grocers of Ill., 1948-50; pres. Sprague Warner div. Consol. Grocers Corp., 1952-54; pres. Central Distributing div. Consol. Foods Corp., 1954—; v.p., dir. Consol. Foods Corp. Clubs: South Shore Country, Lake Shore (Chgo.). Home: 6901 Oglesby Av., Chgo. 49. Died Oct. 7, 1957.

SARTON, George (Alfred Leon) (sär'tŭn), science historian; b. Ghent, Belgium, August 31, 1884; s. Alfred and Léonie (Van Halmé) S.; B.Sc., U. of Ghent, 1906, Sc.D., 1911; medallist in chemistry, 4 Belgian univs., 107; L.H.D., Brown U., 1934; LL.D., Harvard, 1935; Ph.D., Goethe U., Frankfurt-am-Main, 1948; Sc.D., Kenyon Coll., 1951; HH.D., U. Chgo., 1952; Doctor Tech. Sciences, Technion Hafia, 1953; m. Eleanor Mabel, dau. of R. Gervase Elwes, June 22, 1911; 1 dau., Eleanor May. Came to U.S., 1915, naturalized citizen, 1924. Lecturer on history of science, George Washington U., 1915-16, Harvard, 1916-18 and 1920—, Radcliffe, 1927—; prof. history sci. Harvard, 1940-51; Lowell lectr., Boston, 1916; asso. Carnegie Instn., Washington, D.C., 1918-48; Colver lecturer Brown Univ., 1930; spent yr. 1931-32 in Near East and N. Africa for study of Arabic and Islam; Hitchcock professor, University of California, 1932; Elihu Root lecturer, Washington, D.C., 1935; Fielding H. Garrison lecturer, 1941; lectr. in London, Paris, Bruxelles, Liége, Geneva univs., 1948; Kaiser lectr. Library of Congress, 1950; founder, 1912, and editor of Isis, an international review devoted to the history and philosophy of science; founder, 1936, and editor of Osiris, studies on history and philosophy of science and on history of learning and culture. Decorated Knight Order of Leopold, Belgium, 1940. Mem. advisory council, Yenching U., Peiping. Mem. Internat. Acad. History of Science (Paris); pres. Internat. Union of History of Sci., 1950—. Fellow A.A.A.S. (v.p.), Am. Acad. Arts and Sciences, Am. Philos. Soc., Am. Oriental Soc., Mediaeval Acad., Am. Assn. History of Medicine (hon.), Royal Asiatic Soc. (London), Royal Soc. of Edinburgh (hon.), Swedish Soc. for History of Astronomy (hon.); mem. Am. Hist. Assn., History of Science Soc. (hon. pres., 1938—), Swedish Soc. Historical Astronomy, India and Pakistan Society, Newcomen Soc., Deutsche Akademie der Naturforscher, Gesellschaft für Gesschichte d. Med., Soc. Statistique Paris, Soc. Histoire Médecine (Paris), Société asiatique (Paris), Academia de la historia (Madrid), Swedish Linnaean Soc., Gesellschaft für Geschichte der Pharmazie, Soc. italiana di storia d. scienze; United States rep. and pres. III Internat. Congress History of Science, Portugal, 1934. Mem. Institut de phiologie et d'histoire orientales (Bruxelles), American Philol. Association, Belgian Com. History of Science (Bruxelles), South East Asia Inst. (N.Y.), Hakluyt Soc. (London), Turkish Oriental Soc. (Ankara); hon. mem. history of sci. socs. in Belgium, Eng., Germany, Holland, Italy. Awarded Prix Binoux, Académie des Sciences, Paris, 1915 and 1935; awarded Haskins medal by Mediaeval Acad., 1949. Clubs: Faculty (Cambridge, Mass.); Harvard (Boston); Athenaeum (London). Author: Introduction to the History of Science (Vol. 1, From Homer to Omar Khayyam, 1927; Vol. 2, From Rabbi Ben Ezra to Roger Bacon, 1931); The History of Science and the New Humanism, 1931; The Study of the History of Science, 1936; The Study of the History of Mathematics, 1936; Science and Learning in the Fourteenth Century (2 vols.), 1947; The Life of Science, 1948; Science and Tradition (with bibliography of history of sci.), 1951; Horus. A Guide to the History of Science, 1952; Ancient Science through the Golden Age of Greece, 1952; Ancient Science and Modern Civilization, Galen of Pergamon, 1954; Appreciation of ancient and medieval sci. during Renaissance, 1955; Six wings—men of science in the Renaissance, 1957; A history of science—Hellenistic science and culture in the last three cneturies B.C., 1959; papers on History and Philos. of Sci., New Humanism, Asiatic Art, Arabic culture, etc. Home: 5 Channing Pl., Cambridge 38, Mass. Died Mar. 22, 1956; buried Mt. Auburn Cemetery, Cambridge.

SARTORIUS, Irving A., banker; b. N.Y. City, July 21, 1893; s. Abraham and Helen (Smith) S.; B.S., Yale, 1914; m. Joan Cady, Mar. 3, 1945. Partner Sartorius & Co. since 1918. Regent Long Island Coll. Hosp., Brooklyn. Clubs: Century (White Plains, N.Y.); Yale (N.Y. City). Home: 915 Black Rock Turnpike Easton, Conn. Died July 9, 1959. Office: 39 Broadway, N.Y. City 6.

SASS, Herbert Ravenel (săs), author; b. Charleston, S.C., Nov. 2, 1884; s. George Herbert and Anna (Ravenel) S.; B.A., Coll. of Charleston, 1905, M.A., 1906, Litt.D., 1922; m. Marion Hutson, June 4, 1919; children—Elizabeth Elliott, Herbert Ravenel, Marion Hutson. Mem. Kappa Alpha, Phi Beta Kappa. Episcopalian. Author: The Way of the Wild, 1926; Adventures in Green Places, 1926, 2d edit., 1935; Gray Eagle, 1927; War Drums, 1928; On the Wings of a Bird, 1929; Look Back to Glory, 1933; A Carolina Rice Plantation of the Fifties (with Alice R. H. Smith), 1937; Fort Sumter (with DuBose Heyward), 1938; Hear Me, My Chiefs, 1940; Emperor Brims, 1941; Outspoken (A History of the Charleston News and Courier), 1953; The Story of the South Carolina Low Country, 1956. Contbr. articles and stories to mags. Home: 23 Legare St., Charleston 2, S.C. Died Feb. 18, 1958.

SATERLEE, Gerald Britton, telegraph co. exec.; b. Newberry, Pa., Feb. 18, 1893; s. Britton Whitfield and Eda Livona (Managan) S.; ed. pub. schs. Pa.; m. Carrie Magdalena Beck, Nov. 21, 1914; 1 son, Britton Whitfield. With Phila. & Reading Ry. Co., 1907-17; with The Central R.R. Co. of N.J., 1917-33; with The Western Union Telegraph Co., 1933-—, successively sec. to pres., asst. to pres., corporate sec., 1940—; also exec. officer numerous subsidiary cos. mem. at large, Greater N.Y. Council, Boy Scouts Am. Mem. Am. Soc. Corporate Secs., Inc., Newcomen Soc., Pa. Society, Friends of Franklin. Republican. Baptist. Mason. Club: Railroad-Machinery (N.Y.C.). Home: 1821 N. Gate Rd., Scotch Plains, N.J. Office: 60 Hudson St., N.Y.C. 13. Died Apr. 7, 1957; buried Cressona, Pa.

SATTERFIELD, M(illard) H(arrison), univ. professor; b. Dardanelle, Ark., Jan. 7, 1904; s. William Riley and Margaret Elizabeth (Carter) S.; A.B., U. of Kan., 1928; A.M., U. of Neb., 1930, Ph.D., 1933; student American Univ., Washington, D.C., 1935-36; m. Florence Beers, Dec. 23, 1935; children—Burdette Harrison, Rodney Millard. Grad. asst. U. of Neb., 1933-34; asst. state dir. Resettlement Adminstrn., 1934-35; regional management rep., 1935-36; field rep. Am. Municipal Assn. (all at Lincoln, Neb.), 1935; research asst. Tenn. Valley Authority, Knoxville, Tenn., 1936-38; pub. adminstrn. analyst, 1938-42; budget analyst (both T.V.A.) 1942-48. Prof. polit. sci., Vanderbilt U., since 1948, acting head of dept., 1948-49. Mem. Am. Polit. Sci Assn., Am. Soc. for Pub. Adminstrn., Southern Polit. Sci. Assn., Nat. Municipal League, Pi Sigma Alpha, Kappa Sigma. Author: County Government and Administration in the Tennessee Valley States, 1940; Tennessee Valley Resources—Their Development and Use, 1947. Home: 2501 Kensington Pl., Nashville 4, Tenn. Died Apr. 24, 1949.

SATTERTHWAITE, Livingston (săt'tĕr thwāt), fgn. service officer; b. Phila., Mar. 12, 1909; s. George and Inez Helen (Lord) S.; grad. Phillips Exeter Acad., 1927; A.B., Yale, 1931; Fgn. Service Sch., 1932; m. Adelaide Bristol, Jan. 6, 1933 (divorced); children—George, Henry Bristol; m. 2d, Kathleen Charlton, July, 1955. Apptd. fgn. service officer, unclass., 1932; vice consul, Mexico City, 1932, San Jose, Costa Rica, 1932-34, 1934-37, Port Limon, temp., 1934, Caracus, 1937-39, to State Dept., 1939-43 as desk officer, Am. Republic Div. and as asst. chief div. internat. communications, 1943-48; civil air attache, London, also Dublin, 1944; govts. Belgium, Aug.-Sept. 1944, Czechoslovakia, 1944-45, Norway, 1944-45, Poland, 1944-45, Yugoslavia, 1944-45, Netherlands, 1944 (all established in London); U.S. rep. Discussion of Internat. Air Transport Policy, London, 1946; also cons. and 1st sec. and cons. at London, Dublin, and The Hague, 1948-49; vice chmn. U.S. del. Conf. on Civil Aviation between U.S. and Can., N.Y., 1949; Chief, British Commonwealth Div., Dept. of State, 1948-49; vice chairman U.S. delegation International Civil Aviation Orgn., Montreal, 1950; dep. dir. Office British Commonwealth and Northern European Affairs, Washington, 1949; grad. Nat. War Coll., 1952; counselor of Embassy, Ankara, Turkey, 1952-53; polit. advisor U.S. European Command, 1953-54; dep. exec. officer Operations Coordination Bd., 1955; dir. Office Transport and Communications Policy, Dept of State, 1956-57; counselor embassy, Copenhagen, 1958—. Home: Ambler, Pa. Office: Dept. of State, Washington 25. Died Aug. 26, 1959.

SAUD III, ibn', ibn' abd-al' Aziz ibn' Abd-al Faisal, King of Saudi-Arabia, (sōō-ōōd'): b. Rivadh, 1880; son of Abd-al-Rah-man, Wahabi sultan of Nejd; has 32 sons, 6 oldest prominent in govt. are—Saud, Faisal, Mohammed, Khalid, Mansur, Nasir. Driven by civil war into exile, 1891; succeeded father on throne, 1901; organized force that seized Riyadh, 1901, and established dominance of Wahabis in Nejd, 1906; through able adminstrn. built up strength of Nejd, replacing Arab patriarchal system by nationalism, 1906-14; in World War I sided with Britain against Turks; added outlying regions to Nejd, 1919-22; invaded and conquered the Hejaz, 1924-25, forcing abdication of King Husein and his son Ali, proclaimed himself King of Hejaz, 1926; signed treaty with Great Britain by which independence of his country was recognized, 1927; changed title from sultan of Nejd to King of Hejaz and Nejd, 1927; proclaimed official name of Hejaz and Nejd as Kingdom of Saudi Arabia, 1932: introduced order in tribal relations and made pilgrimages to Mecca safe for all Mohammedans; after discovery of oil, 1938, granted extensive concessions to Standard Oil Co. of Calif.; remained neutral but friendly to British at outbreak of war, 1939. Address: royal Place, Riyadh, Saudi-Arabia. Died Nov. 9, 1953.*

SAUER, LeRoy Dagobert, artist; b. Dayton, O., Feb. 17, 1894; s. George Adam and Harriet May (Sauerbrun) S.; grad. Cleveland (O.) Sch. of Art, 1917; student Art Acad. Cincinnati, 1913-15, Western Reserve U., 1917, Am. Art Training Center (Paris), 1919, U. of Dayton (O.), 1921; m. Charlotte T. Theobald, Aug. 15, 1919; children—Richard Joseph, Janet Elizabeth. Established, 1919, and since conducted L. D. Sauer Studios, Dayton, O.; teacher commercial art, Dayton Art Inst., 1925-33; represented by 3 prints in permanent collection Library of Congress; prints in permanent collection Royal Ontario Mus. Awarded prizes for block prints: Best black and white, Florida, 1940, purchase prize Library of Congress, 1943. Served with U.S. Army, 1918-19. Organizer Dayton Soc. of Etchers, 1921 (pres., 1921—), Ohio Print Makers Soc., 1926. Internat. pres. Civitan Internat., 1945-46. Home: 506 Volusia Av., Dayton 9. Died Feb. 6, 1959; buried Woodland Cemetery.

SAUER, William Emil (sour), physician, univ. prof.; b. Evansville, Ill., Apr. 17, 1875; s. Nicholas and Elizabeth (Gerlach) S.; Shurtleff Coll., Alton, Ill., 1891-93; M.D., Wash. U. Med. Sch., St. Louis, Mo., 1896; m. Mary Irene Borders, Dec. 18, 1901; 1 son, William Nicholas. Otolaryngologist in St. Louis since 1900; instr. diseases of the ear, nose and throat, Wash. U. Med. Sch., 1905-13; prof. and dir. dept. otolaryngology, St. Louis U. Sch. Medicine, 1925-45, Distinguished Service prof. otolaryngology, 1945. Capt. Medical Corps, 1918-19. Member Am. Bd. Otolaryngology. Mem. Am. Laryngol. Soc., Am. Otol. Soc., Am Laryngol., Rhinol. and Otol. Soc. (vice chmn.), Pan-Am. Med. Soc. (chmn. sect. otolaryngology, 1935), Acad. Ophthalmology and Otolaryngology, Alpha Omega Alpha; hon. mem. Nat. Acad. of Medicine of Brazil. Presbyterian. Republican. Clubs: University, St. Louis Country. Home: 6309 McPherson Av., University City 5, Mo. Office: 3720 Washington Blvd., St. Louis 8. Deceased.

SAUNDERS, Arthur Percy, chemist; b. London, Ont., Can., Mar. 22, 1869; s. William and Sarah Agnes (Robinson) S.; B.A., Toronto U., 1890; Ph.D., Johns Hopkins, 1894; U. of Göttingen, 1896; U. of Berlin, 1897; L.H.D., Hamilton College, 1943; m. Louise S. Brownell, Aug. 30, 1900; children—Silvia, Olivia (Mrs. Robt. Wood), William Duncan (dec.), Percy Blake. Instr. chemistry U. of Wis., 1894-96; research fellow at Cornell University, 1899-1900; asst. prof. chemistry Hamilton Coll., 1900-01, prof. 1901-39, dean, 1909-26, emeritus, 1939—. Fellow A.A.A.S.; mem. Am. Peony Soc. (dir.), Phi Beta Kappa, Sigma Phi. Address: Clinton, N.Y. Died Aug. 14, 1953.

SAUNDERS, Lowell Waller, oil geologist; b. Red Bluff, Cal., Sept. 30, 1901; s. Edgar Waller and Frances Elvira (Swain) S.; A.B., Stanford, 1922, grad. student, 1923; m. Edna Mae Sells, Dec. 5, 1923; children—Edward William, Diane (Mrs. Don C. Lake), Doska, Susan Gene. Surveyor, draftsman Nat. Coal Co., Price, Utah, 1920; drilling dept. Ethel D. Oil Co., Maricopa, Cal., 1923; insp. Cal. State Mining Bur., Taft, Cal., 1924, Los Angeles, 1925, engr. Long Beach and Huntington Beach, 1926; resident geologist Hugh B. Evans, Inc., Taft, 1927; geologist Cal. Petroleum Corp. and The Texas Co., 1927-28; geologist The Ohio Oil Co., Bakersfield, Cal., 1929-35; cons. geologist KCL Bldg., Bakersfield, 1935-39; with Intex Oil Co. since 1939, v.p., 1939-48, pres., 1948-52, chmn. bd. since 1953. Councilman, Bakersfield. Mem. Am. Assn. Petroleum Geologists, Soc. Econ. Geologists, Am. Soc. Mil. Engrs. Clubs: Stockdale; Los Angeles Petroleum. Home: 2731 18th St. Office: 531 California Av., Bakersfield, Cal. Died June 20, 1954.

SAUNDERS, Samuel James, prof. physics; b. Nanticoke, Ont., Can., Aug. 3, 1862; s. Samuel and Catherine (Lindsay) S.; A.B., U. of Toronto, 1888, A.M., 1894; Sc.D., Cornell U., 1894; m. Jennie A. Stewart, Dec. 29, 1887; children—Samuel Hugh (dec.), Jennie Alma (wife of Dr. H. W. Thompson), Stanley Stewart. Fellow in mathematics, Cornell, 1888-89, in physics and mathematics, 1889-90; instr. in physics, Cornell, 1890-92; became prof. physics, Hamilton Coll., 1892, now prof. emeritus, registrar, 1907-32. Mem. Phi Beta Kappa, Sigma Xi. Republican. Presbyn. Home: Tucson. Deceased.

SAUNDERSON, Henry Hallam (sawn'dĕr-sŭn), clergyman, writer; b. near Ottawa, Ont., Can., May 20, 1871; s. Rev. Edward Alexander and Laura Julia (Allen) S.; prep. edn., high sch. and normal sch., Napanee, Ont.; Ph.B., Hamline U., St. Paul, Minn., 1896, D.D., 1924; A.B., Harvard, 1898, A.M., 1901; married Rosa V. Bennis, Nov. 16, 1898 (died Aug. 8, 1943); married 2d, Laura Howland Dudley, of Cambridge, Mass., Nov. 29, 1945. Came to U.S., 1892, naturalized citizen, 1898; ordained ministry Waverly (Mass.) Unitarian Ch., 1898; pastor Channing Ch., Boston, 1900-03, Third Congl. Ch., Cambridge, 1903-14, Jarvis St. Ch., Toronto, Ont., 1914-15, College Av. Ch., Somerville, Mass., 1915-19, First Parish Ch., Brighton, Boston, since 1919. Founder of Wayside Pulpit, 1917, and editor, 1917-31. President Boylston Chem. Club in Harvard U., Boston Browning Soc.; mem. N.Y. Browning Soc., Boston Assn. Ministers, Cambridge Assn. Ministers, Brighton-Allston Assn. of Ministers (pres.); Mass. Audubon Soc., Mass. Horticultural Society. Governor Thomas Dudley Family Association. Decorated 1930, by Governor Allen of Mass. "for distinguished service to the commonwealth." Republican. Mason. Clubs: Authors, Union Camera, Boston Manuscript, Puddingstone, Appalachian Mt., Harvard Faculty. Author: The Power of an Endless Life, 1924; The Living Word—The Bible Abridged, 1924; Charles W. Eliot—Puritan Liberal, 1928; Modern Religion from Puritan Origins, 1930; Puritan Principles and American Ideals, 1930; Pulpit and Parish Manual, 1930; His Word Was with Power, 1952; The Way Called Heresy, 1956. Home: 24 Avon Hill St., Cambridge 40, Mass. Died Dec. 17, 1957.

SAUVE, Paul, premier of Que.; b. St. Benoist, Can., Mar. 24, 1907; s. Arthur Suave; student St. Therese Sem., also Coll. Ste. Marie, Montreal; hon. degree Bishop's U., Lennoxville, 1951, also Laval U., Que.; m. Luce Pelland, 1936. Admitted to bar, 1930; elected mem. Que. Legislature, 1930, speaker, 1936; minister youth and social welfare, 1946-59; adminstr. Pub. Assistance Act, 1957; prime minister Province of Que., 1959—. Served from lt. to lt. col., Fusiliers Mont Royal, Canadian Army, 1940-43, Fusiliers Mont Royal, Eng., 1943-46. Decorated Croix de Guerre with silver star (France); Efficiency Medal. Address: Parliament Bldg., Quebec City, Que., Can. Died Jan. 3, 1959.

SAVAGE, Theodore Fiske, clergyman; b. Berkeley, Cal., June 8, 1885; s. Charles Albert and Mary Fidelia (Fiske) S.; A.B., Harvard, 1906, A.M., 1907; student Union Theol. Sem., 1908-11; D.D., N.Y. U., 1933; m. Mary Halsted Terry, May 29, 1913; children—Elizabeth Terry (Mrs. Cornelius W. Wickersham, Jr.), Eric Dutton, William Halsted. Ordained to ministry Presbyn. Ch., 1911; pastor Christ Presbyn. Ch., New York, 1911-22; exec. sec. and church extension sec. Presbytery of New York, 1922—. Pres. Greater New York Fed. of Churches, 1939-41; elected first gen. presbyter of N.Y., 1952. Clubs: University (N.Y.C.); Cold Spring Harbor Beach. Author: The Presbyterian Church in New York City, 1949. Home: 320 E. 72nd St., N.Y.C. Died Feb. 15, 1957.

SAWYER, C. Adrian, Jr., constrn. exec.; b. Chgo., Aug. 19, 1881; s. Charles Adrian and Florence Clifton (Ames) S.; student Chicago Manuel Tng. Sch., 1895-98; B.S., Mass. Inst. Tech., 1902; m. Clara Lucille Zeiss, Sept. 15, 1906; 1 dau., Florence Elizabeth. Vice pres. George A. Fuller Co., builders, 1917-18; pres. and treas. Sawyer Constrn. Co., 1924—; bldgs. erected at Northeastern U., Mass. Inst. Tech., Mass. Gen. Hosp., Mass. Meml. Hosp. Served as lt. Mass. State Guard, 1918. Trustee N.E. Peabody Home for Crippled Children, Hahnemann Hosp., N.E. Deaconess Hosp. Mem. Corp. Mass. Inst. Tech., Mass. Hosps. Adv. Com.; chmn. bd. of appeal, City of Newton, Mass. Pres. Mass. Inst. Tech. Alumni Assn., 1949-50. Mem. Mayflower Soc., S.A.R., Am. soc. C.E. Republican. Mem. Union Ch., Waban. Clubs: Brae Burn (past pres.), St. Botolph, Boston Yacht. Home: 57 Dorset Rd., Waban, Mass. Office: 31 St. James Av., Boston. Died Jan. 29, 1952.

SAWYER, Prince Edwin, physician; b. Phillips, Me., June 1, 1874; s. Prince A. and Alvira C. (Oakes) S.; student Bates Coll., Lewiston, Me., 1889-1890, U. of Northwest, Sioux City, Ia., 1889-91; M.D., U. of Ia., 1895; m. Cornelia Johnson, Sept. 6, 1899. Physician and surgeon, 1895-1909; gen. surgery, 1909—. Served as maj. M.C., U.S. Army, A.E.F. Fellow A.C.S.; mem. A.M.A., Ia. (pres. 1936-37), Sioux Valley, Mississippi Valley med. socs., Alpha Omega Alpha. Republican. Mason, Elk. Home: 2020 Nebraska St. Office: Toy Nat. Bank Bldg., Sioux City, Ia. Died Jan. 17, 1954.

SAWYER, Samuel Woodson, lawyer; b. Independence, Mo., Oct. 1, 1878; s. Aaron Flint and Sallie W. (Woodson) S.; A.B., Yale, 1899; LL.B. cum laude, Harvard, 1902; m. Adelina M. Richards, Nov. 18, 1914; children—Martha Ann (Mrs. Blackwell), Samuel Locke. Entered office Lathrope, Morrow, Fox & Moore, 1902, name changed to Lathrop, Crane, Reynolds, Sawyer and Mersereau, 1928, to Lathrop, Crane, Sawyer, Woodson & Righter, 1945; mem. firm, 1910; asst. atty. Kansas City Terminal Ry. Co., 1910, gen counsel since 1918; v.p. Chrisman-Sawyer Bank; dir. Richards and Conover Hardware Co. Mem. Am. and Kansas City bar assns., Lawyers Assn. (past pres.). Democrat. Presbyn. Clubs: Kansas City Country, University. Home: 1249 W. 58th St. Office: Land Bank Bldg., Kansas City 6. Died June 25, 1949.

SAWYER, Wilbur Augustus, pub. health; b. Appleton, Wis., Aug. 7, 1879; s. Wesley Caleb and Minnie Edmea (Birge) S.; Univ. of California, 1898-99; A.B., Harvard, 1902; M.D., Harvard Medical School, 1906; LL.D., University of California 1945; m. Margaret Henderson, Oct. 14, 1911; children—Margaret (Mrs. J. Wallace Carroll), Gertrude (Mrs. R. W. Howell), Ruth Henderson (Mrs. D. P. Yeuell, Jr.), Wilbur Henderson. Interne Mass. General Hospital, 1906-08; medical examiner, University of California, 1908-11; director Hygienic Laboratory, 1910-15, sec. and exec. officer, 1915-18, Calif. State Bd. of Health; lecturer in hygiene and preventive medicine, 1914-16, clin. prof., 1916-19, U. of Calif. Med. Sch. On active duty as capt. and maj., M.C., U.S. Army, Feb. 6, 1918-May 31, 1919; chief of sec. on combating venereal diseases, Surgeon Gen.'s Office, War Dept., actg. mem. Interdepartmental Social Hygiene Bd., actg. dir. of social hygiene div. of Commn. on Training Camp Activities, and acting gen. sec. Am. Social Hygiene Assn., 1918-19; lt. col. M.R.C., 1919-20. Apptd. state dir. Internat. Health Bd., New York, June 1, 1919; dir. Australian hookworm campaign, 1919-22; adviser in pub. health, Australian Ministry of Health, 1922-24; asst. regional dir. for the East, 1923-24, dir. Public Health Lab. Service, 1924-27, Internat. Health Bd. of Rockefeller Foundation; also asso. dir. Internat. Health Division of Rockefeller Foundation, 1927-35, director, 1935-44; director of health, U.N.R.R.A., 1944-47; secretary general 4th International Congress Tropical Medicine and Malaria, Washington, 1948; member West African Yellow Fever Commission, Rockefeller Foundation, 1926-27, in charge Yellow Fever Lab., 1928-35; mem. Nat. Adv. Health Council of U.S. Pub. Health Service, 1937-40; mem. subcom. on Tropical Diseases, Nat. Research Council, 1940-44 (chmn. 1940); dir. commn. on tropical diseases, Army Epidemiol. Bd., 1942-44; hon. cons. to med. dept., U.S. Navy, 1941-44; mem. Ethnogeog. Bd., 1942-44; dir. Rockefeller Foundation Health Commn., 1940-44; convener Sect. Viruses and Viral Diseases, Third Internat. Congress for Microbiology, 1939; mem. adv. sci. bd., Gorgas Memorial Inst., 1944-46 (dir. 1946-49). Methodist. Fellow Am. Pub. Health Assn., A.A.A.S., N.Y. Acad. Medicine, Washington (D.C.)

Acad. Medicine, Royal Soc. Tropical Medicine and Hygiene (hon.); mem. Am. Found. Tropical Med., Assn. of Am. Physicians, Am. Acad. Tropical Medicine (pres. 1936-37), Am. Soc. Tropical Medicine, (pres. 1943-44), Am. Epidemiol. Soc., Am. Soc. Exptl. Pathology, Sigma Xi, Alpha Omega Alpha; hon. mem. Société Belge de Médicine Tropicale; corr. mem. Société de Biologie (Paris); hon. life mem. Conf. of State and Provincial Health Authorities of N. Am., Tenn. Pub. Hlth. Assn. U.S. del. Pan Am. San. Conf., Bogotá, 1938. Decorated Knight 1st Class Order of St. Olav (Norway) 1926; Gran Oficial Order of Carlos J. Finlay (Cuba), 1940. Awarded Leon Bernard prize (League of Nations), 1939; Richard P. Strong medal, 1949. Clubs: Cosmos (Washington); Commonwealth (San Francisco); Berkeley, Faculty (Berkeley). Contbr. on yellow fever, internat. health, etc. Home: 2565 Rose St., Berkeley 8, Cal. Died Nov. 12, 1951.

SAXE, John Godfrey, lawyer; b. Saratoga, N.Y., June 25, 1877; s. John Theodore and Mary (Bosworth) S.; B.A., McGill U., 1897, M.A., 1914; LL.B., Columbia, 1900; LL.D., Middlebury, 1916, Vermont, 1940; m. Mary Sands, June 10, 1909. Admitted to N.Y. bar, 1900; mem. Saxe, Bacon & O'Shea. Mem. N.Y. Senate, 1911, 12; counsel to Gov. Glynn, 1914; mem. Constl. Conv., N.Y., 1915. Served as chmn. law com. Dem. State Com. Chmn. or mem. many state commns. and bar assn. coms.; chmn. exec. com. Bar Assn. City of New York, 1928-29, 34-35; first chmn. Joint Com. of all N.Y. City bar assns. 1930-33. Trustee Met. Mus. Art. Pres. N.Y. State Bar Assn., 1935-37; mem. Phi Upsilon. Episcopalian. Clubs: Manhattan (pres. 1925-27, 29-31), Links, Downtown, Columbia University, Oakland Golf, Links Golf, National Golf Links of America; Fort Orange (Albany); St. James (Montreal), Travellers (Paris); Tin Whistles (Pinehurst, N.C.); Author: Saxe's Manual of Elections, 1918; Genealogy of Saxe Family in America; Charitable Exemptions in New York State; Inter-State Divorce, New York System of Charities; The Jones Golf Swing. Home: 525 Park Av. Office: 102 Maiden Lane, N.Y.C. Died Apr. 1953.

SAXON, Lyle, writer; b. Baton Rouge, Sept. 4, 1891; s. Hugh and Katherine (Chambers) S.; B.A., La. State U., 1912; unmarried. Reporter, New Orleans, and Chicago, 1912-26; feature writer New Orleans Times-Picayune, 1918-26; La. state dir. Federal Writers' Projects, Works Progress Adminstrn., compiling La. sect. Am. Guide. Mem. P.E.N. Author: Father Mississippi, 1927; Fabulous New Orleans, 1928; Old Louisiana, 1929; La Fitte, the Pirate, 1930; Children of Strangers, 1937. Contbr. short stories and articles to mags.; stories were chosen for O. Henry Meml. Award, 1926, O'Brien's Best Short stories, 1927. Editor: New Orleans City Guide, 1938. Home: Melrose, La.; also St. Charles Hotel, New Orleans. Died Apr. 1946.

SAYERS, Dorothy Leigh (sârs), Brit. author; b. Oxford, Eng., 1893; d. Rev. Henry and Helen Mary (Leigh) Sayers; M.A., Oxford U., 1915; honorary D.Litt., Durham University; m. Atherton Fleming, 1926 (dec. 1950). Mem. Ch. of Eng. Club: Detection (London). Author: Cloud of Witness, 1927; Dawson Pedigree, 1928; Lord Peter Views the Body, 1929; Strong Poison, 1930; Unpleasantness at the Bellona Club, 1930; Suspicious Characters, 1931; Unnatural Death, 1931; Have His Carcass, 1932; Whose Body?, 1932; Hangman's Holiday, 1933; Murder Must Advertise, 1933; Nine Tailors, 1934; Gaudy Night, 1936; Zeal of Thy House, 1937; Busman's Honeymoon, 1937; Greatest Drama Ever Staged, 1938; Devil to Pay, 1939; Strong Meat, 1939; In the Teeth of the Evidence, 1940; Begin Here: A Wartime Essay, 1940; The Mind of the Maker, 1941; The Just Vengeance (play), 1946; Creed or Chaos?, 1946; Unpopular Opinions, 1947; Man Born To Be King (radio play), 1943; Dante: Inferno (translation), 1949; Unpleasantness at the Bellona Club, 1956; Clouds of Witnesses, 1956; New Sayers Omnibus, 1956. Home: 24 Great James St., London, Eng., W.C. 1; 24 Newland St., Witham, Essex, Eng. Died Dec. 18, 1957.

SAYLER, Oliver Martin, dramatic critic; b. Huntington, Ind., Oct. 23, 1887; s. Samuel Martin and Luella C. (Daily) S.; A.B., Oberlin, 1909; m. Lucie V. Reichenbach, Sept. 18, 1920 (div. July 1942); 1 dau., Ida Lou (Mrs. Warren Glass). On staff Indpls. News, 1909-20; corr. Boston Evening Transcript, 1915-20. On leave of absence studied European theatres, 1914, Russian theatres, 1917-18; lectr. on the theatre and on Russia; conductor "Footlight and Lamplight" weekly dramatic and literary review, broadcast over radio, 1924-29; founded Oliver M. Sayler, Inc., 1928; partner Marjorie Barkentin. Revisited Russian theatres, 1924, 33; Am. rep. Moscow Art Theatre and other theatres of Russia. Mem. bd. dirs., exec. com. Am. Theatre Wing War Service, Inc., 1942—; mem. Emergency Council of Legitimate Theatre 1942—. Mem. Assn. Theat. Press Agents and Mgrs. Union, A. F. of L., 1938—; v.p., 1941-42; bus. agent 1942—. Contbr. to mag. Mem. Phi Beta Kappa Fraternity. Author: Russia, White or Red, 1919; The Russian Theatre Under the Revolution, 1920 (revised and enlarged as The Russian Theatre, 1922); The Russian Players in America, 1923; Our American Theatre, 1923; Inside the Moscow Art Theatre, 1925; Revolt in the Arts, 1930. Editor: The Moscow Art Theatre Series of Russian Plays, Series I, 1922, Series II, 1923; The Eleonora Duse Series of Plays, 1923; Max Reinhardt and His Theatre, 1924; Plays of the Moscow Art Theatre Musical Studio, 1925. Co-producer Ulysses in Nighttown (N.Y.), 1958. Home: 112 Harmon Dr., Larchmont. Office: 25 W. 45th St., N.Y.C. Died Oct. 19, 1958, buried Ferncliff, Hartsdale, N.Y.

SAYLES, John Manville, educator; b. Mexico, N.Y., June 17, 1877; s. Manville F. and Ollie Newton (Antisdel) S.; A.B., Colgate U., 1900; Pd.B., N.Y. State Coll. for Teachers, 1902; Pd.D. (hon.), Colgate U., 1937; m. Grace Inglehart, June 25, 1902; 1 son, Charles Inglehart. Prin. Richmondville (N.Y.) High Sch., 1902-05, Glens Falls High Sch., 1905, Model High Sch. at N.Y. State Coll. for Tchrs., Albany, 1905-06, Milne (Practice) High Sch., Albany, 1906-20; dir. tchr. tng. N.Y. State College for Teachers, 1920-39, pres., 1939-47. Dir. Farmers and Mechanics Bank. Sec. State of New York Dormitory Authority, apptd. by Legislature, 1944. Trustee Dudley Obs.; chmn. Benevolent Assn., N.Y. State Teachers Coll.; mem. bd. mgrs. Albany Home for Children. Mem. N.E.A., Nat. Soc. Tchrs. Edn., Acad. Principals Assn. of New York State (president 1937), Middle States Assn. Colls. and Secondary Schs., Eastern States Assn. Profl. Schs. for Tchrs., Am. Assn. Tchrs. Colls., Assn. Colls. and Univs., State of N.Y., chmn. Com. on Evaluation of Teaching Efficiency, Council of Supts., 1944. Secondary, Teacher and Albany Adult edn. councils, Fgn. Policy Assn. (hon. vice chmn.), Phi Beta Kappa, Delta Upsilon, Kappa Phi Kappa. Pres. Star Lake Hotel Co. Inc. (N.Y.), 1937. Republican. Presbyn. (elder, trustee). Mason. Clubs: Rotary (pres. 1937-38), University (past pres.), Albany Country. Contbr. to ednl. mags. Frequent speaker at ednl. meetings. Formulated program for ednl. theory through 2 yr. integrated course of extracurricular activities, required of freshmen and sophomores, and illustrated in the sch. of practice. Home: 681 Hudson Av., Albany, N.Y. Died Dec. 3, 1956; buried Albany.

SAYRE, Daniel Clemens, aeronautical engr.; b. Columbus, O., Feb. 1, 1903; s. Joel Grover and Nora (Clemens) S.; grad. Columbus Acad., 1919; B.S., M.S., Mass. Inst. Tech.; m. Ann Hamilton, Sept. 10, 1925; m. 2d Rosamond Foster, Sept. 5, 1931. Organizer, dir. Boston Airport Corp., 1925-28; instr., later asst. prof. aeronautical engring. Mass. Inst. Tech., 1928-32; asst., later asso. editor Aviation Mag., 1933-39; aviation editor Newsweek mag., 1934-39; dir. statistics and information, later chief safety regulations U.S. Civil Aeronautics Authority, 1939-41; organizer, chmn. dept. aeronautical engring. Princeton, 1941-51, apptd. dir. James Forrestal Research Center, 1951; asso. clean engring., 1955—. Fellow Inst. Aeronautical Scis.; mem. Am. Rocket Soc. Author articles profl. and popular mags. Home: Forrestal Rd., Princeton, N.J. Died Oct. 19, 1957.

SAYRE, Farrand, ret. army officer; b. Lewis County, Mo., June 17, 1861; s. Emilius Kitchell and Elizabeth Stanford (Pierson) S.; B.S., U.S. Mil. Acad., 1884; U.S. Inf. and Cavalry Sch., 1905; hon. grad. Army Staff Coll., 1906; A.M., Johns Hopkins, 1936, Ph.D., 1938; Army War Coll., 1916-17; m. Kate Hamlin Phelps, May 10, 1888; children—Elizabeth Stanford (Mrs. Robert H. Kilbourne). Service in Indian Wars, 1885-86, Spanish-Am. War, 1898-99, World War I, 1917-19; comd. Brownsville Dist. Texas frontier, 1917-20; brig. gen., comdg. 1st Cav. Brigade, 1918-19, ret. from active service, 1925; instr. Army Service Schs., 1906-13; comd. dist. in Panama Canal Zone, 1920-26; in charge Reserves, 1st Corps area, Boston, 1922-25; parole agt. State of Mass., 1925-31. Mem. Assn. of Grad. U.S. Mil. Acad., Assn. Vets. of 8th U.S. Cavalry. Author: Map Maneuvers, 1912; Diogenes of Sinope, 1938; The Greek Cynics, 1948. Home: 325 Padington Rd., Balt. 12. Died Apr. 17, 1952; buried Lexington, Ky.

SAYRE, Morris (sâr), president Corn Products Refining Co.; born at Montrose, Pa., Nov. 27, 1885; s. Samuel Huntting and Annie W. (Morris) S.; B.S. and B.A., U. of Richmond, 1906, honorary Doctor of Science, granted in 1948; M.E., Lehigh Univ., 1908; m. Anna M. Hand, Sept. 18, 1912; children—John M., William M. With Corn Products Refining Co. since 1908, mgr. of Granite City, Ill., plant, 1914-16, mgr. of Argo, Ill. plant, 1916-27, gen. mgr. with headquarters in N.Y. City, 1928-36, v.p., 1933-45, exec. v.p., 1942-45, pres. since 1945, dir. since 1929; director New England Grain Products Company, N.Y. Trust Co. Trustee Univ. of Richmond, Phi Gamma Delta Educational Found. Treas. and trustee Nutrition Found. Dir. Found. Am. Agr., Chicago. Mem. Nat. Assn. Mfrs. (pres. 1948, chmn. bd. 1948-50), Phi Gamma Delta, Phi Beta Kappa, Tau Beta Pi, Omicron Delta Kappa. Episcopalian. Mason. Home: 36 Prospect Av., Montclair, N.J. Office: 17 Battery Pl., N.Y.C. Died Mar. 7, 1953 at Zongulak, Turkey; buried Montrose, Pa.

SAYRE, Paul, prof. law; b. Hinsdale, Ill., July 26, 1894; s. Rockwell and Susan (Lombard) S.; A.B., Harvard, 1916, S.J.D., 1925; J.D., U. Chgo., 1920; m. Grace Geyer, Sept. 22, 1924; children—Susan, Mary (Mrs. Arthur H. Abel), Lombard. Admitted to the Illinois State bar, 1920, practiced Chgo., 1920-24; prof. law, Ind. U., 1925-28; research fellow, 1928-29, lecturer on civil procedure, 1929-30, Harvard Law Sch.; prof. law, State U. of Ia., 1930—. Reporter on succession to property Internat. Congress on Comparative Law, The Hague, 1937; del. to State U. Ia. to Internat. Conf. on Higher Edn., Paris, 1937; pres. Nat. Conf. on Family Relations, 1937-39; comparative law congress, Paris, France, 1954. Editor: Interpretations of Modern Legal Philosophies, 1947; Selected Essays on Family Law, 1950. Author: Life of Roscoe Pound, 1947; Introduction to a Philosophy of Law, 1951; Philosophy of Law, 1953; Justice, 1959. Contbr. to legal and philos. jours. Home: 336 Magowan Av. Office: Law Bldg., Iowa City, Ia. Died Aug. 10, 1959.

SAYRE, Theodore Burt, author, playwright; b. N.Y.C., Dec. 18, 1874; s. Theodore H. and Mary E. (Hartwell) S.; student of University Grammar School; Ph.G., New York College of Pharmacy, 1892; m. Laura Helen De Gumoens, April 6, 1904. Play reader and critic for Charles Frohmann, 1899-1914. Club: The Lambs. Author: (novels) Two Summer Girls and I, 1898; The Son of Carleycroft, 1900; Tom Moore, 1902; (plays) The Wife of Willoughby, 1896; Charles O'Malley, 1897; Two Rogues and a Romance, 1898; The Son of Carleycroft, 1900; A Classical Cowboy, 1900; Manon Lescaut, 1901; Tom Moore, 1901; The Bold Soger Boy, 1903; Edmund Burke, 1905; Eileen Asthore, 1906; O'Neill of Derry, 1907; The Commanding Officer, 1910; The Wearing of the Green, 1910; Love's Young Dream, 1912; Ransomed, 1913; The Irish Dragoon, 1915; The Irish Fifteenth, 1916; Lucky O'Shea, 1917. Home: 469 Washington Av., Bklyn. Died Nov. 1954.

SBARRETTI, Donatus, archbishop; b. Montefranco, Italy, Nov. 12, 1856; studied in Sem. of Archdiocese of Spoleto; completed theol. course at Coll. of St. Apollinaris, Rome; ordained R.C. priest, Apr. 12, 1879. Previous to ordination had been prof. ad interim, and afterward was for 8 yrs. prof. speculative and moral philosophy in Coll. of the Propaganda, Rome; also served as minutante, or sub-sec. of Propaganda in affairs pertaining to U.S.; arranged proceedings of 3d council of Baltimore for presentation to com. of cardinals, and was made pvt. chamberlain to Leo XIII, with title of Monsignore; 1st auditor Apostolic Legation at Washington, 1893-1900; consecrated bishop of Havana, Feb. 4, 1900; extraordinary Apostolic del. to P.I., Sept., 1901; titular archbishop of Ephesus, Dec. 16, 1901; del. Apostolic to Canada, Nov., 1902—. Address: Ottawa, Can. Died Apr. 1, 1939.

SCAIFE, Alan Magee (skāf), manufacturer; b. Pittsburgh, Pa., Jan. 10, 1900; s. James Verner and Mary (Magee) S.; prep. edn., Shadyside Acad., Pittsburgh; Ph.B., Sheffield Scientific School (Yale), 1920; LL.D., U. Pitts., 1950; m. Sarah C. Mellon, Nov. 16, 1927; children—Cordelia M. (Mrs. C. Scaife May), Richard Mellon. With Scaife Co., steel tank mfrs., Pittsburgh, since 1920, now chmn.; dir., member executive committee, Gulf Oil Corp.; dir. Consolidated Coal Company, Mellon Nat. Bank and Trust Co., Pullman-Standard Car Mfg. Co., M. W. Kellogg Co., Trailmobile, Inc., Pullman, Inc., Air Reduction Company, also director Washington-Waynesburg Railroad, Bell Telephone Co. of Pa., T. Mellon and Sons. Served in U.S.N.R., World War I; lt. col., United States Army, World War II. Trustee Elizabeth Steel Magee Hospital, Mellon Institute of Indsl. Research, Carnegie Hero Fund Commn. (all of Univ. Pitts. (pres. board). Fellow Yale Corp. Republican. Clubs: Pittsburgh, Pittsburgh Athletic Assn., Pittsburgh Golf, Duquesne, Allegheny Country (Pitts.); Racquet and Tennis, The Lins (N. Y.C.); Rolling Rock (Ligonier, Pa.). Home: Ligonier, Pa. Office: 525 William Penn Pl., Pitts. Died July 24, 1958; buried Allegheny Cemetery, Pitts.

SCAIFE, Roger Livingston, author, pub.; b. Boston, Aug. 14, 1875; s. Lauriston Livingston and Helen Amelia (Sprague) S.; A.B., Harvard, 1897; student Harvard Law Sch.; m. Ethel May Bryant, May 26, 1906; children—Lauriston Livingston, Elizabeth Lincoln (Mrs. Albert J. Beveridge, Jr.), Roger Marvin. Began with Houghton, Mifflin Co., pubs., Boston, 1898, later dir.; became v.p. and dir. Little, Brown & Co., 1934; formerly dir. Harvard U. Press. Mem. Mass. N.G., 4 yrs. Mem. Soc. Colonial Wars. Republican. Episcopalian. Club: Somerset (Boston). Author: The Confessions of a Debutante, 1913; Muvver and Me, 1917; What Daddies Do, 1916; The Land of the Great Outdoors, 1920; Cape Coddities, 1920; The Reflections of a T.B.M., 1922 (all pub. anonymously). Home: The Tudor, Joy and Beacon Sts., Boston. Died Oct. 19, 1951; buried Milton, Mass.

SCALA, Norman Philip (skä'lä), ophthalmologist; b. Washington, D.C., Jan. 21, 1894; s. Francis Maria (capt. U.S.M.C.) and Olivia Octavia (Arth) S.; student Washington Coll. of Music, 1906-09; pupil of Joseffy, piano, 1909-15, Goldmark, harmony, 1910-11, Saenger, voice, 1911-12; A.B., George Washington U., 1916, M.D., 1920; LL.B., Georgetown U., 1924; grad.

work, Harvard, 1922, U. of Vienna, 1924, 26, 28, 29, 30, 31, N.Y. Polyclinic, 1925, U. of Gratz, 1936; m. Emily Kolb, June 12, 1924 (died 1934). Began as concert pianist, 1906; teacher of music, 1906-16; teacher of music Hall Noyes' Sch., Washington, D.C., and Washington pub. schs., 1910; chemist Nat. Canning Assn., 1916. Piano soloist and oboist, U.S. Marine Band, 1917-19; interne Gallinger Hosp., Washington, D.C., 1918-19; resident physician Children's Hosp., Washington, D.C., 1920; surgeon U.S. Pub. Health Service, 1920-23; alienist, 1923-24; interne eye clinic, U. of Vienna, 1929-30; ophthalmologist, Providence Hosp., Washington, D.C., 1932-34, Emergency Hosp., 1936-39; instr. in ophthalmology, Georgetown U., 1932-36; in gen. practice, Washington, D.C., 1920-23, neuro-psychiatry, 1923-25, eye, ear, nose and throat, 1925-34, ophthalmology only since 1934; ophthalmologist Doctor Hosp., Washington, since 1940, also to Office of Civilian Defense, Washington, D.C., and to U.S. Army retraining and induction station, Ft. Myer, Va. Apptd. mem. med. adv. bd. Selective Service, 1941. Mem. A.M.A., Assn. for Research in Ophthalmology, Dist. of Columbia Medical Society, Washington Ophthal. Society, Montgomery Medical Society, Maryland, Pan American Medical Society, Pan American Assn. of Ophthalmology, Internal Med. Club, American Legion, St. Bernard Club of America (library com.), South Atlantic St. Bernard Club (bd. govs.), George Washington U. Alumni; life mem. A.M.A. of Vienna (officer 1929). Loyal Knight of the Round Table. Clubs: Arts, University. Contbr. to Neurology of the Eye, Ear, Nose and Throat, by Drs. E. A. Spiegel and I. Sommer; numerous articles to med. jours. Composer of several musical compositions. Received key from U. of Vienna, 1929, for completing over 9 mos. study in Vienna. Address: 901 20th St. N.W., Washington. Died Jan. 20, 1953; buried Congressional Cemetery, Washington.

SCALES, A(rchibald) H(enderson), naval officer (ret.); b. Greensboro, N.C., Apr. 14, 1868; s. Junius Irving and Euphemia Hamilton (Henderson) S.; B.S., U.S. Naval Acad., 1887; LL.D., St. John's Coll., 1920; master naval sci., Penn. Mil. Coll., 1924; m. Harriet Pierce Graham, July 11, 1899 (dec. May 8, 1925); children—Harriet Graham (Mrs. A. G. Cook), Aroostine Henderson (Mrs. F. L. Riddle), Effie Irving (Mrs. A. L. Thompson). Commd. ensign USN, 1889, and advanced through grades to rear adm., 1919; retired from active service, 1926. Awarded Sampson medal, Spanish-Am. war, D.S.M., World War I; decorated Comdr. Order of Leopold (Belgium). Episcopalian. Club: Yacht (N.Y.). Address: care Capt. F. L. Riddle, Naval Gun Factory, Washington 25. Died Feb. 16, 1952; buried U.S. Naval Acad. Cemetery, Annapolis, Md.

SCANDRETT, Henry Alexander, ry. exec.; b. Faribault, Minn., Apr. 8, 1876; s. Henry Alexander and Jane Whiting (Whipple) S.; grad. Shattuck Mil. Sch., Faribault, Minn., 1894; B.L., U. Minn., 1898, LL.B., 1900; m. Frances Hochstetler, Mar. 11, 1928; 1 son, Henry Alexander. Claim adjuster U.P. R.R. Co., 1901, asst. atty. for Kan. and Mo., 1901-11; asst. interstate commerce atty., U.P. System and S.P., 1911-12; interstate commerce atty. U.P. System and S.P. Co., 1912-13; interstate commerce atty. U.P. System, 1913-18, also asst. dir. traffic, Jan.-July 1918; traffic asst., Central Western Region, U.S. R.R. Adminstrn., 1918-19; valuation counsel and commerce counsel U.P. System, 1919-25, vice-pres., in charge valuation, commerce matters, land and public relations dept., 1925-28; pres. C.,M.,St.P.&P. R.R., 1928-38, trustee, 1936-45, again pres. 1945-47. Recipient Outstanding Achievement award U. Minn., 1952. Mem. Delta Kappa Epsilon, Republican. Episcopalian. Clubs: Chicago; Glen View Golf (Ill.). Home: 425 Grove St., Evanston, Ill. Died Mar. 20, 1957; buried Meml. Park, Evanston.

SCANLON, David Howard, clergyman; b. Staunton, Va., Mar. 27, 1875; s. Michael and Mary Eliza (Garret) S.; A.B., Shenandoah Normal Coll., Va., 1896, A.M., 1897; B.D., Union Theol. Sem., Va., 1900; A.M., Ill. Wesleyan U., 1903, Ph.D., 1906; D.D., Davidson Coll., 1923; m. Turissa May Gruver, June 4, 1896; children—Wilko Gruver, Helen Setszer, Margaret Elizabeth, Mary Cuyler David Howard. Ordained to ministry Presbyn. Ch. 1900; pastor Berryville Va., 1900-08; First Ch. Richmond Ky., 1908-13, First Ch., Meridian, Mississippi, 1913-18, Moore Meml. Church (now Westminster Church), Nashville, 1918-20; pastor First Church, Durham, N.C., 1920-38, pastor emeritus, 1938—; dept. editor Presbyterian of South 1939—. Commr. to Gen. Assembly, 1918, 25, 34; del. to Fed. Council of Chs., Phila., 1908; mem. Gen. Assembly Fgn. Mission Com., 1918-20, Pan Presbyn. Alliance, 1929; former mem. bd. Davidson Coll. Mem. Pi Gamma Mu, Omicron Delta Kappa. Author: Biography of Dr. Charles Scanlon, 1929; Thirty and Eight Years in the King's Service, 1938; I Am of Ireland, 1939; History of Shenandoah Normal College, 1941; also author numerous monographs. Contbg. editor, Presbytreian Outlook. Traveled and lectured in the Mediterranean lands and Europe, 1923, 27, 30, 35. Home: Franklin Court, Durham, N.C. Died Dec. 16, 1950; buried Durham.

SCANLON, Thomas E(dward), ex-congressman; b. Pitts., Sept. 18, 1896; s. Edward Andrew and Elizabeth (Berkins) S.; student Forbes Sch., Epiphany and Duquesne U.; m. Eva Marie Matters, Jan. 20, 1920; 1 son, Edward Andrew. Pressman, Pitts. newspapers, 1914. Mem. Allegheny County Bd. for the Assesment and Revision of Taxes, 1936-41. Mem. 77th and 78th Congresses, 16th Pa. Dist. Served in U.S. Army, World War I. Mem. Am. Legion. Democrat. Roman Catholic. Home: 1601 Federal Bldg., Pitts. Died Aug. 8, 1955.

SCARBOROUGH, Robert Bethea, congressman; b. Chesterfield C. H., S.C., Oct. 29, 1861; s. Rev. Lewis S.; ed. Mullins (S.C.) Acad.; m. Mary J. Jones, Dec. 15, 1882. Read law while teaching school; admitted to bar, May 27, 1884; has since practiced at Conway, S.C.; elected S.C. senate, 1896; pres. pro tem. same, 1898; lt.-gov. S.C., 1899; mem. Congress 1901-05, 6th S.C. Dist. Democrat. Home: Conway, S.C. Died Nov. 23, 1927.

SCATTERGOOD, Alfred Garrett; b. Moorestown, N.J., Sept. 10, 1878; s. Thomas and Sarah (Garrett) S.; B.A., Haverford Coll., 1898; B.A., Harvard, 1899; m. Mary Cope Emlen, Apr. 27, 1904. Began with Provident Life & Trust Co., 1900, assistant treasurer, 1917, v.p. Provident Trust Co., 1923-45, now director; Saving Fund Society of Germantown, Pa. Mgr. Friends Hosp.; treas. William Penn Charter Sch.; mem. bd. mgrs. Pa. Hosp.; chmn. bd. trustee Phila. Gen. Hosp. Mem. Soc. of Friends. Clubs: University, Rittenhouse (Phila.). Home: 6120 Ardleigh St., Phila. 38. Office: 1632 Chestnut St., Phila. Died Aug. 10, 1954.

SCHAAF, Clarence W., business exec.; b. Burlington, Ia., 1892; s. Gustav and Ray (Herschler) S.; student mil. acad.; m. Hortense Ebeling, 1922; children—Richard E., Charles Edward. Started with Wilson Bros.; later with C.B.&Q. Ry. Co., Chicago, Ill.; with Florsheim Shoe Co., Chicago, since 1910, v.p., sec., dir., now ret. Republican. Clubs: Standard (Chgo.); Lake Shore Country (Glencoe, Ill.). Office: 130 S. Canal St., Chgo. Died June 17, 1958.

SCHAAP, Michael (shäp), ret. chmn. bd. Bloomingdale Bros., Inc.; b. N.Y.C., Mar. 20, 1874; s. Maurits and Esther (Digtmaker) S.; LL.B., N.Y. U., 1896; m. Stella Hammerslough, April 27, 1914. Practiced law, N.Y.C., 1895-1917; progressive ("Bull Moose") Party leader in N.Y. Assembly, 1913-14; v.p. and gen. mgr., L. Bamberger & Co., Newark, N.J., 1917-1929; pres. and gen. mgr. Bloomingdale Bros., Inc., N.Y.C., 1929-44, formerly chmn. bd., chmn. exec. com., 1944—. Trustee, Inst. for Advanced Study (Princeton, N.J.). Mem. Harmonie Club: Grand Street Boys. Democrat. Jewish religion. Home: 33 E. 48th St. Office: Lexington Av. & 59th St., N.Y.C. 22. Died Dec. 23, 1957.

SCHACHNER, Nathan (shack ner), author; b. N.Y.C., Jan. 16, 1895; s. Bernard and Dora (Selden) S.; B.S., City Coll. N.Y., 1915; J.D., N.Y.U., 1919; m. Helen Lichtenstein, June 28, 1919; 1 dau., Barbara (Mrs. Ludwig Brunner). Chemist dept. of health, N.Y.C., 1915-17; admitted to N.Y. bar, 1919, practiced in N.Y.C., 1919-33; writing and hist. research, 1933—; editorial cons. Am. Jewish Com., 1945-51; dir. public relations Nat. Council Jewish Women, 1954-55. Served in chem. warfare service, U.S. Army, 1917-18. Mem. Am. Rocket Soc. (pres. 1933), Aaron Burr Assn. Author: Aaron Burr, 1937; The Medieval Universities, 1938; By the Dim Lamps, 1940; The King's Passenger, 1942; The Sun Shines West, 1943; The Wanderer, 1944; Alexander Hamilton, 1946; Church, State and Education, 1947; The Price of Liberty, 1948; Thomas Jefferson, vols. 1 and 2, 1951; Alexander Hamilton, Nation Builder, 1951; Space Lawyer, 1953; The Founding Fathers, 1954. Contbr. articles and fiction to nat. mags. Home: 1749 Grand Concourse, N.Y.C. 53. Died Oct. 2, 1955; buried Mount Hope Cemetery, Hastings-on-The-Hudson, N.Y.

SCHAEFER, Edgar F(rederick) (shay-fur), company exec.; b. Quincy, Ill., Feb. 20, 1896; s. Chris and Caroline (Weinbecker) S.; A.B., U. Ill., 1916; m. Ruth Ferris, Aug. 22, 1922. Joined Gardner Denver Co., Quincy, 1919, pres. since 1947. Dir. Blessing Hosp., Anna Brown Home for Aged, Woodland Home for Orphans. Mem. Quincy Indsl. Assn., Compressed Air Inst. (past pres.), Ill. C. of C. (dir.). Club: Country (Quincy, Ill.). Home: 1443 Maine St. Office: Gardner Dnever Co., Quincy, Ill. Died May 2, 1954.

SCHAEFER, Frederic, engr., mfr., inventor; born Stavanger, Norway, Sept. 8, 1877; s. Capt. Thomas Michelsen and Rachel Johanna (Clausen) S.; student Stavanger Tech. Sch.; M.S., hon., U. Pittsburgh, 1929; m. Sarah Beatrice Bubb, Sept. 5, 1912; children—Jane (Mrs. A. L. Whittemore, Jr.), Frederic Michelsen, Katharine (Mrs. Louis A. Foy). Came to U.S., 1894, naturalized, 1902. Mech. engr., Boston; design engr., Westinghouse Elec. Co., Pitts. and Le Havre France, 1902-06; mech. engr. Summers Steel Car Co., Pittsburgh, 1906-14; organized, pres. Schaefer Equipment Co., since 1914. Exec. asst. Chief Dist. Ordinance Officer. Trustee Carnegie Inst. since 1935; trustee, vice pres. Am. Scandinavian Found. Republican. Episcopalian. Clubs: Duquesne, Rolling Rock, Pittsburgh Golf, Wianno, H.Y.P., Fox Chapel. Decorated Knight of St. Olaf, Comdr. of St. Olaf (Norway). Home: Park Mansions, Pitts. 13. Office: Koppers Bldg., Pitts. 19. Died Feb. 20, 1955.

SCHAEFFER, Albert Charles (shā-fĕr), univ. prof.; b. Belvidere, Ill., Aug. 13, 1907; s. Albert John and Mary Plane (Herrick) S.; B.S. in C.E., U. of Wis., 1930; Ph.D. in mathematics, Mass. Inst. Tech., 1936; m. Caroline Juliette Marsh, Sept. 25, 1931; children—John Alden, Marsha Mary, Raymond Charles. Highway engr, 1930-33; instr., Purdue U., 1936-39; instr., Stanford, 1939-41, asst. prof., 1941-42, asso. prof., 1943-46, acting dept. chmn., 1945-46, prof., 1946-47; prof., Purdue U., 1947-50; prof. mathematics University of Wis., 1950-57, chairman of the department, 1957—. Joint recipient Bocher prize, Am. Math. Soc. Mem. Am. Math. Soc. (asso. sec. 1945-47), Sigma Xi, Delta Sigma Phi. Author: (with D. C. Spencer) Coefficient Regions of Schlicht Functions. Editor Proc. Am. Math. Soc., 1949-56, Duke Math. Jour., 1957—. Home: 730 Seneca Pl., Madison, Wis. Died Feb. 2, 1957.

SCHAEFFER, George W., chemist; b. Oak Park, Ill., Dec. 12, 1917; s. George W. and Catherine M. (Carroll) S.; B.S. in Chemistry, Central YMCA Coll., 1940; Ph.D. in Chemistry, U. Chgo., 1946; m. Rita Ann Mulhern, June 14, 1947; children—Daniel, Monica, Maria, Dominic, Benet. Lecturer in chemistry at the Central YMCA Coll., 1941-42; assistant in chemistry at University of Chicago, 1942, instr., 1942-47, asst. prof., 1947-49, with metall. lab., 1942-45; acting asst. prof. Stanford, 1947; asso. prof. chemistry St. Louis University, 1949-53, prof., 1953—, dir. dept., 1949—; chemist, radiation lab. U. of California, summer 1956. Fellow American Institute of Chemists; member of Am. Chem. Soc., A.A.A.S., Am. Assn. U. Profs., Sigma Xi, Alpha Phi Omega. Contbr. Jour Am. Chem. Soc., Jour. Chem. Physics, also Ency. Britannica. Home: 914 Woodshire Lane, Creve Coeur 41, Mo. Office: 1402 S. Grand Blvd., St. Louis 4. Died Aug. 17, 1959; buried Sacred Heart Cemetery, Florissant, Mo.

SCHAFER, Mac Henry, govt. ofcl.; b. Chgo., Feb. 23, 1906; s. Carl W. and Viola (Boardman) S.; Ph.B., U. Chgo., 1932, M.A., 1934; grad. student Harvard, 1949; m. Gertrude Herrick, Mar. 23, 1935; children—Carl W., Margaret, Ruth. Radio sales, credits Stromberg Carlson Telephone Mfg. Co., Chgo., 1924-30; tchr. English, Oak Park, River Forest high schs., 1934-35; mem. trust dept. real estate div. Northern Trust Co., Chgo., 1935-39, employment mgr., 1939-43, dir. employee relations, 1943-47, 2d v.p., dir. employee relations, 1947-53 2d v.p. adminstrv. dept., 1953, 2d v.p. banking dept., 1953; dir. personnel U.S. Dept. Agr., 1954—. Personnel com. Chgo YMCA, 1945-54 Commr. parks, River Forest, Ill. Mem. Indsl. Relations Assn. of Chgo. (pres. 1953), Soc. Personnel Adminstrn. Ill. C. of C., Am. Inst. Banking (chmn. Chgo. 1950-51), U. Chgo. Alumni Assn., Belles Lettres Soc., Phi Beta Kappa, Phi Kappa Sigma. Clubs: River Forest Tennis, Harvard Business School (Chgo.). Home: 4844 Old Dominion Dr., Arlington, Va. Office: U.S. Dept. of Agr., Washington 25. Died Apr. 20, 1956.

SCHAFF, William Frank, r.r. exec. Vice Pres. New York Central R.R. Co., ret. as exec. v.p., 1943. Home: 515 E. Rockwell St., Arlington Hts. Office: LaSalle St. Station, Chgo. Died May 1, 1957.*

SCHAFFER, Aaron, coll. prof.; b. Baltimore, Md., May 18, 1894; s. Schepschel and Anna (Lapiduth) S.; A.B., Johns Hopkins, 1914, Ph.D., 1917; student Sorbonne, Coll. of France, Sch. of Higher Studies, France, 1919-20; m. Dorothy Grant, Sept. 10, 1923. Instr. Romance langs., Johns Hopkins, 1918-19; instr. Romance langs., Univ. of Tex., 1920-23, adj. prof., 1923-25, asso. prof., 1925-28, prof. and mem. grad. faculty since 1928, chmn. dept. of Romance langs. since 1946; fellow University Texas Research Council, 1951-52. Decorated Officier D'Academie (Palmes Academiques), 1938; Chevalier de la Légion d'Honneur, 1956. Fellow American Council of Learned Socs., summer 1934. Mem. Am. Assn. Univ. Profs. (pres. Univ. of Tex. chapter 1937-38), Am. Assn. Teachers of French (mem. exec. com. 1940-47), Modern Lang. Assn. of Am. (1st pres., South Central Assn., 1940-41), Societe des Textes Francais Modernes, Sigma Alpha Mu, Phi Beta Kappa. Independent Dem. Jewish religion. Club: University of Austin, Tex. (pres. 1942-44). Author: Georg Rudolf Weckherlin, 1918; Parnassus in France, 1929; The Genres of Parnassian Poetry, 1944. Editor: French plays and novels. Contbr. to numerous learned and semi-popular periodicals. Home: 414 W. 32d St., Austin 5, Tex. Died Feb. 24, 1957; buried Hebrew Congregation Cemetery, Balt.

SCHARL, Josef (shärl), artist; b. Munich, Bavaria, Dec. 9, 1896; s. Josef and Therese (Prechtl) S.; student Sch. for Decorators, Munich, 1910-14, Bavarian State Acad. Fine Arts, 1919-21; m. Magdalene Gruber, Jan. 12, 1922; 1 son, Alois Otto. Apprentice, then journeyman in decoration firm, Munich,

1910-15; mil. service in World War I, 1915-18; workman in Munich Tapestry Works, 1918-19; independent artist, 1921—; had one-man shows at Die Juryfreien, and Graphisches Kabinett, Munich, 1930; last exhibition in Germany at Nierendorf Gallery, Berlin, 1933; One-man show, Amsterdam, 1934; arrived in U.S., Jan. 1939; 1st one-man show in U.S. at Nierendorf Gallery, N.Y. City, Apr. 1941; one-man shows, University, Louisville, Ky., Nierendorf Gallery, New York, 1943; Pinecotheca, N.Y.; Mus. Art, San Francisco, Nierendorf Gallery, Hollywood; Munson William Proctor Inst., Utica, N.Y., 1944; one-man show of Bible drawings, Nierendorf Gallery, New York, 1947; one-man shows, Muenster, Germany (Brit. zone), Karlsruhe (Am. zone), 1947; one-man show, New Art Circle, N.Y., 1949, Gallery Franke-Munich (Am. zone), 1949, Museum Heidelberg (Am. zone), 1949, Kunstverein Karlsruhe (Am. zone), 1949, Am. House, Munich, 1950, Heidelberg Kunstverein, 1951, Cologne Kunstverein, 1951, Boston Mus. Art, 1952, Princeton Gallery, Munson, 1952, Munich Pavillon, 1953, Geneva 6, Moos Gallery, 1953, Gallery St. Etienne, 1953-54; works at Museum Rochester, N.Y., Museum of Art, San Francisco, Staats-Galerie-Munich (Am. zone), Stadtische Galerie, Munich (Am. zone), Public Library, N.Y. City. Mus. Tel-Aviv-Israel, Albertina-Vienna-Austria, Academia Tedesca-Rome-Italy, Illustrations for English version of "Grimm's Fairy Tales,"; illustrations for Adalbert Stifters, Rock Crystal; monography, Josef Scharl, by Alfred Neumeyer. Awards: Albrecht Durer award of City of Nuremberg, 1929, Rome prize (trip to Rome), 1930; City of Munich prize, 1930; Prussian Foerderer preis, 1931; Dr. Mond Foundation Prize, 1931. Home: 160 Claremont Av., N.Y.C. Died Dec. 6, 1954; buried Ferncliff Cemetery, Hartsdale, N.Y.

SCHARNAGEL, Isabel Mona (shär'nā-gl), physician and surgeon; b. Henryetta, Okla., May 10, 1906; d. Charles and Belle C. (Phillips) Scharnagel; A.B., U. of Ala., 1926; M.D., Rush Med. Coll., 1930; m. George Sokolay, Apr. 5, 1941; children—Marc Phillips, Elise Roberts. Asst. surgeon Memorial Cancer Center, N.Y. City since 1940; surgeon Strang Clinic, N.Y. Infirmary, since 1933; instructor surgery Cornell Medical College. Award of Merit, Alumnae Assn. U. of Ala., 1950. Fellow A.M.A., N.Y. Acad. Medicine, Am. Coll. Surgeons; mem. Am. Med. Women's Assn. (sec. 1946, 1949), Women's Med. Assn. N.Y. City (sec. Mary Putnam Jacobi Fellowship com. since 1946), Am. Radium Soc., Am. Soc. Cancer Research, N.Y. State and County med. socs., City, Nat., State and Internat. women's med. socs., Alpha Omega Alpha, Phi Beta Kappa. Address: 139 E. 36th St., N.Y.C. 16. Died Nov. 25, 1953.

SCHATZ, Nathan Arthur, judge; b. N.Y.C., Apr. 27, 1893; s. Arthur and Rose (Weinstein) S.; A.B., LL.B., Cornell U., 1915; m. Dora Goldberg, Mar. 24, 1916; children—Arthur H., S. Michael, Davida (Mrs. Joseph H. Edelson). Admitted to Conn. bar 1916, Fed. Cts., 1918, U.S. Supreme Ct., 1921; trial counsel, 1920-35; judge Hartford Police and City Cts., 1923-29, Juvenile Ct., 1924-29, Westbrook Probate Ct., 1949-56; mem. firm Schatz & Schatz, Hartford, 1917—, sr. mem., 1925—. Dir. Bush Mfg. Co., Edward Balf Co., Texon, Inc., Robinson & Wright, Inc.; counsel Conn. Bank & Trust Co., Sage-Allen & Co., Somersville Mfg. Co. Mem. Rep. Town Com., Hartford, 1933-39, chmn., 1938-39; mem. State Rep. Com., 1939-42, Town Com., Westbrook, 1942-56. Trustee Hobby Country Day Sch., Inc., Emanuel Synagogue. Mem. State Bar Assn. Conn., Am., Fed., Hartford County, Middlesex County bar assns. Elk, Mason. Home: Chapman Beach, Westbrook, Conn. Office: 750 Main St., Hartford 3, Conn. Died Mar. 16, 1956; buried Emanuel Cemetery, Wethersfield, Conn.

SCHAUB, Edward Leroy, educator; b. Decorah, Ia., Aug. 13, 1881; s. Frederick and Mary (Strohm) S.; student Charles City (Ia.) Coll., State U. Ia.; Sage fellow Cornell U., 1908-10, Ph.D., 1910; studied U. of Berlin, 1911; m. Alma de Vries, Dec. 28, 1910; children—Frederick de Vries, Elizabeth Ann (dec.), Jean Aleida; m. 2d, Amy Tupper, Dec. 25, 1937. Instr. philosophy Cornell U., 1910-11; asst. prof. philosophy Queen's U., Kingston, Ont., 1911-12; acting prof. philosophy State U. of Ia., 1912-13; prof. of philosophy Northwestern U., 1913-46. emeritus, 1946—. Mem. Am. Theol. Soc., Am. Philos. Assn. (pres. Western div. 1922-23), Am. Assn. U. Profs., Phi Beta Kappa. Methodist. Club: University. Translator: Wundt's Elements of Folk Psychology, 1915, Editor: Immanuel Kant, 1724-1924 (essays), 1925; Philosophy Today, 1928; Spinoza: The Man and His Thought, 1933; William Torrey Harris, 1935-1935, 36; Progressis, 1937. Editor of The Monist (mag.), 1926-36. Contbr. to various philos. jours. Home: 429 N.E. 11th Av., Fort Lauderdale, Fla. Died May 24, 1953; buried Cedar Park Cemetery, Chgo.

SCHAUB, Robert C., newspaper editor; b. Decatur, Ill., Feb. 12, 1904; s. Howard C. and Winnifred (Weiennett) S.; A.B., Princeton, 1928; m. Louise E. Denz, Feb. 1, 1930; children—Robert C., Lisette. Reporter, The Review, Decatur, 1928-33; city editor, mng. editor E. St. Louis Jour., 1933-34; mng. editor The Review, 1934-46; exec. editor Decatur Herald and Review, 1945-56, gen. mgr., editor, 1956—; dir. E. Shore Newspapers, Inc., Ill. Broadcasting, Inc., Lindsay-Schaub Newspapers, Inc. Dir., v.p. Decatur YMCA, 1948-52, pres., 1952-54; dir. Decatur Assn. Commerce, 1942-45. Conglist. Clubs: Decatur; University. Home: 450 W. Forest St. Office: 365 Main St., Decatur, Ill. Died Jan. 17, 1958.

SCHEFF, Fritzi, prima donna; b. Vienna, Austria, 1882 (baptized Fritzi Scheff); daughter Gottfried Scheff (M.D.) and Anna Jager, a noted singer; sang in ch. choir at 5; completed vocal studies at Frankfort, Germany; m. Baron Fritz von Bardeleben (capt. in German Army); m. 2d, John (William) Fox, Jr., 1908; m. 3d, George Anderson. December 25, 1913 (div. Mar. 10, 1921), Début in Martha, Munich, 1900-01; sang the leading roles in Faust, La Boheme, Munich, 1900; 1st appearance in U.S. at Met. Opera House, N.Y.C., in Fidelio, Jan., 1902; prima donna there in various operas, under Maurice Grau, 1900-03; debut in comic opera in Babette, Broadway Theatre, N.Y.C., Nov. 1903; in leading operas to 1913; in vaudeville, 1913-18; in Glorianna, 1918—. Home: N.Y.C. Died Apr. 14, 1954; buried Actors Fund Cemetery, Kensico, N.Y.

SCHEIN, Marcel (shin), physicist, educator; b. Trstena, Czecho-Slovakia, June 9, 1902; s. Henry and Hermina (Messinger) S.; student U. Wurzburg, Germany, 1921-23; Ph.D., U. Zurich, Switzerland, 1927; m. Hilde Schoenbeck, June 2, 1927; 1 son, Edgar H. Came to U.S., 1938, naturalized, 1943. Asst. physics dept., U. Zurich, 1926-29, dozent, 1931-35; prof. exptl. physics, U. Odessa, 1935-37; fellow Rockefeller Found., U. Chgo., 1929-30, research in cosmic rays, 1938-42, asst. prof., 1942-45, prof. physics 1946—; cons. Research Lab., Gen. Elec. Co., 1945-46, Fermi Inst. Nuclear Studies, 1946; vis. prof. Princeton U., spring 1946, Stanford, summer 1948; cons. Manhattan Dist., 1945-46; dir. Task Order 18, Office of Naval Research project, U. Chgo., 1947—; charge cosmic ray research dept. of physics; vis. prof. Brazilian Center Phys. Research, 1951. Numerous expedns. on cosmic rays to Colo. (Mt. Evans, Climax); research on Mt. McKinley, Alaska, 1947, in B-29 planes, Aircraft Carrier (balloon flights); Balloon ascensions from Chgo. to study cosmic-rays close to the top of our atmosphere, 1940—; expdn. to Guam, 1957; worked with Berkeley Bevatron on K-mesons and hyperons, 1956—. Awarded prize, Schnyder von Wartensee Stiftung, Zurich, 1928. Fellow Am. Phys. Soc., N.Y. Acad. Sci., A.A.A.S.; mem. Ill. Acad. Sci., Swiss Phys. Soc, Brazilian Acad. Sci. Club: Quadrangle (Chgo.). Author: Problems in Cosmic Ray Physics, 1946. Home: 5650 Dorchester Av., Chgo. 37. Died Feb. 20, 1960.

SCHELL, Ralph Garfield, clergyman; b. Vaughan Twp., Ont., Canada, May 24, 1892; s. George Washington and Rosanna (Baker) S.; student Beamsville Bible Sch., Ont., Can., 1908-13, Central Business Coll., Toronto, 1913-14; also studied with 4 pvt. tutors, 1913-14; D.D., Northern Bapt. Theol. Sem., Chicago, 1933; m. Olivette Pearl Leggett, Jan. 6, 1915; children—Olive Pearl, David Lloyd George, Phyllis Halcie Bertha. Came to U.S., 1922, naturalized, 1931. Teacher, 1912-13; pastor Ch. of Christ (Disciples) at Toronto, Can., 1920-22, at Portland, Me., 1922-25; ordained Ministry Bapt. Ch., 1925; pastor at Biddeford, Me., 1925-26; asst. pastor Tremont Temple Ch., Boston, Mass., 1927-28, Second Ch. of Chicago, 1928-39; lecturer Northern Bapt. Theol. Sem. of Chicago, also trustee. Has conducted many evangelistic campaigns in East and Middle West. Mem. com. on Theol. edn., bd. of edn. of Northern Baptist Conv. (chmn. com. for orgn. Ministers Council; pres., Ministers Council, 1935-38); executive secretary Illinois Baptist State Conv., 1939-43; pastor Morgan Park Bapt. Ch., Chgo., 1943-53. Mem. bd. mgrs. Am. Bapt. Fgn. Mission Soc., 1944-54. Mem. Bd. Trustees Greater Chicago Ch. Fedn., 1944-55; v.p. Chgo. Bible Soc., 1953—; exec. dir. Chgo. area Midwest World Council Assembly Com., 1953, 54; producer Festival of Faith, Chgo., 1954; mem. Staff 2d Assembly World Council Chs., 1954; exec. dir. United Ch. Canvass, Church Fedn. Greater Chgo., 1956—. Republican. Mason. Address: 1400 S. Douglas St., Springfield, Ill. Died Feb. 10, 1958.

SCHENCK, Edgar Craig (skěnk), museum dir.; b. Hot Springs, N.C., Dec. 6, 1909; s. Norman Craig and Dorothy Jean (Robinson) S.; A.B. Princeton U., 1931; M.F.A., Princeton U. Grad. Coll., 1934; m. Belle Lupton Pike, Oct. 21, 1934; children—Mary Lupton, Andrew Craig. Instr., U. of Hawaii, 1934—; asst. dir., Honolulu Acad. of Arts, 1934, acting dir., 1935, dir., 1936-46; dir. Smith Coll. Mus. Art, Northampton, Mass., 1946-49; dir. Albright Art Gallery, Buffalo, 1949-54; dir. Brooklyn Museum, 1954—. Member Archaeological expedition to Angers, France, 1931, Minturno, Italy, 1932, Syria, 1933. Mem. Coll. Art Assn., Am. Assn. Museums, Assn. Art Mus. Dirs. (pres. 1958—), Phi Beta Kappa. Contbr. articles to mags. Address: Brooklyn Museum, Eastern Parkway and Washington Av., Bklyn. Died Nov. 16, 1959.

SCHENCK, Eunice Morgan, retired coll. prof.; b. Brooklyn, N.Y., Dec. 8, 1884; d. Nathaniel Pendleton and Elizabeth (Morgan) Schenck; A.B., Bryn Mawr Coll., 1907, Ph.D., 1913. Asso. in French, Bryn Mawr Coll., 1913-16, dean, 1916-17, associate professor of French, 1917, professor, 1925-48, professor emeritus since 1948; dean of Graduate School, 1929-42. Asso. dir. under American Red Cross of the Jardin d'Enfants Unit, France, summers, 1920, 1921. Chmn. Com. of Bryn Mawr Alumnae that furnished U. of Paris with a library of Am. Literature and established a permanent fund to maintain it. Officier d'Académie (France), 1929; Chevalier de la Legion d'honneur, 1934. Mem. Modern Lang. Assn. Am., Am. Assn. Univ. Women, Am. Assn. Univ. Profs., Alliance Francaise, Philadelphia (honorary); foreign corr. de l'Académie de Besançon. Clubs: Cosmopolitan, Bryn Mawr (New York); Alliance Francaise (Phila.). Home: Shoreham, L.I., N.Y. Died May 7, 1955.

SCHENCK, Martin A., lawyer; b. Montgomery, N.Y., Aug. 14, 1882; s. Ferdinand S. and Ellen (Haring) S.; A.B., Rutgers, 1904, A.M., 1906; LL.B., N.Y. Law Sch., 1906; m. Janet W. Daniels, Aug. 11, 1916. Admitted to N.Y. State bar, 1906, and since practiced in N.Y. City; mem. firm of Davies, Auerbach and Cornell since 1921, Davies, Auerbach, Cornell and Hardy since 1940, mem. firm of Davies, Hardy, Schenck & Soons, 1949—; member firm Davies, Hardy & Schenck, 1953—; director F. W. Woolworth Co. Mem. Holland Soc., Bar Assn. City of New York, N.Y. State bar Assn., Phi Beta Kappa, Chi Psi. Republican. Clubs: University, Down Town Assn., Knickerbocker. Home: 1165 Park Av. Office: One Wall St., N.Y.C. 28. Died Jan. 30, 1956.

SCHERER, John Jacob, Jr., clergyman; b. Marion, Va., May 6, 1881; s. John Jacob and Katharine (Killinger) S.; student Marion Coll., 1888-97, Fishburne Mil. Sch., Waynesboro, Va., 1897-98; A.B., Roanoke Coll., Salem, Va., 1900, D.D., 1917; B.D., Gettysburg (Pa.) Luth. Theol. Sem., 1904; LL.D., Coll. William and Mary, 1954; m. Anna Belle Downtain, Dec. 13, 1906; children—John Jacob III, James Grotius (dec.), Harriet Anna Belle, Katharine Elizabeth, Mary Grace. Ordained ministry Evang. Luth. Church, 1904; pastor Grace Luth. Ch., Fairmont, W.Va., 1904-06, First Evang. Luth. Ch., Richmond, Va., 1906—. Asso. justice Juvenile and Domestic Relations Court, Richmond, 1916—; sec. religious sect. Va. State Council of Defense, World War I. Member board directors Richmond Community Council (ex-pres.). Trustee Roanoke College, Marion Jr. College, Richmond Professional Institute of College of William and Mary (a founder; pres.), Konnarock Training Sch. (dir.), Iron Mountain School for Boys. Mem. Evang. Luth. Synod of Va. (pres. 1919-22). Luth. Synod of Va. (pres. 1926-48; mem. exec. com., 1926—); v.p. bd. Family Service Soc. Richmond; mem. exec. bd. United Luth. Ch. Am.; dir., past pres. Va. Mental Hygiene Soc.; elected del. World Conf. of Lutherans, Copenhagen, Denmark, 1929, World Council of Chs., 1954; commr. to Nat. Luth. Council; pub. mem. Nat. War Labor Bd., Region IV; vice chmn. Nat. W.S.B., Region IV; chmn. adv. bd. Va. Bd. Pub. Welfare, Richmond City Tax Commn.; mem. Merit Council Commonwealth of Va.; charter mem. Nat. Acad. Arbitrators. Democrat. Club: Torch. Home: 1603 Monument Av., Richmond, Va. Died Jan. 14, 1956; buried Hollywood Cemetery, Richmond.

SCHERER, Walter H(enry), dental surgeon; b. Newport, Ky., Sept. 15, 1880; s. Henry and Fredericka (Weber) S.; D.D.S., U. of Cincinnati, 1900; unmarried. Prof. oral medicine, Sch. of Dentistry, U. of Texas, 1920-45; in private practice as dental surgeon, Houston, Tex., since 1900. Served as major, Dental Corps, U.S. Army, World War I. Mem. bd. regents, U. of Tex. Fellow Am. Coll. Dentists; mem. Tex. State Dental Soc. (pres. 1918), Houston Dist. Dental Soc. (pres. 1913), Am. Dental Assn. (pres. 1945-46), Am. Acad. Periodentology (pres. 1936), Ill. State (life) and Chicago dental socs., Internat. Assn. Research, Houston Chamber of Commerce (mem. bd. dirs.), Psi Omega, Omicorn Kappa Epsilon. Mem. Christ Episcopal Ch. Mason (Shriner, K.T.), Rotarian. Clubs: Houston, Houston (Tex.) Country. Author: Dentistry National and International, Present and Postwar, 1945. Contbr. numerous articles to professional jours. Home: Montrose Blvd. Apartments. Office: Medical Arts Bldg., Houston 22. Deceased.*

SCHEUERMANN, Hugo E., banker; b. Jersey City, Mar. 19, 1887; grad. high sch., Passaic, N.J., 1905. With Merc. Nat. Bank and Liberty Nat. Bank, N.Y. City, 1909-12; with Nat. Park Bank, 1912-29, asst. cashier, 1919-20, asst. v.p., 1920-22, v.p., 1922; following merger of the bank with Chase Nat. Bank, became v.p. Chase Nat. Bank, 1929, sr. v.p., 1947-56. Clubs: Metropolitan (N.Y.C.); Pine Valley Golf (Clementon, N.J.); Montclair (N.J.) Golf. Home: 273 Valley Rd., Montclair, N.J. Office: Chase Nat. Bank, 18 Pine St., N.Y.C. 15. Died Apr. 1, 1957.

SCHEVILL, Ferdinand (shě-vil'), college prof.; b. Cincinnati, Nov. 12, 1868; s. Ferdinand and Johanna (Hartmann) S.; B.A., Yale, 1889; Ph.D., U. of Freiburg, Germany, 1892. Asst. in history and German, U. of Chicago, 1892-93, asso. in history, 1893-95, instr., 1895-99, asst. prof., 1899-1904, associate professor, 1904-09, prof. modern history, 1909-37, Author: Political History of Modern Europe, 1899; Siena, 1909; The Making of Modern Germany, 1916; Karl Bitter, a Biography, 1917; History of the Balkan Peninsula, 1922, revised edit., 1933; A History of Europe (From 1500), 1925, 30, 37, 46; History of Florence, 1936; The Great Elector, 1947; The Medici, 1950; Six Historians, 1956. Clubs: Quadrangle, University. Home: Duneland Beach, Michigan City, Ind. Died Dec. 10, 1954.

SCHIEFFELIN, William Jay (shĕf'lĭn), chemist; b. New York, N.Y., Apr. 14, 1866; s. William Henry and Mary (Jay) S.; Ph.B., Columbia Sch. Mines, 1887; Ph.D., Munich, 1889; m. Louise Shepard, Feb. 5, 1891; children—William Jay, Margaret, Mary, John Jay, Louise, Bayard, Elliott, Barbara, Henry. Civ. service commr., 1896; adj., 12th N.Y. Inf., Spanish-Am. War, 1898. Chemist, Schieffelin & Co., 1889, vice-pres., 1903-06, pres., 1906-22, chmn. bd., 1922-29. Mem. London Chemical Soc., pres. Nat. Assn. Wholesale Druggists, 1910; chmn. Am. Friends of Czecho-Slovakia; president American Mission to Lepers; v.p. Am. Bible Soc. Trustee Hampton Inst. Tuskegee Inst.; director Me. Seacoast Mission. Col. 15th N.Y. Inf., 1918. Pres. Emeritus Huguenot Soc., Chmn. Emeritus Citizens Union. Clubs: Century, City, Church. Home: 620 Park Av., N.Y.C. Died Apr. 29, 1955.

SCHIFF, Leo F(rancis), physician; b. N.Y.C., Feb. 28, 1885; s. Solomon J. and Minnie (Steiner) S.; M.D., Cornell, 1906; m. Fanny Schiff, Oct. 27, 1909; children—Leonard Joseph, Caroline Janet (Mrs. H. L. Schlesinger). Intern Harlem Hosp., N.Y.C., 1906-08; pvt. practice since 1908, specializing in urology, Plattsburg, N.Y., since 1924; organizer, 1922, Clinton Co. Lab. dir. to 1953; health officer, Plattsburg, 1924-53. Mem. A.M.A. (v.p. 1952-53), N.Y. State Med. Soc. (v.p. 1951-52), Am. Pub. Health Assn., Am. Soc. Clin. Pathology. Elk (past exalted ruler). Mason (past master). Address: 157 Broad St., Plattsburg, N.Y. Died Mar. 7, 1957.

SCHIFFER, Herbert Michael, educator; b. N.Y. City, Oct. 20, 1890; s. George Philip and Catherine Frances (Burns) S.; ed. High Sch. of Commerce, Harlem Prep. Sch.; B.C.S., N.Y. Univ., 1916, M.B.A., 1932; m. Anna Kelleher, Feb. 10, 1918 (died Mar. 17, 1932); children—Anita, Maurice, Doris Marie, Herbert Michael; m. 2d Ann O'Meara Jackman, July 10, 1940. Clerk, S. H. Wetmore Co., mfrs. of druggists sundries and surgical glassware, served in various capacities in prodn. and marketing, salesman, sales mgr. v.p.; resigned Aug. 1926; pres. of Glass, Inc., 1924-30; asst. dir. Day Div., Sch. of Commerce, asst. prof. marketing, 1926-30, asso. prof., 1930-34, prof., 1934, asst. dean, 1937; lecturer on marketing, New York University Evening Sch., 1920-26; lecturer on salesmanship K. of C. Vets. Sch., evenings, 1920-22; lecturer on business fundamentals, Coll. of Sacred Heart, Manhattanville, N.Y., 1928-29; prof. marketing, Newark Univ., N.J., 1930-40. Served as chief petty officer, U.S. Navy, May 1, 1917; commd. ensign, Oct. 1917, lt. Oct. 1918. Mem. Am. Marketing Assn., Acad. Polit. Sci., Am. Assn. Univ. Profs., Am. Acad. Polit. and Social Science, Alpha Kappa Psi, Theta Nu Epsilon, Beta Gamma Sigma, Alpha Phi Sigma, Alpha Delta Sigma, Sphinx, Arch and Square, Sigma Eta Phi, Mu Kappa Tau, Psi Chi Omega. Roman Catholic. K.C. Club: Catholic (N.Y.). Received N.Y. Univ. Alumni Meritorious Service award, 1938. Contbr. numerous bus. and profl. articles. Home: Apt. 2D, 240 W. 98 St., N.Y. City 25. Office: New York University School of Commerce, 100 Washington Square, N.Y.C. 3. Died Feb. 1, 1952.

SCHIFFNER, Carl Edmund, banker; b. St. Paul, Feb. 2, 1891; s. Joseph and Rose S.; student Harvard; m. Gladys Norton, Oct. 2, 1915; 1 dau., Jean Erma (Mrs. W. C. Manchester). Began as messenger First Nat. Bank of Chicago, 1907, ret. vice pres. Methodist. Mason. Clubs: Chicago Athletic Assn., Oak Park Country (Chgo.). Home: 555 Keystone Av., River Forest, Ill. Died Oct. 23, 1953.

SCHILLER, Max, business exec.; with Superheater Co. since its organization in 1910; pres. and dir. Am. Throttle Co.; dir. Air Preheater Corp. Home: 23 W. 73rd St., N.Y.C. 23. Office: 200 Madison Av., N.Y.C. Died July 29, 1952; buried Mt. Hope Cemetery, Westchester County, N.Y.

SCHILLING, Joseph T(ravis), utilities exec.; b. State Center, Ia., Oct. 21, 1893; s. Edward Henry and Flora Ellen (Travis) S.; student Ia. State Coll., 1915; m. Lela Bodkin, Sept. 24, 1947. Successively sales dept., comml. mgr., sec., sr. v.p. Ia. Power & Light Co. (formerly Des Moines Electric Light Co.), 1915-43, dir. since 1946, exec. v.p. since 1949; dir. Home Fed. Savs. & Loan Assn., Homes, Inc. Mem. Iowa Utilities Association (president 1955); member Better Bus. Bur., Des Moines C. of C. Presbyn. Elk. Clubs: Wakonda, Des Moines (Des Moines); Mchts. and Mfrs. (Chgo.). Home: 3440 Grand Av. Office: 823 Walnut St., Des Moines, Ia. Died Oct. 1957.

SCHINDLER, Raymond Campbell, investigator; b. Mexico, Oswego, N.Y., s. John Franklin and Isabelle (Campbell) S.; ed. high sch., Milwaukee; children—Dorothy, Ruth, Raymond. Assisted in San Francisco graft investigation, 1907-09; owner, Schindler Bureau of Investigation, New York, since 1912; associated with Dr. Le Moyne Snyder, Clark Sellers, William Harper in Scientific Evidence, Inc.; one of founders and member Court of Last Resort. Fellow Am. Geog. Soc.; mem. Am. Polar Soc., Executives Assn. of Great Britain, Ltd. (hon.), British Detective Assn. (hon.). Clubs: Artists and Writers, Circus Saints and Sinners, Explorers, Adventurers, Canadian (New York); Tavern (Chicago); Jonathan, Authors (Los Angeles). Author: (with Rupert Hughes) The Complete Detective. Contbr. articles to several nat. mags. Home: Spratt Estate, Tarrytown, N.Y. Office: 7 E. 44th St., N.Y.C. 17. Died July 1, 1959.

SCHIROKAUER, Arno C(urt), philologist, medievalist; b. Cottbus, Germany, July 20, 1899; s. Moritz and Louise (Moser) S.; student univs. of Berlin, Halle, Florence, Munich, 1918-21; Ph.D., U. of Munich, 1921; m. Erna Selo-Moser, Aug. 28, 1926; children—Conrad, Annette. Came to U.S., 1939, naturalized, 1946. Asst. librarian, Deutsche Buecherei Leipsic, 1924-27; dir., dept. cultural relations, German Broadcasting Co., Leipsic, 1928-33; asst. prof. Southwestern, Memphis, 1939-41; research fellow, Yale, 1941-43, 1944-45; visiting prof. of German, Kenyon Coll., 1943-44; lecturer, Johns Hopkins U., 1945, prof. German philology, 1946—; vis. lectr. U. Frankfurt-am-Main, 1953. Faculty prize, Univ. of Munich, 1921; stipend of the State of Bavaria for the preparation of habilitation, 1922. Mem. Modern Lang. Assn., Medieval Acad., Goethe-Soc. of Md. and D.C. (pres.). Author: Middle High German Rhyme-grammar, 1923; Expressionism in lyric poetry, 1924; Otfrid v. Weissenburg, 1926; Lassalle, 1928; Merseburger Zauberspruch, 1941; Deutsche Kulturepochen, 1949; Early New High German, 1951; Armer-Heinrich-Studien, 1951; Buchdruck und Gemeindeutsch, 1951; Texte zur Geschichte d. altdeutschen Tierfabel, 1952; Place of Esop in Medieval Literature, 1953. Editor: Corona, testimonial in honor of Singer, 1941; Modern Language Notes since 1952. Home: Mystic, Conn. Died May 24, 1954.

SCHLARMAN, Joseph H., bishop; b. Breese Twp., Ill., Feb. 23, 1879; s. Bernard J. and Philomena (Keyser) S.; ed. Quincy (Ill.) Coll. and U. of Innsbruck, Austria; Dr.Ph. and Dr. Canon Law, Gregorian U., Rome, 1907. Ordained priest R. C. Ch., 1904; asst. pastor Belleville (Ill.) Cathedral, 1907-09; pastor and chancellor Belleville diocese, 1909-30; consecrated Bishop of Peoria, June 17, 1930; apptd. asst. at the Pontifical Throne, Nov. 16, 1950; named Archbishop, Ad Personam, June 27, 1951. Chmn. Gov. Horner's Commn. for Study of Prison Problems; pres, Nat. Catholic Rural Life Conf., since 1943. Author: From Quebec to New Orleans, 1930; Why Prisons?, 1937; Catechetical Sermon Aids, 1942; Mexico, A Land of Volcanoes, 1949. Home: 740 N. Glen Oak Av., Peoria, Ill. Died Nov. 10, 1951.

SCHLERETH C(harles) Q(uinby) (slâr'ĕth), mining engr.; b. Denver, Colo., July 10, 1884; s. Peter M. and Justina C. (Eberst) S.; E.M., Colo. State Sch. of Mines, 1906; m. Florence Louise Barrett, Jan. 12, 1915. Successively chemist, surveyor, engr., chief engr. Compania Minera de Penoles, Durango, Mexico, 1906-11; asst. mgr. Summit Copper Co., Globe, Ariz., 1911; examining engr. Penoles Exploration Co., Mexico, 1911-14; mgr. Bonanza Mines, Ltd., Nicaragua, 1914; asst. gen. supt. Ojuela Mines, Durango, Mexico, 1915, gen. supt., 1916-17; asst. gen. mgr. Mapimi Unit of Ojuela Mines, including lead smelter, arsenic plant, power plant and railway, 1917-18; gen. supt., subsidiaries of Am. Metal Co. (9 metal mines, 2 coal mines), Monterrey, Mexico, 1918-21; gen. mgr. San Francisco Mines of Mexico, Ltd., San Francisco del Oro, Mexico, 1921-23; cons. engr. San Francisco Mines of Mexico and gen. consulting practice, New York, 1923-24; gen. mgr. Potosi Mining Co. and Calera Mining Co., Chihuahua, Mexico, 1924-25; cons. practice Mexico, U.S., Wales, Greece, Venezuela, Australia, etc., since 1925. Mem. Am. Inst. Mining and Metall. Engrs., Mining and Metall. Soc. America, Colo. Mining Assn. Club: Denver. Home: 99 S. Downing St. Office: Equitable Bldg., Denver. Died Nov. 12, 1950.

SCHLEY, Evander Baker (shlī); business exec.; b. New York, N.Y., 1883; s. Grant Barney and Martha Elizabeth (Baker) S.; grad. St. Paul's Sch., Concord, N.H.; Ph.B., Yale, 1904; m. Sophie Duer, Mar. 27, 1931. Entered mining business, 1905; now pres. Howe Sound Co., New York, N.Y. Address: 730 Fifth Av., N.Y.C. Died Jan. 6, 1953.

SCHLEYER, O. L., chmn. bd. Am. Automobile Ins. Co., Am. Automobile Fire Ins. Co., St. Louis, Asso. Indemnity Corp., San Francisco. Home: 63 Ridgemoor Dr., Clayton 5, Mo. Office: 1400 Pierce Bldg., St. Louis. Died Dec. 18, 1954.

SCHLOERB, Rolland Walter (shlûrb), clergyman; b. Oshkosh, Wis., Mar. 1, 1893; s. Albert Peter and Sarah M. (Hammetter) S.; student Marquette U., 1910-11; B.A., North Central Coll., Naperville, Ill., 1915; B.D., Evang. Theol. Sem., 1917; S.T.B., Union Theol. Sem., N.Y., 1920; M.A., Northwestern U., 1921; student U. Chgo., 1928-29; D.D., North Central Coll., Naperville, Ill., 1936; m. Edith Gransden, June 12, 1920; children—Geraldine (Mrs. F. R. Meyer), Robert Gransden. Ordained ministry Evangelical Ch., 1918; pastor Highland Park, (Ill.) Evang. Ch., 1920-21, First Evang. Ch., Naperville, Ill., 1921-28, Hyde Park Bapt. Ch., Chgo., 1928—. Trustee George Williams Coll., Bapt. Theol. Union. With Y.M.C.A. at outbreak of World War (mem. bd. mgrs.; Chgo.); chaplain U.S. Army, 1918-19. Fellow Nat. Council for Religion in Higher Edn. Author: God in Our Lives, 1938, The Preaching Ministry Today, 1946, The Interpreter's Bible, 1955. Club: Quadrangle (Chgo.). Contbr. articles to religious publs. Home: 5812 Stony Island Av., Chgo. Died Mar. 15, 1958.

SCHLOSS, Oscar Menderson, physician; b. Cin., June 20, 1882; s. Hugo and Aurelia (Menderson) S.; S.B., Ala. Poly. Inst., Auburn, 1901; M.D., Johns Hopkins, 1905; m. Rowena Farmer, Oct. 2, 1912; 1 son, Oscar Menderson. Practiced at New York, also prof. diseases of children Cornell Med. Coll., to 1920; attending pediatrist Children's Hosp., med. dir. Infants' Hosp., Boston, and prof. pediatrics Harvard Med. Sch., 1920-23; prof. diseases of children Cornell Med. Coll., also dir. children's service, N.Y. Nursury and Child's Hosp., New York, 1923-32; pediatrician in chief New York Hosp., 1932-34, attending pediatrician, 1934-38, cons. pediatrician, 1948—; cons. physcian Willard Park Hosp., North Country Community Hosp., N.Y. Infirmary for Women and Children; prof. clin. pediatrics Cornell U. Med. Coll., 1934-49. Mem. Am. Acad. Pediatrics, Am. Pediatric Soc., Am. Soc. Clin. Investigation, Am. Soc. for Serology and Hematology, Soc. for Exptl. Biology and Medicine. Republican. Home: 142 E. 71st St. Office: 125 E. 72d St., N.Y.C. Died Oct. 13, 1952.

SCHLOTTMAN, Richard Henry, steel mfr.; b. Tremont, Pa., Dec. 14, 1888; s. Charles A. and Margaret E. (Ramer) S.; student pub. schs., Pa.; m. Mae Ida Lebengood, Sept. 17, 1914; children—Elizabeth (Mrs. Donald B. Mancke), Virginia (Mrs. Truman S. Fuller, Jr.), Richard Henry. Various positions Eastern Steel Co., Pottsville, Pa., 1905-07, accounting dept., 1907-12; chief clk. Spanish-Am. Iron Co., Felton, Cuba, 1912-14; with Pa. Steel Co., Phila., 1914-16; with Bethlehem Steel Corp., 1916—, asst. comptroller, 1923-53, v.p., comptroller, dir., 1953—. Mem. Controllers Inst. Am., Am. Iron and Steel Inst. Clubs: Saucon Valley Country (v.p.), Bethlehem; Beaver Run Hunting and Fishing of Marshalls Creek (v.p., treas.). Home: 838 Tioga Av., Bethlehem, Pa. Died Apr. 11, 1955.

SCHLUETER, Edward Benjamin (shlē'tĕr), clergyman; b. Watertown, Jefferson County, Wis., Aug. 28, 1880; s. John Henry and Emilie (Kresensky) S.; A.B., Northwestern Coll., Watertown, Wis., 1900; student Theological Seminary of Wisconsin Synod, Wauwatosa, Wis., 1900-03; married Helene W. Boerner, July 28, 1916; children—Edward Arthur (maj. United States Army Air Force), Catherine Emilie (Mrs. William Arthur Karr), Helene Marie Schlueter (Mrs. J. Cary Bachman). Ordained to ministry of Lutheran Church, 1903; pastor, Kingston Paris, Green Lake County, Wis., 1903-09, St. John's Evangelical Luth. Congregation, Markesan, Wis., 1909-21, Grace Evan. Luth. Congregation, Oshkosh, Wis., since 1921. Mem. Mission Bd. of Northern Wis. dist., 1920-24; pres. Northern Wis. Dist., 1924-28 and 1930-36. First vice pres. Evan. Luth. Joint Synod of Wis. and other states, 1931-45, chmn. Spiritual Welfare Comm. since 1941; pres. Evan. Luth. Synodical Conf. of North America since 1944. Mem. Wis. State Hist. Soc. Home: 904 Nebraska St., Oshkosh, Wis. Died Mar. 9, 1952; buried Oshkosh.

SCHLUETER, Robert Ernst (shlē'tĕr), surgeon; b. St. Louis, Mo., June 9, 1872; s. Ernst and Elizabeth (Pullmann) S.; Ph.G., St. Louis Coll. Pharmacy, 1891; M.D., Mo. Med. Coll., 1895; grad. study in Europe, 1909-10; m. Katharyne B. Weber, Sept. 19; 1916. Asst. in physiology, Mo. Med. Coll., 1896-99; lecturer in pharmacy, Mo. Med. Coll., 1897-99; instr. in surgery, Washington U., 1899-1916; asso. prof. of surgery, St. Louis U. Sch. of Medicine, since 1923; asst. surgeon, St. John's Hosp., 1899-1903; surgeon, O'Fallon Dispensary, 1903-12, visiting surgeon, St. Louis City Hosp., 1912-16; surgeon, Luth. Hosp. since 1911, St. Louis Mullanphy Hosp., 1920-30, De Paul Hosp. since 1930, Deaconess Hosp. since 1932, St. Anthony's Hosp. since 1933. Hon. cons. Army Med. Library, Wash., 1944-52. Fellow Am. College Surgeons (life), A.M.A. (Mo. del. 1921, 22, 1940-53); mem. St. Louis Med. Soc. (pres. 1911), Mo. State Med. Assn. (president 1918), American Bd. Surgery (founders group), St. Louis Surg. Soc. (pres. 1941), So. Med. Assn., Hist. of Science Soc., St. Louis Acad. Science, Med. Library Assn. (v.p. 1940-41), A.A.A.S., Société Francaise d'Histoire de la Medicine. Served as maj. Med. Corps, U.S. Army, World War I. Republican. Mason. Club: University. Contbr. numerous articles to med. jours. Home: 245 Union Blvd. Office: 3839 Lindell Blvd., St. Louis 8. Died 1955.

SCHMIDT, Elmer Frederick Edward, business exec., engr.; b. Binghamton, N.Y., May 15, 1889; s. Max B. and Clara (Kelley) S.; C.E., Cornell, 1912; m. Lucille English Brawley, Oct. 4, 1916; children—

Charles Donnally, Elmer Frederick. Inventory engr. Ohio Fuel Supply Co., Charleston, W.Va., 1912-13, Northwestern O. Natural Gas Co., Toledo, 1913-14, Fayette County Gas Co., Uniontown, Pa., 1914-15; engr. Ohio Fuel Supply Co., Columbus, 1915-18; gas measurement engr. Lone Star Gas Co., Dallas, Tex., 1918-22, chief engr., 1922-25, gen. supt., 1925-35, vice pres., gen. mgr., dir., 1935-54; v.p., dir. Lone Star Producing Co., 1935-54, ret.; opened natural gas consulting office, Dallas, 1954; president Overland Oil, Incorporated, Denver, 1955—. Dir. Dallas Mus. Natural History. Mem. Am. Soc. M.E., Am. Soc. Testing Materials, Am. Gas Assn., Am. Petroleum Inst., Pacific Coast Gas Assn., Independent Natural Gas Assn., Independent Petroleum Assn. of Am., Tex. Soc. Professional Engrs., Inc., Tex. Mid-Continent Oil and Gas Assn. Republican. Presbyterian. Mason (Scottish rite, Shriner). Clubs: Petroleum, Athletic, Country, Brookhollow Golf (Dallas); Hole-in-One (Professional Golf Assn.). Home: 3605 Princeton, Dallas 5. Office: 5738 N. Central Expressway, Dallas 6. Died Jan. 15, 1959; buried Restland Meml. Park, Dallas.

SCHMIDT, Emil G., educator; b. Osceola, Wis., July 6, 1900; s. Gust and Angelina (Montedura) S.; B.S., U. of Wis., 1921, M.S., 1923, Ph.D., 1924; LL.B., U. of Md., 1936. Biochemist Mercy Hosp., Baltimore, 1925-32; instr. biol. chemistry U. of Md. Sch. Medicine, 1925-32, asst. prof., 1933-40, asso. prof., 1941-46, prof., head dept. since 1947. Mem. Am. Chem. Soc., Soc. Exptl. Biology, Medicine, American Society of Biological Chemists, Alpha Chi Sigma, Phi Lambda Upsilon, Sigma Xi, Gamma Eta Gamma. Home: 2 West University Parkway, Balt. 18. Died Sept. 1958.

SCHMIDT, Karl P., zoölogist; b. Lake Forest, Ill., June 19, 1890; s. George Washington and Margaret Jane (Patterson) S.; student Lake Forest (Ill.) Coll., 1906-07; B.A., Cornell University, 1916; D.Sc. (honorary), Earlham College, 1952; married Margaret Rosanna Wightman, July 3, 1919; children—John Mungo, Robert George. Research asst. Am. Museum of Natural History, N.Y. City, 1916-22; curator of reptiles, Chicago Natural History Museum, 1922-40; chief curator of zoölogy, 1941-55; curator of zoology emeritus, 1955; member of the Cornell Geological Expedition to San Domingo, 1916; Survey of Puerto Rico, 1919; Marshall Field Central Am. Expdn., 1923; Marshall Field Brazilian Expdn., 1926; Crane Pacific Expdn., 1928-29; Mandel Guatemala Expdn., 1933-34; Magellanic Expdn., 1939. Served in U.S. Army, Camp Grant, and Camp Taylor, 1918. Mem. A.A.A.S., American Society Ichthyologists and Herpetologists (president 1942-46), American Society of Mammalogists, Biological Society Washington, Am. Acad. Arts and Sciences, National Academy of Sciences, Ecological Society of Am. Fellow of the John Simon Guggenheim Foundation, 1932. Democrat. Author: Homes and Habits of Wild Animals, 1934; Friendly Animals and Whence They Came, 1938; Field Book of Snakes (with D. D. Davis), 1941; Principles of Animal Ecology (co-author), 1949; Ecological Animal Geography (co-author), 1951; also many scientific papers on amphibians and reptiles and on animal distbrn. Sect. editor for reptiles of Biological Abstracts. Home: 1751 Cedar Rd., Homewood, Ill. Address: Chicago Natural History Museum, Chgo. 5. Died Sept. 26, 1957.

SCHMIDT, Louis Ernst, surgeon; b. Chgo., Jan. 8, 1869; s. Ernst and Theresa (Weikert) S.; Ph.G., Chgo. Coll. of Pharmacy, 1889; B.S., U. Mich., 1892; M.S. Northwestern U., 1895, M.D., 1895, Sc.D., 1942; post-grad. study univs. of Berlin and Vienna; Paris, Breslau and London, 1896-98; m. Marie Mansfield, June 1, 1905 (dec.); children—Hildegarde (dec.), Mansfield. Prof. genito-urinary surgery, Northwestern U. Med. Sch., emeritus prof. after 50 yrs. service; dir. L. E. Schmidt Clinic; sr. attending urologist St. Luke's Hosp., Chgo.; cons. urologist Passavant and Grant hosps. Pres. Ill. Social Hygiene League. Fellow Am. Pub. Health assn.; mem. German, French, Am. and Internat. urol. assns., Clin. Soc. Genito-Urinary Surgeons, Am. Assn. Genito-Urinary Surgeons, Am. Social Hygiene Assn., Nu Sigma Nu. Clubs: Chicago Athletic, University. Home: 113 Bellevue Pl. Home and office: 316 Ruder St., Wausau, Wis. Died July 12, 1957; buried Graceland Cemetery, Chgo.

SCHMIDT, Paul Gerhard, choir mgr.; b. St. Louis, Mo., May 14, 1876; prep. edn., St. Olaf Sch., Northfield, Minn., 1886-91, Minneapolis (Minn.) Acad., 1891-92; A.B., U. of Minn., 1897, A.M., 1898, grad. study summer 1907; LL.D., Luther College, Decorah, Ia., 1945; married Sophie Marie Jorgensen, June 22, 1899; children—Dorothy Allworth, Gertrude Katharine, Paul Gerhard, Frederick Augustus. Pres. and mgr. St. Olaf Lutheran Choir (60 voices; 2 European and annual Am. tours) since 1902; sec. and treas. St. Olaf Coll., 1907-13, acting pres., 1909-10; mgr. Lutheran Tours. Decorated Medal of Order of St. Olaf (Norway). Mem. Phi Beta Kappa. Home: 1200 St. Olaf Av., Northfield, Minn. Died July 27, 1957; buried Oaklawn Cemetery, Northfield, Minn.

SCHMIDT, Petrus Johannes (shmit), U.N. official; b. Arnhem, The Netherlands, Nov. 23, 1896; student Univ. of Utrecht in economics and constitutional law; pvt. lessons in Latin and Greek; received certificate for Municipal and Departmental Adminstrn., 1918, also certificate for Journalism, Univ. of Utrecht. In municipal and civil service, Netherlands East Indies, Thailand (chancellor Netherlands Legation at Bangkok), 1915-21; editor and press corr. Indische Courant (at Soerabaya and Batavia), 1922-24; spl. corr. on staffs of Netherlands and Indonesian newspapers, China, Japan, Canada, Vienna and London; chief Publs. and Documentation of Trade Unions, 1924-28. Member central executive of Social Democratic Labor Party, 1928-31; chmn. Independent Socialist Party, 1932-34; mem. Municipal Council of Amsterdam, 1934-41; mem. Province of N. Holland, 1934-41. During war mem. of Resistance Movement in The Netherlands; editor of Je Maintiendrai one of leading underground papers; author of several anti-fascist pamphlets and manifestoes; a founder of the Netherlands People's Movement. Since the liberation of The Netherlands, editor in chief of Je Maintiendrai and exec. mem. of The Netherlands People's Movement; sec. to prime minister; Netherlands del. exec. com. of Preparatory Commn. of United Nations, Aug., 1945; del. Preparatory Commn. and adviser Netherlands delegation to Gen. Assembly of U.N., and asso. chief of Econ. and Social Sect., London. Sec. of Commn. on Human Rights, U.N.; prin. sec. U.N. Commn. on Korea, Jan.-June 1948; chief European Affairs, UN Security Council Dept., 5 yrs.; prin. sec. UN Commn. for Eritrea, Dec. 1949-June 1950; prin. sec. UN Rep. for India and Pakistan, June-Dec. 1951; dir. Disarmament Affairs Group, Dept. Security Council Affairs, UN. Address: Dept. Security Council, UN, Lake Success, L.I. Died Dec. 2, 1952; buried Westerveld, The Netherlands.

SCHMIDT, Richard Ernst, architect; b. Ebern, Bavaria, Germany, Nov. 14, 1865; s. Dr. Ernst and Theresa (Weikard) S.; brought to U.S., 1866; student M.I.T., 1883-85. Practiced Chgo., 1887—; member Schmidt, Garden & Martin, 1906-26, Schmidt, Garden & Erikson, 1926—; planned Michael Reese, Alexian Brothers and Lying-In Hosps., Tower Building, annex of Chgo. Athletic Assn., Montgomery Ward & Co.'s plant, Cook County Hosp. (all Chgo.), etc. Fellow A.I.A.; mem. Chgo. Historical Society, Am. Astronomical Society, Loyal Legion. Member Ill. Humane Society Chgo. Astronomical Society. Clubs: Chgo. Athletic, University, Cliff Dwellers (Chgo.). Co-author: The Modern Hospital, 1913. Home: 113 Bellevue Pl., Chicago 11. Office: 104 S. Michigan Av., Chicago 3, Ill. Died Oct. 1959.

SCHMIDT, Walter Seton, realtor; b. Cin., July 4, 1885; s. Frederick A. and Appolline Guildford (Tetedoux) S.; A.B., Xavier U., Cin., 1905, Ph. B., 1906, Am., 1908; student Cin. Law Sch., 1909-12; unmarried. Editor Round Table (mag.), 1905-06; began in realty bus., 1905; founder, 1913, and since pres. Fredk. A. Schmidt, Inc.; pres. Leibold Farrell Bldg. Co.; pres., 1932, Lelanau Realty Co., Southwestern Ohio Realty Co.; v.p. Punshon Engineering Co., Foundation Investment Co.; dir. Cin. Enquirer. Chmn. indsl. Council, trustee Urban Land Inst., Soc. Indsl. Realtors. Pres. Cin. Coll. Music. Mem. Nat. Assn. Real Estate Bds. (pres. 1935, dir.). Republican. K.C. Clubs: The Pillars, Queen City. Home: Grasmoor House, 2376 Madison Rd., Cin. 8. Office: 5th and Main Sts., Cin. 2. Died July 16, 1957.

SCHMIDT, William, Jr., public utilities exec. chmn. bd., chmn. exec. com., director Consol. Gas Electric Light & Power Co. of Balt.; dir., mem. exec. com., mem. trust com. Fidelity-Balt. Nat. Bank & Trust Co.; dir., mem. exec. com. Md. Casualty Co. dir. Eutaw Savs. Bank. Home: 5202 St. Albans Way, Homeland, Baltimore 12. Office: Lexington and Liberty Sts., Balt. 3. Died Feb. 18, 1955.

SCHMITT, Cooper Davis, univ. dean; b. Woodstock, Va., Dec. 4, 1859; s. Bernadotte and Barbara S.; grad. Univ. of Va., 1884 (M.A., 1884); m. Rose V. Everly, June 15, 1885; children—Bernadotte Everly, Ralph Scribner. Math. master Pantops Acad., Va., 1884-89; prof. math. U. Tenn., 1899—, dean Univ., 1907—; statist. agt. for Tenn., Ky., U.S. Dept. Agr., 1895-98. Democrat. Presbyn. Contbr. at times to Am. Math. Monthly. Address: 1302 White Av., Knoxville, Tenn. Died Dec. 6, 1910; buried Massanutten Cemetery, Woodstock, Va.

SCHMITT, Oscar C., electric mfg. exec.; b. St. Louis, 1894. Pres. and dir. Emerson Electric Mfg. Co., St. Louis. Mason. Home: Sappington, Mo. Office: 8100 Florissant Av., St. Louis. Died Apr. 21, 1953.

SCHMITT, Rupert P., church decorator; b. Milw., Mar. 27, 1890; s. Conrad and Mary D. (Hemmi) S.; student Marquette U., 1905-07; m. Elizabeth Debes, Oct. 26, 1920; children—Elizabeth (Mrs. Warren P. Jennerjahn), Elaine (Mrs. John Urbain), Conrad, II, Rupert P. Asso. with father (founder) Conrad Schmitt Studios, Milw., since 1907, pres., since 1940; assisted in reviving ancient fresco technique for ch. murals and decoration, revived medieval style and technique of making stained glass; outstanding works include Sacred Heart Ch., Tampa, Fla., Trinity Episcopal Ch., Columbus, Ga., St. Peter's Episcopal Ch., Chgo., St. Cecelia's Ch., Los Angeles, Epiphany Cath. Ch., San Francisco, St. Florian's Cath. Ch., Detroit, (in collaboration with Ralph A. Cram) St. Jean Baptiste Ch., Que.; pres. C.S. Realty Corp.; lectr. schs., colls. and learned socs. Mem. Wauwatosa (Wis.) Sane Fourth Commn. Mem. Civilian Naval Cruise, 1916; service with U.S. Merchant Marine, 1918. Recipient Craftsmanship award for stained glass windows in Balt. Old Cathedral, Balt. Bldg. Congress. Mem. Am. Stained Glass Assn. (pres. 1950-52), Milw. Soc. Decorators (founder). Catholic. K.C. (4°). Clubs: Wauwatosa (pres. 1939-40), City (Wauwatosa, Wis.); Kiwanis (charter mem.), Serra. Home: 8212 Rockway, Wauwatosa, Wis. Deceased.

SCHMUS, Elmer Ezra (shmōōs), banker; b. Naperville, Ill., May 10, 1892; s. William and Ellen Elizabeth (Goessele) S.; student pub. schs., Chicago, Ill.; m. Louise Enfield Melsome, Sept. 7, 1929; 1 son Robert Enfield (dec.). Messenger and clerk bond dept. First Nat. Bank of Chicago, 1909-19, mgr. bond trading div., 1919-25, asst. cashier, 1926-31, asst. v.p., 1931-37, v.p. 1937-45, v.p. and cashier since 1945. Republican. Methodist. Clubs: Bankers, Chicago Athletic (Chicago); Skokie Country (Glencoe, Ill.). Home: 1445 N. State Pkwy. Office: 38 S. Dearborn St., Chgo. Died Dec. 8, 1959; buried Memorial Park Mausoleum, Evanston, Ill.

SCHNABEL, Artur (shnä'bĕl), pianist, composer; b. Lipnik, Austria, Apr. 17, 1882; s. Isidor and Ernestine (Labin) Schnabel; studied piano with Leschetizky, Vienna, 1891-97, theory with Mandyszewsky; hon. Mus.D., U. Manchester, Eng., 1933; m. Therese Behr, June 9, 1905 (dec.); children—Karl Ulrich, Stefan, Elizabeth. Tchr. music, 1895—; hon. prof., Berlin, 1919 (by govtl. decree); was with State Acad. of Music, Berlin, 1925-30; lectured at University of Chicago, 1940, University of Michigan, 1943; concert appearances throughout Europe since 1896; toured United States, 1921-22, 1930, and since 1933, Australia, 1939, Egypt, Palestine, 1935; lecturer, U. of Chicago, 1945. Composer of 3 symphonies, chamber music, compositions for piano, voice, mixed chorus and orchestra. Edited piano works of Beethoven; has made recordings of all Beethoven's piano compositions, also works of other composers. Author: Reflections on Music, 1936; Music and the Line of Most Resistance, 1942. Home: 2 W. 86th St., N.Y. City. Died Aug. 15, 1951; buried Schwyz, Switzerland.

SCHNEE, Verne H(iggs) (snā), research exec.; m. Cleveland, O., Mar. 24, 1898; s. Robert G. and Amy (Higgs) S.; B. Chem., Cornell U., 1920; m. Evelyn Hieber, July 21, 1923; 1 dau., Anne. Welsbach fellow, U.S. Bur. of Mines, 1921; instr., Cornell U., 1922; v.p. and metallurgist, Cleveland Worm & Gear Co., 1922-29; v.p., Rhodes & Schnee, Inc., Cleveland, 1929-34; metallurgist and asst. dir., Battelle Meml. Inst., 1934-49; dir., U. of Okla. Research Inst. and v.p., U. of Okla., 1949-52; dir. Materials Advisory Bd. Nat. Acad. of Sciences, 1952—, consulting metallurgist, 1925—. Served as 2d lt., Coast Art., O.R.C., U.S. Army, 1918-19; chmn. products research com., div. 18, O.S.R.D., 1942-45; chmn. Com. on Ship Constrn., Nat. Research Council, 1943-46. Recipient Presidental Certificate Merit, 1948. Member Alpha Tau Omega. Episcopalian. Clubs: Cosmos (Washington); Cornell (N.Y.), Rotary, Faculty (Norman, Okla.), Tourbillion (Quebec). Home: 2122 Massachusetts Av. N.W., Washington 8. Died Sept. 22, 1957; buried Arlington Nat. Cemetery.

SCHNEEBELI, G. Adolph, congressman, mfr.; b. Neusalz, Prussia, May 23, 1853; s. Adolph and Emilie (Engeler) S.; ed. Bethlehem and Nazareth, Pa.; m. Loyal Oak, O., Sept. 10, 1878, Carrie E. Schneider. Engaged in business pursuits from youth; mfr., 1886—; pres. G. A. Schneebeli & Co.; sec. Nazareth Waist Co.; v.p. Nazareth Nat. Bank; pres. State Belt Elec. Ry. Co. Mem. Congress, 26th Pa. dist., 1905-07. Republican. Moravian; sec. trustees Nazareth Hall. Address: Nazareth, Pa. Died Feb., 1923; buried Nazareth, Pa.

SCHNEIDER, Edward Christian, biologist; b. Wapello, Ia., Aug. 21, 1874; s. John George and Augusta J. (Bauersfeld) S.; B.S., Tabor Coll., Ia., 1897; Ph.D., Yale, 1901; Sc.D., U. of Denver, 1914; M.P. E., International Y.M.C.A. Coll., 1923; Sc.D., Colorado Coll., 1932; m. Elsie M. Faurote, June 24, 1902; children—Edwin George, Marion Elsie (Mrs. R. E. Joyce). Instr. chemistry, 1897-99, prof. biology and physiol. chemistry, 1901-03, Tabor Coll.; prof. biology, 1903-07, head prof., 1907-19, Colo. Coll.; Daniel Ayres prof. biology, Wesleyan U., Conn., 1919-44, retired June 1944. John Jeffries award for contrbts. to aeromedicine Inst. Aeronautical Sciences, 1942. Member and sec. board control Conn. Agrl. Expt. Station, New Haven, Conn. Physiologist in charge of dept. Med. Research Lab., Air Service, U.S. Army, and later, officer in charge same to Aug. 1918; capt. Sanitary Corps, Dec. 1917, maj., June 1918; mem. Med. Research Bd. No. 1, A.E.F., Aug. 1918-Mar. 1919. Dir. physiology, Sch. of Aviation Medicine, Mitchel Field, L.I., N.Y., 1919-26; lt. col., S.R.C., 1920-30. Fellow A.A.A.S., Am.

Phys. Edn. Assn.; mem. Am. Physiol. Soc., Am. Soc. Biol. Chemists, Am. Pub. Health Assn., Soc. Exptl. Biology and Medicine, Soc. Am. Bacteriologists, Sigma Xi, Phi Beta Kappa, Beta Theta Pi. Author: Physiology of Muscular Activity, 1933, revised edition, 1939 revised (with P. K. Karpovick), 1948. Part Author: Report of Pike's Peak Expdn., 1911; Manual of the Med. Research Laboratory, Air Service, publishing chiefly studies of the influence of high altitudes and low oxygen on mankind, aviation physiology, and effects of physical exercise and training. Home: 25 Gordon Pl., Middletown, Conn. Died Oct. 3, 1954.

SCHNEIDER, Walter Arthur, physicist, educator; b. East London, S. Africa, Jan. 2, 1899; s. Richard and Frieda (Schroeder) S.; B.S., U.S. Africa, 1920; M.S., U. Mich., 1922, Ph.D., N.Y.U., 1927; E.E., Brooklyn Poly. Inst., 1936; m. Beatrice Haines, Aug. 8, 1925; 1 dau., Julia. Came to U.S., 1920, nturalized, 1932. Instrument tester Duquesne Light Co., Pittsburgh, 1920-21; asst. physics U. Mich., 1921-22; instr. Brooklyn Poly. Inst., 1929-35; instr. N.Y. U., 1922-27, asst. prof., 1927-29, asso. prof., 1929-46, prof. physics since 1947, dir. physics labs. since 1929; research photoelectricity, di-electric constants, nuclear physics. Civilian with A.E.C., 1942-46. Mem. Am. Phys. Soc., Am. Assn. Physics Tchrs., A.A.A.S., Sigma Xi, Sigma Pi Sigma. Author: Experimental Physics for Colleges (with L.B. Ham), 1932. Home: 68 Edgars Lane, Hastings on Hudson, N.Y. Office: 100 Washington Sq. E., N.Y.C. 3. Died Nov. 20, 1956.

SCHNERING, Otto, business exec.; b. Chicago, Ill., Oct. 9, 1891; s. Julius and Helen Elizabeth (Curtiss) S.; Ph.B., U. of Chicago, 1913; m. Dorothy Russell, Mar. 15, 1927; children—Robert B., Philip B., Barbara (Mrs. William David McFarland). Founder Curtiss Candy Co., Chicago, 1916, pres. and chmn. bd. dirs., since 1916; pres. and chmn. bd. dirs. Bireley's Beverages of Chicago; founder, pres. and chmn. bd. dirs. Equipment Finance Corporation; founder of the Curtiss Candy Company Employees Profit-Sharing Retirement Fund; founder, president and chmn. bd. dirs. Helen Curtiss Schnering Ednl. Foundation, Julius Schnering Ednl. Foundation; founder and chmn. bd. dirs. Otto Schnering Assos.; v.p. and chmn. bd. dirs. Evanston (Ill.) Boy Scouts; mem. regional com. of region seven, Boy Scouts of Am. Clubs: University, Chicago Athletic Assn., Fin and Feather, Chicago Farmers, Am. Guernsey Cattle (Chicago). Home: Cary, Ill. Office: 3638 Broadway, Chgo. 13. Died Jan. 10, 1953; buried Meml. Park, Evanston, Ill.

SCHOEMAKER, Daniel Martin, educator; b. Muscatine, Ia., Oct. 7, 1867; s. Christopher and Dora Gesina (Nyenhuis) S.; student German Am. Acad., Rochester, N.Y., 1889-92; B.S., U. Chgo., 1898; M.D., Rush Med. Coll., Chgo., 1904; unmarried. Instr. German, Des Moines Coll. (affiliated with U. Chgo.), 1893-96, asst. in anatomy, 1898-99, fellow, neuroanatomy, 1899-1900; Rockefeller Inst. med. research Scholar, 1902-03, asso. prof. St. Louis U. Sch. Medicine, 1904-05, 1907-11, prof. 1911-46, dept. dir. 1930-46, prof. emeritus of anatomy and dir. emeritus of dept., 1946; intern St. Louis City Hosp., 1905-06; asst. city bacteriologist, St. Louis, 1906-07. Physician, 16th Ward Draft Bd., 1917-18. Mem. A.A.A.S., Am. Assn. Anatomists, Sigma Xi, Alpha Omega Alpha, Nu Sigma Nu. Baptist. Author (with Dr. A. C. Eycleshymer): A Cross Section Anatomy, 1938; Anatomical Names Especially the Basle Nomina Anatomica (BNA), 1917. Home: 216 S. Maple Av., Webster Groves, Mo. Office: 1402 S. Grand Blvd., St. Louis. Died May 27, 1951; buried Muscatine, Ia.

SCHOENBERG, Arnold, composer and teacher composition; b. Vienna, Austria, Sept. 13, 1874; s. Samuel and Pauline (Nachod) S.; student Realschule, Vienna, 1885-91; studied with Zemlinsky; m. Matilde von Zemlinsky, Sept. 1901 (dec. 1923); children—Mrs. Gertrude Greissle, Georg; m. 2d, Gertrud Kolisch, Aug. 26, 1924; children—Nuria, Ronald, Lawrence. Taught music in Berlin, Amsterdam and U. Cal., Los Angeles; retired, 1944. Works: four string quartettes; Verklaerte Nacht (sextette for strings); Kammersymphonie; Klavierstuecke (piano); Gurre-Lieder; Pierrot Lunaire; Peace on Earth (chorus); Erwartung, Die Glueckliche Hand, Von Heute and Morgen (operas): Pelleas and Melisande (symphonic poem); Kol Nidre (chorus and orchestra); Quintet for winds; Variations for organ; Variations in Wind band; 2d Chamber Symphony; Ode to Napoleon Bonaparte; Piano Concerto; Harmonielehre; Models for Beginners in Composition; Moses and Aaron (opera); Jacobsladder (oratorio); Moderne Psalmen; Briete; Style & Idea. Served in Austrian Army, World War. Jewish religion. Inventor 12-tone harmonic system. Home: 116 N. Rockingham Av., Los Angeles 49. Died July 13, 1951.

SCHOENFELD, H(ans) F(rederick) Arthur (shĕrn'fĕld), diplomatic service; b. Providence, R.I., Jan. 31, 1889; s. Prof. Hermann and Johanna (Richter) S.; A.B., George Washington U., 1907, A.M., 1909; law, 1907-10; m. Aïda Marion Reid, Sept. 22, 1915; children—Douglas Reid, Arthur Derek Reid, Marion Reid, John Short Reid, Aïda Reid, Scott Reid. Asst. and instr. history, George Washington U., 1907-10; appointed consular agent at Caracas, Venezuela, Sept. 1910; confidential clerk to the asst. sec. of State, Jan. 1912; apptd. 3d sec. of Embassy at Constantinople, Turkey, Feb. 1912; sec. of Legation to Paraguay and Uruguay, Aug. 1913; sec. of Legation at Montevideo, July 1914; chargé d'affaires, Feb.-June 1915, and Nov. 1915-Mar. 1916; sec. of Legation at Christiania, Apr. 1916 (chargé d'affaires, July-Oct. 1918); sec. of Legation at Bucharest, Mar. 1919 (chargé d'affaires, June-Oct. 1919); sec. of Legation at Copenhagen, Nov. 1919 (chargé d'affaires, Dec. 1919-June 1920); sec. of Embassy at Rio de Janeiro, July 1920; 1st sec. of Legation at Vienna, 1921 (chargé d'affaires various times); counselor of Embassy, Mexico City, Mar. 1924 (chargé d'affaires various times); apptd. Am. minister to Bulgaria, July 17, 1928, to Costa Rica, Dec. 5, 1929; Am. minister to Dominican Republic, Aug. 1931, Finland, Apr. 1937-June 1944, Sec. Commn. of Inquiry and Conciliation, Bolivia and Paraguay, 1929, resigned from Foreign Service, Mar. 1930; asst. to pres. Internat. Gen. Electric Co., 1930; apptd. U.S. rep. for Hungary, Jan. 1945, Minister to Hungary, Dec. 1945, ret. Aug. 1, 1947; professorial lecturer in diplomatic history, George Washington U., since 1947; apptd. fgn. affairs officer Dept. of State, Dec. 1949. Received Alumni Achievement Award, George Washington U., 1943. Mem. Theta Delta Chi. Episcopalian. Club: Cosmos (Washington). Contbr. to profl. publs. Home: 3301 36th St., N.W., Washington. Died Mar. 2, 1952.

SCHOENFELD, William Alfred (shĕrn'fĕlt), orgn. cons.; b. Limbach, Saxony, Germany, Sept. 16, 1888; s. Gustavus Adolphus and Amalia (Mueller) S.; brought to U.S., 1890, naturalized, 1894; B.S.A., U. Wis., 1914; M.B.A., Harvard Grad. Sch. Bus. Adminstrn., 1922; student U. Berlin, 1925-26; Harvard Grad. Sch., 1926-27; m. Mabel Pearl Wagner, July 25, 1913; children—Arthur Raymond, Robert William (dec.), Benjamin Franklin (dec.) Harold Paul, Barbara Ruth. Civil engr. apprentice with Milwaukee Light, Heat, Traction Co., 1904-07; civil engineer assistant and transitman with U.S. Reclamation Service, Ariz., 1907-10; asst. instr. U. Wis., 1911-13, exec. sec. agrl. expt. Sta., 1913-14; lecturer on agrl. economics, U. Tex., 1914-15; vice dir. extension service, U. Tenn., 1915-20; asst. to war food adminstr., 1917-19, sec.-mgr. New Eng. Research Council, 1920-22; lecturer on business statistics, Mass. Inst. Tech., 1921-22; asst. and acting chief Bur. Agrl. Economics, U.S. Dept. Agr., 1922-25, chmn. European commn., same, 1924-26, Pacific Northwest rep., same, 1926-30; chmn. U.S. Crop Reporting Bd., 1922-24; agrl. commr. for Northern Europe, U.S. Dept. Agr., 1924-26; confidential agrl. adviser Inter-allied Reparations Commn., Berlin, 1924-26; dean and director of agr., Ore. State System of Higher Edn., 1931-50; dir. Ore. Agrl. Expt. Sta., 1931-50; dir. Ore. Agrl. Extension Service, 1934-50; director Regional Agrl. Credit Corporation, Portland Br., 1935-37; v.p. and trustee Ore. Rural Rehabilitation Corp., Agrl. Research Found., Agrl. Engring. Research Found., 1934-35; chmn. bd. dirs. Farm Credit Bd., Fed. Land Bank, Fed. Intermediate Credit Bank, Production Credit Corp., Bank for Co-operatives, 1934-55; Asso. chmn. bd. govs., Refrigeration Research Foundtion, 1943. U.S. delegate to Internat. Agrl. Congress, Warsaw, Poland, 1925; Internat. Inst. of Agr., Rome, Italy, 1926; Pacific Science Congress, Vancouver, B.C., 1933; head of mission of agrl. scientists and administrators to British Isles, 1946; cons. Commn. on Orgn. Exec. Br. of Govt., 1948, cons. Dept. State, 1951-53, Bur. Indian Affairs, 1950-56, retired; now govtl. orgn. cons.; cons. Gov. of Hokkaido prefecture, Japan 1959. Awarded Von Eyth medal by German Agrl. Soc., 1925. Mem. Sigma Xi, Alpha Zeta, Gamma Delta Sigma, Epsilon Sigma Phi. Author of govt. reports and research bulletins. Home: Winter Park, Fla. Died Nov. 13, 1959; buried Oakland Cemetery, Corvallis, Ore.

SCHOEPFLE, Chester S(eitz) (shĕp'flĕ), coll. prof.; b. Sandusky, O., Mar. 13, 1892; s. Fred and Christina (Seitz) S.; B. Chem. Engring., U. Mich., 1914, Sc.D., 1918; m. Inez McKee, June 20, 1919; 1 dau., Barbara Ann. Instr. organic chemistry U. Mich., 1916-19, asst. prof. 1919-24, asso. prof., 1924-36, became prof., dept. chmn., 1936. Sergt., Gas Def. Div., C.W.S., 1918-1919. Fellow A.A.A.S.; mem. Am. Chem. Soc., Sigma Xi, Tau Beta Pi, Phi Kappa Phi, Phi Lambda psilon, Alpha Chi Sigma. Home: 2022 Vinewood Blvd., Ann Arbor, Mich. Died Jan. 24, 1957; buried Woodmere Cemetery, Detroit.

SCHOFIELD, Charles Edwin (skō'fēld), editor; b. Geneva, Neb., April 18, 1894; s. Joseph Robert and Lura Adelia (Stockton) S.; B.A., U. of Neb., 1917; S.T.B., Boston U. Sch. of Theology, 1920; D.D., U. of Denver, 1935; LL.D., Boston University, 1938; married Nora May Elizabeth Fullerton, Aug. 19, 1919; children—Robert Edwin, Mary Lea (Mrs. Max W. Garrett, Junior). Methodist pastorates, Grover, Colorado, 1913, Rockford, Nebraska, 1913-17, West Roxbury, Mass., 1917-20, Inavale, Neb., 1920-22, Wesley Foundation Ft. Collins, Colo., 1922-24, Pueblo, Colo., 1924-25, Casper, Wyo., 1925-29, Fort Collins, Colo., 1929-32; dist. supt. Meth. Ch., Grand Junction, Colo., 1932-34; pres. Iliff Sch. Theology, Denver, Colo., 1934-42; pres. Southwestern Coll., Winfield, Kan., 1942-45; editor Adult Publs., editorial dir., bd. edn., Meth. Ch., 1945—. Pres. Assn. Meth. Theol. Sems., 1938-40; sec. Bd. Publ., Meth. Ch., 1940-45. Mem. S.W. Soc. for Biblical Study and Research, Am. Assn. Sch. Adminstrs., Am. Assn. Adult Edn., Phi Beta Kappa Assos., Phi Beta Kappa, Delta Sigma Rho, Pi Gamma Mu, Schoolmasters Club. Mason (32°). Author: The Gospel of Opportunity, 1925; The Church Looks Ahead (editor), 1930; Aldersgate and After, 1938; We Methodists, 1939; A Manual for the Training of Church Members, 1940; The Methodist Church, 1941. Contbr. numerous articles to various religious periodicals. Home: 1008 Estes Rd. Office: 810 Broadway, Nashville. Died June 28, 1951.

SCHOLL, John William (shŭl), prof. German; b. near Springfield, O., Aug. 17, 1869; s. Harrison and Catharine (Ryman) S.; A.B., Valparaiso (Ind.) Coll., 1896; A.B., U. of Mich., 1901, A.M., 1902, Ph.D., 1905; m. Clara Harwood, Dec. 20, 1896; children—Evelyn Harwood, Dorothy Mayhew, Catherine Daggett. Prof. modern langs., Chattanooga Normal Sch., 1896-1900; instr. German, 1902-12, U. of Mich., asst. prof., 1912-22, asso. prof., 1922-39, emeritus since 1939. Mem. Modern Lang. Assn. America, Phi Beta Kappa, Modern Lang. Research Assn. of Eng., Mich. Acad. Science, Arts and Letters (v.p. sect. for letters, 1922-24), Michigan Authors' Assn. (exec. council; pres. 1932-34). Detroit Philosophical Soc., Mich. Poetry Soc. Club: Research (Ann Arbor). Republican. Unitarian. Author: The Light-Bearer of Liberty, 1899; Social Tragedies, and Other Verse, 1900; Ode to the Russian People, 1907; Hesper-Phosphor and Other Poems, 1910; Children of the Sun (poems), 1916; Scholl, Sholl, Shull Genealogy, 1930; Edith—A Sonnet Sequence, 1930; The Nymph and the Rose, 1931; In Gæa's Garden, 1932; The Rose Jar, 1936; The Thinker, 1940; On the Road to Joyeuse Garde, 1942; Yellow Dwarf and Haughty Rose, 1942; Strenae, 1943; The Unknown Soldier and Other Poems, 1950. Contributor of notable letters to New York Times, from beginning of the war, 1914, advocating complete identification of German-Americans with Am. interests and ideals. Lecturer on patriotic topics. Home: 917 Forest Av., Ann Arbor, Mich. Died Sept. 2, 1952.

SCHOMP, Albert L. (skŏmp), chmn. Am. Bank Note Co.; b. Somerset County, N.J., May 21, 1880; s. Winfield S. and Arabella (VanDerveer) S.; grad. Plainfield (N.J.) High Sch., 1900; m. Charlotte Cave, Jan. 14, 1909; 1 son, Albert L. Clerk, 1904-08; with Am. Bank Note Co., 1908—, asst. treas., 1912-15, v.p., 1915-29, 1st v.p., 1929-35, pres., 1935-52, chmn. bd., 1952—. Mem. N.Y. C. of C. Republican. Presbyn. Clubs: Union League, City Midday (New York); Plainfield Country. Home: 978 Madison Av., Plainfield, N.J. Office: 70 Broad St., N.Y.C. 4. Died July 7, 1957; buried Hillside Cemetery, Plainfield, N.J.

SCHÖNHARDT, Henri (shĕrn'härt), sculptor, painter; b. Providence, R.I., Apr. 24, 1877; s. Louis and Catherine (Gräfenstein) S.; ed. pub. schs., Providence; grad. R.I. Sch. of Design, 1898; Académie Julian, École des Arts Decoratifs and École des Beaux Arts, Paris, 1898-1903; pvt. pupil of Ernest-Dubois, Paris; m. Catherine Connor, Jan. 26, 1909. Worked with Dubois on monument of Bossuet exhibited at 1900 exhbn., Paris, also portraits of Madame Agache and Roger de Sitivaux de Greiche, Paris; instr. modeling R.I. Sch. of Design, 1903-09. Prin. works: meml. to Gov. Elisha Dyer, St. Stephen's Ch., Providence; meml. to Col. Henry Harrison Young, City Hall Park, Providence; colossal group, Inspiration, Thetis inspiring Achilles; Soldiers' and Sailors' Monument, Bristol, R.I.; Cadmus and Clytie, R.I. School of Design Musuem; also The Struggle, group marble, haut relief; life size portrait of William Grosvenor, in marble; meml. to Col. Henry Tillinghast Sisson, Little Compton, R.I.; colossal Indian head in granite, Sprit of Wildacres, at Quidnessett; bronze statue of General Nathaniel Greene, R.I. State House; Peace, bust; portrait busts, bas reliefs, etc.; figure painter, Eastern Morn, painter of portraits, landscapes, and miniatures on ivory. Exhibitor Société des Artistes Français: Le Salon des Champs-Elysées, Hon. mention in sculpture Paris Salon, 1908. Club: Providence Art. Address: 21 Audubon Av., Providence 8. Died Mar. 10, 1953.

SCHOONHOVEN, Helen Butterfield (Mrs. John J. Schoonhoven), lecturer; b. Pompey Center, N.Y., Oct. 21, 1869; d. Otis and Martha (Bogardus) Butterfield; B.L., U. of Ill., 1891, M.L., 1894; grad. student Radcliffe, 1893-94; m. John J. Schoonhoven, June 16, 1897; 1 son, George Otis. In charge English dept., Mattoon (Ill.) High Sch., 1891-93; instr. English, U. of Ill., 1894-97; pres. domestic science dept., Brooklyn Inst. Arts and Sciences, 1906-16; ednl. sec. The Auxiliary of Children's Museum, Brooklyn, 1916—. Lecturer summer session U. Chgo. 1916, N.Y. pub. lecture course, Brooklyn Inst. Lecturer N.Y. U. Graduate Sch., summers 1936, 37. Mem. N.Y. Bd. of Edn., 1904-08. Mem. Colonial Daughters of the 17th Century. Republican. Conglist.

Clubs: Brooklyn Woman's (pres. 1922-24), Urban, Ex-Presidents', Phi Beta Kappa. Home: 773 Eastern Parkway, Brooklyn, N.Y. Died Mar. 1958.

SCHOONOVER, Draper Talman (skōōn'ō-vēr), coll. pres.; b. near Beverly, W.Va., Feb. 26, 1872; s. Marshal and Eliza Belle (Louk) S.; A.B., Washburn Coll., Topeka, Kan., 1899, L.H.D., 1929; Ph.D., U. Chgo., 1907; student Am. Sch. for Classical Studies, Rome, 1901-02; LL.D., Marietta (O.) Coll., 1948; m. May Haines Bowen, Aug. 26, 1903; children—Alice Ruth (dec.), Emma Louise, Lois Margaret (Mrs. Louis R. Kent). Tchr. Morgan Park High Sch., 1902-04; Beaver Coll., 1904-06; asso. prof., Latin, Marietta (O.) Coll., 1907-09, prof, 1900—, registrar, 1910-22, dean coll., 1908-10, 1919-42, acting pres., 1942, pres. 1942-45, pres. emeritus 1945—. Mem. Classical Assn. Middle West and South, Archaeol. Inst. Am. Republican. Methodist. Mason. Club: Rotary. Home: 624 3d St., Marietta, O. Died Feb. 9, 1956.

SCHORLING, Raleigh, educator; b. Batesville, Ind., Aug. 15, 1887; s. Henry and Catherine (Kammeyer) S.; grad. Ind. State Normal, Terre Haute, 1909; A.B., U. of Mich., 1911; A.M., U. Chgo., 1914; Ph.D., Columbia, 1924; m. Marie Louise Oury, July 26, 1916; children—Ruth Mary, Clark, Otis William. Tchr. pub. schs., 1904-07; prin. high sch., 1907-08; prin. Lincoln Sch., exptl. sch. of Tchrs. Coll. (Columbia), 1917-22; organizer, 1922, and prin. Univ. High Sch. (exptl. sch.), Ann Arbor, until 1926. Fellow A.A.A.S.; mem. Phi Delta Kappa, Phi Beta Kappa, Phi Beta Kappa Assos. Methodist. Author: Fundamental Mathematics, Books 1 and 2, 1944; Modern School Algebra, First Year and Second Year, 1942; Modern School Geometry, 1943; Mathematics in Life, 1946; Swords Into Plowshares, 1946; Mathematics for the Consumer, 1947; A Bill of Rights for Teachers, 1947; Student Teaching, 1949; First Year Algebra, 1949. Contbr. on ednl. problems. Home: 403 Lenawee Dr., Ann Arbor, Mich. Died Apr. 22, 1950; buried Forest Hill Cemetery, Ann Arbor.

SCHORSCH, Alexander Peter (shôrsh), clergyman, educator; b. Nagy Szent Miklos, Hungary (now Rumania), February 19, 1882; s. Anthony and Mary (Czagany) S.; came to U.S., 1895; B.A., St. Mary's Sem., Perryville, Mo., 1904, M.A., 1906; Ph.D., U. of Louvain, Belgium, 1925. Joined Congregation of the Mission (C.M.), 1901. On the faculty of high sch. at St. Mary's Sem., 1906-09; St. Thomas Theol. Sem., Denver, Colo., 1909-14; St. Louis (Mo.) Prep. Sem., 1914-20; St. Mary's Theol. Sem., Perryville, 1920-23 and 1925-27; Coll. Liberal Arts, De Paul U., Chicago, 1927, dean Grad. Sch., 1928-51, dean emeritus and dir. internal research since 1951. Member Am. Sociol. Soc., Am. Assn. Univ. Profs., Am. Cath. Philos. Assn., Medieval Acad. of America, Pi Gamma Mu. Author (with Sister Dolores Schorsch) Jesu-Maria course in religion, consisting of guidebook and workbook for each grade, with First Communion Book, 1954-56, Our Lady—the Glory of Her People, and of 12 pamphlets giving methods of using the course. Contbr. to Jour. Religious Instruction; Proceedings of Am. Catholic Philos. Association. Researches in education and philosophy. Address: 2233 N. Kenmore Av., Chgo. Died Aug. 10, 1957; buried Calvary Cemetery, Chgo.

SCHOTT, Max, corp. exec.; b. Russelsheim, Germany; came to U.S. at age 17; married; children—Herman F., Walter M., Mrs. Alice Richards, Mrs. Helen L. Pedotti, Mrs. Katherine A. Peake, Mrs. Mary L. Dangerfield. Started career as office boy with Am. Metals Co., became regional mgr., Colo. and St. Louis, later mem. bd. dirs.; one of founders, gen. mgr. Climax Molybdenum Co., 1917, forced to retire because of illness, 1920, rejoined co. ten yrs. later and became pres., resigned as pres., 1946, but remained a dir. Home: 40 E. 88th St., N.Y.C. Died Nov. 10, 1955.

SCHREIBER, Carl Frederick (shrī'bēr) prof. German, bibliographer, curator; b. Saginaw, Mich., Mar. 21, 1886; s. Hugo Friedrich and Adelaide (Rueter) S.; A.B., U. Mich., 1907; A.M., N.Y.U., 1910; Ottendorfer Meml. traveling fellow and student Leipzig and Munich, 1911-12; Ph.D., Yale, 1914, hon. M.A. (privatim), 1926; L.H.D., U. Mich., 1954; L.H.D., Middlebury Coll., 1954; m. Estelle Brand Martin, June 6, 1911; children—Barbara-Ann (Mrs. George Stearns), Carl F., Richard Martin. Instr. German, Bloomington (Ill.) High Sch., 1907-09, N.Y.U., 1909-13, Yale, 1913-17; registrar Sheffield Scientific School, 1917-19; asst. prof. German, Yale, 1917-23, asso. prof., 1923-26, prof., 1926-54, emeritus 1954, chmn. dept., 1928-32, 1944-54, Leavenworth prof., 1936-54; curator the William A. Speck Collection of Goetheana 1928—; sec. Yale Coll. faculty, 1951-52. Sterling Meml. traveling fellow, 1927-28. Decorated Comdr.'s Cross, Order of Merit (Fed. Republic Germany); fellow Barkeley Coll. and by virtue of this association guest-fellow of Kings Coll., Cambridge; recipient Hindenburg medal für Kunst und Wissenschaft. Mem. Modern Lang. Assn. Am. (exec. council), Am. Assn. U. Profs., Goethe-Gesellschaft, Carl Schurz Meml. Found., New Haven Colony Hist. Soc., Edgar A. Poe Shrine, The Questioners, St. Elmo Soc., Torch Honor Soc., Phi Sigma Kappa. Republican. Presbyterian. Clubs: Graduate and Faculty (New Haven); Andiron; Elizabethan. Author: Fiction and Fantasy of German Romance (with F. E. Pierce); Minimum German (with N. G. Sahlin); Gotheana, a Centenary Portfolio; Goethe's Works with the Exception of Faust, a Catalogue (editor). Contbr. articles on Goethe and Poe to literary jours. and to Dictionary Am. Biography. Home: 65 Elmwood Rd., New Haven. Died Mar. 2, 1960.

SCHREIBER, Walter, lawyer, ex-mayor of Berlin; b. Pustleben (Harz), Germany, June 10, 1884; s. Adolf and Margarethe (Rockstroh) S.; student univs. Grenoble, Munich, Berlin, and Halle; recipient of doctor's degree, University of Halle, 1910, doctor's degree in economic science (hon.), University of Berlin, 1928; m. Margaret Rüffer (dec.); children—Klaus-Dietrich (killed in World War II), Waltraut Klostermann; m. 2d, Ada Lewin-Traeger, Sept. 13, 1947. Admitted to bar, Halle, 1911, practiced in Halle, 1911-14; elected dep. in Prussian Diet, 1919; Prussian Minister for Commerce, 1925-33; practice of law, Berlin, 1934-51; mem. Ho. of Reps., Berlin, 1946—; mayor of Berlin, 1951-55; governing mayor, 1953-55. Co-founder Christian Dem. Union, 1945, chmn. dist. Berlin, 1947. Served as officer, World War I. Mem. Stuben Schurz Soc. Home: Wernerstrasse 14a, Berlin-Grunewald, Germany. Died June 30, 1958; buried Dahlemer Walj-Friedkof, Berlin.

SCHRENK, Hermann von, see Von Schrenk, Hermann. Died Jan. 30, 1953.

SCHRIBER, Louis (shrīb'ēr), banker; b. Oshkosh, Wis., Apr. 7, 1878; s. Charles and Jennie S.; ed. Oshkosh pub. schs.; m. Floretta Elmore, May 19, 1909; children—Susan Samuella, Charles. Started as messenger boy 1897; v.p. First Nat. Bank, Oshkosh, 1918-24, pres. since 1924; vice-pres. U.S. Motors Corp., Oshkosh, Wis.; dir. Wis. Bank Shares Corp., Milwaukee; trustee Northwestern Mutual Life Ins. Co., Milwaukee. Republican. Methodist. Club: Oshkosh Country (Oshkosh). Home: "Shadowlawn," Oshkosh. Office: 130 Main St., Oshkosh, Wis. Died Apr. 19, 1952.

SCHRIEVER, William (shrē'vēr), physicist; b. Dakota City, Neb., Jan. 16, 1894; s. Fred and Elizabeth (Winkhaus) S.; A.B., Morningside Coll., Sioux City, Ia., 1916; M.S., Univ. Iowa, 1917, Ph.D., 1921; m. Lucille E. Weisenbach, Aug. 16, 1922; Children—William W., Elinor Marie. Asst. prof. physics, U. of Okla., 1919-24, asso. prof., 1924-27, prof. since 1927, chmn. dept. physics, 1942-52, dir. Sch. Eng. Physics, 1942-48; research fellow Am. Petroleum Inst., 1927-29. Served in sci. and research div., Signal Corps, U.S. Army in Airplane Radio Development, 1918. Fellow Am. Phys. Soc., A.A.A.S., Okla. Acad. of Sci. Dir. State Bureau of Standards since 1942. Mem. Soc. of Exploration Geophysicists, Am. Assn. Physics Teachers, Am. Geophys. Union, Sigma Xi (1st pres. Okla. chpt., 1930-31), Gamma Alpha, Sigma Gamma Epsilon, Sigma Pi Sigma. Author: Origin of The Carolina Boys; Magnetic Susceptibilities; Electric Currents Caused by Metallic Dental Fillings; Streaming of Potentials. Home: 910 Chautauqua Av., Norman, Okla. Died Nov. 20, 1958; buried Odd Fellow Cemetery, Norman, Okla.

SCHROEDER, Bernard A., patent lawyer; b. Wilmette, Ill., Sept. 19, 1900; s. Carl S. and Frances (Cornelisen) S.; B.S. in Mech. Engring., U. Ill., 1924; LL.B., Chgo. Kent Coll. Law, 1929; m. Mary Seright, June 22, 1929; 1 son, James Bernard. Signal dept. C.&N.-W. Ry., 1918-19; engring. dept. H. M. Byllesby Co., Chgo., 1923-24; safety engr. Hartford Accident & Indemnity Co., 1924-29; admitted to Ill. bar, 1929; mem. U.S. Supreme Ct. bar; engaged in practice of patent law; became partner Dyrenforth, Lee, Chritton & Wiles, 1937, now Schroeder, Hofgren, Brady & Wegner. Capt., U.S. Cav. Res., 1923-40. Mem. Am., Ill., Chgo. bar assns., Bar Assn. City N.Y., Western Soc. Engrs., Am., Chgo. patent law assns., Theta Kappa Phi, Phi Alpha Delta. Republican. Clubs: Union League, Chicago, Illini (past pres.), Tower (Chgo.); Westmoreland Country (Wilmette, Ill.). Home: 636 Garland Av., Winnetka, Ill. Office: Opera Bldg., Chgo. 6. Died Oct. 1957.

SCHROEDER, John Charles (shrōd'ēr), prof., clergyman; b. New York, N.Y., Apr. 22, 1897; s. Charles and Kittie (List) S.; B.S., Coll. City of N.Y., 1917; B.D., Union Theol. Sem., 1921; studied Columbia, 1917-21, Harvard, 1921-23; D.D., Bowdoin, 1933; LL.D., U. of Maine, 1934; S.T.D., Ripon Coll., 1948; m. Katharine Taylor, Sept. 15, 1921; 1 d., Anne Neil. Ordained ministry Congl. Ch., 1921; asso. minister Central Ch., Boston, 1921-23; minister Community Ch., Bogota, N.J., 1923-26, First Congl. Ch., Saginaw, Mich., 1926-30, State St. Ch., Portland, Me., 1930-37; prof. homiletics and pastoral theology, Yale U., 1937-46, chmn. dept. religion since 1946, John A. Hoober professor of religion since 1950; master of Calhoun Coll., Yale, since 1942; lecturer Biblical literature, Bowdoin Coll., 1934-37. Served with Am. Red Cross in France, 1918-19. Trustee Wellesley College. Mem. Delta Kappa Epsilon. Clubs: Faculty (New Haven); Yale (New York). Author: The Task of Religion, 1936; Modern Man and the Cross, 1940. Contbr. to Interpreter's Bible, 1952. Home: 116 College St., New Haven 11. Died Nov. 16, 1954.

SCHROEDER, Rudolph William (shrō'dēr), aviation; b. Chgo., Aug. 14, 1886; s. John August and Nora Ann (Reidy) S.; student Crane Tech. High Sch., Chgo. (about), 1906-07. Engaged in airplane exhbns., 1910-16; aviation engr., Underwriters Labs., 1920-25; supt. Ford Airline, 1925-27; Guggenheim Safe Aircraft Competition, 1927-29; mgr., Chgo. Curtiss Flying Service, 1928-30, Skyharbor Airport, 1930-33; chief airline insp. and asst. dir., Bur. of Air Commerce, 1933-37; v.p. in charge safety, United Airlines, Chgo., 1937-42, now retired. Served in U.S. Army Air Corp., 1916-20; rank of maj.; made seven-mile flight into stratosphere, Feb. 1920; awarded Army Air Force Citation; Distinguished Flying Cross, 1945. Mem. Inst. Aeronautical Science. Methodist. Home: 4136 N. Melvina Av., Chgo. 34. Died 1952.

SCHUCHARDT, William Herbert (shū'shärd), architect; b. Milw., Apr. 28, 1874; s. Louis and Rosalie (Winkler) S.; student, U. Wis., 1891-93; B.S. in Arch., Cornell U., 1895; LL.D., Occidental Coll., 1941; m. Gertrude Nunnemacher, Nov. 4, 1911 (died 1919); m. 2d, Mildred Fraser, Nov. 17, 1928. Archtl. draughtsman, successively with R. E. Schmidt (Chgo.), Cope and Stewardson (Phila.), Cass Gilbert (N.Y.), W. G. Rantoul (Boston), 1895-1905; pvt. practice, Milw., 1905-25; gen. mgr. Pelton Steel Co., Milw., 1917-20; prof. architecture, city planning, Cornell U., 1925-28; ret. to Cal., 1929. Mem. Bd. Public Land Commrs., Milw., 1918-25; pres. City Planning Commn. of Los Angeles. Trustee Occidental Coll., Los Angeles; trustee Milwaukee Downer College, 1912-25, Milwaukee Art Institute, 1910-25, Layton Art Gallery, 1915-25; mem. bd. of governors, Los Angeles County Mus. of Art, Sci. and History. Fellow Am. Inst. of Architects; mem. Pacific Southwest Acad., Cal. Hist. Soc. Clubs: Los Angeles Univ., Bel-Air Bay. Home: 1110 Fallen Leaf Rd., Arcadia, Cal. Died Apr. 17, 1958.

SCHUETTE, Walter Erwin, clergyman; b. Delaware, O., Nov. 14, 1867; s. Conrad Herman Louis and Victoria Mary (Wirth) S.; grad. Capital University Academy, Columbus, O., 1881; A.B., Capital University, 1885, D.D., 1925; graduate Lutheran Seminary Columbus, 1888; married Clyda Pearl Helsel, June 26, 1890; children—Helen Beatrice (dec.), Faith (Mrs. Harmon W. Eibling), Jessie Ruth (Mrs. Raymond F. Crump), Winona Emma (deceased), Conrad Herman Louis, Corine Louise (Mrs. William F. Hamman), Walter Erwin. Ordained Luth. ministry, 1888; pastor successively Detroit, Mich., Bellevue and Toledo, O., until 1914; editor The Lutheran Standard, Columbus, 1909-15, The American Lutheran Survey, 1914-17; pastor Wheeling, W.Va., 1917-22; pres. Eastern Dist. Joint Synod of Ohio and Other States, 1922-30; pres. Eastern Dist. Am. Lutheran Church, 1931—; vice-pres. American Lutheran Church, 1936-44; mem. American Lutheran Conference Commission on Church Unity, 1940—; editor Pastor's Monthly, 1922-28; adv. council American Bible Society, 1938—; lecturer. Hon. mem. International Mark Twain Society, 1944. Author: Her Place Assigned, 1896; The Devotional Life of the Ch. Worker, 1921; God Is Faithful, 1925; Moments with God, 1925; The Best Possible Sunday School, 1928; God Save the Home, 1940; Keeping the Faith, 1941; also 19 juvenile stories and 8 playlets. Home: 235 Bank St., Sewickley, Pa. Died Aug. 10, 1955; buried Sewickley Cemetery.

SCHULER, Hans, sculptor; b. Morange, Lorraine. Germany, May 25, 1874; s. Otto and Amalia (Arndt) S.; brought to U.S., 1880; grad. Md. Inst. Sch. Art and Design (first medal), 1894; grad. Rinehart Sch. Sculpture, (winning $4,000 scholarship), 1898; grad. Julian Acad., Paris, (all honors), 1900; m. Paula M. Schneider, January 15, 1905 (deceased September, 1957); children—Charlotte Agnes, Hans Carl. Awarded three medals Julian Academy, also Salon Gold medal, third class, 1900; Silver medal St. Louis Expn., 1904; Medal Md. Inst.; Civic award Fine Arts and Lit., 1937. Prin. works: "Arladne", Walter's Gallery, Balt.; "Memory," "Life Is But the Turning of a Leaf," and many other tomb figures; portrait statues of Samuel Smith, Pinkney White, etc.; portrait busts of Maj. Walter Reed, Dr. Osler; Buchanan meml., Washington; bust and medallion of Henry Walters, 1931; "Four Horsemen of the Apocalypse," Walters Gallery, Balt.; statue "Freedom of Conscience," St. Mary's City, Md.; Md. Tercentenary medal and half dollar; monument to Johns Hopkins; Heroic statue of Martin Luther, Balt.; bust J. M. T. Finney, M.D.; monument to Sidney Lanier, Balt., 1941; bust Sidney Lanier, Hall of Fame, N.Y. U., 1946; heroic size statue to Ignatius Loyola, Blakefield, Md.; heroic relief to Pulaski. Dir. Md. Inst., 1925-51, awarded Gold Medal of Honor, 1950. Former mem. Nat. Sculpture Soc. Mason. Club: Charcoal (Balt.). Home: 5 E. Lafayette Av., Balt. 2. Died Mar. 30, 1951; buried London Park Cemetery, Balt.

SCHULGEN, George Francis, army officer; b. Traverse City, Mich., Apr. 23, 1900; B.S. in Mech. Engring., Mich. Agrl. Coll., 1922; m. Lillian Jacob, May 14, 1932. Commd. 2d lt. Air Service, 1924, and advanced through the grades to brig. gen., 1943; became asst. chief Inspection Sect., Air Corps Material Div., Wright Field, Dayton, O., June 1939; with Operations and Tng. Div. G-3, War Dept. Gen. Staff, Washington, 1941-42; became asst. sec. of the Gen. Staff, 1942; named wing comdr. First Air Force, Phila. Air Defense Wing, Phila., July 1943. Rated command pilot, combat observer, aircraft observer. Chief of staff, First Air Force, Oct. 1943; assigned to Southwest Pacific Theater, Jan. 1944, to Southeast Asia Command as dir. Plans Air, Sept. 1944; dep. dir. Civil Affairs Div., War Dept. Special Staff, July 1945; chief Air Intelligence Requirements Div., Hdqrs. A.A.F., asst. chief of air staff—Jan. 2, 1947. Address: Suttons Bay, Mich. Died Feb. 17, 1955; buried Arlington Nat. Cemetery.

SCHULMAIER, A(dlai) Talmage, clergyman, educator; b. Berwick, Me., Mar. 1, 1893; s. Henry R. and Lillian Mabel (Thompson) S.; grad. Tilton (N.H.) Sch., 1919; S.B., Boston U., 1923, A.M., 1924; S.T.B., Boston U. Sch. of Theology, 1925; Th.D., Webster U., Atlanta, 1933; m. Lotta F. Johnson, Aug. 27, 1919. Served as sgt. Aviation Corps, U.S. Army, Dec. 1917-Jan. 1919. Ordained M.E. ministry, 1923; pastor successively West Thornton and Laconia, N.H., Trinity Ch., North Cohasset, Mass., Rockland and Hebronville until 1925; field sec. and tchr. East Greenwich (R.I.) Acad., 1923-27, pres., 1927-30; pres. Genesee Wesleyan Sem., Lima, N.Y., 1930-38; dean Vt. Jr. Coll., 1938 until retirement. Pres. R.I. Council of Religious Edn., 1929-31; also pres. Livingston County Council of Religious Edn. and Livingston County Orgn. for Prohibition. Mem. N.E.A., Am. Edn. Assn., Nat. Bibl. Instrs. Assn. Mason (K.T.). Home: Lima, N.Y. Deceased.

SCHULMAN, Samuel (schōōl'mân), rabbi; b. Russia, 1864; s. Tanhum and Rachael Deborah (Alterman) S.; brought to America at the age of 4; B.A., Coll. City of New York, 1885; pvt. tutelage in Hebrew and Judiacs; student Hochschule fuer die Wissenscaft des Judenthums, and U. of Berlin, Germany, 1885-89; D.D., Jewish Theol. Sem. America, 1904; D.H.L., Hebrew Union Coll., 1925; m. Emma Weinberg, Nov. 1, 1890. Rabbi, New York, 1889, Helena, Mont., 1890-93, Kansas City, Mo., 1893-99; rabbi Temple Beth-El, New York, 1899-1927 (presented with gift of $20,000 on 20th anniversary at Beth-El); rabbi Congregation Emanu-El, New York, a consolidation of Temple Emanu-El and Temple Beth-El, 1927-34, rabbi emeritus Congregation Emanu-El, 1934—— (given dinner to celebrate his 50 years rabbinate in U.S., 1939). Pres. Central Conf. of Am. Rabbis, 1911-13 (hon. pres. 1934); pres. Assn. Reform Rabbis of New York and Vicinity, 1921-26; pres. Alumni Coll. City of N.Y., 1930-32. Mem. Council of World Union for Progressive Judaism; mem. bd. of editors Jewish Publication Soc's. English translation of the Bible; mem. of publn. com. Jewish Publn. Soc.; mem. bd. of editors Jewish Classics; of Jewish Publn. Com. on Commentaries; of Ednl. Commn. of Union of Am. Hebrew Congregations; of Synagogue Council of America (chmn. 1934-36); chmn. governing bd. Hebrew Union Coll. Sch. for Teachers; v.p. Y.M. Hebrew Assn. of New York; mem. Interfaith Com. Greater N.Y. and Vicinity; chmn. Com. on Youth Education of Am. Hebrew Congregations; non-Zionist member Jewish Agency, 1929——; mem. exec. com. Am. Jewish Com. Mem. Phi Beta Kappa. Club: City (N.Y.) Author of Tract on Jewish Ethics and Essay on Israel; also of many articles and pamphlets of religious subjects; contbr. to Universal Jewish Ency. Used phrase, "the Melting Pot," in a sermon, Mar. 30, 1907; believed to be first use of this phrase as a symbol of America. Address: 1 E. 65th St., N.Y.C. Died Nov. 2, 1955; buried Beth-El Cemeteries, Bklyn.

SCHULTE, William Henry, clergyman, educator; b. New Vienna, Ia., Oct. 6, 1889; s. B. W. and Mary (Forkenbrock) S.; student St. Joseph Acad. (Dubuque), Loras Coll., U. Fribourg (Switzerland); M.A., U. Ia., 1923, Ph.D., 1931. Ordained priest R.C. Ch., 1913; instr. Latin and Greek, Loras Coll., 1913-20, prof. classical langs., 1920-23, head dept. classical langs., 1923-41; prof. religion and philosophy Clarke Coll., 1941-51; vis. lectr. U. Ia., summer 1935; domestic prelate, 1947; pastor Immaculate Conception Ch., Cedar Rapids, Ia., 1951——; dean Cedar Rapids Deanery, 1951——. Dean examiners jr. clergy, also synodal examiner; chmn. Archdiocesan Music Commn.; nat. sec. Laymen's Cath. Retreat Conf. Dir. Loras Inst. Liturgical Music. Mem. Classical Assn. Middle West and South. K.L., Elk. Author: Approved List of Catholic Church Music, 1937; Index Verborum Valerianus, 1935; Benediction Manual, 1940; The Burial Service and Funeral Mass, 1946. Editor Retreat Bull., 1949——. Address: 857 Third Av. S.E., Cedar Rapids, Ia. Died Apr. 17, 1957.

SCHULTZ, Clifford Griffith, transportation exec.; b. Alta, Ia., May 9, 1890; s. Henry Frederick and Carrie (Griffith) S.; A.B., U. Minn., 1911, M.A., 1912; LL.B., Harvard, 1915; m. Mae Wangler; children—Genevieve Schultz Ayers, Frederick Henry. Admitted to Minn. bar, 1915, practiced in Mpls., 1915-17, 19-21; treas. Jefferson Highway Transportation, 1921-24; organized Union Bus Co., Fla., 1924, v.p., 1924-36, pres. 1936-42; chmn. bd. dirs. Southeastern Greyhound Lines since 1942; dir., mem. exec. com. Greyhound Corp.; dir., Bushnell Steel Co., Barnett Nat. Bank. Served as lt. CAC, U.S. Army, 1917-18. Clubs: Timuquana Country, Florida Yacht, Biltmore Country, Everglades, River, Mountain City. Home: 3644 Richmond St. Office: Schultz Bldg., Jacksonville, Fla. Died Mar. 21, 1958.

SCHULTZE, Leonard (shōōl'tsē), architect; b. Chicago, Ill., Dec. 5, 1877; s. Edward and Ida Kate (Leonard) S.; student Coll. City of New York, 1892-94; pupil of E. L. Masqueray, of N.Y. City and Architectural Sch. of Met. Museum of Art; m. Agnes Frances Briggs, Nov. 25, 1903; children—Kathryn Marion (Mrs. Robert D. Lambert), Frances Elizabeth (Mrs. John H. S. Candee). Practiced in N.Y. City since 1900; mem. Schultze & Weaver (now Leonard Schultze & Associates) since 1921; firm designers of New Waldorf-Astoria Hotel, Pierre Hotel, Park Lane Hotel, Sherry-Netherland Hotel (all of N.Y. City), The Breakers Hotel (Palm Beach, Fla.), Roney Plaza (Miami Beach, Fla.), Los Angeles Biltmore, Biltmore Theatre (Los Angeles), Clift Hotel (San Francisco), Springfield (O.) Daily News Bldg., White Plains (N.Y.) Hosp., housing developments for Met. Life Ins. Co., in Los Angeles and San Francisco, Calif., Alexandria, Va., new home office bldg. Met. Life Ins. Co., N.Y. City; also many others. Sergt. 1st Battalion, 2d Regiment U.S. Volunteer Engineers, 1898, Spanish-Am. War. Fellow Am. Inst. Architects; mem. Architectural League of New York, Beaux Arts Inst. of Design, Society Mayflower Descendants, Phi Gamma Delta. Republican. Clubs. American Yacht; Scarsdale Golf and Country. Home: 18 Autenrieth Rd., Scarsdale, N.Y. Office: 119 E. 40th St., N.Y.C. 16. Died Aug. 25, 1951; buried Kensico Cemetery, Westchester County, N.Y.

SCHULZ, Edward Hugh (shōōlts), army officer; b. Wheeling, W.Va., Jan. 23, 1873; s. Henry John and Gertrude (Niesz) S.; Sc.B., U.S. Mil. Acad., 1895; m. Katherine Julia Muhleman, Oct. 12, 1898; children—Gertrude Adams (Mrs. Wm. A. Hausman), Katherine Louise (Mrs. Albert W. Bruce), Caroline Edward (Mrs. John S. Service). Commd. add. 2d lt. Engrs., June 12, 1895; advanced through grades to col., July 1, 1920. Asst. river, harbor and fortifications, Charleston, S.C., 1895-96, New London, Conn., 1899-1901; submarine defense, Hampton Roads and Charleston, S.C., 1898-99; recorder Bd. of Engrs., New York, 1901-05, in charge New York dist. river and harbor works, 1904-05; forts, Guantanamo, Cuba, 1905-07; river and harbor works, Sioux City, Ia., and Kansas City (Mo.) district, 1907-12; consulting engineer Kaw Valley Drainage District, Kansas City, Kan., 1909-12; New Orleans district, 1912-16, St. Paul and Duluth districts, 1916-17; commander 109th Engrs., Camp Cody, N.M., and 604th Engrs., Vancouver Barracks, Wash., and Camp Leach, D.C., 1917-18; in charge Milwaukee dist., 1919-20, Seattle dist., 1920-23; div. engr., comdr. 3d Engrs., Schofield Barracks, Hawaii, 1923-26; in charge Chicago dist. and corps engr. 6th Corps Area, 1926-28; div. engr., Lakes Div., Cleveland, O., 1928-29; comdg. officer Ft. Humphreys, Va. (now Ft. Belvoir, Va.), also of Engr. Sch., Ft. Humphreys, 1929-33; mem. Bd. Engrs. Rivers and Harbors, 1929-33; engr. 9th Corps Area, San Francisco, and supervising Golden Gate Bridge approaches through Presidio, Fort Scott and Fort Baker, mil. reservations, 1934-37, retired. Engaged in translations for War Dept. and Corps of Engrs., informal, 1940-45. Was member of Mississippi River Commission, Great Lakes Ship Canal Board, Ill., and Bd. on Diversion Channels Mississippi River, 1927-29. Mem. Am. Soc. C.E., Soc. Am. Mil. Engrs. Conglist. Clubs: Army and Navy (Washington); Union League (San Francisco). Author: Use of Search Lights, 1904; Report on Missouri River, 1909; Report on South West Pass, 1916; Diversion Channels of Mississippi River (all publs. U.S. War Dept.); also rept. of Miss. River Commn. on Flood Control, 1927. Contbr. to Engring. News Record, Mil. Engr. Address: 204 El Camino Real, Berkeley 5, Calif. Died Mar. 3, 1951; buried Presidio of San Francisco Nat. Cemetery, San Francisco.

SCHULZE, Paul, Jr., mfr.; b. Chgo., Mar. 1895; s. Paul and Ida (Johl) S.; Ph.B., Yale, 1916; m. Grace Cook, June 30, 1923; children—Idamae (Mrs. John A. Metheany) (dec.), Paul III, Walter II; m. 2d, Rheba G. Thompson, July 17, 1943. Gen. sales mgr. Schulze Baking Co., Chgo., 1921-23; v.p., treas. Paul Schulze Biscuit Co., Chgo., 1923-25, pres., 1935-40; pres. Schulze and Burch Biscuit Co., Chgo., 1940-54, chmn. exec. com., 1954——; dir. Dist. Nat. Bank Chgo., Farmer Seed & Nursery Co., Faribault, Minn. Mem. citizens com. on memls. Chgo. Park Dist. Served as 1st lt., U.S. Cav., Mexican Border, 1917-19. Mem. Am. Legion, Vets. Fgn. Wars, Municipal Art League (dir.), Phi Gamma Delta. Republican. Presbyn. Clubs: Economic, Saddle and Cycle, Cliff Dwellers, Arts, Chicago Yacht, Chicago Athletic Assn. (Chgo.); Yale (N.Y.C.); Mory's Assn. (New Haven); Palette and Chisel, 1020, Wine and Food. Author: The Peace Messenger. Home: 1420 Lake Shore Dr., Chgo. 10. Office: 1133 W. 35th St., Chgo. 9; also Palmolive Bldg., Chgo. 11. Died Sept. 6, 1959.

SCHUMM, Herman Charles, orthopedic surgeon; b. Fort Wadsworth, Staten Island, N.Y., Nov. 23, 1889; s. Herman C. and Anna (Kilshaw) S.; B.S., U. of Pa., 1911, M.D., 1914; m. Sarah Jane Johnson, Apr. 20, 1918; children—Herman Charles, David Kilshaw. Began practice as surgeon, Chicago, 1914; orthopedic surgeon. Lt., later capt. Med. Corps, U.S. Army, 1918-19; specialist in orthopedic surgery, Milwaukee, Wis., 1919——; asso. prof. orthopedic surgery, U. of Wis., 1926——, Marquette U., 1930——, dir. dept. of orthopedics, Marquette U., 1938——. Licentiate Am. Bd. Orthopedic Surgery. Fellow Am. Coll. Surgeons, Am. Acad. Orthopedic Surgeons; mem. Am. Orthopedic Soc., Clinical Orthopedic Soc., Milwaukee Surg. Soc., Milwaukee Acad. Medicine, Alpha Mu Pi Omega, Phi Gamma Delta. Republican. Clubs: University, Milwaukee, Oconomowoc Lake. Contbr. to med. jours. Home: R.D. 5, Oconomowoc, Wis. Office: 1024 E. State St., Milw. Died Dec. 21, 1955.

SCHUTTE, Louis Henry (shōō'tē), educator; b. Wilmington, N.C., Nov. 26, 1874; s. Frederick Arthur and Meta (Hashagen) S.; grad. Mt. Hermon (Mass.) Sch., 1895; A.B., Yale, 1899, A.M., 1902; m. Anna Rutherford Metcalf, June 29, 1918; children—William Metcalf, Louis Henry. Taught in Delaware Acad., Delhi, N.Y., 1899-1901, Carteret Acad., Orange, N.J., 1902-04; headmaster Rumsey Hall, 1905-41; headmaster Indian Mountain School, 1941-46. Republican. Conglist. Clubs: Yale (New York); University (Litchfield County, Conn.). Home: Cornwall, Conn. Died Apr. 17, 1957.

SCHUTZE, Martin, educator, author; b. Germany, Dec. 21, 1866; Ph.D., in German, English and Norse lits., U. Pa., 1899; m. Eva Lawrence Watson, 1901 (dec. 1935); m. 2d, Frieda Bachmann, 1937. Came to U.S., 1891, naturalized, 1899. Prof. emeritus German lit. U. Chgo. Mem. Am. Assn. U. Profs. (charter member), Modern Lang. Assn. of America, Hist. Soc. of Woodstock, N.Y.; hon. corr. mem. German Acad., Munich; corr. mem. Schiller Acad., Munich. Founder and dir. Byrdcliffe Afternoons, Woodstock, N.Y. Author: Crux Aetatis and Other Poems, 1904; Hero and Leander, a Poetic Tragedy in Five Acts, 1908; Judith, a Poetic Tragedy in Five Acts, 1910; Poems and Songs, 1914; Studies in the Mind of Romanticism, 1918-19; The Fundamental Ideas in Herder's Thought, 1920-26; The Cultural Environment of the Philosophy of Kant; Herder's Psychology; Goethe as a Lyrical Poet (in Goethe Centenary Papers), 1932; Academic Illusions in the Field of Letters and the Arts, 1933; Toward a Modern Humanism, 1934; An Approach to an Understanding of Art, 1938; Johann Gottfried Herder: His Significance in the History of Thought, 1944; Considerations of Principles and Aims of general Education, 1946; lit. essays and studies for mags., reviews and books of reference. Editor: Grillparzer's Des Meeres und der Liebe Wellen, with an essay on the dramatic art of Grillparzer, 2d edit., 1915; Goethe's Poems, with an essay on Goethe's poetic art and view of life, 1917; Goethe Centenary Papers, 1932; Deutsches Dichten in Amerika (a quar. of German-Am. poetry); Byrdcliffe Afternoons (2 vols. containing the lectures delivered at the Byrdcliffe Afternoons, Woodstock, N.Y.), 1938, 39. Home: Woodstock, N.Y. Died July 19, 1950; buried Woodstock.

SCHUYLER, Daniel J., lawyer; b. Chicago, September 28, 1873; son Daniel J. and Mary (Byford) S.; student Harvard Prep. Sch.; LL.B., Northwestern, 1896; m. Sybil Moorhouse, Feb. 27, 1906; children—William Moorhouse, Daniel Merrick. Admitted to Ill. bar, 1896; mem. firm Schuyler, Richert & Stough and predecessors. Mem. Am., Ill. and Chicago bar assns., Phi Delta Phi. Republican. Clubs: Union League, University (Chicago); Oconomowoc Golf. Home: 1500 Lake Shore Dr., Chicago 10. Office: 100 Monroe St., Chgo. 3. Died Nov. 11, 1952; buried Oakwoods Cemetery, Chgo.

SCHUYLER, Montgomery, diplomatic service, retired; b. Stamford, Conn., Sept. 2, 1877; s. Montgomery and Katherine Beeckman (Livingston) S.; A.B., Columbia, 1899, A.M., 1900; univ. scholar in Indo-Iranian langs., Columbia U., 1899-1900, univ. fellow, 1900-02; m. Edith Lawver, Aug. 22, 1906. Second sec. Am. Embassy at St. Petersburg, Russia, 1902-04; sec. legation and consul-gen. at Bangkok, Siam, 1904, chargé d'affaires, 1905; chargé d'affaires to Roumania and Servia, Sept. 1906-May 1907; 1st sec. and chargé d'affaires Am. Embassy at St. Petersburg, 1907-09; at Tokyo, Japan, 1909-11, at Mexico City, Mex., 1911-13; E.E. and M.P. to Ecuador, March 1913; spl. agt. of U.S. to Russia, 1914-15; apptd. chief of Russian div. Dept. of State, April 1921; E.E. and M.P. to Salvador, 1921-Dec. 1925. Partner Schuyler, Earl & Co., members N.Y. Stock Exchange, 1926-31; pres. Roosevelt & Schuyler Co., Ltd.; pres., chmn. exec. com. Nat. Bank of Yorkville, N.Y. City, 1934——; v.p. Century Bank; dir. various banks and corps. Trustee Am.-Scenic and Historic Preservation Soc. Commd. capt. U.S. Army, 1918; service in Ordnance Dept., trench warfare, May 1918; duty Intelligence Div., Gen. Staff, July 1918; chief intelligence officer of A.E.F. at Omsk, Siberia, Oct. 1918-May 1919; hon. disch., Aug. 26, 1919; commd. maj. R.C., Dec. 1919. Col., chief of staff, N.Y. City Patrol Corps, 1942-45. Mem. Am. Oriental Soc., Am. Soc. Inetrnat. Law, Siam Soc., Mayflower Soc., Descendants of Colonial Governors (v.p.), Huguenot Soc., Order of Colonial Lords of Manors (pres.), Mil. Order World Wars, Am. Immigration Soc., Grange, Nat. Trust, Bill of Rights Soc. Clubs: Century, India House (New York). Episcopalian. Author: Index Verborum of the Fragments of the Avesta, 1901; Bibliography of the Sanskrit Drama, 1906; also many articles on Oriental and lit. subjects and colonial history in periodicals. Home: 192 E. 75th St., N.Y.C. 21. Died Nov. 1, 1955; buried Greenwood Cemetery, Bklyn.

SCHWAB, Harvey A., architect; b. New Philadelphia, O., Apr. 4, 1887; s. Jacob and Sophia (Fegthling) S.; B.S. in Architecture, U. Pa., 1908; student Ecole des Beaux Arts, Am. Acad. in Rome; m. Helen Ruth Eshelman, June 18, 1921; children—Charles Richard, Robert Harvey. Stewardson traveling fellowship, 1909-10; instr. U. Pa., 1910; asst. prof. Carnegie Inst. Tech. 1911-13; practice of architecture 1913—. Mem. bd. Pitts. Concert Soc., Bach Choir of Pitts. Fellow A.I.A. (vice chmn. com. on practice 1953); mem. Sigma Xi. Republican. Episcopalian. Home: 732 Hill Av., Pitts. 21. Office: Century Bldg., Pitts. 22. Died Jan. 12, 1956; buried William Penn Meml. Cemetery.

SCHWABACHER, James Herbert, business exec.; b. San Francisco, Dec. 13, 1881; s. Ludwig and Carrie (Fleishhacher) S.; m. Sophie Dinkelspiel, Oct. 16, 1917; children—James Herbert, Marie Louise. Partner Schwabacher & Co., San Francisco; pres. Schwabacher-Frey Company; member board of dirs., Roos Bros., Inc., Spring Canyon Coal Co., Standard Coal, Inc., Royal Coal Co. Home: 2520 Pacific Av. Office: 735 Market St., San Francisco. Died Dec. 21, 1958.

SCHWABE, George Blaine, congressman; b. Arthur, Mo., July 26, 1886; s. George Washington and Emily Ellen (Mose) S.; LL.B., U. of Mo., 1910; m. Jeannette Eadie Simpson, June 10, 1914 (died 1939); children—George Blaine, Robert Vernon, John Leonard, Emily Jeannette, William Henry; m. 2d, Barbara Yirsa McFarland, July 23, 1943. Admitted to Mo. bar, 1910, Okla. bar, 1911 and since engaged in practice of law, Nowata and Tulsa, Okla; served as mayor, city atty. and member bd. edn. of Nowata, 8 yrs.; mem. Okla. State Legislature, 2 terms, speaker Ho. Reps., 1 term; mem. 79th-82d Congresses (1945-53) 1st Okla. Dist. Home: 1547 N. Denver St. Office: Hunt Bldg., Tulsa. Died Apr. 2, 1952; buried Tulsa.

SCHWAMM, Harvey, banker; b. N.Y.C., Oct. 26, 1904; s. Moritz and Dora (Eckstein) S.; m. Lillian Tverskoi, Mar. 14, 1924; children—Jay Marc, Judith Dawn. Real estate broker, operator, 1919-30; sr. partner H.L. Schwamm & Co., underwriters, distbrs. state and municipal bonds, 1930-42; pres., chmn. bd. Nat. Bronx Bank, N.Y.C., 1944-50; pres. Am. Trust Co., N.Y.C., 1950-54, chairman of the board of directors, 1957—. Director of Bronx Board Trade. Mem. nat. adv. com. U.S. Senate Banking and Currency Com. Served as maj. U.S. Army, 1942-44. Recipient Knights of Pythias Marc Antony ann. award, 1941. Mem. internat. (U.S. council), U.S., N.Y., U.S.-Mexican (dir., mem. exec. com.) C.'s of C., Nat. Fgn. Trade Council, Bankers Assn. Fgn. Trade, Am. Bankers Assn., Pan Am. Soc. U.S., Consular Law Soc. (hon. fellow; U.S.-Mexico Good Neighbor Policy award 1953), Bronx Soc. Prevention Cruelty to Children (trustee). Republican (exec. com. N.Y. County 1940-42; del. Rep. Conv. State N.Y. 1951; presdl. elector N.Y. 1952, 56). Mason. Clubs: Lotos, National Republican, Manhattan, Economic, Bankers, Saints and Sinners (N.Y.C.). Home: 4650 Fieldston Rd., Riverdale 63, N.Y. Office: 70 Wall St., N.Y.C. 5. Died Aug. 15, 1958.

SCHWARTZ, Hans Jorgen, physician; b. Quebec, Can., May 28, 1876; s. Wilhelm Anton and Alette (Norregaard) S.; M.D., McGill U., 1898; m. Margaret Kilgour, Apr. 30, 1906; children—Margaret Evelyn, Alette, Marie, Jean Else. Mem. faculty Cornell Med. Sch., 1907—, clin. instr., prof. dermatology, 1920-41, prof. emeritus 1941—; specialist dermatology N.Y. Hosp., 1924-32, attending physician, 1932-41; cons. dermatologist 1941—; cons. dermatologist Meml. Hosp. for Cancer and Allied Diseases, 1921-35, N.Y. Eye and Ear Infirmary 1922—, Booth Meml. Hosp., Reconstruction Unit Post-Grad. Hosp. Diplomate Am. Bd. Dermatology and Syphilis; fellow N.Y. Acad. Medicine; mem. N.Y. State and County med. socs., A.M.A., Am. Dermatol. Assn., N.Y. Dermatol. Soc. Rep. Episcopalian. Contbr. articles on dermatology to med. jours. Home: Shelton Hotel, 49th and Lexinston, N.Y.C. 17. Deceased.

SCHWARTZ, Herbert J., business exec.; b. New Orleans, 1887. Pres., dir. City Stores Mercantile Co., N.Y.C., City Stores Co.; chmn., dir. Maison Blanche, New Orleans; chmn. exec. com., dir. B. Lowenstein & Bros., Memphis, Loveman, Joseph & Loeb, Birmingham, Richard Store, Miami, Kaufman Straus Co., Louisville, Franklin Simon, N.Y.C., Oppenheim Collins, N.Y.C.; dir. Am. Broadcasting-Paramount Theatres, Bankers Security Co., Phila., Hearn Dept. Store, N.Y.C., Swern & Co., WSMB Broadcasting Sta., New Orleans, Hoving Corp. Home: Hotel Roosevelt, New Orleans. Office: 132 W. 31st St., N.Y.C. Died Apr. 11, 1955; buried Metairie Cemetery, New Orleans.

SCHWARZ, Frank Henry, mural painter; b. N.Y.C., June 21, 1894; s. Franz Heinrich and Gertrude (Esser) S.; student Art Inst. Chgo., 1908-18; fellow Am. Acad., Rome, Italy, 1921-24; m. Lilian Prentiss, July 2, 1926 (dec. 1935); children—Cornelia Mary, Henrietta Prentiss; m. 2d, Evelyn van der Veer, 1937; 1 son, Allen van der Veer. Designer, comml. artist, student teacher in Art Inst. Chicago, 1907-18; mural painter N.Y.C., 1925-26; Guggenheim fellow, 1926-27; teacher, Columbia, 1928-31. Represented by murals in the rotunda, friezes in the Senate and House of Reps. Chambers and mural in the Senate Chamber, Ore. State Capitol Bldg.; Pioneer Monument, Harrodsburg, Ky., also in Brooklyn Museum and U. of Neb.; triptych, altar, Little Chapel, Lake Joanna, Minn.; reredos, altar, Stations of the Cross, Ch. of the Ascension, Montreal; reredos, altar, S.S. Timothy-Matthew, New York; triptych, altar, Ch. of the Ascension, Seattle; altar, St. Joseph's Ch., West Orange, N.J.; murals in Domestic Relations and Juvenile courts, Phila. Awarded Prix di Rome, 1921; Isidor black and white prize Salmagundi Club. Served as sgt. Ordnance Research Camouflage Corps, 1918-19. Asso. Nat. Academician, 1934; fellow Royal Soc. Arts (London); mem. Nat. Arts Club, Alumni Assn. of Am. Acad. in Rome. Democrat. Address: 221 E. 50th St., N.Y.C. Died Sept. 5, 1951.*

SCHWARZ, Otto Henry, obstetrician, gynecologist; b. St. Louis, June 15, 1888; s. Henry and Laura (Forster) S.; student Yale, 1906-08; M.D., Washington U., 1913; m. Vivian Rowe, June 17, 1916; children—Henry, Thomas Rowe, Otto Edward, Robert, Vivian Rowe. Intern and resident physician Barnes and Washington U. hosps., 1913-15; asso. and asso. prof. of obstetrics Washington U., 1921-26, prof. obstetrics, 1927-28, prof. obstetrics and gynecology, 1929-40, prof. clinical obstetrics and gynecology, 1940-49, full times prof., 1949—; gynecologist in chief and obstetrician in chief St. Louis Maternity and Barnes hosps., 1929-40. Mem. A.M.A., Am. Gynecol. Soc., Am. Assn. of Obstet., Gynecol. and Abdominal Surgeons, Nu Sigma Nu, Sigma Xi, Alpha Omega Alpha. Roman Catholic. Contbr. to med. mags. Home: 4915 Lindell Blvd. Office: 630 S. Kingshighway, St. Louis. Died Aug. 19, 1950.

SCHWARZSCHILD, William Harry (shwärs'-shild), corp. official; b. Richmond, Va., May 17, 1879; s. Harry and Bella (Nelson) S.; ed. pub. schs.; m. Rosalie Held, Mar. 12, 1902; children—William Harry, Louise Mae (Mrs. Leon I. Gubin), Richard I., Rosalie Belle. Began as jewelry merchant, 1907; organized Schwarzschild Bros., Inc., now pres. and treas. same; organized Central Nat. Bank with associates, 1911, pres. and dir., now chmn. bd.; dir. Lakeside Holding Corp., Richmond Hotels, Inc.; mem. bd. dirs. Va. Elec. & Power Co.; dir. and v.p. Hebrew Cemetery Bd.; past pres. Richmond Clearing House Assn.; mem. bd. visitors Med. Coll. of Va.; mem. bd. dirs. and exec. com. Retail Merchants Assn. of Richmond; dir. Hebrew Home for Aged and Infirm of Richmond; treas. and dir. Richmond Chpt., Va. Assn. of Workers for the Blind, Inc.; treas. Democratic State Central Com., 1924-50; mem. sponsoring com. United Service Orgns.; mem. bd. Am. Jewish Joint Distbn. Com., Richmond Port Commn.; mem. hon. bd. govs. Nat. Conf. Christians and Jews, 1947; mem. bd. trustees Ladies Hebrew Benevolent Assn., Richmond Area Community Chest; past treasurer Virginia Society (Richmond chapter) for Crippled Children and Adults; member advertising committee Richmond Committee for Econ. Development; mem. Nat. Council Hebrew Union Coll. since 1945; mem. nat. com. Jewish Statistical Bur. since 1945; mem. Richmond Round Table Conf. of Christians and Jews, Am. Arbitration Assn., Coop. Edn. Assn. (state adv. council), Mental Hygiene Soc. of Va., Am. Jewish Com., Richmond C. of C., Am. Planning and Civic Assn., Nat. Conf. of Investors. Democrat. Jewish religion. Clubs: Jefferson-Lakeside, Automobile of Va. (hon. mem.). Home: 2710 Monument Av. Office: Central Nat. Bank, 3d and Broad Sts., Richmond 15, Va. Died June 8, 1952; buried Hebrew Cemetery, Richmond, Va.

SCHWEDTMAN F(erdinand) Charles (shwĕt'-măn)), elec. engr.; b. Hanover, Germany, May 13, 1867; s. William and Bertha (Vanderwald) S.; came to U.S., 1882; ed. Hanover and New York; m. Cora H. Gehner, Jan. 18, 1904. Chief engr. Mo. Electric Light & Power Co., 1889-99; founder and gen. mgr., 1891-1904, Wagner Electric Mfg. Co.; v.p. Racine-Sattley Co., Springfield, Ill., 1912-15; industrial expert Nat. City Bank of New York since 1915, v.p. since 1917; chmn. exec. com. Nat. City Foundation since 1932; special partner Baker, Weeks & Harden since 1931. Apptd. commercial and industrial adviser to the Chinese Rep. by the Minister of Agr. and Commerce; apptd. by Pres. Taft, mem. Commn. on Industrial Relations, Dec. 17, 1912. Decorated by the King of Sweden as Comdr. of Vasa, 1922, and by President of Finland as Comdr. White Rose, 1925. Clubs: Union League, India House (New York). Home: Hotel Pierre. Office: 1 Wall St., N.Y.C. Died Feb. 2, 1952; buried St. Louis.

SCHWEGLER, Raymond Alfred (shwăg'lẽr), educator; b. Hergiswyl, Switzerland, Dec. 4, 1874; s. Joseph and Frances (Meyer) S.; A.B., Brown U., 1899; A.M., Ottawa U., 1906; student Leipzig U., 1911-12; Ph.D., Columbia U., 1928; m. Eula Leigh Dunn, July 3, 1906; 1 son, Raymond Allen. Instr. in Hebrew, Brown U., 1898-99; prof. Latin and Greek, Indian U., Bacone, Ind. Ty., 1899-1901; prof. Greek and edn., Ottawa U., 1901-07, acting pres., 1905-06; ordained ministry Bapt. Ch., 1903; asso. prof. edn., U. of Kan., 1907-14, prof. since 1914, acting dean Sch. of Edn., 1923-27, dean, 1927-41, dean emeritus since 1941, dir. summer session, 1923-1941. Fellow A.A.A.S.; mem. N.E.A. (life), Nat. Soc. for Study of Edn., Soc. Coll. Teachers Edn., Phi Beta Kappa, Phi Delta Kappa, Acacia. Republican. Mason (33°, K.T.). Clubs: University, Kan. School Masters, Rotary; Lawrence Knife and Fork. Author: A Teachers' Manual for the Use of the Binet-Simon Scale of Intelligence, 1914; A Study of Introvert-Extrovert Responses to Certain Test Situations, 1929. Lecturer on psychology and edn. Condr. Personality Clinic. Home: 805 Missouri St., Lawrence, Kan. Died Oct. 17, 1952; buried Lawrence.

SCHWEIZER, Albert Charles, coll. adminstr., city planner; b. N.Y.C., Jan. 28, 1900; s. Albert Conrad and Charlotta Gaudineer (McTerney) S.; B.S., City Coll. N.Y., 1920; B.S. in Architecture, Mass. Inst. Tech., 1923, M. Architecture, 1924; grad. studies, Columbia, N.Y. U.; studied housing and planning in Europe, 1926; m. Jean Ford, Feb. 11, 1928; children—June Joyce, Ann Gaudineer. Engring. draftsman, 1920; archtl. designer in N.Y. and Boston, 1923-29; instr. architecture Mass. Inst. Tech., 1923-25; successively instr., prof. and dir. Sch. Architecture and Allied Arts, N.Y.U., 1927-43; practice as registered architect, New York, 1929-43; principal planning technician Nat. Resources Planning Bd., 1942-43; planning cons. CAA, 1943. Served from capt. to maj. Mil. Govt. European Civil Affairs Div. Army, 1943-45; dir. Civil Adminstrn. Div. for Office Mil. Govt. for Bavaria, in charge govt. and polit. affairs, 1946-49. Vice chmn. Post War Reconstruction Com., A.I.A. Mem. Am. Soc. Planning Ofcls., Am. Inst. Planners, Archtl. League of N.Y., Delta Alpha. Club: Lotos. Co-author: You Can Design, 1939; Action for Cities, 1943. Home: 390 W. End Av., N.Y.C. Died Oct. 10, 1949.

SCHWELLENBACH, Edgar Ward, judge; b. Frederick, S.D., Mar. 16, 1887; s. Frank W. and Martha (Baxter) S.; Grad. law school, spl. student U. of Wis., 1924; m. Ethel Hoagland, June 15, 1918; children—Baxter Ward, Martha. Admitted to Wis. Bar, 1924, to Wash. State Bar, 1925, and practiced in Seattle, Wash., 1925-26; city atty. Ephrata, Wash., 1927-35; prosecuting atty. Grant Co., Wash., 1931-39; judge of Superior Ct., Douglas and Grant cos., Wash., 1939-46; judge Supreme Ct., State of Wash., since 1946, chief justice, 1951, 1952. Mem. Washington and American bar associations, American Legion, 40 and 8, Phi Delta Phi. Episcopalian. Mason. Home: 504 E. 17th St. Office: Temple of Justice, Olympia, Wash. Died Sept. 22, 1957.

SCHWENTKER, Francis Frederic, prof. pediatrics; b. Schenectady, N.Y., Feb. 13, 1904; s. Frederic Ferdinand and Marie Rose (Bildhauser) S.; B.S., Union Coll., Schenectady, N.Y., 1925, D.Sc.; M.D., Johns Hopkins Medical Sch., Balt., 1929; m. Madalyn Elphic Crockett, July 2, 1932; children—Frederic Noel, Ann Cole, Edwards Park. Interne pediatrics, Johns Hopkins Hosp., 1929-30; asst. resident pediatrician, 1930-31, resident pediatrician, 1934-35, prof. pediatrics, 1946—, pediatrician-in-chief, 1946—; asst. Rockefeller Inst. for Med. Research, 1931-34; resident physician Sydenham Hosp., Baltimore, 1935-36, asso. dir.; dir. med. research, Baltimore City Health Dept., 1936-38; staff mem. Internat. Health Div., Rockefeller Found., 1938-46. Mem. Rockefeller Health Commn. to Europe, 1940. Cons. to sec. of War on epidemic diseases, 1940-42; now consultant in pediatrics U.S. Navy. Served as med. officer, U.S. Naval Res., 1942-46. Mem. Am. Bd. of Pediatrics, Am. Acad. of Pediatrics, Soc. for Pediatric Research, Am. Pediatric Soc., Society Am. Bacteriologists, Interurban Clin. Soc., Assn. Am. Physicians, Sigma Xi, Alpha Kappa Kappa. Author about 36 articles in med. literature. Home: 209 Tunbridge Rd., Baltimore 12. Office: Johns Hopkins Hosp., North Broadway, Balt. 5. Died Nov. 8, 1954.

SCISM, Don (sĭz'm), newspaper editor; b. Bloomfield, Mo., Sept. 1, 1893; s. William Luther and Bertha (Reed) S.; grad. high sch., Bloomfield; grad. S.E. Mo. State Teachers Coll., Cape Girardeau, Mo.; m. Opal Osman, July 17, 1922 (dec. 1954); children—Ruth Elizabeth, Robert Bruce, Nancy Jane. Prin. ward sch., South St. Louis, Mo., 1915-17; reporter Evansville (Ind.) Courier, 1920-22, city editor, 1922-24, editor, 1924—. Pres. Boehne Hosp.; former mem.

Ind. Flood Control Commn. Served as pvt. U.S. Army in Co. M, 138th Inf., 35th Div., in France, World War. Mason (32°). Member Am. Soc. Newspaper Editors, Ind. Asso Press (past pres.). Club: Evansville Country. Home: 512 S. Weinbach Av. Address: Evansville Courier, Evansville, Ind. Died Mar. 2, 1954; buried Oak Hill Cemetery, Evansville.

SCLATER, John Robert Paterson, clergyman; b. Manchester, Eng., Apr. 9, 1876; s. Rev. John and Ellen Gentle (Paterson) S.; student Owens Coll., Manchester, Eng., 1893-95; B.A., Emmanuel Coll., Cambridge U., 1898; M.A., 1900; student Westminster Theol. Coll., 1900-02; D.D., St. Andrews U. (Scotland), 1917, Queen's U. (Can.), 1934, Victoria U. (Can.), 1942; LL.D., U. of Toronto (Can.), 1944; m. Nora Christian Turnbull, July 19, 1904; children—John Arthur Cecil, Gilbert Turnbull (dec.), Mary Lindsay. Moved to Can., 1923. Ordained to ministry Presbyn. Ch. of Eng., 1902; pastor, Greenhill Presbyn. Ch., Derby, Eng., 1902-07, New North Ch. (Church of Scotland), Edinburgh, Scotland, 1907-23, Parkdale Presbyn. Ch., Toronto, Can., 1923-24, Old St. Andrew's United Ch., Toronto, 1924—; Warrack lectr. Scottish Theol. Colls., 1922; Lyman Beecher lectr. Yale, 1928; Dudleian lectr. Harvard, 1937. Moderator United Church of Can., 1942-44, chmn. commn. on reunion of churches, 1942—. Served as chaplain, 9th Bn. (Highlanders), Royal Scots (Great Britain), 1909-23; served on Forth Defenses, 1915; with YMCA, France, 1916-17; twice mentioned by War Office, Governor, St. Andrew's Coll. (Ont.); regent, Victoria U. (Toronto). Pres. Cambridge Univ. Union, 1899. Clubs: Arts and Letters, York (Toronto). Author: The Sons of Strength, 1909; The Enterprise of Life, 1910; John Cairns—A Biography, 1912; The Eve of Battle, 1914; God and the Soldier (with Dr. Norman Maclean), 1919; Modernist Foundamentalism, 1926; The Public Worship of God, 1928; commentary on Psalms 1 to 41 for Interpreter's Bible. Home: 23 Elm Av., Toronto 5. Office: Old St. Andrew's Church, Toronto, Can. Died Aug. 24, 1949; buried Grange Cemetery, Edinburgh, Scotland.

SCOGGINS, Charles Elbert, writer; b. Mazatlan, Sinaloa, Mexico, Mar. 17, 1888 (parents Am. citizens); s. Jefferson Davis and Catharine Josephine Minerva (Grant) S.; grad. high sch., Denton, Tex.; student engring. U. of Tex., 1905-07; m. Lois Lovett Durham, Dec. 26, 1913; 1 dau., Nancy Josephine. On revision of location S.P.R.R. in Mexico, 1907; constrn. Mexican Central R.R., 1908, Colima Lumber Co., railroad and dam of Mexican Light & Power Co., 1909; engaged as machinery salesman in Mexico, 1909-12; saw salesman in Mexico and C.A., also Ga., Fla. and Cuba, 1912-20; novelist and story writer, 1920—, specializing in life of Americans in Latin countries. Dir. of 1st Nat. Bank of Boulder. Mem. Authors League America, Phi Gamma Delta. Protestant. Clubs: Cactus, Denver Country, Town and Gown. Author: The Proud Old Name, 1925; The Red Gods Call, 1926; White Fox, 1928; John Quixote, 1929; The Walking Stick, 1930; The House of Darkness, 1931; Flame, 1931; Tycoon, 1932; The House of Dawn, 1934; Pampa Joe, 1935; Lost Road, 1941; The Strangers, 1945. Address: Sea Horse Hill, Boulder, Colo. Died Dec. 6, 1955.

SCOTT, Charles L., ret. army officer; b. Oct. 22, 1883; B.S., U.S. Mil. Acad., 1905; grad. Mounted Service Sch., 1912, Command and Gen. Staff Sch., 1929, Army War Coll., 1933; married; 1 son, Dean Robert. Commd. 2d lt., June 13, 1905; promoted through grades to maj. gen. (temp.), Oct. 1, 1940; served as lt. col. Quartermaster Corps, 1918-20; mem. Gen. Staff Corps, 1939-40; comdg. 2d Armored Div., July-Nov. 1940, 1st Armored Corps, 1940-42, sr. U.S. mil. observer in Middle East, Mar.-Aug. 1943; comdg. Armored Force Replacement Training Center, 1943-45. Decorated D.S.M. (U.S.); Hon. Comdr., Most Excellent Order Brit. Empire. Address: 4000 Massachusetts Av., Washington. Died Nov. 27, 1954; buried Arlington Nat. Cemetery.

SCOTT, D. R., univ. prof.; b. Monticello, Mo., Oct. 24, 1887; s. David Roland and Eliza (Shanks) S.; A.B., B.S. in journalism, U. Mo., 1910; Ph.D., Harvard, 1930; m. Carrie Lind Pancoast, Apr. 28, 1920; 1 son, Wallace Pancoast. Newspaper work with Detroit Times, 1912-14; instr. U. Mo., 1914-17; asst. prof., 1917-19, asso. prof., 1919-20, prof. 1920—. Served as statistician, U.S. Army, Sta. Br., Gen. Staff, 1918-19, Hdqrs. S.O.S., Tours, France. Mem. Am. Econ. Assn., Am. Accounting Assn., Am. Assn. Univ. Profs., Kappa Tau Alpha, Beta Gamma Sigma, Alpha Pi Zeta, Alpha Kappa Psi. Democrat. Clubs: Dunbar (Harvard); University (Columbia). Author: Theory of Accounts, Vol. I, 1925; The Cultural Significance of Accounts, 1931; articles in professional pubs. Home: 301 Edgewood Av., Columbia, Mo. Died Feb. 8, 1954; buried Valhalla Mausoleum, St. Louis.

SCOTT, Donnell Everett, hosiery mfr.; b. Graham, N.C., Mar. 3, 1887; s. John Levi and Fannie Logan (Brady) S.; B.S., Davidson Coll., 1907; m. Margie Norwood Gray, Oct. 7, 1916; children—Jean Gray, Donnell Everett. Cotton goods mfr., Graham, N.C., 1907-29; hosiery mfr., Graham, N.C., 1929—; pres. Scott Hosiery Mills, Inc.; dir. Nat. Bank of Almance. Mem. Nat. Guard of N.C. 1904—, beginning as private; commd. 2d lt., 1906, and advanced through the grades to brig. gen., 1927; comdg. 60th Brig.; inducted into Fed. service, 1940; served as maj., lt. col. and col., 120th Inf., U.S. Army, World War; with A.E.F., 1918-19; awarded Silver Star for bravery. Mem. Kappa Alpha. Presbyn. (deacon). Address: Graham, N.C. Died Feb. 10, 1955.

SCOTT, Elmer, former exec. sec. Dallas Civic Fedn.; b. Jefferson County, O., Apr. 13, 1866; s. Wesley and Nancy (Welday) S.; ed. Ohio Wesleyan U., Delaware, O., 1885-89; LL.D. (honorary), Southern Methodist U., 1948; married Anna Coble, Sept. 1893; 1 dau., Helen Elizabeth. In employ Sears, Roebuck & Co., Chicago and Dallas, Tex., 1895-1913; with Dept. Pub. Welfare Dallas, 1915-17; organized Dallas Civic Fedn., exec. sec., 1917-51; hon. cons. Dallas Council on World Affairs, 1951—. Dir. Bradford Memorial Hosp., Community Guidance Clinic; mem. Dallas Symphony Orchestra; mem. Adult Edn. Assn. U.S., Am. Acad. Polit. and Social Sci., Fgn. Policy Assn., Nat. Com. for Mental Hygiene, Nat. Edn. Assn., Tex. Soc. for Mental Hygiene, Nat. Conf. of Social Work, Tex. Social Welfare Assn. (ex-pres.), Southwestern Social Science Assn. (ex-pres.), Dallas Lyric Theatre, Dallas Council of Social Agencies, Dallas Historical Soc., Tex. Philos. Soc., Delta Tau Delta (Distinguished Service Chapter). Address: 2419 Maple Av., Dallas 4. Died Apr. 20, 1954; buried Hillcrest Mausoleum, Dallas.

SCOTT, Emmett Jay, author; b. Houston, Tex., Feb. 13, 1873; s. Horace L. and Emma (Kyle) S.; M.A., Wiley U., Marshall, Tex., 1901; LL.D., Wiley U. and Wilberforce U., Ohio, 1918; m. Eleonore J. Baker, Apr. 14, 1897; children—Emmett Jay, Mrs. Evelyn Payne, Mrs. Clarissa Mae Delany (dec.), Lenora Kyle, Horace Clifford. Connected with the Houston Daily Post, 1891-94; editor Texas Freeman (Negro), 1894-97; became sec. Booker T. Washington, 1897; sec. Tuskegee Inst., 1912-19; sec.-treas. Howard University, 1919-32, sec., 1933-38; now cons. in public relations, Washington, D.C. Sec. Nat. Negro Bus. League, 1900-1922; mem. Am. Commn. to Liberia, 1909; sec. Internat. Conf. on the Negro, 1912. Spl. asst. to Sec. of War to advise in matters affecting Negro soldiers, 1917-19. Mem. National Council Y.M.C.A.; mem. Nat. Conf. on Colored Y.M.C.A. Work, and of Interstate Com. Y.M.C.A. of Md., Del. and D.C. Mem. Rep. State Com. for D.C. Mem. Bd. of Indeterminate Sentence and Parole, 1932—. Author: (with Booker T. Washington) Tuskegee and Its People, 1910; (with Lyman Beecher Stowe) Booker T. Washington, Builder of a Civilization, 1916; The American Negro in the World War, 1919; Negro Migration During the War (monograph study for Carnegie Endowment for Internat. Peace), 1920. Club: Mo-So-Lit. Address: 609 F St., N.W., Washington, D.C. Died Dec. 12, 1957.

SCOTT, Ernest Findlay, prof. theology; b. Towlaw, County Durham, Eng., Mar. 18, 1868; s. Ernest and Elizabeth (Couttie) S.; M.A., Glasgow U., 1888; B.A., Balliol Coll. (Oxford U.), 1892; studied U.P. Theol. Hall, Edinburgh; D.D., St. Andrews U., 1909, Amherst College, 1939; LL.D., Queen's U., Kingston, Ont., Can., 1920; m. Annie Roxburgh Dunlop, Apr. 29, 1902; 1 dau., Nora Elizabeth. Minister Prestwick United Free Ch., Scotland, 1895-1908; prof. N.T. lit., Queen's U., Kingston, Can., 1908-19; prof. N. T. lit. Union Theological Seminary, New York City, 1919-38, professor emeritus, 1954—. Author: The Fourth Gospel, 1906; The Apologetic of the New Testament, 1907; The Kingdom and the Messiah, 1911; The Religious and Historical Value of the Fourth Gospel, 1911; The Beginning of the Church, 1914; The New Testament Today, 1921; The Epistle to Hebrews, 1922; The Spirit in the New Testament, 1923; The Ethical Teachings of Jesus, 1924; The First Age of Christianity, 1925; The Gospel and Its Tributaries, 1928; The Epistle to Ephesians, 1930; The Kingdom of God, 1931; The Literature of the New Testament, 1933; The Validity of the Gospel Record, 1937; The Nature of the Early Church, 1941; The Varieties of New Testament Religion, 1943; Man and Society in the New Testament, 1946; The Lord's Prayer, 1951; The Crisis in the Life of Jesus, 1952; I Believe in the Holy Spirit, 1958. Address: 445 Riverside Dr., N.Y.C. Died July 21, 1954.

SCOTT, Fitzhugh, architect; b. Milw., Nov. 9, 1881; s. Frederick Meyer and Mary Evelyn (Caswell) S.; B.S. in Architecture, Columbia, 1905; m. Elise Marshall Landrum, Dec. 9, 1908; children—Fitzhugh, William F., Elise (Mrs. Robert Swansen). Works include Blatz Temple of Music, Milw., Milw. Childrens Hosp., Allen-Bradley Co. plants in Milw. and Galt Can., YMCA's in Milw. and Racine, Milw. Country Day Sch. Served as capt. Q.M.C., U.S. Army, World War I. Fellow A.I.A. Home: 7800 N. River Rd., Milw. 17. Office: 5623 N. Lake Dr., Milw. 17. Died Oct. 12, 1957.

SCOTT, Frederick Hossack, dry goods merchant; b. Ottawa, Ill., Apr. 10, 1879; s. John Edwin and Harriet Emma (Hossack) S.; B.S., Princeton, 1900; m. Helen C. Webster, Dec. 2, 1902; children—Virginia (dec.), Emily S. Hubbard (dec.), Isabel L. (Mrs. Charles C. Fitzmorris, Jr.), Frederick H., Edward W. (dec.). In retail dry goods bus., Ottawa, 1900-01; with Carson, Pirie, Scott & Co., pres. 1939-46, chmn. bd., 1946-52, formerly chmn. finance com.; dir. Quaker Oats Co. Served as treas. Nat. War Work Council of Nat. Y.M.C.A. for Central Army Dept., World War, also chmn. Personnel Com. of same region. Mem. Ill. State Assn. Y.M.C.A. many yrs. (pres. 1917-20), Chgo. Assn. Commerce (v.p. 1916, 27). Pres. Wholesale Dry Goods Inst., 1933-34; served as chmn. of Code Authority of Wholesale Dry Goods Trade. Alumni trustee Princeton, 1927-31; one of original dirs. North Shore Country Day Sch.; pres. Indsl. Club, 1926. Republican. Conglist. Clubs: Commercial (sec. 1931-33), University, Princeton (Chgo.) (twice pres.), Casino, Nassau (Princeton N.J.). Home: 175 Sheridan Rd., Hubbard Woods, Ill. ffice: One S. State St., Chgo. 3. Died Mar. 14, 1958; buried Rosehill Cemetery, Chgo.

SCOTT, Garfield, lawyer; b. Phila., Pa., Sept. 25, 1881; s. William Henry and Martha Jane (Parr) S.; student Germantown (Pa.) Acad., 1889-99; A.B., Princeton, 1903; LL.B., U. Pa., 1906; m. Grace Louise Nevin, Aug. 13, 1925; children—Hugh Nevin, Donald Allison. Admitted to Pa. bar, 1906, and in gen. practice at Phila., 1906-14; legal dept. United Gas Improvement Co., Phila., 1914, gen. counsel 1922—. Republican. Presbyn. Clubs: Union League, Midday, Phila. Cricket. Home: 403 Gate Lane, Phila. 19. Office: 1401 Arch St., Phila. 5. Died June 17, 1955.

SCOTT, Jack Garrett, lawyer; born at Oberlin, Kansas, September 28, 1895; s. Tully and Harriet Isabel (Hunter) S.; A.B., U. Colo., 1917; LL.B., U. Denver, 1921; m. Emma Moore, Dec. 27, 1921; 1 son, Tully. Admitted to Colo. bar, 1921, practiced in Colo., 1921-33; asso. counsel, acting gen. counsel N.R.A., 1933-35; chief atty. Bur. Motor Carriers, I.C.C., 1935-42; gen. counsel Office Def. Transportation, 1942-44; pvt. law practice, limited to transportation law, Washington, 1944-52; under-sec. of commerce for transportation, 1952-53; chmn. transportation and storage com. O.D.M.; private law practice, 1953—. Mem. Am. Bar Assn., Am. Soc. Traffic and Transportation, Assn. I.C.C. Practitioners (gen. counsel), Nat. Assn. Motor Bus Operators. Mason. Home: 3038 P St. N.W., Washington. Office: 839 17th St. N.W., Washington 6. Died May 2, 1956; buried Arlington Nat. Cemetery.

SCOTT, John Addison, coll. pres.; b. Houston, Va., July 9, 1852; s. Rev. John Andrew (D.D.) and Mary Carter (McClelland) S.; Washington and Lee U.; A.B., Hampden-Sidney Coll., 1870; B.D., Union Theol. Sem., Va., 1874; (D.D., Hampden-Sidney, 1903); m. Lucy Payne Waddell, July 8, 1880. Ordained Presbyn. ministry, 1874; pastor chs. at Warrenton and Salem, Va., 1874-81, Hat Creek, Diamond Hill and Rustburg, 1881-89, Point Pleasant and Pleasant Flats, W.Va., 1889-93, Uniontown, Ala., 1893-98, Gainesville, Ala., 1898-1900; pres. Statesville Female Coll., N.C., 1900—. Democrat. Mem. Chi Phi. Mason, K.P. Address: Statesville, N.C. Died Nov. 3, 1950.

SCOTT, Joseph, lawyer; b. Penrith, Cumberland County, Eng., July 16, 1867; s. Joseph and Mary (Donnelly) S.; ed. Ushaw Coll., Durham, England, 1880-88; matriculated in honors London U., 1887; came to U.S., 1889; A.M., St. Bonaventure's Coll., Allegany, N.Y., 1893; Ph.D. (hon.), Santa Clara Coll., Cal., 1907; LL.D., St. Bonaventure Coll. Allegany, N.Y., 1914, Notre Dame U., 1915, Georgetown U., 1939; m. Bertha Roth, June 6, 1898. Admitted to bar, 1894, and since in practice at Los Angeles; dean emeritus of Law School, Loyola Coll., Los Angeles. Mem. Sch. Bd., 1904-15, pres. bd., 1906-11. Dir. Los Angeles C. of C., 1907-18 (pres. bd. 1910); hon. v.p. Panama P.I. Expn., San Francisco, 1915; mem. Charter Revision Com., 1902; ex-pres. Southwest Mus., 1929-30; pres. Los Angeles Community Chest, 1931-35; pres. Cal. Conf. Social Work, 1935-36; apptd. chmn. of Los Angeles County Emergency Relief Com., under fed. and state relief program, 1933; chmn. Los Angeles Boys' Week Com. 1931—; chmn. Citizens Com. for the Army and Navy, Inc.; dir. United Service Orgns., Los Angeles War Chest. Apptd. by Pres. Hoover, mem. U.S. George Washington Bicentennial Commn., 1932. Mem. Los Angeles, Calif., and Am. bar assns. Catholic. Clubs: California, Newman, Sunset (pres. 1923-24), Uplifters, Los Angeles Athletic, Pasadena Athletic. Chmn. Dist. Draft Bd., Southern Dist. of Cal., 1917-18. Spl. commr. for Knights of Columbus on duty in France and Eng., 1918. Awarded Laetare medal by U. of Notre Dame, 1918 for "conspicuous work in the cause of edn., public service and nation-wide platform campaign to eliminate religious prejudice"; gold watch from Los Angeles Realty Bd. as "Los Angeles' Most Useful Citizen in 1931"; Gaudete medal by the St. Bonaventure University, Allegany, N.Y., June 1936, as outstanding layman for that year in the field of Catholic Action in the U.S.; Vercelli Medal at annual conv. Holy Name Soc., in Boston, Oct. 1947; Am. Irish Hist. Medal, for scholarly contributions to work of Soc., 1948. One of four internat.

lay speakers at Eucharistic Congress, Chgo., 1926; one of internat. lay speakers at Eucharistic Congress, Buenos Aires, Argentine, 1934; one of the lay speakers to address Gen. Assembly Nat. Eucharistic Congress, Cleveland, Sept. 1935; only English speaking layman to address Internat. Eucharistic Congress, Manila, 1937; apptd. rep. of Am. laity and speaker at Internat. Eucharistic Congress, Budapest, 1938. Pres. Los Angeles Archdiocesan Soc. for Perpetual Adoration and formerly pres. Los Angeles Archdiocesan Union of the Holy Name Soc. Created Knight of St. Gregory by Pope Benedict, 1920, for work during World War I; Knight Commander of St. Gregory with star of Pope Pius XI. Appointed Privy Chamberlain of the Sword and Cape by Pope Pius XII. Knight of Malta, Knight of Holy Sepulchre. Home: 1119 S. Orange Grove Av., Pasadena, Cal. Office: 791 Chamber of Commerce Bldg., Los Angeles 15. Died Mar. 24, 1958.

SCOTT, Martin J., clergyman; b. N.Y.C., Oct. 16, 1865; s. Thomas E. and Margaret M. (Cooney) S.; A.B., Holy Cross Coll., 1884; A.M., Woodstock (Md.) Coll., 1899. Joined Soc. of Jesus, 1884; ordained priest R.C. Ch., 1899; prof. Latin, Holy Cross Coll., 1891-93; asst. pastor St. Ignatius Loyola Ch., New York, 1901-14; lectr. Boston Coll., 1915. Author: God and Myself, 1917; The Hand of God, 1918; Convent Life, 1919; Credentials of Christianity, 1920; You and Yours, 1921; The Boy Knight, 1921; The Divine Counsellor, 1922; For Better or Worse, 1923; Man, 1923; Mother Machree (novel); Christ or Chaos; The Virgin Birth; Evolution Kelley (novel); Religion and Common Sense, 1926; Things Catholics Are Asked About, 1927; Father Scott's Radio Talks, 1928; Christ's Own Church, 1929; Happiness, 1930; The Altar Boys of St. John's (novel), 1931; Why Catholics Believe, 1932; Religious Certainty, 1933; The Church and the World, 1934; What Is Heaven, 1936; Answer Wisely, 1938; Introduction to Catholicism, 1939; Jesus as Men Saw Him, 1940; All You Who Are Burdened, 1946. Lecturer on Apologetics, Fordham U. Address: College of St. Francis Xavier, 30 W. 16th St., N.Y.C. Died Nov. 29, 1954.

SCOTT, Norman, naval officer; b. Aug. 10, 1889; entered U.S. Navy, June 1907; advanced to rear admiral, July 1939. Awarded Navy Cross, Congressional Medal of Honor. Address: Indpls. Died Nov. 13, 1942; went down with his ship U.S.S. Atlanta at Guadacanal.

SCOTT, Oreon Earle, real estate, investment banker, lawyer; b. McClellandtown, Pa., Nov. 11, 1871; s. Clark B. and Catherine C. (Gilmore) S.; A.B., summa cum laude, Bethany (W.Va.) Coll., 1892; LL.B., U. of Michigan, 1894; LL.D., Drake University, Des Moines, Ia., 1933, Texas Christian U., 1948, Bethany Coll., 1949; honorary LL.D., Culver-Stockton, 1951; married Mabel Crabbe, July 17, 1895 (died Dec. 20, 1928); children—Margaret L. (Mrs. L. Avon Blue, Jr.), Katharine M. (Mrs. Theodore M. Wall), Mary E. (Mrs. Charles C. Skinner) (dec.). Financial agt. Bethany Coll., 1892; admitted to bar, St. Louis, 1894; bus. mgr. Christian Courier, Dallas, Tex., 1895; in business as Scott Adv. Co., Cincinnati, 1895-96; mem. firm Oreon E. & R. G. Scott, real estate, etc., St. Louis, 1896—; dir. Universal Watch Co. Trustee of Bethany College; life trustee, mem. exec. com. Drake U.; dir. St. Louis Pub. Library; v.p. Majestic Mfg. Co.; pres. St. Louis Zool. Soc., Secretary official bd. Union Avenue Christian Ch., 1904-38; pres. Lenoir Memorial Home, Christian Bd. of Publication; president Bd. of Church Extension of Disciples of Christ, 1928—; v.p. Pension Fund of Disciples of Christ; mem. exec. com. Internat. Conv. Disciples of Christ, 1940; pres. Nat. City Christian Ch., Washington; dir. and mem. exec. com. Nat. Benevolent Assn. of Christian Ch.; trustee and mem. exec. com. Internat. Council of Religious Education, 1946; pres. U. of Mich. 1894 Law Class; mem. Alumni Advisory Council of Bethany Coll., W.Va.; Alumni Advisory Council U. of Mich. Mem. bd. mgrs. Protestant World. Trustee Culver-Stockton Coll. Mem. Am. Bus. Men's Research Foundation. Member Am., Mo. State and St. Louis bar assns., Archaeol. Inst. America (executive committee St. Louis chap.), Am. Philol. Assn., Mo. Hist. Assn., St. Louis Acad. Science, Nat. Aeronautics Assn., St. Louis Humane Soc., St. Louis Real Estate Bd., St. Louis C. of C., St. Louis Chapter U. of Mich. Alumni Assn.; Am. Judicature Society, S.A.R., Newcomen Society of North America. Independent Republican. Mason (32°, K.T., Shriner). Clubs: Lawyers (Ann Arbor, Mich.); Noonday, Mo. Athletic, Scottish Rite, Advertising, Contemporary, Public Question, St. Louis Automobile, Ambassador. Mem. Christian (Disciples) Ch. Established Oreon E. Scott, Found., 1950. Home: 5211 Westminster Pl. Office: Scott Bldg., 800 Chestnut St., St. Louis. Died Jan. 9, 1956; buried Bellefontaine Cemetery, St. Louis.

SCOTT, Paul Whitten, lawyer; b. Middleport, O., Aug. 25, 1869; s. Hugh Bartlett and Anna Haddon (Whitten) S.; A.B., Marietta (O.) Coll., 1893; m. Dolores Pearl McNeill, Dec. 5, 1908; 1 dau., Anna Pauline. Admitted to W.Va. bar, 1890, and began practice at Huntington; mem. Williams & Scott, 1893-97, Williams, Scott & Lovett, 1897-1923, Scott, Graham & Wiswell, 1923-38, Scott & Ducker since Jan. 1, 1939; treas. Huntington Sand & Gravel Co., Duncan-Scott-Wiswell Co. Solicitor, Huntington, 1900-07. Mem. of Judicial Council of West Va. since 1934, present term expires 1950. Pres. Cabell County Bar Assn., 1921-22; v.p. Foster Foundation. Mem. Phi Beta Kappa, Alpha Sigma Phi. Republican. Presbyterian. Home: Hawthorne Way, Park Hills, Huntington, W.Va., and 7 Gracie Sq., N.Y. City. Office: First Nat. Bank Bldg., Huntington, W.Va. Died Dec. 28, 1950.

SCOTT, Robert Lindsay, dry goods mcht.; b. Ottawa, Ill., May 26, 1873; s. John Edwin and Harriet Emma (Hossack) S.; m. Ethel Grey, Oct. 11, 1899 (dec.); children—Margaret Grey (Mrs. J.A. Moller), Robert Lindsay. Began in dry goods business at Ottawa; removed to Evanston, 1892, and became connected with Carson, Pirie, Scott & Co., Chicago; admitted to partnership in the firm, 1907, ret. 1949. Honorary trustee University of Chicago, Baptist Theological Union; trustee First Baptist Church of Evanston; served as dir. Evanston Pub. Library, Evanston Hosp. Assn., as dir., v.p. and pres. Evanston Y.M.C.A. Republican. Baptist. Clubs: University, Quadrangle (Chicago); Glenview (Evanston). Home: 144 Greenwood Blvd., Evanston, Ill. Office: 1 S. State St., Chgo. Died Apr. 10, 1953.

SCOTT, Roy Wesley, physician, educator; b. New Albany, Ind., Mar. 20, 1888; s. James McClintock and Ada (Norrington) S.; A.B., Ind. U., 1910; M.D., Western Reserve U., 1913, A.M., 1917; grad. study U. of Vienna, 1924-25; m. Florence Mellette, June 8, 1914; children—Josephine Katherine (dec.), Rowena J. Lahr. Demonstrator of medicine Western Res. U., 1914-15, instr. in physiology, 1915-17, asso. in physiology, 1917-18, instr. in medicine, 1918-20, sr. instr., 1920-22, asst. prof., 1922-25, asso. prof., 1925-29, prof. clin. medicine, 1929—. Fellow A.A. A.S., A.C.P.; mem. Assn. Am. Physician, Am. Physiol. Soc., Am. Soc. Clin. Investigation, Am. Heart Assn. (past pres.), Soc. for Exptl. Biology and Medicine, Am. Soc. Pharm. and Exptl. Therapeutics, A.M.A., Central Soc. for Clin. Research (past pres.). Home: 2721 Sherbrooke Rd., Shaker Heights, O. Office: City Hospital, Cleve. Died May 26, 1957.

SCOTT, Walter Canfield, clergyman; b. Barry, Ill., Feb. 6, 1869; s. David Richard and Julia (Canfield) S.; student Northwestern Normal Sch (Geneseo, Ill.) and Jennings Sem. (Aurora, Ill.); Northwestern U. and Garrett Bibl. Inst., 1893-97; D.D., Philomath Coll., Ore., 1919; m. Edith Blanche Jones, Nov. 19, 1898; children—Mildred Mae (Mrs. E. S. Townsend), Mabel Edith (Mrs. C. Hortley Buke), Walter Brockway, David Frederick. Ordained to ministry M.E. Ch., 1891; pastor Batavia, Ill., 1911-15, Naperville, Ill., 1912-15, Normal Park Ch., Chgo., 1915-19, Sheridan Rd. Ch., Chgo., 1919-22; staff rep. Bd. of Edn. of M.E. Ch., dept. finance, Chgo., 1922-25; field sec. Ch. and Institutional Financing, also of Meth. Ministers' Sons and Daus. Soc.; counselor for personal and estate memls. and memls. with a perpetuity. Lecturer. Dir. Schiller Piano Co. (Oregon, Ill.). Republican. Mason (K.T., 32°, Shriner; decorated by Supreme Council for Meritorious Service, 1939), Odd Fellow. Club: Hamilton (Chgo.). Home: 115 May Av., Monrovia, Cal. Died Dec. 8, 1951.

SCOTT, Walter Dill, educator; b. Cooksville, Ill., May 1, 1869; s. James Sterling and Henrietta (Sutton) S.; grad. Ill. State Normal U., 1891; A.B., Northwestern U., 1895; grad. McCormick Theol. Sem., 1898; Ph.D., University of Leipzig, 1900, (honorary), Northwestern University; LL.D., Cornell Coll., 1921; LL.D., U. of Southern Calif., 1932; m. Anna Marcy Miller, July 21, 1898; children—John Marcy, Sumner Walter. Asso. prof. psychology and edn., and dir. psychol. lab., Northwestern U., 1901-08, prof. psychology, 1908-20, pres., 1920-39, pres. emeritus, 1939—; dir. Bureau of Salesmanship Research, Carnegie Inst. Tech., 1916-17. Pres. The Scott Co., consultants and engrs. in industrial personnel, 1919-21. Dir. com. on classification of personnel in the army, 1917-18; col. U.S. Army, 1918-19; now col., U.S.R. Awarded D.S.M. for "devising, installing and supervising the personnel system in the U.S. Army." Cross Legion of Honor (France), 1933, Chevalier, 1938. Trustee Wesley Memorial Hosp., Presbyn. Theol. Sem. of Chicago; mem. bd. trustees of Century of Progress, 1933, 34. Chmn. solid fuels advisory war council 1941-46; chmn. editorial board, American Peoples Ency., 1948. Mem. Am. Council on Edn., (chmn. 1927), Am. Psychol. Assn. (pres. 1918-19), Phi Beta Kappa, Delta Mu Delta, Sigma Xi, Phi Delta Kappa, Am. Legion. Presbyterian. Clubs: University (Chicago, Winter Park, Evanston); Commercial, Union League; Glenview Golf; etc. Author: Die Psychologie der Triebe, 1900; Theory of Advertising, 1903; Psychology of Public Speaknig, 1907; Psychology of Advertising, 1908; Influencing Men in Business, 1911; Increasing Human Efficiency, 1911; Psychology of Advertising in Theory and Practice, 1921; Science and Common Sense in Working with Men, 1921; Personnel Management, 1941; The Life of Charles Deering, 1929; Biography of John Evans, 1939; Life of John Evans; Life of Charle Deering. Joint Author: The Personnel System of the U.S. Army, Vol. I, History of the Personnel System, Vol. II, The Personnel Manual, 1919; Personnel Specifications, 10 vols., 1918-19; Dwellers by the Road, 1911; Aids in Selecting Salesmen, 1916; Stabilizing Business, 1923; Man and His Universe, 1929; Society Today, 1929; Life of Walter P. Murphy, 1947. Home North Shore Hotel, Evanston, Ill. Died Sept. 23, 1955; buried Meml. Park Cemetery, Evanston.

SCOTT, Walter E(dwin), Jr., mining engr.; b. Black Hawk, Colo., Nov. 7, 1895; s. Walter Edwin and Annette (Gilhooley) S.; student Regis Prep. Sch.; B.S., Regis Coll.; m. Nora Beardsley Livingston, Dec. 19, 1925; 1 dau., Margaret Annette. Various engring. and exec. positions mining cos., Ariz., Cal., Colo., Ida., Mo., Nev., Can., and Alaska, 1917-37; cons. mining engr. pvt. office, Central City, Colo., 1937-50; city engr. City Central, 1938-48; co. engr. Gilpin Co., Colo., 1938-42; commr. mines State Colo., 1950-59, ret. 1959; chmn. Colo. Geol. Survey Bd. 1950—; sec.-treas., dir. Dumont Investment Co.; owner mining properties, Clear Creek and Gilpin cos., Colo. Chmn. Colo. Mineral Resources Bd., 1938-50; mem. Colo. Metal Mining Fund Bd., 1950. Registered profl. engr., Colo. Mem. Am. Inst. Mining and Metall. Engrs., Am. Mining Congress, Colo. Mining Assn. (past v.p.), Colo. Sci. Soc., Colo. Soc. Engrs. Mason (Shriner). Mining editor of the Register-Call, 1940—. Contbr. profl. jours. Home: Central City, Colo. Office: Museum Bldg., Denver 2. Died July 25, 1959; buried Bald Mountain Cemetery, Central City, Colo.

SCOTT, William Kerr (car), senator; b. Haw River, N.C., Apr. 17, 1896; s. Robert Walter and Elizabeth (Hughes) S.; B.S., N.C. State Coll., 1917; m. Mary Elizabeth White, July 2, 1919; children—Osborne W., Mary Kerr (Mrs. A. J. Lowdermilk), Robert W. Agent emergency food prodn., U.S. Dept. of Agr., 1917; farm agent, Alamance Co., 1920-30; master N.C. State Grange, 1930-33; regional dir. Farm Debt Adjustment Program of Resettlement Adminstrn., 1934-36; state commr. agr., elected for 4 yr. terms, 1936, 1940, 1944; elected gov. of N.C., 1948; elected U.S. Senator from North Carolina, 1954. Mem. Am. Jersey Cattle Club (pres. N.C. branch), N.C. Rural Electrification Authority, N.C. Dairy Assn. (pres.), State Farmers Conv. (pres. 1934), N.C. Cotton Growers Cooperative Assn. (adv. bd.), Originator Tobacco Adv. Council, Tobacco Adv. Bd. (chmn. 1945), Nat. Assn. Commrs., Sec. and Commrs. of Agr. (pres. 1947), Nat. Adv. Com. Agrl. Research and Marketing, 1946-48, Jr. Order Am. Mechanics. Served as pvt., F.A., World War I. Awarded Man of the Year by Progressive Farmer, N.C. Agrl. leader, 1937, by N.C. Grange, 1949. Democrat. Presbyn. (elder, 1933-48). Home: Haw River, N.C. Died Apr. 16, 1958; buried Hawfields Presbyterian Church Yard, Alamance County, N.C.

SCOVIL, Samuel (skō'vil), chmn. bd. Soc. for Savings; b. Kingston, N.B., Can., Sept. 13, 1857; s. Rev. William E. and Frances (Lee) S.; student pub. schs., Kingston; m. Emily Hartman, 1890 (dec. 1916); children—Richard, Malcolm. In investment banking, N.Y. City, 1881-94; with Soc. for Savings in the City of Cleve., 1903—, mem. finance com., 1909-37, now chmn. bd.; pres. and mgr. Cleve. Elec. Illuminating Co., 1894-1918. Trustee Huron Rd. Hosp. Republican. Episcopalian. Club: Union (Cleve.). Home: 2717 Edgehill Rd., Cleveland Heights, O. Office: Society for Savings, 127 Public Sq., Cleve. Died Mar. 29, 1950.

SCOVILLE, Samuel, Jr. (skō'vil), lawyer, author, lecturer; b. Norwich, N.Y., June 9, 1872; s. Samuel and Harriet E. (Beecher) S.; A.B., Yale, 1893; LL.B., U. of State of N.Y., 1895; m. Katharine Gallaudet Trumbull, Oct. 17, 1899; children—Samuel (dec.), Gurdon Trumbull, William Beecher, Henry Ward Beecher (dec.), Alice Trumbull (Mrs. Stuyvesant Barry). Admitted to N.Y. bar, 1895; mem. law firm Beecher & Scoville, 1898; admitted to Phila. bar, 1903, and since maintained prin. office there; admitted to Supreme Ct. of U.S., 1910. Trustee Wagner Inst. Mem. council Boy Scouts of America. Mem. Law Assn. Philadelphia, Del. Valley Ornithol. Club, New England Society of Pa. (past pres.), Athenaeum of Phila., Library Co. of Phila., Friends of Haverford College Library (past president), Delta Kappa Epsilon. Presbyn. Clubs: Franklin Inn (hon. pres.), University, Triplets (Philadelphia); Ends of Earth, Yale (N.Y.). Author: Brave Deeds of Union Soldiers, 1915; Abraham Lincoln, His Story, 1918; The Out-of-Doors Club, 1919; Boy Scouts in the Wilderness, 1919; The Blue Pearl, Everyday Adventures, 1920; The Inca Emerald, Wild Folk, 1922; More Wild Folk, 1924; The Red Diamond, 1925; Man and Beast, Runaway Days, 1926; Lords of the Wild, 1928; Wild Honey, 1929; The Snakeblood Ruby, 1932; Alice in Blunderland, 1934. Contbr. to magazines. Law editor and contbr. of daily column, Evening Bulletin. Books translated into German, Hungarian, Norwegian and Finnish. Home: Haverford, Pa.; (summer) "Treetop," Cornwall, Conn. Offices: Harrison Bldg., Philadelphia. Died Dec. 4, 1950; buried Cornwall, Conn.

SCRANTON, Worthington, business exec.; b. Scranton, Pa., Aug. 29, 1876; s. William W. and Katherine M. (Smith) S.; A.B., Yale, 1898; LL. B., Harvard, 1901; m. Marion Margery Warren, Apr. 11, 1907; children—Marion M. (Mrs. Edward B. Mayer), Katherine S. (wife of Dr. H. M. Rozendaal), Sara (Mrs. James A. Linen III), William W. Admitted to Pa. bar, 1901; never practiced law; pres. Ridge Row Corp.; v.p. Scranton Gas and Water Co., 1905, pres., 1906-28; pres. Ridge Row Corp.; dir. First Nat. Bank of Scranton, Scranton Elec. Co., Hudson Coal Co. Mem. 13th Regt., Pa. Inf., 1903-13, disch. as capt. Trustee Community Chest; pres. (several yrs.) Scranton C. of C. Republican. Presbyn. Clubs: University, Yale (N.Y.C.); Graduates (New Haven); Scranton (Pa.); Scranton Country, Clarks Summit (Pa.); Seminole Golf (Palm Beach, Fla.). Home: Marworth, Waverly, Pa. Office: 800 Linden St., Scranton, Pa. Died Feb. 13, 1955.

SCRIBNER, Charles, publisher; b. N.Y. City, Jan. 26, 1890; s. Charles and Louise (Flagg) S.; student St. Paul's Sch., 1904-09; A.B., Princeton, 1913; m. Vera Gordon Bloodgood, May 26, 1915; children—Julia Scribner Bingham, Charles. With Charles Scribner's Sons since 1913, sec., 1918-26, v.p., 1926-32, president since 1932; director Bantam Books. Incorporated, Grosset & Dunlap, Inc. First lt. Remount Service, Q.M.C., World War. Trustee Skidmore Coll., Blair Acad. Republican. Episcopalian. Clubs: Racquet and Tennis, Century Association, Grolier, Westminster Kennel, Essex Fox Hounds. Home: Far Hills, N.J. Office: 597 5th Av., N.Y. Died Feb. 11, 1952.

SCRIPPS, William Edmund, publisher; b. Detroit, Mich., May 6, 1882; s. James Edmund and Harriet Josephine (Messinger) S.; ed. prep. schs. and Mich. Military Acad.; m. Nina A. Downey, June 27, 1901; children—James E. (dec.), William J., Robert Warren, Mary Ann. Pres. Evening News Assn., pubs. Detroit News; v.p. James E. Scripps Corp.; pres. Scripps Motor Co., mfrs. of marine gasoline engines. Founder, Station 8MK (now known as WWJ—The Detroit News), broadcasting regularly since Aug. 1920 and television station WWJ-TV on March 4, 1947. Mem. Associated Press, Detroit Bd. of Commerce. Republican. Episcopalian. Clubs: Detroit, Detroit Athletic, Country Club of Detroit, Bloomfield Hills Country. Home: Molton Manor, Wildwood Farms, Lake Orion, Mich. Office: 615 Lafayette Av., West, Det. 31. Died June 12, 1952.

SCROGGS, William Oscar, economist; b. Monroe, N.C., Mar. 30, 1879; s. William Junius and Lucy (Pearsall) S.; B.S., Ala. Poly. Inst., Auburn, Ala., 1899, M.S., 1900; grad. student, Harvard, 1904-07, A.M., 1905, Ph.D., 1911; unmarried. Librarian and instr. in English, Ala. Poly. Inst., 1900-04; fellow, Harvard, 1905-07; mem. editorial staff, Ency. Britannica (11th edit.), 1907-08; asst. prof. history and economics, La. State U., 1908-11, asso. prof., 1911-12, prof., 1912-13, prof. economics and sociology, 1913-19; financial writer, New York Evening Post, 1920-24; sr. statistician Western Electric Co., 1924-25; editorial staff N.Y. World, 1925-31; dir. of information service, Council on Foreign Relations, 1931-41; dean Grad. Sch., Louisiana State Univ., 1941-49. Served as trade expert with U.S. Shipping Board, 1918-19. Author: Filibuster sand Financiers, 1916; The Story of Louisiana, 1924; A Century of Banking Progress, 1924; (with Walter Lippmann, W. H. Shepardson and Charles Merz) United States in World Affairs, 1932, 33, 34-35, 36, 37, 38, 39, 40, 41. Contbr. hist. and economic subjects to Encyclopaedia Britannica and to various periodicals. Address: 2918 Lake Forest Dr., Augusta, Ga. Died Aug. 21, 1957; buried Fort Valley, Ga.

SCRUGGS, Anderson M., univ. prof., poet; born West Point, Ga., Feb. 18, 1897; s. William Edgar and Talullah Eugenia (Watson) S.; D.D.S., Emory U., 1925; m. Leila Smith, Nov. 23, 1921; 1 dau., Eugenia Elizabeth (Mrs. Otis J. White, Jr.). Asso. prof. histology Atlanta-Southern Dental Coll., 1926-39, asso. in bacteriol. and pathol., 1936-44, asso. in tech. composition, 1936-37, prof. histol., Dental Coll., 1939-44; prof. histol., Sch. of Dentistry, Emory University, 1944-49, associate bacteriol. and pathol., 1944—, prof. tech. composition, 1944, professor of dentistry, 1950—. Fellow American Coll. Dentists; mem. Poetry Soc. of Am., Poetry Soc. of Ga., Am. Dental Assn., Ga. Dental Assn., No. Dist. Dental Assn., Omicron Kappa Upsilon, Psi Omega. Baptist. Author: (poems) Glory of Earth, 1933; Ritual for Myself, 1941; (poem) I Hear Them in the Dawn (set to music by William Naylor), pub. 1948; other poems included in anthologies and textbooks, including Prose, Poetry and Drama for Oral Interpretation, 1936; The Desk Drawer Anthology, 1937; The World's Great Catholic Poetry, 1939; Adventures in Poetry, 1946; The Story of Jesus in the World's Literature, 1946; Masterpieces of Religious Verse, 1948; author: What Shall the Heart Remember?, 1951. Home: 11, The Prado, N.E. Office: Atlanta 3. Died Jan. 28, 1955; buried Westview Cemetery, Atlanta.

SCRUGGS, William Marvin, surgeon; b. Spartanburg, S.C., Aug. 8, 1889; s. Robert Pinckney and Della Ford (Tisdale) S.; B.S., Wake Forest (N.C.) Coll., 1912; M.D., U. of Pa., 1914; grad. study in surgery, German Hosp. and Dispensary, N.Y. City, 1914-16; m. Helen Florence Briggs, Nov. 22, 1922; 1 son, William Marvin. Asso. surgeon, Rutherford Hosp., Rutherfordton, N.C., 1916-17; practices at Charlotte, N.C.; chief of surg. staff Presbyn. Hosp. (chmn. exec. bd.); cons. surgeon Charlotte Memorial Hosp., attending surgeon Mercy Hosp., Good Samaritan Hospital (all of Charlotte). Served as captain in Medical R.C., U.S. Army, Base Hospital, Camp Greene, N.C.; chief surgeon Base Hosp. No. 6, A.E.F., Aug. 1917-May 1919. Fellow Am. Coll. Surgeons, A.M.A.; mem. Southern, Tri-State, 7th Dist., N.C. State and Mecklenburg County med. socs. Southeastern Surg. Congress, Am. Assn. for Study of Goitre. Democrat. Baptist. Club: Charlotte Country. Home: 143 Queens Rd. Office: 301 Hawthorne Lane, Charlotte, N.C. Died May 18, 1951; buried Oaklawn Cemetery Mausoleum, Charlotte.

SCUDDER, Edward Wallace, publisher; b. Newark, N.J., Jan. 15, 1882; s. Wallace McIlvaine and Ida (Quinby) S.; grad. Newark Acad., 1899; A.B., Princeton, 1903; m. Katherine Hollifield, June 4, 1907; children—Dorothea (Mrs. Edward A. Foote), Edward W., Richard B., Katherine Ida (dec.). Pub. of Newark Evening News, 1931-50; chmn. bd. Evening News Publishing Co., director National Newark and Essex Banking Co., Nat. Newark Bldg. Corp.; chmn. bd., North Jersey Radio, Inc. Trustee Newark Museum, Newark Safety Council; dir. Newark Hosp. and Home for Crippled Children; chapter mem. Trinity Cathedral. Episcopalian. Clubs: Essex, Orange Lawn Tennis, Rumson Country, Seabright Beach. Home: Windfall, Red Bank, N.J. Died Feb. 19, 1953.

SCUDDER, Townsend, judge; b. Northport, Suffolk Co., N.Y., July 26, 1865; s. Townsend and Sarah M. (Frost) S.; attended prep. schs. in Europe; LL.B., Columbia, 1888; m. Mary Dannat Thayer (she died Jan. 2, 1924); children—Atala Thayer (Mrs. Wilbert C. Davison), Elizabeth Hewlett (Mrs. Wadleigh Capehart), Townsend III; m. 2d, Alice Booth, d. James McCutcheon, Jan. 18, 1927. Admitted to N.Y. bar, 1889; corpn. counsel for Queens County, N.Y., 1893-99; elected as a Democrat to 56th Congress (1899-1901); declined nomination to the 57th Congress; elected to the 58th Congress (1903-05); justice of Supreme Court of New York, 2d Jud. Dist., 1907-20; resumed the practice of law in N.Y. City, 1920; state park commr. and v.p. L.I. State Park Commn., 1924-27; apptd. to Supreme Court bench by Gov. Alfred E. Smith; Feb. 1927; nominated for the full term by Dem. and Rep. parties to succeed himself, and elected Nov. 8, 1927; served in appellate div. Supreme Court, 1928-36. Grand Master of Masons, State of N.Y., 1907-08. Home: Glen Head, L.I., N.Y.; and Round Hill Rd., Greenwich, Conn. Died Feb. 22, 1960.

SCUDDER, Vida Dutton, coll. prof.; b. Southern India, Dec. 15, 1861; d. David Coit and Harriet L. (Dutton) Scudder; A.B., Smith Coll., 1884, A.M., 1889; L.H.D., 1922; LL.D., Nashotah House, Nashotah, Wis., 1942; grad. study at Oxford, and Paris. Connected with formation coll. settlements; asso. prof. English lit., Wellesley Coll., 1892-1910, prof., 1910-27, prof. emeritus, 1927—. Author: The Life of the Spirit in the Modern English Poets, 1895; The Witness of Denial, 1896; Social Ideals in English Letters, 1898, 1922, 1923; intro. to the Study of English Literature, 1901; A Listener in Babel, 1903; Selected Letters of St. Catherine of Siena (translated and edited), 1905; The Disciple of a Saint, 1907, 1921, 1927; Socialism and Character, 1912; Church and the Hour, 1917; Morte d'Arthur of Sir Thomas Malory, Introduction to Arthurian Romance, 1917; Social Teachings of the Christian Year, 1921; Brother John—A Tale of the First Franciscans, 1927; The Franciscan Adventure, 1931; On Journey (autobiography), 1937; The Privilege of Age: Essays, Secular and Spiritual, 1939; Father Huntington, 1940; My Quest for Realty, 1952. Editor: Macaulay's Lord Clive, 1889, Introduction to the Writings of John Ruskin, 1890, Shelley's Promethus Unbound, 1892; Works of John Woolman, Everyman's Library, 1910; Bede's History of England (Everyman's Library), 1911; English Poems (Lake English Classics), 1915. Address: 45 Leighton Rd., Wellesley, Mass. Died Oct. 9, 1954; buried Newton (Mass.) Cemetery.

SCULLY, C(harles) Alison, banker; b. Pitts., Oct. 17, 1887; s. Charles D. and Mary (Scott) S.; B.S., U. Pa., 1909, LL.B., 1912; m. Elizabeth G. Williams, Nov. 2, 1920; children—Scott Williams, David Williams, Elizabeth Alison, John Alison. Admitted to Pa. bar, 1912, and practiced in Phila., 1912-17; trust officer Corn Exchange Nat. Bank of Phila., 1920-23; 2d v.p. Nat. Bank of Commerce, N.Y.C., 1923-26, v.p., 1926-29; v.p. Bank of the Manhattan Co., N.Y.C., 1929-42; exec. v.p., dir. Corn Exchange Nat. Bank & Trust Co. of Phila., 1942-51; pres. Corporate Fiduciaries Assn. of N.Y. C., 1932, 33. Served as capt. and adj. 51st Inf. 6th Div., U.S. Army, later Courier Service with AEF, 1917-19. Mem. S.R., Soc. Colonial Wars, Am. Acad. of Polit. and Social Science, Assn. Bar City of N.Y., Phila. Bar Assn., Phila. Orchestra (dir.), Pa. Academy Fine Arts (dir.), Psi Upsilon. Republican. Presbyn. Clubs: University, Century (N.Y.C.); Philadelphia, Rittenhouse, Orpheus, University Barge, Merion Cricket (Phila.). Author: Insurance Trusts, 1927; Busines Life Insurance Trusts (with F. W. Ganse), 1930; The Course of the Silver Greyhound, 1936; The Purchase of Common Stocks as Trust Investments, 1937. Home: Boxwood, Conestoga Rd., Box 127, Bryn Mawr, Pa. Died Nov. 8, 1954.

SEABURY, David (sē'bûr-ĭ), psychologist, lecturer; b. Boston, Mass., Sept. 11, 1885; s. Julius Alphonsus and Annetta (Seabury) Dresser (legally adopted mother's maiden name as surname); prep. edn. Chauncy Hall Sch., Boston, until 1898, Scuola Bettini Recasoli, Florence, Italy, 1898-99; studied under pvt. tutor, 1900-04; spl. research Harvard, 1905-07, London, 1907, Paris, 1908-09, 1911-12, Munich, 1910, Rome, 1913; Ph.D., Pacific International U., 1950; m. Evelyn Uhler, Mar. 3, 1945. Began practice as psychologist, N.Y.C., 1914; cons. psychologist, Culver (Ind.) Mil. Acad., 1915-16; psychol. examiner and lecturer, Ft. Benjamin Harrison, R.O.T.C., 1916; in practice as cons. psychologist, N.Y.C., 1921—; lecturer on psychol. subjects. Founder of Centralist Sch. of Psychology; founder and pres. David Seabury School of Psychology, Incorporated; pres. of Seabury U. Adult Edn. Author: Unmasking Our Minds, 1924; Growing Into Life, 1928; What Makes Us Seem So Queer, 1934; Keep Your Wits, 1935; How to Worry Successfully, 1936; Help Yourself to Happiness, 1937; The Art of Selfishness, 1937; Build Your Own Future, 1938; How to Get Things Done (with Alfred Uhler), 1938; Adventures in Self-Discovery, 1938; See Yourself As Others See You, 1939; Why We Love and Hate, 1939; How Jesus Heals Our Minds Today, 1939; High Hopes for Low Spirits, 1955; The Art of Living Without Tension, 1958. Home: Olga, Washington. Office: 1656½ S. Western Av., Los Angeles 6. Died Apr. 4, 1960.

SEABURY, Samuel, lawyer; b N.Y.C., Feb. 22, 1873; s. Rev. William Jones (D.D.) and Alice Van Wyck (Beare) S.; ed. by father, also attended Trinity Sch. and Wilson and Kellogg Sch., N.Y.C.; LL. B., N.Y. Law Sch., 1893, post grad. course, 1893-94; L.H.D., Hobart Coll., 1931; LL.D., Colgate U., 1931, Washington and Jefferson Coll., 1932, Harvard, 1932, U. Mich., 1933, Muhlenberg Coll., 1933, Columbia, 1933, U. Rochester, 1933, Princeton, 1933, Rutgers U., 1934, Dartmouth, 1934; LL.D., Wabash Coll., 1947; m. Josephine Maud Richey, June 6, 1900 (dec.). Admitted N.Y. bar, 1894; elected justice City Ct., N.Y.C., 1901, elected justice Supreme Ct., N.Y., 1906, term of 14 yrs. resigned 1914); elected asso. judge Court of Appeals, State of N.Y., Nov. 1914; resigned 1916, and was nominated by Dem. Party as candidate for gov. of N.Y. State, 1916. Apptd. referee of Appellate Div., 1st Judicial Dept., N.Y., 1930, to investigate conditions of the magistrate courts in that dept.; apptd. 1931, to hear charges filed against the dist. atty. of N.Y. County; designated as counsel to Joint Legislative Com., 1931, to investigate affairs of N.Y.C. Pres. N.Y. Law Inst., 1937-50. Mem. Assn. Bar City of N.Y. (pres. 1939-41), N.Y. State Bar Assn. (pres. 1932-34), Am. Bar Assn., N.Y. County Lawyers assn. (pres. 1925-27). Episcopalian. Clubs: Manhattan, Down Town, Harvard, Century Assn., Church, Wall Street (N.Y.C.); Nat. Golf Links of America (Southampton, N.Y.); Maidstone Club (East Hampton, N.Y.). Home: 840 Park Av., N.Y.C.; also East Hampton, L.I., N.Y. Office: 31 Nassau St., N.Y.C. Died May 7, 1958.

SEACHREST, Effie M., author; b. Independence, Mo.; d. Ephraim G. and Mary Caroline (Meek) Seachrest; grad. Central High Sch., Kansas City, Mo.; spl. courses in English, U. Chgo. and under pvt. tutors; art under Brumidi and Webster, and at Fine Art Sch., Portland, Ore. Mem. D.A.R. Christian Scientist. Author: Storyland, 1912; Legendary Lore and Peeps at Pictures, 1913; Greek Photoplays, 1916; Egyptian Photoplays, 1921. Contbr. to Youth's Companion, Kansas City Star, etc. Owner of "Little Gallery in the Woods," at home address. Home: 4928 Troostwood Rd., Kansas City, Mo. Deceased.

SEALS, Carl H., army officer; born Eufaula, Ala., Dec. 31, 1882; commd. 1st lt. Inf., Ala. Nat. Guard, July 1904, and advanced to maj. 1914; called into Fed. service, 1916, duty on Mexican Border; overseas, World War I. Comd. maj. Inf. Regular Army, Sept. 1920, and advanced to brig. gen., Jan. 1942; served with Mil. Intelligence Div., War Dept. Gen. Staff, Washington, D.C., 1931-35, also chief of Pub. Relations Br. and for 2 yrs. in charge of War Dept. Press Section; ordered for duty as adjutant gen., Philippines, Sept. 1935-37; on duty in Hdqrs., Fourth Corps Area, Atlanta, Ga., 1937-40; returned to Fort William McKinley, as adjutant gn. of the Philippine Div., Philippine Islands, June 1940; brig. gen., Army U.S., since Jan. 1942; Adjt. Gen. U.S. Army Forces in the Far East, Manila, July 1941 to surrender May 1942; prisoner of war, Japanese army, May 1942-Sept. 1945. Awarded Distinguished Service Medal. Ret. Oct. 1946. Mem. Am. Legion. Mason (Shriner). Home: 314 Riverview Blvd., Daytona Beach, Fla. Died Oct. 29, 1955.

SEAMAN, Augusta Hulell (Mrs. Francis P. Freeman), author; b. N.Y.C., Apr. 3, 1879; d. John Valentine and Augusta Cheeseman (Curtis) Hulell;

A.B., Hunter Coll., 1900; m. Robert Reece Seaman, Oct. 3, 1906 (dec. Mar. 1927); 1 dau., Helen Roberta; m. 2d, Francis P. Freeman, Mar. 1928 (dec.). Began as contbr. to mags., 1907, and later became regular contbr. juvenile serials to St. Nicholas (mag.), subsequently published in book form, Ind. Democrat. Presbyn. Club: Pen and Brush. Author: Jacqueline of the Carrier Pigeons, 1910; When a Cobbler Ruled the King, 1911; Little Mamselle of the Wilderness, 1913; The Boarded-up House, 1915; The Sapphire Signet, 1916; The Girl Next Door, 1917; Three Sides of Paradise Green, 1918; Melissa-Across-the-Fence, 1918; The Slipper Point Mystery, 1919; The Crimson Patch, 1920; The Dragon's Secret, 1921; The Mystery at Number Six, 1922; Tranquility House, 1923; The Edge of Raven Pool, 1924; Sally Simms Adventures It, 1924; Bluebonnet Bend, 1925; The Adventure of the Seven Keyholes, 1926; The Secret of Tate's Beach, 1926; The Shadow on the Dail, 1927; The Disappearance of Anne Shw, 1928; The Book of Mysteries, 1929; The Charlemonte Crest, 1930; The House in Hidden Lane, 1931; The Brass Keys of Kenwick, 1931; The Stars of Sabra, 1932; The Mystery of the Empty Room, 1933; The Riddle at Live Oaks, 1934; Bitsy Finds the Clue, 1934; The Figurehead of the Folly, 1935; The Strange Pettingill Puzzle, 1936; Voice in the Dark, 1937; The Pine Barrens Mystery, 1937; The Vanderlyn Silhouette, 1938; The Mystery at Linden Hall, 1939; The Curious Affair at Heron Shoals, 1940; The Missing Half, 1941; The Case of the Calico Crab, 1942; The Mystery of the Folding Key, 1943; The Half-Penny Adventure, 1945; The Mystery of the Other House, 1947. Address: Seaside Park, N.J. Died June 4, 1950.

SEAMAN, Eugene Cecil, bishop; b. Galveston, Tex., Dec. 9, 1881; s. William Henry and Sophia (Baldwin) S.; grad. Ball High Sch., Galveston, 1900; B.A., U. of the South, Sewanee, Tenn., 1903, B.D., 1906, D.D., 1925; m. Henrietta Morgan, Apr. 11, 1912; children—Eugene Cecil (dec.), Mary Henrietta, Henry Frederick. Ordained to ministry P.E. Ch., deacon, 1906, priest, 1907; asst. minister Christ Ch., Houston, 1906; rector Christ Ch., Temple, 1907-11; archdeacon and gen. missionary in N. Tex., 1911-16; rector St. Andrew's Ch., Amarillo, 1916-20, Ch. of the Holy Comforter, Gadsden, Ala., 1920-25; exec. sec. Diocese of Ala., 1923-24; consecrated 2d bishop of North Texas, Jan. 18, 1925. Mng. editor Alabama Churchman 2 years. Trustee University of the South. Mem. Ho. of Deps., Gen. Conv. P.E. Ch., 1910-19, House of Bishops, 1925-28; retired Jan. 31, 1945. Mem. Pi Kappa Alpha. Mason (K.T., Shriner); grand prelate, Tex. Grand Commandery of K.T., 1937-38. Home: 318 W. Edgemont Av., Phoenix. Died Nov. 22, 1950.

SEAMAN, John Thompson, banker; b. N.Y.C., May 2, 1898; s. Edwin Francis and Bertha Hanford (Smith) S.; student Pace & Pace Sch. Accountancy, 1915-16, Columbia, 1919; m. Cecile E. Kane, Feb. 13, 1918; 1 dau., Cecile E. (Mrs. Hotaling); m. 2d, Emily A. Talbot, June 29, 1943. Auditor Battery Park Nat. Bank, N.Y.C., 1915-23, Bank of Am., N.Y.C., 1923-29, Internat. Germanic Trust Co., 1929; auditor Internat. Trust Co., 1929-31, also dir.; auditor Continental Bank & Trust Co., 1931-35, comptroller, 1935-46, v.p., 1946-48, pres. since 1948; dir. Continental Safe Deposit Co., since 1945; trustee, treas. Downtown Hosp., 1944-47. Served with U.S.N.R., 1917-19. Mem. St. Nicholas Soc., Vet. Corps Arty. Soc., Soc. War of 1812. Club: N.Y. Athletic (gov. 1949-51). Home: Bellport, L.I., N.Y. Died May 8, 1955; buried Oakwood Cemetery, Mt. Kisco, N.Y.

SEARING, Hudson Roy, executive; b. N.Y. City, May 3, 1895; B.S. in E.E., Cooper Union, 1916; m. Geraldine Kendrick, Dec. 13, 1917; children—Jean L. (Mrs. C. E. Hoppin), Doris K. (Mrs. Paul A. D. Busch). Pres., Consol. Edison Co. of N.Y., Inc., 1949—, trustee, 1944—, chmn. bd., chief exec. officer; mem. bd. mgrs. D.L.&W. R.R.; trustee Greenwich Savings Bank of N.Y.C. Trustee Cooper Union. Mem. council N.Y.U. Mem. Newcomen Soc. Club: Pinnacle. Address: 4 Irving Pl., N.Y.C. 3. Died June 1957.

SEARLE, Augustus Leach, grain elevator exec.; b. Lyons, N.Y., Mar. 20, 1863; s. Seth Craw and Rosabella Almira (Leach) S.; student pub. schs.; m. Elizabeth Francis Finkler, 1882 (dec.); children—Stewart Augustus, Mrs. Forence Searle Gilchrist (dec.), Mrs. Rosabella Searle Leach; m. 2d, Helen Smith Gardner, 1914 (dec.). Sec., Central Elevator Co., Mpls., 1894-96; gen. mgr. Belt Line Elevator Co., 1896-1907; v.p., mgr. Globe Elevator Co., 1898-1923; v.p. Peavey Duluth Terminal, 1900-23; pres. Port Arthur Elevator Co., 1906-23, Nat. Elevator Co., 1909-23; chmn. bd. Searle Grain Co., Ltd., Northland Elevators and Searle Terminal, Ltd. (Winnipeg, Can.); pres. Searle Grain Co.; dir. Northwest Bancorp. Mem. New York C. of C., U.S. C. of C., Chgo. Bd. Trade, Winnipeg, Mpls. (pres. 1924-25) grain exchanges. Vice pres., trustee Mpls. Inst. Arts; dir. Mpls. Symphony Orchestra, Mpls. Found. (chmn. exec. com.), San Diego Fine Arts Soc., Art Center of LaJolla; hon. v.p. LaJolla Musical Arts Soc. Mem. Nat. Soc. S.A.R., N.E. Historic Geneal. Soc., Acad. Polit. Sci., Order Founders and Patriots of America, Am. Geog. Soc.; only hon. mem. Can. Seed Growers Assn. Patron Smithsonian Inst.; dir. San Diego (Cal.) Fine Arts Soc. Republican. Mason (K.T., Shriner). Clubs: Minneapolis, Minikahda (Mpls.); Manitoba (Winnipeg); LaJolla (Cal.) Beach and Tennis; Cuyamaca (San Diego); Bankers of America (N.Y.C.). Home: 1917 Logan Av. S.; (winter) 6019 Avenida Cresta, LaJolla, (Cal.) Office: Minneapolis Grain Exchange Bldg., Mpls. Died Feb. 2, 1955.

SEARS, Charles Brown, ex-judge; b. Bklyn., Oct. 16, 1870; s. Hector and Leora C. (Brown) S.; grad. Adelphi Acad., Bklyn., 1888; A.B., Yale, 1892; studied U. of Berlin, 1892-93; LL.B., Harvard, 1896; LL.D., Middlebury (Vt.) Coll., 1930, Columbia, 1936, Yale, 1936, St. Lawrence U., 1939, Syracuse U., 1940, Hobart College, 1942; m. Florence Gilbert, Oct. 20, 1896 (dec. Oct. 3, 1939); m. 2d, Mary V. Hun, Nov. 24, 1946. Admitted to N.Y. bar, 1895, and practiced in Buffalo, 1895-1917, apptd. justice Supreme Court of N.Y., Jan. 1917, and elected for terms, 1918-31, 32-40; assigned to Appellate Div. 4th Dept., for term 1922-26, reassigned, 1927-31; presiding justice, 1929-40; asso. judge Court of Appeals, 1940, ret. Dec. 31, 1940; now official referee; presiding judge 4th Mil. Tribunal, Germany, 1947, also Tribunal Four, or Flick Case, Nuremberg, 1947. Chmn. Mayor's Com. on Community Relations, 1943-45; chmn. bd. of community relations for City of Buffalo, 1945-46; chmn. State War Council on Discrimination in Employment, 1941-45; chmn. Buffalo Council State Commn. Against Discrimination, 1945-46; chmn. Enemy Alien Hearing Bd. for Western N.Y. State, 1941-45. Del. N.Y. Constnl. Conv., 1915 (judiciary com.), chmn. judiciary com., 1938. Vice chmn. and mem. council U. of Buffalo; pres. Buffalo Fine Arts Academy (Albright Art Gallery), 1916-17, 29-32, now trustee; trustee Grosvenor Library; ex-chmn. Buffalo branch Fgn. Policy Assn.; pres. Buffalo Philharmonic Orchestra Society, 1941-42, now trustee; pres. Buffalo Joint Charities; trustee Community Chest; pres. Internat. Inst., Buffalo, 1934-42, 46—; life mem. Buffalo Library. Recipient Chancellor medal U. Buffalo, 1944. Mem. Am., N.Y. State, Erie County (pres. 1915-16) bar assns., Am. Law Inst., American Judicature Soc., Judicial Council of New York (chmn. 1940). Episcopalian. Clubs: Buffalo (pres. 1938); Century, University (New York); Genesee Valley (Rochester). Home: 849 Delaware Av. Office: Erie County Hall, Buffalo. Died Dec. 18, 1950.

SEARS, Frank Irving, shoe company exec.; born Boston, Apr. 23, 1872; s. Albert M. and Caroline (Ellis) S.; married Edna Haywood Sears, March 29, 1937; children (by previous marriage)—Emily Villiers Stuart, Richard Niles. Joines Bates Shoe Co., Webster, Mass., 1902, treas. since 1906, chmn. bd. since 1943. Home: 824 School St., Webster, Mass. Died Feb. 17, 1956.

SEARS, Fred Coleman, pomologist; b. Lexington, Mass., May 11, 1866; s. Thomas Bartlett and Mary Katherine (Wellington) S.; B.S., Kan. Agrl. Coll., 1892, M.S., 1896; D.Sc., Kan. State Coll., 1937; m. Ruth T. Stokes, Oct. 19, 1897; children—Florence Hart and Elizabeth Kent (twins). Asst. horticulturist Kan. Expt. Sta., Manhattan, 1892-96; prof. horticulture Utah Agrl. Coll., 1897; dir. Nova Scotia Sch. of Horticulture, Wolfville, N.S., 1897-1904; prof. horticulture Nova Scotia Agrl. Coll., Truro, N.S., 1904-07; prof. pomology Mass. Agrl. Coll., 1907-36. Republican. Conglist. Mason. Author: Productive Orcharding, 1914; Productive Small Fruit Culture, 1920; Fruit-Growing Projects, 1928. Has spent each summer working with Sir Wilfred Grenfell, in Labrador, 1928-39. Home: Amherst, Mass. Died Oct. 1949.

SEARS, Laurence, educator; b. Oneida, N.Y., Apr. 10, 1896; s. Albert and Imogene (Holt) S.; A.B., Princeton, 1918; student Union Theol. Sem., 1920-23; Ph.D., Columbia, 1930; m. Christine Seward, Dec. 31, 1930; children—Peter, John. Sec. Princeton-in-Peking, 1918-20, 1924-27; prof. philosophy Ohio Wesleyan U., 1930-45; instr. U.S. Army U., Biarritz, France, 1945; prof. Am. philosophy and polit. theory Mills Coll., Oakland, Cal., 1946—; vis. prof. Am. polit. theory U. Cal., 1949-51. Fellow Nat. Council on Religion in Higher Edn. Mem. Am. Philos. Assn., Am. Polit. Sci. Assn. Author: Responsibility, 1932; The Development of American Philosophy (with Water Muelder), 1940. Contbr. articles to jours. Home: 2275 Eunice St., Berkeley 9, Cal. Died Feb. 15, 1958.

SEARS, Philip S., sculptor; b. Boston, Nov. 12, 1867; s. Frederick R. and Albertina H. (Shelton) S.; A.B., Harvard, 1889, LL.B., 1892; m. Mary Cabot Higginson, Feb. 2, 1898; children—Philip Mason, David (dec.). Practiced law at Boston, 1892-98; devoted attention to sculpture, 1919—. Prin. works: war memorial, Manchester, Mass.; Indian statue, Harvard, Mass.; bust of Guy Lowell, County Court House, N.Y.C., and Boston Museum of Fine Arts, of Percy Haughton, Varsity Club, Harvard, of W. A. Gardner, Groton (Mass.) Sch., of Senator Lodge, State House, Boston; also garden figures. Trustee Farm and Trade School, Boston; mem. Town Meeting, Brookline, Maj. Adj. Gen's. Dept., U.S. Army Res. Mem. Guild of Boston Artists, Boston Soc. Sculptors; asso. mem. Nat. Sculpture Soc. Episcopalian. Clubs: Somerset, Tennis and Racquet, Athletic Assn. (Boston); Porcellian, Varsity (Cambridge); Myopia Hunt (Hamilton, Mass.). Home: 260 Heath St., Brookline, Mass. Died Mar. 10, 1953.

SEARS, Taber, artist; b. Boston, 1870; s. George Snow and Caroline Augusta (Taber) S.; Boston Museum Fine Arts Sch. of Art; Julian Sch., Paris, as pupil of Jean Paul Laurens and Luc Olivier Merson; also studied in Florence and Rome; m. Florence Warner, Dec. 1909; 1 dau., Anne Franklin (Mrs. Moreau Yeomans). Mural paintings; Triptych, Adoration of the Magi, Church of the Intercession; Joshua Crossing the Jordan, Grace Ch. Choir Sch.; Te Deum, reredos, Old First Presbyn. Ch.; The Transfiguration, St. James Episcopal Ch.; The Resurrection, St. Thomas' Church; New York Among the Nations, N.Y. City Hall (all in N.Y.C.); Holy Innocents in Glory, Ch. of the Holy Innocents; Consecration Ceremony of Bishop Manning in Cathedral of St. John the Divine, N.Y.C.; frieze of the Apostles, and series of stained glass windows, Ch. of the Nativity (both in Bklyn.); Triptych, Christ with the Doctors, Trinity Church, Buffalo; Christ Enthroned, Presbyn. Ch., Newville, Pa.; two episodes in life of Saint Vincent, for St. Vincent's Church, Los Angeles; The Sermon on The Mount, Ch. of The Ascension, New York. Exhibited in Paris salons, Phila. Acad. of Fine Arts, N.A.D. Has held several one-man shows of water colors in New York. Mem. Art Commn., State of New York, 1926-28. Recipient Delano prize N.Y. Water Color Club, 1928. Mem. Archtl. League of New York (past v.p.), Am. Artists Profl. League (treasurer 1940-43); Am. Water Color Society, Rotary Exhibitions, Allied Artists of America, Nat. Soc. Mural Painters (ex-treas.), Municipal Art Soc. of N.Y. (ex-pres.), Artists' Fellowship, New York Water Color Club. Clubs: Church (trustee 1920-22), Century (trustee 1914-27), Salmagundi (N.Y.C.). Home: 1060 Park Av., N.Y.C. 28. Died Oct. 18, 1950.

SEASHORE, Robert Holmes, prof. psychology; b. Iowa City, Ia., June 14, 1902; s. Carl Emil and Mary Roberta (Holmes) S.; B.A., U. of Ia., 1923, M.S., 1924, Ph.D., 1925; m. Marjorie Christine Moore, June 14, 1926; children—Walter Richard Patrick, Norman Holmes, Marjorie Jean. Instr. psychology, Ohio State Univ., 1925-26; nat. research council fellow in biol. sciences, Stanford U., 1926-28; asso. prof. psychology, U. of Ore., 1928-34; summer faculty, Stanford U., 1929; visiting prof. psychology, U. of Southern Calif., 1934-35; prof. psychology, 1936-37; visiting prof. psychology, Northwestern U., 1936-37, asso. prof., 1937-40; summer faculty, U. of Ore., 1939; prof. psychol., Northwestern U., since 1940; chmn. dept. since 1946. Civilian specialist cons., A.A.C., 1941-43; contractor in design bldg., research instruments, A.A.F.; and Armored Forces, 1941-43; co-dir., Nat. Defense Research Council, spl. project in mil. physiol. psychology, 1942. Mem. White House Conf. on Child Health and Protection, 1930; mem. Pacific Coast Social Sci. Research Conf., 1930-34. Fellow A.A.A.S., charter fellow Am. Psychol. Assn. (mem. council, 1943-47, president Division of General Psychology 1948-49), Midwestern (pres. 1942-43), Western (v.p. 1935), Ill. (pres. 1949-50) psychol assns., Sigma Xi (pres. U. Ore. chpt. 1933; v.p. Northwestern chapter, 1942-43, pres. 1943-44), Sigma Alpha Epsilon. Clubs: Psychology (pres. 1939-40; Chgo.); University (Evanston). Author: Studies in Motor Rhythm, 1926; Stanford Univ. Skills Unit 1928; development of Motor Skills in Later Youth, 1932; Elementary Experiments in Psychology, 1935; Work Methods: An Often Neglected Factor Underlying Individual Differences, 1939; (with L. D. Eckerson) The Measurement of Individual Differences in General English Vocabulary, 1940; Experimental and Theoretical Analysis of Motor Skills, 1940. Editor: Fields of Psychology, 1942. Contbr. articles to profl. jours. Home: 1310 Maple Av., Wilmette, Ill. Office: Dept. of Psychology, Northwestern U., Evanston, Ill. Died Aug. 27, 1951.

SEAWELL, Aaron Ashley Flowers (sōō'ĕl), judge; b. Moore County, N.C., Oct. 30, 1864; s. Aaron Ashley Flowers and Jeannette Anne (Buie) S.; Ph.B., U. of N.C., 1889; studied law pvtly. and at U. of N.C.; (hon.) LL.D., U. of N.C., 1937; m. Bertha Alma Smith, Apr. 12, 1905; children—Elizabeth Lee, Aaron Ashley Flowers, Malcolm Buie, Donald Ray, Sarah Jeannette, Edward Harding. Admitted to N.C. bar, 1892, and snice practiced in Sanford; mem. State Ho. of Rep., 1901, 13, 15, 31; mem. State Senate, 1907, 25; former atty. gen. of N.C.; now asso. justice Supreme Court of N.C. Mem. N.C. Bar Assn., Order of Coif, Newcomen Soc., Phi Delta Phi. Democrat. Presbyn. Mason (K.T., Shriner). Clubs: Raleigh History, Torch. Home: Carolina Hotel. Address: Supreme Court Bldg., Raleigh, N.C. Died Oct. 14, 1950; buried Buffalo Cemetery, Sanford, N.C.

SEAY, George James (sē), banker; b. Petersburg, Va., Mar. 10, 1862; s. Robert Moore and Henrietta

James (Williams) S.; desc. Abram Seay (formerly Saye or Say), the Huguenot, who settled in Va., 1700; m. Effie Hall Lewis, of Pittsburgh, Pa., Apr. 26, 1905. With Petersburg Savings and Ins. Co., 1878-1903, cashier, 1894-1903; mem. firm Scott & Stringfellow, bankers, Richmond, Va., 1903-09; governor Federal Reserve Bank of Richmond, Nov. 14, 1914-Mar. 1, 1936; now retired. Mem. Va. Bankers Assn. (pres. 1902). Former mem. Westmoreland, Commonwealth Country Club of Va., Richmond, and Torirelli Fish and Game Club, Laurentian Mountains, Can., Bar Harbor. Writer on banking and railroad finance. Home: 1219 W. Franklin St., Richmond, Va. Died Nov. 12, 1952; buried Hollywood Cemetery, Richmond.

SEAY, Harry Lauderdale, life ins.; b. Gallatin, Tenn., Nov. 25, 1872; s. George Edward and Mary (Lauderdale) S.; student Vanderbilt, 1890-93; LL.B., Georgetown U., 1894; m. Margaret Ballentine, Dec. 17, 1902; 1 son, Harry L. In practice of law, Dallas, Tex., 1894-1915; pres. Southland Life Ins. Co., 1915-38; dir. Tex. Power & Light Co., Rio Grande City Ry. City commr., Dallas, Tex., 1907-11; manager of Magnolia Farms, Sardis, Miss. President American Life Conv., 1917-18; pres. State Fair of Tex., 1939-45; now dir.; chmn. committee presenting summer operas in Dallas; former chmn. State Dem. Exec. Com.; mem. Kappa Alpha. Democrat. Member Christian Church. Mason (32°, Shriner). Clubs: Dallas Athletic, City. Home: Sardis, Miss. Died Aug. 28, 1957.

SEBAST, Frederick Martin (see'bast), educator; b. Albany, N.Y., Apr. 13, 1892; s. Martin and Charlotte (Fullgraff) S.; E.E., Rensselaer Poly. Inst., 1913, D.Eng., 1916; m. Ruth Cecelia Hotaling, Dec. 24, 1917; 1 dau., Charlotte Emma (Mrs. William H. Wink). With Rensselaer Poly. Inst. since 1916, prof. since 1933, head dept. elec. engring. since 1951. Fellow Am. Inst. E.E.; mem. Am. Soc. Engring. Edn., Sigma Xi, Eta Kappa Nu, Tau Beta Pi, Pi Kappa Phi. Mason, Odd Fellow, Rotarian. Home: 218 2d Av., Troy, N.Y. Died July 15, 1955; buried Oakwood Cemetery, Troy.

SEBELIUS, Sven Johan, clergyman, educator; b. Tvaaker, Sweden, Apr. 4, 1874; s. Sebelius and Trina (Simonsdotter) Anderson; brought to U.S., 1879, naturalized, 1892; A.B., Augustana Coll., 1901; B.D., Augustana Theol. Sem., 1904; student U. Chgo., 1908, Columbia, 1922, Leipzig, Germany, 1923, Lund U., Sweden, 1924; D.D., Gustavus Adolphus Coll., 1926; m. Emily Anderson, Sept. 25, 1906. Ordained to ministry Luth. Ch., 1904; pastor Blue Island and Ebenezer Luth. Ch., Chgo., 1904-08; prof. of Christianity, Augustana Coll., Rock Island, Ill., 1909-20; prof. of homiletics and Christian edn. Augustana Theol. Sem., Rock Island, 1920-45, acting dean, 1935-36, dean, 1936-45; v.p. Augustana Coll. and Theol. Sem., 1938—. Del. to 1st Luth. World Conf., Eisenach, Germany, 1923; mem. Bd. of Elementary Christian Edn. and Lit., Augustana Synod, 1924—; mem. Lutheran Mission on Faith and Life, 1937—. Author: Outlines of Church History for Luther Leagues, 1914; Studies in I and II Corinthians, 1926. Editor: A Faith for These Times (a collection of 24 sermons by contemporary Lutheran preachers in America), 1942. Contbr. to church periodicals; asso. editor Augustana Quar., 1924-32. Home: 1647 37th St., Rock Island, Ill. Deceased.*

SECORD, Arthur Wellesley (sē'kôrd), educator; b. Emporia, Kan., Nov. 7, 1891; s. James Monroe and Cora Belle (Surface) S.; A.B., cum laude, Greenville (Ill.) Coll., 1916; A.M., U. Ill., 1920, Ph.D., 1923; fellow Guggenheim Foundation for study abroad, 1927-28; m. Minta Irene Tenney, Sept. 8, 1920; children—Marvin, Muriel, Kristin. Ins.t English, U. Ill., 1923-25, asso. English, 1925-26, asst. prof. and sec. dept. English, 1926-27, asso. prof., 1936-45, prof., 1945—. Lt. Inf., U.S. Army, 1917-18. Trustee Greenville Coll. Mem. Modern Lang. Assn., Am. Geog. Soc., Phi Beta Kappa, Phi Kappa Phi. Secretary edn. commission of Free Methodist Church. Author: Studies in the Narrative Method of Defoe, 1924. Co-editor: Literary Studies, 1929. Editor: Defoe's Journal of the Plague Year, 1935; Defoe's Review (22 vols.), 1938. Co-compiler: Worship in Song, 1935; cooperating editor Jour. English and Germanic Philology, Robert Drurys' Journal and other Essays, 1960. Home: 102 S. Lincoln Av., Urbana, Ill. Died May 16, 1957.

SEDGWICK, Henry Dwight, author; b. Stockbridge, Mass., Sept. 24, 1861; s. Henry Dwight and Henrietta Ellery (Sedgwick) S.; m. Sarah Minturn, Nov. 7, 1895 (dec. Jan. 26, 1919); children—Henry D. (dec.), Robert Minturn, Francis Minturn; married 2d, Gabriella May Ladd, May 18, 1953. Admitted to bar, 1884; practiced at N.Y., 1885-98. Fellow Am. Acad. Arts and Scis.; mem. Acad. of Arts and Letters, Mass. Hist. Soc. Club: Tavern. Author: Letter of Captain Cuellar, 1896; Life of Father Hecker, 1897; Life of Samuel Champlain, 1901; Essays on Great Writers, 1902; Life of Francis Parkman (American Men of Letters Series), 1904; A Short History of Italy, 1905; The New American Type and Other Essays, 1908; Italy in the Thirteenth Century, 1912; An Apology for Old Maids, and Other Essays, 1917; Dante, 1919; Marcus Aurelius, 1921; Pro Vita Monastica, 1923; Life of Ignatius Loyola, 1923; A Short History of Spain, 1925; Cortés, 1926; Life of Lafayette, 1927; Short History of France, 1928; Henry of Navarre, 1930; Alfred de Musset, 1931; The Black Prince, 1932; The Art of Happiness, 1923; Dan Chaucer, 1934; In Praise of Gentlemen, 1935; The House of Guise, 1937; Vienna, 1939; Madame Récamier, 1940; Memoirs of an Epicurean, 1942; Horace, 1947. Address: Stockbridge, Mass. Died Jan. 5, 1957.

SEEBIRT, Eli Fowler, lawyer; b. near St. Clairsville, O., Apr. 12, 1878; s. John H. and Adelia (McCleary) S.; A.B., Mt. Union Coll., Alliance, O., 1901; LL.B., U. Mich., 1904; LL.D., Notre Dame U., 1924; m. Edith Elizabeth Gunn, Nov. 9, 1909; children—Mrs. Mary Elizabeth Bradford, Mrs. Lucy Rosemonde Christman. Admitted to Ind. bar, 1904, also to Mich. and Ind. bars; since practiced at South Bend, Ind., city atty. South Bend, 1913-17; mayor, 1922-26; mem. Seebirt, Oare & Deahl. Pres. Ind. Municipal League, 1922-23; dir. Epworth Hosp. Mem. Am. Bar Assn. (mem. bd. govs. 1944-47), Ind. State Bar Assn. (pres. 1933-34), St. Joseph Co. Bar Assn. (pres. 1918), Am. Law Inst., Am. Acad. Polit. and Social Sci., Am. Judicature Soc. (dir.), Ind. Soc. Chgo., South Bend C. of C. (pres. 1924), Alpha Tau Omega, Phi Delta Phi. Republican. Episcopalian. Mason (32°). Club: University. Home: 1315 E. Wayne St. N. Office: Associates Bldg., South Bend, Ind. Died Feb. 11, 1955; buried Riverview, South Bend, Ind.

SEEGER, Edwin W(ilbur), engr.; born Bucyrus, O., May 22, 1892; s. John Adam and Nora B. (Crise) S.; M.E. in E.E., Ohio State U., 1913; m. Florence J. Sherer, Aug. 10, 1912; 1 son, John Roland. Mem. shop and engring. dept. Cutler-Hammer Co., Milwaukee, 1913-22, gen. supervisor engring. dept., 1922-28, asst. chief engr., 1928-38, chief engr., 1938, mgr. development, 1939-45, vice pres. and asst. sec. 1945—. Mem. bd. of regents Milwaukee School of Engring. Fellow Am. Inst. E.E. (chmn. Milwaukee sect. 1929-30, vice pres. Dist. No. 5, 1948-50, director, 1948-50). Mem. National Society Professional Engineers, Army Ordnance Association, Navy League to United States, International Association Electrical Insps., Nat. Fire Protection Assn. (mem. com. which prepares the Nat. Elec. Code; mem. adv. com. for Wis. State Elec. Code), Am. Standards Assn. (mem. sect. com. for elevator safety code), Wis. Soc. Prof. Engrs. (2d vice pres. 1944, 1st v.p. 1945, pres. 1946), Engrs. Soc. of Milwaukee (dir. 1934, 35. 36, pres. 1943-44), Wis. State C. of C. (v.p., Tau Beta Pi, Eta Kappa Nu. Triangle, Sigma Xi. Republican. Episcopalian. Mason (32°, Shriner). Registered prof. engr., State Wis. Holder 100 patents on electro magnetic devices and control systems. Home: 9702 Harding Blvd., Milw. 13, Office: 315 N. 12th St., Milw. 1. Died Aug. 28, 1955; buried Wisconsin Meml. Park.

SEEGER, Stanley Joseph, surgeon; b. Manitowoc, Wis., June 21, 1889; s. Louis F. and Wilhelmina (Bleser) S.; M.D., Northwestern U., 1911; M.Sc., Marquette U., 1936; m. Helen Buchanan, Oct. 1, 1918; children—Mary (Mrs. John W. O'Boyle), Hannah (Mrs. Wirt Davis, II), Stanley Joseph. In practice at Milwaukee, 1917-41; chief of staff Milwaukee Children's Hospital, 1934-41; chief of staff Columbia Hosp., 1928-41. Pres. Nebo, Bodcaw, Grant oil cos.; dir. Texarkana (Tex.) Nat. Bank, 1st Nat. Bank of Dallas. Pres. The William Buchanan Found. First lt. M.C., U.S. Army, 1918-19. Alumni Merit Award, Northwestern University, 1937. Mem. Founders Group American Board of Surgery. Consultant United States Public Health Service. Fellow American Coll. Surgeons; mem. A.M.A. (chmn. council on industrial health), Wis. State Med. Soc. (ex-pres.), Mayo Foundation Alumni Assn. (ex-pres.), Western Surg. Assn. Clubs: University, Milwaukee, Milwaukee Country. Contbr. to med. pubs. Home: 10444 Strait Lane. Office: Mercantile Bank Bldg., Dallas. Died June 20, 1952; buried Wisconsin Meml. Park, Milw.

SEELEY, Frank Barrows, clergyman; b. Richfield Springs, N.Y., May 10, 1872; s. Frank Hiram and Martha (Weeks) S.; prep. edn., Delaware Acad., Delhi, N.Y., 1882-89; A.B., Middlebury (Vt.) Coll., 1893, D.D., 1920; Union Theol. Sem., N.Y. City, 1893-96; m. Virginia St. Clair Boice, June 4, 1896; children—Louise Caroline (dec.), Virginia St. Clair (Mrs. Delancey A. DeGraff). Ordained ministry Presbyterian Ch. in U.S., 1896; stated supply First Presbyterian Ch., Margaretville, N.Y., 1896-97; supplied pulpit, Gardiner, N.Y., 1897-98; pastor Fair St. Reformed Ch., Kingston, N.Y. since 1898. Pres. Gen. Synod Reformed Chs. in America, 1931-32; pres. and treas. Bd. of Domestic Missions of same organization. Mem. bd. mgrs. Kingston Hosp., Ulster County Tuberculosis Hosp. Republican. Mason, Rotarian. Home: 96 Maiden Lane, Kingston, N.Y. Died Dec. 26, 1951; buried Family Mausoleum, Wiltwyck Cemetery, Kingston.

SEELY, Herman Gastrell, financial editor, writer; b. Chicago, Ill., Sept. 27, 1891; s. Herman Barker and Frances Anna (Edsall) S.; grad. Hyde Park High Sch.; spl. courses Northwestern U.; m. Gladys Frackelton, June 30, 1920; 1 dau., Marcia. Reporter, Chicago Herald, 1915-17; feature writer, Chicago Eve. Post, 1919-31, covering nat. politics editorially, 1920 and 1924 campaigns, asst. editorial writer, 1932-35, financial editor, 1925-30, chief editorial writer, 1931; with Chicago Daily News as editorial and financial writer since 1932 (following merger of Post and News); financial editor Chgo. Daily News, 1943-57, ret. Mem. 1st O.T.C., Ft. Sheridan, Ill., 1917; enlisted later in year, overseas 13 mos., winning commn. as 2d lt., Ordnance Corps, U.S. Army, 1918. Mem. Kenilworth Village bd. trustees, 1934-45, chmn. planning commn. since 1947. Mem. Westerners. Episcopalian. Clubs: Chicago Press Veterans Assn., Am. Legion, Wilmette Post No. 46. Author: A Son of the City (1917); Sagebrush Dentist (with Will Frackelton), 1941. Contbr. financial articles to various magazines, ann. supplement World Book Encyclopedia, and American Peoples Encyclopedia. Speaker on business subjects. Home: 700 Kent Rd., Kenilworth, Ill. Office: Chicago Daily News, 400 W. Madison St., Chgo. Died Feb. 17, 1958; buried Forest Home Cemetery, Milw.

SEELYE, Elizabeth Eggleston, author; b. St. Paul, Dec. 15, 1858; d. Edward and Elizabeth (Smith) Eggleston; ed. by pvt. tchrs.; m. Elwyn Seelye, Nov. 21, 1877. Author: Brandt and Red Jacket; Tecumseh, Montezuma, Pocahontas (with Edward Eggleston); The Story of Columbus; The Story of Washington; Lake George in History; Saratoga and Lake Champlain in History; also short stories in The Century and other mags. Address: Joshua's Rock, Lake George, N.Y. Died Nov. 11, 1923.

SEFRIT, Frank Ira., editor, pub.; b. Wheatland, Ind., Aug. 29, 1867; s. Moses Lark Benson and Eleoner (McDonald) S.; high sch. edn.; m. Ethel Leonard, June 10, 1891; children—Irene (Mrs. James R. Bowers), Charles Leonard, Ben Harrison. With Washington (Ind.) Gazette (now Herald), 1880-1903; postmaster, Washington, Ind., 1898-1903; bus. mgr. and gen. mgr. Salt Lake Tribune, 1904-11; gen. mgr. Salt Lake Telegram, 1908-11; editor and pub. Bellingham (Wash.) Herald, 1911—; v.p. Bellingham Pub. Co. Del. Rep. Nat. Conv., 1920. Curator, Wash. State Hist. Soc. Mason (32°, Shriner). Clubs: Washington, Hobby, Washington State Press, Mountaineers. Home: 415 13th St. Office: Herald Bldg., Bellingham, Wash. Died May 27, 1950.*

SEIBEL, George, dir. of library; b. Pitts., Sept. 13, 1872; s. Nicholas and Margaret (Eidan) S.; ed. pub. schs.; m. Helen Hiller, Sept. 6, 1894; 1 daughter, Mrs. C. B. Yorke. Editor Youth's Journal, 1893, Gazette Times, 1896-1911, Volksblatt Freiheits-Freund, 1912-25; dramatic and lit. editor Pittsburgh Sun Telegraph, 1927-36; judge Morals Court, 1939; professor of poetry and drama Fillion School; dir. Carnegie Free Library of Allegheny 1939-54, ret. Sec. Pitts. Morals Efficiency Commn.; nat. pres. Am. Turnerbund, 1923-37. Author: The Fall, 1918, 2d edit., 1923; The Wine Bills of Omar Khayyam, 1919; The Mormon Saints, 1899, 2d edit., 1919; Bacon vs. Shakespeare, 1919; The Religion of Shakespeare, 1924; Hauptmann and Sudermann, 1925; The Concert (sonnet cycle), 1934. Wrote pageant, "The Vision of She-Who-Knows," for 125th anniversary University of Pittsburgh, 1912; The Leper, drama, 1913, revived, 1920, 29; Appomattox, 1947; The Stories He Told, 1947; Book and Heart (poems), 1951. Delivered address at Johnstown, Pa., 1916, on "The Hyphen in American History," 32d edition, 1929; has lectured in German and British univs. and over 100 Am. cities; has made over 1000 radio broadcasts. Home: 19 Clinton Av., Lynbrook, N.Y. Died July 24, 1958.

SEIBELS, Edwin Granville (sē'bl's), insurance executive; b. Columbia, S.C., Sept. 12, 1866; s. Edwin Whipple and Marie Jane (Smith) S.; A.B. with distinction in Mechanics and Engineering, U. of S.C., 1885; LL.D., Newberry Coll., 1942; D.C.L., University of S.C., 1944; m. Rosamond Kershaw, Jan. 31, 1917. Left school at 14 to become page in S.C. Senate; later reporter, Columbia Register; paid way through coll. by working in ins. office of E. W. Seibels & Son, became partner, 1886; general adjuster fire losses, 1892-97; manager Southern Department, Glens Falls Ins. Co., 1898. Later Royal Exchange Assurance Corp., Colonial Fire Underwriters, Franklin Nat. Ins. Co., South Carolina Ins. Co., Glens Falls Indemnity and Niagara Fire Ins. Co. (America Fore Group) were added to dept., and named changed to Seibels, Bruce & Co., Managers, of which he is chmn. of bd. Organized and apptd. mgr., 1919, of Cotton Fire & Marine Underwriters, writing cotton insurance throughout world; retired from management, 1944. Mem. S.C. Ho. of Reps., 1909-10; organized South Carolina Insurance Co., 1910, pres. and dir., 1910-46, chmn. bd. since 1946. Chmn. bd. trustees U. of South Carolina, 1932-47. Alumni mem. Phi Beta Kappa; mem. Omicron Delta Kappa, Delta Sigma Pi, Blue Key honor fraternities. Invented vertical filing system, 1898, now in general use throughout world; original case deposited in Smithsonian Instn., Washington, D.C. June 1941. Received Am. Legion (S.C Dept.) Distinguished Public Service Award, 1945. Home: 1332 Pickens St., Columbia, S.C. Died Dec. 21, 1954; buried Trinity Church Yard, Columbia.

SEIBERLING, Frank A., rubber mfg. exec.; b. Western Star, O., Oct. 6, 1859; s. John F. and Catherine (Miller) S.; student Heidelberg Coll., Tiffin, O.; m. Gertrude F. Penfield, Oct. 12, 1887; 7 children. Founder, pres., The Goodyear Tire & Rubber Co., Akron, O., 1898-1921; founder, pres. Seiberling Rubber Co., 1921-38, chmn. bd., 1938-50. Trustee Lincoln Meml. U., Heidelberg Coll., Tiffin, O., Western Res. Academy, Hudson, O. Republican. Home: Stan Hywet Hall, Akron, O. Died Aug. 11, 1955.

SEIDEMANN, Henry Peter (sī'dē-măn)), consultant, pub. adminstrn.; b. La Vernia, Tex., Apr. 4, 1883; s. William Joseph and Julia (Curtis) S.; B.C.S., D.C. Coll., 1923, M.C.S., 1925; LL.D., Southeastern U., 1938; m. Mabel Estelle Lyman, Sept. 21, 1910. Chief fiscal insp., U.S. Reclamation Service, 1910-13, chief accountant, 1914-15, chief clk., 1916; chief of accounting staff, Inst. for Govt. Research, 1916-17; tech. dir. Commn. on Pub. Accountancy, Ty. of Hawaii, 1924-27; chief of staff, financial and accounting research, Inst. for Govt. Research, Brookings Institution, 1927-48, retired 1948: treas. Brookings Institution to June 30, 1948; coördinator Federal Social Security Bd., 1935-36; dir. Bureau Old-Age Benefits, 1936-37; consultant Hoover Commn. for reorgn. Fed. Govt., 1948-49; management consultant O.P.S., 1951-52. Assistant treasurer American Red Cross, 1917-18; maj., U.S. Army, European comptroller American Red Cross headquarters, Paris, 1918-19, deputy director, Army Specialist Corps, with rank of brigadier general, 1942-43. Member (Dawes) Dominican Economic Commission, 1929; director survey of state and county government of N.C., 1930, Ala., 1931, N.H., 1932, and participated in other govtl. surveys of state and county govts. of Ia., 1933, Okla., 1935, Montgomery County, Md., 1941. Fellow D.C. Institute C.P.A.; mem. Am. Inst. Accountants, Political Sci. Association, Am. Acad. of Polit. and Soc. Sci., Soc. for Advancement of Management, Am. Inst. of Management (associated), Governmental Research Assn., Vets. of Foreign Wars of the U.S. Decorated Officer Crown of Rumania with swords, and Officer Star of Rumania with swords. Catholic. Club: Columbia Country (Washington). Joint Author: Puerto Rico and Its Problems, 1930. Author: Manual of Accounting and Reporting for the Operating Services of The National Government, 1926; Manual of Accounting, Reporting and Business Procedure for the Territorial Government of Hawaii, 1928; Curtailment of Non-Defense Expenditures, 1941. Assisted in reorganization of financial and accounting methods of American Red Cross to meet war conditions; installed budget and accounting systems in League of Red Cross Socs., Geneva, Switzerland; formulated plan of presentation of 1st and 2d nat. budgets, presented to Congress, 1921, 22; devised uniform accounting and reporting system for comptroller gen. of U.S.; organized auditing, accounting and disbursing depts. of Agrl. Adjustment Adminstrn., 1933; assisted in orgn. of all activities of the Social Security Board and supervised the preparation of all procedures having to do with registration and wage records of the 40 million eligibles under Title II of the Social Security Act; installed budget systems and uniform accounting methods in governments of Ty. of Hawaii, Dominican Republic and State of N.H. Home: The Ontario. Office: 2853 Ontario Rd., N.W., Washington. Died May 1954

SEIFRIZ, William (sī'frĭts), prof. of botany; b. Washington, Aug. 1, 1888; s. Paul and Anna (Schmidt) S.; B.S., Johns Hopkins, 1918, Ph.D., 1920; post-grad. study U. Geneva (Switzerland), Kings Coll. (London, Eng.), Kaiser Wilhelm Inst. (Germany), 1920-22; married. Instr. botany, U. of Mich., 1923-25; prof. botany, U. Pa., 1925—. Mem. Botanical Soc. Am., Ecological Soc., Am. Chem. Soc., A.A.A.S., Phi Beta Kappa, Sigma Xi. Asso. editor Protoplasma, Biodynamica, and Jour. Colloid Science; writer of books and sci. articles on protoplasm, physiology, colloid chemistry and plant geography. Home: 3543 Rhoads Av., Newtown Square, Pa. Address: University of Pa., Phila. Died July 13, 1955; buried Indiana, Pa.

SEINSHEIMER, J. Fellman (sīn'sīm-ĕr), insurance executive; b. Galveston, Texas, September 18, 1881; s. Joseph and Blanche (Fellman) Seinsheimer; student Phillips Exeter Academy and Harvard; m. Irma Kraus, April 24, 1907; children—J. Fellman, Jr., Edna Lee (Mrs. W. C. Levin). Began in the insurance agency business, 1901; pres. and dir. Amer. Indemnity Co., Am. Fire Ins. Co., Tex. Indemnity Ins. Co., Tex. Gen. Indemnity Co., U.S. Securities Corp., Am. Finance Co. of Galveston; v.p. Galveston Corp.; director Texas Prudential Insurance Company, Cotton Concentration Company. Reformed Jewish religion. Home: 2528 Av. O. Office: P.O. Box 1259, Galveston, Tex. Died Jan. 26, 1951.

SELBY, Howard Williams, mgr. agricultural coop. assn.; b. Phila., Pa., Mar. 28, 1891; s. Joseph Wilson and Alice (Williams) S.; B.Sc., Dickinson Coll., Carlisle, Pa., 1913; student Princeton Theol. Sem., 1916-17; married Ethel Wagg, January 1, 1916; children—Howard Williams, John Horace. Sec.-treas. Selby Produce Co., Phila., Pa., 1913-17; gen. mgr. Eastern States Farmers' Exchange, Springfield, Mass., 1917-25; treas. Alfred H. Wagg Organization, Inc., West Palm Beach, Fla., 1925-34; pres. Central Farmers Trust Company, 1926-31; director First Nat. Bank in Palm Beach, 1927-31; general manager United Farmers of New England, Inc., Boston, and Morrisville, Vt., since 1934; trustee Newton (Mass.) Savings Bank. Pres. Walker-Gordon Labs. of New England; dir. Meth. Pub. House, Nashville; director Nat. Coop. Milk Producers Fedn.; pres. Vegetable Growers Assn. of America, 1916-19; trustee and mem. exec. com., Boston U. and New England Deaconess Hosp., Boston; erustee Dickinson Coll., Carlisle, Pa.; pres. Eastern States Expn., Springfield, Mass. Mem. New Eng. Council (dir.), Alpha Chi Rho. Mason (32°), Rotarian. Methodist (elder; mem. Gen. Conf., 1920, 24, 48, 52). Club: Brae Burn Country (West Newton, Mass.). Contbr. various publs. on subject of agrl. cooperation; also lecturer and weekly broadcaster since 1935. Home: 219 Chestnut St., West Newton 65, Mass. Office: 86 Cambridge St., Boston 29. Died Aug. 24, 1953.

SELECMAN, Charles Claude (sē-lĕk-măn), bishop; b. Savannah, Mo., Oct. 13, 1874; s. Isaac Henry and Josephine (Smith) S.; student Central Coll., Fayette, Missouri, 1892-98, 1916; D.D., Central College, Univ. of Southern California and Kentucky Wesleyan Univ.; LL.D., Centenary College, 1923, Austin College, Sherman, Texas, 1924, Baylor Univ., 1933, Southern Methodist Univ., 1939; married Bessie Kyle Beckner, April 27, 1899; children—Francis Asbury, Sarah Josephine (Mrs. D. W. Forbes); m. 2d, Mabel Jack Mason, July 7th, 1945. Entered ministry of the M.E. Ch., S., on rural charge, continuing 2 yrs.; social service work, at Kingdom House, St. Louis, later in New Orleans; pastor Trinity Auditorium, an institutional ch., Los Angeles, Calif., 1913-20, First M.E. Ch., S., Dallas, Tex., 1920-23; pres. Southern Meth. U., Dallas, 1923-38; became bishop Meth. Ch., 1938, ret. Mem. Gen. Hosp. Board; also founder Golden Cross Soc. which is an adjunct of Gen. Hosp. Bd. Served with Y.M.C.A. in U.S., Eng. and France, 1918, World War; field sec. War Work Comm., M.E. Ch., S., 1918; del. World Conf. on Faith and Order, Lausanne, Switzerland, 1927, Edinburgh, Scotland, 1937; chmn. commn. on evangelism, Meth. Ch., 1940—. pres. Council of Bishops, 1945-46. Member Sigma Alpha Epsilon Fraternity. Mason (33°, Shriner); Red Cross of Constantine A.M. & A.M. Author: Christ of Chaos, 1923; The Challenge of Citizenship (with Dr. S. D. Myres), 1933; Methodist Primer, Primer & Evangelism. Home: 6001 Hillcrest, Dallas. Died Mar. 27, 1958; buried Hillcrest Mausoleum, Dallas.

SELF, James C(uthbert), textile exec.; b. Edgefield Co., S.C., July 1, 1876; s. Jas. Anderson and Callie (Holloway) S.; Student Clemson Coll., 1894, Dr. Textile Industry (hon.), 1952; L.H.D., U.S.C., 1952, Lander Coll., 1953; m. Lura Mathews, October, 1915; 1 son, James Cuthbert in cotton mfg. bus. since 1908; pres. Greenwood (S.C.) Mills (a consolidation of Greenwood Cotton Mill, Mathews Mill and Ninety Six Cotton Mill); dir. Piedmont & No. Ry. Co. Chmn. S.C. State Bd. Conciliation. Pres. Self Found. Named Man of the South, 1952. Office: Greenwood Mills, Greenwood, S.C. Died July 21, 1955.

SELIGER, Robert V., cons. psychiatrist; b. New York, N.Y., June 16, 1900; s. Charles M. and Malvine (Wiltschek) S.; student Fordham U.; M.D., U. of Md.; m. Beatrice R. Gorden, Sept. 7, 1926; children—Polly M., Charles R. Asst. visiting psychiatrist, Johns Hopkins Hosp., 1936-46, now asst. neurologist; instr. psychiatry, Johns Hopkins U. Med. Sch., 1936-46, now asst. in neurology; ex-chief staff, Haarlem Lodge Sanitarium, Farm for Patients with Alcoholic Problems; visiting psychiatrist Sinai Hosp., Baltimore, Md.; medical consultant American Graphology Society; executive director Nat. Com. on Alcohol Hygiene, Inc.; pres. Correctional Assn., on affiliate of The Am. Prison Assn.; lecturer in psychiatry for nurses, Seton Inst., Baltimore; mem. Mayor's commn. on problems of Juvenile Delinquency; neuro-psychiatrist Selective Service, med. advisory bd., Baltimore. Fellow Am. Psychiat. Assn., Am. Assn. Mental Deficiencies, Am. Geriatrics Society, International Psychosomatic Society; member American Medical Writers Assn., Am. Psychosomatic Soc., Psychopathol. Society, Southern Psychiatric Society, Maryland Psychiat. Soc., Maryland Private Practicing Psychiatrists Assn., Am. and Southern med. assns. Author: Alcoholics Are Sick People, 1945; A Guide on Alcoholism for Social Workers, 1945; Psychiatry for You, 1945; Contemporary Criminal Hygiene, 1946; Handbook of Correctional Medicine, 1946; It's Smarter Not to Drink, 1949; How to Help an Alcoholic, 1951; The "Dope" on Dope, 1951; For Happier Living, 1952. Contributing editor in psychiatry Current Medical Digest. Feature writer many publs. Mem. editorial staff Alcohol Hygiene; advisory editorial staff Jour. Clin. Psychopathology and Psychotherapy. Home: 2030 Park Av. Office: 2030 Park Av., Baltimore 17. Died April 24, 1953.

SELL, Lewis L., polyglot tech. lexicographer; b. Csenger, Hungary, Aug. 25, 1890; s. Samuel and Kathryn (Mark) S.; B.A., Columbia, 1916, M.A., 1917, Ph.D., 1918; univ. scholar, 1916-17, Drisler fellow, 1917-18; m. Ruth Krugman, Feb. 11, 1927; 1 dau., Kathryn. Came to U.S., 1903, naturalized, 1914. Since graduation from coll. has been operating a profl. translation bur., specializing in tech. catalog translations for Royal Typewriter Co., Wright Aeronautical Corp., Studebaker Export Corp., Gen. Motors, Bethlehem Steel Corp., Civil Aeronautics Adminstrn., Rockefller Found., etc. Lectr. in polyglot technical lexicography at Columbia, 1950-52. Author: De Catulli Carmine Sexagesimo Quarto Quaesitnes Divarsae, 1918; English-French Technical Dictionary of the Automobile and Allied Industries, 1932; Pan American Dictionary and Travel Guide, 1935 (2d edit. 1941); Practical Polyglot Technical Lexicography and the Professional Polyglot Technician, 1945; Comprehensive English-Spanish Technical Dictionary, 1944 (chosen to represent United States at first Pan-American Book Exposition, Washington, 1945); University and Collegiate Syllabus for Formation of Professional Polyglot Technician, 1945; Spanish-English Comprehensive Technical Dictionary, 1949, sect. II, 1959; English-Portuguese Comprehensive Technical Dictionary, 1953; Comprehensive Spanish-English specialist tech. dictionaries for various technical fields, 1955, 1957, 1958; Portuguese-English Comprehensive Technical Dictionary, 1959; Technical translator: Practicum (textbook), 1950. Collaborator: Schloman's English-French-Italian-German Technical Dictionary of Aeronautics, Berlin, 1932 ; Schloman's Hoyer-Kreuter Technical Dictionary in German-English-French, Berlin, 1932. Home: 24 W. 69th St., N.Y.C. 24. Office: 15 Park Row, N.Y.C. 7. Died Dec. 31, 1958; buried Mount Lebanon, Bklyn.

SELLAR, Robert F., humanitarian; b. Philadelphia, Pa., Feb. 10, 1884; s. Robert William and Alwilda (Fisher) S.; ed. Temple Coll., Philadelphia, Pa., class of 1904; m. Letitia Elliot, Sept. 9, 1908; children—Robert Elliot, Dorothy Katherine (wife of Rev. E. Irving Braden); m. 2d Ruth Wilder, Oct. 31, 1933; 1 dau., Jeanne Louise. Engineer Pencoyd Iron Works, Am. Bridge Co. Pittsburgh Testing Lab., 1905-18; associated with Erie County Soc. for Prevention of Cruelty to Animals, Buffalo, N.Y., 1919-23. Humane Soc. of Mo., St. Louis, Mo., 1923-31; pres. Animal Rescue League of Boston, 1931-46; pres. Am. Humane Assn., Albany, since 1947. Served as Y.M.C.A. war sec., France, 1918-19. Mem. Am. Humane Assn. (pres.). Republican. Presbyterian. Clubs: Rotary (Albany, N.Y.), Torch. Home: Leesome Lane, Altamont. Office: 135 Washington Av., Albany 6, N.Y. Died Dec. 18, 1951.

SELSER, James Clyde, Jr., air force officer; b. Alexandria, La., Sept. 10, 1912; s. James Clyde and Ernestine (Gourrier) S.; B.S. in Aero. Engring., Ga. Sch. Tech., 1933; grad. Command and Gen. Staff Sch., Ft. Leavenworth, Kan., 1944, Army-Navy Staff Coll., 1945; m. Mary Garland, Nov. 12, 1935; children—Mary Victoria, James Clyde III, Christopher Garland. Commd. 2d lt., inf., U.S. Army, 1933, 2d lt., AAC, 1936, advanced through grades to maj. gen., 1951; assigned 8th Pursuit Group, Langley Field, Va., 1933-36; flying instr. Randolph Field, Tex., 1936-40; mem. U.S. Air Mission to Brazil, 1940-43; mil. air attache to Brazil, 1943, also sr. Air Force mem. Joint Brazil-U.S. Def. Commn.; assigned G-2 for Air, 10th Army Hdqrs., T.H., 1945; comdr. 444th Bomb Group, Tinian, 1945; comdr. Davis-Monthan Air Force Base, 1946-50; dep. dir. operations Strategic Air Command, Offut Air Force Base, Omaha, Neb., 1950-53; comdr. 7th Air Div., Eng., 1953-54; dep. comdr. 8th Air Force, 1954-56; dep. dir., net evaluation subcom. NSC, 1956—. Decorated Legion of Merit, D.F.C., Bronze Star Medal, Air Medal, Presdl. Unit Citation; Brazilian War Medal, Order So. Cross, Brazilian Order Aero. Merit; Portuguese Order of Avis. Mem. Delta Tau Delta, Omicron Delta Kappa, Pi Delta Epsilon. Roman Catholic. Rotarian. Home: Quarters 84, Bolling Air Force Base, Washington. Died Nov. 18, 1956.

SELTZER, Theodore, business exec.; b. France, 1870; Sedan Coll., 1889. Pres. and dir. Bengue, Inc.; v.p. and dir. Commonwealth Trust Co., Union City, N.J.; dir. Pacquin Inc., N.Y.C. Pres. and dir. French Hosp. of N.Y. Home: 55 King Av., Weehawken, N.J. Office: Bengue Inc., Union City, N.J. Died Jan. 1957.*

SELVIG, Conrad George, ex-congressman; b. Rushford, Minn., Oct. 11, 1877; s. Gunder C. and Marie (Hognestad) S.; apptd. cadet U.S. Mil. Acad., 1896, but did not attend; A.B., U. of Minn., 1907, A.M., 1908; m. Marion E. Wilcox, June 17, 1903; children—Helen Marion, Margaret Elizabeth, Conrad George. Supt. schs., Harmony, 1901-06, Glencoe, 1907-10; supt. U. Minn. Northwest School of Agr. and Agrl. Expt. Sta., Crookston, Minn., 1910-27; mem. 70th to 72d Congresses, 9th Minn. Dist. Served as pvt., Minn. Vols., Spanish-Am. War, 1898. Pres. Red River Valley Live Stock Assn., 1918-36, Red River Valley Winter Shows, 1910-27; gen. chmn. N.W. Minn. Food and Conservation Commn., Minn. div. (Northwestern Sect.) Nat. War Work Council. Mem. Am. Acad. Polit. and Social Sci. Mason (K.T.). Writer, lectr. on social welfare and govt.

Address: 1303 Georgina Av., Santa Monica, Cal. Died Aug. 2, 1953.

SEMAN, Philip Louis (sē'mān), social worker; b. Warsaw, Poland, Nov. 11, 1881; s. Louis and Salka (Geisler) S.; brought by parents to U.S., 1892; B.S., Adelphi Coll., Brooklyn, N.Y., 1902; Washington U. Law Sch., 1908; Ph.D., The Liberal Church of America, 1932; m. Beatrice Prigozen, July 28, 1907; children—Jacob Philip, Louise Salka, Gertrude Rose. In charge club dept., Ednl. Alliance, N.Y. City, 1897-1900; teacher Jewish Orphan Asylum, N.Y. City, 1900-02; club dir. Hebrew Sheltering and Guardian Soc., N.Y. City, 1902-05; supt. Jewish Ednl. and Charitable Assn. of St. Louis, Mo., 1905-10; exec. dir. Fedn. Brooklyn Jewish Charities, 1910-12; asso. dir. Industrial Removal Office, N.Y. City, 1912-13; gen. dir. Jewish community centers, Chgo., 1913-45, now gen. dir. emeritus; pres. People's Jr. Coll., 1933-36; lecturer in sociology, Hebrew Theol. Coll.; faculty U. of Judaism, West Coast br. Jewish Theol. Sem. of Am. Member of faculty of School of Social Economics, Washington University (St. Louis, Mo.), 1908-10. Sec. Missouri Assn. for Prevention of Blindness, 1905-10. Mem. exec. com. White House Conf. on Child Health and Protection, Chgo. area, 1931; v.p. Nat. Conf. Social Work, 1932; mem. Central States Com. of One Thousand, Nat. Public Housing Conf.; mem. adv. bd. Group Health Coop., Inc.; mem. adv. com. Planned Parenhtood Com., Chgo. Woman's Aid; mem. Boys' Workers Assn. Chgo. (ex-pres.), Nat. Conf. Jewish Social Service (pres. 1931), Nat. Assn. Jewish Community Center Soc. (ex-pres.), Jewish Agrl. Soc. Am.; former v.p. Hillel Foundation Commn., now commr. for life; chmn. Chgo. Recreation Commn., 1932-46, now hon. chmn.; served as mem. Chgo. adv. com. N.Y.A.; former dir. Jewish Welfare Bd.; v.p. Assn. Leisure Time Educators; mem. Council of 100 of Am. Assn. for Adult Edn., 1943; adv. mem. Chgo. Plan Commn.; mem. Nat. Group of Ednl. Advisers, O.W.I.; member Selective Draft Board No. 111. Fellow A.A.A.S.; mem. Am. Assn. Social Workers, Pi Gamma Mu. Awarded 40 year service medal Boys' Club Fedn. Am., 1939. Jewish religion. Club: Collegiate. Author: Jewish Community Life, 1924; Jewish Community Center, 1925; Program of a Jewish Community Center, 1926; Problem of the Leisure Hour, 1927; Training for Leadership, 1928; Training for Social Expression, 1929; Social Orientation, 1930; Vision and Experiment in Community Service, 1931; Community Culture in an Era of Depression, 1932. Mem. editorial bd. of Jewish Center; mem. selection com. Dept. Social Instns., Universal Jewish Ency. Asso. editor to Youth Leaders Digest, American Citizen. Contbr. to Social Science, Recreation, The Advocate, The Parent-Teachers' Voice, American Forests, Unity, Character and Citizenship, School Executive, Federal Probation, Nat. Jew. Monthly, Biosophical Review, American Hebrew, World Book Ency., Cal. Youth Authority Quar., Cal. Jour. Secondary Edn., Western Folklore. Home: 536 N. Arden Blvd., Los Angeles. Retired 1945. Died Sept. 25, 1957; buried Mt. Sinai Meml. Park, Los Angeles.

SEMLER, George Herbert, lawyer; b. West Orange, N.J., Aug. 17, 1891; s. George and Bertha (Schedler) S.; LL.B., Harvard, 1917; A.B., Yale, 1914; m. Grace Parker Achelis, Oct. 5, 1923; children—Joan Achelis (Mrs. G. V. Hamilton, Jr.), George Herbert Jr., Gay Parker (Mrs. Albert Pershing Hildebandt), Peter. Admitted to New York bar, 1919; law clk. Winthop & Stimson (now Winthrop, Stimson, Putnam & Roberts), N.Y. City, 1919-26, mem. firm 1926-—; dir. Gen. Telephone Corp., Hartford Electric Steel Corp., Bristol Bearing Corp. Served as 1st lt., 3d Div., U.S. Army, 1917-19; assigned to Gen. McKinstry's Bur., Peace Conf., Paris. Mem. Am. Bar Assn., County Lawyers Bar Assn., Bar Assn. City N.Y. Clubs: University, Yale, Maidstone, Piping Rock, National Golf Links Assn., Lunch (N.Y. City). Home: 1105 Park Av., N.Y. City 28. Office: 40 Wall St., N.Y.C. 5. Died Nov. 10, 1954.

SENANAYAKE, Don Stephen (sä-nä-nä' yä-kä), Prime Minister of Ceylon, agriculturist; b. Botale, Oct. 20, 1884; s. Don Spater and Elizabeth Catherine Perera (Gunasekera) S.; student St. Thomas' Coll., Ceylon; m. Emily Maud Dunuwillie, July 4, 1909; children—Dudley, Robert. Cocoanut, rubber planter, also owner, mgr. plumbago mines; temperance, social worker; interested in politics since 1915; mem. Legislative Council, Ceylon, 1924-31; mem. State Council for Minuangoda Constituency, minister Agr. and Lands, 1931-47; leader State Council, v. chmn. Bd. Ministers, 1942-47; mem. for Mirigama Constituency Ho. Reps. since 1947; 1st Prime Minister, minister Defence and External Affairs since 1947; apptd. Privy Councillor, 1950. Pres. United Nat. Party since 1946. Author: Agriculture and Patriotism. Home: Woodlands, Kanatta Rd., Borrella, Colombo 8, Ceylon. Died Mar. 22, 1952; buried Botale.

SENCENBAUGH, Charles Wilber, banker; b. Aurora, Ill.; s. S. S. and Rebecca R. (Wilber) S.; student U. Mich.; m. Stella M. Smith, Feb. 28, 1911. Sec.-treas. Austin Mfg. Co., Chgo., 1913-34; sec.-treas. Austin-Western Rd. Machinery Co., Chgo., 1913-34; v.p. Wester Wheeler Scraper Co., Aurora, Ill., 1925-29, pres., 1929-34; chmn. bd. Western-Austin Co., 1934-—; chmn. bd. Old Second Nat. Bank, 1933-—; pres. S. S. Sencenbaugh Co., 1925-—. Clubs: Aurora Country; University (Chgo.). Home: R.F.D. Mill Creek, Batavia, Ill. Died Dec. 7, 1950.*

SENEAR, Francis Eugene (sŭn'ẽr), dermatologist; b. Salamanca, N.Y., Nov. 5, 1889; s. Eugene Barker and Alice Lenora (Wellman) S.; B.S., U. of Mich., 1912, M.D., 1914, hon. M.S., 1939; m. Anne E. Seitz, Aug. 6, 1917; 1 son, Allen Eugene. Instr. dermatology, U. of Mich., 1915-16; instr. dermatology, U. of Ill., 1916-18, asso., 1918-20, asst. prof., 1920-21, asso. prof., 1921-22, prof. and head dept. dermatology, 1923-55, emeritus; consulting dermatologist Illinois Central Railroad, 1918-—; attending dermatologist Illinois Central R.R. Hosp. since 1918, Ravenswood Hosp. since 1920, St. Joseph's Hosp. since 1922, Presbyterian Hosp. since 1942; spl. consultant U.S. Public Health Service. Served as 1st lt. M.O.R.C., U.S. Army, since 1916. Mem. adv. com. Chicago Intensive Treatment Center. Mem. American Board of Dermatology and Syphilology 1939-41, pres. 1946 to 51. Member Am. Med. Assn. (sec. section on dermatology, 1930-32; chmn. sect. 1933), Ill. State and Chicago med. socs., Inst. of Medicine of Chicago, Chicago Dermatol. Soc. (pres. 1927-28), Am. Dermatol. Assn. (pres. 1938), Am. Coll. Physicians, Pan-Am. Med. Congress (pres. Dermatological Sect. 1935), Am. Acad. Dermatology (pres. 1949), Alpha Omega Alpha, Sigma Xi, Pi Kappa Epsilon, Nu Sigma Nu; corr. mem. Danish Austrian, and Swedish dermatol. socs.; hon. mem. Australian, British, Italian and Manhattan dermatol. socs.; hon. v.p. Internat. Congress Dermatology, London, 1952. Republican. Episcopalian. Clubs: University, Indian Hill Country. Editor: Year Book of Dermatology (annual editions 1922-30). Home: 592 Cherry St., Winnetka, Ill. Office: 55 E. Washington St., Chgo. Died Jan. 1958.

SENNING, John Peter, univ. prof.; b. Rotenberg, Germany, Aug. 4, 1884; s. William and Anna Katherine (Holle) S.; came to U.S., 1892, naturalized, 1905; A.B., Westmar Coll., LeMars, Ia., 1908; Ph. D., U. of Ill., 1924; student U. of Chicago, 1909-10; fellow in history, Yale, 1914-15; m. Elizabeth Anna Stone, June 18, 1913. Instr. Ill. Coll., Jacksonville, 1910-11, Wesleyan U., Middletown, Conn., 1912-14, U. of Neb., 1916-18, asst. prof. polit. sci., 1918-20, asso. prof., 1920-26, prof. polit. science, 1935-52, chmn. dept. polit. sci., 1920-23 and 1929-39; vis. prof. U. of Tex., summer 1937. Mem. Insterstate Crime Commn., 1935-41; mem. survey com. Neb. Constitutional Conv., 1919-20, mem. com. which drafted constitutional amendment for unicameral legislature, 1934, cons. to legislature in districting state, 1935; mem. Lincoln Bd. Edn., 1947-54; chmn. city-county bldg. planning com., 1948-54. Served as mem. Regional War Labor Bd., 1943-45. Mem. Am. Polit. Sci. Assn. (mem. exec. council 1927-31; dir. state confs., civic edn. and state and local govt. 1931-32), Am. Soc. for Pub. Adminstrn., Nat. Municipal League, Civil Service Assembly, Govtl. Research Assn. (Nat.), Lincoln C. of C., Phi Alpha Delta. Republican. Conglist. Mason (32°). Club: University. Author: The One House Legislature, 1937. Editor and compiler of Survey of Financial Administration of Nebraska Counties, 18 vols. (duplicated), 1938. Contbr. to various professional jours. Home: 2730 Manse Av., Lincoln 2, Neb. Died Dec. 4, 1954; buried Joliet, Ill.

SENSENBRENNER, Frank Jacob (sĕn'sĕn-brenẽr), paper mfr.; b. Menasha, Wis., Dec. 23, 1864; s. Phillip J. and Catherine (Mari) S.; ed. parochial and pubs. schs.; m. Margaret Stilp, Apr. 15, 1885 (deceased 1911); children—John Stilp, Gertrude M. (Mrs. James W. Bergstrom), J. Leslie, Margaret M. (Mrs. George M. Gilbert). Began as clerk in postoffice, Menasha, 1879; bookkeeper Menasha Chair Co., 1880-84, John Strange, lumber and pail mfr., 1884-86, Webster Mfg. Co., 1886-89; became connected with Kimberly-Clark Co., paper mfrs., Neenah, 1889; vice pres., gen. mgr. and dir. Kimberly-Clark Corp., 1905-28, pres. and dir., 1928-42, chmn. bd. and dir., 1942-44, dir. since 1945; pres. Spruce Falls Power & Paper Co., 1920-42, William Bonifas Lumber Co., 1909-42; formerly pres. Neenah-Menasha Water Power Co., North Star Timber Co.; dir. Internat. Cellucotton Products Co., First Nat. Bank (Appleton), First Nat. Bank (Neenah), Wis. Bankshares Corp.; trustee and mem. exec. com. Northwestern Mutual Life Ins. Co. Trustee Marquette U. (bd. govs.), Lawrence Coll.; mem. bd. regents U. of Wis. (pres.); mem. lay adv. com. St. Norbert Coll., West De Pere, Wis. Director Wis. Manufacturers Association, 1911-45. Decorated Knight Commander Order of St. Gregory the Great. Republican. K.C., Cath. Knight of Wis., Modern Woodman. Clubs: Neenah, Menasha, Milwaukee, Chicago Athletic, Union League (Chicago). Office: N. Commercial St., Neenah, Wis. Died July 22, 1952; buried Neenah.

SENTELL, George Washington, merchant; b. Collinsburg, La., Sept. 4, 1863; s. George W. and Mildred A. (Dickson) S.; A.B., Tulane Coll., 1884; m. Maggie L. Sherburne, Sept. 8, 1886; children—Bessie (Mrs. Motte Martin), Newton Washington, James Henry, Eulalie (wife of Dr. Marvin Cappel), Eugenia (Mrs. C. S. Churchill), Marguerite (Mrs. Otis Fleshman), Claudia. Admitted to partnership, G. W. Sentell & Co., 1885, liquidating business of same, 1900-02; located in Avoyelles Parish, 1901; became mgr. Leinster Refinery, 1900; v.p. Avoyelles Wholesale Grocery Co.; propr. G. W. Sentell, gen. mdse. Former mem. Crescent Rifles, La. Field Arty., Washington Arty., all of New Orleans. Mem. La. Live Stock Sanitary Commn., 1908-17; formerly mem. La. State Live Stock Sanitary Board. Mem. La Hereford Breeders' Assn. (v.p.), La. Swine Breeders' Assn. (v.p.), La. Jersey Cattle Club (v.p.), Tulane Alumni Assn. Democrat. Presbyn. Mason. Home: Bunkie, La. Deceased.

SENTELLE, Mark Edgar, educator; b. Greeneville, Tenn., Oct. 6, 1874; s. Gideon Stephens and Rachel Louise (Jones) S.; A.B., Davidson (N.C.) Coll., 1894; A.M., Yale, 1899; grad. study Princeton U. and Princeton Theol. Sem., U. Chgo., Columbia; D.D., King Coll., Bristol, Tenn., 1909; LL.D., Presbyn. Coll. of S.C., 1924; unmaried. Prin. high sch., Davidson, 1894-96; prof. mathematics, King Coll., 1896-98; ordained minister Presbyn. Ch. in U.S.A., 1902, pastor in Tex., 1902-03; prof. philosophy Davidson Coll., 1903-44, dean, 1920-41, prof. emeritus, 1944-—. Mem. Phi Beta Kappa, Omicron Delta Kappa, Sigma Upsilon. Democrat. Club: Philosophy. Home: Davidson, N.C. Died Apr. 13, 1949.

SERLES, Earl R., univ. dean; b. Salem, S.D., Nov. 18, 1890; s. Francis Marion and Sarah Genevieve (French) S.; Ph.G., S.D. State Coll., 1911, B.S. in Pharmacy, 1915, M.S. in Chemistry and Pharmacy, 1917, Doctor of Laws (hon.), 1955; Ph.D., University of Minnesota, 1934; married Daphne Chapman, June 12, 1917. With S.D. State Coll., 1913-40, as student asst. in chemistry and pharmacy, 1913-15, asst. prof. pharmacy, 1916-17, asst. station chemist, summer 1916, prof. and acting head pharmacy dept., 1917-23, dean div. of pharmacy, 1923-40; dean Coll. of Pharmacy, U. of Ill., since 1940. Private 1st class, U.S. Army, 1917-18, Chem. Warfare Service, Med. Unit. Mem. Chicago Nutrition Com., since 1943. Mem. Pharmacopoeia Revision Com., 1930-40; mem. subject matter com., George-Deen program Distbn. Edn. for Retail Pharmacists since 1940; mem. Am. Pharm. Assn. (syllabus com. since 1926; pres. 1946-47), S.D. Acad. Sci., S.D. Pharm. Assn., S.D. Pub. Health Assn. (advisory council 1935-40), Am. Assn. Colleges of Pharmacy, S.D. Med. Assn. (asso.), Soc. Exptl. Biologists (asso.), Am. Legion, Gamma Alpha, Rho Ki, Kappa Psi, Phi Beta Pi, Sigma Xi, Blue Key. Mason (K.T.), Order Eastern Star. Club: Chaos. Home: 7214 Oak Av., River Forest, Ill. Office: 808 S. Wood St., Chgo. Died Mar. 13, 1957; buried Alexandria, S.D.

SERRILL, William Jones, gas engr.; b. Darby, Pa., Nov. 10, 1862; s. William Daniel Humphreys and Frances Paschall (Lloyd) S.; B.S. in M.E., U. Pa., 1883; m. Alice Rush Douglass, Apr. 28, 1898. With United Gas Improvement Co., Phila., 1885-—; engr. of distribution, Phila. Gas Works (leased by United Gas Improvement Co.) 1897-—. Pres. Haverford Tp. Pub. Schs. Mem. Illuminating Engring. Soc. (pres., 1916-17), Am. Gas Inst., Nat. Comml. Gas Assn. Republican. Mem. Friends Ch. Clubs: University (Phila., N.Y.C.); Engineers (Phila.); Merion Cricket (Haverford); Phila. Country. Home: Harverford, Pa. Died May 28, 1952.

SERVICE, Robert William, author; b. Preston, Eng., Jan. 16, 1874; s. Robert and Emily (Parker) S.; ed. Hillhead High Sch., Glasgow, Scotland; m. Germaine Bourgoin, 1913; 1 dau., Iris. Began as bank clerk with Comml. Bank of Scotland, Glasgow, 1888; emigrated to Canada, 1894, and was employed on a farm near Duncan, B.C., 1 yr.; traveled on the Pacific Coast in various occupations for several yrs.; returned to Duncan, B.C., 1902; with Canadian Bank of Commerce, Victoria, B.C., 1905, transferred to Kamloops, B.C., later as teller to Whitehorse, Yukon Ty., then to Dawson, 1907; resigned 1909; spent 8 yrs. in the Yukon and traveled extensively in the sub-artic; war corr. for Toronto (Can.) Star in the Balkans. Served as ambulance driver, Am. Red Cross; later, intelligence officer, Canadian Army, World War I. Author: Songs of a Sourdough (included "The Shooting of Dan McGrew"), 1907 (pub. later as The Spell of the Yukon); Ballads of a Cheechako, 1909; Trail of '98, 1909; Rhymes of a Rolling Stone, 1912; The Pretender (novel); Rhymes of a Red Cross Man, 1917; Ballads of a Bohemian (included "It Is Later Than You Think"), 1920; The Poisoned Paradise (novel); The Rough-neck (novel); The Master of the Microbe (novel), 1926; The House of Fear (novel), 1927; Why Not Grow Young? Or, Living for Longevity, 1928; Ploughman of the Moon (autobiography); Harper of Heaven, 1947; Songs of a Sun-Lover, 1949; Rhymes of a Roughneck, 1950; Lyrics of a Low Brow, 1951; Rhymes of a Rebel, 1952; Songs for my Supper, 1953; Carols of an Old Codger, 1954; Rhymes for My Rags, 1955; More Collected Verse, 1955. Address: Monte Carlo, France. Died Sept. 11, 1958.

SERVISS, Frederick LeVerne, educator; born Telluride, Colo., July 30, 1895; son of Harry LeVerne and Nellie Genevieve (Graham) S.; E.M., Colo. Sch. Mines (fellow civil engring. 1919-20), 1920, M.S., 1922; grad. study George Washington U.; m. Abigail McCarthy, Dec. 26, 1920 (died Feb. 1, 1941); children—Donald, Daniel, Elizabeth, Helen, John, Dorothy, Eileen, Mary Ellen, Margaret. Engr. Colo. Fuel and Iron Co., Utah Fuel Co., 1922-—; cons. Ernest C. Ruebsam, Washington, D.C., 1925-31, Ind. Limestone Co., Bedford, 1931-—, cons. on coal, western div. Penn. R.R. Co., 1944-—. City and water works engr. Trinidad, Colo.; part-time teacher, Catholic U. of Am., 1923-29; mem. faculty, metall., econ. and geol. dept. Purdue U., 1923-25, asst. prof., 1925-29, prof. 1929-34, prof. geology and head of div., 1934-—. Served as pvt., U.S. Army, 1917-19. Fellow A.A.A.S., Am. Geog. Soc.; mem. Am. Inst. M.E., Am. Soc. C.E., N.Y. Acad. Sci., Sigma Xi, Tau Beta Pi, Kappa Sigma. Roman Catholic. Home: 136 E. Stadium Av., West LaFayette, Ind. Died July 23, 1954; buried St. Boniface Cemetery, Lafayette.

SESKIS, I. J., 1st vice pres. and dir. Schenley Distillers Corp. Address: 350 Fifth Av., N.Y.C. 1. Died Mar. 1951.*

SETON, Grace Thompson (Mrs. Gallatin Thompson Seton), writer, lecturer, book designer; b. Sacramento, Cal.; d. Albert and Clemenzie (Rhodes) Gallatin; ed. Packer Collegiate Inst., Bklyn., m. Ernest Thompson Seton, June 1, 1896 (div. 1935); 1 dau., Anya. Began newspaper work in Paris, France, later engaged in designing books. Sec. Conn. div. woman's com. of Council Nat. Defense, 1917-19; organizer and dir. Woman's Motor Unit of La-Bienêtre du Blessé, Woman's City Club, 1917-19, in France. Recipient médaille d'honneur, des Epidémiies, primière classe, and médaille de reconnaissance, by French Govt.; diploma de la Croix Rouge française comite Britannique. Chmn. Washington, D.C. Women's Auxiliary 2d Liberty Loan Com.; v.p. Conn. Women's Suffrage Assn., 1910-20; mem. organizing com. Nat. Soc. of Women Geographers; pres. Nat. League Am. Pen Women, 1926-28, 1930-32; v.p. Nat. Library Assn. for Blind, v.p. Woodcraft League America; del. to Pacific Conf. for Women, Honolulu, 1928, 31, 34, Vancouver, 1937. Fellow Am. Geog. Soc.; mem. Inst. World Affairs, Indian Woman's Assn., Internat. Policewomen, Nat. Inst. Social Sciences (hon.), Soc. of Women Geographers, English-Speaking Union, Authors League America, etc. Historian Field Museum expdn. to Brazil, 1926; as chmn. letters Nat. Council of Women, U.S.A., organized and conducted the Internat. Women Writers Conclave, Chicago, 1933, also Internat. Book Exhibit Century of Progress Expn., 1933, the books now known as Biblioteca Femina, Northwestern U. Internat. vice convener of letters for 41 countries at Internat. Council of Women Triennial, 1934, Paris; headed U.S. del., Edinburgh, 1938. Chmn. ad hoc com. for Participation of 11 countries in Internat. Women's Art Exhbn., N.Y.C., 1939-40; dir. lit. activities, Pan-Am. League, 1941-45; contbr. Writers War Bd., Overseas Div., O.W.I. Recipient literary awards, 1926, 33, 48, 50, 53. Honorary mem. Theta Sigma Phi. Chmn. com. archives, Nat. Council of Women, U.S.A., 1942. Founder Girl Pioneers which became Camp Fire Girls. Explorer Mois country, Indo-China, 1933. Clubs: Colony, Pen and Brush (pres. 1898-1913), Soroptimist (honorary) (New York City); Everglades (Palm Beach, Fla.); Lyceum (London). Conn. chmn. Nat. Poetry Day, editor Poetry Booklet, 1950-55. Author: A Woman Tenderfoot in the Rockies, 1900; Nimrod's Wife, 1907; A Woman Tenderfoot in Egypt, 1923 (selected, 1933, as one of best 100 books by American women during past century); Chinese Lanterns, 1924; Yes, Lady Saheb (winner Washington Book prize contest for best serious books), 1926; Log of the Look-See, 1932; Magic Waters, 1933; Poison Arrows, 1940; The Singing Traveller, 1947; Partial Survey, Women's Archives (in prep); Singing Heart, 1957; also poems and song lyrics, 1946. Contbr. to mags. Address: Binney Lane, Old Greenwich, Conn. Died Mar. 19, 1959; buried Greenwich, Conn.

SETTERFIELD, Hugh E(merson), univ. prof.; b. Shelby, O., May 12, 1900; s. William Gibbs and Lumetta Bell (Dwire) S.; A.B., Wittenberg Coll., 1923; M.Sc. Ohio State U., 1924, Ph.D., 1935; m. Annabella Dean, Aug. 17, 1935; children—Hugh, Suzanne, Elizabeth; m. 2d, Mrs. Maria Voskamp, Dec. 21, 1952. Prof. anatomy, College of Medicine, Ohio State U. since 1934. Mem. Sigma Xi, Kappa Phi Kappa, Gamma Alpha, Nu Sigma Nu, Alpha Epsilon Delta (nat. pres. 1943). Democrat. Home: Route 2, Westerville, O. Office: Ohio State University, Columbus, O. Died Mar. 16, 1953.

SETZE, Julius Adolphus, ret. exec.; b. N.Y.C., June 29, 1871; s. Alphonse Joseph and Mary M. (Crowell) S.; Croton mil. acad., Brooklyn Poly.; m. Sarah Eve Simmons, June 10, 1896; 1 dau., Josephine. Mem. bd. dirs., Tefft Weller & Co., N.Y., 1891-1912; asso. with V. Everit Macy, Esq., N.Y., 1917-23; treas., mem. bd. dirs., P. W. French & Co., N.Y., 1924-29; retired from bus., 1929; dir., chmn. trust and exec. coms. 1st. Nat. Bank & Trust Co., Augusta; dir. Trust Co. of Ga. Assos., Augusta. Trustee, regent, U. of South (hon. Life alumnus), Sewanee, Tenn.; trustee Tuttle-Newton Home, Augusta; adv. bd. Augusta Salvation Army (1st hon. life mem.); Sr. warden. Ch. of Good Shepherd, Augusta, Ga. Mem. standing com., bd. officers and registrar of diocese, Corp. of Diocese of Ga. Home: 635 Gary St., Augusta, Ga. Died May 26, 1955; buried Greenwood Cemetery, Bklyn.

SEVERN, Edmund, musician; b. Nottingham, Eng., Dec. 10, 1862; s. Edmund and Elizabeth (Thornton) S.; brought to U.S., 1866; pub. sch. edn., Hartford, Conn.; studied violin with father, Franz Milcke, Bernhard Listemann and Emanuel Wirth, composition with Philip Scharwenka and George W. Chadwick; m. Minna Sites, May 1900 (died Oct. 1925); m. 2d, Marion Burt Woodsum, Feb. 7, 1927. Composer orchestral, chamber, choral, instrumental and vocal music. Home: 1063 Franklin St., Melrose Highlands, Mass. Died May 14, 1942; buried Melrose, Mass.

SEVEY, Robert (sē'vē), bus. consultant; b. Cleveland, O., July 5, 1898; s. George Edwin and Mary Jane (Murray) S.; ed. pub. and private schs., Chicago, Ill., and Culver, Ind.; student U. of Pa., 1919-23; unmarried. With engring. dept. N.Y. Central Lines, 1923-27; passenger and freight agent U.S. Lines, Chicago, 1927-30; publisher, Histomaps, Chicago, 1930-33; mgr. Chicago office N.R.A. (Ill. and Wis.), 1933-34; dist. mgr. U.S. Dept. Commerce, Chicago, 1934-35; chief, Dist. Office Service, U.S. Dept. Commerce, 1935-42. Served in U.S. Navy, 1917-19. Commd. maj., Air Corps, Sept. 1942; on staff, comdg. gen. Air Transport Command, comdg. gen. E.T.O., London, 1943-44. Adviser to exec. dir., Office of Internat. Trade Operations, Washington, 1945; spl. asst. to Wilson W. Wyatt, housing expediter, 1945-47; consultant to several U.S. bus. firms. Club: Nat. Press (Washington). Home: Westchester Apts., Washington 16. Office: National Press Bldg., Washington. Died Sept. 19, 1951; buried Piqua, O.

SEVIER, Charles Edwin (sē-vēr'), surgeon; born Brownsville, Tenn., May 23, 1889; s. John Henry and Lee (Wagner) S.; B.S., Vanderbilt U., 1912; M.D., Johns Hopkins U., 1916; post grad. work, Switzerland and Germany, 1923-24; orthopedic study Hosp. for Ruptured and Crippled, N.Y. City, 1924-25; unmarried. Intern Johns Hopkins and New York hosps., 1916-18 and 1920; practicing orthopedic surgeon since 1925; asst. orthopedic surgeon, U. of Colo. Med. Sch., 1927-31, became asso. prof. surgery (orthopedic), 1931; now in practice as orthopedic surgeon, Colorado Springs, Colo. Served as captain med. corps, U.S. Army, with A.E.F., 1918-19. Mem. Phi Beta Kappa, Alpha Omega Alpha, Kappa Alpha. Mem. M.E. Ch. Club: Cooking (Colorado Springs). Contributor articles in med. jours. Home: Broadmoor Hotel. Office: Burns Bldg., Colorado Springs, Colo. Died Mar. 8, 1952.

SEVIER, Landers, dir. Associated Industries of Ala.; b. Canton, Miss., Mar. 4, 1866; s. Thomas and Mary O. S.; ed. pvt. schs.; m. Meta Weathersby, Mar. 10, 1887; children—Kirby W., Landers. Clerical work with r.r., New Orleans, 1884-87, Birmingham, 1887-1904; soliciting freight agt. and gen. freight agt. Ala. Great-Southern Rd., 1904-07; v.p. Sea board Air Line, 1907-09; gen. exec. agt. Southern Ry. System, 1909-18; v.p., Sloss Sheffield Steel & Iron Co., Birmingham, Ala, 1918-20; pres Asso. Industries of Ala., 1920-35; dir. Jefferson County Bldg. & Loan Assn., Realty Mortgage Co. of Ala.; trustee Ala. Coll., Montevallo, Ala. Democrat. Presbyn. Clubs: Rotary, Country. Home: Highland Av. and Ash Mt. Office: Webb Crawford Bldg., Birmingham, Ala. Died Nov. 25, 1942.

SEXTON, Sherman J., pres. John Sexton & Co.; b. Chgo., Sept. 12, 1892; s. John and Anna Louise (Bartelman) S.; ed. De Paul U., LL.D.; m. Alice Jordan Conners, Nov. 1, 1916 (now dec.); children—William C., Alice C., Shirley Ann.; m. 2d, Adelaide M. Ross, Nov. 20, 1933 (deceased); m. 3d, Mildred MacMurray, Aug. 29, 1949. With John Sexton & Co., wholesale grocers, Chicago since 1911, pres. since 1926; pres. Deeps, Inc., Long Island City, N.Y.; vice president and dir. Great Lake Transit Co., Buffalo, 1920-33. Mem. exec. com. and bd. trustees, De Paul U.; mem. bd. dirs. and pres. 3 terms Chicago Conv. Bur.; pres. Nat. Instl. Food Supply Dealers Assn.; mem. exec. com. Cath. Charities Chicago since 1921; v.p., mem. bd. dirs. Madonna Center; trustee Tuskegee Inst.; Ill. chmn. Am. Cancer Soc., 1949; dir. Nat. Am. Wholesale Grocers Assn. Dem. Roman Catholic. Clubs: The Chicago, Chicago Athletic Assn., Tavern (Chgo.); Chicago Golf (Wheaton); Everglades, Bath and Tennis (Palm Beach, Fla.); Sankaty Head Golf (Nantucket, Mass.). Home: 1530 N. State Parkway. Office: 500 N. Orleans St., Chgo. Died Mar. 13, 1956.

SEXTON, William Thomas, s.s. owner and operator; b. Jacobstown, N.J., June 20, 1890; s. Wilmer L. and Mary C. (Brown) S.; student pub. schs. of N.J.; m. S. Marguerite Lloyd, July 25, 1912; 1 son, William Thomas. With The Panama R.R. S.S. Co., The Panama Canal, 1910-18, receiving and forwarding agt., 1916-18; with United Fruit Co., 1918-20, States S.S. Co., Portland, Ore., 1920-37, v.p. 1933-37; Pacific Coast mgr. U.S. Lines Co., San Francisco, 1937-47; with Coastwise Line, San Francisco, since 1937, chmn. bd. and dir. since 1949, Sexton Corp. since 1944; pres. Coastwise Bulk Carriers, Inc., since 1948; pres. Pacific Far East Line, 1946-47; v.p. Pacific Tankers, Inc., 1943-47; dir. West Coast Terminals, Inc., Asso. Comml. Co., Ltd., Coastwise Factors, Inc., Golden Gate Scenic S.S. Co., Coastwise Bulk Carriers, Inc., Coastwise Pacific Line. Recipient Theodore Roosevelt Panama Canal award medal with two bars, 1916. Mem. Pacific Am. S.S. Assn. (adv. bd.). Clubs: The Family, Stock Exchange (San Francisco); Arlington, Waverly Country (Portland, Ore.). Home: 2100 Jackson St., San Francisco 15. Office: 141 Battery St., San Francisco 11. Died Jan. 11, 1955.

SEYBOLT, Robert Francis (sē'bōlt), univ. prof.; b. Kearney, N.J., Feb. 25, 1888; s. George Strickland and Mary (Best) S.; Ph.B., Brown U., 1910, A.M., 1911; Ph.D., Columbia, 1916; m. Ottilie Turnbull, Dec. 29, 1913; m. 2d, Frances B. Plummer, Dec. 26, 1926; m. 3d, Leora E. Hopkins, June 7, 1933; m. 4th, Lynn Livingston, June 1, 1950. Instr. history U. Wis., 1913-17, asst. prof., 1917-20; asso. prof. history edn. U. Ill., 1920-26, prof., 1926-46, professor of the humanities since 1946; prof., Harvard Univ., 1st semester, 1925-26 and summers, 1926-27, 1929-35. Fellow Royal Hist. Soc., A.A.A.S., Royal Soc. Arts; corr. mem. Colonial Soc. Mass.; mem Am. Antiquarian Soc., Am. Philol. Assn., Bostonian Soc., Essex Inst., Soc. Preservation New Eng. Antiquities, New Eng. Hist. Geneal. Soc., Soc. Puritan Descendants, Massachusetts Soc. S.A.R., St. Nicholas Soc. of N.Y., Mediaeval Acad. of Am., Soc. of Colonial Wars, Delta Tau Delta, Phi Alpha Sigma; hon asso. mem. New York Hist. Soc. Clubs: Harvard Faculty (Cambridge); Harvard, Authors (Boston); Authors', Connaught (London); Harvard, Brown, Columbia, Cornell, Authors (New York). Author: Apprenticeship and Apprenticeship Edn. in Colonial New Eng. and N.Y., 1917; The Colonial Citizen of N.Y. City, 1918; The Evening Sch. in Colonial Am., 1925; Source Studies in Am. Colonial Edn., 1925; The Public Schools of Colonial Boston, 1935; The Private Schools of Colonial Boston, 1935; The Public Schoolmasters of Colonial Boston, 1939; The Town Officials of Colonial Boston, 1939. Translator: The Manuale Scholarium (from the Latin), 1921; Renaissance Student Life—the Paedologia of Petrus Mosellanus (from the Latin), 1927; The Autobiography of Johannes Butzbach, a Wandering Scholar of the Fifteenth Century (from the German), 1933. Contbr. articles to ednl., hist., lit., philol., med. and scientific jours. and to Dictionary of American Biography, Ency. Social Sciences, etc. Address: 15 Claremont Av., N.Y. City 27. Died Feb. 5, 1951; buried Livingston plot, Maple Grove Cemetery, Kew Gardens, N.Y.C.

SEYFFERT, Leopold (sī'fĕrt), artist; born at California, Mo., Jan. 6, 1887; s. Herman and Emma (Twiehaus) S.; studied art Pa. Acad. Fine Arts, and in Paris and Spain; m. Helen Fleck, June 5, 1911; children— Mary Louise (dec.), Leopold, Peter; m. 2d, Grace J. Vernon, Jan. 4, 1930. Awarded fellowship prize, Pa. Acad. Fine Arts, 1912; hon. mention Carnegie Inst., Pitts., 1913; gold medal Art Club, Phila., 1913; silver medal San Francisco Expn., 1915; Altman prize N.A.D., 1917, Hallgarten prize, 1916, Proctor prize, 1921, Isidor medal; Beck gold medal, 1918, and Temple gold medal Pa. Acad., 1921; Potter Palmer gold medal, Chgo., 1923; F. G. Logan prize, Chgo., 1923; W. R. Hearst prize, Art Inst., Chgo., 1924; silver medal, Municipal Art League, Chgo.; gold medal, Sesquicentennial Expn., Phila., 1926; Stotesbury and Lippincott prizes, Pa. Acad. Fine Arts; medal of honor Allied Arts of Am., 1946. Former instr. Art Inst. Chgo. Represented permanent collections of Art Inst. Chgo., Pa. Acad. Fine Arts, Detroit Art Inst., Meml. Art Gallery, Rochester, N.Y., Carnegie Inst., Pitts., Corcoran Gallery, Washington Art Museum, Los Angeles Met. Mus., N.Y.C., Bklyn. Mus., and in many pvt. collections. Nat. Academician, 1919. Club: Dutch Treat (N.Y.C.). Studio: 1 W. 67th St., N.Y.C. Died June 13, 1956.

SEYMOUR, Alexander Duncan, Jr., architect, educator; b. Bklyn., Feb. 1, 1884; s. Alexander Duncan and Lizzie Vernon (Meekin) S.; B.S. in Architecture, Columbia, 1906; student Ecole des Beaux Arts, Paris, 1906-08; Acad. at Rome, summer 1908; m. Martha Rheinfrank, Apr. 12, 1909; 1 dau., Martha (Mrs. Olindo Grossi). Pvt. practice architecture, N.Y. C., 1909-28; mem. faculty Cornell U., 1928-50, Andrew Dixon White chair of architecture, 1950, prof. emeritus, 1950-—; mem. archtl. adv. bd., Cornell U. Ensign USNR, World War I; civilian instr., Naval Architecture and Seamanship, O.T.S., Cornell, World War II. Won competitions for Portland Pub. Auditorium, 1911, Perry Meml., Lake Erie, 1912 (asso. with H. H. Freedlander, architects). Registered architect N.Y. State. Mem. A.I.A. (emeritus, 1950-—), Am. Soc. Beaux Arts Architects. Clubs: N.Y. Yacht, Cruising of America (charter mem.). Home: (summer) Trevett, Maine; (winter) Oxford, Md. Died Aug. 23, 1957.

SEYMOUR, Charles Milne, lawyer; b. Enterprise, Miss., July 17, 1882; s. Digby Gordon and Josephine Ermine (Douglas) S.; student Sewanee (Tenn.) Mil. Acad., 1897-99; LL.B., U. Tenn., 1903; m. Flora Nell Gloster, June 5, 1906; children—Nell (Mrs. Leo D. Holloway, Jr.), Jane (Mrs. James R. Eckel), Rev. Charles Milne, Josephine (Mrs. Burnham B. Holmes), Arthur Gloster, Richard Caswell, Dorothy (Mrs. Robert C. Harnden), Digby Gordon. Asst. constrn. engr. L.&N. R.R., Knoxville, 1903-05; admitted to Tenn. bar, 1905, since practiced in Knoxville, mem. Cornick, Wright & Frantz, 1905-11, Frantz, McConnell & Seymour since 1911; gen. counsel, mem. bd. dirs., exec. com. Am. Zinc, Lead & Smelting Co. and subsidiaries, St. Louis, since 1930; gen. counsel Tenn. Pub. Service Co., 1932-39; gen. counsel, dir. So. States Portland Cement Co., Rockmart, Georgia, 1928-54; director of the Watauga Stone Company, Wisconsin Zinc Company, Minerals Beneficiation, Inc. Former chairman board Knoxville Planning Commission; trustee Knoxville Library System. Dir. Episcopal Endowment Corp., Chattanooga, Tenn.; former member Bishop and Council, Episcopal Diocese Tenn., now chancellor of the Diocese. Member Knoxville C. of C., Am., Tenn., Knoxville bar assns., Tenn. Soc. S.R. Episcopalian (lay del. to the General Conv., 1940—). Clubs: Executives (pres., dir.), Irving, Cherokee Country. Editor, compiler: History of St. Johns Church, Knoxville, 1947. Contbr. articles newspapers, mags. Home: 1703 Melrose Pl., Knoxville 16. Office: Burwell Bldg., Knoxville, Tenn. Died July 27, 1958; buried New Gray, Knoxville, Tenn.

SEYMOUR, Gideon (Deming) (sē'mōr), editor; b. Arlington, S.D., Aug. 17, 1901; s. Arthur Hallock and Flora (Wilson) S.; student Northern State Teachers College, Aberdeen, S.D., 1916-19, Drake Univ., Des Moines, Ia., 1919-23; hon. D.Litt., Yankton (S.D.) Coll., 1941; m. Agnes Peterson, June 15, 1926; 1 son, Peter Deming. Reporter for Des Moines (Ia.) Register and Tribune, 1919-23; reporter, editor and news exec. for Associated Press in U.S., Argentina, South Africa, Australasia and Europe, 1923-38; editorial page editor, Minneapolis Star, 1939-43; v.p. and exec. editor, Minneapolis Star and Tribune since 1944. Mem. board Minneapolis Orchestra Association. Member board Yankton College. Member American Soc. Newspaper Editors (dir.), Am. Acad. Polit. and Social Science, Sigma Delta Chi, Theta Nu Epsilon. Republican. Conglist. Clubs: Adventurers (New York); Nat. Press, Cosmos (Washington); Mpls., Minikahda, Rotary (Mpls.). Home: 306 E. Minnehaha Parkway. Office: Minneapolis Star and Tribune, 425 Portland Av., Mpls. Died May 20, 1954.

SEYMOUR, Mary Harrison, author; b. Oxford, Conn., Sept. 7, 1935; d. Rev. Abraham and Lucy Maria (Harrison) Browne; acad. edn. at Brooklyn, and Baltimore; m. Storrs O. Seymour, June 20, 1861. Extensive contbr. to children's papers and periodicals. Author: Sunshine and Starlight, 1869; Ned, Nellie and Amy, 1870; Mollie's Christmas Stocking, 1877; Posy Vinton's Picnic, 1877; Every Day, 1877; Recompense, 1881; Through the Darkness, 1893; etc. Address: Litchfield, Conn. Deceased.

SEYMOUR, Storrs Ozias, clergyman; b. Litchfield, Conn., Jan. 24, 1836; s. Origen Storrs and Lucy Morris (Woodruff) S.; A.B., Yale, 1857, A.M., 1860; studied theology, Berkeley Div. Sch., 1859-61; (D.D., Trinity Coll., 1896); m. Mary Harrison Browne, June 20, 1861. Deacon, 1861, priest, 1862, P.E. Ch.; rector St. Peter's, Milford, Conn., 1861-64, St. Thomas, Bethel, Conn., 1864-67, Trinity, Pawtucket, R.I., 1868-74, Trinity, Norwich, Conn., 1874-79, St. Michael's Litchfield, 1878-83, Trinity Hartford, Conn., 1883-93, St. Michael's, Litchfield, 1893—. Trustee Berkeley Div. Sch. Democrat. Address: Litchfield, Conn. Deceased.

SHAFER, Paul W., congressman; b. Elkhart, Ind., Apr. 27, 1893; s. John McClellan and Sarah C. (Werntz) S.; ed. pub. schs., Three Rivers, Mich., and Ferris Inst., Big Rapids, Mich., studied law by correspondence; m. Ila P. Mack, Oct. 31, 1917. Reporter, editor, and pub., 1912-29; municipal judge, Battle Creek, Mich., 1929-36; mem. 75th-83d Congresses 3d Michigan District. Chmn. Rep. Campaign Com. for Calhoun Co., Mich., 1934, Pub. Bronson Jour. Mem. Ind. Nat. Guard, 1917-18. Hon. mem. Vets. of Fgn. Wars; mem. Guild of Former Pipe Organ Pumpers, Royal Order of Jesters. Republican. Presbyterian. Mason (32°, Shriner), Elk. Club: Lions (dist. gov. 1932-33). Home: 38 Woolnough St., Battle Creek, Mich. Address: House Office Bldg., Washington. Died Aug. 17, 1954.

SHAFER, Robert, prof. literature; b. Hagerstown, Md., Dec. 24, 1889; s. Samuel McCauley and Mary Elizabeth (Fahrney) S.; grad. Washington County (Md.) High Sch., 1907, Mercersburg (Pa.) Acad., 1908; A.B., Princeton, 1912, Ph.D., 1916; married Giuditta Grottanelli de' Santi, October 26, 1939. Instructor in English, Princeton University, 1916-17; instr. in English and history, United States Naval Acad., 1917-19; asst. prof. English, Goucher Coll., Baltimore, 1919-20; asso. prof. English, Wells Coll., Aurora, N.Y., 1920-23; asso. prof. of lit., U. Cin., 1923-27, prof., 1927-55, emeritus, fellow Grad. Sch. since 1923; fellow J. S. Guggenheim Memorial Foundation, 1927; gen. editor, Doubleday-Doran Series in Literature, 1934-40. Received Sachs award, Cincinnati Inst. of Fine Arts, 1941. Mem. Modern Lang. Assn. Am., English Assn., Modern Humanities Resrch. Assn., Am. Assn. U. Profs., Phi Beta Kappa. Author: The English Ode to 1660, 1918; Progress and Science, 1922; Christianity and Naturalism, 1926; (with others) Humanism and America, 1930; (with others) Introduction to Western Civilization, 1933, rev., 1939, 1949; Paul Elmer More and American Criticism, 1935; Instructor's course Outline, Survey of English Literature (U.S. Armed Forces Institute), 1945. Editor: Reviews and Critical Papers by Lionel Johnson, 1921; From Beowulf to Thomas Hardy, 1924, revised edition, 1931, new edit. with period introductions, 1939-40, special editions for U.S. Armed Forces Inst., 1944-45; American Literature, 1926; Seventeenth Century Studies, 1933; Workers in the Dawn, by George Gissing, 1935; Seventeenth Century Studies, 2d Series, 1937. Home: Tryon, N.C. Died Jan. 6, 1956; buried Polk Meml. Cemetery, Tryon.

SHAFFER, Joseph Crockett, ex-congressman; b. Wythe Co., W.Va., Jan. 19, 1889; ed. pub. schs. and Plummer Coll.; LL.B., U. Va., 1904; m. Ada Honaker. Admitted to Va. bar, 1904, and began practice at Wytheville; commonwealth atty. Wythe Co., 1908-12; asst. U.S. dist. atty. under Pres. Harding, and U.S. dist. atty. Western Dist. of Va. by apptmt. of Pres. Coolidge, 1924-29; mem. 71st Congress (1929-31), 9th Va. Dist. Republican. Home: Wytheville, Va. Died Oct. 19, 1958*

SHAINWALD, Richard Herman, corp. exec.; b. San Francisco, Oct. 15, 1894; s. Richard S. and Bertha (Loewenthal) S.; children—Barbara, Ruth, Dick (girl). With Pabco Products Inc., since 1914, now dir.; dir. Calif. Ink Co., Inc. Club: Menlo Circus. Home: 145 North Ridge Lane, Woodside Hills, Woodside, Calif. Office: 475 Brannan St., San Francisco. Died Jan. 29, 1955.

SHAINWALD, Richard S. (shän'wâld), chmn. bd. Paraffine Cos.; b. New York, N.Y., June 28, 1862; s. Nathan and Minna (Strauss) S.; prep. edn., pub. schs., N.Y. City; student Coll. City New York, 1875-77; m. Bertha Lowenthal, Jan. 23, 1890; children—Richard Herman, Seville (Mrs. George A. Oppen). In accounting dept. Chas. Zinn & Co., wholesale willow ware, N.Y. City, 1877-79; mdse. business, Boise, Ida., 1879-92; with Pabco Products, Inc., and predecessors since 1892, pres., 1928-37, now hon. chmn. bd.; v.p. Fibreboard Products, Inc., Moore Dry Dock Co.; dir. Wells Fargo Bank & Union Trust Co. Republican. Jewish religion. Clubs: Commonwealth, Concordia-Argonaut, San Francisco Stock Exchange. Home: Hotel Mark Hopkins. Office: 475 Brannan St., San Francisco, Cal. Died May 29, 1954.

SHAKESPEARE, William, Jr., founder, treas. and dir. Shakespeare Co.; pres., dir. Grace Corset Co.; First Fed. Savings & Loan of Brevard Co., Fla.; dir. Ihling Bros. Everard Co., Bard Steel & Mill Supply Co., First Nat. Bank & Trust Co. Home: 2505 Gull Lake. Office: 241 E. Kalamazoo Av., Kalamazoo, Mich. Died June 25, 1950; buried Riverside Cemetery, Kalamazoo.

SHALLBERG, Gustavus Adolphus, exec. Borg-Warner Corp.; b. Moline, Ill., Nov. 6, 1876; s. Andrew and Johanna (Falk) S.; LL.B., U. Mich., 1902; m. Alice Kennedy, June 16, 1909; children—William Grant, Gustavus Adolphus, Betty Alice Quealy. Admitted to Ill. bar, 1902; pvt. practice of law, Moline, 1902-12; mem. law firm Shallberg & Harper, Moline, 1912-16; partner law firm Kenworthy, Shallberg & Harper, 1916-42; now chmn. exec. com. Borg-Warner Corp. of Chgo., Congregationalist. Clubs: Midlothian Country, The Chicago (Chgo.); Detroit Athletic (Detroit). Home: 1550 North State Parkway, Chicago 10. Office: 310 S. Mchigan Av., Chgo. 4. Died Aug. 29, 1959.

SHALLENBERGER, Martin C(onrad), ret. army officer; b. Osceola, Neb., July 6, 1886; s. Ashton Cockayne and Eliza (Zilg) S.; student U. Neb., 1901-04; distinguished grad. Command and Gen. Staff Sch., 1927; grad. Army War Coll., 1931; m. Ina Hamilton Dowdy, May 11, 1910; children—Sarah Elizabeth (Mrs. W. L. Lyons Brown), Martin Conrad. Commd. in U.S. Army from Nat. Guard, 1908; aide de camp to Gen. Pershing, 1915-18; gen. staff officer, 5th Div., 3d Corps, 1918-19; mil. attaché Am. legations, Portugal, Greece, Jugoslavia, 1919-24; sec. Am. Commn. for Tacna Arica Plebiscite, 1925-26; mil. attaché Am. legations, Austria, Hungary, 1933-37; asst. comdt. Command and Gen. Staff Sch., 1939-44; comdg. officer, Camp Sutton, N.C., and Camp Rucker, Ala., 1944-46; retired in rank of gen., Aug. 1946. Decorated D.S.M., Legion of Merit with oak leaf cluster, Order of Commendation with cluster (U.S.), Officer Legion of Honor (France), Officer of Black Star, Officer of White Eagle, Officer of Polonia Resituta, Comdr. of Order of Daneborg, Austrian Order of Merit, Hungarian Order of Merit. Home: Harrods Creek, Ky. Died Feb. 12, 1951; buried Zachary Taylor Nat. Cemetery.

SHAND, S(amuel) James, educator; b. Edinburgh, Scotland, Oct. 29, 1882; s. James and Catherine Grant (Hunter) S.; Ph.D., Munster U., Germany, 1906, Sc.D., St. Andrews U., Scotland, 1910; m. Anna M. J. Davidson, Feb., 1913. Came to U.S., 1937. Geologist, Royal Scottish Mus., Edinburgh, 1907-11; prof. geology, Stellenbosch, S. Africa, 1911-37 prof. geology Columbia, 1937—, Newberry prof. geology, 1945—. Mem. geol. socs. of Am., London, Belgium and S. Africa, mineral. socs. of Am., Great Britain, A.A.A.S., N.Y. Acad. Sci. Author: Eruptive Rocks, 1927, 1943, 1948; The Study of Rocks, 1931, 1948; Earth-Lore, 1933-37. Home: 400 W. 119th St., N.Y.C. 27. Died Apr. 20, 1957.

SHANKS, Henry Thomas, educator; b. Vance County, N.C., Feb. 7, 1896; s. Henry Taylor and Maude (Jenkins) S.; A.B., Wake Forest (N.C.) Coll., 1918, A.M., 1920, L.H.D., 1953; A.M., U. Chgo., 1923; Ph.D., U. N.C., 1929; student Columbia summer 1921; m. Anne Graham, Aug. 31, 1929; 1 son, Alexander Graham. Prof. history, South Georgia State Woman's Coll., Valdosta, Ga., 1920-22; instr. history, U. N.C., 1923-25, 1926-29; asst. prof. history, Birmingham-Southern Coll., Birmingham, Ala., 1929-31, asso. prof., 1932-33, prof. since 1934, dean, 1943-58; prof. history, summers, Eastern Carolina Teachers Coll., Greeneville, N.C., 1923, W.Va. U., 1930, 1931, Emory U., 1934, 35, 38, 39, U. N.C. 1941. Served with U.S. Navy, 1917-19. Awarded Gen. Edn. Bd. fellowship, 1935-36, Grant in Aid, Social Science Research Council, 1935-36. Mem. bd. editors, Jour. So. History, 1946-50. Mem. Assn. Ala. College Administrators (pres. 1956-57), Am., Southern, Ala., N.C. hist. assns., Phi Beta Kappa, Omicron Delta Kappa, Pi Gamma Mu, Pi Kappa Alpha. Dem. Presbyn. Author: The Secession Movement in Virginia, 1847-1861, 1934. Editor: The Papers of Willie P. Mangum, 5 Vols., 1950-56. Address: Birmingham-Southern Coll., Birmingham 4, Ala. Died Dec. 16, 1959.

SHANNON, Effie, actress; b. Cambridge, Mass., 1867. Began stage life as Eva in Uncle Tom's Cabin; took various rôles with Augustin Daly's New York Stock Co., Lyceum Co., etc. Has appeared as ingenue in many popular plays; joint star with Herbert Kelcey, in The Moth and the Flame; His Lord and Master; The Thief; etc. Under management of David Belasco, 1913-14, playing The Years of Discretion, in Winthrop Ames' Children of Earth, 1915; recently in Under Orders, Mamma's Affair, The Detour, David Belasco's mgmt., 1923-24; mgmt. of George Tyler, 1926. Home: Bayport, N.Y. Died July 23, 1954.

SHANNON, Thomas Vincent, clergyman, editor; b. Chicago, Ill., Dec. 11, 1874; s. James and Mary (O'Hara) S.; A.B., St. Ignatius Coll., 1890; Catholic U. of America, 1897-99, S.T.L., 1897; LL.D., Notre Dame, 1922, Loyola, 1922. Ordained priest R.C. Ch., 1897; pastor St. Francis Xavier Ch., Wilmette, Ill., 1912-16, St. Thomas the Apostle Ch., Chgo., 1916—; pastor of St. Mary's, Lake Forest, 1941—. Editor The New World, 1912-36. Served as v.p. 7th Dist., Liberty Loan campaign and as rep. of Archdiocese of Chgo. for A.R.C., World War. Canon of Guadalajara; Knight of St. John de Los Lagos; apptd. domestic prelate to Pope Pius XI, 1925. Republican. Clubs: University, Onwentsia Country. Address: St. Mary's Church, Lake Forest, Ill. Died May 25, 1959; buried St. Mary's Cemetery, Lake Forest, Ill.

SHANTZ, Homer LeRoy, botanist; b. Kent County, Mich., Jan. 24, 1876; s. Abraham K. and Mary E. (Ankney) S., B.Sc., Colo. Coll., Colorado Springs, Colo., 1901, Sc.D., 1926; Ph.D., U. of Nebraska, 1905; m. Lucia Moore Soper, Dec. 25, 1901; children—Homer LeRoy, Benjamin Soper. Inst. botany and zoölogy, Colorado Coll., 1901, 02; instr. botany, U. of Neb., 1903, 04, U. of Mo., 1905, 06; prof. botany and bacteriology, U. of La., 1907; spl. agt. and collaborator, alkali and drought resistant plant investigations, Bur. Plant Industry, U.S. Dept. Agr., summers, 1906, 07, expert, 1908, 09; plant physiologist same, 1910-20, sr. physiologist in charge physiol. and fermentation investigations, 1921-23, physiologist in charge plant geography in its relation to plant industry, 1924-26; prof. botany and head of dept., U. of Ill., 1926-28; pres. U. of Arizona, 1928-36; chief division of wildlife management, Forest Service, U.S. Dept. of Agriculture, 1936-1944; annuitant collaborator U.S. Dept. Agr., 1945—, prof. botany, U. Ariz., 1956, principal investigator Arizona African Expedition, 1956-57. Special lecturer on plant geography, Graduate Sch. Geography, Clark U., 1922-26. Mem. Ariz. State Bd. of Edn., State Bd. of Vocational Edn.; Ariz. State chmn. Rhodes Scholarship Com.; chmn. State Planning Bd. of Ariz. Fellow Am. Soc. Agronomy, Royal Soc. of Arts; mem. Phytog. Soc. Sweden, hon. pres., 7th Internat. Bot. Congress, Stockholm, 1950, also Paris, 1954. Mem. Botanical Soc., Washington, Assn. Am. Geographers, Ecol. Soc. Am., Soc. Plant Physiol. (Charles Reid Barnes life mem.), Wildlife Soc., Soc. pro Fauna et Flora Fennica, Internat. African Inst., Sigma Xi, Phi Kappa Phi (nat. pres., 1935-39), Theta Xi, Theta Alpha Phi, Alpha Zeta, Phi Beta Kappa, Blue Key, Phi Mu Alpha. Congregationalist. Clubs: Explorers (New York City); Federal, Cosmos (Washington, D.C.). Contributor many articles to jours. and publs. of the U.S. Govt., dealing chiefly with wildlife management, plant physiology and with natural vegetation and its value as an indicator of the agrl. capabilities of land, and the plant geography of N.A., S.A. and Africa; agrl. regions of Africa and management of wild animals on the national forests. Spl. detail to determine natural plant resources and crop producing possibilities of large portions of Africa and Latin America for use of Am. Commn. to Negotiate Peace, 1918-19; spl. detail as agrl. explorer with Smithsonian Instn. Africa Expdn., 1919-20; spl. detail as mem. Ednl. Commn. to East Africa under auspices of Phelps Stokes Fund and Internat. Ednl. Bd., 1924. Address: 454 Paseo del Descanso, Santa Barbara, Cal. Died June 23, 1958.

SHARMAN, Jackson Roger, univ. prof.; b. Meridian, Miss., June 22, 1895; s. Jackson Roger and Mary Garland (Trueheart) S.; B.S., U. of Miss., 1917; M.A., Columbia U., 1924, Ph.D., 1929; m. Mildred C. Crook, Dec. 24, 1917; children—Jackson Roger, Jr., Lewis Crook. Teacher, Thomasville (Ga.) High Sch., 1919-21; supervisor phys. edn. and recreation, Mobile, Ala., 1921-23; state dir. health and phys. edn., Ala., 1924-29; asso. prof. phys. edn., U. of Mich., 1930-37; prof. health and phys. edn., and chmn. of dept., U. of Ala., 1937—; principal specialist in physical fitness, United States Office of Education, 1942-43. Served as first lieutenant, 3d Infantry, U.S. Army, 1917-19. Mem. Am. Assn. of Health, Phys. Edn. and Recreation (hon.), N.E.A., Ala. Ednl. Assn., Sigma Alpha Epsilon, Phi Delta Kappa, Kappa Delti Pi, Phi Epsilon Kappa. Presbyterian. Mason. Club: Rotary. Author: Introduction to Physical Education, 1934; A Physical Education Workbook, 1936; The Teaching of Physical Education, 1936; Modern Principles of Physical Education, 1937; Introduction to Health Education, 1948. Home: 15 Audubon Pl., Tuscaloosa, Ala. Died June 18, 1957; buried Memorial Park, Tuscaloosa.

SHARP, Clayton Halsey, physicist, elec. engr.; b. Seneca, Falls, N.Y., Dec. 5, 1869; s. James B. and Martha (Halsey) S.; prep. edn., Mynderse Acad., Seneca Falls, N.Y.; A.B., Hamilton Coll., 1890; Ph. D., Cornell U., 1895; hon. D.Sc., Hamilton Coll., 1941; spl. work, U. Leipzig, 1899-1900; m. Kathleen Hamilton, Malloch, Oct. 27, 1900; children—Dorothy Malloch (Mrs. William Folterman, Jr.), Kathleen Halsey (Mrs. Walker Harden), Marjorie Hamilton (Mrs. William Caldwell), Eleanor Bruen, Mary Elizabeth (Mrs. Robert L. Simpson). Instr. in physics, Cornell U., 1895-1900; test officer for Elec. Testing Labs., N.Y.C., 1901-14, v.p., 1914-33; cons. in light and electricity; also patented various instruments for elec. and photometric measurements. Del. to meetings of Internat. Electrotech. Commn., Turin, 1911, Berlin, 1913, Geneva, 1922, London, 1924, The Hague, 1925, N.Y., 1926, Bellagio and Rome, 1927, Stockholm, 1930, Scheveningen and Brussels, 1935, Torquay-London, 1938, pres. U.S. Nat. Com. of same, 1924-39, hon. pres., 1930—; del. to meetings of the Internat. Commn. on Illumination, Berlin, 1913, Geneva, 1924, Bellagio, 1927, Saranac, 1928, Germany, 1935, and pres. U.S. Nat. Com. of same, 1914-28, v.p., 1928. Fellow Am. Phys. Soc., A.A. A.S., Am. Inst. E.E.; mem. Illuminating Engring. Soc. (pres. 1907-08), Société Française des Electriciens, Alpha Delta Phi, Phi Beta Kappa, Sigma Xi. Republican. Contbr. many technical papers. Home-Office: 294 Fisher Av., White Plains, N.Y. Deceased.

SHARP, George Winters; b. Marlinton, W.Va., June 20, 1882; s. Charles W. and Mary A. (Grimes) S.; A.B., Marshall Coll., Huntington, W.Va., 1907; U. Mich., 1921; m. Beatrice Groves, Aug. 17, 1909. Formerly woodsman and pub. sch. teacher; clk. Circuit Court, Pocahontas Co., W.Va., 1908-20; adminstrn. officer for Game and Fish Commn. of W.Va., 1921, 25; sec. of state, W.Va., two terms ending Mar. 4, 1933. Mem. Theta Chi. Republican. Presbyn. Home: Charleston, W.Va. Died Sept. 1953.

SHARP, Marlay Albert, educator; b. McCook, Neb., May 22, 1889; s. William Marlay and Sarah May (Coleman) S.; B.S., U. of Neb., 1915; M.S., Iowa State Coll., 1928; m. Winnifred Watson, June 30, 1923; children—Watson Marlay, Maywin (Mrs. Robert A. Lauderdale, Jr.). High sch. teacher, Winnebago, Minn., 1915-17; specialist, Neb. State Bd. for Vocational Edn., 1920-21; state supervisor agrl. edn., S. D., 1921-25; asso. prof. agrl. engring., Iowa State Coll., 1925-37; prof. and head agrl. engring. dept., U. Tenn., 1937-59; ret.; specialist in war tng. classes, U.S. Office of Edn., 6 mos., 1941, in farm machinery, Am. Mission for Aid to Greece, 3 mos., 1948; chmn. Farm Machinery Mission to Europe, Econ. Coop. Adminstrn., 3 mos., 1948; survey European Recovery Plan nations; agrl. engr. ICA, Indian Government, State Agricultural College, Madras, India, 1956-58. Member of Alpha Zeta, Sigma Alpha. Mason. Odd Fellow. Author: Teaching Farm Mechanics (with Schmidt and Ross); Principles of Farm Mechanics (with W. M. Sharp), 1930. Contbr. articles to profl. mags. Address: Shelbourne Towers, Knoxville, Tenn. Died Aug. 26, 1959.

SHARP, Thomas Enoch, newspaper editor; b. Butte, Mont., Nov. 6, 1890; s. Jesse James and Sophia (McKnight) S.; student high sch., Cumberland, Md.; m. Alice Gale Bevans, Apr. 14, 1915; children—Thomas Enoch, Daniel Bevens. Reporter various newspapers until 1921; editor daily papers in El Paso, Memphis, Buffalo, Mobile, 1921-40; pres. Prichard Printing Co., Inc., also editor The Citizen, Prichard, Ala. Home: Spring Hill, Ala. Died Sept. 22, 1957. Buried Pine Crest Cemetery, Mobile, Ala.

SHARPE, Henry Dexter, mfr.; b. Providence, R.I., Dec. 12, 1872; s. Lucian and Louisa (Dexter) S.; A.B., Brown U., 1894, hon. A.M., 1920; m. Mary Elizabeth Evans, June 25, 1920 ; 1 son, Henry Dexter. With Brown & Sharpe Mfg. Co., mfrs. of machinery, 1894—, now chairman of bd.; dir. Providence Gas Co., R.I. Hosp. Trust Co., Providence Journal Co.; trustee Providence Inst. for Savings. Chancellor emeritus Brown University. Republican. Associate member American Society M.E.; member Phi Beta Kappa, Alpha Delta Phi. Clubs: University, Hope, Art, Agawam. Home: 84 Prospect St. Office: Brown & Sharpe Mfg. Co., Providence. Died May 17, 1954; buried Providence.

SHARPLESS, Frederick F., mining engr.; b. West Chester, Pa., Jan. 22, 1866; s. Alfred and Elizabeth Cope (Sharples) S.; West Chester State Normal Sch. to 1884; B.S., in Chemistry, U. Mich., 1888; m. Caroline Hawxhurst, June 23, 1892; 1 son, Paul. Prof. metallurgy Mich. Coll. of Mines, Houghton, 1888-93; cons. engr., Mpls., 1893-95; assayer to mgr., various mining cos. in Cal., 1895-97; Am. rep. Consolidated Mines Selection Co., Ltd., London, 1898-1912; cons. mining and metall. engr., 1912-21; sec. Am. Inst. of Mining and Metall. Engrs., 1921-25. Has made examinations and reports in U.S., Alaska, Can., Mexico, C.A., S.A., Asia and Africa. Republican. Mem. Soc. of Friends. Mem. Am. Inst. Mining and Metall. Engrs. Address: Waterbury, N.Y. Died Apr. 11, 1951.

SHATTUCK, Arthur, pianist; b. Neenah, Wis., Apr. 19, 1881; s. Frank Coolidge and Clara A. (Merriman) S.; student pub. schs., Neenah; went to Vienna, Austria, at 13, and studied music under Leschetizsky; unmarried. Has concertized extensively in Europe and U.S. Home: 530 Park Av., N.Y.C. Deceased.

SHATTUCK, Mayo Adams, lawyer; b. Oakland, Calif., Apr. 28, 1898; s. Frank Batchelder and Belle (Little) S.; A.B., Harvard U., 1919, LL.B., 1921; m. Jessie R. Ridge, Oct. 10, 1920; children—John Ridge, Mayo Adams, Jr. Admitted to Me. bar, 1922, Mass. bar, 1923, in practice at Boston; partner firm, Barker, Davison and Shattuck, Boston, 1926-39, Haussermann, Davison & Shattuck since 1939; dir. Hingham Trust Co., Hingham, Mass.; fiduciary advisor, Massachusetts Investors Trust and Massachusetts Investors Second Fund; instructor in trusts, Northeastern University, Boston, 1923-40; lecturer in trusts, U. of Colo., summers 1937, 39, 40; lecturer in trusts to banking and bar assns. Spl. asst. Atty. Gen. of Mass., 1943. Served as lt., j.g., U.S. Naval Res., 1917-19. Trustee Wilder Memorial Charitable and Educational Society, Inc., Hingham, Charity of Edward Hopkins, Estate of Frank Wood; director of Boston Fund, Inc., 1944, Bond Fund of Boston, Inc., 1948; president of Massachusetts Civic League, Inc. Mem. Bd. Bar Examiners, Mass., since 1940. Member Mass. Bar Assn. (pres. 1942-43), American Law Inst., Bar Assn. City of Boston (council since 1948), House of Delegates, American Bar Association, 1944, Harvard Musical Assn. Episcopalian. Clubs: Union, Harvard (Boston). Author: Living Insurance Trusts, 1928; Annotations to Restatement of Law of Trusts for Massachusetts, 1936; Shattuck Revision Loring Trustee's Handbook, 1940; Model Statue Enacting Prudent Man Investment Rule for Trustees; An Estate Planners Handbook, 1948; misc. articles on Trust Adminstrn. and Estate Planning. Home: 712 Main St., Hingham, Mass. Office: 15 State St., Boston 9. Died Nov. 4, 1952; buried Chebeague Island, Me.

SHATTUCK, William, author; b. Great Barrington, Mass., Sept. 19, 1864; s. Aaron Draper (q.v.) and Marian (Colman) S.; acad. edn.; m. Jessie Alice Holcombe, Oct. 19, 1898. Ranchman in Wyo., 1883-93; in printing business at Granby, Conn., 1893—. Author: The Keeper of the Salamander's Order, 1895; The Secret of the Black Butte, 1898; also mag. articles. Address: Granby, Conn. Died Mar. 28, 1946.

SHATZER, Charles Gallatin (shăt'sẽr), educator; b. Shelby, O., Dec. 8, 1877; s. John David and Nancy Jane (Gallatin) S.; A.B., Wittenberg Coll., Springfield, O., 1900, A.M., 1904; grad. study U. Chgo., summers, 1903-09; Sc.D., Susquehanna U., 1921; m. Catharine Susanna Greenawalt, June 14, 1917; 1 dau., Mary Jane. Prin. high sch., Plain City, O., 1900-01; instr. in science and mathematics, Wittenberg Prep. Sch., 1901-04; prof. biology and geology, Wittenberg Coll., 1905-23, also dean college, 1914-23 and 1925 to retirement; prof. geology and geography, 1923-45; now rofessor emeritus. Instructor summer sessions Ohio State U. at Lake Erie Biological Laboratory, 1911-15. Exec. sec. Luth. Laymen's Movement for Stewardship, United Luth. Co. in America, 1923-25. Member A.A.A.S., Ohio Acad. Science, Beta Theta Pi. Republican. Mason. Kiwanian. Home: 1003 Woodlawn Av., Springfield, O. Died Sept. 12, 1959.

SHAUGHNESSY, Gerald, bishop; b. Everett, Mass., May 19, 1887; s. Joseph and Margaret (Colwell) S.; A.B., Boston Coll., 1909; S.T.D., Catholic U. America, 1925; LL.D., Boston College, 1946. Ordained priest R.C. Ch., 1920; professorial and preaching work, 1920-33; consecrated bishop of Seattle, Sept. 19, 1933. Mem. Mediaeval Acad. of America. Author: Has the Immigrant Kept the Faith?, 1925. Editor and translator of To Die with Jesus, 1925, With Jesus to the Priesthood, 1932. Contbr. articles to mags. Address: Seattle. Died May 18, 1950.

SHAVER, Clement Lawrence, b. Marion County, W.Va., Jan. 22, 1867; s. John Riffle and Sarah Cordelia (Cunningham) S.; student Fairmont (W. Va.) State Coll.; LL.B., George Washington U.; m. Catherine Upshur Neale. Tchr. in country schools 10 years; admitted to W.Va. bar, 1899, and practiced at Fairmont; now engaged in framing. Served as chmn. Dem. State Com. and chmn. Dem. Nat. Com. Mem. M.E. Ch., S. Home: Fairmont, W.Va. Died Sept. 1, 1954.

SHAVER, Dorothy, business exec.; b. Howard Co., Ark., July 29, 1897; d. James D. and Sallie Hunter (Borden) S.; ed. U. of Ark., U. Chgo.; LL.D., Syracuse U., 1947, Bates Coll., 1949; D.C.S., N.Y. U., 1950; D.H.L., Russell Sage Coll., 1951, Lafayette Coll., 1952. Dir. Lord & Taylor, N.Y. City, since 1927, v.p., 1931, first v.p., 1937-45, pres., 1946—; v.p., dir. Asso. Dry Goods Corp. Mem. bd. trustees Com. for Econ. Development, N.Y.C.; adv. com. Recruiting and Pub. Information on Civil Def., N.Y.C.; def. adv. com. on Women in the Service, Washington. Mem. women's council N.Y. Pub. Library, organizing com. N.Y.C. for Nat. Assn. for Mental Health; corporation member Crusade for Freedom, New York. Chairman executive committee of Costume Inst. of Met. Mus. Art; trustee Parsons Sch. of Design, Met. Mus. of Art; dir. The Greater N.Y. Fund, Arthritis and Rheumatism Found, Fedn. Protestant Welfare Agencies, Nat. Conf. Christians and Jews; member of the advisory committee Fashion Group, N.Y., Inst. Contemporary Art, Boston; mem. bd. govs. The Menninger Found. Decorated Chevalier of Legion of Honor, France, 1950. Hon. fellow Met. Mus. Art. Home: 160 E. 72d St. Office: 424 Fifth Av., N.Y.C. Died June 28, 1959.

SHAW, Clarence Reginald, banker; b. Niagara Falls, Ont., Can., Mar. 6, 1889; s. John Edward (M.D., C.M.) and Katherine (Acton) S.; grad. Mountain View High Sch., Calif., 1907; m. Lillian B. Snyder, Apr. 30, 1912; 1 dau., Mary. Began in banking business at San Francisco, 1907; v.p., mgr. Seattle Br. Federal Reserve Bank of San Francisco since 1920. Republican. Presbyterian. Mason (K.T., Shriner). Clubs: Seattle Golf and Country, Ranier. Home: 1656 Interlaken Pl. Address: Federal Reserve Bank, Seattle. Died Mar. 20, 1950; buried Acacia Meml. Cemetery, Seattle.

SHAW, Edwin Adams, educator; b. Boston, May 8, 1876; s. Arthur Augustus and Mary M. (Chase) S.; B.S., Tufts Coll., 1898; A.M., Harvard U. Grad. Sch., 1916, Ph.D., 1918; m. Ethel H. Sparrow, Aug. 27, 1906; children—Hester Marie, Edmund Chase. Engaged as civil engr. in railroad work, 1898-1903; teacher and prin. high schs. in New Eng., 1903-16; instr. and asst. prof. Tufts Coll., 1917-20; prof. psychology, sales and advertising, Babson Inst., 1919-20; asst. prof. and asst. dir. Psycho-Edn. Clinic, Harvard U. Grad. Sch. of Edn., 1920-27; prof. edn. and head dept. edn., Tufts Coll., since 1927; lecturer Ednl. Psychology, Perry Kindergarten Normal Sch., Boston, since 1927. V.p. and dir. Middlesex Fed. Savings & Loan Assn. since 1939. Mem. School Bd., Somerville, Mass., 1921-39 (past chmn.); dir. Somerville Y.M.C.A. Fellow A.A.A.S.; mem. Am. Psychol. Assn., Am. Assn. Univ. Profs., Am. Assn Sch. Adminstrs., Mass. Schoolmasters Club (past pres.), Acacia, Phi Beta Kappa, Phi Delta Kappa. Republican. Baptist. Mason, I.O.O.F. Clubs: University (Boston); Rotary of Somerville (past dir.). Home: 63 College Av., Somerville 44, Mass. Died Jan. 8, 1951; buried Highland Cemetery, Ipswich, Mass.

SHAW, Elwyn Riley, judge; b. Lyndon, Ill., Oct. 19, 1888; s. William Henry and Ella Marguerite (Moore) S.; LL.B., U. of Mich., 1910; m. Edith Griffin, June 26, 1913 (dec. 1942); children—Mary Margaret, Joan Milton; m. 2d, Mildred Voigt, 1944. Admitted to Ill. bar, 1910, practicing at Freeport; judge Supreme Court of Ill., 1933-42, chief justice, 1938-39; mem. Nat. Ry. Labor Panel, 1943; chmn. Presdl. Emergency Bds. for settlement nat. labor difficulties; judge U.S. Dist. Ct., No. Ill. Dist., 1944—. Mem. Am., Ill. Stephenson County bar assns. Democrat. Presbyn. Mason. Clubs: Freeport (Ill.) Country; Union League, Standard (Chgo.). Home: Cedarville, Ill. Address: U.S. Court House, Chgo. Died July 22, 1950; buried Oakland Cemetery, Freeport, Ill.

SHAW, Frank L., ex-mayor; b. near Warwick, Ont., Can., Feb. 1, 1877; s. John and Katherine (Roche) S.; brought to U.S., 1883; ed. pub. and pvt. schs., Denver, Colo., and Joplin, Mo.; m. Cora H. Shires, Feb. 5, 1905. Engaged in wholesale and retail merchandising business, 1895-1925; mem. Council of City of Los Angeles, 1925-28; mem. Bd. of

Supervisors, Los Angeles County, 1928-33, chmn., 1932-33; became mayor of City of Los Angeles, July 1, 1933 (all these offices non-partisan). Hon. colonel, 977th Coast Artillery, U.S. Army. Mem. C. of C. (Los Angeles), United Commercial Travelers of Am. Presbyn. Mason (32°, Shriner), Elk, K.P., Moose, Eagle, Maccabee. Clubs: Los Angeles Athletic, Jonathan. Home: 110 W. 59th Pl., Los Angeles, Calif. Died Jan. 1958.*

SHAW, G(eorge) Bernard, author, playwright; b. Dublin, Ireland, July 26, 1856; m. Charlotte Frances Payne-Townshend (died 1943). Playwright, polit. pamphleteer, novelist, critic, lecturer, author of plays, treatises and prefaces on economics, biology, socialism and the fine arts, especially music and the drama. Publications include (novels) Immaturity, The Irrational Knot, Love Among the Artists, Cashel Byron's Profession, An Unsocial Socialist, 1880-83; The Quintessence of Ibsenism, 1891 and 1913; The Sanity of Art, 1893, and The Perfect Wagnerite, 1898 (collected as Major Critical Essays, 1931); Socialism and Superior Brains, 1910; Common Sense About the War, 1914; How to Settle the Irish Question, 1917; The Intelligent Woman's Guide to Socialism and Capitalism, 1928; Adventures of a Black Girl in Search of God, 1932; Pen Portraits and Reviews, 1932; weekly articles on music in the Star, signed "Corno di Bassetto" (collected 1937 as London Music in 1888-89), and in the World (collected 1931 as Music in London in 1890-94); weekly articles in Saturday Review, 1895-98 (collected 1931 as Our Theatres in the Nineties; Doctors' Delusions, Sham Education and Crude Criminology, 1931; The Political Madhouse in America and Nearer Home, 1933; preface to Dickens' Great Expectations and William Morris as I Knew Him, 1936; Everybody's Political What's What, 1942; Plays, Pleasant and Unpleasant (7 plays), 1898; Three Plays for Puritans, 1900; The Admirable Bashville, 1901; Man and Superman, 1903; John Bull's Other Island, 1904; How He Lied to Her Husband, 1904; Major Barbara, and Passion, Poison and Petrifaction (mock tragedy), 1905; The Doctor's Dilemma, 1906; Getting Married, 1908; The Shewing-up of Blanco Posnet, 1909; The Fascinating Foundling, The Glimpse of Reality, 1909; Fanny's First Play, 1911, Androcles and the Lion, Pygmalion, and Overruled, 1912; Great Catherine, 1913; The Music-Cure, 1914; O'Flaherty V.C, The Inca of Jerusalem, 1915; Augustus Does His Bit, 1916; Heartbreak House, Annajanska, 1917; Back to Methuselah (cycle of 5 plays), 1921; Saint Joan of Arc, 1923; The Apple Cart, 1929; Too True to Be Good, 1932; Village Wooing, On the Rocks, 1933; The Six of Calais, The Simpleton of the Unexpected Isles, 1934; The Millionairess, 1936; Geneva, 1938; In Good King Charles's Golden Days, 1939. Mem. Soc. Authors, Playwrights and Composers. Awarded Nobel Prize for literature, 1925. Home: Ayot Saint Lawrence, Welwyn, Herts, Eng. Died Nov. 2, 1950.

SHAW, George Hamlin, lawyer; b. Houlton, Me., Aug. 3, 1890; s. Ransford W. and Mary (Drake) S.; A.B. and LL.B., U. of Colo., 1915; m. May Harding, Dec. 10, 1913; children—Richard Harding, Mary Agnes, Dora Drake; m. 2d, Florence B. Pollak, Aug. 25, 1936. Admitted to Colo. bar, 1915, and began practice at Fort Collins; Denver, 1926; mem. Lee, Shaw & McCreery, 1927—; dir. Cities Service Co., later become vice pres.; dir. Atlas Corporation. Chmn. Rep. State Central Com., Colo., 1922-25; Rep. candidate U.S. senator (Colo.) 1930. Mem. Am., Colo., Denver bar assns. Presbyn. Mason. Clubs: Denver Country; Deepdale Golf, Sand's Point, Turf and Field, River (N.Y.). Home: 435 E. 52d St., N.Y.C.; also Westbury, L.I., N.Y. Office: 60 Wall Tower, N.Y.C. 5. Died Apr. 1956.

SHAW, John Stewart, dir. safety; b. Baltimore, Md., July 17, 1885; s. William Checkley and Leonice M. (Stewart) S.; student Ga. Sch. Tech., 1902; Mich. State, 1903-05; post-grad. work (chemistry) Johns Hopkins U., 1905-06; m. Emma F. Campbell, Aug. 29, 1907 (died Nov. 12, 1934); children—Aileen (Mrs. Roland C. Cardner), John S., William C., III; m. 2d, Mary Lucile Hatcher Northcutt, Sept. 2, 1935. Chemist, duPont Co., 1906-13, Repauno, N.J., 1906, Marquette, Mich., 1907-08, as supervisor chem. operations; asst. acid supt., later supt., Barksdale, Wis., 1908-10, asst. acid supt., Hercules, Calif., 1910-12; asst. supt. operations (acid and explosives) Hercules Powder Co., Calif., 1913-17; gen. supt. Parlin, N.J. plant, Hercules Powder Co. (smokeless powder mfr.), 1917-18, asst. mgr., Explosives Plant "C" (ordnance dept.), Nitro, W. Va., 1918; indsl. research, Hercules Powder Co., Wilmington, Del., 1919-20, asst. gen. mgr. personnel, 1920-25, mgr. safety and service dept. (personnel), 1925-40, dir. safety since 1941. Mem. bd. dirs. Nat. Safety Council, 1948-49, gen. chmn. chem. sect. 1930, 31, 32; pres., Am. Soc. Safety Engrs., 1947-48 (engring. sect. Nat. Safety Council until 1947). Awarded Plaques from Chem. Sect. Nat. Safety Council and Am. Soc. Safety Engrs.; award from War Dept. for work as consultant to chief of safety and security div., Office Chief Ordnance, Nov. 30, 1945. Mem. Am. Soc. Safety Engrs., Veterans of Safety, Y.M.C.A., Civic Assn. of Carrcroft (Wilmington, Del.). Republican. Presbyterian. Mason. Home: "Upton," Carrcroft, Wilmington. Office: Hercules Powder Co., Wilmington, Del. Died Apr. 26, 1952; buried Christiana Cemetery, Newark, Del.

SHAW, Lloyd, folk dance expert; b. Denver, Sept. 29, 1890; s William Goodman and Julia Anne (Banker) S.; A.B., Colo. Coll., 1913, LL.D., 1928; Ed. D., U. Colo., 1937; m. Dorothy Cory Stott, Sept. 3, 1913; children—Doli (Mrs. Donald J. Obee), David Rodney (dec.). Teacher Cutler Acad., Colo. Coll., 1913-14, Colorado Springs High Sch., 1914-16; columnist Colo. Springs Gazette, 1915, 18; supt. Cheyenne Mountain Sch., Colorado Springs, 1916-51; lectr., tchr. of Am. folk dances 1951—; dir. Cheyenne Mountain Dancers and specialist in field of the Am. Sq. dance; dir. sq. dances in motion picture, Duel in the Sun; pres. Lloyd Shaw Recordings, Inc. Mem. Sigma Chi. Episcopalian. Clubs: Kiwanis Winter Night (pres. 1937), Colo. Mountain (founder Pikes Peak br.). Author: Nature Notes of the Pikes Peak Region, 1916; Cowboy Dances, 1939; The Round Dance Book, 1947; Album of Square Dances (Decca); Lloyd Shaw Round Dance Records; The Littlest Wiseman, 1951; also contributor articles to mags. Home: 1527 Winfield Av. Office: P.O. Box 203, Colorado Springs, Colo. Died July 18, 1958.

SHAW, Reuben T(aylor), educator; b. Delaware, O., Oct. 8, 1884; s. William Bigelow and Phoebe Irene (Gardner) S.; B.S., Ohio Wesleyan U., 1905, A.M., 1908, LL.D., 1939; Ph.D., U. of Pa., 1926; m. Mary Margaret Rogers, Apr. 12, 1909; children—Robert Gardner, Henry Van Dyke, Lawrence Willard, Elizabeth Rogers (dec.). Prof. physics and chemistry Temple U., 1905-09; tchr. chemistry and history Radnor High Sch., Wayne, Pa., 1906; prof. Ursinus Coll., summer, 1910; teacher of science Phila. High Schs., 1909-46, head of science dept. Northeast High School, 1929-46, now coordinator of sci. for all Phila. pub. schs. Chmn. Phila. Sr. High Sch. Science Planning Com., 1946-49; chmn. Phila. regional com. on science and mathematics teaching, 1942-46; coordinator for physics Phila. pre-aviation courses, 1942-44; mem. com. on science and mathematics teaching Pa. Dept. Pub. Instsns.; pres. Phila. Sci. Tchrs. Assn., 1942-43. Served as officer Pa. N.G., 1910-13. Del. and tour organizer Conf. of World Fed. of Edn. Assns., Tokyo, 1937, Rio de Janeiro, 1939. Fellow A.A.A.S.; life mem. N.E.A. (chmn. com. on amending charter 1934-37; mem. exec. com. 1937-38; pres. 1938-39; chmn. com. on Affiliated Assns., 1939-40; chmn. Appraisal Com., 1941-43), Pa. Edn. Assn.; chmn. Com. on Secondary Sch. Policy of Council of Higher Schools of Philadelphia; mem. Nat. Sci. Tchrs. Assn. (dir. 1944-48, v.p. 1946-48, chmn. com. on pub. and profl. relations, 1944-46); Middle States Sci. Teachers (chmn. pub. and professional relations com., 1943-46, v.p. 1946-49), Soc. Advancement of Edn., Nat. Geog. Soc., Physics Club of Phila., Nat. Assn. of Secondary Sch. Prins., Pa. Acad. Sci. (chmn. legislative com. 1946-49), Am. Chem. Soc., Beta Theta Pi, Phi Delta Kappa. Republican. Presbyn. Author: Study of Adequacy and Effectiveness of Pennsylvania School Employees' Retirement System, 1927. Contbr. to Jour. of N.E.A., School and Society. Organizer of city and state citizen coms. for support of public schools, 1919-31. Home: Highland Av., Media, Pa. Office: 21st and Parkway, Phila. 3. Died Oct. 25, 1949; buried Arlington Cemetery, Drexel Hill, Pa.

SHAW, Richard, architect; b. Boston, Mass., Sept. 22, 1887; s. Thomas and Abbie (O'Brien) S.; Harvard Grad. Sch. of Design, 1910-11; m. Lillian McMorrow, June 21, 1916. Chief draftsman Maginnis & Walsh, 1912-17; supt. on constrn., U.S. Naval Training Camp, Newport, 1917-19; partner O'Connell & Shaw, architects, 1919-30; private practice since 1930. Member of the Mass. State Art Committee since 1946. Fellow Am. Inst. Architects. Awarded Harleston Parker Gold Medal, Boston Soc. Architects, 1930, 1941-46. Mem. Boston Soc. Architects (dir.), Mass. Charitable Irish Soc., Irish Hist. Soc. Am., Mass. State Assn. Architects (ex-pres., dir.), Boston Architectural Centre (dir.). Clubs: Harvard Clover, Architectural (Boston). Mem. Mass. Bd. Registration of Architects. Home: Bayberry Knoll, Cohasset, Mass. Office: 25 Huntington Av., Boston, Mass. Died Aug. 23, 1958; buried Cohasset, Mass.

SHAW, Robert Sidey, agriculturist; b. Woodburn, Ont., Can., July 24, 1871; s. Thomas and Mary Janet (Sidey) S.; B.S.A., Agrl. Coll., Guelph, 1893; D. Agr., Mich. State Coll. Agr., 1922; m. May Travis, Jan. 2, 1900; children—Robert Linn, Thomas Travis (dec.), Sibyl (dec.), Sarah May. Came to U.S., 1898; dean of agr. and dir. Expt. Sta., Mich. Agrl. Coll., 1908-28, pres. of coll., 1928-41, now pres. emeritus. Mem. Alpha Zeta, Phi Kappa Phi, Sigma Delta Psi. Republican. Presbyterian. Home: 1201 N. Harrison, East Lansing, Mich. Died Feb. 7, 1953; buried Mt. Hope Cemetery, Lansing.

SHAW, Roger, polit. scientist; b. Hastings-on-Hudson, N.Y., Mar. 2, 1903; s. Dr. Albert and Elizabeth L. (Bacon) S.; A.B., Johns Hopkins U., 1925, M.A., Columbia, 1928; LL.D., Rollins Coll., 1945; Ph.D., Fordham U., 1946; m. Eleanor Phillips, 1925 (div. 1934); 1 dau., Carol; m. 2d Elizabeth G. Waller, 1944. Began as reporter Reading (Pa.) Times, 1925; fgn. editor Review of Reviews, 1932-37; Texas Centennial Ranger, 1936; fgn. editor Literary Digest, 1937-38, Current History, 1938-39; radio commentator WNYC, 1939, WOV, 1940, WOR, 1941; with United China Relief, 1941; with Eastern Aircraft, 1943; Nat. Assn. Mfrs., 1944; became prof. internat. relations, Trinity Coll., Hartford, 1946, now ret. Chmn. Hastings War Council. Trustee Rollins Coll. Mem. Am. Com. on Religious Rights and Minorities, Soc. Am. Mil. Engrs. (Toulmin Award, 1949), S.A.R., Mayflower Soc. (gov. 1950-53), Am. Hist. Assn., Founders of Hartford Soc., Beta Theta Pi, Pi Gamma Mu, Pi Delta Epsilon. Mason. Clubs: Town Hall, Veteran Motor Car Club of Am., Sports Car Club, Princeton Court, Overseas Press. Author: Handbook of Revolutions, 1934; Outline of Govts., 1934, 36, 37; 175 Battles, 1937; Mars Marches On, 1944; London Naval Conf. of 1930, 1946; Adam to Atom, 1948, Austro-Frankenstein, 1950. Contbr. polit. articles to European and Am. mags.; also lectr. and columnist. Home: Shandon House, 186 Terry Rd., Hartford, Conn. Died Feb. 21, 1959.

SHAW, Walter Adam, cons. engr.; b. on a farm, 4 miles south Mt. Morris, Ill., Nov. 4, 1866; s. Daniel W. and Vienia (Newcomer) S.; g.s. Adam Shaw, who settled near Oregon, Ogle County, Ill., 1838; prep. edn., Mt. Morris Coll.; B.S., Valparaiso, Ind. Normal Sch. (now Valparaiso University), 1890, C.E., 1891; married Ida M. Barrett, September 15, 1897 (deceased, January 23, 1945); 1 son, Clarence Edward. Taught country school, 1887-88; rodman in city engr. office, Rockford, Ill., 1890-91; village engr. Rogers Park, 1892-93; asst. engr. City of Chicago, 1893-95; mem. firm Alexander & Shaw, 1895-98; asst. engr. tunnel constrn., Chicago, 1898-1901, in charge day labor, 1901-05, chief engr. intercepting sewer div., 1905-07, also in charge Chicago Water Works; pres. Am. Engring. Constrn. Co., Chicago, 1907-13; engring. mem. Rivers & Lake Commn. State of Ill., 1913-14; mem. Illinois Pub. Utilities Commn., 1914-21; mem., later chmn., valuation com. of Nat. Assn. of Ry. and Utility Commrs., 1915-20, pres. of Assn., 1920; cons. practice since 1921; mem. Bd. Supervising Engrs. representing City of Chicago, 1923-34; completed plans in 1933, for separation of all street grades crossing tracks of the C.&N.W. Ry. and Chicago, North Shore and Milwaukee R.R. in Kenilworth, Winnetka, Glencoe and Highland Park, Ill.; apptd. spl. advisor to sr. judge of Dist. Court of U.S. for Northern Dist. of Ill., Eastern Div., in proceedings for reorganization of Middle West Utilities Co., under Federal Bankruptcy Act of 1935; apptd. by same court as dir. Middle West Corp., successor in interest to Middle West Utilities Co., 1936-37; consultant for Pub. Utility Commn. of N.J. in case before Federal Court, cities of Grand Rapids, Mich., and Litchfield, Ill., on bds. of arbitration; Alton Terminal Ry. Co., Ill. Elec. Assn., cities of Peoria, Champaign, Pekin, Ill.; dir. Mortgage and Real Estate Corp.; member reorganization com. for Chicago Rapid Transit Co. properties, 1937; special adviser to judge Dist. Court of U.S. for Northern Dist. of Ill., in proceedings for reorganizing Chicago Surface Lines and Chicago Rapid Transit Co. into one company, April, 1938; chmn. com. to negotiate franchise for transportation lines of City of Chicago, appt. by court chmn. Joint Board of Management and Operation of Chicago Surface Lines, Mar. 1941; served to Oct. 1944; at request of this joint board assumed complete charge of operations of Chicago Surface Lines, Apr. 1942-June 1943; consulting engr. to Chicago Surface Lines, 1944-47; ret. Life mem. Am. Soc. Civil Engrs., Western Soc. of Engrs., Am. Water Works Assn.; mem. Ill. Soc. of Engrs., Am. Pub. Works Assn., Nat. Soc. of Professional Engrs. Protestant. Club: City. Home: 922 Oakwood Ave., Wilmette, Ill. Office: 30 N. LaSalle St., Chgo. 2. Died 1951.

SHAW, William James, contractor; b. Barnet, Vt.; s. John Mefee and Jessie (Abbott) S.; grad. U. Cal., 1901; unmarried. Began in employ of the Atlantic, Gulf & Pacific Co., Manila, P.I., 1901, pres., 1917—; chmn. bd. Peoples Bank & Trust Co., 1926—. Republican. Presbyn. Clubs: University, Rotary, Army and Navy, Manila Golf, Wack Wack Golf and Country. Address: c/o Peoples Bank and Trust Co., Muelle del Banco & T. Pinpin, Manila, P.I. Died Mar. 1, 1939. Buried Cemeterio del Norte, Manila.

SHAY, Frank; b. East Orange, N.J., Apr. 8, 1888; ed. pub. and night schs.; m. Fern Forrester, Jan. 2, 1918; m. 2d, Edith Foley, Dec. 6, 1930. In book business, Brooklyn, N.Y., 1908-11, and since 1916; book auctioneer, 1911-12; mgr. book store, lumber jack and at sea until 1916; propr. Frank Shay's Bookshops, New York and Provincetown, Mass., also proprietor of the Frank Shay's Traveling Bookshop. Served as sergeant Headquarters Co., 312th Inf., U.S. Army, World War; participated in battles of St. Mihiel, Limey sector, Argonne Forest. Author: Iron Men and Wooden Ships, 1924; Here's Audacity!, 1930; Incredible Pizarro, Conqueror of Peru, 1932; Judge Lynch, His First Hundred Years, 1938; The Best Men Are Cooks, 1941; American Sea Songs and Chanties, 1948; Sand in their Shoes, 1951; A Sailor's Treasury, 1951. Address: Wellfleet, Cape Cod, Mass. Died Jan. 14, 1954; buried Snow Cemetery, Trioro, Cape Cod.

SHEA, James R(obert), (shā), paper mfr.; b. Pittsburgh, Dec. 31, 1891; s. John Frances and Ida Maude (Goodman) S.; student pub. schs. of Pittsburgh; m. Sarah Edna (Smith), Feb. 22, 1916 (dec.); children—Walter Earl (dec.), Marjorie (Mrs. R. L. Morgan, dec.), Alice (Mrs. J. M. Ammerman), Kathleen (Mrs. Robert Bathurst), James Robert, Harry David, Norman Andrew. Cashboy, Kaufaman's Dept. Store, Pittsburgh, 1903; with Frick & Lindsay Mill & Supply Co., 1903-07; with W.Va. Pulp & Paper Co., Tyrone, Pa., since 1907, resident mgr. Tyrone mill since 1946, also dir.; dir. Central Bldg. & Loan Assn. Mem. Tyron Borough Council 21 yrs., Pres., 1936-46, and 1949-52. Mem. Evang. United Brethen Ch. Mason. Home: 1551 Pennsylvania Av. Office: Tyrone, Pa. Died Nov. 25, 1952.

SHEAR, John Knox, editor, architect; b. Putnam, N.Y., Mar. 9, 1917; s. Hiram Ray and Mina Belle (Knox) S.; B.Arch., Carnegie Inst. Tech., 1938, M. Arch., 1939; M.F.A., Princeton, 1941; m. Margaret Maddox, May 6, 1944; children—John Knox, Ann Maddox, Thomas Stewart. Instr. architecture Carnegie Inst. Tech., 1941-42, 46, asso. prof. 1947-49, asso. prof. and head dept., 1949-50, prof. and head dept., 1950-55; asst. prof. architecture Princeton, 1946-47; practice architecture, Pitts., 1949—; editor-in-chief Architectural Record, 1955—. Served from ensign to lt., USNR, 1942-46. Mem. A.I.A., Pi Kappa Alpha, Phi Kappa Phi, Tau Sigma Delta, Scarab. Presbyn. Clubs: Century Assn., Princeton (N.Y.C.). Home: 5707 Lynne Haven Rd., Pitts. 17, Pa. Office: 119 W. 40th St., N.Y.C. 18. Died Jan. 10, 1958.

SHEARN, Clarence John, lawyer, b. Leeds, Northampton, Mass.; s. Joseph Henry and Mary Celia (Kearney) S.; B.L., Cornell U., 1890; New York Law Sch., 1891-93; m. Eva Petty (dec. 1929); children—Clarence John, Edith (Mrs. Arthur L. Kerrigan); m. 2d, Mrs. Luella Bouton Mason, Nov. 17, 1932 (dec. Oct. 1938); m. 3d, Mrs. Dorothea Alexandra Troyte-Bullock, Mar. 29, 1940. Admitted to N.Y. bar, 1893; became mem. law firm Einstein, Townsend, Guiterman & Shearn, 1893; mem. Yonge, Brewster & Shearn; apptd. justice of N.Y. Supreme Court, 1st Dist., 1915; elected, 1916, on joint nomination of Dem. and Rep. parties, for 14 yr. term; after 2 yrs. as trial justice, designated by Gov. Whitman an asso. justice of Appellate Div. of Supreme Court, 1st Dept.; resigned 1919 to resume practice (firm Shearn & Hare until death of Mr. Hare in 1932). Mem. Assn. Bar City of N.Y. (pres. 1935-37), N.Y. County Lawyers' Assn. (1st v.p. 1933-38), Am., N.Y. State bar assns. Clubs: Manhattan, Cornell, Recess, Long Island Country, Piping Rock. Home: 740 Park Av., Address: 1 Wall St., N.Y.C. Deceased.

SHEDD, Thomas Clark, prof, structural engring.; b. Worcester, Mass., July 2, 1890; s. Edward Whitten and Jessie (Dexter) S.; student U. of Va., 1908-09; B.S., Brown U., 1913; M.S., U. of Ill., 1932, C.E., 1925; m. Mary Margaret Campbell, Oct. 26, 1916; children—Thomas Clark, Milton Campbell, Harriet Martha. Instr. Brown U., Providence, R.I., 1913-15; Instr. Lehigh U., Bethlehem, Pa., 1917-18; with U. of Illinois, 1922—, professor structural engineering, until 1958, professor emeritus, 1958—; with Phoenix Bridge Co., Phoenixville, Pa., 1915-17, 18-22; Waddell & Hardesty, cons. engrs., N.Y.C., occasionally, 1926-41. Member Ill. Structural Engineers. Examining Com. (chmn.), Profl. Engrs. Examining Com. (chmn. 1945-48). Mem. Nat. Council State Bds. Engring. Examiners, Nat., Ill. socs. professional engrs., International Assn. Bridge and Structural Engineers, Am. Soc. C.E. (dist. dir.), American Ry. Engring. Assn., Am. Concrete Inst., American Soc. for Engring. Edn., Ill. Engring. Council (pres, 1941), Sigma Xi, Tau Beta Pi, Chi Epsilon, Phi Kappa Phi. Republican. Conglist. Club: Exchange (Urbana). Author: Theory of Simple Structures (with Jamieson Vawter), 1931; 2d edition, 1940; Structural Design in Steel, 1934. Home: 706 W. California. Office: Civil Engring. Dept., U. of Ill., Urbana, Ill. Died July 11, 1959; buried Roselawn Cemetery, Champaign, Ill.

SHEEAN, James B., lawyer; b. Anamosa, Ia., Aug. 24, 1863; s. Jeremiah L. and Laura J. (Rawlins) S.; Beloit (Wis.) Coll., 1881-82; A.B., U. Mich., 1885; Mich. Law Sch., 1886-87; m. Emily H. Holman, Nov. 9, 1911; children—Laura, James B. Began practice at Omaha, Neb., 1888; apptd. asst. gen. atty. Fremont, Elkhorn & Mo. Valley Ry. Co., 1897; gen. solicitor C.,St.P.,M.&O. Ry., at St. Paul, Minn., 1905-18; gen. counsel, v.p. C.N.W. Ry. and C.,St.P.,M.O. Ry. Co., Chicago, 1918-24, ret. Mem. Phi Kappa Psi. Episcopalian. Address: Galena, Ill. Died July 14, 1941; buried Galena, Ill.

SHEEDY, Joseph Edward, b. Pembroke, Me., Apr. 17, 1881; s. John E. and Matilda (McIsaac) S.; grad. Mass. Nautical Sch., 1898; m. Ella Burnham, July 20, 1907 (div.); children—Burnham, Betsy Kirby (dec.), Nancy Burnham; m. 2d, Anne Bertner, Apr. 17, 1928; 1 dau., Joanne Elsie. Successively as 3d lt., 2d lt. and engr. USCG, 1903-10; asst. mgr. Inter Island Steam Navigation Co., Honolulu, 1910-15; asst. gen. mgr. Seattle Constrn. Dry Dock Co., 1916-18; gen. mgr. Seattle N. Pacific Shipbuilding Co., 1918-19; asst. to pres. Downey Shipbuilding Corp., N.Y.C., 1919-20, gen. mgr., 1921; European mgr. U.S. Shipping Bd. Emergency Fleet Corp., 1921-22; v.p. in charge operations U.S. Shipping Bd. Emergency Fleet Corp., 1922-24, also trustee; vice pres. in charge European affairs, 1924-27; v.p. Montauck Beach Development Corp., N.Y., 1927-28; pres. U.S. Lines Operations (ocean transportation), 1928-31; consultant on shipping and foreign trade, 1932—. Decorated Comdr. Order of Crown of Roumania. Club: Lotos (N.Y.C.). Home: 110 W. 57th St., N.Y.C. Died Jan. 24, 1955.

SHEEHAN, J. Eastman, surgeon; b. Dublin, Ireland; s. Daniel Stanislaus and Catherine (Eastman) S.; M.D., Yale, 1908; studied at Oxford, London, Paris, Bern, Heidelberg, Berlin, Budapest, Vienna; m. Anastasia Dwyer, May 14, 1914 (dec.); 1 dau., Marguerite Virginia. Prof. plastic reparative surgery N.Y. Polyclinic. Med. Sch. and Hosp.; surgeon to Morrisania and St. Clares Hosps., N.Y., lecturer to Internat. Clinic, Paris, 1922—; guest lectr. univs. of Utrecht, Milan, Parma, Belgrade, Istanbul, Ankara, Rome, Paris, Dublin, Bucharest, Bruxelles, and Guy's Hosp., London; hon. surgeron, N.Y. police dept.; worked at Oxford, 1942; posted to the burns center, Glasgow, 1943; worked under direction Royal Air Force Command, 1944. Apptd. observer at Parliamentary and Congressional groups, Bermuda, Washington, and Ottawa, Can., 1946. Fellow Royal Society of Medicine (London), A.C.S., N.Y. Acad. Medicine; mem. Am. Soc. of Oral and Plastic Surgeons (pres. 1935-36), French Soc. of Pastic and Reparative Surgeons (hon. pres.), French Surg. Soc., Société Française d' Oto-Rhino-Laryngologie, Société Belge d'Oto-Rhino-Laryngologie, Jornadas Medicas de Madrid (hon.), Les Journées Médicales de Bruxelle, Société Academique d'Historie Internationale (corr. editor), Bruxelles Médical (corr. editor), Royal Acad. Spain (corr. editor), French Legion of Honor, N.Y., Belgian Legion of Honor, Legion of Honor of N.Y. Police Dept. Decorated O.B.E. Military, England; service cross, and military cross, Spain, Order Crown of Belgium; Legion of Honor (France); L'umpia (France); Order of Alphonse XII (Spain); Knight Grand Cross Order of Isabella Cahtolica, Spain; Ordre de la Merite Cultural Scientifique, 1st Class (Roumania). Clubs: Bedford Tennis and Golf Club, Yale, British Schools and Universities (v.p. 1938), Oxford Union, St. George's Society, Royal Yacht Club, Devonshire, Royal Automobile, Authors, Public Schools (London); Union Interalliée, Travellers (Paris). Corr. editor: Bruxelles Med. Chirurgie Structive de Bruxelles La Crirurgia Plastica, Roma, Le Journal de la Chirurgie Plastique et Restauratrice, Paris. Author: Plastic Surgery of the Nose, 1925, rev., 1937; Plastic Surgery of the Orbit, 1927; Manual of Plastic Reparative Surgery, 1938; Surgery for War, 1944; General and Plastic Surgery, 1945. Invited by Generalissimo Francisco Franco of Nationalist Army, Spain, to take charge of war wounded; hon. col. Nationalist Forces, Spain; hon. prof. de la academia de Sanidad Militar, Spain; collaboráteur L'Europe, Médicale, Pioneer in applying colour to motion pictures of surgical operations; guest lectr. Oxford U., Eng., 1942; inventor method of rapid skin grafting with aid of tulle and glue. Home: (winter) 211 E. 62d St., N. Y.C. 21; (summer) 47 B Welbeck St., London W1, Eng. Died Jan. 8, 1951.

SHEETS, Frank Thomas, pres. Portland Cement Assn.; b. Lafayette, O., Oct. 5, 1890; s. Edgar Wilson and Gertrude (Williams) S.; B.S., in civil engineering, U. of Ill., 1914. With Ill. State Highway Dept., 1907-33, advancing from clerk to engr. of design, 1907-21, state supt. of highways, 1921-24, chief highway engr., 1924-33; private cons. engring. practice, 1933; cons. engr. Portland Cement Assn., Chicago, 1933-37, pres. since 1937. Del. to 2d Pan-Am. Highway Conf., Rio de Janeiro, Brazil, 1929. Pres. Abraham Lincoln Council, Boy Scouts of Am., 1930-31. Member Am. Soc. of Civil Engrs. (pres. Central Ill. sect. 1925), Am. Assn. of State Highway Officials (pres. 1928), Miss. Valley Conf. of State Highway Officials (pres. 1925), Triangle (pres. 1918), Tau Beta Pi, Sigma Xi. Mason (K.T., Shriner), Potentate, Ansar Temple, 1934. Received Bartlett Award for "outstanding contribution to highway progress," 1941. Clubs: Chicago Athletic, Lake Shore (Chicago). Author booklets pub. by Portland Cement Assn. Home: 850 N. Lake Shore. Office: 33 W. Grand Av., Chgo. Died Nov. 3, 1951; buried Rosehill Mausoleum, Chgo.

SHELBURNE, James M., clergyman; b. nr. Taylorsville, Ky., May 27, 1867; s. John W. and Jane (Goodwine) S.; A.B., A.M., Georgetown Coll., Ky., 1897; Th.M., So. Bapt. Theol. Sem., Louisville, 1900; D.D., Georgetown Coll., 1907; L.H.D., Howard Coll., 1908; m. Martha Washington Crumpton, June 27, 1900; children—Kingman C., Ellen B., James C., Harriet M., Mary Frances, Davis Ryland. Ordained to ministry Bapt. Ch., 1900; pastor College Ch., Birmingham, Ala., 1900-09; 1st Ch., Bristol, Va., 1909-13; pres. Howard Coll., 1913-18; ednl. sec. for War Work Council of YMCA, Camp Wheeler, Macon, Ga., 1917-18; pastor First Ch., Gadsden, Ala., 1918-21, First Ch., Danville, Va., 1921—. Mem. Edn. Bd., So. Bapt. Conv., 1919-21, Bd. Fgn. Missions, 1922-32; mem. exec. com. So. Bapt. Conv., 1932-44; trustee So. Bapt. Theol. Sem., 1914-38, Averett Coll., 1921—; chmn. Interracial Cooperation, 1928—; chmn. local chapter Emergency Peace Campaign, 1935—; asso. justice Juvenile and Domestic Relations Court, 1937—; dir. Public Welfare, 1940—. Emeritus minister to First Bapt. Ch., Danville, 1942—. Author published poems on various themes. Home: 898 Pine St., Danville, Va. Died Oct. 26, 1951.

SHELBY, Robert Evart, broadcasting exec.; b. Austin, Tex., July 20, 1906; s. Lemuel Evart and Mabel Clair (Wright) S.; B.S. in Elec. Engring., U. Tex., 1927, A.B., 1928, A.M. in Physics, 1929; m. Marian Eikel, June 12, 1931; children—Barbara, Jane. With NBC, N.Y.C., 1929—, beginning as engr., successively engr. in charge Empire State TV Lab., supr. TV engring., dir. tech. development. dir. TV tech. development, dir. color TV systems development project, 1929-53, v.p., chief engr., 1954—. Recipient David Sarnoff medal, Soc. Motion Picture and Television Engrs., 1956. Fellow Inst. Radio Engrs. (chmn. TV systems com.), Am. Inst. E.E., Soc. Motion Picture and TV Engrs.; mem. Nat. TV System Com., Phi Beta Kappa, Sigma Xi, Tau Beta Pi, Eta Kappa Nu. Author tech. articles. Holder patents in field. Home: 431 Claremont Av., Teaneck, N.J. Died Dec. 8, 1955.

SHELDON, John Lewis, botanist, bacteriologist; b. Voluntown, Conn., Nov. 10, 1865; s. Samuel H. and Lucy A. (Lewis) S.; B.Sc., Ohio Northern U., 1895, M.Sc., 1899; B.Sc., U. Neb., 1899, A.M., 1901, Ph.D., 1903; m. Clara Adams Fleming, Aug. 21, 1907; 1 son, Earl Fleming. Tchr. pub. schs., Conn., 1885-90, 1895-97; instr. Mt. Hermon (Mass.) Sch., 1892-94; instr. botany, prep. sch. U. Neb., 1898-99; acting head dept. biology, Neb. State Normal Sch., 1899-1900; instr. botany, U. Neb., 1901-03; prof. bacteriology, W.Va. U., and bacteriologist, Agrl. Expt. Sta., 1903-07; prof. botany and bacteriology, 1907-13, rof. botany, 1913-19, W.Va. University. Fellow A.A.A.S., Bot. Soc. Am.; mem. Am. Phytopathol. Soc., Sullivant oss Soc., Am. Genetic Assn., Sigma Xi, Phi Beta Kappa, Theta Kappa Psi. Republican. Contbr. to bot. and agrl. publs.; investigator in plant pathology. Home: 308 Grandview Av., Morgantown, W.Va. Died Jan. 15, 1947; buried Central Village, Conn.

SHELLABARGER, Samuel (shĕl'á-bär'gẽr), author, educator; b. Washington, D.C., May 18, 1888; s. Robert Rodgers and Sarah Rivera (Wood) S.; A.B., Princeton U., 1905-09; student Munich U., Germany, 1910-11; Ph.D., Harvard, 1917; m. Vivan Georgia Lovegrove Borg, June 14, 1915; children—Ingrid Rivera (Mrs. William Holdship Rea), Marianne Jenner (Mrs. John Jeppson), John Eric (dec.). Instr. in English, Princeton U., 1914-16, asst. prof. in English, 1919-23; author, 1923-38; headmaster, Columbus (O.) Sch. for Girls, 1938-46. Served as 1st lt. Ordnance Dept., U.S. Army, 1917; capt. Military Intelligence, as assistant military attaché, U.S. Legation, Stockholm, Sweden, 1918-19. Republican. Episcopalian. Clubs: Tower, Nassau (Princeton); University, Centur Club (N.Y.). Author: The Chevalier Bayard (biography), 1928; The Black Gale (novel), 1929; Lord Chesterfield (biography), 1935; Captain from Castile (novel), 1945; Prince of Foxes (novel), 1947; The Kings Cavalier, 1950; Lord Chesterfield and His World (biography, rev. edit.), 1951; Lord Vanity, 1953; Tolbecken, 1955 (posthumously); The Token, 1956 (posthumously) (mystery stories under name of John Esteven) The Door of Death, 1928; Voodoo, 1930; By Night at Dinsmore, 1935; While Murder Waits, 1937; Graveyard Watch, 1938; Assurance Double Sure, 1939; (novels under name of Peter Loring) Grief Before Night, 1938; Miss Rolling Stone, 1939. Contbr. fiction to McCall's Mag., Cosmopolitan. Home: 107 Library Pl., Princeton, N.J. Died Mar. 20, 1954.

SHELLEY, Henry V(ogel), univ. prof.; born Albany, N.Y., Sept. 26, 1890; s. Henry Vogel and Susan Wilson (Battin) S.; student Boys' High Sch., Brooklyn, 1905-08, Trinity Sch., N.Y. City, 1908-09; A.B., Columbia, 1913; A.M., U. of Pa., 1917, Doctor of Philosophy, 1919; married to Francis Marion Dana, June 28, 1922; children—Dana Wilson (deceased), Richard Henry. Served as a master of Greek and Latin, Kent Sch., Kent, Conn., 1913-15; master of German and French, St. Alban's Sch., Washington, 1915-16; instr. Lafayette Coll., 1919-20, asst. prof. Greek, 1920-27; prof. and head dept. Ancient langs. (Greek and Latin) Washington and Lee U. since 1927. Mem. Am. Philol. Assn. Classical Assn. of Middle West and South, Tau Delta Sigma. Republican. Presbyterian. Clubs: That (Lexington), Rotary. Author: A Study of Piety in the Greek Tragic Chorus, 1919. Pianist and organist. Home: 204 Myers St., Lexington, Va. Died May 27, 1959; buried Lexington, Va.

SHELTON, E(berle) Kost, internist, endocrinologist; b. Bloomfield, Ia., May 19, 1888; s. Eberle Kost and Katherine (Hayes) S.; student U. of Denver, 1907-09; M.D., U. of Colo., 1912, Sc.D., 1944; post grad. student various endocrine clinics, 1927-30; m. Margaret Norine, Feb. 25, 1914; 1 son, Paul Kingsley.

Resident physician, City and County Hosp., Denver, Colo., 1911-13; in gen. practice, 1913; internist, Denver and Antonito, Colo., 1914-26, Santa Barbara, Calif., 1930-40, Los Angeles, Calif., since 1938; asso. clin. prof. medicine, U. of Southern Calif., 1931-51; clin. prof. medicine, U. Cal., Los Angeles since 1951. sr. attending physician Harbor Gen. Hospital, since 1951; dir. endocrine clinic and mem. attending staff of hosp., Los Angeles Gen. Hosp.; mem. cons. staff St. Johns Hosp., Santa Monica, Calif. Diplomate Am. Bd. Internal Medicine. Fellow Am. Coll. Physicians; mem. Am. Med. Assn., Am. Therapeutic Soc., A.A.A.S., Assn. Study Internal Secretions, Los Angeles and Hollywood acads. medicine; Am. Soc. Research in Psychosomatic Problems, Alpha Kappa Kappa. Author of pituitary chapter, vol. VIII, Tice's Practice of Medicine, and editor of endocrine volume, 1935. Author brochures on problems of internal medicine and endocrinology; contbr. to med. text books. Home: 760 North Beverly Glen. Office: 921 Westwood Blvd., Los Angeles 24. Died Feb. 22, 1955.

SHELTON, Orman Leroy, sem. pres.; b. Kingman County, Kan., Mar. 1, 1895; s. Elisha Harvey and Lillian Christiann (Nossaman), S.; A.B., Phillips U., Enid, Okla., 1929, D.D., 1935; student Tex. Christian U., Fort Worth, Tex., 1928-29; m. Ruby Ethel Stratten, Aug. 13, 1913; 1 dau., Orma Le (Mrs. Ervin Laverne Thompson). Ordained to ministry of Christian Church, 1923; pastor, First Christian Ch., Marlow, Okla., 1923-25; pub. relations dir., Phillips U., 1926-28; pastor First Christian Ch., Denison, Tex., 1928-32, Ponca City, Okla., 1932-38, Wichita Falls, Tex., 1938-41, Independence Blvd. Christian Ch., Kansas City, Mo., 1941-44; dean, sch. of religion, Butler U., Indianapolis, Ind., 1944-58, pres. Christian Theol. Sem., Butler U., 1958—. Pres. state conventions Disciples of Christ, Okla., 1937, Tex., 1941; chmn. home and state missions planning council Disciples of Christ, 1938-41, chmn. nat. stewardship com., 1938-44, chmn. Mo. religious edn. commn., 1941-44, chmn. nat. correlation com., 1943-44, chmn. commn. to re-study on edn., on seminaries, mem. bd. higher edn. Pres. Okla. Christian Missionary Soc., 1935-38, chmn. adult work, Disciples of Christ, Tex., 1938-41; mem. bd. mgrs. United Christian Missionary Soc., 1938-41; member board trustees, 1941-44; vice chmn. Kansas City Council of Chs., 1943, vice pres. Internat. Conv. Disciples of Christ, 1953-54; visitor World Council 2d Assembly, 1954; chmn. study com. World Conv., Disciples of Christ; chmn. Bd. of Higher Edn., Disciples of Christ. Member Nat. Evangelistic Assn. (Disciples of Christ), Nat. Assn. of Bibl. Instrs., Internat. Mark Twain Soc.; A.A.A.S.; Am. Acad. of Polit. and Social Sci.; Am. Assn. Univ. Prof., Internat. Theta Phi. Dir. Community Chest, Ponca City, Okla., 1937. Pres. Lions Club, Ponca City, 1937. Author: The Church Functioning Effectively, 1946. Contbg. editor: World Call, 1939, Nat. Stewardship editor, 1939-44. Home: 445 Blue Ridge Rd., Indianapolis 8. Office: Sunset and 46th St., Indpls. Died Mar. 3, 1959; buried Crown Hill Cemetery, Indpls.

SHENK, Hirmna Herr, historian; b Deodate, Pa., Dec. 9, 1872; s. Cyrus Gingrich and Anna R. (Herr) S.; grad. Cumberland Valley State Normal Sch., Shippensburg, Pa., 1894; A.B., Ursinus Coll., Collegeville, Pa., 1899; A.M., Lebanon Valley Coll., Annville, Pa., 1900, LL.D., 1928; grad. study U. of Wis., 1904; m. Bertha Strickler, June 26, 1900; children—Sara Lucile, Ann Esther. Tchr. rural schs., Dauphin County, 1889-93; instr. in polit. sci., Lebanon Valley Coll., 1899-1900, prof. histiry, polit. sci., 1900-16, librarian of coll., 1900-05, registrar, 1906-07, dean, 1907-11; custodian of pub. records, archivist and historian, Pa. State Library, 1916-33. Ednl. sec. Y.M.C.A., Camp Travis, Tex., 1917, 18; instr. Y.M.C.A., Summer Sch., Blue Ridge, N.C., 1916-19, Silver Bay, N.Y., 1919, Lake Geneva, Wis., 1921; instr., Summer Sch., Pa. State Coll., 1925, extension lectr., 1925-26. Sec. Pa. Federation Hist. Socs., 1918-33; exec. sec. Pa. Hist. Commn., 1927-33; prof. Am. history Lebanon Valley Coll. and field sec. alumni, 1933-38. Chmn. com. Pa. hist. exhibits, Sesquicentennial Expn., Phila., 1926. Mem. Am. Hist. Assn., Acad. Polit. Sci., Pa. Hist. Assn., Soc. Pa. Archeology. Republican. Mem. United Brethren Ch. Mason. Club: Torch. Author: History of Lebanon Valley, 1931; Ency. of Pennsylvania, 1932. Joint Author: Pennsylvania History Told by Contemporaries, 1925. Contributor historical monographs, also to Dictionary of Am. History. Home: Annville, Pa. Died May 20, 1954.

SHENK, John Wesley, judge; b. Shelburne, Vt., Feb. 7, 1875; s. John Wesley and Susanna Cake (Brooks) S.; A.B., Ohio Wesleyan Univ., 1900; J.D., U. of Mich., 1903, LL.D., 1955; LL.D., Ohio Wesleyan University, 1930, University of So. California, 1950; m. Lenan R. Custer, June 29, 1907; children—Samuel Custer, John Wesley, III. Admitted to Calif. bar, 1903, and began practice at Los Angeles; dep. and asst. atty., Los Angeles, 1906-10, city atty., 1910-13; judge Superior Ct., Los Angeles, 1913-24; asso. justice Supreme Ct. Cal., 1924—. Mem. Co. K, 4th Ohio Vol. Inf., Spanish-Am. War; served in Puerto Rico. Mem. of Judicial Council of State of Cal. Mem. Am. Bar Assn., bar assns. Los Angeles County and San Francisco, Vets. Fgn. Wars, U.S. War Vets., S.A.R., Beta Theta Pi, Phi Delta Phi, Order of Coif. Republican. Methodist. Mason (33°, K.T., Shriner), Red Cross of Constantine. Clubs: Jonathan (Los Angeles); Commonwealth (San Francisco). Home: Los Altos, Cal. Address: Supreme Court, State Bldg., San Francisco. Died Aug. 3, 1959; buried San Gabriel (Cal.) Cemetery.

SHEPARD, Frank Russell, baking exec.; born Charlestown, Mass., June 29, 1868; s. Charles Dexter and Angeline M. (Sanborn) S.; grad. Charlestown High Sch., 1888; m. Annie Frances Perkins, May 21, 1890; children—Stella Marie, Frances Russell. Treas. and dir. George G. Fox Co., Boston, 1893-1911; chmn. orgn. com., Gen. Baking Co., 1911, 1st v.p., dir. and mem. exec. com., 1911-26, dir. since 1938; ret., 1938; dir. Lexington Trust Co. Chmn. War Emergency Council Baking Industry, World War I. Life mem. Nat. Assn. Master Bakers (now Am. Bakers Assn.; treas. and mem. exec . com., 1897-1903, pres. 1902-03, dir. and mem. exec. com., 1904-06), N.E. Bakers Assn. (past pres. and gov.). Conglist. Mason (32°). K.P. Club: Rotary. Home: 1386 Massachusetts Av., Lexington 73, Mass. Died Oct. 7, 1952; buried Woodlawn, Everett, Mass.

SHEPARD, George Wanzor, naval surgeon; b. Freedom, O., June 11, 1878; s. Sheridan Wells and Fannie Annette (Hopkins) S.; M.D., Western Reserve U. Med. Coll., 1903; m. Frankie Gail Daniels, June 30, 1903; 1 son, Richard Daniels. Surg. intern, Lakeside Hosp., Cleve., 1903-04; in practice, Ravenna, O., 1904-07; commd. asst. surgeon U.S. Navy, Oct. 25, 1907; advanced through grades to capt. Med. Corps, 1929. Med. insp. U.S. Navy, 1921; chief of surg. service, U.S. Naval Hosp., San Diego, Cal., 1922-25; same, U.S. Naval Hosp., Mare Island, Cal., 1927-31; sr. med. officer U.S. hosp. ship Relief, 1931-33; sr. med. officer Am. Embassy Guard, Peiping, China, 1935-37; comdg. officer U.S. Naval Med. Supply Depot, Mare Island, Cal., 1937-42; spent many years at sea on ships of the fleet, ret., 1942. Recalled to active duty in connection with Navy V-12 Training program, 1943. Fellow A.M.A., Am. Coll. Surgeons. Republican. Mason. Address: 115 Camino Alta, Vallejo, Cal. Died Feb. 3, 1958; buried San Bruno Nat. Cemetery, San Francisco.

SHEPARDSON, Frank Lucius, teacher; b. Princeton, Me., Apr. 10, 1861; s. Lucius Franklin and Maria L. (Gage) S.; A.B., Brown U., 1883, A.M., 1886; grad. study University of Chicago, 1913; Litt.D. from Colgate University, 1933; m. Sarah Whidden, of Worcester, Mass., June 25, 1888 (dec. July 11, 1952); children—Whitney H., Margaret. Teacher in pvt. sch., Cumberland, Md., 1883-84; mem. faculty Worcester Acad., 1884-96, acting prin., 1894-95; prin. Colgate Acad., 1896-1912; asso. prof. Greek, and treas., Colgate U., 1912-28, leave of absence for travel and study in Italy, Greece, Near East, 1926, prof. Greek, 1928-34, prof. emeritus since 1934, leave of absence, 1933-34. Examiner in Greek, N.Y. State Dept. Edn., 1922-25. Mem. Phi Beta Kappa, Beta Theta Pi. Baptist. Address: Hamilton, N.Y. Died Aug. 19, 1952.

SHEPLER, Joseph McGuire, clergyman; b. Cumberland, O., Oct. 13, 1869; s. John Irwin and Lydia Louisa (Clark) S.; A.B., Mt. Union Coll., 1896, D.D., 1913; S.T.B., Boston U., 1900, post-grad. work; m. Winifred Johnson, May 30, 1900; children—John Rex, Dwight Clark. Ordained to ministry M.E. Ch., 1896; pastor Finley Ch., Steubenville, O., 1896; asst. pastor Centre Ch., Malden, Mass., 1898-1900; pastor Glendale Ch., Everett, 1900-1906, South St. Ch., Lynn, 1906-08, Hyde Park, 1908-15, Watertown, 1915-20; supt. Meth. chs., Boston Dist., 1920-26; pastor Lafayette St. Ch., Salem, 1926-31, Stanton Av. Ch., Dorchester, Boston, 1931-35, Wincehndon Ch., 1937—. Trustee Boston U.; dir. New Eng. Deaconess Assn. Mem. Sons of Vets. Republican. Mason. Clubs: Boston Itinerants', Kiwanis. Author book chat column Townsend Times. Home: Townsend, Mass. Died Oct. 4, 1951; buried Townsend.

SHERBURNE, Ernest C., play and film reviewer; b. Charlestown, Mass., Apr. 5, 1878; s. George P. and Martha (Tarbox) S.; student Harvard Extension Courses and pvt. instn. under Dr. Alfred H. Hennequin; m. Ethel Karnan, May 20, 1911; 1 dau., Ruth (Mrs. Louis Wicks). Printer and make-up man, Christian Science Pub. Soc., Boston, 1898-1908; reporter Christian Science Monitor, Boston, 1908-09, film and play reviewer since 1909, in New York office, 1929-36, reviewer of art exhibitions, 1910-36, editor weekly magazine section, Boston office, 1936-43, with New York office, 1943-46, retired, 1946; now freelancing. Home: P.O. Box 2084, Carmel. Cal. Died Dec. 8, 1952.

SHERBY, Daniel, business exec.; b. Bridgeton, N.J., July 23, 1908; s. Harry and Kate (Luber) S.; A.B., Washington and Lee U., Lexington, Va., 1931; student law sch., Western Res. U., 1933; m. Clementine Flesheim, Oct. 25, 1934; children—Ann Emily, Ellen Kathryn. Gen. mgr. Zone Cab Corp., Cleve., 1930-53, sec., treas., 1930—; sec., treas. United Garage & Service Corp., 1934—, Yellow Cab Co. of Cleve., Inc., 1934—; v.p. City-Yellow Cab Co., Akron, O.; pres. Ft. Myers Broadcasting Co.; dir. Continental Bank. Mem. nat. adv. heart council U.S.P.H.S. Trustee Mt. Sinai Hosp., Cleve. Zoo. Mem. Nat. Assn. Taxicab Owners (trustee), Cab Research Bur. (treas.), U.S. C. of C. Clubs: Oakwood, Cleveland Advertising. Home: 18501 Shaker Blvd., Shaker Heights 22, O. Office: Leader Bldg., Cleve. 14. Died Aug. 15, 1954; buried Cleve.

SHERIDAN, Thomas Harold, patent lawyer; born Thomaston, Conn., Sept. 26, 1886; s. Thomas Francis and Frances (Ager) S.; student Northwestern U., 1903-04; student Leland Stanford, 1904-05; Lehigh U., 1905-07; George Washington U., 1908-09; LL.B., Nat. U., 1910; student Northwestern U., 1910-11; m. Mary C. Hayes, Aug. 28, 1917; children—Francigene, Thomas Francis II. Admitted to Ill. bar; asst. examiner U.S. Patent Office, 1908-10; engaged in practice of law since 1910; sr. partner law firm Sheridan, Davis & Cargill, specialists in patent law, since 1936. Served as lt. U.S.N.R.F., 1918. Mem. Phi Delta Phi, Sigma Chi. Republican. Clubs: University (Chicago); Exmoor Country (Highland Park, Ill.). Home: 820 S. Linden Av., Highland Park, Ill. Office: 135 S. La Salle St., Chgo. Died July 26, 1952.

SHERMAN, Carl, lawyer, corp. exec.; born Olmutz, Austria, Oct. 16, 1890; s. Sandor and Paula Sherman; LL.B., U. Buffalo, 1910; m. Helena Manheim, Apr. 15, 1915; children—Mildred (Mrs. Alfred M. Zenker), Louis M. Partner Sherman & Goldring, attys., N.Y.C., 1914—; atty. gen. N.Y. State, 1923-24; with Helena Rubinstein, Inc., N.Y.C., 1944—, chmn. bd. dirs., 1947—. Treas. N.Y. State Dem. Com. Chmn. finance com. Ch. Peace Union, Carnegie Found. Democrat. Jewish. Home: 590 West End Av., N.Y.C. Office: 420 Lexington Av., N.Y.C. Died July 17, 1956.

SHERMAN, Charles Lawton, educator; b. Newport, R.I., Feb. 16, 1894; s. Benjamin B.H. and Charlotte A. (Lawton) S.; A.B., Harvard, 1917, Ph.D., 1928; Licenceès-Lettres, U. Grenoble, 1920; m. Dorothy A. Arnold, July 13, 1918 (dec.); children—Charlotte A. (Mrs. Kimball S. Green), Fred A.; m. 2d, Mrs. Mary Burdick Kenly, Mar. 23, 1950. Asst. prof. Greek and Latin, Ohio Wesleyan U., 1920-22; instr. French, Harvard, 1922-23, instr. classics, 1923-29; asso. prof. Latin, Amherst Coll., 1929-34, asso. prof. polit. sci., 1934-40, prof. history and polit. sci., 1940—. Mem. representative town meeting, Amherst. Mem. Am. Philol. Assn., Am. Hist. Assn., Phi Beta Kappa. Club: Harvard (Boston). Editor: John Locke's A Treatise of Civil Government, 1937; Vol. 7 Loeb Classical Library, Diodorus of Sicily, 1952, Vol. 8 (posthumously), to be published. Home: 155 Woodside Av. Office: Amherst College, Amherst, Mass. Died Dec. 22, 1954.

SHERMAN, Ellen Burns, author; b. Montgomery Center, Vt., May 4, 1867; d. Ezra Wright and Harriet Anne (Chase) Sherman; B.Litt., Smith Coll., 1891. Teacher in Feller Inst., Grande Ligne, Que., 1885-86, Birds' Sch., Auburndale, Mass., 1886-87, Greylock Acad., S. Williamstown, Mass., 1887-88. Unitarian. Mem. Mass. Equal Suffrage Assn., Pi Gamma Mu. Author: Taper Lights, 1903; Words to the Wise—and Others, 1907; On the Manuscripts of God, 1918; Volume of Poems, 1936; Balm for Men's Souls, 1953. Contbr. essays, stories and poems. Home: 313 Maple St., Springfield, Mass. Died Jan. 15, 1956; buried Richford, Vt.

SHERMAN, Forrest Percival, naval officer; b. Merrimack, N.H., Oct. 30, 1896; s. Frank James and Grace (Allen) S.; student Mass. Inst. Tech., 1913-14; B.S. (Distinguished Grad.), U.S. Naval Acad., 1917; grad. Naval War Coll., 1927; m. Dolores Brownson, Apr. 2, 1923; 1 dau., Elizabeth Ann. Commd. ensign, U.S. Navy, 1917, and advanced through the grades to Admiral, Nov. 1949, served on U.S.S. Nashville, in Mediterranean, 1917-18, on U.S.S. Murray on French Coast, 1918-19; commd. U.S.S. Barry, 1921; student naval aviation, Naval Air Station, Pensacola, 1922, designated naval aviator; exec. officer Fighting Plane Squadron 2, 1923; Officer in charge combat training, Pensacola, 1924-26; student Naval War Coll., 1926-27; asst. air officer, U.S.S. Lexington, 1927; comd. Scouting Squadron 2, U.S.S. Lexington, 1928-29; staff comdr. aircraft, 1929-30; instr. in flight tactics, U.S. Naval Acad., 1930-31; tactical officer, staff of comdr. of aircraft, U.S. Fleet, 1931-32; wing comdr. Fighting Wing, 1932-33; in charge aviation ordnance, Navy Dept., 1933-36; navigator, U.S.S. Ranger, 1936-37; fleet aviation officer, staff comdr. in chief, U.S. Fleet, 1937-40; office of chief of naval operations, 1940; became deputy chief for operations, December, 1945. Apptd. as U.S. rep. in naval aviation on U.S.-Canadian Permanent Joint Bd. on Defense, Aug. 1940; member Army-Navy Joint Planning Com., 1940, Navy Dept. Research Council, 1940; U.S. naval aviation advisor, Atlantic Conf., 1941; chief of staff, Air Force; Pacific Fleet, 1942; mm. Joint Strategic Com., 1942; comd. U.S.S. Wasp, 1942; Deputy chief of staff, comdr. in chief, Pacific Ocean Areas, 1943; Comd. Carrier Div. One, 1945; Dep. Chief, Naval Operations, 1946; commander of the Naval Forces in the Mediterranean, 1948; commander of the U.S. Sixth Task Fleet, 1948; appointed chief of naval operations,

Nov. 1949. Awarded Navy Cross, D.S.M., Legion of Merit, Purple Heart, Victory Medal, Philippine Liberation Medal, American Defense Medal, American and Asiatic Theater Ribbons, Occupation Medal, U.S. Grand Cross, Order of Phoenix (Greece), Grand Cross Mil. Order of Italy, Companion of the Bath (England), Grand Cross Naval Order of Merit (Brazil), Grand Cross Naval Order of Merit (Chile). Mem. U.S. Naval Inst. Episcopalian. Clubs: New York Yacht; Army and Navy Country (Washington, D.C.). Home: 4611 Kenmore Dr., Washington. Died July 22, 1951.

SHERMAN, Frederick C., ret. naval officer; b. Port Huron, Mich., May 27, 1888; s. Frederick Ward and Charlotte Esther (Wolfe) S.; B.S., U.S. Naval Acad., 1910; grad. Naval War Coll., Jr. Course, 1925, Sr. Course, 1940; rated naval aviator, 1936; m. Fanny Jessop, Nov. 22, 1915; 1 son, John Jessop. Commd. ensign USN, 1912, and advanced through grades to adm.; officer U.S. Submarine 0-7, World War I; became comdr. U.S. Aircraft Carrier Lexington, June 1940, comdg. officer at Battle of Bougainville, Feb. 20, 1942, Battle of Salamaua, Mar. 10, 1942, Battle of Coral Sea, May 7-8, 1942, when Lexington was disabled and sunk; commanded Carrier Task Forces, Pacific area, Nov. 1942-Mar. 1944 and Aug. 1944-Sept. 1945; participated in all major actions in Pacific during this time and surrender and occupation of Japan; comdr. 5th Fleet 1945-46; ret. 1947. Staff writer Chicago Tribune, 1946-48; free lance, 1948—. Decorated Navy Cross (3); Nicaraguan campaign, Mexican campaign, World War I, Nat. Defense and Distinguished Service (3) medals; Asiatic Pacific campaign medal with 17 bronze stars; Philippine Lberation; Presdl. Unit Citation with bronze star. Mason (32°). Clubs: Army and Navy Country (Washington); Cuyamaca (San Diego). Author book on Pacific war. Address: 3118 McCall St., San Diego, Cal. Died July 27, 1957.

SHERMAN, Henry Clapp, chemist; b. Ash Grove, Va., Oct. 16, 1875; s. Franklin and Caroline (Alvord) S.; B.S., Md. Agrl. Coll., 1893; A.M., Columbia, 1896, Ph.D., 1897, D.Sc. (hon.), 1929; m. Cora Aldrich Bowen, Sept. 9, 1903 (dec.); children—Phoebe (dec.), Henry Alvord, William Bowen, Caroline Clapp Sherman Lanford. Asst. in chemistry Md. Agrl. Coll., 1893-95; fellow in chemistry Columbia, 1895-97, asst., 1897-98, lecturer, 1899-1901, instr., 1901-05, adj. prof. analytical chemistry, 1905-07, prof. organic analysis, 1907-11, prof. food chemistry, 1911-24, Mitchill prof. chemistry, 1924—, exec. officer, dept. of chemistry, 1919-39. Asst. in nutrition investigations U.S. Dept. Agr., 1898-99; research asso. Carnegie Instn., 1912-29, 33—. Mem. com. on food and nutrition Nat. Research Council, 1920-28, 40—, chmn. subcom. on human nutrition, 1924-28. Chmn. com. on nutritional problems Am. Pub. Health Assn., 1919-33; pres. Am. Inst. of Nutrition, 1931-33, 1939-40; collaborator U.S. Nutrition Lab., 1940—; chief Bur. of Human Nutrition, Dept. Agr., 1943-44. Fellow A.A.A.S.; mem. Am. Chem. Soc. (v.p. 1907-08), Am. Soc. Biol. Chemists (pres. 1926), Soc. Exptl. Biology and Medicine, Nat. Acad. Science; hon. mem. Harvey Soc. Major and mem. Am. Red Cross mission to Russia, 1917. Medalist Am. Inst. of Chemists, 1933; Nichols medalist Am. Chem. Soc., 1934, Borden award Am. Inst. Nutrition; Franklin medalist and made hon. mem. Franklin Inst., 1946; Chandler medalist Columbia, 1949. Author: Methods of Organic Analysis, 1905, 12; Chemistry of Food and Nutrition, 1911, 8th rev. edit., 1952; Food Products, 4th edit., 1948; The Vitamins (with S. L. Smith), 1922, 2d edit., 1931; Food and Health, 1934 (rev., 1947); Essentials of Nutrition (with C. S. Lanford), 3d edit., 1951; Introduction to Foods and Nutrition (with C. S. Lanford), 1943; The Science of Nutrition, 1943; Foods: Their Values and Management, 1946; Calcium and Phosphorus, 1947; The Nutritional Improvement of Life, 1950. Home: care Mrs. Oscar Lanford, Elmbrook Farm, Castleton-on-Hudson, N.Y. Died Oct. 7, 1955.

SHERMAN, Henry Stoddard, chmn. Soc. for Savs. in City of Cleveland; b. Cleveland, O., Oct. 11, 1879; s. Henry Stoddard and Harriette (Benedict) S.; B.A., Yale, 1902; student Mass. Inst. Tech.; m. Edith McBride, Nov. 21, 1906; children—Henry, John, Elizabeth, Harriette. Chmn. Soc. for Savings in City of Cleveland, 1947—. Trustee Cleve. Clinic Found., St. Luke's Hospital, Laurel School, Western Reserve Hist. Soc.; dir. Ohio Bell Telephone Co. Mem. Ohio Banking Adv. Bd. Clubs: Yale (N.Y.C.); Union, Tavern (Cleve.). Home: 24449 Cedar Rd., Cleve. 24. Office: 127 Public Sq., Cleve. Died Oct. 28, 1956; buried Lakeview Cemetery, Cleve.

SHERMAN, James Morgan, bacteriologist; b. Ash Grove, Va., May 6, 1890; s. Franklin and Caroline (Alvord) S.; B.S., N. Carolina State Coll. of Agr. and Engring., 1911; M.S., U. of Wis., 1912, Ph.D., 1916; honorary D.Agr., University of North Carolina, 1948; m. Gertrude Hendricks, August 3, 1916 (died July 24, 1918); 1 dau., Gertrude Hendricks; m. 2d, Katherine Keiper, June 20, 1928; children—Richard Hinsdale, Thomas Fairchild. Asst. in bacteriology, U. of Wis., 1912-14; asst. prof. bacteriology, Pa. State College, 1914-17; also bacteriologist Pa. Agrl. Expt. Sta.; bacteriologist U.S. Dept. Agriculture, 1917-23; prof. bacteriology, 1923—, head Dept. Dairy Industry, Cornell Univ., 1923-55. Editor-in-Chief, Journal of Bacteriology, 1944-51; editorial com. Ann. Review of Microbiology, 1945-55. Member A.A.A.S., Soc. Am. Bacteriologists (pres. 1937), Am. Chem. Society, Society for Experimental Biology and Medicine, Am. Dairy Science Assn. (pres. 1930), Sigma Xi, Phi Kappa Phi, Kappa Sigma, Gamma Alpha, Alpha Zeta. Club: Cosmos (Washington, D.C.). Home: 223 Willard Way, Ithaca, N.Y. Died Nov. 5, 1956.

SHERMAN, Louis Ralph, clergyman; b. Fredericton, N.B., Can., Aug. 26, 1886; s. Louis Walsh and Alice Maxwell (Myshrall) S.; B.A., U. of New Brunswick, 1907, M.A., 1915, LL.D., 1944; L.S.T., U. of Bishops Coll., Lennoxville, 1909, D.D., 1927; B.A., U. of Oxford, 1911, B.Litt., 1914; m. Carolyn Gillman, Dec. 31, 1919. Ordained deacon, Church of England, 1912, priest, 1913; rector of Holy Trinity Ch., Toronto, 1917-25; dean of Quebec, 1925-27; bishop of Calgary, 1927-43; archbishop of Rupert's Land, Winnipeg, since 1943. Home: 269 Waverley St., Winnipeg, Manitoba. Office: Synod Office, Trinity Hall, Winnipeg, Manitoba, Can. Died July 31, 1953.

SHERMAN, Roger, lawyer; b. Chicago, Ill., Jan. 4, 1872; s. Penoyer L. and Louise A. (Dickinson) S.; B.A., U. of Mich., 1894, also studied law same univ. 1 yr.; LL.B., Northwestern University, 1895; m. Grace T. Buttolph, June 22, 1905; children—Louise Dickinson (Mrs. Philip M. Watrous), Eleanor Buttolph (Mrs. Robert K. Vincent). Practiced law at Chicago, Illinois, since 1895; master in chancery, Superior Ct. of Cook Co., 1906-07; 1st asst. state's atty. Cook County, 1908; now mem. Tenney, Sherman, Bentley & Guthrie. Mem. Am. Bar Assn., Ill. State Bar Assn. (pres. 1923-24), Chicago Bar Assn. (pres. 1922-23), Sigma Phi, Phi Delta Phi. Republican. Episcopalian. Clubs: University, Indian Hill. Home: 213 Linden St., Winnetka, Ill. Office: 120 S. La Salle St., Chgo. Died Jan. 20, 1957.

SHERMAN, William Arthur, business exec.; born Chicago, Feb. 8, 1878; s. Charles Day and Mary Stuart (Arthur) S.; grad. Chicago Manual Training School, 1894; student Ill. Inst. Tech., 1896; m. Bettie Taliaferro, Dec. 7, 1911; 1 dau., Rosalie Taliaferro (Mrs. Joiner Cartwright). Pres. S. Texas Cotton Oil Co., Houston, since 1910, Merchants and Mfrs. Bldg. Corp. since 1936; dir. First Nat. Bank, Am. Comml. Life Ins. Co., Galveston, Houstin & Henderson R.R. Co., Wesson Oil and Snowdrift Co. Vice pres. Ripley Found., Houston, since 1938. Mem. Nat. Cotton Seed Products Assn. Clubs: Houston Country, Tejos, Eagle Lake Rod and Gun. Home: 1002 Bissonnet St., Houston 5. Office: 3405 Collingsworth St., Houston 16. Died Nov. 8, 1950.

SHERMAN, William O'Neill, surgeon; b. Pine Grove, Pa., May 4, 1880; s. Luther Grove and Caroline S.; student Franklin and Marshall Coll., 1894-97; M. D., U. of Pa., 1901; m. Lillian Johnson, Oct. 16, 1910. Practiced at Pittsburgh, 1901—; chief surgeon Carnegie-Ill. Steel Corp., 1900—; chief surgeon H. C. Frick Coke Co. and other subsidiaries of U.S. Steel Corp.; surgeon St. Francis, Children's and Magee hosps.; cons. surgeon Western Pa. dist.; chief, procurement. chemical warfare service, U.S. Army, Pittsburgh district. Fellow Am. Coll. Surgeons; mem. A. M.A., Am. Iron and Steel Inst., Am. Pub. Health Assn., Pittsburgh Acad. Medicine, Pa. Med. Soc. Republican. Mason. Clubs: Duquesne, Pittsburgh Athletic, Longue Vue Country, etc. Home: 4400 Center Av. Office: Carnegie Bldg., Pitts. Died June 20, 1954; buried Greenwood Cemetry, Lancaster, Pa.

SHERRARD, Glenwood John (shĕr-rärd'), hotel operator; b. Dorchester, Mass., July 20, 1895; s. J. Alfred and Catherine M. (McLean) S.; student Moses Brown School, Providence, R.I., 1909-13; D.C.S. (honorary), Boston U., 1951; married Jessie A. Lumsden, Nov. 15, 1924; children—Glenwood J., Jr., Andrew Alfred. Engaged in hotel business continuously since 1914; mgr. Ft. Steuben Hotel, Steubenville, O., 1924; mng. director Hamilton Hotel, Hamilton, Bermuda, 1924-33; pres. The Parker House, Boston, Mass., since 1933, G. J. Sherrard Co. since 1933, Bellevue Hotel Company, 1934—, also president of the Lincolnshire Hotel, Boston. Trustee Suffolk Savings Bank, Boston; now with ODM. Served as enlisted pvt., advancing through the grades to capt. engrs., U.S. Army, 1917-19. Trustee Deaconess Hosp. Mem. Am. (life dir.; past pres.), Mass. (past pres.), N.E. (past pres.) hotel assns., U.S. C. of C. (dir.). Mason, (K.T., 32°, Shriner). Clubs: Algonquin (Boston); Brae Burn (Newton). Home: Buzzards Bay, Mass. Office: The Parker House, Boston. Died Aug. 12, 1958; buried Forest Hills Cemetery, Boston.

SHERRILL, Gibbs Wynkoop, transportation exec.; b. N.Y.C., Mar. 25, 1908; s. Charles Hitchcock and George Barker (Gibbs) S.; grad. Groton Sch., 1927; A.B., Yale, 1931; m. May Gould, Sept. 29, 1934; children—Sarah Barker, Charles Hitchcock, Jane Wynkoop, Georgianna Gibbs, Claire Gould. Sec. to U.S. Senator Peter Norbeck, 1931-34; N.E. passenger agt., dist. rep., regional rep. Am. Export Lines, 1934-50; prof. marine transportation Mass. Inst. Tech., 1949-54; v.p., dir., mem. exec. com. Berkshire, Hathaway, Inc., Providence, 1936—; pres., dir. Louve Ray Corp., 1949—, North Cape Fish Corp., 1949—. Chmn. New Bedford, Woods Hole, Martha's Vineyard, Nantucket S.S. Authority, 1953—. Director Beverly (Massachusetts) United Fund, N.E. Grenfell Association, National Reading Found., Beverly (Mass.) Hosp., Armed Forces YMCA, Charlestown, Mass. Served from lt. (j.g.) to comdr., USNR, 1941-45; capt. Res. Decorated Knight Crown of Italy, Knight White Eagle of Serbia. Mem. Navy League U.S. (pres. Boston), Soc. Naval Architects and Marine Engrs., S.R., Colonial Wars, Mayflower Soc. Republican. Presbyn. Mason. Home: 97 West St., Beverly Farms, Mass. Office: 17 Lewis Wharf, Boston 10. Died July 26, 1957.

SHERRILL, James Winn, dir. Scripps Metabolic Clinic; b. Temple, Tex., Apr. 22, 1890; s. Elisha Winn and Mary Louella (Sample) S.; B.S., Baylor U., 1913; M.D., Johns Hopkins, 1917; m. Lucy M. Heath, Aug. 2, 1924; children—Lucy Sherrill Hartford, James Winn. In practice of medicine, N.Y. City, 1919-24; founder, 1924, since dir. Scripps Metabolic Clinic, La Jolla, San Diego, Cal. Lectr. in medicine U. Cal. Med. Sch.; cons. metabolic diseases, U.S. Naval Hosp., San Diego. Served as lt. M.C., U.S. Army, 1917-19. Presbyn. Writer on diabetes mellitus and metabolic diseases. Home: 1867 Castellana Rd., La Jolla, Cal. Died Jan. 4, 1955; buried Temple, Tex.

SHERRILL, Lewis Joseph, religious edn.; b. Haskell, Tex., Apr. 18, 1892; s. Richard Ellis and Catherine Howard (Taylor) S.; A.B., Austin Coll., Sherman, Tex., 1916, D.D., 1925; B.D., Presbyn. Theol. Sem., Louisville, Ky., 1921; Ph.D., Yale, 1929; grad. study Northwestern U., summers 1925, 26, Yale, 1925, 1927-28, Harvard, 1939-40; Litt.D., Davidson (N.C.) Coll., 1937; m. Helen Hardwicke, May 12, 1921; children—John Lewis, Mary Hardwicke. Ordained ministry Presbyn. Ch. in U.S., 1921; pastor Covington, Tenn., 1921-25; prof. religious edn., Louisville Presbyn. Sem., 1925-50, dean, 1930-50; prof. practical theology Union Theol. Sem. since 1950; exec. sec. Am. Assn. of Theol. Schs., 1935-38, pres., 1938-40, chairman of executive committee; director Religious Education Re-Study, Presbyterian Church U.S., 1945-48. Served as sec. Y.M.C.A., U.S. Army, 1917-18, pvt. F.A., 1918-19. Democrat. Author: Presbyterian Parochial Schools, 1846-1870, 1932; Religious Education in the Small Church, 1932; Adult Education in the Church (with J. E. Purcell), 1936; Family and Church, 1937; Understanding Children, 1939; The Opening Doors of Childhood, 1939 (translated into Spanish 1943); Becoming a Christian (with Helen H. Sherrill), 1943; The Rise of Christian Education, 1944; Guilt and Redemption, 1945 (translated into Japanese); Lift Up Your Eyes, 1949; The Struggle of the Soul, 1951; The Gift of Power, 1955. Home: 99 Claremont Av. Office: Union Theological Seminary, 120 and Broadway, N.Y.C. Died Jan. 30, 1957; buried Louisville.

SHERRILL, R(ichard) E(llis), univ. prof.; born Haskell, Tex., Nov. 12, 1899; s. Richard Ellis and Katherine (Taylor) S.; student, U. of Tex., 1917, Wooster Coll., 1920; B.S. (chem.), Washington and Lee, 1922; M.S., Cornell U., 1928, Ph.D., 1933; m. Mary Lucille Taylor, Nov. 5, 1926; children—Donald Taylor, Richard Ellis IV. Mining engr., Ray, Ariz., 1923-24; prof. Washington and Lee U., 1924-26; field geologist, Marland Oil Co., 1926-27; prof. geol., U. of Pittsburgh, 1928-36, head, dept. oil and gas, 1936-44, head, dept. geol., since 1944; cooperating geol., Pa. topographic and geol. survey, since 1936. Eleanor Tatum Long fellow, structural geol., Cornell U., 1928-1933. Mem. Geol. Society Am., Am. Assn. Petroleum Geol., Am. Inst. Mining and Metall. Engrs., Am. Petroleum Inst., Engring. Soc. Western Pa., Am. Geophys. Union, Phi Beta Kappa, Sigma Xi, Phi Kappa Phi, Sigma Tau, Sigma Gamma Epsilon. Presbyn. Mason. Contbr. articles on Appalachian geol. to sci. and academic publs.; co-author lab. manuel. Home: 7122 Meade St., Pitts. Died Nov. 25, 1953; buried Haskell, Tex.

SHERRILL, Stephen H., ret. army officer; b. East Hampton, L.I., N.Y., Mar. 13, 1893; s. Abram E. and Nettie (Glover) S.; B.S., U.S. Mil. Acad., 1917; post grad. work, Yale, Sheffield Sci. Sch., 1920-21, Command and Gen. Staff Sch., 1930-32, Army War Coll., 1938-39; m. Dorothy M. Roberts, Jan. 26, 1918; 1 son, Stephen H. Commd. 2d lt., 1917, and advanced through grades to brig. gen., 1942; comdg. Troop I, 2d Cav.; instr. equitation Plattsburg Tng. Camp, 1917; AEF, France and Germany, 1918-19; transferred to Signal Corps, 1923; War Dept. Gen. Staff, 1939-42; comdg. gen. Western Signal Corps Tng. Center, Camp Kohler, Sacramento; comdg. gen. Aircraft Warning Unit Tng. Center, 3d Air Force, Drew Field, Fla., Eastern Signal Corps Tng. Center, Fort Monmouth, N.J; ret. 1946. Vice pres. First Nat. Bank of Arlington, Va., in charge Pentagon br. Decorated Legion of Merit with oak leaf cluster, French Legion of Honor. Editor "Signals", 1946—. Home: 3015 45th St., Washington 16. Died June 28, 1956; buried Arlington Nat. Cemetery.

SHERWIN, Belle, b. Cleve., 1868; d. Henry Alden and Frances Mary (Smith) Sherwin; B.S., Wellesley, 1890; LL.D., Western Reserve U., 1930, Denison Coll., 1931, Oberlin Coll., 1937. Pres. Nat. League of Women Voters, 1924-34. Clubs: City (Cleve.); Cosmopolitan (N.Y.C.). Home: Winden, Willoughby, O. Died July 8, 1955.

SHERWIN, Proctor Fenn, educator; b. Suffield, Conn., Nov. 29, 1891; s. A. Proctor and Lillian B. (Fenn) S.; B.A., St. Lawrence U., 1912; grad. study U. Chgo., 1913-14, 19-20, Columbia, 1923, U. Mich., 1938-39; m. Margaret J. O'Leary, Oct. 4, 1913. Prof. English U. N.M., 1914-20, Syracuse (N.Y.) U., 1920-21, U. Dubuque (Ia.), 1921-24, Knox Coll., Galesburg, Ill., 1924, Simonds prof. English since 1928, sec. faculty since 1951; exchange prof. Harvard, 1931. Mem. Modern Lang. Assn. Am., Phi Kappa Phi, Beta Theta Pi. Author: Sources of More's Utopia, 1917. Home: 1233 N. Prairie St., Galesburg, Ill. Died June 9, 1958; buried Evergreen Cemetery, Canton, N.Y.

SHERWIN, Ralph Sidney, chemist; b. Waseca, Minn., Sept. 21, 1876; s. Sidney Orville and Mary Adelaide (Shedd) S.; B.S., U. Okla., 1903; m. Elizabeth Christine Schattgen, Jan. 29, 1908; children—Margaret Elizabeth (Mrs. E. R. Sargent), Ralph Sidney, Charlotte Esther (Mrs. R. M. Toon). With Aluminum Co. Am., 1905-40, process control prodn. alumina, etc., 1932-40; with Reynolds Metals Co., Sheffield, Ala., since 1940, v.p. charge alumina research, 1945, now vice pres. alumina process development, investigation bauxite deposits, aluminum prodn., Europe, 6 yrs.; dir. Reynolds Mining Corp., Reynolds Research Inst. Recipient Certificate Appreciation, Sec. Army, 1951. Mem. Am. Chem. Soc., Am. Inst. Chem. Engrs., Am. Inst. Mining Engrs. (chmn. aluminum and magnesium com. 1950-52). Home: 910 Catalina Pl. Office: Reynold Metals Co., Box 109, Corpus Christi, Tex. Died July 2, 1957.

SHERWOOD, Margaret Pollock, author; b. Ballston, N.Y., Nov. 1, 1864; d. Thomas Burr and Mary Frances (Beattie) Sherwood; A.B., Vassar Coll., 1886; grad. study Zürich and Oxford Univ., 1887-88; Ph.D., Yale, 1898; hon. L.H.D., New York U., 1920; unmarried. Instr., 1889-96, asso. prof. English lit., 1898-1912, prof. same, 1912-31, Wellesley College, prof. emeritus, 1931—. Mem. of Phi Beta Kappa fraternity. Author: An Experiment in Altruism, 1895; A Puritan Bohemia, 1896; Dryden's Dramatic Theory and Practice (doctoral thesis), 1898; Henry Worthington, Idealist, 1899; Daphne—An Autumn Pastoral, 1903; The Story of King Sylvain and Queen Aimée, 1904; The Coming of the Tide, 1905; The Princess Pourquoi, 1907; Whither (pub. anonymously), 1915; The Worn Doorstep, 1916; Familiar Ways, 1917; A World to Mend, 1920; The Upper Slopes (verse), 1924; Undercurrents of Influence in English Romantic Poetry, 1934; Coleridge's Imaginative Conception of the Imagination, 1937; Pilgrim Feet, 1949. Contbr. to Atlantic Monthly, Scribner's, North Am. Rev. Home: 7 Midland Rd., Wellesley, Mass. Died Sept. 24, 1955; buried Ballston, N.Y.

SHERWOOD, Robert Emmet, writer; b. New Rochelle, N.Y., Apr. 4, 1896; s. Arthur Murray and Rosina (Emmet) S.; Harvard Univ., 1914-17; Litt.D., Dartmouth College, 1940, Yale Univ., 1941, Harvard, 1949; D.C.L., Bishop's Univ., 1950; m. Mary Brandon, Oct. 29, 1922; 1 dau., Mary J.; m. 2d, Madeline Hurlock, June 15, 1935. Was dramatic editor of Vanity Fair, 1919-20; associate editor "Life," 1920-24, editor, 1924-28; also motion picture editor "Life" and New York Herald. Enlisted in 42d Batn., Black Watch, Can. Expdn. Force, 1917; hon. disch., Feb. 1919. Spl. Asst. to Sec. of War, 1940, Sec. of Navy, 1945. Served as dir. overseas branch O.W.I.; resigned in September 1944. Clubs: Harvard, Garrick (London). Author: (plays) The Road to Rome, 1927; The Queen's Husband, 1928; Waterloo Bridge, 1929; This Is New York, 1930; Reunion in Vienna, 1931; The Virtuous Knight (novel), 1931; Acropolis, 1933; The Petrified Forest, 1934; Idiot's Delight, 1936; Abe Lincoln in Illinois, 1938; There Shall Be No Night, 1940; The Rugged Path, 1945; Roosevelt and Hopkins (biography), 1948; Miss Liberty, 1949. Contbr. fiction and articles to mags. Pulitzer prize, 1936, 39, 41, gold medal for drama, Nat. Inst. of Arts and Letters, 1941, Bancroft prize for distinguished writings in Am. hist., 1949; Pulitzer prize, 1949. Address: 1545 Broadway, N.Y.C. 36. Died Nov. 14, 1955.

SHERWOOD, Rosina Emmet, artist, illustrator; b. N.Y.C., Dec. 13, 1854; d. William J. and Julia Colt (Pierson) Emmet; pupil William Chase, N.Y., Julian Acad., Paris; m. Arthur Murray Sherwood, June 1, 1887; children—Arthur Murray, Cynthia Townsend, Philip Hyde, Robert Emmet, Rosamond. Silver medal, Paris Expn., 1889; medal, Chicago Expn., 1893; exhibited at Paris Expn., 1900; two bronze medals, Buffalo Expn., 1901; silver medal, St. Louis Expn., 1904. A.N.A.; mem. N.Y. Water Color Club, Am. Water Color Soc. Home: Stockbridge, Mass.; (winter) 141 E. 72d St., N.Y.C. Died Jan. 17, 1948.

SHERWOOD, William (Anderson), painter, etcher; b. Balt., Feb. 13, 1875; s. William Richard and Mary Jane (Anderson) S.; student St. John's Coll., Annapolis, 1889-93, Academie Royale des Beaux Arts, Antwerp, 1898-1901, Academie Julien, Paris, 1901-02; m. Mabel Ffoulkes-Jones, May 7, 1904. Represented in collections of Dowager Queen Elizabeth of the Beligans, Royal Library, Brussels Musée, Musée Royal des Beaux-Arts, Antwerp, Plantin-Moretus, Antwerp; Library of Congress, Nat. Gallery of Art, Washington; Cleve., Detroit pub. libraries; Worcester Free Library; Art Inst. Chgo.; Cal. State Library; City Library, Sacramento; Musée Royal de l'Armée, Brussels. Decorated Chevalier Ordre de la Couronne by King Albert (Belgium). Mem. Am. Fedn. of Arts, Chicago Soc. of Etchers, Print Makers' Soc. of Cal., Societe Royale des Beaux Arts, Société Royale des Aqua-Fortists de Belgique. L'Association des Artistes Professionnels de Belbique. Episcopalian. Home: Balt. Address: "Croix de Bourgogne," rue aux Laines, 47, Bruges, Belgium. Died Aug. 8, 1951; buried Bruges Cemetery.

SHEVELSON, S. Harris, editor; b. Chgo., May 8, 1916; s. Samuel Harris and Solveig Elise (Thompsen) S.; B.A., Yale University, 1938; married Mary Jane Nelson, September 9, 1939 (deceased February 3, 1959); children—Edward Harris, Jo Ann, Mary Lou, James Alan. Circulation promotion dir. Esquire, Inc., 1940; asso. editor Coronet, 1941, co-editor, 1942-44, mng. editor, 1945-47; editor Pageant, 1948-58; editorial dir. Madison Av. mag. and Advt. Trade mag., 1958—; v.p., dir. Hillman Periodicals, Inc. 1951—. Recipient Benjamin Franklin award, 1957. Mem. Alpha Sigma Phi. Conglist. Clubs: Yale, Dutch Treat (N.Y.C.); Weston Field (Conn.). Home: Old Hill Rd., Westport, Conn. Office: 535 Fifth Av., N.Y.C. 17. Died Feb. 3, 1959.

SHEWMAN, Eben B. (shōō'mȧn), suurgeon; b. Richmond, Ind., Mar. 14, 1876; s. Franklin and Harriet F. S.; student Nat. Normal U., Lebanon, O., 2 terms; M.D., Eclectic Med. Coll., Cin., 1898; post-grad. work, U. Ill., Edinburgh, London, Berlin and Vienna; m. Sophronia L. Tobrocke, Aug. 7, 1901; children—Elsie Louise, Evelyn Agnes, Lela Sophronia, Eben Franklin, Marjorie Alice. Gen. practice until 1908; asst. demonstrator anatomy, med. dept. U. Ill., 1908; prof. clin. surgery, Eclectic Med. Coll., Cin., 1910—, dean, 1933-35; mem. sr. surg. staff Bethesda Hosp. Mem. A.M.A., Ohio State Med. Assn., Cin. Acad. Medicine, Nat. and Ohio State electric med. assns., Cin. C. of C., Tau Alpha Epsilon. Republican. Methodist. Elk, Mason. Clubs: Cincinnati Automobile. Home: 3570 Bayard Drive. Office: Doctors Bldg., Cin. Died Feb. 26, 1959.

SHIDELER, W(illiam) H(enry) (shĭd'ler), univ. prof.; b. West Middletown, O., July 14, 1886; s. Leander Pierce and Elizabeth (Helwig) S.; A.B., Miami U., 1907; Ph.D., Cornell U., 1910; m. Katherine Hoffman, June 16, 1900; children—William Watson, James Henry. Instr. zoology and geology Miami U., 1910-11, asst. prof., 1911-19, asso. prof., 1919-20, prof. geology, 1920-57, ret.; field geologist Ohio Geol. Survey, 1917-21, Ky. Geol. Survey, summers 1928-31. Mem. Geol. Soc. Am., Paleontol. Soc., Ohio and Ind. acads. of sci., A.A.A.S., Phi Beta Kappa, Sigma Xi, Phi Sigma, Sigma Gamma Epsilon, Omicron Delta Kappa, Phi Kappa Tau (founder). Republican. Presbyn. Mason (32°, Shriner). Home: 110 S. Campus Av., Oxford, O. Died Dec. 18, 1958; buried Miami U. Plot.

SHIELD, Lansing P., bus. exec.; A.B., Rutgers U., 1917; LL.D. (hon.) Rutgers U., 1952; m. Gladys Byrd, Sept. 24, 1924 (dec. Apr. 4, 1947); children—Lansing P. II (dec.), Evelyn (Mrs. O'Neal); m. 2d, Margaret Gottsberger Karst, Sept. 23, 1948. Pres. and dir. Grand Union Co.; dir. and mem. exec. com. Am. Re-Ins. Co.; dir. Fed. Reserve Bank N.Y., Prudential Ins. Co., Carroll's Ltd., Square Deal Market Co. of Washington, Inc. Eastern Shopping Centers, Inc. Mem. State Chamber Hy. Commn., 1956; nat. campaign chmn. United Cerebral Palsy, 1953; chmn. Puerto Rico Food Commn., 1954. Dir. N.J. Symphony Orchestra; trustee Tobe lecture series, Harvard U., Rutgers U.; mem. Moffett Com. Harvard Bus. Sch. Mem. Hall of Fame in Distbn.; recipient Freedom Found. honor medal, 1951; Cavaliere Ufficiale, Italy, 1956; Rutgers Outstanding Alumni award, 1957; French Legion of Honor, 1958. Mem. Internat. Assn. Chain Stores (pres. 1956—), Nat. Assn. Food Chains (dir., past chmn.), N.J. C. of C. (pres.), Honorary Scholastic Soc. of N.Y.U., Downtown Assn. Clubs: University, Ridgewood Country. Served 2d lt., US AC, 1917-18. Inventor Food-O-Mat. Contbr. to mags. Home: Chestnut Ridge, Saddle River, N.J. Office: 100 Broadway, East Paterson, N.J. Died Jan. 6, 1960.

SHIELDS, Thomas Todhunter, clergyman; b. Bristol, Eng., Nov. 1, 1873; s. Thomas Todhunter and Maria (Davis) S.; ed. Bristol, Eng.; D.D. (hon.), McMaster Univ., Hamilton, Ont., 1919, Temple Univ., Phila., 1917; m. Elizabeth M. Kitchen, 1899 (dec. 1932); m. 2d, Leota Griffin, 1934. Ordained to ministry of Baptist Ch., 1897; pastor, Delhi, Ont., Hamilton, Ont., London, Ont., 1897-1910, Jarvis St. Ch., Toronto, Ont., since 1910; pres. Toronto Baptist Sem. since 1927. Served as vice pres. Home Mission Bd., Baptist Conv. of Ont. and P.Q., thirteen years; pres. Union of Regular Baptist Chs. of Ontario and P.Q., 1937-49. Member board governors McMaster Univ., eight years. Pres. Canadian Protestant League since inception, Oct. 1941. Author: Other Little Ships, 1935; Adventures of a Modern Young Man, 1929; The Plot That Failed, 1936; Christ in the Old Testament, 1923; Most Famous Trial of History, 1928; Russellism, 1923; How to Receive Eternal Life, 1951. Editor The Gospel Witness since 1922. Home: 66 Wells Hill Av., Toronto 10. Office: 130 Gerrard St. E., Toronto 2, Ont., Can. Died Apr. 4, 1955; buried Mount Pleasant Cemetery, Toronto.

SHIENTAG, Bernard Lloyd, judge; b. N.Y.C., Apr. 13, 1887; s. Solomon and Fannie (Jacobs) S.; A.B., Coll. of City of N.Y., 1904; LL.B., Columbia, 1908, A.M., 1908; LL.D., St. Lawrence U., 1941, Columbia, 1947; m. Florence Lorraine Perlow, June 8, 1938. Admitted to N.Y. bar, 1908; asst. counsel New York State Factory Investigating Commn., 1911-15, chief counsel N.Y. State Indsl. Commn., 1919-21; counsel Governor's Labor Bd., 1920; apptd. indsl. commr., 1923; counsel and mem. State Housing Commn., also State Child Welfare Commn., 1923; appt. justice City Ct., N.Y., 1924, elected same, 1925; apptd. justice Supreme Ct. State of N.Y., 1930, elected to same, 1930, reelected, 1944. Designated Appellate Term N.Y. Supreme Ct., 1934-47, justice appellate div., 1st dept., 1947—. N.Y. del. Unemployment Conf., Washington, 1920; chmn. indsl. council Labor Dept., 1923; fed. dir. of employment State of N.Y., 1923; mem. State Adv. Com. for Rehabilitation of Handicapped Persons, 1923; chmn. adv. com. of policyholders in State Ins. Fund, 1924; mem. mediation com. Cloak and Suit Industry, New York, 1923-26. Formerly mem. bd. dirs. Nat. Consumers League; former v.p. and dir. Child Welfare Com. America; former exec. com. Am. Assn. for Labor Legislation; former mem. bd. dirs. Assn. for Old Age Security; former trustee Fedn. for Support Jewish Philanthropic Socs.; former pres. Y.M.H.A.; mem. bd. visitors Columbia Law School. Mem. Am., N.Y. State (chmn. jud. sect. 1947) bar assns. Assn. of Bar City of N.Y., N.Y. County Lawyers Assn., Am. Legal History Soc., City Coll. Alumni Assn. (v.p., mem. bd. dirs.), Phi Beta Kappa (pres. New York Alumni). Democrat. Jewish religion. Mason. Author: The Trial of a Civil Jury Action in New York, 1938; Summary Judgment, 1941; Moulders of Legal Thought, 1943; The Personality of the Judge, 1944. Contbr. to law reviews. Home: 737 Park Av. Address: 400 Park Av., N.Y.C. 22.

SHIER, Calrton S., newspaper editor; b. Ann Arbor, Mich., Jan. 24, 1875; s. William H. and Henrietta A. (Seelye) S.; ed. pub. schs.; m. Maude M. Sexton, Oct. 24, 1900; children—William H., Elizabeth M. (dec.), Louise A., Carlton S., Robert M. Began with Detroit Free Press, 1900, successively reporter, music critic, spl. writer, editorial writer, chief editorial writer, becoming editor same paper, 1926; now ret. Home: 1320 Olivia Av., Ann Arbor, Mich. Died June 3, 1957; buried Highland Cemetery, Ypsilanti, Mich.

SHIGEMITSU, Mamoru, diplomat; b. Minamiakimura, Higashi-Kunizaki-gun, Oita-ken, Japan, July 29, 1887; s. Naomasa and Matsu Shigemitsu; Deg. of Law, Imperial U., Tokyo, 1911; m. Kie Hayashi, Apr. 1, 1923; children—Atsushi, Hanako. Third sec. Japanese Embassy, London, 1916-18; consul, Portland, 1918-21; chief 1st sect. Treaty Bur., 1921-25; 1st sec. legation, China, 1925-27; counsellor of Embassy, Berlin, 1927-29; consul gen., Shanghai, 1929-31; E.E. and M.P., Nanking, 1931-33; vice minister fgn. affairs, 1933-36; A.E. and P., Moscow, 1936-38, London, 1938-41, Nanking, 1941-43; minister fgn. affairs, 1943-44, minister Great Asiatic affairs, 1944-45; mem. House of Peers, 1945; minister fgn. affairs, minister Great Asiatic affairs, 1952; apptd. pres. Progressive Party, 1952; mem. Ho. of Reps., 1952-54; dep. prime minister, minister fgn. affairs, 1954—. Home: 345, 3 chome, Harashuku, Shibuya-ku, Tokyo. Office: 2, 1 chome, Shiba-Tamuracho, Minatoku, Tokyo, Japan. Died Jan. 26, 1957.

SHILOAH, Reuven, diplomat; b. Jerusalem, Israel, 1909; s. Ahron Yitzhak and Sara S.; grad. Hebrew Tchrs. Coll., 1929, Sch. Oriental Studies, Hebrew U., 1933; m. Betty Bordin, Oct. 1936; children—Dov, Nomi. Asst. polit. sec. Gen. Fedn. Jewish Labor, Tel Aviv, 1933-36; also sec. Mixed Arab-Jewish Union Railwaymen; also sec. Union Arab Port Workers, Jaffa; sr. liaison officer Jewish Agy. in Jerusalem, 1936-48; liaison officer between Jewish Agy. and Brit. and Allied Mil. Hdqrs. in Middle East and Mediterranean, 1940-45; spl. adv. Arab affairs to dir. polit. dept. Jewish Agy., 1936-45; observer on behalf Jewish Agy. at UN Charter Conf., San Francisco, 1945; aide to David Ben-Gurion, 1946; spl. adv. to Minister Fgn. Affairs, 1948, also liaison officer between Ministry Fgn. Affairs and Ministry Def.; mem. Israel delegation Rhodes armistice talks, Egypt, 1949, head Isreal delegation, Jordan armistice talks and signatory armistice agreement, 1949; rep. Israel Lausanne Conf. between Israel and Arab states, Palestine Conciliation Commn., 1949; Minister of Israel to U.S. since 1953. Home: 1673 Myrtle St. N.W. Office: Embassy of Israel, 1621 22d St. N.W., Washington. Died May 10, 1959.

SHINN, Everett, artist; b. Woodstown, N.J., Nov. 6, 1876; s. Isaiah Conklin and Josephine (Ransley) S.; ed. Bacon's Acad., Woodstown; studied art at Pa. Acad. Fine Arts, Phila.; m. Florence Scovil, Jan. 26, 1898; m. 2d, Corinne Baldwin; children—Janet, David; m. 3d, Gertrude Chase, Mar. 21, 1924; m. 4th, Paula Downing. Exhibited annually at N.Y. galleries. Represented in Met. Museum, N.Y. C.; Art Inst. Chgo.; Albright Gallery, Buffalo; Whitney Museum;, N.Y.C.; New Briton Museum; Brooklyn Museum; Detroit Museum; Boston Museum; (murals) Belasco Theater, City Hall, Trenton. Elected Nat. Academician, 1942. Has written vaudeville acts which have played 22 years; art dir. for 5 motion pictures; has served on Phila. and N.Y. papers; book illustrator. Address: 26 Washington Sq. N., N.Y.C. Died 1953.

SHIPLE, George J. (shī'p'l), professor; b. Perrysburg, O., June 10, 1891; s. Joseph and Louisa (Schwind) S.; A.B., St. Louis (Mo.) U., 1918, M.S., 1919; D.Sc., Fordham U., 1922; student Woodstock (Md.) Coll., 1922-27. Ordained Roman Catholic priest, 1926; teacher of chemistry and mathematics, St. John's Coll., Toledo, O., 1927-28; study and travel in Europe, 1928-29; asst. biochemistry, Jefferson Med. Coll., Phila., 1929-30; instr. chemistry, U. of Detroit, 1930-31, prof. and dir. dept. chemistry since 1931, regent Coll. of Engring. since 1932, faculty moderator of athletics 1932-46, mem. bd. trustees since 1934, chmn. athletic bd. 1939-46, sec. bd. trustees since 1940. Mem. American Chem. Soc., Electro Chemical Society, Biochemical Society (Eng.), Chem. Soc. (Eng.), Soc. of Chemical Industry (Eng.), Soc. for Exptl. Biology and Medicine, Franklin Inst. Contbr. of articles to Jour. of Am. Chem. Soc., Jour. of Biol. Chemistry, Am. Jour. Physiology. Address: 4133 W. McNichols Rd., Detroit 21. Died May 18, 1958.

SHIPLEY, William Stewart, mfr.; b. Jersey City, Mar. 28, 1879; s. Samuel Shipley and Eliza (McFall) S.; M.E., Cooper Inst. of N.Y.; m. Anna Elizabeth Olsen, Nov. 4, 1903; 1 dau., Ruth Anna (Mrs. Stuart Bruce McNaught). Served apprenticeship with Diehl Motor Co., Elizabethport, N.J., and Nash Gas Engine Co., Bklyn.; machinist York Ice Machinery Corp., 1900-04; salesman of York products with S. J. Shipley Co., Bklyn., 1904-07; v.p., gen. mgr. Shipley Constrn. and Supply Co., 1907-27; v.p., gen. Eastern mgr. York Ice Machinery Corp., 1927-30, pres. 1930-40, chmn. of bd., 1940—; v.p. York-Shipley Co. Fed. Inc. U.S.A. of Shanghai, China; chmn. bd. York-Shipley, Ltd., London; dir. Westerlin & Campbell Co. (Chgo.), Auditorium Conditioning Corp. of N.Y. Dir. Pa. C. of C. (chmn. def. com.); gen. chmn. York Welfare Fedn., 1934-37; dir. York YMCA. Pres. Refrigerating Machinery Assn., 1939-40; past pres. Am. Soc. Refrigerating Engrs.; pres. Mfrs. Assn. of York, 1939; mem. Nat. Assn. Practical Refrigerating Engrs., Engring. Soc. of York County. Republican. Mason. Episcopalian. Clubs: Rotary, Country (dir.), Lafayette (York); Engineers (New York). Home: Bayport, N.Y. Office: York Corp., York, Pa. Died Jan. 13, 1951; buried St. Ann's Cemetery, Sayville, N.Y.

SHIPP, Thomas Roerty, public relations counsel; b. Morristown, Ind.; s. Joseph Vinton and Adelia Elizabeth (Roerty) S.; A.B., Butler U., Indpls., m. Hope Neidig, June 30, 1924. Reporter and staff corr. Indianapolis News; pvt. sec. to U.S. senator; clerk com. on territories, U.S. Senate; editor U.S. Forest Service, Washington; exec. sec. Inland Waterways Commn., Washington; gen. sec. White House Conf. of Govs.; sec. Joint Com. on Conservation between states and Nation; sec. Nat. Conservation Commn.; exec. sec. Nat. Conservation Congress; pres. Thomas R. Shipp, Inc., Washington, 1914—. Conducted Red Cross, YMCA, Plattsburg Tng. Camps and other World War I publicity campaigns. Decorated by Serbia for war relief work. Mem. Ind. bar. Methodist. Mason. Mem. Phi Delta Theta, Kappa Tau Alpha, Delta Sigma Chi. Clubs: Nat. Press, Chevy Chase, Columbia Country, Artists and Writers. Home: 3733 Oliver St., Chevy Chase, D.C. Office: Albee Bldg., Washington. Died Feb. 10, 1952; buried Crown Hill Cemetery, Indpls.

SHIPPEN, Eugene Rodman, clergyman; b. Worcester, Mass., Jan. 30, 1865; s. Rush Rhees and Zoë (Rodman) S.; prep. edn., Roxbury Latin Sch., Boston, and Emerson Inst., Washington; A.B., Harvard, 1887; studied Harvard Div. Sch.; Oxford U., 1893-94; D.D., Meadville Theol. Sch., 1925; m. Elizabeth Herrick Blount, Apr. 18, 1900; children—Harold Blonut, Zoë, Sylvia, Eugene Rodman. Ordained Unitarian ministry, 1892, pastor Wichita, Kan., 1890-93, First Parish, Dorcester, Mass., 1894-1907; McQuaker Trust lectr., Scotland, 1908; pastor Ch. of Our Father, Lancaster, Pa., 1908-10, First Unitarian Congl. Ch., Detroit, 1910-18; spl. rep. War Camp Community Service, 1918-20; pastor Second Ch., Boston, 1920-29, ret. Harvard U. guest preacher, 1925. Incorporator The Ingleside Club, Detroit. Organizer Religious Arts Guild, pres., 1922-28; pres. North End Union (neighborhood house), Boston, 1925-28; pres. Harvard Divinity Sch. Alumni, 1928-29; pres. University Club, Winter Park, 1936-37; founder of Golden Rose Poetry award; hon. mem. Puddingstone Club, Boston; hon. mem. Am. Guild of Organists (Boston chapter), Delta Phi. Democrat. Author: The Nativity and the Consecration of Sir Galahad (pageants); Verses Grave and Gay. Home: Winter Park, Fla. Died Jan. 11, 1959.

SHIPSEY, Edward, clergyman, educator; b. San Luis Obispo, Calif., Dec. 15, 1890; s. William and Anne (Barry) S.; A.B., Gonzaga U., Spokane, Wash., 1915, A.M., 1916, Litt. D., 1935; S.T.L., U. of Innsbruck, Austria, 1926. Entered Society of Jesus, 1908, ordained priest, Roman Cath. Ch., 1925; teacher English, Gonzaga Univ. High Sch., 1916-20; freshman English instr. U. of Santa Clara (Calif.), 1920-22, English instr., theol. studies, Austria, 1922-27; instr. U. of Santa Clara, 1927-31, asst. prof., 1931-36, prof. English since 1936, chmn. English dept. since 1939; lecturer, summer session, Gonzaga Univ., 1929-42, U. of San Francisco, 1944-45. Mem. Nat. Council Teachers of English, San Francisco Bay Area Coll. English Assn. (past pres.). Contbr. articles in various revs. Home: Univ. of Santa Clara, Santa Clara, Cal. Died Dec. 2, 1954; buried Santa Clara (Cal.) Cath. Cemetery.

SHIRLEY, Robert Kirby, business exec.; born Gainesville, Tex., Aug. 15, 1899; s. Robert Newton and Sallie D. (Lauderdale) S.; student pub. schs.; m. Scyrine Carpenter, Nov. 30, 1919; children—Robert, Jane, Marianne. With U.S. War Dept., Washington, 1918-20; with U.S. Treasury Dept., 1920-22; with Freeport Sulphur Co., 1922—, becoming treas., 1934, v.p., 1940, exec. v.p. and dir. 1948, sr. v.p., 1955—. Home: 43 Gateway Drive, Great Neck, N.Y. Office: 161 E. 42 St., N.Y.C. Died Jan. 24, 1956; buried Grand-Saline, Tex.

SHIVELY, Carlton Adamson, financial editor; b. Douglass, Kan., Oct. 18, 1890; s. Jacob Whitefield and Elizabeth (Adamson) S.; A.B., U. Neb., 1911; grad. study, Columbia, 1916-17; m. Marie Leggett, 1927; 1 son, Glenn. Financial writer N.Y. Evening Post, 1920-25; financial writer N.Y. Sun, 1925-30, financial editor, 1930-50; financial writer World Telegram & Sun, 1950—. Mem. Phi Beta Kappa Assos. Clubs: Lotos, City (N.Y.C.); Riverside (Conn.) Yacht. Home: Cottage, Club Road, Riverside, Conn. Office: 125 Barclay, N.Y.C. Died July 8, 1952.

SHOCKLEY, Frank William, ednl. administrator; b. Mooreland, Ind., Oct. 15, 1884; s. John Wesley and Emma (Rhoton) S.; A.B., Indiana Univ., 1917; hon. LL.D., Univ. of Pittsburgh, 1941; m. Borgia Haskett, Aug. 4, 1910; children—Frank (dec.), Maebeth (Mrs. George A. Mock). Elementary teacher, teacher and prin. high schs.; head of Ind. U. Extension center, Fort Wayne, 1917-18; asso. dir. Ind. U. extension div., 1918-20; asst. to dean of univ. extension, U. of Wis., 1920-25; dir. extension and summer session, U. of Pittsburgh since 1925, dir. jr. colls. since 1927, dir. campus evening and Saturday courses since July 1, 1938, acting dean, Sch. of Edn., 1938-40. Mem. Nat. Univ. Extension Assn. (pres. 1934-35), Am. Assn. Jr. Colleges, Assn. for Promotion Adult Edn., Pittsburgh Personnel Assn., Pa. State Edn. Assn., Pa. Assn. for Adult Edn. (pres. univ. extension sect., 1937-38), Assn. Urban Univs. (sec.-treas. 1940-47), Assn. of Univ. Evening Colls., Phi Gamma Delta, Phi Delta Kappa, Delta Mu Delta, Omicron Delta Kappa. Republican. Mason. Club: Faculty (U. Pitts.). Home: 4802 5th Av., Pitts. 13. Died Jan. 12, 1954.

SHOEMAKER, Henry Wharton, newspaper pub.; b. N.Y. City, Feb. 24, 1882; s. Henry Francis and Blanche (Quiggle) S.; ed. private tutors, at Dr. E. L. Lyon's Classical School (now under title of Allen-Stevenson School), New York, and Columbia U., 1897-1900; Litt.D., Juniata Coll., Huntingdon, Pa., 1917, Franklin and Marshall Coll., 1924; m. Beatrice, d George B. Barclay, June 12, 1907; 1 son, Commander Henry F. (U.S.N.R.); m. 2d, Mabelle Ord, May 10, 1913. Began bus. career with C. H. & D. Railway, Cincinnati and N.Y., 1900-04; sec. American Legation, Lisbon, Portugal, 1904; 3d sec. Am. Embassy, Berlin, 1904-05; mem. N.Y. banking house of Shoemaker, Bates & Co., 1905-11; became publisher of daily morning and evening newspapers, Pa. and Conn., 1905; president Altoona (Pennsylvania) Times Tribune, 1912-50, columnist six days weekly, 1915-50; apptd. E.E. and M.P. to Bulgaria, 1930, retired 1933. Officer, New York, later Pa. National Guard, 1907-19; with Gen. Staff U.S. Army, 1918-19; spl. rep. Nat. Guard Pa. in Europe, 1918; lt. col. O.R.C., 1924, col. since 1933; historian Pa. War Memorial Commn. in Europe, 1928; mem. Gov. of Pa.'s Commn. for Nat. Defense, and Com. Pub. Safety, 1917-18. Mem. State Forest Commn. of Pa., 1918-30; comn. State Hist. Commn. of Pa., 1923-30, mem. of commn., 1936-40; mem. State Geographic Bd. of Pa., 1924-30; dir. State Archives of Pennsylvania, 1937-48; dir. Pa. State Division of Folk History, 1948—; director Pa. State Museum, 1939-40; mem. advisory bd. Pennsylvania Council of Nat. Defense, 1941-46. Mem. Pa. Tuberculosis Soc. (2d v.p.), Pa. Parks Assn., Conrad Weiser Park, etc. Decorated Grand Officer Order of the Redeemer (Greece); Grand Cordon Order of Civil Merit (Bulgaria); Comdr. Order of the Crown (Italy); Officer Order of Compassionate Heart (Russia); Knight Order of Nicholas II (Russia); Order of Meritoious Service (Pa.); received War Department citation, 1943. Fellow American Geog. Society, Royal Geog. Society (London); mem. Society Am. Foresters, Netherlands Soc. of Phila. (v.p. 1915-29), Huguenot Soc. of Pa. (pres. 1919-20), Waldensian Hist. Soc. of Pa. (v.p. 1925-30), Pa. Federation Hist. Socs. (pres. 1925-26), Pa. Folk Lore Soc. (pres., 1930—), S.R., Soc. Fgn. Wars, Mil. Order World War, Sons of Union Vets., Am. Legion, Sojourners, Loyal Legion, etc. Mason. Rotarian. Club: Boone and Crockett, Ends of the Earth (all New York). Author: (biographies) General William Sprague, 1916; Chief John Logan, 1917; Gifford Pinchot, 1922; John Brown (in Pennsylvania), 1931; also several books of verse and many books, articles and brochures on Pa. history, Indians, folklore, folksongs, proverbs, old words, wild life. Home: "Restless Oaks," McElhattan, Pa. Office: 911 N. Front St., Harrisburg, Pa. Died July 14, 1958; buried Highland Cemetery, Lock Haven, Pa.

SHOFFSTALL, Arthur Scott (shŏf'stäl), corp. official; b. near Coolsprings, Jefferson County, Pa., Feb. 20, 1876; s. Josiah and Elizabeth Jane (Harmon) S.; B.S., Pa. State Coll., 1900, M.S., 1905; hon. D.Sc., Marshall Coll., 1939; m. Jennie Pearsall, June 17, 1903 (dec.); m. 2d, Lillian Middleton, Feb. 21, 1908 (dec.); children—Arthur Marlin, Mary Jane (Mrs. William H. Smythe), Lillian Isobel (Mrs. Richard H. Cartwright); m. 3d, Mary Louise Griffin, Feb. 24, 1951. Asst. in dept. Pa. State Coll., 1900-01, instr., 1902-05; supt. sulphuric acid plants Repauno Works, E. I. duPont de Nemours, Gibbstown, N.J., 1905-07; supt. acid plants U.S. Bur. of Ordnance Naval Proving Grounds, Indian Head, Md., 1907-08; in operating dept., Internat. Nickel Co., Inc., Orford Works, Bayonne, N.J., 1908-21, gen. mgr. Huntington (W.Va.) Works, 1921 to 1944. Appointed cons. to Head Office in N.Y., 1944; dir. Banks Miller Supply Co. Mem. lay bd. St. Mary's Hosp.; dir. Salvation Army Adv. Bd.; mem. bd. dirs. Y.M.C.A.; gen. chmn. Community Chest Drive, 1936; co-chmn. Community Chest Drive, 1937; chmn. St. Mary's Campaign for Hosp. Funds; pres. United War and Community Chest Fund Huntington and Cabell County, Inc. Mem. Am. Inst. Mining and Metall. Engrs. Am. Iron and Steel Inst.; Mining and Metall. Soc. of Am., W.Va., Mfrs. Assn. (bd. dirs.), Engrs. Soc. of Western Pa., Kappa Sigma, Theta Nu Epsilon, Phi Kappa Phi (hon.). Republican. Presbyn. Mason (K.T., Shriner). Clubs: Huntington Mfrs., Guyan Golf and Country, Nickel Co. Address: 1300 12th St., Huntington, W.Va. Died Feb. W.Va.

SHOLTZ, David (shōlts), former governor; b. Brooklyn, N.Y., Oct. 6, 1891; s. Michael and Anne (Bloon) S.; A.B., Yale, 1914; LL.B., Stetson U., Deland, Fla., 1915, hon. M.A., 1921, LL.D., 1933; hon. D.C.L., U. of Tampa, 1936; m. Agatha M. Roberts, June 1919; m. 2d, Alice Mae Agee, Dec. 28, 1925; children—Mitchell, Carolyn, Lois, Eugene. Admitted to Fla. bar, 1915, Fed. Court, No. Dist. Fla., 1915, U.S. Supreme Ct., 1921, N.Y. bar, 1947; mem. Fla. Legislature, 1917; states atty. 7th Jud. Circuit of Fla., 1919-21; municipal judge, Daytona, 1921; became mem. Sholtz, Green & West, 1925; gov. State of Fla., 1933-37. Director, World Trade Corp.; pres. also director of the Transport Steamship Lines, Incorporated, Florida East Coast Land & Investment Corp.; counsel to law firm of E. Albert Pallot. Ensign U.S. Navy, World War I, now lt. comdr. U.S.N.R. (inactive). Past v. chmn. Laymen's Nat. Com. Past pres. Florida State C. of C., Daytona Beach C. of C., Assn. of Chambers Commerce, East Coast of Fla.; mem. American, Florida State and Volusia County (past pres.) bar assns., Am. Legion, Military Order World Wars (commander-in-chief, 1944-45), 40 and 8, Royal Order Scotland, Nat. Sojourners, Beta Theta Pi, Phi Alpha Delta, Acacia. Democrat. Mason (K.C.C.H., 33°, Shriner); Elk (past grand exalted ruler; treas. Nat. Vets. Service Commn.). Clubs: Bankers, Yale, Nat. Dem., Grover Cleveland Dem. (N.Y.C.); Rotary (past pres.; Daytona Beach); Nat. Press, Army and Navy (Washington); Com. of 100 (Miami Beach, Fla.). Home: 50 Glendale Road, Asheville, N.C.; Star Island, Miami Beach, Fla. Office: DuPont Bldg., Miami 32, Fla., and Savoy Plaza Hotel, 767 5th Av., N.Y.C. 22. Died March 21, 1953.

SHONTZ, Vernon Lloyd (shŏnts), clergyman; b. Kitchener, Ont., Can., June 19, 1889; s. Josiah Eby and Elizabeth (Shantz) S.; student Wilson Acad.; grad. Missionary Inst., Nyack, N.Y.; student U. of Ia., summer, 1929, 1930-32, Divinity Sch. U. of Chicago, summer, 1934; D.D., Northern Baptist Seminary, Chicago, 1936; married M. Bess Reitz, December 12, 1912; (deceased January 1942); children—Vernon Lloyd, Robert Reitz; m. 2d, Claire Beale,

Dec. 27, 1952. Came to U.S., 1909, naturalized, 1923. Ordained ministry Bapt. Ch., 1916; began as supt. of boys, Wilson Acad., later pastor at Chesley, Ont., and Sheraden Ch., Pittsburgh; pastor Central Ch., Williamsport, Pa., 1919-24, First Ch., Beckley, W.Va., 1924-27, First Ch., Muscatine, Ia., 1927-35, Central Ch., Springfield, Ill., 1935—. Pres. Ia. Bapt. pastors Conf., 1929-30; v.p. Ia. Bapt. Conv., 1933-34, pres., 1934-35; mem. bd. mgrs. Am. Bapt. Fgn. Mission Soc., 1935-44; chmn. com. on ordination, Ministers Council, Northern Bapt. Conv., 1937-40, sec., 1940-44; apptd. mem. Ill. Parole and Pardon Bd., 1953. Trustee Northern Bapt. Sem., 1936-48; trustee Shurtleff Coll., Alton, Ill., 1945—; chairman Social Service Exchange Bd., Springfield, 1940-41; mem. exec. com., Council of Social Agencies, Sangamon County, Ill., 1940-41; mem. Pastoral relations com., Ill. Bapt. Ministers Council 1942-46; vice-pres. Ill. Bapt. Conv., 1942-43, pres. 1943-44; mem. com. on cooperative unity, Northern Baptist Conv., 1944-45, pres. Ministers Council, 1944-48; apptd. to Ill. State Com. on Religious Edn., 1942; v.p. N. Bapt. Conv., 1948-49; mem. exec. com. Fed. Council Chs., 1948. Pres. Springfield Council of Chs., 1946-47. Ind. Republican. Club: Lions (pres., 1946-47) (Springfield). Home: 1219 Leland Av., Springfield, Ill. Died Oct. 16, 1954; buried Oak Ridge Cemetery, Springfield.

SHOOK, Glenn Alfred, prof. physics; b. Osgood, Ind., July 16, 1882; s. Alfred Smith and Olive (Gould) S.; student Moores Hill (Ind.) College; A.B., U. of Wis., 1907; Ph.D., U. of Ill., 1914; m. Nellie Switzer, Nov. 15, 1911; 1 dau., Elizabeth Louise. Instr. physics, Purdue U., 1907-11, U. of Ill., 1911-14, U. of Mich., 1914-15, Williams Coll., 1915-18; prof. physics, Wheaton Coll., Norton, Mass., 1918-48, emeritus. Fellow Royal Soc. Arts, A.A.A.S.; mem. Am. Assn. Variable Star Observers, Am. Astron. Soc., Math. Soc. Am., Optical Soc. Am., Sigma Xi. Bahá'í. Author: (with others) Practical Pyrometry, 1917; Mysticism, Sciences and Revelation, (pub. Eng.), 1953. Pioneer worker in mobile color and applied optics. Lecturer. Home: Eliot, Me. Died Aug. 26, 1954; buried Eliot.

SHOOP, Duke, newspaper corr.; b. Abingdon, Ill., Apr. 26, 1905; s. Jesse Campbell and Nellie (Swartzcope) S.; student U.Mo., 1922-27; m. Ruth Agee, Nov. 23, 1931. State capital corr. for Kansas City Star, 1929-34, mem. Washington bur., 1934-53, war corr. ETO, 1943-45, chief Washington corr., 1946—; dir. The Kansas City Star Co., 1952—. Clubs: Gridiron (pres. 1953), Nat. Press, Overseas Writers (Washingotn). Home: 2101 Connecticut Av. N.W. Office: Albee Bldg., Washington. Died Apr. 26, 1957; buried Jefferson City, Mo.

SHORT, Joseph, sec. to Pres. of U.S.; b. Vicksburg, Miss., Feb. 11, 1904; s. Joseph Hudson and Irene Elizabeth (Jones) S.; A.B., Va. Mil. Inst., 1925; m. Beth Campbell, Dec. 27, 1937; children—Alexander Campbell, Stephen Joseph Michael, Victoria Elizabeth. Reporter Jackson (Miss.) Daily News, 1925-26, 27-28, Vicksburg Post and Herald, 1926-27, New Orleans Times-Picayune, 1928-29, Richmond (Va.) Bur. Asso. Press, 1929-31, Washington Bur., 1931-41, Chicago Sun, 1941-43, Washington Bur. Baltimore Sun, 1943-50; press sec. to Pres. of U.S. since 1950. Presbyn. Club: Nat. Press (pres., 1948; Washington). Home: 3407 Gilden Dr., Alexandria, Va. Office: The White House, Washington. Died Sept. 18, 1952.

SHORTRIDGE, Samuel Morgan, ex-senator; b. Mt. Pleasant, Ia., Aug. 3, 1861; s. Rev. Elias W. and Tabitha C. S.; student high sch., San Jose, Cal.; m. Laura Gashweiler, Aug. 3, 1899. Admitted to Cal. bar, 1884, and since practiced at San Francisco; mem. U.S. Senate, 1921-33. Rep. presdl. elector, 1884, 1900, 08. Mason, Elk, Red Man. Clubs: Pacific-Union, Union League, Commonwealth, Press, Masonic, Menlo Country, Bohemian (San Francisco). Widely known as orator on polit. topics and on popular occasions. Home: 202 Elena Av., Ahterton, Cal. Died Jan. 15, 1952; buried Oak Hill Cemetery, San Jose, Cal.

SHOTT, Hugh Ike, former U.S. senator; b. Staunton, Va., Sept. 3, 1866; s. Daniel Webster and Lucy Ellen Bell (Hoy) S.; student pub. schs.; m. Mary Kate Chisholm, Jan. 10, 1894; children—Jas. Howard, Mary Lillian (Mrs. G. C. Brant), Hugh Ike. Learned printers trade, 1882-89; in ry. mail service, 1889-96; pres. Daily Telegraph Printing Co., pubs. of Bluefield Daily Telegraph. Bluefield Sunset News, operators of radio sta. WHIS. Dir. 1st Nat. Bank, Bluefield. Postmaster, Bluefield, 1902-13; mem. Rep. State Co., W.Va., 1908-12; mem. 71st and 72d Congresses, 5th W.Va. Dist. Rep. nominee for U.S. senator, 1936; elected, 1942, to fill term for which defeated in 1936. Mem. So. Newspaper Pubs. Assn., W.Va. Pubs. Assn., Fifty Year Editors Club. Methodist. K.P. Rotarian. Home: Bluefield, W.Va. Died Oct. 12, 1953.

SHOTWELL, Abel V., lawyer; b. Marengo, O., Jan. 7, 1883; s. Hudson Burr and Emma Jane (Noe) S.; student Ohio Wesleyan U., 1900-01; grad. Ohio State University, 1905; m. Hilda E. Condron, June 22, 1907; children—Ruth (Mrs. Tom McAndrews), Hudson Burr (former army officer U.S. Army), Gordon Stewart (parachute officer, killed in action), Anabel (wife of Major Verne Alder). Admitted to Ohio bar, 1904; admitted to Neb. bar, 1905; engaged in gen. practice of law, Omaha, Neb., since 1905; sr. mem. Shotwell, Vance & Marchetti; county atty. Douglas County, Neb., 1919-23. Mem. adv. bd. for registrants, Selective Service Act, 1940. Mem. Rep. State and Douglas County central coms. 1924—; pres. Neb. Rep. Founder's Day, 1943; Nat. Rep. Committeeman for Neb., 1944-56. Mem. Omaha (pres. 1925), Neb. State (mem. exec. council 1940-43, pres. 1949) and Am. bar assns., Omaha C. of C. Member Ak Sar Ben, Mayflower Society, S.A.R., Sigma Chi. Mem. First Presbyn. Ch. Home: 3719 Mason St. Office: Omaha National Bank Bldg., Omaha, Neb. Died Dec. 26, 1958; buried Forest Lawn Cemetery, Omaha, Neb.

SHOUDY, Loyal Ambrose, surgeon; b. Ellensburg, Wash., Sept. 23, 1880; s. John Alden and Mary Ellen (Stewart) S.; A.B., U. Wash., 1904; M.D., U. Pa., 1909; unmarried. Engaged in practice as surgeon, 1910—; intern German Hosp., Phila. (now Lankenau), 1910-13; physician in charge Mary Drexel Childrens Hosp., 1913-14, Phila.; chief surgeon Bethlehem Steel Co., 1914-18, chief med. service, 1918-45, med. dir., 1945—; cons. surgeon St. Lukes Hosps., Bethlehem, Pa. Chmn. com. on indsl. health Am. Iron and Steel Inst.; dir. Nat. Safety Council; pres. Bethlehem area Boy Scouts of America; mem. Health Adv. Council, U.S. C. of C.; Med. Adv. Group, N.A.M. Fellow A.C.S. (mem. fracture com.); mem. Am. Assn. Indsl. Physicians and Surgeons (pres.), A.M.A., Am. Public Health Assn., Conf. Bd. of Indsl. Physicians, Pa. Med. Soc., Phi Gamma Delta, Phi Alpha Sigma. Clubs: University (past pres.). Rotary (hon.), Saucon Valley Country, Bethlehem (Bethlehem). Alumnus Summa Laude Dignatus, U. of Wash., 1943. Author numerous articles on traumatic and indsl. surgery, research on heat sickness and problems of indsl. hygiene. Home: Spring Valley Rd. Office: Bethlehem Steel Co., 701 E. 3d St., Bethlehem, Pa. Died Aug. 30, 1950; buried Ellensburg, Wash.

SHOUP, Earl Leon (shōop), univ. prof.; born Eldorado, Kan., May 1, 1886; s. Levi Harrison and Alice (Campbell) S.; A.B., Washburn Coll., Topeka, Kan., 1911; student Yale, 1913-14; A.M., U. of Chicago, 1919; Ph.D., Harvard, 1923; m. Irene Helena Mehl, Mar. 27, 1919 (dec. July 16, 1943); 1 dau., Rebecca Alice. Asst. prof. history and polit. science, Earlham Coll., Richmond, Ind., 1915-18; instr., polit. science, Stanford Univ., sumer, 1918; prof. hist. and polit. sci., Whittier (Calif.) Coll., 1918-19; asst. prof. polit. sci., Kan. State Teachers' Coll., Emporia, 1919-20; teaching asst. dept. of govt., Harvard, 1920-22; asst. prof. polit. sci., Western Res. Univ., 1922-24, asso. prof., 1924-27, Marcus Alonzo Hanna prof. since 1927, chmn. dept., 1924-50; asst. dean Adelbert Coll., 1925-26. Exec. sec. Cuyahoga County (O.) Charter Commn., 1934-35; draftsman of Proposed County Charter, Cuyahoga Co. Mem. Am. Polit. Sci. Assn., Nat. Municipal League, Am. Soc. for Pub. Adminstrn., Acacia. Republican. Conglist. Author: (with Louis Clinton Hatch) A History of the Vice-Presidency of the United States, 1934; The Government of the American People, 1946; The National Government of the American People, 1948. Contbr. articles to Am. Polit. Sci. Review, Nat. Municipal Review, Western Res. Law Review. Home: 3292 Daleford Rd., Shaker Heights, O. Died Jan. 29, 1953.

SHOUP, Eldon Campbell, mgmt. engr.; b. Whiting, Kan., June 8, 1897; s. Lee Harrison and Alice (Campbell) S.; A.B., Washburn Coll., Topeka, 1920; M.B.A., Harvard, 1922; m. Lucy Botsford Johnson, Feb. 5, 1924; children—Barbara Ann, Penelope, Peter Lee. Marketing specialist U.S. Bur. Agr. and Econs., 1922-24; U.S. agrl. commr. to Germany, 1924-25; editor Fgn. Crops and Markets and asst. chief fgn. service U.S. Dept. Agr., 1926-27; sales promotion mgr. Nat. Blank Brook Co., 1927-31; merchandising mgr. Dennison Mfg. Co., Framingham, Mass., 1932-40; cons. to Dept. of Commerce, 1941—, dir. rationing in New Eng. OPA, 1942-44, regional adminstr. for New Eng., 1944-46; exec. v.p. Associated Universities, Inc., 1946-51; prin. Cresap, McCormick & Paget, mgmt. engrs., N.Y.C., 1951-53, partner, 1953—. Served as ensign USNR, World War I. Former pres. New Eng. chpt. Am. Marketing Assn.; lectr. in marketing and sales mgmt. Home: Barnegat Rd., Pound Ridge, N.Y. Died Oct. 8, 1954.

SHREVE, Forrest, botanist; b. Easton, Md., July 1878; s. Henry and Helen Garrison (Coates) S.; A.B., Johns Hopkins, 1901, Ph.D., 1905; m. Edith Coffin Bellamy, June 1909; 1 dau., Margaret Bellamy. Asst. prof. botany Goucher Coll., Balt., 1906-08; mem. staff Div. Plant Biology, Carnegie Instn., Washington, 1908-43, in charge Desert Lab., Tucson, 1926-39; mng. editor The Plant World, 1911-19. Fellow A.A.A.S. (pres. southwest div., 1928-29); mem. Ecol. Soc. Am. (pres. 1922), Bot. Soc. America, Torrey Bot. Club, Cal. Bot. Soc., Western Soc. Naturalists, Assn. Am. Geographers (v.p. 1940), Assn. Pacific Coast Geographers (pres. 1942), Soc. Am. Foresters, Tucson Nat. Hist. Soc. (pres. 1932-33), Phi Beta Kappa, Sigma Xi (pres. Ariz. chpt. 1932-33). Author: Plant Life of Maryland (with others), 1910; A Montane Rain-Forest, 1914; Vegetation of a Desert Mountain Range, 1915; The Cactus and Its Home, 1931; also numerous papers in sci. jours. Joint author: Distribution of Vegetation in the United States, 1921. Editor: Naturalists Guide to the Americas, 1926. Home: 297 N. Main St., Tucson. Died July 19, 1950.

SHRINER, Charles Anthony, b. Cin., Oct. 14, 1853; s. Bernard and Catherine (Zimmer) S.; student St. Xavier's Coll., Cin., 1868-72; unmarried. Began as reporter and corr. New York Herald, 1877; city editor Paterson Daily Press 14 yrs., also continuing with Herald; founder, 1894, and editor Paterson Sunday Chronicle until its consolidation with the Daily Press, 1910; fish and game protector of N.J. 4 yrs. Author: The Birds of New Jersey, 1896. Compiler: Wit, Wisdom and Foibles of the Great, 1919. Editor of William Nelson's History of Paterson (3 vols.), 1920. Home: 436 Ellison St., Paterson, N.J. Deceased.

SHRIVER, William Payne, b. Lebanon Church, Pa., Sept. 21, 1872; s. Rev. Samuel Smith and Caroline H. (McCluskey) S.; A.B., Johns Hopkins, 1901; Union Theol. Sem., 1904; D.D., Bloomfield Theol. Sem., 1917; m. Margaret Campbell Thompson, Mar. 9, 1909 (dec. Mar. 1958); children—Caroline Hughes (dec.), Robert Campbell. Ordained to ministry Presbyn. Ch., 1904; pastor Northminster Ch., N.Y.C., 1904-09; sec. city, immigrant and indsl. work of Bd. Nat. Missions Presbyn. Ch. in U.S.A., 1910-41. pathfinding service, N.Y. City Mission Soc., 1946-47. Formerly ednl. dir. YMCA, Balt. Mem. Phi Kappa Psi. Author: Immigrant Forces, 1913; What Next in Home Missions, 1928; The Silk Workers of Paterson, 1929; City Church Inventory, 1938; Maltbie Davenport Babcock, Recollections, 1887-1900, 1941; Adventure in Missions, 1946; Mission of the Grass Roots, 1949. Home: 216 Lincoln Av., Ridgewood, N.J. Died Feb. 24, 1957; buried Lorraine Cemetery, Balt.

SHRODER, William Jacob (shrō'dẽr), social and civic worker; b. Cincinnati, O., Nov. 28, 1876; s. Judge Jacob and Bettie (Fechheimer) S.; A.B., Yale, 1898, LL.B., Harvard, 1901; m. Sophia Joseph, June 1, 1908; children—Mary Shroder Aring, William J., Betty Jane Mayersohn. Admitted O. bar, 1901, practiced at Cincinnati; retired, 1921, to devote entire time without compensation to social and civic activities; lecturer Med. Coll., U. of Cincinnati, 1924-38, Coll. of Liberal Arts, same university, 1925-32; pres. of Peoples Bank and Savings Co. since 1934; director Atlas National Bank, Cincinnati. Private, Yale Battery, Spanish-American War, 1898; nat. judge advocate general United Spanish-War Vets., 1905; and comdr. Dept. of Ohio, same, 1906-07; pres. Am. Bd. of Iron Dealers (under War Industries Bd.), 1917-18. Pres. Big Brothers Assn., 1918-19; pres. Jewish Community House, Cincinnati, 1918-22; pres. United Jewish Social Agencies of Cincinnati, 1923-26; chmn. Exec. Budget com. of Community Chest and Council of Social Agencies of Cincinnati and Hamilton County since 1922; chmn. Cincinnati Community Chest, 1939-40; mem. exec. com. Nat. Assn. for Community Orgn., 1923-26; mem. Bd. of Edn., Cincinnati, 1924-34 (pres. 1926-34); mem. Pub. Improvement Program Com. for Cincinnati and Hamilton County, 1927-34, chmn., 1930-34. Pres. Nat. Conf. of Jewish Social Service, 1926-27; chmn. Nat. Appeals Information Service, 1928-32; dir. Am. Jewish Joint Distribution Com., N.Y. City, 1931-39, vice-chmn. since 1939; pres. Nat. Council Jewish Fedns. and Welfare Funds, 1932-38, chmn., 1940-50; mem. exec. com. Cincinnati Defense Fund, 1941; mem. admission and allotment com. and mem. exec. com. Cincinnati War Chest, 1942-46; pres. Cincinnati Govtl. Research Bur., 1934-38; mem. Hamilton County, City of Cincinnati and Cincinnati Sch. Dist. Coördinating Com., 1931-34; mem. City of Cincinnati Charity Solicitation Licensing Commn. to 1938; mem. Hamilton County Pub. Relief Commn. (state local br. for administering unemployment relief) until 1936; mem. board United Service for New Americans, Inc., N.Y.; mem. com. President's War Relief Control Bd. for Allocation of Clothing Collected by United Nat. Clothing Collection. Mem. N.E.A.; Cincinnati Musical Festival Assn., Am. Assn. Social Workers, Pi Gamma Mu. Republican. Club: Yale, The Board, Cincinnati. Address: Hotel Netherland Plaza, Cin. Died July 11, 1952.

SHRYOCK, Joseph Grundy, steel exec.; b. Haddonfield, N.J., Sept. 2, 1880; s. William Knight and Virginia Susan (Schaeffer) S.; grad. Eastburn Acad., Phila., 1897; student Collège Jacques Amyotà Melun, Seine et Marne, France, 1896-97; C.E., Pa. Mil. Coll., Chester, 1900, M.C.E., 1921. Sci. Degree in Engring., 1942; m. Aimé Caroline Picolet d'Hermillon, April 6, 1904; children—Joseph Richard, Raymond de Souville. Draftsman, Am. Bridge Co., 1900-03; designing engr. Va. Bridge & Iron Co., 1903-04; draftsman and checker Belmont Iron Works,

Phila., 1904-06, designing engr. and salesman, 1906-22, chief engr., 1922—, also v.p. and dir., 1926-40, became pres. and chief engr., ret. 1950; inventor Belmont interlocking channel floor, 1933. Life mem. Am. Soc. C.E., Zool. Soc. Phila., Pa. Acad. fine Arts, Welsh Soc. Phila., Colonial Soc. Pa. Republican. Protestant. Clubs: Engineers, Philadelphia Country. Home: New Darlington Rd., Wawa, Pa. Office: Belmont Iron Works, Phila. 46. Died Aug. 29, 1956; buried West Laurel Hill Cemetery, Phila.

SHUBERT, Lee, theatrical mgr.; b. Syracuse, N.Y., Mar. 15, 1883; s. David and Catherine S.; ed. pub. schs. Began with brother, the late Sam S. Shubert, managing small theatrical cos. on tour, with comedies written by Charles H. Hoyt; organized stock co. for Bastable Theatre, Syracuse; became with brother, mgr. Herald Square Theatre, New York, 1900, later the Casino, Princess Hippodrome, Lyric and others; now at head of the Shubert Theatrical Co., controlling many theatres in New York and other cities. Address: 225 W. 44th St., N.Y.C. Died Dec. 25, 1953.

SHUFORD, Forrest Herman, state ofcl.; b. Cleveland Co., N.C., June 3, 1897; s. J. M. and Ella (Copeland) S.; student Berea Coll., 1918-20, N.C. State Coll., 1924, Duke U., 1925; m. May Renfrow, June 3, 1922; children—Forrest Herman, Harry Benjamin. Employed textile mills, R.I. and N.C., 1921-24; prin. high sch., Ellenboro and Spindale, N.C., 1924-26; boys commr. City of High Point, N.C., 1926-33; chief insp. N.C. State Dept. Labor, Raleigh, 1933-38, commr. labor, 1938—; N.R.A. compliance officer for N.C., 1934-35 (on leave from Dept. of Labor). Apptd. by Pres. Roosevelt as adv. to del. Internat. Labor Conf., Phila., 1944, and by Pres. Truman to ILO Conf., Geneva, Switzerland, 1947; pres. N.C. Conf. for Social Service; chmn. N.C. State Bd. Boiler Rules, N.C. State Apprenticeship Council; mem. com. laws and regulations, chmn. sub-com. existing laws and regulations Pres. Conf. Indsl. Safety. Chmn. disaster com. A.R.C. (Wake Co. chpt.). Mem. Internat. Assn. Govtl. Labor Ofcls. (pres., mem. exec. com.), N.C. Council State, Am. Soc. Safety Engrs., Nat. Safety Council (textile sect.), Am. Legion, 40 et 8. Episcopalian (vestryman). Club: Kiwanis. Home: 810 W. Johnson St. Office: N.C. Department of Labor, Raleigh, N.C. Died May 19, 1954; buried Montlawn Cemetery, Raleigh.

SHULER, Ellis W(illiam) (shōō'lẽr), **geologist;** b. Comers Rock, Grayson County, Va., Oct. 15, 1881; s. James Alexander Hamilton and Amanda (Harrington) Shuler; B.A., Emory and Henry College, 1903, LL.D., 1943; M.A., Vanderbilt University, 1907; M.A., Harvard University, 1914, Ph.D., 1915; married Leona Berry Smith, Dec. 31, 1907; 1 son, Ellis William. Assistant in biology, Vanderbilt U., 1908; professor biology and geology, Poly. Coll., Ft. Worth, Tex., 1908-13; fellow Harvard, 1913-14; asst. in geology, Harvard, 1914-15; asso. prof. geology, Southern Methodist U., 1915-17, prof. since 1918, also dean Grad. Sch. since 1926. Mem. Shaler Memorial Expdn. to S. Appalachians, 1916; acting geologist Tex. Bur. Econ. Geology, 1917; geologist Tex. Oil Co., 1918. Fellow Geol. Soc. America, A.A.A.S., Texas Acad. Science; member of the American Association of Geographers, American Association Petroleum Geologists, Sigma Xi, Phi Beta Kappa. Democrat. Methodist. Author: Rocks and Rivers of America, 1945. Contbr. various tech. bulls., also articles in Am. Jour. Science, Scientific American, etc. Home: 3429 Haynie Av., Dallas. Died Jan. 1, 1954; buried Restland Meml. Cemetery.

SHULL, Charles Graves, banker; b. Lexington, Mo., Feb. 18, 1878; s. Charles A. and Phoebe R. (Pearcy) S.; B.S., William Jewell Coll., 1900; LL.B., Washington U., 1902; m. Mamie Smith, Dec. 24, 1903 (dec.); children—Phoebe Jo (Mrs. Jerome V. Jones), Charles Graves; m. 2d, Gladys Madigan, May 29, 1948. Admitted to Okla. bar, 1902; practiced at Hugo, Okla., 1902-05; in banking business, Hugo, 1905-25; Okla. state bank commr., 1927-32; v.p. Federal Land Bank of Wichita, 1933-41, pres., 1941-48. City atty., Hugo, Okla., 1903. Mem. Sigma Nu, Phi Kappa Phi. Democrat. Presbyn. Mason. Club: Rotary (Hugo). Home: Hugo, Okla. Died Nov. 14, 1950; buried Hugo.

SHULL, George Harrison, botanist; b. Clark County, O., Apr. 15, 1874; s. Harrison and Catharine (Ryman) S.; B.S., Antioch Coll., 1901; LL.D., 1940, Ph.D. (botany and zoölogy), U. of Chicago, 1904; Sc.D., Lawrence Coll., 1940, Ia. State Coll. Agr. and Mechanics Arts, Ames, 1942; m. Ella Amanda Hollar, July 8, 1906; 1 dau., Elizabeth Ellen (dec.); m. 2d, Mary J. Nicholl, Aug. 26, 1909; children—John Coulter, Georgia Mary, Frederick Whitney, David Macaulay, Barbara Weaver, Harrison. Bot. asst. U.S. Nat. Museum, 1902; bot. expert U.S. Bur. Plant Industry, 1902-04; asst. plant physiology, U. of Chicago, 1903-04; botanical investigator, Sta. for Exptl. Evolution, Carnegie Instn. of Washington, Cold Spring Harbor, L.I., 1904-15; prof. botany and genetics, Princeton University, 1915-42, emeritus, 1942—; visiting lecturer in genetics, Rutgers University, 1929-30, L. L. Kellogg memorial lecturer, 1931; lectr. in Heterosis Conf., Iowa State Coll., 1950. Member of Princeton Borough Bd. of Education, 1928-44, vice-pres. 1934-36, pres. 1936-44; pres. Mercer County Assn. Boards of Edn., 1934-37; Princeton Old Guard, 1944; member Food Panel of Princeton War Price and Rationing Board, 1944-45. Fellow A.A.A.S.; corresponding member Deutsche Botanische Gesellschaft; corr. mem. Academy Science, Vienna; hon. mem. Gesellschaft fur Pflanzenzüchtung in Wien; hon. mem. John Torrey Club of Princeton; mem. Deutsche Gesellschaft für Vererbungswissenschaft, Société Linnéenne de Lyon, Institut Internat. d'Anthropologie (Paris), Am. Assn. Univ. Profs., Torrey Bot. Club (pres. 1947), Bot. Soc. of Am., Am. Soc. Naturalists (v.p. 1911, pres. 1917), Ecol. Soc. America, Am. Genetic Assn. (chmn. plant sect. 1912, advisory com. 1922—), Eugenics Research Assn. Eugenics Soc. America, Genetics Soc. America, Sigma Xi (1st pres. Princeton chapter, 1932-33), Am. Geog. Soc., Am. Soc. Plant Physiology, Washington Acad. Sciences, Am. Philos. Soc. Hon. pres. Antioch Alumni Assn., 1940—; chmn. Island Beach (N.J.) Nat. Monument Committee, 1945-50. Awarded gold medal by DeKalb Agrl. Assn., 1940, for the invention of hybrid corn. Citation for distinguished service to agr. by New Jersey Bd. of Agr., 1945; John Scott medal and premium, 1946; Marcellus Hartley Medal, Nat. Acad. Science, 1949; mem. Hall of Fame Am. Mechanics Mag. Golden Jubilee, 1952. Lecturer and author of papers on variation, heridity and plant-breeding. Founder and mng. editor of "Genetics" (mag), 1916-25, asso. editor, 1925—; vice-pres. Genetics, Inc., 1940—; first editor genetics sect. of Bot. Abstracts, 1918-22. Home: 60 Jefferson Rd., Princeton, N.J. Died Sept. 28, 1954; buried I O O F Cemetery, Santa Rosa, Cal.

SHULMAN, Harry (shōōl'mȧn), univ. prof., dean; b. Krugloye, Russia, Mar. 14, 1903; s. Simon and Tille (Klebanoff) S.; brought to U.S., 1912, naturalized, 1921; A.B., Brown U., 1923; LL.B., Harvard, 1926, S.J.D., 1927; A.M. (hon.) Yale, 1937; LL.D., Brown U., 1953; m. Rea Karrel, July 10, 1927; 1 son, Stephen Neal. Practice of law, N.Y. City, 1928-29; law clerk to Mr. Justice Brandeis, U.S. Supreme Court, 1929-30; instr. law, Yale, 1930-31, asst. prof., 1931-33, asso. prof. 1933-37, prof. law, 1937-39; Lines prof. law, 1939-40; Sterling prof. law, 1940—, dean Law Sch., 1954—. Special counsel U.S. Railroad Retirement Bd., 1934-36; reporter, restatement of torts, Am. Law Inst., 1937-39. Mem. U.S. Atty. Gen.'s Com. on Administrative Procedure, 1940-41, U.S. Enemy Alien Hearing Bd. for Conn., 1941-42; asso. mem. Nat. War Labor Bd., 1942—, dir. disputes, 1942-43; umpire Ford Motor Co. and United Automobile Workers (CIO), 1943—, Bendix Products div. and United Auto Workers (CIO), Wright Aeronautical Division and United Auto Workers (CIO). Special conciliator, U.S. Conciliation Service. Member bars of R.I. State, N.Y. and U. S. Supreme Court. Author: A Study of Law Administration in Connecticut (with Charles E. Clark), 1937; Opinions of the Umpire, 1945. Editor: Cases on Federal Jurisdiction and Procedure (with Felix Frankfurter), 1937; Cases on Torts (with Fleming James Jr.), 1942; Cases on Labor Relations (with Neil W. Chamberlain). Home: 1100 Ridge Rd., Hamden, Conn. Office: Yale University School of Law, New Haven. Died Mar. 20, 1955; buried Providence.

SHUMATE, Roger V(ernon), univ. prof.; b. near Mexia, Tex., Mar. 21, 1900; s. James MacWooten and Rosa Velva (Ogden) S.; student Tyler (Tex.) Comml. Coll., 1915-16; A.B., Univ. of California, 1928, A.M., 1929; Ph.D., Univ. of Minn., 1933; m. Dessymore Whiting, June 15, 1935; children—Marilyn Rosa, Marcia. Teaching fellow polit. sci., Univ. Calif., 1928-29; instr., Univ. of Cincinnati, 1929-31, teaching asst. and instr., Univ. of Minn., 1931-33, instr., Univ. of Pittsburgh, 1933-37; asso. prof. polit. sci., Univ. of Neb., 1937-44, prof., 1944—, acting chmn. dept. polit. sci., 1948-49; dir. of research, Neb. Legislative Council, 1937—. Served as seaman 2 cl., U.S.N.R. (active duty), 1918-19; seaman and Q.M., U.S. Merchant Service, July 1919-Sept. 1920. Mem. Am. Polit. Sci. Assn., Am. Legion, Phi Beta Kappa, Pi Sigma Alpha. Contbg. author Introduction to Western Civilization, 1933. Editor: Nebraska Blue Book, 1940, 42, 44, 46, 48, 50, 52 (ofcl. manual State of Neb.). Contbr. articles in professional publs.; author 70 research reports on problems of state and local govt. for Neb. Leg. Home: 3050 Puritan Av., Lincoln 2. Offices: Univ of Nebraska, Lincoln 8 and Legislative Council, State Capitol, Lincoln 9, Neb. Died May 22, 1954; buried Wyuka Cemetery, Lincoln.

SHUMWAY, Sherman N(elson) (shŭmway), lawyer; b. Dover, Mass., Dec. 18, 1895; s. Amos Wight and Jennie (Smith) S.; A.B., Bowdoin Coll., 1917; LL.B., Harvard, 1922; m. Agnes Mosher, June 30, 1925; children—Forrest Nelson, Douglas Mosher, John Worthington. Atty. Gower & Shumway, Skowhegan, Me., 1922-27; counsel Bangor Hydro-Electric Co. (Me.), 1927-33; pres. Merrill Trust Co., Bangor, 1933-44; v.p., dir. Signal Oil and Gas Co., Los Angeles, 1944-54. Mem. bd. overseers Bowdoin Coll. Mason. Home: 642 Siena Way, Los Angeles 24. Office: P.O. Box 5840 Metropolitan Sta., Los Angeles 55. Died Apr. 30, 1954.

SHUMWAY, Waldo, college dean; b. New Brunswick, N.J., May 8, 1891; s. Edgar Solomon and Florence (Snow) S.; A.B., Amherst Coll., 1911; A.M., Columbia, 1913, Ph.D., 1916; Mining Engr. (hon.), Stevens Inst. of Tech., 1954; m. Helen Davis, Nov. 20, 1920; 1 dau., Jean (Mrs. Peter Ferguson). Field worker, Amherst Coll. Biol. Expdn. to Patagonia, 1911-12; asst. in zoology, Columbia, 1914-15; asst. in biology, Amherst, 1915-16, instr. in biology, 1916-17; asst. prof. biology, Dartmouth, 1919-22; asso. prof. zoölogy, U. of Ill., 1922-29, prof., 1929-47; asst. dean Coll. Liberal Arts and Scis., 1926-31; dean Stevens Inst. Tech., 1947—, sec. bd. trustees 1947-55, provost, 1955—. Served as 1st lt. inf., U.S. Army, France, 1917-19; maj., lt. col., col. inf. (gen. staff corps since Dec. 1944); assigned to War Dept., Wash., D.C., 1942-46, retired 1951. Decorated Victory medal with 4 battle clasps; Purple Heart, Army Commendation Ribbon, Bronze Star, Legion of Merit. Fellow A.A.A.S.; mem. American Society Zoölogists, American Society Engineering Edn., Am. Soc. Mil. Engrs., Am. Assn. Anatomists, Am. Soc. Naturalists, Am. Soc. Growth and Development, Theta Xi, Phi Beta Kappa, Sigma Xi, Gamma Alpha, Scabbard and Blade. Reserve Officers Assn. Republican. Mason. Clubs: Chaos (Chgo.); University, Amherst, Stevens (N.Y.C.); Cosmos (Washington). Author: Vertebrate Embryology, 1927; The Frog, a Laboratory Guide, 1928; Textbook of General Biology, 1931; Laboratory Manual for Vertebrate Embryology (with F. B. Adamstone), 1939. Contbr. to sci. and ednl. jours. Address: Stevens Inst. of Technology, Hoboken, N.J. Died Mar. 8, 1956; buried Arlington Nat. Cemetery.

SHURCLIFF, Arthur Asahel, landscape architect; b. Boston, 1870; s. Asahel M. and Sarah A. (Shurtfeff) S.; grad. Boston Prince Sch., 1886; Mass. Inst. Tech., 1894; Harvard, 1896; m. Margaret H. Nichols, 1905; children—Sidney N., Sarah P., William A., John P., Elizabeth H., Alice W. Pupil of Charles Eliot; with Olmsted, Olmsted & Eliot, landscape architects, 1896; helped F. L. Olmsted, Jr. establish Harvard Sch. of Landscape Architecture; own office, Boston, 1905; adviser to Mass. Met. Improvements Commn. in preparing first met. plan for an Am. city; adviser to Boston Park Dept., Met. Dist. Commn. Town planner to U.S. Govt. during World War I. Landscape architect for numerous country places also State College, Denton, Tex., Johns Hopkins, Harvard, Amherst, Colgate, Brown and many others; landscape architect for various hosps. and sanitariums. Designer of zoo, Boston and Detroit; landscape architect for Barkhamsted Reservoir and Saville Dam, Hartford, Conn., Quabbin Reservoir. Mass. Landscape architect, Crawford and Franconia Notches of White Mountains. Designer war memorials; designer various mill villages in the South, and in Mass. Town planner for more than 20 eastern cities and towns; designer Plymouth waterfront, south and east shores of Charles River .Basin (Boston); landscape architect for colonial Williamsburg restoration. Mem. Am. Soc. Landscape Architects (pres. 2 terms), A.I.A. (hon.); asso. mem. Boston Soc. Architects, Boston Soc. Civil Engrs., Boston and Mass. Art Commns., Mass. Hort. Soc., Signet Soc. of Harvard. Club: Tavern (Boston). Author: First and Second New England Journal; and other N.E. books. Home: 45 Bromfield St., Boston 8. Died Nov. 12, 1957; buried Mt. Auburn Cemetery, Cambridge, Mass.

SHURTLEFF, Eugene (shûrt'lẽf), physician; b. Russell, Mass.; s. Lyman and Laura L. S.; prep. edn. Williston Sem.; M.D., Coll. Physicians and Surgeons, Boston, 1886; m. Elizabeth M. Mendum, 1888; children—Ernestine M., Laura Edna. Founded, 1888, and supt. North End Dispensary and Hosp., Boston; trustee of Coll. of Physicians and Surgeons. Home: 22 Jones Av., Dorchester 24, Mass. Office: 517 Shawmut Av., Boston 18. Died Oct. 13, 1957; buried Russell Mountain Cemetery, Russell, Mass.

SHUTE, Nevil (Nevil Shute Norway) (shōōt'), author, airplane engr.; b. Ealing, Middlesex, England, Jan. 17, 1899; s. Arthur Hamilton Norway; student Shrewsbury Sch., 1913-16, Balliol Coll., Oxford U., 1921-22 (B.A. in Engring.). Began career as aeronautical designer and engr. with De Havilland Aircraft Co., 1922-24; chief calculator with Airship Guarantee Co., 1924-28, dep. chief engr., 1928-30; mng. dir. Airspeed Ltd., airplanes, 1930-38; first novels pub. 1926. Served as private Suffolk Regt. (inf.), 1918; lt. comdr. Royal Naval Vol. Reserve, 1940-44. Fellow Royal Aero. Soc. Mem. Church of England. Clubs: Oxford and Cambridge (London); also various yacht clubs. Author: Lonely Road, 1930; Kindling, 1938; Ordeal, 1939; Old Captivity, 1940; Landfall, A Channel Story, 1941; Pied Piper, 1942; Pastoral, 1943; Most Secret, 1945; The Chequer Board, 1947; No Highway, 1948; The Legacy, 1950; Round the Bend, 1951; The Far Country, 1952; In the Wet, 1953; Slide Rule, 1954; The Breaking Wave, 1955; Beyond the Black Stump, 1956; On the Beach, 1957; The Rainbow and the Rose, 1958. Home: Langwarrin, Victoria, Australia. Died Jan. 12, 1960.

SIAS, Ernest J. (sī'ȧs), aviation school president; born at Fontanelle, Ia.; son of Jeremiah and Emma

(Aspinwall) S.; student Drake U., Des Moines, Iowa, 1901-02; A.B. Cotner Univ., Lincoln, Nebraska, 1907; m. Alma Demarest; 1 dau., Margaret (Mrs. Wendell Harding). Minister First Christian Ch., Frankfort, Ind., 1907-10; Chautauqua and lyceum lecturer (lectured in 2500 towns), 1910-19; founded Lincoln (Neb.) Airplane and Flying Sch., 1920, and Lincoln Aeronautical Inst., 1935; pres. of both schools which were approved by U.S. Civil Aeronautics Adminstrn. and contractors to U.S. Army Air Forces Training Comd. for training students in aviation; president, Union Air Terminal, Lincoln, Nebraska. Recipient Certificate of Service Award, World War II. Mem. Nat. Aero. Assn. Nat. Aviation Training Assn., Inst. Aero. Sciences, Neb. Hist. Soc., Internat. Lyceum Assn. (charger mem.), Lincoln Chamber of Commerce. Republican. Mason. Clubs: University, Farmers, Lincoln Dinner, Country (Lincoln). Extensively engaged in mod. agr., stock raising, promotion soil conservation. Home: 2645 Van Dorn St. Office: Union Air Terminal, Lincoln, Neb. Died Oct. 4, 1955; buried Grant Evergreen Cemetery, Talmage, Neb.

SIBELIUS, Jean Julius Christian (sĭ-bā'lĭ-ōōs), Finnish composer; b. Hämeenlinna, Finland, Dec. 8, 1865; ed. Berlin, Vienna; hon. prof., dr., Helsinki, Oxford, Yale and Heidelberg Univs.; studied law, U. of Helsinki; studied music with Martin Wegelius; grad. conservatory in Helsingfors, 1889; also studied under Albert Becker and in Vienna under Robert Fuchs and Karl Goldmark; hon. degree, Yale U., 1914; m. Aino Järnefelt. Taught in music conservatory, several yrs.; awarded govt. pension, 1897, and concertized in Europe and U.S.; conducted 4th symphony at Birmingham Festival in England, 1912; composed "Kullervo," a symphonic poem based upon the Kalevala, set for solos, chorus and orchestra and performed in Helsinki, 1892; works include seven symphonies, violin concerto, Saga, Karelia, Lemminkäinen, Finlandia, Valse Triste, Pelleas and Melisande, Luonnotar, Oceanides, Tapiola and other orchestral works; Voces Intimae, Malicnonia and other chamber music; about 200 pianoforte compositions, songs, etc. Hon. mem. Royal Acad. of Music (London), Royal Philharmonic Soc., New York Nat. Soc. of Music, Santa Cecilia Acad., Rome, Franz Liszt-Gesellschaft, Weimar; corr. mem. Acad. des Beaux-Arts, Paris; Akademie der Freien Künste, Berlin; Comitato del Congresso Intern di Musica, Rome; Royal Swedish Acad. Music, etc. Address: Järvenpää, Finland. Died Sept. 20, 1957.

SIBLEY, Frank J., mining engr.; b. Royalton, N.Y., Aug. 11, 1847; s. Jonathan and Ruhamah (James) S.; ed. high schs., with post-grad. courses in sci. and engring.; m. Alice F. Barney, 1866; 2d, Mrs. Mary Charlton Edholm, Sept. 28, 1905. Pres., gen. mgr. Copper Creek (Ariz.) Mining Co.; gen. mgr. Minn.-Ariz. Copper Co. For more than 30 yrs. prominent leader in temperance and prohibtion work. Sec. State Prohibition Com., N.Y., 1876-77, Kan., 1880; Grand Chief Templar, Good Templars of Neb., 1881-86, Ga., 1893-97; chmn. State Prohibition Com. of Cal., 1900; founded several newspapers. Author: What Prohibition Did for Kansas, 1886; Life of John B. Finch, 1888; Templar at work, 1890. Home: Copper Creek, Ariz. Office: 5 Broad St., N.Y.C. Deceased.

SIBLEY, Harper, agriculturalist; b. N.Y.C., Apr. 5, 1885; s. Hiram W. and Margaret (Harper) S.; student Groton (Mass.) Sch., 1898-1903; A.B., Harvard, 1907; LL.B., N.Y. Law Sch., 1909; LL.D., Hobart Coll., 1936; L.H.D., George Williams Coll., 1950; m. Georgiana Farr, June 10, 1908; children—Hiram, Georgiana Sibley Hardy, Anne Sibley Cannon, Elizabeth Sibley Gonzalez, Jane Sibley Auchincloss, Harper, Jr. Dir. Security Trust Co., Rochester; dir. Rochester Savings Bank, N.Y. Life Ins. Co., Western Union Telegraph Co. Operated Sibley Farms, Ill., Mission Ranch, Rancho Marino, Cal., Sibleyville Farms, N.Y. Former pres. C. of C. of U.S., Rochester C. of C. and Rochester Y.M.C.A., Rochester Community Chest, National U.S.O., president Rochester Dental Dispensary; pres. U.S. Com. for Refugees. Trustee Carnegie Endowment for Internat. Peace, U. Rochester, Genesse Hosp., Meml. Art Gallery; past pres. nat. coun. Y.M.C.A.; pres. Church World Service Clubs: Genesee Valley, Rochester Country. Address: 400 East Av., Rochester, N.Y. Died Apr. 24, 1959; Santa Barbara, Cal.

SIBLEY, Robert, engineer, editor; b. Round Mountain, Ala., Mar. 28, 1881; s. Robert Pendleton and Susie (Bolling) S.; B.Sc., Coll. of Mechanics, U. of Calif., 1903, E.E., 1922; grad. work under Harris J. Ryan and Dexter S. Kimball, Stanford, 1930; m. Catharine Stone, Sept. 8, 1904 (died May 29, 1942); 1 daughter, Catharine Sibley Oakes; m. 2d, Carol Rhodes Johnston, December 6, 1943. Chief electrical engineer, Mariposa Commercial & Mining Company, Jan.-Sept. 1903; professor mechanical engineering, U. of Mont., 1903-04, mech. and elec. engring., 1904-07, dean Sch. of Engring., 1903-07; in practice in Mont., as consultant for Chicago, Milwaukee & St. Paul, Bunker Hill and Sullivan mines and other corps., 1907-11; asso. prof. mech. engring., 1911-12, prof. until July 1, 1915, U. of Calif. Pacific Coast editor Electrical World and Electrical Merchandising and editor Journal Electricity, 1919-22; editor Journal of Electricity and Western Industry and pres. McGraw-Hill Co., of Calif., 1919-22; Pacific Coast consultant, McGraw-Hill Co. since 1923. Exec. mgr. Calif. Alumni Assn. since 1923; pres. Fidelity Acceptance Corp. since 1927; dir. Am. Alumni Council since 1939 (pres. 1942-44), chmn. bd. dirs. Bank of Berkeley since 1944. Chmn. bd. dirs. East Bay Regional Parks since 1948. Del. World Power Conf., London, 1924. Fellow Am. Inst. Elec. Engrs., A.S.M.E; mem Delta Upsilon, Phi Beta Kappa, Sigma Xi, Tau Beta Pi, Golden Bear Soc. Mason (K.T., Shriner). Clubs: Bohemian, Commonwealth, Engineers (San Francisco); Faculty (U. of Calif.); Claremont Country (Oakland). Author: A Primer of Applied Thermodynamics: Elements of Fuel Oil and Steam Engineering (with C. H. Delany), 1918; Research Statistics on Undeveloped Water Power Resources of the U.S.; America's Answer to the Russian Challenge, 1931. Editor: Romance of the University of California, 1928, 33; Golden Book of California, 1936; Folio of California Wildflowers, 1939; Folio of The Seasons of California, 1940; Folio Birds of California, 1944, (Coauthor with Carol Sibley) A Treasury of Tradition, Lore and Laughter, 1952. Home: 1777 Leroy. Office: 2333 Shaftuck Av., Berkeley 4, Cal. Died July 22, 1958.

SIBLEY, Samuel Hale, judge; b. Union Point, Ga., July 2, 1873; s. Samuel Hale and Jennie (Hart) S.; A.B., U. Ga., 1892, LL.B., 1893, LL.D., 1925; LL.D. from Oglethorpe U., Atlanta, 1934; m. Florence Weldon Hart, Apr. 29, 1897; children—William Hart, Sara Virginia, Florence Weldon. Began practice at Union Point, 1893; county judge, Greene County Court, 1905-12; judge City Court, Greensboro, 1912-17; dist. atty. Ga. R.R., 1917-19; U.S. dist. judge, No. Dist. of Ga., 1919-31; judge U.S. Circuit Court of Appeals, 5th Circuit, 1931-49; ret. Mem. Chi Phi, Phi Beta Kappa, Alumni Soc. U. Ga. (pres. 1924, trustee 1925-33). Democrat. Presbyn. Moderator Gen. Assembly Presbyn. Ch. in U.S., 1934. Home: Marietta, Ga. Died Oct. 13, 1958; buried Magnolia Cemetery, Augusta, Ga.

SIDAROUSS, Pasha (Sesostris), Egyptian diplomatist; b. Alexandira, Egypt, Jan. 8, 1873; s. Stephen and Galila (Camel-Toueg) S.; ed. St. Andrew's Scotch Sch. and Jesuit Coll., Alexandria; studied law in Cairo and Paris; grad. U. Paris (1st prize in civ. law competition), 1895, LL.D., 1906; m. Clotilde Ghali-Pasha, 1903 (died 1922); 3 children. Began practice at Alexandria; successively pvt. sec. to British judicial adviser, sec. to com. of judicial serveillance of Ministry of Justice, prof. civil law, v. prin. Royal Sch. of Law at Cairo, judge Mixed Court; joined Diplomatic Service, 1923; promoted through grades to minister to Athens and Belgrade, 1929, to Brussels and The Hague, 1930; with mission in London, 1930-31; E.E. and M.P. to U.S., May 25, 1931—. Awarded many honors by Egypt and other countries; created Pasha, 1930. Author or translator books and articles pertainibg to Egypt and the Ottoman Empire; speaks and writes several languages. Clubs: Metropolitan, Chevy Chase, Racquet (Washington), etc. Address: Egyptian Legation, 2301 Massachusetts Av., Washington, D.C. Deceased.

SIDGREAVES, Sir Arthur F., business exec.; b. 1882. Mng. dir. Rolls-Royce, Ltd., 1929—. Maj. R.A.F., 1914-18. Address: Nightingale Rd., Derby, Eng. Died 1946.*

SIDLEY, William Pratt, lawyer; b. Chgo., Jan. 30, 1868; s. William Kirby and Mary Frances (Pratt) S.; A.B., Williams Coll., 1889; LL.B., Union Coll. of Law, Chgo., 1891; student Harvard Law Sch., M.A., Harvard, 1892; m. Elaine Dupee, June 14, 1899; 1 son, William Dupee. Began practice at Chgo., 1891; now mem. Sidley, Austin, Burgess & Smith; former dir. Harris Trust & Savings Bank. Pres. Chgo. Y.M.C.A., 1911; pres. bd. trustees, 1944-48. Former trustee Williams Coll.; trustee Newberry Library. Mem. Chgo. Bar Assn. (pres. 1930-31). Art Inst. Chgo. (gov. mem.). Republican. Ref. Episcopalian. Clubs: Chicago, Commercial, University, Union League, Mid-Day (Chgo.); University (N.Y.); Indian Hill (Winnetka, Ill.). Home: 739 Humboldt Av., Winnetka, Ill. Office: 11 S. LaSalle St., Chgo. Died Apr. 25, 1958; buried Christ Ch. Cemetery, Winnetka, Ill.

SIDLO, Thomas L. (sĭd'lō), lawyer; b. Cleveland, O., Mar. 10, 1888; s. Thomas and Anna Sidlo; student U. Wis., 1906, 07, 08; A.B., Western Res. U., 1909, A.M., 1910, LL.B., 1912, HH.D. (honorary), 1952; married Winifred Morgan, June 27, 1914 (deceased Mar. 11, 1932); m. Elisabeth Avery, June 22, 1935. Asst. street ry. commr. and commr. franchises, Cleve., 1912-13, commr. information and publicity, 1913, dir. pub. service, 1914-15; mem. and sec. city planning commn., 1914-15; mem. power arbitration bd., 1916; counsel, traction arbitration, 1919; partner Baker, Hostetler & Sidlo, later Baker, Hostetler, Sidlo & Patterson, 1916-38; financial dir., controller and gen. counsel Scripps-Howard Newspapers, United Press Assn., Newspaper Enterprise Association. First chairman Friends of Cleveland Orchestra; dir. Metropolitan Opera Assn.; chairman Northern Ohio Assn.; pres. Musical Arts Association; fellow Order of Plum Blossom, China. Past pres., trustee Cleve. Mus. Nat. Hist., Cleve. Inst. Music; past chmn. Cleveland Regional Com., United China Relief; chmn. Cleveland Civil Defense Found.; trustee Newton D. Baker Memorial Fund. Recipient distinguished service award, Community Fund, 1945, gold medal C. of C., Cleve. 1952. Member Am., Ohio and Cleveland bar assns., Am. Judicature Society (director), Council on Foreign Relations (N.Y.), A.A.A.S., Am. Acad. of Polit. and Social Science, American Sociological Society, American Museum Natural History, Fgn. Policy Assn., Adult Edn. Assn., Am. Hygiene Assn., Nat. Econ. League, Cleveland C. of C., Citizens League, Museum of Art, Western Reserve Hist. Soc., Alpha Delta Phi, Phi Delta Phi, Delta Sigma Rho. Clubs: Union, Fifty, Mid-Day, Professional Men's (first pres.), Alpha Delta Phi of New York (life). Home: 12574 Cedar Rd., Cleveland Heights 6. Office: Union Commerce Bldg., Cleve. 14, Ohio. Died May 27, 1955; buried Lakeview Cemetery, Cleve.

SIDO, George Henry (sē'dō), ry. official; b. Edwardsville, Ill., June 20, 1887; s. Fred Cornelius and Katherine Angela (Bange) S.; ed. high sch. and Rankin Training Sch.; m. Sarah Ruth Tanner, Apr. 26, 1916; children—James Harry, George Robert. Clerk Wabash Ry., St. Louis, 1904, chief yard clerk, 1905-07, chief car clerk, 1907-11; chief clerk to supt. S.P. Ry., Houston, and San Antonio, 1911-12; Trainman Wabash, Moberly, Mo., 1913; chief clerk to superintendent of transportation T.& P. R.R., Dallas, 1914-16, trainmaster, 1916-18; chief clerk to pres. Wabash Ry., St. Louis, 1918-20, supt. transportation, 1920-26; gen. mgr. Ann Arbor R.R., Toledo, 1926-29; gen. mgr. Wabash Ry., St. Louis, 1929-37, chief operating officer and gen. mgr., 1937-41, v.p. and gen. mgr. since 1942; vice-pres. and gen. mgr. Ann Arbor R.R. Co.; gen. mgr. Manistique & Lake Superior R.R. Co., N.J., Ind. & Ill. R.R. Co., Lake Erie & Ft. Wayne R.R. Co.; dir. Wabash R.R., Ann Arbor R.R., N.J. R.R., Des Moines Union R.R., Ft. Wayne Union R.R., M.L.S. R.R., M. St. Paul R.R., Det. Western R.R., Wabash Motor Trasit. Presbyn. Mason. Clubs: Glen Echo, Noonday (St. Louis). Home: 7143 Kingsbury. Office: Ry. Exchange Bldg., St. Louis. Died Mar. 30, 1955; buried Oak Grove Meml. Mausoleum.

SIECK, Louis John (sek), seminary pres.; born Erie, Pa., Mar. 11, 1884; s. Henry and Pauline (Stutz) S.; student St. John's Coll., Winfield, Kan.; 1894-95, Concordia Coll., Milwaukee, 1895-1901; grad. Concordia Theol. Sem., St. Louis, 1904, D.D. (hon.), 1939; m. Ottilie Obermeyer, Sept. 21, 1905; children—Lewis William, Charles Arthur. Ordained to ministry of Luth. Ch., Sept. 11, 1904; asst. pastor Hamburg, Minn., 1904-05; asst. pastor Zion Ch., St. Louis, 1905-14, pastor, 1914-43; pres. Concordia Theol. Sem. 1943-52, mem. bd. control 1923-52, chmn. 1939-43; mem. and chmn. bd. dir. Sta. KFUO, Clayton, Mo. Mem. bd. dirs. Valparaiso U., 11 yrs. Chmn. Nat. Adv. Emergency Planning Council Luth. Ch., Mo. Synod; mem. Luth. Publicity Orgn. (organizer and pres. 21 yrs.), St. Louis Pastoral Conf. (pres. 24 yrs.). Mem., Acad. Polit. Sci.; Am. Acad. Polit. and Social Sci., Concordia Hist. Inst. (charter mem.), St. Louis City Mission Soc. (pres. 10 yrs.), State Hist. Soc. Mo. (v.p.), Mo. Social Hygiene Assn., Community Chest Greater St. Louis (bd. dirs.). Club: Mo. Athletic. Author: The Glory of Golgotha (with William C. Burhon), 1944. Contbr. sermons to Concordia Pulpit. Address: 13 S. Seminary Terrace, Clayton 5, Mo. Died Oct. 14, 1952; buried New Bethlehem Cemetery, St.L.

SIEGEL, David Porter (sē'g'l), lawyer; b. New York, N.Y., Sept. 16, 1895; s. Kive and Leah S.; grad. DeWitt Clinton High Sch., 1913; LL.B., N.Y. Law Sch., 1917; m. Rose Jelin, June 28, 1921; children—Kippy, Claire. Admitted to N.Y. bar; was asst. U.S. dist. atty., then chief asst.; now in practice alone, N.Y. City. Mem. Am. Bar Assn., N.Y. County Lawyers Assn., Assn. Bar City of N.Y. Republican. Jewish religion. K.P. Home: 171 W. 57th St. Office: 11 W. 42d St., N.Y.C. Died June 17, 1958; buried Union Field Cemetery, Bklyn.

SIEGEL, David Tevel, mfr.; b. Chgo., Jan. 11, 1896; s. Gershon and Fannie (Freid) S.; B.S., Ill. Inst. Tech., 1925; m. Dorothy B. Haas, Apr. 16, 1931; children—Judith H. (Mrs. Kenneth M. Arenberg), Daniel G. Draftsman, designer Thomas Elevator Co., 1911-17; sales engr. Foster Machine Co., 1919-22; founder, 1925, since pres. Ohmite Mfg. Co. Trustee Ill. Inst. Tech. Served as lt. (j.g.) USN, 1917-19. Mem. Am. Inst. E.E., Inst. Radio Engrs. Club: Standard (Chgo.). Home: 125 Beach Rd., Glencoe, Ill. Office: 3601 Howard St., Skokie, Ill. Died Mar. 8, 1957.

SIEGRIST, Mary (sē'grist), author; b. Jonestown, Pa.; d. Uriah Bowman and Katharine (Dohner) Siegrist; grad. Millersville (Pa.) Normal Coll.; B.S., Teachers Coll., Columbia, 1912, grad. student, 1912-14; m. Myron Townsend, Apr. 1925. Teacher, Lebanon (Pa.), N.Y. City schs., N.Y. Collegiate Inst. (English and Latin) 1913-17. Master Inst. of United Arts, 1925-34; began newspaper writing 1918; wrote column Candle in the Corner, New York Globe, 1919-

21; art editor The Sun, writing Studio and Gallery, 1920-21; free-lance writer N.Y. Times, Forum, Literary Digest; associate editor The Archer Art Magazine; associate editor World Unity Mag.; teacher of poetry and literature, Master Institute, Roerich Museum, 1925-35; book editor the Benevian Ray (magazine); corr. critic for several indusl. firms. Social service work Atlantic Div., Am. Red Cross, 1919. Mem. Fed. Human Rights, Anti-Vivisection Soc., Poetry Soc. Am. (life), World Fellowship of Faiths, Mus. of Nat. History, Yosians-Nature Soc. Group. Mem. Poetry Soc. (London), United World Movement (delegate to UNESCO, Hunter Coll., Dec., 1951), Emergency Conf. (on panel bd.) to Save the Jewish People of Europe (1943-44). Artists of Carnegie Hall, Inc. Poetry award, Jedediah Tingle (Harmon Foundn.); awarded prize World's Fair Anthology of Verse for poem, World Disarmament. Club: Woman's Press (N.Y.; poet laureate). Author: You That Come After, 1927; Sentinel, 1928; Hudson River Boats (children's poems), 1939; Flame Rises on the Mountain, 1943. Translator: Flame in Chalice (from Russian by Nicholas Roerich), 1929; Back to the Nameless One (from German by Friedrich Kettner), 1934. Co-author: Himalaya, 1929. Compiler: The New Humanity (anthology), 1928. Editor and columnist, United World Mag.; contbr. Arts and Decoration, Poetry Review (London), Biosophical Review, Internat. Blue Book, Ency. Am. Biography. Represented in various anthologies, including Principal Poets of the World. Radio recitalist. Poem, The Ongoing, used by British Broadcasting Corp. in "All India" program; also included in anthologies, etc.; poetry set to music by Prof. Charles Haubiel, Dr. Gustave Becker, and other composers. Painting exhbd. Carnegie Art Gallery, since 1945. Address: Carnegie Hall Studios, N.Y.C. 19. Died Mar. 1953.

SIELAFF, Gustav Julius, geologist; b. Gold Hill, Nev., June 18, 1878; s. August Julius Emil and Alwine Augusta (Lietz) S.; B.S., Sch. of Mines, U. Nev., 1900; m. Villa May McDonald, Apr. 15, 1916; 1 dau., Alwine Lorraine. Miner and assayer, Virginia City, Nev., 1900-02; assayer and mill foreman, Abangarez Gold Fields, Costa Rica, 1902-03; gen. mgr. Boston Mines Co., Costa Rica, 1903-05; cons. engr., Reno, Nev., 1906-12; supt. Gongolona & Boston Mines, Costa Rica, 1912-13; gen. mgr. Abangarez Gold Fields, 1914-15; with Southern Pacific Co., 1919-48, chief geologist, 1925-48. Served as capt. Engr. Corps, U.S.A., World War; capt. Chem. Warfare Service, 1919. Mem. Am. Inst. Mining and Metall. Engrs., Seismol. Soc. Am. Republican. Mason (K.T., Shriner). Club: Engineers (San Francisco). Home: 2045 University Av., Berkeley, Calif. Office: 65 Market St., San Francisco. Died Sept. 21, 1956.

SIEMONN, George, composer, pianist, former orchestra dir.; b. Balt., Feb. 12, 1874; s. William Henry and Margaret (Smith) S.; diploma in composition Peabody Conservatory of Music, 1906; m. Mabel Garrison (soprano), June 10, 1908. Violinist, Peabody Symphony Orchestra, 1888-93; taught harmony and composition, Peabody Conservatory of Music, 1903-13; organist, 1905-12; accompanist for wife, 1914-29; conductor Baltimore Symphony Orchestra, 1930-35. Home: Ezesur-mer, France. Died Nov. 21, 1952.

SIEVERS, Fred John (sē'vērz), experiment station dir., agronomist; b. North Milwaukee, Wis., Oct. 1, 1880; s. William and Elizabeth (Oelhafen) S.; B.S. in Agr., U. of Wis., 1910, M.S., 1922; m. Emma C. Behnke, June 12, 1907; children—Jeanette D., Howard R., Frederick J. Instr. soils, U. of Wis., 1909-12; prof. agronomy, Milwaukee County Sch. of Agr. and Domestic Economy, Wauwatosa, Wis., 1912-13, supt., 1913-17; prof. soils, State Coll. of Wash., 1917-28; dir. Mass. Agrl. Expt. Sta. since 1928, also director Grad. Sch., University of Mass., since 1930. Mem. and vice-pres. trustees Cooley-Dickenson Hospital, Northampton, Mass., since 1937. Fellow A.A.A.S.; mem. American Society Agronomy (pres. Pacific sect. 1923-24), Am. Assn. Univ. Profs., Internat. Farm Congress, Internat. Soc. of Soil Science, Am. Soil Survey Assn., Theta Chi, Sigma Xi, Alpha Zeta, Phi Kappa Phi. Conglist. Clubs: Rotary, Amherst Club, Amherst Golf. Author numerous papers on agrl. topics. Home: 100 Fearing St., Amherst, Mass. Died Dec. 25, 1952.

SIGALL, Joseph de, portrait painter; b. Brodi, Poland, May 18, 1892; s. Simon and Martha (Braun) S.; student Lemberg Gymnasium, 1902-09, Imperial and Royal Art Acad., Vienna, 1909-13 (gold medal), Royal Art Acad., Munich, 1913-14; faculty of medicine Vienna U., 1910-13; M.D., (hon.), U. of S.D., 1926; LL.D., Santa Clara (Cal.) Coll., 1934; A.F.D., U. So. Cal., 1934; Litt.D., Webster U., 1935; Ph.D., Universite Philotechnique, Belgium, 1935; Sc. D., Andhra Research U. of India, 1936; m. Mary Stauffer, Sept. 13, 1929 (div. 1933); 1 dau., Mary. Came to U.S., 1922. Began as portrait painter, 1914; painted Emperor Francis Joseph, and Emperor Karl, of Austria, Emperor William of Germany, Admiral Horty (Regent of Hungary), Grand Duke Kirill of Russia, Marcello de Alvear (President of Argentina), President and Mrs. Coolidge, and President and Mrs. Hoover, the mems. of Pres. Hoover's Cabinet and their wives, Senator Phelan and Senator McAdoo of Cal., Archbishop Hanna, Helen Wills Moody, Dr. Ray Lyman Wilbur, mems. of the Chrysler, Stotesbury and Vanderbilt families, and many others in America. Society portrait painter, never sending any portraits to any exhibits in America. Served as capt. 4th Lancer Regt., Austro-Hungarian Army, World War, wounded 3 times; later attached to Marshal Pilsudsky, Poland. Decorated Grand Croix of St. Anna (Russia); Comdr. Constantin de St. Georges; Knight of Franz-Josef of Austria; Iron Crown (Austria); Iron Cross, 1st and 2d class (Germany). Mem. Academie Latine, Arts et Belles Lettres (France), Academia Hispano Americano (Spain), Institut Heraldique de France, Geog. Soc. (Portugal); La Chevalerie, Academia Pontificia Tiberina (Rome); fellow and hon. prof. U. of India. Hon. vice consul of Peru at San Francisco, 1927-34. Home: Saratoga, Cal. Died Sept. 16, 1953.

SIGERIST, Henry Ernest (sĭ'gĕ-rist), med. historian; b. Paris, France, Apr. 7, 1891; s. Ernest Henry and Emma (Wiskemann) S.; student Gymnasium, Zurich, Switzerland, 1904-10, Univ. Coll., London, 1911, Univ. of Zurich, 1912-13, 1915-17, Univ. of Munich, Germany, 1914; M.D., Univ. of Zurich, 1917; D. honoris causa, Univ. of Madrid, 1935; D.Litt., Univ. of the Witwatersrand, 1939; LL.D., Queens Univ., Kingston, Ont., 1941; D.Sc., University of London, England, 1953; married Emmy M. Escher, Sept. 14, 1916; children—Erica Elizabeth, Nora Beate. Came to U.S., 1931. Lecturer history of medicine, U. of Zurich, 1921 to 1923, prof., 1924; prof. history of medicine, U. of Leipzig, Germany, 1925-32; prof. and director of Institute of the History of Medicine, Johns Hopkins University, 1932-47; research associate, Yale University, since 1947; in Switzerland since July 1947; Dwight H. Terry lecturer, Yale, 1938; South African Universities' lecturer, 1939; Messenger lecturer, Cornell, 1940; Heath Clark lecturer, Univ. of London, 1952. Chairman Saskatchewan Health Services Survey Commn., 1944; adviser to Govt. of India, Health Survey and Development Com., 1944. Fellow A.A.A.S. (v.p. sec. L, 1943), Royal Coll. Physicians; corr. fellow Mediaeval Acad. of Am.; hon. fellow Am. Pub. Health Assn., Acad. Med. of Mexico, N.Y. Acad. Med.; mem. American Acad. of Arts and Sciences, International Academy Hist. of Science (Paris), Internat. Soc. History of Medicine (vice pres. since 1938), Am. Assn. History of Medicine (pres. 1937), Am. Philos. Soc., History of Science Society (president 1939-40), Kaiserl. Deutsche Akademie der Naturforscher (Halle), Alpha Kappa Kappa, Delta Omega, Alpha Omega Alpha; correspondent mem. Royal Soc. Medicine of Budapest; Rudolf Virchow Med. Soc. of New York; Soc. of History and Geography of Guatemala; Soc. Paulista de Historia da Medicina, Sao Paulo; hon. mem. Royal Soc. Med. (London), Swiss, Rumanian, Greek, Yugoslavia, Peru, Argentine, Brazil, Dutch, Chinese socs. med. hist., Soc. Med. Hist. N.Y. (hon. pres.); Sect. Med. Hist. Acad. Med. of Richmond, Va., Medical Hist. Society of Tulane University. Awarded Karl Sudhoff medal, 1933; William H. Welch Medal, 1951. Clubs: Tudor and Stuart. Author: Studien and Texte zur fruhmittelalterlichen Rezeptliteratur, 1923; Ambroise Paré, Die Behandlung der Schusswunden, 1923; The Book of Cirurgia of Hieronymus Brunschwig, 1923; Albrecht von Hallers Briefe an Johannes Gesner, 1923; Antike Heilkunde, 1927; Pseudo-Apulei Herbarius (with Ernst Howald), 1927; Man and Medicine (transl. into 7 langs.), 1932; The Great Doctors (German 1932, Spanish 1949), 1933; American Medicine, 1934 (German 1933); Socialized Medicine in the Soviet Union, 1937 (Spanish 1944); Medicine and Human Welfare, 1941 (Spanish 1943.(: Civilization and Disease, 1943 (Spanish 1946); The Earliest Printed Book on Wine, 1943; The University at the Crossroads, 1946 (Chinese edition, 1949); Medicine and Health in the Soviet Union, 1947; A History of Medicine, Volume I, 1951; Letters of Jean DeCarro, 1950; Landmarks in the History of Hygiene, 1956. Editor of many volumes, reports and bulls of fgn. univs.; editor, Bulletin of History of Medicine, 1933-47; pubs. Inst. of History of Med., 1934-47; Am. Review of Soviet Medicine, 1943-48. Address: Casa Serena, Pura, Ticino, Switzerland. Died Mar. 17, 1957; buried Zurich, Switzerland.

SIGLER, Thomas Amon, veterinarian; b. Clinton Township, Putnam County, Ind., Sept. 15, 1879; s. Abner and Artemisia (Cromwell) S.; V.S., Ind. Veterinary Coll., Indpls., 1902; D.V.M., Terre Haute (Ind.) Veterinary Coll., 1912; m. Florence Helen Hughes, July 9, 1932. Began practice at Greencastle, Ind., 1902; prof. animal surgery and restraint, Terre Haute Veterinary Coll., 1909-15; prof. parasitology, Ind. Veterinary Coll., 1911-24; asst. state veterinarian for Ind., 1914-18, fed. appraiser during foot and mouth epidemic, 1914; lectures at state assns., veterinary and agrl. schs. and demonstrates animal surgery at clinics; judge at fairs and horse shows. Mem. State Bd. Veterinary Med. Examiners, 1913-14, 1934; mem. bd. mgrs. Horse and Mule Assn. Am., 1928—; mem. organizing com. 12th Internat. Veterinary Congress, 1934. Trustee Putnam County Hosp., Greencastle, 1932-44, pres. of bd., 1938—. Pres. Nat. Veteran Practitioners Assn., 1942. Mem. Ind. State Vet. Assn. (pres. 1911-12), Ind. State Draft Horse Breeders Assn. (pres. 1923-24), Am. Veterinary Med. Assn. (pres. 1926-27), U.S. Livestock San. Assn., Ind. Soc. Chgo., Soc. Ind. Pioneers; hon. mem. Miss. Vet. Med. Assn., Louisana State Veteran Med. Assn., Alpha Psi. Mason (32°). Democrat (county chmn., 1930-34). Contbr. articles to North Am. Veterinarian and Veterinary Medicine. Apptd. col. on staff of gov. of Ky., 1942. Home: 205 W. Poplar St., Greencastle, Ind. Died June 24, 1957; buried Forest Hill Cemetery, Greencastle, Ind.

SIGNER, Merton I., educator; b. Tonica, Ill., Oct. 25, 1900; s. Ira Grant and Mary (Billings) S.; B.S., Mo. Sch. of Mines, 1923, M.E., 1934; m. Ruth Tresidder, Aug. 20, 1922; children—Merton I., Mary Anne. Mining engr., Princeton Gold Mines, 1922-23; with Ill. Highway Dept., 1924-26, Original M & M Co., 1926-29; instr. Colo. Sch. Mines, Golden, Colo., 1929-32, asst. prof., 1932-36, asso. prof., 1936-43, prof. of mining, 1943-47, dean of the faculty since 1947. Mem. Colo. State Planning Commn. Mem. Am. Inst. Mining and Metall. Engrs., Am. Soc. Engr. Edn., Blue Key, Pi Kappa Alpha, Theta Tau. Mason. Club: University. Home: 950 15th St., Golden, Colo. Died Nov. 17, 1956.

SILKNITTER, G. F., business exec.; b. Centerville, Ia., Dec. 12, 1879; s. Benjamin Franklin and Sarah Elizabeth Silknitter; student pub. schs., Centerville, Ia.; m. Elizabeth Ellen Smith (dec.); children—Frances Elizabeth, Marian Marsden (Mrs. Charles Cunningham); m. 2d, Margaret Ellen Reilly, July 3, 1926; children—Sarah Ellen, George Franklin. Baggageman, C.B.&Q. Ry. Co., Centerville, Ia., 1896-98; timekeeper and clerk Swift & Co., Chgo., 1898-1902, auditor Portland, Ore. and Chicago, 1906-19; clerical work Ore. Ry. & Navigation Co., Portland, 1902-06; sec. Sioux City (Ia.) Stock Yards Co., 1919-25, pres., 1925—; pres. Sioux City Terminal Ry. Co., Ia. Rendering Co.; dir. Live Stock Nat. Bank. Mem. C. of C. Presbyn. Mason, Elk. Clubs: Country, Empire, Gun (Sioux City). Home: 2932 Jackson St. Office: 340 Exchange Bldg., Sioux City, Ia. Died Jan. 28, 1954.

SILL, Frederick Herbert, clergyman, educator; b. N.Y.C., Mar. 10, 1874; s. Thomas Henry and Jane Burges (Miller) S.; A.B., Columbia, 1894, Litt.D., 1924; B.D., Gen. Theol. Sem., 1898, S.T.D., 1928; D.D., Williams Coll., 1931; Litt.D., Rutgers U., 1935. Became deacon, 1898, priest, 1899, P.E. Ch.; curate Mt. Calvary Ch., Balt., 1898-1900; joined Order of the Holy Cross, 1900; founder and headmaster Kent Sch., 1906-41, secretary of corp., headmaster emeritus, 1941—. Founder, 1923, pres. bd. trustees, South Kent Sch., 1923-34. Mem. Alpha Delta Phi (pres. 1934-37). Club: Columbia University (N.Y.C.). Home: Kent, Conn. Died July 17, 1952; buried Kent Sch. Chapel Cemetery, Kent, Conn.

SILLS, Kenneth Charles Morton, ret. coll. pres.; b. Halifax, N.S., Dec. 5, 1879; s. Charles Morton and Elizabeth Head (Ketchum) S.; brought to U.S., 1880; A.B. summa cum laude, Bowdoin Coll., 1901, LL.D., 1934; A.M., Harvard, 1903; student Columbia, 1905-06; LL.D., U. Me., 1916, Bates Coll., 1918, Dartmouth, 1918, Colby Coll., 1920, Williams Coll., 1927, Dalhousie U., 1939, Yale, 1941, Tufts Coll., 1947, Amherst Coll., 1952; L.H.D. (hon.), Boston U., 1949; m. Edith Lansing Koon, Nov. 21, 1918. Asst. in English, Harvard, 1901-03; instr. English, classics, Bowdoin Coll., 1903-04; tutor English, Columbia, 1904-05; adj. prof. Latin, Bowdoin Coll., 1906-07, Winkley prof. Lat. lang., lit., 1907-46, dean, 1910-17, acting pres., 1917-18, pres., 1918-52, pres. emeritus, 1952—; dir. in pub. interest Boston Fed. Home Loan Bank. Mem. bd. vis., U.S. Naval Acad., 1917-21, 1934-35 (pres. bd., 1920-21, 1935); pub. mem. N.E. Regional War Labor Bd., 1943-45; dir. Me. Med. Center, Portland, 1954. Democratic candidate for U.S. Senator, Me., 1916; hon. chmn. adv. council, Me., 1954. Trustee Wellesley Coll., 1927-46 Worcester Acad., 1938-45, Waynflete Sch., 1939-54 (pres. bd. 1954), Athens Coll., Athens, Greece (chmn. 1944-46), Hebron Acad., 1952-54, Episcopal Theol. Sch., Carnegie Found. (mem. commn. survey higher edn. in Canadian Maritime Provinces, 1920-21; chmn. bd., 1939-41), World Peace Found.; pres. N.E. Assn. Colls. and Secondary Schs., 1926; chmn. Brunswick chpt. A.R.C., 1909-19 (fund chmn. Portland chpt., 1954; nat. vice chmn. campaign for members and funds, 1954). Recipient Bowdoin Prize, 1948; Special Award and Citation by Brunswick, Me. for distinguished service to community, 1952; citation for layman Episcopal Church of Me., 1954. Mem. Me. Hist. Soc. (pres. 1922-24), Phi Beta Kappa, Delta Kappa Epsilon (hon. nat. pres. 1929-30), Dante Soc., English Speaking Union (pres. 1954). Protestant Episcopalian (dep. to gen. conv., 12 sessions, 1910-52; del. World Conf., Lausanne, 1927, Edinburg, 1937, World Anglican Congress, Mpls., 1954; mem. Nat. Council, 1940-46). Clubs: Cumberland (Portland); Tavern, Harvard (Boston); Century, University (N.Y.); Rotary (Portland, Brunswick). Author: The First American and other poems, 1911; also reviews and various ednl. addresses. Home: 134 Vaughn St., Portland, Me. Died Nov. 15, 1954; buried Brunswick, Me.

SILSBY, Wilson, artist; b. Chicago, Ill., Oct. 7, 1883; s. Eugene Weston (inventor) and Mary Jane (Redenbaugh) S.; student Lyons Township (Ill.) High Sch., 1895-98; ed. private tutors France and England; 1 son (adopted), Clifford. Designer of stage and motion picture scenery and settings since 1903; art dir. First Nat. Pictures Corp., 1923-24, Fox Film Corp., 1925-26, Pathe Film Corp., 1914-15, Cyrus Williams Productions, 1920-21; art dir. for Harold Lloyd, 1915-17; tech. dir. Universal Pictures Corp., 1913-14, 1918. Represented by etchings in permanent exhbns. at Met. Museum of Art, Rockefeller Foundation (Paris), Art Inst. Chicago, Pa. Acad. of Fine Arts, Boston Museum of Fine Arts, New York Pub. Library, Pa. Museum of Art, Brooklyn Museum, Nelson Gallery (Kansas City), City Art Museum (St. Louis), Cincinnati Museum Assn., Cleveland Museum of Art, Museum of N.M., Oakland (Calif.) Art Gallery, N.J. State Museum, Denver Art Museum, Seattle Art Museum, Springfield (Mass.) Museum of Fine Arts, Fort Worth Museum of Art, Brooklyn (N.Y.) Library, Toledo Museum of Art. San Francisco Museum of Fine Arts, de Young Memorial Museum (San Francisco), Art Assn. of Indianapolis, John Herron Art Inst. Exhibited 64 etchings at Columbus (O.) Gallery of Fine Arts, 1939; exhbtd. Salon d' Automne and Soc. des Artistes Francais, Paris; 3 works acquired by Museo Nacional. Mexico City, 12 dry points acquired by Nat. Museums of Gt. Britain, 11 works in permanent collection of Musee d' Art Moderne, 75 etchings presented by Research Study Club to drs. and scientists over world, 1946. Etchings presented to Library of Congress through Nat. Gallery, 1941. 4 etchings, 1944, Edinburgh, Scotland Mod. Art Society, 3 etchings. Uffizi Gallery, Florence, Italy; The Mr. and Mrs. James Taylor of 83 Silsby etchings and dry-pointes acquired by the British National Gallery for the permanent print collection of the Victoria and Albert Museum, London, 1951. Inventor of the noground etching plate. Discovered the Silsby Mordant, 1941. Author: Etching Methods and Materials, 1943; Etchings and Dry-points of Wilson Silsby, 1945. Home: 14243 Greenleaf St., Sherman Oaks (L.A.), Cal. Died Jan. 17, 1952; buried Forest Lawn Meml. Park, Glendale, Cal.

SILVER, Ernest Leroy, coll. pres.; b. Salem, N.H., Sept. 29, 1876; s. Clinton Leroy and Paulina Clymelia (Ayer) S.; grad. Pinkerton Acad., 1894; B.Litt., Dartmouth, 1899, Pd.D. (hon.), 1924; m. Hattie May Plummer (dec. 1928); m. 2d, Gertrude I. Shaw, 1947. Supt. schs., Rochester, N.H., 1900-04, Portsmouth, 1905-09; prin. Pinkerton Acad., 1909-11; pres. Teachers Coll., Plymouth, N.H., 1911-46, pres. emeritus, 1946—. Mem. N.H. General Court, 1947. Progressive Republican. Mason. Home: Plymouth, N.H. Died Jan. 6, 1949.

SILVERMAN, David, editor; b. Mpls., Apr. 19, 1903; s. Joseph and Hinda (Kantor) S.; ed. Minn. pub. schs.; m. Esther Meshbesher, June 9, 1929; children—Charlotte Rolla, Helene Cecile. With Duluth News Tribune, 1922-24; with Mpls. Star, 1924—, mng. editor, 1934-56, asst. exec. editor, 1956—. Trustee Greater Mpls. Safety Council, Mem. Am. Soc. Newspaper Editors, Asso. Press Mng. Editors, Mpls. Aquatennial Assn., Mpls. Inst. Arts. Jewish religion. Mem. B'nai B'rith. Mason (32°, Shriner). Clubs: Optimist, Standard. Home: 1613 Penn Av. N. Office: 425 Portland Av., Mpls. Died July 14, 1959.

SIMKHOVITCH, Mary Melinda Kingsbury, social economist; b. Chestnut Hill, Mass., Sept. 8, 1867; d. Col. Isaac Franklin and Laura (Holmes) Kingsbury; A.B., Boston U., 1890, L.H.D., 1936; studied Radcliffe Coll., 1 yr.; fellowship from Women's Industrial and Ednl. Union, U. of Berlin, 1 year; Columbia, 1 yr.; L.H.D., N.Y.U., 1938; D.Sc., Colby Coll., 1938; LL.D., Smith Coll., 1951; m. Vladimir Gregorievitch Simkhovitch, Jan. 7, 1899; children—Stephen (dec.), Helena (Mrs. Frank Didisheim). Head worker at College Settlement, New York, Jan.-Nov. 1898, at Friendly Aid House, 1898-1902, Greenwich House, 1902-46, dir. emreitus, 1946—; adj. prof. social economy Barnard College (Columbia), 1907-10; asso. in social economy Tchrs. College (Columbis), 1910-13; lectr. N.Y. Sch. Social Work, 1912-15. Mem. bd. dirs. Nat. Public Housing Conf. Mem. Nat. Fedn. of Settlements, Phi Beta Kappa. Clubs: Cosmopolitan, Town Hall. Author: City Worker's World, 1917; Neighborhood, 1938; Group Life. Co-author of Quicksand, 1942; Here is Gods Plenty, 1949. Home: 27 Barrow St., N.Y.C. 14. Died Nov. 15, 1951; buried Robbinston, Me.

SIMKHOVITCH, Vladimir Gregorievitch, univ. prof.; b. Russia, 1874; Ph.D., Halle, 1898; m. Mary Melinda Kingsbury, Jan. 7, 1899. Prof. econ. history, Columbia, 1904. Interested in settlement work; trustee of Greenwich House, New York. Clubs: Century, Marshall Chess. Author: Marxism versus Socialism, 1913; Toward the Understanding of Jesus and Other Historical Essays, 1921. Contbr. "Approaches to History" in Political Science Quarterly, 1929-36. Has written in English, German and Russian on econ. subjects. Address: 27 Barrow St., New York, N.Y. Died Dec. 10, 1959.

SIMMONS, David Andrew, lawyer; b. Galveston, Tex., May 31, 1897; s. David Edward and Virgilia (Finlay) S.; student U. Texas, 1914-17, 1919-20, LL.B., 1920; LL.D., U. Montreal, 1945, Loyola U. of the South, 1945; m. Elizabeth Daggett, Sept. 7, 1921; children—Elizabeth (Mrs. Philip Masquelette), Andrea. Dep. U.S. marshal, South Tex., 1917, 1919; admitted to bar, Tex., 1919, Mo., 1922, U.S. Supreme Ct., 1925, Interstate Commerce Commn., 1935, U.S. Maritime Commn., 1940; mem. Simmons, Gilmer & Much (and predecessor firms) from 1924; asst. U.S. atty., 1920-22; 1st asst. atty. gen. of Texas, 1926-28; gen. counsel Port of Houston, 1931-49; master in chancery, U.S. Dist. Court, 1934-1934; pres. Old Fort Davis Co. Cons. U.S. delegation U.N. Conf., San Francisco, 1945, and on drafting U.N. charter. Dir. Houston Port and Traffic Bur. Vice chmn. com. on law and legislation Am. Assn. Port Authorities since 1937; mem. panel of arbitrators Inter-Am. Comml. Arbitration Commn. since 1942; mem. nat. adv. council Practising Law Inst. Recipient Freedoms Found. award, 1950, for mag. article, Man's Fundamental Right. Served as lt., Air Service, U.S. Army, 1918. Mem. Houston C. of C. (com. fgn. trade 1942), Am. Acad. Polit. and Social Sci., Am. Bar Assn. (mem. bd. govs. 1937-40, 44-46; mem. House of Delegates 1936-48; pres. 1944-45), Texas Bar Assn. (pres. 1937-38), Houston-Galveston Dist. Bar Assn. (pres. 1933), Am. Law Inst., Tex. Civil Judicial Council, 1937-43, Am. Judicature Soc. (dir. 1931-46, pres. 1940-44), Inter-Am. Bar Assn. (U.S. v.p. 1944-45), Selden Soc. England, Maritime Law Assn., Interstate Commerce Commn. Practitioners Assn., Houston Com. Fgn. Relations (chmn. 1945-46), Nat. Assn. Legal Aid Orgns. (v.p. 1944-45), (hon.) Canadian Bar Assn., Kappa Alpha, Phi Delta Phi. Democrat. Baptist (deacon). Founder, editor Texas Bar Journal, 1937-38; editor Houston Bar Journal, 1930-32; mem. bd. editors Am. Bar Assn. Journal, 1944-45. Contbr. to law journals. Legal adviser Houston Draft Bd. No. 4, 1942-43. Home: 4040 Meadow Lake Lane, Houston. Died Mar. 24, 1951; buried Greenwood Cemetery, Austin, Tex.

SIMMONS, Edward Henry Harriman, stock broker; b. Jersey City, Aug. 21, 1876; s. Charles Dewar and Cornelia Neilson (Harriman) S.; student Stevens Sch., Hoboken, N.J., Drisler Sch., N.Y.C., Columbia Coll. Phys. and Surg.; m. Caroline Comstock, May 15, 1901 (dec. 1920); m. 2d, Mrs. John Mayer, Oct. 4, 1929 (dec. June 1942). Clk. with T. J. Taylor & Co., investment bankers, 1898; clk. Guaranty Trust Co. and Smithers & Reimer, 1899-1900; mem. brokerage firm Rutter & Gross (now E. H. H. Simmons), 1900—; mem. N.Y. Stock Exchange, 1900—, v.p., 1921-24, pres., 1924-30, v.p., 1935. Episcopalian. Clubs: Union, National Golf, Country; Sagaponack (L.I.). Home: 812 Park Av. Office: 50 Broad St., N.Y.C. Died May 23, 1955.

SIMMONS, Geo(rge) Finlay, zoölogist; b. Sherman Tex., Oct. 25, 1895; s. David Edward and Virgilia Octavia (Finlay) S.; student Houston Law Sch., 1913-14, Rice Inst., Houston, 1915-16; B.A., U. Tex., 1921, M.A., 1922; Ph.D., U. Chgo., 1934; m. Armede Victoria Hatcher, Mar. 2, 1922; children—George Finlay II, Robert Macgregor. Was successively stenographer, sec., law clerk, 1913-15; feature writer Houston Post, 1912-15; reporter Houston Chronicle, 1916; sec. of police, Houston, 1916-17; asst. in gen. zoölogy U. Tex., 1919, asst. in comparative anatomy, 1919-21, instr. in zoölogy, 1921-22; asst. editor, later editor-in-chief Longhorn Mag., U. Tex., 1919-22; naturalist, 1921, 22, and chief dep. commr. Tex. Game Fish and Oyster Commn., 1923; sci. leader Blossom South Atlantic Expdn. of Cleve. Mus. Natural History, also capt. 3-masted exploring schooner Blossom, 1923-26; curator of ornithology, same museum, 1926-29; nat. lectr. Alber and affiliated bureaus, 1928-31; lectr. biol. scis. Cleve. Coll. of Western Reserve U., 1927-31; research in zoölogy Hull Zoöl. Lab., U. Chgo., 1931-34, 42-43; asst. prof. zoology Mont. State U., 1934-35, prof., 1936-43, pres., 1936-41; Ridgay fellow in zoology U. Chgo., 1943, also Ency. Brit. fellow in zoology, 1943-44; asst. prof. anatomy Loyola U. Sch. Medicine, 1943-48, asso. prof., 1948—; zoology adviser Ency. Brit., 1944—. Served as private Red Cross Ambulance Co. and Ambulance Corps, U.S. Army and as sergt., hosp. sergt., 2d lt., detachment comdr. and adj. Base Hosp. 130, 1917-18. Mem. A.A.A.S., Am. Ornithologists' Union, Am. Soc. Mammalogists, Am. Soc. Ichthyologists and Herpetologists, Cooper and Wilson ornithol. clubs, Sigma Xi, Phi Beta Kappa, Sigma Delta Chi, Sigma Upsilon, Phi Sigma, Phi Beta Pi, Phi Kappa Psi; hon. mem. Burroughs Nature Club, Can. Camp Fire Club, Sociedade do Oceanographia é Piscicultura do Brazil. Club: Explorers (N.Y.C.). Author: Birds of the Austin Region, 1926. Contbr. to mags. Home: 5424 S. University Av., Chgo. 15. Died July 19, 1955.

SIMMONS, James Stevens, univ. prof., dean, retired army officer; b. Newton, N.C., June 7, 1890; s. James Curtley and Angie Mary (Stevens) S.; B.S., Davidson (N.C.) Coll., 1911, hon. Sc.D., 1937; student Univ. of N.C., School of Medicine, 1911-13; M.D., Univ. of Pa., 1915; grad. Army Medical School, 1917; Ph.D., George Washington Univ. Medical Sch., 1934; Dr. P. H., Harvard School Public Health, 1939; hon. Sc.D., Duke Univ., 1943, U. of Pa., 1943, Marquette U., 1944, U. of N.C., 1946, Harvard, 1952; m. Blanche Scott, June 29, 1920; 1 dau., Frances Scott (Mrs. Frances Simmons McConnell). Resident and chief resident physician U. of Pa. Hosp., 1915; bacteriologist Wm. Pepper Lab., U. of Pa., 1916. Served as 1st lt., M.R.C., 1916, 1st lt., M.C., U.S. Army, 1917, advancing through grades to brig. gen., 1943; retired from service, 1946; dean and prof. Harvard Sch. of Pub. Health, Boston, Mass., 1946—. Served as chief of laboratory services in various U.S. Army hospitals, also as commanding officer of various dept. labs., 1917-24; assistant dir. laboratories, Army Medical Sch., also chief bacteriol. dept. Army Med., Dental and Vet. Schs., 1924-28; pres. Army Med. Dept. Research Bd. Bur. of Science, Manila, 1928-30; mem. Advisory Com. for Control of Leprosy in P.I., 1929; chief of dept. of bacteriology, Army Medical School, 1930-34, also dir. department preventive medicine, 1932-34; dir. of labs. Army Med. Center, 1932-34; president Army Medical Research Board, Ancon, Canal Zone, 1934-35; asst. Corps Area surgeon, I.C.A., 1936-40; chief Preventive Medicine Service, Office of Surgeon Gen., U.S. Army, 1940-46, sr. consultant in preventive medicine to the surgeon gen., 1946—; cons. in epidemiology U.S.P.H.S., in global preventive medicine U.S.A.F., Randolph Field, 1949-52; lecturer on public health Yale Med. Sch., Geroge Washington Univ. Med. Sch., and Univ. of Mich. Sch. of Public Health, 1940-46. Army mem. committee on med. research, Office of Scientific Research and Development, 1941-46; U.S. rep. 8th Am. Sci. Congress, 1940; mem. Div. Med. Scis., Nat. Research Council, 1941-46. Mem. sci. advisory com. Gorgas Memorial Inst., 1941-51; member advisory board, Com. on Health, Institute Inter-Am. Affairs, 1942—; mem. com. on health, Office of Foreign Relief and Rehabilitation; mem. adv. com. Nat. Foundation Infantile Paralysis; mem. Nat. Advisory Health Council, U.S.P.H.S., 1945-46. Mem. Nat. Bd. Med. Examiners, 1933-39, Armed Forces Epidemiol. Bd.; pres Asso. Schs. Pub. Health, 1948-51; chief cons. tropical medicine Vets. Adminstrn., 1946. Acting editor in chief Abstracts of Bacteriology, 1924-26; editor sect., Medical Bacteriology, in Biol. Abstracts, 1926-48; assistant editor Philippine Journal of Science, 1929-30. Fellow A.A.A.S., Am. Coll. Physicians, A.M.A. (mem. bd. on preventive medicine); mem. Assn. Am. Physicians, Assn. Mil. Surgeons, Am. Assn. Pathologists and Bacteriologists, Soc. Am. Bacteriologits, Am. Society Tropical Medicine (pres. 1946), Am. Academy Tropical Medicine (pres. 1946), Am. Foundation Tropical Medicine, Society Experimental Biology and Medicine, D.C. Society Bacteriology (pres. 1932-33), Washington Acad. Sciences, Med. Assn. Isthmian Canal Zone (sec., 1935, pres., 1936), Nat. Malaria Com. (pres. 1942), Council Indsl. Medicine, A.M.A., 1943—; Governing Council, A.P.H.A., 1944-51, Epidemiological Soc., Soc. Colonial Wars, Heroes of '76, Kappa Sigma, Phi Chi, Sigma Xi, Delta Omega. Presbyterian. Author of books and articles on experimental bacteriology, preventive medicine and tropical medicine. Recipient Sternberg medal, 1940; Sedgwick Memorial medal, 1943. U.S.A. Typhus Commn. medal, 1943, Carlos J. Finlay medal, 1943, Walter Reed medal, 1944; D.S.M., 1945; Bruce Medal, 1948; Charles V. Chapin medal, 1952; Gorgas award, Assn. Military Surgeons of United States, 1952. Clubs: Army and Navy (Washington); Harvard (Boston and New York); Tavern (Boston). Home: Longwood Towers, Brookline, Mass. Office: 55 Shattuck St., Boston. Died July 31, 1954; buried Arlington Nat. Cemetery.

SIMMONS, Leo Charles, steel co. exec.; b. DuBois, Pa., Nov. 8, 1900; s. James H. and Margaret (Maloy) S.; student Duquesne U., 1920-23; m. Margaret W. Walker, Sept. 18, 1934; children—Margaret A., Robert L. With Kroger Co., 1930-39; with U.S. Steel Corp., Pitts., 1939—, beginning as gen. works auditor Nat. Tube div., successively asst. controller, controller Nat. Tube div., 1939-55, v.p. accounting of corp., 1956-58, adminstrv. v.p., 1958—; dir. Bessemer Electric Power Co. Dir. Franklin Twp. (Pa.) Sch. Bd. Trustee Seton Hill Coll. Mem. Controllers Inst. Am., Am. Iron and Steel Inst., Pa. Soc., Nat. Assn. Accountants, Duquesne U. Alumni Assn. Clubs: Duquesne, Pitts. Athletic Assn., Lions (Pitts.). Home: R.D. 2, Box 350, Export, Pa. Office: 525 William Penn Pl., Pitts. 30. Died Nov. 21, 1959.

SIMMONS, Thomas J., jurist; b. Crawford County, Ga., June 25, 1837; s. Allen G. and Mary (Cleveland) S.; did not attend coll.; admitted to bar, 1857; served in C.S.A. as 1st lt., lt.-col., col. and brig.-gen. Del. to State constl. conv., 1865; State senator, 1865; re-elected, 1871, 1873, and was pres. of senate. Mem. Constl. Conv., 1877. Chmn. of finance com. and reported present financial article of constitution. Judge of superior cts., 1878-87; asso. justice Supreme Ct. of Ga., 1887-94; chief justice, 1894—. Address: Atlanta, Ga. Died Sept. 12, 1905; buried Rose Hill Cemetery, Macon, Ga.

SIMMONS, Virgil M., newspaper pub.; b. Bluffton, Ind., Nov. 9, 1893; s. Abram and Jennie (Mast) S.;

LL.B., Ind. U., 1917; unmarried. Admitted to Ind. bar, 1918, asst. in office of U.S. dist. atty., Indianapolis, 1917-20; engaged in practice of law, Bluffton, as mem. firm Simmons, Dailey & Simmons, 1921-33; chief administrative officer, dept. of pub. works, and commr. of Conservation, State of Ind., 1933-40; administrative asst. Fed. Security Agency, Washington, D.C., 1941; now pres. Jour.-Gazette Co., Ft. Wayne, Ind. Mem. Ind. Gen. Assembly, 1931-32; mem. bd. directors Virgin Islands Corp., 1949-52. Mem. Ind. Bar Assn., Ft. Wayne C. of C., Indiana Society of Chgo., Ind. Acad. Science, Beta Theta Pi. Democrat. Mason, Elk. Clubs: Indpls. (Ind.) Press; Ft. Wayne (Ind.) Press; Indianapolis Athletic, Indiana University, Bluffton Country, Ft. Wayne Country. Home: Bluffton, Ind. Office: care Journal-Gazette, 701 S. Clinton St., Ft. Wayne, Ind. Died Feb. 19, 1958.

SIMMS, John Field, lawyer; b. Washington, Ark., may 6, 1885; s. Thomas Hamilton and Mary (Field) S.; LL.B., Vanderbilt U., 1906; m. Anne Schluter, Nov. 30, 1915; children—John Field, Albert Gallatin, Frances Anne. Admitted to Ark. bar, 1906, and practiced at Texarkana until 1913, Albuquerque, N. M., 1914-29; justice Supreme Court of N.M., 1929-30; resumed practice at Albuquerque, 1930. Mem. Ark. Ho. of Reps., 1911. Mem. Am., N.M. bar assns. Democrat. Methodist. Home: Rio Grande Blvd. Office: Sunshine Bldg., Albuquerque, N.M. Died Feb. 11, 1954.

SIMMS, Lewis Wesley, mfg. exec.; b. Saint John, N.B., Jan. 7, 1885; s. Thomas Stockwell and Myra (Thompson) S.; student Acadia Acad., Wolfville, N.S.; m. Jessie Pratt Staples, Apr. 12, 1910; children—Thomas Stockwell, Marjorie W. (Mrs. D. G. Poole). Bristle, paint brush dept. T. S. Simms & Co., Ltd. (mfrs. brooms, brushes, mops), St. John, 1902-05, charge shipping dept., 1906, traveling salesman, 1907, pres., 1908—, gen. mgr., 1908-51, chmn. bd., 1951—; dir. T. S. Simms (S.A.), Ltd., Johannesburg, South Africa. Chmn. Maritime Transportation Commn. Chmn. bd. commrs. St. John TB Hosp., 1930-42; chmn. bd. trustees Internat. Council Religious Edn., Chgo., 1924-39. Mem. Canadian C. of C. (chmn. maritime regional com., dir., charter v.p. 1926-28, v.p. 1948-49, mem. Can.-U.S. com. 1951-52, pres. 1952-53), Canadian Mfrs. Assn. (pres. 1928-29), St. John Bd. Trade (pres. 1924-28). Clubs: Canadian, Union. Home: 325 Lancaster Av., Lancaster, N.B. Office: T.S. Simms & Co., Ltd., Saint John, N.B., Can. Died Apr. 3, 1957; buried Saint John.

SIMMS, William Philip, ret. journalist; b. Grantville, Ga., Aug. 28, 1881; s. Benjamin Thomas and Elizabeth (Putnam-Dickinson) S.; student Ga. Sch. of Tech.; LL.B., U. Ga., 1901; m. Blanche Grand, Oct. 7, 1908; 1 dau., Phyllis Jacqueline (Mrs. John D. Scofield). Began as reporter Atlanta Journal, 1902; dramatic editor, city editor, Cin. Post, 1903-08; Paris corr. United Press, 1909-14; war corr. in France, Belgium, Italy and Russia, 1914-16; pres. Anglo-American Press Assn., Paris, 1915-16; with BEF in France, officially attached to G.H.Q., 1916-18; chief of United Press Bur., Paris, during Peace Conf.; mgr. Internat. News Service, Washington, 1919-20; sent to Orient by Scripps-Howard newspapers, 1920, returning to cover Washington Conf., 1921-22, as Far Eastern specialist, fgn. editor in U.S. and abroad until 1950, fgn. editor emeritus, 1950—; visited Japan and China under auspices of Carnegie Endowment for Internat. Peace, 1929. Accredited war corr., French Army, 1940, until fall of Paris; with SHAEF, ETO, 1943-45. Holder of British War, British Victory and Franch Verdun medals; decorated Officer's Cross Order of Polonia Restituta (Poland), Officer Legion of Honor (France), Comdr. Order of Danilo (Montenegro). Fellow Am. Geog. Soc.; mem. Am. Soc. French Legion of Honor, Am. Acad. Polit. and Social Sciences, Acad. Polit. Sci., Nat. Audubon Soc., Ypres League, Pi Gamma Mu. Clubs: Nat. Press, Cosmos, Overseas Writers (Washington); Overseas (N.Y.C.); Gibson Island, Cercle Volney, Anglo-American (Paris). Home: 2101 Connecticut Av., Washington. Died Jan. 16, 1957; buried Rock Creek Cemetery.

SIMON, Sir Francis (Eugene), physicist; b. Berlin, Germany, July 2, 1893; s. Ernst and Anna (Mendelssohn) S.; student U. Munich, 1912, U. Göettingen, 1912-13; Ph.D., U. Berlin, 1921; m. Charlotte Muenchhausen, Aug. 22, 1922; children—Katharina, Dorothee McRae. Prof. U. Berlin, 1927-31; prof., dir. Physikalisch-Chemisches Inst. Breslau, 1931-33; vis. prof. U. Cal., 1932; faculty U. Oxford, 1933—, prof. thermodynamics, 1944—, Dr. Lee's professor experimental philosophy, 1956, mem. Student Christ Church, 1945—. Staff Brit. Atomic Energy Project, 1940. Decorated Comdr. Order of Brit. Empire, 1946, knighted, 1954; recipient Rumford medal Royal Soc., 1948, Kamerling Onnes medal, 1950, Linde medal, 1952. Fellow Royal Soc.; fgn. hon. mem. Am. Acad. Arts and Sci. Author: The Neglect of Science, 1951; Low Temperature Physics (with Kurti, Allen, Mendelssohn), 1952. Contbr. sci. publs. Home: 10 Belbroughton Rd. Office: Clarendon Laboratory, Oxford, Eng. Died Oct. 31, 1956.

SIMON, Leon Charles, merchant; b. New Orleans, La., Sept. 28, 1876; s. Charles and Dora (Kohn) S.; grad. Tulane U. High Sch., 1892; student Soule Coll., 1892; m. Fannie Merz, Nov. 12, 1901; children—Doris Regina (Mrs. Carl Goettinger), Ruth Merz (Mrs. F. Julius Dreyfous), Leone Carol (Mrs. Jacques P. Marks). In mercantile bus., New Orleans, since 1892; now pres. United China and Glass Co.; dir. Fed. Reserve Bank of Atlanta, 1920-36; dir. New Orleans Br. Federal Reserve Bank, 1921-36 (chmn. bd. 1926-36). Chmn. Wholesale Merchants and Mfrs. Bur., 1911; organizer, and 1st pres. New Orleans Assn. Commerce, 1913; dir. Chamber Commerce of U.S., 1914-17; organizer, 1st chmn. Bd. of Guarantors, Coll. of Commerce and Business Adminstrn., Tulane U., 1914. Past chmn. bd. dirs. Isidore Newman Sch.; hon. pres. Jewish Children's Home. Mem. New Orleans Acad. of Scis., Beta Gamma Sigma. Mason (32°, Shriner). Awarded Times-Picayune loving cup "for greatest public service" rendered New Orleans in year of 1913. Home: Pontchartrain Apartment Hotel. Office: 408 Canal St., New Orleans. Died Apr. 13, 1953; buried Metairie Cemetery, New Orleans.

SIMON, Louis A(dolphe), architect; b. Balt.; s. Adolphe Louis and Margaret Elizabeth (Torney) S.; ed. private schs.; Mass. Inst. Tech.; m. Theresa B. McConnor; children—Katharine Hadley, Louise Torney, Hildegarde Elizabeth. Began private practice architecture, 1894; in Office of Supervising Architect, U.S. Treasury Dept., 1896, chief archtl. div., 1905-33; supervising architect, Pub. Bldgs. Adminstrn., 1933-41; retired 1941; returned as archtl. consultant, 1942, retired (second time), 1944. Fellow Am. Inst. of Architects, Assn. of Fed. Architects; mem. Nat. Inst. of Arts and Letters. Unitarian. Club: Cosmos (Washington, D.C.). Home: 1735 New Hampshire Av., Washington, D.C. Died 1958.

SIMONDS, Godfrey Baldwin, investment banker; b. Belmont, Mass., Aug. 13, 1904; s. Philip B. and Persis E. (Godfrey) S.; student Moses Brown Sch., Providence, 1912-23; Middlesex Sch., 1917-18; Harvard, 1927; m. Mary Carolyn Vail, Feb. 22, 1930; children—Carla Godfrey, Linda Vail, Phillis Baldwin. Clerk, Statistical dept. Bodell & Co., Providence, 1927-28, salesman, 1928-30; mgr. Syndicate Dept., 1930-37; partner, 1937-41; pres. Bodell & Co., Inc., 1941-43; mng. partner G.H. Walker & Co., Providence, since 1943; dir. Flightex Fabrics, Inc., Textron, Inc.; Kay's-Newport, Inc., United Public Markets, Inc., Newman Crosby Steel Co., W.N.E.W., So. Clays, Inc.; mem. exec. com. Plantations Bank of R.I. Trustee R. I. Charities Trust. Served as chmn. U.S. Treasury War Finance Com., R.I., 1943-45. Dir. R.I. Children's Friend Soc., Smith Hill Girls' Club. Treas. Little Compton Summer Assn., 1936-50, First Congl. Soc., 1946-1949. Member Newcomen Soc of England. Republican. Unitarian. Clubs: Hope, Agawam Hunt, Turks Head, Providence Art (Providence); Harvard (N.Y. City). Home: 97 Williams St., Providence 6. Office: 15 Westminster St., Providence 3. Died Nov. 25, 1952.

SIMONS, Algie Martin, writer; b. North Freedom, Wis., Oct. 9, 1870; s. Horace B. and Linda (Blackmun) S.; B.L., U. of Wis., 1895 (spl. honors in econs.); m. Eleanor May Wood (May Wood Simons), writer (dec.); children—Lawrence (dec.), Miriam Eleanor. In social settlement and asso. charity work, 1895-99; editor Worker's Call (later Chicago Socialist), Mar. 1899-Jan. 1900; editor Internat. Socialist Review, 1900-06; editor Chicago Daily Socialist, 1906-10, The Coming Nation, 1910-13; editorial staff Milw. Leader, 1913-16; organizer Wis. Def. League, Mar.-Aug. 1917; charge lit. bur. Wis Loyalty Legion, 1917-18. Writer and lit. distbr. for Com. on Pub. Information. Del. Alliance for Labor and Democracy Conv., Oct. 1917, and charter mem. of Alliance; del. Nat. Party Conv., 1917; sec. Am. Sch., Chgo., 1921-30. Research on health ins., Am. Coll. Dentists, 1930-31; with Bur. of Med. Econs., A.M.A., 1932-44 (retired). Chmn. Socialist and Labor Mission to Eng., France and Italy, summer 1918. Charter mem. Social Dem. League. Mem. Am. Econs. Assn., Phi Beta Kappa. Author: The American Farmer, 1902; Class Struggles in America (3d edit.), 1907; Social Forces in American History (4th edit.); Wasting Human Life; The Vision for Which We Fought, 1919; Personnel Relations in Industry, 1921; Production Management, 1922; (with Nathan Sinai) The Way of Health Insurance, 1932. Home: New Martinsville, W.Va. Died Mar. 11, 1950; buried Baraboo, Wis.

SIMONS, George Albert, clergyman, lecturer, writer; b. Laporte, Ind., Mar. 19, 1874; s. Rev. George Henry and Ottilie (Schultz) S.; A.B., Baldwin-Wallace Coll., Berea, O., 1899, A.M., 1906, D.D., 1908; A.B., New York U., 1903; B.D., Drew Theol. Sem., 1905; unmarried. Entered ministry of M. E. Ch., 1899; pastor Prospect Pl. Ch., Brooklyn (succeeding his father, dec.), 1899-1902; asso. pastor 61st St. Ch., New York, 1903-05; pastor Bayside, N.Y. City, 1905-07; supt. Finland and St. Petersburg Mission Conf., 1907-11; sec. Central Conf. of Europe, M.E. Ch., Rome, 1911, and Frankfurt-am-Main, 1922; supt. Russia Mission, 1911-21; supt. of Russia Mission Conf. and Baltic Mission, 1921-24; Baltic and Slavic Mission Conf., 1924-28; pastor Am. M.E. Ch. in Riga, 1922-28; established M.E. Training Inst. for Baltic States, 1923, pres. of same. Mem. Commn. on Continental Europe of World's Sunday Sch. Assn., 1912; del. Gen. Conf. M.E. Ch., Minneapolis, 1912, Des Moines, Ia., 1920, Atlantic City, 1932, reserve delegate Columbus, Ohio, 1936; delegate Ecumenical Conf., London, 1921, Atlanta, Ga., 1931. Editor and pub. Baltic and Slavic Bull. (quarterly); founder and pub. Christiansky Pobornik, Petrograd, pub. later in Riga; manager Baltic and Slavic Methodist Book Concern; chmn. Jubilee Fund of Commn. Baltic-Slavic Conf. since 1927. During World War chmn. Am. Red Cross Com. in Russia; mem. bd. Am. Hosp. for wounded Russian soldiers in Petrograd; testified before U.S. Senate, Feb. 1919, concerning Bolshevik régime in Russia and Bolshevik propaganda in America; accompanied commn. of M.E. Ch., summer, 1919, visiting various European countries; supervised distribution of relief supplies sent by Meth. Episcopal Church to Finland, Russia, winter 1920; Supply Minister Christ Meth. Ch., Glendale, Boro' Queens, New York since Nov. 1933. Chevalier of the Cross, Order of the White Rose of Finland, 1st class; decorated by Russian Red Cross and Esthonian Red Cross; decorated by French Govt. for academic services, 1924; Order of the Three Stars (Latvian Republic). Fellow Am. Geog. Soc. of New York; mem. Anglo-Russian Literary Soc. (London), Hymn Soc. (New York). Republican. Mason (32°, K.T.). Clubs: Town Hall, Indiana Club of New York, Clergy (New York); Authors' (London). Home: 71-29 68th Pl., Glendale, Brooklyn 27, N.Y. Address: Mission Rooms, 150 5th Av., N.Y.C. 11. Died Aug. 2, 1952.

SIMONS, Wilford Collins, newspaper pub.; b. Owatonna, Minn., July 8, 1871; s. Adolphus Ezra and Jennie B. (Gowdy) S.; ed. pub. schs. and Kan. Wesleyan University, Salina, Kan.; married Gertrude Reineke, November 14, 1894 (deceased October 30, 1948); children—Mrs. Blanche S. Maloney, Mrs. Janet S. McNalley, Dolph C., Mrs. Dorothea S. Johnson, John Louis (dec.). Resident of Kansas since 1878; established Lawrence (Kan.) World (now Journal-World), 1892, and since pres. The World Co. Formerly v.p. Kan. State Chamber of Commerce; ex-pres. Kan. State Historical Soc.; mem. Lawrence C. of C. (ex-pres.). Mem. Associated Press, Kan. Press Assn., Audit Bureau of Circulations (formerly rep. small town newspapers on adv. bd.). Dir. and ex-pres. Sunset Home (for aged) and Concordia (Kan.) Hosp.; ex-pres. Lawrence (Kan.) Meml. Hosp.; ex-pres. Douglas County Old Settlers Assn., Sons and Daughters of New England; mem. Kan. Soc. of Mayflower Descendants; dir. and ex-pres. Douglas County Hist. Soc., ex-pres. Kan. Baptist Convention; formerly Kan. state chmn. Baptist Laymen. Mem. Sigma Delta Chi. Republican. Mason (32°, KCCH, Shriner). Clubs: Rotary (1st pres.), University (ex-gov.), Saturday Night. Address: Journal-World, Lawrence, Kan. Died May 15, 1952; buried Oak Hill Cemetery, Lawrence.

SIMPSON, Alfred Dexter, educator; b. Sheffield, Vt., Mar. 24, 1891; s. Herman P. and Mabel Katherine (Dexter) S.; grad. Montpelier (Vt.) Sem., 1909; A.B., Syracuse U., 1913, Pd.D., 1941; A.M., Yale, 1923; Ph.D., Columbia, 1927, A.M., hon., Harvard, 1942; m. Hazel Isabel Fisk, June 26, 1917; children—Isabel Fisk (Mrs. Frederick Williamson Kessler), Priscilla Mabel (Mrs. Norman Boyan) and Dexter Hendee. Teacher of history, Montpelier Sem., 1913-14; prin. Lamoille Central Acad., Hyde Park, Vt., 1914-17; dist. supt. Vt. State Bd. of Edn., 1917; with Conn. State Bd. of Edn. successively as supervising agt., dir. of research and surveys and dir. of teacher preparation, 1917-28; asst. commr. of edn., for finance, N.Y. Edn. Dept., 1928-41; visiting lecturer on edn., Harvard U., 1940-41, asso. prof. edn., 1941-47, prof. edn., 1948—; pres. bd. turstees Vt. Jr. Coll., Montpelier, 1936-47; cons. U.S. Bur. of the Budget, 1942-44; cons. on adminstrn. and finance various assns. and govtl. agys. Corporator Lyndon Inst.; trustees Soc. Advancement Edn., Inc. Mem. N.E.A. (com. on tax edn. and sch. finance 1952—), Am. Assn. Sch. Adminstrs. (mem. 1939, 1945 Yearbook commns., 2d v.p. 1947-49), Am. Ednl. Research Assn. (chmn. com. on finance and bus. adminstrn., 1933-38), Am. Soc. for Pub. Administr., Vt. Hist. Soc., Phi Delta Kappa, Sigma Alpha Epsilon. Republican. Congregationalist. Mason. Club: Harvard Faculty. Author: Financing Edn. in Conn., 1927. Numerous edn. survey reports and tech. studies, especially in sch. finance; contbr. articles on ednl. adminstrn. Home: 984 Memorial Drive, Cambridge 38, Mass.; also, Sheffield, Vt. Died Aug. 24, 1955; buried Sheffield.

SIMPSON, James, Jr., mdse. exec.; b. Chgo., Jan. 7, 1905; s. James and Jessie (McLaren) S.; student Harvard, 1926-27; m. Ella deT. Snelling, 1931; children—Sheila (Mrs. R. I. Cassatt), Diana (Mrs. C. W. Rowley), Sandra (Mrs. T. B. Donnelley); m. 2d, Elisabeth Bonbright, 1940; children—James III, Jessie, Howard. Dir. Marshall Field & Co., Chgo., 1931—, exec. com., 1939—. Mem. U.S. Congress, 1932-34; mem. Ill. Central Com., 1934-40, 1946-52, del. Rep. Nat. Conv., 1936. Admitted to Ill. bar, 1939. Served from 1st lt. to capt.

USMCR, 1942-45. Clubs: Racquet, Tavern (Chgo.); River (N.Y.C.). Home: Stoneybroke Farm, Wadsworth, Ill. Office: 30 W. Monroe St., Chgo. 3. Died Jan. 29, 1960.

SIMPSON, James Inglis, industrialist; b. Elgin, Scotland, June 17, 1885; s. John and Elsie (Inglis) S.; student pub. schs.; m. Jean MacDougall, June 10, 1914. Jr., Brit. Linen Bank, Elgin, 1901-09, Royal Bank of Can., Vancouver, B.C., 1909-11; asst. treas. Dominion Trust Co., Vancouver, 1911-14; with Canadian Industries, Ltd., Vancouver, 1919-32, div. mgr. paint and varnish div., Toronto, 1925-29, gen. mgr. fabrics and finishes group, Montreal, 1929-32; gen. mgr. Dunlop Tire & Rubber Goods Co., Ltd., Toronto, 1932-33, v.p., gen. mgr., 1933-39, pres., 1939-54, chmn., 1953—— (co. name changed, 1954, to Dunlop Canada, Ltd.); dir. Leverage Fund, Ltd., Commonwealth Internat. Corp., Ltd. Mem. Canadian Indsl. Preparedness Assn. (v.p.), Rubber Assn. Can. (pres. 1943-44). Club: Toronto Rotary (pres. 1938). Home: 244 Dunnegan Rd. Office: 870 Queen St. E., Toronto, Can. Died Nov. 14, 1958.

SIMPSON, John R., business exec.; born Richmond, Ind., January 29, 1876; s. Elihu C. and Mary Elizabeth (Ralston) S.; A.B., Miami University, Oxford, Ohio, 1899, LL.D., 1919; m. Mabelle Rose Pratt, June 4, 1902; 1 dau., Mrs. Barbara Pratt Lawrence (dec.). With Western Electric Co., Chicago, 1899-1903; v.p. William Filene's Sons Co., Boston, 1903-17; col. U.S. Army, 1917-19; chmn. bd. Van Raalte Co.; dir. Fiduciary Trust Co. of N.Y., Electric Bond & Share Co., McCall Corp., Tricontinental Corp. Awarded D.S.M. (U.S.); Order de l'Etoile Noire (France). Mem. Beta Theta Pi, Phi Beta Kappa. Independent Republican. Episcopalian. Clubs: University, Down Town, Knickerbocker Country. Home: 207 Chestnut St., Englewood, N.J. Office: 1 Wall St., N.Y.C. Died Dec. 5, 1956; buried Oxford, O.

SIMPSON, Kenneth Miller, cons. engr.; b. Beaver Falls, Pa., Feb. 23, 1882; s. Theodore Parker and Lida (Miller) S.; A.B., Columbia, 1903, A.M., 1903, Engr. of Mines, 1906; m. Mary Donogh Shannon, June 28, 1913; 1 dau., Anne. Engr. Nev. Goldfield Deduction Co., 1906-08; mgr. Longfellow Mining Co. (Colo.), 1908-09; practiced gen. mining and metall. engring., 1909-15; asst. gen. mgr. Goldfield (Nev.) Consol. Mines Co., 1916-19; mgr. Commercial Solvents Corp. (liquidating agent, British War Mission), 1919; cons. engr., N.Y.C., 1919——. Developer copper-iron alloys. Dir. US. Indsl. Alcohol Co. Tech. adviser War Dept., 1918; dep. adminstr. steel, oil and coal codes, NRA, 1933, div. adminstr., div 1, 1934, resigned. Mem. Am. Inst. Mining and Metall. Engrs. Clubs: University, Turf and Field. Author: (with J. G. Baragwanath) All That Glitters, produced 1938. Home: 1150 5th Av., N.Y.C. Died Jan. 13, 1957.

SIMPSON, Richard Murray, congressman; b. Huntingdon, Pa., Aug. 30, 1900; s. Warren Brown and Sue (Miller) S.; A.B., U. Pitts. 1923; LL.B., Georgetown Law Sch., 1943; m. Grace Metz, Sept. 15, 1928 (died March 6, 1945); children—Susan, Barbara; m. 2d, Mae Cox, June 12, 1948. Engaged in insurance, 1923-37; elected to 75th Congress (1937-39), 18th Pennsylvania Dist., at spl. election, 1937; mem. 76th-82d Congresses, 17th Pa. Dist., 83d-86th Congresses, 18th District. Mem. Pa. House of Reps., 1935-37. Served in Tank Corps, U.S. Army, 1918. Mem. Am. Legion. Republican. Presbyterian. Odd Fellow, Patriotic Order Sons of America. Home: Taylor Highlands, Huntingdon, Pa. Office: Huntingdon, Pa. Died Jan. 7, 1960.

SIMPSON, Samuel; b. Centreville, Mich., Nov. 24, 1868; s. Thomas and Sarah (Gibson) S.; A.B., Olivet Coll., 1891, A.M., 1894; B.D., Oberlin Theol. Sem., 1894; post-grad. study in ch. history, Hartford Theol. Sem., 1896-98, Ph.D., 1902; student of history, U. of Berlin, 1900-01; m. Edith Bishop Sumner, Nov. 17, 1898; 1 son, William Sumner. Ordained Congl. ministry, 1894; pastor Garner, Ia., 1894-96, Chardon, O., 1898-1900; asso. prof. Am. ch. history, Hartford Theol. Sem., 1902-09; mem. Conn. Gen. Assembly, 1929-31. Vice pres., dir. Savs. Bank of Tolland, Conn. Mem. Conn. Acad. Fine Arts. Republican. Conglist. Clubs: Salmagundi (N.Y.); Authors' (London). Author: Life of Ulrich Zwingli, Swiss Patriot and Reformer, 1902. Landscape painter; pupil Art Students' League, N.Y. Home: Tolland, Conn. Died Jan. 15, 1955.

SIMPSON, Sid, congressman; b. Carrollton, Ill., Sept. 20, 1894; s. S. Elmer and Martha (Andrews) S.; grad. Carrollton High School; married Edna Oakes, Feb. 1, 1920; children—Martha (Mrs. Arthur Stoffel, Jr.), Janet. Member 78th to 85th Congresses, 20th District of Illinois. Chmn. Greene County Republican Committee; twelve terms; former city treas. Carrollton; dir. Carrollton Public Schs. Mem. Am. Legion (award for attending original Am. Legion caucus, Paris, France), 40 and 8. Address: Carrollton, Ill. Died Oct. 26, 1958.

SIMPSON, Sumner, business exec.; b. Pittsburgh, Pa., May 17, 1874; s. William H. and Sarah E. Simpson; ed. high school; m. Louise E. Vermilya, Aug. 21, 1912; children—William Sumner, Mary Louise (Mrs. B. Franklyn Bulkley). Pres. The Raybestos Co., 1910-29; pres. Combination, Raybestos-Manhattan, Inc., Brigeport, Conn., 1929-48, chmn. bd. since 1948; also pres. of all subsidiaries. Home: 835 Clinton Av., Bridgeport 4. Office: care Raybestos-Manhattan, Inc., Bridgeport, Conn. Died June 13, 1953.

SINCLAIR, Harry Ford, petroleum producer, refiner; b. Wheeling, W.Va., July 6, 1876; s. John and Phoebe (Simmons) S.; ed. pub. schs., Independence, Kan.; course in pharmacy, U. of Kan., 1897-98; m. Elizabeth Farrell, July 20, 1943; children—Mary Virginia, Harry F., Jr. In drug business with father; in oil business, 1901——; pres. Sinclair Oil & Refining Corp. and Sinclair Gulf Corp. until Sept. 22, 1919, when both were consol. as Sinclair Consol. Oil Corp., of which became pres.; was pres. Sinclair Oil Corp., hon. chmn. Apptd. mem. sub-com. on oil, Com. on Raw Materials, Minerals and Metals of Council Nat. Defense, Apr. 1917; mem. Petroleum Industry War Council, 1942-45. Republican. Roman Catholic. Home: 3972 Alta Vista, Pasadena 3, Cal. Died Nov. 10, 1956.

SINCLAIR, John Franklin, financial research, author; b. St. Mary's, Ont., Mar. 7, 1885; s. John (M.D.) and Frances Ann (Henderson) S.; came with parents to St. Thomas, N.D., 1893; A.B., Univ. of Minnesota, 1906, LL.B., 1909; m. Gladys E. Phillips, Oct. 25, 1911; children—Gladys (Mrs. Wright Brooks), Frances Ella (Mrs. Herold W. Larsen). Gen. sec. Y.M.C.A., U. of Minn., 1906-09; asst. gen. sec. same Minneapolis, Minn., 1909-10; sec. central br., Y.M.C.A, Montreal, Can., 1910-11; asst. to Dr. Chas. McCarthy, Wis. Legislative Reference Bureau, Madison, Wis., 1911-12; spl. investigator for State of Wis. in Europe on cooperation among farmers, 1911; with Wells-Dickey Co., bankers, Minneapolis, Minn., 1912-15; spl. lecturer on banking law, U. of Minn., 1913-15; in banking business for self, 1915-22; writer and lecturer on financial and econ. subjects since 1922; econ. and financial editor and writer, North Am. Newspaper Alliance, N.Y. City, 1923-31; also writer of daily syndicated column, "Everybody's Business," for newspapers, 1927-31; now engaged in bus. research, law and writing. Apptd. spl. investigator Farm Credit Adminstrn., completing nat. survey dealing with plans for liquidation of Joint Stock Land Banks, 1933; apptd. mem. Nat. Recovery Review Bd., 1934; Minn. State chmn. LaFollette-Wheeler Presdl. Campaign, 1924; Washington rep. Joint Stock Land Bankers Assn., 1935-37. Mem. Am. Acad. Polit. and Social Science, Am. Econ. Assn., Am. Polit. Science Assn., Delta Sigma Rho, Pi Gamma Mu. Progressive Republican. Clubs: Authors (Hollywood); Town Hall (Los Angeles); Cosmos Club (Wash.). Wrote: Cooperation Among Farmers; Cooperative Credit, Can Europe Hold Together?; Canada in the Making; Can Your Taxes Be Cut?; New Trends in Industry; Studies in Success; Our Financial Governors; Continental Federation (with Walter H. Hull). Home: 426 N. Barrington Av., L.A. 24. Died June 28, 1950; buried St. Mary's, Ont., Can.

SINGER, Edgar Arthur, Jr., prof. philosophy; b. Phila., Nov. 13, 1873; s. Edgar Arthur and Sarah Elizabeth (Phillips) S.; B.S., U. Pa., 1892, Ph.D., 1894, LL.D., 1944; Harvard, 1894-96; m. Helen Bunker, July 5, 1905; children—Edgar Arthur, Richard Bunker. Asst. in phychological dept., Harvard, 1895; prof. philosophy, U. Pa., 1909-29, Adam Seybert prof. philosophy, 1929——. Sgt. First U.S. Vol. Engineers, Spanish-Am. War. Mem. Am. Philos. Assn. Am. Philos. Soc., A.A.A.S., Sigma Xi, Phi Beta Kappa. Democrat. Episcopalian. Clubs: University (Phila.). Author: Modern Thinkers and Present Problems, 1923; Mind as Behavior and Studies in Empirical Idealism, 1924; Fool's Advice, 1925; On the Contented Life, 1936; Mechanism, Vitalism, Naturalism (in Studies in the History of Science), 1941; In Search of a Way of Life, 1948. Home: 4224 Chester Av., Phila. Died Apr. 4, 1954.

SINGER, William H., Jr., painter; b. Pitts., July 5, 1868. Awarded silver medal San Francisco Expn., 1915; Cahn hon. mention, A.I.A., 1916. Principal works: "Mysterius Valley," Stedelyk Museum, Amsterdam; "Gloppen River in September," Royal Museum, Antwerp; "Solitude," Luxembourg Museum, Paris; "The Joy of a Summer Day," Carnegie Inst., Pittsburgh; "Dancing Shadows," Isaac Delgado Museum, New Orleans; "A Summer Sky," Portland Museum; "The Narrow Valley," Carnegie Pub. Library, Fort Worth, Tex.; "Frozen River," Pinakothek Museum, Munich; "June Morning," Brooklyn Museum; "Mysterious North," Metropolitan Museum; "A Summer Evening," Brooks Memorial Art Gallery, Memphis, Tenn.; "Mid-Winter Glow," City Museum of The Hague, also rep. in Milwaukee (Wis.) Art Inst., Washington County (Md.) Museum of Fine Arts, Curtis Inst. of Music (Phila.), Bowdoin Coll. (Brunswick, Me.), etc. Decorated Comdr. Royal Order of St. Olaf with star, by King of Norway; Knight The Legion of Honor (France); Knight The Royal Order of Leopold (Belgium), Nat. Academician, 1931; mem. Pittsburgh Art Soc., St. Lucas Soc. of Art, Amsterdam, Holland. Home:, Olden, Nordfjord, Norway. Address: care Frans Buffa & Sons, 58 W. 57th St., N.Y.. Died 1943.*

SINGMASTER, Elsie (Mrs. Harold Lewars), author; b. Schuylkill Haven, Pa., Aug. 29, 1879; d. Rev. John Alden and Caroline (Hoopes) Singmaster; A.B., Radcliffe Coll., 1907; Litt.D., Pa. Coll., 1916, Muhlenberg Coll., Allentown, Pa., 1929, Wilson Coll., Chambersburg, Pa., 1934; m. Harold Lewars, 1912 (died 1915). Member Delta Gamma, Phi Beta Kappa. Author: When Sarah Saved the Day, 1909; When Sarah Went to School, 1910; Gettysburg—Stories of the Red Harvest and the Aftermath, 1913; Katy Gaumer, 1914; Emmeline, 1916; The Long Journey, 1917; Life of Martin Luther, 1917; History of Lutheran Missions, 1917; Basil Everman, 1920; John Baring's House, 1920; Ellen Levis, 1921; Bennett Malin, 1922; The Hidden Road, 1923; A Boy at Gettysburg, 1924; Bred in the Bone, 1925; Book of the United States, 1925; Keller's Anna Ruth, 1926; Book of the Constitution, 1926; Sewing Susie, 1927; Book of the Colonies, 1927; What Everybody Wanted, 1928; Virginia's Bandit, 1929; You Make Your Own Luck, 1929; A Little Money Ahead, 1930; The Young Ravenels, 1932; Swords of Steel, 1933; The Magic Mirror, 1934; Stories of Pennsylvania, 4 vols., 1937, 1938, 1940; The Loving Heart, 1937; Rifles for Washington, 1938; Stories to Read at Christmas, 1940; A High Wind Rising, 1942; I Speak for Thaddeus Stevens, 1947; The Isle of Que, 1948; I Heard of A River, 1948; also many short stories in mags. Home: Seminary Ridge, Gettysburg, Pa. Died Sept. 30, 1958; buried Macungie, Pa.

SINKLER, John P. B. (sĭn'klẽr), architect; b. Phila., Sept. 10, 1875; s. Wharton and Ella (Brock) S.; grad. Episcopal Acad., De Lancey Sch., Phila.; B.S. in Architecture, U. Pa., 1898; m. Mary P. Gadsden, June 11, 1917; children—Mary D., John P.B., Ella Brock. Began practice at Phila., 1902; mem. Bissell & Sinkler, 1906-32; firm architects for Confederate Meml. Inst., Richmond, Va.; Abingdon (Pa.) Meml. Hosp.; Sun Hill Village, Chester, Pa.; Noreg Village, Gloucester, N.J.; Germantown Municipal Bldg., Chestnut St. Pier, Girard Municipal Piers 3 and 5, all of Phila. City architect, Phila., 1920-24, dir. of city architecture, 1932-35; sec. Phila. Zoning Bd. of Adjustment, 1933-35. Trustee Naomi Wood Collection of Colonial Antiques, Woodford Mansion, Fairmount Park, Phila., Pa. Fellow Am. Inst. Architects, Franklin Inst.; mem. Phi Kappa Sigma. Democrat. Episcopalian. Home: 103 W. Willow Grove Av., Phila. 18. Died Feb. 10, 1959.

SINNOTT, Alfred Arthur, archbishop; b. Victoria, Prince Edward Island, Can., Feb. 22, 1877; s. John and Jane (McAuley) S.; A.B., St. Dunstan's Coll., Charlottetown, Can., 1891-95; grad., Grand Sem., Montreal; D.C.L., Canadian Coll., Rome, 1901. Ordained priest R.C. Ch., Feb. 18, 1900; sec. to Apostolic Del., Ottawa, Can., 1903-16; consecrated bishop, Sept. 21, 1916; archbishop of Winnipeg, 1916-52. Apptd. Asst. to Pontifical Throne by Pope Pius XII, Oct. 21, 1940. Decorated by Polish govt. for care of and interest in Polish people in Am. Address: 353 St. Mary's Av., Winnipeg, Can. Died Apr. 18, 1954; buried St. Mary's Cemetery, Winnipeg.

SIPPY, John Johnson, physician, pub. health adminstr.; b. Venice, Ill., July 13, 1879; s. Benjamin F. and Mary Anne (Mestre) S.; M.D., St. Louis Coll., Phys. and Surg., 1899; m. Grace Aileen Cromwell. Practiced medicine, Belle Plaine, Kan., 1899-1913; pub. health officer Sumner County, Kan., 1908-13; epidemiologist Kan. Dept. Health, 1913-19; epidemiologist Mont. Dept. Health, 1919-22, dir. child welfare, 1922-23; lectr. communicable diseases U. Kan., 1916-19; dist. health officer, San Joaquin, Cal., 1923——; also clin. prof., pub. health and preventive medicine Stanford, 1934——. Sec. Kan. Health Officers Assn., 1909-19; exec. sec. Kan. Tb Assn., 1916-19; sec. Mont. Pub. Health Assn., 1920-23; surgeon res., USPHS, 1919-29; mem. White House Conf. on Child Health and Protection, 1929-30; mem. com. on econ. security, 1934. Fellow A.M. A., Am. Public Health Assn. (pres. 1945-46, pres. Western br. 1941); mem. League of Cal. Cities (pres. 1927), San Joaquin County Med. Soc. (pres. 1925-28), Cal. Med. Assn., No. Cal. Pub. Health Assn. (pres. 1929). Democrat. Protestant. Mason, Rotarian. Contbr. med. jours. Address: Stockton, Cal. Died Mar. 15, 1949.

SISAVANG VONG, King of Laos; b. July 14, 1885; s. King Zakarine and Queen Tiao Thongsi. Crowned King of Luangprabang, No. Laos, 1905, King of Laos, 1946——. Buddhist. Home: Royal Palace, Luangprabang, Laos. Died Oct. 1959.

SISCO, Gordon A., church ofcl.; b. Coaticook, P.Q., Can., Apr. 12, 1891; s. Alfred and Maria (Moyle) S.; student, Wesleyan Theol. Coll., Montreal, 1916; A.B., Queens U., 1925, A.M., 1932, D.D. (honorary), 1937; D.D. (honorary), Am. U., 1947; LL.D., Mount Allison U., 1951; m. Edith Isobel Bothwell, Aug. 16, 1916; children—Norman Alfred, Ruth Geraldine (Mrs. Gordon Birkett). Ordained to ministry of the Methodist Ch., 1916; sec. Gen. Council, The United Ch. of Can., Toronto, since 1936. Mem. World Council Chs. (mem. central com., mem. exec. com.), Internat. Congl. Council, Execs. of World Presbyn. Alliance, Methodist Ecumencal Conf., Canadian Council Chs. (chmn. dept. ecumencal affairs). Home: 12 Relmar Rd., Toronto. Office: 299 Queen St., Toronto 2 (B), Ont., Can. Died Dec. 16, 1953; buried York Cemetery, Toronto.

SISE, Paul F., business exec.; b. Nov. 10, 1879; student Bishop's Coll. School, Lennoxville; B.Sc., McGill U., 1901; m. Phyllis E. F. Porteous, 1905. Vice-pres. Northern Electric Co., Ltd., 1914, pres., 1919-48, chmn. bd. dirs., 1948—. Dir. of many cos. Office: 1050 Beaver Hall Hill, Montreal, Que., Can. Died Aug. 1, 1951.

SISSON, Edward Octavius, educator; b. Gateshead, Eng., May 24, 1869; s. George and Mary (Arnott) S.; B.Sc., Kan. State Coll., 1886, D.Sc., 1930; A.B., U. Chgo., 1893; studied U. of Berlin, 1903-04; Ph.D., Harvard, 1905; Litt.D., U. Mont., 1935; LL.D., Reed Coll. (Portland, Ore.), 1947; m. Nellie May Stowell, Nov. 29, 1899 (dec. Apr. 1945); children—Margaret, Calvin Richard; m. 2d, Astrid Honoria Seron, July 3, 1947. Tchr. and prin. pub. schs., 1886-91; prin. South Side Acad., Chgo., 1892-97; dir. Bradley Poly. Inst., Peoria, Ill., 1897-1904; asst. prof. edn. U. Ill., 1905-06; prof. edn. U. Wash., 1906-12, Reed Coll., Portland, Ore., 1912-13; commr. of edn. State of Ida., 1913-17; pres. State U. of Mont., 1917-21; prof. philosophy Reed Coll., 1921-39, emeritus, 1939—. Lectr. edn. U. Cal., 1923-25, Harvard, summer 1908, 27; vis. prof. philosophy San Jose State Coll., Spring 1942, Reed Coll., 1945-46. Fellow Philosophy of Edn. Soc.; mem. Am. Arbitration Assn., Am. Philos. Assn. (pres. Pacific div. 1939), N.E.A., Am. Assn. U. Profs., Phi Beta Kappa, Phi Delta Kappa, Portland City Club. Author: The Essentials of Character, 1910; Educating for Freedom, 1935; (with others) The Social Emergency, 1913; Principles of Secondary Edudcation, 1914. Received citation for pub. service U. Chgo. Semicentennial, 1941. Address: Carmel-by-the Sea, Cal. Died Jan. 24, 1949; buried Monterey (Cal.) Columbarium.

SKEEN, John A, govt. ofcl.; b. Watonga, Okla., Sept. 21, 1903; s. William Benton and Eliza Lee (Chaney) S.; student Northwestern State Tchrs. Coll., 1922-24; B.C.S., Southeastern U., 1934, M.C.S., 1935; m. Frances Oglesbay, Sept. 20, 1924; children—James Nathan, John Lee, Janice Shirley (Mrs. George Anderson. Printer with U.S. Govt. Printing Office, 1924-27; asst. foreman, office publs. U.S. Forest Service, 1927-33; adminstrv. and budget officer Civilian Conservation Corps, 1933-37, budget and inspection activities, 1940-42; adminstrv. asst. Bighorn and Harney nat. forests, 1937-40; asst. chief equipment supply sect. Bur. of Budget, 1942-44; fgn. program analyst Fgn. Econ. Adminstrn., 1944-45; regional dir. War Assets Adminstrn., 1945-51; regional dir. Gen. Services Adminstrn., Chgo., 1951-56, dir. Acquisition Div., Washington, 1956—. Past chmn. Regional Council Fed. Agencies, Chgo. Mason, Elk. Home: 3027 S. Columbus Av., Arlington 6, Va. Office: General Services Adminstrn. Bldg., Washington 25. Deceased.

SKELLEY, William Charles, educator; b. Cleve., Mar. 18, 1896; s. James Robert and Harriet (Baldwin) S.; B.S., Ohio State U., 1918, M.S., 1923. Instr., Rutgers U., 1919-20, asst. prof., 1920-22, asso. prof., 1923-27, prof. animal husbandry, 1927—; animal husbandman N.J. Agrl. Expt. Sta., 1927—. Mem. New Brunswick C. of C. (dir.), Am. Soc. Animal Prodn., Delta Theta Sigma. Mason (32°), Elks. Clubs: Union, Lions (past pres.), N.Y. Agriculture, Forsgate Country, Lawrence Brook Country. Author of papers and circular on animal husbandry. Home: 119 Livingston Av. Office: N.J. Agrl. Expt. Sta., New Brunswick, N.J. Died Sept. 14, 1950; buried New Brunswick.

SKELLY, William Grove, corp. exec.; b. Erie, Pa., June 10, 1878; s. William and Mary Jane (Sweatman) S.; m. Gertrude Frank, 1904; children—Carolyn Skelly Burford, Joan Skelly Stuart. Chmn. bd. Skelly Oil Co.; pres., owner Southwestern Sales Corp. which owned KVOO Radio; founder, pres. Central Plains Enterprises, Inc., owner, operator KVOO-TV; dir. First Nat. Bank & Trust Co., Atlas Life Ins. Co., Tulsa Stockyards, Sand Springs Textile Mills, Inc. (all Tulsa), Okla. Natural Gas Co., Great Lakes Pipe Line Co. (Kansas City, Mo.). Pres. Internat. Petroleum Expn.; chmn. N.E. Okla. Hereford Assn.; 2d v.p., dir. Magic Empire Jr. Livestock Show Assn., Inc.; chmn. bd. Tulsa Livestock Expn. Chmn. Okla. div. Am. Cancer Soc.; dir. Nat. Conf. Christians and Jews; trustee Midwest Research Inst., Kansas City, Mo. Rep. nat. committeeman for Okla., 1924-40. Hon. life mem. Future Farmers of Am., 4-H Clubs of America. Mem. Chamber of Commerce (president 2 terms, director), American Petroleum Inst. (exec. com., dir.), Mid-Continent Oil and Gas Assn. (dir.), Ind. Petroleum Assn. Am. (dir.), So. States Indsl. Council, Ind. Natural Gas Assn. Am. (dir.), 25 Yr. Club of Petroleum Industry (past pres.), Am.-Irish Hist. Soc. N.Y., Asso. Industries of Okla. (pres. 1946-53). Methodist. Clubs: Tulsa, Tulsa Farm, Southern Hills (Tulsa, Okla.); Kansas City (Mo.); Bankers of Am. (N.Y.C.). Home: 2101 S. Madison, Tulsa. Died Apr. 11, 1957; buried Rose Hill Mausoleum, Tulsa.

SKEWES, James Henry (skew-es), editor, pub.; b. Cornwall, England, Feb. 2, 1888; s. William John and Prudence Jane (Mundy) S.; brought to U.S., 1891; ed. high sch., Racine, Wis., and Wisconsin State Coll., Milw.; m. Grace Clara Buckingham, Feb. 24, 1914. Began as editor Racine Journal-News, 1912; mng. editor Milwaukee Daily News, 1914-17; pub. Danville (Ill.) Press, 1918-22; editor, pub. of Meridian Star since 1922; associated ownership Laurel, (Miss.) Daily Leader-Call, Artesia (N.M.) Advocate and Las Cruces (N.M.) Sun-News as well as other papers in midsouth and southwest; director Alabama Great Southern Railway of Southern Railway System, Mchts and Farmers Bank of Meridian, Lamar Hotel Co. Dir. Miss. Children's Home. Mem. Southern Newspaper Pubs. Association (dir.), Miss. Press Assn. (pres.), Meridian Chamber Commerce (pres. 7 terms), Miss. Highway Assn. (dir.); past gov. Rotary Internat. Club: Milw. Press (past president). Awarded community cup, Meridian, "for most worthwhile civic effort," 1925, 1936. Episcopalian. Mason (Shriner), Elk, K.P. Has received various awards for community service. Home: 1703 23d Av. Address: Meridian Star, Meridian, Miss. Died May 1958.

SKILTON, John Davis, clergyman; b. Monroeville, O., Mar. 15, 1867; s. Alvah Stone and Amanda Jane (Davis) S.; A.B., Kenyon Coll., Ohio, 1888, A.M., 1891; grad. Phila. Div. Sch., 1892, B.D., 1914; S.T.D., Temple U., 1920, and all degrees in course; m. Ida Beistle, June 24, 1902 (dec.); children—Henry Alstone, Jane Davis (dec.), John Davis. Deacon, 1892, priest, 1893; curate St. Paul's Ch., Cleveland 1892-97, Am. Ch., Nice, France, 1897-98; Diocese of O., asst. sec. of Conv., 1893-97, registrar, 1896-98. Prin. Cheltenham Mil. Acad., Ogontz, Pa., 1899-1903; head master Melrose Acad., Oak Lane, Phila., 1903-05; house master Chestnut Hill Acad., Chestnut Hill, Pa., 1905-07; head master and chaplain The Cheshire (Conn.) Sch., 1907-11; prin. School of the Lackawanna, Scranton, Pa., 1911-18; asso. field dir. Am. Red Cross, 1918-19; head master Tower Hill Sch., Wilmington, Del., 1919-23; resident head master, Green Vale Sch., Roslyn, L.I., N.Y., 1923-24; rector St. Peter's Church, Cheshire, Conn., 1924-38, rector emeritus since Dec. 1, 1938; chaplain Conn. Reformatory, Cheshire, Dec. 1924-Jan. 1940. Trustee Episcopal Acad. of Conn. since 1927; dir. Conn. Temperance Union, 1934-44. Sec. Permanent Commn. on Parochial Archives, Diocese of Conn., since 1929, examining chaplain since 1936; dir. Church Scholarship Soc., 1935, sec. 1937; chmn. bd. of trustees, Cheshire Acad., 1941. Mem. Troop A, Ohio N.G., 1893-96; capt. and chaplain 3d Inf., N.G. Pa., 1903-07. Mem. Psi Upsilon, Phi Beta Kappa, S.R., Grange. Mason. Clubs: Monday Evening, University (Phila.); Psi Upsilon, Transportation (New York). Editor of "Dr. Henry Skilton and His Descendants," 1921. Co-editor: (with Henry Alstone Skilton) "The Doctor Henry Skilton House, Southington," 1929. Home: 3282 Congress St., R.F.D. 2, Fairfield, Conn. Died July 9, 1951; buried Riverside Cemetery, Monroeville, O.

SKINNER, Charles Drake, clergyman; b. Wayne County, Pa., Aug. 31, 1874; s. Weston Donaldson and Cora Elizabeth (Blattenberger) S.; A.B., Syracuse U., 1903, fellow in philosophy, 1904, D.D., 1910; m. Alberta Harding, June 10, 1896 (dec.); children—Cora Laila, Mrs. Martha Harding Limburg; m. 2d, Agnetha Rhoda Hanson, Feb. 11, 1925. Asst. in philosophy, Syracuse U., 1904-05; ordained M.E. ministry, 1904; pastor Trinity Church, Auburn, N.Y., 1904-08; pres. Cazenovia Seminary, Sept. 1908-15; pastor Linwood Av. Ch., Buffalo, 1915-17, Central Park Ch., Buffalo, 1917-24, 1st M.E. Ch., Tulsa, Okla., 1924-29, Grand Avenue Temple, Kansas City, Mo., 1929-32, Central Av. M.E. Ch., Indianapolis, 1932-36, First M.E. Ch., La Grange, Ill., 1936-40; supt. Joliet-Dixon Dist., Rock River Conf., Meth. Ch., 1940-46; associate minister St. James Meth. Ch., Chicago; dir. Advance for Christ Trinity Methodist Ch., Chicago, Oct. 1, 1949, to June 13, 1950. Mem. Phi Beta Kappa. Mason (32°). Address: 25 E. Delaware Pl., Chicago. Died June 13, 1950; buried Rosehill Cemetery, Chicago.

SKINNER, Charles Edward, elec. engr.; b. Redfield, Perry County, O., May 30, 1865; s. Thomas Peter and Harriet Newell (Brown) S.; M.E., Ohio State Univ., 1890, D.Eng., 1935; hon. Sc.D., Ohio Univ., 1927; m. Harriet Gladys McVay (B.Ph. and B.Ped., Ohio U., 1889), Apr. 25, 1893; children—Dorothy Harriet, Anna Florence, Charles Edward, Bertha Gladys, Thomas McVay. With Columbus Cash Register Co., June-Aug. 1890; with the Westinghouse Elec. & Mfg. Co., 1890-1933; successively, insulation testing and design, and iron and steel testing, to 1902; engr. insulation div. (phys., chem., elec. labs.), 1902-06; engr. research div., 1906-20; mgr. research dept., 1920-21; asst. dir. engring., 1922-33; elec. engr. Fort Monmouth Signal Lab., U.S. Army, Apr. 1943-45. Mem. Nat. Research Council (exec. com.), 1917-18, engring. div. since 1921, engring council, 1918-20; chmn. Am. Engring. Standards Com., 1925-27; mem. Federated Am. Eng. Soc. and Am. Engring. Council since 1923; chmn. Am. delegation Internat. Electrotech. Commn., Brussels, 1920, Geneva, 1922; del. same, London, 1924, Hague, 1925, Amsterdam, 1926, Bellagio, 1927; del. World's Power Conf., London, 1924; spl. rep. of Am. Inst. Elec. Engrs. at Conf. on Elec. Standards bet. Can., Gt. Britain and U.S., London, Mar. 1915; chmn. orgn. com. Internat. Standards Assn., Apr. 1926, rep. for further orgn., London, Sept. 1926, U.S. mem. council since 1931. Fellow Am. Inst. E.E. (v.p. and mem. exec. com. 1919-20, standards com. since 1910; pres. 1931-32); hon. mem. Am. Inst. Elec. Engrs., May 1945; mem. Am. Physical Soc., A.A.A.S., Am. Soc. Testing Materials, Am. Petroleum Inst., Am. Electrochem. Soc., Engring. Soc., Western Pa., Pittsburgh Acad. Science and Art, Pittsburgh Philos. Soc., Franklin Inst., Beta Theta Pi, Sigma Psi, Tau Beta Pi, Sigma Tau. Mem. John Fritz Medal Bd. of Award, 1931-34, Edison Medal Com., 1929-32. Awarded Lamme gold medal, Ohio State U., 1931. Presbyterian. Iwadare Foundation lecturer, Japan, 1934. Contbr. to tech. press and engring. socs. Home: Ziba's House, Route 1, Athens, O. Died May 12, 1950.

SKINNER, Charles Edward, biologist; b. Brainerd, Minn., Mar. 18, 1897; s. Howard Terrill and Ann (Norrish) S.; B.S., State Coll. of Wash., 1921, M.S., 1923; Ph.D., Rutgers U., 1925; m. Helen Bushnell, May 27, 1933; 1 dau., Helen Anne. Research asst., Rutgers U., 1923-25; postdoctorate research fellow, Rothamsted Station, Eng., 1925-26; instr., U. of Minn., 1926-34, asst. prof., 1934-42, asso. prof., 1942-48; chmn. dept. of bacteriology, State Coll. of Wash. since 1948. Mem. Soc. of Am. Bacteriologists (mem. council, 1946-48), Mycol. Soc. of Am., Phi Beta Pi, Sigma Xi, Gamma Alpha, Phi Kappa Phi, Sigma Alpha Omicron. Democrat. Episcopalian. Club: Kiwanis. Mem. com. med. and vet. mycopathology Internat. Assn. Microbiologists. Author: Henricis Molds Yeasts and Actinomycetes (with Emmons and Tsuchiya), 1947. Contbr. articles and book revs. in tech. bacteriol. jours. Home: 1913 Monroe St., Pullman, Wash. Died May 10, 1958; buried Pullman, Wash.

SKINNER, Edward Holman, radiologist; b. Milwaukee, Wis., Jan. 7, 1881; s. Hoyt Hiram and Caroline Belle (Holman) S.; M.D., St. Louis U., 1904; m. Florence Garrell Schade (died 1906); 1 dau., Florence Schade (Mrs. Joseph H. Farrow); m. 2d, Irene Stowell, Oct. 15, 1912. Chancellor Am. Coll. of Radiology, 1934-42, pres., 1947. Mem. Rad. Soc. N.A. Mem. Am. Roentgen Ray Soc. (pres. 1928), Am. Radium Soc. (pres. 1937), Jackson Co. Med. Soc. (pres. 1931), Kansas City Southwest Clin. Soc. (pres. 1923), British Inst. of Radiology, Phi Alpha Gamma, Alpha Omega Alpha; Independent. Episcopalian. Club: University. Home: 5732 Wyandotte St. Office: Professional Bldg., Kansas City, Mo. Died Jan. 11, 1953.

SKINNER, Eleanor Louise, author; b. Worcester, Eng.; d. Thomas and Emmeline Frances Mary (Benewith) Skinner; spl. student Ohio State U.; studied art at Columbus Art Sch. Vice-principal North High Sch., Columbus, 1920-32. Mem. English-Speaking Union, English Club; hon. mem. Delta Kappa Gamma. Rep. Episcopalian. Author: Tales and Plays of Robin Hood, 1915. Joint author: The Emerald Story Book, 1915; Merry Tales, 1915; Nursery Tales from Many Lands, 1917; The Topaz Story Book, 1917; The Turquoise Story Book, 1918; Children's Plays, 1919; Happy Tales for the Story Hour, 1920; The Pearl Story Book, 1920; The Little Child's Book of Stories, 1922; A Very Little Child's Book of Stories 1923; Our English, 1927; Our English (Junior High School Series), 1927. Co-author: Practice Units in English; Grammar for Daily Use, 1935; Fun in Town and Country, Book I, 1940; Fun in Our Busy World, Book II, 1940. Home: 861 Neil Av., Columbus O. Died Oct. 20, 1951.

SKINNER, James M., business exec.; b. Phila., Feb. 9, 1889; s. Mortimer and Mary Reiff (Stearly) S.; B.S., U. of Pa., 1911; m. Florence Sayre, Sept. 11, 1913; children—James M., Margery Anne (Mrs. Karl de Schweinitz Jr.). Chemical engineer Phila. Storage Battery Co. (Philco), 1911-17, vice pres., 1917-32, pres., 1932-39; dir. Baldwin Locomotive Works, Pa. Co. for Banking and Trusts, Am. Stores Co. Dir. Asso. Hosp. Service of Phila., Germantown Hosp. Trustee U. of Pa. Chmn. exec. com. Community Chest of Phila. and Vicinity since 1942. Recipient Phila. (Bok) award for the most outstanding contbrn. to the welfare of Phila., 1943. Mem. Alpha Chi Rho. Republican. Episcopalian. Clubs: Union League, Midday, Sunday Breakfast, Phila. Country. Home: 7309 Huron Lane, Phila. 19. Office: Fidelity-Phila. Trust Bldg., Phila. 9. Died Feb. 13, 1953.

SKOGMO, Philip Waldo, business exec.; b. Elbow Lake, Minn., Mar. 28, 1896; s. John B. and Mary (Bye) S.; student pub. schs.; m. Florence Moody Gamble, Dec. 26, 1928; 1 son, Donald R. Co-founder of Gamble Stores, Inc. (name now changed to Founders, Inc.) 1925, v.p. and dir., 1925—; co-founder Gamble-Skogmo, Inc., 1928, pres. and dir., 1928—; v.p., dir. Filbert Corp., 1936—; dir. G. R. Herberger's Inc., other Am. and Can. merchandising corps. Vice pres., dir. Mpls. Civic Council; dir. C. of C., Good Will Industries, Union City Mission, Asbury Hosp. Clubs: Minneapolis, Minikahda, Minneapolis Athletic. Home: 4860 W. Lake Harriet Blvd., Mpls. 10. Office: 15 N. 8th St., Mpls. 3. Died Dec. 31, 1949.

SLADE, Caroline McCormick (Mrs. F. Louis Slade); d. William G. and Eleanor (Brooks) McCormick; student Bryn Mawr College, 1892-94; m. F. Louis Slade, Oct. 12, 1907. Mem. College Equal Suffrage League, 1912-17; vice chmn. Woman Suffrage League, 1912-17; vice chmn. Woman Suffrage Party of N.Y.C., 1917-20, League of Women Voters of N.Y.C., 1920-23; chmn. women's div. War Work Council of YMCA, 1917-22; mem. Hoover European Relief Council, 1920; campaign chmn. Nat. Woman's Com. for Hoover, 1928, campaign chmn. women's div. N.Y. Rep. Finance Com., 1932; mem. N.Y. League of Women Voters (state chmn. 1923-25; city chmn. 1928-30; vice chmn. state bd. 1930-34), Nat. Municipal League (mem. council 1924-30; v.p. 1930-33). On various war work coms. during World War. Mem. nat. bd. Girls Scouts, Inc., 1932—, v.p. 1936, acting chmn. nat. bd., 1938; mem. exec. com. Women's Council of Community Service Society, 1939-42; vice chmn. U.S.O., 1941-42 (mem. women's com.); pres. Jr. League of N.Y., 1915-17; mem. nat. bd. English-Speaking Union; dir. and vice chmn. bd. dirs. Bryn Mawr College; exec. com. Am. council Inst. Pacific Relations, 1926-42 (vice chmn. 1933-34); former trustee China Institute in America; mem. Army and Navy Dept. YMCA. Mem. Am. Assn. U. Women, Colonial Dames of America. Anna Howard Shaw lectr. Bryn Mawr College, 1933. Clubs: Cosmopolitan, Colony, Bryn Mawr, Women's National. Republican. Address: 410 N. Michigan Av., Chgo. Died Jan. 12, 1952. Buried Adirondacks.

SLADE William Adams, librarian; b. Fall River, Mass., Sept. 27, 1874; s. Edwin Mial and Susan Elizabeth (Bennett) S.; Ph.B., Brown U., 1898, Litt. D., 1937; m. Gertrude Eugenie MacArthur, May 17, 1923. Asst. in reading room of Library of Congress, 1898-1901, asst., later asst. chief div. of bibliography, 1901-09; librarian Nat. Monetary Commn., 1909-12; chief div. of periodicals, 1912-19, of order division, 1919-23, chief bibliographer, 1923-30—all Library of Congress; dir. Folger Shakespeare Library, 1930-34; reference librarian Library of Congress, 1934-40, reference cons., 1941—. Mem. A.L.A. Bibliog. Soc. of Eng., Bibliog. Soc. of America, Assn. for Study of Negro Life and History, Delta Upsilon, Phi Beta Kappa. Conglist.; mem. Wider Quaker Fellowship. Author of Processional: A Hymn for all Peoples. Editor of Browning's Rabbi Ben Ezra. Compiler of numerous bibliog. lists. Home: 3425 Ordway St. N.W. Address: Library of Congress, Washington. Died May 16, 1950; buried Fall River, Mass.

SLARROW, Malcolm G(ordon), naval officer; b. Belair, Md., May 18, 1891; s. John Morrison and Mary Florence (Gordon) S.; B.S., George Washington U., 1913, C.E., 1915; m. Dorothy Gould, May 6, 1916; children—Dorothy (Mrs. Burbeck Benton Gilchrist), Margaret (Mrs. Alfred Coningsby Jackson). Ensign, Supply Corps, 1916; promoted through grades to rear adm., 1943; now gen. inspector Supply Corps, U.S.N. Mem. Theat Delta Chi. Club: Army and Navy (Washington). Home: Kennedy-Warren Apts., Washington. Died Sept. 29, 1958; buried Arlington Nat. Cemetery.

SLATON, John Marshall, ex-gov. Ga.; b. Meriwether County, Ga., Dec. 25, 1866; s. William Franklin and Nancy Jane (Martin) S.; M.A., U. Ga., 1886 (1st honor); LL.D., U. of Ga., Oglethorpe U.; m. Sarah Frances, d. Capt. William D. Grant, July 12, 1898. Admitted to Ga. bar, 1887; mem. Glenn, Slaton & Phillips, Atlanta, until death of Mr. Glenn, 1899, then Slaton & Phillips, and now by himself. Mem. Ga. Ho. of Reps., 1896-1909 (speaker of House 4 yrs.), State Senate, 1909-13 (pres. 4 yrs.); acting gov. of Ga., Nov. 16, 1911-Jan. 25, 1912, to fill interim after resignation of Gov. Hoke Smith, who was elected to U.S. Senate; elected gov. of Ga., Oct. 1912, for term extending from June 30, 1913-15. Chmn. bd. Law Examiners for State of Ga. Decorated Chevalier Legion d'Honneur (France). Mem. Am. (gen. council, 1933—, Ga. del. to Ho. of Dels., bd. of govs. 1940), Ga. (pres., 1928-29) bar assns., Phi Beta Kappa (pres. Ga.). Democrat. Home: Peachtree Rd. Office: Marietta Bldg., Atlanta. Died Jan. 11, 1955; buried Oakland Cemetery, Atlanta.

SLATTON, Charles Stewart, lawyer, judge; b. Scranton, Tex., March 13, 1895; s. Rev. J. M. and Maggie (Brown) S.; grad. Scranton (Tex.) Acad., 1912; student Stamford (Tex.) Coll., 1912-15; LL. B., Cumberland U., 1923; postgrad. U. Tex. Law Sch.; m. Claudia Baldwin, Oct. 5, 1930; 1 son, Jim A. Admitted to Tex. bar, 1923; atty. Atascosa County, Tex., 1924-25; dist. atty. 81st Jud. Dist., 1926-29; in gen. practice of law, San Antonio, 1930-37; asso. justice Court of Civil Appeals, San Antonio, 1937-40; judge, commn. of appeals, Supreme Court of Tex., Austin, 1940-45; asso. justice, Supreme Court of Tex., 1945-47; gen. atty. for Tex. for Southwestern Bell Telephone Co.; breeder of registered Hereford beef cattle, 1935—, registered Jrsey cattle, 1941—. Pres. bd. dirs. Robert B. Green Hosp., San Antonio, 1936; mem. Capitol Area council Boy Scouts Am., 1944. Mem. state exec. com. Dem. party, 1935, 36. Served overseas with U.S. Army Signal Corps, World War I. Mem. Austin C. of C., Am. Hereford Breeders Assn., Tex. and Travis County bar assns. (pres. judicial sect. State bar, 1942), Am. Legion. Methodist. Mason. Home: 4201 Versailles, Dallas 5. Office: Telephone Bldg., Dallas 2. Died Feb. 23, 1951; buried State Cemetery, Austin, Tex.

SLAUGHTER, Donald, dean, prof. pharmacology; b. Shelby, Ia., July 13, 1905; s. Ura Barkdell and Olive Blanche (Miller) S.; B.S., State Univ. of Ia., Iowa City, Ia., 1929, M.D., 1929; m. Bonita Ilene Brown, July 3, 1931; children—Donald Oliver, Caro Olive, Virginia Ilene. Asst. to instr. pharmacology, U. of Ia., 1929-37; asst. to asso. prof., Baylor U. Coll. of Medicine, 1937-42; prof. pharmacology and physiology, U. of Vt., 1942-43; acting dean, Southwestern Med. Coll., 1943-44, dean of students, prof. pharmacology and chmn. dept. of pharmacol. and physiol., 1944-46; dean and prof. pharmacol., Sch. of Medicine, U. of S. Dak., since 1946. First lt., Med. Corps, U.S. Army, 1929-41. Mem. Dallas C. of C. Fellow A.M.A. (certificate of merit 1942), A.A.A.S.; mem. Am. Soc. for Pharmacology and Exptl. Therapeutics, Soc. Exptl. Medicine and Biology, Am. Assn. Univ. Profs., N.Y. Acad. Science, Am. Chem. Soc., Omega Beta Pi, Alpha Kappa Kappa, Alpha Omega Alpha, Sigma Xi, Ho Din. Research field and interests: cholinergic actions of morphine and med. education. Mason, Rotarian. Home: 24 Harvard South. Office: Dean's Office, College of Medicine, University of South Dakota, Vermillion, S.D. Died June 6, 1952.

SLAVENS, Thomas Horace (slā'vēnz), army officer; b. Portland Mills, Ind., Jan. 18, 1863; s. Zenas L. and Irene (Stanley) S.; B.S., U.S. Mil. Acad., 1887; hon. grad. U.S. Inf. and Cav. Sch., 1893; m. Alice Goodrich, Dec. 3, 1890; 1 son, Stanley G. Commd. 2d lt. 4th Cavalry, 1887; promoted through grades to brig. gen., 1923; ret., 1927. Participated in Ind. campaigns, Spanish-Am. War, Philippine Insurrection, Mexican Punitive expdn., Cuban occupation, World War I. Awarded D.S.M., also war medals and Silver Star citations. Mem. S.A.R., Soc. War of 1812, Soc. Indian Wars in U.S., Soc. Foreign Wars, Mil. Order Carabao, Loyal Legion, Am. Legion. Episcopalian. Part Author: Manual of Military Field Engineering, 1895; Military Topography and Sketching, 1897; History of Military Posts in the United States, 1905. Author: San Carlos, Arizona in the Eighties, the Land of the Apache, 1944, Incidents of Cuban Occupation by U.S. Troops, (1898) 1946; Scouting in Northern Luzon, P.I. (1899-1900), 1947. Address: 234 West King's Highway, San Antonio. Died Dec. 24, 1954; buried Fort Sam Houston Nat. Cemetery, San Antonio.

SLAYMAKER, Philip K(uhns), univ. prof.; b. Kittanning, Pa., July 6, 1877; s. Robert Samuel and Ann Elizabeth Kuhns (Bowman) S.; student Armstrong County Acad., Kittanius, Pa., 1892-94; M. E., Western U. Pa. (now U. Pitts.), 1898; m. Carrie Newel Ridgley, Jan. 2, 1902; children—Robert Ridgley, Frank Harris. Rolling mill and steel works draftsman and engr., Pitts. and Wheeling (W.Va.) dist., 1898-1907; mem. faculty U. of Neb. 1907—, beginning as adjunct prof. applied mechanics and machine design, 1907, prof. machine design, 1917-49. Mem. Am. Soc. M.E., Am. Soc. Engring. Edn., Am. Soc. Univ. Profs., Neb. Acad. Sci., Sigma Tau, Pi Tau Sigma, S.A.R. Presbyn. (elder). Clubs: Lincoln Dinner, Engrs. Author: Revision of Stahland Woods Elementary Mechanism, 1927; Slaymaker's Elementary Mechanism, 1937. Contbr. articles to Machine Design mags. Home: 425 S. 26th St., Lincoln 8, Neb. Died Apr. 20, 1954; buried Meml. Park, Lincoln, Neb.

SLENTZ, Samuel D., lawyer; b. Baraboo, Wis., Apr. 3, 1877; s. Samuel D. and Minnie (Renshausen) S.; LL.B., No. Ill. Coll. of Law, Dixon, 1901; m. Marie Maney, Aug. 31, 1905; children—Eleanore, Marilynne. Admitted to Wash. State bar, 1902, and began practice at Bellingham; active in securing passage of first employees' Compensation law in State of Wash.; atty. for U.S. Compensation Commn., Washington, 1918—. Mem. Wash. State, Whatcom County (Wash.) bar assns. Democrat. Methodist. Home: 3130 Wisconsin Av., N.W., Washinton. Died Feb. 21, 1955; buried Cedar Hill Cemetery, Washington.

SLICHTER, Sumner Huber, economist; b. Madison, Wis., Jan. 8, 1892; s. Charles Sumner and Mary Louise (Byrne) S.; student U. of Munich, 1910; A.B., U. of Wis., 1913, M.A., 1914; Ph.D., U. of Chicago, 1918; hon. LL.D., Lehigh U., 1948; Northwestern U., 1949; U. Wis., 1949, U. Rochester, Harvard, 1949; m. Ada Pence, June 6, 1918; children—William Pence, Charles Pence. Instructor economics, Princeton, 1919-20; asst. prof. economics, Cornell U., 1920-25, prof., 1925-30; prof. bus. economics, Harvard, 1930-40, Lamont univ. prof. since 1940; economic advisor Incorporated Investors since 1946; trustee Teachers Insurance and Annuity Association, 1952-56, College Retirement Equities Fund, 1952-56; dir. Standard and Poor's Corp., 1955—; mem. staff Brookings Instn., Washington, 1925-30, 1955—. Mem. Social Sci. Research Council, 1935-38, research adv. bd. Com. Econ. Development (chmn. 1942-53); chmn. adv. council on Social Security of U.S. Senate, 1947-48. Enlisted U.S. Army, June 18, 1918; commissioned 2d lt., Dec. 1918. Mem. Am. Economic Association (v.p. 1937; pres. 1941), American Philosophical Society, American Assn. University Profs. (vice pres. 1936-37), Industrial Relations Research Assn. (pres. 1949), Delta Sigma Rho, Phi Beta Kappa. Clubs: Cosmos (Washington); Harvard (N.Y.); Harvard Faculty (Cambridge, Mass.); Boston (Mass.) Economic. Author: The Turnover of Factory Labor, 1918; Modern Economic Society, 1931; Towards Stability, 1934; Trade Union Policy and Industrial Management, 1941; Economic Factors Affecting Industrial Relations in Defense, 1941. Present Savings and Postwar Markets, 1943; The Challenge of Industrial Relations, 1947; The American Economy, Its Problems and Prospects, 1948; What's Ahead for American Business, 1951. Contributor to Trend of Economics, 1925; Current Economic Policies, 1934; Financing American Prosperity, 1945; also numerous popular and scientific papers. Home: 10 Wyman Rd., Cambridge 38, Mass. Died Sept. 27, 1959.

SLICK, Thomas Whitten, judge; b. South Bend, Ind., July 5, 1869; s. Thomas J. and Laura A. (Whitten) S.; LL.B., U. Mich., 1893; m. Mollie Grant Falknor, Sept. 20, 1894; children—Glen F., Ralph L. Admitted to Ind. bar, 1893, and began practice at South Bend; pros. atty. St. Joseph County, Ind., 1896-1900; city atty. South Bend, 1918-22; judge U.S. Dist. Ct., No. Ind. Dist., 1925-43. Republican. Mason (32°, K.T., Shriner), K.P. Clubs: Indiana, Union, League, South Bend Country. Home: Chain O'Lakes, R.R. 2, South Bend, Ind. Died Jan. 1959.

SLINGLUFF, Jesse (slĭng'lŭf), lawyer; b. Balt. County, Md., June 7, 1870; s. Charles Bohn and Valerie (von Dorsner) S.; LL.B., U. Md., 1897; m. Kathleen Kernan, Sept. 3, 1902; children—Kathleen Kelso, Jesse, Jr., Silvine von Dorsner (Mrs. Charles C. Savage, Jr.), John Kernan. Admitted to Md. bar, 1897, and since engaged in gen. practice of law at Balt.; mem. firm Marbury, Miller & Evans; dir. Equitable Life Assurance Soc. of U.S., N.Y.C., Balt. Brick Co.; former v.p., dir. Cottman Co., Balt. Served as 1st lt. inf., U.S. Vols. during Spanish-Am. War; maj. 2d Md. Inf., 1918-21. Mem. Am. Bar Assn., Md. State Bar Assn., Bar Assn. of Balt. City. Democrat. Roman Catholic. Clubs: Elkridge, Bachelor's Cotillon (Balt). Home: 2925 N. Calvert St. Office: Maryland Trust Bldg., Balt. 2. Died Apr. 3, 1957; buried Balt.

SLOAN, George A., industrial exec.; b. Nashville, Tenn., May 30, 1893; s. Paul Lowe and Anne (Joy) S.; LL.B., Vanderbilt U., 1915; LL.D. (hon.) U. of Chattanooga, 1945, N.Y.U., 1951; m. Florence Lincol (Rockefeller), Nov. 30, 1929; children—Florence Lincoln, Anne. Admitted to Tenn. bar, 1915; asst. to chmn. Am. Nat. Red Cross, 1919-22; pres. Cotton Textile Inst., 1929-35, chmn. 1932-35; pres. Blue Ridge Mut. Fund, Inc.; chmn. Cotton Textile Code Authority, which submitted 1st Code under N.R. A., July 7, 1933-May 21, 1935; commr. of commerce, New York City, and chmn. Mayor's Business Com., 1940-44; chairman of the board Southern Agriculturist, Oct. 1, 1944-50. Dir. (member finance com.), United States Steel Corp.; dir. Goodyear Tire & Rubber Co., Middle South Utilities, Inc., Distillers Corp.-Seagram, Ltd., Montreal, Great American Insurance Co.; mem. adv. com. Bankers Trust Co. Pres. Metropolitan Opera Assn., 1941-45, chmn. bd. since 1946; pres. and public trustee The Nutrition Foundation, Inc. (New York). Member of President Hoover's Committee on Unemployment Relief, 1931-32; past chmn. U.S. Council Internat. C. of C.; mem. bus. adv. council for Dept. of Commerce, Washington, 1935-42. Served as 1st lt. inf., A.E.F., later capt. inf., U.S. Army, World War I; maj. inf., O.R.C.; col. Gov.'s staff, Tenn. Nat. Guard; lt. col., Gov.'s staff Ga. Nat. Guard. Received Annual Award, Nat. Com. for Music Appreciation, 1940; Chevalier, Legion of Honor (France). Trustee, Milbank Memorial Fund, Inst. for the Crippled and Disabled; member board of trust, Vanderbilt U.; life mem. Corp., Mass. Inst. of Tech.; mem. adv. council So. Research Inst., Birmingham, Ala. Mam. Am. Acad. Polit. Sci., Nat. Inst. Social Sciences, Southern Soc. of N.Y. (pres. 1943-44), Am. Acad. Arts and Scis., Am. Italy Soc. (trustee), Phi Beta Kappa, Kappa Alpha. Episcopalian. Clubs: Century Assn., Downtown Assn., Racquet and Tennis (New York); Maligne River Anglers (Alberta); Round Hill (Greenwich, Conn.); Blind Brook (Port Chester, N.Y.); Metropolitan Opera (hon.); St. Andrews Soc. Writer on economic and social problems. Home: Vineyard Lane, Greenwich, Conn., and 340 Park Av., N.Y. City 22. Office: Chrysler Bldg., N.Y.C. 17, and 14 Wall St., N.Y.C. 5. Died May 20, 1955; buried Greenwich, Conn.

SLOAN, John, artist; b. Lock Haven, Pa., Aug. 2, 1871; s. James Dixon and Henrietta (Ireland) S.; ed. Central High Sch., Phila.; evening classes, Pa. Acad. Fine Arts, under the late Thomas P. Anschutz; m. Anna M. Wall, August 5, 1901 (died 1943); m. 2d, Helen Farr, Feb. 5, 1944. Painter figure and landscape, and etcher of city life subjects; etched plates illustrating Paul de Kock's novels; drawings for Harper's, Collier's, Everybody's, Scribner's, etc. Hon. mention, painting, "The Coffee Line," Carnegie Inst., Pittsburgh, 1905; Carol Beck gold medal for portraiture, Pa. Acad. Fine Arts, 1930-31; rep. by paintings in Met. Mus., Whitney Mus. of Am. Art (New York), Brooklyn Mus. of Art, Corcoran Gallery (Washington, D.C.), Phillips Memorial Gallery (Washington, D.C.), Detroit Mus. of Art, Harrison Gallery, Los Angeles, Art Inst. Chicago, San Diego Art Mus., Barnes Foundation (Merion, Pa.), Mus. of Art and Archaeology (Santa Fe, New Mexico), Pa. State College, Museum of Fine Arts, Boston, Addison Gallery, Phillips (Andover) Academy, Art Museum of Wichita, Kan., Toledo Museum of Art, Pennsylvania Academy of Fine Arts, Phila. Mus. Art, Washington State U., Dartmouth College, Encyclopaedia Britannica Collection, Thomas J. Watson Collection, Clevelandd Museum of Art, and in print collection of Metropolitan Museum of Art, New York Public Library, Cincinnati Museum of Art, Detroit Museum of Arts, Public Library (Newark, New Jersey), Carnegie Art Inst., (Pittsburgh); medal for etchings, Panama P.I. Expn., 1915, Sesquicentennial Expn., Phila., 1926. Instr. Art Students' League, 1914-30, 1932-38; pres., 1930-31. Made etchings for "Of Human Bondage" for Limited Editions Club, 1937. Mural in Bronxville, N.Y., Post Office, 1939. Awarded first prize for prints Artists for Victory Exhbn. Met. Mus., 1943. Author of "Gist of Art," 1939; monographs, "J. S. Paintings" and "J. S. Etchings," 1945. Mem. board of dirs., Sch. of Am. Research and Museum of N. Mex., since 1940. Dir. Soc. Independent Artists; mem. Nat. Inst. Arts and Letters, 1929; asso. Taos Soc. Artists, New Mexico Painters; mem. Am. Acad. of Arts and Letters, 1942. Home-Studio: Hotel Chelsea, W. 23d St., New York 11, N.Y.; (summer) Santa Fe, N.M. Died Sept. 7, 1951.

SLOAN, Thomas Wylie, clergyman; b. Newberry Co., S.C., Nov. 20, 1868; s. Rev. Archibald Strong and Elizabeth Jane (Stewart) S.; grad. Webb Sch., Bell Buckle, Tenn., 1883; B.A., Erskine Coll., Due West, S.C., 1886; grad. Princeton Theol. Sem., 1889; D.D., Davidson, 1907; LL.D., Presbyn. Coll. of S.C., 1924; m. Janie Martin, Nov. 17, 1897; 1 son, James Newton. Ordained ministry Presbyn. Ch. in U.S., 1890; pastor Troy, S.C., Abbeville, S.C., Charlotte, N.C., until 1902, First Ch., Greenville, S.C., 1902-31 (emeritus). Home: Greenville, S.C. Died Aug. 11, 1949.

SLOAN, William Franklin, cons. engr.; b. Bozeman, Mont., July 26, 1879; s. Washington Franklin and Blanche Alpine (Daugherty) S.; B.S. in E.E., Mont. State Coll., 1903, U. of Wis., 1904; m. Mary Elizabeth Moffat, May 22, 1912 (dec.); 1 dau., Mary Elizabeth (now deceased); married 2d, Geneva Groves, December 1940. Successively with Montana Power Co., Union Light and Power Co., of St. Louis, Commonwealth Edison Co., of Chicago, and B. J. Arnold Co., of Chicago, 1904-07; appraisal engr. Wis. R.R. Commn., 1907-13; cons. engr., 1913-55, successively as mem. firms Sloan, Huddle & Co., Sloan, Huddle, Feustel & Freeman, Sloan & Cook, now Sloan, Cook & Lowe, ret.; appraisals of investigations City Los Angeles, City of Louisville, Ky., R.I. Pub. Utilities Commn., Manitoba Commn., Province of Alberta, City of St. John, New Brunswick, etc.; has made appraisals for telephone, telegraph, street railway and power companies; chief equipment prodn. sect., communication div. of War Prodn. Bd., Jan. 1942-45. Served as capt. U.S. Army in aircraft production, and as tech. adviser to Postmaster-Gen. during period of govt. operations of wire system duing World War I. Mem. Am. Inst. E.E. Presbyterian. Mason, K.P. Clubs: Cosmos (Washington, D.C.); Union League (Chgo.). Home: 1550 N. State Parkway, Chgo. Died July 20, 1958.

SLOBIN, Hermon Lester, educator; b. Smolian, Russia, June 19, 1883; s. Joseph David and Annie (Leuchtiger) S.; A.B., Clark U., 1905, Ph.D., 1908; student Cambridge (Eng.) U., 1932; m. Alice Levy, Mar. 30, 1912. Came to U.S., 1895, naturalized, 1905. Instr. mathematics Mich. State Coll., 1908-09, instr. U. Minn., 1909-13, asst. prof., 1913-18; prof. mathematics, head of dept. U. of N.H., 1919-48, dir. summer sch., 1921-28, dean grad. sch., 1927-48, emeritus; lectr. mathematics San Diego State Coll., 1949——. Mem. Am. Math. Soc., Math. Assn. America, Soc. for Promotion Engring. Edn., Am. Assn. U. Profs., Sigma Xi, Phi Kappa Phi. Clubs: Faculty (Durham, N.H.); Authors' (London). Author of researches among which are—Researches on Plane Quintic Curves, Some Transcendental Curves and Numbers, Algebraic and Transcendental Numbers, A System of Algebraic and Transcendental Equations. Co-author: Freshman Mathematics; An Introduction to Calculus; A First Course in Calculus. Home: 3366 Sixth Av., San Diego, Cal. Died Feb. 22, 1951.

SLOCUM, Clarence Alfred, assn. exec.; b. Arnette, Okla., May 16, 1904; s. Ben and Nellie Elizabeth (Griggs) S.; B.S., Okla. A. and M. Coll., 1928, M.S., 1931; Ph.D., Ohio State U., 1953; m. Rose Richardson, Mar. 30, 1934 (dec. 1937); children—Clarence Alfred, Donna Rose. Commerce tchr. Panhandle A. and M. Coll., Goodwell, Okla., 1931-33, Pikeville (Ky.) Coll., 1936-37; tchr. management Kent State U., 1937-47; head management dept. U. Tenn., 1947-50; nat. exec. dir. Soc. Advancement of Management, 1950; editor in chief Advanced Management, 1952; pres. Operations Research Institute, Inc., publisher, mng. editor Management's Operations' Research Digest. Served as lt. comdr. U.S. N.R., World War II. Mem. Acad. Management, Am. Arbitration Assn. Panel, Nat. Management Council, Am. Assn. U. Profs., Beta Gamma Sigma, Delta Sigma Pi, Kappa Kappa Psi, Acacia. Presbyn. Mason. Club: Kiwanis. Contbr. articles profl. jours. Home: 25 Haslet Av., Princeton, N.J. Office: 41 Fifth Av., N.Y. C. 3. Died May 3, 1957. Buried Arlington National Cemetery.

SLOCUM, Lorimer B(ergland), advt. exec.; b. Laconia, N.H., Apr. 24, 1898; s. Joel Byron and Jean (Bergland) S.; A.B., Princeton, 1921; m. Dorothy Gregson, Dec. 25, 1923; children—Robert Gregson, Mary Jean (Mrs. Richard L. Warfield). Vice pres., mgr. Boston office, N. W. Ayer & Con, 1921-36; in charge new bus. J. M. Mathes, Inc., 1937-40; v.p., dir. internat. div. Young & Rubicam, Inc., N.Y. City, 1945——; dir. Young & Rubicam, Ltd., Can. Mexico and Ltd. Co., Eng., 1945——. Mem. bd. trustees Darien (Conn.) Library; dir. Nat. Better Bus. Bur., Internat. Film Found., Darien (Conn.) A.R.C., 1951-55. Mem. Princeton U. Grad. Council, N.E. Soc. in N.Y. City, Princeton Class '21 (pres., 51——). Republican. Presbyn. Clubs: Univ. of N.Y., Wee Burn Country, Univ. Author: The First Fifteen, 1935, The Second Fifteen (30 yr. record class of '21 Princeton). Home: Halter Lane, Darien, Conn. Office: 285 Madison Av., N.Y.C. 17. Died Nov. 19, 1957; buried Wildwood Cemetery, Winchester, Mass.

SLOCUM, Richard William, newspaper exec.; b. Reading, Pa., Apr. 10, 1901; s. Peter Warren and Margaret (Swinglehurst) S.; A.B., Swarthmore (Pa.) Coll., 1922; LL.B., Harvard, 1925, Temple U., 1954; m. Catherine Luden, July 7, 1932; children—Judith Richard, William, Sancha, Catherine, Susan, Jennifer, Gwyneth. Admitted to Pa. bar, 1925, practiced Phila. 1937; exec. v.p., dir. Phila. Bull., 1938——; vice chmn. bd., sec. and dir. radio and television sta. WCAU, Inc., Phila., 1949——. Dir. The Baldwin Sch. Pres. Am. Newspaper Pubs. Association (secretary, director), Phi Beta Kappa, Phi Delta Theta. Presbyn. Clubs: Union League, Philadelphia Country. Home: Lafayette Road, Bryn Mawr, Pa. Office: The Bulletin, Phila. 1. Died Mar. 31, 1957; buried West Laurel Hill Cemetery, Bala Cynwyd, Pa.

SLOMAN, Ernest Gaynor, (slō'mán), coll. dean; b. San Francisco, Calif., Aug. 28, 1895; s. Ernest Gaynor and Josephine (Gough) S.; D.D.S., Coll. of Phys. and Surg., San Francisco, 1921; D.Sc., University of Southern California, 1947; married Phoebe Emelda Lambert, Dec. 19, 1914 (died 1924); m. 2d Mildred Flanagan, June 9, 1936 (died 1947); children—Suzanne, Bonnie Ellen. Instr., Coll. of Physicians and Surgeons since 1921, instr. anatomy, 1921-45, prof. since 1945, lecturer dentistry, 1921-23, asst. prof., 1923-24, asso. prof., 1924-27, supt. coll., 1923-38, comptroller since 1923, lecturer on office management, 1930-38, trustee 1923-44; spl. consultant in dentistry on staff of Men's Health Service, Sch. of Hygiene and Physical Edn., Stanford Univ., 1932-44; lecturer in medicine at Med. School since 1941; administrative mem. Calif. Physicians Service, 1938-1948. Sec. San Francisco Dist. Dental Soc., 1924-39; chmn. finance com., Pacific Coast Dental Conf., 1929-38; councilman Calif. State Dental Assn., to Pacific Coast Dental Conference, 1929-38; dir. Agriculture Workers Health and Medical Association 1938-48; member Nat. Bd. Dental Examiners, 1942-47; mem. bd. dirs. Lick School, San Francisco since 1948. Fellow Am. Coll. of Dentists (regent, 1939-43), Calif. Acad. of Periodontology (hon.); mem. Am. Dental Assn. (2d vice pres. 1941-42), American Assn. of Dental Editors, Ariz. State Dental Soc. (hon.), Pacific Coast Soc. of Orthodontists (hon.), Internat. Assn. Dental Research, A.A.A.S., Psi Omega, Beta Sigma, Tau Kappa Omega (hon. pres.), Epsilon Alpha (hon.), Omicron Kappa Upsilon. Republican. Clubs: Commonwealth of Calif., Lake Merced Golf and Country (pres. 1937-39). Home: 135 Santa Paula Av. Office: 344 14th St., San Francisco 3. Died Apr. 30, 1952; buried Holy Cross Cemetery.

SLOTTMAN, George Vincent, engring. exec.; b. Bklyn., Nov. 22, 1903; s. William Frederick and Helena (Fuchs) S.; B.S., Mass. Inst. Tech., 1925; Ph. D., U. Berlin, 1927; m. Helen McCahill, Mar. 22, 1930. Dir. Buffalo sta. practice Sch.-chem. Engring., Mass. Inst. Tech., 1927-30; iron works mgr. United Steel Cos., Ltd., 1930-34; mgr. tech. sales Air Reduction Co., Inc., N.Y.C., 1934-48, asst. to v.p. sales, 1948-49, dir. research and engring, 1949-52, v.p. research and engring., 1952——. Recipient of the James Turner Morehead medal by the International Acetylene Association, 1956. Member Am. Rocket Soc., Am. Welding Soc., Brit. Iron and Steel Inst., Am. Iron and Steel Inst., Am. Inst. Mining and Metall. Engrs., Tau Beta Pi, Phi Mu Delta. Clubs: Pinnacle, Engineers (N.Y.C.) Author: Oxygen Cutting, 1951; also articles tech. jours. Holder patents. Home: 1 University Pl., N.Y.C. 3. Office: 150 E. 42d St., N.Y.C. Died Apr. 21, 1958.

SLUTZ, Frank D(urward) (slōōts), educator; b. Mount Hope, O., Nov. 27, 1882; s. Stephen Haley and Emma Louise (Schnell) S.; A.B., Mount Union Coll., Alliance, O., 1904, A.M., 1906, L.H.D., 1928; A.M., Harvard, 1911; Litt.D., U. of Denver, 1915; m. Katherine Pierce June 29, 1907; children—Ralph Leland, Donald Pierce, Margaret Louise. Prin. Franklin Sch., Alliance, O., 1904-06, Irving Sch. Pueblo, Colo., 1906-07; instr. dept. of English, Centennial High Sch., Pueblo, 1907-08, 1911-12; prin. high sch., Canon City, Colo., 1908-10; supt. schs., Dist 1, Pueblo, 1912-17; dir. Moraine Park Sch., Dayton, O., 1917-27; ednl. adviser Chicago Teachers Coll., 1927-32; engaged in ednl. counseling and guidance in schools and college, 1932——. Member bd. trustees Mt. Union Coll., Alliance, O. Member Am. Edn. Fellowship, Kappa Delta Pi, Sigma Nu. Rep. Meth. (member of Board of Peace). Club: Rotary. Co-Author: Am I Getting an Education? 1920. Author of Thinking Things Through, 1936; Methodist Men at Work (manual for laymen's activities of the church), 1944. Techniques of Management, 1946; Human Factors in Bus. and Industry, 1947. Contbr. to ednl. lit. of Meth. Ch. Home: 16 Lexington Av., Dayton, O. Died Dec. 16, 1956.

SLYE, Maud, pathologist; b. Mpls., Feb. 8, 1879; d. James Alvin and Florence Alden (Wheeler) Slyde; A.B., Brown U., 1899, Sc.D., 1937; post-grad. work U. Chgo., fellow, 1908-11. Prof. psychology and pedagogy R.I. State Normal Sch., 1899-1905; mem. staff Sprague Meml. Inst., Chgo., 1911-43; instr. pathology U. Chgo., 1919-22, asst. prof., 1922-26, asso. prof., 1926-45, prof. emeritus, 1945——. Research on mice many years to determine the nature of cancer, the relation of heredity to cancer, the laws governing malignancy and its localization, and age at which it will occur. Recipient gold medal A.M.A., 1914; Rickets prize, 1915; gold medal North Am. Radiol. Soc., 1922. Mem. Assn. Cancer Research (past v.p.), Chicago Inst. Medicine, A.A.A.S., A.M.A., Am. Assn. Sci. Workers, N.Y., Ill. acads. sci.; hon. mem. Seattle Acad. of Surgery, So. Cal. Med. Soc., Phi Beta Kappa, Sigma Xi, Sigma Delta Epsilon, Delta Kappa Gamma. Author: 42 brochures on cancer; also Songs and Solaces (poems), 1934; I in the Wind (poems), 1936. Home: 5822 Drexel Av., Chgo. Died Sept. 17, 1954; buried Oak Woods Cemetery, Chgo.

SMALL, Frederick Percival, director of American Express Co.; b. Augusta, Me., Nov. 28, 1874; s. Alonzo Porter and Henrietta (Allen) S.; ed. Cony High Sch., Augusta; Cornell Law School; Eastman Business College, Poughkeepsie, N.Y.; m. Clara J. Cable, June 8, 1898; children—Frederick A., Kathryn Small Conkling. Began with Merchants Dispatch Transportation Co.; with Am. Express Co. since 1896, director since 1918, pres., 1923-44, now director The Am. Express Co., Inc.; mem. adv. com. Chase Manhattan Bank, N.Y.C.; dir. Continental Ins. Co., Remington Rand div. Sperry-Rand Corp., Surety Fire Ins. Co.; trustee Am. Surety Company of New York. Mem. Maine Soc., Empire State Soc., S.A.R. Republican. Mason (K.T., Shriner). Clubs: The Recess (New York); Barnegat Light Yacht (New Jersey). Home: Ridgefield, N.J., and Harvey Cedars, N.J. Office: 65 Broadway, N.Y.C. 6. Died Mar. 1, 1958.

SMALLEY, Frank Mather, assn. exec., former fire ins. exec.; b. Syracuse, N.Y., May 25, 1877; s. Frank and Jennie (Mather) S.; A.B., Syracuse U., 1898, student law, 1898-1900; m. Helen P. Spencer, Dec. 31, 1901; children—Jane Mather, Robert Warren, Margaret Spencer. Began in ins. business with Middle States Inspection Bur., N.Y., 1903; became sec. Glens Falls Inc. Co., 1920, v.p., 1926, pres., 1929-43; exec. sec. Glens Falls C. of C., 1943——; former pres. Commerce Insurance Co.; former v.p. Glens Falls Indemnity Co., Glens Falls Corp.; sec. Glens Falls Hotel Corp.; pres. Glens Falls Savs. & Loan Assn. Trustee Syracuse University, Crandall Library, Glens Falls YMCA. Fellow Insurance Institute America; mem. N.Y. State Hist. Soc., Delta Kappa Epsilon, Phi Delta Phi. Republican. Methoodist. Mason (32°, K.T., Shriner), Rotarian (pres. 3 years). Home: 33 Horicon Av. Address: Glens Falls C. of C., Glens Falls, N.Y. Died June 18, 1957.

SMART, David A., publisher; b. Omaha, Neb., Oct. 4, 1892; s. Louis and Mary (Aronson) S.; student Crane Tech. High Sch., 2 yrs.; m. Gaby Dure, Oct. 1942. Advt. salesman Chgo. Tribune, 1911-14; operated own agy. for prodn. advt. and promotional materials, 1914-17, 18-21, with bro. founded David A. Smart Pub. Co., pres. since 1921, pub. Nat. Men's Wear Salesman, 1997, named changed to Apparel Arts, 1931, Gentleman's Quarterly, 1927; started Esquire: The Mag. for Men, 1933, Coronet, pocket size mag., 1936, both mags. pub. by Esquire, Inc., of which was chmn. bd.; also founded Coronet

Instrnl. Films, 1940, purchased Ideal Pictures Corp., 1949. Served with F.A., A.E.F., World War I. Home: Glenview, Ill. Died Oct. 16, 1952.

SMART, James D., ins. exec.; b. Prince Edward Island, 1882. Pres. N.H. Fire Ins. Co., Granite State Fire Ins. Co.; dir. Amoskeag Nat. Banks, Am. Fidelity Co. of Montpelier (Vt). Pres. N.H. Bd. of Underwriters. Home: 103 Liberty St. Address: Manchester, N.H. Died Aug. 4, 1950.*

SMATHERS, William H(owell), (smă'thěrz), ex-senator; b. Wayneville, N.C., Jan. 7, 1891; s. Benjamin Franklin (physician) and Laura (Howell) S.; student Washington and Lee U., 1907-09, U. of N.C., 1909-11; m. 2d, Mary James Foley, Feb. 9, 1938; children by first marriage—Jayne, Billie, Barbara, Polly, J. B., Ben; children by 2d marriage, James Foley, Virginia Fairfax, William Howell. Admitted to N.C. and N.J. bars, 1912; practicing attorney at Atlantic City, New Jersey, 1912-22; president judge Common Pleas Court of Atlantic County, N.J., 1922-32; commr. N.J. Superior Court, 1923; spl. master in Chancery, 1924; 1st asst. atty. gen. of N.J., 1934, state senator, 1934-36; elected U.S. senator from N.J. for term, 1937-43; mem. law firm Smathers, Scott & Munyan. Awarded Kiwanis Club "Good Deeds" award as most useful citizen of Atlantic City, 1934. Democrat. Home: Margate City, N.J. Office: Boardwalk Nat. Bank Bldg., Atlantic City, N.J. Died Sept. 24, 1955; buried Waynesville (N.C.) Cemetery.

SMEDLEY, Agnes, author; b. Northern Mo., 1894; d. Charles H. and Sarah (Ralls) Smedley; student summer sch. U. Cal., 1915, N.Y.U. night sch., U. of Berlin, 1927-28; divorced. Has spent 23 yrs. in foreign countries, of these, 12 yrs. in China; in war zones of China, with regular and guerrilla armies, and Chinese civilian orgns. engaged in war work, 1937-40; special corr. in Far East for the Frankfurter Zeitung of Germany until Hitler's rise to power; spl. war-time corr. for Manchester Guardian of England, 1938-41. Has ben fgn. corr., field worker for Chinese Red Cross Med. Corps, lectr. in Chinese armies. Interpreter of China to western world and vice versa. Active participant in China's war for liberation. On dealth list of Japanese Secret Service during World War II. Mem. Progressive Citizens of Am., Am. Vet. Com., East and West Asso., P.E.N. Author: Daughter of Earth, 1929; Chinese Destinies, 1933; China's Red Army Marches, 1935; China Fights Back, 1939; Battle Hymn of China, 1943; The Great Road; The Life and Times of Chu Teh (in press); Chapter XI of China, The United Nations Series, edited by Harley F. MacNair. Contbr. to Asia, New Republic, Nation, Vogue, etc. Lecturer. Address: Palisades, N.Y. Died May 6, 1950; buried Peking, China.

SMEDLEY, Graham B., judge; b. Millersburg, Ky., Nov. 10, 1879; s. John G. and Lizzie (Boulden) S.; A.B., A.M., Georgetown (Ky.) Coll., 1901; LL.B., U. of Va., 1904; honorary LL.D., Georgetown (Ky.) Coll., 1950; m. Betty Dunn, December 25, 1907. Admitted to Tex. bar, 1905, practiced, Dallas, 1905-07, Midland, 1907-13; asst. atty. gen. of Tex. at Austin, 1913-18; practiced at Austin, 1918-25, Wichita Falls, 1925-29, Fort Worth, 1929-33; mem. Commn. of Appeals of Supreme Court of Tex., 1933-Sept. 21, 1945; asso. justice, Supreme Court of Tex., Sept. 21, 1945—. Mem. Am. Law Inst., Order of Coif, Raven Soc., Phi Delta Phi, Am. Bar Assn. Democrat. M.E. Church, S. Mason (K.C.C.H., Shriner). Club: Town and Gown (Austin). Author: Digest of Oil and Gas Decisions, 1923. Contbr. articles to law mags. Home: 2305 Woodlawn, Austin 3, Tex. Died June 16, 1954; buried Texas State Cemetery, Austin.

SMITH, Addison Taylor, lawyer; b. Cambridge, O., Sept. 5, 1862; s. Isaac and Jane (Forsythe) S.; grad. bus. sch., 1883; LL.B., Columbian (now George Washington) U., 1895; LL.M., Nat. Law Sch., Washington, 1896; m. Mary A. Fairchild, Dec. 24, 1889 (dec. Feb. 1947); children—Hugh Fairchild, Benjamin Taylor (dec.), Walter Shoup; m. 2d, Mrs. Rose H. Stearns, July 6, 1949. Admitted to D.C. bar, 1899, Idaho bar, 1905; moved to Ida., 1900; registered U.S. Land Office, Boise, Ida., 1907-08; mem. 63d to 72d Congresses, 2d Ida. Dist. Asso. mem. Bd. Vets. Appeals, 1934-42, now ret. Sec. Rep. State Central Com. of Ida., 1904-11. Methodist. Mem. Ohio Soc. (Twin Falls, Ida., and Washington), S.A.R., Rotarian. Home: 3601 Connecticut Av. N.W., Washington. Died July 5, 1956; buried Rock Creek Cemetery, Washington.

SMITH, Albridge Clinton, lawyer; b. Dover, N.J., Nov. 17, 1881; s. Albridge C. and Mary Florence (Wood) S.; A.B., Princeton, 1903; LL.B., New York Law Sch., 1905; m. Frances Dean Halsey, Oct. 20, 1910; children—Margaret Halsey (Mrs. Cornelius H. Smith), Albridge C. III, Frances Dean (Mrs. Fred M. Dudley, Jr.), E. Halsey. Admitted to bar, 1905; engaged in practice of law, in association with father, New York, N.Y., 1905-12; law asst. firm of Byrne & Cutchen, 1912-16; partner, Byrne, Cutchen & Taylor, 1916-20; partner firm of Humes, Smith & Andrews since 1920. Trustee Princeton U. since 1933. Mem. Am. New Jersey, N.Y. City, N.Y. County and N.Y. State bar assns., N.Y. Law Inst. Clubs: University, Downtown Association, Princeton (New York); Orange Lawn Tennis (South Orange, N.J.); University Cottage, Nassau (Princeton). Home: 150 Montrose Av., South Orange, N.J. Office: 50 Broadway, N.Y.C. 4. Died June 4, 1951.

SMITH, Barry Congar, former dir. Commonwealth Fund; b. Pitts., June 28, 1877; s. Horace Plynn and Ella G. (Hobart) S.; B.A., Yale, 1899; grad. N.Y. Sch. Social Work, 1914; LL.D., U. Glasgow, 1946; m. Tryphena Louise Read, June 16, 1920; 1 dau., Barbara Hayden. Teacher, Cutler and Browning schs., New York, 1899-1913; financial sec. New York Charity Orgn. Soc., 1915-18, sec. Bur. Advice and Information, 1917-18; organizer and exec. dir. Nat. Information Bur., 1918-21; gen. dir. Commonwealth Fund, 1921-47, ret. Decorated Chevalier Legion of Honor (France); Das Grosse Ehrenzeichen (Republic of Austria). Mem. Phi Beta Kappa, Beta Theta Pi; hon. mem. Am. Psychiatric Assn. Club: University. Home: 1225 Park Av., N.Y.C. Died Mar. 31, 1952.

SMITH, Benjamin M., army officer; b. Hull, Ala., September 10, 1900; son of Benjamin Alexander and Dovie (Mitchell) Smith; graduate of Company Officer's Course, Ft. Benning, Ga., 1929, Field Officers' Course, 1933, Command and Gen. Staff Sch., Ft. Leavenworth, Kan., 1936; m. Mary Montgomery, Aug. 17, 1927. Served as private, 1919, and advanced through the grades to brig. gen., Ala. Nat. Guard, Jan. 1939; Federal Service since 1939. With Tenn. Coal, Iron and R.R. Co., Birmingham, Ala., 1919-35; Protective Life Ins. Co., 1935-37; Ala. rep., Seagram's Distillery Corp., 1937-39; adj. gen., State Mil. Dept. since 1939, Ala. State dir. Selective Service, 1940-46, retired; now a member G.M.S. General Sales and Mfrs. Agents. Sec. Armory Commn., Ala.; mem. Ala. State Defense Council. Awarded Victory medal, Ala. Faithful Service medal with 5 crosses, Ala. Special Service medal, Ala. Veterans' Service medal. Mem. Ala. State Rifle Assn. (pres.), Nat. Guard Officers Assn. of Ala. Mason (York Rite, Shriner). Club: Country (Montgomery, Ala.). Home: 3294 S. Perry St., Montgomery 6. Office: 811 Shepherd Bldg., Montgomery 4, Ala. Died Apr. 13, 1949; buried Greenwood Cemetery, Montgomery.

SMITH, Blaine Spray, cement mfr.; b. Alta, Ia.; s. William Peter and Christina (Gunn) S.; student pub. schs. of Chgo.; m. Merle Mary Powell, Nov. 15, 1914; children—Barbara Jane (Mrs. Anson W. Krickl), Betty Ann (Mrs. Arthur F. Hetherington). Asso. with C.&N.-W. Ry., Chgo., 1898-1908; salesman Universal Portland Cement Co., Chgo., latterly v.p., 1908-28; pres. Penn-Dixie Cement Corp., New York, 1928-36; pres., dir. Universal Atlas Cement Co., N.Y., 1936—; dir. Walworth Co., U.S. Steel Corp. Dir., past pres. Portland Cement Assn. Mem. U.S. C. of C., Am. Soc. for Testing Materials, Am. Concrete Inst. Republican. Episcopalian. Clubs: Blind Brook (Portchester, N.Y.); Pelham (N.Y.) Country; Union League, Economic, Cloud (N.Y.C.); Shenersek Shore (Rye, N.Y.); Chicago, Chicago Athletic Assn., Tavern (Chgo.). Home: 50 Rockledge Dr., Pelham Manor, N.Y. Office: 100 Park Av., N.Y.C. 17. Died Oct. 27, 1955.

SMITH, Bruce, police adminstrn.; b. Brooklyn, N.Y., May 23, 1892; s. Clarence B. and Jessie A. (Annin) S.; B.S., Columbia Univ., 1914, M.A. and LL.B., 1916; m. Mary Belle Rowell, Oct. 23, 1915; children—Bruce, Miriam Rowell. Staff mem. Institute Public Administration since 1916, manager, 1921-28, sec. 1940—, acting dir. 1941-46, 1950-53, dir. 1954—; counsel for Joint Legislative Com. on Taxation and Retrenchment, N.Y. State, 1922-23; consultant Mo. Assn. for Criminal Justice, 1925, Nat. Crime Commn., 1925-26, N.Y. State Crime Commn., 1926-27, Ill. Assn. for Criminal Justice, 1927, Scientific Crime Detection Lab., 1929-38; Cincinnati Police Dept., 1928, 1930, 1949, Mayor's Advisory Com., Chicago, 1931-33, Westchester County (N.Y.) Commission on Govt., 1934-36, Mass. Spl. Commn. on Taxation and Expenditures, 1937-38; St. Louis, Mo., Police Dept., 1940-41, Baltimore Police Dept., 1940-41; board of Police Commrs., Springfield, Mass., 1941, 1949-50; U.S. Bur. of Budget, orgn. U.S.A.F., 1941-42; War Dept. Price Adjustment Board, 1942; Westchester County, N.Y., Park Commn., 1943, R.I. Public Expenditure Council, 1943-45; Providence Police Dept., 1945; Phila. City Planning Commn., 1945; New Orleans Police Department, 1946-47; dir. Com. on Uniform Crime Records of Internat. Assn. Chiefs of Police, 1928-31; dir. Chgo. Police Survey, 1929-30, N.Y. Police Survey, 1951-52; reorganized Chgo. Police Department, 1931-33, Pitts. Police Dept., 1937-38, also New Jersey Police Department, 1955; organized police mobilization programs of New York, N.J. and Va., 1940; lecturer, Columbia, Yale, Harvard, Wayne, Rutgers, Chgo. univs., U.S. Army, U.S. Navy Schs. of Military Govt., Northwestern U. Traffic Institute and National Police Academy of Federal Bur. Investigation. Editor Uniform Crime Reports, 1930; mem. exec. bd. Am. Inst. Criminal Law and Criminology, 1930-42; mem. N.Y. State Commn. on Administration of Justice, 1931-39; chmn. Com. to Revise N.Y. Code of Criminal Procedure, 1933-39; mem. N.Y. State Law Revision Commn. 1934-45; mem. Governor's Crime Com., N.Y. State, 1935-36; mem. exec. bd. Govtl. Research Assn., 1935-37, 1941-43, 1950-51; member of the board of directors Citizens' Crime Commission of New York, 1937-41; mem. Mayor's Committee on Police Reorganization, San Francisco, 1936-37; chmn. Los Angeles board to select chief of police, 1939, Cincinnati, 1935, Woonsocket, 1943, Connecticut State Police, 1943; N.Y. City board to select city-wide sheriff, 1941; mem. committee on police training and merit systems, American Bar Association, since 1938, chmn. 1943-44; various U.S. Army advisory coms., 1942-43; chmn. adv. com. law enforcement, U.S. Department of Treasury 1954-55. Chairman of Committee on Intergovernmental Relations, 1954-55. Active member of International Assn. Chiefs of Police (advisor. state and provincial section); mem. Delta Tau Delta. Commd. 2d lt. R.M.A. (pilot), U.S. Air Service; with A.E.F., 1917-19. Author: The State Police, Organization and Administration, 1925; A Regional Police Plan for Cincinnati and its Environs, 1932; Rural Crime Control, 1933; Police Systems in United States, rev. 1949; Mobilizing Police for Emergency Duties, 1940; (with others) Uniform Crime Reporting, 1929; Chicago Police Problems, 1931, 34; New Goals in Police Management, 1954; also survey reports on police administration in about 50 leading American cities, 8 states and police systems of England, France, Belgium, Canada and Germany. Contbr. to Encyclopedia Britannica, Encyclopedia Americana, Encyclopedia Social Sciences. Journal of Criminal Law and Criminology, Police Journal (London), The Annals, etc. Clubs: Century (N.Y.); Seawanhaka Corinthia Yacht, Ends of the Earth (N. Y., London). Home: 19 Kensington Rd., Garden City, L.I. Office: 684 Park Av., N.Y.C. 21. Died Sept. 18, 1955.

SMITH, Bruce D(onald), banker; b. Lake Forest, Ill., Aug. 13, 1885; s. Byron Laflin and Carrie Cornelia (Stone) S.; grad. Hill Sch., 1902; B.A., Yale, 1906; m. Pauline Mackay, 1909 (divorced 1920); m. 2d, Florence Mann Fisher, June 1921. With Northern Trust Co., Chicago, 1907-19, resigned as vice pres., 1919; mem. bd. dirs. United Corp., Lehigh Coal and Nav. Corp., South N.J. Gas Co.; dir. Lehigh and New England R.R., 1944-46. Mgr. central div. Am. Red Cross, 1917-18; with Emergency Unemployment Relief Commn., N.Y. City, 1932-33; spl. asst. to chmn. A.R.C., 1933-35; supervisor orgn. and constrn. A.R.C.-Harvard Hosp., 1940-41, in Eng., 1941; asso. N.Y. state adminstr. War Bonds Com., 1941-43; spl. asst. to chmn. War Manpower Commn., 1943-45; cons. to gen. mgr. Atomic Energy Commn., 1948, mem. personnel security review bd., 1949. Served as 1st lt., 1st Ill. F.A., 1914-17; capt. Chem. Warfare Service, 1918-19. Republican. Clubs: Yale, Metropolitan (New York); Chevy Chase, 1925 F Street, Army-Navy (Washington); Reading Room, Clambake, Spouting Rock Beach (Newport, R.I.). Address: Bellevue Av., Newport, R.I.; also 36 E. 72d St., N.Y.C. 21. Died May 29, 1952.

SMITH, Cecil Michener, educator, music critic; b. Chgo., July 12, 1906; s. Gerald Birney and Inez (Michener) S.; Ph.B., U. Chgo., 1927; M.A., Harvard, 1928; m. Louise Shuttles, 1929 (div.). Instr. music U. Chgo., 1929-31, asst. prof., 1931-44, exec. sec., 1938-44, asso. prof. and chmn. music dept., 1944-47; music critic Chicago Tribune, 1936-43, drama critic, 1938-43; music editor New Republic, 1947—; asso. editor Theatre Arts, 1947-48; editor Musical Am., 1948—. Mem. N.Y. Music Critics Circle, Phi Beta Kappa, Delta Sigma Phi. Editor Ravinia Festival program books, 1937-42; v.p. Dalcroze Sch. Music, 1950—. Author: Musical Comedy in America, 1950; Music in America, 1952. Contbr. to The Best Plays of 1938-39, 39-40, 40-41, 41-42, 42-43; also articles to periodicals. Home: 72 University Pl. Office: 113 W. 57th St., N.Y.C. 19. Died May 27, 1956.

SMITH, Charles Carman, index mfr.; b. Junius, Seneca Co., N.Y., Sept. 29, 1866; s. Horace G. and Catharine A. (Carman) S.; student Dansville (N.Y.) Sem., 1879; grad. Doane Acad., Crete, Neb., 1883; B.S., Doane Coll., 1887; Master of Accounts, Eastman Bus. Coll., Poughkeepsie, N.Y., 1888; m. Mary D. Rogers, Oct. 5, 1892; children—Constance Carman, Ruth Dorothea, Lois Babcock, Miriam Rogers. Cashier Bank of Grover (Colo.), 1888-89; asst. cashier First Nat. Bank, Exeter, 1889-97; mfr. index tags and steel guides 1896—; pres. Exeter Cemetery Assn. Mem. Neb. State Senate, 1911-12. Dir. Neb. War Work Council, Y.M.C.A., 1917-18, Neb. State Y.M.C.A., 1917-23; pres. Exeter Red Cross. Trustee Doane Coll. (sec. bd. 1901-15; chmn. bd. 1914-15 and 1925-34); dir. Neb. Congl. Conf., 1918-26. Mem. Asso. Industries of Neb. (pres. 1921), Nat. Stationers Assn. Republican. Home: Exeter, Neb. Died Dec. 29, 1951; buried Exeter, Neb.

SMITH, Charles Howard, engr.; b. Portland, Ore., Sept. 4, 1884; s. Charles Jackson and Elizabeth (McMillan) S.; desc. Richard Smith who came to Mass. with Rogers Williams, 1636; grad. Seattle High Sch., 1901; student Phillips Andover Acad., 1901-02, Yale Sci. Sch., 1902-04; m. Jane Swindell, Sept. 28, 1909; children—Frances Townley (Mrs. Orville Anderson Tyler), Charles Jackson, Robert Fulton, Betsy Jane (Mrs. Jacques Bramhall, Jr.). Engr. Western Coal & Mining Co., St. Louis, 1905; v.p. Davis Coal & Coke Co., Balt., Pitts. Terminal Ry. & Coal Co., Western Coal & Mining Co., Consol. Coal Co., St. Louis; asst. to pres. Western Rd. R.R., 1907-11; v.p., gen. mgr. Durham Coal & Iron Co., 1911-12; expert mining engr., New York, 1913—; cons. engr. Clinchfield Coal Corp., 1913; asso. with Blair & Co., bankers, New York, 1914-21; pres. Internat. Coal Products Corp., Clinchfield Carbocoal Corp., Gen. Oil Gas Corp., Bregeat Corp. of Am., Am. & Automotive Gas Producers Corp., 1915-21; as cons. engr., 1921-27; chmn. bd. Gen. Waterworks & R.R. coal properties, C.&E.I. R.R., Utah Fuel Co., C., M.&St.P. Ry., etc.; organized Chenery & Smith, cons. engr., 1921-27; chmn. bd. Gen. Waterworkd & Elec. Co., 1928-29; pres. Charles H. Smith & Co., Engrs.; cons. engr. Utility Mgmt. Corp., 1937-38; cons. engr. Federal Water Service Co.; pres. Middle States Natural Gas Co., So. Shipbuilding and Dry Dock Corp., 1941, Nat. Armor Co., 1942-43, The Charles H. Smith Co., Engrs., 1944; v.p. South Am. Coal & Iron Co.; pres. Big Inch Gas, Inc. & Big Inch Oil, Inc. which merged Jan 1947 with Big Inch Gas and Oil Corp. During Worlad War I did spl. work for Ordnance Dept., Us. Army, U.S. Fuel Adminstrn., War Indsl. Bd. Inventor of process for converting bituminous coal into a smokeless fuel, also effecting recovery of by-products. Mem. Am. Mining Congress, Am. Inst. Mining and Metall. Engrs., (asso.), Army Ordnance Assn. Republican. Episcopalian. Clubs: Yale (N.Y.); Short Hills (N.J.). Home: 9 Ferncliff Terrace, Short Hills, N.J. Office: 20 Broad St., N.Y.C. 4. Died Dec. 16, 1950.

SMITH, Charles Lavens, banker; b. Franklin, Pa., Mar. 9, 1885; s. Edwin D. and Sophie Jane (Rogers) S.; A.B., Allegheny Coll., 1904; m. Bess McMillan, Sept. 25, 1909; children—Virginia Wadsworth (wife of Dr. Don McCauley Curtis), Raymond McMillan, Edwin David (dec.). Engaged in mfg., Franklin, 1904-07, in mining, Utah and Ariz., 1908-11; partner Ed. D. Smith & Sons, Salt Lake City, 1911-22; v.p. Central Trust Co., 1922-31; pres. Security Nat. Bank, 1931-32; pres. First Nat. Bank, 1932-48; chmn. First Security Bank; dir. First Security Corp., Salt Lake City Branch of Fed. Reserve Bank; mem. Salt Lake City Clearing House Assn. (ex-pres.). Pres. Community Chest of Salt Lake City, 1937-38; mem. adv. com. R.F.C., state chmn. Savs. Bond Div. U.S. Treasury Dept. Treas. U. of Utah. Mem. Salt Lake C. of C. (mem. bd. gov.), Am. Bankers Assn. (mem. econ. policy com.), Utah Bankers Assn., (pres. 1934-35), Reserve City Bankers Assn., Sigma Alpha Epsilon, Phi Beta Kappa. Republican. Presbyn. Club: Alta (pres. 1946). Home: 804 11th Av. Office: First Security Bank, Salt Lake City. Died Feb. 23, 1955; buried Mount Olive Cemetery, Salt Lake City.

SMITH, Charles Lee; b. Wilton, N.C., Aug. 29, 1865; s. Dr. Louis Turner and Nannie G. (Howell) S.; B.S., Wake Forest Coll., 1884, LL.D., 1906; instructor Raleigh Male Acad., 1884-85; associate editor, Biblical Recorder, 1884-85; U. of Halle, Germany, 1888; Ph.D., Johns Hopkins, 1889; m. Sallie Lindsay Jones, Oct. 24, 1889 (died Dec. 26, 1931); children—Howell Lindsay, William Oliver, Katherine Clark (Mrs. Joseph Hammond Hardison), Charles Lee; m. 2d, Celeste Henkel, Mar. 17, 1933 (died Sept. 30, 1935); m. 3d, Cora Antoinette Vaughan, July 12, 1937. At Johns Hopkins successively as univ. scholar, fellow in history and politics, instr. in history, and lecturer on sociology, 1886-91; prof. history and polit. science, William Jewell Coll., Mo., 1891-1905; pres. Mercer U., Ga., 1905-06; exec. dir. Edwards and Broughton Co., pubs., Raleigh, N.C., 1906-15, pres. since 1915; sec. National Conf. Charities and Correction, 1889-90; gen. sec. Baltimore Charity Orgn. Society, 1889-91; mem. administrative council Southern History Assn., 1897-1907. Gay lecturer, Southern Bapt. Theol. Sem., 1901. Trustee, mem. exec. com. and mem. building com., Univ. of N.C., 1911-32; chmn. and mem. exec. com. N.C. Library Commn., 1909-21; mem. adv. bd. N.C. Booklet. Past pres. and chmn. bd. mgrs. N.C. Soc. S.R. Vice chmn. Com. for War Service (N.C.), 1917-18; sometime chmn. Raleigh Municipal Recreation Commission. Mem. Phi Beta Kappa (Delta of N.C.). Author: History of Education in North Carolina; etc. Home: 515 N. Wilmington St., Raleigh, N.C. Died July 14, 1951; buried Oakwood Cemetery, Raleigh.

SMITH, Donald Borden, investment adviser; b. Somerville, Mass., Oct. 5, 1896; s. Reuben Schofield and Lila (Borden) S.; A.B., Mt. Allison U., 1919; M.B.A., Harvard, 1922, Ph.D., 1926; m. Florence Williams, Mar. 27, 1926; children—Cynthia Harvey (Mrs. John A. McFalls), Marilyn Borden (Mrs. James A. Hooper), Dona Charlotte Smith (Mrs. Richard B. Shanklin). Assistant professor Harvard Graduate Sch. Bus. Adminstrn., 1922-27; v.p. Investment Research Corp., 1927-31; investment counsel, gen. partner Scudder, Stevens & Clark, N.Y. and Boston, 1931-51; cons. economist, Boston, 1951—; dir., mem. finance com. Gen. Reinsurance Corp., North Star Reinsurance Corp., Washburn Co.; dir., mem. exec. com. Glens Falls Insurance Company. Member board of trustees of Abbott Academy, Andover, Mass. Chmn. investment adv. com. Ford Found. Served with CEF, 1916-18. Mem. Am. Econ. Assn., Am. Statis. Assn. Clubs: Union (Boston); Harvard, University (N.Y.C.). Home: Starboard Lane, Osterville, Mass. Office: 10 High St., Boston 10, Mass. Died Dec. 1959.

SMITH, Dorman Henry, cartoonist; b. Steubenville, O., Feb. 10, 1892; s. Marion Homer and Carrie (Henke) S.; ed. pub. schs., Columbus, O.; m. Carrie Mae Weed, June 15, 1913; children—Philip Christy, Richard Cherrington, Paul Sannar, Mary Isaphene worker, 1912; advertising artist, Jeffrey Manufacturing Company, Columbus, Ohio, 1917-19; cartoonist, (Mrs. John R. Thompson, Jr.). Began as steel mill Des Moines (Ia.) News, 1919-21, N.E.A. Service, Cleveland, 1921-27, Hearst newspapers in New York, Chicago and San Francisco, 1927-41; now with N.E.A. service, Cleveland, O. Past pres. Marin Art Assn. Member Hammer and Coffin Society of Stanford University (honorary), Eugene Field Society. Represented in Bohemian Club, San Francisco, Huntington Art Gallery, San Marino, Calif., Pa. Hist. Soc., Fed. Bur. of Investigation, Washington, D.C., Cleveland Museum of Art, and in universities, libraries and private collections. Regular exhibitor, water color section in the May show, Cleveland Museum of Art. Sigma Delta Chi award for outstanding achievement in journalism, 1946. Mem. of the Cleveland Soc. of Artists. Democrat. Christian Scientist. Club: Bohemian of San Francisco. Author: 101 Cartoons; Cartooning (course of study); First Steps to a Cartoon Career. Address: Died Mar. 1, 1956.

SMITH, Dudley Crofford, physician, educator; b. Lafayette Springs, Miss., Dec. 15, 1892; s. Dr. John General Marion and Carra (Powell) S.; B.S., U. of Miss., 1914; M.D., U. of Va., 1916; m. Lake Morrow, June 28, 1921; children—Dudley Crofford, Powell Morrow, Marjorie (Mrs. Hamilton Smithey). Intern, resident U. of Va. Hosp.; instr. medicine U. of Va., 1916-17, founded dept. dermatology and syphilology, 1924, prof., 1934-50; special consultant U.S.P.H.S. since 1933; investigator studying and standardizing syphilis treatment with penicillin in collaboration with Nat. Research Council and U.S.P.H.S., 1943-1949. Diplomate Am. Bd. Dermatology and Syphilology (founder). Mem. A.M.A. (chmn. sect. dermatology and syphilology 1950), Am. Dermatol. Assn. (v.p. 1943-45), Am. Acad. Dermatology and Syphilology, Sigma Xi, Kappa Sigma, Alpha Omega Alpha, Phi Beta Pi, Omicron Delta Kappa, Raven Soc., Tilka Soc. Democrat. Baptist. Elk, Mason. Clubs: Rotary, Colonnade, Farmington. Author articles epidemology of syphilis and dermatology profl. jours. Home: 30 University Circle, Charlottesville, Va. Died Aug. 30, 1950; buried University Cemetery, Charlottesville.

SMITH, E. C. E., business exec. Chmn. Rolls-Royce, Ltd. Address: Nightingale Rd., Derby, Eng. Died Oct. 17, 1950.*

SMITH, E. Norman, editor; b. Manchester, Eng.; s. John Walker and Anne (Bourne) S.; ed. schs. of Eng.; m. Elizabeth S. Irving, Apr. 5, 1895; 1 son, Irving Norman; m. 2d, Vessie A. Siddall, Feb. 22, 1922; 1 son, Ross W. Editorial staffs: Toronto Mail, Empire Toronto Globe, 1898-1905; pres. and editor Ottawa Free Press, 1905-16; vice president and president of the Ottawa Journal, since 1917. Pres. The Canadian Press, 1920-25. Chmn. Can. delegation Empire Press Union, S. Africa, 1935. Chmn. trustees, Ottawa Civic Hosp. Mem. Anglican Ch. Clubs: Rideau, Royal Ottawa Golf, Ottawa Country, Seigniory. Home: 454 Laurier Av. E. Office: The Journal Bldg., Ottawa, Ont., Can. Died Oct. 18, 1957.

SMITH, Earl Baldwin, educator; b. Topsham, Me., May 25, 1888; s. Frank Eugene and Nellie Frances (Baldwin) S.; grad. Pratt Inst., Bklyn., 1906; A.B., Bowdoin, 1911, L.H.D., 1931; A.M., Princeton, 1912, Ph.D., 1915; m. Ruth Preble Hall, Jan. 27, 1917 (dec. 1927); children—Mary Baldwin, Lacey Baldwin; m. 2d, Helen H. Hough, June 19, 1930; children—Nathaniel Baldwin, Susan Baldwin. Prof. art and archeology Princeton, 1916—, chmn. 1945; instr. Naval Air Combat Intelligence School, Quonset, R.I.; lectr. on Charles T. Mathews Found., Columbia, 1940. Served as capt., inf., U.S. Army, World War I. Chmn. arts and skills program, Tilton Hosp., Fort Dix; v.p. Princeton Red Cross. Mem. Athenaeum, Archeol. Inst. America, Coll. Art Assn. (dir.), Am. Inst. for Iranian Art and Archeology (dir. 1936-40), Phi Beta Kappa, Psi Upsilon. Clubs: Nassau (Princeton); Princeton (New York); Mountain View Country (ex-pres.). Author: Early Christian Iconography, 1918; Early Churches in Syria, 1929; Egyptian Architecture, 1938; The Dome, 1950; Architectural Symbolism, 1956. Contbr. to Am. Jour. Archeology, Art Studies, Art and Archeology, The Art Bulletin; also chapter on Fine Arts in Roads to Knowledge. Home: 211 Prospect Av., Princeton, N.J. Died Mar. 7, 1956.

SMITH, Edgar Moncena, coll. pres.; b. Livermore, Me., Aug. 4, 1846; s. Charles and Mary (Walker) S.; grad. Wesleyan U., Middletown, Conn., 1871 (A.M.; D.D.); m. Marguerita M. Hauschild, 1875. Pastor, Providence and Newport, R.I., 1875-80; pres. Wesleyan Sem. and Female Coll., Kent Hill, Me., 1882-93; prin. Montpelier Sem., Vt., 1893-98, pres. Ill. Wesleyan U., 1898—. Mem. Gen. Missionary Com., M.E. Ch.; apptd., 1900, mem. U. senate of M.E. Ch. Address: Bloomington, Ill. Died Nov. 10, 1924.

SMITH, Edward G., retired r.r. exec.; b. Buffalo, N.Y., May 11, 1886; s. Albert Bickford and Sarah J. (Flynn) S.; LL.B., N.Y. Law School, 1909; LL.M., N.Y. Univ., 1910; married Nina Neely, 1918, deceased; 1 son, Edward Neely, deceased; married 2d, Mrs. Florence T. Dold, 1949. With N.Y. Central R.R., 1903-07; stenographer Union Pacific R.R., 1907-10, cashier, 1910-18, asst. treas., 1919-20, treas., 1920-52, sec., 1933-52, dir. since 1941, v.p., 1942-52; ret. 1952. Club: Wykagyl Country (New Rochelle, N.Y.). Home: 140 Trenor Drive, New Rochelle, N.Y. Died May 2, 1956; buried Gate of Heaven Cemetery, Valhalla, N.Y.

SMITH, Elmer William, educator; b. Gouverneur, N.Y., Jan. 22, 1868; s. Samuel and Elizabeth (Markwick) S.; A.B., Colgate U., 1891, A.M., 1894, Litt. D., 1936; post-grad. work, U. of Chicago and Harvard; m. Luella Kern, Sept. 3, 1895; children—Markwick Kern, Albert Irving. Asst. in Dept. of English, Colgate, 1891-92; teacher in English and history, Pinkerton Acad., Derry, N.H., 1892-93; head dept. of English, Colgate Acad., 1893-1908; asso. prof. of English, Colgate Univ., 1908-10, prof. pub. speaking and asso. prof. English lit., 1910-17, prof. English lit. and pub. speaking, 1917-36, prof. emeritus of English literature since 1936; lecturer U. of Calif. at Berkeley, 1925, at Los Angeles, 1926, U. of Ore., summer, 1937, Syracuse U., summer, 1932; examiner in English for N.Y. State Edn. Dept., 1912-17; mem. Nat. Commn. on High Sch. Syllabus, N.Y. State Syllabus Com. Mem. Nat. Council English Teachers (dir. 1912-13), N.E.A., Speech Arts Assn., N.Y. State English Teachers' Assn. (pres. 1907), N.Y. State Elocutionists' Assn. (pres. 1914-15), Internat. Torch Assn. (extension sec.), Phi Beta Kappa, Beta Theta Pi. Republican. Baptist. Author: Graded Exercises in Punctuation and Use of Capitals, 1900; Handbook of Debate, 1912; Extemporaneous Speaking, 1931. Associate editor English Jour., 1912-19; editor Colgate Gen. Catalogue. Was lecturer for Redpath Chautauqua, 1915, Radcliffe Chautauquas, 1917, 18, 21, for Y.M.C.A., in A.E.F., France, 1919; dean of College World Tour, 1928-29. Home: 11 E. Kendrick Av., Hamilton, N.Y. Died Oct. 11, 1950; buried Coll. Hill Cemetery, Hamilton.

SMITH, Ethelbert Walton, ry. ofcl.; b. Clarksburg, W.Va., Sept. 21, 1885; s. Mortimer W. and Lucy (Walton) S.; M.E., Va. Poly. Inst., 1905; m. Frances Woodbridge Sprecher (dec.); 1 son, Ethelbert Walton, m. 2d, Mary Shelley Meyer. Shopman Pa. R.R., 1905, advanced through various positions to gen. supt. of motive power, 1922, gen. supt., 1924-26; gen. mgr., 1926-28, regional v.p., Pittsburgh, 1928-31 and 1933-46, became regional v.p. Phila., 1946, now ret.; co-receiver S.A.L. Ry. 1931-32; pres., dir. Baltimore & Eastern R.R. Co., Penna. & Atlantic R.R. Co., Rosslyn Connecting R.R. Co., Harrisburg Warehouse Co.; dir. Camden & Burlington Co. R.R. Co., The Connecting Ry. Co., Cumberland Valley & Martinsburg R.R. Co., Delaware River R.R & Bridge Co., Elmira & Lake Ontario R.R. Co., Lykens Valley R.R. & Coal Co., Merchants Warehouse Co., N.Y., Phila. & Norfolk R.R. Co., N.Y., Phila. & Norfolk R.R. Ferry Co., The Northern Central Ry. Co., Phila. & Trenton R.R. Co., Del., Md. & Va. R.R. Co., Shamokin Valley & Pottsville R.R. Co., Union R.R. Co., Balt., Wilkes-Barre Connecting R.R. Co., York, Hanover & Frederick Ry. Co., Norfolk & Portsmouth Belt Line R.R., Phila. Tidewater Terminals, Inc., Va. Ferry Corp., Washington Terminal Co., Kiptopeake Beach Land Corp., The Del. R.R. Co. Club: Phila. Country. Home: 179 Midfield Rd., Armore, Pa. Office: 409 Pennsylvania Station, Phila. 4. Died June 7, 1958.

SMITH, Ezekiel Ezra, Baptist clergyman; b. Duplin Co., N.C., May 23, 1852; ed. pub. schs.; became a teacher, 1870; grad. Shaw U., 1878; m. Willie A. Burnette, Nov. 17, 1875. Licensed as Baptist preacher, 1879; prin. graded school, Goldsborough, N.C., 1879-83; prin. State Colored Normal Sch., 1883-8; maj. 4th battalion, N.C. Guards, 1880; U.S. minister to Liberia, 1888-90; sec. N.C. State Baptist Conv. 1876-83; pres. State Industrial Assn., N.C., 1892-3; has traveled considerably in Europe and extensively in Africa; adj. 3d N.C. vol. inf., April 27, 1898, to Feb. 8, 1899; editor Carolina Enterprise, 1881-3. Address: Goldsborough, N.C. Died 1933.

SMITH, Ferdinand Conrad, business exec.; b. Portland, Ore., Dec. 19, 1892; s. Charles C. and Clara Smith; student Portland Acad., Milton (Mass.) Acad.; m. Margery E. Hoffman, Jan. 7, 1917. Sales mgr. Peninsula Lumber Co., Portland, Ore., 1919-27; sales mgr. E. A. Pierce Co., Portland, 1927-40, mgr. Portland br., 1938-40; resident partner Portland br. Merrill-Lynch, Pierce, Fenner & Beane, 1940-42, San Francisco br., 1942—; formerly chmn. governing bd. San Francisco Stock Exchange and asso. mem. N.Y. Stock Exchange; spl. asst. to pres. U.S., 1950. Mem. Downtown Assn. (v.p.), C. of C. Clubs: Arlington

(Portland); Burlingame Country; Pacific-Union, Stock Exchange (San Francisco). Home: 825 Francisco St., San Francisco 9. Office: 301 Montgomery St., San Francisco 4. Died Aug. 22, 1958.

SMITH, Ferris, surgeon; b. Pontiac, Mich., Oct. 25, 1883; s. Samuel W. and Alida E. (DeLand) S.; A.B., U. Mich., 1908, M.D., 1910; post-grad. Vienna and Berlin; m. Florence Bannister, June 25, 1913. Began practice at Ann Arbor, 1910; settled in Grand Rapids, Mich., 1913; capt. Royal Med. Corps, Eng., Mar. 1917; facial plastic surgeon Queens Hosp., Eng., World War; prof. plastic surgery Internat. Clinic, Paris, 1923; surgeon Blodgett Meml. Hosp., Grand Rapids. Fellow A.C.S. (gov.); Internat. College of Dentists (hon.); mem. Founders Group Am. Bd. Plastic Surgery, A.M.A., Mich. Med. Soc., Oral and Plastic Surg. Soc. (pres.), Am. Soc. of Plastic and Reconstructive Surgery, Alpha Omega Alpha, Sigma Psi, Delta Tau Delta, Nu Sigma Nu. Co-author: Manual of Plastic and Maxillo-Facial Surgery, Army Med. Corps. Author: Plastic and Reconstructive Surgery, 1950. Home: 639 Plymouth Rd. S.E. Office: Blodgett Med. Bldg., Grand Rapids 6, Mich. Died Sept. 18, 1957; buried Restlawn Meml. Park.

SMITH, Frank Channing, Jr., lawyer, business exec.; b. Worcester, Mass., May 22, 1877; s. Frank Channing and Hattie R. (Chase) S.; A.B., Harvard, 1900, LL.B., 1902; m. Amy Williams; Oct. 5. 1904. Admitted to Mass. bar, 1902, since practiced in Worcester; sr. mem. Thayer, Smith & Caskill since 1914; treas., dir. Worcester Bell Co.; sec., dir. Worcester Telegram Pub. Co., Inc.; trustee Worcester Five Cents Savs. Bank; dir. Baker Lumber Co., Worcester Co. Electric Co., Rice Barton Corp., Mechanics Nat. Bank, Riley Stoker Corp., Baxter D. Whitney & Son, Inc., Bachmann-Uxbridge Worsted Corp. Pres., trustee Worcester Art Mus. Mem. Am., Mass. State, Worcester Co. bar assns. Republican. Unitarian. Clubs: Worcester, Tatnuck Country, Century, N.Y. Harvard; Boston, Soc. Odd Volumns (Boston). Home: 32 Cedar St. Office: 340 Main St., Worcester, Mass. Died Jan. 12, 1952.

SMITH, Frank Grigsby, judge; b. Marion, Ark., Aug. 2, 1872; s. John Franklin and Martha (Gidden) S.; ed. U. of Ark., Searcy (Ark.) Coll., and Davis School, N.C.; m. Clara Webb, June 16, 1897. Admitted to Ark. bar, 1893, and began practice, Marion, Ark.; asso. justice Supreme Court of Ark. since Oct. 31, 1912, present term ending Jan. 1, 1953. Democrat. Methodist. Home: 2200 Gaines St. Address: State House, Little Rock, Ark. Died Oct. 27, 1950; buried Elmwood Cemetery, Memphis.

SMITH, Frank Leslie, b. Dwight, Ill., Nov. 24, 1867; s. John J. and Jane E. (Ketcham) S.; student schs.; m. Ermine Ahern, Feb. 8, 1893. Banker and farmer; collector of internal revenue, Springfield Dist., 1908-12; mem. 66th Congress, 17th Ill. Dist.; chmn. Ill. Commerce Commn., 1918-20, 22-24, 24-26; elected to U.S. Senate, Nov. 2, 1926. Chmn. Rep. State Com., Ill., 1918-24; served as chmn. Rep. State Central Com., 3 times; mem. Rep. Nat. Com. for Ill., 1932-36; del. nat. convs., including 1948; nominee for congressman at large, Ill., 1930. Club: Union League (Chgo.). Home: Dwight, Ill. Died Aug. 30, 1950.

SMITH, Frederick C., ex-congressman; b. Shanesville, O., July 29, 1884. Physician and surgeon in practice at Marion, O., founded Frederick C. Smith Clinic; mayor of Marion, 1935-39; mem. 76th to 81st Congresses, 8th Ohio Dist. Republican. Home: 739 E. Center St., Marion, O. Died July 15, 1956, buried Marion.

SMITH, George Albert, church official; b. Salt Lake City, Utah, Apr. 4, 1870; s. John Henry and Sarah (Farr) S.; student Brigham Young Acad., 1882-83, U. of Utah, 1887-88; Doctor of Humanities (hon.), U. of Utah, 1950; m. Lucy Emily Woodruff, May 25, 1892; children—Emily (Mrs. Robert M. Stewart), Edith (Mrs. George O. Elliott), George Albert. Employed at Grant Odell & Co., Zions Coöp. Mercantile Instn. and Clothing Factory, 1883-91; sec. mission Ch. of Jesus Christ of Latter-day Saints, in Southern states, 1892-94; ex-mem. Quorum of Twelve Apostles (pres. 1943); pres. Ch. of Jesus Christ of Latter-day Saints, since 1945; pres. European mission headquarters England, 1919-21; gen. supt. Young Men's Mutual Improvement Association, 1921-35. Pres. Beneficial Life Ins. Co., Heber J. Grant & Co., Hotel Utah Co., Utah Home Fire Ins. Co., Utah-Idaho Sugar Co., Utah First Nat. Bank, Zion's Savings Bank & Trust Co., Zion's Coop. Mercantile Instn. and Zion's Securities Corp.; v.p. and dir. Utah Savings & Trust Company; director of the Union Depot (Salt Lake City). United States receiver public moneys, special disbursing agent, Utah, 1898-1904; president International Irrigation Congress, 1916-17, Internat. Dry Farm Congress, 1917-18, Internat. Farm Congress, 1918, Utah Pioneer Trails & Landmarks Assn. since 1930; v.p. gen. S.A.R., 1922-27; ofcr. in scouting 20 yrs.; mem. nat. exec. bd. Boy Scouts of Am. since 1931, has traveled extensively in behalf of orgn.; awarded Silver Beaver, 1933, Silver Buffalo, 1934, by Boy Scouts of America. Pres. Soc. Aid of Sightless (pres. since 1934). Dir. Ore. Trail Memorial Assn. Republican. Traveled in Hawaii, Tonga, New Zealand, Australia and Samoa visiting Church missions and Boy Scout councils, 1938. Home: 1302 Yale Av. Office: 47 E. South Temple St., Salt Lake City 5. Died Apr. 4, 1951; buried Salt Lake City.

SMITH, George Hathorn, coll. prof.; b. Harrison, Me., Sept. 25, 1885; s. John Leander and Cedelle (Goss) S.; A.B., Bates Coll., 1909, D.Sc., 1934; A. M., Brown U., 1910, Ph.D., 1914; A.M., Yale, 1926; m. Abbie N. Adams, Sept 3, 1912; children—Allan Hathorn, Bryce Adams, Miriam, Charlotte. Research bacteriologist, Phila., 1912-17; asst. professor, Yale, 1917-23, asso. prof., 1923-26, prof. of immunology since 1926, asst. dean Sch. of Medicine, 1940-45; editor-in-chief Yale Jour. Biology and Medicine since 1927; mem. edit. bd. Am. Jour. Bacteriology. Mem. Soc. Am. Bacteriologists, Am. Assn. Immunologists, A.A.A.S., New Haven Colony Hist. Soc., Cape Sable (N.S.) Hist. Soc., N.E. Hist. and Geneal. Soc., Phi Beta Kappa, Sigma Xi. Republican. Home: 474 Washington Av., West Haven, Conn. Died July July 7, 1952; buried Barrington, N.S.

SMITH, George Hunter, banker; b. at Chillicothe, O., Oct. 12, 1861; s. Amos and Henrietta (Renick) S.; ed. Kenyon Coll., Gambier, O., 1880-83; m. Clara Louise Boggs, Dec. 27, 1888. Began as bookkeeper of coal mining co., 1883; took charge of sales dept. Wellston (O.) Coal Co., 1885, elected a dir., pres. 1892——; interested in several large bus. enterprises. Home: Chillicothe, O. Died Oct. 2, 1939.

SMITH, George L., pres. treas., dir. G. R. Kinney Corp. Home: 6810 Continental Av., Forest Hills, N.Y. Office: 221 4th Av., N.Y.C. 3. Died Nov. 14, 1959.

SMITH, George Milton, surgeon; b. Hong Kong, China, July 5, 1879; s. Jay Henry and Elisabeth (Connor) S.; A.B., Yale University, 1901, honorary LL.D., 1947; M.D., Columbia University, 1905; married Lucy Clare Young, May 21, 1910; 1 daughter, Clare Connor (Mrs. Sidney Webb Noyes, Jr). Came to U.S., as child, parents U.S. citizens. Interne Presbyn. Hosp., and Sloan Maternity Hosp., N.Y. City, 1905-09; asso. prof. pathology Washington U., St. Louis, Missouri, 1909-16; dir. Barnard Free Skin and Cancer Hospital, St. Louis, Missouri, 1916; research asso. rank prof. emeritus Yale since 1948. Served as capt. med. corps mobile hosp. 39, U.S. Army, 1917-19, with A.E.F. Med. dir. Anna Fuller Fund since 1933; mem. bd. sci. advisors Jane Coffin Childs Meml. Fund Med. Research; med. dir. Conn. State Defense Council, 1941-43, Conn. War Council, 1943-45; chmn. sub-com. on armored vehicles, Nat. Research Council, 1942-46; consultant to surg. gen. of Army, 1944-46. Pres. Conn. State Med. Soc., 1943-44. Mem. Nat. Adv. Cancer Council 1939-46; exec. dir. 1944-46; special consultant, 1947——. Recipient citations War Dept.; medal American Cancer Soc., 1949; Bertner Found. award (posthumously), 1952; decorated Cross of Knighthood of Dannebrog (Denmark). Mem. Am. Assn. Anatomists, Pathol. Soc. Great Brit. and Ireland; fgn. corr. French Assn. for Study of Cancer. Episcopalian. Contbr. research papers on cancer to med. jours. Home: Pine Orchard, Conn. Office: 333 Cedar St., New Haven. Died Feb. 26, 1951; buried Center Cemetery, Branford, Conn.

SMITH, G(eorge) Wallace, coll. prof.; born Richmond, Va., Oct. 5, 1894; s. James Wallace and Mary Emily (Waite) S.; B.S. in Elec. Engring., U. of N.C., 1916; M.S.E. in Civil Engring., U. of Mich., 1932, D.Sc., 1936; m. Marguerite Ghent, Dec. 2, 1922; 1 son, George Wallace. Asst. elec. engr. Carolina Shipyards, Wilmington, N.C., 1918-21; asst. instr. engring., dept. of drawing, U. of N.C., 1921-22, instr., 1922-24, asst. prof., 1924-29, asso. prof., 1929-31, 1932-36; asso. prof., head dept. engring. mechanics N.C. State Coll., 1936-37, prof. and head dept. since 1937. Engr., water resources div., N.C. Dept. Conservation and Development, 6 summers, Am. Bridge Co., Pencoyd plant, 1 summer; resettlement adminstrn., Land Utilization Div., 1 summer. Served with U.S. Army, 1917-18. Mem. Am. Soc. C.E., Am. Soc. Engring. Edn., N.C. Soc. Engrs., Raleigh Engrs. Club, Soc. Mayflower Descendants, Sigma Xi, Tau Beta Pi. Episcopalian. Recipient Cain Math. Medal, U. of N.C., 1915. Home: 222 Hawthorne Rd., Raleigh, N.C. Died Sept. 2, 1959.

SMITH, Gerald Hewitt, publisher; b. Swampscott, Mass., Sept. 28, 1912; s. Ormond G. and Grace Hewitt (Pellett) S.; grad. Hotchkiss Sch., 1931; A.B., Princeton, 1936; m. Virginia Ashcraft, Sept. 3, 1936; children—Ann Ashcraft, Ralph Ormond. Sec. Street & Smith Publs., Inc., N.Y.C., 1936-48, pres., dir., 1948——, pub. Mademoiselle, Charm, Living For Young Homemakers, Air Trails. Mem. Mag. Publishers Assn. (dir.). Clubs: Tavern (Chgo.); University Cottage, Nassau; Springdale Golf (Princeton. N.J.). Home: 132 Elm Rd., Princeton, N.J. Office: 575 Madison Av., N.Y.C. 22. Died June 18, 1955.

SMITH, Gilbert Morgan, coll. prof.; b. Beloit, Wis., Jan. 6, 1885; s. Erastus Gilbert and Elizabeth Maria (Mayher) S.; ed. Williston Acad., 1900-03; B.S., Beloit Coll., 1907, D.Sc. (hon.), 1927: Ph.D., U. Wis., 1913; m. Helen Virginia Pfuderer, Aug. 12, 1913. High school teacher, Stoughton, Wis., 1907; asst. in botany, U. Wis., 1909-10, instr., of botany, 1911-15, asst. prof., 1915-17, asso. prof., 1917-25; prof. of botany, Stanford U., 1925-50. Member A.A. A.S. (v.p., 1941), Am. Micros. Soc. (pres., 1928), Botanical Soc. Am. (pres. 1944), Am. Acad., Nat. Acad. Scis., Phi Beta Kappa, Beta Theta Pi, Sigma Xi. Congregationalist. Rep. Club: Menlo Country. Author: Freshwater Algae of U.S., 1933; Cryptogamic Botany, 1938; co-author: A Textbook of General Botany, 1924. Marine Algae of the Monterey Peninsula, Cal.; Manual of Phycology, 1951. Home: 1220 Hobart St., Menlo Park, Cal. Died July 11, 1959.

SMITH, Griffin, judge; b. Laurel Hill, Tenn., July 13, 1885; s. James Robert Napoleon and Ida (Griffin) S.; LL.B., Cumberland U., special work Stanford U.; honorary LL.D., Cumberland University, 1950; m. Amelia Sheffield Daggett, June 15, 1910; children—Sheffield (Mrs. Drew H. Lander), Griffin. Newspaper pub., 1911-21; admitted to the bar, 1923; served as comptroller State of Arkansas, 1932-36; chief justice Ark. Supreme Court since Dec. 31, 1936. Episcopalian. Home: 5315 Sherwood Rd. Office: State Capitol, Little Rock, Ark. Died Apr. 29, 1955; buried Little Rock.

SMITH, Harold Travis, naval officer; b. Mpls., June 7, 1887; B.S., U.S. Naval Acad., 1909, grad. work, 1914; M.S., Columbia, 1915. Commd. as ensign U.S. Navy, 1909, and advanced through the grades to rear admiral, 1945; instr. engring., U.S.S. Fulton, 1915-17; in charge fitting out U.S.S. 0-5, 1917-18; engring. aide on staff comdr. submarine force Atlantic fleet U.S.S. Chgo. flagship, 1918; on duty at periscope sch., Portsmouth, Va., 1918; attached to naval hdqrs., London, Eng., 1918-19; assigned U.S.S. Bushnell, assigned U.S.S. Fulton with spl. duty on German subs, 1919; tour of duty Bur. of Engring., Navy Dept., Washington, 1919-21; in charge outfitting U.S.S. Omaha, Todd Dry Dock & Constrn. Co., Tacoma, 1921-23; engr. officer U.S.S. Omaha, 1923-25; assigned to Navy Yard, Portsmouth, N.H., 1925-26; tour of duty bur. engring., Navy Dept., Washington, 1926-30; aide and engr. officer staff comdr. cruisers, scouting force U.S. Fleet, 1930-32; in charge central draughting office N.Y. Navy Yard, 1932-35; Bur. Engring., Navy Dept., Washington, 1935-39; naval insp. machinery and navigation material, Bethlehem Steel Co., Quincy, Mass., 1939-40; became supervisor shipbuilding and naval insp. of ordnance Betlehem Steel Co., Quincy, Mass. and other shipbldg. and ordnance plants in R.I. and Mass., 1940; now mem. staff Comdr.-in-Chied Pacific Fleet. Decorated Victory Medal, Escort Clasp, U.S. S. Chicago, Am. Defense Service Medal. Address: Navy Dept., Washington. Deceased.

SMITH, Harold Wellington, naval med. officer; b. Boston, Mass., May 30, 1878; s. Wellington and Mary Eleanor (Dodge) S.; student Harvard Coll., 1896-97, M.D., Med. Sch., 1901; m. Mary Currier Eaton, Nov. 10, 1913 (died 1924); children—Margaret (Mrs. W. F. LaMond), Stephen Currier. Commd. asst. surgeon, U.S. Navy, 1904, and advanced through ranks to rear adm., Med. Corps, 1936. Mem. Med. Com. of Office of Scientific Research and Development. Mem. A.M.A. (house of dels.), Assn. Mil. Surgeons (mem. exec. council), Am. Coll. Surgeons (mem. bd. of govs.), Am. Acad. Tropical Medicine (councillor), U.S. Naval Inst. Unitarian. Clubs: Harvard, Army and Navy (Washington). Author med. articles for U.S. Naval Med. Bulletin. In charge of med. research in U.S. Navy. Home: 4000 Cathedral Av. Office: Bureau Medicine and Surgery, Navy Dept., Washington. Died Feb. 4, 1952; buried Forrest Hills Cemetery, Jamaica Plains, Boston.

SMITH, H(arry) Lester, bishop; b. Indiana, Pa., Apr. 15, 1876; s. George W. and Lucy (Shepherd) S.; A.B., Allegheny Coll., 1904, A.M., 1906, D.D., 1913, LL.D., 1921; student Columbia 1 yr.; B.D., Drew Theol. Sem., 1905; LL.D., Albion (Mich.) Coll., 1920, Wilberforce, 1938, Marietta College, 1947; m. Ida L. Martin, June 29, 1899. Began preaching at 20; ordained to ministry M.E. Ch., 1906; pastor Pitcairn, Pa., 1897-1900; asst. pastor, Meadville, 1900-01; pastor Congl. Ch., Corry, 1901-03, M.E. Ch., Leonia, N.J., 1903-05, Bellevue Ch., Allegheny, Pa., 1905-09, Delaware Av. Ch., Buffalo, 1909-12, Central Ch., Detroit, 1912-20; elected bishop, 1920, and apptd. to Bangalore, India, for 4 yrs. in supervision of missionary work; apptd. resident bishop Helena area, 1924, Chattanooga area, 1928, Cin. area, 1932, Ohio area, 1944. Del. Gen. Conf. M.E. Ch., 1916, 20. Mem. Phi Beta Kappa, Delta Tau Delta. Mason (33°). Home: 31 Meadow Park Av., Bexley, Columbus, O. Died Oct. 7, 1951.

SMITH, Harry Pearse, educator; b. Greeley, Ia., May 25, 1885; s. Truman P. and Alice Marion (Pearse) S.; A.B., State U. of Ia., 1909, A.M., 1915; studied 4 summers, U. of Chicago; Ph.D., Columbia, 1925; m. Coleen M. Patterson, Aug. 11, 1915; 1 son, Durwood James. Teacher and supervising principal pub. schs., Ia., 1903-5 and 1906-07; supt. schs., Audubon, 1909-12, Newton, 1912-20; supt. schs., Lawrence, Kan., prof. edn. U. Kan., 1920-24, 25-27; emeritus prof. edn. Syracuse U.; director research Syracuse pub. schs., since 1927; visiting prof. edn.,

Ohio State U., 6 summers to 1938, U. of Southern Calif., Los Angeles, summers 1934, 39, 46, Drake U., Des Moines, Iowa, summers 1940, 41; assisted and directed many sch. surveys in Kan., Ohio and N.Y. State. Mem. N.E.A., American Educational Researcn Association, Educational Research Association N.Y. State (ex-pres.), Am. Assn. Univ. Profs., Nat. Soc. Coll. Teachers of Edn., Phi Beta Kappa, Phi Delta Kappa, Kappa Phi Kappa. Republican. Methodist. Clubs: Faculty, Rotary. Author: Business Administration of a City School System, 1926; Business Administration of Public Schools, 1929; The Emergency Collegiate Centers of Central New York, 1937; Public School Building Program for Syracuse, 1949; Syracuse Youth Who Did Not Graduate, 1950. Contbr. to many ednl. publs. Home: 856 Maryland Av., Syracuse, N.Y. Died Feb. 17, 1953.

SMITH, H(enry) Augustine, coll. prof., author; b. Naperville, Ill., Oct. 17, 1874; s. Henry Cowles and Mary Hittle (Dreisbach) S.; A.B., Northwestern (now North Central) Coll., 1896, A.M., 1910, LL.D., 1936; studied Am. Conservatory of Music and Oberlin Conservatory of Music; Litt.D., Ripon College, 1935; m. Lucia May (Smith) S., Nov. 23, 1916 (died October 8, 1946); children—Henry Augustine, Patricia May. Instructor and professor in hmynology and church music, Chicago Theology Seminary, 1901-16; professor hymnology and church music, Chicago Theol. Sem. and Div. Sch., Univ. of Chicago, 1915, 16; dir. of music and tenor soloist, First Congl. Ch., Chicago, 1901-16; prof. hymnology, Ch. music and pageantry, Boston U. since 1917; dir. fine arts in religion, Boston U. Sch. of Religious Edn., 1921-33; director music, pageantry, art, Daytona Beach Forum and Assembly, 1934, and of dept. of Sacred Music, Boston U. Coll. of Music since 1934; dir. of music, Chautauqua, N.Y., 1921-28; chmn. ch. music Nat. Fedn. of Music Clubs, 1937-1941; church music com. Nat. Educator's Music Conf. since 1939; cond. of Massed Choirs, Boston and Mass. Council of Churches, since 1936. A pioneer in field of ch. music and allied arts; organizer first jr. ch. choirs (new First Congregational Church, Chicago), organizer first multiple choirs in U.S., 1910-16, First Congregational Church, Chicago. Director music and allied arts Religious Edn. Assn. Conv., Boston, 1917; Methodist Centenary, Columbus, 1919; Internat. Council Congl. Chs., Boston, 1919; World Sunday Sch. Conv., Tokyo, Japan, 1920; Gen. Assembly, Presbyn. Ch., Phila., 1920; Internat. Conv. Religious Edn., Kansas City, 1922, Birmingham, Ala., 1926; World and Internat. Christian Endeavor convs., Chicago, 1915, Des Moines, 1922; Internat. Bapt. Y.P. Union, Detroit, 1929; Ecumenical Council, Methodist Ch., Atlanta, 1931; Ref. Churchman's Conv., Harrisburg, 1931; World's Sunday Sch. Conv., Rio de Janeiro, 1932; Ref. Churchmen's Conv., Harrisburg, 1939; Northern Baptist Conv., Los Angeles, 1939; National Fedn. of Music Clubs, Baltimore, 1939, Los Angeles, 1941; N.E.A., Boston, 1941; Southwestern Bible Conf., Shreveport, La., 1944. Organizer-condr., Boston and Mass. Festivals of Choirs, 1935-47, now Fleming H. Revell Co., New York. Mem. Commn. on Worship, Federal Council of Chs. Mem. Hymn Soc. Republican. Conglist. Club: University. Author: (or compiler for D. Appleton-Century Co., New York City) The Hymnal for American Youth, 1919; The Century Hymnal, 1921; The Army and Navy Hymnal, 1922; Hymns for the Living Age, 1923; The American Student Hymnal, 1928; The New Hymnal for American Youth, 1930; Worship in the Church School through Music, Pagentry, Pictures, 1928; Lyric Religion, 1931; Praise and Service, 1932, pub. in Braille by U.S. Govt. for Protestant blind, 1934; Northwestern University Sch. Music Bull. No. 5 on Orgn. and Adminstrn. of Choirs, 1933; The New Church Hymnal, 1937; Ayer Foundation Lecturer, Colgate-Rochester Divinity Sch. on "Expression of Religion in Art-Music." Also pageants and ritual programs—The Immortality of Love and Service, 1918; The City Beautiful, 1919; The Commonwealth of God, 1920; The Stars and Stripes, 1920; The Light of the World, 1922; Chautauqua Sunday Night Services, 1924; A Memorial Armistice Day Service, 1928. Founder of Home Dedicatipm Day. Home: 26 Rockledge Rd., Newton Highlands, Mass.; (summer) 15 Stone Av., Egypt, Mass. Office: 25 Blagden St., Boston. Died Mar. 16, 1952; buried Naperville, Ill.

SMITH, Henry Gerrish, shipbuilder; b. Warrensville, O., Apr. 9, 1870; s. Erastus and Martha (March) S.; grad. U.S. Naval Acad., 1891; studied Royal Naval Coll., Eng., 1891-94; m. Betty Dent, Oct. 9, 1895 (dec.); children—Mrs. Betty Dent Walker, Charles Raymond; m. 2d, Lucy Margaret Gleason, Sept. 24, 1936. Midshipman U.S. Navy, 1887-93; naval constructor U.S. Navy, at Royal Naval Coll., Cramps Shipyard, N.Y. Navy Yard, Bur. of Construction and Repair, Navy Dept., Washington; resigned from Navy, 1903, to become mgr. Fore River Shipbuilding Co. (later Fore River Shipbuilding Corp.), v.p., gen. mgr., 1913-17; mgr. Bethlehem Shipbuilding Corp., Ltd., 1917-21, asst. to pres. 1921, v.p., 1923-32; pres. Shipbuilders Council of Am., 1929-50, chmn. bd., 1950—. Mem. classification Lloyds, U.S. del. to Internat. Conv. of Safety of Life at Sea, London, 1929. Mem. Soc. Naval Architects and Marine Engrs., 1893— (sec.-treas. 1932-39; pres. 1939 and 1940); bd. mgrs. Am. Bur. Shipping. Chmn. Shipbldg. and Ship Repairing Industry Code Authority, 1933-35. Rep. Episcopalian. Home: Bronxville, N.Y. Addresss: 21 West St., N.Y.C. Died June, 1959.

SMITH, Henry Louis, univ. pres.; b. Greensboro, N.C., July 30, 1859; s. Rev. J. Henry and Mary Kelly (Watson) S.; A.B., Davidson, 1881, A.M., 1886; U. of Va., 1886-87, Ph.D., 1890; LL.D., U. of N.C., 1899; m. Julia Lorraine Dupuy, Aug. 4, 1896; children—J. Henry (dec.), Helen Lorraine, Raymond Dupuy (dec.), Julia Dupuy, Louise Watson (Mrs. Robert A. Merritt), Opie Norris, Frank Sampson. Prof. physics, 1887-1901, pres. Davidson Coll. 1901-12, Washington and Lee U., 1912-30 (retired). Pres. N.C. Teachers' Assembly, 1889, Assn. of Va. Colls., 1914-15; mem. Am. Acad. Polit. and Social Science, Am. Soc. for Broader Edn. (dir.), A.A.A.S., N.C., Va. acads. sci., Phi Beta Kappa, Omicron Delta Kappa, Phi Delta Theta, Kappa Phi Kappa. Lectr. on ednl. and sci. subjects. Author: Your Biggest Job, 1920; Enriching One's Vocabulary, 1936; Climbing Upward, 1937; This Troubled Century, 1947. Chmn. Va. delegation to Great Britain, 1921. Pioneer American Scientist in taking X-ray photographs and using X-ray in surgical work. Invented method, highly praised by President Wilson, of using self-deflating rubber balloons in distributing propaganda to Germany, summer of 1918 causing rebellion and the flight of the Kaiser. Home: 208 W. Bessemer Av., Greensboro, N.C. Died Feb. 27, 1951; buried Forest Lawn Cemetery, Greensboro.

SMITH, Henry Michelet, pres. Minneapolis Coll. of Music; b. Dell Rapids, S.D., Feb. 21, 1886; s. Ole Hendrik and Jacobine Alberta (Olsen) S.; student U. of S.D., 1905-06; m. Marie Irene Holland, Aug. 8, 1925. Began as clerk Granite City Bank, Dell Rapids, 1906, cashier, 1907-20; sec. Granite City Investment Co., 1909-21, v.p., 1921-22, pres. and treas. since 1922; sec. Soo Investment Co., 1919-21, v.p., 1921-22, pres. and treas. since 1922; pres. and dir. Minneapolis Coll. of Music since 1928; treas. City of Dell Rapids, 1907-20. Mem. Phi Delta Theta; nat. hon. mem. Phi Mu Gamma; mem. Phi Mu Alpha Sinfonia. Republican. Mason, Odd Fellow. Home: 2441 Sheridan Av. S. Office: 60 S. 11th St., Mpls. Died May 9, 1957; buried Lakewood Cemetery, Mpls.

SMITH, Henry Monmouth, chemist, educator; b. Middletown, Conn., Aug. 31, 1868; s. Samuel George and Sarah Melville (Hunt) S.; B.A., Wesleyan U., Conn., 1891, M.A., 1894; Ph.D., Heidelberg, Germany, 1898; m. Mary Louise O'Brien, May 8, 1909. Asst. chemist Storrs Expt. Sta., Conn. Agrl. Coll., 1891-92, Conn. Expt. Sta., 1892-93; spl. agt. nutrition investigations U.S. Dept. Agr., 1893-95; asso. prof. phys. sci. Hampden-Sidney (Va.) Coll., 1898-99; instr. chemistry Syracuse, 1899-1900, asso. prof., 1900-02, prof., 1902-13; research asso. Nutrition Lab., Carnegie Instn., Washington, 1913-20; prof. chemistry Mass. Inst. Tech., 1920-32. Mem. Am. Chem. Soc., A.A.A.S., Am. Acad. Arts and Sciences, Phi Beta Kappa, Sigma Xi, Alpha Chi Sigma, Beta Theta Pi. Republican. Unitarian. Club: University. Author: Human Vitality and Efficiency Under Prolonged Restricted Diet (with others), 1919; Gaseous Exchange and Physiological Requirements for Level and Grade Walking, 1922 (both bulls.), Carnegie Instn.; Torchbearers of Chemitry, 1948. Home: 25 Cotswold Rd., Brookline 46, Mass. Died Apr. 12, 1950; buried Forest Hills Cemetery, Boston.

SMITH, Herbert Atwood, newspaper pub.; b. Dublin, N.H., July 14, 1878; s. Horace Washington and Emma (Atwood) S.; ed. Norwich (Conn.) Free Acad.; m. Gertrude Aura Shumway, Aug. 12, 1903; 1 son, Herbert Gordon. Reporter Worcester (Mass.) Telegram, 1897-1904; editor Boston Herald, 1904-11; mgr. N.E. dist. Internat. News Service, 1911-20; mng. editor St. Johnsbury (Vt.) Daily Caledonian-Record, 1920—; pres. Caledonian-Record Pub. Co. Mem. St. Johnsbury C. of C., S.A.R. (Vt. chpt.). Republican. Conglist. Mason (Shriner), Elk, K.P. Clubs: Rotary (sec.), St. Johnsbury Country. Home: 35 Cliff St. Office: 25 Federal Av., St. Johnsbury, Vt. Died Apr. 4, 1959; buried Mt. Pleasant Cemetery, St. Johnsbury, Vt.

SMITH, Herman Lyle, univ. prof.; b. Pittwood, Ill., July 7, 1892; s. Church Bruce and Elizabeth (Steward) S.; student U. of Ore., 1911-13, B.S., U. of Chicago, 1914, M.S., 1915, Ph.D., 1926; grad. student Princeton, U. of Minn.; m. Rose Perego, Dec. 31, 1915; children—Tristan Perego, Stewart Ladue. Instr. mathematics Northwestern U., 1915-16; instr. Princeton U., 1916-18; Cornell U., 1918-19; U. of Wis., 1919-21; prof. U. of Philippines, 1921-24, head dept., 1922-24; asst. prof. U. of Minn., 1925-26; successively asst. prof., asso. prof.; prof. La. State U. since 1926. Contbr. research articles to math. jours.; editor Math. Magazine. Mem. Am. Math. Soc. (chmn. La.-Miss. sect. 1936), Math. Assn. Am., Am. Math. Soc., Am. Assn. Univ. Profs., La. Acad. of Sci., Phi Beta Kappa, Sigma Xi (past pres. and a founder). Democrat. Unfinished book on Lensor and Vector Analysts. Home: 4408 Hyacinth Av. Office: La. State U., Baton Rouge 15. Died June 13, 1950.

SMITH, Howard Dwight, architect; b. Dayton, O., Feb. 21, 1886; s. Andrew Jackson and Nancy Evelyn (Moore) S.; C.E. in Architecture, Ohio State U., 1907; B.Arch., Columbia, 1910, Perkins travelling fellow, 1910-11; m. Myrna Theresa Cott, Jan. 24, 1912; children—Marjorie Cott (Mrs. Marion Virgil Packard), Robert Jackson, Howard Dwight, Myrna Hazel (Mrs. Dale Dan Dupler, Jr.), and Priscilla Ruth (Mrs. Eugene C. D'Angelo); m. 2d, Mary Thompson Gramlich, Jan. 17, 1936. Engaged as architectural draftsman in Columbus, O., Washington, D.C., New York City, 1906-14; supervising architect, residence div., Office of John Russell Pope, 1914-18; prof. architecture, Ohio State U., 1918-21 and since 1929; architect Columbus, O., Bd. of Edn., 1921-29; univ. architect Ohio State U., 1929-56, ret.; Fulbright lectr. Alexandria U., Egypt, 1955-56; architectural advisor, Am. Commn. Living War Memorials, since 1943. Principal bldgs. include Ohio Stadium (received Exhibition Gold Medal, Am. Inst. Architects, 1921); Columbus, O., City Hall and West High Sch.; 25 schs. in central Ohio; Marietta, O., City Hall; Springfield, O., Masonic Temple; 50 bldgs. for Ohio State U.; Upper Arlington, O., Elementary Sch. (received Exhibition Gold Medal, Ohio Soc. Architects, 1941). Fellow Am. Inst. Architects; mem. Sigma Xi, Tau Sigma Delta, Sigma Alpha Epsilon. Mason (32°), Rotarian. Clubs: Faculty, Kit Kat (Columbus, O.). Home: 280 Village Dr., Columbus 14, O. Died Apr. 27, 1958; buried Green Lawn Cemetery, Columbus, O.

SMITH, Howard Wayne, denominational sec.; b. Phila., Oct. 9, 1870; s. of William R. and Emma J. (Moore) S.; A.B., Central High Sch., Phila., 1890; Law Dept., U. Pa.; spl. student Johns Hopkins, Crozer Theol. Sem., Chester, Pa.; D.D., Temple U., Phila., 1912; m. Carrie L. Heckman, June 7, 1893. Ordained Bapt. ministry, 1893; pastor Blackwood, N.J., 1893-95, Fulton Av. Ch., Balt., 1895-1902, S. Broad St. Ch., Phila., 1902-05; sec. Phila. Bapt. City Mission, 1905-09; asst. sec. Am. Bapt. Publ. 1909—. Trustee Bapt. Inst. for Christian Workers, Phila. Mem. Am. Acad. Polit. and Social Science, Pa. Soc. S.A.R. Mason. Home: 4107 Pine St., Phila. Died Dec. 28, 1951.

SMITH, Hurlbut William, typewriter mfr.; b. Centre Lisle, N.Y., June 24, 1865; s. Lewis Stevens and Eliza Ann (Hurlbut) S.; student Lisle Acad.; A.M., Syracuse U., 1921; m. Mina Ruma Glazier, Oct. 16, 1889 (dec. Jan. 1935); m. 2d, Gladys A. Morrow, July 1936. Began in gun mfg. works of L. C. Smith, Syracuse, later with Smith Premier Typewriter Co. as treas. until 1903; an organizer, 1903, L. C. Smith & Bros. Typewriter Co., of which was dir. and mem. exec. bd.; pres., treas., chmn. exec. bd. L. C. Smith & Corona Typewriters, Inc.; dir., mem. exec. com. Crucible Steel Co. of America, Syracuse Trust Co.; dir., treas. Great Lakes Steamship Co.; dir. U.S. Hoffman Machinery Corp., Toledo Shipbuilding Co., Syracuse Transit Co. Pres. bd. Syracuse U., Syracuse Public Library; trustee Theol. Sch. of St. Lawrence U.; pres. Onondaga Orphans Home. Mem. Syracuse C. of C. (dir.). Universalist. Mason (32°, Shriner), K.P., Elk. Clubs: Automobile (pres. 33 yrs.), University, Century, Faculty of Syracuse U., Citizens, Rotary, Masonic Temple, Liederkranz (Syracuse), Onondaga Country. Adopted as mem. Seneca Tribe of Indians, 1908. Home: 1111 James St. Office: L. C. Smith & Corona Typewriting Co., Syracuse, N.Y. Died Dec. 16, 1951.

SMITH, Ida B. Wise, former pres. W.C.T.U.; b. Phila., July 3, 1871; d. Robert Emanuel and Eliza Ann (Piper) Speakman; grad. Kindergarten Tng. Sch.; student U. of Neb., 1894; LL.D., John Fletcher Coll., Oskaloosa, Ia., 1927; m. James A. Wise, Sept. 3, 1889 (dec.); 1 son, Carl Edwin; m. 2d, Malcolm Smith, Aug. 15, 1912 (dec.). Began as pub. sch. tchr., 1887; ordained ministry Ch. of Christ (Disciples), 1923. Pres. W.C.T.U. of Ia. 20 yrs. and vice-pres. Nat. W.C.T.U. 8 yrs.; made supt. Christian Citizenship, World's W.C.T.U.; became pres Nat. W.C.T.U., Nov. 1, 1933; voluntarily withdrew, now hon. pres. (life); pres. Iowa State W.C.T.U.; 1st v.p. World's W.C.T.U.; pres. Nat. Temperance Council; pres. bd. trustees Benedict Home (for girls) 25 years. designated by com. apptd. by gov. of Ia as one of ten most honored women of the state, 1925, and by next gov. as most distinguished woman of the state, 1928. Mem. Woman's Com. Council of Defense, World War II. Mem. League of Women Voters, Conf. of Social Agencies, Bus. and Profl Women's Club. Mem. Order Eastern Star. Widely known as lecturer. Clubs: Woman's, Woman's Rotary Woman's City. Died Feb. 16, 1952.

SMITH, Ignatius, coll. dean; b. Newark, N.J., Aug. 25, 1889; s. Michael H. and Maria L. (Gaskin) S.; attended Seton Hall Coll., Dominican Coll. Ph.D., Cath. U. of Am., 1915. Pastor and prior, St Catherine Ch., N.Y. City, 1916-20; prof. philosophy and sociology, Dominican Coll., Washington, D.C. 1920; dir. Preachers' Inst., Cath. U. of Am. 1932 53. dean, sch. of philosophy, 1936—. Radio speaker Pres. Am. Cath. Philos. Assn., 1938. Home: 487 Michigan Av. N.E. Office: Catholic Univ. of America

Washington 17. Died March. 8, 1957; buried Washington.

SMITH, Israel A(lexander), lawyer; born Plano, Ill., Feb. 2, 1876; s. Joseph and Bertha (Madison) S.; student Graceland Coll., 1895-97; LL.B., Lincoln-Jefferson U., 1912; m. Nina Grenawalt, Mar. 4, 1908; children—Joseph Perrine, Don Carlos. Admitted to Mo. bar, 1913, since practiced in Independence. Mem. 34th Gen. Assembly Ia., 1911-12, Constl. Conv. Mo., 1943-44. Trustee State Hist. Soc. Mo. Latter Day Saint (non-Morman) (pres. Reorganized Ch. of Jesus Christ of Latter Day Saints since 1946). Home: 1214 W. Short St. Office: The Auditorium, Independence, Mo. Died June 14, 1958; buried Independence, Mo.

SMITH, J. Paul, business exec. Pres. Visking Corp., Chgo. 1640 E. 50th St., Chgo. 15. Office: 6733 W. 65th St., Chgo. 38. Died May 4, 1955; buried Oakland Cemetery, Warren Pa.

SMITH, Jacob Getlar, artist; b. New York, N.Y., Feb. 3, 1898; s. Morris and Sadie (Getlar) S.; ed. DeWitt Clinton High Sch., New York, 1912-16, Nat. Acad. of Design, 1918-21; m. Adele Harriet Loeffler, Sept. 10, 1923; 1 son, David Loeffler. Artist since 1921; has exhibited in Carnegie Internat., Art Inst. of Chicago; Corcoran Biennial, Virginia Biennial, Pennsylvania Academy, Whitney Museum Am. Art, Museum Modern Art, Baltimore Pan-Am. Century of Progress, Tex. Centennial, Golden Gate Internat. Expn., Latin-Am. Exhbn. of Contemporary Painting in the U.S. Works in permanent collectins: "Self-Portrait," "Approaching Storm," in Whitney Museum Am. Art, "The Broken Bridge," in Mo. State Teachers College: murals in U.S. Post Offices, Nyack, N.Y., and Salisbury, Md. Awarded hon. mention for figure painting, 1926, and Mr. and Mrs. Frank G. Logan prize of $750 for painting, 1930, both at Art Inst. of Chicago; Guggenheim fellowship, 1929. Author: Water Color for Beginners, 1951. Represented by articles in, Water Color Demonstrated, 1945, "Painting in the U.S.A." by Alan Gruskin, 1946; "The Painter's Question and Answer Book" edited by Frederick Taubes, 1947. Mem. Am. Water Color Club, Am. Water Color Soc. (v.p. 1956-57), Nat. Soc. Painters Casein. Contbg. editor Am. Artist mag. Nat. Soc. of Mural Painters. Home: 2 W. 67th St., N.Y.C. Died Oct. 28, 1958.

SMITH, James D., mayor; b. Utica, N.Y., Apr. 16, 1872; s. Thomas T. and Bridget (Dwyer) S.; pub. sch. edn.; m. Clara M. Keiser, Oct. 10, 1901. In street ry. business, 1896-1902; elected assessor, City of Utica, 1909, chmn. Bd. Assessment and Taxation, Jan. 1, 1913; mayor Utica, 1913-19. Democrat. Roman Catholic. Clubs: Democratic, Seneca, Utica Golf and Country, etc. Elk, Moose, K.C., etc. Home: 496 Genesee St., Utica, N.Y. Died Oct. 18, 1955.

SMITH, James W., ophthalmologist; b. Washington, D.C., May 16, 1893; s. Barnet and Mary (Saiber) S.; M.D., College of Medicine, New York University, 1917; m. Sara Pollack, Aug. 28, 1928; children—Barry Frederick, Nancy Doris (dec.). Began as eye surgeon, 1919; clin. prof. ophthalmology Post Graduate Medical School (N.Y.U.-Bellevue Medical Center), clinical director and attending ophthalmologist Hospital for Joint Diseases; consulting ophthalmologist, Goldwater Memorial Hosp., attending eye surgeon University Hosp.; cons. ophthalmologist Nyack Hosp. Served as lt., med. corps, U.S. Army, 1918-19. Mem. bd. of visitors Rockland State Hosp., 1934-44. Received N.Y. U. Alumni Meritorious Award, 1935. Pres. N.Y. U. College of Medicine Alumni Assn., 1939-40; pres. N.Y. Soc. for Clin. Ophthalmology, 1941-42; faculty lectr. Am. Acad. Ophthalmology, 1942-52; member of N.Y.U. Alumni Fedn. (v.p. 1952-54; treas. 1951-52); fellow A.C.S., N.Y. Acad. Medicine. Mem. Am. Med. Assn., N.Y. State and County Med. Socs., Assn. for Research in Ophthal., (hon.) Reading (Pa.) Eye, Ear, Nose and Throat Soc., The Manuscript Society (member of bd. of dirs.), Phi Delta Epsilon (grand consul, 1925, sec. bd. trustees, 1926-46, vice pres. 1947-50, pres. 1950-51). Democrat. Mason. Contributor to ophthal. journals. Home: 12 E. 88th St. Office: 1016 5th Av., N.Y.C. 28. Died Oct. 24, 1955.

SMITH, Jane Norman, feminist; b. Montclair, N.J., Feb. 15, 1874; d. Thomas James and Sophia (Speer) Norman; ed. pub. and pvt. schs., extension univ. courses; m. Clarence Meserole Smith, Dec. 6, 1897; children—Helen, Muriel Smith Wilson. Senatorial dist. chmn. Women's Polit. Union in suffrage campaign of N.Y. State, 1914-15; N.Y. state legislative chmn. Nat. Woman's Party, suffrage campaign, 1915-18, chmn. N.Y. State Br. 1923-27, mem. nat. council, 1927—, chmn., 1927-29; apptd. by Gov. Smith to rep. N.Y. State at Congress of Internat. Women Suffrage Alliance, Paris, 1926; speaker on equal rights treaty (one of two from U.S.) before Pan Am. Conf., Havana, Cuba, 1928; mem. exec. bd. Zonta Club of N.Y.C., 1929-30; 3d v.p. Nat. Council of Women, 1935-37, 2d v.p., 1937-39. Unitarian. Home: West Windsor, Vt. Died Sept. 2, 1953.

SMITH, Joe Frazer, architect; b. Canton, Miss., Mar. 25, 1897; s. Charles Foster and Susan (Cheek) S.; B.S., Ga. Inst. Tech., 1921; m. Ada McDonnell, June 20, 1922; children—Sue Cheek, Margaret Ada. Architect J. Frazer Smith, Inc., Memphis, 1922—; pres. Ark. Housing Corp., 1941, Rivercliff Co., Inc., 1946—, Riverside Development Co., Inc., 1946— (all Little Rock, Ark.). Past pres. bd. trustees Am. Archtl. Found., 1950-53. Fellow A.I.A. Author: White Pillars, 1941. Home: 1635 Peabody Av. Office: 1503 Union Av., Memphis. Died Apr. 13, 1957; buried Calvary Cemetery, Memphis.

SMITH, John Frederick, ins. exec.; b. N.Y. City, Dec. 10, 1860; s. Charles Henry and Mary (Vredenburg) S.; student pvt. schs., Trinity Sch., N.Y. City; m. Abbie E. Crocheron, Sept. 12, 1899; children—Charles Frederick, Dorothy. Clk. Miller & Simonson, ins., West Brighton, S.I., 1877; partner S. D. Simonson & Co., ins., West Brighton, S.I., 1893-98; owner J. F. Smith, real estate, ins., 1898-1908; pres. Richmond (S.I.) Co., Mutual Ins. Co., 1902-06; dir., pres. Richmond Ins. Co. of N.Y., 1906-48; dir. S.I. Bldg. Loan & Savs. Assn., West Brighton, since 1884, treas., 1890-1920; trustee Richmond Co. Savs. Bank since 1893, pres., 1909-46, chmn. bd. since 1946; organizer, dir. S.I. Nat. Bank & Trust Co., 1902, pres., 1928-48, chmn. bd. since 1948, dir. since 1902; pres., dir., Westchester Fire Ins. Co., N.Y. City, since 1948; dir. U.S. Fire Ins. Co., North River Ins. Co., Hutchins Securities Corp. Mem. Rcihmond Co. Bankers Assn. (hon. pres.). Episcopalian. Mason. Home: 1213 Clove Rd., Staten Island 1, N.Y. Office: 110 William St., N.Y.C. 7. Died May 4, 1952; buried Moravian Cemetery, New Dorp, S.I.

SMITH, John Henry, Jr., business exec.; b. Astoria, Ore., Dec. 26, 1894; s. John H. and Minnie (Smith) S.; student pub. schs. in Ore. and Cal.; student U. Cal., 1912-16; m. Margaret O'Malley, June 27, 1927; children—Sarah Jane, John Henry III. Timber mgr. Western Cooperage Co., Portland, 1919-24, asst. gen. mgr., 1924-40, gen. mgr. 1940-48, dir., 1930—; exec. v.p., Hawley Pulp & Paper Co., 1932-40, pres. 1940-48, dir. 1932-48; v.p. Am. Mail Line. Served with U.S. Army during World War I. Trustee Reed College. Mem. Pacific Coast Assn. Pulp and Paper Mfrs. (pres. 1934—), Newcomen Soc. of England, Portland C. of C. (mem. exec. com.), Phi Delta Theta. Republican. Clubs: Arlington, Portland Yacht (Portland); Rainier, Seattle Yacht (Seattle); Bohemian (San Francisco). Home: S.W. Riverwood Rd., Portland 1. Office: American Bank Bldg., Portland, Ore. Died Dec. 15, 1950.

SMITH, John Lawrence, business exec.; b. Germany, Feb. 10, 1889; s. Gottfried Damian (Schmitz) (family name legally changed, 1918) and Johanna (Dollbaum) S.; brought to U.S., 1892, naturalized, 1908; grad. in chemistry Cooper Union, New York, 1910, B.Ch., 1911; m. Mary Louise Pelltier Becker, Sept. 16, 1914; children—Mary Louise (dec.), Dorothy (Mrs Frank Monroe Campbell). Lab. asst. Chas. Pfizer & Co., Inc., Bklyn., 1906-10, chemist, 1910-13; gen. supt. E R. Squibb & Sons, New Brunswick, N.J., Bklyn., 1913-18; works supt. and dir. Pfizer & Co., Inc., 1918-25, sec., 1925-39, v.p., 1929-45, pres., 1945-49, chmn. bd., 1949—; trustee Bushwick Savs. Bank. Part owner and v.p. Bklyn. Nat. League Baseball Club; dir. Montreal (Can.) Baseball Club. Trustee Bklyn. Eye and Ear Hosp., Indsl. Home for the Blind, Bklyn., Bklyn. Pub. Library. Mem. Am. Chem. Soc., Mfg. Chemists Assn., Am. Drug Mfrs. Assn., Brooklyn Chamber of Commerce (dir.), Conglist. Clubs: Drug and Chemical, Chemists, Metropolitan, N.Y. Athletic (N.Y.C.); Montauk (Bklyn.); Huntington (L.I.) Crescent. Home: 25 Prospect Park West, Bklyn. 15. Office: Chas. Pfizer & Co., Inc., 11 Bartlett St., Bklyn. 6. Died July 10, 1950; buried Stonington, Conn.

SMITH, John Lewis, lawyer; b. Washington, Jan. 25, 1877; s. John Ambler and Nannie (Lewis) S.; student Columbian (now George Washington) U.; LL.B., Nat. U., 1902, LL.M., 1903; m. Marie Baggaley, Oct. 1, 1901 (died 1902); 1 dau., Mary Ambler (wife of Brig. Gen. Percy L. Sadler, U.S. Army); m. 2d, Claribel Cassin, June 1, 1909; 1 son, John Lewis. Lawyer, former assistant United States attorney. Began pracece of law, Washington, 1903; president National Tribune Corp. Served as private Dist. Columbia Vol. Inf., Spanish-Am. War; capt. Mil. Intelligence Div., U.S. Army, World War. Mem. Am. Bar Assn., D.C. Bar Assn. (ex-pres.), United Spanish War Vets. (past comdr. in chief, Am. Legion (past dept. comdr.). Republican. Episcopalian. Mason. Clubs: Chevy Chase, Army and Navy. Home: 2424 Tracy Pl., N.W. Office: 729 15th St. N.W., Washington. Died Nov. 9, 1950; buried Arlington Nat. Cemetery

SMITH, Joseph Lindon, painter; b. Pawtucket, R.I., Oct. 11, 1863; s. Henry F. and Emma (Greenleaf) S.; ed. private schs., R.I.; studied in sch. of drawing and painting, Museum of Fine Arts, Boston, and at Académie Julien, Paris; m. Corinna Haven Putnam, Sept. 18, 1899; children—Rebecca Lindon, Frances Lindon, Lois Lindon. Executed mural decorations in Pub. Library, Boston; mural decorations on exterior of Horticultural Hall, Phila. (building since replaced by another, murals no longer exist); work done in Italy, Egypt and Turkey, including copies made for Boston Museum Fine Arts of so-called "Alexander Sarcophagus" in Imperial Museum, Constantinople. Received decoration of the III Order, Medijieh, from Sultan of Turkey. Has taken active part in recent excavations in Egypt, in the Valley of the Kings at Luxor; was present at the discovery of the tomb of the parents of Queen Tiy, 1904-05, and of the tomb of the Queen, 1907; connected with field expdn. of Harvard Univ. and Museum of Fine Arts, Boston; taught 3 yrs. at sch. of Museum of Fine Arts, and at Harvard, 1903 and 1906; teacher painting technique in reproducing exact replicas of sculptured reliefs in tombs, temples of ancient Egypt to Egyptian grads. of Govt. Higher Sch. Art, Cairo, 1946-50; has painted in Japan, Korea, Manchuria, China, Cambodia, Java, Southern India, Central America, Honduras, Yucatan and Persia. Has prod. a number of pageants and masques. Mem. Soc. Mural Painters (New York), Copley Soc., Arts and Crafts Soc. (Boston). Clubs: Century, Coffee House (New York); Tavern, Japan, Naniwa, Harvard Travelers, Boston Thursday Evening (Boston). Relief work in France, Belgium and Italy, 1916-19, serving 1 yr. with Y.M.C.A. as head of soldier talent development. Hon. curator Egyptian dept. Boston Museum Fine Arts. Home: Dublin, N.H. Died Oct. 18, 1950.

SMITH, Joseph Newton, mfr. mechanical rubber goods; b. Lynn, Mass., Mar. 9, 1887; s. Joseph Newhall and Sarah (Fuller) S.; pre. edn., Phillips Acad., Andover, Mass., 1903-05; B.S., Sheffield Scientific Sch. (Yale), 1908; m. Lillie Clark Silver, June 6, 1914; children—Sylvia (Mrs. Usher P. Coolidge), Mary Silver. Sec. and asst. to father in various business interests until his decease, 1912; v.p. Boston Woven Hose & Rubber Co., 1914-28, pres. since 1928, treas., 1927-37; dir. Liberty Mutual Ins. Co., United Mutual Ins. Co.; trustee of various estates since 1913. Served as lt. in the Army Balloon Service, San Antonio, Tex., World War. Republican. Episcopalian. Clubs: Union Club (Boston); Eastern Yacht Club (Marblehead); Salem (Mass.) Country; Yale (New York). Home: 138 Federal St., Salem, Mass. Office: 15 State St., Boston. Died Feb. 5, 1951.

SMITH, Josephine Wernicke (Mrs. Richard Keen Smith), state librarian. Office: State Library, 322 State Capitol, St. Paul. Died June 1953.

SMITH, Lawrence Henry, congressman; b. Racine, Wis., Sept. 15, 1892; s. John Henry and Elizabeth (Tolleson) S.; LL.B., Marquette U., 1923; m. Eleanor J. Rowley, Nov. 10, 1917; children—Betty Eleanor, Alice Elizabeth, John Lawrence. Admitted to Wis. bar, 1923, and began practice at Racine; mem. 77th to 85th Congresses, First Wisconsin District. Served as lt. Inf., World War, 1917-19. Mem. Am. Bar Assn., Racine County Bar Assn. (ex-pres.), Am. Legion (dept. comdr. for Wis.). Republican. Mason. Home: 4510 Spring St., Racine, Wis. Office: House Office Bldg., Washington. Died Jan. 22, 1958.

SMITH, Lemuel Augustus, Sr., judge; b. Holly Springs, Miss., Nov. 19, 1878; s. Lemuel Augustus II, and Carrie (West) S.; ed. St. Thomas Hall, Holly Springs, Miss., and Webb Sch., Bell Buckle, Tenn.; student spl. courses, U. Miss., 1896-99, law sch., 1899-1900; m. Emma Louise Robertson, Feb. 7, 1900; children—Louise Caffey (Mrs. Leonard R. Marbury, Sr.), Lemuel Augustus (officer U.S. Navy), Martha Robertson. Admitted to Miss. bar, 1900, and practiced law, Holly Springs, 1900-36; apptd. chancellor, 3d Chancery Court Dist. of Miss., 1936, reelected, 1939, 1943; asso. justice Supreme Ct., Miss., 1945—. Served with Miss. N.G. Formerly served as mem. county and municipal Dem. exec. coms. Episcopalian (vestryman). Mem. Miss. State Bar Assn., Delta Kappa Epsilon, Phi Delta Phi. Mason (K.T.), Knight of Pythias, Elk. Home: Holly Springs, Miss. Died Oct. 10, 1950.

SMITH, Lemuel F(ranklin), judge; b. Shadwell, Va., Apr. 21, 1890; s. Downing L and Willie Minor (Marshall) S.; A.B., Randolph-Macon Coll., 1910, LL.D., 1951; LL.B., U. Va., 1916; m. Grace Stulting, Oct. 27, 1916. Admitted to Va. bar, 1915; mem. City Council, Charlottesville, Va., 1918-20; mem. Va. State Gen. Assembly, 1920-26; commonwealth atty., Albemarle Co., Va., 1926-30; judge 8th Jud. Circuit, Va., 1930-51, Supreme Ct. Appeals, Va. since 1951. Home: 810 Locust Av. Office: County Office Bldg., Charlottesville, Va. Died Oct. 15, 1956.

SMITH, Leonard Bacon, lawyer; b. N.Y.C., May 18, 1873; s. Eugene and Katharine Wadsworth (Bacon) S.; student Phillips Acad., 1889-90; A.B., Yale, 1894; LL.D. with honor N.Y. Law Sch., 1896; m. Simone Alibert, May 27, 1919; children—Marcel Alibert, Marie Anne (Mrs. Jacques Chabrier), Denyse Bacon, Leonard Eugene, Simone Madeleine. Admitted to N.Y. bar, 1896; mem. firm of Price & Smith, New York, 1897-1908, Strong, Smith & Strong, 1908-19, Smith & Agate, 1919-26; asst. atty. Am. Can Co., 1930-33, gen. counsel, 1933-47; pvt. practice, 1947—. Served with Squadron A. N.G. of N.Y., 1903-13, 1st lt. and capt. 1st F.A., 1913-16, maj. and adj., N.Y.F.A. Brigade, 1916-17; insp.-instr.

F.A. 34th Div., U.S. Army, 1917-18; batt. comdr. 125th F.A., later 127th F.A., 1918-19. Mem. Am. Bar Assn., Assn. Bar City of New York, Am. Fgn. Law Assn. Republican. Clubs: University, Lawyers (N.Y.). Home: 2 Gramercy Park, N.Y.C. 3; (summer) "Willowfield," Norfolk, Conn. Office: 149 Broadway, N.Y.C. 6. Died Apr. 26, 1957; buried Center Cemetery, Norfolk, Conn.

SMITH, Lewis Martin, utility exec.; b. Warrior, Ala., Sept. 3, 1894; s. David N. and Julia (Bibb) S.; B.S., U. Ala., 1916; D.Sc. (hon.), 1956; LL. D., Howard Coll., 1956; m. Mary Moore, Sept. 14, 1918; 1 dau., Mildred Julia (Mrs. T. P. Shumaker). Elec. engr. Tenn. Coal, Iron & R.R. Co., Birmingham, 1916-17, 1920-23; draftsman engring. dept. Ala. Power Co., 1923-39, chief elec. engr., 1939-44, dir. pub. relations, 1944, v.p., 1945-49, dir., gen. manager, 1949-52, pres., 1952-57, vice chairman of the board, 1957—. Member-at-large of National council Boy Scouts Am.; mem. bd. Edison Electric Inst., So. Research Inst., Southeastern Electric Exchange; exec. com. Southern Bapt. Conv.; mem. nat. utilities com. National Fund for Med. Edn. Director Birmingham Board Education, Birmingham Bapt. Hosp.; trustee Howard Coll., Birmingham Civic Symphony Assn. Member Birmingham Chamber of Commerce (past pres.), C. of C. U.S. (mem. bd.), U. Ala. Alumni Assn. (past pres.), Pub. Relations Soc. Am. Democrat. Baptist. Club: Rotary Internat. (past dist. gov.) Home: 2600 Av. T, Fairview, Birmingham 8. Office: Alabama Power Co., Birmingham 3, Ala. Died Mar. 4, 1958; buried Elmwood Cemetery, Birmingham, Ala.

SMITH, Lewis Wilbur, educator; b. West Newton, O., Feb. 13, 1876; s. William Alexander and Sarah Margaret S.; A.B., Denison U., 1902, LL.D., 1928; A.M., U. of Chicago, 1913, Ph.D., 1919; m. Rowena Randall, 1906; children—Lewis Wilbur, Harold William. Instr. in English, Pillsbury Acad., Owatonna, Minn., 1902-03; commercial corr., Chicago, 1903-05; instr. in English, West High Sch., Aurora, Ill., 1905-07; prin. high sch., Kankakee, Ill., 1907-08, Thornton Twp. High Sch., Harvey, Ill., 1908-19; supt. Joliet (Ill.) Twp. High Sch. and Jr. Coll., 1919-28; supt. schs., Berkeley, Calif., 1928-36; dir. Am. Coll. Bur., 1936-41; research fellow, Univ. of California, 1941-51; instructor summer courses in edn., Northwestern U., 1921-22, U. of Chicago, 1923-24, U. of Calif., 1925-26, U. of Mich., 1927, U. of Wash., 1936; lecturer in edn., U. of Chicago, 1936-37. Chmn. Commn. on unit causes and curriculums, North Central Assn., 1922-28. Consultant Presidents' Com. on Vocational Edn., 1937. Fellow A.A.A.S.; mem. Nat. Dept. Secondary Sch. Principals, Nat. Soc. for Study of Edn., Nat. Edn. Assn., Am. Assn. Jr. Colls. (pres. 1926; chmn. research committee 1926-30), Berkeley Art Museum, High School National Commission of National Honor Society, Phi Beta Kappa, Phi Delta Kappa (emeritus). Presbyn. Author: Ill. High Sch., 1917; Planning a Career (with Gideon L. Blough), 1929. Contbr. on ednl. subjects. Home: 98 Alamo Av. Berkeley 8, Cal. Died Dec. 19, 1952.

SMITH, Livingston Waddell, coll. prof.; b. Lexington, Va., May 30, 1876; s. Francis H. and Janetta A. (Waddell) S.; A.B., Washington and Lee U., 1896, A.M., 1898, Ph.D., 1902; student Johns Hopkins, 1903; m. Fanny Gay Catlett, Nov. 11, 1908; 1 dau., Janetta Alexander. Instr. Mass. Inst. Tech., 1904-06; prof. mathematics, Washington and Lee U., 1906—. Democrat. Presbyn. Revised, with C. W. Watts, Nichols' Analytic Geometry, and Nichols' Calculus. Mem. Math. Assn. Am., Phi Kappa Psi, Phi Beta Kappa. Home: Lexington, Va. Died Aug. 9, 1956.

SMITH, Lloyd Gaston, oil exec.; b. Normal, Ill., May 27, 1891; s. Edmund Burke and Florence Metcalf (Gaston) S.; B.S., U. Ill., 1913; m. Lucy Winnifrid Fairhall, Sept. 2, 1916; children—Winnifrid, Ronald, Edmund, Gerald, Lucy, Marjorie, Sarah. Draftsman, engr. Standard Oil Co. Ind., Whiting, Ind., 1913-22, jr. exec., Casper, Wyo., 1922-27; asst. mgr. refineries Pan Am. Petroleum & Transport Co., N.Y.C., 1927-33; gen. mgr. Aruba Refinery, pres. Lago Oil Transport Co., Aruba, Netherlands West Indies, 1933-46; v.p., dir. Creole Petroleum Corp., N.Y.C., 1947—. Mem. bd. appeals, Flower Hill, N.Y. Decorated Knight Comdr. of Orange, Nassau by Queen Wilhelmina, 1946. Mem. Venezuelan C. of C. (dir. N.Y.), Pan Am. Soc. (dir. N.Y.), Am. Petroleum Inst., Bolivarian Soc., Tau Beta Pi. Episcopalian. Home: 607 Chipmunk Lane, Media, Pa. Office: 350 Fifth Av., N.Y.C. Died Sept. 9, 1958.

SMITH, Lloyd Weir, banker; b. Pitts., May 30, 1886; s. Robert Stewart and Mary (McCaslin) S.; grad. Princeton, 1908; m. Gertrude McCormick, Jan. 27, 1914; children—Martha (Mrs. C. W. Cooper), Ann Weir. Chmn. The Union Nat. Bank of Pittsburgh, 1946—. Club: Duquesne. Office: Fourth Av. and Wood St., Pitts. Died Sept. 28, 1950.

SMITH, (Caleb) Lothrop, educator; b. Winterset, Ia., Aug. 14, 1906; s. William Francis and Maud Lothrop (Whedon) S.; B.A., Grinnell Coll., 1928; M.S., State U. Ia., 1929, Ph.D., 1931; m. Geraldine Merryman, Aug. 30, 1937; 1 son, Carver Howe. Asst. in chemistry State U. Ia., 1928-31, instr. chemistry, 1931, 44, 45-48, prof. chemistry, 1948—; head, div. analytical and inorganic chemistry, Manhattan Dist. (atomic bomb) Project, U. Chgo., 1944, Oak Ridge, Tenn., 1945 (C.E.W.-T.E. C.). Mem. Am. Chem. Soc., Optical Soc. Am., Am. Inst. Physics, Am. Assn. U. Profs., Ia. Acad. Sci., Alpha Chi Sigma, Sigma Xi, Phi Lambda Upsilon, Alpha Phi Omega, Triangle. Presbyn. Contbr. to profl. jours. Amateur radio operator (Wo-BZE), 1922—. Home: 224 Fairview Av., Iowa City, Ia. Died Dec. 26, 1949; buried Winterset, Ia.

SMITH, Luther Ely, lawyer; b. Downers Grove, Ill., June 11, 1873; s. Luther Rominor and Adeline (Ely) S.; prep. edn., Thompson's Grove Public School, Monmouth County, N.J.; Emerson Inst., Washington, D.C.; grad. Williston Acad., Easthampton, Mass., 1890; A.B., Amherst, 1894; LL.B., Washington U., 1897; LL.D., Amherst College, 1942; m. SaLees Kennard, Nov. 17, 1909; children—Adeline Ely (Mrs. Ingram F. Boyd, Jr.), Luther Ely, SaLees Kennard (Mrs. John W. Seddon). Teacher English, Smith Academy (Washington Univ.), 1894-98; admitted to Mo. bar, 1897, in practice at St. Louis, 1899—; mem. Gilliam & Smith, 1900-04, Klein & Hough, 1904-07, Smith & Pearcy, 1913-37, Luther Ely Smith & Associates, 1937—; lecturer on contracts, St. Louis U. Law Sch., 1908-13. Served as lt. 3d U.S. Vol. Engrs., Spanish-Am. War, 1898-99; capt. F.A., U.S. Army, 1917. Chmn. Citizens City Plan Com. 1916-22; Civic Development Bur. of St. Louis C. of C., Council Civic Needs, 1929-38; sec. Pageant Drama Assn. of St. Louis,1913-14 ; mem. George Rogers Clark Fed. Sesquicentennial Commn., 1928-40. Chmn. State Orgn. Com., Mo. Non-Partisan Court Plan, 1939-41. Recipient of the St. Louis Award, 1941. Mem Am., Mo., St. Louis (sec. 1905-07) bar assns., Assn. Bar City of New York, Mo. Hist. Soc., Jefferson Nat. Expansion Meml. Assn. (pres. 1934-49), U.S. Territorial Expansion Meml. Commn. (chmn. exec. com., 1934—), St. Louis Bird Club (pres. 1925-27, v.p., 1945—), Civil Service Commn. of St. Louis (vice chmn., 1941-45; chmn., 1945—), 3d U.S. Vol. Engr. Assn. (sec., 1900—), Phi Beta Kappa, Psi Upsilon, Order of the Coif. Republican. Episcopalian. Editor biographies of David DuBose Gaillard, Walter Henry Sanborn. Home: 4969 Pershing Av. Office: 411 N. 7th St., St. Louis 1. Died Apr. 2, 1951.

SMITH, Lynwood H., dairy corp. exec.; b. Slater, Mo., May 28, 1893; s. J. Herbert and Minnie (Tickemeyer) S.; A.B., U. Wis., 1916; m. Arline Chandler, Oct. 14, 1918; children—L. Chandler, Lura Jane, Arline E., Lynwood H. With Am. Dairies, Inc., Kansas City, Mo., since 1928, chmn. bd. since 1929, pres., 1939-50. Republican. Clubs: River, Mission Hills Country, Kansas City, Rotary. Home: Woodlyn Farm, Bucyrus, Kan. Office: 2438 Broadway, Kansas City 8, Mo. Died Oct. 26, 1955.

SMITH, Marion Gertrude, med. research; b. New Brighton, Pa.; d. Perry Alexander and Sula Gertrude (McLean) Smith; B.S., Ohio State, 1920, student grad. sch., 1922-24; unmarried. Undergrad. instr. dept. chemistry, Ohio State Univ., 1917-20, grad. instr., 1922-24; research asst., dept. biophysics, Harvard Med. Sch., 1924-26; research asst. (medicine), Rush Med. Coll., Univ. Chicago, 1928; medicine, clin. phys. therapy research dept., Gen. Electric X-Ray Corp., Chicago, 1926-28. Mem. Am. Bd. of Physical Medicine (asst. sec., treas. since 1947), Am. Soc. Physical Medicine (adv. mem., asst. sec. treas. since 1947), Am. Congress of Physical Medicine (exec. sec. since 1930), Am. Registry of Physical Therapy Technicians (treas. and registrar since 1935); executive secretary Baruch Committee, Phys. Medicine and Rehabilitation, since 1949. Member National Council on Family Relations. Member Theta Phi Alpha. Republican. Roman Catholic. Clubs: Zonta (bd. dirs., 1944-45), Illinois Club of Catholic Women. Home: 1455 E. 56th St., Chicago 37. Office: 30 Michigan Av., Chgo. 2. Died Aug. 19, 1951.

SMITH, Martin F., lawyer and ex-congressman; b. at Chicago, Illinois; May 28, 1891; s. of John F. and Mathilda (Carlson) Smith; married Margaret Genevieve Manty, May 28, 1919 (died 1949); children—Margaret Louise (Mrs. Robert Allan Brown, Marian Eleanor (Mrs. Joseph J. Rudigier, Jr.). Admitted to Washington bar, 1912, bar of U.S. Supreme Ct., 1935; in practice at Hoquiam, Washington, 1912—; municipal judge, Hoquiam, Washington, 1914-17; mem. Hoquiam City Council, 1926-28; mayor same city, 1928-30; mem. 73d to 77th Congresses (1933-43), 3d Wash. Dist.; now special asst. to the atty. gen. and trial atty. antitrust div. U.S. Dept. of Justice; member board of Immigration Appeals, 1943-44. Del. to Dem. Nat. Conv., Phila., 1936. Mem. American, Federal and Wash. State bar associations, United Spanish War Veterans (honorary), Sons of Norway (hon.), Am. Legion 40 and 8. Democrat. Baptist. Elk, Moose, Eagle, Kiwanian. Granger, Redman. Contr. articles to magazines and periodicals on Antitrust Laws; Biblical Law and Trial of Jesus. Lectr. these and similar subjects. Clubs: Washington Athletic (Seattle); National Press (Washington). Address: 4217 Leland St., Chevy Chase, Md. Died Oct. 25, 1954; buried Arlington National Cemetery.

SMITH, Marvin Boren, textile mills exec.; b. Rockingham Co., N.C.; s. Benjamin and Adaline (Meadows) S.; m. Elvira Lowe; children—Marvin (dec.), Harold, Alyse. In manufacturisg bus. High Point, N.C., to 1909; owner, operator M. B. Smith Furniture Store, Burlington, N.C., 1909-44; pres. Burlington (N.C.) Industries, 1923-28, director, 1923-52, also chmn. bd.; dir. Liberty Hosiery Mills, Inc., Alamance Broadcasting Co., Community Fed. Savs. & Loan Assn. Trustee Alamance Hosp., Louisburg (N.C.) Coll., N.C. Meth. Orphanage (Raleigh). Methodist (Trustee Summer Assembly, Lake Junaluska; v.p. Coll. Found.; mem. N.C. Bd. Missions and Church Extension; Bd. Conf. Claimants; mem. local bd. stewards 40 yrs., chmn. 20 yrs., treas.). Home: 1127 W. Davis St., Burlington, N.C. Died May 26, 1952; buried Burlington, N.C.

SMITH, Matthew, pres. Confederated Unions of America, 308 W. Washington St., Chgo. Died Feb. 25, 1958.*

SMITH, Milton Truman, mfr.; b. Hummelstown, Pa., Apr. 9, 1901; s. Robert Richie and Mildred (Hammar) S.; student pub. schs.; m. Elsie M. Thompson, Apr. 14, 1923; children—Robert T., Frank H. Fgn. sales Melchior, Armstrong, Dessau, N.Y.C., 1919-23; sales corr. Comml. Investment Trust, 1924-26; salesman A. M. Byers Co., Phila., 1927-28; fgn. sales Bucyrus Erie Co., N.Y.C. and South Milwaukee, 1928-36, purchasing dept., 1937-38, mgr. purchases, 1939-49, v.p. in charge purchases, 1950-53; v.p., gen. mgr., dir. Marion Power Shovel Co., also Osgood Co., Marion, O., 1953-56, pres., gen. mgr., dir., 1956—. Home: 812 Bedford Av., Marion, O. Died July 11, 1958.

SMITH, Murray, lawyer; b. Troy, O., Mar. 17, 1891; s. Benjamin F. and Alice Caroline (Cromer) S.; student Kenyon Coll., 1911-12; LL.B., U. of Chicago, 1918; m. Katharine McClay, Feb. 16, 1924; children—Murray, Gordon. Admitted to Ohio bar, 1918; in pvt. practice, Dayton, O., 1919-25; partner firm of Craighead, Cowden & Smith, 1925-27, Craighead, Cowden, Smith & Schnacke, 1927-36, Smith, Schnacke & Compton, Dayton, since 1936; gen. counsel, director The Mead Corp. Second lt., A.S., O.R.C., A.U.S., 1918-28. Mem. Am., Ohio and Montgomery County bar assns., Bar Assn. of City of N.Y., Delta Kappa Epsilon, Phi Delta Phi. Republican. Episcopalian. Clubs: Lawyers Club, Ye Buz Fuz, Moraine Country (Dayton); Miami Valley Skeet (Dayton); Cloud (New York City); Miami Valley Hunt and Polo. Home: 250 Southview Rd. Office: 131 N. Ludlow St., Dayton, O. Died Aug. 23, 1955; buried Troy, O.

SMITH, Myrtle Holm (Mrs. Clifford P. Smith), Christian Science practitioner; b. Toledo, May 4, 1875; d. Harry S. and Carrie (Eddy) Holm; grad. Ft. Dodge High Sch., 1893; student, Grinnell Coll., Ia., 1893-94; m. Clifford Pabody, Jan. 31, 1899; children—Muriel Pabody (Mrs. Winter Dean), Alden Holm Smith (dec.). After leaving Grinnell Coll. studied art in pvt. studios; pres. Christian Sc. Ch., Boston, 1945-48; chmn. War Relief Com. Home: Longwood Towers, Brookline 46, Mass. Died Sept. 27, 1951.

SMITH, Oramandal, state ofcl.; b. in Aroostook Co., Me., Dec. 2, 1842; s. Daniel Day and Lucy (Williams) S.; ed. Litchfield Acad. and Waterville Classical Inst.; m. Jennie R. Smith, May 22, 1875 (died 1906). Prin. schs., Litchfield, and Richmond, 1864-77; in charge of schs. of Litchfield, 1863-76; mem. Me. Ho. of Rep., 1870; reëlected, 1896, but resigned; asst. clk. Ho. of Rep., 1874, 1875, clk., 1876, 1877, 1878, and 1880-5; state ins. commr., 1883-5; sec. of state, 1885-91 (3 terms); mem. Exec. Council, 1891-1902; pvt. sec. to Gov. Llewellyn Powers, 1897-1901; state treas., 1901-7 (3 terms); Republican. Trustee and chmn. exec. com., Litchfield Acad., for 25 years.; trustee Me. Sch. for Feeble Minded. Free Baptist. Mem. Patrons of Husbandry. Address: Litchfield, Maine. Died May 21, 1915.

SMITH, Percey Franklyn, mathematician; b. Nyack, N.Y., Aug. 21, 1867; s. James and Maria Jane (Demarest) S.; Ph.B., Yale, 1888, Ph.D., 1891; univs. of Göttingen, Berlin, Paris, 1894-96; m. Julia C. Lum, Dec. 23, 1890; m. 2d, Ethel Harned Gauvran, Nov. 11, 1922. Instr. mathematics, 1888-94, asst. prof., 1895-1900, prof., 1900-36, now emeritus, Sheffield Scientific Sch. Mem. Conn. Acad. Arts and Sciences, Am. Math. Soc. Author: Elements of Differential and Integral Calculus (edith with W. A. Granville), 1904, new edit. (with W. R. Longley), 1934; Elements of Analytic Geometry (with A. S. Gale), 1905; Introduction to Analytic Geometry (with same), 1905; Theoretical Mechanics (with W. R. Longley), 1910; Elementary Analysis (with W. A. Granville), 1910; New Analytic Geometry, revised edit. (with A. S. Gale and J. H. Neelley), 1928. Address: 250 Edgehill Rd., New Haven, Conn. Died June 3, 1956.

SMITH, Peter P., jurist; b. Honesdale, Pa., June 2, 1877, ed. Honesdale pub. schs.; admitted to bar of Wayne and Luzerne cos., Pa., 1874. Dist. atty., Wayne Co., Pa., 1875-8; supervisor of census, 5th dist., Pa., 1880; apptd. additional law judge, Lackawanna, 1892; candidate for co. judge, 1894; judge Superior Court, Pa., 1895—. Address: Scranton, Pa. Died Jan. 2, 1960.

SMITH, Philip Sidney, geologist; b. Medford, Mass., July 28, 1877; s. Sidney L. and Kate (Butler) S.; A.B., Harvard, 1899, A.M., 1900, Ph.D., 1904; m. Lenore W. Kinney, Nov. 26, 1900; children—Sidney Butler, Katharine, Constance Smith Thurrell. Asst. and instr. in geology and physiography Harvard, 1900-06; with U.S. Geol. Survey, 1906-46, successively asst. geologist, geologist, adminstrv. geologist, acting dir., and chief Alaska geologist, retired 1946; engr. Fed. Emergency Adminstrn. of Public Works for Alaska, 1933-34. Chmn. U.S. delegation 17th Internat. Geol. Congress, U.S.S.R., 1937. Fellow Geol. Soc. America, A.A.A.S., Assn. Am. Geographers, Soc. Econ. Geologists, Soc. Am. Mil. Engrs., Am. Geog. Society; mem. Nat. Geographic Soc. (life), Washington Acad. Sciences, Geol. Soc. Washington, Am. Inst. Mining and Metall. Engrs., Am. Polar Soc., Am. Geophys. Union, Soc. Profl. Geographers, Loyal Legion, Nat. Council of American-Soviet Friendship, Inc. (sci. com.), Arctic Inst. of North America. Clubs: Delta Upsilon, Cosmos, Harvard (Washington); Travellers (Harvard); Explorers (New York). Writer various reports on areal, economic and physiographic geology, in publs. U.S. Geol. Survey and tech. jours. Home: 3249 Newark St., Washington; (summer) Philip Smith Landing, Wolfeboro, N.H. Died May 10, 1949; buried Wolfeboro.

SMITH, Ralph M., former dir. selective service; b. Provincetown, Mass., June 23, 1883; s. Franklin N. and Emma M. (Holmes) S.; LL.B., Northeastern Coll. of Law, 1904; m. Ethel M. Coman, June 22, 1907. Admitted to Mass. bar, 1904; in practice of law, Somerville, Mass., 1904-40; special justice, Somerville Dist. Court, since 1922; asst. city solicitor, Somerville, 1923-28; with West Somerville Cooperative Bank (now Middlesex Federal Savings and Loan Assn.) since 1928, successively as treas., v.p., pres., and chmn. of the bd.; dir. Federal Home Loan Bank of Boston. Mem. bd. aldermen, Somerville, 1909-12; mem. Mass. State Legislature, 1913-15. Mem. Mass. Nat. Guard since 1902, advancing through the grades from pvt. to lt. col.; state judge adv., 1920-45; serving with U.S. Army, 1940-45; assigned as state dir. selective service, 1942-46, rank of col.; past pres. U.S. Savs. & Loan Assn.; mem. Council Internat. Union Bldg. Socs. Trustee Follen Ch. Member Somerville, Middlesex, Mass., and Am. bar assns., Judge Advocates Assn. Mason (Shriner, K.T.). Clubs: Boston (Mass.) City; Army and Navy (Washington). Awarded D.S.M. Home: 1162 Massachusetts Av., Lexington 1, Mass. Office: 421 Highland Av. W., Somerville, Mass. Died Oct. 10, 1951.

SMITH, Ray L., prof. law; b. Linden, Ia., May 11, 1886; s. William Dillmon and Mary Elisabeth (Leonard) S.; student, State Univ. of Ia., 1904-05; A.B., Willamette University, Salem, Ore., 1913, LL.B., 1915, recipient Doctor of Laws (honorary), 1954; LL.B., Yale Univ., 1916; m. Gertrude Florence Reeves, Sept. 8, 1915. Gen. law practice, Salem, Ore., 1915-35; prof. law Willamette Univ. Law Sch. since 1916; acting dean, prof. law, 1942-46, emeritus 1948. City atty. Salem, 1921-25; member Salem, Ore., Municipal Water Comm. Mem. Ore., Am. and State bar assns., Am. Assn. Univ. Profs., Delta Theta Pi. Mason. Home: 1895 Center St., Salem, Ore. Died July 16, 1954; buried Belcrest Meml. Park Cemetery.

SMITH, Raymond Underwood, lawyer; b. Wells River, Vt., Sept. 11, 1875; s. Edgar W. and Emma M. (Gates) S.; C.E., Norwich U., 1894; m. Georgie A. Burr, 1922. Admitted to Vt. bar, 1897, N.H. bar, 1900, and practiced at Wells River, later at Woodsville, N.H.; solicitor Grafton County, N.H., 1915-19; U.S. dist. atty., Dist. of N.H., 1922-34; resumed pvt. practice. Referee in bankruptcy for entire state, 1934-44. Admitted to ass. bar, 1943. Mem. Military Service Institution of the U.S. Republican. Mason (K.T., Shriner), Odd Fellow. Home: 2006 Massachusetts Av., Lexington, Mass. Died Sept. 5, 1958; buried Carlisle, Mass.

SMITH, Rex, editor; b. Gate City, Scott County, Va., June 17, 1900; s. William Daniel and Sallie Lou (Minnich) S.; ed. Shoemaker Prep. Sch. (Gate City), U. of Va., Coll. of William and Mary and San Marcos U. (Lima, Peru); m. Alice Buchanan, 1925 (divorced 1929); 1 dau., Sally Lou; m. 2d, Jessie Royce Landis 1937 separated 1940, divorced 1944); m. 3d, Izetta Jewel, 1944; children—Rex, Izetta. With Detroit News, 1918, Washington Herald, 1919-20; entered U.S. Foreign Service and served as vice consul, San Jose, Costa Rica, 1920-21, Lima, Peru, 1922-23; then with San Francisco Examiner, 4 years, Los Angeles Times, 2 years; wrote for motion pictures, Hollywood, 1927; journalistic assignments in Italy, Balearic Islands, Germany, Bavaria, 1929; then corr. for Paris edition, N.Y. Herald-Tribune, France and Europe generally for 2 years; fgn. news editor for Associated Press, 1931; chief of Spanish bur. Asso. Press, Madrid, to 1935; while in Spain organized Asso. Press news service for Europe; became foreign editor Newsweek, 1936, later asst. to pres. and worked out editorial formula, then editor to 1941; editor The Chicago Sun, 1941-42; vice pres. public relations Am. Airlines 1946-58, ret. Served in O.T.C., University of Michigan, World War I; maj. A.C., Apr. 1942; lt. col., asst. to comdg. gen., Air Transport Comd., 1942-44; promoted to col., named chief, office of information, Hdqrs., Army Air Forces, Washington, D.C., 1944. Mem. Kappa Sigma, Sigma Delta Chi. Clubs: National Press (Washington); Overseas Press, Wings (New York), Racquet (Chicago). Address: N.Y.C. Died May 1959.

SMITH, Richard R(oy), publisher; b. Beloit, Wis., Oct. 29, 1885; s. Henry Jennings and Alice C. (Brittain) S.; A.B., Yale, 1908; m. 2d, Evelyn Light, May 15, 1946; one son (by a previous marriage), Richard Emerson. With the Macmillan Co., N.Y.C., 1908-29, mgr. college dept., 1910-29, also mem. bd. dirs.; organizer, 1929, and pres., 1929-33, Richard R. Smith, Inc., pubs.; name changed to Ray Long & Richard R. Smith, Inc., 1931; pres. R&S Motor Corp., New Rochelle, N.Y., 1925-29; organizer, and pres. The Am. Spectator, Inc., pubs. of The American Spectator, a literary mag., 1932-34; v.p. Frederick A. Stokes Co., pubs., 1933-34; pub., and publishers' and authors' consultant, 1934-48; editor Books in Brief, 1937-38; chmn. bd. dirs. Richard R. Smith Pub., Inc., 1948—. Asst. exec. sec. of edn. and spl. training com., war plans div., U.S. Gen. Staff, 1918. Chmn. bd. of review (N.Y.) in charge wartime censorship newsreels and motion pictures, Fed. Office of Censorship, 1942-45. Pres. bd. Larchmont Pub. Library, 1930-34; sec. Class of 1908, Yale Coll., 1918— (editor, pub. Vol. III of class history, 1940). Fellow Berkeley Coll., Yale U.; mem. Yale Assn. Class Secs. (past v.p. and pres.), Am. Econ. Assn., Am. Hist. Assn., Am. Polit. Science Assn., Am. Sociol. Soc., Modern Lang. Assn., Phi Beta Kappa, Beta Theta Pi. Occasional contbr. to mags. Died July 26, 1957.

SMITH, Robert Aura, newspaperman, author; b. Denver, Colo., Jan. 12, 1899; s. Aura and Lily L. (Severinghaus) S.; A.B., Ohio Wesleyan U., 1920; B.A., M.A., Oxford U. (Rhodes scholar), 1924; m. Pauline Crumb, Aug. 16, 1924. Asso. prof. English, Drake U., 1920-21; prof. English, Evansville Coll., 1924-25; mem. editorial staff Cincinnati Commercial Tribune, 1925-29; corr. Christian Science Monitor, 1926-30; news editor Manila Daily Bulletin, 1930-37; staff corr., New York Times, 1930-37, cable desk, 1937-41, Fgn. News Dept., 1945-49, editorial writer, 1949—; Office of War Information, India, 1942-43; O.W.I., N.Y., 1944-45; lecturer, Yale, 1945-46, Barnard Coll., 1946-47. Pvt., Field Hosp. 147, 37th Div., with A.E.F., 1917-19; 2d lt. Mil. Intel. Res., 1934. Chavalier, French Legion of Honor. Mem. Am. Soc. Rhodes Scholars, Phi Beta Kappa, Delta Sigma Rho, Theta Alpha Phi, Alpha Sigma Phi. Author: Our Future in Asia, 1940; Your Foreign Policy, 1941; Divided India, 1947. Home: Timber Lane, Westport, Conn. Office: care N.Y. Times, N.Y.C. Died Nov. 11, 1959.

SMITH, Robert Edwin, author, clergyman; b. Quitman Co., Ga., Feb. 23, 1866; s. John Thomas and Lucinda (Jackson) S.; Baylor U., 1890-94; m. Clara Ara McMahan, Nov. 1, 1893; children—Pauline, Orbie Lee, Carlton Jackson, Hortense, Edwin Moore. Ordained ministry Missionary Bapt. Ch., 1890; pastor Shiloh Ch., McLennan Co., Tex., 1890-96, Crawford, 1896-1900, Meridian, 1900-05, Rule, 1905-10, DeLeon, 1910-16, Lorena, 1916-19, Holland, 1919-22. Dean, Highland Bapt. Ch., Waco, Tex., 1922—. Trustee Bishop Coll., Marshall, Tex. Democrat. Author: Some Things Under the Sun, 1895; Christianity and the Race Problem, 1922; Little Foxes in the Baptist Vineyard, 1923; The Christian Sabbath Restated, 1926. Died Apr. 6, 1941, buried Rose Mount, Waco, Tex.

SMITH, Robert Metcalf, prof. English; b. Worcester, Mass., Mar. 29, 1886; s. Edward Payson and Julia Mack (Church) S.; A.B., Amherst, 1908; A.M., Columbia Univ., 1909, fellow, 1911-12, Ph.D., 1915; m. Agnes Grace Clancy, June 28, 1912. Instr. in rhetoric, U. of Minn., 1910-11; prof. English, Westminster Coll., New Wilmington, Pa., 1912-16; instr. in English, U.S. Naval Acad., 1917-19; prof. English, Drury Coll., Springfield, Mo., 1920-21; prof. English, U. of Wyoming, Laramie, 1921-25; prof. English, Lehigh U., since 1925; summer sessions, Beloit Coll., 1920, U. of Colo., 1921-23, U. of Wyoming, 1924, Lehigh U., 1926-29, Columbia U., 1930, Northwestern U., 1931, Lehigh U., 1932-34, U. of Colo., 1935, Lehigh U., 1936-44. Mem. Modern Lang Assn., Shakespeare Assn. of America, Shakespeare Soc. of Philadelphia, Columbia University English Grad. Union, Phi Gamma Delta, Phi Kappa Phi. Republican. Conglist. Author: Froissart and the English Chronicle Play, 1915. Editor: Types of Philosophic Drama; Types of World Tragedy; Types of Social Comedy; Types of Farce Comedy; Types of Romantic Comedy; Types of Historical Drama; Types of Domestic Tragedy (all 1928); Types of World Literature, 1930; Book of Biography, 1930; Troilus and Cressida, 1932. General editor, Twelve Victorian Bibliographies, 1935; The Shelley Legend, 1945. Spl. research in Shakespeare and other bibliographies; author of various articles on subject. Home: Lehigh Univ. Campus, Bethlehem, Pa. Died Jan. 15, 1952.

SMITH, Rufus D(aniel), prof. politics; b. New York, N.Y., Feb. 5, 1884; s. Rufus E. and Susan Ann (Myers) S.; A.B., Cornell, 1907; A.M., N.Y. U., 1921, LL.D., 1952; LL.D., Ohio No. U., 1936, U. Newark, 1938; m. Georgia L. Burr, Nov. 13, 1909; children—Rufus Burr, Maynard Edwin. Instr. in economics, Cornell U., 1907-09; instr. in sociology, U. of Pittsburgh, 1909-11; also asst. sec. Asso. Charities of Pittsburgh, 1909-11; sec. Asso. Charities, Montreal, Can., 1911-15; asst. in politics, New York U., 1915-16, instr., 1916-20, asso. prof., 1920-26, prof. since 1926, administrative chmn. Dept. of Govt. of Washington Sq. Coll., 1923-32, asst. dean of Coll., 1925-28, asso. dean, 1928-32, dir. Univ. Extension Div., 1926-32, in charge of Evening Division, 1929-32, dean of Washington Square Coll., 1932-34, provost of New York U., 1934, now provost emeritus; acting dean, School of Retailing, 1944-46; vis. Fulbright prof. Chulalongkorn U., Bangkok, Thailand, 1951, 52, 53—. Vice pres. Assn. of Urban Universities, 1931-33; N.E. rep. War Camp Community Service, 1917-19. Former trustee Village of Bellerose, L.I., N.Y. Home: 103 Cedar Shore Dr., Harbour Green, Massapequa, N.Y. Address: 100 Washington Sq. E., N.Y.C. Died Dec. 31, 1953.

SMITH, S(amuel) Archibald, educator; b. Wilton, N.H., Nov. 27, 1870; s. Samuel Wood and Frances Cornelia (Jones) S.; grad. Lancaster (Mass.) Acad., 1890; A.B., U. of Mich., 1894; m. Isabelle Morse Blackburn, Sept. 6, 1898; children—S(amuel)Archibald, George Dimock, Ruth Blackburn (Mrs. Alexander H. Prinz), Jane Wallace (Mrs. Paul Bonynge, Jr.). Prin. high sch., Wilton, 1894-95; instr. English and German, Lancaster (Mass.) Acad., 1895-96; prin. Free Acad., Glastonbury, Conn., 1896-99; master in English, Pingry Sch., Elizabeth, N.J., 1899-1907, headmaster, 1907-15; ednl. work and lecturing, 1915-18; headmaster Friends' Acad., Locust Valley, N.Y., 1918-33; advancement sec. Religious Soc. of Friends, New York, 1933-34; prin. Friends' School, Brooklyn, 1934-37, principal emeritus, 1937—; principal of Friends Seminary, N.Y., 1938-43; engaged in ednl. research, 1943—. Mem. Schoolmasters Assn. (N.Y. City), N.E.A., Nat. Assn. Secondary Sch. Principals, N.H. Hist. Soc., Wilton Hist. Soc. (pres. 1937-38). Republican. Mem. Soc. of Friends. Clubs: Town Hall (New York); Twentieth Century (Brooklyn). Author: Puer Qui Ad Ludum Ire Noluit (Latin play), 1923. Home: Wilton, N.H. Died Sept. 19, 1954; buried Wilton.

SMITH, Sherrill, banker; b. Cuba, N.Y., Nov. 28, 1881; s. Addison W. and Helen A. (McWhorter) S.; ed. Cuba High Sch.; m. Elnora Eaton, Oct. 9, 1907; children—Florence (Mrs. William H. Mountain, Jr.), Russell. Bank clerk Cuba Nat. Bank, 1899-1907; cashier Citizens Nat. Bank, Tionesta, Pa., 1907-09; with Federal Bureau of Investigation, U.S. Dept. of Justice, Washington, 1909; nat. bank examiner, 1910-14; chief nat. bank examiner, Chicago, 1914-19, New York, 1919-21; vice pres. Chase Nat. Bank, 1921-47, ret.; dir. Punta Alegre Sugar Corp. Republican. Presbyterian. Mason. Clubs: Union League (New York); Pelham Country (Pelham Manor, N.Y.). Home: 28 Genesee Parkway, Cuba, N.Y. Died Apr. 10, 1951; buried Cuba.

SMITH, Shirley Wheeler, univ. adminstr. (emeritus); b. Nashville, Mich., May 3, 1875; s. Judge Clement MacDonald and Francis (Wheeler) Smith; B. L., U. Mich., 1897, A.M., 1900, LL.D., 1945; m. Sara Spencer Browne, Sept. 20, 1899; children—Reynolds Rich (dec.), Clement Andrew, Constance Alison (Mrs. V. Blakeman Qua), Donald Shirley, David Wheeler (dec.). Instr. English, U. Mich., 1898-1901; sec. U. Mich. Gen. Alumni Assn. and editor Michigan Alumnus, 1901-04; asst. in president's office, Fidelity Mut. Life Ins. Co., Phila., 1904-08; sec. U. Mich., 1908-27, sec. and business mgr., 1927-30, v.p. and sec., 1930-45, v.p. and sec. emeritus, 1945—. Trustee Teachers Ins. and Annuity Assn., New York; dir. Ann Arbor Bank. Charter mem. (1910) Assn. of Univ. and Coll. Business Officers. Ann Arbor City Councilman, 1945—. Mem. S.A.R., Phi Gamma Delta, Phi Beta Kappa, Phi Kappa Phi. Republican. Conglist. Mason. Clubs: Ann Arbor, University, Rotary. Author: Harry Burns Hutchins and the University of Michigan, 1951; James Burrill Angell: An American Influence, 1954. Home: 1706 S. University Av., Ann Arbor, Mich. Died Feb. 16, 1959.

SMITH, Sidney Earle, govt. ofcl. Can.; b. Port Hood, Nova Scotia, Mar. 9, 1897; s. John Parker and Margaret Jane (Etheridge) S.; B.A., U. of King's Coll., Halifax, N.S., 1915, M.A., 1919, D.C.L. (hon.); LL.B., Dalhousie U., Halifax, N.S., 1920, LL.D.; grad. work, Harvard Law Sch., 1920-21; LL. D., Queen's University, University Manitoba, Laval University, University Ottawa, Univ. Cambridge, U. W. Ont., U. Aberdeen, McMaster U., Princeton, Columbia, Brown University, University of Toronto; D.C. L., McGill U., Acadia U., Bishop's U., Mt. Allison U., m. Harriet Rand, June 29, 1926; children—Sheila Rand, Moyra Jean, Heather Margaret. Lecturer, asst. prof., Dalhousie Law Sch., 1921-25; lecturer, Osgoode Hall Law Sch., 1925-29; dean, Dalhousie Law Sch., 1929-34; pres. The Univ. of Manitoba, 1934-44; principal, University Coll. Toronto, 1944-45; pres. U. Toronto, 1945-57; Canadian sec. of state for external affairs, 1957—. Fellow Royal Soc. Can.; mem. U.N. Assn. Can. (pres. 1948-50), Nat. Council Canadian Y.M.C.A. (pres. 1939-43), Nat. Film Soc. of Canada (pres. 1937-45), Canadian Assn. for Adult Edn. (pres. 1941-44), Nat. Conf. Can. Universities (pres. 1942-44), Canadian Youth Commn. (chmn. 1943-45), Student Christian Movement Nat. Council (chmn. 1954-57). Member board govs., Halifax Ladies' Coll., 1930-34. Served with Royal Canadian Artillery, 1916-18; Royal Flying Corps, 1918-19, W.W. I. Queen's Counsel, Province of Nova Scotia, Province of Manitoba. Mem. Assn. Canadian Clubs (pres. 1954-57), World U. Service Can. (pres. 1955-57). Clubs: Century (N.Y.); York (Toronto); Rideau. Mem. United Ch. Author: Cases on Trusts, 1928; Manual of Canadian Business Law (with J. D. Falconbridge, Q.C.), 1929; Cases on Equity (with H. E. Read, Q.C.), 1932. Asst. editor Canadian Bar Review, 1925-34. Address: Ottawa, Can. Died Mar. 17, 1959.

SMITH, Sion Bass, lawyer; b. Meadville, Pa., Dec. 8, 1865; s. James Wilson and Anna E. (Salisbury) S.; A.B., Allegheny Coll., 1886, M.A., 1889; m. Anna Mae Goff, June 13, 1893; m. 2d, Alice J. Shepler Zimmerman, Nov. 11, 1942. Admitted to Pa. bar, 1889; practiced in Meadville, 1889-1900, Pitts., 1900-44; ret., 1944. Profl. lectr. on Mining Law, Sch. of Mines, Pa. State Coll., 1914-32. Ex-pres. Winfield R.R. Co. Mem. Phi Kappa Psi (past nat. pres.). Republican. Pres. trustees N. Presbyn. Ch., 1914-43, Pitts. Mason (33°). Home: 192 N. Sprague Av., Pitts. 2. Died Jan. 30, 1954.

SMITH, Stevenson, psychologist; b. Phila., Apr. 29, 1883; s. Rev. Henry Augustus (D.D.) and Martha Louise (Stevenson) S.; B.S., U. Pa., 1904, Ph.D., 1909; studied U. of Heidelberg, Germany, 1905, Columbia, 1905-06; m. Ruth Arvilla Norton, Dec. 2, 1920; m. 2d, Dorothy Davidson, Dec. 23, 1925; 1 dau. Bradford. Asst. in psychology Columbia, 1905-06; prof. psychology Hampden-Sydney Coll., Va., 1906-11; prof. psychology U. Wash., 1911—, also head of Dept.; dir. psychol. clinic and Gatzert Found. for Child Welfare; prof. clin. psychology U. Hawaii, 1923-24. Psychologist to Juvenile Court, Seattle. Dir. Inst. of Child Development, of Wash. In charge intelligence testing, 13th Nval Dist., 1918-19. Mem. Am., Western (pres. 1930-31) psychol. assns., Am. Assn. of Clinical Psychologists, Sigma Xi. Club: Faculty (U. of Wash.). Author: General Psychology in Terms of Behavior (with Edwin Guthrie), 1921. Home: 3833 40th Av. N.E., Seattle. Died Nov. 27, 1950.

SMITH, Thurber Montgomery, educator; b. Sioux City, Ia., May 14, 1893; s. Will T. and Sara (Montgomery) S.; A.B., St. Marys (Kan.) Coll., 1913; A.M., Loyola U., Chgo., 1915, LL.B., 1916; student St. Louis U., 1919-23, 30-31, Ph.D., 1931; student Jesuit Sch. of Theology, Hastings, Eng., 1925-26, Lyon, France, 1926-29, Cleve., 1929-30. Entered Soc. of Jesus, 1919; ordained priest R.C. Ch., 1927; instr. history and mathematics St. Ignatius High Sch., Chgo., 1913-14; lectr. polit. sci. Loyola U., 1914-15; investigator Dept. Pub. Welfare, Chgo., 1914-16; admitted to Ill. bar, 1916; instr. English, Creighton U., Omaha, Neb., 1923-25; instr. philosophy St. Louis U., 1931-32, asst. prof., 1932-34, asso. prof., 1934-42, prof., 1942—, dean Grad. Sch., 1933—, sec. univ. bd. trustees, chmn. univ. bd. grad. studies, chmn. Council Regents and Deans; dir. radio station WEW, St. Louis U., 1931-32; gen. dir. studies in coll. of Mo., Province (Soc. of Jesus), 1934-35. Served in U.S. Army, 1917-18. Mem. Nat. Cath. Edn. Assn. (mem. exec. com. Coll. Dept.; chmn. com. on grad. studies, 1936-46), Am. Cath. Philos. Assn., Mo. Acad. Science, Social Justice Commn. of St. Louis. K.C. (4°). Author: The Unemployment Problem, Science and Culture Series, 1932; also articles on philos., social and ednl. subjects. Home: 221 N. Grand Blvd., St. Louis 3. Died Apr. 30, 1950.

SMITH, Vivian Thomas, coll. dean; b. Litchfield, Ill., Aug. 14, 1886; s. Albert Joab and Ella Mae (Enloe) S.; A.B., Greenville (Ill.) Coll., 1916; A.M., University of Illinois, 1929, Ph.D., 1933; LL.D., Cornell College (Iowa), 1943; m. Myrtle Lola Cannon, Dec. 27, 1911; children—Albert Arthur, Julia Mae. Teacher, rural schools, Ill., 1905-06, 1908-10; preceptor, Chili (N.Y.) Sem., 1907-08; supt. of schools, Sparland, Ill., 1911-12, Odell, Ill., 1912-15; prin. Momence (Ill.) High Sch., 1916-18; supt. of schools, Colfax, Ill., 1918-19, Lexington, Ill., 1919-25; building constrn. business, Hollywood, Fla., 1925-28; head dept. of edn., Huron (S.D.) Coll., 1933-36; dean Kan. Wesleyan U., Salina, 1936-38; pres. Upper Iowa U., Fayette, 1938-52; academic dean Coll. of the Ozarks, 1952, later became dean and acting president. Mem. National Education Assn., Phi Delta Kappa, Kappa Delta Pi, Pi Gamma Mu, Beta Kappa. Mason. Methodist. Clubs: Fayette Garden; West Union Rotary. Author: (with W.S. Monroe, and others) Locating Educational Information in Published Sources; Public Junior College Legislation in the United States. Contbr. to ednl. jours. Home: 500 South Campus, Clarksville, Ark. Died Aug. 28, 1953; buried Hillsboro, Ill.

SMITH, W. A., judge; b. Andalusia, Ill., Nov. 19, 1870; s. William and Cynthia (Smith) S.; B.S., Western Coll., Toledo, Ia., 1890; B.S., State U. of Ia., 1898, LL.B., 1898; Doctor of Laws, Coe College, 1956; married Marta G. Lichtenwalter, December 1893; children—Paul F. Head of comml. dept., Western Coll., 1892-93; with electric light and power co., 1894-95; practiced law in New Hampton and Nashua, 1898-1918, Dubuque, 1918-43; justice of Supreme Court of Ia., since 1943. Mem. Chamber of Commerce (pres.), Dubuque Red Cross, Planning and Zoning Commn., Bd. of Adjustment. Dir. Sunnycrest Sanitorium (county hosp.). Mem. Dubuque County, Ia. State (pres. 1941-42), Am. bar assns., Am. Judicature Soc. Home: 1339 Wood St., Dubuque, Ia. Office: Supreme Court, State House, Des Moines, and 609 Bank Ins. Bldg., Dubuque, Ia. Died June 10, 1958; buried Toledo, Ia.

SMITH, Walter Driscoll, army officer; b. Cumberland, Md., Nov. 16, 1875; s. Page John and Sarah Dorothy (Ways) S.; A.B., St. Johns Coll., Annapolis, 1897; B.S., U.S. Mil. Acad., 1901; student Staff Coll., Ft. Leavenworth, Kan., 1922-23, War Coll., Washington, 1921, Naval War Coll., 1924; m. Florence Beverly Egerton, Mar. 27, 1901 (dec. Mar. 8, 1948); children—Beverly Egerton (Mrs. F. B. Kane), Charles Calvert Egerton, Dorothy Egerton (Mrs. R. H. Berry), Page Egerton. Commd. 2d lt., 1901, advanced through grades to brig. gen., 1939; instr. U.S. Mil. Acad., 1905-09, tactics officer, 1915-17; duty on constrn. of Panama Canal, 1909-13; duty with regiment, 1913-15; duty at G.H.Q., France, 1917-19; with Gen. Staff, Washington, 1924-28; instr. and dir. Staff Coll., 1930-31; chief hist. sect. Army War Coll., 1931-35; chief of staff, 82d Res. Div., 1935-39; with U.S. War Dept., 1941-46. Decorated Roosevelt Medal for Constrn. of Panama Canal, Purple Heart; French Legion of Honor. Clubs: Army and Navy (Washington), Army and Navy Country (Arlington, Va.). Home: 1805 Army-Navy Dr., Arlington, Va. Died Sept. 20, 1955; buried Arlington Nat. Cemetery.

SMITH, Warren Du Pré, geologist; b. Leipzig, Germany, May 12, 1880; s. Prof. Charles Forster and Anna Leland (Du Pré) S.; brought to U.S. in infancy; B.S., U. Wis., 1902, Ph.D., 1908; M.A., Stanford, 1904; fellow U. Chgo., 1904-05; m. Phoebe Ellison, July 14, 1910 (dec.); children—James Francis, Warren Ellison, Phoebe Hall. Field asst. Wis. Geol. and Natural History Survey, 1900-02; geologist U.S. Govt. Mining Bur., Manila, 1905-06, Div. of Mines, Bur. of Science, 1906-07; chief Div. of Mines, P.I., 1907-14; pres. Philippine Soc. Engrs., 1912; head dept. of geology U. Ore., 1914-47, ret. 1947; chief div. mines Bur. of Science, Philippine Govt., 1920, 21 (leave of absence from U. of Ore.); cons. geologist on Owyhee Dam, Ore., U.S. Bur. of Reclamation, 1927; ranger-naturalist Crater Lake Nat. Park, 1934, 35. U.S. del. Internat. Geol. Congress, Toronto, 1913; del 1st Pan-Pacific Sci. Conf., Honolulu, 1920; mem. Governor's Spl. Mining Com., Ore., 1935; mem. Philippine com. Pacific Sci. Bd. Fellow Geol. Soc. America (pres. Cordilleran sect. 1925), Pacific Geog. Soc., Ore. Tchrs. Assn. (pres. geog. council 1933), Ore. Mining Congress (pres. 1934), Ore. Acad. Sci. (pres.-elect, 1948), Phi Beta Kappa, Sigma Xi, Sigma Alpha Epsilon. Rotarian. Author: Geology and Mineral Resources of the Philippine Islands; Scenic Treasure House of Oregon, 1941; also about 50 articles and monographs on spl. phases of Philippine and Malayan geology and papers on Ore. and Pacific geology and geography. Editor: Physical and Economic Geography of Oregon, 1940. Home: 1941 University St., Eugene, Ore. Died July 18, 1950; buried Resthaven Meml. Park, Eugene.

SMITH, Warren Robert, state ofcl.; b. Oconto, Wis., July 20, 1888; s. James P. and Katherine (Farrell) S.; student Marquette U., 1912-14; m. Dena A. Besserdich, Mar. 12, 1917; 1 son, Robert (dec.). Accountant, auditor C., M., St.P. and P. R.R., 1923-25; engagd in real estate, 1925-42; with U.S. Army and Navy Ordnance Dept., Milw., 1942-44; insp. Internat. Harvester Co., 1944-58; treas. State of Wis., 1948—. Del. Republican Nat. Conv., 1956. Mem. S. Div. Civic Assn. (Milw.). Lutheran U. Assn. (Valparaiso U.). Lutheran. Home: 2135 University Av., Madison 5, Wis.; also 2601 W. Wells St., Milw. 3. Office: State Capitol, Madison 2, Wis. Died Dec. 4, 1957.

SMITH, Wilbur Cleveland, coll. prof.; b. Independence, Kan., Aug. 9, 1884; s. William Edward and Lucinda Caroline (Parkust) S.; M.D., Univ. Med. Coll., Kansas City, 1908; A.B., Kan. City U., 1911; Sc.D., Wake Forest Coll., 1938; m. Jane Taylor, Jan. 31, 1912. Instr. in anatomy, New York U. and Bellevue Hosp. Med. Coll., 1911-13; head dept. of anatomy, Wake Forest Coll., 1913-16; asst. prof. of anatomy, Tulane U., 1916-18, asso. prof., 1918-33, head of dept. of gross anatomy, 1933-44, dir. of athletics, 1922-44; dean and head dept. anatomy, La. State U. Sch. Medicine, 1945-48; retired. Mem. Orleans Parish Med. Soc., La. State Med. Soc., Southern Med. Assn., A.M.A., Am. Assn. of Anatomists, Alpha Kappa Kappa, Omicron Delta Kappa, Kappa Delta Phi, Alpha Omega Alpha. Republican. Methodist. Mason (Shriner). Clubs: Recess, Metairie Golf (New Orleans). Contbr. to professional jour. Address: Pine Hills, Pass Christian, Miss. Died July 3, 1952; buried Independence, Kan.

SMITH, William Jones, architect; b. Phila., Pa., May 26, 1881; s. Uselma Clarke and Fanny (Mitcheson) S.; B.S. in architecture, U. of Pa., 1903; A.D. G. architecte diplomé par le Gouvèrnement Francais, Ecole des Beaux Arts, Paris, 1907; m. Mary Van Horne, June 30, 1914; children—William Mitcheson, Van Horne, Sidney Stockton. With Cass Gilbert, architect, N.Y., 1907-09; Holabird & Roche, Chicago, 1909-12; mem. firm Childs & Smith, 1912—. firm architects for ins., office, univ. bldgs. such as Northwestern U. Chicago Campus, high and elem. schs. as Davenport, Ia., Freeport and Kankakee, Ill., med. and dental colls., The Mather Home, Evanston, Ill., Hardware and Employers Ins. Bldg., Wis., Marathon Co. Court house, Wausau, Wis., Evanston Schools, asso. prof. in charge of senior design, Armour Inst. Tech., 1924-29. Served as capt. 319th Engrs., U.S. Army, 1917-18; engr. War Dept., 1942-43; field rep. O.S.S., 1944. Licensed architect 14 states. Fellow A.I.A.; mem. Grad's of Beaux Arts, BAID, Ill. Soc. Architects, Pa. Hist. Soc., Art Inst. Chicago, Burnham Library Com., Am. Soc. Testing Materials, Sigma Xi. Episcopalian. Mason. Club: University (Chicago). Home: 435 Linden St., Winnetka, Ill. Office: 20 N. Wacker Dr., Chgo. Died Jan. 22, 1958; buried Churchyard Christ Church, Winnetka.

SMITH, William Skeldon Adamson, b. Dundee, Scotland, June 16, 1860; s. William and Jane (Mitchell) S.; student pub. schs.; m. Zelma Farwell, Oct. 22, 1895; children—Stuart F., R. Graeme. Apprentice at sea, at 14, and at 23 was comdr. in British merchant marine; came to U.S., 1897, and engaged in farming in Ia.; expert in farm practice U.S. Dept. of Agr., 1914-16; mem. Fed. Farm Loan Bd., 1916-22. Republican. Presbyn. Mason. Address: Strath Haven Inn, Swarthmore, Pa. Died Mar. 3, 1953.

SMITH, William W(allace) II, mfr. medicinals; b. Poughkeepsie, N.Y., May 22, 1888; s. Arthur G. and Ida (Lansing) S.; A.B., Williams Coll., 1910; m. Grace Ewing, Jan. 10, 1930; 1 dau., Janet Ewing. With Smith Bros., Inc., Poughkeepsie, 1910—, pres., 1936—; v.p., dir. First Nat. Bank, Poughkeepsie; dir. Central Hudson Gas & Electric Corp. Trustee Samuel & Nettie Bowne Hosp. Mem. Zeta Psi. Clubs: Rotary, Golf and Country. Home: 29 Hornbeck Ridge. Office: 134 N. Hamilton St., Poughkeepsie, N.Y. Died Mar. 6, 1955.

SMITH, Willis, lawyer; b. Norfolk, Va., Dec. 19, 1887; s. Willis and Mary Shaw (Creecy) S.; grad. Atlantic Collegiate Inst., Elizabeth City, N.C., 1905; A.B., Trinity Coll. (now Duke U.), 1910, law sch., Duke Univ., 1912; m. Anna Lee, Apr. 30, 1919; children—Willis, Lee Creecy, Alton Battle, Anna Lee. Admitted to N.C. bar, 1912, and began practice with Col. John W. Hinsdale at Raleigh; practiced alone, 1913; with William B. Duncan, 1915-18, R. C. Maxwell, 1922-24, Col. W. T. Joyner, 1926-32; now mem. Smith, Leach & Anderson. Served in U.S. Army, Fortress Monroe, Va., July-Nov. 1918. Inheritance tax atty., N.C., 1915-20; mem. N.C. Ho. of Rep., 1927, 29, 31 (speaker of House), 1931; now United States Senator from North Carolina; chmn. Dem. State Conv., 1940; del. Dem. Nat. Conv., Chicago, 1944. Mem. com. preparing rules for use Fed. courts in N.C., 1933; mem. Fed. Judicial conf. 4th Circuit. Dir. Occidental Life Ins. Co., Royal Cotton Mill Co., Ocean Ridge Co., Dexdale North Carolina Co. Mem. bd. trustees Patrick Henry Memorial Foundation, Nat. Probation Assn.; mem. adv. council Southern Research Inst.; mem. Am. Bar Assn. (gen. council, 1935-36; state del. 1936-39; board of govs., 1941-44; pres. 1945-46; Observer Nuremburg Trial, 1946; U.S. del. to Interparliamentary Union, 1951, 52, chmn. 1952), (pres. 1941-42), Wake County (pres. 1943-44), 7th Judicial Dist. Bar Assn., Am. Legislators Assn. (mem. bd. mgrs. 1932-33), Am. Law Inst., Am. Counsel Assn., Am. Judicature Soc., International Bar Association, International Association Insurance Counsel (member executive committee 1938-41, pres. 1941-43). Am. Legion (chmn. Child Welfare Dept. of North Carolina 1930-32); President's Amnesty Bd., 1947), Society of Forty and Eight, Sigma Phi Epsilon, Omicron Delta Kappa (Duke U., 1931), Phi Delta Phi, Order of the Coif. Trustee Duke U. (chmn. bd. since 1947). Democrat. Methodist. Clubs: Lawyers, Kiwanis, Carolina Country, Dunes. Office: Security Bank Bldg., Raleigh, N.C. Died June 26, 1953.

SMITH-PETERSEN, Marius Nygaard, orthopedic surgeon; b. Grimstad, Norway, Nov. 14, 1886; s. Morten and Kaia (Ursin) S.; came to U.S., 1903, naturalized citizen, 1924; student Gymnasium, Norway, 1902-03; West Side High Sch., Milwaukee, Wis., 1904-06; U. of Chicago, 1906-07; B.S., U. of Wis., 1910; M.D., Harvard U. Med. Sch., 1914; m. Hilda Dickinson, Sept. 1, 1917; children—Porter Cushing, Morten, Hilda Whitney. After interneships engaged in practice of orthopedic surgery at Boston, Mass., since 1916; asst. instr. orthopedic surgery, Harvard U. Med. Sch., 1920-30, instr., 1930-35, clin. prof. of orthopedic surgery, 1935-46; chief of orthopedic service, Mass. Gen. Hosp., 1929-46. Decorated Grand Cross, Royal Norwegian Order St. Olav. Hon. mem. Brit. and Canadian orthopaedic assns., Italian Soc. Orthopaedics and Traumatol, Royal Med. Soc. Edinburgh; member International Society Surgery, Am. Acad. of Orthopedic Surgeons, Am. Orthopedic Assn., Internat. Soc. of Orthopedic Surgeons, Am. Coll. of Surgeons, Am. Med. Assn., Boston Surgical Soc., Mass. Med. Soc., N.E. Surgical Soc., Phi Beta Kappa. Comdr., Royal Order of St. Olav (Norway), Hon. M.D., U. of Oslo, Norway. Republican. Episcopalian. Club: Harvard (Boston). Home: 32 Farlow Rd., Newton, Mass. Office: 266 Beacon St., Boston, Mass. Died June 16, 1953; buried Newton, Mass.

SMITHWICK, John Harris, congressman; b. Cherokee Co., Ga.; grad. Reinhardt Normal Coll., Waleska, Ga.; LL.B., Cumberland U., Lebanon, Tenn.; m. Jessie Vereen. Moved to Pensacola, Fla., 1906; mem. 66th to 69th Congresses (1919-27), 3d Fla. Dist. Democrat. Home: Pensacola, Fla. Deceased.

SMOLEY, Constantine Kenneth (smō'lē), civil engr., educator; b. Dwinsk, Russia, Apr. 27, 1869; s. Ossip M. and Barbara E. (Radief) S.; C.E., Federal Polytechnicum, Zurich, Switzerland, 1893; m. Pauline B. Sagorin, Feb. 21, 1894 (died Oct. 3, 1926); m. 2d, Florence N. Wood, May 31, 1928. Came to U.S., 1895, naturalized, 1901. Sturctural draftsman, Variety Iron Works, Cleveland, 1895-96; chief draftsman Van Dorn Iron Works, 1896-1902; structural engr. Wilman, Seaver & Morgan Engring. Co., Cleveland, 1902-04; consulting engr. German-Am. Portland Cement Works, La Salle, Ill., 1904-05; sturctural engr. Ill. Steel Co., 1905-06, N.P. Ry. Co., St. Paul, Minn., 1907-09; dir. Schs. of Civ. and Structural Engring. Internat. Corr. Schools, Scranton, Pa., in charge instrn., also preparation textbooks, 1909-26; head of C. K. Smoley & Sons, pubs. Author: Parallel Tables of Logarithms and Squares, 1901; Five-Decimal Logarithmic-Trigonometric Tables, 1908; Handbook of Civil Engineering, 1913; Parallel Tables of Slopes and Rises, 1917; Smoley's Combined Tables, 1919; Graphic Solution of a Right Triangle, 1920; Segmental Functons, 1937. Also many I.C.S. textbooks. Home: 30 School Lane, Scarscale, N.Y. Died Oct. 21, 1952; buried Shady Lane Cemetery, Chinchilla, Pa.

SMUTS, Jan Christiaan, prime minister of South Africa; b. May 24, 1870; s. of J.A. Smuts; student Victoria Coll., Stellenbosch, South Africa; Christ's Coll., Cambridge U.; m. Sybella Margaretha Krige, 1897; 2 sons, 4 daus. Practiced law, Capetown Bar, Johannesburg, 1896; became state atty. of South African Republic, 1898; colonial sec., Transvaal, 1907; minister of interior and minister of mines, South Africa, 1910-12, minister of defense, 1910-20, minister of finance, 1912-13; prime minister and minister for native affairs, 1919-24, minister of justice, 1933-39; prime minister and minister of external affairs and defense, 1939-48; officer comdg. Union Defense Forces since 1930. Served in Boer War; apptd. gen., 1901, comd. Rep. Forces, Cape Colony, 1901; served in World War I; comd. troops in Brit. East Africa, 1916-17; South African rep. Imperial War Cabinet, 1917-18; rep. for South Africa at Peace Conf., Paris, 1919. Chancellor U. of Capetown since 1936. Holds hon. degrees from univs. in Great Britain, U.S., Can. and South Africa. Awarded Companion of Honor, Fellow Royal Soc., Comdr. Legion of Honor, Grand Comdr. of Order of Leopold, Croix de Guerre; recipient of Albert Medal of Royal Soc. of Arts, 1943. Died Sept. 11, 1950.

SMYKAL, Richard, army officer; b. Chicago, Ill., Dec. 29, 1900; s. Edward J. and Bessie (Rusy) Smejkal; B.S. in indsl. adminstrn., U. of Ill., 1922; student Chicago-Kent Coll. of Law, 1923-24; m. Helen Holpuch, Feb. 4, 1925; children—Ralph, Susan. Commd. 2d lt., inf., Officer Res. Corps, 1922, and advanced through grades to maj. gen., 1948; served in China, Burma, India Theatre and in European Theatre of Operations during World War II; assigned comdg. gen., 33d Inf. Div., Ill. Nat. Guard, 1948. Exec. in building industry; pres. Richard Smykal, Inc., Wheaton, Ill., 1924—. Commissioner (chmn.) Community Conservation Bd., Chgo. Awarded Legion of Merit, Bronze Star Medal, Am. Defense Service Medal, Asiatic-Pacific Theatre Medal with 3 bronze stars, European, African, Middle Eastern Theatre, Am. Theatre and Victory medals (U.S.); Breast Order Yun Hwei (Cloud Banner), Army, Navy, Air Forces Medal (China). Mem. Am. Legion, Vets. of Fgn. Wars, Mil. Order World Wars, Lions Internat., Lambda Alpha, Lambda Chi Alpha, Phi Delta Phi, Scabbard and Blade. Presbyterian. Club: University (Chicago). Home: 1010 E. Illinois Street. Office: 100 N. West St., Wheaton, Ill. Died Apr. 4, 1958; buried Wheaton, Ill.

SMYTH, Henry Field (smīth), hygienist; b. Phila., Pa., Nov. 1, 1875; s. Isaac Scott and Catherine Comegys (Mason) S.; prep. edn., Germantown Acad.; certificate in biology. Univ. of Pa., 1893, M.D., 1897, Doctor of Public Health, 1912; studied University Vienna, 1899-1900; married Alice E. Brackett 1902 (deceased 1929); children—Henry Field, Catherine Mason (Mrs. Wilson Brazer); m. 2d, Clara F. Ellis, Oct. 1931. Resident physician Phila. Home for Incurables, July-Dec. 1897, Germantown Hosp., 1898; gen. practice until 1911; pub. health student, U. of Pa., 1911-12, Wood fellow in hygiene, 1912-13, Scott fellow in hygiene, 1913-14; mem. faculty, U. of Pa., 1914—, successively instr. in bacteriology and hygiene, asst. prof. same, asst. professor industrial hygiene, 1921-39, professor of industrial hygiene, 1939-41, emeritus professor, 1942—; acting director Laboratory of Hygiene, 1917-19, director pro tem., 1932-39; dir. of Symth Laboratories, Phila., 1941-45; consultation and investigation of public and industrial health problems. Member Pa. Commn. on School Ventilation, Pa. Commn. on Occupational Disease Compensation. Passed asst. surgeon U.S.P.H. Res., World War; duty in industrial hygiene control, 1917-19. Fellow A.M.A., American Public Health Association (governing council 5 yrs.), Am. Coll. Physicians, Am. Assn. Indsl. Phys. and Surgeons (former dir.); mem. Sigma Xi. Methodist. Pioneer indsl. hygiene research, work in anthrax and carbon tetrachloride toxicity. Author: (with Walter Lord Obold) Industrial Microbiology, 1930. Contbr. scientific articles. Home and Office: Box 232, Pocasset, Mass. Died Oct. 15, 1954; buried Ivy Hill Cemetery, Mt. Airy, Phila.

SMYTH, S(amuel) Gordon, author; b. Penn's Manor, Bucks Co., Pa., July 24, 1859; s. Jonathan and Elizabeth (Ritchie) S.; ed. pub. schs. and acad.; m. Mary Elizabeth, July 24, 1879; children—Francis Alison, Mrs. Marion M. Wertz, S. Gordon. Mem. Co. H. 6th Regt., N.G., N.J., during Pa., riots, 1877; del. Rep. Congressional Conv., 7th Pa. Dist., 1898, Rep. State Conv., 1905. Presbyn. Mem. Hist. Soc. of Pa., Hist. Soc. of Bucks Co., Montgomery Co. Hist. Soc. (ex-pres.), Geneal. Soc. of Pa., Valley Forge Hist. Soc., Scotch-Irish Soc. Author: A Genealogy of the Duke-Shepherd-Van Metre Family, 1909; The Origin and Descent of an American Family, 1923. Editor: Historical Sketches of Montgomery Co., Pa.; also contbr. hist. and biog. articles and monographs. Originator of the federal "service flag," 1917. Home: "Rylmont," W. Conshohocken, Pa. Died Oct. 4, 1930; buried Cold Spring Cemetery, Cape May, N.J.

SMYTHE, J(ohn) Henry, Jr., b. Phila., Oct. 10, 1883; s. Dr. J(ohn) Henry and Ruth Anna (Harrington) S.; grad. Eastburn Acad. Phila., 1901; B.S., in Econs., U. Pa., 1909, student law dept. 1 yr.; bachelor. Founder, 1909, and propr. J. Henry Smythe, Jr., publisher of children's books, New York. Served as lt. A.R.C., overseas, 1918-19; barred from fighting forces by defective vision. Known as "Slogan" Smythe for war slogans; author of over 1,000 slogans and battle cries—"Do Your Bit to Keep It Lit!" "Lend to Defend!" "Keep the Faith!" "Buy and Keep Liberty Bonds!" etc.; managed U.S. Victory Loan Drive in France, 1919; "slogan man" at Rep. Nat. Com. hdqrs., Chgo., 1924; founder of "Franklin Day" and of Nat. Thrift Week's movement to honor Franklin as America's "patron saint of thrift." Mem. Vets. Fgn. Wars, Soc. of Meth. Preachers' Sons, S.A.R., Pi Gamma Mu. Compiler and Editor: The Amazing Benjamin Franklin, 1929. In 1904, with stars and stripes and a megaphone, led the cheering in Rep. Nat. Conv. when Roosevelt was nominated for President; from 1917 led the lay movement in M.E. Ch. for revision of amusement laws which were changed by Gen. conf. in 1924. Chmn. Benjamin Franklin Com. of Nat. Soc. S.A.R.; mem. Mayor LaGuardia's Com. for the Observance of the 150th Anniversary of the Adoption of the U.S. Constitution—supervising Benjamin Franklin Day opening Constitution Month and Statue of Liberty Celebration opening Constitution Week. Remarkable resemblance to the late Pres. Franklin D. Roosevelt attracted widespread attention: impersonated "F.D.R." at U. of Pa. Alumni Day, 1937, Dr. Franklin, 1938. Started movement endorsed by S.A.R. Congress, to put Franklin's image on coins. Led movement for official naming of Printing House Square Park Row, New York. Pub. over 1000 slogans for victory after war was declared, 1941; launched the Flag Pilgrimage of Patriotism, 1942 (the flag went from state to state and a star was sewed on by governor's wife, or others, at public ceremonies), completed flag welcomed at U.S. Capitol, Flag Day, 1943; affiliated with War Finance Com., N.Y. State, special events sect., for 3d War Loan; vol. for Fourth "Go 4th to Victory"; cooperated with Boy Scouts, Girl Scouts and Camp Fire Girls in honoring Franklin, Lee, Lincoln, etc. Hon. Asst. Sgt. at Arms, Rep. Nat. Conv., Chgo., 1944, 52; nominated, 1945, The Unknown Soldier, Lafayette and others for Hall of Fame; secured many governors' proclamations and statements for Franklin's birthday, 1946-53. Address: Room 2120, 60 E. 42d St., N.Y.C. 17. Died Aug. 14, 1956; buried Mount Maria, Phila.

SNARE, Frederick, contracting engr.; b. Huntingdon, Pa., Dec. 4, 1862; s. of Edmund (M.D.) and Adria M. (Ziegler) S.; ed. pvt. and pub. schs.; m. Ellen N. Brown, Dec. 13, 1883. Became asst. to pres. of Huntingdon Car Works at 21; with Pencoyd Iron Co., 1885-98, advancing to v.p.; pres. Snare & Triest Co., contracting engrs., New York, 1900, and of its successor, Frederick Snare Corp. of which is chmn. bd. Republican. A.R.C. service with A.E.F. in France, 1918-19. Clubs: Engineres', Union League, India House, Metropolitan (N.Y.); Havana (Cuba) Country. Office: 114 Liberty St., N.Y.C. Died 1946.

SNEDEKER, Caroline Dale, author; b. New Harmony, Ind., Mar. 23, 1871; d. Charles Augustus and Nina Dale (Owen) Parke; student Coll. of Music, Cincinnati, O.; m. Charles Henry Snedeker, Apr. 29, 1903. Concert pianist, writer of instr. music before marriage. Republican. Episcopalian. Author: The Spartan, 1912; Seth Way, 1914; The Perilous Seat, 1923; Theras and His Town, 1924; Downright Dencey, 1927; The Beckoning Road, 1929; The Black Arrowhead, 1929; The Town of the Fearless, 1931; The Forgotten Daughter, 1933; Uncharted Ways, 1935; The White Isle, 1940; Luke's Quest, 1947; A Triumph for Flavius, 1954. Address: 111 Citizen St., Bay St. Louis, Miss. Died Jan. 22, 1956; buried Pass Christian, Miss.

SNELL, Albert M., physician; b. Lake Park, Minn., June 9, 1896; s. Albert M. and Anna (Markley) S.; B.S., U. Minn., 1916, M.D., 1918, M.S. in Medicine, 1927; m. Alice I. Morrow, Nov. 11, 1944. Grad. work in charge clin. labs. U. Minn. Hosp., Nov. 1919-Mar. 1920; practiced internal medicine, Mankato (Minn.) Clinic, Apr. 1920-Jan. 1924; 1st asst. in medicine, Mayo Clinic, Feb. 1, 1924-July 1925, consultant div. of medicine, July 1925-29, head sect. in div. of medicine since 1929; instr. in medicine, Mayo Foundation Grad. Sch., U. Minn., 1929-32, asst. prof., 1932-35, asso. prof., 1935-39, prof. of med., 1929-50; clin. prof. of medicine U. Cal., 1950-58; clin. prof. of medicine Stanford U., 1958. Entered medical corps., U.S. N.R., lt. (j.g.), served in U.S. Naval Hosp., Great Lakes, Ill., as med. officer and on U.S.S. K. I. Luckenbach, disch. June 9, 1919; entered med. corps U.S.N.R., as comdr., Dec. 29, 1941, served in U.S. Naval Hosp., Corona, Cal. and as sr. med. officer, U.S.S. Tryon, chief of medicine, U.S. Naval Hosp., Oakland, Calif.; disch. rank of capt., Feb. 16, 1946. Mem. professional Services Div. and section chief Vets. Adminstrn. 1946-56, v. chmn. 1948, chmn. 1953. Commended by sec. of navy for meritorious service. Mem. A.M.A., Am. Gastro-enterological Assn., Am. Soc. for Clin. Investigation, Assn. Am. Physicians, Am. Soc. for Exptl. Pathology, Pacific Interurban Clinical Club, Central Soc. of Clinical Research (pres. 1932), Sigma Xi, Alpha Omega Alpha, Alpha Kappa Kappa. Author: two books and numerous articles on med. subjects. Home: 750 Northampton Av. Office: 300 Homer Av., Palo Alto, Cal. Died Feb. 1960.

SNELL, Bertrand H., ex-congressman; b. Colton, N.Y., Dec. 9, 1870; s. Hollis and Flora E. S.; grad. State Normal Sch., Potsdam, N.Y., 1889; A.B., Amherst, 1894; LL.D., George Washington U., 1920, Amherst, 1929; Sc.D., Clarkson Coll., 1943; m. Sara L. Merrick, June 3, 1903; children—Mrs. Helen Cheel, Mrs. Sara Petersen. Began as bookkeeper, later sec., mgr. Racquette River Paper Co., Potsdam, N.Y.; pres. York State Oil Co.; dir. Northern N.Y. Trust Co., Agrl. Ins. Co. (Watertown, N.Y.), Gould Pumps, Inc. (Seneca Falls, N.Y.). Mem. Rep. State Com., 1914-45; mem. 64th to 75th Congresses (1915-39), 31st N.Y. Dist.; del. Rep. Nat. Conv., 7 times to 1940; permanent chmn. Rep. Nat. Conv., 1932, 36. Mem. bd. trustees, Clarkson Meml. Coll., chmn. finance com.; trustee Hepburn Hosp., Ogdensburg, N.Y.; trustee Potsdam State Tchrs. Coll. Mem. Beta Theta Pi. Mason (K.T., Shriner). Episcopalian. Home: Potsdam, N.Y. Died Feb. 2, 1958.

SNEVILY, Henry Mansfield, business exec., editor; b. Bklyn., Oct. 8, 1886; s. Mansfield Buel and Wilhelmina St. Clair (Creevy) S.; student Columbia, 1904-08; m. Marjorie Caswell Clark, Oct. 3, 1911; children—Marjorie Mansfield (Mrs. Roger Sherman), Frances Clark (Mrs. James Johnston). Mem. editorial staff N.Y. Herald, 1909-17; gen. mgr. Bell Syndicate, 1921-51, pres., 1950—, dir., 1927—; pres., dir. St. Clair Oil Co. Served as 1st lt. Inf., U.S. Army, 1917-19; with A.E.F., France. Mem. Sigma Chi. Mason. Home: Stanton, N.J. Office: 229 W. 43d St., N.Y.C. 36. Died Jan. 24, 1954; buried Fairview Cemetery, Westfield, N.J.

SNIDER, Joseph Lyons, coll. prof.; b. Uniontown, Pa., Aug. 25, 1894; s. Frank and Hannah Matilda (Lyons) S.; A.B., Amherst Coll., 1915; A.M., Harvard, 1918, Ph.D., 1923; m. Greta Wood, June 2, 1925; children—Gratia Lowell, Hannah Matilda, Mary Marguerite, Joseph Lyons. Prof. of business economics, Harvard Bus. Sch., Boston, since 1925. Mem. Am. Econ. Assn., Phi Kappa Psi, Phi Beta Kappa, Delta Sigma Rho. Author: Business Statistics, 1929, 1932; Credit Unions in Massachusetts, 1939; Excess Profits Tax Relief: The Cyclical Provisions, 1944; The Guarantee of Work and Wages, 1947. Home: Lincoln, Mass. Office: Harvard Business School, Boston. Died Mar. 4, 1955.

SNODDY, Leland Bradley, educator; b. Hiram, O., Mar. 4, 1898; s. Elmer Ellsworth and Mina (Bradley) S.; student Transylvania (Ky.) Coll., 1914-16, Hamilton (Ky.) Coll., 1916-17, U. Cal., 1923-25; B.S., U. Ky., 1921, M.A., 1923; Ph.D., U. Va., 1929; m. Virginia Halbert Croft, June 16, 1923. Prof. physics Lynchburg Coll., 1925-28; Edison Research fellow Gen. Electric Co., Schenectady, 1929-30, physicist, 1930-33; research fellow U. Va., 1933-36, asst. prof. physics, 1936-40, asso. prof., 1940-43, prof., 1943—. Served with U.S. Army, 1917-19; X-ray technician Base Hosp. Unit No. 40, Southampton, Eng., 1918-19. Fellow Am. Phys. Soc., Am. Optical Soc.; mem. A.A.A.S., Am. Geophys. Union, Am. Assn. U. Profs., Va. Acad. Scis., Am. Phys. Soc. (S.E.sect.), Sigma Xi, Phi Beta Kappa, Alpha Chi Sigma, Sigma Alpha Epsilon. Mem. Disciples of Christ Ch. Club: Colonnade. Contbr. sci. articles to tech. jours. Researcher in transient phenomena in vacuum arc and spark discharge; acceleration of electrons and ions; separation of isotopes by ultra centrifuge. Home: 1102 Rugby Rd., Charlottesville, Va. Died Nov. 12, 1950; buried Lexington, Ky.

SNOW, Charles Henry, educator, engr.; b. N.Y. C., Mar. 24, 1863; s. Charles W. and Mary A. (Smith) S.; C.E., N.Y.U., 1886; Sc.M. (hon.), Western U. Pa. (now U. Pitts.), 1894, Sc.D., 1898; m. Alice Northrop, May 19, 1897 (dec. 1947); children—Helen, Henry, Howard. Surveys, explorations, reports and other work as civil and mining engr., New York, 1886—; dean Coll. of Engring. and Daniel Guggenheim Sch. Aeronautics, N.Y.U., 1897-1931, v.p. univ. senate, 1920-31, now emeritus dean. Civilian dir. Nat. Army Training Detach. and Sect. B, S.A.T.C. ("Fighting Mechanics") N.Y.U., Apr.-Dec. 1918; mem. Mayor Mitchel's Com. for Nat. Def., N.Y., 1915-18, Mayor's com. of citizens to arrange pub. celebration of July Fourth, N.Y.C., 1916-17; War Dep., appraisal expert, aircraft production, service at large, Feb.-July 29, 1919. Recipient N.Y. U. Alumni meritorius service award, 1932. Fellow A.A.A.S.; mem. Am. Inst. Mining and Metall. Engrs. (an incorporator 1904; counsel 1905-06; dir. 1905-10; legion honor, 1940—), Am. Soc. C.E. (life), Soc. for Promotion Engring. Edn., Am. Soc. Mil. Engrs., Soc Mayflower Descs. (bd. of governor's assistants 1928-35), S.R., Phi Beta Kappa, Delta Phi, Iota Alpha (pres. 1921-22); hon. mem. Scabbard and Blade. Presbyn. Republican. Club: New York University Faculty. Author: The Principal Species of Wood, 1903, 2d edit., 1908; Wood and Other Organic Structure Mterials, 1917; Great War Observed from College Campus (a private report); also Marine Wood Borers and other papers in transactions of tech. socs., etc. Home: 12 Lake Av., Yonkers, N.Y. Address: New York University, N.Y.C. Died Oct. 28, 1957; buried Kensico Cemetery, Valhalla, N.Y.

SNOW, J(onathan) Parker, civil engr.; b. Concord, N.H., Nov. 19, 1848; s. Jonathan and Lydia A. (Parker) S.; C.E., Dartmouth, 1875; m. Mrs. Marietta H. Eaton. Instr. civ. engring. Thayer Sch. Civil Engring., Dartmouth, 1877-78, overseer, 1889—; bridge engr. B.&M. R.R.; 1888-1909, chief engr., 1909-11; cons. engr., 1911—. Mem. Am. Soc. C.E. (dir.), Am. Ry. Engring. Assn., Am. Inst. Cons. Engrs., Am. Soc. Testing Materials, Boston Soc. C.E., Thayer Soc. of N.Y. Republican. Universalist. Clubs: Engineers, N.E. Railroad, New Hampshire (Somerville), etc. Home: 58 Chandler St., W. Somerville, Mass. Office: 18 Tremont St., Boston. Died 1934.

SNOW, Leslie W(hitmore), banker; born Snowville, N.H., Dec. 9, 1890; s. Leslie Perkins and Susan E. (Currier) S.; A.B. cum laude, Dartmouth College, 1912; B.S., Mass. Inst. Tech., 1914; m. Emily Royer. June 4, 1921; children—Shirley (Mrs. Douglas King Blue), Janet, Elizabeth (Mrs. Bruce Douglas Knowlton). With Chase Securities Corp., N.Y. City, 1923-31, assistant sec., 1927, assistant vice president, 1928; vice pres. Chase Harris Forbes Corp., 1931-33; 2d vice pres. The Chase Nat. Bank, 1933-45, v.p., 1945-55. Trustee Village of South Orange, N.J., 1949-55. Served as 1st lt., capt. and maj., ordnance dept., U.S. Army, 12 mo. overseas, World War I. Mem. Theta Delta Chi (pres. and dir. Founders Corp.; v.p., trustee Theta Delta Chi Ednl. Foundn.); former mem. Dartmouth Alumni Council. Republican. Presbyterian (elder). Mason. Clubs: Union League, Dartmouth College (N.Y. City); Orange Lawn Tennis (South Orange, N.J.). Home: 49 University Court, South Orange, N.J.; also Snowville, N.H. Died Aug. 15, 1959; buried Rochester, N.H.

SNOW, William Freeman, public health adminstr.; b. Quincy, Ill., July 13, 1874; s. William and Emily M. (Streeter) S.; B.A. in Chemistry, Stanford, 1896, M.A. in Physiology, 1897; M.D., Cooper Med. Coll., San Francisco, 1900; postgrad. Johns Hopkins, 1901-02; m. Blanche Malvina Boring, Aug. 15, 1899; children—William Boring, Richard Boring. Univ. physician, Stanford, 1900-01, asst. prof. hygiene, 1902-03, asso. prof., 1903-09, prof. hygiene and pub. health, 1909-19; gen. dir., chmn. bd. dirs. Am. Social Hygiene Assn., 1914—; pres. Nat. Health Council, 1927-34. Lectr. in health edn. Columbia, 1928-40; spl. cons. USPHS, 1936—; mem. U.S. Interdepartmental Venereal Disease Com., 1942—; mem. nat. adv. com Nat. Youth Adminstrn.; lectr. on preventive medicine N.Y.U., 1930-36. Epidemiologist, 1903-09; mem. and exec. officer Cal. Bd. of Health, 1909-14; lectr. Sch. of Hygiene and Pub. Health, Johns Hopkins, 1920-26. Investigations health adminstrn., Europe, 1912; mem. sec. Gen. Med. Bd., Council Nat. Defense, 1917-19; chmn. exec. com. U.S. Interdepartmental Social Hygiene Bd., 1918, rank of major; lt. col. M.C., U.S. Army, active duty, 1917-19; col. Med. Res. Corps, 1920—. Chmn. League of Nations Com. to Study Traffic in Women and Children, 1924-28. Pres. Union Internationale Contre le Péril Vénérin, 1946, Assn. State and Prov. Bds. Health, 1912-13; fellow Am. Pub. Health Assn., A.A.A.S., A.M.A., N.Y. Acad. Medicine. Clubs: Century, Faculty, Cosmos. Home: 464 Riverside Dr. Office: 1790 Broadway, N.Y.C. 19. Died June 12, 1950.

SNYDER, A(aron) Cecil (snī'dĕr), judge; born Baltimore, Md., Sept. 14, 1907; s. Hyman and Ida M. (Pass) S.; A.B., Johns Hopkins, 1927; LL.B., Harvard, 1930; m. Wanda Gilewicz, Feb. 4, 1938; 1 dau., Ann Cecilia. Admitted to Md. and N.Y. bars, 1930; asso. with Hawkins, Delafield & Longfellow, N.Y. City, 1930-32, with Tydings, Sauerwein, Levy & Archer, Baltimore, 1932-33; U.S. atty. for Dist. of Puerto Rico, 1933-42; acting U.S. dist. judge P.R., 1942, 44, 46, 47, 50, 52, 56; asso. justice supreme ct. P.R., 1942-53, chief justice, 1953—; mem. faculty Seminar for Appelate Judges, N.Y.U., 1957; mem., chmn. at various times of Bd. of Bar Examiners of P.R.; visiting prof., U. of Puerto Rico Law Sch., 1944-45; chmn. Appeals Com., Nat. War Labor Bd., 1943-44; arbitrated labor disputes in railway and sugar industries in Puerto Rico at various times. Chairman committee on criminal law, Bar Association of P.R.; chmn. Judicial Council of P.R.; mem. for P.R. of Nat. Commn. on Uniform State Laws, 1942-44, 1947-50; chmn. Com. on Rules and Procedure, U.S. Dist. Ct. for P.R. Fellow Am. Acad. Arts and Scis.; mem. Am. (Ho. of Del.), Md. bar assns., Am. Soc. Internat. Law, Nat. Panel of Arbitrators, Am. Political Science Association, Bar Assn. of U.S. Dist. Court for Puerto Rico, Colegio de Abogados de Puerto Rico, Phi Alpha, Phi Beta Kappa. Awarded Phi Alpha's Distinguished Alumnus award, 1936. Democrat. Home: Cupey Alto, Rio Piedras. Address: Supreme Court of Puerto Rico, San Juan, P.R. Died Aug. 1959.

SNYDER, Carl J., corp. exec.; b. York, Pa., Nov. 29, 1896; s. Perry J. and Gertrude V. (Herman) S.; student pub. schs. York, Pa., and Det.; m. Elvira Randall Harris, Apr. 23, 1917. Tool, diemaker apprentice Det. Lubricator Co., 1914-19; tool designer, engr. Lincoln Motor Co., 1919-21; joined Chrysler Corp., 1921, operating mgr., 1951-52, v.p. since 1952, dir., 1953—. Home: 1161 Pembroke Dr., Bloomfield Hills, Mich. Office: 341 Massachusetts Av., Detroit 21. Died June 30, 1956; buried Grand Canyon Nat. Cemetery.

SNYDER, Charles Edward, clergyman; b. Hollowville, Columbia County, N.Y., Oct. 13, 1877; s. Marshall and Maria P. (Jones) S.; Life Certificate, U. of State of N.Y., 1900; grad. State Teachers Coll., Oneonta, N.Y., 1901: student Meadville Theol. Sch., 1908-10; Litt.D., Yankton Coll., 1929; LL.D., Morningside Coll., 1931; m. Sara M. Reeder. Aug. 31, 1904; children—Robert Gordon, Betty Beach (Mrs. Joseph E. Nero), Barbara Ives (Mrs. Philip G. Murray, dec.). Teacher district schools; prin. Uniondale Sch., Hempstead, N.Y., 1901-03; sr. master Lakewood (N.J.) Sch. for Boys, 1903-08; minister First Unitarian Ch., Franklin, Pa., 1908-11, North Side Ch., Pittsburgh, 1911-17, First Unitarian Ch., Sioux City, Ia., 1917-31, Davenport, Ia., 1931-47, ret. Sec. Ia. Unitarian Assn., 1918-46; mem. exec. com. Nat. Fed. of Religious Liberals, 1920-34, chmn., 1927-34; mem. fellowship com. Gen. Conf. of Unitarian Chs., 1921-24; dir. Western Unitarian Conf., 1918-25, 1928-32, 1933-37, 1938-1942; 1943-47. Am. Unitarian Assn., 1932-41; chmn. Unitarian Commn. on Planning and Review, 1941-45. Mem. Iowa State Conf. of Social Work (v.p. 1925-27, pres. 1927-28), Ia. State Housing Assn. (chmn. exec. com. 1918-21), Ia. State Tuberculosis Assn. (chmn. housing com. 1922-25), Davenport Council of Social Work (pres. 1934-36); sec. Acad. Science and Letters, Sioux City, 1918-31. Mem. Ia. Acad. Science, S.A.R. (pres. Ia. soc. 1928-30), Soc. War of 1812. Sons and Daughters of the Pilgrims. Mason (32°; Grand Chaplain Ia. Grand Lodge 1922-23; mem. Grand Lodge Library Com. 1934-35; lecturer Masonic Service Com.); mem. Royal Arcanum (grand regent Ia. Grand Council 1922-24), Elk. Clubs: Contemporary, History Round Table, Kiwanis. Home: 934 Iowa Av., Iowa City, Ia. Died May 20, 1950.

SNYDER, Franklyn Bliss, educator; b. at Middletown, Conn., July 26, 1884; s. Peter Miles and Grace (Bliss) S.; A.B., Beloit Coll., 1905, LL.D., 1935; A.M., Harvard, 1907, Ph.D., 1909; L.H.D., Northwestern Univ., 1939; LL.D., Colby College, 1939, University of Pittsburgh, 1940, Wesleyan Univ., 1941, University of Southern Calif., 1945, Knox Coll., 1948, Lake Forest College, 1950; D.C.L., Ripon College, 1948; Litt.D., Illinois Wesleyan University, 1940; Jefferson Med. College, 1944; m. Winifred P. Dewhurst, June 15, 1909; children—Franklin Bliss, Peter Miles, II. Instructor English, Northwestern U., 1909-11, asst. prof., 1911-13, asso. prof., 1913-18, prof. since 1918, dean Grad. Sch., 1934-37, v.p. and dean faculties, 1937-39, pres., 1939-49, emeritus. since 1949. Lectr English, Dartmouth Coll., summer, 1912, U. Cal., summer 1913; Alexander lectr., U. of Toronto, 1936. Director State Bank & Trust Co., Evanston, since 1949. Mem. Modern Language Association of America, Sigma Chi, Phi Beta Kappa, Delta Sigma Rho, Phi Delta Kappa. Trustee Beloit College since 1926, Carnegie Foundation for Advancement of Teaching, 1940-49, Northwestern U. since 1949; mem. bd. mgrs. Presbyn. Hosp., Chgo., 1948-56, pres. 1948-56; dir. Nutrition Found., 1949-56; elector Hall of Fame, 1950, 55; member board directors Evanston Hosp. Assn., 1941-55; hon. mem. governing board Nat. Coll. of Edn., since 1938; mem. bd. of visitors, U.S. Naval Academy, 1940; mem. and pres. 1941, 45; mem. spl. board on Edn. of Naval Officers, 1944. Received U.S.N. Civilian Distinguished Service award. 1949, Significant Sig medal, 1952. Fellow Soc. of Antiquaries of Scotland, 1932. Republican. Congregationalist. Clubs: University (Evanston); Cliff Dwellers, Union League (hon.), Commercial, Glen View. Author of The English of Business (with R. S. Crane), 1921; The Life of Robert Burns, 1932; Robert Burns—His Personality, His Reputation and His Art, 1936. Editor: (with R. G. Martin), A Book of English Literature, 1916, new edits.. 1924, 1932, 1942; A Book of American Literature (with E. D. Snyder), 1927, 1935. Contbr. to English jours. and mags. Home: 1918 Sheridan Rd., Evanston, Ill. Office: 1753 W. Congress St., Chgo. Died May 11, 1958.

SNYDER, Fred Beal, lawyer; b. Mpls., Feb. 21, 1859; s. Simon P. and Mary (Ramsey) S.; B.A., U. Minn., 1881, LL.D., 1940; m. Susan M. Pillsbury, Sept. 23, 1885 (dec. 1891); 1 son, John Pillsbury; m. 2d, Leonora S. Dickson, Feb. 1896 (dec. 1946); 1 dau., Mary Stuart. Engaged in the practice of law in Mpls., 1882—; mem. firm Snyder, Gale, Hoke, Richards & Janes; trustee Farmers & Mechanics Savings Bank. Mem. City Council, Mpls. 1893-96 (pres. 1895-96); mem. Minn. Ho. of Reps., 1897-98, Senate, 1898-1901. Dir. for Hennepin County, Minn. Commn. for Pub. Safety, 1917-18. Author of Torrens land law and advocate of probation law for juvenile offenders in Minn. Regent, chmn. bd. U. Minn. Mem. Am., Minn., Hennepin County (dean) bar assns., Chi Psi, Phi Beta Kappa. Republican. Automobile, Minikahda, Woodhill. Home: 120 W. 22d St., Mpls.; (summer) "Clay Cliffe," Excelsior, Minn. Office: Rand Tower, Mpls. Died Feb. 14, 1951. Clubs: Minneapolis, Civic and Commerce, Lafayette.

SNYDER, Henry George, lawyer; b. Louisa, Ky., Dec. 7, 1879; s. Thomas Jefferson and Sarah Lucrecia (McClure) S.; B.S., Centre Coll., Ky., 1898; law dept., Columbia, 1898-99; LL.B., Yale, 1902; m. Olive Marshall Darrall, Oct. 16, 1907 (died 1910); 1 dau., Olive Darrall; m. 2d, Frances Goudelock, Oct. 11, 1914. Began practice at Lexington, Ky., 1902; moved to Okla. City, 1906; became mem. firm Snyder, Owen & Lybrand, 1907, Asp, Snyder, Owen & Lybrand, 1911, Snyder, Owen & Lybrand, 1923; now mem. firm Snyder & Lybrand. Sec., prof. corp. and constl. law in law dept., Epworth U., 1908-11. Mem. Am. and Okla. bar assns. Ind. Republican. Club: Oklahoma. Compiler: Annotated Constitution of Oklahoma, 1908; Laws of Oklahoma, 1909. Home: 814 N.W. 16th St. Office: Braniff Bldg., Oklahoma City. Died Apr. 1, 1950.

SNYDER, J. Ralph, newspaper pub.; b. Waverly, O., Nov. 24, 1885; s. Henry Richard and Minerva (Burgess) S.; prep. edn., high sch. Urbana, O., and Springfield, Mo.; student Drury Coll., Springfield, 1902-05; m. Edith Turner, June 16, 1910; children—John Turner, Mary Jane. Began as reporter Springfield (Mo.) Republican, 1905; pub. Gary (Ind.) Post and Post Tribune 1910—; business mgr. Memphis Commercial Appeal, 1931; pres. Gary Paper Mills, Inc., 1947—. Chmn. bd. Gary Indsl. Found. 1945—. Methodist. Mason, Elk. Clubs: University, Commercial, Country. Home: 574 Monroe St. Address: Gary Post Tribune, Gary, Ind. Died Feb. 11, 1960.

SNYDER, John Taylor, investment broker; b. Bethlehem, Pa., Dec. 23, 1893; s. Henry Steinman and Mary (Taylor) S.; Ph.B., Yale 1915; m. Laura Ely Jenkins, Apr. 29, 1916; children—Mary Taylor, John Taylor, William Bunker, Robert Jenkins. Began as material engr. Union Iron Works, San Francisco; partner Struthers & Hiscoe, N.Y. City, 1920-24, Ingalls & Snyder since 1924; dir. Tex. & Pacific Coal Oil Co., Empire Trust Co. N.Y. Trustee Moravian Coll. and Theol. Sem. Clubs: Univ., Yale, Downtown Assn. (N.Y. City); Pelham (N.Y.) Country; Litchfield (Conn.) Country. Home: 84 Witherbee Av., Pelham Manor, N.Y. Office: 100 Broadway, N.Y. C. 5. Died Oct. 13, 1956.

SNYDER, William Edward, clergyman, editor; b. Corydon, Ind., Mar. 14, 1877; s. George and Sarah (Kopp) S.; ed. pub. schs. and Ohio Valley Normal Coll., Corydon; D.D., Ind. Central U., Indpls., 1915; m. Grace Jones, Nov. 24, 1903; 1 dau., Freda Lenore. Licensed ministry U.B. Ch., 1899, ordained, 1904; pastor successively Georgetown, Freetown, Dale, Odon—all in Ind.; conf. supt., 1899-1917; later pastor Roanoke and Fort Wayne, Ind.; mem. staff Religious Telescope, Dayton, O., 1921—, chief editor, 1926—. Home: 930 Bryn Mawr Drive. Office: United Brethren Pub. House, Dayton, O. Died Dec. 9, 1949.

SODDY, Frederick, physicist; b. Eastbourne, Eng., Sept. 2, 1877; s. Benjamin and Hannah (Green) S.; student Eastbourne Coll., 1893-94; B.A., Oxford. 1898; M.A., 1910; LL.D., Glasgow; m. Winifred Moller Beilby, Mar. 3, 1908 (dec. Aug. 17, 1936). Demonstrator chemistry McGill U., Montreal, Can., 1900-02; established atomic disintegration of radioactive elements and existence of atomic energy (with late physics prof. Ernest Rutherford); proved spectroscopically the prodn. of helium from radium (with Sir W. Ramsay), 1903-04; London U. extension lectr., Western Australia, 1904; lectr. phys. chemistry, radioactivity, U. Glasgow, 1904-14; prof. chemistry U. Aberdeen, 1914-19, Oxford, 1919-36; ret. 1936. Responsible for conception of isotopes and the displacement law of radioactive change which is at the root of nuclear physics. Awarded Nobel Laureate in chemistry, 1921, Cannizzaro prize by Acad. de Lincei, Rome, 1923. Author: Science and Life. 1920; Interpretation of the Atom, 1932. Applied phys. laws of conservation to econs. and writer on new. econs.: Wealth, Virtual Wealth and Debt, 1926; Store of Atomic Energy, 1949. Address: 39 Overhill Dr., Brighton 6, Eng. Died Sept. 22, 1956.

SODT, William George (sōdt), clergyman; b. Freedom, Mich., Sept. 11, 1893; s. Bernhardt and Mary Anna (Esch) S.; A.B., Wartburg Coll., Clinton, Ia., 1910-14; D.D., Wartburg Theol. Sem., Dubuque, Ia., 1937; m. E. Julia Faur, May 7, 1918; children—William G., Carol Marie, Paul T. Ordained to ministry of Am. Luth. Ch., Berea, O., 1917; pastor Berea, 1917-26, Alpena, Mich., 1926-31; stewardship sec. Am. Luth. Ch., in Columbus, O., 1931-43, vice pres. Am. Lutheran Ch., 1938—; administrator Milwaukee (Wis.) Hosp., 1943—. Mem. Nat. Luth. Council (president 1948), National Luth. Council Service Commn. (1941-47), Nat. Council Boy Scouts of Am. Republican. Club: Rotary. Home: 2566 N. 20th St., Milw. Office: 2200 W. Kilbourn Av., Milw. 3. Died Feb. 24, 1955.

SOERGEL, E. W., vice pres. for traffic C., M., St.P. & P. R.R. Address: 516 W. Jackson Blvd., Chgo. 6. Died Aug. 20, 1949; buried Meml. Park, Skokie, Ill.

SOGGE, Tillman M(orris) (sō'gē), coll. prof.; b. Jackson, Minn., Mar. 10, 1903; s. Lars Larson and Maria (Larson) S.; A.B., St. Olaf Coll., Northfield, Minn., 1924; A.M., U. of Minn., 1931; Ph.D., 1936; m. Adel Anita Madson, Aug. 7, 1926; children—Joanne Marie, Sonja Lynne. Instr. history and econ., Dana Coll., Blair, Neb., 1924-26; supt. schs. Ringsted, Ia., 1926-30; research asst. employment stabilization research inst., U. of Minn., 1931-33, instr. econ., 1933-36; econ. Social Security Bd., 1936-41, Bur. of Census, 1941-45, Bur. of Budget, 1945-47; labor adv. com. War Dept., Tokyo, 1946; industry and commodity classification cons., econ. and sci. sect. Supreme Comdr. for Allied Powers, Tokyo, 1948, 1949, 1951; consultant Bureau of Census since 1950; chmn. dept. econ., sociol., St. Olaf Coll. since 1947. director of college placement bureau 1949-58. Mem. regional enforcement commn. U.S. WSB; former mem. Nat. Luth. Council (com. social trends div. welfare), dir. Child Welfare League Am., Inc. U.S. Govt. Interdeptl. Tech. Com. on Indsl. Classification (former mem. and chmn.), Am. Economic Association, American Sociological Society, American Statis. Assn., Annals Am. Acad. Polit. and Social Science, Indsl. Relations Research Assn., Pi Gamma Mu. Lutheran. Author, co-author, econ. research bulls.; contbr. articles to professional jours., Luth. ch. pubs. Home: 307 Manitou St., Northfield, Minn. Died Dec. 15, 1958; buried Oaklawn Cemetery, Northfield, Minn.

SOKOLOFF, Ruth H. Ottaway, b. Howell, Mich., Oct. 17, 1886; d. John George and Rosetta (Brumm) Haller; Mus. B., Albion (Mich.) Coll., 1906; A.B., U. Mich., 1909; sutdied piano, organ, voice, in Detroit and Ann Arbor; m. Elmer James Ottaway, Aug. 31, 1910 (dec. 1934); 1 son, James Haller; m. 2d, Nikolai Sokoloff, 1937. Began as pianist and organist in Detroit and Ann Arbor; pres. Mich. Fed. Music Clubs, 1921-25; chmn. music Nat. Congress Parents and Teachers, 1927-29; pres. Nat. Fedn. Music Clubs, 1929-33, and its rep. at Anglo-Am. Music Conf., Lausanne, Switzerland, 1929; rep. Nat. Council of Women at Internat. Council, Geneva, 1927, pres., 1935; chmn. music Nat. Council Women, 1931-41; chmn. music Internat. Congress of Women, Century of Progress Expn., Chgo., 1933-34; pres. Nat. Council of Women of U.S., Inc., 1935-41; asst. dir. Fed. Music Project, 1935; chmn. Eastern Preview Bd. for Mus. Films, 1935; exec. chmn. Nat. Am. Artists Contests; vice chmn. Women's Nat. Radio Com.; mem. Nat. Com. for Music in Edn., Nat. Suprs. Conf.; sec. Schubert Meml., 1939-44; mem. bd. Nat. Kindergarten Assn., Nat. Council of Women, Henry St. Settlement, Nat. Fedn. Music Clubs, Musical Arts Soc. of La Jolla, 1940; mem. exec. bd. Nat. Council for Opera in America, 1941; chmn. publicity Nat. Fedn. Music Clubs, 1943. Mem. Am. Assn. U. Women, Kappa Alpha Theta, Sigma Alpha Iota. Methodist. Clubs: Port Huron Musicale (founder-pres.); Tuesday Musicale of Detroit (hon. mem.); Carreno (St. Petersburg, Fla.); also music clubs of Boston, Phila., Bridgeport (Conn.), Providence, Clearwater (Fla.), etc. Editor in chief Music Clubs Mag., 1929-33. Writer of pamphlets; contbr. to mus. jours. Home: Endicott, N.Y.; also La Jolla, Cal. Died July 20, 1955.

SOLBERT, Oscar Nathaniel, army officer, dir. George Eastman House, Inc.; b. Westmanland, Sweden, s. John and Mary (Johnson) S.; came to U.S., 1893; student Worcester (Mass.) Poly. Inst., 1904-06; grad. U.S. Mil. Acad., 1910; student U.S. Engring. Sch. of Application, Washington, 1912-13; m. Elizabeth F. Abernathy, Dec. 25, 1915; children—Peter O. A., Romaine G. Commd. 2d lt., corps of engrs., U.S. Army, 1910, and advanced through grades to brig. gen., 1944; instr. engring. U.S. Mil. Acad., 1914-17; served A.E.F., World War I; mil. attache, Great Britain, 1919-24; presidential mil. aide to Pres. Coolidge, 1924-26; aide to Prince of Wales on U.S. visit, 1924, to Crown Prince of Sweden on U.S. visits, 1926, 1938; resigned 1926; recalled to active duty, 1942, spl. services chief, E.T.O., 1943-45. Asst. to v.p., Eastman Kodak Co., Rochester, N.Y., 1926-49, dir. Eastman House, Inc., 1949—. Decorated D.S.M. Legion of Merit, Bronze star, Commendation, Victory and E.T.O. medals (U.S.); Comdr. St. Michael and St. George, Comdr. Order Brit. Empire (Gt. Britain); Chevalier Legion of Honor, Croix de Guerre (France), Comdr. of Nassau (Netherlands); Comdr. of St. Olaf (Norway); Comdr. of Vasa, Comdr. of Sword, King's medal (Sweden); Polonia Restituta (Poland); Croix de Guerre (Czechoslovakia); Comdr. White Eagle (Yugoslavia); Comdr. Danneborg (Denmark); Croix de Guerre (Belgium). Mem. Theta Chi. Clubs: Metropolitan, Army and Navy (Washington); Genesee Valley, Country of Rochester, Genesee Fox Hunt. Home: George Eastman House, Rochester 7. Office: 900 East Av., Rochester, 7, N.Y. Died Apr. 16, 1958; buried Arlington National Cemetery.

SOLETHER, Pliny Louis (sō'lĕth-ēr), lawyer; b. Jerry City, O., Jan. 17, 1887; s. John Calvin and Lydia Ann (Peters) S.; A.B., Oberlin Coll., 1910; student Harvard, 1910-11, U. of Minnesota, 1911-12; m. Muriel Cadwell, Sept. 12, 1912; children—Grace Lydia (Mrs. Olen C. Hudson), Margaret Ellen (Mrs. Carl T. Johnson), Muriel Frances (Mrs. Milton J. Hadreas), Mary Ellen (Mrs. Robert E. Oestrich), Doris Jean (Mrs. Martin N. Hase). Admitted to Minn. bar, 1913; asso. with S. R. Child and Benjamin Drake, lawyers, Minneapolis, 1913-24; mem. firm Keyes, Pardee & Solether, 1924-36, Keyes, Pardee, Solether & Carr, 1936-42; chief counsel Office Price Adminstrn., Minneapolis, Minn., 1942-43; trustee and counsel for trustees of Duluth, South Shore and Atlantic Ry. Co. and Mineral Range R.R. Co., Minneapolis, Minn., since 1943; v.p. and sec. Duluth S. Shore & Atlantic R.R. Co. Mem. Am., Minn. State (chmn. com. to procure amendment to state constn. removing stockholder's liability clause, 1929-31, chmn. com. to draft new bus. corp. act and secure its passage by legislature, 1931-35) and Hennepin County bar assns., Am. Judicature Soc. Home: 4159 Alabama Av., St. Louis Park, Minn. Office: First National-Soo Line Bldg., Mpls. 2. Died Jan. 2, 1952; buried Lakewood Cemetery, Mpls.

SOLEY, Mayo Hallton, physician, dean; b. Malden, Mass., Apr. 14, 1907; s. Walter Hamilton and Grace Eliza (Mayo) S.; B.S., Bowdoin Coll., 1929; M.D., Harvard, 1933; spl. grad. student U. of Cal. Med. Sch., 1935; m. Karoline Boeker Jump, Feb. 19, 1938; children—Mayo Robert, Charles Hamilton, Jane Elizabeth. Intern Mass. Gen. Hosp., 1933-35; research asst. U. Cal., 1935-37, instr. physiology, medicine, pharmacology, 1937-39, asst. prof. medicine and pharmacy, 1939-42; asst. vis. physician U. Cal. Hosp., 1937-48, San Francisco Hosp., 1938-48, cons. pharmacologist, 1942-44; asst. prof. medicine, lecturer on pharmacology (chmn. div. pharmacology) and toxicology U. Cal., 1942-44, asso. prof., 1942-47, prof., 1947-48, asst. dean, 1944-48; dean, dir. med. services and research prof. medicine State U. Ia. Coll. Medicine, 1948—; cons. pharmacologist Langley Porter Clinic, 1943-44, attending physician, endocrine and metabolic, 1943-48; cons. Letterman Gen. Hosp., San Francisco, 1947-48, Vets. Hosp., Des Moines, Ia., 1948—. Mem. A.M.A., Am. Heart Assn. Assn. for Study Internal Secretions (councilor, 1948-51), Am. Soc. for Clin. Investigation, A.A.A.S., Am. Physiol. Soc., Soc. for Exptl. Biology and Medicine, Cal. Acad. Medicine, Am. Goiter Assn., Am. Fedn. for Clin. Research, Western Soc. for Clin. Research (pres. 1947-48), Assn. Am. Physicians, Sigma Xi. Contbr. numerous articles to med. jours. Specialist in internal medicine and diseases of the thyroid. Home: 1036 Woodlawn, Iowa City, Ia. Died June 21, 1949; buried Mountain View Cemetery, Oakland, Cal.

SOLLOTT, Ralph Preston, govt. ofcl.; b. Phila., June 13, 1908; s. Jacob and Rose (Sclarenco) S.; m. Beatrice M. Mazer, Apr. 9, 1930; 1 son, Paul. Dir. capital budget N.Y. City Planning Commn., 1941-42; staff dir. Conn. Commn. on State Govt. Orgn., 1948-50; management cons. orgn. and fiscal management to pvt. industries, state and fed. govts., 1940—; dir. manpower utilization Dept. Def. 1950—. Home: 3115 Worthington St., N.W., Washington 15. Office: Dept. of Defense, Pentagon, Washington. Died July 10, 1953.

SOLTES, Mordecai, educator; b. Austria, Aug. 27, 1893; s. Judah Leib and Genendel (Schwager) S.; came to U.S., 1899, naturalized, 1905; student Townsend Harris Hall; B.S., N.Y.U., 1915; M.A., Columbia, 1918, Ph.D., 1923; m. Ida Levy, May 1916; children—Avraham Samuel, Aaron Solomon. Tchr., supvr. elementary sch. Talmudical Acad., 1911-13; exec. sec. Downtown Talmud Torah, N.Y., 1913-14; instr., prin. dir. extension activities Bur. Jewish Edn., N.Y.C., 1914-25; nat. dir. edn. Jewish Welfare Bd., 1925-44; lectr. Grad. Sch. Jewish Social Work, 1926-34; lectr. edn., contemporary Jewish history, Tchrs. Inst. Jewish Theol. Sem., 1927-29; exec. dir. Yeshiva U., N.Y.C., 1944—, prof. community Service, 1948—. Chmn. Nat. Jewish Edn. Week, 1936-37. Mem. Jewish Book Council of America (pres. 1941-45, now hon. pres.), National Council Jewish Edn., Nat. Assn. Jewish Center Execs., Jewish Acad. Arts and Sci., League for Safeguarding Fixity of the Sabbath (v.p.). Democrat. Mason. Author: The Yiddish Press, 1925; The Jewish Holidays, 1937; Adjustment of Recent Jewish Immigrants Through the Jewish Community Center, 1939, others. Asso. editor of Jewish Education mag., 1934-35. Home: 596 Riverside Dr., N.Y.C. 31. Office: 186th St. and Amsterdam Av., N.Y.C. 33. Died June 28, 1957.

SOMERVELL, Brehon Burke, business exec.; b. Little Rock, Ark., May 9, 1892; ed. U.S. Mil. Acad.; holds degrees: LL.D., D.Sc., D.Eng., D.M.S.; m. Anna Purnell (died 1942); married second, Louise Hampton Wartmann, 1943; children—Elizabeth Anne (Mrs. Swager Sherley, Jr.), Mary Louise (Mrs. H. P. Van Lear, Jr.), Mary Anne (Mrs. William S. Brenza), Mildred Alice (Mrs. Albert O. Waldon), Susan (Mrs. John W. Griswold), Constance Joscelyn (Mrs. E. M. Matter). Commd. 2d lt., U.S. Army, 1914, advanced through grades. to gen., 1945, ret., 1946. Now chmn. and pres. Koppers Co., Inc., Pittsburgh; dir. Montreal Coke & Mfg. Co., Westinghouse Air Brake Co., Carborumdum Co. Survey on Rhine and Danube Rivers for League of Nations, asst. Walker D. Hines, 1925; collaborated economic survey Turkey, in charge field work, 1933-34. Awarded D.S.C., D. S.M. with 2 oak leaf clusters, Legion of Merit, and other army and navy decorations (U.S.), also several fgn. decorations. Home: 920 E. 5th St., Ocala, Fla. Died Feb. 13, 1955; buried Arlington Nat. Cemetery.

SOMERVILLE, Pearl Cliffe (sŭm'ĕr-vĭl), lectr., educator; b. Milroy, Ind., Jan. 9, 1877; s. Ira Alexander and Elizabeth (Crawford) S.; Ph.B., DePauw U., 1901, A.M., 1902; U. Chgo., summers 1902-09; Ph.D., Ia. Christian Coll., 1912; Ph.D., So. Minn. U., 1917; m. LaRose Colliver, Nov. 30, 1901; children—Vivian Guinevere (dec.), Merlin Parker (dec.), Gareth Geraint, Alfred Alexander; m. 2d, Christine Hildinger, Jan. 9, 1934. Prof. English, Buchanan Coll., Troy, Mo., 1902-03; prof. oratory, Mt. Union Coll., Alliance, O., 1903-05; supt. schools, Troy, Mo., 1905-07; prof. English, Neb. Wesleyan U., 1907-09; prof. English lit. Wesleyan U., Bloomington, 1909-23, registrar, 1912-20; prof. English lit., Kan. Wesleyan U., 1923-31; pub. lectr., 1931—. Mem. Nat. English Tchrs. Assn., New Eng., English Tchrs. Assn., Modern Lang. Assn. Am., Am. Assn. Tchrs. of Journalism, Delta Kappa Epsilon, Phi Kappa Delta, Sigma Tau Delta, Theta Alpha Phi. Ordained M.E. ministry, 1912. Republican. Mason (hon. 33°; sec. Scottish Rite Bodies, Bloomington). Clubs: Kiwanis (ex-pres.), Bloomington Consistory (pres. 4 yrs.), Rotary (past pres.). Widely known as lectr. before pub. meetings, tchrs.' insts. and lyceums on lit., ednl. and civic subjects. Mag. feature writer. Home: Bloomington, Ill. Died Oct. 28, 1954; buried Springhill Cemetery, Milroy, Ind.

SOMERVILLE, Randolph, stage dir.; b. Maryland, N.Y., Apr. 18, 1891; s. Joseph and Isabelle Dalhousie (Whitney) S.; A.B., Columbia, 1914. Instr. in English, N.Y. U., 1915-24, prof. dramatic art, chmn. dept. 1934-57, prof. emeritus, 1957; organizer, dir. Washington Square Players Repertory Co. 1923—; dir. The Duke's Oak Summer Theatre. Club: The Players. Home: 14 Washington Pl., N.Y.C. 3. Died Sept. 5, 1958.

SOMMER, Frank Henry, educator; b. Newark, 1872; student Metropolis Law Sch.; LL.B., N.Y.U., 1893, LL.M., 1900, J.D., 1903. Instr. Metropolis Law Sch., 1893-94; became prof. law N.Y.U., 1895, also dean law faculty, retired as dean, Sept. 1943; practices, Newark, also dep. atty. gen. Recipient gold medal Am. Arbitration Soc., 1939. Home: 156 Heller Pkwy., Newark. Died Aug. 18, 1957.

SOMMER, Henry Getz. Chmn. bd., dir. Keystone Steel & Wire Co.; treas., dir. Mid-State Steel & Wire Co.; dir. Nat. Lock Co. Home: 130 Edgehill Ct., Peoria, Ill. Died Aug. 30, 1952.

SOMMER, William H., pres. Keystone Steel & Wire Co.; b. Tremont, Ill., June 25, 1882; s. Peter and Mary (Preisacker) S.; m. Emma Getz, June 11, 1911; children—Ruth, Hazel, Millard. Pres. Keystone Steel & Wire Co.; dir. Mid-States Steel & Wire Co., Crawfordsville, Ind., Nat. Lock Co., Rockford, Ill. Dir. Am. Iron and Steel Inst. Home: High Point Rd. Office: South Bartonville, Peoria, Ill. Died Dec. 1950.*

SOMMERS, Paul Bergen, pres. Am. Ins. Co.; b. Franklin, O., July 3, 1885; s. Joseph K. and Cornelia (Bergen) S.; grad. Lake Forest U., 1908; m. Florence Adams, Dec. 24, 1914; children—Paul A., Suzanne, Margaret, Otho Lane, Barbara. Spl. agt. Scottish Union Nat. Ins. Co., 1908-18; in local ins. agency on own account, Cleve., 1918-20; asso. with American Ins. Co., Newark, N.J., 1920—, supt. agts., 1920-23, v.p., 1923-35, dir. 1924—, pres. 1935-48, pres., dir. its affiliated cos., Columbia Fire Ins. Co., Dayton, O., Dixie Fire Ins. Co., Greensboro, N.C.; chmn. bd. Bankers Indemnity Ins. Co., Newark, N.J.; dir. Mut. Benefit Life Ins. Co., Reinsurance Corp. of N.Y., Sanborn Map Co., Nat. Newark & Essex Banking Co.; mem. bd. govs. Howard Savings Instn. V.p. and trustee Newark Mus. Assn.; trustee Ins. Execs. Assn., Am. Fgn. Ins. Assn. Dir. Underwriters Laboratories, Fellow Ins. Inst. of Am.; mem. Eastern Underwriters Assn. (v.p.), Fire Cos. Adjustment Bur. (dir.). Address: 425 Ridgewood Rd., Maplewood, N.J. Died June 22, 1958.

SOMOZA, Anastasio, pres. of Nicaragua; b. San Marcos, Nicaragua, Feb. 1, 1896; s. Anastasio and Julia (Garci) S.; B. Scis. and Letters, Instituto Nacional de Oriente, Granada; grad. comml. expert Pierce Sch., Phila.; m. Salvadorita Debayle, 1919; children—Lillian (wife of Dr. Guiller mo Sevilla Sacasa), Luis, Anastasio. Adminstr. taxes, dept. León, 1925; participated in revolution Nationalist Liberal Party, Dept. of Carazo, 1926, soon becoming gov. Dept. León; sec. Gen. Command under Pres. Moncada, 1929, having previously served as ambassador to Costa Rica, undersec. fgn. relations and minister of war; named chief dir. of auxiliary army of Nicaragua, 1932, chief dir. N.G. under Pres. Sacasa; elected pres. Nicaragua, 1939, served to 1947; served as chief dir. N.G., under Pres. Argüelo Barreto; minister of war under presidents Lacayo Sacasa and Victor Roman y Reyes; following death of Pres. Roman y Reyes was named president by the Nat. Congress, reelected pres. on Nat. Liberalist Party ticket, for six year term, 1950. Address: Palacia Presidencial, Managua, Republica of Nicaragua. Died Sept. 29, 1956; buried Cripta para Oficiales G.N., Cementerio de Managua, Nicaragua.

SONDLEY, F. A., lawyer; b. Montreal1a, N.C., Aug. 13, 1857; s. Richard and H. E. (Alexander) S.; A.B., Wofford Coll., Spartanburg, S.C., 1876, LL.D., 1906; LL.D. from U. North Carolina, 1928; unmarried. Admitted to N.C. bar, 1879, also admitted to U.S. courts and the Supreme Court of U.S.; practices at Asheville. Member first N.C. Historical Commn., 1903-05. Author: Descent of the Scottish Alexanders, 1912; Samuel Davidson, 1913; The Indian's Curse, 1915; The Origin of the Catawba Grape and Other Sketches, 1918; The Hickory-nut Gorge, 1917: Asheville and Buncombe County, 1922. Home: R.F.D. 2, Ashville, N.C. Deceased.*

SONES, Warren Wesley David (sōnz), educator; b. Dushore, Pa., Mar. 12, 1888; s. Calvin Low and Rebecca Amanda (Young) S.; B.S., Albright Coll. (Pa.), 1908; A.M., U. of Pittsburgh, 1914; Ph.D., 1925; m. Mary Alice Kennedy, Aug. 11, 1909; children—Warren Wesley David, Jean Elizabeth, Mary Alice. Teacher of Pennsylvania high schools, 1908-13, and high school, Pittsburgh, Pa., 1913-25; teacher U. of Pa., Pa. State Coll., Chautauqua Inst., summer schs. and extension lecturing, 1916-25; prof. edn., dir. practice teaching, and head, Erie Center U. of Pittsburgh, 1925-38; prof. of edn., dir. courses in gen. edn., U. of Pittsburgh, since 1938; consultant Pa. State Dept. Edn., Carnegie Foundation for Teachers. Mem. Pa. State Park and Harbor Commission, 1932-36. Mem. A.A.A.S., Nat. Soc. for Study of Edn., N.E.A., Pa. Edn. Assn., Am. Philatelic Soc., Phi Delta Kappa, Mason. Clubs: University (Pittsburgh); Collectors (New York). Author: Secondary School Achievement Tests, 1928; Youth Education in Practical Living. Home: 123 University Pl. Office: 3704 Cathedral of Learning, Pitts. Deceased.

SONNENBERG, Henry L., coll. pres.; b. Wayne, Neb., Feb. 27, 1915; s. Fred and Minnie (Langenberg) S.; A.B., Union Coll., 1937; Ph.D., Univ. Nebraska, 1945; married Alma Fletcher, September 11, 1938; one son, Craig Meredith. Began as German instr. Walla Walla Coll. Acad., 1938-41; asst. prof. modern lang., Walla Walla Coll., 1942-44, asst. to pres., 1945-46, dean, 1946-54, former trustee bd.; pres. Pacific Union Coll., 1954—. Trustee Walla Walla County Community Chest. Campaign chmn. community chest, College Place, 1948. Mem. Northwest Personnel Assn. Club: Kiwanis. Home: 96 Hillcrest, Angwin, Cal. Died Sept. 1, 1955; buried Montecito, Loma Linda, Cal.

SONNENSCHEIN, Hugo, lawyer; b. Chgo., Nov. 19, 1883; s. Leopold and Charlotte (Stein) S.; B.A., U. Mich., 1905, LL.B., 1907; m. Irene Plaut, May 25, 1915; children—Hugo, Edward, Jane (Mrs. Gerald Fritz). Admitted to Ill. bar, 1907, since practiced law, Chgo., sr. partner Sonnenschein, Berkson, Lautmann, Levinson & Morse. Dir. Chicago Title & Trust Co., Allstate Ins. Co., Bond Stores, Inc. Mem. Am., Ill., Chgo. bar assns., Phi Beta Kappa, Delta Sigma Rho. Clubs: Mid-Day, Tavern, Standard, Lake Shore Country (Chgo.). Home: 2269 Egandale Rd., Highland Park, Ill. Office: 77 W. Washington St Chgo. 2. Died Sept. 2, 1956.

SOPHIAN, Lawrence Henry, physician; b. N.Y.C., June 26, 1903; s. Michael and Cecelia (Frank) S.; B.A., Coll. City N.Y., 1921; M.D., Harvard, 1925; m. Josephine W. Smith, June 25, 1952; children—Celia, Catherine. Instr. Harvard Med. Sch., 1928-29; asso. prof. N.Y. Post-Grad. Med. Sch., 1930; pathologist Roosevelt Hosp., N.Y.C., 1930-39; served from lt. comdr. to capt., USPHS, 1939-52; dir. labs. U.S. Marine Hosps. med. dir. USPHS (ret.); asso. dir. med. lit. Lederle Labs., 1952-53; v.p., med. dir. William Douglas McAdams, Inc., med. advt., N.Y.C., 1953—. Mem. A.M.A., Am. Assn. Pathologists and Bacteriologists, Coll. Am. Pathologists. Club: Harvard (N.Y.C.). Contbr. articles profl. jours. Home: 171 Indian Head Rd., Riverside, Conn. Office: 130 E. 59th St., N.Y.C. 22. Died July 8, 1959; buried Arlington Nat. Cemetery.

SOPHOULIS, Themistocles, premier of Greece. Address: Athens, Greece. Died June 1949.

SORG, (Harrison) Theodore (sôrg), lawyer; b. Newark, N.J., Nov. 22, 1888; s. Frederick and Emma (Albrecht) S.; LL.B., N.J. Law Sch., 1912; D.C.L., Hillsdale Coll., 1939; m. Mildred Hoops, Apr. 12, 1928; children—Winifred Dorothy, Janet Lucille. Admitted to New Jersey bar, 1912, and since in general practice; mem. Sorg and Sorg, 1926—; professor law, New Jersey Law Sch., 1913-35; served with A.E. F. in France, 1918-19 and received Purple Heart. President Hospital Service Plan of New Jersey, Board of Education of American Baptist Convention, Am. Bapt. Publn. Soc., Watchman-Examiner Foundation (publisher of National Baptist weekly). Mem. Am., N.J., N.Y. County and Essex County bar assns. Republican. Baptist. Clubs: Down Town, Essex (Newark); Lawyers (New York); Nassau (Princeton). Home: 1 Haslet Av., Princeton, N.J. Office: 744 Broad St., Newark. Died Dec. 10, 1955.

SOSKIN, William (sŏs'kĭn), pub., literary critic; b. N.Y. City, May 1, 1899; s. Nicolai and Minna S.; A.B., Columbia, 1920; student Columbia Law Sch., 1920-23; married and divorced; 1 son, Richard; m. 2d, Virginia Howell, 1941; 2 sons, David, Nicholas. Reporter, 1921; has been with Wis. News, Chicago Evening Post, N.Y. Evening Mail; was mng. editor N.Y. Call; later news editor N.Y. Evening Post, lit. editor, 1928-33; became lit. critic N.Y. American, 1934; formerly exec. editor Stackpole Sons, pubs.; now editor Book-of-the-Month Club. Home: Darien, Conn. Office: 100 6th Av., N.Y.C. Died Mar. 24, 1952.

SOSMAN, Merrill C(lary) (sŏs'măn) roentgenologist; b. Chillicothe, O., June 23, 1890; s. Francis Asbury and Mollie (Browning) S.; A.B., U. Wis., 1913; M.D., Johns Hopkins, 1917; M.A. (hon.), Harvard, 1949; m. Arline Clark Adams, June 27, 1918; children—John Leland, Barbara Clark. Resident physician, U.S. Soldiers Home Hosp., Washington, 1917; grad. student, Mass. Gen. Hosp., Boston, 1921-22; became roentgenologist in chief, Peter Bent Brigham Hosp., Boston, 1922, now chmn. emeritus; cons. roentgenologist Childrens Hosp., Psychopathic Hosp., N. E. Peabody Home for Crippled Children (Boston), Cape Cod Hosp. (Hyannis). Instr. in roentgenology, Harvard Med. Sch., 1922-28, asst. prof., 1928-40, clin. prof., 1940-44, clin. prof. radiology, 1944-48, became prof. of radiology 1948, now prof. emeritus; now cons. radiology, Mass. Gen. Hosp. Served as 1st lt. Med. Corps, U.S. Army, 1917; capt., 1918-22. Recipient gold medal, Radiol. Soc. of Am. Diplomate Am. Bd. Radiology. Fellow A.A.A.S.; mem. A.M.A., N.E. Roentgen Ray Soc. (past pres.; George W. Holmes lectr., 1947), Radiol. Soc. N.A., Am. Roentgen Ray Soc. (past pres.; Caldwell lectr. 1947), Harvey Cushing Soc. (past pres.), Am. Coll. Radiology, Mexican Soc. Radiol. and Phys. Therapy (hon.), Venezuela Radiol. Soc., Am. Acad. Arts Scis., Sigma Xi., A.O.A. Mason. Clubs: Harvard (Boston); Country (Brookline). Contbr. of numerous articles on diagnosis and treatment of diseases or tumors by X-ray to sci. publs. Home: 24 Lee Rd., Chestnut Hill 67, Mass. Office: 721 Huntington Av., Boston 15. Died Mar. 28, 1959; buried Chillicothe, O.

SOTTER, George William, artist; b. Pittsburgh, Pa., Sept. 25, 1879; s. Nicholas and Katherine (Melder) S.; ed. in art, Pa. Acad. Fine Arts, Phila.; pupil of Chase, Anshutz, Redfield and Henry Keller; m. Alice E. Bennett, Feb. 11, 1907. Has specialized in landscape and stained glass; asst. prof. painting and design, Carnegie Inst. Tech., Pittsburgh, 1910-19. Awarded silver medal, San Francisco Expn., 1915; 1st prize, Asso. Artists of Pittsburgh, 1917; Art Soc. prize Pittsburgh, 1920; hon. mention, Conn. Acad. Fine Arts, 1921, and Flagg prize, same, 1923. Works on permanent exhbn.: "The Hill Road," Reading (Pa.) Museum; "Pennsylvania Country" State College, Pa.; (stained glass): Ch. of Our Lady of Lourdes (New York), St. Agnes Ch., and St. Paul's Monastery and Holy Innocents' Ch. (Pittsburgh), Kendrick Sem. (St. Louis), St. Mark's Ch. (St. Paul), St. Joseph's Cathedral (Wheeling, W.Va.), Sacred Heart Ch. (Pittsburgh), St. Ann's Monastery (Scranton), N.J. State Museum (Trenton), St. James Ch. (Cleveland), St. Michael's Monastery (Union City, N.J.), St. Peter's Ch. (Brownsville, Pa.), Annunciation Church (Cincinnati, O.), St. Mary's Ch. (Akron, O.); hanging metal cross, Sacred Heart Ch. (Pittsburgh), hanging painted cross, Lady of Mt. Carmel (Doylestown, Pa.), etc. Mem. New Hope Art Associates, Asso. Artists of Pittsburgh, Fellowship Pa. Acad. Fine Arts, Conn. Acad. Fine Arts. Club: Salmagundi (N.Y.C.). Home: Ash Mill Rd., Holicong, Bucks County, Pa. Died May 6, 1953; buried Saint Mary's Cemetery, Doylestown, Pa.

SOTZIN, Heber Allen (sŏtz'ĭn), educator; b. Pine Grove, Pa., Sept. 22, 1893; s. Lyman and Lydia (Keefer) S.; student U. Chgo., 1915, 19; A.B., Geo. Wash. U., 1923, A.M., 1929; Ph.D., U. Cin., 1929; m. Anne Henratty, Nov. 10, 1917 (dec.); children—Heber Allen (deceased), Elizabeth Anne (Mrs. Jack Miller); married second, Mrs. Amy E. Burr, June 6, 1958. Pub. sch. teacher, Ind., 1914-16, Pa., 1916-18, Washington, D.C., 1919-27; teaching fellow, U. Cin., 1927-29; head and prof. indsl. arts dept., San Jose (Cal.) State Coll. since 1929, chmn. div. of applied arts; visiting prof., summers U. Cin., 1928, 29, U. Hawaii, 1938, Ohio State U., 1939-41, Stanford, 1932-45, Bradley U., 1949, U. of Utah, 1950. Served with U.S. Navy, 1918-19. Recipient Tchr. of the Year award, Cal. Indsl. Edn. Assn., 1956. Mem. Newcomen Soc. N.A. and Eng., Am. Assn. U. Profs. (pres. San Jose State Coll. chpt.), Am. Indsl. Arts Assn. (v.p., mem. exec. adv. com. nat. scholastic awards), Am. Legion, Am. Vocational Association, Am. Vocational Guidance Assn., Am. Assn. Indsl. Teachers, Cal. Vocational Fedn. (pres.), Northern Cal. Vocational Guidance Assn. (pres.), Phi Delta Kappa, Epsilon Pi Tau (gov. for Western States), Acacia. Mason. Author: An Industrial Arts Curriculum for Grades Four to Twelve Inclusive, 1929; The Function of the School to Foster Economic Competence, 1939; Creed for Industrial Arts Teachers, 1945; A Brief Resume of Industrial Arts Education, 1950; The New Look in Power Tools for Industrial Arts Education, 1950. Contbr. to ednl. and profl. jours. Speaker various bus. and comml. orgns., ednl. orgns. Curriculum and sch. survey consultant. Mem. nat. com. Indsl. Arts, Its interpretation in Am. Schs., 1934—. Home: 1015 Carolyn Av., San Jose 10, Cal. Died Jan. 6, 1960.

SOUCEK, Apollo (sō'chĕk), naval officer; b. Lamont, Okla., Feb. 24, 1897; s. John Gothard and Lydia (Pishny) S.; grad. U.S. Naval Acad., 1921; m. Agnes Eleanor O'Connor, May 27, 1930. Commd. ensign U.S. Navy, 1921, and advanced through grades to capt. capacity of comdg. officer, Oct. 27, 1945, promoted to flag rank, Mar. 2, 1946; qualified as naval aviator Oct. 1924; established world's aircraft altitude record, 39,140 feet, June 4, 1929, seaplane, 38,800 ft. (approximately), June 8, 1929, re-established world's altitude record, any type aircraft, 43,-166 feet, June 8, 1930; commd. aircraft carrier U.S.S. Franklin D. Roosevelt as capt., U.S. Navy, Oct. 27, 1945; air officer U.S.S. Hornet-CV-8, exec. officer when ship sunk, battle Santa Cruz Islands, 1941-42; operations officer Vice Admiral Tower's staff, 1943; comdr. Fleet Air Wing One, 1946-47, asst. chief naval operations for aviation plans, 1949-51; naval attache and naval attache for air London July-Nov. 1951; chief bur. aeronautics Navy Dept., 1953—. Awarded Distinguished Flying Cross, Silver Star medal, Legion of Merit with gold star, Bronze Star medal. Home: Medford, Okla. Died July 22, 1955.

SOULE, Malcolm Herman (sūl), bacteriologist; b. Allegany, N.Y., Dec. 5, 1896; s. Charles M. and Ida May (Ervin) S.; B.S., U. of Mich., 1921, M.S., 1922, D.Sc., 1924; LL.D., St. Bonaventures Coll., 1928; m. Alma Dengler, Sept. 7, 1926; children—Mary Alma, Margaret Laura. Instr. analytical chemistry, U. of Mich., 1919-20; instr. bacteriology, Sch. of Medicine, 1923-25, asst. prof., 1925-28, asso. prof., 1928-31, prof. since 1931, chmn., dept., and Hygienic Lab. since 1935; visiting prof., U. of Chicago, 1931; visiting prof., School Tropical Medicine, Puerto Rico, 1931; leprosy investigation, Leonard Wood Memorial, P.I., 1933-34, chairman Medical Advisory Board since 1944; consultant to director division health and sanitation, Coordinator of Inter-American Affairs since 1942. Del. of U.S. Govt. to 2d Internat. Congress Microbiology, London, 1936, Internat. Congress for Leprosy, Cairo, 1938; 3d Internat. Congress Tropical Medicine and Malaria, Amsterdam, 1938, 9th Pan-Am. Conf. on Health and Sanitation, Rio de Janeiro, 1942, 2d Pan-Am. Conf. on Leprosy, Rio de Janeiro, 1946, Internat. Congress of Cytology, Stockholm, 1947; 4th Congress Microbiology, Copenhagen, 1947; 5th Congress, Leprosy, Havana, 1948, 5th Internat. Congress Microbiology, Rio de Janeiro, 1950; adviser to dir. Leprosy Service and Malaria, Brazil, 1950; mem. med. ednl. mission to Japan, auspices SCAP, Unitarian Services Com., 1951. Member Com. Internat. Affairs, Nat. Research Council. Representative International Biol. Society on UNESCO. Fellow A.A.A.S. (mem. exec. com. since 1947); mem. Am. Assn. Pathologists and Bacteriologists (pres. 1947), Am. Acad. Tropical Medicine (council mem. since 1937), Am. Assn. Pathologists and Bacteriologists (on council since 1940), Am. Assn. Immunologists, Am. Chem. Soc., Am. Micros. Assn., Am. Pub. Health Assn. (fellow), Am. Soc. Exptl. Pathology, Am. Soc. Tropical Medicine (v.p. 1941), Bot. Soc. of America, Internat. Leprosy Assn., Path. So. Great Britain and Ireland, Soc. Exptl. Biology and Medicine, Soc. Am. Bacteriologists, corr. mem. Sociedad Medico-Quirurgica del Guayas, corr. mem. Societe de Pathologie Exotique; hon. mem. Brazilian Leprosy Association; mem. editorial bds., Science; American Jour. Pathology; American Jour. Tropical Med.; mem. Alpha Chi Sigma, Alpha Omega Alpha, Gamma Alpha, Nu Sigma Nu, Phi Kappa Phi, Phi Lambda Upsilon, Phi Sigma, Sigma Xi. Awarded gold medal by A.M.A., 1930. Protestant. Contbr. scientific articles on microbic respiration, microbic dissociation, goitre, undulant fever, leprosy, poliomyelitis, relapsing fever, tropical medicine. Home: 2110 Hill St., Ann Arbor, Mich. Died Aug. 3, 1951.

SOULE, Robert Homer (sōl), army officer; b. Laramie, Wyo., Feb. 10, 1900; s. Justus Freeland and Isabel Dora (Simpson) S.; student U. of Wyoming, 1916-18; grad. Inf. Sch., company officers course, 1927, Command and Gen. Staff Sch., 1940; m. Genevieve Marie Hoffman, Jan. 4, 1922; 1 dau., Genevieve Ann. Commd. 2d lt., inf., U.S. Army, 1918, and advanced through grades to maj. gen., 1950; served with 31st Inf., A.E.F., Siberia and Philippine Islands, 1918-22; Chinese language student and attaché Am. Legation, Peking, China, 1929-33; with War Dept. Gen. Staff, Mar. 1941-Dec. 1942; comdg. officer 11th Airborne Div., 188th Paratroop Glider Inf., 1943-45; became asst. div. comdr. 38th Inf. Div., Mar. 1945, also asst. div. comdr., 11th Airborne Div., Sendai, Japan, 1945-46, mil. attaché Nanking, China, 1946-50; later comdg. gen. 3d Inf. Div., Korea, and then insp. inf., Army Field Forces, Ft. Monroe, Va. Decorated D.S.C. (two), D.S.M., Legion of Merit, Silver Star (two), Bronze Star Medal with oak-leaf cluster, Purple Heart, Combat Inf. Badge, Prachute Badge, Air Medal, Presidential Citation. Mem. Sigma Alpha Epsilon. Mason (Shriner). Home: Carmel, Cal. Died Jan. 26, 1952; buried Arlington Nat. Cemetery.

SOULE, Winsor (sōōl), architect; b. Staten Island, N.Y., Nov. 3, 1883; s. Richard Herman and Ida Helen (Whittemore) S.; grad. St. Paul's Sch., Concord, N.H., 1902; A.B., Harvard, 1906; B.S., Mass. Inst. of Tech., 1907; m. Judith B. de Forest, Oct. 1907; (divorced Oct. 1926); m. 2d, Madeleine Bradbury, Nov. 3, 1926 (dec.); 1 son, Winsor, Jr.; m. 3d, M. Barbara Baker, Apr. 30, 1929; 1 dau. Barbara Ida. Draftsman with Cram, Goodhue & Ferguson, Boston, 1907-08; asso. architect, development Bryn Mawr Coll., 1908-09; draftsman, supt. with Allen & Collens, Boston, 1909-11; practiced architecture with Russell Ray, Santa Barbara, Cal., 1912-17; private practice, 1917-21; with John Frederic Murphy and T. Mitchell Hastings, 1921-25; with John Frederic Murphy, 1925-53; partner Winsor Soule and Glen G. Mosher, architects, 1954—; consultant on ch. architecture to Luth. Synod of So. Calif., 1938-42, to Presbyn. Synod of Calif., so. area, 1945—; supervising architect Santa Barbara coll. U. Calif., 1949-52. Chmn. Bd. Park Commrs., Santa Barbara, 1925; mem. Calif. State Bd. Archtl. Examiners, 1940-50, pres., 1943-45; mem. Calif. Council Architects, 1948-49. Fellow A.I.A. Episcopalian. Clubs: University, Rotary, Harvard, Santa Barbara. Home: 715 Mission Canyon Rd. Office: 116 East Sola St., Santa Barbara, Cal. Died Aug. 19, 1954; buried Santa Barbara Cemetery.

SOUTHALL, Robert Goode, ex-congressman, lawyer; b. Amelia Co., Va., Dec. 26, 1852; ed. Washington acad. and high sch. of Amelia County; grad. law dept., U. Va., 1876; admitted to Va. bar, 1877; del. Dem. Nat. Conv., 1888, 1896; mem. house of delegates, Va., 1899-1903; mem. Congress, 4th Va. dist., 1903-07; judge 4th Judicial Circuit, 1912—. Democrat. Address: Amelia, Va. Died May 25, 1924; buried Amelia, Va.

SOUTHAM, H(arry) S(tevenson), ret. publisher; b. London, Ont., Can.; s. William and Wilson (Mills) S.; B.A., U. Toronto; LL.D. (hon.), Queen's U., Kingston, Ont., 1948; m. Lilias Ahearn; children—Gordon Thomas, Janet (Mrs. D. K. MacTavish), Robert Wilson, Ethel (Mrs. F. H. Toller). With Ottawa Citizen, 1897-53, v.p., pub., 1920-53, ret. June 15, 1953. Chancellor, Carleton Coll., Ottawa. Decorated Companion of St. Michael and St. George. Christian Scientist. Clubs: Rideau, Country, Royal Ottawa Golf. Died Mar. 27, 1954.

SOUTHAM, J(ohn) D(avid), publisher; b. Ottawa, Ont., Can., Apr. 12, 1909; s. Wilson Mills and Henrietta (Cargill) S.; student Upper Can. Coll., Toronto, 1917-22, Ashbury Coll., Ottawa, Trinity Coll. Sch., Port Hope, Ont., 1922-25; m. Marie Elisabeth Roy, Jan. 1932; 1 son, Wilson John Hamilton; m. 2d, Moya Edwards, Oct. 24, 1953; stepchildren—Byron John Edwards, Paul Archibald Edwards. With Royal Bank of Can., 1928-29; del. Kyoto Conf. on Pacific Relations, Japan, 1929; with Ottawa Citizen, 1930-32; with Calgary Herald since 1932, asst. bus. mgr., 1932-35, bus. mgr., 1935-46, pub. since 1946. Served as lt. col. arty., Royal Canadian Army, 1940-45; in command 2d anti-tank regt., Northwest Europe. Mem. Canadian Daily Newspapers Assn. (dir.). Clubs: Royal Ottawa Golf; Ranchmen's, Golf and Country (Calgary). Home: 635 Sifton Blvd., Calgary, Alberta, Can. Died Nov. 28, 1954.

SOUTHERLAND, J. Julien, lawyer; b. Wilmington, N.C., Dec. 9, 1884; s. Capt. Thomas Jefferson and Cornelia (Lamb) S.; ed. pub. and private schs., Wilmington, Washington; LL.B., Georgetown U., 1910; m. Laetitia Mitchell, May 3, 1917. Entered U.S. Civ. Service, 1907; admitted to D.C. bar, 1910; apptd. law clk. Post Office Dept., 1912, atty., 1913; sr. atty. same dept., 1913-18; spl. asst. (counsel) Wire Control Bd., U.S. Telegraph and Telephone Adminstrn., 1918-20, charged with supervision of litigation and adjustment of claims of telegraph and telephone cos. growing out of govt. control of the wires; spl. asst. U.S. atty., N.Y., 1920-21; sr. atty. U.S. Post Office Dept., 1920-21, acting solicitor (chief legal officer), 1921; resigned to join legal staff Western Union Telegraph Co., N.Y.; atty. and asst. gen. atty. same co., 1921-25; resigned to engage in gen. practice of law at Miami, Fla. Mayor Bal Harbor, 1947—; municipal judge Indian Creek Village, 1945—. Mem. Com. of 100 (bd. govs.), Miami Beach. Pres. S. Fla. Crippled Children's Hosp.; trustee St. Frances Hosp. Mem. faculty Georgetown U. Law Sch., 1912-21. Mem. Am Bar Assn, Florida Bar Assn, Dade County Bar Assn., So. Soc. N.Y., S.R., Phi Alpha Delta. Democrat. Episcopalian. Clubs: University (Washington); Bal Harbor (Fla.); The Bath Club, Indian Creek Country (Miami Beach). Home: 5801 Collins Av. Office: 605 Lincoln Road, Miami Beach, Fla. Died Jan. 24, 1950.

SOUTHERN, William Neil, Jr., publisher, editor; b. Morristown, Tenn., Nov. 4, 1864; s. John Nelson and Martha (Allen) S.; ed. pub. schs., Independence, Mo., 1870-81; student Westminster Coll., Fulton, Mo., 1881-84; m. Emma Procter, Feb. 10, 1892; children—Caroline (Mrs. Edward K. Carnes), Mary Frances (Mrs. George P. Wallace). Began as reporter Kansas City (Mo.) Times, 1885; reporter Kansas City Star and Independence Sentinel, 1891-98; founded Jackson (Mo.) Examiner (weekly), 1898; founded Independence Examiner (daily), 1905, since pub. and editor. Mem. Hist. Soc. Mo. (ex-pres.; trustee), Mo. Press Assn. (ex-pres.), Inland Daily Press Assn. (ex-pres.), Independence C. of C. (ex-pres.), Phi Delta Theta, Sigma Delta Chi. Del. World Press Congress, Honolulu, Hawaii, 1921, and Geneva, Switzerland, 1926, Internat. Press Cong., Cologne, Germany, 1928. Awarded D.S.M., 1935, by curators U. Mo. for work in journalism. Democrat. Presbyn. Mason (32°). Author daily column In Missouri Language, in Independence Examiner; syndicates weekly comment Internat. Sunday Sch. Lesson. Home: 639 S. Park Av. Office: 221 W. Lexington St., Independence, Mo. Died Feb. 11, 1956; buried Woodlawn Cemetery, Independence.

SOWELL, Ellis Mast, univ. prof. and dean; b. Chireno, Tex., Apr. 17, 1902; s. James Hilyer and Alma (Mast) H.; B.S., Stephen F. Austin State Tchrs. Coll., Nacogdoches, Tex., 1934; M.B.A., U. of Tex., 1936, Ph.D., 1944; m. Irma Alford, May 6, 1928; 1 son, Ellis Mast, Jr. Began as employee in retail drug store, 1918; with Peoples Drug Store, Chireno, Tex., 1919-20; cashier and dir., Chireno State Bank, Chireno, Tex., 1921-31; instr. Stephen F. Austin State Tchrs. Coll., Nacogdoches, Tex., 1934-35, asst. prof., 1936-37, asso. prof., registrar, 1937-38, 1939-40, prof., registrar, 1941-43; instr., U. of Tex., 1938-39, 1940-41, asst. prof., 1943-44; dean of sch. of bus., prof. of accounting, Texas Christian U., Ft. Worth, 1944-55, distinguished prof. finance, 1955—; adminstr. of staff relations Haskins & Sells Accounting Firm, N.Y.C., 1953-55. Rockefeller Found. Fellow, Grad. Sch. of Bus. Adminstrn., Harvard, June, 1947-Feb. 1948. Certificate as C.P.A., State of Tex. Mem. Am. Accounting Assn., Alpha Chi, Beta Alpha Psi, Beta Gamma Sigma. Mason. Rotarian. Home: 3224 Odessa St. Office: Box 188, Texas Christian University, Fort Worth 9. Died Sept. 10, 1956.

SPACKMAN, Harold Burton, mfg. exec.; b. Sisseton, S.D., June 30, 1899; s. Harry L. and Dora (Wample) S.; student Mil. Sch. and U. Minn.; m. Jane Powell, Feb. 4, 1933; 1 son, Richard. Asso. Northwestern Expanded Metal Co., Chicago, becoming asst. sales mgr.; then dept. mgr. Steel Products U.S. Gypsum Co., Chicago, 1928-37; v.p. and dir. Lyon Metal Products, Inc., Aurora, Ill., 1937-50, pres. since 1950. Mem. C. of C., Delta Tau Delta. Republican. Presbyn. Mason (Shriner). Elk. Club: Union League. Author articles on merchandising, marketing and conversion to war prodn. Home: Rt. 1, Yorkville, Ill. Office: Lyon Metal Products, Inc., Aurora, Ill. Died 1957.

SPAETH, Bernard Anton, estate mgr.; b. Decatur, Ill., Feb. 7, 1885; s. Anton and Clara (Melchior) S.; student St. Francis Coll., Quincy, Ill.; m. Edith K. Nussbaum, July 7, 1914; children—Bernard L., Carl J., Margaret (Mrs. Otto C. Stegmaier), Louis O., James F., Susanne M., Helen (Mrs. Mario Vanni), Anne Marie (Mrs. Joseph K. Hanson), Marie T. (Mrs. H. Dick Nobis), Anton P., and E. Katherine (now Mrs. Daniel A. Molyneaux). President of Spaeth Family Found.; dir. Citizens Building Corporation, Decatur, Ill. Trustee St. Ambrose Coll., Davenport. Mem. Nat. Conf. Christians and Jews (dir.) Home: 720 E. Locust. Office: Kahl Bldg., Davenport, Ia. Died Jan. 30, 1958; buried St. Margaret's Cemetery, Davenport, Ia.

SPAETH, J(ohn) Duncan, educator; b. Phila., Sept. 27, 1868; s. Dr. Adolph and Maria Dorothea (Duncan) S.; A.B., U. Pa., 1888; Ph.D., U. Leipzig, 1892; studied in France and Italy, 1912-13; Litt. D., Muhlenberg Coll., 1918, U. Pitts., 1925; LL.D., U. Ore., 1936, U. Pa., 1938; m. Marie Tinette Haughton, June 19, 1902 (died Apr. 7, 1937); children—Dorothea Duncan, Paul Ernest, Janet Douglas (Mrs. John Stockton de Martelly), John Duncan, Jr.; m. 2d, Amy R. Fielding (nee Williams), Jan. 7, 1942. Asst. prof. English, Gustavus Adolphus Coll., 1893-94; instr., Central High Sch., Phila., 1894-95, prof. English philology, 1895-1905; preceptor in English, Princeton, 1905-11, apptd. prof., 1911, Murray prof. English lit., 1930-35; 1st pres. U. Kansas City, 1933-36, now emeritus; vis. prof. comparative lit., Reed Coll., 1926-27; vis. prof. U. Wichita, 1938, 39, 40. Haverford Coll., 1942-47. Lectr. for University Extension Soc. Bd. Pub. Edn., N.Y.C., 1905-22, Bklyn. Inst. U. Cal.; 4 summers, U. Ore., 9 summers, U. So. Cal., 4 summers, U. Colo., 2 summers, Utah State Coll., 2 summers, Chautauqua Instn., 1921, 23, 32, etc. Mem. bd. mgrs. N.J. State Reformatory, 1923-29. Y.M.C.A. ednl. dir., Camp Wheeler and Camp Jackson, 1918; active in orgn. instrn. for illiterates in army camps, World War. Mem. Modern Lang. Assn. Am., A.A.A.S., Am. Acad. Polit. and Social Science, Nat. Council Nat. Economics League, St. Andrews Soc., Phi Beta Kappa, Psi Upsilon. Amateur coach of Princeton Crews, 1910-25. Clubs: Nassau (Princeton); Princeton (Phila.); Princeton (N.Y.C.); Mazamas (mountaineering, Ore.). Author: Christian Theology in Browning's Poetry; Camp Reader for American Soldiers (several edits.), 1918 (adopted by War Dept. for A.E.F.); Old English Poetry, 1921; American Life and Letters: A Reading List (with J. E. Brown), 1934. Editor (with Henry S. Pancoast) of Early English Poems and transl. of Anglo-Saxon poems in same, 1911. Contbr. articles on Am. Lit. to Am. Year Book, 1926, 27, and on Henry van Dyke, John Grier Hibben and others to Dictionary of Am. Biography, etc. Lectured and wrote on The Humanities in Peace and War, 1943; Woodrow Wilson as I Knew Him and View Him Now, in Woodrow Wilson. Some Princeton Memories (edited by William Starr Myers) 1946. Home: Spring Hollow, R.F.D. Wayne, Pa.; (summer) Rocky Point, Bernard, Mt. Desert, Me. Died July 26, 1954; buried Church of the Redeemer, Bryn Mawr, Pa.

SPAHR, Herman Louis, consular service; b. Macon, Ga., Dec. 18, 1875; s. Herman and Meta Mary (Harbann) S.; A.B., U. S.C., 1895, A.M., 1903; studied U. Heidelberg, Germany, U. Chgo.; m. Zaida Whitman, Sept. 6, 1904. Admitted to S.C. bar, 1899; instr. in modern langs., U. SC., 1900-06; elected prof. German U. Okla., 1906, but resigned to enter consular service; consul at Breslau, Germany, 1906-14, Montevideo, 1914—. Served as 2d lt., Co. C, 2d S.C. Vol. Inf., Spanish-Am. War, 1898. Mem. Chi Phi. Democrat. Episcopalian. Address: Atlanta. Died June 16, 1953.

SPAIN, Will Cook, physician; b. Murfreesboro, Tenn., Aug. 10, 1891; s. Thomas and Annie May (Cook) S.; A.B., U. of Mich., 1914; M.D., Vanderbilt U., 1918; m. Grace Jones, Oct. 12, 1921; children—Joann (Mrs. Arthur Rasmussen), Janet (Mrs. William Spoor). Interne, N.Y. Post-Grad. Hosp., 1918-19, resident physician, 1919; attending physician, N.Y. Hosp., allergy clinic, 1919-29; instr. in immunology, Cornell U. Med. Sch., 1922-24, instr. clin. pediatrics, Cornell U., 1933-35; attending physician and dir., dept. of allergy, N.Y. Post-Graduate Hosp., Columbia U., 1924-48; prof. clin. medicine, N.Y. Post-Grad. Med. Sch., Columbia, 1930-48; chief pediatric allergy clinic, N.Y. Hosp., 1933-35; vis. physician, 1st Div. Welfare Hosp., 1940-41; asst. prof. clin. medicine, N.Y. Med. Coll., 1940-42; attending physician and dir. dept. allergy, U. Hosp., 1948—, prof. clin. medicine, N.Y.U. Post-Grad. Med. Sch., 1948—; vis. physician, 4th Med. Div., Bellevue Hosp., 1949—; cons. in allergy, Mather Meml. Hospital, 1930-53. Served as 1st lt., Med. Res. Corp. 1914. Fellow A.M.A., Am. Coll. Physicians, N.Y. Acad. Medicine, Med. Soc. of State N.Y., Med. Soc. Co. of N.Y.; mem. Soc. for the Study of Asthma and Allied Conditions (sec.-treas. 1924-45), Am. Acad. of Allergy (sec. 1944, v.p. 1946, president 1947); Am. Acad. of Allergy (chmn. com. on edn., 1946-49), N.Y. Allergy Soc. (a founder), A.A.A.S., Am. Bd. Internal Medicine (mem. adv. bd. for allergy 1947-53), Pan Am. Med. Assn. (pres. sect. allergy, 1952-54), N.Y. Post-Grad. Hosp. Alumni Assn., Am. Assn. Immunologists, Phi Chi, Alpha Omega Alpha. Mem. editorial bd. Jour. of Allergy, 1953——. Home: 570 Park Av., N.Y.C. 21. Office: 141 E. 55th St., N.Y.C. 22. Died May 12, 1956; buried Woodlawn Cemetery, N.Y.C.

SPALDING, Albert (spawl'dĭng), violinist; b. Chicago, Ill., Aug. 15, 1888; s. J. Walter and Marie (Boardman) S.; ed. New York, Florence and Paris; m. Mary Vanderhof Pyle, July 19, 1919. Début in Paris, 1905; made tour of principal cities of Europe; Am. début with Damrosch Orchestra, Carnegie Hall, New York, Nov. 8, 1908, followed by concert tour of U.S.; visited Russia, 1910; since then toured Holland, Belgium, Germany, Austria, Italy, Egypt, France, England, Switzerland, Norway, Sweden, Denmark, Cuba, and W.I.; 2d Am. tour, 1912, 3d, 1914, 4th, 1915. Composer of music for violin. Joined Aviation Corps U.S. Signal Service, June 1917, and served as liaison officer; commd. lt.; with OWI, psychol. warfare, Italy, 1944, in chg. radio Rome for Allied Powers, 1944. Mem. Am. Acad. Arts and Letters, Am. Soc. Composers, Authors and Publishers. Club: Century. Address: 3 E. 77th St., N.Y.C. Died May 26, 1953.

SPARGO, John Webster, educator; b. St. Louis, Mo., Mar. 6, 1896; s. John Webster and Sybil Marian (Gray) S.; A.B., Washington U., St. Louis, 1920, A.M., 1921; A.M., Harvard, 1925, Ph.D., in English philology, 1926; student (Irish, Scandinavian), Copenhagen, 1926-27; m. Elsa Vieh, Sept. 20, 1927 (died Jan. 3, 1933); m. 2d, Gladys Raiter, June 15, 1936 (divorced; married 3d Ophelia Hack, Aug. 12, 1950. Resident fellow, Harvard, 1924-25, 1925-26, traveling fellow, summer, 1925. Sheldon traveling fellow, 1926-27; asst. prof. English, Northwestern U., 1927-29, asso. prof., 1929-35, prof., 1935——; Guggenheim fellow (Eng. and Continent), 1930-31, 1936-37; visiting prof. U. of Chicago, summer and autumn, 1928, Harvard, summer 1935, Duke U., summers 1940, 41, Northwestern U., other summers, N.Y. U., summers 1950, 51; vis. lectr. Loyola U., Chgo., 1952-56. Served in U.S. Army, 1917-19, U.S. del. to Internat. Folklore Congress, Paris, 1937. Mem. Folklore Fellows, Modern Lang. Assn. of Am., Mediaeval Acad., Am. Assn. U. Profs., Bibliog. Soc. (London), Bibliog. Soc. of America, Selden Soc., Stair Soc., Phi Beta Kappa. Presbyterian. Author: Chaucer' Shipman's Tale (Helsingfors), 1930; Virgil the Necromancer (Harvard Studies in Comparative Literature X), 1934; Some Reference Books of the 16th and 17th Centuries (Bibliographical Society America), 1937; Bibliographical Manual for Students of Language and Literature of England and the United States, 1939, 41, 56; Juridical Folklore in England, 1944; Imaginary Books and Libraries, 1952. Translator: (from the Danish) Holger Pedersen's Linguistic Science in the Nineteenth Century, 1931. Editor: Northwestern University Studies (30 vols.), 1936-48; Charles Neely, Tales and Songs of Southern Illinois (1938). Club: Caxton (Chicago). Contbr. to learned jours., U.S. and abroad. Address: 1725 Orington Av., Evanston, Ill.; (summer) Belleview, Mo. Died Sept. 6, 1956; buried St. Louis.

SPARKES, Boyden (spärks), writer; b. Cincinnati, O., Jan. 6, 1890; s. Thomas Kinsey and Lillian Cary (Cochnower) S.; student Columbia, 1921-22; m. Bessie Ledford Gore, Jan. 26, 1914; children—Betty Ledford (Mrs. Joseph C. Eagles, Jr.), Dorothy (Mrs. Hugh Primrose). Worked as reporter for Cincinnati Commercial Tribune, 1907, Chicago Examiner, 1910; Chicago Record Herald, 1911, Manila Cable News Am., 1912; San Francisco Call, 1912-13; various editorial positions with Associated Press, 1914-16, New York Evening Sun and New York American, 1917, New York Tribune and New York Herald-Tribune, 1918-24; traveled as Tribune's corr. with Warren G. Harding, 1920-21, with Charles G. Dawes, campaign of 1924; contbr. to mags. since 1924, principally to Saturday Evening Post, also writer of short fiction. Served as lieutenant 1st Illinois Cavalry on Mexican border, 1916. Mason. Clubs: Players, Dutch Treat (New York); Carolina Yacht, Cape Fear Club, Cape Fear Country (Wilmington, N.C.); National Press (Washington). Author: Crime in Ink (with Claire Carvalho), 1929; Hetty Green, A Woman Who Loved Money (with Samuel Taylor Moore), 1930; Customers' Man, 1931; Life a La Henri (with Henri Charpentier), 1934; From Farm Boy to Financier (with Frank A. Vanderlip), 1935; Father Struck it Rich (with Evalyn Walsh McLean), 1936; The Towers of New York (with Louis J. Horowitz), 1937; Life of An American Workman (with Walter P. Chryser), 1937; Dime Store, a Biography of Frank Woolworth (with John K. Winkler), Adventure of a White Collar Man (with Alfred P. Sloan, Jr.), 1941; The Flying Guns (with Lt. Clarence E. Dickinson, U.S. Navy), 1943; Boot Straps: Autobiography of Tom Girdler, 1943; Home Freezing and Storage of Food (revised edit., 1947); Judge Mellon's Sons (with M. L. Mellon), 1948; Life of an American Workman (with Walter P. Chrysler), 1950. Home: Wrightsville Sound, N.C. Died May 18, 1954.

SPARKS, Frank Melville, editor; b. Bangor, Me., Feb. 28, 1877; s. Francis Edward and Laura Jane (Rose) S.; B.A., Bowdoin, 1900; m. Marie McCarty, June 19, 1905 (dec.); 1 dau., Priscilla Marie (Mrs. Bruce C. Swain). Reporter, Daily News, Bangor, 1900; with Detroit Free Press and Detroit Tribune, 1901-02; mng. editor Sault Ste. Marie Evening News, 1902-04; with Grand Rapids Herald, 1904-05, Evening Press, 1905-07; mgr. Daily Sentinel, Holland, Mich., 1907-08; with Grand Rapids Herald, 1908——, now editor. Chmn. Charter Commn., East Grand Rapids, 1927. Dir. Mich. Tourist and Resort Assn. Mem. Am. Soc. Newspaper Editors, Grand Rapids Assn. Commerce, United Spanish War Vets. (hon.), Beta Theta Pi. Republican. Mason (K.T.), Woodman. Clubs: Rotary, National Press, Peninsular, Spring Lake Country. Author: The Business of Government (municipal), 1916; Government as a Business, 1916; Kiltie McCoy, 1918; Reflections of an Editor, 1941. Contbr. to mags. Home: 1722 Burton St. S.E., Grand Rapids, Mich. Died Mar. 7, 1950; buried Woodlawn Cemetery, Grand Rapids.

SPARKS, George McIntosh, coll. pres.; b. Quitman, Ga., Nov. 19, 1888; s. Andrew J. and Julia Catherine (McIntosh) S.; A.B., M.A., Mercer, 1909, LL.D., 1933; grad. work, Emory U., Ga. Tech.; m. Mary Booth, Sept. 16, 1922; children—George McIntosh (dec.), Junelle, Charlene, Robert. With Macon Daily Telegraph and El Pasto Times, to 1920; mil. corr. Camp Harris, Camp Wheeler and Mexican border, Atlanta Constitution, Birmingham Age-Herald, Washington Times; Washington corr. So. newspapers, 1916-18; supt. of publicity and instr. Sch. of Journalism, Mercer U., 1919-23; prof. journalism and advt., Ga. Sch. of Tech., 1924-35, also dir. evening schs.; dir. Atlanta Div., U. of Ga. (formerly Univ. Extension Center) 1035-55; became pres. Ga. State College of Bus. Adminstrn., 1955, now ret. Asst. chancellor U. system of Ga., 1950-51. Chmn. Ga. State Tchrs. Retirement Bd., 1943——; mem. U. System Bldg. Authority, 1950——. Mem. exec. council Battle Haven Bd., 1950——. Mem. exec. council Soc. Bapt. Home Mission Bd., 1950——, Bapt. State Endowment Bd., 1950——. Mem. Mercer U. Alumni Assn. (sec. 1920-24), Am. Assn. of Univ. Evening Colls. (pres. 1942-43), Pi Delta Epsilon (past grand pres.), Alpha Delta Sigma, Phi Sigma Kappa. Baptist. Mason, Odd Fellow. Clubs: National Press (Washington); Ambassadors, Kiwanis. Author: Camp Cotton and Border, 1917; War Activities, 1920; 327th Under Fire, 1923; I's of 327th, 1924. Home: 50 Sheridan Dr., N.E. Office: 33 Gilmer St. S.E., Atlanta. Died Oct. 29, 1958.

SPARKS, Thomas Ayres, clergyman; b. Maysville, Ky., Sept. 11, 1881; s. James William and Minerva Jane Houston (McDowell) S.; A.B., Columbia U., 1912, A.M., 1913; B.D., Gen. Theol. Seminary, 1917, S.T.D., 1943. Engaged in business, 1899-1907. Ordained deacon and priest Episcopal Church, 1913; archdeacon Missionary Dist. of Salina, Kan., and associated positions there, 1913-16; Mayo fellow, Gen. Theol. Seminary, 1916-21; grad. student, Union Theol. Seminary and Columbia Univ., 1916-21; rector St. Clement's Ch., New York, 1918-30, Ch. of Good Shepherd, Rosemont, Pa., 1930-32; priest-in-charge Trinity Ch., New York City, 1932-35; special preacher Holyrood Ch., N.Y. City, 1936-38; on staff of Cathedral St. John the Divine, N.Y. City, since 1938, cathedral pastor, since 1942; canon pastor, 1943-52; sec. Gen. Convention Episcopal Church Committee on Deaconesses. Trustee Gen. Theological Seminary, New York Training School for Deaconesses. Mem. Alumni Assn. Gen. Theol. Seminary (pres. 1925-27), Am. Hist. Assn., King's Crown, Manhattan Neighborhood Assn. (trustee), Pilgrims of U.S., Delta Upsilon. Club: Columbia University (New York). Address: 4 W. 43d St., N.Y.C. 36. Died Nov. 9, 1954; cremated Ferncliffe Cemetery, Valhalla, N.Y.

SPARROW, Stanwood Williston, business exec.; b. Middleboro, Mass., Nov. 18, 1888; s. Samuel J. and Emma J. (Ward) S.; B.S. in Mech. Engring., Worcester Poly. Inst., 1911, D. Engring. (hon.), 1949; Engr. Stevens Duryea Co., 1911-14, Metz Co., 1914-17, Robert T. Pollock Co., 1917-18, Bureau Standards, 1918-26; dir. research Studebaker Corp., South Bend, Ind., 1945——. Mem. Soc. Automotive Engrs., Am. Soc. M.E., Am. Soc. Testing Materials, Soc. Automotive Engrs. (pres. 1949), A.A.A.S., Inst. Aero. Sciences. Republican. Conglist. Contbr. articles in S.A.E. Journal and reports for Nat. Adv. Com. for Aeronautics. Home: Morningside Hotel, South Bend 24. Office: care Studebaker Corp., South Bend, Ind. Died Aug. 14, 1952; buried Central Cemetary, Middleboro, Mass.

SPAULDING, Francis Trow, edn. commnr.; b. Ware, Mass., Nov. 23, 1896; s. Frank Ellsworth and Mary Elizabeth (Trow) S.; A.B., Harvard, 1916, Ed.M., 1921, Ed.D., 1926; A.M., Columbia Tchrs. Coll., 1926; LL.D., Lawrence Coll., 1943, Northeastern U., U. Buffalo, 1946, Alfred U., Rensselaer Polytech. Inst., 1949; Litt.D., Colgate U., 1948; m. Susan Chambers Thompson, June 19, 1922; children—Margaret Montague, Joan Stewart. Tchr., adminstrv. positions, various schs., 1916-17, 1919-24; instr. edn. Harvard, 1924-25, asst. prof., 1926-29, asso. prof., 1929-36, prof., 1936-45, asso. dean grad. sch. edn., 1939-40, dean, 1940-45; commnr. edn., pres. U. State N.Y., 1946——; lectr. secondary edn. Colmbia Tchrs. Coll., 1928-29; specialist in sch. orgn. Nat. Survey Secondary Edn., 1930-32; dir. study secondary edn. N.Y. State Regents Inquiry, 1936-38; trustee Gen. Edn. Bd., 1939-42; mem. Mass. State Adv. Bd. Edn., 1941-44. Sponsor Harvard Found. Advanced Study and Research, 1949——; chmn. div. edn. study Ford Found. on Policy and Program, 1948-49. Mem. War-Navy Commn., USAFI, 1946-47, one of founders USAFI; mem. N.Y. Vets. Affairs Commn., Commn. Accreditation of Service Experiences, Am. Council Edn., 1946-48; mem. VA Adminstrs. Spl. Commn. Vocational Rehabilitation, Edn., Tng. Problems, 1947-50. Mem. Bd. Visitors Air U.; mem. State Dept. Bd. Fgn. Scholarships. Trustee Am. Mus. Natural History. Served in U.S. Army Med. Dept., 1918-19; col. AUS, chief edn. br., 1942-46. Fellow Am. Acad. Arts and Scis.; mem. Am. Assn. Sch. Adminstrs., N.E.A., Nat. Soc. Study Edn., Phi Beta Kapp, Phi Delta Kappa, Kappa Delta Pi. Author numerous monographs, articles and reports on secondary edn. Home: 317 Loudenville Rd., Albany, N.Y. Office: State Edn. Dept., Albany 1, N.Y. Died Mar. 25, 1950.

SPAULDING, Huntley Nowell, ex-gov.; b. Townsend Harbor, Mass., Oct. 30, 1869; s. Jonas and Emeline (Cummings) S.; grad. Phillips Acad., Andover, Mass., 1889; m. Harriet Mason, Aug. 11, 1900. Pres. Internat. Leather Co.; chmn. bd. Spaulding Fibre Co., Inc., mfrs. leatherboard specialties, etc.; dir. United Fruit Co., 1st Nat. Bank, Rochester Trust Co. (Rochester, N.H.). Pres. bd. trustees Lawrence Acad., Groton, Mass.; trustee Tilton Sch., Tilton, N.H., Tufts College, Medford, Mass. Food adminstr. for N.H. during war period; chmn. N.H. Bd. Edn.; gov. of N.H., 1927-28. Received in May, 1944, the Charles Holmes Pettee Meml. Medal, which is awarded for outstanding service to the state, nation, or the world. Republican. Holds hon. degrees, M.A., LL.D., Sc.D. Home: Rochester, N.H. Died Nov. 14, 1955.

SPAULDING, John Cecil, lawyer; b. St. Johns, Mich., Jan. 7, 1879; s. Oliver Lyman and Mary Cecilia (Swegles) S.; A.B., U. Mich., 1897-98; LL.B., George Washington U., 1900, LL.M., 1901; m. Esther Dorothy Roehm, Oct. 25, 1916; children—William Lyman, Robert John. Admitted to Mich. bar, 1903, practiced in Detroit, 1903-51; mem. Miller, Canfield, Paddock Stone, 1927-50, counselor, 1950-51, ret. Mem. Beta Theta Pi. Episcopalian (chancellor Diocese Mich. 1936-53, now emeritus). Club: Detroit Boat. Home: 908 Glynn Ct., Detroit 2. Died Feb. 23, 1954.

SPAULDING, Sumner, architect and town planner; b Ionia, Mich., June 14, 1892; s. Lee Philo and Hannah (Harper) S.; student, U. of Mich., 1911-13; B.A., Mass. Inst. of Tech., 1916; m. Pauline Snyder, Apr. 20, 1918; 1 dau., Rosemary. Archtl. draughtsman, 1920; licensed architect, 1921; traveled and studied in Europe, 1921-26; in Mexico, 1942. Designer of country estates; Catalina Casino for William Wrigley, Jr.; Men's Campus, Pomona Coll.; Sch. of Medicine, Coll. of Med. Evangelists, Los Angeles; chmn. group Am. Inst. of Architects designer of country estates, housing projects, musea, hosps., schools, colleges etc. Mem. Nat. Housing Conf., Inc. Lectr. in architecture, U. of So. Calif. Scripps Coll., Claremont. Fellow A.I.A.; mem. Am. Soc. of Planning Ofcls., Capital Expenditures Com., Los Angeles Community Welfare Fedn. Office: Spaulding, Rex & DeSwart, Architects and Engineers, 3305 Wilshire Blvd., L.A. Died Apr. 10, 1952.

SPEAKMAN, G(eorge) Dixon, lawyer judge; b. Phila., Sept. 3, 1903; s. George Washington and Sarah Jane (Davis) S.; LL.B., Dickinson Sch. Law, 1927; m. Jane Cunningham, July 2, 1932; children—Jane Elizabeth, Ann Cunningham. Admitted to N. J. bar, 1928; partner Toner, Speakman & Crowley, Newark, since 1947; asso. prof. law Newark colls. Rutgers U., 1946-49; counsel, Essex County, 1947-51; judge Essex County Ct., 1951-53; judge Superior Ct. of N.J., 1953——. Mem. Am., N.J. State, Essex Co. bar assns., Lawyers Soc. of Essex (pres., 1936-37), Phi Delta Theta. Republican. Episcopalian. Mason. Clubs: Down Town (Newark); Racquets Short Hills (N.J.); Baltusrol Golf (Springfield, N J.). Asso. editor on N.J. Law Jour., 1946-51. Home: 30 Hillside Av., Short Hills. Office: Court House, Newark 2. Died Nov. 11, 1956.

SPEAR, Lawrence York, pres. Electric Boat Co.; b. Warren, O., Oct. 23, 1870; s. William Thomas and Frances Eliza (York) S.; grad. U.S. Naval Acad., 1890; B.Sc., U. Glastow, Scotland, 1893; m. Lilian Wing, June 2, 1902. Serve on U.S.S. Pensacola, Baltimore and Charleston in South Atlantic and South Pacific, 1890-91; employed in design sect. Bur. Constrn. and repair, 1893; asst. supt. constrn. U.S.S. Oregon and Olympia Union Iron Works, San Francisco, 1893-94; asst. constructor Mare Island Navy Yard, 1894-95; supt. constrn. Moran Bros., Seattle, 1895-98; constructor Bremerton Navy Yard, 1895-98; in charge Post-Grad. Sch. Naval Architecture, U.S. Naval Acad., 1898-99; supt. constrn. Crescent

Shipyard (Elizabeth, N.J.), Gas Engine and Power Co. and Charles L. Seabury & Co. Consol. (Morris Heights, N.Y.), 1899-1902; naval architect, tech. dir. charge design and constrn. Electric Boat Co., 1902-04, v.p., dir., 1904-42, pres., 1942—; chmn. bd., dir. Bed Rock Petroleum Co.; dir. Canadian Ltd. Mem. Am. Soc. Naval Architects and Marine Engrs., Am. Soc. Naval Engrs., Am. Soc. M.E. Clubs: Metropolitan, Wall Street (New York); Thames, Submarine Base Officers (New London, Conn.); Army and Navy (Washington); Army and Navy Country (Arlington, Va.). Home: 105 Gardner Av., New London, Conn. Office: Electric Boat Co., Groton, Conn. Died Sept. 16, 1950.*

SPEAR, Lewis Benson, dentist, educator; b. Evansville, Ind., June 28, 1888; s. Robert and Catherine (Evans) S.; student Purdue, 1905-06; D.D.S., Ind. U., 1917; m. Mary Louise Schrader, Apr. 15, 1925; children—Robert, Eloise, Richard Helton, Rosemary, Lewis Benson. Draftsman, machine design Nordyke & Marmon, Fairbanks, Morse Elec., Indpls., 1907-14; gen. practice dentistry, Indpls., 1917-18, radiodontia and oral diagnosis, 1918—; head dept. radiology Ind. U. Sch. Dentistry, 1920—, chmn. roentgenology, 1946—; cons. VA Regional Office, also VA Hosp. Mem. Am., Ind., Indpls. dental socs., Am. Acad. Oral Roentgenology, Acad. Internat. Dentistry, Delta Sigma Delta, Omicron Kappa Epsilon. Presbyn. Club: Torch International. Home: 4603 Presbyn. Club: Torch International. Home: 716 E. 60th St. Office: School of Dentistry, Indiana U., Indpls. Died Aug. 23, 1959; buried Crown Hill Cemetery, Indpls.

SPEARE, Dorothy, author; b. Newton Center, Mass; d. Edward Ray and Dorothy (Simmons) Speare; A.B., Smith Coll., 1919; grad. work at Radcliffe Coll., 1919-21; m. Franklin Butler Christmas, Nov. 17, 1924; m. 2d, Charles Joseph Hubbard, May 12, 1934. Sang in opera in Italy and France, 1926-27; made Am. debut in Mignon, at Washington, 1927; sang in concert and opera, 1927-30, when forced to abandon career through illness; scenario writer for Hollywood motion picture producers, 1931-34; writer, lectr., 1935—. Mem. P.E.N. Methodist. Author: Dancers in the Dark, 1922; The Gay Year, 1923; The Girl Who Cast Out Fear, 1925; A Virgin of Yesterday, 1925; Prima Donna (play), 1934; The Road to Needles, 1937; Spring on 52nd St., 1947. Contbr. to Sat. Eve. Post, Ladies' Home Jour., Cosmopolitan, Red Book, McCalls. Home: 61 Montvale Rd., Newton Center, Mass. Died Feb. 3, 1951; buried Newton Cemetery, Newton, Mass.

SPEARS, Raymond Smiley, author; b. Bellevue, O., Aug. 2, 1876; s. John R. and Celestia C. (Smiley) S.; ed. pub. schs.; m. C. Eleanor Shepard, July 14, 1904; children—Charles R., John S. Reporter on N.Y. Sun, 1896-1900; N.Y. Herald (summer resorts); walked from Utica, N.Y., to Va., then traveled in skiff down Holston and Tenn. rivers seeking material for articles for Forest and Stream, winter of 1901-02; traveled in skiff down the Mississippi River, later Chesapeake Bay, on Great Lakes, through Bad Lands of Dakota on motorcycle, to California and back by automobile; made 10,000-mile auto tour, 1927, in U.S., gathering facts for departments, fiction articles; connected with the Adirondack field work, Forest Dept. of N.Y., 1909-11; chief Am. Protective League, Herkimer County, N.Y. (Dept. Justice), 1917-18; pres. Am. Trappers' Assn.; mem. Am. Fiction Guild. Author: Camping on the Great River, 1912; Camping on the Great Lakes, 1913; The Cabin Boat Primer, 1913; Trip on the Great Lakes, 1913; The River Prophet, 1920; Diamond Tolls, 1920; Driftwood, 1921; Camping, Woodcraft and Wildcraft, 1924; Helpful Hints for Hikers, 1924; Waltzing Coyotes, 1927; Pete the Gunman (use of rifles), 1927; (motion pictures) Hoarded Assets; Janie of the Waning Glories; How to Be a Fur Trapper. Contbr. many short stories, travel series and articles in mags. On staff various mags. Home: Inglewood, Cal. Died Jan. 1950.

SPEASE, Edward (spēz), educator; b. Dresden, Muskingum County, O., Mar. 31, 1883; s. George Henry and Helena (Cox) S.; Ph.C., Ohio State U., 1905, B.Sc., 1907; Ph.M., Phila. Coll. Pharmacy and Sci., 1936; m. Alice Kelly, June 22, 1911. Began with Ohio State U. as student asst. in pharmacy, 1905, and continued as asst., 1907-08, instr., 1908-14, asst. prof., 1914-16, sec. Coll. of Pharmacy, 1915-16; dean sch. of pharmacy and prof. pharmacy, Western Res. U., 1916-40; dir. profl. relations Nat. Assn. Retail Druggists 1940-44. Registered pharmacist, 1905. Fellow A.A.A.S.; mem. Am. Pharm. Assn., O. State Pharm. Assn., Nat. Assn. Retail Druggists, Cleve. Acad. Medicine, No. O. Druggists' Assn., Phi Delta Chi; 3d v.p. U.S. Pharm. Conv., 1930-40. Directing pharmacist U. Hosps., Cleve., 1932-40; adv. med. advt., Scheel Advt. Agy., Cleve. Republican. Episcopalian. Mason. Author: Lecutres on Pharmaceutical Mathematics; Textbook on Pharmaceutical Mathematics; also author of law setting Ohio standards for pharm. edn. Co-author: Minimum Standards for Hospital Pharmacies, 1936. Home: 12 John Clark Lane, Hudson, O. Died Oct. 12, 1957; buried Dresden. O.

SPEED, Keats, newspaper man; b. Louisville, Ky., Sept. 23, 1879; s. George K. and Jane (Ewing) S.; student U. of Va., 1896-97, Central U. of Ky., 1897-99; m. Florence Chenault, Mar. 17, 1907. Began as reporter in N.Y. City, 1899, later dramatic critic; city editor, 1906-07, mng. editor, 1907-12, New York Evening Journal; editor Hearst's Atlanta Georgian, 1912-14; mng. editor New York Press, 1914-16, and after consolidation of Sun and Press, 1916, mng. editor New York Sun; mng. editor New York Herald, 1923-24; mng. editor New York Sun, 1924-43, exec. editor 1943-50. Died Mar. 1, 1952.

SPEED, Kellogg, surgeon; b. Cleve., Jan. 17, 1879; s. Henry Bryant and Anna (Robb) S.; B.S., U. Chgo., 1901, grad. scholar in chemistry, 1901-02; M.D., Rush Med. Coll., 1904; m. 2d, Margaret Rudd, Mar. 14, 1918; children—(1st marriage) Bertha Brown (Mrs. Wm. J. Pringle, Jr.), Janet Brown (Mrs. Francis Woodworth); (2d marraige) Patricia Rudd, Helen Marjorie (Mrs. Jas. H. Hensinger), Ann (Mrs. E. O. Booth, Jr.). Began practice at Chgo., 1905; former prof. surgery, U. Ill. (Rush), now clin. prof. surgery emeritus; attending surgeon Presbyn. Highland Park, Lake Forest hosps.; cons. surgeon U.S. Naval Hosp., Great Lakes, Ill. Hon. lt. col. R.A. M.C., British E.F., France, in charge surg. div. Gen. Hosp. No. 23, 1916; maj. and lt. col. M.C., A.E.F., in France, 1917-19 Citation U. Chgo. Alumni Assn., 1942. Trustee Rush Med. College. Diplomate Am. Bd. of Surgery (Founder's mem.), Am. Bd. Orthopedic Surgery. Fellow A.C.S. (mem. bd. govs.); mem. Am., Western (pres. 1927-28), Central surg. assns., Chgo. Surg. Soc. (pres. 1925-26), Am. Orthopedic Assn., Am. Assn. for Surgery of Trauma (1st pres. 1938-39). Société Internat. de Chirurgie, Beta Theta Pi, Nu Sigma Nu, Alpha Omega Alpha, Sigma Xi; hon. mem. Los Angeles Mpls., Seattle surg. socs., Am. Acad. Orthopedic Surgeons. Republican. Presbyn. Clubs: University, Tavern, Chicago, Exmoor Country. Author: Text Book of Fractures and Dislocations, 1916 (4 edits.); Taumatic Injuries of the Carpus, 1925; Primer on Fractures for A.M.A. (6 edits). Mem. editorial bd. Ill. State Med. Jour. Home: 1502 Sheridan Rd., Highland Park, Ill.; also 1907 Ocean Way, Laguna Beach, Cal. Died July 2, 1955; buried Chgo.

SPEED, William Shallcross, mfr.; b. Louisville, Ky., Sept. 10, 1873; s. James Breckinridge and Cora A. (Coffin) S.; B.S., Rose Poly. Inst., 1895, M.S., 1897, M.E., 1899, D.E., 1933; Sc.D., University of Louisville, 1950; married Virginia Perrin, November 16, 1904; children—Alice Helen (Mrs. Berry V. Stoll), Virginia Herndon (Mrs. Richard W. Condon). Asst. to pres. Louisville Cement Co., 1895-1904, v.p., 1904-12, pres., 1912-39, chmn. bd., 1939—; pres. Beaver Dam Coal Co.; chmn. bd. Black Star Coal Corporation, Pioneer Coal Company. Trustee Louisville Collegiate School. Mem. American Society Mechanical Engineers, Alpha Tau Omega. Republican. Episcopalian. Clubs: Pendennis, Engineers and Architects, Louisville Country, River Valley, Everglades. Home: 2828 Lexington Rd. Office: 501 S. Second St., Louisville 2. Died Dec. 8, 1955.

SPEER, James Henry, ch. ofcl.; b. Limestone, Pa., June 11, 1867; s. James Washington and Mary Ann (Henry) S.; grad. Park Coll., Parkville, Mo., 1893, D.D., 1908; student Western Theol. Sem., Pitts., 1893-95; grad. McCormick Theol. Sem., Chgo., 1896; m. Mary Catherine Titzel, May 12, 1896 (died Aug. 1898); 1 dau., Mary Catherine; m. 2d, Jessie A. Irvin, Oct. 10, 1900 (died July 1915); m. 3d, Margaret Caldwell Gehrett, Aug. 1, 1917; 1 son, Lloyd Gehrett. Ordained ministry Presbyn. Ch. in U.S.A., 1896; pastor successively Gardner, Kan., North Ch., Denver, Colo., San Bernardino, Cal., First Union Ch., N.Y., Webb City, Mo., Orange, Cal., until 1916; supt. Home Missions, Mo., 1913-14; supt. Los Angeles (Cal.) Presbytery, 1916-19; sec. New Era Movement, Pacific Coast, 1919-21; sec. Eastern Dist. Gen. Council, 1921-24; asso. sec. Gen. Council, 1925-29; exec. sec. Ch. Extension Bd. of Mpls. Presbytery, 1929; formerly pres. Mpls. Ch. Fed., now exec. sec.; pastor Meth. Ch., Mound, Minn., 1940-43; founding minister St. James Presbyn. Ch., 1943-46, pastor emeritus, 1946—. Clubs: Chi Alpha, Automobile. Contbr. to religious publs. Home: 2889 San Pasqual St., Pasadena 10, Cal. Died Feb. 2, 1952; buried Mt. View Mausoleum, Pasadena, Cal.

SPEER, Robert Kenneth, educator; b. Peterboro, Ont., Can., Aug. 11, 1898; s. William Wilson and Mary (Stryker) S.; came to U.S., 1914, naturalized, 1924; B.S., Mich. State Normal Coll., 1921; M.A., Tchrs. Coll. Columbia, 1922, Ph.D., 1928; m. Margaret Helen Harrison, Sept. 1930; children—Robert Michael, Margaret Patricia; m. 2d, Alice Blanche Keenan Hopkins, July 1944; 1 step-son—Bernard Neal. Tchrs., prin. rural schs., Mich., 1915-18; asst. dir. div. reference and research Bd. Edn., Cleve. 1922-23; prin. elementary and jr. high sch., Montclair, N.J., 1923-24; asst. dir. bur. ednl. service Tchrs. Coll. Columbia, 1924-28; asst. prof. Sch. Edn. N.Y.U., 1928-29, asso. prof., 1929-30, prof., 1930-52, mem. div. advanced study, 1952-57, with the department of administration and supervision, 1957—; supr. tng. Sperry Gyroscope Co., 1944-45. Served as cpl. U.S. Army, World War I. Mem. N.E.A., Am. Assn. Sch. Adminstrs., Assn. Supervision and Curriculum Development, Am. Assn. U. Profs., Chi Delta, Phi Delta Kappa, Kappa Delta Pi. Author: Measurement of Appreciation in Poetry, Prose and Art, 1928; Science in the New Education, 1936; Supervision in the Elementary School, 1938; Education and Society, 1942; Living in Ancient Times, 1946; Backgrounds of American Living, 1947; How We Became Americans, 1947. Co-author: Supervision in the Elementary School; Science in the New Education, Education in Society. Editor and co-author: National Achievement Tests, 1940. Editor: Life Around Us, 1948; Better Spelling Series (4 books), 1947-48; City and Country Arithmetic Series (3 books), 1947, 48. Home: 194-01 D 64 Circle, Fresh Meadow, N.Y.C. Died Aug. 9, 1959; buried L.I. Nat. Cemetery.

SPEER, William H., lawyer, banker; b. Jersey City, N.J., Oct. 21, 1868; s. William H. and Eleanor C. (Brinkerhoff) S.; student Hasbrouck Inst., Jersey City; Columbia U., class 1891; LL.D., John Marshall Law Sch., Jersey City, 1930; m. Merretta Kirby, Jan. 10, 1900; children—John Kirby (dec.) William H. (dec.), Eleanor (Mrs. Charles H. Seydel). Admitted to N.J. bar, 1891, and practiced in Jersey City, 1891-1923, Newark 1923—; mem. firm Linn & Speer; judge, Circuit Cts. of N.J., 1908-23; Prosecutor of the pleas for Hudson County, N.J., 1903-08; gen. atty. Pub. Service Corp. of N.J., 1923-48, dir. co. and its affiliates 1924-56; pres., dir. Middlesex Water Co.; pres., dir. Plainfield Union Water Co. until 1957, Counsel, 1957—. Mem. bd. mgrs., exec. com. The Provident Savings Instn. of Jersey City. Trustee and mem. exec. com. The Trust Co. of N.J. Pres. N.J. Inst. for Practicing Lawyers; trustee Stevens Inst. Tech. Mem. Am. and N.J. bar assns. Republican. Presbyn. Clubs: Morristown. Home: Sand Spring Rd., New Vernon, N.J. Office: 80 Park Pl., Newark 1. Died July 8, 1959; buried Brookside Cemetery, Englewood, N.J.

SPEIDEL, Merritt Charles (spi-dĕl), editor, publisher; b. Port Jervis, Orange County, N.Y., May 19, 1879; s. Martin and Hannah Speidel; ed. pub. and private schools, N.Y. State; m. Edna Meredith, Apr. 24, 1912; children—Robert Meredith, Marjorie Jean, (now Mrs. Joseph O. Edy, Junior), and Merritt Charles Junior. Interested in journalism since boyhood; began with Tri-States Pub. Co., Port Jervis, becoming editor Port Jervis Daily Union, then business mgr. and dir. of company; corr. of Asso. Press and N.Y. papers, also wrote for mags.; writer, later editor, Erie Men, 1900; mem. auxiliary editorial bd. Success Mag., 1909; purchased and editor Piqua (O.) Daily Call, 1910-21; purchased Iowa City Press-Citizen, 1921; founder Speidel Newspapers, Inc., national newspaper service and research organ., 1937; a founder, 1932, and since dir. First Capital Nat. Bank, Iowa City; moved to Palo Alto, Calif., 1937; pres. Speidel Newspapers, Inc., 1937-57; pres. emeritus, 1957—, of a transcontinental group, including Visalia (Cal.) Newspapers, Inc., Press-Citizen Co. (Iowa City), Chillicothe (O.) Newspapers, Inc., Salinas (Calif.) Newspapers, Inc., Fort Collins (Colo.) Newspapers, Inc., Reno (Nev.) Newspapers, Inc., Poughkeepsie (N.Y.) Newspapers, Inc. Active in civic affairs in the various states; mem. governing bd. of Nat. Council Boy Scouts Am.; trustee Saints and Sinners; a founder, dir. Culver Fathers Assn. (Culver Military Acad.); life mem. Rotary, Sigma Delta Chi, Beta Gamma Sigma. Member Navy League of U.S., National Editorial Assn., California Press Assn., California Newspaper Editors Assn., Am. Museum Natural History (N.Y.C.), Am. Newspaper Pubs. Assn. Mason (32°, K.T., Scottish Rite, Shriner). Elk. Clubs: National Press (Washington); Illinois Athletic, Press (Chgo.); Commonwealth of California, Press and Union League (life) (San Francisco); Greater Los Angeles Press; Stanford University Associates (Nat.). Office: P.O. Box 270, Palo Alto, Cal. Died Mar. 21, 1960.

SPEIDEL, Thomas D., univ. prof.; b. Iowa City, Ia., Feb. 19, 1908; s. George Paul and Emily Helen (Glenn) S.; D.D.S., U. Ia., 1930, M.S., 1934; m. Edna Warweg, Dec. 27, 1934; children—Thomas Michael, John Joseph, Ann Elizabeth. Research asst. dentistry, pediatrics, U. Ia., 1932-34, asso. prof. orthodontics, 1936-41; asst. prof. orthodontics, U. Tenn., 1934-36; prof. orthodontics Ind. U., 1941-44; dean Sch. Dentistry, Loyola U., New Orleans, 1945-48; prof. orthodontics U. Minn., 1948—. Mem. Am. Dental Assn. (com. on library and indexing), Am. Assn. Orthodontists (chmn. com. research, pres. central sect., 1956-57), Am. Assn. Dental Editors (pres. 1947-48), Am. Coll. Dentists, Sigma Xi, Omicron Kappa Upsilon (nat. pres. 1944-46), Catholic. Editor: Jour. Dental Edn., Am. Assn. Dental Schs., 1940-47; bd. editors, Internat. Assn. for Dental Research. Home: 5062 Garfield Av. S., Mpls. Died Nov. 30, 1957.

SPELLACY, Thomas Joseph (spĕl'á-sī), lawyer; b. Hartford, Conn., Mar. 6, 1880; s. James and Catherine (Bourke) S.; student Holy Cross Coll., Worcester, Mass., 1898-99; LL.B., Georgetown U., D.C., 1901, LL.D., 1920; m. 2d, Elisabeth B. Gill, Aug. 23, 1934; 1 son, Bourke. Practiced law in Hartford since 1903;

mem. Spellacy and Aron, Hartford. U.S. dist. atty., 1915-19; asst. atty. gen. of U.S., 1919-21. Mem. Conn. Senate, 1907-11; del. Dem. Nat. Conv., 1912, del.-at-large, 1920, 23, 1936-40 (chmn. com. on rules 1920). Mayor of Hartford 4 terms, Dec. 5, 1935-June 18, 1943 (resigned); insurance commissioner for state of Connecticut. Dem. nominee for gov. of Conn., 1918; apptd. mem. commn. to demobolize U.S. Navy in Europe; served as legal adviser in Europe to Franklin D. Roosevelt, asst. sec. of Navy, in settlement of naval affairs in Europe, growing out of World War. Eastern mgr. for Dem. Nat. Com., presdl. election, 1924; mem. Metropolitan Dist. Commn. for Hartford County. Chairman Park River Flood Commission. Member of the Am., Conn. State and Hartford County bar assns. Roman Catholic. Home: 422 Farmington Av., Hartford, Conn. Office: 36 Pearl St., Hartford 3, Conn. Died Dec. 5, 1957.

SPENCE, Kenneth Monroe, lawyer; b. N.Y.C., Jan. 18, 1886; s. Lewis Henry and Anna (Tuthill) S.; A.B., Columbia, 1906, LL.B., 1909; m. LaBelle Dunlap, Sept. 6, 1917 (dec. May 22, 1939); children—Kenneth Monroe, Lewis Henry, Patricia; m. 2d Katharine Burns Richards, July 1, 1941. Admitted to N.Y. bar, 1909, since practiced in N.Y.C.; mem. Spence, Hotchkiss, Parker & Duryee, 1915-56; asso. counsel Lowenstein, Pitcher, Spence, Hotchkiss, Amann & Parr; asst. U.S. atty., 1912-15; spl. asst. atty. gen. State N.Y., asso. counsel Austin G. Fox, representing group lawyers who protested nomination Louis D. Brandeis for justice Supreme Ct., 1916. Dir. Internal Elevating Co., Manhattan Eye, Ear and Throat Hosp. Mayor, Lawrence, L.I., 1930-34. Served as 1st lt., A.A.F., World War I; legal staff Gen. Charles G. Dawes, 1918-19. Mem. Am. Coll. Trial Lawyers Assn. Bar City N.Y., Am., N.Y. State bar assns. Clubs: Univ., Century Assn., Downtown Assn. (N.Y. City). Home: 215 E. 72d St., N.Y.C. 21. Office: 25 Broad St., N.Y.C. Died Apr. 1957.

SPENCER, Charles Eldridge, Jr., banker; b. New Brunswick, N.J., Dec. 19, 1882; s. Charles Eldridge and Sarah A. (Conover) S.; ed. Rutger's Prep. Sch.; m. Olive Marion Tuttle, Oct. 10, 1912; children—Margaret Tuttle, Charles Eldridge, III, Patricia Tuttle, Carlisle Tuttle. With National Bank of New Jersey, 1900-03, National Bank of Commerce, New York, 1903-05, National Bank of Commerce, Kansas City, Mo., 1905-06, Trust Co. of America, New York, 1906-07; asst. treas. and treas. Colonial Trust Co., Waterbury, Conn., 1907-18; dep. gov. Federal Reserve Bank of Boston, 1918-20; v.p. First Nat. Bank of Boston, 1920-38, dir. since 1937, pres., 1938-47, chmn. bd. since 1947; pres., dir. First of Boston Internat. Corp. (N.Y.); trustee Am. Optical Co.; chmn. bd., Bay State Corp.; dir. Eastern Malleable Iron Co., United-Carr Fastener Corp., French Am. Banking Corp., Arthur D. Little, Inc., N.E. Tel. & Tel. Co., Reed & Barton, United Shoe Machinery Corp. Trustee of permanent funds, The Mass. Soc. for Prevention of Cruelty to Animals, also dir.; trustee The Children's Hosp.; director Am. Humane Edn. Soc.; trustee Mass. Foundation. Mem. Federal Advisory Council to represent First Federal Reserve Dist. Mem. (life), Corp. of Mass. Inst. Tech.; member com. to visit Dept. Economics, Harvard Coll. Clubs: Algonquin (Boston); Country (Brookline); Union League (New York). Home: 172 Beacon St., Boston 16. Office: 67 Milk St., Boston. Died Jan. 18, 1953; buried Naugatuck, Conn.

SPENCER, Frank E(dwin), business exec.; b. Centralia, Ill., Mar. 13, 1884; s. Nathaniel Walker and Fanny (Still) S.; B.A., Northwestern U., 1905; student Harvard, 1908; m. Mildred Garvin Auten, Feb. 18, 1911; children—Francis Auten, Mildred Still (Mrs. John R. Snyder). Advt. solicitor Chicago Tribune, 1905; instr., coach various boys' schs., 1905-11; salesman and partner W. W. Martin & Co., Chicago, 1911-16; office mgr., later gen. mgr. Anderson & Gustafson, Inc., 1916-21; v.p. Gustafson & Spencer, 1921-22; est. Spencer Petroleum Co., Chicago, pres. since 1922; pres. Spencer Petroleum Div. of Socony Vacuum Oil Co., since 1942; v.p. and dir. Mo. Valley Oil Co., 1926-44. Director Transportation Bank of Chicago, 1920-30. Chmn. Northwestern U. Alumni Foundation, 1935-37; pres. Gen. Alumni Assn., Northwestern U., 1942-43; mem. bd. trustees, 1943-47. Recipient Aladdin's Lamp Award, Oil-Heat Inst. Am., 1945; Merit Award, Northwestern U. Alumni Assn., 1944. Member Petroleum Ind. Twenty-Five Year Club; Ill. Senior Golf Assn.; nat. chmn. Dist. Div. Oil Heat Inst. of Am., 1943-45. Mem. Burning Oil Distribrs. Assn. (pres. 1933-47, dir.), Am. Petroleum Inst.; chmn. Met. Chicago Fuel Oil Industry Com., 1948; chmn. Petroleum Div., Chicago Community Fund, 1942-43. Republican. Methodist. Mason (32° K.T., Shriner). Clubs: Chicago Oil Men's, Chicago Athletic; Bobolink Golf (Highland Park); Executives (Chicago; dir., 1946-48); University (Evanston). Retired 1950. Home: Strawberry Landing on Silver Lake, Wautoma, Wis. Died Nov. 6, 1952.

SPENCER, Frank Robert, physician and surgeon; b. Burlington, Ia., June 12, 1879; s. Dr. Robert Spencer and Alice (Kendall) S.; A.B., U. Mich., 1900, M.D., 1902; m. Edith Clayton, Apr. 5, 1911; children—Donald Clayton, John Robert. Began as physician and surgeon, 1902; asst., Med. Faculty, U. Mich., 1902-04; mem. Med. Faculty, U. Colo., 1905-—; now prof. emeritus otolaryngology. Served as capt., Med. Corps, U.S. Army during World War I. Pres. Colo. State Bd. of Med. Examiners, 1924-26. Fellow Am. Coll. Surgeons, Am. Otol. Soc., Am. Laryngol. Assn. (pres. 1947), Am. Laryngol., Rhinol. and Otol. Soc., Am. Acad. of Ophthalmology and Otolaryngology (pres. 1941; mem. sect. on instrn., 1923-26), Sect. of Laryngology, Otology and Rhinology of A.A. (chmn. of sect., 1928). Charter mem. Am. Bd. of Otolaryngology; mem. Colo. Otolaryngol. Soc. (past pres.). Colo. State Med. Soc. (past pres.), Denver Clin. and Pathol. Soc. (asso.), Sigma Xi, Phi Gamma Delta, Nu Sigma Nu (former mem. exec. grand council). Republican. Episcopalian. Clubs: Boulder Rotary (past pres.). Author of textbook on Laryngeal Tuberculosis; also author more than 75 articles in med. jours.; contbr. to textbook on nose, throat and ear and their diseases; also to Ency. of Medicine. Formerly mem. editorial bd. of Laryngoscope, St. Louis. Home: 427 Pine St. Office: Physicians Bldg., 2111 14th St., Boulder, Colo. Died 1957.

SPENCER, Herbert Lincoln, found. exec.; born Whitney Point, N.Y., July 13, 1894; s. William Henry and Ida Dell (Adriance) S.; B.S., Carnegie Inst. Tech., 1921; LL.D., Pa. Coll. for Women, 1946; M.A., Ph.D., U. Pitts., 1934, LL.D., 1948; L.H.D., Bucknell, 1953; m. Mildred Louise Pollard, June 6, 1916; children—Nancy Lynn (Mrs. L. D. Schaller), Sally Louise. Mech. engr. various indsl. orgns., 1916-21; vice prin. and tchr., Latimer Jr. High Sch., Pitts., 1922-27; vice-prin. Henry Clay Frick Tng. Sch. for Tchrs., Pitts., 1927-28, prin. 1928-34; dean Coll. Liberal Arts and Sciences, U. Pitts., 1934-35; pres. Pa. Coll. for Women, Pitts., 1935-45; pres. Bucknell U. (Lewisburg), 1945-49; exec. v.p. and trustee Samuel H. Kress Found., N.Y.C. 1949-—; dir. Chemecon Corp., Log Cabin Assoc., N.C., N.Y.U. Bellevue Med. Center Coordinator Pitts. Engineering, Science and Management War Training, U.S. Office of Education, 1941-44; ednl. expert for U.S. Army's A.S.T.P.; apptd. to 4th Naval Dist. Navy Manpower Survey Com., U.S. Navy; chmn. coll. and univ. sect. Pittsburgh Defense Council, 1941; chmn. edn. div., blood donors com., Pitts. A.R.C.; mem. Pa. Aero. Commn. Civilian engr., A.C., U.S. Army, World War I. Trustee Bucknell U., Crozer Theol. Sem.; dir. Devitt's Camp. Pres. Pitts. Child Guidance Clinic, Inc., Pitts., Personnel Assn. Dir. Metropolitan Y.M.C.A., Fedn. Social Agencies, Frick Ednl. Commission, Pitts. Acad. Science and Art, Lewisburg Trust & Safe Deposit Bank, Geisinger Hospital; pres. Pa. Assn. Colls. and Univs., 1948; mem. Joint State Govt. Commn. on Higher Education; chmn. Pittsburgh Edn. Com. of Nat. Assn. Mfrs., Exceptionally Able Youths Com., Civic Club of Allegheny County. Mem. N.E.A., A.A.A.S., Pa. State Edn. Assn., mem. Pa. Displaced Persons Commn., Am. Society Mechanical Engineers, Am. Society Engineering Education, Society Advancement Management, Regional War Labor Bd., bd. trustees, Kiskiminetas Springs Sch., Photographic Soc. of Am., Pa. Society of New York, Phi Beta Kappa, Phi Eta Sigma, Phi Delta Kappa, Kappa Phi Kappa, Iota Lambda Sigma, Phi Kappa Phi, Phi Sigma Pi, Delta Tau Deta, Omicron Delta Kappa, Tau Beta Pi, Phi Beta Kappa Assos., Scabbard and Blade. Registered profl. engr. Pa. Mason (33°). Clubs: Century Associates, Rotary (dir.), University (dir.). Home: Newfoundland, Pa. Office: 221 W. 57th St., N.Y.C. Died Jan. 1960.

SPENCER, J. Brookes, business exec.; b. St. Louis, Jan. 15, 1888; s. Selden P. and Mary Susan (Brookes) S.; A.B., Yale, 1910; m. Elma Sanderson, Nov. 3, 1917; children—Susan Elma (Mrs. Thomas T. Brooks, Jr.), Jane Brookes (Mrs. Daniel B. Clark). V.p. Am. Brake Shoe Co. 1937-—. Clubs: Chicago, Cloud, Old Elm (Chgo.); Racquet (St. Louis); Yale, (New York); Woodway Country (Conn.); Princess Anne Country (Norfolk). Home: 15 Park Av. Office: 230 Park Av., New York City 17. Died Nov. 18, 1959.

SPENCER, John, newspaper editor; b. Henrico Co., Va., Feb. 21, 1885; s. Charles and Almedia (Rudd) S.; student Newport News Mil. Acad.; Coll. of William and Mary, 1901-03; m. Florine Bradley, Dec. 13, 1906. Reporter, city editor Newprot News Times-Herald and Daily Press, 1910-17; with Asso. Press, Washington, 1917-24; city editor Norfolk Virginian-Pilot, 1924-41, mng. editor, 1941-—. Mem. Am. Soc. Newspaper Editors, Asso. Press Mng. Editors Assn., Va. Asso. Press (chmn. 1952-53). Club: Norfolk (Va.) Rotary. Home: Apt. 4, 623 Fairfax Av., Norfolk 7. Office: Norfolk Newspapers, Inc., 150 W. Brambleton Av., Norfolk 10, Va. Died Oct. 29, 1957; buried Forestlawn Cemetery, Norfolk.

SPENCER, John Mitchell, business exec.; b. Piqua, O., June 10, 1883; s. Moses G. and Mary Elizabeth (Mitchell) S.; grad. Wooster Coll., 1905; m. Caroline McCulloch, 1906; children—John Mc., David Mc. With Hobart Mfg. Co. 1905-—, beginning as bookkeeper and becoming pres. 1938. Home: Drury Lane. Office: Pennsylvania Av. at Simpson St., Troy, O. Died June 30, 1954.

SPENCER, Kenneth Aldred, mining engr.; b. Columbus, Kan., Jan. 25, 1902; s. Charles Favor and Clara (Hughes) S.; ed. Kan. State Normal, Culver Mil. Acad.; A.B., U. of Kan., 1926; m. Helen Elizabeth Foresman, Jan. 6, 1927. Began as jr. engr., Pittsburg & Midway Coal Mining Co., Kansas City, Mo., 1925, chief engr., 1936-38, gen. mgr. and chief engr., 1938-40, gen. mgr. and treas., 1940-43, pres., since 1943, operating strip coal mines, in Kansas, Mo., Colo., Ky.; pres. Spencer Chem. Co. (formerly Mil. Chem. Works, Inc.), Kansas City, Mo., 1941-59, chairman and chief executive officer, 1959-—; dir. Goodyear Tire & Rubber Co., Internat. Harvester Co., Chgo., Mo.-Kan.-Tex. R.R., St. Louis, Gustin-Bacon Mfg. Co., Kansas City; First Nat. Bank of Kansas City (Mo.), Armco Steel Corp., The Am. Telephone & Tel. Co. Mem. bus. adv. council Dept. Commerce. Awarded citation for outstanding achievement by U. Kan., 1943. Trustee Research Found., U. Kansas. Dir. Nat. Coal Assn.; bd. govs. Midwest Research Inst. Mem. Am. Inst. Mining and Metall. Engrs., Beta Theta Pi, Sigma Gamma Epsilon. Republican. Methodist. Clubs: Kansas City Country, Kansas City, University River (Kansas City); Union League (Chgo.); River, Chemists, Metropolitan, Pinnacle (New York City); Racquet (St. Louis); Metropolitan (Washington). Home: 2900 Verona Rd., Kansas City 15. Office: Dwight Bldg., Kansas City 5, Mo. Died Feb. 20, 1960.

SPENCER, Mrs. Lilian White, writer; b. Albany, N.Y.; d. Frederick William and Catherine Teresa (McGurk) White; ed. in French convents. Mem. Poetry Soc. Am., Colo. Hist. Soc., Denver Art Mus., Archaeol. Soc. N.M., Archaeol. Soc. Colo.; hon. mem. Poetry Soc. Colo., Allied Arts Soc., Sigma Alpha Iota. Began as writer for newspapers, stage and cinema; several plays and moving pictures produced. Author: Astronomy Without a Telescope (textbook), 1925; Pageant of Colorado, prod. Denver, 1927; Pageant of York, produced in York, Pa., 1927; Arrowheads (verse), 1930; The Sun-Bride, grand opera on Pueblo Indian theme (music by Charles Sanford Skilton), broadcast N.Y.C., 1929, also presented before various convs. and by U. Denver, 1935. Nat. broadcast with cast of 60, of "Mesa Verde," romantic play with music (by Charles Wakefield Cadman), 1933. Published series of essays on Am. archaeology and Antiquity of Man in America and many poems on authentic Indian themes. Extensive contbr. of verse to mags. (Atlantic, Forum, Nation, Poetry, North American Review, London Spectator); also many translations of French poetry. Won two nat. poetry prizes. Has made detailed study Am. Indian from poetic and hist. standpoints and is a spl. authority on the great Chief Ouray (Ute—New Mexico—Colorado—1833-1880) and his times. Author: Bright Arrow (biography of chief Ouray). Home: Oceanside, Cal. Died June 23, 1953.

SPENCER, Niles, artist; b. Pawtucket, R.I., May 16, 1893; s. Henry Lewin and Margaret Sterling (Allen) S.; student, R.I. Sch. of Design, Art Students' League; student under George Bellows, Robert Henri. Held one-man exhbns.: Daniel Gallery, 1925, 28; Downtown Gallery, N.Y. City, 1947; rep. collections; Albright Art Gallery, Buffalo; Ann Arbor Art Assn.; Columbus (O.) Museum; Field Foundation; Brooklyn Mus., Metropolitan Mus., Mus. of Modern Art, N.Y. City, and others. Awarded: hon. mention, Carnegie Internat., 1930, purchase prize, Metropolitan, 1942. Mem. Artists Equity, An American Group. Home: Dingman's Ferry, Pa. Died May 15, 1952; buried Pawtucket, R.I.

SPENCER, Samuel Riley, educator; b. Sanger, Tex., July 11, 1874; s. John and Francis (Cowling) S.; grad. Decatur (Tex.) Bapt. Coll., 1905; A.B., Baylor U., 1911; student U. of Chicago 3 summers, Yale, 1915-16; Ph.D., U. of Ia., 1925; m. Cora Penn, Dec. 23, 1900. Prof. physics, Baylor U., since 1917, also dean of coll., 1917-24. Mem. City Commn. Waco, 1925-27; chmn. Waco City Water Bd., 1929-41. Mem. Am. Physical Soc., Sigma Xi. Democrat. Baptist. Mason. Contbr. papers on physical chemistry. Home: 821 Speight Av., Waco, Tex. Died June 18, 1953; buried Decatur, Tex.

SPERRY, Leavenworth Porter, business exec.; born Waterbury, Conn., May 16, 1883; s. Mark Leavenworth and Julia Sherman (Porter) S.; student Waterbury High Sch., 1895-98, Hotchkiss Sch., 1898-99; Ph.B., Sheffield Scientific Sch. (Yale), 1902; grad. student Mass. Inst. Tech., 1902-03; m. Olive Smith, Feb. 15, 1912; children—Richard Smith (dec.), Mark Leavenworth, 2d, Olive Ives (dec.), Catherine Leavenworth (dec.), Leavenworth Porter, Jr. In employ Scovill Mfg. Co., 1903-58, served as pres., treas. and dir. to 1955, chmn. bd., 1955-58, ret.; formerly chairman bd. and dir. A. Scrader's Son, Inc., Hamilton Beach Mfg. Co.; pres. and dir. Mad River Co.; dir. Lone Star Cement Corp., Waterbury Cos., Inc., Citizens and Mfrs. Nat. Bank, Mfrs. Mutual Fire Ins. Co.; mem. Nat. Indus. Conf. Bd. Alderman, Waterbury, Conn., 1910-11; mem. Bd. of Health, 1910-11, mem. Charter Commn., 1929-30. Mem. exec. com. Yale Alumni Bd. Trustee Waterbury Hospital; dir. St. Mary's Hosp. (Waterbury). Mem. Soc. of Cincinnati, Sigma Xi.

Republican. Clubs: Graduate (New Haven); Waterbury, Country (Waterbury); Yale (New York). Address: 154 Buckingham St., Waterbury, Conn. Died Nov. 22, 1958; buried Riverside Cemetery, Waterbury, Conn.

SPERRY, Willard Learoyd, theologian; b. Peabody, Mass., Apr. 5, 1882; s. Willard Gardner and Henrietta (Learoyd) S.; B.A., Olivet (Mich.) Coll., 1903; B.A., Oxford Univ., Eng. (Rhodes scholar), 1907 (1st class honor in Theology); M.A., same, 1912; M.A., Yale, 1909; D.D., Yale, 1922, Amherst, 1923, Brown, 1928, Williams, 1935, Harvard, 1941; D.Litt., Boston U., 1939; m. Muriel Bennett, Dec. 15 1908; 1 dau., Henrietta (Mrs. R. M. Wilson). Ordained Congl. ministry, 1908; asst. pastor 1st Ch., Fall River, Mass., 1908-13, pastor, 1913; pastor Central Ch., Boston, 1914-22; lecturer and prof. practical theology, Andover Theol. Sem., 1917-25; dean Divinity Sch., Harvard, prof. practical theology, 1922—; mem. bd. of preachers, Harvard, 1921—, chmn. bd. and Plummer prof. Christian Morals, 1929—; dean of Nat. Council on Religion in Higher Education, 1927-31. Upton lecturer, Manchester Coll., Oxford (Eng.), 1927; Hibbert lecturer in England, 1927; Essex Hall lecturer, London, 1927; Lyman Beecher lecturer, Yale, 1937; trustee Vassar College, 1942-46. Fellow American Academy of Arts and Sciences, 1927. Clubs: Century (New York City); Faculty (Cambridge, Mass.). Author: The Disciplines of Liberty, 1921; Reality in Worship, 1925; The Paradox of Religion (Hibbert lectures)), 1927; The Divine Reticence, 1927; Signs of These Times, 1929; "Yes, But," 1931; What You Owe Your Child, 1935; Wordsworth's Anti-Climax, 1935; We Prophesy in Part, 1937; Strangers and Pilgrims, 1939; What We Mean by Religion, 1940; Summer Yesterdays in Maine, 1941; Rebuilding Our World, 1943; Those of the Way, 1945; Religion in America, 1946. Frequent contbr. to mags. and religious jours. Home: 984 Memorial Dr., Cambridge, Mass. Died May 15, 1954; buried Mt. Auburn Cemetery, Cambridge.

SPEYER, Leonora, writer; b. Washington, Nov. 7, 1872; d. Count Ferdinand and Julia (Thompson) Von Stosch; ed. pub. schs.; m. 2d, Edgar Speyer, 1902; children—(by first marriage) Enid (Mrs. Robert Hewitt), Pamela (wife of Count Hugo Moy), Leonora, Vivien. Began career as violinist, début with Boston Symphony, 1890; instr. poetry, Columbia, 1937—. Pres. Poetry Soc. Am., 1934-36; mem. Phi Beta Kappa. Author (verse): Canopic Jar, 1921; Fiddler's Farewell (awarded Pulitzer prize 1926), 1926; Naked Heel, 1931; Slow Wall, 1939 (2d edit., 1946). Contbr. verse to leading mags. Awarded Blindman prize, Nation prize, Poetry Soc. Am. prize, 'Chicago Poetry'' prize. Home: 60 Gramercy Park, N.Y.C. Died Feb. 10, 1956.

SPICER-SIMSON, Theodore, sculptor, portrait medallist; b. le Havre, France, June 25, 1871; s. Frederick John and Dora Mary (Spicer) S.; ed. in England, France and Germany; student Ecole des Beaux Arts, Paris, 1892-1894; pupil of sculptor J. Dampt, Paris; m. Margaret Schmidt, July 1, 1896. Draughtsman designer, Gorham & Co., New York, 1896-97; free lance artist, 1897—. Designer of more than 300 portrait medallions, including Franklin D. Roosevelt (ordered by French Govt. mint), William H. Taft, Gen. Horace Porter, Alexander Graham Bell, Henry Ford, Edward Arlington Robinson, Theodore Dreiser, Hervey Allen, George Meredith, G. B. Shaw, H. G. Wells, Lord Rutherford, Georges Courteline, King and Queen of the Belgians, Dr. Selma Lagerlof, etc.; designer Nat. Acad. of Science medals, awarded for outstanding work in oceanography, paleontology, geology, etc., The Guggenheim Aeronautical medal, C. I. Young Princeton University medal, National Tuberculosis Association Medal; commemorative tablets to C. I. Young, Alexander Bell (in Nat. Geog. Bldg., Washington, D.C.), to H.J. Allen (in Am. Mus. of Natural History, N.Y.); life size busts in bronze and marble: Town Hall, Calcutta; Dickinson Coll., Pa.; South Place Chapel, London; Johannesberg Art Mus.; works on permanent exhbn.; Met. Mus. of Art, New York; British Mus., Victoria and Albert Mus., London; Luxembourg, Paris; Kaiser Freidrich Mus., Berlin; Nat. Mus., Prague, etc. Recipient highest awards for medals at the Brussels, Belgium and Grand Internat. Exhbn., 1911-12. Mem. Nat. Soc. Fine Arts, France; fellow of The Nat. Sculpture Soc., New York. Club: Century Assn. (New York). Author: (pamphlets) Portraits and Medals in Relation to Life and Art, 1914; The Artist in His Relation to Coins and Medals, 1936. Home: 3803 Little Av., Coconut Grove, Miami 33, Fla. Died Feb. 1, 1959.

SPIES, Tom Douglas, physician, educator; b. Revenna, Tex., Sept. 21, 1902; s. John Earl and Mary (Love) S.; A.B., U. Tex., 1923; M.D., Harvard, 1927; Sc.D. (hon.), U. of South (Sewanee, Tenn.), 1944. Intern in pathology, Peter Bent Brigham Hosp., Boston, 1928-29; 1st asst. to Dr. F. B. Mallory, Boston City Hosp., 1929-30; intern Lakeside Hosp., Cleve., 1930-31; teaching fellow Western Reserve U., 1931-32, instr. in medicine, 1932-34, senior instr. medicine, 1934-35; asst. prof. medicine, U. Cin. Coll. of Medicine, 1935-36, asso. prof. medicine, 1936-47; vis. prof. medicine U. Ala., 1941—; prof. nutrition and metabolism, chmn. dept., Northwestern U. Med. Sch., 1947—; dir. Nutrition Clinic, Hillman Hosp., Birmingham, Ala., 1936—. Apptd. to Food and Nutrition Bd., Nat. Research Council, 1943; apptd. cons. to Sec. of War on Tropical Medicine Army Med. Sch., Washington, 1945. Recipient John Phillips Meml. award, Am. Coll. Physicians, 1939; Scientific award, Am. Pharmaceutical Mfrs. Assn., 1941; awarded So. Med. Assn. Research medal, 1943; Distinguished Achievement award Modern Medicine mag., 1957; Distinguished Service award of A.M.A., 1957; Oscar B. Hunter Meml. award in Therapeutics, American Therapeutic Society, 1959. Certified by American Board of Internal Medicine. Fellow Am. Coll. Physicians, Royal Soc. Tropical Medicine and Hygiene (Eng.); mem. A.M.A., A.A.A.S., Am. Assn. Pathologists and Bacteriologists, Am. Inst. Nutrition, Am. Soc. Clin. Investigation, Am. Soc. Exptl. Pathology, Assn. Am. Physicians, Am. Soc. Tropical Medicine, Central Soc. Clin. Research, Research Club, Soc. Exptl. Biology and Medicine, So. Med. Assn., Sigma Xi, Phi Beta Kappa. Co-author (with Dr. R. R. Williams) Vitamin B_1 and Its Use in Medicine, 1938; also numerous scientific articles to med. jours. Address: Hillman Hospital, Birmingham, Ala. Died Feb. 28, 1960.

SPILMAN, Robert Scott, lawyer; b. Warrenton, Fauquier County, Va., Mar. 22, 1876; s. William Mason and Heningham Lyons (Scott) S.; B.S., Va. Mil. Inst., Lexington, 1896 (Jackson Hope medal); law student U. of Va., 1899-1900; m. Eliza Polk Dillon, Apr. 4, 1907; children—Robert Scott, Frances Polk (dec.), Edward Dillon, Lisa Polk. Comdt. Sewanee Grammar Sch., 1896-97; asst. prof. English, Va. Mil. Inst., 1897-99; admitted to W.Va. bar, 1900, and practiced since at Charleston; mem. Spilman, Thomas, Battle & Klostermeyer; dir., counsel Kanawha Banking & Trust Co., Chesapeake & Potomac Telephone Co. of West Virginia. Pres. State Board Law Examiners, W.Va., 1919-34; mem. Sch. Bd., Charleston, 1914-32; pres. Charleston Open Forum, 1935-43; pres. Kanawha County War Fund, Inc., 1941-45, United War and Community Fund, Inc., 1943-45. Pres. W. Va. State Chamber of Commerce, 1944-45; dir. Community Chest of Kanawha Valley; trustee Meml. Hosp. Charleston; v.p. V.M.I. Found., Inc. Member Am. Bar Assn., Am. Law Inst., Am. Judicature Soc., W.Va. Bar Assn. (pres. 1919-20), Bar Association of the City of Charleston, Kappa Alpha, Phi Beta Kappa. Democrat. Episcopalian (chancellor diocese W. Va. 1933-56). Mason. Clubs: Edgewood Country, Church, Press. Home: 108 Roscommon Rd. Office: Kanawha Banking & Trust Bldg., Charleston, W.Va. Died May 30, 1958.

SPINGOLD, Nathan Breiter, business exec.; born Chicago, Mar. 6, 1886; s. Kalman and Esther (Breiter) S.; student Chicago Kent Coll. Law; m. Frances Leviton, Nov. 3, 1909. Reporter Hearst's Chicago Examiner, 1903, Chicago Tribune, 1906; gen. publicity dir. William Morris Enterprises, New York, 1909; gen. exec. Columbia Pictures Corp., N.Y. City, 1933-40, dir., 1940-43, vice pres., 1943, v.p. and dir. (in charge publicity advt. and exploitation), 1943-56, v.p., cons., 1956—. Clubs: Hillcrest Golf and Country (Los Angeles); Cavendish (N.Y.C.), Palm Beach (Fla.) Country. Home: 12 E. 77 St. Office: 711 Fifth Av., N.Y.C. Died June 14, 1958; buried Mount Pleasant Cemetery, Hawthorne, N.Y.

SPINNEY, Louis Bevier, coll. prof.; b. Bradford, Stark Co., Ill., May 27, 1869; s. Joseph Oakman Hunt and Julia Hester (Bevier) S.; B.M.E., Ia. State Coll., 1892, B.S. in E.E., 1893; grad. work Cornell U., 1 yr., in 3 periods, 1893-1900; U. of Berlin, 1894-95; Polytechnikum, Zurich, Switzerland, 6 mos., 1895-96; m. Beryl Anna Hoyt, of Carroll, Ia., Aug. 22, 1904; children—Bevier, Beryl. Instr. physics, Ia. State Coll., 1893-97, prof. physics since 1897. Fellow A.A.A.S.; mem. Am. Physical Soc., Am. Inst. Elec. Engrs., Illuminating Engineering Soc., Ia. Acad. Science, Soc. Promotion Engring. Edn., Phi Kappa Phi, Tau Beta Pi. Republican. Author: A Text Book of Physics, 1911, 3d edit., 1925. Home: 2136 Lincolnway, Ames, Ia. Died Jan. 25, 1951; buried Ames Municipal Cemetery.

SPITZ, Leo, lawyer; b. Chicago, Ill., June 30, 1888; s. Henry and Caroline (Horner) S.; grad. South Div. High Sch., 1904; Ph.B., U. Chgo., 1908, J.D., 1910; m. Frankie James. Admitted to Ill. bar, 1910, began practice Chgo.; former mem. law firm Spitz & Adcock (firm dissolved); former pres. Radio Keith Orpheum Corp.; chmn. bd. Internat. Pictures, Inc.; exec. head prodn. Universal Internat. Studio; now ret. mem. Racing Cofmn. of State of Ill., 1932-40, chmn. 1934-40. Mem. Am., Ill. State and Chicago bar assns., Order of Coif. Club: Standard. Address: 1120 La Collina Dr., Beverly Hills, Cal. Died Apr. 16, 1956; cremated Forest Lawn Cemetery, Cal.

SPLINT, Sarah Field; b. Brooklyn, N.Y.; d. Thomas G. and Sarah Field (Weldin) Splint; A.B., Hunter Coll., New York. Asst. editor Delineator, 1907-11; editor Woman's Magazine, 1911-15, To-day's Housewife, 1915-19; chief div. of home conservation, U.S. Food Administration, 1917-18; advt. consultant, 1919-29; asso. editor McCall's Mag., 1929-35; asso. editor Woman's Home Companion, 1935-44. Mem. Society of Friends; mem. staff Am. Friends Service Com.; mem. bd. The Friends Intelligencer. Club: Cosmopolitan. Home: Swarthmore, Pa. Died Dec. 25, 1959; buried Eastlawn Cemetery, Swarthmore, Pa.

SPOEHR, Herman Augustus (spôr), chemist; b. Chicago, Ill., June 18, 1885; s. Charles A. and Frida (Baeuerlen) S.; S.B., U. of Chicago, 1906, Ph.D., 1909, D.Sc., 1929; studied U. of Berlin, 1907, U. of Paris, 1908; m. Florence Mann, Dec. 17, 1910; children—Alexander, Hortense. Swift fellow, U. of Chicago, 1909; asso. in chemistry, same, 1910; became staff mem. Lab. Plant Physiology, Carnegie Instn., Washington, 1910, asst. dir. Coastal Lab. of same, 1926-27, chmn. div. of plant biology, 1928-20; acting prof. chemistry, Stanford, summer 1924; director natural sciences Rockefeller Foundation, 1930-31; chmn. div. plant biology Carnegie Inst., 1932-47, chmn. emeritus, 1947—. Consultant to Sec. of State, 1950-51. Mem. Am. Chem. Soc., Bot. Soc. of Am., A.A. A.S., Am. Academy of Arts and Sciences, Am. Philos. Soc., Am. Soc. Naturalists, Am. Soc. Plant Physiologists, hon. mem. Deutsche Botanische Gesellschaft, Linnean Soc., London. Club: Bohemian. Author of "Photosynthesis," and of numerous papers on photosynthesis and chemistry of carbohydrate metabolism. Home: 464 Coleridge Av., Palo Alto, Calif. Address: Carnegie Institution, Stanford, Cal. Died June 21, 1954.

SPONSLER, Olenus Lee (spons ler), educator; b. Akron, O., June 17, 1879; s. Israel Seymour and Sarah (Lee) S.; A.B., U. Mich., 1909; A.M., U. Neb., 1911; Ph.D., Stanford, 1922; m. Selden Ruger, June 19, 1917 (separated 1921). Asst. prof. botany and forestry U. Neb., 1909-11; asso. prof. forestry U. Mich., 1912-17; asst. prof. botany U. Cal. at L.A., 1922-25, asso. prof., 1925-28, prof., 1928-48, chmn. botany dept., 1933-44, emeritus, 1948; made plywood investigations for airplane constrn. Forest products Lab., Madsion, Wis., World War I. Fellow A.A.A.S.; mem. Am. Bot. Soc. (chmn. Pacific div. 1934-35), Western Soc. Naturalists (president So. California sect. 1924), Am. Soc. Plant Physiologists (Charles Reid Barnes hon. life mem.), Soc. Exptl. Biology and Medicine, Soc. Study Development and Growth, Sigma Xi, Gamma Alpha. Mason. Author: Trees, 1923. Contbr. numerous sci. articles on X-ray determination of molecular structure of biol. materials, such as starch and cellulose, molecular structure studies of protoplasm, electron microscope studies of protoplasmic materials; elect. aspects of protoplasm on molecular level. Home: 15053 Sutton St., Sherman Oaks, Cal. Died March 14, 1953; buried Glen Haven Meml. Park, San Fernando, Cal.

SPOONER, Charles Horace, univ. pres.; b. Charleston, N.H., August 6, 1858; s. Stephen and Sophia L. (Hull) S.; S.B., Norwich U., 1878, completed arts course, 1879 (hon. A.M., 1895; LL.D., U. Vt., 1904); m. Inez G. Davis, Nov. 15, 1882. Instr. English and mil. tactics, St. Augustine's Coll., Benicia, Cal., and maj. N.G. Cal., 1879-81; instr. mathematics and mil. tactics, Vt. Acad., Saxtons River, 1881-89; maj. Vt. N.G., 1888-89; prin. sch. Fitchburg, Mass., 1889-91; instr. mathematics, Manual Tng. Sch. of Washington U., 1891-1904; pres. Norwich U., 1904-15, emeritus, 1916. Address: Charlestown, N.H. Deceased.

SPOTTS, William Bigler, oral surgeon; born St. Louis, June 2, 1888; s. William and Sarah Jane (Knettle) S.; student Arnold Acad., St. Louis, 1907-08; D.D.S., Washington U., 1912; m. Agnes Lonergan, Nov. 27, 1912; children—Jane (Mrs. Jane Spotts Klees), Jack A. Pvt. practice of dentistry, St. Louis, 1912—, specialist in exodontics and oral surgery, 1917—; mem. faculty Wash. U. Sch. of Dentistry, 1916—, prof. anesthesiology, 1942—; mem. staff Barnes, Deaconess and St. Louis City Hosps. Mem. Med. Dental Service Bur., St. Louis, 1940—, vice pres., 1941-42, sec.-treas., 1944-45. Served as mem. sub-com. emergency field med. units (dental), Civilian Defense, 1941. Fellow Am. Coll. Dentists; mem. Internat. Anesthesia Research Soc., Am. Soc. Oral Surgs., Am. Assn. Advancement Oral Diagnosis, Am. Soc. Advance, Gen. Anesthesia in Dentistry, Nat. Geog. Soc., Am. Dental Assn., Midwestern Society of Oral Surgeons (charter mem.), Acad. Sci. of St. Louis, Mo. Dental Assn. (chmn. central history com.), St. Louis Dental Soc. (chmn. pub. dental edn. com., 1936-37, 3d v.p. 1937-38, pres. 1941-42, librarian, 1942-49, life mem.), St. Louis Soc. Dental Sci. (sec.-treas. 1931, 32, 33, pres. 1934), Barnes Hosp. Soc., Evang. Deaconess Soc., Wash. U. Dental Alumni Assn. (pres. 1925-26); Xi Psi Phi, Omicron Kappa Upsilon (pres. 1937-38). Republican. Conglist. Mason (32°). Clubs: Auto of Missouri, Rotary (v.p. 1929-30, pres. 1930-31, dist. gov. 14th dist. 1933-34), Mo. Athletic, University. Author: History of Anesthesia in Dentistry, written for the 75th Anniversary of Wash. Univ. Sch. of Dentistry, 1941. Lecturer on Post-Injection and Post-Operative Complications and their Treatment before dental socs. in Mo. and Ill. Cons. editor Internat. Assn. Anesthesiologists, Inc. Home: 7361 Kingsbury Blvd., University City 5. Office: University Club Bldg., St.

Louis 3. Died Mar. 7, 1957; buried Memorial Park Cemetery.

SPRAGUE, Clifton Albert (sprēg), naval officer; b. Dorchester, Mass., Jan. 8, 1896; s. Henry Bruno and Hazel Williams (Furlow) S.; B.S., U.S. Naval Acad., 1917; m. Annabel Fitzgerald, Apr. 12, 1925; children—Hazel Courtney (Mrs. Daniel Vaughan), Patricia (Mrs. Travis Reneau). Commd. ensign USN, 1917, advanced through grades to rear adm., 1944; comd. jeep carrier div. at Leyte Gulf battle, Oct. 1944; comdr. Alaskan Sea Frontier, comdt. 17th Naval Dist., retired as vice adm., 1951. Address: Quarters B, Naval Station, Kodiak, Alaska. Died Apr. 11, 1955; buried Rosecrans Nat. Cemetery, San Diego, Cal.

SPRAGUE, Oliver Mitchell Wentworth, economist, b. Somerville, Mass., Apr. 22, 1873; s. William Wallace and Miriam (Wentworth) S.; A.B., Harvard, 1894, A.M., 1895, Ph.D., 1897; Litt.D., Columbia, 1938; m. Fanny Knights Ide, June 21, 1905 (died Aug. 4, 1942); children—Katharine Ide, Theodore Wentworth. Instr. econs., Harvard, 1900-04, asst. prof., 1904-05; prof. econs., Imperial U. of Tokyo, 1905-08; asst. prof. banking and finance, Harvard, 1908-13. Edmund Cogswell Converse prof. banking and finance, 1913-41, now prof. emeritus; econ. adv. (under leave of absence) Bank of Eng., 1930-33; financial and exec. asst. to sec. of the Treasury (U.S.) June-Nov. 1933; resigned and returned to Harvard. Author: History of Crises Under the National Banking System, 1910; Banking Reform in the United States, 1911; Theory and History of Banking, 1929; Recovery and Common Sense, 1934. Home: 13 Follen St., Cambridge, Mass. Died May 24, 1953.

SPRAGUE-SMITH, Isabelle Dwight, educator, art instr.; b. Clinton, N.Y., Nov. 11, 1861; d. Dr. Benjamin Woodbridge and Wealthy J. (Dewey) Dwight; ed. Dwight Sch. (her father's sch.), Clinton; studied in Art Students' League, New York, and Paris, 1886-93; L.H.D., Rollins Coll., 1939; m. Charles Sprague-Smith, Nov. 11, 1884; 1 dau., Hilda. Maintained studio and classes in art, New York, 1893-98; art instr., Plainfield Sem., 1895-98; dir. art dept., 1898-1900, prin. 1900-25, The Veltin Sch., New York. Founder and pres. of the Bach Festival Society of Winter Park, Fla. Mem. Fla. Hist. Soc., Audubon Soc., Allied Arts, Met. Museum Art, D.A.R., Nat. Soc. Colonial Dames in State of N.Y. Address: Box 745, Winter Park, Fla. Died Dec. 28, 1950.

SPRECKELS, Rudolph (sprĕk'lz), civic reformer, banker; b. San Francisco, Calif., Jan. 1, 1872; s. Claus and Anna C. S.; ed. pub. schs., San Francisco; m. Eleanor J. Jolliffe, Aug. 5, 1895. At age of 17 was employed in father's sugar refinery in Phila., which was constructed to fight the sugar trust; at 22 became pres. of Hawaiian Commercial & Sugar Co., owner of one of the great sugar plantations of Hawaii; put plantation on a paying basis within a year and sold in 1898; dir., reorganizer San Francisco Gas Co., 1900——. Was mem. of com. of 50 at the time of San Francisco fire and earthquake in 1906, also mem. of exec. com. of five of the San Francisco Relief and Red Cross Funds which managed the entire relief fund of $9,000,000. Organized and financed San Francisco graft prosecution in 1906, and took a prominent part in political uprising against corp. control of state and city govt. Retired from business, 1937; now devoting time to good government cause. Home: 1 W. Santa Inez, San Mateo, Cal. Office: 1901 Willow Rd., Burlingame, Cal. Died Oct. 4, 1958; buried Cypress Lawn.

SPRENGLING, Martin (sprĕng'lĭng), prof. Arabic; b. Centre, Outagamie County, Wis., Oct. 9, 1877; s. Philip and Augusta (Haase) S.; B.A., Northwestern Coll., Wis., 1894; grad. Lutheran Sem., Wis., 1898; Ph.D., U. Chgo., 1914; studied Am. Sch. of Archaeology, Jerusalem; m. Mary Christina Schmidt, Sept. 11, 1914; children—Gerhard, Kurt, Haenne (dec.), Maeda Mary Elisabeth, Uni Aenne Lotte. Prof. classics, Northwestern Coll., 1910-11; instructor Semitic language, Harvard, 1911-15; asst. prof. Arabic language and literature U. Chgo., 1915-25, asso. prof., 1925-26, prof., Oct. 1, 1927——, chmn. dept. Oriental langs. and lit., 1934-36, chmn. com. on archeology, v.p. and editor in chief publs. of New Orient Soc. of Chgo., in cöop, with Open Court 1935-38; editor Jour. Semitic Langs. and Lits. 1932-40, emeritus 1943. Mem. Am. Oriental Soc., Archaeol. Inst. Am., Am. Philol. Assn., Deutsche Morgenlaendische Gesellchaft, Linguistic Soc. Am., Am. Oriental Soc. (pres. Midwestern Br., 1935-36), New Orient Soc. Am., Phi Beta Kappa. Ind. Republican. Author: Descriptive Catalogue of Manuscripts in the Libraries of the University of Chicago (with E. J. Goodspeed), 1912; The Alphabet, Its Rise and Development from the Sinai Inscriptions, 1931; From Persian to Arabic, 1939; Kartir, founder of Sasanian Zoroastrianism, 1940; Shahpuhr I, the Great on the Kaabah of Zoroaster, 1940; The Greek of Sapor K Z, and Roman History, 1945-46; Third Century Iran, 1953; also parts of books pertaining to the Orient, and serials and articles in philological and anthropological journals. Editor: Barnebraeus' Scholia on the Old Testament, Part I, Genesis-II Samuel (with W. C. Graham), 1931. Contbr. to Mathes with Smith Dictionary of Religion and Ethics. Contbr. articles to philol. jours. Address: R.F.D., Tamworth, N.H. Died Sept. 5, 1959; buried Friends Meeting Burial Ground, Sandwich, N.H.

SPRIGLE, Ray (sprī'g'l), newspaper man; b. Akron, O., Aug. 14, 1886; s. Emanuel P. and Sarah Ann (Hoover) S.; student O. State U., 1905-06; m. Agnes Marie Trimmer, Dec. 29, 1922; 1 dau., Mary Rae Jean. Began as reporter for Ohio Sun, Columbus, 1906; worked on papers at Akron, Canton, O., Lansing, Mich., Chicago, St. Louis, Little Rock, Ark., until 1916; joined Pittsburgh Post, later Post Gazette, 1916, London correspondent, 1940. Served as sergeant (Engrs.), U.S. Army, 1918. Award Pulitzer prize for articles on Justice Black and Ku Klux Klan, 1938. Received Headliners medal for series on Black Market at Atlantic City, 1945; posthumously awarded Nat. Mental Health Assn. award, May 8, 1958. Republican. Author: (book) In the Land of Jim Crow, 1949. Contbr. short stories to Red Book, Blue Book, Green Book. Address: 1704 Marmaduke St., Pitts. 12. Died Dec. 22, 1957; buried North Catholic Cemetery.

SPRING, Samuel Newton, college dean; b. Sioux City, Ia., Feb. 5, 1875; s. Winthrop N. and Ellen E. (Newton) S.; B.A., Yale, 1898, M.F., 1903; LL.D., (honorary) Syracuse University, 1944; married Adah E. Bowman, Nov. 29, 1900; children—Ernest Walker, John Bowman, Samuel Gardiner, Charles Peter. Apptd. field asst., Bur. Forestry, 1903; prof. forestry and head of dept., University of Me., 1903-05; forest asst., forest inspector, chief, office of forest extension, Forest Service, U.S. Dept. of Agr., 1905-09; cons. forester, 1909; forester Conn. Agrl. Expt. Sta. and state forester of Conn., 1909-12; prof. silviculture, N.Y. State Coll. Agr., Cornell U., 1912-31; asst. dean N.Y. State Coll. Forestry, Syracuse U., 1932, dean 1933-44; emeritus since 1944. Lecturer, Yale Forestry School, 1910-12 and 1917; member and sec. Connecticut Commission on Investigation of Taxation of Woodlands, 1912. Regional educational adviser Y.M.C.A., with A.E.F., 1918. Dir., treas. Cornell U. Christian Assn., 1922-31; pres. L. A. Fuertes Council Boy Scouts of America, 1931, mem. exec. board Onandaga Council, 1932-44; v.p. Westminster Foundation in N.Y. State, Inc., 1940. Fellow Soc. Am. Foresters (chmn. N.Y. Sect. 1928-30); mem. Alpha Zeta, Phi Sigma Kappa, Alpha Xi Sigma, Sigma Xi, Phi Kappa Phi. Republican. Presbyterian. Author: (with A. B. Recknagel) Forestry, 1929; also numerous repts. and bulls. on forestry topics. Address: 207 Melbourne Av., Syracuse, N.Y. Died Feb. 3, 1952.

SPRINGS, Elliott White, author, mfr.; b. Lancaster, S.C., July 31, 1896; s. Leroy and Grace Allison (White) S.; grad. Culver Mil. Acad., 1913; A.B., Princeton, 1917; student mil. aviation, Oxford U., Eng., 1917; LL.D., U. of S.C., 1949; m. Frances Hubbard Ley, Oct. 4, 1922; 1 daughter, Mrs. H. W. Close, Jr. Test pilot L.W.F. Airplane Co., 1919; flew 1st cross country airplane race, N.Y.C. to Toronto, 1919; began bus. career as cotton weighter, 1919; sec.-treas. Kershaw Cotton Mills, 1920-21, pres., 1931——; pres. Bank of Lancaster, Bank of Heath Springs, Springs Banking & Mercantile Co., Springs Cotton Mills, Columbia Compress, Leroy Springs & Co., Kershaw Cotton Mills, Lancaster Cotton Mills, Fort Mill Mfg. Co., Eureka Cotton Mills, Springsteen Cotton Mills, Springs Mills; dir. Soc. Ry. Mem. N.Y. Cotton Exchange, S.C. Ednl. Finance Commn., 1951. Pvt. aviation sect. S.R.C., 1917; trained with R.F.C., Oxford U., sergeant, 2d lt., 1st lt., flight comdr., squadron comdr., capt. A.C. Res.; served with 85th Squadron R.F.C., 148th Squadron U.S.A.S.; officially credited with destroying 11 enemy airplanes; mil. aviator; capt. Air Corps, 1941; lt. col. 1942; ret. 1942. Exec. officer, Charlotte Air Base. Decorated with D.S.C., Distinguished Flying Cross (British), Medal of Honor (Aero Club of Am.). Pres. Marion Sims Meml. Hosp., 1939. Mem. Quiet Birdmen, Nat. Aeronautical Assn., Res. Officers' Assn., Authors' League Am., Dramatist's Guild, Am. Legion. Democrat. Presbyn. Mason. Clubs: Players, Racquet and Tennis, Princeton (N.Y.C.). Author: Nocturne Militaire, 1927; Leave Me with a Smile, 1928; Above the Bright Blue Sky, 1928; Contact, 1930; In the Cool of the Evening, 1930; The Rise and Fall of Carol Banks, 1931; Pent-Up on a Penthouse, 1931; Warbirds and Ladybirds, 1931; Clothes Make the Man, 1948. Address: Fort Mill, S.C. Died Oct. 15, 1959.

SPRINGS, Holmes Buck, real estate, banker; b. Bucksville, S.C., Aug. 14, 1879; s. Albert Adams and Alice (Buck) S.; student The Citadel, 1895-98; grad. Spartanburg Bus. Coll., 1898; m. Louise Wilson, Oct. 22, 1919; children—Louise Wilson, Holmes Buck, Jr., David Albert, Wilson Baker, Alice Italine, Albert Adams, III. Organizer, pres. Springs & Siau Co., real estate and ins. Georgetown, S.C., 1904-17; organizer, pres. Farmers and Merchants Bank, Georgetown, 1913-19; pres. Serial Bldg. & Loan Assn., 1912-19; mem. Parrish, Gower & Springs, 1919-22; v.p. Woodside Nat. Bank. 1922-29, Pioneer Life Ins. Co., 1925-32; v.p., mgr. Myrtle Beach Investment Co., 1926-32; organizer, pres. H. B. Springs Co., Inc., real estate; State dir. Selective Service, 1940-47; mem. Gov.'s Adv. Counsel Nat. Def., 1940——. Chmn. State Adv. Com. Adult Edn., 1947. Was pres. C. of C. Georgetown and Greenville; mem. S.C. Ins. Commn., 1919——; mem. advisory council Nat. Rivers and Harbors Congress; mem. exec. council Southeastern States Development Commn.; pres. Kings Highway Assn., 1928-35; dir. Atlantic Coastal Hwy. Assn. (1930-35), Ocean Hwy. Assn. Trustee U. S.C., 1919-20; trustee Columbia (Female) Coll., 1940-48. Awarded Presidential citation (Certificate of Merit), 1946; Am. Legion Distinguished Service Plaque, Horry County, 1946. Served as pvt. to col., S.C. Nat. Guard; col., 2d S.C. Inf. on Mexican border, 1916-17; col. Inf. U.S. Army; duty with 30th Div. staff, A.E.F., France, England, Belgium, 1917-19; ret. brig. gen., Apr. 25, 1919; cited for war service. Pres. 2d S.C. Inf. Assn.; mem. 30th Div. Assn. (organizer; 1st pres.). Mem. S.C. Soc. S.A.R., S.C.V., Am. Legion, Ypres League (London), Mil. Order of World War; hon. mem. O.D.K. Leadership Fraternity, 1941. Democrat. Methodist. Mason (K.T., Shriner). Clubs: Rotary, Country, Pinetree Hunt (hon.). Home: Myrtle Beach, S.C. Died Jan. 31, 1951; buried Myrtle Beach, S.C.

SPROUSE, Claude Willard (sprous), clergyman; b. Luray, Mo., Dec. 19, 1888; s. John Fremont and Lottie Belle (Townsend) S.; student Northwestern U., 1910-12, Ph.B., U. of Chicago, 1914, S.T.B., 1916; S.T.D., Seabury-Western Theol. Sem., 1939, Gen. Theol. Sem., 1950; D.D., Mo. Valley Coll., 1948; m. Beryl Varnell, Aug. 30, 1915; children—Claude Willard, Beryl. Ordained ministry P.E. Ch., 1916; successively asst. at St. Johns Cathedral, and rector St. Luke's Ch., both of Denver, St. Mary's Ch., St. Paul, Trinity Ch., Houston, Tex.; dean of Grace and Holy Trinity Cathedral, Kansas City, Mo., since 1931. Pres. Kansas City Council of Churches (2 terms); Chmn. Dept. Missions and pres. Standing Com., Diocese of West Mo. Trustee Church Pension Fund; mem. joint commn. on Ch. Unity of Protestant Episcopal Ch.; dep. to Gen. Conv. 7 times, pres. House of Clerical and Lay Depts., 1949, 52. Chaplain maj. 3d Mo. Inf. Mason. Clubs: River, University, Kansas City Country. Home: 4525 Walnut St. Office: 415 W. 13th St., Kansas City, Mo. Died Sept. 8, 1952; buried Richmond, Ill.

SPURR, Josiah Edward, geologist; b. Gloucester, Mass., Oct. 1, 1870; s. Alfred and Oratia E. (Snow) S.; A.B., Harvard, 1893, A.M., 1894; m. Sophie C. Burchard, Jan. 18, 1899; children—Edward Burchard, John Constantine, William Alfred, Robert Anton, Stephen Hopkins. Mining engr., geologist to Sultan of Turkey, Apr. 1901-May 1902; geologist, U.S. Geol. Survey, 1902-06; chief geol. dept. Am. Smelting & Refining Co., Am. Smelters Securities Co., Guggenheim Exploration Co., 1906-08; Spurr & Cox (Inc.), cons. specialists in mining, 1908-11; v.p. charge mining, Tonopah Mining Co. of Nev., 1911-17; mem. com. mineral imports, U.S. Shipping and War Trade bds., 1917-18; exec. war minerals investigations, chief metal mining engr., Bur. Mines; chief engr., War Mineral Relief, 1918-19; editor Engring. and Mining Jour., 1919-27; prof. geology, Rollins Coll., 1930-32. Mem. Mining and Metall. Soc. Am. (pres. 1921), Am. Inst. Mining and Metall. Engrs., Soc. Econ. Geologists (pres. 1923), Geol. Soc. Am., Am. Geog. Soc., Soc. Mayflower Descendants, Soc. Colonial Wars. Author: The Iron-Bearing Rocks of the Mesabi Range in Minnesota (Minn. Geol. and Nat. Hist. Survey), 1894; Through the Yukon Gold Diggings, 1900; Geology Applied to Mining, 1904; The Ore Magmas, 1923; Geology Applied to Selenology, 1944; Features of the Moon, 1945; Lunar Catastrophic History, 1947; The Shrunken Moon, 1949; also various monographs and reports on econ. geology, etc. Editor: Political and Commercial Geology, 1921. Mt. Spurr peak in Alaska named by U.S. Geol. Survey in honor of his explorations in Alaska, 1896, 98. Home: 324 Henkel Circle, Winter Park, Fla.; also Alstead, N.H. Died Jan. 12, 1950; buried East Alstead, N.H.

SQUIRE, Francis Hagar, educator; born Westfield, Mass., Dec. 23, 1902; s. Francis Freeman and Mertie (DeLaVergne) S.; A.B., Yale, 1925, Ph.D., 1935; m. Marjorie Johnson, Sept. 15, 1932. Instr. in history, U. of Del., 1927-28, asst. prof., 1928-30; instr. in history, Yale, 1930-31; asso.prof. of history, U. of Del., 1932-43, chmn., dept. of history, 1942-43, dean of the univ. and dean sch. of arts and science since Dec. 1945. Served with Naval Aviation Training Command, U.S.Navy, 1943-45; disch. to U.S.N.R. as lt. comdr. Mem. Res. Officers Assn., Am. Hist. Assn., Sons Colonial Wars, Naval Order U.S. Del. Hist. Assn., Omicron Delta Kappa, Phi Kappa Phi, Phi Kappa Tau, Alpha Phi Omega. Clubs: Lincoln (Delaware); Elizabethan (New Haven). Episcopalian. Home: 38 Winslow Rd., Newark, Del. Died Apr. 26, 1956; buried Welsh Tract Cemetery, Newark.

SQUIRES, George Forbes, ry. ofcl.; b. Chgo., June 9, 1894; s. George Dudley and Ida M. (Forbes) S.; student law U. So.Cal., 1917-18; m. Veda M. May, June 15, 1915. With Pacific Electric Ry. Co., Los Angeles, 1908——, beginning in operating dept., successively staff freight traffic dept., gen. mgr. Harbor Belt Line R.R., Los Angeles Harbor, gen. supt. transportation dept., in charge operations, asst. to pres., v.p., 1908-54, v.p., gen. mgr., 1954—. Club: Jonathan. Home: 2445 Monterey Rd., San Marino 9, Cal. Office: 610 S. Main St., Los Angeles. Died Nov. 18, 1956.

ST. JOHN, Theodore Raymond, lawyer; b. Valatie, N.Y., Aug. 28, 1880; s. Theodore L and Caroline A. (Filkins) St. J.; A.B., Columbia, 1902, LL.B., 1905; m. May Irene Kavanagh, July 28, 1919; 1 dau., Mary Caroline (Mrs. Henry H. Villard). Admitted to N.Y. bar, 1905, since practiced in N.Y. C.; partner Hays, St. John, Abramson & Heilbron, 1925—. Mem. bd. mgrs. McBurney YMCA, N.Y.C., 1923-50. Trustee Riverside Ch., N.Y.C., 1943—, pres. of the bd., 1947-55. Mem. C. of C., American Baptist Foreign Mission Society (mem. bd. mgrs. 1924-50), N.Y. Bapt. City Soc. (2d v.p.), Assn. Bar City N.Y., Phi Beta Kappa, Phi Delta Theta. Repub. Bapt. Clubs: Bankers Am. (N.Y.C.); Lake Placid of N.Y. Home: 145 E. 74th St., N.Y.C. 21; summer: Deer Isle, Me. Office: 120 Broadway, N. Y.C. 5. Died Nov. 4, 1958; buried Oakwood Cemetery, Troy, N.Y.

STAAF, Oscar (Emil) (stof), educator, b. Lindsborg, Kan., Dec. 22, 1880; s. Eric Olson and Maria (Wickstrom) S.; A.B., Bethany College, Lindsborg, 1900; A.M., Yale, 1902, Ph.D., 1907; m. Lucia Tuller Magie, Sept. 7, 1907. Asst. instr. French, Yale, 1906-07; instr. Romance langs., Adelbert Coll., Western Reserve U., 1907-08, 1910-14, asst. prof., 1914-20, asso. prof., 1920-25, prof. Romance langs. 1925-52, head dept., 1934-52; chmn. div., prof. Romance langs., U. of Denver, 1908-10. Mem. Modern Lang. Assn., Am. Assn. Teachers Spanish. Baptist. Home: 2440 Overlook Rd., Cleveland Heights, O. Died Dec. 2, 1958.

STACK, Joseph Michael, ex-comdr.-in-chief Vet. of Foreign Wars of U.S.; b. Pittsburgh, May 15, 1895; s. John and Katherine (O'Leary) S.; m. Alice M. Dugan, Aug. 21, 1919; children—Dorothy Alice (Mrs. Thayer G. Wiesner), Irene Elizabeth, Mary Helen. Clerk Arbuthnot Stephenson Co., Pittsburgh, 1910-25; mem. firm Stack and Durning, hatters, Pittsburgh, 1925-27; buyer and dept. mgr., The Rosebaum Co., Pittsburgh, 1927-35; investigator for dist. atty., Allegheny County, Pa., 1935-43; chief Allegheny County Detective Bureau, Pittsburgh, since 1943; commander-in-chief, Veterans of Foreign Wars of U.S., 1945-46; chmn. draft bd. since its inception. Served with Co. F, 357th Inf., 90th Div., A.E.F., U.S. Army, World War I. Former pres. Lincoln Civic Club, Pittsburgh; former vice pres. and mem. bd. mgrs., Soldiers and Sailors Memorial Hall, Pittsburgh. Mem. Pa. Chiefs of Police Assn., Fraternal Order of Police, Am. Legion. K.C., A.O.H. Club: Variety (Pittsburgh). Home: 6929 Churchland St., Pittsburgh 6, Pa. Offices: Broadway at 34th St., Kansas City 2, Mo. 303 Allegheny County Court House, Pitts. Died Mar. 7, 1952; buried Mt. Carmel Cemetery.

STACK, J(oseph) W(illiam), educator; b. Jefferson, O., Feb. 2, 1893; s. Robert Simon and Anna (Murray) S.; B.S., Notre Dame U., 1915, M.S., 1918; m. Helen Elizabeth Dodge, Sept. 6, 1917; children—J(oseph) W(illiam), (Helen) Elizabeth, (Mrs. Alexander Leslie III). Instr. Zoology Mich. State Coll., East Lansing, 1918; asst. prof zoölogy, 1923-26, asso. prof., 1925-42, prof. zoölogy, 1942; curator museum Mich. State Coll. Mus., 1924-41, dir., 1941—; student adviser, 1925—; applied sci. divisional adviser, 1930-33, charge summer sch. of biology, W. K. Kellogg Sch., Battle Creek, 1929-39; Clear Lake, Atlanta, Mich., 1940-41. Served as sec. Mich. Non-game License Commn., 1924-25; merit badge examiner Boy Scouts. Mem. Am. Red Cross (bd. dirs., treas. Ingham County, 1936-38), Inland Bird Banding Assn. (councilor, 1924-26, sec. 1927-30, pres. 1938-39), Mich. Audubon Soc. (adv. bd. 1925-26, exec. bd. 1931-38), Sigma Chi, Phi Kappa Phi (pres. 1941-42), Phi Sigma, Sigma Xi. Roman Catholic. Club: Central Michigan Notre Dame (pres. 1934), Wilson Ornithological (pres. 1930-31). Editor: Inland Bird Banding News, 1929-30; asso. editor bird banding, Jour. Ornithol. Research, 1929-35. Contbr. articles to sci. jours. Home: 1028 Chesterfield Pkwy., East Lansing, Mich. Died Aug. 17, 1954.

STACY, Walter Parker (stā'sĭ), jurist; b. Ansonville, N.C., Dec. 26, 1884; s. Rev. L. E. and Rosa (Johnson) S.; A.B., U. N.C., 1908; studied law same univ., 1908-09, LL.D., 1923; m. Maude DeGan Graff, June 15, 1929 (now dec.). Practiced law, 1910-16; rep. New Hanover County in Gen. Assembly N.C., 1915; judge Superior Court, 8th Jud. Dist., 1916-20; elected asso. justice Supreme Court of N.C. for full term, 1920; apptd. by Gov. A. W. McLean, Mar. 16, 1925, to succeed Chief Justice Hoke (resigned); elected, 1926, chief justice Supreme Court, N.C., reelected 1934, 42, 50. Mem. Am., N.C. bar assns., Gen. Alumni Assn. U. N.C. (pres. 1925-26). Lectr. summers, 1922-25, in Law Sch. U. N.C., tendered deanship in same, 1923; lectr. Northwestern U. Sch. Law, summer sessions, 1926, 27. Named by U.S. Bd. of Mediation, under Ry. Labor Act, as neutral arbitrator to serve on Bd. Arbitration, and later elected chmn. bd., to settle wage controversy between the Brotherhood of Locomotive Engrs. and certain railroads in Southwestern Ty. U.S., 1927-28; apptd. by Pres. Coolidge, 1928, mem. Emergency Bd. under Ry. Labor Act, to investigate and report respecting a dispute between officers and members of Order of Ry. Conductors and Brotherhood of Ry. Trainmen, and certain railroads w. Mississippi River; named by U.S. Bd. Mediation, Jan. 1931, to serve as neutral arbitrator, in controversy between Brotherhood of Ry. Trainmen and N.Y. Central, the "Big Four," and P. & L.E. railroads, and again in Nov. 1931, to serve as neutral arbitrator in controversy between Brotherhood and Ry. and Steamship Clerks, etc., and Ry. Express Agy.; apptd. by Pres. Hoover, 1932, mem. Emergency Bd. of three, later elected chmn. bd. to investigate and report concerning a number of disputes existing between L. & A. and L., A. & T. rys. and certain of their employees; chmn. Commn. apptd. to redraft Constitution of N.C., 1931-32; named by U.S. Bd. Mediation, 1933, to served as neutral arbitrator in several controversies between Boston and Maine R.R. and certain of its employees; apptd. by Pres., 1933, mem. bd. investigation labor dispute Tex. and New Orleans R.R., and 1934, Del. and Hudson R.R.; also apptd. chmn. Nat. Steel and Textile Labor Relations Bds., 1934; apptd. by President Roosevelt, 1938, chmn. emergency bd. of three to investigate and report on threatened strike of railroad employees due to wage reduction controversy on Class 1 railroads; apptd. by Pres. alternate mem. Nat. Def. Mediation Bd., 1941, and asso. mem. Nat. War Labor Bd., also mem. Nat. Ry. Labor Panel, 1942; apptd. by Pres. Truman, chmn. Pres.'s Labor-Mgmt. Conf., 1945. Methodist. Democrat. Home: Wilmington, N.C. Office: Raleigh, N.C. Died Sept. 13, 1951; buried Hamlet, N.C.

STADIE, William Christopher, college professor; b. New York, N.Y., June 15, 1886; s. Charles and Augusta (Kiseo) S.; B.S., New York U., 1907; M.D., Coll. Phys. and Surg., Columbia, 1916; D.Sc. (honorary), University of Pennsylvania, 1959; m. Amanda Brugger, July 28, 1922 (dec. 1956); 1 dau., Elizabeth (Mrs. John Hoopes, II); m. 2d, Catherine Tyler, Dec. 14, 1957. House physician. Presbyn. Hosp., N.Y.C., 1916-18; asst. and asso., Hosp. of the Rockefeller Inst., New York City, 1918-21; asst. prof. medicine, Yale, 1921-24; asso. prof. research medicine, U. of Pa., 1924-41, John Herr Musser prof. research medicine, 1941-56, emeritus, professor research medicine, 1956—. Served as 1st lt., Med Corps, U.S. Army, 1918-19. Awarded John Phillips Meml. Medal of A.C.P., 1940, Kober medal Assn. Am. Physicians, 1955; Banting medal American Diabetes Assn., 1956—. Mem. Am. Philos. Soc., Assn. Am. Physicians, Am. Soc. Clinical Investigation, Am. Soc. Biol. Chemists (treas.; mem. editorial bd. Jour. Biol. Chemistry, 1942-47); Harvey Soc., Phila. Coll. Physicians, Nat. Acad. Science. Author articles profl. jours. Editor Jour. Am. Diabetes Assn. Home: 77 Wynnedale Rd., Narbeth, Pa. Office: Maloney Clinic, 36th and Spruce Sts., Phila. 4. Died Sept. 11, 1959.

STADLER, Lewis John (städ'lẽr), geneticist; b. St. Louis, Mo., July 6, 1896; s. Henry L. and Josephine (Ehrman) S.; B.S.A., U. of Fla., 1917; A.M., U. of Mo., 1918, Ph.D., 1922; grad. work Cornell U., 1919, 26, Harvard, 1925-26; m. Cornelia Field Tuckerman, Dec. 18, 1919; children—Maury Tuckerman, Henry Lewis, David Ross, John Brandeis, Eliot Tuckerman, Joan. Asst. prof. U. of Mo., 1922-25, asso. prof., 1925-36, prof., 1936—; vis. prof. Calif. Inst. Tech. 1940, Yale, 1950. Nat. Research fellow in biology, Harvard, 1925-26; sr. geneticist U.S. Dept. Agr., 1929-36, prin. geneticist, 1936-40, agent, 1940—. Mem. sci. adv. com. Selective Service System; Atomic Energy Commission, Postdoctoral Fellowship Board. Served as 2d lt. F.A., U.S. Army, 1918. Mem. A.A.A.S., Bot. Soc. America, Am. Soc. Agronomy, Genetics Soc. America (pres. 1938), Am. Soc. Naturalists (pres. 1953), Am. Acad. Arts and Scis., Nat. Acad. Scis., Am. Philos. Soc., Sigma Xi (pres.); nat. lectureship, Sigma Xi, 1938, Frank A. Spragg Memorial Lectureship, Mich. State College, 1939. Mem. editorial bd. Exptl. Biology Monographs, Advances in Genetics, American Naturalist, Univ. of Mo. Studies and Genetics. Home: 308 Thilly Av., Columbia, Mo. Died May 12, 1954.

STAFFORD, Geoffrey Wardle, clergyman; b. Birmingham, Eng., Jan. 5, 1898; s. John Thomas Wardle (formerly pres. Meth. Ch. Great Britain and Ireland) and Edith (Hardcastle) S.; educated, Scarborough Coll., 1908-14; B.A., Durham U., 1917, Wadham Coll., Oxford U., 1921; M.A., Oxford U., 1924, U. Dublin, 1944; Litt.D., Wesleyan U., W.Va., 1928; m. Helene, daughter of Bishop John W. Hamilton, Dec. 27, 1933. Came to U.S. 1921, naturalized 1929. Asso. minister First M.E. Ch., Balt., 1922-23; minister Wesley Ch., Milw., 1923-26; Court St. M.E. Ch., Rockford, Ill., 1926-32; lectr. religion Rockford Coll., 1928-32; minister U. Temple Ch., Seattle, 1932-37; guest preacher Stanford U. Meml. Chapel, 1933-36; prof. ch. history Drew Theol. Sem., Madison, N.J., 1937—. Rep. Council of Bishops of Meth. Ch. of N.A. to British Meth. Conf., Central Hall, Westminster, 1946. Guest preacher Egremont Presbyn. Ch., Liverpool, City Temple, London, 1946; Commn. on Internat. Goodwill among Chs. of Fed. Council Chs., Wellington Presbyn. Ch., Glasgow, Scotland, 1947; Ward Chapel, Dundee, Scotland, 1948. Lt. Northumberland Fusiliers (B.E.F.), 1917-19. Author: The Sermon on the Mount, 1927. Home: 52 Hillside Av., Madison, N.J. Died Oct. 27, 1958; buried Forest Hills Cemetery, Boston.

STAFFORD, Maurice L., foreign service officer; b. Windsor, Mo., Apr. 14, 1885; s. M. L. and Elizabeth S. (Patrick) S.; student William Jewell Coll., Liberty, Mo., 1906-07, U. of Calif., 1915; m. Lorna Isabella Lavery, Dec. 31, 1931. Newspaper work, St. Louis, Washington, D.C., Chicago, Atlanta, San Diego, 1907-19; U.S. consul, Santander, Spain, 1919-21, Barranquilla, Colombia, 1921-25, London, Eng., 1925-27, Madrid, Spain, 1927-31; sec. Am. Legation, Santo Domingo, Dominican Republic, 1931-32; charge d'affaires ad interim and consul, Kaunas, Lithuania, 1932-35; consul Cherbourg, 1935-36, Rio de Janeiro, 1936-38, Guadalajara, Mexico, 1938-41; consul and sec. Am. Embassy, Mexico City, 1941, first sec. and consul gen., Sept. 1943-Apr. 30, 1948; ret. Apr. 30, 1948. Research analyst in diplomacy and internat. relations. Mem. Sigma Nu. Home: Paseo de las Palmas 2090, Mexico 10, D.F. Mexico. Address: Dept. of State, Washington. Died July 15, 1957; buried Windsor, Mo.

STALBERG, Jonah (born Ivan Michael Shtalberg), bishop; b. Ossovetz, Russia, Aug. 12, 1894; s. Michael G. and Anna I. (Antonovsky) Shtalberg; cadet Moscow Mil. Acad., 1904-11; student Spl. Michael's Arty. Sch. and Acad., 1911-14, Imperial Acad. Gen. Staff, 1917-18, St. Tikhon's Theol. Sem., 1941-44. Came to U.S., 1923, naturalized, 1940. Laborer line Northwestern Pacific R.R., 1923-24; an establisher St. Nicholas Orthodox Ch., Portland, Ore., 1925-38; reader, sub-deacon San Francisco Cathedral, 1938-41; monk St. Tikhon's Russian Orthodox Monastery, South Canaan, Pa., 1941-44; lectr., provost St. Vladimir's Orthodox Theol. Sem., N.Y. C., 1945-49; dean Holy Trinity Cathedral, San Francisco, 1949-51; consecrated bishop of Washington, Dec. 1951; pres. St. Tikhons Theological Seminar, 1953—. Served as officer, Russian Imperial Army, Poland, Gaeitzia, Turkey-Armenia, Persia-Iran, Iraq, 1914-17, White Army of Siberia, 1918-20. Decorated Cross of St. Vladimir, Cross of St. Anna, Cross of St. Stanislaw (Russia). Mem. Nat. Geog. Soc. Office: 59 E. 2d St., N.Y.C. 3. Died Nov. 24, 1955; buried San Francisco.

STALIN, Joseph Vissarionovich, chmn. Council of Ministers of the U.S.S.R.; b. Gori, Tiflis, Georgia, Russia, Dec. 21, 1879; s. Vissarion and Ekatrina Djugashvili; participated in revolutionary movement from age of 15; ed. Gori Ecclesiastical School, 1888-94, Tiflis Theol. Sch., 1894-99 (expelled for polit. activity); 1st wife died 1917; m. 2d Nadejda Sergeyevana Alleluya (died 1932); children—Vassili, Svietlana. Mem. Tiflis Marxist Social Democratic Organization, 1898-1901; organized Batum Social Democrats, 1901; smuggled revolutionary literature from Lenin in Eng. into Russia; opened first revolutionary printing establishment in neglected crypt in Batum cemetery; first arrest for polit. activity, 1902, being arrested 8 times, exiled 7 times, escaping 6 times, 1902-13; met Lenin at Tammersfors, 1905; played leading role in revolutionary of Caucasus during First Russian Revolution of 1905-06; in accordance with a decision of Prague Conference founded party's paper, Pravda, 1911, editor, 1917; became mem. Party's Central Com. (having joined Lenin after escape from Siberia), Prague, 1912; worked with Bolshevik deputies in Duma, St. Petersburg, 1911-13; with Lenin prepared and led Oct. Revolution, 1917; commissar of nationalities, 1917, commissar of worker and peasant inspection, 1919; participated (military) in Civil War, 1918-20; mem. workers' war council, 1920-23; elected gen. sec. Central Com. of Communist Party of Soviet Union, 1922; suggested plan of Socialist industrialization, 1925, of collectiviation, 1927; adopted Popular Front policy, 1935; Stalin constitution adopted, 1936; purged Russian Army, 1937; chmn. State Defense Com., also People's Commissar for Defense of U.S.S.R., 1941-46; marshal of Soviet Union, 1943-45; Generalissimo of the U.S.S.R. since June 1945; general secretary Communist Party of Soviet Union (Bosheviks); mem. Supreme Soviet of U.S.S.R.; chmn. of the Council of Ministers of the U.S.S.R. and Minister for the Armed Forces. Decorated 1st Order of Red Banner (Civil War), 2d Order of Red Banner (for services in construction of Socialism), Order of Suvorov 1st class, 1943. Hero of Socialist Labor and Order of Lenin, 1939; 1st Order of Victory, 1944; 2nd Order of Victory, 1945; Hero of the Soviet Union, 1945. Author: Marxism and the National Question, 1912; Foundations of Leninism, 1924, section on Dialectical and Historical Materialism, Chapter 4 of the History of the Communist Party of the Soviet Union (Bolsheviks), 1938; first three volumes of 16-volume Collected Works, 1946. Died Mar. 5, 1953; interred Lenin Mausoleum, Moscow.

STALNAKER, Luther Winfield (stăn'â-kẽr), prof. of philosophy; b. Pleasant Hill, Mo., Nov. 27, 1892; s. Ward and Josephine Amanda (Howard) S.; A.B., summa cum laude, Drake U., Des Moines, Ia., 1920; Ph.D., Yale, 1929; m. Margaret Charlotte Fritz, Oct. 28, 1913; children—George Winfield, Margaret Josephine, Howard Lee. Ordained to ministry Disciples of Christ Church, 1915; pastor Brookfield Congl. Ch., Brookfield Center, Conn., 1921-25, Campbell Memorial Ch., Bethany; W.Va., 1926-27; instr. in English, New Haven (Conn.) Commercial High Sch., 1922; asst. prof. of philosophy, Drake U., 1927-29, prof. and head of dept., 1929—; dean coll. of liberal arts, 1940—. As exchange speaker, Internat. Council on Interchange Preachers and Speakers, spoke in Paris, Berlin, England and Scotland, 1938. Mem. bd. dirs. Ia. Civil Liberties Union (State chmn. 1942-1944). Dir. Drake U. Inst. of Pan-Am. Relations, 1941-46. Member of special United States Cultural Science Mission to Japan, Oct. 1948-Feb. 1949; consultant on social scis. to Supreme Comdr. Allied Powers, Japan, 1949-50. Mem. Am. Philosophical Soc., Ia. Philos. Soc., Southwestern Philos. Assn., Am. Acad. Polit. Sci., N.E.A. (higher edn. div.), Am. Adult Edn. Assn., Phi Beta Kappa, Psi Chi, Eta Sigma Phi. Mem. Disciples of Christ Ch. Mason. Clubs: Frontier, University, Lions. Author: Humanism and Human Dignity, 1945. Contbr. to periodicals. Home: 3103 University Av., Des Moines, Ia. Died July 12, 1954; buried Des Moines.

STAMM, John Samuel, bishop; b. Alida, Kan., Mar. 23, 1878; s. George and Mary (Schmutz) S.; grad. Northwestern Coll. Acad., Naperville, Ill., 1906; Ph.B., Northwestern Coll., 1909, Ph.M., 1910; B.D., Evang. Theol. Sem., Naperville, 1910; M.A., U. Chgo., 1926; D.D., Evang. Theol. Sem., Naperville, Ill., 1927; LL.D., Albright Coll., Reading, Pa., 1935; L.H.D., N. Central Coll., Naperville, Ill., 1949; S.T.D., Dickinson Coll., Carlisle, Pa., 1951; m. Priscilla Marie Wahl, Mar. 19, 1912. Entered ministry Evang. Ch., 1899; pastor successively Bloomington and Glasgow, Mo., until 1903, Manhattan, Ill., 1903-07, Downers Grove, Ill., 1907-12, Oak Park, 1912-19; prof. systematic theology, Evang. Theol. Sem., 1919-27, head dept., 1922-27; elected bishop Evang. Ch. 1926, reelected, 1930, 34, 38, 42, 46; elected bishop emeritus by Gen. Conf., 1950; sr. bishop, pres. bd. bishops, Evang. Ch., 1934-46; pres. Evang. Sch. Theology, 1935-41. Pres. Bd. Publ., Bd. Church Extension, Bd. Preacher Pension, all Evang. Ch.; mem. Fed. Council Chs. (mem. exec. com., adminstrv. com.; v.p. 1946-48, pres. 48-50); mem. exec. com. World Council Chs., mem. 1st assembly, 1948, mem. central com., 1948-54, pres. Pa. Council, 1945-49, v.p. Fed. Council, 1946-48, pres., 1948-50, mem. central com., 1948-54. Candidate Prohibition Party for Ill. State Senate, 1911; camp pastor, Camp Grant, Ill., 1918. Mem. exec. com. Ill. State Sunday Sch. Assn., 1916-19; mem. gov. bd. Young People's Work Evang. Ch., 1919-22; gen. sec. of evangelism, Evang. Ch., 1927-34. Lectr., Bible teacher at summer schs., convs., etc. Republican. Author: Evangelical Standard of Evangelism, 1924; Evangelism and Christian Experience, 1930. Address: 428 E. 72d St., Kansas City, Mo. Died Mar. 5, 1956; buried Mount Moriah Cemetery, Kansas City, Mo.

STANBURY, Walter Albert, clergyman; b. Boone, N.C., Jan. 27, 1884; s. John Senter and Alice Theresa (Taylor) S.; A.B., Trinity Coll. (now dept. Duke U.), Durham, N.C., 1908; D.D., Duke U., 1928, also from U. of N.C., 1928; grad. study Columbia, summer, 1929; m. Zula Virginia Bruton, Dec. 29, 1909; children—Walter Albert, John Bruton, Elizabeth Wilson. Teacher Latin, Trinity Park High Sch., Durham, 1908-09; ordained ministry M.E. Ch., S., 1910; pastor Edenton St. Ch., Raleigh, 1909, Tarboro, 1910, Chapel Hill (University Ch.), 1911-12, Clinton, 1913-15, First Ch., Wilson, 1916-19, Grace Ch., Wilmington, 1920-23, Edenton St. Ch., Raleigh, 1924-28, Duke Memorial Ch., Durham, 1929-33, W. Market St. Ch., Greensboro, N.C., 1933-37, Central Ch., Asheville, N.C., 1937-40; Centenary Ch., Winston-Salem, 1940-45; supt. Gastonia Dist., 1945-51; pastor 1st Ch., Asheboro since 1952; prof. practical theology, Duke University, 1929-33. Trustee Duke University; vice chairman North Carolina State Board Correction and Training; member Commn. Interdenom. Relations (M.E. Ch., S.), 1930-34, Federal Council of Chs. of Christ in America, 1930-34; v.p. N.C. Commn. Interracial Relations, 1931-48; pres. N.C. Council Chs., 1940-41, N.C. Conf. Bd. Christian Edn., 1930-33; del. Gen. Conf., M.E. Ch., S., 1930; pres. W.N.C. Conf. Bd. of Missions, 1944-45; del. to Uniting Conf., Meth. Ch., 1939, 1st Gen. Conf., Meth. Ch., 1940, 1944, 1948; mem. Commn. on Entertainment of Gen. Conf., 1940-48. Mem. Judicial Council, Methodist Church. Democrat. Author: with G. T. Rowe and others) The Southern Methodist Pulpit, 1927; Victories of the Cross, 1935. Contbr. to church publs. Home: 224 N. Fayetteville St., Asheboro, N.C. Died Mar. 20, 154; buried Asheboro, N.C.

STANCLIFF, Evert Lee, business exec.; b. North Loup, Neb., Dec. 10, 1887; s. George Washington and Mary Caroline (Ollis) S.; student Nebraska Wesleyan University, 1907-11; A.B., U. of Nebraska, 1913; m. Ruth Johnson, October 5, 1917 (dec. 1949); children—Victor Albert, Theodore Lee, Roger Benjamin (killed in action in Germany, 1945). Vice president and general manager Standard Motors Corporation, Kansas City, Missouri, 1913-18, Crete (Nebraska) Mills, 1918-23, Geo. P. Plant Milling Co., St. Louis, Mo., 1923-28; pres. St. Louis (Mo.) Mart, organizer and developer St. Louis Mart Bldg., 1928-29; head Stancliff & Co., indsl. and bus. management consultant Los Angeles, 1930-41, 47—; president Palm Springs Development Corporation; exec. v.p. Palm Springs Capital Co., Inc., Palm Springs Turf Club. Industrial director War Relocation Authority, installing war industries to employ Japanese evacuees in war prodn., 1942; consultant and adviser on indsl. development, State Dept., Washington, D.C., and Mexico; indsl. adviser to Mexican-Am. Commn. for Econ. Cooperation; rep. State Dept. as mem. of Mexican-Am. indsl. subcom., 1943-45; dir. office of field operation, Dept. of Commerce, Washington, D.C., 1946. Recipient Distinguished Service award, Univ. of Nebraska, June 1945. Member Beta Theta Pi (president and trustee Scholastic Foundation Southern California; distinguished service award So. Cal. alumni 1951), Phi Alpha Tau. Republican. Methodist. Clubs: Rotary, Shadow Mountain (Palm Desert, Cal.). Home: 8 Los Feliz Park, Los Angeles 27. Office: 634 S. Spring St., Los Angeles 14; also Palm Springs, Cal. Died May 22, 1956.

STANDISH, S(herwood) H(ubbard), business executive and engr.; b. Detroit, Mich., June 26, 1883; s. Fred Dana and Carrie M. (Hubbard) S.; grad. Detroit U. Sch., 1901; B.S. in M.E., U. of Mich., 1905; m. Mary Boyd Bransford, Apr. 14, 1910; children—Virginia Caroline (wife of Dr. H. Herman Young), Margaret Richards (Mrs. Abraham Strickle Bickham, Jr.), Sherwood Hubbard, Jr. Began career in foundry, Detroit, Michigan, 1906; foundry exec. in Phila., Pa., Racine, and Milwaukee, Wis., St. Louis, Mo. and Chicago, Ill., 1905-26; gen. mgr. Dayton (O.) Malleable Iron Co., 1926-45, vice pres. in charge engring. since 1945. Professional engr., O. Mem. Psi Upsilon, Sigma Xi. Republican. Protestant Episcopal (sr. warden). Club: Engineers of Dayton (past pres.). Home: 530 Maysfield Rd., Dayton 9. Office: Dayton Mealleable Iron Co., Dayton 1, O. Died Dec. 4, 1953; buried Woodland Cemetary.

STANFIELD, J(oseph) Fisher, univ. prof.; b. Lewisburg, Ky., June 4, 1901; s. Charlie Grant and Mary Martha (East) S.; student Castle Heights Mil. Acad., Lebanon, Tenn., 1918; Milligan Coll., Tenn., 1918-20; A.B., Western State Coll. of Colo., 1927; A.M., Univ. of Colo., 1930; Ph.D., State University of Iowa, 1937; married to Margaret Ellen Cox, August 1, 1939 (deceased September 1956). Teacher of biology at Littleton, Colorado High Sch., 1927-29; summer sch. instr., Univ. of Colo., 1930-31; asst. prof. of biology, Knox Coll., Galesburg, Ill., 1931-33, 1934-39; prof. of botany, Chicago Teachers Coll., 1939-43; research asso., State Univ. of Ia., 1943-44; prof. and head dept. botany, Miami Univ., Oxford, Ohio, since 1944. Fellow A.A.A.S., Ohio State Acad. Sci., Ill. Acad. Sci.; mem. Bot. Soc. of Am. (mem. com on teaching methods, 1941), Am Assn. Biol. Teachers, Am. Soc. for Adv. Edn., Am. Forestry Assn., Am. Soc. Plant Physiol. (chmn. com. on editorial costs 1941, bus. mgr., 1941-44, exec. sec.-treas., since 1944), Am. Soc. Hort. Sci., Am. Assn. Univ. Professors, N.E.A., Phi Sigma, Sigma Xi, Theta Chi, Gamma Alpha. Republican. Presbyterian. Mason. Contributor articles in field of reproduction in plants, physico chem. aspects of sex in dioecious plants, teaching methods in biology pubs. Home: Shadowy Hills, Route 2, Oxford, O. Died May 8, 1958.

STANFORD, Albert Clinton, army officer; b. Chatsworth, Ill., Mar. 25, 1895; s. Fred Clinton and Ettie Nora (Tilden) S.; B.S., U.S. Mil. Acad., 1917; M.S., Yale, 1925; grad. Signal Corps Sch., 1923, F.A., Sch., 1929, Command and Gen. Staff Sch., 1941; m. Florence C. Busbee, Mar. 6, 1918; 1 son, Frederick Clinton. Commd. 2d lt. Cav., 1917; promoted through grades to brig. gen. July 1942; transferred to Signal Corps, 1920, to F.A., 1927; prof. mil. science and tactics, Mich. State Coll., 1936-40; assigned 34th Inf. Div., Aug. 1942; later assigned for overseas station; retired 1946. Home: 301 W. State St., Trenton, N.J. Died Nov. 7, 1952; buried Fort Sam Houston Nat. Cemetery.

STANFORD, Homer Reed, naval officer; b. June 26, 1865; entered U.S. Navy, 1898, and advanced through the grades to rear adm., 1938; retired, 1939. Address: Navy Dept., Washington 25. Deceased.

STANLAWS, Penrhyn (Penrhyn Stanley Adamson), portrait painter; b. Dundee, Scotland, Mar. 19, 1877; s. James and Jessie (Leith) Adamson; came to U.S., 1891; studied art, Paris and London; m. Jean Pughsley, Apr. 30, 1913. Exhibited at Paris Salon, 1904; established studio in N.Y., 1908; built Hôtel des Artistes (largest studio bldg. in Am.), 1916, and another in 1917; pres. Hôtel des Artistes, Inc. Clubs: Princeton (New York); Savage (London, Eng.). Wrote: Instinct (3-act play, prod. London, 1912); The End of the Hunting (1-act play, prod. Yale, 1915). Motion picture dir. for Famous Players Lasky Corp., 1921, 22. Studios: 1127 El Centro Av., Hollywood, Cal.; also The Mission Inn, Riverside, Cal. Died May 18, 1957.

STANLEY, A(ugustus) Owsley, ex-senator; b. Shelbyville, Ky., May 21, 1867; s. Rev. William and Amanda (Owsley) S.; A.B., Centre Coll., Danville, Ky., 1889; m. Sue Soaper, Apr. 29, 1903. Admitted to bar, 1894; began practice at Flemingsburg, Ky., 1894, removed to Henderson, 1898. Presdl. elector, 1900; mem. 58th to 63d Congresses (1903-15), 2d Ky. Dist.; gov. of Ky., term 1915-19; U.S. senator, 1919-25; chmn. Internat. Joint Commn., authorized to settle disputes over boundary waters, etc., between U.S. and Canada, until 1954, ret. 1954; author Clayton Anti-trust Act. Democrat. Home: 1681 31st St. N.W., Washington. Died Aug. 12, 1958; buried Frankfort, Ky.

STANLEY, Edmund, univ. pres.; b. Hendricks Co., Ind., Apr. 7, 1847; s. Harvey and Dorinda (Whicker) S.; acad. edn.; taught sch. in Ind. while studying; hon. A.M., Penn Coll., Oskaloosa, Ia., 1892; LL.D., Fairmount Coll., Wichita, Kan., 1916; m. Martha E. Davis, Sept. 2, 1871. Supt. schs., Lawrence, Kan., 1880-95; state supt. pub. instrn., Kan., 1895-97; pres. Friends U., Wichita, Kan., 1898-1918, pres. emeritus, 1918—. Presiding officer of national five years' meeting of the Friends Church, 1902. Life member NE.A. Author: (with A. R. Taylor) Apple Blossoms, 1897. Address: Wichita, Kan. Died May 21, 1928; buried Maple Grove Cemetery, Wichita, Kan.

STANLEY, Hugh Wright, railway pres.; b. Petersburg, Va., Feb. 13, 1874; s. Washington Hugh and Mary Alice (Bonsack) S.; student Lynchburg (Va.) pub. and high schs.; married. Entered ry. service, May 1890, consecutively telegraph operator, stenographer and chief clerk Norfolk & Western Ry. to 1895; chief clerk to supt. Southern Ry., Knoxville, Tenn., 1895-97; sec. to gen. supt. S.A.L. Ry., 1897-1900, chief clerk to gen. supt., 1900-03, trainmaster, 1903-06, supt. 4th div., 1906-07, supt. transportation, 1907-10, gen. supt. transportation, 1910-11, asst. gen. mgr., 1911-12, gen. mgr., 1912-14, asst. to pres., 1914-16; with special com. Am. Ry. Assn. and asst. to chmn. of Car Service Commn., at Washington, D.C., 1916-17; receiver Tenn. Central Ry., 1917-22, president, 1922-46, chmn. bd. 1946, chairman board, president, 1947-54. Member of American Railway Engring. Assn., Newcomen Soc., Nashville Chamber of Commerce. Clubs: Kiwanis, Executives, Belle Meade Country. Home: 208 Craighead Av. Office: American Trust Bldg., Nashville, Tenn. Died Feb. 7, 1955.

STANLEY, Louise, home economist; b. Nashville, Tenn., June 8, 1883; d. Gustavus Augustus and Eliza Munroe (Winston) S.; B.S., U. of Nashville, 1903; B. Edn., U. of Chicago, 1905; M.A., Columbia, 1907; Ph.D., Yale University, 1911; LL.D., University of Mo., 1940. Instr. home economics, University of Mo., 1907-11, prof. and chmn. dept., 1911-23; leave of absence, 1918, to work as home economics agt. of Fed. Bd. Vocational Edn.; chief Bur. Home Economics U.S. Dept. Agr., Sept. 1, 1923-Feb. 28, 1943; research coordinator Agrl. Research Administration 1943-50. Mem. Am. Chem. Soc., Am. Home Economics Assn., Am. Assn. U. Women, Pi Lambda Theta, Phi Delta Kappa, Omicron Nu. Home: 3725 Macomb St., Washington 16. Died July 15, 1954; buried Mt. Olivet Cemetery, Nashville.

STANLEY, Robert Crooks, mechanical and mining engr.; b. Little Falls, N.J., Aug. 1, 1876; s. Thomas and Ada (Crooks) S.; M.E., Stevens Inst. of Tech., 1899; E.M., Sch. of Mines (Columbia), 1901; Sc.D., Columbia, 1939; D.Eng., Stevens Inst. Tech., 1935; D.Eng., Rensselaer Poly. Inst., 1940; Doctor of Laws, Queen's U. (Kingston, Ont.), 1949; m. Alma Guyon Timolat, June 14, 1912; children—Doris (Mrs. Reuel E. Warriner), Robert Crooks, Jr. Has been with the International Nickel Co. since 1901, gen. supt., 1912-18, 1st v.p., 1918-22, pres., 1922; chmn. bd. dirs., chmn. exec. com. and mem. adv. com., Internat. Nickel Co. of Can., Ltd.; chmn. bd. and dir. The Internat. Nickel Co., Inc.; dir. and mem. finance com. U.S. Steel Corp.; mem. advisory com. The Mond Nickel Co., Ltd. (England); dir. Chase Nat. Bank (mem. exec., fgn., examination coms.), Canadian Pacific Ry. Co., Amalgamated Metal Corp., Henry Gardner & Co. (London), Centre d'Information du Nickel (France). Special trustee for life, Stevens Institute Tech. Mem. Nat. Foreign Trade Council, Am. Inst. Mining and Metallurgical Engineers, Am. Iron and Steel Inst., Am. Mining Congress, Mining and Metallurgical Soc. Am., Chamber of Commerce, State of New York, Institute of Metals (London), British Empire Chamber Commerce in U.S., Canadian Inst. Mining and Metallurgy, Council of Princeton U. Internat. Summer Sch. of Geology and Natural Resources, St. George's Soc. of New York, Copper Development Assn., London (councillor), Nat. Industrial Conf. Board, Inc., Academy of Political Science, Army Ordnance Assn., Canadian Soc. of New York, Newcomen Society of England. Comdr. Order of Leopold conferred by King Leopold at Brussels, Belgium, Apr. 14, 1937. Received Thomas

Egleston medal from Columbia Engring. Schools Alumni Assn., 1939; First Charles F. Rand Foundation gold medal awarded by Am. Inst. Mining and Metall. Engrs., 1941; Gold Medal for Advancement of Research awarded by American Soc. for Metals, 1944; Alumni Award Medallion of Alumni Assn. of Stevens Inst., 1946; His Majesty's Medal for Service in the Cause of Freedom (Eng.), 1947; Platinum Medal of Inst. of Metals, London, 1948. Clubs: City Midday, Mining, Union, New York Yacht, Boca Raton, Richmond County Country; Mount Royal (Montreal); Toronto Club: St. James (London). Home: Country Club Grounds, Dongan Hills, Staten Island, N.Y. Office: 67 Wall St., N.Y. City 5. Died Feb. 12, 1951.

STANLEY, William Eugene, lawyer; b. Wichita, Kan., April 30, 1891; s. William Eugene (15th Gov. of Kan.), and Emma Lenora (Hills) S.; student Baker U., 1908-10; Ph.B., U. of Chicago, 1912, J.D., 1913; m. Margaret Long, Jan. 18, 1922; 1 dau., Margaret Anna. Admitted to Kansas Bar, 1914, practicing at Wichita; mem. Depew Stanley, Weigand & Hook. Served as 1st lt. U.S. Army, 1917; a.d.c., Maj. Gen. Leonard Wood, 1919. Mem. Conf. of Commnrs. on Uniform State Laws (v.p. 1940-43, pres. 1943-44, 46-47, chmn. exec. council, 1945-46). Chmn. Sedgwick Co. A.R.C., 1942-43, mem. bd. 1941-44, 1949-52; mem. bd. Wichita Community Chest, 1949-53. Mem. Am. Bar Assn. (council sect. ins. law 1932-36, chmn. 1935-36; council sect. legal edn. and admissions to bar 1931-40, chmn. 1940-41; council sect. bar orgn. activities 1937-41; chmn. com. on advanced legal edn. 1937-40; mem. house of dels., State del. from Kan. 1937-42; bd. govs. 1942-45; com. rules and calendar, 1945—; committee publications 1944-46; chairman committee ways and means, 1946-—; assembly delegate, 1945—), American Law Inst., Kan. Bar Assn. (sec. 1920-39; editor Jour. of Assn., 1932-39; pres. 1940-41), Wichita Bar Assn., Inter-Am. Bar Assn. (del. Havana, 1941, Mexico City, 1944; mem. council 1941-45), Kans. State Hist. Soc. (v.p. 1941, pres. 1942), U. of Chicago Law Sch. Alumni Assn. (pres., 1943; adv. bd., 1944—), C. of C., Delta Tau Delta. Republican (mem. nat. program com.). Methodist. Mason (32°), I.O.O.F. Clubs: Wichita, Country. Home: 3401 E. 2d St. Office: First Nat. Bank Bldg., Wichita, Kan. Died Sept. 26, 1953; buried Old Mission Mausoleum, Wichita.

STANTON, Frank McMillan, agt. of copper mines; ed. Columbia Grammar School; grad. Columbia Coll. School of Mines, 1887; apptd. agt. pro tem. Central mine, Keweenaw Co., Mich., 1887, mining eng'r Atlantic mine, Houghton Co., Mich., and agt. of same, 1889; had entire charge of construction of stamp mill of 1,800 tons per day, 13 miles railroad, dam 50 ft. high, mining buildings, machinery, water works, etc.; also agt. Baltic Mining Co., Central Mining Co., Phoenix Consolidated Copper Co. Address: Atlantic Mine, Houghton Co., Mich. Deceased.

STANTON, Henry Francis, architect; b. Detroit, Mich., Feb. 7, 1894; s. Robert Lee and Grace M. (Newman) S.; B.Arch., Cornell U., 1916; m. Catharine Pittman, June 28, 1924; children—Annette Newman, Joan Dakin, Kathleen Pittman. Engaged in general practice of architecture, including residential, large scale housing projects, commercial and industrial work, since 1921. Commd. 1st lt., F.A., U.S. Army, 1917, promoted capt., 1918; served with U.S. Army, 1917-19. Trustee Centennial Fund, Diocese of Mich. Episcopal Ch., Fellow Am. Inst. Architects; mem. Mich. Soc. Architects, Engring. Soc. of Detroit, Chi Phi. Clubs: Detroit, Witenagemote, Grosse Ile Yacht. Home: 22003 West River Rd., Grosse Ile, Mich. Office: 1243 Free Press Bldg., Detroit 26. Died Dec. 8, 1953.

STANTON, Henry Thompson, advertising executive; b. Maysville, Ky., 1886; s. Clarence Lyndon and Ida (Pierce) S.; student pub. schs.; m. Louise Collier; children—Henry, Louise, James, Collier. Various positions, then sales mgr. eastern div. Procter & Gamble, Cincinnati, O., 1902-14; with J. Walter Thompson Co., advt., Chicago, Ill., 1914-23, v.p., 1923-25, exec. v.p. and gen. mgr. western div., 1925-—, also dir. Dir. Nat. Blvd. Bank, First Fed. Savings & Loan Assn., Rystan Co., N.Y. City. Republican. Episcopalian. Clubs: Chicago, Tavern (Chicago); Indian Hill (Winnetka, Ill.); Chicago Golf (Wheaton). Address: 840 Manzanita Way, Woodside, Cal. Died Oct. 7, 1954.

STANTON, Timothy William, geologist, paleontologist; b. Monroe County, Ill., Sept. 21, 1860; s. William and Mary A. (Blanchard) S.; B.S., U. of Colo., 1883, M.S., 1895, D.Sc., 1924; Johns Hopkins, 1888-89; Ph.D., Columbian (now George Washington) U., 1897; m. Grace M. Patten, Oct. 12, 1898; children—Grace, Elizabeth, Josephine. Asst. state librarian of Colo., 1885-88; asst. paleontologist, 1889-1900, paleontologist, 1900-03, geologist in charge paleontology, 1903-30, acting chief geologist, 1931, chief, 1932-35, U.S. Geol. Survey; retired. Instructor paleontology and stratigraphic geology, 1894-1905, asst. prof. paleontology, 1906-10, George Washington U. Fellow Geol. Soc. Am. (v.p. 1921), Paleontol. Soc. America (pres. 1921), A.A.A.S.; mem. Washington Acad. Sciences, Phi Beta Kappa, Delta Tau Delta. Republican. Methodist. Club: Cosmos. Has published numerous reports and papers on paleontology and stratigraphic geology. Home: 1017 N. Noyes Dr., Silver Spring, Md. Died Dec. 4, 1953.

STAPLES, Abram Penn, judge; b. Martinsville, Va., Sept. 18, 1885; s. Abram Penn and Sallie Clement (Hunt) S.; grad. high sch., Roanoke, Va., 1904; LL.B., Washington and Lee U., 1908; m. Jean Duncan Watts, Jan. 5, 1911; children—Jean Lee, Allen Watts, Abram Penn III, William Hunt. Began practice at Roanoke, 1908; mem. State Senate, Va., 1928-34; mem. Va. Commn. to Recommend Liquor Control Legislation, 1933; atty. gen. of Va., 1934-47; apptd. judge Supreme Ct. Appeals of Va., 1947; v.p., dir. Interstate Commn. on Crime, 1940-42; chmn. Va. Commn. on Interstate Cooperation, 1936-38; mem. Conf. on State Def.; mem. Fed.-State Joint Conf. Nat. Def.; dir. Council of State Govts., 1941-42 (commn. to draft State war legislation). Mem. com. on law enforcement of Pres.'s Fire Prevention Conf., commn. to revise Va. Code, Commn. on Post Mortem Examinations; Legislative Com. to study taxation of Va. Pub. Utilities. Pres. Nat. Assn. Attys. Gen., 1941-42; mem. Richmond, Va. State, Roanoke (pres. 1924) bar assns., Am. Bar Assn. (house dels., 1941-42), S.A.R., Am. Br. of Newcomen Soc., Am. Judicature Soc., Omicron Delta Kappa, Phi Beta Kappa, Phi Kappa Sigma, Phi Delta Phi, Sigma Ribbon Soc. Democrat. Episcopalian. K.P., Red Man. Clubs: Shenandoah (Roanoke); Commonwealth (Richmond). Home: Monroe Terrace. Address: Supreme Court of Appeals of Virginia, Supreme Court Bldg., Richmond, Va. Died Mar. 21, 1951; buried Fairview Cemetery, Roanoke, Va.

STAPLES, Charles Henry, univ. prof.; b. Downsville, La., June 18, 1885; s. John Baston and Cinderella (Hester) S.; B.S., M.S., La. State U., Tex. Agr. and Mining Coll., 1932; unmarried. Head, dairy dept., La. State U., 1922—. Mem. Am. Jersey Cattle Club (dir., v.p.), La. Dairy Assn. (dir., pres.), Kappa Sigma. Methodist. Elk. Home: 136 W. Chimes St., Baton Rouge 3, La. Died Aug. 13, 1950; buried Rosehaven Cemetery, Baton Rouge.

STAPLES, Percy A., bus. exec.; b. Portland, Me., Mar. 31, 1883; s. Charles Augustus and Maria (Hay) S.; ed. Portland pub. schs., 1889-97, Yonkers (N.Y.) High Sch., 1897-98; Protestant Episcopal Acad., Phila., 1898-1900; Mass. Inst. Tech., 1900-03, B.S., 1905-06; m. Eliza A. Turner, Apr. 21, 1909. Aide, U.S. Coast and Geodetic Survey, 1903-05; C.E. with J. G. White & Co., New York, 1906; with Stone & Webster, management, 1906-13; with W. S. Barstow & Co., New York, 1913-18; partner, L. A. Riley, New York, cons. engring.; comptroller, R.R. and sugar cos., Hershey Interests in Cuba, 1921; gen. mgr., pres. and dir. after 1921; dir. Hershey Chocolate Co., 1927; chmn. bd. and pres. Hershey Chocolate Corp., 1947; chmn. bd. Hershey Corp., Havana, Cuba, 1948—; member board of directors Violeta Sugar Company, Cuban Atlantic Sugar Co., Cia Azc. Atlantica del Golfo, Hershey Nat. Bank, Hershey Cuban Ry. Co., Hershey Terminal R.R., Rosario Sugar Co., Cia Azc. Gomez Mena. pres., Hershey Trust Co., 1944; chmn. bd. and trustee, Milton Hershey Sch. and Hershey Found., Hershey, 1944. Mem. Nat. Fgn. Trade Council, Pa. Chamber of Commerce, Delta Kappa Epsilon. Clubs: American, Havana, Hershey Golf, Central Hershey, Cuba, Hershey Country, Hershey Community (Hershey, Pa.); India House (New York City). Home: Hotel Hershey, Hershey, Pa.; and Central Hershey, Cuba. Offices: Hershey Trust Co., Hershey, Pa.; H. H. Pike & Co., 120 Wall St., N.Y.; also Hershey Corp., Edificio Ambar Motors, Havana, Cuba. Died July 23, 1956.

STAPLES, Thomas S(tarling), coll. dean; b. Roopville, Ga., Apr. 11, 1879; s. Thomas Trammel and Rachel (Stillwell) S.; student Young Harris Coll., 1898-99; Ph.B., Emory Coll., Oxford, Ga., 1900-04; A.M., Central Coll., Fayette, Mo., 1907-08; A.M., Columbia U., 1915, Ph.D., 1918; m. Dove Harton, Dec. 24, 1912. Supt. schs., Lutherville, Ga., 1904-05; instr., Central Coll., Fayette, Mo., 1905-08; prof. hist., Hendrix Coll., Conway, Ark., 1908—, dean, 1928—. Mem. So., Ark., Am. hist. assns. Mem. Ark. State Bd. Edn., Govs. Com. on Edn. Mem. Phi Beta Kappa, Blue Key. Mason (K.T.). Democrat. Club: Executives (Little Rock, Ark.). Methodist (mem. University Senate). Author: Reconstruction in Arkansas, 1923; Political History of Arkansas, 1865-1908, 1930; Our Land and Our People (co-author), 1929; Our America (co-author). Home: 1821 Robinson Av. Address: Hendrix Station, Conway, Ark. Died July 15, 1957.

STAPLETON, Benjamin F., mayor; b. Paintsville, Ky., Nov. 12, 1869; grad. Nat. Normal U., Lebanon, O.; m. Mabel Freeland, June 27, 1917; children—Benjamin F., Lois Jane. Admitted to Colo. bar, 1899, and began practice at Denver; police magistrate, Denver, 1904-15; postmaster, Denver, 1915-21; oil bus. 1921-22; mayor of Denver, 1923-31; auditor for State Colo., 1933-35; again mayor June, 1935-47. Served as volunteer U.S. Army, P.I., 1898-99. Democrat. Mason. Home: 430 Williams St. Address: Municipal Bldg., Denver. Died May 22, 1950; buried Crown Hill Cemetery, Jefferson County, Colo.

STARBIRD, Alfred (Andrews), ret. army officer; b. Paris, Me., July 15, 1875; s. Winfield Scott and Emeline Hardy (Roberts) S.; B.S., U. Me., 1898; m. (Mary) Ethel Dodd, July 20, 1911; children—Alfred Dodd, Catharine Andrews (Mrs. Edward Jennison), Ethel Allan. Enlisted as sgt., 1st Me. Inf., 1898; commd. as 2d lt. U.S. Army, 1898 with artillery; advanced through grades to brig. gen., 1930; saw service in U.S., Philippine Islands, Europe; retired, 1930; genealogist, 1931-41. Awarded Distinguished Service Medal, various campaign medals. Fellow Inst. Am. Genealogy. Republican. Mason (32°). Author: Geneaology of Starbird Family, 1940, 43. Home: R.F.D., Underhill, Vt. Died Dec. 9, 1956.

STARK, Louis, newspaper corr.; b. Tibold Daracz, Hungary, May 1, 1889; s. Adolph and Rose (Kohn) S.; came to U.S., 1891; student N.Y. Training Sch. for Teachers, 1907-08; hon. LL.D., Reed Coll., Portland, Ore., 1937; m. Jennie House, Aug. 17, 1916; 1 son, Arthur. Began as teacher in New York City public schs., 1909; publishing and advertising, 1909-13; reporter, N.Y. City News Assn., 1913-17, N.Y. Evening Sun, 1917, N.Y. Times, 1917—, with N.Y. Times Bur., Washington, specializing in news of labor, 1933-51, editorial dept. N.Y. Times, 1951—. Awarded Pulitzer prize, 1942. Club: Nat. Press, Cosmos (Washington). Home: 325 E. 41st St. Office: N.Y. Times, 229 W. 43d St., N.Y.C. Died May 17, 1954.

STARKWEATHER, Louis Pomeroy, educator, cons. author; b. Plainfield, N.J., Apr. 7, 1898; s. Louis Pomeroy and Jeannette (Nash) S.; B.Sc., Tufts Coll., 1921, M.B.A., N.Y.U., 1925, D.C.S., 1930; m. Ruth Wallace Lecraw, June 28, 1930; children—David Courtney, Louis Pomeroy, Eleanor Widger. Instr. Arlington (Mass.) High Sch., 1921-22; asst. instr. Tufts Coll., 1921-22; with comml. engrs. dept. N.Y. Telephone Co., 1922-23; analyst indsl. dept. Bankers Trust Co., N.Y.C., 1923-24; instr. banking finance N.Y.U., 1924-30, asst. prof., 1930-34, asso. prof., 1934-46, lectr. grad. school business adminstrn. since 1946; adminstv. sec. Wall St. Div., 1926-29; lectr. U. Newark, 1934-41, Summer Inst. Credit N.A.C.A. Babson Inst., 1941; adminstv. asst. Bur. Yards and Docks, U.S.N., 1942; state orgn. officer N.J. OPA, 1942-43; negotiator, expert cons. War Dept., U.S. Army, Q.M. Price Adjustment Bd., 1943-47; prof. finance and ins., chmn. dep. finance Sch. Bus. Adminstrn. Rutgers U., retired, now professor emeritus of finance; visiting prof. commerce U. So. Cal., 1950; vis. lectr. finance, pub. utility execs. course Ga. Inst. Tech., 1953; dir., adv. and cons. to individuals, estates, corps, and mutual funds. Trustee Tufts Coll., 1937-42; meml. trustee, Va. Diocesan Center, Protestant Episcopal Ch. of Va.; chmn. finance com. Plainfield Bd. Edn., 1946-50. Recipient Distinguished Service award Tufts Coll., 1951; Alumni Scroll of Honor, N.Y.U., 1951. Del. to West Point Sesquicentennial, 1952, Tufts Coll. Centennial, 1952. Mem. Nat. Assn. Financial Analysts, Inc., Mem. Am. Econ. Assn., Am. Finance Assn. (secretary-treasurer 1951-52), American Arbitration Assn. (panel member), N.Y. University Men in Finance, Delta Tau Delta, Beta Gamma Sigma, Delta Sigma Pi. Unitarian. Mason. Clubs: University (Wash.); Shelter Island Yacht; Plainfield (N.J.) Country; Newark Athletic. Author: Analysis Industrial Securities, 1930; Questions and Problems in Credit Principles and Practices, 1932; Case Studies in Corporate Financing, 1934; Corporate Financing and Consolidation, 1939; Corporate Readjustment and Reorganization, 1940; Policies and Practices in Corporate Finance, 1951. Contbg. author: Financial Handbook, 1949; Fundamentals of Investment Banking, 1949; Financial Organization & Management (Gerstenberg 3d rev. edit.), 1951; also teaching publs. Address: Oaknoll, 931 Oakwood Pl., Plainfield N.J. Died Aug. 24, 1958.

STARNES, George Talmage, economist; b. Verdi, Scott County, Va., May 31, 1895; s. Peter Johnson and Martha Jane (Morris) S.; B.A., Emory and Henry Coll., 1917; M.A., U. of Va., 1924, Ph.D., 1925; M.A., Harvard, 1925; m. Miriam Maude Thurman, Sept. 15, 1923; 1 son, William Thurman. Prin. high sch., Pungoteague, Va., 1920-21; with U. of Va. since 1922, instr. dept. economics until 1924, asst. prof., 1925-28, asso. prof., 1928-40; prof. since 1940. Served in U.S. Army, May 1918-Sept. 1919; in France 1 yr. Mem. Am. Econ. Assn., Phi Beta Kappa, Beta Gamma Sigma, Tau Kappa Alpha, Alpha Kappa Psi, Delta Sigma Phi. Democrat. Mason. Club: Colonnade. Author: Labor in the Industrial South (with Abraham Berglund and Frank T. de Vyver), 1930; Sixty Years of Branch Banking in Virginia, 1931; Some Phases of Labor Relations in Virginia (with John E. Hamm), 1934; A Survey of the Methods for the Promotion of Industrial Peace (with J. M. McCutcheon and J. M. Stepp), 1939; The Labor Supply of Two Rural Industries (with Wilkins and Wisman), 1951. Home: University, Va. Died July 6, 1955.

STARR, Nathan, physician, surgeon; b. Paris, Ill., Feb. 15, 1860; s. William and Mary Ann (Hess) S.; U. of Ill., 1878-80; M.D., Hahnemann Med. Coll., Chgo., 1889; m. Ida Grace Hall, of Paris, Ill., Dec. 18, 1883. Practiced, Kansas Ill., 1889-90, since at Charleston, Ill.; dir. Charleston Trust and Savs. Bank; mem. Bd. of Edn., Charleston, 1893-99. Mem. Am. Inst. Homoeopathy, Ill. Homoe. Med. Assn. (pres. 1905), Alumni Assn. Hahnemann Med. Coll. (pres., 1905). Republican. Methodist. Address: Charleston, Ill. Deceased.

STARRETT, Paul, builder; b. Lawrence, Kan., Nov. 25, 1866; s. William Aiken and Helen Martha (Ekin) S.; Lake Forest (Ill.) U., 1884-85; m. Anna Therese Hinman, May 25, 1892 (died Aug. 8, 1904); children—Pauline (Mrs. K. D. Pierson), Therese Starrett; m. 2d, Elizabeth Root, June 8, 1920; children—Paul, Daniel, Andrew. With Burnham & Root, architects, Chgo., and successor, D. H. Burnham & Co., 1887-97; with George A. Fuller Co., 1897, pres., 1903-22; with his brothers, Ralph and W. A., founded Starrett Bros., Inc., builders, N.Y., 1922; chmn. bd. The Starrett Corp.; dir. Starrett Investing Corp., Wall & Hanover St. Realty Corp. Erected many notable bldgs., including Pa. R.R. Sta., Plaza, Commodore and Biltmore hotels, N.Y.; Bellevue-Stratford Hotel, Phila.; Blackstone Hotel, Chgo.; Lincoln Meml. Washington, etc. Republican. Clubs: Nat. Arts (New York); Blind Brook, Essex County Country, Greenwich Country. Home: Hillside Rd., Greenwich, Conn. Office: 63 Wall St., N.Y.C. Died July 5, 1957.

STASTNY, Olga Frances, (stăs'nē), b. Wilber, Neb., Sept. 13, 1878; d. Frank John and Theresa (Jurka) Sadilek; M.D., U. of Neb. Med. Coll., 1913; m. Charles Stastny, Oct. 25, 1895 (now dec.); children—Elsa Camilla (Mrs. Ladislav Skocpol), Robert Browning (dec.). Interne New Eng. Hosp. for Women and Children, 1913; began practice at Omaha, Neb., 1914; served with Am. Women's Hosp., in France, 1918-19, Greece, 1921-22, Y.W.C.A., Prague, 1919-21, with Y.M.C.A., 1921-22; established typhus and smallpox quarantine station, Island of Macronissi, Greece, 1922-23; instr. in obstetrics and gynecology, Coll. of Medicine, U. of Neb., 1931-43; now med. dir. Supreme Forest Woodmen Circle Ins. Co., Omaha. Pres. Med. Women's Nat. Assn., 1930-31, nat. treas., 1934-37; nat. health chmn. Business and Professional Women's Fedn., 1929-31; nat. patriotic chmn. Women's Overseas Service League, 1930; dir. Family Welfare Assn., Omaha, 1917-37. Organized Americanization dept., Women's Council of Defense, Neb., World War I. Trustee Doane Coll., Crete, Neb., 1931-48. Mem. A.M.A., Neb. State Med. Soc., Nu Sigma Phi, Order Eastern Star; hon. mem. Mid-West Clin. Soc., Delta Kappa Gamma. Decorated Medaille de Reconnaissance (France); Cross of St. George (Greece), Noguchi medal, 1931; special citation for service with Czechoslovakia Army. Mem. Alpha Lambda Delta. Unitarian. Clubs: Altrusa, Women's Overseas Service League. Address: 308 S. 41st, Omaha 3, Neb. Died Aug. 21, 1952; buried Forest Lawn Crematory, Omaha.

STATON, Harry (Parker), ex-editor and mgr. newspaper syndicate; born Bklyn., November 22, 1879; son Charles Lewis Jesse and Ellen (Parker) S.; ed. pub. schs., Bklyn.; m. Mabel Lydia Qiick, March 9, 1904 (died Feb. 10, 1942); children—Alice Mabel (Mrs. William Kable Russell), Grace Harvey (Mrs. Joseph Xavier DuMond), Harry Parker; married 2d, Elsa Lang, June 4, 1942. With Brooklyn Times, 1894-96; reporter Brooklyn Standard Union, 1896-99, Evening World, 1899-1901, Evening Sun, 1901-04; editor and art director New York Globe, 1904-12; editor and publisher Trend Magazine, 1913-15; publicity Barnum & Bailey Circus, 1916-19, editor and manager New York Herald Tribune Syndicate 1920-47, now retired. Republican. Clubs: Players, Dutch Treat, N. Y.C. Home: 245 20th St., Surf City, N.J. Died July 4, 1959.

STAUB, Albert William (stawb), clergyman, educator; b. Titusville, Pa., Sept. 28, 1880; s. Albert W. and Caroline (Rickert) S.; A.B., Oberlin, 1904; A.M., Columbia, 1907; B.D., Union Theol. Sem., 1907; m. Jane Frederica McIntosh, June 9, 1908; 1 son, Albert W. Ordained Congl. ministry, 1908; ednl. missionary in China, 1908-12; exec. sec. Riverdale Neighborhood Assn., Riverdale-on-Hudson, N.Y., 1912-14; dir. Atlantic Div., Am. Red Cross, 1914-19; Am. dir. Near East Coll. Assn., 1919—; exec. sec. bd. trustees Robert Coll., Am. Univ. of Beirut, Constantinople Woman's Coll., Internat. Coll. (Beirut), Sophia American School, Athens Coll., American College at Baghdad; (trustee of the Town Hall Club, New York City; trustee, The Town Hall, Inc.), Near East Foundation; sec. board trustees Am. Hosp., Istanbul; trustee Oberlin-Shansi Memorial Assn., West Side Presbyn. Church, Ridgewood. Decorated: Edith Cavell Medal, Belgian Red Cross, 1919; Cross of Officer of the Order of St. Sava (Yugoslavia), 1923; Cross of Comdr. Nat. Order of Civil Merit (Bulgaria), 1930; Officer of the Order of the Cedar (Lebanon Republic), 1947. Hon. adviser to Ministry of Industries of the National Govt. (China), 1932. Clubs: Town Hall (New York); Ridgewood Country. Home: 381 Wyola Rd., Santa Barbara, Calif. Retired. Died Jan. 3, 1953.

STAUB, Gordon James, airplane co. exec.; b. Grosse Pointe Park, Mich., Dec. 8, 1919; s. E. Elmer and Emma J. (Flury) S.; student Goshen Coll., 1936-37; A.B., Wittenberg Coll., 1941; student Grad. Sch. Bus. Adminstrn., Cleary Coll., 1952-53; m. Nancy Bingham, Apr. 7, 1945; children—Nancy L., Susanne, Laurie, G. Bradford. With O. E. Thompson & Sons, Ypsilanti, Mich., 1941, 46-52, gen. mgr., 1949-52; v.p., dir. Staub Anderson & Co., mgmt. cons., Detroit, 1948-52; sales rep. mdsg. div. Monsanto Chem. So., 1952-53; spl. asst. to treas. Curtiss-Wright Corp., 1953-54, asst. treas., 1954-55, treas., 1955—; treas. Curtiss-Wright of Can., Curtiss-Wright Europe, Aerophysics Development Co., Utica-Bend Corp. Served with USNR, 1942-46. Mem. Nat. Assn. Cost Accountants, N.Y. State Soc. Security Analysts Ridgewood (N.J.) Assn. Good Schs., Phi Gamma Delta. Presbyn. (chmn. deacons). Clubs: Orpheus. Republican Mens (Ridgewood, N.J.). Comml. illustrator, cartoonist. Home: 204 Spencer Pl., Ridgewood, N.J. Office: care Curtiss-Wright Corp., 50 Rockefeller Plaza, N.Y.C. 20. Died Jan. 28, 1958.

STAUFFACHER, Charles Henry (stouf'făk-ẽr), bishop; b. Cedar Rapids, Ia., Oct. 27, 1879; s. John and Rose (Raymer) S.; B.S., Des Moines U., 1901; attended lectures Coe Coll. and U. of Ia., 1914-18; D.D., Western Union Coll., LeMars, Ia., 1927; LL.D., North Central Coll., 1945; m. Madge Ruth Worthing, Mar. 23, 1905; children—James C., Dean W., Joy (Mrs. Clarence J. Attig), Dale Hillis (dec.). Licensed minister Evangelical United Brethren Church, 1901, ordained, 1903; pastor Belle Plaine, Waterloo, Zearing and Cedar Rapids, Ia., 1901-17; dist. supt., 1917-21; asso. sec. Gen. Missionary Soc., 1921-22; sec. Forward Movement, 1922-26; field sec. Gen. Missionary Soc., 1926-34; bishop Evang. United Brethren Ch. since 1934; now supervisor Southwestern Area including Ia., Mo., Kan., Neb., Colo., Okla., Tex. and Calif., also Oriental missions in China and Japan; general secretary for evangelism, 1922-26 and since 1934, stewardship, 1922-34; organized China Conf., 1937. President Administrative Council of Evang. Church, Sunday Sch. and Tracet Union; v.p. Board of Christian Edn., Bd. of Ch. Extension; mem. exec. com. Bd. of Missions; trustee Bd. of Pubs., Board of Pensions; denominational representative on the Commn. for Army and Navy Chaplains. Pres. Bd. Trustees Western Old People's Home, Cedar Falls, Ia., and Pacific Evang. Home for the Aged, Burbank, Calif.; Westmar Coll., LeMars, Ia., York (Neb.) Coll.; mem. Commn. on Church Fedn. and Union; mem. gen. bd. Nat. Council Chs. Mason (K.T., 33°), K.P., Odd Fellow. Address: 1104 Irving St., Cedar Falls, Ia. Died Nov. 14, 1956; buried Linwood Cemetery, Cedar Rapids, Ia.

STAUFFEN, Ernest, Jr. (stuf'fĕn), banker; b. Balt., Mar. 10, 1883; s. Ernest S.; A.B., Columbia, 1904; LL.B., N.Y. Law Sch., 1905; m. Theodora Barber; 1 dau., Mary Brent. Admitted to N.Y. bar, 1905, and began practice with firm Kirby & Wood, N.Y.C.; mem. Gould & Wilkie, 1908-14; active v.p. United Dry Goods Co., 1910-16; became v.p. Liberty Nat. Bank, 1916 (which became the N.Y. Trust Co.); now chmn. trust com. Mfrs. Trust Co.; dir. Union Oil Co. of Cal., C. G. Gunther's Sons, Nash-Kelvinator Corp., Refrigeration Discount Corp., Sharp & Dohme, Internat. Products Corp., Marine Midland Corp., Mfrs. Trust Co., Stern Bros., Coca Cola Bottling Co., N.Y. and Pacific Lumber Co.; dir. and mem. exec. com. Anchor Hocking Gass Corp.; chmn. bd. trustees Austen Riggs Found.; trustee Central Savs. Bank. Clubs: Columbia University, Union League, Down Town Assn., Lunch, Bankers, Links, Madison Square Garden, Twenty-Nine, Arundel Golf, Bohemian (Cal.). Home: 40 Lincoln St., Englewood, N.J. Office: 55 Broad St., N.Y.C. Died Nov. 29, 1950.

STAUFFER, Donald Alfred (staw'fẽr), prof of English; b. Denver, Colo., July 4, 1902; s. Alfred Vincent and Carrie Ella (Macdonald) S.; A.B., Princeton, 1923, A.M., 1924; Ph.D., Oxford (Rhodes scholar) 1928. Instr., asst. prof., asso. prof., prof., chmn. dept. of English, Princeton, since 1927; summer sessions, U. of Colo., 1938, Bread Loaf Sch., 1941-42, U. of Calif., 1949; George Eastman prof. U. of Oxford, 1951-52. Served with U.S. Marines, capt., major, 1942-45; South and West Pacific as Air Combat Intelligence office, 1934-44. Mem. editorial bd. Princeton U. Press; nat. senator Phi Beta Kappa. Mem. Modern Assn. (mem. exec. council). Club: Nassau (Princeton, N.J.). Author: English Biography Before 1700, 1930; Art of Biography in 18th Century, 1941; The Intent of the Critic, 1941; Nature of Poetry, 1946; Saint and the Hunchback, 1946; The Golden Nightingale, 1949; A World of Images, 1949. Home: 14 Alexander St., Princeton, N.J. Died Aug. 8, 1952.

STAYTON, Edward M(oses), civil engr.; b. Independence, Mo., Sept. 4, 1874; s. Thomas and Louisa Matilda (Corn) S.; grad. Independence High Sch., 1891; student in engring. U. of Mo., 1892-94; m. Bitha Estella Compton, July 26, 1898; 1 son, George Edward. Civil engr. engaged in railroad location and const. in Southwest and in Honduras, 1895-1911; locating and building highway and interurban railways in Kansas City area, 1911-17; building highways in Clay County, 1919-20; mem. bd. control Kansas City Street Ry. Co., 1920-26; design and constrn. Blue River sewer, Kansas City, 1925-27; cons. engr., Jackson County highways, 1928-33; street railway commr., Kansas City, Mo., 1926-40. Served as capt., 1910-14, major, 1914-17, Mo. Nat. Guard; maj. and lt. col. engrs., U.S. Army, with A.E.F., 1917-19; col. engrs. Mo. Nat. Guard, 1920-33, brig. gen., 1933-37, maj. gen., 1938, retired Sept. 1938. Mem. Nat. Defense Com. Mem. U.S. Chamber Commerce 1940-42. Awarded D.S.M. of Society of American Military Engineers; also Missouri Distinguished Service Medal; Master Conservationist Award of Mo. Conservation Commission 1946. Past State Comdr. Am. Legion; dir. Am. Legion Endowment Corp., 1929-42, pres., 1937-41. Delegate to Missouri Constl. Convention, 1943-44. Chmn. Mo. Statewide Forestry Com., 1946-50. Mem. Am. Soc. of Civil Engrs., Soc. of Country, Engineers (Kansas City). Home: 637 Proc-Am. Mil. Engrs., Mo. Acad. Science. Democrat. Mason (32°, Shriner). Clubs: Kansas City, Military ter Pl., Independence, Mo. Died Mar. 2, 1954; buried Woodlawn Cemetery, Independence.

STEAD, William Henry (stĕd) economist; b. Galesburg, Ill., Jan. 22, 1899; s. James R. and Gertrude A. (Wilson) S.; A.B., Beloit (Wis.) Coll., 1920; M.A., U. of Chicago, 1923; Ph.D., U. of Minn., 1926; LL.D., Beloit Coll., 1950; m. Lillian M. Austin, 1922; 1 dau., Margaret Jean (Mrs. Donald B. Stewart). Instr. econs. Beloit Coll., 1921-23, Sch. Business Adminstrn., U. of Minn., 1923-26; asst. prof. economics, Sch. of Business Adminstrn., 1926-32, asso. prof., 1932-33; teacher, St. Paul Labor Coll., 1926-29; asso. dir., chief exec. officer, U.S. Employment Service, Washington, D.C., 1933-39; asst. dir. in charge employment service div., Bur. of Employment Security, Social Security Bd., 1939-40; dean, Sch. of Business and Pub. Adminstrn., Chmn. Dept. of Economics, Washington U., St. Louis, Mo., 1940-45; dir. Inst. for Research and Training in Social Sciences and chmn. dept. bus. adminstrn., Vanderbilt U., Nashville, Tenn., 1945-46. Vice pres. Fed Reserve Bank of St. Louis, 1946-51. Econ. adviser to Sec. of the Inteerir, 1950-51; dir. office natural resources N.S. R.B., 1952-53; resource mgmt. cons., 1953—; dir. bus. edn. Com. Econ. Development, 1958-59. Part-time member staff of Council of Economic Advisers to the President of the United States, 1946-49; spl. consultant to President's Water Resources Policy Commission, also to National Security Resources Board; consultant to Secretary of Labor, 1954—. Official observer for United States Govt., Internat. Labor Conf., Geneva, Switzerland, 1933; U.S. rep. and v.p. Internat. Tech. Placing Conf., Geneva, 1933; U.S. Govt. advisor Internat. Labor Conf., Phila., 1944; sec. Minn. Employment Commn., 1930; exec. sec., Tri-City Employment Stabilization Com., Minneapolis, 1931-33; sec. Minn. Employment Stabilization Research Inst., 1930-33; member of the Regional War Labor Board, 1942-44; consultant War Manpower Commn. 1944-45. Mem. board of directors 8th Dist. Fed. Reserve Bank, 1944-45. Mem. American Economic Association, Phi Beta Kappa, Alpha Kappa Psi, Delta Sigma Rho, Beta Gamma Sigma, Omicron Delta Kappa, Artus. Author and co-author of books, pamphlets, on employment and occupations including, Democray Against Unemployment, 1942; The Tasks of Non-military Defense, 1955; Fomento-The Economic Development of Puerto Rico, 1958. Contributor numerous articles on employment and resources. Home: 357 E. 57th St., N. Y.C. 22. Died June 12, 1959; buried Arlington Nat. Cemetery.

STEARNE, Allen Michener, judge; b. Philadelphia, Pa., Aug. 13, 1882; s. Edwin and Alice (Morris) S.; LL.B. cum laude, U. Pa., 1905, LL.D., 1956; LL.D., Hahnemann Med. Coll., Philadelphia, Pa., 1942; m. Mary H. Simons, June 11, 1907; 1 dau., Dorothy (Mrs. Laird C. Starkey). Admitted to Pa. bar, 1905, and engaged in practice of law, 1905-27; apptd. to bench Orphans' Court of Philadelphia County, 1927, reelected Nov. 1937; elected to Pa. Supreme Court, Nov. 1942, for terms of 21 yrs. Mem. Am., Philadelphia and Pa. bar assns., Am. Acad. Polit. and Social Science, S.A.R. Republican. Swedenborgian. Mason (33°). Clubs: Union League (past pres.) (Philadelphia); Frankford-Torresdale Country. Contbr. articles to legal publs. Home: 1900 S. Rittenhouse Sq., Phila. 3. Office: City Hall, Phila. 7. Died Feb. 28, 1956.

STEARNS, Albert Warren (stûrnz), professor; b. Billerica, Mass., Jan. 26, 1885; s. George Edwin and Helen Maria (Proctor) S.; preparatory education, Howe Sch., Billerica; student Tufts Coll., 1905-06, M.D., Med. Sch. of same, 1910; Sc.D., Tufts College, 1943; married Francis Matsell Judkins, December 28, 1912; children—Albert Warren (dec.), Charles Edward. began practice at Boston, 1910; consultant U.S. Naval Hosp., Chelsea, Mass., 1923-29; prof. psychiatry and dean of Tufts Coll. Med. Sch., 1927-45, commr. of correction, State of Mass., 1929-33; asso. commr. Dept. of Mental Disease, 1935-38; chief of neurology service, Boston Dispensary 1921-45; prof. sociology, Tufts Coll., 1945-55, dean emeritus, 1955-59. Lt. M.C., USN, 1917-19; capt. World War II. Mem. Am. Med. Assn., Boston Soc. Psychiatry and Neurology (pres. 1934), Am. Psychiatric Assn., N.E. Soc. Psychiatry, Mass. Psychiatric Soc. (pres. 1931),

Am. Acad. Arts and Sciences, Mass. Med. Soc. (v.p. 1938-40). Republican. Unitarian. Author: Personality of Criminals, 1931; also monographs in psychiatry and criminology. Home: Billerica, Mass. Died Sept. 24, 1959; buried Fox Hill Cemetery, Billerica, Mass.

STEARNS, Edith Shaffer (Mrs. Clark Stearns), ex-league exec.; b. Chicago; d. Henry Rockwell and Amelie (Countante) Shaffer; ed. pvt. tutors; student St. Mary's Acad., South Bend, Ind., Moravian Coll., Bethlehem, Pa., 1893-95; m. Capt. Clark Daniel Stearns, U.S.N., Nov. 2, 1903 (died May 22, 1944). Mem. bd. of edn., Am. Samoa, 1913-14; hostess for Naval Inter-Allied Commn. of Control and for Armistice Commn., London and Paris, 1919-20; founder Pan American League, Miami, Fla., 1930, and served as president and president international, 1930-48; now lecturer on international events; legislative chmn., mem. bd. dirs. Women's Federation Florida's Republican Clubs. Member national advisory council of 60, Women's Nat. Rep. Com., 1928; mem. adv. bd. City Planning Bd., Miami; citizens adv. bd. Univ. of Miami. Served as vol. nurse Naval Hosp., Portsmouth, N.Y., World War I; served as chmn. Pan Am. com. Nat. Defense for Dade County (Fla.), World War II. Decorated Cavaleiro Order Southern Cross Commanderie, by Brazilian govt., May 1946; Medal of Merit 1st class, by Pan Am. Legion, Mexico, 1945; Diploma de Socio Honorario de Assn. de Intercambio Cult. of State M. Grosso (Brazil); Inst. De Cult. Am., La Plata, Tolosa (Argentina); gold medal from consular corps in Miami, 1933; decorated by Republic of Haiti; Honor of Merit est decérné an Grade de Chevalier, Mai 1947. Fla. del. to Women's Centennial Congress, 1940. Mem. Internat. Council of Women (dir. 1933-35), Asociacion de Escritoras Y Artista Americanos for Cuba (U.S. com.), 1934, Women's Internat. and Nat. (past pres.) aeronautical assns., Southwestern Council of Women (chmn. aeronautics), Air Law Rev. (adv. com.), Dade County Fedn. of Women's Clubs (president), Nat. League American Penwomen, D.A.R. Clubs: Florida Federated Women's (sect. vice pres., 1929-30), Dade County Federation (dir. 1930-32), City of Miami (organized and led city forum; pres. 1931-32). Lecturer. Republican (candidate for U.S. Congress, 4th Congl. district Florida 1944). Consultant Latin-American affairs. Contributor short articles in Inter-American publications. Home: 3555 Poinciana Av., Coconut Grove. Office: The Pan American League, Miami, Fla. Died Mar. 30, 1958.

STEARNS, Foster, ex-congressman; b. Hull, Mass., July 29, 1881; s. Frank Waterman and Emily Williston (Clark) S.; A.B., Amherst, 1903; A.M., Harvard, 1906, Boston Coll., 1915; m. Martha Genung, June 22, 1905. Librarian Mus. Fine Arts, Boston, 1913-17; state librarian of Mass., 1917; 1st lt. inf., U.S. Army, 1917-19; fgn. service officer, 1921-24. Mem. N.H. Ho. of Rep., 1937-38; mem. 76th to 78th Congresses (1939-45), 2d N.H. Dist. Decorated Order of Silver Star and Order of Purple Heart (U.S.), Privy Chamberlain of Sword and Cape to Pope Pius Xi; Knight of Sovereign Mil. Order of Malta, Fgn. Service Ednl. Found., Diplomatic Affairs Found. Regent Smithsonian Instn., 1941-45. Dir. Rumford Printing Co. Fellow Royal Geog. Soc., Soc. of Antiquaries of London; mem. Soc. Mayflower Descendants (dep. gov. gen.), Soc. Colonial Wars, Soc. Cin., Am. Antiquarian Soc., N.E. Hist. Geneal. Soc. (v.p.), N.H. Hist. Soc. (trustee), Alpha Delta Phi. Republican (del. nat. convs., 1940, 48). Catholic. Clubs: Metropolitan (Washington); University, Pilgrims (New York); St. James' (London); Somerset, Odd Volumes (Boston). Home: Exeter, N.H. Died June 4, 1956.

STEARNS, Gustav, clergyman; b. New Richland, Minn., Mar. 23, 1874; s. Halvor and Bergit (Sevats) S.; B.A., St. Olaf Coll., Northfield, Minn., 1896; C.T., Luth. Theol. Sem., St. Paul, Minn., 1899, Master of Theology, 1929; D.D., Augustana Coll., Sioux Falls, S.D., 1931; m. Reidun Moe, June 22, 1920. Ordained ministry Lutheran Ch., June 25, 1899; pastor Evang. Lutheran Church of the Ascension, Milwaukee, 1899-1934; dedicated new church building, 1923; full time U.S. Govt. Vet. Adminstrn. chaplain, Nat. Soldiers Home, Milwaukee, 1934-47. Chaplain, 1st lt., 1st Wis. Inf., Mexican border service, 1916; chaplain, capt., 127th Inf., 32d Div., U.S. Army, 22 mos., World War; overseas 15 mos.; wounded at Badricourt, France, July 12, 1918; engaged in battles, Haute-Alsace sector, May 18-July 21, 1918, Aisne-Marne offensive, July 30-Aug. 6, 1918, Oise-Aisne offensive, Aug. 28-Sept. 6, 1918; chaplain, rank of maj., Wis. Nat. Guard and Reserves, Jan. 1, 1925; lt. col. and chaplain, Nat. Guard of U.S. and State of Wis., 1931-38; v.p. Chaplains' Assn. Army of U.S., 1931, pres., 1932. Awarded service medal by State of Wis. Cited by Gen. Pershing "for gallantry in action" near Juvigny, France, Sept. 1, 1918, in burying dead under heavy shell fire. Decorations (U.S.): Purple Heart medal for wound received in action; Silver Star medal for gallantry in action. In period since 1936, with cooperation of U.S. consuls in foreign service, he assembled largest flag collection in the U.S., including national flags sent from 116 foreign countries. Collection is property of Nat. Soldiers Home Chapel, Wood, Wis. Mem. Am. Legion, Pi Gamma Mu, 1928. Author: From Army Camps and Battlefields, 1919. Contbr. short stories to mags. Home: 1727 South 30th St., Milw. 15. Died Apr. 21, 1951; buried Forest Home Cemetery, Milw.

STEBBINS, Arthur D., business exec., pres. and dir. Merchants & Miners Transportation Co.; vice pres. Century Coal Co. of West Va.; dir. Mercantile Trust Co., Central Savings Bank, Transportation Mutual Ins. Co. Home: Towson, Md. Office: Pier 3, Pratt St., Baltimore, Md. Deceased.*

STEBBINS, Edwin Allen, chmn. Rochester Savings Bank; b. Oswego, N.Y., May 30, 1879; s. Henry H. and Julia (Allen) S.; ed. Phillips Andover Acad. and Yale; m. Elizabeth Sibley, July 9, 1928. Chmn. Rochester Savings Bank; dir. Savings Banks Trust Co., Sibley, Lindsay & Curr Co.; dir. Rochester Bur. Municipal Research; mem. advisory council Rochester Gen. Hosp., Community Chest; commr. Rochester Museum. Clubs: Genesee Valley, Rochester Country (Rochester); University (N.Y. City). Home: 935 East Av. Office: 40 Franklin St., Rochester 4, N.Y. Died June 6, 1954.

STEBBINS, Henry Hamlin, clergyman; b. N.Y.C., June 3, 1839; s. Philander Wright and Marietta (Hamlin) S.; student N.Y.U., 1958-59; A.B., Yale, 1862; Union Theol. Sem., 1864-66; grad. Princeton and Union Theol. seminaries, 1867; D.D., Hamilton 1883; m. Caroline Stanford Van Cott, Jan. 30, 1868 (died Jan. 15, 1876); 2d, Julia Frances Allen, June 11, 1878 (died Dec. 14, 1905). Ordained Presbyn. ministry, Oct. 8, 1867; pastor Riverdale, N.Y., 1867-73, Grace Ch., Oswego, 1874-88, Central Ch., Rochester, 1888-1904; stated supply, 1904—. Pres. bd. of mgrs. Custodial Asylum, Newark, N.Y.; trustee People's Rescue Mission, Rochester; Park Board commr., Rochester; dir. Soc. for Prevention Cruelty to Children; mem. Humane Soc. (exec. com.), Playground League, etc. Was mem. Sanitary Commn., City Point, Va., 1864. Mem. Executive Com. Nat. Progressive Party. Member Rochester Hist. Soc., Psi Upsilon, Skull and Bones (Yale). Clubs: Alpha Chi, Genesee Valley, University. Address: 24 Pine St., Rochester, N.Y. Died July 8, 1952.

STECHSCHULTE, Victor Cyril, educator; b. Leipsic, O., Oct. 2, 1893; s. August and Anna (Rampe) S.; A.B., St. Louis U., 1918, M.S., 1919, A.M., 1920; Ph.D., U. of Calif., 1932. Mem. Soc. of Jesus. Instr. St. Mary's (Kan.) Coll., 1920-23; ordained priest Roman Catholic Ch., 1926; asso. seismology, U. of Calif., 1928-29; prof. physics, dir. seismol. obs., chmn. dept. mathematics and physics, Xavier U., Cincinnati, since 1932. Mem. Am. Geophys. Union, Am. Mathematics Soc., Math. Assn. Am., Seismol. Soc. Am., Assn. Am. Physics Tchrs., Sigma Xi. Address: Xavier University, Cin. 7. Died Mar. 3, 1955; buried Milford Novitiate, Milford, O.

STECK, Daniel Frederic, ex-senator, lawyer; b. Ottumwa, Ia., Dec. 16, 1881; s. Albert Clark and Ada (Washburn) S.; LL.B., U. Ia., 1906; m. Lucile Oehler, June 30, 1908. Admitted to Ia. bar, 1906, and began practice at Ottumwa; U.S. senator from Ia., for term ending 1931 (seated 1926, after contest with Smith W. Brookhart); spl. asst. to atty. gen. U.S., 1933-47. Hon. mem. Internat. Printing Pressmen and Assts. Union N.A. Served in World War as capt. 109th Field Signal Batt., U.S. and France. Mem. Am. Legion; comdr. Dept. Ia., 1921-22; chmn. Nat. Legislative Com. of Am. Legion, 1921-22. Mem. Sigma Nu, Phi Delta Phi. Democrat. Episcopalian. Mason (32°). Home: Ottumwa, Ia. Died Dec. 31, 1950.

STECKEL, Abram Peters, engr., retired; b. Myersdale, Pa., Apr. 1, 1879; s. Lewis Daniel and Barbara (Peters) S.; E.E., Lehigh U., 1899; hon. Eng.D., for "contributions to art and science of steel mfrs." Lehigh University, 1941; married Mabel Rushworth, Sept. 1, 1908 (died 1926); children—Frederick Rushworth, Barbara Ann (Mrs. Thomas Taylor White). Began as engineer, 1900; engaged pvt. research, 1921-26; founded Cold Metal Process Company, Youngstown, O., 1926, retired, 1933. Received Modern Pioneer award by National Assn. of Manufacturers. Unitarian. Club: Saturn (Buffalo). Developed Steckel processes for hot rolling and cold rolling metals; in 1903, in collaboration with Stephen Piek, first handled bulk pig iron with electro magnet and crane, proof of such priority pub. by Bethlehem Steel Co., 1950. In 1942 presented to Lehigh County Hist. Soc. home of great-great-grandfather, Peter Steckel, built in 1756, and provided for restoration and endowment as a Pa. Dutch museum. In 1944 purchased and presented to same Hist. Soc., the home of George Taylor, a signer of the Declaration of Independence; located Catasauqua, Pa.; built 1768. Address: 433 Crandall Av., Youngstown, O. Died Aug. 19, 1954; buried Jamestown, N.Y.

STEDMAN, George Woolverton, lawyer; b. Albany, N.Y., Sept. 9, 1864; s. George L. and Adda Shuler (Woolverton) S.; B.S., U. Rochester, 1885, M.S., 1888; LL.B., Albany Law Sch. (Union U.), 1887; m. Harriet T. Mather, June 18, 1898; 1 son, George W. Mem. firm Stedman, Thompson & Andrews, 1887-95, Stedman & Stedman, 1896—; pres. Albany Morris Plan Co., 1945-46. Mem. N.Y. State Assembly, 1898. Trustee Colgate U., 1893-1938; trustee, pres. Hudson River Bapt. Assn. Mem. Albany County Bar Assn., Delta Kappa Epsilon, Phi Delta Phi, Theta Nu Epsilon. Republican. Clubs: Ft. Orange, Albany University. Home: Loudonville and Albany. Office: 55 State St., Albany, N.Y. Died Nov. 23, 1954.

STEDMAN, John Weiss, insurance; b. Danvers, Mass., Jan. 5, 1880; s. Henry Rust and Mabel (Weiss) S.; A.B., Harvard, 1902; m. Hilda Clifford, Oct. 14, 1905; children—John Weiss, Hilda (Mrs. Eben E. Whitman), Harriet Randall, William Ellery. After about 4 yrs. in operating dept. Pere Marquette Ry., was connected with Clark, Dodge & Co. for more than 10 yrs.; became asst. treas. Prudential Ins. Co., Oct. 1915, 2d v.p., Feb. 1918, v.p. charge investments, Jan. 1924-46; ret. Jan. 1946; chmn. exec. com., dir. St. Louis & San Francisco Ry.; dir. Fed. Ins. Co., Vigilant Ins. Co. Club: Harvard (N.Y.C.). Home: 381 Park Av. Office: 120 Broadway, N.Y.C. Died Dec. 26, 1952.

STEELE, Alfred N., soft drink mfr.; b. Nashville, Apr. 24, 1901; s. Edgar Alfred and Fannie (Bartrum) S.; grad. Northwestern U., 1923; m. Joan Crawford, May 10, 1955. Advt. mgr. Chgo. Tribune, Standard Oil Co. of Ind., Chgo.; mgr. Detroit, CBS; v.p. D'Arcy Advt. Agy., The Coca Cola Co.; pres. Pepsi-Cola Co.; chmn. bd., chief exec. officer Pepsi-Cola Co., N.Y.C., 1955. Mem. Sigma Nu. Home: 3 W. 57th St., N.Y.C. 19. Office: 3 W. 57th St., N.Y.C. Died Apr. 19, 1959.

STEELE, Heath McClung, corp. cons.; born Knoxville, Tenn., Sept. 18, 1884; s. Cornelius Warren and Sarah Rebecca (Heath) S.; ed. pvt. schools; m. Florence Belknap Truman, Feb. 7, 1911; children—Margaret Truman (Mrs. J. Sheridan Fahnestock), Heath Warren, David Truman. Miner in Va., Tenn., and Nev., 1901-11; assisted in appraisal of mines, Mich., 1911-16; cons. engr., N.Y. City; with The Am. Metal Co., Ltd., 1917—, v.p. and dir., 1932-54, retired, now consultant; formerly officer and director in various subsidiary companies, including pres. Compania Minera de Penoles; pres. Cia. Metalurgica de Penoles; chmn. Tsumeb Corp., Ltd.; pres., dir. Southwest Potash Corp.; dir. Consol. Copper Mines, United States Metal Company. Chief of bauxite-alumina branch, Aluminum-Magnesium Div., Office Prodn. Management, Washington, D.C., 1941. Mem. Mining and Metall. Soc. America, Am. Inst. Mining and Metall. Engrs. Episcopalian. Club: Mining (past pres.). Home: Glen Mary Farms, Great Mills, Mc. Retired 1954. Died Feb. 21, 1956.

STEELE, Walter Simeon, publisher, editor; b. Louisville, June 2, 1890; s. Samuel Pottinger and Mary Alice (Johnston) S.; student pub. schs.; m. Valeria Knoob, June 10, 1913; children—Yeteve (Mrs. Alfred J. Owings), Robert K., Patti (Mrs. Robert D. Fuller). Asso. Marion (Ind.) Leader Marion Chronicle, Houston Post, Peru (Ind.) Jour., Logansport (Ind.) Reporter, Indiana State Jour., State Hoosier; acting pub. Muncie (Ind.) Press, 1918-23; bus. mgr. Nat. Republican, Washington, 1924-25, Outdoor Pictorial, Washington, 1924-26; pub., editor Nat. Republic Pub. Co., publishers Nat. Republic Mag., Nat. Republic Lettergram, Nat. Republic News Letter, Nat. Republic Weekly Letter, Washington, 1937—. City alderman, Muncie, Ind., 1916-20; county sec. Rep. Com. Delaware County, Ind., 1916-24; Rep. candidate for mayor, Muncie, 1922. Recipient Am. Citizenship medal Vets. Fgn. Wars; ann. award for contbn. Am. way of life by Freedom Found. of Valley Forge, Pa., 1951, 52, 53; award of merit Nat. Soc. D.A.R., 1956; award Freedoms Found., 1959, Congress of Freedom, 1959, Am. Coalition Patriotic Societies (v.p.), Graffic Arts Assn. Republican. Roman Catholic. Club: Washington Police Boys. Contbr. articles newspapers, mags., books. Home: 6004 Rosland Lane, Luxmanor, Rockville, Md. Office: 511 11th St., Washington 4. Died Mar. 2, 1960.

STEESE, James Gordon (stēs), civil engr.; b. Mt. Holly Springs, Pa., Jan. 21, 1882; s. James Andrew and Anna Zug (Schaeffer) S.; A.B., Dickinson College, 1902, A.M., 1906; B.S. (1st honors), U.S. Mil. Acad., 1907; studied U. of Calif., 1908; grad. U.S. Engr. Sch., Washington, 1910; Sc.D., U. of Alaska, 1932; unmarried. Commd. 2d lt. engrs., June 14, 1907; promoted through grades to col., June 18, 1918; brigadier general and adjutant general Alaska N.G., 1926-27; retired Oct. 1927. Asst. engr. San Diego and San Francisco bays, Calif., 1907-08; asst. engr. Panama Railroad Co. and Panama Canal, 1908-12; chief engr. 5th (expeditionary) Brig., Tex., 1913; instr. and asst. prof. engring., U.S. Mil. Acad., 1913-17; spl. rep. of gen. mgr. West Md. Ry., June-Sept. 1916; organized O.T.C., Ft. Riley, Kan., and instr. Engr. O.T.C., Ft. Leavenworth, Kan., 1917; asst. chief of engrs., U.S. Army, 1917-18; detailed on General Staff and chief of section, Sept. 1918-June 1920; spl. mission to Adriatic and Balkan countries, 1919; pres. Alaska Road Commn., 1920-27, also chief engr., 1924, 27; dist. and acting div. engr. for rivers and harbors, Alaska Dist., 1921-27; cons. engr. Dept. Commerce, 1921-27, also for Ty. of Alaska,

1921-23; mem. spl. commn. to investigate Russian, Japanese, and Am. fur seal rookeries, June-Sept. 1922; dir. pub. works, Alaska, 1923-27; chmn. Alaska R.R., 1923-24, also chief engr., Mar.-Oct. 1923; with Gulf Oil Corp. as gen. mgr. foreign subsidiary co., 1927-32; chmn. bd. and pres. Guajillo Corp. and affiliated cos., 1932-41; pres. Slate Creek Placers, Inc., 1936-41; recalled to active duty, Corps of Engrs., U.S. Army, detailed as asst. engr. of maintenance, Panama Canal, and asst. to 2d v.p. Panama Ry. Co., Jan. 1941-Mar. 1946; asst. to Gov., Panama Canal and asst. to pres., Panama Ry. Co., 1946-47; cons. engr. N. Am. Car Corp., 1947-50; lieutenant gen. a.d.c. to Gov. of Alaska, 1953-55; Brig., general, a.d.c., Alaska National Guard, 1935-37. In charge Pres. Harding's tour of Alaska, 1923. Trustee Dickinson College, 1919—, Amelia S. Givin Free Library, 1921—. Fellow Royal Geog. Soc. (London), Am. Geog. Soc., A.A.A.S.; mem. Am. Soc. C.E. (life), Soc. Am. Mil. Engrs., Phi Beta Kappa, Phi Kappa Sigma, Am. Legion. Decorated Distinguished Service Medal, Legion of Merit (U.S.); Distinguished Service Medal, 2d Class (Panamanian); Officer, later Comdr. Order of Prince Danilo I, and silver medal for bravery (Montenegrin); Croix de Guerre, 2d Class (Grecian); Officer of Public Instruction (French); Khamés de l'Ahal Saxaoul, French Sahara; Knight of Order of Compassionate Heart, Comdr. Imperial Order of St. Nicholas (Russia); Interallied Victory Medal, American Defense Medal with star, and American Theatre Medal (U.S.); specially commended in Senate and House of Rep. of United States, and salary raised by spl. act of Congress, 1926; mil. road from Fairbanks, Alaska, to Yukon River at Circle officially named Steese Highway by War Dept. Del. U.S. Govt. to XIV Internat. Navigatn. Congress, Cairo, Egypt, 1926 (sec. Am. sect.), XV Internat. Navigatn. Cong., Venice, Italy, 1931, XVI Cong., Brussels, Belgium, 1935 XVII Congress, Lisbon 1949 XVIII Congress, Rome Italy, 1953; delegate International Geographic Congress, Paris, France, 1931, XVI Cong., Lisbon, 1949; del. U.S. Govt. to 5th Internat. Congress of Surveyors, London, Eng., 1934 (chmn. Am. section), to Internat. Geog. Congress, Warsaw, Poland, 1934 (pres. sec. I-cartography), to 4th Internat. Congress and Expn. of Photogrammetry, Paris, France, 1934 declined), to Second World Petroleum Congress, Paris, 1937, Internat. Geog. Congress, Amsterdam, Netherlands, 1938. Republican. Episcopalian. Mason (33°), Elk. Clubs: Army and Navy (Washington); West Point Army Mess; University (N.Y.). Author of numerous articles in tech. periodicals and daily press. Address: Mt. Holly Springs, Cumberland County. Pa. Died Jan. 11, 1958.

STEFAN, Karl (stĕ'făn), congressman; b. on farm near Zebravkov, Bohemia, Mar. 1, 1884; s. Karl and Marie (Gazilova) S.; brought to U.S., 1885; ed. public schools, Omaha, Neb.; LL.D., National University, Washington, D.C., 1946; married; children—Dr. Karl F., Ida Mae (Mrs. Robert Askren). Telegraph operator; successively news writer, reporter, city editor, radio news commentator, publs.' agent mags., newspapers; mem. 74th to 82nd Congresses (1935-53), 3d Neb. Dist.; chmn. appropriations com., dealing with Dept. of State, Dept. Commerce, etc. Advisor to United Nations Conf., San Francisco, 1945. Dir. Norfolk Bldg. & Loan Assn. Lieut. in Neb. Nat. Guard; served in telegraph div. Philippine constabulary, 1904-06; hon. brig. gen., Nat. Vols. of Philippines; mem. com. which in 1935 assisted in inauguration of Philippine Commonwealth. Decorated Philippine Military Medal of Merit; Cross of Alfaro by Eloy Alfaro Internat. Found. for workk on good neighbor program; also, Order Nat. Merit Carlos Manual de Cespedes of Cuba. Honorary member Spanish War Vets., mem. Order of Carabao, Rotary, Elks, Odd Fellows. Mason. Mem. bd. of visitors U.S. Naval Acad., 1944. Mem. exec. com. Interparliamentary Union, 1939. Republican. Episcopalian (vestryman Trinity Ch.). Clubs: National Press, Army-Navy. World traveler; speaks numerous fgn. langs. Home: Norfolk, Neb. Address: New House Office Bldg., Washington. Died Oct. 2, 1951; buried Prospect Hill Cemetery, Norfolk, Neb.

STEFFAN, Roger, govt. ofcl.; b. Osborne, Ohio, Jan. 29, 1893; s. Frederick and Amanda (Pfeiffer) S.; B.A., O. State U., 1913; extension student Columbia U., 1927-29; student N.Y.U., 1920-23; m. Martha Allen, Jan. 10, 1916; 1 dau., Pamela. Mem. editorial staff various newspapers, 1913-17; reporter Asso. Press Bur., Washington, 1918-19; dir. pub. relations Ohio Inst. for Pub. Efficiency, Columbus, 1919; ednl. dir. Nat. City Bank of N.Y.C., 1919-23, head business extension dept., 1923-25, asst. v.p., 1926-29, v.p., 1929—; service mgr. Fuller & Smith, Cleveland, 1925-26. Asst. to asst. of President of U.S., 1953—; head econ. adv. group to Nationalist China, 1954. Served as 1st lieutenant, U.S. Inf., 1918. Mem. Phi Beta Kappa, Delta Chi, Sigma Delta Chi. Republican. Mason. Clubs: Union League, New York Athletic (N.Y.C.). Home: Palm Hill Ranch, Vista, Cal. Office: White House, Washington. Died Dec. 27, 1955; buried Forest Lawn Meml. Park, Glendale, Cal.

STEFFENS, Theodore Henry, railway exec.; b. St. Louis, Mar. 1, 1883; s. George and Anna R. (Osberghaus) S.; student Southwestern Bus. Coll.; m. Josie Jones, Aug. 16, 1904; children—Regina I., Marjorie M., Theodora B. With St.L.-S.F. R.R., 1901-11; traffic mgr., later asst. to pres., v.p. Sand Springs Ry., 1911-27, pres. since 1927; dir. Sand Springs Townsite Co., Sand Springs State Bank, Tulsa Stockyards, Sand Springs Textile Co., Citizens Fed. Savs. & Loan Assn. Trustee Sand Springs Home, Meml. Park. Mem. Tulsa C. of C. (dir.), Sand Springs C. of C. (dir.). Mason (Shriner, K.C.C.H.). Clubs: Rotary, Tulsa Traffic. Home: 203 S. Olympia St., Tulsa 5. Office: Broadway and McKinley, Sand Springs, Okla. Died Dec. 19, 1956.

STEGER, Christian Talbot, foreign service officer; b. Danville, Va., Feb. 3, 1893; s. William and Pattie (Carter) S.; B.A., U. of Va., 1913, M.A., 1915; student (summer) U. of Marburg, Germany, 1914; m. Olga Marguerite Anrig, Dec. 27, 1920; 1 son, Henry Carter Pete. Foreign service officer since Jan. 2, 1920; vice consul, Rome, 1920-21; Dresden, Germany, 1921-26; consul, Corinto, Nicaragua, Apr. 1926; Malmoe, Sweden, July 1930, Beirut, Syria, Nov. 1931; Jerusalem, Dec. 1938-Nov. 27, 1944; counselor Embassy and consul gen., Athens, Greece, 1944-45; consul gen., Copenhagen, Denmark, since Dec. 28, 1945. Sergt. 1st class, Engr. Corps, U.S. Army, 1918. Mem. Raven Soc., Phi Beta Kappa. Clubs: Beirut Sporting, Jerusalem Sports, Sodom and Gomorrah Golfing Soc. Retired. Home: 27 8th St., N.W., Pulaski, Va. Died Nov. 1, 1951; buried Oakview Cemetery, Pulaski.

STEGER, Julius (stĕ'gẽr), dir. motion pictures and stage mgr.; b. Vienna, Austria; s. Jacob and Anna S.; ed. high sch., Vienna; Conservatory of Music and Dramatic Art, Vienna. Came to America when very young. Appeared on American stage before entering motion picture field, became star of light opera, and later actor and play producer; in motion pictures first as a star, later as director of production for Fox Film Corp. Club: The Players (New York). Address: Vienna, Austria. Died Feb. 26, 1959; buried Grinzinger Cemetery, Vienna, Austria.

STEIDTMANN, Waldo E(duard) (stīt'măn), botanist; b. Prairie du Sac, Wis., Apr. 27, 1896; s. Charles Frederick and Bertha (Schoenberg S.; Rural Teachers Certificate, Wis. State Teachers College, (Whitewater, 1916; A.B., U. of Wis., 1923; M.S., U. of Mich., 1929, Ph.D., 1935; m. Evelyn Katherine Dressel, Sept. 8, 1930; children—Sally Ann, James Richard. Country sch. teacher, Wis., 1916-17; instr. in botany, Marquette U., Milwaukee, 1923-32; instr. in biology, Wis. State Teachers Coll., La Crosse, 1936; mem. faculty Bowling Green (O.) State U., 1936—, prof. of biology and chmn. biology dept., 1947—. Served in C.A. Corps, 1918-19, overseas in France. Fellow Ohio Acad. Sci. (chmn. plant sci. sect., 1943-44); mem. A.A.A.S., Bot. Soc. of Am., Sigma Xi, Phi Sigma Alpha Tau Omega, Omicron Delta Kappa. Mason. Club: Kiwanis. Research papers in paleobotany. Home: 4 Orchard Circle, Bowling Green, O. Died June 21, 1955; buried Oak Grove Cemetery, Bowling Green, O.

STEIN, Louis P., beauty supply mfr.; b. Warsaw, Poland, Sept. 18, 1893; s. Issac and Basia (Muehlstein) S.; student Univs. of Heidelberg and Warsaw; m. Helene Clarke, 1923; m. 2d, Maxine G. Starr, May 10, 1948. Came to U.S., 1913, naturalized, 1919. Organized Helen Curtis Industries, Chicago, 1927, and served as pres., 1927-47, chmn. bd. since 1947. Interested in charity work, especially with asthmatic children. Mason. Address: 3100 Sheridan Rd., Chgo. Died June 24, 1952; buried Westlawn Meml. Park, Chgo.

STEINBERG, Milton, clergyman; b. Rochester, N.Y., Nov. 25, 1903; s. Samuel and Fanny (Sternberg) S.; A.B., Coll. City N.Y., 1924; A.M., Columbia, 1928; rabbi, Jewish Theol. Sem. Am., 1928, D. H.L., 1946; m. Edith Alpert, June 18, 1929; children—Jonahtan, David Joel. Instr. classical langs., Coll. City N.Y., 1924-25; instr. Jewish history and religion, Teachers' Inst., Jewish Theol. Sem., 1926-28; rabbi Temple Beth El Zedeck, Indpls., 1928-33, Park Av. Synagogue, N.Y.C., 1933—. Served as chaplain (lt. col) N.Y. Guard, 1942-44. Mem. bd. overseers, Hillel Found., 1942-44; mem adminstrn. com. Zionist Orgn. Am., 1942-44. Mem. Rabbinical Assembly Am., Phi Beta Kappa. Author: Making of the Modern Jew, 1934; As a Driven Leaf, 1940 (Hebrew trans. Tel Aviv, 1947); A Partisan Guide to the Jewish Problem, 1945; Basic Judaism, 1947. Editorial bd. Reconstructionist mag., 1936—. Home: 145 E. 92d St. Office: 50 E. 87th St., N.Y.C. 28. Died Mar. 20, 1950; buried Mount Hope, Westchester, N.Y.

STEINDLER, Arthur (stind'lẽr), orthopedic surgeon; b. Vienna, Austria, June 22, 1878; s. Leopold and Caroline S.; M.D., U. of Vienna, 1902; m. Louise Junk, Mar. 1914. Came to U.S., 1907, naturalized, 1914. Prof. orthopedics, State U. of Ia., 1913-49. Prof. extraordinary Nat. U. of Mex.; prof. orthopaedic surgery Coll. Med. Evangelists. Fellow Am. Coll. Surgeons, I.C.S.; mem. Belgian Surg. Soc., Mex. Orthopedic Soc., Brazilian Orthopedic Soc., A.M.A., Ia. State Med. Assn., Am. Orthopedic Assn., Internat. Orthopedic Soc., Belgian Surgical Soc., Am. Acad. of Orthopedic Surgeons, Sigma Xi. Jewish religion. Home: 103 Melrose Av., Iowa City, Ia. Died July 21, 1959; buried Iowa City, Ia.

STEINDORFF, Georg (stin'dôrf), Egyptologist; b. Dessau, Germany, Nov. 12, 1861; s. Louis and Helene (Ehrmann) S.; student univs. of Berlin and Goettingen, 1881-84 (Ph.D., Goettingen, 1884); m. Elise Oppenheimer, Apr. 19, 1887; children—Ulrich, Hilde Hemer. Came to U.S., 1939. Became asst. curator, Mus. Berlin, 1885; prof. Egyptology, U. Leipsig, 1893. Hon. mem. Acad. Hungary, Am. Oriental Soc. Author: Religion of the Ancient Egyptians, 1905; Baddeker's Egypt (8th revised edition), 1929; When Egypt Ruled the East, 1942; Egypt, 1943; also many books pub. in Germany, including Aniba (2 vols.; Cairo), 1935-37. Home: 4420 Ponca Av., North Hollywood, Cal. Died Aug. 28, 1951.

STEINER, Edward Alfred, sociologist; b. Czechoslovakia, Nov. 1, 1866; s. Adolph and Jeanette (Heller) S.; ed. pub. schs., Vienna, gymnasium, Pilsen, Bohemia; U. Heidelberg, 1885; B.D., Oberlin, 1891; post-grad. Göttengen and Berlin univs.; D.H.L. Grinnell Coll.; m. Sara W. Levy, Aug. 31, 1891 (died Jan. 7, 1940); children—Gretchen Henrietta, Henry York (dec.), Richard Morrow; m. 2d, Clara Elizabeth Perry, Oct. 25, 1941. Ordained Congl. ministry, 1891; pastor St. Cloud, Minn., 1891-93, St. Paul, 1893-96, Springfield, O., 1896-99, Sandusky, 1899-1903; spl. rep. The Outlook, Russia, 1903; prof. emeritus; applied Christianity, Ia. (now Grinnell) Coll., Sept. 1903—. Mem. Phi Beta Kappa. Author: Tolstoy, the Man, 1903; On the Trail of the Immigrant, 1906; The Mediator, 1907; The Immigrant Tide, 1909; Against the Current, 1910; The Broken Wall, 1911; The Parable of the Cherries, 1913; From Alien to Citizen, 1914; Introducing the American Spirit, 1915; Nationalizing America, 1916; My Doctor Dog, 1917; Uncle Joe's Lincoln, 1918; Sanctus Spiritus and Company, 1919; Old Trails and New Borders, 1921; The Eternal Hunger, 1925; The Making of a Great Race, 1919. Home: Pilgrim Place, Claremont, Cal. Died June 30, 1956; buried Grinnell, Ia.

STEINER, Robert Eugene, lawyer; b. near Greenville, Ala., May 9, 1862; s. Joseph and Margaret Matilda (Camp) S.; A.B., U. of Ala., 1880, A.M., 881, LL.D., 1919; LL.B., Harvard, 1884; m. May Flowers, Dec. 16, 1884. Practiced in Greenville, 1884-92, since at Montgomery; mem. Steiner, Crum & Weil (now Steiner, Crum & Baker), 1905—; dir. and gen. counsel, Western Ry. of Ala.; dir. and Ala. atty. Central of Ga. Ry.; counsel aa Montgomery for Gulf, Mobile & Ohio R.R. Co., The Seaboard Air Line; dist. atty. for Alabama for L.&N. R.R. Co. Mem. Ala. House of Representatives, 1886, Senate, 1892; city atty., Montgomery, 1895; del. Dem. Nat. Conv., St. Louis, 1904; v. chmn. Ala. State Docks Commission. Served as capt. Greenville Guards and maj. 2d Regt. Ala. N.G.; raised regt. of cav., 1916, apptd. col., and served with it on Mexican border; promoted brig. gen., N.G., Mar. 19, 1917; brig. gen. U.S. Army, Aug. 5, 1917, and comdg. 62d Inf. Brig., 31st Div.; went to France in command 62d Inf. Brig., returned in command of 31st Div. Reapptd. brig. gen. N.G. Ala., 1919, also brig. gen. on reserve, by President, Aug. 1919. Mem. Sigma Nu. Methodist. Mason; Odd Fellow; K.P. Club: Beauvoir Country (Montgomery). Home: 220 S. Hull St. Office: First Nat. Bank Bldg., Montgomery 1, Ala. Died Sept. 26, 1955; buried Montgomery.

STEINWAY, Theodore E. (stīn'wā), piano mfr.; b. New York, N.Y., Oct. 6, 1883; s. William and Elizabeth S.; ed. St. Paul's Sch., Garden City, L.I., N.Y., 1898-1900; m. Ruth Davis, Apr. 6, 1913; children—Theodore D., Henry Z., John H., Frederick, Elizabeth, Lydia. With Steinway & Sons, piano mfrs., New York, since 1899, now pres. Clubs: Century, Players, New York Athletic, Coffee House (New York). Home: 901 Lexington Av. Office: 109 W. 57th St., N.Y. C. Died Apr. 1957.

STELTER, Benjamin F. (stĕl'tẽr), prof. English; b. Delphos, Kan., Dec. 27, 1882; s. John Dietrick and Anna Margaret (Ellermann) S.; B.A., U. of Kan., 1905, M.A., 1908; M.A., Yale, 1909, Ph.D., Cornell U., 1913; m. Rose Edith Taylor, June 2, 1922. Teacher elementary schs., Kan., 1899-1902; asst. in English, U. of Kan., 1905-06; teacher high sch., Leavenworth, 1906-08; univ. scholar, Yale, 1908-10; instr. in English, U. of Kan., 1910-11, Cornell U., 1911-14; asso. prof. English, U. of Southern Calif., 1914-15; prof. English, 1915-18; asst. prof. English, U. of Calif. at Los Angeles, 1918-21; prof. English and head of dept., Occidental Coll., 1921-45; resigned; in business since 1945. Teacher summer sessions and extension lecturer, various univs. Mem. Modern Language Assn. America, Phi Beta Kappa, Sigma Alpha Epsilon. Republican. Co-editor: Concordance to Poems of Keats, 1916; Concordance to Poems of Robert Browning, 1925. Address: 435 W. California St., Pasadena, Cal. Died Feb. 23, 1958.

STEMLER, Otto Adolph, artist; b. Cincinnati, O., Jan. 30, 1872; s. Charles and Caroline (Haehl) S.; student Cincinnati Art Acad.; m. Johanna Whitaker, Oct. 4, 1899. With Standard Pub. Co., Cincinnati, 1906—, all work being reproduced by that co.; has specialized in large colored Bibl. pictures and illustrations for Sunday schools; among notable works are: The Transfiguration; Jesus and the Nations; Timothy Taught by His Mother; Joshua Commands the Sun and Moon to Stand Still; The Man with the Withered Hand; A Living Sacrifice; Christ Called the Four Disciples; Christ Sends Out the Twelve Disciples, Two By Two; The Call to Discipleship; Paul Preaching at His Home in Rome; The Boy Jesus and His Mother, Mary, etc. Presbyn. Home: 5837 Kennedy Av., Cin. Died Aug. 6, 1953; buried Spring Grove Cemetery, Cin.

STEMPEL, Guido Hermann; b. Ft. Madison, Ia., May 18, 1868; s. Hugo Carl and Anna Barbara (Degenhard) S.; A.B., U. of Ia., 1889; A.M., U. of Wis., 1894; U. of Leipzig, 1895-97; m. Myrtle Emmert, June 24, 1895; children—John Emmert, Guido Hermann. Asst. prin. Kendallville (Ind.) High Sch., 1888-89; prin. Litchfield (Ill.) High Sch., 1889-90; instr. German, U. Wis., 1890-91; prin. Oskaloosa (Ia.) High Sch., 1891-94; instr. English, 1894-98, asst. prof., 1898-1904, asso. prof. comparative philol., 1904-22, head of dept., 1906-38, prof., 1922-38, Ind. U., emeritus 1938. Also editorial asst., Henry Holt & Co., N.Y., 1911-15; advisory editor, Benj. H. Sanborn & Co., Chicago, 1915-39. Mem. Modern Lang. Assn. America, Ind. State Symphony Soc. (dir. 1934-37), Am. Assn. Univ. Profs., Linguistic Soc. America, Phi Beta Kappa, Sigma Delta Chi. Democrat. Episcopalian. Clubs: University, Saturday Afternoon (Chicago); Faculty (Bloomington). Contbr. to ednl. mags. and newspapers. Condr. music column, Bloomington Star-Courier, 1926-54 (pub. citation Ind. U. Sch. Music 1954); program annotator Indianapolis Symphony Orchestra, 1933-36. Author: Latin in English (with Myrtle Emmert Stempel), 1940. Editor: A Book of Ballads Old and New, 1917. Consulting editor: General Language by Bugbee et al., 1937. Home: 924 Atwater Av., Bloomington, Ind. Died Dec. 23, 1955; buried Forest Cemetery, Oskaloosa, Ia.

STENGLE, Charles Irwin, congressman; b. Savageville, Va., Dec. 5, 1869; s. Rev. Adam and Elizabeth (Mason) S.; A.B., Goldey Coll., Wilmington, Del., 1890; m. Catherine Ward, Dec. 13, 1899. Chaplain Del. Ho. of Rep., 1898; editor Norfolk Daily Dispatch, 1899, Fredericksburg (Va.) Free Lance, 1900-01, The Chief, N.Y.C., 1910-15; civil service editor Bklyn. Daily Times, 1915-18; sec. Municipal Civil Service Commn., N.Y.C., 1918-23; mem. 68th Congress (1923-25), 6th N.Y. Dist. Hon. v.p. Nat. Assn. Civil Service Employes; mem. Empire City Fraternal Assn., Elks. Author: The Postal Service, 1912; The Customs Service, 1912. Home: 63 Halsey St., Bklyn. Died Nov. 23, 1953.

STEPHAN, Frank Lawrence (stĕf'f'n), lawyer; b. Andrews, Ind., Mar. 18, 1886; s. John and Bridget (O'Rourke) S.; B.S., Marion (Ind.) Normal Coll., 1908; A.B., U. of Mich., 1912, LL.B., 1914; m. Lucile Ridenour, Dec. 1, 1916; 1 son, Robert W. Admitted to Ida. bar, 1914, and began practice at Twin Falls; pros. atty. Twin Falls County, 1917-23; mem. Ida. Ho. of Rep., 1925-26; atty. gen. of Idaho, 1927, 28. Mem. bd. overseers Whitman Coll., Walla Walla, Wash. Mem. Gamma Eta Gamma. Republican. Presbyterian. Mason (Shriner). Home: Twin Falls, Ida. Died Nov. 28, 1953.

STEPHEN, George, ret. ry. exec.; b. Montreal, Que., Can., July 5, 1876; s. George and Ellen Alexandra (Gowan) S.; ed. high sch., Montreal; m. Frances Emma Byrnes, June 1, 1904. Began as jr. clk., Can. Pacific Ry. Co., 1889; clk. fgn. freight dept., Canadian Pacific Ry., Montreal and St. John, N.B., 1889-99; chief clk., gen. freight office, Winnipeg, 1899-1900; traveling freight agt., Manitoba and Sask., 1900; contracting freight agt., Kootenay Ty., B.C., 1901; chief clk., gen. freight office, Winnipeg, 1906-09; apptd. gen. freight agt. west of Port Arthur and Duluth to Pacific, 1909; asst. freight traffic mgr. same dist., 1916, freight traffic mgr. Nov. 1916; freight traffic mgr., Canadian Northwestern, Tor., 1918; resigned; asst. freight traffic mgr., C.P. R.R., lines west of Ft. William, offices at Winnipeg, 1922; freight traffic mgr., all C.P.R. lines, Montreal, 1927, v.p. charge traffic, 1930-47, ret. Pres., dir. Midland Simcoe Elevator Co., Ltd., Midland, Ont.; dir. Aroostook Valley R.R. Co., Canadian Pacific Steamships, Ltd., Can. Pacific Transport Co., Ltd., Canadian Pacific Air Lines, Ltd., Dominion Atlantic Ry., Eastern Abattoirs, Ltd., Grand River Ry. Co., Lake Erie & No. Ry. Co., Pa.-Ontario Transportation Co. Served as asst. rep. Can. Ministry War Transport of United Kingdom, 1939-41. Gov. Montreal Gen. Hosp. Decorated Comdr. Order Brit. Empire. Mem. Montreal Bd. Trade, La Chambre de Commerce du District de Montreal. Clubs: St. James, Canadian (Montreal); Manitoba (Winnipeg); Vancouver (B. C.); Seigniory (pres.) (Montebello, Que.). Home: 3443 Ontario Av., Montreal 25. Office: 317 Windsor Station, Montreal 3, Quebec. Died Jan. 31, 1955; buried Montreal, Quebec.

STEPHENS, George Asbury, economist; b. Topeka, Kan., Aug. 14, 1873; s. Thomas White and Mary Elizabeth (Tyler) S.; A.B., Baker U., Baldwin, Kan., 1899; A.M., U. Chgo., 1906, Ph.D., 1909; m. Anna L. Roosa, June 15, 1911; children—Richard Everett, Margaret Louise. Prin. high sch., Humboldt, Kan., 1900; supt. schs., Attica, Kan., 1900-01; prin. high sch., Manhattan, Kan., 1902-04; tchr. English, high schs., Topeka, 1904-07; fellow and asst. sociology, U. Chgo., 1907-08, fellow and asst. polit. economy, 1908-09; instr. polit. economy, U. Neb., 1909, adj. prof., 1910, asst. prof., 1912, asso. prof., 1915, prof., 1918-19. Investigator social and industrial conditions under Sage Foundation, 1907-08; examiner FTC, Washington, D.C., summer 1916, 1917-19, 1919-33, chief statistician 1933-44; economist, 1944-47; prof. School of Bus. Admin., Am. U., 1921-23; prof. with Baltimore Coll. of Commerce 1921-25. Mem. Am. Econ. Assn., Pi Gamma Mu. Methodist. Clubs: Federal, Round Table. Wrote: The Juvenile Court System of Kan., 1906. Contbr. to economic mags., 1929, to Ency. of Social Sciences and, 1939-—, to Nat. Yearbook. Address: 127 Camaritas Av., South San Francisco. Died May 16, 1952; buried San Francisco.

STEPHENS, Harold Montelle, judge; b. Crete, Neb., Mar. 6, 1886; s. Frank Bray and Lunette (Stebbins) S.; student U. of Utah, 1904-06; A.B., Cornell Univ., 1909; LL.B., Harvard, 1913, S.J.D., 1932; LL.D., (honorary), Georgetown U., 1939, Univ. of Utah, 1950; post graduate work University of California, 1930-31, Harvard, 1931-33; m. Virginia Adelle Bush, Aug. 6, 1912. Admitted Utah bar, 1912, and began practice in Salt Lake City; asst. pros. atty., Salt Lake County, 1915-17; judge Third Jud. Dist. Ct., Utah, 1917-21; mem. Cheney, Jensen, Holman and Stephens, Salt Lake City, 1921-28, Martineau and Stephens, Los Angeles, 1928; appointed by President Roosevelt asst. atty. general U.S. Dept. of Justice, 1933-35; asst. to the atty. gen., 1935; asso. justice, U.S. Court of Appeals for D.C., 1935-48, appointed chief justice by President Truman, 1948; American chairman of Joint Committee on Interchange of Patent Rights and Information with Great Britain (for mutual aid in prosecution of World War II, Dec. 7, 1943-Oct. 1, 1946). Mem. grievance com. Utah State Bar Assn., 1922-23, mem. code commn. to revise Utah Laws, 1928. Acting asso. dir. Am. Coll. Surgeons, 1921; president Salt Lake City Community Clinic and Dispensary, 1923-28. Awarded Medal for Merit by Pres. Truman, 1946. Member Utah, California, Mass. and Dist. Court of U.S. for D.C. bars, bar of U.S. Court of Appeals for D.C., bar of U.S. Supreme Court; mem. Am. Bar Assn., Assn. Bar City of N.Y., American Judicature Society, Washington Nat. Monument Soc., Member of Council, Selden Society (London), Order of Coif, Delta Chi, Phi Beta Kappa, Phi Delta Phi. Clubs: Alta (Salt Lake City); Metropolitan (Washington, D.C.). Author: Administrative Tribunals and the Rules of Evidence, 1933; also contbr. to legal periodicals. Catholic. Home: Wardman Park Hotel. Address: U.S. Court House, Washington. Died May 28, 1955; buried Mount Olivet Cemetery, Salt Lake City.

STEPHENS, Howard V., Rep. nat. committeeman; b. Cincinnati, 1887; Yale, 1909. Chmn. bd. and dir. Johnson-Stephens & Shinkle Shoe Co.; dir. St. Louis Coca Cola Bottling Co., Mercantile Commerce Bank & Trust Co. Rep. Nat. committeeman from Mo. Home: 5165 Lindell Blvd. Office: 4242 Laclede Av., St. Louis. Died Oct. 12, 1952.

STEPHENS, James. Author: Etched in Moonlight, 1928; On Prose and Verse, 1928; Julia Elizabeth (1-act comedy), 1929; Outcast, 1929; Crock of Gold, 1930; Collected Poems, 1930; Strict Joy, 1931; English Poets, Romantic, Victorian and Later, 1938; Kings and the Moon, 1938. Address: care Macmillan Co. of Can., 70 Bond St., Toronto, Can. Died Dec. 26, 1950.*

STEPHENS, Roswell Powell, prof. mathematics; b. Barnesville, Ga., Nov. 4, 1874; s. Roswell Americus and Sarah Frances (Brown) S.; A.B., U. Ga., 1896; Ph.D., Johns Hopkins, 1905; student at Cambridge, Eng., 1924; m. Mabel Chadwick, October 28, 1913; children—Mabel Chadwick (Mrs. R. P. Jacobsen), Corrinne Chadwick (Mrs. Howell C. Erwin, Jr.). Instr. math. Wesleyan U., 1905-07; adjunct prof. math., U. Ga., 1907-09; asso. prof., 1909-19, prof., 1919-45, head math. dept., 1925-45, prof. emeritus, 1945-—; acting dean, 1925-26, dean Graduate Sch., 1928-43, vis. prof., La. State U., 1945-46, U. S.C., 1946-47. Mem. A.A.A.S., Am. Math. Soc., Math. Assn. America, Ga. Acad. Science (an organizer, pres. 1922-23), Phi Delta Theta, Phi Beta Kappa, Beta Gamma Sigma, Phi Kappa Phi. Democrat. Methodist. Contbr. to professional jours. Home: Athens, Ga. Died June 1, 1954.*

STEPHENSON, Carl, educator; b. Fayette, Ia., Aug. 10, 1886; s. Andrew and Julia (Root) S.; A.B., DePauw U., 1907, A.M., 1908; Ph.D., Harvard, 1914; m. Olive Elizabeth Diall, Sept. 15, 1915; children—Richard Montgomery, James Hawley. Asst. in govt. and history, Harvard, 1909-12; acting asst. prof. history, U. Ark., 1912-13; instr. history and govt., Princeton, 1913-15; instr., asst. prof. history, Washington U., St. Louis, 1915-20; asst. prof., asso. prof., prof. history, U. Wis., 1920-30; prof. history, Cornell U., 1930-54; summer appointments at U. Chgo., Columbia, Stanford. C.R.B. fellow, Belgium, 1924-25; Guggenheim fellow, France, 1931. Mem. Am. Hist. Assn. (mem. council 1942-46), Mediaeval Acad. Am., Econ. History Assn., The History Sci. Soc., Phi Beta Kappa, Delta Kappa Epsilon. Author: Borough and Town: A Study of Urban Origins in England, 1933; Mediaeval History: Europe from the Fourth to the Sixteenth Century, 1935, rev. edit. (Europe from the Second to the Sixteenth Century), 1943; A Brief Survey of Mediaeval Europe, 1941; Mediaeval Feudalism, 1942. Editor and translator (with F. G. Marcham): Sources of English Constitutional History: A Selection of Documents from A.D. 600 to the Present, 1937. Contbr. to leading hist. jours. in Am., Eng., France, and Belgium; and to several vols. of essays in same countries. Home: 101 Brook Lane, Ithaca, N.Y. Died Oct. 3, 1954.

STEPHENSON, George Malcolm, author, prof. of history; b. Olds, Ia., Dec. 30, 1883; s. Oliver and Mary (Johnson) S.; A.B., Augustana Coll., Rock Island, Ill., 1905; Litt.D., 1938; B.S., U. of Chicago, 1906; A.M., Harvard, 1911, Ph.D., 1914; Ph. D., honoris causa, Uppsala U. (Sweden), 1938; m. Lilly Sundkvist, Jan. 14, 1918; children—George Malcolm, Gordon Arch. Teacher at Minn. Coll., in Minneapolis, 1907-10; successively member history department, DePauw Univ., Dartmouth Coll., University of Minnesota, 1914-—, professor, 1937-52, professor emeritus, 1952-—; Fulbright professor U. Stockholm, 1954-55; visiting prof. of history, Ohio State U., 1924-25. Mem. bd. of edn. United Lutheran Ch., 1921-29. Mem. bd. dirs. Augustana Coll., 1930-34. Awarded Guggenheim fellowship, 1927-28. Decorated Knight of Royal Order of the North Star by King of Sweden, 1937. Mem. Am. Hist. Assn., Miss. Valley Hist. Assn., Minn. Hist. Soc., Augustana Hist. Soc.; hon. mem. Augustana Inst. Club: Campus. Author: Political History of the Public Lands, 1917; Conservative Character of Martin Luther, 1921; History of American Immigration, 1926; Founding of Augustana Synod, 1927; Religious Aspects of Swedish Immigration, 1932; John Lind of Minnesota, 1935; American History since 1865, 1939; American History to 1865, 1940, Puritan Heritage, 1952; Pilgrim and Stranger, 1953; America's Major Prophetess: Harriet Beecher Stowe, 1953. Editor: Letters Relating to Gustaf Unonius, 1937. Contbr. to Dictionary of Am. Biography and Dictionary of Am. History and historical journals. Editor of publications of Swedish Historical Society of America, 1921-29. Mem. bd. editors of Miss. Valley Hist. Review, 1942-46. Home: 2835 Kyle Av., N., Mpls. 22. Died Oct. 11, 1958.

STEPHENSON, James Pomeroy, educator; b. Chester, O., June 23, 1845; s. James Ebenezer and Lavinia (Norton) S.; A.B., Oberlin, 1867, A.M., 1885; grad. Rochester Theol. Sem., 1871; A.M., Syracuse U., 1891, Ph.D., 1892; U. Chgo. 4 summers; LL.D., Des Moines U., 1919; m. Helen Brooks, June 1874 (died June 1884); children—James Brooks (dec.), Winfred N. (dec.), H. Lavinia (dec.); m. 2d, Florence H. Tyler, of Warren, O., Oct. 7, 1885; 1 dau., Helen Florence (Mrs. Alexander Robertson). Ordained Bapt. ministry, 1871; pastor Warren, O., 1872-76; Ottawa, Kan., 1877-84; Hampton, Ia., 1885-87; prof. Greek, 1887-92, English, 1892-1904, prof. philosophy, 1904-June 1925, Des Moines U. (acting pres. 3½ yrs., and registrar all but 2 years of service there); retired. Republican. Home: 1331 Harrison Av., Des Moines, Ia. Died Jan. 13, 1937.

STEPHENSON, William B., Jr., mfr. author; b. Port Deposit, Md., Nov. 21, 1880; s. William B. and Alice (Hershey) S.; ed. high sch., Cloquet, Minn.; admitted to bar, Alaska and State of Wash.; m. Margaret McClaine, of Spokane, Wash., Dec. 30, 1913 (died June 30, 1916); m. 2d, Hazel Reeves Thompson, Aug. 9, 1926. Builder and operator of saw mills on the Pacific Coast, 1900-09; mgr. Pacific Cold Storage Co., St. Michael, Alaska, 1909-13, also U.S. commr. same period; now mgr. Simplex Mfg. Co., sheet metal work, Fond du Lac, Wis.; pres. Stepenson Chem. Co. Served as 1st lt. Motor Transport Corps, AUS, World War. Mem. Arctic Brotherhood. Republican. Mason. Club: Lake Shore Athletic. Author: The Land of To-morrow, 1919. Home: 195 E. 1st St. Office: 200 N. Main St., Fond du Lac, Wis. Died Aug. 29, 1955; buried Rienzi Cemetery, Fond du Lac, Wis.

STERLING, Donald Justus, newspaperman; born Battle Creek, Mich., Mar. 10, 1887; s. George Carter and Minnie (Justus) S.; A.B., U. of Mich., 1908; m. Adelaide Hannaford Armstrong, Oct. 30, 1926; children—Donald Justus, Harriet Armstrong (Mrs. Edmund Hayes, Jr.). Reporter, Battle Creek (Mich.) Moon-Journal, 1908-09; Sunday editor, Oregon Journal, Portland, Ore., 1909-19, mng. editor, 1919-52; ret. v.p. Journal Pub. Co.; now pub. affairs cons. Pacific Power and Light Co. Consultant on newspaper and publishing industries to Donald M. Nelson, chmn. W.P.B., 1942-43. Pres. Am. Soc. Newspaper Editors, 1939-40. Mem. Delta Upsilon, Sigma Delta Chi. Democrat. Episcopalian. Clubs: Arlington, University, Multnomah, Racquet (Portland); National Press (Washington, D.C.). Home: 3434 S.W. Talbot Rd. Died June 15, 1954; buried Riverview Cemetery, Portland.

STERLING, Frederick Augustine, diplomatic service; b. St. Louis, Aug. 13, 1876; s. Edward Canfield and Cordelia (Seavey) S.; A.B., Harvard, 1898; studied law, Washington U., 1 yr.; m. Dorothy Williams, May 21, 1921; children—John W. Patrick, David, Frederica. Owner, mgr. cattle ranch 8 yrs., mfr. woolen goods 2 yrs.; apptd 3d sec. Embassy, at Petrograd, Russia, 1911, 2d sec., 1912; 2d sec. Legation, Pekin, 1914-15, Petrograd, 1915-16; acting chief and chief Div. Western European Affairs, Washington, D.C., 1916-18; 1st sec., counselor, Am. Embassy, Paris, 1918-21; counselor, Am. Embassy, Lima, Peru, 1921-23, London, 1923-27; E.E. and M.P. to Ireland, 1927-33, to Bulgaria, 1933-36; U.S. commd. to Internat. Expn. on Art and Technique in Modern Life, Paris, France, 1936-37; E.E. and M.P. to Latvia and Estonia, 1937, to Sweden, 1938-42, now ret. Home: Ocean Drive, Newport, R.I. Died Apr. 20, 1957.

STERLING, W. T., business exec.; b. Phila.; Oct. 26, 1906; s. William C. and Mary (Welden) S.; ed. U. Pa. and N.Y. U.; m. Louise M. Deuschle, Jan. 18, 1936; children—Louise M., Barbara J. Tax mgr. Servel Inc., Evansville, Ind., 1925-26, 36-37; with Arthur Andersen & Co., C.P.A.'s, N.Y.C., 1927-36; financial v.p., dir. Brunswick-Balke-Collender Co., Chgo., 1937—, treas. subsidiaries in Canada, Brazil, Mexico and Argentina; certified pub. accountant, N.Y.C.; corp. and estate tax cons. Mem. N.Y. State Soc. C.P.A.'s. Episcopalian. Clubs: Michigan Shores; Men's Garden, Executives, Tam O' Shanter Country (Chgo.). Contbr. articles on taxation to tech. publs. Home: 9 Kent Rd., Winnetka, Ill. Office: 623 S. Wabash Av., Chgo. 5. Died Mar. 24, 1951.

STERN, Bernhard Joseph, sociologist; b. Chgo., June 19, 1894; s. Herman B. and Hattie (Frank) S.; student U. Chgo., 1912-13; A.B., U. Cin., 1916, A.M., 1917; student U. Mich., 1921-22, London Sch. Econs., 1924; Ph.D., Columbia, 1927; m. Charlotte Todes, Aug. 23, 1923; 1 dau., Mira. Tutor, Coll. City N.Y., 1925-26; asst. prof. sociology U. Washington, 1927-30; lectr. sociology, Columbia, 1931—; lectr. anthropology, New Sch. Social Research, 1932-43, 48—; vis. prof. sociology, Yale, 1944-45. Mem. bd. dirs. Am. Com. Protection Fgn. Born. Collaborator, commn. on human relations Progressive Edn. Assn., 1937-38, Com. on Research in Med. Econ., 1938-39, Carnegie Study of the Negro in America, 1939. Mem. Am. and Eastern (sec.-treas. 1943-52), sociol. socs., Am. Anthrop. Soc., N.Y. Soc. Med. History, Am. Assn. Sci. Workers, A.A.A.S. Mem. editorial com., com. on Medicine and the Changing Order, N.Y. Acad. Medicine, 1943-45. Author: Social Factors in Medical Progress, 1927; Lewis Henry Morgan; Social Evolutionist, 1931; The Lummi Indians of Northwest Washington, 1934; Society and Medical Progress, 1941; American Medical Practice, 1945; Philosphy of the Future (with others), 1949; General Anthropology (with Melville Jacobs), 1952; Historical Sociology and Other Selected Papers, 1959. Coauthor: Technological Trends and National Policy, 1937; When Peoples Meet (with Alain Locke), 1937. Asst. editor: Ency. of the Social Sciences (beginning Vol. III), 1930-34. Editor: Young Ward's Diary, 1935; The Family, Past and Present, 1938. Chmn. bd. editors Science and Society. Author numerous articles; contbr. to Am. Sociol. Rev., Am. Anthropologist, annals of Acad. Polit. and Social Science, Social Forces, Science and Society. Home: 423 W. 120th St., N.Y.C. 27. Died Nov. 22, 1956.

STERN, Elizabeth (Eleanor Morton), author; daughter Rev. Aaron and Sarah Leah (Rubenstein) Leven; B.A., U. of Pitt.; M.A. (hon.); student N.Y. Sch. Social Work; m. Leon Thomas Stern, Sept. 26, 1911; children—Thomas Noel, Richard Stephen. Prin. night sch., N.Y. City; organizer, director night sch., Galveston, Tex., 1913. Asst. to dir. Yorkville Community, East Side House Settlement, N.Y. City, 1912, Jacob Schiff Immigration Bur., Galveston, 1913; dir. welfare work, Wanamaker's, Phila., 1919, Community Centre, N.Y. City, 1923; exec. dir. Council House, New York, 1924. Writer Phila. Sunday Press, 1914; columnist Phila. Sunday Record, 1915-19; spl. writer N.Y. Evening World, 1925; columnist Phila. Ledger under name Eleanor Morton, 1926-33, Philadelphia Inquirer, 1933-37; one of organizers Nat. Jail Assn.; adviser, programs and literature, to social service, civic, ednl. agencies and orgns. Mem. Publicity Council for Nat. Defense, Phila.; mem. Pa. Exec. Com. for Amnesty to Political Prisoners; mem. Voluntary Defender Com. of Phila., 1933; mem. joint com. American Friends' Service and Women's Internat. League since 1942; chmn. social problems, Providence Friends' Meeting, since 1942; mem. welfare study com. Armstrong Assn., 1941, chmn. community div. centennary year of Pa. Women's Med. Coll.; chmn. Quaker worship of Old Folks Home adv. com., Friends Center for Older People; member adv. bd. (negro homes) U.S. Housing Authority, Phila., since 1942; mem. State Citizens Com. to Study Negro and the Law, since 1942; Citizens Com. of Phila., 1944. Mem. Women's Internat. League for Peace, Wider Quaker Fellowship, Pa. Historical Society; Armstrong Assn. of Phila. (mem. bd.), adv. com. Delaware Co. Nat. Youth Assn., Tot Lot com. (chmn.) Phila., Citizens Com. to Aid Refugees, Com. to Aid Spanish Loyalists. Mem. bd. of managers, Home for Aged and Infirm Colored People, 1947; mem. exec. com. West Phila. Community Chest since 1952; mem. Friends General Conference since 1952. Mem. Soc. of Friends (Quaker). Club: Women's U. Author: My Mother and I, 1917; A Friend at Court (with Leon Stern), 1923; This Ecstasy, 1927; A Marriage Was Made, 1928; When Loves Comes to Woman, 1929; I Am a Woman and a Jewess, published in 1930; Gambler's Wife, 1931; Not All Laughter, 1937; Sanctuary (short serial), 1939; Vacations from Prison, 1939; Memories: The Life of M.M. Scott, 1943; House of Detention for Adult Prisoneers (for Philadelphia committee), 1944, Josiah White, Prince of Pioneers, 1947; The Women in Gandhi's Life, 1953; Women Behind Gandhi, 1954. Articles on Women Abroad for Philadelphia Inquirer, 1936; series on reeducation of refugees in Am. employment since 1941. Contbr. to mags.; writer, speaker, Am. Friends' Service, 1941-43; lecturer before coll., civic, church groups since 1940; lecturer on America is One, 1944-45. Office: 1806 Spruce St., Phila. 3. Died Jan. 9, 1954; buried Friends Southwestern Burial Ground, Phila.

STERN, Henry Root, lawyer; b. N.Y.C., Sept. 22, 1882; s. Simon Hunt and Sara Stern; grad. Phillips (Andover) Acad., 1899; A.B., Yale, 1903; LL.B., M.A., Columbia, 1906; m. Elsie Weston Lazarus, Apr. 29, 1909 (dec. July 1947); 1 son, Henry Root. Admitted to N.Y. bar, 1905; pvt. practice of law, 1906—; counsel to Sprague and Stern, Mineola, N.Y.; counsel Mudge, Stern, Baldwin & Todd (formerly Mudge, Stern, Williams & Tucker), N.Y.C. Mem. N.Y. Temporary Emergency Relief Adminstrn., 1932-34; chmn. N.Y. Bd. Social Welfare, 1946-54. Treas. N.Y. Rep. State Com., 1934-36; permanent pres. Electoral Coll. N.Y. State. Served from first lieutenant to captain, 311th Infantry, U.S. Army, 1918. Decorated D.S.C. Mem. Am., N.Y. State, Nassau Co. bar assns., Assn. Bar City N.Y., N.Y. County Lawyers Assn., Psi Upsilon. Clubs: Yale, Broad Street, Regency, Adventurers (N.Y.C.). Home: Old Court House Rd., New Hyde Park, L.I. Office: 220 Old Country Rd., Mineola, N.Y. Died May 4, 1959.

STERN, Isaac Farber, cons. engr.; b. Chgo., Nov. 21, 1871; s. Menochem J. and Betty (Farber) S.; B.S. in C.E., U. Mich., 1895; m. Adele Friend, 1916 (died 1918); 1 dau., Adele. Began practice with Gen. William Sooy Smith, Chgo., 1895; successively with bridge dept. I.C. Ry., The Sanitary Dist. Chgo., U.S. Govt. (Milw.), C.&N.W. Ry., until 1905; engr. bridges with C.&N.W. Ry. Co., Chgo., 1905-11; cons. practice, 1912—, on bridges, bldgs., docks, roads, appraisals and gen. adv. service. Served in World War I as cons. engr. and asst. mgr. Dept. Wood Ship Constrn., U.S. Shipping Bd., Emergency Fleet Corp.; expert cons. engr. dept., U.S. World War II. Mem. Structural Engrs. Com. of State Ill. Mem. Am. Soc. C.E., Western Soc. Engrs., Am. Ry. Bridge and Bldg. Assn. Club: Engineers. Home: Hotel Sherry. Office: 38 S. Dearborn St., Chgo. 3. Died Sept. 10, 1949.

STERN, Kurt Guenter, biochemist; b. Tilsit, Germany, Sept. 19, 1904; s. John Kasper and Sonia (Goldberg) S.; student Werner-Siemens Realgymnasium, Berlin, 1912-23; Ph.D., Friedrich-Wilhelms U., 1930; m. Else E. Jacobi, Dec. 24, 1931; 1 son, Rudolph George. Came to U.S., 1935, naturalized, 1946. Carl Duisberg Found. fellow, Rockefeller Inst., N.Y. City, 1930-31; scientific guest Courtauld Inst. Biochemistry, London, 1933-35; vis. lectr., Brown Coxe Research fellow, Yale, 1935-38; research asst. prof. Yale, 1938-42; chief research chemist Overly Biochem. Research Found., N.Y. City, 1942-44; adjunct prof. biochem. Poly. Inst., Bklyn., 1944—. Cons. U.S. AEC Research Project, Montefiore Hosp., N.Y. C. Research cons. to med., indsl. orgns. Recipient Pasteur Medal, Soc. Chem. Biol. Paris, 1952. Fellow Am. Institute of Chemists, New York Academy of Scis.; mem. Am. Chem. Soc., American Soc. Biol. Chemists, Am. Assn. Cancer Research, Harvey Society. Author: General Enzyme Chemistry (with J. B. S. Haldane), 1932; Biological Oxidation (with C. Oppenheimer), 1939; Protoplasm, Ency. Britannica (with R. Chambers), 1948. Contbr. articles to reference books, rev. and exptl. pubs. in field biochemistry. Home: 17 E. 96th St., N.Y.C. 28. Office: Polytech. Inst., Bklyn. Died Feb. 3, 1956.

STERN, Sigmund, investment banker; b. Bavaria, Germany, Dec. 4, 1878; s. Jacob and Rosa (Feldenheimer) S.; student pub. schs. Germany; m. Sybil Cohen, June 29, 1904; children—Judith Claire (Mrs. J.C. Randal), Richard Jay. Came to U.S., 1892, naturalized, 1901. Partner Wise & Stern, 1898 (dissolved); v.p.-treas. Stern & Stern Land Co. since 1902; pres. Stern Bros. & Co. since 1917, Central Coal & Coke Corp. since 1936; v.p. Inland Mortgage Corporation, 1932—; member board of directors and executive committee Employers Reinsurance Corp. since 1928, Central Surety & Ins. Corp. since 1932. Hon. life chmn. Kansas City (Mo.) Community Chest; hon. life pres. United Jewish Social Services; trustee Linda S. Hall Library, U. Kansas City, Children's Mercy Hosp., Menorah Hosp. Exec. mgr. U.S. Treasury Victory Fund Com., 10th Fed. Res. Dist., 1942-43. Mem. Investment Bankes Assn. (past mem. bd. govs.), Kansas City C. of C. (nat. affairs com.). Home: 236 W. 54th St., K.C. Office: 1009 Baltimore Av., K.C. 6, Mo. Died Dec. 31, 1955.

STERNE, Maurice, painter, sculptor; b. Libau, Russia, Aug. 13, 1877; s. Gregor and Naomi (Schlossberg) S.; came to America at 12; studied art, Nat. Acad. Design, New York, in Paris and Rome; m. Mabel Dodge, Aug. 18, 1917; m. 2d, Vera Segal, June 3, 1923. Exhibited Salon de Societe Nat. des Beaux Arts, Paris, The Secession, Berlin, Internat. Soc., London, and in prin. cities U.S. Represented in collections Met. Mus., N.Y.C., Carnegie Inst., Pitts., Mus. Fine Arts, Boston, Cleve. Mus., Detroit Mus., Corcoran Gallery, Washington, Royal Mus., Berlin, Sch. Design, Providence R.I., Art Inst., Chgo., Tate Gallery, London, Uffizi Gallery, Florence, and others. Made Rogers-Kennedy meml., Worcester, Mass.; monument Welcoming the People, Fairmont Park, Phila.; 20 murals The Struggle for Justice, Library, Dept. Justice, Washington. Recipient Corcoran gold medal; 1st William Clark prize Corcoran Gallery for painitng, 1930; Logan prize Chgo. Art Inst., 1927; Clark prize, N.A.D., 1935, Obrig prize, 1936; Walter Lippincott prize Pa. Acad., 1939; Palmer Meml. prize, hon. mention Golden Gate Internat. Expn., 1939. Retrospective exhbn. given by Mus. Modern Art, N.Y., 1933 Academician Nat. Acad.; mem. Commn. Fine Arts, Washington; mem. Am. Soc. Painters, Sculptors and Gravers, Inst. Arts and Letters, Sculptors Guild, New Soc. Artists, Modern Artists Am. Address: Byram Lake Rd., Mount Kisco, N.Y. Died July 23, 1957; buried Sharon Gardens, Valhalla, N.Y.

STERNHAGEN, John Meier, former judge, Tax Court of United States; b. Mt. Vernon, N.Y., March 21, 1888; s. Herman and Christina (Meier) S.; grad. high sch., Mt. Vernon, LL.B., New York U., 1912; m. Gertrude Hussey, Apr. 29, 1927; 1 dau., Frances Hussey. Admitted to N.Y. bar, 1913, began practice N.Y. City; practiced Chicago, Ill., 1921-24; mem. U.S. Bd. Tax Appeals, Washington, D.C., since its creation, July 1924. Served as lt., A.S., U.S. Army, 1918. Mem. Am. Bar Assn., Phi Delta Phi. Episcopalian. Club: Chevy Chase (Washington). Home: 3328 O St. N.W., Washington, 7. Died Sept. 25, 1954.

STETSON, Eugene William, banker; b. Hawkinsville, Ga., Dec. 5, 1881; s. James D. and Eugenia (Pate) S.; ed. Gordon Mil. Inst., Barnesville, Ga.; Mercer U., Macon, Ga., 1898-1901; m. Josephine Shaw, Dec. 28, 1904 (died 1912); m. 2d, Iola Lamar Wise, June 2, 1915; children—Josephine (Mrs. Robert P. Hatcher), Eugene W., Basil, Charles, Iola (Mrs. John M. Hauerstick). Began as clerk Am. Nat. Bank, Macon, 1901; cashier Exchange Nat. Bank, Fitzgerald, Ga., 1904-08; organizer, and cashier, 1908-10, pres., 1910-16, Citizens Nat. Bank, Macon; v.p., dir. and mem. exec. com. Guaranty Trust Co. of N.Y., 1916-41, pres., 1941-44, chmn., 1944-47; dir., mem. executive committee McCrory Stores Corp., McLellan Stores Company, Guaranty Trust Co. of New York; mem. finance com. Coca Cola Co.; chmn. adv. com. French American Banking Corp.; chmn. exec. com. Gulf Atlantic Warehouse Co., I.C.R.R. Co.; dir., mem. exec. com. Air Reduction Co.; dir., mem. adv. com., Tri-Continental Corp.; chmn. Textile Banking Corp.; dir. Tri Continental Financial Corp., United Stores Corp. Arbitrator City of Macon in taking over water system from pvt. corp.; pres. Macon C. of C., 1913-14; v.p. Ga. C. of C., 1914-15; v.p. Ga. State Fair Assn. Mem. Phi Delta Theta. Independent Democrat. Episcopalian. Home: 675 Hull's Farm Rd., Southport, Conn.; also 117 E. 72d St., N.Y.C. Office: 140 Broadway, N.Y.C. Died July 20, 1959; buried Oaklawn Cemetery, Southport, Conn.

STETSON, Henry Crosby, geologist; b. Cambridge, Mass., Oct. 10, 1900; s. Henry Crosby and Eleanor Morland (Gray) S.; A.B., Harvard, 1923, A.M., 1926; m. Edith Williams Reid, Oct. 15, 1927; children—Robert Gray, Thomas Reid, Edith Lincoln. Asst. in geology Harvard, 1924-25, asst. in meteorology, 1925-26, asst. curator paleontology Mus. Comparative Zoology, 1927-34, research asso. paleontology 1934-42, 42-43, research fellow in oceanography, 1943-46, asso. curator oceanography, 1946-48, research oceanographer, 1948—, lectr. geology, 1950—; research asso. Oceanographic Instn., Woods Hole, Mass., 1931-41, submarine geologist, 1941—; Alexander Agassiz fellow in oceanography, 194-42, in oceanography and zoology, 1946—; civilian with OSRD, 1944. Mem. Am. Acad. Arts and Scis., Geol. Soc. Am., A.A.A.S., Am. Geophys. Union, Am. Assn. Petroleum Geologists, Soc Econ. Paleontologists and Mineralogists. Author numerous publs. in field. Home: Belmont, Mass. Died Dec. 3, 1955; buried Mt. Auburn Cemetery, Cambridge, Mass.

STETSON, Raymond Herbert, educator; b. N. Ridgeville, O., Mar. 1, 1872; s. Herbert David and Florence (Simonds) S.; Ph.B., Oberlin Coll., O., 1893, A.M., 1896; Ph.D., Harvard, 1901. Prof. psychology and philosophy Beloit Coll., 1906-09; head dept. psychology Oberlin Coll., 1909-39. Research work in skin sensations, skilled movements, phonetics. Mem. Am. Psychol. Assn., Linguistic Soc. Am., Permanent Internat. Council, Internat. Congress Phonetic Scis. Conglist. Author: Motor Phonetics, Vol. III in Archives Néerlandaises de phonétique expérimentale, 1928; Bases of Phonology, 1945. Home: 157 N. Professor St., Oberlin, O. Died Dec. 4, 1950; buried North Ridgeville, O.

STETTEN, DeWitt, surgeon; b. New York, N.Y., Jan. 22, 1881; s. Joseph and Bella (Rosenthal) S.; M.D., Coll. Physicians and Surgeons (Columbia), 1901; house staff German hosp., New York, 1901-03; studied Vienna, Prague and Breslau, 1904-05; m. Magdalen Ernst, Apr. 23, 1906; children—Margaret (Mrs. Maximilien Vanka), DeWitt, Jr.; m. 2d, Alice Mayer, May 5, 1930. Asst. and attdg. surgeon, German Dispensary, New York, 1905-11; anesthetist, German Hospital, New York, 1905-08; asso. surgeon German Hospital, later Lenox Hill Hospital, New York, 1908-21, actg. attending surgeon, 1921; attending surgeon Lenox Hill Hospital, 1922-46; Beth Israel Hospital, New York, 1930-33; cons. surgeon, Lenox Hill Hospital since 1946; instr. clin. surgery, Coll. Phys. and Surg., 1909-18; clin. prof. surgery, New York University Coll. of Medicine, 1931-46. Member Hospital Corps, 1st Batt., N.Y. Naval Milita, 1898-1902; 1st lt. M.R.C., U.S. Army, 1915-17, capt. 1917-18, maj. M.C., U.S. Army, 1918-19. With Neurol. Sch., U. of Pa., Sept.-Dec. 1917; asst. chief and acting chief of surg. service U.S. Army Gen. Hosp. No. 1, Williamsbridge, N.Y., Jan.-Oct. 1918; chief of surg. service U.S. Army Embarkation Hosp. No. 4, New York, 1918-19; acting comdg. officer same, Feb. 13-22, 1919. Fellow Am. Coll. Surgeons, A.M.A., New York Acad. Medicine, N.A.D., Am. Geog. Soc.; mem. Nat. Audubon Soc., Internat. Soc. of Gastro-Enterology, Am. Gastro-Enterol. Assn., Am. Assn. Thoracic Surgery, Nat. Tuberculosis Assn., Am. Cancer Soc., Assn. Military Surgeons of U.S., A.A.A.S., Acad. Polit. Sci., Fgn. Policy Assn., Med. Soc. State of N.Y., Med. Soc. County of New York (pres. 1929, trustee, 1932-35, chmn. bd. 1935), New York Surg. Soc., N.Y. Soc. for Thoracic Surgery, N.Y. Gastro-Enterological Assn., N.Y. Pathol. Soc., Military Order of the World Wars, Am. Legion, etc. Pres. bd. trustees Blood Tranfusion Assn. of New York; mem. and sec. bd. dirs. United Med. Service, Diplomate founders group Am. Bd. of Surgery. Club: Dachshund Club of America. Contbr. more than 90 papers on surgical subjects. Address: 850 Park Av., New York 21, N.Y.; (summer) White Bridge Farm, Rushland, Bucks County, Pa. Died Nov. 10, 1951.

STEVENS, Adie Allan, lawyer, capitalist; b. Blair Co., Pa., Aug. 20, 1845; s. James and Catharine A. (Agnew) S.; student pub. schs.; m. Mary Mary B. Hazzard, Apr. 29, 1909. Pvt. 15th Pa. Cav. (Anderson's Troop); admitted to bar, 1872; mem. firm of Stevens & Pascoe. Pres. and gen. mgr. Tyrone Gas & Water Co.; v.p. First Nat. Bank (Tyrone); v.p. and general mgr. Am. Lime & Stone Co. Trustee Dickinson Sem. Mem. Nat. Exec. Com. Prohibition Party for 20 yrs. Methodist. Clubs: Art, Lawyers'. Address: Tyrone, Blair Co., Pa. Deceased.

STEVENS, Ashton, dramatic critic, columnist; b. San Francisco, Aug. 11, 1872; s. James William and Hannah Laura (Thompson) S.; ed. pub. sch., Oakland; m. Aleece Uhlhorn, Dec. 4, 1900 (died Mar. 27, 1926); m. 2d, Florence Katherine Krug, June 21, 1927. Dramatic critic, San Francisco News Letter, 1894-95, Morning Call, 1896; dramatic critic, San Francisco Examiner, and editor News Letter and Overland Monthly, 1897; gave up editorship, 1898, devoting entire time to criticisms for Examiner for 10 yrs.; dramatic critic, New York Evening Journal, 1907-10, Herald and Examiner, Chicago, 1910-32, Chicago American (now Herald American) since 1932. Clubs: Cliff Dwellers, Tavern. Author: Actorviews, 1923; (play) Mary's Way Out (with Charles Michelson), prod. Los Angeles, Calif., 1918; articles in magazines and Encyclopaedia Britannica. Address: Herald American, Chicago. Died July 11, 1951.

STEVENS, Charles Brooks, textile mfr.; b. Haverhill, Mass., Oct. 11, 1864; s. George and Harriet Lyman (Brooks) S.; A.B., Harvard, 1886; m. Edith Ames, June 17, 1896; children—Ames, Edith (Mrs. John P. Stevens, Jr.), Harriet (Mrs. A. Alexander Robey), Brooks. In mfg. bus., Mass., 1893—; became pres., treas. U.S. Bunting Co., Lowell, 1900; pres. Lawrence Mfg. Co. (cotton fabrics); treas. Middlesex Co.; pres. Ames Worsted Co.; dir. Union Nat. Bank of Lowell. Asst. in q.m. dept., World War. Pres. Lowell Gen. Hosp. Club: Harvard (N.Y. C. Home: Tewksbury, Mass. Address: Lowell, Mass. Died June 26, 1949.

STEVENS, Daisy McLaurin (Mrs. William Forrest Stevens); b. Raleigh, Smith Co., Miss., June 21, 1875; d. Anselm Joseph and Laura E. (Rauch) McLaurin; grad. Brandon (Miss.) Female Coll., 1890; grad. Belmont Coll., Nashville, Tenn., 1892; m. Judge William Forrest Stevens, Dec. 15, 1896; children—Laurie McLaurin (dec.), Daisy McLaurin, Ann, Delta McLaurin. Pres. Miss. Div. U.D.C., 1907-09; pres.-gen. U.D.C., 1913-15; pres. for Miss. of Southern Commercial Congress, 1911-13; mem. exec. bd. of woman's auxiliary Am. Highway Assn.; regent Mississippi Room of the Confed. Museum, at Richmond, Va.); delivered address presenting Arlington Monument to the U.S. Govt., 1914. Chmn. ex-officio Shiloh Monument Com. and pres. Arlington Monument Assn. of U.D.C., 1913-15; matron of honor for South for Confed. Vets.' annual reunion, 1914-15. County chmn. Woman's Liberty Loan Com., 1917; state pres. Nat. League for Woman's Service; mem. Commn. on Training Camp Activities, woman's com., A.R.C.; state chairman Com. of Mercy for Relief of Belgians, 1914-18. Democratic Nat. Committeewoman Miss., Miss. chairman ladies' auxiliary, Nat. Woodrow Wilson Memorial Assn.; trustee State Univ. and Colls. (Miss.). Methodist. Club: Research (Jackson, Miss.). Home: Brandon, Miss. Deceased.

STEVENS, Edward Francis, librarian; b. Rangoon, Burma, Asia, Sept. 22, 1868; s. Rev. Edward Oliver (D.D.) and Harriet Calista (Mason) S.; B.A., Colby, 1889; grad. Pratt Inst. Sch. Library Sci., Bklyn., 1903; Litt.D., Colby, 1917; m. Sally Field, Sept. 21, 1899. With Baker & Taylor Co., pubs. and booksellers, N.Y., 1889-91, Longmans, Green & Co., 1891-1902; cataloguer Yale U. Library, New Haven, 1903-06; head applied sci. reference dept., Pratt. Inst. Free Library, 1906-09, librarian, 1910-38, ret. June 30, 1938; dir. Pratt Inst. Sch. Library Sci., 1911-38, Mayor of Shoreham, 1927-29. Republican. Baptist. Mem. N.Y. Library Club, Me. Library Assn., Phi Beta Kappa (hon.), Delta Kappa Epsilon. Author: Outline of the History of Printing, The Story of Pratt Institute. Editor, designer and pub. Trollope's "The Warden" (printed for libraries). Home: Miller Place, L.I., N.Y. Died Feb. 25, 1956; buried Kensico Cemetery, Valhalla, N.Y.

STEVENS, Evarts Chapman, chmn. Internat. Silver Co.; b. Wallingford, Conn., Jan. 13, 1885; s. Elizur Seneca and Harriet Amelia (Maltby) S.; ed. private schs. and New Haven (Conn.) High Sch.; m. Lily Garvie, Feb. 12, 1907; children—Evarts Chapman, John Bradford. Began as foreman with Internat. Silver Co., 1906, asst. supt., 1908-19, mgr. 1919-28, vice president, 1929-35, president, 1935-51, chairman board directors since 1951; director Internat. Silver Company of Canada, Ltd.; president Dime Savings Bank (Wallingford); v.p., dir. Home National Bank. Director Manufacturers Association of Connecticut, Inc., 1934-38, National Assn. of Manufacturers, 1935-36. Mem. Wallingford Bd. of Edn., 1917-29, Bd. of Water Commrs., 1924-28; served in Conn. State and Nat. Guard, 1917-22; capt. in O.R.C., 1922-27. Mem. S.A.R. Republican. Conglist. Mason. Clubs: Home (Meriden); Metabetchouan Club (Kiskisink, Quebec); Wallingford, Wallingford Country. Home: Strawberry Hill, Northford Rd., Wallingford, Conn. Office: International Silver Co., Meriden, Conn. Died Nov. 9, 1956; buried "In Memoriam" Cemetery, Wallingford, Conn.

STEVENS, Henry M(eldrum), advt. exec.; b. Portland, Ore., Aug. 12, 1900; s. Harley C. and Pearle (Meldrum) S.; A.B., U. Cal., 1921; M.B.A., Harvard, 1923; m. Stella Riggs, May 28, 1924; children—Henry Meldrum, Sally Riggs, Phyllis. Joined J. Walter Thompson Co., 1923, with Chgo. office, 1923, S.F., 1924-26, 29-34, London, Eng., 1927-28, mgr. St. L. office, 1935, mgr., v.p. N.Y.C. office since 1936, dir. since 1940; pres. Traffic Audit Bur., 1940-45. Spl. study for Treasury Dept. as mem. War. Advt. Council; chmn. advt. and graphics sect. Nat. War Fund, 1943; gen. chmn. United Hosp. Fund, 1948. Dir., chmn. bd. Nat. Outdoor Advt. Bur. Mem. Am. Assn. Advt. Agencies (past treas., now v.p., dir., chmn. bd.), Alpha Delta Phi, Phi Delta Phi. Republican. Conglist. Clubs: Univ. (N.Y.C.); Woodway Country (Springdale, Conn.). Author advt. articles. Home: Ridge Acres Rd., Darien, Conn. Died Aug. 12, 1953.

STEVENS, John Morgan, lawyer; b. Old Augusta, Perry County, Miss., May 27, 1876; s. Capt. Benjamin and Lorena Annette (Breland) S.; student Millsaps Coll., Jackson, Miss., 3 yrs.; B.A., U. of Miss., 1898 (valedictorian); read law at univ., and under bro. Judge William F. Stevens, Carrollton, Miss.; m. Ethel, d. Rev. H. Walter Featherstun, June 7, 1905; children—John Morgan (dec.), Emily White, Joseph Johnston (dec.), Stuart Featherstun (dec.), Ethelwyn Featherstun, Phineas N., Francis Bigelow. Admitted to Mississippi bar, 1899; mem. Southworth & Stevens, Lexington, Miss., 1899-1901, Stevens & Stevens, Hattiesburg, Miss., 1901-06, Stevens, Stevens & Cook, Hattiesburg, 1906-12; apptd. chancellor 8th Chancery Court Dist., by Gov. Earl Brewer, June 1912, and elected to same office without opposition, Nov. 1913; justice Supreme Court of Miss., May 10, 1915-Oct. 1920, resigned; apptd. official reporter, Supreme Court of Miss., Oct. 1923; now senior mem. law firm Jackson, Miss.; apptd. chmn. commn. to recodify all laws of Miss., 1929. Mem. Am. Bar Assn., Miss. State Bar Assn., Kappa Alpha. Democrat. Home: Jackson, Miss. Died Nov. 7, 1951; buried Old Augusta, Perry County, Miss.

STEVENS, Leslie Clark, naval officer; b. Kearney, Neb., Feb. 19, 1895; s. Leslie and Amelia Jane (Phillips) S.; A.B., Neb. Wesleyan, 1913; grad. U. S. Naval Acad., 1918; M.Sc., Mass. Inst. of Tech., 1922; m. Nell Millikin, June 6, 1918; 1 son, Leslie Clark. Served in Queenstown destroyer forces, World War I; naval aviator, 1924; in U.S.S. Langley, 1925-26; in charge ship's installations Bur. of Aeronautics, Navy Dept., Washington, D.C., 1926-30; assembly and repair officer Naval Air Sta., San Diego, Calif., 1930-34; asst. naval attache for air, London, 1934-37; tech. adviser to London Disarmament Conf., 1936; in charge expts. and developments Bur. Aeronautics, 1937-44; staff, comdr. Aircraft Forward Area (Pacfic), 1944; staff, comdr. Aircraft (Pacific), 1944-45; asst. chief Bur. Aeronautics for research development and engring., Washington, D.C., 1946-47; naval attaché and naval air attaché, Moscow, 1947-49; with Joint Chiefs of Staff, 1949-51; chmn. Am. Com. Liberation from Bolshevism, 1952-54; mem. national advisory com. for aeros., 1946-47. Advanced through grades to rear admiral, U.S. Navy, 1946, retired as vice admiral, 1951. Awarded: Legion of Merit, Bronze Star, Commendation Ribbon (United States); Commander Mil. Div. Order of British Empire (Eng.). Mem. Inst. Aero. Sci., Am. Anthrop. Assn., Archaeol. Inst. Am. Clubs: Explorers, New York Yacht (N.Y.C.); P.E.N., Army and Navy, Army-Navy Country (Washington). Author: Russian Assignment. Contbr. publs. Home: 213 King George St., Annapolis, Md. Died Nov. 30, 1956; buried Arlington Nat. Cemetery.

STEVENS, Maltby, business exec.; b. Glastonbury, Conn., Aug. 29, 1895; s. Elizur and Harriet Amelia (Maltby) S.; ed. pub. schs., Wallingford, Conn.; m. Anna E. Lynch, Oct. 12, 1915; various positions with The Internat. Silver Co., Meriden, Conn., 1912-19; foreman, 1921-22, asst. supt., 1922-28, mgr., 1929-45, president since 1951, dir. since 1938; dir. The Internat. Silver Co. of Can., Housatonic P.S. Company. Director Meriden Hosp. Mem. Court of Burgesses, Wallingford, 1920-26. Served on Mexican Border with 5th Conn. Cavalry, 1916, with 102d M.G. Battn., U.S. Army, France, 1917-19. Mem. Mfrs. Assn. of Conn. (dir. 1944-48), Mfrs. Assn. of Meriden (dir.). Republican. Conglist. Clubs: Home (Meriden) (past pres.); Metabetchouan, (Kiskisink, P.Q.); Country, Wallingford (bd. govs. 1936-40). Home: 364 S. Main, Wallingford. Office: The Internat. Silver Co., Meriden, Conn. Deceased.

STEVENS, Patricia, dir. model school; b. Clear Lake, S.D., Apr. 12, 1914; d. James J. and Mary Celia (Kelly) Stevens; student Chicago Bus. Coll., 1930-31; spl. courses in phys. edn., voice, dramatics, and beauty culture; married 2d, Earl Muntz. Model affiliated with John Powers and Harry Conover agys., N.Y.C., 1932-40; organized original Patricia Stevens Models Finishing School, Chicago, May 1942, and later in Hollywood, San Francisco, Kansas City, Detroit, Milwaukee, Indianapolis, Dallas, Minneapolis, Memphis, N.Y.C. and others; pres. Patricia Stevens, Inc. and dir. nat. orgn. of 40 charm, modeling and career schs. and model agencies; founder Patricia Stevens Fashion Show Prodns., Inc., 1946; v.p. Patricia Stevens Franchise Co., Patricia Stevens Cosmetic Co.; star Charm Salon, television program; a pioneer in indsl. charm tng. for Santa Fe R.R., Marshall Field & Co., Henry C. Lyttons, Airlines, etc. Sponsors of local and state contests in Miss America pageants, 1946—. Mem. Ill. State Vocational Schs. Com. Sponsor Jr. Achievement orgn. Mem. C. of C. in all cities where schs. are located, Chgo. Federated Advt. Club, Publicity Club Chgo., Nat. Models Assn., Am. Fedn. Television and Radio Artists, Young Pres. Orgn., Chgo. Photog. Assn., Fashion Group of Chgo. Roman Catholic. Fashion and beauty editor of nat. periodicals and mags. Author: Loveliness Unlimited, 1948, Guide to Good Grooming. Home: 2801 Sheridan Rd. Office: 22 W. Madison St., Chgo. Died June, 1959.

STEVENS, Truman S., lawyer; b. Tama County, Ia., Dec. 20, 1864; s. Ira and Malinda S.; LL.B., State U. of Ia., 1890; m. Cora Patterson, May 13, 1893. Practiced at Hamburg, Ia.; apptd. dist. judge 15th Ia. Dist., Feb. 18, 1917; apptd. acted as asso. justice Supreme Ct. of Ia., May of same yr. and elected to same position 3 times, last term expiring 1934; chief justice, 1922. In practice at Des Moines since 1934; now mem. Cosson, Stevens, Hauge & Cosson. Mem. Ia. State Bar Assn. (pres. 1923). Republican. Baptist. Mason. Address: 1014 Savings and Loan Bldg., Des Moines 9, Ia. Died Aug. 19, 1950; buried Woodland Cemetery, Des Moines.

STEVENS, Wallace, poet, ins. exec.; b. Reading, Pa., Oct. 2, 1879; s. Garrett Barcalow and Mary Catherine (Zeller) S.; student Harvard Univ., N.Y. Law School; married to Elsie V. Kachel, September 21, 1909; one dauguthter, Holly Bright. Admitted to N.Y. bar, 1904, and engaged in gen. practice of law at New York, N.Y.; asso. with Hartford Accident and Indemnity Co., Hartford, Conn., 1916—, v.p., 1934—. Author: (poems) Harmonium, 1924; Ideas of Order, 1936; Owl's Clover, 1936; Man with hthe Blue Guitar, 1937; Parts of a World, 1942; Notes Toward a Supreme Fiction, 1942; The Auroras of Autumn, 1950; The Necessary Angel, 1951. Recipient of Bollingsen Prize in Poetry from Yale University Library, 1949. Member of the National Inst. Arts and Letters, 1946; Transport to Summer, 1947. Home: 118 Westerly Terrace. Office: 690 Asylum Av., Hartford, Conn. Died Aug. 2, 1955; buried Cedar Hill Cemetery.

STEVENS, Wayne Edson, educator, historian; b. Avon, Ill., July 24, 1892; s. Willis Edson and Edith Quincy (Belding) S.; A.B., Knox Coll., 1913; M.A., U. Ill., 1914, Ph.D., 1916; m. Ann Baumler Francis, Sept. 4, 1933. Instr. history U. Minn., 1916-17; sec. war records sect. Ill. State Hist. Library, 1919-20; historian U.S. Army A.S., 1920-21; instr. history Dartmouth, 1921-23, asst. prof., 1923-30, prof., 1930-—; mem. adv. bd. hist. sect. U.S. Army War Coll., 1929-31. Served as 1st lt. U.S. Army, 1917-19, as maj. specialist res., 1929-31. Mem. American Hist. Association, Phi Beta Kappa, Sigma Phi Epsilon. Conglist. Club: Author: The Northwest Fur Trade, 1763-1800, 1928; European Militarism in a New Phase, 1926. Editor: History of the 151st Field Artillery, Rainbow Division (Louis L. Collins), 1924. Contbr. to Dictionary Am. Biography. Home: 4 N. Park St., Hanover, N.H. Died July 20, 1959; buried Pine Knoll Cemetery, Hanover, N.H.

STEVENS, William Chase, botanist; b. Princeton, Ill., Feb. 21, 1861; s. James Thomas and Elizabeth (Flint) S.; A.B., U. Kan., 1885, M.S., 1893; Harvard Summer Sch., 1890, Woods Hole Biol. Lab., 1890, U. Bonn, 1897; m. Ada E. Pugh, July 11, 1888. Prof. botany, U. Kan., 1899-—. Fellow Bot. Soc. Am.; mem. Am. Soc. Naturalists, A.A.A.S., Sigma Xi. Author: Introduction to Botany, 1902; Histological Botany and Micro-technic, 1897; Plant Anatomy, 1915. Address: Lawrence, Kan. Deceased.

STEVENS, William Oliver, author; b. Rangoon, Burma, Asia, Oct. 7, 1878; s. Edward Oliver and Harriet Calista (Mason) S.; A.B., Colby, 1899, Litt.D., 1923; Ph.D., Yale, 1903; m. Claudia Wilson Miles, June 1, 1904; children—Hugo Osterhaus, William Mason. Instr. English, 1903-05, prof., 1905-24, U.S. Naval Acad.; headmaster Roger Aseham Sch., White Plains, N.Y., 1924-27, Cranbrook Sch., Bloomfield Hills, Mich., 1927-35; dean Sch. Lit. and Journalism, Oglethorpe U., 1936-37. Member Phi Beta Kappa, Delta Kappa Epsilon. Episcopalian. Club: Century. Author: The Cross in the Life and Literature of the Anglo-Saxons, 1904; The Young Privateersman (with McKee Barclay), 1910; A Short History of the United States Navy (with others), 1911; Pewee Clinton, Plebe, 1912; Messmates, 1913; The Story of Our Navy, 1914; Boy's Book of Famous Warships, 1915; naval volume of Harper's History of the War (with C. C. Gill), 1919; A History of Sea Power (with Allan Westcott), 1920; Boyhoods of Our Navy Heroes, 1924; Boys' Life of General Grant, 1925; The Correct Thing, 1934; The Right Thing, 1935; Nantucket, The Far Away Island, 1936; Annapolis, Anne Arundel's Town, 1937; Old Williamsburg and Her Neighbors, 1938; Discovering Long Island, 1939; Charleston, Historic City of Gardens, 1939; The Patriotic Thing, 1940; Pistols at Ten Paces, 1940; The Shenandoah and Its Byways, 1941; Forever England, 1941; David Glasgow Farragut, Our First Admiral, 1942; Washington, the Cinderealla City, 1943; Drummer Boy of Burma, 1943; Beyond the Sunset, 1944; Unbidden Guests, 1945; The Quiet Hour, 1947; The Mystery of Dreams, 1949; Famous Women of America, 1950; Famous Men of Science, 1952; Famous Statesmen of America, 1953; Phychics and Common Sense, 1953; Famous Humanitarians, 1953; The Inspirational Reader, 1954; Footsteps to Freedom, 1954. Contbr. newspaper and mags. Home: 26 W. 9th St., N.Y.C. 11. Died Jan. 15, 1955.

STEVENSON, Holland Newton, naval officer; b. b. Cambridge, N.Y., Sept. 3, 1844; s. John M. and Seraph H. S.; C.E., Rensselaer Poly. Inst., 1866; apptd. to Naval Acad. from N.Y. as acting 3d asst. engr., Oct. 10, 1866; grad. spl. course in engring., 1868; 3d asst. engr., June 2, 1868; 2d asst. engr., June 2, 1869; passed asst. engr., Dec. 13, 1874; chief engr., Dec. 14, 1892; comdr., Mar. 3, 1899; capt., Feb. 10, 1903; retired as commodore, June 30, 1905. At Naval Acad., 1866-1868; Navy Yard, N.Y. C., 1867; Dacotah and Saranac, 1868-71; Bur. of Steam Engring., 1871-72; spl. duty, N.Y.C., 1872-74; Swatara, 1874-75; coast and geodetic survey, 1875-78; Morgan Iron Works, N.Y.C., 1878-79; Trenton, 1879-81; Wyo., 1882; coast survey, 1883-87; insp. of machinery, 1888-91; Alliance, 1891-94; Constellation, 1894-95; insp. of machinery, Bath Iron Works, 1895-97; Monterey, 1897-99; insp. of machinery for the Navy at Union Iron Works, San Francisco, 1899-1908. Home: 1482 Sutter St., San Francisco. Died Jan. 11, 1959.

STEVENSON, Howard A., capialist; b. Phila., Jan. 2, 1842; s. Hon. Samuel S.; ed. privately; grad. Coll. of Pharmacy of Phila.; m. Rosalia C. Hunter, Feb. 3, 1870. Mem. 2d regt. 1st brigade Pa. vols., 1861; apptd. to med. dept. U.S.S. State of Georgia, Oct. 31, 1862, and remained until close of Civil War; late dir. Drug Exchange of Phila.; pres. Green and Coates Sts. Passenger Ry. Co., Phila.; late dir. Lombard and South Sts. Passsnger Ry. Co., Phila., West End City Passenger Ry. Co.; pres. People's Passenger Ry. Co., Phila.; dir. Germantown Passenger Ry. Co., Phila., Fire Assn. of Phila., Real Estate Title Ins. and Trust Co., Chelten Avenue Passenger Ry. Co. of Phila., Centennial Passenger Ry. Co. of Phila. In 1890 introduced the 1st bill in Phila. City Council for the passing of an ordinance to operate city street cars by electrical power. Mem. Union League of Phila.; Geo. G. Meade Post No. 1, G.A.R. Summer Address: Hawthorne Villa, Newport, R.I. Home: Cor. Tulpehocken and Green Sts., Germantown, Philadelphia. Deceased.

STEVENSON, Richard Corwine, lawyer; b. Delaware, O., Apr. 25, 1896; s. Richard Taylor and Julia E. (Tevis) S.; A.B., Ohio Wesleyan U., 1918, LL.D., 1952; J.D., U. Chgo., 1925; m. Martha C. Roby, Feb. 24, 1927; children—Sarah Roby, Richard Corwine. Admitted to Ill. bar, 1925, since practiced in Chgo., mem. firm Stevenson, Conaghan, Velde & Hackbert; dir. Ditto, Inc., Elgin Joliet & Eastern Ry. Co. Dir., pres. Immigrant's Protective League. Trustee Ohio Wesleyan U., 1938-43. Served with U.S. Army, 1917-18. Mem. Am., Ill., Chgo. bar assns., Phi Gamma Delta. Republican. Methodist. Clubs: Law, Legal, Lit., Mid-Day, Cliff Dwellers (Chgo.); Glen View (Ill.) Country. Home: 231 Dempster St., Evanston, Ill. Office: 208 S. La Salle St., Chgo. 4. Died Apr. 24, 1958.

STEVENSON, W(illiam) C., engr., oil exec.; b. Boise, Ida., Aug. 10, 1899; s. Charles Clifford and Martha Belle (Black) S.; A.B. in Mech. Engring., Stanford, 1922, postgrad. study elec. engring., 1923; m. Ruby Mae Walser, Mar. 10, 1923; children—William Walser, Joanne (Mrs. Jacob Voogd); m. 2d, Virginia Watt Granberry, Oct. 19, 1957. Elec. engr. City of Los Angeles, 1923-24; asst. supt. chem. plant, Bakersfield, Cal., 1924-25; with Union Oil Co. of Cal., 1925-—, successively in mfg. dept., refinery mgr., asst. to exec. v.p., v.p. indsl. relations, 1952-—. Mem. Civil Def. Nat. Com. Registered mech. engr., Cal. Mem. Pacific Oil Inst., Am. Petroleum Inst., Personnel and Indsl. Relations Assn. Presbyn. Mason. Address: 2575 Deodar Circle, Pasadena, Cal. Died Oct. 22, 1957.

STEVENSON, William Henry, vice dir. Iowa Agrl. Expt. Sta.; b. Freeport, Ill., Sept. 4, 1872; s. Henry Staley and Louisa (Rosenstiel) S.; A.B., Ill. Coll., Jacksonville, 1893, D.Sc., 1923; B.S.A., Ia. State Coll. Agr. and Mechanic Arts, 1905; m. Rosalthea Coffin Scott, June 29, 1904. Asst. in soils U. Ill., 1901-02; prof. soils, 1902-10, prof. farm crops and soils, head dept., 1910-32, Ia. State Coll. Agr. and Mech. Arts; vice dir. Ia. Agrl. Expt. Sta. 1912-48, emeritus; dir. Ia. soil survey, 1910-32. Sec. Ia. Drainage Assn., 1904-13; mem. exec. com. Ia. Drainage. Waterways and Conservation Commn., 1908-10, Ia. State Stocks Com., 1917-18; apptd. by Pres. Harding permanent U.S. del. Internat. Inst. Agr., Rome, 1921-22, spl. rep. U.S. Govt., 1924, 34. Fellow A.A.A.S., Am. Soc. Agronomy; mem. Internat. Soc. Soil Sci., Am. Soc. Agronomy, Am. Soil Survey Assn., Ia. Acad. Sci., Sigma Xi, Phi Kappa Phi, Alpha Zeta, Gamma Sigma Delta, Phi Lambda Upsilon, Pi Kappa Alpha. Republican. Presbyn. Mason (32°, K.T.). Co-Author: Soil Physics Laboratory Guide, 1905. Sr. author of many Iowa soil survey reports and numerous bulls. on soil fertility. Home: 320 Ash Av., Ames, Ia. Died Jan. 7, 1951; buried College Cemetery, Ames, Ia.

STEVENSON, William Patton, clergyman; b. W. Alexander, Pa., Dec. 24, 1860; s. Rev. Josias and Eleanor (Patton) S.; A.B., Westminster Coll., Pa., 1882; Union Theol. Sem., New York, 1882-83; Western Theol. Sem., 1883-85; D.D., Syracuse U., 1902; m. Elizabeth M. Cooper, June 1, 1887. Ordained Presbyn. ministry, 1885; pastor, Avalon, Pa., 1885-87, Mauch Chunk, Pa., 1887-91, Titusville, Pa., 1981-98, Park Ch., Syracuse, N.Y., 1898-1902, 1st Ch., Yonkers, N.Y., 1902-—. Home: 111 N. Broadway, Yonkers, N.Y. Died Nov. 4, 1944.

STEVENSON, William Taylor, utility exec.; b. Leavenworth, Kan., June 10, 1900; s. Horace Saunders and Lottie Belle (Huckins) S.; A.B., U. Kan., 1923; m. Dorothy Moore Ensminger, Mar. 21, 1925; children—William Taylor, Margaret Moore, Charles Hallam. Pres., dir. Texas Gas Transmission Corp., Western Ky. Gas Co. (both Owensboro, Ky.), La. Natural Gas Corp., Lake Charles, La., La. Natural Gasoline Corp., Shreveport, La.; dir. Owensboro Nat. Bank, Walworth Co., N.Y. Mem. Gas Industry Adv. Council, Am. Gas Assn. (dir., mem. exec. com.), Ind. Natural Gas Assn. (dir.), Phi Kappa Psi, Delta Sigma Pi. Clubs: Recess (N.Y.C.); Pendennis (Louisville); Metropolitan (Washington). Home: 1727 Griffith Av. Office: 416 W. Third St., Owensboro, Ky. Died May 22, 1957; buried Owensboro.

STEWART, George, ecologist; b. Tooele, Utah, Nov. 7, 1888; s. William and Ellen (Speirs) S.; A.B., U. of Utah, 1907; B.S., Utah Agrl. Coll., 1913; M.S., Cornell U., 1918; Shevlin fellow U. of Minn., 1924-25, Ph.D., 1926; m. Wynona Barber, Sept. 5, 1918; 1 dau., Betty Ann. Instr. in agronomy, Utah Agr. Coll., 1913-16, asst. prof., 1917-18, asso. prof., 1918-19, prof., 1919-30; became sr. ecologist branch of research U.S. Forest Service, 1930; supervisor Utah State Agrl. Coll.-Fgn. Operations Administration Contract for Agr., Iran, 1954-56; professor botany and agronomy Brigham Young U., 1956-—. With U.S. Dept. Agr., 1951-53. Member Agricultural Commission to Iran (7 year plan), 1949. Chairman Scout committee Church of Latter Day Saints, 1942-48; member Ogden area Scouts council. Recipient Superior Service award, U.S. Department Agr.; Service award, Utah Acad. Science, 1951. Member American Soc. Agronomy, Am. Geog. Soc., Am. Genetic Assn., A.A.A.S., Soc. Am. Foresters, Am. Ecol. Soc., Sigma Xi, Gamma Sigma Delta, Phi Kappa Phi, Alpha Zeta. Mormon (Gen. M.I.A. Board). Author: Alfalfa Growing in U.S. and Canada, 1926. Co-Author: Principles of Agronomy, 1915; second edition of same completely revised, 1930; Development of Collective Enterprise, 1943. Co-editor: Western Agriculture, 1918. Student of crops, soils, and irrigation of intermountain-region, and their social development and of important features in wheat genetics and new varieties, sugar-beet breeding; varieties of vegetation on desert, semi-desert, and foothill ranges, grazing on public lands, reseeding range lands and range conservation. Contbr. to professional jours. Asso. editor: Journal of Forestry, 1939-46. Home: 23 W. 400 North, Orem, Utah. Died Oct. 27, 1957; buried Orem.

STEWART, George James, meat industry exec.; b. Chicago, Sept. 21, 1895; s. George and Mary (Dick) S.; ed. pub. schs.; m. Evelyn O. Bundy, Aug. 16, 1919; children—James B., Robert M. With Swift & Co., Chicago, since 1911, v.p. since 1931, dir. since 1950. Served as ensign U.S.N., World War I. Mem. Am. Legion. Club: South Shore. Home: 5834 Stony Island Av., Chicago 37. Office: 4115 Packers Av., Chgo. 9. Died Oct., 1957.

STEWART, George Walter, physicist; b. St. Louis, Feb. 22, 1876; s. Oliver Mills and Eleanor (Bell) S.; A.B., DePauw U., 1898, Sc.D. (hon.), 1928; Ph.D., Cornell, 1901; Sc.D. (hon.), U. Pittsburgh, 1931; Sc.D., (hon.), Kalamazoo Coll., 1949; m. Dr. Zella M. White, July 7, 1904. Asst. in physics, Cornell, 1899-1901, instr., 1901-03; asst. prof. charge dept. physics, U. of N.D., 1903-04, prof. physics, 1904-09; prof. physics and head dept., U. of Ia., 1909-46, prof. physics (retired), 1946; acting dean, Graduate Coll., State U., 1921-22. Fellow A.A.A.S., Am. Acad. Arts and Scis., Ia. Acad. Sci., Am. Phys. Soc. (pres. 1949) Am. Acoustic Soc.; mem. Soc. for Promotion Engring. Edn., Am. Optical Soc., Nat. Acad. Scis., Am. Assn. Physics Tchrs. (Oersted medalist 1942), Phi Beta Kappa, Sigma Xi (pres. 1930-32), Phi Kappa Phi, Phi Kappa Sigma, Phi Kappa Psi. Author: Introductory Acoustics, 1933; Theoretical Acoustics (with R. B. Lindsay), 1930. Contbr. to current research in physics, upon radiation, archtl. acoustics, sound diffraction, liquid structure. Home: 1010 Woodlawn, Iowa City, Ia. Died Aug. 16, 1956.

STEWART, Gilbert Henry, army officer; b. Wichita, Kan., Nov. 12, 1878; s. Samuel Hamilton and Mary Ibela (Hair) S.; B.S., U.S. Mil. Acad., 1902; grad. Ordnance Sch. of Tech., 1913, Army War Coll., 1922, Army Indsl. Coll., 1932; m. Elizabeth Finley Barnard, June 7, 1909; children—Jane Semple (Mrs. Eric P. Ramee), Sally Finley (Mrs. Alfred J. Ronk), Charles Barnard, Gilbert Henry, Hamilton. Commd. 2d lt., inf., 1902; commd. 1st lt., Ordnance Dept., 1904, and advanced through the grades to brig. gen., 1940; works mgr., Rock Island Arsenal, 1923-26; in command Augusta (Ga.) Arsenal, 1926-28, Hawaiian Ordnance Depot, 1928-31, Watervliet (N.Y.) Arsenal, 1932-38, Springfield (Mass.) Armory, 1938-42; retired June 1942. Awarded Legion of Merit, 1943. Clubs: University (Phila.); Army and Navy (Washington). Home: 142 Randolph Pl., West Orange, N.J. Died Aug. 4, 1957; buried West Point, N.Y.

STEWART, James (Warren), univ. prof.; born Flemington, W.Va., Oct. 2, 1898; s. Alexander Pickens and Ida May (Dilworth) S.; B.S. in E.M., W. Va. U., 1923; M.S., U. of Ill., 1927; m. Marjorie Campbell, Aug. 20, 1941. Asst. mining engr. Consol. Coal Co., Clarksburg, W.Va., 1917-18; mining engr. Soper-Mitchell Coal Co., Morgantown, W.Va., 1923-24; with Nat. (W.Va.) Fuel Co., 1924-25; with Logan County Coal Corp., Lundale, W.Va., 1925-26; instr. mining engring., Pa. State Coll., 1927-31, asst. prof., 1931-37; asst. prof. mining engring. Lafayette Coll., 1937-42; asst. prof. mining engring. U. of Ill., 1942-46; prof. mining engring. and head Sch. of Mines, U. of Ala., since 1946. Registered professional engr., Ala. and Ill. Served as sgt., U.S. Army Artillery Corps, 1918-19, with A.E.F. Mem. Am. Soc. Engring. Edn. (chmn. mineral engring. div. 1942), Am. Institute Mining and Metall. Engrs. (mem. exec. com., edn. div., 1944; chmn. Lehigh Valley Sect. 1945; chmn. membership com., edn. div. 1946; mem. publs. com., edn. div. 1948; programs chmn. 1955), Am. Assn. Univ. Profs., Ill. Mining Inst., Ala. Acad. Sci., University of Alabama Research Council, Sigma Gamma Epsilon, Tau Beta Pi and Sigma Nu. Club: University. Editor: Proceedings of the First Coal Utilization Conference, 1948. Contbr. articles to professional jours.; research in coal mining and utilization. Home: P.O. Box 6175, University, Ala. Died June 18, 1957; buried Arlington Nat. Cemetery, Va.

STEWART, James Garfield, judge; b. Springfield, O., Nov. 17, 1881; s. James Eli and Mary Emily

(Durbin) S.; Ph. B., Kenyon Coll., Gambier, O., 1902; LL.B., U. of Cincinnati Law Sch., 1905; married; children—Irene Potter (Mrs. John Colville Taylor), Potter, Zeph. Admitted to Ohio bar, 1905, in pvt. practice, 1905-1938; mayor, City of Cincinnati, 1938-47, mem. City Council of Cincinnati 1934-47; appointed judge of the supreme Court of Ohio, 1947. Member Alpha Delta Phi, Phi Beta Kappa, Phi Delta Phi. Republican. Episcopalian. Mason (Shriner), Elk, Moose. Clubs: Cincinnati, Literary, Univ., Cincinnati Country. Home: 2348 Grandin Rd., Cin., O. Address: Supreme Ct. of Ohio, Columbus, O. Died Apr. 3, 1959; buried Springfield, O.

STEWART, Paul, ex-congressman; b. Clarksville, Ark., Feb. 27, 1892; s. Charles Jackson and Mary Ellen (Overby) S.; m. Irene Almond Smith, d. Henry and Mary Lottie Almond, June 9, 1938; children—(by previous marriage) Elma Keene, Martha Genia (Mrs. O. J. McKinney); stepchildren—Mary Ellen, Wray Smith. Entered bus. at age 13 in 1905; farmer, merchant, lawyer, pub. and ranchman; owner, pub. Antlers (Okla.) Am., weekly paper, 1929—; owner, operator Paul Stewart Ranch-Farm, Antlers; elected to Okla. House of Reps. in 1922, 24, elected to Okla. State Senate in 1926, 28, 32, 36, 40, majority floor leader 1929-30, pres. pro-tem, 1933-34, resigned from state senate Nov. 1942 to enter Congress; mem. 78th and 79th Congresses (1943-47), 3d Okla. Dist. (not a candidate to succeed himself). Democrat. Presbyn. Mason, Elk. Home: Antlers, Okla. Died Nov. 13, 1950; buried City Cemetery, Antlers.

STEWART, Paul Morton, ret. coast guard officer; b. Belle Center, O., Sept. 5, 1888; s. James Irwin and Rebecca (Perrine) S.; M.D., U. Cin., 1914; m. Norma Pellegrini, Dec. 13, 1919; children—Robert Pellegrini (dec.), Paul Morton, Giovanna, Stewart Kirby, James Alexander. Commd. asst. surgeon US PHS, 1915, passed asst. surgeon, 1919, surgeon, 1926, sr. surgeon, 1935; mem. dir. U.S. Employees Compensation Commn., 1936; asst. surgeon gen., 1939, chief inspector, 1944; chief med. officer, with rank of rear adm. USCG, 1946-52, ret. Fellow A.M.A. Clubs: Columbia Country, Chevy Chase (Washington). Home: 2210 Wyoming Av., Washington. Died Aug. 24, 1957; buried Arlington Nat. Cemetery.

STEWART, Paul William, distribution analyst; b. Bradenville, Pa., Aug. 3, 1899; s. George Murphy and Clara Ann (Lafferty) S.; B.S., U. of Pittsburgh, 1923; m. Winifred Davis Whaley, Jan. 9, 1926. Began as statistician, U.S. Dept. Commerce, 1924, retiring as chief business specialist, 1930; dir. econ. research A. O. Smith Corp., Milwaukee, 1931-32; v.p. Slocum Hat Sales Corp., 1933-34; statistician for several N.R.A. code authorities, 1934-35; dir. research Anderson, Nichols and Assos., 1935-40; pres. Paul W. Stewart & Assos., 1940-44; pres. Stewart, Dougall & Assos., Inc., management consultants and marketing research. Mem. Am. Marketing Assn., Am. Statis. Assn., Am. Econ. Assn. Republican. Presbyterian. Author: Market Data Handbook of the U.S. (received Harvard Bok award), 1929. Co-author: The National Debt and Government Credit, 1937; Does Distribution Cost Too Much?, 1939. Home: 51 Highland Circle, Bronxville, N.Y. Office: 30 Rockefeller Plaza, N.Y.C. Died Feb. 25, 1955.

STEWART, Percy Hamilton, ex-congressman; b. Newark, Jan. 10, 1867; s. Walter E. and Anna G. (Leeper) S.; A.B., Yale, 1890; LL.B., Columbia, 1893; m. Elinor De Witt Cochran, Jan. 11, 1899; children—Eva (Mrs. Harvey Wallace Shaffer), Elinor (Mrs. Edward Lindsley Ayers). Began practice N. Y.C., 1893; mayor of Plainfield, 1912-13; chmn. Union County Dem. Com., 1914; chmn. Washington Rock Park Commn. N.J., 1915-19; mem. N.J. State Bd. Edn., 1919-21; mem. N.J. State Hwy. Commn., 1923-29; del. Dem. Nat. Conv., 1920, 28; elected mem. 72d Congress at spl. election, Dec. 1931 to fill vacancy, 5th N.J. Dist., for term ending Mar. 3, 1933; Dem. candidate for U.S. senator, N.J., 1932. Active in non-combatant mil. affairs, World War; served as civilian aide to adj. gen. of U.S., for N.J.; treas., mem. exec. com. Mil. Tng. Camps U.S. Mem. Delta Kappa Epsilon, Skull and Bones. Presbyn. Clubs: University (New York); Log Cabin Gun (Plainfield); Bath and Tennis (Palm Beach, Fla.). Home: Plainfield, N.J. Died June 30, 1951.

STEWART, Richard Siegfried, petroleum exec.; b. Warren, Pa., Jan. 20, 1912; s. Paul Bryant and Helen Alice (Siegfried) S.; M.E., Cornell U., 1932; m. Ruth Staten, June 6, 1938; children—Richard Burleson, Elizabeth Adair. Refining, Tex. Co., 1932-38; asst. to v.p. mfg. Standard Oil Co. (O.), 1938-45, operations mgr., 1945-49, asst. to pres., 1949-54, v.p., asst. to pres., 1954—; v.p. Sohio Petroleum Co., 1954—; pres. Iricon Agy., Ltd., 1955-56; dir. Iricon Agency, Ltd. Trustee, mem. exec. com. Greater Cleveland chpt. A.R.C., 1955—. Mem. Am. Petroleum Inst., Am. Inst. Mining Engrs., Tau Beta Pi, Phi Kappa Phi, Chi Phi. Clubs: Country (Cleve.); University (N.Y.C.). Home: 2720 Cranlyn Rd., Shaker Heights 22, O. Office: Midland Bldg., Cleve. 15. Died Oct. 6, 1957; buried Lake View Cemetery, Cleve.

STEWART, Robert Giffen, sales counsellor; b. Marion, Ia., Jan. 27, 1892; s. Robert Wright and Josephine (Giffen) S.; student U. Chgo., Tulane U. Med. Sch.; m. Phyllis Shaw, Nov. 22, 1922; 1 dau., Elizabeth Jane; m. 2d, Estelle Finch, May 20, 1935. Began in oil bus., Mpls., 1914; asst. mgr. Standard Oil Co. (Ind.), 1921-23; pres. Pan-Am. Petroleum & Tansport Co., 1927-32; pres. Pan-Am. Foreign Corp., 1932-33; dir. Standard Oil Co. (N.J.), 1933-35. Mem. Beta Theta Pi. Clubs: Valley Club of Montecito (Cal.). Home: Ranco Dos Vientos, Camarillo, Cal. Office: 400 Madison Av., N.Y.C. Died Feb. 1948.

STEWART, Walter W., economist; b. Manhattan, Kan., May 24, 1885; s. Albert Alexander and Ella (Winne) S.; A.B., U. of Mo. 1909, LL.D., 1932, Dartmouth Coll., 1933, Amherst Coll., 1944, Columbia, 1951; Litt.D., Princeton, 1951; married Helen Wynkoop, July 1912; children—Albert W., Helen A., Walter A. Instr. economics, University of Missouri, 1910-11, University of Michigan, 1911-12; assistant prof. economics, Univ. of Missouri, 1913-15; prof. economics, Amherst Coll., 1916-22; mem. price sect. War Industries Bd., 1918; dir. Div. of Research and Statistics, Federal Reserve Bd., 1922-25; v.p. Case, Pomeroy & Co., investment securities, 1926-27, chmn. bd., 1930-37, pres., 1937-38; prof. Sch. of Economics and Politics, Inst. for Advanced Study, 1938-50, emeritus; econ. adviser to Bank of Eng., 1928-30; apptd. Nov. 1931, Am. mem. spl. adv. com., Bank of Internat. Settlements, to investigate ability of Germany to resume reparations payments under the Young Plan; mem. President's Council Econ. Advisers, 1953-55. Trustee Rockefeller Found., 1931-50 (chmn. bd. 1940-50), General Edn. Bd., 1933-50 (chmn. bd. 1942-50), Inst. for Advanced Study, 1933-41, Bennington Coll., 1932-38. Decorated Officer Legion d'Honeur (France). Mem. Am. Philos. Society, American Economic Assn., Phi Beta Kappa. Club: Political Economy (hon. fgn. mem., London). Office: Institute for Advanced Study, Princeton, N.J. Died Mar. 6, 1958.

STEWART, William Alvah, judge; b. Pittsburgh, Aug. 16, 1903; s. William Alvah and Julia Elizabeth (Langworthy) S.; A.B., Amherst Coll., 1925; LL.B., Harvard, 1928; m. Lois Ann Alter, July 11, 1931; children—William Alvah, Foster Ashe. Admitted to Pa. bar, 1928, practiced law, Pittsburgh, 1928-51; partner Weller, Wicks & Wallacs, Pittsburgh, 1946-51; instr. law sch. Duquesne U., 1930; 42; U.S. dist. judge, western dist. of Pa. since 1951. Asst. city solicitor, Pittsburgh, 1934-36, city solicitor, 1938-42, mem. city council, 1946-51; asst. co. solicitor, Allegheny Co., 1936-38; mem. Urban Redevelopment Authority of Pittsburgh, 1947-51. Served Judge Adv. Gen. Dept., U.S. Army, 1942-46. Mem. Judge Adv. Assn., Phi Kappa Psi. Presbyn. (trustee). Club: University (Pittsburgh). Home: 222 Carnegie Pl., Pittsburgh 8. Office: New Federal Bldg., Pittsburgh 19. Died Apr. 9, 1953.

STICKLEY, Ezra Eugenius, lawyer; b. Strasburg, Va., Aug. 30, 1839; s. Levi and Elizabeth S.; ed. Bethany Coll., W.Va., 1860-61; Washington Coll. (now Washington and Lee Univ.), 1863-65; law course U. Va., 1865-66; m. Sophie A. Helm, 1870; m. 2d, Mary B. Cutler, June 27, 1883. Admitted to bar, Oct., 1868; practiced law at Strasburg, 1868-73; Woodstock, 1873—; mem. bd. dirs. W.S. Hosp., Staunton, Va., for past 9 yrs.; Democrat. Was in C.S.A.; lost right arm at battle of Antitam, Md., while on Stonewall brigade staff. Address: Woodstock, Va. Died Nov. 11, 1915; buried Massanutten Cemetery, Woodstock, Va.

STIDLEY, Leonard Albert (stĭd'lē), clergyman, educator; b. Fort Madison, Ia., Dec. 14, 1898; s. Fred and Phoebe (Taylor) S.; A.B., Carthage (Ill.) Coll., 1921; M.S., U. of Ill., 1922; B.D., Union Theol. Sem., 1925; D.D., Carthage Coll., 1939; Ph.D., Columbia, 1944; m. Constance Hill, Aug. 29, 1923; children—Leonard Hill, Constance Hill. Ordained to ministry of Meth. Ch., 1929; dir. religious edn. and asso. pastor 1st Meth. Ch., Decatur, Ill., 1926-30; asso. dir. survey Meth. chs., Manhattan, Bronx, Westchester, N.Y., 1930-31; dir. and pastor, Ch. of All Nations and Neighborhood House, New York City, 1931-37; asst. dir. field work, Union Theol. Sem., 1931-35, 1936-37; asso. prof. of religious edn. and practical theology, Grad. Sch. of Theology, Oberlin Coll., 1937-44, prof. since 1944, dean since 1948; vis. lectr. summers Union Theol. Sem., 1945, Garrett Biblical Inst., 1946, 48, U. of Mich., 1947, Emory U., 1948. Survey for Fedn. of Protestant Welfare Agencies, N.Y.C., 1936-37; chmn. O. Student Y.M.C.A., 1944-46. Served as pvt. 350 infantry A.E.F., France 1918-19. Member Religious Education Association (director since 1943), Nat. Council Chs. Christ in U.S.A. (chmn. prof. adv. sect. 1944-46, 55-56; rep. 1946—), Church Conf. of Social Workers, Nat. Assn. Biblical Instrs. Am. Assn. Univ. Profs., Am. Assn. of Schs. Religious Edn. (pres. 1955-57), Gamma Pi Upsilon, Pi Kappa Delta, Theta Chi Delta. Author: Sectarian Welfare Federation Among Protestants, 1944. Chmn. editorial com. Religious Education, editor, 1946—. Contbr. articles in field of religoius edn. and social work. Home: 29 N. Pleasant St. Office: Oberlin Coll., Oberlin, O. Died May 29, 1958; buried Oberlin, O.

STIGLER, William G., congressman; b. Stigler, Indian Territory (now Oklahoma), July 7, 1891; s. Joseph S. and Mary Jane (Folsom) S.; grad. Northeastern State Coll., Tahlequah, Okla., 1912 (life teacher's certificate); U. of Okla., 1915; student U. of Grenoble, France, 1919; m. Ona Beller, June 7, 1925; children—Denyse, Elaine. Admitted to Okla. bar, 1920; practice before state dist. courts, Supreme Court of Okla., U.S. Dist. Court of Eastern Okla., U.S. 10th Circuit Court of Appeals, U.S. Court of Claims and Supreme Court of U.S.; city atty., Stigler, Okla., 1920-24; elected state senator, 27th senatorial dist. Okla., 1924, reelected, 1928; pres. pro tem. of Okla. State Senate, 1931; nat. atty. for Choctaw Nation (Indian) 1937-44; mem. 78th to 82d Congresses (1944-53), 2d Okla. District. Served with 90th Div., as 2d lt., 357th Inf. A.E.F., during World War I; participated in offensives St. Mihiel and Meuse-Argonne; with Army of Occupation, Germany; lt. col., 45th Div., Okla. Nat. Guard, 1925-38. Mem. Soldiers Relief Commn. of Okla., 1932; former mem. state pardon and parole advisory board; former chmn. war finance com. of Haskell County; an exec. vice pres. Choctaw area council Boy Scouts of America, 1942-45. Nat. pres. 90th Div. Assn., 1935. Mem. Choctaw Tribe of Indians. Mem. Am. Legion (dept. comdr., Okla., 1933; mem. nat. exec. com., 2 yrs.), 40 and 8, Vets. Fgn. Wars, Sigma Alpha Epsilon. Methodist (mem. bd. stewards). Mason (32°) Shriner, Odd Fellow, Modern Woodman. Home: Stigler, Okla. Died Aug. 21, 1952.

STILLMAN, Charles Clark, univ. prof., social worker; b. Troy, N.Y., June 22, 1877; s. Ezra and Elizabeth (Payne) S.; A.B., Williams Coll., 1900; grad. Rochester Theol. Sem., 1904; m. Rachel Schermerhorn, Jan. 1, 1907; children—Ezra Clark, Mary Elizabeth, Huldah, Rachel Florence. Home missionary, Utah and Kan., for Am. Bapt. Home Mission Soc., 1906-11; judge of City Court, Eureka, Utah, 1907-08; dir. research bur., Bd. of Pub. Welfare, Kansas City, Mo., 1912-13; sec. United Charities, St. Paul, Minn., 1913-18; asso. dir. Bur. Civilian Relief, central div., Am. Red Cross, 1918-19; sec. Welfare Union, Grand Rapids, Mich., 1919-29; prof social adminstrn. Ohio State U., since 1929; dir. Sch. Social Adminstrn., 1932-47, emeritus since 1947. Lecturer U. of Minn., 1917-18, Ohio State U., 1925-26. Cons. in relief operations, Ohio State Relief Commn., Apr.-June 1934. Treas. and mem. exec. com. Nat. Conf. Social Work, 1930-34; field rep. (four states) Federal Emergency Relief Adminstrn., 1934-35, dir. in Ohio, 1935, adminstr. Ohio Works Progress Administration, 1935. Special rep. Assn. Community Chests and Councils, New York City, since 1929; mem. Am. Assn. of Social Workers, Phi Beta Kappa, Alpha Kappa Delta. Democrat. Mason (32°). Author: Social Work Publicity, 1927; also Social Service Survey reports for Detroit Dept. Pub. Welfare, 1930, Knoxville, Tenn., 1931, Oklahoma City, Okla., 1931, etc. Home: 1830 Chatfield Rd., Columbus 21, O. Died Jan. 5, 1952; buried Glen Rest Cemetery, Columbus.

STILLMAN, Walter N., business exec.; grad. Yale, 1905. Partner Stillman, Maynard & Co., N.Y.C.; v.p., dir. 642 Park Av. Corp.; dir. N.Y. Trust Co., N.Y.C. Home: 640 Park Av., N.Y.C. 21. Office: 61 Broadway, N.Y.C 6. Died Jan. 6 1956.*

STILWELL, Edmund William, banker; b. Leavenworth County, Kan., Sept. 4, 1880; s. Francis Marion and Sarah (Wade) S.; ed. pub. schs. Andrew County, Mo., and business coll., St. Joseph, Mo.; m. Florence Louise Horne, Mar. 31, 1910; children—Winifred Louise, Elizabeth; married 2d, Marion Speck Hedrick, July 25, 1957. Clk. clothing store, St. Joseph, Mo., 1900; clk. Bonner Springs (Kan.) State Bank, 1900-03; clk. Commercial Nat. Bank, Kansas City, Kan., 1903-13; cashier Commercial Nat. Bank, Emporia, Kan., 1913-16; with Commercial Nat. Bank, Kansas City, Kan., since 1916, now pres. Mem. Kansas City (ex-president), U.S. C.'s of C., president Kansas Bankers Assn. Trustee Bethany Hosp., Kansas City, Kan. Independent Republican. Clubs: Kiwanis of Kansas City, Kan. (ex-pres.), Kansas City Club (Kan.). Home: 2809 Parkwood Blvd. Office: 601 Minnesota Av., Kansas City, Kan. Died Feb. 12, 1957; buried Bonner Springs, Kan.

STIMPSON, George William, newspaperman, author; b. Jones County, near Anamosa, Ia., Nov. 3, 1896; s. John Adams and Anna (Specht) S.; student rural schs., Ia., Valparaiso U., 1916-21, George Washington U. Law Sch., 1922-23; unmarried. Reporter Valparaiso (Ind.) Messenger, 1921-22, Washington Herald, 1922; asso. editor Pathfinder, Washington, D.C., 1922-32; free lance writer, 1932-34; Washington corr. Houston (Tex.) Post, 1934-41; Washington correspondent for various newspapers since 1941; conducted weekly radio feature on politics and science over Sta. WRC, Washington, D.C., 1924-25; author of the daily syndicated newspaper feature "Information Roundup," 1938-48. Member Standing Committee of Correspondents, 77th Congress; mem. bd. dirs. Nat. Press Bldg. Corp., Washington, D.C. Served as pvt. U.S. Army, Sept. 1918, to Feb. 1919. Club: National Press of Washington, D.C. (pres., 1936-37). Author: The Story of Valparaiso University, 1921; Nuggets of Knowledge, 1928; Popular Questions Answered, 1930; Things Worth Knowing, 1932; Uncommon Knowledge, 1936;

A Book About The Bible, 1945; A Book About a Thousand Things, 1946; Information Roundup, 1948; A Book About American History, 1950. Home: George Washington Inn. Office: National Press Bldg., Washington. Died Sept. 27, 1952.

STIMSON, Henry Lewis, former secretary of war; b. N.Y. City, Sept. 21, 1867; s. Lewis Atterbury and Candace (Wheeler) S.; A.B., Yale Univ., 1888; A.M., Harvard Univ., 1889; Harvard Law Sch., 1889-90; m. Mabel Wellington White, July 6, 1893. Admitted to bar, 1891; became mem. Root & Clarke, 1893, Root, Howard, Winthrop & Stimson, 1897, Winthrop & Stimson, 1901, Winthrop, Stimson, Putnam & Roberts since 1927; U.S. atty. Southern Dist., N.Y., 1906-09; Rep. candidate for gov. of N.Y., 1910; sec. of war in Cabinet of President Taft, May 1911-Mar. 5, 1913. Del. at large, New York Constl. Conv., 1915; special rep. of President to Nicaragua, 1927; gov. general of Philippine Islands, 1927-29; sec. of state in Cabinet of President Hoover, Mar. 1929-33; secretary of war in Cabinet of President Roosevelt, July 1940-Apr. 1945, President Truman's Cabinet, Apr.-Sept. 1945; retired Sept. 1945. Chmn. Am. delegation to London Naval Conf., 1930; chmn. Am. delegation to Disarmament Conf., 1932. Commd. maj. judge advocate U.S. Res., Mar. 1917; lt. col. 305th F.A., Aug. 1917; col. 31st F.A., Aug. 1918; with A.E.F. in France, Dec. 1917-Aug. 1918. Republican. Presbyterian. Mem. Am., city and state bar assns., Psi Upsilon, Skull and Bones (Yale). Clubs: Century, University, Republican, Down Town (New York); Metropolitan (Washington). Office: 40 Wall St., N.Y. City. Died Oct. 20, 1950.

STINE, Charles Milton Altland, chemist; b. Norwich, Conn., Oct. 18, 1882; s. Milton Henry and Mary Jane (Altland) S.; A.B., Gettysburg (Pa.) Coll., 1901; B.S., 1903, A.M., 1904, M.S., 1905, Sc.D., 1926; Ph.D., Johns Hopkins, 1907; LL.D., Cumberland U., 1932, Temple U., 1941; Sc.D., U. Del., 1947; m. Martha E. Molly, Feb. 3, 1912; children—Mary Elizabeth (Mrs. F. Samuel Wilcox, Jr.), Barbara Ann (Mrs. J. Seth H. Cruice). Became prof. chemistry Md. Coll. for Women, 1904; fellow Johns Hopkins, 1906-07; joined staff E. I. du Pont de Nemours & Co. (Eastern Lab.), July 1, 1907, in charge organic chem. work, 1909-16; trans. to Wilmington office as head organic div., 1917, made asst. dir. chem. dept., 1919, chem. dir. May 1, 1924-30, v.p. and dir. since 1930, mem. exec. com. 1930-45, retired 1945. Cons. to Chem. Warfare Service since 1942; mem. adv. com., dept. of chem. engring., Princeton U.; mem. bd. trustees The Delaware Hosp., Wilmington, Del.; chmn. bd. trustees Gettysburg Coll.; mem. bd. trustees Tower Hill Sch., Wilmington, U. Del.; mem. exec. com. bd. trustees U. Del.; dir. Acad. Natural Sciences of Phila. Perkin Medalist of Soc. of Chem. Industry, 1940. Mem. Directors of Industrial Research Assn., Am. Chem. Soc. (councillor; mem. com. to cooperate with C. W. S.), Am. Inst. Chem. Engrs. (councillor and pres. 1947), Franklin Inst. (life), Phi Beta Kappa, Gamma Alpha, Tau Beta Pi. Hon. mem. Soc. Chem. Industry, Princeton Engring. Assn., Chem. Engring. Soc. of South Africa, Chem. Engring. Soc. Australia. Clubs: Wilmington Country, du Pont Country (Wilmnigton); Chemical (Johns Hopkins U.); Wilmington (Del.); Everglades (Palm Beach, Fla.). Developer numerous processes and products, many patented, in connection with high explosives, propellent powder, dyes, artificial leather, varnishes, paints, and other inorganic and organic chem. processes and products. Home: 1100 Greenhill Av. Address: E. I. du Pont de Nemours & Co., Wilmington, Del. Died May 28, 1954.

STINE, John William, Jr., educator; b. Stronghurst, Ill., Aug. 5, 1903; s. John William and Mary Elizabeth (Walker) S.; diploma, Columbia Coll. of Expression, 1923; B.S., Northwestern U., 1930; M.S., DePaul U., 1937. Mem. Sprague Players with Redpath Chautauquas, 1923-26; student-dir. Pasadena Playhouse, 1934; dir. speech, Okla. Pub. Schs., Tulsa, 1930-37; chmn. radio dept. Lindenwood Coll., St. Charles, Mo., 1937-42; founder speech dept. DePaul U., chmn. since 1944. Mem. Speech Assn. of Am. Democrat. Served as editor Speech mag.; author series of articles on speech edn. in Instructor mag. Home: 1701 N. Crilly Ct., Chgo. 14. Office: 2322 Kenmore Av., Chgo. Died Jan. 1959.

STIRES, Ernest Milmore (stirz), bishop; b. Norfolk, Va., May 20, 1866; s. Van Rensselaer W. and Lettie M. (Milmore) S.; B.Litt., U. Va., 1888; Episcopal Theol. Sem. Va., 1889-91; D.D., Trinity, 1901; L.H.D., Kenyon Coll., 1903; LL.D., N.Y.U., 1926; D.C.L., King's Coll., Can.; S.T.D., Columbia 1926; m. Sarah McK. Hardwick, Jan. 11, 1894; children—Ernest, Hardwick, Arthur McK., Milmore. Deacon, 1891, priest, 1892, P.E. Ch.; rector West Point, Va., 1891-92, Ch. of the Good Shepherd, Augusta, Ga., 1893, Grace Ch., Chgo., 1893-1901, St. Thomas' Ch., N.Y.C., 1901-25; pres. House of Deputies, gen. conv., Oct. 1925; consecrated bishop L.I., Nov. 24, 1925; ret., Feb. 9, 1942. Chaplain, Richmond Hussars, Augusta, Ga., 1893, Naval Reserves, Chgo., 1897, 1st Ill. Cav., 1901. Mem. Bd. Visitors U.S. Mil. Acad.; mem. Nat. Council. Author: The High Call, 1918; The Price of Peace, 1919. Home: Bolton Landing, N.Y. Died Feb. 12, 1951.

STIX, Ernest William, former president Rice-Stix, Inc.; b. Cincinnati, O., Nov. 16, 1878; s. William and Dinah (Rice) S.; A.B., Harvard, 1900; m. Erma Kingsbacher, Jan. 7, 1907; children—Elizabeth Stix Fainsod, William, Ernest W., John Morris, Thomas Howard. With Rice-Stix, Incorporated, manufacturers and wholesale distributors, St. Louis, since 1900, pres., 1915-54; dir. Merc. Trust Co., Mercantile-Commerce Nat. Bank. Trustee Washington U. Clubs: University, Westwood Country, Columbian (St. Louis); Harvard (N.Y.C.). Home: 6470 Forsythe Blvd., St. Louis. Died Sept. 28, 1955.

STOCK, Chester, educator; b. San Francisco, Jan. 28, 1892; s. John Englebert and Maria Henriette (Meyer) S.; B.S., U. Cal., 1914, Ph.D., 1917; m. Clara Margaret Doud, June 2, 1921 (died Mar. 20, 1934); children—Jane Henriette, John Chester; m. 2d, Margaret Gardner Wood, July 3, 1935; 1 son, James Ellery. Served as asst. in paleontology U. Cal., 1917-19, instr., 1919-21, asst. prof., 1921-26; prof. paleontology Cal. Inst. Tech., 1926—, chmn. div. geol. scis., July 1947—; sr. geologist, War Service appointment, U.S. Geol. Survey, 1943-45; sr. curator in earth scis., Los Angeles County Mus.; research asso., Carnegie Instn. of Washington; vis. prof. zoölogy, U. Cal. at Los Angeles, fall term 1939; fellow of Guggenheim Meml. Found., 1939-40, 40-41. Fellow Am. Acad. Arts and Scis., Am. Philos. Soc., A.A.A.S., Geol. Soc. Am. (mem. council 1944-46), Am. Assn. Petrol. Geologists, Soc. Vertebrate Paleontology (pres. 1947), Wash. Acad. Sci., Paleontol. Soc Am. (pres. 1945); mem. Am. Soc. Naturalists, Am. Soc. Mammalogists, Am. Assn. U. Profs., adv. bd. So. Cal. Acad. Sci.; corr. mem. No. Ariz. Soc. Sci. Club: Athenaeum. Contbr. articles sci. jours. Home: 1420 San Pasqual St. Office: Cal. Inst. Tech., Pasadena 4, Cal. Died Dec. 7, 1950; buried Pasadena Mausoleum, Altadena, Cal.

STOCK, Harry T., clergyman; b. Springfield, Ill., Nov. 10, 1891; s. Thomas John and Mary Catherine (Gerhart) S.; A.B., Knox Coll., 1914; B.D., Chicago Theol. Sem., 1916; A.M., U. of Chicago, 1917; student U. of Ill. Library Sch., 1917; D.D., Piedmont Coll., 1931, Knox Coll., 1939, Chicago Theol. Sem., 1940; m. Grace Bryan Frame, July 24, 1917; 1 dau., Catherine Claris. Ordained Congl. ministry, 1916; instr. in ch. history and librarian, Chicago Theol. Sem., 1917-22; sec. dept. of Young People and Student Life, Congl. Edn. Soc., 1922-38; gen. sec. Div. of Christian Edn., Congl. Bd. of Home Missions, since 1938. Mem. gen. bd. Nat. Council of Chs., and chmn. commn. on gen. Christian edn.; vice chairman International Council of Religious Edn. Mem. Tau Kappa Epsilon, Delta Sigma Rho. Club: City (Boston). Contributing editor, "Christian Education," "The Pilgrim Highroad," "The Missionary Herald. Author: Church Work with Young People, 1927; Training Young People in Worship (with E. L. Shaver); Christian Life Problems, 1927; Problems of Chrisitan Youth, 1928; So This Is Missions, 1933; Better Meetings for the Young People's Society, 1933; Social Issues for Young People, 1933; Young People and Their Leaders, 1933; Social Relationships of Young People, 1930; A Life and a Living, 1936; Preparing for a Life Work, 1936; Christian Education In Our Church, 1944. Home: 30 Jackson Rd., Medford, Mass. Office: 14 Beacon St., Boston. Died Aug. 30, 1958.

STOCKBARGER, Donald C(harles), educator; b. Walkerton, Ind., Oct. 19, 1895; s. Charles Ulysses and Stella (Hurt) S.; S.B., Mass. Inst. Technology, 1919, Sc.D., 1926; m. Hazel Louise Kilbourne, June 22, 1922; children—Jeanne Shirley, Donald Richard. Asst., Mass. Inst. Tech., 1920-23, instr., 1923-27, asst. prof., 1927-35, asso. prof. physics since 1935; dir. Nat. Defense Research Com., research project, Mass. Inst. Tech., 1940-44; dir. U.S. Navy Dept., Bureau Ordnance research project, Mass. Inst. Tech., 1942-44; cons. physicist since 1945, Harshaw Chemical Co. Served as pvt., C.W.S., U.S. Army, 1918. Mem. A.A.A.S., Am. Physical Soc., Optical Soc. of America, Am. Assn. Physics Teachers, Am. Acad. Arts and Sciences, North Am. Yacht Racing Union (N.Y.), Mass. Inst. Tech. Nautical Assn. (faculty advisor), Phi Delta Theta, Alpha Chi Sigma, Sigma Xi. Republican. Methodist Episcopal. Contbr. articles to journals and reports. Home: 290 Payson Road, Belmont 78, Mass. Office: 77 Massachusetts Av., Cambridge 39, Mass. Died Feb. 23, 1952; buried Mount Auburn Cemetery, Cambridge.

STOCKING, Charles Howard, educator; b. Stockbridge, Mich., Aug. 27, 1882; s. Hiram and Mary Ann (Morgan) S.; student Albion (Mich.) College, 1903-04; Ph.C., U. Mich., 1907, B.S., 1909, M.S., 1925; m. Grace A. Cook, Aug. 4, 1909 (died July 2, 1947); children—Charles H., Prescott Norwood; m. 2d, Ethel B. Gregg, Dec. 26, 1949. Prof. pharm., Kansas City Coll. Pharm., 1909-11, dean, 1910-11; research chemist, Upjohn Co., Kalamazoo, Mich., 1911-12; prof. pharm., dean coll. pharm., U. Okla., 1912-17; research chemist, Eli Lilly & Co., Indianapolis, 1917-18; edit. writer, Pharmaceutical Era, N.Y. City, 1918-19; cons. chemist, 1919-20; mem. faculty coll. pharm., U. of Mich., since 1920, acting dir., coll. pharmacy, 1947-49; prof. of pharmacy and dean coll. pharmacy, 1949-52, emeritus dean since 1952. Trustee Prescott Meml. Scholarship Fund, Michigan State Pharmaceutical Association, 1925-51. Fellow A.A.A.S.; member American Pharmaceutical Assn., American Conf. Pharm. Faculties (v.p., 1922-23), Am. Assn. Colls. Pharm. (pres., 1932-33), Phi Delta Chi, Tau Kappa Epsilon, Rho Chi. Methodist. Mason. Author: Emulsification of Oils-Effect of Viscosity, 1917; Business Administration Courses in Colleges of Pharmacy, 1924; Isolation of Alkaloids Aided Medicine, 1924; Fortifying the Prescription Counter, 1927; Michigan's Pharmaceutical Achievement, 1933; Address of the President of the Am. Assn. of Colleges of Pharmacy, 1933; Fundamentals of Pharmacy, Theoretical and Practical (with W. H. Blome), 1939, 2d edit., 1948; Arithmetic of Pharmacy (with E. L. Cataline), 1942, rev., 1952. Home: Britton, Mich. Died Jan. 31, 1958; buried Stockbridge (Mich.) Cemetery.

STOCKTON, Ernest, educator; b. Newbern, Tennessee, Sept. 1, 1888; s. John Selah and Mary Ann (Scobey) S.; A.B., Cumberland U., 1914, A.M., 1915, LL.B., 1916; studied U. of Chicago (summer) and Peabody College, Nashville; LL.D., Centre College, Danville, Ky., 1930; m. 2d, Marvine Frances Bone, June 11, 1924; children—Ernest (by previous marriage), Mary Jean, John Bone. Teacher, Lebanon, Tenn., 1914; instr. English, Cumberland U. Prep. Sch., 1914-16, prin., 1915; prof. English and history, Coll. of Arts and Science, Cumberland U., 1927-41, dean of coll., 1919-26, dir. summer sch., pres. Cumberland U., 1927-41; dir. scholarship interchange, Office of Coordinator of Inter-Am. Affairs, 1941-44; exec. secretary National Cathedral Assn., 1944-48; special attorney Dept. of Justice, 1949-50; consultant House Small Business Committee, 1950—. Mem. N.E.A., Kappa Sigma, Internat. Soc. Theta Phi. Moderator Presbyn. Synod of Tenn., 1937-38; vice chmn. Tenn. com. of Newcomen Soc.; pres. Tenn. Coll. Assn., 1940-41; mem. exec. com. Washington Bible Soc. Author: History Excursions into Tennessee—Its Early Heritage; also articles and addresses. Episcopalian. Mason (K.T.). Lecturer. Home: 832 S. Pitt. St., "Yates Gardens," Alexandria, Va. Office: House Office Bldg., Washington. Died Nov. 4, 1954; buried Mount Comfort Cemetery, Alexandria, Va.

STOCKTON, Kenneth E., business exec.; b. Kansas City, Mo., Jan. 25, 1893; s. Charles W. and Lillian J. S.; Litt.D., Princeton, 1914; LL.B., Columbia, 1917; m. Susette Brevoort, June 21, 1921; children—Susette, Ann, Charles William, 2d, Mary. Law clerk White & Case, N.Y.C., 1917-18, Stetson Jennings & Russell, N.Y.C., 1918-19; partner Stockton & Stockton, N.Y.C., 1919-24; European gen. atty. Internat. Tel. & Tel. Co., 1925-35; v.p., 1935—, also dir.; v.p. Internat. Standard Electric Corp.; pres. Am. Cable & Radio Corp.; dir. Internat. Standard Electric Corp., Am. Cable & Radio Corp., All Am. Cables & Radio, Inc. Home: 830 Linwood Av., Ridgewood, N.J. Office: International Telephone & Telegraph Co., 67 Broad St., N.Y.C. Died May 11, 1950.

STOCKWELL, Walter Lincoln, fraternal orgn. ofcl.; b. Anoka, Minn., Jan. 12, 1868; s. Sylvanus and Charlotte Polly (Bowdish) S.; B.S., U. Minn., 1889; honorary LL.D., U. N.D., 1943; m. Helen H. Tombs, June 27, 1894; children—Walter Lincoln, Helen Frances (dec.). Prin. schs., St. Thomas, N.D., 1889-91; supt. schs., Grafton, N.D., 1891-1903; state supt. pub. instrn., N.D., 1903-11; pres. No. Sch. Supply Co., 1911—. Grand master of Masons, 1902-03; grand sec., recorder Masonic and Knights Templar bodies, N.D., 1910—; librarian Grand Lodge Library, Fargo, 1910—; gen. grand master Gen. Grand Council R.&S.M., 1930-33; editor Grand Lodge Bulletin; chmn. Grand Trustees. Gen. Grand Chapter O.E.S., 1940-49. Pres. bd. Pub. Library, Fargo, 1920—; mem. State Pub. Welfare Bd., 1935-37. Mem. N.E.R. (life), N.D. Edn. Assn. (pres. 1899), Fargo C. of C., Phi Kappa Phi, S.A.R. Clubs: Rotary (pres. 1927-28, dist. gov. 1934-35), Commons (founder). Contbr. to Masonic and ednl. publs. Home: 404 13th St. S. Office: Masonic Temple, Fargo, N.D. Died Dec. 4, 1950; buried Riverside Cemetery, Fargo, N.D.

STODDARD, Francis Russell, lawyer; b. Boston, Mass., July 26, 1877; s. Francis Russell and Mary Frances (Baldwin) S.; prep. edn., schs. in France, Germany, Italy, and Hopkinson Sch., Boston; A.B., Harvard, 1899; law study Harvard and Buffalo law Sch.; m. Eleanor Sherburne Whipple, Nov. 8, 1909; children—Margery Pepperell, Howland Bradford, Anna Bailey (Mrs. Renwick Washington Hurry), Dudley Wentworth, Frances LeBaron (Mrs. Edward Delaney Dunn, Jr.). In law department Brooklyn Rapid Transit Company, 1902-09; with law firm Greene & Hurd, 1909-37, partner, 1915-49; now of counsel in succeeding firm Hamlin, Hubbell and Davis; special deputy attorney general of New York, 1910; mem. New York State Assembly, 1912, 14, 15; deputy superintendent of insurance, in charge New York City office of N.Y. State Insurance Department, 1915-21; state supt. ins., 1921-24; chmn. N.Y. State Pension Commn., 1921-24; chmn. exec. com. Nat. Conv. of Ins. Commrs., 1922-24; employed by N.J. Legislature to reorganize N.J. State Banking and Ins. Dept. and to revise ins. laws, 1925-26; spl. dep. atty. gen. of N.Y., 1925-28; arbitrator, Greater New York, for fidelity and surety companies of U.S., 1927-49, and for casualty companies, 1936-49; member N.Y. State Ins. Bd., 1933—; counsel Eastern Life Insurance Company of N.Y., 1926—, United Mutual Life Ins. Co., 1934—. Vice president of Grant Monument Association. Served in Spanish-American War, 1898, Mexican border, 1916; major 9th Coast Arty., N.Y.G., 1917-18; on artillery mission at front with British and French Armies; maj. 17th Div., U.S. Army, 1918-19; lt. col. Ordnance O.R.C., 1919-23; colonel comdg. 533d C.A., 1923-35; now colonel retired. Organized New York City Patrol Corps; military aide of Mayor La Guardia during World War II. Republican leader 10th Assembly Dist., 1919-27; mem. N.Y. State Rep. Com., 1926-28. Mem. Sons of Revolution, Society Mayflower Descendants in State of N.Y. (ex-gov. and gov. gen. of gen. soc.), Soc. Colonial Wars in N.Y. State (ex-gov. and gov. gen.; now hon. gov. gen. of the gen. soc.), Soc. of the Cincinnati, St. Nicholas Soc. (ex-pres.), Naval and Military Order of Spanish American War, United Spanish War Veterans, American Legion, Military Society of the Loyal Legion, Phi Delta Phi. Episcopalian. Mason. Clubs: Union, Down Town, Badminton of City of N.Y. (ex-president). Author: The Stoddard Family, 1912; War Time France, 1918; The Pilgrims, 1935; The History of Acquisition Cost in the State of New York, 1914; The Truth About the Pilgrims, published, 1952. Contbr. numerous tech. articles on ins. Home: 791 Park Av., New York, N.Y.; and Cold Spring Harbor, L.I. Office: 386 Fourth Av., N.Y.C. 16. Died Oct. 11, 1957; buried Cold Spring Harbor, L.I., N.Y.

STODDARD, (Theodore) Lothrop, author; b. Brookline, Mass., June 29, 1883; s. John Lawson and Mary Hammond (Brown) S.; A.B., Harvard, 1905, A.M., 1910, Ph.D., 1914; J.B., Boston U., 1908; m. Elizabeth Guilford Bates, 1926; m. 2d, Zoya, Klementinovskaya, 1944. Admitted to Mass. bar, 1908. Mem. Am. Hist. Assn., Am. Polit. Sci. Assn., Am. Social Soc., Acad. Polit. Sci., Nat. Inst. Social Scis., Am. Genetic Assn., Galton Soc. Republican. Unitarian. Clubs: Authors, Charles River Country, Harvard, Cosmos. Author: The French Revolution in San Domingo, 1914; Present-Day Europe—Its National States of Mind 1917; The Stakes of the War, 1918; Harper's Pictorial Library of the World War (Vol. 6, The World at War), 1919; The Rising Tide of Color Against White World-Supremacy, 1920; The New World of Islam, 1921; The Evolt Against Civilization, 1922; Racial Realities in Europe, 1924; Social Classes in Post-War Europe, 1925; Scientific Humanism, 1926; Re-Forging American, 1927; The Story of Youth, 1928; Luck—Your Silent Partner, 1929; Master of Manhattan, The Life of Richard Croker, 1931; Europe and Our Money, 1932; Lonely America, 1932; Clasing Tides of Color, 1935; Into the Darkness, 1940. Home: 3418 O St. N.W., Washington. Died May 1, 1950; buried West Dennis, Mass.

STODDARD, Sanford, lawyer; b. Bridgeport, Conn., Oct. 11, 1877; s. Goodwin and Julia Elizabeth (Sanford) S.; student St. Paul's Sch., Concord, N.H., 1891-95; A.B., Yale, 1899; student Harvard Law Sch., 1899-1901; m. Hannah Gould Johnson, June 30, 1903; children—Johnson, Goodwin, David Gould. Admitted to Conn. bar, 1903, since practiced in Bridgeport, mem. Marsh, Stoddard & Day, 1905-35, Boardman, Stoddard & mem. McCarthy since 1941; v.p., trust officer First Nat. Bank Trust Co. Bridgeport, 1935-41; dir. Atlantic Coast Line Co., Turner & Seymour Mfg. Co., U. Club Co., Starring & Co., Inc., Sun, Inc. Dir. Conn. Reformatory, 1927-41; police commr., 1923-25, park commr. (v.p. bd.) since 1927; chmn. grievance com. Fairfield Co., 1921-34; chmn. local draft bd. Div. 3, 1917-19; adminstr. Bridgeport Dist. Office Def. Transportation, 1942-45. Mem. Am., Conn., Bridgeport bar assns., Am. Judiciary Soc., Am. Arbitration Assn. (nat. panel), Soc. Colonial Wars, Conn. League Nations Assn. (pres. 1927-29), C. of C. (pres. 1927-29). Clubs: U. (past pres.) (Bridgeport); Country (past pres.) (Fairfield); Yale (N.Y. City); Lake Placid (N.Y.). Home: 368 Sasco Hill Rd., Fairfield, Conn. Office: 955 Main St., Bridgeport 3, Conn. Died July 11, 1952.

STODDARD, William Leavitt, business exec.; born Northampton, Mass., Nov. 2, 1884; son of John Tappan and Mary Grover (Leavitt) S.; A.B., Harvard, 1907, A.M., 1908; m. Elizabeth Marie Southard, May 1, 1916; children—Elizabeth Marie (Mrs. H. B. Jenkins), Barbara Leavitt (Mrs. R. H. Cunningham, Jr.), John Leavitt, William Carver. Asst. in English dept., Harvard, 1906-07; mem. editorial staff, Atlantic Monthly, 1907-08; an editor Youth's Companion, 1908-10; with Washington bur. Boston Transcript, 1911-16; administrator Nat. War Labor Bd., 1918-19; officer Am. Trust Co., Boston, till 1929. Former owner Stoddard & Co., public relations; pres. and dir. New Eng. Industrial Development Corp., 1941-48; owner Indsl. Development Reports. Vice-pres. Lincoln and Therese Filene Foundation. Author: The Life of William Shakespeare Expurgated, 1910; Everyday English Writing, 1919; The Shop Committee, 1919; Financial Racketeering and How to Stop It, 1931; (with Lincoln Filene) Unfair Trade Practices, 1934. Home: Wayland, Mass. Address: 53 State St., Boston. Died Sept. 13, 1954; buried Northampton, Mass.

STOEHR, Max W. (stěr), wool mfr.; b. Leipzig, Germany, Nov. 8, 1882; s. Eduard and Emmy (Pfeil) S.; ed. Real Gymnasium and Teichmann's Pvt. Schule, Leipzig; m. Elsa C. Bennèche, Nov. 17, 1908; 1 dau., Madeleine E. Came to U.S., 1900, naturalized, 1911. Began, 1900, in mfg. business, at Passaic, N.J., with Botany Worsted Mills (estab. by father); was made sec. and treas. of company, 1915, treas. and chmn. bd., 1923; now chmn. of board Botany Worsted Mills. Republican. Office: 16 W. 46th St., N.Y.C. 19. Deceased.

STOKELY, Jehu Thomas, lawyer; b. Newport, Tenn., Feb. 16, 1878; s. John Burnett and Anne Eliza (Rorex) S.; A.B., U. Tenn., 1900; law study U. Mich., 1900-01, Harvard, 1901-02; m. Kate Smith, Oct. 10, 1906; children—Florence Rorex (Mrs. Edward T. Merry), Kate Devereux (wife of Dr. Hill Carter). Admitted to Ala. bar, 1902, practice of law at Birmingham, 1902-23, 26—; gen. solicitor So. Ry. System Lines, Washington, 1923-26. Served as 2d lt., bn. adj., acting regtl. adj., regtl. ordnance officer, post adj., 4th Tenn. Vol. Inf., Spanish-Am. War, 1898-99. Mem. Am., Ala. State (ex-pres.), Birmingham (ex-pres.) bar assns., Phi Kappa Phi, Phi Delta Phi, Kappa Sigma. Democrat. Baptist. Club: Mountain Brook Country. Home: 2250 Highland Av. Office: Brown Marx Bldg., Birmingham, Ala. Died Aug. 14, 1950.

STOKES, Andrew Jackson, clergyman; b. Orangeburg, S.C., July 25, 1859; s. Joseph and Rosa Anna (Mays) S.; A.B., Benedict Coll., Columbia, S.C., 1884; D.D., Guadalupe Coll., Seguin, Tex.; LL.D., Princeton (Ind.) College, 1912; m. Essie Mae Tucker, Apr., 1884. Ordained Bapt. ministry, 1870; pastor 1st Ch., Montgomery, 1890—; pres. Montgomery Acad.; trustee Nat. Training Sch., Washington, D.C.; editor Helping Hand (weekly); treas. Nat. Bapt. Conv. of America; moderator Spring Hill Dist. Baptist Assn. Mason. Author: Select Sermons, 1913. Home: 716 E. Columbus St., Montgomery, Ala. Died Aug. 29, 1924.

STOKES, Anson Phelps, clergyman, educationist; b. New Brighton, S.I., N.Y., Apr. 13, 1874; s. Anson Phelps and Helen Louisa (Phelps) S.; A.B., Yale, 1896, A.M., 1900; B.D., Episcopal Theol. School, Cambridge, Mass., 1900; D.D., Gettysburg Coll., 1910; LL.D., Yale, 1921, Ill. Coll., Jacksonville, 1927; S.T.D., Kenyon Coll., 1941; Dr. Canon Law, Berkeley Div. Sch., 1952; Doctor of Divinity, Princeton University, 1956; married Caroline Green Mitchell, Dec. 30, 1903; children—Rev. Anson Phelps, Isaac Newton Phelps, Olivia Egleston Phelps (Mrs. John Davis Hatch, Jr.). Traveled around world, visiting China, Java, India, and other countries, 1896-97; also South Pacific, Australasia, Far East, 1920, South America, 1929, Africa (Cape to Cairo), 1932-33. Sec. Yale U., 1899-1921. Deacon, P.E. Ch., 1900, priest, 1925; asst. minister St. Paul's, New Haven, 1900-18, in charge, 1903; canon of Washington Cathedral, 1924-39; Archbishop Ireland Lectr. on Ch. and State, Coll. of St. Thomas, St. Paul, 1951; Pres. Washington Com. on Housing, 1936-39; chmn. Dept. Social Welfare (Washington Diocese), 1938-39; also ex-pres. Washington Family Service Assn.; ex-mem. Gen. Edn. Bd., Internat. Edn. Bd. Rockefeller Foundation, Institute of Internat. Edn., Washington Cathedral Chapter, and ex-chairman Interracial Commn. apptd. by Washington Fed. of Chs.; ex-chmn. bd. trustees Yale in China and Hwachung (Central China) Coll.; ex-trustee Wellesley Coll., Am. Acad. in Rome, Conn. Gen. Hosp., St. Paul's Sch., Tuskegee Inst., Am. Council on Edn. First dir. ednl. dept. YMCA, A.E.F.; proposed and organized Army Ednl. Commn.; a founder Nat. Com. for Mental Hygiene, Lowell House (New Haven Settlement), Yale-in-China, Gaylord Farm Sanatorium; chmn. Com. named by President, 1935, to prepare plan for organizing D.C. Alley Dwelling Authority; pres. emeritus Phelps Stokes Fund (for educational work among Negroes); ex-trustee Brookings Instn.; asso. fellow Trumbull Coll.; Yale U.; trsutee Pleasant Valley Bird Sanctuary of Berkshire County; trustee Lenox Library and Lenox Sch.; chmn. Com. Am. Negroes in Def. Industries; chmn. Com. on Africa and Peace Aims, 1941 (editor of its report "The Atlantic Charter; and Africa from an American Standpoint"). Decorated Chevalier Legion of Honor (France), 1919; recipient Yale medal from corp. of the univ. for service to Yale, 1952. Mem. Phi Beta Kappa, etc. Author: Memorials of Eminent Yale Men (2 vols.); What Jesus Christ Thought of Himself; Educational Plans for the Am. Army Abroad; Tuskegee Institute's First Fifty Years; Booker Washington; a Brief Biography; also author of pamphlets, Historical Prints of New Haven, Christ and Man's Latent Divinity, The Congressional Pork Barrel, Historic Universities in a Democracy, University Schools of Religion, A Visit to Yale in China, Yale and New Haven (a study of the taxation question), Art and the Color Line, The Two Fronts of Freedom, Trinity Church, Lennox Massachusetts, 1793-1943. Published report, entitled Education, Native Welfare and Race Relations in East and South Africa, 1934; History of Lowell House (New Haven) 1946. Engaged in writing "History of Universities from Their Origin to the Present Time"; "Church and State in U.S., 1787-1947," 3 vols., 1950. Clubs: Century, Yale (New York); Graduate (New Haven, Conn.). Carnegie lecturer to universities of Union of South Africa, 1932. Chmn. bd. dirs. Ency. of the Negro, and editor Ency. of the Negro—Preparatory Volume, 1945, rev. edit., 1946. Founder and 1st pres. Stockbridge Bowl Assn., 1946. Gave commencement address (The Happy Mean) Berkshire Div. Sch., 1952. Address: Lenox, Mass. Died Aug. 13, 1958.

STOKES, Francis Joseph, mfr.; b. Philadelphia, Pa., Dec. 24, 1873; s. Francis and Katharine (Evans) S.; A.B., Haverford Coll., 1894; m. Lelia Woodruff, June 28, 1912; children—F. Joseph, Jr., Allen W., Henry W., Alison (wife of Dr. Paul D. MacLean), David E. Machinist apprentice, Robert Shoemaker, Phila., Pa., 1895-96; then purchased the business and operated it as the F. J. Stokes Machine Co., Phila., Pa. (manufacturing chemical and process equipment) 1896, co. incorporated 1920, pres., 1920-48, now chairman. Vice president Ludwick Institute; trustee, director Bryn Mawr College; member of the com. of sponsors American Univ. at Cairo (Egypt); overseer William Penn Charter School. Mem. Franklin Inst., Acad. Natural Sciences, Zool. Soc. of Philadelphia, Am. Chem. Soc., Pa. Acad. Fine Arts, Pa. Forestry Assn. Member of Society of Friends (Quaker). Clubs: University (Philadelphia); Chemists (New York). Home: 629 Church Lane, Germantown, Philadelphia 44. Office: Olney P.O., Philadelphia 20, Pa. Died Aug. 1, 1955.

STOKES, Frank Wilbert, painter; b. Nashville; s. M. S. and Harriet A. (Criswell) S.; ed. pub. schs., Phila. and 1 yr. at Rugby Acad., Phila.; studied music under Hugh Clark, U. Pa.; art under Thomas Eakins, Pa. Acad. Fine Arts, and under Gérôme, at Ecole des Beaux Arts, Paris, 1882; in Paris again, 1884, studied at Colarossi's, under Raphael Collin, at Julian's under Boulanger and Lefèbvre; unmarried. Exhibited in Salon, Paris, for several yrs.; joined Peary relief expn., 1892, as artist for Scribner's; artist mem. of Peary North Greenland expnd., 1893-94; studio in Bowdoin Bay, lat. 77° 44′ N., for 14 mos.; artist mem. Swedish Antarctic expdn. of 1901-02 under Dr. Otto Nordenskjold; artist mem. Amundsen-Ellsworth expdn.; painted "Return of Comdr. Byrd and Floyd Bennett from North Pole," also "Departure of Norge for North Pole." Completed, 1909, for Am. Mus. Natural History, New York, a series of mural decorations illustrating the allegory of the arctic night and day and depicting the life of the Smith Sound Eskimo. Contbr. to mags. Address: 3 Washington Sq. N., N.Y.C. Died Feb. 12, 1955.

STOKES, J(ames) G(raham) Phelps, publicist; b. N.Y.C., Mar. 18th, 1872; s. Anson Phelps and Helen Louise (Phelps) S.; Ph.B., Sheffield Sci. Sch., Yale, 1892; M.D., Coll. Phys. and Surg., Columbia, 1896, grad. work Sch. Polit. Sci., 1896-97; m. Rose Harriet Pastor, July 18, 1905; m. 2d, Lettice Lee Sands, Mar. 13, 1926. Pres. Austin Mining Co., 1897-1900, Nev. Central R.R. Co., 1897-1938, Nev. Central Motor Lines, Inc., 1928-49, The Nevada Co., 1897—, Phelps Stokes Corp., 1927—; v.p. State Bank of Nev., 1899-1904. Many yrs. mem. governing bds. of numerous ednl., philanthropic and sociol. orgns., including governing bds. and coms. of YMCA's in N.Y.C., at Yale, Columbia, and Governor's Island (U.S. Army br.), 1889-1947; founder of Y at Sheffield Sci. Sch., 1892, Coll. Phys. and Surg., 1895, West Side Branch, N.Y.C., 1896; mem. centennial com. YMCA of N.Y., 1944. Mem. bd. trustees Univ. Settlement Soc. of N.Y., 1897-1903, Hartley House, 1896—; chmn. bd. trustees People's Inst., N.Y., 1897-1902; trustee Tuskegee (Ala.) Normal and Indsl. Inst., 1898-1907; dir. Burnham (Berkshire) Indsl. Farm, Cannan, N.Y., 1897-1909, N.Y. Juvenile Asylum (and Children's Village, Dobbs Ferry, N.Y.), 1900-06; treas. Manhattan Trade Sch. for Girls, 1902-03; trustee Northern Dispensary, N.Y.C., 1944—, v.p., 1947—. Treas., exec. com. Outdoor Recreation League of N.Y., 1899-1907; exec. com. Armstrong Assn. (for Hampton Inst., Va.), 1899-1907; mem., treas. N.Y. Child Labor Com., 1902-97; mem. exec. com. Prison Assn. of N.Y., 1899-1906; treas., mem. exec. com. (1904 incorporator) League for Polit. Edn. (later known as Town Hall, Inc.), 1903-07. Treas. Nat. Conf. Charities and Correction, 1904-05; rep. N.Y. Assn. for Improving Condition of Poor, at 1st N.Y. State Conf. Charities and Correction, at the capitol, Albany, N.Y., 1900; apptd. by 1st and 2d confs., mem. for 1901 of com. on care and relief of needy families in their own homes, apptd. by 4d and 5th confs., chmn. com. on preventive social work for 1904, mem. N.Y.C. com. for 6th N.Y. State Conf., 1906. Vice chmn., also its candidate for pres. bd. of aldermen of N.Y., Municipal Ownership League, 1905; v.p. Electoral Laws Improvement

Assn., 1905; vice chmn. Independence League, 1905-06. Presdl. elector Populist ticket, 1904; mem. Socialist Party, 1906-17, mem. nat. exec. com., 1908, mem. state exce. com., Conn., 1911, Party candidate for N.Y. Assembly, 1908, for mayor of Stamford, Conn., 1912; pres. Intercollegiate Socialist Soc., 1907-18 (withdrew from soc. 1918); vice chmn. Nat. Party, 1917; sec.-treas. Social Dem. League of Am., 1917, treas., 1917-19; treas. Am. Alliance for Labor and Democracy, 1917-19. Hon. adviser Roerich Mus., N.Y., 1931-33. Mem. Squadron A, N.Y.N.G., 1898-1901; pvt., cav., U.S. Army, 1898-99; enlisted Vet. Corps of Arty., N.Y., Aug. 1917; trans. to 9th C.A.C., N.Y.G., Oct. 1917; promoted 2d lt., Mar. 1919, 1st lt., Aug. 1919, capt., Dec. 1919; capt. C.A.C., N.Y.N.G, 1920; capt. C.A., O.R.C., U.S., 1922; capt. adj., 244th Arty, C.A.C., U.S., Feb. 1924, maj., May 1924; maj. C.A., U.S., Aug. 1924; trans. to N.Y. State Res. List, 1926, State Ret. List, 1936. Awarded Mil. Cross of State of N.Y. (Conspicuous Service Cross), also N.Y. State decorations for long and faithful service and for service in aid of civil authority, 1922. Hon. councillor Russian Information Bureau in U.S., 1917-22; pres. Constitutional Democracy Assn., 1937-38; mem. adv. bd. Defense Soc., 1937, bd. trustees, 1938-40; mgr. Disaster Relief Service, 6th Precinct, A.R.C., N.Y.C., 1942. Fellow Am. Geog. Soc., N.Y. Acad. Scis.; mem. S.R., S.R. in State of N.Y. (sec. 1925-26), Soc. Am. Wars (sr. vice comdr. 1931), Soc. Colonial Wars, Naval and Mil. Order Spanish-Am. War (council 1953—), N.Y. Soc. Mil. and Naval Officers World Wars (standing com. 1923-26), Soc. Am. Mil. Engrs., Soc. of Massing of the Colors, Am. Mus. Natural History (patron 1906—), Met. Mus. Art, Pilgrims (N.Y. and London), India Soc. (Royal India and Pakistan Soc.) (London), Sulgrave Instn. (founder 1920), N.Y. State C. of C., Mus. of City of N.Y. (founder 1938), Archaeol. Inst. of Am., Société Française des Amis de l'Orient (Paris), Oriental Inst. (U. Chgo.), Am. Oriental Soc., Chelsea Post Am. Legion (hon.), Res. Officers Assn. (mem. council Manhattan chpt. 1941-42), Soc. Ex-members Squadron A, France-Am. Soc., Netherland-Am. Found., Italy-Am. Soc., China Soc. Am. (hon.), Acad. Polit. Sci. (life) Am. Hist. Assn., Am. Acad. Polit. and Social Sci., Delta Psi. Clubs: Century, University, Yale, Columbia, Military-Naval (bd. govs.; chmn. com. nat. defense, 1937-46), City, Drug and Chemical (hon.), Church. Vestryman Grace Episcopal Ch. Traveled around world, 1892-93. Mem. com. apptd. by gov., 1921, to represent State of N.Y. in welcoming to N.Y.C. representatives from European countries arriving in U.S. to attend Internat. Conf. on Limitation of Armaments, Washington. Home: 88 Grove St., N.Y.C. 14. Office: 235 Fourth Av., N.Y.C. 3. Died Apr. 8, 1960.

STOKES, Richard Leroy, journalist; b. Parke County, Ind., Nov. 30, 1882; student 1 yr., Harvard (Class 1904). Reporter, feature writer, St. Louis Post-Dispatch, 1903-14, music and drama critic, 1914-26; music critic N.Y. Evening World, 1926-31; mem. Washington bur. St. Louis Post-Dispatch, 1937-47, accredited war corr. on western front, May 1944-45. Author of libretto of Merry Mount (opera in English), score by Dr. Howard Hanson, dir. Eastman Sch. of Music, prod. by Met. Opera Co., season of 1933-34; Paul Bunyan: a folk comedy; Leon Blum: Poet to Premier (1st full-length biography in any language of France's 1st Jewish and Socialist Prime Minister), Benedict Arnold (drama in heroic couplets). Clubs: National Press, Overseas Writers, Grolier (N.Y.C.). Home: 1331 Madison Av., N.Y.C. Died Aug. 1, 1957.

STOKES, Thomas Lunsford, Jr., newspaper corr.; b. Atlanta, Ga., Nov. 1, 1898; s. Tromas Lunsford and Emma (Layton) S.; A.B., U. of Ga., 1920; m. Hannah Hunt, Jan. 10, 1924; children—Thomas Lunsford, III, Layton (dec.), Reporter, Savannah (Ga.) Press, 1920, Macon (Ga.) News, 1921, Athens (Ga.) Herald, 1921, corr. United Press, Washington, D.C., 1921-33; Washington corr. New York World-Telegram, 1933-36; corr. Scripps-Howard Newspaper Alliance, Washington, D.C., 1936-44. Columnist United Features Syndicate, 1944—. Awarded Pulitzer reporting prize for year 1938; awarded Raymond Clapper Memorial Award for Washington Corr., 1946, spl. citation for journalistic achievement, 1958. Member Am. Acad. Polit. Sci., Phi Beta Kappa Assos., Phi Beta Kappa, Alpha Tau Omega. Clubs: National Press, Gridiron, Overseas Writers, Cosmos (Washington). Author: Chip Off My Shoulder, 1940; The Savannah, 1951. Home: 2019 Hillyer Pl. N.W. Office: 1122 Nat. Press Bldg., Washington 4. Died May 14, 1958; buried Arlington Nat. Cemetery.

STOKES, William Herman, opthalmologist; b. British East India, July 17, 1894; s. Herman and Ellen (Hill) S.; grad. Tubingen Gymnasium, Germany; M.D., U. Mich., 1922; m. Margaret Ann Scott, Sept. 27, 1924. Came to U.S., 1913, naturalized, 1918. Sr. instr. ophthalmology, Med. Sch., U. Mich., 1923-25; asso. prof. ophthalmology, Med. Coll., U. Neb., 1930-36; prof., chmn. dept., 1937-43; practicing oculist, Omaha, Neb., 1930-48; oculist Neb. Meth. Hosp., Bishop Clarkson Meml. Hosp., C.&N.W. Ry., C.B.&Q. Ry.; oculist Mercy Hosp., Cadillac, Mich.; practicing oculist, Lake City, Mich. Served as lt. san. corps, U.S. Army, 1918, with A.E.F. Certificated Am. bd. Ophthalmology. Fellow A.M.A., Am. Acad. Ophthal., A.C.S.; mem. Am. Ophthal. Soc., Sci. Research Soc. Am., Phi Rho Sigma, Sigma Xi. Republican. Mason (32°, Shriner). Club: Omaha. Contbr. articles to med. jours. Address: S. Shore Dr., Lake City, Mich. Died Apr. 8, 1957; buried Lake City, Mich.

STOLAND, Ole Olufson (stō'lănd), educator; b. Beresford, S.D., July 30, 1881; s. Oluf Iverson and Kari (Rambraut) S.; A.B., U. S.D., 1905; M.S., U. Chgo., 1911, Ph.D., 1913; m. Murel Blanche Ross, Sept. 24, 1911; children—Rae Evelyn (Mrs. H. W. Weatherby), Ruth Eleanor, Robert Olaf, Lawrence Iver (deceased). Instr. biology, U. S.D., 1906-11; asst. in physiology, U. Chgo., 1911-13; prof. physiology, U. S.D., 1913-16; prof. physiology and pharmacology, U. Kan., 1916-52, now emeritus, sec. School Medicine. Fellow A.A.A.S.; mem. Am. Physiol. Soc., Kan. Acad. Science, Phi Sigma, Beta Theta Pi, Phi Chi, Sigma Xi, Phi Beta Kappa, Alpha Omega Alpha, Acacia. Republican. Conglist. Mason (32°). Clubs: University, Forum, Country, Williston-ian. Contbr. to Am. Jour. Physiology, Jour. Immunology, Jour. Pharmacology and Exptl. Therapeutics, Archives of Internal Medicine. Home: 1845 Learnard Av., Lawrence, Kan. Died Feb. 24, 1959; buried Memorial Park Cemetery, Lawrence, Kan.

STOLBERG, Benjamin (stōl'bĕrg), author, jouurnalist; b. Munich, Germany, Nov. 30, 1891; s. Michael and Rada (Stolberg) S.; student Real Gymnasium, Munich, 1901-08; A.B., Harvard, 1918, as of 1917; grad. work in socioology, U. Chgo., 1918-19; m. Mary Fox, Jan. 7, 1925 (div. Feb. 18, 1929); 1 son, David Fox. Came to U.S., 1908. Instr. sociology, dir. Sch. of Social Work, U. Okla., 1919-20; instr. sociology, U. Kan., 1920-21; charge of vocational placement Chgo. pub. high schs., 1921-22; acting editor Jour. of the Brotherhood of Locomotive Firemen, 1922-23; asso. editor The Bookman, 1928-29; columnist N.Y. Evening Post, 1932-33. Chmn. N.Y. League Indsl. Democracy, 1925-27; mem. Internat. Commn. of Inquiry into the charges made against Leon Trotsky in Moscow Trials, 1937. Mem. Com. to Defend Am. by Aiding the Allies, 1940; mem. Soc. Am. Historians; v.p. Am. Writers Assn. Club: National Press (Washington). Author: The Economic Consquences of the New Deal (with Warren Jay Vinton), 1935; The Story of the C.I.O., 1938; The Collapse of American Communism, 1939; Tailor's Progress—History of the Women Garment Workers, 1944. Writer on econ. and gen. social topics; to various books, mags., newspapers and syndicates. Lectr. at various colls. and univs. Address: 222 W. 23d St., N.Y.C. Died Jan. 21, 1951.

STOLL, Philip Henry, ex-congressman; b. Little Rock, S.C., Nov. 5, 1874; s. Rev. James C. and Mary (McCollough) S.; A.B., Wofford Coll., 1897; m. Evelyn Cunningham, 1907. Admitted to S.C. bar, 1901, and began practice at Kingstree; mem. law firm Stoll & O'Bryan. Mem. S.C. Ho. pf Rep., 1904-06; solicitor 3d Jud. Circuit, S.C., 1908-17 (resigned); mem. 67th Congress (1921-23), 6th S.C. Dist. Chmn. Dem. County Com., 1908-18. Commd. maj. Judge Adv. Dept., U.S.A., 1917, promoted lt. col, 1918; hon. discharged, Feb. 9, 1919. Democrat. Methodist. Home: Kingstree, S.C. Died Oct. 29, 1958; buried Williamsburg Presbyn. Cemetery, Kingstree, S.C.

STONE, Abraham, physician; b. Russia, Oct. 31, 1890; s. Miron and Amelia (Chamers) S.; M.D., N.Y.U., 1912, B.S., 1915; m. Hannah Mayer, Aug. 17, 1917 (dec. July 1941); 1 dau., Gloria (wife of Dr. Gerard J. Aitken, Jr.). Came to U.S., 1905, naturalized, 1915. Intern Knickerbocker, St. Marks, Bellevue hosps., 1912-15; staff N.Y. City Dept. Health; instr. urology N.Y. Post Grad. Med. Sch., 1923-27; chief urologist Union Health Center, 1929-50; cons. urology Sydenham Hosp., N.Y.C.; asso. clin. prof. preventive medicine N.Y.U., 1951—. Active Margaret Sanger Bur., 1925—, now dir.; active Planned Parenthood Fedn. Am., 1925—, v.p., 1943—; v.p. Internat. Planned Parenthood Fedn., 1953—; dir. marriage consultation center Community Ch. of N.Y.; spl. cons. WHO on family planning, Indian Govt. and Ceylon. NRC del. 1st World Conf. on Family and Population, Paris, France, 1947. Served as 1st lt., M.C., U.S. Army, 1917-20. Recipient Lasker award, 1947. Fellow Am. Soc. Study Sterility, N.Y. Acad. Medicine; mem. A.M.A., Am. Assn. Marriage Counselors, A.A.A.S., Alpha Omega Alpha. Author: (with Dr. Norman Himes) Planned Parenthood (rev. edit.), 1951; (With Dr. Hannah M. Stone) A Marriage Manual (rev. edit.), 1952; (with Dr. Lena Levine) Premarital Consultation, 1956. Editor: Jour. Human Fertility, 1936-49. Contbr. articles profl. and popular publs. Address: 40 Park Av., N.Y.C. Died July 3, 1959.

STONE, Albert Jmes, ry. ofcl.; b. Holly, Mich., Feb. 20, 1873; s. Edson S. and Louis J. (Box) S.; ed. pub. and high schs.; m. Mabel W. Craig, Aug. 4, 1897. Operating dept. Erie R.R., 1888, apptd. asst. to gen. mgr., 1903; gen. supt. Del. & Hudson R.R., 1903-05; asst. gen. mgr. Erie R.R., 1905-07, gen. supt., 1907-13, gen. mgr., 1913-14, v.p. charge operation, 1914—; also v.p. Chgo. & Erie R.R., N.Y., Susquehanna & Western R.R., Wilkes-Barre & Eastern R.R., Bath & Hammondsport R.R., Lake Keuka Navigation Co.; fed. mgr. Erie System and Pitts. & Shawmut R.R., June 1918-Feb. 1920; pres. The Jamestone Co., N.Y., 1920 to retirement. Republican. Presbyn. Club: Congressional Country (Washington). Home: Wilton, Conn. Died Oct. 6, 1950.

STONE, Alfred Holt, tax adminstr.; b. New Orleans, La., Oct. 16, 1870; s. Walter Wilson and Eleanor (Holt) S.; LL.B., U. of Miss., 1891, LL.D., 1916; LL.D., Southwestern, Memphis, 1928; m. Mary Bailey Ireys, June 25, 1896. Cotton planter, 1893-1931; v.p. Staple Cotton Discount Corp., staple cotton co-operative Assn.; dir. Federal Land Bank, Federal Intermediate Credit Bank, Bank for Coops., Production Credit Corp., Farm Credit Administrn.—all of New Orleans, La. Contbr. of studies on Negro problem to mags. and econ. socs., since 1890. Mem. Miss. legislature, 1916-23; chmn. State Tax Commn. of Miss. since 1932. Pres. Miss. Hist. Soc., 1912-13; pres. Nat. Tax Assn., 1938-39; pres. Nat. Assn. of Tax Adminstrs., 1937; chmn. of bd. Fedn. of Tax Administrs., 1943. Mem. Delta Psi Fraternity. Mason. Editor: The Staple Cotton Review. Author: Studies in the American Race Problem, 1908. Home: 817 Arlington St. Office: State Tax Commission, Jackson, Miss. Died May 11, 1955; buried Greenville, Miss.

STONE, Calvin Perry, prof. psychology; b. Portland, Ind., Feb. 28, 1892; s. Ezekiel and Emily (Brinkerhoff) S.; A.B., Valparaiso U., 1913; M.A., Indiana University, 1916, Doctor of Science (honorary), 1954; Ph.D., U. of Minn., 1921; married Minnie Ruth Kemper, June 30, 1917; children—James Herbert, Robert Kemper, Barbara Ruth. High sch. prin. and supt., 1910-14; teaching fellow, U. of Minn., 1916, 1919-21; dir. research Psychol. Lab. of Ind. Reformatory, 1916-17; instr. psychology and histology, U. of Minn., 1921-22; asst. prof. psychology, Stanford, 1922-25, asso. prof., 1925-29, prof. since 1929. Inst. Juvenile Research, 1928-29; research, New York Psychiatric Institute, 1945; Columbia U., summer 1945; U. of Wisconsin, summer 1947. Served as lieut., later capt. U.S. Medical Corps, World War I. Fellow A.A.A.S. (v.p. sect. I, 1938-39); mem. Western Psychol. Assn. (pres. 1931-32), Am. Psychol. Assn. (pres. 1941-42), Am. Assn. Univ. Profs., Am. Assn. on Mental Deficiency, Calif. Acad. Science, Western Naturalists, Soc. Exptl. Biology, Nat. Acad. Science, Sigma Xi. Republican. Author of many articles on exptl. studies of instinct, sex behavior, learning, memory, and genetic psychology. Editor Jour. Comparative and Physiol. Psychology, 1947-50; Annual Review of Psychology since 1948; editor, Comparative Psychology, 1951. Home: 668 Alvarada Row, Stanford, Calif. Died Dec. 28, 1954; buried Alta Mesa Cemetery, Palo Alto, Cal.

STONE, Charles Edwin, mfg. exec.; b. Portland, Mich., Aug. 7, 1887; s. William Harvey and Flora (Wilkes) S.; grad. mech. engring. U. Mich., 1910; m. Queen Robinson, Sept. 9, 1913; 1 son, Charles Wilkes. Engr. Foos Gas Engine Co., Springfield, O., 1910, purchasing agt., 1913-17; purchasing agt. Chain Belt Co., Milwaukee, 1917-20, asst. to pres., 1920-26; treas. Interstate Drop Forge Co., 1920-28, pres., 1928—; dir., mem. exec. com. Sivyer Steel Casting Co., Fed. Malleable Co.; dir. Teutonia Bank. Mem. adv. bd. W.P.B.; panel mem. War Labor Bd.; mem. industry adv. com. N.P.A., 1944-52, chmn. Air Force Forging task group; mem. industry adv. com. O.P.S., 1945-52. Former dir. N.A.M.; former vice president National Assn. Purchasing Agts.; past pres. Am. Drop Forging Inst., Drop Forging Assn.; pres. Milwaukee Employers Assn., 1950-52. Mem. Phi Mu Alpha. Episcopalian. Clubs: Milwaukee, University, Rotary, Milwaukee Country (Milwaukee). Home: 5350 N. Lake Dr., Milw. 11. Office: 4051 N. 27th St., Milw. 16. Died Dec. 20, 1956.

STONE, Charles Newhall, mfg. exec.; b. St. Paul, June 10, 1884; s. Eldridge Kimball and Cora A. (Edison) S.; B.S., U. Ill., 1904; m. Helen A. Loosley, June 29, 1915. With Deere & Co., Moline, Ill., 1904-07, various positions Canadian factory, 1911-20, dir., 1926-52, v.p., 1934-52, ret., now mem. adv. com.; lumberman, B.C., Can., 1907-11; asst. mgr., supt. John Deere Harvester Works, 1920-23, mgr., 1923-34. Home: 4430 Fifth Av. Office: 1325 Third Av., Moline, Ill. Died July 11, 1954.

STONE, Claudius Ulysses, newspaper pub.; b. nr. Middletown, Ill., May 11, 1879; s. William Lee and Johanna (Ohlson) S.; B.S., Western Ill. Normal Coll., 1906; law study U. Mich., George Washington U.; M.A., Bradley U., 1956; m. Genevieve C. Francis, June 18, 1902; 1 dau., Shielagh Day; m. 2d, Alma M. Poppen, Apr. 2, 1925; 1 son, Claude, Ulysses. Tchr., high sch. prin. prior to 1902; county supt. of schs. Peoria County, Ill., 1902-10; admitted to Ill. bar, 1909; Dem. mem. 62dto 64th Congresses 16th Ill. Dist.; postmaster Peoria, 1917-20; practiced law as asso. McGrath, Stone, Daily and Michel in Peoria and Chgo., 1920-25; master in chancery Circu Ct. of Peoria County, 1928-45; editor, pub., mgr. Peoria and Chgo., 1920-25; master in chancery Circuit K., 4th Vol. Inf., 1898-99, 4 mos. in Cuba. Mem. Ill. Archaeol. Soc. (charter mem., pres. 1947-49), Ill. (past v.p.), Peoria (past pres.) acads. sci., Soc. Am. Archaeology, Am., Ill., Peoria bar assns., Am., Ill., Miss. Valley, Peoria hist. socs., Civil War Round Table of Am., Bradley Alumni Assn., Phi Delta Kappa, Phi Alpha Theta. Republican. Presbyn. Mason (Shriner), Odd Fellow, K.P.; mem. Order of Eastern Star. Clubs: Creve Coeur, University, Country. Home: 210 W. Armstrong St., Peoria, Ill. Died Nov. 13, 1957; buried Parkview Cemetery, Peoria, Ill.

STONE, Emerson Law, physician; b. Waterford, N. Y., Apr. 7, 1895; s. Arthur J. and Agnes (Law) S.; A.B., Williams Coll., 1916; M.D., Johns Hopkins, 1920; Mus. B., Yale, 1930; m. Grace E. Kussmaul, July 15, 1926; children—Emerson Law, II, John Arthur, Mary Diana. Resident house officer, Johns Hopkins Hosp., 1920-21; New Haven Hosp., 1921-24; surgeon U.S. Lines, 1924; resident in obstetrics, Johns Hopkins Hosp., 1924-25; asso. prof. obstetrics and gynecology, Yale U. Sch. of Medicine, 1925-27, asso. clin. prof., 1927-44, clin. prof. since 1944; pvt. practice splty. New Haven, Conn., since 1927; consultant various regional hosps. since 1927. Certified Am. Bd. Obstetrics and Gynecology, 1937; mem. Sigma Psi. Club: Graduate (New Haven). Author: The New Born Infant, 1945. Musician. Home: Three Bayberry Rd., Hamden 14. Office: 129 Whitney Av., New Haven 10. Died Jan. 10, 1953; buried West Lawn Cemetery, Williamstown, Mass.

STONE, Fred Andrew, actor; b. Valmont, Colo., Aug. 19, 1873; s. Lewis Preston and Clara (Johnston) S.; ed. pub. schs.; m. Allene H. Crater, Aug. 23, 1904. First appeared on stage at age of 11, at Topeka, Kan.; began traveling with Berry & Sealers Wagon Circus, 1886; later played Topsy in Uncle Tom's Cabin; met David Montgomery, 1895, and associated with him as partner for 22 yrs.; played vaudeville, Palace Thearte, London, Eng., 1899, Herald Square Theatre, New York, 1901; scored success as the Scarecrow, in Wizard of Oz, 1902, and as Con Kidder, in The Red Mill, 1906; toured as Henry Clay Baxter, in The Old Town; played in Jack o'Lantern, 1918-19, 20, 21; has been in pictures, 1934—, appearing in Trail of the Lonesome Pine, My American Wife, Grand Jury, Hideaway, Quick Money, Life Begins in College, No Place to Go. Home: Hollywood, Cal. Died Mar. 4, 1959.

STONE, Fred Denton, clergyman; b. Rock Falls, Ill., Jan. 18, 1875; s. Daniel Delavan and Nancy (Bean) S.; grad. Normal Sch., Dixon, Ill., 1896; student Garett Bibl. Inst., 1896-97, D.D., 1929; LL.D., Ill. Wesleyan U., 1944; m. Dora May Ashby, Oct. 19, 1898; 1 son, Fred Denton. Ordained ministry M.E. Ch., 1897; successively pastor Dixon and Elgin, Ill., and chs. in Chgo.; became pastor Irving Park Ch., 1924; dist. supt. Chgo., 1918-24; pub. agent Meth. Pub. House 1936-48, ret. Trustee Chgo. Tng. Sch. (pres. bd.). Mem. Gen. Conf. M.E. Ch., 1924, 28, 32, 36, 40, 44, and Uniting Conf., 1939. Theta Phi Soc. Republican. Contbr. ch. publs. Home: 729 Eemerson St., Evanston, Ill. Died Oct. 4, 1956.

STONE, Harold, banker; b. Syracuse, N.Y., Oct. 19, 1878; s. Charles L. and Zilla (Sackett) S.; B.A., Yale 1902; LL.B., Syracuse U., 1904; m. Anne Babcock, June 16, 1904. Admitted to N.Y. bar, 1904, practiced law, Syracuse, 1904-17, dir. operations U.S. Employment Service, 1917-19; trustee Onondaga Co. Savs. Bank, Syracuse, since 1920, pres., 1931-43, chmn. bd., 1943—. Club: Century (Syracuse). Home: 213 Highland Av. Office: 101 S. Salina St., Syracuse, N.Y. Died Feb. 22, 1958; buried Oakwood Cemetery, Syracuse, N.Y.

STONE, Herbert Lawrence, editor; b. Charleston, S.C., Jan. 18, 1871; s. William and Mary A. (Taylor) S.; ed. private schs., N.Y. City; m. Redelia Gilchrist. Asst. p.m. N.Y.C. R.R., until 1907; editor Yachting since 1908; president Yachting Publishing Corp. since 1938. Lt. (sr. grade) U.S.N.R.F., April 1917-August 1919; served as navigating officer cruiser Montgomery, transport Pastores; comdr. U.S.S. Onward, Squadron 1, Sub Chasers. Clubs: Cruising Club America, New York Yacht, Larchmont Yacht, Stamford Yacht, Royal Ocean Racing. Author: America's Cup Races, 1914, 30; The Yachtman's Handbook (with others), 1915; Millions for Defense, 1934; The A.B.C. of Boat Sailing, 1946. Editor: Ice Boating, 1916. Home: Pound Ridge, N.Y. Office: 205 E. 42nd St., N.Y.C. Died Sept. 27, 1955.

STONE, Joseph E., business exec.; b. Urbana, O., Dec. 20, 1874; s. John H. P. and Sarah (MacDonald) S.; m. Florence Foote, Dec. 18, 1901; 1 son, John Willard. Began as salesman, Simmons Hardware Co., St. Louis, Mo.; salesman, Stanley Rule & Level Plant, New Britain, Conn., 1907, then made sales manager, 1918; with The Stanley Works, New Britain, Conn., 1920—, vice-pres. in charge sales, 1923, dir. 1927-46, ret.; dir. New Britain Nat. Bank, Stanley Securities Company, New Britain, Three Canadian Plants, The Stanley Works. Served as pres. Am. Hardware Mfrs. Assn., 1930-31. Formerly pres. New Britain Council, Boy Scouts of America. Clubs: New Britain (past pres.); Shuttle Meadow, Indian Hill Country. Home: 1 Ten Acre Rd. Office: New Britain, Conn. Died Feb. 1952.

STONE, Judson F., consultant McCormick Estates; born Canton, Pennsylvania, February 4, 1873; son Judson W. and Ruby (Lilley) S.; student University of Minnesota, 2 years; married to Estella Mayhew, Mar. 30, 1898 (dec.); children—Judson M. (dec.), Fred L., Harry L. Began 1892, with McCormick Harvesting Machine Co., continued with successor, International Harvester Company; now director of International Harvester Company and member executive committee; entered employ McCormick Estates, 1905, mng. agt. same; chmn. Belle City Malleable Iron Co., Racine, Wis.; dir. Wilmette (Ill.) State Bank, Poor & Company, Standard Oil Company of Indiana. Pres. Chgo. Assn. Commerce, 1923. Republican. Presbyn. Mason. Clubs: Commerical, Chicago, Glenview, Mid-Day. Home: 1234 Ashland Av., Wilmette, Ill. Office: 30 N. LaSalle St., Chgo. Died Feb. 20, 1958.

STONE, Kenneth Franklin, lawyer; b. Chippewa Falls, Wis., Mar. 21, 1904; s. Charles Eugene and Amelia (Emerson) S.; A.B., Lawrence Coll., 1925; LL.B., U. of Mich., 1931; m. Ruth Banfield, Dec. 22, 1934; 1 son, John Franklin, II. Admitted N.Y. bar, 1947, Mich. bar, 1931. Clk. No. Trust Co., now No. Minn. Nat. Bank, Duluth, 1925-29; atty. N.Y.C. R.R., Detroit, 1931-40, asst. gen. atty., 1940-48; asst. gen. solicitor, N.Y. City, 1948, asst. gen. counsel, 1949, gen. atty., 1950—, gen. counsel, v.p., 1951—, gen. counsel subsidiaries. Mem. Am., N.Y. State, Mich. State bar assns., Assn. I.C.C. Practitioners, Am. Judicature Soc., N.Y. Law Inst., N.Y. C. of C., Theta Phi, Phi Alpha Delta. Presbyn. Republican. Club: University. Home: 277 Park Av. Office: 466 Lexington Av., N.Y.C. 17. Died Apr. 5, 1952; buried Chippewa Falls, Wis.

STONE, Kimbrough, judge; b. Nevada, Mo., Jan. 15, 1875; s. William Joel and Louise (Winston) S.; Litt.B., U. of Mo., 1895, LL.D., 1928; student law dept., Harvard U., 1895-98; m. Lucy May Cockrill, Oct. 3, 1906; children—Elizabeth Louise, Marjorie May. Began practice at St. Louis, Mo., 1898; judge Circuit Court, 16th Circuit, Mo., 1913-17; judge U.S. Circuit Court of Appeals, 8th Circuit, by appointment of President Wilson, 1917-47, retired, (presiding judge, 1928-47). Democrat. Mem. of Christian (Disciples) Ch. Mem. Am., Mo. and Kansas City bar assns., Beta Theta Pi, Phi Beta Kappa, Phi Delta Phi, Order of Coif. Address: 235 Ward Pky., Kansas City, Mo. Died Feb. 27, 1958.

STONE, Lewis, actor; b. Worcester, Mass., Nov. 15, 1879; s. Bertrand and Lucy S.; student Columbia U.; m. Hazel Woof, Oct. 15, 1930; children—Virginia, Barbara. Starred on stage in N.Y.C., also in Belasco Theatre, Los Angeles; has starred in motion pictures, 1915—; plays in all "Andy Hardy Family Series." Served in U.S. Army in Spanish-Am. War and World War, advancing to rank of maj. Home: San Fernando, Cal. Address: care Metro-Goldwyn-Mayer, Culver City, Cal. Died Sept. 12, 1953.

STONE, Ralph, banker; b. Wilmington, Del., Nov. 20, 1868; s. George W. and Catherine C. (Graupner) S.; A.B., Swarthmore (Pa.) Coll., 1889; LL. B., U. Mich., 1892; m. Mary G. Jeffords, June 1, 1895; children—Ralph, Ruth Waldo Caulkins. Began practice law at Grand Rapids, 1892; trust officer Mich. Trust Co., Grand Rapids, 1893-99; pvt. sec., mil. sec. to Gov. H. S. Pingree, 1899-1900, rank of maj. on staff of gov.; state bank examiner, 1901; asst. sec. Detroit Trust Co., 1901, sec., 1903, v.p., 1912, pres., 1915-27, chmn. bd., 1927-33. Dir. Bur. Trusts for alien property custodian (U.S.), 1917-18. Mem. Mich. State Bar Assn., Am. (exec. council Trust Co. Div., 1929-32), Mich. (exec. com., v.p. 1929-33), Detroit bankers assns., Detroit Bd. Commerce, Mich. Soc. Mayflower Descendants, S.A.R. Republican. Unitarian. Regent, U. Mich., 1923-39; trustee Cranbrook Found., Cranbrook Acad. Art, Cranbrook (girls). Clubs: Detroit, University, Bloomfield brook Sch. (boys and Kingswood Sch., Cran-Hills Country. Home: Garden Court Apts., 2906 E. Jefferson, Detroit 7. Office: Detroit Trust Co., Detroit. Died May 11, 1957.

STONE, Samuel M., mfr.; b. Urbana, O., Feb. 19, 1869; s. John H. P. and Sarah (Mac Donald) S.; ed. grammar and high schs., Urbana; m. Alice Bailey Nov. 16, 1898; children—Henry Taylor, John MacDonald. Began as clk. retail hardware store, Urbana with Simmons Hardware Co., St. Louis, 1891-1905; dir. Phoenix State Bank & Trust Co., Hartford Electric Light Co., Hartford Steam Boiler Ins. Co., Humason Mfg. Co., Peck, Stow & Wilcox, Conn. Mut. Life Ins. Co., Nat. Fire Ins. Co., Hartford County Mutual Fire Ins. Co., Dime Savings Bank, Veeder-Root, Inc., Holo-Krome Mfg. Co. With Colt's Patent Fire Arms Mfg. Co., 1905-45, pres., 1921-45. Trustee Worcester Poly. Inst., Am. Sch. for the Deaf, Y.M.C.A. Republican. Conglist. Mason (32°). Mem. The Newcomen Soc. Clubs: Hartford, Get Together, Congregational, Twentieth Century. Home: 35 Stratford Rd., West Hartford. Office: 17 Van Dyke Av., Hartford, Conn. Died Dec. 9, 1959.

STONE, Theodore Thaddeus, physician; b. Chgo. Aug. 3, 1897; s. Henry and Sarah (Kalish) S.; B.S., M.D., U. Ill., 1919; M.S., Ph.D., Northwestern, 1935; m. Betty Miller, Dec. 31, 1930. Clin. asst., med. sch. Northwestern, 1922-26, instr., 1926-29, asso., 1929-31, asst. prof., 1931-38, asso. prof., 1938-48, prof. nervous diseases since 1948; attending neurologist Michael Reese Hosp., Chgo., 1922-36, Cook Co. Hosp. since 1936; attending neurologist, head dept. nervous and mental diseases Wesley Meml. Hosp. since 1943; 4 lectures U. Whitwaters Rand, Johannesburg, South Africa, 1938, 3 lectures Honolulu Med. Soc. and Honolulu Soc. Nervous and Mental Disorders, 1951. Neurology, psychiatry specialist. Med. Adv. Bd. No. 36, 1941-43. Diplomate Am. Bd. Psychiatry and Neurology. Fellow A.C.P., 1948; mem. 14 med. socs., Sigma Xi. Co-author: Report on Epilepsy, 1936. Contbr. profl. jours. Home: Singing Pine Farm, Route 3, Woodstock, Ill. Died March 5, 1952.

STONE, Walter King, illustrator; b. Barnard, N.Y., Mar. 2, 1875; s. William Talmage and Jenny (Filer) S.; ed. pub. schs., Rochester, Rochester Mechanics' Inst., Pratt Inst., Brooklyn; m. Edith Adams, Aug. 19, 1902; 1 son, Alan. Mural decorator. Asst. prof. arts, Coll. of Architecture, Cornell U., 1920-43, asso. prof. emeritus, 1943—. Unitarian. Club: Savage. Illustrator: The Log of the Sun, 1906; Barn Doors and Byways, 1913; Green Trails and Upland Pastures, 1917; In Berkshire Fields, 1920. Home: "The Byway," Forest Home, Ithaca, N.Y. Died June 21, 1949.

STONG, Philip Duffield (stŏng), author; b. Keosauqua, Ia., Jan. 27, 1899; s. Benjamin J. and Ada Evesta (Duffield) S.; A.B., Drake U., 1919, LL.D., 1947; graduate student, 1924-25; grad. student Columbia, 1920-21, U. of Kan., 1923-24; Litt.D., Parsons Coll., 1939; m. Virginia Maude Swain, Nov. 8, 1925. Athletic dir. and teacher high schs., 1919-23; editorial writer Des Moines (Ia.) Register and instr. debate and journalism, Drake U., 1923-25; wire editor Associated Press, N.Y. City, 1925-26; copy editor North American Newspaper Alliance, 1926-27; with Liberty Magazine, 1928; with Editor and Publisher, 1929; with World, 1929-31. Fellow Am. Geogl. Soc.; Soc. Am. Historians. Club: Authors. Mason (32°, K.T.). Author: State Fair, 1932; Stranger's Return, 1933; Village Tale, 1934; Farm Boy (juvenile), 1934; Week End, 1935; Farmer in the Dell, 1935; Career, 1935; Honk the Moose (juvenile), 1935; No-Sitch! The Hound (juvenile), 1936; Buckskin Breeches, 1937; High Water, (juvenile), 1937; The Rebellion of Lennie Barlow, 1937; Edgar: the 7:58, Young Settler (juvenile), 1938; The Long Lane, 1939; The Hired Man's Elephant (N.Y. Herald-Tribune award), 1939; Cowhand Goes to Town (juvenile), 1939; Horses and Americans, 1939; Ivanhoe Keeler, 1939; Hawkeyes; A Biography of the State of Iowa, 1940; If School Keeps, 1940; Captain Kidd's Cow (juvenile), 1941; The Other Worlds (anthology), 1941; The Princess, 1941; Way Down Cellar (juvenile), 1942; The Iron Mountain, 1942; One Destiny, 1942; Missouri Canary (Juvenile), 1943; Marta of Muscovy, 1945; Censored, the Goat, 1945; Positive Pete, 1947; The Prince and the Porker, 1950; Forty Pounds of Gold, 1951; Hiram, the Hillbilly (juvenile), 1951; Return in August, 1953; Mississippi Pilot, 1954; Blizzard, 1955; Adventure of Horse Barnsby, 1956; Gold in Them Hills, 1957; Mike (juvenile), 1957. Contbr. mags. Home: Keosauqua, Ia. Address: Washington, Conn. Died Apr. 26, 1957; buried Keosauqua, Ia.

STONIER, Harold (stōn'ī-ẽr), educator; b. San Jose, Calif., Jan. 13, 1890; s. Alfred E. and Rella K. (Haynes) S.; Coll. of Pacific, 1909-10; B.A., U. of Southern Calif., 1913, M.A., 1915; postgrad. study U. of Calif. and Columbia; Dr. Business Adminstrn, U. of Southern Calif., 1928; LL.D., Miami U., Oxford, O., 1939; Litt.D., Rutgers Univ., New Brunswick, N.J., 1942; m. Lucille Holderness, Dec. 21, 1917. Teacher economics, Jr. Coll., U. of Southern Calif., 1915-17; in investment business, 1917-18; teacher of economics, U. of Southern Calif., 1918-25, v.p. of univ., 1925-27; nat. ednl. dir. Am. Inst. of Banking, 1927-40; dir. Grad. School Banking, 1935-55, dean, 1955—; was executive manager of the American Bankers Association, 1937-52, exec. v.p., 1952-55. Mem. Com. on Edn. by Radio, 1929-30. Pres. Pacific Advt. Clubs Assn.; v.p. Internat. Adv. Assn.; mem. American Assn. Adult Edn. (treas.), Kappa Alpha, Alpha Kappa Psi, Phi Beta Kappa. Apptd. by President Hoover official del. to Internat. Congress on Commercial Edn., London, 1932. Awarded Call Alumni Trophy by U. of Southern Calif., 1937; Rutgers U. award for service to edn., 1937. Clubs: Union League (N.Y.); Asheville Country (N.C.). Lectr. on bus. and polit. topics. Methodist. Home: 200 N. Griffing Blvd., Asheville, N.C. Office: 12 E 36th St., N.Y.C. 16. Died June 3, 1957; buried Lewis Memorial Cemetery, Asheville, N.C.

STOOKEY, Stephen Wharton, educator; b. Marion, Ia., Apr. 3, 1859; s. Levi J. and Sarah Jane (Clark)

S.; student Cornell Coll., Ia., 1878-81; B.S., Coe Coll., 1884, M.S., 1887, LL.D., 1905; U. Chgo., 1895-96, State U. Ia., 1891-93; m. Isabel Graham, Dec. 23, 1887; children—Robert Marshall, Stanley Clark, Donald Graham, Dorothy Margaret. Supt. city schs., Manchester, Ia., 1884-91; prof. natural sciences, 1892-1900, geology and botany, 1900-08, dean, 1901-08, acting pres., 1904-05, Coe Coll., Ia.; pres. Bellevue (Neb.) Coll., 1908-13; dean Coe Coll., 1913-33, emeritus dean, prof. geology 1933—, acting pres., 1918-19. Asst. on Ia. Geol. Survey, 1906-10; on Neb. Geol. Survey, 1912. Fellow A.A.A.S.; mem. Bot. Soc. Am., Ia. Acad. Sciences, Sigma Xi. Republican. Presbyn. Author: Geology of Iowa County, Iowa; Geology of Poweshiek County, Iowa; New Data on the Upper Devonian of Iowa; Correlation, Upper Devonian of Iowa. Home: 2505 A Av., N.E., Cedar Rapids, Ia. Died Sept. 27, 1951; buried Oak Hill Cemetery, Cedar Rapids, Ia.

STORER, Norman Wilson, elec. engr.; b. Orangeville, O., Jan. 11, 1868; s. Simon Brewster and Lemira (Jones) S.; M.E., Ohio State U., 1891; m. Elizabeth W. Perry, June 14, 1899 (dec. Jan. 14, 1908); children—Norman Wyman, Elizabeth Perry, Morris Brewster, Florence Treadwell; m. 2d, Ruth Esther Beyer, Dec. 7, 1911. Designer direct current generators, motors Westinghouse Electric & Mfg. Co., 1891, successively charge design elec. ry. apparatus, cons. ry. engr., specializing elec. transportation problems, development electric locomotives, electrification of steam rys. until 1936. Awarded Lamme medal Am. Inst. E.E. Fellow Am. Inst. E.E.; mem. Unitarian Layman's League. Home: 6818 Reynolds St., Pitts. Office: Care of American Institute Electrical Engineers, 33 W. 39th St., N.Y.C. Died June 5, 1947.

STOREY, Walter Rendell, critic of decorative art; b. Phila., Pa., June 22, 1881; s. Edwin Adams and Elizabeth (Rendell) S.; student Pa. Museum Sch. Indsl. Arts, Phila., 1900-02, Pa. Acad. Fine Arts, Phila., 1903-08, Academy Julian, Paris, France, under Jean Paul Laurens, 1908-09; m. Muriel Alice Flewitt, Feb. 27, 1914 (died 1918); m. 2d, Helen Edith Anderson, Jan. 1, 1925; children—Hildred Anderson (Mrs. Clifford Geertz), Warren Charles. Exec. sec. Nat. Bd. of Review of Motion Pictures, N.Y. City, 1909-42; with govt. and social orgns., designing ednl. social exhibits, and writing on art, 1913-26; critic of decorative art, N.Y. Times, 1926-49; lectr. decorative art, N.Y. Univ. 1935-43, and Furniture World Ednl. Inst. Silver medal for artistry in ednl. exhibit World's Fair, San Francisco, 1915. Author: Beauty in Home Furnishings; Period Influences in Interior Decoration; A Handbook of Home Decoration (with Helen Anderson Storey); Chippendale: A Sketch of His Life and Works; Hepplewhite; Sheraton; Furnishing with Color; Furnishing with Style. Lecturer. Contbr. to nat. mags. Home: 12 Mountain View Court, Cresskill, N.J. Died Nov. 26, 1953.

STORM, John M(ahley), editor; b. Nevada, Ia., Feb. 26, 1899; s. Jeremiah V. and Anna Frances (Lyons) S.; student Ia. State Coll., 1919-22; m. Evelyn Hershey, July 2, 1928; 1 son, John Hershey. Reporter Des Moines Tribune, 1922-24, Indpls. Star, 1924-26; reporter Cleve. News, 1926-38, asso. editor, head editorial writer, 1938-43; mng. editor of Hospitals (jour. Am. Hosp. Assn.), 1943-51, editor, bus. mgr., 1951—. Mem. Theta Delta Chi, Sigma Delta Chi. Conglist. Home: 124 Seventh Av., La Grange, Ill. Office: 18 E. Division St., Chgo. 10. Died Nov. 4, 1951.

STORRS, Leonard Kip, clergyman; b. Yonkers, N.Y., Nov. 4, 1842; s. Henry L. and Elizabeth (Kip) S.; A.B., Trinity Coll., Conn., 1863, A.M., 1866, S.T.D., 1893; m. Miss Kingsbury, June 1, 1871 (died Dec. 1874); 2d, Mrs. A. F. Adams, Oct. 14, 1906. Deacon, 1869, priest, 1870, P.E. Ch.; rector Hallowell, Me., 1869-71, Pittsfield, Mass., 1871-75, St. Paul's, Brookline, Mass., 1875-1910, now rector emeritus. Address: Brookline, Mass. Died Feb. 17, 1923.

STORY, Walter P., army officer; b. Bozeman, Mont., Dec. 18, 1883; s. Nelson and Ellen S.; ed. pvt. and pub. schs., Mont. and Cal.; Eastman Coll., 1902; Shattuck Mil. Acad., 1903; U.S. Army War Coll., 1933; Leavenworth 9th Corps Area, 1939; Gen. Officers Course, Ft. Benning, 1940; m. Lorenza Lazzarini, May 17, 1923. Enlisted as private in infantry, World War I; commd. capt. Infantry, Calif. National Guard, Dec. 1920, maj., 1921, col., 1922; organized and comd. 160th Infantry; brig. general of the line, July, 1926; comd. Long Beach, Calif. Area, during earthquake, 1933; major gen., July 1937; comd. 9th Army Corps, Ft. Lewis, summer 1940; entered Fed. Service Mar. 1941, assigned command of 40th Div. in training, Camp Merriam, Calif., relieved from comd. due to protracted illness, Sept. 1941, retired from active list July, 1942; maj. gen. Hon. Res., by order of sec. of army placed on A.U.S. ret. list, grade maj. gen., 1948. Decorations: Victory Medal, over 25 yrs. service medal; Medal of Merit; Pre-Pearl Harbor medal; Am. Def. Service Ribbon; Order Crown of Italy. Bookkeeper and teller, Comml. Nat. Bank, Bozeman, Montana; moved to Los Angeles, 1905, managed and pioneered first motor transit lines in West, in Tonopah-Goldfield, Nev., 1906; real estate business, Los Angeles, 1907—; former v.p. L.A. Realty Bd., former mem. L.A. Fire and Police Pension Commn.; former dir. 6th Dist. Agrl. Assn., State of Cal.; chmn. bd. Mullen & Bluett Clothing Co.; pres. Building Owners and Mgrs. Assn. Los Angeles. Mem. S.R., Colonial Wars, Am. Legion (past comdr.), Spanish-Am. War Vets. (hon.), former mil. chmn. Los Angeles C. of C. Clubs: California, Bel Air Bay, Bohemian (San Francisco); Rancho Visitadores (Santa Barbara). Home: Penthouse, Story Bldg.; and 3405 Laurel Canyon Blvd., North Hollywood. Office: Walter P. Story Bldg., 6th and Broadway, Los Angeles 14. Deceased.

STORY, Walter Scott, author; b. Springfield, Mass., June 23, 1879; s. Benjamin Franklin and Jennie Rebecca (Turner) S.; ed. pub. schs.; m. Margaret Helena Healy, Feb. 27, 1908 (died 1937); m. 2d, Elsie Martha Wolcott, Mar. 14, 1940. Began as office boy, Mass. Mut. Life Ins. Co., 1895, later sec. to pres. of Co.; mgr. lit. dept. Mut. Life Ins. Co. of N.Y., 1923-42, editor The Mut. Circle, 1942-46; now ret. (Mut. Life Ins. Co. employee mag.). Mem. Authors' League Am., S.A.R. Republican. Mason. Author: Skinny Harrison, Adventurer, 1922; The Young Crusader; How Richard of Devon Served Richard the Lion-Hearted, 1923; The Unchartered Island, 1926; Boy Heroes of the Sea, 1928; The Missing Million; also about 140 novelletes and short stories. Home: 14 Burnet St., Maplewood, N.J. Died June 23, 1955.

STOTT, Roscoe Gilmore (stŏt), writer, lecturer; b. Franklin, Ind., Oct. 29, 1880; s. William Taylor and Arabella Ruth (Tracy) S.; A.B., Franklin, 1904, hon. A.M., 1916; Litt.D., Lenox Coll., Iowa, 1917; U. of Chicago, 1905-06; m. Isabel Porter, Oct. 2, 1907; children—Isabel Tracy, Gilmore, Edith Porter. Instr., Drury Coll., 1906, Mich. Agrl. Coll., 1908-09; head English dept., Eastern Ky. State Teachers Sch., 1910-16; Lyceum and Chautauqua lecturer since 1910; extension lecturer, Lenox Coll., 1917; mem. faculty Ohio School of the Air, 1930-33; dir. Cleaner Homes Inst., 1935; mem. speakers staff Rep. Nat. Com., dir. Lockyear Forum of Speech and Human Relations (Evansville, Ind.), affiliate Dale Carnegie Inst., N.Y. City, 1945-51; now director Statt Forum of Educational services; mem. speaker staff Rep. Nat. Com., 1936. Mem. Authors League America, Internat. Lyceum Assn., N.E.A., Ky. Ednl. Assn., Phi Delta Theta. Republican. Baptist. Mason. Club: Rotary (hon.). Author: (verse) The Man Sings, 1914; Selling Since Adam; The Smiths Discover America—The Story of Americanization at Work, 1920; Walking Shadows (verse), 1929; How to Win Boys, 1937; Doorway to Dawn (religious novel), 1940; When Boys Ask Questions, 1941; also Somebody's Little Gray Shadow (children's operetta), Happy Home Series (psychology of marriage booklets), songs, mag. articles, etc. Lectures: A Man-size Job; Dying on Third; My Friend—The World; Starving Kings; Paying Caesar; Birds I Would Like to Shoot—and Others; Moving the Machine, and numerous other lit. and ednl. addresses. Editor of Poe's Poems and Tales; asso. editor Lyceum Mag.; cons. editor Mid-West Literary Bur.; contbg. editor Standard Pub. Co., 1934-43; lit. editor Hobson Book Press, Cincinnati-Cynthiana, Ky.), 1943-45; sometime lit. adviser to Gibson Art Co. and Henderson Lithographing Co.; educational advisor to National Teachers Agency of Cincinnati, 1931-32; president Stott Institute of Public Speech, 1932-33. Prominent in National 4-H Club work. Has made over 1,000 high sch. commencement addresses. Author of Fight the Foe (temperance program material), 1939; Dear Shut-In (informational book for invalids), 1944. Contbr. spl. features to The Christian Herald, 1943-45. Address: Patriot, Ind. Died Jan. 12, 1957.

STOUFFER, Gordon A., restaurant ofcl.; b. Cleve., May 7, 1905; s. A. E. and Mahala (Bigelow) S.; student Mercersburg (Pa.) Acad., Cheshire (Conn.) Acad., U. Sch., Cleve.; married 2d, Mary Augusta Biddle, May 7, 1952; stepchildren—Elizabeth Wood, Mary Seton, Christopher Fleming. Exec. v.p., gen. mgr., dir. Stouffer Corp., 1930-53, chmn., 1953—; pres., dir. Portersville (Pa.) Stainless Equipment Corp. Bd. control Cleve. Zool. Park. Mem. Hoover Commn. Task Force on Subsistence Services. Served as col. USAAF, World War II. Decorated Legion of Merit. Mem. C. of C. (del. Internat. C. of C. meeting, Japan, 1955). Episcopalian. Clubs: Union, Pepper Pike Country, Kirtland, The Country, City (Cleve.); Metropolitan, Canadian (N.Y.C.); Cat Key (Cat Cay, Bahamas); Fin 'n Feather (Dundee, Ill.). Home: Rte. 3, Chagrin Falls, O. Office: 1375 Euclid Av., Cleve. 15. Died June 3, 1956; buried Knollwood Cemetery.

STOUGHTON, Bradley, metall. engr.; b. New York, N.Y., Dec. 6, 1873; s. Coll. Charles Bradley (LL.D.) and Ada Ripley (Hooper) S.; Ph.B., Sheffield Scientific School, 1893; B.S., Mass. Inst. Tech., 1896; D.Eng., Lehigh U. 1943; m. Grace A. Van Everen, Jan. 4, 1899 (died Jan. 15, 1905); 1 son, Philip V.; m. 2d, L. Merwin, d. E. P. and Anna P. (Sands) Roe, Nov. 1, 1911; children—Sandroe, Rosamond, Leila Roosevelt. Teacher, Mass. Inst. Tech., 1896; asst. to Prof. H. M. Howe, Columbia U., 1897; metallurgist Ill. Steel Co., S. Chicago, Ill., 1898-99; chief of cost statis. div. Am. Steel & Wire Co., Cleveland, 1900; mgr. Bessemer steel dept., Benjamin Atha & Co., Newark, N.J., 1901; in business as consulting engr., 1902. Instr. adj. prof. and acting head dept. of metallurgy, Sch. of Mines, Columbia U., 1902-08; prof. metallurgy, Lehigh U., 1923—; also dean of Coll. of Engring. until 1939; chief heat treating equipment unit, Tools Section, WPB, 1941-45, acting head foundry equipment sect., 1944-45; London rep. tech. indsl. intelligence com. Fgn. Econ. Assn., July-Sept. 1945. Mem. bd. dir. Lukens Steel Co. Mem. Gen. Engring. Co., Nat. Council of Defense, 1918-19; head of metallurgical division, later v.-chmn. engring. div., Nat. Research Council; mem. welding com., Emergency Fleet Corp., 1918-20. Mem. Am. Inst. Mining and Metall. Engrs. (sec. 1913-21; chmn. iron and steel com., 1922-23), Am. Electrochem. Soc. (chmn. electrothermic div. 1922; pres. 1931), Yale Engring. Assn. (pres. 1922-24), Am. Iron and Steel Inst., Iron and Steel Inst. (Eng.), Am. Soc. for Metals (treas., 1938-39; pres. 1941), Am. Soc. for Testing Materials, Engrs. Club of Lehigh Valley (pres. 1928-29), corr. mem. Canadian Inst. Mining and Metallurgy; hon. mem. Yale Engring. Assn. Inventor converter for making steel castings, and a process for oil melting in cupolas. Club: Cosmos (Washington, D.C.). Author: The Metallurgy of Iron and Steel, 1908; Engineering Metallurgy (with Allison Butts), 1926. Made the field study and wrote technical report used by President Harding in his successful campaign to secure the 8-hour day in the U.S. steel industry, 1922. Awarded Grasselli medal by Soc. of Chem. Industry, 1929. In 1939 Lehigh Valley Chapter of Am. Soc. for Metals established Annual Stoughton Night, and in 1943, the Bradley Stoughton Award for outstanding contbn. to Metall. by a member of Lehigh Valley Chapter. Home: Bethlehem, Pa. Died Dec. 29, 1959.

STOUT, Arlow Burdette, botanist; b. Jackson Center, O., Mar. 10, 1876; s. Hezekiah Milton and Harriet (Bond) S.; grad. State Normal Sch., Whitewater, Wis., 1903; A.B., U. Wis., 1909; Ph.D., Columbia, 1913; m. Zelda Judd Howe, June 22, 1909; children—Elizabeth Bond (Mrs. Herman Rausch), Arlow Burdette (dec.). Instr. botany U. Wis., 1909-11; dir. labs., N.Y. Bot. Garden, 1911-38, curator edn. and labs., 1938-47, emeritus. Recipient Roland medal from Mass. Hort. Soc., William Herbert medal from Am. Amarylis Soc.; Gold medal from Hort. Soc. N.Y.; Bertram Farr award, Am. Hemerocallis Soc.; Distinguished Service award, N.Y. Botanical Gardens. Fellow A.A.A.S., N.Y. Acad. Scis.; mem. Soc. Am. Naturalists, Am. Hemerocallis Society, Baraboo Wis. Hist. Soc., Bot. Soc. Am. Torrey Bot. Club, Am. Soc. Hort. Sci., Am. Amaryllis Soc., Am. Genetic Assn., Genetics Soc. Am., Ohio State Hist. and Archaeol. Soc., Wis. Archaeol. Soc., Hort Soc. N.Y. (hon. life mem.), Pa. Hort. Soc., Royal Hort. Soc., Phi Beta Kappa, Sigma Xi. Spl. fields sci. research, genetics, plant breeding, cytology, sterilities in flowering plants. Home: 4 Grove St., Pleasantville, N.Y. Office: N.Y. Botanical Garden, N.Y.C. Died Oct. 12, 1957; buried Kensico Cemetery, Valhalla, N.Y.

STOUT, Howard A(ckerman), architect; b. Bucks Co., Pa., June 29, 1874; s. Henry S. and Amanda K. (Ackerman) S.; Arch., U. Pa., class 1895; m. Grace D. Morton, Oct. 14, 1901. Practicing architect since 1895. Mem. N. J. State Bd. Architects, 1927-50, pres., 1932-49. Fellow A.I.A. Home: 1105 Shore Rd., Northfield, N.J. Office: Guarantee Trust Bldg., Atlantic City. Died May 19, 1959; buried Laurel Meml. Park, Pomona, N.J.

STOUT, William Bushnell, aero. engr.; b. Quincy, Ill., Mar. 16, 1880; s. Rev. James Frank and Mary L. (Bushnell) S.; ed. Hamline U., St. Paul, 1899-1900; U. Minn., 1901-02; m. Alma E. Raymond, June 16, 1906; 1 dau., Wilma Frances. Tech. and aviation editor Chgo. Tribune, 1912; joined staff of Motor Age and Automobile; founded Aerial Age; moved to Detroit, 1914, as chief engr. Scirpps-Booth Co., advt. mgr., 1915, gen. sales mgr., 1916; apptd. chief engr. aircraft div., Packard Motor Car Co., 1917; during development of Liberty engine. Apptd. tech. adv. to Aircraft Bd., Washington, D.C.; built for bd. the first internally braced cantilever airplane in Am., veneer and wood constrn.; founded Stout Engring. Labs. and built 1st Am. comml. monoplane, known as Batwing, flown at Selfridge field, 1919; undertook contract, 1920, for first metal plane built in U.S., an all metal torpedo plane for U.S. Navy, flown by Eddie Stinson, Selfridge field, 1922; formed, 1922, Stout Metal Airplane Co., to build comml. metal planes. Built air sedan, three seater cabin plane, all metal, and later Liberty engine eight passenger transport; sold Stout Metal Airplane Co. to Ford Motor Co., 1925, and served as v.p., gen. mgr. during development of Ford tri-motored transport plane from the original single engine transport. Started Stout Air Services, 1926, operating first exclusive passenger airplanes in U.S., Detroit to Grand Rapids; on development of tri-motors, transferred line, Detroit to Cleve.,

1927, and added the Detroit to Chgo. route; Stout Air Lines sold, 1929, to United Aircraft and Transport Co., N.Y.; Stout Engring. Labs. revived, 1929, for research and development work in aeros. Built and developed all-metal Sky Car, new type airplane for pvt. owner use; designed and built under a contract with The Pullman Car and Mfg. Corp., a high-speed "Railplane" as a basis of change in r.r. passenger work; recnelty developed new fibreglas automobile with engine in rear, at Graham-Paige Motors Corp., Willow Run, Mich. Commr. Mich. Aero. Commn. Dir. Nat. Aero. Assn. Past pres. Soc. Automotive Engrs., Inst. Aero. Scis.; mem. Detroit Aviation Soc. Clubs: Detroit Athletic, Orchard Lake Country. Home: 1331 W. Edgemont Av. Office: 2211 S. 19th Av., Phoenix. Died Mar. 20, 1956; buried Phoenix.

STOVALL, Wallace Fisher (stō'vål), b. Elizabethtown, Ky., Jan. 4, 1869; s. Jasper and Eliza (Duncan) S.; ed. pub. schs.; widower; children—Minnie (Mrs. J. H. Mason), Wallace O., Susan (Mrs. Richard Mack). Moved Fla., 1886; established the Ind., Lake Wier, Fla., at 16; moved to Ocala, edited, pub. Ocala Free Press; to Sumterville, edited, pub. Sumterville Times; to Polk County, established Polk County News; to Bartow, 1890, and to Tampa, 1893, established Tampa Morning Tribune; sold Tribune, 1925, and devotes attendion to real estate interests; largest individual property owner in Tampa; pres. Crestview Realty Co., Inc.; treas. Lithia Springs, Inc.; dir. Old Peoples Home, Hillsborough County Humane Soc. Democrat. Presbyn. Mason, Elk. Home: 1806 Jetton Av. Office: Stovall's Professional Bldg., Tampa, Fla. Died Apr. 16, 1950.

STOW, Charles Messer, editor, writer; b. Hudson, O., Apr. 10, 1880; s. George William and Charlotte Adelle (Messer) S.; student Stanford, 1900-01, U. Mich., 1901-02; m. 3d Millicent Dingwell Lampee, Nov. 10, 1929. With Grand Rapids (Mich.) Herald, 1899-1900; editorial staff Portland Oregonian, 1906-10, Christian Science Monitor, Boston, 1910-24, exec. editor, 1922-24; editorial staff Boston Eve. Transcript, 1924-29; editor antiques dept. N.Y. Sun, 1929-50; lectr. antiques and culture history; antiquarian editor N.Y. World -Telegram and Sun since 1950. Trustee N.Y. State Hist. Assn., Am. Scenic and Historic Preservation Soc., N.Y. City History Club, Municipal Art Soc., Early Am. Industries Assn. Fellow Rochester (N.Y.) Mus. Arts and Scis.; mem. N.Y. Hist. Soc. (asso.), Am. Hist. Assn., Assn. for State and Local History Am. Inst. Decorators (hon.), Soc. for Preservation N.E. Antiquities, Am. Planning and Civic Assn., Am. Inst. Archaeology, Am. Assn. Adult Edn., Art and Antique Dealers League Am., Bill of Rights Commemoration Soc. (hon.), Am. Designers Inst. (hon.); hon. mem. numerous collectors' clubs. Mason (32°). Clubs: Century, Delta Kappa Epsilon, Grolier (N.Y. City). Compiler: Best Fifty Currier and Ives Prints, large folio, 1933, small folio, 1934. Contbr. antiques and culture history publs. Home: 502 Park Av., N.Y.C. Died May 15, 1952.

STOW, Marcellus H(enry), prof. of geology; b. Washington, D.C., May 19, 1902; s. James Warren and Lizzie R. (Miller) S.; A.B., Cornell U., 1926, A.M., 1927, Ph.D., 1931; m. Grace Wilhelmina Hammond, July 1, 1932. Asst. in geology, Cornell U., 1924-26, instr., 1926-27; asst. prof. geology, Washington and Lee Univ., 1927-34, asso. prof. and acting head dept. geol., 1934-37, Robinson prof. head of dept., 1937—, Thomas Ball prof., 1947—; on leave of absence as dept. dir. mining div. War Production Board, Jan. 1942-Jan. 1946; chief mining branch, Civilian Production Adminstrn., Nov.-Dec. 1945; with U.S. Geol. Survey, summers 1923, 24, 26; Lehigh Valley Coal Co., summer 1925; asst. prof. geology, Cornell U., summers 1929-31; field geology and research Yellowstone-Bighorn Research Assn., summers, 1933—; geol. cons. U.S. AEC, 1953—; geol. cons. to dir. Va. Dept. of Conservation and Development. Awarded scholarship, geology department, Cornell U., 1930-31. Mem. Governor's Adv. Council on Va. Economy, 1948— (chmn. mining com. 1948-49, mem., 1948—). Fellow Geol. Society America, A.A.A.S.; mem. American Association Petroleum geologists, Mineral Soc. Am., Am. Geophys. Union, Am. Inst. Metall. Engrs., Va. Acad. Sci. (mem. council 1939-46, pres. 1942-43, chmn. James River project com., 1941—; chairman long range planning com., 1950-54, chmn. Jamestown Celebration Com.), Geochem. Soc., Wash. Academy Science, Yellowstone Bighorn Research Assn. (council 1935-44, pres. 1939-41, 1944-45); mem. advisory board Virginia Fisheries Lab., Va. State Museum Commn., Southern Assn. Sci. and Industry (exec. com.), Nat. Research Council (sub-committee on pre-doctoral fellowships, 1946), Southern Research Institute (advisory council 1945, board directors, 1945—), Society Am. Mil. Engrs., Soc. Econ. Paleontology and Mineralogy, Sigma Xi, Phi Kappa Phi, Sigma Gamma Epsilon, Sigma Phi Epsilon, Phi Beta Kappa. Received War Dept. citation, Dec. 1945. Club: Cosmos. Author: Mineral Resources and Mineral Industry of Virginia. Editor: The James River Basin—Past, Present and Future. Contbr. to geol. jours. Address: 405 Morningside Heights, Lexington, Va. Died Nov. 27, 1957; buried Stonewall Jackson Cemetery, Lexington, Va.

STOWE, Ansel Roy Monroe (stō), educator; b. Walkerton, Ind., Aug. 30, 1882; s. Dennis Lowery and Leonora Grace (Monroe) S.; Ph.B., Northwestern U., 1903, A.M., 1904; A.M., Harvard, 1905; Ph.D., Columbia, 1909; m. Marjorie Henry, Sept. 5, 1907; 1 son, David Henry. Chicago Harvard Club scholar at Harvard, 1904-05; fellow, Teachers Coll. (Columbia), 1905-06; prin. Central Sch., Darien, Conn., 1906-07; prin. Hyannis (Mass.) Training Sch., 1907-09; prof. history and philosophy of edn., State Normal Coll., Emporia, Kan., 1909-12; supervisor practice teaching, Whitewater (Wis.) Normal Sch., 1912-13; acting prof. edn., DePauw U., Greencastle, Ind., 1913-14; pres. U. of the City of Toledo, 1914-25; prof. education, Randolph-Macon Woman's College, 1926-34; director Lynchburg Extension Center of U. of Va., 1929-30; visiting prof. collegiate edn., Duke U., summers, 1928-34, 37, 41; prof. of education U. of N.H., since 1934, research professor of education since 1950, chmn. Div. Teacher Education, Univ. N.H., 1944-46. Mem. N.E.A., Nat. and New Eng. Coll. Teachers of Edn., Phi Beta Kappa, Pi Gamma Mu, Kappa Delta Pi; corr. academician Royal Acad. Fine Arts and Hist. Sciences, Toledo, Spain. Conglist. Mason 32°. Author: Modernizing The College; Studies in New England College Association; books relating to edn. Home: 10 Madbury Road, Durham, N.H. Died July 16, 1952; buried Lakeview Cemetery, New Canaan, Conn.

STOWELL, Ellery Cory (stō'ăl), educator; b. Lynn, Mass., Dec. 12, 1875; s. George L. and Adeline Tapley (Fuller) S.; A.B., Harvard, 1898; traveled in Orient and Europe, 1901-02, Russia, 1902-03; studied U. of Berlin, 1903-04; U. Paris, 1904-07, Licencié en droit, 1906, Docteur en droit, 1909; grad. Diplomatic Sect., École libre des Sciences Politiques, Paris, 1906; m. Cecile M. Roberts, June 5, 1912; children—Anne Dudley (Mrs. Mairesse), Isabel Roby (Mrs. Pitt), Ellery Cory. Chemist, Diamond Rubber Company, Akron, O., 1898-99; clerk in San Francisco National Bank, 1899-1901; secretary College Polit. Sciences, Washington, 1908-09; instr. internat. law, George Washington Univ., 1908-10; asst. prof. internat. law, U. Pa., 1910-13; lectr. internat. law, 1913-14, asst. prof., 1914-16, asso. prof. internat. law, 1916-18, Columbia U.; prof. internat. law, The American U., 1922—, also chmn. of dept. of internat. affairs, 1935-1944; exchange prof. U. Wash., 1942-43. Pres. Better Government League, Washington, 1935—; sec. adjoint 2d Peace Conf., The Hague, 1907, and sec. of delegation of Panama to same conf.; sec. Am. delegation, Naval Conf., London, 1908-09. Club: Cosmos. Author: Le Consul, 1909; Consular Cases and Opinion, 1909; The Diplomacy of the War of 1914, 1915; Intervention in International Law, 1921; International Law, 1931. Joint Author: International Cases, Vol I, Peace, Vol. II, War and Neutrality. Address: 116 Divisadero St., San Francisco 17. Died Jan. 1958.

STRABEL, Thelma (strā'bĕl), writer; b. Crown Point, Ind.; d. John George and Nannie Hall (Wiley); married Frederick A. Locher, April 19, 1927 (divorced 1937); married second, David P. Godwin, Oct. 25, 1941. Feature writer Associated Editors, Chgo. and N.Y.C., fashion writer Paris (France) Herald; advt. copywriter Abraham & Straus, N.Y.C. Mem. Theta Sigma Phi. Author: Reap the Wild Wind, 1940; Storm to the South, 1944; Caribee, 1957. Contbr. fiction. nat. mags. Home: 1407 31st St., Washington. Died May 28, 1959; buried Charleston, S.C.

STRADLEY, Bland Lloyd, educator; b. Frazeysburg, O., Oct. 29, 1889; s. Howard David and Flora (Fawcett) S.; A.B., Ohio Wesleyan Univ., 1913; LL.D., 1936; grad. student Harvard, 1914-15; LL.D., Ohio Northern University, Ada, Ohio, 1935, Wilberforce University, 1943, Central State College, 1952; D.Ed., U. of Dayton (O.) 1945; m. Elizabeth Cowan, 1917; children—Eliza Bartlit, David Cowan, Prin. high sch., Canal Winchester, 1913-14, Walpole, Mass. 1915-16; Univ. examiner, Ohio State Univ., 1920-44, and dean arts and sciences, 1937-44; vice-pres. Ohio State U., 1944—. Mem. Canal Winchester Bd. Edn.; mem. Acacia, Phi Delta Kappa, Kappa Delta Rho. Methodist (trustee). Mason (33°, K.T., Shriner). Clubs: Faculty, Lions, Torch, Rotary, Columbus, Internat. Gyro (Columbus, O.); Harvard of Central Ohio. Home: Canal Winchester, O. Died Aug. 4, 1957; buried Canal Winchester.

STRADLEY, Leighton Paxton, lawyer; b. Cumberland, Md., Jan. 2, 1880; s. Leonidas P. and Elizabeth (Kettlewell) S.; student St. Paul's Sch.; B.A., U. Pa., 1905, LL.B., 1906; m. Kathryn Wilson, 1907; children—Leighton P., Bentham W., Wilson. Admitted to Pa. bar, 1908; sr. partner Stradley, Ronon, Stevens & Young, Phila., 1926-54; asst. prof. finance U. Pa., 1916-43. Chmn. Pa. Tax Inst., 1947-54. Mem. Am., Pa., Phila. bar assns., S.A.R., Germantown Hist. Soc. (hon. pres.), Am. Sunday Sch. Union (dir.), Phi Sigma Kappa (nat. sec.). Mason. Clubs: Union League, Philadelphia Country (pres. 1949-51) (Phila.). Author: Finance and Investments; (with I. H. Krekstein) Corporate Taxation and Procedures in Pennsylvania, 1940. Address: care Wilson Stradley, Western Saving Fund Bldg., Broad and Chestnut Sts., Phila. 7. Died Apr. 18, 1956.

STRAHM, Victor H., army officer; b. Nashville, Oct. 26, 1895; s. Franz Joseph and Alice Elizabeth (Jones) S.; student Western Ky. Tchrs. Coll., 1911-15, U. Ky., 1915-17, U. Wis., 1919-20, Air Force Engring. Sch., 1923-24, Air Force Tactical Sch., 1931-32, Command and Gen. Staff sch., 1935-36, Army War Coll., 1938-39. Commd. lt. (pilot), Oct. 26, 1917, and advanced through the grades to brig. gen., 1942; Ace (credited with destruction over five enemy aircraft), World War I; comd. 91st Aero Squadron, Army of Occupation, Coblenz, 1919; served in various capacities at Army Air Corps and Air Force stations after World War I; chief of staff, 9th U.S. Air Force, Sept. 30, 1942—; now stationed overseas. Awarded D.S.C., Silver Star, French Croix de Guerre with Two Palms, Legion of Merit. Mem. Sigma Alpha Epsilon. Home: 1349 College Av., Bowling Green, Ky. Died May, 1957.

STRANG, S(amuel) Bartow, lawyer; b. Chattanooga, Tenn., Aug. 7, 1882; s. Samuel Bartow and Frances Gregory (Thornton) S.; LL.B., U. Tenn., 1905; m. Alice Neilson Sharp, June 3, 1913; children—Samuel Bartow, John Sharp, F. Thornton, James Maynard. Admitted to Tenn. bar, 1905 and since practiced in Chattanooga; mem. Strang, Fletcher & Carriger; rep. receiver 1st Nat. Bank of Chattanooga, 1937-45. Mem. Tenn. Bd. Edn., 1939—; mem. Chattanooga Interracial Com., 20 yrs., chmn. 1941-45; past pres. Community Chest; dir. Chattanooga Pub. Library; attended 1st Mobilization for Human Needs at White House, 1933. Mem. Selective Service Draft Bd., World Wars I and II. Decorated for service as govt. appeal agt., World War II. Mem. bd. trustees Baroness Erlanger and Children's Hosp. Mem. Am., Tenn. (past pres.), and Chattanooga (past pres.) bar assns. Republican (Rep. mem. Hamilton Co. Election Commn., 1911, 1913). Episcopalian (chancellor Diocese Tenn.; sr. warden, lay del.). Clubs: Mountain City, Rotary. Home: 220 Lindsay St., Chattanooga E. Office: Hamilton Nat. Bank Bldg., Chattanooga 3. Died Sept. 2, 1954; buried Forrest Hills Cemetery, Chattanooga.

STRANGE, Michael (Mrs. Blanche Marie Louise Oelrichs Twede) (strānj) poet, author, actress; b. N.Y.C., 1890; d. Charles M. Oelrichs; ed. schs. N. Y.C. and Paris; m. Leonard Thomas, 1908; m. 2d, John Barrymore, 1920; m. 3d Harrison Twee, May 23, 1929. Has appeared in Man of Destiny, Importance of Being Earnest, Easter; played Queen Anne in Richard III, Chrysothemis in Electra, L'Aiglon in L'Aiglon; also appeared in Barbara Frietchie. Lectures and gives programs of poetry with music accompaniment. Author: Poems, 1919; Resurrecting Life (poems), 1921; Clair de Lune, 1921; Selected Poems, 1928; Who Tells Me True (autobiography), 1940. Address: 186 East End Av., N.Y.C. Died Nov. 5, 1950.

STRANGE, Robert, lawyer; b. N.Y.C.; Sept. 21, 1888; s. Joseph Huske and Kate (Egbertson) S.; grad. Columbia Sch., South Orange, N.J., 1904; A. B., Princeton, 1909; LL.B., N.Y. Law Sch., 1911; m. Edna Holcomb Bowne, Mar. 7, 1916; children—Betty-Bowne (Mrs. E. C. Rose, Jr.), Nancy (Mrs. J. Harrison Gefaell). Admitted to bars of N.Y., 1911, N.J., 1913; master in chancery of N.J., 1916; organizer, managing exec. and counsel for various transportation and indsl. orgns.; mem. law firm Strange, Myers, Hinds and Wight. Trustee Community House, South Orange. Episcopalian. Clubs: Downtown Assn., Down Town Athletic (N.Y. City); Orange Lawn Tennis (South Orange, N.J.); Bay Head Yacht (Bay Head, N.J.). Home: 171 Grove Rd., South Orange, N.J.; also Bay Head, N.J. Office: 165 Broadway, N.Y.C. Died Oct. 13, 1949.

STRASBURGER, Milton, lawyer; b. Washington, D.C., Nov. 23, 1876; s. Zody and Sara (Ullman) S.; grad. high sch., Washington, D.C.; LL.B., Georgetown U., 1896, LL.M., 1898; D.C.L., George Washington U., 1900; m. Elsa Coblenzer, May 22, 1911; children—Beatrice, Betty. Served as sec. to commn. to revise laws of U.S., under Dept. of Justice, 1900-01; judge Municipal Court of D.C., 1914-18, reapptd. 1918 (resigned 1919); examiner appeal cases Provost Marshal Gen.'s Office, in connection with draft law, World War. Prof. of equity, Nat. Univ. Law Sch. Dir. Security Savings & Commercial Bank, Cofritz Mortgage Co., Ambassador Hotel, Washington. Mem. Bar Supreme Court of U.S., Am. Bar Assn., Bar Assn. of D.C. Democrat. Jewish religion. Mason, Elk. Club: Woodmont. Home: 1629 Columbia Rd. N.W. Office: Tower Bldg., 14th and K Sts. N.W., Washington. Died Feb. 6, 1955.

STRATHEARN, Harold (strā'thĕrn), church official; b. Dudley, Eng., Apr. 30, 1890; s. Alexander and Mary (Turner) S.; student Cliff Coll., Sheffield, Eng., 1908-12; D.D., Los Angeles Bapt. Theol. Sem., 1927; m. Dorothy M. Finn, July 16, 1918; 1 dau., Elizabeth Edith (Mrs. Willis E. Fox). Came to U.S., 1913, naturalized citizen, 1918. Ordained Baptist ministry, 1913; founder Interstate Evangelistic Assn., Inc., 1927 (since exec. sec.), LeTourneau

Evangelistic Center, 1938 (since dir.), LeTourneau Christian Camp, 1935 (since dir.), Christian Refugee Assn., 1943 (since dir.); dir. Winona Lake Christian Assembly, Nat. Bible Inst., All Nations Evangelistic Fellowship. Republican. Baptist. Address: Valley View Rd., Poughkeepsie, N.Y. Died May 15, 1950; buried Elmhurst, Pa.

STRATTON, Clarence, author; b. Phila., Sept. 17, 1880; s. Jacob Brown and Maria Katherine (Williams) S.; B.S., U. Pa., 1901, Ph.D., 1904; studied U. Chgo., Alliance Française, Paris, U. Rome; m. Celeste Warren Clark, Dec. 25, 1915; married 2d, Bernice Marie Reilly, Dec. 29, 1948. Tchr. English, Central High Sch., St. Louis, 1903-21; dir. English, high schs., Cleve., 1921-46. Lectr. Grad. Sch., Western Res. U., 1933-37, 1939-40, Cleve. Coll., 1938-39. Tchr. English, Colo. State Tchrs.' Coll., summer 1918, Western Res. U., summer, 1921-22; instr. pub. speaking, extension dept., Washington U., 1918-21; lectured Stratford-on-Avon, Eng., summer 1923, Bingley Tng. Coll., Eng., summers, 1923, 26. Mem. Nat. Council Tchrs. English, Soc. Midland Authors, Phi Beta Kappa, Rowfant Club. Author: Studies in English (with others), 1917; Public Speaking, 1920; Producing in Little Theaters, 1921; Literature and Life, 1922; Teaching of English in the High School, 1923; A Manual of English, 1925; Bombito; Ruby Red; Paul of France, 1927; Theatron, 1928; Harbor Pirates, 1929; Robert the Roundhead, 1930; In Singapore, 1932; Swords and Statues, 1937; To Read and To Act; When Washington Danced, 1938; Handbook of English, 1940; Improving Your Vocabulary, 1947; (with others) Making Meaning Clear; Expressing Ideas Clearly, 1942; Thinking and Writing Clearly, 1943; Mastering Your Language, 1947; Editor: Great American Speeches, 1920; Stories of Men's Achievements, 1931; Ginn's Modern Literature Series, 1931; Four Plays by Ibsen, 1931; Twelfth Night, 1936; (with others) Modern Short Stories, 1939; Poems for a Machine Age, 1941; Thinking It Through, 1941; Guide to Correct English; New Standard Course in Practical English, 1949; Effective English, 1951. Translator: (from the Spanish) Zaragüeta, 1919; (from the French) On the Margins of Old Books, 1929; Three Gallant Plays, 1929. Contbr. to English and Am. mags. Home: 1864 E. 97th St., Cleve. Died Sept. 13, 1950.

STRATTON, Don B., mfg. exec.; b. Howell, Mich., Mar. 23, 1899; s. L. A. and Ollie (Ford) S.; B.S., U. Mich., 1921; m. Esther L. Lyon, May 14, 1923; 1 son, Robert L. Engr., Nagel Elec. Co., Toledo, 1923 (co. merged with Moto Meter Co., 1926, Electric Auto-Lite Co., 1934), v.p. The lectric Auto-Lite Co., 1937——. Mem. Theta Delta Chi. Mason (K.T., Shriner). Clubs: The Toledo, Inverness (Toledo). Home: 3836 Brookside Rd., Ottawa Hills, Toledo 6. Office: Electric Auto-Lite Co., Toledo 1. Died Mar. 1958.

STRATTON, George Malcolm, psychologist; b. Oakland, Calif., Sept. 26, 1865; s. James T. and Cornelia A. (Smith) S.; A.B., U. of Calif., 1888; A.M., Yale, 1890; A.M., Ph.D., Leipzig, 1896; m. Alice Elenore Miller, May 17, 1894; children—Elenore (Mrs. Robert Fliess), Malcolm, Florence (Mrs. A. Reinke). Fellow in philosophy, 1891-93; instr. philosophy, 1893-96, University of Calif.; mem. Instit für Experimentelle Psychologie, Leipzig, 1894-96; instr., asst. prof. and asso. prof. psychology, 1896-1904, dir. psychol. lab., 1899-1904, U. of Calif.; prof. experimental psychology, Johns Hopkins, 1904-08; prof. psychology, U. of Calif., 1908-35, prof. emeritus psychology since 1935. Captain Aviation, United States Army, 1917; major head of psychology section Medical Research Laboratory, Mineola, Long Island, 1918. President American Psychology Association, 1908; mem. Nat. Research Council, 1921-24; chmn. anthrop. and psychol. div., same, 1925-26; mem. Nat. Acad. of Sciences; hon. mem. Nat. Inst. Psychology; corresponding mem. Am. Inst. of Czechoslovakia. Taylor lecturer, Yale Univ., 1920; lectured in various univs. of U.S., Europe and Orient. Chmn. Round Table Confs., Inst. of Politics, Williamstown, 1931, and at Riverside, Mills College, and elsewhere. Author: Experimental Psychology and Its Bearing upon Culture, 1903; Psychology of the Religious Life, 1911; Theophrastus and the Greek Physiological Psychology Before Aristotle, 1917; Developing Mental Power, 1922; Anger, Its Religious and Moral Significance, 1923; Social Psychology of International Conduct, 1929; International Delusions, 1936; (with J. W. Buckham) George Holmes Howison, Philosopher and Teacher, 1934; Man, Creator or Destroyer, 1952; also contributions to various psychological journals upon perception of change, eye movements, the aesthetics of visual form, railway accidents and the color sense, race, nations, and international action. Home: 2809 Hillegass Av., Berkeley, Cal. Died Oct., 1957.

STRAUS, Aaron, b. Baltimore, Dec. 2, 1864; coll. edn.; employed in furniture bus. with father and brothers after leaving coll.; pres. Reliable Stores Corp., 1925——. Address: 1 S. Howard St., Baltimore 1. Died Jan. 20, 1958.*

STRAUS, Martin L. II, corp. exec.; b. St. Louis, July 19, 1897; s. Louis and Amanda S.; ed. Smith Acad., Dartmouth Coll., U. Ill.; children—Martin L. III (deceased), Nancy Davis Gimble, Phillip B. Identified with advt., retail and investment banking bus. Chgo., 1920-32; former chmn. Eversharp, Inc.; chmn. Bymart-Tintair, Inc., N.Y.C., Marlowe Chem. Corp.; pres. The Advance Corp. Trustee Olivet Inst., Chgo., Nat. Unitarian Service Com. Served as pilot Army Air Service, World War I. Clubs: Stockbridge (Mass.) Golf; Lotus, Bankers, Dartmouth (N.Y.C.). Home: Great Barrington, Mass.; also N.Y.C.; Chgo. Offices: 15 W. 44th St., N.Y.C.; First Nat. Bank Bldg., Chgo. Died July 1958.

STRAUS, Oscar, composer, conductor; b. Vienna, Austria, Mar. 6, 1870; s. Louis and Gabriele (Stern) S.; studied, Vienna Conservatory and with Max Bruch, Berlin; came to U.S., 1925, 1930, 1940; m. Clara Singer, Dec. 9, 1908; children—Erwin, Kitty. Conductor symphony and popular concerts. Composer operettas: A Waltz Dream, The Chocolate Soldier, The Last Waltz, Three Waltzes, etc. Naturalized Am. citizen. Address: 145 W. 58th St., N.Y.C. 19. Died Jan. 11, 1954.

STRAUS, Roger Williams, metal processing exec.; b. N.Y.C., Dec. 14, 1891; s. Oscar S. and Sarah L. (Lavanburg) S.; student Collegiate Sch., N.Y.C., Lawrenceville (N.J.) sch.; Litt.B., Princeton, 1913; L.H.D., Bucknell U., 1936; D.H.L., Hebrew Union Coll., 1943; LL.D., Jewish Theol. Sem., 1950; L.H.D., N.Y.U., 1953; m. Gladys Guggenheim, Jan. 12, 1914; children—Oscar S., Roger Williams, Florence G. (Mrs. Max A. Hart). With Am. Smelting & Refining Co., 1914——, dir., 1916——, pres., 1941-47, chmn. bd., 1947——; dir., chmn. exec. com. Revere Copper & Brass, Inc., Gen. Cable Corp.; dir. N.Y. Life Ins. Co., N.Y. Telephone Co. Hon. pres. Nat. Fedn. Temple Brotherhoods; trustee John Simon Guggenheim Meml Found., Daniel and Florence Guggenheim Found., Theodore Roosevelt Assn., Nat. Found. for Infantile Paralysis; trustee, mem. exec. bd. Union Am. Hebrew Congregations; hon. vice chmn. United Jewish Appeal of Greater N.Y., 1940-56; bd. govs. Am. Financial and Development Corp. for Israel; pres. Fred L. Lavanburg Found.; co-chmn. Nat. Conf. Christians and Jews, chmn. 25th anniversary 1953; gen. chmn. Brotherhood Week, 1953; mem. gen. com. Am. Jewish Com.; mem.-at-large Nat. Council Boy Scouts Am.; Chancellor bd. regents U. State N.Y. Mem. U.S. Delegation 9th session UN Gen. Assembly. Served as capt., intelligence officer, comdg. gen.'s staff in Siberia, World War I; maj. O.R.C., 1920-34. Recipient Am. Soc. for Metals medal for advancement research, 1935, Class Cup (Princeton 1913), 1936. Mem. Am. Inst. Mining and Metall. Engrs., Am. Legion. Jewish religion, (congregation trustee). Clubs: Nat. Republican, Princeton, Bankers of Am., Lotos (N.Y.C.); Cosmos (Washington). Author: Religious Liberty and Democracy, 1939; also articles on religious liberty. Co-editor: The American Way, 1936. Home: 6 E. 93d St., N.Y.C Died July 28, 1957.

STRAUSS, Henry Harrison (strous), univ. prof.; b. Orrville, O., Dec. 3, 1882; s. Henry Harrison and Mary (Leininger) S.; A.B., Wooster (O.) Coll., 1904; A.M., Tulane U., New Orleans, 1909; student U. of Chicago, 1904-05, 1911-12, summers 1906, 07, 08, 10, 12; study in Italy, 1922-23; Doctor of Laws, University of Arkansas, 1956; unmarried. Acting asst. prof. of Latin, Miami (O.) U., 1905-06, summer 1909; acting prof. of Latin and Greek, Upper Ia. U., Fayette, 1907-08; teaching fellow, Tulane, New Orleans, 1908-09, instr. in Latin, 1909-11; acting prof. of Greek, U. of Ky., 1912-13; acting prof. of ancient langs., U. of Ark., 1913-14. prof. and head dept., 1914-48. emeritus. Mem. Classical Assn. of Middle West and South, Am. Assn. Univ. Profs., Acacia, Phi Beta Kappa. Democrat. Presbyn. Mason. Address: 312 E. Lafayette St., Fayetteville, Ark. Died Dec. 4, 1958; buried Orville, O.

STRAUSS, Juliet V(irginia), writer; b. Rockville, Ind., Jan. 7, 1863; d. William Woods and Susan Marcia (King) Humphreys; ed. public schs., Rockville; m. Isaac Rice Strauss. In charge dept. Squibs and Sayings in Rockville Tribune (husband's paper), 1892——; contbr., under title The Country Contributor, to Indianapolis News, 1900——, and Ideas of a Plain Country Woman, in the Ladies' Home Journal, 1905——; formerly connected with Chicago Journal, Indinapolis Journal, and other publs. Socialist. Presbyn. Mem. Nat. Press Assn., Gen. Federation of Women's Clubs, Ind. Woman's Franchise League, Ind. Women's Press Club, Rockville Women's Civic League. Author: Ideas of a Plain Country Woman, 1908. Home: Rockville, Ind. Died 1918.

STRAUSS, Maurice J., dermatologist; born New Haven, Conn., Jan. 3, 1893; s. Jacob and Theresia (Herrman) S.; A.B., Yale, 1914; M.D., Columbia, 1917; m. Carolyn Ullman, June 12, 1923; 1 son, John Steinert. Interne Bellevue Hosp., N.Y. City, 1917-18; pvt. practice of medicine, City of New Haven, 1919——; specialist in dermatology, 1929——; clin. asst. in dermatology and syphilology New York Post-Grad. Hosp. and Med. Sch., 1917-29, asso. attending dermatologist to dispensary, 1929-32; asst. clin. prof. dermatology, Yale U. Sch. of Medicine, 1932-36, asso. clin. prof., 1936-43, clin. prof. of dermatology, 1943-55, emeritus, 1955——; asst. attending physician New Haven Hosp. and Dispensary, 1932-37, attending physician, 1937——; dir. New Haven Venereal Disease Clinic, 1920-45; attending dermatologist Grace Hosp., 1928——. Hosp. of Saint Raphael, 1931——; cons. dermatologist Laurel Heights Sanitorium Shelton, Conn.; consultant in dermatology and syphilology Norwich (Conn.) State Hosp., Newington (Conn.) V.A. Hosp., New Britain (Conn.) Hosp., and consultant in dermatology, Griffin Hosp., Derby, Conn. Diplomate Am. Bd. Dermatology and Syphilology, 1933. Fellow in dermatology and syphilology of N.Y. Acad. of Medicine; mem. A.M.A., Soc. for Investigative Dermatology, Am. Acad. of Dermatology and Syphilology, Am. Acad. of Compensation Medicine; N.E. Dermatol. Soc., Atlantic Dermatologic Conf., Conn. State Med. Soc., Sigma Xi, Phi Beta Kappa. Clubs: Faculty (Yale). Home: 18 Everit St., New Haven 11. Office: 43 Trumbull St., New Haven 10. Died Feb. 2, 1958; buried New Haven.

STRAW, William Parker, pres. Amoskeag Savings Bank; b. Manchester, N.H., June 18, 1878; s. Herman Foster and Mary Onslow (Parker) S.; student Manchester pub. schs., St. Paul's Sch., 1893-95, Harvard U., 1895-99; m. Josephine Perkins, June 6, 1901; children—Ezekiel Albert (dec.), Mary (wife of Dr. Robert Flanders), Josephine (dec.). Engaged in cotton textile mfg., 1899——; agt. Amoskeag Mfg. Co., Manchester, 1921-29; agt. Amoskeag Industries, Inc., 1936——; pres. Amoskeag Savings Bank, 1937——; chmn. of board Amoskeag Savings Bank, 1951——; director Public Service Co. of N.H.; former dir. New England Public Service Co. Served as maj. Q.M. Corps, U.S.A., 1917-18, with A.E.F. in France. Mason. Club: Harvard (Boston). Home: 282 N. River Rd. Office: 875 Elm St., Manchester, N.H. Died Dec. 6, 1953.

STREAMER, A Camp, ret. elec. mfg. exec.; b. Boulder, Colo., Nov. 23, 1885; s. Francis M. and Lula A. (Walker) S.; ed. State Prep. Sch., Boulder, 1899-1903; B.S. in E.E., U. Colo., 1907, hon. D. Eng., 1946; m. Flora E. Goldsworthy, June 1, 1911; children—Flora Ethelyn (Mrs. William A. Mechesney), Douglas Camp (dec.). With Westinghouse Electric Corp., 1907——, tech. apprentice and successively switchboard engr., headquarters sales, asst. dir. sales, mgr. diversified products dept., mgr. transportation div., mgr. switchgear div., 1936-39, gen. mgr. Pitts. divs., 1939-43, v.p. Jan. 1941-Dec. 1946; ret. Jan. 1, 1947. Past pres. Nat. Elec. Mfrs. Assn.; mem. Am. Inst. E.E., Am. Soc. M.E., Newcomen Soc. Presbyn. Mason. Clubs: University, Edgewood Country (Pittsburgh). Home: 310 Overdale Rd., Forest Hills, Pitts. 21. Office: Westinghouse Electric Corp., 306 Fourth Av., Pitts. 30. Died May 4, 1950; buried Boulder, Colo.

STREBEL, Ralph Frederick (strā'bĕl), coll. dean; b. Buffalo, July 26, 1894; s. Frederick J. and Elizabeth Mary (Dickert) S.; B.S., Syracuse U., 1916; A.M., Teachers Coll., Columbia, 1923, Ph.D., 1935; m. Laura M. Roller, Aug. 2, 1919; 1 son, Ralph F. Prin., Alexander (N.Y.) High Sch., 1916-17, Delaware Lit. Inst., Franklin, N.Y., 1917-19, Hamilton (N.Y.) High Sch., 1919-25; instr. Syracuse U., 1925-26, asst. prof. edn., 1926-35, asso. prof., 1935-40, prof. of edn., 1940——, dir. student teaching and dir. teacher placement, 1928-46, acting dean, Sch. of Edn., summer 1937, dean, Utica Coll. of Syracuse U., 1947——. Served as chief in edn. and curricula Am. Mil. Govt., Berlin sector, Berlin, Germany, 1946-47. Asst. sec. ednl. policies commn. N. E.A., on spl. temporary assignment in internat. edn., Apr.-June 1945. Mem. Nat. Inst. Teacher Placement Assn. (past pres. 1940-41), Kappa Phi Kappa (nat. pres. 1943-46), Phi Kappa Phi, Phi Delta Kappa, Alpha Chi Sigma, Phi Gamma Delta. Methodist. Clubs: Rotary, Ft. Schuyler (Utica). Author: The Nature and Meaning of Teaching (with G. C. Morehart), 1929; The Nature of Student-Teaching in Universities, 1935; Institutional Teacher Placement (contbg. author), 1937; A Functional Program of Teacher Education (contbg. author), 1940; Current Practices in Institutional Teacher Placement (chmn. bd. editors), 1941; (pamphlet) Education for International Freedom and Justice, 1943; Education—Keystone of Peace, 1947. Home: 19 Scott St., Utica 3, N.Y. Died Feb. 8, 1959.

STRECKER, Edward Adam, prof. psychiatry; b. Phila., Pa., Oct. 16, 1887; s. Adam and Mary (Weiler); prep. edn., St. Joseph's Coll., Phila., hon. Sc.D., 1935; B.A., LaSalle Coll., Phila., 1907, M.A., 1911, Litt.D., 1938; M.D., Jefferson Med. Coll., 1911; LL.D., Franklin and Marshall Coll., Boston Coll.; L.H.D., St. Bonaventure U., 1956; m. Elizabeth Kyne Walsh, Jan. 1917. Res. physician St. Agnes Hosp., Phila., 1911-15; asst. phys. Pa. Hosp. Dept. for Nervous and Mental Diseases, 1913-17, med. dir., 1917——, and dir. of clinic; staff neurologist, Pa., Phila. and Germantown hosps.; prof. of nervous and mental diseases, Jefferson Med. Coll., 1925-31; prof. and head dept. psychiatry, U. of Pa., 1931-53, emeritus prof. psychiatry Schools of Medicine, clin. prof. psychiatry and mental hygiene, Yale U., 1926-32; chief of service and consultant, Inst. for

Menta Hygiene, Pa. Hosp., Phila.; cons. Sec. War in psy hiatry for Army; cons. surgeon Gen. of Navy, World War II; cons. U.S.P.H.S.; 17th Pasteur lecturer; also consultant to Bryn Mawr Coll., and U.S. Veterans Bureau; Thomas William Salmon Memorial Lecturer, 1939; Pasteur, Menas Gregory Memorial, Bernard McGhie Memorial lectures, 1946; consultant in mental hygiene, U.S.P.H.S. Commd. from 1st lt. to maj., Medical Corps, U.S. Army, 1917-19. Mem. Commn. to administer the U.S.P.H.S. Bill for Psychiatry and Mental Hygiene. Fellow A.C.P.; mem. Am. Neurol. Assn., Am. Psychiatric Assn., Alpha Omega Alpha, Sigma Phi Epsilon, Alpha Kappa Kappa, etc. Republican. Catholic. Author: Clinical Psychiatry, 1925; Clinical Neurology, 1927; Discovering Ourselves, 1931; Practical Examination of Personality and Behavior Disorders, 1936; Alcohol One Man's Meat, 1938; Beyond the Clinical Frontiers (Salmon lecture), 1940; Fundamentals of Psychiatry, 1942; Their Mothers' Sons, 1946; Their Mothers' Daughters (with V. T. Lathbury), 1956; also numerous articles and papers on nervous and mental disorders. Spl. researches in behavior disorder of children and normal and abnormal psychology of childhood. Address: 111 N. 49th St., Phila. Died Jan. 2, 1959; buried Greenmount Cemetery, Phila.

STREET, James Howell, author; b. Lumberton, Miss., Oct. 15, 1903; s. John C. and William Thompson (Scott) S.; ed. Massey Sch. (Pulaski, Tenn.), Southwestern Theol. Sem., Howard Coll.; m. Lucy Nash O'Briant, June 20, 1923; children—James, John, Lucy Ann. Newspaper reporter, Laurel, Miss., 1918-20, Hattiesburg, Miss., 1922-23; Baptist minister, 1923-26; news editor Pensacola (Fla.) Journal, 1926; asst. state editor Arkansas Gazette, Little Rock, 1927; Associated Press corr., Memphis, 1928, Nashville, Tenn., 1929, Atlanta, 1930-33; feature writer Associated Press, Atlanta, 1933, N.Y. City, 1933-34; reporter, columnist New York American, 1934-36; reporter New York World Telegram, 1937; free lance writer. Episcopalian. Author: Look Away—A Dixie Notebook, 1936; Oh Promised Land, 1940; In My Father's House, 1941; The Biscuit Eater, 1941; Tap Roots, 1942; By Valour and Arms, 1944; The Gauntlet, 1945; Tomorrow We Reap, 1949; Mingo Dabney, 1950; The High Calling, 1951; The Velvet Doublet, 1953; The Civil War, 1953; Goodbye, My Lady, 1954; The Revolutionary War, 1954. Home: Chapel Hill, N.C. Died Sept. 28, 1954; buried Chapel Hill.

STRENG, J(ames) Truman, ins. exec.; b. Holland, Mich., May 14, 1896; s. Henry P. and Mary (Cook) S.; student Philadelphia Textile Sch., 1915-16; student Northwestern U. Night Sch., 1932; M.A.I., Am. Inst. of Real Estate Appraisers case study courses, 1940; m. Katherine M. Perkins, Nov. 28, 1931. Entered real estate and mortgage field, Chicago, 1923; joined real estate dept. of Mass. Mutual Life Ins. Co., 1936, successively city property mgr., dist. mgr., vice pres., 1951, managing co's. mortgage loan and real estate dept. in U.S.; non-resident lecturer, U. of Mich. Sch. Bus. Adminstrn. Served as 1st lt., Inf., Am.-North Russian Expeditionary Force, World War I; re-commd. in Res. Corps, 1920, major, 1936. Mem. bd. govs. and mem. New Eng. chapter, Am. Inst. Real Estate Appraisers, Springfield (Mass.) Real Estate Bd. (mem. central bus. dist. council, trustee Urban Land Inst.), Springfield C. of C., Vets. Fgn. Wars; Polar Bear Assn. (past pres.). Conglist. Club: Longmeadow (Mass.) Country. Home: 60 Summit Av., Longmeadow 6, Mass. Office: 1295 State St., Springfield, Mass. Died Apr. 8, 1953.

STRICKLAND, Francis Lorette, educator; b. N.Y. C.; b. May 8, 1871; s. Frank L. and Emily (Clauney) S.; grad. Brooklyn Collegiate and Poly. Inst.; A.B., New York U., 1893; S.T.B., Boston U., 1896, post-grad. work, 1896-97; univs. of Jena and of Berlin, 1897-98; Ph.D., Boston U., 1903, D.D., 1914; m. May Beasley, Sept. 18, 1898 (died Sept. 18, 1900); m. 2d, Antoinette Louise Brown, July 23, 1903; children—Florence May, Mary Edith. Entered N.Y. East Conf., M.E. Ch., 1909; pastor, Flushing, N.Y., 1899-1902, Bayshore, N.Y., 1902-06, Northport, L.I., N.Y., 1906-10; pres. Simpson Coll., Indianola, Ia., 1910-15; prof. philosophy, W.Va. U., 1915-19; prof. history and psychology of religion, Boston U., 1919-40, now emeritus. Mem. Psi Upsilon. Author: Foundations of Christian Belief, 1915; Psychology of Religious Experience, 1924. Home: 1401 Ellis Hollow Rd., Ithaca, N.Y. Died Aug. 26, 1959; buried Cypress Hills Cemetery, Bklyn.

STRICKLAND, Lily, composer, writer; b. Anderson, S.C.; d. Charleton Hines and Teresa (Hammond-Reed) Strickland; spl. student, Converse Coll., Spartanburg, S.C.; Mus.D., 1924; studied Institute of Musical Art, New York, 2 years; m. J. Courtenay Anderson, 1912. Mem. Am. Soc. Composers, Authors and Pubs., Poetry Soc. S.C., Hist. Soc. S.C., Nat. Assn. Composers and Condrs. Author archeol. and music-source papers as mem. Asiatic Research Soc.; poetry and prose for British and Am. periodicals. Specialist Orientalia. Has composed some five hundred musical works, including sacred and secular cantatas and instrumental, orchestra and vocal compositions as operettas and musical playlets for children. Among best known songs: "Lindy Lou," My Lover Is a Fisherman, At Eve I Heard a Flute, St. John the Beloved "Bayou" cycle. Many symphonic, dance and song numbers performed on professional stage, concert platform TV and radio. Lived in India, 1920-29. Address: Rugby Rd., Hendersonville, N.C. Died June 6, 1958; buried Silver Brook Cemetery, Anderson, S.C.

STRICKLER, Thomas Johnson, pub. utility exec.; b. Topeka, Kan., May 21, 1883; s. Jacob Nissley and Mary (Johnson) S.; grad. Wentworth Mil. Acad., Lexington, Mo., 1900, grad. study, 1901; B.S. in C.E., U. Kan., 1906; student of Washburn Law School; m. Lillian Foster, Nov. 14, 1919 (dec.); m. 2d, Margaret Jane Armstrong, Aug. 8, 1929 (dec. Jan. 1958). With U.S. Reclamation Service, 1902-10; asst. mgr. and engr. Fed. Betterment Co., Cherryvale, Kan., 1910-11; asst. engr. Kan. Pub. Utilities Commn., 1911-13, chief engr., 1913-20; admitted to Kansas bar, 1927, consulting engr. Empire Gas & Fuel Co., Bartlesville, Okla., 1920-22, Henry L. Doherty & Co., N.Y. City, 1922-24, at Kansas City, Mo., 1924-25; cons. engr. Gas Service Co., and vice-pres. or dir. 30 subsidiaries in Kan., Okla. and Mo., 1925-27; v.p. and gen. mgr. Kansas City (Mo.) Gas Co. 1927-47; dir. Gas Service Co., 1926-36, v.p., dir., mgr. Kansas City (Missouri) Division 1947—. Served as capt. Engineer Corps, U.S. Army, 1917. Mem. Kansas State Water Commn., 1917-20; gen. chmn. Kansas City Charities Fund campaigns, 1928 and 1929; mem. bd. govs. Am. Royal Live Stock Show, 1928-42; pres. Kan. City Safety Council, 1928, 1929, mem. bd. govs. 1929—; v. chmn. Club Presidents' Round Table, 1929; trustee Liberty Memorial Assn., 1938—, bd. govs., 1951—; Greater K.C. Com. Econ. Development, 1943—: v.p., trustee Kansas City Conservatory of Music, 1934—; mem. bd. of govs. Patriots and Pioneers Memorial Foundation, 1936—, Citizens Regional Planning Council of K.C., 1945—; mem. adv. council, Region No. 7, War Labor Bd., 1942-43; mem. adv. bd. Salvation Army, 1935—; 2d vice pres. Kansas City Art Inst., 1939-49, 1st v. chmn. bd. govs., 1949, chmn., 1952—; mem. exec. com., bd. trustees Kansas City Philharmonic Orchestra, 1933-44; mem. Defense Savings Com., State of Mo., 1941-46; mem. nat. gas and gasoline com., dist. 2, Petroleum Industry War Council 1942-46; mem. com. Internat. Econ. Policy in coop. with The Carnegie Endowment for Internat. Peace, 1943—; pres. Kan. City War Chest Fund, Inc., 1941-46; dir. Mo. War Chest, 1943-47; v.p. Community Chest of K.C., Mo., 1946, mem. exec. com., 1946-48, trustee, 1946—. Registered profl. engr. Mo. and N.Y. Mem. Mo. Soc. Profl Engrs., U.S. C. of C. (dir. 1934-46), Am. Soc. C.E. (v.p. Kansas City Chapter 1931; pres. 1933), Midwest Research Inst. (v. chmn. bd. govs., mem. exec. com., chmn. development com. 1946-48, trustee), Soc. Am. Mil. Engrs., Am. Gas Assn. (pres. 1940-41; chmn. natural gas dept. 1932; nat. advertising com., 1936-42), Mo. Association Pub. Utilities (pres. 1929-30), Kansas City C. of C. (v.p. Civics 1931 and 1934), Am. Legion (comdr. local post 1928; chmn. vets. welfare com. 1929; comdr. Dept. Mo. 1929-30), Forty and Eight, Mil. Order World War (comdr. Kansas City Chapter 1938-39), S.R. (1st v.p. K.C. Chapter 1940-43), Kan. U. Alumni Assn. (pres. 1934-35; bd. dirs. World War II Meml. Bldg., 1951—), Sigma Chi (grand trustee, 1944-48), Tau Beta Pi. Pres. Kan. Engr. Soc., 1915. Mason (32°, K.T., Shriner). Clubs: University (vice pres. 1929), Kansas City, Rotary, Mission Hills Country, Advertising and Sales Executives. Home: 5760 Ward Parkway, Kansas City 2. Office: Scarritt Bldg., 824 Grand Av., Kansas City 13, Mo. Died Nov. 19, 1958.

STRIDE, Joseph Burton, railroad ofcl.; b. Biddeford, Me., Oct. 8, 1894; s. Joseph and Alice Rose (Phillips) S.; A.B., Bowdoin Coll., 1917; m. Irene Sara Haley, June 22, 1918; children—Elaine, Richard Joseph. With Biddeford & Saco R.R. Co., 1919—, successively clk., asst. treas., treas. and v.p., pres. and treas., 1931—; asst. treas. Biddeford Savs. Bank, 1931-39; treas., dir. Mut. Fire Ins. Co., Saco, 1950—; dir. York Nat. Bank, Saco, 1950—; dir. Webber Hosp. Assn., Biddeford, 1921—, treas., 1936-49, trustee, 1930-52, pres., 1950-52; treas., dir. Sweetsor (Found.), Inc., 1939—. Sweetser-Children's Home, 1949—; v.p., trustee Kennebunk (Me.) Hist. Mus.; dir. N.E. Council of Boston, 1949—, Maine chmn., 1952-53; dir. Laurel Hill Cemetery Assn., 1946—, Masonic Bldg. Assn., Biddeford, 1930—; trustee Thornton Acad., Saco, 1950—; adv. bd. Me. Publicity Bur., 1949. Served as pvt. ordnance dept. U.S. Army, 1917-19, 2d lt., 1919. Mem. Am. Legion, S.A.R., U.S. C. of C., A.I.M. (president's council N.Y.C.), Transportation Assn. Am., Am. Newcomen Soc., Delta Upsilon. Conglist. Mason (32°, Shriner). Eastern Star. Clubs: Portland (Me.) Executives; Rotary (Biddeford, Saco); New England Transit of Boston (past pres.). Has been noted in nat. mags. for unique operation of transit co. Home: Rivertide, Ferry Rd. Office: 176 Main St., Saco, Me. Died Jan. 25, 1956; buried Laurel Hill Cemetery, Saco, Me.

STRIJDOM, Johannes Gerhardus (stray dom), prime minister S. Africa; b. Willowmore, S. Africa, July 14, 1893; s. Petrus Gerhardus and Elizabeth Ellen (Nortje) S.; B.A., Stellenbosch U., 1912; LL.B., Pretoria U., 1917, Ph.D. (hon.), 1952; m. Susanna de Klerk, Jan. 13, 1931; children—Estelle, Gerhardus. Farmer, Willowmore, 1912-14; admitted to Cape bar as advocate, 1918; admitted as atty. in Pretoria, 1918; practiced in Nylstroom, 1918-34; farmer, Nylstroom, 1923—; sec. divisional br. Nat. Party in South Africa, Waterberg constituency, 1918-29, mem. Parliament, 1929—; co-leader Herenigde Nasionale Party in Transval, 1939-46, leader, 1946—; leader in chief Nasional Party of South Africa, 1954—; minister lands and irrigation, 1948—, prime minister, 1954—. Chmn. bd. dirs. newspaper Voortrekker Pers. Bpr.; chmn. bd. trustees newspaper Dagbreek Trust Bpr. Mem. Waterberg Agrl. Soc. (pres. 1923-29). Home: Libertas. Brynterion, Pretoria. Office: Union Bldgs., Pretoria, South Africa. Died Aug. 24, 1958.

STRINGER, Arthur (John Arbuthnott) (strĭng'ẽr), author; b. Chatham, Ont., Can., Feb. 26, 1874; ed. Toronto U. and U. Oxford, Eng.; Litt.D., U. Western Ont., 1946; m. Jobyna Howland, 1900; m. 2d, his cousin, Margaret Arbuthnott Stringer, 1914. Editorial writer, Am. Press Assn., 1898-1901; lit. editor of Success, 1903-04. Author: Watchers of Twilight, 1894; Pauline and Other Poems, 1895; Epigrams, 1896; A Study in King Lear, 1897; The Loom of Destiny, 1898; The Silver Poppy, 1899; Lonely O'-Malley, 1901; Hephaestus and Other Poems, 1902; The Wire Tappers, 1906; Phantom Wires, 1907; The Occasional Offender, 1907; The Woman in the Rain, 1907; Under Groove, 1909; Irish Poems, 1911; Open Water, 1912; Gun Runner, 1912; Shadow, 1913; Prairie Wife, 1915; Hand of Peril, 1916; Door of Dread, 1917; House of Intrigue, 1918; Man Who Couldn't Sleep, 1919; Prairie Mother, 1920; The Wine of Life, 1921; Are All Men Alike?, 1921; Prairie Child, 1922; City of Peril, 1923; Diamond Thieves, 1923; Empty Hands, 1924; The Story Without a Name and Manhandled (with Russell Holman); Power, 1925; In Bad with Sinbad, 1926; White Hands, 1927; The Wolf Woman, 1928; A Woman at Dusk and Other Poems, 1928; Cristina and I, 1929; The Woman Who Couldn't Die, 1929; Out of Erin, 1930; A Lady Quite Lost, 1930; The Mud Lark, 1931; Marriage by Capture, 1932; Dark Soil, 1933; Man Lost, 1934; Wife Traders, 1936; Alexander Was Great, 1937; Heather of the High Hand, 1937; The Old Woman Remembers and Other Poems, 1938; The Lamp In The Valley, 1938; The Dark Wing, 1939; The Prairie Omnibus, 1939; The Ghost Plane, 1940; The King Who Loved Old Clothes, 1941; Intruders In Eden, 1942; Star In A Mist, 1943; The Devastator, 1945; Red Wine of Youth, a Biography of Rupert Brooke, 1948; New York Nocturnes, 1948. Contbr. mags. Traveled in S.A., Africa and Europe. Clubs: Canadian in New York; Macaulay, Rockaway River Country, Mountain Lakes; University of Toronto (v.p.) (N.Y.). Chmn. Mountain Lakes Pub. Library Bd.; pres., dir. Mountain Lakes Dramatic Guild; Morris County Library Commr. Home: Mountain Lakes, N.J. Died Sept. 15, 1950.

STRINGFIELD, Lamar, composer, conductor; b. Raleigh, N.C., Oct. 10, 1897; s. O. L. and Ellie (Beckwith) S.; student Wake Forest Coll., N.C.; artist's diploma, Inst. Musical Art, N.Y., 1924 (flute), George Barrere, teacher; and prize in composition, 1924; Percy Goetschius, Franklin Robinson, George Wedge, teachers; studied composition with Nadia Boulanger, Paris, 1928, student of conducting with Chalmers Clifton and Henry Hadley; div.; 1 d., Meredith. Played and conducted N.Y. with chamber music ensembles and major symphony orchestras until 1930; promoted orgn. of Inst. of Folk Music, U. of N.C., 1930; organized N.C. Symphony Soc., 1932; mus. dir., N.C. Symphony Orchestra, 1932-35; asso. condr., Radio City Music Hall, 1938-39; lectr. on Am. folk music Juilliard Summer Sch., 1939-41; teacher composition and orchestration Claremont (Calif.) Coll., summer 1942; mus. dir. Knoxville Symphony Soc., 1946-47; condr. Symphonette of Charlotte, 1947-48; mus. dir. Charlotte Symphony Orchestra, 1948-49. Composed symphonic works based on Am. folk-lore: Indian Legend, 1923; From the Southern Mountains, 1928; A Negro Parade, 1931; The Legend of John Henry, 1932; Moods of a Moonshiner, 1934; From the Blue Ridge, 1937; Mountain Dawn, 1945; (cantata for mixed chorus) Peace (Marian Sims), 1949; About Dixie (chorus and orchestra), 1950; Carolina Charcoal (book and music), 1952. Composed integral music for (plays): Tread the Green Grass (Paul Green), 1931, Potter's Field (Paul Green), 1931, Shroud My Body Down (Paul Green), 1934, Born Climbin' (Cary F. Jacob), 1944; (historical dramas) The Lost Colony (Paul Green), 1937; Shout Freedom (LeGette Blythe), 1948, Thunderland (Hubert Hayes), 1952; Sodom, Tennessee (Berney and Richardson), 1953, Georgia Buck (symphonic band), 1955; Daniel Boone (mil. band), 1956. Served with U.S. Army, Mexican Border and France, World War I. Pulitzer prize for orchestral suite "From the Southern Mountains" 1928. Member American Soc. Composers, Authors and Pubs., Nat. Assn. Composers and Condrs., Composers-Authors Guild, Bohemians. Home: Asheville, N.C. Died Jan. 21, 1959; buried Riverside Cemetery, Ashville, N.C.

STRITCH, Samuel Alphonsus, cardinal; b. Nashville, Tenn., Aug. 17, 1887; s. Garrett and Catherine (Malley) S.; A.B., St. Gregory Coll., Cincinnati, O., 1904; Ph.D., Am. Coll., Rome, 1906, S.T.D., 1910. Ordained priest R.C. Ch., at Rome, 1910; pastor at Memphis and Nashville, 1910-17; apptd. chancellor Diocese of Nashville, 1915; domestic prelate, May 1921; apptd. bishop of Toledo, Aug. 1921, consecrated, Nov. 30, 1921, apptd. archbishop of Milwaukee, Apr. 26, 1930; apptd. archbishop of Chicago, Dec. 27, 1939; apptd. cardinal by Pope Pius XII, Dec. 1945; cardinal pro-prefect congregation for propagation of faith, 1958. Home: 1555 N. State Parkway, Chicago 10. Address: Rome, Italy. Died May 27, 1958.

STRODE, George King (strōd), hygienist; b. Chester County, Pa., Jan. 16, 1886; s. Richard Henry and Hannah Mary (King) S.; Sc.B., Haverford Coll., 1908; M.D., U. Pa., 1912; M.P.H., Harvard, 1927; Sc.D., Haverford, 1942; m. Elizabeth J. Coombs, May 22, 1919 (died 937); m. 2d, Josephine Clark Dillard, June 29, 1944. Hygienist Pa. State Dept. Health, 1915-16 and 1919-20; member International Health Division of Rockefeller Foundation, 1916-17 and, 1920—, rep. in Brazil, 1920-26, also asst. dir. activities in Europe and the Near East, 1927-38, asso. dir., 1938-44, dir. 1944-51, also chmn. Paris (France) office, 1932-38. Served as captain, Med. Corps, U.S. Army, 1917-19. Fellow Am. Pub. Health Assn.; mem. Am. Soc. and Acad. Tropical Medicine, New York Society Tropical Medicine, A.A.A.S., Alpha Omega Alpha, Delta Omega. Hon. fellow Soc. of Med. Officers of Health of Great Britain. Decorated by governments of Norway, Denmark, Bulgaria, Portugal, France, Rumania and Sweden. Presbyterian. Now retired. Died Oct. 27, 1958.

STROH, Donald Armpriester (strō), army officer; b. Harrisburg, Pa., Nov. 3, 1892; B.S., Mich. Agrl. Coll., 1915; m. Annie Imogene Finger, Hickory, N.C., June 13, 1917; children—Imogene Covert (Mrs. Robert H. Stumpf), Harry Richard (killed in action, Aug. 1944). Commd. 2d lt. Cav., June 1917; promoted through grades to maj. gen., 1944; became intelligence officer, G-2, 4th Army hdqrs. Presidio of San Francisco, July, 1940, serving also as aide to Lt. Gen. John L. DeWitt, comdg. gen. 4th Army; mil. observer London, Eng., May-June, 1941, also attended Brit. Intelligence Sch.; returned 4th Army as intelligence officer, July 1941; assigned 85th Inf. Div., comdg. officer 339th Inf., Feb. 1942, upon its activation; assigned 9th Inf. Div., asst. to comdg. gen., July 1942. Served in French Morocco and through campaigns So. and No. Tunisia, Sicily and Normandy; assigned to comd. 8th Inf. Div. July 1944; promoted maj. gen. Aug. 1944. Participated in campaigns of No. France and Germany; transferred to comd. 106th Inf. Div., Feb. 1945. Awarded D.S. M., Legion of Merit with Oak Leaf Cluster, Bronze Star Medal, French Legion of Honor (officer), Croix de Guerre with palm. Home: 3133 Connecticut Av., Washington. Died Dec. 20, 1953; buried Arlington Nat. Cemetery.

STRONG, Austin, dramatist; b. San Francisco, Jan. 18, 1881; s. Joseph Dwight and Isobel Stuart (Osbourne) S.; ed. Vailima, Samoa, Monterey, Cal., and Wellington (New Zealand) Coll.; studied landscape architecture; m. Mary Holbrook Wilson, June 6, 1906. Landscape architect until 1905 (laid out Cornwall Park, Auckland, N.Z.); writer of plays, 1905—. Past v.p. Am. Inst. Arts and Letters; mem. Dramatists Guild of Authors League, Am. Soc. Pilgrims. Clubs: Garick (London); Century (New York); Nantucket Yacht (commodore, 1930, 31). Author: The Exile (with Lloyd Osbourne), prod. London, 1903; The Little Father of the Wilderness (with same), prod. London and New York, 1905; The Drums of Oude, prod. London, 1906; The Toymaker of Nüremburg, prod. New York and London, 1907-08; Rip Van Winkle (new version), produced London, Sept. 1911; adaptation from the French of Madame Rostand's play, Le Bon Petit Diable, prod. N.Y., 1913; Three Wise Fools, prod. N.Y., 1918, London, 1919; Seventh Heaven, prod. N.Y., 1922; A Play Without a Name, produced N.Y., 1928; Liberty; The North Star. Contbr. to Atlantic Monthly, Sat. Eve. Post, Reader's Digest. Address: 717 Madison Av., N.Y.C.; (summer) Nantucket, Mass. Died Sept. 17, 1952; buried Nantucket, Mass.

STRONG, George Frederic, physician; b. St. Paul, Feb. 22, 1897; s. Charles Douglas and Sophia (Haupt) S.; M.D., U. Minn., 1921; D.Sc., U. B.C., 1954; LL.D., U. Toronto, 1955; D.Sc., Laval U., 1956; m. Ruth Nickel, Sept. 9, 1919; children—George Frederic (R.C.A.F.; killed in action), Barbara Jean. Practice of medicine, Vancouver, B.C., 1924—; attending staff Vancouver Gen. Hosp., 1926—, dir. Heart Sta., 1930-54, sr. medicine, 1936—, chief dept. medicine, 1946-51, chmn. med. bd., 1954-56; clin. prof. medicine U. B.C., 1951—. Mem. founding com., 1st pres. Family Service Agy. Greater Vancouver; past pres. Greater Vancouver Health League; past pres., dir. Council Social Agencies and Welfare Found.; mem. founding com., dir., past pres. B.C. Cancer Found.; founder, chmn. med. bd. B.C. Med. Research Inst. Diplomate Am. Bd. Internal Medicine. Fellow A.C.P. (pres. 1955-56), Royal Coll. Physicians Can. and London, Royal Australasian Coll. Physicians; mem. Western Soc. Rehabilitation (v.p., dir.), Canadian Cancer Soc. (dir. B.C. div.), Canadian (pres. 1954-55), Vancouver (pres. 1929-30), B.C. (pres. 1936-37) med. assns., Canadian Heart Association (past president), Alpha Omega Alpha, Nu Sigma Nu, Chi Psi. Home: 1529 W. 37th Av., Vancouver 13. Office: 925 W. Georgia St., Vancouver 1, B.C., Can. Deceased.

STRONG, Harry Allen; b. Republic, O., Sept. 16, 1888. Toledo (O.) Scale Co., 1911-21; vice pres. and gen. mgr. Airway Electric Appliance Corp., Toledo, 1922-31; v.p. and dir. Electrolux Corp., N.Y. City and San Francisco since 1932; v.p. Servel, Inc., Evansville, Ind., 1934-52; dir. Morris Plan Bank, Jorgenson & Co., San Francisco, Household Products Co., Oakland. Clubs: Claremont (Oakland); Commercial, Advertising Press (San Francisco). Home: 17 Westminster Drive, Okland, Calif. Office: 417 Montgomery St., San Francisco 4. Deceased.

STRONG, Hattie Maria, founder Mattie M. Strong Found.; b. South Coventry, Conn., Oct. 24, 1864; d. Henry and Maria (Belknap) Corrin; ed. pvt. schs., N.Y.C.; LL.D., George Washington U., 1937; m. Lester Burchard Lockwood, Tacoma, Oct. 17, 1888 (now dec.), 1 son, Lester Corrin; m. 2d, Henry Alvah Strong (founder of Eastman Kodak Co., Rochester, N.Y.), June 14, 1905 (now dec.). Founder, chmn. Hattie M. Strong Found. to aid young men and women of all countries to secure a higher edn. Donor of chateau and estate at Meussey, France, to Union des Blessés de la Face (of which is hon. v.p.); auditorium to U. Rochester in memory of husband; girls' dormitory to Y.W.C.A. and girls' dormitory to George Washington U., both of Washington; Hall of Government to George Washington U. as tribute to son, 1938; girls' dormitory, Rollins Coll., Winter Park, Fla., 1939; dean's residence, Keuka Coll., Keuka Park, N.Y., 1939; land containing coal mine and bldgs. for Frontier Nursing Service, Wendover, Leslie County, Ky., 1939; Corrin Refectory and renovation of century-old dining hall, Salem Coll., Winston-Salem, N.C., 1940, Hattie Strong (girls) Dormitory, 1941; bldg. to Goodwill Industries, Washington; trade sch. bldg., Farmers' Fedn., Asheville, N.C., 1941; chapel to Brick Presbyn. Ch., Rochester; Corrin Hall, Rollins Coll., Winter Park, Fla.; Strong Day Nursery, New Orleans; Strong Hall, Keuka Coll., N.Y.; Small Hampton Inst., Shuen, So. Africa. Founded Shiloh Indsl. Orphanage, Augusta, Georgia. Trustee George Washington U., Salem Coll.; asso. mem. Home Moravian Ch.; v.p. Inst. Social Scis.; hon. pres., chmn. Anti-Tuberculosis Assn. Shanghai. Hon. alumna George Washington U., Salem Coll., Keuka Coll. Hon. vice-chmn. gen. U.S. Flag. Assn., adv. mem. bd. trustees, Allied Youth, Inc. Hon. chmn. Y.W.C.A., Rochester, N.Y.; mem. Bd. of Frontier Nursing Service. Awarded gold medal, Reconnaissance Francaise, by Pres. of France, 1927; Chevalier Legion of Honor (France), 1930; Order of St. Sava (Jugoslavia); medal of honor, Rollins Coll.; Cross of Honor, Am. Flag Assn., 1931; Girl Scout Medal for Service. Asso. mem. Research Assos. of Mass. Inst. Tech. Vice pres. Am. Forestry Assn., 1942. Republican. Presbyn. Clubs: Republican Women's, National Women's Country, Sulgrave (Washington); Century (Rochester); Nat. Women's Republican (New York); American Women's (London); American Women's (Paris); Sky (Winston-Salem). Address: 2712 32d St. N.W., Washington. Died June 6, 1950; buried Mt. Hope Cemetery, Rochester, N.Y.

STRONG, Ormand Butler, supt. schs.; b. Savannah, Ga., Apr. 3, 1878; s. Charles Hall and Jennie Butler (Rich) S.; student Lawrenceville (N.J.) Sch., 1893-95, Cornell U., 1895-99; m. Ada Marie Blois, May 29, 1899; children—Marie Louise (Mrs. Walter J. Wright), Charles Hall. Tchr. pub. schs., Savannah, 1900, successively prin . and asst. supt., supt., 1926-49. Ga. del. to world ednl. convs. Toronto, Geneva, Dublin. Mem. N.E.A. (dept. superintendence), Chi Psi. Democrat. Episcopalian. Rotarian. Club: Cornell. Home: 215 E. 50th St., Savannah, Ga. Retired. Died May 3, 1954; buried Bonaventure, Cemetery, Ga.

STRONG, Robert Alexander, prof. pediatrics, med. editor; b. New Orleans, Nov. 17, 1884; s. Robert and Joanna (O'Connor) S.; M.D., Tulane, 1907; grad. study, London, and at various German pediatric centers; m. Elmire Delbert, Apr. 3, 1907; 1 son, Delbert. Asst. prof. pediatrics, Tulane U., 1917-20, clin. prof. pediatrics, 1920-23, prof. and head dept. pediatrics, 1929-44, prof., head of pediatrics, Dept. Graduate Studies, 1937-44, on military leave of absence, 1941-44; surgeon, U.S. Pub. Health Service (consultant), 1920-23. Vis. physician Charity and Bapt. hosps., Touro Infirmary. First lt., later capt. and maj., U.S. Med. Corp during World War I; lt. col. Med. Res. Corps, 1919-39, col. 1939—; active duty with rank of col., as med. officer, 3d Mil. Area of the 4th Corps, New Orleans, Apr. 1941—; comdg. officer Station Hosp., Gulfport Field, Miss., 1942-43; inactive Reserve 1943. Pres. La. State Pediatrics Soc., 1930-31; La. state chmn. for Region II, Am. Acad. Pediatrics, 1930-40. Diplomat Am. Bd. of Pedriatics. Fellow and charter mem. Am. Acad. Pediatrics (emeritus 1947); formerly mem. A.M.A., So. Med. Assn., La. Med. Soc., La. and Central States pediatric socs., Alpha Omega Alpha, Phi Rho Sigma, Pi Kappa Alpha. Democrat. Co-author of Tice's Practice of Medicine and Brennemann's Pediatrics. Editor Internat. Med. Digest, 1924—; mem. editorial board Jour. of Pediatrics, 1932-46. Advances in Pediatrics, American Jour. of Syphilis (1930-35), Aviation Medicine (1930-34). Contbr. many articles to professional and assn. jours. Home: 997 East Beach Blvd., Pass Christian, Miss. Died 1955.

STRONG, Samuel M., sociologist; b. London, Eng., Sept. 9, 1906; s. Manasse and Seina (Isaak) S.; grad. Lyceum, Roumania, 1926; A.B., Brown U., 1938; Ph.D., U. Chicago, 1940; m. Mary Symons, Aug. 30, 1940; children—Judith Naomi, David William. Came to U.S., 1927, naturalized, 1935. Research asso., community study U. Chicago, 1938-39; vis. lectr. Howard U., 1940-41, U. Minn., 1941-42; asst. prof. sociology Newcomb Coll., Tulane U., 1942-43; asso. prof. sociology U. Neb., 1945-46; prof. and chmn. dept. sociology Macalester Coll., 1943-45; prof. and chmn. dept. sociology Carleton Coll., Northfield, Minn., 1946-58; assistant prof. sociology U. Alberta, 1958—; vis. prof. sociology Wayne U., summer 1949, U. Nev. summers 1950, 51, 52, 53; post-doctoral research and study, dept. of social relations, Harvard, Feb., March, 1955, dept. indsl. relations U. Chgo., April, May, 1955. Member bd. dirs. Internat. Inst., St. Paul, 1943-45. Chmn. Minn. Com. on Social Work Edn., 1944-45; Mem. speakers panel, Round Table Christians and Jews, Minn. U.N. Com. Mem. Am. Assn. U. Profs., Soc. for Social Research, Am. Sociol. Soc. (nominating com., 1949), Mid-West Sociol. Soc. (exec. com. 1951). Author articles and book reviews in sociol. jours. Address: Univ. Alberta, Edmonton. Alberta, Can. Died Jan. 24, 1959.

STRONG, Wayne F(rederick), mfr.; b. Abilene, Kan., Sept. 22, 1907; s. Frank H. and Maude M. (Aumach) S.; student pub. schs., extension courses U. Ore.; m. Helen Stevenson; children—Lois I., Betty L., Alan F., Dale W. Helper trucking firm, Hillsboro, Ore., 1927-29; with Iron Fireman Mfg. Co., Portland, Ore., 1929—, successively janitor and shipping and prodn. work, organizer planning and prodn. control dept., br. mgr. electronics div., v.p. mfg., pres., dir., 1955—. Tech. counselor engring. exptl. sta. Ore. State Coll., 1955—. Served as sgt. Ore. N.G., 1941-47. Mason (32°). Home: 2912 S.E. Harrison St., Portland. Office: 3170 W. 106th St., Cleve.; also 4784 S.E. 17th St., Portland, Ore. Died Mar. 28, 1957; buried Lincoln Memorial Park Mausoleum, Portland.

STRONG, William Walker, physicist; b. Good Hope, Cumberland County, Pa., May 16, 1883; s. William Harrison and Maria (Garretson) S.; B.S. with honors, Dickinson Coll., 1905; Ph.D., Johns Hopkins, 1908; m. Mary Alberta Kirk, June 17, 1916; children—Walker Albert, Margaret Kirk. Fellow by courtesy, Johns Hopkins, 1908; research asst. Carnegie Instn., Washington, D.C., 1908-11, also asst. Johns Hopkins, 1909-11; fellow Mellon Inst., Pitts., 1911-13, also prof. elec. theory, U. Pitts., pres. Scientific Instrument & Elec. Machine Co., 1912; instr. Carnegie Inst., Pittsburgh, 1914; physicist for Research Corp., 1915, 19; cons. practice. Developed a fume mask for diphenylchlorasin and other poisonous fumes during World War I. Discovered effect of magnetic psychoanalysis, 1921. Sec. Soldiers and Sailors Memorial Park Commn., 1936-49. Fellow A.A.A.S., Am. Phys. Soc.; Tax Justice League of Pa. (v.p.). Democrat. Methodist. Mem. Phi Beta Kappa. Mason. Author: The Absorption Spectra of Solutions (Carnegie Instn.), 2 parts, 1910, 11; The New Science of Fundamental Physics, 1918; The New Philosophy of Modern Science, 1920; also vols. I, II, III, IV of collected papers from phys. and chem. jours.; Immortality in the Light of Modern Thought, 1923; Ourselves and Our Sciences, 1930. Discovered Phoenician letters and words incised on stones in Pa., 1941. Has extended American Phoenician to 400 words. Home: Mechanicsburg, Pa. Died Oct. 25, 1955.

STROUD, William Daniel, physician; b. Villa Nova, Pa., Nov. 20, 1891; s. Morris Wistar and Margaret P. (Rutter) S.; B.S., U. of Pa., 1913; M.D., U. of Pa. Med. Sch., 1916; grad. study, U. of Coll. Hosp., London, 1919-20, St. Andrew's Inst. Clin. Research, Scotland, 1920, L'Hopital de Pitiet, Paris, France, 1920; m. Agnes H. Shober, Sept. 19, 1923; children—William Daniel (dec.), Samuel Shober, Agnes Hutchinson, Magaret Rutter and Charlotte Wistar (twins). Engaged in practice of medicine at Phila. since 1921; chief of staff Children's Heart Hosp., Phila.; cons. cardiologist to Pa. Hosp., Bryn Mawr Hosp., Abington Memorial Hosp., St. Christopher's Hosp., Phila., Norristown State Hosp.; prof. emeritus cardiology, U. Pa. Grad. Sch. Medicine, asst. prof. clinical medicine U. of Pa. Med. Sch. First lt. U.S.M.C., 1917-19. Member bd. dirs. Phila. Health Council and TB Committee, Phila. Fellow A.M.A., Philadelphia College Physicians; member Association American Physicians, American Clinical and Climatological Assn., Interurban Clin. Club, Phila. County Med. Soc., Maine Line Branch Montgomery County Med. Soc., John Morgan Soc. U. of Pa., Delta Psi, Phila. Heart Assn., Am. Heart Assn., Am. Coll. Physicians (Alfred Stengel Meml. award 1957). Republican. Episcopalian. Clubs: Philadelphia, Racquet, Gulph Mills Golf, Mask and Wig, St. Anthony (Philadelphia); St. Anthony (New York). Contbr. articles to med. jours.; also editor The Diagnosis and Treatment of Cardio-vascular Disease, 1957. Home: County Line Rd., Villa Nova, Pa. Office: 1011 Clinton St., Phila. Died Aug. 19, 1959; buried Church of the Redeemer, Bryn Mawr, Pa.

STROUT, Edwin Albert, business exec.; b. Lewiston, Me., Dec. 12, 1871; s. Lester Hale and Martha (Hancock) S.; grad. Maine Wesleyan Sem., 1894, Kent's Hill (Me.) Comml. Coll., 1890; m. Adelia T. Quinn, June 22, 1906; children—Shirley (Mrs. Tempel L. Johnson), Edwin A. School teacher, 1890; salesman Ice Cream Refrigerators, 1895-97, Portland, Maine Factory Window Screens, 1897-98; mgr. advt. and sales, N.Y. Screen Mfrs., 1899-1900; pres. E. A. Strout Realty Agency, Inc., New York City, 1907—; pres. E. A. Strout Western Realty Agency, Inc., of Calif., 1933—; dir. Commuters Homes, Inc., 1925—. Home: Biltmore Hotel, Los Angeles. Died Mar. 28, 1952.

STRUM, Louie Willard, judge; b. Valdosta, Ga., Jan. 16, 1890; s. Louis Henry and Dora Lee (Ramsey) S.; grad. St. Petersburg (Fla.) Mil. High Sch., 1906 (capt. of cadets); LL.B., Stetson U., 1912, LL.D., 1934; m. Ophelia Wilson Gray, June 6, 1917; children—Louie Willard, Charles Gray, Ophelia Gray; married 2d, Grace Hilditch Holt, October 6, 1951. Admitted to Fla. bar, 1912, and began practice Jacksonville; city atty., Jacksonville, 1921-25; justice Supreme Court of Fla., 1925-31; chief justice, Jan.-Mar. 1931; judge U.S. Dist. Court, Southern Dist. of Fla., 1931-50, U.S. Court of Appeals, 5th Jud. Circuit, Oct. 1950—. Served in U.S. Navy, 1906-10; lt. comdr. Apr. 6, 1917-July 2, 1919, World War, Mem. Am. Legion (past post comdr.), Sigma Nu, Phi Delta Phi. Democrat. Episcopalian. Mason (32°, K.T., Shriner). Clubs: Tallahassee Country (Tallahassee); Timuquana, Seminole, Fla. Yacht (Jacksonville). Home: George Washington Hotel. Office: Federal Bldg., Jacksonville, Fla. Died July 26, 1954; buried St. Petersburg, Fla.

STRUTHER, Jan (strŭth'ẽr) **(Joyce Anstruther: Mrs. Adolf Kurt Placzek)**, author; born London, Eng., June 6, 1901; d. Henry Torrens and Eva (Hanbury-Tracy) Anstruther; ed. private schools, London; m. Anthony Maxtone-Graham, July 4, 1923 (div. 1947); children—James Anstruther, Janet Mary, Robert Mungo; married 2d, Adolf Kurt Placzek, March 1, 1948. Writer since 1917. Author: Betsinda Dances and Other Poems, 1931; Sycamore Square and Other Verses, 1932; The Modern Struwwelpeter, 1936; Try Anything Twice, 1938; Mrs. Miniver, 1939; The Glassblower, 1940; Women of Britain, 1941; A Pocketful of Pebbles, 1946. Contbr. prose and verse to many periodicals in Great Britain and U.S.A. Address: care of Curtis Brown, Ltd., 347 Madison Av., N.Y.C. Died July 20, 1953.

STRUTHERS, Robert, business exec.; born South Orange, N.J., Aug. 22, 1879; s. Robert and Sabina R. (Wood) S.; m. Helen Jackson, Nov. 12, 1902. Began with Morton, Bliss & Co., 1895, loan clerk, Morton Trust Co., to 1900; rep. Fisk & Robinson, 1900-05. Organized Libbey & Struthers, 1905, which merged with L. von Hoffmann & Co., 1918; formed Wood, Struthers & Co., of which is limited partner, 1914; dir. Alpha Portland Cement Co., Yale & Towne Manufacturing Company. Fellow (life) Metropolitan Mus. of Art; mem. (life) N.Y. Zool. Soc. (Bronx Zoo), Am. Mus. Natural History, St. Andrew's Soc. Clubs: Union, Down Town Assn., Recess (New York); Special Car, Woodway Country, Wee Burn Country; Stamford (Conn.) Yacht; St. Andrew's, (N.B., Can.) Yacht. Home: Boston Post Rd., Noroton, Conn.; also St. Andrews, N.B., Can. Office: 20 Pine St., N.Y.C. Died May 10, 1951; buried Rosedale Cemetery, Orange, N.J.

STRYKER, Lloyd Paul (strīk'ẽr), lawyer; b. Chicago, Ill., June 5, 1885; s. Melancthon Woolsey and Elizabeth (Goss) S.; A.B., Hamilton Coll., 1906; A.M., 1909, L.H.D., 1933; m. Katharine Truax, Apr. 30, 1910; 1 dau., Katharine S. Dunn. Admitted to N.Y. bar, 1909, and practiced since at N.Y. City; asst. dist. atty. N.Y. County, 1910-12. Served as 2d lt., later 1st lt. and capt., F.A., U.S. Army, World War. Rep. nominee for judge of City Court, New York, 1914; apptd. judge U.S. Dist. Court, Southern Dist. N.Y., by President Coolidge, Mar. 1, 1929, but Senate adjourned without ratifying appointment. Fellow, American College of Trial Lawyers. Member Am. N.Y. State and N.Y. County bar assns., Assn. Bar City New York, New York Hamilton Coll. Alumni Assn., N.Y. Soc. Mil. and Naval Officers of World War, St. Nicholas Society; life mem. Tenn. State Bar Assn. Episcopalian. Clubs: University, Manhattan. Down Town, Piping Rock. Author: Andrew Johnson—A Study in Courage, 1929; Courts and Doctors, 1932; For The Defense (A Biography of Thomas Erskine), 1947; The Art of Advocacy, 1954. Home: 31 E. 72d St., N.Y.C. 21. Office: 40 Wall St., N.Y.C. Deceased.

STUART, Charles T., pub. exec.; b. Elizaville, Ky., Dec. 5, 1883; s. Daniel Ficklin and Mary (Kirk) S.; grad. high sch.; m. Lillie Belle Mortimore, Nov. 17, 1908; 1 dau., Elmira (Mrs. John C. Ingersoll). Clerk Louisville Herald, 1903-07, circulation mgr., 1908-11; asst. merchandise mgr., Lord and Taylor, N.Y. City, 1911-13; v.p. and treas., J. N. Adam and Co., Buffalo, 1913-15; pres. Surety Coupon Co., N.Y. City, 1915-20; v.p., dir. Empire State Finance Corp., 1920-24; v.p., gen. mgr. and dir. Joseph Wild and Co., N.Y. City, 1924-28; dir. Am. Linoleum Co., 1924-28; v.p, .Am. Piano Co., 1928-30; advt. dir. Editor & Publisher (publ.), 1931-40, gen. mgr., 1941-48, dir., sec. and treas., 1934-48, publr. since 1948. Republican. Presbyn. Mason. Clubs: Union League, Advertising (New York); Country (Huntington, L.I.). Home: 44 Gramercy Park, New York 10. Office: Room 1700, Times Tower, N.Y.C. 36. Died July 29, 1958.

STUART, Charles W(illiam) T(homas), mfg. exec.; b. Phila., Aug. 3, 1888; s. Charles and Anne (Thomas) S.; student Drexel Institute Tech.; m. Emily Tyrol, June 22, 1918; 1 dau., Marjorie. With Baldwin Locomotive Works, 1908-09; in motive power dept. Pa. R.R., 1909-24; sales rep. Safety Car Heating & Lighting Co., N.Y. City, 1924-33, south eastern dist. mgr., 1933-43, asst. to pres., 1943-46, v.p. charge sales, 1946-47, exec. asst. to pres., 1947, exec. v.p. 1947-48, pres. since 1948, also dir.; Phila. mgr. Vapor Car Heating Co., 1933-43; dir. Pintsch Compressing Co., Ltd., Spl. Service Co., Vapor Car Heating Co., Ltd., Vapor Heating Corp. Mem. N.Y.R.R., So. and Southwestern R.R., New Eng. R.R. and Central R.R. clubs. Republican. Clubs: Cloud, Canadian, Chicago (New York); Railroad Machinery, Racquet (Phila.); St. Davids Golf (Wayne, Pa.); Seaview Country (Abescon, N.J.); Atlantic Beach (L.I.). Author: Car Lighting by Electricity, 1923. Contbr. to Ry. Age and Ry. Elec. Engr. Home: 307 N. Wayne Ave., Wayne, Pa. Office: 230 Park Av., N.Y.C. 17. Died Oct. 1, 1951; buried West Laurel Hill, Phila.

STUART, Donald Clive, author, playwright; b. Battle Creek, Mich., Apr. 10, 1881; s. Reed and Helen (Soule) S.; A.B., U. Mich., 1903, A.M., 1904; studied U. Paris, 1905-06; Ph.D., Columbia, 1910; m. Herta von Baur, June 12, 1907; children—Donald Clive, Lorna; m. 2d, Martha Slocomb, 1934. Inst. in Romance langs. and lit., 1906-10, asst. prof., 1910-19, prof. of dramatic art, 1919—, Princeton U. Mem. Modern Lang. Assn. America, Phi Beta Kappa, Psi Epsilon. Clubs: Princeton (New York), Nassau (Princeton). Author: Stage Decoration in France in the Middle Ages, 1910; (plays) Sunrise, 1906; A Double Deceiver (prod. at Majestic Theatre, Grand Rapids, 1912); The Development of Dramatic Art, 1929. Contbr. articles on drama. Home: The Western Way, Princeton, N.J. Died June 1943.

STUART, Edward, sanitarian (ret.); b. Boston, Sept. 1, 1888; s. Edward and Emma Sophie (Wornle) S.; S.B., in Sanitary Engring., Mass. Inst. Tech., 1910; studied Technical School of Public Health Harvard, 1914-15; m. Helen Louise Fox, June 21, 1911; children—Edward, Virginia Sedgwick (Mrs. Emmett W. Wood). Sanitary engr. Oklahoma, and Brazil, South America, 1910-14; sanitary engineer, later dir. Am. Red Cross Sanitary Commn. in Serbia, 1915; dir. relief work of Am. Red Cross in the Balkans, 1916-17; with earthquake expn. to Guatemala, 1918; maj. Sanitary Corps, U.S. Army, 1918-19; mem. Rockefeller Tuberculosis Commn. in France, 1919-21; nat. dir. disaster relief, Am. Red Cross, 1922; producer of ednl. motion pictures for Rockefeller Foundation and Internat. Edn. Bd., 1923-25; in charge of malaria control, Cal. State Dept. Pub. Health, 1926-32. Mem. bd. dirs. Am. Yugoslav Soc. Mem. Am. Pub. Health Assn., Beta Theta Pi; asso. mem. Am. Soc. C.E. Episcopalian. Clubs: Explorers (N.Y.C.); Cosmos (Washington, D.C.). Contbr. to Am. Jour. Pub. Health, Nation's Health, etc. Home: 34 Marmion Way, Rockport, Mass. Died Nov. 25, 1953.

STUART, Harry Allen, naval officer; b. Tazewell, Va., June 16, 1882; s. Stuart James and Armie Lee (Miller) S.; student Tazewell Coll., 1898-1900; B.S., U.S. Naval Acad., 1904; m. Marie D. Blandin, Oct. 8, 1913; children—Marie Blandin (Mrs. Thomas J. Wacker), Anna Lee, Valerie Corinne. Commd. ensign, U.S. Navy, 1906, and advanced through grades to rear admiral, May 19, 1939. Democrat. Catholic. Clubs: Army and Navy Country (Washington). Deceased.*

STUART, Holloway Ithamer, banker; b. Knightstown, Ind., Aug. 28, 1865; s. Ithamer Warner and Margaret (Holloway) S.; grad. high sch., Knightstown, 1883; student Earlham Coll., Richmond, Ind., 1883-87; m. Elma Frances Ball, June 17, 1891. Settled in Pasadena, 1887, and since engaged in banking bus.; with First Nat. Bank, 1887-1905, chmn. bd., 1921—; pres. Union Nat. Bank, Union Trust and Savs. Bank, Pasadena, 1905-20; chmn. bd. dirs. First Trust and Savs. Bank of Pasadena, 1921—. Republican. Presbyn. Mason (32°). Clubs: University; Annandale Golf. Home: 1375 E. Mountain St. Address: First Trust and Savings Bank, Pasadena, Cal. Died Aug. 2, 1950.

STUART, Robert Terry, life ins. exec.; b. Kaufman County, Tex., Jan. 24, 1880; s. Champ Terry and Elizabeth (Raines) S.; student M. and F. Inst. (Chico, Tex.), Tex. Coll. (Huntsville); LL.D., Baylor U., 1933; m. Ida Freeny, Aug. 31, 1931; 1 son, Robert Terry. Country sch. teacher and ins. salesman, 1898-1900; organized R. T. Stuart & Co. and pres. of same, 1900-40; chmn. board Am. Investment Corp. (successor to R. T. Stuart & Co.). since 1941; pres. Mid-Continent Life Ins. Co., 1916-54, chmn. board 1954—; dir. Mo. P. R.R. Dir. National Rivers and Harbors Congress. Past pres. Okla. State Chamber of Commerce; chmn. bd. regents Okla. Agricultural and Mechanical Coll.; dir. Okla. City C. of C., Intracostal Canal Assn. of La. and Tex. Democrat. Methodist. Life mem. Masons (32°, Shriner, K.T.); mem. K.P., Elks. Clubs: Oklahoma, Rotary Internat. (Oklahoma City); Oklahoma City Golf and Country. Elected to Okla. Hall of Fame, 1956. Home: 1400 Classen Dr., Oklahoma City; also Stuart Ranch, Caddo, Okla. Office: Mid-Continent Life Bldg., Oklahoma City. Died May 23, 1957; buried Rose Hill Mausoleum, Oklahoma City.

STUBBLEFIELD, Frances Ogden, newspaper pub.; b. Wheeling, W.Va.; d. Herschel Coombs and Mary Frances (Moorhouse) Ogden; A.B., Vassar Coll., 1915; m. Daniel Wilkin Stubblefield, Jan. 9, 1917; children—Frances (Mrs. John Randolph Williams), Ann McEwen (Mrs. Ray Louis Muehlman), Margaret Ogden (Mrs. John Van Etten Hardy). Assistant to father in newspaper publishing business, 1939-43, upon his death became, with sister, publisher of 16 newspapers; president Wheeling News Publishing Co., Fairmount Publishing Co., Elkins Intermountain, Williamson Daily News, Washington (N.C.) Daily News, Point Pleasant Register; vice pres. Parkersburg Pub. Co., Welch Daily News, Hinton Daily News, Weston Times, Martinsburg Daily News. Sec. Kanawha County Rep. Com., 1928-40; Rep. nat. com.-woman W.Va. Mem. Am. Assn. U. Women, W.Va. Press Assn. (pres.). Clubs: Edgewood Country, Charleston Tennis, Kanawha County Women's Republican (Charleston, W.Va.); Fort Henry, Ohio County Women's Republican (Wheeling, W.Va.); National Women's Republican. Home: 5200 Kanawha Av., Charleston, W. Va. Office: News-Register, Wheeling, W.Va. Died Aug. 1959.

STUBBS, Mattie Wilma, author; b. Bucksport, Me., Sept. 10, 1878; d. William Chalmer and Annette Libbie (Morrison) S.; B.A., Colby Coll., Waterville, Me., 1900; studied in Europe, 1908-09. Asst. prin. high sch., Caribou, Me., 1900-06; teacher French and English, high sch., Bristol, Conn., 1908; teacher French, Woodfords High Sch., Portland, Me., 1910. Conglist. Author: How Europe Was Won for Christianity, 1913. Contbr. numerous articles to mags. and jours. Home: 11 Union Pl., Bangor, Me. Died Sept. 10, 1940.

STUBER, William G., company exec.; b. Lousville, Apr. 9, 1864; student pub. schs. of Lsvl.; m. Rose Reutlinger, June 6, 1888; 1 son, Adolph. With Eastman Kodak Co., Rochester, N.Y., 1894—, pres. 1925-34, chmn. bd. 1934-41, hon. chmn. 1941—. Home: Sheraton Hotel. Office: 343 State St., Rochester, N.Y. Died June 17, 1959.

STUDEBAKER, Ellis M., coll. pres.; b. Pearl City, Ill., Sept. 2, 1881; s. Simon and Charlotte (Etter) S.; prep. edn., McPherson (Kan.) Coll. Acad., 1898-1903; student Bethany Bible Sch., Chgo., 1906-09; A.B., McPherson Coll., 1915, D.D., 1927; grad. study U. Wash., summer 1914, U. Kan., summer 1917; A.M., U. Chgo., 1921; m. Lottie Viola Rothrock, Apr. 3, 1902 (dec. 1945); children—Reetha Rowena (Mrs. Paul Kurtz), Lloyd Raymond, Opal Bernice (Mrs. Sidney Miller), Hazel Elma (Mrs. Russell J. Frantz); m. 2d, Ida Schockley. Instr. in Bible, McPherson Coll., 1911-15, prof. N.T. interpretation and Greek, 1915-23; pres. La Verne (Cal.) Coll., 1923-38; insurance bus., 1938-40; adminstr. Bethany Hosp., Chgo., 1940-52, retired. Hon. trustee LaVerne Coll., 1952-54. Mem. gen. ednl. bd., Ch. of Brethren; mem. Nat. Edn. Assn., Cal. Soc. of Secondary Edn. Pres. Assn. of Colls. and Univs. of Pacific Southwest, 1936-37; Western Coll. Assoc. Republican. Club: Lions. Home: Pomona, Cal. Died Dec. 6, 1954; buried Evergreen Cemetery, LaVerne, Cal.

STURDEVANT, Clarence L. (stûr'dē-vănt), army officer; b. Aug. 1, 1885; B.S., U.S. Mil. Acad., 1908; grad. Engring. Sch., 1911; grad. Command and Gen. Staff Sch., 1926, Army War Coll., 1931. Commd. 2d lt., 1908; promoted through grades to maj. gen., 1945; Asst. Chief of Engrs., Washington, D.C., 1940; comdg. gen., New Guinea Base Section, SOS, June 1944; Deputy Chief of Staff, Am. Forces Western Pacific, July 1945; retired in grad of maj., gen., Sept. 1945; supr. Alcan Highway. Legion of Merit; Bronze Star; Distinguished Service Medal. Home: Route 4, Rockville, Md. Died Apr. 1958.

STURDEVANT, William Lommer, newspaper editor; b. North Girard, Pa., July 25, 1885; s. Frank

Watson and Julia (Lommer) S.; ed. high sch., North Girard; student Allegheny Coll., Meadville, Pa., 1904-06; m. Bessie N. Noyes, Oct. 8, 1912; children—Robert Noyes, William Lommer. Began as reporter Geneva, O., 1910; mng. editor Cleveland Press, 1920-22; editor Youngstown Telegram, 1922-27; editor New York Telegram, 1927-29; editor in chief Birmingham Post, 1929-31; editor Louisville Herald-Post, 1933; dir. of information, Tenn. Valley Authority, since 1933. Mem. Phi Gamma Delta. Episcopalian. Club: National Press (Washington). Home: Norris, Tenn. Office: New Sprankle Bldg., Knoxville, Tenn. Died July 2, 1952; buried Girard Cemetery, Pa.

STURGEON, Guy, banker; b. Yale, Kan., Jan. 30, 1901; s. Samuel Grant and Sophronia (Stevens) S.; student U. Neb.; m. Florence Thune, Dec. 10, 1925; children—Phyllis Mary (Mrs. David W. Little), Karen Thune. Pres. and dir. Bank of Commerce, Sheridan, Wyo. Served in U.S. Army, World War I. Mem. State of Wyo. Hosp. Adv. Council; v.p. Northern Wyo. Council of Boy Scouts. Mem. Independent Bankers Assn. Am. (pres.), Am. Bankers Assn. (pres. state bank div.), Am. Legion, Wyo. Bankers Assn., Sheridan C. of C. Elk. Mason (Shriner), Eagle, Moose. Home: 515 W. Burkett St. Office: Bank of Commerce, Sheridan, Wyo. Died Oct. 1, 1955.

STURGES, Preston, playwright, motion picture dir.; b. Chicago, Ill., Aug. 29, 1898; s. Edmund and Mary D'Este (Dempsey) Biden (born Edmund Preston Biden; adopted by Solomon Sturges, stepfather, 1901, and thereafter known as Preston Sturges); student Dr. Coulter's Sch., Chicago, 1906-07, Lycee Janson, Paris, 1907-11, L'Ecole des Roches, Normandy, France, 1911-13, La Villa, Lausanne, Switzerland, 1913-14 (also schools in Dresden, Berlin, Naples between terms), Irving Prep. Sch., N.Y. City, 1914-15; m. Estelle De Wolfe Mudge, 1922; m. 2d, Eleanor Post Hutton, 1930 (divorced 1931); m. 3d, Louise Sargent, Nov. 7, 1938 (div. Nov. 1947); 1 son, Solomon; married 4th, Anne Margaret Nagle, Aug. 15, 1951; children—Preston, Thomas. In cosmetic business, New York City, 1915; with F. B. Keech & Co., brokers, N.Y. City, 1916; with "Maison Desti," 1919-25; inventor, 1925-27; song writer and pub., 1927-28; theater work as assistant stage manager for Brock Pemberton; writer of plays since 1928; dir. motion pictures since 1940. Received Acad. award for best original screen play, The Great McGinty, 1940. Served with Signal Corps, U.S. Army, 1917; U.S. Sch. of Mil. Aeronautics, Austin, Tex., and stationed at Millington, Tenn., and Arcadia, Fla., 1918; commd. 2d lt. Air Reserve, when discharged, 1919. Clubs: Riverside Yacht (N.Y. City); Trans-Pacific Yacht, California Yacht, Pacific Writers Yacht (Los Angeles). Author: (stage plays) The Guinea Pig (also producer), 1928; Strictly Dishonorable, 1929; Recapture, 1930; Well of Romance, 1930, Child of Manhattan, 1932; (motion pictures) The Big Pond, 1929; Fast and Loose, 1930; The Power and the Glory, 1932; The Green Hat, 1933; The Good Fairy, 1934; Thirty Day Princess, 1934; We Live Again, 1934; Diamond Jim, 1935; Hotel Haywire, 1936; Easy Living, 1937; Port of Seven Seas, 1938; If I Were King, 1938; Remember the Night, 1939; The Great McGinty (also dir.), 1940; Christmas in July (also dir.), 1940; The Lady Eve (also dir.), 1941; Sullivan's Travels (also dir.), 1941; The Palm Beach Story (also director), 1942; The Miracle of Morgan's Creek (also dir.), 1943; Hail the Conquering Hero (also dir.), 1944; The Great Moment (also dir.), 1944; The Sin of Harald Diddlebock (also produced and dir.), 1946; Carnival in Flanders, 1953; The Birds and the Bees, 1956; The French They Are a Funny Race, 1957; The Gentleman from Chicago, I Belong to Zozo, 1959. Home: 61 Blvd. Berthier, Paris, France; 7420 Franklin Av., Hollywood 46, Cal. Died Aug. 6, 1959; buried Ferncliff Cemetery, Hartsdale, N.Y.

STURGIS, Charles Inches, retired railway official; b. Paris, France, July 21, 1860; s. Robert Shaw and Susan Brimmer (Inches) S.; prep. edn., St. Mark's Sch., Southboro, Mass.; A.B., Harvard, 1882; m. Margaret Noble, June 6, 1893; children—Robert Shaw, Frank Noble (dec.). In service of the C.,B.&Q. R.R. Co. since 1880, beginning as clk. in freight dept., Chicago, successively in gen. agt.'s office, Denver, 1881, cashier local freight office, Denver, 1882, paymaster's clk., Chicago, 1884, asst. paymaster, Chicago, 1885, paymaster, 1886-88, asst. gen. auditor, 1888-93, gen. auditor, 1893-1918, comptroller, 1918-21, sec. and treas., May 1921, vice pres., sec. and treas., Nov. 1921-Oct. 1938, now dir. Republican. Unitarian. Home: 81 High St., Winnetka, Ill. Died Apr. 24, 1952; buried Mt. Auburn Cemetery, Cambridge, Mass.

STURGIS, R(ichard) Clipston, architect; b. Boston, Dec. 24, 1860; s. Russell and Susan Codman (Welles) S.; A.B., Harvard U., 1881; studied architecture, London, Eng.; m. Esther Mary Ogden, June 22, 1882; children—Richard Clipston (dec.), Dorothy (Mrs. Lester W. Harding). Began practice in Boston, 1887, succeeding to business of John H. Sturgis (dec.); mem. Sturgis & Cabot, 1888-93, Sturgis & Barton, 1904-09, then the Office of R. Clipston Sturgis; consultant to Sturgis Associates, Inc., architects. Franklin Union, Boston; Brookline (Mass.) Public Library; First National Bank Bldg., Boston; Perkins Instn. and Mass. Sch. for the Blind; the Cathedral, Manila, P.I.; also housing for U.S. Housing Corp., Bridgeport, Conn., and for Emergency Fleet Corp., Bath, Me.; architect Federal Reserve Bank, Boston. Chmn. Bd. Sch. House Commr., Boston, 1902-10. Episcopalian. Fellow A.I.A. (pres. 1914-15), Am. Acad. Arts and Sciences. Mem. Colonial Soc. Clubs: Tavern, Union Boat (Boston). Home: Martine Cottage, Portsmouth, N.H. Office: 120 Boylston St., Boston. Died May 8, 1951.

STURTEVANT, Albert Morey (stûr'tē-vănt), educator; b. Hartford, Conn., Feb. 22, 1876; s. Francis Crayton and Hattie Mellen (Ellis) S.; B.A., Trinity Coll., Hartford, Conn., 1898; A.B., Harvard, 1899, A.M., 1901, Ph.D., 1905; student Univ. Berlin, 1906-07, Univ. Christiania, 1907; unmarried. Prof. Germanic languages, U. Kan., 1928—, prof. emeritus 1946—. Mem. Am. Philol. Assn., Modern Lang. Assn. Am., Linguistic Soc. of America, Soc. for Advancement of Scandinavian Study, Am. Assn. Univ. Profs., The Mediaeval Acad. of America. Mng. editor of Scandinavian Studies. Home: 924 Louisiana St., Lawrence, Kans. Died Sept. 22, 1957.

STYGALL, James Henry, physician; b. Buffalo, Mar. 10, 1887; s. James Sadler and Emma (Greiner) S.; M.D., U. Buffalo, 1910; m. Della E. Curry, June 15, 1915; 1 son, James Sadler. Supt. Rocky Chest Sanatorium, Olean, N.Y., 1919-21; med. supt. Ind. Tb Assn., 1921-24, pres., 1928; established Tb clinics in Ind. counties; chief staff Flower Mission Hosp.; Tb controller Indpls. and Marion counties; asst. prof. medicine Ind. U.; staff Meth., St. Vincent's, Gen. hosps. Served as capt. M.C., U.S. Army, World War I; chest cons. Selective Service, 1941-45. Fellow Am. Coll. Chest Physicians (founder council research; pres. 1955-56), A.C.P.; mem. A.M.A., Am. Trudeau Soc., Nat. Tb Assn. Republican. Episcopalian. Kiwanian. Home: 4311 N. Meridian St. Office: 1221 N. Delaware St., Indpls. Died Oct. 19, 1959.

STYKA, Tadé, portrait painter; b. Kielce, Poland, April 13, 1889; s. Jan and Lucie (Olgiatti) S.; studied under tutelage of father, Jan. Styka, Paris; m. Doris Ford, Aug. 12, 1942; 1 dau., Wanda. Naturalized Am. citizen. Exhibited: Grand Salon des Artistes Francais, 1903; Societe Nationale (member), 1913. One-man shows: Georges Petit; Gallery Le Boetie; Knoedler Gallery; Edouard Jonas; Wildenstein; Levy and Acquavella; also Chgo., Detroit, Los Angeles, Argentina, Can., and throughout Europe. Among important portraits painted: Marshal Foch; Gen. M. Wegand; Caruso; Chaliapin; Titto Ruffo; William R. Hearst; Sarah Delano Roosevelt; Pres. Harry S. Truman; I. J. Paderewski; Wm. A. Clark and family; James G. Harbord; H.R.H. King Humberto and Queen Marie José; Maurice Maeterlinck; Dr. and Mrs. Serge Voronoff; Mr. and Mrs. Cornelius Dresselhuys and family. Decorated Officer Legion of Honor. Address: 36 Central Park South, N.Y.C. Deceased.

SUCKOW, Ruth (sōō'kō), author; b. Hawarden, Ia., August 6, 1892; d. William John and Anna (Kluckhohn) Suckow; student Grinnell (Ia.) Coll., 1910-13, Sch. of Expression, Boston, 1914-15; A.B., U. of Denver, 1917; m. Ferner Nuhn, Mar. 1929. Owner and manager The Orchard Apiary, Earlville, Ia., for six years. Author: Country People, 1924; The Odyssey of a Nice Girl, 1925; Iowa Interiors, 1926; The Bonney Family, 1928; Cora, 1929; Children and Older People, 1931; The Folks, 1934; Carry-Over, 1936; New Hope, 1941, Some Others and Myself, A Memoir, 1952; The John Wood Case, 1959. Address: care Viking Press Inc., 625 Madison Av., N.Y.C. 22. Died Jan. 23, 1960. Buried Cedar Falls, Iowa.

SUDLOW, Elizabeth Williams, writer; b. Montreal, Que., Can., Feb. 3, 1878; d. William Porter and Jane Ann (Telfer) Williams; student pub. schs., Montreal and Detroit, also pvt. sch., Eng.; m. Henry Egbert Sudlow, Sept. 26, 1908; children—Phebe Alice, Egbert William, Henry Telfer, Elizabeth Winifred and Harrietta Eleanor (twins). Engaged in work for children, through writing, teaching, lecturing since 1904; popularized Cradle Roll work in Sunday Schs. Presbyn. Author: Primary Problems, Principles and Practice, 1904; All About the Primary, 1909-32; All About the Junior, 1916-23 (trans. Spanish for use in S.A., 1941), Cradle Roll Department, 1915; Cradle Roll Class at Work, 1923; Primary Plans for the Smaller Sunday School, 1928; Cradle Roll Questions Babies, 1929; The Mother's Year, 1929; Career Women of the Bible, 1951; Bible Women from Eve to Eustis, 1955. Contbr. about 5000 articles religious, ednl. mags. Home: 6225 S.W. 50th St., Miami 55, Fla. Died Dec. 4, 1958; buried Miami Memorial Park, Miami, Fla.

SUGG, Redding Stancil (sŭg), dean, Sch. Vet. Medicine; b. Old Sparta, N.C., Oct. 19, 1893; s. William Edgar and Jane Leona (Stancil) S.; student, N.C. State Coll., 1910-13, B.S. in Agr., Ala. Polytech. Inst., 1914, D.V.M., 1915; m. Katherine Maude Miller, Oct. 31, 1918; 1 son, Redding Stancil. Vet. practitioner, 1915-16; with Sch. Vet. Medicine, Ala. Polytech. Inst. since 1916, as instr., bacteriology and pathology, 1916-17, asst. prof. bacteriology, 1919-28, prof., 1930-31; dean of school since 1940; state veterinarian since 1940; extension animal husbandman, Ala. Extension Service, 1928-30, 1931-40. Commd. 2d lt. Vet. Corps, 1917, promoted to capt., 1918; with Officers Reserve Corps, lt. col., 1930; active duty as lt. col., Vet. Corps, 1942; chief, Vet. Service Branch, Camp Shelby, Mississippi, 1942-46; colonel Vet. Reserve, inactive, since 1946. Member American Vet. Med. Assn., U.S. Livestock Assn., Ala. Vet. Med. Assn., Assn. Mil. Surgeons, Alpha Psi. Epsilon Sigma Phi, Phi Kappa Phi, Phi Zeta. Mason. Club: Kiwanis (Auburn, Ala.). Recipient 12th Internat. Vet. Congress award, 1951. Home: 408 W. Magnolia Av., Auburn, Ala. Died Jan. 4, 1958.

SUGRUE, Thomas (shōō-grōō'), writer; b. Naugatuck, Conn., May 7, 1907; s. Michael Patrick and Mary Ann (Doolan) S.; A.B., Washington and Lee University, 1929, A.M., 1930, Litt.D. 1949; married Mary Ganey, October 26, 1935; 1 daughter, Patricia Ann. Reporter and columnist Naugatuck (Connecticut) Daily News, 1930-31; reporter New York Herald Tribune, 1931-34 staff writer, Am. Mag., 1934-38; chmn. editorial bd. Assn. for Research and Enlightenment, Incorporated; contributing editor Tomorrow Magazine. Member Phi Beta Kappa, Phi Kappa Psi, Omicron Delta Kappa, Sigma Delta Chi, Sigma Upsilon, Pi Delta Epsilon. Author: Such is the Kingdom, 1940; There Is a River, 1943; Starling of the White House, 1946; We Called it Music (with Eddie Condon), 1947; Stranger in the Earth, 1948; Watch for the Morning, 1950; A Catholic Speaks His Mind, 1952. Contbr. N.Y. Herald Tribune, Books, N.Y. Times Book Review, Saturday Review of Literature, other mags. Home: 5325 Chevy Chase Pkwy. N.W., Washington 15. Died Jan. 6, 1953; buried Naugatuck, Conn.

SUHR, Otto Ernst Heinrich Hermann, mayor of Berlin; b. Oldenburg, Germany, Aug. 17, 1894; s. Herman and Clara (Runge) S.; Ph.D., U. Leipzig, 1923; m. Susanne Pawel, Feb. 24, 1921. Reporter, 1920-22; labor sec., Kassel, 1922-25; dir. dept. econ. Gen. Assn. Free Employees, Berlin, 1925-33; free-lance economist, writer, 1933; dir. City Aldermen's Assembly, later pres. Congress of Berlin, 1946-54; governing mayor of Berlin, 1955—; prof. polit. theory Free U., 1953; v.p. Bundesrat, mem. German parliamentary council; pres. German City Delegates. Dir. German Coll. Politics, 1948. Mem. Assn. Polit. Sci. (bd.), Max Planck Soc. (senator), Inst. Polit. Sci. (bd.). Social Democrat. Author: The Organization of Employers, The Living Standard of Employees, Die Welt der Wirtschust vom standort des Arbeiters und Viele Einzelabhandlunzen. Home: Hüninger Str. 4, Berlin-Zehlendorf, Germany. Died Aug. 30, 1957; buried Berlin Zehlendorf, Waldfriendhof.

SUHRIE, Ambrose L. (sōōr'ē), educator; b. New Baltimore, Pa., Feb. 28, 1874; s. Francis and Mary (Topper) S.; diploma Cal. (Pa.) State Normal Sch., 1894; Ph.B., John B. Stetson U., 1906, LL.D., 1919; student Wooster Coll., 1903-05, U. Chgo., 1906; A.M., U. Pa., 1911, Ph.D., 1912; Litt.D., Duquesne U., 1941; m. Rosa Ritchie, 1906; children—Lincoln (dec.), Eloise (dec.), Ruth (Mrs. Robert J. Allaway). Tchr., prin., supt. pub. schs., Pa., 10 yrs.; prof. edn. John B. Stetson U., 1906-10; Harrison fellow in edn., U. Pa., 1910-12; dir. normal dept. Ga. State Coll. for Women, 1912-14; head, dept. edn., dir. extension, State Normal Sch., West Chester, Pa., 1914-15; asst. prof. elementary edn., dir. practice teaching, Sch. Edn., U. Pa., 1915-18; dean (head) Cleve. Sch. Edn., 1918-24; prof. Teachers-Coll. and Normal-Sch. Edn., Sch. Edn., N.Y. U., 1924-42; prof. emeritus, 1943—; guest prof. edn., Atlanta U., field cons. Coop. Negro Coll. Study, 1943-44. Lectr. summer sch., U. Pa., 1911-17; lecturer edn. before teachers' insts., chautauquas, univs., tchrs. colls., normal schs. (Has visited all tax-supported teacher-preparing institutions in U.S. and lectured in nearly all of them.) Sec. joint conf. com. Cleve. Sch. Edn., Western Res. U., 1920-24. Life mem. N.E.A. and chmn. City Normal Sch. and Tchrs. Coll. Sect. of Dept. Superintendence, 1921-22; organizer, pres., 1926-32, Eastern States Assn. Profl. Schs. Tchrs.; mem. Soc. Coll. Tchrs. Edn., Am. Acad. Polit. and Social Sci. Council Sociology, A.A. A.S., Nat. Child Health Council, N.Y. Sch. Masters Club, N.Y. Soc. Exptl. Study Edn., Phi Delta Kappa, Kappa Delta Pi. Seventh Day Adventist. Club: Montclair Athletic. Author: The Iductive Determination of Educational Method, 1915; The Spell-to-Write Spelling Series, and Teachers' Manual (with Robert P. Koehler), 1921; The Story World Reading Series—Story Folk, Story Fun, Story Friends and Story Adventures (all with Myrtle Garrison Gee), 1926. Editor: New Possibilities in Education (Am. Acad. Polit. and Social Sci.), 1916; Problems in Teacher-Training, 7 vols., 1926-32; organizer, editor Teacher Education Jour., 1939-42. Asso. editor N.J. Jour. of Edn., 1927-31. Home: Collegedale, Tenn. Died Feb. 19, 1956.*

SULLAVAN, Margaret, actress; b. Norfolk, Va., May 16, 1911; d. Cornelius Hancock and Garland (Council) Sullavan; ed. Chatham Episcopal Inst. (now Chatham Hall), and Sullins Coll., Bristol,

Va.; m. Leland Hayward, Nov. 15, 1936 (div. May 1948); children—Brooke, Bridget, William Leland. Began as understudy in play, Strictly Dishonorable, 1930; appeared on Broadway in leading role, Modern Virgin, 1931, Stage Door, 1936; Voice of the Turtle, 1943; The Dark Blue Sea, 1952; Sabrina Fair, 1953; in motion pictures since 1933, including Only Yesterday; also Three Comrades, Shopworn Angel, The Shining Hour, 1938; Shop Around the Corner, 1939; The Mortal Storm, 1940; So Ends Our Night, Black street, Appointment for Love, 1941; Cry Havoc, 1944, No Sad Songs for Me, 1950; Janus, 1955. Home: Beverly Hills, Cal. Died Jan. 1, 1960.*

SULLENS, Frederick, editor; b. Versailles, Mo., Nov. 12, 1877; s. John Perry and Ann Elizabeth (Waddell) S.; student U. of Mo., 1894-96; m. Anne Kirkpatrick Lemon, Nov. 25, 1903; 1 dau., Ann Kirkpatrick; m. 2d, Barbaara Barber, May 15, 1939. Began with Jackson Daily News, Jackson, Miss., 1904, editor, 1905—. Served as capt. Mil. Intelligence Div., Gen. Staff, U.S. Army, World war; maj. Mil. Intelligence, O.R.C. Mem. Am. Soc. Newspaper Editors. Mem. Associated Press, Southern Newspaper Pubs. Assn., Reserve Officers' Assn. of Miss. Democrat. Presbyn. Clubs: Rotary, Elks, Pioneer, Travelers, Newcomen, National Press, Army and Navy of Washington, Colonial Country, Union League. Home: 3806 Kings Highway. Address: Daily News Bldg., Jackson, Miss. Died Nov. 20, 1957; buried Lakewood Meml. Park.

SULLIVAN, Arthur George, surgeon; b. Eau Claire, Wis., Feb. 27, 1885; s. Florence David and Anna E. (McCarthy) S.; student U. of Wis., 1903-05; M.D., Coll. of Phys. and Surg. (Columbia), 1909; m. Florence D. Stott, Sept. 9, 1908; children—Arthur George, Frances Beale. Began practice in surgery at Madison, Wis., 1909; chief surgeon and cons. surgeon for numerous insurance and industrial cos.; attending surgeon St. Mary's Hosp., Madison Gen. Hosp., St. Mary's Ringling Hosp. (Baraboo, Wis.). Served in Med. R.C. and on Madison Draft Bd., World War I; mem. U.S. Pension Bd., 1916-27. Fellow Am. Coll. Surgeons, Founder's Group, Am. Bd. of Surgery, A.M.A.; mem. Inter-state Post Grad. Med. Assn. (trustee; mng. dir.), Wis. Med. Soc., Phi Delta Theta. Republican. Catholic. Rotarian. Mng. editor, Postgraduate Medicine. Contbr. med. articles. Home: 930 E. Gorham St. Office: Gay Bldg., Madison, Wis. Died Aug. 30, 1954.

SULLIVAN, Florence David, clergyman; b. Dubuque, Ia., Oct. 26, 1883, s. John J. and Honora (Cronin) S.; prep. edn., Jesuit High Sch., New Orleans, B.A., St. Louis U., 1905, M.A., 1906, grad. work, 1910-14; LL.D., Spring Hill College, 1929. Joined Soc. of Jesus (Jesuits) 1898; ordained priest R.C. Ch., 1913; prof. classical langs., Spring Hill Coll., Mobile, Ala., 1906-10; dir. classical studies, Jesuit Normal Sch., Macon, 1915-19; dir. dental dept. Loyola U., 1919-25, dean Coll. Arts and Sciences, 1922-25, pres. Loyola U., 1925-31; asst. editor America, 1931-34; rector of Gesu Ch., Miami, Fla., 1934-45; asso. in Inst. of Social Order, St. Louis, Mo., 1946-47; pastor Sacred Heart Ch., Augusta, Ga., 1947-50; pastor Immaculate Conception Ch., New Orleans, 1950-52, St. Joseph's Ch., Mobile, Ala., since 1952. Home: 808 Springhill Av., Mobile 16, Ala. Died Oct. 28, 1954.

SULLIVAN, Francis Loftus, actor; b. London, Eng., Jan. 6, 1903; s. Michael and Gertrude (Wilson) S.; student Neuchatel, Switzerland, 1911-13, Stonyhurst Coll., Eng., 1914-20; m. Frances Joan Perkins, Mar. 16, 1935. Came to U.S., 1948, naturalized, 1954. Began stage career Old Vic Theatre, London, 1921; with Bernard Shaw Repertory Co., 1925; actor Stratford-upon-Avon Festival, 1928; first appearance N.Y.C. in Many Waters, 1929; appeared as Agatha Christie's Hercule Poirot in Black Coffee, London, 1931, Tovarich, 1935; played role of King, Laurence Oliver's Hamlet, Old Vic Theatre, 1936, title role Oscar Wilde, 1937, role of Bottom in Midsummer Night's Dream, 1939; appeared Duet for Two Hands, N.Y.C., 1947, also Witness for the Prosecution, 1954; motion picture actor, 1931—, pictures include Great Expectations, Oliver Twist, Caesar and Cleopatra, Joan of Arc, Night and the City, My Favorite Spy, The Winslow Boy, The Prodigal; also appeared on TV. Recipient Antoinette Perry award for best featured actor's performance of N.Y. Season, 1955. Address: care Weissberger & Frosch, 120 E. 56th St., N.Y.C. 22. Died Nov. 19, 1956; buried Calvary Cemetery.

SULLIVAN, Francis Paul, architect; b. Washington, D.C., June 25, 1885; s. Thomas Joseph and Mary Katherine (Connolly) S.; A.B., Georgetown U., Washington, D.C., 1904; student George Washington U., 1905-09; m. Villette Anderson, June 28, 1911; 1 dau., Mannevillette. Engaged in practice of architecture, Washington, 1926—. partner with Delos H. Smith and Joseph Whitfield Burnum, 1956—; cons. architect for work on U.S. Capitol, House and Senate office bldg.; asso. architect with David Lynn (architect of the Capitol) and Harbison Hough, Livingston and Larson (cons.) to design reconstrn. of House and Senate Chambers. Principal works; Afghanistan Embassy, Children's Country Home, East Wing Senate Office Bldg., residence of Chief Justice Harlan F. Stone, Canadian Embassy; U.S. Legation, Tirana, Albania (in collaboration with Nathan C. Wyeth); Carrollsburg Housing Project Nat. Sports Center. Served as 1st lt., Ordnance Reserve, 1918-19; capt., Ordnance Dept., U.S. Army, 1919-20, Finance Dept., 1920-22; in charge of audit of war contracts, rep. of sec. of War in settlements with aluminum industry; comptroller, Post Office Dept., 1922-26. Nat. exec. officer Historic American Buildings Survey, 1934. Mem. constrn. code com. N.R.A., 1933. Fellow A.I.A. (2d v.p., 1935-36; chmn. com. Nat. Capital, 1930-42; chmn. com. pub. works, 1936-38; chmn. com. inter-professional relations, 1938-40; pres. Wash., D.C., chapter, 1933), Am. Geog. Soc.; mem. Soc. Archtl. Historians, Thornton Soc., Columbia Hist. Soc., Am. Planning and Civic Assn. (mem. com. of 100 on Nat. Capital), Phi Sigma Kappa. Del. Internat. Congress of Architects, Paris, 1937. Clubs: Cosmos, University (Washington). Author: The Portion of a Champion, 1916; also numerous articles relating to architecture, art criticism and city planning pub. in mags. and newspapers. Home: 3320 Rowland Pl., Washington 8. Office: 808 17th St., Washington 6. Died Feb. 3, 1958; buried Arlington Nat. Cemetery.

SULLIVAN, Gael, exec. dir. Theatre Owners Am.; b. Providence, R.I., Nov. 28, 1904; s. Timothy Joseph and Mary Agnes (Carroll) S.; A.B., Providence (R.I.) Coll., 1926; M.A., Thomas Aquinas U., River Forest, Ill., 1930; Litt.D., Loyola Univ., LL.D., Providence Coll.; m. Anne Burke, July 10, 1930; children—Gael Michael, Bede Carroll, Sheila Ann, Brenda Mary. Asso. prof. and lecturer DePaul U., 1930-31; contact exec. B. A. Holway & Asso. Advt. 1932-33; liaison officer Century of Progress Expn., Chicago, 1933-35; asso. state dir. Fed. Housing Adminstrn., Illinois, 1935-39; administrative asst. to mayor of Chicago, 1939-41; Ill. state dir. Fed. Housing Adminstrn., 1941-43; 2d asst. postmaster general, Washington, D.C., Oct. 1945-Feb. 1947; inaugurated helicopter service in delivery of mails; inaugurated First Flying Post Office, Oct. 1946; exec. dir. Dem. Nat. Com., Feb. 1947-May 1948; exec. dir. Theatre Owners of Am., 1948—. Labor relations adviser on staff of comdg. gen. 6th Service Comd., Chicago. Lectured on methods of mortgage financing and public adminstration Northwestern and Loyola universities. Mem. air coordinating com., Fed. Safety Council; mem. tech. com. on design aircraft Army Air Forces, Air Transport Assn. Served as major, U.S. Army, 1943-45; overseas, participating in North African and Italian campaigns, 18 mos.; chief of labor relations 6th Service Command, Detroit, Mich., 1945. Mem. Am. Soc. Pub. Officials. Roman Catholic, Knight of Malta, First Class, Knight Comdr. of St. Gregory. Home: 1000 Park Av., N.Y.C. 28. Office: 120 W. 42nd St., N.Y.C. 36. Died Oct. 27, 1956; buried St. Francis Cemetery, Pawtucket, R.I.

SULLIVAN, George Hammond, lawyer; b. New York, N.Y., Nov. 20, 1859; s. Algernon Sydney and Mary Mildred (Hammond) S.; LL.B., Columbia, 1884; spl. course Harvard, 1880-81. In practice of law at N.Y. City, mem. firm Sullivan & Cromwell. Mem. Assn. of Bar of City of N.Y., N.Y. County Lawyers Assn.; mem. Harvard Club, Alpha Delta Phi. Home: 16 W. 11th St. Office: 48 Wall St., N.Y.C. Died Nov. 14, 1956.

SULLIVAN, John Berchmans, congressman; born Sedalia, Mo., Oct. 10, 1897; s. Patrick F. and Catherine (Rockford) S.; student Gonzaga Hall of St. Louis U.; A.B., St. Louis U., 1918, LL.B., 1922, LL.M., 1923; m. Leonor Kretzer, Dec. 27, 1941. Admitted to Mo. State bar, July 1921, practiced in St. Louis, 1921-36; mem. firm Sullivan & Sullivan; asso. city counselor, 1936-38, sec. to mayor of St. Louis, 1938-40; spl. asst. to atty. gen. of U.S., 1947-48. Mem. 77th Congress (1941-43), 79th Congress (1945-47), 81st and 82d Congresses (1949-53), 11th Mo. Dist. Panel chmn., Region VIII, W.L.B., 1943-44. Served with U.S. Army, World War I. Mem. Fed., Am., Mo., St. Louis bar assns., Lawyers Assn. of St. Louis (v.p. 1938), Am. Legion (past comdr.; past judge advocate, Dept. Mo.). Home: 2303 Minnesota Av., St. Louis 4. Office: 705 Chestnut St., St. Louis. Deceased Jan. 29, 1951.

SULLIVAN, John Francis, lawyer, univ. prof.; b. Baldwinsville, Mass., Dec. 8, 1900; s. Harry Francis and Nora M. (Courtney) S.; B.C.S., N.Y. Univ., 1922, LL.B., 1926; m. Margaret J. Dwyer, June 7, 1924; children—Jeanne T., John F. Instr. accounting, New York U., 1922-27, asst. prof., 1927-32, asso. prof., 1932-44, prof. accounting since 1943; admitted to N.Y. State bar, 1930 and since practiced in N.Y. City. Chmn. Bd. of Athletic Control, N.Y.U., since 1948. Mem. Am. Assn. Coll. Instrn., Bar State of N.Y., Beta Gamma Sigma, Alpha Kappa Psi, Phi Delta Phi, Alpha Phi Sigma, Spinx Democrat. Catholic. Club: Accountants of America. Author: Legal Aspects of Fiduciary Accounting, 1927; Estate Administration and Accounting (with C. J. Dodge), 1935; Estate Administration and Accounting (professional edit.) (with C. J. Dodge), 1940; Estate Administration and Accounting (student edit.) (with C. J. Dodge), 1940. Home: 130 W. 12th St., New York 11. Office: 150 Nassau St., N.Y.C. 7. Died Sept. 1954.

SULLIVAN, John J(ames), lawyer; b. Phila., Pa., June 29, 1877; s. Jeremiah J. and Ann (Patterson) S.; ed. Notre Dame Acad., Phila.; A.B., St. Joseph's Coll., Phila., 1896, A.M., 1898, LL.D., 1914; LL.B., U. of Pa., 1899; LL.D., Fordham U., 1911; Litt.D., Duquesne U., 1931; unmarried. Admitted to Pa. bar, 1899, and since practiced at Phila.; v.p., trustee Market Street National Bank; president Finance Company of Pa.; director of Dodge Steel Company, Blauner's. Trustee Catholic University of America, Rosemont College, St. Emma Industrial and Agrl. Inst. Rep. Catholic. Clubs: Union League, Merion Cricket. Author: Pennsylvania Business Law, 1906, 14th edit., 1951; American Business Law, 1908, 4th edit., 1937; American Corporations, 1911, 2d edit., 1921. Home: 201 S. 20th St. Office: 2035 Land Title Bldg., Phila. Died Apr. 30, 1958.

SULLIVAN, John Lawrence, lawyer; b. Wilkes-Barre, Pa., July 20, 1891; s. John Martin and Honora (Hurley) S.; LL.B., Georgetown U., 1914; m. Elizabeth Coyne, July 19, 1910 (died Dec. 31, 1927); children—John Francis, Mary Kathleen; m. 2d, Ethel Fisher, Apr. 13, 1936. Admitted to practice law in states of Ariz., Calif., Neb., Ia.; in practice 1915—; county atty. Prescott, Ariz., 1921-23; atty. gen. of Ariz., 1935-36, 44—. Served as 1st lt., later capt. U.S. Army, in France and Germany, World War I; served in Provost Marshal Gen. Dept., U.S. Army, 1942-43. State comdr. Vets. Fgn. Wars, 1922, mem. nat. council of adminstrn., 1923-24, nat. judge advocate gen., 1940-41, now chmn. nat. rehabilitation com. Mem. No. Ariz., Ariz., Cal., Am. bar assns., Am. Legion. Democrat. Catholic. K.C. (State Dept.). Home: 313 W. Granada Rd., Phoenix. Died Oct. 13, 1949; buried St. Francis Cemetery, Phoenix.

SULLIVAN, Mark, author; b. Avondale, Chester Country, Pa., Sept. 10, 1874; s. Cornelius and Julia (Gleason) S.; grad. Normal Sch., West Chester, Pa., 1892; A.B., Harvard, 1900; LL.B., 1903; hon. Litt.D., Brown U., 1927, Dartmouth, 1928; LL.D., Washington and Jefferson, 1936, Bates, 1936, St. John's, 1937; m. Marie McMechen Buchanan, Oct. 31, 1907 (died Dec. 5, 1940); children—Sydney Buchanan (Mrs. Jameson Parker), Mark, Cornelius (dec.), Narcissa Harvey (Mrs. Dale Siegchrist). Author and commentator, Overseer Harvard, 1928-34; Bromley lecturer Yale, 1929; bd. visitors U.S. Naval Acad., 1929. Col. U.S.M.C. Reserve, 1933. Hon. mem. Phi Beta Kappa. Author: Our Times—The United States, 6 vols., 1900-25; The Education of an American (autobiography), 1938. Clubs: Players, Harvard, Century (New York); Metropolitan, Nat. Press, Gridiron (Washington). Address: Avondale, Pa. Died Aug. 13, 1952; buried Balt.

SULLIVAN, Oscar Matthias, atty., author; b. Canal Fulton, O., Jan. 2, 1881; s. Cornelius H. and Catherine (Marx) S.; B.A., Ohio State U., 1905; M.A., U. Pa., 1912; student Minn. Coll. of Law, 1921-23; admitted to Minn. bar, 1923; m. Bessie L. Ness, June 9, 1909 (dec.); children—Oscar Norbert, Ronald Ness, Lindley Dermot; m. 2d, Helen A. Hauser, May 1, 1948. Newspaper reporter, 1901, later asst. city editor Ohio State Journal, Columbus; teacher pub. schs., Minn. and Pa., 1906-12; chief statistician Minn. Dept. of Labor and Industries, 1917; state dir. re-education of disabled persons, Minn. Dept. of Edn., 1919-35; practicing law, Hamilton & Sullivan, 1935-37; Regional Unemployment Compensation Rep. of Social Security Bd., 1937-40; referee (hearing examiner) Soc. Security Adminstrn., 1940-51; retired 1951; practicing law with Sullivan, Stringer, Donnelly & Sharood; spl. asst. to Atty. Gen. U.S., as hearing officer on conscientious objector cases; special agent Federal Bd. Vocational Edn., 1920. Chmn. Governor's Commn. on Rehabilitation of Industrial Cripples, Minn., 1918; mem. Interim Commn. on the Blind, Minn., 1923; pres. Nat. Council for Physically Handicapped, 1935-36. Mem. Am. adv. council of Yenching Univ., Peiping, China. Mem. Am. Vocational Assn. (v.p. 1932), Nat. Rehabilitation Assn. (pres. 1933), Minn. Assn. for Crippled Children, Phi Beta Kappa. Mason (32°); O.E.S. Unitarian. Author: Disabled Persons, Their Education and Rehabilitation (with K. O. Snortum), 1926; The Empire Builder—A Biographical Novel of James J. Hill, 1928. Home: 742 Parkview Av., St. Paul 3. Died Feb. 16, 1955.

SULLIVAN, Owen J., banker; b. St. Louis, Aug. 8, 1878; s. Luther Owen and Melida (Jacquemin) S.; student St. Louis pub. and high schs.; m. Sarah Ott, 1905. With Nat. Stock Yards (Ill.) Nat. Bank since 1900, now chairman of the board and director; director St. Louis Nat. Stock Yards, East St. Louis Junction Ry. Clubs: Glen Echo Country. Home: 27 Cornell Av., University City, Mo. Office: The National Stock Yards National Bank, Exchange Bldg., National Stock Yards, Ill. Died Dec. 7, 1957; buried Valhalla Mausoleum.

SULLIVAN, Paul E., airlines exec.; b. Afton, Ia., Sept. 4, 1900; s. Stephen J. and Helen J. (Coen) S.; B.S., State U. Ia., 1925; LL.B., Loyola of Los

Angeles, 1939. Admitted to Cal. bar, 1959; bookkeeper First Nat. Bank, Creston, Ia., 1919-21, clk., 1921-25, teller, 1925-28; acct. Peat, Marwick, Mitchell & Co., Los Angeles, 1928-30; joined Western Air Lines, Inc., 1930, acct., 1930-35, chief acct., 1935-40, sec.-treas., 1940-45, v.p., sec. since 1945. Mem. Cal. State, Los Angeles bar assns., C. of C. Home: The Miramar Hotel, Santa Monica, Cal. Office: 6060 Avion Dr., Los Angeles 45. Died Sept. 9, 1958; buried Afton, Ia.

SULZER, Hans A., diplomat; b. Winterthur, Switzerland, Mar. 17, 1876; married. Mng. dir. of engrijg. firm of Sulzer Bros., at Winterthur; E.E. and M.P. from Switzerland to U.S., 1917. Address: Winterthur, Switzerland. Died Jan. 1959.

SUMMERALL, Charles Pelot, army officer (ret.) b. Lake City, Fla., Mar. 4, 1867; s. Elhanan Bryant and Margaret Cornelia (Pelot) S.; grad. Porter Mil. Acad., Charleston, S.C., 1885; B.S., U.S. Mil. Acad., 1892; LL.D., Hobart Coll., 1921, Williams Coll., 1927, Coll. of Charleston, 1935, Brown U., 1936; Dr. Mil. Sci., Pa. Mil. Coll., 1927, The Citadel, 1954; m. Laura Mordecai, Aug. 14, 1901; 1 son, Charles P. (U.S. Army). Commd. 2d lt. inf., 1892, transferred to arty., 1893, promoted through grades to col., 1917; brig. gen. N.A., 1917; maj. gen. N.A., 1918; brig. gen. regular army, 1919; maj. gen., 1920; general (as chief of staff), 1929; retired with rank of gen., 1931. A.d.c. to Maj. Gen. Graham, comdr. II Army Corps, 1898, to Brig. Gen. Pennington, comdg. Dept. of Gulf, 1898-99; campaigns, Philippine Islands, 1899-1900; with China Relief Epdn., 1900-01; located and initiated constrn. of Ft. William H. Seward, Alaska, 1902; mem. mil. mission to Eng. and France, Apr.-July 1917; apptd. comdr. 67th F.A. Brig., later 1st F.A. Brig.; joined A.E.F. in France, Oct. 1917; comd. 1st Div., July-Oct. 1918, later V, IX and IV army corps; mem. interallied commn. at Fiume, July-Aug. 1919; on duty with Am. Mission to Negotiate Peace to Aug. 31, 1919; apptd. chief of staff, U.S. Army, 1926. Former mem. Joint Bd. Army-Navy. Pres. The Citadel, Mil. Coll. of S.C., 1931—. Grand Minister of State Supreme Council. Chairman of Florida Canal Authority. Mem. S.C. Rural Electrification Authority. Decorated D.S.C. for gallantry, Battle of Soissons with 1st Div., World War I, D.S.M. for meritorious and distinguished services, Silver Star, 4 War Dept. citations for gallantry in action Philippines and China, 1900, Victory Medal for 5 major operations A.E.F., Spanish-Am. War Philippine and China Relief Epdn. campaign badges (U.S.); Legion of Honor. Croix de Guerre with two palms (France); Grand Officer Crown of Belgium; Comdr. Order of Crown (Italy); Mil. Medal (Panama); Order of Prince Danilo I (Montenegro); Grand Ribbon Polonia Restituta (Poland); Order Military Merit (Cuba). Mem. Soc. of 1st Div. of A.E.F., Am. Legion, S.A.R., Phi Beta Kappa, Omicron Delta Kappa, Blue Key. Episcopalian. Mason (33°); mem. Supreme Council Scottish Rite (grand treas.), grand insp. gen. in S.C. Clubs: Army-Navy (Washington); Rumson (N.J.) Country. Home: Aiken, S.C. Died May 14, 1955; buried Arlington Nat. Cemetery.

SUMMERS, Lewis Preston, lawyer; b. Abingdon, Va., Nov. 2, 1868; s. John Calhoun and Nannie Montgomery (Preston) S.; grad. Wytheville Male Acad., 1886; B.L., U. Va., 1893 (common and statute law), Tulane, 1895 (civil law); m. Katharine Barbee, Feb. 24, 1897; children—Gay White, Jane Douglas, Lewis Preston, Katharine Barbee, John Grant, Andrew Rowan, Olvia Wirt. Postmaster, Abingdon, 1890-94; began practice at Abindon, 1895; commonwealth atty., 1903; collector internal revenue, Western Dist. of Va., 1905-13; U.S. dist. atty. same dist., by apptmt. of Pres. Harding, June 6, 1922. Mem. Va. State Bar Assn. Republican. Presbyn. Author: History of Southwest Virginia and Washington County, 1903; Annals of Southwest Virginia. Home: Abindgon, Va. Died Dec. 10, 1943; buried Sinking Spring Cemetery, Abindon, Va.

SUMMERS, William Henry, cartoonist; b. Springarten, Ill., July 8, 1897; s. Thomas Ira and Cynthia (Willmore) S.; ed. high sch., East St. Louis, Ill.; student The Landon School of Art, Cleveland, O., 1921; m. Katherine Shea, June 22, 1916; children—Dorothy Marguerite (Mrs. Sterling Menke), Daniel Vernon, William Henry (dec.), Harriet Lucille (Mrs. Prentice C. Woodhouse). Began as clerk, later becoming assistant loading superintendent, Armour & Co., St. Louis, 1913-20; with Am. Multigraph Co., Cleveland, 1 yr.; asso. instr. Landon Sch. of Art, 1923-27; joined staff of Cleveland News, 1927, cartoonist, 1930-41; cartoonist Buffalo Evening News, since Mar. 10, 1941. Work on permanent exhbn.: Tex. Christian U. (Ft. Worth), U. of Ga., U. of Ark., Columbus (O.) Gallery of Fine Art, Medill Sch. of Journalism, Northwestern U., Ohio State U., Princeton U., Henry E. Huntington Historical Library and Gallery, San Marino, Calif. Baptist. Mason (32°; Shriner). Compiler: Daily News Reels (book of own cartoons), 1931. Home: 175 Linwood Av. Office: Buffalo Evening News, Buffalo. Died 1951.

SUMMEY, George, clergyman; b. Asheville, N.C., June 3, 1853; s. A. T. and S. R. (Morrison) S.; studied U. of Ga.; A.B., Davidson Coll., N.C., 1870, A.M., 1872; grad. Union Theol. Sem., Va., 1873; D.D., Southwestern Presbyn. U., 1891; LL.D., Davidson Coll., 1900; m. Elizabeth R. Worth, Dec. 15, 1875; children—Mrs. A.B. Dinwiddie, Albert, George, Mrs. C. S. Smith. Ordained Presbyn. ministry, 1873; pastor Bolivar, Tenn., 1873-75. Covington, Ky., 1875-80, Graham, N.C., 1881-84, Chester, S.C., 1884-92; chancellor Southwestern Presbyn. Univ., Clarksville, Tenn., 1892-1903; ed. of Southwestern Presbyterian, 1903-09; pastor Third Ch., New Orleans, 1903-28; became professor systematic theology, Austin Seminary, 1927. Moderator Gen. Assembly Presbyn. Ch. in U.S., 1925. Founder, 1887, and 13 yrs. mng. editor Presbyterian Quarterly; founder, 1890, and 3 yrs. mgr. Presbyterian and Reformed Review; supt. Monteagle Assembly, 1900-03. Hon. v.p. Am. Bible Soc. since 1926. Mem. Pi Kappa Alpha, Phi Beta Kappa Club; Round Table (New Orleans). Received citation for special merit, Davidson Coll., 1948. Home: 3002 DeSoto St., New Orleans. Died Feb. 21, 1954; buried New Orleans.

SUMNER, Clarence (Wesley), librarian; b. Noblesville, Ind., May 2, 1885; s. Charles W. and Mary Ann (Vestal) S.; student Earlham Coll., Richmond, Ind., 1904-07; A.B., U. of Mo., 1909; student Summer Sch. for Librarians, Ind. Library Commn., 1906; m. Florence Gillette, Dec. 25, 1916; 1 son, Clarence Wesley. Asst. Earlham Coll. Library, 1904-07, U. of Mo. Library, 1907-11; librarian, U. of N.D., 1911-17, Pub. Library, Sioux City, Ia., 1917-26; pres. Iowa Library Assn., 1921; librarian Youngstown Pub. Library, Oct. 1926-Feb. 1945. Served as librarian Camp Cody, N.M., Aug.-Nov. 1918, World War. Mem. bd. govs. Youngstown Coll. Mem. World Assn. for Adult Edn., Am. Assn. for Adult Edn., Nat. Council of Parent Edn., A.L.A., Ohio Library Assn. (pres. 1940-41), Ohio Conf. on Adult Edn. Mem. Soc. of Friends. Pioneer and organizer professional library service at bedside of patients in civilian hosps. Founder of Mothers' Room in Youngstown Public Library, 1935. Author: The Birthright of Babyhood, 1936; Books and Babies (with Dr. Garry C. Myers), 1938. Contbr. to ednl., religious and library jours. Lecturer on Parent Education and Child Training to ednl. and civic organizations. Home: R.D. 3, Bates Road, Perrysburg, O. Died Nov. 21, 1952.

SUMNER, G(ee) Lynn, advertising; b. Whitehall, Mich., Apr. 8, 1885; s. George Albert and Clara Jane (Gee) S.; A.B., Albion (Mich.) Coll., 1907, LL.D., hon., 1942; m. Amelia Amann, Oct. 16, 1911; children—Elizabeth June (Mrs. George S. Birdsong), George Warren; m. 2d, Mary Brooks Picken, Nov. 21, 1931. Asso. editor System Magazine, 1907-08; editor book dept., A. W. Shaw Co., Chicago, 1908-09; advertising writer System Service Bureau, Chicago, 1909-10; advertising dept., Internat. Textbook Co., Scranton, Pa., 1910-15; advertising mgr. Internat. Corr. Schs., Scranton, Pa., 1915-25; v.p. Woman's Inst. of Domestic Arts and Sciences, Scranton, Pa., 1916-25; pres., treas. and dir. G. Lynn Sumner Co., advertising agency, New York, 1925-51; v.p. Abbott Kimball Co., advertising agency, since 1951. Awarded medal for distinguished copy in Annual Advertising Awards, 1936. Pres. Advertising Club of New York, 1939-41. Republican. Clubs: Advertising (New York); Quaker Hill Country (Pawling, N.Y.). Author: Abraham Lincoln as a Man Among Men, 1922; We Have With Us Tonight, 1941; Meet Abraham Lincoln, 1946. Home: 11 E. 73d St.; and Quaker Hill, Pawling, N.Y. Office: 250 Park Av., N.Y.C. Died Apr. 7, 1952; buried Pawling, N.Y.

SUMNER, James Batcheller, prof. bio-chemistry; b. Canton, Mass., Nov. 19, 1887; s. Charles and Elizabeth Rand (Kelly) S.; prep. edn., Roxbury (Mass.) Latin Sch., 1900-06; A.B., Harvard, 1910; A.M., 1913, Ph.D., 1914; grad. study U. of Brussels, 1921-22; m. Bertha Louise Ricketts, July 20, 1915 (divorced); children—Roberta Rand, Nathaniel (dec.), Prudence Avery, James Cosby Ricketts, Frederick Overton Burnley; m. 2d, Agnes Paulina Lundkvist, 1931 (div.); m. 3d, Mary Beyer, 1943; children—John Increase, Samuel B. (dec.). Acting prof. chemistry, Mt. Allison College, Sackville, N.B., Can., 1911; research asst. Worcester (Mass.) Poly. Inst., 1911-Jan. 1912; asst. prof. bio-chemistry, Cornell U., 1914-29, prof., 1929—, director of Lab. of Enzyme Chemistry, 1947-55; fellow Commn. for Relief in Belgian Ednl. Foundation, 1921-22; Guggenheim fellow, 1937. Awarded Scheele medal at Stockholm, Sweden, 1937; Nobel Prize in Chemistry, 1946. Mem. Am. Soc. Biol. Chemists, A.A.A.S., Soc. Exptl. Biology and Medicine, Nat. Acad. Science, Am. Acad. Arts and Sciences, Sigma Xi, Phi Kappa Phi. Republican. Unitarian. Author: Textbook of Biological Chemistry, 1927; Laboratory Experiments in Biological Chemistry; Chemistry and Methods of Enzymes, 1943. Co-editor: The Enzymes, Chemistry and Mechanism of Action, 1950-52. Research on enzymes. Home: 508 Cayuga Heights Rd., Itahaca, N.Y. Died Aug. 12, 1955; buried Canton (Mass.) Cemetery.

SUMNER, John D(uncan), economist; b. Ottawa, Kan., May 15, 1904; s. John Stowe and Belle (Allison) S.; student Kan. State Agrl. Coll., 1922-23, U. of Wis., 1923-25; B.S., Northwestern U., 1926, M. B.A., 1926, Ph.D., 1931; Social Sci. Research Coun cil post doctoral fellow, research in Eng., Switzerlan and U.S., 1937-38; m. Marion C. Richter, Aug. 11 1928; 1 dau., Marion Faith. Research asst. Inst. fo Research in Land Economics and Pub. Utilities, 1925 26; lectr. Northwestern U., 1926-27, instr., 1927-28 asst. prof., 1930-31; asst. prof. U. of Buffalo, 1928 35, asso. prof., 1935-38, prof. economics since 1939 chmn. div. of social scis. and philosophy Coll. of Art and Scis. since 1947. Consultant Nat. Resources Com. 1937-38; with O.P.A., 1941-44, price exec. for non ferrous metals, 1942-43, spl. advisor to dep. admin str. for price, 1943-44; advisor on econ. affairs U.S Embassy, China, 1944-45; adviser; Office Financia and Development Policy, Dept. of State, 1945-46 economist Indsl. Mission to China, E.C.A., 1948 chief econ., officer of China Mission, 1948-49; economist, temporary mission to Indonesia, 1950, cons since 1949; economic advisor and dir. economic an finance div. China Mission, E.C.A. and M.S.A., 1951 53; U.S. mem. Capital Mblzn. Com. of U.N. Econ Commn. for Asia and Far East, 1951. Mem. Am Econ. Assn., Conf. on Price Research, Fgn. Polic Assn., Pi Kappa Delta, Sigma Phi Epsilon, Artus Conglist. Author: New York Barge Canal Traffic, 1929 Contbr. to various books also to profl. jours. Home 125 Oakgrove Dr., Williamsville 21, N.Y. Office University of Buffalo, Buffalo 14. Died May 3, 1953 buried Williamsville, N.Y.

SUNDBACK, G., engr., mfg. exec.; b. Jonkoping Sweden, Apr. 24, 1880; s. Otto and Kristina (Klas dotter) S.; M.E.E., Bingen am Rhein, 1903; Allegheny Coll., 1937; m. Marguerite Frances Titus 1916; children—Ruth Margit, Paul Philip, Richar Robert, Eric Henry. Naturalized citizen. Pres., chie engr. Lightning Fastener Co. Ltd., St. Catharines Ont., Can.; dir. Talon Inc., Meadville, Pa. Develope and constructed first slide fastener, Talon, and machinery for its prodn. Home: 502 Chestnut St. Office 950 Grove St., Meadville, Pa. Died June 21, 1954 buried Greendale Cemetery, Meadville.

SUNDELIUS, Marie (ŭn-dă'lĭ-ŭs), soprano; b Karlstad, Sweden; d. Andrew M. and Karolina (For nell) Sundborg; brought to U.S. at 10; studied musi under pvt. teachers; Mas. Doc., Rollins Coll., 1929 m. Gustaf Sundelius, of Stockholm, Sweden. Débu in Boston, 1910; joined Metropolitan Opera Co. 1914; 4 seasons with Antonio Scotti Opera Co.; seasons with Ravinia Opera Co.; 1 season with Th King's Henchman Opera Co. Guest artist Roya Opera, Stockholm, 1923. Awarded decoration of Liter is et Artibus by King Gustave of Sweden, 1923. Mem faculty New Eng. Conservatory of Music, Boston Home: 2 Gardner Road, Brookline 46, Mass. Office New Eng. Conservatory of Music, 290 Huntingto Av. Boston, Mass. Died July 1958.*

SUNDERLAND, Edson Read, b. Northfield, Mass. Aug. 29, 1874; s. Jabez Thomas and Eliza Jan (Read) S.; A.B., U. of Mich., 1897, A.M., 1898 LL.B., 1901; U. of Berlin, 1895-96, U. of Calif. 1898-99; LL.D., Wayne Univ., Detroit, 1929, North estern U., 1933, U. Mich., 1952; m. Hannah De Read, Aug. 23, 1905; children—Thomas Elbert, Alic Luella (Mrs. Harold E. Wethey), Elizabeth Read Teacher various branches of legal procedure, U. o Mich. Law Sch., 1901—, prof. law, 1904-27, prof law and legal research, 1927-44, prof. emeritus 1944—; research asso. on Sterling Foundn., Yal U., 1931-33; vis. prof. U. of Chicago, 1934, U. N.C., 1935, 38, U. of So. Calif., 1936. Advocate o reform in legal procedure; drafted official forms o pleading adopted by Supreme Ct. of Mich., 191 spent six months in Eng. studying court procedure 1924; drafted Mich. Ct. Rules (adopted 1931), Il Civil Practice Act (adopted 1933); mem. Mich. Pro cedure Commn., 1927-29; sec. Nat. Conf. Jud. Coun cils, 1931, chmn., 1932; pres. Assn. Am. Law Sch. 1930; mem. U.S. Supreme Court Advisory Com. fo drafting rules for federal courts, 1935-36; mem. An Arbor Bd. of Edn., 1925-34; mem. bd. dirs. Kings wood Sch., Cranbrook, 1931-43; Mem. Jud. Counc of Mich. (sec., editor, compiler Annual Report 1931-55), Am. Bar Assn., Mich. State Bar Ass. (sec.; editor Mich. State Bar Jour., 1922-24), Am Law Inst., (advisor on restatement of judgments) Am. Judicature Society (dir.), Phi Beta Kappa, Ph Delta Phi, Phi Gamma Delta, Order of Coif; hon mem. bar assns. of Chicago, Kansas City, Tenn., Pa Unitarian. Author: Pleading and Process (Cyclo. o Law and Proc.), 1909; Cases on Trial Practice, 191 Cases on Code Pleading, 1913, 2d edit., 1940, 3 edit., 1953; Cases on Common Law Pleading, 191 2d edit., 1932; Cases on Trial and Appellate Practic 1924, 2d edit., 1941; Cases and Other Materials o Judicial Administration, 1937, 2d edit., 1948; His tory of the American Bar Association and its Wor 1953. Articles on many phases of legal procedure periodicals. Home: 1510 Cambridge Rd., Ann Arbo Mich. Died Mar. 29, 1959.

SUNDERLIN, Charles Algernon, lawyer; b. Chase Mich., Dec. 1, 1883; s. Arthur Vaughan and E. Jenn (Coffin) S.; maternal ancestors came to Mass. abou 1640; mem. same family tree as Daniel Webster an John D. Whittier; great grandson of Hannah Dustin A.B., U. of Neb., 1907; LL.B., George Washingto University, 1908; married Pearl Bragunier Nusbaum ıne 21, 1911; children—Mrs. Geraldine Nusbaum rus, Mrs. Elizabeth-Jayne Hammeraas. Admitted to ·actice before District of Columbia Supreme Court, ›08; spl. rep. United States Dept. Interior investigating land fraud and trying land hearing cases, ›08-11; in federal govt. service in Ore. and Ida. 3 ·s.; practiced in Los Angeles since 1924; lecturer on s., U. of Southern Calif., 1928-33, One of Founders 'orkman's Compensation Ins. law. Member Idaho ate Council of Defense (chmn. legislative com.), orld War. Mem. Am. Bar Assn., State Bar of alif., bar of supreme courts of Ida., Neb. and Calif. ıd of U.S. dist. and circuit cts., Phi Gamma Delta, elta Sigma Rho (founder mem. and nat. officer), .A.R. Democrat. Presbyterian. Mason, Elk. Club: ıwyers (founder Pres.). Author: Sunderlin on Fire ısurance, 1929; Sunderlin on Automobile Insurance, ›29; The New Philosophy of Modernity—God-Science, Philosophy and Religion; The Future of American Democracy; Mysticism of Relativity; Sunderlin's eply to Roosevelt on The Federal Deficit; The Fuıre of American Democracy; also many philosophi-l discourses. Home: 10042 S. Wilton Pl., L.A. 47. ied Nov. 10, 1951; buried Forest Lawn Meml. Park, lendale, Cal.

SUNDSTROM, Swan Reuben (sŭnd'strŭm), pres. a. Greyhound Lines; b. Luleo, Sweden, Feb. 26, ›97; s. John A. and Hilda Sofia (Isaksson) S.; ı. high sch., 1 year; m. Josephine Marie Mattson, 'ar. 31, 1917. Began as bus driver, 1916; with Greyıund Lines since 1928; pres. Pa. Greyhound Lines 33-—. Died Aug., 1956.

SUNDWALL, John, univ. prof.; b. Fairview, Utah, ıne 12, 1880; s. Peter and Anna (Johanson) S.; .S., U. Chgo., 1903, Ph.D., magna cum laude, ›06; M.D., Johns Hopkins, 1912; m. Charlotte ıuline Morton, June 15, 1910. Prof. anatomy and an of Med. Sch., U. of Utah, 1907-09; hygienexpert U.S. Pub. Health Service, Washington, .C., 1910; asst. surgeon same, 1912; prof. anatomy, c. Med. Sch., and dir. Univ. Health Service, U. an., 1913-18; prof. of hygiene and public health, d dir. Univ. Health Service, U. Minn., 1918-21; r. div. of hygiene and pub. health, U. Mich., ›21-41; prof. hygiene and pub. health, 1921-—. em. Selective Draft Examination board, War Dence board, State of Kansas R.O.T.C., Ft. Sherin, World War; in charge med. service S.A.T.C., U. Minn., 1918. Fellow A.M.A., Am. Pub. Health ssn., A.A.A.S., Royal Sanitary Inst., England; em. Mich. Acad. of Science, Am. Student Health ssn. (pres.), Am. Sch. Health Assn. (pres.), N.E. , Michigan Public Health Assn. (pres.), Nat. Tb ssn., Scial Hygiene Assn., Sigma Pi, Alpha Omega pha, Delta Omega (nat. pres.), Phi Delta Kappa, i Gamma Mu, Sigma Delta Psi (nat. pres.), Phi ta Pi. Clubs: University, Rotary, Barton Hills ountry (Ann Arbor). Contbr. to ednl. and scienfic jours. Home: 1520 White St., Ann Arbor, Mich. ied Dec. 13, 1950; buried Mount Olivet Cemetery, lt Lake City.

SURAMARIT, Norodom, King of Cambodia, asnded throne following abdication of son, Norodom hanouk, Mar. 1955. Address: Phnom Penh, Camdia, Indochina. Died Apr. 3, 1960.

SUTHERLAND, Dan A., ex-del. to Congress; b. ape Breton Island, Can., 1869; s. John and Mary (Gwinn) S.; brought to U.S., 1876; ed. pub. hs. Essex, Mass.; m. Hilda Evanston, Oct. 3, ›10; 1 son, Donald. Went to Alaska in 1898 and gaged in mining; mem. Alaska Territorial Senate 8 ars (pres. one session); territorial del. from Alaska 67th to 72d Congresses (1921-33). Republican. onglist. Mem. Pioneers of Alaska. Mason, Odd Felw, Elk. Home: Juneau, Alaska. Died Mar. 25, ›55.

SUTHERLAND, Edward Alexander, educator; b. airie du Chien, Wis., Mar. 3, 1865; s. Joseph and ary (Rankin) S.; B.S., Battle Creek Coll., 1890; .D., Vanderbilt U. and Med. Dept., U. of Tenn., ›14; m. Sallie V. Bralliar, Aug. 13, 1890 (dec. ›53); children—Joseph Edward, Yolanda (wife of . Leonard Brunie); m. 2d, M. Bessie DeGraw, 54. Teacher secondary sch., 1883-86; pres. Walla alla Coll., College Place, Wash., 1892-97, Battle eek Coll., Battle Creek, Mich., 1897-1901, Emanuel Missionary Coll., Berrien Springs, Mich., ›01-04, Madison Coll., Madison College, Tenn., ›04-1946; exec. sec. Seventh-day Adventist Commn. Rural Living, 1946-50; pres. The Layman Founetion, 1924-—; med. supt. Madison Sanitarium and ospital 1914-40. Chairman board of trustees Rural dnl. Assn., 1924-46. Fellow A.M.A.; member Southn Medical Association, Tennessee Med. Assn., Nashle Acad. Medicine. Democrat. Seventh-day Advent. Author: Living Fountains or Broken Cisterns, ›00; also various articles. Editor The Madison Sury (pub. by Madison College), 1919-46. Home: adison College, Tenn. Died June 20, 1955; buried ring Hill Cemetery, Gallatin Pike, Nashville.

SUTHERLAND, Edwin Hardin, sociologist; b. Gibon, Neb., Aug. 13, 1883; s. George and Lizzie Pickett) S.; A.B., Grand Island (Neb.) Coll., 1904; h.D., U. of Chicago, 1913; m. Myrtle Crews, May , 1918; 1 dau., Betty Ann (Mrs. A. B. Sand). Teacher at Sioux Falls (S.D.) Coll., 1904-06, Grand Island Coll., 1909-11; prof. sociology, William Jewell Coll., Liberty, Mo., 1913-19; asst. prof. sociology, U. of Ill., 1919-25, asso. prof., 1925-26; prof. sociology, U. of Minn., 1926-29; prof. sociology, U. of Chicago, 1930-35; prof. sociology, since 1935, head dept. sociology, Ind. Univ., 1935-49; visiting prof. sociology, U. of Kansas, 1918, Northwestern, 1922, U. of Washington, 1942, research associate in criminology, Bureau of Social Hygiene, New York, 1929-30; vis. prof. sociology San Diego State Coll., 1950. Pres. Indiana Univ. Inst. of Criminal Law and Criminology. Mem. Am. Sociol. Soc. (pres. 1939), Am. Prison Assn., Chicago Acad. Criminology (pres. 1932-34), Sociol. Research Assn. (pres. 1940-41). Baptist. Author: Unemployment and Public Employment Agencies, 1913; Criminology, 1924; Principles of Criminology, 1947; An Ecological Survey of Crime and Delinquency in Bloomington, Indiana, 1937; The Professional Thief, 1937; White Collar Crime, 1949. Co-author: Twenty Thousand Homeless Men, 1936; also chapters in Recent Social Trends, 1933, and Young's Social Attitudes, 1931. Author or editor various monographs and papers. Co-editor: Prisons of Today and Tomorrow, 1931. Home: 500 S. Fess Av., Bloomington, Ind. Died Oct. 11, 1950.

SUTHERLAND, Gordon Alexander, musicologist, acad. adminstr.; b. Sacramento, Feb. 4, 1906; s. James Alexander and Beatrice (Wilson) S.; Mus.B., Am. Conservatory Music, 1927, Mus.M., 1930; A.M., Harvard, 1941, Ph.D., 1942; student Harvard Bus. Sch., 1943; m. Lois Smyser, Sept. 3, 1929; children—Gordon Alexander, David Angus, James Martin Hinchman. Asst. prof. music Grinnell (Ia.) Coll., 1930-31; instr. Pomona Coll., 1931-33, asst. prof., 1933-39; personnel dir. Radio Research Lab., Harvard, 1943-46; prof. music and dean sch. fine arts Miami U., Oxford, O., 1946-53; prof. music U. Mich., 1953-—, coordinator grad. studies in music, 1953-—; John K. Paine traveling fellow, Harvard, 1940-42. Member American Musicol. Society (council), Society Music in Liberal Arts College (treasurer 1951), American Association University Professors, Harvard Bus. Sch. Alumni Assn. Presbyn. Contbr. to Musical Quarterly, Music and Letters, New Oxford History of Music. Home: 1614 Granger Av. Address: Sch. of Music, Univ. Mich., Ann Arbor, Mich. Died Aug. 11, 1957; buried Arborcrest Cemetery, Ann Arbor.

SUTHERLAND, Roderick Dhu, ex-congressman, lawyer; b. Scotch Grove, Jones Co., Ia., April 27, 1862; s. Robert and Isabella S.; ed. pub. schs.; m. Ana Laramore, Feb. 8, 1883. Admitted to Neb. bar, 1888; County atty's Nuckolls Co., Neb., 1890-96; mem. Congress from 5th Neb. dist., 1897-1901; Populist with Democratic endorsement. Chmn. Populist State Conv., 1899. Home: Nelson, Neb. Deceased.

SUTPHEN, Duncan Dunbar (sŭt'fĕn), textile mfr.; b. Bedminister, N.J., Jan. 13, 1862; s. Jacob Losey and Christine Dunbar (Brush) S.; B.A., Rutgers, 1883; m. Jane Fraser, Jan. 7, 1904 (died 1919); 1 son, Duncan Dunbar; m. 2d, Elizabeth B. Burgher, June 5, 1929. Began in textile mfg. business, 1883; pres. A. D. Juilliard & Co., Inc.. Trustee Rutgers U. Republican. Club: University. Home: 104 E. 68th St. Office: 40 W. 40th St., N.Y.C. Died Feb. 24, 1953.

SUTPHEN, Henry Randolph, bus. exec.; b. Morristown, N.J., May 13, 1875; s. Morris Crater and Eleanor (Brush) S.; grad. Morris Acad., Morristown, N.J.; m. Susanna Preston Lees, Feb. 16, 1898; children—Preston Lees, Henry Randolph. Chmn. exec. com. Electric Boat Co., N.Y.C., 1947-—; trustee Am. Savs. Bank, N.Y.C., 1934-—. Home: 876 Park Av. Office: 445 Park Av., N.Y.C. Died Dec. 10, 1950.

SUTTER, Harry Blair, lawyer; b. Covode, Pa., May 22, 1891; s. Lafayette F. and Ella (Gourley) S.; B.A., U. Mich., 1914, J.D., 1916; m. Elsie Paul, June 24, 1919; children—William P., Mary (Mrs. John Walter Zick). Admitted to Ill. bar, D.C. bar, 1916; atty. U.S. Food Adminstrn., Washington, 1917-18; spl. atty. Office Solicitor Internal Revenue, Washington, 1919; mem. firm Hopkins, Sutter, Owen, Mulroy & Wentz, Chgo., 1931-—. Dir. Birtman Electric Co., Mandel Bros., Inc. Mem. planning com. Fed. Tax Conf., U. Chgo., 1952. Dir. Gads Hill Center, 1930-—, Evanston (Ill.) Hosp., 1955-—. Mem. Am., Ill., Chgo. bar assns., Law Club Chgo., Legal Club Chgo., Order of Coif, Sigma Chi. Clubs: Chicago, University, Mid-Day (Chgo.); Indian Hill (Winnetka). Home: 84 Indian Hill Rd., Winnetka, Ill. Office: 1 N. LaSalle St., Chgo. 2. Died Nov. 29, 1957.

SUTTON, Claude William, mfr.; b. Vienna, O., Feb. 22, 1883; s. Walter Jermiah and Caroline Phoebe (Murray) S.; acad. edn.; m. Sue Athelia Savage, Oct. 11, 1911. Yard clk., P.&L.E. R.R., 1900; with traffic dept. H. C. Frick Coke Co., 1901-09; indsl. engr. Miller-Franklin-Basset Co., New York, 1909-12; with Am. Vulcanized Fibre Co., 1912-23, pres. 1918-23; mgmt. cons., 1923-42; with Trundle Engring. Co., 1942-—. Mem. Del. adv. bd. Liberty Mut. Ins. Co. of Boston. Republican. Methodist. Mason. Clubs: Wilmington, Wilmington Whist, Wilmington Country, Wilmington Rotary; Manufacturers' (Philadelphia). Home: 1417 Woodlawn Av. Office: Equitable Bldg., Wilmington, Del. Died Aug. 5, 1945; buried Vienna, O.

SUTTON, Richard Lightburn, dermatologist; born Rock Port, Mo., July 9, 1878; s. John Grant and Virginia (Robertson) S.; student U. of Mo., 1898-99; M.D., Univ. Med. Coll., Kansas City, Mo., 1901; student Med. Dept. Geo. Washington U., 1903-04, M.D.; U.S. Naval Med. Sch., 1904; grad. study, Johns Hopkins Med. Sch., and in London, Hamburg, Berlin, Vienna and Paris; LL.D., U. of Mo., 1922; hon. Sc.D., Washburn College, Topeka, Kan., 1925; m. Lena Igel, January 3, 1906; children—Richard Lightburn, Emma Louisa (Mrs. Lewis H. Moore). Asst. surgeon, U.S. Navy (retired); formerly prof. dermatology, U. of Kan., now prof. emeritus; spl. rep. dept. of natural history, U. of Mo., African expdn., 1923-24, and expdns. for same dept. to Indo-China and India, 1925-26; headed African-Asiatic expdn., 1929-30, Arctic expdn., north of Spitsbergen, as spl. rep. dept. of natural history, U. of Kan., 1932; expdns. to New Zealand and Australia, investigating habits of swordfish, 1935, 36, 37, 38, 39, 40, Peru, 1941; with East Arctic Patrol, Northwest Territories, to Ellesmere Island, Somerset Island and Baffinland, summer of 1939. Trustee Kansas City Museum. Served as pvt. 4th Mo. Volunteer Infantry, Spanish Am. War. Mem. bd. dirs. Salvation Army Kansas City, Mo. Corr. mem. Swedish Dermatological Society, 1950. Life fellow Royal Geographical Society, 1924; fellow Royal Soc., Edinburgh, 1925; mem. A.M.A. (chmn. dermatol. sect., 1913-14), Jackson County Med. Soc. (pres. 1913-14), Am. Dermatol. Assn., French Geog. Soc., Alpha Kappa Kappa, Med. Library (pres. 1917-19); corr. mem. British Dermatol. Soc.; hon. mem. Southwest Clin. Assn. Mason (32°). Clubs: American Polar Society (New York); Aransas Pass Light Tackle, Tampico Tarpon, San Pedro Marlin; Bay of Islands, Swordfish and Mako Shark Club (Russell, N.Z.); Tauranga Angler's (Bay of Plenty, N.Z.); Bermagui Big Game Anglers' (Australia); New South Wales' Rod Fishers' Soc. (hon.). Author: An African Holiday, 1924; Tiger Trails in Southern Asia, 1926; The Long Trek, Around the World with Camera and Rifle, 1930; Diseases of the Skin (10th edit., with Richard L. Sutton, Jr.), 1939; An Introduction to Dermatology (4th edit., with Richard L. Sutton, Jr.), 1941; Synopsis of Diseases of Skin (with Richard L. Sutton, Jr.), 1942; An Arctic Safari, 1932; The Silver Kings of Aranas Pass and Other Stories, 1937; A Handbook of Dermatology (with R. L. Sutton, Jr.), 1949; sect. on The Mycoses in Tice's System, 1919, rewritten (with R. L. Sutton, Jr.), 1940-52; Collected Verse, 1946, also numerous sci. articles in Am. and fgn. jours. Contbr. to lay periodicals. Home: McAllen, Tex. Died May 18, 1952; buried Forest Hill Cemetery, Kansas City, Mo.

SUYDAM, Henry (West), newspaper corr.; b. Bklyn., May 19, 1891; s. Frank West and Jane de Hardy (Leigh) S.; student Princeton; m. Anne Hamilton Gordon, Apr. 25, 1925. Attached, 1914-17, to German, Austro-Hungarian, Turkish, British, Belgian, and French armies, and twice to British fleet in North Sea; reported campaigns at Dardenelles, Galicia, Somme, Ancre, and Verdun; reported Irish, Russian, and Chinese revolutions, interviewing leading statesmen; studied conditions and traveled in 30 countries of Europe, Asia, and the Far East; acted as escort for 50 British and French citizens sent into war zone at Gallipoli. Commr. ad interim of Com. on Pub. Information in Gt. Britain, Apr. July 1918; commr. in The Netherlands, July 1918-Mar. 1919; apptd. chief Div. of Current Information, Dept. of State, Apr. 29, 1921; sec. Am. Del. to Conf. on Limitation of Armament, in charge of press matters, 1921-22; Washington corr. Bklyn. Eagle 1922. Contbr. to Life. Home: 1812 19th St. N.W. Office: Colorado Bldg., Washington. Dec. 11, 1955.

SUYDAM, Vernon Andrew (sŭ-dăm'), educator; b. Waupaca, Wis., Mar. 21, 1872; s. George Mead and Elizabeth (Miner) S.; B.Sc., U. Wis., 1896; Ph.D., Princeton, 1912; m. Floy Davis, Oct. 31, 1913; 1 dau., Eleanor Elizabeth. Instr. Rapon (Wis.) High Sch., 1896-1900; supt. Ripon pub. schs., 1900-04; instr. U. Wis., 1904-07, Ind. U., 1907-09; fellow Princeton, 1909-10, instr., 1910-13; prof. physics, head dept., U. N.M., 1913-14, Medico-Chirurg. Coll., 1914-16, U. N.H., 1916-18, Grinnell Coll., 1918-23, Beloit Coll., 1923-43; asso. prof. physics, State U. Ia., 1943. Mem. Sigma Xi. Author: Fundamentals of Electricity and Electro-magnetism. Contbr. articles to Physics Review, Jour. of Franklin Inst. Home: 1224 Porter Av., Beloit, Wis. Died Jan. 23, 1955; buried Pickett, Wis.

SVERDRUP, Harald Ulrik (svâr'drŭp), meteorologist and oceanographer; b. Sogndal, Norway, Nov. 15, 1888; s. Johan Edvard and Maria (Vollan) S.; A.B., U. of Oslo, 1911, A.M., 1914, Ph.D., 1917; LL.D. (honorary), University of California, 1946; m. Gudrun Bronn, June 8, 1928; 1 adopted dau., Anna Margrethe. Came to U.S., 1936. Asst. to Prof. V. Bjerknes in Oslo, 1911-12, in Leipzig, 1913-17; in charge scientific work on Maud Expdn. in Arctic, 1917-25; research asso., Carnegie Instn. of Washington, 1926, 1928-39; prof. meteorology, Geophysical

Institute of Bergen, 1926-30; hon. professor Chr. Michelsen Inst., 1931-40; in charge scientific work on Wilkins-Ellsworth submarine Arctic expdn. on board Nautilus, 1931; prof. of oceanography, U. of Calif. and dir. Scripps Instn. of Oceanography, 1936-48; dir. Norwegian Polar Inst., Oslo, Norway, since 1948. Lieutenant in Reserve of Norway. Decorated Comdr. of St. Olav, Comdr. Dannebrog, Nordstjernen; D.S.M. (U.S.N.); Patrons medal, Royal Geog. Society; Bowie medal, American Geological Society; awarded Vega gold medal, Carl Ritter medal, Bruce memorial, Meteor, Agassiz medals. Member National Academy of Scis., Norwegian Academy of Sciences, American Academy of Arts and Sciences; honorary member Royal Meteorol. Soc., German Meteorol. Soc., Calif. Acad. Sciences, New York Academy Science, Am. Philosophical Soc.; hon. or corr. mem. 7 geog. socs. Mem. Lutheran State Ch. of Norway. Club: Explorer's (N.Y. City). Author: Hos tundra-folket, 1938; also other books pub. in Norway; Oceanography for meteorologists, 1942; The Oceans (with M. W. Johnson, R. H. Fleming), 1942. Editor and contributor scientific reports of Maud Expdn.; contbr. articles to sci. jours.; mem. bd. of editors Jour. of Marine Research. Address: Observatoreigt 1, Oslo, Norway. Died Aug. 21, 1957.

SWACKER, Frank M., lawyer; b. St. Louis, July 1879; s. Howard Wythe and Margaret E. (Walls) S.; ed. pub. schs., pvt. tutors; m. Loretta C. Stark, 1920 (dec. 1946); 1 son, Frank Warren. With various cos., 1892-98, 1898-1912; examiner Interstate Commerce Commn., Washington, 1912; admitted to D.C. bar, 1914; spl. asst. atty. gen. U.S., 1913-20; pvt. practice, N.Y. City since 1915; served as arbitrator, referee, neutral by govtl. appointment on President's emergency bds., bds. Nat. R.R. Adjustment Bd., other arbitrations involving labor relations, r.r., airline matters; mem. Nat. Ry. Labor Panel, 1943, spl. stblzn. bd. Econ. Stblzn. Agy., 1951. Mem. Am. Bar Assn., N.Y. Co. Lawyers Assn., Assn. Practitioners Interstate Commerce Commn., Am. Acad. Polit. Sci., N.Y. So. Soc. Clubs: Lawyers (N.Y. City); Nat. Press (Washington). Office: 120 Broadway, N.Y.C. 5. Died Nov. 29, 1953.

SWAIM, H. Nathan, judge; b. Zionsville, Ind., Nov. 30, 1890; s. Charles Rufus and Alice Elizabeth (Avery) S.; A.B., De Pauw, 1913, LL.D., 1949; J.D., U. Chicago, 1916; m. Clara L. Kenner, July 14, 1917; children—Robert W., Norma Jean Sutter. Admitted to Ind. bar, July 1, 1916, and practiced in Indianapolis, 1916-39; mem. Ogden & Swaim, 1916-39; judge Ind. Supreme Court, Jan. 3, 1939-45; judge U.S. Ct. of Appeals, 7th Circuit, 1949—. Served U.S. Army, 1917-18, disch. as 1st lt. Former pres. bd. of trustees Ind. Soldiers and Sailors Children's Home. Pres. DePauw Alumni Assn. 1944-46; chmn. various President's Emergency Bds. under Ry. Labor Act, 1945-47. Mem. Indpls. Bd. Sch. Commrs., 1947-49. Mem. Am., Ind., Indpls. bar associations, Order of Coif, American Legion, Sigma Nu, Phi Delta Phi. Methodist. Mason. Clubs: Indpls. Athletic, Indpls. Service. Home: 4122 N. Meridian St., Indpls. Office: 1212 Lake Shore Dr., Chgo. 10; also Federal Bldg., Indpls. Died July 30, 1957; buried Crown Hill Cemetery, Indpls.

SWAIN, Philip William, editor; b. Westerville, Ohio, Aug. 26, 1889; s. Richard LaRue and Anna Elizabeth (Shuey) S.; A.B., Syracuse U., 1911; Ph.B., Yale, 1913, M.E., 1915; D.Eng. hon., Case Inst. Tech., 1947; m. Edith Florence Adair, Aug. 21, 1917; children—Jean Adair, Anne Mackintosh (Mrs. Hall F. Overton). Instr. mech. engring. Yale, 1915-16, 16-17; engr. Franklin (Pa.) Mfg. Co., 1919-21; asso. editor Power, McGraw-Hill Pub. Co., 1921-33, mng. editor, 1933-34, chief editor 1934-54, now consulting editor; consultant, lecturer engring., technical writer; assistant director Office Strategic Information, Department of Commerce, 1955; tech. advisor C.B.S. Bikini atom bomb tests, 1946; covered tests for McGraw-Hill papers. Served 2d lt. to 1st lt. with F.A., U.S. Army, 1917-19. Fellow A.S. M.E., Am. Welding Soc., Yale Engring. Assn., Nat. Conf. Bus. Paper Editors, Sigma Xi, Tau Beta Pi, Sigma Delta Chi. Clubs: Yale (N.Y. City); Yacht (Riverside). Address: 95 Club Rd., Riverside, Conn. Died Apr. 27, 1958.

SWAN, Clifford Melville, cons. engr.; b. Boston, Mass., Aug. 6, 1877; s. Reuben Samuel and Emma Augusta (Melville) S.; S.B., Mass. Inst. Tech., 1899; A.M., Harvard, 1908; unmarried. Instr. physics, Mass. Inst. Tech., 1902-11; associated with Prof. W. C. Sabine in pioneer development of science of archtl. acoustics, 1911-18; chief acoustical engr. Johns-Manville Co., 1911-27, dir. co., 1926-27; cons. engr. in acoustics since 1918; cons. bd. of design N.Y. World's Fair, 1939. Past chmn. Nat. Interfraternity Conference Fellow Acoustical Society America; member Harvard Engring. Soc., N.Y. Geneal. and Biog. Society, Soc. Colonial Wars, Soc. Mayflower Descendants, New England Hist.-Geneal. Soc., Delta Upsilon (dir., past pres.). Republican. Episcopalian. Clubs: Century, University, Harvard, (New York); Harvard (Boston); Bohemian (San Francisco). Contbr. articles on archtl. acoustics to Am. Architect, Archtl. Forum, Jour. of Am. Inst. Architects, Architectural Record and other mags. Office: 271 Madison Av., N.Y.C. 16. Deceased.

SWAN, Frank Herbert, lawyer; b. Windham, Me., Aug. 3, 1873; s. John (M.D.) and Elizabeth G. (Dutch) S.; A.B., Bowdoin, 1898; LL.B., Boston U., 1901; LL.D., Bowdoin Coll., 1938; m. Hannah L. Dana, Oct. 30, 1901; children—Woodbury D. (dec.), Elizabeth D., Marshall, Dana M., Frank. Admitted to Me. bar, 1901 and began practice in Portland; city solicitor, Westbrook, 1902-05; asst. U.S. atty. for Me., 1902-05; moved to Providence, 1905; pres. Union Wadding Co.; director Providence Gas Co., Providence Braid Co., R.I. Hospital Trust Co., Brown & Sharpe Mfg. Co.; trustee Bowdoin Coll., Y.M.CA.; ex-pres. Bradley Hosp. Mem. Am. Bar Assn., R.I. Bar Assn. (ex-pres.), Rhode Island Hist. Soc. Republican. Conglist. Mason (K.T.). Clubs: University, Hope, Turks Head. Home: 175 Medway St. Office: Turks Head Bldg., Providence 3. Died June 7, 1954.

SWAN, John Mumford, physician; b. Newport, R.I., Jan. 23, 1870; s. John Mumford and Annie Frances Greene (Taggert) S.; grad. Rogers High Sch., Newport, 1887; M.D., U. Pa., 1893; m. Sara Halyday Raymond, Dec. 16, 1896 (died Oct. 13, 1949). Demonstrator osteology and asst. demonstrator anatomy, U. Pa., 1895-1904; instr. clin. pathology and instr. tropical medicine, Phila., Polyclinic and Coll. for Grades. in Medicine, 1904-10; asso. prof. clin. medicine, Medico-Chirurg. Col. of Phila., 1909-10; med. dir. The Glen Springs, Watkins, N.Y., 1910-12. Commd. 1st lt. Med. Res. Corps, AUS, Dec. 9, 1915; maj., Apr. 9, 1917; lt. col., Aug. 20, 1918; comdg. officer Base Hosp. 19, July 1918 to demobilization, May 1919; active service at Vichy, France; chief med. service Base Hosp., Camp Devens, Mass., May-Aug. 1919; discharged Aug. 18, 1919. Citation from comdg. gen. A.E.F., Apr. 1919, "for especially meritorious and conspicuous service at Base Hosp. 19." Field rep. A.R.C., Dominican Republic and Haiti, 1919-20. Col., Med. Res., U.S. Army, May 1923; col. Auxiliary Res., U.S. Army, Jan. 1934. Awarded Purple Heart. Fellow A.C.P., Coll. Physicians Phila.; mem. Am. Climatol. and Clin. Assn., Am. Acad. Polit. and Social Sci., A.M.A., Am. Cancer Soc. (state sec. N.Y. State Div.), Mil. Order Fgn. Wars, Assn. Mil. Surgeons of U.S. Am. Legion Post No. 194 (comdr. 1942), Am. Soc. Tropical Medicine (pres. 1921). Author: A Manual of Human Anatomy, Arranged for Second Year Students, 1898; A Manual of Human Anatomy, Arranged for First Year Students, 1900; Prescription Writing and Formulary, 1910. Address: 457 Park Av., Rochester 7, N.Y. Died Nov. 22, 1949; buried Arlington Nat. Cemetery.

SWANSEN, Sam T., lawyer b;. Baldwin, Wis., June 4, 1868; s. Torfin and Ragna (Erdahl) S.; B.L., U. Wis., 1890, LL.B., 1892; m. Jessie L. Nelson, July 2, 1902; children—Theodore Lawrence, John Philipps, Sam Torfin (dec.), Robert Coleman. Admitted to Wis. bar, 1892, and began practice at Madison; successively mem. firms Erdall & Swansen; Tennys, Hall & Swansen and Richmond Jackman & Swansen; asst. counsel The Northwestern Mutual Life Ins. Co. of Milwaukee, 1916-29, asst. gen. counsel, 1929-30, gen. counsel, 1930-43, retired. Mem. Am., Wis. and Milwaukee bar assn., Phi Beta Kappa, Phi Delta Phi. Home: 1224 N. Prospect Av., Milwaukee. Died Nov. 18, 1959.

SWANSON, Paul Gustaf, mfg. exec.; b. Rockford, Ill., Oct. 19, 1895; s. Gustaf C. and Ida (Berg) S.; student of public schools; married to Ina M. Anderson, January 17, 1925; 1 daughter, Shirley May (Mrs. Richard E. Dye). Clerk, Nat. Lock Co., Rockford, Ill., 1916, prodn. control, 1917, sales rep., 1918, prodn. control mfg., 1920, night supt., 1921, sales corr., 1922; co-organizer Elco Tool & Screw Corp., Rockford, 1923, sales mgr., 1924-42, pres., gen. mgr., 1942-45, chmn. bd., 1946—; pres. Albert Anderson Clothiers, Inc., Rockford, 1956—. Mem. C. of C., Svea Soner Singing Soc. Republican. Lutheran. Home: 1215 N.E. 97th St., Miami, Fla.; also 1725 Parkview Av., Rockford. Office: 1800 Broadway, Rockford, Ill. Died Dec. 5, 1958; buried Rockford, Ill.

SWANTON, Gerald F(rancis), steamship exec.; b. Bklyn., Sept. 20, 1904; s. Francis X. and Mary (Lynch) S.; LL.M., St. Johns U., 1930; m. Katherine O'Donnell, Dec. 27, 1934; 1 son, Gerald Francis. Admitted to N.Y. bar, 1931, practiced in N.Y.C., 1931-51; sec. Moore-McCormack Lines, Inc., since 1951. Mem. India House. Clubs: Huntington Country, Centerport Yacht, Brooklyn. Home: 7-92d St., Bklyn. 7. Office: 5 Broadway, N.Y.C. 4. Died Apr. 1955.

SWANTON, John Reed, retired ethnologist; b. Gardiner, Me., Feb. 19, 1873; s. Walter Scott and Mary Olivia (Worcester) S.; A.B., Harvard, 1896, A.M., 1897; student Columbia, 1898-1900; Ph.D., Harvard, 1900; m. Alice Barnard, Dec. 16, 1903 (died Sept. 18, 1926); children—Mary Alice, John Reed, Henry Allen. Ethnologist, Bureau Am. Ethnology, Washington, D.C., 1900-44. Mem. Am. Anthrop. Association, Anthrop. Soc., Washington, A.A.A.S., Linguistic Soc. Am., Nat. Acad. of Sciences. Author: Contributions to the Ethnology of the Haida, 1905; Haida Texts and Myths, 1905; Haida Texts—Masse Dialect; Social Conditions, Beliefs, and Linguisti Relationship of the Tlingit Indians; Tlingit Myth and Texts; Indian Tribes of the Lower Mississipp Valley and Adjacent Coast of the Gulf of Mexico (with J. O. Dorsey) A Dictionary of the Biloxi an Ofo Languages; History of the Creek Indians an Their Neighbors; Social Organization and Social Usage of the Creek Indians; Religious Beliefs and Medica Practices of the Creek Indians; Social Conditions an Religious Beliefs of the Chickasaw Indians; Myth and Tales of the Southeastern Indians; (with A. S Gatschet) A Dictionary of the Atakapa Language Source Material for the Social and Ceremonial Life o the Choctaw Indians; Linguistic Material from th Tribes of Southern Texas and Northeastern Mexico Source Material for the History and Ethnology of th Caddo Indians, Indians of the Southeastern U.S. The Wineland Voyages; The Indian Tribes of Nort America, 1952. Chmn. U.S. De Soto Expdn. Commn. 1935—. Swedenborgian. Home: 22 George St Newton 58, Mass. Died May 2, 1958.

SWARTZ, Charles Benjamin, clergyman; b. Wi mington, Del., Sept. 11, 1890; s. William Paley an Florence Allen (Reed) S.; B.A., Lafayette Coll. 1911 (valedictorian); B.A., Merton Coll., Oxford U. Eng., 1914; B.D., summa cum laude, Union Theo Sem., 1917, S.T.M., magna cum laude, 1921; D.D. Blackburn Coll., 1925; m. Ruth Elizabeth Fowler June 14, 1921; children—David Fowler, Barbara Reed Mary Billington. Apptd. Rhodes scholar, Pa., 1911 pastor Forest Hills (L.I.) Ch., 1914-16; ordaine Presbyn. ministry, 1916; student asst. Central Ch. N.Y. City, 1916-17; asst. pastor Bryn Mawr (Pa. Ch., 1917-18; pastor Woodlawn Heights Ch., N.Y City, 1919-24, First Ch., Chicago, 1924-26, First Ch Galesburg, Ill., 1927-31, First Ch., Bloomington, Ind. 1931-44. Dir. student work Indiana U.; instr. i Bible, Knox Coll., 1928-31. With Army Y.M.C.A and dir. religious edn. in colleges, Dept. of the East War Work Council Y.M.C.A., 1918-19. Chmn Commn. on Orgn. of Council of Chs. for Ind., 1937 39; pres. Ind. Pastors Conv., 1937. Mem. bd. mgrs Presbyn. Hosp., Chicago, 1924-26; mem. Gen. Counci of Synod of Ill., 1927-31. Prof. of religion an philosophy, Hanover (Indiana) Coll. 1945; bd. c dirs., Ind. Council of Churches, 1943-50; membe Council of Synod of Ind., Presbyn. Ch., since 1943 Mem. Delta Upsilon, Phi Beta Kappa. Ex-pres Bloomington Kiwanis Club; lt. gov. Kiwanis, 1938 Contbr. to Presbyn. Young Peoples Quarterlies. Home Hanover College, Hanover, Ind. Died Feb. 3, 1951.

SWASEY, Albert Loring (swā'zē), naval architec b. Auburndale, Mass., Sept. 14, 1876; s. Alber Edgar and Ella Cecelia (Wilson) S.; ed. Brist Acad., Taunton, Mass., 1882-94, Mass. Inst. Tec (naval architecture), 1894-98; m. Dorothy Lovering Nov. 26, 1907; children—David Loring, John Loring Draftsman hull depts., Newport News Shipbuildin Co., 1898, Cramp's Shipbuilding Co., 1899, N.Y Shipbuilding Co., Camden, N.J., 1900-05; mem. fir Swasey, Raymond & Page, yacht designers, Bostor 1898-1917; v.p. Herreshoff Mfg. Co., Bristol, R.I. 1917-23; mem. firm Burgess, Swasey & Paine, nava architecture and yacht design, Boston, 1923-27; v.p Henry Gielow Corp., naval architecture and yach design, N.Y. City, 1927-32; marine insurance brok and agent, Boston Ins. Co., 1915-40. Comd. l comdr. Constrn. Corps, U.S., N.R.F., Apr. 2, 1917 comdr., 1919, capt., July 3, 1938; served as sup constrn. U.S. Navy, N.Y. City, Bureau Constrn. an Repairs, Washington, D.C., mem. Appraisal Bd. fo Curtiss Engr. Corpn., mem. sec. of Navy's Bd. o Review, 1917-21; mem. President's Bd. of Commar deering Merchant and Private Vessels, 1917-18; de signed submarine chasers and patrol boats; membe Sec. of Navy's Bd. of Appraisal of Merchant an Private Vessels, 1917-18; retired Sept. 14, 1940; re called to active duty, Dec. 31, 1940; promoted t Commodore, 1944, retired 1945. Decorated Silver Sta for services in designing and building submarin chasers, Legion of Merit. Dir. Taunton Boys Club regional dir. Mass. Sea Scouts Am. Mem. U.S N.R. Assn. (v.p. Mass. U.S.N.R. Assn.), Delta Ps Episcopalian (Junior Warden). Clubs: Exchang (Boston); St. Anthony (New York City); Army an Navy, Metropolitan, Chevy Chase (Washington, D C.); Segreganseet Country (Taunton, Mass.); Edgar town (Mass.) Yacht, Edgartown Reading Room. Cor tbr. to mags. Home: 146 High St., Taunton, Mass Died Jan. 7, 1956.

SWEENEY, Alvin Randolph, med. dir. U.S. P.H.S (retired); b. Grand Chenier, La., Sept. 2, 1881; s George C. Carter and Aurelia (Miller) S.; ed. Acadi Coll., Lake Charles, 1900-02; B.S., Tex. Central U. Greenville, 1904; student Vanderbilt U. Med. Sch 1904-07; M.D., Jefferson Med. Coll., Phila., 1908; m Rilla Adele Ingram, Dec. 1, 1908; children—Gertrud Elizabeth (Mrs. Clarke Eugene Brown), Alvin Ran dolph, Edward Chalmers, Ruth Adele. Physician Lake Arthur, La., 1909-13; asst. surgeon U.S. Pub Health Service, 1913; promoted through grades t Captain Dist. med. 9th Naval Dist., Cleveland served at Ellis Island, New Orleans, Galvestor St. Louis, Port Arthur, Boston. In charge of mar different quarantine stations and hospitals durin ervice; past supt. Gallinger Municipal Hosp., Wash. .C. Mem. Washington Health Council. Fellow Am. Coll. Physicians; mem. Am. Acad. Polit. and Social Science, A.M.A., Washington Med. Soc., Assn. Mil. urgeons, Am. Pub. Health Assn., Acad. Polit. Sci. erved in Army during World War I. Mason (32°). lubs: Washington Board Trade, Boston C. of C. ontbr. articles on health topics. Address: 5126 radley Blvd., Chevy Chase 15, Md. Died Apr. 1954; uried Arlington Nat. Cemetery.

SWEENEY, Orland Russell, coll. prof.; b. Martin's Ferry, O., Mar. 27, 1882; s. Robert Emmet nd Elizabeth (Woods) S.; B.S. in Chem. Engring., hio State U., 1909, M.A., 1910, Chem. E., 1935; h.D., U. Pa., 1916; m. Louella Dubois Smith, ct. 25, 1919; children—Elizabeth Dubois, Jacqueine. Instr. chem. engring., Ohio State U., 1910, . Pa., 1910-16; asso. prof. chem. engring., N.D. grl. Coll., Fargo, N.D., 1916; head dept. chem. ngring., U. Cin., 1919-21, Ia. State Coll. Agr. nd Mechanic Arts, 1921-50 (now Iowa State U.); lso chem. engr. Engring. Expt. Sta. Capt. ordance and maj. C.W.S., U.S. Army, Nov. 22, 1917-eb. 17, 1920; designed, constructed and operated hlorpicrine plant at Edgewood (Md.) Arsenal, World Var. Mem. Am. Chem. Soc., Ia. Engring. Soc., m. Inst. Chem. Engs., Sigma Xi, Tau Beta Pi, hi Lambda Upsilon. Mem. United Presbyn. Ch. Iason. Author: The Commercial Utilization of Agriultural Wastes, 1925. Home: Ames, Ia. Died Apr. 1, 1958; buried Martin's Ferry, O.

SWEENEY, Thomas Bell, Sr., author; b. Wheeling, V.Va., Jan. 19, 1874; s. John F. and Lula (Bell) .; prep. edn., Linsly Inst.; A.B., Washington and efferson Coll., 1895, Litt.D., 1934; martriculated Coll. Phys. and Surg. (Columbia), N.Y.; m. Vellie Katharine Janney, Jan. 15, 1902 (dec.); chilren—Thomas Bell, John F.; m. 2d, Genevieve Bassel Vatson, June 10, 1945. Upon father's death, 1895, ucceeded him as mgr. Equitable Life Assurance Soc. .S. for W.Va. and portions of Ohio, Md. and Va. hmn. Red Cross campaign for D.C., World War; v.p. hildren's Hosp., Washington. Republican. Episcoalian. Clubs: Metropolitan, Chevy Chase (Washingon, D.C.); Pot and Kettle and Kebo Valley Golf, ar Harbor Club (Bar Harbor, Me.). Author: (Tom weeney) Horizon Frames (prose articles and verse), 931; Sunward (verse), 1933; Legend of Leonardo, 936; Life Underwriting as a Professional Career, 940; Flight to Erin, 1945; Makers of War, 1950; aron Burr's Dream for the Southwest (a play), 955. Contbr. verse to periodicals. Home: 1818 Q t., Washington (summer) Bar Harbor, Me. Died eb. 2, 1957.

SWEET, Ada Celeste, writer; b. at Stockbridge, Vis., Feb. 23, 1853; d. Gen. Benjamin Jeffery and ovisa (Denslow) S.; sister of Winifred Black (q.v.). .S. agent for paying pensions at Chgo., 1874-85-—; the first woman ever apptd. as a disbursing ofcer in the U.S.; lit. editor Chicago Tribune, 1886; pened a U.S. claims office in Chgo. 1888-1905; ecame editorial writer on Chicago Journal and occasional contbr. to other newspapers and mags. spl. riter on the National Civic Federation Review, N. .C., 1909-10; mgr. woman's dept. Equitable Life ssurance Soc., Chgo., May, 1911-13. Ex-pres. Muicipal Order League of Chgo.; hon. life mem. and -pres. Chgo. Woman's Club. Prominent in reform nd philanthropic work. Home: 1054 Lombard St., n Francisco. Died 1928.

SWEET, Alfred Henry, professor history; born at Methuen, Mass., Sept. 8, 1890; s. Charles Filkins D.D.) and Matilda (Hill) S.; A.B., Bowdoin, 1913; ongfellow grad. scholar same, 1913-14; A.M., Harard, 1914; Ph.D., Cornell, 1917; research work in ngland, 1916-17; research work in Rome and Engand, 1932, 34; m. Gladys Greenleaf, June 12, 1916; son, Charles Woodbury Greenleaf. Instr. in history, Hobart Coll., Geneva, N.Y., 1916; President White ellow in history, Cornell U., 1916-17; acting asst. rof. English history, same univ., 1917-20; asso. prof. istory, U. of Colo., 1920-21, Washington U., 1921-2; Craig prof. history, St. Lawrence U., 1922-25; rof. European history, Washington and Jefferson College, 1925-27, Linn professor European history, 1927-7, Linn professor history, since 1947; lecturer on hisory, summers, University of California, 1922, Uniersity of Colo., 1923, 24, 27, 31, Pa. State Coll., 928, 29, U. of Pa., 1936, Coll. City of New York, 937, U. of Tex., 1938, 39, 41. Del. Dem. Nat. Conv., 936. Fellow Royal Hist. Soc.; mem. Am. Hist. Assn., Mediaeval. Acad. America, American Association of niversity Profs., Phi Alpha Theta, Beta Theta Pi, hi Beta Kappa. Democrat. Episcopalian. Author: History of England, 1931. Contbr. to National Encyclopedia and hist. revs. Home: 75 S. Watson Av., Washington, Pa. Died Apr. 22, 1950; buried Washington (Pa.) Cemetery.

SWEET, Carroll Fuller, constrn. exec.; born Grand apids, Mich., June 24, 1877; s. Edwin Forrest and ophia (Fuller) S.; grad. St. Marks Sch., 1895; .B., Yale, 1899; m. Agnes Marie Callahan, Feb. , 1908; children—Pauline (adopted, dec.), Carroll uller. With Orizaba & Nogales, r.r. constrn. Mexico 899-1901; mgr. Fuller & Rice Lumber & Mfg. Co., rand Rapids, Mich., 1901-11; treas., gen. mgr. Grand Rapids Lumber Co., 1911-15; exec. v.p. Old Nat. Bank, 1915-29; pres. Morris Plan Bank, Grand Rapids, 1918-26; pres. A. P. Callahan Co., Chicago, 1919-51; financial cons., Grand Rapids, 1930-32; dist. mgr. Home Owners Loan Corp., Mich. Dist. 3 1933-38; exec. sec. Mich. Real Estate Assn., Lansing, Mich., 1939-40; priorities cons. Nat. Housing Authority Chicago and Washington, 1941-43; mgr. Chicago Met. Home Builders Assn., 1943-44; asso. Manilow Constrn. Corp., Chicago, since 1944; dir. Am. Community Builders, Park Forest, Ill.; originator idea which developed into Village of Park Forest (Ill.), 1945. Recipient DeForrest medal, Yale, 1899. Member Grand Rapids Y.M.C.A., Chicago, Grand Rapids assns. commerce, Alpha Delta Phi, Skull and Bones. Episcopalian. Club: Kent Country (Grand Rapids). Address: 350 Oakwood, Park Forest, Ill. Deceased.

SWEET, John Henry Throop, Jr., orthopedic surgeon; b. Hartford, Conn., Nov. 27, 1884; s. John Henry Throop and Sally Jane (Boyd) S.; student Hartford pub. sch. and high sch., 1902-06; B.S., Trinity Coll., 1910; M.D., Tufts College Med. Sch., 1912; m. Henrietta Ketchum Elliott, June 27, 1916; children—Deborah (Mrs. Chester King), Mrs. Barbara Webber, Elliott Boyd (M.D.), Phyllis (Mrs. Douglas A. Carlson). Intern Hartford Hosp., 1912-14; in gen. med. practice, Hartford, 1914-18, practice limited to orthopedic surgery, 1918—; asst. orthopedic surgeon Newington Home for Crippled Children, 1914-29, Hartford Hosp., 1923-35, assn., 1935—, attending, 1940—; orthopedic surgeon McCook Meml. Hosp., 1921-37, cons., 1937—; cons. orthopedic surgeon Inst. Living, 1932—, Middlesex Hosp., 1933—, Manchester Meml. Hosp., 1927—, Windham Community Meml. Hosp., Willimantic, 1933—, New Britain Gen. Hosp., 1946—. Served as 1st lt. M.C., U.S. Army, 1918-19, with A.E.F. in France. Certified by Am. Bd. Orthopedic Surgery. Fellow A.C.S., Am. Acad. Orthopedic Surgeons. A. M.A., Boston Orthopedic Club: hon. mem. N.E. Soc. for Bone and Joint Surgery; mem. Conn. State, Hartford County and Hartford med. socs., Conn. Hist. Soc., Psi Upsilon, Alpha Kappa Kappa. Republican. Baptist. Clubs: Twentieth Century; Barkhamstead Fishing; University (Winter Park, Fla.). Home: 29 Four-Mile Rd., West Hartford, Conn. Office: Medical Bldg., Hartford Hospital, 85 Jefferson St., Hartford, Conn. Died July 30, 1950; buried West Hartford, Conn.

SWEET, Joshua Edwin, prof. surgical research; b. Unadilla, N.Y., Aug. 9, 1876; s. Joshua J. and Emeline G. (Allen) S.; prep. edn., Unadilla Acad.; A.B., Hamilton Coll., 1897, A.M., 1900, hon. Sc.D., 1922; M.D., U. of Giessen, Germany, 1901; studied at Pasteur Inst., Paris, 1901; m. Greta McCauley, June 22, 1904 (died Jan. 2, 1942); 1 dau., Ruth; m. 2d, Florence West, June 6, 1942. With Univ. of Pa., 1906-26, prof. surg. research, 1917-26; prof. research, Cornell U. Med. Coll., 1926-41, emeritus 1941. Lt. col. with A.E.F. in France, as consultant in surg. research, 1917-19; m. staff Base Hosp. No. 10. Fellow Am. Coll. Surgeons; mem. A.M.A., N.Y. State and N.Y. County med. socs., Am. Soc. Exptl. Pathology, Am. Physiol. Soc., Harvey Soc., Society of Exptl. Biology and Medicine, N.Y. Acad. Medicine, N.Y. Surg. Soc., Phila. Acad. Surgery, Surg. Research Soc., Theta Nu Epsilon, Delta Kappa Epsilon, Phi Beta Kappa, Sigma Xi, Alpha Omega, Phi Alpha Sigma. Republican. Presbyterian. Awarded Alveranga prize for essay, "The Surgery of the Pancreas," 1915; delivered annual oration, Phila. Acad. Surgery, 1916; Mütter lecture, "The Gallbladder, Its Past, Present and Future," 1923. Contbr. 75 papers to med. lit. Home: Unadilla, N.Y. Died Apr. 8, 1957; buried Evergreen Hill Cemetery, Unadilla.

SWEET, Louis Matthews, clergyman; b. Southold, N.Y., Oct. 10, 1869; s. Amos Lewis and Sarah Elizabeth (Benedict) S.; B.A., Hobart Coll., 1892, A.M., 1895; grad. Auburn Theol. Sem., 1895; S.T.D., Hobart, 1907; Ph.D., New York U., 1918; m. Margaret Stuart, Sept. 3, 1895; children—Kenneth Stuart, Margaret Elizabeth, Hogarth Stuart, Malcolm Stuart. Ordained Presbyn. ministry, 1895; pastor Union Springs, N.Y., 1896-1901, Warsaw, N.Y., 1901-04, Canandaigua, N.Y., 1905-08, prof. Christian theology and apologetics, Biblical Seminary in New York, 1908-29; mem. faculty Presbyterian Theological Seminary, now McCormick Theological Seminary, Chicago, since June 1, 1929, prof. systematic theology, 1931-39, now prof. emeritus; visiting lecturer in theology, Bibl. Sem. in N.Y., 1940-42; interim pastor, 1st Presbyterian Church, Utica, New York, 1942-43. East Presbyterian Ch., Syracuse, N.Y., 1944-46. Author: Birth and Infancy of Jesus Christ, 1906; The Self-Portrayal of Shakespeare, 1906; Study of the English Bible, 1914; Roman Emperor Worship, 1919; The Verification of Christianity, 1919; The Makin' o' Joe, 1919; To Christ through Evolution, 1925; The Head of the Corner, 1931; The Pastoral Ministry In Our Time (with Malcolm Stuart Sweet). Contbr. Internat. Standard Bible Ency., Chicago, 1915. Lecturer on Smyth Foundation, Columbia (S.C.) Theol. Sem., 1921-22. Mem. Phi Beta Kappa, Order of Founders and Patriots of America (chaplain general 1937). Home: RD No. 1, Clifford, Pa. Died Oct. 3, 1950; buried Lake View Cemetery, Skaneateles, N.Y.

SWEET, William Warren, educator, author; b. Baldwin, Kan., Feb. 15, 1881; s. Rev. William Henry and Rose (Williams) S.; A.B., Ohio Wesleyan U., 1902, Litt.D., 1935; B.D., Drew Theol. Sem., 1906; Th.M., Crozer Theol. Sem., 1907; A.M., U. Pa., 1907, Ph.D., 1912; D.D., Cornell Coll., 1922; m. Louise M. Neill, May 18, 1906; children—Paul R., Elizabeth, Esther, William W., Richard W. Ordained to ministry M.E. Ch., 1906; pastor Willow Grove, Pa., 1906-08, Langhorne, 1908-11; instr. and asst. prof. history Ohio Wesleyan U. 1911-13; prof. history DePauw U., 1913-27, dean Coll. of Liberal Arts, 1926-27; prof. history Am. Christianity, U. Chgo., 1927-46, emeritus 1946; prof. ch. history Garrett Bibl. Inst. 1946-48; vis. prof. and chmn. of faculty Perkins Sch. of Theology, So. Meth. U., 1948—, Jackson lectureship, 1949; vis. prof. McCormick Theol. Sem., 1946-48; prof. history, summers, Northwestern U., 1922, Syracuse U., 1924, 25, U. Wash., 1926, 27; vis. prof. church history Drew U., 1932-34; spl. lectr. on Christian biography; Harris lectr. Bangor Theol. Sem., 1939; vis. prof. and Dudliean lectr. Harvard U., 1944; Beckley lectr., London, Eng., 1946; vis. prof. U. Tex., 1950. Parttime Research Fellow Huntington Library, San Marino, Cal. Del. to Congress on Christian Work, Montevideo, 1925; del. Meth. Ecumenical Conf., Oxford, Eng., 1951. Mem. Am., Miss. Valley and Wis. hist. assns., Am. Soc. Ch. History (pres. 1932), Delta Tau Delta, Phi Beta Kappa. Liberal Republican. Author: The Methodist Episcopal Church and the Civil War, 1912; Circuit Rider Days in Indiana, 1916; History of North Ind. Conf. (with H. H. Herrick), 1917; A History of Latin America, 1929; The Rise of Methodism in the West, 1920; Circuit Rider Days Along the Ohio, 1923; History—A Survey, 1923; Our American Churches, 1924; Community Religion and the Denominational Heritage (J. R. Hargreave, others), 1930; The Story of Religion in America, 1930, rev. edit., 1950; Religion on the American Frontier, Vol. I, The Baptists, 1931; Vol. II, The Presbyterians, 1936; Vol. III, The Congregationalists, 1939; Vol. IV, The Methodists, 1946; A Bibliographical Guide to the History of Christianity (with S. J. Case and others), 1931; Methodism in American History, 1933; Men of Zeal, 1935; Indiana Asbury-DePauw University, 1937-1937; Makers of Christianity; John Cotton to Lyman Abbott, 1937; A Short History of Christianity (with A. G. Baker and others), 1940; Religion in Colonial America, 1942 (a religious Book-of-the-month selective); Revivalism in America: Its Origin, Growth and Decline, 1944; he American Church—An Interpretation, 1947 Der Weg des Glaubens in den USA (pub. in Hamburg), 1951; Religion in the Development of American Culture, 1952 (pulpit Book of the Month Club selection). Contbr. Ency. Brit., Dictionary of Am. Biography. Mem. editorial council and contbr. to Dictionary of Am. History. Winner 1st prize ($1,000), Chicago Tribune, 1930, for best 500-word history of U.S. Chmn. Nat. Groups Div. War Finance Com. of Ill., U.S. Treasury, 1943-45. Home: 2814 Fondren Drive, Dallas, Tex. Died Jan. 3, 1958; buried Restland Cemetery, Dallas.

SWEETS, Henry Hayes, clergyman; b. Elizabethtown, Ky., Oct. 6, 1872; s. Michael and Sarah K. (Matthis) S.; A.B., Centre Coll., Ky., 1894, D.D., 1909, LL.D., 1947; B.D., Louisville Presbyn. Theol. Sem., 1898; D.D., Presbyn. Coll. S.C., 1909; LL.D., Austin Coll., Tex., 1918, Southwestern Presbyn. U., 1923, Davidson, 1923, Erskine, 1939; m. Douschka Martin, Nov. 27, 1907; children—Henry H., Douschka M. (Mrs. Robert V. Ackerman), F. Martin. Ordained Presbyn. ministry, 1897; organizer, 1897, and pastor of James Lees Memorial Church, Louisville, 1897-1904; sec. Bd. Edn. and Ministerial Relief, Presbyn. Ch. U.S., 1904-1943. Mem. Bd. Corporators Presbyn. Ministers' Fund for Life Ins., Phila.; organized Presbyn. Ednl. Assn. of South; one of organizers of Council Ch. Bds. Edn. in U.S. and also Council Secretaries Ministerial Relief and Pensions Am. Moderator Gen. Assembly Presbyn. Ch. U.S., 1935-36, acting moderator, 1936-37; sent to Orient, 1925-26, to study ednl. work in China, Japan, Korea, 1925-26; mem. N.E.A., So. Assn. Colls. and Secondary Schs., Delta Kappa Epsilon. Mason. Filson Club. Author: Planning the Good Life; The Church and Education; Source Book on Christian Education; Source Book on Spiritual Life and Evangelism; also articles on ministry, ministerial relief, Christian edn. and philosophy of life. Cons. Christian Hgher Edn. Presbyn. Ch. in U.S., 1943—. Home: 1633 Beechwood Av., Louisville 4. Office: Urban Bldg., Louisville 2. Died Feb. 26, 1952; buried Cave Hill Cemetery, Louisville.

SWEM, Lee Allan, business exec.; b. Washington, Sept. 20, 1899; s. Edmond Hez and Minnie Lee (Johnson) S.; student George Washington U., 1917-18, 1919; student Mass. Inst. Tech., 1918-21; LL. B., Georgetown Law Sch., 1926; m. Lorraine Serrin Rose, Nov. 1927; children—Lee Allan, Gary Edgar. Examiner, U.S. Patent Office; practiced patent law with The Budd Co., Packard Motor Car Co., and

Standard Oil Co. of New York, 1928-30; in private law practice, N.Y. City, 1930-36; patent counsel Foster Wheeler Corp., 1936-45, asst. to pres. and dir., 1945-48, v.p., asst. to pres., dir. 1948-50, v.p. internat. operations, dir., 1950-53, v.p. since 1953; dir. Bullard Co., Bridgeport, Conn., Thermo Projects, Inc., New York. Registered patent atty. Mem. Bar Dist. of Columbia, N.Y. State, and Fed. courts. Mem. N.Y. State and Am. bar assns., Am. and N.Y. patent law assns., Christian Bus. Men's Committee, Sigma Nu. Republican. Baptist. Clubs: Lawyers (New York); Siwananoy Country (Bronxville, N.Y.). Home: 6 Sunset Av., Bronxville 8, N.Y. Office: 165 Broadway, N.Y.C. 6. Died May 24, 1954.

SWIFT, Elijah Kent, corp. official; b. Eau Claire, Wis., Dec. 10, 1878; s. Elijah and Myra (Evans) S.; prep. edn., Beloit (Wis.) Acad.; A.B., Williams Coll., 1900, L.H.D., 1956; L.H.M., Springfield Coll., 1949; m. Katharine Leland Whitin, Apr. 18, 1911; children—Elisabeth Robinson Swift Whiteside, Katharine Whitin Swift Almy, Anne Whitin Sawyer, Elijah Kent. Began with Whitin Machine Works, Whitinsville, Mass., 1900, now chmn. bd. of dir.; chmn. Seaboard Foundry, Providence, R.I.; president Scott Lumber Co., Burney, Calif.; v.p. Whitinsville Savings Bank (trustee); dir. member of the advisory committee American Mutual Liability Insurance Co., Whitin Machine Works, Whitinsville Nat. Bank, Ashworth Bros., Boston Mfrs. Mut. Insurance, Mass. Mut. Life Ins. Co., Mut. Boiler & Machinery Ins. Co., Pepperell Mfg. Co.; adv. bd. Second Bank-State Street Trust Company (Boston). Past chmn., now mem. Finance Com., Northbridge, Mass.; Zeta Psi. Republican. Conglist. Clubs: Harvard Travellers (Cambridge); Somerset (Boston); and various golf and country clubs. Home: 307 Hill St., Whitinsville, Mass. Died July 17, 1959; buried Pine Grove Cemetery, Whitinsville, Mass.

SWIFT, Harry Ladrew, mercantile exec.; b. Woodcock, Pa., Oct. 9, 1871; s. John Wycoff and Mary Ann (Schlosser) S.; tchrs.' certificate, Tchrs. Coll. of Edinburg, Pa., 19—; m. Alice Philomene McMahon, Sept. 12, 1906; children—Mary Elizabeth (Mrs. E. R. Cullom), Cora Kathleen (Mrs. James I. Miller), Helen Ruth (Mrs. William H. Lewis); m. 2d, Charlotte Louise Keife, Sept. 14, 1926. With The L. B. Price Mercantile Co., St. Louis, 1895—, beginning as salesman, successively div. mgr., purchasing agt., pres., chmn. bd., 1935—, dir., 1926—; dir. Equitable Mut. Homestead Assn. of New Orleans. Mason (K.T., Shriner); mem. Order of Eastern Star. Club: Pass Christian (Miss.) Yacht. Home: 7233 Kingsbury Blvd., University City 5, Mo. Office: 4702 Olive St., St. Louis 8. Died Feb. 11, 1955; buried Medairie Cemetery, New Orleans.

SWIFT, Homer Fordyce, physician; b. Paines Hollow, N.Y., May 5, 1881; s. Charles Fayette and Nancy Maria (Fordyce) S.; Adrian (Mich.) Coll., 1898-1900; Ph.B., Western Res., 1902, student med. dept., 1902-04; M.D., U. and Bellevue Hosp. Med. Coll., 1906; D.Sc., N.Y. U., 1931; received the medallion of Meritorious Service award by Alumni Fedn. N.Y.U., 1933; m. Emma Fordyce MacRae, Apr. 24, 1922; step-dau., Alice MacRae (Mrs. Lester Kissel). Interne Presbyn. Hosp., N.Y., 1906-08; asst. in pathology and dermatology, U. and Bellevue Hosp. Med. Coll., 1908-10; asst. res. physician, Rockefeller Hosp., 1910-12, res. physician, 1912-14; asso. prof. medicine, Columbia, 1914-17; same (on leave), Cornell Med. Coll., 1917-19; asso. mem., Rockefeller Inst., 1919-22, mem., 1922-46, Emeritus mem., 1946—; physician Hosp. of Rockefeller Inst. Med. Research, 1942-46, emeritus mem., 1946—. Mem. Council N. Y.U., 1942-46. Mem. bd. dirs. Russell Sage Inst. Pathology 1923-48; Kober lectr. Georgetown U. Med. Sch., 1949. With A.E.F. in France, May 1917-Apr. 1919, attached to B.E.F., May 1917-May 1918; mem. A.R.C. Trench Fever Commn., also cons. in medicine 1st Army Corps and 3d Army (Army of Occupation), A.E.F.; discharged as col. med. corps, World War I. cons. to sec. of war, 1942-46. Spl. investigator OSRD study of streptococci 1942-45. Has specialized in treatment of syphilis of the central nervous system, and in study of rheumatic fever, streptococcus infections and trench fever. Chmn. gen. adv. com. for the cardiac program, N.Y. State Dept. Health, 1941—. Chmn. Am. Council Rheumatic Fever, 1945-46. Mem. A.M.A., N.Y. State Med. Soc., Assn. Am. Physicians, Am. Soc. Clin Investigation (pres. 1928), N.Y. Acad. Medicine, Soc. Am. Bacteriologists, Am. Soc. Immunology, Harvey Soc. (pres. 1925-26), Alpha Tau Omega, Nu Sigma Nu, Theta Nu Epsilon, Alpha Omega Alpha; fellow A.A.A.S. Club: Century. Collaborator: Trench Fever (report of commn. A.R.C. Research Com.), 1918. Contbr. to Forchheimer's Therapeusis of Internal Diseases, Practical Treatment (Musser and Kelly), Nelson's Loose-Leaf Medicine, Oxford Loose-Leaf Medicine, Text-Book of Medicine (Cecil); Bacterial and Mycotic Infections of Men (Dubos), also numerous articles med. jours. Home: 888 Park Av. Office: Rockefeller Institute Hospital, 66th St. and York Av., N.Y.C. 21. Died Sept. 24, 1953.

SWIFT, Innis Palmer, ret. army officer; b. Fort Laramie, Wyo., Feb. 7, 1882; s. Eben and Susan Bonaparte (Palmer) S.; B.S., U.S. Mil. Acad., 1904; grad. U.S. Mounted Service Sch., 1909, U.S. Cavs. Sch., 1922, Command and Gen. Staff Sch., 1923, Army War Coll., 1930, Army Indsl. Coll., 1931; m. Lucille Genevieve Paddock, Sept. 1908; children—Lucile Paddock (Mrs. Boyd L. Hillsinger), Susanne Palmer (Mrs. Henry Thomas Cherry), Sally Genevieve (Mrs. Ralph Haines, Jr.), Pamela (Mrs. George W. Vaughan). Commd. 2d lt., Cav., U.S. Army, 1904, advanced to maj. gen., 1941; served as maj. of Inf., 1917, lt. col. of cav., 1918, AEF, France. Decorated with campaign medals for service in Philippine Insurrection, Punitive Expdn. Mexico and France, World War I; for service Asiatic-Pacific Theatre, Battle Stars for Bismark Sea, Dutch New Guinea, P.I., World War II; Comd. 8th Cav., 1936-39, 2d Cav. Brigade, 1939-41, 1st Cav. Div., 1941-44; tax force which recaptured the Admiralty Islands, 1944; 1st Army Corps, Dutch New Guinea, 1944-45, during recapture of Luzon, P.I. and occupation of Japan, 1945. Decorated D.S.M. with oak leaf cluster, Legion of Merit, Silver Star Medal for gallantry in action (U.S.); Order of the Aztec Eagle, First Class (Republic Mexico). Episcopalian. Mason (32°, Shriner). Home: 826 Burr Rd., San Antonio 9. Died Nov. 3, 1953; buried Fort Sam Houston Nat. Cemetery, San Antonio.

SWIFT, Lucian, newspaper man; b. Akron, O., July 14, 1848; s. Lucian and Sarah S. (West) S.; grad. Cleveland (O.) High Sch., and U. of Mich., M.E., 1869; m. Minnie Fuller Swift (dec. Aug. 1903); 1 dau. Grace Strong. Located at Minneapolis, 1871; identified with Minneapolis Tribune, 1876-85; asso. with three others in purchasing the Minneapolis Jour., 1885, of which has since been mgr. Pres. Housekeeper Corp'n. Mem. Delta Kappa Epsilon. Clubs: Minneapolis, Commercial, Lafayette, Minikahada, Minnetonka Yacht, Bryn Mawr Golf; and Union League (Chgo.). Residence: 2324 Pillsbury Av. Office: 47 4th St., S. Mpls. Died Oct. 1926; buried Lakewood Cemetery, Mpls.

SWIFT, Nathan Butler, business exec.; b. Chgo., Dec. 17, 1911; s. Alden Butler and Lydia (Niblack) S.; student Yale, 1930-32; m. Janet Herriott; children—Martha, Nathan Butler. With Swift & Co. since 1932, mgr., Watertown, S.D., 1940-42, North Portland, Ore., 1942-47, asst. mgr., Chgo., 1947-49, adminstrv. asst. to pres., 1949-52, asst. v.p., 1952, v.p. in charge pork business since 1952. Episcopalian. Club: Beverly Country (Chgo.). Home: 10848 S. Hoyne Av., Chgo. 43. Office: Union Stock Yards, Chgo. 9. Died July 31, 1953.

SWIGGETT, Douglas Worthington (swĭg'ĕt), editor; b. Morrow, O., Sept. 11, 1882; s. Rev. Edward T. and Eleanor Strode (Mansfield) S.; A.B., Harvard, 1906; unmarried. Teacher Marietta O., U. of Mo. and at Cicero, Ill., until 1908; with Longmans, Green & Co., publishers, 1909-11 editorial writer The Journal, Milwaukee, Wis., 1912-17 and 1919-47. Enlisted in U.S. Army, Aug. 27, 1917; commd. 2d lt., F.A., Nov. 27, 1917; served with 53d Arty., C.A.C., Meuse-Argonne offensive and St. Mihiel and Verdun sectors; discharged, Apr. 1, 1919; capt., O.R.C., 1924-29. Mem. Am. Soc. Newspaper Editors. Presbyterian. Clubs: University, City. Editor: Selections from Malory's Morte d'Arthur, 1909. Received hon. mention for distinguished editorial. Pulitzer award, 1938. Home: University Club. Address: 924 E. Wells St., Milwaukee 2. Died Feb. 12, 1950; buried Spring Grove Cemetery, Cincinnati.

SWINGLE, Walter T(ennyson), botanist, agriculturist; b. Canaan, Wayne County, Pa., Jan. 8, 1871; s. John Fletcher and Mary (Astley) S.; received early schooling at home; B.Sc., Kan. State Agrl. Co., 1890, M.Sc., 1896; U. of Bonn, 1895-96; U. of Leipzig, 1898; D.Sc., Kan. State Agrl. Coll., 1922; m. Lucie Romstaedt, June 8, 1901 (died 1910); m. 2d, Maude Kellerman, Oct. 2, 1915; children—John William, Stella (Mrs. Stanley F. Reed), Frank Anthony, Mary (Mrs. Francis L. Albert, Junior). Asst. boanist Kan. Agrl. Exptl. Sta., 1888; U.S. Dept. Agr., Bur. Plant Industry, 1891-41; collaborator since 1941; cons. tropical botany, U. of Miami, Coral Gables, Fla., since 1941; organizing large scale preparation of serial microtome sections herbarium and fresh material economic plants. Investigated for Dept. Agr. the agriculture and botany of France, Algeria, Morocco, Italy, Spain, Greece, The Balkans, Asia Minor, China, Japan, Philippines, Mexico. Introduced the fig insect into Calif., 1899, thereby rendering possible culture of Smyrna type figs; first successful shipment standard varieties of date palms from Algeria into Calif. and Arizona, 1900, in charge establishment commercial culture of date palm, 1900-34; owns and operates an experimental date garden of Indio, California; helped to establish Egyptian cotton in Arizona; originated by hybridization in Fla., citranges, limequats, tangelos and other new citrus fruits; discovered neophyosis (rejuvenescence of old citrus varieties from nucellar buds seedlings, thereby eliminating all virus infections). First proved existence of centrosomes in plants; originated name and theory of metaxenia for direct effect of pollen on dates, 1928. Introduced many new corp plants alkaloid-yielding species of Ephedra and high-yeilding strains of tropical tung (abrasin). Awarded Meyer medal, 1948; Barbour medal, 1950.
Fellow and life member A.A.A.S.; orig. membe
Washington Academy Sciences, Wash. Acad. Medicin
(past v.p.); mem. Acad. Natural Science (Phila.)
Am. Bot. Soc., Soc. Nat. d'Acelimination de France
corr. mem. Academie d'Agriculture de France; honor
ary life member National Geographical Society. Del
of U.S. Government and Nat. Research Council t
3d Pan-Pacific Science Congress, Tokyo, Japan, 1926
Visited Brazil, Apr.-June 1939, on invitiation of Mir
ister of Foreign Affairs, to advise regarding cultu
of cinchona, tung (abrasin), rubber and other tropica
crops for export to U.S. Author numerous papers o
botany (some 25 on citrus and related genera)
culminating in a complete synopsis of orange sub
family, The Botany of Citrus and Its Wild Relatives
1943; conducting search for new rootstocks immur
to Tristeza, fatal disease of Citrus. Studied econom
plants of China, supervised extensive translations fro
Chinese literature on them; assisted the Librarian c
Congress in building up the largest collection c
Chinese books outside the Orient; wrote annual report
on same, 1915-35; named hon. cons. in developmen
Orientalia Coll., 1947. Club: Cosmos. Author: Ou
Agricultural Debt to Asia, 1945. Home: 4753 Re
servoir Rd. N.W., Washington. Died Jan. 19, 1952

SWISHER, Benjamin Franklin, lawyer; b. Iow
City, Ia., Jan. 21, 1878; s. Lovell and Elizabet
(Leonard) S.; B.Ph., U. Ia., 1899, LL.B., 1900; m
Helen Field Moulton, Nov. 26, 1902; children—Ma
tha Elizabeth (Mrs. Deam E. Horner), Benjamin F
(dec.), Helen Moulton (Mrs. Richard H. Plock)
Charles Franklin. Admitted to Ia. bar, 1900, an
since practiced in Waterloo, Iowa; mem. firm Swishe
Cohrt & Swisher; city solicitor, 1910-15; v.p. ar
general counsel Waterloo. Cedar Falls & Northe
R.R.; general counsel, dir. Rath Packing Co. Pre
Bd. of Edn., Waterloo, 1918-24; pres. bd. truste
Iowa Memorial Union. Lieut. colonel Specialist R
serve. Mem. C. of C. (dir.), Am. Bar Assn., I
State Bar Assn. (pres. 1926-27), U. of Ia. Alum
Assn. (pres. 1927-30), Reserve Officers Assn., P
Kappa Psi, Phi Delta Phi. I Club (U. of Iowa). R
publican. Conglist. (trustee). Elk. Clubs: Rota
(pres. 1942-43), Sunnyside Country (Waterloo)
Home: 410 Sunset Rd. Office: 502-509 Waterl
Bldg., Waterloo, Ia. Died Jan. 22, 1959.

SWOPE, Charles Siegel (swōp), college pres.;
Saltillo, Pa., Mar. 19, 1899; s. Bruce Hudson ar
Anna Elizabeth (Houck) S.; grad. West Chester Sta
Normal Sch., 1921; A.B., Dickinson Coll., Carlisl
Pa., 1925; A.M., U. of Pa., 1929; Pd.D., Dickinso
Coll., 1941; m. Edna M. McAllister, Aug. 19, 192
children—Charles Evans, Richard McAllister. Rur
sch. teacher, Beavertown, Pa., 1916-18; teacher
pvt. sch., Pennington, N.J., 1921-23 and 1925-2
supt. schs., Everett, Pa., 1926-27; teacher West Che
ter State Teachers Coll., 1927-35, pres. since 193
Mem. bd. of dirs. Community Chest since 1939, pres
1941; mem. Franklin Inst.; mem. bd. dirs. Chest
Co. Council Boy Scouts of Am., Inc., since 193
v.p. 1934-1939; pres. 1939-48; member board of d
rectors Chester Co. Historical Society since 193
member board of directors The Chester Coun
Art Asso. since 1940. Mem. board Penningto
(N.J.) Sch. for Boys, West Chester (Pa.) M.E. Ch
Ex-pres. Eastern Dist. Sabbath Sch. Assn., Chest
County, 1933-36. Awarded the Silver Beaver, 194
Silver Antelope, 1950 by the nat. exec. bd. B
Scouts of Am. Mem. Schoolmen's Com.; mem. Aca
Polit. and Social Science, Am. Hist. Assn., N.E.
(ex-officio mem. Ednl. Policy Com. 1937), Pa. Sta
Edn. Assn., Phi Kappa Sigma. Republican. Met
odist. Clubs: Rotary (member board dirs., 1936-4
pres., 1940-41; chmn., Internat. Com., Governo
179th Dist., 1947-48), Elk's Club, X Club, We
Chester, Golf and Country (West Chester), Schoo
men (Philadelphia). Lecturer and author. Hom
Tanglewood, E. Rosedale Av., West Chester, Pa. Di
May 31, 1959.

SWOPE, Gerard, elec. engr.; b. St. Louis, Mo
Dec. 1, 1872; B.S. in E.E., Mass. Inst. Tech
1895; hon. D.Sc., Rutgers, 1923, Union Coll., 192
LL.D., Colgate U., 1927; Dr. Engring., Stevens Ins
Technology, 1929; D.Sc., Washington U., 1932;
Mary Dayton Hill, 1901; LL.D. (hon.), Dartmout
1952; children—Henrietta H., Isaac G., Gerard, D
vid, John. Began as helper Gen. Electric Co., 189
entered employ Western Electric Co., 1895, mgr.
St. Louis, 1899-1906; trans. to Chicago, 1906,
N.Y. as gen. sales mgr., 1908, and elected v.p. a
dir., 1913; elected pres. Internat. Gen. Electric Co
Jan. 1919, chmn. 1922-33, now hon. chmn., pre
General Electric Co., 1922-39, retired, 1939, ho
pres. and dir., 1940-42 and, 1944— (re-electe
pres. 1942-44). Dir. National City Bank, also ma
foreign corps. First pres. and now mem. bd. of gov
of Nat. Elec. Mfrs. Assn.; mem. first Playgrou
Commn. of St. Louis, 1901-03; chmn. of first publ
Bath Commn., St. Louis, 1903-06; chmn. N.Y.
Housing Authority, 1940-42; asst. to sec. of trea
ury, 1942. Mem. gen. staff U.S. Army, World War
served as asst. dir. purchase, storage and traffi
Mem. Indsl. Adv. Bd. of N R.A. (Washington
1933; first chmn. Bus. Adv. and Planning Council f
Dept. of Commerce, 1933; chmn. Coal Arbitratio
Bd., 1933; mem. first Nat. Labor Board, 1933; me

President's Adv. Counil on Economic Security, 1934; mem. Adv. Council on Social Security, 1937-38; chmn. Indsl. Relations Commn. to Great Britain and Sweden, 1938; life mem. corp. and mem. exec. com. Mass. Inst. Tech.; mem. vis. com. Dept. of Astronomy, Harvard, 1927—; former pres. and now dir., Greenwich House (New York); alternate mem. Nat. Defense Mediation Bd., 1941. Chmn. 8th Am. Red Cross Roll Call, 1924; chmn. Nat. Mobilization for Human Needs, 1935-36, gater hon. pres. community chests and councils; organizer and chmn., Com. to Study Budget of Relief Appeals for fgn. countries, 1942; an organizer, mem. exec. com., chmn. and chairman budget com., Nat. War Fund; chmn. Nat. Health and Welfare Retirement Association. F. Am. Inst. Elec. Engrs.; mem. Council on Foreign Relations and various scientific socs.; hon. mem. Tau Beta Pi, 1932. Awarded D.S.M. (for work on procurement program for U.S. Army, 1918), Chevalier Legion of Honor (French); Order of Rising Sun (Japanese). Awarded Gold Medal of Nat. Inst. Social Sciences, 1932; Gold Medal and purse for signal contributions to elec. manufacturing industry, 1932; Hoover medal, 1942, for pub. service in social, civic and humanitarian fields. Clubs: Technology (New York); Mohawk (Schenectady). Author: Stabilization of Industry (often referred to as "Swope Plan"), 1931; Futility of Conquest in Europe, 1943; Some Aspects of Corporate Management. Contbr. papers and articles on unemployment and economic subjects. Home: The Croft, Ossining, N.Y. Office: 570 Lexington Av., N.Y.C. Died Nov. 20, 1957.

SWOPE, Herbert Bayard, journalist, policy consultant; b. St. Louis, Mo.; s. Isaac and Ida S.; L.H.D., Hobart, 1924; Litt.D., Colgate Uuniversity, 1927; married Margaret Honeyman Powell; children—Jane Marion, Herbert Bayard (lt. USNR). Successively reporter on St. Louis Post Dispatch, N.Y. Herald and N.Y. World; war corr. The World and Post Dispatch with German armies 1914-16; in 1914 sent exclusive dispatches of German U-boat U-9, sinking battleships Crecy, Abou-Kir and Hogue; winner Pulitzer prize for best reporting of 1917; upon U.S. war declaration, designated lt. comdr. U.S. Navy; later apptd. to U.S. War Industries Bd., asso. mem. and asst. to B.M. Baruch; chief corr. The World at Paris Peace Conf; chmn. Official Am. Press Delegation; mem. Internat. Press Com. which fought successfully for publicity in conf.; first to publish secret League of Nations Covenant; also first full text of reparation clauses. Exec. editor The World, 1920-29, (during this period paper received 3 Pulitzer medals for pub. service (one for exposure of K.K.K.); retired from The World, 1929; awarded Poor Richard medal, Phila.; U.S. Medal for Merit by President, U.S. Gold Medal by Interfaith in Action, 1950. Major, U.S. Army Res.; personal cons. Sec. of War, 1942-46. Mem. U.S. Delegation to U.N. AEC (Baruch) which prepared Am. plan for Atomic Control. Founder Overseas New Agency; v.p. L.I. Pk. Com.; former chmn. (11 yrs.) N.Y. Racing Com. (voted 3 plaques by turf writers' group for best services to racing); chmn. Turf Com. Am. raising $17,000,000 from Turf for War Relief; a founder and former gov. Am. Soc. Newspaper Editors; dir. Freedom House; sent by Pres. Roosevelt to London Econ. Conf.; exec. com. Citizens Com. Displaced Persons; v. chmn. Citizens Council Civil Rights; cons. Radio Corp. Am., Nat. Broadcasting Company. Chairman God Bless Am. Fund; co. chmn. Greater N.Y. $4,000,000 campaign for Nat. Found. for Infantile Paralysis, 1952; trustee Walt Whitman Birthplace Assn.; dir. United Service for New Americans; dir. 300th Anniversary celebration N.Y.C.; chmn. Mayor's Commn. on Intergroup Relations, N.Y.C.; dir. Nat. Conf. Christians and Jews; mem. Pulitzer Prize Jury for International Reporting, 1957. Decorated Knight Comdr., Republic of Liberia, 1954. Mem. Council Foreign Relations, Vets. Fgn. Wars, Phi Beta Kappa (hon.), Sigma Delta Chi. Clubs: River, Turf & Field, Pilgrims, Overseers Press, National Press, P.E.N. Author nside German Empire; War Censorship; Journalism—an Instrument of Civilization; Free Speech, etc. Home: 1060 Fifth Av., N.Y.C.; and Sands Point. L.I. Office: 745 Fifth Av., N.Y.C. Died June 20, 1958.

SYDNOR, Charles Sackett (sĭd'nôr), univ. dean; b. Augusta, Ga., July 21, 1898; s. Giles Granville and Evelyn Aiken (Sackett) S.; grad. Darlington Sch., Rome, Ga., 1915; A.B., Hampden-Sydney (Va.) Coll., 1918; Ph.D., Johns Hopkins University, 1923; Litt.D., Washington and Lee University, 1948, Princeton, 1953; M.A., Oxford University, 1950; LL.D., Davidson College, 1953; m. Betty Brown, June 2, 1924; children—Charles Sackett, Victor Brown. Instructor, high school, Rome, Ga., January-June 1919; instr., McCallie Sch., Chattanooga, Tenn., 1919-20; prof. history and polit. science, Hampden-Sydney Coll., 1923-25; prof. history, U. of Miss., 1925-36; asso. prof. history, Duke U., 1936-38; prof. since 1938 chmn. dept. history, dean grad. sch. arts and sis. since 1952; vis. prof. Emory U., 1925, 26, Johns Hopkins, 1929, 34, Duke, 1935, 36, Cornell, 1941, U. N.C. 1949, Harvard, 1952; Harold Vyvyan Harmsworth prof. Am. Hist., Oxford U., 1950-51. Mem. Council Inst. of Early Am. Hist. and Culture; mem. adv. com. Office of Chief of Mil. Hist., Dept. of the Army. Recipient awards of Social Sci. Research Council, 1940, and Library of Congress, 1945-46. Mem. Am., Miss. Valley, So. (pres. 1939) hist. assns., N.C. Lit. and Hist. Assn. (exec. com. 1941-44, pres. 1949-50), Hist. Soc. of N.C. (pres. 1949-50), Am. Assn. Univ. Profs., Phi Beta Kappa, Kappa Sigma, Omicron Delta Kappa. Presbyterian. Author: (with Claude Bennett) Mississippi History, 1930, 1939; Slavery in Mississippi, 1933; A Gentleman of the Old Natchez Region: Benjamin L. C. Wailes, 1938; The Development of Southern Sectionalism, 1819-1848 (vol. V of A History of the South), awarded North Carolina Mayflower Cup, 1948; Gentleman Freeholders: Political Practices in Washington's Virginia, 1952. Member of the board editors Journal of Southern History, 1935-38; South Atlantic Quarterly, since 1947. Contributor American Studies in Honor of William Kenneth Boyd, 1940, Dictionary of Am. Biography and to hist. mags. Home: 116 Pinecrest Rd., Durham, N.C. Died Mar. 2, 1954; buried Forest Hills Cemetery, Chattanooga, Tenn.

SYKES, M'Cready, lawyer; b. Isleham, Va., Dec. 25, 1869; s. Rev. Charles L. and Elizabeth Beck (M'Cready) S.; A.B., Princeton, 1894; m. Beatrice M. Evans, Oct. 2, 1912; children—Patricia M'Cready (Mrs. Sykes Terry), Peter M'Cready, Barbara M'Cready, Gresham M'Cready. Admitted to bar, 1891; practiced law, New York City, 1894-1909; fruit grower, Boise, Ida., 1909-16; active in establishment of improved highways in Idaho; editorial writer, Boise Daily Statesman, 1916; editorial staff, Brooklyn Inst. Arts & Scis., 1916-17; resumed practice at N.Y., 1917; mem. firm Stewart & Shearer, ret., 1951. Asso. editor Commerce and Finance, conducted its series, The Obverse Side, 1920-37. Episcopalian. Club: Players. Author: Poe's Run and Other Poems, 1904. Contbr. to mags. Home: 1405 Watchung, Av., Plainfield, N.J. Office: 45 Wall St., N.Y.C. Died Jan. 31, 1952; buried Princeton (N.J.) Cemetery.

SYLVA, Marguerita (Mrs. B. L. Smith); b. Brussels, Belgium; d. Christian (M.D.) and Mathilde (Schearer) Smith; mother of Swiss parentage; studied music at Royal Conservatoire, Brussels; m. Maj. B. L. Smith, U.S.M.C., of Richmond, Va., May 22, 1915 (div.); children—Leslie, Daphne. Came to U.S. in 1897; with Beerbohm Tree's Dramatic Co., then in comic opera, later in grand opera, Paris, France, and other cities Euope; appeared under Oscar Hammerstein, at Manhattan Opera House, N.Y., 1909; also Chgo. Opera Co., Boston Opera Co., and sang in Grand Opera House and Opera Comique, Paris, and other opera houses in Europe; starred with own opera Co.; owned Phila. Grand Opera Co., 1916; opened Hammerstein Theatre in "Golden Dawn," 1927; made concert tour, with Grand Opera Co., 1929; also made concert tours, 1930, 31, 32, 33, 35; The Thrree Waltzes, Majestic Theatre, N.Y.C., 1937-38; has headlined in vaudeville, and has starred in moving pictures; repertoire includes Navairaise, Richard Strauss' Salome, Carmen, Delila, Cleopatra, etc.; gained special notability as Carmen in opera of same name; starred in comedies, The Sky Lark, The Song Bird, Cousin Sonia, Tonight or Never, Camille, Julie, etc. Episcopalian. Home: Glendale, Cal. Died Feb. 20, 1957.

SYMES, J(ohn) Foster (simz), lawyer; b. Denver, Feb. 10, 1878; s. George Gifford and Sophie Elizabeth (Foster) S.; Ph.B., Yale, 1900; LL.B., Columbia, 1903; m. Cynthia Edrington, Jan. 26, 1916 (div. 1928); children—Virginia Bethel (Mrs. John G. McMurtry, Jr.), Cynthia Edrington (Mrs. Claude Maer); m. 2d, Florence J. Wade, Sept. 29, 1931 (died Apr. 1942). Practiced at N.Y.C., 1902-06; moved to Denver, 1906; U.S. dist. atty., Dist. Colo., 1921-22; U.S. Dist. judge, Colo., 1922—. Student 1st Officers' Tng. Camp, Ft. Riley, Kan., Apr. 1917; commd. capt., Aug. 1917; maj., Oct. 1918; served with 355th Inf., 89th Div. and 362d Inf., 91st Div.; hon. discharged, Apr. 1919; participated in St. Mihiel and Argonne operations and Army of Occupation in Germany. Trustee U. Denver. Mem. Am., Colo., and Denver bar assns., Denver Philos. Soc., Mayflower Soc. Republican. Episcopalian. Vestryman St. John's Cathedral. Mason. Clubs: Denver, Denver Country, Mile High (Denver); University (N.Y.C.). Died Apr. 5, 1951.

SYMMERS, Douglas (sĭm'mẽrs), pathologist; b. Columbia, S.C., Sept. 17, 1879; s. George and Jessie (McKay) S.; student U. of S.C. and Univ. Tutorial Coll., London, Eng.; M.D., Jefferson Med. Coll., Phila., 1901; unmarried. Instr. pathology, Bellevue Med. Coll., New York, 1907, Cornell Med. Coll., 1908-11; asst. pathologist, New York Hosp., 1908-13; prof. pathology, Bellevue Med. Coll., 1911-18; dir. labs. Bellevue and Allied Hosps., 1918-29; gen. dir. labs., Dept. of Hosps., N.Y. City, since 1929; cons. pathologist Englewood and Beekman St. hosps. Mem. N.Y. Pathol. Soc. (pres. 2 terms), Assn. Am. Pathologists and Bacteriologists, International Med. Museums, Sigma Alpha Epsilon; fellow New York Academy of Medicine. Episcopalian. Editor Ziegler's General Pathology (5th Am. edit.), 1921. Contbr. about 80 papers on research work. Home: 140 E. 28th St. Address: Bellevue Hospital, N.Y.C. Died Apr. 19, 1952.

SYMONDS, Walter Stout, Christian Science lecturer; b. Atchison, Kan., Oct. 4, 1891; s. Stephen T. and Mary (Dickerson) S.; student Okla. Univ., 1911-12; Harvard, 1913-14; m. Nellie Barry, Dec. 10, 1915; children—Margarette (Mrs. H. N. Copper), Walter S., Robert B. Prin. Granite (Oklahoma) High Sch., 1914-15; editor Ramona (Okla.) Herald, 1915; staff Texas A. and M. Coll. extension dept., 1916-19; pres. Community State Bank, Bristow, Okla., 1924-25; sec. and agency mgr. Beacon Life Ins. Co., Tulsa, Okla., 1934-35; mgr. city office Great Southern Life Ins. Co., Dallas, 1935-36; owner and gen. mgr. Government Personnel Ins. Group, San Antonio, 1938—; Christian Science lectr., tchr., 1950—. Mem. city council Bristow, Okla., 1926-28, mem. bd. edn., 1928-29. Mem. Bristow C. of C. (sec.). Christian Scientist (pres. bd. dirs. and 1st reader First Ch., San Antonio; com. on publication for Tex.). Mason. Club: Lions (sec.). Home: Aurora Apt. Hotel, San Antonio 1. Office: Milam Bldg., San Antonio 5. Died Mar. 28, 1957.

SZE, Sao-Ke Alfred, diplomat; b. Chengtseh, Ku., China, Apr. 10, 1877; A.B., Cornell U., 1901, A.M., 1902; LL.D., St. John's (Shanghai), Toronto, Columbia, Syracuse, Lafayette, Grinnell; m. Alice, d. of Kidson Tng, of Shanghai, 1905. Acting jr. secretary Bd. of Communications, 1906; mng. dir. Peking Hankow Ry., 1906; dir. Northern Rys., 1908; actg. commr. foreign affairs, Kirin, 1910, later jr. and sr. counselor Ministry Foreign Affiars; commr. to Internat. Plague Conf., Muken, Apr. 1911; minister of post and communications and acting minister of finance, 1st Republican Cabinet of China, 1912; apptd. officer of ceremonies, President's Office, 1913; minister from China to Great Britain, 1914-21, 29-32; del. to Peace Conf., Paris, France, 1918-19; minister from China to U.S., 1921-29, ambassador to U.S., 1933-37; mem. adv. com. World Bank, 1945-58; del. to XII Assembly of League of Nations, mem. League Council, 1931; E.E. and M.P. to U.S. chief Chinese del. Washington Conf. on Limitation of Armament and Pacific Far Eastern Questions, 1921. Actg. minister of foreign affairs, 1922; chief Chinese del. to 1st and 2d Internat. Opium Confs., Geneva, Switzerland, 1924-25; chairman board trustees of Peiping Union Med. Coll., China Foundation. Mem. Phi Beta Kappa, Phi Kappa Phi. Author: Addressess: The Geneva International Opium Conferences. Address: 805 Av. Haig, Shanghai, China. Died Jan. 4, 1958.

SZEKELY, Ernest, engr.; b. Debrecen, Hungary, July 24, 1888; s. Julius and Cecilia (Morvay) S.; grad. Archduke Joseph U., 1910; m. Sari Dobo, Sept. 1, 1911; 1 son, George Emery. Came to U.S., 1912, naturalized, 1932. Faculty mem. Marquette U., 1929-43; pres. Bayley Blower Co., Milwaukee, 1940—. Mem. Am. Soc. Heating and Ventilating Engrs. (pres. 1952), Tau Beta Pi, Pi Tau Sigma. Club: Rotary (Milw.). Author technical articles. Home: 6026 W. Washington Blvd., Wanwatosa 13, Wis. Deceased.

SZYK, Arthur (shĭk), artist; b. Lodz, Poland, June 3, 1894; s. Alexander S. and Eugenie (Rogacka) Schick; ed. primary sch. and commercial college, Lodz; student Acad. Fine Arts, Krakow, 1911-12, Sch. of Fine Arts, Paris, 1914; m. Julia Likerman, 1916; children—George, Alexandra Miriam (Mrs. Joseph Braciejowski). Served as pvt., Russian Army, as officer, Polish Army. Decorated Officer of Palms (France), Golden Merit Cross, Commander's Cross of Polonia Restituta (Poland), George Washington Medal (United States). Illustrator: Song of Songs, 1917; Books of Esther, 1922; Temptation of St. Anthony, 1924; Jacob's Well, 1924; Laughing Jew, 1925; Last Days of Shylock, 1926; Statut of Kalisz, 1929; George Washington and His Times, 1931; Rubaiyat, 1939; Hagadah, 1941; New Order, 1942; United Nation Stamps, 1945; Andersons Fairy Tales, 1945; Canterbury Tales, 1946; Pathways Through the Bible, 1946; Ink and Blood, 1946. Designed postage stamps for Liberia, Republic of Israel, Bolivar and his contemporaries, U.S. Declaration of Independence. Home and studio: Weed St., New Canaan, Conn. Died Sept. 13, 1951.

T

TABER, David Fairman, lawyer; b. Valparaiso, Ind., Dec. 29, 1891; s. David Fairman and Catherine (Memler) T.; student Boys High Sch., Brooklyn, N.Y., 1907-11, Tome Sch., Port Deposit, Md., 1911; LL.B., Cornell U., 1916; m. Ann Mary Ambrose, Dec. 28, 1929; children—Mary Ann, David F., Jr., Ruth Waldo. Admitted to Ill. bar, 1916, and since in practice at Chicago; asso. with law firm Isham, Lincoln & Beale, 1916—, partner, 1931—; dir. Brandon Equipment Co., Ideal Roller & Mfg. Co., Robert O. Law Co., Oak Woods Cemetery Assn. Mem. bd. of appeals, 1945-46, Office Contract Settlement. Served as 1st lt., Air Service, R.F.C., World War; overseas, 1917-19. Mem. Am. and Ill. State bar assns. Theta Delta Chi. Clubs: Chicago, Chicago Golf. Home: Hawthorne Lane, Wheaton, Ill. Office: 72 W. Adams St., Chgo. Died July 29, 1958; buried Wheaton (Ill.) Cemetery.

TABER, George Hathaway, Jr., cons. engr. and petroleum refiner; b. Franklin, Pennsylvania,

January 4, 1890; s. George H. and Elisabeth (Fessenden) T.; B.S. in Mech. Engring., University of Pa., 1911; M.S. in Chem. Engring., Mass. Inst. Tech., 1913; m. Elizabeth Irick Brown, Apr. 21, 1917; children—Elizabeth (Mrs. A. Cudahy), George. Tech. asst. chem. engring. dept. Semet-Solvay Co., 1913-15, Gulf Refining Co., 1915-17; mgr. gasoline dept., Sinclair Oil and Gas Co., 1917-19, vice pres., 1919-21, pres. Sinclair Crude Oil Purchasing Co., 1921-22, with Sinclair Refining Co., 1922-48, ret. 1948; now consultant, vice pres., 1923-44, exec. vice president; Trustee United Hosp., Portchester, N.Y.; Mem. American Chem. Engrs., American Society M.E., Am. Chem. Soc., Soc. Automotive Engrs., Am. Inst. Mining and Metall. Engrs. Clubs: Apawamis, Shenorock Shore, Manursing Island (Rye, N.Y.); Racquet (Philadelphia); Rockefeller Center Luncheon (New York). Holder several patents on petroleum refining. Home: Manursing Av., Rye, N.Y. Office: 116 E. 30th St., N.Y.C. 16. Died Aug. 20, 1954.

TABER, Norman Stephen, banking; b. Providence, R.I., Sept. 3, 1891; s. Alfred Henry and Mary Abbie (Weeks) T.; grad. high sch., Providence, 1909; A.B., Brown U., 1913; Rhodes scholar, Oxford, 1913-15; m. Ottilie Rose Metzger, Dec. 2, 1916; 1 dau., Mary. Clerk R.I. Hosp. Trust Co., Providence, 1915-19; trustee or mgr. various private estates and trusts affiliated with John Nicholas Brown Estate, 1920-30; R.I. representative of Brookmire Economic Service, 1930-33; senior mem. Norman S. Taber & Co., consultants on municipal finance, 1933-48; budget dir. Econ. Cooperation Adminstrn., 1948-49; mng. dir. U.S. Council Internat. C. of C. since 1949. Trustee Brown U., Moses Brown Sch. (Providence), Lincoln Sch. Mem. Phi Beta Kappa, Alpha Delta Phi. Rep. Quaker. Club: Rock Spring. Set world's record of 4 minutes 12 3-5 seconds for mile run, Harvard Stadium, 1915. Home: 237 Turrell Av., South Orange, N.J. Office: 103 Park Av., N.Y.C. 17. Died July 15, 1952.

TABOR, Carl Henry, railroad exec.; b. Baptist Valley, Va., Sept. 30, 1893; s. Hugh B. and Rosa B. (Harrison) T.; m. Una Lee Welsh, Mar. 17, 1920. Began as water boy, maintenance of way dept., N. & W. Ry. Co., May 1, 1907, laborer, 1909, timekeeper, 1909, yard clk., 1912, apptd. asst. yardmaster 1919, yardmaster, 1922, gen. yardmaster 1925, asst. trainmaster, 1927, terminal trainmaster, 1933, trainmaster Pocahontas Div., 1934, trans. to Scioto Div., 1936, supt., 1936, trans. Scioto Div. 1938, asst. gen. supt. Western Div., 1939, gen. supt., 1940, gen. mgr. 1942, v.p. and gen. mgr. since 1946; dir. Am. Enka Corp., Cincinnati Union Terminal Co.; v.p., dir. Durham Union Station Co. Methodist. Clubs: Roanoke, Shenandoah, Rotary (Roanoke); Metropolitan (N.Y.). Home: 2706 Jefferson St. S.R., Roanoke 14. Office: 8 N. Jefferson St., Roanoke 17, Va. Died. Jan. 31, 1953; buried Bluefield, Va.

TACKETT, William Clarence, business exec.; b. Champaign, Ill., Oct. 25, 1897; s. Marion Francis and Lura Belle (Fankboner) T.; student Miami Mil. Inst., 1911-13, Rosenbaum Tutoring Sch., New Haven, 1914; student Sheffield Sci. Sch., Yale, class 1918; m. Vera Hutchinson, Feb. 11, 1941; 1 dau., Pamela Ann. Partner Tackett & Drake, Chgo., mortgage banking, 1920-34; pres. W. C. Tackett, Inc., Chgo., 1934-53, Palm Springs, Cal., 1953—, The Center, Inc., Palm Springs, 1953—; dir. First Fed. Savs. & Loan Assn. of Palm Springs, Rexall Drug Co. Mem. C. of C. Palm Springs (dir.). Episcopalian (vestryman). Clubs: Chicago Athletic, Saddle and Cycle (Chgo.); Racquet, Shadow Mountain, Tennis (Palm Springs); Rotary. Home: 535 Tamarisk Rd. Office: 170 N. Palm Canyon Dr., Palm Springs, Cal. Died Apr. 27, 1958.

TAFT, Harry Deward, educator; b. Whitney Point, N.Y., Feb. 13, 1886; s. George C. and Minnie (Bowen) T.; student Homer (N.Y.) Acad., 1902, Cazenovia (N.Y.) Seminary, 1904, Syracuse U., 1907-08; LL.B., De Paul U., Chicago, 1914, LL.M., 1915; Ph.B., U. Chicago, 1933; m. Hazel Stone, Apr. 20, 1911; children—Harriet Elizabeth, Harry D. Teacher dist. sch 1904-07; admitted to Ill. State bar, 1915, and since served as mem. faculty DePaul U., asst. dean, 1925-49, acting dean, 1949-50, dean, 1950-55, prof. pub. law, counsellor coll. adminstrn., 1955—. Advisor to Registration Bd. and Public Panel Mem., W.L.B., World War II. Mem. National Academy of Arbitrators, American Arbitration Association, Am. Law Inst., Am., Ill. and Chicago bar assns., Sigma Phi Epsilon, Delta Theta Phi, Pi Gamma Mu, Phi Beta Kappa. Club: City. Home: 7642 Greenview Av., Chgo. 26. Office: 64 Lake St., Chgo. 1. Died July 16, 1956.

TAFT, Hulbert, newspaper exec.; b. Cin., Sept. 19, 1877; s. Peter R. and Matilda (Hulbert) T.; A.B., Yale, 1900; LL.D., Xavier U., 1940; Litt.D., Cincinnati Conservatory of Music, 1947; m. Nellie Leaman, Apr. 4, 1904; m. 2d, Virginia Kittredge, July 21, 1928; m. 3d Eleanor Gholson, April 9, 1946. Reporter Cincinnati Times-Star, 1901-02; asso. editor, 1902-07, editor, 1907-54, chmn. bd., 1954—; president Times-Star Co., 1930-54. Exec. com. Cin. Summer Opera. Republican. Episcopalian. Clubs: University, Country, Queen City, Camargo. Home: 8125 Indian Hill Rd. Office: Cincinnati Times-Star, Cin. Died Jan. 9, 1959; buried Spring Grove Cemetery, Cin.

TAFT, Robert, prof. chemistry; b. of Am. parents, Tokyo, Japan, Mar. 24, 1894; s. George Wheaton and Jessie (Humpstone) T.; brought to U.S., 1897; A.B., Grand Island (Neb.) Coll., 1916; M.S., U. Ia., 1919; Ph.D., U. Kan., 1925; m. Josephine Miller, Neb., July 24, 1916; children—Robert, Dorothy. Instr. chemistry Grand Island Coll., 1916-17, Gilbert (Minn.) High Sch., 1917-18, U. Ia., 1918-19, Ottawa (Kan.) U., 1919-22; mem. faculty U. Kan., 1922—, asso. prof. physical chemistry, 1930-37, prof., 1937—. Mem. Am. Assn. U. Profs., Kan. Acad. Science (past pres.), Kan. State Hist. Soc. (past pres.). An authority on Am. historical photographs and pictures; lectr. Chmn. Kan. Territorial Centennial Commn., 1952-54. Author: Photography and the American Scene, 1938; Across the Years on Mount Oread, 1941; Pictorial Record of the Old West, 1946; Fifty Years in Bailey Chemical Laboratory, 1950; Artists and Illustrators of the Old West (Bryan Caldwell Smith award), 1953; The Years on Mount Oread, 1955. Editor of Transactions Kan. Acad. of Science, 1941. Contbr. articles to tech. jours. Home: 1713 Louisiana St., Lawrence, Kan. Died Sept. 22, 1955.

TAFT, Robert Alphonso, senator; b. Cincinnati, O., Sept. 8, 1889; s. William Howard (27th President of U.S.) and Helen (Herron) T.; prep. edn., Taft Sch., Watertown, Conn.; B.A., Yale, 1910, M.A., 1936; LL.B., Harvard U., 1913; LL.D., Wittenberg Coll., 1939, Miami U., 1939, Grove City Coll., 1943, Bethany College, 1944, U. of Cincinnati, Ohio Wesleyan Univ. and Kenyon College, 1949, Western Reserve Univ. and William Jewell College, 1951; D.C.L., Marietta College, 1949, Ripon Coll., 1951; D.I.L., Pa. Mil. Coll., 1951; m. Martha Wheaton Bowers, Oct. 17, 1914; children—William Howard, Robert, Lloyd Bowers, Horace Dwight. Admitted to the Ohio State bar, 1913, and began practice at Cincinnati; with firm of Maxwell & Ramsey, 1913-17; mem. Taft & Taft (bro. Charles P. II), 1922, Taft, Stettinius & Hollister 1923-51; director Central Trust Co.; fellow Yale Corp. Assistant counsel U.S. Food Administration, 1917-19; mem. Ohio House of Rep., 1921-26 (speaker of House, 1926), Ohio Senate, 1931-32; mem. U.S. Senate since 1939. Mem. Psi Upsilon Fraternity. Republican. Episcopalian. Clubs: Queen City, Cincinnati, Camargo. Author: A Foreign Policy for Americans, 1951. Home: Station M., R.R. 1, Cincinnati. Home: 1688 31st St., N.W. Address: Senate Office Bldg., Washington, D.C. Died July 31, 1953.

TAFT, Robert Burbidge, radiology; b. Charleston, S.C., Sept. 20, 1899; s. Augustus Robert (M.D.) and Mary Walter (Witsell) T.; student Porter Mil. Acad., Charleston, 1910-17; B.S., Coll. of Charleston, 1923, M.A., 1934; M.D., Med. Coll. State of S.C., 1923; post-grad. study, U. of Mich. and U. of Vienna, Austria, 1929; m. Mary Joyce Steedman, Oct. 6, 1926; 1 dau., Joyce Shannon. Interne Bellevue Hosp., N.Y. City, 1923-24; asst. in radiology to father until his death, 1927, since in pvt. practice; radiologist Baker sanatorium (Charleston); prof. and dir. dept. of radiology Medical Coll. State of S.C., also director of the radioisotope laboratory. Mem. bd. cons. Oak Ridge Inst. Nuclear Studies. Served in U.S. Army, Plattsburg, N.Y., 1918, World War; classed as essential civilian physician World War II. Mem. bd. commrs. Charleston Mus. Licensed as comml. pilot. Awarded silver medal of Am. Roentgen Ray Soc. for research exhibit, 1936, certificate of merit, 1938, 44, silver medal, 1942; Jefferson Medal of South Carolina Academy of Science, 1929. Member A.M.A., Medical Society State of S.C., S.C. State Medical Association, American Roentgen Ray Society (former chairman committee for use and rental of radium; former chmn. com. on safety and standards); American College Radiology (former councillor South Carolina), Radiology Society of North America (2d v.p.; com. on standardization of x-ray measurements; counselor for S.C.), Am. Phys. Soc., S.C. X-Ray Society, S.C. Acad. of Science (former mem. exec. council), Kappa Alpha, Phi Chi. Author: Radium Lost and Found, 1938, 2d edit., 1946. Author numerous articles summarizing his research work and discoveries. Tech. editor Am. Jour. Roentgenology. Home: 135 S. Battery, Charleston 21. Office: 103 Rutledge Av., Charleston 16, S.C. Died Apr. 16, 1951.

TAGGART, Arthur Fay, univ. prof.; b. N.Y., Oct. 1, 1884; s. Jesse and Ophelia (Fay) T.; A.B., Stanford, 1909, E.M., 1910, studied at Mass. Inst. Tech., 1910, Columbia, 1929; Sc.D., Columbia, 1954; m. Alice Ruth Field, Aug. 31, 1911; children—Mary (Mrs. J. Carleton Dillon), Lois (Mrs. Leonard P. Hall, Jr.), Jesse Field. In real estate bus. 1901-05; asst. in math., Stanford, 1906-10, asst. in mining, 1909-10; geol. exploration, Bolivia, 1911; instr. mining, Yale, 1912-16; asst. prof. mining, 1916-19; prof. mineral dressing, Columbia, 1919-51, Vinton prof. emeritus, 1951. cons. engr., 1917—. Trustee, Bd. Edn., Scarsdale, N.H., 1926-42, pres., 1939-41. Recipient Richards award, 1950. Mem. Am. Chem. Soc., Am. Inst. Mining and Metall. Engrs., Sigma Xi, Tau Beta Pi. Club: Scarsdale Golf. Author: Manual of Flotation Processes, 1921; Handbook of Ore Dressing, 1927; Handbook of Mineral Dressing, 1945; Seventy-five Years Progress in Ore Dressing (Anniversary Vol., Am. Inst. Mining and Metall. Engrs.), 1947; also sect. on boring Minings Engineers' Handbook, 1st edit., 1918, sect. on breaking, crushing and sorting ores, and on testing ores, 2d edit., 1927, and 3d edit., 1941. Contbr. articles to tech. and sci. jours. and encys. Home: 19 Donellan Rd., Scarsdale, N.Y. Office: 117th St. and Broadway, N.Y.C. Died Aug. 22, 1959.

TAGGART, Eugene Francis, exec. adminstr.; b. Phila., Jan. 10, 1916; s. Patrick and Bridget (Melley) T.; ed. Phila. Parochial schs.; student Augustinian Prep. Sem., Staten Island, N.Y., 1930-34, Good Counsel Novitiate, New Hamburgh, N.Y., 1935, St. Joseph's Coll. Sch. Social Sci., 1936, Georgetown Sch. Fgn. Service, 1947; m. Kathleen Marie McGarrity, June 7, 1947; children—Kathleen, Eugene F., Maureen J. Supr. Bur. Unemployment Compensation, Harrisburgh, Pa., 1936-38; nat. exec. dir. Cath. War Vets. of U.S.A., Washington, since 1947, mem. nat. exec. com. since 1947, registered lobbyist, 1948—; nat. adj. gen., 1950; U.S. attaché to Yugoslavia, U.S. State Department, 1951—. Entered the military service, 1941, assigned 218th Gen. Hosp., M.C., 1941, advanced to sergt., 1942; served with med. adminstrv. corps as division medical supply officer for 8th Armored Div., later assigned supply officer aboard Jarrett M. Huddleston Hosp. Ship; disch. as 1st lt., 1945. Mem. Holy Name Soc., Augustinian Alumni. Roman Catholic. Author: Officer's Manual (with Thomas Walsh and Donald McQuade), 1950. Home: 1262 S. 50th St., Phila. Office: 711 14th St. N.W., Washington. Died Mar. 21, 1951; buried Holy Cross Cemetery, Phila.

TAGGART, Ralph Enos, corp. ofcl.; b. Leisenring, Pa., Apr. 17, 1887; s. John K. and Mary (Enos) T.; student Phillips Andover Acad.; m. Virginia Howard Bullitt, June 14, 1910; children—Ralph Enos (dec.), Virginia (Mrs. Irving L. Geer), Daniel Reeder. Pres. Phila. & Reading Coal & Iron Co.; dir. Stonega Coke & Coal Co., Va. Coal & Iron Co. Club: Rittenhouse (Phila.). Home: Radnor, Pa. Office: Reading Terminal Bldg., Phila. Died May 1, 1951; buried Big Stone Gap, Wise County, Va.

TAIT, George, foreign service officer; b. Spring Garden, Amherst County, Va., Aug. 14, 1893; s. Robt. and Frances (Adams) T.; ed. U. of Va. Law Sch., 1913-17, Georgetown Sch. Fgn. Service, Ecole Libre des Sciences Politiques, University of Grenoble; married Marjorie Percival, June 5, 1947. Admitted to Virginia bar; practiced law, 1917-18, lecturer Georgetown Sch. Fgn. Service, 1931-33. 2d lt. U.S. Army, 1918-19; vice consul Rio de Janeiro, Nov. 1923, Palermo, July 1925, Algiers, March 1927; Malta, May 1927; consul, Rotterdam, Oct. 1927; Dept. of State, July 1930; consul, Paris, Sept. 1933, Manchester, Apr. 1937, Montreal, May 1941; 1st sec. Bern, Apr. 1942; counselor of Embassy and Consul gen., London, 1946; consul general, Algiers, 1949, Antwerp, 1950—. Address: Dept. of State, Washington. Died Aug. 24, 1952.

TALBOT, Francis Xavier, clergyman, coll. pres.; b. Phila., Jan. 25, 1889; s. Patrick Francis and Bridget (Peyton) T.; A.B., St. Joseph's Coll., Phila., 1909, D.Litt., 1926; A.M., Woodstock Coll., Md., 1913; D.Litt., Boston Coll., 1938; Fordham, U. 1941; D.H.L., Holy Cross Coll., Worcester, Mass., 1941; mem. Soc. of Jesus (Jesuits). Literary editor America, nat. Cath. weekly, 1922-36, editor-in-chief, 1936-44; pres. Am. Press, 1936-44; pres. Loyola Coll., Balt., 1947—. Founder, editor Cath. Book Club, 1929-36, Spiritual Book Assos., co-founder Pro. Parvulis Book Club, 1930-39; founder, dir. Cath. Poetry Soc., 1929-36; editor-in-chief Cath. Mind, 1936-44, Thought, quarterly, 1936-40. Trustee U.S. Cath. Hist. Soc.; chaplain Motion Picture Dept. I.F.C.A. Contbr. Ency. Britannica. Author: Jesuit Education in Philadelphia, 1927; Richard Henry Tierney, 1930; Shining in Darkness, 1932; Saint Among Savages, 1935; Saint Among the Hurons, 1949. Editor: American Book of Verse, 1927; Fiction by Its Makers, 1928. Home: Loyola College, 4501 N. Charles St., Balt. Died Dec. 3, 1953.

TALBOT, George Frederick, judge; b. nr. Ledyard, Conn., Apr. 6, 1859; s. Henry Monroe and Myra Ann (Ayer) T.; ed. pub. schs. Cal., Nev., Ledyard, Conn., and at Dickinson Sem., Williamsport, Pa., 1876-78; m. Rosalind Adams Busing, Nov. 6, 1920. Admitted to bar, 1881; elected dist. atty., Elko Co., Nev., 1884, 86; elected dist. judge, 4th Jud. Dist., Nev., 1884, 98; elected one of four dist. judges from state at large, 1894; justice Supreme Court, Nev., 1902-14 (chief justice, 1906-08, 1913-14); resumed practice. Regent U. of Nev., term 1921-30 inclusive. Pres. Nev. State Hist. Soc., 1914-26. Home: Reno, Nev. Deceased.

TALBOT, Mary White, author; b. at Cambridge, Mass., June 4, 1869; d. John Eaton and Lucy (Nichols) White; student Miss Steer's Sch., New York, Rye (N.Y.) Sem., Cooper Art Sch. and Art Students' League, New York; m. Arthur Dorrance

Talbot, June 11, 1904; children—Dorrance, and John Phillips. Member of the New York Guild of Arts and Crafts, Primitive Arts Club, Brooklyn. Episcopalian. Author: The Book of Games, 1896; How to Make Baskets, 1901; More Baskets and How to Make Them, 1903; The Book of Children's Parties, 1903; How to Do Beadwork, 1904; How to Make Pottery, 1904; The Child's Rainy Day Book, 1905. Home: Monument Rd., Orleans, Mass. Died Mar. 20, 1952; buried Orleans (Mass.) Cemetery.

TALBOTT, Harold E., capitalist, ex-sec. air force; b. Dayton, O., Mar. 31, 1888; s. Harry Elstner and Katharine H. (Houk) T.; prep. edn. The Hill School; student Yale U., 1907-09; married Margaret Thayer, Aug. 11, 1925; children—Margaret T., Pauline, John Thayer, Harold E. III. V.p., gen. mgr. The H. E. Talbott Co., 1911-20, in chg. of hydro-elec. dvlpmnt. and indsl. construction; v.p., gen. mgr. Dayton Metal Products Co., 1914-20; pres. Dayton Wright Airplane Co., 1916-20, Dayton Wright Co., 1919-23; chmn. bd. Standard Packaging Corp., North Am. Aviation Co., 1931-32; vice pres. Talbott Corp., dir. and chmn. finance com. of Mead Corp., Electric Auto-Lite Co.; limited partner Paul B. Mulligan & Company; dir. Baldwin-Lima-Hamilton Corp., Chrysler Corp. (mem. finance com.), Russell Mfg. Co., Madison Square Garden Corp. Dir. aircraft prodn. W.P.B., 1942-43; sec. of Air Force, 1953-55. Served as major Airplane Service, 1918. Eastern chmn. Republican Finance Com., 1934, chmn. for Met. New York, 1943, chmn. Republican national finance com., 1948-49. Republican. Clubs: Deepdale, Cloud, Creek, Madison Square Garden (N.Y.C.); Burning Tree (Chevy Chase, Md.); Capitol Hill (Washington). Dayton, Buzfuz, Miami Valley Hunt and Polo (Dayton, O.); Racquet and Tennis, Meadow Brook, Turf and Field, The River, Piping Rock, The Links (New York). Died Mar. 2, 1957; buried Dayton, O.

TALBOTT, Nelson S., business exec.; b. Dayton, O., 1892; Yale, 1915. Pres., dir. Talbott Corp. Dayton, Midwest Fulton Machinery Co.; v.p., dir. Maxon Constrn. Co.; dir. Specialty Paper Co., Mead Corp., Dayton, Trans World Airlines, Inc., Standard Cap & Seal Corp., Skyline Corp. Home: Hills and Dales, R.F.D. 7, Dayton, O. Died July 6, 1952.

TALLANT, Hugh (tăl'ănt), architect; b. Boston, Sept. 15, 1869; s. Henry Pinkham and Mary Gardner (Coleman) T.; A.B., A.M., Harvard, 1891; Ecole des Beaux Arts, Paris, France, Architecte Diplômé par le Gouvernement Français, 1896; widower. Architect of Bates College Library, Lynbrook Library, Smith College Chemical Laboratory, New Amsterdam Theatre, Lyceum Theatre, Brooklyn Acad. Music, Hurt Building (Atlanta, Ga.), Piccadilly Restaurant (London), Brooklyn Hospital, Martha's Vineyard Hosp., etc. Mem. Société des Architectes Diplômés par le Gouvernement Français, Ga. Soc. Colonial Wars, Phi Beta Kappa. Clubs: Oglethorpe, Harvard. Capt. of Ordnance, U.S. Army, 1917-19; AEF. Home: The DeRenne, Savannah, Ga. Address: 24 E. Liberty St., Savannah, Ga. Died Dec. 7, 1952.

TALMADGE, Norma, actress; b. Niagara Falls, N.Y., May 2, 1897; d. Frederick and Margaret T.; ed. pub. schs., Brooklyn; m. Joseph M. Schenck, of New York, Oct. 1917 (div.); m. 2d, George Jessel, Apr. 23, 1934 (div.); m. Carvel James, 1946. Began in motion pictures at 14, with no previous stage experience; with Vitagraph Co., later with Fine Arts Co., Select Pictures, First Nat. Pictures, United Artists. Motion pictures: The Crown Prince' Double, The Social Secretary, The Law of Compensation, The Secret of the Storm Country, The Ghosts of Yesterday, Her Only Way, The Forbidden City, A Daughter of Two Worlds, The Branded Woman, The Woman Gives, Yes or No, The Passion Flower, The Sign On The Door, Love's Redemption, The Wonderful Thing, Smilin' Through, The Voice from the Minaret, Within the Law, Ashes of Vengeance, Dust of Desire, Secrets, The Lady, Songs of Love, Graustrak, Kiki, Camille, also The Dove, The Woman Disputes, New York Nights (a talking picture), etc. Home: Las Vegas, Nevada. Died Dec. 24, 1957.

TANGUY, Yves, artist; b. Paris, France, Jan. 5, 1900; s. Felix and Therese (Coadou) T.; student Lycee St. Louis; m. Kay Sage, Aug. 17, 1940. Came to U.S., 1939, naturalized, 1948. Exhibited Galerie Surrealiste, Paris, 1927, Hollywood, Cal., 1935, 36, Galerie des Cahiers d'Art, Paris, 1935, Julien Levy, N.Y.C., 1936, Palais des Beaux Arts, Bruxelles, 1937, Galerie Bucher-Myrbor, Paris, Guggenheim Jeune, London, Eng., 1938, Pierre Matisse, N.Y.C., 1939, Arts Club, Chgo., 1940, Wadsworth Atheneum, Hartford, Conn., 1940, San Francisco Mus. Art, 1940; exhibits regularly Pierre Matisse Gallery, N.Y.C., 1939—; paintings in permanent collections prin. museums and galleries of U.S., Paris, Honolulu, Hawaii. Mem. Surrealistes. Home: Woodbury, Conn. Office: care Pierre Matisse Gallery, 41 E. 57th St., N.Y.C. Died Jan. 15, 1955.

TANNER, Fred Wilbur, bacteriologist; b. Buffalo, Feb. 15, 1888; s. Wellington Boughton and Emma Melvina (Olds) T.; B.S., Wesleyan U., 1912, D.Sc., 1943; M.S., U. Ill., 1914, Ph.D., 1916; m. Hope Stuart Montgomery, June 10, 1916 (died 1935); children—Fred Wilbur, Wells Montgomery, Stuart Wellington, Hope Montgomery (dec.); m. 2d, Louise Milliken Pickens, Dec. 27, 1936. Bacteriologist Ill. State Water Survey, 1912-15; with U. Ill., 1915—, prof. bacteriology, 1923—, head dept. bacteriology to 1948; bacteriologist, branch lab. Ill. Dept. Health. Mem. Am. Chem. Soc., Soc. Am. Bacteriologists, Soc. Exptl. Biology and Medicine, Inst. Food Technologists (pres. 1945-46), Internat. Assn. Milk Sanitarians, Alpha Chi Rho, Alpha Chi Sigma, Phi Sigma, Sigma Xi, Pi Gamma Mu; fellow A.A.A.S., Am. Pub. Health Assn.; asso. fellow A.M.A. Republican. Clubs: University, Rotary. Author: Bacteriology and Mycology of Foods, 1919; The Yeats (Guilliermond-Tanner), 1920; Bacteriology, 1929; Practical Bacteriology, 1929; The Microbiology of Foods, 1944; Food-Borne Infections and Intoxications, 1933, also numerous contbr. to sci. jours. Contbr. Ency. Britannica. Editor-in-Chief of Food Research. Home: 921 Lincoln Circle, Winter Park, Fla. Died Feb. 24, 1957.

TANNER, William Vaughn, lawyer; b. at Fairmont, Minn., Apr. 7, 1881; s. John Wolfe and Cora (Edwards) T.; ed. U. Washington, 1896-98. Admitted to Wash. bar, 1902; law clerk to atty. gen. of Wash., 1902-05; asso. in practice with Harold Preston, 1905-09; asst. atty. gen., Wash., 1909-11; apptd. atty. gen. to fill unexpired term, Apr. 1, 1911, elected for terms 1913-21; resigned, March 1, 1919, resumed law practice at Seattle; pub. Seattle Post Intelligencer, 1931-36; mem. firm Tanner, Garvin & Ashley. Republican. Mem. Am. Wash. State, Seattle bar assns. Clubs: Rainier, Seattle Golf. Home: 1017 Minor. Office: Exchange Bldg., Seattle. Died Dec. 3, 1953.

TANSIL, John Bell, lawyer; b. Dresden, Tenn., July 13, 1881; s. Egbert E. and Jackie (Bell) T.; A.B., Vanderbilt U., 1900, LL.B., 1905, A.M., 1906; m. Lillian Summers, Feb. 12, 1908 (died 1914); m. 2d, Helen Fletcher, Aug. 12, 1931. Teacher, 1901-03; admitted to Tenn. bar, 1907, and practiced in Memphis, 1907-15; admitted to Mont. bar, 1915, since practiced in Billings; sr. partner, Tansil, Lamb & Galles; asst. U.S. dist. atty. for Mont., 1918-19; county atty. Yellowstone County, 1923-29; U.S. dist. atty. for Mont. 1935—. Chmn. Yellowstone County Dem. Central Com. several terms; mem. Mont. Dem. State Central Com. 12 yrs. Mem. Alpha Tau Omega, Phi Beta Kappa. Episcopalian. Mason, Elk. Club: Billings Golf and Country. Home: 221 Av. D. Address: Federal Bldg., Billings, Mont. Died Dec. 11, 1952.

TAPPER, Thomas, lecturer; b. Canton, Mass., Jan. 28, 1864; s. Thomas and Ellen (Whalley) T.; F.C.M., Am. College Musicians (N.Y. Univ.); studied music in Europe; Litt.D., Bates Coll., 1911; m. Bertha Feiring Maas, Sept. 22, 1895 (died Sept. 2, 1915); m. 2d, Marie Eugenia Keating, Nov. 20, 1920. Formerly lecturer and instr. Inst. Musical Art, N.Y.; for many yrs. prin. dept. of music, N.Y. Univ.; dir. dept. of edn. J. C. Penney Co., Junior Achievement, Inc.; pres. Nat. Acad. Music; ednl. counsellor and editor West Side Y.M.C.A., N.Y. City. Trustee N.Y. Coll. of Music, Scudder Sch. Mem. editorial bd. the University Society, N.Y.; editor The Dynamo (J. C. Penney Co.), 1916-32, The Musician, 1897-1905. Author: Chats with Music Students, 1890; The Music Life, 1892; Music Talks with Children, 1896; Child's Music World, 1896; The Natural Course in Music (6 vols.); Pictures from the Lives of the Great Composers, 1899; First Studies in Music Biography, 1900; Rhythm of the Fingers (transl. from the French); A Short Course in Music (2 vols.); Harmonic Music Course (7 vols.); One Hundred Rythmical Studies; The Modern Graded Piano Course (19 vols.), and many other text-books; also Efficiency; How to Build a Fortune; Youth and Opportunity; Education of the Music Teacher; Essentials in Music History; The Music Supervisor; Nimble Fingers; First Year Music History; First Year Music Biography; Music Theory and Composition, 6 vols.; Personal Engineering Books (10 vols.); Keyboard Harmony, Text-book on Modulation in Classical and Modern Music; Students Repertoire of Piano Composition (2 vols.). Co-editor University Music Course. Past asso. editorial writer with Arthur Brisbane for Hearst Newspaper Syndicate; also editorial representative, Oliver Ditson Music Publishing Co., Boston. Club: Authors' (London). Home: Colonial Club, 1 Old Mamaroneck Rd., White Plains, N.Y. Office: 330 W. 34th St., N.Y.C. Died Feb. 24, 1958; buried Kensico Cemetery, Valhalla, N.Y.

TAQUINO, George James (tăk-kē-nō), surgeon; b. New Orleans, La., Oct. 19, 1884; s. Thomas P. and Victoria Marie (Guyot) T.; M.D., Tulane University, 1911; D.Sc. (hon.), Loyola University, 1942; married Alice Savich, Mar. 1, 1919; 1 son, George James. Intern Ear, Nose and Throat Hosp., New Orleans, 1911-13; clin. asst. dept. otolaryngology post grad., Tulane, 1913; asst. prof., Tulane, 1915-21; asso. with Dr. Robt. C. Lynch, 1912-22; asst. visiting surgeon Charity Hosp., 1921-26; visiting surgeon, 1926-30, sr. visiting surgeon since 1930; prof. clin. otolaryngology, La. State U., 1931-36, dir. and prof. dept. oto-rhinolaryngology since 1936; prof. bronchoscopy and esophagoscopy La. State U. Med. Center; cons. bronschopist, U.S. Marine Hosp., New Orleans. Served as 1st lt., Gen. Hosp. No. 14, World War. Fellow Am. Acad. of Ophthalmology and Otolaryngology, American Laryngol., Rhinol. and Otological Society, Am. Broncho-Esophagological Society, A.M.A., Am. Coll. of Surgeons, Southeastern Surg. Congress, Internat. Coll. of Surgeons; mem. Orleans Parish, La. State and Southern med. assns., New Orleans Eye, Ear, Nose and Throat Club, Am. Bd. of Otolaryngology, Am. Assn. Mil. Surgeons, Mil. Order World War, Round Table University Club, La. State U. Sch. of Medicine Faculty Club (pres.), Blue Key. Catholic. Clubs: Lions, Metairie Golf, L'Union Francais. Home: 18 Fontainbleau Drive. Office: 1313 Nat. Bank of Commerce Bldg., New Orleans 12. Died Aug. 29, 1953.

TARACOUZIO (Taracous-Taracouzio), Timothy Andrew (tä-rä-kōō'zē-o), educator, author; b. Reval, Russia, Jan. 11, 1897; s. Andrei Ivanovich and Varvara Timofeevna (Alekseev) T.; student law sch., U. of St. Petersburg, 1914; grad. Aviation School, Gatchina, Russia, 1916; M.A., Univ. of Southern Calif., 1927; M.A., Harvard, 1928, Ph.D., 1935; m. Evlin Shaw Coleman, Oct. 14, 1933; 1 son, Lon Anthony. Came to U.S., 1923; naturalized, 1929. Successively manual laborer, bank clerk and translator, 1923-27; bibliog. research asst. and in charge Slavic Dept., Harvard Law Library, 1928-42; lecturer on comparative Law, Harvard Law Sch., 1930-31; mem. Bur. Internat. Research, Harvard Univ. and Radcliffe Coll. 1929-42; with U.S. Govt. in wartime gencies, 1942-1943; capt., to lt. col. A.U.S.; overseas, 1943-46; faculty, Nat. War Coll., 1946-47; asso. prof. U.S. Navy Intelligence Sch., 1947, ret. now professor law U. of Florida, 1956—. Received commn. from Artillery Acad. of Grand Duke Constantin, 1915; grad. Officer's Aviation Sch., 1916; served throughout World War, 1914-17, and Civil War, Russia, 1918-22, successively in arty., air service and Navy, advancing to rank of capt. in the Army. Decorated Order of St. Stanislav (3d and 2d class), Order of St. Anne (4th, 3d and 2d class), Order of St. Validimir (4th class). Mem. American Soc. Internat. Law. Mem. Russian Orthodox. Author: The Soviet Union and International Law, 1935; Soviets in the Arctic, 1938; War and Peace in Soviet Diplomacy, 1940; also articles. Address: Pass-a-Grill, Fla. Died Mar. 4, 1958.

TARBELL, Thomas Freeman, ins. exec.; b. Pepperell, Mass., May 15, 1888; s. Henry F. and Carrie (Swasey) T.; grad. Lawrence Acad.; A.B., Williams Coll., 1910; m. Bessie M. Farley, Feb. 10, 1917. Actuarial work Mutual Life Ins. Co. N.Y., 1910-19; actuary Conn. Ins. Dept., 1919-22; actuary accident dept. Aetna Life Ins. Co., 1922-27; actuary Travelers Ins. Co., Hartford, Conn., 1927-53, v.p. and actuary, 1953-55. Fellow Soc. Actuaries, Casualty Actuarial Soc. (past pres.). Editor, contbr. Insurance Accounting-Fire and Casualty, 1954. Home: 42 Linwold Dr., West Hartford 7, Conn. Office: Travelers Ins. Co., Hartford 15, Conn. Died July 2, 1958; buried Pepperell, Mass.

TARBOUX, Joseph G(alluchat), educator, engr.; b. Juiz de Fora, Brazil, Aug. 15, 1898; s. John William and Sue Frances (Kirkland) T. (Am. Citizens); B.S., Clemson (S.C.) Coll., 1918; E.E., Cornell, 1923, M.E.E., 1926; Ph.D., 1937; m. Isabelle Nicholas, June 12, 1923; children—John William, Emily Joyce. Instr. Clemson Coll., 1918-19; mem. faculty Cornell, 1919-29, prof. elec. engring., 1946-52; prof. elec. engring. U. Mich. since 1952; professor and head dept. elec. engring. U. Tenn., 1929-46; employed with Fla. Power Co., Ala. Power Co., Pub. Service Co. of N.J., Westinghouse Elec. Corp., Gen. Elec. Co.; cons. since 1929. Fellow Am. Inst. E.E. chmn. com. on education, 1946; Hoover medal bd. of award, 1947-53, v.p. dist. 1, 1950-52); mem. Am. Soc. Engring. Edn. Nat. Soc. Profl. Engrs., Inst. Radio Engrs., Engring. Soc. Detroit, Eta Kappa Nu, Sigma Xi, Tau Beta Pi, Phi Kappa Phi. Contbr. to Collier's Engring. Ency., Standard Handbook for Elec. Engrs., various periodicals, publs. Home: 580 Riverview Dr., Ann Arbor, Mich. Died Feb. 6, 1959; buried Knoxville, Tenn.

TARR, Frederick Courtney, educator; b. Balt., May 6, 1896; s. Adam Shoop and Anne (Courtney) T.; student Baltimore City Coll., 1908-11; A.B., Johns Hopkins, 1915, A.M., 1917; Ph.D., Princeton U., 1921; m. Martha Louise Slocomb, Sept. 22, 1917 (div. May 1934); 1 dau., Martha Madeline; m. 2d, Sofia de Yturriaga y Manzano, July 28, 1934. Instr. in Spanish, Princeton U., 1920-22, asst. prof., 1922-28, asso. prof., 1928-37, Emory L. Ford prof. of Spanish, 1937—; vis. prof. Spanish, U. of N.M., 1938. Served from pvt. to capt., U.S. Army, 1917-19. Mem. Modern Lang. Assn. America, Am. Assn. Univ. Profs., Am. Assn. Teachers of Spanish. Awarded John Simon Guggenheim fellowship, 1929-30. Decorated Caballero de la Orden de Isabel la Católica, 1934. Democrat. Asso. editor Hispanic Review. Author: Prepositional Complementary Clauses in Spanish, 1922; A First Spanish Grammar (with C. C. Marden), 1926; A Graded Spanish Review Grammar (with Augusto Conteno), 1933; Impresiones de Espana, 1933; Shorter Spanish Review Grammar, 1937; Romanticism in Spain and Spanish Romanticism, 1939. Contbr. to learned mags. of U.S. and abroad. Home: 1 College Rd., Princeotn, N.J. Deceased.

TASKER, Cyril, engr.; b. Manchester, Eng., Jan. 8, 1899; s. Percy William and Annie E. (Flint) T.; B.S. Tech., Univ. of Manchester, Coll. of Tech. (Foundation scholar), 1921, M.S. Tech., 1923; m. Ada Ruth Brooks, June 19, 1929. Came to U.S., Oct. 1943. With dept. of scientific and indsl. research, Fuel Research Bd., London, Eng., 1924-30; office in charge N. Staffordshire Coal Survey, 1926-30; sr. research fellow Ontario Research Foundation, Toronto, Can., 1930-43; dir. of research Am. Soc. of Heating and Ventilating Engrs., Cleveland, O., since 1943. Served as lt. spl. brigade, Corps of Royal Engrs., 1917-19. Fellow Inst. of Fuel, London; member Inst. of Heating and Ventilating Engrs., London, Eng., Am. Soc. Heating and Ventilating Engrs. (mem. com. on research, 1936-43; mem. council, 1941-43, pres. Ontario chapter, 1941). Presbyterian. Am. corr. Heating and Ventilating Engr. and Journal of Air Conditioning, London, Eng., since 1939. Contbr. many articles on Am. practice, developments and research in field of heating and ventilating. Home: 3538 Edison Rd., Cleveland 21. Office: 7218 Euclid Av., Cleve. 3. Died May 27, 1953; buried Highland Cemetery, Urn Garden, Cleve.

TASKEY, Harry LeRoy, artist; born at Rockford, Indiana, June 9, 1892; the son of Otto and Cora (Pressley) Taskey; was a student Hiram (O.) Coll., 1915-17, Art Students League, 1919-27, Academie Grande Chaumiere, Paris, 1927-29; m. Irene May McMeen. Represented permanent exhbns. Met. Mus. of Art, New York Pub. Library, Syracuse, Museum of Fine Arts, Museum of the City of N.Y., John Herron Inst., Meml. Art Gallery, Library of Congress, represented in exhbns. in New York, Chicago, Phila., Boston and other important art centers since 1931. Served as corpl. 112th Engrs., 37th Div., A.E.F., U.S. Army, World War. Recipient Am. Vets. Soc. of Artists prize, 1954, award 1956. Mem. Delaware Valley Artists, Am. Vets. Soc. of Artists, Audubon Artists, Artists Equity, Asso. Am. Artists, Hunterdon County Art Center. Home: R.F.D. No. 1, Milford, N.J. Died May 9, 1958; buried Presbyn. Cemetery, Milford, N.J.

TATE, James Alexander, school master; b. Maness, Scott Co., Va., Feb. 26, 1860; s. John M. and Martha Rose (Maness) T.; A.B., Milligan Coll., Tenn., 1882, A.M., 1885; m. Laetitia Cornforth, May 17, 1887; children—Rose Eleanor (Mrs. A. B. Stewart), James Alexander (dec.). Pres. West Tenn. Coll., Dyer, 1898-1900; chancellor Am. U., Harriman, Tenn., 1903-08; head master Tate Sch., Shelbyville, Tenn., 1908-33. Asst. to dir. of edn. for Tenn., Nat. Youth Adminstrn., 1935-37. Prominent as temperance and prohibition speaker, 1884—; chmn. Tenn. State Prohibition Com., 1892-1905; mem. Nat. Com., 1888-1905, sec. 1894-1905; nat. organizer, 1902-03; supt. Tenn. Anti-Saloon League, 1928-30; mem. Prohibition Dem. Com. of Tenn.; dir. United Prohibition Forces of Tenn., 1933-36; pres. United Dry Forces of Tenn., Inc., 1937—. Dir. Flying Squadron Foundation, Indianapolis. Mem. Christian Ch. Home: Shelbyville, Tenn. Died Jan. 25, 1951; buried Shelbyville, Tenn.

TATE, John Torrence, physicist; b. Lenox, Adams County, Ia., July 28, 1889; s. Samuel Aaron and Minnie Maria (Ralston) T.; B.Sc., U. of Neb., 1910, M.A., 1912, hon. D.Sc., 1938; Ph.D., U. of Berlin, 1914; hon. D.Sc., Case Sch. of Applied Science, 1945; m. Lois Beatrice Fossler, Dec. 28, 1917 (dec.); 1 son, John Torrence; m. 2d, Madeline Margarite Mitchell, June 30, 1945. Instr. physics, U. of Neb., 1914-15, asst. prof., 1915-16; instr. physics, U. of Minn., 1916-17, asst. prof., 1917-18, asso. prof., 1919-21, prof., 1921-37, dean Coll. Science Lit. and Arts, 1937-43, prof. physics since 1943. Served as 1st lt. signal corps, U.S. Army, 1917-18; chief div. 6, Nat. Defense Research Com., 1941-45. Fellow Carnegie Inst. of Washington. Mem. Am. Phys. Soc. (mng. editor since 1926, pres. 1939); Am. Inst. Physics (governing bd., since 1932, chmn. 1936-39), Nat. Acad. Science, Am. Optical Soc., Am. Philos. Soc., Acoustical Soc. of America, American Assn. Physics Teachers, Sigma Xi, Phi Beta Kappa. Protestant. Clubs: Cosmos, Century Assn. Editor: Physical Review, Review of Modern Physics. Address: 518 Southeast 7th St., Minneapolis. Died May 27, 1950.

TATUM, Arthur Lawrie (tā'tŭm), coll. prof.; b. Wall Lake, Ia., May 17, 1884; s. Elwood and Deborah C. Tatum; B.S., Penn Coll., 1905; M.S., State U. of Iowa, 1907; Ph.D., U. of Chicago, 1913; M.D., Rush Med. Coll., 1914; Doctor Honoris Causa, San Marcos Univ. (Peru), 1948; m. Mabel Webb, Dec. 20, 1908; m. 2d, Celia Harriman, Sept. 9, 1940; children—Edward L., Besse C., Howard J. Instr. physiology, U. Pa., 1915-16; prof. physiology, U. S.D., 1916-17; asst. prof. pharmacology, U. Chgo., 1918-25, asso. prof., 1925-28; prof. pharmacology, U. of Wis., 1928—. Mem. Am. Physiol. Soc., Am. Soc. Pharmacol. and Exptl. Therapeutics (v.p. 1933, 34; president, 1937-38; asso. editor, 1940-50), Inst. Medicine of Chicago; mem. of A.A.A.S., Nat. Malaria Soc., Soc. Exptl. Biology and Medicine, Am. Soc. Anesthesiologists (hon.), Pharm. Revision Com. Xi, Sigma Xi, Alpha Chi Sigma, Phi Chi; mem. A.M.A. Charles Mickle fellowship, U. of Toronto, 1942. Clubs: Chaos, University. Contbr. to med. journals. Address: 1718 Summit Av., Madison 5, Wis. Died Nov. 11, 1955.

TAUB, Sam, partner J. N. Taub & Sons, Houston; chmn. exec. com. and dir. Nat. Bank of Commerce; dir. Houston Lighting & Power Co., Am. Gen. Ins. Co., Am. Life Ins. Co., Am. Gen. Investment Co. Home: 2714 Commonwealth Av. Office: 909 Franklin St., Houston 2. Deceased.

TAYLER, Joseph Henry, banker; b. Green Bay, Wis., Feb. 7, 1859; s. Joseph and Melissa T.; ed. common schs.; m. Eleanor Jane Richardson, June 27, 1889; 1 dau., Eleanor Kennan. Partner McCartney Exchange Bank, Green Bay, 1882-91; pres. McCartney Nat. Bank, 1910—; pres. Northern Bond & Mortgage Co.; v.p. Menominee River Sugar Co.; sec. Green Bay Water Co., 1894-1920; formerly city treas. and mayor, Ft. Howard, Wis.; mayor Green Bay, 1902-04. Treas. and dir. Bellin Memorial Hosp. Republican. Baptist. Rotarian. Address: Green Bay, Wis. Died May 25, 1959; buried Fort Howard Cemetery, Green Bay, Wis.

TAYLOR, Albert Davis, landscape architect, town planner, civil engineer; born Carlisle, Massachusetts, July 8, 1883; son of Nathaniel and Ellen (Davis) Taylor; B.S., Massachusetts State College, 1905, LL.D., 1945; A.B., Boston Coll., 1905; M.S., Cornell University, 1906; Sc.D., Oregon State College, 1940; m. Genevieve Brainerd, June 16, 1917; 1 son, Charles Brainerd. Instructor in landscape architecture, Cornell University, 1906-08; began practice at Boston, 1908; at Cleveland, Ohio, and Orlando, Florida, since 1915; non-resident professor landscape architecture, Ohio State U., 1916-24; lecturer, U. of Mich., since 1938; contbg. editor Landscape Architecture Magazine. Consulting landscape architect, U.S. Forest Service. Landscape architect for Harding, Spanish War, and Roosevelt Warm Springs Memorials, Pentagon Bldg. Site, and Boys Town, and many other pub. and pvt. developments; town planner U. S. Housing Corp., 1917-18; collaborator for the U.S. Nat. Arboretum; consultant for various U.S. Marine hospitals, for War Dept. and for Housing Div.; chief consultant in site planning, War Dept., 1941; site planner for Fla. State Capital development. Mem. landscape architecture jury, Am. Acad. in Rome, Cleveland City Plan Commn., 1928-43; pres. Am. Soc. Landscape Architects, 1935-41 (chmn. committee on bicentennial commn.; ex-pres. O.-Mich. chapter); trustee Lake Forest Foundation Sch., Cambridge Sch. Landscape Architecture. Mem. Am. Inst. Park Execs., City Planning Inst., American Society of Civil Engineers, Phi Kappa Phi, Gamma Alpha, Alpha Sigma Phi. Unitarian. Clubs: Hermit, Cleveland Skating. Author: Shade Trees, Their Care and Preservation, 1908; Plants for Landscape Planting, 1916; Complete Garden, 1920; Landscape Construction Notes, 1928; Problems of Landscape Architecture in the National Forests, 1936; Camp Stoves and Fireplaces, 1937; Landscape Details, 1939. Home: 2178 S. Overlook Rd., Cleveland Heights, O. Office: 7016 Euclid Av., Cleveland. Died Jan. 8, 1951; buried Riverside Cemetery, Cleve.

TAYLOR, Alrutheus Ambush, educator; b. Washington, D.C., Nov. 22, 1893; s. Lewis and Lucy (Johnson) T.; A.B., U. of Mich., 1916; A.M., Harvard, 1923, Ph.D., 1936; m. Harriet Ethel Wilson, Sept. 9, 1919 (died Aug. 19, 1941); m. 2d, Mrs. Catherine Buchanan, September 9, 1943; step-children—Mrs. Leatrice McKissack, Harold, John, Donald and Alrutheus Buchanan. Teacher of English, Tuskegee Inst., 1914-15; social worker, New York Urban League, 1917-18; teacher mathematics, W.Va. Collegiate Inst., 1919-22; asso. investigator, Assn. for Study of Negro Life and History, 1923-25; prof. history, Fisk U., Nashville, Tenn., 1926—, dean of Coll. of Liberal Arts 1930-51, research professor in American history, 1950—. Pres. bd. trustees Nashville Kent Coll. of Law. Fellow Laura Spelman Rockefeller Memorial, 1928-29. Founded Harriet Wilson Taylor Scholarship Fisk U., 1942. Member Assn. Study of Negro Life and History (fellow 1922-23; mem. exec. council 1937-50), Am. and Southern hist. assns., Am. Acad. Polit. and Social Sci. Am. Assn. U. Profs., Planned Parenthood Fedn. of Am., Inc., The Nat. Conf. on Family Relations, Alpha Phi Alpha, Sigma Pi Phi. Author: The Negro in South Carolina During the Reconstruction, 1924; The Negro in the Reconstruction of Virginia, 1926; The Negro in Tennessee, 1865-1880, 1941. Co-author: A Study of the Community Life of the Negro Youth, 1941; Fisk University, A History 1866-1951, 1952. Contbr. to hist. jours. Home: 3602 Batavaia St., Nashville 8. Died June 4, 1954; buried Fowler, Ind.

TAYLOR, Archibald Wellington, educator; b. Linwood, Neb., Apr. 15, 1877; s. Benjamin Francis and Olive Millard (Collins) T.; A.B., Doane Coll., Neb., 1902, LL.D., 1932; A.M., U. Wis., 1908; U. Chgo. and U. Pa., 1909-11; hon. D.C.S., Oglethorpe U., 1932; m. Anna M. Ross, June 1912; children—Archibald W. (dec.), Robert Ross (dec.). Prin Puget Sound Acad., 1902-05; supt. pub. schs., Ritzville, Wash., 1905-07; instr. econs., Purdue U. 1908-09, Ia. State Tchrs. Coll., 1910; instr. finance, U. Pa., 1910-11; prof. econs., head dept econs., sci. and history, Wash. State Coll., 1911-16 asst. prof. econs., dir. Wall Street div., Sch. Commerce, N.Y. U., 1916-18, prof., 1919-44, dea Grad. Sch. Bus. Adminstrn., 1919-44, dean emeritus, 1944—; dir. Edn. C. of C., State N.Y., 1943—. Mem. Am. Econ. Assn., Chamber Commerc N.Y., Alpha Tau Omega, Delta Phi Epsilon, Delt Mu Delta. Conglist. Home: 143 Stanmore Pl., Westfield, N.J. Office: 65 Liberty St., N.Y.C. 5. Die Sept. 25, 1953.

TAYLOR, Charles Gillies, Jr., ins. exec.; b. Petersburg, Va., May 24, 1883; s. Charles G. and Sara Louise (Quee) T.; D.Eng., Stevens Inst. Tech. 1951; m. Kate James Christian, June 21, 1905; children—Katherine (Mrs. Allen Bond Adams), Donal Quee. Actuary, Bur. Ins., Commonwealth Va., 1906-08; sec., actuary, v.p., dir. S. Atlantic Life Ins Co. (now Atlantic Life Ins. Co.), 1908-25; asst mgr., actuary Assn. Life Ins. Pres'., N.Y.C., 1925-32; 3d v.p. Met. Life Ins. Co., 1932, 2d v.p. 1936, v.p., dir., exec. v.p., 1942-51, pres., 1951—; dir. First and Merchants Nat. Bank, Richmond Life Ins. Guaranty Corp., N.Y. Pres. Am. Lif Conv., 1920-21; former dir. Montclair (N.J.) Community Chest, Montclair Council Social Agys., Montclair Y.M.C.A. Trustee Stevens Inst. Tech. Mem. So Soc. N.Y., St. Andrew's Soc. (gov.), Virginians o City of N.Y., Ins. Soc. N.Y. (pres. 1934-35). Republican. Presbyn. Clubs: Union League, Economi (New York); Farmington Country; Hermitage Country (Richmond, Va.). Home: 808 Nottingham Dr., Greensboro, N.C. Office: Jefferson Standard Life Insurance Co. N.Y.C. Died June 9, 1953.

TAYLOR, Edwin, state ofcl.; b. Tecumseh, Mich. July 23, 1844; s. Joshua and Mary (Comfort) T. ed. acad., Adrian, Mich., U. of Mich., 2 yrs.; m Lydia Baldwin Swan, Aug. 19, 1879. Farming i Kan., 1872—; mem. Kan. Sch. Book Commn. 1892-94; mem. Kan. Senate, 1892-96, Ho. of Rep. 1898; pres. Kan. State Hort. Soc., 1906, 1907 pres. Kan. State Bd. of Agr., 1902, 1903; regen Kan. State Agrl. College, 1907-13. Mem. Soc. o Friends. Contbr. North American Review, Rural Nev Yorker, Mail and Breeze, Missouri Stockman. Address: Edwardsville, Kan. Died Dec. 16, 1926 buried Edwardsville Cemetery.

TAYLOR, Floyd, journalist, univ. prof.; b. Riverside, Calif., Mar. 20, 1902; s. John Alva and Ell (Cooper) T.; student Columbia Coll., 1919-23; m Marian Malvina Lockhart, Oct. 9, 1926; children—John Lockhart, Caroline. Reporter N.Y. Herald 1923-24; writing and exec. positions N.Y. Heral Tribune, 1924-31, N.Y. World Telegram, 1931-43 specialist in news editing assigned to China to trai Chinese news editors and edit war news, U.S. Dept of State, 1943-44; editorial writer N.Y. Herald Tribune, 1944-50; asso. professor journalism Columbia 1944-46, prof., 1946—, dir. Am. Press Inst., 1946—, also founder; one founders Internat. Pres Inst.; conducted advanced training program for German publishers under Rockefeller Foundn. grant 1948, for Japanese journalists, 1950. Awarded Victor Medal by the Republic of China, 1944. Mem. Fgn Policy Association, Acad. Political Science, Nationa Conference Editorial Writers, Sigma Chi. Democrat Presbyterian. Club: Overseas Press. Author: chapte on Chungking, China After Seven Years of War 1944. Home: 82 Valley Rd., Plandome, N.Y. Die Aug. 24, 1951.

TAYLOR, Francis Henry, museum dir.; b. Phila. Pa., Apr. 23, 1903; s. Dr. William Johnson an Emily Buckley (Newbold) T.; grad. Kent (Conn. Sch., 1920; A.B., U. of Pa., 1924; L.H.D.; Ar D.; Litt.D.; hon. degrees from Harvard, Yale, Pennsylvania, Columbia, New York, Princeton, Clark Tufts, Miami univs., Amherst, Rollins, Hamilto and Holy Cross, Trinity Colls., 1940-55; grad. stud Univs. of Paris and Florence, Institut d'Estudis Catalans, Barcelona, 1924-26; visiting fellow, Am. Acad in Rome, 1925-26; Carnegie fellow, Grad. Coll. Princeton, 1926-27; Guggenheim fellowship for research, 1931; m. Pamela Coyne, Nov. 3, 1928; children—Pamela (Mrs. James P. Morton), Emily N. John M., Mary B. Asst. curator Phila. Mus. Art 1927-28, curator of medieval art, 1928-31; di Worcester (Mass.) Art Mus., 1931-40; dir. Met. Mus of Art, N.Y.C., 1940-55; elected dir. emeritus an spl. cons. to board trustees; director Worcester A Museum, 1955-58; chairman advisory committee Walters Art Gallery, Baltimore, 1934-44; regional dir for New Eng. States, Federal Art Projects, 1933-34 apptd. chmn. Nat. Council for Art Week, by President Roosevelt, 1940; mem. advisory com. on Art U.S. Dept. of State, lecturing on their behalf i leading S. Am. Art Museums, 1942; mem. Am Commn. for Protection and Salvage of Artistic an Historic Monuments in War Areas, 1943-46; mem adv. council fine and liberal art Notre Dame U Trustee Am. Acad. in Rome, Metropolitan Museu of Art, N.Y.C.; formerly trustee U. of Pa., Archeol

Inst. of Am. (life mem.), Am. Fedn. of Arts (life mem.), Museum of the City of New York. Mem. vis. com. Fogg Art Museum and Dept. Fine Arts, Harvard, Dumbarton Oaks Library and Collection, Dept. Art and Archeology, Princeton and Amherst Coll. Mus. Decorated Comdr. of the Royal Order of Vasa (Sweden); Comdr. of the Order of Merit (Ecuador); Chevalier Order of the Crown (Belgium); Chevalier and officer Legion of Honor (France); Officer Royal Order of Orange-Nassau (Netherlands); Officer Order of San Carlos (Colombia). Fellow Am. Acad. Arts and Sciences (Boston); mem. Am. Philos. Soc., Am. Assn. Mus. (past mem. of council; v.p.), Assn. Art Museum Dirs., Am. Council Learned Societies (mem.-at-large 1955-57), Am. Antiquarian Soc., Mass. Hist. Soc., Colonial Soc. Mass., Delta Psi, Phi Beta Kappa (hon.). Episcopalian. Clubs: Century (N.Y.C.); Tavern, Odd Volumes (Boston); Worcester, Tatnuck (Worcester). Author of The Taste of Angels: A History of Art Collecting from Rameses to Napoleon; numerous monographs and articles on art and archeological subjects. Home: 3 Tuckerman St. Address: Worcester Art Museum, Worcester 8, Mass. Died Nov. 22, 1957; buried Ch. St. James The Less, Phila.

TAYLOR, F(rank) Carroll, lawyer; b. Phila., Nov. 2, 1884; s. Frank Hendrickson and Rebecca Morgan (Nicholson) T.; grad. Haverford (Pa.) Sch., 1902; A.B., Harvard, 1906, LL.B., 1909; m. Marian Warner, Dec. 21, 1912; children—Barbara W. Cummings, David H., George W. Admitted to N.Y. State bar, 1910; sr. mem. Porter & Taylor, N.Y.C., 1921—; gen. counsel, dir. The Yale & Towne Mfg. Co.; gen. counsel, dir. Hans Rees' Sons; dir. Atlantic, Gulf & Pacific Co.; gen. counsel, dir. Alpha Portland Cement Co. Mem. Assn. Bar City of N.Y., Am., N.Y. State bar assns., N.Y. County Lawyers Assn. Republican. Mem. Soc. Friends. Clubs: Harvard, Century Association (N.Y. City). Home: Goodwives River Rd., Noroton, Conn. Office: 60 E. 42d St., N.Y.C. 17. Died Dec. 19, 1949.

TAYLOR, Frank Flagg, banker, b. Lena, Ill., Sept. 26, 1875; s. William Flagg and Elizabeth Lucretia (Cooper) T.; student pub. schs. Chicago, Ill.; m. Bessie M. Strayer, Apr. 19, 1904; children—William Price, Grace Elizabeth (Mrs. J. D. Voelker), Frank Flagg, David George. With Ill. Trust & Savings Bank, Chicago, 1899-1921, asst. sec., 1909-21; sec. Illinois Merchants Trust Co. 1921-24, v.p., 1924-29; vice pres. Continental Illinois National Bank & Trust Co., Chicago, 1929-53, dir. 1942—; vice pres. and dir. Continental Illinois Safe Deposit Co.; dir. Chicago Tunnel Terminal Co. Trustee Old People's Home of Chicago, Denison U., Granville, O., Moody Bible Institute. Mem. Art Institute, Chgo. Natural History Museum. Republican. Presbyterian. Clubs: Bankers, Union League, Attic (Chicago); Pine Lake Golf. Home: 202 Linden Av., Oak Park, Ill. Office: 231 S. La Salle St., Chgo. Died Nov. 4, 1959.

TAYLOR, Frederick R(aymond), physician; born Burlington Co., N.J., July 15, 1887; s. Charles Shoemaker and Rebecca (Hughes) T.; B.S., Haverford Coll., 1909; M.D., U. Pa., 1913; grad. study Boston, 1922, 39; extension courses U. N.C.; m. Rachel Ethel Farlow, Sept. 25, 1914; children—Martha Rebecca (Mrs. W. H. Turner), Mark Hughes, Sarah Merritt (Mrs. W. P. Phillips), Frederick Harvey. Intern Germantown Dispensary and Hosp., Phila., 1913-14; gen. practice medicine, High Point, N. C., 1914-21, practice of internal medicine, spl. interest in psychiatry, since 1922; staff mem., now hon. High Point Meml. Hosp. since 1923; asso. in medicine Bowman Gray Sch. Medicine, Wake Forest Coll., 1941, asso. prof. clin. medicine, 1942-53, prof. med. lit. since 1945. Served as 1st lt., M.C., U.S. Army, World War I; staff mem. Base Hosp. 65, Kerhoun Hosp. Center, A.E.F., 1918. Recipient silver plaque, Guilford Co. (N.C.) Med. Soc., 1934. Diplomate American Bd. Internal Medicine. Fellow A.C.P. (life mem.); hon. mem. Frederick R. Taylor History Medicine Soc.; mem. Guilford Co. Med. Soc. (pres. 1924), N.C. State Med. Soc. (chmn. sect. practice medicine 1925), A.A.A.S., A.M.A., Am. Med. Writers' Assn., Am. Soc. for History of Medicine. Mem. Religious Soc. of Friends (elder). Contbr. med. publs. Home and office: 1113 Johnson St., High Point, N.C. Died Nov. 1, 1955; buried Springfield Cemetery, High Point, N.C.

TAYLOR, Harris, educator; b. West Point, Miss., Sept. 23, 1864; s. Newton Jasper and Mary Frances (Pybas) T.; student Trinity U., San Antonio, Tex., 1884-88, LL.D., 1935, LL.D., Cumberland U., Lebanon, Tenn., 1912; m. Anne Evelyn Butler, 1909 (died 1919). Teacher public schools, 1888-89, Texas School for the Deaf, 1889-94, Pa. Inst. for Deaf, 1894-1906; prin. ednl. dept. Ky. Sch. for Deaf, Danville, Kentucky, 1906-09; supt. The Lexington School for the Deaf, New York, 1909-35; supervisor of edn. of blind and deaf, State of N.Y. Mem. Am. Assn. to Promote Teaching of Speech to Deaf (pres. 1920-29), Volta Bur. for Increase and Diffusion of Knowledge Relating to Deaf (superintendent 1911-12), Nat. Round Table for Improvement of Speech (pres. 1910-11), N. Y. Poetry group; chmn. Conf. Prins. N.Y. Schs. for Deaf, 1918-35; mem. com. on survey of schs. for the deaf of Nat. Research Council; vice-pres. Conv. of Am. Instrs. of the Deaf, 1933-35, pres., 1935-37; mem. advisory council for edn. of the deaf, Columbia U. and N.Y. State Edn. Dept., Albany, N.Y. Episcopalian. Democrat. Clubs: Nat. Arts, Southern. Address: 15 Gramercy Park, N.Y.C. 3. Died July 14, 1952; buried Ellsworth, Me.

TAYLOR, Harry Leonard, judge; b. Halsey Valley, Tioga County, N.Y., Apr. 14, 1866; s. Frederick H. and Hannah C. (Sairs) T.; A.B., Cornell U., 1888, LL.B., 1893; unmarried. Admitted to N.Y. bar, 1893, and practiced in Buffalo; judge Erie Co. Ct., 1906-13; elected justice Supreme Ct., N.Y., 8th Dist., term 1914-27; re-elected, 1927; judge appellate Div., 4th Dept., 1924-37; ofcl. referee Supreme Ct., 1937-44. Republican. Trustee Cornell U., 1903-13. Mem. Phi Beta Kappa. Unitarian. Mason (32°). Clubs: University, Park, Buffalo Athletic. Home: Hotel Lenox, Buffalo. Died July 12, 1955.

TAYLOR, H(arvey) Birchard, M.E., exec. and engr.; b. Phila., Pa., Nov. 17, 1882; s. Charles Tracy and Sophie (Davis) T.; grad. Northeast Manual Training Sch., Phila., 1901; spl. courses Towne Scientific Sch. (U. of Pa.), class of 1905 (class pres. sr. yr.; center, Varsity football team, 1903); m. Florence Bodine, 1908; children—Helen Louise (Mrs. George B. Clothier), Charles Tracy II; m. 2d, Mrs. John McEntee Bowman, 1934; step-children—Clarissa Anne Bowman (Mrs. Ward Sullivan), John McEntee Bowman, Jr. Began with I. P. Morris Co., subsidiary of Wm. Cramp & Sons Ship & Engine Building Co. of Pa., 1905, draftsman, designer and engineer in manufacture high power hydraulic turbine machinery; apptd. asst. hydraulic engr., 1907, hydraulic engr. in charge, 1911; in charge design and mfr. turbine machinery for developments at Niagara, Keokuk, Muscle Shoals, Conowingo in U.S., and Ceders Rapids, Shawinigan and Niagara in Canada. Asst. to pres. Cramp Co., 1915, v.p. and dir., 1917-27; pres. Cramp-Morris Industrials, Inc., Federal Steel Foundry Co., I. P. Morris & De La Vergne, Inc., Pelton Water Wheel Co., Cramp Brass & Iron Foundries Co., 1927-31; exec. v.p. Baldwin-Southwark Corp., 1931-32; exec. mgr. The Phila. Authority, 1939-40; v.p., dir. Cramp Shipbuilding Co., 1940-46; chmn., pres. Phila. Lascala Opera Co., 1946-48; mem. adv. bd. Admiral Farragut Acad. Past trustee U. of Pa., 1934-44; Gen. Alumni Soc. of U. of Pa. (ex-p.). Mem. Phila. Bourse (dir.), Guild of Bracket lecturers of Princeton U. Fellow Am. Soc. Mech. Engineers (v.p. 1924-25); Mem. Am. Inst. E.E., Am. Soc. C.E., Naval Architects and Marine Engrs., Franklin Inst., Atlantic Coast Shipbuilders Assn. (pres. 1920), Navy League of U.S. (ex-pres.), Sandlot Sports Assn. (dir.), Bicentennial Com. U. of Pa. (exec. dir.), Newcomen Soc. of England, Beta Theta Pi, Sphinx Sr. Soc. (U. of Pa.), Soc. Colonial Wars, Colonial Soc. of Pa., S.R., Descendants Knights of Garter, Colonial Society Royal Descent (pres.). Republican. Presbyterian. Clubs: Union League, Rittenhouse, Merion Cricket, Engineers (Phila.). Home: The Barclay, Rittenhouse Sq. East, Philadelphia, Pa. Died Dec. 29, 1959.

TAYLOR, Howard Rice, educator; b. Franklin, Neb., July 9, 1892; s. Frank Collins and Mary Ann (Rice) T.; A.B., Pacific U., Forest Grove, Ore., 1914; A.M., Stanford, 1923; Ph.D., 1928; m. Hazel Mary Davies, Aug. 10, 1916; chidren—Thomas Howard (killed in action), Frances Jean. High sch. tchr., 1914; prin., Port Townsend (Wash.) High Sch., 1916-18, supt. of schs., 1919-22; grad. asst., Stanford U., 1922-24, Cubberley fellowship, 1924-25; asst. prof. psychology, U. Ore., 1925-28, asso. prof., 1929, prof. 1930—, head of dept., 1935-53; asst. dean grad. div. Ore. State System Higher Edn., 1939-42, asso. dean, 1942-47. Fellow Am. Psychol. Assn.; mem. Western Psychol. Assn. (pres. 1939). Home: 1893 Garden Av. Office: 305 Condon Hall, University of Oregon, Eugene, Ore. Died 1954.

TAYLOR, J. Gurney, physician; b. Burlington, N.J., May 23, 1872; s. William Shipley and Julia (Kirkbride) T.; student Haverford Coll.; M.D., U. Pa., 1895; m. Mary Richards; children—Ann Richards, J. Gurney, Jr.; m. 2d, Elizabeth Broughton. Practiced in Phila. 1895-1912, Milwaukee, 1913—; practice limited to internal medicine and pediatrics; cons. physician Milwaukee Children's Hosp., Columbia Hosp., Johnston Emergency Hosp., all Milwaukee. Served as lt. col., med. reserve, U.S. Army, World War I. Chief med. examiner Wis. subsidiary bd. Nat. Bd. Med. Examiners. Fellow A.C.P.; mem. Am. Assn. Med. Milk Commns. (pres., mem. council), A.M.A., Am. Climatol. and Clin. Assn., Am. Acad. Pediatrics, Nat. Tb Assn. (dir.), Wis. Anti-tuberculosis Assn. (dir.), Phi Gamma Delta, Alpha Mu Pi Omega. Episcopalian. Clubs: University, Rotary (Milwaukee). Home: 925 E. Wells St., Milwaukee 2. Office: 324 E. Wisconsin Av., Milwaukee. Died Nov. 30, 1956.

TAYLOR, James Alfred, ex-congressman; b. Lawrence, County, O., Sept. 25, 1878; s. James Clark and Malinda Ann (Bryant) T.; ed. pub. schs. and printing office; m. Bina E. Taylor, July 25, 1900; children—J(ames) Alfred, Louise, Carl Edwards, Paul Bryant, Charles Chilton, Frances Jean. Editor and publisher Alderson (W.Va.) Advertiser, 1900-05; editor Fayetteville Free Press, 1905-08, Fayetteville Sun, 1908-13; editor and propr. Fayetteville Democrat, 1913-16, Mt. Hope Leader, 1917-19, The State Sentinel, 1920—; also pub. Greenbrier Despatch, East Rainelle, W.Va. Corp. and sergt. W.Va. Nat. Guard, 1908-11. Mem. W.Va. Ho. of Del., 1917, 21, 31 (speaker), 37; mem. 68th and 69th Congresses, 1923-27, 6th W.Va. Dist.; Dem. nominee for gov. of W.Va., 1928; Dem. presdl. elector, 1932, serving as chmn. W.Va. Electoral Coll.; now exec. sec. W.Va. Liquor Control Commn. Mem. bd. of dirs. Charleston Union Mission. Presbyn. Mason (Shriner), Moose (ex-pres. state assn.); Eastern Star (past worthy grand patron, mem. bd. of govs. Eastern Star Home). Home: Fayetteville, Va. Office: Liquor Control Commission, Charleston, S.Va. Died June 9, 1956.

TAYLOR, James Henry, clergyman; b. Charleston, S.C., Oct. 2, 1871; s. Frank E. and Clara Scott (Wilson) T.; B.A., Yale, 1894; Presbyn. Sem., Columbia, S.C., 1 yr.; B.D., Presbyn. Sem., Louisville, 1897; D.D., Central U. Ky., 1915. Ordained Presbyn. ministry, 1897; pastor Mt. Sterling, Ky., 1897, Anchorage, Ky., 1898-1905, Macon, Ga., 1905-06, Central Presbyn. Ch. (So.), Washington, Nov. 1906-Oct. 1943, pastor emeritus, Oct. 1943—. Commr. Gen. Assembly Presbyn. Ch. (S.), 1899, 1908, 21, 28, 34, 36, 40, del. Pan-Presbyn. Council, N.Y., 1909, Cardiff, Wales, 1925, Boston, 1929, Belfast, Ireland, 1933, Montreal, 1937; guest preacher, Marylebone Presbyn. Ch., London, Eng., 1934-38. Trustee Union Theol. Sem., Richmond, Va., 1930-48; mem. bd. corporators Presbyn. Minister's Fund for Life Ins., Phila. Mem. N.E. Soc. Charleston, St. Andrews Soc. Charleston (chaplain), Huguenot Soc. S.C. (hon.), Carolina Art Assn. (Charleston), S.R., Soc. Mayflower Descendants (elder D.C. Soc. 1910-12, elder-gen. 1911-12). Democrat. Club: Cosmos. Wrote: The Membership of President Woodrow Wilson in the Central Presbyterian Church; The Spirit and Tradition of the Huguenots; Contributions of Calvinism to Thought and Life; Why I Believe; The Second Advent of Christ; Woodrow Wilson in Church; also pamphlets and contbns. in religious periodicals. Home: 67 Rutledge Av., Charleston, S.C. Died Aug. 6, 1957.

TAYLOR, Joseph Fillmore, business exec.; b. Rochester, N.Y., Feb. 22, 1889; s. Joseph Ward and Clarissa Thompson (Vosburgh) T.; student Yale, 1909-10; m. Hilda Ardelle Drescher, June 24, 1913; children—Joseph William, Hilda Ann (Mrs. Richard Redwood Deupree, Jr.), Thomas Curtiss, Robert Drescher. Began as clerk Bausch & Lomb Optical Co., Rochester, N.Y., 1910, became treas., Apr. 1935, v.p. and treas., 1939, pres., 1949-54, chmn. bd., 1954—; vice pres., dir., Bausch & Lomb Found., Inc., Clarence W. Smith, Inc.; dir. Bausch & Lomb do Brazil, Bausch & Lomb Optical Co., Ltd., Wilmot Castle Co., Lincoln Rochester Trust Co.; trustee Monroe County Savings Bank. Trustee C. of C., Assn. for Blind of Rochester, Rochester Civic Music Assn.; dir. Rochester Community Chest. Mem. Optical Soc. Am., Newcomen Society (England). Republican. Episcopalian. Clubs: Rochester, Country, Genesse Valley, Yale. Home: 1166 Clover St. Office: 635 St. Paul St., Rochester, N.Y. Died June 13, 1956.

TAYLOR, Joseph Richard, educator; b. N.Y.C., Jan. 11, 1858; s. Henry and Caroline Louise (Southard) T.; A.B., Wesleyan U., 1882, Am., 1885; studied U. Leipzig, U. Berlin, archeology in Greece and Italy, 1886-88, Harvard, 1892-96, A.M., 1894; m. Elvira Louise Polhemus, Dec. 25, 1882; children—Mary Katharine, Dorothy Sherwood. Prof. Greek, Hamline U., St. Paul, Minn., 1882-86; instr. in Greek and Latin, Northwestern U., 1888-91; asst. prof. Greek and Latin, Boston U., 1891-96, prof., 1896-1901, prof. Greek, 1901-38, emeritus prof., 1938—; editor Bostonia, 1904-1931. Mem. Phi Nu Theta, Phi Beta Kappa. Republican. Methodist. Author: The Story of the Drama-Beginnings to the Commonwealth, 1930; European and Asiatic Plays, 1936. Translator: The Captives of Plautus, 1896; The Medea of Euripides, 1936; The Menaechmi of Plautus, 1936; The Medea of Seneca, 1936; Dulcitius of Hroswitha, 1936. Editor: Copley Drama Series. Home: 42 Adella Av., West Newton, Mass. Died Aug. 12, 1955; buried Mt. Auburn Cemetery, Cambridge, Mass.

TAYLOR, Maurice, social worker; b. Wigan, Eng., June 1, 1895; s. Louis and Kate (Marcus) T.; came to U.S., 1904, naturalized, 1920; A.B., Harvard, 1916, M.A., 1925, Ph.D., 1931; m. Frances Minevitch, Aug. 18, 1918; 1 son, Arnold Joseph. Agent Mass. Soc. for Prevention of Cruelty to Children, 1916-22; supt. Jewish Welfare Fedn., Columbus, O., 1922-23; dir. Jewish Family Welfare Assn., Boston, 1923-36; exec. dir. Fedn. of Jewish Philanthropies, and United Jewish Fund, Pittsburgh, since 1936. Spl. lecturer Harvard U., Simmons Coll., U. of Pittsburgh, Carnegie Inst. Tech. (Margaret Morrison Sch.). Pres. Nat. Conf. Jewish Social Welfare, 1940-41. Mem. special mission to Israel at invitation Jewish Agency in Jerusalem, 1949. Mem. Am. Social Society, Am. Statis. Assn., Am. Acad. Social and Polit. Science, Am. Assn. Social Workers, Am. Arbitration

Assn. Jewish religion. Mason. Author: The Social Cost of Industrial Insurance, 1933; The Jewish Community of Pittsburgh, 1941. Co-author: Jewish Population Studies, 1943. Home: 5824 Elmer St., Pittsburgh 32. Office: 200 Ross St., Pitts. 19. Died Apr. 15, 1955.

TAYLOR, Montgomery Meigs, naval officer, b. Washington, Oct. 13, 1869; grad. U.S. Naval Acad., 1890. Ensign, July 1, 1892; lt. jr. grade, Mar. 3, 1899; promoted through grade to rear adm., Oct. 1, 1922. Served on Olympia, Spanish-Am. War, 1898; comd. Hopkins, 1903-05, 2d Torpedo Flotilla, 1905-06, receiving ship Wabash, 1906-08; exec. officer Salem, 1908-09, Milw., 1909-10; comdg. Petrel, 1910-11; aide to comdt. Navy Yard, N.Y.C., 1911-13; comd. Buffalo, 1913-15, Balt., 1915; at Naval War Coll., Newport, R.I., 1915-16; apptd. comdr. Me., June 27, 1916; comdg. Fla., 1918-19; staff Naval War Coll., 1919-21; assigned comdr. Control Force, 1923; dir. fleet tng., comdr. divs. in Battle Fleet; vice adm. in command Scouting Fleet, 1926-27; dir. War Plans, 1928-29; apptd. comdr. Asiatic Fleet, 1930; ret., Nov. 1, 1933; apptd. temp. mem. Maritime Commn., 1936. Awarded medals—Manila Bay, Spanish-Am. War, Philippine Campaign, Victory, D. S.M. Address: The Highlands, Connecticut Av. and California St. N.W., Washington. Died Oct. 21, 1952.

TAYLOR, Myron C(harles), lawyer, industrialist, diplomat; b. Lyons, N.Y., Jan. 18, 1874; s. William and Mary Morgan (Underhill) T.; LL.B., Cornell U., 1894; LL.D., Colgate, 1929, St. Johns U., 1945; D.C.S., N.Y.U., 1930; L.H.D., Hobart Coll., 1931; D.C.S., E.C.S.D., U. Rome, 1945; m. Anabel Stuart Mack. Chmn. finance com. U.S. Steel Corp., 1927-34, chmn. bd., chief exec. officer, 1932-38, resigned, now dir., mem. finance com.; dir. Am. Tel. & Tel. Co. Mem. exec. com. President's Nat. Bus. Survey Conf, 1929; chmn. 14th roll call A.R.C., 1930; exec. com. N.Y. Emergency Employment Com., 1930; mem. adv. com., com. on mobilization relief resources President's Orgn. on Unemployment Relief, 1931; gen. chmn., com. on commerce and industry N.Y. Emergency Unemployment Relief Com., 1931-32; mem. indsl. bd. N.R.A., 1933-35; gen. chmn., commerce and industry div. Citizens' Family Welfare Com., N.Y.C., 1933-35; mem. gen. council, bus. adv. and planning council U.S. Dept. Commerce, 1935-37; U.S. rep. to Evian Conf. on Polit. Refugees (rank of ambassador); chmn. conf. 1938; v. chmn. Intergovtl. Com. on Polit. Refugees, 1938-44; personal rep. (rank ambassador) presidents Roosevelt and Truman, to His Holiness Pope Pius XII, 1939-50; rep. Pres. on spl. mission (rank ambassador), 1950-53; cons. Dept. State, also chmn. com. on postwar fgn. econ. policy, and mem. President's adv. com. on postwar fgn. policy, 1942; presided over joint Anglo-Am. discussions of postwar econ. problems, 1943; mem. post-war planning com., v. chmn. adv. council on postwar fgn. policy Dept. State, 1944; apptd. grad. mem., bus. adv. council U.S. Sec. Commerce, 1944. Organizer 1944, chmn. Am. Relief for Italy, Inc.; organizer in Italy, Nat. Com. for Distbn. Relief, 1944; reorganized Italian Red Cross, 1946. Trustee Am. Acad. in Rome, Community Service Soc. N.Y., Cornell U., Lycee Francais de N.Y., Wells Coll.; hon. trustee Met. Mus. Art (fellow), N.Y. Pub. Library, St. Luke's Hosp. (bd. mgrs.); hon. chmn. Underhill Soc. Am. Decorated Medal for Merit (U.S.); Comdr. Order of Crown, Star of Solidarity (Italy); Cross Comdr. Legion of Honor (France); Simon Bolivar Rededication medal (Venezuela); Knight Order of Pius, 1st degree, Knight Grand Cross Saints Mauritius and Lazarus, Knight Order of Malta. Awarded medal, Am. Hebrew mag., 1939; citation for eminent service in field of humanitarian war relief World War II Pres's War Relief Control Bd., 1946; citation Italian Red Cross, 1946; medal for distinguished service, Schroeder Found., 1949; citation for distinguished service, Pres. of Italy, 1940; Italina Red Cross and Nat. Com. for Distbn. Relief in Italy, by Prime Pimister of Italy, 1950; 1st peace medal Third Order of St. Francis in U.S., 1950; resolution of appreciation of services, Am. Nat. Red Cross, 1950; certificate of merit, Vets. Fgn. Wars, 1950; 1st ann. Cardinal Newman award, Newman Club Fedn., 1951; resolution appreciation 30 yrs. service as dir. First Nat. Bank, N.Y., 1953. Hon. citizen, Florence, Italy, 1945, (with Mrs. Taylor) of Anzio and Nettuno, Italy, 1945, Villagio del Fanciullo (Boys Town, Italy), 1946; hon. founder Boys Republic of Italy, 1950. Mem. Am. Iron and Steel Inst., Ancient and Hon. Arty. Co. Mass., N.Y. State Bar Assn., Bostonian Soc., C. of C. U.S., C. of C. State N.Y., Magna Carta Barons, Nat. Indsl. Conf. Bd., New Eng. Hist. and Geneal. Soc. (pres. 1931-35, hon. pres., 1936—), St. Nicholas Soc., Soc Colonial Wars, S.R., Academie Diplomatique Internationale (Paris), Ct. of Worshipful Co. of Goldsmiths (London). Clubs: Bankers, Cedar Creek, Cornell, Down Town, Knickerbocker, Links Golf, N.Y. Yacht, Pilgrims, Piping Rock, Turf and Field, Union, University (N.Y.C.); Metropolitan (Washington); Everglades, Gulf Stream Golf (Fla.); Heatherden, International Sportsmen's, Royal Automotile (Eng.); Travelers, Union Interallice (Paris). Pub. book: Wartime Correspondence between President Roosevelt and Pope Pius XII; sponsored book: Correspondence between President Truman and Pope Pius XII. Home: Killingworth, Locust Valley, L.I., N.Y.; also 16 E. 70th St., N.Y.C.; and Palm Beach, Fla. Died May 6, 1959; buried Locust Valley, N.Y.

TAYLOR, Oliver Guy, civil engr.; b. Boone County, Ind., Oct. 28, 1883; s. Charles Andrew and Margaret Ann (Kern) T.; B.S., in C.E., Purdue U., 1909; m. Marjorie Edwina Macdougall, May 15, 1915. Topographer U.S. Geol. Survey, 1909-13, 1914-17, 1919-20; civil engr., Republic of Argentine, 1914; park engr., Yosemite Nat. Park, 1920-30; civil engr. charge engring. Eastern Nat. Park Areas, 1930-37; chief engr. Nat. Park Service, 1937-43, regional dir. 1943-44, supr. concessions, 1944—. Served as 2d lt., 1st lt. and capt., Engrs., U.S. Army, with A.E. F., 1917-18. Mem. Soc. Civil Engrs. Mason. Club: Cosmos (Washington). Home: 6313 Georgia St., Chevy Chase, Md. Office: National Park Service, Washington 25. Died Aug. 26, 1950; buried Arlington Nat. Cemetery.

TAYLOR, Oury Wilburn, clergyman; b. Calloway County, Ky., Sept. 11, 1885; s. John and Susan Elizabeth (Ford) T.; A.B., Hall-Moody Inst., Martin, Tenn., 1913; A.B., Union U., Jackson, Tenn., 1919, D.D., 1933; m. Virgie B. Glover, Sept. 11, 1917; children—Wilburn Lincoln, Charles Byron (killed in action, 1944). Ordained to Baptist ministry, 1906; pastor of rural churches several years, then successively pastor, Trenton, Franklin, Bolivar (Tenn.); Sturgis, Ky.; Halls, Tenn.; editor, Baptist and Reflector, newspaper of Tenn. Bapt. Conv., 1933-50. Awarded efficiency medal by Union Univ., 1919. Home: Pembroke Av., Nashville 5. Died July 8, 1958; buried Woodlawn Cemetery.

TAYLOR, Samuel Alfred, engr.; b. N. Versailles Twp., Allegheny County, Pa., Oct. 24, 1863; s. Charles Thomas and Elizabeth J. (Maxwell) T.; C.E., Western U. Pa. (now U. Pitts.), 1887; Sc.D., U. Pitts., 1919; m. Anna J. Gilmore, May 17, 1893; 1 dau., Mary Elizabeth (Mrs. W. O. Lytle). Chief draughtsman structural iron dept., Carnegie Steel Co., 1887-88; asst. engr. of constrn., Pa. R.R., 1888-93; in pvt. practice, 1893-1905, cons. engr., 1905—; dean Sch. Mines, U. Pitts., 1910, 12. Tech. adv. to U.S. fuel adminstr., 1917-19. Trustee U. Pitts., Western Pa. Sch. for the Deaf. Mem. Am. Mining Congress (pres. 1912), Am. Soc. C.E., Am. Inst. Mining and Metall. Engrs. (pres., 1926), Internat. Soc. Geologists, A.A.A.S., Engrs. Soc. Western Pa. (pres. 1913-14), Coal Mining Inst. Am. (pres. 1911), etc. Club: Duquesne (Pittsburgh). Author various papers publs. of tech. assns. Home: 617 Whitney Av., Wilkinsburg, Pa. Died Aug. 20, 1950.

TAYLOR, Thomas Nicholls, financier; b. Provo, Utah, July 28, 1868; s. George and Eliza (Nicholls) T.; grad. Brigham Young Acad. (now Brigham Young U.), Provo; m. Maud Rogers, Sept. 18, 1889; children—T. Sterling, Ethel, Lester R., Vesta (dec.), Alden R., Marion R., Victor R., Mary Maud (Mrs. Merrill D. Clayson), Delenna. Gen. mgr. Taylor Bros. Co., dept. stores, Provo, 1890—, pres. 1922—; sr. mem. Taylor's Dept. Store, Provo; dir. Utah Home Fire Ins. Co. Mayor of Provo, Utah, 1900-04; v.p. Utah State Council of Defense, 1917-19; Dem. candidate for gov., Utah, 1920. Counsellor 3d Ward Bishopric, Provo, Ch. of Latter Day Saints, 1891-1900, bishop same, 1900-19; pres. Utah Stake of Zion, 1919-39. Patriarch in Ch., 1939—. Mem. bd. of regents, U. Utah, 1920-24; v.p. bd. trustees, chmn. exec. com. Brigham Young U. Mem. Utah State Bankers Assn. (pres. 1918), Brigham Young U. Alumni Assn. (pres. 1912-13). Home: 342 N. 5th West St. Office: 250 W. Center St., Provo, Utah. Died Oct. 24, 1950.

TAYLOR, Vincent George, clergyman, educator; b. Norfolk, Va., Sept. 19, 1877; s. George Washington and Anna Theodora (Rauh) T.; grad. St. Mary's Parochial Sch., Norfolk, 1893; A.B., Belmont Abbey Coll. and Sem., Belmont, N.C., 1902; D.D. by virtue of office; LL.D., St. Vincent's College, Latrobe, Pa. Joined novitiate of Belmont Abbey, Order of St. Benedict, 1897; ordained priest R.C. Ch., 1902; pastor St. Benedict's Ch., Greensboro, N.C., 1902-24; abbot of Belmont Abbey and ordinary of the diocese 1924—; pres. Belmont Abbey Coll., 1924—; elected 1st visitator Am. Cassinese Congregation of the Benedictine Order, 1929, reëlected, 1932, 35, 38; pres. Southern Benedictine Soc. of N.C., Inc.; also of Benedictine Soc. in Ga. and Benedictine Soc. of Va., Inc. Address: Belmont Abbey, Belmont, N.C. Died Nov. 7, 1959.

TAYLOR, Warner, educator; b. N.Y.C., Apr. 6, 1880; s. John Stephenson and Mary Elizabeth (Steele) T.; grad. Utica (N.Y.) Acad., 1899; B.A., Columbia, 1903, M.A., 1905; m. Clara Bertram Fuller, Aug. 12, 1916; 1 dau., Lucia Fairchild. Asst. in English, Columbia, 1907-08, instr., 1908-11; instr. in English, U. Wis., 1911-15, asst. prof., 1915-22, asso. prof., 1922-27, prof., 1927—. Mem. Modern Lang. Assn. Am., Wilson Ornithol. Club, Phi Kappa Sigma; asso. mem. Am. Ornithol. Union, Wis. Acad. Sciences, Arts and Letters. Unitarian. Club: University. Author (with F. A. Manchester) Freshma Themes, 1918; Study of the Prose Style of Samue Johnson, 1918; Representative English Essays, 1923 Essays of the Past and Present, 1927; National Sur vey of Freshman English, 1928; Types and Times i the Essay, 1932; Varied Narratives, 1932; Literar Masters of England (with N. S. Bushnell and P. M Fulcher), 1936. Contbr. articles on ornithology an pictorial photography. Home: 619 N. Frances St. Madison, Wis. Died March 15, 1958.*

TAYLOR, William C(hittenden), business exec.; b San Francisco, Mar. 3, 1886; s. William and Carri Louise (Chittenden) T., Jr.; student Calif. Sch Mech. Arts, 1900-02, Boston English High Sch. 1903-04, S.B., Mass. Inst. Tech., 1908; Dr. Sc (hon.) Alfred Univ., 1946; m. Alice C. Pratt, Dec 29, 1909; children—Richard G., Marion L. Asst chemist, Corning (N.Y.) Glass Works, 1908-09 chemist, 1910-23, chief chem., 1923-39, dir. glas technol., 1939-47, dir. mfg. and engring., 1947-54 vice pres., 1953-54, honorary vice pres., technica adviser, 1954—; assistant chem. U.S. Dept. Agr Expt. Sta., Mayaguez, P.R., 1909-10; dir. Corhar Refractories Co., Inc. Commodore, charge Se Scouting, Steuben area, Boy Scouts Am., 1938-43 Awarded Potts Medal for radically new type of hea resistant glass, Franklin Inst., 1928; Pioneer of In dustry award, Nat. Assn. Mfrs., 1940. Fellow Am Ceramic Soc., A.A.A.S., Soc. Glass Technol.; mem Am. Chem. Soc., Corning C. of C. Clubs: Rotar (past pres.), Boothbay Harbor Yacht, Cornin Country. Contbr. articles to chem. and glass jour Holder 32 patents, chiefly in field of glass composi tion. Home: 120 E. Fifth St. Office: Corning Glas Works, Corning, N.Y. Died Nov. 2, 1958; burie Corning.

TAYLOR, William Osgood, newspaper pub.; b Nashua, N.H., Jan. 8, 1871; s. Charles Henry and Georgianna O. (Davis) T.; A.B., Harvard, 1893; m Mary Moseley, Mar. 28, 1894; children—Mosele (dec), Eunice (Mrs. N. S. Wyckoff Vanderhoef), Mar garet (dec.), Elizabeth, (Mrs. S. H. Fessenden) William Davis. With Boston Globe since 1893; pres Globe Newspaper Co. since 1921. Home: Marion Mass. Office: 242 Washington St., Boston. Died July 15, 1955.

TEACHENOR, Frank Randall, neurol. surgeon; b Kansas City, Mo., Sept. 1, 1888; s. Richard Bennington and Mary Catherine (Givauden) T.; M.D. U. of Kan., 1911; m. Ethel Glevo Heath, July 3 1920. Interne, Kansas City Gen. Hosp., Kansas City Mo., 1911-12; pvt. practice medicine, Kansas City since 1912, specialist in neurol. surgery since 1920 in research, St. Luke's, St. Mary's, Trinity Luth and Menorah hosps. since 1920; in practice of neurol surgery U. of Kan. Med. Center since 1924; asst in surgery U. of Kan. Med. Sch., 1924-28, asst clin. prof., 1928-35, asso. clin. prof., 1935-39, prof clin. surgery since 1939. Served as capt., M.C., U. S. Army, 1917-19; service in France Certified Am Bd. Surgery, 1937, Am. Bd. Neurol. Surgery, 1940 Fellow A.M.A., A.C.S.; mem. Soc. Neurol. Surgeons, Harvey Cushing Soc. (pres. 1947), Wester Surg. Assn. (pres. 1934), Jackson County Med. Soc (pres. 1936), Mo. State Med. Assn., Southern Med. Assn. Contbr. articles on neurol. surgery to med jours. Home: The Walnuts, 5049 Wornell Road. Office: Plaza Times Bldg., 411 Nichol's Rd., Kansas City 2, Mo. Died Nov. 28, 1953; buried Forest Hil Cemetery, Kansas City, Mo.

TEAGUE, Charles C., agriculturalist; b. Caribou Me., June 11, 1873; s. Milton D. and Clara (Collins) T.; LL.D., U. Calif., 1924, U. of Me., 1931; m Harriet McKevett, Nov. 10, 1897; children—Alice (Mrs. John H. Cox), Milton M., Charles M. Pres. Teague-McKevett Co., Santa Paula, Calif., since 1908 Limoneria Co. since 1917, Santa Paul Water Work Ltd., since 1917, Farmers Irrigation Co. since 1917 Thermal Belt Water Co. since 1917, Calif. Orchar Co., King City, Calif., since 1919, Fruit Grower Supply Co., Los Angeles, since 1920, McKevett Corp. Santa Paul, 1927-33; v.p. Security-First Nat. Ban of Los Angeles since 1928, dir.; v.p. Salinas Lan Co., King City, since 1923; pres. Rancho La Cuesta Ltd., Santa Paula, 1930—; pres. Teague-McKevet Assn., Santa Paula, 1934—, Soledad (Cal.) Ranc Co. since 1936, Calif. Fruit Growers Exchange sinc 1920; Agrl. Council of Calif. (hon. pres., life mem. exec. com., 1919-45); Santa Clara Water Conserva tion Dist., Santa Paula, since 1927; mem. Fed Farm Bd., 1929-31; v.p. Am. Inst. Cooperation 1933-44; pres. Nat. Council Farmer Coop., 1942-43 Cons. prof. cooperating marketing Grad. Sch. o Bus., Stanford, 1935-40. Pres. Calif. Walnut Grower Assn., 1912-42 (now pres. emeritus), Calif. State C. of C., 1932-34. Regent U. of Calif. at Berkele since 1930. Received silver plaque from dir. of Calif Fruit Growers Exchange in appreciation for 25 yrs. service, 1945. Universalist. Mason. Clubs: California University (Los Angeles); Saticoy Country (Saticoy Calif.). Author: Fifty Years a Rancher, 1944. Home 724 McKevett Dr., Santa Paula, Calif. Died March 20, 1950.

TEALL, Gardner (Callahan), author; b. Eau Claire Wis., Mar. 6, 1876; s. William Allen and Kate Gardner (Callahan) T.; ed. Shattuck Sch., Faribault, Minn., U. Minn. Art editor What to Eat, 1895, Good Housekeeping, 1901; asso. editor House and Garden, 1910; editor Travel, mag., 1911, Am. Homes and Gardens, N.Y., 1911-15, Art and Life, 1919-20; Am. corr. La Bibliofilia, Florence, Italy, 1926; art dir. Harper's Bazaar, 1927-28. Illustrated Lewis Carroll's Hunting of the Snark, 1910. Author: The Child's Bookplate, 1904; The Garden Primer, 1910; The Contessa's Sister (novel), 1911; A Little Garden the Year 'Round, 1919; The Pleasures of Collecting, 1920; Book Plates by Sidney L. Smith, 1921; The Art of Sidney Lawton Smith, 1931; The Color Prints of Treeva Wheete, 1935. Lecturer on art, lit., and history. Address: Eau Claire, Wis. Died July 22, 1956.*

TEDESCHE, Leon G(reenfield) (tē-dĕs'kē), bacteriologist; b. Cincinnati, O., Sept. 28, 1878; s. Alexander and Jennie (Greenfield) Tedesche (originally Tedeschi); A.B., University of Cincinnati, 1902, M.D., 1905; unmarried; adopted daughter, Ensign Lucile Elinor Morgan (Mrs. W. P. Steward). Began as assistant bacteriologist to trustees Commissioners Water Works Filtration Experts, 1898-99; experimental work, Louisville, Kentucky, Hornellsville, New York, Chicago Drainage Canal Suit for St. Louis at Grafton, Ill., 1900; instr. pathology, bacteriology and histology, 1902-04, 1906-07, 1913-14, prof. histology and pathology, 1917-18, Cincinnati Veterinary College; asst. bacteriologist, 1902-05, asst. in electrotherapeutics, 1906-07, Med. Coll. of Ohio, Cincinnati; scientific asst. of sec. Smithsonian Instn., 1907; bacteriologist, filtration plant of Cincinnati Water Works, 1907-10; chemist and bacteriologist, Milk Commn. of Cincinnati Acad. Medicine, 1910-12; in charge water sterilization of Hamilton, O., 1913, flood Disaster with State Med. Corps.; prof. physiology, later prof. bacteriology and pathology, Eclectic Med. Coll., 1914-29; prof. physiology, Cincinnati Coll. Dental Surgery, 1917-20; lecturer theoretical pharmacy, Cincinnati Coll. Pharmacy, 1921-24. Volunteer Med. Service Corps, Nov. 9, 1918, essential teacher Surgeon Gen's. office; capt. Med. R.C. (ret.). Instr. A.R.C. First Aid Service for Boy Scout leaders, 1929—; asso. dir. Indsl. Emergency Hosp., 1924-30; dir. West End Indsl. Dispensary, 1939—. Mem. exec. council, U. Cin. Alumni Assn. Mem. Med. Corps, O. Nat. Guard, 1907-17; chmn. health and safety com. Cin. Council Boy Scouts Am., West dist. chmn. troop com., also merit badge counselor Wabash Court of honor; received Silver Beaver award, 1943. Fellow A.M.A., A.A.A.S.; mem. Am. Soc. Social Hygiene, Internat. Philatelic Assn. (sec., treas.), Ohio State Med. Assn., Hamilton County (O.) Acad. Medicine, Am. Pub. Health Assn., Assn. Mil. Surgeons U.S., Daniel Drake Research Soc., Pioneer Philatelic Phalanx (hon. life), Soc. Philatelic Americans (life), Tau Alpha Epsilon, Pi Gamma Mu, Am. Philatelic Soc. (life; bd. of v.p. 1927-29), Com. of 100, U. Cin. Alumni Assn., Am. Nature Assn. V.p. Liberal Art Alumni, B'nai B'rith. Mason (32°, Shriner), Grotto. Patron O.E.S., 1905, 29, 42, 45-46; past asso. pres. Matrons and Patrons Assn., 20th Dist. O., 1939-40; 68 Club (trustee). Rep. Masonic Library. Clubs: Cincinnati Military, Cincinnati Auto; Collectors (New York). Republican. Home: 1016 Valley Lane, Avondale 29 and 2401 Tigertail Av., Miami 33, Fla. Office: 2201 Gest St., Cin. 4. Died Apr. 29, 1956.

TEED, Ralph H., corp. ofcl.; b. Helena, Mont., Feb. 19, 1898; s. H.D. and Anna W. Teed; M.E., Cornell U., 1921; m. Ferol Hawkes, Mar. 16, 1926; children—Ralph H., Richard K., David D. Engr. subsidiary of Fed. Light & Traction Co., Trinidad, Colo., 1923-28; gen. supt. Citizens Electric Co., Hot Springs Water Co., Consumers Gas Co., Hot Springs Street Ry. Co., Hot Springs, Ark., 1928-30, pres., 1938-43; div. mgr. Ark. Power & Light Co., Little Rock, 1943-52, vice president, 1952-56, executive vice president, 1956—; div. manager Hot Springs Municipal Water System, 1943-52; v.p., gen. mgr. Hot Springs Street Ry. Co., 1943—, also dir. Served as pvt., F.A., U.S. Army, World War I. Recipient Medallion award Research Inst. Am., 1955. Mem. Am. Soc. M.E., Phi Gamma Delta. Presbyn. (deacon). Mason (Shriner). Home: No. 1 Gibson Dr. Office: Arkansas Power & Light Co., 4th and Louisiana Sts., Little Rock, Ark. Died May 16, 1958; buried Roseland Meml. Park, Little Rock, Ark.

TEEL, Forrest, corp. ofcl.; b. Delaware County, Okla., May 24, 1904; s. George L. and Elizabeth (Viles) T.; Ph.G., U. Kansas City, 1926; m. Mary Elizabeth Roddy, May 18, 1932; children—Thomas A. With Eli Lilly & Co., 1926—, successively salesman, asst. mgr. export div., exec. v.p. in charge marketing and dir. 1954—; pres. Eli Lilly Internat. Corp., 1948-54, now chmn. Mem. Nat. Wholesale Druggists Assn., Far East-Am. Council Commerce and Industry (dir.), Nat. Fgn. Trade Council, Am. Drug Mfrs. Assn., Indpls. C. of C. Mason (32°). Clubs: Indianapolis Athletic, Indianapolis Country. Home: 5921 Washington Blvd., Indpls. 20. Office: 740 S. Alabama St., Indpls. Died July 31, 1958.

TEETER, Albert A(lexander), business exec.; b. White House, N.J., Sept. 3, 1888; s. David Alexander and Rebecca (Miller) T.; Ph.G., Columbia, 1908; grad. N.Y. Inst. Photography, 1935; m. Agnes Claire Sullivan, Nov. 23, 1915; children—Albert A. Jr., John O., Anne Marie. Chemist, Oliver & Drake Co., Elizabeth, N.J., 1908-13; mgr. Riker-Hegemann Co., Newark and Paterson, N.J., 1913-15; salesman Chas. Pfizer & Co., Inc., N.Y. City, 1915-22, sales mgr., 1922-28, dir. and asst. sec., 1928-34, sec.-treas., 1934, mem. exec. com., 1934-49, sr. vice pres., 1945-49, dir., 1928—; ret. from active bus., 1949; chmn. Indsl. Molasses Corp. Vice chmn. planning bd., Borough of Rumson; dir. vice-pres. and treas. O'Reilly DePanama; Colon; trustee Cath. War Vets, Rumson; chmn. blood donor com. Monmouth County Am. Red Cross, Red Bank, N.J., 1947—; dir. and mem. exec. com. Monmouth Memorial Hosp., Long Branch, N.J., chmn. bldg. fund, 1949; dir Chem. Alliance. Ret. capt., San. Corps, U.S. Army Res. Mem. adv. com. on chemicals Army and Navy Bd., 1939-46; mem. indsl. adv. com. W.P.B., 1942-46; chmn. communications div., Civil Defense Bd., Rumson, 1948—; Rumson Improvement Assn., dir. and treas., N.J. Mem. Internat. Short Wave League (N.J. rep.), Radio Soc. Gt. Britain, Am. Pharm. Assn., A.A.A.S., Armed Forces Communications Assn., Photog. Soc. of Am., Hosp. Assn. of N.J., Am. Radio Relay League, Chemical Salesmans Association, New York Universal Photographers, Institute Radio Engineers (associate member), Army Ordnance Association, Royal Photographic Society Great Britain (asso.), Monmouth Hist. Assn. (trustee and treasurer), N.Y. C. of C., N.Y. Bd. Trade (drug. and chem. sect.; past mem. exec. com.), Drug and Chem. Club of N.Y. (past gov. and treas.). Republican. Roman Catholic. Clubs: Monmouth County Kennel; Beach (Monmouth, N.J.); Rumson (N.J.) Country; Lawn Tennis, Beach (Seabright, N.J.); Twenty Knotty Pines (N.Y.). Advanced photographer (pictures exhibited in leading salons); salon judge in photography. Home: Ridge Rd., Rumson, N.J. Office: 25 Broad St., N.Y.C. Died Sept. 3, 1953; buried Mt. Olivet Cemetery, Middletown, N.J.

TEETS, Harley O, prison warden; b. Terra Alta, W.Va., Nov. 14, 1906; s. Martin Luther and Nancy Ann (Freeland) T.; student U. Md., Ohio State U., Coll. of Marin, Kentfield, Cal.; m. Frieda LaRue Stewart, May 14, 1928 (div.); children—Emma LaRue (Mrs. Walling), Nancy Sue (Mrs. McBride). Staff bur. protection U.S. Steel Corp., Pitts., 1927-35; spl. officer Nat. Park Service, Dept. Interior, 1935-36; lt. Fed. Bur. Prisons, Chillicothe, O., 1936-44; capt. Cal State Prison, Folsom, Represa, Cal., 1944-46; asso. warden, custody Cal. State Prison, San Quentin, 1946-51, warden since 1951. Mem. Am. Prison Assn., Cal. State Employees Assn., San Quentin Employees Mutual Benefit Assn. Mason (Shriner). Home: San Quentin Reservation, P.O. Box 37, San Quentin, Cal. Died Sept. 1, 1957; buried Mount Tamalpais Cemetery, San Rafael, Cal.

TEGARDEN, JB Hollis (tē'gär-d'n), clergyman; b. Summit, Miss., Nov. 19, 1893; s. George Creed and Emma (Goss) T.; A.B., U. of Tenn., 1918; B.D., Meadville Theol. Sch., 1921; A.M., U. of Chicago, 1924; m. Alma Whittle, Sept. 8, 1920; 1 son, William Hollis. Ordained to ministry Unitarian Ch., 1921; minister Unitarian Ch., New Orleans, La., 1921-27, Hopedale Memorial Ch., Hopedale, Mass., since 1927. V.p. Unitarian Ministerial Union, 1938-39; dean Milford-Hopedale Ministerial Union since 1941 (pres. 1939, 1945-46). Trustee Bancroft Memorial Library, Hopedale, Mass. since 1940; mem. of Corp. of Milford (Mass.) Hospital; member of Board of Veterans' Service. Mem. Social Research Society of University of Chicago, Sigma Nu. Club: Hopedale Men's (Hopedale). Author: Why Do We Do As We Do, 1929; also pamphlets, Organic Evolution, Organic Evolution and Christianity, Purpose in Life, The Leadership of Jesus, Catechism on the Bible and Church History. Evacuation officer Hopedale Civilian Defense, 1942-45; disaster officer and dir. local Red Cross. Home: 46 Adin St., Hopedale, Mass. Died Apr. 22, 1954; buried Hopedale, Mass.

TEHON, Leo Roy (tā'h'n), botanist; b. Dumont, S.D., June 21, 1895; s. Patrick John and Bertha (Whittier) T.; student Fremont (Neb.) Normal Sch., 1909, Gregg Sch., Chicago, 1913; A.B., U. of Wyo., 1916; M.A., U. of Ill., 1920; Ph.D., 1934; m. Mary Viola Bruner, Apr. 13, 1918; children—Stephen Whittier, Atha Lee. Asst. in botany, U. of Wyo., 1915-16, U. of Ill., 1916-17, 1924-25; teacher of botany, Arsenal Tech. Sch., Indianapolis, Ind., 1917-18; asst. plant pathologist U.S. Dept. Agr., Ill. State leader in barberry eradication, 1919-20, 1921-22; collaborator, U.S. Dept. Agr. Plant Disease Survey, 1921—; with Mount Arbor Nurseries, Shenandoah, Ia., 1920-21; botanist in charge bot. sect. Ill. State Natural History Survey, 1921-35, head of sect. of applied botany and plant pathology, 1935—; acting chief, 1945-47; prof. plant pathology, U. of Ill., Nov. 1947—; cons. pathologist Davey Tree Expert Co., 1934-42; mem. advisory com. Ill. State Weed Control, 1937-39, of Ill. Seed and Weed Council, 1939—; mem. Nat. Oak Wilt Technical Com., 1949—. Served in U.S. Army, 1918-19. Mem. Central States Forestry Congress, 1933. Pres. Arrowhead Council Boy Scouts of America, 1944-45. Fellow A.A.A.S.; scientific mem. Nat. Shade Tree Conf. (member executive com., 1944—); Midwestern Shade Tree Conf. (mem. exec. comm., 1946—); charter mem. Mycol. Soc. of Am.; mem. Bot. Soc. Am., Torrey Botanical Club, Ecol. Soc. of Am., Am. Phytopathol. Soc., Am. Biol. Soc., Am. Forestry Assn., Ill. State Acad. Sci. (sec., 1943-46, pres., 1946-47), Ill. State Nurserymen's Assn. (hon.), Am. Legion, Phi Beta Kappa, Sigma Xi. Clubs: Am. Coll. Quill (hon.); Exchange (local president, 1932); member national committee on junior exchange 1932-33. Author: The Native and Naturalized Trees of Illinois (with Robert B. Miller); Fieldbook of Native Illinois Shrubs; Drug Plants of Illinois. Contbr. numerous technical monographs, bulletions, reports and articles on botany, plant pathology and mycology; also author of several non-technical pamphlets including "Rout the Weeds!", "Pleasure with Plants" and Ill. Plants Poisonous to Livestock; conductor of column "Diseases of Trees" in Am. Nurseryman magazine, 1940-44. Translator: Targioni-Tozzetti's Alimurgia. Member editorial board Phytopathology, 1945-47. Home: 1003 S. Busey St. Office: Natural Resources Bldg., Urbana, Ill. Died Oct. 17, 1954.

TEMPLE, Henry Willson, ex-congressman; b. Belle Centre, O., Mar. 31, 1864; s. John B. and Martha (Jameson) T.; A.B., Geneva Coll., 1883, A.M., 1890; LL.D., 1913; grad. Allegheny Theol. Sem., 1887; D.D., Westminister Coll., 1902, LL.D., 1914; LL.D., Washington and Jefferson College, 1944; m. Lucy Parr, Apr. 14, 1892; children—John Parr, Martha, William Jameson, Henry Marshall, Edward Lawrence. Ordained ministry R.P. Ch., 1887; pastor Baxter, Pa., 1887-90. First U.P. Ch., Washington, Pa., 1891-1905; adj. prof. polit. science, 1898-1905, prof. history and polit. science, 1905-17, prof. international relations Washington and Jefferson College 1933-48, emeritus. Mem. 63d to 67th Congresses (1913-23), 24th Pa. Dist., and 68th to 72d Congress (1923-33). 25th Dist. Republican. Editorial writer Presbyn. Banner, Pittsburgh, 1898-1900; became asso. editor United Presbyn., Pittsburgh, 1903. Mem. Am. Hist. Assn. Am. Acad. Polit. and Social Science, Am. Soc. Internat. Law (Exec. Council), Am. Polit. Science Assn., etc. Club: Cosmos (Washington, D.C.). Author: William H. Seward (in The American Secretaries of State and Their Diplomacy series); The Battle of Braddock's Field; Colonel Henry Bouquet in Western Pennsylvania in 1758-1765. Contbr. on hist. and econ. subjects. Address: Washington, Pa. Died Jan. 11, 1955; buried Washington (Pa.) Cemetery.

TEMPLETON, Charles Augustus, ex-governor; b. Sharon, Conn., Mar. 4, 1871; s. Theodore and Ella Phoebe (Middlebrooks) T.; ed. pub. schs. and privately; m. Martha Castle, June 17, 1897. Assistant postmaster, Plymouth, Conn., at age of 13; began as bookkeeper, hardware store, Waterbury, Conn., 1888; sec., treas. Hotchkiss & Templeton, 15 yrs.; pres. Charles A. Templeton, Inc., wholesale and retail hardware, 1913—; dir. Waterbury Nat. Bank, Waterbury Trust Co., Diamond Bottling Works. Was alderman and pres. bd., Waterbury; mem. Conn. Senate, 1919-21; del. Rep. Nat. Conv., 1920; lt. gov. of Conn., 1921-23; gov. of Conn., 1923-25. Trustee St. Margaret's Sch. for Girls; ex-pres. Waterbury Chamber Commerce; dir. Conn. Humane Soc.; pres. Waterbury Fish and Game Protective Assn.; pres. Waterbury Eastern League Baseball Club, 1924. Former pres. Conn. State League of Sportsmens Clubs: state dir. Nat. Wildlife Restoration Week, 1938. Mem. Waterbury Y.M.C.A., 1888 (bd. dirs. 6 years; col. in membership campaign 15 consecutive years). Vestryman Trinity P.E. Ch. Mason (33°, Shriner); Past Master Liberty Lodge; Past Comdr. Clark Commandery; Elk, Redman. First pres. Rotary Club; ex-pres. and treas. Waterbury Republican Club; mem. University Club (Waterbury). Address: Hotel Elton, Waterbury, Conn. Died Aug. 15, 1955; buried Riverside Cemetery, Waterbury.

TEMPLETON, Samuel Moore, clergyman; b. Jacksonville, Tex., Dec. 27, 1853; s. David G. and Mary (Moore) T.; A.B., Trinity U., Tex., 1881, A.M., 1886, D.D., 1903, LL.D., 1926; m. Jennie Wofford, Nov. 21, 1882; children—Thomas Wofford, Frances Allen (dec.), David Henry, Anna Louise, Samuel Moore, Jane. Ordained Presbyn. ministry, 1878; pastor Rockwall, Mesquite, Forney, Turner's Point, Tex., 1885-1891, South Dallas, 1891-92, Clarksville, 1892-1914, Rockwall, 1914-27 (retired). Stated clerk Texas Synod, 1888—; moderator Gen. Assembly Cumberland Presbyn. Ch., 1902; mem. Com. on Presbyn. Fraternity and Union, 1903-06, that negotiated reunion with Presbyn. Ch. U.S.A. Trustee Trinity U. (Waxahachie, Tex.). Democrat. Address: Rockwall, Tex. Died June 11, 1935; buried Rockwall Cemetery.

TEMPLETON, Stuart J., lawyer; b. Chicago, Jan. 8, 1889; s. William and Fannie (Cleary) T.; A.B., Williams Coll., 1910; LL.B., Northwestern, 1913; m. Catharine Casselberry, Apr. 26, 1922; children

—Barbara (dec.), Stuart John, Jr., Joan T. Scott. Admitted to Ill. bar, 1913 and since practiced in Chicago; mem. Wilson & McIlvaine; dir. Harris Trust & Savs. Bank, Continental Casualty Co., Continental Assurance Co., Hibbard Spencer, Bartlett & Co. Trustee Williams Coll. Home: 1300 N. Green Bay Rd., Lake Forest. Ill. Office: 120 W. Adams St., Chgo. 3. Died June 1958.

TEMPLETON, Thomas W., ex-congressman; b. Plymouth, Pa.; ed. Wyoming Sem., Kingston, Pa. Admitted to Pa. bar; served as prothonotary of Luzerne Co., Pa.; mem. 65th Congress 1917-19, 11th Pa. Dist. Republican. Home: Plymouth, Pa. Deceased.

TENNEY, Charles H., public utilities. Chmn. bd. Concord Electric Co., Exeter & Hampton Electric Co., Fitchburg Gas and Electric Light Co., Pike County Light & Power Co., Rockland Electric Co., Rockland Light & Power Co., Brocton Gas Light Co., Springfield Gas Light Co., Hotel Kimball Co., Hotel Charles Co.; dir., mem. exec. com., Commodore Hotel, Third Nat. Bank & Trust Co.; dir. Stopperless Water Bottle Co.; pres., dir. The Springfield Nav. Co. Dir. Life Extension Inst., Inc.; Chmn. adv. Bd. Boston Dist. Ordnance, U.S. Army; dir. Army Ordnance Assn.; pres., trustee Tenney Service Vacation Home; trustee Hampstead Properties Trust, Radnor Properties Trust. Address: 35 State St., Springfield, Mass.; and 89 Broad St., Boston. Died Feb. 7, 1951.

TENNEY, Frank Minard, editor; b. Aurora, Ill., Aug. 18, 1870; s. Solomon Amos and Mary Samantha (Cleveland) T.; grad. Jennings Sem., Aurora, 1886; m. Nellie Rice, Oct. 6, 1904 (dec.); 1 son, Minard Rice (dec.). Reporter Aurora Beacon, 1888-90; mgr. Aurora Daily News, 1890-98; reporter Grand Rapids (Mich.) Press, 1898; with Chgo. Press Bur. and Chgo. Daily News, 1899-1900; with Great Falls (Mont.) Leader, 1902—, part owner, 1910-27, editor, 1927—. Mem. Great Falls C. of C. Republican. Episcopalian. Clubs: Advertising (past pres.), Rotary (hon.) (Great Falls). Home: 104 2d Av. N. Office: Odd Fellows Bldg., Great Falls, Mont. Died Sept. 16, 1957; buried Highland Cemetery, Great Falls.

TENNEY, George Lee, choral dir.; b. West Milton, O.; s. Washington Irving and Jennie (Kelly) T.; student Ohio Wesleyan U., 1891-93; A.B., Denver U., 1894, A.M., 1899, Litt.D., 1914; grad. student, U. Chgo., 1898-99; m. Adelaide Brown Miller, June 3, 1896; children—Kathryn Estelle, Walter Irving, Adelaide Ruth. Prin. Manitou (Colo.) High Sch., 1894-96; head Latin dept., Denver Manual Tng. Sch., 1896-98, Manual Tng. High Sch., Denver, 1899-1902; prof. Latin and music, Lewis Inst., Chgo., 1902-41; prof. Latin and English, dean Coll. Music, Fla. So. Coll., 1941-43. Prof. English, U. Notre Dame, Nov. 1943—; tchr. voice, Mid-West Conservatory Music, Chgo., 1943—; dir., owner Tenneyrest Ranch Music School, Grover, Colo. Dir. Lewis Inst. Chrous; tenor, dir. United Choirs, New 1st Conglist. Ch., Chgo.; dir. German Luth. Chorus, Winona Lake Festival Chorus (1,000 voices); chmn. Adv. Com. for Chorus Music for Century of Progress; directed chorus of 5000 for opening of 1933 Century of Progress; directed Handel's Messiah, June 4, 1933, at Court of States, A Century of Progress, with a chorus of 6000, 130 soloists and augmented Chicago Symphony Orchestra; choral dir. of "Wings of a Century'; choral dir. for drama Chgo. on Parade, Soldier Field, and Chgo. Northwestern U. summer schs. Pres. Choral Directors Music Land Festival; spl. lectr. Am. Conservatory, Guild, 1932-34. Breeder pure bred Hereford cattle and pure bred Berkshire pigs; mem. bd. dirs. Ill. Hereford Assn. Mem. Artists Assn., Daedalians, Alpha Tau Omega. Republican. Conglist. Home: Fernwood, R.F.D. 3, Niles, Mich. Died Sept. 11, 1950; buried Silverbrook Cemetery, Niles.

TENNEY, Henry Martyn, clergyman; b. Hanover, N.H., May 16, 1841; s. Adna and Susan Comings (Weld) T.; A.B., Amherst, 1864, D.D., 1889; Union Theol. Sem., 1864-65; grad. Andover Theol. Sem., 1867; m. Ann Elizabeth Parsons, Jan. 12, 1870 (died July 1919); children—Martha Susan (dec.), Frank Parsons, Grace Elizabeth (Mrs. B. J. Olsen), Edward Henry, Faith Wells (Mrs. R. H. Housen). Ordained Congl. ministry, Oct. 21, 1868; pastor, Dorchester, Mass., 1867-70, Winona, Minn., 1870-75, Steubenville, O., 1875-80, 1st Ch., Cleveland, 1880-89, 2d Ch., Oberlin, O., 1889-1910, pastor emeritus, 1910—; dean Schauffler Missionary Training Sch., Cleveland, 1911-13. Trustee Oberlin Coll., 1885—, Oberlin Missionry Home Assn., Congl. Conf. of Ohio. Mem. Psi Upsilon. Home: 546 Oakwood Av., Webster Groves, Mo. Died Feb. 23, 1932; buried Oberlin, O.

TERHUNE, Everit Bogert, publisher; b. Plainfield, N.J., Nov. 5, 1876; s. William Louis and Nellie (Littlefield) T.; Boston Latin Sch., 1895-A.B., Harvard, 1899; m. Charlotte Meinhard, Feb. 14, 1936; children—Everit B., Phillips Glover. Pres. New England Trade Press Assn., 1915; mem. Fgn. Commerce Com., Dept. Commerce, under Secretary Herbert Hoover; rep. Internat. Chamber, Paris, and League of Nations, Geneva, 1923; pres. Assoc. Business Papers, Inc., 1935; vice pres. and dir. Chilton Co., Inc. Trustee Fifth Av.-Flower Hosp. and New York Med. Coll. Pres. Boston Shoe Trades Club, 1916. Mem. Holland Soc. A.F.&A.M. Clubs: Harvard, 40 Plus (founder). Author: Michel Gulpe (1902), Whispering Europe (1921). Home: 160 E. 48th St. Office: 100 E. 42d St., N.Y.C. Died July 24, 1956; buried Forest Hills Cemetery, Boston.

TERMAN, Lewis Madison (tûr'măn), psychologist; b. Johnson County, Ind., Jan. 15, 1877; s. James William and Martha Parthenia (Cutsinger) T.; A.B., Central Normal Coll., Danville, 1898; A.B., Ind. U., 1902, A.M., 1903, LL.D., 1929; fellow in psychology and edn., Clark U., 1903-05, Ph.D., 1905; LL.D., U. Cal., 1945, U. So. Cal., 1949; Sc.D., U. Pa., 1946; m. Anna Belle Minton, Sept. 18, 1899; children—Frederick Emmons, Helen Clare. Prin. high schs., Smiths Valley, Ind., 1898-1901, San Bernardino, Cal., 1905-06; prof. psychology and pedagogy, State Normal Sch., Los Angeles, 1906-10; asst. prof. edn., Stanford, 1910-12, asso. prof., 1912-16, prof., 1916—, exec. head dept. psychology, 1922-42, prof. emeritus, 1942—. Mem. com. Psychol. Exam. Recruits, Com. on Classification of Personnel, U.S. Army, 1918-19; served as maj. in div. of psychology, Surgeon General's Office, Washington. Fellow A.A. A.S., Brit. Psychol. Soc., Ednl. Inst. Scotland (hon.); mem. Am. Psychol. Assn. (pres. 1923), N. E.A., Am. Sch. Hygiene Assn. (pres. 1917), Nat. Soc. Study Edn., Nat. Acad. Scis., Phi Beta Kappa, Sigma Xi. Mem. bd. 5 psychologists appts. to revise Army mental test methods for use in schs.; author of researches on gifted children. Republican. Author: The Teacher's Health, 1913; The Hygiene of the School Child, 1914; (with Dr. E. B. Hoag) Health Work in the Schools, 1914; The Measurement of Intelligence, 1916; The Stanford Revision of the Binet-Simon Intelligence Scale, 1916; The Intelligence of School Children, 1919; The Terman Group Test, 1920; (with T. L. Kelley and G. M. Ruch) The Stanford Achievement Test, 1923; (with others) Genetic Studies of Genius, Vol. I, 1925, Vol. II (with Catharine M. Cox), 1926, Vol. III (with Barbara Burks and Dortha Jensen), 1930; Children's Reading (with Margaret Lima), 1925; Sex and Personality (with Catharine Cox Miles), 1936; Measuring Intelligence (with Maud A. Merrill), 1937; Marital Happiness, 1938; The Terman-McNemar Test of Mental Ability (with Q. McNemar), 1942; The Gifted Child Grows Up (with Melita Oden), 1947; The Gifted Group at Mid-Life (with Melita Oden), 1959. Editor The Measurement and Adjustment Series; asso. editor Brit. Jour. Ednl. Psychology; Jour. Genetic Psychology; Genetic Psychology Monographs. Address: 761 Dolores St., Stanford University, Stanford, Cal. Died Dec. 21, 1956.

TERRELL, Mary Church, lecturer, author; b. Memphis, Tenn., Sept. 23, 1863; d. Robert Reed and Louisa (Ayres) Church; A.B., Oberlin Coll., 1884, A.M., 1888; student France, Germany, Switzerland and Italy, 1888-90; Litt.D., Wilberforce U. (Ohio), 1946; D. H.L. (hon.), Oberlin Coll. (Ohio), 1948, Howard U., 1948; m. Robert Heberton Terrell, Oct. 28, 1891; 1 dau., Phyllis Church. Teacher, Wilberforce (O.) U., 1885-87, High Sch. for Colored Youth, Washington, D.C., 1887-88, 1890-91. Mem. Board Edn., Washington, 1895-1901, 1906-11 (first colored woman to serve on bd.); has represented Am. colored women abroad at internat. confs., including Internat. Congress of Women, Berlin, 1904 (addressed meeting in English, French and German), Women's Internat. League for Peace and Freedom, Zürich, 1919, and World Fellowship of Faiths, London, 1937; apptd. supervisor of work among colored women of Eastern states by Republican Nat. Com. (after 19th amend. passed), 1920, re-apptd., 1932; has lectured widely throughout U.S. at forums, Chautauquas, men's and women's colls. Served as supervisor of work among colored women for War Camp Community Service after World War, traveling throughout country to find women to supervise this work, Del. to Cong. of Women's Internat. League for Peace and Freedom, 1919; formerly sec. race relations com. of Washington Fedn. of Chs., treas. inter-racial com., 1937—; pres. South West Community House, Washington. Received citation for social service, Woman's Centennial Congress, N.Y. City, 1940; award for efforts to abolish segregation presented by Washington br. Ams. for Democratic Action, 1948. First pres. Nat. Assn. of Colored Women, serving 3 terms, 1896-1901, hon. pres., 1901—; mem. Bethel Literary and Hist. Soc. (1st woman pres.). Republican. Conglist. Author: A Colored Woman in a White World, 1940; also numerous articles for mags. throughout U.S. and England and also leading newspapers of U.S. Placed on list of Oberlin Coll's. one hundred most famous alumni and alumnae, 1929, and also spoke at 100th anniversary of founding. Home: 1615 S St. N.W., Washington. Died July 24, 1954; buried Lincoln Meml. Cemetery, Washington.

TERRY, Randall B., mfr., publisher; b. Rockingham, N.C., Jan. 10, 1883; s. Calvin B. and Anne (Hicks) T.; ed. pub. and high schs. and business coll.; m. Nan Carr Heitman, 1908 (died 1928); 1 dau., Nancy Carr (Mrs. A. B. Henley); m. 2d, Mrs. Dorothy Pyle McGrath, Sept. 17, 1931; 1 son, Randall B. Founder, 1905, and owner of Dalton Furniture Mfg. Co.; organizer, 1918, and pres. High Point Underwear Mills; organizer, 1919, and pres. High Point Daily Enterprise; organizer, 1920, and dir. High Point Hotel Co.; organizer, 1920, and v.p. Southern Furniture Expn. Bldg.; organizer, 1922, and chmn. bd. Atlantic Bank & Trust Co.; organizer, 1922, and dir. Atlantic Building & Loan Assn., also Greensboro Joint Stock Land Bank; organizer, 1922, dir. and v.p. Atlantic Ins. & Realty Co.; organizer, 1923, and pres. Premier Furniture Mfg. Co., also Terry-Smith-Rawley Co.; organizer, 1923, and v.p. O. L. Williams Veneer Co.; organizer, 1924, v.p. and dir. H.,P.,T.&D. Ry. Co.; organizer, 1932, and since pub. Daily Times-News (Burlington, N.C.); organizer, 1936, also treas. Premier Silk Mills; pres. WHPE and WHPE-FM Radio Stations. Mem. City Council High Point, 1911-15; del. Dem. Nat. Conv., 1924. Dir. Y.M.C.A. Presbyterian. Clubs: Commercial (ex-pres.), Rotary (past pres.), High Point Country (ex pres.), Sedgefield Country (dir.). Home: Roland Park, High Point, N.C. Died May 27, 1955; buried High Point.

TETER, Lucius, banker; b. Bowling Green, Ind., Sept. 23, 1873; s. Hiram and Frances (Ringo) T.; ed. high school; hon. A.M., Dartmouth, 1920; m. Clara Hahn Lodor, Oct. 23, 1900; 2 children—Elizabeth L., Charles L. Began with Continental Nat. Bank, Chgo., 1892, later with Am. Trust & Savings Bank; an organizer, 1902, of Chgo. Trust Co. (formerly Chicago Savings Bank and Trust Co.) and successively cashier, v.p., pres. and chmn. bd., 1902-31; now chmn. bd. Baird and Warner Corp., real estate. Pres. savings bank sect., Am. Bankers Assn., 1907, trust companies sect. of same, 1925; pres. Chgo. Assn. Commerce, 1918. Pres. Infant Welfare Soc., Chgo., 1910-29, now chmn. bd.; founder Economic Club of Chicago (pres. 1927-33; now hon. chmn.). Republican. Congregationalist. Mason. Clubs: Chicago, Chicago Athletic (pres. 1926), Quadrangle (pres. 1920-21), Mid-Day, Bankers (pres. 1931), Economic (Chicago); Onwentsia, Knollwood (Lake Forest). Home: 1321 E. 56th St., Chgo.; also Lake Forest, Ill. Office: 134 S. LaSalle St., Chgo. Died Oct. 15, 1950.

TETRICK, W(illis) Guy (tĕ'trĭk), newspaper pub.; b. Enterprise, W.Va., Jan. 3, 1883; s. L. Elmer and Sarah Florence (McIntire) T.; student Mountain State Business Coll., Parkersburg, W.Va., and Elliott's Business Coll., Fairmont, W.Va.; m. Virginia Anne Heavner, Feb. 9, 1910; children—Willis Guy (maj. AUS), Catherine V. (Mrs. Maxwell Y. Sutton), Margaret A., James E. Appt. clk. Co. Ct., Harrison Co., W.Va., 1907; elected term 1908-14, pub. Clarksburg, Exponent, 1915-27; gen. mgr. Clarksburg Pub. Co. and pub. Clarksburg Exponent, Clarksburg Telegram and Sunday Exponent-Telegram, 1927-42; mem. firm Heavner and Tetrick. Mem. W.Va. State Legislature, 1945-46, 49-50, 51-52. Author, compiler and pub. Census Returns of Harrison County, (W.)Va. for 1850; Census Returns of Lewis County, (W.)Va. for 1850, Census Returns of Barbour and Taylor County (W.)Va., for 1850, Census Returns of Doddridge, Ritchie and Gilmer Counties, (W.)Va., for 1850, and Calhoun County for 1860, also Obituaries from Newspapers of Northern West Virginia, Second Series, Vols. 1 to 5, covering years 1932 and 1933; Rules and Regulations for Government of the Democratic Party in West Virginia, 1936; republished, S. C. Shaw's Notes on Wood County, W.Va. Presidential elector from 3d W.Va. Dist., 1932, for Franklin D. Roosevelt; mem. W.Va. State Dem. Exec. Com., since 1916, Harrison County Dem. Exec. Com., 1905-15; Democratic mem. W.Va. State Legis., 1945-46, 49-50, 51-52; Dem. Nominee State Senate, 1946 Mem. Commn. on Historic and Scenic Highway Markers in W.Va.; W.Va. War History Commn Mem. Associated Press (Eastern advisory bd., 1925-27), Southern Newspaper Pubs. Assn. (W.Va. dir 1922-27), W.Va. Publishers Assn. (pres. 1922-41) S.A.R. (pres. George Rogers Clark Chapter; registra W.Va. State Soc., nat. genealogist general 1950) Methodist. Odd Fellow, Elk. Collector family history and genealogy of Northern W.Va. families for past 25 yrs. Home: 271 Clay St. Office: Prunty Bldg., Clarksburg, W.Va. Died July 15, 1956; buried The Bridgeport Cemetery, Bridgeport, W.Va.

TEWKSBURY, Donald George (tūks'bûr-ĭ), author educator; b. Peking, China, Apr. 9, 1894; s. Elwood Gardner and Grace (Holbrook) T.; B.A., Columbia 1920, M.A., 1921, Ph.D., 1932; L.H.D., Bard, 1954 m. Helen Taylor Plumb, Aug. 9, 1922; son, John Asst. prof. edn., Yenching U., Peking, 1922-27; lectr Far Eastern Civilization and Culture, Sarah Lawrence Coll., 1928-37 asst. prof. edn. Tchrs. coll. Columbia 1932-33, asso. prof. edn., 1933-38, prof. edn. since 1938, dean of Bard coll., 1933-38; dir. New College (Columbia), 1938-39; vis. prof. New Sch. Social Research, 1949; dep. chief, special training branch Military Training Division, A.S.F., War Dept., 1942-44; visiting prof. polit. sci., edn., U. of Calif. 1949; fgn. students adv., Tchrs. Coll., Columbia, 1954—. Mem. Assn. for Eastern Studies, Nat. Soc. Coll Teachers of Edn., Nat. Council on Religion in Higher Edn.; trustee Inst. Pacific Relations, Lisle Fellowship, China Welfare Appeal, World Study Tours, United Board Christian Colls. in China, Library Inter cultural Studies. Mem. Nat. Assn. of Foreign Students Advs. (pres.), Phi Beta Kappa, Phi Delta Kappa, Sigma Nu, Gamma Theta Upsilon. Democrat. Conglist. Club: Exchange. Author: The Founding of American Colleges and Universities Before the Civil War, 1932; Source Books on Far Eastern Political Ideologies, 1949-51. Home: 400 W. 118th St., N.Y.C.; also Brookfield Center, Conn. Died Dec. 8, 1958; buried New Milford, Conn.

TEWKSBURY, William Davis, physician; b. Hutchinson, Kan., May 7, 1885; s. William Brainard and Minnie (Davis) T.; M.D., George Washington U. Med. Sch., 1908; m. Susan Tidball West, Feb. 25, 1911; children—Jane West, Helen Davis. Began practice at Washington, 1908; resident physician Tuberculosis Hosp., 1908-09; physician in charge Catawba Sanatorium, Va., 1909-11; medical supt. Tuberculosis Hosp., 1911-20; clin. prof. medicine, George Washington U. Med. Sch., since 1915; physician in charge Health Dept. Tuberculosis Clinic, 1915-21; asso. prof. medicine, Georgetown Med. Sch., 1917-19. Mem. Vol. Med. Service Corps. Fellow A.M.A., Am. Coll. Physicians; mem. Am. College of Chest Physicians, Hypocrates Galen Med. Society, Med. Soc. D.C., Tuberculosis Association D.C. (dir.), Sigma Alpha Epsilon, Phi Chi. Episcopalian. Club: Chevy Chase. Contributor of papers on pulmonary disease to Journal of A.M.A., Am. Review of Tuberculosis, Va. Medical Semi-Monthly, etc. Original work in use of artificial pneumothorax in treatment of acute pulmonary abscesses, 1916. Home: 101 E. Lenox St., Chevy Chase, Md. Office: Washington Medical Bldg., Washington. Died Dec. 28, 1956.

TEXTOR, Gordon Edmund, army engr.; b. Kasota, Minn., July 9, 1902; s. Charles E. and Louise (Offenloch) T.; B.A., B.M.S., U.S. Mil. Acad., 1924; C. E., Cornell, 1928; married; children—Mary Louise, Gretchen Elizabeth. Served in U.S. Army, Corps of Engrs., 1928—, advancing to brig. gen., 1945; dir. projects, W.P.A., 1937-39; dir. constrn. and facilitation bur. W.P.B., 1942-43; gen. officer, War Dept. Gen. Staff, 1943-45. Address: 314 Mansion Drive, Alexandria, Va. Died Mar. 30, 1955.

THACHER, Archibald Gourlay, lawyer; b. Boston, Mass., Jan. 16, 1876; s. George and Isabel Gourlie (Gourlay) T.; A.B. magna cum laude, Harvard, 1897, LL.B., 1900; m. Ethel Davies, Aug. 9, 1902 (died Feb. 24, 1935); children—Alice Davies (dec.), Archibald Gourlay (dec.), Isabel Davies (Mrs. Sanford S. Clark); m. 2d, Edna Marston Beeckman, July 29, 1937. Admitted to New York bar, 1900; asst. with Butler, Notman, Joline & Mynderse, New York, N.Y., 1900-05; became partner firm Butler, Notman & Mynderse, 1905, and of successor firms, Wallace, Butler & Brown, 1907-13, Barry, Wainwright, Thacher & Symmers, 1913-51, Thatcher, Proffitt, Prizer & Crawley, 1951—; director Am. and Fgn. Insurance Co., Columbia Ins. of N.Y., Eagle Fire Co. of N.Y., Imperial Ins. Co., Norwich Union, Phoenix, and Sun Indemnity cos., Patriotic Ins. Co. of America, Sun Underwriters Insurance Company of New York, Seamens Bank for Savings in City of N.Y. (trustee). Served as captain 306th inf., 77th Div., A.E.F., 1917; regimental adjutant, 1917-18; promoted major, comdg. 2d Btn., France, 1918; col., inf., O.R.C., 1920; participated in major campaigns Vesle-Aisne and Argonne-Meuse offensive. Decorated Distinguished Service Cross (U.S.), Legion of Honor (France). Nat. co-chmn. Citizens Com. for Universal Mil. Training of Young Men (chmn. advisory com.). Mem. Am. and N.Y. State bar assns., Assn. Bar City of N.Y., (chmn. com. nat. defense; treasurer and mem. executive com. of war com.), American Society International Law, Grotius Soc., London, Council on Foreign Relations, Ins. Soc. of N.Y., Liverpool Underwriters Assn. Clubs: Knickerbocker, Harvard (New York); Southside Sportsmen's (Oakdale, L.I.). Author: Background of The North Atlantic Treaty (monograph); also phamplets relating to history of marine ins. and to universal mil. training. Home: 620 Park Ave., New York, N.Y. Office: 72 Wall St., N.Y.C. 5. Died Jan. 1, 1952; buried Mount Auburn Cemetery, Boston.

THACHER, Thomas Chander, ex-congressman; b. Yarmouth, Mass., July 20, 1858; s. Henry C. and Martha (Bray) T.; grad. Adams (Mass.) Acad., 1878; A.B., Harvard, 1882; m. Maria L. Leavitt, 1890. In wool business, 1882-1908. Dem. candidate for Mass. Ho. of Rep., 1886, for state auditor, 1903, for state treas., 1904, for Congress, 1910; mem. 63d Congress 1913-15, 16th Mass. Dist. Pres. Cape Cod Farm Bur. Mem. New Ch. (Swedenborgian). Writer on business topics. Address: Yarmouthport, Mass. Deceased.

THACHER, Thomas Day, judge; b. Tenafly, N.J., Sept. 10, 1881; s. Thomas and Sarah McCullough (Green) T.; prep education, Taft School, Watertown, Conn., and Phillips Academy, Andover, Mass.; B.A., Yale, 1904, LL.D., Yale, 1930; U. of Wis., 1935; New York U., 1944, Harvard, 1944; Columbia, 1945; student law dept., Yale, 2 yrs.; m. Eunice Booth Burrall, Nov. 9, 1907 (died Jan. 19, 1943); children—Sarah Booth (Mrs. George L. Storm), Mary Eunice (Mrs. Daniel N. Brown), Thomas; married 2d, Eleanor M. Lloyd, July 20, 1945. Admitted to New York bar, 1906, and began practice at New York City; asst. U.S. atty. Southern Dist. of N.Y., 1907-08; asso., later partner firm Simpson, Thacher & Bartlett, of which father was mem. until his death, 1919; judge U.S. Dist. Court. Southern Dist. of N.Y., by apptmt. of President Coolidge, 1925-30; solicitor gen. of U.S., 1930-33; partner Simpson, Thacher & Bartlett, 1933-43; corp. consul of the City of New York, 1943; judge New York State Court of Appeals, 1943-48, ret.; partner firm of Simpson, Thacher & Bartle. Served as maj. Am. Red Cross in Russia, 1917-18. Chmn. N.Y. City Charter Revision Commn.; fellow Yale Corp.; pres. Assn. Bar City of N.Y., 1933-35. Republican. Presbyterian. Clubs: Union, Century, Links, University, Yale (New York); Metropolitan (Washington). Home: 920 Fifth Av., New York; (summer) Northeast Harbor, Me. Office: 120 Broadway, New York 5. Died Nov. 12, 1950.

THACKREY, Lyman Augustus, naval officer; b. Manhattan, Kan., Aug. 6, 1897; s. William Elwood and Bettie (Olsen) T.; student U. N.M., 1915-17; grad. U.S. Naval Acad., 1920, advance course, Naval War Coll., 1949; m. Josephine Murray, Dec. 15, 1930. Commd. ensign U.S. Navy, 1920, advanced through grades to rear adm., 1948; various assignments Atlantic, Pacific, European and Asiatic fleets, 1920-48; command mine sweeper Sunnadin, destroyer Dallas, and Destroyer Div. 63; 1st lt., damage control officer USS North Carolina (participated landing Guadalcanal and Battle Eastern Solomons), 1942, exec. officer rank comdr., 1942; command USS Calvert (APA-32, invasion Sicily), 1943; Naval mem. staff which planned Normandy invasion, London, 1943; U.S. asst. chief staff to Allied Naval Comdr. Expeditionary Force and Sr. Naval planner of Gen. Eisenhower's Supreme Hdqrs., A.E.F., 1943-44; command heavy cruiser U.S.S. Portland, Okinawa, (during surrender Truk), 1945; mem. steering com. formed to give guidance to the Navy Dept. during the period unification of the Armed Services was being negotiated; Secretary's Com. on Unification, 1945-48; command Amphibious Group 4, July 1949-July 1950; comdr. Amphibious Group Three since Aug. 3, 1950; participated amphibious landing Inchon, Korea, Sept. 1950; command amphibious landing Iwon, Oct. 1950; evacuated U.N. forces, Inchon, Jan. 1951; reopened Inchon, Feb. 1951; apptd. chmn. Joint Amphibious Bd., Oct. 1951. Navy dept. liaison officer with Eberstadt Task Force under Hoover Com. studying Modernization govt. structure, 1947-48. Decorated D.S.M., Legion of Merit with Combat V, Navy Unit citation; comdr. Mil. Order of the British Empire; French Legion Honor and Croix de Guerre. Mem. U.S. Naval Inst., Phi Kappa Alpha. Student politicoeconomic systems and part war has played or will play in their establishment. Home: 320 W. Olive St., San Diego, Cal. Office: Care of U.S. Navy Department, Washington 25. Died Apr. 14, 1955; buried Nat. Cemetery, San Diego.

THAYER, Edwin Pope, ex-sec. U.S. Senate; b. Greenfield, Ind., Dec. 15, 1864; s. Hollis B. and Permelia A. (Hart) T.; A.B., DePauw, 1886, A.M., 1889; married; children—George A., Mrs. Roxana H. Smith. In mercantile bus., 1880-1906, irrigated land and mining bus., 1906-16; pres. Arizona Exploration & Development Co. Mem. Ind. N.G. 23 yrs.; served as col. 158th Regt., Ind. Vols., Spanish-Am. War; col. 3d Regt., I.N.G., 1900-12. Chief asst. to sergt. at arms, Rep. Nat. Com., 1904, 08, 12, 16; sergt. at arms, 1920, 24; chief supervisor for U.S. Senate in the Paddy-Mayfield contest (Tex.), 1924, Steck-Brookhart contest (Ia.), 1925, and the Bursum-Bratton contest (N.M.), 1926; sec. of the Senate, 1925-33. Now practicing law, Washington, D.C. Mem. Ind. and D.C. bars. Methodist. Mason (32°). Club: Columbia. Home: Greenfield, Ind. Deceased.

THAYER, Frederick Morris, investment banker; b. Rosemont, Pa., July 17, 1896; s. John Borland and Marian L. (Morris) T.; A.B., Yale, 1918; m. Eliza T. Talbott, Oct. 27, 1923; children—Frederick Morris, Marian (Mrs. Robert Toland, Jr.), Harry E. T., Thurston H., Nelson S. T. Engaged in investment banking; sr. v.p., dir. Harriman Ripley & Co.; dir. Shawmut Bank, Boston, James & Co., Phila., Mead Corp. Served as capt., 310th F.A., U.S. Army, World War I; AEF in France. Died Nov. 16, 1956.

THAYER, Tiffany Ellsworth, author, actor; b. Freeport, Ill., Mar. 1, 1902; s. Elmer Ellsworth and Sybil Madelin (Farrar) T.; ed. pub. schs. Actor dramatic and operatic stock cos., Oak Park, Ill., Indianapolis, Ind., and elsewhere, 1917-18; appeared with Lillian Kingsbury in "The Coward," 1918; newspaper reporter, 1919-20; played in "A Little Mother to Be," "Her Unborn Child," "A Night in Honolulu," "Up the Ladder," etc., 1920-25; asso. with Powner Book Stores, 1925; advertising copy writer, N.Y. City, 1926-30; advertising mgr. Lit. Guild, 1930-32; owner and propr. Old Wine Press Publishers, N.Y. City, since 1932; founder-sec. Fortean Soc., 1931; motion-picture writer, Hollywood, 1932-36; radio writer, J. Walter Thompson, 1938-48; asso. Sullivan, Stauffer, Colwell & Bayles since 1948. Author numerous books since 1930; latest publ.: Tiffany Thayer's Mona Lisa: I-The Prince of Taranto, 1956; writes under several pseudonyms. Editor: (anthologies) 33 Sardonics, Adults' Companion, 1948; also Doubt, the Fortean Soc. mag. Address: Box 192, Grand Central Annex, N.Y.C. Died Aug. 23, 1959; buried Nan Tucket, Mass.

THAYER, William Greenough, head master; b. New Brighton, S.I., N.Y., Dec. 24, 1863; s. Robert H. and Hannah (Appleton) T.; A.B., Amherst, 1885, A.M., 1888; Union Theol. Sem., 1885-86, 1887-88; B.D., Episcopal Theol. Sch., Cambridge, Mass., 1889; hon. A.M., Columbia U., 1906; D.D., Amherst College, 1907; m. Violet Otis, June 1, 1891; children—William Greenough, Mrs. Violet Otis Parker, Sigourney, James Appleton, Robert Helyer, Margaret (Mrs. John R. Suydam, Jr.), John Otis. Teacher, 1886-87, master, 1889-94, Groton (Mass.) Sch.; head master St. Mark's Sch., Southborough, Mass., 1894—. Deacon, 1889, priest, 1890, P.E. Church; pres. standing com. Diocese Mass., 1910-19. Del. Rep. State Conv., Mass., 1904. Mem. Coöperating Com. of War Council, Y.M.C.A.; chmn. Diocesan Com. on Camps. Del. Gen. Conv. P.E. Ch., 1922. Clubs: University, Harvard (New York); Union, Harvard (Boston). Home: Southborough, Mass. Deceased.

THEIS, Edwin Raymond (tīs), educator, chemist; b. Newport, Ky., July 8, 1896; s. Edwin David and Ida Eliza (Holbrook) T.; Ch.E., U. of Cincinnati, 1921, Ph.D., 1926; m. Martha Celestine Pauling, July 2, 1921; children—Edwin Raymond, Richard Carl. Engaged as research asso. and dir. chem. research Dept. Leather Research, U. of Cincinnati, 1921-27; chem. engr., Frederick Stearns & Co., Detroit, Mich., 1927; asst. prof. chem. engring., Lehigh U., Bethlehem, Pa., 1927-30, asso. prof., 1930-38, prof. chem. engring. 1938-45; research prof. chemistry, dir. Div. Leather Technology, Institute of Research, Lehigh University since 1945; has served as consultant to leather and allied industries since 1927; mem. spl. U.S. Govt. com. sent to China and Japan for inspection imported skins, summer 1937; ECA point 4 program Holland, 1950. Served as 2d lt. inf., United States Army, 1918-19; 1st lt. Ordnance Reserve, 1926-31, capt. since 1931. Fellow American Institute of Chemists; Am. Chem. Soc., Tech. Assn. of Fur Industry, Tau Beta Pi, Sigma Xi, Delta Sigma Phi. Republican. Hon. life mem. American Leather Chemists Assn. Co-author: Chemistry of Leather Manufacture (mono-Methodist. Clubs: Lions International, Chemists'. graph). Awarded Moffatt medal by Tanners Council of America, 1943. Invited lecturer to Soc. of Internat. Leather Trades Chemists and to Faraday Soc., London, England, Sept. 1946. Home: 1021 Raymond Av., Bethlehem, Pa. Died Apr. 25, 1953.

THEISS, Paul Seymour, naval officer, ret.; b. Washington, Oct. 6, 1890; s. Capt. Emil Theiss (USN); grad. U.S. Naval Acad., 1912; m. Ellen Elizabeth Wright Macdonald, June 16, 1948. Commd. ensign, U.S.N., 1912, and advanced through grades to commodore, 1944; served in U.S. ships Montana, Prairie, Castine, Brooklyn and South Carolina, 1914-16, U.S.S. Allen, 1917-18, U.S.S. Laub and U.S.S. Ringgold, 1919; comd. U.S.S. Paul Hamilton, 1927-29, U.S.S. Borie, 1929-31, U.S.S. Fuller (formerly S.S. City of Newport News), 1941-42; assigned to command a transportation div. in Pacific area, participating in initial landings on Guadalcanal (1942), on New Georgia Island (1943); chief of staff and aide to comdr. Fifth Amphibious Force, Pacific Fleet, 1943, later becoming chief of staff to comdr. Amphibious Force, Central Pacific to Oct. 1945; command U.S. Naval Training Station, Newport, R.I., 1946-49; rear adm. ret. 1949. Decorated Am. Defense Service Medal with bronze "A," Navy Cross, Legion of Merit with Star, Victory Medal with destroyer clasp, World War I; D.S.M., American area Philippine Liberation and European-African-Middle East campaign medals, Victory Medal World War II. Mexican Service, Haitian Campaign, Yangtze Service and Asiatic-Pacific Area Campaign (with 10 battle stars) medals; Imperial Order of the Rising Sun, Fourth Class, Japan, 1938. Clubs: Cricket, Racquet, Phila. Country. Home: The Kenilworth, Alden Park, Philadelphia 44. Office: General Baking Co., 56th and Market, Phila. Died June 3, 1956.

THIEME, Anthony (tē'mē), artist; b. Rotterdam, Holland, Feb. 20, 1888; s. Karel and Alida Cornelia (Lans) T.; student Acad. of Fine Arts, Rotterdam, 1902-04, Royal Acad., The Hague, 1905, Scuola di Belli Arti, Torino, 1909-10; pupil of Garlobini and Guiseppe Mancini; m. Lillian M. Beckett, 1929. Came to U.S., 1917, naturalized, 1935. Apprentice artist in Dusseldorf, Germany, 1905-08; designer and painter of stage settings in U.S., 1917-27. Represented by seascapes and landscapes in Boston Museum of Fine Arts, Pittsfield (Mass.) Museum, Albany (N.Y.) Museum of History and Art, Dayton (O.) Art Inst., City of New Haven (Conn.) art collection, State U. of Ia. Museum, Met. Museum of Art, Beach Memorial collection (Storrs, Conn.), Metropolitan Museum, N.Y. City, Museum of Art, New Britain, Conn. Awards: 1st landscape prize, Gloucester Art Assn., 1928; Springfield Art Assn., 1928; Springfield Art League prize, 1928; Shaw prize, Salmagundi Club, 1929 and 1931; Delano prize, New York Water Color Club, 1930; Marine prize, North Shore Art Assn., 1930; Atheneum prize, Conn. Acad. of Fine Art, 1930; Mr. and Mrs. Burton Mansfield prize, New Haven Paint and Clay Club; Lucien Powell award; Citizens Jury award, Los Angeles Museum, Purchase prize, Springville High Art exhbn. Purchase prize, Buck Hill Falls Art Assn., 1938. First prize Autumn exhbn. Grand Central Art Galleries, N.Y. City, 1945; Gold medal N.E. Contemporary Show, Boston, 1944, 47, 48. Exhibited Bernheim Jeune Galleries, Paris, 1950. Address: 6 South St., Rockport, Mass.; (winter) St. Augustine, Fla. Died Dec. 7, 1954; buried Rockport, Mass.

THIGPEN, Charles Alston (thĭ'p'n), ophthalmologist; b. Greenville, Ala., Dec. 19, 1865; s. Job and Martha Amanda (Watts) T.; A.M., Howard Coll., Marion, Ala., 1886; M.D., Tulane U., 1889; grad. study Royal London Ophthal. Hosp., 1890-91, U. Vienna, 1892, Augenclinic, Heidelberg, 1892; LL.D., U. Ala.; m. Daisie Lee Bissell, Nov. 17, 1896; children—Dorothy (Mrs. Edmund B. Shea), Elisabeth (Mrs. Wiley C. Hill, Jr.), Charles Alston. Began practice at Montgomery, Ala., 1893. Served as maj. Med. Corps, U.S. Army, 1917-18. Trustee Bryce Hosp., Tuscaloosa, Ala. Fellow A.C.S., A.M.A., Am. Acad. Ophthalmology and Otolaryngology; mem. State of Ala. Med. Assn. (pres.; mem. bd. censors), Montgomery County Med. Assn., World War Vets, Am. Legion. Democrat. Episcopalian. Home: 1420 S. Perry St. Office: 401 S. Court St., Montgomery, Ala. Died Apr. 23, 1958; buried Greenwood Cemetery, Montgomery.

THILL, Frank Augustine (ĭl), bishop; b. Dayton, O., Oct. 12, 1893; s. Bernard J. and Margaret (Schele) T.; A.B., U. Dayton, 1914, Ph.D., 1925; studied philosophy and theology, Mt. St. Mary Sem. of West, Cin., and Angelico U., Rome (J.C.D. 1928). Organizer, 1918, and nat. sec.-treas. Cath. Students' Mission Crusade, 1918-35, exec. counselor, 1935—; ordained priest R.C. Ch., 1920; organizer, 1926, and dir. Soc. to Aid Missions, Cin.; dir. Laymen's Retreat Movement, 1926; chancellor, mem. bd. consultors and Matrimonial Court, Cin., 1937. Mem. bd. dirs. Propagation of the Faith Soc., Holy Childhood Assn. Mem. Flood Prevention Commn., Dayton, 1913. Made hon. Papal chamberlain with title of Monsignor, 1928; made domestic prelate, 1937; consecrated bishop of Concordia, 1938; transferred to Salina, 1944. Knight Comdr. Order of the Holy Sepulchre. K.C. (4°), mem. Phi Kappa Fraternity. Home: 421 Country Club Rd., Salina, Kan. Died May 21, 1957; buried Mount Calvary Cemetery, Salina.

THOM, Charles (tŏm), botanist and mycologist; b. Minonk, Ill., Nov. 11, 1872; s. Angus Sutherland and Louisa Electa (Herrick) T.; A.B., Lake Forest Coll., 1895, A.M., 1897, D.Sc. (hon.), 1936; Ph.D., U. Mo., 1899; grad. study Cornell U., 1902-04; Marine Biol. Lab., summer, 1897; m. Ethel Winifred Slater, Dec. 20, 1906 (dec. Oct. 1942); children—Beatrice (dec.), Charles Richard; m. 2d, Charlotte J. Bayles, Sept. 1944. Sci. tchr. Danville (Ill.) High Sch., 1895-96; instr. biology and botany, asst. prof. botany U. Mo., 1897-1902; asst. in botany Cornell U., 1902-04; mycologist in cheese investigations, dairy div. Bur. Animal Industry, U.S. Dept. of Agr., charge coöperative work in soft and fancy cheesemaking. Agrl. Expt. Sta., Storrs, Conn., 1904-13, Washington, 1913-14; in charge microbiol. lab. Bur. of Chemistry, 1914-27, of soil microbiology, Bur. Chemistry and Soils, 1927-34; with Bureau of Plant Industry, 1934-42, retired Nov. 30, 1942; collaborator U.S. Dept. Agr.; cons. mycologist; lectr. soil microbiology U. Md., 1929-38. Fellow A.A.A.A.; mem. Acad. Medicine (charter), Nat. Acad. Sciences, Washington Acad. Sci. (pres. 1937), Bot. Soc. Am., Am. Naturalists, Internat. Society Soil Sci. Soc. Am. Bacteriologists (pres. 1940), Am. Phytopathological Soc., Sigma Xi, Phi Beta Kappa. Club: Cosmos. Author: The Penicillia, 1930. Co-author: The Book of Cheese; Hygienic Fundamentals of Food Handling; Manual of the Aspergilli, Manual of the Penicillia. Contbr. govt. bulls. Address: Bayles Hill, Port Jefferson, N.Y. Died May 24, 1956; buried Storrs, Conn.

THOM, Corcoran, banker; b. Washington, May 30, 1873; LL.B., George Washington U., 1893, LL.M., 1894; m. Mary Lay; children—Caroline, Corcoran, Huntington. Formerly pres. Am. Security & Trust Co., ret. Dec. 31, 1945, now chmn. bd. Clubs: Metropolitan, Chevy Chase, Alibi. Home: 3244 Nebraska Av. N.W. Office: 15th St. and Pennsylvania Av., Washington. Died Jan. 18, 1956; buried Oak Hill Cemetery.

THOM, Douglas Armour, psychiatrist; b. Boston, Oct. 4, 1887; s. James and Agnes (Russell) T.; grad. Dow Acad., Franconia, N.H., 1907; M.D., U. Vt., 1912, hon. M.Sc., 1935; m. Emily Noyes Barber, Sept. 7, 1919; 1 son, Robert Armour. In practice at Boston, 1920—; asst. pathologist, Monson State Hosp., 1912-16; dir. out-patient dept., Boston Psychopathic Hosp., 1920-23; dir. div. mental hygiene, State Mass., 1923-38; cons. psychiatrist, Smith Coll., 1925-32, and St. Paul's Sch., Concord, N.H., 1928-30; prof. psychiatry, Tuft's Coll. Med. Sch., 1928-47, emeritus; dir. Habit Clinic for Child Guidance, 1921—; hon. cons. to Surg. Gen. in Neuropsychiatry; br. sect. chief in neuropsychiatric tng., U.S.V.A. Served in World War, 1917-19, 8 mos. abroad; col., 1943-47; neuro-psychiatric cons. 2d Service Command, Governors Island, N.Y. Mem. Am. Neurol. Assn., Am. Psychiatric Assn., N.E. Soc. Psychiatry and Neurology, Boston Soc. Psychiatry and Neurology, A.M.A., Am. Psychopathol. Assn., Mass. Soc. Mental Hygiene. Clubs: Army and Navy (Washington); Harvard (Boston); Hoosic-Whisick Golf (Milton). Author: Everyday Problems of the Everyday Child, 1927; The Mental Health of the Child, 1928; Normal Youth and Its Everyday Problems, 1932; Health—Physical, Mental and Emotional (with Dr. Richard Smith), 1936. Contbr. articles jours. Home: 239 Commonwealth Av. Office: 454 Marlborough St., Boston 15. Died Feb. 23, 1951.

THOMAS, Albert Harry, mfg. exec.; b. Richmond, Ind., 1870; Purdue U., 1895. Chmn. bd. and dir. Buckeye Steel Castings Co., Columbus, O.; dir. Huntington Nat. Bank, Midland Mut. Life Ins. Co. Home: 2501 Fair Av., Bexley, Columbus 9. Office: 2211 S. Parsons Av., Columbus 7, Ohio. Died May 29, 1952.*

THOMAS, Benjamin Platt, author; b. Pemberton, N.J., Feb. 22, 1902; s. Benjamin P. and Martha (Johnson) T.; A.B., Johns Hopkins, 1924, Ph.D., 1929; L.H.D. (hon.), Ill. Coll., 1947; LL.D., Knox College, 1953; Litt.D. (honorary), Northwestern University, 1953, Birmingham Southern Coll., 1955; D.Litt. (honorary), Lincoln College, 1953; married Salome Kreider, December 26, 1929; children—George Kreider, Martha Louise, Sarah Hathaway. Asso. editor Abraham Lincoln Quar., 1940-53; editorial adv. bd. Collected Works of Abraham Lincoln, since 1945. Mem. adv. council history dept. Princeton, 1953-56; mem. board of trustees of Illinois College. Awarded Lincoln book of year Lincoln Nat. Life Found., 1947, 52; recipient Lincoln Diploma of Honor, Lincoln Meml. U., 1949. Mem. Am., Miss. Valley hist. assns., So. Hist. Soc., Soc. Am. Historians, Abraham Lincoln Assn. (exec. sec. 1932-36, dir., 1936—), Civil War Centennial Assn. (dir.), Phi Beta Kappa. Phi Beta Kappa Assos. Clubs: Sangamo, Illini Country (Springfield); Johns Hopkins (N.Y.). Author: Russo-American Relations, 1815-1867, 1930; Lincoln's New Salem, 1934; Lincoln 1847-1853, 1936; Portrait for Posterity: Lincoln and His Biographers, 1947; Theodore Weld, 1950; Abraham Lincoln: A Biography, 1952. Editor: Three Years with Grant, 1955. Asso. editor The Lincoln Herald; mem. editorial bd. The Civil War Book Club. Contbr. Atlantic, Look, Am. Heritage, Sat. Rev. Home: 1910 Wiggins Av., Springfield, Ill. Died Nov. 29, 1956.

THOMAS, Cecil Benton, corp. exec.; b. Fredericktown, O., Oct. 12, 1894; s. George Henry and Mary (Chamblaim) T.; student pub. schs., Gibsonburg, O.; m. Glendora Sparling, Jan. 2, 1913 (dec.). Pres., dir. Chrysler Export Corp., 1942—; v.p. Chrysler Corp., Detroit, 1952—, dir., 1953—; dir. Chrysler Motors Ltd., London, Eng., Dodge Bros. (Britain) Ltd., London Societe Anonyme Chrysler Antwerp, Belgium, Chrysler Australia Ltd., Adelaide, Australia. Home: 852 Whittier Blvd., Grosse Pointe Park 30, Mich. Office: 341 Massachusetts Av., Detroit 31. Died June 11, 1956.

THOMAS, Darwin W., judge; b. Malad, Ida., Sept. 5, 1894; s. David M. and Sarah J. (Williams) T.: LL.B., U. Ida., 1925; m. Zilla Lewis, Dec. 22, 1915; children—Robert Dawin, Geraldine. Admitted to Ida. bar, 1925, practiced Pocatello, 1925-26, Malad, Oneida Co., 1926-37; city attorney of Malad, Idaho, 4 years; pros. attorney, Oneida County, six years; asst. atty. gen., Ida. 1937-42; practiced law Boise, 1942-44; asso. Anderson & Thomas, 1944-51; judge Supreme Ct. of Ida. since 1950. Mem. Ida., Dist. bar assns., Am. Judicature Soc. Phi Alpha Delta. Democrat. Mason (Shriner), Elk. Home: 1316 N. 25th St. Office: State Capitol, Boise, Ida. Died Nov. 22, 1954; buried Malad, Ida.

THOMAS, Edward Moseley, ry. officer; b. Richmond, Va., May 31, 1879; s. W. Lucien and Elizabeth Frances (Sheppard) T.; grad. Richmond High Sch., 1896; m. Mary Forrest, Nov. 17, 1909; children—Mary F. (Mrs. William W. Boorse) (dec.), Edward Moseley. Clerk motive power and stores dept., C.&O. Ry. Co., 1897-1900, storekeeper, 1900-02, clerk, auditor of disbursements' office, 1902-08, spl. accountant and statistician, 1908-13, mem. valuation com. in charge of accounting, 1913-18, gen. auditor in charge of corporate accounts, 1918-20, comptroller, 1920-43, comptroller P. M. Ry. Co., 1930-43, N.Y.,C.&St.L. R.R. Co., 1933-43, v.p. these 3 railroads and subsidiary cos., 1943-47; v.p. finance and accounting N.Y.C. & St. L. R.R. Co., 1947-1950; vice president of accounting since October, 1950. Mem. Ry. Accounting Officers Assn., 1920-34 (exec. com. and com. on general accts.; pres. 1924-25); mem. Assn. of Am. Railroads (gen. com., accounting div.). Clubs: Country of Va., Virginia Boat (Richmond); Canterbury Golf (Cleveland); Cleveland Athletic. Home: 11428 Cedar Glen Pkwy. Address: 3100-A Terminal Tower, Cleve. Died April 14, 1951.

THOMAS, Elbert Duncan, ambassador; born Salt Lake City, Utah, June 17, 1883; s. Richard Kendall and Caroline (Stockdale) T.; A.B., U. of Utah, 1906; Ph.D., U. of Calif., 1924; LL.D., U. of Southern Calif., 1935, University of Hawaii, 1951; Litt. D., National U., 1937; m. Edna Harker, June 25, 1907 (died Apr. 29, 1942); children—Chiyo (Mrs. Horton R. Telford), Esther (Mrs. Wayne C. Grover), Edna Louise (Mrs. Lawrence Lee Hansen); m. 2d Ethel Evans, Nov. 6, 1946. Served as missionary of Latter Day Saints' Ch. in Japan, 1907-12; was traveler and student, Asia and Europe, 1912-13; instr. Latin and Greek, U. of Utah, 1914-16, sec.-registrar, 1917-21; fellow polit. science, U. of Calif., 1922-24; prof. polit. science, U. of Utah, since 1924; mem. of U.S. Senate, 1933-51; U.S. High Comissioner Trust Territory of the Pacific Islands with rank of ambassador since 1951. Major Insp. Gen's. Department, Utah Nat. Guard and U.S. Reserves, 1917-26. Mem. Gen. Board Deseret S.S. Union; del. U.S. Senate Interparliamentary Union, Budapest, 1936, Paris, 1937; chmn. Thomas Jefferson Memorial Commn.; dir. Columbia Institute for the Deaf. Aptd. U.S. del., Internat. Labor Organization Conference Philadelphia, 1944, Paris, 1945, Montreal, 1946, Geneva, 1947, San Francisco, 1948. Mem. Am. Assn. Univ. Profs., Am. Soc. Internat. Law (v.p.), Am. Political Science Assn. (v.p. 1940-41), Utah Alumni Assn. (pres. 1913-14), Coun. Am. Learned Socs., Chinese Polit. and Social Science Assn., Am. Oriental Soc., New Orient Soc., Phi Delta Theta, Phi Kappa Phi, Alpha Pi Zeta, Pi Gamma Mu. Mem. Carnegie Internat. Conf. Am. Profs., 1926, Conf. Teachers of Internat. Law, Washington, D.C., 1925-28. Democrat. Club: Timpanogos. Author: (in Japanese) Sukui No Michi; Chinese Political Thought, 1927; World Unity Through Study of History, 1928, Thomas Jefferson—World Citizen, 1942; The Four Fears, 1944; This Nation Under God, 1950. Contbr. on Oriental affairs and internat. relations. Home: 4758 Aukai Av., Honolulu, T.H. Died Feb. 11, 1953.

THOMAS, Elisabeth Finley, author; b. St. Paul; d. Henry Hamilton and Charlotte Augusta (Reynolds) Finley; ed. in France, Germany and Italy; m. Edward R. Thomas, 1912 (deceased); 1 son, Samuel Finley. Began as portrait painter, 1910; exhibited at Nat. Acad. Design, Soc. Am. Artists, Am. Water Color Soc., Woman's Art Club (N.Y.C.), Paris Salon and Royal Acad., London. Writer for 15 yrs. for Morning Telegram (N.Y.C.), of which her husband became owner. Author: Cloak of Dreams (verse), 1913; Tales of Palm Beach and Florida, 1918; Rendezvous, 1926; Empty Shrines, 1927; Nevertheless the Duke, 1929; Light Lady, 1930; Knickerbocker Blood, 1932; Daphne Winslow, 1933; Ladies, Lovers and Other People, 1935. Contbr. to mags. Home: 1 W. 72d St., N.Y.C. Died 1955.

THOMAS, Francis D., patent lawyer; b. Rockville, Md., Oct. 8, 1896; s. Frank E. and Stella (Eagle) T.; LL.B., Georgetown Univ., M.P.L.; m. 1st May Reilly, June 1925 (died); children—Nancy, Hugh Reilly, Francis D.; m. 2d Elizabeth Reilly, Mar., 1933; 1 son, Stephen Larned. Admitted to D.C. bar, and since practiced in Washington, sole proprietor of firm Bacon & Thomas; chmn. Hugh Reilly Co. Member Am. Patent Law Assn., Am. Bar Assn., Newcomen Soc., Delta Theta Phi. Republican. Methodist. Clubs: Columbia Country, Burning Tree, Alfalfa, Sulgrave (Washington). Home: 80 Kalorama Circle, N.W. Office: Shoreham Bldg., Washington. Deceased.

THOMAS, Frank H., ins. exec.; b. Wilmington, Del., Oct. 18, 1899; s. Frank H. and Phoebe T. (Chambers) T.; A.B., Cornell U., 1921; m. Margaret Butler, Apr. 28, 1927; children—Elizabeth Ann, Frank H. III. Vice pres., Standard-Trump Brothers Machinery Co., knitting machine factory, Wilmington, Del., 1921-30; vice pres. and investment officer, Equitable Trust Co., Wilmington, Del., 1930-35; vice pres. Electric Hose and Rubber Co., 1935-36; financial sec. Fire Assn. of Phila. and affiliated companies, The Reliance Ins. Co. of Phila., vice pres., 1939-44, pres. since 1944, dir. since 1941; dir. Electric Hose and Rubber Co. (Wilmington), Electric Bond and Share (New York). Director Chamber Commerce of the United States. Mem. finance com. Phila. Art Museum. Mem. Ins. Soc. of Phila. Clubs: Wilmington (Del.) Country; Down Town, Racquet, Fourth Street (Phila.); Bankers (New York). Home: Greenville, Del. Office: 401 Walnut St., Phila. 6. Died Sept. 24, 1952.

THOMAS, Franklin, civil engr.; b. Red Oak, Ia., May 19, 1885; s. Rev. Thomas D. and Eleanor (Jones) T.; B.E., University of Iowa, 1908, C.E., 1913; studied McGill University, Montreal, Can., 1908-09; Doctor of Engring., U. of Southern Calif., 1949; m. Marie Elizabeth Planck, Sept. 20, 1910; children—William Planck, Richard Erik, Edward Albert (dec.), John Robert (dec.), Eleanor May (Mrs. Lee R. Champion), Margaret (dec.), Katherine (Mrs. Donald G. Langille). Chainman C.B.&O. Ry., 1903-04; with the Mines Power Co., Cobalt, Ontario, Canada, 1909-10; instructor dept. of engring. U. of Mich., 1910-12; with Ala. Power Co., made designs for developments at Lock 18, Coosa River and Muscle Shoals, Tenn. River, 1912-13; prof. civ. engring., Calif. Inst. of Tech. since 1913, also chmn. administrative com. of faculty, 1917, and 1920-21 during absence of president and following his resignation, chairman division engring. 1926-44, Dean of students since 1944. Assistant Engineer U.S. Reclamation Service, while on leave, 1919. Has served as consultant on municipal projects. Commd. 1st lt. Engr. R.C., U.S. Army, 1918. Member and vice chmn. Bd. Dirs. City of Pasadena, 1921-27; pres. Chamber Commerce, Pasadena, 1927; pres. Pasadena Community Chest, 1928; pres. Pasadena Civic Orchestra Assn., 1929-31; mem. bd. Metropolitan Water Dist. of Southern Calif. since 1928, vice chmn. 1929-48; chmn. Colo. River Bd. of Calif. since 1948. Awarded gold medal (Arthur Noble award) for 1939 by City of Pasadena for notable service in promoting welfare of the city. Mem. Am. Soc. C.E. (v.p. 1944-45; pres. 1949; pres. Los Angeles sect. 1924). Am. Soc. for Engring. Edn., American Water Works Association, Sigma Tau, Sigma Xi, Tau Beta Pi. Republican. Conglist. Clubs: Twilight, New Century (Pasadena), Kiwanis. Home: 685 S. El Molino Av., Pasadena 5, Cal. Died Aug. 27, 1953.

THOMAS, Gus (William Augustus), judge; b. Fulton, Ky., Dec. 14, 1863; s. Francis Marion and Laura Lavinia (Taylor) T.; grad. Murray Inst.; LL.B., Valparaiso U. Law Sch., 1888; LL.D., Wilmore Coll.; m. Elizabeth Patterson, July 12, 1892; 1 dau., Anita (Mrs. Kenneth Gooding McConnell). Admitted to Ky. bar, 1889; mem. Smith, Robbins & Thomas, Fulton, 1889-1902; became mem. Robbins & Thomas, Mayfield, 1902, later Robertson & Thomas; atty. I.C.R.R. for 1st Dist. of Ky.; appointed master commr., Graves County, 1900-15; elected judge Court of Appeals, 1915, to fill unexpired term, elected to full term, 1918, and re-elected 4 times since for a full term of 8 years without opposition; was chief justice 4 times. Methodist. Home: 108 W. Third St. Office: The Capitol, Frankfort, Ky. Died June 3, 1951; buried Frankfort Cemetery.

THOMAS, Henry Bascom, orthopedic surgeon; b. Elk Garden, Va., Aug. 17, 1875; s. Thaddeus Peter and Sarah (Price) T.; B.S., U. Chgo., 1899; M.D., Northwestern U., 1903; m. Louise Downing Wendell, 1905. Prof. hygiene and physical edn., med. adviser Armour Inst. Tech., 1903-20; instr. orthopedic surgery, Northwestern U., 1911; prof. and head of dept. orthopedic surgery, U. of Ill. Coll. of Med., now emeritus; sr. cons. orthopedic surg. St. Luke's Hosp., Research and Ednl. Hosp., Ill. Surg. Inst. for Children (dir. in charge); chief orthopedic surgeon Cook County Hosp., 10 yrs., Home for Destitute Crippled Children, 10 yrs.; cons. orthopedic surgeon Municipal Tuberculosis Hosp., Sanitarium and Dispensary, 16 yrs. Orthopedic surgeon, major, U.S. Army, World War. Citation from University of Chicago, St. Luke's Hospital for 25 yrs. of service; certificate of Merit (U.S.A.) for World War II. Mem. A.M.A. (past sec. and pres. orthopedic sect.), Ill., Chicago med. socs., Am. Orthopedic Assn., Chicago Orthopedic Soc. (past pres.), Clinical Orthopedic Soc. (ex-pres.), Am. Acad. Orthopedic Surgery, Inst. of Medicine, Chicago. Mason (Shriner), Elk. Clubs: University, Rotary, City, Olympia Fields Country: Lake Placid (New York). Home: University Club of Chicago, 76 E. Monroe St., Chicago 3. Office: 30 N. Michigan Av., Chgo. Died Mar. 25, 1958; buried Oak Woods Cemetery.

THOMAS, James Bishop, clergyman, writer; b. Petaluma, Calif., Mar. 21, 1871; s. Edward Cady and Emma Amelia (Davies) T.; B.A., Rutgers Coll., 1892; Union Theol. Sem., 1892-93; B.D., Episcopal Theol. Sch., 1895; studied U. Berlin; Ph.D., Halle, 1901; D.D., Rollins, 1934; m. Myra Harris Mott-Smith, July 20, 1895 (dec. Jan. 1930); children—Dorothea, Leslye Ida (Mrs. David Gray Diffin), Clare Rosamond, Virginia St. John, Myra Amelia; m. 2d, Mrs. Jessamine E. Lockwood, July 1, 1931; step dau., Rosamond T. Lockwood (Mrs. B. F. Kyner). Deacon, 1895, priest, 1896, P.E. Ch.; minister St. Stephen's Ch., Cohasset, Mass., 1895-98; curate St. Michael's Ch., N.Y. City, 1901-02; mem. staff Cathedral St. John the Divine, 1902-03; curate Trinity Ch., New Haven, Conn., 1903-06, St. John's Ch., Stanford, 1906-07; rector St. Andrew's Ch., Rochester, N.Y., 1907-14; prof. systematic theology, U. of the South, 1915-19; spl. preacher Ch. of Ascension, N.Y. City, 1919-21; rector All Saint's Ch., Winter Park, 1923-35; prof. Biblical lit. and comparative religion, Rollins Coll., 1926-33. Mem. Allied Arts Soc. of Winter Park, Fla. (v.p.), S.A.R., Sons of Vets., Delta Upsilon, Pi Gamma Mu. Mason. Author: Religion, Its Prophets and False Prophets; A Guide to Kant; A Guide to Bergson. Home: (winter) The Hideout, Winter Park, Fla.; (summer) Christmas Cove, Me. Died Mar. 18, 1946.

THOMAS, John Martin, educator; b. Ft. Covington, N.Y., Dec. 27, 1869; s. Rev. Chandler N. and Marion H. (Martin) T.; A.B., Middlebury (Vt.) Coll., 1890, A.M., 1893; grad. Union Theol. Sem., 1893, grad. student, 1894-95; U. Marburg, 1903; D. D., Middlebury, 1907, Amherst, 1908, Dartmouth, 1909; LL.D., U. Vt., 1911, Jefferson Med. Coll., 1922, Temple U., 1922; Litt.D., Norwich U., 1917; m. Sarah Grace Seely, May 18, 1893 (died Dec. 11, 1948); children—Mrs. Marion T. Fox, Mrs. Huldah T. Gale, Henry Seely, John M., Sarah G. (Mrs. Edgar T. Killary); m. 2d, Eleanor Ross, June 18, 1949. Ordained to ministry Presbyn. Ch., 1893; pastor East Orange, N.J., 1893-1908; pres. Middlebury (Vt.) Coll., 1908-21; pres. Pa. State Coll., 1921-25; pres. Rutgers U., 1925-30; v.p. Nat. Life Ins. Co., Montpelier, 1930-38, also dir.; acting pres. Norwich U., 1938-39, pres., 1939-44. Chmn. Vt. State Bd. Edn., 1910-14; mem. Vt. Commn. Tercentenary of Discovery of Lake Champlian, 1908-11. Served as 1st lt. and chaplain, U.S. Army, 1918-19; lt. col., chaplain, Officers Res. Corps. Expert on mil. edn., U.S. Bur. Edn., 1928-29. Trustee Kimbal Union Acad. Pres. Vt. Hort. Soc., 1935-38, Vt. State C. of C., 1936-38; mem. Chi Psi, Phi Beta Kappa. Mason (Grand Chaplian Grand Lodge of N.J., 1904-06). Republican. Author: The Christian Faith and the Old Testament, 1908. Compiler: (with A. H. Espenshade) Bible Readings for Schools and Colleges, 1925. Home: Mendon, Vt. Office: R.D. 2, Rutland, Vt. Died Feb. 26, 1952; buried Middlebury, Vt.

THOMAS, John Montague, insurance; b. Oxford, Ind., May 7, 1874; s. John Montague and Elizabeth (Fillius) T.; ed. Oxford Acad.; m. Grace Randol, Oct. 1, 1919; children—John Montague, 3d, Jane Randol. Clerical and field work and gen. insurance agency in West and Southwest, 1892-1917; successively sec. Fidelity Phenix Fire Ins. Co., western mgr. Fire Assn. Group, Aetna Ins. Co. group, at Chicago, 1917-27; v.p. and dir. Fire Assn. (Reliance, Victory and Constitution Ins. cos.) at Phila., 1927-30; also v.p. several companies of Home Insurance Co., New York group; chmn. bd. Nat. Union Fire Insurance Company, Pittsburgh, dir. since 1931; pres. and dir. Nat. Union Indemnity Co.; chmn. bd. Birmingham Fire Insurance Co. of Pa.; dir. Fire Cos. Adjustment Co.; past pres. Nat. Bd. Fire Underwriters; vice pres. Ins. Fedn. of Pa.; trustee Underwriters Lab., Inc. (Chicago); former dir. Chamber of Commerce of U.S. Republican. Christian Scientist. Mason. Clubs: Pittsburgh Athletic Assn., Duquesne. Home: Schenley Apts. Office: 139 University Pl., Pitts. Died Mar. 14, 1951; buried Justus Cemetery, Oxford, Ind.

THOMAS, John S(aunders) Ladd, clergyman; b. in South Wales, May 1, 1875; s. Thomas and Jane (Ladd) T.; private schs. and Univ. Coll., London, Eng., 1892-97; came to U.S., 1897; grad. Garrett Biblical Institute, Evanston, Illinois, 1903; S.T. D., Philadelphia Divinity School, 1957; married Catherine Firman, July 1, 1897 (deceased May 29, 1951); children—Howard Wesley, Laura Mildred, Catharine Gwendolyn, Kenneth Arnold, Stuart Austin; married 2d, Mrs. Ethel Eddleman, October 10, 1953. Ordained M.E. ministry, 1902; pastor St. John's Ch., 1902-06, Centenary Church, 1906-09, Austin Church (all of Chicago), 1909-22, First M.E. Church Germantown, Phila., 1922-43; dean Theol. Sch., Temple University, Phila., since May 1943. Chmn. "Billy" Sunday Chicago Exec. Co., 1917-18; pres. trustees Chicago Training Sch., spl. preacher Y.M.C.A. to American soldiers, England and France, Feb.-Aug. 1919. Del. Gen. Conf. M.E. Ch., Des Moines, Ia., 1920, Atlantic City, 1932 and 1940, Columbus, 1936, del. Ecumenical Conf., London, 1921; del. to World Conf. on Faith and Order, Lausanne, Switzerland, 1927, Edinburgh, 1937; del. to Ecumenical Conf. Meth. Ch., Atlanta, Ga., 1931; asso. del. World Conf. on Life and Work, Oxford, 1937. Exchange preacher Great Britain, 1927, 34; pres. Phila. Fedn. of Chs., 1927-29; mem. Bd. Foreign Missions M.E. Ch., 1936-40; mem. Unification Commn. of M.E. Ch., 1932-39; del. Uniting Conf. of Methodist Ch., Kansas City, 1939; member Commission on Worship, Meth. Church. Recipient Russell H. Conwell award Temple U., 1957. Republican. Club: Union League. Contbr. to mags. and religious jours. Home: 346 Green Lane, Roxborough, Phila. 28. Died July 14, 1959.

THOMAS, John W., hon. chmn. bd. Firestone Tire & Rubber Co.; b. Tallmadge, O., Nov. 18, 1880; s. David E. and Fannie E. Thomas; Ph.B., Buchtel Coll. (now Akron U.), 1904; D.Sc. (hon.), University of Akron, 1945; married Bertha A. Hine, October 25, 1906; children—John W., Jr., Robert David, Marjorie Louise (Mrs. Baird Curtis Brookhart), Elizabeth May (Mrs. Joseph Mahan Wells, Jr.), Jean Carolyn (Mrs. Donald Malcolm Lambert). Firestone Tire & Rubber Co. since 1908, chief chemist, 1908-11, gen. supt. of plants, 1911-19, dir., 1916, v.p., 1919-32, pres., 1932-41, chmn. bd., 1941-46, hon. chmn. since 1946; dir. Firestone Bank; also officer and dir. Firestone Steel Products Co., Firestone Textiles, Inc., and other subsidiaries. Received Gold Medal Award, Am. Inst. of Chemists, 1945. Mem. Society of Automotive Engrs., Am. Inst. Chemists, Automobile Old Timers, Inc. Conglist. Clubs: Portage Country, Firestone Country, Surf, La Gorce Golf (Miami, Fla.). Home: 117 Edgerton Rd. Office: 1200 Firestone Parkway, Akron, O. Died Nov. 26, 1951; buried Rose Hill Cemetery, Akron.

THOMAS, Joseph Brown, capitalist; b. Boston, Jan. 3, 1879; s. Joseph B. and Annie M. (Hill) T.; ed. École Monge (Paris), Berkeley Sch., N.Y., A.B., Yale, 1903; m. Clara Fargo; children—Joseph B., Clara Jane Diana. Has traveled extensively Russia and Persia, written much on those countries. Republican; mem. Conn. House Reps., 1907-08. N.Y. chmn. Four-Minute Men, 1917; maj. U.S. Army, 1918-19; furnished French Govt. 11,000 dairy cattle to restock devastated regions. Pres. Thomas Holding Corp., builders co-operative apartments, East River, N.Y., 1924; organized, 1928, Spur Distributing Co. extensive track-side gasoline distributing system—tank car to consumer direct; organized, 1932, the Fgn. Exchange and Trade Inst.—1st orgn. to advocate the gold embargo to preclude operations of British Exchange Equalization Fund. Dir. Pacific Coast Co., Harvard Brewing Co.; pres. Kar-Foam Corp. Mem. Alpha Delta Phi, Scroll and Key. Clubs: Yale, University. Author: Observations on Borzoi, 1912; Hounds and Hunting Through the Ages, 1928. Home: 135 E. 19th St., N.Y.C. Died July 1955.

THOMAS, Lewis F(rancis), educator; b. Pioneer, O., Nov. 1, 1886; s. Heman and Celia Zitella (Drake) T.; B.S., Denison U., 1910; A.M., U. Mo., 1917; Ph.D., U. Chgo., 1925; m. Eleanor Gideon, June 4, 1917; children—Jean Alden (Mrs. Merwin P. Magnin) (adopted), Betty Mae (ex-wife of Carl J. Brock), Bradford Lewis. Cons. S.W. Bell Telephone Co., econ. survey Mo., 1927; civilian cons. to Army-Navy Munitions Bd., underground sites com., summer 1946; prof. Drury Coll., 1912-16; instr. geography U. Mo., 1917-18; asst. prof. Washington U., St. Louis, 1919-23, asso. prof., 1923-39, prof., 1939—, head dept., 1944—; prof. summer sessions, U. Colo., U. Minn.; expert cons. in indsl. geog. Indsl. Coll. of Armed Forces, Nat. War Coll., War Dept., 1944-47. Chmn. City Plan Commn., University City, Mo., 1945—. Served as sgt., 472d engrs., sch. of reconnaissance, topographic mapping, World War I. Cons. Miss. River Div., Nat. Research Bd., 1934; mem. Div. Geol.-Geog. Nat. Research Council, 1936-42. Mem. Assn. Am. Geographers, Am. Soc. Profl. Geographers, Nat. Council Geog. Tchrs., Am. Meteorol. Soc., A.A.A.S., Acad. Sci. (St. Louis), Sigma Xi, Omicron Delta Kappa, Delta Sigma Pi, Sigma Nu. Republican. Conglist. Author: The Climate of St. Louis, 1924; The Geography of the St. Louis Trade Territory, 1924; The City (with Stuart A. Queen), 1939; Global Geography (with George T. Renner), 1944. Home: 7556 Stanford St., University City 5, Mo. Office: Washington U., St. Louis. Died Feb. 13, 1950; buried Oak Grove Cemetery (The Chapel), St. Louis.

THOMAS, Percy H(olbrook), elec. engr.; b. Boston, Mar. 31, 1872; s. James Francis and Lurinda Brown (Holbrook) T.; B.S. in Elec. Engring., Mass. Inst. Tech., 1893; m. Isabelle Mary Patten, 1900. With engring. dept., Westinghouse Electric & Mfg. Co., Pitts., 1893-1902; chief engr. Cooper-Hewitt Electric Co., 1903-07, and consulting engr., 1907-16; consulting elec. engr. Guggenheim Bros., 1916-23; practicing on own account, 1928-34; chief of power requirements div. of Nat. Power Survey of Fed. Power Commn., 1934-37; regional dir. Atlantic office Fed. Power Commn., 1937-41; with Office of Chief Engr., Washington, D.C., 1941-49, ret. Patentee. Fellow American Inst. E.E.; mem. Am. Soc. M.E., Delta Upsilon. Unitarian. Home: 3051 Idaho Av. Office: Federal Power Commn., Washington, D.C. Died Mar. 1957.

THOMAS, Samuel, iron mfr.; b. Yniscedwin, Brecknockshire, N. Wales, March 13, 1927; came to U.S., June, 1938; ed. at Nazareth Hall, Nazareth, Pa.; trained as machinist; became expert in construction of furnaces; supt., 1854-64, and pres., 1864-87, Thomas Iron Co., Catasauqua, Pa.; pres., 1865-94, and since then v.p. Pioneer Mining and Mfg. Co., Birmingham, Ala. Mem., 1871— (v.p. 1880-01) Am. Inst. Mining Eng'rs. Address; Catasauqua, Pa. Deceased.

THOMAS, Stephen Seymour, artist; b. San Augustine, Tex., Aug. 20, 1868; s. James Edwards and Mary Landon (Blount) T.; student Art Students League, 1885-88, Académie Julien, Paris, 1888-91; pupil of Jules Lefebre and Benjamin Constant; A.M., Williams Coll., 1914; m. Helen M. Haskell, Oct. 11, 1892 (died May 5, 1942). Represented by portraits of Lord Bryce, National Liberal Club, London, Eng.; Cardinal O'Connell; Dr. Arthur Noyes and Dr. Frederick Moore, Massachusetts Institute of Technology; General Lew Wallace, John Herron Museum, Indianapolis; President Woodrow Wilson, White House, and State House, N.J.; Mrs. Seymour Thomas "Lady and Dog," Met. Museum of Art; "Lady with Muff," Albright Gallery, Buffalo; Equestrian portrait of Gen. Sam Houston, Houston Art Museum; James Sheffield, U.S. Ambassador to Mexico, Yale Club, New York; Darwin P. Kingsley, pres. of N.Y. Life Ins. Co.; Mrs. Andrew Carnegie private gallery, New York; Dr. Donald Cowling, Carleton Coll., Minn.; Judge Abner Thomas, Surrogate Court, New York; Francis Lynde Stetson, Bar Assn., New York; James Mabon, N.Y. Stock Exchange; Judge William H. Moore, Calumet Club, Chicago; Dr. Geo. Ellery Hale, Acad. of Sciences, Washington, D.C.; Dr. Wm. Wallace Campbell, U. of Calif., Dr. Ellwood Cuberly and Mrs. Cuberly, Stanford U.; group portrait Drs. Robert A. Millikan, George Ellery Hale and Arthur Noyes, Calif. Inst. of Tech.; Bishop Joseph H.

Johnson, Good Samaritan Hosp., Los Angeles; Mrs. John P. Jones, Los Angeles Museum; Mildred Lee, Smithsonian Institution, "Victime Innocente," St. Vincent's Hosp., L.A., Mrs. O'Connor, Dallas Mus. Art, Col. S. W. Blount, Tex. Hist. Soc.; portraits Mr. and Mrs. George H. Maxwell, Maxwell School of Citizenship, Syracuse U.; Mrs. Alex Morrison, of Calif.; Dr. Howard C. Nafziger, pres. Am. Coll. of Surgeons; 2 portraits of Darwin Kingsley, N.Y. Chamber of Commerce and N.Y. Lifs Ins. Co.; Dr. Robert Gordon Sproul, pres. U. of Calif.; Mrs. Joseph Sartori, regent U. of Calif.; F. F. Prentiss, Chamber Commerce, Cleveland; Wm. G. Mather, Cliff Iron Works, Cleveland; 2d portrait of Mr. Mather, Trinity College, Conn.; portrait of Dr. Wm. B. Munro, California, Institute Technology; Dr. Robert G. Cleland, Occidental Coll., Los Angeles; The Black Pearl, Los Angeles Museum. Honorary mention Paris Salon, 1895, gold medal 1901 and 1904; Hors Concours Salon, 1904; bronze medal, Paris Expn., 1900; bronze medal, Buffalo Expn., 1901; Chevalier of the Legion of Honor, 1905; mem. Internat. Jury of Awards, St. Louis, 1904. Mem. Paris Soc. of Am. Painters, Los Angeles Art Assn., Pasadena Art Soc., Acad. of Western Painters. Clubs: Century (New York); Athenæum, University (Pasadena). Home: 4617 Rosemont Av., La Crescenta, Cal. Died Mar. 1956.

THOMAS, Wilbur Kelsey, humanitarian; b. Amboy, Ind., Dec. 21, 1882; son Isaac and Eliza Jane (Shockney) T.; A.B., Friends U., Wichita, Kansas, 1904; grad. study Brown U., 1904-05; B.D., Yale, 1907; Ph.D., Boston U., 1914; LL.D., Friends U., 1939; m. Elizabeth Folger, Aug. 16, 1905; children—Elizabeth Jane, Helen, Thomas Folger. Exec. dir. Am. Friends Service Com. (Quaker), 1918-28; exec. dir. Carl Schurz Memorial Foundation, Inc., 1930-46: trustee Oberlaender Trust since 1931; trustee John Greenleaf Whittier Homestead since 1932; pres. Pa. Forestry Assn. 1939-47; pastor Congregational Church, Otis, Mass., 1947. Home: Monterey, Mass. Died Apr. 15, 1953; buried Corashire Cemetery, Monterey.

THOMAS, William Aubrey, ex-congressman; b. Wales, June 7, 1866; s. John R. and Margaret (Morgan) T.; Mt. Union (O.) Coll., 1883-85; Rensselaer Poly. Inst., 1886-88; unmarried. Chemist in lab. of blast furnace, 1888-90; mgr. Thomas Furnace Co., 1890-98; pres. Minerva Pig Iron Co., 1898-1900, operating blast furnace at Milw., which was taken over by Thomas Furnace Co.; v.p. Thomas Furnace Co., 1900—, Niles Fire Brick Co. Mem. City Council, 1892-96; elected 58th Congress, Nov., 1904, for unexpired term (1904-05, of Charles Dick, reelected 59th to 61st Congresses (1905-11), 19th Ohio Dist. Republican. Address: Talladega, Ala. Sept. 8, 1951.

THOMPSON, Alexander Marshall, judge; b. Canandaigua, N.Y., Sept. 27, 1872; s. Samuel Huston and Martha Jane (McIlwain) T.; A.B., Princeton, 1893; LL.M., U. Pitts., 1918, L.D., 1940; m. Melvina Graff, June 10, 1914. Admitted to Pa. bar, 1897, since practiced in Pitts.; served as 1st asst. city solicitor, Pittsburgh; dean Law Sch., U. Pitts.; judge Court of Common Pleas of Allegheny County, Pa., 1938—; v.p. Scott Graff Lumber Co., Duluth. Minn. Area sec. overseas work, Y.M.C.A. at Inverness, Scotland, World War. Trustee Grove City (Pa.) Coll. Mem. Liquor Control Board of Pa. at organization. Mem. Am. Law Inst., Philos. Soc., Polygon Club. Democrat. Presbyterian. Clubs: Kitchie Gammi, Northland Country (Duluth, Minn.); University, Duquesne (Pitts.); Butler Country (Butler, Pa.). Home: Schenley Apts., Pitts. 13. Office: 707 City County Bldg., Pitts. Died Sept. 21, 1958; buried Homewood Cemetery, Pitts.

THOMPSON, Arthur Scott, lawyer; b. Farlinville, Kan., Apr. 20, 1876; s. John Walker and Nancy Ann (Brown) T.; LL.B., U. Mich., 1902; m. Elsie Peery, June 26, 1904; children—John David (dec.), Virginia (dec.), Joseph Stuart, Daniel Scott. Admitted to Okla. bar, 1902, and since practiced in Miami; specializes in mining and corp. law; gen. counsel Commerce Mining & Royalty Co. Del. Rep. Nat. Conv., 1928. Mem. Am., Okla. State bar assns. Methodist. Mason (32°). Clubs: Rotary, Miami Country. Home: Miami, Okla. Died Oct. 19, 1949.

THOMPSON, Cecil Vincent Raymond, journalist; b. London, Eng., Jan. 3, 1906; s. Edward Raymond and Elsie Mabel (Watts) T.; ed. Taunton School, Somerset, Eng., 1916-19, Westminster School, London, 1919-25; m. Dixie Tighe, April 7, 1934; married 2d, Sallyann Meenan, 1946; children—Susan, E. Raymond. Reporter for the London Daily Express, 1926-28, sub-editor, 1928-29, asst. news editor, 1929-33, Am. corr. since 1933. Pres. Foreign Press Assn., 1944-45. Received Selfridge award for descriptive writing, 1931. Episcopalian. Author: I Lost My English Accent, 1939; Trousers Will Be Worn, 1941; How to Like An Englishman, 1946. Home: Sunset Road, Stamford, Connecticut. Office: 50 Rockefeller Plaza, N.Y.C. Died June, 1951.

THOMPSON, Charles Fullington, army officer; b. Jamestown, N.D., Dec. 11, 1882; s. John Justin and Ida May (Fullington) T.; student U. of Mich., 1899-1900; B.A., U.S. Mil. Acad., 1904; m. Laura Bell Jenks, Apr. 29, 1909; children—Marjorie Fullington (Mrs. Howard Eugene Engler), Barbara Jenks (Mrs. J. Maury Dove, Jr.). Commd. 2d lt., Inf., June 15, 1904; advanced through grades to maj. gen., Oct. 1, 1940, retired Nov. 30, 1945. Inclusive of 10 yrs. overseas, service comprises 18 yrs. with troops, 14 yrs. on high staffs, 2 yrs. as student and 7 yrs. on faculties. Decorated D.S.M., with two Oak Leaf Clusters; Companion Military Division, Most Honourable Order of the Bath (British). Chevalier Legion of Honor (French). Clubs: Chevy Chase (Md.); Army and Navy (Washington). Home: Kenneday-Warren Apts., Washington 8. Died June 15, 1954; buried Arlington Nat. Cemetery.

THOMPSON, Charles Impey, lawyer; b. Mont Clare, Pa., Aug. 25, 1899; s. Joseph Whitaker and Anna (Williamson) T.; A.B., U. Pa., 1921, LL.B., 1924; m. Anna Miriam Farnum, Apr. 5, 1926; children—Charles Impey, Joseph W. II, Henry Farnum. Admitted to Pa. bar, 1924, since practiced in Phila.; partner Ballard, Spahr, Andrews & Ingersoll; lectr. Pa. Law Sch., 1924-31; asst. dist. atty. Phila. County, 1926-29. Dir. Provident Tradesmen's Bank & Trust Co., Fidelity Mut. Life Ins. Co., Tex. Eastern Transmission Corp., Algonquin Gas Transmission Co., Kan., Okla. & Gulf R.R.; trustee Mut. Assurance Co., Stock Ins. Co. of Green Tree; bd. mgrs. Western Savs. Fund Soc. Pres. Fairmount Park Commn.; dir. Phila. Zool Soc.; trustee Phila. Mus. Art; asso. trustee U. Pa.; bd. mgrs. U. Pa. Grad. Hosp. Served with USNRF, World War I; mem. Pa. N.G., 1924-35. Mem. Am., Pa., Phila. bar assns., Lawyers Club, Legal Club. Episcopalian. Clubs: Philadelphia, Union League (Phila.); Racquet, Sunnybrook Golf, Metropolitan (Washington); Shreveport (La.). Home: 8862 Towanda St., Chestnut Hill, Phila. 18. Office: Land Title Bldg., Phila. 10. Died Aug. 3, 1958.

THOMPSON, Charles Nebeker, lawyer; b. Covington, Ind., July 7, 1861; s. William and Hannah (Nebeker) T.; A.B., DePauw U., 1882, A.M., 1885; m. Julia Finch Conner, Oct. 7, 1891 (died Oct. 26, 1928). Admitted to Ind. Bar, 1885, practiced Indpls.; pres. Ind. Savings & Investment Co. Mem. Ind. Senate, 1900-04. Mem. Ind. Library and Hist. Commn., 1925-33; mem. State Library and Hist. Bldg. Commn., 1929-34. Mem. bd. of trustees DePauw U. Mem. Am., Indpls. bar assns., Am. Hist. Assn. (life), Soc. of Ind. Pioneers (life), Ind. Hist. Soc., Phi Kappa Psi, Phi Beta Kappa. Republican. Presbyterian. Clubs: Columbia, Indianapolis Literary, Contemporary. Author: Thompson on Building Associations, 1892-99; Sons of the Wilderness—John and William Conner, 1937. Established and endowed The Julia Conner Thompson Memorial Collection on the Finer Arts of Home Making in Indianapolis Public Library. Home: 3650 Washington Blvd., Indianapolis; (summer) The Meadows, Harbor Springs, Mich. Office: Fletcher Trust Bldg., Indpls. Died Aug. 16, 1949; buried Crown Hill Cemetery, Indpls.

THOMPSON, C(harles) Seymour, librarian; b. Orange, N.J., Nov. 8, 1879; s. Wilmot Haines and Laura Pamela (Garrigues) T.; B.A., Yale, 1902; m. Elizabeth Skirm Howell, June 24, 1909; 1 dau., Olive. With Pub. Library, Brooklyn, N.Y., 1903-11; asst. librarian Pub. Library, Washington, D.C., 1911-16; librarian Savannah Pub. Library, 1916-24; dir. nat. library survey made by A.L.A., 1924-27; reference and asst. librarian Univ. of Pa. Library, 1927-31, librarian, 1931-45; now retired. Mem. Hist. Soc. Pa., Christian Scientist. Editor: A Survey of Libraries in the United States (4 vols.), 1926-27; Life of Robert Montgomery Bird, written by Mary Mayer Bird. Home: 21 President Av., Rutledge, Pa. Died Nov. 22, 1954.

THOMPSON, Clara, physician, psychiatrist; b. Providence, Oct. 3, 1893; d. Thomas Franklin and Clara Louise (Medbery) Thompson; A.B., Brown U., 1916; M.D., Johns Hopkins, 1920. Intern Phipps Clinic, Johns Hopkins Hosp., 1920-21, N.Y. Infirmary for Women and Children, N.Y.C., 1921-22; instr. 29; asst. exec. dir. Washington Sch. Psychiatry, 1943-psychiatry, med. sch. Johns Hopkins, 1924-25; asso. mental hygiene Inst. Euthenics, Vassar Coll., 1928-29; asst. exec. dir. Washington Sch. Psychiatry, 1943-46; exec. dir. William Alanson White Inst. Psychiatry, Psychoanalysis and Psychology, N.YC., 1946—. Pub. lectr. psychiatry and human relations before med. and lay groups. Trustee William Alanson White Psychiatric Found., Washington; trustee, pres. bd. trustees William Alanson White Inst. Psychiatry, Psychoanalysis and Psychology. Fellow Am. Psychiatric Assn.; mem. American Psychoanalytic Assn., American Psychopathological Association, Phi Beta Kappa, Sigma Xi. Author: Psychoanalysis: Evolution and Development, 1950; also numerous sci. papers. Home: 2 E. 86th St. Office: 12 E. 86th St., N.Y.C. 28. Died Dec. 1958.

THOMPSON, Clem Oren, educator; b. Millgrove, Ind., Sept. 28, 1888; s. Andrew and Clara Nesbit (Orndorff) T.; A.B., Ind. State Normal Coll., 1913; A.M., U. Chicago, 1920, Ph.D., 1930; m. Flora Williams, June 29, 1915 (died 1936); m. 2d, Olive LeGassick, Aug. 14, 1937. Rural sch. teacher, Jay and Blackford counties, Ind., 1906-10; teacher Salem (Ind.) High Sch., 1912-16, prin., 1916-18, supt. schs., 1918-19; head dept. edn., dir. summer session and extension activities Hanover (Ind.) Coll., 1920-23; head dept. edn. and chmn. faculty com. on extension activities Ealham Coll., Richmond, Ind., 1923-25; prof. edn., Ball State Tchrs. Coll., Muncie, Ind., 1925-29, acting head dept. edn., 1926-27, dir. extension div., 1930; instr. U. Chicago, 1930-31, asst. prof. edn. and counselor of dept., 1931-37, asst. dean Univ. Coll., 1935-44, asst. dir. Home Study Dept., 1937-44, acting dir., 1944-45, dir. since 1945. Fellow A.A. A.S.; mem. Nat. Univ. Extension Assn. (past mem. exec. com.; chmn. com. on corr. study 1946-48), N.E. A. (life mem.; mem. adult edn. dept.), Ind. Acad. Sci., Adult Edn. Council of Greater Chicago (dir.), Phi Delta Kappa. Club: Quadrangle (Chicago). Author: Extension Program of the University of Chicago 1932; (co author) University Extension Services, 1932; University Extension in Adult Education, 1943. Home: 6011 Kimbark Av., Chgo. 37. Deceased.

THOMPSON, Edward Archibald, clergyman; b. Chandler Twp. (Caseville), Mich., Nov. 25, 1884; s. Neil and Jane (Maxwell) T.; grad. Ferris Inst., Big Rapids, Mich., 1909; Ph.B., Alma (Mich.) Coll., 1913; grad. study, Edinburgh (Scotland) U., 1913-14; B.D., Yale, 1916; grad. study, U. Chgo., summer 1922; D.D., Olivet (Mich.) Coll., 1921; m. Elsie Hanchett, Aug. 6, 1913; children—Jean Maxwell (Mrs. Henry Fredrik Andersson), Katy Mariel (Mrs. Bernard Holmes Bradley). Student asst. and student minister various churches, 1913-16; minister First Congl. Church, Greeley, Colo., 1916-18; Y.M.C.A. sec., U.S. Army camps, 1917-19; minister First Union Congl. Ch., Quincy, Ill., 1919-23; First Congl. Church, LaGrange, Ill., 1923-29, First Congl. Ch., Pasadena, Calif., 1929-33, First (Park) Congl. Ch., Grand Rapids, Mich., 1933-52, emeritus; mem. staff 1st Congl. Ch., Los Angeles, 1952-54. Dir. Chgo. Theol. Sem., 1928-52; pres. bd. trustees, Congl. Conf. of Ill., 1928-29; pres. Tower Hill Assn., 1924-27; chmn. finance com. Congl. Conf. of Southern Calif., 1930-33; pres. advisory bd. Chgo. Congl. Assn., 1927-28; dir. Chgo. Congl. Union, 1928-29; pres. Lions Club, Quincy, Ill., 1922-23; dir. Kiwanis Club, La Grange, Ill., 1927-29, Rotary Club, Pasadena and Grand Rapids, 1930-39; moderator Mich. Congl. Conf., 1938-39; trustee Mich. Congl. Conf., 1940-51; mem. exec. com. Gen. Council Congl. Christian Chs., 1938-44, chmn. finance com. and v. chmn. Republican. Mason (32°, K.T.). Club: Wranglers (Pasadena). Home: 694 Priscilla Way, Claremont, Cal. Retired. Died June 7, 1959; buried Big Rapids, Mich.

THOMPSON, Eliza Jane Trimble, temperance crusader, writer; b. Hillsboro, O., Aug. 24, 1816; d. ex-Gov. Allen Trimble of Ohio; m. Hon. James H. Thompson. Attended 1st Nat. Temperance Conv., Saratoga, 1836. When Ohio crusade against rum was contemplated, 1873, Mrs. Thompson and Mrs. McDowell (wife of Gen. McDowell) led the 1st praying band in the streets of Hillsboro, O., Mrs. Thompson making the 1st prayer in a Hillsboro saloon; is, therefore, known as The Mother of the Crusade. Mem. advisory council, World's Congress of Representative Women, 1893. Author: Hillsboro Crusade Sketches; Family Records. Address: Hillsboro, O. Died Nov. 3, 1905.

THOMPSON, (Mrs.) Elizabeth McArthur, trustee The Christian Science Pub. Soc.; b. Hudson, N.Y.; d. George Powers and Carolyn Lefferts (Webb) McArthur; ed. pub. schs.; special tutors in languages; extension courses in music; C.S.B., Mass. Metaphysical Coll., 1928; m. John Grey Thomson, Sept. 18, 1905; 1 dau., Elizabeth Antoinette (Mrs. Albert D. Swazey). Social service rep., 1907-09; probation officer, Juvenile Court, St. Louis, 1910-12; exec. sec., Food Adminstrn. Office, St. Louis, 1916-18; professional singer in concert and church, 1905—; Christian Science practitioner, 1918, teacher, 1928—, lecturer, 1938-44; mem. bd. of trustees, The Christian Science Pub. Soc., 1945—. Charter mem. League of Women Voters. Clubs: Women's City (Boston); Park Avenue (New York); Republican Women's. Contbr. articles to Christian Science periodicals. Office: 1 Norway Street, Boston 15. Died 1956.

THOMPSON, Frank Abner, lawyer; b. St. Louis County, Mo., Oct. 4, 1880; s. Frank A. and Kate (Edmonstone) Thompson; LL.B., University of Michigan, 1904; m. Olive A. Jacques, Oct. 19, 1910; children—Jacqueline, Frank Abner, Amanda Noel. Admitted to Mo. bar, 1904, and began practice, St. Louis, Mo.; now member Thompson, Mitchell, Thompson & Douglas, St. Louis; chmn. bd. dir. St. Louis & San Francisco Ry. Co., since 1947; director and counsel Bank of St. Louis, Gen. Contract Corp. Dir. Frisco Transportation Co. Dir. Comml. Industrial Bank, Memphis, Tenn. Democratic nominee for Congress, 1908; judge St. Louis Court of Appeals, 1916-17; mem. Bd. of Freeholders, St. Louis and St. Louis County, 1925-26; apptd. spl. asst. to atty. gen. of U.S., 1933; apptd. by judge of U.S. Dist. Court as counsel for trustee St. Louis-San Francisco Ry. Co., apptd. trustee, July 8, 1943. Member American, Missouri State and St. Louis bar associations, Phi Delta Theta, Phi Delta Phi. Democrat. Clubs: Optimist, Noonday, Mo. Athletic, St. Louis Country. Home: 20 N. Kingshighway. Office: 705 Olive St., St. Louis. Died Feb. 7, 1958.

THOMPSON, Frederick Ingate, newspaper pub.; b. Aberdeen, Miss., Sept. 29, 1875; s. Edward P. and Laura (Cox) T.; ed. pub. schs., Aberdeen; m. Adrianna Ingate, Feb. 5, 1900. Editor Aberdeen Weekly, 1892-95, Weekly Commercial Appeal, Memphis, Tenn., 1897-1902; mem. Smith & Thompson, newspaper reps., New York and Chicago, 1902-08; chief owner and pub. Mobile Daily (morning) and Sunday Register, 1909-32; chief owner and pub. Mobile News-Item (evening), 1916-32, Montgomery (Ala.) Journal (evening), since 1922, also Birmingham (Ala.) Daily (morning) and Sunday Age-Herald, 1922-27. Dir. The Associated Press. Apptd. member Ala. Ednl. Commn., 1919. Mem. Dem. Nat. Conv., 1912, 24 and 28. Apptd. commr. U.S. Shipping Bd. by President Wilson, 1920, reappointed by President Harding, 1921, and by President Coolidge, 1923; resigned, Nov. 1925; apptd. by President Roosevelt, mem. Advisory Board on Pub. Works, 1933; apptd. by President Roosevelt Commr. Federal Communications Commn., 1939; mem. Ala. State Docks Commn. since 1935. Pres. Seaboard Investment Co. Episcopalian. Home: 1621 Spring Hill Av., Mobile, Ala. Died Feb. 1952; buried Magnolia Cemetery.

THOMPSON, Guy A., lawyer; b. St. Louis County, Mo., Sept. 29, 1875; s. Frank A. and Kate (Edmonstone) T.; LL.B., U. of Mo., 1898; LL.D., 1932; m. Susan Alexander, June 11, 1903 (now dec.); children—Mrs. Kate Edmonstone Borders, Mrs. Lucy Montfort Smith, Alexander Campbell, Edmonstone Field, Mrs. Susan Elizabeth Peschka; m. 2d, Forence Streett Shields, 1933. Admitted to Mo. bar, 1898; practiced, St. Louis, with Campbell & Ryan, 1898-99; with Hon. Given Campbell, 1899-1903, partner, 1903-05; mem. Thompson & Campbell (Jas. C.), 1905-06; practiced alone, 1906-11; with Judge O'Neill Ryan, mem. firm Ryan & Thompson, 1911-17; with brother Frank A., mem. Thompson & Thompson, 1917-29, Thompson, Mitchell, Thompson & Douglas, 1929—; trustee of Mo. Pacific R.R. System, 1933-56. Mem. 7th Distrist Legal Advisory Draft Bd., 1917-18. Mem. board of curators Missouri State U., 1945-51. Mem. Am. Bar Assn. (pres. 1931-32), Mo. Bar Assn. (ex-pres.), Bar Assn. of St. Louis (ex-pres.), Am. Law Inst., Am. Judicature Soc., Am. Soc. Internat. Law, Seldon Soc. London, St. Louis C. of C., Phi Beta Kappa, Phi Delta Theta, Phi Delta Phi, Order of Coif. Democrat. Presbyterian. Clubs: Noonday, St. Louis Country Club. Has been author of various addresses and articles on legal subjects. One of organizers, and chmn. survey com. Mo. Assn. for Criminal Justice, which made first state-wide crime survey in U.S. Has served as spl. judge of Supreme Court of Mo. Address: 40 North Kingshighway, St. Louis. Died Jan. 26, 1958; buried Fee Fee Cemetery, St. Louis County, Mo.

THOMPSON, Harry LeRoy, naval officer (ret.); b. Gibraltar, Pa., Mar. 18, 1890; s. Heber Clouser and Emma Fawkes (Wicklein) T.; grad. Naval War Coll., 1929, U.S. Naval Acad. Postgrad. Sch., 1930; m. Kathryn Dunleavy, Jan. 5, 1913; children—Harry LeRoy (Comdr. U.S.N.), Leah (Mrs. James Wilbur White), Jordan (M.D.). Enlisted U.S. Navy, 1906, commd. ensign, 1917, advanced through grades to rear adm., 1947; splized. in communications; comdr. U.S.S. Humphreys, 1931-33, U.S.S. Owl, 1930-31, U.S.S. Nevada, 1941-42, U.S.S. Richmond, 1944-45; ret. from active service, Jan. 1, 1947; now engaged in real estate bus. Awarded combat Legion of Merit. Reformed Ch. Home: 1519 Arlington Terrace, Alexandria, Va. Office: 1505 H St., N.W., Washington. Died Aug. 17, 1953.

THOMPSON, James F(razier), drug exec.; b. Covington, Ky., Nov. 7, 1900; s. James F. and Ada (Perry) T.; B.C.H.E., U. Cincinnati, 1923; m. Edna Weaver, July 14, 1925; children—George Weaver, Robert Perry. Joined Sterling Drug, Inc., Cincinnati, 1945, v.p. since 1949; gen. mgr. Hilton-Davis Chem. Co. (div. Sterling Drug) since 1949. Mem. Am. Chem. Soc., Cincinnati Engring. Soc., Photog. Soc. Am., Sigma Alpha Epsilon. Republican. Presbyn. Club: Chemists (N.Y.C.). Home: 2600 Willowbrook Dr., Amberly Village, Cin. 37. Office: 2235 Langdon Farm Rd., Cin. 12. Died Jan. 11, 1956.

THOMPSON, James Stratton, educator; b. Bedford, Ia., Nov. 13, 1899; s. Seth Edward and Adelaide (Stratton) T.; ScB., U. Chgo., 1922, Ph.D., 1930; studied U. Munich, Germany, summer 1930; m. Mildred Bergren, June 26, 1926; 1 son, James Stratton. Began asst. in physics, Armour Inst. Tech. (now Ill. Inst. Tech.), Chgo., 1924, succesively instr., asst. prof., asso. prof., prof. physics, 1934—, also chmn. dept. physics; physicist Simpson-Breed Radium Inst., 1927—. Served as 2d lt. Heavy Arty., O.R.C., 1919-24. Fellow A.A.A.S. Mem. Am. Phys. Soc., Am. Assn. Physics Tchrs., Chgo. Physics Club (pres. 1943), Am. Soc. Engring. Edn., Swedish Engrs. Soc., Am. Assn. U. Profs., Sigma Alpha Epsilon, Sigma Xi. Presbyn. Contbr. tech. articles. Home: 5540 Kenwood Av. Office: 3300 Federal St., Chgo. Died Aug. 5, 1951.

THOMPSON, James Voorhees, religious edn.; b. Rock Springs, Pa., May 25, 1878; s. Johnathan MacWilliams and Anna Sara (Carpenter) T.; A.B., Wesleyan U., Conn., 1902; B.D., Drew Thoel. Sem., 1905; grad. study, U. of Pittsburgh, 1912-14; Ph.D., Northwestern, 1928; m. Nora Gray, Aug. 18, 1909; m. 2d Mary Young Ruffin, Aug. 12, 1951. Student pastor Bronxdale M.E. Ch., N.Y. City, 1903-04; asst. minister and dir. religious edn. (first recorded in U.S.), Christ M.E. Ch., Pittsburgh, 1905-07; ordained ministry M.E. Ch., 1907; teacher Shadyside Acad., Pittsburgh, 1908-12, Peabody High Sch., Pittsburgh, 1912-14; supt. young people's dept. Bd. of Sunday Schs., M.E. Ch., 1914-25; instr. dept. religious edn., Boston U., 1918; agt. World's Sunday Sch. Assn. and Bd. of Sunday Schs. M.E. Ch. in Japan, Korea and China, 1920-21; asso. minister and dir. religious edn., First M.E. Ch., Evanston, Ill., 1925-28; asst. prof. religious edn., Northwestern U., 1928-29, asso. prof., 1929-30; prof. adminstr. in religious edn., Drew Theol. Sem., 1930-48; ret.; counselor div. inter-religious activities Am. Jewish Com., N.Y.C., 1948-52; dir. Coll. of Religious Edn. and Missions, same, 1931-35. Active National Conference Christians and Jews. Served as corporal Spanish-Am. War, 1898; chaplain 325th Inf., 82d Div., A.E.F., June-Oct. 1918, sr. chaplain 2d Army Corps, Oct. 1918-19; mem. O.R.C. Decorated capt. Order of the Silver Palms (France), also Officer of Academy. Mem. Religious Edn. Assn., Internat. Council Religious Edn., Alpha Delta Phi, Phi Delta Kappa, Ind. Rep. Mason (32°). Club: University (Evanston). Author: Handbook for Workers with Young People, 1921; The Daily Vacation Church School (with J. E. Stout), 1923; Studies in Religious Education (with Lotz and others), 1931; Orientation in Education (with Schutte and others), 1932; Great Biographies (with Lotz and others), 1938; Making the Gospel Effective (with Anderson and others), 1944. Editor and author of "The Open Door Series" (guidance pamphlets for adolescents and their leaders). Lecturer on religious edn. Home: 22 Irving Pl., N.Y.C. Died. July 1, 1952; buried State College, Pa.

THOMPSON, John, newspaper publisher; b. Elkton, Ky., Dec. 20, 1873; s. Thomas Edward and Lucy (Smith) T.; ed. public and private schools, Elkton; m. Minnie Herbert; m. 2d, Beatrice Davies; children—John, Jr., Jane Ann, Laura May. Reporter Times-Herald, Chicago, 1899; with business office of N.Y. Time , 1900-08; mng. editor Pearson's Mag., 1908-16; sec. J. J. Little & Ives, New York, book mfrs., 1916-21; publisher Minneapolis Star and Tribune. Methodist. Clubs: Lafayette, Minneapolis, Minikahda, Minneapolis Athletic. Home: 2115 E. Lake of Isles Blvd. Office: 425 Portland Av., Mpls. Died Apr. 17, 1958.

THOMPSON, John Winter, organist; b. Mich., Dec. 21, 1867; s. George and Martha (Cook) T.; grad. Oberlin Conservatory of Music, 1890, Mus.B., 1906; grad. Royal Conservatory, Leipzig, Germany, 1894; Mus.D., Knox Coll., 1909; m. Mary J. Moon, June 11, 1891 (died 1932); children—Edyth, Helen Mildred; m. 2d, Jessie Lynde Hopkins, June 12, 1935. Prof. music, Knox Coll. Conservatory, Galesburg, Illinois, 1890—; organist Central Congl. Ch., Galesburg. Many organ recitals in Middle West. Pres. Ill. Music Teachers' Assn. 3 terms. Republican. Conglist. Composer: Cathedral Echoes (16 organ compositions); A Course in Harmony; A Course in Counterpoint; also songs, anthems, etc. Home: 982 N. Cedar St. Office: Knox Conservatory of Music, Galesburg, Ill. Died Mar. 8, 1951; buried Meml. Park, Galesburg.

THOMPSON, Joseph Addison, coll. pres.; b. Ross Grove, De Kalb County, Ill., Feb. 8, 1860; s. Rev. Samuel F. and Ellen Kerr (Given) T.; A.B., Monmouth Coll., 1882, A.M., 1885; student Allegheny Sem., 1883-85; Princeton Theol. Sem., 1885-86; D.D., Westminster Coll., Pa., 1891; LL.D., Cedarville Coll., 1917; L.H.D., Monmouth Coll., 1939; m. Lillian Esther Logan, Dec. 30, 1886 (died Jan. 2, 1888); m. 2d, Lillie Olivia Woodling, July 14, 1891 (died July 24, 1938); children—Mary Lyon, Mrs. J. J. Osuna, Elizabeth Thompson Koppenaal (M.D.). Ordained U.P. ministry, 1886; pastor Chetopa, Kan., 1886-87; pres. Tarkio Coll., 1887-1930, pres. emeritus 1930—. Moderator 49th Gen. Assembly, U.P. Church, 1901; mem. 9th Gen. Council, Alliance Reformed Chs. Holding the Presbyn. System, New York, 1909; pres. Y.M.C.A. Conf. for Missouri, 1911; trustee Anti-Saloon League Mo., 1910—; mem. conv. Fed. Council Chs. of Christ in America, St. Louis, 1916; mem. Nat. Council Y.M.C.A., 1925-27; treas. Living Endowment Soc., Tarkio Coll.; mem. bd. dirs. Pittsburgh-Xenia Theol. Seminary, 1937-46. Home: 352 S. York St., Elmhurst, Illinois. Died July 11, 1957; buried Tarkio, Mo.

THOMPSON, Joseph Osgood, physicist; b. Weymouth, Mass., July 29, 1863; s. Samuel and Mary Ann (Eaton) T.; student Thayer Acad., S. Braintree, Mass., 1878-79; B.A., Amherst Coll., 1884; Ph.D., U. of Strassburg, Germany, 1891; courtesy fellow, Yale, 1920; m. Lulu Lester Burbank, May 22, 1912; children—Rebecca Burbank, Samuel Mountfort. Teacher of science, Park Coll., Parkville, Mo., 1884-86; asst. in physics, Amherst Coll., 1886-87, instr. in mathematics, 1887-89; instr. in physics, Haverford (Pa.) Coll., 1891-94; asso. prof. physics, Amherst Coll., 1894-1918, prof., 1918-28, emeritus prof., 1928—. Fellow A.A.A.S., Am. Physical Soc.; mem. Phi Beta Kappa. Republican. Conglist. Club: Faculty. Established law of elastic lengthening in metals. Home: 209 Lincoln Av., Amherst, Mass. Died Dec. 12, 1953.

THOMPSON, Lewis Ryers, asst. surgeon gen.; b. LaFayette, Ind., Aug. 6, 1883; s. Lewis Ryers and Laura (Steuben) T.; M.D., Louisville Med. Coll., 1905; married Mabel Cook, February 22, 1908; children—Lewis Ryers, Joyce Ann. Member Philippine Constabulary, 1906-09; United States Public Health Service, 1910—, assistant surgeon, 1910, passed assistant surgeon, 1914, surgeon, 1921, senior surgeon, 1930, asst. surgeon gen., 1930-42; dir. National Institute of Health, 1937-42, inspection officer 1943, asst. surg. gen. Bureau of State Service, 1943-45; dir. med. div., Strategic Bombing Survey of Japan, 1945; rank of brigadier general; consultant medical services of the American Red Cross 1947—. Was scientific dir. Internat. Health Div., Rockefeller Foundn. Mem. div. of med. scis. Nat. Rsrch. Council. Fel. Am. Coll. Dentists; mem. A.M.A., Am. Pub. Health Assn., Indsl. Phys. and Surgs., Phi Chi. Episcopalian. Club: Columbia Country. Author of numerous arts. and bulletins on med. subjects. Home: 3917 Virgilia St., Chevy Chase, Md. Address: U.S. Public Health Service, Bethesda Sta., Washington. Died Nov. 12, 1954; buried Arlington Nat. Cemetery, Va.

THOMPSON, Maurice Wycliffe; b. Crawfordsville, Ind., Aug. 27, 1878; s. Will H. and Ida (Lee) T.; student U. Washington, 1896-97; m. Ada Forsey, Mar. 14, 1907; children—Alma (dec. 1918), Wilda (dec.), Betty (Mrs. Carroll Barton McMath, Jr.). Mem. Washington N.G., 1898—, advanced through grades to rank maj. gen.; appt. adj. gen. State of Wash., with rank of brig. gen., 1914, and served until retirement, 1941; acting adj. gen., 1945-47. Served in adj. gen's. dept. U.S. Army, with rank of maj., World War I. Supt. State Soldiers Home, Orting, Wash., 1941-47; state dir. S.S.S., 1917, 1940-41. Awarded certificate of merit and selective service medal, 1946. Mem. Mil. Order of the World Wars, Am. Legion, S.A.R. Elk. Club: Lions (Orting, Wash.). Address: 9115 Gravelly Lake Drive, South Tacoma, Wash. Died Nov. 3, 1954; buried Lakeview Cemetery, Seattle.

THOMPSON, Reuben Cyril Hill, educator; b. Wasco County, Ore., Apr. 30, 1878; s. Rufus and Adaline (Hill) T.; A.B., McMinnville (Ore.) Coll., 1899; A.B., Harvard, 1901, A.M., 1902; LL.D., Linfield Coll., McMinnville, Ore., 1938; m. Mabel Elizabeth McLeran, June 14, 1905; children—Alfred Lair (dec.), Doris, Bruce, Mary Adaline, Gordon. Teacher of Latin and history, high sch., Boise, Ida., 1902-05, State Normal Sch., Albion, Ida., 1905-08; instr. Latin and Greek, U. Nev., 1908, asst. prof., 1909, asso. prof., 1910, prof., 1914, prof. philosophy, 1915-48, also head of dept., dean of men, 1932-48, retired. Chmn. com. on publs. of war council, U. Nev., 1917; speaker for A.R.C. and Liberty Loan. Mem. Enemy Alien Hearings Bd. for Nev. Mem. Am. Assn. U. Profs., Am. Philos. Assn., Phi Kappa Phi. Democrat. Baptist. Mason, Odd Fellow. Author: Introduction to Philosophy, 1935. Home: 1101 Riverside Av., Reno. Died Sept. 12, 1951.

THOMPSON, Robert LeRoy, clergyman, educator; b. Ticonderoga, N.Y., Feb. 25, 1873; s. Orlo and Emma A. (Preston) T.; prep. edn., Troy Conf. Acad., Poultney, Vt., 1893; student Wesleyan U., Conn., 1893-94; A.B., Middlebury (Vt.) Coll., 1899; D.D., Wesleyan, 1922; m. H. Lillian Adams, Dec. 25, 1894; children—Grace Lillian (Mrs. Robert L. Pallmerine), Mabel Adams (Mrs. Howard S. Maguire), Mildred Ruth (Mrs. Leonard S. Inskip), Alice Elizabeth (Mrs. Charles W. Fuller), Robert LeRoy, Helen Harriett, Orlo Lewis. Entered M.E. ministry, 1899; pastor Brandon (Vt.), Granville, Johnstown and Troy (N.Y.), 1901-19; supt. Albany and Southern dists., Troy Conf. M.E. Ch., 1919-23; prin. Troy Conf. Acad., 1923—. Mem. Delta Kappa Epsilon. Republican. Mason (K.T., Shriner); mem. Modern Woodmen of America. Home: Poultney, Vt. Died Aug. 29, 1937; buried Dalton, Mass.

THOMPSON, Roy Leland, banker; b. Gilsburg, Miss., Jan. 10, 1891; s. John Wilkes and Emma Gertrude (Tate) T.; B.S., La. State U., 1922; M.S., U. of Wis., 1924; Ph.D., U. of Minn., 1929; m. Eunice Holland Pierce, 1916; m. 2d, Douglas May Green, Aug. 1, 1935; children—Sue Ann, John, Wilsie, Roy L. Jr. Prin. high school, Spring Creek, 1915-17, Chesbrough, 1918-19, Centerville, 1922-23; prof. economics, La. State U., 1923-32, prof. and head dept. Economics, 1932-33; field organizer, Production Credit Division of Farm Credit Administration, Regional director, Division Program Planning, Washington, D.C., 1933-34; deputy general agent, Farm Credit Adminstrn., New Orleans, 1934-35, gen. agt., 1935-41; pres. Federal Land Bank of New Orleans, 1938—. Chmn. Price Decontrol Bd., 1946-47. Pvt. U.S. Army, 1917-18. Mem. U.S.D.A. state council for Louisiana. Mam. Alpha Zeta, Delta Sigma Pi, Phi Kappa Phi, Omicron Delta Kappa, Beta Gamma Sigma. Democrat. Baptist. Mason. Club: Boston.

Author agrl. papers. Home: 828 Burdette St. Office: 860 St. Charles, New Orleans. Died Aug. 1, 1955; buried Metairie Cemetery, New Orleans.

THOMPSON, Russell Irvin, coll. adminstr.; b. Reading, Pa., Dec. 29, 1898; s. Dr. Oan Joshua and Sarah Elizabeth (Snyder) T.; A.B., Dickinson Coll., 1920; student Garrett Bibl. Inst., 1920; Ph.D., Yale, 1932; m. Ethel Mae Wright, Aug. 11, 1923. Pastor Grace M.E. Ch., Reading, Pa., 1917-20; vice prin. high sch., Rockwood, Pa., 1921; prof. Greek, psychology Williamsport (Pa.) Dickinson Sem., 1921-24; dir. Wesley House Settlement, New Haven, 1925-28; instr. edn., psychology Dickinson Coll., 1928-31, asso. prof., 1931-40, prof., 1940—, dean sch. family edn., 1933-40, coll. registrar, 1935-41, dir. summer sch. 1942-47, dean, 1947-51, provost, 1951—. Fellow A.A.A.S.; mem. Am. Assn. Collegiate Deans, Am. Acad. Polit. and Social Sci., Pa. Edn. Assn., N.E.A., Phi Beta Kappa, Omicron Delta Kappa, Kappa Sigma. Republican. Methodist. Mason (Shriner). Home: R.F.D. 5, Carlisle, Pa. Died Oct. 20, 1957; buried Mt. Zion Cemetery, Carlisle, Pa.

THOMPSON, Sam(uel) H., farm ofcl.; b. Adams County, Ill., Aug. 18, 1863; s. Samuel and Elizabeth (McConnell) T.; ed. common schs.; m. Lemmie Dickhut, Jan. 23, 1889; children—Charles E., Ray E., Mabel Irene (Mrs. Orrin Crossland), Grace Marie (Mrs. Arthur Tenhouse), Florence, Edith (Mrs. Louis Durst), Samuel R. Farmer in Ill. for many years; served as tax collector, road commr. and mem. sch. bd.; mem. Ill. Ho. of Rep., 1916; pres. Broadway Bank (Quincy, Ill.), Adams County Fair Assn.; dir. Nat. Com. on Boys' and Girls' Work. Chmn. finance com. Adams County War Savings Staff. Formerly pres. Am. Farm Bur. Fedn. and dir. Farmers Nat. Grain Corp., Nat. Life Stock and Meat Bd.; mem. Fed. Farm Bd., 1931-33 (vice-chmn.). Chmn. bd. trustees Layman Trust for Evangelism, Inc., 1940—. Trustee Chaddock Boys' Sch. Republican. Meth. Received award of Am. Farm Bur. Fed., 1932, "for distinguished service to agriculture," and official expression of esteem, U. of Wis., 1935, for same reason; gold plaque for outstanding service to Am. agr. and nat. rural life from Ill. Farm Mgrs. Assn., 1943. Home: 1850 Broadway. Office: 1719 Broadway, Quincy, Ill. Died Apr. 20, 1956; buried Quincy Meml. Park.

THOMPSON, Samuel Hunter, educator; b. Chuckey, Tenn., Apr. 19, 1876; s. William Pinckney and Florence Loretta (Gefellers) T.; B.S., Valparaiso (Ind.) U., 1906, B.Pd., 1907, D.Pd., 1912; m. Bertie Ethel Mottsberger, Aug. 1, 1906. Supr. Fed. Census, 1st Tenn. Dist., 1910; business mgr. Meth. Advocate-Journal, Athens, Tenn., 1910-14; supt. pub. schs., Athens, 1912-13; supt. pub. instrn., Tenn., 1913—; mem. State Bd. Edn., 1911—. Trustee U. Chattanooga; pres. Chattanooga-Athens-Knoxville Hwy. Assn. Mem. N.E.A. (dir.), Tenn. State Teachers' Assn. (pres., 1914-15). Mem. Gen. Conf. M.E. Ch., 1912; mem. Gen. Deaconess Bd. M.E. Ch., 1912-16. Republican. K.T. Author: The Highlanders of the South, 1910; Southern Hero Tales, 1914; Namjika, an Indian Princess, 1915. Home: Washington. Died Oct. 27, 1952.

THOMPSON, Thor Arthur, r.r. ofcl.; b. LaCrosse, Wis., Oct. 19, 1891; s. Ole H. and Helen (Anderson) T.; student pub. schs., Wis.; m. Ethel I. Rinehart, Oct. 16, 1915; children—Thor Arthur, James Rinehart. Clk.-stenographer various railroads; sec., v.p. operations St. Louis & S.W. Ry., Tyler, Tex., 1917; with D.&R.G.W. R.R., 1917—, successively statistician, chief clk. operating dept., chief clk. exec. dept., gen. auditor and asst. comptroller, asst. to pres., corporate sec., 1917-54, v.p., sec., 1954—, also chmn., dir. subsidiaries. Republican. Home: 691 Dexter St. Office: 1531 Stout St., Denver. Died Jan. 2, 1957.

THOMPSON, Willard Chandler, univ. prof. b. Sun Prairie, Wis., Nov. 24, 1890; s. George Ezra and Frances Augusta (Chandler) T.; B.S. in Agr., U. of Wis., 1912; Ph.D., N.Y. Univ., 1934; m. Mabel Clare Bell, June 21, 1920; 1 son, Willard Chandler. Asst. in animal husbandry U. of Ark., 1912-13; instr. in poultry husbandry Rutgers U., New Brunswick. N.J., 1913-21, prof. since 1921; poultry husbandman N.J. Agrl. Expt. Sta., New Brunswick, since 1921; first. dir. Nat. Inst. of Poultry Husbandry, Newport, Salop, Eng., 1924-26. Served as 2d lt., S.C., Med. Div., U.S. Army, 1918; Mem. Alpha Zeta, Sigma Xi. Republican. Member Dutch Ref. Ch. Club: Rutgers of New Brunswick, N.J. (past pres.). Author: Egg Farming, 1936; numerous bulletins and circulars. Home: 133 N. 7th Av. H.P. Office: College Farm, New Brunswick, N.J. Died Jan. 12, 1954.

THOMPSON, Willard Owen, physician; b. Fredericton, N.B., Can., Feb. 17, 1899; s. Samuel Stirling and Mary (Owen) T.; B.A., Dalhousie U., Halifax, N.S., 1919; M.D., Harvard, 1923; m. Phebe K. Christianson, June 21, 1923; children—Willard Owen, Frederic Christianson, Nancy Kirsten, Donald McRae. Came to U.S. 1920, naturalized, 1937. Engaged in practice of medicine since 1925; interne Boston (Mass.) City Hosp., 1923-25; research fellow in medicine Harvard Med. Sch., 1925-28. Henry P. Walcott fellow, 1928-29; fellow Nat. Research Council, 1926-28; grad. asst. in medicine Mass. Gen. Hosp., 1925, research fellow in medicine, 1926-29, in charge metabolism lab., 1926-29; asst. in chemistry, Harvard, 1927; asst. clin. prof. medicine, Rush Med. Coll., U. of Chicago, 1929-35, asso. clin. prof. 1935-41; asso. prof. medicine, U. of Ill. Coll. of Medicine, 1941-43, prof. medicine, 1943-45, clin. prof. medicine since 1945; research asso. in pathology, Cook County Hosp., 1934-40; asso. attending physician, Presbyn. Hosp., Chicago, 1930-46; attending physician, Grant Hosp., Chicago, since 1947; attending physician, sr. staff, Henrotin Hosp., Chicago, since 1947; attending physician, U. of Ill. Research and Ednl. Hosps., 1945—. Mem. exec. forum Chgo. Assn. of Commerce and Industry. Certified by Am. Bd. Internal Medicine, 1937; diplomate, Nat. Bd. Med. Examiners, 1925. Fellow A.C.P., A.M.A., Am. Geriatrics Soc. (pres.) Soc. for Research in Child Development; mem. Assn. Am. Physicians, Am. Soc. Clin. Investigation, Central Soc. Clin. Research, Endocrine Society (vice pres.), Soc. for Exptl. Biology and Medicine, Am. Goiter Assn. (president), A.A.A.S., Am. Assn. History Medicine, American Diabetes Assn., Am. Soc. Research in Psychosomatic Problems, Am. Therapeutic Soc. (v.p.) Gerentol. Soc., Am. Soc. for Study of Sterility, Am. Heart Assn., World Med. Assn., Am. Med. Writers' Assn., Am. Genetic Assn. Am. Acad. Compensation Medicine, Chicago Med. Service (bd. trustees), Association American Medical Colleges, Institute Medicine of Chicago, Chicago Soc. Internal Med., Soc. Med. History of Chicago, Chicago Med. Soc. (pres.), Asso. Diplomates of Nat. Bd. Med. Examiners (pres.), Miss. Valley Med. Soc. (recipient distinguished Service award, 1952; president, trustee executive com.), Ill. State Acad. Sci., Ill. State Med. Soc., Sigma Xi, Pi Kappa Epsilon. Republican. Presbyterian. Clubs: University, Racquet, Harvard (v.p. for Chicago). Contbr. numerous articles to med. jours. and textbooks. Mng. editor Jour. Clin. Endocrinology and Metabolism; editor Journal of Am. Geriatrics Soc., American Lectures in Endocrinology; asso. editor Am. Practitioner; editorial bd. Miss. Valley Med. Journal; adv. editorial bd. Jour. Am. Acad. Gen. Practitioners. Home: 1430 Lake Shore Dr., Chgo. 10. Office: 700 N. Michigan Av., Chgo. 11. Died Mar. 23, 1954; buried Rosehill Cemetery, Chgo.

THOMPSON, William Leland, wholesale druggist; b. Troy, N.Y., Apr. 4, 1871; s. William Augustus and Harriette (Crosby) T.; A.B., Harvard, 1893; LL.D., Rensselaer Poly. Inst., 1931; m. Martha Groome, Jan. 6, 1909; children—William Leland, Martha E., Peter Schuyler. With John L. Thompson Sons & Co., Troy, 1893—, treasurer, 1903, president, 1911-54, chairman of the board, 1954—; chairman of board Nat. City Bank of Troy, Rensselaer Improvement Co., Community Hotel Co.; 1st v.-pres. of the Troy Savings Bank. Rep. candidate for N.Y. Assembly, 1897; mem. Bd. of Edn., Troy, 1906-27 (resgined); regent University State of N.Y., 1927-51. Pres. Associated Sch. Boards of N.Y. State, 1920-22; former pres. board trustees Emma Willard Sch., and Russell Sage Coll.; former mem. bd. Troy Pub. Library; mem. bd. Tuberculosis Relief Assn., Y.M.C.A. Former regent and vice chancellor, Univ. State of N.Y. Mem. Nat. Guard N.Y., 1896-1912, advancing to capt. Co. C, 2d Regt.; served in Spanish-Am. War and as aide to Brig. Gen. Charles F. Roe; aide on staff Gov. Odell of N.Y., 1901-05. Republican. Episcopalian; sr. warden St. John's Church; mem. Standing Com. Diocese of Albany. Mem. N.Y. State Hist. Soc., Am. Assn. Museums, S.R., St. Nicholas Soc., Mil. Order Foreign Wars. Clubs: Institute of 1770, Varsity, Hasty Pudding, Dickey and Spee clubs (Harvard); Harvard (New York); Troy. Home: Red House Farm, Rensselaer, N.Y. Office: 161 River St., Troy, N.Y. Died Oct. 13, 1957; buried Oakwood Cemetery, Troy.

THOMPSON, William Thomas, editor; b. St. John, N.B., Can., Mar. 20, 1861; s. William Elder and Margaret Ray (Scott) T.; ed. pvt. and grammar sch., St. John; m. Elba H. Wilbur, Apr. 19, 1924. Came to U.S., 1887, naturalized, 1897. Reporter St. John Telegraph, 1877-79, St. John Sun, 1880-82, editor Winnipeg Times, 1883-86; mng. editor Duluth Tribune, 1889-89; with St. Paul Pioneer Press, 1890-91; mng. editor Duluth Herald, 1892-1934; editor Duluth Herald, News-Tribune, 1934-41; ret. Republican. Episcopalian. Club: Northland Country (Duluth). Home: 1017 London Road, Duluth, Minn.; (winter) Corpus Christi, Tex. Died Apr. 5, 1951.

THOMSON, David Sidney, ry. exec.; b. Cornwall, Ont., 1895; s. Archibald and Mary Elizabeth (Robertson) T.; student pub. schs.; m. Florence Beatrice McIntyre, 1927; children—David Keith, Elaine Mary. With Canadian Pacific Ry., 1910—, successively jr. clk., clk., sec., statistician, chief clerk, Montreal, assistant superintendent, supt., Smiths Falls, Ont., supt., Trenton, Ont., Brownville Junction, gen. supt. Ont. dist., Toronto, asst. gen. mgr. Eastern region, Toronto, gen. mgr., v.p. Eastern region, v.p. prairie region, Winnipeg, system v.p. operations and maintenance, Montreal, 1953-55, v.p. all lines, 1955-56, vice pres., dir. and mem. exec. com., 1956—; president Canadian Pacific Transport Co., 1955—, Dominion Atlantic Ry. Co., 1955—, Quebec Central Railway Co., 1955—. Clubs: Manitoba (Winnipeg); National (Toronto); Canadian Railway, St. James's (Montreal). Home: 3010 Westmount Blvd., Montreal. Office: Windsor Station, Montreal 3, Que. Died Sept. 16, 1958.

THOMSON, Francis A(ndrew), mining engr., educator; b. London, Eng., Dec. 21, 1879; s. John Alexander and Frances Springett (Wyatt) T.; E.M., Colo. Sch. Mines, 1904, M.S., 1914, D.Sc., 1923; studied Royal Sch. Mines, London, Ecole des Mines, Paris; m. Josephine H. Bruckman, Aug. 16, 1906 (died June 5, 1927); children—Andrew Halleck, Richard Wyatt; m. 2d, Edna L. Michaelsen, July 16, 1928; 1 dau., Jean Louise. Prospector, miner and assayer, Western States and Can., 1895-98; asst. engr. Northwest Smelting & Refining Co., B.C., 1902-03; cons. engr., supt. properties, Colo. and Nev., 1904-07; head dept. mining engring., State Coll. Wash., 1907-17; dean Sch. Mines, U. Ida., 1917-28; dir. Ida. State Bur. Mines and Geology, 1919-28; pres. Mont. Sch. Mines, and dir. State Bur. Mines and Geology, 1928-50, ret.; cons. engr. U.S. Bur. Mines, 1919-28. Mem. Am. Inst. Mining and Metall. Engrs., Mining and Metall. Soc. Am., Am. Mining Congress (bd. govs.), Soc. Promotion Engring. Edn., Mont. Soc. Engrs., Sigma Nu, Sigma Xi, Sigma Tau, Sigma Gamma Epsilon. Episcopalian. Author: Stamp Milling and Cyaniding, 1915. Contbr. numerous articles tech. mining press U.S. and Can. Address: South 1704 Cedar, Spokane. Died Jan. 11, 1951.

THOMSON, Sir Godfrey Hilton, educator; b. Carlisle, Eng., Mar. 27, 1881; s. Charles and Jane (Hilton) T.; B.S., U. Durham (Pemberton fellow), 1903, Sc.D., 1913, D.C.L. (hon.), 1939; Ph.D. summa cum laude, U. Strasbourg, 1906; m. Jane Hutchinson, July 17, 1912; 1 son, Godfrey Hector. Lectr. 1920-25; prof., dir. studies Moray House Tng. Coll,. edn. Armstrong Coll., U. Durham, 1906-20, prof., 1920-25; prof. edn. and dir. studies at Tng. Sch., U. Edinburgh, 1925—; vis. prof. Columbia, 1923-24, Yale, summer 1933; mem. Colonial Social Sci. Research Council, 1944-50; gov. St. George's Sch., Landsdowne House; mem. edn. bd. Merchant Co. of City of Edinburgh. Hon. sec. 12th Internat. Congress Psychology, Edinburgh, 1948. Served with Vol. and Territorial Forces; acting adj., Durham U.O.T.C., 1915-19, in command, 1921-23. Mem. War Office Adv. Com. for Selection Personnel. Decorated Order of Polonia Restituta. Fellow Royal Soc. Edinburgh, Ednl. Inst. Scotland (hon.), A.A.A.S., Swedish Psychol. Soc. (hon.); mem. British Assn. Advancement Science (v.p. 1951), Nat. Acad. Sciences, Am. Acad. Arts and Sciences, British Psychol. Soc. (pres. 1945-46), Internat. Statis. Inst., Population Investigation Com. (London), Scotlish Council Research Edn., Nat. Found. Ednl. Research, Am. Statis. Assn., Inst. Math. Statistics. Author: The Essentials of Mental Measurement, 1921 (with William Brown); Instinct Intelligence and Character, 1924; A Modren Philosophy of Education, 1929; The Factorial Analysis of Human Ability, 1939; The Northumberland Mental Tests, 1921-22; The Moray House Tests, 1932—; The Geometry of Mental Measurement, 1954; articles British and U.S. sci. jours. Joint editor of British Jour. Psychol. Statis. Sect. Home: 5 Ravelston Dykes, Edinburgh 4, Scotland. Ded Feb. 9, 1955.

THOMSON, James McIlhany, editor, publisher; b. Summit Point, Jefferson County, W.Va., Feb. 13, 1878; s. Augustus Pembroke (M.D.) and Elizabeth (McIlhany) T.; B.A., Johns Hopkins, 1897; studied law in office of Gen. John E. Roller, Harrisonburg, Va.; m. Genevieve Champ, June 30, 1915. Mem. staff of Washington Post, 1898; owner and editor Norfolk (Va.) Dispatch, 1900-06; pub. and prin. owner New Orleans Item, 1906-41; retired. Democrat. Episcopalian. Home: Gaylord, Clarke County, Va. Died Sept. 25, 1959.

THOMSON, Reginald Heber, engr.; b. Hanover, Ind., Mar. 20, 1856; s. Samuel Harrison and M. Sophronia (Clifton) T.; A.B., Hanover (Ind.) Coll., 1877, A.M., Ph.D., 1903; m. Sarah Adeline Laughlin, Aug. 29, 1883; children—James Harrison, Marion Wing, Reginald Heber, Frances Clifton. Instr. mathematics, Healdsburg (Cal.) Inst. and Alexander Acad., 1879-81; with F. H. Whitworth, civ. and mining engr., Seattle, and his partner, 1882-86; city surveyor, Seattle, 1884-86; locating engr. mountain div. Seattle, Lake Shore & Eastern R.R., 1886-88, res. engr. at Spokane, 1888-89; designed G.N. Ry. track encircling butte above Scenic, 1889; mining engr. at Seattle, 1889-92; city engr., 1892-1911; chmn. Bd. Pub. Works, 1896-1908, 1900-11. In charge design and constrn. Seattle municipal improvement, 1892-1912, requiring expenditure of over $42,000,000, including gravity water system conveying water from mountain stream, 28 miles distant, etc.; cons. engr. Water Bd., city of Portland, Ore.; mem. Wash. Armory Commn., 1905, 1906; mem. adv. bd. to gov. of Wash., 1909-11; cons. engr. city of Tacoma, city of Prince Rupert, B.C.; chief engr. Seattle Port Commn., 1911-12; cons. engr. Prov. of

Brit. Columbia, 1912-15; spl. engr. Rogue River Valley Canal Co., 1921-23. Mem. Seattle City Council, 1916-22; spl. engr. hydro-electric power constrn., Eugene, Ore., 1922-24; charge water development, City of Bellingham, 1927-33, city engr., Seattle, 1930-31; cons. engr., City of Wenatchee Met. Water System, 1933, Inter-County River Improvement, 1937, engr. State of Wash. Pontoon Bridge Commn. Pres. bd. mgrs. U. Wash. Y.M.C.A., 1905-15. Pres. Pacific N.W. Soc. Civ. Engrs., 1902, 1903, Wash. Good Roads Assn., 1910-11; hon. mem. Am. Soc. C.E., Engring. Inst. Can., W. Coast Mineral Assn., Beta Theta Pi. Club: Arctic. Address: 2404 42d Av. N., Seattle 2. Died Jan. 7, 1949; buried Lake View Cemetery, Seattle.

THOMSON, Roy B., lawyer; b. Versailles, Ky., Nov. 17, 1881; s. Albert W. and Inez (Wilson) T.; B.S., Tulane U., 1903; LL.B., U. Va., 1905; m. Beulah Corbett, Nov. 15, 1913; children—Albert W., William C. Practicing lawyer Kansas City, Mo.; mem. Stinson, Mag, Thomson, McEvers & Fizzell, and predecessors; U.S. commr., 1910-26; lectr. internat. law Kansas City Law Sch., Mem. Mo. Commn. for Blind. Pres. Andrew Drumm Inst. since 1939. Mem. Am., Mo. State, Kansas City bar assns., Lawyers Assn. of Kansas City, Coll. Alumni Assn. Mem. Christian Ch. Clubs: Country, University (Kansas City). Home: 635 W. 66th Terrace. Office: 9 W. Tenth St., Kansas City 5, Mo. Died 1955.

THOMSON, T. Kennard, cons. engr.; b. Buffalo, Apr. 25, 1864; s. William Alexander and Lavinia Day (Newcomb) T.; grad. U. Toronto, 1886 (head of class), C.E., 1892, D.Sc., 1913; m. Mary Julia Harvey, 1888; children—Annis Eveleen, M.D., Mary Marjory, M.D., A. Kennard, W. Glencairn (capt. U.S.N.), H. Stranraer. Large experience in bridge, r.r., deep found. work; chief engr. Arthur McMullen & Co., Found. contrs., 9 yrs.; retained for found. work Comml. Cable Bldg., Mut. Life Bldg., U.S. Express Bldg., 41-story Singer Bldg., Zinn Bldg., Govt. Assay Bldg., Municipal Bldg., Bankers Trust. Seaboard Nat. Bank, N.Y., First Nat. Bank of Jersey City and over forty other bldgs. Has taken out several tunnel and lighthouse patents. Mem. bd. cons. engrs. for Barge Canal (enlargement of old Erie Canal), 1911-14. Built over two hundred bridges; designed bridges to be built over the Niagara River to celegrate the victory of World War; originator of Manhattan extension and belt line ry., also 2,000,000 h.p. Niagara River and St. Lawrence River power development, and made valuation and appraisals; appraised 110 bldgs., Manhattan, 1937; has done much work connection subway constrn.; proposed solution Miss. River problem; proposed Internat. Forest Park from Lake Superior to Pacific Coast to be 20 miles wide in width by 1500 miles long. Founder, life mem. U. Toronto Engring. Soc., 1884; life mem. Am. Soc. C.E. (dir. 1911-14), Am. Soc. M.E., Engring. Inst. Can., Niagara Hist. Soc., N.Y. Profl. Engrs., Past and Present Officers of Am. Soc. C.E.; mem. St. Andrews Soc. N.Y., etc. Republican. Episcopalian. Clubs: Engineers; hon. life mem. Canadian Club of New York (pres. 1912-14) and U. of Toronto Club of New York (ex-pres.). Mason. Proposed elevated streets for Manhattan, airplane landing for Manhattan, 1919. Has written over 200 papers on engring. subjects. Received medal for walking from Dr. John H. Finley, 1936; has walked 15 miles a day every April. Office: 32 W. 40th St., N.Y.C. Died July 1, 1952.

THOREK, Max (tôr'ĕk), surgeon; b. Hungary, Mar. 10, 1880; s. Isaac and Sarah (Mahler) T.; prep. edn., Budapest, Hungary; came to U.S., 1900; M.D., Rush Med. Coll. (U. of Chicago); 1904; hon. LL.D., Lincoln Memorial U., Sc.D., Wesleyan Coll.; Honoris Causa, U. Istanbul, Turkey, 1954; married Fannie Unger, April 16, 1905; 1 son, Philip (M.D.). Practiced at Chgo., 1904—; asst. in gnyecology to late Prof. Henry Banga, for 5 yrs.; prof. clin. surgery, Loyola U., 3 yrs.; chief surgeon to Am. Hosp., Chicago; prof. of clinical surgery, Cook County Grad. Sch. of Medicine; attending surgeon Cook County Hosp., cons. surgeon Municipal Tuberculosis Sanitarium; Cushing lecturer McGill U., Montreal, 1954. Fellow A.M.A., Internat. College Surgeons (life; internat. founder and permanent sec. general; editor in chief of jour.), Nat. Acad. Medicine (Colombia, S.A.), Nat. Gastroenterol. Soc., Internat. Coll. Anesthetists, Royal Soc. of Arts, Royal Photographic Soc. of Gt. Britain, Am. Coll. Gastroenterology; hon. fellow Royal Surg. Society (Sofia, Bulgaria), Internat. Society of Gastroenterologists; hon. member Belgian Society Gastroenterology; corr. fellow Peruvian Surg. Society; mem. Ill. State and Chicago med. socs.; mem. Orden del Sol, Republic of Peru; member American Eugenics Society, Rush Medical Coll. Alumni (life), Mark Twain Society (life); Chicago Historical Soc., Mississippi Valley Medical Society (charter mem.), Internat. Hospital Association, Internat. Soc. of Gastroenterology, Internat. Anesthetic Research Soc., Am. Soc. French Legion of Honor, DePaul Art League, Pi Gamma Mu (Life); hon. mem. Terre Haute Acad. Medicine; corr. academician Nat. Acad. Sciences of Mexico, Surg. Acad. of Mexico; corr. mem. Soc. des Chirurgiens (Paris), Soc. Scientifique Française de Chirurgie Reparatrice, Russian Endocrinol. Assn. (Moscow), Soc. of Neurology and Endocrinology (Jassy, Roumania), Sociedad das Sciences Medicas (Lisbon), Brazilian Coll. Surgeons; asso. corr. mem. Royal Acad. Medicine (Turin, Italy); hon. corr. mem. Egyptian Med. Assn. (Cairo, Egypt); past pres. American Physicians Art Assn.; Collaborator Rassegna Internazionale di Clinica Terapia, Milano, Italy; U.S. del. Internat. Congress Hepatic Insufficiencies, Vichy, France, 1927. Decorated Knight of Legion of Honor (France); Knight Order of Crown of Italy; comdr. Order of St. Alexander (Sofia, Bulgaria); Medal of Honor (Republic of Venezuela); distinguished citizens medal from Vets. of Fgn. Wars of U.S.; Aztec Eagle, Mexican Govt., Gold Medalist Phi Lambda Kappa, 1951; Comdr. Cruzeiro do Sul (Brazil); Grand Officer Order of Merit (Argentina); Comdr. Nat. Order of Merit Carlos J. Finlay, Cuba. Club: Chicago Alumni. Author: The Human Testis and Its Diseases, 1924; Surgical Errors and Safeguards, 1931, 4th editions, 1943; Modern Surgical Technic (3 vols.), 1941; Plastic Surgery of the Breast Abdominal Wall, 1942; A Surgeon's World, 1944. Translator: Surgery of the Brain and Spinal Cord (by Fedor Krause), 1912. Cons. editor: Arquivos de Cirurgia Clinica e Experimental, Sao Paolo, Brazil. Contbr. to surg. lit. Guest lecturer in surgery, Washington U., 1940. Founder Photographic Society of America. Home: 3920 Lake Shore Drive. Office: American Hospital, 850 Irving Park Rd., Chgo. 13. Died Jan. 25, 1960.

THORN, James, U.N. ofcl.; b. New Zealand, 1882; ed. Christchurch Boys High Sch. Active in formation Independent Labor Party, 1904; pres. New Zealand Labor Party, 1929, 1930, sec., 1932-35; elected mem. Parliament, 1935, 38, 43; Parliament undersec. to Prime Minister, 1943; high commr. to Can., 1947-50; New Zealand rep. Econ. and Social Council U.N. (became pres. 1949). Home: 60 Totara Rd., Wellington, N.Z. Deceased.

THORNE, Robert Julius, merchant; b. Chicago, Ill., 1875; s. George R. and Ellen (Cobb) T.; LL. B., Cornell U., 1897; married; 5 daughters. Entered Kansas City br. of Montgomery Ward & Co., 1897, and advanced to mgr.; returned to Chicago and entered main office, becoming pres.; resigned 1920; active restoration Chgo. lake front. Civilian aid, Q.M. Dept., Washington, 1918; appointed asst. to Maj. Gen. Goethals, q.m. gen., April 1918. D.S.M., 1919, "for especially meritorious service in reorganization of service of supply." Mem. Delta Kappa Epsilon. Home: 7723 Ludington Pl., La Jolla, Cal. Died Mar. 20, 1955; buried Rosehill Cemetery, Chgo.

THORNE, William, portrait painter; b. Delavan, Wis.; ed. Nat. Acad. Design, N.Y. (medal), and Julian Académie, Paris, France; married; 1 dau., Margaret Frances. Hon. mention Paris Salon; medal, Buffalo Expn., 1901; picture in Corcoran Gallery, Washington. N.A. Home: 216 N. 4th St., Delavan, Wis. Died Jan. 10, 1956; buried Spring Grove Cemetery, Delavan.

THORNTON, Edwin William, editor, clergyman; b. nr. West Middleburg, O., Aug. 20, 1863; s. James Preston and Amy Catherine (Nash) T.; student U. of Mo., Transylvania Coll., Lexington, Ky.; m. Lucy W. Fitzgerald, June 4, 1890. Ordained ministry Disciples of Christ, 1888; pastor Paola, Kan., 1888-89, Lathrop and Carrollton, Mo., 1890-92, Kansas City, Mo., 1893-99, Mayfield, Ky., 1900-1902, Pittsburgh and Waynesburg, Pa., 1902-05, Long Beach and Los Angeles, Calif., 1905-10; editor-in-chief S.S. lit. for Standard Pub. Co. Address: Standard Pub. Co., Cin. Died Nov. 14, 1940; buried Wilmington, O.

THORNTON, Harrison John, prof., author; born Liverpool, Eng., July 8, 1894; s. Harrison and Isabella (Almond) T.; came to U.S., 1914, naturalized, 1923; A.B., Grinnell (Ia.) Coll., 1925, A.M., 1926; A.M., Harvard, 1927; Ph.D., U. of Chicago, 1929; m. Nadine Hemmingson, Sept. 12, 1928; 1 dau., Norma Nadine. Instr. in history, Grinnell (Ia.) Coll., 1925; fellow, U. of Chicago, 1927; exchange instr., Harvard, 1927-28; prof. history, State U. of Ia., since 1929. Served with Canadian Army, 1916-19, World War I. Mem. Am., Miss. Valley, N.Y. Hist. Assn.; S.D., Ia., Neb., Wis. Hist. Socs., Am. Acad Polit. and Social Sci. Author: History of the Quaker Oats Company, 1933; Theodore Roosevelt-Historian (in Marcus W. Jennegan Essays in Am. Historiography), 1937; Life of Samuel Calvin, 1947; Presidents and Others at Chautauqua (articles), 1945-47. Editor: Univ. of Iowa Centennial Biographies, 1947. Specialist in social and economic history of the American people, and history of the South. Home: 716 River St., Iowa City, Ia. Died Sept. 22, 1952; buried Oakland Cemetery, Iowa City.

THORNTON, Patrick M(oran), gen. contractor; b. St. Paul, Apr. 11, 1884; s. Patrick H. and Margaret Amelia (Moran) T.; student pub. schs.; m. Violet D. King, Sept. 23, 1918; children—Patrick K., James M., John Joseph, Thomas R. With P. H. Thornton, municipal contractor, 1904-07, Copper River-N.W. R.R., Alaska, 1907-08; foreman, supt., v.p. Thornton Bros. Co., St. Paul, 1908-37; prin. owner Thornton Constrn. Co., Hancock, Mich., 1937—. Chmn. Houghton County Infantile Paralysis Drive, 1941, Houghton Co. Def. Council, 1942-45. Mem. bd. control Mich. Coll. Mining and Tech., 1941-47, chmn., 1949—. Mem. Mich. Rd. Builders Assn., Inc. (past pres.), Asso. Gen. Contractors Am. (exec. bd., past chmn. hwy. div.), Mich. Engring. Soc., Soc. Am. Mil. Engrs., Mich. Asphalt Paving Assn., Inc., U.S., Hancock C.'s of C. Roman Catholic. K.C., Elk. Clubs: Great Lakes Cruising (Chgo.); St. Paul Athletic; Miscowaubik (Calumet, Mich.); Onigaming Yacht (Houghton, Mich.). Home: Sheridan Rd., Box 591, Houghton, Mich. Office: 1028 Ethel Av., Hancock, Mich. Died Feb. 17, 1959; buried Forest Hill Cemetery, Houghton, Mich.

THORNTON, William D., mining; b. Deer Lodge, Mont., Apr. 22, 1870; s. John C. C. and Louise (Archer) T.; student Columbia Univ. Pres. Greene Cananea Copper Co., Inspiration Consol. Copper Co.; dir. Raritan Terminal and Transportation Co., Savannah Sugar Refining Corp., Am. Power & Light Co. Clubs: Racquet and Tennis, Links Golf, Whitehall, India House. Office: 25 Broadway, N.Y.C. Died June 1953.

THORP, Willard Brown, clergyman; b. Oxford, N.Y., Jan. 22, 1868; s. John Warren and Charlotte (Brown) T.; A.B., Amherst, 1887; B.D., Yale Div. Sch., 1891; D.D., Pacific School of Religion, 1928; m. Mariel Morris Rushmore, Sept. 13, 1939. Ordained Congl. ministry, 1891; pastor First Ch., Binghamton, N.Y., 1891-99, South Ch., Chicago, 1899-1908, First Ch., San Diego, Calif., 1908-20, First Ch., Palo Alto, 1920-39, retired 1939. Mem. Chi Phi, Phi Beta Kappa. Author: Perspectives of the Spirit, 1910. Address: 1010 Waverley St., Palo Alto, Cal. Died Mar. 2, 1952.

THORPE, Merle, magazine editor; b. Brimfield, Ill., Nov. 1, 1879; s. Joseph and Mayday E. (Smith) T.; A.B., Stanford U., 1905; A.B., U. of Wash., 1908; m. Lilian Isabel Day, Aug. 17, 1909; children—George Day, Merle. Editorial work on Palo Alto (Calif.) Times, 1903-04, Washington Post, 1905-06, Havana (Cuba) Post, 1906-07, Seattle Post-Intelligencer, 1907; adv. mgr. Washington Life, 1905; editor and mgr. The Washington Alumnus, 1907-11; editor Kansas Editor, 1913-16; prof. journalism, U. of Wash., 1907-11, U. of Kan., 1911-16; editor and pub. The Nation's Business, Washington, 1916-44; dir. business development, Cities Service Co., since 1944; former contbg. editor Collier's; dir. National Metropolitan Bank, Chesapeake and Potomac Telephone Company; trustee of the Northwestern Mutual Life Insurance Co. Lecturer on journalism, U. of Calif., summers, 1914, 15. Pres. Am. Assn. Journalism Teachers, 1915-16; sec. Mo. Valley Cost Congress, 1914-16; dir. Nat. Journalism Congress, 1914; asst. dir. President's Unemployment Relief Orgn.; dir. George Washington Bicentennial Commn., Nat. Publishers Assn. Mem. Sigma Alpha Epsilon, Phi Delta Phi, Sigma Delta Chi. Republican. Congregationalist. Clubs: Seigniory (Province Quebec, Can.); Chevy Chase, Metropolitan, Burning Tree, Alfalfa, Overseas Writers (Washington); Wall Street, Artists and Writers, Players, Metropolitan (New York); Chicago (Chicago); Bohemian (San Francisco). Author: The Coming Newspaper, 1915; How's Business,, 1931; Organized Business Leadership, 1931; Neither Purse nor Sword (with James M. Beck), 1936; We Hire a Cook and a Congressman, 1940. Contbr. short stories to nat. mags. Awarded Harvard-Bok prize for writing best individual advertisement in 1925. Home: Hollin Hall, 1275 Ft. Hunt Rd., Alexandria, Va. Offices: Ring Bldg., Washington 6; also 70 Pine St., N.Y.C. Died: Oct. 31, 1955.

THORSON, Nelson Thor, editor, pub.; b. Horby, Sweden, Sept. 16, 1881; s John N. and Hanna Nelson T.; brought to Am., 1887; ed. pub. schs., Lincoln, Neb.; m. Corinne Paulson, Aug. 5, 1923. In hotel and restaurant bus., Omaha, St. Louis; owner and editor Omaha Posten (Swedish weekly), 1910-43. Served as co. treas. Douglas Co., Neb., for Progressive Party, and as member Prog. State and Nat. coms., mem. Rep. State Com.; del. Rep. Nat. Conv., 1928. Treas. Tornado Relief Com., 1913; county treas. Gen. Woods for President campaign, 1919; mem. Congressional Com. on John Ericsson Memorial; nat. treas. John Ericsson Rep. League of America, 1926-30, nat. sec. since 1930; mem. bd. and v.p. Pub. Library; mem. bd. govs. Omaha Symphony Orchestra Assn., 1932-33; v.p. Omaha Auditorium Poultry Show. Mem. Nat. Editorial Assn., Neb. Foreign Lang. Press Assn. (sec. 1916), Am. Numismatic Assn. (ex-chmn. bd. of govs., ex-pres., founding pres. Omaha chpt.), Numis. socs. of America, Sweden, England, Holland, Belgium. Editor: The Monitor (retired); operates coin and stamp exchange. Home: 1109 N. 56th St. Office: 1514 Dodge St., Omaha. Died Nov. 27, 1951; buried Forest Lawn Cemetery, Omaha.

THROCKMORTON, George Kenneth, indsl. cons.; b. Romney, Ind., Nov. 2, 1884; s. Edwin Wolf and Nancy Ann (Webster) T.; student Purdue, 1901-03; Cornell U., 1904-05; m. Mary Clarissa Downin, May 2, 1908. With Link Belt Co., Chgo., beginning as timekeeper, 1903-10, prodn. mgr. Concrete Steel Products Co., Chicago Heights, Ill., 1910; supt. Sears, Roebuck & Co., 1911-22; mgr. mdse. dept.

Herbert H. Frost, Inc., Chgo., 1922-25; v.p., gen. mgr., part owner E. T. Cunningham, Inc., radio tubes, 1926-30, became pres., 1931; exec. v.p. RCA Radiotron Co., 1931-33, RCA Victor Co., 1933-35; pres. RCA Mfg. Co., 1937-41; v.p. RCA, 1942-43; indsl. cons., 1943—. Address: 46 Hayward St., Asheville, N.C. Died Apr. 4, 1953.

THURBER, Caroline, artist; b. Oberlin, O.; d. Alvred Bayard and Melissa (Tenney) Nettleton; student pub. schs.; m. Dexter Thurber, 1885 (dec.); children—Gorham Nettleton (dec.), Luman Tenney. Studied in Paris, 1897-1901, also in Italy and Germany. Exhibited Paris Salon, 1899-1900; Walker Gallery, Liverpool, and New Gallery, London, 1900; Royal Academy, London, 1901. Early work largely portraiture of children, later oils and drawings of professional people and educators. Home-Studio: 620 Tappan St., Brookline, Mass. Deceased.

THURMAN, Hal C., airways exec.; b. Greenfield, Mo., July 29, 1881; s. Berry G. and Lula (Clark) T; A.B., U. of Mo., 1903, LLB., 1904; m. Freda Levy, Sept. 23, 1903; children—Margaret, Harold (dec.), Freda, Estelle. Admitted to Mo. bar, 1904, U.S. Court for Western Dist., Indian Ty., 1905, U.S. Dist. and Circuit courts for Eastern Dist. of Okla., 1907, Supreme Ct. of Okla., 1909; law clerk, allotment contest div., U.S. Commn. to Five Civilized Tribes of Indian Ty., Muskogee, Indian Ty., 1904; apptd. judge Superior Ct. of Muskogee County, Okla. 1914, elected for term 1915-19, resigned 1918; in gen. practice of law, Oklahoma City, 1918-42; dir., mem. exec. com. of bd. and gen. counsel Brainiff Airways, Inc., Dallas, Tex., since 1942. Mem. legal adv. com., apptd. by mayor of Okla. City of $4,000,000 municipal project, 1924-26. Trustee Kingfisher Coll., 1928-42. Mem. Internat. Assn. Ins. Council (v.p. 1941-43), Am., Okla. and Dallas bar assns., Sigma Chi, Phi Delta Phi. Conglist. Mason (K.T.). Clubs: Mens Dinner (Oklahoma City). Home: 5424 Walnut Hill Lane, Dallas 9. Office: Love Field. Dallas 9. Died Aug. 22, 1952; buried Oklahoma City.

THURSTON, Ernest Lawton, educator, writer; b. Fall River, Mass., Feb. 13, 1873; s. Frank Taylor and Ida (Treadwell) T.; high schs., Washington, D. C.; C.E., Columbian University, 1893; A.M., George Washington University, 1914; married Nina Agnes Clayberger, June 30, 1909; children—Dorothy Nelson, Ernest Lawton, Robert Davenport. Bagan as teacher in Business High Sch., Washington, 1894; supt. schs., D.C., Jan. 1, 1914-July 1, 1920. Was many yrs. mem. faculty George Washington U. (later trustee); Editor Iroquois Pub. Co., Syracuse, N.Y., 1926-32, 35-40, now sr. editor. Member Professional Bookmen of America, Pi Gamma Mu. Presbyterian. Author: Mental Commercial Arithmetic, 1897; Practical Tests in Commercial and Higher Arithmetic, 1898; Business Arithmetic for Secondary Schools, 1913; (with G. R. Fowler and M. C. Collister) Our Surroundings, A Complete Course in General Science, 1948; (with M. C. Collister) A Laboratory Guide and Project Book in General Science, 1928; (with G. R. Fowler) A Laboratory Guide in General Science, 1943; (with G. R. Bodley, A. W. Abrams and E. A. Faigle), Iroquois Geography Seris, 1929-44; The Black Shadow, 1934; Tongues of Flame, 1934; The Young Boss of Camp Eighteen, 1935; (with G. W. Fowler and M. C. Collister) Science and You, 1948; Living with Science, 1948; Homelands of the World (with G. C. Hankins); Homelands of the Americas, 1954; Homelands Beyond the Seas, 1955. Speaker and writer on ednl. topics; writer, editorial cons. textbooks and informational material. Home: 708 James St., Syracuse 3. Office: care Iroquois Publishing Co., 333 W. Fayette St., Syracuse, N.Y. Died July 10, 1958; buried Rock Creek Cemetery, Washington.

THURSTON, Lee Mohrmann, educator; b. Central Lake, Mich., Aug. 7, 1895; s. George Lee and Lenore Mary (Mohrmann) T.; A.B., U. Mich., 1918, A.M., 1929, Ph. D., 1935; m. Jessie Holmes Gothro, Dec. 26, 1921; children—Jane, Robert Lee. Tchr. high schs., Boyne City, Manistee, Owosso, Mich.; supt. schs., Perry, Mich., 1926-31; asst. supt. schs., treas. bd. edn., Ann Arbor, Mich., 1931-35, dep. supt. pub. instrn., 1935-38, 1944-48; prof. ed., U. Pitts., 1938-44; lectr. edn. U. Mich., since 1944; dean Sch. Edn., Mich. State Coll., since July 1953; state supt. pub. instrn., Mich., 1948-53; administrative cons. pub. schs., Pittsburgh; staff mem. sch. survey, N.Y.C., 1942-43, Boston, 1944, Wash. State, 1946; adv. U.S. Commr. Edn., 1950-51, 53—, Ednl. Policies Commn., 1950. Pub. sch. adv. com. Nat. Girl Scouts; mem. nat. com. Armed Forces Edn. Program. Served with U.S.M.C., World War I. Mem. Nat. Council Chief State Sch. Officers (pres. 1950-51), N.E.A., Am. Assn. Sch. Adminstrs., Phi Delta Kappa, Kappa Phi Kappa, Phi Kappa Phi. Republican. Club: Rotary. Mem. editorial bd. The Nations Schools. Home: 1519 W. Lenawee St., Lansing 15. Office: U.S. Office Education, Dept. Health, Education & Welfare, Washington 25. Died Sept. 4, 1953; buried So. Cemetery, Central Lake, Mich.

THURSTONE, Louis Leon (thûr'stōn), prof. psychology; b. Chicago, Ill., May 29, 1887; s. Conrad and Sophie (Stroth) T.; M.E., Cornell U., 1912; Ph.D., U. of Chicago, 1917; Ph.D. (hon.), U. Gothenburg, Sweden, 1954; m. Thelma Gwinn, July 17, 1924; children—Robert Leon, Conrad Gwinn, Fredrick Louis. Prof. of psychology, Carnegie Inst. Tech., 1915-23, University of Chicago since 1924; psychologist Inst. for Govt. Research, Washington, D.C., 1923-24, Charles F. Grey distinguished service prof., 1938; now research prof. and dir. psychometric lab. U. of N.C.; vis. prof. of Frankfurt, Germany, 1948; vis. prof. University of Stolkholm, Sweden, 1954. Author of trade tests for occupational classification in U.S. Army, World War I; mem. com. on classification of mil. personnel, Adj. Gen.'s Office, World War II. Editor of intelligence tests of Am. Council on Edn. Recipient Centennial Award Northwestern U., 1951. Fellow A.A.A.S.; hon. fellow British Psychol. Society, Swedish Psychol. Soc.; mem. Am. Philosophical Society, Am. Psychological Assn. (member council; pres. 1932-33), Soc. Promotion Engring. Edn. (council), Nat. Acad. Sciences, Academy of Arts and Sciences, Sigma Xi, Eta Kappa Nu, Phi Delta Kappa, Acacia. Mason. Clubs: Quadrangle. Literary (Chgo.); Cosmos (Washington). Author: The Learning Curve Equation, 1918; The Nature of Intelligence, 1924; Fundamentals of Statistics, 1924; The Measurement of Attitude, 1929; The Vectors of Mind, 1935; Primary Mental Abilities, 1938; (with Thelma Gwinn Thurstone) Factorial Studies of Intelligence, 1941; A Factorial Study of Perception, 1944; Multiple Factor Analysis, 1947. Home: 400 Laurel Hill Rd., Chapel Hill, N.C. Died Sept. 29, 1955.

TIBBALS, Seymour Selden, editor, playwright; b. Cin., Feb. 9, 1869; s. William F. and Frances (Selden) T.; grad. Franklin High School, 1887; m. Minnie Clay Gugle, of Franklin, Ohio, June 14, 1892; m. 2d, Mary Eldridge, Jan. 1, 1917; 1 dau., Mary Frances. In newspaper work, 1889—; editor and owner Franklin (Ohio) Chronicle; postmaster of Franklin, O., 1905-1914. Republican. Club: Rotary (pres. 1925-26). Plays: (produced) A Money Order; The Struggle for Gold; At the State Capital; Corporal Corinne; How Hopper Was Side-Tracked; Somewhere in France; Putting It Up to Patty; Getting Even with Reggy; etc. Home: Franklin, O. Died Jan. 8, 1949; buried Woodhill Cemetery, Franklin, O.

TICE, Frederick, physician; b. near Oshkosh, Wis., July 30, 1871; s. A. B. and Jane (Stephens) T.; M.D., Rush Med. Coll., 1894. Practiced Chgo., 1895—; asst. prof. diseases of chest, prof. clin. medicine, U. Ill., Coll. Medicine, 1903, prof. diseases of chest, 1905-17, prof. medicine, 1916-26, now emeritus; attending physician, pres. of attending staff. Cook County Hosp. until 1938; prof. clin. med., Rush Med. Coll. Ex-pres. bd. dirs. Chgo. Municipal Tb Sanatorium. Ex-v.p. A.C.P.; mem. Am. Congress Internal Medicine, Inst. Medicine, A.M.A., Ill. State, Chgo. med. socs., Miss. Valley Med. Assn., Chgo. Soc. Internal Medicine, Soc. Med. History, Inst. Medicine, Chgo. Tb Soc. Home: 440 Linden Av., Oak Park, Ill. Office: 25 E. Washington St., Chgo. Died Dec. 18, 1953; buried Omro, Wis.

TIEDEMANN, Tudor H. A. (tēd'ȧ-mȧn), industrial relations counselor; b. Seattle, Wash., July 17, 1889; s. Tudor J. A. and Mary J. (Suffern) T.; grad. Stanford U., 1912; m. Maybelle Barlow, Aug. 3, 1912 (divorced, 1919); children—Jane, Tudor Alfred; m. 2d, Alice Irwin Hopper, Dec. 1922; 1 son, Tudor H. A. Fire insurance broker, Los Angeles, 1912-16; pres. Jr. Underwriters Assn., 1916; joined Standard Oil Co. of N.J., 1920, for development of employment and personnel program and employee representation in subsidiary cos.; worked on labor relations in Standard Oil Co. of La., Colonial Beacon Oil Co., Humble Oil Co., Carter Oil Co. and various natural gas cos. and southwestern pipe line units; mem. labor com. Am. Petroleum Inst., 1932, later same for petroleum industry at Washington, D.C.; mng. dir. Indsl. Relations Counselors, Inc., N.Y. City (founded and fostered by J. D. Rockefeller, Jr.), 1934-52; exec. asst. to employers panel. War Labor Bd., Washington, 1942; trustee Indsl. Relations Counsellors, Inc., since 1944. Enlisted Calif. Nat. Guard, 1916; served in Mexico; sergt., 2d lt., 1st lt., Co. B, 160th Inf.; sent to Washington, D.C., for conf. on war risk ins. details; capt. 40th Div., Camp Kearny, Calif.; div. personnel adj. in France, later maj. in Adj. Gen.'s Dept.; replacement officer for 1st Army; returned to U.S. as lt. col. and div. adj. Mem. Phi Kappa Psi. Clubs: Rockefeller Center; Bronxville Field; American Yacht Club (trustee; vice commodore, 1940; commodore, 1941, 42); Stanford of New York (trustee), New York Yacht Shenorock Shore, Tred Avon Yacht. Lecturer on labor subjects. Contbr. articles on labor problems. Home: Bald Eagle Point, Tilghman, Md. Office: Americas Bldg., Rockefeller Center, N.Y.C. Died Apr. 15, 1956.

TIERNEY, William Laurence, congressman; b. Norwalk, Conn., Aug. 6, 1876; s. Jeremiah and Mary Ann (Loughlin) T.; A.B. Fordham U., 1898, M.A., 1916; N.Y. Law Sch., 1900; m. Marie I. Brady; 1 son, William Laurence; m. 2d, Margaret Walsh, Dec. 19, 1925. In practice law, N.Y.C., 1900-—, Greenwich, Conn., 1912-—; at various times associated with De Lancy Nicoll, John R. Dos Passos, and late father. Mem. 72d Congress, 4th Conn. Dist. Clubs: Nat. Democratic Club of New York, New York Athletic; Indian Harbor Yacht, Millbrook Country, Congressional Country. Home: Brookridge Drive, Greenwich, Conn. Office: Chatteau Lafayette Offices, Post Rd., Greenwich, Conn., and 299 Broadway, N.Y.C. Died Apr. 13, 1958.

TIFFANY, Francis Buchanan, lawyer; b. Springfield, Mass., Apr. 26, 1855; s. Francis and Esther (Allison) T.; A.B., Harvard, 1877, LL.B., 1880; m. Nina Moore, Oct. 16, 1889; 1 dau., Esther A. Admitted to Mass. bar, 1881; practiced at Boston, 1882-87, St. Paul, 1887—. Mem. Am. Law Institute. Club: Minnesota. Author: Handbook of the Law of Sales, 1895; Death by Wrongful Act, 1893; Handbook of the Law of Principal and Agent, 1903; Handbook of the Law of Banks and Banking, 1912. Compiler and editor General Statutes of Minnesota, 1913, and Supplement, 1917. Home: 682 Fairmount Av. Office: Endicott Bldg., St. Paul, Minn. Died Oct. 25, 1936.

TIFFANY, J(oseph) Raymond, lawyer; b. Ocean Grove, N.J, Sept. 4, 1888; s. Edward LeRoy and Jseophine Louise (Brown) T.; LL.B., N.Y. Law Sch, 1912; LL.D. (hon.) Tusculum (Tenn.) College; spl. work Columbia U., m. Adeline Ely, Feb. 7, 1912; children—Forrest Fraser, Elizabeth Louise. Admitted to N.J. bar, 1912; also authorized to practice in various Fed. Cts. and U.S. Supreme Ct.; specialized in corp. law and practices before State and Fed. Adminstrn. bodies and cts.; gen. counsel Book Mfrs. Inst., N.Y.; Nat. Small Business Mens Assn. Judge Hoboken (N.J) Dist. Ct., 1918-23; assistant attorney general, New Jersey, 1926-34; spl. counsel N.J. State Water Policy Commn., 1927-32, N.J. State Milk Control Bd., 1928-32, Bd. of Commerce and Navigation, 1926-34, South Jersey Port Commn., 1930-34; gen. counsel Interstate Sanitation Commn. for N.Y., N.J., Conn. since 1935; taught constl. law, U. of Newark, Post Grad. Course, 1934-35. Mem. Hoboken Rotary Club (gov. 36th Dist., 1931-32); mem. mag. com. of Rotary Internat., "Rotarian" and "Revista Rotaria," Dir. and 1st vice pres. Rotary International, 1942-43 American Bar Association, Hudson County Bar Association (former pres.), Assn. of Bar of N.Y., Interstate Commerce Commn. Practitioners Assn. Mem. adv. council Carnegie Inst. of Tech. (Gaphic Arts); mem. exec. com. Nat. Soc. for Crippled Children and Adults, Inc., past pres.; past pres. N.J. Soc. for Crippled Children and Adults. Republican. Baptist. Mason (Shriner), Elk. Clubs: Advertising. Downtown Athletic, Engineers (N.Y.). Home: 10 Crestmont Rd., Montclair, N.J. Office: 25 W. 43rd St., N.Y.C. Died Apr. 9, 1956.

TIFFANY, Nina Moore, author; b. Cin.; d. Augustus Olcott and Harriet Cornelia Moore; m. Francis Buchanan Tiffany, Oct. 16, 1889; 1 dau., Esther Allison. Author: Pilgrims and Puritans, 1887; Colony to Commonwealth, 1889; Samuel E. Sewall, a Memoir; also pamphlets (for school use) on William Lloyd Garrison, Shadrach, Anthony Burns. Joint Author: (with Francis Tiffany and Francis B. Tiffany) Harm Jan Huidekoper, 1904. Joint Editor: (with Susan I. Lesley) Letters of James Murray, Loyalist. Contbr. to mags. Address: 682 Fairmount Av., St. Paul, Minn. Died Sept. 29, 1958.

TIGHE, Laurence Gotzian (tī), education; b. St. Paul, Minn., Mar. 19, 1894; s. Ambrose and Harriet (Gotzian) T.; student U. of Minnesota, 1911; A.B., Yale, 1916, A.M., 1938; m. Hester Smith, Feb. 7, 1918; children—Laurence Gotzian, Patricia. Clerk, Equitable Trust Co., New York, N.Y., 1916-17, Kalman, Matteson & Wood, St. Paul, Minn., 1919; asst. treas., F. H. Swift & Co., Inc., Boston, Mass., 1919-21; sales corr., S. W. Straus & Co., Boston, Feb.-Oct. 1921; rep. Stacy & Braun, Boston, 1921-24; with Brown Brothers & Co. and Brown Brothers, Harriman & Co., Boston and New York, 1924-34, partner, 1930-34; vice pres. and dir., Brown, Harriman & Co., New York and Boston, 1934-38; asso. treas., Yale U., 1938-42, treas. since 1942; dir. Pa. Water and Power Co. (mem. finance committee), Connecticut Light & Power Company, National Sugar Refining Company, First Nat. Bank & Trust Co., New Haven, Conn. (mem. trust com.); trustee, corporator New Haven Savs. Bank. Served as capt., 339th F.A., U.S.A., 1917-19; overseas, 1918-19. Treas. bd. trustees Sheffield Scientific Sch. (Yale); treas. Yerkes Labs. of Primate Biology, Inc., (Orange Park, Fla.), Conn. Acad. Arts and Sciences, Interseminary Commn. for Training for Rural Ministry. Trustee New Haven Orphan Asylum and Children's Center. Dir. Am. Red Cross (New Haven chapter). Mem. Phi Beta Kappa, Delta Kappa Upsilon, Skull and Bones. Clubs: Bond (hon.) (Boston); Lawn, Graduates, Faculty, Mory's (New Haven); Yale (New York); Hammonassett Fishing (Madison, Conn.). Home: 31 Hillhouse Av., New Haven 11. Died Dec. 3, 1954.

TILDEN, Charles Joseph, civil engr.; b. Brookline, Mass., Oct. 3, 1873; s. George Thomas and Alice Olmstead (Butler) T.; S.B. in Civ. Engring., Harvard, 1896; hon. M.A., Yale, 1919; m. Mabel Katherine Myers, Oct. 14, 1902 (died Mar. 8, 1940);

children—Elinor (Mrs. H. G. Hitchcock), Carol (Mrs. D. L. Morris); m. 2d, Linda Palmer Littlejohn of Sydney, Australia, Apr. 6, 1942. Assistant instructor engring., Harvard University, from 1896 to 1897; assistant engineer New York Rapid Transit Commn., 1897-1903; instr. civ. engring., Cornell U., 1903-05; instr., asst. prof. and jr. prof. civ. engring., U. of Mich., 1905-11, prof. and head dept. of engring. mechanics, 1911-13; prof. civ. engring., Johns Hopkins, 1913-19; Strathcona prof. engring. mechanics, Yale, 1919-40, emeritus, 1940—, and fellow of Branford Coll., 1933—. Mem. Conn. Highway Safety Commission, 1936-42. Capt. Engr. O. R. C. 1917-37. With Signal Corps, U.S. Army, 1942-44. Mem. Am. Soc. C. E.; fellow A.A.A.S.; mem. Sigma Xi, Phi Beta Kappa, Omicron Delta Kappa; hon. mem. Tau Beta Pi. Author of various articles in mags., etc. Clubs: Harvard (New York); Graduate (New Haven). Home: Westport, Conn. Office: Strathcona Hall, Yale Univ., New Haven, Conn. Died Nov. 15, 1959.

TILDEN, Josephine Elizabeth, botanist; b. Davenport, Ia.; d. Henry and Elizabeth Aldrich (Field) Tilden; B.S., U. Minn., 1895, M.S., 1896. Prof. botany, U. Minn., to 1938; studied and collected algae in Yellowstone Park, western United States and Canada, Hwaaiian Islands, Society Islands, New Zealand, Australia, Japan, and Minnesota Seaside Station, summers 1901-07, Puget Sound Biol. Sta., summer 1918. Delegate to 1st Pan-Pacific Sci. Conf., Honolulu, 1920; 2d Pan-Pacific Congress, Melbourne, Sydney, Australia, 1923; 3d Congress, Tokyo, Japan, 1926; 1st Pan-Pacific Food Conservation Congress, Honolulu, 1924. Author: (or editor) American Algae, 1894—; Postelsia (the year-book of the Minn. Seaside Sta., 2 vols.), 1902, 1906; South Pacific Algae, 1909—; Myxophyceae of North America, 1910; South Pacific Plants, 1912—; Index Algarum Universalis, 1915—; Bibliography of Pacific Ocean Algae, 1920; Our Richest Source of Vitamins, 1928; A Classification of the Algae, 1933; Standardization of Method of Drawing Algae for Publication, 1934; South Pacific Plants, second series, 1934-35; The Algae and Their Life Relations, 1935-37. Made trip around world with ten grad. students, collecting algae in Australia and New Zealand, 1934, 35. Fellow A.A. A.S., Am. Geog. Soc.; mem. Bot. Soc. Am.; Am. Soc. Naturalists, Am. Microscopical Soc., Nat. Geog. Soc., Bull Torrey Botany Club, Fla. Acad. Science, Sigma Xi. Home: Golden Bough Colony, Hesperides, Lake Wales, Fla. Deceased.

TILLER, Theodore Hance, newspaper corr.; b. Oglethorpe County, Ga., Jan. 1, 1881; s. John Winston and Blanche Corrinne (Hance) T.; ed. pub. schs. and Southern Shorthand and Business U., Atlanta, Ga.; m. Leona Patterson, June 10, 1903; children—Theodore II, Teel. Began with Bainbridge Argus, 1903, owner and editor, 1904-06; polit. writer Munsey newspapers, 1909-17; Washington correspondent of Atlanta Journal, 1918-28, New York Telegram, 1920-27, Macon Telegraph, 1928-30; on Washington staff of Baltimore (Md.) Sun, 1927-28; mem. Capitol staff of Washington Times, 1929-33; with publicity and information office of Home Owners' Loan Corp. and Fed. Home Owners' Loan Orgn. asso. with Com. on Pub. Information, World War I. Mem. Ga. State Soc. of Washington (ex-pres.). Democrat. Christian Scientist. Clubs: Gridiron, Nat. Press (ex-pres.). Home: 3409 Mount Pleasant St. Office: Federal Home Loan Bank Board, Washington, D.C. Deceased.*

TILLETT, Charles Walter, lawyer; b. Mangum, N.C., Feb. 6, 1888; s. Charles W. and Carrie (Patterson) T.; A.B., U. N.C., 1909; student law sch., 1909-10; m. Gladys Avery, July 21, 1917; children—Gladys (Mrs. Coddington), Charles Walter III, Sara (Mrs. Thomas). Admitted to N.C. bar, 1910 and since practiced in Charlotte; mem. Tillett, Campbell, Craighill & Rendelman. Mem. bd. sch. commrs. City Charlotte, 1919-23; mem. Bd. Law Examiners N.C., 1933-44; city atty., Charlotte, 1941-45. Mem. bd. trustees U.N.C., 1932-36. Served as capt. 50th Inf. Regt., World War I. Mem. Am., N.C. (past pres.) and Meclenburg bar assns., Am. Law Inst., Am. Legion, Phi Beta Kappa, Sigma Alpha Epsilon. Democrat (co. exec. com.; del. nat. conv. 1944). Presbyn. Clubs: Charlotte Country, Charlotte City, Rotary. Author articles. Home: 2200 Sherwood Av., Charlotte 7. Office: Law Bldg., Charlotte 2, N.C. Died Dec. 23, 1952; buried Charlotte.

TILLINGHAST, Benjamin Franklin, journalist; b. E. Greenwich, R.I., July 4, 1849; s. Samuel R. and Julia A. (Searle) T.; ed. pub. schs. of Providence, R.I., prep. depts. Beloit Coll. and Monmouth Coll., grad. Monmouth Coll., B.S., 1870; m. Sept. 25, 1878, Nellie Nourse. Editor Coll. Courier at Monmouth Coll., 1868-70; editor Moline (Ill.) Rev., 1872; city editor, Davenport (Ia.) Gazette, 1878; asso. editor, 1882-94, editor, 1904—, Davenport (Ia.) Democrat. Sec. of organization sending relief to Russia, 1892. Independent in politics. U.S. del. to Internat. Conf. of Red Cross, St. Petersburg, Russia, 1902. Author: Rock Island Arsenal, in Peace and War, 1898 X1. Address: Davenport, Ia. Deceased.

TILLINGHAST, Harold Morton, mfg. co. exec.; b. Cambridge, Mass., July 18, 1884; s. Wm. H. and E. Grace (Akin) T.; B.A., Harvard, 1907; m. Dorothy Pratt, 1913; children—William P., Ruth. Chemist Cuban-Am. Sugar Co., Cent. Tinguaro, Cuba, 1907-08, chief chemist, 1908-09; export salesman Grinnell Willis & Co., 1909-10; with R. Hoe & Co., Inc., 1910—, sec., 1920-26, v.p. and dir. 1926-39, pres. and dir., 1939-45, chmn. bd., 1945-50. Dir. Bronx Bd. Trade, 1940-47. Mem. Am. Ordnance Assn. (adv. bd., past pres. N.Y. post; mem. council). Mem. Council of Graphic Arts Research Bur., 1937-38; chmn. Newspaper Printing Press Builders' Code Authority, 1934; chmn. Newspaper Printing Press Builders Assn., 1935; mem. N.Y. Advisory Bd. of Am. Mutual Liability Insurance Co. Clubs: Harvard, Advertising N.Y.); Harvard (New Canaan). Retired. Home: Laurel Rd., New Canaan, Conn. Died Apr. 26, 1958; buried Lakeview Cemetery, New Cauaus, Conn.

TILSON, John Quillin, lawyer, ex-congressman; b. Clear Branch, Tenn., Apr. 5, 1866; s. William E. and Katharine (Sams) T.; A.B., Yale, 1891, LL.B., 1893, M.L., 1894; m. Marguerite North, Nov. 10, 1910; children—John Quillin, Mrs. Margaret Shafer, Mrs. Katharine Murray. In law practice New Haven, Conn., 1898—; Washington, 1933-40. Mem. Conn. Ho. of Reps., 1905-06, 1907-08 (speaker 1907-08); mem. at large, from Conn. 61st and 62d Congresses, 64th to 72nd Congress from 3d Dist.; majority leader Ho. of Reps., 69th, 70th and 71st Congresses. Prof. parliamentary law, Yale. Republican. Served as 2d lt., 6th U.S. Vol. Inf., Spanish-Am. War, 1898; lt. col. 2d Conn. Inf., Mexican border, 1916. Chmn. bd. Save the Children Fed. Received King's Medal for service to Brit. Children; citation French Govt. service to children in liberated France. Mem. Psi Upsilon, Phi Delta Phi. Baptist. Mason (33°). Clubs: Chevy Chase (Washington); Graduate (New Haven). Author: Manual of Parliamentary Procedure; condensed manual: How to Conduct a Meeting. Home: 3 Loomis Pl. Office: 205 Church St., New Haven, Conn. Died Aug. 14, 1958.

TILT, Charles Arthur, bus. exec.; b. Chgo.; June 28, 1877; s. Joseph E. and Sarah Bowes (Thompson) T.; ed. U. Sch.; Chgo. Manual Tng. Sch.; m. Agnes J. Morgan, Nov. 5, 1902; children—Mrs. Morehead Patterson, Mrs. John Wentworth. Pres. Diamond T Motor Car Co. from 1905, now chmn. bd. Clubs: Chicago, Chicago Athletic, Glen View. Home: 1500 Lake Shore Dr. Office: 4401 W. 26th St., Chgo. Died Sept., 1956.

TILTON, John Philip, college administrator; born Dedham, Mass., Dec. 18, 1900; s. John Freeman and Katherine (Berry) T.; A.B., Colby Coll., 1923; Ed.M., Harvard, 1927, Ed.D., 1933; m. Ruth Dinsmore, Sept. 1, 1928; 1 dau., Kay Grace. Teacher of English, Deering High Sch., Portland, Me., 1923-24, Newton (Mass.) High Sch., 1924-26; asst. in edn., Harvard, 1927-29; instr. in psychology, Babson Inst., Wellesley, Mass., 1929-33; instr. in edn., Tufts Coll., 1927-31, successively asst. and asso. prof., dir. grad. studies, dean grad. sch., dir. div. spl. studies, dir. summer sch., chmn. dept. edn., 1931-53, prof., 1947—, provost, 1951—, sr. v.p., 1953—, sec. bd. trustees 1955—; dir. Middlesex County Nat. Bank. Mem. corp. Walter B. Fernald Sch., Lasell Jr. Coll.; mem. adv. com. Simmons Coll. Sch. of Social Work, Lowell Inst. Broadcasting Council; sec.-treas. Ednl. Service Assos.; trustee Csivic Education Found. Mem. A.A.A.S., Harvard Tchrs. Assn., Am. Assn. Sch. Adminstrs., Mass. Schoolmasters Club, Nat. Soc. Coll. Tchrs. Edn., Am. Psychol. Assn., Horace Mann League, Mass. Civic League, Phi Beta Kappa, Phi Delta Kappa, Delta Upsilon. Club: Harvard (Boston). Home: 48 Professors Row, Tufts Univ., Medford, Mass. Died Jan. 15, 1959; buried Belfast, Me.

TIMBERLAKE, Gideon, urologist; b. Charlottesville, Va., Mar. 6, 1876; s. Crawford G. and Sarah (Garland) T.; M.D., U. of Va., 1902; m. Sallie Virginia Helms, Jan. 19, 1922; children—Virginia Helms (Mrs. A. B. Taylor, Jr.), Martha Ann (Mrs. Wm. J. Haymaker, Jr.). Prof. urology, U. of Md. and Coll. of Physicians and Surgeons, Baltimore; urologist to University, St. Agnes and Franklin Square Hosps., Baltimore, Maryland; cons. urologist to Bay View Hospital, Kernan Hospital for Ruptured and Crippled Children and Med. Center of Venice, Florida; surgeon to staff of Church Home and Infirmary and West Baltimore General hosps. (resigned); mem. staff Mound Park and St. Anthony's hosps., St. Petersburg, Fla.; consultant in urology to Vets. Hosp., Bay Pines, Fla.; consultant to Crippled Children's Hosp., St. Petersburg. Organizer, dir. Army Sch. Urol., Ft. Oglethorpe, Ga., 1918; chief of dept. of urology, Walter Reed Hosp.; maj. Med. Corps, U.S. Army, World War. Founder and diplomate Am. Bd. Urology. Fellow Am. Coll. Surgeons; mem. Am. Urol. Assn., A.M.A., Pinellas County Med. Soc. (St. Petersburg, Fla.). Club: Baltimore. Editor: The Urologic and Cutareous Review. Contbr. med. jours. Inventor several urol. instruments. Home: 455 19th Av. N.E., St. Petersburg, Fla. Died Mar. 1, 1951.

TIMBLIN, Louis M., chem. mfr.; b. Midway, Pa., Mar. 11, 1899; s. Monroe J. and Sara M. (McFarland) T.; A.B. Marietta Coll., 1921; m. Irene Norman, Nov. 23, 1932. Tchr., athletic coach Aurelius Twp. High Sch., Macksburg, O., 1921-24; staff F. W. LaFrentz & Co. C.P.A.'s, 1924-39; auditor Charles Pfizer & Co., Inc., 1940-42, asst. treas., 1943-45, dir. since 1943, treas. since 1945, mem. exec. com. since 1948; dir. Lafayette Nat. Bank, Bklyn. Mem. Controllers Inst., N.Y. State Soc. C.P.A.'s, Nat. Assn. Cost Accountants. Clubs: Union League; Drug and Chem. (Bklyn.). Home: Edgewood Av., Smithtown Branch, L.I. Office: 11 Bartlett St., Bklyn. 6. Died Nov. 20, 1955.

TIMME, Walter (tĭm'mĕ), physician; b. New York, N.Y., Feb. 24, 1874; s. Frederick and Emma (Wirth) T.; B.S., Coll. of City of New York, 1893; M.D., Columbia, 1897; grad. student, U. of Berlin, 1912-13; m. Ida Helen Haar, June 27, 1901; m. second Anne C. Auwell, July 28, 1951. Began as physician, 1897; was chief of clinic, Vanderbilt Clinic, N.Y.; sr. attending neurologist, mil. dir. neuroendocrine dept. and consultant in endocrinology, Neurol. Inst. of New York; prof. clin. neurology, Columbia. Fellow N.Y. Acad. Medicine; founder member Assn. for Research in Nervous and Mental Diseases (pres.); mem. Assn. for Study Internal Secretions (pres.), N.Y. Endocrine Soc. (pres.), Am. Neurol. Assn., Assn. of Alumni Coll. of City of N.Y. (pres.), Phi Beta Kappa, Phi Delta Theta, Phi Beta Kappa Associates. Townsend Harris Medal 1948. Clubs: Columbia University, City College, Marshall Chess (New York); Highland Country (Garrison, N.Y.). Author: Lectures in Endocrinology, 1923. Contbr. to volumes of Assn. for Research in Nervous and Mental Diseases; also to med. jours. Home: Cold Spring, N.Y. Died Feb. 12, 1956; buried Timme Mausoleum, Cold Spring.

TIMMONS, Wofford Colquitt, clergyman; b. Lawrenceville, Ga., Sept. 20, 1888; s. Benson Ellison Lane and Margaret Elizabeth (Longden) T.; student Asbury Coll., Wilmore, Ky., 1905-08; A.B., Southwestern Coll., Winfield, Kan., 1913; student Union Theol. Sem. and Columbia, 1915-17, Oxford U., summer 1925; D.D., Chgo. Theol. Sem., 1926; m. Fanny Elizabeth Pray, June 21, 1917; children—James Joseph (dec.), Robert Lansing, John Benson. Asst. pastor Roseville M.E. Ch., Newark, 1914-17; Y.M.C.A. sec., Camp Dix, N.J., 1917-18, Mpls., 1918-20; asso. pastor Plymouth Congl. Ch., Mpls., 1920-22; pastor First Congl. Ch., St. Louis, 1922-32, South Ch., New Britain, Conn., 1932-46, now minister Ch. Wide Fellowship, Southern Pines, N.C. Brit. Am. exchange minister, 1939; moderator Conn. Congl. Conf., 1943-44. Trustee Hartford Theol. Sem. Found.; mem. Nat. Council Congl. Ch.; chmn. Commn. Evangelism, Congl.-Christian Chs.; sec. bd. home missions, mem. exec. commn. evangelism and devotional life; mem. exec. com. dept. evangelism Nat. Council Chs. Christ U.S.A.; mem. Home Missions Council; exec. sec. Commn. Evangelism. Mem. Pi Kappa Delta, Chi Alpha. Democrat. Mason. Clubs: Friars (Hartford, Conn.); Rotary, Nat. Arts (N.Y.C.). Author: The Task of the Church in This Time. Contbr. articles and verse to Advance, Christian Leader, etc. Home: 450 Country Club Rd. Office: Church of Wide Fellowship, Southern Pines, N.C. Died Aug. 29, 1957; buried Waterville, O.

TIMPY, Jack J., mfg. exec.; b. Ludington, Mich., Jan. 4, 1897; s. Martin and Catherine (Ruby) T.; student LaSalle Inst., 1919-23; m. Coletta A. Galvin, June 22, 1926; children—Mary Catherine, Coletta Ann. With Am. Motors Corp. (formerly Nash-Kelvinator Corp.), Detroit, 1922—, successively accountant, comptroller, 1944-54, v.p., 1954—. Mem. Controllers Inst., Nat. Assn. Cost Accountants, Detroit Bd. Commerce, Army Ordnance Assn. Club: Detroit Golf. Home: 17554 Warrington Dr., Detroit. Office: 14250 Plymouth Rd., Detroit 32. Died Jan. 1960.

TINCHER, J. N., ex-congressman; b. Sullivan Co., Mo., Nov. 2, 1878; ed. high sch. Medicine Lodge, Kan.; m. Nellie M. Southworth, of Medicine Lodge, 1901; children—George (dec.), Coreine Albert (dec.), J. N. Admitted to Kan. bar, 1899, practiced law at Medicine Lodge, until 1927, Hutchinson, Kan., 1927—; identified with farming and live stock raising; mem. 66th to 69th Congresses (1917-27), 7th Kan. Dist. Republican. Home: Hutchinson, Kan. Died Nov. 7, 1951.

TINGELSTAD, Oscar Adolf (tĭng'ĕl-städ), educator; b. Hickson, Cass County, N.D., September 20, 1882; s. Bent and Beret (Livdalen) T.; A.B., Luther Coll., Decorah, Ia., 1905; D.D. (honorary) Pacific Lutheran College, 1952; graduate Luther Sem., St. Paul, Minn., 1907; A.M., U. of Chicago, 1913, Ph. D., 1925; fellow in edn., same, 1913-14, instr., 1925; m. Alfield Sophie Tvete, Aug. 4, 1909. Ordained Luth. ministry, 1907; pastor Zion Ch., Seattle, Wash., 1907-09; prof. psychology and edn., 1909-19, prof. edn., 1919-28, registrar, 1914-27, prin. prep. dept., 1917-19, Luther Coll., Decorah, Ia.; pres. Pacific Lutheran Coll., Parkland, Wash., 1928-43; indoctrination instructor, Puget Sound Navy Yard, 1943-

44; prof. philosophy and Bible, Luther Coll. 1944-50, now emeritus. Sec. Young People's Luther League. Norwegian Lutheran Ch., Am., 1917-22. Member N. E.A., Am. Scandinavian Foundation, Soc. Adv. Scandinavian Study, Phi Delta Kappa. Author: Norgesfaerden (with J. C. K. Preus), 1914; Christian Keyser Preus (with O. M. Norlie), 1922; Luther College Through Sixty Years (with others), 1922; The Religious Element in American School Readers, 1925. Home: 309 Center St., Decorah, Ia. Died Apr. 8, 1953; buried Decorah Lutheran Cemetery.

TINGLE, John Bishop, chemist, educator; b. Sheffield, Eng., Nov. 12, 1866; s. Alfred and Mary Elizabeth (Bishop) T.; ed. pvt. sch., Sheffield Royal Grammar Sch.; Owens Coll., Manchester, Eng., 1884-87; Ph.D., U. Munich, 1899; married. Teacher of chemistry, 1889—; came to U.S., 1896; professor chemistry, Ill. Coll., Sept. 1901-04. Asst. in charge organic chemical laboratory, Johns Hopkins U., and sub-editor Am. Chem. Journal, Sept., 1904—. Fellow Chem. Soc., England, German Chem. Soc., Am. Chem. Soc., A.A.A.S. Translated and enlarged: General Organic Chemistry (E. Hjelt), 1890, Spectrum Analysis (J. Landauer), 1898, Determination of Radicles in Carbon Compounds (H. Meyer), 1899, 2d edit., 1903. Application of Some General Reactions to Investigations in Organic Chemistry (Lassar-Cohn), 1904. Address: Johns Hopkins University, Baltimore. Died 1918.

TINGLEY, Louisa Paine (tĭng'lē), physician; b. Providence, R.I., June 14, 1869; d. Charles Edward and Eliza Taylor (Fiske) Paine; studied and traveled abroad, 1886-89, and 1896-97; M.D., Tufts Coll. Med. Sch., 1901; m. Frank Foster Tingley, June 14, 1899 (died 1921). German tutor and instr. in pvt. schs., 1889-97; practicing physician in Providence and Boston since 1901; specialist in opthalmology; ophthalmic surgeon, New England Hosp. for Women and Children (1901-10, New England Deaconess Hosp. since 1901, Mass. Women's Hosp. since 1918; councillor Mass. Med. Soc., 1920-24 and 1931-37. Served on staff New England Deaconess Base Hosp., World War I. Mem. Am. Board Commrs. Foreign Missions. Fellow Am. Coll. of Surgeons; mem. A.M.A., Mass. Med. Soc., R.I. Med. Soc., Providence Med. Assn., New England Ophthal. Society, American Acad. of Ophthalmology and Otolaryngology, Illuminating Engring. Soc., Providence Animal Rescue League (dir.), Am. Unitarian Assn. (life), R.I. Hist. Soc., A.A.A.S., Roger Williams Assn. Republican. Unitarian. Clubs: Mass. Women's Republican, Republican (Boston); R.I. Women's Republican (Providence). Author: Some Sidelights in the Biography of My Great, Great Grandfather, Caleb Fiske, M.D. Contbr. to med. jours. Address: 416 Marlborough St., Boston. Died July 16, 1952; buried Swan Point Cemetery, Providence.

TINKER, Earl Warren, assn. exec.; b. Fenton, Mich., Oct. 28, 1890; s. Clarence and Hattie J. (Perry) T.; B.S., Mich. State Coll., 1913; M.F., Yale, 1915; m. Kathleen Buzard, Nov. 29, 1917; 1 dau., Margaret J. Forester, U.S. Forest Service, Washington, 1915-39; exec. sec., Am. Paper & Pulp Assn., N.Y. City, since 1940. Mem. Soc. Am. Foresters, Tech. Assn. of Paper Industry. Republican. Episcopalian. Clubs: Yale, Uptown (N.Y. City); Metropolitan (Washington). Home: 470 Park Av., N.Y.C. Office: 122 E. 42d St., N.Y.C. 17. Died Aug. 31, 1957; buried Fenton, Mich.

TINKER, Edward Richmond, banker; b. North Adams, Mass., Mar. 10, 1878; s. Giles Knight and Catherine W. (Andrews) T.; A.B., Williams, 1899; m. Marie V. Sollace, Oct. 23, 1909. Clk. Edward Sweet & Co., N.Y.C., 1899, later with Vermilye & Co., and William A. Read & Co.; mem. Rhoades & Co., 1907-12; v.p. Chase Nat. Bank, 1912-20; pres. Chase Securities Corp., 1920-25; chmn. exec. com. Chase Nat. Bank and Chase Securities Corp., 1925-27; pres. Interstate Equities Corp., 1929-32; chmn. bd. Fox Film Corp., 1932-33; engaged in reorganization of theater companies and other corps, 1933—; mem. bd. of dirs. Hat. Corp. of Am., Wilson & Co., Inc., U.S. Hat Machinery Corp., Byrndun Corp. Alternat on Liberty Loan Com., 1917-18; mem. Commrl. Banks and Trust Companies Com., Liberty Loan Com., 1918-19. Fellow Am. Geog. Soc. Clubs: Williams Coll. Club, Racquet and Tennis, Piping Rock, Creek (N.Y.) Bohemian (San Francisco); Bath and Tennis (Palm Beach); Seawanhaka Corinthian Yacht; Deepdale (N.Y.) Golf; Ekwanok Country (Manchester, Vt.). Home: Syosset, L.I., N.Y. Died Mar. 1, 1959.

TINKER, Martin Buel, surgeon; b. Granville, Mass., Mar. 17, 1869; s. Martin Phelps and Margaret Maritta (Smith) T.; S.B., Harvard, 1895; M.D., Jefferson Med. Coll., Phila., 1893; M.D., U. of Berlin, 1899; m. Ethel Louise Bates, May 4, 1905; children—Martin Buel, Alfred Bates, Charity Marshall. Asst. physiology and hygiene, Harvard, 1894-96; demonstrator in surgery and anatomy, Jefferson Med. Coll., 1897-1900; resident surgeon, Johns Hopkins Hosp., 1900-03; lectr. surgery, 1903-08, asst. prof. surgery, 1908-10, Cornell U.; surgeon, Ithaca Meml. Hosp. cons. surgeon, Tioga County Gen. Hosp., Willard State Hosp. Served from maj. to lt. col., Med. Res. Corps., 1917-19. Diplomate Am. Bd. Surgery (founder). Fellow A.C.S., Am. Surg. Assn., Am. Assn. for Study of Goiter, del. to Internat. Goiter Conf.; mem. A.M.A., Am. Acad. Medicine, N.Y. State Med. Soc. (chmn. surg. sect. 1913, pres. 1916), A.A.A.S, N.Y. Acad. Sciences, Société Internat. de Churugie, Deutsche Gesellschaft für Chirurgie, Am. Legion (comdr.), Sigma Xi, Alpha Omega Alpha, Nu Sigma Nu, Pi Gamma Mu, Phi Kappa Tau. Republican. Congregationalist. Clubs: Town and Gown, Country, University, Rotary, Masons, Appalachian Mountain, Green Mountain. Home: The Knoll, Cornell Heights, Ithaca, N.Y. Office: 219 Savings Bank Bldg., Ithaca, N.Y. Died Feb. 26, 1954; buried Granville, Mass.

TINKMAN, George Holden (ting'ăm), ex-congressman; b. Boston, Oct. 29, 1870; s. George Henry and Frances Ann (Holden) T.; A.B., Harvard, 1894; student Harvard Law Sch.; unmarried. Admitted to Mass. bar, 1899; mem. Common Council, Boston, 1897-98, Bd. Aldermen, 1900-02; mem. Mass. Senate, 1910-12; mem. 64th to 77th Congresses (1915-43), 10th Mass. Dist. Mem. Am. Bar Assn., Mass. Bar Assn., Bar Assn. City Boston, N.E. Historic-Geneal. Soc., Hasty Pudding Club (Harvard), Soc. Mayflower Descendants, Co. of Mass. Bay in N.E. Republican. Clubs: Algonquin (Boston); Harvard (New York); National Press (Washington). The 1st Am. to fire shot against the Austrians after the declaration of war by U.S. at Capo d'Argine, on Piave River, Dec. 11, 1917. Did not accept decoration Chevalier della Corona d'Italia conferred, because of constl. provision. Office: Barristers Hall, Pemberton Sq., Boston. Died Aug. 28, 1956; buried Forest Hills Cemetery, Boston.

TINLEY, Mathew Adrian, industrial surgeon; b. Council Bluffs, Ia., Mar. 5, 1876; s. Mathew Hugh and Rose (Dolan) T.; M.D., U. of Neb., 1902; post-grad. work, N.Y. Post Grad. Med. Sch., 1902; m. Lucy Shaw Williams, Oct. 8, 1902; children—Winifred M., Robert E. (officer U.S. Army). Began career as member of staff Janie Edmundson Hospital, 1903; surgeon Union Pacific R.R. since 1905, Wabash R.R. since 1920, C.&N.W. RR. since 1936; examiner for Aetna, Conn. Mutual, Ia. Employers Mut. Insurance cos. Nominated for Vice Pres. of U.S. by Ia. delegation, Dem. Nat. Conv., 1932. Served in U.S. Army, Philippine campaign, 1898-99; col. inf. World War I, comdg. 168th Inf., 42d Div.; retired as maj. gen. U.S. Nat. Guard, Mar. 5, 1940; now lt. gen. Ia. State Guard. Awarded D.S.M., Philippino Congressional Medal (U.S.); Officer Legion of Honor (France); Croix de Guerre (France); gold medal for best act of law enforcement for year U.S. Flag Assn., 1934. Fellow American College, Surgeons; member American Medical Association, Iowa, State Med. Soc. (v.p. 1920), Wabash Surgeons (pres. 1934), Am. Assn. Ry. Surgeons (pres. 1939), Nat. Rainbow Vets. Soc. (pres.), Nat. Guard Assn. America (pres. 1934), Am. Legion (1st dept. comdr. Ia.), Vets. Foreign Wars, Order of Carribao (Phillipine), Newcomen Soc. England, Phi Rho Sigma. Democrat. Catholic. K.C., Elk. Club: Council Bluffs. Home: 520 Third St. Office. Park Bldg., Council Bluffs, Ia. Died Mar. 11, 1956; buried Council Bluffs.

TINSLEY, Gladney Jack, coll. pres.; b. Haynesville, La., June 19, 1896; s. George Munroe and Merrah Belle (McEachern) T.; student, Valparaiso Univ., spring, 1917, U. of Tex., summer, 1923, U. of Chicago, summer, 1930; B.S., La. State Univ., 1924, M.S., 1925; Ed.D., Stanford U., 1931; m. Maud Hood, Aug 13, 1927. Public Sch. teacher, Claiborne Parish, La., 1914-17; prin., Summerfield (La.) High Sch., 1919-23, Rosenthal grammar sch., Alexandria, La., 1924-30; dir. extension, Southwestern La. Inst., Lafayette, 1931-41, head dept. of edn. adminstrn., 1941-45; pres., Southeastern La. Coll., since 1945. Mem. Draft Bd., Lafayett, La., 1942-45. Served U.S. Army, 1917-19. Mem. Am. Legion (comdr., 1942-44), N.E.A (life mem) La. Teachers Assn., Phi Delta Kappa, Kappa Delta Pi. Mason (Shriner). Club: Rotary (pres., Hammond, La., 1948-49). Home: Dakota Av., Hammond, La. Died Dec. 8, 1951; buried Haynesville (Ia.) Cemetery.

TINSLEY, John Francis, loom mfr.; b. Hampton Junction, N.J., July 4, 1880; s. Robert and Elizabeth (Ahern) T.; B.S., Rutgers, 1900, M.S., 1904, D.Sc., 1931; honorary M.A., College of the Holy Cross, Worcester, Mass., 1922, LL.D., 1943; m. Helen Munroe, November 26, 1910; 1 dau., Mary Munroe. With Western Electric Co., N.Y. City, 1900-02, United Electric Co., Newark, N.J., 1902-03; asst. elec. engr., Signal Corps, U.S. Army, 1903-05; with Am. Steel and Wire Co., Worcester, advancing to gen. supt. South Works, 1905-16; v.p. and gen. mgr. Crompton & Knowles Loom Works, Worcester, 1916-38, pres. and gen. mgr. since 1938; pres. and treas. Crompton & Knowles Jacquard & Supply Co.; pres. Hutchison Av. Co., Charlotte, N.C.; dir. Worcester County Trust Co., Peoples Savings Bank, Mass. Bonding & Ins. Co., Worcester Street Ry. Co. (chmn. exec. com.), 2d Nat. Bank of Boston, N.E. Telephone & Telegraph Co. (mem. exec. com.), Mfrs. Mutual Fire Ins. Co., Providence. Chairman adv. board War Department, Boston Ordnance District; governor National Industrial Conference Board; grad. Command and General Staff Sch., U.S. Army. Mem. bd. overseers Harvard Coll. Com. to visit Sch. Bus. Adminstrn., 1945, 1946-50; mem. C. of C. of U.S. Decorated Cavalieri Order of Crown of Italy; Knight of Sovereign Military Order of Malta; Knight Commander Order of Mercy; Officer Legion of Honor (France). Life trustee Rutgers Univ., St. Vincent Hosp.; trustee, Western Massachusetts Co., Springfield, Massachusetts; vice president and director of the Community Chest of Worcester; dir. Worcester Children's Friend Soc.; dir. Worcester Br. Mass. Soc. for the Prevention of Cruelty to Children; director American Society of French Legion of Honor. Fellow of the Royal Soc. of Arts (England). Mem. Layman Advisory Council of Boston Coll. Sch. of Business Administration. Dir. Nat. Assn. Textile Machinery Mfrs. (ex-pres.), National Association of Manufacturers; American Iron and Steel Institute, Am. Soc. for Testing Materials, Asso. Industries Mass. (former pres.), Newcomen Soc., Eng. (Am. branch), New England Council (dir.; ex-v.p.), Nat. Fgn. Trade Council (dir., mem. committee on foreign trade reconstruction), Worcester Chamber of Commerce (ex-pres.), Army Ord. Assn., Phi Beta Kappa, Chi Phi and Tau Beta Pi fraternities. Republican. Catholic. Clubs: Economic (ex-pres.), Worcester, Tatnuck Country (Worcester); Rutgers of New England (pres.); Harvard Faculty (Cambridge); Kiwanis (hon.), University (New York). Author: New Phases of Industrial Management, 1926. Founder of New England Indsl. Research Foundation. Home: 15 Regent St. Office: 93 Grand St., Worcester, Mass. Died Nov. 18, 1950.

TIPTON, Ernest Moss, judge; b. Bowling Green, Mo., Jan. 2, 1889; s. Rev. William Morton and Mary Ann (Moss) T.; LL.B., U. of Mo., 1911; m. Rosalie Bloch, Jan. 19, 1916; children—Dorothy Nell, William Ernest. Admitted to Mo. bar, 1911; in practice at Fulton, 1911-20, at Kansas City, 1920-32; judge Mo. Supreme Court, 1932—, chief justice, 1938-40, 46-48, 55—. Mem. State Bd. of Bar Examiners, 1923-30. Mem. Aberdeen Angus Breeders' Assn. Democrat. Baptist. Mason. Home: Hwy. 50 E., Jefferson City, Mo. Address: Supreme Court Bldg., Jefferson City, Mo. Died Feb. 25, 1955; buried Jefferson City.

TIPTON, Laurence B., educator; b. Selma, Ala., Mar. 27, 1910; s. William Hogan and Mary Wood (Buell) T.; student The Citadel, 1928, 1930; A.B., U. of Ala., 1933; M.A., New York U., 1940, Ed.D., 1941; m. Catharine Randolph, June 2, 1939; children—Laurence B., Catharine. Editor Shelby County (Ala.) Democrat, 1932-33; Ala. state examiner of pub. accounts, 1933-34; Ala. dir. pub. safety, 1934-36; asst. dir. Northwestern U. Safety Inst., 1936-38; prof. and head bur. of safety, Rutgers U., 1938-41; instr. summer sessions, U. of Ala., Penn State Coll., Harvard U., 1936-40; chief training advisor, U.S. Dept. of Labor, 1941-42; lt. col., U.S. Army, assigned as fed. dir. indsl. safety training, 1942-46; ednl. dir. Warner Bros. Pictures, Inc., 1946—; head Laurence B. Tipton & Associates; v.p. Pathe Pictures, Inc. Mem. Phi Beta Kappa, Phi Delta Kappa, Phi Gamma Delta. Democrat. Episcopalian. Author articles, papers, treatises and bulls. in field. Home: 412 Union St., Selma, Ala. Office: 33 W. 60th St., N.Y.C. Died Jan. 20, 1957; buried Live Oak Cemetery, Selma, Ala.

TIRRELL, Frank A., Jr., asso. justice Supreme Ct. of Me. Address: State Capitol, Augusta, Me. Deceased.*

TITUS, Paul, obstetrician, gynecologist; b. Batavia, N.Y., May 6, 1885; s. Rev. John Wentworth and Elma Margaret (Titus) Sanborn; adopted by maternal grandparents, Rev. and Mrs. Wicks Smith Titus; M.D., Yale, 1908; m. Mary Cushing. Asst. Universitäts Frauenklinik, Heidelberg, Germany, 1908-10; asst. in obstetrics, Johns Hopkins Hosp., Baltimore, 1910-11; resident obstetrician and gynecologist, Magee Hosp., Pittsburgh, 1911-12; now obstetrician and gynecologist, St. Margaret Memorial Hosp.; cons. obstetrician and gynecologist, Shadyside Hosp. Sec.-treas. and dir. Am. Bd. of Obstetrics and Gynecology; sec.-treas. Adv. Bd. for Med. Specialists, 1933-41, v.p., 1943-45, pres., 1945-47; mem. adv. editorial bd., Am. Jour. Obstetrics and Gynecology; directing editor, Directory of Medical Specialists, 1937-47. Pres. the Assn. of Yale Alumni in Med., 1942-43. Special agt. for Naval Intelligence, and Mil. Intelligence Sect., War Dept., 1915-19. Consultant to surg. gen., U.S. Army, 1943-44; lt. comdr. to capt., M.C., U.S.N.R., attached to Professional Div., Bur. Med. and Surg., Navy Dept., Washington, 1944-45 and 1946; mem. Reserve Consultants Adv. Bd., Bur. Medicine and Surgery, Navy Dept., since 1946; mem. Armed Forces Medical Adv. Com., 1948-50. Awarded Navy Commendation Ribbon. Fellow Am. Coll. Surgeons, A.M.A., Am. Assn. of Obstetricians, Gynecologists and Abdominal Surgeons (exec. council 1929-35, and 1939-45; pres. 1937-38), Am. Gynecol. Soc. (v.p. 1948-49); mem. Med. Soc. State of Pa., Pittsburgh Acad. Medicine (pres. 1929-30), Allegheny County Med. Soc., Soc. Royale, Belge de Gynécologie et d'Obstetrique, Phi Gamma Delta, Nu Sigma Nu. Awarded Commanders Cross, Order of Merit, Hungary, 1938. Author: Management of Obstetric Difficulties, 1937, 2d edit., 1940, 3d edit., 1945, 4th edit., 1950; Diseases of Women for the

General Practitioner, 1937; Atlas of Obstetric Technic, 1943, 2d edit., 1949. Home: Schenley Apts., 5th Av. Office: Highland Bldg., Pittsburgh 6. Died June 28, 1951.

TOBEY, Charles William (tō'bē), U.S. senator; b. Roxbury, Mass., s. William H. and Ellen Hall (Parker) T.; educated Roxbury Latin School; honorary A.M., Dartmouth, 1929; LL.D., U. of N.H., 1929; m. Francelia M. Lovett, June 4, 1902 (dec.); children—Russell Benjamin, Louise, Francelia, Charles William; m. 2d, Loretta C. Rabenhorst, May 26, 1948. Was pres. F. M. Hoyt Shoe Co. Chmn. Lib. Loan campaigns, N.H., 1917-19. Was mem. N.H. Ho. of Rep. (speaker 1919-20), N.H. Senate (pres. 1925-26); gov. N.H., 1929-30; mem. 73d to 75th Congresses (1933-39), 2d N.H. Dist.; mem. U.S. Senate, term 1939-45. In 1944 was re-elected to U.S. Senate for 2d term ending Jan. 1951. Mem. of U.S. delegation to International Monetary Conference, Bretton Woods, New Hampshire, July 1944. Trustee Colby Jr. Coll., New London, N.H. Pres. Manchester Chamber Commerce. Formerly pres. Bapt. State Conv. Republican. Mason. Club: Rotary (pres.). Home: Temple, N.H. Died July 24, 1953.

TOBIN, Daniel J., labor official; b. Ireland, 1875; s. John and Bridget (Kennelly) T.; ed. in Ireland and in night schools, Cambridge, Mass.; m. Annie E. Reagan (dec.); children—John M., Frank L., Frederick, Edmund P., Joseph, Katherine; m. 2d, Irene Halloran. Came to U.S., 1889; general pres. Internat. Brotherhood Teamsters, Chauffeurs, Warehouseman and Helpers, 1907——; treas. American Fdn. Labor, 11 years, resigned 1928, v.p., 1933——; v.p. Nat. Bldg. Trades Dept. A.F. of L., 1933——; apptd. administrative asst. to Pres. Roosevelt, July 1940, resigned Oct. 1940. Represented Am. Fedn. of Labor at British Trades Union Congress, 1911, 38, 42; del. internat. Fedn. Trade Unions, at Amsterdam, 1918; served in various labor adjustments during World War ; mem. Pres. Wilson's Indsl. Conf.; chmn. of Labor Div. of Nat. Dem. Campaign Com., 1932, 36, 40, 44; declined appointment as Regional Federal Administrator, 1933; sent by Pres. Roosevelt to England, Aug. 1942, as his representative to investigate labor conditions there and report findings to Am. people. Office: 222 East Michigan St., Indpls. Died Nov. 14, 1955; buried Cambridge, Mass.

TOBIN, John Charles, lawyer; b. St. Louis County, Mo., Sept. 6, 1886; s. Thomas Joseph and Mary Cantwell (Cluney) T.; A.B., St. Louis U., 1908, A.M., 1909; LL.B., St. Louis Inst. Law, 1911; grad. study Harvard Law Sch., 1912; m. Pauline Robyn, June 17, 1914; children—Mary Louise, John Charles, Paul Robyn, Thomas Joseph, Virginia Terese. Admitted to Mo. bar, 1912, began law practice, St. Louis, now gen. practice. Past pres. Bd. Edn., St. Louis, 2 terms. Organized Spirit of St. Louis for Col. Lindbergh. Chmn. St. Louis Social Security Commn., Selective Service, Appeal Bd. No. 7; treas. Mo. Soc. Crippled Children; dir. St. Louis Soc. for Blind, St. Louis Grand Opera Assn.; dir. St. Louis Pub. Library. Mem. Am., Mo., St. Louis (v.p.) bar assns., Tb and Health Soc. St. Louis, St. Louis C. of C. Democrat. Catholic. Clubs: University, Noonday, Automobile of Mo. (v.p., dir.), Bellerive Country Bogey Golf. Home: 5 Kingsbury Pl. Office: Security Bldg., St. Louis. Died May 9, 1956; buried Calvary Cemetery.

TOBIN, Maurice Joseph, former Sec. of Labor; b. Roxbury, Mass., May 22, 1901; s. James and Margaret (Daly) T.; LL.D., Boston U., 1940, Portia Law Sch., 1941, U. Mass., 1949, Boston Coll., 1949, John Carroll U., 1949, Sienna and St. John's U., 1950, St. Louis U., 1951, Loras Coll., 1952; m. Helen Noonan, Nov. 19, 1932; children—Helen L., Carol A., Maurice J. With Conway Leather Co.; with N.E. Telephone and Telegraph Co., 1922-37; mayor of Boston, 1938-44; mem. Mass. Ho. of Rep., 1926-28; mem. Boston Sch. Com., 1931-34, 1935-37; gov. of Mass., 1945-47; U.S. Sec. of Labor, 1948——. Mem. Massachusetts Cath. Order of Foresters, K.C. (4th degree), Moose, Owls. Clubs: Commonwealth Country (Brighton); Boston City. Home: 30 Hopkins Rd., Jamaica Plain, Mass. Died July 19, 1953; buried Holyhood Cemetery.

TOBIN, Ralph C., army officer; b. N.Y.C., May 5, 1890; student Coll. City of N.Y.; entered Fed. Service with N.Y. Nat. Guard, June 1916, as pvt. serving at McAllen, Tex., with 7th N.Y. Inf. until Dec. 1916 during border crisis; commd. 2d lt. Inf. Res., Oct. 1918; commd. capt. Inf. N.Y. Nat. Guard, Apr. 1921, and advanced to brig. gen., July 1942; entered Fed. service, Feb. 1941 as comdg. officer 207th Coast Arty. (Anti-Aircraft) Camp Stewart, Ga., 1941-42; in command 44th Coast Arty., Brigade (Anti-Aircraft), July 1942——. Awarded Silver Star, World War I. Address: Washington. Died Aug. 5, 1957.

TOBIN, Richard Montgomery; b. San Francisco, Calif., Apr. 9, 1866; s. Richard and Mary (Regan) T.; ed. St. Ignatius College; honorary LL.D., U. of San Francisco. Dir. Hibernia Bank, 1889; president Association Savings Banks of San Francisco, 1906-27; chmn. San Francisco Group Cal. Bankers Assn., 1922; chmn. Federal Home Loan Bank, 12th Dist., 1933; pres. Hibernia Bank. Chmn. in San Francisco, Nat. Recreation Assn.; lay mem. Roman Cath. Sem. of San Francisco Corp.; v.p. Golden Gate Internat. Expn., 1940 (chmn. Fine Arts Commn.); trustee San Francisco War Memorial 1930-34; regional v.p. 12th Naval Dist. Navy League of U.S., 1943-44; mem. bd. of governors, San Francisco Symphony, 1912-15, 1931-36, v.p. 1931-33, pres. 1934-35; mem. San Francisco Opera Bd. 1930-42. Commd. lt. Class 4, U.S.N.R.F., Dec. 19, 1917; ordered to Paris as rep. of U.S. cable censorship, Jan. 18, 1918; assigned to additional duty as assistant to naval attaché Am. Embassy, Paris, Oct. 13, 1918; attached to Am. Commn. to Negotiate Peace, Paris, Dec. 5, 1918, serving until officially detached, Mar. 25, 1919. E.E. and M.P. to The Netherlands, Mar. 5, 1923-29 (resigned). Home: 1000 Mason St. Address: Hibernia Bank, San Francisco. Died Jan. 23, 1952.

TOBIN, Robert Gibson, naval officer; b. Ronceverte, W.Va., Aug. 17, 1894; s. Robert Emmet and Nellie Theresa (Farrell) T.; student Va. Mil. Inst., 1912-13; B.S., U.S. Naval Acad., 1917; m. Carolyn Cecilia O'Rourke, Jan. 7, 1922; 1 son, Robert G. Commd. ensign U.S. Navy, 1917, and advanced through grades to commodore; served in World War I as engring. and later comdg. officer U.S.S. Hopkins; served on destroyers, cruiser Marblehead, the Pennsylvania, at sea, and the U.S. Naval Acad. and Bur. of Navigation, Washington, D.C.; served as commander 12 destroyers and as commanding officer, U.S.S. Montpelier in the South Pacific Area, World War II; also in London. Awarded 3 Navy crosses, Bronze star, Navy Expeditionary medal, China service, Victory World War I, Purple Heart, Defense medal, Navy Unit commendation, Am. campaign, European campaign, Pacific campaign (7 battle stars), World War II medal. Catholic. Office: 90 Church St., N.Y.C. 7. Deceased.*

TOBITT, Edith, librarian; b. Hawkhurst, Kent, Eng., Jan. 16, 1868; d. George and Ellen (Butcher) T.; brought to U.S. 1872; grad. Pratt Inst. Sch. of Library Science, Bklyn. 1897. Connected with Omaha Pub. Library, 1887-1934, head librarian, 1898-1934. Mem. A.L.A., Neb. State Library Assn., Neb. State Hist. Soc. Home: 3848 Cass St. Address: Public Library, Omaha, Neb. Died July 5, 1939; buried West Lawn Cemetery, Omaha.

TOD, John; b. Youngstown, O., Nov. 29, 1870; s. Henry and Delia (Pollock) T.; ed. Cornell U., 1890-94; LL.D., Youngstown (Ohio) College, 1947; married Alice Wood, Dec. 10, 1895. Sec. and treasurer Falcon Bronze Co., 1895-1900; sec. and treas. Republic Rubber Co., 1900-05; v.p. Brier Hill Iron & Coal Co., 1905-12, pres. since 1919; v.p. Brier Hill Steel Co., 1912-23; pres. Bessemer Limestone Co., 1906-26; pres. David Tod Land Co.; v.p. First Nat. Bank and Dollar Savings & Trust Co., 1920-31; dir. and mem. exec. com. Youngstown Sheet & Tube Co.; dir. Union Nat. Bank, 1930-45. Past pres. Youngstown Hosp. Assn. Mem. Zeta Psi. Republican. Clubs: Youngstown Country. Home: 711 Wick Av. Office: Stambaugh Bldg., Youngstown, O. Died Feb. 14, 1953.

TODD, Clare Chrisman, coll. prof.; b. McMinnville, Ore., Mar. 4, 1880; s. Robert H(arrison) and Amanda Belle T.; B.S., Wash. State Coll., 1906; Ph.D., U. of Chicago, 1914; m. Hilda M. Musgrove, 1916; children—Gordon Musgrove, Leonard Chrisman, Eleanor Olive. With Wash. State Coll. since 1907, successively asst. prof. chemistry, asso. prof. and prof. organic, and physiol. chemistry, also head dept. of chemistry and chem. engring., acting head Grad. Sch., dean Coll. Sciences and Arts, ret. 1949. Mem. Am. Chem. Soc., A.A.A.S. Democrat. Episcopalian. Home: 126 Calle Cabrillo, Redondo Beach, Cal. Died June 6, 1954.

TODD, Laurence, press corr.; b. Nottawa, Mich., Dec. 15, 1882; s. Oliver Hovey and Julia (Farrand) T.; student Mich. U., 1905-08; m. Constance D. Leupp, May 15, 1915; children—David, Alden; m. 2d, Dorothy Haessler, Jan. 8, 1938; 1 dau., Mary. Reporter Kalamazoo Gazette, 1904-05, city editor, 1907; reporter San Francisco Bulletin, 1909; San Francisco News, 1909-12; Scripps corr., Sacramento, 1912; United Press Bur., Washington, D.C., 1912-13; Internat. News Service, 1913-15; sec. to Socialist Congressman Meyer London, 1915-16; corr. for Nonpartisan Leader and labor papers, 1916-19, Federated Press, 1919-33; Telegraph Agency of U.S.S.R., 1923-52; reported UN Conf. on Food and Agriculture, 1943; conference establishing U.N.R.R.A., 1943; at San Francisco Conf., establishing United Nations, 1945. Mem. Socialist Party, 1904-20. Clubs: National Press (N.Y.C.). Home: 4805 Langdrum Lane, Chevy Chase 15, Md. Retired. Died Nov. 30, 1957.

TODD, Michael (Avrom Hirsch Goldbogen), theatrical producer; b. Mpls., June 2, 1909; student pub. schs., Chgo.; m. Bertha Freshman, 1926 (dec. 1946); 1 son, Michael; m. 2d, Joan Blondell, 1947 (div. 1950); m. 3d, Elizabeth Taylor, 1957; 1 dau., Elizabeth. Apprentice pharmacist, Chgo., 1921; founder Coll. of Brickmaking, 1923, Michael Todd Ready-Made Home Co.; builder soundproof stages, various motion picture firms, Hollywood, 1927-29; writer radio skits Olsen and Johnson, Chgo.; creator vaudeville revue Bring on the Dames; creator flame dance Chgo. World's Fair, 1933; prod. musical comedies on Broadway, Call Me Ziggy, The Man from Cairo, 1938, Hot Mikado, 1939, Star and Garter, 1942, Something for the Boys, 1943, Mexican Hayride, Up in Central Park, also dramas, including Catherine Was Great, As the Girls Go, others; founder (with Lowell Thomas) film process Cinerama; development (with Am. Optical Co.) Todd-AO process; producer Around the World in 80 Days; recipient Loah award for best producer, 1956. Acad. award and N.Y. Film Critics award for best picture, 1956), 1956. Civilian cons. spl. services div. U.S. Army, Europe, 1945. Address: Michael Todd Co., Inc., 729 7th Av., N.Y.C. Died Mar. 22, 1958; buried Chgo.

TODD, Thomas, printing exec.; b. Concord, Mass., May 25, 1878; s. Thomas and Rebecca (Wheeler) T.; m. Louise Towle, Oct. 16, 1911; children—Jeannette S. (Mrs. Max W. Sullivan), Thomas Jr. Pres., treas., dir. Thomas Todd Co., Boston, 1924——, also v.p. Middlesex Instn. for Savs., Concord. Served with 6th Mass. Inf. during Spanish-Am. War. Sec., dir. Am. Congregational Assn. Mason (K.T.). Home: 97 Main St., Concord, Mass. Office: 14 Beacon St., Boston 8. Died July 18, 1956.

TODD, William T(homas), Jr., business exec.; b. Pitts., Sept. 25, 1893; s. William Thomas and Mollie (Mackrell) T.; M.E., Cornell U., 1916; m. Elizabeth Alcorn, Apr. 19, 1941; 1 son, Thomas. With Somers, Fitler & Todd Co., Pitts., 1916——, successively laborer, counter salesman, purchasing dept. clk., sales dept. clk., v.p. in charge sales, pres., 1941——. Pres. bd. edn., Pitts. Dir. Americans for Competitive Enterprise System, Inc., Pitts. Newsboys Club; trustee Carnegie Library, Carnegie Inst. Tech., Pitts. Assn. Improvement Poor. Mem. C. of C. Presbyn. Mason (32°). Clubs: Automobile, Duquesne, Pittsburgh Field (Pitts.). Home: 315 S. Linden Av., Pitts. 8. Office: 325 Fort Pitt Blvd., Pitts. 30. Died Sept. 13, 1957.

TOLLEY, Harold Sumner, ex-congressman; b. Honesdale, Pa., Jan. 16, 1894; s. Adolphus Charles and Emma Grace (Sumner) T.; A.B., Syracuse U., 1916; student Drew Theol. Sem. 1 yr.; m. Anna Marguerite Germond, Oct. 6, 1917; children—Douglas Germond, Eleanor Grace, Harold Tolley. Asso. with father in retail shoe bus., Binghamton, as A. C. Tolley & Co., 1919——; mem. 69th Congress (1925-27), 34th N.Y. Dist. Dir. Buffalo area, N.Y. State Social Welfare, 1937-56. Enlisted in R.O.T.C., May 13, 1917; commd. 2d lt. 309th Inf., U.S.A., Aug. 15, 1917; 1st lt. Dec. 31, 1917; capt. May 13, 1918; participated with 1st Army in Meuse-Argonne offensive; hon. discharged, July 25, 1919; capt. inf., O.R.C.; capt. F.A., exec. officer 1st Bn., 104th F. A., N.Y.N.G. (resigned Dec. 1924). Mem. Am. Legion, Delta Sigma Rho, Pi Kappa Alpha. Republican. Methodist. Mason. Home: Kenmore, N.Y. Died May 20, 1956.

TOLLEY, Howard Ross (tŏl'ē), agrl. economics; b. Howard County, Ind., Sept. 30, 1889; s. Elmer E. and Mollie (Grindle) T.; student Normal Coll., Marion, Ind., 1905-06; A.B., Indiana Univ., 1910; m. Zora F. Hazlett, May 8, 1912; children—Edwin Grant, Howard Elmer, George Stanford. Teacher in Ind. high schs., 1906-12; coast and geodetic survey computer, 1912-15; with U.S. Dept. Agr., 1915-30, asst. chief Bur. of Agrl. Economics, 1928-30; dir. Giannini Foundation and prof. agrl. economics, U. of Calif., 1930-36; adminstr. A.A.A., 1936-38; chief Bur. Agrl. Economics, U.S. Dept. Agr., 1938-46; chief economist, economics, statistics, Food and Agr. Orgn. UN, 1946-51; cons. Ford Found., 1951-54; adv. Planning Bd. Pakistan, 1955; cons. Nat. Planning Assn., 1955——; asst. adminstr., dir. food, fiber div. Office of Price Adminstrn., Mar.-Aug. 1941-42. Member American Farm Economics Assn. (ex-pres.), American Statis. Assn., Am. Econ. Society, Am. Polit. Science Association, A.A.A.S., Agricultural History Soc., Econometric Soc., Alpha Zeta (hon.). Made Chevalier du Merite Agricole (France), 1934. Presbyn. Club: Cosmos (Washington, D.C.). Author: The Farmer Citizen at War, 1943. Writer of articles and bulletins on scientific subjects. Home: 212 S. Fairfax St., Aexandria, Va. Died Sept. 18, 1958; buried Ivy Hill Cemetery, Alexandria, Va.

TOLMAN, Ruth S., psychologist; b. Washington, Ind., Oct. 10, 1893; d. Warren C. and Lillie (Graham) Sherman; A.B., U. Calif., 1917, Ph.D., 1937; A.M., Occidental Coll., 1930; m. Richard Chace Tolman, Aug. 5, 1924. Asso., psychology dept., U. Calif., Los Angeles, 1927-29; instr. Occidental Coll., 1930-32, lecturer in psychology, Scripps Coll., 1934; sr. psychology examiner, Los Angeles Co. Probation Dept., 1936-40; asso. social sci. analyst, div. program surveys, U.S. Dept. of Agr., 1941-42; public opinion analyst, O.W.I., 1942-44; clin. psychologist, Office Strategic Services, 1944-45; head, clin. psychology training unit, Vets. Adminstrn., Los Angeles, 1946-54; clin. psychologist VA Mental Hygiene Clinic, Los Angeles, 1954——; clin. prof. psychology U. Cal., Los Angeles, 1953——. Fellow Am. Orthopsychiatric Assn., Am. Psychol. Assn.; mem. A.A.A.S., Cal. State and So. Cal. psychol. assns., Phi Beta Kappa, Sigma Xi. Contbr. articles in psychol. jours. Home: 345 S. Michigan Av., Pasadena 5, Calif. Office: 1031

S. Broadway, Los Angeles. Died Sept. 18, 1957; buried Woods Hole, Mass.

TOLMAN, William Howe (tŏl'măn), social economist; b. Pawtucket, R.I., June 2, 1861; s. William E. and Martha Lee (Howe) T.; A.B., Brown University, 1882, A.M., 1887; Ph.D., Johns Hopkins, 1891; m. Anna C. Gerhold, August 25, 1891; 1 son, George Leighton. General agent New York Association for Improving Condition of the Poor, 1894-98. Founder, 1st director American Museum Safety, 1908-16. Joint organizer Am. Inst. Social Service (dir., 1898-1908). Member Internat. Jury in Social Economy, Paris Expn., 1900; pres. Group and pres. Dept. Jury in Social Economy and mem. Superior Jury, St. Louis Expn., 1904; dir. U.S. Sect. Social Economy, Internat. Expn., Liège, 1905; commr. Am. Sect. Internat. Expn., Milan, 1906; commr.-gen. Am. Sect. Internat. Book and Paper Expn., Paris, 1907; dir. gen. Internat. Safety Expn., New York, 1913, 14; del. U.S. Govt. Internat. Housing Congress, Liège, 1905, London, 1908, Vienna, 1910, The Hague, 1913, Internat. Congress Hygiene and Demography, Berlin, 1907, Internat. Congress Social Insurance, Rome, 1908, The Hague, 1911; del. State of N.Y., Internat. Med. Congress, Budapest, 1909, Internat. Congress Accident Prevention, Milan, 1912. Officier de la Légion d'Honneur (France); Chevalier Order of Leopold (Belgium); Knight Royal Order of the Prussian Crown; Croix de Guerre, Chevalier Order of the White Lion (both Czechoslovakia); Kontorische Ehrenkreuzder Bergenfahrer (Bergen, Norway); Chevalier Order of Crown of Italy; also awarded the Hungarian Cross of Merit. Regional dir. and later publicity dir. for Foyers du Soldat, with French Army, and for Y.M.C.A. in France and Czechoslovakia, 1918-19. Délégué Société France-Amérique, Paris, Ente Naizonale per le Industrie Turistiche, Rome; corr. mem. Hanseatic useum, Bergen, Norway; active mem. Académie du Var, Toulon. Corr. mem. Soc. Polit. Economy, Paris; asso. Statis. Soc. of Paris; dir. Internat. Associates; hon. mem. Hungarian Statis. Society; mem. Phi Beta Kappa (Brown U.), Beta Theta Pi. Author: History of Higher Education in Rhode Island, 1891; Municipal Reform Movements in the United States, 1894; Handbook of Sociological Reference for New York City, 1894; Report on Public Baths and Public Comfort Stations, 1897; The Better New York, 1906; Social Engineering, 1909 (has been transl. into French); Hygiene for the Worker (has been translated into Czecho-Slovak), 1912; Safety, 1913; also wrote Industrial Betterment, a monograph prepared for U.S. Sect. of Social Economy, Paris Expn., 1900; Industrial Betterment in the Economic History of the U.S.; Life and Labor in Rotary Centres in France, 1929. Mason. Clubs: Authors' (London); hon. mem. Rotary (Budapest, Hungary), Nat. Arts Club (N.Y.). Address: 126 Prospect St., Pawtucket, R.I. Deceased.

TOMLIN, Bradley Walker, artist; b. Syracuse, N.Y., Aug. 19, 1899; s. Charles Henry and Matilda (Hollier) T.; B.P., Syracuse U., 1921; unmarried. Represented in art collections: Met. Mus. of Art, Mus. Modern Art (N.Y.C.), Munson-Williams Proctor Inst. (Utica, N.Y.), Whitney Mus. Am. Art, Bklyn. Mus. and Sci., Addison Gallery (Andover, Mass.), Pa. Acad. of Fine Arts, Cranbrook Mus. (Detroit), Iowa State U., Duncan Philips Coll. (Washington), Edward Root Coll., Ency. Britannica collection. Awarded 1st hon. mention Carnegie Internat. Exhibn., 1946. Mem. Fedn. Modern Painters and Sculptors. Address: 149 Bleecker St., N.Y.C. Died May 11, 1953; buried Quidnessett Cemetery, Wickford, R.I.

TOMLINSON, Allen U., church official; b. Bloomingdale, Ind., July 21, 1875; s. Rev. Andrew DeMoss (M.D.) and Milea (Trueblood) T.; student Whittier Coll. prep. dept., 1895-97; A.B., Earlham Coll., Richmond, Ind., 1902; m. Katherine Jenkins, Sept. 12, 1904; children—Frances Esther (Mrs. James L. Bogle), Allen Robert, Harriet Louise (deceased), Andrew DeMoss. Salseman and treas., Whittier Hardware Co., 1903-35; stock brokers agent, Crowell, Weedon & Co., Los Angeles, Calif., 1936—; dir. Whittier Mushroom Growers, Inc. Dir. (for life) Y.M.C.A. (Whittier); councilman, City of Whittier, 1940-48. Clerk, Cal. Yearly Meeting of Friends Ch., 1917-47; Clerk, Five Years Meeting of Friends in Am., 1940-45. Mem. Kiwanis Club (Whittier), University. Club: Address: 142 S. Friends Av., Whittier, Cal. Died Sept. 22, 1956; buried Rose Hills Meml. Park, Whittier, Cal.

TOMLINSON, Charles C(reighton), physician; b. near Villisca, Ia., Aug. 29, 1884; s. Creighton and Sophia (Martin) T.; M.D. U. Neb., 1908; m. Nellie Winn, June 16, 1909; children—Margaret (Mrs. Wm. E. Davis Jr.), Elizabeth. Intern Douglas County Hosp., Omaha, 1908-09; pvt. practice medicine, Wakefield, Neb., 1909-15, Omaha, 1915—, specialist dermatology and syphilology, 1917—; mem. staff Neb. Methodist Episcopal, U. Neb., Clarkson Memorial, Douglas County hosps., 1917— as instr. in dermatology, U. Neb., 1917-27, asst. prof., 1927-35, prof. and chmn. of Dept. dermatology and syphilology, 1935-49, prof. emeritus, 1950—. Mem. A.M.A., Soc. Investigative Dermatology, Am. Acad. of Dermatology and Syphilology, Am. Dermatol. Assn., Neb. State Med. Assn., Omaha Douglas County Med. Soc., Nu Sigma Nu. Republican. Presbyn. Home: 5215 Jackson St., Omaha 6. Office: Medical Arts Bldg., Omaha 2, Neb. Died July 1, 1955.

TOMLINSON, H(enry) M(ajor), author; b. England, 1873; Dr. Laws (hon.), U. Aberdeen; m. Florence Margaret Hammond, 1899; 1 son, 2 daus. Editorial staff, Morning Leader and Daily News, 1904; war corr., Belgium and France, 1914-17; lit. editor, Nation and Athenaeum, 1917-23; writer since 1912. Author: The Sea and the Jungle, 1912; Old Junk, 1918; London River, 1921; Waiting for Daylight, 1922; Tidemarks, 1924; Under the Red Ensign, 1926; Gifts of Fortune, 1926; Gallions Reach, 1927; Between the Lines, 1928; All Our Yesterdays, 1930; Out of Soundings, 1931; Norman Douglas, 1931; The Snows of Helicon, 1933; South to Cadiz, 1934; Below London Bridge (with H. C. Tomlinson), 1934; Mars His Idiot, 1935; All Hands, 1937; The Day Before, 1940, The Wind Is Rising, 1941; The Turn of the Tide, 1945; Morning Light, 1947; Face of the Earth, Malay Waters, 1950; Haunted Forest, London River (illustrated), 1951; A Mingled Yarn, 1953; The Trumpet Shall Sound, 1957. Decorated Officer Brazilian Order So. Cross. Hon. asso. Nat. Inst. Arts and Letters. Address: 1 St. Peter's Sq., London W.6, England. Died Feb. 5, 1958.

TOMPKINS, Charles Hook, constructing engr.; b. Baltimore, Md., Nov. 30, 1883; s. Edward H. and Louise O. (Chappell) Tompkins; student Lehigh U., 1903-04, George Washington University, 1905-06 (hon. D.Eng., 1946); married Lida R. Tompkins, Nov. 30, 1906 (dec.), children—Francis M., Louise C. (Mrs. Andrew Parker), Emma H. (Mrs. Malcolm Matheson, Jr.), Charles H., Jr. Engineer with U.S. Corps Engrs., 1904, E. Saxton, Ry. constr., 1905, D.C. Govt., 1906, Ohio Elec. Ry. Co., 1907-08, Capital Traction Co., 1909, Smithsonian Inst., 1910; constr. engineer under own name, 1911-21; pres. of Chas. H. Tompkins Co., construction engrs., since 1922; builders of many defense projects including Bainbridge Naval Training Sta.; Ft. Belvoir Cantonment and Engr. Bd. bldgs.; Allegheny Ordnance Plant; White Oaks Naval Ordnance Lab.; in Washington, many notable structures such as Dalecarlia Filtration Plant; Garfinckel Dept. Store; Tower Bldg.; World War Red Cross Mem.; District of Columbia National Guard Armory; D.C. Scottish Rite Temple; groups of buildings for Georgetown, George Washington, and American Universities, National Inst. Health, Naval Research Lab., United States Court House, and many others; inventor Concrete Distributing System; pres. and dir. H St. Bldg. Corp.; former chmn. bd. Old Dutch Refining Co.; former pres., dir. Wis. Petroleum Terminals Corp.; dir., mem. exec. com. Woodward & Lothrop; dir., mem. exec. com. Riggs Nat. Bank; gov. and p.p. Washington Bldg. Congress; trustee George Washington U.; mem. bus. adv. com. Am. U.; mem. bd. directors Gallaudet Coll., Washington; mem. exec. com. Fed. City Council; mem. adv. bd. YMCA; mem. Commrs. Planning Adv. Com. Dist. of Columbia; mem. Commn. 100 Fed. City; hon. permanent mem. bd. Children's Hosp.; dir. Centennial Engineering, 1952; mem. council Corcoran Gallery of Art; dir. D.C. adv. bd. A.A.A.; past pres. D.C. chapter, A.G.C.; past pres. Master Bldrs. Assn.; dir. D.C. chapter, A.R.C.; dir. Wash. Boys Club; life mem. Am. Soc. Civil Engrs. mem. Soc. Am. Military Engrs. (dir., past pres. Washington post). Wash. Bd. Trade (econ. development com.), Wash. Soc. Engrs., Theta Delta Chi (trustee ednl. found.) Sigma Tau, Omicron Delta Kappa. Mason (32°, Shriner). Episcopalian. Clubs: Cosmos (member board) Metropolitan. Chevy Chase; Eastern Point Yacht (Gloucester, Mass.); Casanova (Va.) Hunt Lehigh, Rotary. Alfalfa. Home: 3055 Whitehaven St., N.W. Office: 907 16th St., Washington 6. Died Dec. 12, 1956; buried Rock Creek Cemetery, Washington.

TOMPKINS, Juliet Wilbor (Mrs. Juliet Wilbor Tompkins Pottle), writer; b. Oakland, Cal., May 13, 1871; d. Edward and Sarah (Haight) Tompkins; A.B., Vassar, 1891. Asso. editor Munsey's Mag., 1897-1901. Clubs: Onteora, Cosmopolitan. Author: Dr. Ellen, 1908; Open House, 1909; The Top of the Morning, 1910; Mothers and Fathers, 1910; Pleasures and Palaces, 1912; Ever After, 1913; Diantha, 1915; The Seed of the Righteous, 1916; At the Sign of the Oldest House, 1917; A Girl Named Mary, 1918; The Starling 1919; Joanna Builds a Nest, 1920; A Line a Day, 1923; Left in Trust, 1929; also many short stories. Home: 10 Mitchell Pl., N.Y.C. Died Jan. 29, 1956; buried The Little Chapel by the Sea, Pacific Groves, Cal.

TOMPKINS, Leslie Jay, educator, lawyer; b. Salem, Olmstead County, Minn., May 2, 1867; s. Moses J. and Kate M. (Travers) T.; B.S., N.Y. U., 1890, LL.B., 1892, M.S., 1894, LL.M., 1897, J.D., 1903, LL.D., 1940; LL.D., Villanova Coll., 1909; m. Jean Burnet, Feb. 19, 1913 (died 1947); children—Harriet Schurz (Mrs. John K. Thomas), James Burnet. Librarian, N.Y. U., 1892-1901, asst. treas., 1892-1905, registrar, 1895-1904, instr. law, 1898-99, prof. law, 1899—. Mem. N.Y. Assembly, 1905, 06. Trustee, chmn. Am. Def. Soc. Author: The Law of Promissory Notes, Drafts, Checks, etc., 1900; Condensed Cases on Corporations, 1897; A Summary of the Law of Corporations, 1904; Select Cases on the Law of Private Corporations, 1908; The Law of Commercial Paper, 1911; Trial Evidence, 1936. 1st asst. dist. atty. N.Y., Jan. 1916-18. Home: 1165 5th Av. Office: 116 John St., N.Y.C. 7. Deceased.

TOMPKINS, Nathaniel, judge; b. Bridgewater, Me., May 17, 1879; s. Nathaniel and Emma F. (Sargent) T.; student Ricker Classical Inst., Houlton, Me., 1893-98; A.B., Colby Coll., Waterville, Me., 1903; LL.B., Harvard, 1907; m. Ragnhild L. Iversen, June 17, 1913; 1 dau., Sigrid E. Admitted to Me. bar, 1942, gen. practice law, Houlton, Me., 1907-41; apptd. justice Superior Ct. Me., Oct. 9, 1941; asso. justice Supreme Ct. Me., Aug. 1945—. Trustee Houlton Savs. Bank. Trustee Ricker Classical Inst. and Jr. Coll., Houlton, Me. Speaker Mem. House Reps., 1935; pres. Me. Senate, 1941. Mem. Delta Kappa Epsilon. Republican. Mason. Home: 78 Court St. Office: Houlton, Me. Died Apr. 22, 1949.

TOMS, Robert Morrell, jurist; b. La Crosse, Wis., Oct. 14, 1886; s. Frank Phelps and Lark M. (Looney) T.; A.B., U. Chgo., 1907; LL.B., U. Mich., 1910; m. Gladys Bassford Wetmore, Nov. 11, 1914; children—Elinor Bassford (Mrs. Robert M. Jones), Margaret Sprague (Mrs. George C. Cope). Prosecuting atty., Detroit, 1921-29; judge, 3d Judicial Circuit, Mich., 1929—; exec. presiding judge, U.S. War Crimes Courts, Nurnberg, Germany, 1946-47; prof. constl. law, Wayne U., 1932—. Home: 17374 Muirland Av., Detroit. Office: County Bldg., Detroit 26, Mich. Died Apr. 6, 1960.

TONER, James Vincent, corp. exec.; b. N. Attleboro, Mass., Sept. 12, 1888; s. Arthur and Annie (Corr) T.; grad. LaSalle Acad., 1908; A.B., Holy Cross Coll., 1912, A.M., 1926; B.B.A., Boston Univ., 1921; LL.D., Holy Cross Coll., 1942; m. Mary A. Zilch, Aug. 22, 1914; children—Mrs. Mary A. (Toner) Couzens; Col. James V., Jr., Mrs. Elizabeth F. (Toner) Shriner, Catherine V., Jane L. (Mrs. Maynihan), John L., Patricia. Tchr. grade schools, 1912-20; prof. accounting, Boston U., 1920-38; president, treas. Saart Bros. Co. to 1937; asso. with Boston Edison Co. and mem. bd. dirs. since 1937, pres. since 1941, also gen. mgr.; dir. First Nat. Bank of Boston, John Hancock Mut. Life Ins. Co., Attleboro Trust Co., Am. Optical Co., Union Savs. Bank, Am. Enka Corp., N.Y., N.H.&H. R.R. Dir. Nat. Indsl. Conf. Bd.; dir. United Community Services, Northeastern U.; dir. Children's Hosp.; dir. Home for Catholic Children. C.P.A.; mem. Am. Inst. Accountants, Gen. Alumni Assn. of Holy Cross Coll. (dir.). Roman Catholic. Clubs: University, Algonquin, Downtown, City, Clover, Golf. Home: 14 Lockwood Rd., West Newton, Mass. Office: 182 Tremont St., Boston. Died Oct. 19, 1951.

TONKS, Oliver Samuel, educator; b. Malden, Mass., Dec. 27, 1873; s. Alfred and Elizabeth Anne (Dunne) T.; A.B., Harvard, 1898, A.M., 1899, Ph. D., 1903; Charles Eliot Norton fellow, Am. Sch. Athens, Greece, 1901-02; m. Bernice Estabrook, 1905; children—Richard Estabrook (dec.), Robert Estabrook, Gretchen Estabrook, Neal Estabrook. Asst. curator dept. classical art, Mus. Fine Arts, Boston, 1902-03; instr. Greek, U. Vt., 1903-04; lectr. Columbia, 1904-05; asst. prof. art and archaeology, Princeton, 1905-11; prof. art, Vassar Coll., 1911—, also chmn. dept., emeritus, 1944—. Republican. Episcopalian. Author: A History of Italian Painting. Joint Author: The Art Museum and the Pub. Schs., 1912; Vassar Mediaeval Studies, 1923; Classical Studies, 1936; also many articles on art. Home: 69 Raymond Av., Poughkeepsie, N.Y. Died Dec. 25, 1953; buried Great Chebeague Island, Me.

TOOTHAKER, Charles Robinson, curator; b. Phila., May 4, 1873; s. Charles Everett and Zetta (Elder) T.; grad. Central Manual Training High Sch., Phila., 1890; spl. course in geology under E. D. Cope; other spl. courses; m. Martha Taylor McCandless, Sept. 27, 1904. Mineralogist A. E. Foote, Phila., 1890-97; asst. curator Commercial Museum, 1898-1904, curator, 1904-52; pioneered in extending popular museum educational activities; lectr. on comml. geography. Commr. in charge Pa. mining exhibit, Atlanta Expn., 1895. Hon. consul of Czechoslovakia. in Phila.; former consul Columbia. Decorated Officer Order of White Lion, Czechoslovakia. Fellow Mineral Soc. Am., A.A.A.S.; mem. S.R., Mineral Soc. Pa., Acad. Natural Sci., Am. Assn. Mus. Republican. Author: Commercial Raw Materials, 1905. Home: 4260 Chestnut St., Phila. Died May 25, 1952.

TORBETT, Joe Hall (tôr'bĕt), editor; b. Jericho Springs, Mo., Dec. 28, 1899; s. David Hall and Emily Adell (Blake) T.; student Pea Ridge (Ark.) Masonic Coll., 1913-15, U. of Ark., 1915-17, Mass. Inst. Tech., 1918; m. Jessica May Rooks, May 16, 1925; 1 dau., Judith Ann. Proofreader Muskogee (Okla.) Phoenix, 1919; editor Beggs (Okla.) Independent and Okmulgee Life, 1920; with Kansas City (Mo.) Star, 1920-26, Cleveland (O.) Press, 1926-27; city editor Toledo (O.) News-Bee, 1927-28; feature editor N.Y. Telegram and N.Y. World-Telegram, 1928-33; mng. editor Cincinnati Post, 1933-35; news editor Rochester (N.Y.) Times-Union, 1935-37; mng. editor Utica (N.Y.) Daily Press, 1937-38; exec. editor

Utica Daily Press and Utica Observer-Dispatch, 1938-42; mng. editor Knickerbocker News, 1942-43; Washington rep. and corr. Press Assn., Inc. (Asso. Press subsidiary), 1943-47. Author of nat. radio column, "Washington Inside Out." Manager Asso. Press City News Service, Washington, 1946-47; asso. with radio stations KDLK, Del Rio, Tex.; public information officer 2d Army 1949: public relations consultant U.S. Coast Guard. Consultant National Security Resources Bd., 1948. Ex-chmn. Selective Service Bd. No. 428. Served as gunnery sgt. in aviation U.S. M.C., World War I. Col. on staff of Gov. of Ky. Ex-mem. Am. Soc. of Newspaper Editors, Radio Corrs. Assn., Marine Corps League, Am. Legion, Pi Kappa Alpha, Theta Nu Epsilon, Quo Vadis. Clubs: Kenwood Country, National Press. Home: 4818 Morgan Dr., Chevy Chase 15, Md. Office: Hdq., U.S. Coast Guard, Washington. Died Dec. 18, 1954; buried Parkhill Meml. Gardens, Rockville, Md.

TORCHIO, Phillip, Jr., (tor'kiō), electric utility exec.; b. Bronxville, N.Y., July 8, 1908; s. Philip and Angela (de Nova) T.; B.S., Mass. Inst. Tech., 1930; grad. study Columbia, 1932-33, N.Y.U., 1939-40, Harvard, 1952; m. Muriel Farnum, Oct. 15, 1938; children—Marilyn, Philip III. Test engr. Gen. Electric Co., 1931-32; successively engr. generating, distbn., system planning and sales depts., dist. sales mgr., asst. sales mgr. sales mgr., mgr. wholesale bus. bur. Consol. Edison Co. of N.Y., Inc., and affiliated cos., 1932-48; asst. to operating v.p. Am. Gas & Electric Service Corp., 1948-49, comml. v.p., dir., 1952—; asst. to v.p. and gen. mgr. The Ohio Power Co., 1949-50, asst. gen. mgr., 1951-52, dir., 1952—. Served as lt., Amphibious Forces, U.S.N.R., E.T.O. and P.T.O., 1942-45. Registered profl. engr., N.Y. and Ohio. Mem. A.S.M.E., Phi Sigma Kappa. Clubs: Canton, Brookside Country (Canton, O.); Railroad and Machinery (N.Y.C.). Home: 9 Lookout Av., Bronxville. Office: 30 Church St., N.Y.C. Died Aug. 9, 1953; buried Faust, N.Y.

TORRANCE, Stiles Albert, editor; b. Erie Co., N.Y., Sept. 10, 1872; grad. Cornell, 1894; m. Flora E. Chapman, July 18, 1895; 1 son, Charles C. Editorial work on Johnson's Cyclopaedia, 1894-95; editor Am. Book Co. Mason. Home: 165 Buckingham Rd., Yonkers, N.Y. Office: Care American Book Co., Washington Sq., New York. Died Oct. 1, 1953.

TORRENCE, (Frederick) Ridgely, poet, b. Xenia, O.; s. Captain Findley David and Mary (Ridgely) T.; ed. Miami (O.) U. and Princeton; Litt.D., Miami U.; m. Olivia Howard Dunbar, Feb. 3, 1914. Librarian N.Y. Pub. Library, 1897-1903; editor The Critic, 1903; asso. editor The Cosmopolitan, 1905-07, The New Republic, 1920-34; prof. English, Miami U., 1920-21; res. creative writing, Antioch Coll., 1938, Miami U., 1941. Mem. Nat. Inst. Arts and Letters. Clubs: Coffee House, Century. Author: The House of a Hundred Lights, 1900; El Dorado, a Tragedy, 1903; Abelard and Heloise (poetic drama), 1907; Granny Maumee, The Rider of Dreams, Simon the Cyrenian (plays for a Negro theatre), 1917; Hesperides, 1925; Danse Calinda, 1927; The Story of Gio, 1935; Common Sense (play), 1941; Poems (Shelley Memorial Award 1941), 1941; The Story of John Hope, 1947. Awarded $5,000 fellowship Acad. Am. Poets, Apr. 1947. Editor: Selected Letters of Edwin Arlington Robinson, 1940; Last Poems of Anna Hempstead Branch, 1944. Address: 59 Morton Street, N.Y.C. 14. Died Dec. 1950.

TOSCANINI, Arturo (tŏs-kä-nē'nē), conductor; b. Parma, Italy, Mar. 25, 1867; grad. Conservatory, Parma. Started career as 'cellist; conducted for first time at age of 19 in Rio de Janeiro, Brazil, performance of "Aïda"; condr. La Scala, 1898, at Milan, and in other Italian cities; joined Metropolitan Opera Co., New York, 1908, and served as condr. under Gatti-Casazza through 1915; toured U.S. and Can. with La Scala Orchestra, 1921; guest conductor N.Y. Philharmonic-Symphony Orchestra, 1926-28, regular condr., 1928-33, gen. musical dir., 1933-36. European tour with N.Y. Philharmonic-Symphony Orchestra, spring of 1930; guest conductor Philadelphia Orchestra, Phila., Pennsylvania, 1930-31 and 1941-42, 43; condr. Bayreuth Festival, 1930, 31. Salsburg Festival, 1934, 35, 36, Luzern Festival, 1937-39; organizer, and conductor Nat. Broadcasting Co. Symphony Orchestra, 1937-54; South American tour with Nat. Broadcasting Co. Symphony Orchestra, 1940; recordings made with RCA Victor, Camden, N.J. Reopened La Scala theatre, Milan, rebuilt, 1946. Address: Via Durini 20, Milano, Italy. Died Jan. 16, 1957; buried Cimitero Monumentale Milano, Italy.

TOTTON, Frank Mortimer, banker; b. Minneapolis, Minn., May 5, 1890; s. Joseph Mortimer and Mary King (Proud) T.; A.B., Harvard, 1912; LL.B., LaSalle U., 1915; LL.D. (honorary), Missouri Valley College, 1953; m. Gladys Orme Barnes, Oct. 6, 1922; children—David Courtney, Robert Mortimer, Stephen Malcolm, Clerk, Farmers Loan & Trust Co., N.Y. City, 1912-23; trust officer, Chase National Bank, N.Y. City, 1923—, vice president, 1929-54; trustee, Harlem Savings Bank, since 1937. Served as 1st lt., Ord. Dept., U.S. Army, 1917-19. Chmn. West Side branch, Y.M.C.A. of N.Y. City, 1928; vice pres. Y.M.C.A., City of N.Y., 1941, pres. since 1945; pres. N. Y. State Y.M.C.A.'s, 1930, chmn. bd. trustees, 1934; treas. Nat. Child Labor Com., Inc., N.Y. City, 1936. Treas. Goodwill Industries of N.Y., Inc., Wiltwyck Sch. for Boys, N.Y. City, Sydenham Hosp., and Am. Coll., Sofia, Bulgaria, 1942. Pres. bd. trustees, Athens (Greece) Coll., 1946; trustee, Walter Harvey Jr. Coll., N.Y. City, 1946; Dir. Greater N.Y. Council, Boy Scouts of Am., 1943. Foundation of Presbyterian Education U.S. A., Protestant Council, City of N.Y., Fedn. Protestant Welfare Agencies, Travelers Aid Soc. of N.Y., 1944; Andrew Freedman Home, N.Y. City, 1946; nat. chmn. United Negro Coll. Fund, 1946-47; chmn. finance com. Bd. Edn., Mamaroneck, N.Y., 1933-39; vice chmn. Downstate N.Y. War Finance Com., U.S. Treasury, 1939-44. Mem. Am. Inst. Banking (pres. N.Y. chapter, 1922, nat. pres. 1928); Am. Bankers Assn. (chmn. pub. edn. commn. since 1943, also chairman public relations council, 1953); Am. McAll Assn. (treas. 1944), Phi Sigma Kappa. Republican. Presbyterian (chmn. finance com., Gen. Council Presbyn. Ch. in U.S.A., 1945-48, nat. chmn. Presbyn. Restoration Fund, 1945-47). Mason (grand master, New York). Clubs: Harvard (New York); Orienta Beach (Mamaroneck, N.Y.). Home: 139 Rockland Av., Larchmont, N.Y. Office: Chase National Bank, N.Y.C. 5. Died Nov. 1, 1954; buried Kensico Cemetery, Valhalla, N.Y.

TOUR, Reuben S(imkin) (to͝or), chem. engr.; b. Troy, N.Y., Aug. 20, 1889; s. James and Sophia (Simkin) T.; B.S., U. of Mich., 1910, M.S.E., 1915, Ch.E., 1927; m. Margaret Meyer, 1914; 1 son, Robert Louis. Asst. supt., Consolidated Gas Co., N.Y. City, 1911-13; asst. prof. gas engring., U. of Calif., 1913-17; capt. Ordnance Dept., U.S. Army, chief of tech. dept. U.S. Nitrate Plant No. 1, Muscle Shoals, Ala., 1917-19; chem. engr. nitrate div. Ordnance Dept., U.S. Army, 1919-21; prof. chem. engring. and head of dept., U. of Cincinnati, since 1921; cons. chem. engr. (industrial gases). Lt. col. Ordnance O.R.C., to 1942. Mem. Am. Inst. Chemical Engrs., Am. Soc. Engineering Educ., A.A.A.S., Am. Assn. Univ. Profs., Sigma Xi, Tau Beta Pi, Phi Lambda Upsilon. Mason. Contributor of articles on nitrogen fixation and chemical engineering. Address: University of Cincinnati, Cin. 21. Died Aug. 1, 1952.

TOWER, Edwin Briggs Hale, Jr., patent and copyright lawyer; b. Freehold, N.J., Aug. 2, 1879; s. Edwin Briggs Hale and Eleanor Hamilton (Bawden) T.; LL.B., Columbia University, (George Washington U.), 1902; m. Bessie Mather Applegate, May 4, 1909; children—(twin daus.) Jean (Mrs. William R. Rennie), Milbrey. Admitted to Courts: U.S. Supreme Court, 1921; Court of Appeals of D.C., 1908; Supreme Court of D.C., 1908; U.S. Circuit Court of Appeals for 7th Circuit, 1912; U.S. Court of Custom and Patent Appeals, 1931; Supreme Court of State of Wis., 1915; U.S. Dist. Courts for: Eastern Dist. of Wis., 1909; Northern Dist. of Ill., 1909; Western Dist. of N.Y., 1914; Northern Dist. of O., Western Div., 1934; practice of patent, trademark and copyright causes, Milwaukee, Wis., 1908-47, New York, N.Y., 1909-28, and Chicago, Ill., 1909-16. Served in The Am. Protective League, received certificate of exceptional service as operative, military intelligence staff, 1917-19. Author, Public Law 587, 79th Congress. Mem. Nat. Assn. Mfrs. (present mem. research and patents com., present chmn. spl. subcom. on amending revised statutes to expedite recovery of damages in suits of infringement of patents). Wis. Mfrs. Assn., Am. Bar Assn., Assn. of Bar of City of New York, Chicago, Wis., Milwaukee bar assns., Chicago, New York, Am., Milwaukee (past pres.) patent law assns. Clubs: Chicago, University, Tavern, Post and Paddock (Chicago); Bankers of America (N.Y.), Mohawk (Schnectady, N.Y.); Milwaukee. Milwaukee Country (Milwaukee). Home: 2743 N. Lake Dr., Milwaukee 11. Office: First Wisconsin National Bank Bldg., Milw. 2. Died Mar. 27, 1948.

TOWERS, John Alden, business exec.; b. Kansas City, Mo., June 2, 1894; s. John Royal and Anna A. (Vineyard) T.; student Rockingham Acad.; LL.B., University of Missouri, Kansas City School of Law, 1917; married Hazel Mae Foresman, October 28, 1916. Was admitted to the Missouri bar in 1917; atty., O'Brien, Hobart and Perrin, Kansas City, 1917-18, owner, 1918-23; started office on reinsurance and ins., Phila., 1919, Towers-Perrin Co.; merged with Brown, Crosby & Co. and Henry W. Brown & Co., 1930; formed corp. Towers, Perrin, Forster & Crosby, Inc., 1934; pres., vice pres., dir. Alden Park Corp., Chelton Av. Bldg. Corp., Kenilworth Bldg. Corp., Cambridge Bldg. Corp. Served as lt. F.A., U.S. Army, World War I. Member Soc. Mayflower Descendants, Order Constantine; life mem. Sigma Chi (sec. treas. alumni assn., 1918-21; pres. Kansas City alumni chapter, 1921); dir. Volunteers Services for Blind; sponsor Ams. Future; chmn. bd. govs., Sigma Chi Foundation, Union League (Phila., New York). Clubs: Philadelphia Country, Radnor Hunt, Drug and Chemical (N.Y.C.); Bayhead Yacht. Home: Gayhurst, Buttonwood Rd., Berwyn, Pa. Office: 3 Penn Center, Phila. 2. Died Nov. 18, 1956; buried Forest Hill Cemetery, Kansas City, Mo.

TOWERS, John Henry, naval officer; b. Rome, Ga., Jan. 30, 1885; s. William Magee and Mary (Norton) T.; student Ga. Sch. Tech., 1 yr.; grad. U.S. Naval Acad., 1906; m. Lily Carstairs, Oct. 5, 1915 (div.); children—Marjorie, Charles Stewart; m. 2d, Pierrette Anne Chauvin de Grandmont, Aug. 1930. Commd. ensign U.S. Navy, Feb. 12, 1908, promoted through grades to comdr., June 25, 1918, admiral, Nov. 7, 1945. Aviation duty 1911—; one of earliest officers of Navy in aviation service; twice attached to Am. Embassy, London; asst. dir. Naval Aviation, World War; comdr. transatlantic flight, 1919; asst. chief Bur. Aeros., Navy Dept., 1929-31; comdg. officer U.S.S. Saratoga, 1937-38; chief Bur. Aeros., June 1, 1939-Oct. 7, 1942; comdr. Air Force, U.S. Pacific Fleet, 1942-44; deputy comdr. in chief, Pacific Areas, Feb. 1944-Nov. 1945; comdr. in chief Pacific Fleet and Pacific Ocean Areas, Nov. 1945—; adm. ret.; asst. v.p. Pan-American Airways. Decorated Navy Cross, Royal Air Force (British); comdt. Order of Tower and Sword (Portuguese); spl. medals of Congress; Kt. Comdr. Order British Empire. Clubs: Army and Navy, Chevy Chase, Metropolitan (Washington); New York Yacht, Seawanhaka-Corinthian Yacht. Address: Navy Dept., Washington. Died Apr. 1, 1955; buried Arlington Nat. Cemetery.

TOWLE, Charles Brother (tōl), mfr.; b. Clinton, Ia., Sept. 10, 1875; s. Phineas Stewart and Mary (Brother) T.; grad. Williston Sem., 1894; B S., Rensselaer Poly. Inst., 1898; m. Lucy Bonney Curtis, Jan. 4, 1902; children—Mary Katharine (Mrs. John Kenneth Cozier), Priscilla (Mrs. Thomas Tiffany Varney, Jr.), Charles Curtis. Engaged in mining operations in Colo., S.D., Mo., and Mexico, 1893-1900; engaged in railroad construction in Mo., Kan., and Okla., 1900-03; engaged in manufacture of wood work since 1903; v.p. Curtis Companies, Inc.; v.p. C.F. Curtis Co.; dir. First Nat. Bank. Served as corporal 1st Vol. Engrs., U.S. Army, Spanish-Am. War. Member Council of Defense, 1917; mem. State Bd. of Mediaaion, 1921; pres. Lincoln Community Chest, 1927-28; v.p. Great Lakes-St. Lawrence Deep Waterway Assn.; chmn. Com. on Stabilization of Employment. Mem. Nat. Mfrs. Assn. (v.p. for Neb. 1910-20); pres. Neb. Mfrs. Assn., 1912-13; pres. Lincoln Mfrs. Assn., 1925-27; pres. Lincoln Chamber of Commerce, 1922; pres. Lincoln Builders Bureau, 1930. Mem. Nat. Econ. League, Delta Kappa Epsilon. Republican. Mason (Shriner). Clubs: University (ex-pres.), Country Club (ex-pres.), Candlelight, Round Table, Patriarchs. Home: Cornhusker Hotel, Lincoln, Neb. Died Nov. 7, 1951.

TOWLE J(osiah) Norman, newspaper editor; b. Port Hope, Ont., Can., of Am. parents; s. Josiah C. and Katherine (Carveth) T.; ed. pub. schs.; m. Mary Agnes Andrews, Dec. 29, 1892; children—Lillis Katherine, Helen May. Editor and pub. Bangor (Me.) News, 1895—. Home: 44 Forest Av. Office: 170 Exchange St., Bangor, Me. Died 1932.

TOWNE, Arthur Whittlesey, social worker; b. Springfield, Mass., Mar. 13, 1878; s. John and Corena L. (Thomas) T.; B.S., Amherst, 1901; B.A., Harvard, 1902; m. Bertha Vilas Knapp, of Essex, N.Y., July 26, 1905 (died 1934); m. 2d, Rose Kermode, of Syracuse, May 29, 1936. Supt. Syracuse (N.Y.) Boys' Club, 1903-07; sec. Syracuse Asso. Charities, 1904-07; sec. N.Y. State Probation Commn., 1907-13; supt. Brooklyn Society for Prevention of Cruelty to Children, 1913-22; dir. Joint Com. on Methods of Preventing Delinquency (Commonwealth Fund), 1922-23; sec. Milbank Fund Health Demonstration, 1924—; exec. sec. Onondaga Health Assn., 1924-47, cons., 1947-54. Mem., one of organizers Com. for Alcoholics, mem. Wagon Wheel Com. for the Aged. Mem. Phi Kappa Psi. Unitarian. Home: 1030 E. Genesee St. Office: McCarthy Bldg., Syracuse, N.Y. Died July 19, 1954.

TOWNE, Ezra Thayer, economist; b. Waupun, Wis., Apr. 1, 1873; s. William Hammond and Marion (Kingsbury) T.; grad. advanced course, State Normal Sch., Oshkosh, Wis., 1894; B.L., U. of Wis., 1897; studied New York Sch. of Philanthropy, 1898; grad. work, U. of Wis., 1897-99; studied and traveled in Europe, 1901-03; Ph.D., U. of Halle, 1903; H.H.D., University of North Dakota, 1948; married to Alma Louise Ihrig, 1901 (died Jan. 1920); children—Miron Kingsbury, Marion Louise; m. 2d, Grace Elizabeth Rice, June 30, 1921; 1 dau., Frances Elizabeth. Asst. prin. De Pere (Wis.) High Sch., 1894-95; supt. schs., Sharon, Wis., 1899-1901; acting prof. and prof. of economics and polit. science, Carleton Coll., Northfield, Minn., 1903-17; head dept. economics and polit. science, and dir. course in commerce, U. of N.D., 1917-24, dean Sch. Commerce, 1924-48, ret. Expert, Bur. of Census, 1910-11. Sec. University War Com. throughout the war period. Mem. Am. Econ. Assn., Am. Assn. Univ. Profs., Phi Beta Kappa, Beta Gamma Sigma, Alpha Pi Zeta (nat. prsident 1931), Theta Chi, Beta Alpha Psi, Delta Sigma Pi. Congregationalist. Republican. Mason (K.T., Shriner). Clubs: University, Fortnightly, Franklin, Lions. Author: The Organic Theory of Society, 1903;

Social Problems, 1916, 1924, 1932. Editor Quarterly Jour. U. of N.Dak., 1923-28, and 1932-33. Home: 504 S. 6th St., Grand Forks, N.D. Died Feb. 27, 1952; buried Meml. Park Cemetery, Grand Forks.

TOWNE, Robert Duke, editor, pub.; b. Warren, O., Jan. 4, 1866; s. Levi and Mary Ellen (Duke) T.; A.B., St. Lawrence U., Canton, N.Y., 1888; m. Maude Agnes Barackman, June 28, 1888; children—Duke (dec.), Marian E., Bertha V. (Mrs. John Gray). Served in pulpit, Sherman, N.Y., Dubuque, Ia., Marlboro, N.H., and Lewiston, Me., 1888-98; propr. Lewiston (Me.) Daily Sun, 1898; mem. staff Newark (N.J.) Evening News, 1900-05; newspaper columnist, 1905; editor Judge, N.Y., 1905, Judge and Leslie's Weekly, 1906-07; pres. Judge Co., 1907-08; propr. Scranton (Pa.) Tribune, 1908-10, Tribune-Republican, 1910-12; consol. with Scranton Truth, 1912; founded Scranton Daily News, 1915; gen. mgr. National Single Tax League, 1919; director citizenship campaign, Phila. North American, 1920; staff of Public Ledger, 1923-27; pres. Gazette Publishing Co. and Suburban Newspapers, Inc., 1926-32; dir. and treas. Chas. H. Ingersoll Dollar Pen Co., 1928-34; apptd. Federal Receiver North Jersey Dist., 1929-36; editor, mgr. Manufacturers' Jour., Phila.; author series Bus. Leadership, 1938-39; author, pub. Henry George and Site Value; writer articles Publs., 1938-48. Pres. Am. Press Humorists, 1905. Author: Citizenship and Civilization, 1922; also of "The Teddy Bears," "How Old Is Ann?" and many humorous sketches in verse and prose. Writer of syndicated series, "The Great Awakening," appearing in various daily newspapers; editor of mag., The Areo, since 1915. Del. at large from Pa. to Rep. Nat. Conv., 1912; a founder of Progressive Party. Lectr. on civics and economics. Home: Ambler, Pa. Died Feb. 24, 1952; buried Chelten Hills, Phila.

TOWNSEND, Edgar Jerome, coll. prof.; b. Litchfield, Hillsdale County, Mich., Feb. 22, 1864; s. Warren and Henriette (Crocker) T.; Ph.B., Albion (Mich.) Coll., 1890, LL.D., 1915; Ph.M., U. of Mich., 1891; U. of Chicago, summers 1894, 95; A.M., Ph.D., U. of Göttingen, Germany, 1900; m. Phebe Belle Miller, June 24, 1891; children—Mrs. G. L. Alexander, Jerome T. (dec.). Prin. pub. schs., Reading, Mich., 1887-88; county examiner schs., Hillsdale County, Mich., 1887-90; teacher mathematics, Chicago Manual Training School, 1891-93; asst. prof. mathematics, U. of Ill., 1893-95, asso. prof., 1895-1905, prof., 1905, dean Coll. of Science, 1905-13 (now retired). Fellow A.A.A.S.; mem. Am. Math. Soc. (Council, 1905-08), Delta Tau Delta, Sigma Xi, Phi Beta Kappa. Conglist. Author: Functions of a Complex Variable, 1915; Functions of Real Variables, 1929. Co-author: First Course in Calculus, 1910; Essentials of Calculus, 1910; A Layman's View of the Bible, 1954. Translator of: Foundation of Geometry (from the German of Hilbert), 1902. Editor of American Mathematical Series. Contbr. to math. and ednl. jours. Home: 510 John St., Champaign, Ill. Died July 8, 1955; buried Rose Lawn, Champaign.

TOWNSEND, Lawrence, diplomat; b. Phila., Aug. 13, 1860; s. Henry C. and Georgiana Lawrence (Talman) T.; student U. Pa., class 1881; was not grad. owing to illness in sr. yr.; spent 5 yrs. ranching in western Colo.; m. Natalie Hannau, Mar. 8, 1886; children—Yvonne, Lawrence (dec.), Reginald Miers Fisher. Spent 6 yrs. in Europe studying internat. law and history of diplomacy; made several transls. from French and German on those subjects. First sec. U.S. Legation at Vienna, 1893-97; U.S. minister to Portugal, 1897-99, to Belgium, 1899-1905. Address: Pass-a-Grille, Fla. Died Mar. 8, 1954.

TOWNSEND, M. Clifford, ex-governor; b. Blackford County Ind., Aug. 11, 1884; s. David and Lydia (Glancy) T.; ed. Marion (Ind.) Normal sch., 1902-07, Marion Bus. Coll., 1908; B.S., Marion Coll., 1927; m. Nora Adele Harris, 1910; children—Robert Harris (dec.), Max A., Lucile Mae (Mrs. Robert Marshall Jr.), Helen Marie (Mrs. Lemoyne Duncan). Farm boy, later sch. tchr. until 1909; county supt. schs., Blackford County, 1909-19; farmer, 1919-25; mem. Ind. Gen. Assembly, 1923; county supt. schs., Grant County, Ind., 1925-29; dir. orgn., Ind. Farm Bur., 1919-32; lt. gov. Ind., 1933-37, gov., 1937-41; appt. adminstr. Agrl. Conservation and Adjustment Adminstrn., Jan. 1943; chmn. bd. dirs. Fed. Crop Ins. Corp. Democrat. Methodist. Home: Hartford City, Ind. Died Nov. 11, 1954.

TOWNSEND, Mary Evelyn, educator; b. N.Y.C., June 5, 1884; d. Charles and Mary (Mulligan) Townsend; A.B., Wellesley Coll., 1905; A.M., Columbia, 1917, Ph.D., 1921; grad. work U. Wis., U. London, Eng.; unmarried. Tchr. St. Mary's sch., N.Y.C., 1906-12; head history dept., Vail-Deane Sch., Elizabeth, N.J., 1912-17; instr. history, Tchrs. Coll., Columbia, 1918-29, asst. prof., 1928-35, asso. prof., 1935-39, prof., 1939-49. Exchange lectr. Inst. Internat. Edn., Bedford Coll., U. London, Eng., 1921-22. Mem. pub. affairs com. Y.W.C.A. Mem. Am. Hist. Assn, Nat Council Social Studies, Middle States Council Social Studies, English Speaking Union, Union Dem. Action, Fgn. Policy Assn. Democrat. Episcopalian. Pres. Womens Faculty Club (Columbia), 1929. Author: Origins Modern German Colonialism, 1921; The Baltic States; Study Syllabus, 1921; Rise and Fall of the German Colonial Empire, 1930; Guides to study Materials for Social Studies, 1936; European Colonial Expansion Since 1871 (Lippincott), 1941. Home: 39 Claremont Av., N.Y.C. Died May 1954.

TOWNSEND, Willard Saxby, labor leader; b. Cincinnati, O., Dec. 4, 1895; s. William and Beatrice (Townsend) T.; student Royal Coll. of Science, Toronto, Can., 1922-25; LL.D. (hon.) Wilberforce U., 1943; Bachelor of Laws; Doctor of Jurisprudence; married Consuelo Mann, Oct. 1, 1930; 1 son, Willard Saxby. Employed as Red Cap, Cincinnati Union Depot, Cincinnati, O., 1914-16; dining car waiter, Canadian Nat. Ry., Toronto, Canada, 1921-25; Red Cap, Chicago, Northwestern Ry., Chicago, Ill., 1930-36; internat. pres. United Transport Service Employees, C.I.O., since 1940; organized Red Caps into A.F. of L., elected pres. their auxiliary, 1936; organized Independent Brotherhood of Red Caps, elected pres., 1937; Independent Brotherhood Red Caps became United Transport Service Employes, C.I.O., 1940; UTSE-C.I.O. affiliated with C.I.O., 1942. Candidate for Congress, 1st Congl. Dist. of Ill., 1940; v.p. Nat. Urban League, 1945; vice chmn. Mayor's Commn. on Human Relations, Chicago, 1946; vice chmn. Southside Planning Bd., Chicago, 1947; vice chmn. Union for Democratic Action, Chicago, 1944; sec. Nat. C.I.O. com. to abolish discrimination, 1943; exec. bd. Congress Indsl. Orgns., 1942; bd. dirs. Am. Council on Race Relations (exec. com.), 1944; C.I.O. com. on Latin-Am. Affairs, on Housing and Community Development; nat. com., Nat. Citizens Polit. Action com.; labor com. Nat. Planning Assn.; Served as 1st lt., 372d inf., Ohio, World War I. Mem. President's Labor-Management Conf., 1945; U.S. labor adviser to Internat. Labor Office Conf., Apr. 1946, Mexico City, D.F.; C.I.O. fraternal del. to Cuban Fed. of Labor, Havana, Cuba, Dec. 1944; special representative to International Confederation of Free Trade Unions, Japan, 1952; member bd. dirs. Parkway Community Center, Chicago; adv. bd. Municipal Tuberculosis Sanitarium, Chicago; trustee Hampton (Va.) Inst. Statements before House Labor com. for Pepper 65c minimum wage, Nov. 2, 1945; before Senate banking and currency com. for Wagner-Ellender-Taft Housing bill, Dec. 11, 1945. Mem. Comm., World Fed. of Trade Unions to study conditions in Japan, China, Korea, Philippines, and the Malaya States, Feb.-Mar. 1947. Protestant. Democrat. Mem. Omega Psi Phi. Author: (with Dr. Rayford Logan) What the Negro Wants, 1944; articles; Full Employment and the Negro Worker, 1945; Leadership in the Economy of Living, 1945; Japanese handbook, Trade Union Practices (written in Japanese), 1948. Home: 423 E. 60th St. Chgo. Office: 3452 S. State St. Chgo. 16. Died Feb. 3, 1957.

TOY, Harry Stanley, lawyer; b. Elkhorn, W.Va., Jan. 12, 1892; s. James W. and Mary E. (Beals) T.; LL.B., Detroit Coll. of Law, 1913; m. Lorol E. Murray, Dec. 31, 1912; 1 son, James M. Admitted to Mich. bar, 1913; in gen. practice at Detroit, 1913-21 and 1923-30; asst. pros. atty. Wayne County, 1921-23, pros. atty., 1930-35; atty. gen. State of Mich., Jan. 1, 1935-Oct. 24, 1935; justice of Supreme Court Mich., 1935-37; prof. criminal procedure, U. Detroit, 1924-31; police commr. Detroit, 1948-50; partner Toy & Toy; pres. T-W-T Co.; sec.-treas. Howe Hinge Co.; dir. Scullin Steel Co. Served as capt. inf., U.S. Army World War. Mem. Am., Mich. State and Detroit bar assns., Nat. Prosecuting Attys.' Assn. (past pres.), Delta Phi Delta. Republican. Mason (33°). Clubs: Detroit Athletic, Grosse Pointe Yacht. Home: 415 Burns Av. Office: Penobscot Bldg., Detroit. Died Sept. 9, 1955; buried Mausoleum Woodlawn Cemetery Assn., Detroit.

TOZZER, Alfred Marston (tŏz'ĕr), anthropologist; b. Lynn, Mass., July 4, 1877; s. Samuel Clarence and Caroline Blanchard (Marston) T.; A.B., Harvard, 1900, A.M., 1901, Ph.D., 1904; Am. fellow Archaeol. Inst. America, 1902-05; m. Margaret Tenney Castle, Apr. 10, 1913; children—Anne (dec.), Joan. Dir. Internat. Sch. of Archaeology, Mexico, 1913-14; instr. in anthropology, 1905-12, asst. prof., 1912-20, asso. prof., 1920, prof., 1921-45. Harvard, also curator Middle Am. archaeology, and sec. Peabody Mus., Harvard. John E. Hudson prof. archaeology, 1945-47, emeritus 1947. Hon. prof. Museo Nac. Mexico. Fellow Nat. Acad. of Sciences, Am. Philos. Soc., Am. Acad. Soc., Archaeol. Inst. of Am., Am. Antiquarian Soc., Colonial Soc. of Mass.; Mass. Hist. Soc., corr. mem. Société des Américanistes de Paris, Soc. de Historia (Guatemala), Am. Franciscan Hist. Soc., Hispanic Soc. Am. Ethnol. Soc., Am. Anthrop. Assn., Am. Geog. Soc., Boston Soc. Natural History, Harvard Travellers Club, Royal Geog. Soc., Royal Anthrop. Inst. Major Air Service, U.S. Army, World War I. Dir., Honolulu Branch, Office of Strategic Services, 1943-45. Kidder Medal for Am. Arch. Author: A Comparative Study of the Mayas and Lacandones, 1907; Ruins of Tikal, 1911; Ruins of Nakum, 1913; Maya Grammar, 1921; Social Origins and Social Continuities, 1925; Landa's Relación, 1941; The Okinawas, a Japanese Minority Group, 1944; (postumously) Chichen Itza and Its Cennte of Sacrifice, 1957; also numerous pamphlets. Home: 7 Bryant St., Cambridge, Mass. Died Oct. 5, 1954.

TRACY, Daniel William, labor exec.; b. Bloomington, Ill., Apr. 7, 1886. Apptd. 2d asst. sec. labor, July 1940, later becoming 1st asst. sec.; resigned, Jan. 25, 1946; formerly pres. A.F. of L. Elec. Workers Union; presently 11th v.p. A.F. of L. and internat. pres. Internat. Brotherhood Elec. Workers. Home: 2505 Yupon Dr., Houston. Office: care Internat. Brotherhood of Electrical Workers, 1200 15th St., Washington 5. Died Mar. 1955.

TRACY, Henry Chester, author; b. Athens, Pa., Aug. 26, 1876; s. Charles Chapin and Myra (Park) T.; A.B., Oberlin Coll., 1902; A.M., U. Cal., 1910; m. Miriam Lee, Nov. 26, 1906; children—Herbert Lee, Arthur Park. Asst. in zoölogy, U. Cal., 1909-10; biologist, Hollywood (Calif.) High Sch. and Jr. Coll., 1910-23; research and writing, 1923—. Conglist. Author: An Island in Time, 1924; Towards the Open, 1927; The Shadow Eros, 1927; English as Experience, 1928; American Naturists, 1930; The Amateur Writer, 1935. Lecturer for Readers' Book Groups of Calif. and condr. the Bookshelf for Common Ground, Quarterly, New York. Home: 2104 N. Las Palmas, Hollywood 28, Cal. Died Dec. 19, 1958.

TRACY, John Clayton, civil engr.; b. Willimantic, Conn., Nov. 3, 1869; s. John Theodore and Annie (Downer) T.; Ph.B., Sheffield Sci. Sch. (Yale), 1890, C.E., 1892; m. Elizabeth Mary Blakeslee, Oct. 23, 1894 (died Mar. 30, 1934); children—John Blakeslee, Philip Louis (dec.), Thomas North, Delia Elizabeth. Instr., Yale U., 1891-1902, asst. prof. structural engring., 1902-15, prof., May-Nov. 1915, prof. civil engring., 1915-36, emeritus, 1936—. Pres. New Haven C. of C., 1925-26, New Haven Taxpayers, Inc., 1936-37. Mem. Am. Soc. C.E., Soc. Promotion Engring. Edn., Conn. Soc. C.E., Sigma Xi, Tau Beta Pi. Author: An Introductory Course in Mechanical Drawing, 1898; Plane Surveying, 1907; Exercises in Surveying, 1909; Aesthetic Elements in Engineering Design; Some Experiments in Reading Leveling Rods and Stadia Rods, 1908; Bridge Design, 1900; Descriptive Geometry, 1913. Dir. New Haven War Bur. Conn. State Council Def., Jan. 1918-May 1919. Gov. N.E. Kiwanis Dist., 1923. Author: Stresses Statically Determined, 1929; The Enrichment of Experience in the Development of the Teacher, 1932; Contemporary Science and Personal Faith, 1934; Commonplace Mysteries, 1943; Surveying—Theory and Practice, 1947. Address: 345 Winthrop Av., New Haven. Died Nov. 1, 1955.

TRACY, John Evarts, prof. law; b. Green Bay, Wis., Sept. 2, 1880; s. John Jay and Sarah Jane (Moore) T.; A.B., Maryville (Tenn.) Coll., 1901, LL.D., 1921; studied law, U. Wis., 1901-03; m. Margaret Elliott, Dec. 20, 1933. Admitted to bar, 1904; practiced in Menominee and Marquette, Mich., N.Y.C. and Chgo., 1904-30; prof. law, U. Mich., 1930-50; sec., dir. Newberry Lumber & Chem. Co. Served as asst. dir. bur. of exports, War Trade Bd., World War. Mem. Am. and Mich. State bar assns. Republican. Episcopalian. Club: Ann Arbor Golf and Outing. Author: Corporate Foreclosures, Receiverships and Reorganizations, 1939; Corporation Practice (vol. 19 of Fletcher's Cyclo. of Corps.), 1933; Hints on Entering Practice of Law, 1933; Cases and Materials on the Law of Evidence, 1937; The Practice of Law, 1947. Contbr. legal articles. Home: 24 Ridgeway Rd., Ann Arbor, Mich. Died Dec. 31, 1959.

TRACY, Joseph Powell, army officer; b. Washington, Oct. 4, 1874; s. Burr Ridgway and Anna (Putnam) T.; grad. U.S. Mil. Acad., 1896, Sch. Submarine Def., Ft. Totten, N.Y., 1905, Army War Coll., 1920, Naval War Coll., 1921; m. Jeanne West Wood, Apr. 18, 1899; children—Jeanne Wood, Maxwell Wood. Commd. add. 2d lt. arty., U.S. Army, June 12, 1896; advanced through grades to col., June 27, 1920; brig. gen., May 22, 1931. Served in Cuba, Spanish-Am. War, Philippine Insurrection; with C.A. C. and Adj. Gens. Dept., World War. Mem. Gen. Staff Corps, 1907-11, asst. comdt. Army War Coll., 1930-31; asst. chief staff, War Plans Div., 1931-32; comdg. 3d Coast Arty. Dist. and comdt. Coast Arty. Sch., Ft. Monroe, Va., 1932-36; comdg. 9th Coast Arty. Dist., Presidio San Francisco, 1937-38; ret., Oct. 31, 1938. Awarded D.S.M. (U.S.). Episcopalian. Clubs: Army and Navy, Army, Navy and Marine Corps Country (Washington); Chevy Chase (Md.) Address: 2126 Connecticut Av., Washington. Died May 21, 1950.

TRACY, Lyall, pulp and paper mfr.; b. Ivanhoe, Ill., Dec. 12, 1893; s. Isaac B. and Myra Sara (Parker) T.; student U. Minn., 1919-22; m. Lucy Belle Anderson, May 1, 1926; children—John Robert, Raymond Donald. Admitted to Minn. bar, 1922, Wash. bar, 1923; practice of law, Mpls., 1922; office mgr., asst. mgr. Washington Pulp & Paper Co. (now Port Angeles div. Crown-Zellerbach Corp.), Port Angeles, Wash., 1922-29; asst. mgr., div. mgr. Rayonier, Inc., Grays Harbor div. (formerly Grays Harbor Pulp & Paper Co.), Hoquiam, Wash., 1929-46, indsl. relations mgr. since 1946. Dir. pulp, paper and paperboard div. N.P.A., Washington, 1952, dep.

asst. adminstr., chem., rubber and forest products bur., 1952. asst. adminstr., 1953, dep. adminstr. N.P.A., 1953. Member National Defense Exec. Reserve, 1956—. Served as 1st sgt. Co. B., 20th Engrs., France, World War I. Mem. Wash. State Bar Association, U.S. Chamber of Commerce (dir. 1955-56). Republican. Mason, Elk. Club: Grays Harbor Country (Aberdeen. Wash.). Home: 421 W. Fifth St., Aberdeen. Office: P.O. Box 539, Hoquiam, Wash. Died May 29, 1959.

TRAIN, John Lambert, business exec.; b. Batavia, N.Y., July 17, 1883; s. Richard John and Ella (Hayes) T.; LL.B., Syracuse U., 1904; m. Dorothy Tunison, Sept. 17, 1907; children—Elizabeth (Mrs. John Norris MacDonald). Gen. mgr. Utica (N.Y.) Mutual Insurance Company, 1914—, pres., 1935—; president of John L. Train Co., Inc., Utica, 1923—. Director of First Bank & Trust Co., Asso. Industries of N.Y. State. Mem. New York Commn. on Old Age Security, 1929-30. Mem. N.Y. State Unemployment Ins. Adv. Council, 1939—. Mem. Utica (dir.) C. of C. Mem. Bar Assn. N.Y. State, Casualty Actuarial Soc., Nat. Assn. of Mutual Casualty Cos. (past pres.). Republican. Episcopalian. Mason (Shriner). Clubs: Utica Rotary (past pres.), Fort Schuyler, Yahnundasis Golf. Home: 36 Beverly Pl. Office: 185 Genesee St., Utica, N.Y. Died June 12, 1958.

TRANE, Reuben Nicholas, mfg. exec.; b. LaCrosse, Wis., Sept. 13, 1886; s. James A. and Mary (Miller) T.; B.S., U. Wis., 1910; m. Helen Hood, May 11, 1912; children—Reuben James, Helen Elizabeth (Mrs. Wayne Hood), Frank Hood. Sales engr. dept., Kempswith Mfg. Co., Milwaukee, 1910-13; organized The Trane Co., LaCrosse, 1913, and served as president, 1913-51. Chairman of the board since 1951. Charter member. dir., U. of Wis. Found. Mem. Am. Soc. Heating and Ventilating Engrs., C. of C. (past pres.), Pi Tau Sigma. Clubs: University (Chicago); La Crosse, La Crosse Country. Holds 27 patents in heating, ventilating, air conditioning, heat transfer. Home: 137 S. 13th St. Office: 2d and Cameron Av., La Crosse, Wis. Died Sept. 5, 1954.

TRAP, William Martin, educator; b. Muskegon, Mich., Dec. 23, 1887; s. Martin and Dirkje (Roozendaal) T.; student Calvin Coll., and Calvin Theol. Sem., 1905-13; Ph.D., U. Mich., 1925; postdoctoral research inivs. of Amsterdam, Oxford and Heidelberg, 1925-26; m. Johanna Cornelia ten Hoor, June 11, 1913. Ordained to ministry of Christian Reformed Ch., 1913; pastor Willard, O., 1913-16, Chicago, 1916-18, Grand Rapids, Mich., 1919-20, instr. in philosophy U. Mich., 1923-25; asst. prof. Wayne U., 1923-29, asso. prof., 1929-34, prof. of philosophy 1934-58, prof. emeritus, 1958; chmn. dept. of philosophy 1929-58. Served as camp pastor, Camp Grant, Ill., 1917-19. Mem. Am. Philos. Assn., Am. Assn. Univ. Profs., Mich. Acad. Sci., Arts and Letters, Detroit Philos. Soc. (pres.). Author: Divine Personality, 1925. Home: 440 S. York St., Dearborn, Mich. Office: Wayne University, Detroit 1. Died June 28, 1958; buried Woodlawn Cemetery, Grand Rapids, Mich.

TRAPP, Martin Edwin, ex-governor; b. Robinson, Kan., Apr. 18, 1877; s. Charles Franklin and Mary C. (Capps) T.; grad. Capitol City Coll., Guthrie, Okla., 1898; m. Lou Strang, Nov. 7, 1907; 1 s., Martin E. County clk. Logan Co., 1904-07; admitted Okla. bar, 1912; 1st state auditor, Okla., 1907-11; lt. gov. of Okla., 1914, reëlected, 1918-22; became acting gov. of Okla., Oct. 25, 1923, when J. C. Walton was suspended by resolution of Okla. Senate following his impeachment, and succeeded to office of gov., Nov. 19, 1923, for term 1923-27. Engaged in business of crude oil prodn., financing and construction. Member Oklahoma Bar Association, Oklahoma Hist. Soc. Democrat. Roman Catholic. Clubs: Oklahoma, Men's Dinner, Okla. City Golf and Country. Home: 315 N.W. 15th St. Address: Petroleum Bldg., Oklahoma City. Died July 26, 1951; buried Fairlawn Mausoleum, Oklahoma City.

TRASK, John William, physician; b. Bay City, Mich., Feb. 18, 1877; s. William Henry and Ellen Grey (McKim) T.; M.D., U. Mich., 1901; m. Fleta Lawrence, Aug. 23, 1902; children—Elsie Margaret, Ethel Lawrence, John Lawrence. Apptd. asst. surgeon USPHS, 1902; passed asst. surgeon, 1907; asst. surgeon gen., 1909-18; surgeon, 1918; promoted med. dir., 1930. Served at Detroit, Ft. Stanton (N.M.), Washington; charge of U.S. Marine hosps., Buffalo, Balt., Chgo., Boston, also fgn. quarantine and immigration inspection, Charleston, S.C. Editor Pub. Health Reports and charge Div. San. Reports and Statistics, USPHS, 1909-18; med. dir. U.S. Employees' Compensation Commn., 1918-22. Mem. sub-coms. on tb and statistics Com. Hygiene and Sanitation of Gen. Med. Bd. and sub-com. on information and statistics of Com. Labor of Council Nat. Def., 1917-18; commr. pub. health, City of Pittsfield, Mass., Apr. 1942-June 1946. Fellow A.C.P.; mem. A.M.A., Am. Pub. Health Assn. (chmn. sect. vital statistics, 1915-18), Mass. Med. Soc., Phi Rho Sigma. Author: A Digest of the Laws and Regulations of the Various States Relating to the Reporting of Cases of Sickness, 1911; Vital Statistics, 1914; Physiology, Hygiene and Sanitation and Primer of Personal Hygiene (text books), 1923; also chpts. various med. books and articles med. jours., principally on vital statistics, tb, malaria, milk as a factory in the spread of disease; geographic distribution of disease, etc. Address: 30 Sampson Pkwy., Pittsfield, Mass. Died Jan. 6, 1951.

TRAUB, Peter Edward (trawb), army officer; b. N.Y.C., Oct. 15, 1864; grad. U.S. Mil. Acad., 1886. Commd. 2d lt. 1st Cav., July 1, 1886; advanced through grades to col. U.S. Army, July 1, 1916; brig. gen. N.A., Aug. 5, 1917; maj. gen. N.A., June 15, 1918; honorary discharge N.A., June 30, 1919; brig. gen. U.S. Army, Apr. 19, 1928; retired Oct. 15, 1928; promoted maj. gen., ret. June 21, 1930. Served in campaign against Crow Indians, Nov. 1887 and against Sioux Indians in S.D., 1890-91; duty dept. of langs., U.S. Mil. Acad., 1892-98, 1902-04; comd. 1st Platoon, Troop G, 1st Cav., Battle of Las Guasimas, Cuba, June 24, 1898; recommended for bvt. of capt. "for gallantry in action," at Las Guasimas and brevet maj. for gallantry at Battle of San Juan, July 1-3, 1898, and siege of Santiago; acting asst. adj. gen. and asst. adj. gen., Dept. Luzon, 1900-01; secured signed agreement of Gen. Guevara to surrender, Apr. 27, 1902; head dept. of langs., Army Signal Sch., Army Staff Coll., 1904-07; on confidential missions fgn. countries, 1904-05; mem. mission, on invitation of Kaiser, to witness German army maneuvers, Breslau, 1906; appt. asso. prof. modern langs., U.S. Mil. Acad., 1907; mem. mission Isthmus of Panama supervise eection pres. of republic, 1908; in P.I., 1911-17; dist. chief Philippine Constabulary, Mindanao-Sulu, 1914-17; apptd. comdr. 51st Inf. Brig., Aug. 16, 1917; served in France, Sept. 1917-19; comd. 35th Div., July 20-Dec. 26, 1918, 41st Div., to Feb. 20, 1919; comd. Camp Pike, Ark., to July 1, 1919, Ft. Thomas, Ky., Nov. 1921. In charge recruiting drive, Washington, Jan.-Apr. 1920. Silver Star Citation, Purple Heart with Oak Leaf Cluster, for wounds in action in France (U.S.); Croix de Guerre with palm; Comdr. Legion of Honor (French). Home: Augusta, Ga. Died Sept. 1956.

TRAUGOTT, Albert Maser (traw'gŏt), civil engr.; b. Rochester, N.Y., July 31, 1882; s. Frederick George and Maria (Meier) T.; prep. edn., Rochester Free Acad. and Mechanics Inst., Rochester; student Purdue, 1899-1902; m. Myrtle Perkins, Nov. 6, 1920 (deceased July 17, 1942); children—Mary Perkins (Mrs. Townsend Brown), Myrtle Patricia (Mrs. John F. Rixey). Chainman Buffalo, Rochester & Pittsburgh Ry., 1898, Delaware, Lackawanna & West. R.R., 1900; successively rodman, draftsman, instrumentman, Virginian Ry., 1903-07, resident engr., locating engr. and div. engr., 1908-18, acting chief engr., 1919, asst. chief engineer, 1920-26, chief engineer, 1927-47, retired, 1947—. Mem. Rodmasters and Maintenance of Way Association, American Society Civil Engineers, Am. Railway Engring. Assn., Sigma Alpha Epsilon. Mason (Shriner). Clubs: Hampton Roads Engineers, Princess Anne Country, Norfolk Yacht and Country. German. Home: 1516 Blandford Circle, Lochhaven, Norfolk 5, Va. Died Jan. 1, 1954; buried Forest Lawn Cemetery, Norfolk.

TRAVIS, Robert Falligant, army officer; b. Savannah, Ga., Dec. 26, 1904; s. Maj. Gen. Robert Jesse and Rena (Falligant) T.; student U. Ga., 1923; B.S., U.S. Mil. Acad., 1928; grad. A.C. Engring. Sch., Wright Field, 1933; rated sr. pilot, combat observer, expert aerial gunner, celestial navigator and bombardier; grad. Nat. War Coll.; m. Frances Johnson, Aug. 16, 1929; children—Jane Darracott, Robert Falligant, Jr., John Livingston, Roger Bassett. Commd. 2d lt. Air Force, 1928, and advanced through the grades to brig. gen., 1943; at Mitchell Field, L.I., N.Y., 1929-31, Wright Field, Dayton, O., 1932, Langley Field, Va., 1933-39, Hickam Field, Oahu, T.H., 1939-41, MacDill Field, Tampa, Fla., 1941, Gowen Field, Boise, Ida., 1942-43; comdg. officer, 29th Bombing Group, 1940-42, 15th Tng. Wing, 1942-43, 1st Bombardment Command, 1943, 41st Combat Bombardment Wing, 8th Air Force, 1943; 17th Bombardment Wing, 1944-45; 14th Air Force, 1946; Commander of the Pacific Air Command, 1948—. Awarded D.S.C., Silver Star with 2 oak leaf cluster, D.F.C. with 3 oak leaf clusters, Air Medal with 3 oak leaf clusters, Purple Heart; Legion of Honor, Croix de Guerre and palm (France); British D.F.C.; Croix de Guerre and palm (Belgium); also numerous service ribbons; Presdl. Citation. Mem. Sigma Alpha Epsilon (Georgia Beta). Mason. Travis Air Base, Cal. so named in his honor. Address: care Adjutant General, War Dept., Washington. Died Aug. 5, 1950.

TRAVIS, Simeon Ezekiel, lawyer; b. Clarke County, Miss., Aug. 28, 1866; s. James and Susan (Merrell) T.; student Lake Como Inst., Jasper, Miss.; LL.B., with honors, Law Dept., U. Miss., 1892; m. Mattie Hall, Dec. 25, 1890; children—Simeon Ezekiel, Leonidas Erskine (dec.), James Kearney. Practiced Hattiesburg, Miss., 1892—; mem. Watkins & Travis, 1892-98; practcied alone until 1931, since mem. Travis & Travis; gen. counsel Miss. Central R.R. Co., 1898-1908, and 1914-20; pres. Hattiesburg Traction Co., 1908-12; dir. First Nat. Bank. Delegate to Conference on Uniform Legislation, Washington, D.C., 1910; delegate Third Nat. Conservation Congress, 1911; delegate 5th Annual Conv. Southern Commercial Congress, 1913. Pres. Bd. Bar Admissions of Miss. (resigned 1940)) mem. Miss. State Bar Assn. (pres. 1918-19), Am. Bar Assn. Dem. Mason (32°, K.T., Shriner). Clubs: Chamber of Commrce, Kiwanis, Shriners. Home: Hattiesburg, Miss. Died Dec. 31, 1952.

TREADWAY, Charles Terry, mfg. exec.; b. Bristol, Conn., Sept. 8, 1877; s. Charles S. and Margaret (Terry) T.; student Philips Andover Acad., 1896; A.B., Yale, 1900; m. Isabella G. Richards, June 4, 1902. With New Departure Mfg. Co., 1900-19, treas., chmn. bd., 1914-19; v.p. Bristol Nat. Bank, 1905, pres., 1907-29; chmn. bd. Bristol Bank & Trust Co., 1929-47, chmn. exec. com., 1947-54; vice pres. Bristol Brass Corp., 1924-51, now chmn. bd.; dir. Landers, Frary & Clark, Bristol Brass Corp. Vice pres. Bristol Hosp., 1920-51. Mason (32°, Shriner). Clubs: Farmington Country (Hartford); Yale (N.Y.C.); Graduate (New Haven); St. Bernard, Fish and Game (Que.). Home: 228 Belridge Rd. Office: 200 Main St., Bristol, Conn. Died Jan. 6, 1958.

TREANOR, Arthur Ryan (trā'nôr), editor; b. Saginaw, Mich., May 26, 1883; s. Hugh O'Connell and Margaret (Ryan) T.; grad. high sch., Saginaw, 1899; LL.D., Alma Coll., 1934; hon. alumnus, U. of Mich., 1934; m. Margaret Louise Corcoran, Mar. 1, 1927 (deceased); one daughter, Mary Margaret. Began career as reporter, Saginaw Daily News, 1901, editor and mgr. 1913-35; regional dir., 1927-32, Booth Newspapers, in charge Flint Journal, Saginaw News, Bay City Times (all of Mich.); v.p. and editorial counsel Booth Newspapers, Inc., 1935-46; chmn. bd. radio sta. WFDF, Flint, 1947-52; dir. Wood, Grand Rapids, Mich., 1947-52; pres. and dir. Wilson Cypress Co. (Palatka, Fla.); dir. Bancroft Hotel. Dir. of printing and publishing division of WPB, 1943-44; 51-53, cons., 1953. Served as member board of trustees Saginaw County Tuberculosis Sanatorium, 1922-32; director Saginaw Community Chest, Y.M.C.A. President Board of Trustees Saginaw Museum, 1946-49. Mem. Asso. Press (central advisory board, 1923-28; pres. 1927-28); mem. Am. Soc. Newspaper Editors. Mem. Group of Am. Editors visiting European countries, 1927, upon invitation of Carnegie Foundation, to review post-war conditions. Catholic. Clubs: Saginaw, U. of Mich. Press, Saginaw Country, Saginaw Tennis; Detroit Club; National Press (Washington, D.C.). Home: 1571 S. Washington Av. Address: 405 Bearinger Bldg., Saginaw, Mich. Died July 16, 1956; buried Oakwood Mausoleum, Saginaw.

TREAT, George Winfield, banker; b. Livermore Falls, Me., July 21, 1875; s. Winfield S. and Sarah B. (Pierpont) T.; grad. Hebron (Me.) Acad., 1894; B.S., Mass. Inst. Tech., 1898; m. Elsie M. Reynolds, 1926-29, chmn. bd. 1929-31 (retired); dir. and chmn. July 18, 1906. Bridge engr., 1899; with E. H. Rollins & Sons, Inc., investment bankers, Boston, Mass., since 1900, sales mgr., 1910-16, dir., 1914-31, pres., bd. Wickwire Spencer Steel Co. (exec. com. 1937-43) (retired); dir. Fruit of the Loom, Inc., Livermore Falls (Maine) Trust Co., Boston Met. Bldgs., Inc. Vice pres., trustee and chmn. finance com., Hebron Acad.; 2d v.p. and trustee, Mass. Memorial Hosp. (dir. Interscholastic Foundation). Member Boston C. of C. Mason (32°, K.T., Shriner). Clubs: Algonquin, University, Exchange (Boston); Country (Brookline); University (New York); Chapleau (Canada). Home: 56 Monatiquot Av., Braintree, Mass. Office: 75 Federal St., Boston 10. Died Aug. 25, 1952; buried Livermore Falls, Me.

TRECKER, Theodore, bus. exec.; b. LaSalle, Ill., Oct. 5, 1868; s. Theodore and Elizabeth (Franken) T.; student pub. schs.; m. Emma Pufahl, Nov. 24, 1890; children—Theodore Carl, Bertha (Mrs. Paul Powell), Joseph Leonard, Edgar William, Lydia Clara (Mrs. Anthony Busch), Francis Julius. With Wilkin Mfg. Co., Milw., 1897-1891, Kempsmith Co., 1891-93, 95-98; with city fire dept., Milw., 1894-95; co-founder, pres. Kearney & Trecker Corp., 1898-1947, chmn. bd., 1947-48, hon. chmn. bd., 1948—; pres. West Allis (Wis.) Bldg. & Loan Assn., 1919-47; v.p. First Nat. Bank of West Allis, 1920-33. Mem. Nat. Metal Trades Assn. (past pres.). Clubs: Rotary, Athletic, Wisconsin (Milw.). Home: 1735 N. Hi Mount Blvd., Milw. 8. Office: 6784 W. National Av., Milw. 14. Died Dec. 21, 1955; buried Holy Cross Cemetery, Milw.

TREDER, Oscar F. R. (trē'dẽr), clergyman; b. Albany, N.Y.; s. Rudolph and Emma (Helvig) T.; grad. St. Stephen's Coll., Annandale, N.Y., 1901, D.D., 1917; grad. Gen. Theol. Sem., N.Y.C., 1904; m. Lillian E. Howe, Oct. 5, 1904; children—Oscar F. R., Lillian G., John Howe, Rudolph W., Alfred H. G. Ordained to ministry P.E. Ch., 1904; rector St. Luke's Ch., East Hampton, N.Y., 1904-16; dean Cathedral of the Incarnation, Garden City, N.Y., 1916-26; dean St. Stephen's Cathedral, Harrisburg, Pa., 1926-34; rector St. Jame's Ch., Bedford, Pa., 1934-1944, St. Ann's Ch., Smithsburg, Md., 1944-

—. Mem. Sigma Alpha Epsilon. Mason (32°, K.T.). Club: Masonic (New York). Residence: The Rectory, Thurmont, Md. Died 1952.

TREES, Merle Jay, civil engineer; born on farm near Mayview, Ill., June 14, 1883; s. George Washington and Jennie Myrtle (Ray) T.; B.S., U. of Ill., 1907, C.E., 1911; m. Emily Lavinia Nichols, Jan. 2, 1909; children—Katherine, George Spencer. With Chicago Bridge & Iron Co., Oct. 1908—, beginning as estimator, apptd. gen. sales mgr., 1911, dir., 1913, v.p., 1918, exec. v.p., 1942, chmn. bd. 1945, dir. Guardite Corp., International Harvester Co., Am. Lumber & Treating Co., John I. Hay Co., Northern Trust Co., A.T.&S.F. Ry., Horton Steel Works, Ltd., Chgo. Bridge & Iron Wks., Ltd., Sociedad Chibridge de Construcoes Ltd. Has served as pres. bd. dirs. United Charities of Chicago, Chicago Commonwealth Club, U. of Ill. Alumni Assn., Nat. Ry. Appliance Assn.; mem. executive com. Chicago Community Trust; mem. Cancer Research Committee Univ. Chgo.; mem. bd. trustees, U. of Ill. (past pres.), 12 years; mem. bd. trustees Art Inst. of Chicago, 4th Presbyn Ch. Life mem. Chicago Hist. Soc., Art Inst. Chicago, Field Museum of Natural History. Mem. Am. Soc. Civil Engrs., Western Soc. Engrs., Steel Plate Fabricators Assn. (past pres.), U. of Ill. Alumni Assn. (past pres.), Nat. Ry. Appliance Assn. (past pres.), Am. Iron and Steel Inst., Phi Delta Theta. Republican. Mason. Clubs: Chicago, Commercial (past pres.) Commonwealth, University, Illini, Wayfarers, Casino, Economic, Ind. Soc. of Chgo., Glenview (Chgo.). Home: 1500 Lake Shore Dr. Office: 322 S. Michigan Blvd., Chgo. Died Aug. 6, 1954.

TRELEASE, Sam F., plant physiologist; born in St. Louis, Missouri, July 3, 1892; the son of William and Julia Maria (Johnson) T.; A.B., Washington University, 1914; Ph.D., Johns Hopkins, 1917; m. Mrs. Helen Mary Cato Ashton, July 11, 1922. Asst. in plant physiology, Johns Hopkins, 1916-17, instr., 1920-23; asst. prof., U. of Philippines, 1917-19, asso. prof., 1919-20; asst. prof., U. of Louisville, 1923-25; asso. prof., Columbia, 1925-28, prof. botany, 1929-36, Torrey prof. botany, 1937—, exec. officer of dept., 1930—. Mem. bd. mgrs. New York Bot. Garden. Fellow Am. Assn. Advancement Science (asst. sec. 1921-23; sec. council 1921-30; program editor 1923-30; sec. sect. G 1925-36), Bot. Soc. America (sec. 1932; editor Am. Jour. Bot., 1933-39; v.p. 1941), Am. Soc. of Plant Physiologists, Torrey Bot. Club, Soc. Bot. de France, Gamma Alpha, Sigma Xi. Author: Laboratory Exercises in Agricultural Botany, 1919; How to Write Scientific and Technical Papers, 1957; Selenium (with O. A. Beath), 1949. Contbr. various papers on bot. subjects. Home: 520 W. 114th St., N.Y.C. 25. Died Feb. 1, 1958; buried St. Louis, Mo.

TREMAINE, Frederick Orlin, writer, editor; b. Harrisville, N.Y., Jan. 7, 1899; s. Rev. De Witt Charles and Alice Nelson (Dowd) T.; B.O., Valparaiso U., 1921. Editor, Torch, 1920-21; asso. editor Eastern Underwriter, 1921-22; mng. editor Brain Power, Beautiful Womanhood, True Romances, and Metropolitan mags., 1923-24; editor True Story Magazine, 1924; editor Smart Set, 1924-26, Everybody's Magazine, 1931, Clayton Magazines, 1929-30 and 1931-33, Street and Smith Magazines, 1933-38. pres. and editor Orlin Tremaine Co., book pubs., 1939-42, organized and edited mag., Plus, distributed in bulk to war industries, 1941-42; editor spl. govt. manuals on tech. subjects for armed forces, C.C.M. Aeronautical Company, 1943; editor of books, Bartholomew House, 1943-48; editor Southerner mag., 1948-50; cons. and contbg. editor several mags. and orgns. since 1950; editor-in-chief The Biltmore Mags. since 1951. Served as private and non-commissioned officer 307th Cav. and 51st Field arty., U.S. Army, Club: National Press (Washington, D.C.). Author: One Burning Minute, 1926; The First Person Story, 1927; Aviation Conquests, 1931; Short Story Writing, 1949. Contributor numerous short stories, verse, and feature articles to periodicals. Address: Tunder Mountain, Stony Creek, N.Y. Died Oct. 22, 1956; buried Stony Creek.

TRENCH, William Washington, corp. exec.; b. Staten Island, N.Y., Feb. 22, 1892; s. William P. and Lillian Evelyn (Greene) T.; A.B., St. Lawrence U., Canton, N.Y., 1913; LL.B., Brooklyn Law Sch., 1916; m. Edwina Holbrook Corey, Nov. 18, 1919; children—William Corey, Barbara. Asst. sec. Gen. Electric Co., Schenectady, N.Y., 1916-28, sec. 1928—; dir. Electric Mut. Liability Ins. Co., Arkwright Mut. Fire Ins. Co. Sec., chmn. City Planning Commn., Schenectady, 1922-46, sec., dir. Bur. Municipal Research, 1927-46. Served with minesweeper squadron U.S. Navy, on French coast, 1917-19. Mem. Am. Soc. Corporate Secs. (dir.), Beta Theta Pi. Republican. Clubs: Mohawk, Mohawk Golf (dir.) (Schnectady); University (N.Y.C.). Home: 1049 Avon Rd. Office: 1 River Rd., Schenectady, N.Y. Died Sept. 22, 1954.

TRENCHARD, Hugh Montague (1st Viscount Trenchard), British marshal Royal Air Force; b. Feb. 3, 1873; hon. LL.D., Cambridge U.; D.C.L., Oxford U.; m. Katherine Bowlby Boyle, 1920; 1 son, Thomas. Chmn. The United Africa Co., 1936—; dir. Goodyear Tyre & Rubber Co. (Gt. Britain), Ltd. Served with British Army 1893—; in South Africa, 1899-1902, later with Canadian Scouts, West African Frontier Force and in Europe during World War I; promoted maj. gen., 1916; asst. comdt., Central Flying Sch., 1913-14, comdt., 1913-18, became air marshal, 1919, Marshal Royal Air Force, 1927—. Commr. Met. Police, 1931-35. Decorated Comdt. of Legion of Honor, Order of St. Anne (3d class with swords), Order of King Leopold, Distinguished Service Medal (U.S.), Order de la Couronne (Italy), Order Sacred Treasure of Japan, Queen's medal with 3 clasps, King's medal with 2 clasps, companion Distinguished Service Order, Companion of the Bath, Knight Comdr. of the Bath, Knight Grand Cross of the Bath, Knight Grand Cross Royal Victorian Order, Order of Merit. Sometimes known as "father of the R.A.F." Home: 141 Cranmer Court, Sloane Av., S.W. 3, London, Eng. Died Feb. 10, 1956; buried Westminster Abbey.

TRESSLER, Jacob Cloyd, teacher and author; b. Wila, Pa., Mar. 24, 1882; s. Henry Lenig and Catherine Elizabeth (Dum) T.; A.B., Syracuse U., 1906, Pd.D., 1946; student Harvard, summer sessions, 1907-09; M.A., Columbia U., 1912; m. Edith Howard, Dec. 28, 1915. Teacher pub. schs., Newport, Pa., 1900-02, Centenary Collegiate Inst., Hackettstown, N.J., 1906-07, Potsdam (N.Y.) State Normal Sch., 1907-09, Alexander Hamilton High Sch., N.Y. City, 1909-11, Boys High Sch., N.Y. City, 1911-14; head English and Speech Dept., Newtown High Sch., N.Y. City, 1914-26; head English Dept., Richmond Hill High Sch., N.Y. City, 1926-47; instr. Columbia Univ. Extension Sch., 1920-22, New York U. Extension Sch., 1920, Coll. of City of N.Y. Extension Sch. and Sch. of Edn., 1920-30, Syracuse U., summers 1919-29. Mem. N.Y. State Com. to Prepare English Regents, 1925-28 and 1936-39. Mem. New York City Association of Teachers of English (president 1919-21); member of Phi Beta Kappa, Phi Gamma Delta, Delta Sigma Rho. Conglist. Mason. Club: Men's Faculty (Columbia Univ.). Author: (with William Williams) Composition and Rhetoric by Practice, 1923; Grammar in Action, 1928, revised edition, 1938; English in Action, 1929 6th edit., 1955; Grammar Minimum Essentials, 1931; English in Action Practice Books, 1936, 6th edit., 1955; (with Edwin C. Woolley and Frank W. Scott) High School Handbook of Composition, 1931; also, Handbook of Writing and Speaking, 1944; (with Marguerite, Shelmadine) Junior English in Action, 1933, 6th edit., 1956; (with same) Introductory English in Action, 1934; (with George P. Shannon) Philippine Edit. of English in Action, 1929; (with Marguerite Shelmadine) Relating Experiences, also, Building Language Skills, 1944; (with R. W. Bardwell and Ethel Mabie Falk) Making Plans, Sharing Interests, Exchanging Thoughts, Expressing Ideas, 1944; (with Maurice C. Lipman) Business English in Action, 1949, 2d edit., 1957; (with Henry I. Christ) Practice in English Usage, 1952. Address: 8324 Edgerton Blvd., Jamaica Estates 32, N.Y. Died Dec. 24, 1956; buried Willow Dale Cemetery, Bradford, Pa.

TREVOR, John Bond (trĕv′ẽr), lawyer; b. "Glenview," Yonkers, N.Y., Nov. 19, 1878; s. John Bond and Emily (Norwood) T.; prep. edn., Cutler Sch., N.Y. City; B.A., Harvard, 1902, M.A., 1903; LL.B., Columbia U. Law Sch., 1906; LL.D., University of Rochester, 1932; m. Caroline M. Wilmerding, June 25, 1908; children—John B., Bronson. Admitted to N.Y. bar, 1904; spl. dep. atty. gen. State of N.Y., 1919; asso. counsel for sub-com. of Com. on Foreign Relations, U.S. Senate, 1920. With U.S. Army, Nov. 1917-June 1919; 1st lt., later capt. Mil. Intelligence Div., U.S. Army, May 1918-June 1919, in comd. Office of Mil. Intelligence Div., N.Y. City, Dec. 1918-June 1919. Chmn. of board Am. Coalition of Patriotic Socs., 1927-33; pres. Am. Coalition, 1933-50; active in movement to restrict immigration into U.S. Trustee Am. Museum Nat. History, 1908-25; mem. council New York U., 1927-28; mem. bd. mgrs. Empire State Soc., S.A.R., since 1935; mem. bd. dirs. Eugenics Research Assn., 1937-38. Mem. Chamber Commerce of State of N.Y. (mem. exec. com. 1921-23, 1924-27), France-America Soc., New York Soc. Mil. and Naval Officers World War, S.A.R., New York Chap. Soc. Colonial Wars (mem. council), 1942-45), French Inst. in United States, American Society of French Legion of Honor, Institute of 1770 Harvard), Delta Kappa Epsilon. Decorated Chevalier Legion of Honor (France). Republican. Baptist. Club: Union. Wrote: (brochures) An Analysis of the American immigration Act of 1924; Japanese Exclusion—A Study of the Policy and the Law, 1925; The Crisis, 1931; The Recognition of Soviet Russia by the United States—an American Problem, 1932. Home: Paul Smiths, N.Y. Office: 20 Exchange Pl., N.Y.C. Died Feb. 20, 1956; buried Woodlawn Cemetery, N.Y.C.

TRIGG, Ernest T., mfr.; b. Aurora, Ill., Aug. 12, 1877; s. Thomas and Anna M. (Anderson) T.; ed. pub. schs.; m. Alice Gibbons, June 19, 1901 (dec.); children—Helen Alice (Mrs. Charles J. Swain, Jr., dec.), Ernest T., Jr. With Heath & Milligan Mfg. Co., Chgo., 1895-1908; gen. mgr. John Lucas & Co., paints, Phila., 1908, v.p., 1912, pres. until 1933; pres. Nat. Paint, Varnish and Lacquer Assn., 1933-47, now hon. life chmn.; former chmn. Industry Recovery Bd.; dir. Bankers Securities Corp., Lit Bros., The Warner Co. (Phila.); pres., chmn., Savs. & Loan Found.; pres., dir. Land Title Bldg. Corp. Dir., v.p. bd. Land Title Building Corporation. City Trusts, Phila.; trustee, chmn. exec. com. Mercersburg (Pa.) Acad. Pres. Paint Mfrs. Assn., U.S., 1911, Phila. Paint, Oil and Varnish Club, 1918-21, Phila. C. of C., 1918-21; bd. dirs. U.S. C. of C., 1918-30; chmn. ednl. bur. Am. Paint and Varnish Mfrs. Assn. Mem. Pa. Commn. to San Francisco Expn., 1915; regional adv. War Industries Bd.; mem. Pres. Wilson's Indsl. Conf., 1919, Pres. Harding's Unemployment Conf., 1921; chmn. Pres. Hoover's Com. Home Ownership and Home Bldg.; chmn. Fed. Home Loan Bank, 3d Fed. Res. Dist. Hon. life mem. N.E., N.Y., Balt., Paint Varnish and Lacquer assns.; bd. dirs. C. of C. of Greater Phila. Republican. Presbyn. Mason (Shriner). Author: 55 Colorful Years. Clubs: Aronimink Golf (Newton Sq., Pa.); Union League, Bachelors Barge, Radnor Hunt, Kiwanis (Phila.); Duquesne (Pitts.). Home: Hotel John Bartram, Phila. 7; also Malvern, Pa. Office: Land Title Bldg., Phila. 10. Died Aug. 19, 1957; buried Great Valley Presbyn. Ch. Cemetery, Paoli, Pa.

TRIPLETT, Arthur Fairfax, lawyer; b. Pine Bluff, Ark., Aug. 20, 1891; s. Charles Hector and Estelle (Holland) T.; A.B., U. Va., 1912, LL.B., 1914; m. Vashti King, Jan. 16, 1918; children—Tomme Fairfax (Mrs. Samuel Baker Fullerton, Jr.) Instr. law dept. U. Va., 1914-15; admitted to Va. bar, Ark. bar, 1914; pvt. practice, Pine Bluff, Ark., since 1915. Mem. Ark. (pres. 1952-53), Pine Bluff (pres. 1935) bar assns. Home: 912 W. 6th Av. Office: National Bldg., Pine Bluff, Ark. Died Nov. 24, 1958.

TROOST, George Wilbur, business exec.; b. Canaan. Vt., Apr. 25, 1902; s. Peter Jay and Hulda (DuBois) T.; A.B., U. Mich., 1924; m. Louise Schlutt, June 29, 1926; children—George Richard, Mary Louise. Pub. acct. Ernst & Ernst, 1924-35; asst. comptroller Chrysler Corp., 1935-47, comptroller, 1947-53, v.p. since 1949, dir. since 1951, mem. finance com. since 1953. Trustee Grace Hosp. Mem. Am. Inst. Accts., Controllers Inst., Mich. Assn. C.P.A.'s, Phi Beta Kappa, Phi Mu Alpha, Alpha Kappa Psi. Clubs: Golf, Detroit, Athletic (Detroit). Home: 17394 Muirland, Detroit 21. Office: 341 Massachusetts, Detroit 31. Died Jan. 24, 1956; buried Glen Eden Lutheran Cemetery.

TROTT, Stanley B., banker; b. Baltimore, July 21, 1896; s. Frank B. and Margaret L. (Tatum) T.; student Balt. City Coll., 1913; grad. sch. banking Rutgers, 1937; m. Corinthia Caldwell Roberts, Feb. 10, 1950. With Md. Trust Co., Balt., 1913—, pres., 1949-59, chmn., pres., 1959—; pres., dir. Park Central Savs. & Loan Assn., 1929—; director Eutaw Savs. Bank, Balt. Life Ins. Company, Md. Title Guarantee Co., Finance Co. of Am., Archer Laundry Co., Black & Decker Mfg. Co., Maryland Casualty Co. Trustee Western Maryland College. Member Robert Morris Assos., Assn. Res. City Bankers, Balt. Assn. Credit Men. Clubs: Maryland, Baltimore, Country (Balt.) Home: 6100 York Road, Balt. 12. Office: Md. Trust Co., Balt. 3. Died Sept. 25, 1959.

TROTTI, Lamar (trŏt′ē), author; b. Atlanta, Ga., Oct. 18, 1900; s. John Patterson and Emma (Dineen) T.; A.B.J., U. of Ga., 1921; m. Louise Kennedy Hall, Oct. 2, 1928; children—Lamar (dec.), John Hall, Louise Hall. Reporter and city editor, Atlanta Georgian, 1921-25; asst. to Will H. Hays, Motion Picture Producers and Distributors of Am., Inc., 1925-32; producer and writer for 20th Century-Fox Film Co. since 1932; author of following screenplays; Cheaper by the Dozen, I'd Climb the Highest Mountain, Wilson, The Razor's Edge, Captain from Castile, The Ox Bow Incident, Young Mr. Lincoln, and 30 others. Mem. Delta Tau Delta, Sigma Delta Chi fraternities. Democrat. Club: Piedmont Driving (Atlanta). Home: 812 Birchwood Dr., Los Angeles, Claif. Office: 20th Century-Fox Studio, Beverly Hills, Cal. Died Aug. 28, 1952.

TROUT, David McCamel, psychologist and educator; b. Elmira, Mo., Sept. 7, 1891; s. James McCamel and Viola (Utt) T.; A.B., William Jewell Coll., Liberty, Mo., 1916; A.M., B.D., U. of Chicago, 1922, Ph.D., 1924; L.H.D., Hillsdale College, 1939; m. Charlotte Woods, June 20, 1916; children—Maurice Elmore, Elinor Helene, Marjorie Rogene. Teacher pub. schs., 1908-10; ordained ministry, Missionary Bapt. Ch., 1911; student pastor in Mo., 1910-16; pastor Clifton Hill (Mo.) Ch., 1916-17, Park Ch., Brookfield, 1917-20; fellow religious edn., U. of Chicago, 1920-22; with Union Theol. Coll. as instr., 1923-24, prof. Bible and religious edn., 1924-25; prof. psychology, Hillsdale Coll., 1925-37, dean of men, 1926-37; head dept. of edn. and psychology, Central State Teachers Coll., Mount Pleasant, Mich., 1937-40; special consultant to Mich. Secondary Sch. Curriculum Study, 1940-41; head dept. of psychology and edn., Central Mich. Coll. of Edn., 1941-45, dean of students, 1941—; coorindator Mich. Coöperative Teacher Edn. Study, 1942-43; visiting prof. Edn., U.

of Mich., summer 1945. Fellow A.A.A.S.; life mem. N.E.A.; mem. Mich. Edn. Assn., Am. Coll. Pres. Assn., Mich. Assn. Coll. Registrars and Adminstrn. Officers (pres. 1950), Mich. Soc. for Mental Hygiene, Mich. Counselors Assn. (mem. bd. dirs.), Nat. Soc. for Study of Education American Personnel and Guidance Association, Student Personnel Association for Teacher Education, Am. Assn. of University Profs., Mich. Acad. Science, Arts and Letters, Mich. Schoolmasters' Club, Faculty Club, Pi Gamma Mu, Beta Alpha Delta, Kappa Delta Pi. Democrat. Presbyterian. Author: Religious Behavior, 1931. Writer and lecturer on psychology and education. Home: 421 S. Kinney St., Mt. Pleasant, Mich. Died Sept. 14, 1954; buried Riverside Cemetery, Mt. Pleasant.

TROUT, Grace Wilbur (Mrs. George W. Trout); b. Maquoketa, Ia.; d. Thomas and Anne (Belden) Wilbur; ed. pub. schs., specializing under pvt. tutors in dramatic art, lit. and langs.; m. George W. Trout, January 5, 1886; children—4 sons, 1 living, Philip Wilbur, and also an adopted son who was killed in World War. Removed to Chicago shortly after marriage; made an exhaustive study of Mormonism; known as suffrage orator; pres. Ill. Equal Suffrage Assn., 1912-Oct. 1920; was leader of campaign by which woman's suffrage for many offices was enacted by Gen. Assembly of Ill., 1913; leader, 1917, in securing passage of resolution in Ill. legislature, calling for State Constl. Conv. Mem. lobbying com. of Nat. Am. Woman's Suff. Assn., Washington, 1917, 18, 19, until federal suffrage amendment was passed; mem. women's com. Council Nat. Defense, Ill. Div. Settled in Fla., 1921; pres. City Planning Advisory Bd., that secured adoption of city plan for Jacksonville, 1929, re-elected each year since formation of bd. (work of board now centered on aiding defense), elected president emeritus, 1943. Hon. member General Federation Women's Clubs: mem. Illinois Woman's Press Association, Florida Hist. Soc., Fine Arts Soc. (Jacksonville), D.A.R., etc. Clubs: Chicago Woman's (Chicago); Jacksonville Woman's, Garden Club (ex-pres.), Friday Musicale (Jacksonville), Fla. Soc. Desc. of the Mayflower, Fla. Soc. of Colonial Dames of America. Author: A Mormon Wife, 1896. Awarded medal of honor by Am. Legion, Jacksonville, "to the most public-spirited citizen of Jacksonville," in 1928. Home: "Marabanong," Atlantic Blvd., Jacksonville, Fla. Died Oct. 21, 1955; buried Evergreen Cemetery, Jacksonville.

TROY, John Henry, horticulturist; b. Mt. Hissarlik, Co. Kildare, Ireland, Apr. 29, 1856; ed. pub. schs.; m. Margaret Muir Wylie (now dec.); 1 son, William Wylie. Gardener apprenticeship in Ireland and Eng.; attached to Queen Victoria Gardens, Windsor, Eng.; foreman in gardens of Duke of Westminster, Eaton Hall, Cheshire, Eng., 1878-84; rose specialist and landscape plantsman. Came to U.S., 1885; chmn. Bd. Commrs. of Parks, Docks and Harbors, New Rochelle, N.Y., 1910-16; city councilman, New Rochelle, N.Y., 1910-12; pres. New Rochelle Housing Corpn.; dir. New Rochelle Trust Co., Peoples Bank for Savings. Mem. Hort. Soc. of N.Y. (life), C. of C., New York Florists' Club (ex-pres.), Soc. Am. Florists and Ornamental Horticulturists (life). Mason (K.T.). Clubs: City (New York); Rotary (New Rochelle). Home: 257 Mayflower Av., New Rochelle, N.Y. Died Mar. 24, 1931; buried Beechwood Cemetery, New Rochelle, N.Y.

TROY, Peter Henry, telephone exec.; b. Red Hook, N.Y., Jan. 23, 1868; s. Peter and Bridget (Dee) T.; ed. pvt. schs., tutor; m. Matilda Bullock, June 30, 1897; children—Almira, Helen, Frances, Peter. Telegrapher Western Union, 1883; stock broker Boody McLellan & Co., Poughkeepsie, N.Y., 1883-90; telephone exec., 1890; pres. Red Hook Telephone Co. (N.Y.), 1945-50, chmn., 1950—; dir. Poughkeepsie Trust Co., U.S. Fire Ins. Co., U.S. Casualty Co., New Amsterdam Casualty Co. (N.Y.C.). Mem. N.Y. State Automobile Assn. (dir.). Clubs: Bankers, Stock Exchange, Nat. Democratic, Amrita. Home: 1 Dwight St. Office: 9 Cannon St., Poughkeepsie, N.Y. Died Aug. 23, 1958.

TRUE, Allen Tupper, mural decorator; b. Colorado Springs, Colo., May 30, 1881; s. Henry A. and Margaret (Tupper) T.; student U. of Denver 2 yrs.; ed. in art, Corcoran Art Sch., Washington, D.C.; pupil of Howard Pyle, 1902-08, and of Frank Brangwyn (his assistant 2 yrs.); m. Emma Goodman Eaton, June 3, 1915 (divorced 1934); children—Frank Eaton, Jan, Edith Tupper, Allen Tupper. Formerly illustrator for mags.; decorated the New Telephone Bldg., Denver; has executed mural decorations in Wyo. State Capitol, Missouri State Capitol, Colo. State Capitol (8 murals for rotunda), Colo. Nat. Bank, Denver, and in many pub. bldgs. in the West; one man exhbn. circulated in 29 cities by Am. Fedn. of Arts; 72 sketches (murals) exhibited in various Western cities. Fellow Royal Soc. of Arts, England; mem. Mural Painters of America, Beta Theta Pi. Unitarian. Mason. Clubs: Cactus (Denver); Authors (London, Eng.). Consultant for U.S. Bur. of Reclamation in charge of and designing all decoration and color schemes Boulder Dam power plant; now laying out the decorative color scheme for Grand Coulee, Shasta and other power plants; last mural in Student Union Bldg., U. Colo. Address: 2393 Raleigh St., Denver. Died Nov. 8, 1955; buried Evergreen Cemetery, Colorado Springs, Colo.

TRUEBLOOD, Ralph Waldo, editor; b. Richmond, Ind., Nov. 19, 1885; s. William Newby and Emma (Stubbs) T.; B.S., Earlham Coll., Richmond, Ind., 1903; A.M., Haverford (Pa.) Coll., 1905; m. Elsie May Smith, Nov. 9, 1914; children—Jacqueline, Ralph W. Instr. in chemistry, Haverford Coll., 1903-05; instr. in science and langs., high sch., Cranford, N.J., 1905-07; chemist Victor Portland Cement Co., Los Angeles, 1909-10; reporter Los Angeles Times, 1910-12, asst. city editor, 1912-16, city editor, 1916-20, exec. editor, 1920-26, mng. editor, 1926-34, editor in chief, 1934-37, editorial dir., 1938-44, retired Jan. 1, 1945. Mem. Am. Soc. Newspaper Editors, Pi Gamma Mu. Republican. Co-inventor of telephotograver, first device used by newspapers for sending pictures by wire. Home: 131 S. Rockingham Av., Brentwood Park, Los Angeles 49. Died May 6, 1954.

TRUEBLOOD, Thomas Clarkson, educator; b. Salem, Ind., Apr. 6, 1856; s. Jehu and Louisa T.; A.M., Earlham Coll., 1886, Litt.D., 1921; elocution and oratory under James E. Murdock, S. S. Hamill, Charles John Plumptre; m. Carolyn Hoggs; children—Byram Clarkson, Clara Louise. With Prof. Robert I. Fulton founded sch. of oratory in Kansas City, 1879; lectr., U. Mo., Ohio Wesleyan, Ky. U., U. Mich., 1884-89; prof. pub. speaking, U. Mich., 1889-1926 became head dept. speech, 1926, prof. emeritus, 1926—. Pres. Nat. Speech Arts Assn., 2 years. Organized No. Oratorical League, 1890, Central Debating League, 1898, Midwest Debating League, 1914; presided at orgn. Delta Sigma Rho Soc. for honor debaters and orators, 1906. Hon. pres. Nat. Assn. Tchrs. Speech, 1941-42; hon. pres. No. Oratorical League, 1941-42. Author: (with Prof. Robert I. Fulton) Practical Elocution, 1893; Choice Readings, 1884; Patriotic Eloquence, 1900; Standard Selections, 1907; Essentials of Public Speaking, 1909; British and American Eloquence, 1912. Editor: Honor Orations of the University of Michigan, 1898; Winning Speeches in Northern Oratorical League, 1909. Lectr. colls. and univs. Cal., Hawaii and Japan in 1910, univs. Australia and New Zealand, 1917-18, instns. Argentina and Chile, 1927-28, U. So. Cal., 1929, colls. and univs., Union of S. Africa, 1929-30. Pres. Emeritus Club, U. Mich., 1931-37. Organizer of golf as varsity sport in Midwest, 1901; dir. golf, U. Mich., 1901-1936. Address: Ann Arbor, Mich. Died June 4, 1951; buried Forest Hill Cemetery, Ann Arbor.

TRUESDELL, Karl (trōōz'dĕl), army officer; b. Moorhead, Minn., Aug. 27, 1882; s. Julius Augustus and Cornelia Octavia (Riggs) T.; ed. high sch., Washington, D.C., 1901, Army Signal Sch., 1911-12, Sch. of the Line, 1920-21 (hon. grad.), Staff Sch., 1921-22, Army War Coll., 1925-26, Naval War Coll., 1926-27; m. Mary Maurice Smith, Apr. 15, 1907; children—Karl, Cecil Olive (wife of Edgar Thomas Conley III, U.S. Army). Enlisted in U.S. Army, 1901, commd. 2d lt., 1904, advanced through the grades to maj. gen., 1940; served with 33d, 26th and 1st Divs. and V Army Corps, A.E.F., during World War I; in battles of Siechprey, Cantigny, Soissons, St. Mihiel, Meuse-Argonne; chief budget and legislation, War Dept. Gen. Staff, 1927-31; with 15th Inf., Tientsin, China, 1932-35; dir. Mil. Intelligence Dept., Army War Coll., 1935-37; comdg. officer Ft. Jay, N.Y., and 16th Inf., 1937-38; comdg. gen. 12th Brig., 1938-39, First Div., 1940, 6th Army Corps, 1941; dep. comdr. Panama Dept. to Mar. 1942; comdt. Command and Gen. Staff Sch., Ft. Leavenworth, 1943-45; ret. 1946. Am. mem. of Internat. Allied Radio Commn. Decorated Distinguished Service Medal with oak leaf (U.S.); Croix de Guerre (France); Comdr. Order Brit. Empire; Grance official Order Merit Militar, Order Merit Aeronautico (Brazil); Grand officer Mil. Order Ayacuche (Peru); Comdr. Order Polonia Rsestituta (Poland). Mem. Am. and Washington philatelic socs., China Stamp Soc., Council Fgn. Relations, N.Y. Genealogical and Biographical Society, Founders and Patriots (governor D.C. dist.), Soc. of the Cincinnati. Mason. Club: Army and Navy (Washington). Author: Military Policy of the United States, 1921; Tactics and Technique of Separate Branches, 1922; Command and General Staff School Correspondence Courses, 1923-26. Lecturer for Council on Foreign Relations. Address: 6312 Beechwood Dr., Chevy Chase, Md. Died July 16, 1955; buried Arlington Mil. Cemetery.

TRUITT, Max O'Rell, lawyer; b. Millersburg, Mo., Jan. 25, 1904; s. Edwin Thomas and Mary Elizabeth (Hulen) T.; student U. of Mo., 1921-26, National University Law School and George Washington U., 1927-28; m. Marian Frances Barkley, Jan. 20, 1929; children—Max O'Rell, Alben William Barkley, Thomas Hulen, Stephen McKenzie. Admitted to Mo. bar, 1926; asst. clk. Mo. Supreme Court, 1926-27; atty. U.S. Dept. of Justice, 1927-28; practice of law, St. Louis, Mo., 1929-36; solicitor R.F.C., 1935-37; general counsel U.S. Maritime Commission, 1937-38, apptd. mem. Commission, Feb. 1938, to succeed Joseph P. Kennedy; reappointed for 6-year term ending Sept. 26, 1944; resigned Apr. 1, 1941, to reenter practice of law with Cummings & Stanley, Washington, D.C. Trustee Electric Home and Farm Authority, 1935-37; dir. and mem. exec. com. Jefferson Nat. Memorial Assn. Mem. Exec. Com. on Commercial Policy, 1939-40; U.S. Del. to Inter-American Maritime Conference, 1940. Mem. Am. Geog. Soc., Acad. Polit. Science, Am. Polit. Science Assn., Am. Acad. Polit. and Social Sciences, Delta Tau Delta. Democrat. Episcopalian. Clubs: Metropolitan, Burning Tree (Washington). Home: 3100 Que St., Washington 7. Office: 1625 K St., Washington 6. Died Feb. 2, 1956; buried Oak Hill Cemetery, Washington.

TRULLINGER, R(obert) W(illiam) (trŭl'ĭn-gẽr), sci. research administr.; b. Farragut, Ia., Feb. 25, 1889; s. William Barton and Lucy Martha (Butler) T.; B.S., Ia. State Coll, 1910, A.E., 1925; Engr. D. (hon.), Rutgers U., 1941; m. Pearl Maude Jordan, Jan. 24, 1913; 1 dau.. Virginia (Mrs. Roy C. Dawson). Gen. practice civil engring., Clarinda, Ia., and Omaha, Neb., 1910-12; specialist in agrl. engring., Office Expt. Sta., U.S. Dept. Agr., Washington, 1912-17, expt sta. adminstr., 1919-38, asst. chief, 1938-46, chief Office of Expt. Stas. and asst. research administr., since 1946. Served as 1st lt., then capt., U.S. Army, 1917-19; assigned research in arty. ammunition. Awarded John Deere gold medal by Am. Soc. Agrl. Engrs., for distinguished achievement in application of sci. and art to soil, 1941; U.S. Department Agriculture Gold Medal Award, 1951. Fellow Am. Soc. Agrl. Engrs. (pres. 1931); mem. Nat. Research Council, Western Irrigation and Drainage Research Assn. (hon.), Tau Beta Pi, Phi Kappa Phi, Sigma Alpha Epsilon. Mason. Episcopalian. Contbr. articles and bulls. on various aspects of agrl. research and its adminstrn. Home: 7120 Colesville Rd., Hyattsville, Md. Office: Office Experiment Sta., U.S. Dept. Agriculture, Washington 25. Died Nov. 8, 1955; buried Arlington Nat. Cemetery.

TRUMBO, Arthur Cook (trŭm'bō), investments and oil royalties; b. near Columbus Grove, O., Aug. 6, 1866; s. Enoch and Martha Lucretia (Cook) T.; g.g.s. Thomas Corwin, U.S. senator and gov. of Ohio; grand nephew of General Robert B. Mitchell, Union Army; student Ohio Northern U.; Tri-State Normal Coll., Angola, Ind., 1886-88; Wooster Coll., 1890-92; A.B., Stanford, 1894; LL.B., Northwestern U., Chicago, 1896; m. Bess Ethlyn Patterson, Apr. 11, 1901; children—Donald, Elizabeth (Mrs. Herbert L. Branan). Editor Daily Palo Alto during senior year at Stanford. Practiced law, Chicago, 1896-1901; then in banking business Muskogee, Okla., until 1925; now owner and manager farm lands and city properties. Pres. Trans-Miss. Comml. Cong., 1911-12. Pres. Trumbo Investment Co., ex-pres. Muskogee County Tax League; organizer Pioneer Abstract & Trust Co.; mem. Bd. Freeholders that prepared charter for commn. form of govt. for Muskogee. Chmn. Am. Red Cross membership campaign in 10 counties, Okla., World War I. Republican. Mem. Delta Tau Delta, Hi-12 and Real Estate Board. Mason, Elk. Club: Commercial (ex-pres.). Known in Oklahoma as advocate improvement Arkansas River for navigation, lower freight rates, and flood control. Sec. Local Draft Board No. 1, Selective Service, 1940-47, World War II. Home: 1505 Camden Way, Oklahoma City, Okla. Office: 404 Wall St., Muskogee, Okla. Died June 15, 1954.

TRUMPLER, Robert Julius, astronomer; b. Zurich, Switzerland, Oct. 2, 1886; s. Wilhelm Ernst and Luise (Hurter) T.; grad. Gymnasium, Zürich, 1905, student U. of Zürich, 1906-08; student U. Göttingen, Germany, 1908-11, Ph.D., 1910; m. Augusta C. O. De La Harpe, Aug. 5, 1916; children—Cecile Eliane Ramona, Marguerite Caroline Jacqueline, Elizabeth Julie Helen, Robert Hamilton, Alfred Oswald. Astronomer of Swiss Geodetic Survey, 1911-15; came to U.S., 1915, and served as asst. in determination of stellar parallaxes, Allegheny Obs., Pitts., until 1919; Martin Kellogg fellow, Lick Obs., Mt. Hamilton, Calif., 1919-20, asst. astronomer (studies of Mars and star clusters), 1920-26, asso. astronomer, 1926-29, astronomer, 1929-38; prof. astronomy, Berkeley dept., U. Cal., 1938-51, ret. Mem. Am. Astron. Soc., Astron. Soc. of Pacific, Int. Astron. Union, Nat. Acad. of Sciences, Astronomische Gesellschaft, Royal Astron. Soc., Société Astronomique de France hon. mem. Société Helvétique Sc. Nat., Sigma Xi. Unitarian. Author: Statistical Astronomy (with H. F. Weaver), 1953. Made exptl. test confirming Einstein's theory, at Wallal, Australia, 1922, a determination of light absorption in Galactic System, 1930. Address: 620 Bay View Dr., Box 1750, Aptos, Cal. Died Sept. 10, 1956; buried Berkeley, Cal.

TRUSLOW, Francis Adams, lawyer; b. Summit, N.J., May 4, 1906; s. Henry Adams and Jane Kent (Auchincloss) T.; A.B., Yale, 1928; LL.B. Harvard, 1932; Doctor Comml. Sci. (hon.), New York University, 1950; m. Elizabeth Auchincloss Jennings, Nov. 17, 1933; children—Francis Adams, Frederic Jennings, Elizabeth Buck, Sophia Day. Asso. with law firm Duryee, Zunino and Amen, N.Y. City, 1932-34; asst. to gen. counsel, N.Y. Curb Exchange, 1934-41, became gen. counsel, 1941; asso. with law firm Morgan and Lockwood 1934-42; partner in firm, 1936-42; formed law firm Reed, Truslow, Crane and De Give, Mar. 1942; on leave of absence July 1942-Dec. 1945 spl. rep. (area mgr.) to Peru, Rubber Reserve Co. (U.S. Govt. agency), 1942-44; vice pres. and dir. Rubber Development Corp. (govt. agency which succeeded Rubber Reserve Co. in responsibility for accumulation of natural rubber in all regions outside U.S.), Washington, D.C., Mar.-Oct. 1944, pres. Oct. 1944-Nov. 1945; in practice of law Dec. 1945-Mar. 1947; pres. of New York Curb Exchange since 1947. Mem. selection bd. A of U.S. Dept. of State, 1950; chief of Cuban Mission International Bank, 1950; treas. and trustee Am. Com. on United Europe. Awarded Order of El Sol (Peru); Star of Africa (Liberia). Mem. Assn. Bar City of N.Y.; former treas. Pub. Edn. Assn. of N.Y. City; formerly arbitrator of panel Am. Arbitration Assn. Clubs: Univ., Downtown Assn., Anglers' (New York); Nacional Lima, Peru) Metropolitan (Washington); American Alpine Club. Home: 136 E. 95th St., N.Y.C.; also Cold Spring Harbor, L.I., N.Y. Office: 86 Trinity Place. Died July 8, 1951; buried Cold Spring Harbor, L.I., N.Y.

TRYON, James Libby, publicist and educator; b. Boston, Nov. 21, 1864; s. Joseph and Ellen Bigelow (Cummings) T.; A.B., Harvard, 1894; B.D., Episcopal Theol. Sch., Mass., 1897; LL.B., Boston U., 1909, Ph.D., 1910; m. Kate Allen, Sept. 15, 1885; children—James Libby (dec.), Sylvia, Robert Jordan (dec.), Richard Westcott. Reporter Portland Press, 1884; city editor Portland Express, 1885, Bangor Commercial, 1886; night editor Portland Argus, 1887-88; deacon, 1896, priest, 1897, P.E. Ch.; rector All Saints Ch., Attleboro, Mass., 1897-1907, Ch. of St. John the Evangelist, Mansfield, Mass., 1900-07; later serving Grace Ch., Medofrd, Mass. Asst. sec. Am. Peace Society, 1907-11; sec. Massachusetts Peace Soc., 1911-14; dir. New Eng. dept. Am. Peace Soc., 1911-18; sec. Me. Peace Soc. and Me. Prison Assn., 1917-18. Mem. Mohonk confs., 1907-16, Internat. Peace Congress, Munich, 1907, London, 1908, Geneva, 1912, The Hague, 1913; peace congress of Protestant chs., Constance, Germany, 1914; lecturer on internat. arbitration, Episcopal Theol. Sch. Cambridge, 1908-11; lecture tour of Canadian clubs, univs. and chs. to promote the peace centennial, spring, 1911. Lectr. internat. law, U. Me., 1918-19; lectr. Mass. Inst. Tech., 1919-29, asst. registrar, 1920-26, asst. to sec. of faculty, 1926, sec. grad. sch. com., 1920-36, dir. of admissions, 1930-36, asst. prof., 1922, asso. prof., 1923, became prof., 1931, now emeritus. Admitted to bar of Me., 1916. Trustee Westbrook Junior Coll., Portland, Me. Mem. Am. Soc. Internat. Law, Medford Hist. Soc., Twentieth Century Assn., Boston, Alumni Assn. Mass. Inst. Tech. (hon. mem. with fraternal citation, 1944). Republican. Mason. Club: Field and Forest (pres. 1927, 29). Author of pamphlets and articles on internat. orgn.; contbr. on internat. peace and arbitration to the Am. Year Book, to Yale Law Journal and to World Affairs. Visited widely among colleges and univs. of U.S., Canada and Cuba, lecturing on tech. edn. and giving ednl. guidance to students, 1928-36; observations on ednl. policies of instns. visited, summed up in writing reports. Home: 55 Terrace Rd., Medford 55, Mass. Died Dec. 22, 1958.

TRYON, Rolla Milton, educator; b. Knox County, Ind., Jan. 20, 1875; s. Philip and Eliza Ann (Thompson) T.; prep. edn., Vincennes (Ind.) U.; grad. Ind. State Normal Sch., Terre Haute, 1902; A.B., Ind. U., 1907, A.M., 1912; Ph.D., U. Chgo., 1915; m. Agnes Carey Polk, Sept. 19, 1907; children—Philip Freeland, Rolla Milton. Prin. schs., Edwardsport, Ind., 1902-04; prin. ward sch. Vincennes, 1905-07; tchr. history, high sch., Vincennes, 1907-08; prin. high sch., Madison, Ind., 1908-09; supt. schs., Madison, 1909-11; critic tchr. history, high sch., Bloomington, 1911-12; with U. Chgo., 1912—, becoming prof. social sciences, prof. emeritus, July, 1940—. Mem. N.E.A., Nat. Council Social Studies, Am. Assn. U. Profs. Republican. Methodist. Mason (K.T.). Author: Household Manufactures in the United States (1640-1860), 1916; The Teaching of History in Junior and Senior High Schools, 1921; (with Prof. C. R. Lingley) The American People and Nation, 1927; The American Nation Yesterday and Today (with C. E. Lingley and Frances Morehouse); Tryon Illustrated American History Maps; The Social Sciences as School Subjects, 1935. Editor: (with C. R. Lingley) Tryon and Lingley History Series. Home: Freelandville, Ind. Died Nov. 10, 1954.

TSCHIRKY, Oscar (Oscar of the Waldorf) (shĕr-kĭ); b. Locle, Canton of Neuchâtel, Switzerland, Sept. 28, 1866; s. August and Antoinette (Fassbind) T.; ed. Gymnasia, Chaux-de-Fonds, and at Fribourg; m. Sophie Bertisch, Sept. 18, 1887; children—August, Leopold, Clover. Came to U.S., 1883, naturalized, 1888. Began with old Hoffman House, N.Y.C., later with Delmonicos', also with Waldorf-Astoria since opened, 1893; owner of model 1,000 acre farm near New Paltz, N.Y.; said to know more people from all over the world than any other person in America. Decorated Chevalier of the Crown (Belgian); Chevalier of the Crown (Roumanian); Chevalier de Mérite Agricole (French). Address: Waldorf-Astoria, N.Y.C. Died Nov. 6, 1950; buried New Paltz, Ulster County, N.Y.

TSCHUDY, Arnold Nord, (choo'di), banker; born Billings, Mont., Feb. 7, 1902; s. Otto August and Georgia (Nord) T.; student Univ. of Mont., 1919-21, Univ. of Wash., 1921-22; A.B. Univ. of Calif., Berkeley, 1925; Dr. of Laws (hon.), Univ. of Sao Paulo, Brazil, 1946; m. Adelheid Schraft, Sept. 20, 1930; children—Heidi, Gay, Nina. Entered employ of General Motors Acceptance Corp., Los Angeles, Calif., 1926, served as mgr. for Spain at Madrid and Barcelona, 1929-33, for Hawaii at Honolulu, 1933-35, for Japan at Osaka, 1935-38, and for Brazil at Sao Paulo, 1938-45; Council for Inter-American Cooperation, Inc., New York, N.Y., executive vice pres. Apr. 1, 1946-47; cons. Inter-Am. coml. and pub. relations, 1947-49; vice pres., New York rep. Bank of Am. since 1950. Served as dir. Office of Coordinator of Inter-Am. Affairs in Sao Paulo (on war service leave of absence from Gen. Motors Acceptance Corp., 1943-45. Mem. Am. C. of C. of Sao Paulo (pres. 1941-42, U.S. nat. councillor; hon. life mem. since 1946). Awarded Order of the Southern Cross by Brazilian govt., 1945. Hon. mem. Sao Paulo Advt. Men's Assn., Consular Soc. of Sao Paulo, Sao Paulo Artists League, Sao Paulo Press Assn., Brazilian-Am. Cultural Union. Mem. Sigma Chi., Phi Delta Phi, Pi Delta Epsilon. Conglist. Club: University, Ardsley on Country, Bond. Home: Field Terrace, Ardsley-on-Hudson, N.Y. Office: 40 Wall St., N.Y.C. Died Mar. 12, 1955.

TUBBS, Edward, corp. exec.; b. Chicago, Sept. 39, 1900; s. Frank and Ellen (Helquist) T.; student Northwestern U. extension courses, 1917-23; m. Elsie Jerrick, Nov. 3, 1923; children—Phyllis Joyce (Mrs. Donald Paulsen), Ronald Edward. Pub. accountant Price, Waterhouse & Co., 1920-22, Arthur Young & Co., 1933-42; treas. Am. Electric Co., 1923-32; comptroller Internat. Minerals & Chem. Corp., Chicago, 1943-56; exec. v.p. Engineered Nylon Products, Inc., So. Bend, Ind.; treas. Internat. Agrl. Corp., Ltd.; treas. Innes, Speiden & Co., Inc., N.Y. City, Millen (Ga.) Fertilizer Co.; dir. Fla. Mining Co. President Controllers Institute of America, 1954-55 (director 1950-51); member of the National Assn. Cost Accountants, Clarendon Hills (Ill.) Civic Assn. (pres. 1948). Presbyn. Mason. Clubs: Executives, Electric (Chicago); Hinsdale (Ill.) Golf. Home: 613 E. Jefferson Blvd. Office: 1318 S. Olive St., So. Bend, Ind. Deceased.

TUBERMAN, Walter H(endrix), state ofcl., grain dealer; b. Montgomery Co., Ill., Apr. 19, 1879; s. Isaih and Mary (Harris) T.; student pub. schs. Fillmore, Ill.; m. Estelle Short, Oct. 1, 1904; 1 son, Walter Isaih. In grain bus., St. Louis, 1904—; pres. Toberman Grain Co.; clk. Circuit Ct., St. Louis, 1943-45; Sec. of State, State Mo., 1949—. Mem. St. Louis Bd. Aldermen, 1933-43. Guarantor Municipal Opera, St. Louis. Mem. St. Louis Mchts. Exchange, Nat. Grain Dealers Assn., Nat. Hay Assn. Club: Missouri Athletic (St. Louis). Home: 3439 Pestalozzi, St. Louis. Office: Merchants Exchange Bldg., St. Louis; also Secretary of State, Capitol Bldg., Jefferson City, Mo. Died Feb. 14, 1960.

TUCKER, C(larence) M(itchell), univ. prof.; b. Centralia, Mo., Oct. 28, 1897; s. Joseph Davis and Lena Theophilus (Swinney) T.; B.S., U. of Mo., 1920, Ph.D., 1930; m. Helen Baskwell Jones, Sept. 15, 1920; 1 dau., Jacqueline Lee (Mrs. James C. Dowdy). Prof. plant pathology, U. of Puerto Rico, 1920-23; plant pathol., Puerto Rico Agr. Expt. Sta., 1923-30; asso. plant pathol., U. of Fla., 1930-31; asso. prof. botany, U. Mo., 1931-37, prof., chmn. dept., 1937—, acting dean, 1952. Served with U.S. Marine Corps, 1918-19. Mem. Am. Phytopath. Soc. president 1950; mem. editorial bd., 1946-48), Am. Soc. Botany, Mycol. Soc. Am., A.A.A.S., Mo. Hist. Soc. Democrat. Episcopalian. Club: Rotary (pres. Columbia, Mo., chapter, 1938). Contbr. articles on plant diseases and fungi to sci. jours.; research monographs on genus-phytophthora, 1931-32. Research in taxonomy and physiol. of Phytophthora, breeding plants for disease resistance. Home: 310 Thilly Av., Columbia, Mo. Died Feb. 3, 1954.

TUCKER, Henry St. George, bishop; b. Warsaw, Va., July 16, 1874; s. Beverley Dandridge and Anna Maria (Washington) T.; M.A., U. Va., 1895, D.D., 1911; m. Mary Lillian Warnock, Apr. 18, 1911; children—Henry St. George, James W. Deacon and priest, P.E. Ch., 1899; sent as missionary to Japan, 1899, and soon afrerwards placed in charge of Episcopal missions in Aomori Province; pres. St. Paul's College, Tokyo, 1903-12; bishop Diocese of Kyoto, Mar. 25, 1912; retired, 1923; bishop coadjutor Diocese of Va., 1926; bishop of Va., 1927-44; presiding bishop P.E. Ch. in U.S.A. 1938-46. Pres. of the Fed. Council of Chs. of Christ in Am., 1942-44. Mem. Pi Kappa Alpha. Mason. Author: Reconciliation through Christ, 1910; Providence and the Atonement, 1934; Episcopal Church in Japan. Served Am. Red Cross Commn. in Siberia as maj. in charge of civilian refugee work. Home: 6501 Three Chopt Rd., Richmond, Va. Died Aug. 8, 1959.

TUCKER, Katharine Dickinson (Mrs. Collingwood Tucker); b. Cumberland, Md., Mar. 18, 1873; b. Laurence Thomsen and Nannie Hill (Tidball) Dickinson; ed. pvt. schs. and under tutors; m. George Collingwood Tucker, May 3, 1893. Student negro folk songs since childhood; has given lecture recitals, leading cities of U.S. and before many univs. and socs.; made phonographic records of many Afro-Am. folk songs for Harvard U. collection; sang with success in Paris. Democrat. Episcopalian. Address: Hilliard Manor, Beesley's Point, Ocean City, N.J. Died May 7, 1957.

TUCKER, Preston Thomas, bus. exec.; b. Capac, Mich., Sept. 21, 1903. Office boy Cadillac Motor Co., 1916-20; with Ford Motor Co., 1920-24; successively as wholesale and retail sales mgr., Studebaker, Chrysler distbrs., Memphis, zone mgr. Pierce-Arrow Motor Car Co., Buffalo, Packard distbr., Indpls., 1925-37; owner, operator cos., identified with automobile and aviation industries, 1942; gen. mgr. Ypsilanti Machine & Tool Co., 1944-46; became exec. v.p., gen. mgr. Higgins-Tucker Motor Co., Inc., 1945-46; organized Tucker Corp., 1946, now pres. Home: Drake Hotel. Office: 7401 S. Cicero Av., Chgo. Died Jan. 7, 1957.

TUCKER, Richard Blackburn, industrialist; b. Norfolk, Va., June 3, 1886; s. Bishop Beverley D. and Anna Maria (Washington) T.; ed. Norfolk (Va.) Acad.; student U. Va., m. Elinor Hilliard, October 12, 1909 (deceased January 21, 1948); children—Elinor Hilliard (Mrs. Cornelius D. Scully, Jr.), Richard B., Jr., Isota Ashe (Mrs. W. Perry Epes); m. 2d Mary Williamson Foster (Jackson), May 24, 1949. Manager of the John D. Gordan Co., Camaguey, Cuba, 1907-08; v.p. and gen. mgr. Building Supplies Corp., Norfolk, Va., 1908; mgr. Plate Glass Sales, Standard Plate Glass Co., Pitts., 1925; pres. Standard Plate Glass Co., 1926; mgr. glass sales, 1929; dir. glass sales, 1940; dir., 1942—; v.p., 1944; exec. v.p., 1947-54; v.p., dir., mem. exec. com. Pittsburgh Plate Glass Co., 1956; ret. 1956; dir. J. W. Fecker & Co., Pitts. Trustee, mem. exec. com. Jamestown Glasshouse Found., Inc., Jamestown, Va.; gov., mem. bd. gov., Jamestowne Soc. Descs. Signers Declaration Independence (2d v.p. gen., dir.) Soc. of the Lees of Va. (dir.), Baronial Order of Magna Charta (dir.), Soc. Descendants Knights of the Garter, Officer del 'Ordre Leopold II, Soc. of the Cincinnati (dir.), Alpha Tau Omega. Episcopalian. Clubs: Manhattan (N.Y.), Colonnade (University, Va.), Princess Anne Country (Virginia Beach, Va.); Commonwealth (Richmond, Va.), Farmington Country (Va.). Home: Kingston Hall, Port Haywood, Va. Died Nov. 1959.

TUCKER, Richard Hawley, astronomer, retired; b. Wiscasset, Me., Oct. 29, 1859; s. Capt. R. H. and Mary (Armstrong) T.; C.E., Lehigh U., 1879, Sc.D., 1922; m. Ruth Standen, Apr. 29, 1914; children—Mary Ronald, Jane Standen. Astron. work, Dudley Obs., 4 yrs.; instr. mathematics and astronomy, Lehigh U., 1883-84; at Argentine Nat. Obs., Cordoba, 9 yrs.; at Lick Obs., 1893-1908; dir. So. Obs., Carnegie Instn., San Luis, Argentine, S.A., 1908-11, Lick Obs., 1911-26. Mem. Albany Inst., Astron. Soc. Pacific, A.A.A.S., Astronomische Gesellschaft, Soc. Astronomique de France, Am. Seismol. Soc., Am. Philos. Soc. Author: Vol. IV, 1900, Vol. VI, 1903, Vol. X, 1907, Vol. XV, 1925, Lick Obs. publs.; contbr. astron. jours., etc. Address: 1525 Waverly St., Palo Alto, Cal. Died Mar. 31, 1952; buried Wiscasset, Me.

TUCKERMAN, Arthur, author; b. N.Y.C., Jan. 6, 1896; s. Fleming and Edith Adele (Cozzens) T.; prep. edn., Cutler Sch., N.Y.C., U. Sch., Washington, Cheltenham Sch., Eng.; B.A., Christ Ch., Oxford U., 1921; m. Elise Strother, Jan. 20, 1927. Writer numerous short stories, novels, travel articles for leading Am. and European publs. Dir. Public Relations, Am. Car & Foundry Co. Home: 103 E. 86th St., N.Y.C. Died Oct. 5, 1955.

TULLIS, H(eber) H(icks), bus. exec.; b. Blanchester, O., May 18, 1901; s. Abram Walter and Norma (Hicks) T.; m. Vivian Stuff, Sept. 1924 (divorced Apr. 1935); m. 2d, Elizabeth Harding Renick, Oct. 15, 1936. With Armco Steel Corp. 1928—, v.p., cont., 1947-55, admin. v.p., 1955-57, ret.; dir. mem. exec. com. First Nat. Bk. of Middletown. Republican. Clubs: Moraine Country (Dayton, O.); Queen City, Camargo (Cincinnati); Union (Cleveland). Home: 1004 S. Main St. Office: Armco Steel Corp., Middletown, O. Died Apr. 14, 1958; buried Woodside Cemetery, Middletown, O.

TULLOSS, Rees Edgar (tŭl'ŏs), coll. pres. emeritus; b. Leipsic, Ohio, July 26, 1881; s. Rees Pierce and Almira D. (Weaver) T.; B.A., Wittenberg College, 1906, L.H.D., 1949; B.D., Hamma Div. Sch., Springfield, O., 1909; Johns Hopkins, 1915-16; Ph.D. Harvard, 1918; D.D., Lenoir Coll., 1921; LL.D., Muhlenberg, 1923; m. Alpha D. Miller, in 1908 (dec. Oct. 1956); children—Frances Louise (dec.), Alice Miller, Mary Elizabeth (dec.), Nancy Martha, Rees Edgar. Founder, 1901, and pres. until 1917, Tulloss School of Touch Typewriting, Springfield; pastor Messiah Lutheran Ch., Constantine,

Mich., 1909-15, First Ch., Mansfield, O., 1918-20; pres. Wittenberg Coll., 1920-49, pres. emeritus; gen. dir. United Luth. Ch. of Am. Six Million Dollar Christian Higher Edn. Appeal, 1949-52. Pres. First Nat. Bank & Trust Co., 1930-40, chmn. board, 1940—; dir. and mem. exec. com. Ohio C. of C., 1939-49, life dir., 1949—. Dir. Ohio State Life Insurance Co., 1939—; dir. Wm. McCulloch Sons Co., 1946—, treas., 1951—. Psychologist, U.S. Naval Radio Sch., Cambridge, Mass., 1917-18. Mem. gen. bd. Nat. Coun. Y.M.C.A., 1921-31; mem. exec. com. Liberal Arts Coll. Movement, 1930-34, chmn. 1933; mem. exec. com. Nat. Conf. Ch.-Related Colls., 1934-44, chmn. 1930; mem. com. Assn. Am. Colls., on Christian Higher Edn., 1944-48; sec., Nat. Lutheran Ednl. Conf., 1922-27, and chmn. 1928; mem. exec. bd. United Lutheran Church, 1930-38, and 1940-48; mem. com. Investments, U.L.C.A., 1937-54, mem. commn. Adjudication, 1954—; commissioner Nat. Luth. Council, 1938—, pres. 1945-48, sec. 1951-54. Fellow of the Royal Soc. of Arts, A.A.A.S.; mem. O. Hist. Soc. (pres. 1956—), Phi Kappa Psi, Kappa Phi Kappa, Psi Chi, Tau Kappa Alpha, Tau Pi Phi, Phi Eta Sigma, Blue Key, Rotary Club. Author Tulloss Touch Typewriting, 1901; New Way in Typewriting, 1912; Instruction Book in Radio Operating (for use in U.S. Navy), 1918. Republican. Lutheran. Home: 1617 Woodedge Rd. Address: Parkside Bldg., Springfield, O. Died June 8, 1959.

TUMULTY, Joseph Patrick (tŭm'ŭl-tĭ), ex-sec. to the President; b. Jersey City, May 5, 1879; s. Philip and Alice T.; B.A., St. Peter's Coll., Jersey City, 1899; studied law in office of Bedle, McGree & Bedle, and Gilbert Collins, ex-justice Sup. Court of N.J.; m. Mary Byrne, June 1, 1903. Admitted to N.J. bar, 1902, and practiced law in N.J. Mem. N.J. Assembly, 1907-10; apptd. pvt. sec. to Gov. Wilson, 1910, and apptd. clk. of Sup. Court, N.J., 1912; served, without compensation from the State, as sec. to Gov. Wilson until latter resigned to become Pres. of the U.S.; sec. to President, Mar. 5, 1913-Mar. 4, 1921; resumed practice, Washington, 1921. Mem. Thomas Jefferson Memorial Commn. since 1935. Democrat. Catholic. Author: Woodrow Wilson as I Know Him, 1921. Home: Olney, Md. Office: 1317 F St. N.W., Washington. Died Apr. 8, 1954.

TUNISON, George McGregor (tŭ'nĭ-sŭn), lawyer; b. Parkersburg, Ia., Dec. 20, 1882; s. James Wellington and Catherine (McGregor) T.; A.B., U. of Neb., 1906, LL.B., 1908; m. Otis Wakefield Hassler, Aug. 4, 1915; children—Mary Elizabeth (wife of Lieut. James F. Addington), Catherine McGregor (wife of Capt. Charles H. Pillsbury). Admitted to Nebraska bar, 1908, and since practiced in Omaha; became member of firm of Jefferis, Howell & Tunison; now mem. firm of Tunison & Joyner; atty. for Shoshone Tribe of Indians of Wyo. in U.S. Supreme Court cases, resulting in recovery for their lands taken from them by the U.S.; atty. for Flathead Tribe of Indians of Mont. Mem. Omaha Bd. of Edn., 1933—. Trustee Presbyn. Theol. Sem., Omaha. Mem. Omaha Bar Assn. (pres. 1933-34), Am. Bar Assn., Omaha Chamber of Commerce, Delta Upsilon, Phi Delta Phi. Republican. Presbyterian. Mason. Club: Omaha Country, Omaha Athletic. Home: 5115 Webster St. Office: First National Bank Bldg., Omaha, Neb. Died Dec. 3, 1954.

TUNKS, Walter F., clergyman; b. Adrian, Mich., Oct. 31, 1886; s. Charles Randolph and Jane (Fuller) T.; Ph.B., Kenyon Coll., 1910; D.D., Bexley Hall Theol., 1915; m. Anne D. Parsons, Oct. 17, 1917 (deceased); m. 2d, Helen Marie Roberts, June 5, 1920; 1 dau., Mary Anne (Mrs. William P. Steffens); married 3d, Mrs. Ferne Adams, April 12, 1947. Curate St. Paul's Church, Cleveland, O., 1915; rector, St. Paul's Ch., Muskegon, Mich., 1917-30; rector St. Paul's Ch., Akron, O., 1930—. Trustee Kenyon Coll. Mem. Phi Beta Kappa, Delta Tau Delta. Mason (K.T.). Address: 2896 Hastings Rd., Cuyahoga Falls, O. Died Jan. 14, 1958.

TUNSTALL, Robert Baylor (tŭn'stŭl), lawyer; b. New York, N.Y., Feb. 9, 1880; s. Richard Baylor and Isabel Mercein (Heiser) T.; B.A., and M.A., U. of Va., 1899, LL.B., 1902; LL.D., Washington and Lee U., 1930; m. Virginia Hunter Lyne, June 28, 1916. Practiced at Norfolk, Va., 1902-27; div. counsel, Southern Railway Co., 1907-24; general solicitor in charge of fed. valuation, Virginian Ry., 1920-27; asst. gen. counsel, C. & O. Ry. Co. (Richmond, Va.), 1927-35, gen. counsel, Cleveland, O., 1935-42, vice-president and gen. counsel, 1942-43; gen. counsel N.Y.C.&St.L. R.R. Company, 1939-42, vice-pres. and gen. counsel, 1942-43; vice president Pere Marquette Ry. Co., 1942-43; returned to gen. law practice at Norfolk, Virginia, Dec. 1943. V.p. Common council Norfolk, and chmn. finance com., 1908-10; mem. Norfork Water Com., 1911-13; chmn. Norfolk Chap. Am. Red Cross, 1917-18. Enlisted in F.A.C.O.T.S., Camp Zachary Taylor, Ky., Sept. 10, 1918, commd. capt. F.A.R.C., Dec., 1918. Trustee citation, 1948, Am. Library Assn. (one of two in U.S.). Trustee Norfolk Acad. (ex-pres.); mem. Alumni Bd. Trustees, U. of Va.; chmn. Va. State Library Board, 1935-49; mem. board Norfolk Pub. Library, Norfolk Mus. Arts and Sciences; chmn. Norfolk Tax Commn., 1946-47. Mem. Am. (v.p. 1935-36), Va. State (ex-pres.), Norfolk and Portsmouth (ex-pres.) bar assns., Am. Law Inst. (mem. council), Alumni Assn. Univ. of Va. (ex-pres.), Delta Psi, Phi Beta Kappa, Raven Society of U. of Va. (recipient Raven award, 1940). Democrat. Episcopalian; chancellor Diocese of Southern Va., 1927. Clubs: Colonnade, Farmington Country (U. of Va.); Virginia (Norfolk). Home: 1401 Graydon Pl. Office: Citizens Bank Bldg., Norfolk, Va. Died Dec. 30, 1956; buried Norfolk.

TUOHY, Edward Boyce (too'e), physician; b. Duluth, Minn., March 17, 1908; s. Edward Leo and Ida Mary (Boyce) T.; B.S., U. of Minn., 1925-29; M.D., U. of Pa., 1929-32; M.S. in Anesthesiology, Mayo Foundation Grad. Med. School, U. of Minn., 1933-36; m. Dorothy A. Johnson, April 11, 1934; children—Barbara, Michael, Patrick. Fellowship in anesthesiology, Mayo Foundation; Mayo Clinic staff, 1935, consultant 1935-47; prof. of anesthesiology, Georgetown Med. Center 1947-51; prof. surgery (anesthesiology) U. So. Cal. 1953; pvt. practice anesthethesiology. Mem. Reserve Corps. U.S. Army; active duty, May 1942; disch. rank maj., 1945; cons. USAF, 1954-56. Diplomate Am. Bd. Anesthesiology (mem. bd. 1950-56, del. A.M.A. 1951-55). Mem. Am. Soc. Anesthesiology for Pharmacology and Exptl. Therapeutics (pres. 1947), A.A.A.S., Sigma Xi, Nu Sigma Nu, Chi Psi. Roman Catholic. Contbr. chapters to Surgery and Dental Science and Dental Art by Dean Lewis; also over 100 articles to jours. Address: 2485 Sherwood Rd., San Marino, Cal. Died Jan. 12, 1959; buried Calvary Cemetery, Los Angeles.

TURLINGTON, Edgar, lawyer; b. Smithfield, N.C., Oct. 24, 1891; s. Ira Thomas and Hortense Mary (Rose) T.; A.B., U. of N.C., 1911; Rhodes scholar, Oxford U., Eng., 1911-14, M.A. and B.C.L., 1914 (1st class in Honor Sch. of Jurisprudence, 1913); m. Catherine Hackett, June 18, 1926; children—Sylvia (Mrs. Gerard K. O'Neill), Ellen Rigby (Mrs. Eugene Johnston), Barbara. Instr. in Latin and English Univ. N.C., 1915-17; spl. asst. Dept. of State, Washington, D.C., 1918-20, asst. solicitor, 1920-25, asst. chief, Div. of Near Eastern Affairs, 1925; detailed to Lausanne as legal adviser to Am. delegation to Conf. on Near Eastern Affairs, 1923, to Constantinople as legal adviser to Am. High Commr., 1923; research asso. Columbia U. Com. on Research in Latin America, 1925-28; spl. counsel U.S. Agency, U.S.-Mexican Claims Commns., 1928-30; legal adviser Am. ambassador, Habana, Cuba, 1930-32; acting prof. history and internat. relations, Clark U., 1932; Am. mem. Joint Com. under U.S.-Mexican Conv., 1934, chief counsel Spl. Mexican Claims Commn., 1935-38; mem. adv. com. Harvard Research in Internat. Law, 1935-42; chmn. D.C. bar, Commn. to Study the Orgn. of Peace, 1944-45. Mem. Roberts & McInnis, Washington, D.C., 1940-45, Peaslee, Turlington & Cowles, 1946-47, Peaslee & Turlington, 1947-53; legal adv., Imperial Ethiopian Government, 1953—; lectr. Georgetown U. Lectr. Inter-American Academy of comparative and International Law, Habana, 1950. Mem. Ala. Bar, Am. Soc. Internatl. Law (mem. bd. editors Am. Jour. of Internat. Law), Am. Bar Assn. (chmn. sect. internat. and comparative law, 1945-46; mem. ho dels. 1952), Internat. Law Assn., Am. Peace Soc., Inst. World Polity, Phi Beta Kappa, Sigma Upsilon, Alpha Tau Omega. Democrat. Unitarian. Clubs: Cosmos, Torch (Wash., D.C.). Author: Mexico and Her Foreign Creditors, 1930; Neutrality: The World War Period, 1936. Home: 2 Via Giovanni Chiarini. Office: Imperial Palace, Asmara, Eritrea. Died Sept. 1959.

TURNBULL, J(ohn) Gordon, engr.; b. San Francisco, Nov. 8, 1891; s. Alexander and Margaret (Noakes) T.; specialized tng. engring. U. Louvain, 1907-10; m. Susan Aycock, 1938; children—John Gordon, Alexander, Susan Gay. Draftsman, San Francisco, 1911-13; engr., Portland, Ore., 1913-15; partner W. A. Kramer Co., Portland, and co-adventurer Hans Pederson Co., Seattle, constn. Nisqually Dam, Tacoma Power Plant and transmission lines, Lake Washington Canal Locks, 1915-17; cons. archtl., indsl. engr. for Ford, G.M., Paige, Dodge, Hudson & Packard Motor cos., Curtis-Wright, Chance-Vought Airplane cos., Pratt-Whitney Engine Co., and others, 1918-37; cons. engr. G.M. Corp. (Detroit Diesel, Allison Engine, Electro-Motive plants), 1938-41; pres., chmn. bd., chief cons. J. Gordon Turnbull, Inc., 1941—, designing and supervising constrn. synthetic rubber plants including, Rubber Res Corp.; tire plants including, Goodyear, U.S. Rubber, Kelly Springfield; aircraft plants including, N.A. Aviation, Lockheed, Goodyear); aluminum reduction and extrusion plants including, Reynolds Metals Co.; def. installations including, Canol Project comprising airfields, highways, pipelines, refineries and dockage: airfields at Ferry Island Groups, Honolulu to New Guinea; master plans U.S.A.F. bases, U.S.A., Eng., and Japan; and other engring. projects for U.S. C.E., AEC, Air Force; headed spl. engring. mission to Europe for U.S. State Dept., Army, Navy and Air Force, 1948. Mem. Am. Soc. C.E. Clubs: Rainier (Seattle); Union (Cleve.). Home: 11499 Bellagio Rd., Los Angeles. Died Apr. 1, 1953; buried Glen Haven Meml. Park, San Fernando, Cal.

TURNEAURE, Frederick Eugene (tûr-nûr'), engineer; b. Freeport, Ill., July 30, 1866; s. Giles and Clarissa (May) T.; C.E., Cornell, 1889; studied engring. abroad, 1895-96; Dr. Engring., U. of Ill., 1905; m. Mary D. Stewart, Aug. 25, 1891 (died 1916); 1 son, Frederick Stewart. Instr. Washington U., 1890-92; prof. bridge and sanitary engring., U. of Wis., 1892-1902, acting dean Coll. Engring., 1902-03, dean and prof. engring., 1903-37, dean emeritus since 1937. Mem. ex officio Wis. State Highway Commn., 1911-29; city engr. Madison, 1900-02. Mem. A.A.A.S., Soc. for Promotion Engring. Edn. (pres. 1908-09), Western Soc. Engrs., Am. Ry. Engring. Assn., Am. Soc. of Civil Engineers (hon.), American Concrete Institute, American Society Testing Materials. Author: Theory and Practice of Modern Framed Structures (with J. B. Johnson and C. W. Bryan), 1893; Public Water Supplies (with Dr. H. L. Russell), 1900; Principles of Reinforced Concrete Construction (with Edward Rose Maurer), 1907. Investigations on stresses in bridges under moving train loads, also on strength of steel columns, Trans. Am. Soc. Civ. Engrs., 1899, 1927, 31; Bulletins of Am. Ry. Engring. Assn., 1910-17. Home: 166 Prospect Av., Madison, Wis. Died Mar. 31, 1951.

TURNER, Claude Allen Porter, consulting engr.; b. Lincoln, R.I., July 4, 1869; s. John M. and Elizabeth (Darling) T.; C.E., Lehigh U., 1890; m. Mary E. Burns, June 6, 1894 (died 1941); children—Margaret E. H., William M.; m. 2d, Kathleen Flavin, 1943. With N.Y. and N.E. Ry., 1890-91, Edgemore Bridge Co., of Wilmington, Del., 1891; asst. engr. Columbus Bridge Co., 1892; draftsman Pittsburgh Bridge Co., 1893, Berlin Bridge Co., 1894-95; asst. engr. Pottsville Iron & Steel Co., 1896, Gillette-Herzog Co., Minneapolis, Minn., 1897-1900; engr. western contracting dept. Am. Bridge Co., Minneapolis, 1901; consulting practice, Minneapolis, since 1901; took over bus. founded by Theo. A. Wegener in 1941; cons. bridge engr. for Soo Line R.R., 15 yrs. prior to World War; also cons. engr. for tunnel under Bunker Hill, St. Paul; designed structure and power plant of Electric Steel Elevator, Minneapolis, and dam for Manistique (Mich.) Pulp & Paper Co. Originator and patentee of flat slab "mushroom system" of floor constrn. and spiral mushroom floor constrn., a type embodied in hundreds of buildings and many important bridges. Designer of Missouri River Bridge between Bismarck and Mandan, N.D.; series of arches over St. Croix River for the Soo Line; series of concrete arches over the Minnesota River at Ft. Snelling; development of the theory of ultimate economy in steel frame trusses. Author: Elasticity, Structure and Strength of Materials (Part I develops the exact stress mechanism of beams, shafts and plates for the first time and contains an introduction to the theory of thermo-elasticity which is so developed in Part III that physical properties of materials are coordinated with atomic weights and numbers, melting and vaporization temperatures, specific heat and density; chem. mechanics is developed in Part III so that the heat of formation of reversible chem. compounds of all classes may be calculated by thermal theory, coordinating with melting and vaporization temperatures. Physical problems, the permanence of solar heat, nature of gravity and electrical energy are accounted for by thermo-elasticity which explains in detail the molecular vibration of heat energy); Natural Philosophy of the Science of Physics, Chemistry and Engineering, 1947; Educational and Industrial Problems With Intermolecular Forces Analyzed in Engring., Physics and Chemistry, 1948; A Research in Natural Phenomena, 1951; Revision of Thermal Mechanics, 1952. Home: 1007 Delaware Av. Address: 964 N. High St., Columbus, O. Died Jan. 10, 1955.

TURNER, Edward Crawford, judge; b. Columbus, O., Mar. 26, 1872; s. Robert M. and Jane L. (Crawford) T.; LL.B., Ohio State U., 1901, LL.M., 1903; m. Nan A. Jahn, Dec. 11, 1902; 1 son, Carl Robert. Admitted to Ohio bar, 1901, and practiced at Columbus; pros. atty., Franklin County, 1911-15; atty. gen., Ohio, 1915-17, 27-29; judge Ct. Common Pleas, 1939-40; judge Supreme Ct., Ohio, 1940—. Republican. Mason (33°), Elk, Columbus Club. Home: 4309 W. Broad St. Address: State House, Columbus, O. Died Sept. 13, 1950.

TURNER, Edward Lewis, med. adminstrn.; b. Alton, Ill., Aug. 9, 1900; s. John and Rettie Clara (Haight) T.; B.S., U. Chgo., 1922, M.S., 1923; M.D., U. Pa., 1928; m. Katherine Ensminger, June 1, 1923; children—John Ellis, Edward Lewis, Leslie Dean. Asst. in anatomy, U. Chgo., 1922-23; adjunct prof. physiology, Am. U., Beirut, Lebanon, 1923-26, asso. prof. physiology, dept. head, 1928-30, asso. prof. medicine, 1931-33, prof., 1933-36, head dept., 1931-36; prof. medicine, head dept. Meharry Med. Coll., Nashville, 1936-38, prof. medicine, head dept. and pres., 1938-44; pvt. practice, Bradford, Pa., 1944-45; prof. medicine and dean sch. medicine, U. Wash., 1945-53; sec. council med. edn. and hosps., A.M.A., 1953-59; dir. div. sci. activities, 1959—; cons. education, training div., Office Surgeon General, U.S. Army 1954—; bd. med. edn., U. Pa., 1955—; cons. in med. edn. Madigan Gen. Hosp.; cons. tropical medicine V.A. area 11, 1946-48 mem. med. adv. panel, Office Rehabilitation, 1955; mem.

Wash. Hosp. Planning Council, 1948-53; mem. Surgeon General's USPHS Committee on Medical Manpower Needs, 1958-59. Diplomate Am. Bd. of Internal Medicine. Fellow Am. College Physicians; member A.M.A. (sec. council on med. edn., hosps. 1953-59), Nat. Inst. Health (training Grants Com., nat. adv. council), Soc. Exptl. Biol. and Medicine, Assn. Am. Physicians, Ill. Med. Assn., Chgo. Med. Soc., Am. Med. Edn. Found., Assn. Am. Med. Colls. (v.p., 1950-51; exec. council mem. 1950-53; nat. adv. heart council 1952-55), Phi Rho Sigma, Sigma Xi, Alpha Omega Alpha. Club: Oval. Contbr. articles to profl. jours. Home: 2140 Glen Oak Dr., Glenview, Ill. Office: 535 N. Dearborn St., Chgo. Died Feb. 1960.

TURNER, Farrant Lewis, govt. ofcl.; b. Hilo, Hawaii, July 16, 1895; s. Lewis Farrant and Jessie (Curtis) T.; B.S., Wesleyan U., Middletown, Conn., 1917, M.A. (hon.), 1947; m. Helen Van Inwegen, May 20, 1921; 1 son, Albert Farrant. With sugar plantation, Hawaii, 1919-22; v.p. Building Supply House, Honolulu, 1922-53; sec. Territory of Hawaii, 1953-58; branch manager Small Business Adminstrn., 1958—. Served from 2d lt. to capt., U.S. Army, 1917-19; lt. col. AUS. 1940-44. Decorated Inf. Combat Badge, Medaille Militaire (Italy), Legion of Merit. Mem. Honolulu C. of C. (past pres.), Psi Upsilon Conglist. Rotarian. Home: 4644 Kolohala St. Office: Finance Factors Bldg., Honolulu. Died Mar. 19, 1959.

TURNER, Harold Rhoades, textile mfr.; b. Greenville, S.C., Jan. 1, 1898; s. William Stephen and Lottie (Rhoades) T.; student Furman U., 1915-16, Clemson Coll., 1919-20; m. Anne Elizabeth Schade, June 21, 1926; children—Harold Rhoades, Robert James. With Dunean Mills, 1922—, supt., 1931-39, asst. gen. mgr., 1939-46, gen. mgr., 1946-52; asst. exec. officer Dunean Mills, Watts Mills, gen. mgr. Greer, Monaghan, Victor plants, div. J. P. Stevens & Co., Inc.; v.p. J. P. Stevens & Co., Inc. 1952—, gen. mgr. mfg. synthetics div., 1958—; dir. Textile Hall Corp., Greenville. Trustee Greenville County Found., 1957, chmn., 1958. Served with co. A, 1st S.C. inf., Mexican Border Service, U.S. Army, 118th Inf., Belgium, France, 1918. Mem. Phi Psi Eta. Episcopalian (vestryman). Home: Paris Mountain, R.F.D. 5, Box 433. Office: Dunean Mills, Div., J. P. Stevens & Co., Inc., Greenville, S.C. Died Jan. 1960.

TURNER, Helen M., artist; b. Louisville, Ky.; d. Mortimer and Helen Maria (Davidson) T.; diploma, Teachers Coll. (Columbia), 1902; pupil Art Students' League, New York. Awards: Elling prize, Woman's Art Club, 1910; Julia A. Shaw Memorial prize, Nat. Acad. Design, 1913; arts prize, Association Women Painters and Sculptors, 1913; Altman prize, Nat. Acad. Design, 1921; Nat. Arts Club prize for painting, 1922; Nat. Arts Club prize, 1927; prize for portraiture, spring exhbn., Nat. Acad. Design, 1927. Represented in Met. Museum of Art, Corcoran Gallery (Washington), Detroit Museum, Phillips Memorial Gallery (Washington), Nat. Arts Club (N.Y.), Delgado Museum (New Orleans), Museum Fine Arts, Houston, Tex., Highland Park Soc. Arts, Dallas, Tex., Norfolk (Va.) Museum, Vanderpoel Gallery (Chicago) and pvt. collections. Episcopalian. Asso. Nat. Acad., 1913, Nat. Academician, 1921; asso. mem. N.Y. Hist. Soc.; mem. New York Water Color Club, Nat. Arts Club, Grand Central Art Galleries (New York), Am. Artists Professional League. Address: National Arts Club, New York. N.Y.; also 343 Broadway, New Orleans, La. Died 1958.

TURNER, Henry Chandlee, bldg. constrn.; b. Betterton, Md., Oct. 16, 1871; s. Richard T. and Martha E. (Birch) T.; B.S., Swarthmore Coll., 1893, C.E., 1903, D.Eng., 1923; m. Charlotte Haines Chapman, Oct. 11, 1899; children—Henry Chandlee, Katharine, Howard Haines, Robert Chapman, James Sinclair. Organizer, 1902, pres. to 1941, Turner Constrn. Co., one of largest Am., now ret. Mem. Am. Soc. C.E., Am. Soc. for Testing Materials, Am. Concrete Inst., Phi Kappa Psi, Sigma Xi, Beta Kappa. Trustee Swarthmore Coll. Republican. Quaker. Clubs: St. Andrews Golf; Highland Park (Fla.). Home: Pierrepont St., Bklyn. Died June 5, 1954.

TURNER, James, lawyer, corp. exec.; b. Lansing, Mich., July 18, 1878; s. James M. and Sophie Porter (Scott) T.; A.B., U. Mich., 1902, LL.B., 1904; m. Pamela Tappey, Oct. 30, 1907; children—Ernest T., John D., Pamela W., Richard H. Practice of law in Detroit, 1904—; mem. Angell, Turner, Dyer & Meek, 1909—, senior mem., 1932—; counsel and dir. Surety Savings and Loan Assn.; gen. counsel, v.p. and dir. Detroit & Cleveland Navigation Co.; dir. and mem. exec. com. Mich. R.Rs. Assn. (rep. Pa. R.R. Co.). Served as maj. Gen. Staff, US. Army, A.E.F., 1918-19. Mem. Am., Mich., Detroit bar assns. Clubs: Yondotega, University, Detroit, Detroit Athletic, Detroit Country (Detroit); Grosse Pointe (Grosse Pointe, Mich.); Huron Mountain, Fontinalis, St. Clair Flats Shooting, St. Luke's. Home: 330 Provencal Rd., Grosse Pointe Farms, Mich. Office: 2103 Dime Bldg., Detroit 26, Mich. Died Aug. 15, 1947.

TURNER, J(ames) Walter, coll. dean; b. Colby, Kan., Sept. 21, 1892; s. James William and Mary (Johnston) T.; A.B., Phillips U., 1918; A.M., Peabody Coll. 1933; Ed.D., N.Y.U. 1940; m. Lillian M. Barbour, June 25, 1936. Head history dept., U. Prep. Sch., Tonkawa, Okla. 1919-21; supt. schs., Newkirk, Okla., 1921-23; pres. Southwestern Okla. Tchrs. Coll., 1923-27; supervising prin. Union Free Schs. Dist., Dobbs Ferry, N.Y., 1936-42; dean Shurtleff Coll., 1943-45; dean Culver Stockton Coll., 1945-47, dean Ark. State Coll., 1947-54; dean of basic edn., Arkansas State College, 1954—. Dir. Okla. Soc. for Crippled Children, 1923-27; chmn. Northeastern Dist. Mo. Assn. for Socal Welfare; mem. state exec. com., 1945-47; cons. Nat. Com. on Music Curriculum for High Schs., 1944; chmn. of the Arkansas Conf. on Higher Edn., 1956-57. Mem. C. of C. Mem. N.E.A., Phi Delta Kappa, Kappa Delta Pi, Ark. Edn. Assn. Mem. Christian Ch. Mason (K.T.). Club: Rotary. Office: Arkansas State College, Jonesboro, Ark. Died Oct. 13, 1957; buried Tower of Memories, Denver.

TURNER, John Roscoe, economist; b. Matville, W.Va., Feb. 13, 1882; s. William and Martha Dolliver (Hinchman) T.; student W.Va. Conf. Sem., 1897; B.S., Ohio Northern U., Ada, O., 1901, M.S., 1903; Ph.D., Princeton U., 1913; LL.D., W. Va. Univ., 1928, U. Southern Calif., 1933; m. Effie Eleanor Vertner, Aug. 23, 1905; 1 dau., Elizabeth. Instructor history, St. Joseph (La.) High Sch., 1903-04; asst. prin. Willie Hassell Coll., Vinita, I.T., 1904-05; prin. Sandy Valley (Ky.) Sem., 1905-08; instr. and lecturer, Cornell U., 1908-12; fellow in economics, Princeton, 1912-13; asst. prof. economics, Cornell U., 1913-16; prof. economics, 1916-28, head of dept., 1920-23, and dean Washington Sq. Coll., New York U., 1917-28; pres. W.Va. Univ., 1928-35; dean of men, College City, N.Y.C., 1935-42, prof. econ., 1942-44; economics expert for Alexnader Hamilton Inst., 1944—. Chief economist and chairman advisory bd. U.S. Tariff Commn., 1923-24. Mem. Am. Econ. Assn., Phi Beta Kappa. Del. to Nat. Rep. Conv., 1932. Meth. Club: Southern. Author: Ricardian Rent in American Economics; Introduction to Economics; Economics—The Science of Business. Home: 3358 North Mountain View Dr., San Diego, Calif. Died Mar. 25, 1960.

TURNER, Kenneth B(urlen), physician; born Lynchburg, Va., Jan. 29, 1901; s. Hartley and Josephine (Burlen) T.; A.B., Hamilton Coll., 1922; M. D., Harvard, 1926; m. Helen Forbes McIlvaine, June 9, 1925; children—Alan Forbes, Laura Averell, Alison McIlvaine. Interne, Presbyn. Hosp., N.Y. City, 1927-28, asst. physician, 1928-38, asst. attending physician, 1938-45, asso. attending physician 1945, now attending physician; director dept. cardiology, 1954—. Pvt. practice medicine, N.Y. City, 1948—; asst. in medicine Coll. Phys. and Surgs., Columbia, 1928-30, instr. in medicine, 1930-35, asso. in medicine, 1935-39, asst. prof. of medicine, 1939-48, asso. prof. clinical medicine since 1949. Served as liaison officer in London for Com. on Med. Research, Office of Sci. Research and Development, 1942-43, chief, records sect. Com. on Med. Research, 1944-45, consultant, 1946-47; civilian consultant in internal medicine to Surgeon Gen. since 1947. Recipient Presidential Certificate of Merit, 1948. Mem. Assn. Am. Physicians, Am. Soc. Clin. Investigation, Soc. Exptl. Biology and Medicine, Harvey Society, A.M.A., Am. Heart Assn., A.A.A.S. (fellow), Century Assn., Co. and State of New York med. socs., Alpha Omega Alpha, Phi Beta Kappa, Psi Upsilon. Republican. Episcopalian. Clubs: University, Collectors, Century Assn. Home: 21 E. 87th St., N.Y.C. 28. Office: 180 Fort Washington Av., N.Y.C. 32. Died Oct. 9, 1955; buried Putnam Cemetery, Greenwich. Conn.

TURNER, Maurice Clark, lyceum mgr.; b. Monroe, Mich., Apr. 7, 1878; s. Jacob and Eliza Clotilda (Spaulding) T.; grad. high sch., Monroe, 1896; LL.B., U. of Mich., 1900; m. Epsie Walden, Aug. 11, 1908; 1 son, Maurice Clark. Began as lyceum mgr. at Louisville, Ky., 1901; moved to Dallas, Tex.; owner and pres. Dixie Bureau; director Affiliated Lyceum and Chautauqua Bur., Chicago; pres. Southwestern Musical Bur. Has arranged tours for many notables. Vice chmn. Speakers Bureau, 4th Liberty Loan, and chmn. Speakers Bur. Victory Loan, 11th Fed. Reserve Dist., World War I. Dir. Am. Platform Guild. Mem. Pi Gamma Mu. Republican. Methodist. Mason (32°, Shriner). Clubs: University, Athletic, Dallas Country. Home: 3820 Gillon Av., Highland Park. Office: Wilson Bldg., Dallas. Died Mar. 22, 1953; buried Hillcrest Meml. Park, Dallas.

TURNER, Samuel Gilbert Hathaway, banker; b. Elmira, N.Y., June 18, 1878; s. Robert Tifft and Helen E. (Boyd) T.; A.B., Union College, Schenectady, N.Y., 1898; Albany Law School, 1900; m. Helen Maude MacCaul, June 15, 1907; children—Hathaway, Lucy, Alexander MacCaul, Helen Elizabeth. In banking business since 1913; hon. chmn. Elmira Bank & Trust Co.; chmn. bd. L. C. Smith & Corona Typewriters, Inc.; dir. Shepard-Niles Crane & Hoist Corp.; v.p. and dir. Insular Lumber Co.; director, Thatcher Glass Mfg. Co., L. C. Smith & Corona Typewriters, Inc., Moore Corp., Ltd., Marine Midland Corp., Elmira Floral Products, Inc., Chemung Foundry Corp., Moore Business Forms, Inc. Mem. Phi Upsilon, Phi Beta Kappa. Republican. Episcopalian. Club: Elmira City. Home: Montour Falls, N.Y. Office: 150 Lake St., Elmira, N.Y. Died Feb. 27, 1953.

TURPIN, Edna Henry Lee (tûr'pĭn), author; b. "Echo Hill," Mecklenburg County, Va., July 26, 1867; d. Edward Henry and Petronella (Lee) Turpin; ed. chiefly at home; grad. lit., Hollins Inst. (now coll.), Va. Prin. Hope (Ark.) Inst., 1893-95. Presbyterian. Mem. Authors League America, Am. Hist. Assn., U.D.C., Colonial Dames Va. Author: History of the American People, 1911; Honey Sweet, 1911; Happy Acres, 1913; Abram's Freedom, 1913; Peggy of Roundabout Lane, 1917; Treasure Mountain, 1920; The Old Mine's Secret, 1921; Whistling Jimps, 1922; Cotton, 1924; Echo Hill, 1933; Echo Hill (Dramatized), 1933; Three Circus Days, 1935; Lost Covers, 1937; Zickle's Luck, 1938; Littling of Gaywood, 1939; Zickle's Puppy Dog, 1942; Story of Virginia, 1949; Our History, 1949. Joint author: (with Andrew M. Soulě) Agriculture (sch. textbook), 1907; (with Catherine T. Bryce and Rose Lees Hardy) The Newson Readers, 1927-29. Editor of various sch. and coll. textbooks. Clubs: Virginia Writers, Nat. Arts, Woman's. Home: 303 N. Allen Av., Richmond 20, Va.; (summer) Hariot Cottage, Biological Sta., Mountain Lake, Va. Died June 7, 1952; buried Hollywood Cemetery, Richmond, Va.

TURRENTINE, Samuel Bryant, clergyman, educator; b. Chatham County, N.C., Nov. 15, 1861; s. William Holt and Annie Amy (Strowd) T.; A.B., U. N.C., 1884, A.M., 1887; theol. studies, Vanderbilt U., about 2 yrs.; corr. course Yale, and U. Chgo., 1 yr.; D.D., Trinity Coll. (now Duke), 1900; m. Sallie Leonora Atwater, Jan. 4, 1888 (died Jan. 4, 1943); children—Samuel Bryant, Mrs. Annie Leonora Simmonds, Carney Gray (dec.), Wilbur Clinton (dec.), Julian Atwater, Walter William. Ordained ministry M.E. Ch., S., 1890; pastor Centenary Ch., Winston-Salem, 1891-95; Tinity Ch., Charlotte, 1895-97; presiding elder Charlotte Dist., 1897-1900; pastor West Market Ch., Greensboro, N.C., 1900-04; presiding elder Greensboro Dist., 1904-08; pastor First Ch., Salisbury, 1908-10; presiding elder Shelby Dist., 1910-13; pres. Greensboro Coll. (for Women), 1913-35, pres. emeritus, 1935—, prof. of Bible, 1935-39, also spl. lectr. in Bible, 1940—. Sr. mem. bd. trustees, Duke. Del. Gen. Conf., Meth. Ch., S., Dallas, Tex., 1902; Gen. Conf, M.E. Chs., Birmingham, Ala., 1906. Democrat. Mason. Grad. work summer session, Columbia, 1921. Author: A Romance of Education—A Narrative Including Recollections and Other Facts, Connected with Greensboro College, 1946. Co-organizer N.C. Coll. Conf., 1921. Home: 219 N. Spring St., Greensboro, N.C. Died Apr. 11, 1949; buried Green Hill Cemetery, Greensboro.

TURTON, Franklin E., copper co. exec.; b. Oakland, Calif., June 15, 1891; s. Frederick Richard and Mary (Alumbaugh) T.; student U. Pacific, 1911; A.B., U. Calif., 1915; m. Emma Jean Baker, Apr. 20, 1930; children—Robert Lawrence, Patricia Mae. With Braden Copper Co., 1915—, in Chile, 1951-52, gen. mgr., 1944-51, v.p., Santiago, Chile, S.A., 1951-52. Mem. Am. Inst. Mining and Metall. Engrs. Club: Union (Santiago). Home: Coya via Rancagua, Chile. Office: Augustinas 1389, Santiago, Chile, S.A. Died Dec. 21, 1952; buried Mausoleum of Braden Copper Co. General Cemetery, Santiago.

TUTTLE, Arthur Lemuel, mining engr.; b. Salt Lake City, Oct. 30, 1870; s. Rt. Rev. Daniel S. and Harriet M. (Foote) T.; E.M., Washington U., 1893; m. Mary E. Hackley, Oct. 8, 1896; 1 son, Arthur Lemuel. Instr. mining dept., Washington U., 1893-94; ore buyer and mine supt. La Gran Fundicion Nacional Mexicana, Mexico, 1894-97; supt. Conrey Placer Mining Co., Virginia City, Mont., 1897-98; supt., mgr. Catherine Lead Co., Fredrickton, Mo., and Columbia Lead Co., Flat River, Mo., 1899-1902; gen. supt. Jimulco Mining Co., and Continental Mining Co., Mexico, 1902-16; asst. mgr. and gen. mgr. Tenn. Copper Co., Copperhill, Tenn., 1916-19; consulting engr. Tenn. Copper Chem. Co., N.Y..C, 1919-23; engr. and resident mgr. in Mexico of Gen. Development Co., 1923-26; practicing at Danville, 1926—. Mem. Am. Inst. Mining and Metall. Engrs. Republican. Episcopalian. Address: 212 N. 3d St., Danville, Ky. Died Jan. 21, 1958.

TUTTLE, Henry, pub. utilities exec.; b. nr. Detroit, Jan. 29, 1897; s. Charles Joseph and Minnie E. (McGrann) T.; corr. student Columbia, 1926-27, U. Mich., 1943-44; m. Marjorie Mendenhall, Dec. 31, 1934. Gas service man Mich. Consol. Gas Co., 1920, then accounts and treasury depts., 1920-37, v.p. and controller, 1940-45, v.p. and treas., 1945-49, exec. v.p. 1949-52, pres., 1952; dir. 1944—; dir. Am. Natural Gas Co.; cons. gas planning div. Petroleum Adminstrn. for Def., Dept. Interior. Trustee Detroit Ednl. Found., Inst. Econ. Edn., Inc., Citizens Research Council; dir. Detroit Conv. and Tourist Bur., United Found.; dir. chmn. Detroit Internat. Riverama. Mem. Bd. Commerce (dir. Detroit), Traffic Safety Assn. (dir.), Am. Ordnance Assn. (dir.), Am. Gas Assn. (dir.), Ind. Natural Gas Assn., Mich. Gas Assn. (past pres.). Mason (K.T.). Clubs:

Press (Lansing); Aero, Detroit, Economic (dir.), Detroit Golf, Detroit Athletic. Home: 1650 Balmoral Dr., Detroit 3. Office: 415 Clifford St., Detroit 26. Died Mar. 26, 1959; buried Grand Lawn Cemetery, Detroit.

TUTTLE, Morton Chase, constrn. engr.; b. Milford, N.H., June 29, 1875; s. Charles Bell and Cornelia (Chase) T.; B.S., Dartmouth Coll., 1897, A.M., 1925; m. Alice Kidder, June 4, 1907. Gen. mgr. Aberthaw Constrn. Co., Boston, 1896-1923; pres. Morton C. Tuttle Co., engrs., Boston, since 1923; dir. State Street Trust Co. Mem. emergency constrn. com., War Industries Bd., later mgr. supply production div., later consol. supply div., Emergency Fleet Corp., World War. Republican. Conglist. Clubs: Brae Burn Country (Boston); Country (Brookline); Army and Navy (Washington). Home: Newton Centre, Mass. Office: Park Square Bldg., Boston. Died July 19, 1957.

TUTWILER, Temple Wilson, corp. exec., b. Cincinnati, O., Jan. 5, 1879; s. Edward Magruder and Mary (Jeffray) T.; grad. of U. of Ala. Supt. Vanderbilt Furnace, 1899-1901; supt. Tennessee Coal, Iron and Railroad Co. furnaces, Sheffield, Ala., 1901-04; with U.S. Steel Corp., South Chicago, Ill., 1904-06; supt. Virginia Iron, Coal & Coke Co. furnaces, 1906-09; with U.S. Steel Corp., Gary, Ind., 1909-11; supt. Tata Iron & Steel Co., Ltd., blast furnaces, Jamshedpur, India, 1911-13, gen. supt., 1913-15, gen. mgr., 1915-25; dir. and pres. Black Creek Coal & Coke Co., Leeds Improvement Company, Tutwiler Investment Company, Ridgely Operating Company, dir. and mem. exec. com., Cities Service Co., Cities Service Oil Co. (Pa.), Empire Gas & Fuel Co. (Del.); dir. Ark. Fuel Co., Ark. La. Gas Co., Ark. Natural Gas Corp., Ark. Pipeline Corp., Birmingham Fire Ins. Co., Buffalo Rock Co., Cities Service Defense Corp., Cities Service Oil Co. (France), Cities Service Refining Corp., Dominion Natural Gas Co., Ltd., Frst Nat. Bank (Birmingham, Ala.), Orange State Oil Co., Penn-York Gas Corp., Petroleum Advisers, Surface Combustion Corp., Sixty Wall St. Mem. Ala. State Docks Commn., 1931-36; past pres. Birmingham C. of C., Ala. State Fair Assn.; mem. Birmingham Community Chest, Am. Gas Assn., Am. Iron & Steel Inst., Am. Inst. of Mining & Metall. Engrs., Am. Petroleum Inst. Clubs: Mountain Brook Country, Country (Birmingham); Deepdale (L.I.); American (London, Eng.); Oakfield (New Market, Eng.); Royal Calcutta Turf (Calcutta, India). Office: Suite 430 Brown-Marx Bldg., Birmingham, Ala. Died Nov. 9, 1950; buried Birmingham.

TWADDELL, William Powell (twŏ-dĕl'), musician; b. Phila., Pa., Aug. 17, 1879; s. Jacob Horter and Nancy Hartshorn (Freeman) T.; married to Emily May Fawcett, June 21, 1905 (died Oct. 1918); children—William Freeman, Mary-Jo, John Fawcett; m. 2d, Anna Elizabeth Dunnock, Oct. 13, 1919 (died Feb. 1926); 1 dau., Elizabeth Spilman; m. 3d, Vera Gladys Carr, Mar. 7, 1927. Organist and musical dir. St. Andrew's Ch., West Phila., 1899-1903, Christ's Ch., Rye, N.Y., 1903-07, St. John's Ch., Bridgeport, Conn., 1907-10, Bapt. Temple, Phila., 1910-16, Eutaw Pl. Bapt. Ch., Baltimore, 1916-20; dir. of music, Bessie Tift Coll., Forsyth, Ga., 1920-21; organist and musical dir. First Presbyn. Ch., Durham, N.C., since musical dir. First Presbyn. Ch., Durham, N.C., 1921-47; also musical dir. and organist, Temple Bapt. Ch., 1922-24; dir. dept. of music, Durham city schs., since 1922; musical dir. St. Philips' Episcopal Ch. 1937-46. Choral dir. and adjudicator of State Music Festivals in Va., Ky., Tenn., S.C., Ga., and Fla., 1936-47, N.C., 1949. Founded Durham Children's Choir Sch., 1924; sec., treas. Twaddell Pvt. Sch.; prof. organ, piano, voice, Twaddell Sch. of Music. Clubs: Rotary, Executives. Recipient Civic Honor Award, 1934, by Durham C. of C., "in recognition and appreciation of splendid and unique services in enriching the cultural life of the city." Home: 707 S. Duke St., Durham, N.C. Died Aug. 14, 1949.

TWEEDY, Henry Hallam, theologian; b. Binghamton, N.Y., Aug. 5, 1868; s. Asa Raymond and Sara Amelia (Pratt) T.; B.A., Yale, 1891, M.A., 1909; student, Union Theol. Sem., 1893-96; U. Berlin, 1896-98; D.D., Lebanon Valley Coll., 1921, Middlebury Coll., 1940; m. Grace H. Landfield, Aug. 12, 1902; children—Helen Landfield, Gordon Bradford. Ordained Congl. ministry, 1898; pastor Plymouth Ch., Utica, N.Y., 1898-1902, South Ch., Bridgeport, Conn., 1902-09; prof. practical theology, Yale Div. Sch., 1909-37, emeritus, 1937—. Mem. Psi Upsilon. Joint author: Moral and Religious Training in the School and Home; Religion and the War; Training the Devotional Life; The King's Highway Series, also others. Editor: Christian Worship and Praise, hymnal. Home: 112 Huntington St., New Haven. Died Sept. 11, 1953.

TWENHOFEL, William Henry (twĕn'hōf-el), geologist; b. Covington, Ky., Apr. 16, 1875; s. Ernst August Herman Julius and Helena (Steuwer) T.; B.A., Nat. Normal U., Lebanon, O., 1904; B.A., Yale, 1908, M.A., 1910, Ph.D., 1912; m. Virgie Mae Stephens, Sept. 10, 1899; children—Lillian Helena, Helen Vivian, William Stephens. Tchr. village and country schs., Ky., 1896-1902; tchr. sci. and mathematics, E. Tex. Normal Coll., Commerce, Tex., 1904-07; asst. and asso. prof. geology, U. Kan., 1910-16; state geologist of Kan., 1915-16; asso. prof. geology, 1916-21, U. Wis., prof., 1921—, chmn. dept., 1940—, ret., 1945. Prof., summer session, Stanford U., 1930. Chmn. Com. on Sedimentation, Nat. Research Council, 1923-31, chmn. Div. Geology and Geography, 1931-34, chmn. com. on Paleocology, 1934-37, geol. work in Kan., St. Lawrence, Baltic regions, Upper Miss. Valley. Mem. Geol. Soc. Am., Paleontol. Soc. Am. (pres. 1930), A.A.A.S., Wis. Acad. Sci., Am. Assn. Petroleum Geologists, Soc. Econ. Paleontologists and Mineralogists (pres. 1935); chmn. research com., 1938—, Rotary Internat., Sigma Gamma Epsilon, Sigma Xi, Phi Beta Kappa, Phi Kappa Phi, Sigma Alpha Epsilon. Conglist. Contbr. on sedimentation, stratigraphy and paleontology. Home: Rt. 3, Woodsmere, Orlando, Fla. Died Jan. 4, 1957; buried Orlando.

TWOMBLY, Henry Bancroft, lawyer; b. Albany, N.Y., Nov. 10, 1862; s. Alexander Stevenson and Abigail Quincy (Bancroft) T.; grad. Boston Latin Sch., 1880; A.B., Yale, 1884; law, Harvard, 1884-86; m. Frances Doane, Sept. 12, 1889; 1 son, Edward Bancroft. Admitted to N.Y. bar, 1887, N.J. bar, 1894, Md. bar; sr. mem. Putney, Twombly, Hall, & Skidmore; dir. and gen. counsel Internat. Salt Co., Lobsitz Mills Company, Berkshire Industrial Farm. Member of Am. and N.Y. State bar associations, New York Law Inst., N.Y. County Lawyers Assn., University Assn. (pres.), Playhouse Assn. (Summit), S.A.R., Phi Beta Kappa, Psi Upsilon, Skull and Bones. Republican. Presbyterian. Clubs: Lawyers, Republican (New Jersey); Athenaeum, Graduate (New Haven), Touchdown. Home: 226 Hobart Av., Summit, N.J. Office: 165 Broadway, N.Y.C. Died Feb. 28, 1955; buried Fairmount Cemetery, Chatham, N.J.

TYLER, Charles A. (tī'lẽr), newspaper pub.; b. Bristol, Pa., Oct. 14, 1877; s. George F. and Mary E. (Young) T.; student Drexel Inst., Phila.; m. Isabel Thompson, June 21, 1906. Manager steamship and travel cos., 1897-1914; v.p. Public Ledger, Phila., 1914-34; pres. and treas. The Phila. Inquirer, 1934-43; chairman since 1943, gen. mgr., 1943-49; director Tradesmen's National Bank & Trust Co., Liberty Mut. Ins. Co.; trustee Cyrus H. K. Curtis Estate. Republican. Episcopalian. Mason (32°). Clubs: Union League, Racquet, Midday, Phila. Country; Seaview Country (Absecon, N.J.). Home: The Kenilworth, Wissahickon and Chelten, Philadelphia 44. Office: 400 N. Broad St., Phila. 1. Died Aug. 1, 1952.

TYLER, Cornelius Boardman, lawyer; b. Plainfield, N.J., Nov. 15, 1875; s. Col. Mason Whiting and Eliza Margaret (Schroeder) T.; 9th generation from Gov. William Bradford of Mayflower; prep. edn., Williston Sem.; A.B., Amherst, 1898, Pope Fellow in Physics, 1899; LL.B., Columbia, 1901 (studied physics, mathematics also); m. Susan Tilden Whittlesey, Dec. 29, 1908; children—John, David, Caroline (Mrs. L. E. Creo). Mem. firm Tyler & Tyler (with brother Wm. S.), N.Y.; pres. Rossendale Reddaway Co. (Newark, N.J.); dir. and mem. exec. com. Plainfield Trust Co.; was active in developing apple raising on Lake Chelan, Washington; with sons, John and other partners owns and operates Wood Brook Farms (certified milk plant), Metuchen, N.J.; dean bd. dirs. Plainfield Trust Co.; officer or dir. various corporations. Pres. Plainfield Pub. Library, Social Service Center, Community Chest of Plainfield, 1922-36. Chmn. Price Com. of Food Adminstrn. for N.J., World War I. Active in affairs of Amherst Coll., chmn. alumni fund, 1926-28, chmn. exec. com. alumni council, 1933-34. Fellow Am. Geog. Soc.; mem. Mayflower Soc., Mil. Order Loyal Legion, Acad. of Polit. Science, Shakespeare Soc. of Plainfield, Phi Beta Kappa, Psi Upsilon, Phi Delta Phi. Independent Republican. Presbyterian. Clubs: The Century Association (New York); Country (Pittsfield). Author: Genealogical Appendix to Autobiography of W. S. Tyler, D.D., LL.D. (grandfather), 1912; (with Rollin U. Tyler) Tyler Genealogy (2 vols.), 1912; Essays on Moral Philosophy, 1952. Crossed Am. continent 49 times, traveled in Europe, other parts of world. One of founders Columbia Law Review. Home: 525 W. 7th St., Plainfield, N.J.; (summer) Eastern Point, Gloucester, Mass. Died Mar. 27, 1955.

TYREE, Lewis (tī'rē), lawyer; b. Salem, Va., May 18, 1892; s. Cornelius and Nan Taylor (Abrams) T.; A.B., U. of Va., A.M., 1912; LL.B., Washington and Lee U., 1915; m. Winifred Scott West, July 28, 1921; children—Lewis, Mary West, Scott West. Dean, Fork Union Mil. Acad., 1912-13; engaged in practice of law, Richmond, Va., 1915-17; prof. law, Washington and Lee U., 1919-25, Rutgers U. Law Sch. (and predecessor sch), 1925—; district price attorney, O.P.A., Newark, N.J., 1942-46, dist. counsel Office Price Administration since 1951. Ensign, U.S.N.R.F., 1915-17. Mem. Alpha Chi Rho, Omicron Delta Kappa, Phi Alpha Delta, Raven Soc. Democrat. Baptist. Author: Chancery Practice in New Jersey, 2d edit., 1947; also miscellaneous articles. Address: Mulberry Hill, Lexington, Va. Died Jan. 27, 1957; buried Lexington.

TYSON, Carroll Sargent, (tī'sŭn), artist; b. Phila., Nov. 23, 1877; s. Carroll S. and Clara (Reeves) T.; student Forsyth's Sch., DeLancey Sch., Royal Acad., Munich, Germany, 1899-1901; m. Helen Roebling, Oct. 16, 1912; children—Charles Roebling, Helen (Mrs. Louis Madeira). Artist, 1896—, specializing in landscapes and birds; exhibited in N.Y., Boston, Phila., Wilmington, Washington, London, Eng.; dir. Phoenix Iron Co., Little Schuylkill Navigation and Coal Co., Del. & Bound Brook R.R. Co. Dir. Zoöl. Soc. Phila., Fairmont Park Assn., Pa. Mus. N.A. Decorated with two medals Legion of Honor (France). Republican. Episcopalian. Clubs: Racquet, Art, Philadelphia, Sunnybrook (Phila.). Home: 8811 Townda St., Chestnut Hill, Pa. Died Mar. 19, 1956.

U

UDALL, Denny Hammond (ū dawl), veterinarian; b. Craftsbury, Vt., Feb. 9, 1874; s. Socrates and Martha Freeman (Hovey) U.; B.S.A., U. Vt., 1898, hon. D.Sc., 1938; D.V.M., Cornell, 1901; m. Mary Elizabeth Taylor, Sept. 10, 1903; children—John Taylor, Mary Catherine, Robert Hovey. Practiced at St. Johnsbury, Vt., 1901-03; asso. prof. surgery, Ohio State Univ. Vet. Coll., 1903-08; prof. vet. medicine and head of dept. in charge ambulatory clinic, Cornell U., 1908-42, prof. emeritus since 1942. Served as pvt. 1st Vermont Volunteers, Spanish-Am. War; maj. Vet. Corps, div. veterinarian, 86th Div.; comd. vet. hosps. Nos. 7 and 18, France. Mem. Sigma Xi, Sigma Nu. Author: Veterinarians' Handbook of Materia Medica and Therapeutics, 1912; The Practice of Veterinary Medicine, 1947. Home: 106 Brandon Pl., Ithaca, N.Y. Died Sept. 8, 1955; buried Pleasant Grove Cemetery, Ithaca.

UEHLING, Edward A. (ū'lĭng), mech. engr.; b. Richwood, Dodge County, Wis., June 3, 1849; s. Frederick and Anna Margareth (Krug) U.; Northwestern U., Watertown, Wis., winters, 1871, 1872; M.E., Stevens Inst. Tech., 1877 (hon. D.Eng.); m. Jeannette Mertz, Dec. 25, 1881; children—Fritz Frederic, Gretchen (dec.), Edward. Began as asst. to Dr. Thurston, Stevens Inst. Tech., 1877-78; on ry. survey and draftsman, Douglas Furnace Co., Sharpsville, Pa., to 1880; operated commercial lab., Sharpsville, 1880-83; chief chemist Bethlehem Iron Co., Pa., 1883-85; supt. Sharpsville Furnace Co., 1885-87; supt. blast furnaces, Bethlehem Iron Co., 1887-90, Sloss Iron & Steel Co., 1890-95; started Uehling Instrument Co., mfrs. recording instruments, pres., 1896-1919. Inventor pneumatic pyrometer (the pioneer autographic recording pyrometer), Uehling pig iron casting machine (now in use in all large iron-making plants), a recorder which continuously records per cent of carbon dioxide in flue gas, and about 25 other inventions. Introduced pig casting machine in prin. European countries. Recipient Stevens Inst. Notable Achievement Medallion, 1951. Fellow Am. Soc. M.E.; mem. Am. Inst. Mining and Metall. Engrs., Engineers' Soc. of Milwaukee, Delta Tau Delta, Tau Beta Pi. Contributor many papers to tech. publs. and socs. Author: Heat Loss Analysis. Home: 2360 S. 81st St., West Allis, Wis. Died Dec. 21, 1952.

UHLER, Horace Scudder (yōōl'ẽr), physicist; b. Balt., Aug. 5, 1872; s. Philip Reese and Sophia (Werdebaugh) U.; B.A., Johns Hopkins, 1894, Ph.D., 1905; M.A., Yale, 1937; m. Beatrice Drummond Ward, Nov. 24, 1897 (died Nov. 10, 1920); m. 2d, Minnie Ida Fleischer, July 12, 1922. Instr. Acad. of Northwestern U., 1896-97; dir. Lab. of U. Sch., Balt., 1897-1902; Carnegie asst. in physical chemistry, Johns Hopkins, 1905; instr. physics, 1906-09, asst. prof., 1909-22, asso. prof., 1922-25, Yale; dir. dept. physics, Gettysburg Coll., 1925; asso. prof. physics, Yale, 1926-37, prof., 1937-41, spl. lectr. physics, 1941-43, prof. emeritus, 1941—. 1st lt. R.O.T.C.; tchr. firing data, S.A.T.C., at Yale, 1 yr. Fellow A.A.A.S., Am. Phys. Soc.; mem. Am. Math. Soc., Am. Math. Assn.., Optical Soc. Am., Phi Beta Kappa, Sigma Xi; life mem. Société Française de Physique. Disproved Thiele's Theory of band spectra and established a fundamental formula in prism theory. Formerly asso. editor Am. Jour. Sci., Phys. Review, Am. Math. Monthly, Jour. Optical Soc. Am. Author: Atlas of Absorption Spectra, 1907. Contbr. variosus papers on geometrical optics, spectroscopy, X-rays and pure mathematics. Translator of Haas' Die Welt der Atome, 1927, also of his contributions to vol. 2 of Special Commentary on the Work of J. W. Gibbs, Table of 1/n! to 475 Decimals, 137-place Logarithmic Tables, and Exact Values of the First 300 Factorials. Home: 12 Hawthorne Av., Hamden 14, Conn. Died Dec. 6, 1956.

UIHLEIN, Edgar John, beverage co. exec.; b. Chicago, June 30, 1877; s. Edward Gustav and Augusta (Manns) U.; B.S., Cornell, 1900; m. Paula Huck, June 10, 1911 (dec. 1931); children—Paula Huck (wife of Dr. Fred Hunt), Edgar John. With Jos. Schlitz Brewing Co., Milwaukee, since 1900, as clk., asst. mgr. and mgr., Chicago br., v.p., now mem. bd. dirs.; dir. Diamond T. Motor Car Co., 1905-42. Trustee and treas. Chicago Latin School, 1926-27; treas. Grant Hosp., Chicago, 1930-31. Breeder of registered Hereford cattle at Brush Creek Ranch, Saratoga, Wyo., 1923-50. Clubs: Chicago Commercial, University, Athletic, Shoreacres, Old Elm. Home:

Sheridan Road, Lake Bluff, Ill. Office: 65 East Randolph St., Chgo. 1. Died Oct. 1, 1956.

UIHLEIN, Robert A., business exec.; b. Milw., 1888; student Cornell U. v.p., sec., dir. Joseph Schlitz Brewing Co., Milw.; pres., dir. Alaska Land Co.; v.p., dir. Alhambra Realty Co.; dir. Wis. Bankshares Corp., First Wis. Nat. Bank, First Wis. Trust Co.; trustee Northwestern Mut. Life Ins. Co. Home: 3252 N. Lake Dr., Milw. 11. Office: 235 W. Galena St., Milw. 1. Died Feb. 28, 1960.

UIHLEIN, Robert August, brewing co. exec.; b. Milw., Jan. 26, 1883; s. August and Emily (Werdehoff) U.; LL.B., Cornell U. Law Sch., 1905, Wahl-Henius Inst., Alfred Joergenson Lab.; LL.D., Marquette U.; m. Mary Ilsley, Sept. 18, 1913; children —Robert August, Mary (Mrs. Robert B. Trainer). Vice pres., sec., director Jos. Schlitz Brewing Co., Milw.; pres., dir. Alaska Land Co.; dir. Wis. Bankshares Corp., First Wis. Nat. Bank, First Wis. Trust Co.; trustee Northwestern Mut. Life Ins. Co. Mem. bd. govs. Marquette U.; dir. U. Wis. Found. Home: 3252 N. Lake Dr., Milw. 11. Office: 235 W. Galena St., Milw. 1. Died May 13, 1959; buried Milw.

UKERS, William Harrison, (ū kērz), author, editor, publisher; b. Germantown, Pa., July 30, 1873; s. George and Amy (Leonard) U.; ed. Central High Sch., Phila., A.B., 1893, M.A., 1922; m. Helen Scholefield Degraff, 1912. Began with Phila. North Am., later Phila. Record, New Haven Union-Palladium, N.Y. Times, Paper Trade Jour.. House-furnishings Review, Spice Mill; editor, pub. Tea and Coffee Trade Jour., N.Y., since 1901. World traveler and promoter of good will and better understanding by press, lecture and radio, between tea and coffee producing countries and U.S.; drafted original Standards of Practice of Asso. Bus. Papers, Inc., adopted by Asso. Advt. Clubs of World, 1914; drafted personal creed for advt. men, London, 1924; a founder Asso. Bus. Papers, Inc. and Audit Bur. of Circulation, Inc. Mem. Nat. Editorial Assn., Authors League of Am., Pan-Am. Soc., Am.-Brazilian Assn., China Soc., Colombian-Am. C. of C. Awarded by Brazil gold medal for book, All About Coffee; gold medal for All About Tea, by China; bronze plaque for distinguished service to business journalism by Asso. Bus. Papers, Inc., 1926; Officer Order Southern Cross, Brazil, 1936; Order of Jade, China, 1937. Author: All About Coffee, All About Tea, The Romance of Tea, Coffee Merchandising; The Tea and Coffee Industries; Little Journeys to Brazil, Japan-Formosa, India, Ceylon, Java-Sumatra, China; Rosemary and Briar Sweet; The Romance of Coffee. Dept. editor Standard Dictionary. Contbr. ency. Brit. and sci. publs. Home: 52 Gramercy Park. Office: 79 Wall St., N.Y.C. 5. Died Jan. 19, 1954.

ULIO, James Alexander (ū'lĭ-ō), army officer; b. Walla Walla, Wash., June 29, 1882; grad. Command and Gen. Staff Sch., 1921, Army War Coll., 1934; hon. degree, Villanova, 1943. Enlisted as private in Regular Army, 1900; commd. 2d lt. Inf., 1904, and advanced through the grades to brig. gen., 1939, major gen., 1942; served with 1st Inf., P.I., 1906-08, Vancouver Barracks, Wash., 1908-12, Hawaii, 1912-16; with 23d Inf. in U.S., 1917-18; asst. chief of staff for personnel, 35th Div., France, May-June 1918, for IV Corps, July-Nov. 1918; chief Statis. Div., Central Records Office, adjutant General's Office, A.E.F., 1918-19; asst. chief of staff for supply, Mission to Armenia, 1919-20; chief Administrative Div., Am. Red Cross, Athens, 1923; asst. to adjutant gen., 2d Corps Area, N.Y., 1924-26; in Adjutant General's Office, 1926-29, 1931-33, exec. officer, same, 1934-35; aide to comdg. gen. Hawaiian Dept., Honolulu, 1935; chief Service Command Sect., Hawaiian Dept., 1936, chief of staff, 1936-37; asst. adjutant gen., 2d Corps Area, N.Y., 1938; exec. officer, Office of Adjutant Gen., 1938-39, asst. adjutant gen. (brig. gen.), 1939-42, adjutant gen. of the Army (major gen.), 1942-46; retired; v.p. Food Fair Stores, Inc., Phila., 1945-49. Awarded D.S.M., Oak Leaf Cluster (U.S.); Chevalier French Legion of Honor; Comdr. Order of Prince Danillo (Montenegro); Order of White Eagle with swords (Serbia); Knight Order of the Redeemer (Greece); Order of the Crown (Italy); Abdon Calderon, 1st class (Ecuador); La Salidaridad (Panama). Address: The Adjutant General, Dept. of the Army, Washington. Died July 30, 1958; buried Arlington Nat. Cemetery.

ULREY, Albert Brennus, biologist; b. N. Manchester, Ind., Dec. 31, 1860; s. Samuel S. and Phebe (Miller) U.; grad. Ind. State Normal Sch., 1885; studied Woods Hole, Mass., summer, 1892; A.B., Ind. U., 1892, A.M., 1894; student Rush Medical Coll., Chgo., 1900-1. Instr. zoölogy, Ind. U., 1892-4; prof. biology, Manchester Coll., 1895-9, U. Southern Cal., since 1901; prof. biology, Summer Sch. of Biology, Warsaw, Ind., 1895; instr. histogenesis, biol. sta. Ind. U., summers, 1896-97. Mem. A.A.A.S., Southern Cal. Acad. of Sciences (chmn. Biol. Sect). Author of several zoöl. publs. Address: 1435 W. 23d St., Los Angeles, Cal. Died Dec. 21, 1932.

UMBERGER, Harry John Charles (ŭm'bêr-gêr), agriculturist; b. Hymer, Kan., Sept. 27, 1881; s. Martin David and Sarah Stephania Ernestine (Hart-

ert) U.; B.S., Kan. State Coll., 1905; m. Rachel M. Kolck, June 12, 1909; children—Grace Kolck (Mrs. Ralph Marshall), John David, Pauline Ernestine (Mrs. John C. Pierce, Jr.); m. 2d, Marguerite V. Harper, Aug. 11, 1934. Scientific assistant Bureau of Soils, United States Dept. of Agriculture, 1906, Bureau of Plant Industry, U.S. Dept. of Agr., 1907-11; established and supt. Expt. Sta., Moro, Ore., 1909-11; asst. in charge cooperative experiments, Kan. State Coll., 1911-12; farmer, Chase County, Kan., 1912-15; demonstration supervisor and asst. county agt. leader, Div. of Extension, Kan. State Coll., 1915-17, county agt. leader, 1917-19, acting dean, 1919, dean since July 1, 1919. Dir. Kan. Crop Improvement Assn., 1909-20; sec. Kan. State Farm Bur.. 1919-20; chmn. radio com. Land Grant Coll. Assn., 1929-40 and 1943; v.p. Nat. Com. on Edn. by Radio since 1929; mem. Kan. Agrl. advisory Council, 1933; chmn. Regional Advisory Com. on Land Use Practices in Southern Great Plains Area, 1935-44; mem. Southern Great Plains Regional Agrl. Council, 1940-42; mem. Upper Ark. River Drainage Basin com. Nat. Resources Planing Bd., 1941, Lower Mo. Drainage Basin Com., 1942; mem. State adv. com. United Service Orgns., 1942; vice-pres. American Country Life Assn., 1937; chmn. extension sub-sect., Land Grant Coll. Assn., 1924; mem. com. on extension organization and policy, Land Grant College Assn., 1938-41; chairman, Northern Great Plains Council, 1946. Mem. Manhattan Chamber of Commerce. Mem. Kan. Hist. Soc., Farm House Fraternity, Phi Kappa Phi, Alpha Zeta, Gamma Sigma Delta, Epsilon Sigma Phi (com. on academic standing, 1939; vice-grand dir. nat. frat., 1944-45; grand dir., 1946-47). Democrat. Mason. Club: Rotary (Manhattan). Contbr. articles on "Farming and You" in Kansas newspapers. Awarded certificate for Distinguished Service Ruby, also Ruby for distinguished work in extension at National Epsilon Sigma Phi meeting, 1942. Home: 1412 Leavenworth St., Manhattan, Kan. Died Oct. 1, 1951.

UMSTEAD, William Bradley (ŭm'stĕd), governor; born Durham County, N.C., May 13, 1895; s. John Wesley and Lulie Elizabeth (Lunsford) U.; A.B., U. of N.C., 1916; legal edn., Trinity Coll. (Duke U.); m. Merle Davis, Sept. 5, 1929; 1 dau., Merle Bradley. Taught sch., 1916-17; admitted to N.C. bar, 1920. Pros. atty. Durham County Recorder's Court, 1922-26; solicitor 10th Jud. Dist. of N.C., 1926-33; mem. 73d to 75th Congresses, 6th N.C. Dist.; U.S. senator, 1946-48; gov. of N.C. since 1953. Trustee, Greater University of N.C. Served with A.E.F., World War I. Chmn. State Dem. Exec. Com., 1944-47. Mem. Vets. of Foreign Wars, Am. Legion. Democrat. Methodist. Mason. Home: 807 Hermitage Ct., Durham, N.C. Died Nov. 7, 1954; buried Mount Tabor Meth. Ch., Durham County, N.C.

UNDERHILL, Charles Reginald, electrical engr.; b. Chappaqua, N.Y., Nov. 2, 1874; s. Joshua Bowron and Elizabeth (Green) U.; desc. of Capt. John U.; on account of deafness did not attend college; largely self-ed., specializing through corr. and textbooks, in mathematics, physics, and engring.; m. Ella Howell Johnson, Apr. 6, 1898; children—Charles Reginald, Marguerite Allaire. Employed in inspection dept. Western Electric Co., N.Y. City, 1892-1900; chief elec. engr. Varley Duplex Magnet Co., Jersey City, N.J., and Providence, R.I., 1900-04; consulting elec. engr. N.Y. City, 1904-09; editor and tech. writer, Westinghouse Electric & Mfg. Co., Pittsburgh, 1909-10; chief engr., Am. Electric Fuse Co., Muskegon, Mich., 1910-11; chief elec. engr., Acme Wire Co., New Haven, Conn., 1911-21; cons. elec. engr., 1921-26; with Wappler Elec. Co., Inc., L.I. City, 1926-29, developing surg. and other high frequency machines. Has made extensive researches in the actions of electromagnets, the results of which have been published largely in Electrical World and Trans. Am. Inst. Elec. Engrs. Lectured on "Electromagnets," in leading colleges and univs. of U.S. Inventor of wireless telegraph printing system and other telegraphic and signaling devices. Commd. capt., Aviation Sect., Signal R.C., 1917; officer in charge radio tests in flight, Langley Field, on flying status; transferred to Air Service, 1918; served as radio officer, Sch. for Aerial Observers, Langley Field, also as radio statis. officer, Air Service Mil. Aeronautics. Fellow A.I.E. E., A.A.A.S.; mem. Mil. Order World War, Am. Legion, National Society Puritan Descendants, Pi Gamma Mu. Democrat. Author: The Electromagnet, 1903; Wireless Telegraphy and Telephony (with W. W. Massie), 1908; Solenoids, Electromagnets and Electromagnetic Windings, 1910; Magnets, 1924; Coils and Magnet Wire, 1925; Power Factor Wastes, 1926; Electrons at Work, 1933. Contbr. to Standard Handbook for Electrical Engineers since 1913. Discovered connections between elec. resistivity and heat content of metals. Address: Lower Bank, N.J. Died Oct. 3, 1950.

UNDERHILL, James, mining engr.; b. N.Y.C., Apr. 9, 1871; s. James and Louise Fuller (Johnson) U. grad. Phillips Exeter Acad., 1890; B.A., Harvard, 1894; M.A., U. Colo., 1905, Ph.D., 1906; m. Lucy Caroline Stoller, Dec. 18, 1899. Cons. practice Idaho Springs, Colo., 1896-——; asso. prof. mining. Colo. Sch. Mines, 1919-46; ret. Geologist. Colo. Geol. Survey, 1907-08; mem. State Bd. Examiners Engrs.,

1924-——. County food adminstr. Clear Creek Co., Colo., World War I. Capt., Engrs. O.R.C., 1923-——. Mem. Am. Inst. Mining and Metall. Engrs., Theta Tau, Tau Beta Pi, Kappa Sigma, Scabbard & Blade. Mason (Shriner). Author: Mineral Land Surveying, 1906. Home: Idaho Springs, Colo. Died Apr. 22, 1954.

UNDERWOOD, Felix Joel, state health officer; b. Nettleton, Miss., Nov. 21, 1882; M.D., U. of Tenn., 1908; m. Sarah Beatrice Tapscott, Nov. 21, 1904; children—Virginia Christine (dec.), Felix J. In private practice medicine, and part-time health officer of Monroe County, Miss., 1904-18; dir. Monroe County Health Dept., 1918-21; mem. staff of gov. of Miss., 1920-23; dir. Bur. of Child Hygiene, Miss. State Bd. of Health, 1921-24; state health officer of Miss. since 1924; mem. bd. dirs. Standard Life Ins. Co. since 1929; mem. staff Bapt. Hosp. since 1931. Mem. exec. com. State Bd. Pub. Welfare, 1933-35; gen. chmn. Miss. Council for Child Health and Protection; sec. bd., trustees Miss. State Tuberculosis Sanatorium since 1924; mem. board of trustees Miss. Children's Home Society 1928-——; pres. 1941-——; mem. State Commn. for the Blind, 1928-38; official delegate to 7th Pan Am. Child Congress, Mexico, 1935, 8th in Washington, 1942; formerly mem. White House Conf. on Child Health and Protection, Gulf and South Atlantic Mosquito Congress, Conf. of State and Provincial Health Authorities of N. America (exec. com.), Nat. Malaria Com.; mem. State Vocational Bd., 1936-45; mem. State sub-com. of Am. School Health Assn., 1945; mem. bd. dirs. Miss. Safety Council; pres. State bd. examiners for nurses since 1931; mem. bd. trustees So. Med. Assn., 1931-37; mem. State Consumer Adv. Council, O.P.A., 1942; mem. Children's Bur. Adv. Com. on Maternal and Child Health, 1935; member medical and health survey committee of American Red Cross; mem. adv. bd. on health services, and com. on pub. health, Am. Red Cross, 1945-49; pres. State and Provincial Health Authorities, 1939; mem. bd. sci. dirs. Rockefeller Found. 1938-40; mem. bd. dirs. Am. Cancer Soc., 1947, 50-52, state fund raising chmn. Miss. div. 1945-56, hon. pres. for life Miss. div., 1954; mem. Nat. Commn. on Children and Youth, 1946-50; mem. (hon.) State Dental Assn.; mem. pub. health com., Commonwealth Fund; pres. State Conference on Social Work, 1936; pres. Miss. Pub. Health Assn., 1937; mem. planning com. and report coms., White House Conf. on Children in a Democracy, 1939; mem. adv. com. Nat. Orgn. for Pub. Health Nusring, 1939-44; chmn. State exec. com. for Control of Cancer 1940-54; mem. bd. dirs. Am. Social Hygiene Assn., 1945-49; mem. governing council, Am. Pub. Health Assn., 1946-49; mem. standing Com., State Program and State Confs., Nat. Citizens Com. White House Conf., 1940. State fund raising chmn. Nat. Foundation for Infantile Paralysis 1938-——; mem. health adv. council U.S. Chamber Commerce, 1943. Diplomate Am. Bd. Preventive Med. and Pub. Health (past vice chmn.). Fellow Am. Coll. Phys., Am .Pub. Health Assn. (council of Southern br.; pres. southern br., 1941, pres. A.P.H.A., 1944); mem. Am. Med. Assn., Southern Med. Assn. (past pres. and trustee 1931-37), Miss. State Med. Assn. (past pres.), Miss. Tuberculosis Assn. (exec. com.), Nat. Tuberculosis Assn. (dir. at large, 1942-44). Presbyn. Mason (Shriner). Rotarian. Hon. life mem. Alpha Epsilon Delta. Author: History of Public Health and Medical Licensure, Vol. I, 1798-1937, vol. II, 1938-47 (with Whitfield). Recipient Arthur T. McCormack award, 1950; Lasker award, 1945, 53. Home: 1058 N. Congress St., Jackson, Miss. Died Jan. 9, 1959.

UNDERWOOD, Joseph Merritt, nurseryman; b. Palmyra, N.Y., Nov. 10, 1844; s. Daniel and Chloe (Durfee) U.; student pub. schs.; m. Anna Bingham Sargeant, May 4, 1871. In nursery bus., Lake City, Minn., 1867-——; pres. The Jewell Nursery Co.; v.p. Lake City Bank. Mem. Minn. State Hort. Soc. (pres. 1892-8), Minn. State Agrl. Soc. (pres. 1909-10). Republican. Episcopalian. Mason, K.T. Club: Lake Pepin Country. Address: Lake City, Minn. Deceased.

UNDERWOOD, Thomas Ingle, lawyer; b. Chgo., Aug. 27, 1898; s. William Thomas and Georgie (Lovell) U.; A.B., U. Mich., 1921, LL.B., 1923; diploma econs. and polit. sci., Oxford U., 1924; m. Frances Coonley Rawson, Apr. 25, 1932; 1 dau., Nancy R. (Mrs. Walter Luscher). Admitted to Ill. bar, 1925; asso. Winston, Strawn, Smith & Patterson, Chgo., 1924-42, partner, 1942-——. President, dir. Welfare Council of Met. Chgo.; chmn. Lyric Opera of Chgo. Served as 2d lt., AC, World War I. Mem. Mil. Tng. Camps Assn. (nat. sec.), Chgo. Commons Assn. (past pres.), Am., Ill., Chgo. (chmn. corp. law) bar assns., Psi Upsilon, Phi Delta Phi. Presbyn. (trustee). Club: Legal, Commercial (Chgo.); Casino, Saddle and Cycle (past pres.), Shoreacres. Home: 1550 N. State Pkwy., Chgo. 10. Office: 38 S. Dearborn St., Chgo. 3. Died Aug. 14, 1957.

UNDERWOOD, Thomas Rust, ex-senator, editor; b. Hopkinsville, Ky., Mar. 3, 1898; s. Thomas C. and Frances Pettus (Rust) U.; student U. Ky., 1915-17, LL.D. (hon.) 1949; m. Eliza McLean Piggott, June 20, 1925; children—Thomas Rust, Jr., Walter

Piggott. Gen. mgr. Lexington (Ky.) Herald, 1931-35, editor since 1935. Asst. to dir. Fred M. Vinson, Officer of Econ. Stabilization, 1943. Mem. 81st and 82d Congresses from 6th Ky . dist. Sec. Ky. State Racing Commn., 1931-43, 1947-48; mem. Nat. Assn. State Racing Commrs., 1934-48. Mem. bd. trustees Julius Marks Tuberculosis Sanitorium. Mem. Ky. State Crippled Children's Commn., 1935-39, Ky. State Planning Bd., 1931-35. U.S. Senator, from Ky., 1951-52. Mem. U.S. delegation Inter-Parliamentary Union, Bern, Switzerland, 1952. Mem. Lexington Y.M.C.A. Board. Member American Legion, 40 and 8, Lexington Bd. Commerce (past pres.), Ky. Press Assn. (past pres.). Democrat (past chmn. state central exec. com.), Phi Delta Theta. Episcopalian. Elk. Clubs: National Press, Blue Grass Automobile (past pres.), Lexington Optimist (past pres.), Lexington Country, Idle Hour Country, Thoroughbred Club of America. Editor: Thoroughbred Racing and Breeding, 1945; Call Me Horse, 1946. Home: 233 Woodspoint Rd. Office: Lexington Herald-Leader, Lexington, Ky. Died Jan. 29, 1956; buried Lexington Cemetery.

UPDEGRAFF, Harlan, educator; born Sigourney, Iowa, August 22, 1874; the son of Ambrose and Hannah (Harlan) U.; Ph.B., Cornell Coll., Ia., 1894; A.M., Columbia, 1898, Ph.D., 1908; fel. tchrs. Coll. Columbia, 1906-07; LL.D., Syracuse U., 1926; m. Gertrude Bartholomew, 1901 (died Oct. 3, 1939); children—Ruth, Harlan, Jr.; m. 2d, Lucina Borton Rodi, 1942. Principal and superintendent public schools, Ia., 1894-97, 1898-1900; asst. in philos. and edn., Columbia, 1900-02; prin. Girls' Latin Sch., Baltimore, 1902-05; chief Alaska div. U.S. Bur. Edn., 1907-10; chief div. sch. adminstrn., U.S. Bur. of Edn., 1910-12; prof. edn. Northwestern U., 1912-13; prof. ednl. administration, U. of Pa., 1913-23, chmn. gen. com. in charge Schoolmen's Week, 1915-23, dir. Bur. Ednl. Measurements, 1917-23, pres. Cornell Coll., Mt. Vernon, Ia., 1923-27 (hon. trustee since 1940); vis. prof., Swarthmore Coll., 1927; prof., summers, Univ. of Ohio, 1917, U. of Calif., 1927, Cornell Univ., 1937; dir. New Jersey Ednl. Survey Commn., 1928-29; dir. of studies Nat. Adv. Com. on Edn., 1930; sometime ednl. cons. U.S. Office of Edn., Am. Council of Edn., Brookings Instn., Youngstown (O.) C. of C., N.Y. State Dept. Edn., Pa. Dept. of Pub. Instrn., Am. Youth Commn. Mem. Nat. Inst. of Social Scis., N.E.A., Nat. Soc. Study Edn., Soc. Coll. Tchrs. of Edn., Nat. Assn. Dirs. Ednl. Research, Sigma Xi, Phi Beta Kappa, Phi Delta Kappa, Sigma Nu. Mason. Neighborhood Ch. (Liberal), Pasadena. Author: Rise of Moving School in Mass., 1907; Teachers' Certificates Issued under Gen. State Laws and Regulations, 1911; Study of Expenses City Sch. Systems, 1911; Administrative Coöperation in the Making of Courses of Study, 1919; Financial Support of Rural Schools of New York, 1923; A Survey of the Fiscal Policies of the State of Pennsylvania in the Field of Education, 1923; Inventory of Youth in Pennsylvania, 1936. Coauthor: Research Problems in School Finance, 1933 Collaborator on surveys of city school systems of Baltimore, Maryland, 1911, Brookline, Mass., 1917, Phila., Pa., 1921, rural schs. of Pa., 1913, N.J. Tax Survey Report, 1931, and Miss. State and Local Govt. Survey, 1931; director financial sect. N.Y. State Rural Sch. Survey, 1921. Home 1596 E. Mountain St., Pasadena, Calif. Died April 14, 1953.

UPDEGRAFF, Paul Walter, lawyer; b Berta, Ark., Oct. 1, 1906; s. Walter Everett and Ella (Lawhorn) U.; LL.B., U. of Okla., 1930; m. Ruth Foreman, Aug. 3, 1930; children—Elizabeth, Paul Walter. Admitted to Okla. State bar, 1930; Fed. Court, 1936; U. S. Circuit Ct. of Appeals, 1943; U.S. Supreme Ct., 1948; county atty., Cleveland Co., 1933-35; in practice of law, Norman, Okla., 1935-44 and since 1946. Served as lt. (j.g.) to lt., U.S.N.R., 1944-46; E.T.O.; gunnery officer. Mem. bd. govs. Am. Nat. Red Cross. Member American Bar Association (member house of delegates), American Judicature Soc., Phi Delta Phi. Democrat. Baptist. Am. Legion (comdr. Norman Post 88); Vets. Fgn. Wars. Club: Lions (past pres.). Home: 324 Emelyn St., Norman, Okla. Died Mar. 16, 1959; buried I.O.O.F. Cemetery, Norman, Okla.

UPDIKE, Edward Lafayette, lawyer; b. Browntown, Va., Dec. 16, 1899; s. Byrd Franklin and Mary Bennet (Leach) U.; student Va. Polytech. Inst., 1918; B.C.S., Southeastern U., 1921, student Am. U., 1922-23; LL.B., George Washington U., 1926; m. Laela Eugenie Mattingly, Jan. 18, 1933; children—Jon Edward, Mary Sue. Auditor and accountant, Bur. Internal Revenue, 1920-30; admitted to District Columbia bar, 1926, U.S. Supreme Ct. bar, 1938, U.S. Ct. of Claims, U.S. Tax Ct., 1942; special attorney office chief counsel, Bureau Internal Revenue, 1931-42; associate, Miller and Chevalier, 1942-49, partner McClure & Updike, 1949—. Served with U.S. Army, 1918. Mem. Am., D.C. bar assns. Methodist. Mason. Address: 7553 Alaska Av. N.W., Washington. Died June 8, 1953; buried Arlington Nat. Cemetery.

UPDIKE, Ralph E., Sr., ex-congressman; b. Brookville, Ind., May 27, 1894; s. Harvey and Celia J. U.; LL.B., U. Indpls., 1919; m. Mrs. Charlotte Davis, Nov. 28, 1918; children—Ralph Eugene, Arthur Thomas. Admitted to Ind. bar, 1919, and began practice with firm Robinson, Symmes & Melson, now alone; served as spl. judge Superior Ct. and City Ct.; elected to Ind. Ho. Rep., 1922; mem. 69th and 70th Congresses (1925-29), 7th Ind. Dist. With 74th Co., U.S. Marines, in France, World War; wounded in action 5 times and gassed twice; $7,000,000 during Victory Loan Drive, N.Y. Republican. Mem. Christian Ch. Mason, Red Man. Club: Columbia. Home: 2843 Washington Blvd., Indpls. Died Sept. 16, 1953.

UPHAM, Roy, physician; b. Dartmouth, Mass., Mar. 16, 1879; s. Joseph Kellog and Sarah Condon (Davis) U.; M.D., N.Y. Med. Coll., 1901; grad. study N.Y. Post Grad. Hosp., 1912, N.Y. Polyclinic Med. Sch., 1913, Ryks Hosp., Copenhagen, 1912, Vienna (one month each), 1922, 23, 24, 26, 28, 30, St. Marks Hosp., London, 1933, 34, Kasr-el-Aini Hosp., Cairo, Egypt, 1934; m. Edna Norma Tingley, Aug. 16, 1916. Intern Hahnemann Hosp., N.Y. City, 1901-03; practice in N.Y. City since 1903, specializing in gastroenterology since 1910; asst. attending surgeon Cumberland Hosp., New York, 1908-14; attending gastroenterologist, Cumberland Hosp., 1904-26, Carson Peck Hosp., 1921-26, Prospect Heights Hosp., 1910-26; attending physician and head of gastroenterology sect. Met. Hosp.; cons. gastroenterologist Jamaica, New York Ophthalmic, Flower-Fifth Av. hosps.; chief of gastro-intestinal clinic, outpatient dept. Met. Hosp., Flower-Fifth Av. Hosp.; cons. gastroenterologist Evang. Luth. Hosp., Brooklyn; asso. N.Y. Med. Coll., 1903—, successively demonstrator histology, lectr. gastroenterology, assistant and associate professor, professor of clinical medicine, 1953—, chief of gastroenterology section since 1935; hon. mem. staff Utrecht Homeo. Hosp., Utrecht, Holland, 1946. Diplomate Am. Bd. Internal Medicine (sub-splty. gastroenterology), Internat. Bd. Surgery. Fellow Am. Acad. Proctology (hon.), A.C.S. Internat. Coll. Surgeons; mem. Am. College Gastroenterology (sec.-gen.), Am. Med. Assn., Acad. Pathol. Science, Nat. Gastroenterological Assn. (sec. gen.), Am. Med. Assn. of Vienna (life), N.Y. Academy. Medicine, N.Y. State Med. Soc., N.Y. Co. Med. Soc., N.Y. State, N.Y. Co. and Kings Co. Homeo. med. socs.; hon. mem. Monroe Co. and Albany Co. homeo. med. socs., Gen Homeo. Society Germany, Italian Gastroenterological Assn.; Internat. Homeo. League (hon. pres.); mem. (hon.) Argentine Homeo. Med. Soc., British Homeo. Assn. (hon. v.p.). Club: Lotos. Mason (32°, Shriner). Contbr. articles to med. jours. Address: 45 E. 74th St., N.Y.C. 21. Died 1956.

UPSHAW, William David, ex-congressman; b. Newman, Ga., Oct. 15, 1866; s. Isaac and Addie (Stamps) U.; student Mercer U., 1895-97; L.H. D., (honorary), Lanier-Milton Univ. married Margaret Beverly, May 5, 1909; children—Margaret Adeline, Charlotte Beverly. Injured spine by fall while working on farm. and consned to bed 7 yrs.; wrote book while in bed and paid expenses at coll. by sale of book and lectures delivered from rolling chair; founder, 1906, and editor The Golden Age (mag.), Atlanta, Ga. Mem. 66th to 69th Congress (1919-27), 5th Ga. Dist., carrying every county in dist. at last election; now pres. Nat. Citizenship Found. Democrat. A leader in closing of saloons in Ga.; v.p. Anti-Saloon League Am.; addressed legislatures and audiences in various parts of country in behalf of prohibition. Trustee Bessie Tift Coll. for Women, Forsyth, Ga.; raised money to build dormitory, as meml. to mother, Addie Upshaw Hall. Formerly vice pres. Southern Baptist Conv. Mem. Layman's Speech Inst. America (vice president). Kiwanian. Author: Earnest Willie, or Echoes from a Recluse, 1893 (11 edits.); Clarion Calls from Capitol Hill (patriotic and religious addresses), 1923. Advocate of total abstinence of all ofcl., social and civic leaders as the proper interpretation of the 18th Amendment and a safe and wholesome example of Am. youth. Left Democratic Party because of dissatisfaction with stand of both old parties on liquor question and was nominated by Prohibition Party for President, 1932. Home: Santa Monica, Cal. Died Nov. 21, 1952.

UPSTON, John Edwin, air force ofcr.; b. Tawas City, Mich., Sept. 9, 1890; s. Marshall J. and Frederica (Smith) U.; grad. A.C. Tactical Sch., 1935, Command and Gen Staff Sch., 1937, Army War Coll., 1939; m. Claudia J. Smith, July 7, 1934; 1 son, John Edwin. Enlisted as aviation cadet, aviation sect. Signal Corps, 1917; commd. 2d lt., 1918; promoted through grades to brig. gen. Dec. 1942, to major gen. January, 1950; chief African and Middle Eastern Theater Unit, Operations Div.; dep. chief theatres group, operations div., War Dept. Gen. Staff, Mar. 1942-Feb. 1944; apptd. chief of African and Middle Eastern Theater Unit, Operators Div, War Dept. Gen. Staff, Mar. 1942; operations officer and chief of staff XX Bomber Command; overseas in China-Burma-India Theater, Mar. 1944-Feb. 1945; comdg. gen. 72d Fighter Wing, Mar.-Sept. 1945; assigned Hdqrs. Army Air Forces, Sept. 1945; staff duty Hq. A.F., Sept. 1945-Jan. 1948; apptd. comdg. gen. 4th Air Force, Jan. 1948. Awarded: Distinguished Service Medal; Air Medal; Legion of Merit; rated command pilot, combat observer, Mason (32°, Shriner). Clubs: Army and Navy Country (Arlington, Va.), Columbia Country (Chevy Chase, Md.); Army-Navy (Washington); Bohemian, St. Francis Yacht (San Francisco). Home: Sonoma, Cal. Address: Hamilton Air Force Base, Hamilton, Cal. Died Aug. 18, 1952; buried Presedio Nat. Cemetery, S.F.

UPTON, Clifford Brewster (ŭp'tŭn), univ. prof.; b. Detroit, May 10, 1877; s. Albert B. and Esther A. (Johnstone) U.; grad. Mich. State Normal Coll., Ypsilanti, Mich., 1898; A.B., U. of Mich., 1902; A.M., Columbia, 1907; student U. of Göttingen, 1907, U. of Paris, 1908-10; m. Siegried Maia Hansen, Sept. 14, 1905. Instr. Arthur Hill High Sch., Saginaw, Mich., 1898-1900; instr. mathematics, Mich. State Normal Coll., Ypsilanti, Mich., 1901; instr. and head dept. of mathematics, Horace Mann High Sch., Teachers Coll., Columbia, 1902-10; instr. mathematics, Teachers Coll., Columbia, 1907, asst. prof., 1910, asso. prof., 1917, prof., 1927-42, prof. emeritus since 1942, secretary Teachers College, 1911-19, and provost, 1919-24. Member International Commission on Teaching Mathematics, Am. Math. Soc., Math. Assn. America, Nat. Council Teachers of Mathematics, Assn. for Symbolic Logic. Director Am. Book Co. Author: Modern Calculating Machinery, 1907; Standardized Tests in Mathematics for Secondary Schools, 1923; Studies in the Teaching of Arithmetic, 1927; The Strayer-Upton Arithmetics (with G. D. Strayer), 1928; The Strayer-Upton Junior High School Mathematics (with same), 1929; Modern Algebra, 1930; A Series of 8 Arithmetic Workbooks for Elementary Schools, 1932, 39; Number Primer, 1933; First Days with Numbers, 1946; Practical Arithmetics (with G. D. Strayer), 1934; Practical Junior Mathematics (with same), 1935; Practical Algebra, 1936; Social Utility Arithmetics, 1937, 1951; Adventures in Arithmetic, 8 volumes, 1938-40; Air Navigation Workbook (with Lt. A. D. Bradley, U.S.N.R.), 1943; Short Course in Arithmetic, 1953; Arithmetics, Grades 3 to 8 (with K. G. Fuller), 1945-47, 1956; Junior Mathematics, 2 books, 1951; Arithmetic Workshop, Books 1 to 8 (with M. Uhlinger) 1949-51; American Arithmetics, Grades 3 to 8 (with K. G. Fuller, 1957-58. Contbr. to yr. books Nat. Council Tchrs. of Mathematics. Home: 501 W. 120th St., N.Y. City. Address: Teachers College, Columbia U., 525 W. 120th St., N.Y.C. 27. Died Sept. 1957.

UPTON, Louis Cassius, corporation exec.; b. Fredonia, N.Y., Oct. 10, 1886; s. Cassius M. and Carrie A. (Bodgett) U.; ed. Lake Forest Acad.; m. Elizabeth Fogg, June 13, 1914; children—Robert C., Judith Upton Hoyt, Philip O. (dec.), Sarah Elizabeth. With Commonwealth Edison Co., 1908-12; organized the Upton Machine Co., 1912, pres., 1912-29; v.p. Nineteen Hundred Corp. (merger of Nineteen Hundred Washer Co. and Upton Machine Co.), 1929-33, pres. since 1933; chmn. bd. Whirlpool Corp.; dir. Clark Equipment Co., Monroe Calculating Machine Co.; pres. Upton Found., Inc. Dir. durable goods industries, W. P.B., Washington, 1942. Alderman, City of St. Joseph, and mayor pro tem. Former pres. of Mich. Mfrs. Assn., now dir. Pres. Berrien-Cass Area, Council Boy Scouts of Am. and mem. Nat. Council, received Beaver Award. Nat. councillor Chamber of Commerce of U.S. Former pres. St. Joseph Chamber of Commerce; mem. Council, U.S. Assos. Internat. Chamber of Commerce; pres. Am. Washer & Ironer Mfrs. Assn., 1945-46; trustee Kalamazoo Coll.; trustee Com. Econ. Development; pres. Economic Club of Southwestern Michigan; dir. Nat. Assn. Mfrs. Clubs: Chicago, Union League (Chicago); Berrien Hills Country; Westmoreland Country; Quadrangle (Univ. of Chicago). Home: 298 Ridgeway St., St. Joseph, Mich.; also Scottsdale, Ariz. Office: Whirlpool Corp., St. Joseph, Mich. Died Oct. 9, 1952.

URICE, Jay Adams (ū'ris), ret. YMCA exec. b. Garrison, Ia., Mar. 13, 1891; s. George Nathaniel and Alice (Pavey) U.; B.S., Coe Coll., 1912, LL.D., 1937; student Union Theol. Sem., and Columbia U., 1918-27; m. Marguerite Nesbit, Aug. 4, 1915; children—George Nesbit, Janet Alice, Jay Adams. In Y.M.C.A. work since 1912, beginning as sec.; ednl. dir., Honolulu, 1912-17, mem. personnel bd., War Work Council, 1917-20, Europe, 1920-21, personnel bureau, Internat. Com., 1921-25, home div., Nat. Council, 1925-34; asso. gen. sec., 1934-54, gen. sec., 1954-56; lectr. Yale Divinity School, 1957—; ednl. cons. Inst. Pacific Relations, Honolulu, 1925. Dir. Silver Bay Assn., Silver Bay, N.Y.; dir. U.S.O., Inc., World War II. Democrat. Presbyn. Clubs: Columbia University, Arkwright. Author: The Theory of the YMCA, 1922; Committees and Board in the Early History of the New York City YMCA, 1929; Working Together, 1940. Home: 38 East View Av., Pleasantville, N.Y. Died Sept. 7, 1957; buried Ticondaroga, N.Y.

URICH, Walter K., probation officer; b. Lima, O., Feb. 13, 1902; s. George and Anna (Klein) U.; A.B., Heidelberg Coll., 1925; student Central Theol. Sem., 1925-26, McCormick Theol. Sem., 1926-27; B.D., Chgo. Theol. Sem., 1928; m. Louise Marie Miller, Feb. 14, 1929; children—Bruce, David, Walter K. (dec.), Carol Louise, Robert Walter.

Worked in various indsl. fields while gaining edn.; student pastor, recreation leader rural community; dir. community center Chgo. Bd. Edn., 1929-31; tchr. high schs., Chgo., 1929-32; case worker Unemployment Relief Service, also investigator fraud cases, 1932-35; apptd. chief probation officer U.S. Dist. Ct. of No. Ill., 1935; acting parole executive U.S. Bd. Parole, 1939, parole exec., 1940-52. Mem. bd. dirs. Nat. Council on Edn. for Character and Citizenship; past mem. exec. com. Chgo. Acad. Criminology. Mem. Am. Assn. Social Workers, Nat. Probation Assn. Conglist. Home: 5809 Annapolis Rd., Hyattsville, Md. Died June 3, 1952; buried Fort Lincoln Cemetery, Washington.

URNER, Mabel Herbert (Mrs. Lathrop Colgate Harper), author; b. Cin., June 28, 1881; m. Lathrop Colgate Harper, Mar. 12, 1912. Creator of Helen and Warren characters; for over 30 yrs. the Helen and Warren stories have been syndicated in prin. newspapers throughout the U.S. Can., Eng. Clubs: National Arts, Pen and Brush, Authors League (New York); Authors, Playwrights and Composers (London). Author: Journal of a Neglected Wife, 1909; The Price Inevitable, 1912; The Woman Alone, 1915; The Married Life of Helen and Warren, 1925; Helen and Warren Guidelet to Europe, 10th edit., 1939. Collector Am. and European samplers of 17th and 18th centuries; also collector amber viniagrettes, snuff boxes, pocket compasses and sundials. Home: One Lexington Av., N.Y.C. 10. Died Mar. 1957.

URQUHART, Leonard Church (ûr'kĭt), structural engr.; b. Cleve., Oct. 24, 1886; s. William and Belle (Church) U.; student Western Reserve U., 1903-05; C.E., Cornell U., 1909; m. Jane Dalziel McKelway, June 10, 1915 (div. 1936); children—Edmond Ragland, Leonard Church, Junior (deceased); married second, Augusta Packard Graff, June 25, 1936; one daughter, Sylvia. Engr. Nickel Plate R.R., Cleve., 1909; with Cornell U., 1911-46 (on leave 1941-46), as instr., asst. prof., prof. structural engring. 1925—; prof. civil engring. Drexel Inst., Phila., 1925, prof. engring. U. Hawaii, 1940, with engring. branch constrn. div. O.Q.M.G., Washington, 1941; now consulting engr. Porter, Urquhart, McCreary & O'Brien (Newark, Los Angeles, Sacramento, San Francisco). Served as 2d lt., engineers, July 1918-Mar. 1919, World War I; col. Engrs. Corps, Chief, Engring. Div., Office Chief Engrs., Washington, D.C., World War II. Decorated Legion of Merit. Mem. Am. Soc. Civil Engrs., Am. Concrete Inst., Beta Theta Pi, Phi Kappa Phi. Republican. Baptist. Author: Design of Concrete Structures, 1923, 6th edit., 1958; Stresses in Simple Structures, 1926, 2d edit., 1932; Design of Steel Structures, 1930. Editor in chief of Civil Engineering Handbook, 1934, 4th edit. 1959; Elementary Structural Engineering, 1941. Home: 94 Knollwood Rd., Short Hills, N.J. Office: 415 Frelinghuysen Av., Newark. Died Mar. 1960.

UTASSY, George d', publisher; b. Phila., Nov. 5, 1870; s. Anton W. and Laura Wood d'U.; A.B., Harvard, 1898; m. Florence Chapman, Oct. 8, 1904; children—Chapman, Babette. Began with Harper & Bros., 1898; was pub. Motor, Cosmopolitan Mag., Motor Boating, Hearst's, Mag., Harper's Bazar, Good Housekeeping, Nash's Mag., (London), Illustrated Daily News; subsequently pub. Daily Mirror, N.Y. Democrat. Episcopalian. Mason. Clubs: University, Harvard, Rockaway, Hunt. Home: Cedarhurst, L.I., N.Y. Deceased.

UTTER, George Benjamin, pub., editor; b. Westerly, R.I., Apr. 11, 1881; s. George Herbert and Elizabeth Lavina (Brown) U.; prep. edn., Riverview Mil. Acad., Poughkeepsie, N.Y.; student Amherst Coll., 1901-05, honorary Master of Arts, 1946; married Katherine Latham Wilbar, January 17, 1916; children—Charles Wilbar (capt. U.S. Army), George Herbert, Jean Chilton. Reporter Westerly Sun, 1905, city editor, 1906-13, mng. editor, 1913—; treas. Utter Co., pubs., printers, 1911—. Mem. Westerly Town Council, police commr., 1922-26; mem. R.I. Ho. of Rep., 1925-26; mem. Children's Law Commn. of R.I. (mgr. before Gen. Assembly which passed 21 of 27 laws presented). Mem. Rep. Town Com., Westerly, 1908-15; mem. Rep. State Central Com. and Rep. State Exec. Com., 1915-28; alternate Rep. Nat. Conv., 1940. Trustee Westerly Memorial and Pub. Library, Westerly Hosp. (sec.; chmn. campaign com. which raised $752,000); trustee of the Rhode Island Boy Scouts; member R.I. advisory committee on aviation; member exec. R.I. Tercentenary Committee; incorporator R.I. Roger Williams Memorial Assn.; pres. Westerly Chamber of Commerce; State director Civilian Defense; chairman Westerly United Service Orgns. com. Recording sec. Seventh Day Bapt. Missionary Soc.; pres. Seventh Day Bapt. General Conf.; mem. New England Council; R.I., mem. New Eng. Trails Conf.; pres. R.I. Camps, Inc.; chmn. State Advisory Com. on Roadside Control; pres. of New Eng. Daily Newspaper Publishers Assn. Mason. Club: Appalachian Mountain. Author: Old Westerly; "The First Hundred Years"; Nicholas Utter (genealogy); author of Westerly highway commn., caucus, zoning and accounitng laws (state caucus law, similar to Westerly law, adopted, 1930). Home: 40 Grove Av. Office: The Westerly Sun, Westerly, R.I. Died Nov. 12, 1955; buried River Bend Cemetery, Westerly.

UTTLEY, Clinton B(ennett), govt. official; b. O'Neill, Neb., Feb. 13, 1887; s. Howell Mosier and Alberta Merriam (Ensign) U.; ed. pub. schs. of Holt Co., Neb.; m. Mary Gertrude Floyd, May 12, 1911; 1 son, George Bennett; m. 2d, Gertrude Dositheus Shea, Dec. 25, 1937. Post office clerk, Muskogee (Indian Territory), Okla., 1907, city delivery carrier, 1911, post office clerk, 1914-20; post office insp., Chicago and St. Louis Divs. 1920-33; post office insp. in charge, San Francisco Div., 1933-34; supt. Post Office Service, 1934-43; dep. 1st asst. postmaster gen., 1943-50; exed. dir. Bur. of P.O. Operations since 1950. Democrat. Home: 7700 Blair Rd., N.W., Washington 12. Office: Post Office Dept., Washington 25. Died June 30, 1953; buried Rock Creek Cemetery.

V

VACHON, Alexandre (vă-shōn), archbishop of Ottawa; b. St. Raymond, Portneuf, Que., Can., Aug. 16, 1885; s. J. Alexandre and Mary (Davidson) V.; student Petit Seminaire de Quebec and Grand Seminaire de Quebec; student 2 yrs. Harvard U. and Mass. Inst. Tech.; M.A., Laval U., 1906, Licentiate in Philosophy, summa cum laude, 1907, Licentiate of Theology, summa cum laude, 1909, Th.D., 1910, M.A., 1916; hon. Sc.D., U. of Montreal and Laval Univs.; Dr. Ut. Juris, Univ. of Ottawa; LL.D., McGill and Queen's Univs. Ordained to priesthood, Saint Raymond, Quebec, May 22, 1910; apptd. teacher of chemistry, Laval Univ., 1912; prof. chemistry, 1916; dir., Ecole Supérieure de Chimie of Laval, 1926-37, then dean of Faculty of Science; elected superior gen., Seminary of Quebec and rector of Laval Univ., Apr. 11, 1939; apptd. titular archbishop of Achrida and coadjutor archbishop of Ottawa, Dec. 1939; consecrated in Cathedral-Basilica of Ottawa, Feb. 2, 1940; Archbishop of Ottawa, May 22, 1940. Roman Court Assistant to the Pontifical Throne. Traveled extensively in Europe, South America, Africa and all of N. Am. as far as Alaska and the Polar Circle. Serves on National Research Council of Canada. Chancellor of Ottawa University. Fellow Canadian Institute of Chemistry (president, 1933-34, 1934-35); Fellow Royal Soc. of Can.; mem. Canadian Chem. Assn. (pres., 1929), Can. Acad. St. Thomas Aquinas, Societe Chimique de France; hon. mem. Engring. Inst. of Can. Former chaplain Fifth Signal Corps; holds rank of major in Army. State Provincial Chaplain for Quebec of the Knights of Columbus. Author of textbook on chemistry; collaborated on textbook on mineralogy and geology; research work at Atlantic Biological Sta., St. Andrew's, N.B. Address: Archbishop's Residence, 145 St. Patrick St., Ottawa, Ont., Can. Died Mar. 30, 1953; buried Ottawa.

VAIL, Curtis Churchill Doughty, coll. prof.; b. Brooklyn, N.Y., Feb. 27, 1903; s. Henry Noxon and Martha Rhoda (Doughty) V.; A.B., Hamilton Coll., 1924; A.M., Columbia, 1929, Ph.D., 1936; student U. of Munich, 1929; m. Faith Newbrook Ely, June 21, 1930; 1 son, Van Horn. Instr. German and Spanish, Port Jervis (N.Y.) High Sch., 1924-25; head of modern lang. dept., Massanutten Acad., Woodstock, Va., 1925-26; part time instr. of German, Columbia, 1926-27; instr. of German, U. of Buffalo, 1927-32, asst. prof., 1932-38, asso. prof., 1938-39; prof. of Germanic langs. and lit. and exec. officer of dept., U. of Wash., 1939—; acting dir. div. of adult edn., 1944-45; member of the faculty, Hunter College, summer 1930, Teachers Coll., Columbia, 1938. Chmn. N.Y. State German Syllabus Com., 1932-34, N.Y. State Com. for Accrediting Teachers of German, 1933-38; examnier in German, Coll. Entrance Exam. Bd., 1937-38; consultant U.S. Armed Forces Institute, 1953; adv. council Junior Year in Munich, 1953—; dir. Students Internat. Travel Association, 1952—; consultant Brittanica World Dictionary, 1953. Carl Schurz fellow in Germanic langs. and lits., Columbis U., 1930-31; director Western Washington Key Center of War Information and Training, 1942-45; visiting prof. of Germanic languages and literatures, Columbia Univ., winter 1945. Mem. of American Assn. of Teachers of German (president 1947), Modern Language Assn. Am. (exec. council 1955-58), Eugene Field Soc. (hon.), Mark Twain Society (hon.), Modern Humanities Research Assn., Philol. Assn. of the Pacific Coast (v.p. 1953, pres. 1954), Delta Chi, Delta Phi Alpha. Episcopalian. Club: Faculty (U. of Wash.). Author: Lessing's Relations to the English Language and Literature, 1936. Compiler: Basic German Word and Idiom Lists, 1933; Scientific German for Science and Premedical Students, 1938; Graded German Short Stories, 1941. Asso. editor of The German Quarterly, 1937-41, managing editor, 1942-45; co-author German for Beginners, 1958; co-editor of The Modern Language Quarterly. Contbr. to lang. jours. Home: 4552 52d Av. N.E., Seattle 5, Wash. Died Sept. 19, 1957; buried Acacia Meml. Park, Seattle.

VAIL, Richard B(achelor), ex-congressman; b. Chgo., Aug. 31, 1895; s. Richard B. and Mary (Joyce) V.; student Chgo. Tech. Coll., 1914, John Marshall Law Sch., 1917. Chmn. bd. Vail Mfg. Co., Chgo., since 1940; pres. Nat. Autostitch Corp. since 1951, E. H. Hotchkiss Co. since 1953. Elected 80th United States Congress, 1946; member 82d Congress. Served as lieut., Inf., U.S. Army, World War I. Mem. Am. Legion. Clubs: South Shore Country, Olympia Fields Country (Chicago). Home: 6946 S. Bennet Av., Chgo. Died July 29, 1955; buried Holy Sepulchre Cemetery.

VAILE, Rawson, business exec.; b. Kokomo, Ind. Sept. 22, 1888; s. Joseph E. and Isabelle (Voiles) V.; B.S., Purdue U., 1909; m. Elizabeth Smith, Mar. 3, 1927; 1 dau., Elizabeth R. Engr. Penberthy Injector Co., Detroit, 1909-10; mech. engr. Canadian Bridge Co., Windsor, Ont., Can., 1910-12. Am. Blower Corp., Detroit, 1912, mgr. sales dept., 1919-21, sec., 1921-32, exec. v.p., treas., 1932—; v.p., treas., dir. Canadian Sirocco Co., Ltd., Windsor, 1937—. Dir. Detroit Citizens League. Served as 1st lt., U.S. Army, World War I. Mem. St. Dunstans Guild, Phi Gamma Delta. Mem. Christ Ch. Clubs: Boat, Economic, Orchard Lake Country (Detroit). Home: 864 Pilgrim Rd., Birmingham. Office: Box 58, Roosevelt Park Annex, Detroit 32. Died June 19, 1954.

VALASEK, Otakar, cartoonist; b. Moravany, Bohemia, Feb. 28, 1884; s. Joseph and Frances V.; came to U.S. at 17; ed. in Bohemia, and at Art Inst. Chgo.; m. Maud Powell, July 3, 1910. In comml. art adv. bus., Chgo., 1914-17; with Chgo. Herald, Aug. 1917-Apr. 1918; staff Com. on Pub. Information until end of the war. Author: (cartoons) American War Cartoons, 1917; 100 Cartoons—200 Years of Slavery (Slavic), 1918. Serial cartoons Creepers on the Earth, published in Russia, 1919. Address: 926 Belden Av., Chgo. Died 1950.

VALE, Roy Ewing, clergyman; b. Ewington, O., May 18, 1885; s. Fremont Fordyce and Margaret Ella (Ewing) V.; prep. edn. Ewington Acad.; A.B., Washington and Tusculum Coll., 1909; grad. Princeton Theol. Sem., 1912; D.D., Washington Coll. (Tenn.), 1917, Wooster Coll., 1945, Tusculum Coll., 1945; LL.D., Maryville Coll., 1922, Washington and Jefferson Coll., 1944, Ind. Central Coll., 1945; m. Jess N. Dobson, Oct. 17, 1912; children—Dorothy May (Mrs. John R. Kissinger), Marjorie Jean (Mrs. Robert Harrison Wilson). Ordained Presbyn. ministry, 1912; pastor successively, Lambertville, N.J., Second Ref. Ch., Somerville, N.J., Second Ch., Knoxville, Tenn., until 1921, First Ch., Oak Park, Ill., 1921-30, Woodward Av. Ch., Detroit, 1930-40; pastor Tabernacle Ch., Indpls., 1940-55, pastor emeritus 1955—. New era chmn. Synod of Tenn., 1919-21; mem. ch. extension bd., Chgo. Presbytery, 1921-30; pres. Detroit Pastors Union, 1936-37; pres. Alumni Assn., Princeton Theol. Sem., 1937-38; mem. permanent jud. commn. Presbyn. Ch., U.S.A., 1936-44, moderator Gen. Assembly, 1944-45, chmn. spl. com. pastoral relocation, 1944-48, mem. spl. com. on structure and organization of the church, 1947-50. Dir. Maryville Coll.; mem. adv. bd. Beaver Coll. for Women; mem. greater Indpls. Bd. Week-Day Religions Edn. Served as sec. Army YMCA, 1918. Recipient Constructive Citizenship award from nat. soc. S.A.R., 1951; Award of Merit from D.A.R., 1954. Democrat. Mason (K.T., 32°). Clubs: Rotary (life mem. Oak Park); Benham (Princeton); Indianapolis Athletic, Torch, Literary (Indpls.). Author chpt. on ch. govt. Address: 235 W. 54th St., Indpls. 8. Died Apr. 3, 1959.

VALENTA, Frank Louis, investment banker; born N.Y. City, Jan. 26, 1906; s. Joseph and Margaret (Hurt) V.; grad. N.Y. Univ., 1931; m. Elizabeth Celia Middlebrook, June 27, 1931 (dec.); children—Bettina Middlebrook, Frank Louis; m. 2d, Lucy McColl, July 26, 1957. Research dept. N.Y. Stock Exchange firm Shearson, Hammill & Co., N.Y. City, 1927-33; head research dept. and account exec., Lionel D. Edie & Co., 1933-35; organized and mgr. investment adv. dept. Shearson Hammill & Co., 1935-39; v.p. charge research and management Distributors Group, Inc., Investment Bankers, 1939-49, dir., 1941-49; v.p. and dir. Group Securities, Inc., Jersey City, N.J., 1941-49; organizer and pres. Natural Resources Fund, Inc., N.Y. City, 1949—; organizer and head Frank L. Valenta & Co., Inc., N.Y. City. Dir. Automobile Banknig Co., Phila.; lecturer on mutual funds N.Y. Inst. Finance, N.Y. City; guest lecturer dept. finance, Rutgers U., Sch. Bus. Adm., Newark, N.J. Organizer and president of Natural Resources Fund of Canada, Inc. Member Newcomen Society England, Am. Statis. Assn., N.Y. Soc. Security Analysts, Am. Mil. Engrs. Elk. Clubs: Bankers (Am.), Athletic (N.Y.). Author: (with Dr. Louis P. Starkweather) Five Cents on the Dollar, 1934; Avoiding Doomed Investments, 1934; Causes of Corporate Failures, 1934; Detecting Corporate Failure Tendencies, 1935; Reverse Split-ups in Stocks—Devaluation and Decapitalization, 1935; Real Cost of Bankruptcy, 1934. Contbg. author: Retail Salesmanship of Mutual Funds, 1949. Address: View St., Saranac Lake, N.Y. Died Sept. 17, 1957.

VALENTINER, William Reinhold (văl'ĕn-tĭn-ĕr), art historian; b. Karlsruhe, Germany, May 2, 1880; s. Wilhelm and Anna (Lepsius) V.; student University of Leipzig; Ph.D., University of Heidelberg, 1905;

married Cecilia Odefey, Dec. 10, 1919; 1 dau., Brigitta. Assistant to Prof. H. Thode, Heidelberg U., 1904-05, Dr. C. Hofstede de Groot, The Hague, 1905-06, Dr. W. von Bode, Kaiser Friedrich Mus., Berlin, 1906-08; curator decorative arts, Met. Museum Art, 1908-14; adviser, Detroit Institute Arts, 1921-23, director, 1924-44; director and consultant, Los Angeles County Museum, 1946-49; cons. in art, 1949-54; dir. Getty Museum, Los Angeles, 1954; dir. North Carolina Mus. of Art, Raleigh, 1955-58, ret. General Masterpieces of Art Exhibit New York World's Fair, 1939. Author: Rembrandt und seine Umgebung, 1905; Rembrandt in Bild und Wort (with Dr. W. von Bode), 1906; Catalogue Raisonné of the Works of the Most Important Dutch Painters of the Seventeenth Century, Vol. I (with Dr. C. Hofstede de Groot), 1907; Handzeichnungen altholländischer Genremaler (with W. von Bode), 1907; Rembrandt—Des Meisters Gemäld, 1909; The Art of the Low Countries, 1914; The Late Years of Michelangelo, 1914; Umgestaltung der Museen, 1919; Zeiten der Kunst und der Religion, 1919; Schmidt-Rottluff, 1920; Georg Kolbe, 1922; Rembrandt Handzeichnungen (vol. I), 1923; Rembrandt, Wiedergefundene Gemälde, 1923; Frans Hals, 1923; Nicolaes Maes, 1924; Jacques Louis David, 1929; Pieter de Hooch, 1930; Rembrandt Paintings in America, 1931; Rembrandt Handzeichnungen (vol II), 1934; Tino di Camaino, 1935; Frans Hals paintings in America, 1936; Letters of John B. Flannagan, 1942; Origins of Modern Sculpture, 1945; The Bamberg Rider, 1956; also catalogues of Johnson, Goldman, Mackay, Widener and other important collections, Hudson-Fulton Exhibition, 1909, Rembrandt Exhibition, 1930, etc. Editor: Unknown Masterpieces, 1930; editor Art in America, 1913-31, Art Quarterly, 1938-49. Contbr. to U.S. and European periodicals. Address: Raleigh, N.C. Died Sept. 6, 1958.

VALLANCE, Harvard Forrest, educator; b. Adams Co., O., Nov. 12, 1879; s. James W. and Clarissa (Brooks) V.; B.S., Ohio Northern U., 1902; A.B., Ohio State U., 1908, A.M., 1915, Ph.D., 1936; m. Maude M. Perkins, Aug. 2, 1904; children—Charlotte Lillie (Mrs. William H. Thomas), Virginia Perkins (Mrs. F. M. Randolph), Theodore R. Tchr. rural schs., Brown Co., 1898-1900; supt. schs. Center Village, O., 1902-03; Ostrander, O., 1903-05; prin. high sch. Plain City, O., 1905-06; teacher mathematics and history North High Sch., Columbus, O., 1908-18; prin. Indianola Jr. High Sch., Columbus, 1918-33; asso. prof. edn. Miami U., 1933-38; dir. bur. of recommendations 1933-50, prof. edn., 1938-50, dean grad. sch., 1946-50, emeritus since 1950; lectr. edn. Wesleyan Coll., 1950, dean school fine arts, 1951-53, retired. Mem. Ohio Edn. Assn. (mem. exec. com., 1929-35, pres. 1947, mem. edn. council, 1939-46, pres. council, 1945-46), Southwestern Ohio Teachers Assn. (mem. exec. bd. 1936-40, pres. 1940); Ohio Instl. Teacher Placement Assn. (organizer and pres. 1935, 38), Nat. Instl. Teachers Placement Assn. (pres. 1947), N.E.A., Midwestern Conf. on Grad. Study and Research, Acacia, Phi Delta Kappa. Republican. Mason (32°). Club: Kiwanis. Author: chapter on William James, Ten Famous Educators, 1933; History of Antioch College, 1936; collaborator Current Teacher Placement Practices; contbr. jours. Address: 198 E. Torrence Rd., Columbus, O. Retired. Died Oct. 27, 1956.

VAN, Billy B., actor, sales educationalist; b. Pottstown, Pa., Aug. 3, 1870; s. George W. and Henrietta (Detweiler) Vandergrift; ed. pub. schs.; m. Grace Visgar Walsh, Sept. 2, 1922; children—Mary Ann, Billy B., Bonnie Grace. Began as actor, 1893; comedian, appearing in The Dream Girl, The Errand Boy, Little Nemo, Have a Heart, Words and Music, Rainbow Girl, Sunny Days, etc.; also motion picture actor; ret. from stage 1925; pres. Pine Tree Products Co., 1925-38; now pres. Billy B. Van Sales Co.; lectr. sales promotion before advt. clubs, C. of C.'s, etc. Mayor town of Newport, N.H.; sponsor Children's Sunshine Club of Newport. Mem. Internat. Sales Execs. Assn., N.E. Council and Advt. Fedn. Republican. Conglist. Mason (32°, Shriner). Clubs: Friars (New York); Boston Advertising (Boston). Author: The Seriousness of Being Funny, 1925; Snap Out of It, 1933. Contbr. sales publs. and trade mags. Home: Newport, N.H. Died Nov. 16, 1950.

VAN ALEN, William, architect; b. Brooklyn, Aug. 10, 1882; s. Jacob and Eleda (Squire) Van A.; ed. Pratt Inst. (Brooklyn), Beaux Arts Inst. of Design, Ecole des Beaux, Atelier Laloux (Paris); m. Elizabeth B. Van Alen, Jan. 18, 1916. Introduced Garden Apts. in N.Y. City, 1912; pioneered in design for skyscraper without cornice (Albemarle Bldg.), 1912; pioneered in use of stainless steel and aluminum as part of archtl. design when building Chrysler Bldg., 1929. Dir. sculpture Beaux Arts Inst. of Design, 4 yrs. Recipient numerous U.S. and fgn. awards and honors in architecture. Mem. Am. Inst. Architects, Beaux Arts Inst. of Design, Nat. Acad. of Design. Inventions include different methods of pre-fabricated constrn. During World War I, introduced the Pentz Airplane Compass for use by Air Service, U.S. Army. Home: 27 Prospect Park W., Bklyn. 15. Office: 139 E. 52d St., N.Y.C. 22. Died May 24, 1954.

VAN-ALLEN, John W(arren), lawyer; b. Le Ray, N.Y., Aug. 12, 1876; s. Warren and Lucia (Barnes) Van A.; Ph.B., Hamilton Coll., Clinton, N.Y., 1902; LL.B., Albany Law Sch. (Union U.), 1904; m. Gertrude Sweet, Feb. 14, 1907; children—Lucia, Eleanor, Marjory. Admitted to N.Y. bar, 1904, and began practice with firm Bissell, Carey & Cooke, at Buffalo; mem. Wilcox & Van Allen since 1908; gen. counsel Liberty Bank of Buffalo; gen. counsel Buffalo & Fort Erie Public Bridge Authority ("Peace Bridge"); dir. gen. counsel Ellicott Square Co.; gen. counsel emeritus Radio Mfrs. Assn. Mem. Am., N.Y. State bar assns., Chi Psi. Republican. Presbyterian. Club: Buffalo. Home: 100 Chapin Parkway. Office: Liberty Bank Bldg., Buffalo. Died July 28, 1958.

VAN AUKEN, Wilbur Rice, naval officer; b. Utica, N.Y., Mar. 13, 1882; s. Myron W. and Caroline (Rice) Van Auken; B.S., M.S. U.S. Naval Acad., 1903; Naval War Coll., 1927; m. Pauline Thompson, June 16, 1909; 1 dau., Rosalie (wife of Comdr. Francis Blouin). Promoted through grades to captain, 1926; served as gunnery officer on Flagship Rhode Island (Mexican campaign, 1914) and later on Texas; in World War I, in charge fire control, Bureau Ordnance; naval ordnance observer on staff of Admiral W. S. Sims in Europe; command of Stribling in Mediterranean and Adriatic seas; head of Ordnance and Gunnery Dept. at U.S. Naval Acad., 1921-24; command of Aircraft Tender Aroostook, 1924-26; head Training Div., Bureau of Navigation, 1927-29; command of U.S.S. Vestal, 1929-31; staff of Naval War Coll., 1931-34; in command of Oklahoma, 1934-35; on Naval Examining Bd. Navy Dept., 1935-39; retired 1939; entered investment banking business, Washington, D.C.; returned to active duty (on leave from Merrill Lynch Pierce Fenner & Beane) as chief of naval personnel, Bur. of Ordnance, Navy Dept., Jan. 1941-Sept. 1945. Retired, inactive duty, Navy 1941-Sept. 1945. Retired, inactive duty, Navy Dept., since Sept. 1, 1945. Awarded Mexican Campaign Victory, Army Occupation of Austria, 1918, National Emergency medals; World War II medals and Commendation Ribbon, citation from Sec. of Navy. Mem. Naval Hist. Foundn., Naval Inst., National Geographic Soc., Herkimer Co. (N.Y.) Hist. Soc., Fairfield Sem. Alumni Assn. Former pres. Washington Philatelic Soc. Rep. Presbyterian. Mason. Clubs: Army and Navy, Country, Chevy Chase (Washington, Country,); N.Y. Yacht Club. Former mem. Bd. of Control. Naval Inst.; former mem. bd. of mgrs., Navy Relief Soc.; mem. bd. dirs. Navy Mutual Aid Assn., since 1942; chmn. restoration com. Fairfield Coll. and Sem. Chapel. Author: (textbooks) Technical Ordnance; Gunnery and Strategy Textbooks for Navy, Revised "Naval Ordnance," 1942 Edition Encyclopedia Britannica; "Notes on Half Century of U.S. Naval Ordnance, 1939"; Top of the Hill (with Thomas O'Durell) 1953. Contributor articles on naval subjects to mags. Speaker in colls. and Navy training schs., during World War II. Home: Quebec House, 2800 Quebec St. N.W., Washington; Fairfield, Herkimer County, N.Y. Office: 815 15th St., Washington 5. Died Aug. 15, 1953; buried Arlington Nat. Cemetery.

Van BEINUM, Eduard, orchestral condr.; b. Arnhem, The Netherlands, Sept. 3, 1900; s. Eduard Alexander and Antonia (Polman) Van B.; student Conservatorium Musik, Amsterdam; Mus.D., Rutgers U., 1954; m. Josepha Antonia Anna Maria Jansen, July 12, 1927; children—Eduard, Bartolomeus. Appeared as violinist with Arnhem Philharmonic Orchestra, 1917; leader Schiedam and Zutphen choirs; condr. Haarlem Orchestra, 1927, also Haarlem Roman Cath. Choir; successively 2d condr., condr., mus. dir. Concertgebouw (Concert Hall), Amsterdam, 1931; guest condr. orchestras throughout Europe; tour Soviet Union with Leningrad Philharmonic Orchestra, 1937; guest condr., later 1st condr. London Royal Philharmonic Orchestra, 1949; North Am. debut with Phila. Orchestra, 1954; Am. debut with Concertgebouw, Carnegie Hall, 1954; formerly condr. San Francisco Orchestra; condr. in Chief Concertgebouw Orchestra, musical dir. Los Angeles Symphony Orchestra, 1958—. Grand officer Order Orange Nassau (Netherlands). Roman Catholic. Address: Joh Verhulststraat 37, Amsterdam, The Netherlands. Died Apr. 13, 1959.

van BUREN, Maud, anthologist; b. Montfort, Wis., Dec. 9, 1869; d. Martin and Rosina (Buhlmann) van B.; grad. Pratt Inst. Library Sch., Brooklyn, N.Y., 1902; studied under private teachers, 1894-1901. Teacher grade schs., Black Earth, Wis., 1889-91, Dodgeville, Wis., 1891-93, Carl von Linne Sch., Chicago, 1894-1901; librarian Owatonna Pub. Library, 1902-06; head cataloguer State U. Ia. Library, 1906; librarian Mankato (Minn.) Pub. Library, 1906-11; instr., Wis. Library Sch., and library visitor for Wis. State Library Commn., 1911-13; instr. in Summer Library Schools of Minn., Iowa, Mo., and Wis. univs. at various times; chmn. dept. jr. civics, Am. Civic Assn., 1913-17; exec. and field sec. State Council Child Welfare of Woman's Com. N.J., Council of Defense, 1918; librarian Owatonna Pub. Library, 1920-36. Mem. Am. Library Assn., Minn. Library Assn. (pres. 1904). Republican. Conglist. Co-author: The Essentials in Library Administration (with Ethel Farquhar McCullough), 1931. Co-editor (with Katharine Isabel Bemis); Christmas in Storyland, 1927; Christmas in Modern Story, 1927; Mother in Modern Story, 1928; Thanksgiving in Modern Story, 1928; Easter in Modern Story, 1929; Father in Modern Story, 1929. Editor: Quotations for Special Occasions, 1938. Contbr. articles to professional publs. Home: 1125 S. Cedar St., Owatonna, Minn. Died Jan. 2, 1959.

VAN BUREN, Robert, city ofcl.; b. N.Y.C., March 25, 1843; grad. Rensselaer Polytechnic Inst., 1865; m., Louise Aymar, Feb. 4, 1875. Rodman Brooklyn water works 1865, and by successive promotions reached position as chief engr., 1877, so remaining until 1894, when he resigned because of poor health; recalled to same office, 1898. Designated most of the sewer plans, the intercepting sewer system, and the most important additions to the water supply of Brooklyn, and many other public works. Has also acted as consulting engr. for many important works. Mem. Am. Soc. Civ. Engrs. Residence: Norwalk, Conn. Office: Municipal Bldg., Bklyn. Died Dec. 16, 1919.

VANCE, Estil, banker; b. Queen City, Tex., July 18, 1906; s. Steve Harod and Beatrice (Smith) V.; B.S., Tex. A. & M., Coll., 1927; M.B.A., Harvard, 1929; m. Murle Block, Aug. 11, 1932; children—Estil, Richard. With State Nat. Bank, Texarkana, Ark., 1929-47; v.p. Ft. Worth Nat. Bank, 1947-52, pres., dir., 1952—; pres. Fort Worth Air Terminal, Inc.; dir. State Res. Life Ins. Co., International Service Life Ins. Co., Ft. Worth, T.&P. Ry. Mem. Tex. Bar Assn., Sigma Alpha Epsilon. Presbyn. Mason (Shriner). Clubs: Lions, Ft. Worth, River Crest Country, Colonial Country (Ft. Worth). Home: 601 Rivercrest Dr. Office: P.O. Box 2050, Ft. Worth 1. Died Mar. 16, 1959; buried Greenwood Cemetery.

VANCE, Harold Sines, govt. ofcl.; b. Port Huron, Mich., Aug. 22, 1890; ed. pub. schs.; LL.D., U. Notre Dame; m. Agnes M. Monaghan, June 17, 1922; children—Patricia (Mrs. George Morgan), Barbara (Mrs. John C. Chatterton), John and William. Held various positions Studebaker Corp., 1911-54, chmn. bd., 1933-53, pres. 1948-54; prodn. engr. Bethlehem Steel Co., 1918-19; mem. AEC, 1955—. Cons. Office Def. Moblzn., 1952-55. Republican. Episcopalian. Home: 2539 Massachusetts Av. Office: AEC, 1901 Constitution Av., Washington 25. Died Aug. 31, 1959.

VANCE, Johnstone, editor, pub.; b. New Britain, Conn., Dec. 21, 1890; s. Robert Johnstone and Matilda (O'Connor) V.; ed. high sch. (New Britain), Fishburne Mil. Acad. (Waynesboro, Va.), University Sch. (New Haven, Conn.); m. Anne Gauer, Aug. 24, 1921. Mng. editor and pub. New Britain Herald since 1915; pres. of corporation since 1938. Served as ensign, later lt. j.g., U.S.N.R.F., World War. Mem. Am. Soc. Newspaper Editors, Associated Press, Conn. Newspaper Publishers' Assn. Episcopalian. Mason (K.T., Shriner). Clubs: New Britain, Shuttle Meadow; Lotos (New York); Nat. Press (Washington, D.C.). Home: "Birchwood," New Britain. Address: New Britain Herald, New Britain, Conn. Died Apr. 11, 1951; buried Fairview Cemetery, New Britain, Conn.

VANCE, Joseph Anderson, clergyman; b. Sullivan County, Tenn., Nov. 17, 1864; s. Charles Robertson and Margaret (Newland) V.; A.B., King Coll., Bristol, Tenn., 1885; B.D., Union Theol. Sem., Hampden-Sidney, Va., 1888; D.D., Huron Coll., S.D., 1902, King Coll., Bristol, Tenn., 1904; LL.D., Austin Coll., Tex., 1917; LL.D., King Coll., 1919; Wayne U., 1936; m. Mary B. Forman, Jan. 15, 1890; children—Dorothy, Joseph A., Mary F. Ordained Presbyn. ministry, 1888; pastor Woodland Av. Ch., Louisville, 1888-91, Maryland Av. Ch., Baltimore, 1891-99, Hyde Park Ch., Chicago, Ill., 1899-1911, First Church, Detroit, Sept. 1, 1911-Jan. 1, 1940, now pastor emeritus; minister in charge Royal Poinciana Chapel, Palm Beach, Fla., Dec. 1939-May 1941; acting pastor Grosse Pointe Woods Presbyterian Church, Detroit, 1942-43; interim preacher, Immanuel Presbyn. Ch., Los Angeles, 1943-44, First Presbyn. Ch., Bristol, Tenn., 1944-45, Westminster Presbyn., Detroit, 1945-46; Central Presbyn., Denver, 1947-48; Kirk-in-the-Hills, Detroit, 1948. Director and mem. exec. committee Charity Organization Society while at Baltimore; ex-moderator Maryland Presbytery and of Chicago Presbytery; ex-pres. Presbyn. Ministers Assn. of Chicago; mem. Ch. Federation Council of Chicago; ex-pres. Detroit Fedn. of Chs.; ex-pres. Nat. Bd. Missions Presbyn. Ch. U.S.A.; moderator Detroit Presbytery; moderator Gen. Assembly Presbyn. Ch., U.S.A., 1935-36. Author: Westminster Assembly and Its Confession for God, 1897; Home, 1900; Religion and Money, 1903; American Problems, 1904; The True and the False in Christian Science, 1904; Consider Christ Jesus, 1913; Why We Are Going to War, 1917; Christianity and Capital Punishment; America's Future Religion, 1927; The Way of the Cross, 1936; The Upward Way, 1945; The Glory Way, 1949. Home: 15 E. Kirby St., Detroit. Office: 39 E. Edmund Place, Detroit 1. Died June 11, 1951; buried Woodlawn Cemetery, Detroit.

VANCE, Robert Cummings, editor, pub.; b. New Britain, Conn., Feb. 21, 1894; s. Robert Johnstone and Matilda (O'Connor) V.; Ph.B., Yale, 1921; married Arline Dorothy Story, July 7, 1928; children—Joanne E., Robert (deceased). With New Britain Herald, 1921—, successively political editor, treas., bus. mgr., pres., editor and pub., 1951—. Served with Am. Field Service, French Army, 1917, U.S. Army, 1917-20. Mem. Am. Soc. Newspaper Editors, Am. Newspaper Pubs. Assn., Am. Legion (a founder), Vets. Fgn. Wars, Chi Phi. Catholic. Mason, Elk, Eagle. Moose. Clubs: Lions, Shuttle Meadow Country (New Britain); Graduates (New Haven). Home: 588 Lincoln Rd. Office: One Herald Sq., New Britain, Conn. Died Nov. 4, 1959.

VAN CLEAVE, Harley Jones (văn-klēv'), zoölogy; b. at Knoxville, Ill., Oct. 5, 1886; s. Jasper McMurtry and Mary (Jones) Van C.; B.S., Knox Coll., Galesburg, Ill., 1909; M.S., U. of Ill., 1910, Ph.D., 1913; m. Bernice Ford, Aug. 1, 1914; children—Mrs. Dorothy Lincicome, Philip Ford. Began as instr. zoölogy, U. of Ill., 1913, asso. 1916-19, asst. prof., 1919-22, asso. prof., 1922-29, prof., 1929-48, research prof., 1948-52, emeritus, 1952—, acting head zoology, chmn. div. biol. scis., 1938-39; mem. staff Ill. State Normal U., summers, 1913-15, Puget Sound Marine Sta., summer, 1916; asst. U.S. Bur. Fisheries, summers, 1919, 21; field naturalist Roosevelt Wild Life Expt. Sta., Syracuse, N.Y., 1929-34. Mem. staff Cold Spring Harbor Biol. Lab., summer 1936; Isles of Shoals Zoöl. Lab., summer 1939. Received Knox Coll. first Alumni Achievement award, 1938. Fellow A.A.A.S. (council 1925-31, 1944), mem. Am. Micros. Soc. (ex-pres.), Am. Soc. Zoölogists, Am. Soc. Parisitologists (past v.p.; pres. 1947), American Fisheries Society, Am. Soc. Naturalists, Ecol. Soc. of America, Illinois State Academy of Science (pres. 1928), Limnol. Soc. of America, Wild Life Society, Helminthological Soc. of Washington, Am. Assn. University Profs. (pres. Ill. chapter 1932-33), Sigma Xi (pres. of Illinois chapter 1924), Phi Beta Kappa (president Illinois chapter, 1942-43), Kappa Delta Pi, Phi Sigma, Beta Beta Beta, Phi Kappa Phi, Gamma Alpha, Alpha Kappa Lambda. Conglist. Club: University. Author: Invertebrate Zoölogy, 1924; A Textbook in General Zoölogy (with Linville and Kelly), 1929; Laboratory Directions for an Elementary Course in General Zoölogy (8th edit.), 1930; Biological Principles in General Zoölogy (with Linville and Kelly), 1930. Editor Trans. Am. Micros. Soc., vols. 44-50, 1925-31. Mem. editorial bd. Ill. Biological Monographs. Biological Abstracts, Bios, American Mid. Nat. Contbr. numerous articles in mags. Home: 713 W. Indiana Av., Urbana, Ill. Died Jan. 2, 1953.

Van COTT, Waldemar Quayle, lawyer; b. Salt Lake City, Apr. 11, 1889; s. Waldemar and Ella (Quayle) Van C.; A.B., Cornell, 1911; LL.B. cum laude, Harvard, 1914; m. Beth Baldwin, Jan. 17, 1920; children—Elizabeth (Mrs. Thomas Sothern Shreve), Barbara (Mrs. William Dean Agnew, Jr.). Admitted to Utah bar, 1914, since practiced in Salt Lake City. Served as capt., inf. U.S. Army, World War I. Mem. Supreme Ct. U.S., Supreme Ct. Utah, U.S. Circuit Cts. Appeals 8th, 9th, 10th circuits, U.S. Dist. Cts. Utah, Nev., Cal., Mont., Interstate Commerce Commn., U.S. Treasury Dept. bars, Am. Law Inst., Am., Utah (pres. 1938) bar assns., Chi Psi. Home: 105 E. South Temple St., Salt Lake City 1. Office: Walker Bank Bldg., Salt Lake City 1. Died Nov. 14, 1953.

VANDENBERG, Arthur Hendrick, senator; b. Grand Rapids, Mich., Mar. 22, 1884; s. Aaron and Alpha (Hendrick) V.; grad. Grand Rapids High Sch.; student law dept. U. Mich., 1901-02, hon. A.M., 1925; LL.D., Hope Coll., Holland, Mich., 1926, Alma Coll., Alma, Mich., 1937, Syracuse U., 1939; D.C.L., Union Coll., Schenectady, N.Y., 1938; D.H.L., Albion Coll., 1941; hon. degree, Dartmouth; m. Elizabeth Watson, 1905 (dec. 1916); children—Arthur Hendrick, Barbara, Elizabeth; m. 2d, Hazel H. Whittaker, June 14, 1918 (dec. 1950). Formerly with Collier's Weekly; editor Grand Rapids Herald, 1906-28. Apptd. U.S. senator to fill vacancy, 1928, and elected, 1928, for term ending Mar. 3, 1935, re-elected for term ending 1941 and for terms ending 1947 and 1953; nominee of Republican senators for pres. pro tem, Senate, 1933, 35, 41, 43, elected pres. pro tem, 1947; received 76 votes for Rep. presdl. nomination, Phila., 1940, 62 votes, 1948; U.S. del. San Francisco UN Orgn., 1945, 1st and 2d gen. assemblies UN, 1946; U.S. rep. Council Fgn. Ministers and Peace Conf. Paris, 1946; apptd. adv. to Sec. Byrnes at Big Four fgn. ministers' meeting in Paris Apr. 25, 1946. Am. del. Rio Pact Conf., Rio de Janeiro, Brazil, 1947. Mem. Grand Rapids Charter Commn., 1910; mem. Rep. State Central Com., 1912-18; chmn. Rep. State Conv., 1916, 28. Mem. S.A.R., Loyal Legion, Delta Upsilon. Conglist. Mason (33°, Shriner), Elk, Woodman. Clubs: Peninsular, Kent Country, Masonic Country (Grand Rapids); Authors' (London, Eng.). Author: Alexander Hamilton, the Greatest American, 1921; If Hamilton Were Here Today, 1923; The Trail of a Tradition, 1925. Contbr. mags. Chmn. Mich. commn. to erect statue of Zachariah Chandler in Washington, 1913, and delivered dedicatory address. Home: 316 Morris Av., Grand Rapids, Mich. Died Apr. 18, 1951; buried Oak Hill Cemetery, Grand Rapids.

VANDENBERG, Hoyt Sanford, air force officer; born Milwaukee, Jan. 24, 1899; s. William Collins and Pearl (Kane) V.; student Columbian School, 1918-19; B.S., U.S. Mil. Acad., 1923; student A.C. Tactical Sch., 1934-35, Command and Gen. Staff Sch., 1935-36, Army War Coll., 1936-39; m. Gladys Rose, Dec. 26, 1923; children—Gloria Rose, Hoyt Sanford. Commd. 2d lt., 1923, U.S. Army Air Corps; promoted through grades to lieut. gen., Mar. 1945, gen., 1947; instr. Fighter Tactics, A.C. Tactical Sch., 1936-38; asst. chief of staff A.A.F., 1940-41; chief of staff, Northwest African Strategic Air Force, 1942-43; dep. chief of staff, 1943; head of air mission to Russia, 1943-44; apptd. dep. comdr. in chief, A.E.F., Apr. 1944; made comdg. gen. U.S. 9th Air Force in France, Aug. 1944; became asst. chief of staff G-2 (Intelligence), War Dept. Gen. Staff, Feb. 1946; apptd. U.S. dir. Cent. Intelligence, June 1946; became dep. comdr. A.A.F. and chief of air staff A.A.F., 1947; vice chief of staff U.S. Air Force, October 1947, chief of staff 1948-53. Awarded Distinguished Service Medal (with Oak Leaf Cluster), Silver Star, Distinguished Flying Cross, Air Medal (4 Oak Leaf Clusters), Legion of Merit, Bronze Star. Home: Washington. Died Apr. 2, 1954.

Van den BROEK, Jan A., engr., educator; b. Middleharnis, Holland, Mar. 6, 1885; s. Christian Jan Hagen and Peternella (Van den Broek); B.S., U. Kan., 1911; Ph.D., U. Mich. (Carnegie scholar), 1918; m. Wendelina Pot, Dec. 1920; m. 2d, Helen Margaret Olbrych, June 12, 1929. Came to U.S., 1905, naturalized, 1924. Surveyor, Colo. Bell Telephone Co., 1910-11, also Caribou Willow River Ry., B.C.; detailer Boston Bridge Works, 1911-12; designer bridge dept. C.P. Ry., 1913-14; faculty mem. U. Mich. since 1914, prof. engring. mechanics since 1926. Awarded Norman medal, Am. Soc. C.E., 1941. Mem. Am. Soc. C.E., Engring. Inst. Can., Am. Soc. Engring. Edn. Author: Elastic Energy Theory, 1942; Theory of Limit Design, 1945; articles in Am. and fgn. profl. jours. Home: 785 Arlington Blvd., Ann Arbor. Died Apr. 20, 1959; buried Arborcrest, Ann Arbor.

VANDERBILT, Arthur T., chief justice; b. Newark; July 7, 1888; s. Lewis and Alice H. (Leach) V.; A.B., Wesleyan U., Middletown, Conn., 1910, A.M., 1912; LL.B., Columbia, 1913; LL.D., Tulane, Wesleyan, Western Reserve, U. of British Columbia, 1938, Tusculum Coll., 1939, Am. Univ., 1941, Univ. of Michigan, 1942; Northeastern U., 1944, Marietta Coll., U. of Pa., 1945; D.C.L., Boston U. 1945; LL.D., Rutgers U., 1948, Lafayette Coll., 1948, Washington and Lee U., 1949, Bowdoin Coll., O. Wesleyan University, Pennsylvania Mil. Coll., 1950, St. Peters College, 1952; D.C.L., McGill University, New York Univ., 1948; m. Florence A. Althen, Sept. 12, 1914; children—Jean A. (Mrs. Christian L. Swartz), Virginia Elizabeth (Mrs. Lemuel Bannister, Jr.) Lois Dorothy (Mrs. George C. Brainard, Jr.), Robert Althen, William Runyon. Admitted to New Jersey bar, 1913; counsellor at law, 1916; prof. of law, New York U. Law Sch., 1914-48; dean, 1943-48; counsel Essex County, N.J., 1922-48; chmn. Judicial Council, N.J., 1930-1940; judge Circuit Court, N.J., November 1947-Sept. 1948; chief justice Supreme Court since September 1948. President Essex County Republican League, 1919-47. Chairman of National Conference Judicial Councils, 1933-37 and chairman of its executive com., 1937—; chairman United States atty. gen's. com. to confer with com. of senior circuit judges appointed by Chief Justice Hughes to draft the bill for the administrative office of the U.S. Courts, 1938-39; mem. of atty. general's com. on administrative procedure, 1939-41; chmn. advisory com. apptd. by U.S. Supreme Court to draft Rules of Criminal Procedure for Fed. Cts., 1941-44; chmn. adv. com. of War Dept. on Military Justice, 1946; mem. N.J. State Constitution Revision Commn., 1941-42; spl. asst. atty. gen., N.J., to defend validity of referendum on Constitutional Revision, 1942-43. John Randolph Tucker Meml. lectr. Washington and Lee U., 1950, Frank Irvine lectr. Cornell U. 1950; Pitcairn Crabbe lect. U. Pittsburgh, 1951. Mem. American Bar Assn. (gen. council 1932-34; chmn. insurance law sect. 1933-34; mem. executive committee 1934-35; bd. govs. 1935-37; pres., 1937-38; dir. survey of legal profession, 1947; gold medal, 1948; life member American Law Institute; hon. mem. Canadian Bar Assn., 1938; mem. American Polit. Science Assn., Acad. of Polit. Science, Delta Kappa Epsilon (hon. pres., 1939-40), Phi Beta Kappa (pres. Phi Beta Kappa Associates, 1939-41, senator 1942-47), Phi Delta Phi, Order of Coif (hon., Geo. Washington U., 1938). Mem. Rep. Nat. Conv., 1936, 1940, 1944; chmn. Nat. Com. on Traffic Law Enforcement, 1938—. Mem. President's Highway Safety Conf., 1945—. Trustee Wesleyan U., 1934—(pres. bd. of trustees 1946-47); mem. council N.Y.U., 1948—; pres. N.Y.U. Inst. Jud. Adminstrn., 1952—, Law Center Found., 1948—; trustee Rutgers U., 1948—; chmn. Citizenship Clearing House, 1947—; trustee Nat. Foundation for Edn. and Nat. Foundation for Edn. in Am. Citizenship. Republican. Methodist. Clubs; University, N.Y. University Faculty (New York); Short Hills (Short Hills, New Jersey); Down Town (Newark). Author: Studying Law 1945; Men and Measures in the Law, 1949; Minimum Stanards of Judicial Administration, 1949; Cases and Other Materials on Modern Procedure and Judicial Administration, 1952; The Doctrine of the Separation of Powers—Its Present-Day Significance, 1952. Editor (with Carl McFarland) Cases and Materials on Administrative Law, 1947. Home: Hobart Av., Short Hills, N.J. Office: 744 Broad St., Newark. Died June 16, 1957.

VANDERBILT, O(liver) DeG(ray), business exec.; b. East Orange, N.J., Aug. 23, 1884; s. O. DeG. and Emily Augusta (West) V.; B.S., Princeton, 1906; m. Madelon Emma Weir, Feb. 17, 1912; children—Oliver DeGray, Barbara (Mrs. Peck), Lefreda (Mrs. Schenider). With Frank Presbrey & Co., N.Y. C., 1906-12; pres. Weir Frog Co., Cin., 1912-26, Camargo Bank of Madeira, 1926-50, Weir Kilby Corp., Cin., 1926—; chmn. bd. Taylor Wharton Iron & Steel Co., Cin., 1950-54; dir. Adams Express Co., 1912-15, First Nat. Bank of Norwood 1914—. Gen. chmn. Community Chest, Cin., also Hamilton Co., 1940, War Chest, 1943. Pres. Children's Home of Cincinnati Ohio and Hamilton County, 1937-53, chmn. bd., 1954—. Member Master of Foxhounds Assn. Am. (exec. com.). Episcopalian (sr. warden 1945-50). Clubs: Am. Foxhound (dir.); Princeton, Racquet and Tennis (N.Y.C.); Racquet (Phila.); Queen City, Camargo Comml. (Cin.); Ivy (Princeton, N.J.). Home: 7200 Drake Rd., Indian Hill, Cin. 43. Office: Taylor Wharton Iron & Steel Co., Norwood 12, O. Died Jan. 22, 1960.

VANDERBLUE, Homer Bews, economist; b. Hinsdale, Ill., Dec. 24, 1888; s. Frank J. and Mary (Bews) V.; A.B., Northwestern, 1911, A.M., 1912; Ph.D., Harvard, 1915; unmarried. Instr. economics, Harvard, 1914-15; asst. prof. transportation, 1915-16; asso. prof., 1916-20, prof., 1920-22, Northwestern U.; research dir. Denver Civic Commercial Assn., 1920-21; prof. business economics, Harvard U., 1922-29, also served as economist, Harvard U. com. on economic research, and dir. Harvard Economic Service; v.p. Tri-Continental Corp., 1929-37; cons. economist Gen. Motors Corp., 1938; curator Kress Library of Business and Economics, Harvard, 1938-39; prof. bus. economics and dean Sch. of Commerce, Northwestern U., 1939-49. Hon. curator of early econ. lit., Baker Library, Harvard University since 1936. Director of Minn., St.P. & S.S. Marie Railroad, since 1944. Student 1st O.T.C., Ft. Sheridan, Ill., 1917; hon. disch. as capt., Dec. 19, 1918. Chmn. Library Com. Coll. of William and Mary, 1936-42; mem. Com. on Economic Bibliography of the British Acad., 1937. Mem. Am. Econ. Assn., Business Hist. Soc., Econ. History Soc., American Branch of Newcomen Soc. of England, Sigma Nu. Clubs: Tavern (Chicago); Harvard (New York); University (Chicago and Evanston); Minneapolis. Author or co-author books relating to field. Contbr. to econ. and bus. publs. Home: 2629 Stewart Av., Evanston, Ill.; also Penwood Farm, Everett, Pa. Died July 12, 1952.

VANDERLIP, Kelvin Cox, land developer; b. Scarsborough, N.Y., Apr. 15, 1912; s. Frank Arthur and Narcissa (Cox) V.; student Scarborough Sch., 1919-29; B.S., Princeton, 1933; m. Elin Regine Brekke, Nov. 19, 1947; children—Kelvin Cox, Narcissa Cox. Real estate and investment bus. N.Y.C., 1933-41; U.S. govt. sr. housing specialist for So. Cal., So. Nev., Ariz., Los Angeles, 1941-44; pres., gen. mgr. Rancho Palos Verdes (12,000 acres), Los Angeles County, Cal., 1944—; pres. Palos Verdes Corp. Filiorum Corp., 1944-50, dir., 1944—; pres., dir. Rancho Mut. Water Co. 1944—; exec. v.p., dir. Reynolds Development Co. of Ore., Coos Bay, 1945—; dir. Los Molinos Land Co., Barker Bros. Corp., Scarborough Properties Corp. Vice pres., dir. Home Builders Inst. Los Angeles, 1948. Trustee Palos Verdes Coll., Chadwick Sch. Decorated Knight, Order of Orange Nassau. Netherlands, 1948. Served as chmn. Los Angeles Co., Queen Wilhelmina Fund and Am. Relief for Holland, 1942-49. Mem. bd. mgrs. Army-Navy Y.M. C.A.; Residential Research Com. Los Angeles, 1942—, chmn., 1948-49. Mem. Nat. Assn. Real Estate Bds., Los Angeles Real Estate Bds., Cal. Real Estate Assn., Nat. Inst. Real Estate Brokers, Los Angeles C. of C., San Pedro C. of C., Home Builders Inst. Los Angeles (dir., v.p. 1948). Republican. Clubs: Lawyers (New York City); California, Los Angeles Yacht (Los Angeles); Colonial (Princeton, N.J.); Portuguese Bend (Palos Verdes) (pres. 1948—). Home: Portuguese Bend, Palos Verdes Estates. Office: Rolling Hills, Cal. Died Aug. 21, 1956.

VANDERPLOEG, Watson H. (văn'dėr-plōō), pres. Kellogg Co.; b. Marion County, Ia., Dec. 24, 1888; s. Ruard and Pietje (Terpstra) V.; student Central Acad., Pella, Ia., 1903-06; m. Eva Van Houweling, June 1, 1910; children—Florence, Ruard. Began as bank clerk, 1906; cashier Farmers & Merchants Bank and Farmers Nat. Bank, Pella, 1912-24; mem. Iowa State Banking Dept., Des Moines, 1925-30; pres. Washington Park Nat. Bank, Chicago, Ill., Jan.-June 1931; v.p. Harris Trust & Savings Bank, Chicago, 1931-39; exec. v.p. Kellogg Co., Battle Creek, Mich.,

1939, pres., 1939—; chmn. bd. Detroit br. Fed. Res. Bank of Chgo.; dir. Bankers Life Co. (Des Moines, Ia.). Chmn. R.R. Consolidation Bd., Battle Creek. Trustee W. K. Kellogg Found. Republican. Baptist. Mason. Clubs: Chicago (Ill.); Battle Creek Saddle and Hunt, Gull Lake Country. Home: Augusta, Mich. Office: Porter and Stiles Sts., Battle Creek, Mich. Died Mar. 28, 1957; buried Lakeview Cemetery, Yorkville, Mich.

VANDERPOEL, Robert P. (văn'dēr-pōōl), financial columnist Chicago Sun-Times; born Chicago, January 10, 1894; s. John and Henrietta (Van Vlissingen) V.; Ph.B., U. of Chicago, 1916; m. Helen M. Waid, June 4, 1921; children—Waid Richard, Robert P., Jr. Instr. economics and English, Ashtabula Harbor (O.) High School, 1916-17; reporter Chicago Journal, 1917-18; with Am. Red Cross, 1918-19; financial editor Chicago Daily Journal, 1920-29; financial editor and columnist Chicago Evening American, 1929-39, Chicago Herald-American, 1939-50; corp. consultant on finance and economics; consultant U.S. Treasury Dept., Washington, 1942-45. First lt. Am. Red Cross, later with League of Red Cross Socs., World War I. Fellow American Inst. of Management. Member of Economic Club of Chicago, Merchants & Manufactures Club, U. of Chicago Alumni. Contbr. to financial and trade mags. Home: 5844 N.W. Circle Av., Norwood Park, Chicago (31). Office: Chicago Sun-Times, 211 W. Wacker Dr., Chgo. Died Jan. 20, 1955.

VAN DEVENTER, John Herbert (văn'dē-vĕn-tēr), engr., editor; b. Paramus, N.J., Apr. 24, 1881; s. Rev. John Cornelius and Eliza Jane (King) Van D.; M.E., Sibley Coll. (Cornell), 1903; m. Isabelle M. Stone, Feb. 23, 1905; children—John Herbert, Mrs. Helen Law, Mrs. Mary Sweeney, Henry Cornelius, George Mather, Mrs. Jane Godley, Mrs. June Rickard, Peter, Arthur. Supt. prodn., cost manager Goulds Mfg. Co., Seneca Falls, N.Y., 1905-07; gen. supt., factory mgr. Buffalo Forge Co., 1907-14; asso. editor Am. Machinist, 1915, editor in chief, 1917-20; editor Indsl. Management, The Engring. Mag., Industry Illustrated, 1921-26; pres. Engring. Mag. Co., N.Y.C., 1921-26; cons. editor McGraw-Hill Pub. Co., 1927-28; editor The Iron Age, 1930-46, pres., editorial dir., 1939-46; v.p. Chilton Co. until Nov. 1946; dir. information Com. for Econ. Development, 1947-49, trustee, 1945-54. Chmn. bus. papers industry, 1943-46; ret. 1950. Called to Washington, Sept. 1917, to assist in organizing Ordnance Dept.; maj., U.S. Army, 1917-18. Organized Army Ordnance Assn., 1919; chmn. N.Y. Bus. Pubs. Assn., 1923-24, pres., 1924-25. Guest of Brit. govt. on tour of United Kingdom war plants, 1944. Republican. Roman Catholic. Presented paper on Mass Prodn. at World Engring. Congress, Tokyo, Japan, 1929. Home: R.F.D., Brewster, N.Y. Died Mar. 5, 1956.

VANDEVENTER, William Luther, lawyer; b. Garrison, Mo., May 16, 1889; s. Daniel Oliver and Annie Elizabeth (Cummings) V.; LL.B., Benton Coll. of Law, St. Louis, 1915, LL.M., 1916; m. Cora Casey, Mar. 1, 1911; children—Lancey Wilber, Mildred Joyce; married second, Elizabeth Randall, September 19, 1925. Admitted to Missouri bar, 1915, and began practice at Ozark; pros. atty. Christian County, Mo., 1917-20; asst. atty. gen. of Mo., 1924-25; asst. U.S. dist. atty. Western Dist. of Mo., 1926-29, U.S. atty. same, 1929-34. Mem. Mo. Ho. of Reps., 1921-22. Apptd. judge Springfield Court of Appeals, 1944, elected judge, same court, for 12-year term, 1946. Mem. Am. Mo. and Greene Co. bar assns. Republican. Mason. Co-author: (with Robert W. Otto) Instructions to Juries in Criminal Cases, Indictments and Informations in Missouri Felonies, 1925. Home: 823 University Av., Springfield, Mo. Office: Woodruff Bldg., Springfield, Mo. Died Nov. 1953.

van DIEST, Edmond Cornelis (vān-dēst'), cons. engr.; b. Buitenzorg, Java, Aug. 13, 1865; s. Pieter Hendrik and Josine (Gude) van D.; came to U.S., 1871, naturalized, 1888; E.M., Colo. State Sch. Mines, 1886; hon. Dr. Mining Engring., 1936; m. Anna Louise Meyer, May 4, 1890; children—Alice Elfrieda, Annette Josine (Mrs. Ralph E. Weldie), Eloise Margaret (Mrs. David M. Skilling, Jr.). Engr. charge Monument Valley Park and Glen Eyrie, Colo., 1903-19; mgr. Costilla Estates, 1886-1906; pres. Western Pub. Service Co., 1909-26, Gen. Service Corp., 1927—; pres. Rito Seco Gold Mines Co., Colo. Concrete Co., Hygienic Service Co. Mem. Bus. Adv. Planning Council for Dept. Commerce until July 1936; trustee Colo. Coll. Mem. Am. Inst. Mining and Metall. Engrs., Colo. Engrs. Soc., Alpha Kappa Psi. Republican. Episcopalian. Elk. Club: El Paso. Home: 1730 N. Cascade Av. Office: Mining Exchange Bldg., Colorado Springs, Colo. Died Aug. 1, 1950; buried Evergreen Cemetery, Colorado Springs.

VANDIVER, J. S., educator. State supt. edn., Miss., until 1945; pres. Chamberlain-Hunt Acad., Port Gibson, Miss., 1945-50. Address: Port Gibson, Miss. Died Feb. 28, 1950; buried Baldwyn, Miss.

VAN DOREN, Carl (văn'dō'rĕn), editor, author; b. Hope, Ill., Sept. 10, 1885; s. Charles Lucius and Dora Anne (Butz) Van D.; A.B., U. Ill., 1907; Ph.D., Columbia, 1911, Litt.D., 1940; L.H.D., U. Pa., 1940; m. Irita Bradford, 1912; children—Anne (Mrs. Jerome Davis Ross), Margaret (Mrs. Tom Torre Bevans), Barbara (Mrs. Spencer A. Klaw); m. 2d, Jean Wright, 1939 (died 1945). Asst. in rhetoric U., Ill., 1907-08; instr. English, Columbia, 1911-14, asst. prof., 1914-16, asso. in English, 1916-30; headmaster The Brearley Sch., N.Y., 1916-19; lit. editor The Nation, 1919-22, The Century Mag., 1922-25; editor The Literary Guild, 1926-34; chmn. Readers Club, 1941-44; editor The Living Library, 1946—. Mem. com. on mgmt. Dictionary Am. Biography, 1926-36. Author: The Life of Thomas Love Peacock, 1911; The American Novel, 1921, rev. edit., 1940; Contemporary American Novelists, 1922; The Roving Critic, 1923; Many Minds, 1924; James Branch Cabell, 1925, rev. edit., 1932; Other Provinces, 1925; (with Mark Van Doren) American and British Literature since 1890, 1925, rev. edit., 1939; The Ninth Wave, 1926; Swift, 1930; Sinclair Lewis, 1933; American Literature—An Introduction, 1933 (reissued as What Is American Literature?, 1935); Three Worlds, 1936; Benjamin Franklin, 1938 (Pulitzer prize for biography, 1939; Franklin medal from Am. Philosophical Soc., 1943), Secret History of the American Revolution, 1941; Mutiny in January, 1943; Portable Library Carl Van Doren (selected writings), 1945; (with Carl Carmer) American Scriptures, 1946; The Great Rehearsal, 1948; Jane Mecom, the Favorite Sister of Benjamin Franklin, 1950. Editor Modern Am. Prose, 1934; An Anthology of World Prose, 1935; The Borzoi Reader, 1936; Benjamin Franklin's Autobiographical Writings, 1945; Letters and Papers of Benjamin Franklin and Richard Jackson, 1947; The Portable Swift, 1948; The Letters of Benjamin Franklin and Jane Mecom, 1950. Translator: Hebbel's Judith, 1914. Mng. editor Cambridge History of American Literature, 1917-21; A Short History of American Literature, 1922. Address: 41 Central Park W., N.Y.C. 23. Died July 18, 1950.

VAN DOREN, Harold Livingston, industrial designer; b. Chicago, Ill., Mar. 2, 1895; s. Charles Luther and Harriet (Clark) Van D.; ed. Williams Coll., 1913-17 (A.B., 1917), Art Students League, New York, 1920-21, Académie de la Grande Chaumière, Paris, 1922-24, Ecole du Louvre, Paris, 1922-23; also private art teachers; m. Mary Huggins, Apr. 15, 1933; 1 dau., Patricia. Art editor Survey Graphic, New York, 1919-20, field service fellowship in history of art, and lecturer Musée du Louvre, Paris, 1921-22; writer for mags., 1924-27; asst. dir. Minneapolis Inst. of Arts, 1927-30; industrial designer, 1930—. Member bd. govs. Phila. Mus. Sch. Art. Served as 1st lieut. Ambulance Service, U.S. Army, 1917-1919. Decorated Croce di Guerra (Italy). Awarded 1st in commercial and industrial class, Nat. Alliance Art and Industry, 1932; 1st in commercial class, Modern Plastics competition, 1936; Lord & Taylor's Am. Design award Philco refrigerator, 1941. Fellow Royal Soc. Arts Eng., Am. Soc. Indsl. Designers (v.p. 1946-47, pres. 1949-50, member bd. of governors 1950—); member of the Phi Beta Kappa and Chi Psi. Author: Industrial Design—A Practical Guide, 1940, rev. 1954. Translator: Cézanne—His Life and Art (from the French by A. Vollard), 1923; Renoir—An Intimate Record (from the French by A. Vollard, R. T. Weaver, co-translator), 1925. Contbr. Saturday Evening Post, House and Garden, The Arts, Encyclopedia Americana Annual, and many tech. and trade publs. Home: Crosby Brown Road, Gladwyne, Pa. Office: 1717 Sansom St., Phila. 3. Died Feb. 3, 1957.

van DRUTEN, John William (văn-drōō'tĕn), author; b. London, Eng., June 1, 1901; s. Wilhelmus and Eve van D.; student Univ. Coll. Sch., London, 1911-17; LL.B., U. of London, 1923; unmarried. Spl. lecturer English Law, Univ. Coll. of Wales, Aberystwyth, 1923-26. Author: (plays), Young Woodley, 1925; Diversion, 1927; After All, 1930; London Wall, 1931; There's Always Juliet, 1931; Behold, We Live, 1931; Somebody Knows, 1932; The Distaff Side, 1933; Most of the Game, 1935; Flowers of the Forest, 1935; Gertie Maude, 1937; Leave Her to Heaven, 1940; Old Acquaintance, 1940; The Voice of the Turtle, 1943, I Remember Mama (from Kathryn Forbes' book) 1944, The Mermaids Singing, 1945; The Druid Circle, 1947; Hollywood Holiday (with B. W. Levy), 1931; The Damask Cheek (with Lloyd Morris), 1942; Make Way for Lucid (adapted from E. P. Benson), 1948; Bell, Book and Candle, 1950; I Am a Camera (adapted from Berlin Stories by Christopher Isherwood) directed the King and I, 1951; (novels) Young Woodley; A Woman on Her Way; And Then You Wish; (autobiography) The Way to the Present; I've Got Sixpence, (a play), 1952; Playwright at Work, (a text), 1953; Dancing in the Chequered Shade, 1955; The Vicarious Years (novel), 1956; Anatomy of Murder, adapted novel of Robert Traver, 1957. Home: A J. C. Ranch, Thermal, Cal. Office: care Monica McCall, 457 Madison Av., N.Y.C. Died Dec. 19, 1957; buried Coachella Valley Cemetery nr. Indio, Cal.

VAN DUSEN, Charles B(elden) (văn-dōō'sĕn); b. Detroit, Jan. 28, 1871; s. Charles Theron and Jessie (Mackay) Van D; ed. grammar schs., Detroit; M.S. Coll. City of Detroit (now Wayne U.); m. Minnie Thornton Buick, July 1, 1895; children—David Lowry, Charles Theron, Bruce Buick (dec.), William Douglas. Newsboy, telegraph messenger, wholesale dry goods business, 20 yrs.; with S. S. Kresge Co. from 1905, pres., 1925-38, co. operating stores in over 100 cities in U.S. Republican. Presbyn. Mason (33°, K.T., Shriner). Clubs: Detroit Athletic, Players, Detroit Boat, Detroit, Bloomfield Hills Country. Home: 1830 Baltimore Dr., Detroit 3. Died Aug. 16, 1958; buried Woodlawn Cemetery, Detroit.

VAN DYCK, Ernest-Marie Hubert, opera singer; b. Antwerp, Belgium, April 2, 1861; ed. Coll. Jesuits, Antwerp, Univs. of Louvain and Brussels; m. Augusta Servais, 1886. Has sung several yrs. at the Wagner Bayreuth performances; also at Imperial Opera House, Vienna. Created Lohengrin, Tannhauser and Walkure (Siegmund), in Paris; sung several seasons at Covent Garden, London, and in U. S. Knight Order of Leopold; mem. Legion of Honor of France, etc. Address: Chateau de Berlaer nr. Lierre, Belgium. Died Aug. 31, 1923.

VAN DYKE, Tertius, clergyman; born at New York, N.Y., Jan. 18, 1886; son of Henry and Ellen (Reid) van D.; B.A., Princeton U., 1908 (Phi Beta Kappa); B.A., Magdalen Coll. (Oxford U.), 1910, M.A., 1917; B.D., Union Theol. Sem., 1913; D.D. Princeton U., 1948; m. Mary Elizabeth Cannon, Nov. 15, 1924; children—Dorothea Atherton (Mrs. Frederic Maccabe, Jr.), Henry, Paul Cannon. Ordained Presbyn. ministry, 1913; pastor Spring St. Ch., N.Y., 1913-16; sec. to father, Am. minister at The Hague, Feb.-May 1915 and Nov. 16-May 1917; pastor Park Av. Ch., New York, 1918-26, Congl. Ch., Washington, Conn., 1926-35; headmaster Gunnery School, Washington, Conn., 1936-42; acting dir. Bureau Student Aid, Princeton, 1942-43; dean Hartford (Conn.) Theological Seminary, 1943-54, emeritus, 1954—; interim pastor Congregational Ch., Washington, Connecticut, 1955, active pastor emeritus, 1956—. Member of the Board Foreign Missions Presbyn. Ch. U.S.A., 1923-26; dir. Am. Waldensian Aid Soc., 1922—; trustee of Hartford Sem. Foundation, 1928-43, Berkshire Sch., Sheffield, Mass., 1952—; pres. Me. Sea Coast Missionary Soc., 1947—. Member S.R. Democrat. Clubs: Princeton, Century. Author: Songs of Seeking and Finding, 1920; Light My Candle (with father), 1926; Henry van Dyke (a biography), 1935; also, with father, "The Guidepost" (syndicated newspaper articles), 1924-26. Contbr. articles and verse. Home: Washington, Conn. Died Feb. 28, 1958.

Van DYKE, William Duncan, Jr., corp. exec.; b. Milw., Dec. 13, 1893; s. William Duncan and Gertrude H. (Goodrich) Van D.; grad. The Hill Sch., 1913; A.B., Princeton, 1917; m. Helen Bagley Buttrick, June 9, 1923; children—Helen Bemis (Mrs. Paul V. Godfrey), Olive Bagley (Mrs. Thomas F. Scannell, Jr.), William Duncan III. Pres., dir. Mineral Mining Co., Milw., 1938—; trustee, mem. finance and exec. coms. Northwestern Mut. Life Ins. Co.; dir., mem. finance com. Marine Nat. Exchange Bank, Northwestern Nat. Ins. Co.; dir. Western Lime & Cement Co. Served as capt., F.A., U.S. Army, World War I. Mem. Am. Inst. Mining and Metall. Engrs., Am. Legion. Presbyn. (trustee). Republican. Clubs: University, Milwaukee Country, Milwaukee, Beach (Milw.). Home: 7272 N. Bridge Lane, Fox Point, Milwaukee County, Wis. Office: Wells Bldg., Milw. 2. Died Apr. 29, 1959.

VAN ES, Leunis, animal pathologist; b. Melissant, Netherlands, Oct. 3, 1868; s. Jacob and Maatje (Zaayer) Van E.; grad. Govt. Sch. of Agr., Wageningen, Netherlands, 1886; Vet. Surgeon, Ont. (Can.) Vet. Coll., 1893; M.D., Med. Coll. Ala., 1898; Sc. D., U. Pa., 1935; m. Alice E. Wilson, July 11, 1894; children—Jacob, Maatje (wife of Dr. W. C. Zulauf), Marie (Mrs. Charles Rumbolz). Came to U.S., 1889, naturalized citizen, 1899. In practice of vet. surgery, 1893-1903; demonstrator in bacteriology and microscopic anatomy, Med. Coll. Ala., 1898-1903; prof. vet. science, N.D. Agrl. Coll., 1903-18; also chief state veterinarian, N.D., 1903-07, dir. N.D. Serum Inst., 1909-18, and acting dir. N.D. Agrl. Expt. Sta., 1918; prof. animal pathology and hygiene, U. Neb., since 1918. Mem. Am. Vet. Med. Assn., A.A.A.S, U.S. Live Stock Sanitary Assn. (pres. 1927), Nat. Assn. Study and Preventive of Tuberculosis, Am. Pub. Health Assn., Soc. Netherlands' Scholars in N. America, Conf. of Research Workers in Animal Diseases of N. America. Sigma Xi, Gamma Sigma Delta, Alpha Zeta, Phi Zeta. Author: Principles of Animal Hygiene and Preventive Veterinary Medicine, 1932. Contbr. many articles on animal diseases and rural hygiene to agrl. jours. expt. sta. publs., etc. Address: 3335 W Street, Lincoln, Neb. Died 1956.

VAN ETTEN, Nathan Bristol, M.D.; b. Waverly, N.Y., June 22, 1866; s. Solomon and Maria (Bristol) Van E.; M.D., Bellevue Hosp. Med. Coll., 1890; m. Josephine Swinton, of Port Jervis, N.Y., May, 1893 (died 1912); children—John Swinton, Eleanor Swinton, Katherine Swinton; m. 2d, Elizabeth Read, July, 1918 (died 1939). Practiced in N.Y. City, 1890—; cons. phys. Morrisania City Hosp., Bronx Eye and

Ear Infirmary; visiting phys. Union Hosp., 1906—, became v.p., 1919, pres., 1936. Fellow Am. Coll. of Physicians, New York Acad. of Medicine; mem. Am. Med. Assn. (speaker, 1936; pres., 1940), Med. Soc. of State of N.Y. (past pres. and trustee), Greater New York Med. Assn. (past pres.), Bronx Co. Med. Soc. (past pres.), Bronx Borough Med. Soc. (past pres.), New York Soc. Med. Jurisprudence (past pres.), Med. Alumni New York U. (past pres.), Holland Soc., Kappa Alpha, Phi Alpha Sigma. Republican. Presbyn. Home: 300 E. Tremont Av., N.Y.C. Died July 23, 1954.

VAN ETTISCH, Raymond Treder (văn-ĕt'ĭsh), newspaper editor; b. La Junta, Colo., June 21, 1886; s. Oscar and Lena (Treder) Van E.; ed. pub. and pvt. schs., Denver and Pueblo, Colo.; m. Elsie Kirkpatrick, Mar. 3, 1929; children—Dorothy Mildred, Rae. Began as reporter Pueblo Chieftain, 1903, state editor, 1904; asst. city editor Rocky Mountain News, Denver, 1905-06; news editor Grand Junction (Colo.) Daily News, 1907-08; corr. Associated Press, 1907-08; city editor Los Angeles (Calif.) Examiner, 1908-18, day mng. editor, 1919-30; mng. editor Seattle (Wash.) Post-Intelligencer, May 1, 1930-June 1, 1933; day mng. editor Los Angeles Examiner, June 1-Sept. 1, 1933, editor and mng. editor, 1933-50, ret., 1950. Served as 1st lt. Chem. Warfare Service, U.S. Army, 1918. Nat. vice comdr. Chem. Warfare Vets. Assn. of U.S. Mem. Am. Soc. Newspaper Editors, Soc. Am. Mil. Engrs., U.S. Infantry Assn., Am. Numismatic Assn., Propeller Club of U.S., Am. Legion, Sigma Delta Chi. Clubs: Los Angeles Athletic, Pacific Coast. Episcopalian. Home: 1609 Bayside Dr., Corona-del Mar, Cal. Died Oct. 24, 1951; buried Forest Lawn Meml. Park, Glendale, Cal.

VAN FLEET, Frederick Alvin, pub. relations counsel; b. Cambria Mills, Mich., June 12, 1874; s. James Alvin and Fanny Marthesia (Lyon) Van F.; grad. pub. high sch. Springfield, Ill., 1890; m. Kathryn Cameron Norrie, Sept. 1, 1900 (died Oct. 1937); 1 son, Frederick McKay (dec.). Printer, 1890-94; reporter Detroit Tribune, 1894-1900, Detroit Jour., 1902-03; mgr. yachting mag., 1904-07; asst. city editor, Detroit Jour., 1908-09; sec. to mayor of Detroit, Phil Breitmeyer, 1910-11; mgr., Wolverine Motor Supply Co., 1912-15; financial editor, Detroit Times, 1915-16; editor, State Journal, Lansing, 1916-25; advt. mgr., Peerless Motor Car Co., 1925-28; public relations counsel since 1928; pres. Advertising Associates, Inc. Mem. Society Mayflower Descendants (head Cleveland orgn. 5 yrs., O. orgn. 2½ yrs.; nat. governor gen., 1942-48; has emphasized Mayflower Compact as beginning and fundamental foundation of Am. dem. govt.). Republican. Presbyterian. Mason. Home: Cleveland Athletic Club. Office: Union Commerce Bldg., Cleve. Died June 25, 1952; buried Evergreen Cemetery, Detroit.

van GELDER, Robert, writer, editor; b. Baltimore, Md., Oct. 19, 1904; s. Peter and Alice LeMaitre (Harlan) van G.; grad., Columbia U. Sch. of Journalism, 1928; m. Dorothy Scarborough Lampe, Aug. 1, 1935; 1 stepson, John Lampe. Reporter, New Haven (Conn.) Times-Leader, 1921-22; New Haven Register, 1922-23; copywriter, Wilson H. Lee Advt. Co., 1923-24; reporter, New Haven Jour.-Courier, 1924-26; became reporter, New York Times, 1928, editor, The N.Y. Times Book Review, 1943-46. Democrat. Club: P.E.N. Author: Front Page Story, 1937; Smash Picture, 1938; Marjorie Fleming, 1939; The Enemy in the House, 1940; Writing and Writers, 1945 (includes interviews with many famous contemporary authors); (novel) Important People, 1948. Editor for Crown Publishers. Home: 399 Park Av. Office: 419 4th Av., N.Y.C. Died Apr. 3, 1952.

VAN HOOK, La Rue, prof. Greek; b. Illiopolis, Ill., Jan. 20, 1877; s. William Russell and Matilda (Weller) Van H.; A.B., U. Mich., 1899; Ph.D., U. Chgo., 1904; student Am. Sch. Classical Studies, Athens, Greece, U. Halle, Germany; m. Edith vom Baur, June 14, 1910; children—Katrina, Elise. Acting prof. Greek, U. Colo., 1902-03; instr. Greek and Latin, Bradley Inst., Peoria, Ill., 1904, Washington U., St. Louis, 1905; preceptor in classics, Princeton, 1905-10; asso. prof. Greek and Latin, Barnard Coll., 1910-20, prof., 1920-30; ann. prof. Am. Sch. Classical Studies, Athens, Greece, 1930-31, also sec. mng. Com., 1938-45; Jay prof. Greek, Columbia, 1931-42; emeritus prof., 1942—; spl. lectr., 1942-45; mem. Agora Comm. charge of excavation of ancient market place in Athens, 1931-39. Fellow Am. Acad. of Arts and Scis.; mem. Am. Philo. Assn., Am. Archaeol. Inst., British Classical Assn., Phi Beta Kappa. Club: Century. Author: Greek Life and Thought—A Portrayal of Ancient Greek Civilization, 1924. Isocrates, Vol. 3 (Loeb Classical Library), 1945. Contbr. various publs. field of classics. Home: 39 Claremont Av., N.Y.C. 27. Died 1951.

VAN HOOSEN, Bertha (văn-hōō'sĕn), surgeon; b. Rochester, Mich., Mar. 26, 1863; d. Joshua and Sarah Ann (Taylor) Van Hoosen, B.A, U of Mich, 1884, M.D., 1888, hon. M.A., 1910; LL.D., Loyola, 1929. Began practice at Chicago, 1892; attending gynecologist Provident Hosp., 1895-1929, Woman's Hosp, 1900-07, Mary Thompson Hosp., 1911-19, Cook County Hosp., 1913-20, Frances E. Willard Hosp., 1919-27; attending obstetrician Cook County Hosp., 1920-26; cons. obstetrician Oak Park Hosp., 1919-29; prof. gynecology and embryology, Woman's Med. Coll., Northwestern U., 1894-1902; prof. clin. gynecology, U. of Ill. Med. Sch., 1902-12; prof. and head Dept. Obstetrics, Loyola University Medical School, 1919-37, professor emeritus since 1937; consultant to Women and Children's Hospital, Lewis Memorial Hospital. Asst. editor Narcotic Review. Fellow A.C.S., Internat. Coll. Surgeons; mem. A.M.A., Ill. State, Chgo. med. scos., Asso. Anesthetists of U.S. and Can., Ill. Acad. Science, Chicago Pathol. Soc., Med. Woman's Nat. Assn., Med. Women's Internat. Assn., D.A.R. Clubs: Chicago Woman's, Women's City, Business and Professional Women's, Author: Petticoat Surgeon. Address: 1005 Romeo Rd., Rochester, Mich. Died June 7, 1952; buried Stoney Creek Cemetery-Avon Township, Oakland County, Mich.

VAN HORN, Francis Joseph, clergyman; b. Northfield, O., Oct. 18, 1865; s. Milton Andrew and Harriet (Thompson) Van H.; A.B., Oberlin (O.) Coll., 1890; B.D., Oberlin Theol. Sem., 1893; D.D. Berea Coll., 1902; m. Amy Belle Richards, June 23, 1892; children—Robert Bowman, Gladys (Mrs. F. C. Arnold) (deceased), Francis Dane, Faith (Mrs. G. L. Knox), Paul Beverly, Theodora (Mrs. Harold Jenkins), Amy (Mrs. Franklin Metz), Richard Milton, Philip Roland; m. 2d, Lois C. Nelson, 1934. Ordained to the Congl. ministry, 1893; pastor Columbia Ch., Cin., 1893-95, Dane St. Church, Beverly, Mass., 1895-99, lymouth Ch., Des Moines, Ia., 1899-1902, 1895-99, Plymouth Ch., Des Moines, Ia., 1899-1902, Old South Ch., Worcester, Mass., 1902-06, Plymouth Ch., Seattle, 1906-14, 1st Ch., Oakland, Cal., 1914-22, 1st Ch., Tacoma, Wash., Nov. 1922-29, again pastor 1st Ch., Oakland, 1929-33; acting pastor Old South Ch., Worcester, 1933, 1st Congl. Ch., Los Angeles, 1934, Pilgrim Ch., Pomona, Cal , 1936, Plymouth Congl. Ch., Seattle, 1936, 1st Congl. Ch., Glendale, Cal., 1937-38, Plymouth Congl. Church, Oakland, Cal., 1939-40, First Congl. Church, San Diego, Cal., 1940, First Congl. Ch., Tacoma, Wash., 1941, Plymouth Congl. Ch., Seattle, 1941, Pilgrim Congl. Ch., Seattle, 1942, First Congl. Ch., Everett, Wash., 1943, Pilgrim Congl. Ch., Pomona, Cal., 1945. Trustee Pacific Sch. of Religion. Mem. Nat. Council Congl. Chs. Home: 503 W. Crockett St., Seattle, Wash. Died Jan. 20, 1949.

VAN HORNE, John, prof. Spanish and Italian; b. Brooklyn, N.Y., Mar. 14, 1889; s. John Douglass and Mary Van H.; A.B., U. of Va., 1908; A.M., Harvard U., 1909, Ph.D., 1913; m. Margaret Varney, Sept. 15, 1915; 1 dau., Margaret (Mrs. David Oswell Walter). Master, Baylor U. Sch., Chattanooga, Tenn., 1909-10; teacher of Spanish, German and Latin, Jefferson Sch. for Boys, Charlottesville, Va., 1912-13; teacher of Spanish, French, German and Latin, Riverview Acad., Poughkeepsie, N.Y., 1913-14; instr. in Romance langs., State U. of Ia., 1914-17; instr. Romance langs., U. of Ill., 1917-19, asso., 1919-20, asst. prof., 1920-27, asso. prof., 1927-34, prof. of Romance langs., 1934-39; prof. of Spanish and Italian and head of dept., 1939—. Cultural relations attaché Am. Embassy, Madrid, Spain, 1943-46. Decorated Cavaliere della corona d'Italia. Diploma of Honor Mexican Acad. Corresponding mem. Hispanic Soc. Am.; mem. Modern Lang. Assn. America (mem. exec. council, 1938-41), Am. Assn. Teachers of Italian, Am. Assn. Teachers of Spanish. Club: University (Urbana). Author: Elementary Spanish Grammar (with Arthur Hamilton), 1925; El Bernardo of Bernardo de Balbuena, 1927; La Grandeza Mexicana de Bernardo de Balbuena, 1930; Amici di Scuola (with V. Cioffari), 1938; Raccontini (with V. Cioffari), 1940; Bernardo de Balbuena. Estudio biográfico y crítico, 1940. Editor: Tres Comedias of Benavente, 1917; Short Stories of Antonio de Trueba, 1921; Il Risorgimento, 1924; Zaragoza by Benito Pérez Galdós, 1923; Scènes de la vie de Bohème by Murger, 1929. Editor of Italica, 1933-42; editor of Heath-Chicago Italian series since 1937. Contbr. to professional jours. Home: 713 W. Pennsylvania Av., Urbana, Ill. Died June 21, 1959.

van HOUTEN, Jan; dir. Am. Crystal Sugar Co., Denver Nat. Bank, Nev.-Cal. Electric Corp. Address: 2605 S. Sheridan Rd., Denver 10. Died Mar. 8, 1949; cremated.

VANIMAN, Roy Lawrence, sales exec.; b. Girard, Ill., Dec. 12, 1889; s. Daniel B. and Emma (Snell) V.; B.S., U. of Ill., 1912; m. Helen Francis, Nov. 14, 1914; 1 dau., Elizabeth. Cons. engr. Hudson Bay Co. and Can. Pacific R.R., Vancouver, B.C., 1914-15; pres. and dir., Produce Terminal Corp., Chicago, 1915-19; gen. mgr. F. W. Russum Co., Detroit, 1919-23; asst. to pres., Chrysler Export Corp., 1929-33; dir. and gen. mgr., Chrysler Motors, Ltd. and Dodge Bros., Ltd., London, Eng., 1933-35; spl. asst. chmn. bd. Chrysler Export Corp., Detroit, 1935-39; exec. mgr. African div., Johannesburg, 1939-41; dir. automotive div., W.P.B., Washington, 1942-43; v.p. Fruehauf Trailer Co., N.Y.C., 1944-53; pres. Vaniman Internat. Services, Inc. since 1953. Mem. Tau Beta Pi, Sigma Xi. Address: 6 Great Oak Rd., Manhasset, L.I., N.Y. Died Feb. 18, 1956.

VAN INGEN, Philip (văn ĭng'gĕn), physician; b. Washington, Conn., July 31, 1875; s. E. H. and Mary L. (McLane) Van I.; A.B., Yale, 1897; M.D., Coll. Physicians and Surgeons, Columbia, 1901; unmarried. House physician, Presbyn. Hosp., N.Y.C., 1903, N.Y. Foundling Hosp., 1904; attending cons. (pediatrics), Roosevelt Hosp., 1938—; cons. physician Willard Parker Hosp., 1921—; prof. clin. pediatrics, Columbia, 1921-30. Served as lt. col. Med. Dept., U.S. Army, World War; A.E.F., 1918-19. Fellow N.Y. Acad. Medicine, Am. Pub. Health Assn., Am. Acad. Pediatrics (former pres.); mem. A.M.A., Am. Pediatric Soc. (former pres., Am. Child Hygiene Assn. (ex-gov.), Phila. Pediatric Soc. (hon.). Home: 157 E. 72d St., N.Y.C. Died Mar. 28, 1953.

VAN INGEN, W(illiam) B(rantley), mural painter; b. Phila., 1858; s. William Henry and Sarah (Fairlamb) Van I.; studied under Christian Schuessele and Thomas Eakins, Pa. Acad. Fine Arts; John La Farge, Francis Lathrop and Louis C. Tiffany, N.Y.; Leon Bonnât, Paris, France; m. Bertha Sequard, 1915. Panels in the Congl. Library, Washington; U.S. Mint, Phila.; State Capitol, Harrisburg, Pa.; State Capitol, Trenton, N.J.; U.S. Court House and Postoffice, Indpls. and Chgo.; series of mural decorations, U.S. Govt. Adminstrn. Bldg., Panama, C.Z., N.Y. State Coll. Tchrs., Albany, N.Y., etc. Commd. by late Charles T. Yerkes to make Japanese room for his N.Y. residence, visited Japan and made extensive studies in Japanese art. Mem. Fellowship Pa. Acad. Fine Arts, Phila., Archtl. League (N.Y.), Soc. Mural Painters, Artists' Aid Soc., Artists' Fund Soc. Lectr. on art and landscape architecture. Home: 330 E. 19th St., N.Y.C. Died Feb. 6, 1955.

Van KIRK, Lawrence E(dward), dentist, univ. dean; b. Freeport, Pa., May 6, 1895; s. Thomas Campbell and Ariadne (Hathaway) V.; A.B., Washington and Jefferson Coll., 1916; D.D.S., U. of Pittsburgh, 1919, M.S., 1931; m. Virginia Reams, Oct. 20, 1924; children—Virginia H. Hilborn, Lawrence Edward. Pvt. practice of dentistry, Pittsburgh, 1919-47; instr. Sch. of Dentistry, U. of Pittsburgh, 1919-42, dean since 1947; organized dental dept. Presbyn. Hosp., Pittsburgh, 1920; staff mem. Presbyn. and Women's hosps., since 1920. Mem. Pittsburgh Bd. of Edn., 1947; pres. Pittsburgh Council Intercultural Edn., 1947. Dir. Fedn. Social Agencies, Pittsburgh, 1945-48, Pittsburgh Y.M.C.A. (past pres.), Child Guidance Center, Am. Service Inst. of Pittsburgh. Fellow Am. Coll. Dentists; mem. Odontological Soc. of Western Pa. (dir.; pres. 1946), Pa. Dental Soc., Am. Dental Assn., Pittsburgh Acad. Dentistry, A.A.A.S., International Association for Dental Research, National Research Council (committee on dentistry), Phi Beta Kappa, Sigma Xi, Phi Delta Theta, Psi Omega, Omicron Kappa Upsilon, Omicron Delta Kappa. Baptist. Mason. Clubs: Kiwanis, University (Pittsburgh); Rotary. Contbr. articles on dental edn. and sci. to dental publs. Home: 3 Bayard Rd., Pitts. 13. Died Aug. 26, 1953; buried Uniondale Cemetery, Pitts.

VAN KIRK, Walter William, clergyman; b. Cleveland, O., Nov. 11, 1891; s. Henry Elson and Kittie (Cochran) Van K.; grad. Doane Acad., Granville, O., 1913; A.B., Ohio Wesleyan U., 1917, D.D., 1934; S.T.B., Boston University School of Theology, 1920; LL.D., Dennison University, 1946; honorary Doctor of Humanities, Catawba Coll., 1948; married Gladdys Evelyn Stuber, May 13, 1918; 1 daughter, Marcia. Ordained ministry M.E. Ch., 1919; pastor Parkman St. Ch., Dorchester, Mass., 1919, Needham Heights, 1920-22, Lynn, 1922-25; secretary Dept. of Internat. Justice and Goodwill, Federal Council Chs. of Christ in America, 1925-50; exec. dir. dept. international affairs, National Council Churches of Christ in U.S.A. since 1950; Earl lectr. Pacific School of Religion, 1951. Member North Eastern Annual Conf., Meth. Ch. Dir. Nat. Peace Conf., 1930-35; sec. Commn. on a Just and Durable Peace; mem. Am. Seminar, Pan Am. Conf., Lima, Peru, 1938; conslt. to Am. del. United Nations Conf., San Francisco, 1945; mem. Conf. on Peace Aims, Oxford, England, 1942, Christian deputation to Japan, 1945; sec., Internat. Conf. of Religious Leaders on Problems of World Order, Cambridge, England, 1946; cons. Amsterdam Assembly, World Council Chs., 1948; accredited observer Gen. Assembly U.N., Paris, 1948. Mem. Am. Academy Political and Social Science, Council on Fgn. Relations, Pi Delta Epsilon, Delta Sigma Rho, Sigma Phi Epsilon. Author: Youth and Christian Unity, 1927; Highways to International Goodwill, 1930; Religion Renounces War, 1934; The Lima Conference, 1939; Religion and the World of Tomorrow, 1941; A Christian Global Strategy, 1945. Radio commentator Religion in the News, 1936-49. Home: 421 E. Sidney Av., Mt. Vernon, N.Y. Office: 297 4th Av., N.Y.C. 10. Died July 6, 1956; buried Ferncliffe, Hartsville, N.Y.

VAN LAER, Arnold Johan Ferdinand (văn lär), archivist; b. Utrecht, Holland, Oct. 21, 1869; s. Johannes Renatus Eugenius (Ph.D.) and Johanna Gerardina (Neuman) van L.; M.E., Poly. Inst., Delft, Holland, 1897; B.L.S., N.Y. State Library School,

1899; m. Naomi, d. late Rev. George van Deurs, of Phila., Dec. 27, 1897. Archivist, N.Y. State Library, 1899-1915; archivist, div. of archives and history, N.Y. State Edn. Dept., 1915-39. Retired. Edited Van Rensselaer-Bowier Manuscripts and various other publs. of N.Y. State. Home: 433 Western Av., Albany, N.Y. Died Mar. 25, 1955.

VAN LEER, Blake Ragsdale (văn-lēr′), college pres.; b. Mangum, Tex., now Okla., Aug. 16, 1893; s. Maurice Langhorne and Mary (Tarleton) Van L.; B.S., in Elec. Engring., Purdue U., 1915, M.E., 1922; M.S. in Mech. Engring., U. of Calif., 1920; student U. of Caen, France, Feb.-June 1919, U. of Munich, Germany, 1927-28; Sc.D. (hon.) Washington and Jefferson U., 1943; D. Engring. (hon.), Purdue U., 1944; m. Ella Wall, Sept. 6, 1924; children—Blake Wayne, Maryly (Mrs. Jordan Brown Peck), Samuel Wall. Instructor and assistant professor hydraulics, University of California, 1915-28; engineer with S.P. Ry. Co., Byron-Jackson Pump Co., 1922-26; asst. sec. Am. Engring. Council, 1928-32; dean engring., U. of Fla., 1932-37, consolidated colls. of engring. of U. of N.C. and N.C. State Coll., Raleigh, N.C., 1937-44; pres. Ga. Inst. Tech., since July 1, 1944; Florida representative U.S. Coast and Geodetic Survey, 1933-35; tech. adviser Fla. Emergency Relief Adminstrn., 1934-35; tech. adviser Fla. State Planning Bd., 1934-37; water consultant Nat. Resources Com., 1936; vice-pres. Fla. State Bd. Engr. Examiners, 1937. Mem. United States Commn. for UNESCO, 1945-49. Served as 1st lt. Co. F, 316th Engr. Corps, U.S. Army, with A.E.F., 1917-19; maj. Engrs. Res. Corps, 1928-42; lt. col. Army of U.S., May 17, 1942-Oct. 1943, col. Gen. Staff Corps, Oct. 1943-July 1944; chief facilities branch Army Specialized Training Division. Former member N.C. Defense Council; regional advisor, engineering, science and management. Defense Training, Virginia, North Carolina, South Carolina. Chmn. Ga. State Ports Authority, 1945-49. Pres. S.E. Conf. Intercollegiate Athletics, 1949; v.p. National Collegiate Athletics Assn., 1948-49. Registered professional engineer, Fla., N.C. and Ga. Awarded Croix de Guerre (France); awarded Freeman traveling scholarship for study of hydraulics in Europe by Am. S.M.E., 1927-28. Fellow and Life Mem. A.S.M.E. Mem. Am. Society of Engring. Edn. (mem. council 1933-36; pres. S.E. sect. 1939-40), Soc. Am. Mil. Engrs., Fla. Engring. Soc. (v.p. 1937-38), N.C. Soc. of Engrs., Ga. Engring. Soc., Ga. Soc. Professional Engrs., Atlanta; Pine Burr, Newcomen Soc., Am. Legion, Tau Beta Pi, Sigma Tau, Sigma Xi, Alpha Tau Omega, Eta Kappa Nu, Omicron Delta Kappa, Scabbard and Blade; honorary member of A.I.A. Democrat. Episcopalian. Mason (32°). Clubs: Cosmos, Army and Navy Country (Washington); Atlanta Rotary Internat., Capital City (Atlanta). Contbr. of articles on hydraulics to engring. jours. Home: 292 10th St., N.W., Atlanta. Died Jan. 23, 1956; buried Marietta Nat. Cemetery.

VAN METER, Ralph Albert, univ. pres.; b. Columbus Grove, O., Oct. 4, 1893; s. George Shriver and Hannah Mariah (Reeder) Van M.; B.S., O. State U., 1917; M.S., U. of Mass., 1930; Ph.D., Cornell U., 1935; LL.D. Amherst College, 1949, U. Mass., 1954; married Eudora Farnham Tuttle, July 6, 1918; children—David, Helen Lucile, James Tuttle, Marcia Elizabeth. Specialist in food conservation, U. of Mass., 1917-18, extension splist. in pomology, 1919-23, prof. pomol., 1923-48, dean, Sch. of Horticulture, 1931-48, dean in charge Army Training Programs, 1942-45, acting pres., 1946-47, pres., 1948-54, emeritus, 1954—. Vice pres. Mass. Forest and Park Association. Served World War I, 1918-19. Recipient Silver Star award. Member of the American Pomological Society, American Society for Horticulture Science, Mass., Worcester hort, socs., Sigma Xi, Phi Kappa Phi, Delta Theta Sigma, Alpha Tau Gamma. Conglist. Clubs: Green Mountain; Appalachian Mountain; Rotary. Home: Mockingbird Lane, Box 142 Harwich, Mass. Died July 26, 1958; buried Amherst, Mass.

VAN NORDEN, Warner Montagnie; b. Feb. 7, 1873 (tenth generation of Van Nordens, New York City); s. Warner and Martha A. (Philips) Van N.; A.B., Columbia U., 1894; New York U. Law Sch.; LL.D., Wheaton (Ill.) Coll., 1922; m. Grace T., d. James and Henrietta Talcott, April 16, 1898; 2 sons, Montagnie and James Talcott. Pres. Van Norden Trust Co., Van Norden Safe Deposit Co., 19th Ward Bank, Fifth Av. Estates, Van Norden Magazine; retired 1910. Dir. Halmemann Hosp., Legal Aid Soc., Shantung Christian Coll., rest for convalescents. Fellow Royal Soc. for Encouragement Arts, London. Member Royal Asiatic Society, London and Shanghai, Highland Cattle Soc., Am. Asiatic Soc., Hackluyt Soc., China Soc., Sulgrave Instn., League of Audubon Socs., Authors League of America, Hist. Assn. of London, Holland Soc., N.Y. C. of C. Presbyn. Union (v.p.) Am. Bison Soc., Metropolitan Mus., National History Mus., N.Y. Zoological Soc., N.Y. C. of C., Soc. of Psychical Research, Presbyn. Hist. Soc. of America, N.Y. Hist. Society, Bibliophile Soc. Republican. Clubs: Metropolitan, Grolier, Columbia Univ., Republican, D.K.E., Authors, New York Athletic, Travel, Automobile, Explorers, Riding, West Side Tennis, New York Yacht (N.Y.); Balsam Lake; Clove Valley Rod and Gun; Lake Mohonk Tennis; Rockwood Hall; Westfield Tennis; Shackamaxon; Royal Arts (London, Eng.); Westchester Hunt, Apawannis, Fencer's, Am. Yacht, Compiler N.Y. Chinese "Who's Who." Author: Chinese Music and Musical Instruments, 1918; The Fatness of Thy House, 1953. Contributor articles on Chinese archeology and customs to jours. Traveled 2 yrs. in interior of China and Indo-China. Importer of herd of Highland cattle, headed by "Sir Andrew," champion of Scotland; Grevy zebras from Abyssinia, Bohemei zebras from South Africa, zebus from India. Experiments in Telegony Breeding. Owner of Gamin II, Madison Square Garden Champion French Bulldog. Student of Greek, Latin and Early English pastoral drama. Owner of Sand Pond, Ulster County, N.Y., fishing and shooting lodge. Home: 7 W. 57th St., New York, N.Y. Died Dec. 1959.

VAN NORMAN, Louis Edwin, author, economist; b. Quebec, Can., Aug. 3, 1869; s. Edwin M. and Elizabeth Eleanor (Healey) Van N.; A.B., Coll. of City of N.Y., 1891, A.M., 1896, New York U.; m. Daniela Kotnowska, Oct. 4, 1903. Journalist, 1890-91; magazine editor and review writer. Tokok extended tour of Europe and Asia, 1900, and wrote for mags., chiefly on internat. politics and economics; authority on Slavonic subjects (Russia and Poland); editor of civic improvement publs., Springfield, O., 1902; went to Europe to study Russia and Scandinavia for Am. mags.; asso. editor Chautauquan, 1902; foreign editor Literary Digest, 1900; asst. editor Review of Reviews, in charge foreign dept., 1904-14; editor The Nation's Business, monthly mag. of Chamber of Commerce, U.S.A., 1915-16; editor Capital Publishers, Inc., and advisory editor Sea Power, for Navy League, Art and Archeology for the Archeol. Inst. America, and others, 1916-17; organized div. of information for War Trade Bd. and took charge of its publicity, Sept. 1917; apptd. trade commr. to Rumania (hdqrs. Bucharest), by Bur. Fgn. and Domestic Commerce, Jan. 1919; apptd. resident trade commr. to the minister at Warsaw, Poland, Sept. 1919; transferred to Bucharest Nov. 1921; apptd. commercial attaché to Legation at Bucharest, Mar. 1925, transferred for duty in Washington, D.C., 1925; as spl. rep. Bur. Foreign and Domestic Commerce; with U.S. Daily, Washington, D.C., 1930-33, 1934-36; rep. Dept. of Commerce of information com. for negotiation of reciprocal trade agreements. Hon. mem. Polish Patriotic Internat. Soc.; mem. Phi Delta Theta, Phi Beta Kappa. Decorated Cross of Polonia Restituta (Poland). Author: Poland, the Knight Among Nations. Translator and editor: States-General, from the Story of a Peasant (of Erckmann-Chatrian), 1903. Reviser Dury's History of the World. Editor: Tales from the Italian and Spanish, 1913. Has lectured U.S. and abroad on economic, literary and social subjects. Address: 1763 Titus St., San Diego, Cal. Died Sept. 16, 1956.

VAN ORMAN, F. Harold, hotel man; b. Flint, Mich., Sept. 26, 1884; s. Fred and Demaris M. (Paddock) Van O.; prep. edn., Phillips Exeter Acad. (N.H.), Stone Sch. (Boston); A.B., Harvard, 1908; m. Susie Beeler, 1913; children—F. Harold, Jr., Jerome Beeler, William Henry; married second, Harriet Hodgini; November 9, 1935; 1 son, Richard Albert; married third to Kitty Clark. Became associated with father in hotel business, Evansville, Indiana, 1908; now pres. Van Orman Hotels, Hotel McCurdy (Evansville), Hotel Van Orman, Ft. Wayne, all belonging to same chain. Member Indiana State Senate, 1920-24; lt. gov. of Ind., 1924-28. Del. to Rep. Nat. Conv., Chicago, 1932. Dir. Royal Order of Jesters. Ky. Colonel. Pres. Am. Hotel Assn. Mem. Hotel Men's Mut. Benefit Assn. (pres. 1922-24), C. of C. (dir. 8 yrs.), Hotel Greeters of Am., Ind. Soc. of Chgo. (v.p.), Ind. Hotel Assn., Ohio Hotels Association (life), Hotel Sales Mgmt. Association, Delta Sigma Pi. Republican. Episcopalian. Mason (K.T., 32°); past potentate Hadi Shrine, Evansville; past exalted ruler Evansville Lodge of Elks. Clubs: Tavern (Chicago), Rotary (ex-pres.), Columbia (Indianapolis); Automobile of Evansville (dir.), Evansville Country. Address: Hotel McCurdy, Evansville, Ind. Died Jan. 6, 1958; buried Oak Hill Cemetery, Evansville.

VAN PATTEN, Nathan, librarian; b. Niskayuna, N.Y., Mar. 24, 1887; s. John and Jennie (Boughton) Van P.; ed. Union Classical Inst.; Litt.D., Dartmouth College, 1936; m. Mabel Waite, June 20, 1910; 1 dau., Dolores. Teacher, pub. schs., also bookseller, 1907-17; librarian Wolcott Gibbs Library, Coll. City of New York, 1917-20; reference librarian, Mass. Inst. Tech., 1920-21, asst. librarian, 1921-23; chief librarian, Queen's U., Kingston, Ont., Can., 1923-27; dir. univ. libraries, Stanford, 1927-47; professor of bibliography, 1947-52, prof. emeritus since 1952, curator Meml. Lib. Music since 1952; lectr. Library Sch., McGill U., Montreal, Canada, 1928; lecturer chemistry department, Stanford U., 1928-52; lecturer U. Calif. Medical School since 1931. Adviser on World War Collection, Yale library. Counselor Hoover Library on War, Revolution, and Peace. Hon. cons. in Canadiana Library of Congress. Fellow Library Association (Great Britain); Royal Soc. of Arts; mem. Bibliog. Soc. of Am., Bibliog. Soc. U. of Va., Theta Chi, Phi Lambda Upsilon, Sigma Delta Pi. Repub. Presbyterian. Clubs: Grolier (N.Y.C.); Roxburghe (San Francisco); Rowfant (Cleveland). Author: Bibliography of the Corrosion of Metals, 1923, 24; Literature of Lubrication, 1926; Coöperative Cataloging of the Medical Literature, 1926; Concerning "Condensed Novels," by Bret Harte (introd. and bibliog. notes), 1929; Index to Bibliographies and Bibliographical Contributions Relating to the Work of American and British Authors (1923-1932), 1933; Printing in Greenland, 1939; Catalogue of the Memorial Library of Music at Stanford University, 1951. Contbr. to bibliog., chem. and med. jours. Home: 579 Alvarado Row, Stanford, Cal. Died Mar. 17, 1956.

VAN POOLE, Chalmer Melanchton, physician; b. Salisbury, N.C., Sept. 2, 1854; s. Otho and Lucretia Katherine (Lentz) van P.; A.M., N.C. Coll., 1878; M.D., Coll. Phys. and Surg., Baltimore, 1880; postgrad. work, N.Y.U., 1909-11; m. Mary Eliza Linn, Oct. 22, 1885. Practiced, Salisbury, since 1880; capt., Med. Reserve Corps, 1917. Pres. Rowan Mut. Fire Ins. Co.; dir. Vance Cotton Mills, China Grove Cotton Mills, Inc., Rowan Cotton Mills, Inc. Trustee N.C. Coll., Mont Amoena Female Sem. Mem. N.C. Med. Soc. (treas. 1888-93, pres. 1910-11), Rowan Co. Med. Soc. (twice pres.), N.C. Anti-Tuberculosis Soc. ; Pres. N.C. S.S. Assn., 1909-10. Democrat. Lutheran. Address: Salisbury, N.C. Died July 28, 1933; buried Chestnut Hill Cemetery, Salisbury.

VAN SAUN, Walter (văn-sawn), clergyman, educator; b. Cherry Grove, Cin., Sept. 22, 1889; s. John and Rosa (Monjar) Van S.; A.B., Otterbein Coll., Westerville, O., 1913; student Lane Sem., Cin., 1915-17; B.D., Bonebrake Sem., Dayton, O., 1918; Ph.D., U. Cin., 1929; m. Juliana Schipler, Sept. 12, 1911; children—Dorothea (Mrs. H. C. Ringenoldus), Martha Rose (Mrs. D. A. Lam). Began as tchr. pub. schs., Hamilton County, O., 1908-10; ordained to ministry of United Brethren Ch., Vandalia, O., 1918; transferred to Reformed Ch., Am., 1930; pastor United Brethren Ch., Harrison, 1913-17, North Bend, 1918-22, New Hope, 1922-23, Mt. Airy, Cin., 1923-27; prof. philosophy Hope Coll., Holland, Mich., 1929—. Mem. Am. Philos. Assn., Mich. Acad. Sci., Arts and Letters. Republican. Mem. editorial com. Intelligencer-Leader (now Church Herold), 1934-36. Contbr. article, Some Permanent Contbrs. of St. Augustine to Christian Thought, Evangelical Quarterly, July, 1934. Home: 58 W. 12th St., Holland, Mich. Died July 26, 1950; buried Pilgrim Home Cemetery, Holland.

Van SICKLE, Kenneth Ardean, corp. exec.; b. Olpe, Kan., Aug. 6, 1911; s. William Harrison and Essie Mae (Ellis) Van S.; m. Mary A. Boterf, Apr. 15, 1936. Pres. Kenneth A. Van Sickle, Inc., 1940-51; dir. Chgo., Aurora & Elgin R.R., 1950—; pres. Westport Properties Corp., Kansas City, Mo., 1954—; pres., dir. Tri-State Warehousing & Distbg. Co., C. A. & E. Properties, Inc. Home: R.R. 1, Highgrove Farm, Grandview, Mo. Office: Commerce Bldg., Kansas City, Mo. Died Feb. 1, 1960.

VANSITTART, 1st Baron, of Denham, Robert Gilbert (văn-sĭt′ärt), British diplomat; (cr. 1941, P.C.), b. June 25, 1881; s. Captain Robert Arnold V.; ed. Eton Coll., Windsor, Eng.; Litt.D. (hon.), U. Reading (Eng.); LL.D. (hon.), Aberdeen; m. Gladys Heppenheimer (dau. Gen. William C. Heppenheimer, of N.J.), 1921; 1 dau.; m. 2d, Sarita Enriqueta Ward Barclay (widow of Sir Colville A. de R. Barclay), 1931. Brit. diplomatic service, 1902-0, as attaché 1902; 3d sec., 1905; 2d sec., 1908; asst. clerk Brit. Foreign Office, 1914; 1st sec., 1919; counsellor, 1920; stationed at Paris, 1903-05; Teheran (Persia), 1907; Cairo, 1908; Stockholm, 1915; Paris, 1919; pvt. sec. to Marquis Curzon (Brit. sec. of state for fgn. affairs), 1920-24; asst. undesrsec. state in Fgn. Office, 1928; pvt. sec. to prime minister, 1928-29; permanent undersec. of State in Brit. Fgn. Office, 1929-38; chief diplomatic adv. to Brit. Govt. 1938-41; known as the grand old man of Brit. fgn. policy; has played an important diplomatic role for United Kingdom for many years. Decorated: Order of the Bath (Companion, Comdr., Grand Cross), Order of St. Michael and St. George (Companion, Grand Cross), Royal Victorian Order. Mem. de I'Académic des Sciences Morales et Politiques. Author: Singing Caravan, 1932; Collected Poems, 1934; Black Record, 1941; Lessons of My Life, 1943; Green and Grey, 1944; Bones of Contention, 1945; Events and Shadows, 1949; Even Now, 1949. Address: Denham Place Denham, Bucks, Eng. Died Feb. 14, 1957.

Van SPLUNTER, John Marcus, engr.; b. Grand Rapids, Mich., July 2, 1881; s. James and Nellie (Van Dam) Van.S.; B.S., U. Mich., 1904. Engring. dept. Sargent & Lundy, cons. engrs., Chgo., 1904-06; sales, constrn. engr. Stanley G. I. Electric Co., Pittsfield, Mass., 1906-08; sales engr. Gen. Electric Co., Chgo., 1908-12; chief engr. Elec. Engrs. Equipment Co., Chgo., 1912-14; sec., elec. engr. Gen. Devices & Fittings Co., Chgo., 1914-24, pres., sec., Grand Rapids, 1924—. Pres., owner Grand Rapids Baseball Club; pres. Olympic Athletic Club. Served as lt. comdr. USN, 1917-19. Mem. Am. Inst. E.E. Home: 930 Lafayette Av. S.E., Grand Rapids 7. Office: 1450 Buchanan Av. S.W., Grand Rapids 2, Mich. Died 1957.

VANSTON, W(illiam) Justus K(eough), investment banker; b. Dorchester, Ont., Can., Sept. 10, 1881; s. William T. N. and Florence (Scott) V.; A.B. cum laude, U. Toronto, 1904; m. Daisy M. Crampton, Aug. 28, 1908 (died May 10, 1927); children—Elizabeth (Mrs. C. W. Morgan) (died May 3, 1958), Margaret (Mrs. C. O. Braatz). Came to U.S., 1904, naturalized, 1915. Reporter Wall Street Jours., N.Y.C., 1904-06; head research dept., Moffatt & White and successor firm of White, Weld & Co., 1906-12, gen. partner, 1912-54, ltd. partner, 1954—; dir. Ont. Natural Gas Storage & Pipe Lines, Ltd., Geo-Sci. Prospectors, Ltd., Toronto, El Paso Natural Gas Co., McCall Corp., Union Gas Co., Ltd., Can., Western Natural Gas Co. Republican. Episcopalian. Clubs: Orange Lawn Tennis (S. Orange, N.J.); N. Fork Country (Cutchogue, L.I., N.Y.); Downtown Association, Canadian (N.Y. City) Megantic Fish and Game (Me.) Home: 14 Glenside Rd., S. Orange, N.J. Office: 20 Broad St., N.Y.C. 5. Died Nov. 28, 1957; buried Rosedale Cemetery, Orange, N.J.

VAN VLECK, William Cabell, law school prof.; b. Washington, D.C., Nov. 11, 1885; s. William Henry and Martha R. (Shinn) Van V.; A.B., Geo. Wash. U., 1908, LL.B., 1911, LLD., 1948; S.J.D., Harvard, 1921; m Jennie Moyer, July 1, 1914. Instr. law, Geo. Washington U., 1912-16, asst. prof., 1916-19, prof. law since 1919, sec. law dept., 1912-20, actg. dean, 1923-24, dean, 1924-48; acting prof. law, summers, U. Mich., 1924, 29, Stanford U., 1927, U. Chgo., 1934. Mem. com. of advisers to report on conflict of laws, Am. Law Inst.; mem. exec. com. Assn. American Law Schools, 1944; mem. Am. Bar Assn., Sigma Phi Epsilon, Phi Delta Phi, Order of Coif. Author: Administrative Control of Aliens, 1932. Clubs: Rotary, Cosmos (Washington); Harvard (Washington, D.C.). Home: 4120 Harrison St., Washington, D.C. Died Oct. 12, 1956; buried Parklawn Cemetery, Rockville, Md.

VAN VOORHIS, Daniel (van-vōr'ēz), army officer; b. Zanesville, O., Oct. 24, 1878; s. Henry Clay and Mary Ann (Brown) Van V.; ed. Ohio Wesleyan U. and Wasihington and Jefferson Coll.; grad. Inf.-Cav. Sch., 1905, Mounted Service Sch., 1910, Army War Coll., 1929; m. Edith Burbank, Jan. 11, 1911; children—Daniel, Betsy Bell. Enlisted as pvt., 10th Pa. Vol. Inf., Spanish-Am. War, 1898; commd. 2d lt. Cav., U.S. Army, Feb. 1, 1900, and advanced through the grades to brig. gen., 1936, maj. gen., 1938, lt. gen., 1940; served as col. of cavalry, during World War. Decorated D.S.M., Navy Cross, Silver Star (U. S.); Legion of Honor (France); Order of the Sun (Peru); Legion of Merit (Ecuador). Mem. Phi Kappa Psi. Club: Chevy Chase (Md.) Country. Home: Van Voorhis Farm, Nashport, O. Address: War Dept., Washington. Died Jan. 9, 1956; buried Meml. Park, Zanesville, O.

VAN WICKEL, Jesse Frederick, foreign service officer; b. Bklyn., June 11, 1890; s. Jesse and Rosina (Versfelt) VanW.; ed. N.Y. pub. schs. and bus. schs.; m. Lilian Perry, July 26, 1913; children—Doris Lilian, Jesse Frederick, Jr. Code expert, 1906-12; traffic mgr., export mgr., purchasing agt., 1912-18; branch mgr. in Shanghai for trading companies, 1918-22; special asst. to sugar corp. in Cuba, 1922-23; trade commr. at Batavia, 1923; commercial attaché at The Hague, Sept. 1926; del. 5th Internat. Congress for Sci. Mgmt., Amsterdam, 1932; del. 8th Internat. Road Congress, The Hague, 1938; consul and sec. in the Diplomatic Service, 1939; consul at Batavia, 1940, Sydney, 1942; detailed to the Dept. of Commerce, 1942, Dept. of State, 1942; 1st sec. American Embassy, London, 1944-45; comml. attaché Am. Embassy, The Hague, 1945-47; consul general at Amsterdam since 1947. Clubs: Rotary, Am. Businessmens (both Amsterdam), Royal Netherlands Automobile (The Hague). Address: Am. Consulate, Amsterdam, Netherlands. Died Mar. 1958.

VAN WYCK, William (văn-wīk'), author; b. Terre Haute, Ind., Mar. 10, 1883; s. William and Harriet Reynolds (Early) Van W.; A.B., A.M., Litt.D., U. of Southern Calif.; Pd.M. and sometime fellow and scholar, New York U.; A.M., U. of Calif; m. Jessica Davis Nahl, Mar. 13, 1922. Lecturer in English, U. of Calif. Extension Div. Phi Beta Kappa, Phi Kappa Phi. Officer d'Académie (France). Clubs: Bohemian (San Francisco); Faculty (Berkeley); Authors (London); Interallied (Paris). Author: Florentines, Savonarola, Chaucer's Canterbury Tales, Ronsard's Sonnets for Helen, The Sinister Shepherd, Rostand's Cyrano de Bergerac and Chanteclair (with Clifford H. Bissell); How to Enjoy Poetry, 1956. Contributor to American and European periodicals. Home: Hotel Claremont, Berkeley 5, Cal. Died Dec. 11, 1956; buried Mountain View Cemetery, Oakland, Cal.

VARDELL, Charles Graves, college president; b. Charleston, S.C., Feb. 12, 1860; s. William Gildersleeve and Jane Dickson (Bell) V.; student Oberlin (O.) Coll., 1883-85; A.B., Davidson (N.C.) Coll., 1888, D.D., 1903; grad. Princeton Theol. Sem., 1891; m. Linda Lee Rumple, Oct. 27, 1891; children—Charles Gildersleeve, Elizabeth (Mrs. William B. McNett), Jane Dickson (Mrs. J. J. Murray), Margaret (Mrs. Alexander Sprunt, Jr.), Ruth (Mrs. Gaston Gage), Mary Linda (Mrs. Ellison Smyth). Ordained Presbyn. ministry, 1891; pastor Newbern, N.C., 1891-96; a founder, 1896, and since pres. Flora MacDonald Coll. Trustee Davidson Coll., 1892-99; regent Presbyn. Home, Barium, N.C. Democrat. Mason. Mem. Gaelic Soc., Inverness, Scotland, 1922; pres. Scottish Soc. America, 1922-24; hon. mem. Clan Macneil Assn. of America. Club: Rotary (pres. 1926-27). Home: Red Springs, N.C. Died May 3, 1958; buried graveyard 2d Presbyn Ch., Charleston, S.C.

VARDEN, George, clergyman; b. E. Dereham, Norfolk Co., Eng.; s. William and Mary Ann (Kent) V.; came to America, 1852; A.B., Georgetown Coll., Ky., 1858, A.M., 1861, Ph.D., 1866; D.D., 1872, LL.D., 1877, William Jewell Coll., Mo.; m. Mrs. Mattie Stephens Gilman, June 25, 1858; 2d, Emily Greene, Oct. 21, 1896. Ordained Bapt. ministry, 1858; pastor Paris, Ky., 1858-70; then at Falmouth, Cynthiana, and Colemansville. Asso. editor Bapt. Monthly, Covington, Ky., 1866-68, Western Recorder, Louisville, Ky., 1872-81, Am. Bapt. Flag, St. Louis, 1879, and Central Bapt., St. Louis; corr. Journal and Messenger, Cin., since 1869. Sch. commr. of Bourbon Co., 1863-9; prin. Paris High Sch., 1857, of Bourbon Gymnasium, 1869-74; instr. Greek and practical surveying, Edgar Coll. and Mil. Inst.; instr. English lit. and Latin, Bourbon Female Coll.; examiner of teachers for Bourbon Co., 1886-1902; commr. of William Garth Ednl. Fund, 1894-1902; trustee Georgetown Coll., 20 yrs. Mem. Am. Acad. Polit. and Social Science. Extensive contbr. to religious press. Address: Paris, Ky. Died May 1, 1917.

VARGAS, Getúlio, pres. of Brazil; b. São Borja, Rio Grande do Sul, Brazil, Apr. 19, 1882; s. Manuel do Nascimento and Candida (Dornelles) V.; student Ouro Preto, Minas Gerais and Escola Preparatória e de Táctica, Rio Pardo, 1899-1902; LL.B., U. Porto Alegre, 1907; m. Darcy Sarmanho, 1911; children—Luthero, Jandira, Alzira, Manuel Antônio Getúlio (dec.). Practiced law, Porto Alegre, 1907-08, São Borja, 1908; state dep. Rio Grande do Sul, 1909-13, re-elected, 1917, becoming majority leader in legislature; elected fed. dep., 1923; minister finance, 1926-27; gov. State of Rio Grande do Sul, 1928-30, pres. of Brazil, 1930-45, since 51; nat. senator from Rio Grande do Sul, 1946. Founder Partido Trabalhista Brasiliero, 1946. Catholic. Author: A Nova politica do Brasil (9 vols.). Address: Rio de Janeiro, Brazil. Died Aug. 24, 1954.

VARIAN, Russell Harrison, physicist; b. Washington, Apr. 24, 1898; s. John Osborne and Agnes (Dixon) V.; A.B., Stanford, 1925, M.A., 1927; D.Eng. (hon.), Poly. Inst. Bklyn., 1943; m. Dorothy Hill, 1947; children—George Russell, Charles John, Susan Aileen. Research physicist Humble Oil & Refining Co., 1929, Farnsworth Television Co., 1930-33; pvt. research 1934-35; research asso. Standford, 1937-40. 46—; research engr. Sperry Gyroscope Co., 1940-46; pres. Varian Associates, mfrs. ultra-high frequency microwave tubes, 1948-56, chmn. bd. 1956—. Awarded John Price Wetherill medal, Franklin Inst., 1950. Fellow Inst. Radio Engrs., Cal. Acad. Sci., Am. Phys. Soc., A.A.A.S.; mem. Sigma Xi. Inventor klystron radio tube for prodn. waves in range of one to a few centimeters; patentee approximately 100 devices in microwave, applied physics field. Home: 10114 Crescent Rd., Cupertino. Office: 611 Hansen Way, Palo Alto, Cal. Died July 28, 1959.

VAUGHAN, Floyd Lamar, educator; b. Paris, Tex., June 29, 1891; s. Morrison Cornelius and Caledonia Anderson (Speairs) V.; student N. Tex. Teachers Coll., 1908-10; B.A., U. Tex., 1913, M.A., 1914; Ph.D., U. Wis., 1917 (scholarship and fellowship); m. Margaret Adelle Du Puy, Dec. 22, 1923 (died 1930); children—Margaret Adelle, Floyd Lamar (dec.), Baby (dec.); m .2d, Wilma English, June 9, 1936; children—Robert Lamar, John Charles, Virginia. Asst. in econs., Tex., 1912-14, U. Wis., 1916-17; examiner Federal Trade Commn., 1917-19; asst. prof. econs., Brown U., Providence, R.I., 1919-23; prof. econs., U. Okla., 1923—. Mem. Am. Marketing Assn., Southwestern Social Science Assn. Presbyn. Club: Faculty. Author: The Grain Trade, Vol. I, Country Grain Marketing (with W. H. S. Stevens and B. P. Parry), 1920; Economics of Our Patent System, 1925; Marketing and Advertising, 1928; Marketing, 1942. Home: 915 Lahoma Av., Norman, Okla. Died Feb. 20, 1955.

VAUGHAN, John Russell, physician; b. Huntsville, Mo., Mar. 16, 1888; s. William Walter and Ella Mary (Peery) V.; M.D., Washington U., 1910; m. Sara Elizabeth Thomas, Mar. 6, 1912; children—John Russell, William Edward. Intern, Washington U. Hosp., St. Louis, 1910-11; pvt. practice, specializing in obstetrics and gynecology, St. Louis since 1912; staff St. Louis City and Barnes hosps., 1921-35, St. Luke's Hosp. since 1921. Mem. Med. Civil Def., St. Louis, 1941-45, dep. chief, 1943-45, med. exec. com., 1951; mem. Sch. Bd., University City, Mo., 1929-34, pres., 1933-34. Served as capt., med. corps U.S. Army, 1918-19; chief surgery Camp Colt, Gettysburg, Pa., 1918, Base Hosp. 103, Dijon, France, 1918-19. Mem. A.M.A., St. Louis Gynecol. Soc., Mo. State and St. Louis med. socs., Phi Beta Pi, Sigma Nu. Mason. Club: University (St. Louis). Office: 634 N. Grand Blvd., St. Louis 3. Died Dec. 4, 1952.

VAUGHAN, John Samuel, coll. pres.; b. nr. Knoxville, Tenn., Nov. 29, 1885; s. Edward Fredrick and Alice (Kennedy) V.; A.B., U. Okla., 1923, A.M., 1927; m. Eunice Lewis, June 30, 1914; 1 dau., Marice. City supt. schs., Kingston and Wapanucka, Okla., 1907-17; mem. Okla. State Senate, 1917-21; dean, registrar Southeastern State Tchrs. Coll., 1919-21, 23-25, acting pres., 1926; exec. sec. Okla. Ednl. Survey, 1923; acting pres. Okla. state supt. pub. instrn., 1927-36. Mem. Okla., State Bd. Edn., 1927-36; pres. Northeastern Tchrs. Coll., 1936—. Mem. N.E.A. (v.p. 1927), Okla. Ednl. Assn. (dir. 1920-27). Democrat. Baptist. Mason (33°, Shriner). Club: Kiwanis. Home: Tahlequah, Okla. Died Jan. 21, 1951; buried Tahlequah.

VAUGHAN, Richard Miner, theologian; b. Bangor, Wis., Aug. 28, 1870; s. John J. and Mary A. (Thomas) V.; A.B., Brown U., 1895, D.D., 1913; B.D., U. of Chicago, 1898; m. Eleanor J. Farries, June 24, 1897 (died July 12, 1938); children—Wayland Farries, Richard Farries. Ordained Bapt. ministry, 1897, pastor Warren Av. Ch., Detroit, Mich., 1899-1901; 1st Ch., Janesville, Wis., 1901-08; dean Pacific Coast Bapt. Theol. Sem., Berkeley, Calif., 1908-09; instr. Pacific Theol. Sem., 1910-12; pastor 1st Ch., Berkeley, Calif., 1909-12; prof. Christian theology, Newton Theol. Instn. (now Andover-Newton Theol. Sch.) since Sept. 1, 1912, prof. emeritus since 1940; pastor Community Ch., Babson Park, Fla. 1940-48. Mem. bd. mgrs. Am. Bapt. Home Mission Soc., 1913-32; pres. Am. Theol. Soc., 1930. Mem. Phi Beta Kappa. Author; The Significance of Personality. Contbr. to religious jours. Home: Hotel Dwellere. 304 E. Central Av., Orlando, Fla. Died Dec. 28, 1954; cremated; in chapel, Mt. Auburn Cemetery, Cambridge, Mass.

VAUGHAN, T(homas) Wayland, geologist, oceanographer; b. Jonesville, Tex., Sept. 20, 1870; s. Dr. Samuel Floyd and Annie R. (Hope) V.; B.S., Tulane U., 1889, D.Sc., 1944; A.B., Harvard, 1893, A.M., 1894, Ph.D., 1903; LL.D., U. of B.C., 1933, U. of California, 1936; studied mus. in Europe; married Dorothy Q. Upham, March 22, 1909 (deceased, August 18, 1949); one daughter, Caroline Ely (Mrs. James H. Fortune, Jr.). Engaged in geologic and paleontologic researches, with U.S. Geol. Survey, 1894-1923; geologist in charge Coastal Plain investigations, 1907-23, sr. geologist 1924-28, prin. scientist, 1928-39; retired. Custodian of Madreporarian corals, U.S. Nat. Museum, 1903-23; asso. in marine sediments, 1924-42, in paleontology since 1942; dir. Scripps Inst. of U. of Calif., La Jolla, 1924-36, dir. emeritus since 1936. Specialist on tertiary geology, fossil and recent corals, larger Foraminifera, and marine sediments. Decorated Order of Rising Sun, 3d class, Japan, 1940; awarded Agassiz medal for research in oceanography, Nat. Acad. of Science, 1935; Mary Clark Thompson medal for geology and paleontology, 1945; Penrose Medal, Geol. Soc. of America, 1946. Fellow Am. Academy Arts and Sci., Am. Philos. Soc., Calif. Acad. Sciences, A.A.A.S. (pres. Pacific div. 1930-31), Geol. Soc. America (1st v.p. 1938, pres. 1939), Assn. Am. Geographers, Paleontol. Soc. (pres. 1923), Washington Acad. Science (pres. 1923); San Diego Soc. Natural History (pres. 1926); mem. Nat. Acad. Sciences, Am. Geophys. Union (chmn. oceanography sect. 1926-28), Geol. Soc. of Washington (pres. 1915); Oceanographic Soc. of the Pacific (pres. 1935-36); Philos. Soc. Tex.; corr. mem. Zoölogical Soc. of London, Acad. Natural Sciences Philadelphia, Konk. Nat. Ver. Nederl.-Ind., Soc. Geograf., Cuba, fgn. mem. Linnean Soc., fgn. fellow Geol. Soc., London; hon. mem. Geological Soc., Peru. U.S. del. 1st Pan-Pacific Science Conf., Honolulu, 1920 (chairman sect. geology); del. U.S., Nat. Acad. Sciences, etc., to 2d Pan-Pacific Science Congress, Melbourne and Sydney, Australia, 1923; 3d Pan-Pacific Science Congress, Japan, 1926; 4th Pacific Science Congress, Java, 1929, 5th Congress, Victoria and Vancouver, 1933; mem. div. geology and geography, Nat. Research Council, 1919-26; chmn. Internat. Com. Oceanography of Pacific, Pacific Science Assn., 1926-35; chmn. sect. geol. sciences, 8th Am. Sci. Congress, Washington, 1940. Clubs: Cosmos (Washington); Faculty (Berkeley). Author: The Eocene and Lower Oligocene Coral Faunas of the United States (Monograph 39, U.S. Geol. Survey); Recent Madreporaria of Hawaiian Islands and Laysan (Bull. 59, U.S. Nat. Museum); Contributions to the Geology and Paleontology of the Canal Zone, Panama (Bull. 103, U.S. Nat. Mus.); Geologic Reconnaissance of the Dominican Republic; International Aspects of Oceanography; and more than 300 other scientific papers. Made trip around world, 1932-33, to study provisions for oceanographic research for Nat. Acad. Science. Home: 3333 P St. 7. Office: U.S. National Museum, Washington 25. Died Jan. 16, 1952.

VAUGHAN WILLIAMS, Ralph, composer; b. Down Ampney, Gloucestershire, Eng., Oct. 12, 1872; Mus. Doc., Cambridge, 1901; student Royal Coll. Music, studied with Max Bruch, Berlin, Maurice Ravel, Paris;

Organist St. Barnabas Ch., South Lambeth, 1895-99; tchr. composition Royal Coll. Music, condr. Bach Choir; dir. concert Norfolk Music Festival, U.S., 1922; tchr. nat. music Bryn Mawr Coll. Hosp. orderly Territorial Royal Army Mil. Corps, France and Macedonia, World War I, also with Arty. Decorated Order of Merit, 1935. Mem. English Folk Dance Song Soc. Compositions: In the Fen Country, 1904, Fantasia on a Theme by Thomas Tallis, 1910, On Wenlock Edge, Hugh the Drover (opera), London Symphony, 1913, The Lark Ascending, 1914, Pastoral Symphony, 1921, Shepherds of the Delectable Mountains, 1922; Old King Cole (ballet), 1923, Riders to the Sea (opera), 1937, Fifth Symphony, Concerto for Oboe and Orchestra, 1941, Thanksgiving for Victory, 1945, Sixth Symphony, 1947, Pilgrim's Progress, 1950; Sinfonia Antarctica, 1952; 8th Symphony, 1955; 9th Symphony, 1958. Author: The Making of Music, 1955. Address: 10 Hanover Terrace, London N.W. 1, Eng. Died Aug. 26, 1958.

VAUGHN, Robert Gallaway, banker; b. Madison, N.C., Mar. 10, 1868; s. Joseph Mitchell and Casandra (Black) V.; ed. U. of N.C. and Bryant and Stratton Business Coll., Balt.; m. Margaret Virginia Smith, June 7, 1893; children—Mary Watson (Mrs. John W. McAlister), Josephine M. (Mrs. Charles W. Angle), Robert Gallaway, Margaret S. (Mrs. C. M. Vanstory, Jr.), Cynthia Norris. Entered banking business at Reidsville, N.C., 1885; pres. Am. Nat. Bank and Trust Co., Greensboro, N.C., 1911; bank merged with N.C. Bank & Trust Co., 1929, and now with other cos. in liquidation. Mem. Sigma Alpha Epsilon. Democrat. Presbyn. Home: Greensboro, N.C. Deceased.

VAUGHT, Edgar Sullins, (vawt), judge; b. Cedar Springs, Wythe County, Va., Jan. 7, 1873; s. Noah Trigg and Minerva (Atkins) V.; B.S., Carson and Newman Coll., Jefferson City, Tenn., 1899; grad. study at Emory and Henry Coll., Emory, Va.; LL.D., Oklahoma City U., 1929, Florida Southern College, 1956; m. Mary Holtsinger, Nov. 1, 1899; children—Mary Eleanor (Mrs. Marquis Stone Morris), Edgar Sullins, Jr., Ruth Loretta (Mrs. Wayman J. Thompson). Teacher public sch., Tenn., 1891-95; county supt. of schs., Jefferson County, 1895-1901; prin. high sch., Oklahoma City, Okla., 1901-02; supt. schs., Oklahoma City, 1902-06; admitted to Okla. bar, 1906, began practice at Oklahoma City; mem. firm Everest, Vaught & Brewer, 1918-28; U.S. dist. judge, Western Dist. Okla., since 1928. Mem. Okla. Ty. Bd. of Edn., 1903-06, Okla. Ty. Bd. of Regents for Normal Schs., 1907-08; del. Rep. Nat. Conv., Cleveland, 1924. Trustee Oklahoma City U. Distinguished Service Citation, U. Oklahoma, 1951. Mem. Oklahoma City C. of C. (ex-pres.). Republican. Methodist. Mason (Shriner). Clubs: Lions (pres. Oklahoma City br., 1922; internat. pres., 1922-23); Oklahoma, Oklahoma City Golf and Country, Men's Dinner (pres.). Home: 1422 W. 36th St. Office: Federal Bldg., Oklahoma City, Okla. Died Dec. 12, 1959.

VEASEY, Clarence Archibald (vēz'ē), ophthalmologist; b. Pocomoke City, Md., Aug. 9, 1869; s. Thomas Jefferson and Marietta (Richards) V.; student Western Md. Coll., Westminster, 1885-87, A.M., 1896; M.D., Jefferson Md. Coll., Phila., 1890; interne Jefferson Med. Coll. Hosp., 1890-91; student European hosps., 1891; m. Gertrude Mabel Clogg, June 20, 1894; children—Clarence, Archibald (M.D.), Winona Gertrude. In practice at Phila., 1890-08, at Spokane, Wash., 1908——. Clinical asst. Wills Eye Hosp., 1891-92; asst. demonstrator surgery, Jefferson Med. Coll., 1891-92; consulting ophthalmologist, Phila. Lying-in-Charity Hosp., 1892-1908; clin. asst. ophthal. dept. Jefferson Med. Coll. Hosp., 1892-94; chief clin. asst., and asst. ophthal. surgeon, 1894-1905, demonstrator diseases of the eye, 1897-1903, asst. prof. ophthalmology, 1905-08, Jefferson Med. Coll.; asst. ophthalmologist, Jefferson Med. Coll. Hosp., 1905-08; instr. operative ophthalmology, Phila. Polyclinic, 1894-95; adj. prof. diseases of the eye, Phila. Polyclinic, 1895-1900; ophthalmic surgeon M.E. Hosp., Phila., 1901-08. Retired. Member of American Ophthal. Society, Am. Acad. Ophthalmology and Oto-Laryngology, Pacific Coast Oto-Ophthalmol. Soc. (pres. 1916-17), Spokane Acad. Ophthal. and Otolaryn. (pres. 1943-44), Western Ophthalmol. Soc., Assn. for Research in Ophthalmology, A.M.A., Wash. State Med. Soc., Spokane County Med. Soc.; fellow Coll. Physicians of Phila., Am. Acad. Medicine, Am. Coll. of Surgeons; hon. mem. Alpha Kappa Kappa (Epsilon). Clubs: Spokane City University. Author: Ophthalmic Operations as Practiced on Animals' Eyes, 1896; A Manual of Diseases of the Eye, 1903; also many essays and monographs on affections of the eye. Home: 1118 W. 9th Av., Spokane 4, Wash. Died Aug. 11, 1957; buried Spokane.

VEDDER, Beverly Blair, lawyer; b. Rushville, Ill., Jan. 6, 1877; s. Isaac N. and Emma (Bulkley) V.; A.B., U. Mich., 1909, J.D., 1912; m. Helen Morse, May 17, 1923; children—Blair, Nancy (Mrs. Daniel G. Quirk). Admitted to Ill. bar, 1912, since practiced in Chgo.; formerly partner Butler, Lamb, Foster & Pope and succeeding firms, until 1952, now partner Vedder, Price, Kaufman & Kammholz. Conglist. Club: Univ. Home: 590 Willow Rd., Winnetka. Office: 105 S. LaSalle St., Chgo. 3. Died 1955.

VEDDER, Edward Bright, dir. med. edn.; b. N.Y. C., June 28, 1878; s. Henry C. and Minnie (Lingham) V.; Ph.B., U. Rochester, N.Y., 1898, D.Sc 1924; M.D., U. Pa., 1902, M.A., 1903; honor grad. Army Med. Sch., 1904; m. Lily S. Norton, June 22, 1903; children—Sibyl Norton, Henry C. 1st lt., asst. surgeon Med. Corps, U.S. Army, July 1903; advanced through grades to col., 1929. Served at various stas., U.S. and Pi., 1904-10; mem. U.S. Army Bd., for study tropical diseases, 1910-13; asst. prof. pathology, Army Med. Sch., Washington, 1913-19; charge So. Dept. Lab., Ft. Sam Houston, Tex., 1919-22; chief, med. research div., Edgewood Arsenal, Md., 1922-25; sr. mem. U.S. Army Bd. Med. Research, 1925-28; dir. Army Med. Sch., 1930-32; ret., 1933; prof. exptl. medicine, George Washington U., 1933-42; dir. med. edn., Alemeda County Hosp., 1942-47. Fellow A.C.P., A.C.S., A.M.A., A.A.A.S.; mem. Am. Soc. Tropical Medicine, Acad. Tropical Medicine, Washington Acad. Scis., Washington Acad. Medicine, Assn. Mil. Surgeons U.S., Delta Kappa Epsilon, Sigma Xi. Clubs: Army and Navy. Author: Beriberi, 1913; Sanitation for Medical Officers, 1917; Syphilis and Public Health, 1918; The Medical Aspects of Chemical Warfare, 1925; Medicine—Its Contribution to Civilization, 1929; also many papers med. jours. Home: 1090 Ardmore Av., Oakland, Cal. Died Jan. 30, 1952.

VENABLE, William Mayo, engineer; b. Cincinnati, O., Feb. 14, 1871; s. William Henry and Mary Ann (Vater) V.; B.S., U. of Cincinnati, 1892, M.S. (electricity), 1893, C.E., 1909; m. Jessie Genevieve Tuckerman, Dec. 26, 1901; children—Henry, John Ellinwood, Emerson. Mgr. Nat. Contracting Co., sect. A, East Boston Tunnel, and portion of New Orleans drainage system, 1900-04; mgr. Municipal Engring. Co. and Sanitary Engring. Co. of New York, 1904-06; div. engr. Fla. East Coast R.R. building Long Key Viaduct, 1906-08; in charge of sewer work for Ferro-Concrete Constrn. Co., 1908-09; mgr. Blackstaff Engring. Co., Louisville, 1909-10; engr. Blaw-Knox Co., Pittsburgh, since 1912. Mem. Am. Soc. C.E., A.A.A.S., Optical Society Am.; American Astronomical Society; vice president American Rights League, 1916. Author: The Second Regiment of United States Volunteer Engineers, 1899; Interior Wiring, 1900; Garbage Crematories in America, 1906; Methods and Devices for the Bacterial Purification of Sewage, 1908; The Sub-Atoms, 1933; The Spectrum of Hydrogen, 1942; The Interpretation of Spectra, 1948; Hydrogen in Chemical Atoms, 1950. Also has written various engineering papers and contributions to knowledge of color and of the structure of hydrogen and of helium; pamphlets on spectra, 1951 and 1952. Home: 6111 Fifth Av., Pitts. 32. Died June 3, 1955; buried Spring Garden Cemetery, Cin.

VENEMANN, H(enry) Gerald, univ. prof.; born Avon, Mass., Mar. 3, 1884; s. Robert Theodore and Jennie Adelle (Gerald) V.; student Purdue U., 1903-06; B.S. in Mech. Engring., U. of Colo., 1907; student Grad. Sch. Applied Sci.; Harvard, 1909-10; m. Elizabeth Frey Doughty, Dec. 28, 1910; children—Elizabeth Marie (Mrs. Wm. M. Lyles, Jr.), Minnie Adelle (Mrs. Dexter A. Smith). Engr., Colo. Ice and Cold Storage Co., Denver, 1911; chief engr. El Paso Ice & Coal Co., Colo. Springs, 1912-16, Des Moines Ice & Cold Storage, Des Moines, Ia., 1916-17; sales engr. Baker Ice Machine Co., Omaha, 1918-21, sales mgr., 1921-24, dist. mgr., Phila., 1924-28; sales engr. Frick Co., Pitts., 1929; prof. refrigeration Purdue U., 1929——. Sec.-treas. Ind. State Sr. Golf Assn., 1940——. Charter mem. Lafayette Little Theatre. Mem. Am. Soc. Refrigerating Engr., Nat. Assn. Practical Refrigerating Engrs. (chmn. ednl. com.), S.A.R., Ind. Soc. Mayflower Descendants, Phi Kappa Tau, Alpha Phi Omega, Pi Tau Sigma, Sigma Xi. Progressive Democrat. Episcopalian. Mason (Shriner), Elk. Author: Refrigeration Theory and Applications, 1942. Editor of question box, Ice and Refrigeration, 1942——. Home: 269 Littleton St., West Lafayette, Ind. Died Oct. 15, 1954; buried Fairmount Cemetery, Lamar, Colo.

VEREEN, William Jerome, mfr.; b. Wheeler County, Ga., June 11, 1885; s. William Coachman and Mary (McNeill) V.; grad. Ga. Mil. Acad., College Park, Ga., 1902; m. Lottie Thompson, Dec. 29, 1908; children—Mary Ellen (Mrs. Thomas A. Huguenin), Rosalind Eugenia (Mrs. George H. Lanier, Jr.), William Coachman, Thompson Jerome. With Moultrie Cotton Mills, 1903——, became vice president and treasurer, 1917, president, February 1943——; president Riverside Mfg. Co.; vice pres., dir. Moultrie Banking Co.; dir. 1st Nat. Bank, Atlanta. Mayor, City of Moultrie, 1916-17; mem. Industrial Advisory Bd., NRA, 1933-34; mem. Business Advisory Council of U.S. Dept. Commerce, 1933-36; chmn. Ga. Dem. Exec. Com., 1920-21; mem. Bd. Regents, Univ. System of Ga., 1933-35; pres. Cotton Mfrs. Assn. of Ga., 1919; mem. Am. Cotton Mfrs. Assn. (pres. 1925-26); pres. Southern Garment Mfrs. Assn., 1937-43, chmn. bd., 1943——. Democrat. Presbyn. (chmn. bd. deacons 25 yrs.). Clubs: Rotary of Moultrie (hon.), Capital City (Atlanta). Address: Moultrie, Ga. Died Oct. 1, 1952; buried Moultrie.

VERNON, James William, physician, psychiatrist; b. Person Co., N.C., July 21, 1886; s. Charles R. and Corinna Josephine (Henry) V.; B.S.; Wake Forest (N.C.) Coll., 1907; M.D., Jefferson Med. Coll., 1909; m. Sarah Cole Taylor, July 17, 1919; children—James Taylor, Livingston, Charles Robertson. Interne, Polyclinic Hosp., Philadelphia, Pa., 1910; asst. physician, Broadoaks Sanatorium, Morganton, N.C., 1910-17, supt. since 1921; cons. psychiatrist Morganton State Hosp.; psychiatrist to Grace Hosp., Morganton; company surgeon to Southern Ry., Morganton. Dir. First Nat. Bank, Morganton. Mayor of Morganton, 1933-37. Examining physician Burke County (N.C.) Local Bd. No. 1 since 1940; N.C. Hospitals Bd. Control (advis. comm.) since 1945. Served as 1st lt., M.C., U.S. Army, 1917, capt. 1918, major 1918; with A.E.F., France. Diplomate Am. Bd. Psychiatry and Neurology. Fellow A.C.P., A.M.A., Am. Psychiatric Assn.; mem. Southern Med. Assn., Fellow Med. Soc. of N.C. (pres. 1943-44), Assn. Southern Ry. Surgeons, Burke County Med. Soc. (pres. 1936), Tri-State Med. Assn., Catawba Valley Med. Soc., N.C. Bd. of Med. Examiners (pres. 1938), N.C. Neuropsychiatric Soc. (pres. 1938), Southern Psychiatric Assn., Am. Ornithologists Union, A.A.A.S., N.C. Academy Science, National Committee for Mental Hygiene, American Legion. Democrat. Presbyterian. Mason (32°). Clubs: Kiwanis, North Carolina Bird. Author: Circular Psychosis, 1926; Psychoneurosis, 1933; Psychiatry and the General Practitioner, 1926; Some Preventive Aspects of Mental Hygiene, 1943; A Challenge to the Doctors of North Carolina, 1944. Home: 209 Valdese Av. Office: Broadoaks Sanatorium, Morganton, N.C. Died July 16, 1955; buried Morganton.

VERNOR, Richard Edward, fire prevention b; Detroit, June 19, 1890; s. Frank Alanzo and Elsie C. (Shepard) V.; A.B., Albion (Mich.) Coll., 1913; m. Edith Ruth Begley, Sept. 24, 1927; 1 step-son, Harry Raymond Begley. Surveyor Mich. Inspection Bur., Jackson office, 1915; spl. agt. Liverpool & London & Globe Ins. Co., Detroit, 1919-20, state agt., 1920-22; mgr. fire prevention dept. Western Actuarial Bur., Chicago, since Oct. 1922. Member-at-large national council Boy Scouts of America. Chmn. Annual Fire Dept. Instrs. Conf. (Memphis); mem. fire service adv. com. Fed. Civil Defense Adminstrn.; chmn. Fire Waste Contest Com. Mem. Nat. Fire Protection Assn. (chmn. bd. dirs.), Am. C. of C. Executives, Internat. Assn. Fire Chiefs, Internat. Assn. Fire Fighters, Honorable Order Blue Goose International, Michigan Fire Chiefs Association, United States Chamber of Commerce, Chgo. Trade Assn. Execs. Forum, Greater Chicago Safety Council, Am. Legion, Sigma Chi. Republican. Methodist. Mason (32°). Clubs: Union League, Rotary (internat. treas. since 1946). Home: 40 E. Oak St. Office: 222 W. Adams St., Chgo. 6. Died June 3, 1958; buried Marshall, Mich.

VERRALL, Richard P(ercy), C.S. lecturer; b. Falmer, Sussex, Eng., Dec. 19, 1868; s. Richard Relfe and Mary Elizabeth (Gorringe) V.; student pvt. schs., Crystal Palace Engring. Sch., 1885, Instn. C.E., 1886; m. Gertrude Morris, Oct. 5, 1916. Came to U.S., 1893, naturalized, 1911. Apprentice Naysmyth & Wilson's Machine Tools, Manchester, Eng., 1887; with Laird's Shipbldg. Yards, Birkenhead, Eng., 1888; engring. staff Manchester Ship Canal, 1889; at sea African SS. Co., 1890; with Atlantic Transport Line, 1891; supt. Washington Ironworks, N.Y.C., 1893; joined First Ch. of Christ Scientist, N.Y.C., 1893, librarian C.S. Reading Room, 1894-1903, apptd. mem. com. publ. for C.S. chs. State N.Y., 1903, 1st reader, 1911-14, trustee First Ch. C.S., N.Y.C., 1924-26, 37, Chmn., 1938, 39; chmn. released time religious edn. com. C.S. chs. of Greater N.Y., 1940-45; apptd. to C.S. bd. lectureship The Mother Ch., First Ch. of Christ, Scientist, Boston, since 1945. Home: Hotel Devon, 70 W. 55th St., N.Y.C. 19. Office: 366 Madison Av., N.Y.C. 17. Died Dec. 20, 1952.

VERRILL, Alpheus Hyatt (vĕr'rĭl), author, illustrator, naturalist, explorer; b. New Haven, July 23, 1871; s. Addison Emery and Flora L. (Smith) V.; ed. Hopkins Grammar Sch.; Yale Sch. Fine Arts; spl. course in zoölogy under father; m. Kathryn L. McCarthy, Jan. 21, 1892; children—Dorothy I. (Mrs. Russell Rhodes), Eric E. (dec.), Loyola K. (Mrs. F. Cintron, Jr.), Valerie G. (Mrs. P. A. C. Ellis) (dec.); m. 2d, Lida Ruth Shaw, Nov. 11, 1944. Illustrated natural history dept. Webster's Internat. Dictionary, 1896; Clarendon Dictionary; many sci. reports, and other publs. Invented autochrome process (photography in natural colors), 1902. Extensive explorations in Bermuda, West Indies, Guiana, Central America, Panama, 1889-1920. Rediscovered supposedly extinct Solenodon parodoxus in Santo Domingo, 1907. Resided Dominica, British West Indies, 1903-06, British Guiana, 1913-17, Panama, 1917-21. Author of 105 books on adventure subjects natural history, travel and books for boys, latest being The Real Americans, 1954. Contbr. mags. Made enthnological expeditions to Panama, Peru, Bolivia, Chile and Surinam, 1916-

28; archaeological explorations, Central America, 1924-27; discovered remains of unknown prehistoric culture and carried on extensive excavations, Panama, 1924-27; engaged in making series of oil paintings of South and Central Am. Indians from life, 1926-28; archaeol. expdns., Peru and Bolivia, 1928-32; in charge of expdns., 1933, 34, slavaging Spanish galleon sunk in West Indies in 17th Century; expdn. to Brit. West Indies, 1948; expdn. to Mexico, 1953. In 1940 established the Anhiarka exptl. gardens and Natural Sci. Mus. at site of the ancient Indian village of Anhiarka where De Soto made his first settlement in Fla., 1944, established shell business, Lake Worth, Fla. Home: Route 1, Box 254, Chiefland, Fla. Died Nov. 14, 1954; buried Chiefland Cemetery.

VERSFELT, William H(olly), paper company exec.; b. Bklyn., July 7, 1898; children—William Holly, Jay Stuart, Suzanne. Joined St. Regis Paper Co., N.Y.C., 1921, treas. since 1935, dir. since 1939, v.p. since 1945; sec., dir., treas. Eastern States Corp.; v.p., treas., dir. Norwood & St. Lawrence R.R., St. Regis Timber Co., Ltd., St. Regis Paper Co. of Can., Ltd. Trustee, mem. police com. Village of Garden City. Republican. Clubs: Union League (N.Y.C.); Garden City Golf. Home: Garden City, L.I. Office: 230 Park Av., N.Y.C. 17. Died Sept. 4, 1956.

VER STEEG, Karl (vĕr-stēg'), geologist; b. Pella, Ia., Mar. 10, 1891; s. Nicholas and Marguerite (Van der Zyl) Ver S.; B.S., Central Coll., Pella, Ia., 1914; M.S., U. of Chicago, 1926; Ph.D., Columbia, 1930; Honorary D.Sc., Central College, Pella, Ia., 1946; m. Helena Martha Erdman, May 31, 1919. Began as instr. in science, Pella High Sch., 1914; served as principal, instr. in science, and as dir. of athletics in high schs.; instr. in geology and geography, U. of Ida., 1920-21; prof. geology and head of dept., Wis. Sch. of Mines, Platteville, Wis., 1921-23; prof. geology, Coll. of Wooster, 1923-26, prof. and head dept. since 1926, dir. civil pilot training program, 1940-41; special lecturer in meteorology and geography, Army pre-flight training program, Mich. School of Mines and Technology, Houghton, Michigan, summer, 1943; consulting geologist for various corporations and industries, consulting geologist for Texas Co., summer 1944. Served as director of athletics, Army Y.M.C.A., Camp Dodge, 1918. Mem. industrial water supply and conservation and flood control sub-coms., Ohio Chamber of Commerce ground water table com., 1940-41. Mem. National Affairs Committee of U.S. Chamber Commerce, of Western Ohio Bd. Trade, 1943-45. Fellow Geol. Soc. America, A.A.A.S., Ohio Acad. Sci. (past v.p.); mem. Ohio Athletic Conf. (v.p. 1945-47, pres. 1947-49), N.Y. Acad. Arts and Sciences; Seismological Soc. Am., Am. Assn. of U. Professors, Am. Soc. Professional Geographers, Nat. Aeronautic Assn., Ohio Forestry Assn., Sigma Xi. Republican. Presbyn. Mason. Author: (monograph) Wind Gaps and Water Gaps of the Northern Appalachians, Their Characteristics and Significance, 1930; co-author, Water Supplies of Ohio, Bulletin, 44, Ohio Geological Survey; also writer of publications on the buried topography of Ohio and parks of Ohio, jointing in the coal beds of Ohio, structural geology of Ohio, and contbr. scientific articles and reviews to jours. Home: 1105 Quinby Av., Wooster, O. Died Oct. 10, 1952; buried Pella, Ia.

VEST, Samuel Alexander, Jr., physician, eduacator; b. Almanace County, N.C., Jan. 21, 1905; s. Samuel Alexander and Gertrude (Roberts) V.; A.B., Duke; M.D., Johns Hopkins; m. Sarah Elise Thompson, Aug. 1, 1931. Research fellow Johns Hopkins, then asso. urology; practice of medicine, specializing urology; prof., head dept. urology U. Va. Mem. A.C.S., Am. Urol. Assn, Am. Assn. Genito-Urinary Surgeons, Clin. Soc. Genito-Urinary Surgeons. Home: Route 2, Greencroft, Charlottesville. Office: University of Virginia Hospital, Charlottesville, Va. Died Apr. 6, 1958; buried Monticello Meml. Park, Charlottesville.

VESTAL, Samuel Curtis, author, army officer; b. Cloverdale, Ind., Apr. 6, 1873; s. William B. and Isis M. (East) V.; grad. U.S. Naval Acad., 1895, Army Staff Coll., 1906, Army War Coll., 1915, Gen. Staff Coll., 1920; m. Olive S. Miller, of Greencastle, Ind., Mar. 29, 1899 (died 1943); children—Mildred (Mrs. M. V. Seeds), William Miller; m. 2d, Bertha Kimmel, Feb. 3, 1946. Pvt., corpl. and sergt., Co. E, 2d Inf., 1895; 2d lt. 7th Artillery, 1898; promoted through grades to colonel, 1920; retired, 1937. With siege train, Spanish-American War; in Puerto Rico, 1903-04; in Philippines, 1909-11, 1924-27; comdr. 339th Regiment F.A., Aug. 1917; arrived in France, Sept. 1918; participated in Meuse-Argonne offensive; insp. 6th Corps, after Armistice; instr. Army War Coll., 1920-24; asst. comdt. Coast Arty. Sch., 1927; chief of historical sect. Army War Coll., 1928-30; prof. mil. science and tactics, Mass. Inst. Tech., 1930-37; asso. mem. Walter Hines Page Sch. of Internat. Relations, Johns Hopkins U., 1929-33. Mem. Am. Hist. Assn., Am. Legion. Mason. Author: The Maintenance of Peace, 1920; Washington, The Military Man, 1931; also numerous mag. articles on mil. and internat., subjects. Home: 554 E. Howard St., Pasadena 6, Cal. Died Nov. 21, 1958.

VIALL, Ethan (vil), editor, cons. engr.; b. Kalamazoo, Mich., Aug. 17, 1873; s. Ethan and Mary Ophelia (Conklin) V.; high sch., tech. edn., Bloomington, and Chicago, Ill.; m. Evia Mae Sickles, Dec. 26, 1898 (dec.); children—Alda Sickles (dec.), Mrs. Eloise Brittingham, Mrs. Verda Isabelle Dell; m. Fern L. Parks, Jan. 28, 1939. Mech. apprenticeship, Chgo., 1893-98; foreman, supt. and mgr. various machine shops until 1908; began writing as corr. Am. Machinist, Machinery. Power, Am. Blacksmith; asso. editor Machinery, 1909-11; asso. editor, Am. Machinist, 1911-13, western editor, 1913-17, mng. editor, 1917-19, and editor-in-chief, 1919-21; gen. mgr. T. W. Minton & Co., 1921-22; special corr. Am. Machinist, and feature writer, 1922-26; editor Motor Service Magazine, Chicago, 1927-30, field editor since 1937. Is regarded as an authority on fine tool and die work, broaching and automatic machinery. Mem. Am. Soc. M.E., Am. Inst. Elec. Engrs., A.A.A.S., Franklin Inst, Soc. Automotive Engrs., Am. Soc. Testing Materials, Am. Steel Treaters Soc., Am. Assn. Business Paper Editors. Clubs: Engineers, Motor (Cincinnati); Commonwealth (New York). Republican. Mason (32°, K.T., Shriner), Odd Fellow, Woodmen of the World (thrice consul comdr., Cincinnati). Author: United States Artillery Ammunition, 1917; (with others) Manufacture of Artillery Ammunition, 1916; United States Rifles and Machine Guns, 1917; Broaches and Broaching, 1917; Welding and Cutting, 1920; Electric Welding, 1921; Gas-Torch and Thermit Welding, 1921; Grinders and Grinding, 1924; Mechanical Forging, 1924; also articles on Machine Tools, Thermit and Thermit Welding, Gas-Torch Welding, etc., for 12th and 13th edits. Ency. Britannica; also numerous tech. articles. Home: Knox, Ind. Died Dec. 15, 1949; buried Crown Hill Cemetery, Knox.

VICTOR, John Harvey, business exec.; b. Chicago, Ill.; married; children—Irene (Mrs. O. W. Clifton), George Edward, William Francis, Elaine Gay (Mrs. N. E. Berglund). Chmn. Victor Mfg. & Gasket Co., Chgo. Clubs: Union League (Chgo.); Glen View (Golf, Ill.); Michigan Shores (Wilmette, Ill.); Indian Creek Country, Surf (Miami Beach, Fla.). Home: 1046 Michigan Av., Wilmette, Ill. Office: 5750 Roosevelt Rd., Chgo. 50. Died Dec. 8, 1957.

VIETOR, Karl (vē-ā'tor), univ. prof.; b. Wattenscheid, Germany, Nov. 29, 1892; s. Karl Ludwig, and Laura (Clewing) V.; grad. Gymnasium Wiesbaden, 1912; student U. of Geneva, 1912, U. of Munich, 1912-13, U. of Berlin, 1913-16; Ph.D., U. of Frankfurt, 1919; A.M. (hon.), Harvard, 1942; m. Alice Beatrice Perner, July 10, 1919. Came to U.S., 1937, naturalized, 1944. Privatdozent U. of Frankfut A-M, 1922-25, prof. German literature of Giessen, Hesse, 1925-37; Kuno Francke prof. of German art and culture, Harvard, since 1937; vis. prof. U. of Amsterdam, 1930, Columbia, 1932, Harvard, 1935, 36, Stanford, 1941. Award Scherer-Preis Berlin Acad., 1923. Fellow Am. Acad. Arts and Scis.; mem. Modern Lang. Assn. Lutheran. Author: Die Lyrik Hoelderlins, 1921; Geschichte der deutschen Ode, 1923; Probleme d. Barockliteratur, 1928; Der junge Goethe, 1930, G. Buechner als Politiker, 1939; Goethe, 1949, G. Buechner, 1949. Home: 7 Shady Hill Sq., Cambridge 38. Office: Widener Library 446, Cambridge 38, Mass. Died June 7, 1951.

VIETT, George Frederic, author; b. Boulogne-sur-mer, France, Jan. 17, 1868; s. George Richard and Alice Blanche (Cook) V.; ed. pub. schs.; m. Georgia May Cunningham, of Gainesville, Ga., Aug. 25, 1898; 1 dau., Mrs. Vivienne Hancock. Came to U.S., 1876. Editor Galaxy Magazine, Norfolk, 1907-13. Episcopalian. Author: (verse) Thou Beside Me Singing, 1900; The Deeper Harmonies, 1905; New Rubaiyat from a Southern Garden (answer to Rubaiyat of Omar Khayyam), 1914; The Western Front, and Other Poems, 1915; Divae Memoriae, 1927; (prose) The Famous Hardy Murder Trial, 1910; The Advent of Reason, 1911; (drama) Pocahontas, prod. Norfolk, Va., 1907. Contbr. prose and verse to newspapers and mags. Owner and compiler lit. scrap collection, said to be largest and best pvt. collection in the country. Designer new aquatic sport, "Splash-Bunt," and pres. S.B. Sports Corpn. Home: 204 Park Av., Norfolk, Va. Deceased.

VILLA-LOBOS, Heitor (vēl'yä-lō bōs), Brazilian musician and composer; b. Rio de Janeiro, 1884; s. Raul Villa-Lobos and Noemia Monteiro; ed. Colegio Pedro II, 1897-1901; Colegio São Bento, 1900; Inst. of Music, 1901; m. 2d, Arminda d'Almeida. Dir. Lamoureux and Colonne concerts of Paris, and orchestras of Brussels, Barcelona, U.S., London, Rome, Buenos Aire, Rio de Janeiro, São Paulo, Paris; director of Villa-Lobos orchestra organized in Rio, 1933; now dir. Conservatory Nat. of Canto Orfeonico of Ministry of Edn.; had contact with Teatro Colón, Buenos Aires to direct 10 concerts and 4 ballets, 1935; del. to Internat. Congress of Musical Edn., Prague; del. to Internat. Meeting of Melody and Piano, Vienna, 1936. Honors: Decorated by Belgium, Spain and Portugal; hon. dir. various music insts. in Brazil and abroad. Mem. Conservatoire International (Paris), International Inst. of Intellectual Co-operation, Académie Internationale de Beaux-Arts (Paris), Society Contemporary Music, Instituto musical (Mexico), Inst. of Music (Bahia), Brazilian Assn. of Edn., Brazilian Press Assn., Brazilian Syndicate of Orchestral Professors, Carioca Society of Education. Author: Compositions: Operas, "Izaht," "Zoe," "Malazarte." Ville-Lobos utilizes native folklore. Address: Rue Aranjo Porto Alegre 5, Rio de Janeiro, Brazil. Died Nov. 17, 1959.

VINCENT, Clinton Dermott, U.S. Army officer; b. Borden Co., Tex., Nov. 29, 1914; s. Carvin Wyoming and Rose Loins (Burgess) V.; B.S., U.S. Mil. Acad., 1936; grad. Air Corps Advanced Flying Sch., 1937; m. Margaret Thayer Hennessey, Feb. 10, 1938; children—Thayer Ann, Patricia Thayer. Commd. as 2d lt. U.S. Army, 1936; and advanced to lt. col., 1942; mem. 19th pursuit sqdn., Wheeler Field, Hawaii, 1937-40; comdg. officer air base sqdn., Moffet Field, 1940; sqdn. comdr. fighter sqdn., Hamilton Field, Cal., 1940, later group operations officer, group exec., group comdr., 1940-42; exec. to Brig. Gen. F. M. Brady, India, 1942; operations officer, later exec., China air task force, acting chief staff 14th air force under Maj. Gen. Chennault, China, 1943; comdg. officer forward echelon 14th air force and C. G. 68th composite wing since May 1943, participating in fighter and bomber combat missions, combat record 6 Japs planes confirmed, 4 probably destroyed. Spl. mission to U.S., Sept.-Nov. 1943. Decorated Silver Star, Legion Merit, Distinguished Flying Cross with oak leaf cluster, Distinguished Service Medal, Air Medal with 3 oak leaf clusters, (U.S.); Golden Air Hero Medal, Order of Precious Tripod, Order of the Cloud Banner, Spl. Order of Yun Ma (China). Democrat. Methodist. Home: 232 W. Hollywood, San Antonio. Office: care Adjutant General, Washington. Died July 6, 1955.

VINCENT, Earl W., ex-congressman, lawyer; b. Keota, Ia., Mar. 27, 1886; s. George G. and Teressa (Wright) V.; A.B., Monmouth (Ill.) Coll., 1909, A.M., 1913; LL.B., State U. of Ia., 1912; m. Madge Lee, June 8, 1916; 1 dau., Marjorie Lee. Admitted to Ia. bar, 1912, and began practice at Guthrie Center; mem. firm Batschelet & Vincent; county atty. Guthrie County, 1919-22; mem. Ia. Ho. of Rep., 1923-26; mem. 70th Congress (1928-29), 9th Ia. Dist.; resumed practice. Judge of District Court of Iowa since 1945. Mem. Am. Bar Association, Iowa State Bar Assn., Sigma Alpha Epsilon, Phi Delta Phi, Sigma Delta Phi. Republican. Presbyn. Club: Lions (dist. gov. Lions Clubs of Ia., 1931-32). Home: Guthrie Center, Ia. Died May 22, 1953; buried Union Cemetery Guthrie Center.

VINSON, Frederic Moore, former Chief Justice of the U.S.; born in Louisa, Ky., Jan. 22, 1890; son of James and Virginia (Ferguson) Vinson; grad. Kentucky Normal Coll., 1908; A.B., Centre Coll., Ky., 1909 (Ormond Beatty alumni prize); LL.B., 1911 (Jacobs Jr. law prize and Sr. law prize), LL.D., Centre College 1938, U. of Ky., 1944, Mercer U., Washington and Lee U., Bethany Coll., Princeton, U. Louisville, 1947; Dickinson Coll., 1948; m. Roberta Dixon, Jan. 24, 1923; children—Frederick Moore, James Robert. Began law practice at Louisa, 1911; city attorney, Louisa, 1913; commonwealth attorney 32nd Judicial District, Kentucky, 1921-24; mem. 68th-70th and 72d Congresses (1923-29, 1931-33), 9th now 8th, Ky. Dist., 73d Congress (1933-35), Ky. at large 74th and 75th Congresses (1935-39), 8th Ky. Dist.; resigned May 12, 1938; asso. justice U.S. Court of Appeals for D.C., 1938-43; apptd. by Chief Justice Harlan F. Stone as chief judge U.S. Emergency Court of Appeals, Mar. 2, 1942; resigned as asso. justice of U.S. Court of Appeals, Washington, May 27, 1943; dir. Office Economic Stabilization, May 28, 1943-Mar. 4, 1945; apptd. fed. loan administrator, Mar. 5, 1945; apptd. dir. Office War Mobilization and Reconversion, April 2, 1945; apptd. secretary of the treasury July 23, 1945. Nominated Chief Justice of the United States by President Truman, confirmed by the Senate on June 20, 1946 and took his seat June 24, 1946. Recipient Presidential Medal for Merit; Distinguished Service Medal, American Legion, 1947. Member American, Kentucky State and Boyd County bar assns., Phi Delta Theta, Omicron Delta Kappa. Democrat. Methodist. Mason. Died Sept. 8, 1953.

VINSON, William Ashton, lawyer; b. White Oak, S.C., Dec. 22, 1874; s. John and Mary Elizabeth (Brice) V.; B.A., Austin Coll., Sherman, Tex., 1896, hon. LL.D., 1925; m. Ethel Clayton Turner, Dec. 19, 1900; children—Virginia (Mrs. James Griffith Lawton), Julia Elizabeth (Mrs. Charles William Dabney, Jr.), Martha Brice (Mrs. Dean Emerson, Jr.). Admitted to Texas bar, 1899; became member of the firm of Wilkins & Vinson, Sherman, Texas, 1900-09, Lane, Wolters & Storey, Houston, Tex., 1909-15, Townes & Vinson, Houston, 1915-17, Vinson & Elkins, 1917; mem. Vinson, Elkins, Weems & Francis, Houston, since 1936, also predecessor firms; dir. and gen. counsel Great Southern Life Ins. Co. Apptd. by Supreme Court mem. of com. to prepare Code of Civil Procedure for all Tex. Civil Courts, 1940; chmn. Com. on Interpretation of Rules of Civil Procedure. Pres. bd. trustees Houston Pub. Library since 1925. Mem. Am. and Tex. State bar assns., Am. Judicature Soc., Alpha Tau Omega. Democrat. Presbyterian (elder 1st Presbyn. Ch., Houston). Mason. Clubs: Houston, Houston Country, Bayou (Houston). Home: 1110

Lovett Blvd. Office: Esperson Bldg., Houston 2. Died Oct. 26, 1951.

VIPOND, Jonathan, bus. exec.; pres., dir. Scranton Tobacco Co., Inc.; pres., dir. Auburn Tobacco Co.; dir. Bayuk Cigars, Inc.; officer other cos. Dir. Nat. Assn. Tobacco Distbrs. Home: 1717 N. Washington Av. Office: Spruce St. and Franklin Av., Scranton, Pa. Died Nov. 12, 1954.

VIR DEN, Ray, advt. exec.; b. Wheeler, Ind., Dec. 3, 1895; s. Rev. Alanson Moody and Docia Grace (Hawk) Vir D.; student music and fine arts, N.Y.C., 1919-21; m. Frances Alda, Apr. 14, 1941. Singer light opera and concert, 1921-26; jr. partner Smith, Graham & Rockwell, members N.Y. Stock Exchange, 1926-30; joined Lennen & Mitchell, Inc., 1930, pres., 1947—, also dir. Served with U.S. Navy, 1917-19. Mem. Soc. Illustrators, Artists and Writers, Am. Assn. Advt. Agys., S.A.R. (former 2d v.p. N.Y. chpt.). Republican. Methodist. Clubs: Dutch Treat (pres.), Players, Cloud (N.Y.C.); Dauntless (Essex, Conn.); Deepdale (Great Neck, L.I.). Home: 510 E. Shore Rd., Gt. Neck, L.I. Office: 17 E. 45th St., N.Y.C. 17. Died Nov. 27, 1955.

VIRKUS, Frederick Adams, editor, pub., writer; student pub. schs., Chgo.; m. Nellie Moore, Apr. 9, 1902 (dec. May 24, 1951); children—George Frederick, Lorene Elizabeth (Mrs. Edwin Harper Lane), Robert Moore. With A. N. Marquis & Co., Chgo., 1892-1924; pres. Embossing Process Co., Chgo., 1912-14; v.p., treas. Wood, Nathan & Virkus Co., mfrs. Virkotype process, N.Y.C., 1914-17; pres. The Virkus Co., pubs., Chgo., since 1925. Rep. candidate for Congress, 6th Dist. Ill., 1936, Ill. at large, 1938; chmn. Cook Co. Congl. candidates and treas. Cook Co. Central Campaign Com., 1936; elected mem. Ill. Gen. Assembly, 7th Senatorial Dist., 1943-44, 45-46, chmn. Ill. legislative commn. small bus., 1943-47; del. Rep. Nat. Conv., 1948-52; chmn. exec. com. Nat. Rep. Roundup Com. since 1949. Mem. President's Conf. Indsl. Safety since 1947; bus. adv. bd. President's Council Econ. Advisors, 1948-53; small bus. task force Nat. Securities Resources Bd., 1948-50; adv. coms. Def. Transport Adminstrn. and Mut. Security Adminstrn. Delegated to make ind. survey econ. and monetary policies of Marshall Plan countries in Europe, 1950, drafted bill (H.R. 4036), 83d Congress to return U.S. to gold standard and redeemable currency. Organizer, chmn. City Mgr. Com., Chgo., 1934-36; mem. All Chgo. Council, 1936-38; mem. def. savs. and war finance coms. Ill., 1942-45. Mem. adv. bd. Progress Found. (Cal.), Patriotic Education, Inc. (Mich.). Mem. 1st Joint Orientation Conf. of Nat. Mil. Establishment, 1948. Enlisted in 1st Ill. Vol. Cav., Spanish-Am. War, 1898; served in Council Nat. Def., Washington, World War I; mem. adv. bd., and chief small facilities sect. Chgo. Ordnance Dist., World War II. Fellow Inst. Am. Genealogy; mem. Ill. Small Bus. Men's Assn. (pres. since 1939), Am. Small Bus. Orgns. (chmn. conf. since 1942), Am. Order Pioneers (hon. v.p.), Brit. Record Soc. (London), Deutscher Roland, Verein für Deutschvolkische Sippenhunde (Berlin), Zentralstelle für Deutsche Personan und Familiengeschichte (Leipzig), Gesellschaft Adler für Familien und Wapenkunde (Vienna); hon. mem. Koninklijk Nederlandsch Genootschap voor Geslachten Wappenkunde (The Hague), De la Soc. Suisse d'Heraldique (Lausanne), Inst. Araldico Romano (Rome), Genealogiska I Finland (Helsingfors), Dansk Genealogisk Inst. (Copenhagen), Real Sociedad Hispano-Americana de Genealogia y Heraldica (Mexico City), Union Heraldique Internationale (Brussels), Inst. Argentino de Ciencias Genealogicas (Buenos Aires), Kolgeun Heraldyczne (Warsaw), da Acad. Nacional de Heraldica e Genealogia (Oporto, Portugal), Luxembourg, Costa Rica, and many other Am. geneal., hist., civic socs. Mason. Club: Union League. Editor: Compendium of American Genealogy since 1917, Magazine of American Genealogy, 1928-30, Handbook of American Genealogy since 1932. Home: 350 Blackstone Av., La Grange, Ill. Office: 407 S. Dearborn St., Chgo. 5. Died Jan. 24, 1955.

VISSCHER, J(ohn) Paul, prof. biology; b. Holland, Mich., Sept. 19, 1895; s. Johannes W. and Everdena (Bolks) V.; A.B., Hope Coll., Holland, Mich., 1917; A.M., Johns Hopkins, 1920, Ph.D., 1924; m. Grace Yeomans, June 14, 1921; children—Marideen Julia, Paul Hummison. Instr. zoölogy, Washington U., St. Louis, 1920-22; spl. investigator, U.S. Bur. Fisheries, 1920-25; asst. prof. biology, Western Res. U., 1924-26, asso. prof., 1926-31, prof., 1931—, chmn. div. biology 1937-45; instr. Marine Biology Lab., Woods Hole, Mass., summer 1919-23. On leave absence as consultant, Chmn. Div., Naval Research Lab., Washington, 1945-46. Served as lt., Chem. Warfare Service, U.S. Army, 1917-18; spl. investigator, div. constrn. and repair, U.S. Navy, 1935-36. Bruce fellow, Johns Hopkins, 1918-19. Trustee Cleve. Mus. Natural History, Cleve. Bird Club. Fellow Ohio Acad. Sci. A.A.A.S.; mem. Zoölogy Soc. Am., Cleve. Regional Sci. Tchrs. Assn., Am. Soc. Naturalists, Ornithol. Union. Clubs: Wild Flower and Conservation (pres.), Professional Men's (past pres.) (Cleveland). Author: Nature and Extent of Fouling of Ships' Bottoms, 1928. Home: 2859 Scarborough Rd., Cleveland Heights, O. Office: 2080 Adelbert Rd., Cleve. Died Feb. 11, 1950; buried Pilgrim Home Cemetery, Holland, Mich.

VITTUM, Harriet E. (vĭt'ŭm), social worker; b. Canton, Ill., Feb. 14, 1872; d. George B. and Delia (Burrell) Vittum; ed. pub. schs.; hon. M.A., Knox Coll., 1924, Northwestern U., 1936. Engaged social welfare work, Chgo., 1893—; head res. Northwestern U. Stettlement, 1906-47. Ind. candidate for alderman 17th Ward, Chgo., 1914; Progressive Party candidate for mem. Bd. County Commrs., Cook County, Ill., 1914; mem. Progressive State Senatorial Com., Ill., 1914-16; del. Progressive Nat. Conv., 1916; charge woman's work for Rep. Nat. Com., campaign, 1916. Treas. City Gardens Assn., 5 yrs.; ex-pres. Social Service Club; pres. League No. 10, Juvenile Protective Assn.; dir. Ill. Div. Woman's Com., Council Nat. Def., May 1917-Feb. 1918. In charge women's dept. in Leonard Wood's campaign for Rep. presdl. nomination, 1920. Club: Woman's City. Home: 53 E. Elm St., Chgo. Died Dec. 1953.

VIVIAN, John Frederick; b. Phoenix Mine, Mich., Dec. 9, 1864; s. Joseph and Mary (Tresdder) V.; student pub. schs.; m. Addie E. Higgins, Aug. 27, 1886. Cattle raiser; pres. Jefferson County (Colo.) Republican Pub. Co. Mayor of Golden 3 terms; has been postmaster of Golden, surveyor gen. of Colo., collector of customs at Denver; register State Bd. Land Commrs., Colo., 8 yrs.; served as sec. and chmn. Rep. State Com., Colo.; mem. Rep. Nat. Com., 1920-24. Federal prohibition dir. for Colo., 1923-25; Federal prohibition administrator 18th Dist. 1925-33. Mason, K.P., Woodman. Home: Golden, Colo. Office: Mercantile Bldg., Denver, Colo. Died Aug. 12, 1954; buried Golden, Colo.

VOGEL, Charles W., U.S. Pub. Health Service; b. Baltimore, Aug. 8, 1870; s. Philip R. and Maria (Mueller) V.; grad. Knapp's Inst., Baltimore, 1886; Md. Coll. of Pharmacy, 1892; M.D., U. Md., 1895; widower; one son. Commd. asst. surgeon U.S.PH.S., 1899, passed asst. surgeon, 1904, surgeon, 1912, med. dir. 1930, retired, 1935. Mem. A.M.A., Baltimore Med. Soc., Assn. of Mil. Surgeons. Lutheran. Contbr. articles to med. jours. Home: 104 W. University Parkway, Baltimore. Died July 23, 1950.

VOIGT, Irma Elizabeth (voit); b. Quincy, Ill., Sept. 1, 1882; d. Henry and Mary (Tuffli) Voigt; grad. State Normal U., Normal, Ill., 1902; A.B., U. Ill., 1910, Ph.D., 1913. Dean of women, Ohio U., Athens, Ohio, 1913-49. Mem. Sherwood Eddy European Seminar, 1928; mem. Oxford Summer Sch., for Am. Univ. Women, 1932; del. to Internat. Fedn. Univ. Women, 1932. Mem. State bd. Ohio Deans Assn., 1942-46; mem. State bd. Ohio div. Am. Assn. Univ. Women, 1941-44. Mem. Am. Assn. U. Women (pres. Ohio State Fedn., 1929-31; dir. N.E. Central Sect. 1933-41; mem. Nat. bd.), N.E.A. (life), Am. Assn. Univ. Profs., Nat. Assn. Deans of Women (chmn nat. finance policies com. 1933-34, pres. 1935-37), Am. Council Guidance and Personnel Assn. (chmn. 1938-39; policy com. 1939-40), Soc. for the Advancement of Education, Ohio College Assn., Y.W.C.A., Nat. Collegiate Players, Sigma Kappa, Delta Sigma Rho, Kappa Delta Pi, Mortar Board, Methodist. Author: Life and Works of Mrs. Theresa Robinson: (with others) Deans at Work and Undergraduates; Housing College Students. Lecturer. Home: 35 Park Pl., Athens, Ohio. Died 1953.

VOLINI, Italo Frederick (vō-lē'nē), physician; b. Chgo., May 24, 1893; s. Camillo E. (M.D.) and Virginia (Botto) V.; A.B., U. Chgo., 1917; M.D., Rush Med. Coll., 1917; m. Marcella Ringwald, Nov. 4, 1925; children—Marcella Coletta, Gloria, Italo Frederick, Virginia, Yolanda, Camillo, Dolores, Francis, Patricia Anne, Thomas Anthony. In practice, 1917—; prof., head dept. medicine Loyola U. Sch. Medicine, 1929—; attending physician Cook County; cons. St. Mary's Hosp., Gary, Ind., Holy Cross, Columbus, Oak Park, St. Anne's, St. Bernard's and St. Elizabeth's, Mercy, Columbus hospitals; staff mem. Dept. Medicine Grant Hosp., St. Josephs Hosp., U. Hosp.; hon. pres. staff Mother Cabrini Hosp.; prof. medicine Chgo. Coll. Dental Surgery, Loyola U. Vice pres., trustee, prof. medicine, Cook County Grad. Sch. Medicine; chmn. dept. medicine Mercy Hosp., Chgo.; former dean Loyola U. Sch. Medicine. Mem. exec. bd. Cath. Charities Chgo.; v.p., mem. exec. bd. Cook County Hosp.; former mem. Chgo. Bd. Edn. Decorated Chevalier Order of Crown of Italy, 1930. Chevalier Officiale, 1934. Fellow A.C.P., Am. Coll. Chest Physicians; mem. A.M.A., Ill. State, Chgo. med. socs., Am. Heart Assn., Am. Bd. Internal Med., Chgo. Tb Soc., Chgo. Heart Assn. (dir.), Chgo. Soc. Internal Medicine (past pres.), Inst. Medicine, Italian Acad. Medicine (pres.), Dante Alighieri Soc. (p. pres.), Assn. Study Internal Secretions, Miss. Valley Med. Soc., Med. Adv. Council Hematology Research Found., Central Soc. Clin. Research, Am. Legion, Phi Beta Pi, Alpha Omega Alpha, Blue Key. Mem. K.C., Knight of St. Gregory. Club: Lake Shore Athletic. Address: 1511 N. Dearborn Parkway, Chgo. Died June 24, 1950.

VOLLMER, August, criminologist; b. New Orleans, Mar. 7, 1876; s. John and Philippine V.; student New Orleans Acad.; m. Millicent Fell, July 23, 1924. Served as pvt., G. Battery, 3d Arty., U.S. Army, Spanish-Am. War and Philippine Insurrection, June 23, 1898-Aug. 1899. Chief police, Berkeley, Cal., 1905-32; organized police dept., San Diego, 1917, Los Angeles, 1923-24; some time prof. police adminstrn., U. Chgo., U. Cal. Police cons. Detroit, Kansas City, Mpls. and Havana, Cuba. Mem. Internat. Assn. Chiefs Police (pres. 1921-22). Republican. Unitarian. Author: The Criminal, 1949; Police and Modern Society; (with A. E. Parker) Crime and the State Police; Crime, Crooks and Cops. Mem. adv. editorial council, Jour. Inst. Criminal Law and Criminology. Home: 923 Euclid Av., Berkeley, Cal. Died Nov. 4, 1955.

VOLLMER, Lula, playwright; b. Keyser, N.C.; d. William Sherman and Virginia (Smith) Vollmer; educated at Normal and Collegiate Institute (now Asheville College), Asheville, North Carolina. Member Dramatists Guild of Authors League America. Episcopalian. Author: Sunup, a play of the North Carolina mountains, produced at Provincetown Theatre, N.Y., May 24, 1923, later in Chicago, London, Amsterdam, Holland, Paris and Budapest, raising over $40,000 for ednl. work among mountain people; The Shame Woman, play of N.Carolina mountains, prod. New York, Oct. 16, 1923; The Dunce Boy, prod. New York, Apr. 5, 1925; Trigger, prod. New York, Dec. 6, 1927; Sunup pub. in book form, 1925; Moonshine and Honeysuckle, radio serial, started July 1930, and continued until Apr. 30, 1933; Sentinels, play of the South, prod. Biltmore Theatre, New York, Dec. 25, 1931. Wrote radio serials: Grits and Gravy, on air 6 mos., 1934; The Widow's Son, on air, 1935-37; The Hill Between (a play produced New York, 1938); also stories in The Saturday Evening Post, 1939, 41 and 42, Collier's, 1946; The American Story, Radio Series Nat. Assn. Mfrs., 1949. Home: 1 MacDougal Alley, N.Y.C. Died May 2, 1955; buried Attalla, Ala.

VOLWILER, Albert Tangeman (vŏl'wĭ-lẽr), prof. history; b. Cincinnati, O., Aug. 25, 1888; s. Jacob and Dorothea (Tangeman) V.; A.B., Miami (O.) U., 1910; A.M., U. of Chicago, 1911; Harrison scholar, fellow and research fellow, U. of Pa., 1920-23, Ph.D., 1922; m. Ada Ethel White, June 26, 1913; 1 son, Wade. Teacher, high sch., Hibbing, Minn., 1911-14, Evanston, Ill., 1918-20; instr. in history, U. of North Dak., 1914-18; prof. of history, Wittenberg Coll., Springfield, Ohio, 1923-33, also head of dept., 1926-33; asso. prof. history, Ohio University, 1933, prof. since 1934; chmn. department of history, 1947-55; acting prof. history (leave of absence), Indiana University, 1925-26; prof. of history, summers, Miami U., 1922, Johns Hopkins, 1923, W.Va. U., 1925, 38, U. of Pittsburgh, 1926, Pa. State U., 1931, 35, 50, U. Pa., 1928, 32, Coll. of the City of N.Y., 1941, Washington U., 1945, U. Mo., 1947, Mich. State U., 1950, San Francisco State Coll., 1956, U. So. Cal., 1957. Trustee Cooper Ohioana Library, 1946-57. Cons. Pres. Hayes Memorial Library. Fellow (Brit.) Royal Hist. Soc.; mem. Soc. Colonial History, Society American Historians, American and Mississippi Valley (exec. com. 1946-49) hist. assns., Phi Beta Kappa Tau Kappa Alpha, Phi Kappa Tau, Acacia. Awarded research grant by American Council Learned Societies, 1927 and 28, and a grant in aid by Social Science Research Council, 1929, and by the Am. Philos. Society, 1937. President of the Ohio Acad. of History, 1939; member Ohio War History Commission, 1942-47. Methodist. Author: George Croghan and the Westward Movement, 1741-82, 1926. Editor: Correspondence between Benjamin Harrison and James G. Blaine, 1940; contbd. sect. The Shaping of American Diplomacy, 1956. Mem. bd. editors Ohio Archaeol. and Hist. Quarterly, 1935-57. Contbr. to Am. Hist. Rev., Miss. Valley Hist. Rev., Scottish Hist. Rev., Dict. of Am. Biography, Collier Ency. Spl. cons. and contbr. to New Century Cyclopedia of Names, Nat. Ency. Home: 32 2d St., Athens, O. Died June 25, 1957.

VON HUTTEN, Baroness Bettina, author; b. Erie, Pa., Feb. 14, 1874; d. John S. and Kate (Howard) Riddle; ed. in Miss Peebles' and Miss Thompsons' Sch., N.Y.C.; m. Florence, Italy, Freiberr von Hutten zum Stolzenberg, Apr. 29, 1897. Author: Miss Carmichael's Conscience, 1898; Marred in Making, 1900; Our Lady of the Beaches, 1901; Violett, 1903; Pam, 1905; What became of Pam, 1906; The Halo, 1907; also Julia, Mrs. Drummond's Vacation. Address: London, Eng. Died Jan. 26, 1957.

von MISES, Richard (mē'zĕs), scientist; b. Austria, April 19, 1883; son Arthur Edler and Adele (Landau) von M.; Dr. tech., Tech. Univ. of Vienna, 1907; Dr. honoris causa, U. Brussels, 1935, Tech. U. Vienna, 1951, U. Istanbul, Turkey, 1952; M.A. honoris causa, Harvard Univ., 1945. Lecturer on mechanics, Tech. Univ. of Brno, 1908-09; asso. prof. of applied mathematics, Univ. of Strasbourg, 1909-18, Univ. of Frankfurt, 1918-19; prof. of strength of materials, Tech. Univ. of Dresden, 1919-20; prof., dir. of inst. of applied mathematics, Univ. of Berlin, 1920-33; prof. mathematics, U. Istanbul (Turkey), 1933-39; prof. of applied mathematics, Harvard

Univ. since 1939, Gordon McKay prof. of aerodynamics and applied mathematics, 1944-53; founder and editor Zeitschrift für Angewandte Mathematik und Mechanik, 1920-33; editor Differential und Integralgleichungen der Mechanik und Physik (with Philipp Frank), 1925-30. Served with Austro-Hungarian Air Force, 1914-18; built 600 horsepower plane of the Austrian Army, 1915. Fellow Am. Acad. of Arts and Sciences, Inst. of the Aeronautical Scis., Inst. Math. Statistics, and numerous other hon. socs. Author: Elemente der technischen Hydromechanik, 1914; Fluglehre, 1918; Wahrscheinlichkeit, Statistik und Wahrheit, 1928; Wahrscheinlichkeits-Rechnung und ihre Anwendungen, 1931; Kleines Lehrbuch des Positivismus, 1939; Theory of Flight, 1945; also numerous scientific papers, 1905-53. Editor: (bibliography) Rilke in English, 1946; 3 collections of writings in Rainer Maria Rilke (pvtly. printed); Advances in Applied Mechanics, Vols. I-III. Home: 10 Chauncy St., Cambridge 38, Mass. Died July 14, 1953.

VON NEUMANN, John (fŏn-noi'man), mathematics; b. Budapest, Hungary, Dec. 28, 1903; s. Max and Margaret (Kann) V.; student Berlin U., 1921-23, Zurich Inst., 1923-25; Ph.D., Budapest, 1926; D.Sc. Princeton, 1947, U. Pa., Harvard, 1950, Case Inst. Tech., U. Istanbul, 1952, U. Md., 1952, Munich Inst. Polytechnics, 1953, Columbia U., 1954; m. Mariette Kovesi, Jan. 1, 1930; 1 dau., Marina; m. 2d, Klara Dan, Dec. 18, 1938. Privatdozent mathematics, Berlin U., 1927; visiting prof. mathematical physics, Princeton U., 1930, prof., 1931-33, prof. Institute for Advanced Study, 1933. Mem. and consultant various Army, Navy, O.S.R.D., AEC, Committees, 1940-—; appointed to membership AEC, October, 1954. Received Medal for Merit and Distinguished Civilian Service award, 1947; Medal of Freedom, 1956, Albert Einstein award, 1956, Enrico Fermi award, 1956. Fellow Am. Physical Society; mem. Am. Math. Soc. (pres. 1951-53), American Mathematical Association, National Academy of Scis., Am. Philos. Soc., Am. Acad. Arts and Scis.; corr. mem. Royal Dutch Acad. Scis. (The Hague), Istituto Lombardo (Milan, Italy); associate mem. Academia Nacional de Ciencias Exactas, Lima, Peru. Mem. Sigma Xi. Clubs: Nassau (Princeton), Cosmos (Washington). Contbr. articles on math. subjects. Editor Annals of Mathematics (Princeton). Co-editor Compositio Mathematica (Amsterdam, Holland). Home: 26 Westcott Rd. Address: Institute for Advanced Study, Princeton, N.J. Died Feb. 8, 1957; buried Princeton.

VONNOH, Bessie Potter (Keyes) (vŏn'nō), artist, sculptor; b. St. Louis, Aug. 17, 1872; d. A. C. and Mary (McKenney) Potter; pupil Art Inst. Chgo.; m. Robert William Vonnoh, Sept. 17, 1899; m. 2d, Dr. Edward L. Keyes, June 26, 1948. Bronze medal, Paris Expdn., 1900; gold medal, St. Louis Expn., 1904, Nat. Acad. Design, 1921. Represented in Met. Mus. Art, Art Inst. Chgo. Corcoran Art Gallery (Washington), Bklyn. Mus. Made Roosevelt meml. bird fountain, Oyster Bay, L.I., 1925; Children's Garden fountain group, Central Park, N.Y.C. N.A., 1921; mem. Nat. Sculptrure Soc., Nat. Inst. Arts and Letters. Home: 33 W. 67th St., N.Y.C. Died Mar 9, 1955.

von PRITTWITZ und GAFFRON, Friedrich Wilhelm, diplomat; b. Stuttgart, Germany, Sept. 1, 1884; s. Arwed and Baroness Sara Schott von Schottenstein von P.; prep. edn., Baden-Baden; student univs. Bonn and Berlin; LL.D., Leipzig, 1906; referendar, Dist. Ct., Frankfurt-on-the-Main, 1906; student comml. coll., same city, 1906-07; LL.D., Syracuse U., 1929, U. Mo., 1930, Columbia, 1930, Atlantic U., 1931; m. Marie-Louise, nee Countess von Strachwitz, Dec. 20, 1920; 1 dau., Marie-Elisabeth. With br. Dresdner Bank, Frankfurt, 1906-07; began service in Fgn. Office, Berlin, 1908; attaché German Embassy, Washington, 1908-09; in Fgn. Office, Berlin, 1910; 3d sec., later 2d sec., St. Petersburg, Russia, 1911-14; army service, World War; wounded and transferred bur. Fgn. Office, later to Chancellery of The Reich; consul, Trieste, 1920; counselor Embassy in Rome (Quirinal), 1921-27; German A.E. and M.P., Washington, 1928-—. German del. Internat. Agrl. Inst. in Rome, 1924-26. Co-editor Die Deutsche Nation, 1919-25. Protestant. Clubs: Metropolitan, Racquet (Washington); Union (Berlin). Home: Tutzing, Oberbayern, Germany. Address: Personnel Department of the German Foreign Office, Bonn, Koblenzerstrasse 15, Germany. Died Sept. 1, 1955.

VON SCHRENK, Hermann (vŏn-shrĕnk), timber engr.; b. College Point, L.I., N.Y., March 12, 1873; s. Prof. Joseph and Anna (Bandtke) V.; B.S., Cornell, 1893; A.M., Harvard, 1894; Ph.D., Washington U., 1898; m. Mary Jane Kimball, Feb. 22, 1909. Instr. plant diseases, Shaw Sch. Botany, Washington U., 1896-1903; pathologist charge Miss. Valley Lab., Bur. Plant Industry, U.S. Dept. Agr. 1898-1907, charges investigations on timber diseases and timber preservation; spl. agt., chief div. forest products, Bur. Forestry, 1901-05; lectr. diseases of trees and timber preservation, Yale Forest Sch., 1902-09; lectr. plant pathology, U. Wis., 1909. Cons. timber engr., R.I., Frisco and C.&E.I. rys., 1907-12; Kansas City So., 1907-—, D.,L.&W. Ry., 1909-19; Lehigh Valley Ry., 1909-11; N.Y.C.&H.R. R.R., Lake Shore, Big Four, 1910-26; Mo. Pac., 1912-—, M., K.&T., 1915-—; N.Y., N.H.&H. R.R., 1921-30; Boston & Me., 1923-25; Wabash R.R., 1920-—; N.Y. Central Lines, 1926-—; Eric Railroad, 1927-46; St.L. S.W. Railroad, 1917-—; T.&P.R.R., 1920-—; St. Louis & San Francisco Lines 1946-—; Nickel Plate Ry., 1916-43; Fla. E. Coast Ry., 1941-43; engr. Nat. Lumber Mfrs. Assn., 1914-18. Chmn. Mo. State Forest Commn., 1908-12; lectr. timber preservation, Baltimore Forest Sch., 1906-14; pathologist, Mo. Bot. Garden, 1907-—. Sec. Am. bd. editors Botanisches Centralblatt, 1908-14, engaged in investigations of diseases of fruit trees and forest trees, and timber preservation. Author: The Decay of Timber and Methods for Preventing It, 1902; Seasoning of Timber, 1903; Diseases of Hardwood Trees, 1909; Protection of Ties Against Mechanical Wear, 1930; also papers on kindred subjects. Mem. sub-com. forest products s.w. region, U.S.R.R. Adminstrn., 1919-20. Del. Internat. R.R. Congress, Madrid, 1930. Home: 289 St. Denis St., Florissant, Mo. Office: Tower Grove and Flad Avs., St. Louis. Died Jan. 30, 1953; buried Florissant, Mo.

VON STROHEIM, Erich (Oswald, Hans Carl Maria von Nordenwall) (fŏn-strō'hīm), motion picture dir., actor, author; b. Vienna, Austria, Sept. 22, 1885; s. Benno and Johanna (Von Bondy) Von S.; grad. Imperial and Royal Mil. Acad., Wiener-Neustadt, 1902; m. Marguerite Knox (dec.); m. 2d, May Jones; 1 son, Erich; m. 3d, Valerie Marguerite Germonprez, Oct. 16, 1920; 1 son, Josef Erich. Came to United States 1909, naturalized citizen, 1926. Wrote, acted leading part and directed motion pictures—Blind Husbands, Foolish Wives; wrote and directed Devil's Passkey, Merry-Go-Round, Greed, The Merry Widow; also wrote, acted leading part and directed The Wedding March, for P. A. Powers-Famous Players-Lasky Corp., 1925-27; starred in Three Faces East, The Lost Squadron; supported Greta Garbo in As You Desire Me; wrote Tempest, Walking Down Broadway, Her Highness, Queen Kelly, Between Two Women, The Alienist (stage play), The Great Gabbo; portrayed Rommel in Five Graves to Cairo, 1943; appeared in North Star, 1945, Sunset Blvd., 1949. Was elected in 1926, by All American Critics in contest as best director. In France working in motion pictures (La Grande Illusion, most notable), 1936-39, 1945; in I Was an Adventuress, So Ends Our Night, 1940; stage appearance in Arsenic and Old Lace, 1941. Served as second and first lieutenant in the Imperial and Royal Austrian Army and as pvt. Squadron "C," 1st Cav., N.Y.N.G. Decorated Officier Palmes Academiques of France; Mil. Cross of Merit. Mem. Acad. Motion Picture Arts and Sciences, Actors Guild, Writers Guild, Directors Guild (Eng., France), Actors Equity. Catholic. Author: Paprika (book), 1935; Feux de la St. Jeane, 1951. Address: care Jean Loudon. 65 Champs Elysés, Paris, France. Died May 12, 1957.

VON TUNGELN, George Henry, educator; b. Golconda, Ill., July 30, 1883; s. Gerhardt and Kathrine (Manson) V.; Ph.B., Central Wesleyan Coll., Warrenton, Mo., 1909; M.A., Northwestern U., 1910; Ph.D., Harvard, 1926; m. Maude Mildred Drew, of Caldwell, Kan., Sept. 2, 1914. Teacher rural sch., Ill., 2 yrs., instr. English, Mich. State Agrl. Coll., 1910-11; teaching scholar, 1911-12, Robert Treat Paine fellow, 1912-13, Harvard; asst. prof. sociology, 1913, asso. prof., 1914, prof. 1919-—, Ia. State Coll. Agr. and Mechanic Arts. Mem. Am. Economic Assn., Am. Sociol. Soc., Nat. Country Life Assn. (state dir.), Am. Farm Economics Assn., Nat. Conf. Social Work, Pi Gamma Mu, Gamma Sigma Delta; life fellow Royal Economic Soc., London. Mem. Nat. Com. Boys' and Girls' Club Work in America. Methodist. Joint Author: Persistent Public Problems, Unemployment, and Social and Industrial Righteousness, 1916; also monographs on rural social service. Home: Ames, Ia. Deceased.

VOORHIES, Paul Warren (vôr'ēz), lawyer; b. Plymouth, Mich., Dec. 17, 1875; s. James Warren and Jennie (Gillespie) V.; B.L., U. of Mich., 1898, LL.B., 1900; m. Faye Bodmer, Aug. 28, 1902; children —Jeanne Eleanor, Pauline. Admitted to bar, Michigan, 1900, N.Y. State, 1901; began practice at Detroit; asst. pros. atty. Wayne County, Mich., 1912-18, pros. atty., 1921-24; atty. gen. of Mich., term 1931-33; prosecuting atty., Wayne County, Mich., 1940; member Voorhies, Long, Ryan and McNair; pres. and trustee Kresge Foundation; pres. First Federal Savings & Loan Assn. Mem. Mich. Public Utilities Commn., 1935-36; dir. Plymouth United Savings Bank. Mem. Am. Mich. State and Detroit bar assns. Republican. Methodist. Mason. Clubs: Detroit, Detroit Golf, Rotary. Home: 1180 Longfellow Av. Office: Penobscot Bldg., Detroit. Died Jan. 8, 1952; buried Plymouth, Mich.

VOORHIS, Warren Rollin, lawyer; b. Indpls., Dec. 6, 1873; s. William Manning and Anna Christine (Cox) V.; student Central Normal Coll., Nat. U., Ind. Teachers Coll.; LL.B., Ind. Law Sch., 1896; m. Edna Curlee, June 22, 1895 (dec.); children—Harold O., Manning C., Dorothy A. (Mrs. Alden DeHart), Margaret Virginia (Mrs. F. Willoughby Frost). Admitted to Ind. bar, 1896; gen. practice in Ind., 1896-1918; pros. atty. Howard Circuit Court, Ind., 1903-05; city atty., Kokomo, 1907-11; spl. practice of rate and valuation law for pub. utilities, 1918-41; now retired from all pub. utility bds. and offices; v.p. and dir. American Water Works and Electric Co., Inc.; v.p. and dir. West Penn Electric Co.; dir. West Pen Power Co., Monogahela West Penn Pub. Service Co., Potomac Edison Co.; v.p. and dir. Medallic Art Co. Mem. Acad. Polit. Science, Soc. of Medalists. Republican. Presbyn. Mason. Clubs: The Holland Society (New York); Plainfield Country. Contbr. articles on finance and pub. utility management to jours. Home: Rahway Road, Plainfield, N.J. Died Aug. 31, 1953; buried Jerome, Ind.

VOS Geerhardus, theologican; b. Heerenveen, The Netherlands, Mar. 14, 1862; s. Jan Hendrik and Aaltje (Beuker) V.; grad. Gymnasium, Amsterdam, 1881; student theol. sch., Holland Christian Reformed Ch., Grand Rapids, Mich., 1881-83, Princeton Theol. Sem., 1883-85; Hebrew fellow, Princeton Sem., 1885; student, U. Berlin, 1885-86, Strassburg, 1886-88, Ph.D., 1888; D.D., Lafayette, 1893; m. Catherine Frances Smith, Sept. 7, 1894. Ordained Presbyn. ministry, 1894. Prof. theol. sch., Holland Christian Reformed Ch., Grand Rapids, 1888-93; prof. Bibl. theology, Princeton Theol. Sem., 1893-1932, now emeritus. Author: The Mosaic Origin of the Pentateuchal Codes, 1886; De Verbondsleer in de Gereformeerde Theologie, 1891; Die Kämpfe und Streitigkeiten Zwischen den Banu Ummajja, und den Banu Hashim, 1888; The Teaching of Jesus Concerning the Kingdom of God and the Church, 1903; Spiegel der Genade (verse in Dutch), 1922; Grace and Glory, 1922; Self-Disclosure of Jesus, 1926; Spiegel der Natuur (verse in Dutch), 1927; The Pauline Eschatology, 1930; Charis (verse in English), 1931; Spiegel des Doods (verse in Dutch), 1932; Western Rhymes, 1933; Zeis en Garve (verse in Dutch), 1934; Old and New Testament Biblical Theology, 1948. Home: 1341 Colorado Av. S.E., Grand Rapids 7, Mich. Died Aug. 13, 1949; buried Roaring Branch, Pa.

VOTER, Perley Conant, educator; b. Farmington, Me., Apr. 30, 1889; s. Warren Tyler and Ella Eliza (Conant) V.; A.B., Bowdoin Coll. (Charles Everett fellow), 1909; A.M., Harvard, 1911; m. Anne Mabel Crossland, Aug. 13, 1913; children—Muriel Anne (Mrs. Carroll M. Williams), Roger Conant. Austin teaching fellow Harvard, 1910-12, 19-20; in str. chemistry Middlebury (Vt.) Coll., 1912-13, asst. prof., 1913-19, prof. since 1919, chmn. dept. chemistry since 1919, chmn. div. natural scis. since 1947, Burr prof. natural history and chemistry since 1952. Trustee Battell Park Trust. Mem. American Chem. Soc., Societé Suisse Chimie, Soc. Chem. Industry. Republican. Conglist. Mason (33°). Home: 20 College St., Middlebury, Vt. Died June 1953.

VUILLEUMIER, Ernest Albert (vē'ūm-yā), prof. chemistry; b. New City, Rockland County, N.Y., Mar. 1, 1894; s. Charles and Matilda (Barny) V.; B.S. in Chemistry, U. of Pa., 1914; grad. student, same, 1915-16; Ph.D., U. of Berne, Switzerland, 1918; m. Frances E. Smith, Dec. 27, 1924. Analytical and control chemist, Powers-Weightman-Rosengarten Co., Phila., 1914-15; instr. chemistry, Drexel Inst., Phila., 1915-16; Rosengarten traveling scholarship, U. of Pa., at Berne, 1916-18; research chemist Powers-Weightman-Rosengarten Co., 1919-20; became head dept. chemistry, Dickinson Coll., 1920-58, dean of the junior class, 1927-28, the freshman class, 1928-33, acting dean of the college, 1933-35, dean 1935-47, also C. Scott Althouse prof. chemistry, 1951-—. With A.E.F. in France, 1918-19. Acting Swiss consul, Pa., N.J., and Del., summer 1923. Fellow Am. Inst. Chemists, A.A.A.S.; mem. Am. Chemical Society (chmn. S.E. Pa. section 1951-52), American Electrochem. Society, Verein für Chemiker der Universitaet Berne, Pa. Acad. of Science (pres. 1941-42), Phi Beta Kappa, Omicron Delta Kappa. Republican. Methodist. Author of articles presenting investigations in electrodeposition, analysis of alcoholic liquids, etc. Inventor Dickinson alcohometer and Dickinson solids-hydrometer; co-inventor of contractometer for study of peeling of nickel-plating. Address: Dickinson College, Carlisle, Pa. Died Oct. 6, 1958; buried Halifax, Pa.

VYSHINSKY, Andrei Yanuarievich, U.S.S.R. del. to United Nations; b. Odessa, 1883; grad. in law, Kiev Univ., 1913; awarded Dr. of State and Social Sciences, 1935. Joined revolutionary movement, 1905; organized Social-Dem. militant group in Caucases; became sec. Baku Council of Workers Deputies; subjected to deportations and arrests and imprisoned for one year for activities in connection with Dec. Railway strike, 1905. Engaged in literary work and teaching, 1913-17; leetured at Moscow U., 1921-22; prosecutor Div. of Criminal Cases, Supreme Ct. of U.S.S.R., and also prof. of criminal law procedure, Moscow U., 1923-25; rector Moscow State U., 1925-28; mem. Collegium of People's Commissariat for Edn., of R.S.F.S.R., 1928-31; prosecutor of Russian Republic, 1931-33; dep. prosecutor of U.S.S.R., 1933-35, prosecutor, 1935; prosecutor in trials, Trotskyite-Zinoviev Terrorist Center, 1936, Anti-Soviet Rightist-Trotskyite Bloc, 1938; dir. U.S.S.R. Acad. of Sciences Law Inst.

and editor Soviet State and Law mag., 1937-41; mem. Central Exec. Com., U.S.S.R., 1935-37; mem. Supreme Soviet of U.S.S.R. since 1947; elected mem. Central Com. of Communist Party of Soviet Union at 18th congress of the party; senior dep. Peoples Commissar for Fgn. Affairs of U.S.S.R., 1940-46; dep. minister fgn. affairs for general questions, 1946-49, became minister for fgn. affairs 1949; now U.S.S.R. delegate to U.N. Elected candidate mem. Presidium of Communist Party of Soviet Union by XIX Congress of Communist Party, Soviet Union. Member Consultative Council for Italy, 1943-44; mem. Soviet del. to Crimea and Berlin confs., 1945; mem. Conf. Ministers of Fgn. Affairs, Moscow, 1943, 45; mem. Paris Peace Conf., 1946; mem. Council Fgn. Ministers, N.Y. City, Moscow, London; head Soviet del. to U.N. Gen. Assembly, London, 1946, N.Y. City, 1947, Paris, 1948, N.Y. City, 1949; mem. Council Fgn. Ministers, Paris, 1949. Awarded Order of Lenin 4 times; Order of Red Banner of Labor; Defense of Moscow medal; medal for Valiant Labor in Patriotic War of 1941-45. Author: Theory of Court proves in the Soviet Law (Stalin Prize laureat, 1st grade). Address: The Kremlin, Moscow, U.S.S.R.; also care U.N., 610 Fifth Av., N.Y.C. Died Nov. 25, 1954.

W

WACH, Joachim, educator, scholar; b. Chemnitz, Germany, Jan. 25, 1898; s. Felix and Katharina (Von Mendelssohn-Bartholdy) W.; student U. of Munich, 1917, U. of Berlin, 1919-20; Ph.D., U. of Leipzig, 1922; Th.D., U. of Heidelberg, 1929; unmarried. Came to U.S., 1935, naturalized, 1946. Prof. history of religions, U. of Leipzig, 1924-35; vis. prof. Brown U., Providence, 1935-37, asso. prof., 1937-46; prof. of history of religions, U. of Chicago, 1946—. Mem. Am. Ch. History Soc., Phi Beta Kappa (hon. mem.). Episcopalian. Author: Das Verstehen (3 vols.), 1926-32; Sociology of Religion, 1944; Types of Religious Experience, 1951. Home: Casa Bagatella, Orselina, Locarno, Switzerland. Died Aug. 27, 1955; buried Orselina, Locarno, Switzerland.

WACK, Henry Wellington, lawyer, author, artist; b. Baltimore, Md.; s. Charles G. A. and Elizabeth W. (Noss) W.; ed. pvt. instrn. and univ. course; admitted to New York bar, 1897; m. Lillian Tremere de Blois, Apr. 18, 1899; children—John T. de Blois, Audrey Wellington, Damon de Blois. Writer St. Paul Globe, and on Dispatch; founder and first editor Field and Stream; vice chairman and managing dir. A. J. White, Ltd., London; advertising dir. Murphy Varnish Co., 1916-18; mem. law firm Dunne, Rutherford & Wack, N.Y. City. Counsel in Cook-Peary North Pole controversy. Mem. Minn. Nat. Guard 5 yrs. Del. New York Press Club to Internat. Press Congress, Vienna, 1904; mem. Royal Geog. Soc. (life fellow), Am. Geog. Soc., Medico-Legal Soc. (chmn. sect. on eugenics), Nat. Editorial Assn., Am. Bar Assn., Nat. Shakespeare Fedn. (pres.), Baconian Soc. America (pres.). Asso. editor Medico-Legal Journal, 1910-17. Exec. adviser Com. of One Hundred, Newark, N.J., and mgr. Newark's 250 Anniversary Celebration, Pageant, etc., 1915-16; chmn. com. on pub. comfort stations, Newark. Asso. publicity dir. Y.M.C.A. War Work Council, 1918; "four-minute" speaker, World War; mng. director of seized corps. for alien property custodian during World War I; camp, travel, ednl. editor Red Book Mag., 1923-27; chmn. Little Theatre Guild, Newark, N.J.; dir. Berkshire Nature Trail, Lakeville, Conn.; mem. advisory board Sportsmanship Brotherhood. Abroad 8 yrs.; painter of landscapes; works on exhibition in Am. museums. Past pres. Brooklyn Soc. of Artists, Brooklyn Painters and Sculptors (dir.), Shakespeare Memorial Circle of New York (pres.). Clubs: Royal Socs., Wimbledon Golf, Antiquarian (London); Press, Authors (life), Athletic, Nat. Arts, Salmagundi (New York); Kishawana Country. Canadian Camp; Authors (London). Author: The Fish and Game of Florida, 1897; In the Snow of the Alps, 1901; The Bachelor Book, 1902; The Story of the Congo Free State, 1905; The Romance of Victor Hugo and Juliette Drouet, 1905; In Thamesland, 1906; Feminism and Divorce, 1912; Newark Anniversary Poems, 1917; Four Minute Year Book, 1918; Hive Farm Ballads, 1918; The Right Hon. Arthur James Balfour, 1918; The New Soul of the Nations, 1919; Foundations of American Liberty, 1921; Summer Camps—Boys and Girls, 1923; The Camper's Creed, 1923; The Camping Ideal—a New Human Race, 1924; You and I and Life, 1925; A University of Leisure, 1926; Songs of the Trail, 1926; Tableaux of the Trail, 1927; Ten Commandments of the Trail, 1927; Travelgrams, 1929; Explorations in Friendship, 1930; The Romance of Trees, 1933; Early History of Field and Stream, 1949. Radio speaker for City of New York, 1926-32; cruise lecturer for Cunard-White Star Line; also lecturer on civics, art, camping and travel. Was travel editor Arts and Decoration, 1929-31; asso. editor Camp Life Mag. Psychologist, Round-up Lodge for Boys, Mt. Princeton, Colo. Spl. writer for New Eng. and Pacific Coast newspapers. Formerly asso. editor of Field and Stream. Home: 175 Butterfly Lane, Santa Barbara, Cal. Retired. Died Dec. 13, 1954.

WACK, Otis, engr.; b. Lansdale, Pa., Dec. 11, 1880; s. David and Susan (Fetterolf) W.; degree in C.E., LaFayette Coll., Easton, Pa., 1906; m. Bessie Wier Manee, June 25, 1910; children—Edwin Otis, Virginia Annabell (Mrs. M. A. Heagy), Elaine Manee (Mrs. C. M. Maffie). Engring. in and around N.Y. C., 1906-13; work mgr., v.p. Wentworth Gypsum Co., Gypsum Packet Co., Newport Plaster Mining and Mfg. Co., Hillsboro Plaster Mining Co. (Canadian subsidiaries J. B. King and Co.), 1913-24; operating mgr. in Can., U.S. Gypsum Co., 1924-36; chief engr., 1936-46, v.p., 1946—. Mem. Engring. Socs. Can. and N.S. Mason (K.T., Shriner), Rotarian. Home: 3039 Payne St., Evanston, Ill. Office: United States Gypsum Co., 300 W. Adams St., Chgo. Died Feb. 21, 1951.

WADE, Frank Bertram, educator, author; b. New Bedford, Mass., July 8, 1875; s. Joseph Bennett and Mary Bradford (Gooding) W.; B.S., Wesleyan U., Conn., 1901 (spl. honors in chemistry); research study at Lewis Inst., Chicago, 1901-03; m. Ethel Alberta Nicholson, Aug. 19, 1908; children—Lucille Winkley, Nicholson Gooding. Asst. teacher of science, New Bedford (Mass.) High Sch., 1894-97; instr. in chemistry, Lewis Inst. Chicago, 1901-03; with Shortridge High Sch., Indianapolis, 1903-49, now head chemistry dept. Editor (for chemistry) School Science and Mathematics, Chicago. Fellow Ind. Acad. Scis. (pres. 1926-27); mem. Ind. Sect. Am. Chem. Soc. (twice pres.; mem. com. on chem. edn. and Senate of Chem. Edn. of Am. Chem. Soc.), Central Assn. Sci. and Mathematical Teachers (pres. 1922-23), C. of C., A.A.A.S. (com. on place of science in the curriculum), Phi Beta Kappa, Psi Upsilon. Republican. Quaker. Mason. Clubs: School Men's of Indianapolis, Scientech Club of Indiana. Author: Foundations of Chemistry (with A. A. Blanchard), 1914; Laboratory Exercises in Chemistry, 1917; Teachers' Hand Book (with A. A. Blanchard), 1915; Diamonds—A Study of the Factors that Govern Their Value, 1916; A Text-Book of Precious Stones, 1917; How to Buy Diamonds Wisely, 1921; Fundamental Facts in Regard to Industrial Diamond Setting, 1923; The Teaching of Science and the Science Teacher (with Prof. Herbert Brownell), 1925. Home: 5241 College Av., Indpls. Died Oct. 3, 1950.

WADE, George Garretson, business exec.; b. Cleve., Aug. 29, 1882; s. Jeptha Homer and Ellen (Garretson) W.; prep. edn. Univ. Sch., Cleveland; student Yale, 1904; m. Irene Elizabeth Love, June 2, 1909. Pres. Wade Realty Co., Montreal Mining Co.; dir. Columbia Transportation Co., Wyoming Pocahontas Coal & Coke Co., Cleveland Quarries Co., Cleveland Cliffs Iron Co., Mogul Mining Co., Medusa Portland Cement Co., Toledo, Angola & Western Ry. Co., Pringle Barge Line Co. Clubs The 50, Tavern, Kirtland, Union, Chagrin Valley, Hunt. Home: 10804 Magnolia Dr. Office: Union Commerce Bldg., Cleve. Died June 29, 1957.

WADE, Herbert Treadwell, editor, author; b. New York, N.Y., Sept. 2, 1872; s. Daniel Treadwell and Margaret Anna (Munroe) W.; prep. edn., J. H. Morse's pvt. sch., New York, A.B., Columbia Coll., 1893; m. Mrs. Ethel G. Jacquelin Stout, July 3, 1931 (deceased March 25, 1951). Assistant in physics, Columbia University, 1893-99; office editor (technology) New International Encyclopedia, 1900-03; advisory editor and contbr. applied science and technology, 2d edit., and supplement same, 1913-24, editor, 1925-32. Mng. editor Nelson's Ency., 1905-07; editorial dept. Am. Review of Reviews, 1907; editor Engineering Index Annual, 1909-10; lit. editor Photographic History of Civil War, 1911; editor, adviser and contbr. New Internat. Year Book, 1907-24, editor in chief, 1925-32. Mem. bd. trustees of Grant Monument Assn., N.Y. City. Commd. capt. Ordnance Dept., U.S. Army, June 14, 1918; in charge Spl. Reports Br., Information Sect., Office Chief of Ordnance; hon. discharged Mar. 22, 1919; capt. ordnance, O.R.C., promoted maj., Oct. 14, 1924; maj. Inactive Reserves, 1939. Mem. Army Ordnance Assn., Society of Colonial Wars (gov. N.Y. Society, 1944-45; Deputy Governor General, 1945), Sons of the Revolution, Military Order of Foreign Wars, Military Order World War, Society of Older Graduates of Columbia (pres. 1939-40), Phi Beta Kappa. Republican. Episcopalian. Clubs: University, Columbia University. Author: Evolution of Weights and Measures, and The Metric System (with Wm. Hallock), 1906; Astronomy (with W. Kaempffert), 1909; Everyday Electricity, 1924; Scales and Weighing—Their Industrial Applications, 1924; The Colonial Wars in America, 1942, illustrated edit., 1948; also numerous articles in magazines. Advocate of the metric system. Home: "Cedarmarch," New Canaan, Conn.; also University Club, 1 W. 54th St., N.Y.C. 19. Died Mar. 18, 1955.

WADSWORTH, Alfred Powell, newspaper editor; b. Rochdale, Eng., May 26, 1891; hon. M.A., Manchester U., 1932; m. Alice Lillian Ormerod, July 1, 1922; 1 dau., Janet Rosemary. Trained as journalist Rochdale Observer; with Manchester Guardian, 1917—, successively spl. corr., labour corr., leader writer, asst. editor, editor, 1944—; dir. Manchester Guardian and Evening News, Ltd. Gov., John Rylands Library. Mem. Ct. Manchester U. Author: (with Julia de Lacy Mann) The Cotton Trade and Industrial Lancashire 1600-1780, 1931. Home: 30 Broadway, Withington, Manchester 20. Office: The Guardian Office, Manchester, Eng. Died Nov. 4, 1956.

WADSWORTH, Eliot, ex-asst. sec. treasury; b. Boston, Mass., Sept. 10, 1876; s. Oliver Fairfield and Mary Chapman (Goodwin) W.; A.B., Harvard, 1898; LL.D. (honorary), University of Rochester, 1921, Northeastern U., 1947; A.M., Harvard, 1923; m. Mrs. Nancy Scull, 1922 (dec. Aug. 1958); 1 dau., Nancy Elizabeth. Began in employ Planters' Compress Co., Boston; became connected with Stone & Webster, elec. engrs., admitted as partner, 1907; retired from firm, Dec. 31, 1916, now mem. bd. dirs.; v. chmn. central com. Am. Nat. Red Cross, 1916-19; mem. central com., 1921-42, nat. treas. A.R.C., 1921-26, asst. sec. treasury, 1921-25, chairman of the retirement board, 1937-56; chmn. bd. commrs. Sinking Fund, City of Boston, 1926-29 and 1934-40; vice-pres., director Franklin Savings Bank, 1908-43; John Hancock Mutual Life Ins. Co., 1927-42, United Shoe Machinery Corp., 1934-50, U.S. Smelting, Refining and Mining Company, 1933-43; Am. Woolen Co., Central Aguirre Sugar Co., 1932-44. Am mem. League Loans Com., London, since 1932. Sec. World War Foreign Debt Commn., 1923-25; mem. Mass legislature, 1926-32. Represented U.S. Government at Paris for the settlement of the cost of the American Army of Occupation on the Rhine, from Feb. to June 1923. President Hoover's rep. to investigate conditions after hurricane, Santo Domingo, 1930; chmn. com. on coöp. with nat. groups and assns., President's Orgn. on Unemployment Relief; rep. of U.S. at Geneva Conf. for Rewriting Red Cross Conv., 1929, and new Prisoners of War Convention (12 yrs.). Overseer of Harvard (pres. bd. of overseers, 1929), and chmn. of exec. com. Harvard Endowment Fund Com. member bd. of dirs. Ellis Memorial House; pres. Boston C. of C., 1933-39; chmn. Am. sect. International Chamber of Commerce, 1937-45; dir. Chamber of Commerce U.S., 1934-40; trustee, Carnegie Endowment for International Peace; mem. Loyalty Review Bd. U.S. Civil Service Commission. Awarded D.S.M.; Comdr. Order of the Crown (Belgium). Member Delta Phi. Member Battery A, Mass. Vol. Militia, 3 yrs. Clubs: Tavern, Engineers, Harvard, Somerset (Boston); Downtown, Harvard, Knickerbocker (New York); Metropolitan (Washington, D.C.). Traveled widely in Europe, Russia and the Balkans, 1915, as member Rockefeller Foundation, European Relief Commn. Home: 2416 Tracy Place, Washington. Died May 27, 1959; buried Mt. Auburn Cemetery, Cambridge, Mass.

WADSWORTH, George, U.S. ambassador; b. Buffalo, N.Y., April 3, 1893; s. Henry Cowles and Mabel (Miller) W.; B.E., Union U., 1914, M.A., 1934; m. Dorothy Maynard Lasell, May 21, 1921 (died Nov. 20, 1928); children—George, Caroline Long; m. 2d, Norma Mack, May 1, 1936 (died 1946). Instr. Am. University, Beirut, 1914-17; clerk to Am. Consulate General, Beirut, 1916-17; v. consul, Nantes, France, 1917-19; Constantinople, 1919-20, Sofia, 1920, Alexandria, 1920-21, Constantinople, 1921-22; consul, Cairo, 1922-24; detailed for duty in Dept. of State, 1924-28; first sec. of Legation and consul, Cairo, 1928-31; first sec. of Legation, Teheran, 1931-33; assigned first sec. of Legation, Bucharest, 1933, counselor of Legation and consul gen., 1935; consul gen. at Jerusalem, 1936-40; counselor of Embassy, Rome, 1941-42; diplomatic agent and consul gen. to Syria and Lebanon, 1942-44, E.E. and M.P., 1944-46; ambassador to Iraq 1947-48; ambassador to Turkey, 1948-51; mem. Policy Planning Staff, Dept. of State, 1952; apptd. U.S. ambassador to Czechoslovakia, 1952, Saudi Arabia, 1954-57; assigned State Dept., 1957—. Mem. Alpha Delta Phi. Presbyn. Clubs: Metropolitan, Chevy Chase (Washington). Address: care Dept. of State, Washington. Died Mar. 5, 1958.

WADY, Clifton Sanford, editor; b. Westport (Fall River), Mass., Aug. 19, 1860; s. John Howland and Malvina Fitzland Bowen (Sanford) W.; student pub. schs., bus. coll.; m. Eleanora Anderson Harmon, June 1, 1888. Printer, N.Y.C., 10 yrs.; advt. writer, Boston and N.Y.C.; asso. editor American Printer, N.Y.C., 1900-10; owner and editor Pacific Printer and Publisher, San Francisco, 1910-17; owner and editor The Letter, Swedenborgian. Author: Poems, 1916. Song writer. Editor Paper & Ink, monthly. Home: East Pepperell, Mass. Office: Fahringer Engraving Co., 56 Market St., Wilkes-Barre, Pa. Died Aug. 11, 1936; buried Oak Grove Cemetery, Fall River, Mass.

WAGGENER, Leslie, banker; b. Russellville, Ky., Dec. 4, 1876; s. Leslie and Fannie (Pendleton) W.; LL.B., U. Tex., 1898; m. Annie Venable Nelson, Jan. 1900; children—Leslie (dec.), Nelson, William. Engaged in practice law, Dallas, 1898-1915; active Tex. Farm Mortgage Co., 1906-24; elected v.p., dir. Republic Trust & Savs. Bank, dir. Republic Nat. Bank, 1924; became exec. v.p. Republic Nat. Bank & Trust Co. (merger), 1929; chmn. exec. com., 1931, vice chmn. bd., 1945—. Mem. exec. com., dir. Texas Employers Ins. Assn.; dir. Nat. City Bank of Tex., Republic Nat. Bank of Dallas, Oak Cliff Bank & Trust Co., Southwestern Life Ins. Co. Mem. bd. regents U. Tex., 1931-42 (chmn. finance com. 1931-41, chmn. bd. 1942). Mem. Philos. Soc. Tex., Tex. Folk Lore

Soc. (life), Dallas Hist. Soc. (fellow and trustee), Dallas Art Assn. (treas.); hon. life mem. Tex. State Hist. Assn. (chmn. ways and means com.); mem. Critic Club, Beta Theta Pi. Democrat. Episcopalian. Home: Oak Hill, White Rock Lake. Office: Dallas. Died Jan. 1, 1951; buried Hillcrest Mausoleum.

WAGNER, Charles L., impressario; b. Charleston, Ill.; s. Charles David and Bertha (Wenzler) W.; ed. pub. schs.; unmarried. Began as sec. Slayton Lyceum Bur., Chgo., 1898, mgr. mus. artists, 1909; mgr. St. Paul Symphony Orchestra, 1910-11; removed to N.Y., 1911; has been mgr. for John McCormack, Rudolph Granz, Emmy Destin, Amelita Galli-Curci, Frances Alda, Alice Neilsen, Will Rogers, Mary Garden, Jeanette MacDonald, Miliza Korjus, Walter Gieseking, Egon Petri and Nicola Moscona. Republican. Pub. his autobiography, Seeing Stars, 1940. Home: 50 Park Av. Office: 511 Fifth Av., N.Y.C. Died Feb. 25, 1956.

WAGNER, Frederick Runyon, clergyman; b. New Market, N.J., May 30, 1873; s. George William and Agnes (Runyon) W.; student Missionary Inst., Selinsgrove, Pa.; A.B., Wittenberg Coll., Springfield, O., 1898, A.M., 1901; B.D., Luth. Theol. Sem., Gettysburg, Pa., 1901; D.D., Susquehanna U., 1917; m. Sarah B. Toot, Oct. 10, 1901; children—Agnes Elizabeth (Mrs. Ralph A. Beebe), Harriet Frances (Mrs. W. F. Warren), John Frederick, Richard Harman. Ordained ministry Luth. Ch., 1901; pastor St. Pauls Luth Ch., Frostburg, Md., 1901-10, St. James Luth. Ch., Huntingdon, Pa., 1910-20, St. Johns Luth. Ch., Martinsburg, W.Va., 1920-—. Pres. Allegheny Synod. Luth. Ch., 1916-18. Mem. S.A.R. Republican. Mason. Rotarian. Home: 305 W. Martin St., Martinsburg, W.Va. Died Jan. 24, 1953; buried Rosedale Cemetery, Martinsburg.

WAGNER, Henry Raup, historian; b. Phila., Sept. 27, 1862; s. Jacob Frederick and Eliza (Kemp) W.; A.B., Yale, 1884, LL.B., 1886, L.H.D., 1946; D. Litt., Pomona Coll., Claremont, Cal., 1935; LL.D., U. Cal., 1949; m. Blanche Henriette Collet, July 17, 1917. Admitted to Mo. bar, 1887, practiced at Kansas City; with Globe Smelting & Refining Co., Denver, 1890, later E. P. Allis Co., mfrs. mining machinery, Milw., at Mexico City; visited S.A., rep. M. Guggenheim's Sons, N.Y., 1898, after consolidation of bus. with Am. Smelting & Refining Co., served the co. in London, Eng., in sale of silver, 4 yrs., mem. exec. com., so. dept., 1907-11, gen. mgr., Mexico City, 1911-15; res. dir. Am. Smelting & Refining Co., Chile Exploration Co. and Braden Co., at Santiago, Chile, 1915-17; mem. exec. com. Am. Smelting & Refining Co., N.Y., 1918-20, v.p., 1920-21. Fellow Royal Geog. Soc. (London); mem. Am. Antiquarian Soc. Republican. Clubs: Grolier (New York); Zamorano, Sunset (Los Angeles). Author: Sir Francis Drake's Voyage Around the World—Its Aims and Achievements, 1926; Spanish Voyages to the Northwest Coast of America in the Sixteenth Century, 1929; Apocryphal Voyages to the Northwest Coast of America, 1931; Spanish Explorations in the Strait of Juan de Fuca, Santa Ana, 1933; The Cartography of the Northwest Coast of America to the year 1800, 1937; Bullion to Books (autobiography), 1942; The Rise of Fernando Cortes Los Angeles, 1944; Nueva Bibliografia Mexicana del Siglo XVI, Mexico, 1946. Compiler: Irish Economics (1700-1783), bibliography with notes, 1907; The Plains and the Rockies (bibliography of original narratives of travel and adventure), 1800-1865, 1921, 2d edit. 1937; California Imprints (Aug. 1846-June 1851), 1922; The Spanish Southwest (annotated bibliography, 1542-1794), 1924, 2d edit. 1937; California Voyages (1539-1541), 1925; Manuscript Maps of Battista Agnese, 1931; Joaquin Garcia Icazbalceta (Am. Antiquarian Soc. Proc.), 1935; New Mexico Spanish Press, 1834-1845 (N.M. Hist. Rev. Jan. 1937); The Grabhorn Press, catalogue of imprints in his collection, Los Angeles, 1938; Commercial Printers of San Francisco from 1851 to 1880 (Papers Biblio. Soc. Am.), 1939; Juan Rodriguez Cabrillo, 1941; The Discovery of Yucatan; also The Discovery of New Spain (both Cortes Soc.), 1942. Home: 1135 Winston Av., San Marino, Cal. Died Mar. 28, 1957.

WAGNER, Martin, architect; b. Koenigsberg, Prussia, Germany, Nov. 5, 1885; s. Carl and Johanna (Hardt) W.; Diploma as engr., Technische Hochschule, Dresden, Germany, 1910; Dr. Engring. Technische Hochschule, Berlin, 1915; m. Gertrud Sandow, April 29, 1911; children—Irmgard Wagner Schüle, Bernhard, Sabine. Began as town planner of the City of Berlin-Weissensee, 1910; with City of Hamburg, 1910-12; chmn. bldg. dept., City of Wilhelmshaven, 1911-14; chief of planning bur., City of Berlin, 1914-18, chmn. bldg. dept., 1926-33; organizer German Bldg. Guilds, 1920-26; prof. housing, regional planning, Harvard, 1938-50, prof. emeritus 1950-—. Served as pvt., Germany Army, during World War I. Received Iron Cross, 1918. Fellow Am. Acad. Arts and Sciences. Mem. Prussian Acad. of Arts, 1931. Author: Städtische Freiflächenpolitik, 1916; Amerikanische Bauwirtschaft, 1925; Städtebauliche Probleme in Amerikanischen Städten, 1929; Das Wachsende Haus, 1932; Wirtschaftlicher Städtebau, 1951. Also author articles. Home: 33 Bowdoin St., Cambridge, Mass. Died May 28, 1957; buried Mt. Auburn Cemetery, Cambridge.

WAGNER, Robert Ferdinand, ex-senator; b. Nastatten, Hesse-Nassau, Germany, June 8, 1877; brought to U.S. in childhood; B.S., Coll. City of N.Y., 1898; LL.B., New York Law Sch., 1900; widower; 1 son, Robert F., Jr. Practiced at N.Y. City; mem. N.Y. Assembly, 1905-08, Senate, 1909-18; chmn. New York State Factory Investigating Commn., 1911; lt. gov. of N.Y., 1914; justice Supreme Court of N.Y., 1st Dist., 1919-26; assigned to Appellate Div., 1st Dept., 1924 (resigned); member of U.S. Senate, 1927-49; resigned; author Wagner Labor Relations Act; chmn. Senate Committee on Banking and Currency. Dem. leader, N.Y. Constitutional Conv., 1938. Introduced National Industrial Recovery Act, Social Security Act, National Labor Relations Act, Ry. Pension Law, U.S. Housing Act of 1937, and other social and econ. legislation in Senate. Democrat. Roman Catholic; received Pope Leo XIII award of Sheil School of Social Studies, 1947. Home: 530 E. 86th St., N.Y.C. Died May 5, 1953.

WAGNER, Russell Halderman, educator; b. Greenville, O., June 4, 1894; s. William J. and Ida Bird (Halderman) W.; A.B., Monmouth (Ill.) Coll., 1915; A.M., Cornell, 1923, Ph.D., 1928; m. Helen Friend, Sept. 9, 1920; 1 dau., Flavia (Mrs. R. L. Stutz). Instr. Jefferson High Sch., LaFayette, Ind., 1915-17; prin. Fairmont High Sch., Dayton, O., 1919; asst. prof. Adrian (Mich.) Coll., 1919-22, Davidson (N.C.) Coll., 1922-23; asst. prof. to asso. prof., acting chmn. dept. of speech Ia. State Coll., Ames, 1923-26; instr. to asso. prof. speech Cornell, 1926-47; prof. of speech, chmn. sch. speech and drama, U. Va., since 1947. Sgt. Air Service and Machine Gun Officers Tng. Sch., U.S. Army, 1917-18. Mem. Speech Assn. Am., Eastern Pub. Speaking Conf. pres. 1948), Phi Kappa Phi, Theta Alpha Phi, Sigma Upsilon. Clubs: Colonnade (U. Va.); Farmington Country (Charlottesville, Va.). Author: Handbook of Argumentation, 1936; Handbook of Group Discussion (with Carroll C. Arnold), 1950. Editor: Problems and Opinions (with A. M. Drummond), 1931. Editor: Speech Monographs, 1941-47. Contbr. to jours., books. Home: Piedmont, Charlottesville, Va. Died Jan. 9, 1952; buried University of Virginia Cemetery, Charlottesville.

WAGNER, Steward, architect; b. Marlin, Tex., Dec. 26, 1886; s. Herbert and Ella (Miller) W.; private instructions; course in architecture International Correspondence Schools, 1901-05; special course, drawing, design, Columbia U., 1907-09; Beaux Art Inst. of Design, Atelier Hornbostel, N.Y. City, 1907-10; m. Irma Frederica Brion, Oct. 24, 1914; 1 dau., June (Mrs. Armand Nazzaro). Archtl. draftsman in office, Howard Messer, Fort Worth, 1901-04, Sangoinet and Staats, Fort Worth, 1904-07, Harry Allan Jacobs, N.Y. City, 1907-09; archtl. dept., Bd. Edn. Newark, N.J., 1909-10; architect with H. Van Buren Magonigle, N.Y. City, 1910-12, Tracy and Swartwout, N.Y. City, 1912-14; private practice, N.Y. City, 1914-21; partner with Alfred Fellheimer, N.Y. City, since 1921 (specialized on ry. stations, grade crossing eliminations, large bldgs. of all types, indsl. research labs., bank and office buildings (S.A. and U.S.), hosps., school and coll. bldg., large housing projects, U.S. Govt. buildings, etc. Fellow A.I.A.; mem. Soc. Beaux Art Architects, Archtl. League, N.Y., N.Y. Soc. Architects. Baptist. Republican. Clubs: Cloud, Metropolitan (N.Y.); West Side Tennis (Forest Hills, N.Y.). Home: 54 Continental Av., Forest Hills. Office: 155 E. 42d St., N.Y.C. 17. Died June 28, 1958.

WAINWRIGHT, Guy Alwyn, mfg. exec.; b. Noblesville, Ind., Nov. 29, 1889; s. Lucius and Victoria (Gray) W.; B.S., Purdue U., 1911; m. Jeanette Harvey, Jan. 3, 1922; children—William Harvey, Stephen Andrew. Pres., gen. mgr. and dir. Diamond Chain Co., Inc., Indpls., 1931-—. Served as lt. col., U.S. Army, World War I. Decorated Croix de Guerre with Palm. Mason. Mem. Sigma Xi, Sigma Chi, Tau Beta Pi. Club: Rotary. Home: 4139 N. Capitol St., Indpls. 8. Office: 402 Kentucky Av., Indpls. 7. Died Sept. 26, 1956.

WAINWRIGHT, Jonathan Mayhew, army officer; b. Walla Walla, Wash., Aug. 23, 1883; s. Major Robert Powell Page (U.S. Cav.) and Josephine (Serrell) W.; B.S., U.S. Mil. Acad., 1906; m. Adele Howard Holley, Feb. 18, 1911; 1 son, Jonathan Mayhew V. (officer United States Merchant Marine and U.S. Naval Reserve Force). Commd. 2d lt. cav., 1906; promoted through grades to brig. gen., 1938; temp. rank of maj. general, 1940, lieut. general (temp.), Mar. 19, 1942, promoted to general, September 1945. Served with 1st Cav., Tex., 1906-08; with expedition against Moros, Philippines, 1909-10; with 1st Cav., Ida., Vt., Wyo., 1910-15; attended Mounted Service Sch., Fort Riley, 1915-16; adjutant 1st O.T.C., Plattsburg, N.Y., 1917; with gen. staff, 76th Nat. Army Div., Aug. 1917, sailing for France, Feb. 1918; gen. staff 82d Div. at Toul, St. Mihiel and Meuse-Argonne; gen. staff 3d Army, Germany, Nov. 1918-20; instr. Cav. Sch., Fort Riley, 1920-21; Gen. Staff War Dept., 1921-23; with 3d Cav., Fort Myer, Va., 1923-25; Chem. Warfare Sch., Cavalry Sch., Command and Gen. Staff Sch., 1928-31; Army War Coll., 1933-34; asst. comdt., Fort Riley, 1934-36; comd. 3d Cav., Fort Myer, 1936-38, 1st Cav. Brigade, Fort Clark, Tex., 1938-40; assigned duty in Philippines, Oct. 1940; comd. Philippine Div., Oct. 1940; served throughout the Bataan campaign and assumed command when Gen. MacArthur went to Australia; prisoner of war of Japanese govt.; rescued from Jap prison camp, Manchuria, Aug. 1945; became comdr. 4th Army, Jan. 1946; retired Aug. 31, 1947. Decorated D.S.M., 1920; D.S.C. Feb. 1942; Oakleaf Cluster for D.S.M., Nov. 1942; received Congressional Medal of Honor, Sept. 1945. Now chmn. bd. Hom-Ond Food Stores; mgr. Alamo Stock Farm; v.p. Acme Sash Window Balance Co. Home: Fiddlers Green, 500 Elizabeth Rd., San Antonio. Died Sept. 2, 1953; buried Arlington Nat. Cemetery.

WAINWRIGHT, Samuel Hayman, clergyman; b. Columbus, Ill., Apr. 15, 1863; s. Rev. Daniel Thomas and Amanda Fitzallen (Agee) W.; M.D., Mo. Med. Coll., 1886; D.D., Central Coll. of Fayette, Mo.; m. Margaret M. Todd, Dec. 30, 1886 (dec.); children—Daniel (dec.), Samuel Hayman, Elizabeth Agee. Practiced, Pierce City, Mo., 1886-87; went to Japan under Bd. Fgn. Missions, M.E. Ch., S., 1888; licensed to preach by Japan Annual Conf., 1893; prin. Kwansei Gakuin, Kobe, 1890-1906; twice elected pres. Japan Annual Conf.; del. Gen. Conf. Am., 4 times; pastor Centenary Ch., St. Louis, during Dr. W. F. McMurry's unexpired term, 1906; trans. St. Louis Ann. Conf., 1907, presiding elder St. Louis dist., 1907-11; pastor U. Meth. Ch., St. Louis, 1911-12; gen. sec. (gen. mgr.), Christian Literary Soc. Japan, 1912-39; ret. 1939. Acting pastor Hong Kong Union Ch., 1899, Kobe Union Ch., 1905-06, Tokyo Union Ch., 1916. Vice pres. Am. Assn. Tokyo, 1917, pres., 1926; pres. Am. Peace Soc. Japan, 1920-21; v.p. Asiatic Soc. Japan, 1922-29, pres., 1930, 31; del. Ecumenical Conf. of Methodism, London, 1921; mem. exec. com. Am.-Japan Soc., Tokyo; chmn. Fgn. Auxiliary to Japan Nat. Temperance League, 1933. Decorated Fourth Order of the Rising Sun, 1930. Hon. Adv. Christian Lit. Soc., 1940-41. Pres. Evang. Alliance, St. Louis, 1910; hon. life mem. Am. Bible Soc., Fondren Lecturer, 1927. Mem. Meth. Ch. Democrat. Club: Tokyo. Author: Campaigning for Christ in Japan; Social Japan in Japanese Literature; A Commentary on the Gospel of John (in Japanese), 1929; Principles of Protestantism (in Japanese), 1937. Translator of Wesley's Sermons and J. W. Lee's "Making of a Man" into Japanese; Kokwa Jichiroku (A Buddhist treatise on Casuistry), into English; "Tanka' or Short Poems; The Methodist Mission in Japan. Contbr. to mags. and revs. on Oriental and religious subjects; versed in Oriental classical lit. Address: 5349 College Av., Oakland 18, Cal. Died Dec. 7, 1950; buried Mountain View Cemetery, Oakland.

WAITE, Clark Francis, publisher; b. Harvard, Neb., Oct. 26, 1877; s. William James and Mary Elizabeth (McCoy) W.; m. Ruth M. Massey, June 21, 1903 (died June 6, 1941); children—Alden Clark, Marjorie Ruth (Mrs. B. C. Wanglin; dec. Aug. 27, 1949); m. 2d, Esther S. Chaffee, Oct. 2, 1943. Pub. San Pedro (Calif.) Daily Pilot, 1909-28, San Pedro News-Pilot, 1928-32, Long Beach (Calif.) Morning Sun, 1930-32; pres. So. Calif. Asso. Newspapers, 1932-47, chmn. bd. since 1947; v.p. and dir. San Pedro Printing and Publishing Company; treasurer and director Fullerton Publishing Company. Director So. Calif. All Year Club. Mem. Calif. Newspaper Pubs. Assn. (pres. 1935), Sigma Delta Chi. Republican. Mason. Club: Press (Los Angeles). Home: 507 N. Maple Drive, Beverly Hills, Cal. Office: 801 N. Moraga Dr., Los Angeles 49. Died Apr. 7, 1958.

WAITE, Edward Foote, judge; b. Norwich, N.Y., Jan. 15, 1860; s. John and Betsey Newton (Foote) W.; A.B., Madison (now Colgate) U., Hamilton, N.Y., 1880; LL.B., Columbian (now George Washington) U., 1883, LL.M., 1884; m. Alice Maud Eaton, May 5, 1892 (died 1935); 1 son, Bradford (dec.). With U.S. Pension Bur., 1880-97; in charge of investigations, involving extensive system of pension frauds in Ia. and Minn., 1893-95; practiced law, Mpls., 1897-1904; asst. city atty., Mpls., 1901-02 supt. police, Mpls., 1902-03; judge Municipal Court, Mpls., 1904-11; judge Dist. Court, Mpls., (with exclusive charge of juvenile court to Sept. 1921 and Jan. 1931-—), 1911-41; retired. Spl. asst. to U.S atty. gen. for hearing cases of conscientious objectors in Minn., Apr. 1942-—. Lectr., dept. sociology, U. Minn., 1926-34. Pres. Minn. State Conf. Charities and Corrections, 1913; chmn. Minn. Commn. for Revising Laws Relating to Children, 1916-17. Pres. Minn Acad. Social Sciences, 1913; many articles in sociological and legal periodicals. Mem. Am. Bar Assn. Am. Law Inst., Am. Judicature Soc., Am. Assn. Social Workers, S.A.R., Delta Kappa Epsilon, Phi Delta Phi, Phi Beta Kappa. Republican. Conglist. Mason. Clubs: Athletic, University, Six o'Clock Lions. Home: 2009 Queen Av. S., Mpls. Died Apr 27, 1958; buried Lakewood Cemetery, Mpls.

WAITE, Frederick Clayton, coll. prof.; b. Hudson ^., May 24, 1870; s. Nelson and Cynthia (Post) W. grad. Western Reserve Acad., Hudson, 1888; B.Litt. Western Reserve University, 1892, A.M., 1894, Doctor of Humanities, 1943; A.M., Harvard University

1896, Ph.D., 1898; married December 24, 1916, (Mrs.) Emily Bacon (Fisher). Asst. in biology, Western Reserve, 1892-95; Morgan fellow, 1896-97, demonstrator zoölogy, 1897-98, Harvard; instr. biology, high schs., New York, 1898-1900, New York U., 1899-1900; asst. in anatomy, Rush Med. Coll., Chicago, 1900-01; asst. prof. histology and embryology, 1901-04, asso. prof., 1904-06, prof., 1906-40; emeritus prof. since 1940, sec. of med. faculty, 1907-17, Western Reserve U. Capt. Sanitary Corps, U.S. Army, Jan. 1918-Feb. 1919; maj. Reserve Corps, U.S. Army. Fellow A.A.A.S.; mem. Assn. Am. Anatomists, Am. Soc Naturalists, Am. Soc. Zoölogists, Am. Micros. Soc. (v.p. 1913), Boston Soc. Natural History, Ohio Acad. Science (pres. 1930), Cleveland Acad. Medicine, Internat. Dental Research Assn., Cleveland Dental Soc. (hon.), Mass. Historic Geneal. Soc., N.H. Hist. Soc., Vt. Hist. Soc., N.E. Soc. of the Western Reserve (president 1932), American Assn. History of Medicine, S.A.R., Society of Colonial Wars, Sigma Xi, Phi Beta Kappa, Alpha Omega Alpha; v.p. Assn. Am. Med. Colls., 1905-06; asso. fellow A.M.A. Clubs: University, Rowfant (Cleveland, O.). Author: History of the School of Dentistry of Western Reserve University, 1940; History of Western Reserve University—The Hudson Era, 1826-1882, 1943; Story of a Country Medical College, 1945; Western Reserve University: Centennial History of the School of Medicine, 1843-1943, 1946: The First Medical Coll. in Vermont, Castleton, 1818-1862, 1949; History of the New England Female Medical College, 1848-1874, 1950. Home: 144 Locust St., Dover, N.H. Died Mar. 30, 1956.

WAITE, J(ohn) Herbert, ophthalmologist; b. Bellefonte, Pa., Nov. 24, 1889; s. John Sitman and Mary Lucetta (Bottorf) W.; student Pa. State Coll., 1907-08; Sc.B., in Biology, Bucknell University, 1911, Sc.M., 1919, Sc.D. (honorary), 1936; M.D., Harvard U. Med. Sch., 1916; m. Marion S. Kennedy, Feb. 4, 1916 (died 1917); children—(twins) John H. and Joanne (wife Dr. David H. Scott); m. 2d, Florence E. Long, Sept. 20, 1919; 1 dau., Elinor (Mrs. Bruce A. MacDonald): In Far East service, Rockefeller Foundation, 1916-19; interne, resident, teaching fellow in ophthalmology, Mass. Eye and Ear Infirmary, 1920-24; instr. in ophthalmology, Harvard, 1925-29, asst. prof., 1930-34, clin. prof. and head of dept., 1934-40, lecturer in ophthalmology since 1941; ophthalmic chief of staff Mass. Eye and Ear Infirmary, 1931-41, cons. surgeon in ophthalmology since 1941; consultant in ophthalmology Peter Bent Brigham, Children's and Infants', N.E. Deaconess, N.E. Baptist, N.E. Peabody Home for Crippled Children, Winchester, and other hospitals. Fellow Mass. Med. Soc.; fellow Boston Med. Library; mem. Am. Med. Assn., A.A.A.S., Am. Ophthalmol. Society, N.E. Ophthalmol. Society; associate Guild of Boston Artists; mem. Phi Beta Kappa, Phi Gamma Delta, Nu Sigma Nu. Mem. editorial bd. Archives of Ophthalmology, 1929-42; mem. bd. hon. consultants Army Med. Library, 1946. Contbr. to Dictionary of Am. Biography. Home: 1731 Beacon St., Brookline, Mass. Office: 7 Bay State Rd., Boston. Died Feb. 23, 1957.

WAITE, Sumner, army officer; b. Westbrook, Me., Sept. 6, 1888; s. John L. and Annie (Gowen) W.; A.B., U. of Maine, Orono, Me., 1911; grad. Inf. Sch., Ft. Benning, Ga., 1923, Command and Gen. Staff Sch., 1926, Army War Coll., 1932; Ecole Superieure de Guerre, Paris, France, 1928; Master of Arts, George Washington University, 1950; m. Elizabeth Carrison, Nov. 7, 1923; children—Elizabeth C., Sumner, Jordan C. Commd. 2d lt., 5th Inf., U.S. Army, 1911, promoted through the grades to brig. gen., 1944. Decorated D.S.M., Commendation Ribbon, Legion of Merit (U.S.); Commander Legion of Honor, Croix de Guerre with palm (France), Croix de Guerre, Mil. Cross 1st Class (Belgium). Mem. Phi Gamma Delta. Club: Army and Navy (Washington). Address: care The Adjutant General's Office, War Dept., Washington 25. Died June 7, 1952.

WAITE, Warren C., univ. prof.; b. Seattle, May 1, 1896; s. William W. and Sarah Genevieve (Thompson) W.; A.B., U. of Minnesota, 1919, A.M., 1921, Ph.D., 1924; m. Aurel A. Warner, Oct. 5, 1921; children—William Warren, Jean Frances, Aurel Louise. Instr. in agrl. economics, U. of Minn., 1922-24, asst. prof., 1924-27, asso. prof., 1927-28, prof. since 1930; sr. agrl. economist, U.S. Dept. Agr., 1928-29. Prin. marketing specialist Agrl. Adjustment Adminstrn., Surplus Marketing Adminstrn. and War Food Adminstrn., 1933-45 (intermittently). Economic consultant Province of Alberta, Can., 1938. Mem. League of Nations Conf. on Relation of Agr. and Nutrition, 1936. Mem. bd. dirs. Nat. Bureau Economic Research, 1944; pres. Am. Farm Econ. Assn., 1950. Editor Jour. of Farm Economics, 1944-49. Author: Economics of Consumption, 1928; The Consumer and the Economic Order (with Ralph Cassady, Jr.), 1938; Introduction to Agricultural Prices (with H. C. Trelogan), 1948. Home: 2352 Bourne Av., St. Paul 8. Died Nov. 11, 1950; buried Lakewood Cemetery, Minneapolis.

WALCOTT, Frederic Collin, ex-senator; b. New York Mills, N.Y., Feb. 19, 1869; s. William Stuart and Emma (Welch) W.; prep. edn., Andover (Mass.) Acad., A.B. Yale, 1891, hon. A.M., 1917; D.Sc., Trinity Coll., Hartford, Conn., 1928; m. Mary Hussey Guthrie, Apr. 3, 1907 (died May 27, 1931); children—Alexander Guthrie, William Welch. Investment banker and mfr., 1907-15; officer and dir. many corps. until 1922. Engaged in Belgian and Polish relief work, 1915-17; served as mem. U.S. Food Adminstrn., 1917-19. Mem. Conn. State Senate, 1925, 27 (pres. pro tempore 1927); pres. Conn. State Bd. Fisheries and Game, 1923-28; chmn. Conn. State Water Commn., 1925-28; U.S. senator from Conn., term 1929-35; welfare commr. of State of Conn., 1935-39. Mem. exec. com. Carnegie Instn. of Washington; trustee Am. Geog. Soc., Bethune Cookman Coll., Daytona, Fla., Trinity Coll., Conn. College; chmn. board trustees, Jane Coffin Childs Memorial Fund for Med. Research; mem. advisory com., Human Welfare Group, Yale U.; pres. American Wild Life Foundation; regent Smithsonian Inst. Decorated Legion of Honor (France); Officer's Cross (Poland). Republican. Has made several scientific exploration trips to South America, etc. Home: Norfolk, Conn. Died Apr. 27, 1949.

WALCOTT, Gregory Dexter, college prof.; b. Dexter Lime Rock, Lincoln, R.I., Aug. 29, 1869; s. Charles Stuart and Mary Catherine (Leary) W.; grad. Worcester (Mass.) Acad., 1893; A.B., Brown U., 1897, A.M., Columbia, 1899, Ph.D., 1904; B.D., Union Theol. Sem., New York, 1900; univs. of Bonn and Berlin, 1901; Litt.D., Long Island U., 1958; m. Helen Rebecca Steward, June 17, 1944. Assistant minister Central Congl. Church, Providence, R.I., 1902-03; acting minister Sayles Memorial Congl. Ch., Saylesville, R.I., 1903-04; prof. Greek and Latin, Blackburn College, Carlinville, Ill., 1904-05, prof. Greek and philosophy, also dean, 1905-07; prof. philosophy and psychology, Hamline U., 1907-21; prof. philosophy, 1921-28; asso. prof. philosophy, Long Island Univ., 1928-29, prof., 1929-54, emeritus; prof. psychology and lecturer on ethics, Tsing Hua Coll., Peking, China, 1917-18. Mem. A.A.A.S., History of Science Soc. (council 1928-31, 1937-40; del. to Am. Council of Learned Socs., 1937-40), Am. Assn. U. Profs., Am. Philos. Assn., Royal Inst. of Philosophy, Delta Upsilon, Phi Beta Kappa, P.B.K. Assos. Baptist. Author: The Kantian and Lutheran Elements in Ritschl's Conception of God, 1904; Tsing Hua Lectures on Ethics, 1919; An Elementary Logic, 1931; The Rationality of the World, 1950; Logic and Sceitific Method published in 1952. Contributor reviews. Originator and general editor of the Source Books in the History of the Sciences, 1924—— (2 vols. issued, 1929, 1 vol., 1935, 39, 48, 51, 52), and articles in sci. philos. and other jours. Home: 106 Monringside Dr., N.Y.C. 27. Died Mar. 20, 1959; buried Swan Point Cemetery, Providence, R.I.

WALCOTT, Robert, lawyer; b. Cambridge, Mass., Oct. 17, 1874; s. Henry Pickering and Charlotte Elizabeth (Richards) W.; grad. Browne and Nichols Sch., Cambridge; A.B., Harvard, 1895; LL.B., 1899; m. Mary T. Richardson, Oct. 12, 1907 (died Apr. 15, 1953); children—Mary (Mrs. H. M. Keyes), Robert, John Cotton (killed at Salerno, Nov. 18, 1943), Maurice Richardson. Pres. emeritus Cambridge Savs. Bank. Mem. Mass. Constl. Conv., 1916-18. Mem. Mass. Hist. Soc., Mass. Audubon Soc., Cambridge Hosp., Trustees (Mass.) Pub. Reservations; pres. Colonial Soc. Mass.; trustee Nuttall Ornithol. Club. Chmn. Mass. Selective Service Bd. No. 47, 1941-46. Republican. Unitarian. Home: 152 Brattle St., Cambridge, Mass. Office: Barristers Hall, Boston. Died Nov. 11, 1956.

WALD, Abraham, educator; b. Cluj, Romania, Oct. 31, 1902; s. Melchior and Dora (Glasner) W.; Ph.D., U. Vienna, 1931; m. Lucille Lang, Oct. 31, 1941; children—Betty, Robert. Came to U.S., 1938, naturalized, 1943. Research fellow Columbia, 1938-39, lecturer, 1939-42, prof. math. statistics, 1942——. Fellow Inst. Math. Statistics (pres. 1948), Econometric Soc., Am. Statis. Assn. (v.p. 1948); mem. Am. Math. Soc. Author: Sequential Analysis, 1947. Home: 241 108 St., N.Y.C. 25. Died Dec. 13, 1950.

WALDECK, Herman, banker; b. Germany, Nov. 19, 1871. Began as asst. cashier, now exec. v.p. and dir. Continental Ill. Nat. Bank & Trust Co.; dir. Am. Automobile Insurance Company. Director Passavant Hosp.; treas. Ill. Soc. Prevention of Blindness. Clubs: Union League; Mid-Day; Attic; Lake Shore Country. Home: Drake Hotel. Office: 231 S. La Salle St., Chicago 90, Ill. Mar. 22, 1960.

WALDO, George C(urtis), newspaper editor; b. Bridgeport, Conn., Feb. 2, 1888; s. George Curtis and Annie (Frye) Waldo; educated in grade and high schools, Bridgeport; married Ethel Donaldson, October 16, 1915 (died September 15, 1945); children—Annie Lou, Susan Frye. Reporter Bridgeport Standard, 1904-09; city editor Bridgeport Telegram, 1912-18; editor in chief Bridgeport Post and Telegram since 1918; pres. Post Pub. Co. since 1939; v.p. Bridgeport-Peoples Savings Bank. Chmn. Conn. State Park and Forest Commn. Chmn. Greater Bridgeport Red Cross War Fund drives, 1942, 43, 44; mem. exec. com. Bridgeport Hosp. Mem. Am. Assn. Variable Star Observers. Home: Greenfield Hill, Fairfield, Conn. Office: Post and Telegram, Bridgeport, Conn. Died Sept. 30, 1956.

WALDO, Selden Fennell, lawyer; b. Gainesville, Fla., Mar. 1, 1915; s. George Selden and Myrtle (Fennell) W.; A.B., U. of Fla., 1937, LL.B., 1939; m. Tommy Ruth Blackmon, Oct. 28, 1941; children—George Selden, Andrew Blackmon. Admitted to Fla. State bar, 1939; partner firm Gray, Waldo & Chandler, Gainesville, Fla., since 1940; municipal judge, Gainesville, 1942-46; prof. law (part time), U. of Fla. since 1947. Mem. commn. to re-write common law procedure of Fla. State pres. jr. sect. Fla. Bar Assn., 1944-45 (mem. bd. govs. since 1944); pres. 8th Judicial Bar Assn., 1945-46; state pres. Fla. Jr. Chamber of Commerce, 1943-44, nat. dir. U.S. Jr. Chamber of Commerce, 1944-45 (chmn. governmental affairs com., 1944-45, nat. v.p., 1945-46, designated outstanding nat. dir., 1944, pres., 1946-47); mem. Fla. state Bd. Law Examiners; dir. Fla. State C. of C. Awarded gold key for outstanding civic activity by Fla. State Chamber of Commerce, 1944. Home: 719 N.E. 1st St. Office: Baird Bldg., Gainesville, Fla. Died Nov. 8, 1950; buried Evergreen Cemetery, Gainesville.

WALDRON, Arthur Maxson, r.r. exec.; b. Plainfield, N.J., Feb. 10, 1884; s. Randolph and Laura Ellen (Groff) W.; student pub. schs., Bklyn.; m. Stella Brown, May 9, 1918. Asst. cashier Southern Pacific Co., N.Y., 1901-10; cashier C.&O. Ry. Co., N.Y., asst. treas., Cleveland, 1934; treas. N.Y.C. &St.L. R.R. Co., Cleveland, 1947——. Mem. Ohio C. of C., Brotherhood of St. Andrew in U.S. (nat. treas.), Assn. Am. R.R.'s (chmn. treas. div.), Newcomen Soc. Eng. Republican. Epis. Mason. Clubs: Union Mid-Day (Cleve). Home: 1595 Arthur Av., Lakewood, O. Office: Terminal Tower, Cleve. Died May 13, 1959; buried Waynesville, N.C.

WALDRON, Jeremy Richard, lawyer; b. Somersworth, N.H., Oct. 1, 1889; s. Augustus Scott and Sarah Higgins (Mullen) W.; grad. Tilton (N.H.) Sch., 1908; student U. N.H., 2 yrs., and Boston U. (non-grad.); m. Helen Staples Walker, Aug. 1920; children—Jeremy Richard, Ann. Admitted to N.H. bar, 1914, began practice at Portsmouth; mem. firm Waldron, Boynton & Waldron; city solicitor, Portsmouth, 1915-16, 19-20; Rockingham county solicitor, 1921-24; served atty. gen. of N.H., 1925-29. Trustee U. N.H., 1945——. Served as sgt. Co. A, 14th Engrs., 1917, sgt., Co. B, 127th Inf., 32d Div., 1918. Mem. Am., N.H. State (pres. 1939), Rockingham County, York County (Me.) bar assns., Theta Chi, Gamma Eta Gamma. Republican. Conglist. Mason. Clubs: Rotary, Country (Portsmouth). Home: Portsmouth, N.H. Died Oct. 20, 1949.

WALKER, Alexander Stewart, architect; b. Jersey City, N.J., Oct. 8, 1876; s. James H. and Emeline (Tate) W.; grad. St. Paul's Sch., Concord, N.H., 1894; B.S., Harvard, 1898; m. Sybil Kane, Oct. 27, 1906; children—Alixe, Grenville. Began as architect, 1906, forming partnership with Leon N. Gillette as Walker and Poor. Served as lt. j.g., Overseas Transportation Service, U.S. Navy, during World War. Works: Industrial Trust Bldg., Providence, R.I.; First Nat. Bank, New York; 3 East River Savings bank; 15 Nat. City banks; Playland and Grasslands Hosp., Westchester County, N.Y., New Aircraft Assembly Plant-Grumman Aircraft, Calverton, Ill.; residences for William Goadby Loew, George F. Baker, Thomas W. Lamont, H. P. Davison, etc. Firm has been awarded medal for apt. house design by Am. Inst. Architects, 1910; gold medal by Archtl. League of N.Y., 1922; gold medal by Am. Inst. Architects, 1925; 2d prize for Nat. City Bank Bldg., Canal and Broadway for best building built in downtown New York, 1927; medal for best two-story alteration on Fifth Av. Mem. Archl. League of New York, Am. Inst. Architects (New York Chapter), Beaux Arts Inst. of Design. Club: Knickerbocker (New York). Home: 132 E. 72d St. Office: 787 Fifth Av., N.Y.C. 22. Died June 10, 1952.

WALKER, Arthur Lucian, metallurgist; b. New York, N.Y., Jan. 14, 1863; s. Thomas George and Lucy (Holbrook) W.; student Charlier Inst., New York; Morris Acad., Morristown, N.J.; E.M., Columbia, 1883. Chemist, Old Dominion Copper Co., Ariz., 1883-85, engr., 1885-87; gen. supt., 1887-93; mgr. Baltimore Electrolytic Refining Co., 1893-99; mgr. Perth Amboy (N.J.) plant of Am. Smelting & Refining Co., 1899-1906; dir. same, 1906-07; prof. metallurgy, Columbia, 1908-29. Spl. lecturer in metallurgy, Post-Grad. Sch., U.S. Naval Acad., 1912, new engring. sch., Harvard, 1919. Invented, 1898, the Walker mech. casting machine which revolutionized methods used for casting refined copper into shapes and obviated hard labor; invented new system, 1902, for tank room arrangement in electrolytic copper refining plants; designed many copper casting installations and/or electrolytic refining tank rooms for plants in the U.S., Can., S. America, Australia, Russia and Africa; cons. metallurgist-at-large for ordnance, War Dept., 1917-18. Received Egleston Medal from Columbia U. for distinguished engring. achievements, 1939. Mem. Am. Inst. Mining and Metall. Engrs., Mining and Metall. Soc. America, Sigma Xi, Tau Beta Pi. Clubs: Century, Columbia Univ., Psi Upsilon, Mining; Richmond County Country. Contbr. articles to mining, metall.

and hist. jours. Address: Whippany, N.J. Died Sept. 30, 1952; buried Woodlawn Cemetery, N.Y.C.

WALKER, Clifford Mitchell, ex-gov.; b. Monroe, Ga., July 4, 1877; s. Billington Sanders and Alice (Mitchell) W.; prep. edn. Ga. Mil. Inst.; A.B., U. Ga., 1897; m. Rosa Carter Mathewson, Apr. 29, 1902; children—Clifford (dec.), Harold M., Sanders J. (dec.). Admitted to Ga. bar, 1897; sr. mem. Walker & Kilbride, Atlanta; mayor Monroe, 1905-07; solicitor gen. Western Jud. Circuit, Ga., 1909-13; atty. gen. Ga., 1914-19; gov. Ga., 1923-27; resumed practice of law. Pres. Woodrow Wilson Coll. Law. Gen. counsel Ga. Bur. Unemployment Compensation. Democrat. Baptist. Trustee Mercer U. (Macon, Ga.), U. Ga., Athens. Mem. Ga. Bar Assn., Phi Beta Kappa, Sigma Alpha Epsilon. Address: 318 McDaniel St., Monroe, Ga. Died Nov. 9, 1954, buried Walker Family Cemetery, Monroe.

WALKER, Curtis Howe, educator; b. Orange, Conn., Aug. 14, 1877; s. James and Martha Hall (Johnstone) W.; A.B., Yale, 1899, Ph.D., 1905; m. Lillian Luke, Aug. 22, 1912; 1 dau., Virginia Johnstone. Instr. history, Amherst Coll., 1903-04, Yale, 1905-09, Chgo., 1909-11; asst. prof. history, Univ. Chgo., 1911-18; lecturer on European history, Rice Inst., Houston, Tex., 1919-27; prof. of European history, Vanderbilt U., 1927-48, emeritus. Mem. Am. Hist. Assn., Mediaeval Acad. America, Hist. Assn. Great Britain, Houston Open Forum (v.p., 1926-27; hon. v.p., 1927—). Conglist. Contbr. to Rice Inst. Pamphlet on Dante, F. E. Compton's Children's Encyclopedia, article on the middle ages to The March of Time and various learned periodicals, notably the English Hist. Review. Author: A(e)leanor of Acquantaine. Home: 3311 Love Circle. Address: Vanderbilt University, Nashville, Tenn. Died Oct. 28, 1956.

WALKER, Dougal Ormonde Beaconsfield, clergyman; b. Layou St. Vincent, Brit. West Indies, Jan. 5, 1890; s. George Oswald and Maria (Jeffers) W.; student Howard U., 1909-11; S.T.B., Boston U., 1914; student Andover Div. Sch., Harvard, 1914-15; A.B., Shaw U., 1924; A.M., Western Reserve U., 1932; grad. student Western Reserve U., 1932-36; D.D., Allen U., Columbia, S.C., 1932; LL.D., Campbell Coll., Jacksonville, Miss., 1942; married Eva Revallion, Apr. 21, 1915; 1 dau., Deon Yvonne. Came to U.S., 1908, naturalized, 1930. Ordained ministry African M.E. Ch., 1914; minister People's Ch., Chelsea, Mass., 1911-15, Bethel Ch., New Bedford, Mass., 1915-20, St. James Ch., Winston-Salem, N.C, 1920-21, St. Paul Ch., Raleigh, N.C., 1921-25, Bethel Ch., Wilkes-Barre, Pa., 1925-26, St. James Ch., Cleveland, O., 1926-36; pres. Wilberforce (O.) U., 1936-41; minister Bethel A.M.E. Ch. since Oct. 1941; elected 66th bishop A.M.E. Ch., 1948, apptd. to 5th Episcopal Dist. Trustee Wilberforce U. since 1929. Mem. Sen Mer Rekh, Alpha Phi Alpha. Democrat. Mason, Odd Fellow, K.P., Elk, Forester. Address: P.O. Box 305, Wilberforce, O. Died June 28, 1955.

WALKER, Elisha, banker; b. N.Y.C., Oct. 8, 1879; s. Isaac and Charlotte Mary (Parker) W.; A.B., Yale, 1900; B.S., Mass. Inst. Tech., 1902; m. Adele D'Orn, Oct. 12, 1904; children—Robert, Adele, Louis, Elisha, Bayard. With Fisk & Robinson, bankers, N.Y., 1902-04, William Salomon & Co., 1904-20, partner, 1910-20; pres. Blair & Co., Inc., title changed, 1929, to Bancamerica-Blair Corp., pres., 1920-30; chmn. bd. Transamerica Corp., 1930, 32; became partner Kuhn, Loeb & Co., Jan. 1933; dir. Diamond Match Co., Armour & Co., Tidewater-Asso. Oil Co. Industria Electrica de Mexico, S.A., Inversiones Latinas, S.A. Hat Corp. of Am., U.S. Lines Co., Petroleum Corp. of Am., Moore-McCormack Lines, Inc., Rockwell Mfg. Co. Chmn., dir. Beckman-Downtown Hosp. Mem. Council on Fgn. Relations; dir. Boys' Clubs Am. Clubs: The Recess, The Creek, Piping Rock, University. Address: Syosset, L.I., N.Y. Died Nov. 8, 1950.

WALKER, Frank Comerford, ex-postmaster general, lawyer; b. Plymouth, Pa., May 30, 1886; s. David and Ellen (Comerford) W.; student Gonzaga U., 1903-06, LL.D., 1937; LL.B., U. Notre Dame, 1909, LL.D., 1934; LL.D., Montana Sch. of Mines (Butte), 1934, Georgetown U., 1942, Manhattan Coll., 1943; Litt.D., St. Francis Coll. (Loretto, Pa.) 1944; m. Hallie Boucher, Nov. 11, 1914; children—Thomas Joseph, Laura Hallie (Mrs. James S. Jenkins). Admitted to Mont. bar, 1909; mem. Walker & Walker; chairman board Meco Realty Company, Scranton, Pa.; member board of directors Grace Nat. Bank of New York City. Assistant county attorney Silver Bow Co., Mont., 1909-12; member of the Montana legislature, 1913; exec. sec. Pres. Exec. Council, 1933, exec. dir., Nat. Emergency Council, 1935; postmaster gen. U.S., 1940-45. Mem. Dem. Nat. Com. (treas. 1932, chmn. 1943-44). Served as 1st lt., U.S. Army, 1918, A.E.F. Mem. bd. of lay trustees, U. Notre Dame; regent U. Scranton. K.C., Knight of Malta. Awarded Laetare Medal, U. Notre Dame 1948. Democrat. Mem. Am., Mont. State and N.Y state bar assns. Apptd. alternat rep. U.S. to 1st part of 1st session, Gen. Assembly, U.N., London, Jan. 1946. Home: New York, N.Y. Address: 1600 Broadway, N.Y.C. 19. Died Sept. 13, 1959.

WALKER, George Abram, railroad exec.; b. Toronto, Ont., Can., Oct. 8, 1879; s. William and Mary (Martin) W.; student Wellesley Sch., Toronto; grad. Osgoode Hall, Toronto, 1906; Doctor of Civil Law, Bishop's University, 1950; married Gladys Graves, Sept. 5, 1928; 1 dau., Gladys June. Called to bar, Ont., 1906, Alberta, 1911, Brit. Columbia, 1913. Barrister C.P. Ry. Co. Toronto, 1906-11, solicitor Calgary, Alberta, 1911-34, asst. gen. solicitor, Montreal, 1934-36, gen. solicitor, 1936-45, vice pres. and gen. counsel, Montreal, 1945-47, sr. vice pres., 1947-48, dir. and mem. exec. com., 1947, chmn., 1948-55, now director; dir. Canadian Pacific Steamships, Can. since 1948; dir. W. Kootenay Power & Light Company, Ltd. Member of the law socs. of Upper Can., Alberta and British Columbia. Mem. Can. Colonization Assn. (dir.). Created King's Counsel, 1915. United Ch. Can. Clubs: Mount Royal, University, Royal Montreal Golf (Mont.); Rideau (Ottawa); Ranchmen's (Calgary). Home: 3940 Cote des Neiges Rd., Montreal, P.Q. Office: Windsor Sta., Montreal, P. Q., Can. Died June 7, 1959.

WALKER, Harry Bruce, agrl. engr.; b. Macomb, Ill., Apr. 13, 1884; s. Henry Boyd and Margaret Alcinda (Yeast) W.; preparatory edn., Highland Park (Ia.) Coll.; B.S. in C.E., Ia. State Coll., 1910, C.E., 1920; post-grad., Kan. State Coll., 1925; LL.D. U. Cal., 1954; m. Coralie Harris Walker, Sept. 11, 1912; children—Mary Margaret, Boyd Wallace. Topographer C.,B.&Q.R.R., 1906-07; asst. drainage engr. Humboldt County, Ia., 1909, 10; with Kan. State Agrl. Coll., drainage and irrigation engr., 1910-17, extension engr., 1919-21, head dept. agrl. engring., and agrl. engr., Engring. Expt. Sta., 1921-28; state irrigation engr., Kan., 1913-17; engr. Kan. Water Commn., 1917-26; dir. research mech. farm equipment, U.S. Dept. Agr., 1927-28; with U. Cal., head of dept. agrl. engring., agrl. engr., Agrl. Expt. Sta., 1928-47, prof. agrl. engring., 1947-51, prof. emeritus, 1951—, agrl. engr. in Expt. Sta., 1947—; cons. agrl. engr., 1951—. Capt. engrs., U.S. Army, 1917-19; asst. div. engr. 78th Div., A.E.F., 13 mos.; in St. Mihiel and Meuse-Argonne offensives. Awarded John Deere medal for distinguished achievement in application of sci. and art to soil, by Am. Soc. Agrl. Engrs., 1939. Fellow Am. Soc. Agrl. Engrs. (acting pres., 1924-25; pres., 1942-43), A.A.A.S., mem. Am. Soc. C.E., Am. Soc. Engring. Edn., Am. Soc. Sugar Beet Technologist (v.p. 1942-43), Sigma Xi, Sigma Tau, Tau Beta Pi, Phi Kappa Phi, Alpha Zeta, Gamma Sigma Delta, Delta Tau Delta. Del. World Engring. Congress, Tokio, 1929. Republican. Presbyn. Author pamphlets, bulls., etc. Club: Commonwealth (San Francisco). Home: 54 College Park, Davis, Cal. Died July 27, 1957.

WALKER, Harry Leslie, architect; b. Chicago, Ill., Feb. 20, 1877; s. Charles Frost and Nancie Ann (Doolittle) W.; student Armour Inst. Tech., Chicago, and at Art Inst., Chicago, 1897-98; B.S. in architecture, Mass. Inst. Tech., 1900; m. Jessie Eloise Blanchard, Nov. 26, 1903; children—John Blanchard, Elizabeth Nancy (Mrs. James C. Mouzon). In practice architecture, Atlanta, Ga., 1902-10, N.Y. City, 1910—; mem. architectural board design, Ten Eyck Houses, Brooklyn, N.Y. Architect of First Presbyn. Ch., Passaic, N.J.; Reformed Ch., Bronxville, N.Y.; Christian Herald House, N.Y. City; Pub. Library, Bronxville; Passaic Nat. Bank & Trust Co.; Henry W. Putnam Memorial Hosp., Bennington, Vt.; Proctor Memorial Bridge, Proctor, Vt.; Pub. Sch., Bronxville, etc. Past pres. bd. trustees Pub. Library, past mem. and sec. Village Planning Commn., Bronxville. Bus. mgr., Dist. 2, Com. on Edn. and Spl. Training, U.S. war Dept., during World War I. Mem. A.I.A. (past pres. Atlanta chapter), Church Archtl. Guild of America (past pres.), Archtl. League of N.Y., Am. Arbitration Assn., Delta Upsilon. Republican. Dutch Reformed Ch. Clubs: University (N.Y. City); St. Andrews Golf (Hastings, N.Y.). Author and illustrator (brochure): The English Parish Church, 1930; also author articles on church architecture, cost accounting and filing for architects. Lecturer on medieval churches, ecclesiastical symbolism, early Am. architecture. Home: 30 Elm Rock Rd., Bronxville, N.Y. Office: 126 E. 38th St., N.Y.C. 16. Died Jan. 6, 1954.

WALKER, Henry Yonge; b. Moncton, N.B., Can., July 30, 1879; s. James Joseph and Lucy (McSweeney) W.; ed. grammar sch.; m. Katherine Paradice, June 1, 1903. Came to U.S., 1897. With M. Guggenheim's Sons Smelter interests, 1897-1901; with American Smelting & Refining Co., Denver, 1901-04, Everett, Wash., 1904-07; Tacoma, Washington, 1907-23; gen. mgr. Am. Smelting & Refining Co., plants in Colo., Utah, Mont., Calif. and Wash., 1922-28, v.p. in charge of all smelters and refineries 1928, pres. 1947. Mem. Mining and Metall. Soc. America, Am. Inst. Mining and Metall. Engrs. Home: 360 Forest Av., Palo Alto, Calif. Office: 405 Montgomery St., San Francisco 4. Died July 2, 1955; buried Holy Cross Cemetery, San Francisco.

WALKER, James Wilson Grimes, civil engr.; b. Salem, Mass., Sept. 22, 1868; s. Rear-Adm. John Grimes (U.S. Navy) and Rebecca White (Pickering) W.; prep. edn. St. Paul's Sch., Concord, N.H., Neuchatel, Switzerland, Pont Levoy, France, and Heidelberg, Germany; civil engring. Mass. Inst. Tech.; Nina Chinn, Feb. 24, 1897; children—Elizabeth Grimes (Mrs. John Williams Davis), John Grahame, Robert Serrell Wood, Herbert Wood. Employed gen. engring. work, bridge constrn., ry. location, constrn. and mgmt., 1890-97; charge surveys by Nicaragua Canal Commn., beteen Lake Nicaragua and Pacific Ocean, 1898; commd. civil engr. USN, 1898; resigned 1912. Mem. Am. Soc. C.E., N.H. Soc. Cin., Acad. Polit. Sci., Naval Hist. Found. Author: Ocean to Ocean, an Account, Personal and Historical, of Nicaragua and Its People, 1902. Address: Brownfield, Me. Died Nov. 2, 1950; buried Mt. Auburn Cemetery, Cambridge, Mass.

WALKER, John Earl, lawyer; b. Cooper, Mich., Apr. 5, 1886; s. Cyrus Alexander and Lydia Orel (Earl) W.; B.S., Kalamazoo Coll., 1907, LL.D., 1927; B.S., U. Chgo., 1907; LL.B., George Washington U., 1916; m. Vara Millicent Muffley, Oct. 11, 1913 (dec. Apr. 1944); m. 2d, Mrs. Ernestine Hall Rolls, Feb. 11, 1947. Clk., ways and means com. Ho. of Reps., 1915-19; dep. commr. Internal Rev. Bur., 1919; spl. atty. Office of Solicitor of Internal Revenue, 1919-21; admitted to D.C. bar, 1920; practiced in Washington, 1923; chief U.S. Senate br. of Legislative Drafting Service, 1921-22; spl. asst. to Sec. of Treasury, 1925-26; pvt. practice law as mem. firm Walker, Rice, English & Grabber, 1946-50; counsel Am. Econ. Assn. Mem. Nat. Tax Assn., D.C. Bar Assn. Clubs: Cosmos, Columbia Country (Washington). Home: 2852 Northampton St., Washington 15. Office: Tower Bldg., 14th and K Sts. N.W., Washington. Died Oct. 6, 1955.

WALKER, John Moore, bishop; b. Macon, Ga., Nov. 24, 1888; s. John Moore and Clara Pruyn (Roosevelt) W.; B.A., U. of Georgia, 1910; B.D., U. of the South, Sewanee, Tenn., 1913, D.D., 1941; m. Julia Benedict, June 1, 1915; children—Anne Rodgers (Mrs. Blake T. Newton), John Moore. Bishop Protestant Episcopal Diocese of Atlanta. Mem. Phi Beta Kappa, Sigma Alpha Epsilon (U. of Georgia). Home: 108 N.E. 17th St., Atlanta, Ga. Died July 16, 1951; buried Riverside Cemetery, Macon, Ga.

WALKER, Kenneth N., army officer; b. Cerrillos, N.M., July 17, 1898; grad. Air Service Observation Sch., 1922, Air Corps Tactical Sch., 1929, Command and Gen. Staff Sch., 1935; rated, command pilot, combat observer. Enlisted as private 1st class, Aviation Sect., Signal Enlisted Reserve Corps, 1917, called to active duty 1918; commd. 2d lt., U.S. Army, 1918, and advanced through the grades to brig. gen., 1942; served as comdr. 5th Bomber Command, Solomon Islands; reported missing in action leading bombing attack on Japanese shipping at Rabaul, New Britain, Jan. 5, 1943. Awarded Congl. Medal of Honor for conspicuous leadership and Personal valor and intrepidity at an extreme hazard to life, Mar. 1943. Died Dec. 12, 1945.†

WALKER, Kenzie Wallace, army officer; b. LaGrange, Tex., Dec. 25, 1870; s. William Wallace and Emma (Routh) W.; grad. U.S. Mil. Acad., 1893; m. Helen Hobart Whitman, Oct. 17, 1895 (dec.); children—Augustine Whitman (dec.), Dorothy Whitman. Commd. add. 2d lt. cav., 1893; 2d lt., 1893; promoted through grades to col. of inf., N.A., 1917, and to col. of cav., U.S. Army, 1920; apptd. chief of finance, U.S. Army, with rank of brig. gen., 1922; reappted. chief of finance, with rank of maj. gen., 1925; retired 1928. Cited for service in Spanish-Am. War; D.S.M., World War. Mem. Mil. Order Fgn. Wars, M.O. World War, Am. Legion, Sojourners. Mason. Clubs: Army and Navy (Washington, D.C. and New York); Chevy Chase (Chevy Chase, Md.). Home: 2962 2d Av., North, St. Petersburg, Fla. Died June 18, 1958; buried Arlington Nat. Cemetery.

WALKER, Ramsay M(ilton), Dem. Nat. committeeman; b. Poke Co., Ia., Dec. 29, 1867; s. Joel Milton and Louise (Ramsay) W.; ed. schs. Howard, Kan.; m. Abbie S. Smith, Apr. 19, 1908. Engaged in banking 1890-94, 1911-31; merchandising, 1894-1909; engaged in farm operating, 1923—. Dir. Wallace Bank & Trust Co., Lincoln Hardware and Implement Co., Wallace Nat. Bank. Mem. Ida. State Bd. Edn. Mem. Dem. Nat. Com. from Ida., 1936—. Mem. Am. Bankers' Assn. (exec. council). Home: Coeur d'Alene, Ida. Died Jan. 3, 1959.

WALKER, Robert, actor; b. Salt Lake City; s. Horace and Zella (McQuarrie) W.; ed. pub. schs., Salt Lake City, San Diego Army and Navy Acad., Am. Acad. Dramatic Arts; m. Jennifer Jones, Jan. 9, 1939 (div. 1945); children—Robert, Michael; m. 2d, Barbara Ford, July, 1948. Has appeared on radio and with midwest stock co. Pictures include: See Here, Private Hargrove, Since You Went Away, 30 Seconds Over Tokio, 1944; Her Highness and the Bellboy, The Clock, 1945; What Next Corporal Hargrove?, The Sailor Takes a Wife, Blue Skies, Song of Love. Mem. Lambs Club (New York). Author of radio scripts. Address: care M-G-M Studios, Culver City, Cal. Died Aug. 28, 1951.*

WALKER, Robert Coleman, lawyer, ins. exec.; b. Richmond, Va., June 2, 1889; s. William James and Josephine Irving (Coleman) W.; student St. Paul's Sch., 1904-07; A.B., Yale, 1911; LL.B., Harvard, 1914; m. Kate Ewing Eaches, June 16, 1913; children—Robert Coleman, Jr., James Ewing; m. 2d Elizabeth Travers Eaches, Aug. 4, 1944. Admitted to Pa. bar, 1914 and since practiced in Phila.; asso. Montgomery, McCracken, Walker & Rhoads and predecessor firms, 1914—, partner, 1923—; chmn. bd. Life Ins. Co. of Va., 1949—. Treas. Phila. Tuberculosis and Health Assn. Chmn. acting com. Corp. for Relief of Widows and Children of Clergymen in Communion of P.E. Ch. Commonwealth of Pa. Mem. Soc. of the Cincinnati. Clubs: Gulph Mills Golf, Philadelphia, Midday. Home: Montgomery Av. and Valley Rd., Ardmore, Pa. Office: 1421 Chestnut St., Phila. 2. Died Dec. 21, 1954.

WALKER, Robert E(lisha), investment banker; b. N.Y.C., July 11, 1906; s. Elisha and Adele (D'Orn) W.; Ph.B., Yale, 1929; m. Muriel Lowe, May 12, 1930; children—Muriel Anne (Mrs. Charles A. Chidsey), Wendy (Mrs. Dulaney Glen). Statistician Blair & Co., N.Y.C., 1929-32, R.F.C., Chgo., 1932-33; asso. with Kuhn, Loeb & Co., N.Y., 1935—, partner, 1949, now limited partner; pres. L.I. Co., Ltd., 1951—. Served as lt., U.S.N., 1942-45; assigned port dir. Third Naval Dist.; lt. comdr., U.S. N.R., 1945—. Republican. Roman Catholic. Knight of Malta. Clubs: Recess, Wall St., Downtown Assn. (N.Y.C.); Piping Rock (Locust Valley, L.I.); South Side (Islip, L.I.). Home: Muttontown Rd., Syosset, N.Y. Office: 46 Cedar St., N.Y.C. 5. Died Mar. 16, 1958.

WALKER, Roger A. P., business exec.; b. Petersburg, Va., Dec. 24, 1879; s. Francis T. and Mary Blair (Pryor) W.; student Va. Mil. Inst., 1896-1900; m. Sophie Berney White, Jan. 17, 1914; 1 dau., Sophie. President, dir. Bush Terminal Bldgs. Co., 1937—; gen. traffic mgr. Am. Cotton Oil Co., gen. agent C. & O. Ry. Co. Mem. Brooklyn Chamber of Commerce, Real Estate Bd. of New York, Brooklyn Real Estate Bd., Merchants and Manufacturers Assn. of Bush Terminal. Club: Union League. Home: 33 Fifth Av., New York 3. Office: 100 Broad St., N.Y.C. 4. Died Jan. 6, 1955; buried Richmond, Va.

WALKER, Rollin Hough, univ. prof.; b. Columbus, Ohio, Dec. 19, 1865; s. Benjamin Blake and Charlotte (Hough) W.; A.B., Ohio Wesleyan U., 1888; S.T.B., Boston U., 1892, Ph.D., 1908; studied New Coll., Edinburgh, 1900, United Free Church College, Glasgow, and U. of Halle, 1907, also U. of Zurich, 1929; unmarried. One of founders of Epworth League House (social and evangelistic settlement), Bosotn, where remained 1892-95; instr. Foltz Mission Inst. (training sch. for fgn. missionaries), 1896-99; made tour of missions of Eastern Asia, 1898; prof. English Bible, Ohio Wesleyan U., 1900—. Methodist. Mem. Phi Beta Kappa. Author: (with Prof. Russell B. Miller) Studies in the Prophets of Israel, 1909; A Study of John's Gospel by the Questionnarie Method (handbook), 1919; A Study of Luke's Gospel by the Questionnaire Method, 1921; A Study of Genesis and Exodus by the Questionnaire Method, 1923; Men Unafraid, A Study of Amos, Hosea, Isaiah, and the Herald of the Restoration, 1923; Picturesque Interviews with Jesus, 1926; Jesus and Our Pressing Porblems, 1930; Paul's Secret of Power, 1935; The Modern Message of the Psalms, 1938; An Old Letter With a Modern Message, 1940. He has also been a contributor to the Sunday School Journal series of advanced lessons on the Synoptic Gospels, also a series of articles on Books of the New Testament, the latter forming a complete teachers' introductory course to the N.T.; contbr. to internat. Standard Bible Ency.; weekly contbr. to Christian Advocate. Home: 173 N. Sandusky, Delaware, O. Died Aug. 4, 1955; buried Columbus, O.

WALKER, Theodore Penfield, pres. Commercial Solvents Corp.; b. Penfield, O., Sept. 4, 1886; s. Theodore C. and Emma Louise (Catt) W.; B.S., Drury Coll., 1908; LL.D., Drury Coll., 1939; student Philippine Constabulary Acad., 1908; m. Eugenie Grandblaise Revel, May 7, 1919. Officer of Philippine Constabulary, 1908-16; with Standard Oil Co. of N.Y., Dutch East Indies, 1916-17, Am. Metals Co., Ltd., Java, 1919-22; with Commercial Solvents Corp. as exec. v.p. and dir., 1922-38, pres., dir., 1938-47, chmn. bd. since 1947; chmn. bd. Thermatomic Carbon Co.; dir. Corn Products Refining Company. Served as lieutenant, advancing to captain, major, Air Corps, U.S. Army, during World War. Mem. bd. of trustees, Drury College. Member Manufacturing Chemists Assn., Kappa Alpha, Phi Lambda Upsilon. Clubs: Creve Coeur (Peoria, Ill.); Uptown, University (New York). Home: 710 Park Av. Office: 17 E. 42d St., N.Y.C. Died Nov. 28, 1951; buried Blue Hill, Me.

WALKER, Walter, ex-senator, editor and pub.; b. Marion, Ky., Apr. 3, 1883; s. Robert Clement and Martha (Brown) W.; student grade and high sch., Marion, Ky.; m. Kathie Woods, Nov. 2, 1903; 1 son, Robert Preston (associated with his father in newspaper business). Began as reporter Crittenden County Press (paper owned by father), Marion, 1899, later mgr. same; with Grand Junction (Colo.) Daily Sentinel since 1903, editor and publisher since 1911. Democratic state chairman for Colorado, 1930-32; apptd. U.S. senator, Sept. 26, 1932, by gov., to fill vacancy caused by death of Senator C. W. Waterman, term expired Dec. 7, 1932; del. to Dem. Nat. Convs., 1924, 28, 32, 36, 40, 48, 52; mem. sub-com. to draft Nat. Dem. platform Phila. conv., 1936; presidential elector, Colo., 1936. Recipient Distinguished Service award, U. Colo., 1954. Mem. Newcomen Soc. England (Am. branch). Democrat. Mem. Elks, Woodmen of World. Clubs: Rotary (Grand Junction); Democratic, Press (Denver). Home: Grand Junction, Colo. Died Oct. 8, 1956. Buried Grand Junction.

WALKER, Walton Harris, army officer; b. Belton, Tex., Dec. 3, 1889; s. Sam Sims and May Lydia (Harris) W.; B.S., U.S. Mil. Acad., West Point, N.Y, 1912; grad. Field Arty. Sch., 1920, Inf. Sch., 1923, Command and Gen. Staff Sch., 1926, Army War Coll., 1936; m. Caroline Victoria Emerson, Mar. 18, 1924; 1 son, Sam Sims. Commd. 2d lt., U.S. Army, 1912, advanced through ranks to maj. gen., 1942; participated in Vera Cruz, Mexico, expedition, 1914; with A.E.F., 1918-19, engaged in Saint Mihiel and Meuse-Argonne campaigns; served in China, 1930-33; maj. gen. comdg. IV Armored Corps, Sept. 1942-Oct. 1943; comdg. XX Corps, 1943-45; European Theater of Operations, 1944-45; promoted lt. general Apr. 1945; commanding gen. Sixth Service Command, 1946; commanding gen. Fifth Army, 1946-48; comdg. general of Eighth Army in Japan since 1948. Participated in Normandy, France and Germany campaigns. Awarded Distinguished Service Cross with oak leaf cluster, D.S.M. with oak leaf cluster, Distinguished Flying Cross with oak leaf cluster, Air Medal, Legion of Merit, Silver Star medal with 2 oak leaf clusters; Bronze Star (U.S.), Legion of Honor (officers class), Croix de Guerre with Palm (French); Order of War for the Fatherland (Russia); Order of Oak Leaves in the Ducal Crown, Croix de Guerre (Luxembourg). Made 4-star general posthumously, Jan. 2, 1951. Mason (32°, K.T., Shriner). Club: Army-Navy Country (Washington). Home: 340 N. Pearl St., Belton, Tex. Died Dec. 23, 1950 (in Korea); buried Arlington Nat. Cemetery.

WALKER, William S., advt. exec.; b. Grand Rapids, Mich., July 20, 1889; s. William Samuel and Stella (Riley) W.; student Carnegie Inst. Tech., 1905-08; m. Elsie W. Williams, Oct. 25, 1919. Propr. Walker & Downing, Pitts., 1917—. Mason. Home: R.D. 9, South Hills, Pa. Office: Oliver Bldg., Pitts. 22. Died Nov. 24, 1955.

WALLACE, Addison Alexander, clergyman; b. Independence, Mo., Dec. 25, 1862; s. Rev. Joseph William and Jessamine (Young) W.; A.B., Westminster Coll., Fulton, Mo., 1884, A.M., 1887, LL.D., 1944; B.D., McCormick Theol. Sem., 1887; D.D., Central U., Richmond, Ky., 1900; m. Annie Lacy Marquess, May 16, 1888; children—Marquess, Josephine, Mildred (Mrs. Knut T. Wernstrom), Anne Lacy. Became pastor 1st Presbyn. Ch., Mexica, Mo., 1888. Temp. supply, 1st Presbyn. Ch., Fulton, Mo., Sept. 1942-June 1943. Moderator Synod Mo. 1898. Trustee Westminster Coll., 1890—; mem. Mexico Pub. Library Bd., 1913—. Commr. Gen. Assembly Presbyn Ch. U.S., 5 Times to 1939, mem. spl. com. on missions, 1930; mem. western sect. Alliance of Ref. Chs., Atlantic City, N.J., 1929; mem. com. to survey fields occupied by Presbyn. Ch. in U.S. and Presbyn. Ch. U.S.A., 1929. Mem. Beta Theta Pi. Author: Outline History of the First Presbyterian Church in Mexico, Mo.; Memoirs and Gospel Testimony, 1945. Home: 132 Princeton St., Nutley 10, N.J. Died Nov. 21, 1954; buried Mexico, Mo.

WALLACE, Daniel Alden, farm editor; b. Winterset, Ia., Dec. 23, 1878; s. Henry and Nannie (Cantwell) W.; B.S. in Agr., Ia. State Coll. Agr. and Mechanic Arts, 1901; m. Grace V. Roshon, Dec. 23, 1920 (dec. Aug. 1933); m. 2d, Cecelia McCarthy, July 2, 1935. With Webb Pub. Co., St. Paul, Minn., 1905-35; directing editor The Farmer, 1905-35, The Farmer's Wife, 1919-35. Dir. Farm Foundation; mem. Council Minn. Inst. of Government Research. Mem. Phi Gamma Delta, Sigma Delta Chi. Republican. Presbyn. Home: Walker, Minn. Died Feb. 12, 1954.

WALLACE, David Duncan, college prof.; b. Columbia, S.C., May 23, 1874; s. William Henry and Alice A. (Lomax) W.; A.B., Wofford Coll., S.C., 1894, A.M., 1895; Ph.D., Vanderbilt U., 1899; Litt.D., Presbyn. Coll. S.C., 1924; LL.D., U. Sc., 1924; m. Sophie W. Adam, Jan. 10, 1900; 4 children; m. 2d, Maud S. Orr, Oct. 6, 1937. Taught in Carlisle Fitting Sch. of Wofford Coll., 1896-98; prof. history, econs., Wofford Coll., Spartanburg, S.C., 1899—; acting prof., Am. history, U. Mich., ½ yr.; vis. prof. history and polit. sci., Emory U. and Coll. Charleston, 1947-50. Mem. and sometime chmn. S.C. State Bd. Charities and Corrections and State Bd. Pub. Welfare. Has made special study of manuscript records of S.C. history. Author: Constitutional History of South Carolina, 1725 to 1775, 1899; Civil Government of South Carolina and The United States, 1906; Life of Henry Laurens, 1915; Government of England, Central, Local and Imperial, 1915; The South Carolina Constitution of 1895, 1927; also monographs and rev. articles on S.C. history and conditions in the South; 3-vol. History of S.C., 1934; S.C., a Short History, 1520-1948, 1951; History of Wofford College 1854-1949, 1951. Editor of series maps on hist. of S.C., 1935. Now preparing History of William Gregg and the first Hundred Years of the Graniteville Co. Home: Spartanburg, S.C. Died Apr. 29, 1951.

WALLACE, Donald H., economics; b. West Chester, Pa., June 29, 1903; s. B. Holmes and Frederica (Cross) W.; A.B., Harvard, 1924, M.A., 1928, Ph.D., 1931; m. Marcia Lincoln, Aug. 17, 1927; children—Marcia, Donald Keith. Instr. Suffield, Conn., Sch., 1924-25; instr. economics U. of Vt., 1925-26; asst. economics Harvard, 1926-27, instr., tutor, 1927-36; study in Europe, Social Science Research Council, 1931-32; asst. prof. economics Harvard, 1937-39; asso. prof. econ. Williams Coll. 1939-45; economist U.S. Dept. of Labor (part time basis), 1939, Nat. Defense Adv. Commn., price stabilization div., 1940, Office of Price Adminstrn., 1941, dir. indsl. mfg. price div., 1942-43; acting dep. adminstr. for price, OPA, June-Aug. 1943; econ. adv. to dep. price adminstr., 1943-46, mem. staff Council of Econ. Adv., 1946-47, consultant, 1947-48; dir. grad. program, and prof. economics Woodrow Wilson Sch. of Pub. and Internat. Affairs, Princeton U. since 1947. Mem. bd. dirs. Nat. Bureau Econ. Research. Mem. Am. Econ. Assn. Author: Market Control in the Aluminum Industry, 1937; International Control in Non-Ferrous Metals (with William Y. Elliott and others), 1937; Industrial Markets and Public Policy (in Public Policy, edited by E. S. Mason and C. J. Friedrich), 1940; Economic Standards of Government Price Control (editor and with Ben W. Lewis and others), 1941; (with L. V. Chandler) Economic Mobilization and Stabilization, 1951; Economic Controls and Defense, 1953; also articles. Contbr. articles to Quarterly Jour. Econs., Am. Econ. Review. Home: 120 Fitz Randolph Rd., Princeton, N.J. Died Sept. 19, 1953.

WALLACE, George Macdonald, banker; b. Oakland, Calif., Apr. 15, 1885; s. Hugh and Janet (Sinclair) W.; ed. pub. schs.; m. Juliette Boileau, July 29, 1915; children—George Sartori, Margaret (Graham). Began as messenger, 1901, with Security Savings Bank of Los Angeles, title later changed to Security Trust & Savings Bank and now Security-First Nat. Bank; was made asst. cashier, 1914, cashier 1920, mem. bd. dirs. and v.p., 1921, pres. 1934, chmn. bd. since 1946; president and dir. So. Realty Co., Los Angeles Trust & Safe Deposit Co., Pacific Southwest Realty Co.; dir. Union Oil Co., Founders Ins. Co.; adv. bd. American Mutual Fund, Inc.; mem. adv. com. California Community Found., 1953. Trustee, Barlow Sanatorium. Mem. Adv. Finance com. Henry E. Huntington Library and Art Gallery. Mem. Fed. Advisory Council, Fed. Reserve System, 1941-45. Mem. Am. Bankers Assn. (commerce and marine commn. 1935-39), Assn. Reserve City Bankers (com. on Fed. fiscal policy, 1944-45, com. on Fed. relationships, 1946). Republican. Presbyterian. Clubs: California, Automobile of Southern Calif. (dir.), Los Angeles Athletic, Los Angeles Country. Home: 332 S. Oxford Av. Office: Security-First Nat. Bank, 6th and Spring Sts., Los Angeles. Died May 17, 1957.

WALLACE, Harold Ayer, trade assn. exec.; b. Wyoming, Ill., Aug. 22, 1902; s. James Blair and Cora (Butler) W.; LL.B., Ill. Wesleyan U., 1926; m. Mildred Luellyn Brown, Sept. 18, 1926; children—Diane Mildred Mrs. James V. Piet), Beverly Jean (Mrs. R. Richard Straub). Mgr. Credit Bureau of Bloomington, Ill., 1923-28; gen. mgr. Credit Bur. of Will Co., Joliet, Ill., 1928-44; pres. Asso. Credit Burs. of Am., 1939-40, gen. mgr., 1944-46, exec. v.p., treas., 1946—; mgmt. lectr. univs. N.C., Ill., Kan., Tex., Mich. State, Stanford. Member C. of C. of U.S. (trade assn. com.), Am. Soc. Assn. Execs. (pres., dir.), Am. Retail Assn. Execs., Phi Delta Phi, Tau Kappa Epsilon. Republican. Mason. Clubs: Moolah Temple, Rotary (St. Louis); Missouri Athletic, Algonquin Golf; National Executives (Washington). Contributor articles to trade journals, Ency. Brit. Home: 45 Glen Rd., Webster Groves, Mo. Office: 7000 Chippewa St., St. Louis 19. Died Nov. 6, 1958; buried Oak Hill Cemetery, Webster Groves, Mo.

WALLACE, Harry Brookings, corp. exec.; b. St. Louis, Mo., Aug. 6, 1877; s. Asa A. and Mary Jane (Brookings) W.; ed. Smith Acad., St. Louis, Mo., 1885-95; A.B., Yale, 1899; Doctor of Laws, Washington University, 1947; married Mary R. Kennard, Oct. 29, 1902; children—John Kennard, Anne Kennard (Mrs. Chapin S. Newhard). With Cupples Co., St. Louis, Mo., since 1899, sec., 1910, pres., 1917, chmn. of the bd. since 1942; pres. of the corp. Washington Univ., since 1942. Dir. Southwestern Bell Telephone Co. since 1946. Served as maj. in command of Am. Red Cross at the Am. front in France, World War I. Coordinator O.P.M. Eighth Fed. Reserve Dist., 1941; acting chancellor, Washington Univ., 1944-46. Trustee Washington Univ., Brookings Inst., Mercantile Library, Methodist Orphans' Home. Clubs: Log Cabin, Noonday, St. Louis Country, Racquet, Round Table. Home: 4976 Pershing Av., 8. Address:

7th and Spruce Sts. 2, St. Louis. Died Aug. 11, 1955.

WALLACE, Hugh D., banker; b. Desdemona, Tex., June 25, 1892; s. Edwin R. and Mary Edna (Davis) W.; ed. high sch. and Poly. Coll., Ft. Worth; m. Jackie Lucille Jennings, Jan. 11, 1916 (died Mar. 20, 1951); children—Marion Alice (Mrs. H. Howard Cockrill), Evelyn Bel (Mrs. Ben Rand, Jr.). Cashier, Rule Cotton Oil Co., Rule, Tex., 1913-15; v.p. Arlington (Tex.) State Bank, 1915-21; bank examiner State of Tex., 1921-29; v.p. Mercantile Nat. Bank, Dallas, 1929-32; v.p. Fed. Home Loan Bank of Little Rock, Ark., 1932-44, pres. since 1944. Methodist. Club: Little Rock Country. Home: Albert Pike Hotel. Office: 110 E. 7th St., Little Rock, Ark. Died Apr. 20, 1953.

WALLACE, Robert Charles, exec. director Arctic Institute of N.A.; b. Orkney, Scotland, June 15, 1881; s. James and Mary (Swanney) W.; M.A., Edinburgh U., 1901, B.Sc., 1907, D.Sc., 1912; Ph.D., Gottingen U., 1909; student St. Andrews U., 1909-10; hon. LL.D., Univ. of Manitoba, 1928, Queen's Univ., 1930, Univ. of Toronto, 1933, Univ. of Saskatchewan, 1936, McMaster Univ., 1936, McGill Univ., 1938, U. of Western Ont., 1938, Temple U., 1940, St. Lawrence U., 1942, Harvard, 1944, U. Buffalo, 1946, U. Edinburgh, 1947, U. Ottawa, 1948, U. N.B., 1950, U. Alberta, 1951; D.Sc., Mich. Coll. Mining and Tech., 1942, Queen's U., Belfast, 1949; Laval U., 1951; D.C.L., Bishop's U., 1945, Oxford U., 1948; m. Elizabeth Harcus Smith, May 7, 1912; children—Ronald Stuart (deceased), Sheila Craigie (Mrs. David Woodsworth), Brenda Swanney (Mrs. Hiley Addington), Elspeth Harcus (Mrs. Charles Baugh). Lecturer in charge of dept. geology and mineralogy, U. of Manitoba, Winnipeg, 1910-12, prof., 1912-28; pres., U. of Alberta, 1928-36; prin. and vice chancellor, Queen's Univ., 1936-51; pres. Research Council of Ontario, 1948-51; executive director Arctic Institute of North America. Commissioner for Mines and Natural Resources, 1926-28; commr. Northern Manitoba, hdqrs. at The Pas, 1918-21. Mem. bd. of trustees, Carnegie Foundation Advancement of Teaching, 1938-51. Chmn. Nat. Adv. Com. for Children from Overseas 1941-46; mem. Commn. for Investigation of Cancer Remedies in Ont., mem. Com. on Reconstrn.; chmn. sub-com. Conservation and Development of Nat. Resources, 1940-43; former chmn. Ont. Research Commn. Fellow Royal Soc. of Canada (pres. 1940-41), Geological Soc. of London, Soc. Economic Geologists, Geological Soc. of Am., Mineralogical Soc. of Am.; mem. Canadian Inst. Mining and Metallurgy (pres. 1924-25), Manitoba Edn. Assn. (pres. 1925-26), Assn. Canadian Clubs (pres. 1930-31); hon. mem. Engring. Inst. of Can. Companion of St. Michael and St. George, 1944. Club: Rotary (Canada). Member United Church of Can. Author: The Burwash Lectures, A Liberal Education in a Modern World, 1932; Religion, Science and the Modern World, 1952; also tech. papers. Address: 4 Centre St., Kingston, Ont., Can. Died Jan. 29, 1955; buried Cataraqui Cemetery, Kingston.

WALLACE, Robert Minor, ex-congressman; b. New London, Ark., Aug. 6, 1857; s. William J. and Susan Ann (Williams) W.; A.B., Arizona Coll., La., 1876; m. Minnie Pennington, 1879; m. 2d, Jennie Kelso, 1895. Admitted to bar, 1877, under Judge U. M. Rose, Little Rock. Mem. Ark. Ho. Rep., 1881; post-office insp., 1887-89; pros. atty. 13th Circuit, 1890-1902; asst. U.S. dist. atty. at Texarkana, Ark., 1895; mem. 58th to 61st Congresses, 7th Ark. Dist. Democrat. Mem. Ark. Good Roads Assn., (pres.), Nat. Good Roads Assn. (v.p. 1903). Platform and chautauqua lectr. Now engaged in spl. campaign, state and nat. platform and orgn. work, for prohibition. Address: Magnolia, Ark. Died Nov. 9, 1942.

WALLACE, Thomas Ross, consul; b. Phila., Pa., Oct. 20, 1848; s. William and Jane (Ross) W.; ed. pub. schs. and commercial coll.; studied law; m. Margaret Gill, Oct. 6, 1874. Teacher, lawyer; served as clk. dist. and circuit courts of I.A. 3 terms; mayor of Atlantic, Ia., 3 terms; consul at Crefeld, Germany, 1901-07, Jerusalem, 1907-10, Marinique, W.I., June 24, 1910—. Mason (K.T.), Odd Fellow, Elk. Republican. Home: Atlantic, Ia. Died Dec. 6, 1929.

WALLACE, William Henry, mfg. exec.; b. Moorestown, N.J., Aug. 25, 1887; s. Charles and Ella (Shivler) W.; student Rutgers U., 1905-09; m. Beatrice Morrison, Aug. 11, 1921; children—Paul K., William Henry, Nancy Linda. Sales engr., Eaton Mfg. Co., Detroit, 1919-25, sales mgr. 1925-31, div. mgr., 1931-42, v.p. directing the spring div., since 1942. Mem. Soc. Automotive Engrs. Clubs: Grosse Pointe (Mich.) Yacht: Lochmoor (Grosse Pointe Woods). Office: 9771 French Rd., Detroit 13. Died Aug. 23, 1951; buried White Chapel Meml. Cemetery, Birmingham, Mich.

WALLER Cecile Howell (Mrs. Littleton W. T. Waller, Jr.), American Red Cross exec.; b. Philadelphia, Pa., Oct. 6, 1893; d. Charles Harkness and Anne Margaret (Fitler) Howell; ed. Agnes Irwin Sch., Phila., Pa.; m. William Overington Rowland, Jr., Nov. 3, 1917 (died Aug. 1, 1934); children—William Overington 3d (dec.), Anne; m. 2d, Maj. Gen. Littleton W. T. Waller, Jr., May 15, 1948. Ward chmn., Southeastern Pa. chapter Am. Red Cross Roll Call., 1926-32, dist. chmn., roll call, 1932-38, volunteer chmn. roll call, 1938-42, chmn. vol. special services, 1939-46, mem. nat. com. on vol. spl. services, 1938, vice chmn. Southeastern Pa. chapter, 1941; mem. central com., Am. Nat. Red Cross, 1943, chmn. nat. com. on insignia, uniforms and awards, Jan. 1945, mem. bd. govs., 1947; vice chmn., 1948-52. Mem. Emergency Aid of Pa.; hon. member Junior League of Philadelphia. Clubs: Acorn, Huntingdon Valley Country. Home: Washington Lane and Welsh Rd., Meadowbrook, Pa. Died Aug. 21, 1953; buried All Saints Church, Torresdale, Phila.

WALLER, Curtis L., judge; b. Silver Creek, Miss., Jan. 9, 1887; s. William Mikell and Clara Cordelia (Longino) W.; Ph.B., Miss. Coll., 1908; LL.B. Millsaps Coll., 1910; grad. Sch. Mil. Aeros., Tex., 1918; m. Lucy McGinn, Dec. 8, 1920; 1 dau., Mary Ann. Admitted to Miss. bar, 1910; pvt. sec. to Pat Harrison, mem. Congress, 1911; mem. firm Gex and Waller, Bay St. Louis, Miss., 1914-27; Waller and Pepper, 1930-37, Waller and Meginniss, 1937-40, Tallahassee, Fla., apptd. U.S. Dist. judge, No. and So. dists. Fla., 1940; apptd. U.S. circuit judge, Fifth Circuit, 1943. Served in World War I; lt. col. U.S. Res. Corps. Mem. Miss. Legislature, 1924, Fla. Legislature, 1933; states atty., Fla., 1932. Mem. Fla. State, Am. bar assns., Kappa Alpha; hon. mem. Phi Alpha Delta, Elks, Am. Legion. Club: Army and Navy (Washington). Home: 416 E. Williams St. Office: Federal Bldg., Tallahassee, Fla. Died July 11, 1950; buried Tallahassee.

WALLIS, Frederick Alfred, former govt. ofcl.; b. Ky., Mar. 13, 1869; s. Allan M. and Albertine R. W.; ed. pub. and pvt. schs., Ky.; m. Nannie Williams Clay, Apr. 1901. Sr. mem. Wallis & Co., ins., N.Y. Formerly dep. police commr. City of N.Y.; U.S. commr. immigration, Ellis Island, 1918-22; became commr. correction, N.Y.C., 1922; mem. exec. com. Nat. Com. of 10,000 on Law Enforcement. Former chmn. finance com. N.Y. State Dem. Party; mem. N.Y. County Dem. Com. (finance com.). Vice pres. People's Hosp.; treas. for many years Com. for Care and Betterment of Immigrant Population of Greater N.Y.; chmn. Com. Instl. Work for Foreigners; etc. Pres. N.Y. State Christian Endeavor Union; trustee, ex-pres. N.Y. Presbyn. Union; trustee Council Federated Chs. Am.; pres. Ruling Elders' Assn. N.Y., N.Y. State Christian Endeavor Fedns., Internat. Narcartics Rescue League; nat. supt. citizenship Com. United Soc. Christian Endeavor; trustee Beekman St. Hosp., Centre Coll., Danville, Ky.; chmn. Onward Ky. Expn. Com., Ky. Dept. Pub. Welfare, Ky. State Dem. Campaign and finance coms. Mem. Ky. Soc. (dir.), Tenn. Soc., etc. Served as col., staff gov. of Ky. Clubs: Bankers, Broadway Assn., Nat. Democratic, Civitan (v.p.). Address: 616 Pleasant St., Paris, Ky. Died Dec. 21, 1951.

WALLS, David Crawford, lawyer; b. Breckinridge County, nr. Hardinsburg, Ky., Sept. 26, 1882; s. Leander and Mary Dorcus (Lyons) W.; student Hardinsburg Normal Sch., 1901-02, Teacher's Tng. Sch., 1903-04, Bowling Green Tchrs. Coll., 1905-06, 1907, Jefferson Sch. Law, 1912-13; m. Lillian Ewing Alexander, Mar. 15, 1913. Tchr. pub. schs., Breckinridge Co., 1901-12; dep. clk. Breckinridge Ct., 1906-08, master commr., 1929-31; admitted to Ky. bar, 1913; active practice of law, 1914—; first asst. atty. gen., State of Ky., 1933-36; 1st asst. U.S. atty., Western Dist. Ky., 1939-45, acting U.S. atty., 1946, U.S. atty., 1946—. Mem. Ky. State and Ky. Ninth Jud. Dist. bar assns. Democrat. Methodist. Home: Hardinsburg, Ky. Office: Federal Bldg., Louisville 2. Died Dec. 11, 1958.

WALRATH, Florence Dahl, humanitarian; b. Chicago, Ill., Oct. 18, 1877; d. H. Lawrence and Betsy Louisa (Anderson) Dahl; ed. North Div. High Sch., Chicago, 1892-96; m. William Bradley Walrath, June 29, 1897; children—Hester (Mrs. H. H. Hunter), Helen (Mrs. J. B. Sanborn), Comdr. William B., II (U.S.N.R.), Gretchen (Mrs. Arthur Oehl). Founder, mng. dir. emeritus The Cradle Society, Evanston, organized in 1923 for the purpose of receiving and preparing homeless babies for adoption into permanent homes—a work in which she had been engaged for several yrs. prior to 1923. Over 6000 babies adopted in homes in the U.S. and in some foreign countries as result of her work and that of The Cradle Society. Has assisted in development of improved technique for care of babies where considerable number are cared for in one place, resulting in an unusually low death rate. Episcopalian. Home: 1615 Hinman Av. Address: The Cradle Society, 2049 Ridge Av., Evanston, Ill. Died Nov. 7, 1958; buried Rosehill Cemetery, Chgo.

WALSH, Correa Moylan, author; b. Newburgh, N.Y., Sept. 23, 1862; s. Joseph Correa and Anna (Wood) W.; A.B., Harvard, 1884; studied univs. Berlin, Paris, Rome and Oxford. Mem. Am. Econ. Assn., Am. Acad. Polit. and Social Sci., Royal Econ. Soc., Royal Statis. Soc., Soc. for Psychical Research, Am. Math. Soc., Math. Assn. America, A.A.A.S. Club: Harvard Union (Cambridge, Mass.). Author Measurement of General Exchange-Value, 1901; Fundamental Problem in Monetary Science, 1903; Doctrine of Creation, 1910; Political Science of John Adams, 1915; Climax of Civilization, Socialism, and Feminism, 1917; Problem of Estimation, 1921; Four Kinds of Economic Value, 1926; An Attempted Proof of Fermat's Last Theorem by a New Method, 1932. Editor of Shekespeare's Complete Sonnets, 1908. Home: Bellport, L.I., N.Y. Deceased.

WALSH, Edmund (Aloysius), clergyman, educator; b. Boston, Mass., Oct. 10, 1885; s. John Francis and Catherine (Noonan) W.; ed. Boston Coll., and Jesuit sems., at Frederick, and Woodstock, Md., and Poughkeepsie, N.Y.; spl. studies London U., Dublin U., U. of Innsbruck, Austria, and other European univs.; A.B., Ph.D., Georgetown U., A.M., Woodstock; LL.D., U. of Delaware; D.Litt., Georgetown U. Joined Soc. of Jesus (Jesuits), 1902; ordained priest R.C. Ch., 1916; teacher of lit., Georgetown U., 5 yrs.; apptd. dean arts and sciences, Georgetown, May 5, 1918, but called by War Dept. as mem. spl. com. to administer S.A.T.C. to supply officers to U.S. Army; served as asst. ednl. dir. same, N.E. states (32 colls.); resigned Jan. 1, 1919; organized, 1919, and regent Sch. of Foreign Service (Georgetown U.); vice president Georgetown University since 1924. In Europe, 1921-22, making econ. study of schools of polit. science and commerce; also pursuing other studies in France. Entered Soviet Russia in Mar. 1922, for famine relief work, representing Am. Catholics on Am. Relief Administration; named by Vatican, June 1922, dir. gen. Papal Relief Mission to Russia and apptd. rep. to treat with Soviet Govt. regarding Catholic interests in Russia; pres. Catholic Near East Welfare Assn., 1926-31; conducted preliminary negotiations, 1931, for founding of Baghdad College, Baghdad, Irak; assisted, with Dwight Morrow, to bring about peace between Catholic Ch. and Mexican govt., 1929; lecturer, Acad. of Internat. Law, The Hague, 1935, 1939. Consultant, office of chief of counsel, U.S.A., at Nürnberg, 1945-46; mem., The President's Adv. Commn. on Universal Training, 1946-47. Fellow American Geographical Soc.; mem. Am. Economic Association, Council on Foreign Relations. Decorated with Medal of Pub. Instruction (Venezuela), 1921; Comdr. of the Crown (Rumania); Knight Order of Isabella La Catolica (Spain). Club: Cosmos. Author: The Fall of the Russian Empire, 1928; The Last Stand—An Interpretation of the Soviet Five-year Plan, 1931; Ships and National Safety, 1935; Woodcarver of Tyrol, 1935; Total Power, 1948; Total Empire, 1951; also numerous periodical articles on Geopolitics. Lectr. on Russia. Address: Georgetown University, Washington. Died Oct. 31, 1956; buried Community Cemetery, Georgetown U.

WALSH, Gerald Groveland, clergyman, editor; b. S. Norwalk, Conn., Nov. 9, 1892; s. Michael Francis and Mary (O'Rourke) W.; B.A., London (Eng.) U., 1916; M.A., 1st class honors, Oxford U., 1924; student theology, Woodstock Coll., 1925-28; Ph.D., S.T.D., Gregorian U., Rome, Italy, 1929. Mem. Soc. of Jesus since 1910; ordained priest R.C. Church, 1926; prof. of church history and librarian, Woodstock (Md.) Coll., 1929-34; grad. prof. medieval history, Gregorian U., Rome, 1934-36; head grad. dept. Italian studies, Fordham U., 1937-38, grad. prof. medieval history, 1938-40; editor Thought (Fordham University Quarterly) since 1940. Lowell lecturer, 1945. Medalist Royal Geographical Society (London), England), 1910; Cobden Club prizeman in economics, 1910; Gibbs scholarship in modern history and Marquis of Lothian prizeman, Oxford U. (England), 1923. Member American Historical Association, Am. Catholic Hist. Assn., Mediaeval Acad. of America, Am. Acad. Polit. and Social Science, Am. Assn. Teachers of Italian, Oxford Soc., Dante Soc. Author: Emperor Charles IV, 1924; (with Felix Fellner and others) The Catholic Philosophy of History, 1936; (with Dr. Frank Kingdon and others) Faith for Today, 1941; Medieval Humanism, 1941; (with John A. Mackay and others) Great Religions of the Modern World, 1946; Dante Alighieri: Citizen of Christendom, 1946; (with F. X. Glimm and J. M. F. Marique) The Apostolic Fathers, a New Translation, 1947; The City of God, a New Translation (with D. Zema and J. R. O'Donnell, 1948; The Philosophy of Catholic Higher Education (with others), 1948; Church and State in the United States (with J. M. O'Neill), 1948. Asso. editor The Fathers of the Church, a new translation, 1946; translator and editor Christian Answers to Social Problems, by Cardinal Verdier, 1940; contributor to scholarly publs. Address: Keating Hall, Fordham University, N.Y.C. 58. Died Dec. 17, 1951; buried St. Andrew-on-Hudson, Poughkeepsie, N.Y.

WALSH, James Lawrence, assn. exec.; b. Boston, May 6, 1886; s. James Lawrence and Rose (Raycroft) W.; student Mass. Inst. Tech., 1903-05; grad. U.S. Mil. Acad., 1909; m. Mazie Porcher, June 29, 1918; 1 son, James Lawrence (dec.). Commd. 2d lt. U.S. Army, June 11, 1909; promoted through grades to maj. regular army, June 23, 1917; served in World War as lt. col. and col. (temp.); retired Nov. 4, 1922. Became connected with Bankers Trust Co., New York, 1922, asst. v.p., 1926-27; v.p., dir. McGraw-Hill Pub. Co., 1927-28; later v.p. Nat. Bank of Detroit. Dir. and trustee Am. (formerly Army) Ordnance Assn., pres. since Jan. 1947; founder and first editor Army Ordnance Mag., 1920-22; dist. chief N.Y. Ordnance Dist., 1923-32; special advisor to chief of ordnance, U.S. Army, 1942-46. Chmn. War Prodn. Com. Am. Soc. Mech. Engrs., 1939-45, mem. bd. pub. affairs since 1947; vice chmn. Nat. Tech. Adv. Commn. since 1940. Awarded D.S.M., Victory medal, Mexican Border Service medal, Mexican medal (U.S.); Comdr. Saints Maurice and Lazarus (Italy); Crozier Medal by Army Ordnance Assn., 1941. Clubs: Army and Navy, Metropolitan (Washington); University (New York). Founder and first editor Logistics, 1945-47. Address: 1 W. 54th St., N.Y.C. Died June 11, 1952.

WALSH, John Gaynor, v.p., Southern Pacific Co.; b. Albany, N.Y., May 19, 1891; s. Michael Francis and Margaret Genevieve (Gaynor) W.; student Christian Brothers Acad., Albany High Sch.; B.A., Harvard Coll., 1913; m. Mary Frances Reilly, Nov. 20, 1916; children—John Gaynor, Mary Reilly. Examiner Pub. Service Commn., Albany, N.Y., 1913-17; asst. to v.p. financial dept., Erie R.R., 1917-23; asst. v.p., 1923-26, treas., 1926-37, sec-treas., 1937-38; vice president, finances, Southern Pacific Company, since 1938, dir. since 1943; pres., dir. 620 Park Avenue Corporation, N.Y.; dir., mem. exec. com., v.p. St. Louis Southwestern R.R. Co., Wm. E. Walsh & Sons, Inc., Albany, N.Y.; dir. Ry. Express Agy., Inc. Mem. Newcomen Soc. Eng. Roman Catholic. Knight of Malta. Clubs: Recess, Harvard, Bankers (New York). Home: 620 Park Avenue, N.Y.C. 21. Office: 165 Broadway, N.Y.C. 6. Died Aug. 28, 1953.

WALSH, Raycroft, aircraft mfg.; b. Boston, Mass., Nov. 14, 1888; s. James Lawrence and Rose (Raycroft) Walsh; student Mechanic Arts High Sch., Boston, 1902-05, Mass. Inst. Tech., 1908-09, Columbia U., 1909-10; m. Emma L. Wupperman, Sept. 14, 1920; children—Mary Louise, Raycroft, Jr., Emmy Lu. Commd. second lt., U.S. Army, and advanced through grades to maj., 1910-26; resigned as maj., Air Corps, with rating as airplane pilot from Sept. 1917; lt. col. Air Reserve, U.S. Army, since 1932; with McGraw-Hill Pub. Co., 1926-28, Cheney Bros., silk mfrs., 1928-30; with United Aircraft Corp. since 1930, dir. since 1936, vice pres., 1936-43, senior vice pres., 1942; vice chairman, 1943; gen. mgr. Hamilton Standard Propellers Division, 1930-40; director of the United Aircraft Export Corporation. Member Institute Aeronautical Sciences, Phi Kappa Psi. Roman Catholic. Clubs: Hartford (Conn.); Hartford Golf (West Hartford, Connecticut). Home: 35 Westwood Rd., West Hartford 5, Conn. Office: United Aircraft Corp., East Hartford 8, Conn. Died Aug. 17, 1952; buried Arlington Cemetery, Washington.

WALSH, Thomas Joseph, archbishop; b. Parker's Landing, Penn., Dec. 6, 1873; s. Thomas and Ellen (Curtin) W.; ed. College and Sem. of St. Bonaventure (Allegany, N.Y.), U. of St. Appollinaris, the Pontifical Roman Sem., Rome, Italy, receiving S.T.D. and J.C.D.; LL.D., St. Bonaventure, 1913. Ordained priest R.C. Ch., 1900; 3d asst. rector St. Joseph's Cathedral, Buffalo, N.Y., Jan.-June 1900; pvt. sec. to Bishops Quigley and Colton, 1900-15, also chancellor of the diocese; rector St. Joseph's old Cathedral, 1915-18, and reapptd. chancellor of the diocese upon installation of Bishop Dougherty, serving 1916-18; consecrated bishop Diocese of Trenton, July 25, 1918; made asst. at Pontifical Throne, Mar. 13, 1922; transferred to See of Newark, Mar. 7, 1928; apptd. first archbishop of Newark, Dec. 11, 1937. Home: 552 S. Orange Av., South Orange, N.J. Address: 31 Mulberry St., Newark. Died June 6, 1952.

WALSON, Charles Moore, army officer; b. Delaware, Aug. 24, 1883; s. George W. and Minnie S. (Collins) W.; M.D., Jefferson Med. Coll., Phila., 1906; grad. Army Med. Sch., 1912; m. Bonnie Miller, June 2, 1915; children—Charles W. (officer U.S. Army), Elizabeth W. (wife of Lt. Col. George W. Bixby). Commd. 1st lt., Med. Corps, U.S. Army, 1912, and advanced through the grades to brig. gen., 1945; surgeon, Expeditionary Forces, Vera Cruz, Mexico, 1914; during World War I served successively at Honolulu and Schofield Barracks, T.H.; camp surgeon, Camp Lewis, Wash.; div. surgeon, 15th Div., Camp Logan, Houston, Tex.; comdg. officer, Gen. Hosp. 33, Fort Logan H. Roots, Little Rock, Ark.; asst. to chief surgeon, A.E.F., France; at station hosp. Am. Forces in Germany, Coblenz, Germany; hosp. inspector and exec. officer, Walter Reed Gen. Hosp., 1922-26; asst. to corps area surgeon, 7th Corps Area Surgeon's Office, Omaha, Neb., 1926-31; surgeon, Station Hosp., Fort Benjamin Harrison, Ind., 1931-35; in Surgeon Gen.'s Office, Washington, D.C., 1935-39; asst. to corps area surgeon, II Corps Area, 1939, corps area surgeon, 1940-42; Service Command surgeon Aug. 1942-June 1946, surgeon of 1st Army since consolidation of 1st and 2d Service Commands. With St. Joseph Infirmary, Fort Worth, Texas, 1906-07, St. John's Hospital, St. Louis, Mo., 1907-08; asst. to clinical professor surgery, St. Louis U., 1908-11; assts. to city health officer, St. Louis, 1909-11; lecturer on vital statistics Creighton U., 1926-30, on tropical medicine, Indiana U. Med. Sch., 1930-34. Adminstr. Am. Red Cross Blood Program, Greater N.Y., 1947-51, Washington, 1951——. Decorated Mexican Service, Victory,

Army Occupation of Germany medals, Am. Defense Ribbon, Am. Theater Campaign Medal, Victory Medal World War II, Legion of Merit, Army Commendation Ribbon. Fellow Am. Coll. Surgeons; mem. A.M.A., Assn. Mil. Surgeons of U.S.A., Am. Hosp. Assn., Phi Rho Sigma. Mason. Club: Army-Navy Country (Washington). Home: Washington, D.C. Died May 14, 1959.

WALSTER, Harlow Leslie, dean of agr.; b. Troy Twp., Sauk County, Wis., Apr. 20, 1883; s. George Albert and Mary Etta (Stelzman) W.; B.S.A., U. of Wis., 1908; A.M., Harvard, 1913; Ph.D., U. of Chicago, 1918; m. Ada Georgene Meadows, June 15, 1921; 1 dau., Eunice Mary. Instr. in soils, U. of Wis., 1908-15, asst. prof., 1916-19; agronomist N.D. Agrl. Expt. Sta., Fargo, N.D., 1919-34; dean, div. of agr., N.D. Agrl. Coll., Fargo, 1924——, dir. agrl. extension service, 1934-37, dir. Agrl. Expt. Sta. 1934-37 and 1939——; consultant to Bureau of Reclamation, U.S. Dept. of Interior, 1944——; v.p. Fargo Sch. of Religious Edn., N.D. Agrl. Coll. Fellow A.A.A.S.; mem. Am. Soc. Agronomy, Am. and Internat. Society Soil Science, American Agricultural Historical Society, N.D. Academy of Science, Phi Beta Kappa, Phi Kappa Phi, Alpha Zeta, Phi Lambda Upsilon, Gamma Alpha, Alpha Gamma Rho. Conglist. Mason. Clubs: Lions, Commons (Fargo). Author: Soils and Soil Fertility (with A. R. Whitson), 1912. Author of many agrl. expt. station bulletins. Home: 1130 4th St. N., Fargo, N.D. Died Oct. 7, 1957; buried Mount Pleasant Cemetery, Lodi, Wis.

WALTERS, Carl, ceramic sculptor; b. Fort Madison, Ia., June 19, 1883; s. Nelson Peter and Emily Elizabeth (Larson) W.; student Minneapolis Art Sch., 1905-07, Chase Sch. of Art and Henri Sch. of Art (New York), 1908-09; m. Helen Lawrence, 1912. Designed and executed glass doors in Whitney Museum. Represented in Met. Museum of Art, Whitney Museum of Am. Art, Art Inst. Chicago, Minneapolis Inst. of Arts, Portland (Ore.) Art Assn., Detroit Inst. of Arts, Davenport (Ia.) Municipal Art Gallery, Cincinnati museums, Museum of Modern Art, N.Y. City, Phillips Memorial Gallery, Washington, D.C. Awarded Guggenheim fellowship, 1936 and 37; purchase prize Metropolitan Museum, 1942. Home: Woodstock, N.Y. Died Nov. 12, 1955; buried Aritsts Meml. Hill, Woodstock.

WALTERS, Charles S., utilities exec.; b. Monroe, Wis., Oct. 12, 1871; s. Henry and Catherine Walters; student pub. schs.; m. Edith Sykes, June 20, 1904 (dec. Dec. 1948). Messenger, Western Union, 1880-84; trainmaster's clk. C.R.I., 1885-87; various positions Ia. Central Ry., 1887-1902; gen. agt., passenger dept. M. & St.L. R.R., 1903-05; gen. agt. Ore.-Electric Ry., 1909-10; v.p., gen. mgr. Walla Walla Valley Ry., 1911-23; dist. mgr. Pacific Power & Light Co., 1919-23; v.p., gen. mgr., dir. Asheville Power & Light Co., 1923-26; now v.p., Western div. mgr. Carolina Power & Light, also dir., 1926——. Served with Wash. N.G., World War I. Mem. Asheville C. of C. (pres. 1943-44). Elk, Mason (32°). Clubs: Asheville Rotary (pres. 1937-38), Asheville Country. Home: 198 Kimberly Av. Office: Public Service Bldg., Asheville, N.C. Died Aug. 23, 1959.

WALTERS, Francis Marion, Jr., metallurgist; born Monticello, Ind., Apr. 25, 1888; s. Francis M. and Jennie Elizabeth (Horning) W.; A.B., U. of Mo., 1911, A. M., 1914, Ph.D., 1920; m. Roma Crow, Nov. 16, 1916; children—Jane (dec.), Francis Marion, III, John Linton, Thomas Charles. In charge of dept. of physics U. of Mont., 1915-16; instr. in physics, Central H.S. and Jr. Coll., St. Joseph, Mo., 1916-18; asst. physicist Bur. of Standards, Washington, 1918-20, asso., 1920-21; prof. physics, St. John's Univ., Shanghai, China, 1921-22; asso. physicist, Bur. of Standards, 1922-24; dir. Bur. of Metall. Research, 1924-32; physicist Metals Research Lab., Carnegie Inst. Tech., 1932-34; research engr. Youngstown Sheet & Tube Co., 1935-38; cons. metallurgist, 1938-39; metallurgist, Naval Research Lab., 1939-40, sr. metallurgist and acting supt., div. of phys. metallurgy, since 1940, prin. metallurgist, 1942, head physicist and supt. div. of physical metallurgy 1943-46; asso. div. leader chemistry metallurgy div., Los Alamos Sci. Lab. since 1946. Awarded Henry Marion Howe medal, Am. Soc. for Steel Treating, 1932; Navy Distinguished Service Award, 1946. Fellow Am. Phys. Society; member Washington Philosophical Society, Am. Inst. of Mining and Metall. Engrs., Am. Soc. for metals Iron and Steel Inst., Gamma Alpha, Sigma Xi, Phi Beta Kappa. Presbyterian. Research in spectroscopy, photography, metallurgy. Home: 4911 Trinity Dr., Los Alamos, N.M. Died April 18, 1953; buried Warrensburg, Mo.

WALTERS, George Alexander, inventor; b. Canfield, Ont., Can., Nov. 11, 1872; s. John Comstock and Margaret (MacDonald) W.; brought to U.S., naturalized, 1898; LL.B., Detroit Coll. of Law, 1912; m. Ethelwyn Taylor, Nov. 28, 1900 (dec. 1945); children—Margaret (Mrs. Herbert Noxon), George (died Nov., 1946). Editor Kingsville (Ont.) Reporter, 1891-97; representative Sun Life Insurance Co., China, 1903; vice consul general, Central China, Hankow, 1903-05; editorial and feature writer Detroit

News, Detroit Journal, Detroit Free Press, 1905-12; admitted to Mich. bar, 1912; dep. police commr. Detroit, 1912-22; v.p. Great Lakes Land Co., 1930-34; office mgr. Lawrence Aero. Corp., Linden, N.J., 1940-44; personnel mgr. Gen. Motors Corp., Linden, 1944-45. Invented, developed stop and go traffic signal; writer Negligent Homicide Act; pioneer in establishment accident investigation bur., safety zones, safety edn. programs for schools and public. Sheriff, Wayne County, Mich., 1922-26; councilman, Detroit, 1926-30. Served with Mich. Inf. Vol., Spanish-Am. War, 1898. Mem. Delta Theta Phi. Republican. Presbyn. (deacon). Mason (Shriner, 32°). Clubs: Detroit Yacht, Detroit Rotary; St. Clair River Country. Home: 58 E. 79th St., N.Y.C. 21. Died Jan. 1, 1960.

WALTERS, Leon L(ouis), taxidermist; b. Portland, Ind., May 1, 1888; s. Charles Evans and Martha Ann (Woten) W.; student Art Institute Chicago; m. Ethel Agnes Dow, March 19, 1915; children—Allen Dow, David William. Staff taxidermist Chgo. Museum of Natural History, 1911——; mem. Marshall Field Expedition to Central America, 1923, to Ga., 1925; Field Mus. Expdn. to S.W. U.S., 1937, to Fla., 1939; Leon Mandel-Field Mus. Expdn. to Galapagos, 1941; discoverer of a basic principle of coloring in connection with making reproductions of animal and plant life; inventor processes in taxidermy and model making. Mem. Am. Soc. of Mammalogists, Chicago Ornithol. Soc. Author: (brochure) New Uses of Celluloid and Similar Material in Taxidermy, 1925; also scientific papers. Sculptor and artist. Home: 12142 Harvard Av. Address: Chicago Natural History Museum, Chgo. Died June 7, 1956; buried Mt. Hope Cemetery, Chgo.

WALTERS, R(ea) G(illespie), educator, textbook author; b. Baltimore, Jan. 22, 1888; s. Jacob Harry and Emma (Shuman) W.; student Mercersburg Acad., 1906; B.S. in commerce, U. of Cincinnati; student, Eastman Sch. of Bus., 1908; m. Rose Marie Schall, April 1, 1909 (deceased); 1 d., Rose Emma (Mrs. William S. McKay, Jr.); m. 2d Marie Fields, July 14, 1951. Teacher, Wood Business School, N.Y., 1908-10; teacher, prin., Aspinwall (Pa.) High Sch., 1910-18; head dept. commerce, Grove City (Pa.) Coll., 1919-27, dir. pub. relations, personnel officer, since 1930; advt. mgr. Southwestern Pub. Co., 1927-30. Pres., Grove City C. of C. 1922, 1932; chmn. Grove City 50th Anniversary Celebration, 1933, State Rep. Com., 1925-27. Trustee Pa. Soldiers Orphan Sch., 1924-27, Warren State Hosp., since 1946; dir., Grove City Hosp., 1935-47. Mem. Nat. Bus. Teachers Assn. (past pres.), Nat. Assn. of Bus. Teacher Training Instns. (past pres.), Tri-State Bus. Edn. Assn. (past pres.), Eastern Commercial Teachers Assn. (formerly exec. com.), Pa. Bus. Edn. Assn., Pi Gamma Mu, Omicron Delta Kappa, United Bus. Edn. Assn. Republican. Methodist. Mason. Club: Grove City Rotary (pres., 1939). Author: High School Commercial Education, 1922; One Hundred Lessons in Spelling, 1916; Fundamentals of Selling (with J. W. Wingate), 1948; Retail Merchandising (with J. W. Wingate, J. P. Weiner), 1951; How to Find and Apply for a Job 1947; Word Studies (with C.A. Nolan), 1949; Principles and Problems of Business Education, 1950; coordinated bus. edn. terms, Dictionary of Edn. Home: 507 Stewart Av., Grove City, Pa. Died Nov. 11, 1952.

WALTMAN, Harry Franklin, artist; b. Killbuck, O., 1871; s. Elmore and Mary E. (Schatzel) W.; studied at Washington, D.C., and Julian Acad., Paris; m. Carolyn Lee Fetter, July 1916. Rep. in Butler Museum of Art, Youngstown, O. Awarded Isidor prize for portrait, 1909, for landscape, 1916, Salmagundi Club; Nat. Arts Club prize, 1927. Asso. Nat. Acad., 1917. Clubs: Salmagundi, Nat. Arts. Home: Dover Plains, N.Y. Died 1951.

WALTMAN, William DeWitt, mining engr.; b. Kendallville, Ind., Feb. 8, 1875; s. Martin Van Buren and Catherine (Aller) W.; E.M., Colo. Sch. of Mines, Golden, Colo., 1899; m. Eula C. Hamilton, Mar. 24, 1927; 1 son, Wm. DeWitt, Jr. Began as mining engr., Cripple Creek, Colo., 1900; editor of Hills Manual of Cripple Creek Mines, 1901; prin. asst. city engr., Colorado Springs, 1901-04; supt. mining, Panama Canal, 1905-06; supt. constrn., Culebra and Porto Bello divs., Panama Canal, 1906-09; chief engr. Costilla Estates Development Co., San Acacio, Colo., 1910-11; gen. mgr. Fanco Wyo. Oil Co., 1912-19; corp. pres. petroleum Producing Cos., U.S. and Mexico, 1919-25; pres. dir. and gen. mgr. in charge of U.S. operations of Franco Wyoming Oil Co., 1926——; pres. and dir. Franco Western Oil Co., Franco Central Oil Co., Franco Wyoming Securities Corp., McElroy Ranch Company, Arzaco, Inc., Oil Producers Agency Calif.; ret., 1951. Capt. U.S. Army, Chem. Warfare Reserve. Mem. Am. Soc. Civil Engrs. (life), Am. Assn. Petroleum Geologists, Am. Inst. Mining and Metall. Engrs., Society of American Military Engineers, American Petroleum Inst., Am. Numismatic Soc., Colo. Soc. Engrs., Calavo Growers Assn. Past pres. bd. of trustees, Colo. Sch. of Mines. Awarded Roosevelt Panama medal, Medal of Individual Merit and Honor, Colo. Sch. of Mines (first medal ever granted by this institution), 1942. Republican. Methodist. Mason. Clubs:

California, Jonathan (Los Angeles). Home: 325 S. Plymouth Blvd., Los Angeles 5. Died Feb. 14, 1955; buried Colorado Springs, Colo.

WALTON, Albert Douglass, lawyer; b. Dundee, N.Y., Feb. 22, 1886; s. Griffin B. and Emma (Douglass) W.; LL.B., U. of Mich., 1907; m. Harriet G. Lund, June 23, 1915; children—Elizabeth Ann, Ruth Mildred, William Griffin. Began practice at Penn Yan, N.Y., 1907; moved to Cheyenne, Wyo., 1910. Chmn. Rep. Central Com., Laramie County, Wyo., 1916-22; mem. exec. com. Rep. State Central Com. since 1918, vice chmn., 1932-36; city atty., Cheyenne, 1918-19; U.S. atty., Dist. of Wyo., 1921-33; associated with spl. govt. counsel in prosecution of "Teapot Dome" case. Presbyterian. Mason (33°, Shriner). Club: Lawyers (New York). Home: 102 W. 27th St. Office: Majestic Bldg., Cheyenne, Wyo. Died Apr. 3, 1951; buried Lakeview Cemetery, Cheyenne.

WALTON, Frank Richmond, business exec.; born Richmond, Va., July 25, 1886; s. Frank Henry and Josephine (McMasters) W.; ed. pub. and high sch.; m. Dorothy Douglass Miller, Feb. 12, 1919; children—Mary Josephine (Mrs. Frederick O. Schweizer), Humphries Miller, Nancy McMasters (Mrs. George H. Follansbee). Began with Union Supply Co. (subsidiary of U.S. Steel Corp.), Mar. 1902, purchasing dept., purchasing agt. 1919, pres., 1933-55, ret.; dir. Gunnison Homes, Inc.; trustee The Dollar Savings Bank. Dir. South Side Hosp. Dir. Pitts. chpt. A.R.C., chairman of disaster committee. Member American Iron and Steel Institute and Pittsburgh Athletic Assn. Episcopalian. Republican. Clubs: Duquesne (dir.), University, Oakmont Country (dir.). Home: Schenely Apartments, Pittsburgh 13. Office: Union Supply Co., Pitts. 3. Died May 12, 1956; buried Allegheny Cemetery, Pitts.

WALTON, William Randolph, entomologist; b. Bklyn., Sept. 23, 1873; s. Walter and Susan (MacArdell) W.; ed. pub. schs. and Stevenson Sch. Art, Pitts., 1904-05 (prize student); m. Mary Agnes Becher, June 9, 1904; children—Walter F., M. Margaret, Wm. R., Henry V., John M. Telegraph operator Erie R.R., 1890; later with engring. depts. various rys., N.Y. and Pa., and with engring. firms until 1906; specialist, artist, Pa. State Div. Econ. Zoölogy, Harrisburg, Pa., 1906-10; with Bur. Entomology, U.S. Dept. Agr., 1910—, entomologist charge cereal and forage insect investigations, 1917-23, sr. entomologist, 1923-43, now ret. Specializes in dipterology, families of Syrphidae, Asilidae, and Tachinidae. Fellow Entomol. Soc. Am., A.A.A.S.; mem. Entomol. Soc. Washington, Am. Assn. Econ. Entomol. Author illus. papers on taxonomy of Muscoidean and other flies, including illustrated glossary of terms used in describing them; publs. on insects affecting cereal and forage crops, also many articles on fresh-water fishing and lure making. Home: 4323 Madison St., Hyattsville, Md. Died Oct. 20, 1952.

WALZ, John Albrecht, educator; b. Kirchheim, Germany, Dec. 19, 1871; s. John and Charlotte (Neumann) W.; came to U.S., 1889; A.B., Northwestern U., 1892; Ph.D., Harvard, 1897; U. of Berlin, 1897-99; D.Litt., Northwestern U., 1941; m. Esther Sellholm, June 30, 1901; children—Hans Gunnar, John Albrecht (dec.), Erik. Teacher Latin and German, Northwestern Acad., Evanston, Ill., 1892-94; instr. German lang. and lit., Harvard, 1895-97, Western Reserve U., 1899-1901; asst. prof. German lang. and lit., Harvard, 1905-10, prof., 1910-38, prof. emeritus, 1938—. Mem. Modern Lang. Assn. America (pres. 1941), Goethe Soc., Phi Kappa Psi, Phi Beta Kappa; corr. mem. Deutsche Akademie, Munich. Author: German Influence in American Education and Culture, 1936. Author numerous articles philological jours. Home: 42 Garden St., Cambridge, Mass. Died Apr. 16, 1954.

WAMBAUGH, Sarah (wăm'baw), internat. affairs; b. Cincinnati, O., Mar. 6, 1882; d. Eugene and Anna S. (Hemphill) Wambaugh; A.B., Radcliffe, 1902, A. M., 1917; studied Sch. of Economics, London U., and at Oxford, 1919-20; LL.D., Ohio State and Western Reserve univs., 1935; L.H.D., Tufts Coll., 1935; Dr. en Soc., U. of Geneva, 1935; LL.D., Columbia, 1936, Russell Sage Coll., 1938. Asst. in history and govt., Radcliffe, 1903-06; instr. in history, Wellesley, 1st semester, 1921-22. Mem. administrative commns. and minorities sect. of League of Nations Secretariat, 1920; expert adviser to the Peruvian Govt. for the Tacna-Arica plebiscite, Lima, Arica, Washington, 1925-26. Professeur Académie de Droit International, The Hague, 1927; lecturer, Institut Universitaire de Hautes Etudes Internationales, Geneva, 1935. Apptd. by League of Nations one of 3 experts to draft regulations for Saar plebiscite, 1934, and as tech. adviser and dep. mem. Saar Plebiscite Commn., 1934-35. Consultant to dir. Enemy Branch, Foreign Econ. Adminstrn., Washington, 1945; adviser to chief U.S. Mission to Observe Elections in Greece, Washington, Athens, 1945-46; plebiscite procedure adv. U.N. Plebiscite Mission for Jammu and Kashmir, Lake Success; 1949. Fellow American Academy of Arts and Sciences. Mem. American Soc. Internat. Law, Am. Polit. Sic. Assn., Acad. Polit. Sci., Grotius Soc. (London), Sociedad Geografica de Lima, Phi Beta Kappa (hon.); member Com. to Study the Orgn. of Peace. Awarded gold decoration of City of Arequipa, 1926; Knight Cross, first class, Austrian Order of Merit, 1935; Officer Order of the Sun, Peru, 1937; Herladic Order of Christopher Columbus of the Dominican Republic, 1940. Knight, Royal Order of Phoenix of Greece, 1949. Wrote: Monograph on Plebiscites, with a collection of official documents, 1920; La pratique des plébiscites internationaux, 1928; Plebiscites Since the World War, 1933; The Saar Plebiscite, 1940; contbtd. to World Organization, 1942; Greece of Tomorrow, 1943; Regionalism and World Organization, 1944; Pioneers in World Order, 1944; also contbr. to Current History, Atlantic Monthly, etc. Home: 22 Berkeley St., Cambridge 38, Mass. Died Nov. 12, 1955.

WANN, Frank B(urkett), coll. prof.; b. Warsaw, Ind., Apr. 18, 1892; s. Lucius Cacius and Retta Mary (Burkett) W.; A.B., Wabash Coll., Crawfordsville, Ind., 1914; student Washington U., St. Louis, 1914-15; Ph.D., Cornell U., 1920; Nat. Research fellow in biol. scis., 1923-26; m. Elizabeth Berrells, Nov. 20, 1920 (died Sept. 28, 1948), Instr. botany Cornell U., 1920-23; asso. prof. botany Utah State Agr. Coll., 1926-46, prof. botany, 1946—. Mem. Bot. Soc. of Am., A.A.A.S., Am. Soc. Plant Physiologists, Am. Soc. Hort. Sci., Sigma Xi, Phi Beta Kappa, Phi Kappa Phi, Lambda Chi Alpha. Presbyterian. Home: 544 E. 4th N. St., Logan, Utah. Died Jan. 11, 1954; buried Aurora, N.Y.

WANN, Louis (wān), writer; born in Claypool, Ind., Aug. 30, 1885; s. Lucius Cassius and Mary Auretta (Burkett) W.; A.B., Wabash Coll., Crawfordsville, Ind., 1908; grad. study U. of Marburg, 1909, U. of Lausanne, 1910; A.M., Columbia, 1912; Ph.D., U. of Wis., 1919; m. Irma Estel Neff, June 25, 1913 (dec.); children—Mary Caroline, George Edward; m. 2d, Alberta W. Metzger, Dec. 18, 1950. Instr. in English, Robert Coll., Constantinople, Turkey, 1908-11; scholar in English, Columbia U., 1911-12; asst. prof. English, Heidelberg U., Tiffin, O., 1912-14; instr. in English, U. of Wis., 1914-18; head of dept. English, Lawrence Coll., Appleton, Wis., 1918-19; prof. English lang. and lit., U. of Southern Calif., 1919-51, emeritus prof. English since 1951, chmn. of dept., 1927-30, 1937-40; engaged in cultural history of Pacific Coast since 1947; exchange professor English, New York University, 1925-26; acting prof. English, Stanford U., summer 1937; visiting prof. English, U. of Brit. Columbia, summer 1942; editor in chief The Parchment, 1926-30; asso. editor, The Personalist, since 1941. Mem. Modern Lang. Assn. of Am., Philol. Assn. Pacific Coast (pres. 1938-39), Am. Assn. Univ. Profs., Am. Coll. Quill Club (high vice chancellor; member High Witan, 1926-30), Phi Beta Kappa (president Epsilon Calif. chapter, 1930-31), Phi Kappa Phi. Democrat. Episcopalian. Clubs: Faculty (past pres.); 65 of U. So. Cal. (pres.). Author: The Prepartion of Course Papers in the Field of Literature, 1922, 28; Effective English—A Handbook of Composition, 1932. Editor: Century Readings in the English Essay, 1926, rev. edit., 1939; The Rise of Realism (Vol. III of Am. Literature—A Period Anthology) 1933, rev. ed., 1949. Contbr. chiefly in fields of English drama, Am. lit. and Eng. essay, to Shakespeare Studies (U. of Wis.), 1916, U. of Wis. Studies in Lang. and Lit., 1918, Anglia, Modern Philology, Modern Lang. Notes, etc. Co-editor: (with Allison Gaw and Roy T. Thompson) University of Southern California Poems, 1930. Home: 5386 Village Green, Los Angeles 16. Died Apr. 21, 1956; buried Melrose Abbey Meml. Park, Santa Ana, Cal.

WANVIG, Chester Odin (wăn'vĭg), mfr.; b. Milwaukee, Wis., Dec. 7, 1890; s. John D. and Annie (Christensen) W.; ed. high sch., Milwaukee, and Mich. Coll. Mines, Houghton; m. Engring. (hon), Michigan College of Mining and Tech.; LL.D. (honorary), Marquette University; married Jean Wallace, Aug. 31, 1912; children—Mavis, Chester Odin. Gen. mgr. and sec. Wallace & Smith Co., 1910-21; treas. Globe-Union, Inc. (formerly Globe Electric Co.), 1921-25, pres., 1925-49, now press. and chmn.; chmn. bd. Peerless Machine Co.; dir. Milw. Gas Light Co., Milsco Mfg. Co. Mem. bd. govs. Marquette U.; pres. Milw. Country Day Sch., 1934-37. Clubs: Chicago; University, Milwaukee, Milwaukee Country, Milwaukee Athletic. Home: 9120 N. Upper River Rd., River Hills. Office: 900 E. Keefe Av., Milw. Died Mar. 18, 1959; buried Forest Home Cemetery, Milw.

WARBEKE, John Martyn, college prof.; b. Marion, N.Y., May 28, 1879; s. Cornelius and Elizabeth (Dykstra) W.; A.S., Bradley Poly. Inst. (U. Chgo.), 1900; A.B., Princeton, 1903; Ph.D., Leipzig, 1906; m. Norah McCarter, July 15, 1908; 1 dau., Adana. Instr. German and philosophy, Williams Coll., 1906-12; asso. prof. philosophy, 1912-16, prof. Mt. Holyoke Coll., 1916—; prof. ad interim, Amherst, 1919-20. Mem. Am. Philos. Assn., Browning Soc. (New York). Co-founder Holyoke League Arts and Crafts, Woodrow Wilson Award. Author: Das Homogenitäts-prinzip in der Spencer-ischen Psychologie; The Searching Mind of Greece, 1930; The Power of Art, 1951. Contbr. chiefly on philos. subjects. Home: South Hadley, Mass. Died May 21, 1950.

WARBURTON, Barclay Harding; b. Phila., Apr. 1, 1866; s. Charles E. W., founder Phila. Evening Telegraph; ed. pvt. schs. in Pa., U. Pa., Christ Ch. Coll., Oxford, Eng.; m. Mary Brown, June 13, 1895. Pub. Phila. Evening Telegraph, Jan. 1894-1911, pres. Evening Telegraph Co., Oct. 1899-Feb. 2, 1911, now ret.; gen. mgr. E. F. Hutton & Co., Fla. offices, 1923-30. Capt. Light Battery A, N.G. Pa., Jan. 17, 1898-1908; capt. U.S.V., May 5-Nov. 12, 1898, serving in P.R. campaign, command of battalion of Pa. arty.; commd. maj. U.S.A., 1917; asst. mil. attaché, Am. Embassy, London, 1917-18; mil. attaché, Am. Embassy, Paris, 1918-19; discharged June 25, 1919; commd. lt. col. U.S.R., Aug. 25, 1919. Address: Phila. Died Dec. 5, 1954.*

WARBURTON, Stanton, ex-congressman; b. Sullivan Co., Pa., Apr. 13, 1865; s. James A. and Sarah (Bedford) W.; A.B., Coe Coll., 1888; m. Iris Brockway, Sept. 30, 1890. Admitted to bar, 1888, and since in practice at Tacoma, Wash.; splty. ins. law. Mem. Wash. Senate, 2 terms, 1896-1904; mem. 62d Congress, 2d Wash. Dist. Republican. Elk. Clubs: Columbia Country (Washington), Union, Country (Tacoma). Address: Tacoma, Wash. Died Dec. 24, 1928.

WARD, Arch, sporting editor; b. Irwin, Ill., Dec. 27, 1896; s. Thomas Stephen and Nora Gertrude (O'Connor) W.; prep. edn., Columbia Acad., Dubuque, Ia.; student Columbia Coll., Dubuque, 2 years, and 2 years at Notre Dame; m. Helen Carey, June 22, 1921; children—Ruth Helen (dec.), Thomas Edward. Sports editor Dubuque Telegraph-Herald, 1919; athletic publicity dir. Univ. of Notre Dame, 1920-21; sports editor Rockford (Ill.) Star, 1921-25, Chicago Tribune since Apr. 14, 1930. Catholic. Home: 5848 N. Washtenaw Av. Address: Tribune Tower, 435 N. Michigan Av., Chgo. Died July 9, 1955.

WARD, Charles Allen, calendar mfg. exec.; b. Seattle, Wash., May 29, 1886; s. George and Pauline (Kuntz) W.; ed. Denny Hill High Sch., Seattle; m. Mrs. Yvette Hennig Saunders, Feb. 29, 1940; children—Allen, Vida, Herbert. With Brown & Bigelow, May 1925—, engring. dept., foreman, 1926-27, supt. 1927-28, gen. supt., 1928-29, asst. gen. mgr., 1929-31, v.p., 1931-33, pres., gen. mgr., dir., 1933—; chmn. bd. and dir. Graphic Arts Engraving Co., Herb-Shelly, Inc., Farmington, Minn., The Beissel Co., Consol. Printing Ink Co., Quality Park Box Co., Inc., Quality Park Envelope Co., Century Envelope Co., Brown & Bigelow Agy., Inc.; pres., dir. Hudson Development Co. (Wis.), Western Lithograph Co., Los Angeles; dir. Midway Nat. Bank of St. Paul; owner Northwestern Land & Development Co., Rancho Roca Roja, Rimrock, Ariz., Seven Lazy T Ranch, Camp Verde, Ariz. Mem. Am. Soc. M.E. Mason (K.T. 32°, Shriner; Jester), Elk. Clubs: Minnesota, Athletic, Town and Country, University (St. Paul); Army and Navy (Washington). Home: Quality Park Farm No. 2, Hudson, Wis. Office: 1286 University, St. Paul. Died May 25, 1959; buried Willow River Cemetery, Hudson, Wis.

WARD, Charles Carroll, teachers coll. pres.; b. Port Allegany, Pa., Sept. 25, 1891; s. John Lester and Gretta (Kinney) W.; B.S., Bucknell U., 1918; M.A., Teachers Coll. (Columbia), 1930; Ph.D., N.Y. University, 1934, LL.D., Bucknell University, 1943; married Ann Louise Buckley, June 26, 1915 (died 1930); 1 daughter, Janet Louise; m. 2d, Eleanor L. Miller, July 16, 1932; 1 dau., Nan Gaylord. Teacher rural schs. McKean County, Pa., 1909-13; instr. high sch., Port Allegany, Pa., 1914; instr. and prin. model sch., State Normal Sch., Mansfield, Pa., 1914-16; head dept. history, New Paltz (N.Y.) State Normal Sch., 1918-20, dir. of training, 1920-32; dir. teacher training, N.Y. State, 1932-33; prin. N.Y. State Normal Sch., Plattsburg, N.Y., 1933-42; pres. State Teachers Coll., Plattsburg, N.Y., since 1942. Twice mayor New Paltz, N.Y. Mem. Registrants Adv. Bd.; mem. Clinton Co. Vocational Bd.; mem. bd. dirs. Asso. Hosp. Service of Capital Dist.; mem. N.Y. State Teachers Assn. (past pres.), Delta Sigma. Republican. Club: Rotary (pres. 1935). Contbr. to ednl. jours. Died Feb. 28, 1952.

WARD, Fannie (Mrs. Joseph Lewis), actress; b. St. Louis, Nov. 23, 1875; d. John Buchanan; m. Joseph Lewis, 1905. Début as Cupid, in Pippino, Broadway Theatre, N.Y., Nov. 26, 1890; début in London, in The Shop Girl, 1895; has frequently toured in U.S., appearing in A Marriage of Reason, A Fool and a Girl, The New Lady Bantock, Madam President, etc., also in vaudeville. Address: 3 Berkeley Sq., London, Eng. Died Jan. 1952.

WARD, Florence Jeanette Baier, writer; b. Mpls., Aug. 21, 1886; d. Leo and Florence C. (Nichols) Baier; student Pillsbury Acad., Owatonna, Minn., 1899-1901, pvt. tutor, 1901-02; A.B., U. Minn., 1906; m. Clifford Earle Ward, Feb. 23, 1907; 1 son, Earle Jay. Field agent, Federal Bur. of Labor, 1906-08; later v.p. charge personnel, Campana Corp. Mem. Soc. of Midland Authors, Am. Assn. U. Women, P.E.N., Art's Club (Chicago). Republican. Episcopalian. Author: The Singing Heart, 1920; Phyllis Anne, 1922; The Flame of Happiness, 1925; Spread Circles, 1927; Second Eden, 1929; Stormy Fires, 1931; Wild Wine, 1932; Women May Learn, 1933; Dalesacres, 1939. Home: Batavia, Ill. Died Mar. 27, 1959.

WARD, Frank Edwin, organist, composer; b. Wysox, Bradford County, Pa., Oct. 7, 1872; s. Cyrenus Osborne and Stella Aurelia (Owen) W.; High Sch., Washington, D.C., 1888-91; New York Coll. of Music (piano and theory), 1896; Scharwenka Conservatory of Music (organ), 1896-97; Columbia U. Dept. of Music, 1898-1903, fellow in music, 1902-03; m. May Louise Corby, Feb. 24, 1897. Organist and choirmaster, Columbia U., 1902-13, Temple Israel, New York, 1902-—, Ch. of Holy Trinity, 1906-—, retired 1946; associate in music, Columbia, 1909-19; teacher harmony and counterpoint, Trinity School of Church Music, 1915-18; established his own school for piano, organ and theory, 1919. Head of Theory Dept. Guilmant Organ School, 1937-42. Mem. Am. Guild Organists. Clubs: St. Wilfrid, Governors Island, The Bohemians. Author: Sonata for Piano and Violin, op. 9, 1904; Peter Pan Scherzo (for orchestra), op. 13; Sonata No. 1 for organ, op. 15; Quartet for piano and strings, op. 18; The Savior of the World (cantata), op. 20, 1909; The Divine Birth (cantata), op. 23, 1910; Symphony, Shakespearean Moods, op. 25; Soleumn Mass in G minor, op. 29; Organ Sonata No. 2, op. 37; Ocean Rhapsody (for orchestra), op. 31, 1915; String Quartet in C Minor, op. 22, 1917 (awarded prize of Nat. Federation Music Clubs, 1917); Trio for Piano and Strings, op. 44; String Quartet, No. 2, op. 46; Organ Sonata, No. 3, op. 49; Serenade Miniature, p. 51, for string orchestra; Second Symphony in F minor, op. 52, 1921; Overture, Theodora, for orchestra, 1922; Five American Dances for Orchestra, op. 53, 1923; Lilith, a symphonic poem, op. 57, 1924; grand opera Theodora, op. 60, 1926; Foursome Suite for piano, op. 62; Violin Sonata No. 3 in F inor, op. 67, 1936; etc.; also many songs, anthems, piano, organ and violin pieces. Home: 924 West End Av., New York 25, N.Y.; (summer) Jackson, N.H. Died Sept. 15, 1953.

WARD, George Gray, gynecologist; b. London, Eng., Aug. 15, 1868; s. George Gray and Marianne (Smith) W.; brought to America, 1874; ed. Bklyn. Collegiate and Poly. Inst., Holbrook Mil. Acad. (Ossining, N.Y.); M.D., L.I. Coll. Hosp., 1891; studed U. Berlin, 1892-93, also London and Paris; m. Edith Wigham, June 23, 1898. Prof. diseases of women, N.Y., Post-Grad. Med. Sch., 1905-16, sec. faculty, 1910-16; prof. obstetrics and gynecology, Cornell U. Med. Coll., 1916-34, emeritus; chief surgeon Woman's Hosp., 1918-38, emeritus; prof. clin. obstetrics and gynecology, Columbia; formerly attending gynecologist, Bellevue Hosp.; con. gynecologist, N.Y. Post-Grad. Hosp., N.Y. Hosp., Monmouth Meml. Hosp., Lawrence Hosp., Home for Incurables, Booth Meml. Hosp. Mem. 7th Regiment, Nat. Guard, N.Y., 8 yrs.; capt., asst. surgeon, 12th Regt., 1895-98; maj. surgeon, 1898-1902; maj. surgeon 12th Regt. Inf., N.Y. Vols., Spanish-Am. War. Founder, fellow A.C.S.; fellow Am. Gynecology Soc. (ex-pres.), N.Y. Acad. Medicine; hon. fellow Edinburgh Obstet. Soc., Royal Coll. Obstetricians and Gynecologists, Royal Med. Soc. Budapest; hon. mem. British Congress Obstetrics and Gynecology; mem. A.M.A. (chmn. sect. obstetrics and gynecology), Med. Soc. State N.Y., N.Y. County Med. Soc. (ex-pres.), N.Y. Obstet. Soc. (ex-pres.), Hosp. Grads.' Club (ex-pres.), Phi Alpha Sigma, Alpha Omega Alpha, Mil. Order Fgn. Wars, Naval and Mil. Order Spanish-Am. War. Rep. Episcopalian. Clubs: Union, Century, Riding, Racquet (New York); Rumson Country; Army and Navy (Washington), Travellers (Paris). Co-author: Gynecology in Operative Therapeusis, 1915; Kelly's Gynecology, 1928; Lewis Practice of Surgery, 1928; Curtis Obstetrics and Gynecology, 1933; Davis Gynecology and Obstetrics, 1933; and numerous monographs on gynecology and obstetrics. Home: 1175 Park Av. Office: 101 E. 80th St., N.Y.C. Died Dec. 21, 1950; buried Greenwood, Bklyn.

WARD, Grant Eben, surgeon; b. Lorain County, O., Aug. 28, 1896; s. Fletcher DeLay and Harriett Grace (Walker) W.; A.B., Baldwin-Wallace Coll., Berea, O., 1917; M.D., Johns Hopkins Med. Sch., 1921; hon. D.Sc., Baldwin-Wallace Coll., Berea, O., 1940; married Lillian Anderson Hersperger, August 16, 1922; children—Mary Grace (Mrs. George Storey Wheaton, Jr.), Margaret Lucille. Resident house officer, Johns Hopkins Hospital, 1921-22; associate, Howard A. Kelly Hosp., Baltimore, 1922-27; instr. surgery, U. of Md. Med. Sch., 1930-35, associate in surgery, 1935-37, asso. prof. surgery, 1937-51; asst. in surgery, Johns Hopkins Med. Sch., 1927-32; instr. in surgery, 1932-38, associate in surgery, 1938-45, asst. prof., 1945-49, asso. prof., 1949-—; asst. vis. surgeon Johns Hopkins Hospital, 1935-45, visiting surgeon, 1945-—, lecturer oral oncology, Baltimore College Dental Surgery, U. Md. Dental School 1934-54; co-founder, dir. Tumor Clinic, Johns Hopkins (named Grant E. Ward Tumor Clinic 1958); consulting surgeon Walter Reed General Hospital; consultant in treatment of tumors at U.S. Marine Hospital, Baltimore. Co-organizer, 1930 (with Dr. J. Mason Hundley, Jr.) and co-director Oncology Clinic, Univ. of Maryland Med. Sch. Mem. bd. dirs., Baltimore Goodwill Industries, Inc. Served in S.A.T.C., 1918. Pres. Methodist Social Union of Baltimore, 1935-37; pres. Ohio Society of Baltimore, 1936. President Md. div. of the American Cancer Soc., 1949-52, chmn. bd., 1952-56. Diplomate Am. Bd. Surgery. Fellow A.C.S.; mem. A.M.A., Soc. Head and Neck Surgeons (pres. 1957-58 founding mem.), Balt. Med. Soc. (pres. 1956), Am. Acad. Phys. Medicine (v.p. 1930-32), Am. Congress Phys. Therapy (v.p. 1935), So. Surg. Assn., Southeastern Surg. Congress, S.A.R., Alpha Omega Alpha, Phi Kappa Phi. Vice pres. Med. Chirurg. Faculty of Md., 1945-46, 57-58. Republican. Methodist. Club: Faculty (Johns Hopkins U.). Author (with H. A. Kelly) Electrosurgery, 1932; Tumors of the Head and Neck (with J. W. Hendrick), 1950; author or co-author articles in field. Mem. adv. bd. Am. Jour. of Surgery. Home: 602 W. University Pkwy., Balt. 10. Office: 15 E. Biddle St., Balt. 2. Died Feb. 16, 1958; buried Druid Ridge Cemetery, Balt.

WARD, J. H., dir., v.p. Bethlehem Steel Corp.; dir. Chicago Pneumatic Tool Co. Address: 25 Broadway, N.Y.C. Died July 12, 1958.

WARD Leo L(ouis), clergyman, coll. prof.; b. Otterbein, Ind., Jan. 6, 1898; s. Thomas and Ellen (Kirk) W.; Ph.B., Univ. of Notre Dame, 1920, theol. student Holy Cross Coll., Cath. Univ., Washington, D.C., 1923-27; reading and study, Oxford Univ. 1930-31. Ordained priest Roman Catholic Ch., 1927. Teacher in dept. of English, Notre Dame, since 1927, prof. of English; head dept. of English since 1935. Mem. Congregation of Holy Cross, Cath. teaching order in charge of Notre Dame. Author: (with John T. Frederick) Good Writing, 1934, Reading for Writing, 1937; short stories in various mags., (included in Best Short Stories 1931, 1932); poetry in various mags. Editor: Uses of Knowledge, 1949. Home: University of Notre Dame, Notre Dame, Ind. Died Jan. 21, 1953; buried Notre Dame.

WARD, Ralph Ansel, missionary; b. Leroy, O., June 26, 1882; s. Fletcher DeLay and Harriet Grace (Walker) W.; A.B., Ohio Wesleyan U., 1903, A.M., 1906, D.D., 1919, LL.D., 1940; S.T.B., Boston U., 1906; D.D., 1946; D.D., Baldwin-Wallace Coll., Berea, O., 1919; m. Mildred May Worley, Sept. 7, 1905 (died 1947); children—Imogene Grace, Gladys Walker; m. 2d, Katherine Boeye, Aug. 25, 1948. Ordained ministry M.E. Ch., 1906; pastor chs. in Mass., 1906-08; field sec. Mass. Anti-Saloon League, 1907-08; missionary M.E. Ch., Foochow, China, 1909-16; asso. sec. Missionary Centenary, M.E. Ch., 1916-19; asso. sec. for Eastern China, Bd. Foreign Missions, M.E. Ch., 1919-24; exec. sec. China Soc. America, 1921; pres. Anglo-Chinese Coll., Foochow, 1925-27; exec. sec. World Service M.E. Church, 1928-32; city missionary M.E. Ch., Nanking, 1933-37; elected bishop Meth. Ch., 1937; resident bishop Meth. Ch., Chengtu, China, 1937-41, Soochow Univ., Shanghai, China, 1941-—; interned 1941-46. Mem. bd. mgrs. U. of Nanking. Clubs: Masonic, Rotary. Writer of pamphlets and articles on Nanking and China. Address: Hong Kong. Died Dec. 6, 1958.

WARD, Robert William, army officer; b. Cin., Mar. 2, 1905; s. Robert G. and Katie (Enderes) W.; student mech. engring., U. Cin., 1924-25; B.S., U.S. Mil. Acad., 1929; student Inf. Sch. 1932, Command and Gen. Staff Coll., 1942, Armed Forces Staff Coll., 1947, Nat. War Coll., 1951, Command Mgmt. Sch. 1956. Guided Missiles Sch., 1956; m. Marjorie H. Leward, June 7, 1930; 1 dau., Marjorie (Mrs. Frederick L. Munds, Jr.). Commd. 2d lt. inf., U.S. Army, 1929, advanced through grades to maj. gen., 1955; task force operations officer North African landings, 1942; comdr. 135th Inf. Regt., 34th Inf. Div., Tunisian, Italian campaigns, 1943-44; chief plans and policy, orgn. and tng. div. War Dept. Gen. Staff, 1945-47; staff Office Sec., Def., 1951; chief SHAPE Tng. Mission to Royal Netherlands Army, 1952-55; comdg. gen. Army Replacement Tng. Center, Ft. Dix, N.J., 1955; dep. chief staff for plans Hdqrs. Far East Command, 1956-57. Decorated Legion of Merit with cluster, Bronze Star medal, Purple Heart, Combat Infantryman's badge; comdr. Order Orange Nassau (Netherlands). Club: Army-Navy (Washington). Home: 2301 River Rd., West Point Pleasant, N.J. Office: Detachment of Patient, Walter Reed Army Hosp., Washington. Died Apr. 1, 1960.

WARD, Stevenson E., banker; b. Mansfield, O., July 22, 1879; s. Marion D. and Mary (Stevenson) W.; ed. pub. schs., Mansfield, and U. Mich.; m. May Sullivan, Oct. 4, 1904; children—Katherine, Stevenson E., James Alexander. Clk., later cashier, Bank of Mansfield, 1902-12; with Nat. Bank of Commerce, N.Y.C., 1912-—, successively asst. cashier, cashier, v.p., pres. from 1923 to date of merger with Guaranty Trust Co.; now dir. Comml. Union Fire Ins. Co. of N.Y., Columbia Casualty Co., 1st Fed. Savs. & Trust Co. of N.Y.; mem. Am. bd. Ocean Accident & Guaranty Corp., Ltd., Comml. Union Assurance Co., Ltd. Republican. Clubs: Bankers Club of America, Metropolitan; Siwanoy Country Club, Bronxville, N.Y.; Everglades (Palm Beach, Fla.); Wianno (Wianno, Mass.). Home: 8 Governors Rd., Bronxville, N.Y. Died June 16, 1950.

WARD, Wilbert, bank exec.; b. South Bend, Ind., Dec. 5, 1888; s. Wilbert and Alice (Clearhart) W.; A.B., DePauw, 1910; LL.B., Columbia, 1913; m. Emily McKernan, Apr. 7, 1951. Admitted to N.Y. bar, 1913, and practiced, N.Y.C., until 1917; retired as vice pres. First Nat. City Bank of New York, 1951. Mem. adv. com. Fgn. Econ. Admnstrn., exec. sec. U.S. delegation to Internat. Bus. Conf., Rye, N.Y., 1944. Past pres. Bankers Assn. for Fgn. Trade, dir. Nat. Council Am. Importers, Nat. Fgn. Trade Council, chmn. subcom. on fgn. funds control Fgn. Exchange Com. N.Y., mem. administrative com. fgn. credit interchange bur. Nat. Assn. Credit Men, mem. internat. transport com. U.S. Chamber of Commerce; chmn., com. on banking techniques, comml. documentary credits and fgn. remittances of the U.S. Assos., Internat. C. of C., exec. dir. U.S. council Internat. C. of C. Author: American Commercial Credits, 1923; Bank Credits and Acceptances, 1931. Home: Setauket, L.I., N.Y. Office: 103 Park Av., N.Y.C. Died Jan. 15, 1959.

WARD, Wilbur, gynecologist, obstetrician; b. Bloomfield, N.J., Jan. 4, 1879; s. Theodore Hastings and Elizabeth (Potter) W.; A.B., Williams Coll., 1900 M.D., Coll. Phys. and Surg., Columbia, 1904; m. Edith Richards, Sept. 18, 1916 (died Jan. 1937); 1 dau., Elizabeth; m. 2d, Mrs. Mabel Park Baker, Sept. 9, 1939. Interne St. Luke's Hosp., 1904-07; interne Sloane Hosp., 1907-09, resident obstetrician, 1909-11, attending gynecologist, 1911-18, attending obstetrician, gynecologist and dir., 1918-19; attending obstetrician City Hosp., 1913-30; prof. of obstetrics and gynecology, N.Y. Polyclinic, 1922-24; formerly cons. obstetn. Mt. Vernon and Mountainside hosps., Montclair, N.J., Lawrence Hosp., Bronxville, N.Y., Nassau Hosp., Mineola, L.I.; cons. gynecologist Nassau Hosp.; retired from active practice, June 1939. Diplomate Am. Board of Obstetrics and Gynecology. Fellow A.C.S., N.Y. Acad. of Medicine (former chmn. obstetrics and gynecology sect.); mem. Quiz Med. Soc., Hospital Graduates, Harvey Soc., A.M.A., N.Y. Path. Soc., New York Obstet. Soc. (former pres.), Soc., Alumni Assn. St. Luke's Hosp., Alumni Assn. Sloane Hosp., Delta Upsilon, Nu Sigma Nu. Republican. Presbyterian. Clubs: Williams, University (New York). Contbr. to med. jours. Home: 700 Prospect Blvd., Pasadena, Cal. Died Sept. 1954.

WARD, William I.; clergyman; b. Fairhaven, Mass., Nov. 3, 1857; s. William D. and Elizabeth T. (Sisson) W.; ed. Fairhaven High Sch., Wesleyan Acad., New Bedford High Sch. and Sch. of Theology, Boston U.; m. Emma L. Thomas, May 18, 1881; children—Elizabeth H. (dec.), Marjorie L. Snyder, Katherine C. (dec.), Eldoretta (Mrs. Ellsworth A. Hawkes). Ordained to ministry of Methodist Ch., 1879; pastor or dist. supt., Methodist Ch., 1878 to 1923, retired, 1923-—. Hon. trustee (formerly trustee) Boston U., 1907-—. Home: Main St., Sandwich, Mass. Died Sept. 7, 1956; buried Union Cemetery, South Carver, Mass.

WARD, William Rankin, physician; b. Newark, Dec. 9, 1870; s. William Rankin and Mary Robinson (Meeker) W.; grad. Newark Acad., 1888; student N.Y. Homeopathic Med. Coll. and Hosp., 1890-92; M.D., Hahnemann Med. Coll. Phila., 1893; m. Jennie Warren Prentiss, June 16, 1903; children—Carolyn P., Elisabeth B. (Mrs. Frederick L. Trowbridge), William Rankin, C. Prentiss, Marion M. (Mrs. Max Kronstein). Intern, Hahnemann Hosp., Phila., 1894; practicing physician, Newark, 1893-1905; asst. med. dir. Mut. Benefit Life Ins. Co., Newark, 1905-12, med. dir., 1912-46, med. dir. emeritus, 1946-—. Founder, Florence Crittenton Home of Newark, 1901, pres., 1901-53; dir., past pres. Newark Y.M.C.A.; Essex Co. chmn. Good Will Council of N.J., 1941; chmn. Citizens's Housing Council, Newark, 1941; N.J. chmn. Commn. for Displaced Persons, 1949-53. Mem. Newark C. of C. Trustee Hosp. Service Plan N.J., Clara Maass Memorial Hosp., Newark, Am. Waldensian Aid Soc., Bloomfield Coll. and Sem., Welfare Fedn. Newark (past pres.), Newark U. (1941), Temperance League N.J.; dir. China Famine Relief of U.S.A., 1934; mem. adv. bd. Rutgers U; v. chmn. Weequahic Adult Sch. Mem. Assn. Life Ins. Med. Dirs. Am. (pres 1923-24), Acad. Medicine N.J., N.J. Med. Soc., Essex Co. Med. Assn., S.A.R. (past pres. N.J. soc.), Soc. for Relief Widows and Orphans Med. Men of N.J. (pres. 1951), N.J. Med. Club, Washington Assn. N.J., N.J. Hist. Soc. (trustee, past pres.), Abraham Lincoln Assn., Am. Sunday Sch. Union (hon. v.p.), Essex Co. Council Chs. (trustee), Lord's Day Alliance U.S. (hon. v.p.). Presbyn. (ruling elder, past moderator Presbytery of Newark). Club: Rotary. Author: Down the Years, 1932. Named Outstanding Citizen of Newark by Advt. Club of Newark, 1941. Home: 112 Chancellor Av., Newark 8. Died Feb. 10, 1955; buried Evergreen Cemetery, Hillside, N.J.

WARDELL, Morris L., prof. of history; b. Lawrence County, Ill., June 19, 1889; s. William Chapman and Melissa (Shinn) W.; A.B., Univ. of Okla., 1919; A.M., Harvard, 1922; Ph.D., Univ. of Chicago, 1936; m. Jessie Alma Bardin, June 9, 1920; children—Margaret Ann (Mrs. John Joseph Dulin), Melissa Alice (Mrs. John McKeeth Sowle). Principal Geary (Oklahoma) High School, 1912-13; teacher rural school of Texas County, Oklahoma, 1913-15, Panhandle Agrl. Coll., Goodwell, Okla., summers 1914-15; prin. Guymon (Okla.) High Sch., 1915-17, Pawhuska (Okla.) High Sch., 1919-21; teacher of history Tulsa Central High Sch., 1922-25; mem. dept. of history, Univ. of Okla., since 1925, acting dean of men, 1925-29, asst. to the pres., 1937-41, chmn. dept. of history 1945-47, David Ross Boyd prof., 1946. Served in air service, Kelly Field, Tex., 1917-18. Chairman United States Savings Bonds, Dist. 3, 1951. Dir. Survey Fed. Archives in Okla., 1935-36; regional dir. Coll. N.Y.A., 1941-42; one of six adminstrs. chosen by Carnegie Corp. of N.Y. to study adminstrative problems in colls. and univs. of choice, 1939-40. Mem. Okla. Soc. Welfare Assn. (dir., past pres.). Mem. N.E.A. (exec. com. dept. higher edn. 1949-51, v.p. 1950-51), Am. Cancer Soc. (pres. Okla. div. 1950), Norman Chamber of Commerce (bd. dirs.), Okla. Alumni Assn. (life mem.), Okla. Hist. Soc. (life mem.), Miss. Valley Hist. Assn., Assn. of Univ. Prof., Southwestern Social Sci. Assn., Soc. of Am. Archivists, Cleveland County Childrens' Clinic, Am. Legion, Am. Indian Inst., Blue Key, Phi Beta Kappa, Phi Eta Sigma (nat. grand historian). Democrat. Presbyn. Clubs: Wabunaki Study, University of Okla. Faculty, Harvard of Oklahoma, Lion's (internat. counsellor). Author: A Political History of the Cherokee Nation, 1838-1907, 1938; report to Carnegie Corp. on "Trends in Higher Education, (unpub.), 1940. Joint author (with E. E. Dale) History of Oklahoma, 1948. Contbr. weekly book reviews. Home: 730 Chautauqua. Office: University of Oklahoma, Norman, Okla. Died Feb. 5, 1957; buried I.O.O.F. Cemetery, Norman.

WARDEN, Oliver Sherman, pub.; b. North Haverhill, N.H., Aug. 19, 1865; s. Alexander and Lucy A. (Flint) W.; B.A., Dartmouth, 1889; LL.D., U. Mont., 1937; m. Etta A. Scott, Jan. 22, 1895 (died Mar. 1, 1919); children—Alexander, Robert D., Helen E. (Mrs. Dan B. Carroll) (died Oct. 31, 1941), Gertrude N. (Mrs. G. A. Hansen), Virginia M. (Mrs. Rowe Morrell), Jock F.; m. 2d, Florence A. Warden, Oct. 16, 1920; m. 3d, Eleanor McRae, May 23, 1936. Newspaper reporter, 1889; part ownership Great Falls Tribune, 1895—, pub., 1920—; pres. N. Mont. State Fair; dir. Mont. Taxpayers Assn.; chmn. Mont. State Water Bd.; pres. Great Falls Park Bd. Dir. Asso. Press; mem. Am. Soc. Newspaper Editors, Psi Upsilon, Phi Beta Kappa, Sigma Delta Chi. Mem. Dem. Nat. Com. from Mont. Mason. Club: Meadow Lark Country; National Press (Washington, D.C.). Home: Great Falls, Mont. Died Mar. 12, 1951; buried Highland Cemetery, Great Falls.

WARDWELL, Allen, lawyer; b. New York, N.Y., Oct. 4, 1873; s. William Thomas and Eliza (Lanterman) W.; A.B., Yale, 1895; LL.B., Harvard, 1898; m. Helen Rogers, Oct. 14, 1903; children—Edward Rogers, Clarissa (Mrs. Francis L. Pell, Jr.). Practiced law, N.Y., 1898—; mem. firm Davis Polk Wardwell Sunderland & Kiendl. and predecessor firms since 1909; trustee Bank of N.Y. Commr. Red Cross Mission to Russia, 1917-18; chmn. Gov.'s Unemployment Relief Commn., 1934-35; chmn. Red Cross Delegation to Russia, 1941. Trustee and president Juilliard Musical Foundation, Metropolitan Opera Assn., Juilliard School of Music (director), State Charities Aid Assn., Legal Aid Soc. Mem. New York State Bar Assn., Assn. of Bar of City of New York (pres. 1943-45). Democrat. Clubs: Century, University, Yale (N.Y.); Rockaway Hunting. Home: Ocean Av., Lawrence, L.I., and 1021 Park Av., N.Y.C. 28. Office: 15 Broad St., N.Y.C. 5. Died Dec. 5, 1953.

WARE, Mary S., author; b. Raymond, Hinds Co., Miss., Dec. 27, 1842; d. Augustine L. and Elizabeth (Smith) Dabney; student pvt. schs.; m. William L. Ware, planter, 1864 (dec.); children—Sedley Lynch, Augusta Lee (dec.). No experience as a writer until 1912; at age of 70, started on tour of 3 yrs. through countries of the Orient; at age of 79, 1921-22, visited Central Europe, the Balkans and the Near East, and wrote letters from those countries under title A New World Through Old Eyes. Author: The Old World Through Old Eyes, 1917. The entire proceeds of this book contributed to the wounded soldiers of France. Home: Sewanee, Tenn. Died 1933.

WAREHAM, Harry P(ercival), philanthropic exec.; born Maple Grove, Md., May 8, 1883; s. George Edward Menges and Laura Agnes Anne (Wentz) W.; ed. pub. schs.; student, Baltimore Bus. Coll., 1900-01; m. Pleasant Pearl Matthews, June 1, 1904; children—Dorothy (Mrs. Arthur M. McCoy), Marjorie, Harry Percival, Jr., James Matthews, John Douglas, Sarah Jane. Pvt. sec. Citizens Nat. Bank, Baltimore, 1901-07; lay asst. Marble Collegiate Ch., Fifth Av., N.Y. City, 1907-13; bus. mgr. re-organized financial structure, Camp Dudley, Westport-on-Lake Champlain, N.Y., 1909-13; bus. mgr., installed system of bus. management Y.M.C.A., Rochester, N.Y., 1913-19; originated team quota system for short term financial campaigns, 1917; mgr. Rochester (N.Y.). Community Chest, (originator the term Community Chest), 1919-46; exec. v.p. Nat. War Fund, N.Y. City, 1942; exec. v.p. Am. Hearing Soc., Washington, since 1946; organized and directed 131 financial campaigns for various philanthropic, ednl. orgns., netting more than $250,000,000. Mem. Community Chests and Councils of Am. (mem. bd. dirs. 1921, 1931-36, 1941-46; chmn. adv. com. 1930-35; mem. exec. com. 1942-44; v.p. 1942-45; chmn. nat. quota com. 1942; mem. nat. budget com. 1942), mem. bd. dirs. Nat. Informaton Bur., N.Y. City, 1941-49; mem. bd. trustees Nat. Health and Welfare Retirement Assn. since 1945; mem. bd. dir., Nat. Health Council since 1948. Republican. Episcopalian. Mason. Home: 31 Sutton Pl. S., N.Y. City. Office: 817 14th St. N.W., Washington. Died June 11, 1951.

WARFIELD, David, actor; b. San Francisco, Nov. 28, 1866; pub. sch. edn.; m. Mary Gabrielle Bradt, Oct. 5, 1899. First appearance at the Wigwam Theatre, San Francisco, 1889; went to N.Y.C., 1890; played in Casino Theatre and Weber and Field's Music Hall, N.Y.C., 1898-1900; starred by David Belasco in The Auctioneer, 1900-03, The Music Master, 1903-07, 17-18, A Grand Army Man many seasons from 1907; Vanderdecken in The Flying Dutchman; then Shylock in The Merchant of Venice. Address: 135 Central Park West, N.Y.C. Died June 27, 1951.

WARING, Clarence Henry (wâr'ĭng), pub. health officer; b. Ray County, Mo., June 2, 1882; s. George Washington and Sara Tommie (LaFayette) W.; M.D., Miss. Med. Coll., Meridian, 1907; m. G. Louise Stewart, Dec. 14, 1907; children—George S., Clarence H., Bettye Jeanne. Pvt. practice, 1907-13; apptd. asst. surgeon USPHS, 1914, passed asst. surgeon, 1918, surgeon 1922, sr. surgeon 1934, med. dir., 1940; chief quarantine officer U.S. Quarantine Sta., New Orleans, June 9, 1941—; on field duty, 1914-18; at Newport News, Va., 1918-19; supr. 6th Dist., New Orleans, 1919-21; supt. Hot Springs Nat. Park, Ark., 1922-24; charge Mobile (Ala.) Quarantine Sta., 1925-27; med. adv. Am. Consulate Gen., Antwerp, Belgium, 1928-31; med. dir. 1st Dist., Indian Field Service, Mpls., 1931-33; med. dir. 2d Dist. Indian Field Service, Spokane, 1934-Aug. 1935; exec. officer, U.S. Marine Hosp. Stapleton, S.I., N.Y., 1935-36; med. officer charge U.S. Marine Hosp., Evansville, Ind., 1936-38; chief med. officer, U.S. Penitentiary Hosp., Leavenworth, Kan., July 1, 1938-Apr. 1, 1940; med. adv. U.S. Consulate Gen., Havana, Cuba, Apr. 1, 1940-June 1, 1941; chief quarantine officer Panama Canal, 1944-46. Mem. A.M.A. Democrat. Episcopalian. Mason, Elk. Address: 939 E. Beach, Pass Christian, Miss. Died Feb. 26, 1949.

WARING, James Howard, educator; b. Tyrone, Pa., Sept. 4, 1889; s. Edmund and Lydia Ramey (Beyer) W.; B.S., Pa. State Coll., 1920, M.S., 1921; Ph.D., Mich. State Coll., 1930; m. Iva Althea Stanley, June 17, 1918. Mem. faculty Pa. State Coll., 1920-25, asst. prof. pomology, 1923-25; mem. faculty U. Me., 1925—, prof. horticulture, 1925—, head dept. horticulture, 1925-51. Served in United States Infantry, 1917-18. Fellow A.A.A.S.; mem. Am. Soc. Hort. Sci., Am. Pomol. Soc., Am. Assn. U. Profs., Sigma Xi, Phi Kappa Phi. Methodist. Author articles on pomology. Home: 24 University Pl., Orono, Me. Died Apr. 18, 1959; buried Monmouth Ridge Cemetery, Monmouth, Me.

WARING, Malvina Sarah, author; b. Newberry, S.C., Nov. 12, 1842; d. John Blair and Elizabeth Ann (Sheppard) Black; ed. pvt. schs. and City Acad., Columbia, S.C., and grad. Limestone Coll., S.C., 1859, followed by post-grad. course; m. William Morena Gist (dec.); m. 2d, Clark Waring, Feb. 5, 1867. Mem. D.A.R. (organized 1st chapter in state, 3 yrs. state regent, 2 yrs. v.p.-gen., 3 yrs. mem. Continental Hall com., one of exec. com. and now mem. Revolutionary Relics com., Columbia Hosp. Assn., Columbia Art League, Pub. Library Assn.; alternate lady mgr. Chgo. Expn.; del. to Congress World's Fair Auxiliary of Representative Women; lady mgr. Charleston Expn.; pres. Columbia Choral Soc., 2 yrs., Derthick Club, 2 yrs.; pres. Limestone Coll. Alumnae Assn.; ex-regent Wade Hampton Chapter Daughters of the Confederacy; mem. Colonial Dames Am.; pres. Assembly (social), 3 yrs. Episcopalian. Author: The Lion's Share, 1888, That Sandhiller, 1904; also various serials, short stories, lectures and poems. Address: 1428 Laurel St., Columbia, S.C. Died 1930.

WARING, Roane, lawyer; b. Memphis, Tenn., July 20, 1881; s. Thomas Roane and Elizabeth (Ashe) W.; LL.B., U. of Va., 1902; m. Grace Titus Ford, Oct. 17, 1906; children—Mary Elizabeth (Mrs. Coe Stone), Grace Ann, Roane, Jr. Admitted to bar, 1902; pres. and gen. counsel Memphis St. Ry. Co., ret., now director and member executive committee; mem. of law firm Waring, Walker, Cox & Lewis. Elected nat. comdr. Am. Legion, Sept. 21, 1942. Served as maj. Inf., 30th Div., and later lt. col. asst. chief of staff, 33d Div., World War I; later col. Inf. Reserve. Awarded Silver Star medal, World War I. Mem. Am., Tenn. State bar assns., Am. Transit Assn., Memphis C. of C. (pres.). Clubs: Rotary, Memphis Yacht. Home: 170 Williford Pl. Office: 2410 Sterick Bldg., Memphis. Died Sept. 9, 1958.

WARNER, Charles, chmn. Warner Co.; b. Wilmington, Del., Apr. 22, 1877; s. Alfred D. and Emalea (Pusey) W.; ed. Friends Sch. (Wilmington), Stevens Inst. Tech., Drexel Inst. Tech.; m. Ethel Eden Bach, Jan. 4, 1900; children—Dorothy (Mrs. Edward M. Kenworthey (now dec.), Charles, Frederick. With Charles Warner Co., and successor Warner Co., since 1899, beginning as engr. and asst. to pres., became pres., spring 1915, pres. and chmn. of bd. at death father, 1915, chmn. bd., 1948-56; dir. Fed. Home Loan Bank. Pitts., First Fed. Savs. & Loan Assn. of New Castle County, Balt. & Eastern R.R. Trustee Drexel Inst. Tech., Phila. Chmn. Delaware Rep. State Com., 1920, 22; chmn. Del. Rep. Finance Com., 1922. Mem. Acad. Polit. Science, Am. Acad. Polit. and Social Science, Am. Planning and Civic Assn., Phila. Chamber of Commerce, Drexel Alumni. Unitarian. Clubs: Union League, Engineers, Midday (Phila.); Wilmington Club. Home: Indian Field Rd., Wilmington, Del. Office: 1721 Arch St., Phila. 3. Died Dec. 11, 1956.

WARNER, Edward (Pearson), engr., internat. ofcl.; b. Pittsburgh, Nov. 9, 1894; s. R. L. and Anne (Pearson) W.; B.A., Harvard, 1916, B.S., 1917; B.S., Mass. Inst. Tech., 1917, M.S., 1919; hon. D.Sc., Norwich Univ., 1938; m. Joan, d. of William H. Potter, Feb. 13, 1931; children—Sandra, Barry. Instr. aeronautical engring., Mass Inst. Tech., 1917-18; aero. engr. U.S. Army, 1918; chief physicist Nat. Advisory Com. for Aeronautics, 1919-20; tech. attaché N.A.C.A. in Europe, 1920; asso. prof. aeronautical engineering, Mass. Inst. Tech., 1920-24, prof. aeronautical engineering, 1924-26; asst. sec. Navy for aeronautics, 1926-29; editor of Aviation, 1929-34; vice chmn. Fed. Aviation Commn., 1934-35; cons. engr., 1935-38; mem. Civil Aeronautics Board, 1939-45; (v. chmn. 1943 45); resigned 1945; pres. Interim Council of Provisional Internat. Civil Aviation Orgn., 1945-47; pres. council Internat. Civil Aviation Orgn., 1947-57. Lend-lease staff, U.S. Embassy, London, Mar.-June 1941. Mem. N.A.C.A., 1929-45 (chmn. com. on aerodynamics and operating problems). Decorated Comdr. Mil. Order of Christ (Portugal); Order of Francisco de Miranda (Venezuela); Order of Cedars (Lebanon); Knight comdr. Order of Falcon (Iceland); Comdr. Legion of Honour (France); Order of Duarte, Sanchez and Mella (Dominican Republic); Comdr. Order Crown (Belgium); Grand Officer Order Aero. Merit (Brazil); Order Sacred Treasure (Japan); Comdr. Royal Order of St. Olav (Norway); Comdr. Order Al Merito (Italy); Comdr. Dannebrog (Denmark); recipient Wright Bros. medal Soc. Auto. Engrs., 1932; Daniel Guggenheim medal for achievement in aeronautics, 1950; FAI Gold Medal, 1952; Flight Safety Found. award, 1956; Wright Bros. Meml. Trophy, 1956. Hon. fellow Canadian Aero. Inst., Aeronautical Soc. of India, Institute Aero-Sciences, Royal Aeronautical Society; mem. Am. Soc. Mech. Engrs., Soc. Automotive Engrs. (pres. 1930), International Society of Aviation Writers (honorary). Clubs: Harvard (Boston); Royal Aero. and Anthenaeum (London); Cosmos (Washington); Harvard, Wings (New York City); University (Montreal). Author: Aerostatics, 1926; Airplane Design—Aerodynamics (awarded medal of Aero Club de France as leading work in aviation of year), 1927; Aviation Handbook, 1931; Airplane Design-Performance, 1936. Wilbur Wright Lectr., Royal Aeronautical Soc., 1943. Address: Duxbury, Mass. Died July 12, 1958.

WARNER, Gertrude Bass (Mrs. Murray Warner), art dir.; b. Chicago, Ill., May 14, 1863; d. Perkins and Clara (Foster) Bass; ed. Madame Rapp's Sch., Paris, later at Misses Grant Sch. (Chicago), Ogontz Sch. (Phila.) and Vassar Coll.; hon. M.A., U. of Ore., 1929; m. George F. Fiske (M.D.), 1888; children—Samuel Bass, George F.; m. 2d, Murray Warner, Oct. 1, 1904. Founded museums at St. Mary's Hall (P.E. sch., part of St. John's Coll.), Shanghai, 1908, and at Internat. Inst., Shanghai; donor collections of oriental art, Smithsonian Instn., 1920; gave large oriental collection of paintings, prints, bronzes, porcelains, etc., started by husband and self, to State of Ore., placed in U. of Ore., at Eugene, also donated library of books on China and Japan to the Museum of Art, of which has been dir. since May 1921; 6 expdns. made to Japan and China to increase collection. Del. to Conf. of Inst. of Pacific Relations, Kyoto, Japan, 1929. Mem. Am. Federation Arts, Am. Assn. Museums, A.A.A.S., N. China Br. Royal Asiatic Soc., Asiatic Soc. of Japan, Meiji Japan Soc., Soc. Colonial Dames, S.A.R. Christian Scientist. Home: 56 Grove St., Peterborough, N.H. Address: 2401 Calvert St. N.W., Washington 8. Deceased.

WARNER, Glenn Scobey, football coach; b. Springville, N.Y., Apr. 5, 1871; s. William Henry and Adeline (Scobey) W.; grad. Griffith Inst., Springville, 1889; LL.B., Cornell U., 1894; m. Tibb Loraine Smith, 1899. Admitted to N.Y. State Bar, 1894; football coach U. of Ga., 1895-96, Cornell U., 1897-98, Carlisle (Pa.) Indian Industrial Sch., 1899-1903 Cornell U., 1904-06, Carlisle, 1907-14, U. of Pittsburgh, 1915-23, Stanford, 1924-32, Temple U. Phila., 1933-38, San Jose (Cal.) State Coll., 1939-40. Pres. All Am. Football Bd., 1925—. Hon. mem. Am. Football Coaches Assn., Rotary Club; mem. Phi Delta Phi. Republican. Methodist. Mason (32° K.T.), Elk. Clubs: Olympic Athletic (San Francisco) Multnomah Athletic (Portland, Ore.). Author: Football for Players and Coaches, 1912; Football for Coaches and Players, 1927; Pop Warner's Book fo

Boys, 1934, revised edition, 1942. Home: 1623 Escobita Av., Palo Alto, Cal. Died Sept. 7, 1954; buried Springville, N.Y.

WARNER, Harry Jackson, physician; b. Prophetstown, Ill., July 19, 1880; s. Nathan Cole and Euphemia Hester (Dias) W.; B.S., U. Ill., 1901; M.D., George Washington U., 1907; m. Edmonia Francisco, Dec. 21, 1912; children—Murray Byrd, Hugh Francisco. Chemist U.S. Dept. of Agr., 1902-07; commd. asst. surgeon U.S.P.H.S., 1908, passed asst. surgeon, 1912, surgeon, 1920, sr. surgeon, 1930, med. dir. 1934; med. officer in charge, U.S. Quarantine Station, Boston, 1936-39; med. dir. Dist. 2, U.S. Indian Service, Spokane, Wash., 1939-40; liaison officer, Hdqrs., 7th Corps Area, U.S. Army, Omaha, Neb., Nov. 1940-May 1942; chief quarantine officer, Port of Baltimore, 1942-44, retired 1944. Mem. A.M.A., Assn. Mil. Surgeons, George Washington U. Med. Soc., Kappa Sigma, Phi Lambda Upsilon, Alpha Kappa Kappa. Episcopalian. Mason (32°). Address: 7815 Mt. Vernon St., Lemon Grove, Cal. Died July 26, 1954; buried Greenwood Meml. Park, San Diego, Cal.

WARNER, Harry Morris, motion picture exec.; b. in Russia, Dec. 12, 1881; s. Benjamin and Pearl (Eichelbaum) W.; brought to U.S., 1890; ed. pub. schs.; m. Rea Levinson, Aug. 20, 1907; children—Lewis J. (dec.), Doris Ruth, Betty, Lita (guardianship). Pres. Warner Bros. Pictures. Sponsored development of talking pictures (vitaphone) and of full-length and color motion pictures to 1956, retired 1956. Trustee Montefiore Hosp., Hebrew Orphan Asylum. Jewish religion. Club: Hillcrest Country (Los Angeles). Home: 355 St. Cloud Road, Bel-Air, Los Angeles, Calif. Office: 321 W. 44th St., N.Y.C. Died July 25, 1958.

WARNER, Harry O., prof., dir. dept. elec. engring. Coll. Engring., U. Detroit. Address: 17578 Ohio Av., Detroit 21. Died Sept. 16, 1950; buried Holy Sepulchre Cemetery.

WARNER, Joseph Everett, lawyer; b. Taunton, Mass., May 16, 1884; s. Richard Everett and Ida Evelyn (Briggs) W.; A.B., Harvard, 1906, student Law Sch., 1905-08; unmarried. Admitted to Mass. bar, 1909, and began practice at Taunton. Mem. city council, 1907-11; mem. Mass. Ho. of Rep., 1913-20 (chmn. ways and means com. 1916-18; speaker 1919-20); asst. atty. gen., Mass., 1923-28, atty. gen., 1928-35; associate justice Superior Court of Mass. since Oct. 1940. Trustee Taunton Pub. Library, Mem. Sigma Alpha Epsilon. Republican. Episcopalian. Mason, Odd Fellow, K.P., Elk. Home: 52 Church Green, Taunton, Mass. Died May 30, 1958.

WARNER, Langdon, archeologist; b. Cambridge, Mass., Aug. 1, 1881; s. Joseph B. and Margaret Woodbury (Storer) W.; A.B., Harvard, 1903; LL.D., U. Cal.; m. Lorraine d'O. Roosevelt, May 14, 1910; children—Lorraine, Margaret, Caleb. Mem. Pumpelly-Carnegie Expdn. to Trans-Caspia, 1904-05; asst. curator Oriental art, Mus. Fine Arts, Boston, 1906-13; dir. Am. Sch. Archeology, Peking under auspices of Smithsonian Instn. and Am. Archeol. Inst., 1913-14; field agent Cleve. Mus. Art, 1925; dir. Pa. Mus., Phila., 1917-23; field fellow, Fogg Mus., Harvard U., 1923-50. In charge 1st and 2d China expdns. for Fogg Art Mus.; lectr. div. fine arts, Harvard; dir. Art of Pacific Basin exhbn. at Golden Gate Expn., San Francisco. Spl. agt. Dept. State, Nov. 1917-Jan. 1919. Expert cons. arts and monuments sect. Civilian Information and Edn., G.H.Q., Supreme Comdr. Allied Powers, Japan, Apr.-Sept. 1946. Fellow Royal Geog. Soc. Home: 64 Linnaean St., Cambridge, Mass. Died July 9, 1955.

WARNER, Lucien Thompson, mfr.; b. N.Y.C., Apr. 18, 1877; s. Lucien Calvin and Keren Sarah Thirza (Osborne) W.; A.B., Oberlin (O.) Coll., 1898; LL.B., Columbia, 1901; m. Mary Barbour Whitman, Apr. 29, 1903; children—Arthur Whitman, Agnes Howland. Admitted to N.Y. bar, 1901; mem. firm The Warner Bros. Co., 1901—; now chmn. bd. Bridgeport Hydraulic Co. (exec. com.); trustee Bridgeport-Peoples Savs. Bank (exec. com.). Mem. exec. com., chmn. war personnel bd., Nat. War Work Council, YMCA, 1917-19; mem. ex-chmn. Army and Navy Com.; Nat. Board, internat. bd., mem., trustee internat. com., YMCA; dir., trustee and ex-pres. Bridgeport YMCA; mem. trustees YMCA Retirement Fund Dir. Bridgeport Hosp. (ex-pres.); trustee Oberlin Coll.; chmn. trustees Bordman-Beardsley Home. Mem. Phi Beta Kappa, Phi Gamma Delta, Phi Delta Phi. Republican. Conglist. Rotarian. Clubs: University, Black Rock Yacht (Bridgeport); University, Phi Gamma Delta, Columbia University (New York); Adirondack League. Home: 61 Broad St. 4. Office: The Warner Brothers Co., Bridgeport 2, Conn. Died Mar. 6, 1950; buried Woodlawn Cemetery, N.Y.

WARNER, Milton Jones, corp. mgmt. cons.; b. Salisbury, Conn., Jan. 9, 1873; s. Milton J. and Maria B. C. W.; A.B., Yale, 1894; m. Olive Young, Oct. 19, 1899. Chmn. bd. Nazareth Cement Co.; treas., dir. Alden M. Young Co.; pres., dir. Pine Orchard Improvement Co., Securities Equity Co. Trustee Rollins Coll., Winter Park, Fla. Republican. Conglist. Clubs: Pine Orchard, Quinnipiack (New Haven). Home: Pine Orchard, Branford, Conn. Died July 9, 1952.

WARNER, Richard Ambrose, Naval officer; b. Washington, D.C., July 4, 1878; s. John and Katherine Theresa (Keating) W.; student, Lehigh U., 1896-97; M.D., Georgetown U., 1901; m. Mary Cathcart Ransdell, Sept. 26, 1907; 1 dau., Mary Cathcart. Practicing physician and surgeon, Washington, (D.C.); Pekin (Peiping, China). Commd. M.C., U.S. N., 1905, commodor, M.C., U.S.N 1944—. Fellow Am. Coll. Surgery. Clubs: Army and Navy (Washington, D.C.), 1901-05. Home: 3716 49th St. N.W. Office: Navy Dept., Washington 25, D.C. Died Jan. 5, 1955.

WARNER, Thor, geologist; b. near Gottenburg, Sweden, Spet. 15, 1883; s. John Jacob Anderson and Lizzie (Johnson) W.; prep. edn. in Europe; studied evening schs., also U. of Calif., 1922-23; unmarried. With U.S. Steel Corp., Negaune, Mich., until 1903; mem. discovery party of Cobalt, Can., 1903-04; jr. mem. Leighton & Warner, Haileybury, Ont., Can., 1909-12; comdr. Canadian Sub-Arctic Expdn., 1914-15; comdr. geol. expdn. to headwaters of Amazon River, 1919-20; cons. geologist, specializing on petroleum, Los Angeles, Calif., 1920—. Vol. with assigned rank as 2d lt. Engr. Corps, U.S. Army, World War. Mem. Am. Inst. Mining and Metall. Engrs., Seismol. Soc. America, Am. Anthrop. Assn. Democrat. Author: Earth's Story of Evolution, 1920; The Siege of Lopeno, 1954. Contbr. to Am. Anthropologist, Art and Archaeology, etc. Discoverer Rio Puerco ruins, an ancient city (500 rooms), at Rio Puerco, N.M., 1925. Home: St. Anthony Hotel, San Antonio. Died Jan. 20, 1956; buried San Jose Burial Park, San Antonio.

WARNOCK, Arthur Ray, ret. coll. dean; b. Mason City, Ill., Dec. 4, 1883; s. George William and Charlotte Emma (Costain) W.; A.B., U. Ill., 1905; student U. Ill., Sch Law, 1905-07, 1908-09; m. Geraldine Grace Fouche, Sept. 4, 1915; children—Arthur Ray, John Fouche. Asst. in English Lit., U. Ill., 1905-07, asst. dean men, 1910-19; tchr. Smith Acad., St. Louis, 1907-08; admitted to practice law State Ill., 1910; dean men, Pa. State College, 1919-49, ret. Mem. Exec. Com. Nat. Interfraternity Conf., chmn. 1950-51; mem. Beta Theta Pi, Phi Beta Kappa, Phi Delta Phi. Republican. Methodist. Rotarian. Aughor: History of the Pennsylvania State College, 1940. Editor for 27 yrs. of newspaper column, The Daily Half Colyum, Centre Daily Times of State College, Pa. Address: Puddlintown Rd., R.D. 1, State College, Pa. Died Nov. 4, 1951; buried Rose Hill Cemetery, Petersburg, Ill.

WARNSHUIS, Abbe Livingston (wärns'hois), missionary sec.; b. Clymer, N.Y., Nov. 22, 1877; s. John William and Hendrika Johanna (Oonk) W.; A.B., Hope Coll., Holland, Mich., 1897, A.M., 1900, D.D., 1916; New Brunswick Theol. Sem., 1900; m. Anna De Vries, July 11, 1900 (died October 26, 1941); m. 2d, Margaret Chambers Halsey, Nov. 13, 1942. Ordained to ministry of the Reformed Church in America, 1900; missionary, Amoy, China, 1900-15; nat. evangelistic sec. China Continuation Com., Shanghai, 1915-20; sec. Internat. Missionary Council, London, 1921-24, New York, 1925-43, in Far East, 1930-31; foreign counsellor of Church Com. on Overseas Relief and Reconstruction, 1943-45; exec. v.p. Church World Service, Inc., 1946-48. Vice-pres. General Synod Ref. Ch. in Am., 1909, 34, 43, 44, treas., since 1943; pres. Foreign Missions Conference N. Amer. 1943-44. Former member exec. com. Fgn. Policy Association, World's S.S. Assn.; consultant, U.S. delegation to Opium Confs., Geneva, 1925. Trustee Nanking Theol. Sem., Yenching U., Peiping, and Hua Chung Coll., Wuchang, China. Mem. board of managers, Am. Bible Soc.; member bd. dirs. New Brunswick Theological Sem.; American Committee for World Council of Churches; com. on Religious Liberty, com. on a Just and Durable Peace; secretary of American Council of Voluntary Agencies for Foreign Service, 1943-45. Republican. Clubs: Aldine, Clergy. Author: Language Lessons in Amoy Vernacular, 1911. Editor of Talmage's Dictionary of Amoy Vernacular (revision) and compiler and translator various books; editor of Directory of Foreign Missions, 1933. Editor, The Christian Message for the World Today, 1934. Coeditor: The Madras Series, 1940. Visited Palestine, 1909, 1928, Japan, Korea, China, Philippines, 1930-31, India, 1938-39. Visited England, France, Switzerland, Nov.-Dec. 1944. Home: 48 Valley Rd., Bronxville 8, N.Y. Offices: 156 Fifth Av., N.Y.C. 10. Died Mar. 17, 1958.

WARREN, Avra Milvin, foreign service officer; b. Ilchester, Md., Aug. 26, 1893; s. Frederick and Mary Jane (Myers) W.; A.B., Johns Hopkins 1915; m. Mary Nicols Newnam, Apr. 7, 1924; children—Geoffrey Spencer, Anna Maria Lloyd. Consul, Cape Haitien, Haiti, 1920-22, Karachi, India, 1922-23, Nairobi, Kenya Colony, 1924-25, St. John's Newfoundland, 1926-30; consul gen., Buenos Aires, 1932-35; adviser Pan. Am. Commercial Conf. Buenos Aires, 1935; chief of visa div., Dept. of State, 1938-41; ambassador to Dominican Republic, July 1942-Apr. 1944; ambassador to Panama, June 1944-Jan. 1945; dir. Office of American Republic Affairs, Dept. of State, 1945; minister to New Zealand, 1945-46, Finland, 1948-49; ambassador to Pakistan, 1950-53, to Turkey, 1953-56. Served in O.T.C., Fort Meyer, Virginia, 1917; 2d lt. 310 Inf. Machine Gun Co., 78th Div., U.S. Army, with A.E.F.; disch. as 2d lt. Air Corps, Aug. 1919. Mason (K.T.). Clubs: Sind (Karachi, India); Metropolitan (Washington); Brook (N. Y.C.). Address: 5014 Waneta Dr., Dallas. Died Jan. 21, 1957; buried Old St. Paul's, Kent County, Md.

WARREN, Charles, lawyer; b. Boston, Mass., Mar. 9, 1868; s. Hon. Winslow and Mary Lincoln (Tinkham) W.; A.B., Harvard U., 1889, A.M., 1892; student at Harvard Law School, 1889-92; LL.D., Columbia U., 1933; m. Annie Louise, d. William Henry Bliss, Jan. 6, 1904. Admitted to bar, 1892, and practiced at Boston; asso. in practice with Moorfield Storey, 1892-93; pvt. sec. to Gov. William E. Russell, 1893; asso. in law practice with Gov. Russell until the death of the latter in 1896; sr. mem. Warren & Perry, Boston, 1897-1914. Chmn. Mass. Civil Service Commn., 1905-11; assistant attorney general of the United States, Washington, 1914-18; apptd. spl. master by U.S. Supreme Court in case of New Mexico vs. Texas, 1924, United States vs. Utah, 1929, Texas vs. New Mexico, 1936, Stafford Little lecturer, Princeton, 1924; Cutler lecturer on Constitution, U. of Rochester, April 1927; Bacon lecturer on same, Boston U. Law School, Feb. 1928; James Schouler lecturer on history, Johns Hopkins, 1928; William H. White lecturer on jurisprudence, Univ. of Va., Jan. 1932; Julius Rosenthal Foundation lecturer on law, Northwestern U. Law School, Nov. 1934; Norman Wait Harris lecturer on neutrality, U. of Chicago, 1936; Frank Irvine lecturer, Cornell U., 1937; Cutler lecturer on Constitution, College of William and Mary, 1940. Appointed by President Roosevelt as Am. mem. Trail Smelter Arbitral Tribunal, 1937 (final decision filed 1941), Am. mem. Conciliation Internat. Com. under Treaty between U.S. and Hungary; mem. President's War Relief Control Bd., 1943-46. Member Board of Overseers, Harvard Coll., 1934-40; pres. Harvard Alumni Assn., 1941-42; trustee N.E. Conservatory of Music. Mem. Mass. Hist. Soc., Am. Soc. Internat. Law (hon. v.p.), Nat. Inst. of Arts and Letters (1925), Am. Acad. Arts and Letters (1937), Am. Philos. Soc. (1939); mem. com. management Dictionary of American Biography. Clubs: Metropolitan, Cosmos (Washington, D.C.); Harvard, Saint Botolph (Boston); Century, Harvard (New York). Author: The Girl and the Governor, 1902; History of the Harvard Law School and Early Legal Conditions in America (3 vols.), 1909; History of the American Bar, Colonial and Federal, to 1860, 1911; The Supreme Court in United States History (3 vols.), 1922; awarded Pulitzer prize ($2,000), 1923, for best book on American history pub. in 1922, new edit., 2 vols., 1926; The Supreme Court and Sovereign States, 1924; Congress, the Constitution and the Supreme Court, 1925, enlarged edit., 1935; The Making of the Constitution, 1928, 2d edit., 1937; Jacobin and Junto, 1931; Congress as Santa Claus—The General Welfare Clause, 1932; Bankruptcy in United States History, 1935; Odd Byways in American History, 1942. Class sec. Harvard class of 1889. Home: 1527 18th St. N.W., Washington. Died Aug. 16, 1954; buried Vine Hills Cemetery, Plymouth, Mass.

WARREN, Charles Hyde, mineralogist; b. Watertown, Conn., Sept. 27, 1876; s. Charles Alanson and Frances Maria (Hyde) W.; Ph.B., Sheffield Sci. Sch. (Yale), 1896, Ph.D., 1899; m. Charlotte Wardner Lamson, June 17, 1903; children—Richard, Allen Johnson, William Lamson. Asst. in chemistry and mineralogy, Sheffield Sci. Sch., 1896-99, instr., 1899-1900; instr., asst., asso. prof. mineralogy, Mass. Inst. Tech., 1900-12, prof., 1912-22; dean Sheffield Sci. School, Yale, and prof. mineralogy, 1922-45; master Trumbull Coll. of Yale U., 1938-45; ret. June 1945. Fellow Geol. Soc. Am., Am. Acad. Arts and Scis.; mem. Am. Philos. Soc. Author: Manual of Determinative Mineralogy, 1910. Contbr. Am. and German tech. jours. Home: Litchfield, Conn. Died Aug. 16, 1950; buried Watertown, Conn.

WARREN, Fred D., editor; b. Arcola, Ill., Mar. 24, 1872; s. J. J. and Harriet D. (Mains) W.; common sch. edn.; m. Hattie Barton, June 12, 1895. Learned printing trade and established Rich Hill Tribune (Republican), 1890; joined Social Dem. party, 1898, and established Bates County Critic; asso. editor Appeal to Reason, 1899-1901; reëstablished Coming Nation, 1902, and consolidated it with Appeal to Reason, 1904, of which is now editor. Indicted by Federal Court, Kan. Dist., for mailing offer of reward for Ex-Gov. Taylor Ky., and sentenced to jail for 6 mos. by Judge Pollock, July, 1909; appeal taken to U.S. Circuit Ct., St. Paul; judgment of lower ct. affirmed, Nov. 21, 1911; Pres. Taft, Feb. 1, 1911, issued unsolicited pardon, commuting jail sentense and reducing fine from $1,500 to $100. Author of a number of pamphlets on socialism. Address: Girard, Kan. Died Mar. 25, 1959.

WARREN, Henry Ellis, inventor, corp. exec.; b. Boston, May 21, 1872; s. Henry and Adelaide Louise (Ellis) W.; S.B., Mass. Inst. Tech., 1894; D.Sc., Rutgers, 1950; m. Edith B. Smith, Jan. 19, 1907. Elec. engr., Saginaw Valley Traction Co., Mich.,

1897-1902; supt., engr. Lombard Governor Co., Boston and Ashland, Mass., 1902-20, pres. 1937—; pres. Warren Telechron Co. (formerly Warren Clock Co.), 1914-43; cons. engr. Gen. Electric Co., 1919-40. Awarded Wetherill Medal by Franklin Inst., 1935. Chmn. Ashland (Mass.) selectmen, 1907-09, water commrs., 1910-17, Ashland Town Forest Com., 1937—. Trustee Middlesex County Extension Service in Agr. and Home Econs., 1936-45, pres., 1945-53; trustee Framingham Union Hosp. Chmn. Summer Inst. Social Progress, Wellesley, 1938-47, vice-chmn., 1948—. Trustee Algonquin Council Boy Scouts Am., Salvation Army. Fellow (life) Am. Inst. E.E. (Lamme medalist, 1935). Contbr. of papers to engring. publs. Home: 531 Chestnut St., Ashland, Mass. Died Sept. 21, 1957; buried Mount Auburn Cemetery.

WARREN, James Carey, investment banker; b. Cleve., Oct. 18, 1896; s. Frederick Morris and Estelle (Carey) W.; B.A. magna cum laude, Amherst Coll., 1918; m. Josephine Jenks, June 8, 1923; children—James Carey, Penelope (Mrs. Emil Caccavo), Zoe; m. 2d, Priscilla Murdock Gibb, July 1, 1946. Mfr., 1919-21; with Lee Higginson & Co., 1921-23, Jenks, Gwynne & Co., N.Y.C., 1923-38; with A. M. Kidder & Co., N.Y.C., 1938—, gen. partner in charge underwriting and syndicate depts., 1942-56, v.p., dir A. M. Kidder & Co., Inc., 1956—; dir. Felmont Petroleum Corp. Vice pres. bd. trustees Knickerbocker Hosp., N.Y.C., 1938—. Served as corpl., F.A., U.S. Army, 1918. Mem. Phi Beta Kappa. Episcopalian. Clubs: Century Assn., Downtown Assn. (N.Y.C.); Piping Rock (L.I., N.Y.). Home: Cove Rd., Oyster Bay, N.Y. Office: 1 Wall St., N.Y.C. 5. Died July 6, 1959.

WARREN, James E(win); born in Beech Grove, Tenn., Dec. 3, 1878; s. Andrew Johnson and Elizabeth Jane (Stephenson) W.; studied U. of Nashville, 1897-1900; m. Mary E. Houston, Oct. 10, 1905 (now dec.); children—Mary Elizabeth (wife of Dr. J. C. Read), James Ewin. Began as stenographer with Cumberland Telephone & Telegraph Co., 1900, gen. supply and purchasing agt., 1907-18, plant supt., 1918-19, asst. to pres., 1919-25; gen. plant mgr., 1925-28, gen. mgr., 1928-30, v.p., 1930-35; dir. Southern Bell Telephone and Telegraph Co. since 1930, pres., 1935-43, chmn. of bd., Jan. 1, 1943-Jan. 1, 1944. Presbyn. Mason. Club: Capital City (Atlanta). Home: 42 Brookhaven Drive. Office: Hurt Bldg., Atlanta. Died Apr. 22, 1952.

WARREN, Leonard, baritone; b. N.Y.C., Apr. 21, 1911; s. S. and Sarah Warren; ed. pub. schs. and Columbia; m. Agatha Leifflen, Dec. 27, 1941. Sang with Radio City Music Hall Glee Club for 3 yrs.; with Met. Opera Co., N.Y.C., 1938—; Cin. Summer Opera, 1940; Nat. Opera, Puerto Rico, 1940; Grand Opera Festival, Montreal, 1941; Robin Hood Dell, Phila., 1940; Cleve. Summer Music Soc., 1941; leading baritone Teatro Municipal, Rio de Janeiro and Teatro Colon, Buenos Aires, summers, 1942-45; sang role of High Priest in the New York premiere of Gluck's Alcest, Jan. 1941; sang role of Ilo in world premiere of Menotti's Island God, Met. Opera Co., Feb. 1942; title role of Rigoletto, Dec. 1943, same role LaScala Opera, Milan, 1953, Lewisohn Stadium Concerts, 1956; appeared in Falstaff, also Simon Bocconegra at San Francisco, 1956. Has also sung over the radio in the series Echoes of New York, 1939-40, Musical American, 1940, Ford's Sunday Evening Hour, 1941, 42, Treasury Hour, 1943, Coca Cola program, Pause that Refreshes, 1943, Ford Hour, 1945, also Voice of Firestone, Telephone Hour, NBC spectacular Festival of Music. Songs on Victor records. Died Mar. 4, 1960.‡

WARREN, William Marshall, univ. dean; b. Bremen, Germany, Nov. 4, 1865; s. William Fairfield and Harriet Cornelia (Merrick) W.; A.B., Boston U. 1887, Ph.D., 1892; studied Tübingen, Jena, Berlin; studied and traveled in Europe and Egypt, 1890-92; m. Sara Bainbridge Shields, June 9, 1896; children—Shields, Virginia Fairfield (Mrs. Edward Ellis Allen, Jr.). Prof. philosophy, Boston U., 1896-1942, acting dean, 1904-05, dean Coll. of Liberal Arts, 1905-37, dean emeritus since 1937. Editorial writer. Pres. New Eng. Coll. Entrance Certificate Bd., 1922-37; Trustee of Donations for Edn. in Liberia since 1922. Mem. Beta Theta Pi, Phi Beta Kappa, Am. Philos. Assn.; Soc. for the Preservation of New Eng. Antiquities, Rockport Art Assn., Copley Soc. of Boston. Author: Beacon Hill and Boston University. Home: 28 Hawthorn Rd., Brookline, Mass. Died Apr. 16, 1953.

WARTENBERG, Robert, neurologist; b. Grodno, Lithuania, Russia, June 19, 1887; s. James and Mnucha (Pikower) W.; M.D., U. Rostock, 1919; m. Baroness Isabelle von Sazenhofen, Aug. 30, 1929. Physician-in-chief Nerve Clinic, prof. neurology U. Freiburg im Breisgau, 1935; faculty U. Cal., 1936—, now clin. prof. neurology. Corr. mem. German Rio de Janeiro socs. of Neurology; hon. mem. neurol. socs. Spain, Italy, Yugoslavia and Vienna, Association of German Neuopathologists, German Society of Neurosurgery. Author: Examination of Reflexes, 1945 (translated into Italian, Spanish, French, German, Serbian, Japanese); Hemifacial Spasm, 1952; Diagnostic Tests in Neurology, 1953; Neuritis, Sensory Neuritis, Neuralgia, 1957; also sci. articles. Editorial bd. Jour. Nervous and Mental Disease, Confinia Neurologica, Neurology, Neuropsiquiatria (Buenos Aires). Address: University of Cal., San Francisco 22. Died Nov. 16, 1956.

WARTON, Frank Riggs, food co. exec.; b. Appleby, Eng., Aug. 5, 1889; s. Richard and Anne (Rigg) W.; ed. in Eng.; m. Elizabeth Hines, Aug. 18, 1927; children—John, Patricia, Anne (Mrs. William C. Douglas), Rigg Frank. Came to U.S., 1906, naturalized, 1914. Former pres. Allied Packers, Inc.; became v.p. Quaker Oats Co., 1942, ret., now cons. Home: 900 N. Michigan Av., Chgo. 11. Office: Quaker Oats Co., Merchandise Mart Plaza, Chgo. 54. Died Oct. 21, 1959.

WARWICK, C. Laurence, civil engr.; b. Phila., Pa., July 29, 1889; s. Charles F. and Emily N. (Meyers) W.; B.S., U. of Pa., 1909, C.E., 1926; m. Mary E. Orem, Jan. 25, 1915; children—C. Laurence, Robert O., Mary Elizabeth. Instr. and asst. prof. structural engring., civil engring. dept. U. of Pa., 1909-19; editorial asst. Am. Soc. for Testing Materials, 1909-17, assistant secretary, 1917-19, sec.-treasurer, 1919-45, executive secretary since 1945. Consultant and chief specifications branch (later, materials branch), conservation div. War Production Bd., 1941 to Sept. 1943, consultant to dir. conservation div. and chief specifications staff Sept. 1943 to June 1944, engaged in conserving critical materials; adminstr. nat. emergency steel specifications project War Prodn. Bd., 1941 to 1944. Commr. Radnor Twp., Del. Co., since 1937. F. of A.A.A.S., assoc. mem. Am. Soc. C.E.; mem. A.S.T.M., A.S.M., Sigma Xi Soc., hon. mem. Sigma Tau. Republican. Presbyterian. Clubs: Engrs. (Phila.), St. David's Golf Home: 418 Woodland Av., Wayne, Pa. Office; 1916 Race St., Phila. 3. Died Apr. 23, 1952; buried Valley Forge Gardens, King of Prussia, Pa.

WASHBURN, Reginald, mfr.; b. Worcester, Mass., Oct. 13, 1871; s. Charles F. and Mary Elizabeth (Whiton) W.; A.B., Harvard, 1894; m. Dorcas Lockwood Bradford, Aug. 26, 1903; children—Dorcas (Mrs. Donald W. Campbell), Phoebe (Mrs. Charles B. Barnes, Jr.), Mary Elizabeth (Mrs. Stuart W. Cragin). With the Wire Goods Co., Worcester, 1898—, became treas., 1900, pres., 1906—; treas., gen. mgr. The Washburn Co., 1922, pres., 1928, chmn. bd., 1941, also pres. Andrews Wire Works of Can., Ltd., Watford, Ont., Mich. Wire Goods Co., 1928-41, now dir. both; trustee Worcester County Instn. for Savings to 1954; dir. Worcester County Trust Co. Trustee Bancroft Scholarship Fund, Worcester, 1909-54, chmn., 1920-54; trustee Groton Sch., 1928—; dir. Worcester Boys' Club, 1907—, pres., 1912-45; dir. Boys' Clubs of Am., Inc., 1918-50. Awarded Silver Keystone, 1948. Mem. Am. Antiquarian Soc., Nat. Inst. Social Scis., Newcomen Soc. Republican. Episcopalian. Clubs: Worcester, Century Association (N.Y.C.). Home: 253 Salisbury St. Office: 28 Union St., Worcester, Mass. Died May 12, 1955.

WASHBURN, Stanley, war corr., author; b. Minneapolis, Feb. 7, 1878; s. U.S. Senator William Drew and Elizabeth M. (Muzzy) W.; A.B., Williams Coll., 1901, hon. Dr. Humane Letters, 1921; attended Harvard Law Sch., 1901; m. Alice Langhorne, Nov. 27, 1906; children—Fawan, Stanley, Langhorne. Attached Minneapolis Journal, 1901-02; on staff Minneapolis Times, 1902-04; war corr. Chicago Daily News, 1904-06. Covered Russo-Japanese War, operated dispatch boat "Fawan" 4 mos., at fall of Port Arthur; with Nogi's army before Port Arthur; served with 3d Japanese Army until end of war; organized news service in Far East and India; operated dispatch boat in Black Sea, Dec. 1905, carrying British and U.S. Govt. official dispatches, mail and refugees; covered Russian Revolution, 1905; went again to Europe, Aug. 1914, as corr. Collier's Weekly, to Russia, Sept. 1914, as spl. corr. London Times, attached to Russian Army for 26 mos., only Am. having access to whole Russian front; also with French at Verdun, Apr. 1916, and attached to Roumanian Army 2 mos., 1916. Wrote foreign policy of Russia for Russian Govt., 1916; wrote case of Roumania for King, 1916; attached to Sec. of State Lansing as mil. advisor, 1917. Commd. maj. Minn. N.G., Apr. 1915, col., Feb. 1916, as aide on gov.'s staff; apptd. maj., cav., O.R.C., May 5, 1917; active duty May 9, as mil. aide to John F. Stevens, adv. railroad mission to Russia; transferred at Vladivostok to Root diplomatic mission to Russia as mil. aide and asst. sec. of mission; G2 of 26th Div., in France, Apr. 1, 1918; served in Toul and Chateau-Thierry sectors with that div.; invalided home, Sept. 1918; hon. disch., Jan. 27, 1919; lt. col. Mil. Intelligence Dept., June 10, 1931; mil. aide to Queen Marie of Roumania during visit U.S., 1926. Before leaving for France, by request Russian Embassy, detailed by State and War depts. to make speaking tour through 35 states presenting case of Russia in the war. Decorated by Emperor of Japan, Order Imperial Crown, 1907; by Czar, Order of St. Anna, 1915; by Gen. Brossilov, Order of St. George, 1916; by King of Roumania, Comdr. Order of Crown; awarded Am. Service Ribbon with 2 silver stars, 1919. Hon. mem. Japanese Red Cross Soc. Del. Rep. Nat. Conv., Chicago, 1912. Apptd. by State Dept. to secretariat of Am. Delegation to Disarmament Conf., to do liaison between Am. and Japanese delegations, Washington, 1921. Pres. Washburn Lignite Coal Co., Wilton, N.D., 1926-29. Pres. N.D. Coal Operators Assn., 1925-35; v.p. and nat. councilor Greater N.D. Assn.; dir. Nat. Security League; chmn. Russian com. Nat. Civic Fedn., 1920-35; trustee Am. Defense Soc. Mason, Elk. Pres. Willkie Club of Lakewood, 1940; chmn. affiliated Rep. Clubs, Lakewood. 1936. Clubs: University, Century (N.Y.C.); Delta Psi. Member of the American Legion, also member of the Veterans Foreign Wars. Made 1000 speeches in 42 different states since 1917; war corr. or soldier with 20 armies; covered approximately 100 battles since 1904. Author: The Cable Game, 1911; Nogi—The Man Against the Background of a War, 1913; Field Notes from the Russian Front, 1915; The Russian Campaign, April to August, 1915; The Russian Offensive, 1917. Writer of propaganda for British, Russian and French, 1939-40; speaker and broadcaster on morale, mil. and naval intelligence, etc. Contbr. to newspapers. Home: Inverfirs, Lakewood, N.J. Died Dec. 14, 1950; buried Arlington Nat. Cemetery.

WASHINGTON, Thomas, naval officer; b. Goldsboro, N.C., June 6, 1865; s. James A. and Virginia N. W.; grad. U.S. Naval Acad., 1887; m. Genevieve F. Clement, June 12, 1900; children—John Clement, Primitive Secret Societies, 1908, rev. edit., 1932 Thomas. Commd. ensign, July 1, 1889; lt., jr. grade, Sept. 5, 1897; lt., Mar. 3, 1899; lt. commdr., July 1, 1905; commander, July 1, 1909; captain, April 9, 1914; rear admiral, August 10, 1918; admiral, October 11, 1923. Served on board Indiana, 1898-99, during Spanish-American war; on board Illinois, 1902. Hydrographer, in charge of Hydrographic Office, Washington, 1914-16; comdg. Florida, June 1916-Nov. 1918, serving with British Grand Fleet in the North Sea, Nov. 1917-Nov. 1918; comd. 3d Div. Atlantic Fleet, 1919; chief Bur. of Navigation, Navy Dept., 1919-23; comdr.-in-chief Asiatic Fleet, 1923-25; commanding 12th Naval Dist., San Francisco, Nov. 19, 1925; retired June 6, 1929; gov. U.S. Naval Home, Phila., 1931-37. Medals: Santiago, West India, Philippine, Nicaraguan (campaigns), D.S.M. (U.S.); Medaille Militaire (Belgium); Order of Bolivar (Venezuela). Mem. Order of the Cincinnati; Order of Washington, Baronial Order of Magna Charta. Episcopalian. Mason. Club: Army and Navy. Home: 1725 Monterey Av., Coronado, Cal. Died Dec. 15, 1954; buried Arlington, Va.

WASON, Robert Alexander, author; b. Toledo, O., Apr. 6, 1874; s. Robert Alexander and Gertrude Louise (Paddock) W.; high schs., Delphi, 1 yr.; m. Emma Louise Brownell, May 11, 1911; children—Charles Brownell, Jane (Mrs. Francisco J. Llanso), Robert Alexander. Clerk in gen. store 8 yrs., varied by tramping and "roughing it" in the West; served 9 mos. in Light Battery D, 5th U.S. Arty., 1898-99. Author: Babe Randolph's Turning Point, 1904; The Wolves, 1908; Nachette (with Ned Nye), 1909; Happy Hawkins, 1909; The Steering Wheel, 1910; The Knight Errant, 1911; The Dog and the Child and the Ancient Sailor Man, 1911; Friar Tuck, 1912; And Then Came Jean, 1913; Happy Hawkins in the Panhandle, 1914; Knute Ericson's Celebration, in The Grim Thirteen, 1917; also vaudeville sketches, a comic opera, and short stories in popular mags. Home: Mountain Lakes, N.J. Died May 11, 1955.

WASON, Robert R. (wä'sŭn), business exec.; b. Ashtabula, O., May 1, 1888; s. Samuel and Anna Ross (Wallace) W.; grad. Harbor High Sch., Ashtabula, O., 1905; m. Hilda Bradford, Aug. 28, 1922. Began as longshoreman, 1905; dir. merchandising, v.p. Proctor & Collier, Cin., 1920-23; sales mgr. A. S. Boyle Co., Cin., 1923-25; with Proctor & Collier, 1925-28; gen. mgr., Clark Lighter Co., 1929-30; pres., dir., mem. exec. com., Manning, Maxwell & Moore, Inc., N.Y.C., 1931—; dir., mem. exec. com. Zonite Corp., N.Y.C., 1939—, also pres., 1935-39. Dir. N.A.M., 1944—, pres., 1946, chmn. bd., 1947; chmn. Reconversion Council, 1945; chmn. adv. com. econ. policy, 1942-45; hon. vice chmn., Laymen's Nat. Com., 1946; dir. Nat. Indsl. Conf. Bd., 1948; trustee America's Future, 1947-48. Mem. Ohio Soc. N.Y. Lectr. marketing and merchandising methods U. Cin., 2 yrs. Home: One Gracie Sq., N.Y.C. 28. Office: care Manning, Maxwell & Moore, Inc., 405 Lexington Av., N.Y.C. 17. Died June 7, 1950.

WASON, William J., Jr. (wä'sŭn), chmn. Kings Co. Trust Co.; b. Port Jefferson, L.I., N.Y., Dec. 7, 1872; s. William J. and Sarah E. (Connor) W.; student Bryant & Stratton Business Coll., Brooklyn, N.Y.; m. Jennie M. Stephens, Mar. 11, 1897; children—Mildred E., William J., 3d, Dorothy I. With Kings County Trust Co. since Jan. 2, 1895, now chmn. and trustee; dir. The Brooklyn Citizen, Brooklyn Union Gas Co., Dime Savings Bank of Brooklyn, N.Y. Dock Co., N.Y. Dock Trade Facilities Corp. Clubs: Brooklyn, Bankers. Home: 136 Stratford Rd. Office: 342 Fulton St., Bklyn. Died Feb. 2, 1958.

WASSAM, Clarence Wyckliffe, educator; b. Black Hawk Co., Ia., Oct. 23, 1887; s. Daniel J. and Lucinda (Cain) W.; M.Di., Ia. State Teachers Coll.,

Cedar Falls, Ia., 1900; B.Ph., State U. of Ia., 1903, M.A., 1904; Ph.D., Columbia, 1908; unmarried. Instructor economics, State U. of Ia., 1905-07; fellow N.Y. Sch. of Philanthropy, 1907-08; asst. prof. economics and sociology State U. of Ia., 1908-—. Mem. Am. Econ. Assn., Internat. Tax Assn., Nat. Conf. Charities and Correction. Mem. Progressive Brethren. Author: Salary Loan Business in New York City, 1908. Wrote pamphlet on Organized Charity in Iowa, 1904. Address: Iowa City, Ia. Deceased.

WASSON, George Savary, artist, author; b. Groveland, Mass., Aug. 27, 1855; s. David Atwood and Abby A. (Smith) W.; ed. Medford (Mass.) High Sch., and in private instn.; took course 3 yrs. Royal Würtemberg Art Sch.; m. Amelia Bullock, 1885. Began career as marine artist in Boston; built house and studio at Kittery Point, Me., 1889, in order to study sea. Author: Cap'n Simeone's Store, 1903; The Green Shay, 1905; Home from Sea, 1908. Contbr. to leading mags. Died Apr. 28, 1931; buried Bangor, Me.

WATERBURY, Henry S., architect. Senior partner Delano and Aldrich. architects. Mem. American Inst. Architects since 1924, fellow since 1935. Address: Delano and Aldrich, 126 E. 38th St., N.Y.C. Died 1953.

WATERHOUSE, George Booker, metallurgical engr.; b. Sheffield, Eng., May 25, 1883; s. Joseph J. and Mary E. (Booker) W.; B.Met., U. of Sheffield, 1901; post-grad. work same univ., 1901-03; Ph.D., Columbia U., 1907; Dr. Metallurgy, U. of Sheffield, 1937; D.Eng., Nova Scotia Technical College, 1949; married Eleanor F. Wood, June 29, 1909 (died Dec. 16, 1935); m. Germaine S. Souverain, June 15, 1938. Came to U.S., 1903, naturalized citizen, 1910. With Lackawanna Steel Co., as metallographist, metallurgist and metall. and insp. engr., until 1922; prof. metallurgy, Mass. Inst. Tech., 1922-45; was prof. emeritus; cons. practice; mem. research adv. bd. Westinghouse Electric & Mfg. Co.; dir. Belmont Trust Co.; mem. Corp. Belmont Savings Bank; cons. engr. U.S. Bur. Mines. Served as mem. 74th Regt. N.Y. Nat. Gd., hon. discharged as 1st lt., May 1919. Mem. Am. Iron and Steel Inst., Am. Inst. Mining and Metall. Engrs. (chmn. iron and steel div. 1929; dir. 1933-1939), Am. Soc. for Testing Materials, Am. Soc. for Metals (trustee since 1934, prres. 1937-38), Am. Foundrymen's Assn., Sigma Xi, Scabbard and Blade, also Iron and Steel Institute and Cleveland Institute Engineers (all of Great Britain); chairman metallurgical advisory committee U.S. Bureau Standards. 1920-43; chmn., dir. research, iron alloys com. of Engineering Foundation, 1929-42; spl. staff consultant Office Prodn. Management, June 1941-Dec. 1941, steel div. of War Prodn. Bd., Dec. 1941-Aug. 1942, Office Lend-Lease Adminstrn. since Aug. 1942, Office Fgn. Econ. Adminstrn., Dec. 1943-May 1945. Mem. Belmont (Mass.) Sch. Com. (chmn. 1934, 36, 37). Republican. Mason. Contbr. numerous scientific papers and articles; export witness in suits relating to iron and steel. Home: 16 Fairmont St., Belmont 78, Mass. Died May 10, 1952; buried Bergen (N.Y.) Cemetery.

WATERMAN, Earle Lytton, univ. prof.; b. Glover, Vt., Sept. 1, 1885; s. Darwin Samuel and Nora (Willey) W.; B.S. in C.E., U. Vt., 1907, C.E., 1913; m. Florence Votey, Dec. 21, 1910; 1 dau., Anne. Successively asst. instr., asst. prof., asso. prof. hydraulic and san. engring., Pa. State Coll., 1907-19; asso. prof. pub. health, extension div., U. Ia., 1919-22; asso. prof. san. engring., Coll. Engring., 1922-25, prof., 1925-—; head Dept. Civil Engring., 1944; asst. state engr., Mich. State Dept. Health, 1916-17; in pub. health engring. and cons., summers 1923-40; state san. engr., Vt. Dept. Pub. Health, summers 1931-40. Served as lt., capt., San. Corps, U.S. Army, 1918-19. Chmn. City Plan Commn., Iowa City, 1930-—; pres. Social Service League, Iowa City, 1925-29. Recipient Fuller Award, 1945. Mem. Am. Soc. C.E. (mem. exec. com. san. engring. div., 1936-40; chmn. 1940; former pres. Ia. sect.), Am. Water Works Assn. (dir. 1938-41; sec. Mo. Valley sect., 1929-45), Am. Pub. Health Assn., Soc. Promotion Engring. Edn., Ia. Engring. Soc. (former pres.), Ia. Wastes Disposal Assn. (past pres.), Federated Sewage Works Assn. (dir. bd. control), Boulder Soc., Triangle, Sigma Xi, Chi Epsilon, Tau Beta Pi, Phi Delta Theta. Episcopalian. Republican. Clubs: Engineers; Mt. View Country (Greensboro, Vt.). Home: 24 Heat's Bridge Rd. Concord, Mass. Office: Eliot-Pearson Sch., Tufts, Mass. Died July 30, 1951.

WATERMAN, Warren Gookin, prof. botany; b. Southport, Conn., Sept. 3, 1872; s. Edwin Southworth and Martica (Gookin) W.; A.B., Yale, 1892, A.M., 1907; Ph.D., U. Chgo., 1917; m. Anna Sarah Mueller, June 14, 1898 (died Feb. 23, 1944); children—Warren G., Alice Southworth, John French. Instr. natural sci., Fisk U., Nashville, 1896-1902, prof. geology, 1903-11; asst. prof. biology, Knox Coll., Galesburg, Ill., 1912-15; asst. prof. botany, 1917-23; asso. prof., 1923-33, prof., 1933-37, Northwestern U., chmn. dept., 1928-37, ret.; formerly fellow A.A.A.S.; formerly mem. Bot. Soc. Am., Ecol. Soc. Am., Ill. State Acad. Sci. (ex-pres.), Ill. Bd. Mus. Advs., Conservation Council Chgo., Sigma Xi, Mich. Acad. Sci., U. Clubs of Chgo. and Evanston. Republican. Conglist. Author: Plant Communities (mimeograph edit.), 1924; also articles on plant communities, especially in bog and dune habitats. Home: R.F.D., Frankfort, Mich. Died Nov. 1952.

WATERS, Eugene A(lbertus), educator; b. Wellsville, Kan., Nov. 4, 1899; s. Charles C. and Minnie (Hays) W.; B.S., Kan. State Coll., 1925, M.S., 1929; Ph.D., Columbia, 1941; m. Mildred Thornburg, May 27, 1926; 1 son, Richard Lyle. Tchr. sci., math. secondary schs., Kan. and Okla., 1922-39; tchr. chemistry, physics, Tulsa, 1929-30, prin. Sapulpa High Sch., 1931-33, dir. sci. pub. schs., 1934-36; asst. prof., chmn. sci. com. U. Sch., Ohio State U., 1937-38; chmn. grad. com., coordinator research U. of Tenn., 1940-48, became dean grad. sch., 1948, vice president university, 1953-—; member staff Southern Study conducted by Southern Assn. Colls. and Secondary Schs., 1938-41, consultant Secondary Commn's. revision sch. standards, 1947-51; consultant survey higher edn., Miss., 1944; co-dir. Tenn. State survey pub. edn., 1945-46. Fellow American Association Advancement Science; member Am. Ednl. Research Assn., Nat. Assn. for Research Sci. Edn., Am. Acad. Polit. and Social Scis., Bur. Ednl. Research in Sci. Edn. Columbia, Phi Delta Kappa, Phi Kappa Phi, Omicron Delta Kappa. Author numerous articles and reports. Home: 15 Highland Hills, Knoxville 16, Tenn. Died Dec. 6, 1956.

WATERS, Samuel M(athew), mortgage banker; b. Minneapolis, Minn., Mar. 22, 1883; s. Murray Randolph and Martha (Nicholson) W.; LL.B., U. of Minn., 1906; m. Nora Barnett, Nov. 6, 1907; children—Murray Barnett, Lenore (Mrs. Russell Fredsall). Admitted to Minn. bar, 1906; v.p. State Bank of Bethel and State Bank of Lonsdale, Minn., 1906-09; asso. with M. R. Waters & Sons, Inc. (mortgage bankers), Minneapolis, since 1909, v.p., 1909-35, pres. since 1935. Pres. Mortgage Bankers Assn. of Am., 1938-39; chmn., ways and means com., Mortgage Bankers Assn. of America. Mem. National Agrl. Credit Com. Mem. Christian Ch. Clubs: Minneapolis, Minnesota; Union League (Chicago). Home: 4315 E. Lake Harriet Blvd. Office: 1036 Baker Bldg., Mpls. 2. Died July 4, 1952; buried Lakewood Cemetery, Mpls.

WATERS, William Laurence, engr.; b. London, Eng.; s. Rev. William and Ellen (Turnbull) W.; Central Technical College (London University), C.E. and M.E., 1898; m. Hilda Johnston, Milwaukee, Wis., 1906; 1 dau., Carolinda; m. 2d, Mildred M. Warner, Baltimore, 1942. With L. & S. Ry., London, Eng., 1898-1901; chief engr., Nat. Brake & Electric Co., Milwaukee, 1901-05; consulting engr., Westinghouse Air Brake and Canadian Westinghouse and Westinghouse Electric & Mfg. cos., Pittsburgh, 1905-13; consulting engr. in pvt. practice, N.Y. City and Montreal, Can., since 1913; partner in Bury & Waters, consulting engrs., New York and London, Eng., with Sir George Bury (formerly sr. v.p. Canadian Pacific Ry.). Episcopalian. Mem. Am. Inst. E.E., Am. Soc. M.E., Am. Soc. C.E., Engr. Inst. of Can. Clubs: University (Milwaukee and Pittsburgh); Bankers, Economic, Sleepy Hollow Country (New York). Home: 3 Westview Av., White Plains, N.Y. Died 1956.

WATERS, William P., communications exec.; b. N.Y.C., Mar. 21, 1886; s. Hugh and Sarah (Sullivan) W.; B.C.S. cum laude, N.Y.U., 1918; N.Y. Post Grad. Sch. Accountancy, 1920; m. Adelaide Hamill, Sept. 7, 1910; children—Marion (Mrs. Curtis Nunn), Virginia (Mrs. Allen Gein). Treas. The Western Union Telegraph Co., N.Y.C., 1949-—, Teleregister Corp., 1949-—; asst. treas. Am. Dist. Telegraph Co., N.Y.C., 1940-—; dir. N.Y. Mut. Telegraph Co., So. and Atlantic Telegraph Co., Gold & Stock Telegraph Co., Internat. Ocean Telegraph Co. Mem. N.Y. Stock Transfer Assn., Beta Gamma Sigma. Elk, K.C. Home: Two Hillside Terr., Packanack Lake, N.J. Office: 60 Hudson St., N.Y.C. 13. Died May 6, 1957.

WATKIN, William Ward, architect; b. Boston, Mass., Jan. 21, 1886; s. Fred Ward and Mary Mathilda (Hancock) W.; grad. high school, Danville, Pa., 1903; B.S. in Architecture, University of Pa., 1908; studied and traveled in Europe; m. Annie Ray Townsend, June 1, 1914 (died Paris, France, Mar. 2, 1929); children—Annie Ray (wife of Lt. Col. Carl Biehl), Rosemary (wife of Lt. Nolan Barrick, U.S.N.), William Ward (maj., U.S. Army); m. 2d, Josephine Cockrell Watkin, Oct. 19, 1933. Practiced with Cram, Goodhue and Ferguson, architects, Boston and N.Y., 1908-10; assoc. architect, Rice Inst., Houston, Tex., 1910-14; instr. in architecture, Rice Inst., 1912-15, asst. prof., 1915-22, prof. since 1922. Architect for Chem. Lab., Faculty Club and Stadium, Rice Inst.; Museum of Fine Arts; Public Library; Palmer Memorial Chapel; Golding Chapel, Christ Church, Central Ch. of Christ, etc., Houston; St. Mark's Ch., Beaumont; cons. architect Houston Public Schools, 1923-25; Methodist Hospital, Houston, 1951; associate architect Y.W.C.A. Buildings, Beaumont, Galveston and Houston, Tex.; cons. architect Fondren Library, Abercrombie Engring. Lab., Rice Inst., and Tex. Tech. Coll., Lubbock, Tex. Del. Hispano-Am. Expn., Seville, Spain, 1929. Mem. Bd. Archtl. Consultants on Federal (triangle) Bldgs., Washington, D.C., U.S. Treasury Dept. Mem. spl. adv. com. Sch. of Fine Arts, U. of Pa., 1949. Fellow American Institute Architects; mem. Houston Philos. Soc. (pres. 1931), Tex. Philos. Soc. Pres. Southwest Athletic Conf., 1920; v.p. A.A.A.E., 1941. Episcopalian. Republican. Clubs: Faculty (ex-pres.), Torch, Houston Country. Author: Impressions of Modern Architecture, 1931; The Church of Tomorrow, 1935; Planning and Building the Modern Church, 1951; also numerous articles in professional jours. Home: 5009 Caroline St. Office: Rice Institute, Houston 1. Died June 24, 1952.

WATKINS, Arthur Charles (wŏt'kinz), educator; b. Sandy Creek, N.Y., Nov. 30, 1873; s. Charles and Lucy Almira (Woodruff) W.; A.B., Johns Hopkins U., 1895; grad. student (Fogg honor scholar) Yale, 1897-99; grad. student, Columbia, 1899-1900; B.D., Union Theol. Sem., New York, 1900; grad. student same, 1900-01; m. Florence Elizabeth Van Auken, August 19, 1896; 1 daughter, Olive Lucy (Mrs. F. G. Leasure). Church and social work, and lecturing, New York, 1900-04, and 1910-16; dir. Beth-Eden Community House, Philadelphia, 1918-19; pres. Northern Liberties Community Workers, Philadelphia, 1918-19; owned and operated pvt. press, New York, 1899-1904; organized, owned and operated The Univ. Press, Sewanee, Tenn., 1904-06; editor Mt. Pleasant Press, Harrisburg, Pa., 1916-18; editor Forest Service, U.S. Dept. Agr., Washington, D.C., 1919-24; asso. sec. Nat. Council for Prevention of War, Washington, 1924-38; organizer and dir. Nat. Student Forum on the Paris Pact since 1929; operated The Two Oaks Press since 1943; spl. lecturer, summer session, Columbia U., 1922, 23, summer conf., Isles of Shoals, 1922, 23, 24; instr. and lecturer on internat. relations, summer 1933, Univ. of Utah. Mem. N.E.A. (dept. secondary sch. principals), Phi Kappa Psi, Beta Delta Beta. Presbyterian. Clubs: Cosmos, Chevy Chase Citizens Assn. (Washington). Author: The Paris Pact, 1931-32; The Story of the Paris Pact, 1934; The Paris Pact and International Relations in American High Schools, 1934-38; America Stands for Pacific Means, 1937; Does America Stand for Pacific Means?, 1947. Frequent contbr. to ednl. jours. Home: 3365 Rittenhouse St. N.W., Washington 15, D.C. Died April 24, 1953.

WATKINS, Elton, Sr., lawyer; b. Newton, Miss., July 6, 1881; s. M. M. and Virginia (Williams) Watkins; A.B., Washington and Lee U.; LL.B., Georgetown U.; Master's Degree, George Washington Law Sch.; m. Daniela Ruth Sturges, Nov. 26, 1918; children—Eton, Wilma Virginia (Mrs. Frederick Earl Weber, Jr.). Admitted to Ore. bar; active law practice, Portland, 1912-—; asst. U.S. atty. for Ore., 1919. Dem. presdl. elector from Ore., 1920, 36 and 44; mem. 68th Congress, 3d Ore. Dist. Democrat. Baptist. Home: 2686 S. W. Vista Av. Office: Failing Bldg., Portland, Ore. Died June 24, 1956; buried Greenwood Cemetery, Portland.

WATKINS, Everett C., newspaper corr.; b. Lincoln, Cass County, Ind.; s. Benjamin Franklin and Ora L. (Conner) W.; ed. pub. schs.; unmarried. Reporter, later mng. editor Marion (Ind.) Chronicle; then polit. reporter Indpls. Star, Washington corr. 1917-—. Alternate del. from Ind. to Rep. Nat. Conv., 1928. Mem. White House Corrs. Assn., Sigma Delta Chi. Club: National Press. Home: 716 S. Gallatin St., Marion, Ind. Died Nov. 6, 1955.

WATKINS, Frank Thomas, naval officer; b. Provo City, Utah, Dec. 15, 1898; s. Charles Frederick and Mary Elizabeth (Kearney) W.; B.S., U.S. Naval Acad., 1922; m. Margaret Ruth Orem, July 11, 1925; children—Frank Thomas, John O. Commd. ensign, USN, 1922, advanced through grades to vice adm., 1957; chief staff to comdr. submarines Pacific Fleet, 1946-47; comdg. officer U.S. Naval Sch., Monterey, Cal., 1948-49; asst. chief naval personnel Navy Dept., Washington, 1949-51; comdr. cruiser div. 2 U.S. Atlantic Fleet, 1951; comdr. mine for Atlantic Fleet, 1952-53; dep. chmn. naval operations, 1953-54; comdr. submarines Atlantic Fleet, 1954-57, comdr. Anti-Submarine Force, Atlantic Fleet, 1957-—. Decorated Legion of Merit, B.S.M. Mem. Phi Sigma Kappa. Home: 1549 N. Harvard Blvd., Hollywood, Cal. Office: Bureau of Naval Personnel, Navy Dept., Washington. Deceased.

WATLING, John Wright, investment banker; b. Ypsilanti, Mich., June 17, 1883; s. John A. and Eunice W. (Wright) Watling; A.B., U. of Mich., 1904; m. Sallie Rice, 1906; children—John W. Jr., Palmer, William B.; married 2d Roxane Loud Pierson, December 26, 1928. Entered the security business as a bond salesman, 1904; manager of the Detroit office, Bolger, Mosser & Willaman (Chicago), 1908-15; partner Watling, Lerchen & Co., since 1915. Mem. bd. govs. Investment Bankers Assn. of America, 1939-42, Assn. of Stock Exchange Firms, 1942-44; mem. bd. management, W. L. Clements Library, Univ. of Mich.; former dir. Detroit chapter A.R.C., campaign chmn. War Fund of 1943. Vice chmn. Michigan War Finance Com. (banking div.), during World War II. Mem. bd. trustees, Brookside, Cranbrook and Kingswood Schools; chairman of the executive com. of

The Clements Library Associates. Director Kingswood School, Cranbrook. Member Phi Kappa Psi. Republican. Episcopalian. Clubs: Detroit, University, Bond, Economic (Detroit); Bloomfield Hills (Mich.) Country; Groiler (New York). Home: Long Lake Rd., Bloomfield Hills, Mich. Office: 3d Floor, Ford Bldg., Det. 26. Died Dec. 22, 1951.

WATROUS, Richard Benedict, b. Black River Falls, Wis., July 19, 1869; s. Jerome Anthony and Ellen Mary (Benedict) W.; student Lawrence University, Appleton, Wis.; m. Clara Crowther Noble, Apr. 18, 1895; children—Ada Marcella (Mrs. W. D. Collins, dec.), Jerome Anthony, Richard Benedict (dec.). Associate editor, bus. mgr. Milwaukee Telegraph, 1890-1900; sec Citizens Business League, Milwaukee, 1900-09; sec. Am. Civic Assn., 1909-17; sec. Nestle's Food Co., 1919-21; sec. Providence C. of C., 1922-41; sec. R.I. Div. New England Council. Pres. Civic Improvement and Park Assn., Providence, 1935—. Mem. N.Y. Commandery Loyal Legion; hon. mem. R.I. chapter Am. Inst. Architects. Republican. Episcopalian. Mason. Clubs: Turks Head, Providence Art (Providence); Army and Navy (Washington, D.C.). Home: 68 Charles Field St. Office: Chamber of Commerce, 162 Westminster St., Providence, R.I. Deceased.

WATSON, Albert, lawyer; b. Mt. Vernon, Ill., Apr. 15, 1857; s. Joel F. and Sarah M. (Taylor) W.; B.S., McKendree Coll., Lebanon, Ill., 1876, LL.D., 1928; m. Mary E. Way, Aug. 12, 1880; children—Mrs. Marine W. Frazier, Joel F., Alice E., Isabel (dec.), Stanley. Admitted to Ill. bar, 1880, and since practiced in Mt. Vernon; dir. and atty. King City Federal Savings and Loan Assn.; city atty., 1881; master in chancery, 1890; states attorney, 1892; judge Illinois Supreme Court, 1915; pres. Ill. State Board Law Examiners, 1915-35. Democrat. Methodist. Member Knights of Pythias (past grand chancellor of Illinois). Home: 402 N. 10th St. Office: 908 Main St., Mt. Vernon, Ill. Died Nov. 25, 1944; buried Oakwood Cemetery, Mt. Vernon.

WATSON, Archibald Robinson, lawyer, pub. official; b. Holly Springs, Miss.; s. James Henry and Annah Walker (Robinson) W.; B.L., U. of Va., 1894; m. Margaret Percival O'Neil, Aug. 3, 1904; children—Nancy, Archibald R. Practiced law, N.Y. City, since 1902; corp. counsel under Mayor Gaynor, 1910-14; founder Bench & Bar, 1905, editor 10 yrs.; founder New York Law Rev., 1923, now dir. corp.; former owner, pub., cons. editor Living Age mag., U.S. Law Review; editor N.Y. Law Journal 1932—. Clk. Supreme Court of N.Y. and county clerk of N.Y. County, 1937—. Del. Dem. Nat. Conv., 1912; presdl. elector, N.Y. State, 1940, 44; del. 20th Congl. Dist. Dem. Nat. Conv., 1944. Mem. Am., N.Y. State, bar assns., Assn. Bar City of N.Y., N.Y. County Lawyers' Assn., Soc. Mayflower Descs., S.R., Order of Runnemede, Kappa Alpha, Phi Delta Phi, Phi Beta Kappa. Democrat. Episcopalian. Club: Metropolitan. Address: 60 Centre St., N.Y.C. 7. Died Oct. 26, 1957; buried Smithtown, L.I., N.Y.

WATSON, Drake, lawyer; born New London, Mo., Mar. 28, 1885; s. Fontaine B. and Sallie Mariah (Priest) W.; LL.B., Mo. Univ., 1907. Admitted to Mo. bar, 1907, and practiced in New London since; asst. atty. gen. of Mo., 1935-39, 46-47; spl. asst. U.S. atty., 1941-44; U.S. atty. for Eastern Judicial Dist., Mo., 1947-51; mem. Mo. legislature for 3 terms, 1913, 15, 17, speaker of House, 1917; engaged in farming, New London, since 1907. Chmn. Legal Adv. Bd., World War I; govt. appeal agt., World War II; regent, Northeast Mo. State Teachers Coll., 1919-25; procured passage of law creating Mo. Univ. trust fund for students, 1915; dir., Ralls Co. State Bank. Mem. Mo. Bar Assn., 10th Judicial Dist. Bar Assn. (past pres.). Democrat. Baptist. Mason. Home: New London, Mo. Died Dec. 25, 1951; buried Barkley Cemetery, New London, Mo.

WATSON, Edith Sarah, artist; b. East Windsor Hill, Conn., Nov. 9, 1861; d. Reed and Sarah (Bolles) W.; ed. pvt. schs. Water color artist, photographic illustrator. Exhibited Boston Art Club; San Francisco Expn., 1915; every winter in Bermuda. Many photographs in newspapers and mags. Democrat. Episcopalian. Collaborator with Victoria Hayward in Romantic Canada, 1922. Home: East Windsor Hill, Conn. Deceased.

WATSON, Emile Emdon, consulting actuary; b. nr. Miami, Saline County, Mo., Feb. 7, 1885; s. Benjamin Frank and Sarah Ellen (Hawk) W.; B.A., William Jewell Coll., 1908, M.A., 1909; grad. work, Univ. of Chicago, 1909-11; LL.D., Florida Southern Coll., 1945; L.H.D. (honorary), Philathea College, London, Ontario, 1946; Litt. D. (honorary), St. Andrews University, 1954; Ph.D. (honorary), Chatham Hill Coll.; married Melisse Baye Wadlington, Aug. 16, 1911; children—Benjamin Wayne, Emile Enoch, William Wallace, Sallie Melisse, Gwendolyn Rita. Began as statistician, Chicago, 1910; moved to Columbus, O., 1911; actuarial work for states of N.Y., Md., W.Va., Ohio, Illinois, N.D., Ore., Idaho, also Ill. Mfrs. Mut. Casualty Assn., Associated Industries of Mo. and a large number of employers' assns. and industrial corps. Cons. actuary to Bur. War Risk, U.S. Treasury Dept., and adviser to com. on ins., War Dept., World War I; upon invitation of the gov. of Puerto Rico has made 4 actuarial surveys of the island, 1926, 1931, 1935 and 1951, consultant actuary to Puerto Rico Workmen's Compensation Plan, 1935-41; cons. actuary State Ins. Fund of Puerto Rico, 1952—; governmental actuarial survey for Hawaii, 1954; survey for Brazil, 1954. Assisted the War Department in connection with Ohio war industries; mem. Ohio Production for Victory Committee; advisory services on absenteeism and loss of man power during World War II. General chairman for Ohio, 1st birthday ball for President Franklin D. Roosevelt, January 30, 1934, director organization of National Committee of 2d birthday ball for the President, Jan. 30, 1935, also mem. Nat. Com.; chmn. Survey of Infantile Paralysis for Warm Springs Foundation, 1934-35; made personal study of social ins. plans of leading countries of Europe, 1935; cons. New York Unemployment Insurance Plan, 1935. Received Citation for Speical Achievement, William Jewell Coll., 1945, Silver Medallion of Merit, Am. Internat. Acad. N.Y.C., 1954; Diploma & Medallion, Found. Internat. Elroy Elfaro of Panama, 1955. Fellow Consular Law Soc. N.Y.; mem. Am. Soc Internat. Law, National Social Sci. Honor Society, Am. Internat. Acad. (acad. council and senate), Am. Sociological Society, Acad. Political Science, Ohio Society of New York, Lambda Chi Alpha; associate member International Assn. of Industrial Accident Bds. and Commns., Royal Society of St. George, London, Pi Gamma Mu. Mason. Clubs: Columbus Rotary, Columbus Athletic, Scioto Country, Business Men's (Columbus); Cincinnati. Rl. est. in Florida, Ohio and Canada. New Admnstrn. bldg. at Fla. Southern Coll. dedicated in his honor. Author: Is Civilization Gaining or Losing Ground, 1948; Compulsory Military Training, 1945; Dynamic Power of Educational Training, 1949; Can Man Use This Earth, 1949; The Human Value World, 1950; Godless Stalinism—Whose Will Shall Be Done?, 1951; meditations of Joseph Stalin, 1952; An Actuarial Analysis of Man. Home: 1801 Roxbury Rd., Upper Arlington. Office: LeVeque-Lincoln Tower, Columbus, O. Died Jan. 31, 1958.

WATSON, F(rank) B(ingley), army officer (retired); b. Sharp's Wharf (now Sharps), Va., Feb. 9, 1870; s. Charles Clark and Mary (Wheeler) W.; B.S., U.S. Mil. Acad., 1895; grad. Army Sch. of the Line, 1912; grad. Army War College, 1921; married to Sara Maria Wetherill Dunn, November 1, 1898 (deceased May 10, 1952); one son, Numa Augustin. Apprentice and journeyman printer National Standard Printing office, Salem, New Jersey, 1886-91; commd. additional 2d lt. 19th inf., U.S. Army, 1895, and advanced through grades to brig. gen., Aug. 8, 1918; served in U.S., 1895-98, Puerto Rico, 1898-99 and Philippines, 1899-02, Alaska, 1904-06; Philippines, 1909-11, comd. 3d inf. detachment in expdn. against hostile natives, Mindanao, 1910; capt. Q.M. corps, asst. to constructing Q.M. and comdr. Army Service Detachment, West Point, N.Y., 1912-15; Mexican border, 26th Inf., 1915-17; 153d Depot Brig., Camp Dix, N.J., 1917; comd. 115th inf. 29th div., Camp McClellan, Ala., 1917-18; War Dept. gen. staff, 1918; comd. 13th div. and 26th brig., Am. Lake, Washington, 1918-19; comd. U.S. Troops, Butte, Mont., 1919; comdr. Presidio of San Francisco, Calif., 1919; col., asst. to constructing Q.M. and comdr. army service detachment, West Point, N.Y., 1919-20; comd. 52d inf., camp exec. and acting chief of staff 6th div., Camp Grant, Ill., 1921; comd. 2d inf., Ft. Sheridan, Ill., 1921-23; 1st corps area recruiting officer, Boston, 1923-27; sr. instr., Md. Nat. Guard, 1927-31; comd. 35th inf. Schofield Barracks, Hawaii, 1931-34; ret. brig. gen., Feb. 28, 1934. Mem. Assn. of Grads. of U.S. Mil. Acad. (sr. v.p., 1950), Army Athletic Assn., (U.S. Mil. Acad.), U.S. Inf. Assn., Am. Legion, 29th Div. Assn., Wash. chapt. No. 3, Nat. Sojourners Lodge 51 (charter mem., gov. 1940-50), Salem County Historical Soc., Heroes of 76 (New Eng.) D.C. chpt. Military Order World Wars, New Jersey State Society, Mil. Order of the Carabao. Republican. Presbyn. Clubs: Army and Navy (Boston, Washington). Mason (32°. Home: 317 Atlantic St., Bridgeton, N.J. Died July 24, 1955; buried West Point, N.Y.

WATSON, Frank Dekker, prof. sociology; b. Phila., June 28, 1883; s. Edward Hagner and Margaret (Halfman) W.; grad. Central High Sch., Phila., 1902; B.S. in Economics, Wharton Sch. Finance and Commerce, U. of Pa., 1905; Ph.D., U. of Pa., 1911; m. Amey Brown Eaton, Mar. 19, 1913; children—Mason Hagner, Roger Eaton, Curtis Brown, Peter Dekker. Asst. prin. schools, Quakertown, Pa., 1905-06; instr., Wharton Sch. Finance and Commerce, 1906-11; acting instr., Swarthmore (Pa.) Coll., 1908-11; mem. permanent staff New York Sch. of Philanthropy, 1911-14; prof. sociology and social work, Haverford Coll., 1914-49, emeritus; dir. relief and rehabilitation in Greece, Congl. Christian Service Com., Am. Bd. Commrs. for Fgn. Missions, 1950-53; dir. Pa. Sch. of Social Service, 1918-21; lecturer, Temple U., 1924-25. Dir. Red Cross institutes, southeast Pa. chapter, and member fuel commn., Delaware County, Pa., World War. Trustee White-Williams Foundation, 1920-30, pres. bd., 1921-26; dir. Race Relations Inst., Swarthmore, Pa., 1935; special labor economist Dept. of Labor and Industry, Commonwealth of Pa., 1937-38; lecturer, Pub. Service Inst., Dept. of Pub. Instruction, Commonwealth of Pa., 1938-39. Panel chairman Regional War Labor Board, 1943-45. Mem. Am. Sociol. Soc., Am. Acad. Polit. and Social Science (editor May 1918 Annals), Phi Btea Kappa, Sigma Phi Epsilon, Delta Sigma Rho, Pi Gamma Mu. Democrat. Quaker. Club: Mountain View Country (Greensboro, Vt.). Author: Economics (with Scott Nearing); The Charity Organization Movement in the United States, 1922. Home 36 Railroad Av., Haverford, Pa. Died Feb. 22, 1959, buried Phila. Meml. Park, Malvern, Pa.

WATSON, George Henry, mining; b. Hancock, Mich., Apr. 30, 1883; s. James and Julia (Harrington) W.; ed. pub. schs., Hancock; m. Agnes Kisselburgh, Oct. 5, 1911; children—Agnes Braid, Alta Patricia (dec.). Pres., mgr., Geo. H. Watson & Co., mines and minerals, Alta United Mines Co. Mayor of romantic Alta, Utah (old silver mining camp). Awarded medal by U.S. Govt. for extraordinary service rendered during Victory Loan drive, Salt Lake City, World War I. Organizer and scribe of Great Am. Prospectors Assn.; dir. Salt Lake City Winter Sports Assn. Donated 1800 acres of Alpine mountain land in and surrounding the old silver mining village of Alta, Utah, to U.S. for development of winter and summer recreation (internat. experts have pronounced this one of the finest ski and mountain climbing areas in the world). Mem. Salt Lake City Chamber of Commerce. Republican. Elk, K.C. Home Alta, Utah. Office: 22½ E. First South St., Salt Lake City. Died Mar. 28, 1952; buried Mt. Calvary Cemetery, Salt Lake City.

WATSON, Harry Legare, editor, pub.; b. Phoenix Greenwood County, S.C., July 11, 1876; s. Johnson Sale and Charlotte Louisa (Moseley) W.; Furman U. 2 yrs.; A.B., U. of North Carolina, 1899; hon. Litt.D. U. S.C., 1938; m. Ella Dargan, June 27, 1900 (dec.) children—Louise M., John D., Elizabeth S. (Mrs. J F. Potter), Johnson Sale (dec.), Margaret J., Ell Virginia (Mrs. W. H. Logan, Jr.). Began wit Greenwood Index, later consolidated with Greenwoo Journal, 1900; president Index-Journal Co.; admitte to the bar of S.C., 1908. Del. to Dem. Nat. Conv. 1912, 20; fuel adminstr., Greenwood County, 1917 19; member Greenwood County Highway Commn. mem. advisory bd. for S.C. of N.Y. World's Fair 1939. Lt. col. on staff of Gov. Wilson G. Harvey Trustee Furman U., 1912-24; chmn. bd. Greenwoo public schools 1915-52. Past Ex-president South Caro lina Press Association Furman University Alumni As sociation; mem. South Carolina Hist. Assn., S.A.R. Pendleton Farmers Soc., Southern Hist. Assn., P Gamma Mu, Kappa Alpha. Baptist. Mason (K.T. Shriner). Clubs: National Press; Rotary. Home: 42 Taggart St., Greenwood, S.C. Died Nov. 6, 1956 buried Magnolia Cemetery, Greenwood.

WATSON, James Gray, editor; b. Crosshouse, Ayr shire, Scotland, Mar. 14, 1886; s. John and Agne (Gray) W.; B.S., Ia. State Coll., 1913, hon. M.S Agr., 1921; m. Priscilla Morris Scott, June 26, 1920 1 son, Donald Scott. Came to U.S. 1906, naturaliz ed, 1921. Asst. prof. of dairy extension, Ia. Stat Coll., 1913-15; asso. prof. of dairy extension, U of Mo., 1915-16; dir. of extension Ayrshire Breeder Assn., Brandon, Vt., 1916-17, sec.-treas., 1917-22 live stock sales mgr. and commn. agent, 1922-23 live stock editor New England Homestead, Spring field, Mass., 1923-32, editor, 1932—; president an partner New England Homestead Company. Organize and developed sheep dog trials in United States judge of dairy cattle at state fairs and expns.; speak er on agrl. topics. Trustee and mem. exec. com Eastern States Exposition, Springfield, Mass. Pres Am. Agrl. Editors Association, 1943. Mem. Amer can Society Animal Production. Dairy Science Ass Republican. Conglist. Mason (K.T., Shriner) Founded Ayrshire Quarterly (now Ayrshire Digest) Home: 192 Converse, Longmeadow, Mass. Office: 2 Worthington, Springfield 3, Mass. Died Aug. 8, 1956 buried Brandon, Vt.

WATSON, James Sibley, banker; b. Rochester, N Y., Mar. 11, 1860; s. Don Alonzo and Carolir (Manning) W.; B.S., U. Rochester, 1881; m. Emi Sibley, 1891; 1 son, James Sibley. Began bankin bus., Rochester, 1882; pres. Security Trust Co Rochester Savs. Bank; dir. Eastman Kodak Co. Club University, Knickerbocker, New York Yacht (Ne York); Genesee Valley (Rochester). Home: 11 Prin St. Office: Security Trust Co., Rochester, N.Y. Die May 4, 1951.

WATSON, James Webster, coll. prof.; b. La Cross Wis., Jan. 16, 1879; s. Aaron Martin and Jenn (Webster) W.; B.S., U. of Wis., 1902; m. Eth Churchill, Sept. 12, 1910; children—Charles Churc ill, Robert Webster, James Webster, Richard Churc ill. Instr. elec. engring., Univ. of Wis., 1903-0 asst. prof., 1908-20, asso. prof., 1920-28, prof. sin 1928, chmn. dept. elec. engring. since 1939. Di Beecroft Bldg. Assn. Mem. Am. Inst. Elec. Engrin Soc. for Promotion Engring. Edn., Madison Techn cal Club, Tau Beta Pi, Pi Kappa Sigma. Clu University (Madison). Protestant. Republican. Hom 2116 Monroe St., Madison, Wis. Died Oct. 4, 195

WATSON, John B(roadus), psychologist; b. Greenville, S.C., Jan. 9, 1878; s. Pickens Butler and Emma K. (Roe) W.; A.M., Furman U., 1900; grad. student in psychology U. Chgo., 1900-03, Ph.D., 1903; LL.D., Furman U., 1919; m. Mary Ickes, Oct. 1, 1904; children—Mary I., John I.; m. 2d, Rosalie Rayner, Dec. 31, 1920; children—William Rayner, James Broadus. Prin. Batesburg Inst., 1899-1900; asst. in exptl. psychology U. Chgo., 1903-04, instr., 1904-08; prof. exptl. and comparative psychology, dir. psychol. lab., Johns Hopkins, 1908-20; became v.p. J. Walter Thompson Co., N.Y., 1924; v.p. William Esty & Co., N.Y., 1936. Editor Psychol. Rev., 1908-15, Jour. Exptl. Psychology, 1915-27. Commd. maj. Aviation Sect., Signal Corps, U.S.R., 1917; on duty, Washington, Mineola, and with A.E.F. Fellow Am. Acad. Arts and Scis.; mem. Am. Psychol. Assn. (pres. 1915), Am. Physiol. Soc., Sigma Xi, Phi Beta Kappa, Kappa Alpha (Southern). Author: Animal Education, 1903; Behavior, 1914; Homing and Related Activities of Birds, 1915; Suggestions of Modern Science Concerning Education, 1917; Psychology from the Standpoint of the Behaviorist, 1919; Behaviorism, 1925, rev. edit., 1930; Ways of Behaviorism, 1928; Psychological Care of Infant and Child, 1928. Contbr. on neurology, animal and infant psychology. Home: Park Rd., Woodbury, Conn. Died Sept. 25, 1958; buried Willowbrook Cemetery, Westport, Conn. Died Sept. 25, 1958, buried Willowbrook Cemetery, Westport, Conn.

WATSON, John Thomas (J. Tom), lawyer; b. Danville, Va., Nov. 20, 1885; s. George Alanson and Sallie Ross (Keen) W.; LL.B., Washington and Lee U., 1911; m. Mary Wicks Boisseau, Nov. 11, 1915; children—Patrick Boisseau, John Thomas, Jr., Deane Carrell. Supt. Havana-Am. Cigar Co., Tampa, Florida, 1903-08; admitted to Fla. and Va. bars, 1911; began practice; municipal judge, Tampa, 1913-15; mem. Fla. Legislature, 1931; U.S. spl. atty. Dept. of Justice, 1935-38; atty. gen., Florida, 1940-48; now practicing attorney at Tampa, Fla. Pres. Nat. Assn. Attys. Gen., 1948. Mem. Phi Delta Theta, Phi Delta Phi. Presbyn. Elk, Mason (32°, K.T., Shriner). Home: 850 S. Newport Av., Tampa. Office: Stovall Prof. Bldg., Tampa, Fla. Died Oct. 24, 1954; buried Danville, Va.

WATSON, Thomas John, chmn. IBM Corp. and IBM World Trade Corp.; b. Campbell, N.Y., Feb. 17, 1874; s. Thomas and Jane (White) W.; ed. Addison (N.Y.) Acad. and Elmira Sch. of Commerce; LL.D., Lafayette Coll. and Rutgers U., 1934, Colgate U., 1936, Cumberland U., 1936, Syracuse U., 1940, Hendrix Coll., 1941, Northeastern U., 1944, Mt. Allison U. (Can.), 1945, Tusculum Coll., 1946, U. State N.Y., 1946, U. Fla., 1952, Elmira College, 1952, U. Vt. and State Agrl. Coll., 1952, Bucknell U.; L.H.D. (Humanities), Rollins Coll., 1935, Boston U., 1943; Bryant College, 1945; D.Eng., Stevens Inst. of Tech., 1936; D.Sc., Alfred U., 1936, Universidad Nacional Mayor de San Marcos (Lima, Peru), 1950, Genoble (France) U., 1950, Georgetown U., 1951, Colo. State Coll. Edn., 1951; D.Bus.Admn., U. So. Cal., 1940; D.Social Sc., Fla. So. Coll., 1949, U. Liege (Belgium), 1952; D.C.S., Ogelthorpe U., 1939, Drexel Inst. Tech., 1944, N.Y. U., 1950; hon. rector, U. Dubuque, 1948-49; A.F.D., Kan. City Art Inst. and Sch. of Design, 1950; D.C.L. h.c., Union College and University, 1953; m. Jeannette M. Kittredge, Apr. 17, 1913; children—Thomas J., Jane (Mrs. John N. Irwin, II), Helen Mary (Mrs. Walker G. Buckner), Arthur Kittredge. Connected for 15 yrs. with Nat. Cash Register Co. as br. mgr., spl. rep. and gen. sales mgr.; pres. and dir. Internat. Bus. Machines Corp., 1914-49, chmn. bd., chief exec. officer, 1949-56, chmn. bd., 1956—; dir. Guaranty Trust Co. of N.Y., Niagara Fire Ins. Co., Fidelity-Phenix Fire Ins. Co. of New York; dir. Am. Assn. for U.N., Inc.; mem. Am. Brazilian Assn.; hon. mem. Am. Businessmen's Club (Amsterdam); mem. Am. C. of C. in France; life trustee Am. Scandinavian Found.; member British Commonwealth Chamber of Commerce in U.S.; hon. trustee Carnegie Endowment for Internat. Peace; mem. Council on Foreign Relations; gov. Dunford House Assn. (England); sponsor Folke-Bernadotte Meml. Found.; dir., France-America Soc., Norwegian-Am. C. of C., Swedish C. of C. of United States; honorary member United States Council and hon. pres. Internat. C. of C. (past pres.); trustee Koskiuszko Found.; mem., Nat. Foreign Trade Council, hon. pres., Am. Soc. of U.S., Inc.; charter mem. Peruvian-Am. Assn.; mem. nat. adv. bd. Am. Merchant Marine Library Association; International Commissioner Boy Scouts of America; trustee, Brick Presbyterian Church, Columbia U., Cordell Hull Found. for Internat. Edn., Nat. Fund for Med. Edn., Religious Edn. Assn. of Nat. Council of Chs. of Christ in U.S.A., vice pres. bd. of trustees Lafayette Coll.; mem. sponsors com., Christian Laymen for Youth of Nat. Council of Chs. of Christ in U.S.A.; life mem. New York State Congress of Parents and Tchrs. (Endicott, N.Y.); v.p., dir. Fedn. of Protestant Welfare Agencies; dir. Internat. Assn. of Daily Vacation Bible Sch. Sportsmanship Brotherhood; mem., Laymen's Movement for Christian World, Inc.; sponsor Nat. Conf. Christians and Jews; mem. Nat. Council Chs. Christ in U.S.A.; trustee Religious Edn. Assn.; mem. N.Y. Acad. Sci.; trustee, life mem. Air Force Acad. Soc.; nat. sponsor, Disabled Am. Vets. Service Found.; council mem. Eye Bank for Sight Restoration, Inc.; dir., Salvation Army Assn. N.Y., Travelers Aid Soc. N.Y.; nat. patron hon. Mil. Order Purple Heart; trustee Nat. Found. for Inf. Paralysis; life mem. Navy League, U.S., Inc., v.p., dir. Acad. Polit. Sci.; mem. Advertising Club of N.Y., Am. Acad. of Polit. and Social Sci. (Phila.), C. of C. of U.S. (past dir.), Commerce and Industry Assn. of N.Y., Inc. (past pres.), Commonwealth Club of Cal., Economic Club of N.Y. (past pres.), Ind. Adv. Assn. of N.Y., Inc., Nat. Assn. Mfrs., Sales Exec. Club N.Y.; dir. Am. Arbitration Assn.; life mem. and commr. U.S. sect. Canadian-Am. Comml. Arbitration Commn.; hon. chmn. Inter-Am. Commn.; trustee, Am. Heritage Found., Nat. Safety Council, Vassar Brothers Hosp. (Poughkeepsie, N.Y.); trustee Roosevelt Hosp.; council mem. Am. Ordnance Assn.; grad. mem. Bus. Adv. Council of Dept. of Commerce; dir., Fifth Avenue Assn., Greater N.Y. Safety Council, Inc.; councillor Nat. Indsl. Conf. Bd.; v.p. Nat. Inst. of Social Sci.; dir. Am.-Italy Soc., Inc., Franklin D. Roosevelt Meml. Found., Met. Opera Assn., Inc., Syracuse (N.Y.) Mus. of Art; sponsor Acad. of Am. Poets; mem. Am. Assn. of Mus.; Am. Friends of Lafayette, Am. Shakespeare Festival Found., Mus. City N.Y., Met. Opera Guild, Inc., Municipal Art Soc. N.Y., Mus. of Modern Art, Newark (N.J.) Mus., Newcomen Soc. of England (Am. branch), Philharmonic-Symphony Soc. N.Y., The Pilgrims, Rochester Hist. Soc., St. Andrews Soc. State N.Y., Soc. for the Advancement of Scandinavian Study; hon. trustee Am. com. Am. Library in Paris, Inc.; patron Am. Mus. Natural History; v.p., dir. Am. Soc. of French Legion of Honor; trustee Binghamton (N.Y.) Mus. Fine Arts, Grand Central Art Galleries, Kansas City Art Inst.; hon. trustee, Met. Mus. Art; fellow in perpetuity Nat. Acad. Design; hon. v.p. Nat. Arts Club; life mem. Pen and Pencil Club (Phila.), Pa. Acad. of Fine Arts; founding fellow Pierpont Morgan Library; fellow Rochester Mus. of Arts and Sciences; honorary mem. Society of American Graphic Arts, Inc.; vice president and trustee Thomas Alva Edison Found. Decorated Medal for Merit, U.S. War Dept., 1947; Order of the Crown of Belgium, Comdr., 1937, Grand Officer, 1946; Condor de los Andes, Bolivia, 1943; Nat. Order of So. Cross, Comdr., Brazil, 1939; Hon. Comdr., Most Excellent Order of the Brit. Empire, 1947; Grande Croix de Cambodge, Cambodia (Indo-China), 1939; Grand Officer, Bernardo O'Higgins Order of Merit, Chile, 1951; Order of Ching Hsin (Auspicious Star), Special Class, China, 1948; Knight, Order of Boyaca, Colombia, 1945; Comdr., Order of Carlos Manuel de Cespedes, Cuba, 1946; Comdr. 1st Grade Royal Order of Dannebrog, Denmark, 1939; Order of Juan Pablo Duarte, Dominican Republic, 1944; Officer Nat. Order of Merit, Ecuador, 1940, Grand Officer, 1943; Comdr. 1st Class Order of the White Rose, Finland, 1938; Chevalier of the Legion of Honor, France, 1934, Officer, 1935, Comdr., 1937, Grand Officer, 1950; Comdr., Royal Order of George I, Greece, 1938; Grand Officer of the National Order of Republic of Haiti, 1944; Cordon of Grande Croix, Hungary, 1939; Grand Officer, Grand Ducal Order of the Crown of Oak, Luxembourg, 1946; Order of the Aztec Eagle, Mexico, 1947; Officer, Order of Orange-Nassau, Netherlands, 1946; Comdr., Cross with Star, Royal Order of St. Olav, Norway, 1945; Eloy Alfaro Internat. Found. Cross, Republic of Panama, 1949; Comdr., Nat. Order of Merit, Paraguay, 1946; Grand Officer, Order of the Sun, Peru, 1943; Comdr., Ancient and Most Noble Mil. Order of Christ, Portugal, 1939; Comdr., Order of Vasa, Sweden, 1937; Knight, Royal Order of North Star, Sweden, 1937; Comdr., Order del Libertado, Venezuela, 1945; Insignia II Degree with Star, 1936 and Comdr. I Class, 1937, Order of the Yugoslav Crown; Hon. Citizen, Athens, Greece, 1945, Fontainbleau, France, 1948, Lima, Peru, 1950; Medal of City of Ghent (Belgium), 1950; six medals of the Province and City of Liege (Belgium), 1948 (Province of Liege, Liberation of City of Liege, Assn. of Eng. Montefiore Elec. Inst., U. of Liege, Liege Eng. Soc., and Honor Medal of Grads. U. of Liege). Received Captain Robert Dollar award, 1940; first Western Hemisphere arbitration award given by Inter-Am. Comml. Arbitration Commn., Am. Arbitration Assn. and Canadian-Am. Comml. Arbitration Commn., 1943; gold key of Delta Phi Epsilin for work in interest of world trade, 1940; first Internat. Award of Am. Arbitration Assn. for distinguished service in advancement of world peace through world trade, and arbitration as an Am. way of life, 1950; Silver Buffalo, Boy Scouts of Am., 1944; award N.Y. Acad. Pub. Edn., 1944; Russell Colgate Distinguished Service citation Internat. Council Religious Edn., 1947; Kansas City Art Inst. Medal, 1941; Gold Medal of Cuban C. of C. in U.S., 1947; Gold Medal of Nat. Inst. Social Scis., 1947; Gold Insigne of Pan Am. Soc. of the U.S. for "distinguished service in cause of Pan Americanism," 1947. Clubs: Automobile Old Timers (life mem. and dir.), Bankers (gov.), Columbia University, Dutchess Golf and Country (Poughkeepsie, N.Y.), Explorers, Jefferson Island (Sherwood, Md.), Kiwanis International (hon. mem.), Lafayette (Ind.) Country, Lotos, Metropolitan (former gov.) New Canaan (Conn.) Country, New York Yacht, Ohio Society of N.Y. (res. v.p.), River, Salmagundi, Union, Woodway Country (Stamford, Conn.). Presbyn. Home: 4 E. 75th St., N.Y.C. also New Canaan, Conn. Office: 590 Madison Av., N.Y.C. 22. Died June 19, 1956.

WATSON, William Franklin, scientist, traveler; b. N.B., Can., May 11, 1861; s. George Corey and Isabella (Byron) W.; A.B., Colby Coll., 1887, A.M., 1890, Sc.D., 1924; student univs. of Pa. and Chicago; m. Clara Norwood, June 24, 1889 (died Aug. 30, 1935); children—Ethel Drysdale (Mrs. Arthur L. Collins), Lucia Norwood (Mrs. Norman C. Mendes); m. 2d, Anette M. Phelan, Oct. 14, 1938. Prof. of chemistry, Furman U., Greenville, S.C., 1887-1912, of biology, 1898-1912, curator of museum, 1902-1912, sec. of faculty, 1904-11, lecturer, 1911-14. Mem. commn. apptd. by Nat. Civ. Fedn. to inspect ednl. instns. of Great Britain; lecturer on scientific subjects and travel. Experimenter in photographing with lenses from the eyes of insects and higher animals; originator of new methods in photo-micrography. Received medal of Charleston Expn., 1902, for invention of a method for concentration of monazite sand. Mem. Am. Microscopical Soc. (v.p., 1906), Navy League of U.S., Am. Nature Study Soc., Internat. Lyceum Assn., Am. Health League (advisory com), Ga. Acad. Science, Phi Delta Theta, Atlantic Union of London, London Teachers Assn., Royal Soc. of Arts, London, Société Linnéenne de Lyon, France; fellow A.A.A.S., Science League America. K.P. Clubs: Club of Thirty-nine of Greenville, S.C. (pres.), British Empire Club of London (hon.). Author: Children of the Sun (poems), 1887; Textbook on Experimental Chemistry, 1901; Laboratory Courses in Chemistry, 1895. Contbr. to periodicals, London, Paris, Madrid, and in U.S. Made tour of the world, 1912-13. Lecturer for Dept. of Edn., New York City, 1914-15. Address: 1539 3d Av., Bradenton, Fla. Died Mar. 22, 1953.

WATTERS, William Henry (wŏt'tĕrz), physician; b. Mechanic Falls, Me., June 23, 1876; s. William and Judith (Nichols) W.; A.B., McGill U., 1897; M.D., Boston U., 1900, M.A., 1907, Ph.D., 1909; m. Gertrude Hepburn, 1904; children—Preston Hepburn, Doris Nichols. Practiced, Boston, 1900—; prof. pathology, Boston U., 1903-25, prof. preventive medicine, 1925-35; emeritus prof. preventive medicine 1936—; asso. dept. legal medicine, Harvard Med. Sch.; founder med. dir. Boston-Miami Clinic, Coconut Grove, Miami, Fla.; asso. med. examiner Suffolk County. Republican. Fellow A.C.P.; mem. A.M.A., Am. Assn. Pathologists and Bacteriologists, Am. Assn. Clin. Pathologists, Mass. Med. Soc., Mass. Medico-Legal Soc. (pres. 1929-30), Mass. Surg. and Gynecol. Soc., Internat. Assn. Med. Museums. Mason. Clubs: Highland (West Roxbury); Com. of One Hundred (Miami Beach); Century (Coral Gables, Fla.); Harvard (Boston). Home: Coconut Grove, Miami, Fla. Died Oct. 11, 1949; buried Searsport, Me.

WATTLES, Willard Austin (wŏt'l'z), educator, author; b. Bayneville, Kan., June 8, 1888; s. Harvey Austin and Jennie (Fay) W.; A.B., Univ. of Kansas, 1909 (Phi Beta Kappa), M.A., 1911; LL.D., Rollins Coll., 1945; m. Mary Brownlee, June 17, 1926; 1 son, Austin Brownlee. Instr. in English, Leavenworth (Kan.) High Sch., 1909-10; fellow in English, U. of Kansas, 1910-11; instr. in English, Mass. State Coll., 1911-14, U. of Kan., 1914-20. Grad. student Princeton, 1920-21; asst. prof. English, Conn. State Coll., 1921-25; asst. prof. English, Oregon State Coll., 1925-27; prof. English, Rollins College since 1927; on staff Breadloaf School of English, 1929, Blowing Rock School of English, 1937; exchange prof. U. of Fla., 1930, Mass. State Coll., summer 1936. Mem. 10th Div. U.S. Army. Mem. Am. Editorial Assn., Poetry Soc. of America, MacDowell Assn., Kansas Authors' Club, N.E. Poetry Club, Oregon Writers League, Press Club (Portland), The Poets Club (New York), Grange, Am. Assn. Univ. Profs., Omicron Delta Kappa. Conglist. Mason. Compiler: (also contbr.) Sunflowers—A Book of Kansas Poems, 1914. Author: Lanterns in Gethsemane, 1918; The Funston Double-Track and Other Poems, 1919; A Compass for Sailors, 1928. Contbr. to "Songs from the Hill," 1911; contbr. to mags. Address: 455 Melrose Av., Winter Park, Fla. Died Sept. 25, 1950.

WATTS, Charles Henry, corp. exec.; b. Thamesville, Ont., Can., Apr. 27, 1881; s. Edward T. and Mary D. (Dickison) W.; ed. pub. schs. of Can., Mich.; m. Mabel Lamborn, Oct. 2, 1925; 1 son, Charles Henry II. Came to U.S., 1893, naturalized citizen. With Household Finance Corp., 1898-1925, supervisor Phila., 1925; pres., dir. Beneficial Management Corp., Newark, 1925-44, chmn. bd. and dir. since 1944; chmn. bd. and dir. Bankers Nat. Life Ins. Co., Beneficial Loan Corp. since 1944; dir. Firemen's Ins. Co., Newark. Chmn. bd. and dir. Nat. Better Bus. Bur., N.Y.; dir. N.J. State C. of C. Clubs: Metropolitan, Bankers (N.Y. City); Essex

(Newark); University (Phila.). Home: 1015 Cordova Rd., Fort Lauderdale, Fla. Office: 15 Washington St., Newark 2. Died Aug. 18, 1955.

WATTS, H. Bascom, bishop; b. Yellville, Ark., Nov. 6, 1890; s. John Henry and Mary T. (Sims) W.; A.B., Southwestern U., 1913, D.D. (hon.), 1932; B.D., So. Meth. U., 1918; m. Minnie Keyser, Aug. 20, 1913; children—Ewart Goodell, Dorothy Dell (Mrs. Sterling F. Wheeler). Ordained to ministry Methodist Ch., 1918; pastor Univ. Meth. Ch., Austin, Tex., 1926-30, Laurel Heights Meth. Ch., San Antonio, 1930-36, First Meth. Ch., Little Rock, Ark., 1936-39, Boston Av. Meth. Ch., Tulsa, 1939-50; dist. supt. Meth. Ch., Tulsa, 1950-52; bishop of Neb. Area, 1952-—. Address: 4045 Mohawk St., Lincoln 10, Neb. Died Nov. 3, 1959; buried Tulsa, Okla.

WATTS, Harry Dorsey, business construction; b. Baltimore, Md., Apr. 28, 1885; s. John H. C. and Mary Dorsey (Mitchell) W.: B.S., U. of Md., 1904; m. Idoline L. Austell, Nov. 30, 1907 (deceased); children—Idoline L. W. (Mrs. Thomas Crabbe), Harry D., Audrey W. (Mrs. Harold McTigue), Evelyn W. Fiske; m. 2d, Elise Sparrow Yawkey, Dec. 2, 1944. Timekeeper and engr., Wells Brothers Co., 1905, vice pres., 1909-15; pres. H. D. Watts Co., 1915-23; with James Stewart & Co., construction, since 1924, beginning as mgr. southern territory and asst. to pres., vice pres., 1926, exec. vice pres. 1937, pres. 1940, chmn. of bd. and pres., 1942-46; pres. and dir. One East End Av. Corp. (N.Y. City), Pryor St. Corp. (Atlanta, Ga.), N.Y. Bldg. Congress, Canadian Stewart Co., Ltd. Erected notable bldgs., including: United States Chamber Commerce Dept. Labor bldgs., Home Owners Loan bldg. (Washington, D.C.); U.S. Court House, N.Y. City Post Office, Federal bldg., New York Central bldg., 60 Wall Tower, West Side Express Highway (New York); Cincinnati Union Station, Trinidad Naval Air Base, Republic Steel Plant, Chicago. Awarded U.S. Navy's Meritorious Civilian Service Emblem, 2 Army-Navy "E" awards. Mem. U.S. Chamber of Commerce, Sigma Alpha Epsilon. Clubs: Deepdale, Metropolitan, Cloud, Clove Valley Rod and Gun, Atlantic Beach, Devon Yacht, Lawyers, Pilgrims (New York); Maidstone Golf (Easthampton); Maryland (Baltimore); Elkridge (M.D.); Piedmont Driving (Atlanta); Metropolitan (Washington). Home: 1 East End Av. Office: 1 East End Av., N.Y.C. Died July 27, 1952.

WATTS, Joseph Thomas, church official; b. Raleigh, N.C., Mar. 19, 1874; s. Josiah Turner and Annie Eliza (McIver) W.; student Southern Bapt. Theol. Sem., 1903-05; D.D., Wake Forest (N.C.) Coll., 1916; m. Neva Hawkins, July 2, 1895; 1 dau., Elizabeth (Mrs. W. Emory Trainham). Sec. to gen. freight agent, and traveling freight agt. I.C.R.R. until 1903; ordained ministry Bapt. Ch., 1903; pastor and asst. pastor successively Aberdeen, Miss., Louisville, and Ashland, Ky., Lexington, N.C., and S.C. sec., Ky., 1906; S.S. and Bapt. Young People's Union sec., Va., 1909-27; co-dir. Bapt. Coöperative Program, 1919-27; gen. sec. Md. Bapt. Union Assn., Baltimore, 1927-48, now emeritus. Democrat. Author: Convention Adult Bible Classes, 1914; Home and Extension Department, 1930 (revision 1936), The Growing Christian, 1937. Contbr. on religious subjects. Home: Homewood Apts. Office: 330 N. Charles St., Baltimore. Died Feb. 7, 1957.

WATTS, Roderick John, editor; b. Dodge, Tex., Mar. 18, 1904; s. John Henry and Dohris Wilhelmina (Clark) W.; student Sam Houston State Tchrs. Coll., 1921-22, U. Tex., 1923-24, summers 1924, 25; m. Annie Elsbeth Giese, Aug. 16, 1930; children—Roderick Kent, Annie Elsbeth. Reporter Houston Press, 1926-27; with Houston Chronicle, 1927-—, reporter, polit. writer, staff corr., 1927-37, asst. city editor, 1937-45, city editor, 1945-48, mng. editor, 1948-—; mem. bd. dirs. Fairbanks State Bank, Houston. Judge nat. picture contest Asso. Press, 1950; newsphoto chmn. Asso. Press Mng. Editors, 1951, nat. dir., 1953-56, newsfeatures chmn., 1954, chmn. membership participation com., 1955, nat. treas. and Tex. pres., 1956, chmn. domestic news com., 1957, vice chmn. continuing study coms. 1958, gen. chmn., 1959); participated in Am. Press Inst. seminar for mng. editors Columbia, 1950. Dir. Tex. Election Bur., 1949-—, Houston-Harris County Tb. Assn., 1952-—, Harris County Polio Assn., 1952-—, Houston Youth Symphony, 1952-58; Houston adv. bd. mem. Salvation Army, 1955-—; pres. Sam Houston Meml. Assn., 1956-58, dir., 1956-—. Mem. C. of C., Sons Republic Tex. Clubs: Variety, Press, Houston Yacht, Old Capitol, Cork, Tidelands (Houston). Home: 6134 Lake St., Houston 5. Office: Houston Chronicle, Houston 2. Died Sept. 16, 1959; buried Forest Park Cemetery, Houston.

WATTS, Thomas Joseph, church official; b. Raleigh, N.C., Mar. 19, 1874; s. Josiah Turner and Annie E. (McIver) W.; student Southern Bapt. Theol. Sem., Ky., 1903-05; D.D., Furman (S.C.) U.; m. Margaret Glenn Whitelaw, Aug. 15, 1894; children—Mary Emily, Emily Mary (twins); m. 2d, Sarah Jenkins Graves, Oct. 6, 1934; 1 son, George Berry. Pharmaceutical chemist until 1899; ordained ministry So. Bapt. Ch., 1899; pastor Forsyth, Ga., 1900-03; student pastor Louisville, Ky., 1903-06; pastor New Liberty, Ky., 1906-09; field rep. Southern Bapt. Theol. Sem., 1909-10; field sec. Bapt. Edn. Soc. of Ky., 1910-12; gen. sec. S.S. Bapt. Gen. Assn. of Mo., 1912-14; exec. sec. S.S., B.Y.P.U. and Colportage, Bapt. State Conv. of S.C., 1914-25; asso. sec. Relief and Annuity Bd., So. Bapt. Conv., Dallas, Tex., 1925-27, exec. sec., 1927-47. Corr. sec. B.Y.P.U. of the South, 1906-11; gen. sec. Bapt. Summer Assembly System, S.C., 1915-25; lesson writer, B.Y.P.U. Quarterly, 1916-21; publicity dir. for S.C., Bapt. 75 Million Campaign, 1919-25; pres. Field Workers' Assn. of So. Bapt. Conv., Louisville, Ky.; pres. Louisville Bapt. Ministers' Conf., 1904; pres. Ch. Pension Conf. of U.S. and Can. (interdenom.), 1934-35. Democrat. Author: Twenty-one Years of Ministry to Ministers; The Rich Fruitage of a Tree of Life (brochure). Author of 80-page brochure Silver Anniversary Relief and Annuity Bd., Southern Bapt. Conv. Home: 1906 S. 5th St., Waco, Tex. Dec. 20, 1948.

WATTS, William Carleton, naval officer; b. Phila., Pa., Feb. 14, 1880; s. Ethelbert and Emily (Pepper) W.; grad. with honors, U.S. Naval Acad., 1898; m. Julia F. Scott, Apr. 16, 1902. Ensign, Apr. 4, 1900; promoted through grades to rear adm., Apr. 1, 1931. Served on U.S.S. Columbia during Spanish-Am. War; judge advocate gen. of Navy, with rank of capt., Jan. 6, 1917-Apr. 15, 1918; apptd. comdr. U.S.S. Albany, Apr. 24, 1918; engaged on convoy escort duty to end of World War I; retired for physical disability, Dec. 1, 1940; served on active duty, Navy Dept., Jan. 1942-Aug. 1943. Episcopalian. Club: New York Yacht. Home: Ringwood Rd., Rosemont, Pa. Died Jan. 5, 1956; buried Arlington Nat. Cemetery.

WAVELL, Archibald Percival (The Earl Wavell), British Field Marshal; b. Colchester, Essex, Eng., May 5, 1883; s. Maj. Gen. Archibald Graham and Eliza (Percival) W.; ed. Winchester Coll.; Royal Mil. Coll., Sandhurst; Staff Coll., Camberley; m. Eugenie Marie Quirk, Apr. 22, 1915; children—Archibald John A. (Viscount Keren), Pamela (Lady Pamela Humphrys), Felicity (Lady Felicity Longmore), Joan (Lady Joan Gordon). Commd. 2d lt., May 8, 1901, apptd. to Black Watch (Royal Highland Regt.), 1901; served in S. African War, 1901-02, Indian frontier, 1908, World War I, 1914-18, Palestine, 1937-38, World War II, 1939-43; comdr. 6th Inf. Brigade, 1930-34, 2d Div., 1935-37, troops in Palestine, 1937-38; gen. officer So. Command, 1938-39; comdr.-in-chief Middle East, 1939-41, India, 1941-43; viceroy of India, 1943-47. Mem. Privy Council. Decorated: Knight Grand Gross of the Bath, Knight Grand Comdr. Star of India, Knight Grand Comdr. Indian Empire, Companion St. Michael and St. George, Mil. Cross constable of Tower of London, 1948, lord-lt. County of London, 1949 (Eng.); Comdr. Legion of Honour; Order of Nile; Order of El Nahda; Order of George I (Greece); Order St. Vladimir; Order St. Stanislas; Virtuti Militari (Poland); Czechoslovak Mil. Cross; Greek Mil. Cross; Seal of Solomon (Ethiopia); Order of Orange-Nassau (Holland); Comdr. Order of Merit; Star of Nepal, Chancellor Aberdeen Univ., 1945. Mem. Royal Soc. Lt. (pres.), Kipling Soc. (pres.), Ch. of England. Clubs: United Service, Athenaeum, Royal and Ancient, Marylebone Cricket. Author: The Palestine Campaign, 1928; Allenby: A Study in Greatness, 1941; Allenby in Egypt, 1943; Other Men's Flowers: An Anthology of Poetry, 1944; Generals and Generalship; Speaking Generally; The Good Soldier, 1947. Address: 23 Kingston House South, London, Eng. Died May 24, 1950; buried The Charity Garth, Winchester Coll.

WAVERLEY, Viscount (Sir John Anderson); b. Edinburgh, Scotland, July 8, 1882; s. David Alexander Pearson and Janet Kilgour (Briglmen) A.; student George Watson's Coll., Edinburgh, 1888-99, Edinburgh U., 1899-1903; M.A. and B.Sc., Leipzig U., 1903, hon. LL.D. U. of Aberdeen, 1927, Cambridge U., 1938, St. Andrews U., 1939, Edinburgh U., 1943, Leeds U., 1946, Liverpool U., 1947, Sheffield U., 1948, Queens U. of Ontario, 1946; D.Sc., McGill U., 1946; m. Christina Mackenzie, Apr. 1907 (died May 1920); children—Alastair, Mary; m. 2d, Ava Wigram, Oct. 1941. British civil servant, 1905-32, becoming under-sec. of state, Home Office, 1922-32; gov. of Bengal, 1932-37; mem. Parliament for Scottish Univs., 1938-50; mem. British Cabinet and of Winston Churchill's War Cabinet, 1938-45. Held in succession office of Lord Privy Seal, Home Sec., Lord Pres. of Council, and Chancellor of Exchequer, 1943-45, Chmn. Parliamentary Scientific Com. since 1946. Chmn. Port of London Authority since 1946. Director Imperial Chemical Industries, Canadian Pacific Ry., Hudson's Bay Co., Employers Liability Assurance Corp. Chmn. Convent Garden Opera Trust, Post Grad. Med. Fedn. Decorated Knight Grand Cross of the Bath, Knight Grand Comdr. of Star of India, Knight Grand Comdr. Indian Empire, Knight of St. John, Grand Officer Legion of Honor, Crown of Italy, St. Anne of Russia, Knight Grand Cross Order of St. Olaf (Norway), Order of North Sea (Sweden), Military Order of Christ (Portugal), Also Order of Dannebrog (Denmark). Created Viscount Waverly, 1952. Fellow Royal Society of London. Presbyterian. Clubs: Brooks, Athenaeum. Address: 4 Lord North St., London S.W. 1, Eng. Died Jan. 4, 1958.

WEADOCK, John C., lawyer; b. St. Marys, O., Feb. 18, 1860; s. Lewis and Mary (Cullen) W.; m. Helena F. Bertch, Sept. 15, 1886. Admitted to Mich. bar, 1883; practiced in Mich., 1883-1907, in N.Y.C., 1907-—; corp. counsel. Mem. Am. Bar Assn., Assn. Bar of City N.Y. Democrat. Elk, K.C. Clubs: Lambs, Bankers, Lawyers, New York Athletic. Home: 225 Central Park W. Office: 20 Pine St., N.Y.C. Died Sept. 10, 1950.

WEAGLY, Mrs. Roy C. F. (Maude E. Weagly) (wā'glē), federation exec.; b. near Hagerstown, Md., Aug. 8, 1886; d. Nathan C. and Charlotte R. (Gaver) Eccard; pvt. summer course in preparation of teaching, recevied certificate, 1904; m. Roy C. F. Weagly, Nov. 26, 1908; 1 son, Roger Funk (dec.). Teacher rural schs., Washington Co., Md., 1904-08. Dir. Md. Farm Bur., Inc., Am. Farm Bur. Fedn. (mem. nat. health com.). Mem. Associated Women of Am. Farm Bur. Fedn. (nat. sec. 1937-40, nat. vice pres. 1940-44, nat. pres., 1944-—), Md. Farm Bur. (state sec. home and community com., 1931-36, state chmn., 1936-39), served as mem. Westren Dist. Md. Council of Defense, 1942-43; mem. adv. council Famine Emergency Com., Apr. 1946-—; mem. U.S. Nat. Commn. for UNESCO, 1946-—. Mem. Grange, N.E. A., Nat. Com. for Traffic Safety, Nat. Commn. for Children and Youth (children's bur.), Fed. Security Agency (mem. women's adv. com. Social Protection div.), War Dept. Bur. Pub. Relations (mem. women's interests sect.), Washington County Council Homemaker Clubs (legislative chmn.); vice pres. Women's Christian Missionary Soc. of Md. Teacher Bible class. Democrat. Mem. Disciples of Christ Ch. Clubs: Rural Women's Short Course, Univ. Md. Home: Route 1, Hagerstown, Md. Died Aug. 16, 1957; buried Beaver Creek Cemetery.

WEAVER, Claude, lawyer; b. Gainesville, Tex., Mar. 19, 1867; s. W. T. G. and Nancy Wilkin (Fletcher) W.; LL.B., U. Tex., 1887; m. Leila Ada Reinhardt, May 13, 1891; children—Mrs. Floy Barrier, Mrs. Amelia Capshaw, Mrs. Barbara James, Mrs. Lucy Cinningham, Claude, Mrs. Julio Zumeta. Practiced law at Gainesville, 1887-95, Pauls Valley, I.Ty., 1895-1903; moved to Oklahoma City, 1908. A leader to fight for constl. prohibition of liquor traffic in Okla. and in movement for commn. form of city govt.; author of charter of Oklahoma City which embodies commn. form of govt.; mem. 63d Congress, Okla. at-large; (mem. Banking and Currency Com., which framed Fed. Reserve Act); mem. Dem. National Congl. Com., 1913-15; postmaster of Oklahoma City, 1915-23. Speaker on Liberty Loan campaigns, World War. Founded, with the late Congressman J. B. Thompson, the 1st system of pub. schs. in Ind. Ter., 1899. Dem. nominee for 66th Congress, to fill vacancy, 1919. Legal adviser and sec. to Gov. Murray of Okla., 1931-34; judge 13th District of Okla., 1934. Methodist. Mem. Beta Theta Pi. Mason. Author: A Century of Progress; Why I Go to Church (essay); Memoir of W. T. G. Weaver; Life's Darkest Moment or The Dobbs Murder Trial. Editor of Literary Remains of Green Weaver. Home: 1620 N.W. 17th St., Oklahoma City. Died May 17, 1954; buried Fairlawn Cemetery, Oklahoma City.

WEAVER, George Calvin, ret. naval officer; b. Mill Hall, Pa., Aug. 6, 1905; s. Jasper Daniel and Jessie Fremont (MacGregory) W.; B.S., U.S. Naval Acad., 1926; M.S., Mass. Inst. Tech., 1931; m. Irene Streeter, Sept. 7, 1930; children—Calvin George, Jeanne. Commd. ensign USN, 1926, advanced through grades to rear adm., 1954; submarine design, constrn., Navy Yard, Portsmouth, N.H., Electric Boat Co., Groton, Conn., Mare Island Navy Yard, Vallejo, Cal.; supr. shipbuilding, constrn. fleet-type submarines and LCT landing craft, Manitowoc, Wis., World War II; head submarine br. Bur. Ships, 1945-49; prodn. officer Phila. Naval Shipyard, 1949-52; comdr. Naval Shipyard, Long Beach, Cal., 1952-54; vice chief naval material Navy Dept., Washington, 1954-55, ret. Aug. 1956; asso. prof. mech. engring. George Washington U., 1957-—. Decorated Legion of Merit. Mem. Am. Soc. Naval Engrs. Home: 3709 Woodstock St. N., Arlington 7, Va. Office: George Washington U., Washington. Died Mar. 1960.

WEAVER, Powell, organist, composer; b. Clearfield, Pa., June 10, 1890; s. Paul F. and Jennie (McCullough) W.; student Inst. of Musical Art, N.Y. City; studied organ 3 yrs. under Gaston Dethier, composition under Percy Goetschius, also privately under Pietro Yon (1 yr. N.Y. and 1 yr. Italy); studied composition under Ottorino Respighi, St. Cecelia Acad., Rome, Italy, organ under Rimigio Renzi (Vatican organist); m. Mary Watson, 1938; 1 son, Thomas Watson. Toured as accompanist with Johanna Gadski, Julia Claussen, Paul Althouse, Mario Chamlee and others; organist and director of Music, First Baptist Ch. since 1937, and Temple B'Nai Jehudah, Kansas City, Mo., since 1927. Has given organ recitals all over America and in Italy; orchestral compositions have been played by the Boston Philharmonic Orchestra, Minneapolis Symphony, St. Louis Symphony, Kansas City Symphony, Ill. WPA Orchestra. Denver Symphony and Oklahoma Symphony Orchestra. Mem.

The MacDowell Colony, Am. Composers Alliance, Am. Soc. Composers. Authors and Publishers, Am. Guild of Organists, Soc. of Native Am. Composers. Composer: Moon-Marketing, The Squirrel, and many others. Presbyterian. Home: 5535 Central St. Address: First Baptist church, K.C., Mo. Died Dec. 22, 1951; buried Mt. Moriah Cemetery, K.C.

WEBB, Carl N(athan), univ. prof.; b. Montague, Mich., Sept. 11, 1900; s. Nathan Hunt and Belle (Chase) W.; B.S., Northwestern, 1925, M.S., 1926, Ph.D., 1935, A.M., Harvard, 1928; m. Albertine Newton, Dec. 17, 1932; 1 dau., Beverly Elizabeth. Asst., Northwestern, 1930-31, Harvard, 1926-27, half-time instr. in organic lab., 1927-28; instr. in chemistry, Miami Univ., Oxford, Ohio, 1928-29, asst. prof., 1930-37, asso. prof., 1937-47, prof. of chemistry since 1947. Mem. A.A.A.S., Am. Chem. Soc., Ohio Acad. Sci., Alpha Chi Sigma, Phi Beta Kappa, Phi Lambda Upsilon. Republican. Methodist. Specializes in organic chemistry—pyrolysis of aryl allyl ethers, etc. Home: 326 W. Vine St., Oxford, O. Died Dec. 14, 1951.

WEBB, Daniel Clary, lawyer; b. Culleoka, Tenn., Apr. 7, 1881; s. William Robert and Emma (Clary) W.; prep. edn. Webb Sch., Bellbuckle, Tenn., 1895-99, and Lawrenceville (N.J.) Sch., 1900; student Vanderbilt U., 1900-02; A.B., U. of Chicago, 1907; m. Maud Lindsay, Apr. 6, 1912 (died Sept. 14, 1914); 1 son, Daniel Clary (dec.); m. 2d, Julia McCulley, Apr. 3, 1917; children—William Robert III, George McCulley, Margaret Johns. Admitted to Tenn. bar, 1907; in practice at Knoxville, Tenn.; mem. Green, Webb & McCampbell since 1918; judge Juvenile Court, 1912-18. Special Judge of Supreme Court of State of Tennessee. Mem. State Bd. Charities, 1918-22, charter mem. Asso. Charities (pres. 1931-33); mem. bd. Y.M.C.A., Boy Scouts Council (pres.); chmn. Tenn. Valley Commn.; vice chmn. Tenn. State Planning Bd. Mem. Knox County (pres. 1939), Am. and Tenn. State bar assns., Delta Kappa Epsilon, Phi Delta Phi. Received citation for pub. service from Alumni Assn., Univ. of Chicago, June 1943. Democrat. Presbyterian (elder). Rotarian (ex-pres.). Home: R.F.D. 15, Knoxville. Address: Burwell Bldg., Knoxville, Tenn. Died Feb. 24, 1954.

WEBB, Edwin Yates, ret. judge; b. Shelby, N.C., May 23, 1872; s. Rev. G. M. and Priscilla J. (Blanton) W.; A.B., Wake Forest Coll., 1893; law student U. N.C., 1893-94, U. Va., 1896; m. Miss Willie Simmons, Nov. 15, 1894; m. 2d, Mrs. Alice Pender Taylor, Oct. 28, 1928. Admitted to bar, 1894; chmn. Senatorial Dem. Exec. Com., 1896; chmn. County Dem. Exec. Com., 1898-1902; temp. chmn. Dem. State Conv., May 1900; elected state senator, 1900; mem. 58th to 66th Congresses (1903-21), 9th N.C. Dist. U.S. dist. judge, Western Dist. N.C., 1919-48, ret. Home: Shelby, N.C. Died Feb. 7, 1955; buried Shelby.

WEBB, Ernest Clay, clergyman, educator; b. Webb City, Mo., July 4, 1887; s. Elijah Thomas and Emma Isabella (Hayden) W.; grad. Webb Bros. Prep. Sch., Bellbuckle, Tenn., 1904; B.A., Vanderbilt, 1908; S.T.B., Yale Div. Sch., 1911; grad. work in theology, economics and anthropology, same univ., 1911-13; D.D., Southwestern U., 1927; m. Elenora Wilson Smith, Aug. 3, 1911; children—Thomas Hall, Alice Robertson. Ordained ministry M.E. Ch., S., 1910; pastor Kansas City, Mo., 1913-14, Pleasant Hill, 1914-15, St. Louis, 1915-20, Joplin, 1920-21; dir. Wesley Bible Chair of M.E. Ch., S., at U. of Tex., 1921-33; prof. religion and head dept. in Coll. of Arts and Sciences, Southern Meth. U., since 1933. Approved instr. in Pastors' Schs. and Teacher Training Work, Meth. Ch. Mem. Ednl. Assn. Meth. Ch. Mem. Religious Edn. Assn., Nat. Assn. Biblical Instrs., Am. Assn. Univ. Profs., Sigma Nu, Pi Gamma Mu, Theta Phi. Democrat. Mason, Elk. Club: Faculty (Southern Meth. U.). Contbr. to church pubs. Home: 3501 University Blvd., 5. Office: Box 203 S.M.U. Station, Dallas 5. Died Apr. 30, 1952.

WEBB, James Avery, lawyer; b. Memphis, July 2, 1868; s. M. D. and Minerva Caroline (Meadows) W.; grad. Lauderdale Inst., Ripley, Tenn., 1886; LL.B., Vanderbilt U., 1889; m. May Folk, June 21, 1907. Admitted to bar, 1889; practiced in St. Louis, 1896-1920; in real estate N.Y.C., 1920—. Mem. St. Louis Bar Assn. Democrat. Club: Missouri Athletic. Author: Webb on Interest and Usury, 1899; Webb on Passenger and Freight Elevators, 1901; Webb's Pollock on Torts, 1900. Compiler: (with Return J. Meigs) Webb and Meigs' Digest of Tennessee Decisions, 1898. Home: 101 W. 85th St., N.Y.C. Died Aug. 28, 1953.

WEBB, Joseph James, lawyer; b. Salinas, Cal., Dec. 9, 1878; s. William Henry and Augustias A. (Abrego) W.; ed. pub. schs.; m. Nancy B. Turner, Dec. 31, 1912. Accountant until 1904; admitted to Cal. bar, 1904, and practiced since at San Francisco. Served as maj. Am. Red Cross, overseas, World War. First pres. State Bar of Cal.; chmn. Adult Probation Bd., San Francisco. Mem. Am. Bar Assn., Bar Assn. of San Francisco, Am. Judicature Soc. (v.p.), Audubon Assn. of Pacific. Democrat. Mason. Club: Commonwealth. Home: 2736 Lyon St. Office: 519 California St., San Francisco. Died Mar. 1, 1958.

WEBB, Robert H(enning), educator; b. Suffolk, Va., Feb. 21, 1882; s. Joseph Prentis and Annie Jordan (Darden) W.; A.B., Hampden-Sydney Coll. 1901, A.M., 1902; A.M., U. Va., 1904; Ph.D., Harvard, 1909; m. Blanche Farrington Miller, June 26, 1912; 1 son, Joseph Prentis, II. Teaching fellow in Greek, Hampden-Sydney Coll., 1901-02, instr. Latin, U. Va., 1904-06; instr. Latin and Greek, Harvard, 1909-12; prof. Greek, U. Va., 1912-50; mem. mng. com., Am. Sch. Classical Studies at Athens. Mem. exec. com., Va. Music Festival; mem. bd. dirs. Tuesday Evening Concert Group (Charlottesville, Va). Mem. Am. Philol. Assn., Classical Assn. (British), Raven Soc., Pi Kappa Alpha, Phi Beta Kappa. Democrat. Episcopalian. Clubs: Colonnade (U. of Va.); Farmington Country (Charlottesville, Va.). Hbme: 928 Rugby Rd., Charlottesville, Va. Died Nov. 2, 19 Rugby Rd., Charlottesville, Va. Died Nov. 2, 1952; buried Suffolk, Va.

WEBB, Ulys Robert, naval officer; b. Jan. 18, 1874; grad. Naval War Coll. Entered U.S. Navy, Oct. 21, 1901; promoted through grades to rear admiral, Med. Corps, Feb. 1, 1933; retired Feb. 1, 1938. Deceased.*

WEBB, Vanderbilt, lawyer; b. New York, N.Y., Apr. 23, 1891; s. William Seward and Eliza Osgood (Vanderbilt) W.; grad. Groton Sch., 1909; A.B., Yale, 1913; student Balliol Coll., Oxford, Eng., 1912-13; LL.B., Harvard, 1916; m. Aileen Osborn, Sept. 11, 1912; children—Derick Vanderbilt, William Osborn, Barbara, Alexander Stewart (dec.), Richard Humphrey. Admitted to N.Y. bar, 1916; asso. with Root, Clark, Buckner & Howland, 1916-17, 1919-22, Webb & Patterson and Webb, Patterson & Hadley, 1922-29; mem. Murray, Aldrich & Webb, 1929-31, Milbank, Tweed, Hope & Webb, 1931-38, Curtis, Belknap & Webb, 1938-39; Patterson, Belknap & Webb since 1947; dir. Phelps Dodge Corp. Dir. Williamsburg Restoration, Inc. Trustee N.Y. Trust Co. Dir., v.p. Rockefeller Center, Inc. Mem. Taconic State Park Commn., 1925-47. Served as capt. Judge Adv. Dept., with A.E.F., 1917-19. Trustee Metropolitan Museum of Art, Frick Collection, 1939-51, Am. Univ. of Beirut, Groton Sch., Colonial Williamsburg, Inc. Mem. Phi Beta Kappa, Delta Kappa Epsilon,Scroll an d Key (Yale). Episcopalian. Clubs: Century, Knickerbocker, Racquet and Tennis, Rockefeller Lunch, (Yale). Down Town. Home: 66 E. 79th St. Office: 1 Wall St., N.Y.C. Died June 17, 1956.

WEBBER, James Benson, Jr., mdse. exec.; b. Detroit, Sept. 25, 1911; s. James Benson and Marana (Chase) W.; grad. Detroit U. Sch., 1930; A.B., Trinity Coll., 1934; M.B.A., Harvard, 1936; m. Nancy Scarborough, May 30, 1942; children—Nancy Chase, Elizabeth Brett, James Benson, Mary Hudson. With The J. L. Hudson Co., Detroit, since 1936, dir., 1940—, now exec. v.p.; vice chmn. Associated Merchandising, 1948—; dir. Ford Motor Co., National Bank of Detroit. Trustee Trinity Coll., Grosse Pointe U. Sch., Harper Hosp.; dir. United Community Services Met. Detroit, chmn. 1946 campaign. Mem. Advt. Council Inc. (industries adv. com.), U.S. C. of C. (national distribution council), Am. Retail Fedn. (vice chmn.), United Foundation (dir., vice president), Detroit Symphony Orchestra, Inc., United Health and Welfare Fund of Mich. (dir.), Mich. Retailers Assn. (chmn. war savings com., 1942-46, treas.), Retail Merchants Assn. Detroit (dir.), Detroit Bd. Commerce. Clubs: Turtle Lake (Hillman, Mich.); Yondotega, University, Athletic (dir.), Econ., Detroit (Detroit); St. Anthony (N.Y. City); Triton Fish and Game (Quebec); The Grosse Pointe, Hunt (Grosse Pointe, Mich.). Mem. Newcomen Society. Home: 226 Provencal Rd., Grosse Pointe Farms 30, Mich. Office: 1206 Woodward Av., Detroit 26. Died Aug. 28, 1956.

WEBER, Alfred, educator; b. Erfurt, Germany, 1868; s. Maximilian and Helene (Fallenstein) W.; student Kaiserin Augusta Gymnasium, Berlin, Bonn U., Tübingen U.; Ph.D., U. Berlin, 1895. Privatdozent U. Berlin, 1899; prof. ordinarius Prague U., Czechoslovakia, 1904; faculty polit. economy, social sci., sociology Heidelberg U., emeritus, 1933—. Fgn. mem. Am. Acad. Arts and Scis. Author: Kulturgeschichte als Kultursoziologie, 1950; Der Dritte oder der Vierte Mensch, 1953; others. Address: Bach Str. 24, Heidelberg, Western Germany. Died Feb. 1958.

WEBER, Frederick Theodore, painter, sculptor, etcher; b. Columbia, S.C., Mar. 9, 1883; s. Heinrich Christian Ludwig and Anna Julia (Nixon) W.; grad. Königliches Joachimsthalsches Gymnasium, Berlin, 1903; student Academie Humbert, Paris, 1905-06, Julian Academy, Paris, 1910-11, École Nationale des Beaux Arts, Paris, 1910-13; m. Mary Louise Brown, July 6, 1936. Painted portraits of Miss Minnie Macfeat, Winthrop Coll., S.C., Mrs. John King Van Rensselaer, Mus. of City of N.Y., Dr. Patterson Wardlaw, Univ. of S.C., Mayor T. P. Stoney, City Hall, H. F. Welch, S.C. Soc., Charleston, Dr. Frederick Tupper, U. of Vt.; painting in Virginia House, Richmond; etchings in permanent collections of Met. Museum, Brooklyn Museum, Library of Congress, U.S. Nat. Museum, New York Pub. Library, Bibliothèque Nationale (Paris). Mem. Soc. of Am. Etchers, Am. Water Color Society. Episcopalian. Clubs: Quill (New York); Nat. Arts. Wrote article on portrait painting Ency. Britannica (14th edit.). Home: 86-11 34 Av., Jackson Heights, N.Y. Died Jan. 1, 1956; buried Magnolia Cemetery, Charleston, S.C.

WEBER, Harry M(athew), physician, radiologist; b. Lewistown, Mont., June 30, 1899; s. Matt and Anna Barbara (Nickol) W.; student St. John's U., 1918-21; B.S., U. Minn., 1924, M.B., 1925, M.D., 1926; m. Kathleen Osborn, Feb. 16, 1937; children—Harry Osborn, Frederic William, George Osborn. Intern St. Joseph's Hosp., 1925, Ancker Hosp., 1926 (both St. Paul); fellow radiology U. Minn. Mayo Found., 1927-30, successively instructor, assistant and asso. professor, professor radiology, 1952—; head section of roentgenology at Mayo Clinic and affiliated hosps., since 1951. Served as lt. comdr., M.C., U.S.N.R., 1942. 1st award for sci. exhibit by 5th Internat. Congress of Radiology, 1937. Fellow Am. Coll. Radiology; mem. A.M.A., Olmsted-Houston-Fillmore-Dodge Co. Med. Soc., So. Minn. Med. Assn., Minn. Radiol Soc., Detroit Roentgen Ray Soc. (hon.), St. Louis Med. Soc. (hon.), Am. Roentgen Ray Society (president 1953-54, dir section instruction 1948-56), Rocky Mountain Radiol. Soc., Radiological Society of North America, Am. Gastroenterol. Assn., Assn. Resident and Ex-Resident Physicians of Mayo Clinic, Sociedad de Radiolgia y Fisioterapia (hon., Havana, Cuba), Sigma Xi, Phi Rho Sigma. Roman Catholic. Author numerous med. papers and treatises. Home: 1219 7th St. S.W. Office: 200 1st St. S.W., Rochester, Minn. Died Oct. 6, 1958; buried Calvary Cemetery, Rochester, Minn.

WEBER, Paul, clergyman; b. Switzerland, Aug. 28, 1884; s. Henry and Marie Anna (Eichenberger) W.; came to U.S., 1893, naturalized, 1914; A.B., William Jewell Coll., 1909, D.D., 1937; student Ia. State U., 1909-10, Newton (Mass.) Theol. Inst., 1910-11; m. Bettie Bell Rose, Jan. 4, 1909; children—Frank, Paul, Grace. Ordained to the ministry of Baptist Ch., 1906; pastor, Three Rivers, Mass., 1910-11, St. Charles, Mo., 1911-15, Poplar Bluff, Mo., 1915-20, First Bapt. Ch., Jefferson City, Mo., 1920-40; supt. St. Louis Bapt. Mission Bd. since 1940. State mem. Home mission Bd., Southern Bapt. Conv. Trustee William Jewell Coll.; dir. Kansas City Bapt. Theol. Sem. Moderator Mo. Bapt. Gen. Assn., 1936-38; Mo. leader of the Bapt. Hundred Thousand Club; mem. council on missionary cooperation Am. Baptist Conv.; sec. exec. com. of bd. of mgrs. Mo. Bapt. Hosp. since 1941; sec.-treas. Associated Hospitals of St. Louis; state vice pres. Temperance League of Mo. Mem. Pi Gamma Mu. Home: 7028 Glades Av. Office: 919 N. Taylor Av., St. Louis. Died Nov. 26, 1954; buried Laurel Hills Cemetery, St. Louis.

WEBSTER, Edwin Sibley, engr.; b. Boston, Aug. 26, 1867; s. Frank G. and Mary (Messinger) W.; B.S., Mass. Inst. Tech., 1888; LL.D., Northeastern U.; m. June de Peyster Hovey, June 1, 1893. Organizer with Charles A. Stone, 1889, firm of Stone & Webster (later Stone & Webster, Inc.), engrs. and mgrs. pub. service cos.; ret. as chmn. bd. 1946; dir. traction, light, power and other cos., Life Mem. Corp. Mass. Inst. Tech.; mem. exec. com. Mass. Inst. Tech.; trustee Mus. Fine Arts. Mem. Am. Inst. E.E. Unitarian. Clubs: Somerset, Union, St. Botolph, Engineers, University, Down Town (Boston); Eastern Yacht; The Country (Brookline). Home: Chestnut Hill, Mass. Office: 49 Federal St., Boston. Died May 10, 1950.

WEBSTER, Edwin Sibley, Jr., investment banker; b. Newton, Mass., Dec. 24, 1899; s. Edwin S. and Jane de Peyster (Hovey) W.; S.B., Harvard, 1923; M.B.A., Harvard sch., of Bus. Adminstrn., 1925; m. Jean Bennett, Jan. 10, 1942; children—Edwin Sibley III, Jean, Mary. With Stone & Webster, Inc., 1926-30, v.p., 1929-30, dir.; partner Kidder, Peabody & Co., 1931—; dir. many corps. Presbyn. Clubs: Somerset (Boston); Country (Brookline, Mass.); Norfolk Hunt (Medfield, Mass.); River (N.Y.). Home: 159 E. 65th St., N.Y.C. 21. Office: 17 Wall St., N.Y.C. 5. Died Nov., 1957.

WEBSTER, Harold Tucker, cartoonist; b. Parkersburg, W.Va., Sept. 21, 1885; s. James Clarence and Fannie Marsh (Tucker) W.; ed. pub. schs.; m. Ethel Worts, Aug. 2, 1916. Began on Denver Republican, 1902; with Chicago Daily News, 1903-05; polit. cartoonist, Chicago Inter-Ocean, 1905-08, Cincinnati Post, 1908-10; settled in N.Y. City, fall of 1911 and began drawing cartoons for Asso. Newspapers; joined staff of New York Tribune, 1919, of New York World, 1923, of New York Herald Tribune, 1931. Mem. Soc. of Illustrators. Clubs: Dutch Treat, Players, Coffee House. Author: Our Boyhood Thrills and Other Cartoons, 1915; Boys and Folks, 1917. Co-author: Webster's Bridge, 1924; Webster's Poker Book, 1925; The Timid Soul, 1931; The Culbertson Webster Contract System, 1932; Who Dealt This Mess, 1948; How to Torture Your Wife, 1948; How to Torture Your Husband, 1948. Creator of the series, Life's Darkest Moment, The Timid Soul, The Thrill That Comes Once in a Lifetime, The Boy Who Made Good, They Don't Speak Our Language, How To Torture Your Wife, Poker Portraits, The Unseen Audience; co-author Life With Rover, 1949. Home: Shippan Point, Stamford,

Conn. Died Sept. 22, 1952; buried Lake View Cemetery, New Canaan, Conn.

WEBSTER, Hutton, univ. prof.; b. Malone, N.Y., Mar. 24, 1875; s. David and Helen E. (Hutton) W.; A.B., Leland, Stanford Jr. U., 1896, A.M., 1897; A.M., Harvard, 1903, Ph.D., 1904; m. Winifred Sophie Fry, Aug. 14, 1903; children—David H., Wilfrid, Sophie E., Winifred, Hutton, Cedric, Douglas. Asst. in economics, Stanford U., 1899-1900; Austin teaching fellow in economics, Harvard, 1902-04; asst. prof. economics, Williams, 1904-07; prof. of social anthropology, U. of Neb., 1907-33; lecturer in sociology, Stanford U., 1933-40. emeritus, 1940—. Associé de l'Institut International de Sociologie; fellow Royal Anthropological Inst., A.A.A.S.; mem. Am. Anthrop. Assn., Am. Folklore Soc., Am. Sociological Society, Phi Beta Kappa, Pi Gamma Mu. Author: (Japanese transl. 1915; Italian transl. 1922); Rest Days, 1916; World History, 1923; History of Civilization, 1940; Taboo, 1942; Magic, 1947; also 15 textbooks of ancient, medieval, and modern history for high schs. and colls. Clubs: Harvard (New York); Cosmos (Washington, D.C.); Commonwealth (San Francisco). Home: 2025 Cowper St., Palo Alto, Cal. Died May 20, 1955.

WEBSTER, Hutton Jr., artist; b. Lincoln, Neb., Feb. 11, 1910; s. Hutton and Winifred (Fry) W.; ed. U. of Neb., Princeton U., and Nat. Acad. of Design; studied with Leon Kroll, N.A.; m. Janet Catherine Nelson, Oct. 20, 1941; children—Michael Ion, Peter H. Studied in Greece, Italy, Spain, France and Eng.; worked in Canal Zone and Puerto Rico; painter and etcher, 1931—, also teacher of art. Represented in collections: Library of Congress, New York Pub. Library, Met. Museum of Art, Stanford and Princeton Univs., U. of Neb. and in pvt. collections. Awarded 1st prize Nat. Acad., 1931, 1932; 2d Hallgarten prize Nat. Acad., 1932; fellowship Tiffany Foundation, 1932; Pulitzer prize ($1500), 1933-34; fellowship, Research Studio, Bok Foundation, 1940, citation Nat. Society for Crippled Children, 1952. Mem. Calif. Soc. Etchers, Printmakers Soc. of Calif., Southern Printmakers Soc., Soc. Am. Etchers (Talcott prize 1942). Home and studio: R.D. 6, Box 46, 5380 Genematas Dr., Tucson. Died Jan. 30, 1956.

WEBSTER, James R., dermatologist; b. Chgo., Oct. 16, 1906; s. Ralph Waldo and Grace Burleigh (Nye) W.; B.S., U. Chgo., 1927; M.D., Rush Med. Coll., 1932, postgrad. study dermatology; student dermatology, Vienna; m. Ruth Marion Burtis, Sept. 4, 1930; children—James R., Stephen B. Practice of medicine, specializing in dermatology, 1937—; prof. dermatology Northwestern U. Med. Sch., 1950—; sr. attending dermatologist Wesley Meml. Hosp. attending dermatologist Cook County Hosp., Chgo. Served as maj., M.C., AUS, 1942-46; theater skin cons. Southwest Pacific area, 1945; cons. Surgeon Gen., Dept. of Army, 1948. Chief del. U.S. to Internat. Congress Dermatology, Stockholm, Sweden, 1957. Decorated Bronze Star. Diplomate Am. Bd. Dermatology and Syphilology. Fellow A.M.A., Am. Acad. Dermatology and Syphilology (pres. 1957-58); mem. Am. Dermatol. Assn., Chgo. Dermatol. Soc. (past pres.), Inst. Medicine Chgo., Phi Beta Kappa, Alpha Omega Alpha, Delta Kappa Epsilon, Nu Sigma Nu. Home: 1120 N. Lake Shore Dr., Chgo. 11. Office: 55 E. Washington St., Chgo. 2. Died Feb. 28, 1958; buried Oakwood Cemetery.

WEBSTER, Paul Kimball, accountant; b. South Royalton, Vt., Oct. 17, 1905; s. Walter E. and Katherine O. (Kimball) W.; B.S., U. So. Cal., 1926; m. Harriet L. Boardman, Jan. 15, 1927; children—Judith K. (Mrs. Philip E. Barton), H. Joyce (Mrs. William O. Hetts), Steven K. Instr. accounting U. So. Cal., 1927-28; accountant Haskins & Sells. Los Angeles, 1926-40, mem. firm, San Francisco, 1940-53, partner charge San Francisco office, 1951-53, Los Angeles office, 1953-54, 55—; asst. commr. Internal Revenue, Washington, 1954-55. Treas., dir. community chest, San Francisco, budget chmn., San Mateo County; v.p. Peninsula YMCA. Trustee San Mateo Elementary Schs. Mem. Cal. Bd. Accountancy, Am. Inst. Accountants, Am. Accounting Assn., Assn. C. P.A. Examiners, Fed. Govt. Accountants Assn., Cal. Soc. C.P.A.'s (pres. 1948-49), Cal. C. of C. (tax com.). Conglist. Clubs: California. University (Los Angeles). Author articles in field. Home: 965 Fallen Leaf Rd., Arcadia, Cal. Office: 523 W. Sixth St., Los Angeles 14. Died June 29, 1957.

WECTER, Dixon (wĕk'tẽr), writer, prof. Am. history; b. Houston, Jan. 12, 1906; s. John Joseph and Eugenia (Dixon) W.; A.B., Baylor U., 1925, Litt. D., 1945; A.M., Yale, 1926, Ph.D., 1936; B.Litt., Merton Coll. (Rhodes scholar), Oxford, Eng., 1930; LL.D., Rockford Coll., 1950; m. Elizabeth Farrar, Dec. 28, 1937. Instr. English, U. Denver, 1933-34; asst. prof. English, U. Colo., 1934-36, asso. prof., 1936-39; prof. U. Cal. at Los Angeles, 1939-49; Margaret Byrne prof. U. Cal. at Berkeley, 1949—; vis. prof. Am. history, U. Sydney, 1945, as first prof. of subject in Australia; Walgreen Found. lectr., U. Chgo., 1946; Harris Found. lectr., 1947. Research fellow, Henry E. Huntington Library, San Marino, Cal., 1939-49, asso. in research, 1943-49, chmn. permanent research staff, 1946-49; John Simon Guggenheim Meml. fellow, 1942-43; literary editor Mark Twain estate, 1946—; asso. editor Literary History of the U.S., 1948. Fellow Soc. Am. Historian; mem. Am. Acad. Polit. and Social Sci., Am. Hist. Assn., Am. Antiquarian Soc., Am. Acad. Arts and Scis. Democrat. Episcopalian. Clubs: Cactus (Denver); Faculty; Valley Hunt, Twight (Pasadena). Author: The Saga of American Society, 1937; Edmund Burke and His Kinsmen, 1939; The Hero in America, 1941; (with William Matthews) Our Soldiers Speak, 1943; When Johnny Comes Marchine Home, 1944; The Age of the Great Depression, 1948. Editor Mark Twain's Letters to Mrs. Fairbanks, 1949; Report from Paradise, 1949; Love Letters of Mark Twain, 1950. Contbr. Atlantic Monthly and other jours. Office: U. of Calif., Berkeley, Cal. Died June 24, 1950.

WEDDELL, Donald J., author, scientist, educator, adminstr.; b. Sault Ste. Marie, Mich., Sept. 25, 1903; s. John Wesley and Katherine Isabelle (Metzgar) W.; B.S. in Forestry, Mich. State Coll., 1928, M.S. 1932; m. Winifred Mildred Tornblom, Mar. 23, 1932; children—Mary, Caroline, James. Forester Goodman (Wis.) Lumber Co., 1928-32; nurseryman Fla. Forest Service, Tallahassee, 1932-34; asst. prof. forestry Ala. Poly. Inst., Auburn, 1934-39; acting dir. div. forestry Dept. Natural Resources, Alanta, 1939; dean sch. forestry U. Ga., 1939—. Mem. Soc. Am. Foresters (sr. mem., chmn. S.E. sect. 1940), Assn. So. Agrl. Workers (chmn. 1948-49), Ga. Forestry Council (sec. 1940, 54, 55), Ga. Forestry Assn. (v.p. 1940), So. Assn. Sci. and Industry (exec. com. 1944-46), Forest Farmers Assn. (dir. 1951-54), Phi Kappa Phi, Omicron Delta Kappa, Xi Sigma Pi, Phi Sigma, Phi Kappa Tau, Blue Key. Clubs: Gridiron, Kiwanis (past pres. Athens, lt. gov. 7th dist., chmn. internat. com. on agr. and conservation). Author articles in profl. jours., bulls. and mags. Home: 270 Cloverhurst Av., Athens, Ga. Died May 31, 1956; buried Evergreen Meml. Park, Athens.

WEED, Hugh Hourston Craigie, carburetor mfr.; b. Stamford, Conn., Oct. 17, 1883; s. Hezekiah and Ella Belle (Craigie) W.; B.A., Amherst Coll., 1905; m. Faith Potter, Dec. 27, 1909; children—Hugh Hourston Craigie, Phoebe Andrew, Catharine Andrew. Timekeeper Am. Car & Foundry Co., Madison, Ill., 1905-09; asst. supt. St. Louis Basket & Box Co., 1909-13; v.p., gen. mgr. Carter Carburetor Co., 1913-21; v.p., gen. mgr. Carter Carburetor Corp., St. Louis, 1921-46, pres., 1946-54, chmn. bd., 1954—. Republican. Episcopalian. Clubs: University, Noonday (St. Louis); University, Athletic (Detroit). Home: 9 Ridgewood Rd., Clayton, Mo. Office: 2850 N. Spring Av., St. Louis 7. Died Jan. 5, 1957.

WEED, Lewis Hill, anatomist; born Cleveland, O., Nov. 15, 1886; s. Charles Henry and Mary Frances (Lewis) W.; A.B. Yale, 1908, A.M., 1909, M.D., John Hopkins, 1912; Sc.D., U. of Rochester, 1929; Univ. of Pennsylvania, 1942. Washington Univ. (St. Louis), Lafayette Coll., 1944, U. of Western Ont., 1947; LL.D., Duke, 1938, Tufts College, 1943, Tulane University, 1944, Birmingham U., England, 1947; unmarried. Fellow in charge of Laboratory of Surgical Research, Harvard Medical School, 1912-13; Arthur Tracy Cabot fellow, same school, 1913-14; instructor, asso. and asso. prof. anatomy, Johns Hopkins U., 1914-19, professor, 1919-47, dean medical faculty, 1923-29, director School of Medicine 1929-46. Served as capt., Med. Corps, U.S. Army, Aug. 1917-May 1919; was mil. dir. Army Neuro-Surg. Lab. at Johns Hopkins Med. Sch. Research asso. Carnegie Instn. of Washington, 1922-35. Trustee Inst. for Advanced Study since 1930; trustee Carnegie Instn. of Washington since 1935; mem. Med. Fellowship Board, Nat. Research Council, 1935-39, chairman Division of Medical Sciences, same, 1939-49; successor fellow Yale Corp. Mem. Health and Med. Com., Council of Nat. Defense, 1940-41; mem. and v. chmn. Com. on Med. Research, Office of Scientific Research and Development, 1941-47. Chmn. med. and health advisory com. Am. Red Cross, 1943-44, chmn. advisory bd. for The Health Services, 1945-47. Mem. bd. of honorary consultants Army Med. Library since 1944. Mem. Am. Assn. Anatomists, A.A.A.S., Am. Physiol. Soc., Am. Philosophical Soc. Author of monographs and original articles on anatom. and neurology subjects. Research in experimental neurlogy. Clubs: Cosmos (Washington); Century Assn. (New York). Received Medal for Merit, 1946; Order British Empire. Home: 720 Centre Av., Reading, Pa. Died Dec. 21, 1952; buried Cleve.

WEEKS, Benjamin D., clergyman, educator; b. Auburn, Mo., Sept. 27, 1881; s. John H. and Annie L. (Wilson) W.; grad. Buchanan Coll., Troy, Mo.; student Mo. Valley Coll., Marshall; D.D., Ottawa U., 1926; m. Grace E. Berger, Oct. 26, 1914; 1 son, Roger C. Ordained ministry Bapt. Ch., 1902; pastor successively Plattsburg and Monroe City, Mo., Washington Av. Bapt. Ch., Oklahoma City, Okla., Compton Heights Ch., St. Louis, Mo., and Woodland Park Bapt. Ch., St. Paul, Minn., until 1917; pres. Bacone (Okla.) Coll., 1917-41; gen. sec. The Clara Barton-Sequoyah Found. (for Indian edn.); supt. Murrow Indian Orphans' Home, Bacone, until 1941. Republican. Mason (32°). Home: Bacone, Okla. Died Oct. 4, 1950.

WEEKS, H. Hobart (wēks), architect; b. N.Y.C. Aug. 12, 1867; s. Alfred Monroe and Cecilia (Ketcham) W.; student Trinity Church Sch., N.Y., 1876; m. Adele Frank, Aug. 17, 1899; children—Hobart Godfrey, Helen Adele (Mrs. James F. McKernon, Jr.). Traveled in U.S. and Europe studying architecture and sculpture, 1883-86; draughtsman and designer for McKim, Mead and White, N.Y., 1886-99; former partnership Hiss and Weekes, N.Y., 1899, (The office practice was general in character works include churches, banks, apartment houses and large residences including B. F. Jones and J. F. Byers, Sewickley, Pa., Percy A. Rockefeller, (Greenwich, Conn.); dissolved partnership, 1933. Mem. A.I.A., 1902—. Made Fellow in 1927. Club: S.R. (New York). Home: Oenoke Ridge, New Canaan, Conn. Died Dec. 13, 1950; buried Lakeview Cemetery, New Canaan.

WEEKS, John L., business exec.; b. Baltimore, Aug. 27, 1882; s. Alexander Kirkland and Lulu (Richards) W.; m. Margaret Louise Clabaugh, 1902. Partner Luke Banks & Weeks since 1909; dir. Barber Oil Co., Hotel Waldorf-Astoria Corp. Clubs: National, Golf Links of America, The Maidstone. Home: Lily Pond Lane East Hampton, L.I., N.Y. Office: 52 Wall St., N.Y.C. 5. Died Jan. 18, 1951; buried Camden, S.C.

WEEKS, Ralph Emerson, educator, pub.; b. Skaneateles, N.Y., Feb. 9, 1878; s. William Thomas and Martha M. (Cuddeback) W.; ed. high schs., Skaneateles; m. Elizabeth Porter, Nov. 22, 1904 (died 1940); children—Clara Porter (Mrs. Nelson Hardie), John Porter, Eleanor Porter (Mrs. R. R. Kearton), Ann Porter (Mrs. M. L. White, Jr.); m. 2d, Elizabeth W. Morse, Nov. 27, 1943. Pres. of International Textbook Co., International Correspondence Schools, International Correspondence Schools, Canadian, Ltd., The Haddon Craftsmen, Inc.; pres. and dir. Northeastern Industries, Inc.; v.p. Williams Bakery; treas. and dir. U.S. Lumber Co., Miss. Central R.R. Co.; dir. J. J. Newman Lumber Co., Ralph E. Weeks Co., Hudson Coal Co., Internat. Ednl. Pub. Co., Internat. Corr. Schs., Ltd., London Internat. Schs. Co. of Latin America, First Nat. Bank (Scranton), Scranton-Lackawanna Trust Co., Wesel Manufacturing Co., Syndicate Realty Co., Bell Telphone Co. of Pa. Pres. Scranton Bd. of Trade, 1913-14; chmn. Scranton Chapter Am. Red Cross, 1916-20; trustee Community Welfare Assn., Scranton Public Library (v.p.), Wyoming Sem. (v.p.), Community Chest, Scranton-Keystone Jr. Coll., Y.W.C.A., First M.E. Ch. (pres. bd. trustees); dir. Pa. State Chamber of Commerce, Scranton Y.M.C.A., Am. Red Cross. Republican. Methodist. Clubs: Scranton, Scranton Country. Home: 544 Jefferson Av. Office: 525 First Nat. Bank Bldg., Scranton, Pa. Died Sept. 28, 1950.

WEEKS, Raymond, author; b. Tabor, Ia., Jan. 2, 1863; s. Joseph Van Rensselaer and Imogene (Cookson) W.; A.B., Harvard, 1890, A.M., 1891, Ph.D., 1897; m. Mary Arnoldia, Mar. 3, 1885. Instr. French, U. Mich., 1891-93; prof. Romance langs., U. Mo., 1895-1908, U. Ill., 1908-09, Columbia, 1909-29. Mem. Modern Lang. Assn. Am. (pres. 1922), Am. Dialect Soc. (pres. 1910), Spelling Reform Assn. (pres.). Author: Ode to France, Boys' Own Arithmetic, French by Sound, Hound-Tuner of Callaway, Chevalier de la Legion d'Honneur. Club: Harvard (New York). Unitarian. Address: Manakin, Va. Died Feb. 16, 1954.

WEESE, A(sa) O(rrin) (wēs), zoölogist; b. Hutchinson, Minn., Nov. 7, 1885; s. Peter Chester and Alice Martha (Van Buskirk) W.; B.A., Univ. of Minn., 1909; M.A., U. of Ill., 1917, Ph.D., 1922; m. Josephine Mousley, June 2, 1915. Prof. biology, U. of N.M., 1911-22; prof. biology, James Millikin U., 1922-24; prof. zoölogy, University of Oklahoma since 1924, dean Graduate College, 1946-47, David Ross Boyd professor zoology since 1948; professor ecology, Rocky Mountain Biological Lab., since 1928; pres. bd., 1938-54; ecologist, Okla. Biol. Survey since 1928, also editor of its publications. Mem. Nat. Research Council Com. on Ecology of Grasslands, 1933-50; mem. Grasslands Research Found. (pres. 1941-47; v.p.). Fellow A.A.A.S.; mem. Ecol. Soc. of America (sec. 1920-30; pres. 1931), British Ecol. Soc., Am. Soc. Zoölogists, Wildlife Soc., Okla. Acad. Science (pres. 1931, permanent sec. since 1946), The Nature Conservancy, Sigma Xi, Phi Kappa Phi, Phi Sigma. Episcopalian. Contbr. to scientific publs. Home: 809 W. Brooks St. Address: Univ. of Okla., Norman, Okla. Deceased.

WEGENER, Theodore H., investment banker, mem. Rep. Nat. Com.; b. Deshler, Neb., Nov. 26, 1892; s. Frederick D. and Clara E. (Werner) W.; student Concordia Coll., 1908-12, Creighton U., 1913-16; m. Mabel A. Steward, May 1, 1916 (dec.); children—Jean (Mrs. James Free), Donnabeth (Mrs. Francis Cannon; m. 2d, Frieda Wilts, May 18, 1941. Pres. Wegener & Daly Corp., Boise, Ida., 1932—; partner Wegener & Daly; v.p., mgr. Broadway Holding Co. Ida. state chmn. Crusade for Freedom, 1949-54; pres. Ida. Soc. Crippled Children, 1948-54, Boise

Community Chest, 1934-35, Boise area council Boy Scouts Am., 1932-47, Ida. Hosp. Service, 1945—; president National Society for Crippled Children, 1956-57, also vice pres. executive committee, 1953—. Chmn. Ida. Rep. Finance Com., 1950-55. Mem. Rep. Nat. Com., 1954—. Mem. Boise C. of C. (past pres.), Investment Bankers Assn. (mem. N.W. exec. com.), Pacific N.W. Development Assn., Ida. Wildlife Fedn. (pres.), Am. Automobile Assn. (nat. dir.). Clubs: Knife and Fork (past pres., v.p. and dir. internat.), Rotary (past dist. gov. internat.) (Boise). Home: 914 Houston Rd. Office: First National Bank Bldg., Boise, Ida. Died Nov. 19, 1958; buried Morris Hill Cemetery, Boise, Ida.

WEHLE, Louis Brandeis (wā'lē), lawyer; b. Louisville, Ky., Sept. 13, 1880; s. Otto A. and Amy (Brandeis) W.; A.B., Harvard, 1902, A.M., 1903, LL.B., 1904; m. Mary Gray Patterson Liddell, May 17, 1911; children—Mark Liddell, Louis B., Mary Field. Admitted to Ky. bar, 1904; practiced in state and federal courts, also before ICC, N.Y.C., 1921—; mem. legal com. Gen. Munitions Bd., also of legal com. War Industries Bd., Council of Nat. Defense, at Washington, D.C., 1917; originator of plans adopted by U.S. Govt. to prevent strikes in building of cantonments and ships; spl. asst. to sec. of war, 1917; counsel of Cantonment Labor Adjustment Commn., June 1917; of counsel U.S. Shipping Bd. Emergency Fleet Corp., Aug. 1917-Mar. 1919; organizer and counsel Fed. Shipbuilding Labor Adjustment Bd., Sept. 1917; gen. counsel War Finance Corp., Mar. 1919-Nov. 1920; apptd. by Pres. Wilson mem. Federal Electric Rys. Commn., May 1919. Mem. President's White House Conf. on Power Pooling, Sept. 1936. Mem. Am. Com. at Internat. Congress of Comparative Law and gen. reporter at The Hague, 1937. Head U.S. Foregin Economic Adminstrn's. overseas mission to the Netherlands, and associated by State Dept. designation with U.S. Ambassador to the Netherlands (acting in Holland and in Eng., 1944-45). Mem. Am. Bar Assn., Am. Law Institute, Am. Soc. Internat. Law (executive council). Clubs: Cosmos (Washington); Harvard (New York). Author: Hidden Threads of History; Wilson Through Roosevelt, 1953; also many articles. Home: 1150 Fifth Av., N. Y.C. 28. Office: 14 Wall St., N.Y.C. 5. Died Feb. 13, 1959.

WEHLER, Charles Emanuel, educator; b. nr. New Oxford, Pa., Oct. 18, 1864; s. Levi and Catherine (Mummert) W.; Millersville (Pa.) Normal Sch., 1881-2; Palatinate Coll., Pa., 1882-3; A.B., Ursinus Coll., Pa., 1887, A.M., 1890; grad. Ursinus Sch. of Theology, 1889; U. Tenn., summer term, 1910; (D.D., Catawba Coll., N.C., 1906); m. Bertha Hendricks, Dec. 18, 1889. Ordained ministry Ref. Ch. in U.S., 1889; pastor Boehm's Ref. Ch., Blue Bell, Pa., 1889-93, Manheim, Pa., 1893-9, Dayton, O., 1899-1902; in editorial work, 1902-4; pastor Newton, N.C., 1904-9; organizer and supt. graded schs., Newton, 1905-6; teacher of history and polit. science, Catawba Coll., Newton, 1905-6, acting pres., 1907; pastor Presbyn. Ch., Ingleside, Ga., 1909-10; v.p. and prof. history and bible, 1911—, acting pres., 1919-20, Hood Coll., Frederick, Md. Y.M.C.A. service, Washington (D.C.) Barracks, 1918. Mem. N.E.A., Am. Hist. Assn., Frederick Y.M.C.A. (dir.), etc. Democrat. Mason (K.T., 32°). Studied Harvard, summer, 1919. Author: Why I Am a Church Member. Home: Frederick, Md. Deceased.

WEHRLE, William Otto Joseph, educator; b. Pittsburgh, July 4, 1896; s. Daniel Virgil and Margaret K. (Bloeser) W.; grad. St. Michael Sch., Pittsburgh, 1909, U. of Dayton Prep Sch., 1914; A.B., U. of Dayton, 1918; M.A., Cath. Univ. of America, 1931, Ph.D., 1933. Entered Soc. of Mary, 1909; teacher 5th grade, St. Barbara Sch., Brooklyn, 1916-17; teacher West Catholic High Sch., Phila., 1917-18, Cathedral Latin Sch., Cleveland, 1918-21, St. Joseph High Sch., San Jose, Calif., 1921-24, 1926-28, St. James High Sch., San Francisco, 1924-26, St. Mary High Sch., Stockton, 1928-30; prof. of English, U. Dayton, 1933—, head English dept., 1935-57. Mem. Modern Lang. Assn., Cath. Poetry Soc., Coll. English Assn. Republican. Author: The Macaronic Hymn Tradition in Medieval English Literature, 1933; History of the University of Dayton, 1937; Vocabulary Drill Book, 1939. Editor: Visual Education English Vocabulary Cards. Home: University of Dayton, Dayton 9, Ohio. Died Dec. 23, 1959.

WEIDLER, Albert Greer (wīd'lēr), clergyman, educator; b. Erie, Pa., Jan. 24, 1882; s. Albert Wright and Margaret Luella (Pollock) W.; desc. Martin W., who came from Switzerland, 1697; B.A. summa cum laude, Westminster Coll., New Wilmington, Pa., 1902, M.A., 1905; Ph.D., U. of Pittsburgh, 1910; Th.B., Pittsburgh Theol. Sem., 1911; B.D., Western Theol. Sem., 1911, S.T.M., 1924; M.A., Harvard, 1927; M. Josephine Mary Corbin, Aug. 24, 1911. Tutor prep. dept. Westminster Coll., 1901-02; asst. prin. graded schs., Erie, Pa., 1902-03; founder, and prin. high sch., Harborcreek, Pa., 1903-05, East Millcreek, 1905-08; teacher high sch., Homestead, 1908-09; ordained ministry U.P. Ch., 1911; pres. Frenchburg (Ky.) Jr. Coll., 1911-18, and pastor at Frenchburg; founder Frenchburg Hosp., 1914; admitted to Ky. bar, 1918; prof. econ., dean of labor, Berea Coll., 1918-52, emeritus dean, 1950—; chmn. dept. econ. and sociology, 1920-25; chmn. dept. econs., 1925-40; and bus., 1940-52; implemented student-labor program, 1919; brought student labor to self-supporting basis, 1922; inaugurated schollabor contests, 1923, to dignify student labor; organized Berea Credit Union, first credit union to be operative within a group of undergraduates, 1923, adapting prins. to student loans; organized, directed econ., ednl., health, religious and social survey of Menifee County, Ky., 1915. Federal fuel adminstr., Menifee County, Ky., 1917-18; Coll. and Secondary Fed. Emergency Relief Adminstr., 1934-36; Nat. Youth Adminstr., 1936-42; pres. Berea Community Coop; founder, pres. Berea Bldg. & Loan Assn., 1923-48; dir. Berea Credit Union; dir. Berea Bank & Trust Co., 1925-42; gen. agent in Ky. for Cuna Mutual Ins., 1940—; librarian Berea Pub. Schs., Berea, Ky., 1950—. Mem. Fellowship of Reconciliation. Mem. Ky. Bar Assn., Ky. Credit Union League (pres. 1934-37, now dir.); pres. Ky. League Credit Union, 1940-48; mem. Credit Union Nat. Assn. (dir. 1939-43; treas. exec. com. 1940-42), S.A.R., Fellowship of So. Churchmen, Pi Gamma Mu (nat. v.p. 1924-30; gov. for Ky.), Tau Kappa Alpha (mem. Nat. Honor Chapter), Ky. Acad. Social Scis., Am. Assn. U. Profs., Berea Honor Soc., Phi Kappa Phi. Mason (chaplain). Club: Faculty (Berea). Editor, pub. The Agitator, 1916-18. Awarded Tau Kappa Alpha special distinction medal, 1928; citation of work and philosophy in U.S. Dept. of Edn. Bulletin for "college projects for aiding students," 1938; Berea (Ky.) Coll. Labor award, 1952; also Western Hemisphere Credit Union award, 1952. Made travel study of cooperative movement in 35 countries, 1929-30; study tours of European folk schs., youth hostels and labor centers; asso. with Internat. Peoples Coll., Elsinore, Denmark, summer 1929, with Am. Peoples Coll., Oetz in Tirol, Austria, Summer 1934. Mason. Home: 26 Center, Berea, Ky. Died Oct. 8, 1957.

WEIDLER, Victor Otterbein, bishop; b. Highspire, Pa., Jan. 27, 1887; s. Zur Abner and Lydia Alice (Harp) W.; A.B., Lebanon Valley Coll., Annville, Pa., 1910, D.D., 1935; m. Dora Henrietta Houskeeper, Jan. 27, 1920. Instr., Waynesboro (Pa.) High Sch., 1910-13; pastor, Frewsburg, N.Y., 1913-16; pastor, Buffalo, 1916-26; pastor, Mpls., 1926-34; exec. sec., Home Mission and Ch. Erection, United Brethren Ch., 1934-38; bishop, United Brethren Ch., 1938—, and Evang. United Brethren Ch. (former by merger of United Brethren and Evang. chs. 1946), 1946—. Address: 3814 The Paseo, Kansas City 3, Mo. Died Aug. 5, 1950; buried Bowling Green, O.

WEIDMAN, Frederick Deforest (wīde-man), dermatologist; b. Bristol, Conn., Oct. 16, 1881; s. Herman C. and Eva Lucinda (Stone) Wiedenmann; M.D., U. Pa., 1908; m. Florence L. Krewson, 1919; children—Allen F., Dorothy Mary (Mrs. Robert B. Burr); m. 2d, Lillian E. Hawk, May 21, 1937. Intern Delaware Hosp., 1909-10; pvt. practice, Phila., 1909-14; asst., later asso. pathologist Phila. Zool. Gardens, 1910-54; prof. pathology Woman's Med. Coll. of Pa., 1914-17; prof. dermatol. research U. Pa., 1923-45, prof. research in dermatology and mycology, 1945-49, emeritus, 1949—; chief dermatology staff Phila. Gen. Hosp., 1920-47, Grad. Hosp. of U. Pa., 1934-46. Diplomate Am. Bd. Dermatology and Syphilology. Mem. Am. Acad. Dermatology and Syphilology (pres. 1954), Am. Dermatol. Assn. (pres. 1944-46), Soc. for Investigative Dermatology (pres. 1944). Home: 20 Tenby Rd., Havertown, Pa. Office: Dermatology Clinic, University Hosp., 36th and Spruce Sts., Phila. 41. Died Aug. 30, 1956.

WEIK, Jesse William, author; b. Greencastle, Ind., Aug. 23, 1857; s. Louis and Katharine (Schmidt) W.; A.B., Asbury (now DePauw) U., 1875, A.M., 1883; m. Frances A. Hayes, Dec. 1, 1890 (died Mar. 1911); children—John Edward, Mary Hays. Admitted to bar, 1880, never practiced. After graduation from coll. spent several yrs. in and around Springfield, Ill., where became deeply interested in the history and career of Abraham Lincoln; formed a lit. connection with William H. Herndon, who was Lincoln's law partner for many years; carefully interviewed Lincoln's contemporaries and many others who had known him intimatley; also visited Ky., where Lincoln was born, and Southern Ind., where he spent his boyhood, studying his development from every point of view. Pioneered telphone communications. Author: (with William H. Herndon) Herndon and Weik's Life of Lincoln, 1889, revised edit. in 2 vols., 1892; History of the Republican, 1908. Contbr. to Century, Outlook, American, and other mags. on Lincoln incidents and other hist. topics; has one of the largest and most valuable collections of Lincoln letters and MSS. in the country; now The Jesse W. Weik Collection, Library of Congrss. Author: The Real Lincoln, 1922; History of Putnam County, Indiana. Mem. Am. Hist. Assn., Western Writers' Assn., Lincoln Fellowship of New York, Authors' Club, London, Ind. Lincoln Route Commn. Address: Greencastle, Ind. Died Aug. 19, 1930; buried Forest Hill Cemetery, Greencastle, Ind.

WEIL, Adolph Leopold (wil), lawyer; b. Petaluma, Cal., Jan. 8, 1876; s. Moritz and Mary (Poehlmann) W.; Ph.B., U. Cal., 1897, LL.B., 1899; m. Florence Greenbaum, Nov. 29, 1895 (died 1932); children—Martin John, Mary Elizabeth (Mrs. Jack Voscamp), Elizabeth Anne (Mrs. Edward Coney). Admitted to Cal. bar, 1899, and practiced in San Francisco to 1934, then in Los Angeles; pres. Gen. Petroleum Corp. of Cal., 1934-41. Dir. Am. Soda Products Co. Asso. Cal. Inst. Tech. Dir. Goodwill Industries; pres. Cal. Coll. in China Found. Chmn. commn. for reorgn. of City Govt., Los Angeles; treas., dir., mem. exec. com. Cal. Taxpayers Assn; gen. chmn., dist. 5 Petroleum Industry for War, 1941-42; mem. Petroleum War Council, 1942. Mem. Am., Cal. State and San Francisco bar assns., Acad. Polit. Sci., Delta Sigma Rho. Republican. Mason. Clubs: Jonathan, Los Angeles Yacht, Olympic, Commonwealth. Editor of Rose's Notes in U.S. Reports (1st edit., 12 vols.), 1899. Address: 324 S. June St., L.A. Died Feb. 25, 1952.

WEIL, Frank L., lawyer; b. New York, N.Y., Mar. 6, 1894; s. Leopold and Rebecca (Rosenstein) W.; B.S., Columbia Coll., 1915; LL.B., Columbia Law Sch., 1917; D.H.L., Hebrew Union College, 1945; m. Henrietta A. Simons, July 7, 1924; children—John William, Thomas Alexander, Peter Henry. Director B. T. Babbitt, Inc., Dorothy Draper, Inc., Leon-Ferenbach, Incorporated. President of the Y.M.H.A. (92d St.), N.Y. City, 1932-40; co-founder, dir., United Service Orgns., 1940-50, v.p., member exec. com. and policy com., 1940-47; pres. Nat. Jewish Welfare Bd., 1940-50, honorary pres., 1950—; pres. World Fedn. Y.M.H.A. and Jewish Community Centers, 1947—; v.p. Asso. Youth-Serving Orgns., 1943-48; mem. Nat. Exec. Bd., Boy Scouts America, 1940—, v.p., 1957—, also chmn. Div. of Personnel, and recipient Silver Beaver, Silver Antelope, Sliver Buffalo awards; chmn. nat. exec. com. Nat. Social Welfare Assembly, 1946-49, pres. 1949-51; chmn. bd. govs. Hebrew Union Coll. Trustee Congregation Emanu-El., 1933—, chmn. Religious Sch. Com., 1935-40, v.p., 1949—; dir. Lincoln Center for Performing Arts, 1956—; formerly mem. bd. dirs. Am. Jewish Com., Union Am. Hebrew Congregations, N.Y. State Citizens Council. Mem. U.S. Nat. Commn., UNESCO, 1946-48. Chairman of the President's com. on Religion and Welfare in Armed Forces, 1948-51; dir. co-chmn. Asso. Services for A.F., 1950; chmn. Nat. Citizens' Com. for United Nations Day, 1952; pres. Nat. Inst. Social Relations, 1946-48; trustee Shapiro Found.; mem. Pres. Truman's Nat. Famine Emergency Council; held office in many other civic orgns. Employer rep. N.Y. Unemployment Ins. State Adv. Council 1935-49; mem. N.Y. State Temporary Com. Against Discrimination, 1944-45. Mem. American, New York State bar associations. Bar Association of the City of New York, New York County Lawyers Assn. Democrat. Jewish religion. Mason. Clubs: Manhattan, Uptown, Harmonie, Centuy Country, Standard (Chicago); Cosmos (Washington). Contributed to periodicals of articles on Social Security, activities of U.S.O. and the Jewish Welfare Bd. Public speaker, interested in youth-serving orgns. Awarded Medal for Merit by Pres. Truman, 1946. Home: 635 Park Av. Office: 60 E. 42d St., N.Y.C. Died Nov. 10, 1957; buried Kensico Cemetery, Valhalla, N.Y.

WEIL, Louis A., newspaper editor; b. Brooklyn, N.Y., June 19, 1878; s. Abram and Caroline (Strauss) W.; grad. Port Huron (Mich.) High Sch., 1896; m. Blanche Alpine Granger, Sept. 15, 1904; children—Louis A., Frank Granger, William Lee. Reporter Detroit Tribune, 1897-98, Detroit Free Press, 1898-1900; established Port Huron Herald, 1900, and editor and pub., 1900-10; editor and pub. Port Huron Times Herald 1910—; v.p. Federated Publs., Inc., pubs. of Grand Rapids Herald, Lansing State Journal, Battle Creek News; pres. Times Herald Co. Mem. Am. Society of Newspaper Editors, Mich. U. Press Club. Club: National Press (Washington, D.C.). Author of "Bill Goes Abroad and We Go, Too," 1937; "For Grandparents Only," 1947. Home: 4344 Gratiot Av. Office: The Times Herald, Port Huron, Mich. Died Dec. 10, 1959.

WEIL, Richard, Jr., dept. store exec.; b. N.Y.C., Dec. 5, 1907; s. Richard and Minnie (Straus) W.; student Hotchkiss, 1921-25, Yale, 1925-38; m. Allene Hall, Jan. 5, 1935; children—Richard, III, Martha. With R. H. Macy & Co., 1928-36; v.p. L. Bamberger & Co., 1936-39, pres., 1939-45; v.p. R. H. Macy & Co., Inc., 1945-49, pres. Macy, N.Y., 1949-53; dir. E. J. Korvette, Inc., Intercultural Publs., Inc. Served as lt. col., AUS, World War II. Decorated Legion of Merit, 1945. Italian Star of Solidarity, 1952. Clubs: Yale, Grolier, Regency. Author: The Art of Practical Thinking, 1940. Home: 540 Park Av., N.Y.C. Died May 10, 1958.

WEILAND, Christian Frederick van Leeuwen (wī'lānd), elec. engr.; b. Rotterdam, Netherlands, Feb. 19, 1887; s. Johannes and Clazina Johanna (van Leeuwen) W.; student Acad. of Creative Arts and Tech. Sciences, and Tech. Crafts Sch., The Hague, 1902-05; E.E., Rhenish Engring. Coll., Bingen, Germany, 1910; married Alida Jeanne Jacoba Briedé, March 13, 1913; 1 son, Johannes; m. 3d, Elise Cunningham, November 22, 1942. Came to U.S., 1924, naturalized, 1936. Began as machinist apprentice, 1905; successively engr. testing lab. Garbe Lahmeyer Co., Aix-la-Chapelle, Engr. Algemeene Electriciteits My, Amsterdam; engr. in charge lit. and advertising dept. "Heemaf," Holland, chief engr. in charge sales dept. Machine Works, Breda, Holland; held various engring. positions in U.S., 1924-29, foreign lang. and tech. editor Engineering Index, Inc., 1929-40; chief elec. engr. Todd Shipyards Corp., 1940-43; now chief elec. engr. Slocum & Fuller, New York. Mem. Am. Inst. Elec. Engrs. Protestant. Cllub: Netherland. Author of tech. publs. published in Europe. Home: 3875 Waldo Av., Riverside, N.Y.C. 63. Died Jan. 13, 1953.

WEILL, Kurt, composer; b. Dessau, Germany, Mar. 2, 1900; s. Albert and Emma (Ackerman) W.; student U. of Berlin, State Acad. for Music, Berlin; studied with Ferruccio Busoni and others; m. Lotte Lenya, Jan. 28, 1926. Composer operas and musical plays. Lived in Berlin until 1933, Paris, 1933-34, U.S., 1935—. Mem. Am. Soc. Composers, Authors, and Publishers, Dramatists, Guild, League of Composers; dir. Playwrights Company. Compositions: (operas) Magic Night (children's ballet), 1923; Protagonist, 1926; Royal Palace, 1927; The Czar Photographs Himself, 1927; The Lindbergh Flight, 1927; Three-Penny Opera (with Bert Brecht), 1928; Mahagony, 1930; Jasager, 1930; Die Buergschaft, 1931; Happy End (musical play with Bert Brecht), 1929, The Silverlake, 1933; Deadly Sins (ballet), 1933; The Silverlake, 1933; Anna Anna (ballet), 1933; Marie Galante (musical play), 1934; My Kingdom For a Cow (operetta), 1935; The Eternal Road (with Max Reinhardt), 1936; Johnny Johnson (with Paul Green), 1937; Knickerbocker Holiday (with Maxwell Anderson), 1938; Railroads on Parade (N.Y. World's Fair), 1939; Lady In the Dark (with Moss Hart and Ira Gershwin), 1941; One Touch of Venus (with S. J. Perelman and Ogden Nash), 1943; A Flag Is Born, 1944; The Firebrand of Florence (with E. J. Mayer and Ira Gershwin), 1945; Street Scene (opera based on Elmer Rice's play), 1947; Down In the Valley (folk opera; with Arnold Sundgaard), 1948; Love Life (with Alan J. Lerner), 1948; Lost In The Stars (with Maxwell Anderson), 1949; (motion picture scores) You and Me, Where Do We Go From Here?, Lady In the Dark, Knickerbocker Holiday, One Touch of Venus; (chamber music) Concerto for violin and wind instruments, 1925; String quartet, 1925; The New Orpheus, cantata for soprano, solo violin and orchestra, 1926; (song) Three Songs by Walt Whitman; Symphony Nos. 1 and 2. Home: Brook House, S. Mountain Rd., New City, N.Y. Office: 630 Fifth Av., N.Y.C. Died Apr. 3, 1950; buried New City, N.Y.

WEIMAN, Rita (wī'măn), author, playwright; b. Phila., Pa.; d. Charles and Jennie (Bash) Weiman; grad. Friends Central Sch., Phila.; studied in Paris, France, later at Art Students League, New York; m. Maurice Marks, Nov. 27, 1924. Retains maiden name. Writer since sch. days; was asso. editor The Blue and Gray and contbr. to Phila. Evening Bulletin; spl. writer, N.Y. Sunday Herald. Mem. Authors League of America, the Dramatists Guild, Woman Pays Club, Am. Arbitration Assn. Awarded U.S. Treasury citation for participation in War Finance Campaign. Author: (books) Footlights (collection of theatrical stories), 1923; What Manner of Love (novel), 1935; Last of the House of Robsart (novel), 1943; Paths of Judgment, 1945; Dangerous Heritage, 1947; Mist, 1949; (only woman collaborator) The President's Mystery Story, 1935; Headline News, 1939; (plays) The Watch Dog; The Co-Respondent; The Acquittal (prod. in New York, 1920, England, 1928); Moon Magic; Breakfast with the Prince (with Maurice Marks); The Witness Chair. Television prodn. Mist, The Target, Here Is My Life, Be Just and Fear Not, The Acquittal. Contributor articles, novels, short stories and novelettes to Am., Brit. and Continental mags.; contbr. to Writers War Bd. Home: Cedar Hills, R.F.D. 1, Westport, Conn. Died June 23, 1954.

WEIMER, Claud F., newspaperman; b. Mason City, Neb., June 18, 1902; s. Curtis E. and Kitty (Foster) W.; student State Coll., Kearney, Neb., 1920-22, Wooster (O.) Coll., 1924-25; m. Lillian Marston, Dec. 8, 1928; children—Robert, Alice. Reporter, dept. editor several Neb. and Ohio newspapers, 1919-25; editorial exec. Scripps-Howard Newspapers in Toledo, Cleve., Columbus, O., 1926-42; asso. pub. St. Petersburg (Fla.) Times, 1952-54; pres. Weimer Orgn., pub. relations advisors, Columbus, O., 1946—, Pomeroy (O.) Daily Sentinel, 1951—. Area mgr. War Finance Com., 1943-45. Mem. Pub. Relations Soc. Am., Sigma Delta Chi. Home: 12009 Sunshine Lane, St. Petersburg 6, Fla. Office: 51 N. High St., Columbus 15, O. Died July 20, 1955.

WEINMAN, Adolph Alexander (wīn'măn), sculptor; b. Karlsruhe, Baden, Germany, Dec. 11, 1870; s. Gustave and Katharina (Weingaertner) W.; ed. Volkschule, Germany, pub. schs., New York, Cooper Inst., Art Students League; pupil in sculpture of Martiny and Augustus St. Gaudens; m. Margaret Lucille Landman, Nov. 23, 1898; children—Howard Kenneth, Katherine Jane, Robert Alexander. Engaged professionally as sculptor since 1901. Awarded silver medal, St. Louis Expn., 1904; won competition for monument to Gen. Alexander Macomb, Detroit, 1906; Md. Union Soldiers and Sailors Monument, Baltimore, 1907; Lincoln Memorial, Hodgenville, Ky.; Lincoln Memorial, Madison, Wis.; Lincoln statue, rotunda of State Capitol, Frankfort, Ky., 1911; statue of Col. William F. Vilas, of Wis., now in Vicksburg Nat. Mil. Park, Vicksburg, Miss.; other works: pediment, Senate wing, Wis. State Capitol; Maybury Memorial, Detroit, Mich., 1912; sculptures façade of Municipal Bldg., New York, 1912-13; fountains of the "Rising" and the "Setting Sun" for Court of the Universe, Panama P.I. Expn., 1915; pair of monumental sphinxes flanking entrance to Scottish Rite Temple, Washington, 1915; designed the new dime and new half dollar, 1916. Victory button for U.S. Army, 1919, Dominican campaign medal, U.S. Navy, 1923; designed pediment sculpture for Mo. State Capitol Bldg., and monumental fountain for Capitol grounds; designed Monument to Mayor William Jay Gaynor, Brooklyn, N.Y.; monumental frieze, Elks Nat. Memorial, Headquarters Bldg., Chicago, 1928; statue of Gov. William C. C. Claiborne, La. State Capitol, 1931; designed pair of monumental groups, Bronx County Bldg., 1932; all sculpture for façade, Post Office Dept. Bldg., Washington, 1933; monumental frieze for Supreme Court Room, Supreme Court Building, Washington, 1933; pediment sculpture for Archives Building, Washington, 1933; bronze door, American Academy Arts and Letters Building, 1937, "Riders of the Dawn" group for Brookgreen Gardens, Brookgreen, S.C., 1944, statue of Alexander Hamilton and De Witt Clinton for Museum of City of N.Y., 1940; pediment group for Thomas Jefferson Nat. Memorial, Washington, 1941. Mem. Internat. Jury of Awards, Panama, Pacific-Internat. Exposition, San Francisco, 1915. Awarded silver medal, Brussels International Exposition, 1910; gold medal of honor in sculpture, Archtl. League, New York, 1913; J. Sanford Saltus award medal of Am. Numismatic Soc., 1920; George D. Widener gold medal, Pa. Acad. Fine Arts, 1924; fine arts medal, A.I.A., 1929. Nat. Academician, 1911; Nat. Arts Club Sculpture Prize, 1942; Elizabeth W. Watrous Gold Medal, Nat. Acad. of Design, 1945; Medal of Honor, National Sculpture Society, 1949; mem. Nat. Inst. Arts and Letters, Am. Acad. Arts and Letters, Nat. Sculpture Soc. (pres. 1927-30; hon. pres. since 1946), Archtl. League, Am. Numis Soc. (medal 1920). Mem. Nat. Commn. Fine Arts (1928-32); mem. N.Y. City Art Commn., 1924-28. Clubs: Century, Nat. Arts. Studio: 234 Greenway S., Forest Hills, N.Y. Died Aug. 8, 1952.

WEIR, Ernest Tener (wēr), mfr.; b. Pittsburgh, Pa. Aug. 1, 1875; s. James and Margaret (Manson) W.; ed. public schs., Pittsburgh; m. Mary Kline, 1901; children—Mrs. Coleman C. Carter, Henry K. and Ernest T. (twins); m. 2d, Mrs. Aeola Dickson Siebert, 1926 (divorced); m. 3d, Mary E. Hayward, Dec. 11, 1941; 1 son, David M. II. With Braddock Wire Co., 1891; with Oliver Wire Co., 1892; apptd. chief clk. Monongahela Tin Plate Mills, 1901, later supt., also mgr. Monessen Mills, 1903, both belonging to the Am. Tin Plate Co.; asso. with J. R. Phillips, 1905; in organizing the Phillips Sheet & Tin Plate Co. (Clarksburg, W.Va.), of which became pres., 1908, title changed, 1916, to the Weirton Steel Co., which became a subsidiary in 1929 of the Nat. Steel Corp. of which he was founder and is now chmn. of bd. and chief exec.; also officer and dir. Wierton Steel Co., Great Lakes Steel Corp., Hanna Iron Ore Co., Hanna Furnace Corp., Midwest Steel Corp., Weirton Coal Co., Bank of Weirton and numerous other corps. Dir. American Iron and Steel Institute. Mem. advisory bd. Transportation Assn. America; dir. Pittsburgh Regional Planning Assn.; v.p. Pittsburgh Symphony Soc., Engrs. Society of Western Pennsylvania Pittsburgh Chamber of Com. merce; vice chairman Maurice and Laura Falk Foundation. Trustee East End Christian Ch. (Pittsburgh). Clubs: Duquesne, Civic Club of Allegheny County, Fox Chapel (Pittsburgh); Long Vue Club of Verona, Pa. (gov.); Williams Country (Weirton, West Virginia); Detroit Club (Detroit); Racquet and Tennis, River, Links, Cloud (N.Y.); Seminole Golf (Palm Beach, Fla.). Home: Park Mansions. Office: Grant Bldg., Pitts. Died June 26, 1957.

WEIR, William Figley, clergyman; b. Augusta, O., Dec. 28, 1861; s. Andrew D. and Emily S. (Figley) W.; A.B., Washington and Jefferson Coll., 1886; Western Theol. Seminary, Pitts., 1886-90; Union Theol. Sem., N.Y.C., 1887-88; D.D., Coll. of Wooster, 1905; LL.D., Macalester Coll., St. Paul, Minn., 1930; m. Martha J. Barr, Oct. 30, 1889 (died Jan. 1931); children—John Barr, William Thomas, LeRoy Moffat; m. 2d, Sadie M. Galloway, June 27, 1933. Ordained Presbyn. ministry, 1889; pastor Mingo Junction, O., 1889-92, Toronto, O., 1893-98, Cambridge, O., 1899-1902, Ashtabula, O., 1903-12; coll. pastor, Coll. of Wooster, 1912-16; gen. dir. Dept. of Men's Work and dist. sec. of Bd. of Christian Edn., Presbyn. Ch. in U.S.A., 1916-31; later became head Dept. of Ch. Adminstrn., Presbyn. Coll. of Christian Edn., Chicago; retired, 1942, becoming pastor emeritus Deerfield Presbyn. Ch., Apr. 1942. Mem. Interdenom. Council of Men's Work; mem. Nat. Council, Boy Scouts of America. Mem. bd. of trustees, Coll. of Wooster; trustee Western Theol. Sem., Pittsburgh, 1909-28. Club: University (Chicago). Author: Giving the Men a Chance, 1931; The Program of the Local Church, 1932; The Lay Leader Looks at the Presbyterian Church, 1934. Home: Deerfield, Ill. Died Mar. 2, 1949; buried Wooster, O.

WEISER, Harry Boyer (wī'sẽr), prof. chemistry coll. dean; b. Greencastle, O., Sept. 5, 1887; s. Calvin Walace and Mary (Boyer) W.; B.A., Ohio State U., 1911, M.A., 1912; Ph.D., Cornell, 1914; m. Hazel Eleanor McKean, Sept. 18, 1915; children—Dorothy Boyer (Mrs. W. W. Seale, Jr.), Marjorie McKean (Mrs. H. T. Witherspoon, Jr.). Instr. chemistry, U. Tenn., 1914-15; instr. chemistry, Rice Inst., Houston, 1915-18, asst. prof., 1918-19, prof., 1919—, dean 1933—. Capt. Chem. Warfare Service, 1918; chief of Catalytic Unit, Research Div.; chmn. com. on chemistry of colloids div. of chemistry and chemical technology, NRC, 1925-1943. Fellow Am. Acad. Arts and Sciences, A.A.A.S., Am. Inst. Chemists; mem. Am. Chem. Soc. (sec. div. of physical and inorganic chemistry, 1925, chmn. 1926; chmn. div. of colloid chemistry, 1927; chmn. colloid symposium committee, 1934-46); mem. The Faraday Society, Phi Beta Kappa, Sigma Xi, Phi Lambda Upsilon, Alpha Chi Sigma fraternities. Democrat. Presbyn. Mason. Author: The Hydrous Oxides, 1926; The Colloidal Salts, 1928; Inorganic Colloid Chemistry—Volume I, The Colloidal Elements, 1933, Vol. II, The Hydrous Oxides and Hydroxides, 1935; Vol. III, The Colloidal Salts, 1938; Colloid Chemistry, 1939. Also numerous articles on photo-chemistry and colloid chemistry. Editor Colloid Symposium Monograph; asso. editor Jour. of Physical Chemistry, 1927-28, 31-32, 36-37, 45-46; editor Colloid Chemistry, Jour. of Phys. and Colloid Chemistry, 1947—. Home: 1320 Milford, Houston, Texas. Died Sept. 27, 1950; buried Forest Park Cemetery, Houston.

WEISGERBER, William Edwin, educator; b. Luthersburg, Pa., Nov. 10, 1881; s. Henry and Theresa (Schindele) W.; B.S., Franklin and Marshall Coll., 1912, M.S., 1913, Sc.D., 1944, M.S., U. Pa., 1928; m. Margaret M. Kryder, June 10, 1914; children—W Eloise (dec.), Wilma E. Mem. faculty Franklin and Marshall Coll., 1912—, prof. chemistry, 1929—, head dept., 1946—. Mem. Am. Chem. Soc., Pa. Acad. Sci., Phi Beta Kappa, Phi Kappa Tau. Mem. Evang. Ref. Ch. Home: 615 N. President Av., Lancaster, Pa. Died Aug. 3, 1953.

WEISS, Lewis Allen (wīs), **business exec.; b. Chicago, Ill., May 8, 1893; s. Joseph Ignatius and Regina (Buchs) W.; student Kent Coll. of Law, 1912-15, U. of Southern Calif., 1926-29 (extension course in advanced economics); m. Sue C. Stephenson, April 22, 1922; 1 dau., Patricia Sue (Mrs. John Austin Armitage). Chairman board directors Mutual Broadcasting System; director and president of Don Lee Broadcasting System. Pacific Northwest Broadcasting Co.; pres., dir. Calif. Broadcasters, Inc.; pres. T. S. Lee Enterprises; dir. Organic Chemicals. Asst. adminstr. Nat. Production Authority 1951-52. Mem. Los Angeles Airport Commn. Served as capt. 4th U.S. Cavalry, 1915-19. Dir. Los Angeles Chamber of Commerce (v.p.); mem. Hollywood Chamber of Commerce, Merchants and Mfrs. Assn. (dir.), Mil Order of the World War, Television Broadcasters Assn. (dir. 1944-45), Delta Theta Phi, Alpha Delta Sigma. Clubs: Los Angeles Rotary (dir., 1943-45), University (Los Angeles). Home: 9917 Durant Dr., Beverly Hills, Cal. Died June 15, 1953; buried Forest Lawn Cemetery, Los Angeles.**

WEISS, Louis Stix (wis), lawyer; b. N.Y.C., Feb. 7, 1894; s. Samuel William and Carrier (Stix) W.; Horace Mann Sch., 1900-11; B.A., Yale, 1915; LL. B., Columbia U., 1920; m. Aline Pollitzer, June 6, 1919; children—Elizabeth (Mrs. Edwin L. Goldwasser), Barbara (Mrs. Robert S. Merrill), Katherine, William Pollitzer. With legal div., War Industries Bd. of U.S., 1917-18, U.S. Housing Corp., Dept. Labor, 1918-19; with Simpson, Thacher and Bartlett, attys., 1920-23, Weiss and Wharton, 1923-27; dep. atty. gen. N.Y. in Nassau County, 1924-25; mem. Cohen, Cole, Weiss & Wharton, 1927-46, Paul, Weiss, Wharton & Garrison, 1946—; gen. counsel, sec., dir. Field Enterprises, Inc., New York Star, Inc.; dir. Seeman Bros., Inc., Duffy-Mott Co., Inc., Simon & Schuster, Inc., Pocket Books, Inc., Louis G. Cowan, Inc., U.S. Com. for Care of European Children, Inc. (also v.p.), Field Foundation (also sec.), New School for Social Research (chmn. bd.). Dir. Am. Council on Race Relations. Trustee Nat. Opinion Research Center. Mem. Assn. Bar New York City, New York County Lawyers Assn. Clubs: Yale, City, Lawyers (New York City). Home: 262 Central Park West 24. Office: 61 Broadway, N.Y.C. 6. Died May 13, 1950.

WEISS, Samuel, business exec.; b. New York, Nov. 3, 1892; s. Simon and Rosa W.; graduate Cornell U., 1913; m. Mildred M. Atkins, Sept. 23, 1913, (dec. 1933); m. 2d, **S. Winifred Wilson, July 8, 1933. Civil engr. Otis Steel Co., Cleveland, 1913-14; salesman Semet-Solvay Co., Detroit, 1914-24, dist. sales mgr., Cleveland, O., 1924-25, div. sales mgr.,**

Buffalo N.Y., 1925-41; indsl. analyst, O.P.A., Washington, 1941-42, chief fuel sect. steel div., W.P.B., 1942-45; chief coke div., Solid Fuels Adminstrn. for War, 1944-45; exec. sec., Am. Coke and Coal Chemicals Inst., 1945-53, pres., 1953—. Mason. Home: 2480 16th St., Washington 9. Office: 711 14th St., Washington 5. Died Nov. 17, 1956.

WEISS, William, lawyer; b. Hungary, July 10, 1887; s. Jacob and Nina (Weinberger) W.; came to U.S., 1896; naturalized, 1902; LL.B., Brooklyn Law Sch., 1908; LL.M., New York Law Sch., 1909; m. Mildred Roth, Dec. 17, 1916; (dec. 1955); children—Beatrice Fine, Florence. Admitted N.Y. bar, 1909, and since practiced N.Y.C.; sec.-treas. Ambassador Holding Corp., Manville Constrn. Co., Inc.; secretary Triangle Warehouse Corp.; gen. counsel Ind. Order Brith Abraham, 1936-37, 1943-46; spl. asst. atty. gen., N.Y.; condemnation appraisal commr. (chmn.) Delaware River Aqueduct & Reservoir for N.Y.C., 1947-49; pub. mem. N.Y. State Minimum Wage Bd., 1952. advisory counsel Village of Hunter, N.Y. Hon. (formerly nat.) pres. Union Orthodox Jewish Congregations America; hon. sec. Synagogue Council Am.; hon. pres. Congregation Ohab Zedek (N.Y.); pres. Beth Hillel Hebrew Inst.; pres. board review and conciliation N.Y.C. Hebrew Schs.; dir. N.Y. Jewish Edn. Com.; former del. Am. Jewish Conf.; mem. adminstrv. and exec. bds. Am. Jewish Com.; formerly mem. administrative Commn. Am. Jewish Congress; formerly chmn. bd. govs. Council of Fraternal and Benevolent Orgns. of N.Y. Jewish Fedn.; trustee Jewish Memorial Hosp. of N.Y.; editor of mag. Orthodox Union, 1933-42; author of Civil Rights and Anti-Bias Laws of the State of New York; mem. and chmn. sch. bd. Borough of Manhattan, N.Y. City, 1916-32. Recipient Ednl. Alliance Hall of Fame award, 1954. Editor Mem. Am. Bar Assn., N.Y. County Lawyers Assn. (legislative and workmen's compensation coms.), Grand St. Boys Assn. Past consul Modern Woodmen Am. Home: 231 Seaman Av., Rockville Centre, L.I., N.Y. Office: 1440 Broadway, N.Y.C. 18. Died May 10, 1958.

WEIZMANN, Chaim (vītz'măn kī'ĭm), Zionist leader, scientist; b. Motol, Prov. of Grodno, Russia, Nov. 27, 1874; s. Reb Oiser and Rachel (Czerminsky) W.; ed. Pinsk High Sch. and U. of Berlin; D.Sc., U. of Freiburg, 1900; Sc.D., U. of Manchester, 1909, LL.D., 1919; m. Dr. Vera Chatzmann, 1906; children—Benjamin, Michael (dec.). Became naturalized Brit. subject, 1910; adjured Brit. citizenship on establishment of new State of Israel, of which is now citizen. Lecturer in organic chemistry U. of Geneva, 1901-04; became reader in biochemistry U. of Manchester; dir. Brit. Admiralty Labs., 1916-19, Elected president of the state of Israel, 1949; chairman 1st Zionist Commn., recognized by Brit. Govt. as adv. body to Brit. authorities in all Jewish questions, 1918; pres. World Zionist Orgn., 1921-29, Extended Jewish Agency for Palestine, 1929-31, 1935-46; obtained League of Nations ratification of mandate for Palestine, which also provided for severance of Trans-Jordan from Palestine area; pres. English Zionist Fedn., 1931-48; presided at World Zionist Congress, London, Aug. 1945; head Jewish delegation at meeting of U.N. Special Com. on Palestine, Lake Success, N.Y., Oct. 1947; chmn. bd. Hebrew U., Jerusalem, since 1932; dir. Daniel Sieff Research Inst., Rehovoth; elected pres. provisional govt. of new State of Israel, 1948. Author: Trial and Error (autobiography), 1949. Address: Hakirya, Israel. Died Nov. 9, 1952.*

WELCH, George Martin, telephone official; b. St. Charles, Ill., Jan. 29, 1881; s. George and Julia Ann (Lawler) W.; grad. Met. Bus. Coll., Chicago, 1900; Dr. Bus. Adminstrn., U. Mich., 1941; m. Sarah F. McElligott, Aug. 3, 1912; children—Margaret (Welch) Townsend, George Martin, James Arthur, Julia Ann (Welch) Yantis. Began as stenographer Northwestern Telephone Co., Mpls., 1904; chief clerk and office asst. to gen. mgr. 1905-07, asst. sec., asst. to gen. mgr., 1907-08; began with Mich. Bell Telephone Co., 1908, successively contract agt., commercial supt., gen. mgr., v.p. and gen. mgr. to 1934, pres. 1934-46, dir. to 1951. Mem. Detroit Bd. of Commerce (dir. 1926-28, 1931-32; 1st v.p. 1928-29; pres. 1929-30); Telephone Pioneers of America (pres., 1942). Republican. Catholic. Clubs: Detroit, Detroit Athletic, Detroit Economic, Engineering Society of Detroit. Home: 27 Oakland Park Blvd., Pleasant Ridge, Mich. Died Mar. 15, 1955.

WELCH, Howard A., business exec. Chmn., dir. Union Nat. Bank of Youngstown; asst. treas., dir. Youngstown Bldg. Material & Fuel Co.; dir. Shangri-La, Lowellsville, O., Albert H. Buehrie Co., Youngstown. Home: 32 W. Philadelphia St. Office: 6 W. Federal St., Youngstown, O. Died Feb. 20, 1957.

WELCH, Paul R., business exec.; b. Phila., Pa., July 20, 1882; s. Dr. Charles E. and Jennie (Ross) W.; LL.B., Columbia U. Law Sch., 1905; m. Mary Babcock, 1914 (dec.). With Welch Grape Juice Co. as v.p., 1903-14, v.p. and treas., 1914-28, became pres. and gen. mgr. 1928, now chmn. of bd. and dir. Mason. Clubs: Columbia University, Buffalo Athletic. Home: 203 E. Main St. Office: Westfield, N.Y. Died Nov. 22, 1952.

WELCH, Roy Dickinson, prof. music; b. Dansville, N.Y., Jan. 19, 1885; s. Enam Dickinson and Alice (Conable) W.; diploma U. of Mich. Sch. of Music, 1907; A.B., U. of Mich. Coll. of Literature, Science and Arts, 1909; hon. Mus.M., 1927; studied U. of Munich, 1930-31, U. of Vienna, 1931-32 (under Guggenheim fellowship); m. Mildred Scott, Aug. 11, 1911 (died July 23, 1917); m. 2d, Sylvia Eastman Spencer, June 16, 1920; children—Anne Spencer, Catherine Conable, Spencer, Roy Dickinson. Instr. in piano, U. of Mich. Schl. of Music, 1907-10; instr. history of music and composition, same, 1912-14; asst. prof. music, Smith Coll., Northampton, Mass., 1914-18, asso. prof., 1918-21, prof., 1921-35, also chmn. dept. of music, 1923-30 and 1933-34; visiting prof. music, Harvard, summers, 1923-34; visiting prof. music, Princeton U., 1934-35, prof and chmn. music dept. since 1935. Mem. bd. dirs. Naumburg Foundation since 1938; dir. Am. chapter of Internat. Soc. Contemporary Music, 1943-46; co-founder, chmn. bd. Soc. for Music in Liberal Arts Coll. Cons. expert War Finance Div. U.S. Treasury, June 1942-Sept. 1943. Mem. music adv. com. Joint Army-Navy Com. on Welfare and Relief, 1943. Served as capt. Am. Red Cross in France, 1918-19. Mem. Music Teachers Nat. Assn., Am. Musicol. Soc., Am. Assn. Univ. Profs., Phi Beta Kappa, Trigon (Univ. of Mich.). Author: The Study of Music in the American College, 1925; The Appreciation of Music, 1927, revised edit., 1945, 47; essays, chpts. in Roads to Knowledge, On Going to College. Also articles in mags. Home: 34 Allison Rd., Princeton, N.J. Died Jan. 8, 1951; buried Dansville, N.Y.

WELCH, Thomas Anthony, bishop; b. Faribault, Minn., Nov. 2, 1884; s. Thomas Joseph and Helen (Deasy) W.; grad. St. Thomas Coll., St. Paul, Minn., 1903; studied philosophy and theology at St. Paul Sem., 1903-09. Ordained priest R.C. Ch., 1909; sec. to Archbishop John Ireland, 1910-18; chancellor Archdiocese of St Paul, 1918-23; vicar general of Archdiocese of St. Paul; apptd. bishop of Duluth, Dec. 17, 1925, consecrated, Feb. 3, 1926. Home: 2215 E. Second St. Office: 215 W. 4th St., Duluth, Minn. Died Sept. 9, 1959.

WELCH, Vincent S., ins. exec.; b. Rochester, N. Y.; ed. Dean Acad., Franklin, Mass., and U. of Pa.; married; children—Mary Jane Straub, Vincent P. Football, baseball and basketball coach, Hobart Coll., Geneva, N.Y., 1919-28; with the Equitable Life Assurance Soc. since 1928 as agent, Rochester, N.Y., then group supervisor in home office; became div. mgr. Greater N.Y. dept., 1931, mgr. group dept. for all U.S., 1933; later 2d v.p. in charge central and Eastern Dept., Chicago; agency v.p. in charge ordinary and group depts., and since 1950, exec. vice pres. Served as lt., infantry, overseas with 81st Div. Home: 10 Davis Rd., Port Washington, L.I., N.Y. Office: Equitable Life Assurance Society, 393 7th Av., N.Y. City 1. Died Aug. 3, 1951.

WELCH, W(alter) S(cott), lawyer; b. nr. Collins, Miss., July 10, 1877; s. James N. and Mary Anise (Rogers) W.; B.S., A. and M. Coll. of Miss., 1898, M.S., 1901; LL.B., Millsaps Coll., 1906; m. Alice Tracy, Oct. 16, 1901; children—James Tracy, Walter Scott, David Cannon, Margaret Mills. Admitted to Miss. bar, 1906, since practiced Laurel, mem. Welch, Gibbs & Butts; city atty., 1909-10, 35-42, 49—; v.p. First Nat. Bank of Laurel, 1941—, Laurel Oil & Fertilizer Co., 1939—; dir., mem. exec. com. Merchants Co., Hattiesburg. Democratic presdl. elector, 1944. Mem. Am., Miss., Jones County bar assns., C. of C. Democrat. Rotarian. Home: 820 Fourth Av. Office: First Nat. Bank Bldg., Laurel, Miss. Died June 14, 1956; buried Laurel, Miss.

WELD, J. Linzee, corp. exec.; b. Milton, Mass., Nov. 10, 1896; s. C. Milnot and Marian (Linzee) W.; A.B., Harvard, 1918, M.B.A., 1920; m. Barbara Foster, Oct. 31, 1925 (died 1952); children—Barbara W. (Mrs. George Putnam), Jane L.; married second, Rose C. Weld. With Boston Mfg. Co., 1920-22; asst. treas. Suncook Mills, 1922-36, treas., 1936-43, pres., treas., 1941-43; v.p., dir. Textron, Inc., since 1943; dir. Am. Mut. Life Ins. Co., Allied Am. Mut. Fire Ins. Co., Amoskeag Co. Home: Charles River, Mass. Office: 1407 Broadway, N.Y.C. Died Feb. 19, 1956.

WELD, William Ernest, ex-coll. pres.; b. Marysville, O., Jan. 21, 1881; s. Theodore Dwight and Matilda Cochran (Smith) W.; A.B., Coll. of Wooster (O.), 1903, LL.D., 1927; A.M., Princeton, 1909; student Princeton Theol. Sem., 1906-09; Ph.D., Columbia, 1920; m. Margaret Elizabeth Elder, Aug. 26, 1909; children—Helen Elder, William Ernest, Frances Mary. Instr. economics and commercial law, Am. U., Beirut, Syria, 1903-06; ordained ministry Presbyn. Ch., 1909; prof. economics, Allahabad Christian Coll., Allahabad, India, 1909-18; asso. in economics, Columbia, 1919-21, asst. prof., 1922-24, asso. prof., 1924-27, prof., 1927-29, also asst. to dean, 1922-27; prof. economics and dean of coll., U. of Rochester, 1929-36; pres. Wells College, Aurora, New York, 1936-46. Lectr. on pub. fiance, Amherst, 1924 and 1927. Kahn Found. traveling fellow, 1927-28. Student Christian Movement in N.Y. State; trustee Wells Coll., Aurora, N.Y., 1931-47; trustee Cazenovia Junior College; mem. commn. on Istns. of Higher Edn., 1936—; president Middle States Assn. of Colls. and Secondary Schools, 1941-42. Consultant Com. on Need state university, 1946-47. Mem. Academy on Polit. Science, Am. Acad. Polit. and Social Science, Am. Econ. Assn., Phi Beta Kappa, Alpha Tau Omega. Clubs: Fortnightly, Humdrum. Author: India's Demand for Transportation, 1920; A Case Book for Economics (with Alvin S. Toslebe), 1927; Standard Economics (with others), 1922. Address: The Brunswick, Waterville, N.Y. Deceased.

WELFLE, Frederick Edgar (wĕl'flā), univ. pres.; b. Hamler, O., Aug. 21, 1897; s. Joseph and Catherine (Kaple) W.; B.A., Gonzaga U., 1922, M.A., 1923; M.A., St. Louis U., 1930; Ph.D. (history), O. State U., 1940. Entered Soc. of Jesus, 1916; ordained Roman Catholic priest, St. Louis, 1929. Instr. English and classical languages, Loyola Acad., Chicago, 1923-25, St. John's High Sch., Toledo, 1925-26; instr. Latin, history and religion, St. Xavier High Sch., Cincinnati, 1931-32; asst. prof. history, Xavier U., Cincinnati, 1932-37; prof. history and head of dept., John Carroll U., 1940-46, dir. grad. work, 1944-46, pres. since 1946. Trustee, Council on World Affairs. Mem. Am. Hist. Assn., Catholic Hist. Assn., Jesuit Hist. Assn., Ohio Coll. Assn. (exec. com. 1952). Address: John Carroll University, University Heights, Cleve. 18. Died Aug. 17, 1956.

WELKE, Edward Arthur (wĕl'kĕ), clergyman; b. Eau Claire County, Wis., Feb. 22, 1889; s. August W.; student Concordia Coll., St. Paul, Minn., 1903-07, Concordia Sem., 1907-11, U. Wis., 1912-13; D.D., Capital U., 1938; m. Amanda Weissbrodt, July 2, 1911; children—Theophil Eslie, Leo August William, Dorothy Amanda. Ordained to ministry of Luth. Ch., 1913; pastor Madison, S.D., 1913-19, Belmond, Ia., 1920-21, Halloway, Minn., 1921-23, Pine Island, Minn., 1923-30. Pres. Minn. Dist. Joint Synod of Ohio, 1928-30; pres. Minn. Dist. Am. Luth. Ch., 1930—; chmn. Bd. Home Missions, Am. Luth. Ch.; vice pres. American Lutheran Church; mem. Minn. State Bd. of Parole. Home: 588 N. Lexington Parkway, St. Paul 4, Minn. Died Dec. 3, 1949; buried Elmhurst Cemetery, St. Paul, Minn.

WELKER, Herman, ex-U.S. senator; b. Cambridge, Ida., Dec. 11, 1906; s. John Thornton and Ann Zella (Shepherd) W.; LL.B., U. Ida., 1929; m. Gladys Pence, Sept. 20, 1930; 1 dau., Nancy. Admitted to Ida. bar, 1929; pros. atty., Washington Country, 1929-35; gen. practice law, Los Angeles, 1936-43, Payette, Ida., 1944-50. State senator from Payett Ceounty, Ida., 1948-50; U.S. Senator from Ida., 1951—. Served with U.S.A.A.F., 1943-44. Mem. Am. Legion, Sigma Chi, Phi Alpha Delta. Republican. Episcopalian. Elk, Mason (Shriner). K. P. Address: 3300 Kootenai, Boise, Ida. Died Oct. 30, 1957; buried Arlnigton Nat. Cemetery.

WELKER, William Henry, teacher, investigator; b. Red Hill, Pa., Aug. 20, 1879; s. William Alexander and Angelina (Wile) W.; A.C., Lehigh U., 1904; Ph.D., Columbia, 1908; Sc.D., Franklin and Marshall College, 1942; m. Evie M. Hutchinson, June 1904 (dec. June 3, 1950); 1 dau., Dr. Dorothy Hutchinson (Mrs. Joseph Greengood); m. 2d, Grace Day, Dec. 1953. Asst. in biol. chemistry, Columbia, 1904-07; pathol. assistant in obstetrics, Sloane Maternity Hosp., New York, 1906-07; demonstrator physiol. chemistry, U. Pa., 1907-10; chemist to German Hosp., New York, 1910; asso. in biol. chemistry, 1910-11, asst. prof., 1911-12, Columbia; asst. prof. physiol. chemistry, U. Ill. Coll. Medicine, 1913, asso. prof. 1919-21, prof., 1921-31, prof., head of dept., 1931-47, emeritus; mem. grad. teaching faculty, U. Ill., 1916—, mem. exec. faculty, Graduate Sch., 1946—. Fellow A.A.A.S.; charter mem. Am. Soc. Biol. Chemists; mem. Radium Inst. America, Soc. Exptl. Biology and Medicine, Harvey Soc., Tau Beta Pi, Sigma Xi, Alpha Omega Alpha; fellow Inst. of Medicine Chicago (v.p. 1947); asso. fellow A.M.A.; mem. Am. Pub. Health Assn., Ill. Acad. Science, Internat. Assn. for Dental Research, Am. Congress on Internal Medicine; F.A.C.P.; affiliated mem. of the Chicago Allergy Society. Gibbs prize, $2,000, N.Y. Academy Medicine, 1907 (with Dr. Dittman) for essay on nephritis. Contbr. to scientific jours. Home: 534 N. Elmwood Av., Oak Park, Ill. Died July 7, 1956; buried East Greenville, Pa.

WELLER, Carl Vernon, pathologist; b. St. Johns, Mich., Feb. 17, 1887; s. Martin and Emma (Pulfrey) W.; A.B., Albion (Mich.) Coll., 1908; M.D., U. Mich., 1913, M.S., 1916, D.Sc., Albion College, 1956 (honorary); graduated study in pathology, Vienna, Austria, 1925; m. Elsie Huckle, June 26, 1913; children—Thomas Huckle, John Martin. Mem. faculty, U. Mich., 1911—, instr. pathology, 1911-16, asst. prof., 1916-21, asso. prof., 1921-24, prof., 1924—, asst. dir. pathol. labs., 1924-31, dir., 1931-37, chmn. dept. of pathology, 1938—, also mem. exec. com. Med. Sch., 1934-37, 1946-49. Mem. sci. adv. bd. Armed Forces Inst. Pathology, 1950—. Fellow Am. Geriatrics Soc., A.C.P.; member N.Y. Acad. Scis., Nat. Research Council (com. on pathol.

1947-50), Am. Assn. Cancer Research, Am. Assn. Pathologists and Bacteriologists (ex-pres.), A.M.A., Assn. Am. Physicians (emeritus), Fedn. of Am. Socs. for Exptl. Biology, Internat. Assn. Geographic Pathology, Internat. Assn. Med. History (Am. sect.), Internat. Assn. Med. Museums (ex-pres. Am.-Canadian sect.), Am. Cancer Soc. (mem. edn. com. 1946-47), Sociedad Argentina de Argentina de Anatomia Normal y Patologica, Mich. Pathological Soc. (ex-pres.), U. Mich. Research Club (ex-pres.), Soc. Experimental Biology and Medicine, American Soc. for Exptl. Pathology (ex-pres.), Galens, Alpha Omega Alpha, Sigma Xi (Mich. ex-pres.), Phi Sigma, Gamma Alpha, Nu Sigma Nu. Author: (with A. S. Warthin) Medical Aspects of Mustard Gas Poisoning, 1919; Hemolymph Node Chapter in Handbook of Hematology, 1938. Editor: Contributions to Medical Science, 1927; Annals Internal Medicine, 1931-33; Am. Jour. Path., 1941—. Mem. editorial bd. of Physiol. Reviews, 1941-44. Contbr. many articles to med. jours. Home: 1130 Fair Oaks Parkway, Ann Arbor, Mich. Died Dec. 10, 1956.

WELLER, Frank I., newspaperman; b. Vincennes, Ind.; s. Willard E. and Nora B. (Johnson) W.; student Indiana U.; m. Marcella V. Rielly; 1 daughter, Rita Ann. Reporter Seymour Democrat, Seymour Republican, Columbus (Ind.) Republican, 1919-21; news editor Peru (Ind.) Tribune, 1922-23; telegraph editor St. Petersburg (Fla.) Times, 1924; asst. mgr. Internat. News Service bureau, Indpls., 1924-25, bureau mgr., Springfield, Ill., Columbus, O., 1925-26; feature writer Gary (Ind.) Post Tribune, Kokomo (Ind.) Dispatch, 1926; news editor Ind. Tribune (Dem. party tabloid), Indianapolis, 1926; chief of State House staff, Ill. State Register, Springfield, 1926; with The Associated Press, 1926—, as chief of legislative staff, Springfield bureau, 1926, farm editor, Washington, D.C., 1926-32, corr. Brit. Econ. Conf., Ottawa, Can., 1932, feature editor Washington, D.C., 1932-36, wire photo editor, 1937; gen. staff, special writer, 1937-46; chief Wisc. Rapids Daily Tribune Washington bur., 1946—. His summary "First Ten Months of the New Deal" voted best financial story of 1933 by The Associated Press membership (later published in book form); won Nat. Headliners Club award for feature stories, 1941. Newspaper, magazine and radio contributor. Clubs: National Press, National Headliners (Washington, D. C.). Address: 1701 H St. N.W., Washington. Died Apr. 19, 1951.

WELLES, Kenneth Brakeley, clergyman; b. Scranton, Pa., June 18, 1886; s. Charles Hopkins and Hannah (Sherrerd) W.; A.B., Yale, 1908; student Union Theol. Sem., 1909-10, 1911-12, New College, Edinburgh, 1910-11; D.D., Union Coll., 1937; m. Margaret Whittemore, Dec. 9, 1913; children—Atossa Frost, Sherrerd Belin, Owen Watkins, Lucie Margaret. Ordained Presbyn. ministry, 1912; pastor Manlius, N.Y., 1912-16, Congl. Ch., Old Lyme, Conn., 1916-18, Edwards Ch., Northampton, Mass., 1919-28, Westminster Presbyn. Ch., Albany, N.Y., since 1928. Chaplain U.S. Army, Camp Lee, Va., 1918-19. Mem. Delta Kappa Epsilon. Republican. Home: 118 S. Pine Av., Albany, N.Y. Died Aug. 21, 1953.

WELLFORD, Edwin Taliaferro, clergyman; b. Gloucester County, Va., Dec. 6, 1870; s. Beverley Randolph and Susan Seddon (Taliaferro) W.; student Richmond U.; A.B., Hampden-Sydney Coll., 1891, D.D., 1910; student Union Theol. Sem., 1890-92; m. Courtenay Brooke Selden, Apr. 2, 1892. Ordained ministry Presbyn. Ch. in U.S., 1892; pastor First Presbyterian Ch., Newport News, Va., 1892-1941, pastor emeritus, September, 1941—; began with mission station, 25 members, and has received about 3,000 into ch.; built or remodeled 7 structures and sent off 3 colonies. Served as moderator Synod of Va., also first moderator Presbytery of Norfolk; host to Synod of Va., 1900, to Gen. Assembly Presbyn. Ch. in U.S., 1915; frequently speaker before Gen. Assembly and member 7 times; former pres. Newport New Ministerial Assn. Mem. defense council Presbyn. Ch., U.S. (chmn. chaplains com.); mem. Judicial Com. Presbyn. Ch. U.S., 1943—. Trustee Union Theol. Sem., Va. pres. bd.), Va. Children's Friends Soc., Hampden-Sydney Coll.; v.p. Va. Seamen's Friend Soc.; past pres. Va. Anti-Saloon League. Mem. S.C.V. (chaplain), Va. Sons Confederate Vets., Newport News Chamber Commerce; chaplain Newport News Pioneers Soc.; mem. Kappa Sigma. Mem. Western sect. Alliance of Reformed Chs. and del. several times to world confs.; mem. commn. on Cooperation and Union Presbyn. Church U.S. Democrat. Author: Lynching of Jesus, 1905; Crime and Cure, 1930. Delivered opening prayer, Yorktown Sesqui-centennial, 1931. Home: 66 33d St., Newport News, Va.; and Glen Roy, Gloucester County, Va. Died Nov. 26, 1956; buried Peninsula Meml. Park.

WELLINGTON, Charles Oliver, accountant; b. Belmont, Mass., Oct. 1, 1886; s. Arthur Jeduthan and Helen Augusta (Hill) W.; A.B., Harvard Coll., 1907; m. Helen Cushing Underwood, Sept. 26, 1912 (div.); children—Margaret (Mrs. George Parsons), Roger Underwood, Jane (Mrs. Roger Merrill, Jr.), Martha (Mrs. George C. Cunningham Jr.), Florence Cushing (Mrs. Martin Rudolph Haase); m. 2d Lucile Pierce Rohde, Apr. 19, 1930; children—Elizabeth Ann (Mrs. Dennis Puleston), Nancy (Mrs. Knute Lee), Patricia (Mrs. Robert Barron). Joined the staff Eastern Audit Co., Boston, 1907, later with Gunn, Richards & Co.; became asso. with Clinton H. Scovell & Co., 1911, partner, 1913; name of firm changed to Scovell, Wellington & Co., sr. partner since 1926. Trustee Brookhaven Library. Mem. Am. Inst. Accountants (pres. 1940-41), N.Y. and Mass. socs. certified pub. accountants, Am. Soc. Mech. Engrs., Am. Econ. Assn., Nat. Assn. Cost Accountants. Assn. Cons. Management Engrs. (pres. 1935-37). Republican. Unitarian. Clubs: Harvard, Down Town Assn., West Side Tennis (New York); Apawamis (Rye, New York); Bellport Yacht, Old Inlet (Bellport, New York); Longwood Cricket (Boston). Gulf Stream Golf (Fla.). Author; lectr. accounting bus. and econ. subjects. Home: 169 E. 78th St., N.Y.C. 21. Office: 111 Broadway, N.Y.C. Died Feb. 6, 1959; buried Mt. Auburn Cemetery, Cambridge, Mass.

WELLMAN, Beth Lucy, prof. child psychology; b. Clarion, Ia., June 10, 1895; d. Alonzo and Hannah Esta (Nichols) Wellman; A.B., State U. of Iowa, 1920, Ph.D., 1925; student U. of Chicago and Columbia U. Research asst. Iowa Child Welfare Research Station, 1921-24; asso. in research, Lincoln Sch., Teachers Coll., Columbia U., 1924-25; research assistant professor Iowa Child Welfare Research Sta., 1925-29, research asso. professor, 1929-37, prof., 1937—, chmn. administrative com., 1949-51. Fellow Soc. Research Child Development, A.A.A.S.; mem. Nat. Soc. Study of Edn. (mem. year-book com.), Am. Pschol. Assn., Midwestern Psychol. Assn., Nat. Assn. Nursery Edn., N.E.A., Sigma Xi. Author: Child Psychology (with George Dinsmore Stoddard), 1934; Manual of Child Psychology (with George Dinsmore Stoddard), 1936. Contbr. original researches on mental and motor development of children. Contbg. editor: Jour. Exptl. Edn. Home: Iowa City, Ia. Died Mar. 22, 1952.

WELLMAN, Hiller Crowell, librarian; b. Boston, Mar. 2, 1871; s. Joseph Hiller and Ellen Maria (Crowell) W.; A.B., Harvard, 1894; Litt.D., Am. Internat. Coll., 1945; m. Emily A. Whiston, Sept. 20, 1900; children—Bertram, Constance, Katharine (dec.), Margaret, Ellen. Asst. in Boston Athenaeum, 1894-96; supervisor branches Boston Pub. Library, 1896-98; librarian Brookline (Mass.) Pub. Library, 1898-1902; librarian City Library Assn., Springfield, 1902-49, consultant. Mem. Mass. Free Pub. Library Commn., 1909-39. Pres. Springfield Adult Ednl. Council. Contbr. periodicals on library topics. Sec. 1897-99, pres. 1901, Mass. Library Club; pres. American Library Assn., 1914-15; mem. Phi Beta Kappa (Harvard). Home: 125 Atwater Rd. Office: City Library, Springfield, Mass. Died Feb. 3, 1956.

WELLS, Agnes Ermina, educator, polit. worker; b. Saginaw, Mich., Jan. 4, 1876; d. Edgar S. and Julia H. (Comstock) Wells; student Bryn Mawr Coll., 1 yr.; A.B., U. Mich., 1903; A.M., Carleton Coll., 1916; Ph.D., U. Mich., 1924. Prin. high sch., Crystal Falls, Mich., 1904-05; teacher mathematics Duluth High Sch., 1905-06, head math. dept., 1907-14; instr. mathematics, Carleton Coll., Northfield, Minn., 1915-16; social dir. Helen Newberry Residence U. of Mich. dormitory, 1917-18; acting dean of women, U. Mich., summer 1917 and yr. 1918; dean of women, Ind. U., 1919-38, prof. mathematics, astronomy, 1938-44, emeritus dean of women, 1944—. Mem. Nat. Assn. Deans of Women (pres. 1923, 24, 1924-25; 2d v.p. 1925-27), Ind. Assn. Dean Women (pres. 1933-35; vice-pres. 1936), Am. Assn. Univ. Women (1st v.p. 1926-29), Am. Assn. Univ. Profs., Ind. Acad. Sci., Nat. Ednl. Assn., D.A.R (regent Bloomington, Ind, chapt. 1945-46), Phi Beta Kappa, Sigma Xi, Pi Lambda Theta, Gamma Phi Beta. Republican. Episcopalian. Clubs: Indiana Sch. Women's Club, Business and Professional Women's Club (state ednl. chmn. 1936; state pres. Ind. Fed. 1938-39), mem. Nat. Woman's Party, 1943—, Nat. Council, 1945—, Chmn. College Women's Com., Nat. Women's Party, 1944—), Woman's Club of Bloomington; Ind. U. Women's Faculty Club (pres. 1940-41). Home: 111 South Granger St., Saginaw West Side, Mich.; (summer) Upper Jay, N.Y. Died July 6, 1959.

WELLS, Arthur Register, lawyer; b. Corning, Ia., Dec. 1, 1873; s. Arthur Lee and Lucina (Register) W.; A.B., Princeton U., 1895; student State U. of Ia. Law Sch., 1895-96; m. Helen Wilson, Apr. 28, 1897; children—Mary (dec.), Theodore Arthur. Admitted to Ia. bar, 1896; in practice at Corning, Ia., 1896-1907, at Omaha, Neb., 1913—; atty. for C.,B.&Q. Ry., Omaha, 1907-13; mem. of firm Wells, Martin & Lane, Omaha, and its predecessors, 1913—; counsel for Omaha Nat. Bank. Served as capt., Army Service Corps, U.S. Army, 1918. Mem. Omaha Bd. of Edn., 1917-21. Mem. Am. Neb. State, Douglas County bar assns. Republican. Presbyn. Mason (K.T., Shriner). Club: Omaha. Home: 113 N. Happy Hollow Blvd. Office: Omaha National Bank Bldg., Omaha, Neb. Died Jan. 5, 1955; buried Corning, Ia.

WELLS, (Grant) Carveth, explorer, author, lecturer; b. Barnes, Surrey, Eng., Jan. 21, 1887; s. Thomas Grant Wells, of Bermuda, and Anna Carkeet, of Cornwall; Civil and Mech. Engineer, London U., 1909; m. 2d, Zetta Robart, Mar. 7, 1932; 1 dau., Francis Virginia. Engineer on the original survey of Grand Trunk Pacific Railway, Canada; later assistant professor civil engineering, London Univ.; sent to Malay Peninsula by British Govt. and lived in the jungle for 6 yrs. surveying route for East Coast Ry., and making study of flora, fauna and people of the peninsula; came to U.S., 1918, taking out naturalization papers; made expdn. to Arctic Lapland for Swedish Govt. and Am. Museum Natural History; traveled in Morocco, Syria, Palestine, Egypt, China, Japan, Manchukuo, India; Chicago del. to Centenary of Royal Geog. Soc., London; leader of Massee expdn. to Mountains of the Moon (Ruwenzori) for Chicago Geog. Soc.; leader of Milwaukee Museum expdn. to Kenya and Tanganyika, and of Massee expdn. to Caribbean Sea; leader Chicago Geog. Soc. Expdn. to Russia Caucasus Mts. and Mt. Ararat, 1932, expdn. to Panama and Mexico, 1935; expdn. to Hokkaido, Japan, study of Hairy Ainus; also returned to Malay Jungle, auspices Nat. Geog. Soc., Chicago Geog. Soc., Nat. Travel Club, 1939; expedition to Kashmir, Pakistan and India, 1950. Has lectured widely in the U.S., Great Britain, Norway and Sweden; civilian orientation lecturer to soldiers about to go abroad, U.S. War Dept., 1942 and 1943. Pioneer radio television broadcaster; producer of motion pictures, "Hell Below Zero," "Cockeyed Animal World," "Russia Today," "Lapland." Fellow American Geog. Soc., Royal Geog. Soc.; asso. mem. Instn. Civ. Engrs. (Eng.); elected patron Chicago Geog. Soc., 1930. Mem. Ch. of England. Clubs: Ends of the Earth, Explorers, Nat. Arts, Circumnavigators, Authors, Adventurers, Faculty Club of Columbia U., Dutch Treat (New York); Old Pauline, British Commonwealth. Royal Socs. Club (London); Penang (Straits Settlements); Mandalay (Southampton, Bermuda); Explorers (N.Y.). Author: Field Engrs. Handbook, 1913; Six Years in the Malay Jungle, 1925; A Jungleman and His Animals, 1925; Let's Do the Mediterranean, 1928; In Coldest Africa, 1929; Adventure, 1931; Kapoot, 1933; Exploring the World, 1934; Bermuda in Three Colors, 1935; Pana-mexico, 1937; Around the World with Bobby and Betty, 1939; North of Singapore, 1940; Raff, The Jungle Bird, 1941; Introducing Africa, 1943; Raffles The Bird Who Thinks He's A Person, 1945. Home: "Mandalay," Southampton, Bermuda. Address: Explorers Club, N. Y. City; also "Mandalay," Southhampton, Bermuda. Died Feb., 1957.

WELLS, Frederick Brown, corp. official; b. Am. parentage, Menton, France, Apr. 21, 1873; s. Thomas Bucklin and Annie Elizabeth (Jonas) W.; student U. Minn., 1889-90, Yale, 1890-93; m. Mary Drew Peavey, Sept. 19, 1898; children—Thomas B. (dec.), Mary (Staples) (dec.), Frank H. (dec.), Frederick Brown, Jr.; m. 2d, Grace Louise Broadfoot, June 17, 1936. Began career as clerk, 1891; pres. F. H. Peavey & Co.; dir. First National Bank & Trust Co. Served as colonel on general staff, U.S. Army, 1917-19. Awarded D.S.M., 1919. Dir. Minn. Inst. Arts, Mpls. Symphony Orchestra. Republican. Episcopalian. Clubs: Minneapolis; Cloister (Yale); Manitoba (Winnipeg); Woodhill Country. Home: Bloomington, Minneapolis. Office: Grain Exchange Bldg., Mpls. Died Aug. 3, 1953.

WELLS, George Miller, cons. engr.; b. New Brunswick, Can., July 4, 1879; s. Asael James and Apphia (Moore) W.; student U. of Wash., 1893-96, Mich. Coll. of Mines, 1901, non-resident extension course, U. of Chicago, 1902-03; m. Elizabeth Gibson Bradley, July 7, 1909; children—George Calhoun, Thomas Moore. Jr. civil engr., sea coast defenses, U.S. Engr. Corps, 1902-04; asst. engr. in charge surveys, Panama Canal, Atlantic Coast to continental divide, 1904-06, office engr. in charge Atlantic div. designs, 1908-13, resident engr. in charge municipal division and bldg. div., 1913-16; partner Geo. W. Goethals Co., cons. engrs., 1916-23; pres. Solvay Process Co., Semet Solvay Co., Atmospheric Nitrogen Co., Brunner-Mond Co. of Can.; vice pres. Allied Chem. and Dye Corp., 1923-32; pres. Union Sulphur Co., 1932-45; in private practice, 1945—; dir. and mem. exec. com. Va. Carolina Chem. Corp., Congoleum Nairn Corp.; dir. Daystrom, Inc., Heyden Chem. Corp. Mem. Am. Soc. C.E. Rep. Episcopalian. Clubs: Recess, Union League (New York); Upper Montclair (N.J.) Country. Home: 152 Clarewill Av., Upper Montclair, N.J. Office: 67 Wall St., N.Y.C. Died May 3, 1957; buried Newton, Mass.

WELLS, Hermon J(oseph), ry. atty. and official; b. Salt Lake City, Utah, Sept. 22, 1891; s. Joseph S. and Anna (Sears) W.; B.A., Univ. of Utah, 1916; LL.B., George Washington U., 1929; LL.M., Harvard, 1930; married Carolyn Augusta Ivins, July 30, 1917; children—Anthony Ivins, Hermon Manning, Jane Fairfax (Mrs. Roger G. Harder), Barbara Ivins. Teller, Utah Lt. & Ry. Co., 1910-11; represented church in Eng., 1911-13; Univ. of Utah, 1914-17 (Editor Utah Chronicle, 1914-15; student-body pres., 1915-16); prin. Milford, Utah high sch., 1917-18; sec.-treas. Insulation Mfg. Co., 1918-22; head English dept., L.D.S. Coll., 1922-27; George

Washington U., 1927-29; also audit clerk Dept. of Justice, 1927-28; U.S. Civil Service examiner, 1928-29; Harvard Law Sch., 1929-30; law examiner and acting sec., Civil Service Commn., 1930; tax counsel, N.Y. N.Y.&H.R.R.Co., 1931-35, solicitor, 1935-38, asst. gen. counsel, 1938-43; handled for trustees of Co., bulk of litigation in reorgn. proceedings, U.S. Dist. Ct. for Conn. and appellate cts.; vice pres. and gen. counsel, 1943—, in charge law and of finance; v.p., gen. counsel and dir., The Connecticut Co.; Berkshire St. Ry. Co., New England Transportation Co.; v.p. and gen. counsel N. E. Steamship Co.; gen. counsel and dir., So. Manchester R.R. Co.; gen. counsel, N.Y. Connecting R.R. Co., County Transportation Co.; counsel and dir., Hartford & Conn. Western R.R. Co.; dir., gen. counsel, N.Y. & Stamford Ry. Co.; v.p., dir. Old Colony R.R. Co., Providence Securities Co.; gen. counsel N.Y. Westchester & Boston Ry. Co.; v.p., N.E. Car Co. Mem. YMCA; Law Com. of A.A.R.; Conf. of Ry. Counsel; Am., Conn., bar assns., Phi Alpha Delta, Tau Kappa Alpha (hon.). Mormon. Clubs: Graduates, New Haven Country (New Haven); High Lane (Hamden) (pres. 1939-42); New Haven R.R. (pres. 1941-42); Social Science, Benchers (New Haven). Home: 135 Spring Glen Terrace, Hamden, Conn. Office: 71 Meadow St., New Haven. Died Dec. 17, 1950; buried Salt Lake City.

WELLS, Joel Cheney, trustee Am. Optical Co.; b. Southbridge, Mass., Nov. 11, 1874; s. George Washington and Mary Eliza (McGregory) W.; ed. Worcester Acad.; m. Florence Winifred Morse, Nov. 20, 1901; children—John Morse, Gertrude Alice, Florence (dec.); m. 2d, Marion Hengerer Hollister, July 20, 1942. With Am. Optical Co., Southbridge, 1893—, clerk, 1902-03; sec., 1903-08, dir. 1908—, v.p., 1913-30, exec. v.p., 1930-37, trustee 1912—, President and trustee Wells Hist. Museum, dir. Megantic Fish & Game Corp. Member Massachusetts S.A.R. Republican. Baptist. Mason (32°). Clubs: Country (Brookline); Union (Boston); Fishers Island; Southbridge; Cohasse Country. Home: 5815 La Jolla Mesa Dr., La Jolla, Cal. Died Jan. 6, 1960; buried Southridge Oak Ridge Cemetery. Office: care American Optical Co., Southbridge, Mass.

WELLS, Kenneth Robert, banker; b. Breckenridge, Minn., Mar. 15, 1904; s. Robert Joseph and Sarah E. (Langford) W.; A.B., U. Minn., 1929; diploma Grad. Sch. Banking Rutgers U., 1944; m. Dorothy P. Kenning, Feb. 2, 1929. Asst. credit mgr. Mpls. dist. B. F. Goodrich Co., 1927-29; with Comml. Investment Trust, Inc., Chgo., 1929-39; with Am. Nat. Bank & Trust Co., Chicago, since 1939, asst. cashier, 1942-44, asst. v.p., 1944-48, v.p. indsl. loaning div. since 1948; lectr. finance Northwestern U., 1947-52, Central States Sch. Banking U. Wis., 1950. Mem. Chgo. Assn. Commerce and Industry (dir. 1952-53), Chgo. Credit Mens' Assn. (treas., dir. 1953-54, American, Illinois (president of installment lending division 1952-53) bankers associations, Nat. Constrn. Machinery Credit Group (treas.), Robert Morris Assos., Theta Xi. Baptist. Clubs: Union League, Bankers (Chgo.); Park Ridge Country, Park Ridge University (pres. 1951-52). Author articles on installment credit. Home: 700 N. Overhill Av., Park Ridge, Ill. Office: 33 N. LaSalle St., Chgo. 90. Died June 7, 1958; buried Sunset Meml. Park, Mpls.

WELLS, Orlando William, map pub.; b. Southold, L.I., N.Y., Oct. 7, 1878; s. Oscar Lewis and Caroline Frances (Coffin) W.; direct desc. of William Wells of Southwold, Eng., one of original settlers of Southold, N.Y., 1640; grad. Southold High Sch., 1896; Eastman Business Coll., Poughkeepsie, 1897; m. Mae Schoenk Daemish, Oct. 7, 1905; children—William Daemish, Francis Drake, Mildred Mae (Mrs. Harold K. Hughes). With Robert Crooks & Co., New York, 1897-98; with Simpson, Spence & Young, New York, 1898-1902; asst. sec. Barber Asphalt Paving Co., Phila., 1902-20; with Carib Syndicate, Ltd., New York, 1920-22; with Internat. Map Co., Inc., New York, since 1922, pres. since 1925; pres. and dir. Southern Exploration Co., Inc.; v.p. and dir. Wichita River Oil Corp.; sec., treas., dir. Venezuelan Holding Corp. Fellow Am. Geog. Soc.; mem. Am. Inst. Mining and Metall. Engrs., Am. Gas Assn., Pan-Am. Soc. Republican. Methodist. Club: Explorers (New York). Home: 189 Weaver St., Larchmont, N.Y. Office: O. W. Wells & Co., 90 West St., N.Y.C. Died Jan., 1956.

WELLS, Oscar, banker; b. Platte County, Mo., Feb. 6, 1875; s. Wesley W. and Rosa A. (Mock) W.; student Bethany (W.Va.) Coll. to end of jr. yr.; m. Hallie Hurst Jacob, Oct. 11, 1900. Asst. cashier, Wells Banking Co., Platte City, Mo., 1898-99; pres. Bank of Edgerton, Mo., 1899-1902; cashier Carthage (Mo.) Nat. Bank, 1903-05, Ft. Worth (Tex.) Nat. Bank, 1905-09, Commercial Nat. Bank, Houston, 1909-12; v.p. Union Nat. Bank, Houston, 1912-13, 1st Nat. Bank, Houston, 1913-14; gov. and dir. Federal Reserve Bank, Dallas, Oct. 16, 1914-Mar. 1, 1915 (resigned); pres. 1st Nat. Bank, Birmingham, Ala., 1915-30, chmn. bd. since 1930; dir. Woodward Iron Co., Birmingham Fire Ins. Co., Louisville & Nashville R.R. Co., U.S. Fidelity & Guaranty Co., Baltimore, Md., Ala. Power Co. Mem. Fed. Adv. Council, 6th Dist., 1920, 24, 25; pres. Am. Bankers Assn., 1925-26; dir. U.S. Chamber of Commerce, 1928-32, treas., 1931-32, dir. since 1939. Mem. Beta Theta Pi. Democrat. Presbyterian. Mason (32°, K.T.). Club: Mountain Brook. Home: 3830 Crescent Rd., Mountain Terrace, Birmingham. Office: First National Bank, Birmingham, Ala. Died May 30, 1953.

WELLS, Walter Farrington, pub. utility official; b. Rahway, N.J., Jan. 10, 1870; s. William Edmund and Anna Potter (Woodruff) W.; prep. edn., Pingry Prep. Sch., Elizabeth, N.J.; student Rutgers Coll., 1890-92, hon. E.E., 1915; m. Elizabeth Stephens, Oct. 5, 1898; children—Donald Stephens (dec.), Margery (Mrs. Kenneth M. Bevier). Draftsman, later elec. supt., Edison Electric Illuminating Co. of Brooklyn, 1892-97; was asst. gen. mgr. Manhattan Electric Light Co., Harlem Lighting Co., supt. Mount Morris Electric Light Co., dist. supt. N.Y. Edison Co., 1897-1905; gen. supt. Edison Electric Illuminating Co. of Brooklyn, 1905-13; v.p., gen. mgr. and dir. Kings County Electric Light & Power Co., 1913-19; was 1st v.p., gen. mgr. and dir. Brooklyn Edison Co.; v.p. and dir. Amsterdam Electric Light, Heat & Power Co., Edison Constrn. Co.; treas. and dir. Elec. Testing Labs. until retired, 1935. Fellow Am. Inst. E.E.; mem. Am. Soc. M.E., Nat. Electric Light Assn. (past pres.), Assn. Edison Electric Illuminating Cos. (past pres.), N.Y. State Chamber Commerce, Brooklyn Chamber Commerce, Delta Kappa Epsilon. Clubs: Engineers, Crescent Athletic, Cherry Valley, Madison Beach. Home: 458 Washington Av., Brooklyn. Died Aug. 31, 1958.

WELLS, William Calvin, lawyer; b. Raymond, Miss., Sept. 9, 1878; s. William Calvin and Mary Eliza (Miller) W.; A.B., U. Miss., 1899; LL.B., Millsaps Coll., Jackson, Miss., 1901; m. Rosa Farrar Watkins, Dec. 8, 1904; children—Alice Watkins, William Calvin, Rosa Farrar, Mary Miller, Erskine Watkins. Admitted to Miss. bar, 1901, and practiced since at Jackson; mem. firm Wells, Wells, Newman & Thomas pres. Walthall Hotel Co.; general counsel and dir. Lamar Life Ins. Co., Miss. Fire Ins. Co.; counsel and dir. Jackson State Nat. Bank; dir. Mortgage Bond & Trust Co. Formerly mem. Miss. Nat. Guard; maj. judge advocate, U.S. Army, 1918-19. Pres. bd. trustees Belhaven Coll. for Young Ladies; former mem. bd., State Instns. of Higher Learning of Miss. Mem. Am. Bar Assn., Miss. State Bar Assn., Hinds County Bar Assn., Miss. Hist. Soc., Phi Delta Phi, Delta Psi. Democrat. Presbyterian. Home: 1333 N. State St. Office: Lamar Life Bldg., Jackson, Miss. Died Dec. 22, 1957; buried Greenwood Cemetery, Jackson, Miss.

WELSHIMER, Helen Louise (wĕl' shim-ẽr), writer; b. Millersburg, O.; d. Pearl Howard and Clara (Hornig) Welshimer; A.B., Hiram Coll., 1923; student Columbia, 1924-25; unmarried. Newspaper reporter and feature writer on Canton (O.) Daily News, 1925-28, Akron Beacon Journal, 1929; feature writer and woman's editorial writer, Newspaper Enterprise Assn., 1929-37; writer for King Features, also syndicates and mags., 1937—. Mem. Ohio Newspaper Women's Assn. (pres. 1929-31). Trustee Milligan (Tenn.) Coll. Republican. Mem. Disciples of Christ Ch. Author: Souvenirs (poems), 1932; Candlelight (poems), 1935; Singing Drums (poems), 1937; Talks to Girls, 1936; Girlhood Today, 1937; Society Editor, 1938; The Question Girls Ask, 1939; Shining Rain (poems), 1943. Contbr. articles fiction, verse to mags. and newspapers. Home: 211 13th St. N.E., Canton, O. Died Dec. 22, 1954.

WELSHIMER, Pearl H., clergyman; b. York, Union County, O., Apr. 6, 1873; s. Samuel and Louisa (Wilson) W.; A.B., Ohio Northern U., 1894; A.B., Hiram (O.) Coll., 1897; D.D., Butler U., Indpls., 1926; D. Litt., Cincinnati Bible Sem., 1929; m. Clara Hornig, May 15, 1900; children—Helen Louise, Mildred Katherine, Ralph H. Ordained ministry Christian (Disciples) Ch., 1897; pastor Millersburg, O., 1897-1901, First Ch., Canton, O., 1902—. Pres. Disciples Congress, 1913, 19, 20; pres. of North Am. Christian Conv., 1940; dir. Ohio Christian Missionary Soc. Pres. Phillips Bible Inst., Canton, O., 1912-17. Del. for Christian Churches of N. America, to Nat. Conv. of Church of Christ of British Isles, Manchester, Eng., July 1938. Trustee Ohio Anti-Saloon League, Lake James Assembly, Angola, Ind. Trustee of Johnson Bible Coll., Kimberlin Heights, Tenn., and Minnesota Bible Sem., Mpls., Bethaney College, Bethaney, West Virginia, member of Re-study commn. of Disciples of Christ. Mem. bd. of North Am. Evangelistic Assn. Republican. Author: Bible School Vision, 1909; Concerning the Disciples, 1935; also a volume of sermons, 1928, and various tracts. Contbr. editor The Lookout, 1911—. Home: 211 13th St. N.E., Canton, O. Died Aug. 1957.

WELTE, Carl Michael, mfr., inventor, musician; b. Norwich Town, Conn., Aug. 8, 1872; s. Emil and Emma M. (Foerstner) W.; student various pianists, 1886-90, City Coll. N.Y., 1888-92, Packard Bus. Sch., 1893 94; m. Annie Morgan, Nov. 12, 1903. Joined grandfather's firm M. Wolte & Sons (mfrs. mus. instruments), 1894, mem. firm, 1901-32. Trustee estate of Phillipina Young, Emma M. Welte, Annie E. Morgan, Empire Tin Mining Co. of Nome, Alaska. Inventor pneumatic valve action, 1900, driving control, 1917, control mechanically, 1918, playing control mus. instruments, 1919. Democrat. Lutheran. Mason. Home: 34 E. Town St., Norwich Town, Conn. Died Mar. 25, 1955.

WENDELL, Arthur Rindge, corp. exec.; b. Quincy, Mass., Feb. 22, 1876; s. George Blunt and Mary Elizabeth (Thompson) W.; prep. student Greenleaf St. Sch., Quincy, Mass., 1881-87, Adams Acad., Quincy, 1887-92; A.B., Harvard, 1896; m. Grace Frances Peck, Nov. 8, 1902; 1 dau., Eleanor Sherburne. Office mgr. Health Food Co., N.Y. City, 1896-1903; dir. The Wheatena Corp., Rahway, N.J. since 1903, now pres. and dir.; v.p. and dir. Highspire Flour Mills, Inc., since 1920; trustee and mem. adv. com. Individual Underwriters since 1916; trustee and chmn. Fireproof Sprinklered Underwriters since 1925; trustee and mem. adv. com. Met. Inter-Insurers since 1928; chmn. bd., dir. Arex Indemnity Co. since 1936; dir. Rahway Savs. Instn. since 1913, v.p. since 1921; pres. Indsl. Bldg. & Loan Assn., Rahway, 1910-38; Commr. and v.p. Union Co. Park Commn., Elizabeth, N.J., since 1921 (formerly sec., v.p. and pres.); commr. Rahway Civic Commn., 1910; pres. Rahway Bd. of Trade, 1914-16; sinking fund commr. and treas. City of Rahway, 1916-25; chmn. Citizens' Com. for Rahway Valley trunk sewer since 1932; formerly trustee Morristown (N.J.) Sch. Mem. U.S. Trade Mark Assn. (dir.), Holland Soc. N.Y. (trustee), N.J. Soc. Founders and Patriots Am., St. Nicholas Soc. N.Y., Netherlands Soc. Phila., N.Y. Pilgrims, Pi Eta. Republican. Unitarian. Mason (royal and select master). Clubs: University, Harvard, Harvard of New Jersey; Baltusrol Golf (Springfield). Home: 111 Beekman Terrace, Summit, N.J. Office: 1839 Elizabeth Av., Rahway, N.J. Died May 31, 1952.

WENDELL, James Isaac, educator; b. Schenectady, N.Y., Sept. 3, 1890; s. Irving and Ida Van Hyning (Lamb) W.; prep. education Townsend Harris Hall, N.Y.C., 1903-06, Mt. Hermon Sch., Mass., 1906-09; B.A., Wesleyan U., Conn., 1913, hon. M.A., 1930; hon. M.A., U. Pa., 1938; LL.D., Lafayette, 1938; m Marjorie Potts, June 11, 1915; children—James, Jr., John Potts, Harlan Leonard Potts. With The Hill School, 1913—, successively instr. in English, asst. headmaster, treas., dean of administration, asso. headmaster, to 1928, headmaster 1928-52, headmaster emeritus, 1952—. Co-founder Business Officers Assn. of Eastern States Prep. Schs. Trustee Wesleyan U., 1931-43. Mem. com. examination ratings and mem. exec. com., Coll. Entrance Examination Bd.; Pa. State adv. com. Commn. on Secondary Schools. Republican. Episcopalian. Held world's record in 220 yards low hurdles, 1913-23; holder of intercollegiate record of 220 yds. low hurdles; mem. Am. Olympic Team (2d in 110 metre hurdles), Stockholm, 1912. Address: The Hill School, Pottstown, Pa. Died Nov. 22, 1958; buried Edgewood Cemetery.

WENDT, Edwin Frederick (wĕnt), consulting engr.; b. New Brighton (Pittsburgh), Pa., May 12, 1869; s. Christian Ihmsen (M.D.) and Agnes (Scott) W.; g.g.s. Frederick Wendt, glass mfr. Pittsburgh, 1800, and of David Scott, q.m. Army of Gen. Anthony Wayne, 1792; A.B. Geneva (Pa.) Coll. (valedictorian), 1888, D.Sc., 1913. Began engring. work on Pittsburgh & Lake Erie R.R. (N.Y. Central Lines), 1888, successively rodman, transitman, inspector, locating engr. and resident engr.; asst. (chief) engr. in charge of engring. parties, maintenance of way, constrn. and contract work, 1898-1913 (road reconstructed during his service, developed from single track to 4-track road); engr. in charge constrn. Lake Erie & Eastern R.R. (Youngstown, O.), 1911-13; mem. N.Y. Central Lines Engring. Com., 1907-13; mem. Govt. Commn. which inspected Alaska R.R. (500 mi.) under constrn., 1917, and the coal deposits available for development; mem. engring. bd., Interstate Commerce Commn., 1913-21; also chief engr. in charge Eastern dist., Bur. of Valuation, investigated 600 R.R.s and prepared estimate of cost values and depreciation; cons. engr. since 1921; in general practice particularly the valuation, appraisal and cost analysis of railroads and public utilities. Admitted to practice before Interstate Commerce Commn., 1929. Mem. bd. trustees Geneva Coll. (10 yrs.), Beaver Falls, Pa. Charter mem. Am. Ry. Engring. Assn. (pres. 1913-14; member committee accounts, signals and waterways). Member American Society C.E. (chairman executive committee engineering economics division, 1935, 36, 37; mem. com. on valuation procedure), Am. Inst. Cons. Engrs. (pres. 1936-37), Engrs. Soc. of Western Pa., Washington Soc. of Engrs. (pres. 1918), A.A.A.S., Signal Sect. of A.A.R., Ry. Club of Pittsburgh, Am. Economic Assn., Washington Acad. Sciences, Historical Soc. of Western Pa. United Presbyterian. Clubs: Cosmos (Washington); University (Pittsburgh). Author numerous reports and articles on engring., transportation, depreciation and valuation. Home: 5860 Solway St., Pittsburgh 17, Pa. and 1470 3rd Av., New Brighton, Pa. Office: Union Trust Bldg., Pitts. Died Sept. 30, 1952.

WENE, Elmer H., ex-senator; b. Hunterdon Co., N.J.; s. Emanuel S. and Mary J. (Kiley) W.; ed. pub. schs. and spl. course in agr., Rutgers U. Lectured at various agrl. colleges; member N.J. State Bd. of Agr., 1925-34, pres., 1929-34; pres. Cumberland County Bd. of Agr., 1922-36; owner Wene Chick Farms, also Wene Poultry Laboratories. Pres. radio station WSNJ (Bridgeton, N.J.), radio station WTTM (Trenton, N.J.). Dir. Vineland Savings & Loan Assn. Member 75th, 77th and 78th Congresses (1937-39 and 1941-45), 2d N.J. Dist.; elected mem. Bd. of Chosen Freeholders of Cumberland County, 1939; exec. adv. to U.S. Sec. of Agr., Clinton P. Anderson, 1945; elected N.J. state senator from Cumberland County for 3 years, 1946; elected del. from Cumberland County to N.J. State Constitutional Conv., serving on the Taxation and Finance Com. as well as the Com. on Pub. Relations and Information, 1947. Mem. bd. dirs. Newcomb Hosp., Vineland, N.J. Pres. Vineland-Landis Twp. Chamber of Commerce, 1934. Pres. Vineland Rotary Coub, 1932. Democrat. Methodist. Mason, Elk, Grange. Address: Vineland, N.J. Died Jan. 25, 1957; buried Quakertown, N.J.

WENGER, Oliver Clarence (wĕng ẽr), sr. surgeon, U.S.P.H.S.; b. St. Louis, Mo., 1884; s. George and Mary (Siegwart) W.; student O'Fallon Poly. Inst., 1902-04; M.D., St. Louis U, 1908; m. Elsie Isenman, Jan. 15, 1915; 1 dau., Audrey Louise. Asst. in med. clinic, Alexian Bros. Hosp., St. Louis, 1909-10; asst. diagnostician St. Louis Health Dept., 1910-12, 1916-17; pvt. practice in St. Louis, 1915-16, specialist in div. venereal diseases, U.S. Public Health Service, 1919-45; retired; now med. administrative consultant, Nat. Arthritis Research Foundation. Fellow A.M.A. Am. Coll. Phys. Member Soc. of Mil. Surg., Ark. State and Garland County Med. Socs.; London Acad. Medicine; hon. mem. Most Excellent Order of the British Empire. Address: Dugan Stuart Bldg., Hot Springs, Ark. Died Jan. 6, 1958.

WENIGER, Willibald, physicist, coll. prof.; born Milwaukee, Wis., June 20, 1884; s. Heinrich Wilhelm and Carolina (Taubert) W.; A.B., U. of Wis., 1905, A.M., 1906, Ph.D., 1908; m. Myrtle Elizabeth Knepper, May 13, 1918 (died April 23, 1950); 1 son, George Edward. Teacher of algebra and physics, Wis. Acad., Madison, Wis., 1903-05; computer Washburn Obs., Madison, 1904-06; asst. and fellow in physics, Univ. of Wis., 1906-08; head dept. physics, Ore. State Coll., 1908-14, and 1920-49, asst. dean, Grad. Sch., 1933-47, dean, 1947-49; prof. physics, University of Alaska, College, Alaska, 1951-55; head of the department of physics and elec. engineering, 1952-55; acting dir. agr., engring., forestry, Idaho State College, 2d semester 1956-57; physicist, Nela Research Lab. Gen. Elec. Co., East Cleveland, O., 1914-20. Fellow Am. Phys. Soc., A.A.A.S.; mem. Optical Soc. of Am., Illuminating Engring. Soc., Am. Assn. Physics Teachers, Ore. Acad. Sci., Phi Beta Kappa, Sigma Xi, Phi Kappa Phi, Sigma Pi Sigma. Republican. Episcopalian. Mason (Shriner). Author: Fundamentals of Physics, 1940. Contbr. articles to physics jours. Address: 1010 N. 29 St., Corvallis, Ore. Died Mar. 13, 1959; buried Masonic Cemetery, Corvallis, Ore.

WENNER, Frank (wĕn'ẽr), physicist; b. Garrison, Ia., Jan. 18, 1873; s. Christian and Margaret (Cokely) W.; B.S., Knox Coll., Galesburg, Ill., 1899, Sc.D., 1942; student U. Wis., 1900-02; Ph.D., U. Pa., 1909; m. Lottie Louisa Ward, Jan. 1, 1903. Instr. physics, Ia. State Coll., 1902-05, U. of Pa., 1905-07; with Nat. Bureau of Standards, 1907-43, 51-54; cons. physicist Carnegie Inst. of Washington, 1943-46, and of Rubicon Co., Phila., 1943-51. Mem. panel of com. on Geophysics. Research and Development Bd., National Mil. Establishment, 1947-48. Fellow Am. Inst. E.E., Am. Phys. Soc., Washington (pres. 1937), Am. Geophysical Union, Sigma Xi. Delegate to 4th and 7th General Assembly of the International Geodetic and Geophysical Union; del. 2d Pan-American Science Congress. Mason (32°, Shriner). Clubs: Cosmos, Federal. Author of numerous papers on galvanometers and electric resistance measurements; researches on the theory of seismometers having electromagnetic magnification and electromagnetic damping; control for guns on airplane (World War I); the distribution of current in systems of linear electrical conductors; potentiometers; fundamental or absolute measurement of electrical resistance; apparatus for study of ground movements within the destructive area of major earthquakes; land and sea mines, their detection in offensive operations and use in defense operations (World War II). Home: 5614 32d St., Washington. Died Feb. 7, 1954; buried Evergreen Cemetery, Vinton, Ia.

WENTWORTH, Edward Norris, livestock historian, specialist; b. Dover, N.H., Jan. 11, 1887; s. Elmer Marston and Elizabeth Tilton (Towne) W.; B.S., in Agr., Ia. State Coll. Agr. and Mechanic Arts, 1907, M.S., 1909; grad. study Cornell U. and Harvard; m. Alma B. McCulla, June 14, 1911; children—Edward Norris (dec.), Raymond Howard (dec.). Asst., asso. prof. animal husbandry, Iowa State Coll. Agr. and Mech. Arts, 1907-13; asso. editor Breeder's Gazette, also prof. zoötechny, Chicago Vet. Coll., 1913-14; prof. animal breeding, Kan. State Agrl. Coll., 1914-17; public relations dept., Armour and Co., Chgo., 1919-20, Bur. of Agrl. Research und Economics, 1920-23; ir. Armour's Livestock Bur., 1923-54, retired 1954; lectr. U. Chgo., 1923-31. Served as capt. F.A., U.S. Army, and mil. dir. Coll. Agr., A.E.F. Univ., Beaune, France, World War I; col., Honorary Reserve; mem. advisory com. to Q.M. General. Mem. Am. Farm Economics Assn., Am. Genetic Assn., Am. Soc. Animal Production, A.A.A.S., Am. Soc. Naturalists, Am. Econ. Assn., Am. Statis. Assn., S.A. R., Soc. of Piscataqua Pioneers, Am. Legion, Mil. Order World Wars (past commander in chief), Miss. Valley Hist. Assn., Reserve Officers' Assn. U.S., Sigma Alpha Epsilon, Alpha Zeta, Alpha Psi, Sigma Delta Chi, Phi Kappa Psi. Decorated Officer du Merite Agricole (French). Republican. Clubs: University, Saddle and Sirloin, Army and Navy Club, Army and Navy (Washington, D.C.); Town and Country Equestrian Assn. (pres.). Author: Portrait Gallery of Saddle and Sirloin Club, 1920; America's Sheep Trails, 1948. Co-author: Progressive Beef Cattle Raising, 1920; Progressive Hog Raising, 1922; Marketing Live Stock and Meats, 1924; Progressive Sheep Raising, 1925; Cattle Breeding, 1925. Co-author with Charles W. Towne, Shepherds' Empire, 1945; Pig's Progress, 1949. Home: R.R. 3, Box 285, Chesterton, Ind. Address: Armour and Co., Chgo. Died Apr. 21, 1959.

WENTWORTH, Franklin Harcourt, author; b. Chgo., Mar. 27, 1866; s. Charles Roberts Powers and Marilla (Brunton) W.; ed. pub. schs. and Oakland High Sch., Chgo.; m. Marion Jean Craig, Mar. 31, 1900; m. 2d, Alice Chapman, Nov. 6, 1912. In service of I.C. R.R., Chgo., 1882-93; traveled and studied social and polit. economy, 1894; asst. sec. and corr. Underwriters' Labs., Chgo., 1895-1900; ed. and pub. The Socialist Spirit, 1900-03; studied social conditions in Italy, France, Germany, Holland, Belgium, Switzerland, Eng., 1903; Washington corr. for Socialist press, 1904-05; sec.-treas. and editor Nat. Fire Protection Assn., 1909-39. Pres. Chicago Single-tax Club, 1897-98. Mem. Salem (Mass.) City Council, 1910. Mem. Housing Adv. Council, Fed. Housing Adminstrn., 1934-35. Hon. mem. Institut Francais de Prevention du Feu, Dominion Fire Prevention Assn., Fire Waste Council C. of C. U.S.A., Nat. Fire Protection Assn., Internat. Assn. of Fire Chiefs, Dominion Assn. of Fire Chiefs, Pacific Coast Assn. of Fire Chiefs, Fire Chiefs' Club of Mass. Mem. Poetry Soc. Am. Author: The Pride of Intellect, 1901; Forgings of the New, 1907; Wendell Phillips, 1908; The Woman's Portion, 1910; Factories and Their Fire Protection, 1910; Syllabus for Public Instruction in Fire Prevention, 1912; Decreasing the Fire Hazard, 1930; Automatic Sprinklers in Apartment Houses, 1935. Home: 1104 Esplanade, Redondo, Cal. Died Oct. 4, 1954.

WENTWORTH, John, ret. architect; b. Chgo., Sept. 24, 1892; s. Moses Jones and Lizzie (Hunt) W.; A.B., Harvard, 1914, student Mass. Inst. Tech.; m. Mary Tilt, 1938; 1 son, Eric. With Rebori, Wentworth & Dewey, architects, Chgo., 1923-33; self employed as John Wentworth, investments, Chgo., 1933-—; dir. Commonwealth Edison Co., Chgo. Former vice chmn. Chgo. Plan Commn.; chmn. Chgo. Med. Center; dir. Brookfield Zool. Soc. Address: 1260 Astor St., Chgo. 10. Died June 20, 1958.

WENZEL, Caroline, librarian; b. San Francisco; d. George Francis and Jennie (Brown) Wenzel; student Cal. State Library Sch., 1914. Library asst., Cal. State Library, 1914-33; supervising librarian, Cal. Dept., Cal. State Library, 1933-52; now engaged in hist. research for 1957 Centennial edition of the Sacramento Bee. Mem. Sacramento Historic Landmarks Commission. Mem. bd. sponsors Cal. Hist. Found.; Coll. of Pacific. Mem. Am. Pioneer Trails Assn.; Alumni Assn. of U. Cal. and Cal State Library Sch., Cal. Hist. Soc., Am. Library Assn., Calif. Library Assn., Business and Professional Womens Club, Nat. League for Woman's Service, Sacramento Co. Hist. Soc. Republican. Clubs: Sacramento Book Collectors. Contbr. hist., profl. publs.; authority Calif. history and lit. Home: 723 17th St. Address: 723 17th St., Sacramento, Cal. Died Mar. 24, 1959.

WERBE, Thomas Chandler, Sr., corp. exec.; b. Indianapolis, Sept. 7, 1883; s. Henry G. and Anna (Chandler) W.; student pub. schs. of Indianapolis; m. Cleo Edwards, Apr. 5, 1913; children—Thomas Chandler, Richard Henry. Pres., Dice Machine Co., 1909-28, treas. Lynch Glass Machine Co., 1917-28, two above cos. consol. to form Lynch Corp., Anderson, Ind., 1928 and since served as pres., chmn. bd. dirs. since 1950; chmn. bd. Lynch Internat., London, Eng., since 1950; v.p. and dir. Citizens Banking Co. Chmn. bd. dirs. Anderson Community Chest; dir. Anderson Y.M.C.A. Trustee Hanover Coll. Mem. Ind. Mfrs. Assn. (dir.). Republican. Presbyn. Mason. Clubs: Anderson Country; Columbia (Indianapolis); Bath and Tennis (Palm Beach). Home: Woodlawn Heights, Anderson. Office: Lynch Corp., Anderson. Ind. Died Dec. 5, 1951; buried Crown Hill, Indpls.

WERNER, Henry Paul, business exec.; b. Buffalo, Nov. 17, 1874; s. Paul and Melanie (Graf) W.; student Buffalo Bus. U., 1889-92; m. Grace Clara Brinker, Apr. 25, 1900; 1 dau., Barbara (Mrs. Oliver Holmes Matinzi). Became pres. Meadville (Pa.) Distilling Co. (subsidiary Fleischmann Co.), 1912, H-O Co., Hecker-H-O Co., 1919; chmn. Best Foods, Inc., ret., now dir. corp. and its various coms.; indsl. cons. Def. Plant Corp.; dir. Fidelity Trust Co., Mfrs. & Traders Trust Co., 1923-33. Mem. Script Money Commn., 1933; mem. State Council of Parks; commr., pres. Niagara State Park Commn.; mem. Grand Island Commn.; chmn. Niagara Authority. Asst. chmn. community chest campaign; vice chmn. Red Cross campaign. Bd. govs. Millard Fillmore Hosp., Buffalo Sem. Democrat. Presbyn. Mason (32°). Clubs: Buffalo (past pres.), Country (Buffalo); Eastword Ho Country, Chatham Beach, Stage Harbor Yacht (Cape Cod, Mass.). Home: 70 Penhurst Park, Buffalo 22. Office: Marine Trust Bldg., Buffalo 3. Died Oct. 24, 1955.

WERNER, Max (pseudonym) (real name: Alexandre Schiffrin), writer; b. Kharkov, Russia, 1901. Political editor of daily paper, Mannheim, Germany, and special writer for periodicals in Berlin and Vienna; lived in Paris, 1933-40. Author: Military Strength of the Powers, 1939; Battle for the World, 1941; The Great Offensive, 1942; Attack Can Win in 1943, 1943. Address: care S. J. Greenberger, 11 W. 42d St., N.Y.C. Died Jan. 8, 1951.

WERNER, Oscar Emil Wade, reporter; b. Harvey, Ill., Jan. 31, 1893; s. Dietrich and Agnes (Zernecke) W.; grad. Los Angeles High Sch., 1910; student Occidental Coll., Los Angeles, 1910-11; B.A., U. of Calif., 1916; m. Mary Eckles, June 15, 1916; children—Miles Allen, George Carleton. Began as reporter Los Angeles Evening Herald, 1911; reporter Prescott (Ariz.) Evening Courier, 1920-22; connected with Associated Press, 1922-—, successively editor on Los Angeles staff, state capitol corr. at Sacramento, Hollywood film feature editor, feature editor in London, Eng., staff writer at Berlin, chief of bureau, Vienna (covering Feb. and July revolts, 1934); staff writer Berlin bureau, 1935-37; chief of Moscow bureau, 1938-39. Baltic bureau, Copenhagen, 1939; corr. at front Russian-Finnish War, Jan.-Mar. 1940; Ottawa, 1940-41; Washington, 1941-43; E.T.O., 1943-45; signed dispatches "Wade Werner." Served as pvt., 126th Regt., C.A., Mar.-Dec. 1918, World War I. Retired. Address: 1018 Camino Ramon, San Jose, Cal. Died Dec. 28, 1953.

WERNER, William M., mfg. exec.; b. Richmond, Ind., Feb. 11, 1898; s. Andrew A. and Mary A. (Wehner) W.; student U. Dayton, 1916; m. Josephine E. Westerheide, June 2, 1920; children—Mary Kay (Mrs. William Donauer), Irene B. (Mrs. Richard Woeste) William J. Vice pres. Avco Mfg. Corp., N.Y.C., 1949-—, gen. mgr. New Idea div., Coldwater, O., 1949-—; pres. New Idea Farm Equipment Co., Coldwater, Horn Mfg. Co., Ft. Dodge, Ia., (Avco subsidiaries). Served as sgt. major, 61st Inf., 5th Div., 1917-19. Mem. Farm Equipment Inst. (v.p.), Vets. Fgn. Wars, Am. Legion. Home: P.O. Box 26, Coldwater, O. Died Sept. 13, 1958; buried St. Elizabeth Cemetery, Coldwater.

WERRENRATH, Reinald (wâr'ĕn-räth), baritone, vocal teacher, condr.; b. Bklyn., Aug. 7, 1883; s. George and Aretta (Camp) W.; A.B., New York U., 1905, Dr. Mus. (hon.), 1932; studied singing with father, and with Dr. Carl Dufft, Frank King Clark, Dr. Arthur Mees, Percy Rector Stephens, Victor Maurel; m. Ada Petersen, Dec. 6, 1909; children—George Hans, Dorothy (Mrs. Carleton B. Hutchins, Jr.), Reinald; m. 2d, Frances M. Aston, March 25, 1942. Made debut at Metropolitan Opera House, New York, as Sylvio, in Pagliacci, Feb. 19, 1919. Appeared, 1907-— in recitals and oratorios in leading cities of U.S.; starred in operetta, Music in the Air, 1932-33. Vocal supervisor Nat. Broadcasting Co., 1929-32; has taught singing at U. of Miami, Peabody Conservatory of Music (summer), Baltimore, and De-Paul U., Chicago; now teaching in own studio Carnegie Hall, N.Y.; Washington (D.C.) Musical Inst.; Albany (N.Y.) Conservatory of Music and Art; Troy Conservatory of Music. Conductor Mendelssohn Club of Albany, N.Y., 1941-—; N.Y.A.C. Glee Club, N.Y., 1942-47, Nat. Press Club Chorus, Washington, D.C., 1943-—. Lectures on American Song and Songs of the British Isles, 1935-—. Mem. Psi Upsilon, Republican. Episcopalian. Mason. Clubs: Dutch Treat, New York Athletic, Automobile Ol Timers, University Glee, American-Irish Historical Soc., Sleepy Hollow Country, Psi Upsilon (New York). Pres. N.Y. Univ. Arts and Engineering Alumni Assn., 1940-44. Awarded N.Y.U. Alumni Meritorious Service Medal, 1945; King Christian X's Medal of Liberation, 1946. Compiler and editor The New Arion for Male Voices, 1916, One Hundred Modern Scandinavian Songs, 1925. Composer several male choruses. Address: 131 Riverside Dr., N.Y.C. Died Sept. 12, 1953; buried Greenwood Cemetery, Bklyn.

WERTENBAKER, Charles Christian (wẽr'tĕn-bā-ker), editor, author, fgn. correspondent; b. Lexington, Va., Feb. 11, 1901; s. William and Imogen (Peyton) W.; student University of Virginia, 1919-21, and 1923-25; m. Henrietta Hoopes, Sept. 25, 1926 (divorced 1935); m. 2d, Nancy Hale (Hardin), Sept. 21, 1935 (divorced 1941); 1 son, William; m. 3d, Lael Tucker (Laird), September 1942; children—Christian Tucker, Lael Louisiana Timberlake. Reporter, Washington Star, other newspapers, 1922-23, 1925-28; traveled in Europe and contributed to Saturday Evening Post, etc., 1928-31; contributing editor Time, 1931-33; associate editor Fortune, traveling in Central and South America, 1933-36; asso. editor and foreign corr. Time, 1938-39, foreign news editor, 1940-43, war editor, 1951-43; chief military corr. and chief of Paris bur., Time and Life, 1944-45, chief of foreign corrs., 1945-46; chief European corr., 1947. Mem. Phi Kappa Psi Fraternity. Democrat. Episcopalian. Author: Boojum, 1928; Peter the Drunk, 1929; Before They Were Men, 1931; To My Father, 1936; A New Doctrine for the Americas, 1941; Invasion, 1944; Write Sorrow on the Earth, 1947; The Barons, 1950. Home: Sneden's Landing, Palisades, N.Y. Died Jan. 8, 1955; buried Ciboure, France.

WERTHEIM, Maurice (wert'him), investment banker; b. N.Y.C., Feb. 16, 1886; s. Jacob and Hannah (Frank) W.; A.B., Harvard, 1906, A.M., 1907; m. Alma Morgenthau, 1909; children—Mrs. Josephine W. Pomerance, Mrs. Barbara W. Tuchman, Mrs. Anne W. Langman; m. 2d, Ruth White Warfield, Mar. 1930; m. 3d, Cecile B. Seiberling, June 1944. V.p. and sec. United Cigar Mfrs. Co. (now Gen. Cigar Co.), 1907-13; mem. N.Y. State Industrial Bd., 1913-15; entered investment banking with Hallgarten & Co., 1915-19, mem. firm, 1919-26; founder Werthiem & Co., investment bankers, 1927, and since sr. partner; dir. Underwood Corp., Cuban Atlantic Sugar Co., Hat. Corp. of America, Bond Stores Co. Pres. Am. Jewish Com., 1941-42; served in Washington with War Production Bd. (mem. requirements com.), 1941-43, later with War Dept. One of the founders and former director, Theatre Guild of N.Y.; publisher, The Nation, 1935-37; pres. Manhattan Chess Club; hon. trustee, Fed. of Jewish Philanthropies of N.Y.; trustee, Mt. Sinai Hospital; trustee Am. Wildlife Found.; mem. adv. com. N.Y. Univ. Inst. of Fine Arts, member com. to visit dept. of fine arts, Harvard. Home: 33 E. 70th St. Office: 120 Broadway, N.Y.C. Died May 27, 1950.

WESCOTT, James Barney, lawyer; b. Lacon, Ill., Mar. 20, 1887; s. William L. and Emily (Barney) W.; LL.B., Northwestern U., 1909; m. Mary Hotchkiss, Aug. 26, 1913; 1 dau., Jean (wife of Dr. James B. Hurd). Admitted to Ill. bar, 1909, since practiced law, Chgo.; partner Miller, Gorham, Wescott & Adams; dir. Diamond T Motor Car Co., Acme Aluminum Foundry Co., 1900 Lake Shore Dr. Bldg. Corp. Asst. counsel Emergency Fleet Corp., U.S. Shipping Bd., 1918; mem. adv. bd. to Dept. of Ins. of Ill., 1955—. Mem. Am., Ill., Chgo. bar assns., S.A.R., Phi Kappa Psi. Clubs: Chicago, Midday, Post and Paddock (Chgo.); Glen View (Golf, Ill.); Bohemian (San Francisco); Everglades, Old Guard Soc. Palm Beach Golfers (Palm Beach, Fla.). Home: 1500 Lake Shore Dr., Chgo. 10. Office: 1 N. LaSalle St., Chgo. 2. Died Apr. 27, 1957.

WESSON, Charles Macon, army officer; b. St. Louis, July 23, 1878; s. Charles Macon and Caroline Moye (Dancy) W.; B.S., U.S. Mil. Acad., 1900; grad. Ordnance Sch. of Technology, 1911, Army War Coll., 1925; Dr. Eng., Stevens Inst., 1941; married. Commd. 2d lt. cav., U.S. Army, 1900, and advanced through the grades to maj. gen., 1938; served in Cuba and Ft. Riley, Kan., with cav.; instr. in dept. of philosophy, West Point, 1903-07; served in ordnance dept. in Watertown and Watervliet arsenals and with A.E.F. in France; comdg. officer Aberdeen Proving Ground, 1925-29; chief of tech. staff. Office Chief of Ordnance, 1930-34; chief of ordnance, 1938-42; Office of Lend-Lease Adminstr. and Fgn. Econ. Adminstr., 1942-45. Decorated D.S.M. with 2 oak leaf clusters (U.S.); Officer Black Star (French); hon. comdr. British Empire. Clubs: Army and Navy, Chevy Chase (Washington, D.C.); St. Botolph (Boston). Home: The Westchester, Washington 16. Died Nov. 24, 1956; buried West Point, N.Y.

WEST, Charles Cameron, shipbuilder; b. Chicago, Ill., Sept. 22, 1877; s. John and Annie (Ladd) W.; Chicago Manual Training Sch.; M.E., Cornell U., 1900; m. Julia Bernice Dunham, June 10, 1905; children—John Dunham, Robert Dunham, Sylvia, Ruth (Mrs. Clark). Engaged in shipbldg., 1900—; founder Manitowoc Shipbldg. Co., 1902, pres. 1920—, (now known as The Manitowoc Co., Inc.); dir. several corps. Mem. Bd. Edn., 1925-31; pres. local Boy Scouts Am., 1933—. Selected indsl. leader by Inst. Research in Biography, 1936. Naval constructor U.S. Navy, 1917-18. Mem. Instn. Naval Architects, Shipbuilders Council Am. (dir. 1943), Am. Soc. Naval Architects and Marine Engrs., Beta Theta Pi. Republican. Episcopalian. Mason. Home: Manitowoc, Wis. Died Oct. 3, 1957.

WEST, DuVal, judge; b. Austin, Tex., Nov. 13, 1861; s. Charles Shannon and Florence (DuVal) W.; grad. Tex. Mil. Inst., Austin, Tex., 1879; B.L., Cumberland U., Lebanon, Tenn., 1890; m. Isabella Clerc Terry, of New Orleans, La., Apr. 7, 1891. Began practice at San Antonio, Tex., 1890; personal representative of Pres. Wilson in Mexico, Feb.-May 1915; judge U.S. Dist. Court, Western Dist. of Tex., 1917-32 (retired). Adj. 1st Tex. Vol. Inf., Spanish-Am. War. Democrat. Episcopalian. Home: San Antonio, Tex. Deceased.

WEST, Edward Augustus, exec. engr.; b. Wiarton, Ont., Can., Nov. 5, 1882 (parents U.S. citizens); s. Henry Gilder and Annie Alice (Masters) W.; student Bromfield-Pearson Engring. Sch., Tufts Coll. 1905-09; Lowell Sch. for Indsl. Foremen, Mass. Inst. of Tech., 1907-09; m. Charlotte Barton, Mar. 1907; children—Barton Gilder, Franklin Griffith, Edward Wilford; m. 2d, Marion Maxwell Kirkland, Apr. 27, 1923. Constr. engr. Portland (Ore.) R.R., Light & Power Co., 1909-12, efficiency engr., 1912-16; chief engr. Denver Tramway Co., 1916, gen. supt., 1918-25; vice-pres., gen. mgr. and dir. Utah Light & Traction Co., 1925-36; exec. v.p., dir. Fla. Power & Light Co., Miami, 1936-37; v.p. Miami Water Co.; v.p. Miami Beach R.R.; v.p., gen. mgr. Consumers Water Co.; exec. v.p. Denver & Rio Grande Western R.R. Co.; pres. Rio Grande Motorway, Larsen Transport Co.; pres. Salt Lake City Union Depot & R.R. Co., Denver Union Terminal R.R.; dir. Pueblo Union Depot & R.R. Co., Denver Market & Produce Terminal, Denver Nat. Bank. Served as chief petty officer, U.S. Navy, 1901-04, and ensign, U.S. Naval Res., 1912-16. Mem. C. of C., Timpanogas (Salt Lake City), Newcomen Soc., Soc. Military Engrs., Theta Delta Chi, Spanish Am. War Vets. Clubs: Denver, Denver Athletic, Press, Country, Civic (Denver), Country, Alta (Salt Lake City). Contbr. to professional jours. Originator of modern trolley coach and application of the rear engine principle to mass transportation vehicles. Address: 1919 Yalecrest St., Salt Lake City. Died Feb. 22, 1955.

WEST, Judson S., judge; b. in Mich., 1855; s. David S. and Hannah W.; ed. common schs. and U. of Kan.; m. Mollie Sympson, 1882 (deceased); 2d, Mattie Nold, 1886. Admitted to bar at Fort Scott, Kan., 1881; co. atty., 1884; dist. judge, 1889-94; asst. atty-gen. 4½ yrs.; asst. U.S. atty., 5 yrs.; justice Supreme Ct. of Kan., for terms 1911-17, 1917-23. Republican. Baptist. Club: Saturday Night. Address: Topeka, Kan. Deceased.

WEST, Olin, sec. A.M.A.; b. Gadsden, Ala., July 12, 1874; s. Anson (D.D.) and Sarah Bryant (Kittrell) W.; ed. Howard College, Ala.; Ph.C., Vanderbilt, 1895, M.D., 1898; m. Susie P. Hunter, July 25, 1906; children—Robert Hunter, Olin. Practiced at Nashville, Tenn., 1898-1910; instr., later asso. prof. Vanderbilt Med. Dept., 1895-1910; dir. for Rockefeller Sanitary Commn. and Internat. Health Bd. in Tenn., 1910-18; sec. and exec. officer Tenn. State Bd. of Health, 1918-22; field sec. A.M.A., 1922, sec., 1922-24, sec. and gen. mgr., 1924-46, elected pres.-elect, 1946 (resigned because of ill health, 1946). Member Chicago Inst. Medicine, Nashville Academy Medicine, Tenn. State Med. Assn., Sigma Alpha Epsilon. Democrat. Methodist. Mason. Club: University (Chgo.). Sec., editor Jour. of Tenn. State Med. Assn., 1914-22. Home: Helena Court, Belle Meade, Nashville 5, Tenn. Died June 20, 1952; buried Mt. Olivet Cemetery, Nashville.

WEST, Roy Owen, lawyer; b. Georgetown, Vermilion County, Ill., Oct. 27, 1868; s. Pleasant and Helen Anna W.; A.B., DePauw U., 1890, A.M., 1893, LL.B., 1890, LL.D., 1938; studied law at Chicago; m. Louisa Augustus, June 11, 1898 (died Nov. 4, 1901); 1 son, Owen Augustus; m. 2d, Louise McWilliams, June 8, 1904 (died June 8, 1942); 1 daughter, Helen Louise. Admitted to bar, 1890; head of law firm of West, Leaton & West, ret. Was asst. county attorney, Cook County, Illinois, 1894; city atty., Chicago, 1895-97; mem. Bd. of Review of Cook County, 1898-1914; elected chmn. Rep. State Central Com., 5 times; mem. Rep. Nat. Com., 1912-16, 1928-32, sec., 1924-28; atty. for South Park Commrs., Chicago, 1917-24; sec. of interior, July 25, 1928-29; spl. asst. to atty. gen. of U.S. to hear cases of conscientious objectors to mil. service, 1941-53. Western treas. Rep. Nat. Com., 1928. Pres. emeritus bd. trustees DePauw U. Mem. Bd. of Edn., M.E. Ch., 1936-40. Mem. Am., Ill. and Chicago bar assns., S.A.R., Delta Tau Delta, Phi Beta Kappa, Phi Delta Phi. Methodist. Mason. Clubs: Chicago, Union League, Law. Home: 5633 Woodlawn Av. Office: First Nat. Bank Bldg., Chgo. Died Nov. 29, 1958.

WESTCOTT, Allan Ferguson (wĕst'kŏt), educator, writer; b. Alexandria Bay, N.Y., Nov. 22, 1882; s. Wilson Henry and Isabel (Thomson) W.; Ph.B., Brown U., 1903, A.M., 1904; Ph.D., Columbia, 1911; m. Mary Townsend, June 29, 1905 (died 1922); children—Lois Townsend, William Allan, Ruth Isabel; m. 2d, Elizabeth Cravena, Aug. 25, 1923; children—Emily Craven, Allan Cravdn. Instr. English, Brown U., 1903-04, Columbia, 1906-11; instr. English, U.S. Naval Acad., 1911-18, asso. prof., 1918-20, prof., 1920-48, Senior prof., 1942-48, emeritus; special duty with historical section, Office of Naval Intelligence, Washington, summer 1918. Mem. and asst. editor Monthly Proc. of U.S. Naval Inst. Mem. Soc. Stukely Westcott Desc. America (pres.), Kappa Sigma, Phi Beta Kappa. Democrat. Mem. Dutch Ref. Ch. Author: (with Prof. W. O. Stevens) A History of Sea Power, 1920, revised edit., 1937; (with Prof. C. S. Alden) The United States Navy, a History, 1943. Editor: New Poems, by James I of England, 1910 (the original MS. found by the editor in the British Museum); Mahan on Naval Warfare, 1918, revised edit., 1941; Dana's Two Years Before the Mast; Southey's Life of Nelson; Four Centuries of Literature, 1925. Editor and co-author: American Sea Power since 1775, 1947. Home: 1 Thompson St., Annapolis, Md. Died May 2, 1953; buried U.S. Naval Acad. Cemetery, Annapolis.

WESTCOTT, Thompson Seiser, physician; b. Phila., June 11, 1862; s. Thompson and Mary (Seiser) W.; ed. Friends' Sch. of Phila., 1869-77; grad. Univ. Pa., 1882, med. dept. same, 1886; m. Oct. 11, 1893, Marie Louise. Asso. in diseases of children, Univ. Pa., 1896—; vis. physician Meth. Episcopal Hosp., Phila., 1893—. Mem. Phi Kappa Psi, Phi Beta Kappa Fraternity. Fellow Coll. Physicians of Phila., Am. Pediatric Soc., Pathol. Soc. of Philadelphia, Pediatric Soc. of Phila., County Med. Soc. Asst. editor American Textbook of Diseases of Children, 1894, 1898. Contb'r to med. jours. Address: 1720 Pine St., Phila. Died Jan. 28, 1933.

WESTERGAARD, Harald Malcolm (wĕs'tẽr-gärd), prof. civil engring.; b. Copenhagen, Denmark, Oct. 9, 1888; s. Harald Ludvig and Thora Alvilda (Koch) W.; B.S. in C.E., Royal Tech. Coll., Copenhagen, 1911; U. of Gottingen, spring, 1913; Technische Hochschule, Munich, spring 1914, Dr. Ing., 1925; Ph.D., U. Ill., 1916; Dr. Techn., Royal Tech. Coll., 1929; D.Sc., Lehigh, 1930; m. Rachel Talbot, Sept. 15, 1925; children—Mary Talbot, Peter Talbot. Naturalized U.S. citizen 1920. In engineering work, chiefly reinforced concrete design, Copenhagen, Hamburg, London, 1911-14; fellow Am.-Scandinavian Foundation, 1914-15; instr. in theoretical and applied mechanics, U. Ill., 1916-19, asso., 1919-21, asst. prof., 1921-24, asso. prof., 1924-27, prof., 1927-36; Gordon McKay prof. of civil engring., Harvard, 1936—, dean of Grad. Sch. of Engring., Harvard, 1937-46. With U.S. Bur. of Pub. Roads, summers, 1923, 26, 28, 29 and 32, U. of Mich., summers, 1931, 32, 34 and 36; sr. mathematician, U.S. Bur. of Reclamation, on Boulder Dam, 1929-30, cons. engr. on same, 1930-32; cons. structural engr., Bureau of Yards and Docks, Navy Dept., 1935-37; cons. U.S. Army, airfield pavements. Lt. comdr., Civil Engr. Corps., U.S.N.R., 1936-39, comdr., 1939, capt., 1946; on active duty, intermittently, 1942-46; mem. Bureau of Yards and Docks mission to Japan, 1945. Consultant to Panama Canal, 1946-47. Trustee Am. Scandinavian Found., 1938—. Fellow Am. Acad. Arts and Scis.; mem. Am. Soc. M.E., Am. Soc. E.E., Am. Concrete Inst., Am. Soc. Engring. Edn., Danish Instn. Engrs., Dansk Selskab for Bygningstatik, Am. Philos. Soc., Phi Beta Kappa, Tau Beta Pi, Sigma Xi. Awarded Wason medal, Am. Concrete Inst., 1922, J. J. R. Croes medal, Am. Soc. Civil Engrs., 1934. Recipient Thomas Fitch Rowland prize, 1950. Clubs: Harvard Faculty (Cambridge); Harvard (Boston); Harvard (N.Y.); Cosmos (Washington, D.C.). Contbr. papers to tech. jours. and publs. of tech. socs. Home: 33 Pinehurst Road, Belmont 78, Mass. Address: Pierce Hall, Harvard University, Cambridge 38, Mass. Died June 22, 1950; buried Belmont, Mass.

WESTERMANN, William Linn, coll. prof.; b. Belleville, Ill., Sept. 15, 1873; s. Louis and Emma Hilgard (Tyndale) W.; B.A., U. of Neb., 1894, M.A., 1896, LL.D., 1938; Ph.D., U. of Berlin, 1902; H.L.D., U. of Chicago, 1941; LL.D., U. of Mo., 1943; m. Avrina Davies, June 15, 1912; 1 son, Evan Davies. Asst. in Latin, U. of Neb., 1894-96; teacher Latin, high sch., Decatur, Ill., 1896-99; instr. Latin and Greek, U. of Mo., 1902-04, asst. prof., 1904-06; asst. prof. history, U. of Minn., 1906-08; asso. prof. history, U. of Wis., 1908-14, prof. history, 1914-20; prof. ancient history. Cornell U., 1920-23; prof. history, Columbia, 1923-48, emeritus. Adviser, Turkish affairs, and chief Div. of Western Asia, Am. Commn. to Negotiate Peace, Paris; del. on Greek Territorial Commn., Peace Conf., Paris, 1918-19; mem. commission reporting to State Dept. on Armenian boundary decision, 1920. Round Table leader on Near East, 3d Williamstown Inst. of Politics, 1923; mem. bd. trustees Am. Acad. in Rome, 1922-33; prof. in charge, Sch. of Classical Studies, Am. Acad. in Rome, 1926-27; vis. prof. Farouk I Univ., Egypt, 1949; prof. ancient history Alexandria U., Egypt, 1953, 54. Mem. Am. Hist. Assn. (pres. 1944), Classical Assn. Middle West and South, Phi Delta Theta, Phi Beta Kappa, Phi Eta. Clubs: Men's Faculty, Columbia University; Scarsdale Golf. Democrat. Author: Story of the Ancient Nations, 1912; Westermann and Kraemer, Greek Papyri in the Library of Cornell University, 1926; Upon Slavery in Ptolemaic Egypt, 1929; Westermann and Keyes, Columbia University Series, Greek Papyri II, 1931; Westermann and Hasenoehrl, Greek Papyri III, 1933; Westermann, Keyes and Liebesny, Greek Papyri IV, 1940. Contbr. to Am. and foreign philol. and hist. jours. Editor Westermann's Classical and Historical Map Series, 1918. Home: 23 Donellan Rd., Scarsdale, N.Y. Died Oct. 4, 1954.

WESTERVELT, William Irving, b. Corpus Christi, Tex., Sept. 11, 1876; s. G. W. and I. F. W.; grad. U.S. Mil. Acad., 1900; m. Dorothy Jocelyn, Dec.

26, 1918; children—Peter Jocelyn, Dirck de Ryee, Jane. Commd. 2d lt. 1st Arty., June 13, 1900; promoted through grades to lt. col., Nov. 3, 1910; brig. gen. N.A., 1918. Served in Dept. of Tex. and Philippines; instr. dept. of philosophy, U.S. Mil. Acad., 1904-06; insp. ordnance Midvale Steel Works, 1906-07; mem. Field Arty. Bd., 1910-11; in Philippines, 1913; arrived in France, July 10, 1917; served as brigade adj., 1st Arty. Brigade, material officer, army arty., 1st Army, and as asst. to chief of arty., A.E.F.; returned to U.S., Mar. 1919; Gen. Staff, Aug.-Nov. 1919; Watervliet Arsenal, Nov. 1919-Sept. 1923, and in command, June 1921-Sept. 1923; attaché for ordnance, Am. Embassy, Paris, 1923-27, retired; tech. dir. Sears, Roebuck & Co., 1928-38. Dir. processing and marketing, A.A.A., June-Dec. 1933; mem. Exec. Commercial Policy Com., 1933. Decorated D.S.M.; Officer Legion of Honor (French); Companion St. Michael and St. George (British); Comdr. of Crown (Italian); also Victory medal, Philippine Campaign medal, and service ribbons Spanish-Am. War and Mexican border. Mem. Am. Soc. M.E. Clubs: University (New York); Army and Navy (Washington). Address: 441 Lexington Av., New York, N.Y.; also 83 Summit St., Burlington, Vt. Died Mar. 2, 1960.

WESTERVELT, William Young, mining engr.; b. Jersey City Heights, N.J., July 30, 1872; s. Richard Henry and Mary (Welsh) W.; E.M., Sch. Mines Columbia, 1894; m. Mary Westervelt Young, Sept. 12, 1900 (died 1926); m. 2d, Henrie Whiting McIlwaine, July 27, 1929. Chemist, surveyor, engr. and supt. mines, Ducktown Sulphur, Copper & Iron Co., 1894-98, cons. 1898—, responsible for development of Ducktown Co.'s mines to 1923; cons. engr. Anglo-Am. Copper Co., of London, 1905, and developed the Ray (Ariz.) property to the point of sale to present owners; apptd. consulting engr. Grasseli Chem. Co., of Cleveland, O., 1909, developed and organized its New Market (Tenn.) zinc property, Butte and Superior Mines, Butte, Mont.; apptd. consulting engr. Wilkes-Barre Dredging Co., 1914, organized the gold property of the co. at Folsom, Calif.; prepared report on pyrites resources of the world, 1916; selected, 1917, by Am. Inst. Mining Engrs. and the Mining and Metall. Soc. American mem. War Minerals Com., Washington, D.C., was chmn. of com.; organizer and pres. Copper Pyrites Corp., of Ducktown Mining Dist., Tenn., 1919; in 1927 purchased control of Ducktown Chemical & Iron Co. for Ducktown Pyrites Corp. Head consultant on mining Office of Dep. Dir. Gen., Industry Div., War Production Bd., 1942-44. Author of various articles on mining in tech. journals and of section on Mine Examinations, Valuations, and Reports, in Peele's Mining Engineer's Handbook. Fellow A.A.A.S., Royal Soc. of Arts (London, England); mem. Am. Inst. Mining and Metall. Engrs., Mining and Metall. Soc. America (v.p. 1920-22), Electrochem. Soc., Am. Mining Congress, Holland Soc., others. Clubs: Century, Columbia University (New York); Arts (Washington); Royal Societies (London). Presbyterian. Home: 4103 N. State St. (30). Office: Lamar Life Bldg., Jackson 2, Miss. Died Oct. 8, 1958.

WESTFALL, Alfred R(ensselaer), educator; born Darlington, Okla., June 25, 1889; s. George R. and Albertine (Maxwell) W.; A.B. cum laude, Park Coll., Mo., 1911; Ph.D., U. of Mo., 1930; m. Dollie Mae Towne, Aug. 18, 1914; children—Alfred R., Ralph L., Eleanor W. (Mrs. O. L. Holmes), Richard S. Mem. faculty, English dept., Colo. State Univ., Fort Collins, 1913—, prof. of English and head of dept., 1923—; vis. prof., U. of Mo., 1947-48. Mem. Modern Lang. Assn. of Am., Am. War Dads (state pres.), Fort Collins Writers Club (pres., 1951), Colo.-Wyo. Acad. of Letters, Pi Kappa Delta (nat. pres., 1924-28). Democrat. Presbyn. Mason. Author: Winning Intercollegiate Debates and Orations, Vol. I, 1926, Vol. II, 1928; American Shakespearean Criticism, 1939. Editor The Forensic of Pi Kappa Delta, 1924-28, 1930-47. Contbr. articles in popular and profl. publs. Home: 214 Elizabeth St., Fort Collins, Colo. Died Apr. 11, 1953; buried Ft. Collins.

WESTFALL, W(ilhelmus) D(avid) A(llen), univ. prof., mathematician; b. Montague, N.J., Jan. 27, 1879; s. Wilhelmus and Hanna Jane (Everett) W.; A.B., Yale, 1901; Ph.D., Goettingen U., 1905; m. Frederica Kees, Mar. 24, 1904 (dec. Jan. 22, 1917); 1 dau., Frederica (Mrs. Leon Barkman) m. 2d, Ruth Rollins, Dec. 22, 1921; children—David, Ellen. Instr. U. Mo., 1905-08, asst. prof., 1908-14, asso. prof., 1914-21, prof., 1921—. Home: 11 S. Glenwood, Columbia, Mo. Died Apr. 18, 1951.

WESTON, Edward, photographer; b. Highland Park, Ill., Mar. 24, 1886; s. Edward Burbank, and Alice Jeannette (Brett) W.; m. Flora Chandler, 1909; children—Chandler, Brett, Neil, Cole; m. 2d, Charis Wilson, 1946 (div.). Has given more than 75 One-man shows, 1920—; faculty mem. Cal. Sch. of Fine Arts, San Francisco, 1947—. Workd represented in permanent collections of Huntington Library, Smith Coll., Museo del Estado, Ualisco, Mexico; Los Angeles Mus.; Mus. of Modern Art, N.Y. City; Brooklyn Mus.; Los Angeles Pub. Library; San Francisco Mus. of Art; m. H. dl Young Mus., San Francisco; Fine Arts Gallery, San Diego, Calif.; and numerous others in schs. and pvt. collections. Awarded John Simon Guggenheim Memorial Found. Fellowship, 1937. Author (with Charis Wilson); California and the West, 1940; The Cats of Wildcat Hill, 1947. Illustrator: Leaves of Grass, 1942; The Art of Edward Weston (by Merle Armitage and E. Weyhe), 1932. Home: R.F.D., Carmel, Cal. Died Dec. 31, 1957.

WESTON, James Francis, ins. exec.; b. Gagetown, N.B., Can., Apr. 12, 1868; s. George and Frances W. (Dingee) W.; m. Bessie P. D. Allingham, Jan. 27, 1923. Local agt. Mfrs. Life Ins. Co., St. John, N.B.; insp. for Maritime Provinces; supt. of agencies, head office, Toronto, 1894-1913; gen. mgr. The Imperial Life Assurance Co. of Can., 1913-14, mem. bd. since 1914, mng. dir., 1914-34, v.p., 1934-36, pres., 1936-47, chmn. bd. since 1947; v.p. Colonization Finance Corp. of Can., Ltd. Mem. Canadian Life Ins. Officers Assn., Dominion Mortgage and Investments Assn. Mason. Clubs: Royal Canadian Yacht, York, Granite, Toronto Hunt. Home: 242 Douglas Dr. Office: 20 Victoria St., Toronto 1, Ont., Can. Died Aug., 1950.*

WESTON, Karl Ephraim, college prof.; b. Winchendon, Mass., Oct. 7, 1874; s. Irving Ephraim and Harriet Louisa Augusta (Mason) W.; A.B., Williams, 1896, A.M., 1898, L.H.D., 1940; student Am. Sch. Classical Studies in Rome, winter of 1896-97; spl. courses, Johns Hopkins and Princeton; Sorbonne, Paris, 1904-06; m. Ruth Mary Sabin, Apr. 7, 1921. Instr. Romance langs., Williams Coll., 1900-04, asst. prof. 1904-11, prof. 1911-12, prof. fine arts, 1912-40; founder, 1927, and dir. Lawrence Art Mus., Williams Coll., 1927-48. Alumni trustee Williams Coll., 1941-47. Mem. College Art Assn., Archeol. Inst. of America, Am. Acad. of Arts and Scis., Am. Assn. Univ. Prof., Phi Beta Kappa, Phi Delta Theta. Cavaliere Order of Saints Maurizio e Lazzaro (Italy), 1922. Conglist. Home: Thornwood, Williamstown, Mass. Died May 4, 1956.

WESTWOOD, Horace, clergyman; b. Wakefield, Eng., Aug. 17, 1884; s. Rev. John and Emma (Ogden) W.; ed. pub. schs., Grimsby, Eng.; student Garrett Bibl. Inst., Evanston, Ill., 1908-09, Meadville Theol. Sch., 1909, Div. Sch., U. of Chicago, 1909-10; D.D., Lombard Coll., 1914; m. Florence Wright, 1905 (died 1919); children—Lucy Emma (Mrs. Leonard C. Gifford), Florence Ashby (Mrs. T. P. Scott), Horace Frederick; m. 2d, Elizabeth A. Farrow, August 1920; 1 son, Arnold Farrow. Preacher, Primitive Methodist Ch., at 16; in charge ch. at Pelee Island, Ont., Can., 1904; at Ewen, Mich., 1905, Saulte Ste. Marie, Mich., 1906, 07; received spl. ordination by Bishop McCabe of M.E. Ch., 1906; joined Unitarian Ch., 1910; pastor First Ch., Youngstown, O., 1910-12, All Souls' Ch., Winnipeg, Can., 1912-19; sec. Canadian Unitarian Assn., 1913-19, First Ch., Toledo, O., 1919-1927. Ministerial del. Trades and Labor Council, Winnipeg, 1913-18; mem. Social Welfare Council of Manitoba, 1914-19; mem. Canadian Invalided Soldiers Commn. Vocational Advisory Com., Winnipeg, 1917-19. Mission preacher Unitarian Laymen's League, 1927-33; founder and brother dir. of The Mission Brotherhood, first liberal preaching order in modern religion; minister-at-large Universalist Ch.; chmn. Gen. Conf. Com. Am. Unitarian Assn., 1925-27; minister 1st Ch., Berkeley, Calif., 1934-45; minister Unitarian Ch., Charleston, S.C., 1945-49. Member faculty and v.p. of trustees Pacific Unitarian School for the Ministry, acting dean, 1943 (now Starr King School for the Ministry). Regional vice pres. Am. Unitarian Assn., 1944-46. Mem. Am. Acad. Polit. and Social Sci. Mason (32°). Author: This Do and Live, 1938; Seven Ways of Life; Prophets of Darkness and Apostles of Light; Legends from Genesis, The World of Today, 1948; So You Never Pray, 1948; There is a Psychic World, 1949; also numerous pamphlets on modern interpretation of religion. Contbr. "Saturday Sermons" to Toledo Blade, 1919-27. Home: 704 Bruce Av., Clearwater Beach, Fla. Died Dec. 24, 1956.

WETMORE, Maude A. K., civic worker; b. Paris, France, Feb. 7, 1873; d. George Peabody and Edith Malvina (Keteltas) Wetmore; ed. pvt. schs. Is actively interested in numerous civic and patriotic organizations. Episcopalian. Clubs: Colony, Woman's Nat. Republican. Home: Newport, R.I. Died Nov. 3, 1951.

WETMORE, Monroe Nichols, coll. prof.; b. Lebanon, Conn., Nov. 10, 1863; s. William Augustus and Abby Frances (Peckham) W.; B.A., Yale, 1888, M.A., 1900, Ph.D., 1904; m. Helen Green Leonard, Mar. 26, 1889 (died Dec. 4, 1941); 1 adopted son, Howard William (died Sept. 17, 1953). Asst. prin. Naugatuck (Conn.) High Sch., 1888-89; prin. Brunson (S.C.) graded schools, 1889-90; associate principal Harrisburg (Pa.) Academy, 1890-95; instr. Greek and Latin, Staten Island Acad., 1895-1902; Foote fellow in Latin, Yale, 1902-04; instr. Latin, Williams Coll., 1904-05, asst. prof., 1905-11, asso. prof., 1911-13; prof., 1913-32. Republican. Conglist. Mem. Am. Philol. Assn., Classical Assn. of New Eng. (sec.-treas. 1918-34, pres. 1935-36, Am. Assn. Univ. Profs. Editor for New Eng. of Classical Journal, 1913-20. Author: Index Verborum Vergilianus, 1911, 30; Index Verborum Catullianus, 1912. Contbr. to classical periodicals. Collaborating editor: A Selection of Latin Verse, 1914; Notes to same, 1915. In Italy and Greece, 1920-21, Europe, 1927-28. Home: 21 Moorland St., Williamstown, Mass. Died Nov. 18, 1954; buried Lebanon, Conn.

WETTEN, Albert Hayes, real estate; b. Downers Grove, Ill., July 26, 1869; s. Valentine and Hulda (Bartel) W.; m. Marion, daughter John H. Batten, June 20, 1901; children—Mildred (Mrs. T. Lloyd Kelly), Eleanor (Mrs. James S. Pennington, Jr.). Engaged in real estate business at Chicago since 1888; mem. firm of Rounds & Clough, 1890-96, Rounds & Wetten, 1896-1902; alone, doing business as Rounds & Wetten, 1902-12, alone, as Albert H. Wetten & Co. since 1912; dir. First Nat. Bank, Commonwealth Edison Co., Children's Memorial Hosp. Trustee Chicago Natural History Museum, Newberry Library, St. Luke's Hosp. Pres. Chicago Real Estate Bd., 1909; mem. Chicago Assn. Commerce, Art. Inst. Chicago (life). Republican. Episcopalian. Clubs: Chicago, Union League, Commercial, Mid-Day, Attic, Glenview. Home: 209 Lake Shore Drive. Office: 141 W. Jackson Blvd., Chgo. Died Sept. 3, 1953.

WEYERHAEUSER, John Philip, Jr., president Weyerhaeuser Timber Co.; born Rock Island, Illinois, Jan. 18, 1899; s. John Philip and Nellie (Anderson) W.; B.A., Yale; m. Helen Walker, Oct. 25, 1922; children—Ann, John Philip, III, George, Elizabeth. Had various jobs in lumber industry, 1920-22; sales mgr. Rutledge Timber Co., 1922-24; gen. mgr. Clearwater Timber Co., Lewiston, Idaho, 1925-31; pres. Potlach Forests, Inc., Lewiston, Idaho, 1931-32; exec. vice pres. Weyerhaeuser Timber Co., Tacoma, Wash., 1933-47, pres. since June 1947. Presbyterian. Office: Tacoma Bldg., Tacoma. Died Dec. 8, 1956.

WEYGANDT, Cornelius (wī'gănt), writer; b. Germantown, Phila., Dec. 13, 1871; s. Cornelius N. and Lucy E. (Thomas) W.; student Germantown Acad., 1882-87; A.B., U. Pa., 1891, Ph.D., 1901, Litt.D., 1931; Litt.D., Franklin and Marshall, 1930; LL.D., Susquehanna U., 1933; m. Sara Matlack Roberts, June 19, 1900; children—Cornelius N., Ann Matlack. Engaged in newspaper work with Philadelphia Record and Philadelphia Evening Telegraph, 1892-97, instr. English, U. Pa., 1897-1904, asst. prof., 1904-07, prof., 1907-42, emeritus prof., 1942—. Mem. Modern Lang. Assn. Am., Am. Ornithologists' Union, Del. Valley Ornithological Club. Author: Irish Plays and Playwrights, 1913; A Century of the English Novel, 1925; Tuesdays at Ten, 1928; The Red Hills, 1929; The Wissahickon Hills, 1930; A Passing America, 1932; The White Hills, 1934; The Time of Tennyson, 1936; The Blue Hills, 1936; The Time of Yeats, 1937; New Hampshire Neighbors, 1937; Philadelphia Folks, 1938; The Dutch Country, 1939; Down Jersey, 1940; November Rowen, 1941; The Plenty of Pennsylvania, 1942; The Heart of New Hampshire, 1944; On the Edge of Evening: An Autobiography, 1945. Home: 6635 Wissachickon Av., Germantown, Phila. Died Aug. 1957.

WEYL, Hermann (vīl), mathematics; b. Elmshorn, Germany, Nov. 9, 1885; s. Ludwig and Anna (Dieck) W.; ed. univ. of Munich and Göttingen; Ph.D., Göttingen, 1908; hon. Dr. Philosophy, University of Oslo, 1929; hon. Dr. Technology, Hochschule, Stuttgart, 1929; D.Sc., University of Pennsylvania, 1940, Columbia, 1954; Dr. Math. (honoary), Tech. Hochschule, Zürich, 1945; Dr., Université de Paris, 1952; married Helene Joseph, Sept. 1, 1913 (dec.); children—Fritz Joachim, Michael; m. 2d Ellen Baer Lohnstein, Jan. 7, 1950. Privatdozent U. of Göttingen, 1910-13; professor mathematics Tech. Hochschule, Zürich, 1913-30; Jones research prof. in mathematical physics, Princeton, 1928-29; prof. mathematics, U. of Göttingen, 1930-33; prof. mathematics Inst. for Advanced Study, Princeton, since Dec. 1, 1933. Mem. National Adademy, American Academy Arts and Sciences, American Philosophical Society, American Math. Society, and mem. or hon. mem. various European socs. including Royal Soc. of London, Pontificial Acad. of Sciences. Award Lobatschefsky prize, Kazan, 1925. Research work in differential equations, topology, relativity, theory, infinitesimal geometry, group theory, philosophy of mathematics, etc. Author of 8 books pub. in Europe, and 7 books pub. in U.S.—The Open World, 1932; Mind and Nature, 1934; The Classical Groups, 1939; Algebraic Theory of Numbers, 1940; Meromorphic Functions and Analytic Curves, 1943; Philosophy of Mathematics and Natural Sci., 1949; Symmetry, 1952; also articles in mags. Address: 284 Mesces St., Princeton, N.J. Died Dec. 8, 1955.

WEYMOUTH, Thomas Rote, gas engr.; b. Lock Haven, Pa., Mar. 16, 1876; s. George and Effie Pamelia (Rote) W.; S.B. in E.E., Mass. Inst. Tech., 1897; m. Josephine Goettel Loomis, Apr. 8, 1913; 1 step-son, William Goettel Loomis. Draftsman, Met. St. Ry. Co., N.Y.C., 1898; elec. engr., Internat. Hydraulic Co. (subsidiary of Emerson McMillin Co.), 1898-1903; asst. chief engr., Nat. Transit Co., Oil City, Pa., 1903-11; chief engr., United Natural Gas Co., Oil City, Pa., and Pa. Gas Co., Warren, Pa., 1911-23; pres. Iroquois Gas Corpn., Iroquois Building Corpn., Peoples Gas Light & Coke Co., 1923-28; pres. Am. Natural Gas Corpn., Okla. Natural Gas Corpn., Okla. Natural Building Co., Texokan Oil Corpn.,

Western Natural Gas Corpn., 1928-30; v.p. in charge of operations, Columbia Gas & Electric Corpn. and subsidiaries 1930-41, retired 1941. Formerly pres. Bd. Edn., Oil City, Pa. Mem. Am. Soc. M.E., Am. Gas Assn., Delta Upsilon, Royal Arcanum. Republican. Presbyn. Clubs: Saturn, Country (Buffalo). Author of Weymouth Formula for measuring flow of gas in pipe lines; inventor fluid measuring devices; contbr. on professional subjects. Address: 930 Park Av., N.Y. C. Died Sept. 23, 1958.

WEYRAUCH, Martin Henry (wī'rŏk), lawyer, educator, editor; b. New York, N.Y., Aug. 28, 1885; s. Henry M. and Sarah (Widmer) W.; Ph.B., Union Coll., Schenectady, N.Y., 1908; LL.B., Brooklyn Law School, St. Lawrence University, 1911; L.H.D., Union Coll., 1936; 1 dau., Elizabeth Thornton (Mrs. R. S. Pearsall). Began as reporter for Brooklyn (New York) Daily Eagle, 1908, later feature writer, dramatic editor, asso. city editor until 1923; successively city editor, mng. editor, business mgr., editor and pub. N.Y. Evening Graphic; pub. Daily Investment News, 1926-29; v.p. Macfadden Publs., 1923-30; circulation dir. Brooklyn Eagle, 1932-34, mng. editor, 1934-36; prof. law, Brooklyn Law Sch., since 1936. Corp. Counsellor, Village of Freeport, N.Y., 1947-55. Edgar Truman Brackett lectr., Union Coll., 1947. Mem. legal advisory staff Selective Service Adminstrn., N.Y. Vol. War Activities; chmn. newspaper division, Liberty Loan campaign; legal adviser, Flatbush Draft Bd., World War I. Member New York State Crime Commn., 1929-31. Special asst. atty. general and chief legal asst., Legislative Investigation, N.Y. State, 1944-45; special hearing officer, U.S. Dept. Justice, 1956. Mem. American, N.Y. State, Brooklyn bar associations, American Society International Law, National Panel of Arbitrators, Am. Arbitration Assn., Delta Upsilon, Phi Delta Phi, Pi Delta Epsilon. Republican. Methodist. Mason. Elk. Clubs: Fraternity, Rotary. Republican. Wrote: Pictorial History of Brooklyn, Brooklyn Historical Pageant, Crossroads House, Fundamentals of Labor Law; Richardson on Contracts (6th edit.), 1951; Fundamental Cases and Materials on Labor Law, 1954; Weyrauch on Labor Law, 1956. Home: 80 Connecticut Av., Freeport, N.Y. Office: 375 Pearl St., Bklyn. Died Feb. 1, 1958.

WHALEN, Robert E., lawyer; b. Ballston Spa, N.Y., July 29, 1874; s. Seth and Debby Anna (Murphy) W.; student Albany (N.Y.) Acad., 1887-92; A.B., Yale, 1896; student Albany Law Sch., 1897-98; m. Louise B. Herrick, Oct. 14, 1919. Admitted to N.Y. bar, 1898, since in practice at Albany; mem. Whalen, McNamee, Creble & Nichols, 1931—; dir. State Bank of Albany, 1910—, v.p., 1939—; trustee Mechanics and Farmers Savings Bank of Albany; dir. Hudson Valley Paper Co.; counsel for N.Y. Central, Boston & Albany, Boston & Me., West Shore, L.I. and Erie R.R. cos. Mem. Albany draft bd. during World War. Del. N.Y. State Constnl. Conv., 1938. Mem. Am., Albany County and City N.Y. bar assns. Democrat. Episcopalian. Clubs: Fort Orange, University (Albany). Home: 352 State St. Office: 75 State St., Albany, N.Y. Died Aug. 12, 1951.

WHALEY, Richard Smith, chief justice; b. Charleston, S.C., July 15, 1874; s. William B. and Helen (Smith) W.; Episcopal High Sch., Alexandria, Va.; LL.B., U. of Va., 1897. Admitted to S.C. bar, 1897; elected mem. S.C. Ho. of Rep., 1900, and reelected five successive times (speaker of House 2 terms); presiding officer Dem. State Conv., 1910; delegate Democratic Nat. Conv., Baltimore, 1912, and San Francisco, Calif., 1920; elected mem. 63d Congress (1913-15), 1st S.C. Dist., to fill vacancy caused by death of Hon. George S. Legaré; reelected to 64th to 66th Congresses (1915-21); chmn. Rent Commn. of D.C., 1923-25; commr. U.S. Court of Claims, 1925-30; judge of Court of Claims, 1930-39, chief justice since June 28, 1939. Home: Charleston, S.C.; also Washington. Died Nov. 8, 1951; buried Magnolia Cemetery, Charleston, S.C.

WHARTON, Carol Forbes, journalist; born Baltimore, Oct. 2, 1907; d. James Harris and Mary Armstrong (Craig) Forbes; ed. Bryn Mawr Sch., Corcoran Sch. of Art (Washington), Md. Inst., Peabody Inst., Nat. Sch. of Fine and Applied Arts (Washington); m. Col. James P. Wharton, Aug. 9, 1929. Professional miniature painter since 1928; freelance writer for newspapers, 1933-40; news and feature writer Baltimore Evening Sun since 1942; also art critic and columnist, since 1945. Democrat. Episcopalian. Club: Women's Advertising (Baltimore). Home: 106 West University Parkway, Baltimore 10. Office: The Sunpapers, Balt. 3. Died June 30, 1958.

WHEELER, Charles Gardner, author; b. Peabody, Mass., Sept. 21, 1855; s. Charles H. and Elen G. (Gage) W.; grad. Bowdoin Coll., 1876; high sch. teacher several yrs.; also designer of decorative woodwork. Unmarried. Editor and joint compiler of works of reference; Who Wrote It? 1881; Familiar Allusions, 1882. Author: The Course of Empire, 1884; Woodworking for Beginners, 1900; The A B C of Woodworking, 1911. Address: 4 Topsham St., Topsham, Me. Died Sept. 19, 1946; buried Riverview Cemetery.

WHEELER, Esther Willard, Rep. nat. committeewoman; b. South Chatham, Cape Cod, Mass., Oct. 1, 1898; d. Edward and Elizabeth (Nickerson) Willard; grad. Miss Miller's Finishing Sch., Brookline, Mass.; m. Raymond Wheeler, June 15, 1917. Mem. Malden (Mass.) Licensing Commn., 1941-48; vice chmn. Malden Rep. City Com., 1940-45; mem. Rep. State Com., 1945-54, vice chmn., 1945-52; Rep. nat. committeewoman from Mass., 1952—. Incorporator Malden Hosp.; past pres. Malden YWCA; past chmn. Am. citizenship, also past chmn. legislation Mass. State Fedn. of Women's Clubs. Club: Malden Women's. Home: 105 Summer St., Malden, Mass. Office: 8 Beacon St., Boston. Died Feb. 24, 1959; buried East Harwich, Cape Cod, Mass.

WHEELER, Harold Francis, newspaperman; b. Boston, Mass., July 27, 1888; s. Alvaro Santos and Helen Lee (Hall) W.; ed. pvt. schs.; m. Olive McGuire, June 27, 1921. Reporter on Boston newspapers, 1907-20; Sunday editor Boston Herald, 1921-22; mng. editor Boston Traveler, 1922-53. Member American Society Newspaper Editors. Mason. Episcopalian. Clubs: Lexington Golf, Old Belfry. Wrote biography of Gen. Pershing for newspaper syndication. Home: 12 Tower Road, Lexington, Mass. Office: 80 Mason St., Boston. Died Feb. 15, 1956; buried Westview Cemetery, Lexington, Mass.

WHEELER, Howard Duryce, editor, writer; b. Montclair, N.J., Nov. 3, 1880; s. Francis Augustus and Maria Dodd (Crane) W.; student Columbia, 1900-01, Stanford, 1902-04; m. Hazel Dorothy Davis, Apr. 18, 1925; 1 dau., Mary Patricia; m. 2d, Katherine Winders Stockton, Apr. 20, 1936. Reporter Bakersfield (Cal.) California, 1904, later with San Francisco Call; editor San Francisco Daily News, 1906-08; editor, Pacific Coast mgr. Newspaper Enterprise Assn., 1908-14; mng. editor Harper's Weekly, N.Y.C., 1914-15; editor in chief Everybody's Mag., 1915-19; gen. mgr. Science Service, Washington, 1920-21; gen. mgr. McClure Newspaper Syndicate N.Y.C., 1922-26; editor Condé Syndicate, 1928-32; chief editorial writer N.Y. Daily Mirror, 1932-36; cons. Office of Coordinator of Information, Washington, 1941; dir. information Inter-Am. Student Forum. Pan-Am. Union, 1942-43; editor-writer U.S. Office Inter-Am. Affairs, 1943-45; commd. lt. comdr., apptd. editor The Mast. U.S. Maritime Service, 1945, comdr., 1946; editor Retirement Life, 1955-56; editorial consultant various govt. depts., 1948—. Mem. Am. Academy of Polit. and Social Science, Phi Gamma Delta. Author: Are We Ready?, 1915; Interludes, 1934; Know Your Neighbor (Pan-Am. Union), 1942; Cordell Hull (U.S. Office Inter-Am. Affairs), 1943. Address: 322 1st St. S.E., Washington 9. Died Feb. 25, 1958.

WHEELER, Howard V., banker; s. Oscar G. W.; ed. pub. schs.; m. Mary Sluss, Nov. 9, 1898; 1 son, Winston. Pres. Wheeler, Kelly, Hagny Trust Co., Wichita, Kan. Home: 4 Lynwood. Office: 120 S. Market St., Wichita, Kan. Died Jan. 15, 1951.

WHEELER, James Everett, lawyer; b. New Haven, Dec. 24, 1870; s. Edwin Saxton and Ella Marion (Welch) W.; grad. Hillhouse High Sch., New Haven, 1887; student Robert Coll., Constantinople, Turkey, 1887-88; A.B., Yale, 1892, LL.B., 1894; m. Edith Pemberton Williams, Nov. 30, 1898 (died Sept. 17, 1953); children—Mary Pemberton, Lucy Miner (Mrs. Franklin Beardsley), Robert (dec.). Admitted to Conn. bar, 1894, since practiced in New Haven; clerk, later partner Alling, Webb & Morehouse, 1894-99; practiced alone, 1899—; councilman New Haven, 1900-04, mem. Bd. of Edn., 1904-08, Bd. of Finance, 1908-18; sec. Acme Wire Co.; treas. Conn. Bar Examining Com., 1907-51; receiver of Conn. Mortgage & Title Guaranty Co., 1930-39, Mechanics Bank of New Haven, 1932-35; dir. Andrew B. Hendry Co., Bradley & Scoville, Inc., Dextone Co. Served as chmn. Draft Bd. No. 6, New Haven, 1917. Chmn. Municipal Legal Aid Com., City of New Haven; mem. Conn. Jud. Council, 1927-47. Mem. New Haven County Law Library Assn., Am., Conn. (sec.-treas. 1908-43), New Haven County (treas. 1920-49) bar assns., Am. Law Inst., New Haven County Hist. Soc. (dir.), Soc. Colonial Wars, Wolf's Head Soc. (Yale), Alpha Delta Phi, Phi Beta Kappa, Phi Delta Phi. Mem. exec. com. Yale Alumni Bd., 1932-35. Clubs: Graduate, Elizabethan, New Haven Lawn. Author: Connecticut Administrative Officers, 1903. Home: 82 Edgehill Rd. Office: 42 Church St., New Haven, Conn. Died Feb. 16, 1954.

WHEELER, John Taylor, educator; b. Towanda, Pa., Jan. 15, 1886; s. Marshall Bullock and Florence (Stratton) W.; student Pa. State Coll., 1912-13; B.S., U. Wis., 1916, M.S., 1924; Ph.D., Cornell U., 1930; m. Evelyn Grigson, Aug. 24, 1916; children—Evelyn, John Taylor, Marshall Bullock, Gene Stratton, Joyce. Prin. of rural school, Osceola, Pa., 1910-11; instr. Mansfield (Pa.) State Tchrs. Coll., 1911-12; supt. pub. schs., Westfield, Pa., 1913-14; prof. horticulture Mass. State Coll., 1916-17; asso. prof. edn. U. Ga., 1917-19, prof., 1919—, head div. of vocational tchr. tng., 1928—. Served as 1st lt. San. Corps., U.S. Army, 1918-19; Reserve officer, 1919-29. Mem. agrl. council Near East Found., 1930—. Mem. Am. Farm Bur. Fedn., N.E.A., Ga. Edn. Assn., Am. Vocational Assn., Pi Kappa Phi, Phi Kappa Alpha, Alpha Zeta. Author: Methods in Farm Training, 1926; Curriculum in Agricultural Colleges, 1931; History of Georgia (with Sell), 1942; Two Hundred Years of Agricultural Edn. in Georgia, 1948. Co-author: Contributions of Ten Leading Americans to Edn., 1933; Contributions of Leading Americans to Agr., 1940. Spl. editor Agricultural Education mag., 1928-30. Home: 520 University Dr., Athens, Ga. Died May 17, 1950; buried Oconee Hill Cemetery, Athens.

WHEELER, Maxwell Stevenson, business exec., lawyer; b. Chicago, Ill., Feb. 13, 1874; s. Lester and Genevra Leslie (Newell) W.; A.B., magna cum laude, Harvard U., 1894; LL.B., Buffalo Law Sch., 1896; m. Gertrude Morgan Leibee, Feb. 11, 1903; 1 son, Henry Leibee. Admitted to N.Y. bar, 1896; and practiced in Buffalo; asso. with Larkin Co., Inc., 1904-39; v.p. and gen. counsel same and Larkin Co. of Ill., Larkin Co. of Pa., Larkin Co. of America, Larkin Warehouse, Inc., Kenland Co., Inc., Larkin Gasoline Co., Buffalo Pottery for many yrs.; treas. Gen. Drop Forge Co., Hubbell Realty Co.; v.p. Granger & Co.; dir. Hard Mfg. Co. Pres. Asso. Industries of N.Y. State, 1924-35; mem. Nat. Industrial Conf. Bd., 1924-35; mem. nat. advisory council Nat. Assn. Mfrs., 1924-35; mem. nat. council NRA; mem. advisory council Federal Housing Adminstrn., Federal Employment Service, N.Y. State Employment Service; mem. Gov. Roosevelt's Commn. on Stabilization of Employment; mem. Pres. Hoover's Commn. on Illiteracy; mem. N.Y. State Indsl. Council, 1924-44. Trustee, v.p., dir. Buffalo Y.M.C.A.; trustee Buffalo Y.W.C.A. (pres. bd.), De Veaux Sch.; treas., mem. exec. council Episcopal Diocese of Western N.Y.; mem. advisory council Buffalo Children's Hosp.; mem. nat. council Boy Scouts of Am. and pres. Buffalo council, 1940-41, pres. Merchant Sailors' League, Inc.; vice chmn. Buffalo chapter American Red Cross; member board Buffalo United Service Orgns.; mem. exec. bd. United War and Community Fund; pres. Buffalo Council Social Agencies; mem. Policy Holders Adv. Council of N.Y. State Ins. Fund; dir. Buffalo Municipal Research Bureau; mem. Erie County Bar Assn., Newcomen Soc., Phi Delta Phi. Republican. Episcopalian (vestryman; recipient Bishop's Cross as outstanding layman, 1953). Clubs: Harvard (pres.), Automobile, Country, University, Turtle Lake Fish and Game (Buffalo). Address: 42 Saybrook Place, Buffalo. Died Mar. 17, 1956; buried Middletown, O.

WHEELER, Post, ex-ambassador; b. Owego, N.Y., Aug. 6, 1869; s. Henry and Mary (Sparkes) W.; A.B., Princeton, 1891, univ. fellow, 1891-93; Litt.D. 1893; LL.D., Temple U., 1937; matriculated med. dept. U. Pa., 1893-94, Sorbonne, Paris, 1894-95; Ph.D., Andhra U., Vizianagram, South India, 1939, Thirtha Pandita (hon. fellow) of Univ.; m. Hallie Erminie Rives, Dec. 29, 1906 (died Aug. 15, 1956). Corr. in Paris and Morocco of Westminster Gazette and N.Y. Evening Post; editor N.Y. Press, 1896-1900; col. judge adv. gen. staff of Gov. Meade of Wash.; pres. Camelot Pub. Co., N.Y.C., 1902-05. Spent some time among the Tukudh Indians in the Arctic regions and has written extensively concerning them. Second secretary Am. Embassy at Tokyo, 1906-09; sec. Embassy, St. Petersburg, 1909-11, Rome, 1912-13, Tokyo (charge d'affaires), 1914-16; counselor of Embassy at Tokyo, 1916-17, of Legation Stockholm, 1917-20, of Embassy, London, 1921-24, of Embassy, Rio de Janeiro (charge d'affaires), 1929; E.E. and M.P. to Paraguay, 1929-33; special ambassador to inauguration of pres. Ayala, 1931; E.E. and M.P. to Albania, 1933-34, ret. Decorated Grand Cross and Cordon of St. Anne, Russian; Grand Cross, Comdr. Order of Prince Danilo I. Montenegrin; Plaque de Justice, and Grand Cross, Comdr. Order of St. Lazarus of Jerusalem; Imperial Order of St. Nicholas Miracle-Worker, 1st Class, Russian; Plaque of Fedn. of Chivalric Orders; Imperial Coronation Medal of Emperor Taisho, Japanese Grand Cross Grand Prix Humanitaire Belge; Grand Cross, Comdr. Coûrosane de Charlemaque; Khillats Star of Jeypore. Fellow Am. Geog. Soc., Royal Geog. Soc. (London); mem. Asiatic Soc. Japan, Japan Soc. London, Loyal Legion, Phi Delta Theta, Pi Gamma Mu; pres. Jr. Order Soc. of Army of Potomac. Mason (33°). Clubs: Century (New York); St. James's (London). Author: The Writer, 1893; Reflections of a Bachelor, 1897; Love-in-a-Mist (poems), 1901; Poems, 1902; Russian Wonder Tales, 1910; Albanian Wonder Tales, 1936; The Golden Legend of Ethiopia, 1936; Ho-Dan-Zo (10 vols.), 1938; Hathoo of the Elephants, 1943; India Against the Storm, 1944; Dragon in the Dust, 1946; Hawaiian Wonder Tales, 1946; The Sacred Scriptures of the Sun-Folk, 1948. Address: 102 Mt. Herman Way, Ocean Grove, N.J. Died Dec. 23, 1956; buried Hopkinsville, Ky.

WHEELOCK, Ward, company exec.; b. Phila., Feb. 20, 1896; s. Louis W. and Blanche (Toulon) W.; student Cornell, class of 1917; m. Margot Trevor Williams, Oct. 20, 1927 (deceased 1949); children—Margot Ward, Ian Ward, Keith Ward; m. Clay Borden, 1953. Advertising dept. Phila. Inquirer, 1914-15; with F. Wallis Armstrong Co., 1915-38, 1938 purchased co., changing name to Ward Wheelock Co., pres. 1938-51, chmn. bd. since 1951. Served as 1st lt., aviation sect., Signal Corps, World War I; fighter pilot attached Royal Flying Corps, 1917-19; col., A.U.S., A.C., 1942-44; service in Eng., Africa, chief in Control Office Hdqrs., Air Service Command, P. T.O. Decorated Legion of Merit. Recipient British Life Saving Medal, World War I. Republican. Episcopalian. Clubs: Union League, Racquet, Merion Cricket, Philadelphia Country (Phila.); Edgartown Yacht; Army and Navy (Washington); Sunday Breakfast. With Margot T. Wheelock, originated and operated Packages for Britain; originated, financed, and with Edward R. Murrow runs, This I Believe, radio program, newspaper syndicate, and books; originated, developed plans for Eisenhower Fellowships, mem. bd. trustees and selection committee. Office: Phila. Nat. Bank Bldg., Phila. 7. Died Jan. 24, 1955.

WHELAND, Edward F(ranklin) (whee-land), mfg. exec.; b. Chattanooga, Tenn., Jan. 30, 1878; s. George Washington and Emily Leville (Windsor) W.; student Southwestern Coll., 1897-1900; m. Minnie Newman, May 17, 1904 (dec. May 1941); children—George Edward, Charles Windsor. Vice pres., gen. supt. Wheland Co., 1910-28, pres., 1929-45, chmn. bd., 1945—; sec.-treas. Yates Bleachery Co., Flintstone, Ga., 1920-43. Home: 216 Belleview Av., Chattanooga 9. Office: Wheland Co., Chattanooga, Tenn. Died Feb. 16, 1959.

WHELAND, Zenas Windsor (hwē'lănd), mfr.; b. Athens, Tenn., Nov. 20, 1873; s. George Washington and Emily Leville (Windsor) W.; student Univ. of Chattanooga, Chattanooga, Tennessee, 1891-92; M.E., Cornell Univ., 1896; m. Lena Beck Willard, Dec. 1, 1897 (she died July 25, 1941); children—Mary Emily (Mrs. Arch Calder Willingham), Dorothy Eleanor (Mrs. Edward Dudley Lynde), Frances Elizabeth (Mrs. Douglas Fisher Wall), George Willard. Sales engr. Wheland Co., 1896-1900, treas., 1900-35, chmn. bd., 1935-46, sec. since 1946; v.p. Purse Co.; pres. Yates Bleachery Co. to 1945; v.p. Title Guaranty & Trust Co., Chattanooga, Tenn. Trustee U. of Chattanooga. Mem. Quill & Dagger. Republican. Methodist. Clubs: Mountain City Club, Golf and Country. Home: 1331 Dallas Rd. Office: The Wheland Co., Chattanooga, Tenn. Died Dec. 31, 1957.

WHELCHEL, B. Frank, ex-congressman; b. Lumpkin Co., Ga., Dec. 16, 1895; ed. pub. schs., Gainesville, Ga.; studied law in Gainesville pvtly.; m. Ruth Johnson, Dec. 15, 1943. Admitted to Ga. bar, 1925, and since practiced in Gainesville; judge of City Court of Hall County 1932-34; mem. 74th and 75th Congresses (1935-39) 9th Ga. Dist. Democrat. Home: 1195 Cherokee Rd. Gainesville, Ga. Died May 11, 1954; buried West View Abbey, Atlanta.

WHERRY, Kenneth S. (hwâr'rĭ), U.S. senator; b. Liberty, Neb., Feb. 28, 1892; s. David Emery and Jessie (Comstock) W.; B.A., U. of Neb., 1914, student Harvard, 1915-16; m. Marjorie Colwell, Sept. 15, 1920; children—Mrs. Marilynn Latta, David. Began as businessman, atty. 1915, U.S. senator from Neb., term 1943-51; Senate minority whip, 1944-46, Republican whip, 1944-48, Rep. floor leader since 1949. With U.S. Naval Flying Corps, 1917-19. Mem. 2 regular and 2 spl. sessions, Neb. legislature, 1929-32; Rep. state chmn., 1939-42; Rep. Midwest dir. for 22 states, 1941-42; mayor Pawnee City, 1929-31, 1938-43. Mem. Neb. State and Am. bar assns., Am. Legion, Beta Theta Pi. Presbyterian. Republican. Mason (Shriner). Home: Pawnee City, Neb. Died Nov. 29, 1951; buried Pawnee City, Neb.

WHICHER, George Frisbie, educator, writer; b. Lawrenceville, N.J., Nov. 5, 1889; s. George Meason and Lillian (Frisbie) W.; A.B., Amherst, 1910; A.M., Columbia, 1911, Ph.D., 1915; m. Harriet Fox, June 20, 1914; children—Stephen Emerson, Edward Fox (dec.), John Fox. University fellow Columbia, 1913; instr. English, U. Ill., 1913-15; asso. prof. English, Amherst, 1915-22, prof., 1935—; vis. prof. U. Hawaii, 1947, U. Minn., 1950; Turnbull lectr. Johns Hopkins, 1947. Fulbright vis. prof. U. Istanbul, Turkey, 1952-53. Trustee Jones Library, Amherst, Mass., Marlboro (Vt.) Coll. Mem. Modern Lang. Assn. Am., Phi Beta Kappa, Theta Delta Chi. Club: Century. Author: (verse) On the Tibur Road (with George M. Whicher), 1911; The Life and Romances of Mrs. Eliza Haywood, 1915; This Was a Poet, 1938; Alas, All's Vanity, 1942; Walden Revisited, 1945; The Goliard Poets, 1949; Mornings at 8:50, 1951. Editor: Borrow's Lavengro; Hammond's Remembrance of Amherst; Thoreau's Walden, Selected Poems of Horace; Poetry of the New England Renaissance, 1790-1890; William Jennings Bryan and the Campaign of 1896, Amherst Graduates' Quarterly, 1919-32; editorial bd. The American Scholar until 1950. Contbr. to Cambridge History of American Literature, Dictionary of American Biography, and articles, verse, reviews to various mags. Home: 272 Amity St., Amherst, Mass. Died Mar. 7, 1954.

WHIGHAM, Henry James (hwig'ăm), author, editor; b. Ayrshire, Scotland, Dec. 24, 1869; s. David Dundas and Ellen Murray (Campbell) W.; grad. Queen's Coll., Oxford, Eng.; m. Frances Macdonald, Nov. 1909 (died Feb. 1954); 1 dau., Sybil Whigham Young. Dramatic critic, Chgo. Tribune, 1896; war corr. for Chgo. Tribune and London Standard in Spanish-Am. War; present at battle of San Juan; imprisoned by Spaniards in Mantanzas; went to Boer War, S. Africa, for London Morning Post, also to Boxer rising, 1899-1900, Macedonian rebellion, 1903, Russo-Japanese War (on Russian side), 1904; fgn. editor London Standard, 1906-07; joined editorial staff of Metropolitan Mag., 1908, editor, pub., 1919-22; editor Town and Country, 1909-35; editor Internat. Studio, 1928-31. Clubs: The Links, Coffee House. Author: How to Play Golf, 1897; The Persian Problem, 1903; Manchuria and Korea, 1904. Home: 471 Park Av., N.Y.C. Died Mar. 16, 1954.

WHIPPLE, Charles John, chmn. Hibbard, Spencer, Bartlett & Co., b. Chicago, Ill., July 10, 1885; s. Charles Backus and Almira Elizabeth (Hayward) W.; prep. edn., Chicago Manual Training School; B.S., in E.E., U. of Mich., 1907; m. Elsa Kempf, Apr. 2, 1910; children—Pauline Elizabeth (Mrs. John W. Todd, Jr.), Charles John. Apprentice Western Electric Co., Chicago, 1907-08; with Hibbard, Spencer, Bartlett & Co., wholesale hardware, Feb. 1908—, salesman, 1908-12, superintendent, 1913-16, general manager, 1916-20, vice president, 1920-26, president, 1926-46, chairman, 1946—. Director First Nat. Bank of Chicago, Protection Mutual Fire Ins. Co., Atchison, Topeka & Santa Fe Railway Company, Western Electric Co.; pres., trustee Northwestern Mut. Life Ins. Co. Mem. com. on personnel, U.S. Army, 1917-18. Dir. Chgo. Home for Friendless. Pres. Bd. of Education, 1947. Member Alpha Delta Phi, Tau Beta Pi. Republican. Clubs: Chicago, University, Tavern, Economic, Commercial, Old Elm, Glen View. Contbr. to hardware trade journals. Home: 335 Sheridan Rd., Winnetka, Ill. Office: 2201 W. Howard St., Evanston, Ill. Died Oct. 28, 1958; buried Memorial Park, Evanston.

WHIPPLE, Harvey, journalist; b. Ovid, Mich., Aug. 2, 1884; s. Henry Bulkley and Ada (Eggabroad) W.; ed. pub. schs. of Port Huron, Mich.; m. Ina Frances Wright, Sept. 1, 1909; children—Frances Wright (Mrs. Oscar Karrel), Jane Wright (Mrs. Edwin A. Brown), Elizabeth Wright (Mrs. Millard Lampell). Reporter Port Huron (Mich.) Times, 1903-04, Detroit News, 1904-05, Detroit Free Press, 1905-10; successively asso. editor, mgn. editor, editor mag. Concrete (later Concrete-Cement Age), Detroit, Mich., 1910-25; successively sec., sec. and treas., sec.-treas. American Concrete Inst., Detroit, since 1919; editor Journal of the Am. Concrete Inst. since 1929. Contbr. gen. mag. and to specialized publs. Editor compilations in field of concrete. Mem. Engring. Soc. of Detroit. Club: Torch of Detroit. Home: 46280 W. Main St., Northville, Mich. Office: 18263 W. McNichols Rd., Detroit 19. Died Sept. 6, 1952; buried Ovid, Mich.

WHIPPLE, Lucius Albert, coll. pres.; b. Harmony, R.I., Jan. 29, 1887; s. Charles Lucius and Cora Sayles (Mowry) W.; student R.I. Sch. Design, 1902-04; B.S., R.I. State Coll., 1908; A.M., Brown U., 1928; hon. Ed.D., Providence Cath. Coll., 1940; hon. Sc.D., R.I. Coll. Pharmacy and Allied Sciences, 1940; LL.D., R.I. State Coll., Providence Coll., 1950; Ed.D., Bryant Coll., 1950; m. Mabel G. Ranger, June 19, 1912; 1 dau., Dorothy Sayles. Tchr. Abbott Sch., Farmington, Me., 1908-11; teacher, Pawtucket (R.I.) High Sch., 1911-13; prin. Sr. High Sch., 1922-31; supt. schs., Lincoln, R.I., 1913-17, R.I. State Home and Sch. Supt., 1917-22; dir. surveys and research R.I. Dept. Edn., 1931-35; exec. sec. Pawtucket and Blackstone Valley Community Chest, Inc., 1935-39; pres. R.I. Coll. Edn., 1939—. Past Pres. R.I. State Coll. Alumni Assn., former mem. bd. mgrs. former treas. Mem. R.I. Inst. of Instrn. (past pres.), Pawtucket Congl. Ch. (moderator). Mem. N.E.A., Am. Assn. Tchrs. Colls., N.E. Teacher-Preparation Assn. (pres. 1944), Eastern States Assn. Profl. Schs. for Tchrs. (treas.). Mason (32°, Shriner). Clubs: Lions (Pawtucket) (past pres. local, past dist. gov. of Conn. and R.I.); Barnard Club (pres.). Home: Greenville, R.I. Died Apr. 20, 1952.

WHIPPLE, Oliver Mayhew, life ins. exec.; born New Haven, Sept. 21, 1901; s. Harry V. and Elizabeth (Young) W.; grad. Phillips Andover Acad., 1919, A.B., Yale, 1923; grad. work, Harvard, 1923-24; m. Alice Elizabeth Heath, Sept. 14, 1928; children—Joan Elizabeth, Oliver Mayhew. Asso. with Kidder, Peabody & Co., N.Y. City, 1924-28; asst. financial mgr., Mutual Life Ins. Co. of N.Y., 1929-34, asso. financial mgr., 1934-44, 2d v.p., June 1944, v.p. and mgr. securities investment, 1944-47, v.p. and mgr. of investments, 1947-48, financial v.p. 1948—; v.p., dir. Union Securities Corp., 1953-54; v.p. Gulf Life Ins. Co., Jacksonville, Fla., 1955—. Mem. Soc. Colonial Wars. Clubs: Yale, University (N.Y.); Farmington Country (Charlottesville, Va.); Ponte Vedra (Fla.). Home: San Juan Dr., Ponte Vedra Beach, Fla. Office: care Gulf Life Ins. Co., Jacksonville, Fla. Died Apr. 26, 1959; buried Mather Cemetery, Darien, Conn.

WHIPPLE, Ralph W(heaton), geologist; b. Phila., Oct. 5, 1890; s. Fenner E. and Anna Elizabeth (Murray) W.; grad. Dean Acad., Franklin, Mass., 1910; B.S., Amherst Coll., 1914, A.M., 1917; student U. Paris (Sorbonne), 1929; m. Marjorie Davis, June 19, 1919; children—Ann, James Wheaton. Asst. in geology Amherst Coll., 1914-17; instr. in geology Marietta (O.) Coll., 1919-20, asst. prof., 1920-23, prof., 1923-25, Ebenezer Baldwin Andrews prof. natural scis. and curator of museum, 1925—. Served with U.S. Ambulance Service, French Army, 1917-19; with Civilian Defense, also AC cadet tng. Marietta Coll., 1942-43. Decorated Croix de Guerre (France). Mem. A.A.A.S., Ohio Acad. Sci., Geol. Soc. Am., Sigma Delta Rho. Republican. Unitarian. Contbr. to sci. jours. Home: 214½ Fifth St., Marietta, O. Died Dec. 3, 1954.

WHITAKER, Alma (Mrs. Jerome Reynolds), writer (syndicate); b. London, Eng.; d. Dr. Wotton and Marian (Hopkins) Fullford; ed. in 32 schs. in 9 countries including St. Michael's Convent, Blomfontein, S. Africa, St. Ursuline Convent, Belgium, Normal School, Cape Town, etc.; m. Harold Whitaker, Dec. 6, 1906 (dec.); 1 son, Colin Whitaker; m. 2d, Jerome Reynolds, Dec. 12, 1918; 1 son, Jerome Byrd (lt. AC, reported missing Sept. 1943). Came to U.S., 1906, naturalized citizen, 1915. Mem. staff Los Angeles Times, 1910—; with McClure's Syndicate, 1924-40. Republican. Episcopalian. Author: Trousers and Skirts, 1924; Bacchus Behave, 1933; The Governor's Wife Pays a Call (play). Home: 1038 C Linden Av., Glendale, Cal. Died Nov. 23, 1956.

WHITAKER, John Albert, congressman; b. Russellville, Ky., Oct. 31, 1901; s. Arthur and Annie B. (James) W.; ed. public schools and Bethel Coll., Russellville, and U. of Ky.; m. Helen Dent, 1931. County atty., Logan County, Ky., 1928-48; elected mem. 80th Congress, 1948, to fill unexpired term; mem. 81st Congress (1949-51), 2d Ky. Dist. Mem. Am. Legion, Sigma Alpha Epsilon. Democrat. Methodist. Rotarian. Home: Russellville, Ky. Office: House Office Bldg., Washington. Died Dec. 15, 1951; buried Maple Grove Cemetery, Russellville, Ky.

WHITAKER, Nelson L., mfg. exec.; b. Fulton, N.Y., Aug. 31, 1878; s. Charles and Clarissa W. (Moss) W.; ed. pub. schs. of N.Y.; m. Ivy F. Pierce, June 12, 1934; children—Mrs. Kurt H. Reinhold, Gaylord C. Pres. Oswego Country Trust Co., Fulton, N.Y., 1928-44; with Graflex, Inc., Rochester N.Y., since 1928, pres., gen. mgr. and dir., 1928-49, chmn. bd., dir. since 1949; dir. Security Trust Co. of Rochester. Member bd. of directors Rochester Inst. Tech. Mem. C. of C., Newcomen Soc. Clubs: Genesee Valley, Rochester. Home: 50 Ambassador Dr., Rochester 10. Office: 3750 Monroe Av., Rochester 3, N.Y. Died June 9, 1958; buried Mt. Hope Cemetery, Rochester, N.Y.

WHITE, Albert Beebe, prof. history; b. East Randolph (now Holbrook), Mass., Sept. 11, 1871; s. Edmund and Sarah (Beebe) W.; grad. Boston Latin Sch., 1889; B.A., Yale Univ., 1893; U. of Leipzig, Germany, 1897; Ph.D., Yale, 1898; m. Mabel White Jones, Oct 1, 1893 (died Dec 10, 1928); 1 son, Richard Beebe; m. 2d Mary Tower Jones, July 19, 1930. Teacher Siglar's Preparatory School, Newburgh, N.Y., 1893-95, Hillhouse High Sch., New Haven, Conn., 1898-99; instr. in history, U. of Minn., 1899-1900, asst. prof., 1900-07, prof., 1907, prof. emeritus since 1940. Mem. Am. Hist. Assn., Phi Beta Kappa; fellow Royal Hist. Soc. Author: The Making of the English Constituion, 1908, 1925; Source Problems in English History (with Wallace Notestein), 1915; Self-Government at the King's Command, 1933. Contbr. to hist. periodicals. Exchange prof. at U. of Mich., 1921-22; visiting prof. at Yale, 1930-31; prof. of history, summer, U. of Chicago, 1911, Columbia, 1913, 1940. Home: 311 Seymour Av. S.E., Minneapolis 14, Minn.; (summer) Rowe, Mass. Died May 10, 1952; buried Holbrook, Mass.

WHITE, Alfred Holmes, chem. engr.; b. Peoria, Ill., Apr. 29, 1873; s. Samuel Holmes and Jennie (McLaren) W.; student McGill U., 1889-90; A.B., U. Mich., 1893, B.S., 1904; grad. study Polytechnicum, Zurich, Switzerland, 1896-97; Sc.D., Northwestern, 1942; Eng.D. (hon.) U. Detroit, 1948; m. Rebecca Mason Downey, July 28, 1903; children—Alfred McLaren (dec.), Mary Julian. Asst. chemistry U. Ill., 1893-96; instr. chem. tech., U. Ch., 1897-1904, asst. prof. U. Mich., 1904-07, prof. chem. engring., 1907-43, prof. emeritus, 1943—, head dept. chem. engring., 1914, chmn. dept. chem. and metall. engring., 1938-42; cons. engr. U.S. Bur. Mines, 1907-20. Served from capt. to lt. col. Ordnance Dept., U.S. Army, 1917-19; chief research sect., asso. chief nitrate div., 1917-19; lt. col., Ordnance R.C., 1919, col., 1925; cons. chem. engr., Ordnance Dept., U.S. Army, 1919-22. Mem. Am. Gas Assn., Am. Inst. Chem. Engrs. (pres. 1929-31), Am. Soc. Testing Materials, Am. Chem. Soc., Soc. Promotion Engring. Edn. (pres. 1941-42), Phi Beta Kappa, Sigma Xi, Tau Beta Pi, Phi Lambda Upsilon, Alpha Chi Sigma, Phi Sigma Kappa. Republican. Unitarian. Clubs: Chemists (N.Y.C.); Cosmos (Washington); Rotary (Ann Arbor). Author: Technical Gas and Fuel Analysis, 1913; Engineering Materials, 1939. Contbr. tech. jours. Home: 120 E. 30th St., N.Y.C. Died Aug. 25, 1953.

WHITE, Aubrey Lee, writer; b. Hodgdon, Me., Feb. 17, 1869; s. George and Jane Marie (Beardsley) W.; student Houlton Acad. and Ricker Classical Inst., Me.; m. Ethelyn Binkley, 1906; children—Mary Jane, Elizabeth Binkley, Ethelyn Louise, Harriet Beardsley. Settled at Spokane, Wash.; served as officer or dir. Eden & Crescent Mining Co., Inland Empire R.R. Co., Grandby Mining & Smelting Co., Spokane & Eastern Trust Co., Northwestern Wall Paper & Paint Co. Pres. Park Bd., Spokane, Meml. Auditorium Assn.; organized park system and City Museum; mgr. Spokane Parkway Assn.; dir. Spokane Art Assn.; mgr. Spokane River Parkways Assn.; hon. life mem. Spokane C. of C., Spokane Hist. Soc.; Boy Scout commr.; sec. Constl. Govt. League; dir. Izaak Walton League Am.; dir. Am. Green Cross; dir. Arboretum Bd. of U. Wash., Wash. State Roadside Counsel, Wash. Federated Garden Clubs, Wash. State Soc. Conservation Wild Flowers and Trees; mem. State Adv. Council on Parks and Recreational Survey of Wash. Distinguished service award, Nat. House Planting Bureau, 1932; eminent service award State Coll. of Wash. Republican. Episcopalian. Mason (32°, K.T., Shriner), life mem. Blue Lodge, consistory and commandery; mem. K.P. Clubs: Spokane City, Rotary (hon. life), Spokane Athletic (life), Press, Early Birds. Writer of Garden Column, and in charge department on civic development, Spokesman-Rev., Spokane. Home: 617 E. 13th, Spokane, Wash. Died Sept. 1949.

WHITE, Charles Daniel, bishop; b. Grand Rapids, Mich., Jan. 5, 1879; s. Patrick and Catherine (Bolger) W.; grad. St. Francis Sem., Milwaukee, Wis., 1905; Ph.D., Coll. of Propaganda, Rome, 1907, S.T.D., 1911. Ordained priest R.C. Ch., 1910; instr., St. Joseph's Sem., Grand Rapids, Mich., 1911-19, rector, 1919-27; also asst. pastor St. Andrew's Cathedral, Grand Rapids, 1911-18; made domestic prelate by Pope Pius XI, 1925; installed as bishop of Spokane, Wash., 1927. Home: 238 E. 13th Av., Spokane 3. Office: 317 S. Howard St., Spokane 4, Wash. Died Sept. 25, 1955.

WHITE, Charles Henry, geologist; b. Yadkin County, N.C., Aug. 13, 1865; s. William and Sarah Catherine (Nicholson) W.; Licentiate of Instrn. diploma, Peabody Coll., 1887; student Vanderbilt U., 1887-88; S.B., U. N.C., 1894; S.B., Harvard, 1897, A.M., 1902; m. Josephine Pope, June 5, 1890 (died Jan. 4, 1919); m. 2d, Sarah Elizabeth MacDonald, June 4, 1920 (dec. Aug. 20, 1946); m. 3d, Marjorie Mills, Feb. 23, 1950. Asst. prof. mining and metallurgy Harvard, 1905-15, prof., 1915-17, chmn. dept., 1909-14; cons. geologist San Francisco, 1917—; has travelled in many countries for engring. and mining cos., mainly in search of copper mines. Commd. capt. Ordnance R.C., U.S. Army, and assigned to Watertown Arsenal, Feb. 14, 1918; discharged, Jan. 11, 1919; commd., Feb. 24, 1919, capt. Engrs. R.C. for 7 yrs. Mem. Am. Inst. Mining and Metall. Engrs., Soc. Econ. Geologists, Le Conte Geol. Club, Acad. Polit. Science, Calif. Acad. Sciences, Seismol. Soc. of Am., Harvard Engring. Soc., Phi Beta Kappa. Fellow Am. Geog. Soc., Royal Geog. Soc. Club: Commonwealth. Author: Methods in Metallurgical Analysis, 1915, 2d edit., 1920; Structural Geology, with Special Reference to Economic Deposits (with B. Stoces), 1936. Contbr. to tech. and scientific jours. Address: 3440 Clay St., San Francisco 18. Died Mar. 17, 1952; buried Cypress Lawn Cemetery, San Francisco.

WHITE, Charles Thomas, author, editor; b. White's Valley, Pa., Jan. 19, 1863; s. Samuel Frebun and Elizabeth Clarissa (Peck) W.; student pub. schs.; m. Mary Mendall, Nov. 22, 1888 (died 1946); children—Viola Chittenden, Mrs. Maude White Hardie. Tax commr. N.Y.C. under Mayors Gaynor and Mitchel, 1910-18; political news writer; with Herald Tribune, 1898-1932; asso. editor The Hancock (N.Y.) Herald, 1932-52. Republican. Methodist. Mason. Club: Kings County Republican. Author: Lincoln the Comforter, 1916; Lincoln and Prohibition, 1921; Lincoln and the Newspapers, 1924; Lincoln the Athlete and Other Stories, 1930. Owner of a valuable collection of Lincolniana. Home: Hancock, N.Y. Died Jan. 25, 1954.

WHITE, Compton Ignatius, ex-congressman; b. Baton Rouge, July 31, 1877; s. John Edward and Roberta Henrietta (Bowman) W.; student Met. Bus. Coll., Chgo., and Gonzaga Coll., Spokane, Wash.; m. Josephine Elizabeth Bunn, Nov. 24, 1915; children—Compton Ignatius, Enid Mary. Ry. telegraph operator, 1897-1903, trainman, 1903-06, conductor, 1906-10; agrl., lumbering and mining work, 1910—; mgr., v.p., dir. Whitedelph Mining & Developing Co. Former chmn. bd. trustees town of Clarksford; mem. 73d to 79th Congresses, 1st Ida. Dist. Mem. Am. Order Ry. Conductors, Farmers Union, Grange, Pomona Grange. Democrat. Catholic. Elk, Eagle, Modern Woodman. Contbr. to newspapers. Home: Clark Ford, Ida. Died 1956.

WHITE, Dudley Allen, publisher; b. New London, O., Jan. 3, 1901; s. Albert Union and Bertha (Triffit) W.; ed. pub. schs. of New London; hon. LL.D., 1940; m. Alice Davenport Snyder, June 28, 1924; children—Alice Mack, Dudley Allen. Pub. and editor Reflector-Herald, Norwalk, O.; pres. and gen. mgr. Sandusky Newspapers, Inc.; pub. The Register-Star-News, Sandusky, O.; pres. Sandusky Broadcasting Co.; dir. Citizens Nat. Bank, Norwalk; dir. The Northern Ohio Telephone Co.; mem. 75th and 76th Congresses (1937-41), 13th Ohio Dist. Mem. Ohio Citizens Narcotics Adv. Com., Gov.'s Traffic Safety Committee. Delegate National Republican Convention, 1928-48, alternate, 1932. Director Speakers Bureau, Rep. Nat. Committee, 1940. Exec. dir. U.S. Commn. on Intergovernmental Relations, 1953. Enlisted in USN, 1918; World War II as dir. recruiting and induction of U.S. Navy, rank of capt., USNR. Member New York Academy of Political Science, American Legion State comdr. 1929-30), Am. Newspaper Pubs. Assn. (chmn. postal com.), Ohio Newspaper Assn., Inter-Am. Press Association, Sigma Delta Chi. Republican. Episcopalian. Mason (32°). Clubs: The Capitol Hill Club, Army-Navy Country, National Press (Washington, D.C.); Union (Cleveland, O.). Home: 27 Edgewood Dr., Norwalk, O. Address: The Register-Star-News, Sandusky, O. Died Oct. 14, 1957.

WHITE, Edmund Valentine, educator; b. Mt. Lebanon, La., Aug. 11, 1879; s. Joseph V. and Laura Josephine (Woodard) W.; B.S., U. of Tex., 1914; M.A., Baylor U.; LL.D., Hardin-Simmons U.; m. Ollie Martin, Feb. 2, 1905; children—Edmund V., William L., Mary Josephine. Began teaching, 1896, and served as prin. and supt. schs. in Tex., county supt. schs., state insp. high schools in dept. of extension, U. of Tex.; dean Texas State College for Women, Denton, Tex., 1915-48, also prof. mathematics. Now retired; dean emeritus Tex. State Coll. for Women. Pvt. 23d U.S. Inf., Spanish-Am. War; in Philippine Campaign, 1898-99. Democrat. Baptist. Mason. Author: (with E.E. Davis) Survey of Rural Schools in Texas (U. of Tex.), 1914; Mental Arithmetic, 1921; Chocolate Drops from the South; Folks Are Funny; Let's Laugh; Senegambian Sizzles; also numerous ednl. articles and bulls. Joint author of high sch. and coll. algebras. Home: 904 Avondale Rd., Austin, Tex. Died Apr. 1955.

WHITE, Edwin, investment banker; born Chicopee, Mass., Sept. 26, 1882; s. William Gardner and Carolyn (Hall) W.; student Phillips Andover Acad., 1899-1902; A.B., Yale, 1906; m. Anne Turney, Oct. 10, 1914; children—Barbara (Mrs. Judson Bemis), Lt. (j.g.) William Gardner (killed in action at Chichi Jima, Sept. 2, 1944). Salesman Eugene M. Stevens & Co., Minneapolis, 1906-07; owner Edwin White & Co., 1907-13; partner White, Grubbs & Co., 1913-19; partner, Gates, White & Co., 1919-21; partner Kalman & Co., Inc., St. Paul, since 1921, chmn. bd. since Jan. 1948. Dir. Northwest Airlines, Inc., Am. Hoist & Derrick Co., Gen. Trading Corp., Northwestern States Portland Cement Co. Pres. bd. dirs., Charles T. Miller Hosp., St. Paul. Dir. St. Barnabas Hosp. (Minneapolis), Minneapolis Symphony Orchestra. Capt. Minn. N.G., 1917-18; candidate for commn., F.A., Central O.T.C., Fort Taylor, Ky., 1918. Mem. Newcomen Soc. of England. Republican. Episcopalian. Clubs: Minnesota (St. Paul); Minneapolis; White Bear Yacht (White Bear Lake, Minn.). Home: White Bear Lake 10. Office: Endicott Bldg., St. Paul 1. Died Oct. 22, 1951.

WHITE, Florence Donnell, educator; b. Alna, Me., Jan. 22, 1882; d. Henry Kirke and Jane Caroline Donnell White; B.A., Mt. Holyoke, 1903, M.A., 1907; Ph.D., Bryn Mawr Coll., 1915; student U. Paris, 1903-04. Tchr. French, Springfield (Mass.) Classical High Sch., 1904-06; instr., asst. prof., asso. prof., Vassar, 1908-21, prof., 1921—, chmn. dept. French, 1918—, prof. emeritus, 1947. Decorated Chevalier de la Légion d'Honneur, 1934. Mem. Modern Lang. Assn. Am., Assn. Tchrs. French, Am. Assn. U. Profs., Am Assn. U. Women, D.A.R., Colonial Dames of America, Phi Beta Kappa. Democrat. Conglist. Author: Voltaire's Essay on Epic Poetry, A Study and an Edition, 1915. Home: Vassar Coll., Poughkeepsie, N.Y. Died Dec. 15, 1950; buried Sheepscot, Me.

WHITE, Francis W(ilford), bus. exec.; b. Plymouth, Mass., July 22, 1893; s. Leo L. and Mary H. (Sampson) W.; ed. pub. schs. of Plymouth; m. Katherine Hickey, July 12, 1922; children—Katherine A., Francis W., Mary E., John R., Anne. Apprentice Standish Worsted Co., Plymouth, 1910-14; designer Puritan Mills of Am. Woolen Co., 1914-25; head designer Cleveland Worsted Mills, 1925-27, mgr. supt., 1927-28, gen. supt., 1928-36; supt. Atlantic mill. of A. D. Juilliard & Co., Providence, 1936-46, asst. resident mgr. Wood Worsted Mills of Am. Woolen Co., Lawrence, Mass., 1946-48; resident mgr., 1948-49; v.p. charge Worsted div. Am. Woolen Co., N.Y.C., 1949-50, became pres., 1950; mem. N.Y. adv. bd. Liberty Mut. Ins. Co.; gov. Wool Assos. of N.Y. Cotton Exchange; dir. Nat. Shawmut Bank of Boston. Served as capt., Co. D, 2d Machine Gun Bn., A.U.S., overseas, World War I. Knight of Malta, Knight of Holy Sepulchre. Mem. Am. Legion, 40 and 8. Club: Algonquin (Boston). Address: Manter's Point, Plymouth, Mass. Died Apr. 29, 1957.

WHITE, George, ex-gov. Ohio; b. Elmira, N.Y., Aug. 21, 1872; s. Charles W. and Mary S. (Back) W.; A.B., Princeton U., 1895; m. Charlotte McKelvy, Sept. 25, 1900; m. 2d, Mrs. Agnes Hofman Baldwin, Apr. 15, 1936. Mined in the Klondike, 1898-1900; oil producer, Marietta, O., 1902—; v.p., dir. The Peoples Banking & Trust Co. Mem. 77th Ohio Gen. Assembly, 1905-08; mem. 62d and 63d Congresses (1911-15), and 65th Congress (1917-19), 15th Ohio Dist.; governor of Ohio, 2 terms, 1931-35. Chmn. Dem. Nat. Com., 1920-21. Chmn. Northwest Territory Celebration Commn. Trustee Marietta College. Home: Marietta, Ohio; (winter) Hobe Sound, Fla. Died Dec. 15, 1953; buried Oak Grove Cemetery, Marietta, O.

WHITE, George Avery, pres. State Mutual Life Assurance Co.; b. Worcester, Mass., May 14, 1896; s. A. Avery and Mary F. (Stowell) W.; grad. Worcester South High Sch., 1914; student Williams Coll., 1915-17 and 1919 (certificate of matriculation and war service); served as enlisted man on destroyer, U.S. Navy, in home and fgn. waters, 1917-18, commd. ensign, 1918, retired as lieut. U.S.N.R.; LL.B., Harvard U. Law Sch., 1922; m. Katharine Bradley, Sept. 6, 1921; children—George Avery, Janet. Admitted to Mass. bar, 1922, in gen. practice at Worcester; asso. with Smith, Gage & Dresser, becoming partner in firm Gage, Hamilton, June & White in 1925 when firm name was changed, 1922-35; withdrew from firm to become pres. and dir. Worcester County Trust Co., pres. until 1942, still a dir. Pres. State Mutual Life Assurance Co. since 1942, dir. since 1933. Director United States Envelope Company since 1947. Vice-pres. and dir. Community Chest of Worcester; dir. Worcester County Musical Assn., Inst. of Life Ins.; trustee Williams College; exec. com. Am. Life Conv. Past pres. Mass. Bankers Assn.; mem. Gargoyle Soc. (Williams), Phi Gamma Delta, Am. Legion (past comdr. Devens Post). Clubs: University, Williams (N.Y. City); Worcester (pres. 1940-41), Tatnuck Country (Worcester); hon. mem. Rotary Club. Episcopalian. Home: 28 Westland St. Office: 340 Main St., Worcester, Mass. Died Sept. 12, 1951; buried Pine Grove Cemetery, Boylston, Mass.

WHITE, Georgia Laura, educator; b. Nashville, Tenn., Apr. 28, 1872; d. George Leonard and Laura Amelia (Cravath) W.; student Fredonia (N.Y.) State Normal Sch., 1881-84, 1887-89, Lake Erie Coll. for Women, Painesville, O., 1889-94; Ph.B., Cornell U., 1896, Ph.D., 1901; grad. study, Halle-Wittenberg U., Halle, Germany, 1899-1900; unmarried. Teacher, high sch., Newcastle, Ind., 1896-98; head teacher, Walnut Lane Sch., Germantown, Pa., 1901-03; asso. prof. economics and sociology, Smith Coll., 1903-11; dean of women, Olivet (Mich.) Coll., 1911-13; same and dean of home economics, Mich. Agrl. Coll., 1914-18; dean of women, Cornell U., 1918-26; same, Carleton Coll., Northfield, Minn., 1926-30; prof. English, Fisk U., Nashville, Tenn., 1934-36. Mem. Women's War Bd. of Michigan, mem. exec. com. Women's Council of Defense, home economics dir. Food Administration for Mich. and chmn. Women's Com. for Prevention of Venereal Disease, Mich. State Bd. of Health, World War. Trustee Lake Erie Coll., and of Fisk U., Nashville, Tenn. Mem. Am. Assn. Univ. Women, Nat. Assn. Deans of Women, Alpha Phi, Omicron Nu, Pi Lambda Theta, Phi Kappa Phi. Republican. Conglist. Home: 313 Commonwealth Av., Boston, Mass. Died May 15, 1949.

WHITE, Harry, bus. exec.; b. Guelph, Ont., Canada, Nov. 24, 1878; s. Harry and Sarah M. (Morrison) W.; student business coll., Chicago, 1902-04; m. Hazel M. Johnson, Aug. 25, 1915; children—Hazel Mary, Ruby Virginia. Brought to U.S., 1879, naturalized, 1899. Entered service Alton, B.&O. predecessor co., 1895, gen. auditor's office, Chicago, 1900-12, various traveling auditor clearing house agt., 1902-05, chief clerk, 1910-12, chief clerk in joint office of vice pres. B.&O. R.R. and pres. B.&T. Chicago Terminal R.R., 1912-47; one of 5 signers for Alton R.R. Co. charter, 1931, dir., 1931—, vice pres., 1943—; ret. 1948. Mason. Home: 1030 Wenonah Av., Oak Park, Ill. Office: Grand Central Station, Chgo. 7. Died May 19, 1955.

WHITE, Henry Adelbert, coll. prof., editor; b. Oran, N.Y., Apr. 8, 1880; s. Edward Albert and Gertrude (Candee) W.; A.B., Wesleyan U., 1904, A.M., 1905; A.M., Yale, 1908; A.M., Harvard, 1912; Ph.D., Yale, 1924; studied U. of Chicago; m. Henrietta Davidson, June 28, 1916; children—Muriel G., Donald D., Frank A. (dec.). Instr. English, Purdue U., 1906-07, 1909-11; actg. prof. English, McMaster U., Toronto, Can., 1912-13; prof. English, Lombard Coll., 1913-17; Wallace prof. rhetoric and pub. speaking, Washington and Jefferson Coll., 1918-26; prof. English, U. of Neb., 1926-50. Adviser for Neb., radio com. of Am. Acad. Arts and Letters, 1929-36. Sec. Pa. Intercollegiate Debating Assn., 1923-24, pres. 1924-25; editor Gavel, 1926-33. Mem. Modern Lang. Assn. Am., London, Am. Bibliog. Soc., Society Midland Authors (v.p. for Neb., 1929-32), Neb. Com. on Enrichment of Adult Life, Delta Sigma Rho (v.p. 1924-39), Delta Tau Delta, Pi Delta Epsilon, Sigma Tau Delta. Methodist. Author: English Study and

English Writing, 1922; Walter Scott's Novels on the Stage, 1927. Edited Stevenson's Master of Ballantrae, and assisted Fanny J. Crosby, blind hymnist, in writing her autobiography; revisory editor New Century Book of Facts since 1925. Home: 2350 Sumner St., Lincoln 2, Neb. Died Nov. 25, 1951; buried Oran, N.Y.

WHITE, Henry Middleton, ex-govt. ofcl.; b. Lewis County, W.Va., Apr. 9, 1874; s. Alexander Perry and Mary Catharine (Fetty) W.; A.B., W.Va. U., 1899, LL.B., 1899; m. Ada Baxter Caldwell, Jan. 31, 1914; 1 son, Henry Middleton, (naval air pilot). Began practice in Bellingham, Wash., 1900; mem. Brown & White, 1906-08, Brown, White & Perringer, 1908-13; city atty. Bellingham, 1901-06; elected mem. com. to frame charter for Bellingham, 1903; candidate for judge Superior Court of Whatcom County, 1908; mem. Wash. Senate, 1910-12; Dem. candidate for congressman-at-large, 1912; commr. of immigration at Port of Seattle, 1913-21. Was commr. of conciliation U.S. Dept. Labor, dist. sec. U.S. Employment Service, and agt. Nat. Adjustment Commn. during war. Pres. Bellingham C. of C., 1906, 07. Formerly atty. in charge Seattle office FTC. Mem. Sigma Chi. Home: 4883 Terrace Dr., Seattle 5. Died Oct. 10, 1950; buried Rose Hill Terrace Mausoleum, Seattle.

WHITE, John Chanler, bishop; b. Laurens County, S.C., May 21, 1867; s. Thomas Grimke and Martha Phoebe (Edings) W.; desc. Gen. Francis Marion and John C. Calhoun, and g.s. John Blake White, artist; A.B., St. Stephen's Coll., Annandale, N.Y., 1888; grad. Gen. Theol. Sem., 1891; D.D., St. Stephen's; S.T.D., Gen. Theol. Sem.; m. Katherine Dresser, September 10, 1891; children—Thomas Dresser (gen. U.S. Air Force), Katherine Virginia. Deacon, 1891, priest, 1892, P.E. Ch.; rector St. Paul's Church, Rantoul, Illinois, and St. Thomas' Ch., Thomasboro, Ill., 1891-93; chaplain and private sec. to Bishop Seymour, Springfield, with charge of Christ Ch., Waverly, Ill., 1893-97; rector Holy Trinity Ch., Hartwell, O., 1898-1900, St. Paul's Ch., East St. Louis, Ill., 1900-09; gen. missionary, Diocese of Springfield, 1909-16; rector Trinity Ch., Lincoln, Ill., 1916-24; elected bishop of Springfield, Feb. 19, 1924; consecrated 4th bishop of Springfield, May 1924; ret. Maj. chaplain U.S.R. Mem. Sigma Alpha Epsilon. Democrat. Mason (32°, K.T.). Club: Country. Home: 119 S. Walnut St., Springfield, Ill. Died Feb. 11, 1956; buried Oak Ridge Cemetery, Springfield.

WHITE, John W., business exec.; b. Indianapolis, Ind., Jan. 6, 1889; s. Clarence R. and Nellie (Porter) W.; student Randolph-Macon Coll., 1903-05, Carnegie Inst. Tech., 1905-07; m. Pia Maria Libera, Feb. 5, 1937; children—Pia Maria, Joanna Libera, John W. Sales engr. Westinghouse Electric Co., Pittsburgh, Pa., 1907-12, Allis-Chalmers Mfg. Co., Milwaukee, Wis., 1912-17; with Westinghouse companies since 1918, successively mgr., Cuba, 1918-24, gen. mgr., Japan, 1925-30, vice pres., Argentina, 1930-36, vice pres. and gen. mgr. Westinghouse Electric Internat., New York, 1937-43, pres., gen. mgr. and dir., 1943-46, pres., dir. Industria Electria de Mexico S.A., Mexico City, 1946-51, ret. Clubs: Metropolitan, India House, Wall Street (New York); Westhecster (N.Y.) Country; Bankers, Mexico City Country (Mexico City, Mexico). Home: Calle Colima 194, Colonia Roma, Mexico, D.F. Died Aug. 29, 1951.

WHITE, Joshua Warren, physician; b. Charlotte County, Va., 1875; s. Capt. Joshua Warren and Bessie (Morton) W.; student Va. Polytech. Inst.; A.B., Hampden Sydney Coll., 1895; M.D., Med. Coll. Va., 1901; m. Emily Fuller Johnston, 1911; children—Robert Johnston, Alan Johnston (Lt. U.S.N.S.C.), Joshua Warren, Jr. (lt. comdr. U.S.N.R.), Intern and house doctor St. Vincent de Paul Hosp., Norfolk, Va., 1901-02; asst. and house surgeon Manhattan Eye, Ear and Throat Hosp., 1913-15; surgeon oculist S.A.L. R.R., 1939—; chief opthalmological and otolaryngological dept. St. Vincent's Hosp., Norfolk, Va., 1917—; (past pres. med. staff); mem. vis. staff Norfolk Gen. Hosp.; cons. St. Vincent DePaul Hosp., 1948—. Diplomate Am. bds. Ophthalmology and Otolaryngology. Fellow A.C.S., Am. Acad. Ophthal. and Otolaryn., Am. Laryngological, Rhinological and Otological Soc., A.M.A., Soc. Ex-House Surgeons, Manhattan Eye, Ear, Throat Hosp., Va. State Med. Soc. (past 1st v.p.), Norfolk County Med. Soc. (past pres.), Norfolk chpt. A.R.C. (dir.), Anti-Tb. League (dir. Norfolk chpt.), Assn. S.A.L. Ry. Surgeons; honorary member Omicron Delta Kappa. Awarded Algernon Sydney Sullivan medallion. Served as chief, Ophthalmological Dept., Base Hosp. 90 (G.H.Q.), Chaumont, France, and as capt. U.S. Army Med. Corps, World War I. Presbyterian. Trustee Hampden-Sydney Coll., 1943, chmn. alumni fund, 1943-50. Mem. com. on ednl. instns. Synod of Va., 1946-49. Democrat. Contbr. many articles to med. jours. Home: 527 Fairfax Av. Office: Medical Arts Bldg., Norfolk, Va. Died Mar. 4, 1953; buried Elmwood Cemetery, Norfolk.

WHITE, Lawrence Grant, architect; b. New York, N.Y., Sept. 26, 1887; s. Stanford and Bessie Springs (Smith) W.; A.B., cum laude, Harvard, 1907; diploma Ecole des Beaux Arts, Paris, France, 1913; honorary Doctor of Fine Arts, Union College; married Laura Astor Chanler, June 19, 1916; children—Frederick Lawrence Peter, Elizabeth Stuyvesant, Robert Winthrop, Alida Mary, John Chanler, Cynthia Margaret, Sarah Matilda, Ann Octavia. Began as architect, 1914; mem. McKim, Mead & White since 1919, now sr. partner. Principal works: Pa. R.R. Station, Newark, N.J.; 52 Wall Street, New York; Regimental Barracks, Governors Island, N.Y., Hotel National, Havana, Cuba; Girard Trust Co. Offices, Phila. Dir. Garden City Co., Hempstead Plains Co.; trustee Manhattan E.E. & T. Hosp., N.Y., Met. Mus. Art; Tiffany Found.; pres. Nat. Acad. of Design; trustee Parsons Sch. of Design; member Smithsonian Art Commn.; v.p. Nat. Sculpture Society. Served as lt. (s.g.) U.S.N.R.F., World War I; naval aviator No. 176; naval aide to Pres. Wilson, 1919; commd. lt. (s.g.), U.S.N.R., 1942, and advanced to rank of lt. comdr. Decorated Chevalier Crown of Italy, Naval War Cross, Knight Officer Order SS. Maurice and Lazarus (Italy); Chevalier Legion of Honor (France). Fellow American Inst. Architects, Society Architects Diplomes by French Government, Phi Beta Kappa. Republican. Episcopalian. Clubs: Harvard, Century Assn. (New York); Missequogue Beach (Smithtown, L.I.). Author: Sketches and Designs by Stanford White, 1920; Translation of Dante's Divine Comedy, 1948. Home: St. James, L.I., N.Y. Office: 101 Park Av., N.Y.C. Died Sept. 8, 1956.

WHITE, Lazarus, civil engr.; b. Rochester, N.Y., Feb. 26, 1874; s. Max A. and Ann (Lewine) W.; student N.Y.U., 1892-93; C.E., Columbia, 1897; m. Marie Emelin, June 23, 1904; children—Felicia Marie (wife of Dr. Hans Peter Gossman), Edward Emelin, Robert Emelin. Inspector U.S. Engrs. Key West, Fla., 1897-98; rodman Pa. R.R., Jersey City, 1898-1900; asst. engr. Rapid Transit Commn., N.Y., 1900-06; div. engr. Bd. of Water Supply, New York, 1906-14; engr. Smith, Hauser & MacIsaac, 1914-19; pres. Spencer, White and Prentis, Inc., 1919-50, ret.; pres. Pleasantville Construction Co.; mem. exec. com. Dry Dock Associates. Recipient Egleston medal Columbia, 1941. Mem. Soc. for Ethical Culture, Am. Acad. Science, Am. Soc. for Testing Materials, Am. Soc. C.E. (dir.), Sigma Xi. Clubs: Engineers, Columbia University (N.Y.C.); Faculty (Harvard U.). Author: Catskill Water Supply of New York City, 1911. Co-author: (with E. A. Prentis) Modern Underpinning, 1917; Underpinning, 1929; Cofferdams, 1940. Contbr. to mags. Home: 28 Pryer Lane, Larchmont, N.Y. Died July 30, 1953; buried Mt. Pleasant Cemetery, Hawthorne, N.Y.

WHITE, Leonard Dupee, polit. science; b. Acton, Mass., Jan. 17, 1891; s. John Sidney and Bertha H. (Dupee) W.; B.S., Dartmouth, 1914, M.A., 1915, Litt.D., 1946; Clark U. and Harvard; Ph.D., U. Chicago, 1921; LL.D. (honorary), Princeton University, 1952; m. Una Lucille Holden, June 17, 1916; 1 dau., Marcia Robinson. Instr. in govt., Clark Coll., Worcester, Mass., 1915-18; instr., later asst. prof. polit. science, Dartmouth, 1918-20; became asso. prof., prof. polit. science, U. of Chicago, 1920; now Ernest DeWitt Burton Distinguished Service professor pub. adminstrn. Guggenheim Fellow, 1927-28; mem. Chicago Civil Service Commn., 1931-33; mem. Civil Service Commn. and Central Statis. Bd., Washington, D.C., 1934-37; mem. President's Com. on Civil Service Improvement, 1939-41; v.p. Nat. Civil Service Reform League, 1939-—. Special Investigator for Nat. Research Council (states relation div.), 1923, 25, Chicago Citizens Police Com., 1929-31; investigator Personnel Policy Com. of Hoover Commn., 1948-49, mem. personnel task force 2d Hoover Commn., 1953-55; U.S. Civil Service Commn. 7th Regional Loyalty League since 1939. Special investigator for Nat. Re-Hoover Commn. on Social Trends, 1930-31; mem. Improvement, 1939-41; v.p. Nat. Civil Service Reform Bd. 1948-50, U.S. Civil Service Commn. Loyalty Review Bd., 1950-52. Comdr. Order Leopold II (Belgium); recipient Bancroft prize; Woodrow Wilson award. V.p. Institut Internat. des Sciences Administratives, 1938-47, hon. v.p. since 1947; mem. Political Sci. Assn. (pres. 1944), Am. Acad. Arts and Scis., Am. Soc. Pub. Adminstrn. (pres. 1947), Phi Beta Kappa, Delta Sigma Rho. Republican. Club: Quadrangle (Chicago, Ill.). Author: The Status of Scientific Research in Illinois, 1923; Evaluation of the System of Central Financial Control of Research in State Governments, 1924; Introduction to Study of Public Administration, 1926, revised edit., 1948; The City Manger, 1927; Prestige Value of Public Employment in Chicago, 1929; Further Contributions to the Prestige Value of Public Employment, 1932; Whitley Councils in the British Civil Service; Trends in Public Administration, 1933; Government Career Service, 1935; Politics and Public Service (with T. V. Smith), 1939; The Federalists, 1948. Editor: Civil Service in the Modern State, 1930; The New Social Science, 1930; Chicago, an Experiment in Social Sciences Research (with T. V. Smith), 1929; Future of Government in the United States, 1942; The Federalists, 1948; The Jeffersonians, 1951; The Jacksonians, 1954; The Republican Era, 1958. Editor in chief Public Administration Review, 1940-43. Home: 5626 Dorchester Av., Chgo. Died Feb. 23, 1958; buried Acton, Mass.

WHITE, Llewellyn Brooke, author; b. Battle Ground, Ind., Oct. 3, 1899; s. Harry S. and Lulu Yeager (Stretch) W.; A.B., U. of Kansas, 1923; grad. studies, U. of Paris; m. Susannah Smith Moody, Aug. 25, 1925; 1 son, Robert Ogden; m. 2d, Marjorie Elinor Taggart, May 14, 1940. City editor Courier, Winfield, Kans., 1922; reporter Chicago American, 1923; chief editorial writer Kansas City Kansan, 1923-24; reporter San Francisco Examiner, 1924; sports editor Kansas City Journal, 1925-26; asst. mng. editor N.Y. Herald, Paris, France, 1927-29; Paris corr. United Press, 1930-31; regional editor Asso. Press, N.Y. 1931-32; day copy chief N.Y. Herald Tribune, 1932-36; asst. mng. editor Literary Digest, 1936-37; nat. affairs editor Newsweek, 1938-41; editor editorial pages and Washington columnist, Chicago Sun, 1941-42; chief news and features bur., overseas br. O.W.I., 1942-44; spl. advisor to dir. O.W.I., 1944; asst. dir. Commn. on Freedom of the Press, 1945-46; spl. asst. to asst. sec. of State, 1946; 1st sr. counsellor for mass media, UNESCO, 1946; mng. editor, The Reporter, 1948-51; chief program div. The Press Service, Internat. Information Adminstrn.; Dept. of State, 1951-55; asso. dir. Plans bd. U.S. Information Agy., 1953-55; Great Issues lectr. Dartmouth Coll.; now engaged in free lance writing. Served with 137th Inf., Co. H, 1917-19, World War I. Mem. Acad. Polit. Sci., Alpha Tau Omega, Sigma Delta Chi. Club: Nat. Press. Author: Peoples Speaking To Peoples (with Robert D. Leigh); 1946; The American Radio, 1947; Ground Zero, 1955; The Azure Mountain, 1956; Kitty Somebody, 1957; Small Symphony for Two Violas, 1958; Up the Rebels!, 1959; The Impact of Europe, 1959. Home: 9 W. 82d St., N.Y.C. 24. Died May 15, 1959; buried Porter Lake, Strong, Me.

WHITE, Luke Matthews, clergyman; b. Huntsville, Ala., Oct. 18, 1877; s. David Irvine and Lucy (Matthews) W.; B.A., U. Va., 1902, M.A., 1902; D.D., Va. Theol. Sem., 1905; m. Jane Tucker, June 27, 1905; children—Beverly Tucker, David Irvine, Luke Matthews. Ordained to ministry P.E. Ch., 1905; rector St. John's Ch., Warsaw, Va., 1905-06, Christ Ch., Pulaski, Va., 1906-10, St. Mark's Ch., Shreveport, La., 1910-16, St. Luke's Ch., Montclair, N.J., 1916-46; retired. Home: 48 Union St., Montclair, N.J. Died Oct. 1, 1955.

WHITE, Lynn Townsend, clergyman, educator; b. Knoxville, Tenn., July 12, 1876; s. William Orlando and Letitia Dalton (Lynn) W.; B.A., Univ. of Tenn., 1897; sec. Southern Biblical Assembly, 1897; Y.M. C.A. sec. 4th Tenn. Vols., Spanish-Am. War, 1898; grad. Union Theol. Sem., 1901; studied Columbia Univ., 1900; D.D., Occidental Coll., Los Angeles, Calif., 1916; M.A., Columbia Univ., 1927; m. Mary A. Tarrant, Dec. 31, 1904; 1 son, Lynn Townsend. Ordained Presbyn. ministry, 1903; pastor Fall River Mills, Calif., 1903-05; superintendent ch. extension, Presbytery of San Francisco, Calif., 1906-08; pastor 1st Church, San Rafael, Calif., 1908-20; Margaret S. Dollar professor Christian Social Ethics, San Francisco Theol. Sem., 1920-48, emeritus. Served as Y.M.C.A. sec. in France (5th Marines) Jan.-Dec. 1918. Awarded Croix de Guerre (French). Past chaplain, Grand Lodge of Calif., F.&A.M. Del. to Pan-Presbyn. Council, Cardiff, Wales, 1925; attended Institute of Internat. Relations, Geneva, Switz., 1925; del. Presbyn. Ch. of U.S.A., World Conf. on Christian Life and Work, Stockholm, Sweden, 1925; frequent commr. to Gen. Assembly, Presbyn. Chs. of U.S.A.; chmn. com. on soc. edn. and action, Synod of Calif., since 1943; mem. commn. on worship, commn. on social service, Federal Council of Churches of Christ in America. Former chmn. sections on delinquency, industrial relations, hot cargo and secondary boycott, Quarterly Luncheon chmn., Commonwealth Club of Calif. Member. Phi Gamma Delta. Contbr. articles to religious periodicals. Mason. Clubs: Commonwealth of Calif., Meadow. Home: 265 Crescent Rd., San Anselmo, Cal. Died Mar. 6, 1953; buried Tamalpias Cemetery, San Rafael, Cal.

WHITE, Nelia Gardner, author; b. Andrews Settlement, Pa., Nov. 1 1894; d. John Adrian and Anna Amelia (Jones) Gardner; student Syracuse, 1911-13, Emma Willard Kindergarten Sch., 1913-15; m. Ralph Leon White, Aug. 11, 1917; children—Ralph, Mrs. Barbara Yedlin. Kindergarten teacher, Kenmore, N.Y., 1915-18. Author: Mary, 1925; Marge, 1926; And Michael, 1927; Jen Culliton, 1927; Joanna Gray 1928; David Strange, 1928; Kristin, 1929; Tune in the Tree, 1929; Toni of Grand Isle, 1930; Hathaway House, 1931; Mrs. Green's Daughter-in-Law, 1932; This, My House, 1933; Family Affairs, 1934; The Fields of Gomorrah, 1935; The Heaths and the Hubbells, 1937; Daughter of Time, 1941; Brook Willow 1944; No Trumpet Before Him, 1948; The Pink House, 1950; Woman at the Window, 1951; The Merry Month of May, 1952; The Spare Room, 1954; The Thorn Tree, 1955; A Little More Than Kin, 1956; The Gift and The Giver, 1957. Contbr. to leading mags. Home: R.F.D. 1, New Hartford, Conn. Died June 12, 1957; buried Old Town Hill Cemetery, New Hartford.

WHITE, Paul W., editor; b. Pittsburg, Kan., June 9, 1902; s. Paul Welrose and Anna (Pickard) W.;

student U. Kan., 1920-21, Columbia Coll., 1922; B. Litt., Columbia U. Sch. of Journalism, 1923, M.S., 1924; m. Margaret Miller; Children—Mrs. Joan Jenkens, Toni Susanne. Reporter Pittsburgh Headlight, 1918, Salina (Kan.) Jour., 1919; telegraph editor Kansas City Jour., 1920; reporter N.Y. Evening Bulletin, 1924; contbr. N.Y. Sunday World, 1924; staff corr. United Press, N.Y.C. (editor United Feature Syndicate, 1 year), 1924-30; publicity dir. CBS, 1930-33; v.p., gen. mgr. Columbia News Service, 1933-34; dir. of public affairs CBS (supervision of all Columbia news programs including war broadcasts) 1934-46; asst. prof. of journalism Columbia School of Journalism, 1939-46; asso. editor San Diego Journal, 1948-50; exec. editor, KFMB and KFMB-TV, 1951—; mng. editor Am. Broadcasting Co.'s Polit. Conv. Staff, 1952. Recipient CBS Peabody award for news coverage, 1945. Mem. Delta Upsilon, Sigma Delta Chi. Author: News on the Air. Home: 4545 45th St. Office: KFMB, San Diego, Cal. Died July 9, 1955.

WHITE, Robe Carl, lawyer, ex-govt. ofcl.; b. on farm, Delaware County, Ind., Aug. 27, 1869; s. Samuel Simpson and Mary (Andrews) W.; grad. high sch., Iola, Kan., 1887; grad. Bryant & Stratton Business Coll., Chgo., 1889; LL.B., U. Minn., 1896; m. Agnes L. McSorley, June 10, 1896 (died May 20, 1916); m. 2d, Lillian A. Austin, June 4, 1920. Began practice at St. Paul, 1896; moved to Muncie, Ind., 1899; now mem. firm White & Mansfield. City atty. Muncie, 1906, 07; postmaster Muncie, 1907-12; chmn. Ind. State Speakers Bur., Prog. Party, 1914; chmn. Rep. County Com., Delaware County, Ind., 1918, 19; chmn. Bd. of Review, Dept. of Labor, Washington, 1922; 2d asst. sec. of Labor, in charge immigration, 1922-25, asst. sec. of Labor, 1925-33; mem. firm White & Snyder. Presbyn. Mason, Elk, Moose, Woodman. Home: Muncie, Ind. Died Jan. 1951.*

WHITE, Thomas Holden; b. Cleveland, O., Aug. 4, 1894; s. Windsor Thomas and Delia Bulkley (Holden) W.; grad. University Sch., Cleveland, 1912; S.B., Harvard, 1917; m. Kathleen York, Aug. 16, 1917; children—Windsor Thomas II, Robert York, Thomas Holden, Jr. With White Motor Co., Cleveland, beginning 1919, production mgr., 1920, v.p. of mfg., 1921-24, v.p. and gen. mgr., 1924-27; pres. Commonwealth Securities, Inc., 1928-44. Joined Reserve Officers Training Corps, Ft. Benjamin Harrison, May 1917; commissioned 2d lieutanant C.A., Aug. 1917; 1st lt. A.S., Feb. 1918; hon. disch., Dec. 31, 1918. Trustee Cleveland Museum Natural History, Hawken School, Western Reserve University. Independent Republican. Unitarian. Clubs: Union, Chagrin Valley Hunt, Harvard (Cleveland); University, Harvard (New York). Home: care Halfred Farms, Chagrin Falls, O. Office: Union Commerce Bldg., Cleve. Died Oct. 26, 1951.

WHITE, Trentwell Mason, college pres., editor; b. Boston, Mass., May 15, 1901; s. Harry Mason and Ivonetta G. (Marten) W.; B.S., Norwich University 1922, M.A., 1928, Litt.D. (honorary), 1951; graduate study, Harvard University, 1925-26; D.A., Staley Coll., 1936; L.H.D., Maryland Coll., 1940; Ed.D. (honorary), Calvin Coolidge College, 1956; m. Helen Thompson Hawley, June 22, 1926 (divorced 1936); children—Merideth Thompson, Trentwell Mason, Jr.; 2d, Alma Hortense Carvill, July 22, 1939. English master, Hotchkiss Sch., 1922-23, Williston Acad., 1923-26; dir. English, Dedham (Mass.) pub. schs., 1926-28; asst. prof. English and dir. of ednl. research, Northeastern U., 1928-30; lecturer on creative writing, Breadloaf Sch. of English, Middlebury Coll., 1930, Curry Sch., 1930-39; Mass. Dept. of Edn. (Harvard), 1930-58; pres. Curry College, Boston, 1935-39; headmaster, Tome School, Port Deposit, Md., 1939-41; vice-president Mt. Ida Junior College, Newton Centre, Mass., 1941-44; pres., Lesley College, since 1944; associate editor Education Magazine, 1930-50; contbg. editor The Writer, 1930-37; asso. editor D. C. Heath & Co., 1930-34; pres. and editorial dir. Lothrop, Lee & Shepard Co., 1934-35; editor-in-chief, Pitman Pub. Corp., 1935-37; editor-in-chief Egmont Press-Sovereign House, 1937-39; dir. of edn., Inst. for Industrial Progress, 1937-39. Trustee and corp. mem. Curry Coll., 1930-46, chmn. bd., 1935-39. Trustee Norwich U. Gen. Alumni Assn., 1937-40. Lesley College; mem. adv. bd. Mt. Ida Jr. Coll., 1941-44; regent Am. Found. for Greece. Mem. N.E.A. (life member), Am. Acad. Polit. and Social Science, Cambridge Tb. and Health Assn. (pres. 1955-57), Norwich U. Club of N.Y. (pres. 1937-38), Authors League Am., Boston Authors Club, Cum Laude Soc., Mass. Schoolmasters Club, Delta Psi Omega, Pi Gamma Mu. Mason, Odd Fellow. Clubs: Norwich (bd. govs.) (Boston); Harvard Faculty, English Lunch, Rotary. Author: Opportunity Ahead! (with C. H. Ernst), 1929; Three Rookies at Morton, 1929; Writers of Colonial New England (with P. W. Lehmann), 1929; The Thing in the Road, 1930; Famous Leaders of Industry (Series III), 1931; How to Write for a Living, 1937. Contbr. to mags. of fiction and nonfiction. Home: 27 Everett St., Cambridge 38, Mass. Died Sept. 18, 1959; buried Riverside Cemetery, Winchendon, Mass.

WHITE, Wallace Humphrey, Jr., ex-senator; b. Lewiston, Me., Aug. 6, 1877; son Wallace and Helen (Frye) W.; A.B., Bowdoin Coll., 1899, LL.D., 1928; studied law Columbian U., and with Cotton & White, Washington, D.C.; LL.D., Bates College, 1938; m. Nina L. Lunn, Nov. 1, 1917. Served as asst. clk. U.S. Senate Com. on Commerce, later sec. to pres. of Senate and private sec. to Senator William P. Frye; admitted to bar, D.C., 1902, Maine, 1903; began practice at Lewiston with White & Carter, of which father was sr. mem.; mem. 65th to 71st Congresses (1917-31); U.S. senator from Me., 1931-49, ret., Senate minority leader, later majority leader; chmn. com. on merchant marine and fisheries, House of Rep., 1927-31; del. Pan Am. Electrical Communications Conf., Mexico City, 1924, to Internat. Telegraph Conf., Paris, 1925; apptd. unofficial observer of U.S. at Internat. Juridical Conf. on Wireless Telegraphy, Geneva, Switzerland, 1927, later elected mem. conf. and pres. Am. sect.; del. Internat. Radio Telegraphic Conf., Washington, 1927; chmn. U.S. delegation to Internat. Conf. on Safety of Life at Sea, London, 1929; chmn. U.S. delegation to meeting of Internat. Tech. Cons. Com. on Radio Communications, Copenhagen, 1931; chmn. U.S. delegation Telecommunications Conf., Cairo, 1938; U.S. commr. New York World's Fair. Regent Smithsonian Instn. Mem. Am. Group Interparliamentary Union. Mem. Bd. Overseers, Bowdoin. Republican. Conglist. Home: Auburn, Me. Died Mar. 31, 1952; buried Mount Auburn, Auburn.

WHITE, Walter (Francis), author; b. Atlanta, Ga., July 1, 1893; s. George W. and Madeline (Harrison) W.; B.A., Atlanta U., 1916, LL.D., 1943, Howard U., 1939; m. Leah G. Powell, Feb. 15, 1922 (div.); children—Jane, Walter Carl Darrow; married 2d, Poppy Cannon, July 6, 1949. Asst. sec. Nat. Assn. for Advancement of Colored People, 1918-29, acting sec., 1929-30, sec., Mar. 1931—. Del. 2d Pan-African Congress, England, Belgium and France, 1921; mem. N.Y. Apptd. by President Roosevelt, mem. Advisory Council for Govt. of Virgin Islands, resigned, 1935. Mem. Am. Com. on Economic Policy; former mem. board visitors N.Y. State Training School for Boys; mem. Governor's Commn. on Constl. Conv., New York, 1938; consultant to organizing conf. of U.N., 1945; consultant to U.S. delegation to U.N. Gen. Assembly, Paris, 1948; mem. exec. com. Nat. Health Assembly, 1948; mem. exec. com. Nat. Com. for Prevention and Control of Juvenile Delinquency, 1947; mem. N.Y. Mayor's Adv. Com. on Atomic Edn., 1948; mem. Com. for Commemoration Golden Anniversary (N.Y.). Awarded Spingarn medal, 1937; Sir James Jeans award, New London Junior College, 1950; Order of Honor and Merit (Haiti), 1950. Member American Center of the P.E.N. Club. Author: Fire in the Flint, 1924; Flight, 1926—both novels; Rope and Faggot—A Biography of Judge Lynch, 1929; A Rising Wind—a report on the Negro Soldier in the European Theatre of War—1945; A Man Called White (autobiography), 1948; How Far The Promised Land, 1955. Fellow of John Simon Guggenheim Meml. Found., for creative writing in prose, in France, 1927-28. Contbr. to mags. Home: Breakneck Hill, West Redding, Conn.; also 242 E. 68th St., N.Y.C. Office: 20 W. 40th St., N.Y.C. 18. Died Mar. 21, 1955.

WHITE, Wilbur Wallace, ex-univ. pres., educator; b. Topeka, Kan., June 4, 1903; s. John Pressly and Anna May (Philips) W.; A.B., Ohio State U., 1924; M.A., U. Chgo., 1929, Ph.D., 1935; m. Edwarda Jane Curran Williams, June 14, 1936; children—William Wallace, James Wilson, Marsha Curran. Tchr. Twinsburg (O.), High Sch., 1922-23, Assuit (Egypt) Coll., 1924-25; asst. prof. polit. sci. Macalester Coll., St. Paul, 1933-35, instr. Western Reserve U., 1935-37; asst. prof., 1937-39, asso. prof. and dean Adelbert Coll., 1939-41, prof. and dean Graduate School, 1941-48, on leave, 1943; engaged in special research, Div. of Polit. Studies, Dept. of State, Washington, 1943; dir. Civil Affairs Tng. Sch. for U.S. Army, Western Reserve Univ., 1943-44; asst. dir. Cleveland Foreign Affairs Council, 1940-42. Special writer or columnist for Cleveland Plain Dealer, 1943-45; vis. prof. dept. polit. sci. U. Chgo., summer 1945; pres. U. Toledo, 1948-50; M. D. Anderson prof. polit. sci. The Rice Inst., Houston, 1950—. Mem. Am. Polit. Science Assn., Am. Society Internat. Law, Am. Acad. Polit. and Social Science. Club: City (dir. 1943-45; pres. 1945) (Cleveland). Author: The Measurement of Good Will (with L. W. Bartlett), 1932; The Process of Change in the Ottoman Empire, 1937; The United States and World peace, 1947; White's Political Dictionary, 1947. Contbr. mags. Home: Houston. Died Nov. 14, 1950.

WHITE, William Chapman, author; b. Reading, Pa., Feb. 20, 1903; s. William and Margaret (Dye) W.; B.A., Princeton, 1923; M.A., U. of Pa., 1926; studied Moscow University, 1927-29; married Ruth Morris, 1936; 1 son, William M. Instructor in European history, University of Pennsylvania, 1923-24; teacher private schs., 1924-27; Penfield scholar U. of Pa. for research work in Russia, 1927-30; foreign corr. Germany-Poland, 1930-31; with scenario dept., Metro-Goldwyn-Mayer, 1934, 39; with Office of War Information, New York and London, 1942-45; Am. corr. for British "News Review" 1946-50; columnist N.Y. Herald Tribune, 1952-55. Dir. Saranac Lake Library, Saranac Lake Hosp. Author: These Russians, 1931; B.E.F., 1933; Lenin, 1937; The Pale Blonde of Sands Street, 1946; Adirondack Country, 1954; Tin Can on a Shingle, 1957; numerous children's books. Contbr. to mags. Home: Camp Intermission, Saranac Lake, N.Y. Died Nov. 28, 1955; buried St. John's in the Wilderness, Paul Smith, N.Y.

WHITE, William Lawrence, botanist; b. Salina, Pa., May 29, 1908; B.S., Pa. State Coll., 1934; Ph.D., Cornell U., 1940; A.M. (hon.), Harvard, 1948. Asst. curator fungi Garlow Herbarium, Harvard, 1940-45; sr. mycologist, supv. mycol. lab., Q.M.C., Phila., 1946-48; dir. Farlow Library and Herbarium, also asso. prof. botany, Harvard, 1948—; cons. research and development labs. Q.M.C., U.S. Army, 1948—. Mem. Mycol. Soc. Am., Bot. Soc. Am. Home: 45 Hillcrest St., Arlington, Mass. Died July 30, 1952.

WHITE, Windsor T., chmn. bd. Park Drop Forge Co.; b. Orange, Mass., Aug. 28, 1866; s. Thomas H. and Almira (Greenleaf) W.; B.S., Worcester Poly. Inst., 1890; m. Delia Bulkley Holden, Sept. 14, 1892; children—Thomas Holden, Mrs. Delia Vail, Windsor Holden. Pres. White Motor Co., 1906-21, chmn. bd., 1921-27; chmn. bd. Park Drop Forge Co., Cleve. Republican. Unitarian. Clubs: Union, Mid-Day, Chagrin Valley Hunt, Winous Point. Home: Halfred Farms, Chagrin Falls, O. Office: Union Commerce Bldg., Cleve. Died Apr. 9, 1958; buried Cleve.

WHITEAKER, Robert O., army officer; b. Texas, Dec. 16, 1882; enlisted Tex. Nat. Guard, Inf., July 1899; commd. capt. Cav. Tex. Nat. Guard, Mar. 1916 and entered Fed. service for Mexican border crisis, May 1916; commd. maj. Tex. Nat. Guard, F.A., Oct. 1922, and advanced to brig. gen. of the line, Apr. 1938; entered Fed. service, Nov. 1940, and in command of 72d Field Arty. Brigade, 36th Div. in training at Camp Bowie, Brownwood, Tex.; retired 1948. Address: 1716 Justin Lane, Austin. Tex. Died Apr. 26, 1959; buried Meml. Cemetery, Cleburne, Tex.

WHITEHEAD, Donald Strehle, retail pharmacist; b. Three Oaks, Mich., Oct. 10, 1888; s. William Searing and Louise M. (Strehle) W.; B.S., U. of Ida., 1907; m. Muriel Shaw, Nov. 17, 1909; 1 dau., Beth (Mrs. Frank Streebel). Retail pharmacist under own name, 1908—; farmer, Boise, 1928. Mem. Ida. Ho. of Reps., 1923-24, 27-28, speaker of the house, 1929-39; lt. gov. and pres. of senate, 1939-40, and 1946-50. Member Beta Theta Pi, Phi Beta Kappa. Episcopalian. Mason (33°). Home: 1000 Houston Rd. Office: 800 Main St., Boise, Ida. Died Jan. 2, 1957.

WHITEHEAD, John Boswell, elec. engr.; b. Norfolk, Va., Aug. 18, 1872; s. Henry Colgate and Margaret Walke (Taylor) W.; EE., Johns Hopkins, 1893, A.B., 1898, Ph.D. 1902; m. Mary Ellen Colston, Apr. 14, 1903; children—Clara (dec.), Margaret Walke, Joan Boswell. Elec. engr. Westinghouse Electric & Mfg. Co., 1893-96, Niagara Falls (N.Y.) Power Co., 1896-97; instr. applied electricity Johns Hopkins, 1897-1900, asso., 1901-04, asso. prof., 1904-10, prof., 1910—, dean, 1919-38, dir. Sch. Engring., 1938-42, prof. emeritus, 1942—; exchange prof. to France, 1926-27. Lab. asst. U.S. Bur. Standards, 1902; research asst. Carnegie Instn. Washington, 1902-05. Edison medalist, 1941. Fellow Am. Inst. E.E. (pres. 1933-34); Am. Phys. Soc., A.A.A.S.; mem. Nat. Acad. Scis., Nat. Research Council, Société Française des Electriciens, (hon.), Phi Beta Kappa, Tau Beta Pi, Delta Phi, Commd. maj. Engr. R.C., 1917. Democrat. Episcopalian. Clubs: Maryland, Johns Hopkins. Author: Electric Operation of Steam Railways, 1909; Dielectric Theory and Insulation, 1927; Impregnated Paper Insulation, 1935; Electricity and Magnetism, 1939; also many researches in field of high voltage insulation. Home: 3100 St. Paul St., Balt. 18. Died Nov. 16, 1954.

WHITEHOUSE, Horace, organist, conductor; b. West Bromwich, Eng., Jan. 25, 1881; s. Walter William and Mary Lees (Davis) W.; was brought to U.S. in infancy; grad. New England Conservatory of Music, Boston, 1904; post-grad. work, same, 1906, and abroad, 1911; student Washburn Coll., 1917-18; hon. Dr.Mus., Washburn Coll., Topeka, Kan., 1938; m. Emma Rempfer, Feb. 3, 1916; children—Robert Rempfer (dec.), Barbara, Martha, Horace Davis, Rempfer Lees, Philip Krein, Adelaide, Agatha, David Rempfer. Asst. organist and choirmaster, Trinity P.E. Ch., Boston, 1904-09; dean fine arts dept. Washburn Coll., Topeka, Kan., 1909-18; was condr. Musical Arts Soc., Topeka; guest prof. Univ. of Calif., 1917; dir. Coll. of Music, Ohio Wesleyan Univ., 1918-21, and organist Christ P.E. Ch.; condr. Indianapolis Oratorio Soc., 1921-26; dir. Coll. of Music, Univ. of Colo., 1926-27, and organist 1st Bapt. Ch., Boulder, Colo.; prof. organ and church music, Northwestern Univ., 1927-47, and organist and choirmaster Christ Ch. (Prot. Episcopal), Winnetka, Ill., 1932-45; choral conductor Chicago North Shore Musical Festival, 1931; organist Chicago Choirmasters Assn., 1935; condr. male choir Garrett Biblical Inst., 1947—. Pipe organ recitalist; pipe organ and choral compositions. Mem. Am. Guild Organists, Am. Assn. Univ. Profs., Phi Mu Alpha, Pi Kappa Lambda. Home: 1742 Asbury Av. Address: Northwestern University, Evanston, Ill. Died July 27, 1958; buried Parkston, S.D.

WHITENER, Paul A(ustin) W(ayne) (white-ner), museum dir.; b. Lincoln County, N.C., Sept. 1, 1911; s. William Alexander and Sadie Eustice (Kidd) W.; student Duke, 1931-35, Ringling Sch. Art, Little Switzerland, N.C., summer 1945; pvt. pupil Wilford S. Conrow, Frank Stanley Herring, Donald Blake; m. Mildred M. McKinney, Aug. 22, 1936. Founder, dir., sec.-treas. Hickory Mus. Art, 1943; profl. portrait, landscape artist, 1937—; art staff Hickory High Sch. Adv. com., exhbn. council Asheville (N.C.) Art Mus.; ofcl. art examiner Hickory Boy Scouts, Girl Scouts; art council Duke. Mem. Am. Artists Profl. League (nat. exec. com., dir., N.C. state chmn.), N.C. State Art Soc., Kappa Pi. Moose. Clubs: Salmagundi (N.Y.C.); Rotary (Hickory); Catawba County Country (Newton). Author newspaper articles on art. Home: 215 7th St. S.E. Office: 514 3d Av. N.W., Hickory, N.C. Died May 19, 1959; buried Oakwood Cemetery, Hickory, N.C.

WHITESIDE, Horace Eugene, lawyer; b. Bell Buckle, Tenn., June 5, 1891; s. Samuel R. and Kate (Tune) W.; A.B., U. Chgo., 1912; LL.B., Cornell, 1922; S.J.D., Harvard, 1927; m. Esther Versey, Mar. 31, 1913 (died, 1950); children—Anne Esther (Mrs. Leo F. Wynd), Horace E. (dec. 1954); m. 2d, Ruth Kinyon, Jan. 20, 1951. Teacher, East Waterloo (Iowa) High School, 1912-14; athletic director, Earlham College, 1914-17; captain 67th Artillery, C.A.C., in France, 1918-19; lecturer and secretary, Cornell, Law School, 1922-24, assistant professor, 1924-27, professor, 1927-51, J. DuPratt White professor of law since 1951. Research consultant, New York State Law Revision Commn., on property, consideration and the seal; consultant with Whitman, Ransom, Coulson & Goetz, New York City, since 1939. Member of the American, New York State and Tompkins County bar assns., Order of Coif, Delta Theta Phi, Phi Kappa Phi. Republican. Clubs: Country (Ithaca, New York) also the Cornell (New York City). Author: Statutory Rules Against Perpetuities and Accumulations, 1957. Editor: Huffcut's Cases on Agency (3d edit.), 1925; Kales' Cases on Future Interests (2d edit.), 1936. Contbr. to legal jours. and N.Y. Annotations to Restatement of Contracts. Co-author: American Law of Property, 1951. Home: Highland Road, Ithaca, N.Y. Office: Myron Taylor Hall, Ithaca, N.Y. Died June 9, 1956; buried Arlington Nat. Cemetery.

WHITFORD, Edward Everett, prof. mathematics; b. Brookfield, N.Y., Jan. 31, 1865; s. Calvin and Emeline (Burch) W.; A.B., Colgate, 1886, A.M., 1890; Ph.D., Columbia, 1912; m. Lilla E. York, July 31, 1890 (dec. May 1943); 1 son, Robert Calvin. Teacher, Colby Acad., New London, N.H., 1886-91, Keystone Acad., Factoryville, Pa., 1891-98; bank cashier, Brookfield, N.Y., 1898-1900; prin. high sch., Brookfield, 1900-02, Commercial High School, Brooklyn, 1902; prof. mathematics, College of the City of New York, 1905-35, prof. emeritus, 1935—. Served in Y.M.C.A. educational work, Eng. and Scotland, 1918, Army Ednl. Corps, France, 1919. Mem. Am. Math. Soc., Math. Association America, Delta Upsilon, Phi Beta Kappa. Republican. Seventh Day Baptist. Author: The Pell Equation, 1912. Home: Brookfield, N.Y. Died May 3, 1946.

WHITHORNE, Emerson (hwi'thôrn), composer; b. Cleve., Sept. 6, 1884; s. Charles and Emma (Pillars) W.; studied piano with James H. Rogers, Cleveland, and piano with Theodore Leschetizky, and composition with Robert Fuchs, Vienna; m. Jane Reynolds, June 1932. Teacher, composer, musical criticism, London, 1907-15; exec. editor Art Publ. Soc., St. Louis, 5 years; then v.p. Composers Music Corp.; music composition, 1922—. Compositions: Greek Impressions (string quartet); New York Days and Nights (orchestra; rep. U.S. at Salzburg Festival, 1923); Poem (piano and orchestra; Chicago Symphony, 1927); Fata Morgana (N.Y. Philharmonic, 1928); Moon Trail (Boston Symphony, 1933); Dream Pedlar (Los Angeles Orchestra, 1931); Fandango (Sir Thomas Beecham, condr., 1932); Sierra Morena (Nat. Broadcasting Co. Symphony, 1939); 2 Symphonies; (chamber music) Piano Quintet; String Quartet; (voice and chamber orchestra; Saturday's Child; Grim Troubadour (voice and string quartet); (ballet) Sonner or Later; Violin Sonata; Stroller's Serenade for String Orchestra, 1943. Wrote incidental music for Marco Millions, 1925. Awarded publ. prize by Julliard Foundation for Second Symphony, 1939. Died Mar. 25, 1958.

WHITING, Edward Elwell, writer; b. Springfield, Mass., Feb. 18, 1875; s. Charles Goodrich and Eliza Rose (Gray) W.; prep. edn., Williston Sem.; student Harvard 3 yrs.; m. Margaret Webster, Oct. 3, 1906 (dec.); 1 dau., Margery Rose; m. 2d, Margaret Robbins, September 1, 1943. Learned journalism from father, who was associate editor Springfield Republican many yrs.; began newspaper work with Springfield Homestead (weekly); became connected with Boston papers, 1903; formerly editor Boston Evening Record; writer 'Whiting's Column'' in Boston Herald, ''Beacon Hill'' in Worcester (Mass.) Telegram; etc.; chmn. Boston Elevated Ry., 1927-47; political consultant. Trustee Deaconess Hosp., Boston; mem. advisory council, School Practical Art, Boston. Member Theta Delta Chi. Republican. Episcopalian. Mason. Clubs: Puddingstone, City. Authors (Boston); Iota (Boston and Cambridge); Saturday, Tuesday, Central, (Newtonville). Author: President Coolidge, A Contemporary Estimate, 1923; Calvin Coolidge—His Ideals of Citizenship, 1924; Changing New England, 1929. Lecturer on polit. subjects and current events. Home: 148 Highland Av., Newtonville 60, Mass. Died Dec. 24, 1956; buried Springfeld (Mass.) Cemetery.

WHITING, Fred T., business exec.; born Knoxville, Ia., Dec. 27, 1890; s. Fred S. and Emma E. (Allum) W.; B.S. in M.E., Iowa State Coll., 1913; E.D. (honorary), Iowa State Unversity, 1953; m. Rhoda A. McFeatters, Mar. 24, 1919. Asso. with Westinghouse Electric Co., Chicago, since 1913, v.p. since 1943; dir. Am. Steel Foundries since 1946. Mem. Western Soc. Engrs. (trustee), Electric Assn., Chgo. Assn. Commerce (past v.p.). Republican. Presbyn. Clubs: Executives, Tower, Economic, Merchants and Manufacturers, Tower, Fin 'n Feather, Chicago Engineers, The Chicago (Chicago); Bob O'Link Golf (Highland Park, Ill.). Home: 5335 N. Magnolia Av., Chgo. 40. Office: Merchandise Mart Plaza, Chgo. 54. Died Aug. 20, 1953.

WHITING, Gertrude, assn. exec.; b. N.Y.C.; d. William Dunbar and Anna Phillips (Stickney) Whiting; student Rye (N.Y.) Sem., 4 yrs.; grad. Hollins (Va.) Coll., 1899; agrégée Institut Professionel Neuchâtelois de Dentelles, 1909; studied Tchrs. Coll., Columbia and N.Y. univs., Oxford U. Formerly director Auxiliary Society of New York League of Girls' Clubs, National and New York Leagues of Women Workers, and of Hotel Irvin for Women, Inc.; treas. Manhattan Trade Sch. for Girls; treas. The Virginia Hotel; pres. Mutual Benefit Ins. Fund. Was founder, corr. sec. and v.p. Rye Sem. Asso.; founder and former pres. Needle and Bobbin Club, also The Spinster. Worked indexed samples of 145 lace grounds, hanging in Met. Museum, N.Y.C. Hon. fellow Met. Museum of Art; fellow Royal Soc. Arts; Master Craftsman, 1939, Boston Soc. Arts and Crafts; mem. Authors' League America, Les Amis du Louvre. Episcopalian. Author: A Lace Guide for Makers and Collectors, 1920; Tools and Toys of Stitchery, 1927. Collaborator on Antique Laces of American Collectors, 1926. Contbr. to mags. Home: 1 W. 72d St., N.Y. C. 23. Died Apr. 14, 1951.

WHITING, William Alonzo, prof. biology; b. Meadville, Pa., June 15, 1890; s. John Xenophon and Anna Hayward (Smith) W.; B.S., Allegheny Coll., 1914; Ph.D., Cornell U., 1921; m. Marion Bright, Sept. 11, 1918; children—John Irwin, Allan Bright. Instr. bacteriology, Cornell Univ., 1917-21; prof. biology, Birmingham-Southern College, 1922-55, also chmn. div. natural sciences. Fellow A.A.A.S.; mem. Alabama Academy of Science. Beta Beta Beta, Omicron Delta Kappa, Theta Chi Delta, Lambda Chi Alpha. Dem. Meth. Co-Author: Variations in Bacteria Counts from Milk as Affected by Media and Incubation Temperature, 1922. Author: The Relations between the Clumping of Bacteria and the Utensil Flora, 1924; Laboratory Manual in General Zoölogy, 1925; Flora of the Birmingham District, 1927; Laboratory Manual in General Biology, 1931. Home: 715 8th Av. W., Birmingham 4, Ala. Died Feb. 2, 1957; buried Elmwood Cemetery, Birmingham.

WHITMAN, Alfred Freeman, social worker; b. Worcester, Mass., Mar. 20, 1882; s. Frederick Augustus and Emily Ives (Coumans) W.; A.B., Harvard, 1908; student Simmons Coll. Sch. Social Work, 1907-08; m. Bessie Hitchcock, Sept. 12, 1908 (died 1920); children—Emily, Mahala (Mrs. Austin L. Starrett); m. 2d, Fannie Marie Whitman, Oct. 16, 1924; 1 son, Robert F. With Mass. Soc. Prevention Cruelty to Children, 1908-19; exec. sec. Pa. Soc. Prevention Cruelty to Children, 1920-22; exec. sec. Children's Aid Assn., Boston, 1922—; instr. social ethics, Harvard, 1923-24. Dir. Greater Boston Community Fund, Unitarian Service Com., U.S. Com. for Care European Children, Children to Palestine. Mem. Child Welfare League of Am. (v.p.), Am. Assn. Social Workers (dir. 1924-26), Mass. Com. on Public Safety (chmn. on day care), Am. Unitarian Assn. (dir. 1938-41). Republican. Unitarian. Clubs: Boston City; Cambridge. Home: 27 Everett St., Cambridge. Office: 41 Mount Vernon St., Boston. Died Feb. 26, 1951.

WHITMAN, Arthur Dudley, coll. prof.; b. Boston, Nov. 21, 1884; s. James Dean and Isabel (Horsfield) W.; A.B., Harvard, 1906, A.M., 1907; Ph.D., Columbia, 1926; m. Ellen Allwell Irwin, Aug. 26, 1915; 1 son, James Irwin. Inst., Black Hall Sch., Lyme, Conn., 1906-08, Mohegan Lake (N.Y.) Sch., 1908-12, Tome Sch., Port Deposit, Md., 1912-15; head of dept. of English, New Bedford (Mass.) High Sch., 1915-20; instr. Teachers Coll. (Columbia), summers, 1920, 21; teacher English, Lincoln Sch. of Teachers Coll. (Columbia), 1921-24, asst. prin., 1925-26; asst. prof. edn., School of Edn., N.Y. Univ., 1926-28, asso. prof., 1928-30, prof., 1930-52, serving as chairman of Grad. Com. and head dept. English edn., Sch. Edn.; retired, 1952; instr. U. of Ark., summer, 1928; dir. Sch. of Education, Chautauqua, N.Y., 1930-32, and 1940, 41; acting dean Nassau Coll. (N.Y.U.), 1935-36, dean Hofstra Coll., 1936-39. Editor of Junior-Senior High Sch. Clearing Ho., 1929-35. Author: Value of College Entrance Examinations as Prediction of Success in College, 1926. Home: Washington, Conn. Died Feb. 17, 1957; buried Washington, Conn.

WHITMAN, Hendricks Hallett, textile mfr., mcht.; b. Brookline, Mass., Feb. 27, 1884; s. William and Jane Dole (Hallett) W.; grad. Volkmann Sch., Boston, Mass., 1902; A.B., Harvard, 1906; m. Pauline Danforth, Sept. 6, 1933; children—Rose Farwell, Nancy, Hendricks Hallett. Began as pvt. sec. to pres. of bank, 1907; salesman, William Whitman Co., 1909-13, treas., 1913-20, v.p. since 1920, treas. and dir. since 1936; chmn. Whitman Co., Inc., since 1946; pres. Nonquitt Mills, Monomac Spinning Co.; dir. Calhoun Mills, Arlington Mills (Lawrence, Mass.), Washington Trust Co. (Westerly, R.I.). Capt., F.A., U.S. Army, World War I. Mem. Chamber Commerce, State of N.Y. Republican. Clubs: Somerset (Boston); Harvard, Racquet and Tennis (New York); Harvard, Travellers'. Home: Stonington, Conn. Office: 261 5th Av., N.Y. City 16. Died Mar. 18, 1950; buried Mt. Auburn Cemetery, Cambridge, Mass.

WHITMORE, Carl, executive; b. Oakland, Cal., Sept. 27, 1884; s. Welles and Bertha (Nusbaumer) W.; student U. Cal., 1904-08; m. Elma Edwards, Aug. 24, 1911; children—Jane (Mrs. Raymond H. Keeler), Edwards Clay, Barbara Lin, Nancy Franc (Mrs. R. N. MacKinnon). Fieldman Pacific Telephone and Telegraph Co., San Francisco, 1911-13, engr. Portland, Oregon, 1913-21, div. plant supt., 1921-23; division supt. installation, Western Electric Co., San Francisco, 1923-26, general supt. installation in Chgo., 1926-27, general mgr. installation in New York, 1927-35; gen. plant mgr., New York Telephone Co., Albany, N.Y., 1935-36, vice pres. and gen. mgr. in Long Island, 1936-40, vice pres. personnel, 1940-41, operating v.p. 1941-44, pres., 1944-49, chmn., 1949—. Pres., dir. Empire City Subway Co., Ltd.; dir. Holmes Elec. Protective Co.; trustee Brooklyn Saving Bank, United Hosp. Fund of New York, Brooklyn Hosp., Brooklyn Bur. of Social Service. Dir. U.S.O., nat. campaign chmn., 1947. Dir. Commerce and Industry Assn. of N.Y., N.Y. Conv. and Visitors Bureau, N.Y. Heart Assn. Mem. Am. Inst. Elec. Engrs., Newcomen Soc., New York State C. of C. (v.p.), Chi Psi. Clubs: Garden City Golf (N.Y.); Rembrandt (Brooklyn); Seaview Country (Absecon, N.J.). Home: 140 Remington Rd., Manhasset, N.Y. Office: 140 West St., N.Y.C. 7. Died Oct. 13, 1958.

WHITNEY, Allen Sisson, educator; b. Mt. Clemens, Mich., June 16, 1857; s. Samuel and Ann (Stroup) W.; A.B., U. of Mich., 1885; student Cornell U., summer 1893, univs. of Jena, and Leipzig, 1896-97; LL.D., Syracuse Univ., 1921; Dr. of Edn., U. Michigan, 1939; m. Maybelle E. Howe, June 10, 1916; 1 dau., Elizabeth Howe. Supt. schs., Mt. Clemens, Mich., 1875-92, Saginaw, 1892-99; prof. edn., 1899-1921, actg. dean Sch. of Edn., 1921-23, dean, 1902-29, U. Mich. Mem. Beta Theta Pi, Phi Beta Kappa, Phi Kappa Phi, Phi Epsilon Kappa. Republican. Episcopalian. Mason. Author numerous brochures. Served as pres. Mich. schoolmasters Club, Mich. Assn. of Superintendents and School Bds., Mich. State Teachers' Assn., Soc. of Coll. Teachers of Edn. Author: Training of Teachers, University of Michigan, 1879-29, 1931. Home: 930 Church St., Ann Arbor, Mich. Died Sept. 9, 1944.

WHITNEY, Charles Smith, cons. engr.; b. Bradford, Pa., Nov. 4, 1892; s. Henry Parker and Myra (Allen) W.; C.E., Cornell, 1914, Master C.E., 1915; m. Gertrude Schuyler, June 19, 1920; children—James S., Lillian R., Charles A. Asst. engr. John Parkinson, architect, Los Angeles, 1916-17; chief engr. A. C. Eschweiler, architect, Milwaukee, 1919-20; chief engr., mgr. Hool & Johnson, engrs., Milwaukee office, 1920-22; cons. and designing engr. city planning, design and supervison bldgs., bridges, sewer and water systems, and numerous other municipal improvements, Milw., 1922—; chief architect, planning Camp McCoy, Wis., 1941; partner Ammann & Whitney, cons. engrs., N.Y.C., Milw., 1946—; designer or cons. numerous structures including hangars, expressways, bridges, theatres, office bldgs., hosps., chs., Am. Airlines, TWA hangers, Chgo., Onondago Meml. Auditorium, Syracuse, N.Y., Montgomery (Ala.) Livestock Coliseum, Pitts. Civic Light Opera Amphitheatre, Milw. expressway system, N.Y. Throughway, New Jersey, Connecticut and Ohio Turnpikes. Development of plastic theory reinforced concrete design, method of design of structures to resist atomic bombs and earthquakes, design air raid shelters. Served as sgt., 25th C.E., U.S. Army, 1917-19; AEF. Awarded J. James R. Cross medal 1925, Am. Soc. C.E.; Fuertes Grad. medal, Cornell, 1925, 37; Wason medal, Am. Concrete Inst., 1932-53; Alfred E. Lindau award, Am. Concrete Inst., 1951;

Ammann & Whitney recipiensts 1st ann. award. Concrete Reinforcing Steel Inst., 1949. Registered profl. engr., Wis., N.Y., Conn., Ohio, Mo., Cal., Tex., Colo., Mich., Fla.; structural engr. Ill. Mem. Am. Soc C.E (pres. Milw. sect. 1930), Am. Concrete Inst. (v.p. 1953-54, pres. 1955), Am. Inst. Cons. Engrs., Wis. Soc. Profl. Engrs., Am. Assn. Airport Execs, Inst. Aero. Scis., Internat. Assn. Bridge and Structural Engring., Soc. Exptl. Stress Analysis, Am. Ry. Engring. Assn., Am. Road Builders Assn., A.I. A., Sigma Xi, Tau Beta Pi. Clubs: University (Milw.); Engineers (N.Y.C.). Author: Bridges, 1929; Concrete Designers Manual. Numerous reports, articles tech. jours. Home: 2710 E. Bellevue Pl., Milw. 11. Offices; 724 E. Mason St., Milw. 2; 111 Eighth Av., N.Y.C. 11. Died Oct. 25, 1959; buried Forest Home Cemetery, Milwaukee.

WHITNEY, Edwin Morse, interpreter of plays; b. Parma Centre, N.Y., Mar. 17, 1877; s. Rev. Edwin J. and Myra C. (Bentley) W.; grad. high sch., Castile, N.Y., 1896; grad. Emerson Coll. Oratory, Boston, 1902; m. Foss Lamprell, Sept. 8, 1904 (died Jan. 1923); m. 2d, Emma Miller Bolenius, July 29, 1933. Began as vocalist and reader, Whitney Bros. Quartette, 1902; reader of plays, also radio actor, 1928—; founder, 1914, and dir. Whitney Studios of Platform Art; has filled over 5,000 engagements in public recitals; program dir. with Nat. Broadcasting Co., N.Y.C., 1928-43, with Blue Network 1943-44. Enlisted in Arizona, 1898, as member Co. A, 1st Territorial Volunteer Infantry, Spanish-American War, and advanced to 1st Sergt. Republican. Methodist. Mason (32°, Shriner). Home: Quaker Lake, Pawling, N.Y. Died June 5, 1957.

WHITNEY, Paul Clinton, hydrographic engr.; b. Washington, D.C., Aug. 28, 1882; s. Arthur Pierce and Margaret Jane (Milburn) W.; student George Washington U., 1900-03; m. Jeannette B. Prescott, Dec. 17, 1908; 1 daughter, Margaret Jeannette (Mrs. Margaret Adams); married 2d, Barbara Schmitt, Sept. 24, 1932. With United States Coast and Geodetic Survey, 1902—; commd. hydographic and geodetic engr., 1917; participated in and directed surveys, coasts of Alaska and Philippine Islands, and Pacific and Atlantic coasts, 1903-17; chief of Sect. of Coast Pilot, Washington, D.C., 1919-25; insp. San Francisco Field Sta., 1925-28; chief Div. of Tides and Currents, Washington, 1928-42, supervisor, S.E. District 1942-46. Magnetic observer on first magnetic cruise, Pacific Ocean, under auspices of Carnegie Instn., 1905. Served as lt. and lt. comdr. U.S. Navy, World War I; now capt. U.S. C. and G. S. (retired.). Mem. Washington Soc. Engrs., Philos. Soc. of Washington, Poetry Society of Virginia, American Geophysical Union A.A.A.S., Wash. Academy of Science. Author of various technical government publications, and articles on tides and ocean currents. Club: Cosmos. Home: 1306 Rockbridge Av., Norfolk, Va. Address: U.S. Coast and Geodetic Survey, Washington. Died June 9, 1954; buried Hillsboro, N.D.

WHITNEY, Robert Bacon, banker; b. N.Y. City, Dec. 16, 1916; s. George and Martha B. (Bacon) W.; A.B., Harvard, 1939; m. Adelaide Weld, Sept. 14, 1939; children—Hope, Robert Bacon; Stephen Weld, Willia mMichael. Joined J.P. Morgan & Co., Inc., N.Y. City, 1939, asst. v.p. since 1949; dir. Merc. Stores Co., Inc. Dir. L.I. Y.M.C.A., Soc. Prevention Cruelty to Children (Nassau Co., N.Y.). Served as lt. comdr., U.S. Navy, 1940-45; lt. comdr., U.S.N.R. Republican. Protestant Episcopalian. Home: Old Westbury, L.I. Office: 23 Wall St., N.Y.C. Died Dec. 24, 1952.

WHITNEY, Wheelock, transportation exec.; b. St. Cloud, Minn., Aug. 28, 1894; s. Albert G. and Alice (Wheelock) W.; student Phillips Acad., Andover, 1913; B.S., Yale, 1916; m. Katharine Kimball, Jan. 7, 1922; children—Sally (Mrs. George S. Pillsbury), Wheelock, John Kimball. Vice pres. St. Cloud (Minn.) Pub. Service Co., 1919-24; div. mgr. St. Cloud div. No. States Power Co., 1925-42; pres. Whitney Land Co., Whitney Securities Co. since 1936; dir. Springfield (Mass.) Street Railway Co., Worcester (Mass.) Bus Co., Jacksonville (Fla.) Coach Co., Truax-Traer Coal Co., Chicago North Shore Systems, Susquehanna Corporation (Chicago), Charlotte City Coach Lines (North Carolina), Grand Rapids City Coach Lines, Incorporated, City Coach Lines, Flint Trolley Coach Co., Evansville City Bus Lines, Tucson Rapid Transit Co., Northwest Airlines, St. Paul. Mem. nat. council Boy Scouts Am.; asst. regional mgr. local transport div. Office Def. Transportation, Chgo., regional mgr., Cleve., 1942-45. Mem. Nat. Assn. Motor Bus Operators. Clubs: Minneapolis, Chicago, University. Home: Wayzata. Office: Box 398, St. Cloud, Minn. Died Mar. 23, 1957.

WHITNEY, Willis Rodney, chemist; b. Jamestown, N.Y., Aug. 22, 1868; s. John J. and Agnes (Reynolds) W.; S.B. Mass. Inst. Tech., 1890; Ph.D., Univ. of Leipzig, 1896; hon. Sc.D., Union U., 1919; Ch.D., U. of Pittsburgh, 1919; Sc.D., U. of Syracuse, 1926, U. of Mich., 1927; LL.D., Lehigh, 1929; m. Evelyn Jones, June 26, 1890; 1 dau., Mrs. Evelyn Schermerhorn. Asst. instr., asst. prof. to 1904, nonresident asso. prof., 1904-08, nonresident prof. theoretical chemistry since 1908, Mass. Inst. of Tech.; dir. Research Laboratory of General Electric Co., Schenectady, N.Y., 1900-28, v.p. in charge of research, 1928-41, now honorary vice-president General Electric Co. Hon. mem. American Steel Treaters' Soc., Franklin Inst.; mem. U.S. Naval Consulting Bd. since 1915; mem. advisory com. U.S. Bur. of Standards, 1925-30, Nat. Research Council. Trustee Albany Med. Coll., Union Coll.; mem. Corp. Mass. Inst. Tech. Willard Gibbs medal, Am. Chem. Soc., 1916; Chandler medal, Columbia U., 1920; Perkin medal, Am. Sect. of Soc. Chem. Industry, 1921; Franklin medal, 1931; Edison medal, 1935; Pub. Welfare medal, Nat. Acad. Sciences, 1938. Chevalier Legion d'Honneur (France), 1937; receved John Fritz medal, 1943; medal of Industrial Research Institute, 1946. Member of National Academy of Sciences; fellow American Academy of Arts and Sciences, A.A. A.S., Am. Chem. Soc. (pres. 1910), Am. Electrochem. Soc. (pres. 1911), Am. Inst. Mining and Metall. Engrs., Am. Inst. E.E., Am. Philos. Soc., Am. Phys. Soc., etc. Presbyterian. Republican. Translator of M. Le Blanc's Electro-Chemistry, 1896. Home: Box 2684 Troy Rd., Schenectady. Died Jan. 9, 1958; buried Parkview Cemetery, Schenectady.

WHITT, Hugh, air force officer; b. Catlettsburgh, Ky., Aug. 3, 1888; s. John Bunyan and Julia (Ball) W.; m. Jewel Burnett, Apr. 14, 1935; 1 son, Hugh Pelham. Enlisted U.S. Army, 1907, advanced through grades to brig. gen., USAF, 1948; served in Mexican Punitive Expdn. under John J. Pershing; served in France, World War I; finance officer Tng. Command, USAAF, World War II; became dir. finance USAF, 1947; retired as brig. gen. USAF, 1948, and entered pvt. bus. in Atlanta as founder and pres. NAMAC Corp. Republican. Baptist. Mason, Sojourner; mem. Heroes of '76. Club: Army and Navy Country (founder mem.). Home: 1711 Westwood Av. S.W., Atlanta. Died Feb. 1, 1955; buried Greenwood Cemetery, Atlanta.

WHITTAKER, Edmund Boyd, ins. exec.; b. Cambridge, Eng., Aug. 5, 1902; s. Sir Edmund T. and Lady Mary (Boyd) W.; student Fettes Coll., Edinburgh, 1916-20. U. Edinburgh, 1921-22; m. Nancy Livingstone, Sept. 12, 1927; children—Jean, Douglas, Diana. Came to U.S., 1926, naturalized, 1935. Actuarial apprentice Scottish Widows Fund, Edinburgh, Scotland, 1921-26; actuarial dept., New York Life Ins. Co., N.Y. City, 1926-29; with Prudential Ins. Co. of Am., Newark, since 1929, as mathematician, 1929-35, asst. actuary, 1935-41, asso. actuary, 1941-43, 2d v.p., 1943-46, v.p. since 1946. Mem. Adv. Council on Disability Benefits. Mem. St. Andrew's Soc. N.Y., Comml. Bridge League of Northern N.J. Club: Montclair Golf. Contbr. actuarial papers in ins. pubs. Home: 150 Highland Av., Montclair, N.J. Office: 763 Broad St., Newark 1. Died Mar. 10, 1958.

WHITTAKER, Miller F. (hwĭt'tā-ēr), coll. pres.; b. Sumter, S.C., Dec. 30, 1892; s. Johnson Chestnut and Page (Harrison) W.; B.S. in Architecture, Kansas State Coll., 1913, M.S., 1928; LL.D., Allen U., Columbia, S.C. Prof. and dir. mechanic arts State Agr. and Mech. Coll., Orangeburg, S.C., 1913-32, pres., 1932—; registered architect, S.C., 1918, Ga., 1928; pres. Conf. Land-Grant Colls., 1936-37. Served as 2d lt., 371st and 368th Inf., U.S. Army, AEF, 1917-18. Mem. Palmetto State Tchrs. Assn. Am. Legion. Mason. Home: Orangeburg, S.C. Died Nov. 14, 1949.

WHITTEMORE, Clark McKinley (hwĭt'ē-mōr), lawyer, banker; b. New York, N.Y., May 2, 1876; s. Clark F. and Annie (McKinley) W.; ed. high sch., Elizabeth, N.J.; m. Regina G. Baremore, June 12, 1915; children—Patricia, Jean, Ann Randel, Clark McKinley, Margaret, John Rae. Admitted to N.J. bar, 1897, and began practice at Elizabeth; mem. Whittemore & McLean, 1922-29, now Whittemore, Porter & Pollis; president Union County Trust Company, 1922-34, now chairman of board; president El Mora Realty Co.; dir. Linden Trust Co., Am. Gas Accumulator Co., Elastic Stop-Nut Corp.. Judge Dist. Court, Elizabeth, 1908-13. Pres. board Elizabeth Free Pub. Library. Mem. Am., N.J. State, Union Co. (pres. 2 yrs.) bar assns., N.J. Bankers Assn. Republican. Episcopalian. Mason. Clubs: Rotary, Elizabeth Town and Country. Home: 135 Malden Terrace, Hillside, N.J. Office: 125 Broad St., Elizabeth, N.J. Died May 18, 1953.

WHITTEMORE, Herbert Lucius, mech. engr.; b. Milw., Oct. 1, 1876; s. Lucius Lorenzo and Charlotte Elizabeth (Hanson) W.; B.S. in Mech. Engring., U. Wis., 1903, M.E., 1910; m. Elizabeth Amanda Kittredge, Mar. 31, 1923; children—William Kittredge, Nancy. Asst. supt. Sullivan Machinery Co., Claremont, N.H., 1902-04; engr. A. P. Hanson Co., Berlin, Germany, 1905; prodn. engr. British Westinghouse Electric & Mfg. Co., Manchester, Eng., 1906; instr. engring. mechanics U. Ill., 1906-10; engr. of tests Watertown Arsenal, Mass., 1910-12; instr. mechanics Columbia, 1912-16; prof. mechanics U. Okla., 1916-17; chief engring. mechanics sect. Nat. Bur. Standards, Washington, ret. 1946. Recipient Morehead medal Internat. Acetylene Assn., 1927; Longstreth medal Franklin Inst., 1937. Mem. Am. Soc. M.E., Washington Acad. Sciences. Unitarian. Club: Cosmos (Washington). Author of many bulletins pub. by govt. Home: 3906 McKinley St. N.W., Washington. Died July 11, 1954.

WHITTEMORE, Thomas, archeologist; born Cambridge, Mass., Jan. 2, 1871; s. Joseph and Elizabeth (St. Clair) W.; A.B., Tufts Coll., 1894; studied Harvard Grad. Sch., and Oxford U., Eng. Formerly prof. English, later prof. fine arts Tufts College; asst. prof. fine arts N.Y.U.; Am. rep. Egypt. Exploration Fund, 1911—; served as lectr. Byzantine and Coptic art, Columbia and N.Y. univs. Officer French Red Cross, 1914-15; dir. Com. for Edn. of Russian Youth, 1915-31; now dir. Byzantine Inst. Decorated Officer Légion d'Honneur (France). Fellow Royal Geog. Soc., London; keeper of Byzantine coins and sales, Fogg Museum, fellow for research in Byzantine art, Harvard; fellow Society of Antiquaries, London; mem. Archaeol. Inst. Am., Am. Numis. Soc., Clubs: Faculty (Cambridge, Mass.); St. Botolph, Harvard (Boston); Harvard, Century (New York); Oxford Union (Oxford, Eng.); St. James's, Gargoyle, Athenaeum (London). Author: Poss Luminia; The Mosaics of St. Sophia. Contbr. on archeol. subjects to many jours. and periodicals. Address: Room 712, 199 Washington St., Boston 8. Died June 8, 1950.

WHITTEMORE, William John, artist; b. N.Y.C.; s. Charles and Maria F. (Kimball) W.; student pvt. schs., New York; pupil in art of William Hart, N.A. D. and Art Students' League, N.Y., Jules Lefebvre and Benjamin Constant, Paris; m. Alice Vaud Whitmore, 1895 (died 1911); m. 2d, C. Helen Simpson, 1921. Portrait painter. Recipient silver medal Paris Expn., 1889; bronze medal Atlanta Expn.; Proctor prize N.A.D., 1917; Lloyd C. Griscom prize Am. Water Color Soc., 1927; Isidor water color prize Salmagundi Club, 1927; Weyrich meml. prize, Balt., 1928; McCarthy prize, Pa. Soc., Miniature Painters, 1934; hon. mention Calif. Soc., Miniature Painters, 1940, 2d hon. mention, 1941, Medal of Honor, 1942. Represented at Columbia U.; State House, Montpelier, Vt.; State House, Trenton, N.J.; Franklin Inst., Phila.; Brooklyn Museum; Boston Art Club; Detroit Club; Lotos Club, New York; Wesleyan Coll., Macon, Ga.; Essex Club, Newark, San Diego Gallery of Art, etc., A.N.A.; mem. Am. Water Color Soc., N.Y. Water Color Club, Am. Soc. Miniature Painters, Calif. Soc. Miniature Painters, Allied Artists Am. Clubs: Century, Salmagundi. Address: East Hampton, N.Y. Died Feb. 7, 1955.

WHITTLESEY, Derwent (Stainthorpe) (hwĭt'-l-sĭ), geographer; b. Pecatonica, Ill., Nov. 11, 1890; s. Joseph Henry and Sophia Jane (Derwent) W.; Ph.B., U. of Chicago, 1914, M.A., 1915, Ph.D., 1920; hon. M.A., Harvard, 1942; D.Sc. (honorary), Beloit College, 1953. Acting assistant professor history, Denison U., 1915-16; successively instr., asst. prof. and asso. prof. geography, U. of Chicago, 1919-28; asst. prof. geography, Harvard, 1928-31, asso. prof., 1931-43, prof. since 1943; consultant to U.S. State, War and Navy Depts., and Office of Strategic Services, 1940-46; mem. panel Research and Dev. Bd. Dept. of Defense, 1948-53; com. chmn. div. geol. and geog. National Research Council, 1937-43, and 1948-53. Fulbright Research Scholar in Tropical Africa, 1951. Served as private, ordnance sergeant and 2d lt., U.S. Army, 1918-19. Hon. fellow and gold medalist. Chicago Geographic Society, fellow American Academy Arts and Sciences; member Assn. Am. Geographers (pres. 1944, hon. pres. 1954), Sigma Alpha Epsilon, Sigma Xi. Club: Harvard Faculty. Author: Major Geographic Regions of North America (with M. C. Stark), 1923; Introduction to Economic Geography (with W. D. Jones), 1925; The Earth and the State, 1939; German Strategy of World Conquest, 1942; Geografia Politicia, 1948; Environmental Foundations of European History, 1949; Wall Map of Agricultural Regions of the World, 1951; Regional Study with Special Reference to Geography, 1952. Contbr. to Geographic Aspects of International Relations, 1937; War as a Social Institution, 1941; Makers of Modern Strategy, 1943; Ten Eventful Years, 1947; Goode's School Atlas, 1949; Ency. Brit. World Atlas 1945, 51, and Ency. Brit. since 1946; American Geography: Inventory and Prospect, 1954; also to mags. Home: 20A Prescott St., Cambridge 38, Mass. Died Nov. 25, 1956; buried Twelve Mile Grove Cemetery, Seward, Ill.

WHORF, John, artist; b. Boston, Mass., Jan. 10, 1903; s. Harry and Sarah (Lee) W.; student of art at age of 14, Boston Museum of Fine Arts Sch., later at Provincetown, Mass., Paris, Spain; M.A. (honorary), Harvard Univ., 1938; married to Viviene Wing, Mar. 31, 1925; children—Carol, John, Nancy, Michael. Paints mainly in watercolor; has exhibited widely, most recently at Milch Galleries, N.Y. City, 1942. Awarded hon. M.A., Harvard U., 1938; prizes from R.I. Sch. of Design, Baltimore Museum of Arts; special room for his work, Internat. Watercolor Exhbn., Chicago Art Inst., 1939; Munroe prize for watercolor in Sanity in Art exhbn., Chicago, 1939, 41; Waldo Logan watercolor prize in Sanity in Art exhbn., Chicago, 1941; represented in collections of Brooklyn Museum of Art, Metropolitan Museum of Art, Whitney Museum of Am. Art (N.Y. City), Fogg Art Museum (Harvard U.), Harkness

Memorial Museum (Yale U.), Chicago Art Inst., Herron Art Inst. (Indianapolis), Boston Museum of Fine Arts, R.I. Sch. of Design (Providence). Nat. Academician, 1947. Mem. Am. Watercolor Soc., Fla. Watercolor Soc. (hon.). Address: 8 W. Vine St., Provincetown, Mass. Died Feb. 13, 1959; buried Provincetown, Mass.

WHYTE, Frederick William Carrick (hwīt), mining engr.; b. Biggar, Scotland, July 27, 1863; s. Robert and Catharine (Carrick) W.; grad. High Sch., Stirling, 1878; mining course, night sch., Glasgow; m. Adeliza Crichton, Mar. 23, 1892; 1 son, Keith Carrick. Apprentice with Johnstones & Rankine, Glasgow, 1878-83; in Office of Pub. Works, Glasgow, 1883-85; asst. engr. Johnstones & Rankine, 1885-87; came to America, 1887; asst. and resident engr., work on location and constrn., in Mont., G.N. Ry., 1887-92; chief engr. constrn., Butte, Anaconda & Pacific Ry., 1892-94; engr. at Belt Coal Mines, for Anaconda Copper Mining Co., 1895-96, gen. mgr. coal dept., 1896-1936; cons. engr., 1936—; gen. mgr. Diamond Coal & Coke Co., 1899-1936. Mem. Am. Inst. Mining and Metall. Engrs., Mont. Soc. Engrs. Presbyn. Club: Anaconda Country. Home: Anaconda, Mont. Died Sept. 15, 1949.

WHYTE, Jessel Stuart, business exec.; b. Chicago, Ill., Nov. 25, 1890; s. George Stuart and Anne (Jessel) W.; student Univ. high school, Chicago; Cornell, 1909-13; post grad., Univ. of Sheffield (Eng.). 1913-14; m. Ruth Johnson, Oct. 9, 1915; children—Harriet Louise, Anna Jessel (Mrs. George C. Wilder), Helen (Mrs. Frank J. Griffith), Ruth. Dir., pres. and gen. mgr. MacWhyte Co., Kenosha, Wis.; dir. First Nat. Bank, Kenosha, Northwestern Loan and Trust Co., Am. Hoist and Derrick Co., St. Paul, Minn. Dir. Kenosha Co. Am. Red Cross; treas. Kenosha Co. Republican Com.; pres. State Bd. Vocational and Adult Education (Wis.); pres. bd. trustees, Stout Inst. (Menomonie, Wis.), Kemper Hall (Kenosha). Mem. Am. Legion, Psi Upsilon. Mason (32° Shriner), Elk, Eagle, Moose, Baptist. Republican. Clubs: Chicago Athletic Assn.; Kenosha Country (treas.); Cornell of New York and Chicago. Home: 6926 Second Av. Office: care of MacWhyte Co., Kenosha, Wis. Died May 28, 1952.

WHYTE, John, educator; b. Watertown, Wis., Nov. 30, 1887; s. William Foote and Florence Adelaide (Kohn) W.; B.A., Northwestern Coll., Watertown, Wis., 1905; B.A., U. of Wis., 1906, M.A., 1907, Ph.D., 1915; studied univs. Leipzig and Berlin, 1908-11, Columbia, 1919, New Sch. for Social Research, 1920; m. Isabel Van Sickle, June 13, 1913; 1 son, William Foote. Ottendorfer memorial trav. fellow, 1908-09; instr. German, N.Y. U., 1911-12, Ohio State U., 1912-13; instr. of German, N.Y. Univ., 1913-15, asst. prof., 1915-19; actg. dir. Div. of Pub. Works and Construction Development, Washington, D.C., Jan.-July 1919; dir. research and edn., Nat. Assn. Credit Men, 1919-24, asst. prof. German, Coll. City of New York, 1924-28, asso. prof., 1928-32; prof. German, Brooklyn Coll., since 1937, also chmn. dept.; teacher, summers, U. of Wis., 1928, Western Reserve, 1931. Asst. sec. Emergency Com. in Aid of Displaced German Scholars, 1935-37; lectured at U.S. Information Centers in Germany under auspices of the State Dept., 1951. Mem. Modern Lang. Assn. Am. (treas. 1928-31), Goethe Soc., America (sec. 1928-31), Am. Assn. Teachers of German, Am. Assn. Univ. Profs. Club: Town Hall (N.Y. City). Author: Young Germany in Its Relations to Britain, 1917. Co-author: Economics of the Construction Industry, 1919; The Undistributed Earnings Tax, 1920; (with J. H. Tregoe) Effective Collection Letters, 1925; American Words and Ways, 1943; Heine Poems in Their Musical Settings, 1945. Contbr. on literature, economics and edn. Home: 657 E. 26th, Bklyn 10. Died Mar. 30, 1952; buried Greensboro, Vt.

WICHER, Edward Arthur (wĭch'ĕr), theologian; b. Peterborough, Ont., Dec. 14, 1872; s. Rev. John Woodmore and Elizabeth Mary (Lowry) W.; B.A., U. Toronto, 1895, M.A., 1896; B.D., Knox Coll., Toronto, 1899; studied U. Halle, Germany, 1899-1901; D.D., Park Coll., Mo., 1907; m. Elizabeth Gordon Langlois, Feb. 11, 1901 (died Dec. 1919); children—Herbert Woodmore, Edward Arthur, Mary Langlois, Elizabeth Langlois; m. 2d, Ida Lucy Oberbeck, Jan. 17, 1922. Ordained Presbyn. ministry, 1901; pastor Union Ch., Kobe, Japan, 1901-04, St. Stephen's Ch., St. John, N.B., 1904-05; prof. N.T. interpretation, San Francisco Theol. Sem., 1905-45, also v.p.; prof. emeritus, 1945—. Special religious sec. of Y.M.C.A. with British Army in Palestine, 1918-19. Annual prof. Am. Sch. of Oriental Research, Jerusalem, 1928-29. Moderator Synod of Cal., 1937. Mem. Soc. Bibl. Exegesis, Am. Philos. Assn., Am. Archeol. Institution. Republican. Clubs: Rotary, Chi Alpha. Author: Presbyterian Church in Californa; The Same Yesterday, Today and Forever; The Temptation of Our Lord. Contbr. to religious periodicals. Home: 2399 South Court, Palo, Alto, Cal. Deceased.

WICKER, John Jordan, educator; b. Lynchburg, Va.; s. Ambrose and Anna Maria (Reid) W.; Richmond (Va.) College, 1887-91; Th.G., Southern Bapt. Theol. Sem., Louisville, Ky., 1895; D.D., U. Richmond, 1916; m. Elizabeth Pumphrey, Apr. 19, 1892; children—Elizabeth (wife of Maj. G. Heyward Mahon, Jr.), John Jordan, James Caldwell. Pastor Bapt. Ch., Baltimore, Md., 1895-1900, First Ch., Trenton, N.J., 1900-05, Leigh St. Ch., Richmond, Va., 1910-20; pres. Wicker Tours, Richmond, 1908-—; pres. Fork Union (Va.) Millitary Acad., 1930-45, now president emeritus. Editor Atlantic Baptist, 1897-98; asso. editor The Commonwealth, 1898-1900. Mem. State Mission Board, Education Commission and Virginia Foreign Mission Bd. of Southern Bapt. Conv.; v.p. Bapt. Gen. Assn. of Va. Republican. Mason. Author of The March of God; Into Tomorrow. Contbr. to denominational publs. and various mags. Lecturer, evangelist, world traveler. Home: Ford Union, Va. Died Mar. 17, 1958.

WICKHAM, Henry Taylor, lawyer; b. Hickory Hill, Va., Dec. 17, 1849; s. Williams Carter and Lucy Penn (Taylor) W.; A.B., Washington and Lee U., 1868; LL.B., U. Va., 1870; LL.D., Washington and Lee U., 1935; m. Elise Warwick Barksdale, Dec. 17, 1885; children—Williams Carter, George Barksdale. In practice at Richmond, 1870—; asst. atty., 1874-78, asst. counsel, 1875-85, C.&O. Ry. Co., and Newport News and Miss. Valley Co., 1885-86; gen. solicitor in charge of law dept., and dir., 1886-1909, and 1909-18, v.p. and gen. counsel, Chesapeake & Ohio Ry. Co.; gen. solicitor in charge of law dept. C.&O. R.R., under U.S. R.R. Administration, 1918-20; v.p. and gen. counsel C.&O. Ry. and Hocking Ry., 1920-23, and since advisory counsel. Also receiver for U.S. Circuit Court, of Va. Passenger & Power Co., Richmond Passenger & Power Co. and Richmond Traction Co. Elected to Va. House of Dels. as a Debt-Payer, 1879; elected to Va. Senate 10 times since 1888 and pres. protem; 1897-1907; acting lt. gov. 1939-41; mem. Va. Debt. Commn., 1890; mem. Va. Debt Commn. in controvelsy with W.Va., 1896-1920; chmn. Dem. conf. of Senate and of finance com., 1896-1907. Was mover of Senate resolution, 1890, under which Va. state debt was settled on present basis. Episcopalian. Mem. S.A.R., S.C.V., Va. Hist. Soc. Club: Commonwealth. Home: Hickory Hill, Hanover Co., Va. Office: First Nat. Bank Bldg., Richmond, Va. Died Mar. 5, 1943; buried Hollywood Cemetery, Richmond.

WICKMAN, Carl Eric, a founder, former chmn. Greyhound Corp.; chmn. bd. Central Greyhound Lines, Pacific Greyhound Lines, Southwestern Greyhound Lines, New England Greyhound Lines, Inc., Pa. Greyhound Lines, Great Lakes Greyhound Lines, Inc., Richmond-Greyhound Lines, Inc., Western Canadian Greyhound Lines, Inc.; v.pres. Tropic-Aire, Inc., dir. Interstate Transit-Lines, Atlantic Greyhound Corp., Capitol Greyhound Lines, Dixie Greyhound Lines, Inc., Ill. Greyhound Lines, Inc., Pan-Am. Greyhound Lines, Inc., Northland Greyhound Lines, Inc., retired 1953. Home: 16 Canterbury Court, Wilmette, Ill. Office: Board of Trade Bldg., Chgo. Died Feb. 5, 1954.*

WICKS, Frank Scott Corey, minister; b. Millville, Mass., Feb. 15, 1868; s. Joseph Francis and Eunice (Corey) W.; grad. Peekskill (N.Y.) Mil. Acad., 1887, Meadville Theol. Sem., 1894, Harvard Div. Sch., 1895; D.D.; m. Elizabeth Goodnow, June 20, 1899 (she died, 1929); children—Coryenne Clevenger, Warwick, Lynton Peirce; married 2d, Katharine Gibson, July 22, 1932. Ordained to the Unitarian ministry, 1895; pastor Passaic, N.J., 1895-98, Boston, 1898-1905, All Souls' Church, Indianapolis, since 1905. Works chiefly along sociol. lines; frequently lectures on literary and sociol. subjects. Clubs: Indianapolis Literary, Athenæum (Indianapolis). Mason (32°). Home: 111 E. 44th St. Office: 1453 N. Alabama St., Indpls. Died Dec. 21, 1952.

WICOFF, John Van Buren, lawyer; b. Plainsboro, N.J., June 9, 1878; s. John and Catharine Lucretia (Britton) W.; prep. student State Model Sch., Trenton, N.J., 1891-96; A.B., Princeton, 1900; student N.Y. Law Sch., 1900-01, 1903; m. Lavinia Ely Applegate, June 8, 1904; children—John Edward, Douglas Britton, Dorothy Applegate (Mrs. W. M. Bennett), Catharine Lavinia, Evelyn Elizabeth, Marjorie Frances (Mrs. E. W. Cooper), Lavinia Applegate. Admitted to N.J. bar, 1903; partner, late Judge William M. Lanning, 1903-04; practice alone, 1904-11; mem. Wicoff & Lanning since 1911; pres., dir. and counsel Broad St. Nat. Bank of Trenton; pres., dir. Trenton Bone Fertilizer Co.; counsel and dir. Walker-Gordon Lab. Co.; dir. Trenton Savs. Fund Soc. Chmn. twp. com. Plainsboro Twp. since 1922, pres. bd. edn., 1919-50; mem. Middlesex Co. Vocational Sch. Bd., 1914-40; Rep. candidate for state senator from Middlesex Co., 1936; chmn. Mercer Co. com. on character and fitness of bar candidates through Supreme Ct. appt., 1923-50; fed. food adminstr. Mercer Co., N.J. and City of Trenton, World War I; mem. legal adv. bd. and mem. War Manpower Commn. for Trenton area, World War II. Mem. Am., N.J. State and Mercer Co. bar assns., S.R. (former N.J. chancellor), Soc. Colonial Wars (dep. gen. gov.), Order Founders and Patriots of Am. (gov. gen. 1941-42), Holland Soc. N.Y., St. Nicholas Soc. City N.Y. Republican. Presbyn. Mason (K.T., Shriner). Clubs: Rotary, Trenton, Princeton (Trenton); Nassau and Cannon (Princeton). Home: 1900 Princeton Rd., Plainsboro, N.J. Office: 143 E. State St., Trenton 8, N.J. Died Feb. 25, 1952.

WIDEMAN, Francis James (wīd'mȧn), lawyer; b. Micanopy, Fla., Oct. 21, 1891; s. John Waller and Julia Elizabeth (Edwards) W.; A.B., Stetson U., 1913; LL.B., Stetson U., 1914; m. Pattie Dickson Holmes, Dec. 8, 1920; children—Francis J., Jane Dickson, Patricia Holmes. Admitted to Florida bar, 1914; was states atty., 1921-24; partner law firm Wideman, Wideman & Wardlaw, 1924-33; asst. U.S. attorney gen., June 1933-Feb. 1936; now in charge Washington office of firm of Wideman, Caldwell, Pacetti & Robinson, Palm Beach. Mem. City Council, Jacksonville, Fla., 1919-20; del. Nat. Dem. Conv., 1932; mem. Fla. State Bd. of Control, 1929-33. Lt. U.S. Army, 1917-18. Mem. Am. and Fla. State bar assns., Sigma Nu. Shriner. Episcopalian. Clubs: Everglades (Palm Beach); Metropolitan, Burning Tree, Chevy Chase, National Press (Washington). Home: 3232 Woodley Rd., Washington, D.C. Office: 815 15th Street, Washington. Died Sept. 28, 1952; buried Jacksonville, Fla.

WIDTSOE, John Andreas (wĭd'sō), educator; b. on Island of Froyen, Norway, Jan. 31, 1872; s. John A. and Anna C. (Gaarden) W.; grad. normal dept. Brigham Young Coll., Utah, 1891; B.S., Harvard, 1894; A.M., Ph.D., U. of Göttingen, 1899; Polytechnicum, Zürich, 1900; traveling fellow of Grad. Sch. of Harvard U., 1898-1900; LL.D., Utah Agrl. Coll., 1914, U. of Utah, 1921; m. Leah Eudora Dunford, June 1, 1898; children—Anna G., Leah Eudora. Chemist, Utah Expt. Station, 1894-1905; prof. chemistry, Utah Agrl. Coll., 1895-1905; dir. Utah Expt. Sta., 1900-05; prin. School of Agr., Brigham Young Univ., Provo, Utah, 1905-07; pres. Agrl. Coll. of Utah, 1907-16; pres. U. of Utah, 1916-21; mem. Council of Twelve Apostles Latter Day Saints Church since Mar. 17, 1921; pres. European Missions of Ch. of Jesus Christ of Latter Day Saints, 1928-33. Pres. Internat. Dry-Farming Congress, 1912. Author: Dry-Farming, 1911; Irrigation Practice, 1914; Rational Theology, 1915; Success on Irrigation Projects, 1927; In Search of Truth, 1930; Seven Claims of the Book of Mormon (with F. S. Harris), 1936; Program of the Church of Jesus Christ of Latter-Day Saints, 1936; The Word of Wisdom (with Leah D. Widtsoe), 1938; Priesthood and Church Government, 1940; In the Gospel Net, 1941; Evidences and Reconciliations, 1943; Man and the Dragon, 1944; How the Desert Was Tamed, 1947. Numerous sci., popular articles, papers, books. Address: 47 E. South Temple St., Salt Lake City. Died Nov. 29, 1952; buried Salt Lake City Cemetery.

WIEAND, Albert Cassel (wē'ănd), educator; b. Wadsworth, Medina County, O., Jan. 17, 1871; s. David Rauch and Elizabeth (Cassel) W.; A.B., McPherson (Kan.) Coll., 1895, A.M., 1900; grad. Columbia Coll. of Expression, 1899; student Div. Sch., U. of Chicago, 1899-1901; Ph.B., U. of Chicago, 1901; grad. studies, U. of Jena, 1902-03, U. of Leipzig, 1905, Columbia, 1903-04, and summer 1921, Boston U., spring 1923 and 1924, Harvard, summer 1923, Yale, spring 1925; D.D., Manchester Coll., North Manchester, Ind., 1916, Juniata College, Huntingdon, Pa., 1925; B.D., Th.D., Bethany Bibl. Sem., Chicago, 1921; m. Katherine Grace Broadwater, June 16, 1909; children—Cassel B., David John, Alberta Katherine, Ruth Elizabeth, William Winton. Prof. English, McPherson Coll., 1895-98; prof. religious edn., Bibl. Sem., N.Y. City, 1902-05; founder and pres. Bethany Bibl. Sem., 1905-32, prof. of bibl. lit. and devotional life, 1932-46; retired, 1946. Author: Analytic Outline and Diagram of the Life of Christ, 1914; Foundation Truths, 1918; The Child's Life of Christ, 1918; The Prayer Life and Teachings of Jesus, 1931; Studies in the Gospel According to Matthew, 1929; Studies in the Gospel of Mark, 1932; Studies in the Gospel According to John, 1946, Gospel Records of The Message and Mission of Jesus Christ, 1947; The Gospel of Prayer, 1953. Home: 2320 Fourth St., La Verne, Cal. Office: 3435 Van Buren St., Chgo. Died July 24, 1954.

WIEBOLDT, William A., merchant, philanthropist; b. Altenbruch, Hanover, Germany, Mar. 8, 1857; s. Johann and Anna Catherine (von Bergen) W.; m. Anna Louise Krueger, 1883; children—Werner A., Raymond C., Elmer F., Mrs. Florence Wieboldt Sieck, Mrs. Ada Wieboldt Straub. Formerly chmn. bd. dirs. Wieboldt Stores, Inc. (dept. stores), Chgo., now resigned. Established Wieboldt Found. 1921, with gift of $5,000,000. Mem. Chgo. Mus. Natural History, Art Inst. Chgo., Chgo. Hist. Soc., German Club of Chgo. Lutheran. Home: Homestead Hotel Evanston, Ill. Died Dec. 9, 1954.

WIECZOREK, Max (vĕ-ȧ-chŏr'ĕk), artist; b. Breslau, Germany, Nov. 22, 1863; s. Joseph W. and Bertha (Gärtner) W.; studied Karlsruhe Art Acad. under Ferdinand Keller, and Weimar Art Acad. under Max Tedy; m. Ida Luer; children—Anny Bertha Caroline (Mrs. Robert O. Beardsley), Maxine (Mrs. Henry M. Watts, Jr.); m. 2d, Gertrud Besser, Mar. 14, 1929. Came to U.S., 1893, naturalized, 1921. Works on permanent exhbn. in Library of Union Chaffey High Sch., Ontario, Calif.; Engineers' Club, N.Y. City; Denshawn Sch. of Dancing, N.Y. City;

Los Angeles Museum, Library of Virgil Jr. High Sch., Los Angeles; City Hall, Los Angeles. Pres.-founder Foundation of Western Art. Awarded silver medal, Panama-Calif. Expn., 1915; William Preston Harrison prize, Calif. Art Club, 1918; merit prize, Laguna Beach (Calif.) Art Assn., 1920; merit prize, Ariz. State Exhbn., 1920-22; A. J. Ackerman prize, Calif. Art Club, 1920; H. E. Huntington prize, Calif. Water Color Soc., 1923; award of merit, Bookplate Assn. Internat., 1926; 2d prize, Calif. State Fair, 1927; 2d prize Los Angeles County Fair, 1927; gold medal, Pacific Southwest Expn., Long Beach, Calif., 1928. Mem. Am. Federation of Arts, Am. Water Color Soc., Am. Artists Professional League, Calif. Water Color Soc., Calif. Art Club, New York Water Color Club, Laguna Beach Art Assn., Painters' and Sculptors' Club, Chicago Galleries Assn., Painters of the West, Bookplate Assn. Internat., Artland Club, Fine Arts Soc. (San Diego). Clubs: Los Angeles Athletic; hon. mem. Los Angeles Commercial. Contbr. to Am. Mag. of Art, Art Digest, Calif. Graphic, etc. Home: 1590 Lombardy Rd., Pasadena, Calif. Studio: Hollingsworth Bldg., Los Angeles. Died Sept. 25, 1955; buried Rose Hills Cemetery, Whittier, Cal.

WIEGAND, Gustave Adolph, artist; b. Bremen, Germany, Oct. 2, 1870; s. Daniel Ludwig and Dorothea Charlotte (Heine) W.; came to U.S., 1883; prep. edn., Remberti Sch., Bremen; art edn., Pratt Inst., Bklyn.; pupil of William M. Chase, Bklyn. Art Sch., Eugen Bracht, Royal Acad. of Dresden; m. Anna Margarethe Abresch, June 14, 1906; 1 dau., Phyllis Dorothea (Mrs. Paul Tilson). Represented in Bklyn. and Newark museums. Recipient bronze medal for landscape St. Louis Expn., 1904; 2d Hallgarten prize N.A.D., 1904-05; hon. mention Allied Artists Exhbn., 1937. Mem. Allied Artists Am., N.Y. Soc. Painters. Clubs: Nat. Arts (life), Salmagundi (N.Y. C.); Brooklyn Art; Lake Sunapee Yacht (N.H.). Home: Old Chatham, N.Y. Died Nov. 3, 1957.

WIEGMAN, Fred Conrad (wēg'măn), clergyman; b. Wellsburg, Ia., Feb. 15, 1899; s. Frederick and Bertha (Hammerschmidt) W.; student Midland Coll., Fremont, Neb., 1919-24, Litt.D., 1957; student Western Theol. Sem., Fremont, 1924-27; D.D., Wittenberg Coll., 1930; m. Mary Clarinda Rangeler, June 8, 1927; 1 dau., Mrs. Herma Jean Weir. Apprentice Howells (Neb.) Jour., 1911-12; proofreader Lincoln (Neb.) Jour., 1916; asst. mgr. Fisk Rubber Co., Memphis, 1916-18; dept. mgr. Kirkendall Shoe Co., Omaha, 1918-19; pastor First Luth. Ch., Nebraska City, 1927-30, North Platte, 1930-37, Salem Luth. Ch., Fremont, 1937-39; pres. Midland Coll., Western Theol. Sem., 1939-45; pastor Evangelical Luth. Ch. of the Holy Trinity, Akron, O., 1945-57; pres. Ohio Synod United Luth. Ch. in Amm, 1957—. Served in U.S. Army, 1918. Sec. Nat. Luth. Ednl. Conf. Received Nebraska City Distinguished Service award, 1939, Fremont Man of the Year, 1940. Trustee Wittenberg Coll., Springfield, O. Mem. Bd. Am. Missions, United Luth. Ch. Am. Dir. Akron United Fund; mem. Salvation Army Adv. Bd. Mem. Family Service Soc., C. of C. (dir.). Rotarian. Home: 20 S. 3d St., Columbus 15, O. Died Dec. 3, 1957; buried Akron, O.

WIELAND Arthur J., business exec.; b. Sandusky, O., May 11, 1895; s. Jacob Charles and Amelia (Winterstellar) W.; student Ohio State U., 1914-17; Toledo U., 1947-48; m. Bianca Scheuer, Aug. 21, 1920; 1 dau., Alice Clare; m. 2d, Zella Holaday Smith, August 16, 1952; 1 daughter, Cynthia Kelly. With Hearst Pubs., 1920-24; assistant to president General Motor Export Company, 1925; managing director General Motors International, Denmark 1926, Near East, Egypt, 1927; regional sales mgr. Gen. Motors Export Co., Europe, 1928-29; mng. dir. Gen. Motors, Berlin, Germany 1929-30; dir. and sales mgr. Adam Opel A/G (Gen. Motors subsidiary) Germany 1930-33; vice pres. and sales mgr. Gen. Motors overseas operations, 1933-37; regional mgr. Gen. Motors Overseas, European Area, 1937-39, Far Eastern Area, 1939-40, European-Indian Area, 1940-46; v.p. and dir. Willys-Overland Motors Toledo, O., 1946, mem. bd. dirs., 1946-49, exec. v.p., 1948; chmn. bd. Wilson Foundry, 1948-49; gen. mgr. Ford internat., 1949—, v.p., 1950—, mem. adminstrn. com., chmn. fgn. operations com. Ford Motor Co., 1950—, v.p., 1950—. Recipient citation by War Dept., for Civilian Aid in Middle East and European Theatre of War, World War II 1948. Mem. Phi Kappa Psi. Clubs: Apawamis Country (Rye, N.Y.); Gipsy Trail (Carmel, N.Y.); University (N.Y.). Contbr. several articles and papers to tech. periodicals. Home: Dearborn Inn. Office: Ford Internat., American Rd., Dearborn, Mich. Died Mar. 21, 1957.

WIELAND, G(eorge) R(eber), paleontologist; b. Boalsburg, Pa., Jan. 24, 1865; s. Washington Frederick and Margaret (Reber) W.; B.S., Pa. State Coll., 1893; studied U. Göttingen, 1894; U. Pa., 1896-97; Yale U., 1899, Ph.D., 1900; m. Edla Kristina Andersson, 1891 (deceased); 1 son, Hans Leonard. Asso. Carnegie Inst.; asso. prof. paleobotany, Yale. Mem. Wilderness Soc. Author: Polar Climate in Time the Major Factor in the Evolution of Plants and Animals, 1903; Osteology of Protostega, 1906; Armored Dinosauria, 1911; La Flora Liasica de la Mixteca Alta (in the Spanish), 1914; American Fossil Cycads, Vol. I, 1906, Vol. II, 1916; New North American Cycadeoids, 1921; Antiquity of the Anglosperms, 1926; A New Cycad from the Mariposa Slates, 1929; Raumeria of the Zwinger of Dresden, 1934; The Cerro Cuadrado Petrified Forest, 1935; Cycadeoid Types of the Kansas Cletaceous, 1942; The Carpathian-Black Hills Cycadeoid parallel, 1941; Fossil Cyad National Monument, 1944; The Yale Cycadeoids, 1945; also Chemistry of Petrifaction; Ancient Flower and cone-bearing Plants; The World's two greatest Petrified Forests; Land Types of the Trinity Beds; Mesaverde Cycadeoids; Wood Opalization Origin of Angiosperms; Ancient Climates; Dinosaur Extinction, etc. Awarded Archeuke Rainer medal, Vienna, 1914; Bologna, 1907. Mem. N.Y. Acad. Sci.; hon. mem. Botanical Society of India, 1935. Proposed establishment "Fossil Cycad National Monument" of the Southern Black Hills, donating site of 320 acres including the world's finest flowering petrified forest, 1922; brought to light there, Nov. 1935, aided by the C.C.C. over one ton of in situ cycadeoids, proving a three-fold value—evolutionary, chemic, and stratigraphic. Discovered the giant fossil turtle Archelon in 1895, various paleontologic explorations in the West, Mexico and S. America. Democrat. Home: Anawan Rd., West Haven, Conn. Died Jan. 18, 1953.

WIELAND, Heinrich Otto, chemist; b. Pforzheim, Baden, Germany, June 4, 1877; s. Theodor Wolfgang and Elise (Blum) W.; Phil.D., U. München, 1901; Dr.Ing., Technische Hochschule, Darmstadt, 1925; Dr.Med. (hon.), U. Freiburg, 1926; Dr.Phil., U. Athenes, 1932; m. Josephine Bartmann, Mar. 31, 1908; children—Eva (Mrs. F. Lynen), Wolfgang, Theodore, Otto. Prof. chemistry Technische Hochschule, Munchen, 1917-21, U. Freiburg, 1921-25; prof. U. München, 1925-52, retired. Recipient Nobel prize for chemistry, 1927, Otto Hahn prize, 1955. Address: Schiesstättstr 12, Germany. Died Aug. 5, 1957.

WIER, Jeanne Elizabeth (wēr), prof. emeritus history and political science; b. Grinnell, Ia., Apr. 8, 1870; d. Adolphus William and Elizabeth (Greenside) W.; B.Di., Iowa State Tchrs. Coll., 1893; B.A., Stanford, 1901; studied summers, U. Cal.; LL.D., U. Nev., 1924. Teacher pub. schs., Ia., 1889-92; asst. prin. high sch., Heppner, Ore., 1893-95; acting asst. prof. history U. Nev., 1899,, asso. prof., 1901, prof. history and polit. science, 1907, prof. history, 1917-21, prof. history and polit. science, 1921—, acting head of dept., 1899-1901, head dept., 1901-40. Founder, 1904, and sec. Nev. State Hist. Soc.; called first woman suffrage meeting in Nev., 1911, in campaign leading to suffrage adoption. Mem. Am. Hist. Assn. (v.p. Pacific Coast br. 1915-16), Am. Polit. Science Assn., N.E.A., Reno br. Nat. League Am. Pen Women, Am. Pioneer Trails Assn. (life), Am. Assn. for State and Local History, Soc. Am. Archivists, Am. Assn. U. Profs., Am. Collegiate Doctor's Degree Assn., Reno Business and Profl. Women's Club, Phi Beta Kappa, Phi Kappa Phi, Pi Gamma Mu; hon. mem. Nev. Fedn. Women's Clubs. Republican. Conglist. Compiler and editor of all Nevada Hist. Soc. Publs., also author of many articles in those publs.; article on Nevada in sup. to Ency. Britannica, World Ency.; contbr. to Dictionary of Am. Biography, Dictionary Am. History. Author of chpt. Nevada Politics, in Rocky Mountain Politics, 1940. Sponsor of Nevada: a Guide to the Silver State, and all publs. of W.P.A. hist. records survey in Nevada; gathering Nevada World War II records. Address: 120 E. 9th St., Reno, Nev. Died Apr. 7, 1950; buried Reno.

WIGGAM, Albert Edward (wĭg'ăm), author, lecturer; b. Austin, Ind.; s. John and Harriet Small (Jackson) W.; ed. pub. schools, Vernon, Ind.; entered Moore's Hill (Ind.) Coll. at age 14; B.S., Hanover (Ind.) Coll., 1893, M.A., 1903, LL.D., 1932; chemical control Belle Terre Sugar Factory, Donaldsonville, La., season, 1891-92; student in philosophy Colo. Coll., Colorado Springs, 1894; hon. D.Sc., Colgate U., 1929; LL.D., U. Vt., 1940; m. Elizabeth M. Jayne, Apr. 9, 1902 (died Jan. 26, 1943); m. 2d, Helen Scott Holcombe, Sept. 17, 1944. Assayer and mine supt., Boulder, Colo., 1895-96; editorial writer Mpls. Jour., 1899-1900; lyceum and Chautauqua lecturer and writer, 1901-19; editorial dir. Nat. Newspaper Service, Nat. Sci. Writers Assn. Trustee Hanover Coll., 1945. Mem. Internat. Lyceum Assn., A.A.A.S., Am. Genetic Assn., Assn. for Study of Human Heredity (v.p. 1933, dir.), Am. Eugenics Society, Nat. Community Foundation (adv. council), P.E.N. Independent Republican. Clubs: The Dutch Treat, Muscatatuck Country, Rotary. Author: The New Decalogue of Science, 1923; The Fruit of the Family Tree, 1924; The Next Age of Man, 1927; Exploring Your Mind, 1927; The Marks of an Educated Man, 1930; New Techniques of Happiness, 1948. Writer illustrated newspaper column Let's Explore Your Mind. Contbr. to mags., periodicals. Address: 340 16th St., Santa Monica, Cal. Died Apr. 1957.

WIGGIN, Albert Henry, banker; born Medfield, Mass., Feb. 21, 1868; s. Rev. James Henry and Laura (Newman) W.; grad. Dwight Sch., Boston, Mass., 1882, English High Sch., 1885; LL.D., Middlebury (Vt.) Coll., 1922, Kenyon Coll., 1929, Columbia, 1932; m. Jessie Duncan Hayden, Oct. 4, 1892; children—Marjorie (Mrs. Sherburne Prescott), Muriel (Mrs. Lynde Selden). Bank clerk, 1885-91; asst. nat. bank examiner, Boston, 1891-94; asst. cashier Third Nat. Bank, Boston, 1894-97; v.p. Eliot Nat. Bank, Boston, 1897-99; v.p. Nat. Park Bank, Mt. Morris Bank and Mutual Bank, New York, 1899-1904; v.p. Chase Nat. Bank, New York, 1904-11, pres., 1911-17, chmn. bd., 1917-21, chmn. bd. and pres., 1921-26, chmn. bd., 1926-30, chmn. governing bd., 1930-33, retired, 1933; trustee American Surety Company; director American Express Company, Am. Express Co., Inc.; dir. Am. Locomotive Co., Am. Woolen Co., Internat. Paper Co., Otis Elevator Co., Stone & Webster, Surety Fire Ins. Co., Underwood Corp. U.S. fuel administrator for State of N.Y., 1917-18; trustee, 1910-36, and treas., 1917-33, United Hosp. Fund of New York; trustee Middlebury Coll.; trustee and treas. Roosevelt Memorial Assn.; treas. Boys' Clubs of America, Inc.; life mem. Corp. of the Mass. Inst. of Tech. Mem. Two Hundred Fifty Associates of Harvard Business School. Chamber of Commerce, New York, The Pilgrims, New England Soc. Republican. Unitarian. Clubs: Metropolitan, Union League, Recess, Century, Bankers, New York Yacht, The Links, Blind Brook, Grolier (New York); Union (Boston). Home: 660 Park Av., New York; (summer) Greenwich, Conn. Office: 65 Broadway, N.Y.C. Died May 21, 1951; buried Putnam Cemetery, Greenwich, Conn.

WIGGINS, William D., civil engr.; b. Richmond, Ind., Apr. 28, 1873; s. Philamon and Henrietta (McCullough) W.; grad. Rose Poly. Inst., Terre Haute, Ind., 1895; m. Lula J. Daft, 1910; children—Jane Wiggins Spencer, William D., Jr. (USNR). Entered service of Pa. Lines West of Pitts., engring. dept., 1895, has held various positions including div. engr., div. supt., valuation engr., chief engr. maintenance of way, chief engr. Central region, acting v.p. engr., and chief engr. Pa. R.R., 1935-43, v.p. engring., 1943, retired. Mem. Am. Soc. C.E., Am. Ry. Engring. Assn. Republican. Episcopalian. Clubs: Union League, Merion Golf (Phila.). Home: Merion, Pa. Died June 12, 1949.

WIGHT, E(dward) Van Dyke (wīt), clergyman; b. New Hamburg, N.Y., Mar. 13, 1869; s. Rev. Joseph Kingsbury and Elizabeth (Van Dyke) W.; A.B., Princeton U., 1892, M.A., 1895; student Chgo. Theol. Sem., 1892-94; grad. Princeton Theol. Sem., 1895; D.D., Hastings Coll., 1903; m. Kate O. Wilkerson, Aug. 28, 1895; children—Edward V. D., Elizabeth A., William K. Ordained Presbyn. ministry, 1895; pastor Wayne, Neb., 1895-97, Hastings, Neb., 1897-1907, also pres. Hastings Coll., 1901-1907; pastor Webb Horton Memorial Presbyn. Ch., Middletown, N.Y., 1907-36, pastor emeritus, 1936—. Served as Y.M.C.A. religious sec., France, World War. Moderator Synod of New York, 1915; mem. bd. of ch. erection. Republican. Clubs: University, Rotary, Historical. Author of "Revelation in Stained Glass" and a number of religious paper articles; lecturer at Evang. Sem., San Juan, Puerto Rico, 1933. Home: Snowden Lane, Princeton, N.J. Died Dec. 14, 1957.

WIHT, Thomas, architect; b. Halifax, N.S., Can., Sept. 17, 1874; s. Robert Adam and Emmaline (MacLean) W.; ed. pub. schs., Can.; archtl. study, Italy and Greece; m. Grace S. Sheridan, Oct. 3, 1905; children—Helen MacLean (Mrs. Glen Edward Riley), Dorothy Mary (Mrs. Delmer M. Buckley), Marjorie Sheridan (dec.). Came to U.S., 1891, naturalized citizen, 1913. With McKim, Mead & White, architects, N.Y.C., 1892-1904; began practice at Kansas City, Mo., 1904; owner Wight & Wight. Among important bldgs. designed and supervised by him are: William Rockhill Nelson Gallery of Art, Atkins Museum of Fine Arts, Kansas City Life Ins. Co. Bldg., St. Joseph Hosp., Wyandotte County Court House (winner of competition), First Nat. Bank Bldg., Jackson County Court House (exterior design), all Kansas City. Chmn. Art Commn., Kansas City, 1906-07. Mem. A.I.A., C. of C. Club: Kansas City. Home: 3863 Holmes St. Office: 923 Baltimore Av., Kansas City, Mo. Died Oct. 6, 1949; buried Forest Hill Pantheon.

WILBER, Edward Bacon, govt. ofcl.; b. Fairport, N.Y., Sept. 24, 1902; s. Thomas Cornelius and May Louise (Meade) W.; A.B., Union Coll., 1925; m. Georgia Horend, Aug. 19, 1929; children—Edward Bacon, Paul Horend, Marcia Jeanne. Management consultant, pvt. enterprise, 1928-36; pub. adminstrn. consultant local, state and fed. govts., 1936-41; asst. chief budget examiner, chief bus. methods br., administrative management div. U.S. Bur. Budget, 1941-48; advisor and consultant on orgn. exec. br. govt. Hoover Commn., 1948; management cons., chief orgn. and div. budget State Dept., 1948-50; became dir. budget and finance, budget officer, 1950; now dep. asst. sec. for adminstrn., Dept. of State; guest lectr., instr. management subjects Am. U. and Dept. Agr. Grad. Sch.; speaker management and administrative subjects profl. socs. Mem. Soc. Advancement Management (former pres., nat. dir.), Am. Soc. Pub. Adminstrn., Am. Polit. Sci. Assn., Chi Psi. Lutheran (sec., pres.; bus. mgr., dir. Nat. Com. Christian Leadership 1948-50). Home: South Glen Rd., Potomac, Md. Office: State Dept., Washington 25. Died Jan. 2, 1956; buried Parklawn Cemetery, Rockville, Md.

WILBUR, Curtis Dwight, judge; b. Boonesboro, Ia., May 10, 1867; s. Dwight Locke and Edna Maria (Lyman) Wilbur; grad. U.S. Naval Academy, 1888; B.S. (by act of Congress, 1937); LL.D., U. of Southern California, 1923, Occidental College, 1924, Penna. Military College, Chester, Pa., 1927; m. Ella T. Chilson, Nov. 9, 1893 (died Dec. 6, 1896); m. 2d, Olive Doolittle, January 13, 1898 (died February 15, 1942; children—Edna May, Lyman Dwight, Paul Curtis, Leonard Fiske (deceased). Resigned from navy, 1888; began practice of law at Los Angeles, Cal., 1890; chief dep. dist. atty. Los Angeles, Co., 1899-1903; judge Superior Court, same co., 1903-18; asso. justice Supreme Court of Cal., term 1919-31, chief justice, 1922-27, resigned; sec. of the Navy, by apptmt. of President Coolidge, 1924-29; judge 9th U.S. Circuit Court of Appeals, May, 1929—, senior circuit judge 1931-45; retired, 1945. Organized Juvenile Court of Los Angeles and drafted several juvenile court laws of Cal. Republican. Conglist. Club: Commonwealth. Home: Pine Lane, Los Altos, Cal. Died Sept. 8, 1954.

WILBY, Ernest, architect; b. Ossett, Yorkshire, England, June 6, 1868 (Am. entry, 1872); s. Oliver and Martha Ann (Wilson) W.; Wesley Coll., Harrogate, England, 1881-85; m. Kathleen Olga Hirst, Mar. 17, 1921. Followed profession in Toronto, 1886-1890; London, 1891-95; New York City, 1896-1903; Detroit, 1904-10; became associate architect with Albert Kahn, Detroit, 1910; instr. architecture U. of Mich., 1922-25, prof. 1926-30, lecturer, 1930-43. Fellow, Am. Inst. Architects; fellow, Royal Soc. of Arts, London; hon. life mem. Mich. Soc. of Architects; Ontario Assn. Architects; hon. fellow (life) Royal Architectural Inst. of Canada. Hon. pres. Windsor Art Asso. Life mem. Tau Sigma Delta and Alpha Rho Chi. Mem. Anglican Ch. Home: 1567 Ouellette Av., Windsor, Ontario, Can. Died Dec. 10, 1957; buried St. Mary's Churchyard, Walkerville, Ont., Can.

WILCOX, Clarence E(dward), lawyer; b. Adrian, Mich., Dec. 14, 1880; s. Isaac Lamar and Mary Elizabeth (Rogers) W.; student Adrian Coll., 1899-1901; LL.B., U. of Mich., 1905; m. Marguerite Belle Arnett, Dec. 30, 1908 (dec.); children—Edward A., James H., Josephine M. Admitted Mich. bar, 1905, since practiced in Detroit; asso. with Harlow P. Davock, U.S. referee in bankruptcy, 1905-06; with Anderson & Rackham, 1906-09; mem. firm Anderson, Rackham & Wilcox, 1909-15, Anderson, Wilcox, Lacy & Lawson, 1915-47, Wilcox, Lacy, Lawson, Kirkby & Hunt since 1947; corp. counsel City of Detroit, 1920-24, 1928-33, serving under 8 mayors; dir. Wabeek State Bank of Detroit; life trustee, chmn. Children's Fund of Mich. (trust fund created by Senator James Couzens); life trustee and sec. Horace H. Rackham and Mary A. Rackham Fund (trust fund created by Horace H. Rackham); mem. Madge Sibley Hoobler Foundation; life mem. bd. govs, Horace H. Rackham Sch. of Grad. Studies, U. of Mich. (Ann Arbor). Mem. exec. com. School Soc. Sciences and Pub. Adminstrn., U. of Mich. Grad. Sch. (Detroit). Mem. Wayne County Legal Adv. Draft Bd., 1918-19; chmn. Wayne Co. Draft Bd. 32, 1941-47. Dir. Detroit Citizens Housing and Planning Council. Counsel, Ford Motor stockholders forty million dollar tax case, Mellon vs. Couzens, et al; counsel, City of Detroit refunding program (four hundred million dollars). Mem. Am., Mich., Detroit bar assns., Am. Inst. Archaeology, Detroit Symphony Soc., Detroit Bankers, Torch, Engineers Soc. of Detroit (hon.), Alpha Tau Omega. Republican. Baptist. Mason (K.T., Shriner). Clubs: University (Ann Arbor); Thomas M. Cooley, Economic, Detroit Athletic, Detroit Golf, Ingleside (Detroit); University Lawyers (U. of Mich.); Harbor Beach Resort (Harbor Beach, Mich.). Author: Detroit Metropolitan Authority. Excess condemnation and co-drafter of Detroit Port Authority Constitutional Amendments; also many municipal legislative laws. Home: 18666 Fairway Drive, Detroit 21. Office: Buhl Bldg., Detroit 26. Died Nov. 21, 1958.

WILCOX, Herbert Budington, physician; b. Bklyn., July 1, 1874; s. George and Mary (Budington) W.; A.B., Yale, 1898; M.D., Columbia, 1902; m. Louise Geer, Nov. 23, 1905; children—Herbert Budington, Jarvis Geer, George Gunton, Mrs. Louise W. Knowlton. Interne St. Luke's Hosp., 1902-04; asso. in pediatrics Coll. Phys. and Surg., 1904-20, Carpentier prof. diseases of children, 1921-31, prof., 1931-39, prof. emeritus, 1939—; attending physician Children's Med. Div., Bellevue Hosp., 1909-20, dir., 1920-25; physician in chief Babies Hosp., 1925-31; cons. pediatrician Sloane Maternity, Presbyn., New Rochelle, Manhattan Eye, Ear and Throat, New York Neurological hosps. to 1940. Trustee Am. Child Health Assn.; dir. Normal Child Development Study, Babies Hosp., 1935-39, N.Y. Acad. of Medicine, 1939-46. Mem. Am. Pediatric Soc., A.M.A., N.Y. Quiz and Pathol. Assn., St. Luke's and Babies hosps. alumni socs. Republican. Conglist. Club: Century Assn. (N.Y.C.). Author: Infant and Child Feeding, 1928. Contbr. articles on child health to jours. Home: Orford, N.H. Died Feb. 1, 1955; buried Green Wood Cemetery, N.Y.C.

WILCOX, J(ames) Mark, ex-congressman; b. Willacoochee, Ga., May 21, 1890; s. Jefferson and Marion (Hinson) W.; Emory Coll., 1906-08; LL.B., Mercer U., Macon, Ga., 1910; m. Christine Helm, Nov. 25, 1914; children—James Mark, Joel Conley. Began practice at Hazelhurst, Ga., 1910; removed to Brunswick, Ga., 1919, West Palm Beach, Fla., 1925, Miami, Fla., 1938; mem. firm Hudson & Cason; served as county solicitor Jeff Davis County, Ga., 1911-18; apptd. city atty. West Palm Beach, 1928; counsel for Fla. League of Municipalities, 1930—; mem. 73d to 75th Congresses, 4th Fla. Dist. Mem. taxation com. of President Hoover's Conf. on Home Ownership, 1931. Mem. Ga., Fla. State, Dade County bar assns. Civitan award of merit for most outstanding service to his community, West Palm Beach, 1929. Pres. Everglades Nat. Park Assn. Democrat. Mason, Elk, Moose, Kiwanian. Mem. M.E. Ch. Author: Finance and Taxation Problems of Florida Municipalities, 1930; Nat. Air Frontier Defense Act, Municipal Bankruptcy Act. Home: 1710 Granada Blvd., Coral Gables, Fla. Office: Seybold Bldg., Miami, Fla. Died Feb. 2, 1956.*

WILCOX, LeRoy T., r.r. exec.; b. Chgo., May 30, 1876. Mail boy, C.R.I.&P., Chicago, 1891, later chief clerk commercial office, Kansas City; with Union Pacific-Southern Pacific R.R., as rate clerk, tariff clerk, 1902-07; traffic asst. to Interstate Commerce atty., 1907-18; traffic asst. Central Western Region, U.S. Ry. Adminstrn., World War I; with Union Pacific R.R., 1920—, as asst. to commerce counsel, 1920, asst. to freight traffic mgr., 1920-27, asst. freight traffic mgr., Omaha, 1927-40, gen. freight traffic mgr., Omaha, 1940-43, asst. v.p. in charge of traffic, Omaha, Oct. 1943—. Home: 5223 Western Av. Office: Union Pacific R.R., Omaha, Neb. Deceased.*

WILCOX, Perley S., business exec.; b. Mexico, N.Y., June 18, 1874; s. Luzern H. and Mary E. (Smith) W.; M.E., Cornell U., 1897; m. Isabelle V. Blake, July 14, 1904. Mech. draftsman Swift & Co., Chicago and St. Joseph, Mo., 1897-98; mech. engr. Eastman Kodak Co., Rochester, N.Y., 1898-1901, supt. roll coating dept., Kodak Park Works, 1901-06, asst. mgr., 1906-20; gen. mgr. Tenn. Eastman Corp., Kingsport, Tenn., 1920-33, dir. since 1920, v.p. 1921-33, pres. 1933-44, chmn. bd. dirs. since 1944; dir. Eastman Kodak Co., Rochester, N.Y., since 1935, chmn. bd. 1945-52, ret. 1952. Mem. Am. Soc. Mech. Engrs., Am. Chem. Soc., Sigma Xi. Clubs: Genesee Valley, Country (Rochester, N.Y.). Home: 1218 Linville St. Office: Tennessee Eastman Corp., Kingsport, Tenn.; also Eastman Kodak Co., Rochester, N.Y. Died May 17, 1953; buried Riverside Cemetery, Rochester, N.Y.

WILCOX, Walter Dwight, author; b. Chgo., Sept. 24, 1869; s. Sextus Newell and Sarah (Adams) W.; A.B., Yale, 1893; m. Nanna White Lawson, Nov. 27, 1901. Traveled and made scientific investigations in Canadian Rockies, Hawaiian Islands, Cuba, etc.; engaged in developing timber lands in Cuba, 1905—. Rep. of War Trade Bd., in Cuba, Feb. 1918-19. Fellow Royal Geog. Soc., 1898; sec. Am. Alpine Club, 1920—; hon. mem. Alpine Club of Can. Clubs: Metropolitan, Chevy Chase. Author: Camping in the Canadian Rockies, 1896; Picturesque Landscapes in the Canadian Rockies, 1898; The Rockies of Canada, 1900; A Guide Book to the Lake Louise Region, 1909; Caoba, the Mahogany Tree, 1924. Has written on geol. and geog. subjects in Geographical Journal of Royal Geog. Soc. Address: Chevy Chase Club, Chevy Chase, Md. Deceased.

WILDE, Percival, author, playwright; b. N.Y. City, Mar. 1, 1887; B.S., Columbia, 1906; married Nadie (Rogers) Marckres, June 30, 1920 (deceased February 9, 1952); children—Roger Marckres, Dana Brooks (deceased). Connected with banking business, 1906-11; began writing as book reviewer, New York Times, New York Post, etc.; upon publication of first story, 1912, received many requests for dramatic rights, and turned to play writing. Mem. Bd. of Edn., Sharon, Conn., 1926-29; member Associated Friends of Rutgers U. Library, New Brunswick, N.J. Mem. Authors' League America, Drama League America, New York Theatre Guild (advisory bd., 1918-19), American Dramatists (dir., sec. 1921-36), Mystery Writers of America (mem. advisory bd.), Royal Photographic Soc. of London (asso. fellow), Societé des Auteurs et Compositeurs Dramatiques; mem. editorial board, Religious Drama Guild. Member Board Sponsors, Foster Parents Plan for War Children, N.Y. City. Clubs: Authors (London); Players, Camera (New York); Committee of One Hundred (Miami Beach); Sharon Country; Nassau (Princeton). Chief machinist's mate U.S. N.R.F., Aug. 22, 1917; commissioned ensign, Oct. 14, 1918; ordered to inactive duty, Jan. 3, 1919; honorably discharged, May 10, 1921. Author: (book) The Line of No Resistance, 1913; Dawn, and Other One Act Plays of Life Today, 1915; Confessional, and Other American Plays, 1916; The Unseen Host, and Other War Plays, 1917; (books) Dawn, The Noble Lord, Playing with Fire, The Traitor, A House of Cards, The Finger of God, Confessional, The Villain in the Piece, A Question of Morality, The Beautiful Story, 1919; (plays) The Woman in Room 13 (in collaboration), prod. 1919; First Is Last (in collaboration), comedy in 3 acts, 1919; Tomorrow's Price (in collaboration), prod. 1920; The Aftermath, play in 4 acts, prod. 1921; Eight Comedies for Little Theatres, 1922; The Craftsmanship of the One-Act Play, 1923; The Inn of Discontent, and Other Fantastic Plays, 1924; The Reckoning, 1924; The Toy-Shop (children's play), 1924; Reverie (children's play), 1924; The Sequel, 1925; The Previous Engagement, 1925; The Dyspeptic Ogre, 1925; In the Net, 1925; A Wonderful Woman, 1925; Catesby, 1925; His Return, 1925; Embryo, 1925; The Enchanted Christmas Tree, 1925 (last 12 titles pub. in separate vols., but prod. on earlier dates); Kings in Nomania, 1926; Alias Santa Claus, 1927; Three-Minute Plays, 1927; The Giftie, comedy in 3 acts, prod. 1928; Rogues in Clover (stories), 1929; The Devil's Booth (novel), 1930; Ten Plays for Little Theatres, 1931; There Is a Tide (novel), 1932; (plays) In the Ravine, 1932; Lady of Dreams, 1932; The Luck-Piece, 1932; Mothers of Men, 1932; Pawns, 1932; Gadgets, 1933; The Lost Elevator, 1933; Lot's Wife, 1933; The Moving Finger, 1933; The Short Cut, 1933; Standish Pride, 1933; The Thing, 1933; What Never Dies, 1933; June Harvest (novel), 1933; The One-Act Plays of Percival Wilde, First Series, 1933; Little Shot, 1935; Comrades in Arms and Other Plays for Little Theatres, 1935; Glamour, 1937; Over the Teacups, 1937; An Affair of Dishonour, 1937; World Without End, 1937; Blood of the Martyrs (based on a Story by Stephen Vincent Benét), 1937, Mystery Week-End (novel), 1938; Ordeal by Battle (play), 1938; Inquest (novel), London, 1939; New York, 1940; Design for Murder (novel), 1941; Mr. F (play), 1941; Hocus Focus series (on photography) in Consumers' Digest, 1938-41. Editor: Contemporary One-Act Plays from Nine Countries, 1936. Editor and adaptor: The Corridors of the Soul (N. N. Evréinov), 1936; With Discretion (A. v. Orbók), 1936; Refund (Fritz Karinthy), 1936; The Next War (Hans Gross), 1936; Saul (A. Lernet-Holenia), 1936; To Kill A Man (Gabriel Timmory), 1936; Nanny (Henri Duvernois), 1937; The Silent Sex (Gabriel Timmory), 1938; Among Friends (Gabriel Timmory and Jean Manoussi), 1950; The Gossip Shop (Gabriel Timmory), 1950; Tinsley's Bones (novel), 1942; Bridge Blackouts, 1942; one-act version of Lillian Hellman's "Watch on the Rhine" for Writers' War Board, 1942; P. Moran, Operative (short stories), 1947; Racketeering in Hearing Aids, 1948; The Sportsman, 1950; The Craftsmanship of the One-Act Play (revised) 1951; The One-Act Plays of Percival Wilde, new series, London, 1953; The Miracle of Sister Ursula. Contbg. editor Minicam Photography, 1943-45. Contbr. Nat. Ency.; also photoplays. Said to have had more plays produced in American "Little Theatres" than any other author; represented in 94 collections of one-act plays or stories. Home: "Wildeacre" Sharon, Conn. Address: 225 W. 86th St., N.Y.C. Died Sept. 19, 1953.

WILDER, Laura Ingalls, author; b. Pepin, Pepin County, Wis., Feb. 7, 1867; d. Charles Philip and Caroline Lake (Quiner) Ingalls; ed. dist. schs. of Minn. and Dak. Ty.; m. Almanzo J. Wilder, Aug. 25, 1885; 1 dau., Rose (Mrs. Rose Wilder Lane). Writer on children's stories, 1932—. Author: Little House in the Big Woods, 1932; Farmer Boy, 1933; Little House on the Prairie, 1935; On the Banks of Plum Creek, 1937; By the Shores of Silver Lake, 1939; The Long Winter, 1940; Little Town on the Prairie, 1941; These Happy Golden Years, 1943. Home: Rocky Ridge Farm, Mansfield, Mo. Died Jan. 10, 1957; buried Mansfield Cemetery.

WILDER, Wilbur Elliott, army officer; b. in Mich., Aug. 16, 1856; s. Elliott S. and Sylvia (Gilkey) W.; grad. U.S. Mil. Acad., 1877; m. Violet Blair Martin, 1884; children—Throop M., Wilbur E., Sylvia, Cornelia M., Violet B. Commd. 2d lt., 4th Cav., 1877, promoted through grades to col., 1911; ret., 1920; brig. gen. by spl. act. of Congress, 1927; served as brig. gen. N.A., 1917-19; served on frontier until 1895, in many Indian campaigns and engagements. Adj. U.S. Mil. Acad., 1895-98; supt. Yellowstone Nat. Park, comdg. Ft. Yellowstone, Wyo., Mar.-June 1899; in Philippine Islands, comd. Macabebe Scouts 1899-1900 and supt. of police, Manila, 1901; comdr. 168th Inf. Brigade, Camp Taylor, Ky., 1917; in France, 1918-19. Bvtd. capt., 1890, for gallant service in action agsinst Indians, at Horse Shoe Canyon, N.M., 1882. Decorated Congl. Medal of Honor for most distinguished gallantry in action. Mem. Soc. Indian Wars, Legion of Valor. Clubs: University (N.Y.C.); Army and Navy, Army and Navy Golf and Country (Washington). Address: University Club, 1 W. 54th St., N.Y.C. Died Jan. 30, 1952

WILDMAN, Clyde Everett (wīld'măn), educator; b. Greensburg, Ind., Mar. 8, 1889; s. John William and Jean (Chapman) W.; A.B., De Pauw, 1913; S.T.B., Boston U., 1916, Ph.D., 1926; fellow United Free Ch. Coll., Glasgow, Scotland, and Basel (Switzerland) U., 1919-20; D.D., Cornell Coll., Mt. Vernon, Ia., 1927; LL.D., Northeastern U., 1937, Wabash College, 1938; S.T.D., Northwestern Univ., 1940, D.Sc. in Edn., Boston University, 1944, Litt. D., Rose

Polytechnic Institute, Terre Haute, Indiana; married Forest Kyle, June 18, 1917; 1 daughter, Sarah Jean (Mrs. John R. Long). Professor of Bible and religion, Cornell College, Mt. Vernon, Ia., 1920-24, dean, 1924-26; prof. English Bible, Syracuse U., 1926-30; prof. O.T. history and religion, Boston U. Sch. of Theology, 1930-36; pres. De Pauw U., 1936-51, pres. emeritus since 1951, vis. prof. So. Meth. U. and Garrett Bibl. Inst., 1952; vis. prof. English Bible, Dickinson Coll., Carlisle, Pa., since 1953. Pres. Ind. Assn. of Independent and Church-related Colls., 1940-41; president Nat. Assn. Meth. Colleges, Universities and Secondary Schs., 1944-45; member commn. on instns. of higher edn. North Central Assn. of Colls. and Secondary Schs. (v.p., 1949-50); mem. University Senate Methodist Ch. (vice chairman 1948-51); dir. Pennsylvania Heart Assn., 1953—; pres. Indiana Conference of Higher Edn.; member Nat. Adv. Arthritis and Metabolic Diseases Council; member Indiana Conference of Methodist Church; member Ind. War Hist. Com., chmn. Div. Social Forces; mem. Am. Assn. Univ. Profs., Phi Beta Kappa. Republican. Methodist. Author: Fifteen years at DePauw. Contbr. of arts. on religious and ednl. topics. Home: 325 W. High St., Carlisle, Pa. Died Nov. 1, 1955.

WILDS, George James, Jr., plant breeder; b. Longtown, Fairfield County, S.C., Sept. 19, 1889; s. George James and Mary Leslie (Crawford) W.; A.B., U. of S.C., 1913, LL.D., 1946; A.M., Cornell U., 1917; D.Sc., Clemson Coll., 1937; m. Ruth Lawton, June 8, 1918; 1 son, George James III. Asst. plant breeder Coker's Pedigreed Seed Co., Hartsville, S.C., 1908-11, plant breeder, 1913-15, 17-19, dir. plant breeding since 1919, pres. and mng. dir., 1938-47, pres., treas. and mng. dir. since 1947. Awarded testimonial for distinguished service to agrl. development of S.C., Clemson College, 1932; medallion Assn. Southern Agricultural Workers, for years of distinguished service in Southern agr., 1947; Man of the Year in Service to S.C. Agr., Progressive Farmer Mag., 1947; American Legion Plaque for Distinguished Service to South Carolina, 1948. Member A.A.A.S., S.C. Academy Science, American Phytopathol. Soc., S.C. Seedsmens Assn. (pres. 1947), Darlington County Agriculture Soc. (pres. 1945-47), Southern Agricultural Workers Assn., Omicron Delta Kappa, Phi Beta Kappa, Sigma Xi. Democrat. Presbyterian (elder). Mason. Club: Rotary (Hartsville). Breeder of full length, wilt-resistant short staple cottons and upland long staple cottons; breeder of smut, cold and rust resistant oats, mildew and rust resistant wheat. Home: 1210 Home Av. Office: Coker's Pedigreed Seed Company, Hartsville, S.C. Died Oct. 26, 1951; buried Hartsville.

WILDS, William Naylor, pres. Am. Crystal Sugar Co.; b. Fernandina, Fla., Dec. 28, 1879; s. Wesley Curtis and Mary Rebecca (Higginbotham) W.; m. Eoline Cassibry, Oct. 27, 1910 (died Jan. 11, 1945); 1 dau., Mary Eoline (wife of Dr. Howard Palmer Gilbert). With Am. Crystal Sugar Co. since 1908, pres. since 1934; pres., Ventura County Ry. Co. Republican. Protestant. Club: Denver. Home: Park Lane Hotel, Denver, Colo.; (winter) Grand Bay, Ala. Office: Boston Bldg., Denver. Died Nov. 20, 1951.

WILEY, Herbert V(ictor), naval officer (ret.); b. Wheeling, Mo., May 16, 1891; s. Joel Augustine and Minnie Alice (Carey) W.; B.S., U.S. Naval Acad., 1915; m. Marie F. Scroggie, Oct. 20, 1917 (dec. 1930); children—Gordon Scroggie, David Carey, Marie Elinor; m. 2d Charlotte Mayfield Weeden, Sept. 21, 1935. Commd. ensign U.S. Navy, 1915, and advanced through grades to rear adm., 1947; jr. officer, Pacific fleet, 1915-17; destroyer duty, 1917-21; instr., Dept. of Electricity, U.S. Naval Acad., 1921-23; service on lighter than air airships, Shenandoah and Los Angeles, 1923-30, battleship U.S.S. Tennessee, 1930-31, airship, Akron (only officer to survive crash of Akron), 1932-33; comdr. airship Macon, 1934-35; served on cruisers U.S.S. Cincinnati, Pensacola, and cargo transport Sirius, 1933-37; instr. English Dept., U.S. Naval Acad., 1937-39; served on U.S.S. Mississippi, 1940-41; comdr. destroyer squadron, Asiatic fleet, P.I., Java, Australia, 1941-42; head, dept. of electricity, U.S. Naval Acad., 1942-43; comdr. U.S.S. West Virginia, 1944-45, Atlantic fleet training unit, Guantanamo Bay, Cuba, 1945; ret. with rank of rear adm., Jan. 1, 1947; asst. to dean of engring., U. of Calif., 1947—. Awarded Navy Cross, 1944, Bronze Star, 1945, Navy and Marine Corps medal (for saving life of fellow officer), 1935. Mem. U.S. Naval Inst. Episcopalian. Club: Union League (San Francisco) Pioneer in airship operations, developing mooring methods, airplane hook-on and carrying, 1923-30. Home: 43 Parkside Dr., Berkeley, Cal. Died Apr. 28, 1954; buried Golden Gate Nat. Cemetery, San Bruno, Cal.

WILEY, Robert Hopkins, newspaper editor; b. Gridley, Illinois, May 31, 1886; son Reverend William Richard and Gertrude Margaret (Green) Wiley; student of Augustana College, Rock Island, Illinois, 1905; m. Harriett Abernathy, Feb. 26, 1920 (dec. 1950). Sports editor, Rock Island Argus, 1906; legislative correspondent Houston Post, 1907; editorial staff, Davenport Times, 1908-09; editor, San Angelo Standard, 1910; editorial staff, Ft. Worth Star-Telegram, 1911-12, St. Louis Republic, 1912-13; news editor, Chicago Evening American, 1916-27; news editor, New York Evening Journal, 1927-37; managing editor New York Journal-American, 1937-45; exec. editor Chicago Herald-American 1945-47, supervising editor Pittsburgh Sun-Telegraph and Detroit Times 1947-49; editor of the Pittsburgh Sun-Telegraph, 1949-51. Served with Artillery Officers Training Corps, Camp Zachary Taylor, 1918. Republican. Methodist. Mason. Mem. American Legion. Home: Hotel Schenley, Pitts. Died Jan. 30, 1952; buried Oakwood Cemetery, Macomb, Ill.

WILEY, William Ogden, publisher; b. East Orange, N.J., Dec. 27, 1862; s. Charles and Julia (Halsted) W.; student New York U., 1878-80; A.B., Columbia, 1882, A.M., 1887; m. Kate Root Quimby, Apr. 26, 1897; children—Cynthia (Mrs. Hamilton D. Darby), Julia Halsted (Mrs. John Porter Gilbert). Engaged in business as clerk in commission dry goods, 1882-90; with John Wiley & Sons, Inc., publishers, 1890—, president, 1925-41, chmn. of bd., 1941-56; ret. Awarded Alumni medal, Columbia U., 1933. Trustee Bridgehampton, Public Library, L.I., N.Y. Mem. Soc. Engring. Edn. (treas. 1907-42: now hon. mem.), Theta Xi. Clubs: Columbia University, Engineers (N.Y.). Home: 1192 Park Av., N.Y.C. 28. Office: 440 4th Av., N.Y.C. 16. Died Jan. 15, 1958.

WILKER, Arthur V(ictor), business exec.; born Berea, O., Mar. 11, 1888; s. Victor and Caroline C. (Schultz) W.; B.S., Baldwin Wallace Coll., Berea, 1906, M.S., 1907, Sc.D., 1949; B.S., Case Inst. Tech., 1909, D.Eng., 1948; H.H.D., Willamette Coll., 1954; L.L.D., Evansville Coll., Texas Christian U., m. Mabel McKelvey, Nov. 9, 1912; children—Thomas Arthur, Edith Carolyn (Mrs. Richard B. Korsmeyer). Prof. of chemistry, Moores Hill (Ind.) Coll., 1909-10; research Assoc. Natural Carbon Co., Cleveland, 1910-13; prof. of chemistry, Baldwin-Wallace Coll., 1913-17; asst. supt., Nat. Carbon Co., Inc., 1918, supt., 1919, gen. supt., 1923, works mgr., 1927, v.p., 1932, pres., 1944-50; v.p. Union Carbide & Carbon Corp., N.Y.C., 1944-53, now ret.; dir., trustee Union Carbide Ednl. Fund; industrial adviser, spl. projects, Bur. of Ordnance, Dept. of Navy, 1951. Trustee Baldwin-Wallace Coll. Mem. Sigma Xi, Lambda Chi Alpha, Alpha Chi Sigma. Clubs: Chemists, Uptown, Cloud (N.Y. City); Golf (Scarsdale, N.Y.). Hybridizes flowers (gladiolus). Home: Ten Kensington Rd., Scarsdale, N.Y. Office: 30 E. 42d St., N.Y. City. Died Feb. 7, 1960.

WILKERSON, Marcus Manley, publisher, journalist; b. Boyce, Rapides Parish, La., Jan. 10, 1896; s. Columbus F. and Martha Jane (Cudd) W.; A.B., La. State U., 1924, A.M., 1926; Ph.D., U. of Wis., 1931; m. Helen Crowell, Sept. 14, 1922. Instr. journalism La. State U., 1924-26, asst. prof. advancing to prof., 1926—, dir. univ. press, 1935—; vis. prof. U. Tex., 1941-42; legislative corr. New Orleans State and Shreveport Times, 1926; Asso. Press, 1928-30, editor La. Leader, 1933-42; asso. editor Journalism Quarterly, 1938—. Mem. book pub. and mfg. industry advisory com. W.P.B., 1942-43. Member research council in charge monographs Am. Assn. Schs. and Depts. Journalism, 1938—; mem. Am. Legion, Am. Assn. U. Profs., Am. Assn. U. Presses, Am. Assn. of Teachers of Journalism (pres. 1947), S.A.R., Sigma Delta Chi, Phi Kappa Phi, Sigma Chi. Democrat. Presbyterian. Clubs: Faculty, Baton Rouge Rotary. Author: Public Opinion and the Spanish-American War: A Study in War Propaganda (La. State U. Press), 1932; Thomas Duckett Boyd: The Story of a Southern Educator, 1935. Address: 2330 Kleinert Av., Baton Rouge. Died Mar. 14, 1953; buried Roselawn Meml. Cemetery.

WILKES, John, ret. naval officer; b. May 26, 1895; entered USN, 1912, grad. U.S. Naval Acad., Annapolis, 1916; m. Winifred Jarvis; 1 son, John. Advanced through grades to rear adm., 1943; stationed in Pacific at outbreak of World War II, escaped from Corregidor aboard submarine Swordfish, then reassembled U.S. underseas forces from base in Java; retired 1951. Decorated D.S.M., Legion of Merit. Address: Navy Dept., Washington 25. Died July 20, 1957; buried Arlington Nat. Cemetery.*

WILKIE, Harold McLean (wĭl'kē), lawyer; b. Fond du Lac, Wis., Oct. 28, 1890; s. James A. and Annie (Lange) W.; A.B., Ripon (Wis.) Coll., 1910; LL.B., U. Wis., 1913; m. Vivian Marie Jones, June 18, 1913; children—Edwin M., James M., Horace W., John A., Mary Isabelle, Harold W., Vivian R. Admitted to Wis. bar, 1913, practiced in Milw., 1913-17; mem. Doe, Ballhorn & Wilkie, later Doe, Ballhorn, Wilkie & Doe, 1914-17; mem. Richmond, Jackman, Wilkie & Toebaas, Madison, Wis., 1917-39; sr. mem. Wilkie, Toebaas, Hart, Kraege and Jackman, 1939—; mem. faculty law sch. U Wis., 1915-19; spl. counsel for State of Wis. in various matters, 1928—; state counsel Wis. Mutual Ins. Alliance; gen. counsel, mem. bd. Northern Paper Mills, Green Bay, Wis. Mem. bd. regents U. Wis., 1931-39, pres., 1934-39; former chmn. Council of Boy Scouts, Madison. Recipient Silver Beaver. Mem. Am., Wis. bar assns., Am. Law Inst., Am. Acad. Polit. and Social Sci., Am. Judicature Soc., Order of the Coif, Phi Delta Phi. Conglist. Mason (32°, Shriner), Elk. Club: Madison. Contbr. to Norton's Handbook of the Law on Bills and Notes, 4th edition, 1914. Author: Winslow's Forms of Pleading and Practice, 3d edit., 1934. Home: 126 Forest St., Madison 5. Office: 111 S. Hamilton St., Madison 3, Wis. Died May 4, 1950.

WILKINS, Horace M., banker; b. Brenham, Tex., Jan. 9, 1885; s. W. G. and Eunice W.; student A. and M. Coll.; LL.D. (hon.), Baylor U.; m. Mary Wallace, May 14, 1914. Exec. v.p. First Nat. Bank in Houston, now retired, dir. since 1946. Trustee Anderson Found., Houston, Tex. Med. Center. Democrat. Episcopalian. Mason. Clubs: Houston, River Oaks Country. Home: 912 Kipling St. Office: 201 Main St., Houston. Died Sept. 13, 1953.

WILKINS, Sir Hubert, explorer, scientist, lecturer; b. South Australia, Oct. 31, 1888; s. Harry and Louisa (Smith) W.; ed. Australian State Sch. and Adelaide (S. Australia) Sch. of Mines and Industries; m. Suzanne Bennett, Aug. 1929. Employed as elec. engr. and meteorologist; cine photographer and theater manager, 8 years; second-in-command Stefansson's Canadian Arctic Expdn., 1914-17; navigator England Australia flight, 1919; second-in-command British Imperial Antarctic Expedition, 1919-20; naturalist Shackleton "Quest Expdn.," 1921-22; comdr. Australian Islands Expdn., 1922-25; comdr. Detroit Arctic Expdns., 1925-28, making 1st trans-arctic flight by airplane; comdr. Wilkins Hearst Expdns. to Antarctic, making pioneer flight in Antarctica, discovering 5 new islands, more than 500 miles of coast line and several large glaciers, 1928-30, Nautilus submarine expdn. to Arctic, making pioneer submarine trip under Arctic ice, 1931; mgr. Ellsworth expdns., Antarctica, 1932-39; comdr. Soviet search expdn. for Levanevsky, covering 170,000 sq. miles never before seen by man, 1937-38. Consultant to Mil. Planning Div., U.S. Army, 1942-54, cons. to U.S. Army Q.M. Research and Engring. Command, 1954-57, USN Office Sci. Research, 1946-47, Weather Bur., 1946-48. Councilor Arctic Institute of N.A., 1947. Served as capt., Australian Flying Corps, 1917-19; overseas in Aleutians, also service with Office Strategic Services, World War II. Created Knight Bachelor, 1928. Decorated Order St. Maurice and St. Lazarus (Italy); Mil. Cross with bar; numerous citations; recipient Founders Medal Royal Geog. Soc., Finley-Breeze-Morse medal Am. Geog. Soc., also gold medals from foreign geog. socs. and aero. socs. of France, Norway, Denmark, International League of Aviators; Explorers Club medals; 16 honor medals from various socs. Mem. Royal Meteorol. Soc., Royal Geog. Soc., Am. Meteorol. Soc., Geophys. Union, Ornithologists Union, A.A.A.S. Clubs: Explorers, Adventurers, Circumnavigators, Royal Socs., City (N.Y.). Author: Undiscovered Australia, 1925; Flying the Arctic, 1928; Under the North Pole, 1931; (with Harold M. Sherman) Thoughts Through Space, 1942. Contbr. to scientific jours., mags. and newspapers. Lecturer McGill Summer Sch. of Geography, 1947-48, Nat. Defense Coll., Can., 1948-50. Home: Walhalla, R.D. 4, Montrose, Pa. Office: 37 W. 53d St., N.Y.C. 19. Died Dec. 1, 1958.

WILKINS, J. Ernest, former asst. sec. labor; b. Farmington, Mo., Feb. 1, 1894; s. Henry and Susie Olivia (Douthit) W.; A.B. with spl. honors in mathematics, U. Ill., 1918; J.D., U. Chgo., 1921; LL.D., Lincoln U., 1941, Southwestern Coll., 1957, Ohio Wesleyan U., 1958; m. Lucile Robinson, November 23, 1922; children—J. Ernest, John Robinson, Julian Byrd. Admitted to Ill. bar, 1921, practiced in Chgo., 1921-54; vice chmn. President Com. on Government Contracts, 1953; asst. sec. of labor, 1954-58; mem. bd. fgn. service, Dept. of State; Pres'. Com. on Govt. Employment Policy; U.S. Rep. on Governing Body of ILO, 1954-57; U.S. del. and head of delegation to ILO Confs., 1954-57. Trustee Provident Hosp. Chgo., Dillard U., Wesley Theol. Sem. Dir. Am. Council on Human Rights, 1948-54; member of the Civil Rights Commission, 1957—. Mem. Ill., Chgo., Cook Co., (pres. 1941-42), Am., Nat. bar assns., Am. Judicature Soc., U. Chgo., Alumni Assn., Phi Beta Kappa, Kappa Alpha Psi (grand keeper records and exchequer, 1922-47; grand polemarch, 1947-50), Sigma Pi Phi. Republican. Meth. (mem. commn. on world service and finance, 1942-48; exec. com. gen. commn. on world service and finance, 1944-48; judicial council, 1948—); conf. lay leader, Lexington Conf., 1942-48; sec. judicial council 1953-56, pres., 1956; del. gen. conf. Meth. ch. 1948, Central Jurisdictional Conf., 1940, 44, 48; mem. exec. com. Meth. World Council). Mason, K.P. Clubs: City, Illini (Chgo.). Home: 4708 Blagden Terrace N.W., Washington 11. Died Jan. 19, 1959; buried Lincoln Cemetery, Chgo.

WILKINS, John A., physician; b. New York, May 1, 1843; s. Archibald and Mary (Robinson) W.; ed. Denison Univ.; grad. Starling Med. Coll., Columbus, O.; m. Ruth Rebecca Shull, May 12, 1873. Served in Ohio Vols., U.S.A., 1861-65; was State senator in Ohio 1880-81; med. dir. Dept. Ohio, G.A.R., 1897; surgeon-gen. G.A.R., 1900; mem. Am. Med. Assn., Ohio State Med. Soc.; Gold Democrat. Address: Delta, Ohio. Deceased.

WILKINS, Vaughan (vôrn wilkins), author; b. London, Eng., Mar. 6, 1890; s. Rev. William Henry and Lena Charlotte (Law) W.; student Merchant Taylors Sch., 1900-07; m. Mary Isabel Powell, Feb. 27, 1930; children—William, Christopher. Fgn. editor London Standard, 1914; editor Daily Call, 1915; spl. writer Pall Mall Gazette, 1920; asst. editor Daily Express, 1929-33, Sunday Referee, 1933-34, News Chronicle, 1934. Served as lt. Royal Army Service Corps, Egypt, Palestine, France, 1915-19; billeting officer Nat. Def., Eng., intelligence officer Welch Regt. (Home Guard), World War II. Author: Industrial Evolution, 1925; And So—Victoria, 1937; Endless Prelude, 1938; Seven Tempest, 1942; Being Met Together, 1944; After Bath, 1945; Once Upon a Time, 1949; The City of Frozen Fire, 1951; Crown Without Sceptre, 1952; A King Reluctant, 1953; Fanfare for a Witch, 1954; Valley Beyond Time, 1955; Lady of Paris, 1957. Home: The Instead, Pencraig, Ross-on-Wye, Herefordshire, Eng. Died Feb. 8, 1959.

WILKINS, William James, ry. exec.; b. Roanoke, Va., Oct. 22, 1898; s. Oscar Perry and Eleanor Caroline (Lusk) W.; ed. pub. schs. of Roanoke; prep. edn., Washington; m. Emma Franklin, Dec. 11, 1920; 1 dau., Emily Ann (Mrs. Thomas Boyd Mason). Spl. schooling traffic dept., Southern Ry. System, Washington; freight traffic rep., N.Y. City, 1927-33, dist. freight and passenger agt., 1933-36; div. freight and passenger agt., St. Louis, 1936-39, asst. freight traffic mgr., Memphis, 1939-40, Eastern traffic mgr., N.Y. City, 1940-43, Western traffic mgr., St. Louis, 1943-45, freight traffic mgr., Cincinnati, 1945-49, v.p.-resident exec. officer since 1949; v.p. and dir. Cincinnati, New Orleans & Texas Pacific Ry. Co.; pres. and dir. Cincinnati Union Terminal Co.; dir. Ky. and Ind. Terminal R.R. Co. (Louisville), Cincinnati, Burnside & Cumberland River Ry. Co. (Cincinnati), Central Transfer Ry. & Storage Co. (Louisville). Mem. Newcomen Soc., Cincinnati and Ky. c.'s of c. Clubs: Associated Traffic of America, Cincinnati Traffic, Queen City (Cincinnati). Home: 2372 Madison Rd., Cincinnati 8. Office: Transportation Bldg., 307 E. 4th St., Cin. 2. Died Dec. 30, 1950.*

WILKINSON, Charles Fore, Jr., educator, physician; b. College Park, Ga., Mar. 30, 1912; s. Charles Fore and Martha Inez (Hardin) W.; B.S., Ga. Sch. Tech., 1932; grad. study U. N.C., 1932-33; M.D., Emory U., 1937; m. Frances Elizabeth Wallace, Apr. 22, 1939; children—Charles Fore, Martha Wallace, Robert Gage. Intern dept. internal medicine U. Mich. Hosp., 1937-38, asst. resident, 1938-39, resident, instr., Upjohn fellow clin. investigation, 1939-40; asst. prof. internal medicine, coordinator grad. med. edn. U. Mich., 1946-49; civilian cons. internal medicine Percy Jones Gen. Hosp., Battle Creek, Mich., 1946-49; asso. dir. div. medicine W. K. Kellogg Found., Battle Creek, 1948-49; prof., chmn. department of medicine, post-grad. med. sch. N.Y.U., N.Y. City, since 1949; vis. physician, dir. 4th Med. N.Y.U. div. Bellevue Hosp., med. service U. Hosp., 1949-—; cons. in internal medicine, Manhattan V.A. Hospital. Served as 1st lt. to col. with M.C., A.U.S., 1940-46. Diplomate Am. Bd. Internal Medicine. Fellow N.Y. Acad. Medicine, A.A.A.S., A.C.P.; mem. Harvey Soc., Am. Fedn. Clin. Research, Am. Genetic Assn., N.Y. Medico-Surgical Society, American Therapeutic Soc., Society for Experimental Biology and Medicine, American Society of Human Genetics, Am. Soc. Study of Arteriosclerosis, Am., N.Y. heart assns., Soc. Biol. Research, Sigma Xi. Author tech. and sci. articles med. jours. Home: 24 Ellery Lane, Westport, Conn. Office: New York University Post-Graduate Medical School, 550 First Av., N.Y.C. Died Sept. 29, 1959.

WILKINSON, Ford L(ee), Jr., coll. pres.; b. Elkton, Ky., Aug. 15, 1895; s. Ford and Sue (Russell) W.; prep. dept., Ga. Sch. Tech., 1911-12; U. of Ga., 1912-13; grad. U.S. Naval Acad., 1917, post-grad. course, 1923-24; M.S., Columbia U., 1925; D.Eng., U. of Louisville, 1947; m. Lois Smyer, October 27, 1927; 1 dau., Walta. Ensign, 1917; convoy and transport duty, 1917-18; U.S.S. Delaware, 1918-21; Submarine Service, 1921-27; sales engr. Wilson, Weesner, Wilkinson Co., Nashville, 1927-28; chief engr. bur. smoke regulation, Knoxville, 1928-30; with Riley Stoker Corp., Worcester, Mass., 1930-33; asst. prof., mech. engring., U. of Tenn., 1933-34, asso. prof., 1934-35, head dept., 1935-38; dean, Speed Scientific Sch. U. of Louisville, 1938-47; pres. Univ. of Louisville Inst. of Indsl. Research, 1944-47; academic dean U.S. Naval Postgraduate Sch., 1947-49; pres. Rose Polytech. Inst., Terre Haute, Ind., 1949-—. Mem. Am. Soc. Mech. Engrs., v.p. 1943-45; Am. Soc. for Engring. Edn. (mem. council, 1943-46); Acad. Polit. Science, Tau Beta Pi, Phi Kappa Phi, Sigma Tau. Methodist. Clubs: Columbia (Indpls.), Country (Terre Haute). Address: 335 Robinwood Rd., Terre Haute, Ind. Died Sept. 1, 1958; buried Elmwood Cemetery, Birmingham, Ala.

WILKINSON, George Lawrence, patent lawyer; b. Washington, D.C., Sept. 9, 1868; s. A. George and Lue Burnam (Wilson) W.; B.S., Columbian (now George Washington) U., 1888, LL.B., 1891, LL.M., 1892; m. Adele Enloe, Oct. 30, 1895; children—Frances Ashworth (Mme. Augusto Rosso), Lawrence, Lucian, Enloe. Examiner in U.S. Patent Office, 1889-1901, law clk. 1901; registrar of Columbian Univ., 1888-89; patent atty., Chicago, 1901-—; mem. Chamberlin & Wilkinson, 1902-07, Sheridan & Wilkinson, 1907-09, Sheridan, Wilkinson & Scott, 1909-16, Wilkinson & Huxley, 1917-20, Wilkinson, Huxley, Byron & Knight, 1920-—. Mem. Am. and Chicago bar assns., Am. and Chicago patent law assns., Phi Kappa Psi, Phi Delta Phi. Baptist. Clubs: University, Glenview (Chicago); Cosmos (Washington, D.C.). Home: 1027 Greenwood Av., Evanston, Ill. Office: First Nat. Bank Bldg., Chgo. Died Oct. 26, 1958.

WILKINSON, Ignatius Martin, dean law school; b. New York, N.Y., Jan. 6, 1887; s. Peter A. and Elizabeth (Martin) W.; B.A., Coll. of St. Francis Xavier, New York, 1908; LL.B., summa cum laude, Fordham, 1911, M.A., 1913, LL.D., 1924; Doctor of Laws, St. John's Univ., 1949; m. Agnes McGivney, 1914 (died February 16, 1944). Admitted to New York bar, 1910; member of the law firm King and Wilkinson, New York City, 1913-31; lecturer in law, Fordham U. Sch. of Law, 1912-15, asso. prof. law, 1915-19, prof. law since 1919, dean Fordham U. Sch. of Law since 1923, on leave of absence, July 1943-Jan. 1946. Chmn. spl. com. apptd. by Mayor La Guardia to study labor relations on transit system of the City of N.Y., Jan. 1943-Apr. 1943; corp. counsel of City of N.Y. by appointment of Mayor La Guardia, June 1943-Dec. 30, 1945. Mem. Am. Bar Assn., N.Y. State Bar Assn., Assn. Bar City of N.Y., N.Y. County Lawyers Assn. (pres. 1944-46), Coll. of St. Francis Xavier Alumni Assn., Fordham U. Alumni Assn. Democrat. Roman Catholic. Clubs: University, Catholic. Home: 1001 Park Avenue. Office: 302 Broadway, N.Y.C. Died June 22, 1953; buried Gate of Heaven Cemetery, N.Y.

WILKINSON, Joseph A., farmer, mayor; b. Autaugaville, Ala., Oct. 23, 1851; s. Joseph Brady and Elizabeth Ann (Nicholson) W.; student Emory and Henry Coll., Va., 1869-70; m. Rebecca Howard, Dec. 23, 1897. Merchant at Autaugaville, 1876-90; farmer, 1890-—. Mem. Ala. Ho. of Rep., 1903; state commr. of agr., 1907-10; mayor of Autaugaville, 1914-—. Mem. Gen. Conf. M.E. Ch. S., 1906; pres. Autauga Co. Sunday Sch. Assn., 15 yrs.; pres. Autaugaville Agrl. Club. Democrat. Address: Autaugaville, Alabama. Died Jan. 1930.

WILKINSON, Robert Johnson, surgeon; b. Campbell County, Va., July 12, 1888; s. Beverly Jasper and Sarah Jane (Traylor) W.; prep. edn. Mary Agnes Inst., Brookneal, Va.; under private tutors and in public schs.; M.D., Med. Coll. of Va., 1912; m. Elizabeth Lewis Richmond, Apr. 6, 1916; children—Robert J., Elizabeth Traylor (Mrs. Howard Ross Crews), Walter Richmond. Telegraph operator Southern Railway Company, 1904-07; owner of general merchandise business, Lynch Station, Virginia, 1907-08; Interne Memorial Hospital, Richmond, 1912-13; asso. in gen. surgery with Dr. C. C. Coleman, Richmond, Va., 1913-15; surgeon in charge C.&O. Ry. Employees Hosp. Huntington, W.Va., 1915-—; sr. surgeon Wilkinson Surgical Clinic, Huntington on surgical staff St. Mary's Hospital; assistant chief surgeon C.&O. Railway Employees Hospital Assn., sr. partner Wilkinson and Asso., clinic and hosp. cons. Trustee Huntington Clin. Found., Inc.; trustee and chmn. board Wilkinson Clinic Foundation, Inc. Served in 1st Vt. Med. Corps, U.S. Army World War. Fellow Am. Coll. Surgeons, Internat. Coll. Surgeons; hon. fellow American College Clinic Adminstrs.; member World Medical Association (dir.), A.M.A., Southern Medical Association (pres. 1952), W.Va. State Med. Assn. (pres. 1942-43), Cabell County Med. Soc. (ex-pres.), C.&O. Ry. Surgeons (ex-pres.), W. Va. Hosp Assn. (dir.). Democrat. Presbyterian. Mason (32°, Shriner), Elk. Clubs: Guyandotte, Guyan Country. Contbr. articles on surg. diseases and treatment to W.Va. State Med. Jour., Southern Med. Jour., Southern Surgeon. Office: Wilkinson Clinic, 1119 6th Av., Huntington, W.Va. Died Sept. 14, 1953.

WILKINSON, William John, educator; b. North Stamford, Conn., Nov. 29, 1874; s. Robert Henry and Caroline (Miller) W.; B.Litt., William and Mary Coll., 1902; grad. work, Princeton, 1905-06; M.A., Columbia, 1908, Ph.D., 1924; LL.D., Washington College, 1920; hon. M.A., Wesleyan U. Conn., 1923; hon. L.H.D., Colby College, 1945; m. Mary Doak Bradshaw, June 12, 1912. Instr. Latin and Greek, William and Mary College, 1902-03; dean Washington College, 1909-18; lectr. history, Wesleyan U., 1919-23; prof. history Colby, 1924-28, U. Vt., 1928-29; prof. history, Colby, 1929-1945, now emeritus. Y.M.C.A. ednl. dir. Camp Hancock, 1918; with Army Ednl. Corps, Beaune, France, 1918-19. Mem. council Nat. Economic League; chmn. Waterville World Court Com.; chmn. Nat. Youth Adminstrn. Coll. Work Council of Me. and mem. regional com. Nat. Youth Adminstrn. Mem. Am. Hist. Assn., Am. Political Science Assn., N.E. Hist. Assn., Foreign Policy Assn., Kappa Sigma, Phi Beta Kappa. Democrat. Conglist. Author: Tory Democracy, 1925. Compiler: A Guide to Historical Literature, 1931. Lecturer on internat. affairs, European problems, etc. Sponsor Good Neighbor League, Humanity Guild, Jewish Peoples Com. for United Action Against Fascism and Anti-Semitism. Home: 405 E. Unaka Av. Johnson City, Tenn. Died Apr. 7, 1950; buried Salem Presbyn. Ch., Washington Coll., Tenn.

WILL, Arthur Percival, lawyer; b. Walter's Falls, Ont., Can., Jan. 11, 1868; s. Rev. Phineas Drake and Caroline Annie (Collins) W.; ed. collegiate insts., Brantford, Ont., and Toronto; LL.B., U. Mich., 1891, LL.M., 1892; m. Flora Maude Quigley, 1895; children—Arthur Joseph, Percival Drake. Admitted to Mich. bar, 1891, later, N.Y., and Cal. bars. Lectr. law dept. U. Minn., 1895, 96; removed to N.Y.C., 1901; associated with W. D. Guthrie and Paul D. Cravath, 1904-07, with J. C. McReynolds, 1908-09, in prosecution of cases brought by U.S. under anti-trust law; asst. gen. counsel N.Y. Life Ins. Co., 1909; editor-in-chief Standard Ency. of Procedure, 1910-13; law lectr. U. So. Cal., 1910-14. Chmn. exec. com. Prog. Party, Los Angeles County, 1912-13, appointed by Gov. Hirma W. Johnson to be first chief Cal. Legislative Counsel Bur., 1914-20; fed. dir. Cal. U.S. Pub. Service Res. during World War; sec. legislative com. to investigate edn., 1919-20; referee Superior Court, 1920-33. Pres. Altadena Citizens Assn., 1927. Chmn. legislative clearing house com. of Cal. State Bar, 1930-31; cons. Cal. Legislative Counsel Bur., 1935, 37, 39, 41, 43, Los Angeles rep., 1943-44. Editor: Cooley's Elements of Torts, 1895; Circumstantial Evidence, 1896; Will's Gould on Pleading, 1909. Home: Altadena, Cal. Died Aug. 26, 1950.

WILLARD, DeForest P., orthopedic surgeon; b. Phila., Feb. 20, 1884; s. Dr. DeForest and Elizabeth (Porter) W.; B.S., U. of Pa., 1905; M.D., 1908; m. Margaretta Miller, Dec. 11, 1926. Asst., orthopedic service, Univ. Hosp., also Orthopedic Hosp., Phila., 1910-17; orthopedic surgeon, Graduate, Bryn Mawr and Abington hosps., 1920-47; cons. in orthopedics, Pa., Babies and Chestnut Hill hosps.; vice dean orthopedics Grad. Med. Sch., U. of Pa., 1920-47, prof. orthopedics 1926-47, emeritus. Commd. 1st lt., M.C., U.S. Army, 1917-19; with A.E.F., France and England; dicsh. with rank lt. col., Army Res. Corps, 1935. Mem. Am. Orthopedic Assn. (sec. 1912-33; pres. 1935), Am. Surg. Assn., Am. Acad. Orthopedic Surgeons, Internat. Orthopedic Assn., A.M.A., Phila. Acad. Surgery, Phila. Coll. Physicians, Delta Psi. Clubs: Philadelphia, University (Phila.); Gulph Mills Golf. Contbr. numerous articles to med. jours. Home: "Redleaf," 514 Lancaster Av., Wynnewood, Pa. Office: 1726 Spruce St., Phila. 3. Died Dec. 1957.

WILLARD, Frank H., comic artist; b. Anna, Ill., Sept. 21, 1893; s. Francis William and Laura (Kirkham) W.; ed. Union Acad. of Southern Illinois, Ill. Acad. of Fine Arts, Chicago, 1913; m. 3d, Marie O'Connell, Jan. 7, 1933; children by former marriage—Priscilla Alden, Frank Henry, Jr. Cartoonist Chicago Herald, 1914-18; enlisted in U.S. Army, Oct. 3, 1917; with Hdqrs. Co., 343th Inf., 86th Div.; transferred to Co. A, 3111th Engrs., same div., May 1918; served with A.E.F. Sept. 21, 1918 to July 2, 1919; with King Features Syndicate, 1920-23; joined Chicago Tribune-N.Y. News Syndicate, June 19, 1923. Creator "Moon Mullins," "Kitty Higgins." Member Artists and Writers Golf Assn.; National Cartoonist Soc., The Willard Family Assn., Soc. Illustrators. Presbyn. Club: Wilshire Country. Home: 308 N. Sycamore, Los Angeles 36. Address: Chicago Tribune, Chgo., Chicago Tribune-N.Y. News Syndicate, 220 E. 42d St., N.Y.C. Died Jan. 11, 1958; buried Anna, Ill.

WILLARD, Julius Terrass, chemist; b. nr. Wabaunsee, Kans., Apr. 9, 1862; s. Julius F. and Mary E. (Terrass) W.; B.S., Kan. State Coll. Agr. and Applied Science, 1883, M.S., 1886, D.Sc., 1908; Johns Hopkins, 1887-88; m. Lydia P. Gardiner, Aug. 6, 1884; 1 son, Charles Julius. Asst. in chemistry, Kan. State Coll. Agr. and Applied Science, 1883-87, asst. prof., 1891-96, asso. prof., 1896-97, prof. applied chemistry, 1897-1901, prof. chemistry, 1901-18, dean div. gen. science, 1909-39, v.p., 1918-36, college historian since 1936; asst. chemist Agrl. Expt. Sta., 1888-97, chemist, 1897-1918, dir., 1900-06, vice-dir., 1907-18. Fellow A.A.A.S.; mem. Am. Chem. Soc., Kan. Acad. Science, Nat. Edn. Assn., Kan. State Teachers Assn., Sigma Xi, Phi Kappa Phi, Alpha Zeta, Gamma Sigma Delta, Phi Lambda Upsilon, Acaci. Mason (32°). Republican. Rotarian. Author: Organic Compounds of Every-day Life, 1894; History of the Kansas State College of Agriculture and Applied Science, 1940; also numerous Expt. Sta. publs. and hist. articles. Home: 1207 Houston St. Address: Kansas State College, Manhattan, Kan. Died July 26, 1950; buried Sunset Cemetery, Manhattan.

WILLARD, Leigh, business exec.; b. New Berlin, N.Y., Feb. 14, 1880; s. Marcus Salanes and Emma Estelle (Allendorf) W.; student Providence Manual Training High Sch., 1894-97; D. Engring. (hon.), Mich. Coll. of Mines and Tech.; m. Ellen Petronella Froberg, Nov. 1, 1905; children—Karine Annette (Mrs. Colyer Garre), Ellen Estelle (Mrs. Robert Lockwood). Began as draftsman, 1897; chief engr. W. J. Rainey, 1911-18, gen. supt., 1918-22, industrial engr., 1922-27; pres. Semet-Solvay Co. since 1927, dir, mem. exec. com. since 1942, pres., dir. Interlake Chem. Corp., Interlake Iron Corp.; v.p., dir. Dalton Ore Co., Black Mountain Coal Co.; Chicago Short Line R.R., Allis-Chalmers Mfr. Co. Fire commr., Village of Pelham, N.Y., 5 yrs.; trustee of village, 3 yrs. Mem. Am. Soc. M.E., Am. Iron and Steel Inst. (dir.). Am. By-Product Coke Institute (pres., dir.). Clubs: Union (Cleveland); Chicago (Ill.); Union League (N.Y.C.); Detroit (Mich.); Duquesne (Pitts.); Kitchi Gammi (Duluth, Minn.). Office: Union Commerce Bldg., Cleve. Died Dec. 5, 1951.

WILLCOX, Mary Alice, zoölogist; b. Kennebunk, Me., Apr. 24, 1856; d. William Henry (D.D., LL.D.) and Annie Holmes (Goodenow) Willcox; student State Normal Sch., Salem, Mass., 1875; student Mass. Inst. Tech., and Boston Soc. of Natural History, 1878-80, Newnham Coll., Eng., 1880-83; Ph.D., U. of Zürich, 1898. Teacher Frederick (Md.) Female Sem., 1875-76, Charlestown High Sch., Boston, 1876-78; prof. zoölogy, Wellesley Coll., 1883-1910, prof. emeritus, 1910. Mem. Boston Soc. Natural History, Sigma Xi, Mass. Audubon Soc., National Assn. Audubon Societies. Author: Pocket Guide to Common Land-Birds of New England, 1895; also various papers on zoöl. subjects. Chmn. sub-com. on Americanization, Mass. Federation of Women's Clubs, 1914-19; dir. Newton League of Women Voters, 1940—; chmn. com. on interracial relations, 20th Century Assn., Boston, 1940-45. Home: Pocasset, Mass. Deceased.

WILLFORD, Albert Clinton, ex-congressman; b. Vinton, Ia., Sept. 21, 1877; s. Samuel and Rebecka (Henkle) W.; student Vinton High Sch.; student, Tilford Acad., Vinton, 1892-94; m. Edna Tharp, Sept. 15, 1898; children—Charlott (dec.), Berl Clinton. Chief engr. Electric Light, Power & Water Co., Vinton, 1900-07; organizer, 1907, Artificial Ice Co., Waterloo, supt., 1907-10; owner and mgr. Willford Seed and Feed Co. 1910—. Mem. 73d Congress, 3d Ia. Dist. Pres. Ia. dist. Izaak Walton League, 1927-29; mem. Court of Honor, Boy Scouts of Am., 1917-33. Democrat. Mason (32°, pres. Consistory Club of Waterloo). Home: Waterloo, Ia. Deceased.

WILLGING, Joseph C. (wil'ging), bishop; b. Dubuque, Ia., Sept. 6, 1884; s. Henry Philip and Elizabeth (Hanover) W.; A.B., Loras Acad. and Coll., Dubuque, Ia., 1905, LL.D., 1913; S.T.B., St. Mary's U., Baltimore, Md., 1908; student Catholic U. of America, 1908-12, U. of Chicago, 1913. Ordained priest of Roman Catholic Ch., 1908; prin., St. Aloysius Inst., Helena, Mont., 1909; treas. and instr., Carroll Coll., Helena, 1910-14; sec. to bishop of Helena, and chancellor Diocese of Helena, 1914-27; pastor, Immaculate Conception Parish, Butte, Mont., 1927-41; apptd. vicar general Diocese of Helena, 1939; created papal chamberlain by Pope Benedict XV, 1921, domestic prelate by Pope Pius XII, Dec. 6, 1939; elected first Bishop of Pueblo by Pope Pius XII, 1941; consecrated bishop, Feb. 24, 1942, installed, Mar. 12, 1942. Home: 325 W. 15th St., Pueblo, Colo. Died Mar. 3, 1959.

WILLIAMS, Albert Frank, lawyer; b. Appleton City, Mo., July 18, 1876; s. Luke Allen and Jennie Jane (Wylie) W.; grad. high sch., Lamar, Mo., 1894; m. Kate Weisenbarker, Dec. 18, 1904; children—Margaret A. (dec.), June C. Admitted to bar, 1897; practiced, Columbus, Kan. Pres. Al. F. Williams Drug Corp. Co. atty. Cherokee Co., Kan., 1903-07; U.S. dist. atty. for Kan., by apptmt. of Pres. Harding, 1921, reapptd. by Pres. Coolidge, 1926. Mem. Am., Kan. State bar assns. Served as 1st lt. Co. F, 22d Kan. Vols., Spanish-Am. War. Republican. Methodist. Mason (32°, Shriner, life member Imperial Council); past president Internat. High Twelve Clubs (Masonic); K.P., Elk, Woodman. Home: 2506 W. 10th St., Topeka, Kan. Office: New England Bldg., Topeka, Kan. Died Sept. 11, 1958.

WILLIAMS, Alexander Elliot, army officer; b. Linden, N.C., Mar. 12, 1875; s. William L. and Mary Eliza (Elliot) W.; grad. U.S. Mil. Acad., 1898, Army War Coll., 1923; m. Janie McBryde, Dec. 29, 1899. Commd. 2d lt. inf., 1898; advanced through grades to col., detailed brig. gen. Q.M.C., 1920-21. In Santiago campaign, 1898, and in Cuba until 1900; in Philippines, 1900-02; detailed in Q.M.C., 1907, and in charge water transportation in Philippines; q.m. Militia Bur., Washington, 1916-17; in charge depot at Montoir, France, 1918-19; detailed as chief q.m. 3d Army, 1919, and went into Germany; asst. to q.m. gen., Washington, 1919-22; at War Coll., 1922-23, Field Arty. Sch., 1923-24; chief of staff, 82d Div., 1924-26; q.m. duties, 1926-30; handled pilgrimage of War Mothers, N.Y., 1930-31; apptd. asst. to q.m. gen. for 4 yrs. from 1931, with rank of brig. gen. Presbyn. Clubs: Army and Navy (Washington), Army and Navy (Manila). Author: Manual for Quartermaster, 1915; Company Supply Manual, 1916. Address: War Dept., Washington. Died Mar. 1948.

WILLIAMS, Alford Joseph, Jr., aviator; b. N.Y. C., July 26, 1896; s. Alford Joseph and Emma Elizabeth (Madden) W.; A.B., Forham U., 1915; LL. B., Georgetown U., 1925; m. Alice Helen Ort Toomey; 1 foster son, John E. Pitcher N.Y. Giants, Nat. League baseball team, 1916-17; enlisted as aviator USN, 1917, research aviator, 1917-30, advanced through grades to lt.; tested planes, developed aerial acrobatics for air combat, specialized in hish speed research; Navy entrant Pulitzer Trophy Races, winner 1923, speed 243 mph; established world's absolute speed record of 266.7 mph in 1923; held Am. speed record 8 consecutive yrs.; unofcl. world's speed records, 302 mph in 1925, 322 mph in 1927; developed improvements for standard combat planes; performer Nat. Air Races, frequent winner Aerobatic trophy; headed 1st Internat. Aerobatic Team, Chgo., 1930; winner trophy for outstanding individual airmanship; Rickenbacker Airmanship trophy, Miami, 1935; inspected European Aero. centers, 1930-38; inaugurated ann. Lightplane Air Cavalcades to Miami Air Maneuvers, 1936-41; weekly commentator NBC radio Flying With Al Williams, 1933-36; pioneered establishment separate air force; pilot Gulfhawk aerobatic-fighter enshrined in Smithsonian Instn.; lectr. Nat. War Coll., NACA, Inst. Aero. Sci., the mil. univs., others; retired to cattle ranch The Eyrie, Elizabeth City, N.C., 1949; admitted to N.Y. bar, 1926; lectr. aero. engring. U. Pitts.; mgr. aviation dept. Gulf Oil Corp., 1933-49. Served as major U.S. Marine Corps Res., 1935-40. Decorated Distinguished Flying Cross (USN); trophy of Am. Soc. M.E., 1929. Comdr. Scripps-Howard Jr. Aviators numbering 485,000; daily aviation columnist Scripps-Howard newspapers. Mem. N.Y. State Bar Assn., Nat. Aero. Assn. Author: Airpower, 1940; contbr. nat. periodicals and aero. jours. Inventor vertical dive-bombing, 1923. Address: The Eyrie, R.D. 1, Elizabeth City, N.C. Died June 15, 1958; buried Arlington Nat. Cemetery.

WILLIAMS, A(rthur) J(oseph), govt. ofcl.; b. Washington, Mar. 15, 1898; s. William Handy and Hannah (Jackson) W.; student pub. schs. and bus. coll., Washington; Phila. School of Fine Arts, 1918-19; married to Faye Skiles, July 7, 1921; children—Arthur Joseph, William Handy, Vivien Lois Burns (stepdau.). Rail transportation work, Washington Terminal Co., 1916-18; with U.S. Shipping Bd. Mcht. Fleet Corp., since 1918; sec., U.S. Maritime Commn. 1943-50, commn. divided into U.S. Maritime Bd. and Maritime Administration, secretary, 1950—; former War Shipping Administration. Trustee and dir. Govt. Services, Inc.; former trustee Washington Community Chest; dir. U.S. Maritime Commn. Welfare Soc. Recipient distinguished service award, Dept. of Commerce, 1955. Mason. Home: 1507 Otis St. N.E. Office: U.S. Maritime Commission, General Accounting Office Bldg., Washington 25. Died Nov. 22, 1956; buried Ft. Lincoln Cemetery, Washington.

WILLIAMS, B. Y. (Mrs. Karl H. Williams), author, editor; b. Hamersville, O.; d. Elsberry and Eleanor Belle (Smith) Young; m. Karl Howland Williams, 1907; children—Anne Bernice (Mrs. W. Massey Foley), Thomas Young (dec.). Co-founder and co-editor (with Annette Patton Cornell) of poetry mag., Talaria, 1936. Mem. League of Am. Pen Women (past president for Ohio; national chairman poetry, 1946-47), Poetry Society of America, Writers' League of Greater Cincinnati, Cincinnati Woman's Press Club (past president), Cincinnati Woman's Club, Cincinnati MacDowell Soc. Recipient of numerous awards for literary work. Author: House of Happiness (verse), 1928; Apples of Gold (verse), 1932; Far Is the Hill (verse), 1939; For Each a Star (Zodiac Sonnets), 1942; What Else Matters (verse), 1949. Co-author: Garland for a City, 1946. Contbr. verse to Cincinnati Times-Star, New York Times, Ladies' Home Jour., Good Housekeeping, Saturday Evening Post, London Poetry Review, etc. Home: The Phelps, 506 E. 4th St., Cin. Died Feb. 1951.

WILLIAMS, Ben Ames, author; b. Macon, Miss., Mar. 7, 1889; s. Daniel Webster and Sarah Marshall (Ames) W.; A.B., Dartmouth College, 1910; Litt.D., Colby College, 1942, Dartmouth, 1946, Batts Coll., 1951; m. Florence Trafton Talpey, Sept. 4, 1912; children—Roger Chilton, Ben Ames, Penelope Ann. Newspaper writer until 1916. Member Delta Tau Delta Fraternity. Club: Country. Author: All the Brothers Were Valiant, 1919; The Sea Bride, 1919; The Great Accident, 1920; Evered, 1921; Black Pawl, 1922; Thrifty Stock, 1923; Audacity, 1924; Sangsue (pub. England), 1923; The Rational Hind, 1925; The Silver Forest, 1926; Immortal Longings, 1927; Splendor, 1927; The Dreadful Night, 1928; Death On Scurvy Street, 1929; Touchstone, 1930; Great Oaks, 1930; An End to Mirth, 1931; Pirate's Purchase, 1931; Honeyflow, 1932; Money Musk, 1932; Pascal's Mill, 1933; Mischief, 1933; Hostile Valley, 1934; Small Town Girl, 1935; Crucible, 1937; The Strumpet Sea, 1938; Thread of Scarlet, 1939; The Happy End, 1939; Come Spring, 1940; The Strange Woman, 1941; Time of Peace, 1942; Amateurs at War, 1943; Leave Her to Heaven, 1944; It's a Free Country, 1945; House Divided, 1947; Fraternity Village, 1949; Owen Glen, 1950; The Unconquered, 1953. Home: 124 Chestnut Hill Rd., Chestnut Hill, Mass. Died Feb. 4, 1953.

WILLIAMS, Ben J., cotton mcht., ret.; b. New Orleans, Sept. 20, 1891; s. Benjamin and Leontine (Maine) W.; ed. pub. sch., New Orleans; m. Edna Ayraud; 1 dau., Nell Pape, M.D. (wife of William W. Waring, M.D.). Office boy, Edward Eisenhauer & Co., cotton mchts., New Orleans, 1906, mem. of firm, 1916; organizer firm Pape, Williams & Co., 1917, partner, 1917-50, ret. Member New Orleans Pub. Belt Railroad Commn., 1920-37 (chmn. exec. com. 8 yrs.). Vice pres. New Orleans Cotton Exchange, 1923-24; v.p. Southern Cotton Shippers Assn., 1936, pres., 1937; v.p. New Orleans Assn. of Commerce, 1937, pres. 1938; v.p. Am. Cotton Shippers Assn., 1940, pres. 1941, now dir. Bur. Govtl. Research New Orleans, Nat. Cotton Council Am.; nat. councillor U.S. C. of C. Member panel of arbitrators, Inter-Am. Comml. Arbitration Commn., N.Y. Dir., New Orleans chapter Am. Red Cross (chmn. Am. Red Cross Roll Call, 1941; chmn. A.R.C. War Fund campaign, 1942). Clubs: Country, Lake Shore (New Orleans). Contbr. articles to various publs. Home: 6120 Marquette Pl., New Orleans 18. Office: 820 Union St., New Orleans 12. Died May 19, 1956; buried New Orleans.

WILLIAMS, Berkeley; b. Richmond, Va., Oct. 13, 1878; s. John Langbourne and Maria Ward (Skelton) W.; desc. on paternal side of Col. John Dandridge, father of Martha, the wife of George Washington, and on the maternal side from Edmund Randolph, atty. general of United States in Washington's cabinet; grad. McGuire's University Sch., Richmond, 1895; University of Va., 1897; m. Huldah Justice Steel, Feb. 4, 1903; children—Berkeley, Huldah Justice (Mrs. Barron Proctor Lambert); m. 2d, Kate Harris Skipwith, Feb. 17, 1937. Clerk in superintendent's office Richmond Traction Co., 1898-99; purchasing agt., Rys. & Light Co. of America, 1899-1904; dist. supt. Md. Life Ins. Co., 1904-06; investment broker, 1906-13; v.p. The Alabama Co., 1912-13; pres. Richmond Mica Co., 1913-25; partner John L. Williams & Sons, investment bankers, 1913-28; postmaster, Richmond, Va., 1931-33; pres. Derby Oil Co., Wichita, Kan., 1935-38; now pres. Brown Oil Co.; v.p. Va. Bldg. and Loan Co.; dir. Williamsburg Packing Co., Bank of Commerce & Trusts, Virginia Mutual Ins. Co. Pres. Va. Better Trade Assn., 1925-39; organizer Anti-Diphtheria League of Va. Republican. Episcopalian. Clubs: Va. Boat, Country Club of Va. (Richmond), Newcomen Soc. Eng., Wolf Scaffold Hunt. Home: 6101 Three Chopt Rd., Address: 302 E. Grace St., Richmond 19, Va. Died Nov. 29, 1954.

WILLIAMS, Bert(ice) C(larence), educator; b. 1909; A.B., DePauw U., 1933; M.A., Ind. U., 1940, Ph.D., 1946. Mem. faculty U. Ala., 1945—, prof. biology, 1951. Mem. Am. Bot. Soc., A.A.A.S., Am Assn. U. Profs., Am. Soc. Profl. Biologists, Ala. Ednl. Assn., So. Assn. Sci. and Industry, Sigma Xi. Author sci. articles. Home: 89 Cedar Crest, Tuscaloosa, Ala. Died July 6, 1954.

WILLIAMS, Carl, editor; b. Porter County, Ind., Mar. 30, 1878; s. Abraham Lennington and Julia Ann (Williams) W.; ed. pub. and normal schs.; Dr. Agr., Okla. Agr. and Mech. Coll., 1930; m. Mabel Bates, July 14, 1906. Reporter, editor city newspapers, 1895-1903; sec. Scientific Farming Assn., Colo., 1904-05; farming and irrigation work, 1905-13; became editor Okla. Farmer-Stockman, Oklahoma City, 1913, now retired. Was an organizer of Okla. Cotton Growers' Assn. (dir.), Am. Cotton Growers' Exchange (ex-pres.), Southwest Wheat Growers' Assn. (ex-pres.), Am. Agrl. Editors' Assn. (ex-pres.), Nat. Council Farmers Coöperative Marketing Assn. (v. chmn.). Former mem. U.S. Bd. of Mediation; mem. Federal Farm Bd., 1929-33. Democrat. Conglist. Home: Fort Pierce, Fla. Died June 7, 1953.

WILLIAMS, Charles Bray, educator; b. Shiloh, N.C., Jan. 15, 1869; s. Simeon Walston and Mary (Bray) W.; A.B., Wake Forest (N.C.) Coll., 1891; B.D., Crozer Theol. Sem., 1901; A.M., U. Chicago, 1908; Ph.D., 1909; D.D., Baylor U., 1917; m. Alice Julia Owen, Jan. 2, 1899 (died Jan. 23, 1925); children—Charles Weston, Eunice Lois, John Broadus (dec.); m. 2d Mrs. Lucile Adams Bruner, Dec. 26, 1925; m. 3d Edith Stallings, Aug. 26, 1934; 1 dau., Charlotte Edith. Ordained to ministry of Bapt. Ch., 1890; pastor North Chester Ch., Chester, Pa., 1898-1900, Olive St. Ch., Texarkana, Tex., 1902-04, Rock Dale, Tex., 1904-05; prof. Greek, Southwestern Bapt. Theol. Sem., Ft. Worth, 1905-19; dean, 1913-19, financial agt., 8 yrs.; pres. Howard Coll., Birmingham, 1919-21; prof. N.T. interpretation Mercer U., 1921-25; prof. Greek and ethics Union U., Jackson, Tenn., 1925-38; pastor First Bapt. Ch., Bruceton, Tenn., 1938-39, Shiloh (N.C.) Bapt. Ch., 1941-46; ret.; mng. editor Southwestern Jour. Theology, 1917-19. Mem. Soc. Bibl. Lit. and Exegesis, Am. Research Soc., Victoria Inst. (Gt. Britain). Democrat. Mason. Club: Rotary. Author: History of the Baptists in North Carolina, 1901; The Participle in the Book of Acts, 1910; The Function of Teaching in Christianity, 1913; New Testament History and Literature, 1916; Citizens of Two Worlds, 1919; Introduction to Christian Ethics, 1925; The Evolution of New Testament Christology, 1928; Introduction to New Testament Literature, 1929; A Translation of the New Testament in the Language of the People, 1937;

Syllabus, Bible Readings in Public Schools, 1940; (posthumously) Life and Letters of Paul. Address: R.F.D. 5, Box 1426, Lakeland, Fla. Died May 4, 1952; buried Elizabeth City, N.C.

WILLIAMS, Charles Finn, ins. ofcl.; b. Cin., Apr. 23, 1873; s. William Gregory and Mary Ellen (Donovan) W.; LL.B., U. Cin., 1897; LL.D., Xavier U., Cin., 1932; m. Elizabeth Ryan, May 26, 1906; children—Mary Elizabeth, Margaret Mary, Charles Matthew, William Joseph, James Ryan. Began practicing law alone, Cin., 1897, later mem. firm Shay, Cogan & Williams, later Williams, Ragland, Dixon & Murphy; chmn. Hamilton County delegation to Ohio legislature, 1901-06; spl. pros. atty. of milk and food violators, 1906; dep. atty. gen. of Ohio, 1906; dep. U.S. atty. gen. for So. Ohio, 1907-11, later spl. counsel to George W. Wickersham, atty. gen. of U.S.; v.p. and gen. counsel, 1910, of The Western and Southern Life Ins. Co., with brother, W. J. Williams (founder of the co.) acquiring control of entire capital stock of company; pres. The Western and So. Life Ins. Co., 1931-—; dir. and trustee Rookwood Pottery. Gen. chmn. Cin. Community Chest, 1932, chmn. bd., 1932-33; apptd. chmn. Ohio State Tax and Mortgage Delinquency Commn., 1932; Cin. mem. Nat. Citizens Com. of Welfare and Relief Mobilization, 1932; orgn. com. of Nat. Economy League, 1932; Ohio dir. Century of Progress Expn., Chgo., 1933-34, serveda as Ohio Day mgr. at the Expn., July 15, 1933; elected gen. of NRA for Cin. and Hamilton County, 1933; elected mem. Building Com. for New Wing to Art Mus., 1933; chmn for Pres. Roosevelt's birthday celebration in Cin., 1934, for benefit of Ga. Warm Springs Foundation; mem. Ins. Com. Ohio C. of C., 1934; dir. A.R.C.; 1934; hon. life mem. Cin. chpt. Res. Officers Assn. U.S.; trustee Cin. Museum Assn.; chmn. Cancer Control Council of Coll. of Medicine, U. Cin., all 1934; pres. Catholic Youth Orgn. of Cin. Archdiocese, 1934; dist. chmn. A.R.C. Roll Call in Cin. Area, 1935; trustee Cin. Inst. of Fine Arts. Mem. Nat. Economy League (nat. council), New Eng. Historic-Geneal. Soc. Hon. col. 445th F.A., U.S. Army. Decorated Knight Comdr. Order of St. Gregory the Great, by Pope Pius XII, 1934. Republican. Catholic. Office: 4th St. and Broadway, Cin. Died Sept. 11, 1952; buried Gate of Heaven Cemetery, Cin.

WILLIAMS, Charles Mallory, dermatologist; born Brooklyn, N.Y., Oct. 16, 1872; s. Charles Phelps and Fanny Elizabeth (Mallory) W.; A.B., Brooklyn Collegiate and Poly. Inst., 1890; Ph.B., Yale, 1892, post-grad. work, 1892-94; M.D., Coll. Physicians and Surgeons (Columbia U.), 1898; hon. D.Sc., U. of Vt., 1932; m. Margaret Dows Worcester, Feb. 25, 1904 (died March 30, 1941); children—Mary Low (wife of Dr. Macdonald Dick, of Duke U.), Margaret (wife of Billings B. Fairbrother); m. 2d, Edith Bramhall Cullis, Apr. 14, 1942. Intern Roosevelt Hosp., 1898-1900, Sloane Hospital 1900; specialized in dermatology since 1902; served in dispensaries Vanderbilt Clinic, North-Western Dispensary, and Bellevue Hospital, and New York Skin and Cancer Hospital; prof. dermatology, University of Vermont, 1913-30; attending physician New York Skin and Cancer Hospital, 1920-34, president med. bd. same, 1928-34; served as consulting dermatologist Memorial Hosp.; prof. clin. dermatology and syphilology, Post-Grad. Med. Sch. (Columbia), 1934-35; retired, 1935. Entered U.S. Army as 1st lt. M.C., 1917; advanced to lt. col., 1919; originated and put into practice segregation of venereal cases in separate battalion, in training camps; with 79th Div. in Meuse-Argonne; citation for services in World War I. Mem. A.M.A., Am. Dermatol. Assn. (pres. 1934-35; dir. 1935-39), New London County (Conn.) Medical Society, Medical Advisory Board (Connecticut), Society Colonial Wars, Century Assn. Republican. Episcopalian. Mason (32°). Clubs: Yale (New York); Graduate, Beaumont Med. (New Haven); Wadawanuck Country (Stonington, Conn.). Contbr. on dermatology, especially in connection with fungus diseases. Home: Stonington, Conn. Died Nov. 12, 1951; buried Stonington, Conn.

WILLIAMS, Charles Page, hydraulic and irrigation engr.; b. Chillicothe, Mo., Feb. 3, 1866; s. Charles Andrew and Ann Catherine (Page) W.; B.S., Topog. Engr. and Prin. of Pedagogy, cum laude, U. Mo., 1890; m. Lena Leigh Johnson, Jan. 5, 1892; children—Ben Charles, Catherine Elizabeth (Mrs. Robert L. Templeton); m. 2d, Rose Conklin Klinzing, July 10, 1927. Instr. in mathematics, Mo. Mil. Acad., Mexico, Mo., 1890-91; topographer, U.S. War Dept., 1891-92; agt. St. Louis Bridge & Iron Works, 1893; draftsman, U.S. Engrs. Office, Sioux City, Ia., 1894; draftsman, St. Extension Dept., D.C., 1895-97; jr. engr. and supt. constrn. seacoast defs., Portland, Me., and New London, Conn., 1897-1903; with U.S. Reclamation Service, successively engr. design for irrigation works, Wyo. and Mont., mgr. Huntley Irrigation Project, Mont., asst. to supervising engr. northern div., mgr. Milk River and Sun River projects, Mont., and Shoshone Project, Wyo., asst. chief engr. and cons. engr., 1904-24; cons. engr. Hidalgo County (Tex.) Flood Control Com. and La Feria, Pharr-San Juan and El Jardin water improvement dists., 1924-26; cons. engr., Los Angeles, 1926-35; cons. engr. J. G. White, and Co., irrigation development, Baja, California, Mexico, 1927-28; cons. engr. Comisión Nacional de Irrigación of Mexico, water development, Baja California, Mexico, including Rodriguez Dam, highest dam of the Ambursen type in the world, 1928-35; cons. engr. in office that commission, Mexico City, 1936-38, engr. Ambursen Engring. Corp., N.Y., proj. engr. Possum Kingdom Dam and Power House, Brazos River Conservation and Reclamation District, Texas, 1938-40; resident engr. San Vicente Dam, City of San Diego, 1941-43; resident engr. Lake Loveland Project, Sweetwater Falls Dam, Alpine, Cal., 1943-45; cons. engr. Ambursen Engring. Corp., N.Y. and Houston, 1945-46; pvt. work. Mem. Am. Soc. C.E., S.A.R., Phi Delta Theta. Democrat. Mason (32°). Address: 1269 Law St., San Diego 9, Cal. Died Dec. 28, 1955.

WILLIAMS, Charles Parker, lawyer; b. Mansfield, La., Jan. 8, 1872; s. Thomas Jefferson and Florence (Parker) W.; A.B., Vanderbilt U., 1895, M.A., 1897; m. Mabel Annette Megginson, June 3, 1903; children—Mrs. Sara Bosman, Florence Parker (Mrs. Andrew Marshall). Began practice in St. Louis, 1899; pros. atty., 1902-06; asso. city counselor, 1906-10; police commr., 1913-15; spl. asst. to U.S. atty. gen. for War Work, 1917-18; regional counsel, U.S. Railroad Adminstrn., 1919-20; chmn. St. Louis Election Bd., 1936-37; lectr. Washington U. Law Sch., 1912-19. Annual award, St. Louis Lawyers' Assn., 1947. Mem. Mo. Bar Assn., St. Louis Bar Assn., Phi Beta Kappa, Phi Delta Theta. Mason. Club: Noonday. Protestant. Ind. Democrat. Author: Federal Practice, 1914, 2d Edition, 1927. Home: 6215 Washington Av. Office: 220 N. 4th St., St. Louis. Died May 8, 1951; buried Bellefontaine Cemetery, St. Louis.

WILLIAMS, Clarence Stewart, naval officer (ret.); b. Springfield, O., Oct. 7, 1863; s. Orson Bennett and Pamela (Floyd) W.; B.S., U.S. Naval Acad., 1884; m. Anna Marie Miller, June 6, 1888; 1 son, Edgar Miller. Commd. ensign, U.S. Navy, 1886, and promoted through grades to rear adm., 1918, vice adm. (temp), 1919, ret. with rank rear adm., 1927, vice adm. (ret.), 1930, adm. (ret.), 1942; pres. U.S. Naval War Coll., 1922-25; comdr. U.S. torpedo boat Gwin, 1898, U.S.S. Albany, 1910-11, U.S.S. Rhode Island (Mex. campaign), 1912-15; chief of staff, Battleship Force, Atlantic Fleet, 1916-17, Battleship Force 2, 1917; comdr. Battle Squadron 1, Pacific fleet, 1919, Battleship Force, Pacific Fleet, 1920; comdr. in chief U.S. Asiatic Fleet, 1925-27. Mem. party which pioneered hydrographic survey for cable sta. on Midway Islands, 1901. Decorated D.S.M., Spanish Campaign, Cuban Pacification, Mexican Campagn, Victory and Yangtze Service medals. Mem. U.S. Naval Inst. Club: Army-Navy (Washington). Address: Meadowbrook Heights, Charlottesville, Va. Died Oct. 24, 1951; buried Arlington Nat. Cemetery.

WILLIAMS, Claude Allen, oil exec.; b. Big Sandy, Tex., Jan. 1, 1904; s. Herbert A. and Fanny (Lacy) W.; student U. Tex., 1921-22, U. So. Cal., 1923-25; LL.B., Cumberland U., 1932; m. Clara Boyle Williams, June 3, 1930. Ind. oil and gas operator since 1930; admitted to Tex. bar, 1933, practiced Longview, 1933-34, 1935-38, 1945-47; dist. atty., Gregg Co., 1934-35; asst. sec. state, Tex., 1938-40; chmn., exec. dir. Tex. Unemployment Compensation Commn., Austin, 1940-45; pres. Transcontinental Gas Pipe Line Corp., Houston, since 1945. Pres. Interstate Conf. Employment Security Agencies, 1943-44. Mem. Ind. Natural Gas Assn. Am. (dir.). Democrat (co. chmn. 1937-38). Baptist. Home: 2432 Stanmore Dr., Houston 19. Office: City National Bank Bldg., Houston 2. Died Oct., 1957.

WILLIAMS, Clyde, ex-congressman; b. Jefferson County, Mo., Oct. 13, 1873; prep. edn. high sch., De Soto, Mo., and State Normal Sch., Cape Girardeau; A.B., U. Mo., 1901, also LL.B.; m. Lola Marsden, Apr. 26, 1905; children—Eleanor Doyne, Merle Lee, Evan Duane. Admitted to Mo. bar and began practice at Hillsboro; pros. atty. Jefferson County, Mo., 1902-08; mem. 70th and 72d Congresses, 13th Mo. Dist., 73d Congress, Mo. at large, and 74th to 77th Congresses, 8th Mo. Dist. Democrat. Home: Hillsboro, Mo. Died Nov. 12, 1954.*

WILLIAMS, (Robert Perry) Dean, business exec.; b. Reynoldsville, Pa., July 11, 1891; s. John Calvin and Permelia Adel (Dean) W.; B.S., Pa. State Coll., 1915; m. Wilma Elizabeth Chamberlin, Nov. 16, 1918; children—John Chamberlin, Robert Dean, Neil Saxton. Chemist and supt. Clawson Chem. Co., 1919-21; chief chemist U.S. Leather Co., 1940-44, v.p. in charge of prodn. and dir., 1944-50; technical dir. L. H. Lincoln & Son, 1950-—, v.p., 1955-—, sole leather cons., 1944-—. Received Alsop Award, Am. Leather Chemists Assn., 1948. Fellow Am. Inst. Chemists; mem. Am. Leather Chemists Assn. (past pres., editor Jour.), Am. Chem. Soc., Soc. of Chem. Industry, Internat. Soc. of Leather Trades Chemists, also member of Sigma Pi, Phi Lambda Upsilon. Republican. Presbyterian. Mason. Club: Chemists (N.Y.). Home: 219 Park Av., Ridgway, Pa. Office: Coudersport, Pa. Died Aug. 14, 1955; buried Ridgway, Pa.

WILLIAMS, Edmund Randolph, lawyer; b. Richmond, Va., May 1, 1871; s. John Langbourne and Maria Ward (Skelton) W.; prep. edn., McGuire's Univ. Sch., Richmond; LL.B., U. of Va., 1893; m. Maud Lathrop Stokes, Nov. 22, 1900; children—Edmund Randolph (dec.), John Langbourne (dec.), Margaret Pickett (Mrs. John Lee McElroy), Maude Stokes (Mrs. Thomas Harcourt Urmston). Admitted to Virginia bar, 1893, and practiced at Richmond since 1896; v.p. and gen. counsel Va. Ry. & Power Co., 1918-25; dist. counsel S.A.L. Ry., 1900-20; mem. Hunton, Williams, Anderson, Gay & Moore; gen. counsel Richmond, Fredericksburg & Potomac R.R. Co. until 1951, adv. counsel, 1951-—; director of the First & Mchts. Nat. Bank of Richmond, Va. Electric & Power Co.; dir. Children's Home Soc. Va.; v.p. Virginia Museum of Fine Arts. Mem. Am. Bar Assn., Va. State Bar Assn., Assn. Bar City New York, Va. Hist. Soc. (dir.), Delta Psi. Club: Country Club of Va. Home: Windsor Farms. Office: Electric Bldg., Richmond, Va. Died June 9, 1952.

WILLIAMS, Ednyfed H. (ed - nĕv - ed williams), lawyer; b. Carnavon, Wales, May 25, 1882; s Daniel H. and Annie (Williams) W.; brought to U.S., 1887, naturalized, 1917; LL.B., Chicago-Kent Coll. Law, 1907; grad. work Northwestern U. Law Sch., 1908; m. Edna Blum, Oct. 5, 1922. Admitted to Ill. bar, 1907, and since practiced in Chicago; member of the firm Williams and Leonard; pres. R.S.V.P., Ltd., Chicago, since 1937; v.p. Kester Soldier Co. since 1929, Charles W. Wrigley Co., 1922-—; dir. Laminet Cover Co., Maybelline Company. President Nat. Assn. State Racing Commrs., 1943-45; chmn. Ill. Racing Bd., 1941-48; chmn. Selective Service Appeal Board Number 8, Cook County, 1941-45; member War Board Contract Adjustment, 1919. Member Chicago Republican Conv. Committee, and asst. to western treas., 1912, 1916, 1920; regional dir. rep. clubs under Rep. Nat. Com., 1920; liaison officer to Gov. Dwight H. Green with War Agencies and Activities, 1941-45. Chevalier d'honneur de Notre Ordre Imperial Constantinien Militaire de Saint George. Mem. Delta Chi. Mason (32°, Shriner, Jester), Elk. Clubs: Tavern, Mid-day, Illinois Athletic, Executives; Racquet Club (Palm Springs, California). Author: Liability of Manufacturers and Retailers of Electrical Appliances, 1933. Home: Ambassador West Hotel, Chicago 10. Office: 7 S. Dearborn St., Chgo. 3; also 64 Bis Rue De Monceau, Paris Ville, France. Died Sept. 1958.

WILLIAMS, Emmons Levi, b. Binghamton, N.Y., Jan. 10, 1854; s. Aaron and Rebecca B. W.; student pub. schs.; m. Nettie S. Crans, Mar. 5, 1878; m. 2d, Mary T. E. Cornell, Nov. 26, 1907. Asst. treas., Cornell U., 1872-79; treas. 1879-1914, comptroller, 1914-19, retired 1919. Address: 608 E. State St., Ithaca, N.Y. Deceased.

WILLIAMS, Frank Backus, ret. lawyer, city planner; b. Phila., Dec. 17, 1864; s. J. Austin and Anna (Backus) W.; A.B., Harvard, 1888, A.M., LL.B., 1891; student N.Y. Sch. Philanthropy, 1909. Began practice law, Hartford, Conn., 1892; moved to N.Y. C., 1909; mem. staff Legislative Drafting Bur., Columbia U., 1910; began practice of law of city planning and zoning, 1912; mem. staff Heights of Buildings Commn., which zoned N.Y.C., 1913; sent abroad by City of New York to investigate building regulations and zoning, 1913, again in 1914; reported on plans for Bridgeport, Conn., Akron, Ohio, etc. Mem. Common Council, Hartford, 1898. Mem. Nat. City Planning Conf. Mem. Am. Inst. of Planners, Am. Soc. Planning Officials, Citizens Union of New York (city planning commn.), Phi Beta Kappa. Clubs: City (vice pre.), Harvard, Salmagundi, Bar Assn. Author: The Law of City Planning and Zoning, 1922. Co-Author: Airports, Their Location, Administration and Legal Basis, 1930, and Model Laws for Planning and Zoning Cities, Counties and States, 1934 (Harvard City Planning Studies). Contbr. articles in mags. Editor Harvard Law Review, Zoning Bull. of Regional Planning Assn. Formerly asso. dir. legal dept., Regional plan of N.Y and environs. Address: 300 E. 57th St., N.Y.C. Died Dec. 1954.

WILLIAMS, Frank Eugene, lawyer; b. nr. Saginaw, Mich., July 6, 1892; s. George Gordon and Anna (Irland) W.; student U. Mo., 1913-14; LL.B., U. Mich., 1917; m. Grace Ellen Edwards, June 1919; 1 dau., Shirley (Mrs. Lincoln Dulaney); m. 2d Clara Irene Brown, Feb. 18, 1940. Admitted to Mo. bar, 1917, Mich. bar 1920; practiced St. Louis, 1917-20, 1922-51; partner firm Fordyce, White, Mayne, Williams and Hartman, 1930-51; Fordyce, Mayne, Hartman, Renard & Stribling, of counsel, 1950-—; private practice in Detroit, Michigan, 1920-21; chmn. bd. Loose Leaf Metals Co., St. Louis; counsel, sec. and dir. Reardon Co., 1942-—; counsel and dir. Municipal Theatre Assn. of St. Louis, 1947-—; dir. Lambert Phamacal Co., Millman Lumber Co. Mem. Legal Adv. Bd., St. Louis, World War I; mem. Draft Appeals Bd., World War II. Mem. Am., Mo. State, Mich. State and St. Louis bar assns., Nat. Jr. C. of C. (a founder), Jr. C. of C. of St. Louis (dir.), Big Brother Organization (dir.). Presbyn. Mason. Clubs: Midland Valley Country, Glen Echo Country, Missouri Athletic, Civitan, Contemporary (St. Louis),

Yacht, Bahama Shores Yacht, Ambassador (St. Petersburg, Fla.). Home: 5815 Bahama Shores Dr., St. Petersburg 5, Fla. Office: 506 Olive St., St. Louis 1. Died Feb. 13, 1957; buried Royal Palm Cemetery, St. Petersburg, Fla.

WILLIAMS, Fred Lincoln, lawyer; b. Fincastle, Ind., May 31, 1879; s. James Crittenden and Mary Alice (Bridges) W.; Ph.B., DePauw U., 1902; student Ind. Law Sch., Indpls., 1902-03; m. Mary Ethel Jones, June 20, 1906. Began practice at Joplin, Mo., 1903; apptd. Supreme Court commr. by Supreme Court of Mo., 1913, and reapptd. 1915; asso. justice Supreme Court of Mo., 1917-21; now mem. Williams. O'Bryen & Schlafly, St. Louis. Democrat. Home: 24 Cornell Av. Office: Boatmen's Bank Bldg., St. Louis. Died May 20, 1949.

WILLIAMS, Frederic Arlington, textile mfr.; b. Flowery Branch, Ga., Mar. 6, 1883; s. Horace M. and Margaret (Bruce) W.; ed. pub. schs., Ga.; m. Ruth Cowan, Nov. 17, 1921 (div. Nov. 1928); 1 dau., Margot Bruce (Mrs. Robert E. McCann); m. 2d, Pauline P. Wood, Aug. 4, 1933. Began as telegraph operator, 1900; bookkeeper Gibson Mfg. Co., Concord, N.C., 1904-08; with Cannon Mills, Inc., 1908—; beginning as salesman, v.p., 1923-33, pres., 1933—; v.p. and dir. Cannon Mills. Co. Dir. Assn. of Cotton Textile Merchants. Republican. Clubs: Merchants (N. Y.C.); Apawamis (Rye, N.Y.); Wyantenuck (Great Barrington, Mass.). Home: Rye, N.Y. Office: 70 Worth St., N.Y.C. Died May 24, 1953.

WILLIAMS, Frederick Ballard, artist; b. Brooklyn, N.Y., Oct. 21, 1871; s. John K. and Jennie C. (Williams) W.; ed. pub. schs., Bloomfield and Montclair, N.J., art edn. in Cooper Inst., New York Inst., Artists and Artisans, Nat. Acad. Design, etc., under John Ward Stimson, William Hamilton Gibson, C. Y. Turner, Edgar M. Ward; m. Marion Gerry Duncan, Oct. 16, 1901; children—Duncan B., F. Ballard. Landscape and figure painter; exhibitor at important art exhbns. in U.S. and in London, Paris, Venice and Rome. Pictures in Met. Museum of Art (New York), Nat. Art Gallery (Washington), Brooklyn Inst. Arts and Sciences (purchased N.A.D. figure picture, 1909), Herron Inst. (Muskegon, Mich.), St. Louis Museum, Albright Gallery (Buffalo), Arnot Gallery (Elmira, N.Y.), Los Angeles Museum, Nat. Arts Club, Lotos Club, Engineers' Club (New York), Art Inst. Chicago, Montclair (N.J.) Art Museum, Milwaukee Art Inst., Grand Rapids Art Assn., Ft. Worth Museum of Art, Nat. Gallery (Lima, Peru), etc. Recipient bronze medal. Pan-American Expn.; Inness prize, Salmagundi Club; Isador gold medal, Nat. Acad. Design, 1909; Medal of Honor, Salmagundi Club, 1943. Nat. Academician, 1909. Mem. New York Water Color Club; Council Nat. Acad. Design, 1910-11, asst. treas., 1930-38, treas. 1940-41; nat. chmn. Am. Artists Professional League; pres. Montclair (N.J.) Art Assn., 1919-21. Mem. Mayors Municipal Art Com. of 100 for New York City, Municipal Planning Committee, Glen Ridge, N.J. Clubs: Lotos, Salmagundi (pres. 4 terms), Nat. Arts, Glen Ridge Country. Studio: 31 Highland Av., Glen Ridge, N.J. Died Dec. 11, 1956.

WILLIAMS, Frederick Crawford, textile exec.; b. Pawtucket, R.I., Feb. 6, 1890; s. Albert Nathaniel and Margaret Burns (Kinloch) W.; Sc.B., Brown U., 1913; m. Dorothy M. Sayer, Aug. 30, 1916; children—Janet Searle (Mrs. Draper W. Phillips), Malcolm Davis, Frederick Crawford. U.S. asst. engr., Corps of Engrs., Newport, R.I., Muscle Shoals, Ala., 1913-23; hydro elec. engr., Hugh L. Cooper & Co., 1923-25; city engr., Pawtucket, R.I., 1925-32, budget dir., 1932-34; engr. to Supreme Ct. Commn. on Tidal Flowed Lands R.I. since 1932; budget director of Berkshire-Hathaway, Incorporated, Providence, since 1933, dir. since 1935; v.p. Berkshire Fine Spinning Corp. since 1947; engr. Burrillville Racing Assn., Inc., 1943—; engr. Twenty Nine Palms Assos. Mem. Govs. Conf. on Unemployment Relief, R.I., 1932; mem. water resources com., N.E. Council. Mem. Acad. Polit. Sci., The Quartermaster Assn., Soc. of Am. Mil. Engrs. Episcopalian. Home: 217 Raleigh Av., Pawtucket, R.I. Office: 704 Hospital Trust Bldg., Providence 2. Died Oct. 11, 1957.

WILLIAMS, George, ry. official; b. Caribou, Colo., July 18, 1873; s. James Henry and Martha (Dalley) W.; ed. high sch., Boulder, Colo.; m. Jennie Francis Andre, Sept. 27, 1897; children—Addison LeClerque, Martha Eleanor, Florence Jane. Began as stenographer passenger dept. U.P. Ry., 1892, later with U.P.,D.&G. Ry., St.L.&S.F. and C.S. rys.; chief clk. to traffic mgr. C.S. Ry., 1900-10, asst. gen. freight agt., 1910-11, asst. gen. freight and passenger agt., 1911-20; gen. freight agt. D.&R.G. Ry. and its successor D.&R.G. Western R.R. until 1925; freight traffic mgr., D.&R.G. Western R.R., 1925-35, gen. traffic mgr., 1935-39, traffic counsel, 1939-48, ret. Republican. Congregationalist. Clubs: Traffic, Motor (Denver); Commerce (Pueblo, Colo.); Optimist-Weber (Ogden, Utah). Home: 1107 Steele St. Office: Rio Grande Bldg., Denver. Died Mar. 11, 1951; buried Fairmont Cemetery, Denver.

WILLIAMS, George Orchard, newspaperman; b. Phila., July 14, 1890; s. Antipas Freeborn and Margaret W.; ed. pub. schs., Balt.; m. Dora Ellen Greening, June 30, 1915; 1 son, Roger G. Began as reporter Baltimore World, 1908; newspaper reporter Johnstown, Pa., 1917-18, Pitts., 1918-20; city editor Buffalo Times, 1921-22; mng. editor Albany Times Union, 1928—. Democrat. Episcopalian. Home: Niverville, N.Y. (Chatham Center, R.F.D.). Office: 24 Sheridan Av., Albany, N.Y. Died Nov. 8, 1952.

WILLIAMS, George S(eth), utility exec.; b. Augusta, Me., Sept. 9, 1882; s. William H. and Frances E. (McMaster) W.; student U. Me., 1902-03; m. Marian Phillips, June 10, 1943; children—William H., George Seth Jr. Gen. supt. Central Me. Power Co., 1917-25, v.p., gen. mgr., 1925-47, exec. v.p., dir. since 1947. Chmn. exec. com., chmn. bd. trustees, mem. maintenance and control com. technol. adv. com. U. Me.; trustee Windsor Sch. Dist.; dir. N.E. Council; mem. adv. com. Me. Publicity Bur. Industry mem. War Labor Bd., World War II. Home: Ridgeway Farms, Windsor. Office: 9 Green St., Augusta, Me. Died May 27, 1953.

WILLIAMS, Griff (Griffith E.), musician, orchestra leader; b. The Dalles, Ore., May 16, 1908; s. Carleton P. and Helen (Goss) W.; A.B., Stanford, 1932; married to Dorothy Bostwick, on January 7, 1936; children—Holly, Wendy, Lynne, also Griff III. Organized dance orchestra under own name, San Francisco, 1934; appeared at Hotel Mark Hopkins, San Francisco, 1935-38, 1946, Stevens Hotel, Chicago, 1937-41, Palmer House, Chicago, 1941-43, 1946-47, Waldorf-Astoria, New York, 1946-47; appeared on radio programs, Fitch Bandwagon 1943, Moose Family Fireside, 1943; records for Sonora, 1946—; partner Nat. Water Co. and Alhambra Water Co., San Francisco, 1938—; v.p. Haywood Publishing Company, 1954—. Served as lieutenant U.S.N.R., Jan. 21, 1944; as officer in charge band music, entertainment div., U.S.N.T.C., Great Lakes, Ill., disch. 1946. Mem. Ram's Head, Musician's Union. Republican. Roman Catholic. Club: Variety. Home: 1331 Forest Av., Evanston, Ill. Office: Haywood Pub. Co., 6 N. Michigan, Chgo. Died Feb. 23, 1959.

WILLIAMS, Harold E(ugene), news co. exec.; b. Weymouth, Mass., Feb. 27, 1892; s. Lyman C. and Mary Pratt (Lowell) W.; student pub. schs. of Weymouth, Mass.; m. Bertha May Smith, May 29, 1914; 1 dau., Elizabeth Virginia (Mrs. I. Vincent Gage). With The Am. News Co. and brs. since 1909, v.p. charge book operation, N.Y. City, since 1939. Home: Marcotte Lane, Tenafly, N.J. Office: 131 Varick St., N.Y.C. 13. Died Dec. 3, 1955.

WILLIAMS, Harrison, officer of electric corps.; b. Avon, O., Mar. 16, 1873; s. Everett E. Williams; ed. pub. schs.; m. Katharine Gordon Breed, Aug. 4, 1900 (dec.); m. 2d, Mona Strader Bush, July 2, 1926. Chmn. bd. dirs. North Am. Co. (exec. com.); mem. board of dirs. Am. Gas & Electric Co. (exec. com.). Mem. central council Community Service Soc.; benefactor and mem. bd. mgrs., New York Zoöl. Soc.; fellow Met. Museum of Art. Mem. Soc. Colonial Wars, S.R., Ohio Soc. of New York. Clubs: Metropolitan, Recess, New York Yacht (New York); Piping Rock, National Golf Links of America, The Creek (Long Island); Metropolitan (Washington); Union Interalliée. Home: Bayville, Long Island, N.Y. Office: 60 Broadway, N.Y.C. Died Nov. 10, 1953.

WILLIAMS, Henry A(ugustus), publisher; b. Paterson, N.J., Jan. 15, 1895; s. Robert and Alice Winslow (Ingham) W.; A.B., Newark Acad., 1912, Princeton, 1916; student N.Y. Law Sch., 1916-17; m. Peggy Dodds, Jan. 23, 1933; children—Maxine Harriet (by former marriage), Joan Carroll (adopted), Henry Alexander. Admitted to N.J. bar, 1920, and practiced in Paterson, N.J., 1920-45; sec. and counsel Dalzell Trucking Co., Paterson, 1923-48; sec. and treas. (1923), editor-in-chief (1945), Call Printing and Publishing Company, became publisher and president, 1953 (pubisher Paterson Morning Call newspaper). Elected to N.J. Senate while under Constl. age, admitted by spl. resolution, 1924; founder and treas. Call Save-a-Child Fund; v.p. YMHA Music Foundation; apptd. a commissioner of State Bd. Edn., 1952. Enlisted in United States Army, April 1917, and served with A.E.F., advancing from second to first lieut.; France, 1918-19. Received Nat. Gold medal award for fire prevention, Nat. Bd. Fire Underwriters, 1943; Outstanding Citizen award, Paterson, 1947. Mem. Disabled Am. Vets., Vets. Fgn. Wars, Am. Legion, Woodstock (N.Y.) Art Assn., N.J. Press Assn., Am. Soc. Newspaper Editors; hon. life mem. N.J. Patrolmen's Ebenvolent Assn., N.J. Firemen's Mutual Benevolent Assn., Post Office War Veterans Legion, American Publishers Association. Presbyterian. Clubs: Woodstock Country; Princeton Elm. Composer of We're on the Way to Get Der Fuehrer, 1942; Hymn to Victory, 1943; Happy Birthday, 1946. Woodstock club golf champion, 1942. Home: 300 E. 35th St. Office: 33 Church St., Paterson 4, N.J. Died Mar. 23, 1958.

WILLIAMS, Horatio Burt, physiologist; b. Utica, N.Y., Sept. 17, 1877; s. Horatio Olin and Julia Amanda (Pierce) W.; A.B., Syracuse U., 1900, M.D., 1905, Sc.D., 1925; m. Abbie Prentiss Schermerhorn, 1905 (died January 27, 1944). Interne New York Hospital House of Relief, 1905-06; engaged in medical practice, N.Y. City, 1907-11, asst. in physiology, Cornell U., Med. Sch., 1907-11; asso. in physiology, Columbia, 1915-16, asst. prof., 1916-22, Dalton prof. and executive officer of department, 1922-37, Dalton prof., 1937-42, professor emeritus since Sept. 17, 1942; consultant Greenwich (Conn.) Hosp.; dir. and tech. adviser Cambridge Instrument Co., Inc.; registered engr., Conn. Served as capt., Corps of Engrs., U.S. Army 1917-19; instr. Engr. Sch., U.S. Army, 1919; capt. Engr. Res. Corps, 1919-39. Mem. com. on safety, Am. Inst. E.E., Nat. Com. Radiation Protection, Am. Physiol. Soc. Am. Phys. Soc., Phys. Soc. of London, Optical Soc., Acoustical Soc. of America, Math. Society, A.M.A. (former mem. council phys. med.), New York Academy of Medicine, Society Am. Mil. Engrs., Am. Inst. Elec. Engrs., Am. Soc. Anesthetists (hon.), Nat. Soc. Professional Engrs., Conn. Soc. Professional Engrs., Society of Experimental Biology and Medicine, Saint Nicholas Soc. of N.Y., Psi Upsilon, Nu Sigma Nu, Sigma Xi (v.p. Columbia Chapter, 1939-40; pres. 1940-41), Alpha Omega Alpha. Republican. Clubs: Faculty, Engineers, University (N. Y. and Chgo); Cosmos (Washington). Contbr. sci. articles to publs. Home: Dingletown Rd., Greenwich, Conn.; (summer) Woodstock, N.Y. Died Nov. 1, 1955; buried St. Marks Ch. in the Bouwerie, N.Y.C.

WILLIAMS, Irving, editor, author; b. Watertown, Wis., Aug. 4, 1873; s. Dr. Thomas George and Adella Paulina (Coe) W.; student Purdue U., 1893, 95; unmarried. Lumber buyer, with Russe & Burgess, Cairo, Ill., 1895-96; with Rough Notes Co., Indpls., 1897—, editor, sec., v.p., retired. Mem. C. of C., Ind. Pond Blue Goose, Internat. (sec., 1906—). Republican. Presbyn. Author: Insurance Definitions, 1903; Mistah Robinson's Remembery Book, 1913 (juveniles) Big Wallace, 1914; Joe Manning, 1915; Bruce Wright, 1916; Insurance Policy and Forms Analyses Service; Insurance Coverages Applicable, 1938. Died Sept. 1957.

WILLIAMS, Jack, editor, pub.; b. Castle Hayne, N.C., July 26, 1879; s. Thomas and Ellen Elizabeth (Johnston) W.; prep. edn. Cape Fear Acad., Wilmington, N.C., grad. Oak Ridge (N.C.) Inst., 1904; m. Ethel Katharine Woodard, June 19, 1912; children—Jack, Katharine Lee, Ruth Winifred, Betty Louise, Eva. In purchasing dept. A.C.L. R.R., Wilmington, and Waycross, Ga., 1899-1903; same positing with Atlanta, Birmingham & Atlantic R.R., Waycross, 1905-06; gen. storekeeper, same r.r., Fitzgerald, Ga., 1906-07; mgr. pub. Co., Boston, 1909-11; editor, owner and pub. Waycross Daily Journal-Herald and Waycross Weekly Journal, 1915—, also pub. Blackshear Times, 1924-26, Hogansville News, 1925-26, and LaGrange Reporter, 1924-27; pres. Waycross Journal-Herald Pub. Co., Radio Station WAYX; vice-pres. Ga. Loan and Savings Co., 1939-41; pres. Merchants & Mechanics Loan Co., 1941—; Waycross Bldg. & Loan Assn., Waycross Hotel Co., Progressive Life Ins. Co., president First Federal Savings and Loan Association. Served as state senator, 1937-38 and 1943-44; member state legislature, 1939-41 and 1942-47. Lieut. Col. on Gov.'s Staff. Mem. City Bd. of Edn.; pres. Kings Daughters Home for Children, 1935-36. Pres. Georgia Press Assn.; mem. Eleventh Dist. Press. Assn. (pres.); pres. Advisory Bd. Salvation Army; v.p. Waycross R.R. Y.M.C.A.; v.p. Ga. Forestry Assn.; pres. Waycross and Ware Co. Chamber of Commerce, 1936-37, 1945-47. Awarded Sutlive Trophy, Ga. Press Assn., 1925, "for greatest service to community" of any paper in the state; Baynard Knight Cup, Kiwanis Club, 1923, "for greatest service to community"; Miller medal "for having rendered greatest service to his city and county during year 1932." Democrat. Presbyterian. Mason (Shriner), Elk. Clubs: Kiwanis (v.p. 1928; pres. 1929), Okefinokee Golf (sec.), Dovers Bluff Fishing (pres.). Farmer, dairyman and stock raiser. Home: Cherokee Drive, Waycross, Ga. (summer St. Simons Island). Address: Journal-Herald Bldg., Waycross, Ga. Died Dec. 2, 1957; buried Waycross.

WILLIAMS, James Robert, cartoonist; b. Halifax, N.S., Can., Mar. 30, 1888; s. Thomas Edward and Helena (McKee) W.; brought to U.S. in infancy; ed. pub. schs., Detroit, Mich., and Conneaut, Ohio; student Mt. Union Coll., Alliance, O.; m. Lida Keith, Sept. 24, 1911; children—Helen Jean, Robert Keith. Engaged in various occupations, as fireman on Pa. R.R., ranch work in West, mem. U.S. Cav., later worked in factories and as loader of freight cars; drew animated cartoons for motion pictures; connected with NEA Service, Cleve., 1922—; producer of Out Our Way, a daily feature in more than 700 newspapers; a full-page weekly comic, The Willets, etc. Home: 1221 Virginia Rd., San Marnio, Cal. Address: NEA Service, 1200 W. 3d St., Cleve. Died June 17, 1957; buried Mountain View Cemetery.

WILLIAMS, Jerome Oscar, clergyman; b. Clanton, Ala., Mar. 29, 1885; s. Joseph Lebingston and Lelia (Brown) W.; A.B., Howard Coll., 1912, D.D., 1925; Th.M., Southern Bapt. Theol. Sem., Louisville, Ky., 1915, grad. study, 1921-22; m. Kathleen Jeanette Akans, Nov. 16, 1915 (died Apr. 14, 1922); children—Jerome Otis, Margarette Jeanette; m. 2d, Ethel Hudson, June 29, 1927. Began preaching, 1909; ordained to the ministry of the Baptist Church, 1916;

pastor Sylacauga, Ala., 1916-17, First Church, Athens, Alabama, 1919-23, First Church, Bessemer, Alabama, 1923-26, Fourth Av. Ch., Louisville, Ky., 1926-32, First Ch., Bowling Green, Ky., 1932-34; business manager S.S. Board of Southern Baptist Convention, 1934-43, educational secretary since 1943. Served as chaplain A.E.F., 1918-19. Member Pi Kappa Alpha. Democrat. Mason (Shriner). Rotarian. Author: The Gospel of Christ, 1935; Definite Decisions for New Church Members, 1936; Pastors Record of Weddings, 1937; Pastor's Record of Funerals, 1938; Sermons in Outline, 1943; Seed for Sermons, 1945; Heart Sermons in Outline, 1949; The Gospel Preacher and His Preaching, 1949; Evangelistic Sermons in Outline, 1951; Spiritual Truth in Personal Experiences, 1952. Contributor to denominational publications, 1934-46. Home: Stokes Lane. Office: 161 N. 8th Av., N., Nashville. Died Nov. 26, 1953; buried Woodlawn Meml. Cemetery, Nashville.

WILLIAMS, John Alonzo, illustrator; b. Sheboygan, Wis., Mar. 23, 1869; s. Bille and Elizabeth Hannah (Brooks) W.; pub. schs., Sheboygan; studied art at Art Students' League and Met. School of Art, New York; unmarried. Awarded Zabriski prize, Am. Water Color Soc.; Shaw prize, Salmagundi Club, 1934, 1936; Isidor prize, 1939; Church Osborn purchase prize, 1946. Nat. Academician (water color), 1947. Mem. Am. Water Color Soc.; hon. life mem. Artist Guild, Soc. Am. Illustrators. Club: Salmagundi (hon. life). Home-Studio: 39 W. 67th St., N.Y.C. 23. Died 1951.

WILLIAMS, John Castree, business exec.; born N.Y. City, May 31, 1903; s. Dr. Percy H. and Alice (Castree) W.; ed. Princeton, 1925, Harvard Bus. Sch., 1927; m. Virginia Cooper, Oct. 19, 1928; children—Joan Cooper, Ann Herbert. Began as rug buyer Macy & Co., Inc., 1927, mdse. councillor, 1930, advt. mgr., 1933; mdse. adminstr. and exec. v.p. L. Bamberger & Co., Newark, 1938-39, v.p., sec. 1939-43, later acting pres., pres., elected chmn. bd. 1954; pres. Williams & London Advt., 1956; sr. v.p. Fuller & Smith & Ross, Inc., 1958-—; dir. Fidelity Union Trust Co., Firemen's Ins. Co., N.J. Bell Telephone Co., Princeton Inn Co., Trustee Princeton U. Recipient Outstanding Citizen award, Newark, 1946; N.J. Bus. Statesman award, 1954. Mem. Advt. Fedn. Am. (dir.), N.J. C. of C. (pres., dir.). Home: 120 Winant Rd., Princeton, N.J. Office: 230 Park Av., N.Y.C. Died Mar. 30, 1960.

WILLIAMS, John Howard, theol. sem. pres.; b. Dallas, July 3, 1894; s. Daniel Paul and Emma Julia (Bozeman) W.; student So. Meth. U., 1915-18; A. B., Baylor U., 1918, D.D., 1932; Th.M., Southwestern Bapt. Theol. Sem., 1922; grad. study So. Bapt. Theol. Sem., 1921-23; m. Floy Ettys Kelly, June 23, 1920; children—Martha Genne (Mrs. Frank Farwell Sandford), Carolyn Lee (Mrs. Joseph T. Mason), John Howard, Kelley Dan, Floy Kate (Mrs. Marshall D. Woodruff). Ordained to ministry, Baptist Ch., 1914; pastor Bapt. chs. successively in Dallas, Venus, Tex., Middletown, Ky., Sulphur Springs, Tex., Corsicana, Amarillo, 1914-40, Oklahoma City, 1940-45; exec. sec. Bapt. Gen. Conv. of Tex., 1931-36, 46-53; pres. Southwestern Bapt. Theol. Sem., Fort Worth, 1953-—. Pres. Bapt. Gen. Conv. Tex., 1938-39; to Orient as spl. rep. fgn. bd., So. Bapt. Conv., 1956; pres. bd. trustees Okla. Bapt. U., 1944-45; mem. exec. com. So. Bapt. Conv., 1940-45, pres., 1944-45; mem. exec. com. Bapt. World Alliance, 1953-—. Served as 1st lt. Chaplain Corps, U.S. Army, 1918. Mem. C. of C. Clubs: Knife and Fork, Rotary (Fort Worth). Author: The Importance of the Church to the Child, 1946. Home: 4441 Stanley, Fort Worth 15. Office: Southwestern Baptist Theological Seminary, Fort Worth 15. Died Apr. 20, 1958; buried Laurel Land, Fort Worth.

WILLIAMS, John Powell, physician; born Richmond, Va., Oct. 25, 1894; s. William Reid, Sr. and Caroline (Henderson) P.; student McGuire's U. Sch., Richmond, Va., 1902-11, U. of Va., 1912-14, Med. Coll. of Va., Richmond, 1919-21; A.B., M.D., U. of Va., 1923; m. Virginia Pittman Marshall, July 15, 1928; 1 son, John Powell, Jr. Instr. mathematics and German, McGuire's U. Sch., 1914-16; resident physician St. Luke's Hosp., N.Y. City, 1923-25. Fellow McGuire Clinic, Richmond, 1925-28; mem. adjunct faculty Med. Coll. of Va., 1925, asst. prof. med., asst. physician to hosp. div., instr. physical diagnosis and clin. pathol., 1932. Pres. Richmond Acad. Med., 1940, chmn. bd. trustees, 1941; asso. prof. Medicine, Med. Coll. of Va., 1942, unit dir. and chief med. service of affiliated unit, 45th Gen. Hosp.; chief med. service Kennedy Gen. Hosp., Memphis, Tenn., 1945-46; prof. clin. medicine, Med. Coll. of Va., 1945; chief med. service, acting chief professional services, McGuire Vet. Adminstrn. Hosp., Richmond, 1946; col. and unit dir. comdg. officer Postwar 45th Gen. Hosp., since 1948. Served as pvt. Inf., 1914-15; lance corpl. 1st Va. Cavalry, Mexican border, 1916-17; instr. practical geometry and trigonometry, R.O.T.C., Fort Myer, Va., 1917; reconnaisance and telephone officer, F.A., Camp Lee, Va. and France; promoted to 1st lt. during combat, St. Mihel and Meuse-Argonne offensives, France chief med. service 45th Gen. Hosp., Camp Lee, Va., N. Africa, Italy, 1942-46; promoted to col. Med Corps, 1944. Awarded Legion of Merit for outstanding clinical investigation in infectious hepatitis and trench foot. Diplomate Am. Bd. Internal Med. Fellow A.C.P., A.M.A., Am. Psychosomatic Soc.; mem. Richmond Acad. Med., Med. Soc. of Va. chmn. com. on emergency med. service), So. Med. Assn.; Phi Beta Kappa, Alpha Omega Alpha, Raven Hon. Soc. Contbr. sci. papers to med. jours. Instrumental in developing second liver extract produced for treatment of pernicious anemia. Active in developing Blue Cross Plan, Richmond and Va. (mem. bd. trustees, 1941). Democrat. Episcopalian. Home: 3614 Seminary Av., Richmond 22. Office: McGuire Veterans Adminstrn. Hosp., Richmond 19, Va. Died Sept., 1954; buried Holywood Cemetery, Richmond, Va.

WILLIAMS, Judith Blow, educator; b. N.Y.C., Aug. 1, 1890; d. Thomas Marion and Elizabeth (Dickey) Williams; A.B., Vassar Coll., 1912; A.M., Columbia, 1913, Ph.D., 1916. Am. Assn. U. Women European fellow, 1915-16; faculty Wellesley Coll., 1916-56, successively instr., asst. and asso. prof., prof., 1935-56, chairman of the Department of history, 1942-48, Alice Freeman Palmer history prof., 1945-56, prof. emeritus, 1956-—. Guggenheim fellow, 1927-28, 29-30. Mem. Am. Hist. Assn., Econ. History Assn., Phi Beta Kappa. Episcopalian. Author: A Guide to the Sources of English Social and Economic History, 1750-1850, 1926; also articles, reviews. Home: 2 Lawrence Dr., North White Plains, N.Y. Died Oct. 16, 1956; buried Kensico Cemetery, Valhalla, N.Y.

WILLIAMS, Keith Shaw, artist; b. Marquette, Mich., Oct. 7, 1905; s. Herbert Howard and Mabel Keith (Shaw) W.; studied Nat. Acad. of Design, N.Y. City, Pa. Acad of Fine Arts, Phila.; m. Ruth Moore, Oct. 7, 1933; 1 dau., Judith; married 2d, Katherine Kernan, December 14, 1946. Painter in oil and water color, etcher, mural painter; instr. in painting and life drawing, Grand Central Sch. of Art, 1935-41. Served in camouflage batn., U.S. Army, 1942-45. Rep.: (by etchings) Library of Congress, Rollins Museum Library, Norfolk Museum; (by paintings): Cornell Club, Salmagundi Club, Nat. Acad. of Design, New York Hist. Soc. Received Hallgarten prize, Nat. Acad. of Design, 1935; gold and bronze medals, Allied Artists; Nat. Arts Club purchase prize; Samuel Shaw, black and white purchase prizes, Library of Congress purchase prize, etc. Awarded Montclair Art Assn. medal. Academician, Nat. Acad. of Design, 1942; mem. Baltimore and Am. Watercolor socs., Soc. Am. Etchers, Allied Artists of America, Grand Central Art Galleries, Chicago Soc. of Etchers. Clubs: Salmagundi, Nat. Arts (life). Home: 235 W. 11th St., N.Y. City 14. Died Feb. 11, 1951.

WILLIAMS, Kenneth Powers, mathematician, historian, educator; b. Urbana, O., Aug. 25, 1887; s. John H. and Eva Augusta (Powers) W.; student Clark Coll., Worcester, Mass., 1905-06; A.B., Ind. U., 1908, A.M., 1909; Ph.D., Princeton, 1913; m. Ellen Laughlin Scott, Aug. 30, 1920. With Ind. U., 1909-—, instr. mathematics until 1914, asst. prof., 1914-19, asso. prof., 1919-24, prof., 1924-—, chmn. dept., 1937-44. Served as 1st lt. Indiana National Guard, Mexican Border, 1916; captain Field Artillery, United States Army, with A.E.F., 1917-19; maj. F.A., Ind. Nat. Guard, 1921-24, lt. col., 1924-31, col. and chief of staff, 38th Div., Nat. Guard, 1931-39, col., Q.M.C., comdg. 113th Q.M. Regt., and Q.M., 38th Div., in fed. service, 1941. Received Gold Medal Soc. of Libraries of N.Y.U., Diploma of Honor Lincoln Memorial U., and others. Fellow A.A.A.S.; mem. Am. Math. Soc., Math. Assn. Am. (mem. bd. govs., 1945-47, chmn. commn. on place of math. in secondary edn. 1934-40), Am. Astron. Soc., Société Astronomique de France, Am. Assn. Univ. Prof. (chmn. com. required courses in education 1931-35, council, 1946-48), Phi Beta Kappa, Sigma Xi, Scabbard and Blade. American Legion. Republican. Mason. Author: Dynamics of the Airplane, 1921; College Algebra, 1928; The Calculation of the Orbits of Asteroids and Comets, 1934; The Mathematical Theory of Finance, 1935, revised edit., 1947; Lincoln Finds a General, Vol. I, II, 1949, III, 1952; math. and astron. papers. Home: 702 E. 10th St., Bloomington, Ind. Died Sept. 25, 1958; buried Columbus, Ind.

WILLIAMS, Louis Coleman, coll. adminstr.; b. Lincolnville, Kan., July 9, 1892; s. Francis Buckner and Lucy Lakin (Coleman) W.; B.S. (horticulture), Kan. State Coll., 1912, B.S. (agr.), 1922; m. Jean Nelson, Mar. 2, 1932. Teacher Tecumseh (Neb.) High Sch., 1913-14; asst. supt. of Insts., Kan. Agrl. Extension Service, 1915-17, asst. state club leader (conducted by Kan. State Coll. and U.S. Dept. of Agr.), 1917-20, horticultural specialist, 1920-24, supervisor of agrl. specialists, 1924-36; asst. dean and dir. Extension Kansas State Coll., 1936-47, dean and dir., Sept. 1947-—. Mem. Kan. Hort. Soc. (hon. life mem.), Kan. State Coll. Alumni Assn., Chamber of Commerce, Phi Kappa Phi, Gamma Sigma Delta, Epsilon Sigma Phi. Mason. Home: 1855 Anderson Av., Manhattan, Kan. Died Aug. 25, 1955; buried Sunset Cemetery, Manhattan.

WILLIAMS, Louis Laval, sanitarian; b. Georgetown, S.C., 1859; M.D., S.C. Med. Coll., 1880. Apptd. asst. surgeon, U.S.P.H.S., 1885; passed asst. surgeon, 1888; surgeon, 1899; sr. surgeon, 1916; married; children—Charles Laval, Louis Laval, Frederick Ford. In charge pub. health various immigrant stations many yrs.; asst. surgeon gen. at large, 1920-24, retired 1924; made med. dir. by act of Congress, 1930. Home: 46 Panola St., Asheville, N.C. Deceased.*

WILLIAMS, Michael, author; b. Halifax, N.S., Feb. 5, 1877; s. Michael and Anne (Colston) W.; ed. St. Joseph's Coll., N.B.; hon. Litt.D., Gonzaga Coll., D.C.; m. Margaret Olmsted, 1900; children—Margaret Anne, Philip Hale. Reporter, Boston Post, New York World, and Evening Telegram, New York, until 1904; city editor San Francisco Examiner, 1906 (during earthquake and fire); spl. corr. in Mexico, Internat. News Service, 1913; editor Nat. Catholic War Council Bulletin, 1919-20; editor The Commonweal; mem. bd. dirs. Pontificial Inst. of Sacred Music. Mem. Authors' League of America, Am. Com. of Religious Rights and Minorities, American Conf. of Jews and Christians, K.C. Chairman Calvert Associates, Inc. Clubs: Overseas Press (New York); National Press (Washington); Center. Recipient of Catholic Action Gold Medal, St. Bonaventure College, 1935. Author: Good Health and How We Won It (with Upton Sinclair), 1909; The Book of the High Romance, 1918; American Catholics in the War, 1921; The Little Flower of Carmel, 1926; Little Brother Francis of Assisi, 1926; Catholicism and the Modern Mind, 1928; The Shadow of the Pope, 1932; The Catholic Church in Action, 1935. Mem. editorial staff Brooklyn Eagle. Contbr. to Sunday newspapers, lit. and popular mags. Investigated religious persecution in Germany, for New York Herald Tribune, 1933; reported election at Vatican City of Pope Pius VII, New York Times; Spanish Civil War for New York American; Archbishop Spellman's mission to Europe and Orient for Brooklyn Eagle. Home: Roseville Rd., Westport, Conn. Died Oct. 12, 1950.

WILLIAMS, Neil Hooker, prof. of physics; b. Almont, Mich., Oct. 23, 1870; s. Rev. Horace Robbins and Amelia (Robbins) U.; B.S., in elec. engring.; U. of Mich., 1893; M.S., 1895; Ph.D., 1912; m. Elizabeth McDonald, Aug. 8, 1899; children—Donald Hooker, Howard Robbins. Teacher, West Bay City (Mich.) High Sch., 1895-98, Central High Sch., Detroit, 1898-1901, Shortridge High Sch., Indpls., 1901-03; asst. prof. Rose Poly. Inst., Terra Haute, Ind., 1903-08; instr. of physics, U. Mich., 1908-12, asst. prof., 1912-16, asso. prof., 1916-19, prof., 1919-41, now prof. emeritus. Fellow A.A.A.S., Am. Phys. Soc.; mem. Inst. Radio Engring. Republican. Conglist. Author: General College Physics (with H. M. Randall and W. F. Colby), 1929, revised edit., 1937; Electron Tubes, 1935. Contbr. articles to scientific jours. Home: 1020 Olivia Av., Ann Arbor, Mich. Died Nov. 26, 1956.

WILLIAMS, O(scar) B(rown), univ. prof.; b. Kosse, Tex., Sept. 17, 1895; s. William Alfred and Matilda (Lowrey) W.; A.B., U. Tex., 1921, A.M., 1923; Ph.D., U. Cal., 1928; m. Frances Rowe, Dec. 14, 1923; children—Oscar Brown, Katherine Rowe. City water bacteriologist, Austin, Tex., 1921-23; instr. U. Tex., 1922-25, adjunct. prof., 1925-27, asso. prof., 1927-35, became prof. bacteriol. 1941, now chmn. dept. and athletic council; bacteriol. Research Lab., Nat. Canners Assn., Washington, 1935-41. Served in Med. Corps, U.S. Army, 1917-19; sgt. 1-c. Mem. subcom. on animal products Nat. Research Council. Mem. Soc. Am. Bacteriol. Inst. Food Technol., Am. Pub. Health Assn., A.A.A.S., Chi Phi, Phi Beta Kappa, Sigma Xi, Gamma Alpha, Phi Sigma, Alpha Epsilon Delta. Democrat. Methodist. Mem. editorial bd. Advances in Food Research, McGraw-Hill series in food technol, 1944-—, Jour. of Bacteriology, 1951-—. Home: 2509 Spring Lane, Austin 21, Tex. Died Sept. 23, 1959.

WILLIAMS, Robert, publisher; born Paterson, N. J., Jan. 27, 1892; s. Robert and Alice Winslow (Ingham) W.; A.B., Princeton, 1915; LL.B., N.J. Law Sch., 1919; married, Frances A. Roche, January 1, 1938; children—Robert, Helena (by former marriage), Giles, Rachelle. Admitted to N.J. bar, 1920, and practiced, 1920-48; v.p. Call Printing and Pub. Co. (pubs. of Paterson Morning Call), 1919-20, sec.-treas., 1920-23, pres. and pub. since 1923, chmn. bd. of dirs.; lit. editor Paterson Morning Call since 1931. Lecturer on newspaper and printing history, book and autograph collecting and rare books. Mem. adv. council, N.J. State Mus., Trenton, since 1945, Mayor's Civic Group for Preservation of Civic Archives; commr. and pres. Passaic Co. (N.J.) Bd. of Taxation, 1925-36, 43-46; boxing coach, Princeton U., 1934-38, Paterson Y.M.C.A., 1935-38; del. to Rep. Nat. Conv., 1928; air raid warden Paterson, World War II; chmn. Paterson Natural History Mus., 1927-48. Trustee Paterson Library System, 1925-52 (pres.), Paterson Orphan Asylum Assn. Served in U.S. Army, 1916-18. Apptd. U.S. Commr. 1924, but declined. Fellow Am. Geog. Soc.; mem.

Passaic Co. Soc. for Prevention of Cruelty to Children, Passaic Co. Historical Soc. (exec. com.), N.J. Association Amateur Athletic Union (v.p. 1932; hon. life member), Morning Call Athletic Assn., pres., Passaic County Bar Assn., North Jersey Mineral Soc., N.J. Press Assn., Asso. Press, Paterson Forum, Chamber of Commerce, N.J. Library Assn. Republican. Presbyterian. Clubs: Paterson Charter, Manuscript. Author: In Fields Afar with Traveler, 1927; Rare Books from an Old Library, 1930; Pageant of Printing in Picture and Prose, 1938; The Viking's Daughter (1-act play), 1928; Adventures of an Autograph Collector, 1952; Compiler of local historical data for newspaper anniversary edits. Collector oldtime banjo music (1860-1920). Home: 394 E. 30th St., Paterson 4. Office: 33 Church St., Paterson 1, N.J. Died 1953.

WILLIAMS, Robert Carlton, designer; b. Chicago, June 4, 1893; s. Augustus and Rose (Hahn) W.; student Lewis Inst., 1907-09; m. Edna M. Gerard, Mar. 5, 1927. Designer, arthctl. consultant, ticket offices U.P. R.R., N.Y. City, Chicago, Denver, Omaha, San Francisco, Washington, Kansas City, (Mo.), Portland (Ore.), Seattle, Los Angeles, San Diego (Calif.), 1937-46, design consultant spl. cars, 1935-46; collaboration furniture designs, rooms and colors, Sun Valley, Ida., 1935; interiors car ferry City of Midland, Manitowoc, Wis., 1940; furniture designs United Fruit Ships, 1946; practice indsl. and interior designing, Chicago, 1947—. Decorated Commemorative medal (Italy). Mem. Indsl. Designers Inst. (nat. sec.). Clubs: Port, Propellor (Chicago). Address: 707 Roscoe St., Chgo. 13. Died Mar. 12, 1956; buried Eden Cemetery, Chgo.

WILLIAMS, Robert E(dwin), indsl. exec.; b. Mulberry, Ind., Mar. 6, 1912; s. James Milton and Elizabeth Jane (Wainscott) W.; B.S., Purdue, 1934; M.A., Columbia, 1952, Ph.D., 1956; m. Laura E. Telenius, June 10, 1950; 1 dau. Rebecca Wainscott. Marine designer for Gibbs and Cox, Inc., N.Y. City, 1934-36; assistant editor American Inst. E.E., 1936-38; spl. exec. asst. Westinghouse Electric Corp., Pitts., 1938-43; dir. ednl. service Standard Oil Co. (N.J.), 1946-50; indsl. management cons., N.Y.C., 1950-52; became exec. sec. Assn. Cons. Mgmt. Engrs., 1952; mgr. Norris & Elliott, Inc., N.Y.C., 1954—; asst. dir. Consumers Union U.S., Mt. Vernon, N.Y., 1955-56; vice pres. Disogrin Industries, 1956—. Served as lt., USNR, 1943-46. Mem. A.A.A.S., Am. Marketing Assn., Soc. Advancement Mgmt., Am. Psychol. Assn., Sigma Xi. Clubs: Hudson River Country, Columbia University. Author books and articles. Editor: Electronics Reference Book, 1946. Home: 19 Lawrence Park Crescent, Bronxville, N.Y. Office: 510 S. Fulton Av., Mt. Vernon, N.Y. Died Apr. 11, 1959.

WILLIAMS, Robert Purcell, Jr., cons. engr.; b. Columbia, Ala., Feb. 25, 1908; s. Robert Purdy and Mamie Drake (Purcell) W.; B.S., Ga. Inst. Tech., 1931; M.S., Yale, 1933; m. Sylvia Ethel Lantz, Mar. 7, 1942. Engr. Ala. Public Service Commn., 1935-40; joined Rheem Mfg. Co., 1942, mgr. Washington office, 1943-52, v.p., 1952-57; founded Williams Engring. Co., 1957, pres., 1957—. Tech. advisor cartridge case com. NATO, 1952. Served as lt. Ordnance Corps, AUS, 1940-42. Mem. Am. Ordnance Assn., Am. Soc. Naval Engrs., Nat. Security Indsl. Association, Armed Forces Chem. Assn., Yale Engineering Association (vice president). Presbyterian (deacon). Clubs: Army and Navy, Congressional Country (Washington); Yale (N.Y.C. and Washington). Home: 1306 36th St., Washington 7. Office: 839 17th St., Washington 6. Died Feb. 14, 1958; buried Arlington Nat. Cemetery.

WILLIAMS, Roger Henry, banker, lawyer; b. Ithaca, N.Y., July 27, 1874; s. Henry Shaler and Harriet H. (Wilcox) W.; Ph.B, Cornell U., 1895; M.A., Yale, 1903; LL.B., New York U., 1912, J.D., 1913; m. Frances Page Coleman, 1901; children—Coleman Shaler, Gordon Page, Roderick Otis, Douglas. Began in banking business with N. W. Harris & Co., New York, 1898, later with N. W. Halsey & Co.; admitted to N.Y. bar, 1913, and practiced, N.Y. City; mem. Williams, Glover & Washburn, 1914-19; v.p. Nat. Bank of Commerce, 1919-22; partner Estabrook & Co., New York and Boston, since 1922; dir. and officer various corps. Officer 9th Coast Arty. Corps, N.Y. Nat. Guard, 1917-19. Pres. board of trustees Internat. Com. Y.M.C.A., also mem. executive committee Y.M.C.A.; trustee and mem. finance com. Nat. Council Y.W.C.A.; trustee and pres. Schepp Foundation, Lenox Fund; trustee emeritus Cornell Univ. Mem. Am. Bar Assn., American Econ. Association, National Inst. Social Sciences, Civil Service Reform Assn. (treas. exec. com.), Phi Beta Kappa, Kappa Alpha (nat. pres. 10 yrs.; nat. council), English-Speaking Union. Presbyterian. Clubs: Century, University, Yale, Cornell, Down Town, Cruising Club of America; Pequot Yacht. Home: 107 E. 48th St. Office: 40 Wall St., N.Y. City. Died Oct. 26, 1950; buried Ithaca, N.Y.

WILLIAMS, Samuel Hubbard, soap mfr.; b. Glastonbury, Conn., Sept. 28, 1864; s. James Baker and Jerusha (Hubbard) Williams; A.B., Amherst, 1885; post-grad. chemistry, Sheffield Scientific School, Yale U., 1 year; m. Frances Anna Scudder, January 9, 1889; children—Carol Scudder (Mrs. Douglas Horton; died 1944), Frances Rousseau (Mrs. Hugh C. Burr), Martha Huntington, James Baker. With the J. B. Williams Co. soap manufactuers, 1886—, became dir., 1892, sec., 1898, treas., 1908, v.p., 1910, pres., 1922, chmn. bd., 1935; retired, 1939. Chmn. Sch. Com. Glastonbury, 1909-29; mem. Conn. Ho. Reps., 1901. Trustee Hartford Sem. Found.; pres. Conn. Sunday Sch. Assn., 1902-14; exec. com. Internat. Sunday Sch. Assn., 1905-18. Mem. Soc. Chem. Industry, Am. Hist. Assn., Am. Acad. Polit. and Social Science, Foreign Policy Assn., League of Nations Assn., S.A.R., Chi Phi. Republican. Conglist. Mason (32°). Club: University (Hartford). Home: Glastonbury, Conn. Died Feb. 18, 1951.

WILLIAMS, Sidney Clark, editor; b. Wells, Me., Mar. 2, 1878; s. S. Sumner and Ellen M. (Clark) W.; ed. pub. schs. and under private tutors; unmarried. Began as spl. writer on Lewiston (Me.) Journal; later reporter Portland (Me.) Evening Express; editorial paragrapher Boston Evening Record, 1908-14; lit. editor and dramatic critic Boston Daily Advertiser, 1902-14; lit. editor Boston Herald, 1914-19, Phila. North American, Apr. 1920-25; became lit. editor Philadelphia Inquirer, 1925. Clubs: Union Boat, Papyrus, Newspaper (Boston); The Players, Dutch Treat, Century Assn. (New York); Univ. Barge, Franklin Inn Club, Phila. Art Alliance (Phila.). Author: A Reluctant Adam, 1915; The Eastern Window, 1918; An Unconscious Crusader, 1920; The Body in the Blue Room, 1922; In the Tenth Moon, 1923; Mystery in Red, 1925; The Drury Club Case, 1927; The Murder of Miss Betty Sloan, 1935; The Aconite Murders, 1936. Home: Alfred, Me. Died May 24, 1949; buried Portland, Me.

WILLIAMS, Sidney James, engr.; b. Milwaukee, Wis., May 12, 1886; s. Gavin Perry and Fannie (West) W.; B.S., U. of Wis., 1908, C.E., 1915; m. Margaret Frankenburger, Sept. 6, 1909; children—Dorothy Ann, Barbara. Asst. engr. Utah Gas & Coke Co., Salt Lake City, Utah, 1906-07; supt. for R. B. Hartman, building contractor, Milwaukee, 1908-13; engr. Industrial Commn. of Wis., Madison, 1913-18; chief engr. Nat. Safety Council, Chicago, 1918-24, dir. of pub. safety div., 1924-43, gen. mgr., 1943-45, asst. to pres. since 1945. Dir. of safety Fed. Civil Works Administration, 1933-34; consultant to various federal agencies. Beecroft Memorial Lecturer, Society Automotive Engrs., 1950. Chairman safety and industrial health advisory board, Atomic Energy Commn., 1947—. Received C.I.T. Safety Foundation grand award for greatest contribution to pub. safety, 1938, Arthur Williams Memorial Award, 1954. Mem. Am. Soc. C.E., Inst. Traffic Engrs., Soc. Automotive Engrs., Alpha Delta Phi, Phi Beta Kappa, Tau Beta Pi. Conglist. Author: The Manual of Industrial Safety, 1927; (with W. W. Charters) Safety (high sch. text), 1940. Contbr. articles on safety, traffic, etc., and lecturer. Home: 2501 McDaniel Av., Evanston, Ill. Office: 425 N. Michigan Av., Chgo. 11. Died Aug. 5, 1956; buried Forest Home Cemetery, Milw.

WILLIAMS, Stanley Thomas, author, educator; b. Meriden, Conn., Oct. 25, 1888; s. Charels Merriam and Emeline Beaumont (MacFarland) W.; B.A., Yale, 1911, M.A., 1914, Ph.D., 1915; studied Sorbonne, Paris; m. Mary Lee Rockwell, June 9, 1917; children—Charles Rockwell, David Lee, Mary Lee. Instr. English, 1915-17, 1919-20, asst. prof., 1920-26, asso. prof., 1926-32, prof., 1932—, Yale. War service U.S. Army, 1917-18. Mem. Modern Lang Assn. of America, Colonial Society of Massachusetts, American Antiquarian Society, Zeta Psi. Congregationalist. Club: Elizabethan. Author: Life and Dramatic Works of Richard Cumberland, 1917; Studies in Victorian Literature, 1923; The American Spirit in Letters, 1925; American Literature, 1933; The Life of Washington Irving, 1935. Editor: Timon of Athens, 1920; King John, 1927; Irving's Notes While Preparing Sketch Book, and Tour in Scotland, 1927; Letters from Sunnyside and Spain, 1928; Journal of Washington Irving (1823-1824), 1931; Washington Irving and the Storrows, 1933; Journal of Washington Irving (1803), 1934; Journal of Washington Irving (1828), 1937; Letters of Jonathan Oldstyle, Gent., 1941. Joint editor: Sketches of Eighteenth Century America, 1925; Irving's History of New York, 1927; Courses of Reading in American Literature, with Bibliographies, 1930; Washington Irving on the Prairie, 1937; The American Mind, 1937; Joarnal of Emily Foster, 1933; Around the Horn, 1944. Gen. editor of Am. Authors' Series, 1925-29. Contbr. on lit. topics. Home: 152 Waite St., Hamden, Conn. Died Feb. 4, 1956; buried Rocky Hill (Conn.) Cemetery.

WILLIAMS, Wayne Cullen, lawyer; b. near Indianola, Ill., Sept. 20, 1878; s. Daniel Jackson and Katherine (Stockton) W.; grad. Decatur (Ill.) High School, 1897; student in liberal arts University of Denver, 1898-1900, LL.B., 1906; m. Lena B. Day, Dec. 1, 1909 (died Aug. 14, 1932); children—Daniel Day, Roger Withrow, Wayne De Armond, Jerre Stockton. Reporter Rocky Mountain News, Denver, 1906; admitted to Colo. bar, 1906, and began practice at Denver. Elected county judge, Denver County, 1912; asst. dist. atty., Denver, 1913-15; mem. Colo. Industrial Commn., 1915-17; atty. gen., Colo., 1923-25; apptd. spl. asst. to atty. gen. of U.S., July 25, 1933. Lecturer on labor problems, Sch. of Commerce, U. of Denver. Mem. Meth. Gen. Conf., 1916, Methodist World Service Commn., 1925-28; former mem. Meth. Bd. of Temperance, Prohibition and Pub. Morals, Methodist Council for Men (Denver). Regional counsel Office of Price Administration. Served as Four-minute man, World War I. Member Denver and Colo. state bar assns., Sigma Alpha Epsilon, Phi Delta Phi, Phi Beta Kappa. Democrat. Author: Study of William Jennings Bryan, 1923; The Life of William Jennings Bryan, 1935; American Tomorrows, 1939; Life of Gov. Wm. E. Sweet, 1943; A Rail Splitter for President, 1950. Contbr. to Christian Century and other mags. Office: Equitable Bldg., Denver 2. Aug. 15, 1953.

WILLIAMS, William Horace, engring. exec.; b. Fort McIntosh, Laredo, Tex., June 18, 1882; s. Maj. William Morrow (U.S. Army) and Eugenie Lelia (Simon) W.; preparatory edn., high sch., Detroit, and Doane Acad., Granville, O.; student Denison U. to 1902; m. Ruby Ionia Mugnier, Dec. 30, 1908 (dec.); children—Elizabeth Ionia, William Horace, Eugenie Lorrance, Robert Milton; m. 2d, Viola Bloch, October 26, 1923; children—Robert Howard (dec.), John Wesley. On preliminary surveys, Pa. R.R., 1901-02; with U.S. Army engrs., on constrn. breakwaters, Lorain, O., in charge levees, New Orleans to Gulf of Mexico, 1903-04; resident engr. Christie & Lowe, civ. engrs., jetty constrn., Miss. River, 1905-07; mem. Doullut & Williams, 1908-21; sec.-treas. and gen. mgr. Doullut & Williams Shipbuilding Co., 1918-21; pres., gen. mgr. Doullut & Williams, Inc., 1921-24; becmae pres., gen. mgr. W. Horace Williams Co., Inc., 1925, pres., dir., 1933-40, pres., gen. mgr., 1950-51, chmn. bd., 1951—; mem. firm, gen. mgr. W. Horace Williams Co., 1940—; v.p. Merritt-Chapman & Scott Corp., 1931-32; pres., gen. mgr. Merritt-Chapman & Williams Corp., 1931-33; pres., dir. Baronne Howard Realty Co., Inc.; dir., mem. exec. com. Whitney Nat. Bank, New Orleans. Mem. La. Engring. Soc. (past pres.; life mem.), Am. Soc. C.E., Am. Soc. Mil. Engrs., Beta Theta Pi. Mason (Shriner). Clubs: Bankers (N.Y.), Internat. House (New Orleans); various carnival orgns. Home: Galabank-on-the Jourdan, Star Route, Bay St. Louis, Miss. Office: 833 Howard Av., New Orleans. Died Feb. 6, 1957; buried Metairie Cemetery, New Orleans.

WILLIAMS, Wilson, former mem. Rep. Nat. Com.; b. Woodbury, Ga., Nov. 6, 1893; s. Wilson and Lula (Holloway) W.; educated Atlanta College of Pharmacy, 1910-11; m. Julia Gill, Dec. 5, 1916; children—Rochelle, Alexa. Engaged in farming in Georgia. Chmn. and pres. Medley Mfg. Co., Columbua, Ga.; vice pres. Gastonia Roller Flyer & Spindle Co., Gastonia, N.C.; dir. Warren Foundery & Pipe Corp., Warren Pipe Co. of Mass., Inc., N.Y. Mem. State Planning Bd., 1941-43; mem. Agrl. and Indsl. Development Bd. of Ga., 1943-47; Republican Nat. Committeeman, 1940-48. Meth. Clubs: Columbus Country, Columbus Rotary. Home: Green Island Hills, Columbus, Ga. Office: P.O. Box 1319, Columbus, Ga. Died Jan. 1950.

WILLIAMS, Wynant James, prof. elec. engring.; b. Port Dover, Ont., Can., Mar. 9, 1884; s. Benjamin and Christine (Alexander) W.; student Heriot Watt Coll., Edinburgh, Scotland, 1899-1900; B.S. in Civil Engring., Rensselaer Poly. Inst., Troy, N.Y., 1905; student Technische Hochschule, Berlin, 1909-10; m. Alice Louise Carpenter, Dec. 28, 1912; children—Wynant James, Ruth Louise. Asst. in physics and elec. engring. Rensselaer Poly. Inst., 1905-06, instr., 1906-13, asst. prof., 1913-34, prof., 1934-40, head of elec. engring. dept., 1940—. Mem. Am. Inst. E.E., Soc. Engrs. Eastern N.Y., A.A.A.S., Sigma Xi, Tau Beta Pi. Presbyn. Home: 40 Norwood Av., Albany, N.Y. Died May 1, 1950.

WILLIAMS, Wythe, writer; b. Meadville, Pa., Sept. 18, 1881; s. Wilbur Garrettson and Caroline (Wythe) W.; student Ohio Wesleyan U., 1898-1900; m. Viola Irwin, Mar. 22, 1913; children—Wilbur M., David Irwin, Ian Wythe. Reporter Mpls. Tribune, 1905, Milw. Sentinel, 1906, Chgo. Examiner and Daily News, 1907-08, N.Y. World, 1909, London corr., 1910-12, N.Y. Times, 1912-13, trans to Paris, 1913, and war corr. Times, 1914-17; spl. corr. Collier's Weekly, in Europe, 1918, London Daily Mail, at Berlin, 1919; returned to U.S. as dir. propaganda of Am. Com. for Devasted France; Retrned to Europe as Paris corr. Pub. Ledger; corr. on European politics, for Staurday Evening Post, 1915-26; spl. corr. N.Y. Times, at League of Nations, 1927-28, chief corr. of Berlin Bureau, same, 1929; chief corr. Hearst newspapers and Universal Service, London, 1931; editor and general manager, Greenwich Time, 1937-40; political commentator, WOR-Mutual Broadcasting System, 1940-41. Special assistant to bd. dir., Reconstruction Finance Corp., 1945-46. With American Ambulance, Paris, France, 1914; corr. with Allied armies throughout World War I. Mem. Sigma Chi, Nat. Inst. Social Sciences; pres. Anglo-Am. Press Assn. of Paris, 1922; pres. Internat. Assn. of Journalists accredited to League of Nations, 1928.

Pres. Overseas Press Club of Am., 1944-45. Decorated Chevalier Legion of Honor. Republican. Clubs: Players, Dutch Treat, Lotos, Advertising (New York); Cercle Artistique et Litteraire, Racing Automobile, Sporting Club de France. Author: Passed by the Censor, 1916; When Chenal Sings the Marseillaise, 1917; This Flesh, 1931; Dusk of Empire, 1937; Adaption of Cahen's Men Against Hitler, 1939; Washington Broadcast, 1944; The Tiger of France, 1949; (with Albert Parry) Riddle of the Reich, 1941; (with William Van Narvig) Secret Sources, 1943. Address: 15 Boulevard East, Weehawken, N.J. Died July 13, 1956.

WILLIAMSON, George Emery, paper manufacturer; b. Worcester, Mass., Sept. 11, 1878; s. Frank E. and Ida M. (Moore) W.; ed. Worcester public and high sch.; B.S., Worcester (Mass.) Polytechnic Inst., 1900, Doctor of Engineering (hon.), 1950; m. Alice May Lytle, June 9, 1903 (dec.); children—Mrs. Elizabeth W. Sharkey, Mrs. Harriet W. Easton; m. 2d, Florence Sargeant Clark, Sept. 7, 1938. With Am. Writing Paper Co., 1901; chemist, foreman, engr. of works Union Metallic Cartridge Co., Bridgeport, Conn., 1902-11; chief engr. and asst. to pres. Strathmore Paper Co., 1911-28, treas., 1928-46, v.p., 1942-46, pres., 1946-48, now chmn; dir. Rising Paper Co., asst. treas., 1928-38, treas., 1939-45; treas. and dir. Premoid Products, Inc., 1928-45, pres. and dir. since 1945; president Agawam Chemicals, Inc., 1945-48. Cons. engr., Ordnance Dept., U.S. Army, 1918. Treas. and trustee Eastern States Expn., 1928-42, v.p., chmn. exec. com. and trustee, 1942-46, v.p., mem. exec. com. and trustee since 1946; dir. Springfield Nat. Bank, Boston Mfrs. Mut. Fire Ins. Co. Former trustee Worcester Poly. Inst., Springfield Coll. Pres. Springfield Y.M.C.A., 1940-45, dir. since 1928; hon. pres., dir. Hampden County Improvement League; dir., clk. Junior Achievement, Inc., 1926-46. Member Engring. Soc. Western Mass. (pres. 1921-22), Tech. Assn. Pulp & Paper Industry (pres. 1921-22), Writing Paper Mfrs. Assn. (exec. com.), Associated Industries of Mass. (exec. com.), Nat. Assn. Mfrs. (bd. dirs., 1944-45), Am. Soc. M.E. (1906-31), American Paper and Pulp Association (vice pres.), Sigma Alpha Epsilon. Clubs: Colony, Rotary, Reality (Springfield); Metropolitan (New York). Republican. Conglist. Mason (32°). Home: 22 Maplewood Terrace, Springfield, Mass. Office: West Springfield, Mass. Died July 3, 1951.

WILLIAMSON, Mary Lynn, educator, author; b. nr. Charlottesville, Va., May 4, 1850; d. Peachy Rush and Mary Frances Harrison; ed. Farmsville Female Coll. and Richmond Female Coll.; m. White-Williamson, Nov. 2, 1874. Teacher, 1869—. Author: Life of Gen. Robert E. Lee (in Easy Words for Children), 1895 J8; Life of Gen. T. J. (Stonewall) Jackson, 1898 J8; Life of Washongton, 12; Life of J. E. B. Stuart, 1914. Address: New Market, Va. Died Feb. 6, 1923; buried St. Matthews Cemetery, New Market, Va.

WILLIAMSON, Thomas, lawyer; b. Staunton, Ill., May 19, 1867; s. Thomas and Elizabeth (Creighton) W.; student Northern Ind. Normal Sch., 1887, St. Louis Law Sch., 1890-91; m. Martha L. Binney, Oct. 14, 1891; children—Bessie Eleanor, Jessie Christine, Thomas Binney (vice admiral, United States Navy), and Robert Warnock. Began practice at Mt. Olive, Illinois, 1891; moved to Edwardsville, 1899; member firm of Warnock, Williamson & Burroughs; master in chancery, 1919-22; asst. atty. gen. of Ill., 1919-21; U.S. atty., Southern Dist. of Ill., by apptmt. of President Harding, July 1, 1922-Aug. 1, 1926; asst. dir. Dept. Purchases and Constrn., 1930-33; referee in bankruptcy Southern Dist. of Illinois. Dir. Bank of Edwardsville. 1917-32. President Board of Education, Edwardsville, 16 yrs.; chairman Council of Defense, World War. Presbyterian. Mason (33°), K.P. (Grand Chancellor), Woodman. Clubs: Madison County, Rotary of Edwardsville (pres.). Del. to Internat. Rotary Conv., Belgium; dist. governor of Rotary International, 1930-31. Originator of the legal system for road constrn. in Illinois. Author: Madison County Hard Road System: Origin of the Flag; A Little Journey Beyond the Sea; "This Nation Shall Not Perish"; The Founding of a Nation. Home: 800 St. Louis St., Edwardsville, Ill. Died Apr. 3, 1956; buried Valley View Cemetery, Edwardsville, Ill.

WILLIFORD, Forrest Estey, army officer; b. Coffeen, Ill., Jan. 22, 1882; s. Hiram Henry and Mary Alice Ann (McWilliams) W.; B.S., U.S. Mil. Acad., 1906; grad. Coast Ary. Sch., regular course, 1915, advanced course, 1925; M.S., Mass. Inst. Tech., 1917, M.S., Harvard U., 1917; grad. Army War Coll., 1920, 30; Command and Gen. Staff Sch., 1926; m. Fredrika Martin, Dec. 29, 1908; 1 dau., Fredrika Martin (Mrs. William L. McPherson). Commd. 2d lt., U.S. Army, advanced through grades to brig. gen., 1940; retired, 1944. Served as private, Ill. Nat. Guard, 1900-02. Awarded Distinguished Service medal and Victory medal, 1920; decorated Officer Legion of Honor (France), 1920. Mason. Address: Box 23, Blacksburg, Va. Died Mar. 17, 1955.

WILLINGS, George Carke, publisher; b. Liverpool, England, May 16, 1888; s. Thomas Radley and Lucy Anne (Clarke) W.; B.A., Coll. of Preceptors, England, 1906; m. Georgia I. Renshaw, 1911; 1 dau., Frances Georgia (Mrs. Henry G. Wells, Jr.). Successively clk. L.&N. R.R. Louisville, contracting agt., Mobile, Ala., traffic mgr. Gulf, Fla. & Ala. R.R.; now exec. v.p. Jacksonville Jour., Panama City Herald, Pensacola Jour., Pensacola News, Pensacola Broadcasting Co., Innerarity Island Recreational Estates; v.p. Intertype corpns. of N.Y., London, Cal., So. N.Y. Power and Ry. Corpn., Olean Bradford and Salamanca Ry. Dir. Jacksonville C. of C.; chmn. Social Welfare Bd., Duval Co., Fla.; mem. exec. com. Community Chest, Jacksonville; dir. Tourist and Conv. Bur., Jacksonville. Lt. col. on staff gov. of Fla. Mem. Asso. Press, So. Newspaper Pubs. Assn. Catholic. Clubs: Rotary, Timuquana Country, Florida Yacht (Jacksonville); Escambia (charter mem.); Pensacola Country (pres. 1930); Asso. Advertising Clubs of World. Home: 1847 Greenwood Av. Office: Jacksonville Jour. Bldg., Jacksonville, Fla. Deceased.

WILLIS, Edwin Caldwell, lawyer, state ofcl.; b. Cave City, Ky., June 4, 1906; s. Michael Owsley and Mary (Smith) W.; A.B., U. Mich., 1929; student Harvard, 1929-30; LL.B., U. Louisville, 1934; m. Helen Beard, Aug. 4, 1941. Admitted to Ky. bar, 1933, since practiced Louisville; practice limited to civil litigation; asst. city atty., Louisville, 1937-41, atty. Dept. Pub. Wks., 1942; commr. indsl. relations Commonwealth of Ky., since Dec. 1949; mem. Ky. Agrl. and Indsl. Development Bd. since Jan. 1950. Mem. bd. aldermen City of Louisville, 1943; Dem. nominee for co. judge, Jefferson Co., Ky., 1945; apptd. mem. Jefferson Co. Election Commn., 1946. Mem. Am., Ky. State, Louisville bar assns. Mem. Christian Ch. Club: Mose Green Democratic (Louisville). Home: 2224 Lauderdale Rd., Lsvl. 5. Office: Kentucky Home Life Bldg., Louisville. Died Oct. 31, 1953; buried Cave Hill Cemetery, Louisville.

WILLIS, Raymond Eugene, ex-senator, publisher; b. Waterloo, Ind., Aug. 11, 1875; s. Frank Welcome and Josephine (Dickinson) W.; A.B., Wabash Coll., 1896, hon. A.M., 1901; m. Mary Adelaide Taylor, June 15, 1902. Began as printers apprentice Waterloo (Ind.) Press, 1889; editor, pub. Angola Magnet, 1898-1907, Steuben Republican, 1907—; pres. Steuben Printing Co.; postmaster, Angola, 1910-11. Pres. Angola C. of C., 1924-25; dir. Steuben County chpt. A.R.C., 1920—; chmn. Steuben County Council of Defense, 1917-18. Mem. Ind. State Legislature, 1919-21, floor leader, 1920; Rep. nominee for U.S. senator, 1938; elected to U.S. Senate 1940, for term ending Jan. 3, 1947. Mem. Ind. Rep. Editorial Assn., Phi Delta Theta, Sigma Delta Chi. Conglist. Mason (33°). Clubs: Rotary (dist. gov. 20th dist., 1934-35); Indiana Society (Chgo.). Home: 212 S. West St., Angola, Ind. Died Mar. 21, 1956.

WILLKIE, E(dward) E(verett), foods exec.; b. Elwood, Ind., Dec. 25, 1896; s. Herman F. and Henrietta (Trish) W.; grad. U.S. Naval Acad., 1921; m. Faye Hollingsworth, Apr. 8, 1922; children—Marion Elizabeth, Edward Everett, Frederick Rew. Joined Libby, McNeill & Libby, Chgo., 1923, v.p., 1939-52, dir., 1944-52; pres. Pacific Am. Fisheries, Inc., Bellingham, Wash., 1952—, Cedergreen Frozen Pack Corp., 1953—. Apptd. mem. fish industry adv. com. WPB. Served as ensign, USN, 1921-22. Mem. Nat. Canners Assn. (pres. 1954), Beta Theta Pi. Republican. Baptist. Mason. Clubs: Rainier (Seattle); Yacht (Bellingham). Home: 219 Hawthorn Rd. Office: 401 Harris Av., Bellingham, Wash. Died Oct. 15, 1956; buried Bronswood Cemetery, Hinsdale, Ill.

WILLKIE, Herman Frederick, business consultant, born Elwood, Ind., September 30, 1890; son of Herman F. and Henrietta (Trisch) Willkie; Bachelor of Arts, Indiana U., 1912; m. Helen F. Hall, June 10, 1944; children—H. F. II, Arlinda, Julia, Hall Francis. Admitted Indiana bar. Control chemist, later soil and fertilizer chemist, chief chemist Fajardo Sugar Company, Puerto Rico, 1911-16; assistant chief chemist, Great Western Sugar Co., 1911-12; mgr. research Lab. and mfr. spl. products, Celluloid Co. of Am., 1916-17; research chemist U.S. Indsl. Alcohol Co., 1917-24; asst. plant mgr. Canadian Indsl. Alcohol Co., 1924-27; gen. supt., Hiram Walker & Sons, Ltd., 1927-33; v.p., prodn. mgr. and builder Peoria Distillery and designer of Dumbarton, Scotland, Distillery, 1933-37; v.p. and dir. Distillers Corp.-Seagrams, Ltd., since 1937; now dir. and cons. Mem. Am. Inst. C.E., A.A.A.S. Mason. Clubs: University, Chemists (N.Y. City); Creve Coeur (Peoria); Pendennis (Louisville); Cosmos (Washington, D.C.). Author: (books) A Rebel Yells; An Outline for Industry; Food for Thought; Fundamentals of Distillery Practice. Contbr. articles to jours. Address: 4270 N. Meridian St., Indpls. 8. Died Dec. 28, 1959.

WILLOUGHBY, Barrett, writer; b. Alaksa; d. Martin and Flornace (Clink) Barrett; ed. in convents and under pvt. tutors; m. Robert H. Prosser, Oct. 19, 1927 (died 1928); m. 2d, Capt. Larry O'Connor, July 17, 1935 (div. 1942, resumed former married name). Writes exclusively of Alaska. Mem. P.E.N. Author: Where the Sun Swings North, 1922; Rocking Moon, 1925; Gentlemen Unafraid, 1928; Trail Eater, 1929; Sitka, Portal to Romance, 1930; Spawn of the North, 1932; Alaskans All, 1933; River House, 1935; Sondra O'Moore, 1939; Alaska Holiday, 1940; The Golden Totem, 1945. Contbr. to Cosmopolitan, American Mag., Saturday Evening Post, Reader's Digest. Home: 8816 Saturn St., Los Angeles 35. Died Aug. 1959.

WILLOUGHBY, Charles Grant, camera store exec.; b. Oceola, Ohio, Dec. 13, 1866; s. Jonathan Burke and Sarah Lucinda (Montpier) W.; ed. pub. schs., Mich.; m. Elli Ojala; 1 dau., Jessie Marguerite (Mrs. Arthur F. Schlobohm). Teacher Edgewood, Mich., 1886; messenger and apprentice, The Detroit, Lansing & Northern R.R., Ithaca, Mich., 1888, station agt., telegrapher, 1888-95, ticket agt. Detroit, 1895; dealer Vive Camera Co., as agent in Detroit, 1896-97, N.Y. rep., 1897-98; orgn. photographic supply bus. under own name, 1898-16; founder Charles G. Willoughby, Inc., N.Y. City, 1916, pres., 1916-26, chmn. bd., Willoughby Camera Stores, Inc., since 1926; pres. Willoughby Bond & Mortgage Co. since 1922. Hon. life mem. Nat. Photo Dealers Assn. Clubs: Siwanoy Country, Oval Table Society, Canadian of N.Y., Morse Telegraph of America, Inc. Home: Hotel Ansonia. Office: 110 32d St., N.Y. City 1. Died June 7, 1951.

WILLOUGHBY, Edwin Eliott, librarian; b. Phila., Nov. 5, 1899; s. Frank Faul and Annie (Smith) W.; A.B., Dickinson Coll., 1922; A.M., U. of Chicago, 1924; Ph.D., 1932; Litt.D., Dicksinson Coll., 1940. Sr. asst. Newberry Library, Chgo., 1922-28, reference librarian, 1929; European study as follow of John Simon Guggenheim Meml. Found., 1929-31; prof., acting head library sci. dept., Coll. of William and Mary, 1932-35; European study on grant from Am. Council of Learned Socs., summer 1934; chief bibliographer Folger Shakespeare Library, 1935-58, ret. 1958. Fellow Royal Soc. of Lit. (London). Mem. A.L.A., Bibliog. Soc. Am., Bibliog. Soc. (London), Shakespeare Assn. (London), Am. Legion, Phi Beta Kappa. Republican. Club: Grolier (N.Y.). Author: The Printing of the First Folio of Shakespeare, 1932; A Printer of Shakespeare; The Times and Books of William Jaggard, 1934; Fifty Printers Marks, 1947; The Making of the King James Bible, 1956. Contributor to Library Quarterly (adv. editor); contbd. to Encyclopedia Britannica and to Britannica Jr. Advisory editor Comptom's Picture Encyclopedia. Home: 414 W. Holly Av., Pitman, N.J. Died Oct. 2, 1959; buried Richwood, N.J.

WILLS, George Stockton, educator; b. Halifax County, N.C., Apr. 3, 1866; s. Richard Henry and Ann Louisa (Norman) W.; Ph.B., U. of N.C., 1889, Ph.M., 1896; A.M., Harvard, 1898; Litt.D., Western Maryland Coll., 1935; married Georgia M. Chidester, June 24, 1903 (died Feb. 25, 1943); children—Katharine Walker (dec.), Richard Norman, Merillat Chidester (Mrs. A. Vail Frost, Jr.). Instructor, Oak Ridge (N.C.), Military Inst., 1889-94; instr. English, University of North Carolina, 1894-96, and summer term, 1900; instr. English, Battle Ground Acad., Franklin, Tenn., 1900-01; prof. of English, Western Maryland College, 1898-1900, 1901-04, head department English, Western Maryland College, Sept. 1, 1922-44; prof. emeritus (same), Sept. 1, 1944—; prof. English, Greensboro Woman's Coll., N.C., 1904-07; instr. English, Baltimore Poly. Inst., 1907-12, and 1914-22, actg. head dept. of English and German, 1911-12, head of dept., 1914, head dept. of English, 1920-22. News editor Atlantic Ednl. Jour., Baltimore, 1908-11. Special instructor English, Univ. of Md., 1918-20; prof. English Western Md. Coll., summers 1945-50. Member American Association University Prof., S.A.R., Phi Beta Kappa, Sigma Nu. Wrote sketch of life and bibliography of works of Sidney Lanier, 1899; papers on Southern history and literature to Publs. of Southern History Assn., and biographies for Ashe and Van Noppen's Biographical History of North Carolina. Author: (with D. W. Hendrickson, J. D. Makosky and Evelyn W. Wenner) Freshman Handbook in English; History of Western Maryland College (1866-1886), 1949; History of Western Maryland College (1886-1951), 1952. Episcopalian. Home: Westminster, Md. Died Feb. 27, 1956; buried Druid Ridge Cemetery, Pikesville, Md.

WILMER, Cary Breckinridge, clergyman; b. Williamsburg, Va., June 2, 1859; s. George Thornton and Mary Barbara (Saunders) W.; B.A., William and Mary Coll., Va., 1875; Theol. Dept., Kenyon Coll., 1883-84; D.D., University of South, Sewanee, Tenn., 1906; married Mrs. Kate Phillips Ammons, January 23, 1905 (deceased, April 27, 1950); 1 son, Cary Breckinridge. Deacon, 1884, priest, 1886, P.E. Church; rector Grace Ch., Ocala, Florida, 1884-89, Ch. of Resurrection, Fernbank, O., 1889-91; supt. Colored Orphan Asylum, Lynchburg, Va., 1891-98; rector, Ch. of Epiphany, Lynchburg, 1892-93, Ch. of Nativity, Cincinnati, 1898-1900, St. Luke's Ch., Atlanta, 1900-24, now rector emeritus; prof. of practical theology, Univ. of the South, 1924-32 (retired). Chaplain, retired, 5th Regt. Ga. Nat. Guard. Recipient loving cup as Pioneer in Inter-racial Good Will from Colored People of Atlanta, Ga. Delegate General Conv. P.E. Ch. 6 times to 1925. Charter mem. Ga. Nat. Child Labor Com. (hon. mem.); charter mem. The Southern Regional Council, Inc. since Jan. 6, 1944. Mem. Elks, Pi Kappa Alpha, Phi Beta Kappa. Author mag. articles, book reviews and tracts on religious subjects; writer on Atlanta Jour. Sunday Mag., 1919-40; also collaborator in a number of books; lecturer; author prize essay on The Name of the Church; contributing to revision of Book of Common Prayer. Special speaker for Y.M.C.A. with A.E.F. in France, 1919. Lecturer at College of Preachers, Washington, D.C., and Clergy Conf., Kanuga, N.C. Home: 101 South Armenia Av., Tampa, Fla. Died Jan. 1958.

WILMETH, James Lillard (wĭl'mĕth); b. Chewalla, McNairy County, Tenn., Oct. 10, 1870; s. Benjamin F. and Isabella Bruce (DePoyster) W.; student Christian Coll., Howard County, Ark., 1890-93; LL.B., Nat. U., Washington, D.C., 1906; m. Alpha B. Moore, Nov. 5, 1896; children—James L., Clyde Fairfax, Janice Louise. Became connected with office of auditor of Post Office Dept., Washington, D.C., 1895; lawyer in office of comptroller of the Treasury, 1906-10; chief clerk of Treasury Dept., 1910-17; dir. Bur. of Engraving and Printing, 1917-22; national sec. Jr. Order United Am. Mechanics, 1923-51, also editor Junior American, retired, 1951; consultant since July 1951. As chief clerk assisted in reorganizing the Treasury Department; directed the making of moneys, bonds and securities for financing World War I; visited Europe at outbreak of war, in charge of relief voted by Congress for Am. Citizens. Mem. Nat. Fraternal Congress (past pres. press sect.). Mem. Pa. Acad. Fine Arts, Pa. Hist. Soc., Geneal. Soc. of Pa., Sigma Nu Phi, Legal, Franklin Institute. Mem. of Christian (Disciples) Church; past pres. Pa. Christian Missionary Soc. Mason, Modern Woodman. Democrat. Author of Wilmeth, Wilmoth, Wilmot Genealogy; also Book of Addresses. Home: School Lane House, 5450 Wissahickon Av. Office: 3025-29 N. Broad St., Phila. Died Apr. 24, 1959.

WILMOT, R(oyal) J(ames), horticulturist; b. Rochester, N.Y., Jan. 9, 1898; s. Louis George and Gertrude (Bennett) W.; B.S.A., U. Tenn., 1922; M.S.A., U. Fla., 1931; m. Gladys Gallaher, Nov. 14, 1922; 1 son, Royal James. With Agr. Exp. Sta., Gainesville, Fla., 1927—. Sec. Am. Camellia Soc., 1945—; editor Am. Camellia Yearbrook, 1946-49. Served as 2d lt., F.A., U.S. Army, 1918. Mem. Fla. State Hort. Soc., Sigma Nu, Alpha Zeta, Phi Sigma, Phi Kappa Phi, Thrysus. Democrat. Presbyterian. Club: Mens Garden (Gainesville, Fla.). Contbr. articles to profl. and sci. publs. Specialist in ornamental horticulture and fumigation research. Home: Box 2397, Gainesville, Fla. Died May 7, 1950.

WILNER, Robert Franklin, bishop; b. Forty Fort, Pa., Apr. 10, 1889; s. George Mortimer and Lillian Isabel (Price) W.; ed. Wilkes-Barre (Pa.) Business Coll., 1905-06, Bloomsburg (Pa.) State Teachers Coll., 1907-09, Temple U. (med. dept.), 1909-10, 1911-12, Philadelphia Divinity Sch., 1927-28; D.D., Philadelphia Divinity Sch., 1947; m. Alfaretta Amburn Stark, Apr. 10, 1917; children—Alfaretta Isabel, Robert Edson, George Amburn (killed in action in Germany, Nov. 14, 1944). Ordained deacon Episcopal Ch., 1928, priest, 1929. Stenographer, Wilkes-Barre, 1906-07, 1910-13; sec. to George W. Bailey, of Phila., 1913-15; apptd. missionary to China by Bd. of Missions Episcopal Ch., 1915; asst. treas. China Mission, Shanghai, later Hankow, 1916-26; staff St. Stephens Mission to Chinese, Manila, P.I., 1928-29; chaplain Brent Sch. (for Am. boys and girls) 1929-31; rector Easter Sch. (for Igorot boys and girls), asst. priest Ch. of Resurrection, Baguio, P.I., 1929-37; elected suffragan bishop, P.I., Oct., 1937, consecrated bishop Jan. 25, 1938. Address: All Saints Mission, Bontoc, Mt. Prov., Philippines. Died Mar. 1960.

WILSHIRE, Joseph (wĭl'shīr), mfr.; b. Cincinnati, O., Dec. 18, 1879; s. Joseph White and Ada (Van Hamm) W.; ed. pub. schs.; m. Helen Seely, 1907 (died 1914); 1 son, Joseph White III; m. 2d, Helen Payne, 1919. Began with Arctic Ice Co., Cincinnati, later apprentice Bullock Electric Co.; entered employ of The Fleischmann Co., 1898, and continued with same as salesman, supervisor of agencies Western div., gen. sales agt. in Mexico, asst. mgr. Western div., gen. mgr., v.p., 1919, 1st v.p. and asst. to pres., 1920, pres. from Mar. 12, 1925, until merger into Standard Brands, Inc., 1929; pres. Standard Brands, Inc., 1937-40; chmn. bd. Continental, Inc., Danbury, Conn., at time of death (co. cited by U.S. govt. for achievements World War II). Mem. Mil. Order Loyal Legion. Clubs: United Hunts Racing Assn. (New York); Masters of Fox Hounds Assn. (Boston); Round Hill (Greenwich, Conn.). Home: Wilshire Farms, Round Hill Rd., Greenwich, Conn. Office: 595 Madison Av., N.Y. City. Died Nov. 17, 1951; buried Spring Grove Cemetery, Cincinnati.

WILSON, Albert Dwight, mfr. brass; b. Forestville, Conn., Feb. 5, 1877; s. John O. and Caroline (Beach) W.; student Huntsinger Business Coll., Bristol, Conn.; m. Cherrie Ward, June 22, 1904; 1 dau., Estelle (Mrs. Frank M. Jerman). Clk. for Muzzy Bros. & Co., Bristol, 1895-1902; with Bristol Brass Corp., mfrs. sheet brass, rod and wire, 1902—, serving successively as clk., bookkeeper, cashier, asst. treas., v.p. and treas., until 1935, then pres. and treas., now chmn. Republican. Mason (32°). Clubs: Chippanee Country (Bristol); Farmington Country. Home: 209 Woodland St. Office: 580 Broad St., Bristol, Conn. Died Jan. 18, 1951.*

WILSON, Alexander, army officer; b. Farmington, Mo., Nov. 11, 1886; midshipman, U.S. Naval Acad., 1906-08; resigned to accept commn. as 2d lt. Inf. Regular Army, 1911, and advanced through the grades to brig. gen., 1942; became exec. officer, Edgewood Arsenal, 1927; Transferred to C.W.S., 1929 and assigned as chief of Training Div. of Office of C.W.S., Washington, D.C.; became executive officer in Office of Chief of C.W.S., 1931; began tour of duty as chemical officer, Hawaiian Dept., Ft. Shafter, 1933; moved to hdqrs. 7th Corps Area, Omaha, Neb., as Corps Area chemical officer, 1934; assigned as pres. of Chem. Warfare Bd., Edgewood Arsenal, Md., 1938; with Air Force Combat Command, Bolling Field, D.C., 1941; with Office, Chief of Chem. Warfare Service, Washington, D.C., 1942; named commnadant of Chem. Warfare Sch., Edgewood, Md., Oct. 1942. Died July 1, 1952.*

WILSON, Arthur Riehl, ret. army officer, author; b. Cherokee, Cal., July 18, 1894; s. Alexander M. and Agnes Matilda (Sorenson) W.; A.B., U. Cal., 1919; grad. Field Arty. Tech. Sch., 1922, Command and General Staff Sch., 1934, Field Officers' course, Chem. Warfare Sch., 1935; Army War Coll., 1935. Instr. Comd. and Gen. Staff Sch., 1935-37; promoted maj. gen., 1944, retired 1946; v.p. Trans World Airlines, 1946-47; v.p. Indsl. Products Trading Co., Zurich, 1947—. Mason (K.T.). Clubs: Bachelordon (Berkeley, Cal.); Faculty (U. Mo.); Army and Navy (Washington). Author: Field Artillery Manual (2 vols.), 1925; Field Artillery Manual (2 vols.), 1940; Drill and Ceremonies for Field Artillery, 1941. Home: 2470 Quincy Rd., Oroville, Cal. Died Aug. 11, 1956; buried Cherokee, Cal.

WILSON, Benjamin, organizer and pres. Converse Coll.; b. Mayesville, S.C., March 12, 1862; s. Benjamin F. and Rebecca E. W.; grad. Davidson Coll. (medallist), 1884 (A.M.); grad. Princeton Theol. Sem., cum laude, 1887; student in Germany, 1888; m. Sallie Gist Farrar, July 30, 1890. Ordained to Presby'n ministry, 1887; pastor 1st Presby'n Ch., Spartanburg, S.C., 1887-90. Organized and became first pres. Converse Coll. (endowed undenaminational coll. for women), 1889; Independent Democrat; mem. Sigma Alpha Epsilon; hon. mem. Literary Soc., Princeton Univ. Author: Christology of Genesis, 1888; Ethical Application of Materialism, 1900, both in Quar. Rev.; also numerous addresses and articles on ee'n. Address: Spartanburg, S.C. Deceased.

WILSON, Burwell L., farmer, bus. exec.; b. Barren Co., Ky., Nov. 24, 1861; s. Willis L. and Evalyn C. (Mosby) W.; common sch. edn.; m. Lizzie King, Sept. 29, 1887. Began as shipper of live stock, 1882, since also engaged in farming on extensive scale, and in other lines of business; owner of farms in Barren, Warren and Rock Castle cos., Ky.; mem. Wilson Bros., B. L. Wilson & Son, farming and live stock; pres. Lewis-Wilson-Hicks Co., lumber; dir. H. Y. Davis Nat. Bank, Cave City, Ky. Trustee Liberty Coll., Glasgow, Ky. Democrat. Baptist. Mason. Address: Cave City, Ky. Died July 16, 1936.

WILSON, Carroll Louis, director of finance; born in Minneapolis, Minn., March 16, 1900; s. Louis Blanchard and Mary Elizabeth (Stapleton) W.; A.B. cum laude, Harvard, 1920, A.B. in Mechanical Engineering, magna cum laude, 1922; m. Harriot Boynton Sawyer, June 20, 1923; children—Katherine, Constance Bird. Began as apprentice Westinghouse Electric Mfg. Co., 1922; heating engr. in sales dept. and later gen. engr., 1922-28; industrial analyst Investment Research Corp., Detroit, 1928-29; dir. research and mem. investment policy com. Scudder, Stevens & Clark, Boston, 1929-39; spl. asst. to U.S. Sec. of Commerce, 1939-40; exec. asst. to dir. Bur. of Fgn. and Domestic Commerce, 1939-40, asst. dir. Sept.-Dec. 1940, acting dir. Dec. 1940-Mar. 1941, dir. Mar., 1941-Aug. 1943; consultant to U. S. sec. of commerce, 1943-45; consultant to Nat. Patent Planning Commn., 1943-45; sec. Com. for Econ. Development, Sept. 15, 1942-Oct. 1, 1944, Venture Counsel, 1944-47; dir. of finance Champion Paper and Fibre Co., Hamilton, O., since 1947. Served as mem. Harvard R.O.T.C., 1916-18, Harvard S.A.T.C., 1918. Mem. Tau Beta Pi, Am. Legion. Sec. Harvard Club of Mich., 1928. Episcopalian. Clubs: Harvard (Washington); Queen City, Harvard, Bankers (Cincinnati). Author of article on elec. furnaces in Mech. Engrs. Handbook, 1930 edit. Home: 501 Dick Av., Hamilton, O. Died Jan. 30, 1958.

WILSON, Charles Scoon, ex-mem. Federal Farm Bd.; b. Hall, N.Y., Dec. 11, 1879; s. Thomas Burrell and Margaret Ann (Scoon) W.; grad. Canandaigua (N.Y.) Acad., 1900; A.B., Cornell U., 1904, M.S. in Agr., 1905; m. Ada L. Miller, Sept. 4, 1907; children—Margaret Scoon, Thomas Miller. Prof. pomology N.Y. State Coll. Agr., Cornell U., 1905-15; state commr. agr., N.Y., and dir. N.Y. State Expt. Sta., Geneva, 1915-20; mem. N.Y. State Fair Commn., 1915-20; farmer, fruit grower, 1920-29; mem. Federal Farm Bd., 1929-33; farmer, 1933—. Pres. N.Y. State Hort. Soc.; sec. Western N.Y. Fruit Growers Coöp. Packing Assn. Trustee Cornell U., 1915-20; pres. Finger Lakes council, Boy Scouts Am., 1935-37, mem. nat. rural scouting com., 1937—. Mem. N.Y. Grange, Alpha Zeta. Republican. Conglist. Odd Fellow. Home: Hall, N.Y. Died Jan. 1954; buried Hall.

WILSON, David Cooper, educator; born Clarinda, Ia., Jan. 30, 1882; s. David C. and Abigail (Thome) W.; A.B., Princeton, 1904, A.M., 1910; Ph.D., U. Mich., 1928; m. Mary Scott Spencer, Aug. 8, 1916; 1 son, David Spencer. Prof. Greek Whitworth (Wash. Coll., 1904-06; tchr. Latin and Greek Broadway High Sch., Seattle, 1906-09; prof. Latin Sterling (Kan.) Coll., 1913-14; asso. headmaster Moran Sch. for Boys, Seattle, 1914-21; prof. Green Hampden-Sydney Coll., 1923-57, dean, 1939-54, ret. Mem. Mid-West, South classical assns. Presbyn. Club: Lions. Home: Hampden-Sydney, Va. Died July 17, 1958; buried College Church Cemetery, Hampden-Sydney.

WILSON, Edgar Bright; b. Chapel Hill, Tenn., July 27, 1874; s. James A. and Mary (Graves) W.; prep. edn., Chapel Hill Acad.; student Cumberland U., Lebanon, Tenn., 1892-93; m. Alma Lackey, Mar. 1903; children—Sue Alexander (Mrs. William S. Cutchins), Edgar Bright, Alma (Mrs. T. Ames Wheeler). Admitted to Tenn. bar, 1896, and began practice at Gallatin; mem. Tenn. Ho. of Rep., 1899-1903 (speaker 1901-03); moved to N.Y. City, 1904. Dollar-a-year man, War Trade Bd., World War. Retired. Democrat. Presbyterian. Mason. Home: 1801 16th St. N.W., Washington. Died Feb. 2, 1953.

WILSON, Edward Harlan, orthopaedic surgeon; b. Columbus, O., May 31, 1891; s. Edward J. and Ida Sarah (Tudor) W.; ed. Central High Sch., Columbus, O., 1908-11; B.S., Dartmouth Coll., 1915; M.D., Harvard, 1920; m. Dorothy Hewitt, October 7, 1922; children—Edward Harlan, Jr., Dorothy Elizabeth, Priscilla. Intern surg. service, Mass. Gen. Hosp., Boston, Mass., 1920-22; orthopaedic service, Mass. Gen. and Boston Children hosps., 1923; entered pvt. practice of orthopaedic surgery, Columbus, O., 1924; prof. orthopaedic surgery and head dept. Coll. of Medicine, Ohio State U., Columbus, O.; dir. orthopaedic surgery University Hosp. Childrens Hosp. and Mt. Carmel Hosp. (both Columbus); dir. Midland Mutual Life Ins. Co., Columbus, O. Resident dir. Am. Hosp. in Britain, Oxford, 1942. Hon. fellow Exeter Coll. Oxford, Eng. Fellow Am. Coll. Surgeons; mem. Am. Acad. Orthopaedic Surg., Am. Orthopaedic Assn., Am. Bd. Orthopaedic Surg. (1936), Buckeye Orthopaedic Assn., Clin. Orthopaedic Soc., A.M.A., Professional Advisory Com. on Rehabilitation (chmn.), Advisory Com. on Cerebral Palsy, Polio, and Crippled Children, Phi Delta Theta (Dartmouth), Dragon Sr. Soc. of Dartmouth, Phi Rho Sigma. Conglist. (Shriner, Mason Scottish Rite). Clubs: Columbus, Rocky Fork Hunt and Country, Rotary, Robert Jones of England. Home: 181 Stanbery Av., Columbus 9. Office: 380 E. Town St., Columbus 15, O. Died Dec. 14, 1952; buried Greenlawn Cemetery, Columbus.

WILSON, Edward Taylor, petroleum corp. exec.; b. Ballston Spa, N.Y., Jan. 25, 1869; s. John Robert and Susan Patience (Taylor) W.; ed. pub. schs.; m. Susie Milne, Feb. 4, 1902; children—Mrs. Isabel Wilson Johnson, Edward Taylor, Laurence Raeburn, Mrs. Elsie Wilson Blackwell, Robert Bruce. Clerk, gen. offices of Standard Oil Co., N.Y.C., 1886; held various positions with the Standard companies in Middle and Western States, and served as pres. West India Oil Co.; at time of dissolution of the Standard Oil Co., 1911, was pres. Continental Oil Co., the distributing agency for the Rocky Mountain region, until meger, 1924, of Continental Oil Co. and Mutual Oil Co., as Continental Oil Co., of which was made chmn. bd.; title of co. changed upon merger, 1929, with Marland Oil Co., to Continental Oil Co. (Del.), of which was elected chmn. bd., retired 1932; dir. U.S. Nat. Bank (Denver); retired. Mem. Am. Petroleum Inst. Baptist. Clubs: Denver, Mile High, Denver Country; Bankers of Am. (N.Y.); Point O'Woods Club, Point O'Woods Yacht. Home: 180 Franklin St., Denver, Colo.; (summer; Point O'Woods, L.I., N.Y. Died Dec. 1957.

WILSON, Ernest Dana, coll. prof.; b. Harlan, Ia., Nov. 2, 1890; s. Charles Henry and Harriet Elizabeth (Dana) W.; B.S., U. of Neb., 1913; Ph.D., U. of Chicago, 1915; research associate physical chemistry Massachusetts Institute Technology, 1913-14; m. Avilda Downing Moore, Dec. 29, 1915; children—Robert Downing, Avilda Dana. Fellow Mellon Inst., Pittsburgh, Pa., 1916-18; chief engr., Graton & Knight Mfg. Co., Worcester, Mass., 1918-20; chief, comml. research, George Batten Co., N.Y. City, 1920-21; dept. head, Am. Cyanamid Co., N. Y. City, 1922-33; consultant, Barsky and Wilson, N.Y. City, 1934-36; pres., Zialite Corp., N.Y. City, since 1936; prof. chem. engring., and chemistry, and head dept., Worcester Poly. Inst., 1940—; dir. Zialite Corp. Mem., past chmn. Mass. State Board Registration Profl. Engrs. Fellow A.A.A.S., mem. Am. Inst. Chem. Engrs., Am. Soc. Engring. Edn., Am. Chem. Soc., Electrochem. Soc., Am. Soc. Profl. Engrs., Am. Assn. U. Professors, Society Chem. Industry (British), Pi Delta Epsilon, Sigma Xi, Tau Beta Pi, Gamma

Alpha, Alpha Chi Sigma, Phi Gamma Delta. Baptist. Republican. Clubs: Engineers (Boston); Worcester (Mass.) Country. Home: 33 Flagg St. Office: Worcester Poly. Inst., Worcester 9, Mass. Died Oct. 19, 1958; buried Beechmont Cemetery, Centerville, Mass.

WILSON, Francis Cushman, lawyer; b. Winchester, Mass., June 8, 1876; s. John Thomas and Pleasantine (Cushman) W.; student Harvard, 1893-98; LL.B., Columbian (now George Washington) Law Sch., 1903; m. Charlotte Lansing Parker, July 2, 1902; children—Frances Charlotte (Mrs. Millard S. Peabody), Parker. Began practice, Dist. of Columbia, 1903; at Santa Fe, New Mexico, since 1907; retired from active practice, 1942; member Hanna & Wilson, 1909-13; president Wilson Oil Company; member New Mexico State Tax Commission, 1917-18; interstate river commissioner for New Mexico, 1927-31; mem. Com. on Conservation and Administration of Public Domain, May 1930-50. Served with Mass. Heavy Arty., May-Nov. 1898, Spanish-Am. War, Past dept. comdr. N.Mex., United Spanish War Vets.; member board trustees Roosevelt Memorial Assn. Mem. Am. Bar Assn., N.M. State Bar Assn. (pres. 1913), N.Y. Soc. Mayflower Descendants, S.A.R. (past State pres.). Republican. Episcopalian. Mason (32°, K.C.C.H., K.T.). Clubs: Harvard (New York); University (Wash.). Contbr. on Problem of Public Domain. Interstate Compacts and various legal articles. Home: 316 Buena Vista Rd. Office: 40-47 Sena Plaza, Santa Fe. Died Jan. 17, 1952; buried Santa Fe Nat. Cemetery.

WILSON, Francis Servis, judge; b. Youngstown, O., Feb. 7, 1872; s. Hon. David M. (lawyer) and Grisselda E. (Campbell) W.; ed. Western Reserve Acad., Hudson, O.; LL.B., Western Reserve U., 1896; m. Caroline E. Siegfried, Nov. 18, 1903; children—David, Francis Servis, Jr. Admitted to Ohio bar, 1896; nominated for judge of Probate Court, Mahoning County, O., 1896; removed to Chgo., 1897; nominated for judge Municipal Court of Chgo., on independent ticket, 1906; county atty. Cook County, 1911-12; for a number of yrs. mem. Darrow, Masters & Wilson; mem. Felsenthal & Wilson until 1920; became judge Circuit Court of Cook County, 1920; apptd. justice Appellate Court, 1st Ill. Dist., 3d Div., 1927, presiding justice, 1930; justice Supreme Court of Illinois, 1935, chief justice, 1939. Mem. Ill., Chgo. bar assns., Legal Club Chgo., Chgo. Law Inst., S.A.R., Ohio Soc. (dir.), Dekta Kappa Epsilon. Democrat. Served in World War as chmn. Legal Advisory Bd., Div. 17, 1917; capt., judge advocate U.S. Army, Camp Sherman, 1918; maj. O.R.C. Clubs: University, Commonwealth, Flossmoor Country, Chikaming Country. Home: 1340 E. 48th St. Office: 30 N. Michigan Av., Chgo. Died March 14, 1951; buried Meml. Park Cemetery, Evanston, Ill.

WILSON, Frank N., physician; b. Livonia, Mich., Nov. 19, 1890; s. Norman O. and Mary (Holtz) W.; B.S., U. of Mich., 1911, M.D., 1913; m. Juel A. Mahoney, Aug. 6, 1914; 1 dau., Julia Ann. Asst. in medicine, Univ. of Mich., 1913-14, instr. 1914-16, asso. prof., 1920-24, professor, 1924—; instructor, Washington University, 1916-20. Henry Russel lecturer, Univ. of Mich., 1939-40; Dr. honoris causa, Escola Paulista Medicina (Brazil); hon. mem. Faculta de Biologia y Ciencia Médicas de la U. de Chile; Soc. de Med. de Montevideo; Soc. Medicine de Santigo de Chile; Uniao Cultural Brasil-Estados Unidos; corr. mem. Acad. Nacional de Med. do Brasil; Soc. Argentina de Cardiologia; hon. mem. Cardiac Soc., Great Britain and Ireland. Fellow Am. Coll. Physicians, A.A.A.S., A.M.A.; mem. Assn. Am. Physicians, Am. Soc. Exptl. Pathology, Soc. Exptl. Biology and Medicine, Am. Soc. Clin. Investigation, Central Soc. Clin. Research, Am. Heart Assn., Alpha Omega Alpha, Sigma Xi. Served as lt. and capt., Med. Corps, U.S. Army, 1917-19. Author 100 articles on electrocardiography; lectured in Brazil, Uruguay, Argentina, Chile, Peru. Address: Route 2, Stockbridge, Mich. Died Sept. 11, 1952.

WILSON, George Allison, ex-U.S. Senator; b. Menlo, Ia., Apr. 1, 1884; s. James Henderson and Martha Green (Varley) W.; student Grinnell Coll., 1900-03, State U. Ia., 1904-07; m. Mildred Elizabeth Zehner, Dec. 8, 1921; children—James Henderson, George Allison, Jr., John David, Mary Ann. Admitted to Ia. bar, 1907, began practice in Des Moines; asst. county atty. Polk County, 1912-14, county atty., 1915-16; dist. judge, 1917-21; gov. of Ia., 1939-43; U.S. senator, 1943-49. Mem. State Senate, 1925-35. Mem. Am., Polk County bar assns., Sigma Chi, Moose. Home: 4220 Grand Av., Des Moines, Ia. Office: Senate Office Bldg., Washington. Died Sept. 8, 1953.*

WILSON, George Grafton, publicist; b. Plainfield, Conn., Mar. 29, 1863; s. Archibald A. and Betsey L. (Brown) W.; A.B., Brown U., 1886, A.M., 1888, Ph.D., 1889, LL.D., 1911; LL.D., U. Vt., 1911, U. Hawaii, 1937; studied at Heidelberg, Berlin, Paris and Oxford, 1890-91; m. Elizabeth Rose, June 30, 1891; children—Grafton Lee, Miriam (Mrs. Paul Harrison Arthur), Rose (Mrs. Harry Gray Anderson), Bayton Fuller (dec.). Principal schs., Groton, Conn., 1886-87, high sch., Rutland, Vt., 1889-90; asso. prof. social and polit. scis. Brown U., 1891-94, prof., 1894-1910; prof. internat. law Harvard, 1910-36, now emeritus, lectr. internat. law, 1907-10; prof. internat. law, U.S. Naval War Coll., 1900-37; prof. internat. law, Fletcher Sch. of Law and Diplomacy, 1933—; spl. counsel, U.S. Maritime Commn., 1941—; lectr. internat. law U. Hawaii, 2d semester, 1937. Am. del. plenipotentiary Internat. Naval Conf., 1908-09; counselor Am. Legation, The Hague, early period of war, 1914; exchange prof. to France, 1912-13; lecture, Académie de Droit Internat., The Hague, 1923; Am. mem. Internat. Commn., U.S. and Netherlands, 1928; designated by Nicaragua, mem. Internat. Central Am. Tribunal, 1928. Mem. bd. editors Am. Jour. Internat. Law, 1907—, Law editor in chief 1924-43, hon. editor in chief, 1943—; dir. Revue de Droit International, 1913—. Membre de l'Institut de Droit International; fellow Am. Acad. Arts and Sciences (v.p.); v.p. Am. Soc. Internat. Law (exec. com.); mem. Am. Political Science Assn., Am. Philos. Society, Delta Phi. Clubs: Faculty (Cambridge); Harvard (Boston); Harvard (N.Y. C.); Cosmos (Washington). Author: Town and City Government in Providence, 1899; Insurgency, 1900; Submarine Telegraph Cables in Their International Relations, 1901; International Law Situations (U.S. Naval War Coll.), 36 vols., 1902-37; International Law (with George Fox Tucker), 1901, 10th edit., 1937; L'Insurrection, 1902; International Law, Hornbook series, 1910, 3d edit., 1939; The Hague Arbitration Cases, 1915; The First Year of the League of Nations, 1921. Editor of centenary edition of Wheaton's Internat. Law (Carnegie classics), 1936. Contbr. mags. Legal adviser U.S. mission for return of Dutch ships, 1919; mem. legal staff Washington Conf. on Limitation of Armament, 1921-22. Address: 38 Kirkland St., Cambridge, Mass. Died Apr. 30, 1951; buried Grafton, Vt.

WILSON, G(eorge) Lloyd, prof. transportation and public utilities; b. Phila., Pa., July 10, 1896; s. George Pepper and Margaretta R. (Duckett) W.; A.B., Swarthmore (Pa.) Coll., 1918; A.M., U. of Pa., 1924, Ph.D., 1925, M.B.A., 1926; graduate in transportation law, Temple U., 1929; LL.B., U. of Pa., 1940; m. Florence Platt Cornman, June 29, 1918; children—G(eorge) Lloyd, Marjorie Eleanor. Began as industrial traffic mgr., 1918; served as traffic manager Chester Shipbuilding Co., Ltd., and Merchant Shipbuilding Corp.; was commercial agent Southern S.S. Co., research director Nat. Freight & Delivery Co., and lecturer Temple U.; mem. faculty U. of Pa. since 1922, instr. in transportation, 1922-25, asst. prof., 1925-28, prof. since 1928, also dir. bureau of public affairs, University of Pennsylvania, 1935-37, chairman transportation and public utilities department since 1945; consultant to federal coördinator of transportation; consultant transportation economist; research dir. Federal Communications Commn., 1938-40; head economist, Nat. Resources Planning Bd., 1940-41; dir. Transportations Div., OPA, 1941; dir. and consultant, Div. of Rates, Office of Defense Transportation, 1941-47; research cons. U.S. Steel Corporation since 1944. Member Associated Traffic Clubs of Am. (v.p.; chmn. coms. edn. and research; editor publs.), Atlantic States Shippers Advisory Bd. (chmn. coll. relations com.), Transportation Soc., Am. Econ. Assn. (chmn. transportation and pub. utilities sect. 1946-47), Am. Acad. Polit. and Social Sci., Assn. of Practitioners before Interstate Commerce Commn., Am. Assn. Traffic and Transportation (v.p., dir. edn.), Indsl. Transporation Assn. (England), Institute of Transport (Great Britain). Book and Key, Kwink, Phi Beta Kappa, Beta Gamma Sigma, Phi Sigma Kappa, Pi Gamma Mu, Pi Alpha Epsilon, Alpha Lambda Sigma, Institut Scientifique d'Etudes des Communications et des Transport (France). Baptist. Mason. Clubs: Duquesne, Traffic. Author: Organization and Management Industrial and Commercial Traffic, 1925; Traffic Management, 1926; (with E. R. Johnson and G. G. Huebner) Principles of Transportation, 1928; Motor Traffic Management, 1928; Coordinated Motor-Rail-Steamship Transportation, 1930; The Transportation Crisis, 1933; Public Utility Industries (with J. M. Herring and R. B. Eutsler), 1936; Public Utility Regulation (with Herring and Eutsler), 1938; Transportation and Traffic Management, 1938; Transportation: Economic Principles and Practices (with E. R. Johnson and G. G. Huebner), 1940; Traffic Management; Industrial and Commercial, 1941; Interstate Commerce and Traffic Law, 1947; Nationalization of Transport in Great Britain, 1948; also of a series of monographs on Industrial Traffic Management, and monographs on Railroad Freight Services, Motor Freight Transportation, and Air Transportation. Editor: (with F. C. James) Banking and Transportation Problems, 1934. Editor, "Railroads and Government," 1936; "Ownership and Operation of Public Utilities," 1939, Transportation: War and Post-war, 1942, American Academy Political and Social Science. Contributor many articles to economic, transportation and traffic publs. Home: 474 Gerhard St., Roxborough, Phila. 28. Died Apr. 11, 1956.

WILSON, Grove, author, editor; b. Greenville, O., Dec. 6, 1883; s. Henry and Matilda L. (Willis) W.; ed. pub. schs., Minn.; m. Berenice Moncrieff, June 10, 1933. Reporter Winona (Minn.) Independent, 1900-03; city editor Minneapolis Tribune, 1903-08; editorial writer Baltimore American, 1908-10; political editor St. Paul Dispatch, 1910-13; city editor New York Call, 1917-18; editor Live Stories, N.Y. City, 1919-21; asso. editor Hearst's International and Smart Set, 1921-28; asso. editor Popular Science Monthly, 1930-34. Club: Stockdale Golf (Bakersfield). Author: Man of Strife, 1925; Sport of the Gods, 1926; The Mysterious Wife, 1927; Human Side of Science, 1929 (translated into Korean, Malayalam, Portuguese, Norwegian and Dutch); Temperamental Jane, 1931; The Monster of Snowdon Hall, 1932; Sneckles of Mowbrey Street, 1933; The Defiant Corpse, 1946. Home: R.R. 2, Box 502, Atascadero, Cal. Died Oct. 11, 1954; buried Atascadero Cemetery.

WILSON Halsey William, publisher; b. Wilmington, Vt., May 12, 1868; s. John Thompson and Althea (Dunnell) W.; ed. Univ. of Minn., 1885-92; Litt.D., Brown U., 1939; m. Justina Leavitt, Aug. 15, 1895. Began in retail bookselling while a student in coll., and continued in it until success of Cumulative Book Index, first published in 1898, and of other bibliographical publs. based on his origination of cumulative indexing of books and periodicals, necessitated disposing of it in order to move his growing publishing business East in 1913; organized H. W. Wilson Co., of which is now chairman of the board, issuing Cumulative Book Index, United States Catalog, Readers' Guide to Periodicals, Book Review Digest, and over dozen subsidiary, supplementary or allied services in addition to reference works, and conducting large back-number periodical dept. Recipient Outstanding Achievement medal, U. of Minn., 1948. Mem. (life) A.L.A., Phi Kappa Psi, Scottish Rite Mason. Address: 950-72 University Av., N.Y.C. Died Mar. 1, 1954.

WILSON, Harold Kirby, educator; b. Clark County, Mo., March 6, 1900; s. Isaac James and Amanda Ellen (Beidman) W.; B.S., Ia. State Coll., 1918-24; M.S., Univ. of Illinois., 1925; Ph.D., 1927; m. Florence Helen Munson, Aug. 24, 1921 (dec.); m. 2d, Eva Grace Donelson, Dec. 22, 1947. Instr. natural sci., Ia. State Teachers Coll., summers 1925, 26; asst. prof. and asst. agronomist, Univ. of Minn., 1927-31; asso. prof. and asso. agronomist, 1931-36; prof. and agronomist, 1936-45; acting chief of div. agronomy and plant gen., 1932-33, 1936-37, 1941-42; collaborator U.S. Dept. Agr., 1935-45; head dept. agronomy Pa. State U., 1945-47, vice dean, dir. resident instrn., 1946-49, dean of men, 1949-52, director Div. Intermediate Registration, 1949-57, prof. agronomy, 1950—, asso. dean of admissions for research and development, 1957—. Served U.S. Army, 1918. Chief agrl. research, Nat. Resources sect., Gen. Hdqrs., Supreme Commd. Allied Powers, Tokyo, 1947. Fellow A.A.A.S., Am. Soc. Agronomy. Mem. Am. Soc. Plant Physiology, Am. Assn. Univ. Profs., Minn. Acad. of Sci. (sec. 1933-41), Farm House Nat. (vice president, 1954-56, secretary, treasurer, 1956—), Higher Education Association, N.E.A., Am. Coll. Personnel, American Legion, Phi Epsilon Phi, Omicron Delta Kappa, Sigma Xi, Alpha Tau Alpha, Delta Theta Sigma, Alpha Zeta, Phi Kappa Phi, Gamma Sigma Delta, Phi Sigma, Gamma Alpha, Phi Delta Kappa. Methodist. Mason (32°, Shriner). Club: University (State Coll., Pa.). Author: (with A. Boss and W. E. Petersen) American Farming Agriculture I, 1939; Agr. II, 1940; Agr. III, 1941; Agr. I (rev.), 1944; Agr. IV, 1944; (with A. H. Larson) Identification and Judging, 1940; Grain Crops, 1955; Field Crop Production (with Will M. Myers), 1954. Editor Pearls and Rubies, 1958—. Contbr. many articles to various jours. Home: 256 E. Irvin Av., State College, Pa. Died Nov. 26, 1958; buried Maple Hill Cemetery, Birmingham, Ia.

WILSON, Henry Braid, ret. naval officer; b. Camden, N.J., Feb. 23, 1861; s. Henry B. and Mary A. W.; grad. U.S. Naval Acad., 1881; married; children—Mrs. Patrick B. Hurley, Henry Braid. Commd. ensign (j.g.) USN, 1883, advanced through grades to adm., 1919; on Bancroft, Spanish-American War, 1898; duty Bur. of Navigation, 1904-08; comd. Chester, 1908-09; mem. Bd. Inspection and Survey, Navy Dept., 1909; asst. Bur. of Navigation, 1910-11; comd. North Dakota, 1911-13; pres. Bd. Inspection and Survey, 1913-16; comd. Pennsylvania, 1916-17; comdr. Patrol Force, Atlantic Fleet, 1917-18; apptd. comdr. U.S. Naval Forces in France, 1918; comdr.-in-chief Atlantic Fleet, 1919; supt. U.S. Naval Acad., 1921-25 (retired). Address: 35 Fifth Av., N.Y.C. Died Jan. 30, 1954; buried Arlington Nat. Cemetery.

WILSON, Howard Stebbins, life ins. exec.; b. Lincoln, Neb., Nov. 16, 1894; s. William Cook and Adele Almira (Stebbins) W.; A.B., U. of Neb. 1917; married Louise Maxwell Baker, Sept. 18, 1952. President Bankers Life Insurance Co. of Neb., 1919—; dir. Beatrice (Neb.) Nat. Bank. Enlisted as seaman, 2d class, served later as chief boatswain's mate, U.S.N.R.F., 1917-19. Mem. Lincoln Hosp. Bd., 1936-47; pres. U. of Neb. Found. 1946-50; trustee at large Nat. Soc. for Crippled Children and Adults, 1950-54, mem. nat. exec. com., 1951-54; mem. Bd. Govs., Am. Nat. Red Cross 1947-51; mem. com. fed. finance of U.S. C. of C., 1948-50; mem.

City Planning Adv. Com. Received Boy Scouts Am. Silver Beaver Award for distinguished service 1942, U. of Nebraska Distinguished Service Medal 1944. Mem. Am. Life Conv. (exec. com.), Newcomen Soc., C. of C., Am. Legion, Phi Kappa Psi. Republican. Congregationalist. Mason (33°, Scottish Rite, Shriner). Clubs: University, Lincoln Country. Home: 1230 Crestdale Rd., Lincoln 10. Office: Bankers Life Bldg., Lincoln 8, Neb. Died Mar. 14 1958.

WILSON, I. H., b. Columbia, Tenn., exec. v.p. and dir. Union Planters National Bank and Trust Co.; dir. Bluff City Abstract Co., Union Planters Title Guaranty Co., Dyersburg Cotton Products, Inc. Home: 450 N. McLean Blvd., Memphis. Died 1953.*

WILSON, John G., business exec.; b. Alma, Ill., Aug. 17, 1900; s. Edward E. and Rachel E. (French) W.; ed. U. of Ill., U. of Wis., and Northwestern U.; m. Hazel Lillian Anderson, Apr. 27, 1920; children—Jean, Shirley, John E. With Price Waterhouse & Co., Chgo., 1920-24, Blackhawk Press, 1924-27, Montgomery Ward & Co., 1927-30, Goldblatt Bros., Inc., 1940-43, United Wallpaper Factories, Inc., 1944; v.p., gen. mgr. R.C.A. Victor div. R.C.A., 1944-49, exec. v.p., 1949—; dir. Goldblatt Bros., Inc., R.C.A. Victor Co., Ltd. (Montreal, Can.). Mem. N.J. C. of C., Controllers Inst. Am., Soc. Naval Engrs. Republican. Episcopalian. Club: Penn Athletic. Home: 405 Montgomery Av., Wynnewood, Pa. Office: Front and Cooper Sts., Camden, N.J. Died June 1, 1950.

WILSON, John Henry, engr.; b. Honolulu, T.H., Dec. 15, 1871; s. Charles Burnett and Evaline Malvetta (Townsend) W.; ed. pub. and pvt. schs. in Hawaii; student Stanford, 1891-94; m. Jennie Kapahu, May 8, 1909. Joined engring. staff, Oahu Ry. & Land Co., Ltd., 1896; connected with Dept. Pub. Works under Republic of Hawaii, 1897; formed firm of Wilson and Whitehouse, civil engrs. (with L. M. Whitehouse), 1897; constructed internationally famous Pali Road, Lahaina (Maui) waterworks system, and numerous other works, partnership dissolved 1900; supt. hwys. Island of Maui and supt. streets Honolulu, 1908-11; engaged in pvt. practice; pres. Wilsonite Brick Co., Ltd., Honolulu. City engr. of Honolulu, 1919, mayor, 1920-23, 24-27, 29-30, 47-48, 49-54, postmaster, 1934-39, dir. Dept. Pub. Welfare, 1939-46. Dem. Nat. Committeeman for Hawaii, 1912-40. Charter member Engring. Assn. of Hawaii (1st pres. 1920-21); mem. Order of Kamehameha. Home: 1551-A Oili Rd. Address: City Hall, Honolulu 43, Hawaii. Died July 2, 1956.

WILSON, John P., lawyer; b. Chgo., Oct. 7, 1877; s. John P. and Margaret C. (McIlvaine) W.; grad. St. Paul's Sch., Concord, N.H., 1896; A.B., Williams Coll., 1900, LL.D., 1953; LL.B., Harvard, 1903; m. 2d, Alice B. Keep, July 15, 1916; children—(by previous marriage) John P., Cynthia; m. 3d, Nina M. Bingham, Mar. 8, 1952. Practiced in Chgo., 1903—; mem. Wilson & McIlvaine; dir. Marshall Field & Co., Internat. Harvester Co., First Nat. Bank. Trustee Children's Meml. Hosp., Newberry Library, Chgo. Natural History Mus. Mem. Am. Ill. State and Chgo. bar assns., Chgo. Law Inst., Alpha Delta Phi. Clubs: University, Mid-Day, Attic, Chicago, Commercial, Old Elm, Casino (Chgo.). Home: 1260 Astor St. Office: 120 W. Adams St., Chgo. Died July 26, 1959.

WILSON, Joseph G., psychiatrist; b. Guernsey County, O., June 23, 1874; s. Benjamin and Mary Ann (French) W.; M.D., U. of Pa., 1898; m. Carmen Iriarte, July 28, 1900; children—Martha Ann (Mrs. Leo McCarthy), Josephine Carmen (Blum), Dolores; m. 2d, Mary Flowers, May 17, 1913 (died 1948); 1 son, Gregory. Intern St. Christophers Hosp. for Children, Phila., 1898; practicing physician, 1899-1906; acting asst. surgeon U.S. Pub. Health Service, 1906, and advanced to sr. surgeon, 1934, now retired; engaged in medical and psychiatric service to federal prisoners from 1930; became director div. of hospitals and mental hygiene, Dept. of Welfare, State of Ky.; psychiatrist N.J. Mental Hygiene Bur.; contract surgeon, U.S. Army, Span.-Am. War; dep. state health officer and city health officer and in charge of extra-cantonment zone sanitation at Leavenworth, Kan., World War. Mem. A.M.A., Am. Prison Assn., Am. Psychiatric Assn., Med. Correctional Assn., Retired Officers Assn., Ky. Psychiatric Assn. (hon. life mem.). Am. Geriatrics Society Alcohohlics Information Center. Author: (with M. J. Pescor) Problems in Prison Psychiatry, 1939; Are Prisons Necessary?, 1950; Eight Times Ten, 1954. Author med. papers. Mem. editorial cons. bd. Sexology Mag. Address: 1123 Chapin St., Beloit, Wis. Died Feb. 2, 1957.

WILSON, Joseph Robert, lawyer; b. Liverpool, Eng., Sept. 6, 1866; s. Joseph and Mary Amanda Victoria (Hawkes) W.; Alsopps' Prep. Sch., Hoylake, Cheshire, Eng.; Liverpool Inst.; Dr. Steele's Strathallan Hall, Douglas, Isle of Man; University of Sydney, New South Wales, 1884; LL.B., University of Pennsylvania, 1902; married to Cora Irene Shaw, Phila., May 14, 1890 (deceased 1951); children—Mary Michelet (Mrs. P. E. Dieperveen, Rotterdam, Holland), John Hawkes, Sydney Violet (Mrs. Francis Thibault Boyd), Cora B. H. (Mrs. Horace T. Greenwood, Jr.). In engring. business with Thomas Shaw, prior to admission to bar, 1902; since practiced at Phila. First lt., New South Wales V Infantry, 1885. Trustee American Oncologic Hosp. Chairman Legal Advisory Bd. for the Selective Service, 20th Div., Phila., 1917-18; spl. Registrar for Selective Service, U. of Pa., 1917-18; spl. counsel Ordnance Dept., Phila., and mil. dir. for Manayunk and Roxborough Dist., Phila., 1917-18; chairman War Savings Div. Treasury Dept., Bernalillo County, N.M., 1919. Dir. education and social economy, Sesquicentennial Internat. Expn., 1925-26. Officer Order of White Lion (Czechoslovakia), 1929; Comdr. Royal Order Isabel la Catolica (Spain), 1930; Comdr. Royal Order Crown of Italy, 1931. Mem. Am. Acad. Polit. and Social Science, Trans-Atlantic Soc. America (gov. 1909-21), Hist. Soc. Pa., Am. Bar Assn., Pa. Bar Assn., Phila. Bar Assn., Law Acad., Phila., Law Alumni Soc. U. of Pa. (bd. mgrs. 1906-16), Miller Law Club U. of Pa. (pres.), Delta Upsilon, Acacia (nat. pres. 1908-10; chmn. trustees University of Pa. Chapter; hon. mem. Harvard Yale and Columbia Chapters); mem. Rice Leaders of the World, 1930. Clubs: Lawyers, Cosmopolitan, University of Pa., National Sojourners (pres. Phila. Chapter 1935-36), Church Club of Phila. (bd. govs. 1934-38), Delta Upsilon (dir.), Acacia, Philobiblon, Poor Richard (Phila.); University (Washington, D.C.). Author: A Chapel in Every Home, 1898, 1922, 1936, 1946; The Santa Fe Trail, 1921. Home: Moorestown, N.J. Died Feb. 1, 1957; buried Trinity Episcopal Ch., Moorestown.

WILSON, Julian DuBois, naval officer; b. Clarksburg, W.Va., July 2, 1896; s. Henry Tyson and Lucy Snow (Hart) W.; student Columbian Prep. Sch., 1913-14; B.S., U.S. Naval Acad., 1917; m. Hazel Hamilton, Dec. 23, 1922; children—Henry Hamilton, John R., Juliana DuBois (Mrs. William Foss Thompson). Commissioned ensign in United States Navy, 1917, advanced through grades to rear adm., 1950; served on gunboats, destroyers as convoy escort, European waters, 1917-18; staff comdr. U.S. Naval Force in France, 1918-19; sea duty, 1919-23, 25-28, 30-33; instr. dept. marine engring. naval constrn. U.S. Naval Acad., 1923-25, 28-30, dept. ordnance and gunnery, 1933-35; comdg. officer destroyer Goff, Pacific, 1935-37, Worden, 1937-38, U.S. Naval Tanker in Atlantic overseas convoys, 1940-43; insp. ordnance N.Y. Shipbldg. Corp., Camden, N.J., 1938-40; comdr. Task Force 32, Atlantic, 1943; served fleet maintenance div. Office Chief Naval Operations, Washington, 1943-44; comdg. officer U.S.S. Md., Pacific (participated Battle Okinawa), 1944-45; staff comdr. 19th Fleet, Pacific Coast, 1945-46; on ship characteristics bd. Office Chief Naval Operations, Washington, 1946-49, exec. mem., 1947-49; supt. Mass. Maritime Acad., Buzzards Bay, Mass., 1949—; ret. active duty, June 30, 1950. Decorated Order of Sun (Peru); Bronze Star medal with combat insignia, Sec. Navy Commendation. Pres. Cape Cod council Boy Scouts Am. Mem. Am. Soc. Mil. Engrs. (pres.), U.S. Naval Inst., Mil. Order World Wars (past comdr. Cape Cod chpt.), Cape Cod Power Squadron, Naval Order of U.S. Baptist. Clubs: Hyannis Yacht, Army and Navy (Washington); Rotary (Hyannis). Home: 64 Harbor Rd., Hyannis, Mass. Office: Mass. Maritime Acad., Buzzards Bay, Mass. Died Sept. 1, 1958; buried Arlington Nat. Cemetery.

WILSON, L. B., ex-banker, broadcasting exec.; b. Covington, Ky., May 20, 1891; s. Wes Berry and Louise (Miles) W.; ed. high sch., Covington; m. Jean Oliver, Oct. 7, 1929. Began in banking, 1918; formerly pres. Peoples Liberty Bank & Trust Co.; pres. L. B. Wilson, Inc. (Radio Sta. WCKY), Covington-Cincinnati Cities Bridge Corp., Stanwood Boiler Corp., Doerman-Roher Co., Cin.; owner of motion picture theatre circuit, Covington. Pres. Covington C. of C. Republican. Mason (Shriner), Elk. Address: Sheraton Hotel Gibson, Cin. Died Oct. 29, 1954.*

WILSON, Lawrence Glass, business exec.; b. Alexandria, Scot., Oct. 26, 1890; s. Robert and Mary (Glass) W.; student pub. schs.; m. Gertrude Treatch, May 4, 1933. Came to U.S., 1912, naturalized, 1927. With Rayonier, Inc., since 1936, comptroller, treas. since 1944. Home: 450 E. 63d St., N.Y.C. 21. Office: 161 E. 42d St., N.Y.C. 17. Died Dec. 17, 1954.

WILSON, Leroy A(ugust), business exec.; b. Terre Haute, Ind., Feb. 21, 1901; s. Garrett August and Rose May (Kerschner) W.; B.S., Rose Polytechnic Inst., Terre Haute, Ind., 1922; m. Blanche Willhide, Sept. 1, 1928; 1 dau., Shirley Ann. Traffic student Ind. Bell Telephone Co., Indianapolis, 1922, dist. traffic supt., 1923-29; engr. Am. Telephone & Telegraph Co., New York, 1929-38; directory engr., 1939, rate engr., 1940-41, comml. engr., 1942-44, vice pres., 1944-48, pres., dir. since 1948; dir. Chase Nat. Bank, Metropolitan Life Insurance Co. Trustee East River Savings Bank, Carnegie Corp., Dennison Univ.; mem. bd. mgrs. Rose Polytech. Ins. Mem. Nat. Interfrat. Conf. (past chmn.), Tau Beta Pi, Theta Kappa Nu (past pres.), Lambda Chi Alpha. Methodist. Clubs: University, Links. Home: 17 Fairfield Dr., Short Hills, N.J. Office: 195 Broadway, N.Y. City 7. Died June 28, 1951.

WILSON, Lyman Perl, lawyer, educator; b. Leslie, Ia., Jan. 21, 1883; s. John and Amanda (Phillippi) W.; B.S., Knox Coll., 1904, LL.D., 1924; J.D., U. Chgo., 1907; m. Edith Marks, Jan. 21, 1910; children—Mary Esther, Florence Lea. Admitted to Ill. bar, 1907, began practice at Galesburg, asso. prof. law U. Ida., 1911-13, prof., 1913-14; prof. law U. Okla., 1914-20, George Washington U., 1920-21, Cornell U., 1921—. City atty., Galesburg, 1909-11. Mem. Am. Bar Assn., Am. Law Inst., Am. Judicature Soc., Delta Sigma Rho, Phi Gamma Delta, Phi Alpha Delta, Order of Coif, Phi Kappa Phi. Democrat. Methodist. Rotarian. Author: Cases on Torts, 1928, 2d edit., 1939. Home: 106 Oak Hill Pl., Cayuga Heights, Ithaca, N.Y. Died Apr. 20, 1951.

WILSON, Mary Elizabeth, educator; b. Helena, Mont., 1869; d. Enoch Henry and Joanna Halsted (McIntire) Wilson; B.L., Smith Coll., 1891, L.H.D., 1931; M.L., U. Cal., 1896. Tchr. of English, Miss Murison's Sch., San Francisco, 1895-1906; tchr. English, Anna Head Sch., 1907-09, prin. and owner, 1909-38. Mem. Am. Assn. U. Women, Assn. Collegiate Alumnae (v.p. Pacific coast 1912-15), Nat. Assn. Prins. Schs. for Girls (pres. 1932), Presbyn. Clubs: Smith Coll. of Northern California (pres. 1915-18); Fortnightly of San Francisco (prs. 1922-24); Town and Gown of Berkeley (prs. 1925); Woman's Athletic (Oakland); Orinda Country. Translator: Intellectual and Moral Development of the Child, 1896; Later Infancy of the Child, 1902. Home: 757 Alvarado Rd., Berkeley 5, Cal. Died Mar. 5, 1949.

WILSON, Mira Bigelow, ret. educator; b. Andover, Mass., Jan. 13, 1893; d. Frederick A. and Florence N. (Nason) Wilson; A.B., Smith Coll., 1914, LL.D., 1938; S.T.B., Boston U., 1918; L.H.D., Wilson College, 1951. Tchr. Curtis-Peabody School, Boston, 1914-15; hostess Girls' Vacation House Assn., Princeton, Mass., 1915-22; instr. sch. of edn. Boston U., 1918-19; with Smith Coll., 1919-29, filling positons as sec. Christian Assn., instr. and asst. prof. dept. religion and biblical lit., dean class of 1927, and dir. religious and social work; prin. Northfield (Mass.) Sch. for Girls, 1929-52, ret. Alumnae trustee Smith Coll.; trustee Abbot Acad.; dir. Girls' Vacation House Assn.; mem. bd. dirs. Edward W. Hazen Found., Haddam, Conn. Recipient Northfield award for significant service, 1952. Mem. Headmistresses Assn. of East, Nat. Assn. Prins. of Schs. for Girls. Club: College (Boston). Address: Kenarden Hall, Northfield School for Girls, East Northfield, Mass. Died Apr. 5, 1953; buried Andover, Mass.

WILSON, Philip Whitwell, ex-mem. Brit. Parliament, author; b. Kendal, Westmorland, Eng., May 21, 1875; s. Isaac Whitwell and Anne (Bagster) W.; ed. Clare Coll., Cambridge; m. Alice Selina Collins, Apr. 25, 1899 (dec.); children—Oliver Whitwell, Theodora Whitwell, Philip Whitwell (dec.), Elizabeth Mary Whitwell, Christopher Whitwell, David Alan Whitwell; m. 2d, Mary Elizabeth Cross, May 27, 1944. Editorial staff London Daily News, 21 yrs.; also spl. corr. N.Y. Times and contbr. to revs.; mem. British House of Commons for South St. Pancras, 1906-10. Ex-pres. Cambridge Union Soc. and of Assn. Fgn. Corrs., N.Y.; hon. life mem. Am. Bible Soc. Clubs: City, Clergy (N.Y.C.); Nat. Liberal (London). Author: The Unmaking of Europe, 1915; The Christ We Forget, 1917; The Church We Forget, 1919; The Vision We Forget, 1921; The Layman's Confession of Faith, 1924; An Unofficial Statesman (Life of Robert C. Ogden), 1924; George Peabody, Esq., 1926; An Explorer of Changing Horizons (biog. of William Edgar Geil), 1927; Life of Evangeline Booth, 1938; Newtopia, 1941; Bride's Castle, 1944; Black Tarn, 1945; Old Mill, 1946. Editor: The Greville Diary (2 vols.), 1927; William Pitt, the Younger, 1929; Is Christ Possible?, 1932; The Romance of the Calendar, 1937. Home: Linden House, Spuyten Duyvil, N.Y.C. Died June 1956.*

WILSON, Respess S., lawyer; b. Hempstead, County, Ark., Dec. 20, 1886; s. Thomas Webster and Mattie (Miller) W.; student Ark. State Teachers Coll., Conway, Ark., 1908-09 and 1914-15, Ark. State U., Fayetteville, Ark., 1917; m. Anna Florence Sadler, Dec. 26, 1945; 1 son by previous marriage, Charles Newell. Supt. of schools, 1915-18; in gen. mercantile business, 1919-23; county judge Crawford County, Ark., 1923-27; admitted to bar, 1924; dist. prosecuting atty., 15th Judicial Dist. of Ark., 1927-31; in pvt. practice, Van Buren, Ark., 1931-45; chief atty. Ark. State Dept. of Revenues, 1945-46; U.S. dist. atty. Western Dist. of Ark.; since 1946; sec. Van Buren Freezing Plant, Inc.; sr. mem. Wilson & Starbird, attys. Served as capt., Des Arc, Ark., Home Guards, 1918. Awarded medal for services to Selective Service System, World War II. Mem. Ark. and Federal bar assns., Van Buren (Ark.) Chamber of Commerce (pres.). Democrat. Baptist. Mason (Scottish Rite, past monarch Amrita Grotto). Club: Lions (past pres.) (Van Buren, Ark.) Home: 505 N. 14th St., Van Buren, Ark. Office: Federal Bldg., Fort Smith, Ark. Died July 4, 1954; buried Rose Lawn Cemetery, Fort Smith, Ark.

WILSON, Robert Cade, magazine pub.; b. Burlington, Ia., Nov. 25, 1870; s. Henry and Henrietta

(Gall); attended Mt. Hermon School, class 1888; m. Ada Bell, Oct. 5, 1893; children—Robert Cade, Jr., Marcus Bell (d), Donald Beckles, Meredith Bourne, John Kenneth Collier. Mgr. Atlanta, branch Am. Press Assn., 1890-93; pub. Atlanta Daily Commercial, 1893-95; v.p. Frank Leslie Pub. Co., N.Y. City, 1895; pubs. of American Mag., v.p. Phillips Pub. Co., 1906-10; gen. mgr. Scientific American, 1910-13, Phila. Pub. Ledger, 1913-14; founder and dir. Popular Science Pub. Co. since 1915 (pub. Popular Science Monthly and Outdoor Life); dir. McCall Corp. (pub. McCall's Mag., Red Book Mag., Blue Book Mag.) since 1917. Former mem. Am. Newspaper Pub. Assn., Asso. Press, Periodical Pubs. Assn. of Am. (founder and pres. 1920-26). Democrat. Episcopalian. Club: Baltusrol Golf. In 1932 suggested to Pres. Hoover the idea in detail for Fed. Deposit Ins. (F. D. I. C.); creator in 1938 of plan in detail for labor courts to insure settlements without strikes. Home: Dalkeith Estate, Summit, N.J. Died Dec. 10, 1954.

WILSON, Robert Lee, elec. and mech. engr.; b. Shelbyville, Ill., Jan. 29, 1871; s. William G. (M.D.) and Frances Anna (Lee) W.; student State U. Iowa, 1 yr.; B.S. in M.E.. Rose Poly. Inst., 1892; post-grad. work in elec. engring., Johns Hopkins, 1894; m. Fanny Hampton Jeffers Kennard, Nov. 15, 1900; children—Robert L., Eloise Hampton. With Gen. Electric Co., Schenectacy, N.Y., 1892; with Westinghouse Electric & Mfg. Co., 1894—, successively as engineer, supt., gen. supt., works mgr., asst. v.p. and gen. mgr., asst. to pres.; superintended original electrification of the Manhattan Elevated R.R. and New York Subway; built and installed equipment for electrification of N.Y., N.H.&H. R.R. and the St. Clair Tunnel of Grand Trunk R.R.—the first two important alternating current r.r. electrifications in the U.S.; directed mfg. operations of Westinghouse Electric & Mfg. Co. at East Pittsburgh, 1914-31, then consultant to same; retired 1938. Fellow Am. Inst. E.E.; mem. Engrs.' Soc. Western Pa., S.A.R. Republican. Methodist. Clubs: University, Edgewood Country (Pittsburgh); Engineers' (New York). One of the first to advocate workman representation in works councils (joint conf. coms.); frequent speaker upon industrial relations. Home: Bel Air, Md. Died Dec. 2, 1957.

WILSON, Roy William, business exec.; b. Chgo., Nov. 13, 1894; s. Frank Ernest and Emma Christina (Kraetsch) W.; student Northwestern U., 1914; m. Hildur Charleston, 1914 (died 1924); 1 dau., Bettyjean (Mrs. Galloway); m. 2d, Phyllis Frederica Rietz, June 15, 1929. Accountant, purchasing agt. G. S. Blakeslee & Co., Cicero, Ill., 1912-19; partner Advance Pattern & Foundry Co., Chgo., 1919—, dir., 1919-36, sec.-treas., 1936—, dir., sec. Super Maid Cookware Corp. (subsidiary), Chgo., 1924-36; dir., pres. Super Maid Corp., and successor firm Advance Aluminum Castings Corp., 1928—; dir. Am. Nat. Bank of North Miami, Fla., 1951—. Mem. Swedish Engrs. Soc. Mason (Shriner). Clubs: Swedish, South Side Swedish (Chgo.). Home: 550 Woodland Av., Hinsdale, Ill. Office: 2742 W. 36th Pl., Chgo. 32 Died Nov. 29, 1954.

WILSON, Rufus Rockwell, author; b. Troy, Pa., Mar. 15, 1865; s. Hiram and Mary (Rockwell) W.; ed. high sch.; m. Anna Otilie Erickson, June 2, 1934; children—Marion Elizabeth (dec.), Edward Strong. Journalist in Pitts., Washington, N.Y.C., 1883-91; mag. writer and newspaper syndicate mgr., 1891-1906; on staff Bklyn. Eagle, 1906-08; editor and pub. Malden (Wash.) Herald, 1908-09; lit. and polit. reform work, 1911; sec. Seattle Comml. Club, 1911; sec. Humboldt Development Co., Eureka, Cal., 1912-13; community advt., N.Y.C., 1914-16; sec. Nat. Assn. Cotton Mfrs., 1917-21; organizer and gen. sec. First World Cotton Conf., New Orleans, 1919; engaged in mining, 1921-29; now pres. Primavera Press, Inc., Wilson Book Co. Author: Rambles in Colonial Byways, 1900; Washington, The Capital City, 1901; New York, Old and New, 1902; Lincoln in Caricature, 1903; New England in Letters, 1904; The Sea Rovers, 1906; A Noble Company of Adventurers, 1908; What Lincoln Read, 1932; Out of the West, 1932; Lincoln in Portraiture, 1936; Lincoln Among His Friends, 1942; Intimate Memories of Lincoln, 1945; Lincoln in Caricature (new edit.), 1946; New York in Literature, 1947. Editor: Burnaby's Travels Through North America, 1904; Heath's Memoirs of the American War, 1904; Moultrie's Memoirs of the American Revolution, 1905; The Golden Year, 1932; Across the Plains and Among the Diggings, 1936; Jedediah Smith: Trader and Trail Breaker, 1936; Lincoln's First Years in Illinois, 1946; Uncollected Works of Lincoln—A Supplement to Nicolay and Hay, 1947. Home: 610 W. Church St., Elmira, N.Y. Died Dec. 14, 1949.

WILSON, Samuel Bailey, lawyer; b. Price's Branch, Mo., May 12, 1873; s. Charles and Rebecca (Sutherland) W.; grad. Mankato (Minn.) Normal Sch., 1894; LL.B., U. Minn., 1896; m. Daisy Sheehan, June 21, 1898; children—Samuel Bailey, Jr. (dec.), Phyllis (Sloss), Corol (Blethen). Admitted to Minn. bar, 1896; judge Probate Ct., Mankato, 1898; county atty. Blue Earth County, Minn., 1900-06; pres., dir. Mankato Citizens Telephone Co.; dir. Nat. Citizens Bank; chief justice Supreme Ct. of Minn., 1923-33; resigned 1933 to practice law at Mankato. Dir. Safety Commn., Blue Earth County, World War, also Govt. appeal agt., food adminstr., dir. Bur. War Industries for the dist., and field agt. Bur. War Risk Ins.; pres. Blue Earth County Safety Assn. and mem. Legal Advisory Bd. Mem. Am., Minn. State and Blue Earth County bar assns. Republican. Presbyterian. Mason (32°), K.T., Elk, Woodman, etc. Club: University, Home: Mankato, Minn. Died Jan. 24, 1954.

WILSON, Samuel Knox, clergyman, educator; b. Chicago, Ill., Aug. 20, 1882; s. Samuel Knox and Mary Cecilia (Gaynor) W.; ed. St. Mary's (Kan.) Coll. and Loyola U., Chicago, until 1901; B.A., St. Louis U., 1908, M.A., 1909; studied divinity same univ., 1914-18; Ph.D., Christ Coll. (Cambridge U.), 1924. Joined Soc. of Jesus (Jesuits), 1902; ordained priest R.C. Ch., 1917. Instr. in history St. Xavier High Sch., Cincinnati, 1909-13, St. Mary's Coll., 1913-14; asso. prof. history, Loyola U., 1918-21, prof. Am. history, 1924-25, research prof. Am. history, 1925-29; prof. Am. history, Loyola U., 1929-30, head Dept. History and Polit. Science, 1930-33, dean Grad. Sch., 1932-33, pres. 1933-42; exec. mem. Jesuit Edn. Assn.; dir. admissions, U. of Detroit, North Central Asso. Colls. and Universities (mem. bd. review). Mem. Am. Hist. Assn., Miss. Valley Hist. Assn., Ill. State Hist. Soc., Chicago Hist. Soc., Jesuit Edn. Assn., Nat. Cath. Ednl. Assn. (sec. coll. dept.), Assn. Am. Colleges. Research professor of Am. Hist., Univ. of Detroit, August, 1943—. Editor, The College Newsletter. Home: Univ. of Detroit, Detroit 21. Died Apr. 2, 1959.

WILSON, T. B., pres., dir. Louisville Gas & Electric Co., Ohio Valley Transmission Corp.; dir. Citizens Fidelity Bank and Trust Co. Home: 2140 Bonnycastle Av., Louisville 5. Office: 311 W. Chestnut St., Louisvllie 2. Died May 24, 1957.

WILSON, Thomas Edward, packer; b. London, Ont., July 22, 1868; s. Moses and Mary Ann (Wilson) W.; came with parents to Chicago, 1877; ed. pub. and high schs.; LL.D., U. of Western Ontario London, Can., 1945; LL.D. (honorary), Coe Coll., Cedar Rapids, Ia., 1951; m. Elizabeth L. Foss Nov. 1, 1899; children—Mary Harry J. Williams, Edward Foss. Began with C.,B.&Q. R.R., 1886; became connected with Morris & Co., packer, 1887, v.p., 1906-13, pres., 1913-16; elected pres. Sulzberger & Sons Co., 1916, name changed same yr. to Wilson & Co., plants in Chicago, Dothan, Ala., Oklahoma City, Kan. City, Kansas, Omaha, Los Angeles, Cedar Rapids, Ia., Albert Lea, Minn., Columbus, Ga., Buenos Aires, Sao Paulo, Australia, New Zealand, and branches in prin. countries of Europe as well as branches in U.S. resigned as chairman bd. Wilson & Co., 1953. One of the organizers and first pres., American Meat Inst.; chmn. National Life Stock and Meat Board, 1935-39, now mem. bd. dirs.; dir. International Live Stock Expn., Ill. Central Ry., Live Stock Nat. Bank of Chicago, The Sherwin-Williams Co.; past dir. 1st Nat. Bank, U.S. Chamber Commerce; director Am. Shorthorn Soc.; mem. Chicago Assn. Commerce (sr. council), Chicago Mus. Natural Hist. (life); charter mem. Chicago Horticultural Soc. Awarded Silver Buffalo, Boy Scouts of Am., 1938. An organizer and chairman National Committee on Boys and Girls Club Work; awarded Rosenberger medal of University of Chicago for "work devoted to extending programs of 4-H Clubs," 1940. Received Chicago Merit Award, National, from Rotary (Chicago), Jan. 1945. Republican. Mason. Moose, Woodman. Clubs: Chicago, Commercial, Forty, Union League (hon.), Chgo. Athletic, Saddle and Sirloin, Old Elm, Post and Paddock, Knollwood Country (Chicago); American (London, Eng.). Home: Edellyn Farms, Wilson (Lake County), Ill. Died Aug. 4, 1958; buried Lake Forest (Ill.) Cemetery.

WILSON, Walter K., army officer; b. Oct. 7, 1880; B.S., U.S. Mil. Acad., 1902; grad. Coast Arty. Sch., 1910 (advanced course 1911), Army War Coll., 1922; m. Evangeline Taylor; children—Walter K. (U.S. Army), John N. (killed in action). Commd. 2d lt. U.S. Army, 1902, advanced through grades to maj. gen., 1940; comd. 3d Army Corps, Monterey, Cal., 1940-41; assigned command 9th Coast Arty. Dist., San Francisco, 1941, 11th Army Corps, 1941-42, No. Cal. sector under Western Def. Command, 1942-44; exec. dir. Army Emergency Relief, Washington, 1944-46, ret. 1944, recalled to active duty until Nov. 30, 1946, continued as exec. dir. as civilian, resigned 1951. Decorated D.S.M. with oak leaf cluster, Legion of Merit. Home: 1661 Crescent Pl., Washington 9. Died Jan. 20, 1954; buried Arlington Nat. Cemetery.

WILSON, Wilbur M., engring. research; b. West Liberty, Ia., July 6, 1881; s. Mathias and Ruth (Mosher) W.; B.M.E., Ia. State Coll., 1900, C.E., 1914; M.M.E., Cornell U., 1904; Dr. Engring., Ia. State Coll., 1942; m. Teresa May Stewart, June 28, 1905; children—Grace, Matt. Fellow Cornell, 1903-04; asst. prof., asso. prof. mech. engring., Ia. State Coll., 1904-07; pvt. practice, 1908-13; asst. prof. structural engring. U. Ill., 1913-17, asso. prof., 1919-20, research prof., 1921—. Observer, Bikini Atom Bomb Test, 1946. Student 1st O.T.C., 1917; capt. engrs. O.R.C., 1917; maj. N.A., 1918; served as regtl. supply officer 109th Engrs., testing engr. concrete ship sect. U.S. Shipping Bd. and in charge of building of concrete ships at Wilmington, N.C.; hon. disch., 1918; col. O.R.C. Mem. Am. Soc. C.E. (dir. 1946-47), Am. Soc. Engring. Edn., Am. Soc. Testing Materials, A.A.A.S., Am. Ry. Engring. Assn., Western Soc. Engrs., Am. Welding Soc., Internat. Assn. for Bridge and Structural Engring., Ill. Soc. of Engrs., Am. Concrete Inst., Sigma Xi, Theta Tau, Tau Beta Pi. Author of numerous bulls. pub. by U. of Ill. Engr. Expt. Sta. Awarded the Chanute medal (twice), Western Soc. Engrs.; J. James R. Croes medal, Am. Soc. C.E.; Wason medal, Am. Concrete Inst.; Anson Marston award, Ia. State Coll., 1949. Conglist. Home: 807 S. Busey Av. Office: 118 Talbot Lab., U. of I., Urbana, Ill. Died Nov. 28, 1958; buried Oak Ridge Cemetery, West Liberty, Ia.

WILSON, William Oliver, mfg. exec.; b. Hardwick, Mass., June 25, 1884; s. John J. and Janet B. (Neilson) W.; student pub. schs.; m. Caroline M. Goth, July 28, 1909. With Jeanesville Iron Works, Hazelton, Pa., 1898-1911, Worthington Corp., Harrison, N.J., 1914-53, successively erecting supt., salesman, dist. sales mgr., regional sales mgr., comml. v.p., 1943-53; dir. Electric Machinery Mfg. Co., Mpls., 1946-53. Presbyn. Mason (Scottish Rite, Shriner). Clubs: Chicago, Sunset Ridge Country (Winnetka, Ill.). Home: 1316 Maple Av., Evanston, Ill. Died Oct. 13, 1955; buried Bethlehem, Pa.

WILSTACH, Paul, (wĭl'stăk), writer; b. Lafayette, Ind., July 1, 1870; s. John Augustine and Elbra Cecilia (Patti) W.; A.B., St. Viateur's Coll., Bourbonnais, Ill., 1889. Clubs: Players (N.Y.C.); Metropolitan, Army and Navy (Washington). Lt. comdr. USNRF, 1917, on inactive list, 1919. Plays: Bridget, Bluff, A Gay Deceiver (Washington), 1897; A Partial Eclipse (New York), 1898; A Capitol Comedy (Columbus, O.), 1901; Polly Primrose, 1903; Keegan's Pal (Chicago), 1909; Thais (New York), 1911; The Poor Rich, 1911; What Happened at 22 (New York), 1914. Author: Richard Mansfield, the Man and the Actor, 1908; Mount Vernon, Washington's Home and the Nation's Shrine, 1916; Potomac Landings, 1921; Along the Pyrenees, 1925; Jefferson and Monticello, 1925; Islands of the Mediterranean, 1926; Patriots Off Their Pedestals, 1927; An Italian Holiday, 1928; Tidewater, Virginia, 1929. Editor Correspondence of Adams and Jefferson, 1925; Tidewater, Maryland, 1931; Hudson River Landings, 1933. Contbr. to Scribner's, Atlantic, Dictionary of Am. Biography, Nat. Geog. Mag., etc. Address: Army and Navy Club, Washington. Died Feb. 10, 1952.

WILTSEE, William Pharo, civil engr.; b. Cin. May 30, 1878; s. Charles Spinning and Ida Bell (Hood) W.; ed. grammar and high schs.; m. Viola Bertha Day, Jan. 24, 1900 (died Aug. 1942); children—Virginia Agnes (Mrs. Walter L. Young), Donald Lee, Mary Lee (Mrs. Peyton R. Keller); m. 2d Agnes Gray, Sept. 1, 1943. Rodman, transitman draftsman, resident engr., etc., for various lines 1895-1901; with Norfolk & Western Ry. Co., 1901—successively draftsman, chief draftsman to engr. o br. lines, asst. engr. with engr. br. lines, 1903-12, asst. engr. maintenance and constrn., 1912-16, asst engr. assigned to office of chief engr. on spl. maintenance of way matters, etc., 1916-22, prin. asst. engr., 1922, acting chief engr., 1923, chief engr 1924-1949, ret. In charge of extensive tide-water improvements at Norfolk, Va., 1912-15, and improvements calling for large expenditures annually from 1925. Dir. First Fed. Savs. & Loan Assn. of Roanoke; past pres. Roanoke Hosp. Assn., Hosp. Service Assn. of Roanoke. Life mem. Am. Soc. Civil Engrs.; mem. Am. Soc. for Testing Materials, Am. Wood Preservers Assn., Roadmasters and Maintenance of Way Assn. (ex-pres.), Am. Ry. Engring. Assn. (v.p., dir., chmn. com. on track 1918-25, pres 1933-34), Holland Soc. (New York). Episcopalian. K.P. Club: Cincinnati (Cin.). Home: 2818 Avenham Av., Roanoke, Va. Died Feb. 3, 1958; buried Evergreen Cemetery, Roanoke, Va.

WIMAN, Charles Deere (wī'mán), mfr. agrl. implements; b. Staten Island, N.Y., Feb. 11, 1892; s. William Dwight and Anna Caroline (Deere) W.; student Hill Sch., Pottstown, Pa.; Ph.B., Sheffield Scientific Sch. (Yale), 1914; m. Pattie Harris Southall, Apr. 12, 1920; children—Mary Jane Deere, Patricia Deere. With Deere & Co., mfrs. agrl. implements, Moline, Ill., 1915—, pres., 1929—; dir. Moline Nat. Bank, Continental Ill. Nat. Bank & Trust Co., Protection Mutual Fire Ins. Co. C., R.I. & P. R.R., Hilton Hotels Corporation. Served as second lieutenant, first lieutenant, capt. F.A., A.U.S., May 1917-Aug. 1919, 13 mos. in France. Comd. col. Ordnance Dept., June 17, 1942; chief prodn. Farm Implement Branch, War Prodn. Bd.; released Jan. 18, 1944. Dir. Ill. Mfrs. Assn. Awarded Legion of Merit, Dec. 1945. Republican. Episcopalian. Mason (32°). Clubs: Chicago, Saddle and Cycle, Racquet (Chicago); Yale (New York). Home: 817 11th Av. Address: Deere & Co., Moline, Ill. Died May 12, 1955; buried Riverside Cemetery, Moline.

WIMBERLY, Lowry Charles, prof. English; b. Plaquemine, La., Dec. 25, 1890; s. Charles Perry William and Betty Beeman (Lowry) W.; student Woodbine (Ia.) Normal Sch., 1905-09, Morningside Coll., summer, 1911; A.B., U. Neb., 1916, A.M., 1920, Ph.D., 1925; studied Columbia, summer, 1918; m. Ida May Boynton, Feb. 14, 1910; children—Ruth Lucille (Mrs. D. V. Sarbach), Steve Boynton, Martha May (Mrs. Eugene Penton), Ben Lowry. Has been connected with U. Neb., 1917—; instr. English until 1925, asst. prof., 1925-27, asso. prof., 1927-28, prof., 1928-56, prof. emeritus, 1956; prof. English, U. S. Dak., summer, 1931. Original researches in folk-lore of English and Scotch popular ballads. Mem. Modern Lang. Assn. Am., Am. Folk-Lore Soc., Am. Assn. Univ. Profs., Neb. Writers Guild, Midland Authors, Tau Kappa Epsilon, Sigma Upsilon, Phi Beta Kappa, Kappa Tau Alpha. Democrat. Presbyn. Mason. Club: Cosmopolitan. Author: Death and Burial Lore in the English and Scottish Popular Ballads, 1927; Folklore in English and Scottish Ballads, 1928. Co-author Using Better English, 1937. Compiler and editor Famous Cats of Fairyland, 1938. Editor: Essays on Agriculture, 1921; Ideals and Models, 1935; Prairie Schooner Caravan, 1943; Mid Country, 1945. Editor in chief Prairie Schooner until 1956. Co-editor of Dominant Types in British and American Literature, 1949. Contbr. to mags. Home: 3201 R St., Lincoln, Neb. Died July 8, 1959.

WINCHELL, Alexander Newton, coll. prof.; b. Minneapolis, Mar. 2, 1874; s. Newton Horace and Charlotte Sophia (Imus) W.; B.S., U. of Minn., 1896, M.S., 1897; Sc.D., U. of Paris, 1900; m. Clare Edith Christello, May 29, 1898 (died Apr. 12 1932); children—Vira Frances, Ima C., Alexander Vaughn, Clare Bernice and Horace; m. 2d, Florence M. Sylvester, May 31, 1934. Prof. geology and mineralogy, Mont. Sch. of Mines, 1900-07; prof. mineralogy and petrology, U. of Wis., 1908-44, chmn. dept. geology, 1934-40; resident cons. Am. Cyanamid Co., Stamford, Conn., 1945-48; mineral expert, U.S. Commn. to Paris Expn., 1900; dir. Mont. Mineral exhibit, St. Louis Expn., 1904, Portland Expn., 1905; field asst., 1901-06, asst. geologist, 1907-12, U.S. Geol. Survey; geologist, Ore. Bur. of Mines and Geology, 1913-14; vis. prof. geology, U. Va., 1948-49, Columbia, 1949-50. Recipient Roebling Medal, Mineraol. Soc. Am., 1955. Fellow Geol. Soc. America (v.p. 1932), Mineral Soc. America (pres. 1932), A. A.A.S.; mem. Am. Inst. Mining and Metall. Engrs., Wis. Hist. Soc., Minn. Hist. Soc., Wis. Acad. of Sciences, Arts and Letters, Phi Gamma Delta, Phi Beta Kappa, Sigma Xi Independent Republican. Methodist. Club: University. Author: Elements of Optical Mineralogy (with father), 1909, 5th edit., 1937; Microscopic Characters of Artificial Minerals, 1927; Elements of Mineralogy, 1942; Optic Properties of Organic Compounds, 1943; also reports and articles. Home: 88 Vineyard Rd., New Haven 14, Conn. Died June 7, 1958.

WINCHESTER, Benjamin Severance, clergyman; b. Bridport, Vt., Feb. 26, 1868; s. Warren Weaver and Catherine Mary (Severance) W.; A.B., Williams, 1889; B.D., Chicago Theol. Sem., 1895 (fellowship); student of theology, U. of Halle, Germany, 1895-97; spl. student of O.T., U. of Chicago, 1905; D.D., Chicago Theol. Sem., 1909; m. Pearl Adair Gunn, Aug. 31, 1897; children—Margaret, Katharine (Mrs. Edward T. Wakeman), Pauline (Mrs. Robert G. Inman), Alice, John Henry. Instructor and prof. natural science, Whitman College, Walla Walla, Wash., 1889-92; ordained Congregational ministry, 1897; pastor Snohomish, Wash., 1897-1900, Hassalo St. Ch., Portland, Ore., 1900-01; asso. pastor, New England Ch., Chicago, 1901-03; pastor Winnetka, Ill., 1904-09; editor and ednl. sec. Congl. Sunday Sch., Sch. and Pub. Soc., 1910-15; asst. prof. religious edn., Yale Sch. of Religion, 1915-18; pastor Greenfield Congl. Ch., Fairfield, Conn., 1918-25. Actg. sec. commn. on Christian edn., Federal Council Chs. of Christ in America, 1917-20 (exec. sec. 1925-28; ednl. sec. of council 1929-31); pastor Gilbert Memorial Congl. Ch., Georgetown, Conn., 1931-38; retired 1938. Mem. Hymn Soc. of America (editor source material), John Milton Foundation. Lecturer on religious edn.; asso. editor Congregational Pub. Soc., 1922-24, 1931-32. Author: The Youth of a People, 1914; The Master Teacher; Religious Education and Democracy, 1917; The Church and Adult Education, 1930; also articles on Sunday School work. Editor: The Encyclopedia of Sunday Schools and Religious Education, 1915; (hymnal) Worship and Song. Home: Newtown, Conn. Died Apr. 29, 1955; buried Newtown.

WINDINGSTAD, Ole, symphony condr.; b. Norway, 1886; s. Thorleif and Elsie (Christoffersen) W.; ed. Oslo Conservatory and Leipzig Conservatory. Conductor, Scandinanvian Symphony Orchestra, Carnegie Hall, New York City, and Acad. of Music, Brooklyn, N.Y., 1913-29; Oslo Philharmonic, 1923, 1926; Philadelphia Sesquicentennial Exposition, 1926; Richard Wagner Symphony Orchestra of N.Y., 1930; Brooklyn Symphony Orchestra, 1930-32; Promenade Concert Symphony Orchestra, Mecca Auditorium, New York, 1931; N.B.C. Symphony Orchestra, 1935; N.Y. Civic Orchestra, 1936; L.I. Little Symphony, Westchester Philharmonic and Brooklyn Symphony, 1937; Knickerbocker Symphony Orchestra, Albany, 1937-39; Federal Symphony Orchestra of New York, 1938; Metropolitan Opera Orchestra, 1939; New York Civic Orchestra in Concerts and broadcasts, including appearances at N.Y. World's Fair, 1939; New Orleans Symphony Orchestra, 1940-44; N.Y. Philharmonic Orchestra, 1943, 1945, Albany Symphony, 1945-48, Duchess County Philharmonic, 1945—; toured Norway, 1955, conducting symphony orchestras in Oslo, Bergen, Drammen, Trondheim and Sandefjord. Knight Order of St. Olaf. Composer symphonic works for orchestra. Home: Skytop Lodge, Kingston, N.Y. Died June 3, 1959.

WINDSOR, Wilbur Cunningham, oil exec.; b. Boonville, 1906-10, U. Mo., 1910-13; LL.D. (honorary) Austin Coll., 1955. Student Kemper Mil. Sch., Boonville, 1906-10, U. Mo., 1919-23; m. Gertrude Buckley, 1916; children—Wilbur C., Gertrude Anne (Mrs. Will Mann Richardson). In charge land dept. Humphreys Interests, Powell and Mexica, Tex., 1920-23; ind. oil bus., Tyler, Tex., 1923—; chmn. Windsor Properties, Century Post Co., Nat. Bank of Boonville; dir. Citizens Nat. Bank (Tyler), Lone Star Steel Co., Carlton Hotel Corp., Mid-Continent Oil & Gas. Dir. Community Chest, Salvation Army, 1949—; chmn. Tex. Prison Bd., 1946-52; mem. Tyler Park Bd., 1946-47. Chmn. bd., trustee Austin Coll.; chmn. bd. dirs. Kemper Mil. Sch., Boonville, Mo.; v.p., chmn. development com., mem. bd. curators Stephens Coll.; trustee East Tex. Symphony Orchestra. Served as 1st lt., inf., U.S. Army, 1917-18. Mem. Ind. Petroleum Assn. An. (dir.), Tex. Mid-Continent Oil and Gas Assn., Tex. Ind. Producers and Royalty Owners Assn. (v.p., mem. exec. bd.), Tex. Rose Festival Assn. (past pres.), Panola County Royalty Owners Assn., Nat. Anxiety 4th Hereford Breeders (pres.), East Tex. Fair Assn. (dir.), Tyler C. of C. (past pres.), Sigma Nu, Scabbard and Blade. Presbyn. (ruling elder). Mason (32°). Clubs: Rotary (hon., Tyler, Tex.); Industrialists (hon.), Petroleum (Dallas); Willowbrook Country, The Austin. Home: Tyler, Tex. Office: Fair Found. Bldg., Tyler, Tex. Died Sept. 10, 1958; buried Walnut Grove Cemetery, Boonville, Mo.

WINE, William E., ry. equipment inventor and mfr.; b. Bridgewater, Va., Sept. 20, 1881; s. John H. and Jennie (Berry) W.; B.S., Va. Poly. Inst., 1904, M.E., 1905; D.Engring. (hon.), Bridgwater Coll., 1950; m. Eleanor Worts, Apr. 5, 1924 (dec. Dec. 15, 1949); m. 2d, Margarite Kommer, Dec. 26, 1950. Instr. Va. Poly. Inst., 1904-05; draftsman S.A.L. R.R., A.B. & C. R.R., A.C.L. R.R., 1905-10; shop engr. .C.L. R.R., 1910-12, chief mech. draftsman, 1912-13; pres. Wine Ry. Appliance Co., 1913-37; v. p. Indsl. Steel Casting Co., 1920-37; chairman of the board Unitcast Corporation, Wine Ry. Appliance Co., Indsl. Steel Casting Co. since 1937. Army E, prodn., 1943. Mem. exec. com. R.S. M.A., 1926-37, Am. Soc. M.E. Pres. Va. Poly. Inst. Alumni Assn., 1929-30. Rector bd. visitors Poly. Inst., 1948-53. Mem. Omicron Delta Kappa, Phi Kappa Phi. Clubs: Commonwealth (Richmond, Va.); Toledo (O.); Castalia (O.) Trout. Home: Bramblewood, Berryville, Va. Office: Munsey Bldg., Washington. Died Nov. 3, 1955.

WING, John Durham, bishop; b. Atlanta, Nov. 19, 1882; s. John Durham and Sallie (Peeples) W.; ed. U. Ga. and William and Mary Coll., Va.; D.D., U. Ga., 1918, Va. Theol. Sem., 1926, Univ. of the South, 1927; LL.D., Rollins Coll., Winter Park, Fla., 1932; m. Mary Catherine Ammons, Mar. 31, 1913; children—Mary Catherine (Mrs. Douglas Carter), Rev. John Durham, Breckenridge Wilmer (M.D.), Sarah Peeples (Mrs. David C. Wilson). Deacon, 1909, priest, 1910, Protestant Episcopal Church; rector Ch. of the Holy Comforter, Atlanta, 1910-12, Ch. of the Incarnation, Atlanta, 1913-15, Christ Ch., Savannah, 1915-22, St. Pauls' Ch., Chattanooga, 1923-25; consecrated bishop coadjutor of S. Fla., Sept. 29, 1925, became bishop, 1932; now retired Dep. to Gen. Conv. P.E. Ch., 1919-22. Mem. Newcomen Soc., Chi Phi. Democrat. Home: 1021 Lincoln Circle, Winter Park, Fla. Died Feb. 1960.

WING, Orlon N., educator; b. Capron, Ill., Apr. 28, 1891; s. Hans and Emma Jane (Nelson) W.; student Northern Ill. State Teachers Coll., 1910-12; B.A., U. of Ill., 1916; grad. work U. of Chicago, 1927, Northwestern U., 1939-40; m. Eloise Rosenburger, July 7, 1923 (died 1944); 1 daughter, Lucille (Mrs. Ray Lauless); married second, Mrs. Fischer Perkins, 1945. Principal of pub. sch., Poplar Grove, Ill., 1912-14; supt. schs., Windsor, 1915-17, Barry, 1917-18, Rochell, 1918-22; prin. Central Y.M.C.A. Coll. Day Sch., Chicago, 1922-35, prin. Day and Evening High Schs. and Secretarial Sch., 1935-37, dean high schs. since 1937, dir. div. secretarial practice, 1940-45. Director Central YMCA High Schs., ret. 1956. Del. Nat. Council Ind. Schs., 1954. Captain Inf. Reserve, 1918-51. Awarded Citation, Pvt. Schs. Assn. of Central States, 1957. Organizer Chicago Pvt. Sch. Athletic League, 1931, sec., 1931-33; mem. Pvt. Schs. Assn. of Central States (pres., 1946), Chicago Assn. of Commerce (edn. com., agr. com.), Adult Edn. Council (bd.), Nat. Assn. Secondary Sch. Prins., Acacia. Republican. Methodist. Mason (K.T., 32°, Shriner), Sword of Bunker Hill. Clubs: Army and Navy, Chicago Farmers; Quadrangle (Chgo.). Home: 400 Laurel Av., Wilmette, Ill. Office: 19 S. La Salle St., Chgo. Died Sept. 27, 1957; buried Capron, Ill.

WINGER, Maurice Homer (wĭng'ēr), lawyer; b. nr. Polo, Mo., Jan. 23, 1875; s. Carey Jefferson and Nancy M. (Cooper) W.; student William Jewell College, 1892-95; LL.B., Kansas City Sch. Law, 1902; hon. LL.D., William Jewell College, 1944; m. Nora E. Ribelin, Oct. 15, 1895; children—Alice Maurine, George Jefferson, Robert Alexander, Maurice. Admitted to Mo. bar, 1899; practiced at Polo, 1901-07; asso. firm Karnes, New & Krauthoff, later New & Krauthoff, Kansas City, 1907-15; mem. New, Miller, Camack & Winger, 1915; sr. mem. firm Winger, Barker & Winger; dir. and gen. counsel W. S. Dickey Clay Mfg. Co., Missouri Mapes Corp., Industrial Paper Stock Co., Merry Investment Co., Eleventh and Baltimore Corp.; counsel Sinclair Coal Co., Hume-Sinclair Coal Mining Co., Huntsville Sinclair Mining Co., Delta Coal Mining Co. Pres. The Helping Hand Inst.; trustee, v.p. trustees William Jewell Coll.; chmn. legislative com. C. of C., Kansas City; ex-pres. Alumni Assn. of William Jewell Coll. Mem. Am., Mo., Kansas City bar assns., Phi Gamma Delta. Democrat. Baptist. Mason. Clubs: University, Mission Hills Country. Home: 229 Ward Parkway. Office: Waltower Bldg., Kansas City, Mo. Died Dec. 6, 1949.

WINKELMAN, Nathaniel William, neuropsychiatrist and neuropathologist; b. Phila., Pa., Oct. 28, 1891; s. Frank N. and Frieda (Cohen) W.; M.D., (with honor), U. of Pa., 1914; m. Lillie Gabel, Sept. 16, 1919; children—Nathaniel William (M.D.), Alean G. (dec. 1942). Interne, Allegheny Gen. Hosp., 1914-15; resident neuropsychiatrist, Pittsburgh City Hosp., 1915-18; post grad. study U. of Hamburg, Germany, 1925-26; apptd. to teaching staff, U. of Pa., 1919 advancing through grades to asst. prof. neurology, 1929; prof. neuropathology, U. of Pa., grad. sch. of medicine, 1927—; prof., head of dept. neurology, Temple U. Med. Sch., 1929-36; neurologist, Mt. Sinai Hosp., 1930-35; neurologist, Jewish Hosp. (now Albert Einstein Med. Center, No. div.), 1932—; visiting neurologist, Phila. Gen. Hosp., 1933-35; asso. editor in charge of neurology, Jour. of Syphilis and Neurology, 1933-38; dir., John L. Eckel Lab., U. of Pa., grad. sch. of medicine, 1936—; medical director Phila. Psychiatric Hospital, 1937-53, vice president medical affairs, 1953—; cons. St. Joseph Hosp., Reading, Pa., 1940—. U.S. Army Med Corps, neurologist to base hosp., 87, Toul, France, 1918-19. Established and directed dept. of neuropathology, Phila. Gen. Hosp., 1920-35. Awarded medal and diploma, Athens Med. and Surg. Soc., 1952. Diplomate Am. Bd. Psychiatry and Neurology. Fellow A.M.A., Am. Psychiat. Assn., Coll. of Physicians of Phila., Am. Academy of Neurology; life mem. N.Y. Acad of Science; mem. Phila. Neurological Soc. (past pres.), Phila. Pathological Soc., Phila. Psychiat., Soc., Am. Neurological Assn. (2d vice president 1944-45), Am. Assn. of Neuropathologist (past pres.), Assn. for Research in Nervous and Mental Diseases, Nat. Mental Hygiene Com. Pa. Chapter, Phila. Med. Soc., Pa. State Med. Soc., Pa. Psychiatric Soc., Med.-Surg. Acad. Athens, Sigma Xi. Author: Chronic Syphilitic Poliomyelitis, 1932; Progressive Pallidal Degeneration, 1932; Brain Trauma; Histopathology during the Early Stages, 1934; Residual Lesions in the Brain in Cases of Old Head Injury, 1936; Syphilis of the Spinal Cord, 1936; Cerebral Fat Embolism, 1942; Scarlatinal Encephalomyelitis, 1942; Neurohistologic Findings in Experimental Electric Shock Treatment, 1944; Observations on the Histopathology of Schizophrenia I. The Cortex, 1949; Neurologic Symptons Following Accidental Intraspinal Injection, 1951. Degeneration, 1932, called Winkelman's Disease. Address: 1911 Spruce St., Phila. 3. Died Feb. 13, 1956; buried Mt. Sinai Cemetery, Phila.

WINKLER, John K(ennedy), author; b. Camden, S.C., Feb. 3, 1891; s. Cornelius Lawrence and Sarah Doby (Kennedy) W.; ed. pub. schs. and high schs. of S.C. and N.Y.; m. Marion Worthington Marsh. Mem. staff N.Y. American, 1908-25; war corr. in Mexico, 1914; magazine writer and biographer since 1925; European mag. assignments, 1926. Author of a series of "Profiles," biographies of famous people, appearing in The New Yorker, 1926-31. Author: Hearst: An American Phenomenon, 1928; John D., A Portrait in Oils, 1929; Morgan, The Magnificent, 1930; Incredible Carnegie, 1931; Woodrow Wilson: The Man Who Lives On, 1933; The First Billion: The Stillmans and the National City Bank, 1934; The du Pont Dynasty, 1935; Mind Explorers (with Walter Bromberg, M.D.), 1938; Five and Ten: The Fabulous Life of F. W. Woolworth, 1940; Tobacco Tycoon: The Story of James Buchanan Duke, 1942; William Randolph Hearst, A New Appraisal, 1955; The Great Manipulator (biography Thomas F. Ryan). Special writer, Hearst newspapers, 1937; contbr. articles and fiction to Collier's, Cosmopolitan, Liberty, Red Book, Saturday Evening Post, etc. Home: 49

Bayview Av., Port Washington, N.Y. Died July 31, 1958.

WINKWORTH, Edwin David, mfr.; b. at Syracuse, N.Y., Jan. 21, 1877; s. John W. and Anna S. (Sweeting) W.; ed. pub. schs.; m. Prudence May Brindley, of Syracuse, Aug. 30, 1905. Began as messenger in employ Solvay cos., Syracuse, 1892, and advanced through various offices to pres. Semet-Solvay Co., 1921; became pres. Solvay Process Co. (now div. Allied Chem. & Dye Co.), 1922, now ret.; pres. Atmospheric Nitrogen Corpn., Solvay Bank, Wing & Evans, Inc., Tully Pipe Line Co., Pa. Solvay Coke Co., Utah Salduro Co., Brunner, Mond Water & Gas Co., Delray Connecting R.R. Co.; v.p. Brunner, Mond, Can., Ltd.; dir. By-Products Coke Corpn., Edgewater Coal Co., Ashland By-Product Coke Co., Ashland By-Product Gas Co., Ironton By-Product Coke Co., Kingston Land Co., Kingston Pocahontas Coal Co., Steel & Tube Co. America; trustee First Trust & Deposit Co., Syracuse Savings Bank. Dir. Music Festival Assn., Boys Club. Republican. Methodist. Mason, Elk. Clubs: Bankers' (New York), Century, Rotary, Citizens, Automobile, Onondaga Golf and Country, Bellevue Country (ex-pres.), etc. Home: Barclay Rd., Solvay, N.Y. Died Nov. 15, 1955.

WINSLOW, Arthur Ellsworth (winz'lō), prof. civil engring.; b. Berlin, Vt., June 15, 1877; s. John Fenno and Ella A. (Bosworth) W.; B.S. in C.E., Norwich U., Northfield, Vt., 1898, C.E., 1901; C.E., Thayer Sch. of Civil Engring. (Dartmouth), 1903; m. Lois Electa Tarbell, July 16, 1901. Asst. engr. Central Vt. R.R., June-Sept. 1898; asst. prof. engring., Rose Poly. Inst., Terre Haute, Ind., 1898-99; asst. engr., Everett, Mass., 1899-1900; prof. civil engring., Norwich U., since 1900, head dept. civil engring. since 1925, became dean of University, 1933, now dean ermeritus; assistant engineer of New York Water Supply, summer, 1906; general practice since 1900. Mem. Soc. for Promotion of Engring. Edn., Vt. Soc. Engrs. (pres.); asso. mem. Am. Society C.E. Democrat. Universalist. Home: 49 Central St., Northfield, Vt. Died Oct. 16, 1950; buried Mount Hope Cemetery, Northfield.

WINSLOW, Carroll Dana, broker; b. N.Y.C., May 30, 1889; s. Francis Dana and Emma (Carroll) W.; Ph.B., Sheffield Scientific School (Yale), 1910; m. Rose O'Neil Kane, Feb. 17, 1912. With Aristos Co., N.Y.C., automobile accessories, 1910-13; with Winslow & Co., stock brokers, 1913-15, now partner same. Served in French Aviation Corps, 1915-17; 1st lt. Signal O.R.C., Aviation Sect., 1917-18; joined aviation force of U.S. Marine Corps.; discharge, 1918. Mem. Book and Snake Soc. (Yale). Episcopalian. Clubs: University, Tuxedo, Yale, Racquet and Tennis (New York). Author: With the French Flying Corps, 1917. Home: Tuxedo Park, N.Y. Office: 20 Nassau St., N.Y.C. Died Dec. 1932.

WINSLOW, Charles-Edward Amory, sanitarian; b. Boston, Feb. 4, 1877; s. Erving and Catherine Mary (Reignolds) W.; B.S., Mass. Inst. Tech., 1898, M.S., 1899; A.M., Yale, 1915; Dr.P.H., N.Y.U. 1918; m. Anne Fuller Rogers, 1907; 1 dau., Anne. Asst. health officer, Montclair, N.J., 1898; spl. work in engrs. office, Mass. State Bd. Health, summers of 1899-1902; asst. 1900-01, instr. sanitary bacteriology, 1902-05, asst. prof. sanitary biology, 1905-10, Mass. Inst. Tech., and biologist-in-charge Sanitary Research Lab., same, 1903-10; asst. prof. bacteriology, U. of Chicago, winter term, 1910; asso. prof. biology, Coll. City of New York, 1910-14; curator of pub. health, Am. Museum Natural History, New York, 1910-22; dir. Div. Pub. Health Edn., N.Y. State Dept. Health, 1914-15; Anna M.R. Lauder prof. public health, Yale Medical School, 1915-45, professor emeritus since 1945; director John B. Pierce Laboratory of Hygiene, 1932-47. Senior sanitarian, U.S.P.H.S. (reserve); Rosenberg lecturer, University of California, 1941. Member board of scientific directors of Internat. Health Div., Rockefeller Foundation, 1929-30. Pres. Nat. Assn. Housing Officials, 1942-43. Received Sedgwick Memorial medal American Public Health Association, 1942; W. Paul Anderson medal, A.S.H.V.E., 1949; Léon Bernard medal, WHO, 1952; Lasker award 1952; Nat. Inst. Social Sci. Medal, 1941; Lemuel Shattuck Medal, Mass. Tb. Pub. Health Assn., 1951; Elizabeth S. Prentiss Award, 1945. Fellow Am. Public Health Assn. (ex-pres.), A.A. A.S. (ex-chmn. sect. K); hon. fellow Royal Soc. Health, Soc. Med. Officers Health (London); member of Conn. Society of Civil Engineers, Army Medical Library, also Society History of Medicine (Peru). Conn. Acad. of Arts and Sciences, Society of Exptl. Biology and Medicine, Soc. Am. Bacteriologists (ex-pres.), Am. Society Naturalists, New England Water Works Assn., American Soc. Heating and Ventilating Engrs. (president 1945), chairman New York State Commn. on Ventilation, 1917-23, 1926-31; mem. Am. Red Cross mission to Russia, July 1917; mem. Pub. Health Council Conn., 1917-51; editor-in-chief Journal Bacteriology, 1916-44; editor American Journal of Public Health, 1944-54. Gen. med. director League of Red Cross Socs., Geneva, 1921; expert assessor Health Committee, League of Nations, 1927-30; chmn. Housing Authority, New Haven, since 1938. Clubs: Century (N.Y. City); Graduate (New Haven). Author: Magda (translation Herman Sudermann's Heimath), 1896; Elements of Water Bacteriology (with S. C. Prescott), 1904; Elements of Industrial Microscopy, 1905; Systemaitc Relationships of the Coccaceae (with Anne Rogers Winslow), 1908; Sewage Disposal (with L. P. Kinnicutt and R. W. Pratt), 1910; Healthy Living, 1917; Health Survey of New Haven, Conn. (with J. C. Greenway and D. Greenberg), 1917; The Land of Health (with Grace T. Hallock), 1922; Nursing and Nursing Education in the United States (chmn.), 1923; Report of the New York State Commission on Ventilation (chmn.), 1923; The Evolution and Significance of the Modern Public Health Campaign, 1923; A Pioneer of Public Health—William Thompson Sedgwick (with E. O. Jordan and G. C. Whipple), 1924; The Laws of Health and How to Teach Them (with Pauline Brooks Williamson), 1925; Fresh Air and Ventilation, 1926; The New Healthy Living (with Mary L. Hahn), 1929; Life of Hermann M. Biggs, 1929; The Road to Health, 1929; Health on the Farm and in the Village, 1931; A City Set on a Hill, 1934; Health Under the "El" (with Savel Zimand), 1937; The Conquest of Epidemic Disease (Princeton U. Press), 1943; The Cost of Sickness and the Price of Health, 1951; Man and Epidemics, 1952. Home: 313 St. Ronan St., New Haven. Died Jan. 8, 1957.

WINSLOW, Guy Monroe, educator; b. Browningtom, Vt., July 1, 1872; s. James M. and Mary A. emeritus; instr. in histology, Tufts Coll. Med and er science, 1898-1908, pres. Lasell Jr. Coll., 1908-47, (Powers) W.; A.B., Tufts Coll., 1895, Ph.D., 1898; m. Clara M. Austin, June 10, 1903; children—Richard Austin, Marjorie, Donald James, Priscilla. Teacher science, 1898-1908, pres. Lasell Jr. Coll., 1908-47, emeritus; instr. in histology, Tufts Coll. Med. and Dental Sch., 1903-13. Mem. Bd. of Aldermen of Newton, 1913-18; mem. Mass. Constl. Conv., 1917-19; trustee and v.p. Newton Savings Bank; dir. Auburndale Cooperative Bank, 1910-47. Mem. Mass. Bd. of Collegiate Authority, 1943-46; ret. Trustee Tufts College. Mem. Am. Assn. Jr. Colls. (v.p. 1935-36). Republican. Conglist. Home: 145 Woodland Rd. Address: 5 Philip St., Medfield, Mass. Died Oct. 17, 1957.

WINSLOW, Thacher, govt. official; b. Newton, Mass., Sept. 16, 1907; s. Andrew Nickerson and Gertrude (Laverack) W.; A.B. cum laude, Harvard, 1929, grad. work history, 1930; m. Frida Frazer, June 24, 1938; children—Thacher, Belinda, David. Real estate agent Winslow Real Estate Trust, 1930; Council on Fgn. Relations (research asst.), 1932-33; research and library sec. to Oswald Garrison Villard, 1933-35; chief pub. relations div., asst. to dep., adminstr. and asst. to adminstr., Nat. Youth Adminstrn., 1935-42; asst. to adminstr., acting dept. adminstr., and deputy adminstr., 1942-46; wage-hour and pub. contracts div., U.S. Dept. Labor; asst. to under-sec. of labor, 1947-50; Dir. Washington branch International Labor Office. Author: Youth—A World Problem, 1937. Editor American Youth, An Enforced Reconnaissance (with Frank P. Davidson), 1940. Home: 3432 Newark St., N.W. Office: 1262 New Hampshire Av., N.W., Washington. Died Jan. 9, 1955.

WINSOR, James Davis, Jr., broker; b. Radnor, Pa., Sept. 6, 1876; s. James Davis and Rebecca (Chapman) W.; grad. Haverford Sch., U. Pa.; m. Marion Harding Curtin, June 16, 1904; children—Curtin, James Davis III, Marion (Mrs. Henry D. Mirick). Partner Yarnall, Biddle & Co., Phila., 1953—; dir. Insurance Co. North Am., Indemnity Ins. Co. North Am., Phila. Fire & Marine Ins. Co., Life Ins. Co. Am., Parkway Co., Stock Ins. Co. of the Green Tree, Westmoreland Coal Co., Westmoreland, Inc.; trustee Mutual Ins. Co. Mgr. Phila. Savs. Fund Soc.; pres. Merchants Fund, Oliver Fund. Mem. N.Y. Stock Exchange. Club: Rittenhouse (Phila.). Home: 101 Cherry Lane, Ardmore, Pa. Office: 1528 Walnut St., Phila. Died Jan. 11, 1957.

WINSOR, Mulford, state govt. official; b. Jewell City, Kan., May 31, 1874; s. Mulford and Caroline Hannah (Kelly) W.; ed. pub. schs. of Jewell City and Fort Smith, Ark.; m. Clara Beatrice Brown, Dec. 25, 1903; children—Eleanor (Mrs. L. H. Davis), Margaret (Mrs. V. E. Blalack), Mulford. Editor and pub. and founder, The Yuma (Ariz.) Sun, 1896-1901; mgr. and co-pub. Daily Citizen, Tucson, Ariz., 1901-03; editor and pub. Evening Enterprise, Phoenix, Ariz., 1903-05; editor, pub. and founder The Morning Sun, Yuma, 1905-08; editor and pub. The Daily Globe (Ariz.), 1909; first occupant office of Ariz. historian, 1909; exec. sec. to 1st gov., 1912; chmn. and organizer State Land Commn., 1912-15; mem. Ariz. State Senate, 1917-28, pres., 1923-28; dir. State Dept. Library and Archives since 1932; owner Persian Gardens, Yuma, Ariz. (producer many varieties of dates) since 1916. Mem. A.L.A., Am. Acad. Polit. and Social Sci., Council of State Governments (bd. mgrs.), Nat. Council of Commrs. on Uniform State Laws. Democrat. Elk. Author: Guide to Legislative Drafting in Arizona, 1941; monographs on legislative procedure. Home: 1402 W. Washington, Phoenix. Offices: State Capitol, Phoenix; (legal) Yuma, Ariz. Died Nov. 5, 1956.

WINSTON, Garrard Bigelow, lawyer; b. Chicago, Ill., July 25, 1882; s. Frederick Seymour and Ada (Fountain) W.; B.A., Yale, 1904; B.L., Northwestern U., 1906; unmarried. Former mem. law firm of Winston, Strawn & Shaw, Chicago; undersecretary of the treas., 1923-27; sec. Am. Debt Funding Commn.; mem. firm of Shearman & Sterling & Wright, New York. Former treas. Am. Red Cross. Commd. maj. arty., O.R.C., U.S. Army, Aug. 1917. President The Roosevelt Hosp.; pres. New York Trade Sch.; v.p. Osborne Memorial Home. Mem. Am. and N.Y. bar assns., Soc. of the Cincinnati. Republican. Episcopalian. Clubs: Chicago (Chicago); Links, Nat. Golf, Recess. Home: 7 E. 92d St., New York 28. Office: 20 Exchange Pl., N.Y.C. 5. Died July 28, 1955.

WINTER, Andrew, artist; b. Estonia, April 7, 1892; s. George and Anna (Klaas) W.; student Nat. Acad. Design, 1921-25; m. Mary Taylor, Dec. 24, 1928. Came to U.S., 1916, naturalized, 1921. Exhibited at Nat. Acad. Design, Salmagundi Club, Corcoran Gallery, Pa. Acad., Chgo. Art Inst., Toledo Mus., Am. Fedn. of Art, Rotary Exhibition, Golden Gate Internat. Expn., Artists for Victory (Met. Mus. of Art) Carnegie Inst. Awarded Mooney Travelling Scholarship, 1925, J. Frances Murphy Meml. prize, 1930; Mrs. Louis Betts prize, 1933; Salmagundi Club prize, 1934; Isidor gold medal, 1935; hon. mention, Allied Artists Am., 1936; Salmagundi Club Prize, 1937, 40, Lay prize, 1938, 1st Lay prize, 1941; awarded anonymous prize Allied Artists Am., 1939, 40, popular prize, 1940; Buck Hill Falls (Pa.) Art Assn. purchase prize, 1940; Edwin Palmer meml. prize Nat. Acad., 1940; Best Watercolor prize, Currier Gallery, 1941; Albert H. Soan Meml. Water Color prize, Salmagundi Club, 1942; Edwin Palmer memorial prize, Nat. Acad., 1942, 49, 54; for outstanding contbn. in field of art by Am. citzien of foreign birth was included in "Wall of Fame," N.Y. World's Fair, 1940. 1st Lay Prize—Salmagundi, 1945; 1st Altman Prize Nat. Acad., 1944; Lempert Meml. Purchase Prize; Frank B. Williams Prize, 1948; Lucile Dingley Popular Prize, 1948; Certificate of Merit, 1949; Saltus Gold Medal of Merit, N.A.D., 1956; Lee Eaton Prize, 1954; Portland Art Festival Prize, 1957; Popular Art Festival Prize, 1958; Jane Peterson Prize, 1958. Member International Institute of Arts and Letters, Saluigundi, National Academy, National Arts Club (life), Artists Fellowship, Inc., Louis Comfort Tiffany Foundation, Salmagundi Club, Am. Water Color Soc., Grand Central Art Galleries, Inc. Home: Monhegan Island, Me. Died Oct. 27, 1958; buried Monhegan Island, Me.

WINTER, John Garrett, univ. prof.; b. Holland, Mich., Feb. 14, 1881; s. G. and Janet (de Weerd) W.; A.B., Hope Coll., Holland, 1901; A.M., U. of Mich., 1904, Ph.D., 1906; m. Johanna Anthonette Riemens, Feb. 20, 1911. Instr. in Greek and Latin, Hope Coll., 1901-03; instr. in same, U. of Mich., 1906-11, asst. prof., 1911-15, asso. prof., 1915-19, professor, 1919-28, professor Latin Language and literature, 1928-51, prof. emeritus Lat. lang. and lit. 1951—, chmn. dept., 1928-46; dir. Museum of Archeology 1928-51; dir. Institute of Fine Arts. 1928-46. Lecturer on Thomas Spencer Jerome foundation, Am. Acad. in Rome, 1929, Russel lecturer, U. of Mich., 1935-36. Mem. mng. com. Am. Sch. Classical Studies, Athens, Greence; mem. adv. council Am. Acad. in Rome. Mem. Société Royal Egyptienne de Papyrologie, Soc, Promotion of Byzantine and Modern Greek Studies, American Phil. Assn. (pres. 1944), Association Internationale de Papyrologues, Archeological Inst. Am., Am. Assn. Univ. Professors, Netherland American University League, Mich. Acad. Scis., Arts and Letters, Research Club of U. of Mich., Phi Beta Kappa. Author: Myth of Hercules at Rome, 1910; Prodomus of Nicolaus Steno, 1916; Life and Letters in the Papyri, 1933. Contbr. to classical jours. Editor: T. S. Jerome's Aspects of the Study of Roman History, 1923; Michigan Papyri (vol III), 1936 (vol. VIII with H. C. Youltie), 1951. Gen. editor U. of Mich. Studies (Humanistic Series), 1928-50. Home: 901 S. Forest Av., Ann Arbor, Mich. Died Mar. 23, 1956; buried Arborcrest Cemetery, Ann Arbor.

WINTER, Thomas Daniel, ex-congressman; b. Columbus, Kan., July 7, 1896; s. Louis Henry and Florence (Blake) W.; grad. Cherokee Co. High Sch., Columbus, Kan., 1916; m. Blanche Naomi Gracey, Sept. 9, 1922; children—Robert Gracey, John Louis. Stenographer in law office of Chas. Stephens, Columbus, Kan., 1921; ofcl. court rep. 38th Judicial Dist. of Kan., 1922-27; studied law, 1921-27; admitted to Kan. bar, 1926; asst. county atty., Crawford County, Kan., 1927-28, county atty., 1929-30; engaged in gen. practice of law, Girard, Kan., 1931—; commr. pub. utilities, Girard, Kan., 1933-35; commissioner of Finance, Girard, 1936-38; mem. 76th to 79th Congresses, 1939-47, 3d Kan. Dist. Served in U.S. Air Service, Kelly Field, San Antonio, Tex., World War. Mem. Crawford County Bar Assn., Am. Legion. Republican. Presbyterian. Mason (Shriner), Elk. Home: Girard, Kan. Died Nov. 7, 1951; buried Columbus, Kan.

WINTER, William D., chmn. executive com. Atlantic Mutual Ins. Co., Centennial Ins. Co.; trustee

Bank of N.Y. Seamen's Bank for Savings. LL.D., Hamilton Coll. Author: Marine Insurance. Home: 61 Prospect Hill Av., Summit, N.J. Office: 49 Wall St., N.Y.C. Died Mar. 8, 1955.

WINTERBOTHAM, Joseph, indsl. engr.; b. Joliet, Ill., Feb. 24, 1878; s. Joseph and Genevieve Fellows (Baldwin) W.; Yale, 1900; M.A. (hon.) Univ. of Vt., 1941; m. Eleanor Hall, 1902 (dec.); 1 dau., Louise (Mrs. George McKay Schieffelin); m. 2d, Harriot Lee, Mar. 1929. Industrial exec. and engr., now retired from a large part of business activities; formerly served as pres. Perth Amboy Terra Cotta Co., Mitchell-Lewis (now Nash) Motor Co., Muller Export Co.; formerly vice-pres. Paramount (now Bear Brand) Knitting Co., Racine Rubber Co.; formerly chmn. bd. Atlantic Terra Cotta Co.; dir. Bear Brand Knitting Co., J. H. Winterbotham & Sons, J. C. Pennoyer Co., Tenak Products, Inc., Pennoyer Merchants Transfer Co., Muller Export Co., Nash Motor Co. Perth Amboy Terra Cotta Co., New England Indsl. Development Co., Vt. Soy Bean Assn., Inc. Chmn. Vt. Agrl. and Indsl. Products Commns. since 1939. Supervisor of art and consultant Fleming Museum, U. of Vt., 5 yrs.; governing mem. and mem. spl. com. Art Inst. of Chicago. Mem. exec. bd. regional (Boston) Boy Scouts of America. State chmn. British Relief Soc. Trustee Old Ladies Home, Burlington, Vt. Chmn. housing administrn., planning bd., post war planning bd., Burlington, Vt. Chmn. Vermont Indsl. Agrl. Products Commn. Mem. exec. bd. Nat. Seaway Council, Washington, D.C. Clubs: University, Tavern, Arts, Casino (Chicago); Century Assn. (N.Y. City). Home: Burlington, Vt. (summer); Roosevelt Hotel, New Orleans, La. (winter). Office: 8 S. Dearborn St., Chgo. Died Apr. 19, 1954.

WINTERNITZ, Milton Charles (wĭn'tẽr-nĭts), pathologist; b. Baltimore, Feb. 19, 1885; s. L. Carl and Jennie (Kittner) W.; A.B., Johns Hopkins U., 1903, M.D., 1907; M.A. (hon.), Yale, 1917, LL.D., 1952; m. Helen Watson, M.D., Mar. 20, 1913 (died Apr. 1930); children—Elizabeth Watson, Jane Kimball, Thomas Watson, Mary Watson, William Welch; m. 2d, Pauline Webster Whitney, Apr. 6, 1932. Fellow, asst. instr. and asso. prof. pathology, Johns Hopkins Med. Sch., 1907-17; asst. resident pathologist, Johns Hopkins Hosp., 1910-13, asso. pathologist, 1913-17; pathologist to City Hosp., Baltimore, 1910-17; prof. pathology and bacteriology, Yale, Sept. 1917-25, Anthony N. Brady prof. of pathology, 1925-50, prof. emeritus, 1950—; dean Yale Med. Sch., 1920-35; asso. dir. Inst. Human Relations, Yale, 1931-50. Mem. Commn. Orgn. Exec. Br. Govt., 1953-55. Mem. bd. Gaylor Farm Sanatorium, Grace-New Haven Community Hosp.; dir. bd. sci. advisers Jane Coffin Childs Meml. Fund for Med. Research, 1948—; chmn. Div. of Med. Scis., Nat. Research Council, Wsahington, 1950-53. Captain and major United States Medical Corps, 1918. Recipient Newell Sill Jenkins Meml. medal, 1932; King's Medal for Service in Cause of Freedom, 1948; Pres.' Certificate of Merit, 1948; Yale Medal, 1952. Fellow Royal Soc. Medicine, A.M.A., A.A.A.S.; mem. Am. Soc. Experimental Pathology, Assn. Bacteriologists and Pathologists, New Haven Medical Society, Society for Experimental Biology, National Com. for Mental Hygiene, Conn. Society for Mental Hygiene, New Haven Co. Med. Assn., Conn. Birth Control League. Clubs: Yale, N.Y. Graduates, New Haven Lawn; Cosmos. Author: The Pathology of Influenza, 1919; The Biology of Arteriosclerosis, 1937. Compiler: Collected Studies on the Pathology of War Gas Poisoning, 1919; Pathology of Vascular Disease. Home: 2126 Connecticut Av., Washington 8. Died Oct. 3, 1959.

WINTHROP, Henry Rogers, b. Newport, R.I., July 2, 1876; s. Buchanan and Sarah Helen (Townsend) W.; A.B., Yale, 1898; m. Alice Babcock, Oct. 3, 1905. Mem. N.Y. Stock Exchange; dir. Met. Opera Assn.; dir. Long Island R.R., Loew's Inc., U.S. and Fgn. Securities Corp., U.S. and Internat. Securities Corp. Maj. U.S. Army, 1918-19; now col. U.S. Res. Corps. Decorated Distinguished Service Order; Comdr. British Empire (British); Comdr. Royal Order of Crown (Italian). Mem. Delta Kapa Epsilon. Republican. Episcopalian. Clubs: Knickerbocker, Piping Rock. Home: (legal) Woodbury, L.I.; (winter) 474 Arlington Av., Sarasota, Fla. Office: Shearson, Hammill & Co., 14 Wall St., N.Y.C. Died Nov. 1958.

WINTNER, Aurel, mathematician; b. Budapest, Hungary, Apr. 8, 1903; s. Edward and Charlotte (Hirschfeld) W.; student U. Vienna, U. Göttingen; Ph.D., U. Leipzig, 1929; m. Dr. Irmgard Hölder, Sept. 11, 1930; 1 son, Claude Edward. Came to U. S., 1930, naturalized, 1937. Mem. faculty Johns Hopkins, 1930—, prof. mathematics, 1946—. Rockefeller Found. fellow U. Rome, 1929, Copenhagen Obs., 1930; mem. Inst. for Advanced Study, Princeton, 1937-38; John Simon Guggenheim Meml. Found. fellow, 1941. Mem. Astronomische Gesellschaft, London Math. Soc., Edinburgh Mathematical Society, Palermo Mathematical Society. Author: Spektraltheorie der unendlichen Matrizen, 1929; Beweis des E. Strömgrenschen dynamischen Abschlussprinzips der periodischen Bahngruppen im restringierten Dreikörper-problem. Publikationer og mindre Meddelelser fra Köbenhavns Observatorium, 1931; Sortengenealogie, Hekubakomplex und Gruppenfortsetzung, 1931; Lectures on asymptotic distributions and infinite convolutions, 1938; Analytical Foundations of Celestial Mechanics, 1941; Eratosthenian Averages, 1943; Theory of Measure in Arithmetical Semi-groups, 1944; The Fourier transforms of probability distributions, 1947. Asst. editorial bd. of Mathematische Zeitschrift and of Jahrbuch über die Fortschritte der Mathematik, 1927-29; asso. editor Am. Jour. Mathematics, 1936-39, editor, 1943—, sec., 1954—; cons. editor Rendiconti Del Circolo Matematico Palermo, 1951—. Contbr. articles math. jours. Address, Johns Hopkins U., Balt. 18. Died Jan. 15, 1958.

WIRE, G. E., librarian; b. Dryden, N.Y., Feb. 6, 1859; s. Rev. T. D. and N. B. W.; ed. Northwestern U. Acad., Evanston, Ill.; M.D., Northwestern U., 1883; LL.B., Kent Coll. of Law, Chgo., 1895; grad. N.Y. State Library Sch., 1889, B.L.S., 1913; m. E. A. Clark, Apr. 16, 1903. In Northwestern U. Library, Evanston, Ill., 1885-88, Columbia Library, N.Y., 1888-90, Newberry Library, Chgo., 1890-95; in expert work, 1895-98; in Worcester County (Mass.) Law Library, 1908—. Made law and med. classifications pub. by C. A. Cutter, Forbes Library, Northampton, Mass.; contbr. to Library Jour., Pub. Libraries, etc. Mem. A.L.A. (life), A.A.L.L., Mass. Library Club, Appalachian Mountain Club, Green Mountain Club. Address: Worcester County Law Library, Worcester, Mass. Died Feb. 23, 1936.

WIRTH, Louis, sociologist, educator; b. Gemünden, Germany, Aug. 28, 1897; s. Joseph and Rosalie (Lorig) W.; brought to U.S., 1911, naturalized, 1924; Ph.B., U. of Chicago, 1919, M.A., 1925, Ph.D., 1926; m. Mary L. Bolton, Feb. 14, 1923; children—Elizabeth, Alice. Began as social worker, 1919; dir. delinquent boys div., Bur. of Personal Service, Chicago, 1919-22; instr. in sociology, U. of Chicago, 1926-28, asst. prof., 1931, asso. prof., 1932-40, prof. since 1940, also associate dean social science division, 1940-46; assistant professor of sociology, Tulane University, New Orleans, Louisiana, 1928-29, associate professor, 1929-30; research fellow in Europe of Social Science Research Council, 1930-31; consultant Nat. Resources Planning Bd., 1935-43, regional chairman, Region 4, 1942-43; dir. of planning Ill. Post-War Planning Commn., 1944. Mem. Am. Sociological Soc., (sec., treas. and mng. editor, 1932; pres. 1947); Am. Council Race Relations (pres.), Soc. for Social, Research, Am. Soc. Planning Officials, Am. Assn. Univ. Profs., Institut Internat. de Sociologie, Phi Beta Kappa. Club: Quadrangle. Asso. ed. Am. Jour. of Sociology, 1926-28 and, 1931—. Author: (with R. E. Park and others) The City, 1925; The Ghetto, 1928; Our Cities: Their Role in the National Economy (with others), 1937; Urban government (with others), 1938; Urban Planning and Land Policies (with others), 1939; Local Community Fact Book, 1939; Community Planning for Peacetime Living, 1946. Editor: Contemporary Social Problems, 1939; 1126: A Decade of Social Science Research, 1940. Contributor articles on sociology and social research in various journals. Address: 5727 Kimbark Av., Chgo. 37. Died May 3, 1952.

WIRTZ, Alvin J. (wirts), lawyer; b. Columbus, Tex., May 24, 1888; s. Lewis M. and Dora (Dent) W.; LL.B., U. of Tex., 1910; m. Kitty Mae Stamps, Nov. 18, 1913; 1 dau., Ida May (wife of Dr. James C. Cain). Admitted to Tex. bar, 1910; practiced in Colorado County, 1910-17, Guadalupe County, 1917-34; member firm Powell, Wirtz and Rauhut of Austin Tex., since 1934; specializes in oil and water law; under sec. Dept. of Interior, Jan. 2, 1940-May 24, 1941; dir. Austin Housing Authority; organized and served as gen. counsel Lower Colorado River Authority; chmn. state advisory bd. Nat. Youth Adminstrn. for Tex. Mem. Tex. State Senate, 1922-30. Del. Dem. National Conv., Houston, 1928, Chicago, 1932 and 1940. Democrat. Baptist. Mason, Elk. Club: Austin Country. Home: 2307 Woodlawn. Office: Brown Bldg., Austin, Tex. Died Oct. 27, 1951; buried Texas State Cemetery, Austin, Tex.

WISE, Arthur Chamberlin, investment banking; b. Boston, Mass., Jan. 6, 1876; s. Daniel Webster and Mary Anna (Chamberlin) W.; grad. Brookline (Mass.) High Sch., 1896; m. Marion Strong Somers, Oct. 9, 1902; children—Barbara, John. In brokerage and investment business since 1896; formerly partner Millett, Roe & Hagen; now president Wise, Hobbs & Seaver, Inc.; treas., dir. Boston Garden-Arena Corp.; dir. Boston Sand Gravel Co., Hingham Trust Co., Hingham Coöp. Bank, Internat. Braid Co. Chmn. Hingham Red Cross Committee during World War. Trustee and dir. New Hampshire Jockey Club. Republican. Unitarian. Clubs: Algonquin, Boston Garden (Boston); Hingham Yacht (Hingham); Cohasset Golf (Cohasset). Home: 37 Fearing Rd., Hingham, Mass. Office: 15 Congress St., Boston. Died June 26, 1952; buried Old Ship Cemetery, Hingham, Mass.

WISE, Harold A., publisher; b. Bklyn., 1896; married; children—Mrs. Daniel Kelly, Jr., Betty Lou, Robert B. (dec.). Joined Macfadden Co., 1920, became v.p., advt. dir., later gen. mgr. Liberty mag., 1941, sr. v.p. co., 1945-50, pres., 1951, chmn. bd., dir., 1951—. Home: Onancock, Va. Office: 205 E. 42d St., N.Y.C. 17. Died Dec. 1954; Keosico Cemetery, Valhalla, N.Y.

WISE, Jonah Bondi, rabbi; b. Cincinnati, O., Feb. 21, 1881; s. Isaac M. and Selma (Bondi) W.; B.A., U. of Cincinnati, 1903; grad. as rabbi, Hebrew Union Coll., 1903, LL.D. (hon.); studied U. of Berlin and U. of Berne, Switzerland; LL.D., New York U., 1932; m. Helen Rosenfeld, June 23, 1909; children—David, Elsa, Joan. Rabbi Mizpah Temple, Chattanooga, Tenn., 1904-06, Beth Israel Temple, Portland, 1906-25, Central Synagogue, New York, Sept. 1925—. Nat. chmn. of fund raising campaign of the Am. Jewish Joint Distribution Com., 1931-32. Founder, condr. Message of Israel, radio program, ABC, 1934-59. Editor The American Israelite. Contbr. to religious and spl. jours. Address: Central Synagogue, 35 E. 62d St., N.Y.C. Died Feb. 1, 1959; buried Linden Hill Cemetery, Bklyn.

WISE, Marion Johnson, ry. ofcl.; b. St. Louis County, Mo., Aug. 16, 1883; s. George Ricketts and Olive Anna (Brown) W.; student Barnes Bus. Coll., St. Louis, 1899-1900; m. Anna Grace Scudamore, Apr. 25, 1906; 1 son, Marion J. Began as clerk Mobile & Ohio R.R., 1901-11; supt. Southern Ry. Co., Columbus, Miss., 1911-13; asst. to gen. mgr. Mobile & Ohio R.R., Mobile, Ala., Southern Ry., Miss., 1913-18; staff officer in charge of operations, Mobile & Ohio R.R., Southern Ry., Miss., G., M.& N. R.R., Mobile, Ala., 1918-20; mgr. dept. material and supplies U.S. R.R. Adminstrn., 1920-23; officer on staff of pres. S.P. Co., 1923-26, asst. to vice chmn. S.P. Co., N.Y.C., 1926-32, asst. to pres. San Francisco; pres., dir. S.P. Land Co., Coos Bay Ore. Coal Co.; dir. San Diego & Arizona Eastern Ry., Interurban Electric Ry., Visalia Electric Co.; asst. to pres. Northwestern Pacific R.R., Petaluma & Santa Rosa R.R., San Diego & Ariz. Eastern Ry. Co., 1932-43; pres., dir. Ocean Staemship Co., Savannah, pres., dir., Central of Ga. Ry. Co., Savannah, Ga., 1948—; dir. Wadley Southern R.R., Louisville & Wadley R.R., Savannah Bank & Trust Co. Mem. adv. council Southern Research Inst. Dir. Savannah Tumor Clinic. Mem. Savannah C. of C. (dir.), S.A.R., Soc. Colonial Wars, Newcomen Soc., Ga. Forestry Assn. (dir., 1st v.p.). Baptist. Clubs: Golf, Oglethorpe, Rotary (Savannah); Pacific Railway (San Francisco). Home: Hotel De Soto. Office Address: 233 W. Broad St., Savannah, Ga. Died Apr. 26, 1950; buried Pine Crest Cemetery, Mobile, Ala.

WISE, William Frederic, business exec.; b. Lima, O., Dec. 19, 1895; s. William Henry and Jane (Pugh) W.; student Western State Normal Sch., Kalamazoo, Mich.; m. Ione O. Truax, 1928. Production engr. Excello Corp. (Detroit, Mich.), later v.p. and gen. sales mgr.; then pres. Republic Products Corp. (Detroit, Mich.), Aviation Mfg. Corp. (Williamsport, Pa.); Am. Propeller Corp. (Toledo, O.); exec. v.p., Avco Mfg. Corp. (New York); now pres. Scotten Mfg. Corp., Republic Realty Corp., Shop Tools, Inc., Detroit. Mem. Soc. of Automotive Engrs. Mason. Club: Detroit Athletic. Home: 27400 Rainbow Circle, Lathrop Village, Mich. Office: 24275 Mound Rd., Centerline, Mich. Died Apr. 18, 1958.

WISEMAN, Bruce Kenneth, physician; b. South Bend, Ind., Mar. 1, 1897; s. Samuel Judson and Virginia McKee (Galentine) W.; student Butler Coll., 1922-24; B.S., Ind. U., 1926, M.D., 1928; m. Adah Viola Quinlan, Oct. 25, 1921. House officer, Indianapolis City Hosp., 1927-29; asst. dept. bacteriology and pathology Rockefeller Inst. for Med. Research, 1929-30; mem. faculty O. State U. 1930—, prof. and chmn. dept. medicine, 1944—. Awarded Ravdin medal by Ind. U., 1928. Fellow A.C.P..; mem. Am. Soc. Exptl. Pathology, Soc. Exptl. Biology and Medicine, A.M.A., Central Soc. Clin. Research, Columbus Acad. Medicine, Sigma Xi, Alpha Omega Alpha. Home: 2180 Tremont Rd., Columbus 21, O. Died Mar. 1960.

WISLOCKI, George Bernays (wĭs-lŏk'ĭ), anatomist; b. San Jose, Calif., Mar. 25, 1892; s. Stanislaus and Lily C. (Bernays) W.; A.B., Washington U., 1912, Sc.D. (hon.), 1951; M.D., Johns Hopkins, 1916; A.M., (hon.), Harvard U., 1942; m. Florence Clothier, Feb. 13, 1931; children—Louis Clothier, Johanna, George Stanislaus, Edith Ball. Anatomist, Johns Hopkins, 1916-31; Parkman prof. of anatomy, Harvard U., 1931-1941, James Stillman prof. of comparative anatomy since 1941, and Hersey professor of anatomy, 1947—, mem. faculty Mus. Comparative Zoology, 1952—. Served as 1st lieutenant U.S. Med. Corps, 1917-18. Mem. Harvard Infantile Paralysis Com., Ella Sachs Plotz Foundation, Elizabeth Thompson Science Fund; mem. Scientific Advisory Bd., Wistar Inst. of Anatomy and Biology, 1939-40. Trustee emeritus Forsyth Dental Infirmary. Fellow A.A.A.S., Zool. Society London (hon. fgn.); member Anatomical Soc. Great Britain and Ireland (honorary), National Academy of Sciences, American Academy Arts and Sciences, Am. Assn. Anatomists, Histochemical Society (president 1950-51), American Physiological Society, Am. Soc. Zoölogists, Institut internat. d'embryol., Phi Beta Kappa, Sigma Xi, Alpha Omega Alpha. Asso. editor Johns Hopkins Hosp. Bulletin, 1926-31; associate editor American Journal Anatomy, 1939-46, Journal of Histochemistry, 1953—; editor Am. Anatomical Memoirs. Author of papers on embryology, histology and endocrinology. Clubs:

14 W. Hamilton St. (Baltimore); Med. Exchange, Harvard (Boston). Home: 148 Hillside St., Milton, Mass. Office: Harvard Medical School, 25 Shattuck St., Boston. Died Oct. 22, 1956; buried Walnut Hill, Brookline, Mass.

WIST, Benjamin Othello, university dean; b. St. Paul, Minn., Aug. 7, 1889; s. Johannes B(enjamin) and Josephine (Aasve) W.; student Luther Coll., Decorah, Ia., 1906-09; A.B., Spokane Coll., 1910; M.A., U. of Hawaii, 1924; Ph.D., Yale, 1937; student U. of California, 1911; m. Blanche Carmen Canario, Dec. 28, 1912; children—Zoe Aasve (Mrs. Hubert V. Everly), Lois Joem (Mrs. S. Carl Wright), Corrine Ann (Mrs. Charles E. Cherry). High school teacher, Almira, Washington, 1910-11; principal elementary schools (T.H.), Kaiwiki, 1911-12, Pahala, 1912-14, Honokaa, 1914-15, Kamehameha III (Lahaina), 1915-21; pres. Terr. Normal, Honolulu, 1921-31; dean, teachers college, University of Hawaii, 1931-48, emeritus; vis. prof. University of Calif., summer 1935, Yale, 1936-37. Chmn. Survey Commn. Am. Samoa, 1932-33; dir. Honolulu Edn. Council; delegate Hawaii State Constitutional Convention, 1950; mem. Hawaii Statehood Commission since 1951. Regent U. of Hawaii. Mem. N.E.A., Oahu Edn. Assn., Hawaii Edn. Assn. (pres. 1925), Phi Kappa Phi, Pi Gamma Mu, Phi Delta Kappa. Lutheran. Club: Public Question. Author: A Century of Public Education in Hawaii, 1940. Home: 2322 Maile Way, Honolulu 14, Hawaii. Died Oct. 26, 1951; buried Nuuanu Meml. Park Cemetery, Honolulu, Hawaii.

WISWALL, Richard H., lawyer; b. Providence, Jan. 8, 1886; s. Herbert and Marie R.E. (Gerber) W.; A.B., Harvard, 1907, LL.B., 1910; m. Katharine Coggin, Dec. 29, 1913; children—Richard H., Hope (Mrs. Thomas McLean Griffin). Admitted to Mass. bar, 1910; mem. Hill, Barlow, Goodale & Wiswall, Boston, since 1918; trustee, v.p. Salem (Mass.) Five Cents Savs. Bank. Trustee Peabody Mus., Salem Hosp., Bertram Home for Aged Men. Mem. Am., Mass. State bar assns., Am. Law Inst. Unitarian. Home: 14 Broad St., Salem, Mass. Office: 53 State St., Boston. Died Mar. 12, 1955.

WITHAM, Ernest C. (wĭth'ăm), educator; b. West Gray, Me., Oct. 6, 1880; s. Alphonso Nelson (M.D.) and Mary Lizzie (Pennell) W.; B.S., Tufts Coll., 1904; M.A., New York U., 1933; m. Lillian Emma Davis, Dec. 24, 1908; children—Pennell Davis, Elizabeth Clair (Mrs. Chester A. Brewer). Principal John A. Andrew School, Windham, Me., 1904-05; submaster Hudson (Mass.) High School, 1905-06; principal boys' department Perkins Institution for the Blind, Mass., 1906-09; supt. schs. Conway-Bartlett-Madison Dist., N.H., 1909-12; supt. schs., Southington, Conn., 1912-22; supt. schs., Putnam, Conn., 1922; dir. of research, pub. schs. of Wilmington, Del., 1922-29; instr. N.H. State Normal Sch., Keene and Plymouth, several summers; instr. U. of Del. Summer School, 1927; prof. edn., Rutgers U., 1929-52. Pvt. Conn. State Guard, 1917-19. Mem. of the Bd. of Edn. of Raritan Township. Mem. N.E.A., Am. Assn. School Adminstrs., Ednl. Research Assn., Nat. Soc. for Study of Edn., Theta Delta Chi, Phi Delta Kappa (treas. of Alpha Pi chpater), Kappa Phi Kappa. Republican. Elder Reformed (Dutch) Ch. Mason. Author: Standard Geography Tests; Witham Silent Reading and English Vocabulary Tests; Standard Arithmetic Tests; Witham's Fraction Drill Cards (oral); Hall of Fame Test; Standardized History Tests; New Series of Witham Geography Tests; School Administration Forms; Tests on Essential Language Habits; series of ten articles on Types of School Administration in the various states, 1934-35; Problem Studies in School Administration, 1936; also numerous essays and articles on edn. and other subjects. Home: Central Av., Stelton, N.J. Address: Rutgers University, New Brunswick, N.J. Died Feb. 20, 1958.

WITHERS, Garrett Lee, congressman; b. Providence, Ky., June 21, 1885; s. Francis Gooch and Sarah Catherine (Imboden) W.; student Providence M. and F. Acad.; Southern Normal Sch., Bowling Green, Ky.; m. Mabel Hammack, Feb. 12, 1912; children—Thomas Lee, Dr. John Carroll, Helen (Mrs. Robert B. Griffith). Practicing atty., Webster County, from 1911; served as clerk circuit court, also commr. in chancery and referee in bankruptcy, Webster County; became mem. Hunt & Withers, Dixon, Ky.; now member of the firm of Withers, Lisman & Withers, Dixon; member congress, 1952—. Past pres. Peoples Bank, Clay, Ky.; dir. Dixon Bank & Trust Co. Commr. highways State of Ky., 1947-49, mem. Ky. State Highway Commn. since 1932. Home: Leeper St., Dixon, Ky. Address: Congressional Hotel, Washington. Died Apr. 30, 1953.

WITHERS, Harry Clay (wĭth'ĕrz), newspaper man; b. Denton, Tex., Nov. 20, 1880; s. John Allen and Mary (Coleman) W.; student Denton (Tex.) Pub. Sch., 1886-95, Haskell Inst., 1897-99; Litt.D. (hon.), Southwestern U., 1947; m. Annie Sinclair, Jan. 23, 1907. City editor Denton Record-Chronicle, 1901-03; staff correspondent Houston (Tex.) Post, 1903-04; reporter Dallas (Tex.) News, 1904-06, sports editor, 1906-11, city editor, 1911-14, columnist, 1938-39, managing editor, 1939-50, and executive editor since 1950; city editor Dallas Journal, 1914-18, mng. editor, 1918-38; director A. H. Belo Corporation. Served as pvt., 33d U.S. Vol. Inf., in P.I., 1899-1901. Member English-speaking Union, Dallas Hist. Soc., Civic Federation. Democrat. Methodist. Clubs: Dallas Athletic, Dallas Rotary, Town and Gown. Home: 3331 Southwestern St. Office: Dallas News, Dallas. Deceased.

WITHERS, Robert Edwin, aluminum exec. (ret.); b. Danville, Va., Mar. 13, 1865; s. Dr. Robert Enoch and Mary Virginia (Royall) W.; ed. pvt. schs. of Richmond, Alexandria and Wytheville, Va.; grad. Va. Mil. Inst., 1885; m. Mary Cloyd Kent, June 2, 1892; children—Robert Edwin, Kent Cloyd. Sec. to father, U.S. consul to Hong Kong, 1885; apptd. vice and dep. consul, 1886; mem. staff Keystone Bank, Pittsburgh, 1893; chief clerk Pittsburgh Reduction Co. (now Aluminum Co. of Am.), New Kensington, Pa., 1895, became treas. and asst. sec., 1898, v.p. in charge of finance, 1922, dir., 1927, sr. v.p., 1931, also dir. and officer numerous subsidiary cos.; resigned v.p., retired, 1946; helped establish St. Andrews Episcpal Ch., New Kensington. Organizer, past dir. New Kensington Y.M.C.A.; past pres. bd. trustees Citizens Gen. Hosp. of New Kensington; mem. bd. of trustees of P.E. Diocese Pittsburgh; v.p. and trustee Shady Side Acad. Mem. Va. Soc. of Cincinnati, Sigma Chi. Mem. Calvary Episcopal Church, Pittsburgh (past rep. to Diocesan convs.; past pres. Brotherhood). Mason. Clubs: Duquesne, University, Oakmont Country, Fox Chapel Golf, The Wytheville Golf. Author: Ancestry of Robert Edwin Withers, III, 1947. Address: 924 S. Aiken Av., Pittsburgh; also "Ingleside," Wytheville, Va. Died Dec. 29, 1952; buried East End Cemetery, Wytheville, Va.

WITHERSPOON, Archibald William, lawyer; b. Detroit, Mich., June 11, 1876; s. William Wallace and Isabella (Grant) W.; grad. high sch., Spokane, Wash., 1894; m. Eda Mauseth, Nov. 11, 1901 (dec.); children—Margaret Eda (Mrs. Forest Watson), William Wallae, Helen Elizabeth (Mrs. Neal Fosseen); m. 2d, Ruth Warner, Jan. 23, 1947. In law office Forster & Wakefield, Spokane, 1895-1906; admitted to Wash. bar, 1899; mem. Wakefield & Witherspoon, 1906-35 (W. J. C. Wakefield, dec. 1931); firm reorganized as Witherspoon, Witherspoon & Kelley. Chmn., dir. Old Nat. Bank of Spokane, White Pine Sash; pres., dir. Finch Investment Co., Old Nat. Corp., Old Nat. Bank Bldg. Co., Investment and Securities Co.; v.p. Pend Oreille Mines & Metals Co.; dir. Greenough Investment Co., First Nat. Bank Spokane, Centennial Flouring Mills Co., G.N. Ry. Co. Mem. Am., Wash. State, Spokane Co. bar assns. Clubs: Spokane City, Spokane Country. Home: W 538 Sumner Av., Spokane. Office: Old Nat. Bank Bldg., Spokane 8, Wash. Died Dec. 2, 1958.

WITHERSPOON, Thomas Casey, physician, surgeon; b. Natchez, Miss., May 25, 1868; s. Thomas Casey and Mary A. D. (Conner) W.; St. Louis High Sch.; St. Louis Coll. of Pharmacy; M.D., Mo. Med. Coll., 1889; m. Nina H. Butler, Oct. 2, 1890; children—Thomas Casey (dec.), Evelyn Butler (Mrs. Fred W. Baldwin); m. 2d, Rita De Courney, Dec. 15, 1922. Practiced, Butte, Mont., 1889-93, St. Louis, 1893-1906, then at Butte; chiff surgeon Murray Hosp., for many yrs. from 1907. Lt. col., Med. Res. Corps, World War I; A.E.F. Fellow A.C.S.; mem. Western Surgical and Gynecological assns. Club: Los Angeles Country. Address: 12518 Helena St., Los Angeles. Died May 15, 1957; buried Hollywood Meml. Park Cemetery.

WITHINGTON, Robert, coll. prof.; b. Roxbury (Boston), Mass., June 7, 1884; s. Charles Francis (M.D.) and Georgiana (Bowen) W.; grad. Roxbury Latin School, 1902; A.B., Harvard, 1906, A.M., 1909, Ph.D., 1913; m. Helen Frances Small, Mar. 21, 1925; children—Elizabeth, Joan. "Lecteur" at Univ. of Lyons, France, 1909-10; asst. in English, Harvard U., 1910-12; Rogers traveling fellow (Harvard), in Europe, 1913-14; instr. English, Ind. U., 1914-17; asst. prof., asso. prof. and prof. English lang. and lit., Smith College, since 1917; prof. Biarritz American Univ., France (2 terms) 1945; visiting prof. (summers) U. of Colo., 1931, 32; Harvard U., 1933-37; Wesleyan University, 1944, 46; University of Vermont, 1947, Johns Hopkins University, 1948. Member commission for Relief in Belgium, 1916; cap. American Red Cross in France, 1918; commd. 2d lt. inf., U.S. Army, liaison service, Sept. 1918; hon. disch., Apr. 14, 1919. Mem. Modern Lang. Assn. America, Am. Assn. Univ. Profs. (council, 1944-46), Belgian-Am. Edn. Fdn., Am. Vet. Assn. Decorated Knight Order of Crown (Belgian); Officier d'Académie and Officier de l'Instruction Publique (French). Independent. Episcopalian. Club: Garrick (London). Author: English Pageantry, 1920; Excursion in English Drama, 1937. Author, contbr., editor or co-editor publs. relating to field since 1918. Address: 37 Prospect Heights, Northampton, Mass. Died Aug. 31, 1957; buried Spring Grove Cemetery, Northampton, Mass.

WITHINGTON, Winthrop, business exec.; b. Jackson, Mich., Nov. 30, 1878; s. William Herbert and Julia C. (Beebe) W.; ed. Phillips Acad.; Chateau de Lancy, Geneva, Switzerland; Univ. of Michigan; married Jane Wilkins, Feb. 14, 1920; married 2d, Sara V. Rau, June 12, 1946. With Withington & Cooley Mfg. Co., Jackson, Mich., until its merger with The Am. Fork & Hoe Co., dir. and in various positions until 1926, now v.p. and mfg. dir.; chmn. b. Sparks-Withington Co., Jackson, Mich. Mem. Psi Upsilon, Cleveland C. of C. Clubs: Union, Tavern, Mayfield Country, Pepper Pike Country, Country of Cleveland, Detroit Athletic. Home: 17915 Shaker Blvd. Office: 1910 Keith Bldg., Cleve. Died Sept. 5, 1953.

WITMER, Lightner, psychologist; b. Phila., June 28, 1867; A.B., U. of Pa., 1888; studied dept. of law, U. of Pa., 1888-89, dept. philosophy, 1889-91; A.M., Ph.D., U. of Leipzig, 1892; Sc.D., U. of Pa., 1937; m. Emma Repplier, June 11, 1904. Instr. English and history, Rugby Academy of Phila., 1888-91; director lab. of psychology, U. Pa., 1892-1937; founded psychol. clinic, 1896, orgnized psychol. lab. and clinic as dept. U. Pa., 1909, dir. to 1937, professor emeritus, 1937—. Lecturer on psychology, and established the psychol. lab. Bryn Mawr Coll., 1896-98; psychologist of Pa. Training Sch. for Feebleminded Children, Elwyn, Pa., 1896—; prof. psychology, and established the psychol. lab., Lehigh Univ., 1903-05; founder of the Witmer School for the psychol. diagnosis and enl. treatment of mental retardation and deviation, 1907. Founder and editor The Psychological Clinic, 1907. Mem. A.A.A.S., Am. Philos. Soc., Am. Psychol. Assn., N.E.A.; mem. Nat. Council of Edn., 1899, 1900; v.p. Nat. Inst. Criminal Law and Criminology, 1909-10; mem. Orthopsychiatric Assn.; Phi Beta Kappa, Sigma Xi. Mem. First Troop Phila. City Cav.; served in P.R., 1898. Club: Century (New York). Author: Analytical Psychology, 1902. Editor: Experimental Studies in Psychology; The Special Class for Backward Children. Contributor to technical and educational reviews on topics in experimental and clinical psychology. Major and deputy commissioner of Am. Red Cross to Italy, 1917-18. Home: Lincoln Court, Overbrook, Phila. Died July 19, 1956.

WITTIG, Gustav Frederick (wĭt'ĭg), editor, educator; b. New Brunswick, N.J., Sept. 15, 1876; s. Fritz and Babette (Steger) W.; B.S., Rutgers, 1896; E.E., Columbia, 1904; m. Gladys Fellows, June 1, 1909; children—Frederick Emory, Donald Roscoe. Tchr. pub., pvt. schs., 1896-1901; instr., asst. prof. elec. engring., U. Me., 1906-09; head dept. physics and elec. engring., U. Ala., 1908-18; div. elec. engr., Camp McClellan, Ala., summer, 1917; mem. faculty, Sch. for Tng. Officer Candidates for U.S. Signal Corps, Yale, 1918; asst. prof. elec. engring., Yale, 1919-26; statis. editor, Electrical World, 1926-41; mem. faculty Def. Tng. Inst., 1941-43; ret. Asso. Am. Inst. E.E. (life), Phi Beta Kappa, Tau Beta Pi. Co-author: Principles Underlying Radio Communication (Govt. Printing Office). Contbr. to Am. Year Book, hist. chpater U.S. Census of Electric Light and Power, 1927; year-end surveys light and power industry, annual supplements giving data of maj. systems, etc. Home: R.R. 1, Mooresville, Ind. Died May 30, 1950; buried New Brunswick, N.J.

WITTMER, John L., physician, pub. utilities exec.; b. Brooklyn, Aug. 26, 1895; s. George A. and Bertha (Hicks) W.; student U. Chicago, 1914-15, Fordham U., 1916-17; M.D., Long Island Coll., 1922; m. Dorothy L. Burgoyne, July 24, 1901; children—Craig J., Bruce H. Interne L.I. Coll. Hosp., Brooklyn, 1922-23; physician Brooklyn Edison Co., 1924-28, supervising physician, 1928-30; supervising physician, N.Y. Edison Co., 1930-33; med. dir. Consol. Gas Co., 1933-35, Consol. Edison Co. of N.Y., Inc., 1936-38, also dir. personnel, 1938-46, asst. v.p., indsl. relations, 1946-49, v.p. employee relations since 1949. Mem. Mayor's Adv. Com. on Puerto Rican Affairs since 1948; adv. com. to dept. health, Civil Defense Program, 1950. Mem. Am. Assn. Indsl. Phys. and Surgs., A.M.A., Am. Pub. Health Assn., Health Ins. Plan of Greater N.Y., Visiting Nurse Service of N.Y., Green Mt. Lake Found. Contbr. to pub. health and indsl. relations jours. Home: 160 Henry St., Brooklyn. Office: 4 Irving Pl., N.Y. City 3. Died May 19, 1951.

WOEHLKE, Walter Victor (wĕl'kē), writer, editor; b. Hanover, Germany, Feb. 17, 1881; s. Rudolph H. and Louise M. (Riechers) W.; ed. Oberrealschule, Hanover and U. of Göttingen; widower; 1 dau., Dorothea (Mrs. Edward F. Crofut). Came to U.S., 1898; city editor Volkszeitung, St. Paul, Minn., 1902-05, San Diego Union, 1905; mng. editor San Bernardino (Calif.) Index, 1906-07; contbg. editor, 1912-14, later mng. editor, Sunset Magazine. Asst. to commr. of Indian Affairs, 1934-48; state dir. Cal. Indian Agy., 1948—; dir. Phoenix area Indian Bureau, 1949-51. Clubs: Commonwealth, Bohemian. Author: Water as Wealth, 1908; Autobiography of a Hyphenated American, 1916; Union Labor in Peace and War, 1918; The Mooney Case, 1919. Contbr. to mags. Home: 1908 Capitol Av., Palo Alto, Calif. Office: P.O. Box 7007, Phoenix. Died Aug. 16, 1954.

WOFFORD, Kate Vixon (wŏf'ford), professor edn.; b. Laurens, S.C.; d. John Albert and Cleo (Cunningham) Wofford; A.B., Winthrop Coll., Rock Hill, S.C., 1916; A.M., Cornell U., 1931; Ph.D., Columbia, 1934. Teacher high sch., Laurens, 1917-23; county supt. schs., 1923-30; prof. and dir. rural edn. State Teachers Coll., Buffalo, N.Y., 1943-47; head prof. elementary edn., Coll. of Edn., U. of Fla., since July 1947; visiting prof. Columbia University Summer Sch., 1939, 40, U. of Minn., 1941, 42, 44, U. Chgo. 1943; vis. lectr. on invitation Turkish Ministry Edn., Ankara, 1951. Mem. S.C. State Tchrs. Assn. (pres. 1926-27), N.E.A. (sec. bd. trustees 1927-34; pres. rural edn. dept., 1931-32; mem. exec. com. on rural edn., 193-34; chmn. yearbook com., rural edn. dept., 1936—), Pi Lambda Theta, Kappa Delta Pi (Educators award best professional writing 1947), Pi Gamma Mu. Del. to Internat. Conf. on Edn., Geneva, Switzerland, 1929; member of U.S. Educational Mission to Korea, 1948. Democrat. Author: History of the Status and Training of Rural Teachers in the U.S. (1860-1930), 1934; Modern Education in the Small Rural Schools, 1938; Teaching in Small Schools, 1946. Editor of 1938, 1939 and 1941 yearbooks of Rural Edn. Dept. of N.E.A. Editor: Instructional Leadership in Small Schools, 1951. Address: 4 Lake Ridge Rd., Gainesville, Fla. Died Oct. 31, 1954; buried New Prospect Cemetery, Lamens, S.C.

WOHL, David Philip, shoe mfr.; b. St. Louis, Aug. 24, 1886; s. Philip and Lena (Samisch) W.; ed. pub. schs., St. Louis; m. Carlyn Hartman, Mar. 25, 1917; children—Francelle, Elizabeth, David (dec.). With a St. Louis shoe concern in 1900; later rep. eastern mfrs. in middlewest; organizer, pres. Wohl Shoe Co., St. Louis, 1916-51, merged Brown Shoe Co., St. Louis; dir. Merc. Trust Co., Merc.-Commerce Nat. Bank. Mem. Mo. Penal Survey Com., 1954; Govtl. Research Inst. Served on Retail Shoe Adv. Com., World War II. Trustee Wohl Found.; dir. Washington U.; dir. Bernard Free Skin and Cancer Hosp., Neighborhood Assn.; dir. St. Louis City and County units Am. Cancer Soc., St. Louis A.R.C. Past pres. St. Louis Council, Boy Scouts of Am. Recipient T. Kenyon Holly Meml. Award, 1954, W. Scott Johnston Meml. award, Mo. Health Assn., 1951. Mem. C. of C. Clubs: Missouri Athletic, Westwood Country. Home: 6400 Forsythe Blvd., Clayton, Mo. Office: 1601 Washington Av., St. Louis 3. Died Mar. 2, 1960.

WOHLENBERG, Walter Jacob (wō'lĕn-bĕrg), prof. mech. engring.; b. Lincoln, Neb., Feb. 17, 1888; s. Peter Jacob and Gretchen (Tychsen) W.; B.S. in M.E., U. of Neb., 1910, hon. D.Engring., 1937; M.S., U. of Illinois, 1914; hon. M.A., Yale Univ., 1928; m. Charlotte Alvarita Spangler, June 24, 1918 (dec.); 1 dau., Barbara (dec.); m. 2d, Eleanor B. Hutchins, Sept. 6, 1950. Asst. prof. mechanical engring. U. Okla., 1914-16, U. of Mont., 1916-18; asst. prof. same, Yale. 1918-25, asso. prof., 1925-28, prof. since 1928, Sterling professor mech. engring. since 1930, dean sch. engring. 1948-55, researcher; chairman mechanical engineering dept., Yale, 1946; spl. lecturer on heat transfer by radiation, Purdue Univ., 1940; cons. engr. on steam generating equipment since 1920. Mem. Div. Engring. and Indsl. Research, Nat. Research Council, 1930-32. Fellow A.S.M.E. (life mem.; chmn. fuel test code com. 1930-45, spl. research com. on radiation in boiler furnaces, 1934-41; main com. power test codes; mem. com. on meetings and programs 1936-41, chmn. 1941; v.p. 1943-45; member main committee on furnace performance factors; sub-committee on heater in furnaces). Society for Promotion Engineering Education, Yale Engineering Assn., Sigma Xi, Sigma Tau. Clubs: Graduate (New Haven); Yale (New York). Widely known for theoretical work in heat transfer, leading to a rational basis for design of furnaces. Author of tech. papers. Home: 1220 Ridge Road, Hamden, Conn. Address: 400 Temple St., New Haven. Died Aug. 8, 1956.

WOLBACH, Edwin J(osephus) (wōl'bäk), banker, b. Grand Island, Neb., Oct. 31, 1877; s. Samuel N. and Rosa (Stein) W.; B.S., Harvard, 1899; m. Jeannette Heinsimer, Nov. 3, 1909; children—Louise Pettinger (dec.), Samuel N. Chemist Am. Beet Sugar Co., 1899-1900; in mercantile business, 1900-30; pres. First Nat. Bank, Grand Island, since 1930; treas. Equitable Bldg. and Loan Assn.; pres. Wolbach Realty Co. Pres. Grand Island Chamber of Commerce; chmn. Red Cross; trustee Grand Island Coll.; pres. bd. Grand Island Pub. Library; president Hall County Historical Society. Member American Society Chemists, Hall County Hist. Soc. (pres.), Newcomen Soc. of Eng. Republican. Episcopalian. Mason (32°, Shriner). Clubs: Harvard (N.Y. City and Neb.); Lincoln University. Home: 619 S. Clay St. Office: First National Bank, Grand Island, Neb. Died Sept. 18, 1959; buried Grand Island Cemetery.

WOLBACH, Simeon Burt, pathologist; b. Grand Island, Neb., July 3, 1880; s. Samuel N. and Rosa (Stein) W.; student Lawrence Scientific Sch., Harvard, 1897-99; M.D., Harvard, 1903; m. Anna F. Wellington, 1914; children—William, John Gray, Edmund (dec.). Shattuck prof. emeritus pathol. anatomy, Harvard U. Med. Sch. since 1947; pathologist emeritus to Peter Bent Brigham, Children's, Infants' and Boston Lying-In hospitals, also Free Hosp. for Women, since 1947; dir. Div. Nutritional Research of The Children's Hosp. since 1947; cons. AEC Div. Biology and Medicine, Armed Forces Institute of Pathology, Boston Lying-In Hosp., Free Hosp. for Women. Dir. League Red Cross Socs. Research Commn. on Typhus Fever to Poland, 1920. Recipient of the Howard Taylor Ricketts Award, 1950. Fellow American Academy of Arts and Sciences, Royal Society of Tropical Medicine and Hygiene; member Association of American Physicians, Society for Exptl. Pathology (ex-pres.), Am. Assn. Pathologists and Bacteriologists, Am. Assn. for Cancer Research (ex-pres.), Soc. Exptl. Biology and Medicine, National Academy of Sciences; American Academy of Tropical Medicine; corresponding mem. Société de Pathologie Exotique. Comdr. 3d class Order of Polonia Restituta. Hon. mem. Harvey Soc., Alpha Omega Alpha, Sigma Xi. Clubs: St. Botolph, Harvard, Harvard Travelers; Country (Brookline); Millwood Hunt. Author of medical papers, and monographs on Rocky Mountain spotted fever and typhus fever; Pathology of the Deficiency States. Home: Sudbury, Mass. Office: 300 Longwood Av., Boston 15. Died Mar. 19, 1954.

WOLF, H. Carl, assn. exec.; b. Edwardsville, Ill., Oct. 28, 1891; s. Herman E. and Mary Harriet (Handlon) W.; B.S., Univ. of Ill., 1913, M.S., 1914, E.E., 1920; m. Louise Burroughs, Sept. 24, 1919; 1 son, Robert Burroughs. Asst. engr. Ill. Pub. Utilities Commn., Springfield, Ill., 1914-16; supt. Edwardsville (Ill.) Water Co., 1916-17; engr. Griffinhagen & Assos., Chicago, 1919-21; asst. chief engr. Pub. Service Commn. of Md., Baltimore, 1921-22, chief engr., 1922-29; asst. to vice pres. Central Pub. Service Corp., Chicago, 1929-33; vice pres. Consolidated Electric & Gas Co. and subsidiaries, New York, N.Y., 1933-34; pres. and dir. Central Ind. Gas Co. and assos., Muncie, Ind., 1934-38, Atlanta Gas Light Co., Atlanta, Ga., 1938-45, Mobile Gas Service Corp., 1938-45, Fla. Public Utilities Co., 1938-44; mng. dir. Am. Gas Assn., N.Y., 1945-54, now cons. Mem. Atlanta area management-labor com., War Manpower Commn., 1943-45; mem. gas industry minimum wage com., Wage-Hour Div. U.S. Dept. of Labor, 1943; regional chmn. 6th dist. Com. for Econ. Development, 1943-45, trustee since 1945, co-chmn. Atlanta Community and War Fund Appeal, 1943, chmn. Atlanta Community Fund Appeal, 1940. Served lt. to capt. U.S. Engrs. Reserve, 1917-19, 18 mos. in France; lt. col. gov.'s staff, 1944-45. Mem. Am. Inst. Elec. Engring., Am. Soc. for Metals, Am. Gas Assn. (pres. Ind. Gas. Assn., 1937-38, Southern Gas Assn., 1941-42), Atlanta Junior Chamber of Commerce (hon. life), Atlanta Chamber of Commerce (pres. 1942), Am. Legion, Acacia, Eta Kappa Nu, Sigma Xi. Protestant Episcopalian. Mason (32°, Shriner). Clubs: Engineers of Baltimore (pres. 1928-29); Capital City, Univ. (N.Y.); Scarsdale Golf, Town, Shenorock Shore; Engineers, Rotary (president Muncie, Ind., 1938, dir. Atlanta, 1940-41) (New York). Home: 19 Woodland Place, Scarsdale. Office: 420 Lexington Av., N.Y.C. Died June 26, 1955; buried Woodlawn Cemetery, Edwardsville, Ill.

WOLF, Irwin Damasius, merchant; b. Paragould, Ark., July 8, 1894; s. Joseph and Ida (Goldman) W.; grad. high sch., Paragould, 1908, Western Mil. Acad., Alton, Ill., 1910; student Washington U., St. Louis, 1910-11; m. Martha C. Kaufmann, June 26, 1917; children—Irwin Damasius, John Morris, Betty Kaufmann. Began as retail clk. for S. L. Joseph Mercantile Co., Paragould, 1911, advancing to gen. mgr.; partner Wolf and Bascho Cotton Co., also chmn. bd. S. L. Joseph Mercantile Co., 1919-22; with Kaufmann Dept. Stores, Pitts., 1922—, v.p., 1935-55, pres., gen. mgr. Kaufmann Dept. Stores, 1955—; v.p., dir. The May Dept. Stores Co., Allegheny Broadcasting Corp.; dir. Pittsburgh and Lake Erie Railroad. Organized and was chairman Allegheny County war price and rationing bd. of OPA, represented retail trade as mem. wholesale and retail inventory policy com. WPB, was also mem. retail adv. com. OPA; now mem. retail industry advisory committee OPS; member National Distribution Council. Chmn. Allegheny Co. Transit and Traffic Commn.; dir., past pres. Allegheny Council Boy Scouts Am.; mem. governing com. Arthritis and Rheumatism Found.; dir. Community Chest Allegheny Co.; mem. bus. adv. com. American University; former state chmn., now mem. exec. com. Nat. Found. Infantile Paralysis; dir. United Cerebral Palsy Assn. Pitts. dist. Mem. President's adv. bd. Duquesne U.; dir. United Negro Coll. Fund of Pitts.; trustee, chmn. exec. com. Irene Kaufmann Settlement. Served as 2d lt. Signal Corps, later capt. A.S., World War I; maj. Res. A.S. Mem. Am. Management Assn., Civic Light Opera Assn. (pres., dir.), Labor Standards Assn. (v.p.), Marketing Execs. Soc. (past pres.), National Retail Dry Goods Assn. (dir., chmn. exec. com.), Package Designers Council, Pitts. Convention Bureau (director v.p.), Fedn. Jewish Philanthropies (president, member exec. committee), Health and Welfare Assn. Allegheny Co. (treas.), Montefiore Hosp. Assn. Western Pa. (pres.), Nat. Conf. Christians and Jews, Inc. (dir.), Vis. Nurse Assn. Allegheny Co., Inc. (dir.), Young Men's and Women's Hebrew Assn. (dir.), Annual Packaging Conf. (originator and donor ann. award for best package design). Democrat (delegate to national conventions since 1944). Hebrew. Mason. Clubs: Concordia, Westmoreland, Harmonie (N.Y.C.); Downtown, Green Oaks, Palm Beach Country. Author: (with W. J. Donald) Handbook of Business Administration, 1931; also Survey on Simplification and Standardization Progress during 1942, and Survey of the Progress Made in Simplification and Standardization of Distribution in War-Time, and an Evaluation of the Problems Facing Distributors (both for WPB). Contbr. to bus. publs. Home: Morewood-Fifth Apts., Pitts. Office: 400 Fifth Av., Pitts. Died Apr. 18, 1956.

WOLF, Joseph, realtor; b. Fort Edward, N.Y., Aug. 6, 1874; s. William Wallace and Ada (Ives) W.; ed. dist. sch., Todd County, Minn.; m. Hannah Abrahamson, Sept. 7, 1898; children—Helen I., William Wallace, Marguerite Ann. In lumber business with father, 1890-98; hotel mgr., 1898-1904; in grocery business, 1904-06; in real estate business, 1906—; v.p. Peoples State Bank, Staples, Minn., 1929—. Mayor of Staples, 1909-13; postmaster, Staples, 1914-22. Del. to Dem. Nat. Conv., 1912, 24, 28; chmn. Dem. State Com., Minn., 1922-24; mem. Dem. Nat. Com., 1924-36. Home: Staples, Minn. Died May 31, 1948.

WOLF, Paul Alexander, army officer; b. Kewanee, Ill., Dec. 23, 1868; s. William and Margaret W.; grad. U.S. Mil. Acad., 1890, Inf. and cav. Sch., 1897; Army War Coll., 1920; m. Minnie Otis, d. Col. Charles Hobart, U.S. Army, July 22, 1897; 1 dau., Margaret Hobart. Commd. 2d lt., 1890, promoted through grades to brig. gen., 1925; served as brig. gen. N.A., 1918-19. Participated in Sioux Indian Campaign, 1890-91, campaign against Santiago de Cuba, 1898; duty in Philippine Islands, 1898-1901, 1903-05, 1908-09; exec. officer U.S. Mil. Prison, Ft. Leavenworth, Kan., 1909-13; duty on Tex. border, 1913-17; was chief of pub. works, Vera Cruz Expdn., 1914; comdg. officer 1st and 2d Plattsburg mil. training camps, 1917; comdr. 66th Brigade Inf., 33d Div., A.E.F., 1918; comd. 9th Inf., 1920-22; O.C. N.A. 8th Corps Area, 1922-25; comdg. gen. 5th Brigade, 3d Div., and comdg. Vancouver Barracks, Wash., 1925-26; then comdg. gen. 21st Brigade, Schofield Barracks, Hawaii, and, Oct. 6, 1929—, comdg. general 5th Brigade, 3d Divison, Vancouver Barracks. Distinguished marksman, U.S. Army, 1906; mem. of winning U.S. Infantry National Rifle Team, 1906, 08; shooting mem., 1913, Palma Rifle Team, champion long distance shots of the world; coach inf. rifle team which won nat. match, Camp Perry, 1920. Awarded D.S.M. (U.S.); Officer Legion of Honor (French); Croix de Guerre with Palm (French); Companion of The Bath (British). Episcopalian. Retired Jan. 1, 1933. Home: 147 Corey Av., San Antonio 2, Tex. Died Jan. 12, 1954; buried Fort Sam Houston Nat. Cemetery.

WOLF, Robert Bunsen, mech. engr.; b. Newark, Del., May 1, 1877; s. Theodore R. and Rose (Kohler) W.; B. Elec. Engring., Delaware Coll. (now U. of Del.), 1896, M.E., 1916; m. Harriette Couch, Sept. 18, 1901; children—Robert Bunsen, Theodore R., Ann, Margaret (Mrs. Frederick T. Wolverton). Employed in pulp and paper mills in N.Y. and N.E., 1896-99; in constrn. and maintenance dept. Internat. Paper Co.; later, supt. Piercefield Sulphite Pulp Mill; became asst. chief engr. Union Bag and Paper Co., 1900; designer and supervisor constrn., later becoming mill supt., Fenimore Sulphite Mill; mgr. Burgess Sulphite Fibre Co., Berlin, N.H., 1906-17; mgr. Spanish River Pulp and Paper Mills, Ltd., Sault Ste. Marie, Ont., 1917-18; organized R. B. Wolf Co., specializing in design, constrn. and operation of pulp and paper mills, 1919; pres. Pulp Bleaching Corp., N.Y.C., 1923; mgr. pulp div. Weyerhauser Timber Co., Longview, Washington, 1931-47; now indsl. cons. Served as staff asst. to v.p. U.S. Emergency Fleet Corp. 1918. Recipient Frederick W. Taylor Key, Soc. Advancement Management, 1946. Fellow Am. Soc. M.E.; mem. Tech. Assn. Pulp and Paper Industry (gold medalist 1942), Canadian Tech. Sect. Pulp and Paper Industry, Am. Pulp and Paper Mills Supts. Assn., A.A.A.S., U.S. Pulp Producers Assn. (dir.), Pacific Coast Assn. Pulp and Paper Mfrs. (vice pres.), Sigma Phi Epsilon, Tau Beta Pi. Mem. Engineers Club (N.Y.C.). Author of numerous tech. articles pub. in trade and profl. jours. Received patents covering method and apparatus for processes used in pulp and paper industry. Home: 84 Weed St., New Canaan, Conn. Died Nov. 10, 1954.

WOLFE, Clayton A., business exec.; b. Webster, N.Y., Apr. 14, 1893; s. William and Sarah K. (Volzel) W.; student Cornell; m. Gertrude C. Wright, Sept. 26, 1925. With fine chem. div. Mathieson Alkali Works, 1919-29; supr. Monsanto Chem. Co., St. Louis, 1929-31, asst. dir. purchases, 1931, dir. purchases, 1932-39, dir. purchasing and traffic dept. since 1939, v.p. since 1947. Served with U.S.N., World War I. Mem. Nat. Assn. Purchasing Agts. Clubs: Univ., Cornell (St. Louis); Cornell (N.Y.C.). Home: St. Louis. Office: Monsanto Chemical Co., St. Louis 4. Died Oct. 20, 1953.

WOLFE, Edgar Thurston, co-publisher Ohio State Journal; v.p. Columbus Dispatch; chmn. bd. WBNS Radio Inc., Agr. Lands, Inc.; dir. Bank Ohio Corp., Wolfe Wear-U-Well Corp. Home: 2511 Bryden Rd. Office: 62 E. Broad St., Columbus, O. Died Feb. 2, 1957.*

WOLFE, James H., judge; b. Skippackville, Pa., Apr. 26, 1884; s. Samuel and Emma Jane (Seipt) W.;

student Central Manual Tng. Sch., Phila., 1898-1901; M.E., Lehigh U., Bethlehem, Pa., 1905; LL. B., U. of Pa., 1910; m. Carolyn S. Williams, Apr. 16, 1918; children—Samuel, Emma Katherine, James H., Russell, George. Began as engr., 1905; admitted to Utah bar, 1910, Pa. bar; 1st asst. atty. gen. of Utah, 1917-21; judge of 3d Jud. Dist. Ct., 1929-35; justice Supreme Ct. of Utah, 1935-55, chief justice, 1943-44, 1951-55. Served as private, Nat. Guard, Mexican border, 1916; maj. judge advocate Nat. Guard, Utah, 1917; lt. Air Service, U.S. Army, World War, 1918. Served on Gov. Dern's Relief Com. of 100, and as Adv. Com. of Distribution of R.F.C. Funds; v. chmn. Adv. Com. to draft state liquor control legislation; dir. Credit Union Nat. Assn.; mem. council Nat. Municipal League, 1915-16; regent U. of Utah, 1925-29; rep. State of Utah, Valley Forge Utah Day, 1935; dir. Family Service Soc., Salt Lake City, 20 yrs. Served as referee mem. Nat. R.R. Adjustment Bd. and Express Adjustment Bd. No. 1; appointed to Nat. Ry. Labor Panel and several R.R. Emergency Bds.; mem. Non-Ferrous Metals Fact Finding Bd.; chmn. Alien Enemy Hearings Bd. for Utah; mem. Spl. Enemy Alien Hearings Bd. (nat.); mem. bd. of appeals for leave clearance, War Relocation Authority. Chmn. Utah com. selection candidates Root-Tilden Scholarships, N.Y. U. Law Sch. Mem. Council Conf. of Chief Justices. Charter mem. Nat. Acad. Arbitrators, Indsl. Relations Research Assn.; mem. Am., Utah State and Salt Lake County bar assns., Am. Law Inst., Nat. Lawyers Guild (v.p.), Am. Legion, Sigma Chi, Phi Delta Phi. Unitarian (regional v.p. Am. Assn. 1931-38). Democrat (del. to Dem. Nat. Conv., 1916). Editor Utah Survey, 1914-16, and frequent contbr. to the Survey. Mem. bd. editors Nat. Guild Quarterly. Contributor to The Humanist, Rocky Mountain Law Rev., Columbia Law Jour. Home: 361 Chase St., Sonoma, Cal. Died Mar. 25, 1958.

WOLFE, Lawrence, architect; b. Kansas City, Mo., Mar. 23, 1890; s. Thomas Barnes and Alice Evelyn (Moore) W.; Allegheny Prep. Sch., 1904-09; B.S. in Architecture, U. of Pa. 1913; m. Mary Harper Clark, May 22, 1917; children—Lawrence Clark, Lindsay Harper, Anthony Lee. Partner with father, 1919-23; own firm, 1923-41; on staff of chief architect, Pentagon Bldg., and War Production Bd., Washington, D.C., 1941-45; practice in Pittsburgh. Fellow Am. Inst. Architects; mem. Asso. Artists of Pittsburgh, Rotary, Sigma Xi, Kappa Alpha. Democrat. Methodist. Home: 309 Walnut Rd., Ben Avon, Pittsburgh 2. Office: 119 E. Montgomery Av., Pitts. Died Mar. 4, 1953.

WOLFER, John A., surgeon; b. Decatur, Ill., Dec. 7, 1880; s. Louis and Catherine (Ullrich) W.; grad. high sch., Decatur, 1899; M.D., Northwestern U. Med. Sch., 1908; m. Maude Hanaford, Sept. 11, 1923. Intern Cook Co. Hospital, 1908-09; began teaching surgery, Northwestern U. Med. Sch., 1910, successively clin. asst., instr., asso., asst. prof., asso. prof. surgery, prof., now prof. emeritus; attending surgeon Cook County Hosp., 1913-20; mem. surg. staff Wesley Meml. Hosp., 1911-31; attending surgeon Passavant Memorial Hosp., 1931-47, now attending surgeon emeritus; cons. surgeon VA Hosp., Hines, Ill.; chief out-patient surg. clinic, Northwestern U., 1927-29, dir. tumor clinic, 1932—; gov. Northwestern U. Found. during its existence. Am. chmn. gen. surgery sect., Pan-Pacific Surg. Congress, Honolulu, 1939; mem. exec. com. med. and sci. com., Ill. div., Am. Cancer Soc.; mem. adv. bd. to div. of cancer control dept. of health, State of Ill. Fellow Am. Surg. Assn., Am. Coll. Surgeons (chmn. exec. com. Clinical Congress, 1940); mem. Central Surg. Assn., A.M.A., Ill. State Med. Soc., Chgo. Med. Soc., Chgo. Surg. Soc. (pres. 1939-40), Northwestern U. Med. Sch. Alumni Assn. (pres. 1934-39), Nu Sigma Nu, Alpha Omega Alpha, Sigma Xi. Republican. Protestant. Club: Lake Shore. Author of numerous articles pub. profl. jours.; co-author 1 book and contrbr. to 2 profl. books. Home: 3000 Sheridan Rd., Chgo. 14. Office: 700 N. Michigan Av., Chgo. 11. Died Nov. 1955.

WOLFERMAN, Fred (wŏl'fĕr-măn), retail foods b. Cassel, Germany, Sept. 13, 1870; s. Louis and Friedericke (Herrmann) W.; brought to America, 1881; grad. high sch., Kansas City, Mo., 1887; m. Etha Paxson, Jan. 5, 1912; children—Ethelberg Paxson, Elsa Janet, Barbara, Frederica, Burleigh, Reed. Estab. retail food business in Kansas City, 1888, under name of Fred Wolferman, Inc., store also at Tulsa, Okla.; pres. Fred Wolferman Bldg. Co.; owner Twin Sycamore Farms. Trustee Kansas City Art Inst., Kansas City Philharmonic Orchestra and Kansas City Museum. Clubs: Kansas City, Mission Hills Country. Home: 5725 State Line Rd., Kansas City 2; and Robles del Rio, Calif. Office: 118 W. 47th St., Kansas City 2, Mo. Died Oct. 2, 1955; buried Mt. Washington Cemetery, Kansas City, Mo.

WOLL, Matthew, labor leader; b. Luxemburg, Jan. 25, 1880; s. Michael and Janette (Schwartz) W.; came to U.S., 1891; student pub. schs., Chicago; student Coll. of Law, Lake Forest U., 1901-04. Learned photo-engraver's trade; pres. International Photo-Engravers' Union N.A., 1906-29, now 1st v.p.; 1st v.p. AFL-CIO; chmn. nat. defense, postwar problems com.; co-chmn. internat. affairs com., AFL-CIO; mem. civil rights, legislative, econ. policy, political education, community services, public relations coms., AFL-CIO; president of Union Label Trades Dept.; chmn. Workers Edn. Bureau; pres. Union Labor Life Insurance Company; trustee and American Federation of Labor rep. of radio station WCFL (Chicago); dir. and mem. exec. com. N.Y. World's Fair, Inc. Served as mem. War Labor Board and as assistant to Samuel Gompers, chmn. Committee on Labor of Council National Defense; mem. Nat. War Labor Board, 1942; Pres. Truman's Labor Management Conference, 1945. Editor of The Am. Photo-Engraver; has served as editor The American Federationist. Fraternal del. to British Trade Union Congress, Birmingham, Eng., 1915, 16; del. Internat. Federation of Trade Unions, Warsaw, 1937; rep. of labor to Internat. Labor Orgn., Oslo, 1938; del. International confederation of Free Trade Unions, London, 1948, also Milan, Italy, 1951. Trustee Public Education Association (Chgo.), Chgo. Tuberculosis Inst., Nat. Tuberculosis Assn.; dir. Nat. Bur. Econ. Research; pres. Labor League for Human Rights, United Nations Relief; mem. Nat. War Fund, Nat. Com. on Prisons and Prison Labor. Mem. Nat. Acad. Political Science, New York State Insurance Advisory Board. Member Modern Woodmen of America, K.C.; member President Harding's Unemployment Conference. Author: Labor Industry and Government, 1935. Writer and speaker on labor and economic topics. Address: 200 E. 70th St., N.Y.C. Died June 1, 1956; buried Fort Lincoln Cemetery, Washington.

WOLSEY, Louis (wŏol'zē), rabbi; b. Midland, Mich., Jan. 8, 1877; s. William and Frances (Krueger) W.; A.B., U. Cin.; rabbi, Hebrew Union Coll., Cin., 1899, D.D., honoris causa, 1939; grad. study U. Chgo., Western Reserve U., U. of Pa.; m. Florence Helen Wiener, June 12, 1912 (dec.); children—Allon L., Jonathan L. (dec.); m. 2d, Helen Frank Meyers, Mar. 7, 1943. Rabbi Congregation B'nai Israel, Little Rock, Ark., 1899-1907, Euclid Av. Temple, Cleve., 1907-25, Congregation Rodeph Shalom, Phila., 1925-47, emeritus, 1947—. Chaplain, Ark. Nat. Guard, 1906-07. Mem. Bd. Edn., Little Rock, Ark., 1906-07. Mem. Central Conf. Am. Rabbis (pres. 1925-27; chmn. revision of Union Hymnal), Fedn. Jewish Charities, Phila. (trustee), Am. Council for Judaism (v.p., founder). Mem. exec. bd. Commn. on Jewish Edn. Chmn. Mayor's Crime Commn., Phila. 1937. Clubs: Philmont, Ashborne. Home: Mayfair House 44. Office: 615 N. Broad St., Phila. 23. Died Mar. 4, 1953.

WOMBLE, John Philip, Jr., naval officer; b. Atlanta, Dec. 13, 1900; s. John Philip and Mary Venable (Thompson) W.; B.S., U.S. Naval Acad., 1920; LL.D. (hon.), Ursinus Coll., 1944; m. Mary Brainie, Nov. 7, 1924; 1 dau., Mary Elizabeth (Mrs. Arthur O. Spaulding); m. 2d, Lillian Cobb, May 19, 1934; 1 son, John Philip II. Commd. ensign, U.S. Navy, June 4, 1920, and advanced through grades to rear admiral, Sept. 1947; exec. officer, U.S.S. Dobin, Pearl Harbor, 1941; dir. field adminstrn. tng. activities, Bur. Naval Personnel, 1942-44; comdr. Destroyer Squadron 52 and Task Flotilla 2, and served as screen comdr. for fast Carrier Task Group in Task Forces 38 and 58, 1944-45; comdr. Cruiser Springfield, Feb.-Nov. 1946; commanded Support Group Naval Forces Far East, 1948-49; commander United States Naval Station and Naval Training Center, San Diego, Calif., 1947-48; dep. dir. for intelligence, Joint Staff Office of Joint Chiefs of Staff, 1949-50, comdr. Mine Force U.S. Atlantic Fleet, 1950-52, assigned Office Sec. Def., 1952-55; comdr. Service Force, Atlantic Fleet, 1955—. Decorations: Silver Star medal, 3 Legion of Merit medals, Bronze Star medal; spl. commendation letter from Sec. Navy, The Pacific-Asiatic Service ribbon with 9 engagement stars, Philippine Liberation ribbon (2 stars). Home: 2575 Habersham Rd., N.W., Atlanta, Ga. Office: Office of the Secretary of Defense, the Pentagon, Washington. Died Oct. 5, 1956; buried Arlington Nat. Cemetery.

WOMER, Parley Paul (wō'mĕr), educator; b. Osceola, Pa., May 29, 1870; s. David Porter and Jane Elizabeth W.; student Allegheny Coll., Meadville, Pa., 1888; Ohio Wesleyan U., 1889-91; B.D., Yale Div. Sch., 1895, U. Minn., 1911-12; grad. student Univ. Glasgow, 1903; LL.D., Washburn Coll., Topeka, Kan., 1930; m. Verna Elaine Bing, Oct. 9, 1895. Pastor St. Matthew's United Free Ch., Glasgow, Scotland, 1902 to 1903, Danforth Congl. Ch., Syracuse, N.Y., 1903-07, Plymouth Ch., St. Paul, Minn., 1907-14; pres. Washburn Coll., 1915-31, prof. Am. citizenship and pub. affairs, 1931-39; dir. Citizenship Program Nat. Municipal League, 1939-46; mem. Am. Acad. Social and Polit. Science, 1925. Fellow Am. Geogl. Soc., 1945, Euclid fellow Royal Soc. of Arts (London), 1939; fellow American Acad. Polit. Science, 1947; mem. (hon.) Eugene Field Soc. Authors, 1947. Author: The Relation of Healing to Law, 1908; A Valid Religion for the Times, 1909; The Coming Creed, 1911; The Church and The Labor Conflict, 1913; Citizenship and the New Day, 1945. Home: Washburn Campus, Topeka, Kan. Died Oct. 16, 1957; buried Mt. Hope Cemetery Mausoleum, Topeka, Kan.

WOOD, Arthur B(arton), ins. exec.; b. Knowlton, P.Q., Can., Oct. 28, 1870; s. Hannibal Whitney and Jane Margaret (Barton) W.; A.B., McGill U. (Anne Molson gold medal for mathematics), 1892; m. Hetty Georgina Daviss, Apr. 22, 1808. Chief clerk actuarial dept. Sun Life Assurance Co. of Can., Montreal, 1893-1900, asst. actuary, 1900-08, actuary, 1908-23, v.p. and actuary, 1923-32, v.p. and mng. dir., 1932-34, became pres. 1934, now chmn. bd.; dir. Crown Trust Co., Howard Smith Paper Mills, Ltd. Gov. McGill U., Montreal Gen. Hosp. Fellow Inst. of Actuaries (Eng.), Actuarial Soc. Am. Inst. Actuaries, Casualty Actuarial Soc. Mem. Anglican Ch. Clubs: St. James, University, Royal Montreal Golf, Royal Montreal Curling, Rotary. Home: 1227 Sherbrooke St., W. Office: Dominion Sq., Montreal, P.Q., Can. Died June 14, 1952; buried Mount Royal Cemetery, Montreal.

WOOD, Arthur D., newspaper pub., penologist; b. Little Falls, Minn., Oct. 3, 1876; s. A. DeLacy and Julia (Langford) W.; ed. pub. schs.; m. Sophia E. Goupelle, Oct. 14, 1899; children—Grace M. (Mrs. F. F. Mumford), Thelma M. (Mrs. William Barsanti), Mercedes (Mrs. George McIntyre), Arthur D. Newspaper reporter, later editor and pub. Grand Marais (Mich.) Herald and Munising (Mich.) News, 1894-1927; juvenile judge of Alger Co., 1908-27, commissioner of pardons and paroles, State of Mich., 1927-30; chmn. U.S. Bd. Paroles, 1930-47; spl. asst. to the atty. gen. of U.S., Mar. 1-Oct. 31, 1947; retired. Now adviser in penal and parole matters. Chmn. Alger County Chapter A.R.C., Alger County War Relief Bd., World War. Founder Am. Parole Assn.; dir. Am. Prison Assn., Washington Child Guidance Clinic, Washington Inst. of Mental Hygiene; mem. exec. bd. Am. Inst. Criminal Law and Criminology; mem. advisory council Osbourne Foundation. Mem. Nat. Econ. League, Mich. Acad. of Science and Arts, Mich. Prosecuting Atty's. Assn., Central States Parole Assn., Am. Probation Assn. Catholic, K.C. Home: 221 E. Onota St., Munising, Mich. Died Apr. 1958.

WOOD, Clement, author; b. Tuscaloosa, Ala., Sept. 1, 1888; s. Sterling Alexander and Ida May (Richardson) W.; A.B., U. of Ala., 1909; LL.B., Yale, 1911; m. Mildred Mary Cummer, Oct. 31, 1914 (divorced 1926); children—Janet, John Thornton; m. 2d, Gloria Goddard, Apr. 2, 1926. Practiced law at Birmingham, Ala., 1911-12, asst. city atty., 1912-13; recorder, Birmingham, 1913; teacher, Pingry Sch., Elizabeth, N.J., 1914-15; with Barnard Sch. for Boys, N.Y. City, 1915-20, principal Upper Sch. of same, 1919-20; vice-principal Dwight Sch. N.Y. City, 1920-22; sec. N.Y. Preparatory Sch., 1920-23; v.p. Bankers Financial Trust since 1934; visiting lecturer Div. of Gen. Edn., New York Univ., 1939, instr. in versification, 1940; instructor in versification, Richmond Professional Institute, 1941-42; resident poet, College of William and Mary, Richmond Division, 1941-42; founder, director, Bozenkill School of Creative Writing. Vice-president Service Kits, Inc., since 1941. Pres., Special Social Services, Inc., since 1942; member Schoolmasters Association of New York, Poetry Society America, Catholic Poetry Society America, Songwriters Protective Association, The Writers, Bookfellows, Am. Literary Assn. (pres. 1924-26), Poetry Soc. Ala., Poetry Inst. of America (dir.), Poetry Soc. of Va., Nat. Poetry Soc. of Am. (mem. acad.), Am. Soc. of Composers, Authors and Publishers, Southern Soc. of New York, Sons of Confederate Vets. (mem. hdqrs. camp, Richmond; asst. historian in chief since 1933), Order Stars and Bars (asst. historian-gen. 1938), Phi Beta Kappa, Phi Gamma Delta, Theta Nu Epsilon, Delta Sigma Rho. Author: (poems) Glad of Earth, 1917; The Earth Turns South, 1919; Jehovah, 1920; Mountain (novel), 1920; The Laugher, 1922; Nigger (novel), 1922; The Tide Comes In (poems), 1923; For Walt Whitman (with Mildred Cummer Wood), 1923; The Stone Age, 1923; Poets of America, 1924; Folly (novel), 1925; The Eagle Flies (poems), 1925; The Greenwich Village Blues, 1926; Amy Lowell—A Critical Life, 1926; A Slang Dictionary (with Gloria Goddard), 1926; The Outlone of Man's Knowledge, 1927; Don't Tread on Me—A Study of Aggressive Legal Action for Labor Unions (with Arthur Garfield Hays), 1927; The Shadow From the Bogue, 1928; Ivanhoe (comic opera), prod. 1927; Cipher Stories Puzzle Book, 1928; The White Peacock (verse), 1928; King Henry the Rake, 1929; The Craft of Poetry, 1929; Hunters of Heaven—The American Soul as Revealed by Its Poetry, 1929; Flesh, and Other Stories, 1929; The Sociology of Lester Ward, 1930; Six Indiscreet Lovers, 1930; Macfadden, the Conqueror, 1930; Dreams—Their Meaning and Practical Interpretation, 1931; The Tabloid Murders, 1931; Honeymoon, 1931; The Woman Who Was Pope, 1931; The Man Who Killed Kitchener, 1932; Warren Gamaliel Harding—An American Comedy, 1932; Herbert Clark Hoover—An American Tragedy, 1932; Your Dreams, and What They Mean, 1933; Deep River (novel), 1934; If There Is a Hell (novel), 1934; The Life of a Man—A Biography of John R. Brinkley, 1934; A Popular History of the World, 1935; A Complete History of the United States, 1935; The Glory Road; an Autobiography (collected poems), 1936; The Complete Rhyming Dictionary and Poet's Craft Book, 1936; A History of he World (5 vols.), 1937; Lays for the Laity, 1937; Games for Two (with Gloria Goddard), 1937; Carelessness: Public Enemy No. 1, 1937; The Complete Book of Games (with Gloria Goddard), 1938; Let's Have a Good Time Tonight: an Omnibus of Party Games (with Gloria Goddard), 1938; Let's Play the Game: The Complete Book of Charades, 1939; Tom Sawyer Grows Up, 1939; The Strange Death of Adolf Hitler (published anonymously), 1939; More Power to Your Words, 1940; More Adventures of Huckleberry Finn, 1940; Poets Handbook, 1940; The 1941 Quiz Book (with Gloria Goddard), 1941; Ripe Olives (poems), 1941; The Unabridged Rhyming Dictionary and Complete Formbook for Poets, 1943; The Sensualist (novel), 1941; Efil: A Masque, 1942; The Eagle Sonnets, 1942; The United States of the World: Permanent Global Peace the American Way, 1943; The Poetry Workshop: Writing and Marketing Poetry, 1943; Death in Ankara, 1944; Death on the Pampas, 1944; The Corpse in the Guest Room, 1945; Emily Dickinson, the Volcanic Heart, 1945; The Song of Sapph. 1945; The Art and Technique of Versification, 1945; Global Quiz Book, 1946; Double Jeopardy, 1947; The Eagle Returns, 1947; Rombstone: The Town Too Tough to Die, 1947; The Ballad of Jonathon Swain and Other Poems, 1947; The Ballad of Sally Skull and the Corpus Christi Squite, 1948; Poet and Songwriters Guide: the Complete Book of Sansion, 1948; The Glory Road and The Eagle Sonnets, 1950; many novels over the pseudonym of Alan Dubois, Alvin Winston, etc. Biographical Forewards on Poe, Whitman, Lanier, Emerson, Kilmer, and others, to the annual Muse anthologies since 1940; also over sixty-five books in Haldeman-Julius "Little Blue Books," on literature and scientific themes. Editor: Summaries of Buckle and Lacky, The Vanguard Series. Writer of The Glory Road, Gwine to Heaven, Short'nin' Bread, and Five Songs on Negro Themes, and also Cahawba Days, a song cycle, 1933, also Carry Me Home and Weeping Mary (with Leonard Thomas), 1935, The Dummy Line and If the Seas Dry (with Carroll Ely), 1935; The Lord's Baptizing (with David Guion), 1939. Contbg. editor Voices, The Circle, The Harp, The New Leader, Popular Biography, Better English, Interchange, Poetry Caravan, The Southern Literary Messenger, Kansas City Poetry Mag., etc. Publisher and editor The Bozenkill Breeze, since 1929; Publisher, The Bozenkill Press. Awarded first prize for poem, The Smithy of God, by Newark (New Jersey), Committee of 100, 1916; awarded one of the three Lyric prizes of $500 each for poem, Jehovah, by The Lyric (New York), 1919. Contributor verse, articles, and short stories to magazines. Teacher of versification by correspondence since 1920. Writer, "What Your Dreams Mean," N.Y. Mirror, 1930-31; staff writer for Physical Culture, 1930, for Liberty, 1931. Editor-in-chief, The Lantern Library, 1935. Editor, Looking Ahead, 1945. Home: Dream House, Bozenkill, R.D. 2, Delanson, N.Y. Address: care Blue Ribbon Books, 14 W 49th St., N.Y. City. Died Oct. 27, 1950.

WOOD, David Muir, lawyer; b. Bklyn., Nov. 22, 1892; s. Joseph Storey and Jean (Andersen) W.; LL.B., N.Y. Law Sch., 1913, LL.M., 1914; m. Anna C. Wehrum, Apr. 25, 1917; children—Anna C. (Mrs. Edward E. Ingraham), Jean M. (Mrs. Donald E. Runyon), Marjorie A. (Mrs. James M. Robertson). Admitted to N.Y. bar, 1914; sr. partner Wood, King & Dawson, N.Y.C., 1926—; bond counsel for many states, T.H., counties and municipalities. Mem. Am. (chmn. sect. municipal law 1954-56; mem. ho. of del., 1956-58), N.Y. State bar assoc. Bar Assn. City of N.Y., N.Y. State C. of C., Municipal Finance Officers Assn. U.S. and Can., Pa. Municipal Authorities Assn., Bankers Club Am., N.Y. (pres. 1942-44), Chgo. (hon.) municipal bond clubs. Episcopalian (vestryman). Club: Wheatley Hills Golf (East Williston, L.I.). Author Fed. Municipal Bankruptcy Act. Home: 3 Chestnut Dr., Great Neck, L.I., N.Y. Office: 48 Wall St., N.Y.C. 5. Died Mar. 9, 1960.

WOOD, Edgar Liberty, lawyer; b. Davenport, Ia., Sept. 23, 1869; s. Harrison Reuben and Mary Jane (Hilton) W.; LL.B., University Wisconsin, 1892; LL.D., Carroll College, Wisconsin; married Loretta Belle Haseltine, July 19, 1894 (dec.); 1 dau., Dorothy Belle (Mrs. Elliott J. Neal). Admitted to Wis. bar, 1892 and since practiced in Milwaukee, specializing in corp. law and management; sr. partner Wood, Warner, Tyrrell & Bruce, now named Wood, Brady, Tyrrell & Bruce, 1928—; pres. and dir. Chicago N. Shore & Milwaukee R.R., 1938-46, dir., 1946-48; pres., dir. Chicago & Milwaukee Electric Ry., 1934—; member of bd. directors. Security bldg. & Investment Company, Chain Belt Co., Interstate Drop Forge Co., Grede Foundries, Inc., Sivyer Steel Casting Co., Metro-Nite Co., Pres. City Civil Service Commn., Milwaukee, 1900-02. Vice pres., dir. Ole Evinrude Found. Mem. Selden Soc. (Law) London (Eng.), Am., Wis. State and Milwaukee Co. bar assns., Newcomen Soc., English Speaking Union, Wis. Alumni Assn., Order of Coif, Phi Delta Phi. Republican. Presbyn. Mason, Forester, Royal League Modern Woodman. Clubs: Milwaukee, National Republican, City, Half Century, University, Gun (Milwaukee); Madison (Wis.); Golf, Lake, Gun (Oconomowoc, Wis.). Home: 11 Beach Rd., Oconomowoc Lake, Oconomowoc, Wis. Office: 756 N. Milwaukee St., Milw. Died Dec. 9, 1958; buried Forest Home Cemetery, Milw.

WOOD, Floyd Bernard, air force officer; b. Richland Springs, Tex., May 18, 1908; s. Claud Bernard and Helena (Askew) W.; B.A., N. Tex. State Coll., 1927; M.S., Mass. Inst. Tech., 1937; grad. U.S. Army Air Corps Flying Sch., 1929, Air Corps Tech. Sch., 1931, Air Corps Tactical Sch., 1939; m. Nancie Allen, Sept. 20, 1930. Commd. 2d lt. USAAC, 1929, advanced through grades to maj. gen. USAF, 1954; served in Panama, South Pacific, South Atlantic theaters, World War II; various positions in mgmt. Air Force Research and Development, 1947—; dep. comdr. research and development Air Research and Development Command, Balt., 1952—. Decorated Legion of Merit with oak leaf cluster, Air Medal (U.S.); Brazilian Aero. Order of Merit, Brazilian War Medal. Mem. Air Force Assn. Home: Richland Springs, Tex. Office: 5 W. Baltimore St., Balt. Died Apr. 3, 1956; buried Arlington Nat. Cemetery.

WOOD, Francis Carter, pathologist; b. Columbus, O., Dec. 30, 1869; s. Henry Raynor and Annie (Carter) W.; B.S., Ohio State U., 1891; M.D., Coll. Physicians and Surgeons (Columbia), 1894; studied at Berlin, Vienna, 1896; B.S. (hon.), Tufts, 1925, Ohio State U., 1931; m. Edith Warren Sterling, 1901; children—Eleanor Carter, Edith Sterling, Mary Lydia, Francis Carter, Winifred Warren. Inten, 1894-96, pathologist, 1897—, attending physician St. Luke's Hosp., N.Y.C., 1909-38, cons. physician 1938—; dir. pathol. lab., 1910—, dir. radiotherapeutic dept., 1921—; asst. in clin. pathology, Coll. Physicians and Surgeons, Columbia, 1896-98, instr., 1898-1904, adj. prof., 1904-06, prof., dir. dept. clin. pathology, 1906-12; prof., dir. Inst. Cancer Research (founded by George Crocker), Columbia, 1912-40, now emeritus; v.p. Internat. Union Against Cancer, 1935—. Mem. Am. Assn. Pathologists and Bacteriologists, Soc. Exptl. Biology and Medicine, N.Y. Pathol. Soc., A.M.A., Am. Cancer Soc., Am. Assn. Cancer Research, Assn. Am. Physicians, Radiol. Soc. N.A., Beta Theta Pi, Sigma Xi, Phi Beta Kappa, Radiol. Soc. of the Scandinavian Countries (hon.). Mem. Legion of Honor (France); Belgian Order of the Crown. Club: Century. Republican. Episcopalian. Author: Clinical Diagnosis, 1899; Chemical and Microscopical Diagnosis, 1905; Delafield and Prudden's Text-Book of Pathology, 16th edit., 1935; also numerous med. papers. Editor Am. Jour. of Cancer, 1930-41. Home: 110 Lydecker St., Englewood, N.J. Died Jan. 5, 1951; buried Brookside Cemetery, Englewood, N.J.

WOOD, Frederic Taylor, motor bus transportation exec.; b. Bangor, Me., Dec. 19, 1874; s. George Frederic and Jeannie Emery (Butler) W.; A.B., Williams Coll., 1898; m. Mary Cotton Kimball, June 15, 1904. With War Dept., Washington, D.C., 1898-1901 and 1902-03; mem. Chicago Bd. of Trade, 1901-02; with Met. St. Ry. Co., N.Y. City, and successors, 1903-22; pres. Fifth Av. Coach Co., 1922-35, chmn., 1936-39, vice chmn., 1939-55; chmn. N.Y.C. Omnibus Corp., 1936-39, vice chmn., 1939-55; pres. Champlain Coach Lines, Inc., Frontier Coach Lines, Inc., 1929-39; president Gray Line Motor Tours, Inc., N.Y. City, 1926-38; dir. Fifth Av. Coach Co., N.Y.C. Omnibus Corp., Surety Fire Ins. Co.; trustee Am. Surety Co. of N.Y. Director The Fifth Avenue Assn., Twenty-third St. Assn., Broadway Assn., Inc., West Side Assn. of Commerce in City of N.Y., Inc., Greater New York Safety Council, Inc., West of Central Park Association; trustee emeritus Williams College. Mem. The Pilgrims of U.S., The Newcomen Soc. of England, Am. Ordnance Assn., Am. Transit Assn., Met. Mus. of Art Acad. of Polit. Sci., Regional Plan Assn., Inc., Fed. Grand Jury Assn. So. District of New York, Gargoyle Society, Phi Beta Kappa, Sigma Phi. Member Chamber of Commerce of State of New York. Joint author of Transportation Facilities of London and Paris as of October 1913; editor, Williams College in the World War. Clubs: Williams (pres. 1918-20), Century, University, City Club of New York. Home: 438 Washington Av., Pelham, N.Y. Office: 605 W. 132d St., N.Y.C. 27. Died Sept. 28, 1955; buried Mt. View Cemetery, Camden, Me.

WOOD, Guy Bussey, ry. official; b. Hot Springs, Ark., Nov. 3, 1878; s. James Bussey and Harriet Gray (Scott) W.; ed. Hot Springs, Ark., pub. schs., and U. of Ark. (A.B., 1899); m. Kate Berenice Barry, Dec. 24, 1900; 1 dau., Lelia Jeannette (Mrs. Robert H. Mann). Clk. in traffic dept., Kansas City Southern Ry. Co., Texarkana, Tex., 1899-1902, commercial agent, 1902-04, gen. agent, Texarkana, 1904-06, Shreveport, La., 1906-09, Mena, Ark., Jan.-Sept. 1910, asst. gen. freight agent, Texarkana, 1910-17, asst. to pres., Beaumont, Tex., 1917-18, Kansas City, Mo., 1918-28, gen. freight agent, Kansas City, 1928, freight traffic mgr., 1929-37, v.p. in charge traffic since 1937; also v.p. in charge traffic La. & Ark. Ry. since 1939. Mem. Sons of Revolution, Mayflower Soc., Sigma Alpha Epsilon. Episcopalian. Mason. Club: Kansas City. Home: 229 Ward Parkway. Office: Kansas City Southern Ry. Bldg., Kansas City, Mo. Deceased.

WOOD, Hart, architect; b. Phila., Dec. 26, 1880; s. Thomas Hart Benton and Margaret (Spencer) W.; student pub. schs. West Denver; m. Jessie Eliza Spangler, Nov. 21, 1906; children—Hart de Wit, Benton Spangler, Kenneth Donald, Thomas Laurence. Designer, Bliss & Faville, architects, San Francisco, 1905-14; architect, Bd. Water Supply, Honolulu, T.H., Alexander & Baldwin Bldg., Chinese Christian Ch., residences and other bldgs., Honolulu, 1919—. Mem. Honolulu City Planning Commn., 1925, Territorial planning Bd., 1937-41, Govs. Postwar Planning Div., Dept. Pub. Works, T.H. Fellow A.I.A. (organizer, past pres. Hawaii chpt.); mem. Engring. Assn. Hawaii. Christian Scientist. Mason. Home: 5113 Maunalani Circle. Office: Wood, Weed & Assos., Hawaiian Life Bldg., Honolulu, Hawaii. Died Oct. 6, 1957.

WOOD, Horatio Charles, Jr., physician, pharmacologist; b. Phila., Pa., Feb. 26, 1874; s. Horatio C. and Eliza H. (Longacre) W.; grad. William Penn Charter Sch., Phila., 1890; student lit. dept. U. of Pa. 2 yrs.; M.D., U. of Pa., 1896; research work, U. of Berne, 1897-98, U. of Turin, 1898; m. Alice L. Lovell, Dec. 19, 1899; children—Horatio C. III, Florence L. Demonstrator in pharmacodynamics, U. of Pa., 1898-1907; asso. prof. pharmacol., 1907-10; prof. pharmacol. and therapeutics, Medico-Chirurg. College, Phila., 1910-16; prof. same, U. of Pa., 1916-42; prof. pharmacology, Phila. Coll. of Pharmacy and Science, 1921-50. Asst. visiting physician to Phila. General Hosp., 1904-08; mem. Com. on Revision of U.S. Pharmacopoeia, 1910-40; vice-pres. U.S. Pharmacopoeia Convention, 1941. Fellow A.A. A.S.; mem. Am. Soc. Pharmacology, Am. Pharm. Assn. Presbyterian. Editor: Therapeutics, Its Principles and Practice, 11th to 13th edits. (with father), 1899; United States Dispensatory, 20th edit., 1918, 21st edit., 1926, 22d edit., 1937, 23d edit., 1943. Author: A Text Book of Pharmacology, 1912. Home: 319 S. 41st St., Phila. Died Mar. 31, 1958; buried West Laurel Hill Cemetery, Phila.

WOOD, James Madison, college pres.; b. Hartville, Wright County, Mo., Oct. 2, 1875; s. James Thomas and Mary Elizabeth (Smith) W.; grad. State Normal Sch., Warrensburg, Mo., 1901; A.B. and B.S. in Edn., U. Mo., 1907; A.M., Columbia, 1911; LL.D., Hiram (O.) Coll., 1930, William Jewell Coll., Liberty, Mo., 1943; LL.D., Alfred U.; m. Lela Raney, Dec. 24, 1896; 1 son, James Madison. Teacher and prin. schs., Mo., 1894-1904; supt. schs., Edina, Mo., 1904-06, Fredericktown, 1907-10; with Dept. of Edn., State Normal Sch., Springfield, Mo., 1911-12; pres. Stephens College for Women, Columbia, Mo., 1912-47, ret. Pres. Women's Foundation, N.Y.C. Pres. Am. Assn. Jr. Colls., 1922-24; mem. N.E.A., Phi Delta Kappa, Phi Beta Kappa. Baptist. Mason (32°, K.T.). Home: 1205 Maple St., Santa Monica, Cal. Died Sept. 28, 1958.

WOOD, John Scott, banker; b. nr. Monroe City, Mo., Dec. 29, 1872; s. John Oliver and Elizabeth Boardman (Broadley) W.; ed. Christian U. now Culver-Stockton Coll., Canton, Mo., 1888-91; m. Ella Jane Strode, Oct. 16, 1899; children—Dorothy Jane (Mrs. Chester A. Sunder), John Scott, Mary Elizabeth (dec.), Anna (dec.). Bookkeeper Ralls County Bank, New London, Mo., 1893-95; asst. cashier Bank of New London, 1895-1913; state bank examiner for Mo., 1913-16; nat. bank examiner, 1916-20; chief nat. bank examiner, 8th Federal Res. Dist., 1920-30; chmn. bd., Federal Reserve Bank of St. Louis, 1930-36, v.p. 1936-39; now retired. Trustee Culver-Stockton Coll. Democrat. Mem. Christian (Disciples) Ch., trustee Nat. Benevolent Assn. of same. Mason. Clubs: Mo. Athletic, Noonday. Home: New London, Mo. Died Nov. 23, 1957.

WOOD, John Travers, congressman; b. Calder Grove, Yorkshire, Eng., Nov. 25, 1878; s. William and Sarah Ann (Heaton) W.; brought to U.S., 1889, naturalized, 1901; M.D., Detroit Coll. Medicine, 1904, post-grad. courses Wesley Meml. Hosp., Chgo., 1926, U. of Pa. Postgrad. Hosp., 1949, Bellevue Hosp., N.Y.C., 1949; also studied under Dr. Edward Rosenberg, Chgo., 1949; m. Margaret O'Deil Thomson, June 5, 1907; children—William Travers, George Edward. Pub. sch. tchr., N.D., 1897-99; gen. practitioner, Hannah, N.D., 1904, gen. practice and contract surgery, Coeur d'Alene, Ida., 1906—, specialized in arthritis, 1940—; surgeon C.M.&St.P. R.R., 1910—; a founder and 1st pres. Coeur d'Alene Hosp. Co., 1908. Pres. bd. trustees Northwest Medicine. Mem. 82d Congress, 1st Ida. Dist. Served as mayor of Coeur d'Alene, 1911-12. Served as 1st lt., U.S. Army, World War I. Mem. Ida. State Med. Assn., Kootenai County (Ida.) Med. Soc., Athletic Round Table. Republican. Presbyn. Elk, Mason (past grand master; 33°, Shriner). Clubs: Spokane (Wash.) City; Rotary (hon. life mem. Coeur d'Alene). Discovered (with Dr. D D. Drennan) Rocky Mountain Tick fever paralysis, 1914. Pub. speaker. Home: 817 Sherman St., Coeur d'Alene, Ida. Office: House Office Bldg., Washington 25. Died Nov. 2, 1954; buried Forest Cemetery, Coeur d'Alene, Ida.

WOOD, John Walter, architect, airport cons.; b. Short Hills, N.J., June 5, 1900; s. John Walter and Nathalie (Wilmer) W.; grad., Middlesex School, Concord, Mass., 1919; B.S., Harvard, 1922, M.Arch., 1927; student Oxford U., 1923, Ecole des Beaux Arts, 1928; m. Suzanne Jane Cort, Mar. 1, 1938; children—Michèle, John. Engaged in architecture and airport design since 1931; partner Poor & Wood, airport cons., N.Y.C., 1937-42; architect outdoor aquariums, Marine Studios, Inc., St. Augustine, Fla., tech. schs. for A.A.F., Denver; cons. airports Asst. Sec. Commerce, various agencies, and airlines; airport analyst Port of N.Y. Authority, 1943-45; chief layout and safety unit, airport engring. and development br., Hdqrs. A.A.F., 1945; asso. prof. architecture U. Ill. since 1948. Served with C.A.C., U.S. Army, 1918. Finalist Rome prize in architecture, 1926. Chmn. graduate committee Harvard Flying Club, 1927-29. Fellow Am. Geog. Soc., Inst. Aeronautical Sciences (associate); mem. Am. Inst. Architects, Liturgical Arts Soc. (founding mem.; director), New York State Association Architects, Scarab. Club: Harvard (New York City). Author: Airports—Some Elements of Design and Future Development, 1940; Airports and Air Traffic, 1948. Contbr. airport sect. to City-Planning Housing, 1938. Contbr. airport articles profl. jours. Holder airport patents in U.S., Can., Eng., France. Office: Dept. of Architecture, University of Illinois, Urbana, Ill. Died Nov. 1958.

WOOD, Lewis (Gaynor), newspaperman; b. Columbia, S.C., Jan. 3, 1880; s. Lewis G. and Fannie Baylor (Portlock) W.; student U. of S.C., 1897-98, U. of the South, 1900-01; m. Katharine Fauntleroy, Sept. 7, 1918. Reporter The State, Columbia, S.C., 1902-09, New York Tribune, 1909-16, mem. London Bureau of same, 1912-14; reporter New York American, 1916; mem. Washington Bureau of Internat. News Service, 1916-18; Washington Bur. New York Times 1918-51, ret. 1951. Mem. White House Correspondents Assn. (pres. 1930), Sigma Nu, Sigma Delta Chi. Episcopalian. Clubs: Gridiron (pres. 1942, and 1943, first time in 24 yrs. a pres. has held the office twice successively), Nat. Press (chmn. board govs. 1925), Overseas Writers (pres. 1928); Chevy Chase (Md.); Alfalfa (Washington). Home: 2559 Waterside Drive. Office: 711 Albee Bldg., Washington, D.C. Died June 7, 1953.

WOOD, Mary I., assn. exec; b Woodstock, Vt, Jan. 18, 1866; d. John and Jean Ainsworth (Brand) Stevens; ed. Vt. Acad.; pvt. instrn. in economics, ethics and psychology; hon. A.M., U. N.H., 1935; m. George A. Wood, Oct. 14, 1884; children—Helen Margaret (Mrs. Gordon McKay Campbell), Albert James, Mary Elizabeth (Mrs. R. L. Lamont, dec.), Keith Ainsworth. Mgr. Bur. Information Gen. Federation Women's Clubs 14 yrs.; ex-pres. N. H. Federation Women's Clubs now hon. v.p.; ex-chmn. N.H. Woman's Citizenship Com.; ex-chmn. N.H. League Women Voters; ex-pres. Civic Assn., Portsmouth Dist. Nursing Assn.; councilor Girl Scouts; chmn. woman's committee N.H. Div. of Council Nat. Defense, World War, and home economics dir. for N.H. under Federal Food Administrator; state chmn. N.H. Woman's Citizenship Com.; mem. Bd. of Pub. Instrn.; official parliamentarian State Fed. Women's Clubs; County v.p. Soc. for Protection N.H. Forests. Mem. bd. overseers Stoneleigh Coll.; trustee N.H. Memorial Hosp.; dir. Animal Rescue League of Rockingham County. Unitarian. Clubs: Women's City, Business and Professional Women's. Lecturer on edn., citizenship for women, etc.; teacher of parliamentary law and citizenship; formerly editor New Hampshire Mag., also The Northern (official organ State Federation of Women's Clubs in Me., N.H. and Vt.). Author: History of General Federation of Women's Clubs. Editor women's club dept. Ladies' Home Journal for several yrs. Home: 845 South Rd., Portsmouth, N.H. Deceased.*

WOOD, Paul Spencer, coll. prof.; b Chicago, Ill., July 12, 1882; s. William Henry and Selina (Spencer) W.; student Wittenberg Acad., Springfield, O., 1895-98, Wittenberg Coll., 1898-1900, 1904-05; Ph. B., U. of Chicago, 1908, student, same, summers 1909, 10, 11; Ph.D., Harvard, 1922, Dexter traveling scholar, Oxford U., Eng., 1922-23; m. Irene Lucile Biggs, Sept. 1, 1910; children—Mary Elizabeth (Mrs. Nathaniel Lawrence), Margaret Spencer (Mrs. Milton Anderson). Began as newspaper reporter, Springfield (O.) Sun, 1908-09; teacher Marshall (Ill.) High Sch., 1909-10; successively asst. prof., asso. prof. and prof. of English, U. of Southern Calif., 1910-20; asst. in English, Harvard, 1920-21; Ames prof. of English and chmn. of dept. Grinnell College, 1923-47, chairman div. language and literature, 1940-44; chmn. of faculty, 1944-47, emeritus; first holder of Trustees' Honor Professorship, 1946-47; acting head of dept., Trinity College, Hartford, Conn. (on leave of absence from Grinnell), 1927-29; prof. of English, Breadloaf Summer Sch. of English, 1928; visiting prof. of English, U. of Mo., summer 1927, 29, 30-33, 35, 39; lecturer in English, Columbia University, 1947——. Mem. Modern Lang. Assn. America, Assn. University Professors, Iowa Colleges Conference on English (pres. 1937-38, 1944-46), Guild of Scholars in Episcopal Church, Phi Beta Kappa. Democrat. Edi-

tor: Descriptive and Narrative Prose (with Willoughby Johnson), 1933; English Prose and Poetry, 1660-1800 (with Odell Shepard), 1934; Masters of English Literature, Vol. I, 1942, Vol. II, 1943. Contbr. to jours. Home: 11 Niles Av., Madison, N.J. Died Jan. 11, 1955; buried Hanover, N.J.

WOOD, Pierpont Jonathan Edwards, lawyer; b. Stoughton, Wis., Aug. 12, 1890; s. William Squier and Caroline (Pierpont) W.; student State U. Ia., 1912-13; m. Helen Jeffris, Oct. 27, 1915; children—Steven P. J., Carolyn Wood Haumerson, Malcolm Jeffris. Admitted to Mont. bar, 1913, Wis. bar, 1919; mem. law firm now known as JMOW&C, 1919——; chmn., dir. The Burdick Corp., Milton, Wis.; chmn. v.p., dir. Warner Electric Brake & Clutch Co., South Beloit, Ill.; treas., dir. Gilman Engring. & Mfg. Co., Janesville, Wis.; pres., dir. Daily News Pub. Co., Beloit, Bostwick Realty Co., Janesville; sec.-treas., dir. Janesville Realty Co.; dir. Cunningham Bros., Inc., Beloit Iron Works (Beloit), Marine Nat. Exchange Bank (Milw.), Hough Mfg. Corp., Parker Pen Co., Rock River Woolen Mills, Solie Lumber Co., Frank H. Blodgett, Inc. (Janesville, Wis.), Mohawk Lumber Co., Ltd. (B.C., Can.). Wis. vice chmn. A.R.C. campaigns for mems. and funds, 1954, 55. Dir. U. Wis. Found.; mem. citizens com. Beloit Coll.; trustee U. Wis. YMCA. Mem. Wis. State Council Def., during World War II. Wis. mem. Rep. Nat. Com., 1936-40, mem. Rep. State Finance Com. of Wis., 1938-53. Served as pvt. F.A., U.S. Army World War I. Mem. Am., Wis., Rock County bar assns., Acad. Polit. Sci., State Hist. Soc. Wis. (life). Am. Legion, Navy League U.S., Newcomen Soc. N.A., Beta Theta Pi, Phi Delta Phi. Episcopalian. Mason, Elk. Clubs: Tavern. University (Chgo.); University, Milwaukee (Milw.); Janesville Country, Kiwanis (Janesville); Lake Geneva Country; Canadian (N.Y.C.). Home: 7722 Sanderling Rd., Siesta Key, Sarasota, Fla.; (summer) Williams Bay, Wis. Died Nov. 12, 1956; buried Oak Hill Cemetery, Janesville, Wis.

WOOD, Ralph (Frederic), naval officer (ret.); b. Goshen, Ind., July 6, 1890; s. Franklyn Wellington and Clara (Wilson) W.; student, N.Y. Nautical Sch., 1905-06; B.S., U.S. Naval Acad., 1911; grad. Naval War Coll., 1934; m. Irene Porter, Oct. 20, 1914; children—Joy (wife of Lt. Comdr. Stuart H. Smith), Elaine. Commd. ensign U.S. Navy, 1911, and advanced through grades to rear adm., 1942; comdr. submarine Shark, Far East, 1913-15; served in Siberia, Japan, U.S. France and aboard U.S.S. Buffalo and L-8, 1917-19; erected 1st helium inflated airship and flew over arms conf., 1921; comdr. Naval Air Sta., Canal Zone, 1922-24; with 1st Naval flights to Colombia and Venezuela, 1924; staff comdr., air force, 1924-25; Naval air attache, Am. Embassy, Rome, 1926-28; served in carriers Lexington and Saratoga, 1928-30, 1934-36; at Naval Air Sta., Pensacola, Fla., 1931-33; aviation aid, 9th Naval Dist., 1936-38; comdr. U.S.S. Wright and Ranger, 1938-40, Naval Air Sta., Seattle, Wash., 1940-42; comdr. Naval Air Forces, S.W. Pacific, 1942-43, Fleet Air, Seattle, 1943-44; comdt. 17th Naval Dist., Alaska, and dep. comdr., N. Pacific forces, 1944-45; comdr. N. Pacific forces, also comdr., 4th wing and task force comdr., 1945-46; ret. from active service, Oct. 1, 1946. Awarded Legion of Merit and various service medals from both World Wars. Mem. U.S. Naval Inst. Protestant. Clubs: Army Navy Country (Arlington, Va.), Athletic (Seattle), Desert (Borrego Springs, Calif.). Home: Cloudy Moon Drive. Office: Borrego Springs County, Borrego Springs, Cal. Died Nov. 29, 1959.

WOOD, Reuben Terrell, ex-congressman; b. Green County, Mo., Aug. 7, 1884; s. Henry N. B. and Martha A. (Wood) W.; ed. pub. schs., Springfield, Mo.; m. Mary Ellen Eshman, Dec. 31, 1936. Began as cigarmaker, 1898; labor orgn. officer, 1902-39; became pres. Mo. State Fed. of Labor 1912, now pres. emeritus; mem. 73d Congress (1933-35), Mo. at large, 74th to 76th Congresses (1935-41), 6th Mo. Dist. Democrat. Home: 1530 N. Douglas St., Springfield, Mo. Died July 16, 1955.*

WOOD, Robert Williams, physicist; b. Concord, Mass., May 2 ,1868; s. Dr. Robert Williams and Lucy J. (Davis) W.; A.B., Harvard, 1891; student Johns Hopkins, 1891-92, U. Chgo., 1892-94, U. Berlin, 1894-96; LL.D., Clark U., 1909. U. Birmingham, 1913, U. Edinburgh, 1921; Ph.D., honoris causa, U. Berlin, 1931; D.Sc., honoris causa, Oxford U., 1948; m. Gertrude Ames, Apr. 19, 1892; children—Margaret, Robert Williams, Elizabeth, Bradford (dec.). Instr. physics U. Wis., 1897-99, asst. prof., 1899-1901; prof. exptl. physics, Johns Hopkins, 1901-38, prof. emeritus, 1938, later reappointed research professor. In 1898 originated method now in general use of thawing frozen street mains and service pipes by passing an electric current through them. Awarded John Scott Legacy premium and medal Franklin Inst., Phila., for color-photography; Rumford prem'um, a gold and a silver medal, by Am. Acad., 1909, for researches on theory of light; silver medal London Soc. Arts for color-photography process; gold medal for physics for 1918, Societa Italiana delle Scienze (delta dei XL). Rome; Ive's medal

Optical Soc. of Am., 1933; Rumford gold medal Royal Soc., London, 1938; Henry Draper gold medal Nat. Acad. of Sci. for distinguished contbns. to astronomy, 1940. Served as cons. in development of atom bomb; with Manhattan group in New York during World War II; served at Aberdeen proving ground, and as cons. in Navy Experiments on shock waves under water. Commd. major, Signal O.R.C., Aug. 1917; with A E.F.; developed methods for secret signaling. Fgn. mem. Royal Soc., London, Acad. Sci., Leningrad.; Royal Swedish Acad. (1932); hon. fellow Royal Micros. Soc., London, London Phys. Soc. (1933); hon. mem. London Optical Soc., Royal Instn., London, Am. Optical Soc. (1945); corr. mem. Königliche Akademie der Wissenschaften du Göttingen; fgn. asso. Academia dei Lincei, Rome; fellow Am. Acad. Arts and Sciences; mem. Nat. Acad. Sciences, Am. Philos. Soc., Am. Phys. Soc. (pres. 1935); hon. fgn. mem. Indian Assn. for Cultivation of Science, Calcutta, 1931. Author: Physical Optics, 1905, rev. edits., 1911, 34; Researches in Physical Optics, 2 vols.; (fiction) The Man Who Rocked the Earth, and the Moon-Maker (with Arthur Train), 1915. Illustrated nonsense verses, How to Tell the Birds from the Flowers and other wood-cuts. Researches in optics, spectroscopy, atomic and molecular radiation, supersonics improvements in diffraction gratings recorded in some 260 papers in European and Am. tech. jours. Complete bibliog. on all papers at end of William Seabrook's biography, "Dr. Wood," pub. 1941, translated into Russian by V. Vavilov, introduction by Sergei Vavilov, 1946. Home: 1023 St. Paul St., Balt. 2. Died Aug. 11, 1955; buried Concord, Mass.

WOOD, Stella Louise, educator; b. Chgo., Sept. 2, 1865; d. Abraham Wilder and Abie Fales (Walker) Wood; student Chicago Froebel Assn., 1884-86; U. Mich., 1890-91, U. Minn., 1910. Kindergaretn tchr., Chgo., Muskegon, Mich., 1891-93, Dubuque, Ia., 1895; supt. Mpls. Kindergaretn Assn. Normal Sch. (later Miss Wood's Kindergarten Primary Training Sch., Inc.), 1896-1905, prin., 1905——. Mem. Assn. for Childhood Edn., N.E.A. (pres. kindergarten sect.), Minneapolis Froebel Club, Delta Gamma, Delta Kappa Gamma. Conglist. Home: Hampshire Arms Hotel. Address: 2017 Bryant Av. S., Mpls. Deceased.

WOOD, Thomas Denison, prof. health edn.; b. Sycamore, Ill., Aug. 2, 1865; s. Thomas H. and Katharine Hannah (Allen) W.; A.B., Oberlin Coll., 1888, A.M., 1891; M.D., Coll. Physicians and Surgeons (Columbia), 1891; m. Abbie W. Alden, June 25, 1891. Prof. physical edn., Columbia, 1901-27, prof. health edn., 1927-32, now prof. emeritus. Chmn. Commn. on Welfare of Tchrs., N.Y. State Tchrs'. Assn., 1913-16; chmn. Joint Com. on Health Problems in Edn., N.E.A., A.M.A., 1911-38, now chmn. emeritus; chmn. health sect. of Internat. Fedn. of Home and Sch., 1928-36; chmn. Com. on Sch. Child, White House Conf. on Child Health and Protection, 1929-32. Home: 501 W. 120th St., N.Y.C. Died Mar. 19, 1951; buried Sycamore, Ill.

WOOD, Thomas John, lawyer; b. Louisville, Apr. 25, 1899; s. George Twyman and Helen (Veech) W.; student Centre Coll., 1916-17; A.B., Princeton, 1920; LL.B., Harvard, 1923; m. Ellen Robinson Barret, Dec. 2, 1926; children—Ellen B., Mary Lee, Thomas J. Admitted to Ky. bar, 1923, since practiced Louisville; partner Stites, Wood, Helm & Peabody and predecessor firms, 1927——. Dir. Community Chest of Louisville and Jefferson County, pres. 1942-45; member of Louisville Board of Education, 1940-48; trustee YWCA Children's Hosp. of Louisville. Trustee Louisville Collegiate Sch., Louisville Presbyn. Theol. Sem. Mem. Am., Ky., Louisville bar assns., Am. Law Inst., S.A.R., Soc. Colonial Wars, Beta Theta Pi. Republican. Presbyn. Clubs: Pendennis, Louisville Country, Wynn-Stay, Filson (Louisville). Home: 1648 Cherokee Rd., Louisville 5. Office: Kentucky Home Life Bldg., 239 S. Fifth St., Louisville 2. Died Dec. 19, 1956.

WOOD, William Elliott, pub. utility exec.; b. Aiken, S.C., June 21, 1887; s. Ezekiel Jeremiah Charles and Mary (Abercrombie) W.; B.S. in E.E. Ga. Tech., 1907; m. Ruth Johnson, Oct. 8, 1913; children—Mary Louise (Mrs. T. T. Adams, Jr.), Ruth Ellen (Mrs. William Thompson, dec.). Student engr. Jacksonville (Fla.) Traction Co., 1907-13; supt. transportation, same company, 1913-16; general superintendent El Paso (Texas) St. Railway, 1916-18; manager Houston Electric Company, 1918-25; v.p. Va. Elec. Power Co , 1925-27, pres., 1927-29; v.p. Engrs. Pub. Service Co., N.Y. City, 1929-38, v.p. Stone & Webster Service Corp., 1938-40; pres. Va. Pub. Service Co. Alexandria, Va., 1941-44; exec. vice pres. Virginia Electric & Power Co. Richmond, Va., 1945-54; chmn. Richmond-Petersburg Turnpike Authority (Va.), 1954-57. Mem. Am. Transit Assn. (pres. 1933-34), Beta Theta Pi. Mason (Shriner). Clubs: Commonwealth, Hermitage (Richmond); Belle Haven (Alexandria). Author: Wandering in the Wilderness. Died Feb. 1, 1957; buried Hollywood Cemetery, Richmond, Va.

WOOD, William Hamilton, educator; b. Ontario, Can., Feb. 11, 1874; s. Sterling Williams and Catherine Amelia (Hamilton) W.; A.B., U. of Toronto,

1901, B.D., Victoria U., 1904; B.D., Yale, 1905, A.M., 1906, Ph.D., 1909; studied Am. Sch. Archeology, Jerusalem, and univs. Göttingen, Berlin and Paris; m. Mabel Munson, Nov. 1, 1911 (dec. 1951); children—Frances May, Catherine, Beulah Beach, William Hamilton. Prof. Bibl. lit. Birmingham (Ala.) Coll., 1910; acting prof. of Bibl. lit., Allegheny Coll., Meadville, Pa., 1914; prof. Bibl. lit. and religious edn., Hamline U., 1915-16; prof. Bibl. lit. and history, Dartmouth 1917-43, retired. Mem. Religious Edn. Assn., Assn. Biblical Teachers America, Am. Oriental Soc., Am. Hist. Assn., N.H. State Sunday Sch. Assn. (pres.). Republican. Mason. Club: Graduate (Hanover, N.H.). Author: International Sunday School Graded Lessons, Senior Grade, 1912; The Religion of Science, 1922. Contbr. to periodicals. Home: W. Hartford, Conn. Died Sept. 1, 1953.

WOOD, Word Harris, banker; b. Elkin, N.C., Apr. 28, 1873; s. Warwick Whitfield and Juriah (Lucretia) W.; student Univ. of N.C., 1891-92; grad. business coll., Baltimore, 1893; m. Louisiana Gibson, July 9, 1909; 1 dau., Mrs. Louisiana Wood Simpson; m. 2d, Mrs. Frances Brack Fitzsimons, Jan. 13, 1938. Began with Wachovia Loan & Trust Co., Winston-Salem, N.C., 1893; with Am. Trust Co., Charlotte, since 1901, pres., 1917-43, chmn. bd. since 1943. Home: 925 Harvard Pl. Office: American Trust Co., Charlotte, N.C. Died Dec. 26, 1951; buried Charlotte, N.C.

WOODBINE, George Edward, prof. history; b. Boston, Apr. 29, 1876; s. Mark and Maria (Townshend) W.; grad. Phillips Acad., Andover, Mass., 1898; B.A., Yale, 1903, Ph.D., 1909, LL.B., 1919; studied in Europe, 1907, 08; m. Helen Norton, June 16, 1920. With Yale, 1906——; successively instr., asst. prof. history, 1906-15, asst. prof. Yale Sch. of Law, 1919-23, asso. prof., 1923-24, prof., 1924-27, George Burton Adams prof. hist., 1927-44, prof. emeritus, 1944——. Fellow Medieval Acad. Am., Am. Geographical Society; member of the Royal Historical Society, also Phi Beta Kappa, Phi Delta Phi, Order of the Coif. Conglist. Specialist, medieval English law. Author: Four Thirteenth Century Law Tracts, 1910; Bracton—De Legibus, Vol. I, 1915, Vol. II, 1922, Vol. III, 1940, Vol IV, 1942 (awarded Haskins medal); Glanvill—De Legibus Angliae, 1932; many articles in legal periodicals. Home: Clapboard Hill, Guilford, Conn. Died Aug. 20, 1953; buried Nut Plains Cemetery, Guilford, Conn.

WOODBRIDGE, Homer Edwards, prof. English; b. Williamstown, Mass., Sept. 28, 1882; s. Luther Dana and Abigail Marvin (Mather) W.; A.B., Williams, 1902; A.M., Harvard, 1904, Ph.D., 1919; m. Isabelle Worthington Strong, Aug. 22, 1906; children—Dorothy (Mrs. Gordon Hill), Margaret (Mrs. William S. Jackson), Dana Mather. Instr. Dow Acad., Franconia, N.H., 1902-03; asst. in English, Harvard, 1904-05, instr., 1906-08, asst. prof., 1908-10, prof., 1910-17, Colo. Coll., Colorado Srpings; vis. prof. English, U. of Ill., 1917-19; asso. prof. English, Ind. U., 1919-20; prof. English, Wesleyan U., 1920——; lectr. summer schs., U. Colo., Ind. U., U. of N.H., Northwestern U., Harvard, U. Mich., U. Me., U. Ore.; exchange prof. Harvard, 1913-14. Mem. Middletown Sch. Bd. Trustee Russell Library. Mem. Mod. Lang. Assn. Am., Am. Assn. Univ. Profs., Phi Beta Kappa. Author: Essentials of English Composition, 1920; Life and Letters of Stuart P. Sherman (with Jacob Zeitlin), 1929; Sir William Temple, the Man and His Work, 1940. Editor: Lamb's Essays of Elia, 1927. Contbr. articles and reviews to various periodicals. Home: 178 Cross St., Middletown, Conn. Died Jan. 21, 1958; buried Middletown, Conn.

WOODMAN, Frederic Thomas, ex-mayor; b. Concord, N.H., June 28, 1872; s. Alfred and Maria T. (Gallap) W.; grad. high sch., White River Junction, N.H., 1895; studied law in office Hon. John L. Spring, Lebanon, N.H.; m. Etta M. Sanborn, Feb. 6, 1908 (died Apr. 16, 1916); m. 2d, Katherine P. Winter, Feb. 2, 1921. Began practice at Concord, 1899; mem. N.H. Ho. of Rep., 1901-03; removed to Los Angeles, 1908; pres. Harbor Commn., 1912-16; apptd. mayor of Los Angeles, 1916, elected for term 1917-19; resumed law practice; pres. Woodman-Gray Co.; chmn. adv. bd. Bank of Am. Pacific League of Cal.; gov. Soc. Colonial Wars for Cal. Mem. Am. Bar Assn., Cal. State Bar Assns., Founders of Am., S.C. W., S.A.R., Sons of Vets., Soc. Am. Royal Descent, Descs. Knights of the Garter. Republican. Pres. Mason (32°), Odd Fellow. Clubs: California, Los Angeles Country. Home: 514 Shatto Pl., Los Angeles 5. Died Mar. 25, 1949; buried Rosedale Cemetery, Los Angeles.

WOODROW, Jay W(alter), prof. physics; b. Rock Co., Minn., Apr. 3, 1884; s. Joseph Thomas and Della Erbain (Kennedy) W.; A.B., Drake U., Ia., 1907; B.A., Rhodes scholar from Ia., Oxford U., 1910; Ph.D., Yale, 1913; m. Flora Bernice Williams, June 23, 1915; 1 dau., Margaret Williams. Instr. physics, U. Ill., 1910-12; fellow in physics, Yale, 1912-13; research engr. Western Electric Co., N.Y.C., 1913-14; instr. physics, U. Colo., 1914-15, asst. prof., 1915-18, prof., 1918-21; prof. physics, Ia. State Coll. Agr. and Mechanic Arts, 1921——; Guggenheim fellow for study in Europe, 1927-28. Mem. Am. Phys. Soc., Soc. Promotion Engring. Edn., A.A. A.S., Phi Beta Kappa, Sigma Xi and Gamma Alpha. Mem. Christian (Disciples) Ch. Home: Ames, Ia. Deceased.

WOODRUFF, Elmer Grant, cons. geologist; b. Bradford County, Pa., June 9, 1872; s. George W. and Katherine (De Reamer) W.; B.S., U. of Neb., 1901, M.S., 1904; m. Amy Grace Bucklin, Sept. 19, 1907 (died 1925); children—Vivian Grant, Edith Amy, Elaine Bucklin, Eva May; married 2d, Anna S. Wolfe, 1936. Austin fellow, Harvard University, 1906-07; with Neb. Geol. Survey, 1899-1904, U.S. Geol. Survey, 1904-14; chief geologist Tex. Oil Co., 1914-18, Okla. Producing & Refining Corp. since 1918; mem. Woodruff & Eches; geologist U.S. Army Engrs., Memphis, Tenn., 2 mos., 1935, Conchas Dam, Tucumcari, New Mex., 9 mos. to June, 1936, Memphis, Tenn. and Little Rock, Ark., Dists. since 1936. Served as lt. Third Neb. Vol. Infantry, Spanish-Am. War. Mem. Geol. Soc. America, Am. Assn. Petroleum Geologists, Tulsa Geol. Soc. (pres.), Sigma Xi. Mason. Author repts., also articles in tech. and trade jours. Home: 1611 S. Detroit St., Tulsa. Died June 25, 1952; buried Rose Hill Burial Park, Tulsa.

WOODRUFF, Frederick William, banker; b. Joliet, Ill.; s. Frederick William and Nellie (Davis) W.; student U. of Pa.; m. Katherine Miller, Jan. 3, 1927; 1 dau., Katherine. Asst. cashier Citizens Nat. Bank, Joliet, 1908-09, v.p., 1909-10; v.p. First Nat. Bank, Joliet, 1910-21, pres., 1921-52, chmn. bd. 1952——. Served as capt., AUS. Chmn. Will County chapter A.R.C. Mem. Delta Kappa Epsilon. Republican (del. nat. conv. 1952). Presbyn. Clubs: Racquet, Attic, Casino (Chicago); Seminole (Palm Beach, Fla.). Home: Fairway Farm, Joliet, Ill.; also Hobe Sound, Fla. Office: First National Bank, Joliet, Ill. Died May 20, 1959.

WOODRUFF, Roy Orchard, former U.S. congressman; born at Eaton Rapids, Michigan, on March 14, 1876; the son of Charles and Electa A. (Wallace) W.; D.D.S., Detroit Coll. of Medicine, 1902; m. 2d, Daisy E. Fish, June 11, 1921; children—Mrs. Ronald Houck, Devere H. (lt. col. U.S. Army, Philippines). Began practice Bay City, Mich., 1902; mayor Bay City, 1911-13; mem. 63d Congress (1913-15), and 67th to 82nd Congresses (1921-53), 10th Michigan Dist. Corporal Co. G, 33d Michigan Volunteer Inf., Spanish-American War; served 2 years, advancing to major infantry; with A.E.F., World War I. Mem. Am. Dental Assn., Mich. State Dental Soc., United Spanish War Vets., Am. Legion, Vets. Foreign Wars, Delta Sigma Delta. Republican. Presbyterian. Mason, Elk, I.O.O.F. Clubs: Bay City Country, Bay City, Midland Country. Home: George Washington Inn, Washington. Died Feb. 12, 1953; buried Bay City, Mich.

WOODRUM, Clifton Alexander, ex-congressman; b. Roanoke, Va., Apr. 27, 1887; s. Robert H. and Anna (T.) W.; ed. pub. schs.; student law dept. Washington & Lee U.; hon. M.A., Roanoke; m. Lena Hancock, 1905; children—Clifton A., Jr., Martha Anna. Admitted to bar, 1908, and began practice at Roanoke; commonwealth atty., 1917-19; judge Corp. Court, Roanoke, 1919-22; mem. 68th to 78th Congresses (1923-45), 6th Va. Dist.; pres. Am. Plant Food Council since Dec. 1945. Democrat. Methodist. Mem. Phi Delta Phi (hon.), Omicron Delta Kappa, Sigma Chi. Mason (33°, Shriner). Was orator. Home: 2507 Stanley Av., Roanoke, Va. Office: 910 17th St. N.W., Washington 6. Died Oct. 6, 1950; buried Fairview Cemetery, Roanoke.

WOODS, Alfred W., architect; b. St. Clair Co., Ill., Jan. 30, 1857; s. Robert and Elizabeth H. (Short) W.; ed. common schs. and business coll., Quincy, Ill.; m. Haidee Finney, of Lincoln, Neb., Dec. 30, 1885; children—Mary E., Robert E., Ethel J., H. Lucille, Alfred W. (dec.), Edna L. Practiced architecture, Quincy, 1881-82, Lincoln, Neb., 1885-1933; splty. ch. work. Author: Square Root Delineator, 1894; Key to the Steel Square, 1902; Master Key to the Steel Square, 1933. Joint Author: Steel Square and Its Uses (2 vols.), 1907, Radford's Cyclopedia of Construction, 1909. Inventor of the standard foot decimal scale, 1921. Home: 2311 S. 14th St., Lincoln, Neb. Died Dec. 29, 1942; buried Wyuka Cemetery.

WOODS, Baldwin Munger, univ. exec., professor; b. Lampasas, Tex., Sept. 22, 1887; s. Michael L. and Eloise (Munger) W.; E.E., U. of Tex., 1908; M.S., U. of Calif., 1909, Ph.D., 1912; studied U. of Paris, fall and winter, 1912-13, U. of Munich, summer 1913; hon. Dr. of Engineering, S.D. State Sch. of Mines, 1941; hon. Sc.D., College of Osteopathic Physicians and Surgeons, Los Angeles California, 1942; married Bessie Harshman, June 1918; children—Baldwin Charles, Robert Harshman, Ronald Munger. Assistant in applied mathematics, U. of Tex., 1907-08; John W. Mackay Jr. fellow in E.E., U. of Calif., 1908-10; with U. of Calif., successively asst. in mathematics, Jan.-June 1910, instr., 1910-14, instr. in theoretical mechanics, 1914-15, asst. prof., 1915-19, prof. aerodynamics, 1919-30, prof. mech. engring. since 1930, also rep. in ednl. relations, 1923-30, asst. dean, 1923-25, asso. dean, 1925-30, chmn. dept., 1930-37, prof. engring., 1947——, dir. Univ. Extension, 1942——, vice pres. univ. extension, 1950——, vice chmn. University War Council, 1942-44. President academic board and director U.S. School of Mil. Aeronautics, U. of Calif., 1917-19, World War; chairman National Committee for the Award of W. E. Boeing Scholarships, 1930-38, National Committee for the award of United Air Lines scholarships, 1939-42; member California State Planning Board, 1934-35; chairman Region 8 of National Resources Planning Bd., 1936-43; mem. state Council of Defence, 1940-43; chmn. Water Resources Com., Nat. Resources Planning Bd., 1941-43; mem. advisory com. on Engineering, Science, Management War Training, 1940-45; chmn. adv. bd. for aeronautics U. of Ill., 1944-46. Consultant in Survey of Fed. Research for the Nat. Resources Committee for year 1937-38. Fellow A.A.A.S., A.S.M.E.; mem. Engrs. Council Profl. Development, Nat. Planning Assn., Nat. U. Extension Assn., Adult Edn. Assn., Am. Assn. U. Profs., Assn. Land-Grant Colls. and Univs., Am. Society Planning Officials (pres. 1941), Am. Soc. Heating and Air Conditioning Engrs. (pres. 1947), American Soc. for Engineering Education (2d v.p. 1942-43), U.S. Naval Institute, Institute of Aeronautical Sciences (founder member), Alpha Chi Rho, Sigma Xi (pres. Calif. chapter, 1931), Tau Beta Pi, Phi Delta Kappa; asso. member Eta Kappa Nu. Methodist. Clubs: Engineers (San Francisco); Faculty, Commonwealth, Jonathan (Los Angeles). Author: Logarithms of Hyperbolic Functions to Twelve Significant Figures (with Frederick E. Pernot), 1916; Dynamics of Airplanes (with John E. Younger), 1931. Introduction to Engineering Economy (with E. Paul DeGarmo), 1942. Home: 249 The Uplands, Berkeley 5, Cal. Died Sept. 7, 1956.

WOODS, Bertha Gerneaux (Davis), writer; born Penn Yan, N.Y.; d. Charles W. and Harriet (Winton) Davis; ed. pub. and high schs., Washington; m. Albert Fred Woods, June 1, 1898 (dec.); children—Charles Frederick (dec.), Albert Frederick (dec.), Mark Winton, Winton de Ruyter. Mem. League Am. Pen Women, Audubon Society. Presbyterian. Club: Progress. Contbr. poems and short stories. Author: Verses, 1908; Verses by Three Generations (with Harriet Winton Davis and Mark Winton Woods), 1921; The Guest and Other Verse, 1926; The Patient Scientists and Other Verse, 1928; The Little Gate (poems), 1935; World Communion and Other Verse, 1943. Awarded Near East Relief prize for Golden Rule Sunday poem published in Youth's Companion, 1925. Home: 4001 Quintana St., Hyattsville, Md. Died Feb. 14, 1952; buried Rock Creek Cemetery, Washington.

WOODS, Edgar Hall, lawyer, plantation operator; b. Kemper Co., Miss., Apr. 18, 1864; s. Hervey, Jr., and Callie (Sanders) W.; student Southwestern Presbyn. U., Clarksville, Tenn.; LL.B., U. Miss., 1886; m. Elizabeth Bullus Scott, Dec. 27, 1893 (died 1903); children—Charles Scott (dec.), Edgar Hall II; m. 2d, Ida Lyell, June 3, 1912. Admitted to Miss. bar, 1887, and practiced at Rosedale; mem. firm Woods & Woods, Meridian, Miss., 1892-96, Chas. Scott & E. H. Woods, 1896-1911; retired from practice, 1911, and began stock raising nr. Lucas, Ky., 1914; owner and operator 2,500 acre stock and grain farm until summer of 1929 (disabled by illness); chmn. Louisville Br. of Federal Reserve Bank of St. Louis, 1924-34; sr. supervising atty. Home Owners Loan Corpn., Louisville, 1934-35; now owner and operator cotton plantation. Served as captain U.S. Volunteers, Spanish-American War, and as brigadier general Miss. N.G.; was chief of Ky. div. American Protective League, also chmn. 5th Ky. Dist., United War Work Campaign, World War; mem. Com. of Four, agrl. loans of War Finance Corpn., 1921. Formerly mem. Dem. State Exec. Com., Miss. An organizer Am. Farm Bur. Federation (dir. until 1924; exec. com., 1922-23), Ky. Farm Bur. Federation (pres. 6 terms); apptd. by U.S. Chamber Commerce mem. com. to study development of waterways and coördination of rail and waterway service, 1923. Mem. Am. Bar Assn., Ky. Tax Reform Assn. (pres.), Sigma Alpha Epsilon. Presbyn. Club: XV. Home: Rosedale, Miss. Died Mar. 7, 1939.

WOODS, Frank Henry; b. Boone County, Ill., Feb. 1, 1868; s. Col. Fred M. and Eliza (Eddy) W.; B.Litt., University of Nebraska, 1899, LL.B., 1892, LL.D., 1945; graduate student Columbia University Law Sch.; m. Nelle Cochrane, 1894 (dec. 1950); children—Henry C., Thomas C., Frank H. Admitted to Neb. bar, 1892, and practiced at Lincoln as mem. Hall, Woods & Pound until 1910; counsel Woods, Aitken & Aitken, since 1919; chmn. bd. Addressograph-Multigraph Corp., Cleveland; pres. Lincoln Telephone & Telegraph Co., 1909-45, chmn. bd. since 1945; pres. Frank H. Woods & Co.; director Sahara Coal Co. (president 1920-44), Chicago. Member of Am. and Neb. State bar assns., Nat. Independent Telephone Assn. (pres. 1910) Beta Theta Pi. Republican. Congregationalist. Home: 2501 Sheridan Blvd., Lincoln. Office: Telephone Bldg., Lincoln, Neb.; and 59 E. Van Buren St., Chgo. Died Apr. 1, 1952; buried Wyuka Cemetery, Lincoln, Neb.

WOODS, Frederick Shenstone, mathematician; b. Monson, Mass., Mar. 8, 1864; s. Frederick and Sarah

H. (Shenstone) W.; A.B., Wesleyan U., Conn., 1885, A.M., 1888; Ph.D., U. Göttingen, 1894; m. Ethel M. Eager, June 20, 1899; children—Emily, Helen. Asst. in physics and astronomy, Wesleyan U., 1885-86; tchr. mathematics, Lima, N.Y., 1886-90; instr. mathematics, 1890-95, asst. prof., 1895-1903, asso. prof., 1903-06, prof. mathematics, 1906-34, Mass. Inst. Tech. emeritus prof., 1934—, hon. lecturer, 1934-35. Lectr. mathematics, Harvard, 1898-99; editor Annals of Mathematics, 1900-11. Mem. American Math. Soc., Math. Assn. of America, Psi Upsilon fraternity. Author: (with F. H. Bailey) Plane and Solid Analytic Geometry, 1897; (with E. B. Van Vleck and H. S. White) Boston Colloquium Lectures on Mathematics, 1905; (with F. H. Bailey) A Course in Mathematics for Students of Engineering and Applied Science, 1908; (with F. H. Bailey) Analytic Geometry and Calculus, 1917; Higher Geometry, 1922; (with F. H. Bailey) Elementary Calculus, 1922; Advanced Calculus, 1926. Editor: Journal of Mathematics and Physics. Home: 123 Sumner St., Newton Centre 59, Mass. Died Dec. 1, 1950.

WOODS, George Benjamin, educator; b. Morris Grundy County, Ill., Nov. 14, 1878; s. Benjamin Franklin and Augusta (Clark) W.; A.B., Northwestern U., 1903; A.M., Harvard, 1908, Ph.D., 1910; Litt.D., American U., 1945; m. Helen Smith, July 14, 1904; children—Katharine, John Lucius, Margaret Jane. Instr. English, Twp. High Sch., LaSalle, Ill., 1903-04; instr. English and pub. speaking, Pacific U., Forest Grove, Ore., 1904-05; instr. English and debating and asst. prin., Evanston (Ill.) Acad., 1905-07; prof. English, Miami U., Oxford, O., 1910-13, Carleton Coll., Northfield, Minn., 1913-25; dean Coll. Arts and Sciences and professor English, American University, 1925-44, prof. English, 1925—. Mem. Phi Beta Kappa, Delta Sigma Rho, Sigma Nu, Omicron Delta Kappa. Methodist. Clubs: Federal Schoolmen, Torch (internat. pres. 1937). Editor: English Poetry and Prose of the Romantic Movement, 1916, rev. edit. 1950; Poetry of Victorian Period, 1930, rev. edit., 1955. The Literature of England (with H. A. Watt and George Anderson), 2 vols., 1936, rev. edit., 1953. Author: College Handbook of Writing, 1922; Manual of English (with Clarence Stratton), 1925; Drills in English, 1931; A Guide to Good English, 1934; The Odyssey Handbook and Guide to Writing (with W. Arthur Turner), 1954; Versification in English Poetry, 1958. Home: 3718 University Av., Washington 16. Died Nov. 8, 1958.

WOODS, Robert Patterson, engr.; b. Buffalo N.Y., Mar. 4, 1870; s. Thomas Hamilton and Margaret Jane (Patterson) W.; grad. Buffalo Central High Sch., 1890; m. Bertha Dicken, Oct. 10, 1894; children—Dorothy (Mrs. Lester D. Castle), Robert Dicken (dec.), Helen (Mrs. Ansel N. Mitchell). With Henry L. Lyon, civ. engr., Buffalo, 1888-91, as asst. engr.; chief engr., Queen City Electric Ry., Marion, Ind., Mar.-Sept. 1891; city engr., Wabash, Ind., 1891-1901, and during same period in private practice on water works, bridge work and sewer design; chief engr. constrn. Wabash River Traction line (19 miles), 1900, Indianapolis, Shelbyville, Southeastern Traction line (27 miles), 1901, Indianapolis & Northwestern Traction line (92 miles), 1902-04 Lebanon-Thornton Traction Co. (10 miles), 1905, Indianapolis & Western Ry. Co. traction lines (74 miles), 1906-08; irrigation projects in N.M., 1910-11; chief engr. construction electric roead Kansas City to St. Joseph, Mo., and Kansas City to Excelsior Springs, Mo. (80 miles), 1911-13; mem. bd. of control Kansas City Rys. Co., 1914-20; pres., gen. mgr. K.C.,C.,C.&St.J. Ry. Co., 1920-30, receiver 1930-36; pres. Consumers Tie Service Co.; practicing as cons. engr. Pres. Midwest Electric Ry. Assn. 1931-32; president Research Hospital, 1922, 23; director, 1917—; mem. and v. chmn. City Plan Commn., 1920-40; street railway commr. and dir. Kansas City Public Service Co., May 20, 1940—; local War Transportation adminstr., 1942-46. Awarded Collingwood prize American Society C.E., 1900, for paper on "Street Grades and Cross-Sections in Asphalt and Cement." Mem. Am. Soc. C.E. (pres. Kansas City sect. 1936), Ind. Engring. Soc. (twice pres.), Am. Wood Preservers Assn., Mo. Soc. of Professional Engrs., Kansas City C. of C. Presbyterian. Republican. Clubs: K.C. Engrs., Kansas City Club. Registered professional engr., Mo. Home: 5527 East Mission Dr., Kansas City 15, Mo. Office: 1627 Main St., Kansas City 8, Mo. Died May 20, 1958; buried Forest Hills Cemetery, Kansas City, Mo.

WOODS, Rufus, editor, pub.; b. Surprise, Neb., May 17, 1878; s. Lebbeus B. and Mary (Morrison) W.; grad. high sch., Ulysses, Neb., 1898; student Grand Island (Neb.) Coll., 1900, Vashon Coll., Wash., 1901; LL.B., U. of Neb., 1903; Litt.D., Whitman Coll., 1933; m. Mary Greenslit, May 1, 1909; children—Wilma Cecelia (dec.), Walter Greenslit (dec.), Willa Lou (Mrs. Walter F. Hiltner), Wilfred Rufus, Kathryn Adelle (Mrs. R. G. Haley). Editor Wenatchee (Wash.) Republic, 1904, Wenatchee Advance, 1905; sec. Wenatchee C. of C., 1906-07; editor, pub. Wenatchee Daily World, 1907—. Del. Rep. Nat. Conv., Cleve., 1924, Chgo., 1932. Chmn. Prog. Rep. League of Wash., 1908. Chmn. Wash.-N. Idaho div. Asso. Press, 1926-27; dir. Wash. State C. of C., 1928-29; pres. Columbia River Development League, framing program for Grand Coulee Dam, 1931-34; mem. State Columbia Basin Commn. (authorized to build Grand Coulee Dam), 1933-37; pres. Strategic Industries Bd. of Central Wash., 1942, Decentralization League of Eastern Wash., 1942; mem. State Columbia Basin Commn. (represent state in Columbia River Valley power, irrigation, development program; 1943—; mem. Bonneville Adv. Council, 1943—. Sec.-treas. Northwest Chemurgy Coop., mfg. concern, 1942—. Methodist. Syndicate articles and addresses, Roamin' Round Russia, 1930-32; Among the Dictators, 1938; Undeclared War in the Orient, 1939; Riding the Wings around South America, 1941; 25 Year Battle for Grand Coulee Dam, 1946; Round the Rim of the Northwest, 1946; hist. articles, Three Glamorous Decades in the Great Northwest, 1932. Home: Wenatchee, Wash. Died May 29, 1950; buried Wenatchee, Wash.

WOODS, Sam Edison, diplomat; b. Starville, Tex., May 15, 1892; s. Roderick Sam and Annie Lee (Palmer) W.; B. Manual Arts, U. of Valparaiso, 1913; student U. of Wis., 1914, Mass. Inst. Tech., 1917-18; B.S., Miss. State Teachers Coll., 1920; m. Katie Rose Anderson, Aug. 2, 1917 (died Sept. 14, 1918); 1 daughter, Katie Rose; m. 2d, Milada P. Vondracekova, December 1, 1923; married 3d, Wilhelmina Busch, 1948. Head of Mannual Arts Department, Miss. State Teachers Coll., 1917-19; dir. extension work Grenada (Miss.) Bank, 1920; supervised and constructed playgrounds, Czechoslovak Govt., 1921; supervisor of rehabilitation, Miss. State Dept. Edn., 1922-28; asst. trade commr., assigned to Prague, 1928-34; commercial attaché, Prague, 1934-37; commercial attaché at large, Berlin, 1937-39; commercial attaché, Berlin, 1939-41; interned by German Govt. and later exchanged with other diplomatic personnel; consul gen., Zurich, Switzerland, 1942-45, 1945-46, Istanbul, Turkey, 1945; consul general with personal rank of minister, Munich, Germany, 1947-52, ret. Member Marine Aviation, Corps, 1918; in charge vocational endeucational work, United States Army Education Corps, 6th Army Area, France, 1919. Mem. Am. Econ. Assn., Acad. Polit. Sciences, Miss. Ednl. Assn., Am. Legion. Methodist. Club: Metropolitan. Home: Hattiesburg, Miss. Address: American Consulate General, Munich, Germany. Died May 22, 1953.

WOODS, Thomas Cochrane, lawyer, corp. exec.; b. Lincoln, Neb., Oct. 24, 1895; s. Frank Henry and Nelle (Cochrane) W.; A.B., Yale, 1918; LL.B., Harvard, 1921; m. Sarah Ladd, Sept. 9, 1918; children—Thomas Cochrane, Shirley Ladd. Admitted to Neb. bar, 1921; mem. Woods Aitken & Aitken, Lincoln; pres., dir. Lincoln (Neb.) Telephone & Telegraph Co.; member bd. dirs. Addressograph-Multigraph Corp., Cleve., 1932, chmn., dir., mem. exec. com., 1952—; v.p., dir. Sahara Coal Co., Inc., Chgo.; pres. W-K Realty Co., Lincoln, Woods Charitable Fund, Incorporated; director of Addressograph-Multigraph of Can., Ltd., Addressograph-Multigraph Ltd. of London, Anglo-Canadian Telephone Co. of Montreal, Asso. Telephone & Telegraph Co., Chgo., First Nat. Bank, Lincoln, Woodmen Accident Co., Securities Acceptance Corp., Omaha. Served as first lieutenant, 101st F.A., 51st Brigade, U.S. Army, World War I. Mem. Ind. Telephone Pioneer Assn. Am., Am., Lancaster Co. bar assns., Beta Theta Pi. Republican. Conglist. Clubs: Univ., Country (Lincoln, Neb.); Chicago (Chgo.); Union (Cleve.). Home: 2475 Lake St. Office: 1342 M St., Lincoln, Neb. Died Mar. 22, 1958.

WOODS, Walter Orr, ex-treas. of the U.S.; b. Carlinville, Ill., Oct. 31, 1873; s. Joseph Poley and Mary (Holliday) W.; student U. Kan.; LL.B., George Washington U., 1906; m. Elizabeth T. Woods, Dec. 12, 1912. Admitted to D.C. bar, 1906; partner firm Woods Bros., operators of Holliday Farm, Macoupin Co., Ill., 1914—; apptd. capt. finance dept., U.S. Army, 1921; mem. War Loan Staff, U.S. Treasury, 1923-27; register U.S. Treasury, 1927-29; treas. of U.S., 1929. Served as pvt. U.S. Vols., Spanish-Am. War; capt., later maj. ordnance dept., U.S. Army, World War I. Mem. Phi Delta Theta. Republican. Elk. Author: The Story of Uncle Sam's Money. Home: 3740 Kanawah St. N.W., Chevy Chase, D.C. Office: U.S. Treasury Dept., Washington. Died June 7, 1951.

WOODSIDE, John Thomas, corp. ofcl.; b. Balt., Feb. 19, 1890; s. William Shepard and Josephine (Coulter) W.; student pub. schs. of Balt.; m. Margaret McGiveran, June 25, 1924; children—Margaret Joan, William S. Mdse. mgr. Weco Products Co., 1920-24, v.p., gen. mgr., 1924-30, pres., gen. mgr., 1930—; pres., gen. mgr. Weco Products Co. Ltd. of Can., 1930—; chmn. Owens Brush Co., Toledo. Gov. Chgo. Heart Assn. Served as lt. 7th N.Y. Inf., C.W.S., 1916-18. Clubs: Chicago Athletic, Tower (Chgo.); Knollwood (Lake Forest, Ill.). Home: 209 Lake Shore Dr., Chgo. Office: 20 N. Wacker Dr., Chgo. 6. Died Jan., 1956.

WOODSIDE, Robert I., banker; b. Woodville, S.C., Mar. 30, 1873; s. Dr. John L. and Ellen (Charles) W.; ed. pub. schs., Clemson (S.C.) Coll., Eastman Bus. Coll., Poughkeepsie, N.Y.; m. Lula B. Woodside, Apr. 23, 1902. Cashier Chicora Savs. Bank, Pelzer, S.C., 1898-1903; sec. Southern Trust Co., asst. cashier Am. Nat. Bank, Spartanburg, S.C., 1903-05; rep. George H. McFadden Bros. Agency; organized Farmers and Merchants Bank, Greenville, S.C., 1907; organized, pres. Woodside Nat. Bank, Greenville, S.C., 1919-29, Farmers & Merchants Bank (Greenville)—both sold to Peoples State Bank of S.C., 1929; pres. Securities Investment Co., The Robert I. Woodside Co. (investmt. bankg.), Woodside Realty Co., Woodside Travel Service, Woodside Securities Co., Farmers Loan & Trust Co., Home Bldg. & Loan Assn.; dir. Peoples State Bank of S.C., Easley Cotton Mills Co., Woodside Cotton Mills Co., Myrtle Beach Development Co. Mem. Am. Commn. to Europe to study rural banking systems and coop. marketing systems, 1913; visited Europe, 1928, studying br. banking systems. Mem. Am. Arbitration Assn., Nat. Econ. League, Am. Bankers Assn. (agrl. commn.), S.C. Bankers Assn. (pres. 1924-25). Served as 2d lt. S.C. Militia, 1902-03; chmn. first Liberty Loan campaign. Vol. for World War, 1918; now lt. col. O.R.C. Pres. Greenville, S.C. Chpt. U.S. Organized Res'. Democrat. Presbyn. Clubs: Poinsett, Kiwanis, Elks, Chess, Sans Souci Country, Thirty-nine. Home: 115 Crescent Av. Address: Poinsett Hotel Bldg., Greenville, S.C. Died Dec. 24, 1949.

WOODSON, Aytch P., business exec.; born Platte City, Mo., Sept. 4, 1881; s. Stephen C. and Margaret (Perrin) W.; ed. U. of Mo.; LL.B., Kansas City Sch. of Law, 1906; m. Leigh Yawkey, Aug. 15, 1911. Chmn. bd., dir. Marathon Electric Mfg. Corp., Wis. Valley Trust Co., Wausau, Wis., Burke Electric Co., Erie, Pa.; pres., dir. Bay West Paper Co., Green Bay, Wis., Clark Realty Co., Colby, Wis., Mosinee Paper Mills Co. (Wis.), Woodson Fiduciary Corp., Wilmington, Del., Yawkey Lumber Co., Wausau, Wis.; v.p., dir. Employers Mutual Liability Ins. Co., Employers Mutual Fire Ins. Co., Wis. Box Co., Wausau, Wis., The McCloud River Lumber Co. (Cal.), Mont.-Dakota Utilities Co., Mpls., Western Exploration Co., Silverton, B.C.; sec., dir. Masonite Corp., Chgo., Wausau Theatres Co., Wausau So. Lumber Co.; dir. Am. Box Board Co., Inc. (Grand Rapids, Mich.), Hall Garage Corp. (Wausau), Longview Fibre Co. (Wash.), Lumbermen's Underwriting Alliance (Kansas City, Mo.), Marathon Corp. (Menasha, Wis.), Marathon Improvement Co. (Earlville, Ill.), Marshall & Ilsley Bank (Milw.), Marsh Wall Products, Inc. (Dover, O.). Pres., dir. The Aytchmonde Woodson Found., Inc., Wausau Cemetery Assn. Home: 1100 Highland Park Blvd. Office: First Am. State Bank Bldg., Wausau, Wis. Died Oct. 8, 1958; buried Pine Grove Cemetery, Wausau, Wis.

WOODSON, Carter Godwin, editor, author; b. New Canton, Buckingham County, Va., Dec. 19, 1875; s. James Henry and Anne Eliza (Riddle) W.; Litt.B., Berea (Ky.) Coll., 1903; studied La Sorbonne, Paris; A.B., U. Chgo., 1907, A.M., 1908; Ph.D., Harvard, 1912; LL.D., Va. State Coll., 1941. Teacher high schs., Washington, 1908-18; prin. Armstrong Manual Tng. High Sch., D.C., 1918-19; dean Sch. of Liberal Arts, Howard U., 1919-20; dean W.Va. Collegiate Inst., Institute, W.Va., 1920-22; dir. (exec.) Assn. for Study of Negro Life and History; pres., chmn. bd. Asso. Pubs., Inc.; founder, 1916, editor Jour. of Negro History (quar.); founder, 1937, editor Negro History Bull. Recipient Springran medal, N.A.A.C.P., 1926. Baptist. Author: The Education of the Negro Prior to 1861, 1915; A Century of Negro Migration, 1918; History of the Negro Church, 1921; The Negro in Our History, 1922; Negro Orators and Their Orations, 1925; Free Negro Owners of Slaves in the United States in 1830, 1925; Free Negro Heads of Families in the United States in 1830, 1925; The Mind of the Negro as Reflected in Letters During the Crisis, 1925; African Myths, 1928; Negro Makers of History, 1928; The Rural Negro, 1930; The Negro Professional Man and the Community, 1934; The Story of the Negro Retold, 1935; The African Background Outlined, 1936; African Heroes and Heroines, 1939. Joint author: The Negro Wage Earner; The Negro as a Business Man; editor: The Works of Francis J. Grimke, 1942. Address: 1539 Ninth St. N.W., Washington. Died Apr. 3, 1950; buried Lincoln Meml. Cemetery, Washington.

WOODSON, Omer Lee, aviation exec.; b. Dalton, Ky., Apr. 26, 1895; s. William H. and Leila (Wyatt) W.; m. Margaret Horne, Dec. 31, 1917; children—Margaret (Mrs. Terence Nolan), Jayne, Marsha. With Service Aviation & Transport Co., Wabash, Ind., 1919-21; U.S. mail service, 1921-25; mfg. comml. airplanes, 1925-32; with Northrup Aircraft Corp., Los Angeles, 1934-36; Curtis Airplane Div., Curtiss Wright Corp., Buffalo, 1936-39; v.p., asst. gen. mgr., Bell Aircraft Corp., Buffalo, 1936-39; v.p., asst. gen. mgr., Bell Aircraft Corp., 1939-43; v.p., mgr., Ga. div. Bell Aircraft, 1943-44; v.p., gen. mgr. Ryan Aero. Corp., 1944-45; operating O. L. Woodson Co., indsl. cons., engring., 1945-47; dir. research Radioplane Co., Van Nuys, Cal., 1948, now v.p. mfg. and research. Served with Signal Corps, 1917; non-commissioned officer U.S. Air Service, A.

E.F., France, 1917-19; learned to fly in France, 1917; rated mil. aviator; 1,600 logged hours. Patented an idea to teach flying without dual instrn., in successful operation, 1941—, and has taught 420 students to fly. Designed and built first 6-passenger closed cabin airplane in Am., 1919. Mem. Inst. Aero. Scis., Soc. Automotive Engrs., Nat. Aero. Assn., Vets. of Foreign Wars, Quiet Birdmen, Modern Woodmen of Am. Protestant. Clubs: Wings, La Jolla Beach and Tennis (La Jolla, Cal.). Contbr. to tech. jours. Home: 339 Stocker St., Los Angeles 43. Office: 7901 Woodley Av., Van Nuys, Cal. Died Feb., 1951.

WOODWARD, Allan Harvey (wood'wẽrd), iron mfr.; b. Wheeling, W.Va., Sept. 16, 1876; s. Joseph Hersey and Martha B. (Metcalfe) W.; U. of South, 1892-95, Mass. Inst. Tech., 1896-99; m. Annie Hill Jemison, Nov. 1, 1904. Began with Woodward Iron Co., as gen. supt., 1899, pres., 1918, chmn. bd., 1918—; vice chmn., dir. Wheeling Steel Corp.; v.p. Southern Assn. Baseball Clubs. Mem. Alpha Tau Omega. Episcopalian. Clubs: Woodward (Ala.) Golf; Country (Birmingham). Home: Birmingham, Ala. Address: Woodward, Ala. Died Nov. 23, 1950.

WOODWARD, Frederic (Campbell), v.p. emeritus U. Chgo.; b. Middletown, Orange County, N.Y., Feb. 23, 1874; s. Benjamin C. and Harriet M. (Campbell) W.; LL.B., Cornell, 1894, LL.M., 1895; hon. A.M., Dickinson, 1902, LL.D., 1932; LL.D., Northwestern U., 1929; m. Elizabeth Raymond, July 28, 1904; 1 d., Mrs. Donald Horn; m. 2d, Mrs. Harriet Walton Freund, Jan. 5, 1937; step-children—Nancy (Mrs. W. W. White), Emma Louise Ditterling; m. 3d, Gabrielle Verbrugghen Hyldahl, Apr. 4, 1952. Engaged in practice of law, N.Y., 1895-98; prof. law, Dickinson Coll., 1898-1902; prof. law, Northwestern U., 1902-07, Leland Stanford Jr. U., 1907-16, dean Law Sch., 1908-16; prof. law, U. Chgo., 1916-39, v.p., 1926-39, acting pres., 1928-29; vice chmn. Laymen's Foreign Missions Inquiry Commn., 1931-32; pres. bd. trustees Country Home for Convalescent Children, Chgo., 1928-56; pres. Chgo. Council on Foreign Relations, 1942-43. Editor in chief Ill. Law Rev., 1906-07. With U.S. Food Adminstrn., Washington, 1917; maj., judge advocate U.S. Army, 1917-19; duty in Office of Provost Marshal Gen., Washington. Clubs: Quadrangle, University, Tavern. Author: The Law of Quasi-Contracts, 1913; Cases on the Law of Sales of Goods, 1913, 2d edit., 1925. Contbr. to law jours. Home: Breamar, Grand Beach, Mich. Died Jan. 17, 1956; buried Middletown, N.Y.

WOODWARD, George, physician; b. Wilkes-Barre, Pa., June 22, 1863; s. Stanley and Sarah (Butler) W.; A.B., Yale, 1887, Ph.B., 1888; M.D., U. of Pa., 1891; m. Gertrude Houston, Oct. 9, 1894; children— Henry Howard Houston (killed in action, World War), George, Stanley, George H., Gertrude Houston (dec.). Mem. Phila. Bd. of Health, 1897-1900; mem. Com. of 70; mem. Permanent Relief Com.; ex-pres. Children's Aid Soc., Bur. Municipal Research; trustee Chestnut Hill Acad. (sec., treas.). Mem. Pa. State Senate, 1918-46. Republican. Episcopalian. Mem. Phila. Art Alliance (ex-pres.), Art Alliance Am. (v.p.), Yale Alumni Assn. (ex-pres.). Club: University. Home: Mermaid, cor. McCallum St. Office: Girard Trust Bldg., Phila. Died May 25, 1952; buried St. Thomas (P.E.) Ch. Ground, Whitemarsh, Pa.

WOODWARD, Robert Strong, artist; b. Northampton, Mass., May 11, 1885; s. Orion LeRoy and Mary Eliza (Strong) W.; student Bradley Poly. Inst., Peoria, Ill., 1900-04; unmarried Landscape painter in oil, 1918—; rep. in Springfield (Mass.) Art Museum, Stockbridge (Mass.) Pub. Library, Williston Acad. (Easthampton, Mass.), Northfield Seminary (East Northfield, Mass.), Putnam Memorial Hospital (Bennington, Vt.), Forbes Library (Northampton, Mass.), Syracuse (N.Y.) Museum of Fine Arts, Mass. State Coll., Art Gallery of Mt. Holyoke Coll., Art Gallery of Canajoharie (N.Y.), Yale U. Gallery of Fine Arts, Pasadena (Calif.) Art Inst., Fine Arts Gallery, San Diego, California, Gardner (Mass.) High School. Awarded 1st Halgarten prize at Nat. Acad. of Design, N.Y. City, 1919; hon. mention Concord (Mass.) Art Assn., 1920; 1st landscape prize Springfield (Mass.) Art League, 1927; gold medal of honor Tercentenary Exhibition, Boston, 1930; 2d prize with bronze medal Boston Art Club, 1932; 2d landscape prize Albany (N.Y.) Inst. of History and Fine Arts, 1937; hon. mention Jordan Marsh Exhibition, 1941. Member Am. Water Color Soc., Springfield (Mass.) Art League, Pittsfield (Mass.) Art League, Grand Central Art Galleries of N.Y. City, The Guild of Boston Artists. Episcopalian. Clubs: Salmagundi (N. Y. City); Boston Art (Boston). Home: Buckland, Mass. Address: Shelburne Falls, Mass. Died June 26, 1957; buried Arms Cemetery.

WOODWARD, Roland Beavan; b. Hubbard, O., July 23, 1873; M.A., U. Wooster, 1895; post-grad. work various univs.; LL.D., U. Rochester, 1932; m. Anne Murray Curr; children—Roland Beavan, Anne Murray, John Gordon Harper. Supt. schs., Shreve, O., 1895-97; with Rochester Mechanics Inst., as supt. depts. of mechanics, arts and sciences, 1900-09; apptd. gen. sec. Rochester C. of C., 1909, exec. v.p. since 1929; v.p. Symington-Chicago Corp., mfrs. war munitions, 1918; v.p., later pres. Defender Photo Supply Co., Rochester, 1919-21. Mem. Bd. of Regents, Univ. State of N.Y. Home: 1 Argyle St. Address: 55 St. Paul St., Rochester, N.Y. Deceased.

WOODWARD, Samuel Bayard, physician, banker; b. Worcester, Mass., Aug. 24, 1853; s. Samuel and L. E. R. (Treadwell) W.; A.B., Harvard, 1874, M.D., 1878; m. Margaret Perley, Sept. 16, 1884. Practiced at Worcester, 1881-1921; cons. surgeon City Hosp., 1903—; surgeon Memorial and St. Vincent's hosps.; pres. Worcester County Instn. for Savings, 1913-38, chmn. trustees, 1938—; ex-pres. Washington Mills Emery Co. Pres. Harvard Medical Alumni Assn., 1912-15; pres. Mass. Med. Soc., 1916-19; pres. bd. trustees Memorial Hosp., 1917-28; pres. Worcester C. of C., 1921-23; ex-treas. Antiquarian Soc.; mem. Worcester Fire Soc. Fellow A.A.A.S. Republican. Unitarian. Clubs: Harvard, Bohemian, Worcester, etc. Home: 58 Pearl St. Office: 365 Main St., Worcester, Mass. Died Jan. 29, 1946.

WOODWARD, William E., author; b. Ridge Spring, S.C., Oct. 2, 1874; s. Thomas J. and Etta (Gunter) W.; grad. Citadel Mil. Coll., Charleston, S.C., 1893; Litt.D. (hon.), 1932; m. Helen Rosen, 1913. Was on staff Atlanta Constitution, 1896-98; advt. agy. exec., N.Y.C., 1899-1916; established first nat. lit. review syndicate, 1912; v.p. Industrial Finance Corp., 1916-20; ret. from bus. to devote attention to writing. Mem. Bus. Adv. Council of Dept. of Commerce, 1933-36. Author: Bunk, 1923; Lottery, 1924; Bread and Circuses, 1925; George Washington—The Image and the Man, 1926; Meet General Grant, 1928; Money for Tomorrow (a work on economics), 1932; Evelyn Prentice, 1933; A New American History, 1936; Lafayette (a biography), 1938; The Way Our People Lived, 1944; Tom Paine—America's Godfather, 1945; The Gift of Life (autobiography), 1947; Years of Madness, 1951. Collaborator: Crowded Years (memoirs of William Gibbs McAdoo), 1931. Address: care Harold Ober, 40 E. 49th St., N.Y.C. Died Sept. 27, 1950.

WOODWORTH, Herbert Grafton, author; b. Boston, Feb. 27, 1860; s. Alfred Skinner and Anna Gorton (Grafton) W.; A.B., Harvard, 1882; m. Grace Greenleaf Taylor, Oct. 29, 1884. Mem. Robinson & Woodworth, tea importers, Boston, 1886-1926. Mem. U.S. Tea Bd. by apptmt. of U.S. Govt., to regulate importation of tea, 1897 (chmn. 1914-26), retired 1926. Formerly member com. of classics dept. Harvard. Trustee Home for Aged Women, Boston (v.p., 1929—). Club: St. Botolph. Author: In the Shadow of Lantern Street, 1920; Where the Twain Met, 1935. Home: Brewster, Mass. Deceased.

WOODWORTH, Kennard, investment exec.; b. Boston, Apr. 5, 1905; s. Arthur Vernon and Margaret (Kennard) W.; A.B., Harvard, 1926; student Bus. Sch., 1927-28; m. Adelaide Rice, Oct. 12, 1934; children—Adelaide, Kennard, Martha. Asst. to pres. Boston Ins. Co., 1930-43; v.p., dir. Eaton & Howard, Inc., Boston, 1945-53; pres., dir. Mass. Hosp. Life Ins. Co. and Mass. Life Fund, Boston, 1953—; trustee Mass. Savs. Bank. Mem. Lend-a-Hand Soc. (treas.), Nat. Fedn. Financial Analysts Socs. (pres. 1947-49, sec.-treas. 1951-53), YWCA. Home: Strawberry Hill St., Dover, Mass. Office: 50 State St., Boston 9. Died June 24, 1956.

WOODWORTH, Melvin J., pub.; b. Fenner, N.Y., Mar. 8, 1880; s. Melvin and Ellen M. (Loomis) W.; ed. Cazenovia (N.Y.) Sem. and Eastman Bus. Coll., Poughkeepsie, N.Y.; m. May C. Armstrong, Sept. 6, 1906; 1 son, Walter V. Successively stenographer, reporter, solicitor N.Y. News Bur., 1902-24, controlling owner, pres., 1924—; financial editor The Spur, 1913-29; pres. Central News of Am., affilated with Doremus & Co. advt. agy. 1936—; owner, pres. Ticker Topics, Inc. (N.Y.C.). Republican. Episcopalian. Club: Bankers (N.Y.C.). Home: 300 Park Av. Office: 120 Broadway, N.Y.C. Deceased.

WOODY, Walton L., mfg. exec.; b. Terre Haute, Ind., Feb. 10, 1891; s. Albert and Elizabeth (Vimont) W.; B.S., Rose Poly. Inst., 1914, Rose Poly. Inst., 1953; E.D. (hon.), 1953; m. Nellie May Flesher, Nov. 27, 1914; children—Elizabeth Jane, Walton L., Robert F., Richard Alan. With Nat. Malleable & Steel Castings Co., 1914—, chemist Cleve. plant, 1915-22, asst. gen. supt. Cleve. plant, 1922-26, plant mgr. Cleve. plant, 1926-38, Sharon (Pa.) plant, 1938-42, Sharon and Melrose Park (Ill.) plants, 1942-43, v.p. co. charge mfg., 1943—, dir., 1944—; v.p., dir. Capitol Foundry Co., Phoenix; dir. First Nat. Bank, Sharon, Pa. Mem. Cleve. C. of C. Mem. Am. Foundrymen's Soc. (pres.), Am. Mgmt. Assn., Nat. Assn. Mfrs., Iron and Steel Inst., Nat. Casings Council, Steel Foundry Soc., Malleable Foundry Soc., Tau Beta Pi. Baptist. Clubs: Univ. (Cleve.); Union League (Chgo.); Athletic (Indpls.). Home: 19100 Shaker Blvd., Shaker Heights, O. Office: 10600 Quincy Av., Cleve. 6. Died Oct. 30, 1954.

WOODYATT, Rollin Turner (wood'yät), physician; b. Chgo., June 3, 1878; s. William Henry and Clara (Burnham) W.; grad. Chgo. Manual Tng. Sch., 1897; Cornell, 1897-98; M.D., Rush Med. Coll., 1902; B.S., U. Chgo., 1906; studied European labs., 1906-08; spl. work U. Chgo., 1908-09. Intern. Presbyn. Hosp., 1902-04, later attending physician; apptd. asso. prof. medicine, Rush Med. Coll., 1912; clin. prof., U. Chgo., chmn. dept. medicine, Rush Med. Coll.; now clin. prof. emeritus, U. Ill. Mem. A.M.A., Assn. Am. Phys. (pres. 1935), Am. Soc. Clin. Investigation (pres. 1916), Am. Soc. Biol. Chemists, Am. Chem. Soc., Sigma Xi, Sigma Chi, Phi Rho Sigma. Clubs: University, Cliff Dwellers, Tavern. Contbr. studies in metabolism and nutrition. Home: 237 E. Delawar Place. Office: 700 N. Michigan Av., Chgo. Died Dec. 17, 1953.

WOOLFOLK, William Gordon, cons. engr., corp. exec.; b. Columbus, Ga., Aug. 16, 1877; s. Joseph Washington and Josie (Wilkins) W.; student Sheffield Scientific Sch., Yale, 1899; m. Emma Ward, Apr. 29, 1909; 1 dau., Emma Ward. Practiced in Chicago, 1914—; pres. William G. Woolfolk & Co., 1919-30; president and chairman of executive committee Michigan Consolidated Gas Company, 1932—; chmn. Mich.-Wis. Pipe Line Co., Am. Natural Gas Co. Mem. Chi Phi. Democrat. Episcopalian. Mason (K. T.). Clubs: Chicago (Chicago); Detroit, Detroit Athletic, Bloomfield Hills Country, Grosse Point (Detroit); Yale, The Links, Recess (New York). Home: 415 Burns Drive, Detroit. Office: Michigan Consolidated Gas Co., Detroit, Mich.; Am. Natural Gas Co., N.Y.C. Died Apr. 20, 1954.

WOOLLEN, Evans, Jr., banker; born Indianapolis, Mar. 15, 1897; s. Evans and Nancy (Baker) W. Sr.; grad. Hotchkiss Sch., 1916; A.B., Yale, 1920; LL. D., Hanover Coll., 1948; m. Lydia Douglas Jameson, Oct. 4, 1924; children—Evans, Jameson, Katharine. Joined Fletcher Trust Co., Indpls., 1920, vice pres. 1930-35, pres., dir., 1935-47, chmn. bd., 1948 until consolidation with Am. Nat. Bank, now chmn. of new co. American Fletcher National Bank and Trust Company; dir. State Life Ins. Company. Corporator Crown Hill Cemetery. Trustee of Long College for Women; Mem. bd. govs. James Whitcomb Riley Memorial Hosp. Pres. Indianapolis Bd. Pub. Health and Charities, 1931; board school commissioners, 1941, Community Fund, 1946. Served as 2d lt., 73rd F.A., U.S. Army, 1918. Pres. American Bankers Assn., 1948-49. Democrat. Presbyn. Club: Woodstock. Home: 6800 Dean Rd., Indpls. 20. Office: 108 N. Pennsylvania St., Indpls. 9. Died Jan. 25, 1959.

WOOLLEY, Charles H., pres. Sunset Mag., Inc.; b. near Cincinnati, Feb. 4, 1872; s. George Washington and Blanche (Lyons) W.; ed. pub. schs.; m. Bertha Davis, Oct. 12, 1897; 1 son, Davis (dec.). Began in adv. dept. Scripps-McRae League of Newspapers, 1893; adv. mgr. Cincinnati Post, 1898-99, business mgr., 1899; business mgr. Kansas City (Mo.) World, 1900; same, St. Louis Chronicle, 1901-02, Cleveland World, 1903-05; in stock and bond business, Cincinnati, 1905-11; business mgr. Cincinnati Commercial Tribune, 1912-13; v.p. and business mgr. Sunset Mag., Inc., 1917-25, pub. and pres., 1925-28, pres. since 1928. Republican. Conglist. Mason. Office: 605 Market St., San Francisco 5, Cal. Died Apr. 11, 1952.

WOOLLEY, Helen Bradford Thompson, educator; b. Chgo., Nov. 6, 1874; d. David W. and Isabella P. (Foxon) Thompson; Ph.B., U. Chgo., 1897, fellow dept. of philosophy, 1897-1900, Ph.D., 1900; fellow, Assn. Collegiate Alumnae, U. of Berlin, U. of Paris, 1900-01; m. Paul Gerhardt Wooley, Aug. 8, 1905; children—Eleanor Faxon, Charlotte Gerhardt. Instr. psychology, 1901-02, prof. psychology, dir. psychol. lab., 1902-05, Mt. Holyoke Coll.; experimental psychologist to Bur. of Edn., P.I., 1905-06; instr. philosophy, U. Cin., 1909-11; dir. Bur. for Investigation of Condition of Working children, Cin., 1911-14; dir. vocation bur. pub. schs. of Cin., 1914-21. Research fellow Helen S. Trounstine Found., Cin., 1921-22; asst. dir., psychologist, Merrill-Palmer Sch., Detroit, 1922-26, 1926-30; dir. Child Development Inst., prof. of edn., Tchrs. Coll., Columbia. Del. to 9th Internat. Congress of Psychology, Yale, 1930; del. 3d Conf. of Nursery Sch. Workers, Chgo., 1929; del. 1st Internat. Congress on Mental Hygiene, Washington, 1930; del. White House Conf. on Child Health and Protection, 1930. Fellow A.A.A.S.; mem. Am. Psychol. Assn., Phi Beta Kappa, Laureate Chpt. Kappa Delta Pi. Author: The Mental Traits of Sex, 1903; Mental and Physical Measurements of Working Children, 1914; Diagnosis and Treatment of Young School Failures, 1922; An Experimental Study of Children, 1926; Education and the Pre-School Child (Proceedings of First Internat. Congress on Mental Hygiene), 1930; (chpt. 2) Eating, Sleeping and Elimination—A Handbook of Child Psychology, 1931. Contbr. numerous papers to sci. jours. Address: Kent, Conn. Deceased.*

WOOLLEY, Herbert Codey, physician; b. Monmouth County, N.J., Aug. 27, 1881; s. Levi L. and Nellie (Codey) W.; grad. Temple U., 1900; M.D., Jefferson Med. Coll., Phila., 1904; m. Agnes Hibinbotham, Aug. 24, 1908; children—Richard George, Herbert Codey; m. 2d, Henrietta Croft Beman, Apr. 3, 1937. Began practice at Phila., 1909; clin. dir. St. Elizabeth's Hosp., 1924-29, asst. supt., 1929-37; supt. Pennhurst State Sch., 1937-40; supt. Phila. State

Hosp., 1938-41. Commd. 1st lt. M.R.C., U.S. Army, 1908, and promoted through grades to col.; served as post surgeon Ft. Davis, Alaska, and Ft. Sill, Okla.; fed. examiner State of Okla., 1917; tng. officer personnel 35th Div. (Med. Dept.); organized and comd. 110th Sanitary Train; comd. 1st Sanitary Train, 1st Div., A.E.F.; mil. comdr. Hilschid and Syne areas in occupied Germany; comdg. officer 364th Med. Regt.; col. U.S. Army Reserve. Fellow Am. Psychiatric Assn.; mem. Washington Soc. Mental and Nervous Diesases (ex-pres.), U.S. Power Squadron, Am. Legion (past comdr.), Jefferson Med. Coll. Alumni Assn. (ex-pres.), Chester County and Pa. State Med. socs., Am. Med. Assn., Am. Assn. on Mental Deficiency, Soc. of First Div., U.S. Army, Phi Beta Pi. Republican. Methodist. Clubs: Army and Navy, Army-Navy Country, Internat. Med. Club, Eau Gaillie Yacht. Address: Sea Girt, N.J. Died Aug. 28, 1954; buried Arlington Nat. Cemetery.

WOOLLEY, Robert Wickliffe, lawyer; b. Lexington, Ky., Apr. 29, 1871; s. Frank W. and Lucy (McCaw) W.; student U. Ky., 1886-87, LL.D., 1955; Fordham U., 1887-89; m. Marguerite Holmes Trenholm, Apr. 24, 1900 (died July 1936); children—Marguerite Trenholm, Lucy de Graffenreid (Mrs. Clarence S. List), Florence Trenholm Wicliffe (Mrs. Herbert A. McKee), Frances Howard (Mrs. James S. Robb). Began newspaper work Lexington Leader, 1893; sporting editor Chicago Tribune, 1896-97; on staff of N.Y. World, New York and Washingtpn, D.C., 1897-1905, and 1907-09; chief investigator for Stanley Com., investigating affairs of U.S. Steel Corp., 1911-12; chief of Bur. of Publicity, Dem. Nat. Com., 1912, also editor Dem. campaign textbooks, 1912 and 1914; auditor of the Treasury for the Interior Dept., 1913-15; dir. of the Mint, 1915-16; dir. publicity and mem. Dem. Nat. Campaign Com., 1916; dir. publicity 1st Liberty Loan of 1917; mem. Interstate Commerce Commn., 1917-21; mem. law firm Esch, Kerr, Woolley, Taylor & Shipe, 1929-34; chmn. N.Y. Stockholders' Protective Com. of Mo.-Kan. Pipe Line Co., 1934-37. Del. to Dem. Nat. Conv., 1936-40; chmn. Nat. Dem. Council of D.C., 1935-36. Trustee Frontier Nursing Soc. Mem. Ky. Soc. of Washington, S.R. Episcopalian. Democrat. Clubs: University, Alfalfa, National Press (Washington); Silurians, Kentuckians (New York); Filson (Louisville). Home: The Dresden, 2126 Connecticut Av., Washington 8. Died Dec. 15, 1958; buried Fairfax (Va.) Cemetery.

WOOLMAN, Henry Newbold; b. Phila., Pa., Sept. 3, 1875; s. Edward W. and Rebecca S. (Townsend) W.; student William Penn Charter Sch., 1886-92; B.S., U. of Pa., 1896, hon. Sc.D., 1931; m. Mary S.C. Boude, Nov. 19, 1902 (now deceased); 1 son, Henry Newbold; m. 2d, Mary Lillian Murr, Sept. 24, 1942. Clerk in father's milk business, 1896; joined Supplee Wills Jones Milk Co. (now merged with Nat. Dairy Products Corp.), 1919, now honorary vice-pres.; president Mantua Building Association No. 2. Honorary member Philadelphia Dairy Council. Member Appalachian Trail Conf.; mem. Nat. Com. on Hiking in National Parks. Director of exhibits Sesqui-Centennial Commn. of State of Pa., 1926. Life trustee, mem. exec. bd., chmn. Valley Forge Bd., U. of Pa.; overseer William Penn Charter School; director Pennsylvania State Council, American Youth Hostels, Incorporated; director Wharton Sch. Alumni Soc. of U. of Pa. (pres. 1927-35), Gen. Alumni Soc. of U. of Pa. (pres. 1926-30); mem. Hist. Soc. of Pa., Friend Hist. Soc., Am. Acad. Polit. and Social Science, Phila. Milk Exchange (hon.; pres. 1914), Internat. Assn. of Milk Dealers, Phila C. of C., Centenary Firms of America, Psi Upsilon (exec. council), Beta Gamma Sigma. Republican. Mem. Religious Soc. of Friends. Clubs: Union League, University, Pickering Hunts, Horseshoe Trail (pres.). Home: 132 St. George's Rd., Ardmore, Pa. Died Dec. 27, 1953.

WOOLSON, Abba Louisa Goold, author, farmer; d. Windham, Me., April 30, 1838; d. Hon. William and Nabby Tukey (Clark) Goold; grad. 1856 (valedictorian) Girls' High School, Portland, Me.; m. 1856, Moses Woolson, prin. of that school, who died, 1896. Lecturer on literature and history; founder and hon. pres. Castilian Club, of Boston. Author: Woman in American Society, 1873, Dress Reform, 1874, Browsing Among Books, 1881, George Eliot and Her Heroines—A Study, 1886. Residence; (farm and summer home) Windham Centre, Me.; (winter) Boston. Deceased.

WOOSLEY, John Brooks, prof. economics; b. Asheboro, N.C., Jan. 20, 1892; s. John Evander and Pauline Sophia (Fishel) W.; A.B., Guilford Coll., 1912; A.B., A.M., Haverford Coll., 1914; Ph.D., U. of Chicago, 1931; m. Oma Gray, July 22, 1926. Prof. history and economics, Guilford (N.C.) Coll., 1914-17; prin. Jamestown (N.C.) High Sch., 1919-20; asst. prof. economics U. of N.C., 1920-22; asst. in polit. economy U. of Chicago, 1922-24; asso. prof. economics U. of N.C., 1924-29, prof. since 1930, head depart. of economics and commerce since 1946. Served as lt., U.S. Army, 1917-19. Economic analyst for research com. North Carolina Bankers Assn. since 1937. Mem. Am. Econ. Assn., Am. Finance Assn., Southern Econ. Assn. (v.p. 1934 and 1939, pres. 1940), Beta Gamma Sigma, Sigma Nu. Methodist. Author: State Taxation of Banks, 1935; also reports, articles and monographs, including, The Taxation of Banks (N.C. Tax Commn.), 1928; The Permanent Plan for the Insurance of Bank Deposits, 1936; Differential Elements in North Carolina Banking, 1939; The Capital Problem of Small and Medium Sized Businesses, 1941 (all pub. in Southern Econ. Jour.); eight monographs: Trends in North Carolina Banking (N.C. Bankers Assn.), 1938-45. Address: Box 628, Chapel Hill, N.C. Died Feb., 1956.

WOOTEN, June Price, lawyer; b. Russellville, Ark., Sept. 25, 1878; s. William Price and Mary Elizabeth (Stockard) W.; U. of Ark., 1894-95; grad. Draughon's Business Sch., Nashville, Tenn.; LL.B., U. of Ark., 1902; m. Nelle Palmer, Nov. 11, 1914. Began practice at Little Rock, 1904; mem. Dem. State Com., 1912-20, 1934-40, since 1942, chmn., 1937-38; mem. Dem. Co. Com., Pulaski Co., since 1908; 1st judge Municipal Ct., Civil Div., Little Rock; U.S. atty., Eastern Dist. of Ark., 1919-22; mem. Bd. Law Examiners of Supreme Court of Ark., 1934-35; spl. asso. justice Supreme Court of Ark., 1937. Del. to Dem. Nat. Conv., 1932, 48; Dem. Presidential elector, 1932. Mem. Policemen's Pension Bd., Little Rock, 1931-47. Chmn. Bar Assn. of Ark. Com. on War Work 1944-46. Mem. Am., Ark. and Little Rock bar assns., Phi Alpha Delta. Democrat. Baptist. Contbr. to legal publs. Home: 2908 Gaines St. Office: Pyramid Bldg., Little Rock, Ark. Died Dec. 15, 1950; buried Roselawn Meml. Park, Little Rock, Ark.

WOOTEN, William Preston, ret. army officer; b. LaGrange, N.C., Feb. 14, 1873; s. Shadrach Isler and Henrietta Louise (Harper) W.; Ph.B., U. of N.C., 1893; grad. U.S. Mil. Acad., 1898, Army Engr. Sch., 1902, Army War Coll., 1922; m. Katherine Longworth Clay, Jan. 2, 1904; 1 son, Col. Sidney Clay. Commd. 2d lt., Corps of Engrs., U.S. Army, 1898, and advanced through grades to brig. gen., 1930; during Philippine Insurrection comd. Co. A Bn. of Engrs., 1899-1900, served as engr. officer on Gen. Arthur MacArthur's Staff; served as dist. engr., Dallas, 1905-08; instr. U.S. Mil. Acad., 1908-11; dist. engr., Honolulu, 1911-14; comd. U.S. Engr. Sch., 1914-16; organized and comd. 14th Engrs.; took regiment to France, 1917; made engr., 3d Corps, 1918, Army of Occupation, 1919; dist. engr., Newport, R.I., 1919-20, Detroit, 1920-21; instr. Army War Coll., 1922-26; div. engr. Gulf Div., 1926-27; chmn. Spillway Bd. which submitted plans for Bonnet Carre Spillway and other devices for reducing floods in Lower Miss. River, 1927; dir. procurement, U.S. Army, 1927-30; ret. at own request, 1930. Decorated Order of St. Michael and St. George (Great Britain), Distinguished Service Medal (U.S.). Mem. Soc. Cin., Order of Stars and Bars, Am. Soc. C.E., Soc. Am. Mil. Engrs. (sec. 1931-39), Phi Beta Kappa. Co-author: Wooten-Bowden report of 1921, submitting plans for improvement St. Lawrence River. Editor: The Military Engineer (Soc. Am. Mil. Engrs. jour.), 1931-39. Home: 2540 Massachusetts Av. N.W., Washington. Died Dec. 12, 1950.

WORCESTER, Alfred (wŏŏs'tẽr), physician; born Waltham, Mass., June 22, 1855; s. Benjamin and Mary Clapp (Ruggles) W.; A.B., Harvard U., 1878, A.M., 1881, M.D., 1883; Sc.D., Tufts Coll., 1931; m. Elizabeth Joy Hill, Oct. 19, 1886. Practiced at Waltham, Mass., since 1883; trustee Mass. Hosp. for Consumptives, 1897-1901 (the first state sanatorium for tuberculous patients); founder Waltham Training Sch. for Nurses; chmn. Mass. Commission on Maternity Benefits, 1920. Prof. hygiene, Harvard, 1925-35, prof. emeritus since 1935; one of earliest surgeons to operate for appendicitis. Dep. commr. rank of maj., Am. Red Cross for Switzerland, June 1918-Feb. 1919. Mem. Mass. Med. Soc. (pres. 1919-21), Obstetrical Soc. of Boston, Harvard, Med. Alumni Assn. (ex-pres.). Decorated Officer Order Leopold II by King Albert of Belgium. Mugwump. Episcopalian. Author: Monthly Nursing, 1886; Small Hospitals, 1894; Nurses for Our Neighbors, 1913; Nurses and Nursing, 1927; Selected Medical Papers, American Red Cross Service in Switzerland; Hygiene for Freshman; Sex Hygiene; The Care of the Aged, the Dying and the Dead. Home: Waltham, Mass. Died Aug. 28, 1951.

WORCESTER, Charles Henry (wŏŏs'tẽr), lumberman; b. Detroit, Mich., Sept. 23, 1864; s. Ira and Caroline C. (Cooper) W.; ed. pub. schs., Detroit; m. Mary F. Southwell, Jan. 3, 1894. In employ Farrand, Williams & Co., wholesale druggists, Detroit, 1882-89; mgr. Peninsula White Lead and Color Works, Detroit, 1889-92; investment securities and real estate business, Chicago, 1892-95; in lumber business, 1895-—; now pres. C. H. Worcester Co.; chmn. bd. Munising Paper Co.; director Masonite Corporation, Consolidated Naval Stores Co. (Jacksonville, Fla.). Served in World War as vice chmn. Lumber Com. of Council of Nat. Defense, which later became Lumber Dept. of War Industries Bd. Mem. bd. of trustees of Lawrence College, Appleton, Wis. Hon. pres., and trustee Art Inst. Chicago (chmn. com. coördinating the Inst. with Chicago World's Fair, 1933; chmn. painting and sculpture com.); founder mem. Century of Progress Exposition (Chicago World's Fair 1933); mem. Field Museum of Natural History (life). Republican. Clubs: Chicago, Union League, Attic, Cliff Dwellers, Palette and Chisel, Glenview Golf. Home: 1323 N. State St., Chicago, Ill.; and Chassell, Mich. Office: 135 S. La Salle St., Chgo. Died Mar. 23, 1956.

WORKS, George A., educator; b. Augusta, Wis., May 14, 1877; s. Obadiah and Clarasia (Perry) W.; Ph.B., U. of Wis., 1904, M.S., 1912; Ed.D., Harvard U., 1925; hon. LL.D., Wittenberg Coll., 1934, Luther Coll., 1938, Southwestern, 1939; m. Saidee B. Coerper, Aug. 10, 1904; children—Helen Works Hathcock, Janet Works Reece, Ruth Works Kincheloe, George Alan, David Perry. Supt. of schools, Wisconsin, 1899-1902, 1906-11; instr. rural edn., U. of Wis., 1912-13; asst. prof. rural edn., Univ. of Minn., 1923-14; prof. rural edn., 1914-26, chmn. of div. of edn., 1926-27, Cornell U.; dean of Grad. Library Sch., U. of Chicago, 1927-29; pres. Conn. Agrl. Coll., 1929; prof. Sch. of Edn., U. of Chicago, 1930-42, also dean of students and univ. exam., 1931-41, ret. July 1, 1942. Dir. Nat. Roster Science and Specialized Personnel, 1944-46; sec. United Chapters of Phi Beta Kappa, 1946-47. Dir. rural sch. survey of N.Y., 1921-22; dir. ednl. survey of Tex., 1923-24; dir. surveys of higher edn. in N.C., 1931-32, Ga., 1932-33, 1941-43; dir. survey of Phila. pub. schs., 1936-37. Mem. Montgomery County Governmental and ednl. Survey Board, 1939-40; survey of college and seminaries of the Presbyterian Church, U.S., 1941-42; survey of Minneapolis Public School System, 1942-43; survey of Louisville Public Sch. System, 1942-43; survey for Commn. on Higher Edn. Facilities in Ill., 1944; dir. Survey of Higher Ednl. Instns., 1945-46; survey of De Paul University, 1950. Consultant to Henry Strong Educational Foundation, 1948-50. Secretary Commission on Instns. of Higher Edn., North Central Assn. Colls. and Secondary Schs., 1931-38, president, 1939-40. Fellow American Association for the Advancement of Science, Am. Geog. Soc.; mem. Nat. Soc. for Study of Edn., Delta Upsilon, Phi Beta Kappa, Alpha Zeta, Phi Delta Kappa. Methodist. Mason. Author gen. report and joint author of Organization and Administration, Financial Support, Higher Ed.—Tex. Ednl. Survey, Report; joint author of A Report to the Rural School Patrons, and of Administration and Supervision of the Rural School Survey of New York State; also author College and Univ. Library Problems; joint author The Land Grant Colleges; Rural America Today; also co-author numerous reports on ednl. surveys. Home: 242 Gateway Rd., Ridgewood, N.J. Died Dec. 13, 1957.

WORLEY, John Stephen, cons. engr.; b. Jackson Co., Mo., Apr. 19, 1876; s. Albert Harrison and Mary Elizabeth (Campbell) W.; ed. Odessa (Mo.) Coll.; U. Mo., 1896-97; B.S., and M.S., U. Kan., 1904, C.E., 1922; m. Mayme Lee Baker, Dec. 22, 1897; 1 dau., Mary Louise Symons. Various positions in design and construction of pub. utility plants, steam and interurban rys. in Mo., Kan., Ark., Okla., Mich., Ohio and Ind., 1904-09; bur. of Valuation, 1913-20; federal receiver, exec. v.p. and gen. mgr. Habirshaw Electric Cable Co. and affiliated cos., 1921-27; cons. engr. City of Detroit, 1932-40; cons. engr. U.S. Engr. Corps., 1945-46; cons. engr. econ. and engring. problems cities, states, and Province of Ontario, with appearances before committees of Congress and state legislatures, 1922-53; prof. transportation engring. and curator Transportation Library, U. Mich., 1922-46. Lt. Col., Specialist Res., U.S. Army. Mem. Am. Soc. C.E., Am. Ry. Engring. Assn., Sigma Xi, Tau Beta Pi, Phi Kappa Phi, Sigma Chi, Scabbard and Blade. Methodist. Author of numerous articles and pamphlets on transportation and related subjects. Address: Engineering School, University of Michigan, Ann Arbor, Mich. Died May 25, 1956.

WORMSER, I(saac) Maurice (wûrm'zẽr), lawyer, prof. of law; b. N.Y. City, May 26, 1887; s. Maurice and Lucie Marie (Dahlman) W.; A.B., Columbia, 1906, LL.B., 1909; LL.D., Fordham, 1924; m. Florence Werner, July 20, 1911; children—Franklin Charles, Janice. Practiced in N.Y. City, 1908-11; asst. prof. law, U. of Ill., 1911-13; prof. law, Fordham, 1913-—; consulting and appellate counsel, 1913-—; editor of New York Law Journal, 1919-31. Spl. asst. U.S. atty. and govt. appeal agt. in N.Y., World War; spl. counsel to Transit Commission of New York in 1927; cons. legal counsel to Kings County (N.Y.) Crime Investigation, 1938-41. Mem. N.Y. State Bar Assn., Bar Assn., City of New York, N.Y. Law Inst., Phi Beta Kappa, Phi Alpha Delta, Tau Epsilon Phi; former vice pres. Federal Bar Assn. Author: Wormser on Private Corporations, 1913; Cases on Corporations, revised edit., 1955; Cases on Mortgages, 1925; The Disregard of the Corporate Fiction, 1928; Frankenstein, Inc., 1931. Co-Author: Wormser and Crane's Cases on Private Corporations, 1948. Editor: Keener's Cases on Contracts, 3d edit., 1933; Clark on Corporations, 3d edit., 1916. Home: 168 W. 86th St. Office: 60 Wall St., N.Y.C. 5. Died Oct. 22, 1955; buried Westchester Hills Cemetery.

WORNER, Jno. (John), business exec.; b. New Orleans, May 21, 1888; s. John and Pauline (Frohn) W.; student pub. schs. New Orleans; m. Clara Lindner, Oct. 25, 1909; children—Jno., Mrs. John Boensel. Clk. retail hardware store, 1902; asst. to cons.,

1907; asst. to cons. and buyer wholesale hardware house, 1912-17, cons., buyer, 1917-32; organized Jno. Worner & Son, builders hardware, 1932; partnership since 1942; dir. Union Savs. & Loan Assn. Mem. Nat. Contract Hardware Assn. (past pres.), Am. Soc. Archtl. Hardware Cons. (past pres.), Constrn. Industries Assn., Inc. Elk. Club: New Orleans Athletic. Home: 4168 Iberville St., New Orleans 19. Office: 401-405 Decatur St., New Orleans 16. Died June 15, 1957; buried New Orleans.

WORRELL, William Hoyt (wôr'ĕl), orientalist; b. Toledo, O., Apr. 28, 1879; s. William Clifford and Alta (Hoyt) W.; A.B., U. Mich., 1903; U. Berlin, 1903-04; B.D., Hartford Theol. Sem., 1906; U. Leipzig, 1906-07; Ph.D., U. Strassburg, 1909. Instr. Semitics, U. Mich., 1908-10; instr. Oriental langs. and Hellenistic Greek, Hartford Theol. Sem., 1910-12; in Egypt and Syria, 1912-13; asso. prof. phonetics and instr. Oriental langs., Kennedy Sch. of Missions, Hartford Sem. Foundation, 1913-16, prof., 1916-24; asso. prof. Semitics, U. Mich., 1925-31, prof., 1931-49, emeritus. Dir. Am. Sch. Oriental Research, Jerusalem, 1919-20; Gustav Gootheil lecturer Semitic langs., Columbia, 1921-24; Henry Russel lecturer, U. of Mich., 1941-42. Corr. mem. Société de Archéologie Copte; mem. Mich. Acad. Sci., Arts and Letters, Am. Oriental Soc. Contbr. on Coptic and Semitic philology. Editor: The Coptic Manuscripts in the Freer Collection, 1923; Documents from the Cairo Genizah in the Freer Collection (with Richard Gottheil), 1927; The Proverbs of Solomon in Sahidic Coptic, 1931; Coptic Texts from the U. of Mich. Collection (with collaborators), 1942. Author: Coptic Sounds, 1934; A Short Account of the Copts, 1945. Address: Melbourne Beach, Fla. Died Jan. 1953.

WORST, John H., agriculturalist; b. in Ashland Co., O., Dec. 23, 1850; s. George and Margaret (Martin) W.; ed. Salem Coll., Ashland U. (LL.D.); m. Susan Wohlgamuth, Oct., 1872. Was country sch. teacher, farmer, in mercantile business and editor Fairfield Co. (O.) Republican. Removed to N.D., county supt. schs., Emmons Co., 1883-89; state senator, 1889-94; lt.-gov., 1895-97; pres. N.D. Agrl. Coll., 1895-1916. Republican. Address: Agricultural College, N.D. Died Sept. 25, 1945; buried Inglewood Cemetery, Los Angeles.

WORTH, William E., formerly exec. vice pres. Internat. Harvest Co., ret. 1947. Mem. Nat. Safety Council (past v.p., treas.). Mem. Ill. Mfr. Assn. (past chmn. indsl. com.). Home: 180 N. Michigan Av., Chgo. Deceased.

WORTHAM, James Lemuel, educator; b. Paris, Tex., Nov. 10, 1911; s. James Lemuel and Mazie (O'Neill) W.; A.B., U. Cal. at Los Angeles, 1933; M.A., U. Cal., 1934; Ph.D., Princeton, 1939; m. Mary Aurora Harper, Dec. 31, 1942; children—James Lemuel, Mary Ann, Linnea. Instr. English Occidental Coll., Los Angeles, 1939-42; instr. English U. Cal. at Los Angeles, 1946-48, asst. prof., 1946-50; prof. English, U. Kan., 1950—, chmn. dept., 1950-56. Served as lt. USNR, 1943-46. Mem. Modern Lang. Assn., Nat. Council Tchrs. English, Theta Delta Chi. Home: 615 Louisiana St., Lawrence, Kan. Died Jan. 26, 1958.

WORTHEN, George, justice Utah Supreme Ct. Address: Utah Supreme Court, Salt Lake City. Died Apr. 1958.*

WORTMAN, Denys (wôrt'măn), cartoonist; b. Saugerties, N.Y., May 1, 1887; s. Denis and Jessie (Babcock) W.; student Blair Acad. 1903-04; Stevend Inst. Tech., 1904-05, Rutgers U., 1905-06, N.Y. Sch. of Fine and Applied Art, 1906-09; m. Aimee Kempe, 1913; m. 2d, Hilda Juliet Renbold, 1927; 1 son, Denys. Cartoonist N.Y. World, 1924-30, N.Y. World Telegram and Sun, and United Features Syndicated Papers, 1930-54. Complete collection of proofs of all drawings kept by Metropolitan Museum of Art and N.Y. Pub. Library; painting in New Britain (Conn.) Mus. Art. Portrayed George Washington in re-enactment of his inaugural journey, 1939. Served in U.S. Navy 1918. Mem. Nat. Academy of Design. Mem. Soc. of Illustrators of N.Y. (pres. 1936-37), Nat. Inst. of Arts and Letters, Delta Upsilon. Clubs: Dutch Treat (N.Y. City). Author: Mopey Dick and the Duke, their life and times. Home: Vineyard Haven, Martha's Vineyard, Mass. Died Sept. 20, 1958; buried Reformed Protestant Dutch Church, Hopewell Junction, N.Y.

WRAGG, Samuel Holmes, bus. exec.; b. Needham, Mass., June 9, 1882; s. William and Mary (Holmes) W.; student public schools, Needham, Mass.; m. Henrietta Beless, Aug. 28, 1906; 1 son, William Henry. Errand boy, Samuel Ward Co., Boston, 1895; with John G. Holmes, Phila., 1897-1900, with Frank W. Gorse, Needham, Mass., 1900-17; court officer, County of Norfolk, Mass., 1917-36, sheriff, 1939—; pres. Charles Walton & Son, mfrs., 1933—; dir. Norfolk County Trust Co., Needham Coop. Bank, Norfolk-Dedham Mutual Fire Insurance Co., 1948—. Selectman, Needham, 1914-20; mem. Mass. House of Rep., 1919-24, state senate, 1925-38 (pres. 1937-38). Pres. Middlesex U., Boston, Mass., 1942-45. Moderator, Needham, 1931—. Chmn. Masonic Service Assn. Mason, Grand Master of Masons in Mass., 1946-47 (Shriner, 33°); Odd Fellow. Address: 74 High St., Needham 94, Mass. Died May 13, 1959.

WREDEN, Nicholas (vrä'dĕn), editor; b. St. Petersburg, Russia, Nov. 30, 1901; s. Roman and Emily (Rosinsky) W.; ed. Russian Imperial Naval Acad.; m. Sophie Dalmas, Apr. 14, 1923 (divorced); children—Phyllis (Mrs. C. Richard Harholdt), Nicholas, Peter; married Patricia Clement, Dec. 21, 1945; children—Merrell Clement, Robert Derrick, and James Ramsay. Came to the United States, 1920, naturalized, 1926. Pubs. rep., 1926-31; asst. mgr. Doubleday Doran book shops, St. Louis, Mo., 1932-36, Detroit, Mich., 1936-39; mgr. Scribner book store, New York, N.Y., 1939-44, dir. Charles Scribner's Sons, New York City, 1941-44; vice pres., editor in chief, dir., E. P. Dutton & Co., 1944-54; dir. Chekhov Pub. House; editor in chief, dir. Little, Brown & Company, 1954—, vice president, 1955—. Member of the American Booksellers Assn. (president 1942-43). Club: The Players. Author: The Unmaking of a Russian, 1935. Translator: Dog Lane (Goomilovsky), 1928; Fifth Seal (Aldanov), 1943; Tolstoy and His Wife (Polner), 1945; For Thee the Best (Aldanov), 1945; I'll Never Go Back (Kouakov), 1948; The Specter of Alexander Wolf (Gazdanov), 1950; Taming of the Arts (Jelagin), 1951; Buddha's Return (Gazdanov), 1951; To Live as We Wish (Aldanov), 1952. Home: 89 Abbot St., Andover, Mass. Office: 34 Beacon St., Boston. Died Aug. 6, 1955.

WREN, William Clinton, editor; b. N.Y.C., Aug. 5, 1891; student U. Cal., 1914-16; m. Helen Rolph, 1921; 1 son, William Arnot. Began as newspaper office boy, 1905; city editor San Francisco Examiner, 1924-36, mng. editor since 1936. Served as lt. 312th Inf., 78th Div., U.S. Army, 1917-19. Mem. Sigma Alpha Epsilon. Home: 3 Twelfth Av., San Francisco. Office: San Francisco Examiner, San Francisco 19. Died Aug. 10, 1956; buried Forest Lawn Cemetery, San Francisco.

WRENN, Henry S., newspaperman; b. Belton, S.C., Oct. 22, 1907; s. James Thomas and Elizabeth (Cheek) W.; ed. Greenville (S.C.) High Sch., 1922-25; m. Kathleen Brown, Nov. 29, 1929; children—Elizabeth Sue (adopted), Barbara Kay. Office boy, reporter, Greenville (S.C.) News, 1923; telegraph editor, Wilmington (N.C.) Star; mng. editor, Pensacola (Fla.) Jour.; editor and corr. Asso. Press., 1931-43; pub. Tallahasse News-Democrat, 1943-49; dir. Fla. Legislative Reporters, Inc., 1949—. Mem. Tallahassee C. of C. Elk. Club: Tallahassee Exchange. Home: 1010 Washington St. Office: Center Bldg., Tallahassee. Died June 9, 1958; buried Tallahassee.

WRIGHT, Alfred, lawyer; b. Modesto, Calif., Apr. 26, 1889; s. Christopher Columbus and Mary Ann (Swain) W.; student Stanford, 1906-10, U. Chicago, 1908, U. So. Calif., 1910-12; m. Marie Frances Bobrick, Oct. 30, 1912; children—Gabrielle (Mrs. John Lockwood Bradley), Alfred, Marion Bobrick. Admitted to Calif. bar, 1912 and since practiced in Los Angeles; partner Wright & Garrett 1947, now Wright, Peeler and Garrett. Member American Judicature Soc., American and Los Angeles bar assns., So. Calif. Symphony Assn. (bd. dirs. and exec. com.), Los Angeles Civic Light Opera Assn. (v.p. and dir), Zeta Psi. Republican. Mason. Clubs: Men's Garden (dir.), California, Stock Exchange (Los Angeles); Annandale Golf (Pasadena); Burlingame (Calif.) Country. Home: 2007 Ashbourne Dr., South Pasadena, Calif. Office: 621 S. Hope St., Los Angeles 17. Died Sept. 30, 1952; buried Calvary Mausoleum, Los Angeles.

WRIGHT, Boykin Cabell, lawyer, army officer; b. Richmond, Va., Sept. 20, 1891; s. Boykin and Constance (Cabell) W.; A.B., U. of Ga., 1911; LL.B., Harvard, 1914; m. Miriam Harriman, Sept. 9, 1926; children—Alan H., Boykin C. Mem. firm Wright and Wright, Augusta, Ga., 1914-17; Am. sec. to Supreme Econ. Council at Peace Conf., Paris, 1919; practiced law, N.Y. City since 1919; mem. Cotton and Franklin, 1922, and its successor firms; senior member of Wright, Gordon, Zachry, Parlin & Cahill when re-entered army, Mar. 1943, retired Apr. 1944; resumed law practice; mem. firm, Shearman & Sterling & Wright, since Feb. 10, 1945. Entered 1st Officers Training Camp, 1917; commd. capt., Inf., promoted to major overseas with 82d Div.; brig. gen., May 1943; dir. Internat. Div. Army Service Forces, Washington, 1943-44. Dir. Georgia-Pacific Corp., First Railroad & Banking Co. of Ga., Corning Glass Works, Investors Management Co., Inc., N.Y. City Omnibus Corp., Fifth Av. Coach Lines, Inc., Gray Line Motor Tours, Inc., Augusta Newspapers, Incorporated, Home Insurance Company. Mem. Bar Assn. of the City of New York; mem. bd. mgrs. Memorial Hosp. of N.Y.; dir. Nassau Hosp. of Mineola, Long Island, New York, also the John and Mary Markle Found. Mem. N.Y. Co. Law Assn., Am. and N.Y. State bar assns., Chi Phi. Decorations: Legion of Merit, Silver Star and Victory medals. Democrat. Episcopalian. Clubs: Union, Knickerbocker, Piping Rock, Brook, Links, Down Town (New York); Southside Sportsmen's (L.I.); Laurentian (Can.); Metropolitan (Washington, D.C.). Home: 680 Madison Av., N.Y.C. 21; also Syosset, L.I., N.Y. Office: 20 Exchange Place, N.Y.C. 5. Died Nov. 9, 1956. Buried Locust Valley Cemetery, Locust Valley, L.I., N.Y.

WRIGHT, Charles Henry Conrad, educator; b. Chgo., Nov. 16, 1869; s. Charles Henry and Margaret Barker (Upham) W.; A.B., Harvard, 1891; B.A., Trinity Coll., Oxford U., 1895, M.A., 1899; m. Elizabeth Longfellow Woodman, Apr. 17, 1914; children—Walter Woodman, Charles Conrad, Brooks. Tchr. Harvard, 1895—, prof. French lang. and lit., 1913-36, prof. emeritus, 1936—. Fellow Am. Acad. Arts and Scis.; mem. Modern Lang. Assn. Am., Phi Beta Kappa. Author: A History of French Literature, 1912, rev. edit. 1925; A History of the Third French Republic, 1916; French Classicism, 1920; The Background of Modern French Literature, 1926. Editor: A. France's Le Crime de Sylvestre Bonnard, 1899; Selections from Michelet, 1901; Selections from Rabelais, 1903; Racine's Les Plaideurs, 1906; Molière's Tartuffe, 1906; Selections from Montaigne, 1914; French Lyric Verse of the Sixteenth Century, 1916; Molière's Femmes Savantes, 1920; Selections from Bossuet, 1930; Four Plays of Corneille, 1934. Home: 9 Lowell St., Cambridge 38, Mass. Died May 16, 1957.

WRIGHT, Charles Lovel, banker; b. Orange, Cal., Aug. 27, 1885; s. Charles L. and Clara Alma (Warren) W.; ed. pub. schs.; m. Ellen Louise Andrews, 1936. Began as messenger with Nat. Bank of Cal., Los Angeles, 1901, made chief teller, 1910; asst. cashier First Nat. Bank of Long Beach, Cal., 1912-16; asst. mgr. Long Beach Clearing Housee Assn., 1912-16; cashier Security Nat. Bank of Pasadena, Cal. (title changed 1940 to Union Nat. Bank of Pasadena), 1916-20, v.p. 1920-24, pres., 1925—. Chmn. Ednl. Commn. Cal. Taxpayers Assn., 1926-34; founder, chmn. Pasadena Unit, Cal. Taxpayers Assn., 1926-32; former mem. adv. com. Pasadena Community Chest; dir., v.p. Pasadena C. of C., 1926-29; founder mem., dir., treas. of Pasadena Civic Orchestra, 1929-31; dir. Pasadena Hosp. Assn., 1929-36, treas., 1936; mem. investment com. Huntington Meml. Hosp., 1936—; dir. Pasadena Improvement Assn., 1941-43; gen. chmn. 50th Anniversary Conv. Com., Cal. Bankers Assn., 1941; pres. Pasadena Clearing House Assn., 1941, '47, '51; mem. Town Hall, 1941—; pres. Pasadena Merchants Assn., 1941-42, dir. 1941-47. Rep. Episcopalian. Mason. Clubs: Valley Hunt (Pasadena); Bel Air Bay (Santa Monca). Home: 421 Prospect Square. Office: Union National Bank of Pasadena, Pasadena, Cal. Died May 27, 1954; buried San Gabriel Cemetery, San Gabriel, Cal.

WRIGHT, Donald S(tevenson), lawyer; b. Grenada, Miss., May 16, 1897; s. William Benjamin and Jeanie George (Highgate) W.; B.S., U. Miss., 1918, LL.B., 1920. Admitted to Miss. bar, 1920; pvt. practice law, Greenwood, Miss., 1920-26; co. judge Leflore Co., Miss., 1926-29; atty. G., M. & O. R.R., 1929-40, gen. atty., 1940-46, gen. counsel, 1946-54, vice pres., gen. counsel, 1954—; vice pres., gen. counsel Mobile Investment Co., New Orleans G.N. Ry., GM&O Land Co. Served with aviation detachment U.S.M.C., World War I. Mem. Am., Mobile Co. bar assns., Am. Legion, Phi Delta Theta. Presbyn. Mason (Shriner). Club: Kiwanis. Home: 1306 Dauphin St., Mobile. Office: 104 St. Francis St., Mobile 13, Ala. Died June 5, 1956; buried Grenada, Miss.

WRIGHT, Edward R., judge; b. Skaneateles, N.Y., June 23, 1877; s. Arthur Merrill and Ellen (Reynolds) W.; A.B., Hamilton Coll., Clinton, N.Y., 1898, A.M., 1906; LL.B., New York Law Sch., 1900; m. Eleanor Morison, Nov. 10, 1906 (dec.); 1 dau., Norma Louise (Mrs. W. Hoover). Practiced law at New York, 1900-01, Santa Rosa, N.M., 1901-10, Santa Fe, N.M., 1912-51. Dist. atty., Guadalupe and Quay counties, 1907-10; apptd. asso. justice Supreme Court N.M., term 1910-11; chmn. bd. dirs. and atty. First Nat. Bank of Santa Fe, N.M., 1934-55. Republican. State senator, Santa Fe County, 1921-25. Pres. N.M. State Bar Assn., 1923-25; chmn. State Board Bar Examiners, 1923-31; mem. State Bd. Penitentiary Commrs., 1927-33, chmn. bd., 1927-31. Mem. Phi Beta Kappa, Chi Psi. Mason (33° Hon.); Dep. Supreme Council (Scottish Rite) in N.M., 1929-35. Home: 165 E. Houghton St., Santa Fe. Died May 22, 1956.

WRIGHT, Fielding Lewis, ex.-gov.; b. Rolling, Fork, Miss., May 16, 1895; s. Henry James and Fannie (Clements) W.; ed. Webb Sch., Belbuckle, Tenn., Univ. of Ala.; m. Nan Kelly, July 16, 1917; children—Fielding Lewis, Elaine. Admitted to the Miss. bar; served as Miss. state senator, 1928-32; mem. Miss. House of Reps., 1932-40, speaker of the House, 1936-40; lt. gov. of Miss., 1944-46, governor of Miss. Nov. 1946-Jan. 1948 (to complete term of Governor T. L. Bailey), and 1948-52, now practicing law Jackson and Rolling Fork, Miss. Methodist. Home: Rolling Fork, Miss. Office: Deposit Guaranty Bank Bldg., Jackson, Miss. Died May 4, 1956; buried Rolling Fork, Miss.

WRIGHT, Frank James, geologist; b. Bridgewater, Va., Nov. 22, 1888; s. Robert Joseph and Alice Mary (Sanger) W.; A.B., Bridgewater (Va.) Coll., 1908, LL.D., 1947; A.M., U. of Va., 1911; Ph.D., Columbia, 1918; m. Anna Catherine Zigler, Aug. 15, 1914; children—Robert James, Harold Douglas. Prof.

geology, Bridgewater Coll., 1911-24, dean, 1921-24; prof. geology Denison U., 1924-49, emeritus; vis. asso. in physiography, Columbia, 1923-24, teacher, summers, 1918, 1920-26, 28, 30, 31, 36, 37, 38, 1940-43. Director Mutual Cold Storage, Incorporated, Broadway, Va., 1918-45. Mem. Virginia House of Delegates, 1916-20. Mem. bd. editors, Geol. Society of Am. 1943-46. Awarded Walker Memorial Prize by Boston Soc. Natural History, 1922; A. Cressy Morrison Prize in Natural Science by N.Y. Acad of Sciences, 1931. Fellow Geol. Soc. America, A.A.A.S.; mem. Assn. of Am. Geographers, Ohio Acad. of Science (v.p. 1931, 38), Am. Assn. of Univ. Profs., Phi Gamma Delta, Phi Beta Kappa (pres. Denison chapter, 1935-38), Sigma Xi, Omicron Delta Kappa. Republican. Mem. Ch. of the Brethren. Author various bulletins and papers on geol. subjects, especially the Southern Appalachians. Home: Granville O. Died Sept. 5, 1954; buried Oak Lawn Cemetery, Bridgewater, Va.

WRIGHT, Frank Lee, prof. edn.; b. Bronson, Kan., Mar. 16, 1884; s. John Lewis and Laura Ann (Wilson) W.; life diploma, Kan. State Teachers' Coll., Emporia, Kan., 1908, A.B., same, 1910; A.M., U. of Wis., 1915; Ed.M., Harvard, 1924; Ed.D., 1925; m. Nancy Leota Busenbark, Aug. 10, 1910; children—Homer Lee, Frank Leon, Evan Leonard. Teacher rural schs. of Kan., 1902-04; teaching fellow Kan. Teachers' Coll., 1907-08; head of normal training dept. Emporia High Sch., 1909-10; supt. schs., Bucklin, Kan., 1910-14; asst. in edn., U. of Wis., 1914-15; prof. edn., State Teachers Coll., Greeley, Colo., 1915-23; prof. ednl. psychology Sam Houston Teachers' Coll., Huntsville, Tex., summer, 1920; lecturer on edn., Boston U., 1923-24; prof. edn. and head of dept., Washington University, St. Louis, 1924-53, dir. summer session, 1941-49. Lecturer in edn., New York U., summer, 1933, U. of Washington, summer, 1939. Past pres. Board of Edn. of Webster Groves, Mo., Mo. Assn. of Sch. Boards; member St. Louis Bd. of Edn., since 1951. Mem. N.E.A., Nat. Soc. for Study of Edn., Nat. Soc. Coll. Teachers of Edn., Mo. Ednl. Assn., Am. Assn. of Sch. Adminstrs., Phi Delta Kappa, Kappa Delta Pi (exec. pres. council), Pi Kappa Delta, Pi Gamma Mu. Methodist. Contbr. to edn. jours. on sch. bd. problems. Home: 5947 Waterman Av., St. Louis 12. Died Nov. 10, 1953; cremated; Bronson, Kan.

WRIGHT, Frank Lloyd, architect; b. Richland Center, Wis., June 8, 1869; s. William Russell Cary and Anna Lloyd (Jones) W.; student civil engring., U. of Wis., 1884-88; m. Catherine Lee; children—Lloyd, John, Catherine, David, Frances, Llewellyn; m. 2d, Miriam Noel; m. 3d, Olga Lazovich, Aug. 25, 1928; 1 dau., Iovanna. Began practice at Chicago, Ill., 1893; architect of Imperial Hotel, Tokio, Japan, and numerous other buildings of note; work characterized in America as "The New School of the Middle West" and in Europe as "The American Expression in Architecture." Phi Delta Theta; hon. mem. Academie Royale des Beaux Arts d'Anvers, 1927, Nat. Acad. of Cuba, 1927, Nat. Acad. of Brazil, 1932, Royal Inst. British Achitects, 1941, Nat. Acad. Architects, Mexico, 1943, Nat. Acad. of Finland, 1946; hon. mem. Nat. Acad. and Society of Architects (Uruguay), 1942; extraordinary hon. mem. Akademie der Kunst (Royal Acad.), Berlin, 1929; hon. mem. Am. Inst. Decorators, Am. Nat. Inst. Arts and Letters; life member American Academy Arts and Letters. Honored guest of the Soviet Republic, 1937. Awarded Royal Gold Medal for Architecture by King George VI, 1941; Gold Medal of A.I.A., 1948. Hon. Doctor of Fine Arts, Princeton, 1947, M.A., Wesleyan U., 1939. Architect Imperial Household, Japan, 1914; high honors, Holland and Switzerland, 1921; Gold Medal by Am. Inst. Architects, 1949; Star of Solidarity (Italy). Clubs: Players (N.Y.); Tavern (Chicago). Author: An Interpretation of Japanese Prints, 1912; In the Cause of Architecture (essays), 1909-23; Experimenting with Human Lives, 1923; Ausgeführte Bauten und Entwürfe, 1909, Sonderheit, 1910; Wendingen, 1925 (last three pub. in Europe); Modern Architecture (Kahn lectures at Princeton), 1931; The Nature of Materials, 1932; An Autobiography—Frank Lloyd Wright, 1932, later revised, expanded and brought up to date, 1943; The Disappearing City, 1932; Architecture and Modern Life (with Baker Brownell); Frank Lloyd Wright on Architecture, 1894-1940 (edited by Frederick Gutheim); In the Nature of Materials (edited by Henry-Russell Hitchcock), 1941; When Democracy Builds, 1946; Genius and the Mobocracy, 1949. The founder and the conductor of the "The Taliesin Fellowship," a cultural experiment in the arts, by way of a non-profit organization entitled The Frank Lloyd Wright Foundation situated at "Taliesin" in Wis. (Apr.-Nov.) and Ariz. (Dec.-Mar.), about 40 apprentices participating. Editor of "Taliesin," Fellowship magazine, pub. 6 times a year; and The Taliesin Square Papers pub. from time to time at Taliesin. Home "Taliesin," Spring Green, Wis.; and "Taliesin West," Paradise Valley, Phoenix, Ariz. Died Apr. 9, 1959.

WRIGHT, Frederick Eugene, geologist; b. Marquette, Mich., Oct. 16, 1877; s. Charles Eugene and Carolyn Alice (Dox) W.; grad. Ann Arbor High Sch., 1895; student Realgymnasium, Weimar, Germany, 1895-96; Ph.D., U. of Heidelberg, 1900; hon. Sc.D., U. of Mich., 1940; m. Kathleen Ethel Finley, June 16, 1909; children—Kathleen Margaret (dec.), Frederick Hamilton, Mary Helen, William Finley, Kenneth Aldro. Instr. petrology, Mich. Coll. of Mines, 1901-04; asst. state geologist of Mich., 1903-04; asst. geologist, 1904-05, geologist, 1906-17, U.S. Geol. Survey; petrologist Geophys. Lab., Carnegie Instn., Washington, 1906-44, ret. Commd. capt. Ordnance Res. Corps, 1917; maj. U.S. Army, 1918-19; lt. col., Ordn. Res. Corps, 1919, col., 1928; chief physicist, A.S.F., War Dept., Jan. 1942 to Jan. 1946. Awarded exceptional service medal, U.S. Army, 1945. Fellow Am. Acad. Arts and Sciences, Phys. Soc. London, A.A.A.S.; mem. Nat. Acad. Sciences (v.p. 1927-31; home sec. 1931-51), Mineral. & Geology (foreign member) socs., London, Am. Philos. Soc., Mineral. Society America (pres. 1941, Roebling Medal, 1952), Geological Society America, American. Phys. Soc. Optical Soc. America (pres. 1917-19), Astron. Soc. America, Washington Acad. Sciences, Am. Inst. Mining and Metall. Engrs., Army Ordnance Assn., Nat. Research Council, Am. Geophys. Union, Sigma Xi. Republican. Baptist. Clubs: Cosmos. Writer of papers of petrologic and phys. nature. Home: 2134 Wyoming Av., Washington 8. Office: 1530 P St., Washington 5. Died Aug. 25, 1953.

WRIGHT, George Hand, artist; b. Fox Chase, Pa., Aug. 6, 1872; s. William Hamilton and Elizabeth W.; ed. pub., private schs.; studied art at Acad. Fine Arts, Spring Garden Inst., Phila.; m. Anna Boylan, Feb. 6, 1906. Began as illustrator, Phila., 1892. Mem. Soc. of Illustrators (pres. 1925-26), Artists' Guild, Soc. Am. Etchers; A.N.A., 1936, N.A., 1939. Clubs: Salmagundi (pres.), Dutch Treat (New York). Home: Westport, Conn. Died Mar. 13, 1951.

WRIGHT, Graham, lawyer; b. Rome, Ga., Feb. 22, 1892; s. Seaborn and Anna (Moore) W.; LL.B., U. of Ga., 1911; m. Mary Ann Tucker, May 5, 1913 (div. Jan. 1941); children—Bettye Ann (Mrs. Donald Livingston), Graham, James Aiken; m. 2d, Aline Tatum Thompson, Jan. 1941. Admitted to Ga. bar, 1911, since practiced in Rome; now mem. firm Wright & Glover; asst. atty. gen. of Ga., 1919-20. Mem. Ga. State Bd. of Bar Examiners 1936-53. Mem. Ga. Bar Assn. (pres. 1934-35), Sigma Alpha Epsilon, Phi Delta Phi. Presbyterian. Home: 307 4th Av. Office: Baron Bldg., Rome, Ga. Died Oct. 13, 1958; buried Mrytle Hill Cemetery, Rome, Ga.

WRIGHT, Hamilton Mercer, writer; b. New Haven, Conn., Dec. 29, 1875; s. Hamilton M. and Anne Dana (Fitzhugh) W.; student U. of Mich., 1895, U. of Colo., 1896, LL.B., 1899; m. Cora Elizabeth Pease, 1900; children—Hamilton Mercer, Eugene Pease, Richard Wm., Peter Craig. Instr. Law Sch., U. of Southern Calif., 1899-1900; on staffs Los Angeles Times, Herald, Saturday Post until 1903; with Bur. Information Calif. Promotion Com., 1903-05; wit . Pacific Commercial Museum in Philippine Islands, 1905-06; editor Overland Monthly, 1907; staff San Francisco Examiner, 1907-11; editor in chief San Francisco Expn., 1911-15 (gold medal of honor); toured Central and S. America, contributing to Pan-Am. Union, 1916-17; corr. in France, 1918; information dir. Fla. E. Coast Railway, 1922-29, City of Miami, 1927-31, Govt. of Egypt, 1932-40, 1947-49; Atlantic Coast Line Railroad, 1940-42; pres. Hamilton Wright Organization, publicizing Canadian industries, 1942-47; editing, distributing news reels for British govt., 1944-46, state of Florida, 1946, P.R., 1948-52, govt. of Chile, 1949-51, commonwealth of Puerto Rico, 1948-—, govt. of Venezuela, 1951-—. Vice pres. Fla. State C. of C., 1931-32, 33, 34; toured Nile Valley Basin (studying government irrigation scheme), 1933-35. Republican. Episcopalian. Author: Handbook of Philippines, 1905; America Across the Seas (with John F. Stevens and others), 1912. Regular contbr. to mags. and newspapers. Home: 620 Winters St., West Palm Beach, Fla. Office: 30 Rockefeller Plaza, N.Y.C. Died Apr. 10, 1954; buried West Palm Beach, Fla.

WRIGHT, Horace Melville, farmer, fox rancher; b. Bedeque, Prince Edward Island, Jan. 7, 1879; s. Thomas and Mary Alice (Hooper) W.; ed. Bedeque Sch., 1897, Prince of Wales Coll., 1897-1899; m. Minnie M. Ross, June 20, 1904; children—William Ross, Winnifred I., Horace M., John Sidney, Pres., Malpeque Oyster Co., Ltd., v.p., P.E.I. Potato Growers Assn. Chmn. Workmen's Compensation Bd., Prince Edward Island. Mem. Provincial Legislature; pres. Exec. Council, 1940-43. Chmn. Regional War Labor Bd. and minister in charge of evacuee children, World War II. Liberal Party. Mem. United Ch. of Can. Home: Bedeque, Prince Edward Island, Can. Died Jan. 21, 1951; buried Lower Bedeque Cemetery.

WRIGHT, James Lloyd, newspaper corr.; b. New Hampton, Ia., Oct. 12, 1885; s. George Cyrus and Mary Jane (Hamilton) W.; grad. high sch., New Hampton, 1903; m. Marie A. Johnson, Oct. 20, 1916; children—Richard Hamilton, Donald. Printer New Hampton (Ia.) Gazette, 1902-03; became a reporter Waterloo (Ia.) Reporter, 1905; same, Sioux City Journal, 1908, Des Moines Register and Leader, 1909-10, Washington (D.C.) Times, 1911; asst. Washington corr. for Detroit News, 1911-15, Cleveland (O.) Plain Dealer, 1915-27; Washington corr. Buffalo Evening News since 1927; pres. Nat. Press Bldg. Corp. Assigned to cover trip of President-elect Hoover on "Good Will" tour to Latin-America, 1928-29; assigned to Germany, France, England for series of articles, 1935; as newspaper correspondent with naval convoy with U.S. troops to Iceland, 1941, prior to U.S. entry into World War II; on U.S.S. Philadelphia for initial "Magic Carpet" trip bringing troops home from France by warship, Nov. 1945. Member Nat. Press Club (bd. of govs.); chmn. standing com. of corrs. controlling press galleries of Congress, 1924-25. Republican. Mason. Clubs: Gridiron (ex-pres.), Columbia Country, Nat. Press, Overseas Writers, Alfalfa, Variety. Contbr. to magazines. Home: 3115 44th St. N.W. Office: National Press Bldg., Washington. Died Dec. 7, 1952.

WRIGHT, John Womack, army officer, writer; b. Kirkwood, Mo., July 10, 1876; s. Brig. Gen. Marcus Joseph (Confederate Army) and Pauline (Womack) W.; student William and Mary Coll., 1892-95, LL.D. (hon.) from same, 1947; LL.B., George Washington University, 1898; graduate Army School of the Line, 1921; m. Helen Elizabeth Hyde, Sept. 1905; 1 dau., Pauline Hyde. Commd. 1st lt. and adjutant, 5th U.S. Vol. Inf., 1898; promoted capt., 1899, serving on staff of Gen. Leonard Wood at Santiago de Cuba; apptd. 2d lt. 5th U.S. Inf. Regular Army 1899, advancing through the grades to col., 1923; retired, 1940; recalled to active duty, 1941, assigned sec. of hist. sect. Army War College; comdt. Baracoa Mil. Dist. under mil. govt. of Cuba, 1899-1902; while there and in Puerto Rico, directed restoration and improvement of ancient fortifications, barracks and other edifices. Chief of information div. Army of Cuban Pacification, 1906-09; asst. chief of staff, G-3, Services of Supply, A.E.F., Tours, France, 2 yrs.; comdr. 5th U.S. Inf. and Harbor Defenses, Portland Me. Aug. 1925-Sept. 1929; prof. mil. science and tactics, U. of Mo., 1929-33; comdr. 65th Inf. and U.S. forces in Puerto Rico, 1936-39. Decorated Distinguished Service Medal, Spanish-Am. War, Cuban Occupation, Cuban Pacification, Mex. Expeditionary Force and World War I campaign medals (U.S.), Officer Legion of Honor (France); Comdr. Order of Isabel the Catholic (Spain). Hon. citizen of Baracoa (Cuba) and San Juan (Puerto Rico). Presented sword by city of Portland, Me. Mem. Soc. of the Cincinnati, Am. Hist. Assn., Phi Beta Kappa, Kappa Sigma. Episcopalian. Clubs: Army and Navy (Washington, D.C., and Governor's Island, N.Y.). Author: Road Notes on Cuba, 1909; The Organization of the Services of Supply in the A.E.F., 1921; Warfare, a Study of Military Methods from the Earliest Times (with others), 1935; Development of Bastioned Fortifications from 1500 to 1800, 1946. Co-author: History of the Second Division A.E.F., 1937-38. Contbr. to William and Mary Coll. Quar., Am. Hist. Rev. and Dictionary of Am. Biography. Home: 1851 Columbia Rd. N.W., Washington. Died Feb. 2, 1952; buried Arlington Nat. Cemetery.

WRIGHT, Louis Tompkins, surgeon; b. LaGrange, Ga., July 23, 1891; s. Ceah Kentchen and Lulu (Tompkins) W.; A.B., Clark U., Atlanta, Ga., 1911, D.Sc., 1937; M.D., Harvard, 1915; m. Corinne M. Cooke, May 18, 1918; children—Jane Cooke, Barbara Penn. Interne, Freedmens Hosp., Washington, D. C., 1916-17; began practice of surgery, N.Y. City, 1919; mem. surg. staff Harlem Hosp. since 1920, also surg. dir.; police surgeon, N.Y. City Police Dept.; pres. Crisis Pub. Co.; pres. med. bd. Harlen Hosp.; mem. exec. com. and adv. council, Dept. of Hosps., City of New York; med. advisor to N.Y. City dir. Selective Service. Served as lt., later captain, Medical Corps, A.E.F., with Field Hosp. 366, during World War I; formerly lt. col. Med. Res. Corps. Decorated Purple Heart; Springarn Medallist. Diplomate Am. Bd. of Surgery; hon. fellow Internat. Coll. of Surgeons; fellow Am. Coll. Surgeons, A.M.A., N.Y. Surgical Soc., Am. Acad. Compensation Medicine; mem. A.A.A.S., N.Y. Academy of Science, Nat. Assn. Advancement Colored People (chmn. bd. dirs.), N. Y. County, N. Y. State and Manhattan med. socs., Uptown Med. Center Assn. (past sec.). A founder John A. Andrew Clin. Soc. (Tuskegee, Ala.); founder Harlem Surg. Soc. Author chapter on head injuries, Treatment of Fractures by Scudder, 11th edit. Contbr. numerous articles on med. and surg. subjects to various publs. Pioneered in use aureomycin in humans. Address: 218 W. 139th St., N.Y.C. 30. Died Oct. 8, 1952.

WRIGHT, Norris N., mfg. exec.; b. Newark, Del., Mar. 29, 1886; s. Samuel J. and Isabel (Pilling) W.; student at University of Delaware also Swarthmore Prep. School; married Fleta Robertson, June 3, 1921; children—Eugenia Isabel, Martha. Vice pres. and dir., Continental-Diamond Fibre Co., 1929-47, pres. since 1947; v.p. and dir. Newark Trust Co. Served as state senator, 1934-38. Mem. State Bd. Edn., 1933-35. Mason. Clubs: Union League, Wilmington, Wilmington Country. Office: 70 S. Chapel St., Newark, Del. Died Mar. 27, 1951; buried Newark, Del.

WRIGHT, Walter Henry, educator, dentist; born southwest Pa., Feb. 18, 1893; s. Elmer Henry and Martha (Dean) W.; D.D.S., U. Pittsburgh, 1917,

B.S., 1931, M.S., 1932, Ph.D., 1934; m. Esther Emily Prugh, Mar. 31, 1916; 1 son, David Walter (U.S.N.). Practice of dentistry, Pittsburgh, 1935-46; lecturer anatomy, 1918-19; asst. prof. anatomy and clin. prosthesis, 1919-20; asso. prof. prosthetic dentistry, 1933-37, prof. of anatomy and prosthesis, 1938-June, 1946, U. Pittsburgh Sch. of Dentistry; prof. of prosthetic dentistry and dean N.Y.U. Coll. Dentistry since 1946; dental cons. to surgeon gen. U.S. Army, also cons. to Vets. Adminstrn. Served as dental consultant to surgeon gen. U.S. Army, World War II. Advisor Health Council Greater N.Y. Fellow Am. Coll. Dentists (past pres.); mem. Am. Dental Assn. (past chmn. prosthetic sect.), A.A. A.S., Am. Assn. Anatomists, Am. Acad. Cleft Palate Prosthesis (pres. 1946), Am. Assn. Univ. Profs., Am. Assn. Dental Schs. (chmn. plans and projects com.), Internat. Assn. for Dental Research, Nat. Soc. Denture Prosthesis (past pres.), Nat. Bd. Dental Examiners, Odontol. Soc. of Western Pa., Pa. State Dental Soc., N.Y. Acad. of Dentistry, Omicron Kappa Upsilon (past pres.), Omicron Delta Kappa, Sigma Xi, Phi Sigma, Delta Sigma Delta. Contbr. about 65 articles on the teaching and practice of dentistry, dental edn., research reports in dental jours. Past dir. Men's Glee Club, U. Pittsburgh. Home: 43 Fifth Av., N.Y.C. 3. Office: N.Y.U. Coll. of Dentistry, 209 E. 23d St., N.Y.C. 10. Died Dec. 31, 1951.

WRIGHT, Warren, capitalist; b. Springfield, O., Sept. 25, 1875; s. William Monroe and Clara Lee (Morrison) W.; ed. pub. grammar and high schs. and business coll. Began as office boy with the Calument Baking Powder Co., 1890, and since identified with the company in various capacities, becoming pres., 1899; propr. Warren Wright, investment securities. Owner of Calumet Farm, Lexington, Ky., thoroughbred horse breeding and racing. Republican. Presbyterian. Clubs: Chicago Athletic Assn.; Jockey, Bath, Indian Creek (Miami Beach, Fla.); Idlewild Country (Lexington, Ky.). Home: Miami Beach, Fla. Office: 33 N. La Salle St., Chicago. Died Dec. 28, 1950; buried Rosehill Cemetery, Chicago.

WRIGHT, William Hammond, astronomer; b. San Francisco, Nov. 4, 1871; s. Selden Stuart and Joanna Maynard (Shaw) W.; B.S., U. Cal., 1893, grad. student, 1894-96, U. Chgo. (Yerkes Obs.), 1896-97; D.Sc., Northwestern U., 1929; m. Elna Warren Leib, Oct. 8, 1901. Asst. astronomer Lick Obs., 1897-1908, astronomer, 1908-44, emeritus, 1941—, dir., 1935-42, in charge obs.' expdn. to So. Hemisphere, 1903-06. Served as capt. Ordnance U.S. Army, 1918-19. Fgn. asso. Royal Astron. Soc. London; mem. Nat. Acad. Sci.; Am. Philos. Soc., Am. Astron. Soc. Contbr. astron. publs. Address: 60 N. Keeble Av., San Jose 26, Cal. Died May 16, 1959; buried Oak Hill Cemetery, San Jose, Cal.

WRIGHT, William Kelley, prof. philosophy; b. Canton, Ill., Apr. 18, 1877; s. Nathaniel Stephen and Laura (Kelley) W.; grad. Lake Forest (Ill.) Acad., 1895; student Amherst Coll.; A.B., U. of Chicago, 1899, Ph.D., 1906; studied U. of Freiburg, 1909, univs. of Oxford and London, 1912-13; m. Gertrude Beryl Sly, June 21, 1916; children—Lois Laura (Mrs. S. C. Brown), Stanley Proctor (1st lieut., U.S.M.C., killed in action, 1943). Dry goods business, Canton, Illinois, 1899-1903; instructor philosophy, U. of Tex., 1906-07, U. of Chicago, 1907-09, U. of Wis., 1909-11, Ind. U., 1911-12, Cornell U., 1913-16; asst. prof. philosophy, Dartmouth, 1916-23, prof., 1923-47, emeritus, 1947—. Mem. Am. Philos. Assn. (pres. 1945), American Theological Society (president 1937), Phi Gamma Delta. Republican. Conglist. Club: Graduate. Author: Ethical Significance of Feeling, Pleasure and Happiness, 1907; A Student's Philosophy of Religion, 1922, revised edit., 1935, General Introduction to Ethics, 1929; A History of Modern Philosophy, 1941. Editor: (with T. V. Smith) Essays in Philosophy, 1929. Contbr. to Religious Realism, 1931. Home: Hanover, N.H. Died Mar. 29, 1956; buried Hanover.

WRIGHT, William Ryer, cons. engineer; b. N.Y. City, July 31, 1888; s. William Franklin, M.D., and Marie Louise (Ryer) W.; grad. Stevens School, Hoboken, N.J., 1907; E.M., Sch. of Mines (Columbia Univ.), 1911; m. Agnes R. Mackenzie, Feb. 18, 1913; children—Agnes Louise, William Ryer, Jr., Barbara Ashley. Began practice in N.Y. City, 1905; on Hudson Tunnel constrn., 1907; engr. with Braden Copper Co., 1911-12, Stafford & Wright, 1912-14, W. & W. F. Crockett, 1914-15, Aetna Explosives, Inc., 1916-17, Smith & Serrell, 1919-21; Chicago manager (partner) Ford, Bacon & Davis, Inc., consulting engrs., 1921-50 (retired from business activity with firm, July 1950, retaining connection as stockholder-partner); now in private practice as cons. engr.; State of Ill., since Nov. 1945. Served as 1st lt. Ordnance Dept., U.S. Army, 1917-19; formerly lt. col. Ordnance Reserve. Fellow, Am. Geographical Soc. Mem. Am. Institute Mining and Metallurgical Engineers (past dir.) Mining and Metall. Soc. of Am., Western Soc. Engineers, English-speaking Union, Acad. Polit. Science, S.R., Fraunces Tavern (N.Y. State), Army Ordnance Assn. (dir. Chicago Post), Delta Kappa Epsilon. Republican. Presbyterian. Mason. Clubs: University, Exmoor Country. Home: 1167 Lincoln Av. S., Highland Park, Ill. Died Nov. 27, 1952.

WRIGHT, William Thomas, Jr., asst. surgeon gen. ret.; b. Rue, Va., Feb. 25, 1891; s. William Thomas and Annie Jackson (Bundick) W.; D.D.S., U. Md., 1914; m. Jean Boteler, Oct. 25, 1919; children—John Boteler, Joanne Louise. In practice of dentistry, Balt., 1914-17; commd. officer U.S. Pub. Health Service, 1920, advanced through grades to asst. surgeon gen.; chief dental officer in charge of all dental activities in U.S.P.H.S., Coast Guard, Maritime Tng. Service, Indian affairs, Fed. Correctional and Penal Insts., 1941-48. Served as dental officer with 2d div. in 5 maj. engagements; with Army of Occupation in Germany, World War I. Decorated Fourragere (France). Del. Am. Dental Assn. Mem. Xi Psi Phi, Omicron Kappa Upsilon (hon. mem.). Democrat. Episcopalian. Mason. Home: 4704 Locust Hill Circle, Bethesda 14, Md. Died Mar. 20, 1954; buried Arlington Nat. Cemetery.

WRIGHTSMAN, Charles John, lawyer, oil producer; b. Dayton, O., Sept. 7, 1870; s. Peter R. and Elizabeth (Witter) W.; LL.B., Georgetown U., 1890, LL.D., 1955; m. Edna Wrightsman, Jan. 1894; 1 son, Charles Bierer. Admitted to bars of territorial, various states and fed. courts; active practice at Oklahoma City, 1890; elected territorial senator from Pottawatomie County to 2d Legislative Assembly, 1892; county atty. Pawnee Co. (with jurisdiction over Osage and Otoe Indian reservations), 1893; U.S. commr., 1895-99; engaged in practice of law, Tulsa, Oklahoma, 1906-12; entire time given to oil and gas interests, 1912—; moved to Ft. Worth, 1936. Originator depletion allowance of oil, gas and other minerals, also proratable taking of gas from producing wells. Pres. bd. regents U. Okla., 1923-26; chmn. Ty. Dem. convs., 3 times; chmn. Okla. delegation Dem. Nat. Conv., Kansas City 1900, also v.p. of conv. (for Okla. Ty.). Mason. Clubs: Ft. Worth, Rivercrest Country, Ridglea Country, Exchange. Home: 935 Hill Crest. Office: W. T. Waggoner Bldg., Ft. Worth. Died May 30, 1959; buried Hillcrest Mausoleum, Dallas.

WRONG, H. Hume, Can. pub. service; b. Toronto, Ont., Can., Sept. 10, 1894; s. George M. and Sophia (Blake) W.; student Upper Can. Coll., Toronto, Ridley Coll., St. Catharines, Ont.; B.A., U. of Toronto, 1915; M.A., B.Litt., Oxford U., 1921; m. Joyce Hutton, Dec. 22, 1922; children—Dennis, June. Became lectr., asst. prof. history, U. of Toronto, 1921-27; apptd. 1st sec. Can. Legation in Washington, 1927; promoted counsellor, 1930; apptd. permanent del. of Can. to League of Nations, Geneva, 1937; spl. econ. adviser, Can. House, London, 1939-40; minister counsellor, Can. Legation, Washington, 1941-42; asst. undersec. of State for External Affairs, Ottawa, 1942; asso. undersec., 1944-46; Canadian ambassador in Washington, 1946-53; undersec of state for external affairs, Ottawa, 1953—. Served in Inf. and Air Force, World War I, 1915-19, capt. on demobilization. Club: Rideau (Ottawa); Metropolitan, Chevy Chase (Washington). Author: The Government of the West Indies: Sir Alexander Mackenzie, Explorer and Fur Trader. Address: 603 Besserer St., Ottawa, Can. Died Jan. 24, 1954.

WUNDHEILER, Alexander Wundt (voond'hiler), educator; b. Warsaw, Poland, Apr. 6, 1902; s. Felix and Celia (Halperson) W.; M.Sc., U. Warsaw, 1927, Ph.D., 1932; m. Luitgard Natorp, June 13, 1952. Came to U.S., 1939, naturalized, 1945. Instr. mechanics U. Warsaw, 1927-39; spl. lectr. Mass. Inst. Tech., also instr. mathematics Tufts Coll., 1940-41; instr. physics Coll. City N.Y., 1942-44; asst. prof. physics U. Rochester, 1944-45; physicist Bur. Ordnance, Navy Dept., 1945-48; research prof. mechanics Ill. Inst. Tech., 1948—. Cons. Air Force Intelligence Center, 1950-51. Mem. Am. Assn. U. Profs., Sigma Xi. Editor of Applied Mechanics Reviews, 1948-50; asso. editor Indsl. Labs., 1952-55. Home: 6031 S. Dorchester Av., Chgo. 37. Died Aug. 6, 1957.

WURZBURG, Francis Lewis, pub.; b. Grand Rapids, Mich., May 10, 1877; s. Frederic William and Anna Louise (Druecke) W.; student Canisius Coll., 1892-95, U. of Mich. Law Sch., 1898; m. Evelyn Noble Craw, Dec. 26, 1905; children—Elinor (Mrs. William V. Lawrence), Evelyn (Mrs. J. Hampton Barnes, Jr.), Francis, Frederic. Textile and fgn. mgr. Root Newspaper Assn., N.Y. (United Pubs. Assn., 1910—), 1899-1908; advt. mgr. Style Books, Home Pattern Co., N.Y., 1908-12; gen. mgr. Automotive Publs. (dv. United Pubs., N.Y.C., Chgo., 1912-14; promotion mgr. N.Y. Times, 1914-15; pub. Cosmopolitan mag., N.Y.C., 1915-18; formerly v.p., Conde Nast Publs., Inc., dir., vice chmn. bd., 1918—. Dir., sec. Nat. Pubs. Assn. Republican. Roman Catholic. Clubs: Metropolitan, Dutch Treat (N.Y.C.); Long Island Country. Home: 10 Brooklands, Bronxville, N.Y. Died Apr. 24, 1954; buried Kensico Cemetery.

WYANT, Paul Byron, financial exec.; b. Salem, W. Va., Jan. 16, 1905; s. Harvey M. and Stella M. (Sommerville) W.; B.S. in Econs., Wharton Sch. U. Pa., 1928; m. Myrne M. Whipple, Apr. 29, 1929. Investment banking and brokerage bus., 1928-41; investment adviser, N.Y.C., 1941-54; treas. Scott Paper Co., Chester, Pa., 1954—; dir. Phila. Mfrs. Mutual Ins. Co. Mem. Theta Delta Chi. Club: Overbrook Golf (Byrn Mawr, Pa.). Home: 230 Arden Rd., Broomall, Pa. Office: Scott Paper Co., Chester, Pa. Died June 14, 1958.

WYATT, Edith Franklin, author; b. Tomah, Wis., Sept. 14, 1873; d. Franklin Osmon and Marian (La Grange) W.; ed. Higher Sch. for Girls, Chicago, 1884-91, Bryn Mawr Coll., Pa., 1891-93. Author: Every One His Own Way, 1901; True Love, 1903; Making Both Ends Meet, 1911; Great Companions; The Wind in the Corn, 1917; The Invisible Gods, 1923; The Satyr's Children, 1939; Community Gardener. Contbr. to mags. Home: 222 E. Chestnut St., Chgo. Died Oct. 1958.

WYATT-BROWN, Hunter, bishop; b. Eufaula, Ala., Feb. 14, 1884; s. Eugene L. and Serena (Hoole) Brown; his surname legally changed to Wyatt-Brown, 1941; B.A., U. of South, 1905, B.D., 1908; Litt.D., U. of Ala., 1915; D.D., St. John's Coll., 1921, U. of South, 1933; LL.D., Dickinson Coll., Carlisle, Pa., 1933; m. Laura Little, Sept. 5, 1911; children— Hunter Jr., Charles Matthews, Laura Serena, Bertram III. Deacon, 1908, priest, 1909, P.E. Ch.; asst. St. John's Ch., Montgomery, Ala., 1908-09; rector All Saints' Ch., Mobile, Ala., 1909-13; Trinity Ch., Ashville, N.C., 1913-15, Ch. of Ascension, Pitts., 1915-20, Ch. of St. Michael and All Angels, Balt., 1920-28; lectr. on Pastoral Theology, Va. Theol. Sem., 1927-28; dean St. Paul's Cathedral, Buffalo, 1928-31; elected bishop of Harrisburg, 1931; consecrated bishop, St. Stephen's Cathedral, Harrisburg, Pa., 1931; ret. as bishop of Harrisburg, 1943, because of physical infirmity. Dep. to Gen. Conv., 1919, 25, 28; mem. Gen. Bd. Missions, 1917-19. Mem. Phi Delta Theta. Democrat. Mason (K.T.); Grand Prelate Grand Commandery K.T. of Pa., 1935-37. Clubs: Monterey Country; Waynesboro Golf. Author: Chasing Foxes and Other Sermons. Home: Sewanee, Tenn.; (summer) Denystead, Blue Ridge Summit, Pa. Died Apr. 24, 1952.

WYER, James Ingersoll (wir), librarian; b. Red Wing, Minn., May 14, 1869; s. James Ingersoll and Rosabel E. (Shear) W.; U. of Minn., 1895-96; B.L. S., Univ. of the State of N.Y., 1898; M.L.S., 1905; Pd.D., New York State Coll., 1919; m. May Tyner, May 3, 1894; children—William, Margaret; m. 2d, Leah O. Roys, June 29, 1938. Asst. cashier and dir. First Nat. Bank, Red Lake Falls, Minn., 1887-89; asst cashier 1st Nat. Bank, Concordia, Kan., 1889-95; asst. in Pub. Library, Minneapolis, 1895-96, N.Y. State Library, Albany, 1897-98; librarian and prof. bibliography, U. of Neb., 1898-1905; reference librarian, N.Y. State Library and vice-dir. N.Y. State Library Sch., 1906-08; dir. N.Y. State Library Sch., 1908-26; dir. N.Y. State Library, 1908-38; lecturer on bibliography and govt. publs., Columbia, summer, 1928, 30, U. of Chicago, summer, 1931; with Walker Bank, Salt Lake City, Utah, 1943-49. Pres. N.Y. State Library Sch. Assn., 1926-47; life mem. and sec. Am. Library Assn., 1902-09, v.p., 1909-10, pres., 1910-11. Trustee City Library, Lincoln, Neb., 1902-05; pres. Neb. Pub. Library Commn., 1901-05. Mem. Bibliog. Soc. Am. Club: Collectors (N.Y.C.). Author: Bibliography of the Study and Teaching of History, 1900; Annual Bibliography of Education, 1899-1907; United States Government Documents, 1906, 33; The College and University Library, 1921; Reference Work, 1930; Some Descendants of Edward Wyer of Charlestown, Mass., 1935; The Nantucket Wyers, 1911. Also many professional papers. Chairman of war service com. of A.L.A., which raised over $5,000,000 and maintained libraries in all army and navy camps, vessels, posts, etc., at home and overseas during the war, 1917-20. Home: 1331 E. 6th South St., Salt Lake City 2. Died Nov. 1, 1955; buried Albany Rural Cemetery, Albany, N.Y.

WYER, Samuel S., cons. engr.; b. Wayne County, O., Feb. 18, 1879; s. David and Katherine (Eicher) W.; M.E., Ohio State U., 1903; m. Pauline L. Conover, June 16, 1904; children—Jean, Neal, Ramon; m. 2d, Eva Armstrong, Apr. 29, 1926. Practiced at Columbus, O., 1905—. Chief of Natural Gas Conservation, U.S Fuel Adminstrn., during war period. Mem. Am. Soc. Mech. Engr., Am. Inst. Mining Engrs., A.A.A.S., Am. Gas Assn., Sigma Xi. Republican. Unitarian. Club: Athletic. Author: Producer Gas and Gas Producers, 1905; Catechism on Producer Gas, 1906; Gas Engines and Gas Producers (textbook), 1910; Regulation, Valuation and Depreciation of Public Utilities, 1913; Natural Gas—Its Production, Service and Conservation (Bull. 102, Smithsonian Instn.); The Smithsonian Instn.'s Study of Natural Resources Applied to Pa.'s Resources; Living Together in a Machine Civilization; reports on Niagara Falls, Power Possibilites at Muscle Shoals; Living-Together in a Power Age, also many reports on corp. problems. Retired temporarily and giving all time to research and pub. speaking on changing social order problems. Home: 1325 Cambridbe Blvd., Columbus, O. Died Nov. 30, 1955; buried Columbus, O.

WYLES, Tom Russell (wēlz); b. Prince Edward County, Va., 1872; s. Tracy Robert and Anne (Trickett) W.; ed. at Allesley, Warwickshire, Eng.; m.

Mary Richards, Feb. 12, 1900; children—Tom Russell, Jr., Mary Caroline (wife of Dr. Anthony B. Day), Anne (wife of Willis Prague Coleman), Eben Richards. Clerk, Wabash R.R. Co., 1890, later with the M.P. Ry. until 1897; salesman, with Detroit Graphite Co., paint mfrs., 1897, v.p., 1916-31; salesman Armstrong Paint and Varnish Co., and exec. dir. Steel Plate Fabricating Assn. Sec. Code Authority, Steel Plate Fabricating Industry under N.R.A.; civilian aid to sec. of Army. Asst. camp quartermaster Madison Barracks, N.Y. World War; capt. q.m. Officers' Reserve, U.S. Army. Pres. Citizens Mil. Training Camp Assn. Republican. Episcopalian. Clubs: Engineers, Exmoor, Union League. Home: 360 Park Av., Highland Park, Ill. Office: 37 W. Van Buren St., Chgo. Died June 16, 1959.

WYLIE, Ida Alexa Ross, author; b. Melbourne, Australia, Mar. 16, 1885; d. Alexander Coghill and Ida Millicent (Ross) Wylie; student Cheltenham Coll. Writer, 1898—. Mem. Cosmopolitan Club (N.Y.C.). Author: Dividing Waters, 1911; Daughter of Brahma, 1912; Five Years to Find Out, 1914; Hermit Doctor of Gayda, 1916; Holy Fire, 1922; Toward Morning, 1922; Ancient Fires, 1924; Black Harvest, 1926; Mad Busman, 1926; Silver Virgin, 1929; Some Other Beauty, 1930; Feather in Her Hat, 1934; To the Vanquished, 1934; Furious Young Man, 1936; My Life with George, 1940; The Young in Heart, 1941; The Keeper of the Flame, 1942; Flight to England, 1943; Strangers Are Coming, 1941; Ho, the Fair Wind, 1945; Storm in April 1946; Where No Birds Sing, 1947; Candles for Therese; Undefeated, 1957. Regular contbr. Sat. Evening Post, Good Housekeeping, Collier's, Ladies Home Journal. Home: Trevenna Farm, Belle Mead, N.J. Died Nov. 4, 1959.

WYLIE, Robert Bradford, educator; b. Maquoketa, Ia., Mar. 28, 1870; s. Edmund Burke and Elizabeth (McConnell) W.; B.S., Upper Ia. U., Fayette, Ia., 1897; studied U. Minn., 1898; Ph.D., U. Chicago, 1904; m. Ada M. Blatherwick, June 27, 1900; 1 dau., Helen Janet. Prof. biology, Morningside Coll., Sioux City, Ia.; 1897-1906; asst. prof. botany, State U. Ia., 1906-08, prof. morphol. botany, now emeritus, head dept. of botany 1919-40; fellow in botany, U. of Chicago, 3 yrs., also taught at Marine Biol. Lab., Woods Hole, Mass., Marine Biol. Lab., Friday Harbor, Washington, and Ill. State Normal Sch.; mem. U.S. Kelp expdn. to Alaska, 1913, State U. Ia. expdn. to Fiji Islands and New Zealand, 1922. Fellow A.A.A.S. (chmn. sect. G, 1925), Ia. Acad. Science (pres. 1921-22); mem. Bot. Soc. Am. (chmn. gen. sect. 1924-25, 1934-35), Sigma Xi, Gamma Alpha. Republican. Author of numerous bot. papers chiefly on morphology of plants. Home: 1047 Woodlawn, Iowa City, Ia. Died June 9, 1959; buried Oakland Cemetery, Iowa City.

WYMAN, Alfred Lee (wī'măn), judge; b. Yankton, S.D., Dec. 9, 1874; s. Frank D. and Mattie C. (Carlton) W.; grad. high sch., Yankton, 1893; studied law in office French & Orvis, Yankton; m. Bessie M. White, Dec. 8, 1900; children—Leila Grace (Mrs. Casper O. Pfefferle), Gale Burdette, Frank D., W. Keith, Ernest Blake, William Ward, Lyle K. (dec.). Admitted to S.D. bar, 1896, and began practice at Yankton; partner of Eldon W. Clark, 1927-29. States atty., Yankton County, 1905-08, 1915-18; city atty., Yankton, 1909-14; mem. S.D. Ho. of Rep., 1909, State Senate, 1911; mayor of Yankton, 1914-24; apptd. judge, U.S. Dist. Court, Dist. of S.D., 1929 now ret. Republican. Episcopalian. Mason (33°, K.T., Shriner). Rotarian. Home: 1220 S. Main Av. Address: Federal Bldg., Sioux Falls, S.D. Died Dec. 15, 1953; buried Yankton, S.D.

WYMAN, Levi Parker, prof. chemistry; b. Skowhegan, Me., July 12, 1873; s. Augustine H. and Sarah (Parker) W.; grad. high sch. Skowhegan, 1891; A.B., Colby Coll., 1896, A.M., 1899; Ph.D., U. of Pa., 1902; Sc.D., Pa. Mil. Coll., 1930; m. Ida M. Rich, Dec. 31, 1896; 1 son, Newton Augustine. Tchr. pub. schs. of Mass. 4 yrs., Pa. State Coll., 1903-04; prof. chemistry, Pa. Mil. Coll., 1905—, dean, 1920-43, dean emeritus, 1943—, v.p. 1930—. Lt. col. Pa. Nat. Guard, 1930. Mem. Phi Delta Theta. Republican. Baptist. Author: The Gooden Boys Series (9 vols.), 1920; The Lakewood Boys Series (5 vols.), 1924; The Hunniwell Boys Series (7 vols.), 1929-30; Donald Price's Victory, 1930; The Mystery of Eagle Lake, 1931; After Many Years, 1941. Home: 115 West 24th St., Chester, Pa. Died Apr. 16, 1950; buried Chester (Pa.) Rural Cemetery.

WYMAN, Phillips, publisher; b. Evanston, Ill., May 24, 1895; s. Edward Frothingham and Katharine Lovela (Easter) W.; A.B., Cornell U., 1917; m. Mildred Sutton, June 8, 1918 (dec. May 31, 1932); children—Phillips, Katharine (Mrs. H. Baekgland Roll), Ruth (Mrs. Carl Kaufmann); m. 2d, Nina Baekeland, May 8, 1936. With U.S. Food Adminstrn. under Herbert Hoover, 1917-20; bus. mgr. paint and varnish industry, Save the Surface campaign, 1920-22; exec. sec. Periodical Pubs. Assn., 1921-23; with McCall Corp. since 1923, successively circulation dir., vice pres., dir., dir. publ. selling; pres. and dir. S-M News Co., Inc.; pres. Nat. Mag. Service Corp.; publisher of Redbook and Blue Book magazines. Chairman bd. Periodical Publishers Assn. Am., Mag. Advt. Bur., 1949-53; dir. Audit Bureau Circulations, 1938-50; mem. Greater Cornell Committee Cornell U.; former dir. Cornell Alumni Assn.; chmn. pub. com., Cornell Alumni News, 1939-48; chmn. ednl. com., Nat. Better Bus. Bur., sponsoring consumer edn. study of Nat. Assn. Secondary Sch. Prins., 1942-44, 1946-48. Mem. Zeta Psi. Clubs: Cornell, University. Author: Mag. Circulation—An Outline of Methods and Meanings, 1936. Home: Redding, Conn. Office: 230 Park Av., N.Y.C. 17. Died May 28, 1955.

WYNEGAR, Howard LaVerne (wī'nĕ-gär), comml. banker; b. Greenville, Ind., July 1, 1884; s. David A. and Mary E. W.; prep. edn., high sch., Moorse Hill (Ind.) Coll.; LL.B., Ind. U., 1907; m. Elizabeth Page, June 21, 1924. Pres. Comml. Credit Corp., N.Y., 1922-49, chmn. adv. com., dir., 1949—. Pres. Comml. Credit Co., Balt., 1930-48, v. chmn. 1948-49; pres. Comml. Credit Corp. of Can., Ltd., 1922-49; ret. from active officer; dir. Agar Packing & Provision Corp.; Croname, Inc., Chgo. Mem. War Industries Bd., 1918-19. Mem. Kappa Sigma, Phi Delta Phi. Rep. Clubs: Cloud, Sleepy Hollow Country, University (N.Y.). Home: 375 Park Av. Office: 100 E. 42 St., N.Y.C. 17. Died Apr. 13, 1957.

WYNN, William Thomas, educator; b. Henry Co., Ga., Oct. 30, 1874; s. Winfrey Lockett and Emma (McCarty) W.; A.B., Emory U., 1900; student U. Tenn., U. Chgo., Columbia; A.M., Peabody Coll. Tchrs., 1920; Litt.D., Central U., Indpls., 1928; m. Mary Floyd, Feb. 13, 1902; children—William Thomas, Winfrey Irving, Floyd Ellison, Mary Mildred, Lawrence. Prof. mathematics, English S.E. Ala. Agrl. Sch., 1901-05; supt. schs., Enterprise, Ala., 1905-08; pres. Martin Coll., Pulaski, Tenn., 1908-19; prof. State Tchrs. Coll., Murfreesboro, Tenn., 1920-25; prof. English Ga. State Coll. for Women, Milledgeville, 1925-47, dean, 1927-33, sub-dir. div. gen. extension, 1935-43, prof. emeritus, 1947—. Mem. Ga. Edn. Assn., Doctors Acad., Phi Beta Kappa, Kappa Alpha, Phi Delta Kappa. Democrat. Methodist. Mason (32°, Shriner). Clubs: Kiwanis (Milledgeville); Low Twelve (Nashville). Author: Grammar Essentials, 1934. Editor: Readings in Georgia Literature, 1937; Grammar of the English Language (rev. edit.), 1946; Smile With Me, 1950. Author articles ednl. subjects. Home: 402½ W. Montgomery St., Milledgeville, Ga. Died Apr. 13, 1954; buried Milledgeville.

WYNNE, Thomas Neil, mech. engr.; b. Indianapolis, Ind., June 24, 1890; s. Thomas Alfred and Mary Isabel (Neil) W.; prep. edn., Culver (Ind.) Naval Sch. and Indianapolis Manual Training High Sch.; student Cornell U., 1912; B.S. in Mech. Engring., U. of Wis., 1914, M.E., 1926; m. Hazel Black, Nov. 8, 1915; children—Catherine Jane, Mary Elizabeth, Thos. Neil, Martha Ann, John Watterson. With Indianapolis Light & Heat Co., 1914-26, becoming chief engr.; in business under title of Thos. N. Wynne & Associates, as pub. utility adviser and expert, since 1926; pres. Poll Mines, Inc., Metal Furnace Block Corp., Am. Public Service Corp., Wynnedale Constrn. Corp.; president, director, National Uniforms, Inc.; trustee Thomas A. Wynne Estate. Inventor and patentee Wynne Metal Furnace Block. Organized Town of Wynnedale, 1939, former trustee and pres. bd. (acting). Served as capt. Co. B, Ind. State Militia; organizer 113th Ind. Engrs., 1917; mgr. Chicago Dist. War Prodn. Bd., 1942. Fellow Am. Geog. Society; organizer Ind.-Ky. sect. Amateur Athletic Union (past pres.); mem. Am. Soc. M.E. (past pres. Ind. sect.), Am. Inst. E.E., Nat. Electric Light Assn., Ind. Engring. Society, Acad. Polit. Science, Nat. Aeronautical Soc., Ind. Electric Light Assn. (past pres.), Nat. Assn. Purchasing Agents (past pres. Ind. sect.). Republican. Episcopalian. Mason (32°, K.T., Shriner). Clubs: Hoosier Motor, Highland Golf, Optimist (hon. life mem. and past pres.). Author: Facts on Indiana Coal, 1926. Inventor various mech. appliances. Designer of subaqueous coal storage pit. Home: 2110 W. 42d St., Indpls. Died Jan. 30, 1953.

Y

YAGER, Vincent, banker; b. Clamar, Ia.; s. William V. and Emma (Shipley) Y.; A.B., Grinnell Coll., 1920, A.M., 1940; m. Juanita Cook, June 12, 1924; children—Vincent Cook, Judith Anne. With credit dept. Harris Trust & Savs. Bank, Chgo., 1920, asst. cashier, 1930-33, asst. v.p., 1933-40, v.p. 1940—. Mem. C. of C., Robert Morris Assos. (dir., past pres.), Phi Beta Kappa. Conglist. Clubs: University, Skokie Country. Contbr. articles on credit subjects to profl. jours. Home: 290 Bernon St., Glencoe, Ill. Office: 115 Monroe St., Chgo. 90. Died May 7, 1957.

YANNEY, Benjamin Franklin (yăn'ē), educator; b. Dundee, O., Sept. 11, 1859; s. Jacob and Nancy (Strome) Y.; A.B., Mt. Union Coll., Alliance, O., 1885, A.M., 1888; Ph.D., U. Chgo., 1923; m. Linnie May Goodin, July 15, 1886 (died 1901); m. 2d, Lulu Carolyn Hock, June 1, 1905; children—Reginald Hock, Cecilia Hock (Mrs. Oldrich Jicha). Instr., 1886-88, prof. Latin, 1888-92, prof. mathematics, 1894-1908, Richard Brown prof. mathematics, 1908-11, Mt. Union Coll.; Johnson prof. mathematics, Coll. of Wooster, 1911-40, emeritus, 1940—. Asst. in revision of math. text-books, and contbr. to math. jours. Fellow A.A.A.S.; mem. Am. Math. Soc., Math. Assn. America, Phi Beta Kappa. Trustee Mt. Union Coll., 1929-39. Club: Century (emeritus). Address: Wooster, O. Died Aug. 9, 1958.

YARDLEY, Farnham, mfr. valves; b. Yonkers, N.Y., Aug. 8, 1868; s. Charles Burleigh and Margaret Tufts (Swan) Y.; grad. Ashland High School, East Orange, N.J., 1885, Phillips Acad., Andover, Mass., 1886; m. Harriet Mullett Jenkins, Apr. 2, 1907; 1 son, Alfred Jenkins. Formerly insurance broker, N.Y.C.; elected v.p. Jenkins Bros., 1911, pres., 1917-47, now chmn.; chmn. Jenkins Bros., Ltd., Montreal, First Nat. Bank (West Orange); pres. Bartlett Carry Realty Co. Mayor, West Orange, 1915-16; councilman, East Orange, 1902-06, also chmn. water com. Rep. presdl. elector, N.J., 1924. Paymaster U.S.S. Portsmouth, Spanish-Am. War; was aide to comdg. officer N.R. N.J., rank of lt. j.g., 1894-99; now on retired list. Active in World War I work; chmn. Defense Com., West Orange; fed. food adminstr. of Oranges; chmn. or vice chmn. various Liberty Loan Campaigns, West Orange; trustee West Orange High Sch. Scholarship Fund, Llewellyn Park (West Orange), Marcus L. Ward Home (Maplewood, N.J.), House of Good Shepherd (Orange, N.J.), The Record Ambulance (ex-pres.), Metcalf Meml. Assn., Orange, N.J. (v.p.). Mem. Acad. Polit. Sci., Assn. for Protection of Adirondacks (v.p.), N.J. N.J. Hist Soc., N.E. Soc. of Oranges, Founders and Patriots Am., Soc. Colonial Wars, S.A.R., Soc. of the Cincinnati, C. of C., State of N.Y., C. of C. and Civics of the Oranges and Maplewood, N.J. Community Chest, the Oranges and Maplewood (ex-pres. and mem. adv. com.), Assn. Residents on Upper Saranac Lake (ex-pres.), Am. Supply and Machinery Mfrs. Assn. (ex-pres., mem. adv. bd.). Episcopalian (warden). Clubs: Essex County Country, Rock Spring (N.J.); Union, Merchants, Racquet and Tennis (N.Y.C.). Home: Llewellyn Park, West Orange, N.J. Office: 100 Park Av., N.Y.C. 17. Died Dec. 30, 1956.

YARDLEY, Herbert O(sborn), writer; b. Worthington, Ind., Apr. 13, 1889; s. Robert Kirkbride and Emma (Osborn) Y.; ed. Worthington, Ind. high sch.; m. Hazel Milam, 1914; 1 son, Jack. Entered U.S. Dept. of State, 1912; advised new diplomatic cipher code for dept., 1914; in charge cryptographic dept. (so-called Black Chamber), 1919-29; lectr. in cause of world peace. Served U.S.A. War Coll., as capt. Signal Corps, 1917, maj., 1918; chief of mil. intelligence No. 8, 1917-18; mil. observer staff Gen. Pershing, Aug., 1918; in charge mil. intelligence C-17 at Peace Conf., 1918; rec'd Distinguished Service medal, 1919; hon. discharged, 1919. Author: The American Black Chamber, 1931; The Blonde Countess, 1934; Red Sun of Nippon, 1934. Address: Worthington, Ind. Died 1958.

YARNELL, Harry Ervin, naval officer; b. nr. Independence, Ia., Oct. 18, 1875; s. Ervin and Catherine (Countryman) Y.; B.S., U.S. Naval Acad., 1897; grad. Naval War Coll., 1915; D.Eng., Stevens Inst. Tech., 1941; LL.D., U. Cal., 1941, Brown U., 1942, Clark U., 1942; m. Emily Carroll Thomas, Sept. 15, 1903; children—Ruth (wife of John Sylvester, U.S.N., dec.), Philip (officer U.S.N.R.). Ensign U.S. Navy, 1899; promoted through grades to adm., 1942. Served in U.S.S. Oregon, Spanish-Am. War; in U.S.S. Yorktown in Philippine Insurrection and Boxer Campaign; took part in occupation of Vera Cruz, 1914; patrol duty, Gibraltar, in command U.S.S. Nashville, 1917; on staff of Admiral Sims, London, 1918; 1st comdg. officer U.S.S. Saratoga, 1927-28; apptd. chief of Bur. of Engring., Navy Dept., Sept. 24, 1928; comdr. Aircraft Squadrons, Battle Fleet, 1931-1933; comdt. Pearl Harbor Naval Sta., 1933-36; commander-in-chief of Asiatic Fleet, 1936-39; retired 1939. Mem. tech. staff Am. delegation Conf. on Limitation of Armaments, London, 1930. Naval aviation observer. Gold medalist U.S. Naval Inst.; awarded Distinguished Service Medal by Act of Congress, 1939; Navy Cross, 1919; Comdr. Order of British Empire, 1919, Cloud Standard, 2d class of China. Mem. Soc. Navl Engrs. Mem. Council on Foreign Relations. Episcopalian. Clubs: Army and Navy Country (Washington); New York Yacht. Home: 62 Ayrault St., Newport, R.I. Died July 7, 1959; buried Berkeley Meml. Chapel, Newport, R.I.

YARROW, Philip (Walter), clergyman; b. London, Eng., Apr. 7, 1872; s. Rev. William Henry and Emma (Radwell) Y.; Mount Hermon School for Boys, 1892; A.B., Princeton, 1896; Hartford Theol. Sem., 1899; m. Georgiana Robinson, Aug. 8, 1900; children—Paul Warren, Dorothy Dunbar Brook (Mrs. Alexander Hamilton), Philip Robinson. Ordained to ministry Congl. Ch., 1899; pastor Fosston, Minn., 1899, Montevideo, Minn., 1900-02. Olive Branch Ch., St. Louis, 1902-08, also supt. St. Louis City Missionary Soc., 1902-08; pastor Waveland Av. Ch., Chgo., 1908-12; asso. supt. Chicago City Missionary Soc., 1912-14; pastor Morgan Park Ch., 1914-20; state supt. Ill. Vigilance Assn., 1922—; pastor Auburn Park (Chgo.) Federated Ch., 1923-27, Auburn Park Community Ch., 1934-37, Pilgrim Mayflower Congl. Ch., 1937-42. Pres. Gospel League, Inc., 1936-38; pres. Chicago Young People's Civic League, 1915-21; gen. supt. Dry Chicago Fedn., 1916-18; former mem. Chicago Recreation Commn.; chmn. civic relations commn. and trustee of Chicago Ch. Fedn., 1925-43. Trustee Morgan Park Mil. Acad. Mem. Am. Acad. Polit. and Social Science, Pi Gamma Mu. Lectr. to high sch. students and parents orgns. Author: Fighting the Debauchery of Our Boys and Girls, 1922. Home: 315 N La Grange Rd., La Grange, Ill. Died June 1954.

YATES, Eugene Adams, pub. utility exec.; b. Elizabeth, N.J., Nov. 7, 1880; s. Joseph Johnson Yates and Elizabeth Ann (Whaley); B.S. Rutgers U., 1902; m. Margaret Wendell Polk, 1914; children—Eugene Adams, Margaret Polk, Mrs. Elizabeth Y. Shepard. Chmn. The Southern Co.; v.p., dir. Ala. Power Co., Ga. Power Co., Gulf Power Co., Miss. Power Co. Mem. Am. Soc. C.E., Beta Theta Pi. Republican. Episcopalian. Clubs: Mountain Brook (Birmingham, Ala.); Capitol City (Atlanta); Metropolitan (Washington); Bankers, University, Union (N.Y.C.). Home: 765 Park Av., N.Y.C. 21; and Nantucket, Mass. Office: 250 Park Av., N.Y.C. 17. Died Oct. 5, 1957; buried Westview Cemetery, Atlanta.

YATES, Julian Emmet, army chaplain; b. Chatham County, N.C., Oct. 23, 1871; s. James Dallas and Abbie Cornelia (Olive) Y.; M.A., Wake Forest (N.C.) Coll., 1894; B.D., U. Chgo., 1900; D.D., Wake Forest Coll., 1930; m. Pauline Norvell, Aug. 6, 1900 (died July 1909); 1 dau., Norvell Pauline; m. 2d, Janet Wier, Oct. 11, 1911. Ordained Bapt. ministry, 1893; asst. pastor Immanuel Ch., Chgo., 1899-1900; pastor First Ch., Olathe, Kan., 1900-02; appointed chaplain U.S. Army, grade of captain, 1902; promoted through grades to col., 1929. Served in the Philippines, 1902-04; chaplain Atlantic Coast defense forts, 1904-17; assigned to 53d Regt. Railway Arty., A.E.F., 1917; arrived in France, 1917; chaplain 53d Regt. in Aisne-Marne section to 1918; base chaplain Base Sect. No. 5, Service of Supply, Brest, 1918; chaplain 52d Regt. Ry. Arty., 1919; with Gen. Staff, War Dept., 1919-20; with 3d Cav., Ft. Myer, Va., 1920-22; exec. officer Office Chief of Chaplains, 1922-26; with 6th Cav., Ft. Oglethorpe, Ga., 1926-29; chief of Chaplains, U.S. Army, 1929-33; retired, 1935. Decorated Purple Heart; Medaille d'Honneur des Epidemies (France). Mem. Mil. Order Caraboa, Mil. Order of the World War, Spanish War Vets., Am. Legion, Heroes of '76, Sojourners. Republican. Mason (K.T.). Home: 3803 Huntington St. N.W., Washington, D.C.; (summer) Nantucket, Mass. Died May 24, 1953; buried Arlington Nat. Cemetery.

YEATMAN, Pope, mining engr.; b. St. Louis, Aug. 3, 1861; s. Thomas and Lucretia (Pope) Y.; M.E., Washington U., 1883; m. Georgie Claiborne Watkins, June 28, 1894 (dec. Jan. 1941); children—Jane Bell (Mrs. Ernest C. Savage), Georgina Pope, Pope. In mining in Mexico, Mo., N.M., Colo., 1883-95; mining engr. Consol. Gold Fields of S. Africa, Ltd., and mgr. Robinson Deep Gold Mining Co., Johannesburg, South Africa, 1895-99; also gen. mgr. Simmer and Jack Proprietary Gold Mining Co. Ltd., 1899; gen. mgr. and cons. engr. Randfontein Estates Gold Mining Co., Ltd., Transvaal, South Africa, 1899-1904; cons. engr. M. Guggenheim's Sons Co., and Guggenheim Exploration Co.; also cons. engr. Nev. Consol. Copper Co., Steptoe Valley Smelting & Mining Co., Chile Exploration Co., of Chile, Braden Copper Co., of Chile, 1906-16; ind. cons. practice since 1916. Vol. for service of U.S. in World War, Aug. 1917; cons. engr., later chief non-ferrous metals div. War Industries Bd., Washington, until Jan. 1919. Decorated D.S.M. Mem. Am. Inst. Mining Engrs., Am. Soc. C.E., Instn. Mining and Metallurgy (London), Engrs.' Society St. Louis, Mining and Metall. Soc. of America. Republican. Home: 520 East Gravers Lane, Chestnut Hill, Phila. Office: 70 Pine St., N.Y.C. 3. Died Dec. 5, 1953.

YEATON, Arthur Charles, teacher; b. Dover, N.H., Aug. 25, 1871; s. Charles Wesley and Sarah Ann (Wentworth) Y.; A.B., Bates Coll., 1893; m. Ella Adams Sylvester, July 25, 1900. Tchr. history and Latin, Nichols Latin Sch., Lewiston, Me., 1891-92; chemist Agrl. Dept., Chicago Expn., 1893, prin. Lebanon Acad., W. Lebanon, Me., 1894; teacher science, 1894-1912, bursar, 1902-1911, president, 1907-1912, Westbrook Sem., Portland, Me.; head sci. dept. Edward Little High Sch., Auburn, Me., 1914-36. Treas. Lisbon Falls, Me., 1939-51. Mem. Am. Chem. Soc., Me. Hist. Soc. Address: Lisbon Falls, Me. Died Aug. 23, 1955.

YEOMANS, Charles, mfr. pumping machinery; b. Orange, N.J., Nov. 16, 1877; s. Alfred and Elizabeth B. (Ramsay) Y.; prep. edn., Lawrenceville (N.J.) Sch.; A.B., Princeton, 1900; m. Maud Gernon, May 1, 1907 (dec.); m. 2d, Florence M. White, Oct. 19, 1921; children—John Ramsay, Caroline White. Entered firm of Yeomans Bros. Co., mfrs. pumping machinery, Chgo., 1900, now chmn. bd. and treas. Mem. Art Inst. Chgo. Clubs: Chicago Literary, University. Home: 1173 Tower Rd., Winnetka, Ill. Office: 1999 N. Ruby St., Melrose Park, Ill. Died Aug. 28, 1959.

YEPSEN, Lloyd Nicoll, psychologist; born Princeton, Ill., Nov. 24, 1896; s. John N. and Caroline (Karstensen) Y.; A.B., Carthage (Ill.) Coll., 1921, LL.D., 1942; univ. scholar, Ohio State U., 1924, Ph.D., (fellow), 1931; m. Ethel Dale Miller, Sept. 3, 1924; 1 dau., Carolyn Dale (Mrs. M. Lee Walton). Research asst., chief clinician, Dept. of Research, Training Sch., Vineland (N.J.), 1921-29; advisor to Minister of Edn., Santiago, Chile, 1929-30; chief clin. psychologist, Mental Hygiene Clinic, Greystone Park, N.J., 1931-32; asst. prof. edn., N.Y. U., 1932-36; lecturer, Miami U., 1931, Dana Coll., Newark U., 1934-38, Rutgers U., 1937-39, Temple U., 1942-46, N.Y. U., 1946-50; dir., Div. of Classification and Edn., Dept. of Institutions and Agencies, Trenton, N.J., 1934-52, director Div. of Mental Deficiency, 1952, chief psychologist, 1945-50; superintendent N.J. State Colony, New Lisbon, 1952——. Served with A.E.F., 1918-19. Recipeint Medalle de Merito (Chile). Diplomate Clin. Psychology (chairman conference state societies, 1944-46) Fellow Am. Psychol. Assn.; mem. N.J. Psychol. Assn. (president, 1934), N.J. Guidance and Personnel (v.p., 1937), Med. Soc. of N.J. (hon.), Correctional Edn. Association (treas. 1947), Policy and Planning Board. 1945-46, Am. Assn. on Mental Deficiency (v.p. 1942-43, pres. 1947-48, exec. v.p. since 1948), Internat. Cong. on Mental Deficiency (sec.. since 1948). Lutheran. Research and author articles on mental deficiency, clin. psychology, special edn., delinquency, crime. Home: Washington Crossing, N.J. Office: N.J. State Colony, New Lisbon, N.J. Died Aug. 1, 1955; buried Ewing Cemetery, Trenton, N.J.

YERBY, William James, consular service; b. Oldtown, Phillips Co., Ark., Sept. 22, 1867; s. Robert Milton and Clementine Y.; A.B., Roger Williams U., Nashville, Tenn.; M.D., Meharry Med. Coll., Nashville, 1898; m. Cecilia Kennedy, June 30, 1897; children—Mrs. Edwyna Y. Church, Clementine. Engaged in publishing and printing business 6 yrs.; practiced medicine 8 yrs.; apptd. consul at Sierra Leone, Africa, June 28, 1906, Dakar, Senegal, 1915, La Rochelle, France, 1925, Oporto, Portugal, 1926, Nantes, 1930; ret. 1932. Mem. South Center Community Council, Citizens Civic and Economic Welfare Council (both Chgo.). Baptist. Address: 4756 Champlain Av., Chgo. Died July 30, 1950.

YERGIN, Howard Vernon, clergyman; b. Jordan, N.Y., Sept. 4, 1885; s. Rev. Vernon Noyes and Harriet Adell (Swetland) Y.; A.B., Yale, 1908; B.D., Auburn, (N.Y.) Theol. Sem., 1913; immigrant fellow Presbyn. Bd. of Home Missions in Italy, 1913-14; m. Ida Flohr, May 13, 1913 (dec. 1950); children—Gladys (Mrs. S. Arthur Voelker), Ruth, Helen (Mrs. Lowell H. Brown), Alice (Mrs. Raymond Zacchera), Howard Vernon, Paul Flohr. Ordained to ministry of Presbyn. Ch., May 8, 1913; travel fellowship, Italy 1913-14; dir. Boyle Memorial Centre, St. Louis, Mo., 1914-18; exec. Am. Parish, Presbyn., New York, N.Y., 1918-24; lecturer on Immigration, Teachers Coll., Columbia, 1918-22; pastor Ch. of the Covenant, N.Y. City, 1924-36; exec. Synod of New York (state) 1936-49; sec. for field service, Presbyn. Bd. Nat. Missions since 1949; rep., Italy, The World Council of Churches, 1946. Dir. Auburn Theol. Sem., Union Theol. Sem. Mem. New York State Council of Chs. (pres. 1938-42, vice pres. since 1946), Am. Waldensian Aid Soc. (pres.), Phi Beta Kappa. Author: Growing as Jesus Grew, 1920. Contbr. articles to religious periodicals. Home: 1635 Edison Av., New York 61. Office: 156 Fifth Av., N.Y. City 10. Died July 28, 1951.

YERKES, Robert Mearns (yĕr'kēz), psychobiologist; b. Breadysville, Pa., May 26, 1876; s. Silas Marshall and Susanna Addis (Carrell) Y.; A.B., Ursinus, 1897; A.B., Harvard, 1898, A.M., 1899, Ph. D., 1902; LL.D., Ursinus, 1923; D.Sc., Wesleyan U., 1923; hon. M.A., Yale, 1931; m. Ada Watterson, 1905; children—Roberta Watterson, David Norton. Began as teacher and investigator at Harvard, 1901, asst. prof. comparative psychology, 1908-17, psychologist to the Psychopathic Hosp., Boston, 1913-17; prof. psychology and dir. Psychol. Lab., U. of Minn., 1917-19 (absent on mil. duty); chmn. research information service, Nat. Research Council, 1919-24 (chmn. com. for research in problems of sex, 1921-47); prof. psychology, Inst. Psychology, Yale, 1924-29; prof. psychobiology, Yale 1929-44, emeritus, 1944——; organized and dir. Yale Labs. of Primate Biology, Orange Park, Fla., 1929-41, named Yerkes Labs. of Primate Biology, 1942. Chief, division of psychology, office Surg. Gen., A.U.S., 1917-18. Consulting services War Dept. and Nat. Research Council, World War II. Fellow Am. Acad. of Arts and Sciences, A.A.A.S.; mem. Nat. Acad. Sciences, Am. Philos. Soc., Am. Psychol. Assn. (pres., 1916-17), American Physiological Society, American Society Naturalists (pres. 1938), Soc. of Mammalogists. Club: Cosmos. Author: The Dancing Mouse, A Study in Animal Behavior, 1907; Introduction to Psychology, 1911; Methods of Studying Vision in Animals (with J. B. Watson), 1911; Outline of a Study of the Self (with D. W. La Rue), 1914; A Point Scale for Measuring Mental Ability (with R. S Hardwick and J. W. Bridges), 1915; The Mental Life of Monkeys and Apes—A Study of Ideational Behavior, 1916; Psychological Examining in the U.S. Army (with others), 1921; Chimpanzee Intelligence and Its Vocal Expressions (with B. W. Learned), 1925; Almost Human, 1925; The Mind of a Gorilla, 1927; The Great Apes (with A. W. Yerkes), 1929; Chimpanzees: A Laboratory Colony, 1943; published papers chiefly on physiology of the nervous system, animal behavior, comparative psychology and mental measurement. Especially interested in psychobiological research, mental engineering, and problems of population. Home: 4 St. Ronan Terrace, New Haven. Died Feb. 3, 1956.

YODER, Jocelyn Paul, b. Galena, Kan., Jan. 14, 1884; s. Jocelyn Z. and Phebe Ellen (Tallman) Y.; ed. Washington; m. Leona Edgar Kidwell, Oct. 17, 1911; 1 dau., Mrs. Leona Jacqueline Sangster. Newspaper reporter, Washington, N.C., Chgo., etc.; toured country with Roosevelt, campaign of 1916; served as bur. mgr. and rep. United Press Assn.; sec. Fed. Trade Commn., 1919-22; dir. of publicity Dem. Nat. Com., at Chgo., 1924; dir. advertising and publicity, City of Miami, Fla., 1927; dir. publicity for Coral Gables (Fla.) Corp.; asst. gen. news mgr. Internat. News Service; dir. publicity, Chatham Phenix Nat. Bank & Trust Co., N.Y., 1930; asst. dir. of publicity Fed. Housing Adminstrn., 1934——; dir. public relations Morris Plan Bankers Association and Consumer Banking Institute, 1941. Dir. publicity, Office of Surgeon General U.S. Army, 7 mos.; adj. Mobile Hosp. Unit 104, in France, rank of captain, 6 months; captain, M.D., A.O.R.C. First post commander, Coral Gables Post, No. 98, Am. Legion; past chef de gare 40 and 8, Miami, Fla. Club: Nat. Press (Washington). Home: 4910 Rock Spring Road, Arlington, Va. Office: 1025 Connecticut Av. N.W., Washington. Died Sept. 30, 1950.

YODER, Robert McAyeal, newspaperman; b. Gibson City, Ill., Aug. 18, 1907; s. Milo Franklin and Lyda (McAyeal) Y.; student U. Ill., U. Wis., U. Ill. Law Sch.; m. Virginia Lipscomb, June 20, 1932; children—Judith Ann, Robert McAyeal, John. Reporter Decatur (Ill.) Herald reporter Chgo. Bur. of Asso. Press, 1933-36; reporter Chgo. Daily News, 1936-40; writer of editorial column, "Sharps and Flats,' Chgo. Daily News, 1940-44; asso. editor Sat. Evening Post, 1945-49. Served as lt. U.S.N.R., World War II. Mem. Nat. Press Club, Sigma Alpha Epsilon. Democrat. Presbyn. Author: There's No Front Like Home, 1944. Home: 327 Kent Rd., Cynwyd, Pa. Died Nov. 1959.

YOKOYAMA, Taiwan (Hidemaro), Japanese painter; b. Ibaraki-ken, Aug. 1868; grad. Tokyo Sch. Fine Arts. Founder Nihon Bijitsu-in (Fine Arts Assn.), with late Tenshin Okakura, 1898; taught Japanese painting in India, 1903; visited Europe, Am., 1904; exhibited Japanese paintings in Italy, 1923. Decorated by Italian Govt. Mem. Imperial Acad. Fine Arts. Address: 19 Kayacho 2-chome, Taito-ku, Tokyo, Japan. Died Mar. 1958.

YONGE, Philip Keyes, ret. lumber mfr.; b. Marianna, Florida, May 27, 1850; s. Chandler Cox and Julia Ann (Cole) Y.; A.B., U. Ga., 1871, A.M., 1872, LL.B., 1872; LL.D., U. Fla., 1921; m. Lucie C. Davis, Dec. 13, 1876; children—Archie Louise (Mrs. Peter Amos Buck), Julien Chandler, Philip Keyes (dec.), John Eayres Davis, Henry Matthew (dec.), Malcolm Roland, Ethel Wilmer (dec.), Chandler Cox, Marjorie Jean. Sec. Muscogee Lumber Co., Pensacola, 1876-89; asst. mgr. So. States Land & Timber Co., Ltd., 1889-98; v.p. and mgr. Southern States Lumber Co., 1898-1903, pres., mgr., 1903-1930. Alderman, Pensacola, 4 yrs.; chmn. War Camp Community Service, World War; mem. Bd. Pub. Instruction, Escambia Co., 10 yrs.; chmn. bd. trustees sch. tax Dist. 16, Escambia Co. 1921——; mem. Bd. of Control, State of Fla., 1905—— (except 4 yrs.), chmn. 18 yrs. Mem. C. of C. (past pres.), Phi Beta Kappa, Phi Kappa Phi. Democrat. Episcopalian, Odd Fellow, K.P.; mem. Knights of Honor. Home: 1924 E. Jackson St., Pensacola, Fla. Died Aug. 9, 1934.

YORK, Amos Chesley, lawyer; b. Rockport, Mass., Oct. 11, 1884; s. Charles Frederick and Marietta (Lufkin) Y.; grad. high sch., Gloucester, Mass., 1903; LL.B., cum laude, Boston U., 1905; Litt.D., Portia Coll., 1937; D.A.O., Staley College, 1948; LL.D., Windsor U., 1950; m. Hortense Eloise Stanhope, Sept. 3, 1913. Began practice at Boston, 1906; now mem. firm Devine, York & Volpe. Govt. appeal agt. Selective Service, 1917-18 and since 1940; city solicitor, Medford, 1918-21, 41-50; asst. atty. general of Massachusetts, 1921-Jan. 1927; resigned and apptd. asst. U.S. atty., Dist. of Mass., Feb. 1927, continuing until 1934; prof. law Suffolk Univ. Law Sch. since 1908, Portia Law Sch. (for women) since 1910; pres. bd. trustees and dean, Portia Law Sch. and Calvin Coolidge Coll. of Liberal Arts. Mem. Am. Bar Assn., Soc. Mayflower Descendants, Mass. Law Soc., Soc. for Preservation of New Eng. Antiquities, Medford Hist. Soc., Gamma Eta Gamma. Republican. Conglist. Mason, Elk. Club: Boston City. Lecturer on legal and world travel topics. Home: Medford, Mass. Office: 11 Beacon St., Boston. Died Jan. 10, 1952; buried Rockport, Mass.

YORK, Francis Lodowick, musical dir.; b. Ontonagon, Mich., 1861; s. Lodowick Clark and Frances DeGrace (Collester) Y.; B.A., U. Mich., 1882, M.A. summa cum laude, 1883; Doctor of Music (honorary), Hillsdale College, Hillsdale, Michigan, 1922; studied organ, composition with Alex. Guilmant, Paris, 1892, 1898; m. Mary O. Albright, Sept. 6, 1883 (dec.); children—Kate Ethel, Satia F., Leila Dorothea. Tchr. piano, organ, composition, U. Sch. Music, Ann Arbor, Mich., 1892-96; head piano dept. State Normal Conservatory, Ypsilanti, Mich., 1896-1909; represented Mich. as concert organist, Buffalo Expn., 1901; chmn. music com. Detroit City Bi-Centenary, 1901; city mus. historian, 1901; dir. Detroit Conservatory Music, pres. of corp., 1902-27; alternated with Alex. Guilmant, Paris, organ concerts, St. Louis Expn., 1904; municipal organist, City of Detroit, 1927; curator of music, Municipal Art Inst., Detroit; chmn. bd. Detroit Inst. Musical Art, 1927-43; lectr. Detroit Pub. Library, 1939-45; dean Detroit Conservatory of Music, 1943-51, honorary dean, 1951-—; as an organist he gave numerous recitals and concerts until about 1945. Member of Music Tchrs. Nat. Asn. (sec. 4 terms; v.p. 1921), Am. Guild Organists (dean Mich. chpt., 1927-28), Music Assn. Great Britain, Detroit Orchestral Assn., Founders Soc., Mich. Music Tchrs. Assn., Adult Choristers St. Paul's Cathedral, Detroit Composers Guild (pres. 1935-36), Mich. Composers Club (pres. 1937-38), Mich. Grand Opera Soc., (pres. 1944-45), Phi Beta Kappa, Beta Theta Pi. Clubs: Bohemians (past pres.); Authors (London); Acanthus, Composers. Author: Harmony Simplified, 1900; Counterpoint Simplified, 1907; History of Music in Detroit for Mich. State Hist. Commn. Prepared report on conservatories, organ instrn. in Am. for Frnech Govt., 1905. Composer of piano, organ, orchestral, choral music. Editor for Schirmer's Lib. Contbr. to mags. Lectr. on music. Recognized as authority on interpretation of music of Chopin. Home: 3922 N. Main St., Royal Oak, Mich. Died Jan. 13, 1955; buried Roseland Park Cemetery Mausoleum, Royal Oak.

YORK, Harry Clinton, author, educator; b. Lebanon, Conn., Dec. 18, 1878; s. Benjamin Franklin and Lucy Adelaide (Peckham) Y.; prep. edn. Bacon Acad., Colchester, Conn., and Norwich Free Acad.; B.A., Yale, 1905, M.A., 1906, Ph.D., 1908; B.D., Yale Sch. of Religion, 1914 as of 1908; m. Olive Rogers, July 17, 1908; children—Alan Clinton, Raymond Rogers, Robert Sefton, Richard (dec.). Vice prin. Jaffna Coll., Ceylon, 1908-13; asso. prof. Bibl. lit. and history, Mt. Holyoke Coll., 1914-17; ordained Congl. ministry, 1917; prin. Blanche Kellogg Inst. (for young women), Santurce, P.R., 1917-22, also lecturer Evangelical Sem. of P.R.; prof. sociology and economics, Hood Coll., Frederick, Md., 1922-26; prof. religious edn., Elmira (N.Y.) Coll., 1926-32, also dean Sch. of Religious Education, 1928-44, dean emeritus, 1944-—. Sociologist of the New York State Reformatory, Elmira, N.Y., 1932-33. Chemung County (N.Y.) Dept. Pub. Welfare, 1934-—. Y.M.C.A ednl. dir. Camp Las Casas, and O.T.C., P.R., World War. Mem. Am. Oriental Soc., Soc. Bibl. Lit. and Exegesis, Religious Edn. Assn., Am. Sociol. Soc., Am. Acad. Polit. and Social Science, Am. Assn. Univ. Profs., Phi Beta Kappa, Pi Gamma Mu, Alpha Chi Rho. Republican. Author: Bible Stories from the Old and New Testaments, 1912; also articles in Jour. of Semitic Lang and Lit., Jour. of Bibl. Lit., etc. Home: R.F.D. 2, Elmira, N.Y. Died Aug. 28, 1948; buried Thurmont, Md.

YOST, Gaylord, violinist, composer; b. Fayette, O., Jan. 28, 1888; s. Charles E. and Ada Virginia (Purcell) Y.; student Toledo Conservatory of Music, 1903-04, Detroit Conservatory of Music, 1905-06, later in Berlin, Germany, with Issay Barmas; self-taught in composition; Mus.B., Detroit Cons. of Music, 1931; Mus.D., Waynesburg Coll., 1936; m. Rose Natalie Strebe, Apr. 18, 1917; m. 2d, Ruth Margaret Steuernagel, Mar. 30, 1931. Concert tours in Europe, Central America and U.S., 1907-11; head of violin dept. Ind. Coll. of Music and Fine Arts, Indpls., 1915-21; head of violin department Pitts. Musical Institute, 1921-42; also appears frequently as soloist. Pres. Pitts. Violin Teachers' Guild. Composer: (violin and piano) Reverie; Abendlied; Serenade; Novellette; American Rhapsody; Berceuse; Canzonetta; Humoresque; Danse Characterisque; La Coquette; From the South; Evening; Firefly; Farfalls; Nostromo; Prelude; Song and Dance; also transcriptions of famous composers and pedagogical works; (piano) Prelude Solonnelle, Improvisation; Etude; Caprice Excentrique; Vistas; (songs) A Love Note; Love's Count; My Heart Must Break; (orchestra) Louisiana Suite; many manuscript compositions. Hon. mem. Litteraire e Artistique Institute de France. Founded the Yost String Quartet, 1925, and also an annual chamber music series of concerts in Pittsburgh; condr. Fed. Symphony Orchestra of Pitts. Made revolutionary discoveries regarding violin technic in 1932, incorporated in a book, The Yost System, author of Basic Principles of Violin Playing. String Quartet album of arrangements and three original compositions published in 1940; Yost Violin Method in 3 vols., 1946-47; Contrition; Arlette for Violin and piano, 1947; Bow and Finger Magic for Violin, 1948. Joint recitals with Barre Hill, 1935-36. Home and Studio: 1430 Barnesdale St., Pitts. Died Oct. 10, 1958.

YOST, Mary, dean of women; b. Staunton, Va., Sept. 25, 1881; d. Jacob and Mary Spillman (Young) Yost; student Mary Baldwin Sem. (Mary Baldwin College), Staunton, Va., 1899-1900; A.B., Vassar College, 1904, A.M., 1912; Ph.D., Univ. of Michigan, 1917; LL.D., Mills College, 1946; unmarried. Assistant in English dept., Wellesley College, Mass., 1906-07; instr. English, Vassar Col., 1907-13; fellow in rhetoric, U. of Mich., 1913-15; asst. prof. English, Vassar Coll., 1915-21; dean of women and asso. prof. of English, Stanford Univ., 1921-30, dean of women and lecturer in English, 1930-46, emeritus, 1946-—. Home: 676 Alvarado Row, Stanford, Cal. Died Mar. 4, 1954; buried Staunton, Va.

YOUNG, Benjamin E., banker; b. Carthage, Mo., Sept. 27, 1897; s. Charles Henry and Alice (Lionberger) Y.; student pub. schs. of Ark.; LL.D., Wayne U., 1949; m. Madelyn Flanery, Feb. 7, 1920; children—Shirley Ann, Joan Carol. Clerk Commerce Trust Co., Kansas City, Mo., 1915-24; comptroller, 1924-33; asst. to pres. Nat. Bank of Detroit (Mich.), 1933-34, gen. v.p., 1935-52, retired, dir. since 1950; pres. B. E. Young & Associates; chmn. Indsl. Enterprises, Inc.; dir. Am. Natural Gas Co., Detroit Steel Corp., Standard Accident Ins. Co., Mich. Consol. Gas Co., Penobscot Bldg., Inc. Trustee Earhart Fund., Henry Ford Hosp., Found. Econ. Edn., Relm Found.; dir. Un'ted Found. Detroit. Served in A.C., U.S. Army, 1917-18. Republican. Clubs: Country, Detroit, Athletic, Witenagemote, Bloomfield Hills Country. Author: Bank Cost Control, 1933. Home: 4120 Echo Rd., Bloomfield Hills, Mich. Office: Nat. Bank Bldg., Detroit 26. Died July 31, 1957.

YOUNG, Charles Duncanson, ry. official; b. Washington, May 19, 1878; s. Thomas H. and Annie Cowden (Forster) Y.; M.E., Cornell U., 1902; m. Florence Booth, June 8, 1904; children—John R., Marjorie B. (Mrs. Drew W. Hiestand; dec.), Anne F. (Mrs. Nelson Y. Ruth). Began as spl. apprentice Columbus (O.) shops, Pa. R.R., 1900; successively asst. motive power inspector, asst. master mechanic, asst. engr. motive power, engr. tests, supt. motive power, div. supt., gen. supervisor stores, stores mgr., gen. purchasing agt., asst. v.p. Apr. 1932-Sept. 1938, v.p. purchases stores and insurance, and dir. and v p. in charge real estate, purchases and ins., 1938, dir. and v p., 1939, became v.p. in charge purchases, stores and ins., 1946; now ret.; inventor many devices asso. with mech. arts; dir., mm. exec. com. Norfolk and Western Ry. Co.; dir. Corn Exchange Nat. Bank & Trust Co., Phila. Served with U.S.N., Spanish-Am. War; lt. col. U.S. Army Transportation Corps, World War I; col., 304th Engrs., U.S. Res.; col., Engrs. Corps, U.S. Army Res.; promoted brig. gen., 1941; dir. procurement and distrbn. Services of Supply; dep. dir. Office Defense Transportation, 1943-45. Awarded Edward Longstreth medal Franklin Inst., 1915, for work on locomotive superheaters, George R. Henderson medal, 1948, for contbns. to sci. advancement in Steam locomotives. Trustee Drexel Ins. Tech. Fellow Am. Soc. M.E.; mem. Am. Soc. Testing Materials (chmn. various coms. 1913-21, pres. 1921-22), Am. Ry. Assn. (chmn. Div. VI, purchases and stores, 1925), S.A.R., Scotch-Irish Soc., Hist. Soc. of Pa., Soc. Am. Mil. Engrs., Mil. Order of World War, Pa. Soc. of N.Y., Beta Theta Pi, Sphinx Head, Aleph Semach. Republican. Episcopalian. Clubs: Racquet (Phila.); No. 1925 F St. (Washington). Home: 1941 Panama St., Phila. 3. Died May 13, 1955; buried Exton, Pa.

YOUNG, Clarence Hoffman, educator; b. N.Y.C., Dec. 24, 1866; s. James Baxter and Julia A. O. (Wells) Y.; A.B., Columbia, 1888, A.M., 1889, Ph. D., 1891; student Am. Sch. Classical Studies, Athens, Greece, 1891-92; m. Ada I. Young, Aug. 1891 (died Jan. 25, 1932); 1 son, J. Donald; m. 2d, Anita E. Klein, May 30, 1933. University fellow in Greek, Columbia, 1888-91; successively with same univ., instr., Greek, 1892-1902, adj. prof., 1902-05, prof., 1905-19, prof. Greek archeology, 1919-37, also exec. officer dept. Greek and Latin, 1911-37, prof. emeritus of Greek archeology, 1937-—. Mem. mng. com. Am. Sch. Classical Studies, Athens, 1908-—. Mem. Archeol. Inst. America, Am. Philol. Assn., Classical Assn. Atlantic States, Am. Assn. U. Profs., New York Classical Club. Episcopalian. Club: Columbia University. Home: 312 W. 88th St., N.Y.C. 24. Died Apr. 1957.

YOUNG, Francis Brett, author; b. Eng., June 29, 1884; s. Thomas Brett and Annie Elizabeth (Jackson) Y.; M.B., Ch.B., U. Birmingham, 1906; m. Jessie Hankinson, 1908. Began as a physician, 1906. Served under Gen. Smuts in East Africa, 1915-18; maj. Royal Army Med. Corps. Club: Garrick (London). Author: Underwrowth (with E. B. Young), 1913; The Dark Tower, 1914; The Crescent Moon, 1918; Marching on Tanga, 1918; The Young Physician, 1919; Poems, 1919; The Tragic Bride, 1920; The Black Diamond, 1921; The Red Knight, 1921; Pilgrim's Rest, 1922; Woodsmoke, 1924; Cold Harbour, 1924; Sea Horses, 1925; The Key of Life, 1928; My Brother Jonathan, 1928; Black Roses, 1929; Mr. and Mrs. Pennington, 1931; The House Under the Water, 1932; The Cage Bird, 1933; This Little World, 1934; White Ladies, 1935; Far Forest, 1936; They Seek a Country, 1937; Dr. Bradley Remembers, 1938; The City of Gold, 1939; Mr. Lucton's Freedom, 1940; Cotswold Honey, 1940; A Man About the House, 1942; The Island, an English Epic, 1944. Died Mar. 28, 1954.*

YOUNG, George (Benham), lawyer; b. Cleve., Feb. 17, 1894; s. Cornelius Clark and Ella Coburn (Benham) Y.; student Adelbert Coll. of Western Reserve U.; A.B., Dartmouth Coll., 1915; LL.B., Western Reserve U., 1919; m. Agnes Raymond Brooks, Nov. 27, 1920. Admitted to Ohio bar, 1919, since practiced law in Cleve.; mem. firms Andrews & Belden, 1927-32, Belden, Young & Beach, 1932-36, Day, Young, Veach & LeFever, 1936-38, Jones, Day, Cockley & Reavis, 1939-—; dir., sec. S. P. Mfg. Corp., Rex Products Co. Served as 1st lt., A.S., World War I. Mem. Am., Ohio, Cleve. bar assns., Phi Beta Kappa, Beta Theta Pi, Phi Delta Phi. Republican. Club: Union. Home: 12309 Fairhill Rd., Cleve. 20. Office: Union Commercial Bldg., Cleve. 14. Died July 3, 1957.

YOUNG, George, Jr., banker; b. Clifton, N.J., Jan. 12, 1892; s. George and Mary Catherine (McNamara) Y.; B.S., Dartmouth Coll., 1914; M.C.S., Amos Tuck Sch. of Administration and Finance, Hanover, N.H., 1915; m. Bertha Bennett, Apr. 28, 1922; 1 son, George III. Sec. Bd. of Trade, Passaic, N.J., 1915-17; with Passaic-Clifton Nat. Bank & Trust Co. since 1920, dir. since 1932, pres. since 1935; director N.J. Manufacturers Ins. Companies. Served as capt. 33d Arty. Brig., U.S. Army, 1917-19. Vice-chmn. Passaic Am. Red Cross; v.p. Passaic Gen. Hosp. Mem. Delta Tau Delta. Episcopalian. Mason. Clubs: Arcola Country (Ridgewood, N.J.); Bankers (N.Y. City); Pennington (Passaic, N.J.). Home: 225 Aycrigg Av. Office: 657 Main Av., Passaic, N.J. Died June 13, 1956.

YOUNG, George Gilray, newspaper ofcl.; b. Mar. 15, 1876; s. George Anderson and Annie Maria (Clarke) Y.; student pub. schs.; m. Juliette Helen Hogan, June 18, 1908; 1 son, Guy George. Came to U.S., 1899, naturalized, 1917. Began as reporter Winnipeg Free Press, 1894; free lance advt. writer, N.Y.C., 1900-03; with Hampton Advt. Agy., 1903-07; with Hearst newspapers, 1907-38, gen. mgr. Los Angeles Examiner, 1921-38. Clubs: Sunset, Uplifters, Authors. Home: Manhattan Beach, Cal. Died July 2, 1950.

YOUNG, Gordon, author; b. Mo., Sept. 27, 1886; s. A. Howard and Hettie (Kincaid) Y.; ed. pub. schs. Author: Savages, 1921; Wild Blood, 1922, Hurricane Williams, 1923; Men in the Night, 1924; Days of '49, 1925; Seibert of the Island, 1925; Dangerous Men, 1926; Hurricane Williams' Vengeance, 1926; Pearl Hunger, 1927; Gaboreau, 1927; Gaboreau the Terrible, 1927; Wastrel, 1927; Treasure, 1928; There Is Nought But Courage, 1928; Standish of the Star Y, 1928; LaRue of the Eighty-Eight, 1928; Tajola, 1932; The Devil's Passport, 1933; The Fighting Fool, 1933; Red Clark O'Tulloco, 1933; Red Clark Rides Alone, 1933; Red Clark of the Arrowhead, 1935; Huroc the Avenger, 1937; Red Clark on the Border, 1937; Red Clark Range Boss, 1938; Poems in Prose, 1938; Red Clark Two Gun Man, 1939; Mr. Beamish, 1940; Iron Rainbow, 1941; Red Clark Takes a Hand, 1941; Trouble Rides Double, 1942; Tall in the Saddle, 1943; Red Clark to the Rescue, 1946; Red Clark in Paradise, 1946; Red Clark at the Showdown, 1947; Crooked Shadows, 1947; Quarter Horse, 1947; Wanted, Dead or Alive, 1948. Home: 2325 Vestal Av., Los Angeles 26. Died Feb. 10, 1948.

YOUNG, James Nicholas, editor, writer; born San Marcos, Texas, Aug. 6, 1885; s. Adam Moore and Margaret Moore (Coleman) Y.; student U. of the South, 1902-04, Columbia, 1908, Harvard, 1909-11; m. Katharine Whipple Strong, Dec. 10, 1917 (dec. May 11, 1942); children—James Nicholas, Katherine Whipple. Mem. editorial staff Baltimore American, 1912, New Orleans Times-Picayune, 1913; Los Angeles Tribune, 1914, Los Angeles Examiner, 1914-17; mng. editor Leslie's Weekly, 1919-22; dir. Better Homes in America movement, 1922; asso. editor Am. Legion Weekly, 1923-24; asso. editor Collier's Weekly, 1924-53. Grad. R.O.T.C., The Presidio, San Francisco, 1917; commd. successively as 2d and 1st lt., 91st Div., Camp Lewis, Wash., 1917-18; grad. Army Sch. of the Line, Langres, France, 1918; mem. Gen. John J. Pershing's staff, G.H.Q., Chaumont, France, 1918-19; commd. capt., Regular Army, 1918. Elected Officier d'Academie, Ordres des Palmes (France), 1919; awarded Purple Heart by Gen. Pershing. Mem. Delta Tau Delta. Episcopalian. Author: 101 Plots Used and Abused, 1945. Contbr. articles and fiction to mags. Home: 455 E. 51st St., N.Y.C. Died Apr. 3, 1959; buried Arlington Nat. Cemetery.

YOUNG, Joseph Hardie, ry. official; b. Salt Lake City, Utah, Jan. 17, 1864; s. Judge Le Grand and Grace (Hardie) Y.; student St. Mark's Sch., Salt Lake City, and Univ. of Utah; m. Katherine Kimball Lawrence, Sept. 21, 1898; children—Jeanette Lawrence, Katherine. Began in engring. dept. of what is now Ore. Short Line R.R., 1881, and occupied various positions with same ry. and U.P. until 1886; traveling pass. agt. C.&N.W. Ry., 1886-89; gen. agt.

and gen. supt. Utah Central Ry., 1889-91; supt. Utah div. of U.P., 1891-1902; gen. supt. Rio Grande Western Ry. (now part of D.&R.G. Ry.), 1902-04; gen. supt. and gen. mgr. C.&S. Ry., 1904-07; gen. supt. St.L.&S.F. R.R.; gen. supt. S.P. Co., 1907-10; pres. Alaska S.S. Co.; v.p. Copper River & North Western Ry. and various other cos. and gen. rep. of the Alaska Syndicate in the Northwest, 1910-12; became pres. Spokane, Portland & Seattle Ry. Co., May 1912; also pres. Ore. Trunk Ry. Co., Pacific & Eastern Ry. Co., Ore. Electric Ry. Co., United Rys. Co., Spokane & Inland Empire R.R. Co., Dallas, Portland & Astoria Navigation Co., Ruth Trust Co., until 1914; pres. Norfolk Southern R.R. Co., 1914-18; apptd. federal mgr. Virginia R.R., May 18, 1918; also federal mgr. Norfolk Southern R.R.; apptd. sr. asst. dir., Div. of Operation of U.S. Railroad Administration, Washington, D.C., 1919; pres. Norfolk Southern R.R. Co., 1920-21; pres. and receiver D.R.G. Western R.R. Co., 1921-23; pres. Rio Grande Southern R.R. Co., 1923-25; mem. R.R. Mgrs. Com. Train Service Bd. Adjustment, Western Region; asst. to pres. Westinghouse Air Brake Co. and Union Switch & Signal Co., Jan. 1927—. Mason (32°). Clubs: Union League, Chicago, Saddle and Cycle, Westmoreland Country (Chicago); Recess (New York). Home: 1448 Lake Shore Drive. Office: Peoples Gas Bldg., Chgo. Died Nov. 15, 1958.

YOUNG, Lewis Emanuel, cons. engr.; b. Topeka, Oct. 1, 1878; s. William O. and Martha (Lebegern) Y.; B.S., Pa. State Coll., 1900; E.M., Ia. State Coll., 1904; Ph.D., U. Ill., 1915; D.Engring., Mo. Sch. Mines, 1947, Colo. Sch. Mines, 1951; m. Mabel E. Webb, July 1, 1903 (dec.); children—Edwin Webb, Lewis Eugene (dec.); m. 2d, Elizabeth Whipple, Oct. 3, 1927. Instr. mining Ia. State Coll., 1900-03; prof. mining Colo. Sch. Mines, 1903-07; cons. engr., Denver, 1903-07; dir. Mo. Sch. Mines, 1907-13; spl. field work Ill. Geol. Survey, 1913-17; asst. prof. bus. adminstrn. U. Ill., 1915-18; mining engr. Union Colliery Co., St. Louis, 1918-22, gen. mgr., 1922-26; prodn. v.p. Pitts. Coal Co., 1927-39; cons. mining engr., Pitts., 1939. Mem. Am. Inst. Mining and Metall. Engrs. (dir. 1937-42, v.p. 1942-45, pres. 1949), Canadian Inst. Mining and Metallurgy, Mining and Metall. Soc. Am., Am. Mining Congress, Coal Mining Inst. Am., Inst. Mining Engrs. (Eng.), Sigma Xi, Tau Beta Pi, Kappa Delta Pi, Beta Gamma Sigma, Phi Kappa Phi. Mason (Shriner). Clubs: Duquesne (Pitts.); Mining (N.Y.C.); University. Home: Schenley Park Apts., Fifth Av., Pitts. 13. Office: Oliver Bldg., Pitts. 22. Died Dec. 27, 1953; buried Homewood Cemetery, Pitts.

YOUNG, Mahonri (Mackintosh), sculptor, painter, etcher; b. Salt Lake City, Aug. 9, 1877; s. Mahonri M. and Agnes (Mackintosh) Y.; pupil J. T. Harwood, Salt Lake City; student Art Students League, N.Y.C., Julian, Colarossi and Delacluse acads., Paris; m. Cecilia Sharp, Feb. 19, 1907 (dec.); children—Cecilia Agnes (Mrs. Oliver Lay), Mahonri Sharp; m. 2d, Dorothy Weir, Feb. 17, 1931. Important works: statues Brigham Young (U.S. Capitol), Joseph Smith and his brother Hiram, Sea Gull Monument (all Salt Lake City), Father Kino Monument (Tucson), Monument to the Dead (Am. Pro Cathedral, Paris); designed and executed medals Pony Express for Philatelist Soc., The Builders for Medalic Art Soc.; Habitat groups Navahoes, Hopis, Apaches in Am. Mus. Natural History. Represented in: Met. Mus., Bklyn. Mus., Newark Library, Peabody Inst. (Balt.), Corcoran Gallery Art (Washington), Smithsonian Inst., Phillips Meml., Addison Gallery, Utah State Art Coll. Pres. Tiffany Found. Recipient state prizes for painting and sculptor, Utah Arts Inst., 1906; Helen Foster Barnett prize N.A.D., 1911, prize for portrait, 1931; silver medal for sculpture Panama P.I. Expn., 1915; 1st prize for sculpture Olympic Games, Los Angeles, 1932. Mem. A.N.A., 1912, N.A., 1923. Mem. Am. Acad. Arts and Letters, Am. Soc. Graphic Arts, Art Students League, Nat. Sculpture Soc. (v.p.), Inst. Arts and Letters, N.Y. Water Color Club. Clubs: Utah Artists (past pres.); Century, Nat. Arts (N.Y.C.). Home: 36 W. 44th St., N.Y.C. Died Nov. 2, 1957.

YOUNG, Percy S(acret), pub. utilities exec.; b. London, Eng., Dec. 19, 1870; s. Richard and Sarah Anne (Sacret) Y.; B.C.S., N.Y.U., 1908; m. Grace Whiting Mason, Dec. 7, 1904; children—Percy S. Jr., Mrs. Malcolm R. Warnock, George Wooldridge, William Clements, Thomas Rumsey, Mrs. Robert B. Cheney, Katharine (Mrs. Gordon B. Davis), Mrs. Leonard L. Shertzer, Jr. Began with Omaha Gas Co., 1890-95; traveling auditor United Gas Improvement Co., 1895-98, asst. agt., 1898-99; asst. treas., later sec. Hudson County Gas Co., 1899-1903; comptroller Public Service Corp. of N.J., 1903-14, treas., 1914-17, v.p., dir., 1917-39, chmn. exec. com., 1939-47, ret.; dir. Fireman's Ins. Co., Fidelity Union Trust Co., Brighton Mills, Inc., Walter Kidde & Co., Inc. Mem. council N.Y.U.; trustee Rutgers U. Episcopalian. Clubs: Essex (Newark); Montclair (N.J.) Golf; Plymouth (Mass.) Country; Yeamans Hall (Charleston, S.C.). Home: 97 Warren Pl., Montclair, N.J. Died Nov. 15, 1950.

YOUNG, Philip, trustee and real estate management; b. Portsmouth, N.H., Nov. 16, 1874; s. Aaron and Louisa Blaisdell (Paige) Y.; A.B., Dartmouth, 1921; m. Ella Margaret Bender, May 22, 1909 (died May 2, 1937; m. 2d, Ann Marie Kettell, Bucksport, Me., Sept. 11, 1944. With E. H. Rollins & Sons, 1894-1902; partner Montgomery, Rollins & Co., 1902-04; mem. Baker, Ayling & Co., 1904-10, Baker, Ayling & Young, 1910-19, Baker, Young & Co. (fiscal agts. for many cos.) since 1919; dir. Republic Service Co., Atlantic Ice Mfg. Co. since 1926, The Mead Co. Mem. Alpha Delta Phi. Republican. Congregationalist. Club: Union (Boston). Home: 8 Louisburg Sq. Office: 209 Washington St., Boston. Died Feb. 2, 1953.

YOUNG, Philip Endicott, rubber goods mfr.; b. Dorchester, Mass., Dec. 1, 1885; s. George H. and Elizabeth (Endicott) Y.; B.S., Mass. Inst. Tech., 1909; m. Edith B. Ames, May 11, 1910; children—Edith E. (Mrs. David H. Harris), Richard B. Pres. Acushnet Process Co., 1910—; dir. First Nat. Bank of New Bedford. Mem. Delta Kappa Epsilon. Clubs: Country, Wamsutta; Riviera Country (Coral Gables, Fla.). Home: 8 Fort St., Fairhaven. Office: Acushnet Process Co., New Bedford, Mass. Died June 17, 1955; buried Riverside Cemetery, Fairhaven, Mass.

YOUNG, Robert Ralph, corp. officer; b. Canadian, Tex., Feb. 14, 1897; s. David John and Mary Arabella (Moody) Y.; student Culver Mil. Acad., 1912-14, U. of Va., 1914-16; m. Anita Ten Eyck O'Keeffe, Apr. 27, 1916; 1 dau., Eleanor Jane Young. With du Pont Company, 1916-20, Allied Chem. Corp., 1921-22, Gen. Motors Corp., 1922-29; treas. Pierre du Pont and John Raskob Holding Co., 1929-31; partner Young, Kolbe & Co. (mems. N.Y. Stock Exchange), 1932-37; chmn. board of dirs. Alleghany Corp.; chmn. bd. Chesapeake & Ohio Ry. Co. 1942-54; chmn. bd. N.Y. Central System, 1954—. Clubs: Newport Country, Spouting Rock Beach Assn., Clambake, Reading Room, Ida Lewis Yacht (Newport, R.I.); Everglades Seminole. Contbr. mags. Founder Fedn. for Ry. Progress, 1947. Home: Fairholme. Newport, R.I. Office: 230 Park Av., N.Y.C. 17. Died Jan. 25, 1958.

YOUNG, Roland, actor; b. London, Eng., Nov. 11, 1887; s. Keith Downes and Emily Cornelia Y.; student Sherborn Sch. and Univ. Coll., London; Tree's Acad. of Dramatic Art; m. Marjorie Kummer, Sept. 5, 1921. Came to U.S., 1912, naturalized, 1918. First appeared on stage in London, 1908. Prin. rôles: Rollo in Rollo's Wild Oat; General Burgoyne in The Devil's Disciple; Neil Macraé in Beggar on Horseback; Lord Dilling in The Last of Mrs. Cheyney; etc. Clubs: Coffee House (N.Y.C.); Cliff Dwellers (Chgo.). Author: Actors and Others. Home: 230 W. 59th St., N.Y.C. Died June 5, 1953.*

YOUNG, Roy Odo, M.D., indslist; b. Youngsville, La., July 31, 1870; s. Nicholas Dominique (M.D.) and Carmelite Idea (Roy) Y.; B.S. La. State U., 1890; M.D., Tulane, 1894; m. Nita Regina Scranton, Sept. 30, 1897. House surgeon Houston & Tex. Central R.R. Hosp, Houston, Tex., 1894-95; practiced Youngsville, 1895-1907; financier and agriculturist; chmn. bd. Bank of Lafayette & Trust Co., Lafayette, La.; pres. Young's Land Co., Youngsville; chmn. exec. com. Broussard (La.) Cotton Oil Co.; 1st v.p. State Agr. Credit Assn., New Orleans; mng. dir. Youngsville Sugar Co., Milton Cane Products, Home Land Co.; mng. dir. and treas. Duplex Co., Inc., R. O. Young, Inc., Young's Motors, Inc.; gen. mgr. La. Coast Furs. Mem. Constitutional Conv. of La., 1921; v.p. La. State Chamber Commerce (ex-pres.); chmn. State Bankers Agrl. Com., 1913—. Mem. Bd. of Supervisors La. State Univ. and Coll. Mem. Kappa Sigma. Republican. Methodist. Mason, Elk. Home: Youngsville, La. Died May 26, 1951.

YOUNG, Thomas Gorsuch, banker; b. Baltimore; s James and Sarah Jane (Gorsuch) Y.; student Pa. Mil. Coll., 1901-02; spl. course mech. engring. U. Pa., 1902-05; m. Isabel Evans Mundy, Jan. 14, 1909; 1 son, Thomas Gorsuch. Dir., v.p. Broadway Savs. Bank, 1936; propr. Auto Supply Co., jobbers, 1909-40; chmn. bd., mem. exec. com., dir. Fidelity Trust Co., 1951—; rpes. Calvert Bank (merged with Fidelity Trust), 1944—; pres. Oak Lawn Cemetery Co. Mem., pres. City Service Commn., 1925-28; city and state tax collector for Balt., 1932-44. Past sec., now pres. bd. mgrs. Maryland Inst.; mem. bd. dirs. Gen. German Orphans Home; mem. bd. trustees St. Paul's Sch. Mem. Sigma Nu. Mem. St. Paul's Ch. (vestryman). Odd Fellow, Mason. Clubs: Automobile of Md. (past treas.), Univ., Country, Mchts. (Balt). Home: 1305 Park Av., Balt. 17. Office: Fidelity Trust Co., Balt. 3. Died Mar. 11, 1953; buried Greenmount Cemetery, Balt.

YOUNG, Thomas Kay, clergyman; b. Sewell, W. Va.; s. William Wilson and Elizabeth (Kay) Y.; A.B., Hampden-Sydney Coll., 1908, D.D., 1920; B.D., Union Theol. Sem., Va., 1911; student Washington and Lee U., 1919-23; D. Litt., Southwestern at Memphis, 1946; m. Harriet Rebecca Cox, Sept. 21, 1911 (died July 10, 1939); children—Tom Kay, William Benjamin, Helen L., Mary Elizabeth; m. 2d, Estelle Bond Neusum, July 26, 1942. Grew up in coal camp on W.Va.; miner, mule driver and blacksmith; ordained ministry Presbyn. Ch. U.S.; home mission work in coalfields, 1 yr.; successively pastor Covington, Lexington and Roanoke, Va.; pastor Idlewild Ch., Memphis, 1930—. Trustee Union Theol. Sem., 1918-30, Stonewall Jackson Coll., Abingdon, Va., 1925-29. Mem. Exec. Com. on Foreign Missions, 1931—, Permanent Judicial Com. of Gen. Assembly; com. Cooperation and Union; moderator Gen. Assembly, 1945-46. Mem. Kappa Sigma, Omicron Delta Kappa. Democrat. Mason. Home: 587 S. Belvidere St., Memphis. Died Mar. 23, 1954; buried Memphis Meml. Park.

YOUNG, Victor, composer, musical dir.; b. Chgo., Aug. 8, 1900; s. William and Rose Young; grad. Conservatory, Warsaw, Poland, 1917. Debut as violinist Orchestra Hall, Chgo., 1921; violinist Grauman's Million Dollar Theatre, Hollywood, 1922, Central Park Theatre, Chgo., 1929; became condr., arranger, dir., Texaco, Shell Oil, Westinghouse radio music program and recordings, 1929; mus. dir. Decca Records; mem. mus. staff Paramount Pictures, Inc., from 1935; composer mus. score for more than 100 films, including Golden Earrings, Three Coins in the Fountain, The Greatest Show on Earth, Frenchmen's Creek, Shane, Johnny Guitar, Country Girl, Drum Beat, For Whom the Bell Tolls, Scaramouche, Samson and Delilah, The Story of Will Rogers, Little Boy Lost, The Star, About Mrs. Leslie, Quiet Man, Around the World in Eighty Days; composer of music for opening of TV program Medic, 1954; composer, mus. dir. Music for Seventh Heaven (play), 1955. Mem. Musicians Union (N.Y.C., Chgo., Los Angeles). Died Nov. 10, 1956.*

YOUNG, William Lindsay, clergyman; b. Braidwood, Ill., Feb. 2, 1893; s. Hugh Gold and Lillias Kilpatrick (Walker) Y.; grad. Moody Bible Inst., 1916; A.B., Carroll Coll., Waukesha, Wis., 1920; B.D., Manitoba Coll., Winnipeg, Can., 1922; M.A., U. Mont., 1926; LL.D., Waynesburg (Pa.) Coll., 1932, Litt.D. (hon.), 1941; D.D., Carroll Coll., 1935; L.H.D., Lincoln Coll., 1941; LL.D., Johnson C. Smith U., Charlotte, N.C., 1943; PhD., U. Pitts., 1947; m. Tess Elizabeth Krueger, August 10, 1916; children—William Hugh, Robert Lindsay, Tess Elizabeth. Ordained ministry Presbyn. Ch., 1918; pastor Beaver Dam, Wis., 1918-22; sec. Y.M.C.A., U. Wis., 1922-23; pastor U. Mont., 1923-28, dir. Sch. of Religion; 1924-29; gen. dir. dept. of univ. work, Presbyn. Bd. of Christian Edn. in U.S.A., 1929-34, gen. dir. dept. of colls., theol. sems. and tng. schs., 1934-36; was also gen. dir. Dept. of Religion in Higher Edn., and chmn. div. of univ. work of Council Ch. Bds. of Edn.; pres. Park Coll., Parkville, Mo., 1936-43; regional dir. Nat. Conf. of Christians and Jews for Western Pa. and W.Va., 1944; v.p. Nat. Conf. Christians and Jews, 1945—; dir. World Conf. Christians and Jews. Served as 1st lt. and chaplain, U.S. Army, World War I. Trustee Omaha Theol. Sem. Moderator Gen. Assembly Presbyn. Ch. in U.S.A., 1940-41. Mem. Am. Assn. Univ. Profs., Alpha Kappa Delta, Phi Alpha Tau. Republican. Mason; mem. Order of Eastern Star. Asso. editor Presbyn. Tribune. Contbr. to religious and ednl. jours. Home: 406 S. Hamel Rd., Los Angeles 48. Office: 3335 Wilshire Blvd., Los Angeles 5. Died Aug. 1959.

YOUNGER, John Elliott, engr., prof. engring.; b. Canyon, Tex., Mar. 7, 1892; s. James Beauregard and Mary Ella (Elliott) Y.; student West Tex. State Teachers Coll., 1911-12, U. of Tex., 1914-15; B.S., U. of Calif., 1923, M.S., 1924, Ph.D., 1925; m. Nancy Brunette Francis, June 3, 1919; children—John Francis, Nancy Ella. Prin. Abernathy (Tex.) High. Sch., 1912-14; teacner Philippine Islands, 1914-17; teacher of mech. engring., U. of Calif., 1923-27; sr. aeronautical engr. U.S. Army Air Corps, 1927-29; prof. of mech. engring., U. of Calif., 1929-38; prof. mech. engring., head dept., U. of Md., 1938-47, since 1948; prof. Structures, Inst. Tecnológica de Aeronáutico, Brasil, 1947-48. Served as 2d lt., Res. mil. aviator, Air Serv., U.S.A., 1917-19. Stud. aeronautl. developments in round-the-world tour, 1936; lectured before Royal Aeronaut. Soc. of Great Britain, London, on high altitude flying, 1938. Recipient of Spirit of St. Louis Gold medal for contributions to science of aviation, 1941. Fellow Inst. Aeronautical Sciences; mem. A.S.M.E., Am. Soc. Engring. Edn., American Assn. of Univ. Profs., Sigma Xi, Tau Beta Pi. Author: Dynamics of Airplanes (with B. M. Woods), 1931; Airplane Construction and Repair, 1931; Structural Design of Metal Airplanes, 1935; Airplane Maintenance (with A. F. Bonnalie and N. F. Ward), 1937; Mechanics for Engineering Students, 1938; Mechanics of Aircraft Structures, 1942; Advanced Dynamics, 1958. Contbr. many papers to jours. of scientific socs. Home: 4124 Woodbery St., Hyattsville, Md. Office: U. of Md., Coll. Park, Md. Died Dec. 29, 1958; buried Arlington Nat. Cemetery.

YOUNG-HUNTER, John, artist; b. Glasgow, Scotland, Oct. 29, 1874; s. Colin Hunter and Isabella Ratray (Young) H.; ed. Clifton Coll., Royal Academy Schools, London, and U. of London; studied art under his father and Sir William Orchardson, Sir Lawrence Alma-Tadema and John S. Sargent. Exhibited yearly, 1900— at Royal Acad., London; came to

U.S., 1913; exhibited in New York; Washington, Buffalo, Toledo, Boston, Chicago, Kansas City (Mo.), Okla. City. Hon. mention Paris Salon, 1910, silver medal, same, 1914; gold medal, Allied Artists of Am., 1932; hon. mention, Western State Coll. Colo., 1943; cash prize, 1944. Prin. works: "My Lady's Garden," Nat. Tate Gallery, London; "The Dream." Musée de Luxembourg, Paris; "Two Voices," Walker Art Gallery, Liverpool, Eng.; "Judith Shakespeare," Art Museum, Wellington, New Zealand; portrait of President King, Oberlin (O.) Museum; portrait of Raymond Henneker-Heaton, Worcester (Mass.) Art Museum; portrait sketch, Museum of Art, Dayton, O.; portrait of Scott Skinner, Museum of Art, Dundee, Scotland; portrait, Duke of Argyle, Govt. House, Ottawa, Can.; portraits: Pres. F. Knapp, Texas Tech. Coll., Clifford B. Jones, Pres., Texas Tech. Coll. Pres. William M. Whyburn of Tex. Tech., Dr. Thomas Grover of U. Kan., Profs. Edwin Grant Conklin, Charles F. W. McClure, Princeton U.; Prof. Jacob H. Hollander, Prof. Barnet, Johns Hopkins; Andrew Carnegie, Harvard. Mem. Am. Water Color Soc., Conn. Acad. Fine Arts, Allied Artists of America. Clubs: Salmagundi (New York); Chelsea Arts (London). Studio: Taos, N.M. Died Aug. 9, 1955.

YOUNGQUIST, G(ustaf) Aaron, lawyer; b. Skarabors Lan, Sweden, Nov. 4, 1885; s. Andrew and Margareta (Abrahamson) Y.; brought to U.S., 1887; LL.B., cum laude, St. Paul Coll. Law, 1909; m. Scharlie M. Robertson, June 29, 1915; children—Robertson, John, Margaret (Mrs. John R. Goetz), Scharlie (Mrs. Dale R. Wikman). Admitted to Minn. bar, 1909; county atty. of Polk County, 1914-18; asst. atty. gen. of Minn., 1921-27, atty. gen., 1928-29; asst. atty. gen. U.S. in charge of Tax Div., 1929-33; now in practice Mpls., mem. firm. Youngquist, Comaford, Fassett & Clarkson; argued some 70 cases before Supreme Ct. of U.S. Mem. faculty St. Paul Coll. of Law, 1924-29. Mem. adv. com. on Rules of Criminal Procedure, apptd. by Supreme Ct. of U.S. Mem. bd. dirs. Minn. Valley Natural Gas Co., First Fed. Savs. & Laon Assn. Trustee Mpls. Soc. Fine Arts; chmn. adv. com. Rules of Civil Procedure, apptd. by Minn. Supreme Ct. Capt. Minn. Nat. Guard, 1918, capt. Army Service Corps, U.S. Army, 1918. Mem. Am., Minn., Hennepin County Bar Assns., Am. Law Inst., Am. Legion. Republican. Conglist. Clubs: Minneapolis, Woodhill Country. Contbr. to Am. Bar Assn. Jour., Nat. Tax Mag. Decorated Comdr. Order of Vasa (Sweden). Home: 1700 Dupont Av. S., Mpls. Office: Northwestern Bank Bldg., Mpls. 2. Died Oct. 29, 1959.

YOUTZ, Lewis Addison (ūtz), chemist; b. Canton, O., July 21, 1864; s. Reuben J. and Harriett (Miller) Y.; Ph.B., Simpson Coll., Indianola, Ia., 1890, Ph.M., 1893, M.S., 1902; Ph.D., Columbia, 1902; m. Eva I. Moore, Nov. 3, 1892. Science teacher high sch., Des Moines, Ia., 1891-93 asso. prof. chemistry; and biology, Simpson Coll., 1893-99; prof. science, Montana Wesleyan U., 1899-1900; prof. chemistry, Lawrence Coll., Appleton, Wis., 1902-— and of Inst. Paper Chemistry, 1930-—; former chemist, Riverside Paper and Fiber Co., Great Lakes Chem. Co., Patten Paper Co. (all of Appleton). Mem. Am. Chem. Soc., Phi Kappa Psi, Phi Beta Kappa. Republican. Methodist. Author: Laboratory Outline of General Inorganic Chemistry, 1904. Home: 843 E. South St., Appleton, Wis. Died Nov. 19, 1947.

YOWELL, Everett Irving, astronomer; b. Cin., Jan. 2, 1870; s. Richard Chase and Sarah Louisa (Lloyd) Y.; C.E., U. Cin., 1891, M.S., 1893, Ph.D., 1911; studied U. Göttingen, 1894-95; m. Elizabeth Cabell Carrington, May 30, 1912; children—John Lloyd, Mary Tucker, Everett Carrington, Elizabeth Morton. Instr. mathematics, U. Cin., 1891-94, 1895-97; asst. in Cin. Obs. (part of U. Cin.), 1897-1901, U.S. Naval Obs., 1901-06; instr. in mathematics, U.S. Naval Acad., 1906-09; 1st asst. Cin. Obs., 1909-30, acting dir., 1930-31, dir. and head dept. of astronomy, 1931-40, acting dir., 1943-46; v.p., chmn. math. sect., Ohio Acad. Sci., 1944-46. Fellow A.A.A.S. (v.p., chmn. astronomy sect., 1939); mem. Am. Astron. Soc., Am. Math. Soc., Math. Assn. Am., Nat. Inst. Social Scis, Sigma Alpha Epsilon, Sigma Xi. Mem. Naval Obs. eclipse party, 1900, 05; Internat. Latitude observer, 1910-16; in charge Cin. Obs. eclipse party, 1932. Ind. Republican. Author of various publs. of Cincinnati Observatory. Home: 3127 Griest Av., Cincinnati 8, O. Died Mar. 13, 1959.

YUDKIN, Arthur M(eyer), ophthalmologist; born at Ansonia, Connecticut, December 31, 1892; son of Michael and Minnie (Zandler) Y.; Ph.B., Yale University, 1914, M.D., 1917; married Adele I. Weissman, Jan. 25, 1920; children—Gerald S., Marvin H. Asst. resident physician, New Haven Hosp., 1917-18, interne ophthalmology, 1918; clin. asst. ophthalmology and laryngology, Yale Sch. of Medicine, 1918-21, clin. instr. ophthalmology, 1921-25, asst. clin. prof., 1925-28, asso. clin. prof., 1928-34, clin. prof. ophthalmology since 1934; attending surgeon ophthalmology, Grace-New Haven Community Hosp. Univ. Service, attending ophthalmologist St. Raphael Hosp.; cons. ophthalmologist Griffin Hosp., Derby. Conn., Bristol Hosp. and Meriden Hosp., also to Nat. Soc. for Prevention of Blindness. Major Med. Res. Corp, 1943. Mem. Am. Acad. Ophthal. and Otol., A.M.A. (sect. ophthalmology), Am. Ophthol. Soc., Assn. Resrch. in Ophthol., Nat. Soc. Prevention Blindness, Soc. Exptl. Biol. and Medicine, N.Y. Acad. Medicine, N.Y. Soc. Clin. Ophthol., A.A.A.S., Sigma Xi, Sigma Alpha Mu. Clubs: Milford Yacht; Racebrook Country; Faculty (Yale). Co-editor: Practitioners Library of Medicine and Surgery, Vol. 11, 1939. Contbr. articles to med. jours. Home: Tallwood Rd., Woodbridge. Office: 257 Church St., New Haven 10, Conn. Died May 1957.

YUNGBLUTH, Bernard Joseph (yŭng'blōōth), railway pres.; b. Marquette, Mich., Aug. 29, 1882; s. Conrad and Anna Marie (Derra) Y.; ed. pub. schs. and by taking spl. courses; m. May M. Lieblein, Apr. 20, 1904; children—Marie A., Bernard J., Lenore A. (Mrs. Ralyea), George C., Clyde F., Grace (Mrs. Frawenheim), Rita (Mrs. Gibson). Began 1899, at $15 a month, in employ of Duluth, South Shore & Atlantic R.R., at Marquette; with Mineral Range R.R., 1900-05, L.S.&M.S. R.R., at Cleveland, 1905-06, L.E.&Western R.R., Lima, O., 1906-10; connected with Pittsburgh Rys. Co., electric service, 1910, continuing 10 years; Phila. Rapid Transit Co., 1920-25, serving as member coordinating committee, supervisor of purchase and supplies, asst. v.p. of traffic and assistant vice president of finance; elected vice president in charge operation, Internat. Railway Company, urban and interurban transportation, Buffalo, N.Y., 1925, president, 1926-—, also chmn. bd., 1943-47, ret. 1947; former tchr. transportation U. Pitts.; former lectr. pub. utilities Temple U. Mem. Engineering Soc. of Buffalo. Republican. Catholic. Clubs: Buffalo Athletic, Rotary (ex-pres.), Automobile. Home: 418 Parker Av., Buffalo 16. Died Apr. 18, 1957; buried Mt. Olivet Cemetery, Kenmore, N.Y.

YUST, Walter (ūst), editor; b. Phila., May 16, 1894; s. Robert and Rose Dorothy (Bauer) Y.; A.B., U. Pa., 1917; m. Ruth McClintock Barker, Feb. 15, 1923; children—Jane Ann, Larry Barker. Sec. in charge, YMCA, Camp Hill, Newport News, Va., 1917-18; with Phila. Evening Ledger, 1917, Phila. Press, 1918-20, Memphis Press, 1921, New Orleans Item, 1922; mng. editor Double Dealer, 1923; asso. editor Literary Review, editor Literary Lobby, New York Evening Post, 1923-26; literary editor Phila. Pub. Ledger, 1926-30; advt. mgr. Ency. Britannica, Inc., 1930-32; asso. editor Ency. Britannica and Britannica Junior, 1932-38, editor-in-chief of all Britannica publs., 1938-—. Mem. Phi Beta Kappa, Alpha Chi Rho. Club: Caxton (Chicago). Home: 2760 Eastwood Av., Evanston, Ill. Office: 425 N. Michigan Av., Chgo. Died Feb. 29, 1960.

Z

ZABRISKIE, Edwin G., (zȧ-brĭs'kĭ), physician: b. Flatbush, L.I., N.Y., Oct. 7, 1874; s. John Lloyd and Eliza (Garvin) Z.; Erasmus Hall, 1880-90; Columbia U., 1890-94; M.D., Long Island Coll. Hosp., 1897; Faculty of Med., U. of Berlin, 1898-1900; Faculté de Medécin, U. of Paris, 1900; m. Blanche arnaud, Dec. 29, 1919. Began medical practice, 1901; Arnaud, Dec. 29, 1919. Began medical practice, 1901; Goldwater Memorial Hosp.; consulting neurologist —Hartford (Conn.) Retreat, Lawrence Hosp., Ossining, N.Y., Manhattan Eye and Ear Hosp., Mount Vernon (N.Y.) Hosp., St. John's Riverside (Yonkers), St. Joseph's Hosp. (Rockaway); hon. surgeon, N.Y. Police Dept. Served as contract surgeon U.S. Army, Aug. 1917 capt.; to lt. col., Med. Corps, 1917-18. Mem. A.M.A. (pres.), Am. Neurological Assn., Assn. for Research in Nervous and Mental Disease, Am. Psychiat. Assn., N.Y. Soc. for Clin. Psychiat., N.Y. Acad. of Med. (fellow), N.Y. County Med. Soc. Clubs: Bohemian (San Francisco); Garden City Golf (Garden City, N.Y.); Pine Valley Golf (N.J.); Union, Century, Bohemian Musicians (N.Y. City). Home: 1185 Park Av. Office: 115 E. 61st St., N.Y.C. Died Jan. 1959.

ZABRISKIE, George Albert, flour mcht.; b. N.Y. C., Dec. 7, 1868; s. John Albert and Martha L. (Knox) Z.; student pub. schs.; LL.D., Rollins Coll.; unmarried. Began in flour business, N.Y.C., 1883; now dir. Columbia Baking Co. Pres. U.S. Sugar Assn., U.S. Sugar Equalization Bd. Sugar and flour adminstr., World War I. Decorated Knight Order of the Crown (Belgian); Icelandic Falcon (Iceland); Order of Polonia Restituta (Poland). Mem. N.Y. Produce Exchange; past pres. N.Y. Hist. Soc.; mem. Soc. Colonial Wars, S.R. in State of N.Y., Soc. War of 1812, etc. Democrat. Episcopalian. Clubs: Salmagundi, India House, New York Athletic, Rockland Country, Grolier, Garden City Golf. Home: 222 Central Park South. Office: 21 West St., N.Y.C. Died Jan. 2, 1954; buried Brookside Cemetery, Englewood, N.J.

ZADEIKIS, Povilas (zä-dā-ĕ'kēs), diplomat; b. in Lithuania, Mar. 14, 1887; s. Juozas and Teofile (Klimas) Z.; grad. Imperial Univ. of St. Petersburg, Russia, 1912; m. Marē Radzevičaite, Aug. 30, 1923; 1 dau., Mirga-Zita. Mem. Lithuanian mission in Leningrad, 1918; minister nat. defense, 1919; v.p. Lithuanian finance mission in United States, 1920; mem. Lithuanian Military Delegation in France, 1923; consul in Chicago, 1924-28; consul gen. in N.Y. City, 1928-35; E.E. and M.P. from Lithuania to U.S., since July 1935. Served as lt. col. Engrs. Corps, Lithuanian Army Reserve. Awarded Order of Vytautas the Great and Gediminas (Lithuanian). Home: 2622 16th St. N.W., Washington. Died May 11, 1957.

ZAHM, Albert Francis, educator; b. New Lexington, O..; s. J. M. and M. E. (Braddock) Z.; A.B., U. of Notre Dame, Ind., 1883, A.M., 1885, M.S., 1890; M.E. Cornell, 1892; Ph.D., Johns Hopkins, 1898. Prof. mathematics U. Notre Dame, 1885-89, mathematics and mechanics, 1890-92; asso. prof. mechanics Cath. U. Am., 1895-1907, prof., 1907-08; chief research engr. Curtiss Aeroplane Co., 1914-15; dir. Aerodynamical Lab., USN, 1916-29; in charge aero. div. Library of Congress, 1930-46, occupying the Guggenheim chair of aeronautics. Del. Internat. Conf. Aerial Navigation, 1893, 1900. Recipient Laetare medal U. Notre Dame, 1925, Mendel medal Villanova Coll., 1930. Mem. Am. Soc. M.E., Philos. Soc. Washington, Washington Acad. Sciences, Inst. Aero. Scis. Author: Treatise on Aerial Navigation; booklet on Early Powerplane Fathers; also many tech. papers on aerial research. Address: Cosmos Club, Washington. Died July 23, 1954; buried Community Cemetery, Notre Dame, Ind.

ZANTZINGER, Clarence Clark (zănt'zĭng'ẽr), architect; b. Phila., Aug. 15, 1872; s. Alfred (M.D.) and Sarah Crawford (Clark) Z.; Ph.B., Yale, 1892; B.S., in Architecture, U. of Pa., 1895; A.D.G., École des Beaux Arts, Paris, 1901; m. Margaret S. Buckley, Oct. 24, 1903; children—C. Clark, Alfred, Sarah Z. Groome, Mary-Vaux Z. Wurts. Practiced, Phila., 1901-51, retired. Fellow Am. Inst. Architects, 1911, National Academician, 1945. Mem. Am. Inst. Arts and Letters, Art Alliance, Soc. Beaux Arts Architects, Société des Architects Diplomés, Pa. Soc. S.R., Soc. Colonial Wars in State of Pa. Officer Legion d'Honneur (France). Clubs: Yale, Century Assn. (New York). Address: 8500 Seminole Av., Chestnut Hill, Phila. Died Sept. 26, 1954; buried St. Thomas Churchyard, Whitemarsh, Pa.

ZAPFFE, Frederick Carl, physician; b. Milw., Mar. 16, 1873; s. August and Babette (Weiss) Z.; student grammar and high schs., Milw.; M.D., Coll. Phys. and Surg. (U. Ill.), 1896; m. Mazie A. Stolba, Oct. 21, 1896. Mem. A.M.A., Ill., Chgo. med. socs., Assn. of Am. Med. Colleges (sec.). Lt. comdr. USN Med. R.C.; retired. Author of Zapffe's Manual of Bacteriology. Contbr. to med. jours. Home: 832 Washington Blvd., Oak Park, Ill. Office: 5 S. Wabash Av., Chgo. Died 1951.

ZAPOTOCKY, Antonin, president of Czechoslovakia; b. Zakolany, Czechoslovakia, Dec. 19, 1884; s. Ladislav and Barbara (Dolejsová) Z.; ed. at pub. schs.; m. Sklenickova, Sept. 22, 1910; children—Marie, Jirina. Gen. sec. Communist Party of Czechoslovakia, 1923; dep. Nat. Assembly, 1925-38; gen. sec. Revolutionary Trade Union orgn. of Czechoslovakia, 1928-38; chmn. United Revolutionary Trade Union Movement in Czechoslovakia since 1945; dep. of the Provisional Nat. Assembly since 1945; dep. Constituent Nat. Assembly since 1946; chmn. Central Council of Trade Union, U.R.O., since 1946; dep. prime minister, 1948, prime minister; now president of Czechoslovakia. Mem. presidency Central Com. of the Communist Party of Czechoslovakia. Author: The Fight for the Unity of the Union Movement; We Cannot Live the Old Way; New Trade Union Policies; The Revolutionary Trade Union Movement after February 1948; The Unity of the Trade Unions a Support for the Fight for Socialization; (novels) New Fighters Will Arise; Stormy Year; Fiery Light over Kladno. Address: Prague, Czechoslovakia. Died Nov. 13, 1957.

ZAROUBIN, Georgi N., Soviet diplomat; b. May 6, 1900; ed. Stalin Indsl. Acad. and Moscow Textile Inst.; m. Elizaveta V. Dir. Molotov Indsl. Acad., 1931-35; chief central bd. edn. People's Commissariat for Light Industry, 1935-38; dep. commissar gen., chmn. Art Council of Soviet Pavilion, Internat. Exhbn., N.Y.C., 1938-40; joined Soviet Diplomatic Service, 1940, ambassador to Can., 1944-46, Gt. Britain, 1946-52, U.S. 1952-58; dep. minister fgn. affairs USSR, 1958-—. Served with Red Army, 1918-24. Home and office: 1125 16th St. N.W., Washington. Died Nov. 24, 1958.

ZDANOWICZ, Casimir Douglass (stăn'ō-vĭch), coll. prof.; b. Gallatin, Tenn., Sept. 14, 1883; s. Casimir and Juliet Glass (Douglass) Z.; A.B., Vanderbilt U., 1903; A.M., Harvard, 1905, Ph.D., 1906; Officier d'Académie; studied, Paris, Madrid, Florence, 1906-07; m. Frederica E. McBain, Feb. 3, 1933. Instr. Romance langs., U. of Wis., 1907-10, asst. prof., 1910-19; prof. Romance langs., Randolph-Macon Woman's Coll., Va., 1919-21; asso. prof. Romance langs., U. of Wis., 1921-23, prof. since 1923, chmn. dept., 1923-30. French dir. Army Y.M.C.A., Fort Oglethorpe, Ga., 1918; pvt. U.S. Inf., 1919; (prof. English) Foyers du Soldat, Centre de Préparation, Metz, 1919. Decorated Chevalier Legion d'Honneur. Mem. Modern Lang. Assn. Am. (mem. exec. council 1945-48, v.p. 1952), Nat. Fedn. Modern Lang. Teachers (pres. 1931), Am. Assn. Teachers, French (pres., 1939-40, 1944-46), Modern Humanities Research Assn., Wisconsin Academy Sciences Arts and Letters, Société des anciens textes, Société des textes modernes, Soc. des Am. de la Bib. Nat. (exec. sec. Am. Group), Fed. Internat. des Prof. de Lang. Viv. (v.p.), Am. Assn. Univ. Profs., Wesley Foundation of Wis. (pres. 1931-44), Phi Beta Kappa, Alpha Tau Omega. Methodist. Club: University. Co-author: Liberty French, 1918. Editor of college texts. Contbr. on philol. topics. Home: 2214 Commonwealth Av., Madison 5, Wis. Died Jan. 7, 1953; buried Gallatin, Tenn.

ZEDER, Fred Morrell (zē'dĕr), vice-chmn. bd. dirs. Chrysler Corp.; b. Bay City, Mich., Mar. 19, 1886; s. Rudolph J. and Matilda (McKendry) Z.; B.Sc.M.E., U. of Mich., 1909, hon. Master Engring., 1933; Dr. of Engring., 1944; m. Lucille Monroe, Sept. 10, 1918; children—Dorothy June, Fred Monroe, Priscilla Ann, Margaret Lucille. Engr., mfg. corps., Milwaukee and Detroit, 1909-13; cons. engr. with Studebaker Corp., 1913, chief engr., 1914-20; pres. Zeder-Skelton-Breer Engring. Co., 1921-24; became v.p. in charge engring., Chrysler Corp., 1924, now vice-chmn. bd. Mem. national exec. bd., Boy Scouts of America. Member Am. Soc. M.E., Am. Soc. C.E., Engring. Society of Detroit, American Society for Testing Materials, Soc. Automotive Engrs., The Franklin Inst., National Inventors Council, Tau Beta Pi, Sigma Xi. Republican. Catholic. Knight of Malta. Clubs: Athletic, Golf, Detroit, Grosse Pointe, Grosse Pointe Yacht, Detroit Country. Home: 17500 E. Jefferson St., Grosse Pointe, Mich. Office: 341 Massachusetts Av. (Highland Park), Detroit. Died Feb. 24, 1951.

ZEHRING, Blanche, educator; b. Miamisburg, O., Apr. 24, 1867; d. Lewis Henry and Elizabeth (Gebhart) Z.; B.S., Ohio Wesleyan U., 1890; grad. student, Yale, 1894-7, Ph.D., 1897; studied in Germany, 1903-4, U. Chgo., traveled in Palestine, Egypt, Asia Minor, Turkey and Greece, for archaeological study, 1909. International and state secretary of YWCA, Chgo., 1890-4; prof. English lit., Coll. for Women, Columbia, S.C., 1897-8; prof. N.T. and philosophy, Nat. Training Sch., Washington, 1899-1903; prof. Bibl. lit. and Semitic history, Wells Coll., Aurora, N.Y., 1904-1915. Mem. Phi Beta Kappa, Soc. Bibl. Lit. and Exegesis, Religious Edn. Assn., Assn. Collegiate Alumnae; mem. D.A.R., Am. Hist. Assn. Lecturer, Bibl. history, geography, Mohammedan history, etc. Home: Miamisburg, O. Died Aug. 12, 1950.

ZEIGLER, Lee Woodward, artist; b. Baltimore, May 7, 1868; s. Daniel and Laura (Woodward) Z.; student Baltimore public schools, Maryland Institute and Art Sch. of Charcoal Club, Baltimore; m. Mary Stuart, d. William J. and Mary Stuart (Norton) Roe, Oct. 16, 1909; 1 dau., Audrey (Mrs. Richard M. Archer-Shee). Contributor drawing of society subjects to Life, New York, 1889-94, also to several mags. Has illustrated editions de luxe of works of Charles Kingsley, Thèophile Gautier, Jane Austin and Honoré de Balzac; mural decorations; St. Thomas Ch., New Windsor, N.Y.; Public Library, St. Paul; Maryland Inst., Baltimore, Md.; Trinity Luth. Ch., Ft. Wayne, Ind.; All Saints-by-the-Sea, Monticito, Calif.; Ch. of St. John the Evangelist, N.Y. City; Crucifixion, St. Michael's R.C. Ch., N.Y. City; Ch. of St. Francis of Assisi, Phelps, N.Y. Museum, Stony Point, N.Y.; St. Mary's R.C. Ch., Auburn, N.Y.; Chapel, Reformatory, Elmira, N.Y.; "Faerie Queene" decoration (eighteen panels 8 feet high, above book shelves) Enoch Pratt Free Library, Baltimore; many portraits. Exhibited Am. Water Color Soc., Water Color Club, Nat. Acad. Design. Gold medal, exhbn. of Northwestern Artists, 1915. Dir. St. Paul (Minn.) Inst. Sch. of Art, 1910-18. Fellow Royal Soc. of Arts (London); mem. N.Y. Southern Soc., N.Y. Md. Soc., Hudson Highland Art Assn., Medieval Acad. America, Nat. Temple Hill Assn. (v.p.), Nat. Soc. Mural Painters. Home: "Fanewood," New Windsor-on-Hudson, P.O Newburgh, N.Y. Died June 16, 1952; buried St. Georges Cemetery, Newburgh.

ZELENY, John, physicist; b. Racine, Wis., Mar. 26, 1872; s. Anthony Herbert and Josephine (Pitka) Z.; B.S., U. Minn., 1892, Ph.D., 1906; student U. of Berlin, 1897; A.B., U. of Cambridge, Eng., 1899; M.A., Yale, 1915; m. Carolyn S. Rogers, June 21, 1905 (died Dec. 13, 1936); children—Elizabeth Rogers, Henrietta Carolyn; m. 2d, Clara Rogers Dunn, Dec. 26, 1938. Instr. physics, U. Minn., 1892-96, asst. prof., 1896-1900, asso. prof., 1900-08, prof. and head dept., 1908-15, acting dean Grad. Sch., 1912-13; prof., chmn. dept. and dir. grad. studies in physics Yale, 1915-40, emeritus since 1940, lecturer, 1941-43. Mem. Am. Phys. Soc., Am. Philos. Soc., A.A.A.S., Am. Acad. Arts and Sciences, Am. Assn. U. Profs., Am. Assn. Physics Tchrs., Phi Beta Kappa, Sigma Xi, Berzelius, Aurelian. Club: New Haven Country. Writer of monographs and articles on subjects in physics, especially on elec. conduction through gases, and related topics. Home: 44 Cold Spring St., New Haven. Died June 19, 1951.

ZELLER, Walter Philip, business exec.; b. Waterloo Co., Ont., Can., Oct. 21, 1890; s. Philip and Marie (Riener) Z.; student pub. schs., Kitchener, Ont.; m. Nettie E. Lewis, Sept. 1913; 1 son, Carl Edward Staff F. W. Woolworth Co., Ltd., Can., 1912-15; asso. various variety store corps., Can., U.S., 1915-31; founder Zeller's, Ltd., Montreal, 1931, chmn. bd. dirs., 1931—; dir. Nat. Trust Co. Ltd., Toronto, Tolhurst Oil Ltd., Montreal. Pres. Shawbridge Boys' Farm; dir. Montreal Y.M.C.A. Mem. Newcomen Soc. Mason (Shriner). Clubs: Kiwanis, Seigniory, Canadian Engineers, St. Denis, Mount Stephen, Kanawaki Golf. Home: 753 Lexington Av., Westmount, Montreal 6. Office: 5115 Trans-Island Av., Montreal 29, Can. Died Aug. 25, 1957; buried Montreal.

ZERBAN, Frederick William (zĕr'băn), chemist; b. Oppenheim-on-Rhine, Germany, Oct. 20, 1880; s. Alexander and Mathilde (Witterstaetter) Z.; prep. edn., Gymnasium, Darmstadt, Germany, 1893-99; Ph.D., U. of Munich, 1903; m. Helen Regan, Aug. 18, 1908. Came to U.S., 1904, naturalized citizen, 1920. Carnegie research asst., Coll. City of New York, 1904-06; chemist La. Sugar Expt. Sta., 1906-08; dir. Sugar Expt. Sta., Lima, Peru, 1908-09; sub-dir. Agrl. Expt. Sta., Tucuman, Argentina, 1909-10; research chemist, Porto Rico Sugar Planters Expt. Sta., Rio Piedras, 1911-12; mgr. agrl. office, Potash Syndicate, New Orleans, 1913-17; research chemist La. Sugar Expt. Sta., New Orleans, 1917-20; dir. research, Penick & Ford, Ltd., New Orleans, 1920-23; chemist in charge New York Sugar Trade Lab. since 1923. Fellow A.A.A.S., Am. Inst. Chemists, Am. Inst. Chemical Engineers; member American Chemical Society, Inst. Food Technologists, International Soc. Sugar Cane Technologists (pres.), Assn. des chimistes de sucrerie de France; corr. mem. Nat. Acad. Sciences of Peru; hon. fellow Sugar Technologists of India; honorary mem. of Sugar Technologists of Peru; mem. Internat. Sugar Commn. Republican. Club: Chemists. Author: System of Cane Sugar Factory Control. Co-author: Sugar Analysis. Contbr. to chem. and tech. sugar trade jours. Home: 50 Commonwealth Av., Boston 16. Office: 113 Pearl St., N.Y.C. 4. Died Aug. 31, 1956; buried Westport, Conn.

ZIEGLER, William, Jr., pres. Great Island Holding Corp.; b. Muscatine, Ia., July 21, 1891; s. William and Electa Matilda (Curtis) Z.; grad. Haverford (Pa.) Sch., 1910; student Columbia and Harvard; children by first marriage—Elizabeth Virginia, Barbara; m. 2d, Helen Martin Murphy, Jan. 5, 1927; children—William III, Helen Martin. Pres., dir. Great Island Holding Corp., Park Av. Operating Co., Inc.; chmn. bd. Am. Maize Products Co., Huttig Manufacturing Co., Southworth Management Corp., Realty Administration Corp. Trustee Parson's School of Design, New York City. Exec. sec. War Credits Board, later company comdr. Motor Transport Corps, U.S. Army World War. Pres. E. Matilda Ziegler Foundation for Blind; sec. Boys' Clubs of Am.; pres. and dir. Am. Foundation for Blind; dir. pres. Nat. Industries for the Blind; pres. American Foundation Overseas Blind, Inc.; dir. Nat. Society for Prevention of Blindness, Inc., The Eye-Bank for Sight Restoration, Inc. Comdr., Legion of Merit, Italian Republic, 1956; Gold Medal, Italian Red Cross, 1956. Member of Psi Upsilon. Republican. Episcopalian. Mason. Clubs: Harvard, The Brook; Columbia, Rep., Racquet and Tennis, River, Union League, Uptown, N.Y. Yacht (New York); Metropolitan (Washington); Chevy Chase, Wee Burn, Ox Ridge Hunt. Home: 116 E. 55th St. Office: 250 Park Av., N.Y.C. 17; buried Woodlawn Cemetery, N.Y.C.

ZIFF, William Bernard, publisher; b. Chicago, Ill., Aug. 1, 1898; s. David and Libby Mary (Semco) Z.; ed. Crane Tech. High Sch., Chicago; student Art Inst. of Chicago, 1915-17; m. Denea Fischer, July 25, 1923; 1 dau., Sylvia Antoinette; m. 2d, Amelia Morton, Apr. 27, 1929; children—William Bernard, Priscilla Rae, David Morton. Cartoonist and commercial artist, Chicago, 1918-20; pres. W. B. Ziff Co., newspaper reps., Chicago, since 1920; pres. E. C. Auld Co., Chicago, pubs., 1923-32; chmn. Ziff-Davis Pub. Co., pubs., since 1946; editor Am. Humor Mag., 1928-30; editor Aeronautics Mag., 1931-33; publisher of Photography, Modern Bride, Radio and Television News, Amazing Stories, Fantastic Adventures, also Flying Magazine. Served with 202d Aero Squadron, U.S. Army, 1918-19. Chmn. Interracial Soc., 1928-31. Co-leader and ethnologist, expdn. to Honduras, 1934; cons. to U.S. Department of Justice, 1942-43; lecturer. Candidate for congressman, 2d Ill. Dist., 1932. Mem. Am. Legion. Clubs: Advertising, Wings, Lotos (New York); Overseas Press, Nat. Press (Washington); Sarasota Bay Country. Author: The Rape of Palestine, 1938; The Coming Battle of Germany, 1942; The Gentlemen Talk of Peace, 1944; Two Worlds; He, The Maker (poem), 1948. Contbr. to jours. Home: The Fitz Tower, N.Y.C. Office: 366 Madison Av., N.Y.C.; also 185 N. Wabash Av., Chgo. Died Dec. 20, 1953; buried Arlington Nat. Cemetery.

ZILBOORG, Gregory, psychiatrist; b. Kiev, Russia, Dec. 25, 1890; s. Moses and Anne (Braun) Z.; grad. Realschule, Kiev, Russia, 1911; M.D., Psychoneurological Inst., St. Petersburg, Russia, 1917; M.D., Coll. Phys. and Surg., Columbia, 1926; m. Ray Leibow, Dec. 14, 1919 (div. 1946); children—Gregory, Nancy; m. 2d, Margaret Stone, August 19, 1946; children—Caroline Crawford, John Talcott, Matthew Stone (step-son). Came to U.S., 1919, naturalized, 1925. Physician in Russian Army, 1915-16; participated in first revolution in Petrograd, 1917; sec. to ministry of Labor in Cabinets of Lvov and Kerensky, 1917; editor daily paper, Kiev, until Germans occupied So. Russia, in 1918; forced to leave Russia and came to U.S., 1919; engaged in lecturing, journalism, and theater, 1919-22: Grad. Coll. Phys. and Surgeons, N.Y.C., 1926; staff Bloomingdale Hosp., 1926-31; asst. Psychoanalytic Inst., Berlin, 1929-30; pvt. practice in psychiatry and psychoanalysis, N.Y.C., 1931—; sec., dir. of research, com. for the Study of Suicide; Noguchi lectr. history of medicine, Johns Hopkins U., 1935; asso. in psychiatry, Catholic U. of Am., 1944-46; Gimbel lecturer, U. Cal., 1947; cons. in research and psychotherapy, Butler Hosp., Providence; asst. prof. clin. psychiatry, N.Y. Med. Coll., Flower and Fifth Av. Hosp., N.Y. Chmn. Consulting Delegation on Criminology to United Nations; asso. vis. psychiatrist, Kings Co. Hosp., N.Y.; clin. asso. prof. psychiatry college of medicine State U. of N.Y. Mem. A.A. A.S., Am. Assn. of History of Medicine, Am. Bd. of Psychiatry and Neurology (diplomate), A.M.A., Am. Orthopsychiatric Assn., Am. Psychiatric Assn., Am. Sociological Soc., American Psychoanalytic Assn., American Soc. for Research in Psychosomatic Problems, Assn. for Research in Nervous and Mental Diseases, Research Council on Problems of Alcohol, History Sci. Soc., Internat. Psychoanalytic Soc., Medical Correctional Assn., Med. Soc. County of N.Y., N.Y. Acad. Medicine, N.Y. Med. Soc., N.Y. Neurol. Soc., N.Y. Psychoanalytic Soc. (sec. 1933), N.Y. Soc. Clin. Psychiatry, N.Y. Soc. for Med. History (pres. 1944-45), Pan-Am. Med. Assn.; corresponding mem. Argentine Soc. of Neurology and Psychiatry, Argentine Society of the History of Medicine, Argentine Psycho-analytic Society, Brazilian Institute of the History of Medicine. Clubs: Lotos, Cosmos. Author: The Medical Man and the Witch During the Renaissance, 1935; A History of Medical Psychology (co-author with George Henry), 1941; Mind, Medicine and Man, 1943; Sigmund Freud, 1951; The Psychology of the Criminal Act and Punishment, 1954; Freud and Religion, 1959. Translator: He, the One Who Gets Slapped (by Andreiev), 1921; We (by Zamiatin), 1924; The Criminal, the Judge and the Public (by Alexander and Staub, from the German), 1931; Outline of Clinical Psychoanalysis (by Fenichel), 1934. Asso. editor: One Hundred Years of American Psychiatry, 1944. Contbr. numerous articles to med. jours. and drama mags. Office: 33 E. 70th St., N.Y. C. 21. Died Sept. 17, 1959; St. Francis, Mt. Kisco, N.Y.

ZIMMER, H. Ward, pres. Sylvania Electric Products, Inc.; v.p. Emporium Trust Co. Home: 126 W. 6th St., Emporium, Pa. Office: 1740 Broadway, N.Y. C. 19. Died Jan. 28, 1955; buried Emporium, Pa.

ZIMMER, John Todd, museum curator, ornithologist; b. Bridgeport, O., Feb. 28, 1889; s. Franklin Pierce and Ida Virginia (Todd) Z.; B.S., U. of Neb., 1910, M.A., 1911, D.Sc., 1943; m. Margaret Louise Thompson, 1917; children—Ida Elizabeth (Sprague), Lawrence Thompson. Field expert in entomology, Nebraska Expt. Sta., 1911-13; asst. entomologist, P. I. Bur. of Agr., 1913-16; agrl. expert Ter. Papua, 1917-21; asst. curator birds, Field Museum Natural History, 1922-30; associate curator birds of Western Hemisphere, Am. Museum Natural History, 1930-34, acting curator, 1935, executive curator, 1936-42, curator, 1942—, became chairman, 1954. Fellow of the American Ornithologists' Union (council 1937-38, 1939-41; com. check list since 1930; Brewster Award com., 1940-45, chmn., 1942-45; recipient Brewster Award Medal, 1952). Fellow A.A.A.S., New York Zoological Soc.; mem. Society Systematic Zoology, Society for Study of Evolution, American Society of Mammalogists, Biol. Society of Washington, Neb. Ornithol. Union (hon.), Sigma Xi. Clubs: University (White Plains); Explorers (N.Y.). Mem. John Burroughs Memorial Award Com. since 1942. Republican. Presbyn. Author: Catalogue of Edward E. Ayer Ornithological Library (2 vols.), 1926; Birds of Marshall Field Peruvian Expedition, 1930; Studies of Peruvian Birds, Nos. 1-52 (cont.), 1931—; various papers on tropical Am. birds, P. I. birds, birds and insects of Neb., etc. Editor The Auk, 1942-47. Home: 112 Ralph Av., White Plains, N.Y. Office: Am. Mus. Natural History, N.Y.C. Died Jan. 6, 1957.

ZIMMERMAN, Charles Fishburn, banker; b. Duncannon, Pa., June 21, 1878; s. Lucien Calvin and Clara Reed (Steele) Z.; A.B., Princeton, 1900, grad. work, 1901; m. Eleanor Graydon Hinckley (direct desc. of Elder William Brewster of the Mayflower), Sept. 10, 1903; children—Charles Hinckley, Edward Bailey, Eleanor Graydon. Clerk First Nat. Bank, Harrisburg, Pa., 1901, Steelton (Pa.) Trust Co., 1902-07, treas., 1907-12; treas. Lebanon County (Pa.) Trust Co., 1912-26; pres. First Nat. Bank, Huntingdon, Pennsylvania, 1926-52; chairman of the board since 1952; member of Regional Advisory Committee, Defense Contract Service, O.P.M., for 3d Federal Reserve District, 1941; mem. State of Pa. Defense Council, 1941. Sec-treas. J. C. Blair Memorial Hospital since 1940. Secretary Pa. Bankers Assn., 1921-49;

mem. Am. Bankers Assn. (pub. edn. commn. 1924-31; econ. policy commn. 1931-36; exec. com. nat. bank div. 1931-36; com. on banking studies 1934-36; exec. council 1936-37); mem. Research Council, 1937-40; Com. on Am. System of Banking, mem state Bank Div., Am. Bankers Assn., 1940-43 (member of the executive council, 1943-46). Member Delta Upsilon. Mem. of board of dirs. U.S Chamber Commerce, 1938-42, Pa. State Chamber Commerce 1937-48; chmn. U.S. Treasury War Loan, Banking and Investment Com. for Huntingdon County, Pa., 1942-45 Republican. Presbyterian. Mason. Club: Nassau (Princeton). Address: Huntingdon, Pa. Died Oct. 9, 1954; buried Duncannon, Pa.

ZIMMERMAN, Fred R., state sec.; b. Milw., Nov. 20, 1880; s. Charles Emil and Augusta (Fiesenhaeuser) Z.; ed. grade and high schs. and business coll., Milw.; m. Amanda Freedy, Sept. 8, 1904; children—Robert Charles, Frederick Underwood. Served as dir. indsl. relations, Nash Motors Co.; engaged in bldg. materials and supply bus., Milw., 1910-20; mem. Wis. Assembly, 1909-10; mem. Rep. Nat. Com. many yrs.; sec. of state, Wis., 1923-26, 38—; gov. of Wis., term 1927-28. pptd. by President Hoover, del. to World's Expn., Seville, Spain, 1929. Progressive Republican. Mem. Evang. Ch. Mason (32°, Shriner), Odd Fellow, K.P. Club: Hi Noon. Home: 2995 South Shore Drive. Office: Capitol, Madison, Wis. Died Dec. 14, 1954.

ZIMMERMAN, Henry Martin, lawyer; b. Marine City, Mich., July 7, 1867; s. Frederick and Charlotte (Allman) Z.; LL.B., U. Mich., 1895; LL.M., Yale, 1896; m. Carrie L. Carver-McElroy, Mar. 30, 1898 (dec.); children—Bradley Maynard, Helen Mary (Mrs. Albert E. Betteley, dec.). Admitted to Mich. bar, 1895, practicing at Pontiac, Mich.; commr. of banking, Mich., 1907-11; chmn. United Savings Bank, Detroit. Mem. Mich., Oakland County bar assns. Republican. Presbyn. Mason. Clubs: Rotary (Pontiac); Bankers (Detroit). Office: Riker Bldg., Pontiac, Mich. Deceased.

ZIMMERMAN, Percy White, plant physiologist; b. Manito, Ill., Feb. 23, 1884; s. Henry and Elizabeth Ann (Singley) Z.; student Eastern Ill. State Normal Coll., 1907-10; B.S. and M.S., U. of Chicago, 1916, Ph.D., 1925; m. Patti C. Martin, Aug. 16, 1911; children—Jack Lois (Mrs. Wm. Gerow), Robert Louis. Supt. sch., Westville, Ill., 1910-13; asst. in botany, U. of Chicago, 1916; asso. prof. botany, U. of Md., 1916-17, actg. dean div. plant industry, 1917-18, prof. botany and dean coll. agr., 1918-25, prof. botany and asso. dean on part time, 1925-27; plant physiologist on part time, Boyce Thompson Inst. for Plant Research, 1925-27, plant physiologist, 1927—. Fellow A.A.A.S.; mem. Am. Soc. for Hort. Science Botanical Soc. of America, Torrey Botany Club (pres. 1946), Am. Chem. Soc., Am. Soc. Naturalists, Internat. Mark Twain Soc. (hon.), Sigma Xi, Alpha Zeta, Phi Kappa Phi, Pi Alpha Xi (honorary). Awarded (with others) A Cressy Morrison prize in exptl. biology by N.Y. Acad. Sciences, 1932. Awarded with Dr. A. E. Hitchcock $1000 prize of A.A.A.S. for research on plant hormones, 1935; Vaughn award of Am. Soc. for Hort. Science, 1946. Republican. Protestant. Author: Plant Hormones, 1946; and many scientific publs. on physiology of plants, etc. Contbr. to bot. and hort. jours. Home: 18 Greystone Pl., Yonkers 3, N.Y. Died Aug. 14, 1958.

ZIMMERMAN, Rufus Eicher, v.p. U.S. Steel Corp. of Del.; b. Mt. Pleasant, Pa., Nov. 26, 1886; s. Simon P. and Mary (Eicher) Z.; Ph.B., Franklin and Marshall College, 1908, D.Sc., 1938; S.B., Mass. Inst. Tech., 1911; LL.D., Thiel Coll., Greenville, Pennsylvania, 1942; m. Anna Burns, Sept. 7, 1911; children—Margaret Burns (Mrs. W. S. Nuckols) and Anne Burns (Mrs. N. O. Price). Instructor physical chemistry, Massachusetts Institute of Technology, 1911-14; research associate Am. Sheet & Tin Plate Co., Pittsburgh, 1914, asst. dir. research lab., 1915-17, actg. dir., 1917-19, dir., 1919-22, asst. to v.p., 1922-32; asst. to pres. U.S. Steel Corp., N.Y.C., 1932-33, v.p., 1933-37; dir., mem. exec. committee U.S. Steel Corp. of Delaware, 1938-51; v.p., dir., chmn. research policy com. U.S. Steel Company, 1951—. Cons. chemical engineer, United States Bur. Mines, World War. Mem. metallurgical advisory bd. Carnegie Inst., mem. of Corp. Mass. Inst. Tech.; trustee Hood Coll., Franklin and Marshall Coll.; past pres. Am. Standards Assn.; mem. engineering advisory council, Princeton U. Mem. research com. Army Ordnance Assn., Com. on Standards, U.S. Dept. of Commerce. Dir. Air Hygiene Inst. Member American Iron and Steel Institute, American Chemical Soc., The Electrochem. Society, American Inst. Mining and Metall. Engrs., Am. Soc. for Metals, Welding Research Com., Phi Kappa Psi, Phi Beta Kappa. Mem. Ref. Ch. of U.S. Home: 102 Stewart Rd., Short Hills, N.J. Office: 71 Broadway, N.Y.C.; 525 William Penn Place, Pitts. Died June 21, 1955.

ZIMMERMANN, Herbert George, bus. exec.; b. Little Ferry, N.J., July 16, 1900; s. George and Elizabeth (Dare) Z.; student N.Y.U., 1923; m. Pauline Wächtershauser, June 20, 1923. Jr. clerk Clyde Mallory Lines, 1920; v.p. Atlantic Gulf & West Indies Steamship Lines, New York City, Cuba Mail Steamship Co., Agwilines, Inc., 1946—. Dir. Agwilines, Inc., Internat. Airways, Inc. Pres. Security Bur., Inc., 1949—. Served as maj. to lt. col., AUS, 1943-46; E.T.O. Awarded Legion of Merit, Army Commendation ribbon, Am. campaign medal, European African Middle Eastn campaign medal, N.Y. State Conspicuous Service cross. Mem. Steamship Hist. Soc. of Am., Reserve Officers Assn., Soc. Philatelic Americans, U.S. Power Squadron, Army Transportation Assn., Maritime Assn., Port of N.Y., Inst. Navigation, Am. Legion. Clubs: Propeller of U.S., Fort Hamilton Officers, Whitehall, Richmond County Country. Home: 9949 Shore Rd., Bklyn. 9. Office: Pier 34, North River, N.Y.C. 13. Died July 9, 1949.

ZIMMERN, Sir Alfred, polit. scientist; b. Surbiton, England, Jan. 26, 1879; s. Adolf and Mathilda Sara (de Neufville Eckhard) Z.; student Winchester Coll., 1892-98; M.A., New Coll., Oxford University, 1905; LL.D., Universities Aberdeen, Melbourne; D.Litt., University Bristol, Trinity College, Hartford, Connecticut; married Lucie Anna Hirsch, Mar. 31, 1921. Fellow, tutor Greek history New Coll., 1903-09; visited U.S., 1911-12; founder, dir. Geneva Sch. Internat. Studies, 1923-39; dep. dir. Internat. Inst. Intellectual Coop., Paris, 1925-30; prof. Internat. relations Oxford U., 1930-44, now emeritus; fellow Ednl. Inst. Scotland, 1947. Fellow of the American Academy of Arts and Sciences. Was Created Knight, 1936. Author: The Greek Commonwealth, 1911; Nationality and Government, 1918; Europe in Convelescense, 1921; Learning and Leadership, 1926; The Prospects of Democracy, 1929; Solon and Croesus, 1929; The League of Nations and the Rule of Law, 1936; Spiritual Values and World Affairs, 1939; The American Road to World Peace, 1953. Editor: Modern Political Doctrines, 1929. Address: Country Club Rd., Avon, Conn. Died Nov. 24, 1957.

ZINNECKER, Wesley Daniel, educator; b. Portsmouth, O., Dec. 11, 1878; s. Christian Henry and Lea Lydia (Jahraus) Z.; A.B., Baldwin-Wallace Coll., Berea, O., 1903; grad. study, Leipzig and Berlin U.; Ph.D., Cornell U., 1912; m. Margaret Agatha Aichele, June 16, 1908 (died Dec. 14, 1937); children—Katharine Agatha, Margaret Anne. Instr. in modern langs. Peekskill (N.Y.) Mil. Acad., 1903-05; instr. German, Cascadilla Sch., Ithaca, N.Y., 1905-08, Cornell U., 1909-18; asst. prof. German, N.Y.U., 1918-19, asso. prof., 1919-22, prof., 1922-42, emeritus prof. 1942—; sec. gen. N.Y.U. Sch. of Fine Arts in Berlin, 1927; instr. Institut für Ausländer, Berlin U., 1927. Mem. Modern Lang. Assn. America, Andiron Club of N.Y. City, Phi Beta Kappa. Author: Deutsch für Anfänger, 1915; Gerhart Hauptmann, Hanneles Himmelfahrt; Thomas Mann, Königliche Hoheit. Editor: Prentice-Hall German Series. Home: 4422 Third Av., N.Y.C. 57. Died Sept. 1952.

ZINSSER, Rudolph, business exec.; born New York City, Oct. 5, 1889; s. William H. and Frida (Scharman) Z.; A.B., Princeton, 1910; A.M., Columbia, 1911; m. Dorothy Douglas, Sept. 13, 1924; children—Roderick Douglas, Joan Colville. Asso. Wm. Zinsser & Co., New York and Chicago, shellac mfrs. (founded by grandfather in 1849), 1911—, sec. and treas., 1915—. Pres. board of trustees Buckley Country Day School, Great Neck, N.Y., 1941-46; trustee Village of Kings Point, L.I., N.Y., mayor, 1953—. Mem. grad. council Princeton U. Clubs: University, Piping Rock, Cedar Creek, Princeton, Beaver Dam. Home: Leeward, Kings Point, Great Neck, N.Y. Office: 516 W. 59th St., N.Y.C. 19. Died Aug. 14, 1955.

ZISKIN, Daniel E., prof. of dentistry; b. Grand Forks, N.D., Apr. 27, 1895; s. Harris and Minnie (Griver) Z.; D.D.S., U. Minn., 1917; m. Ann Lucinda Lilienfeld, June 26, 1926; children—Margaret Field, Harriet Wilma. Asst. prof., U. Minn., 1918-30; chief of staff, dental clinic, Minneapolis Gen. Hosp., 1920-30; asst. prof., Columbia U. Sch. Dental and Oral Surgery, 1931-36, asso. prof., 1936-45, prof., 1945—; head div. oral diagnosis, 1931-45, head clin. research lab. 1946—, head div. grad. studies 1945—; attending dentist, Presbyn. Hosp. Consultant in dentistry, N.Y. Diabetes Assn. Fellow A.A.A.S.; mem. Internat. Assn. Dental Research, Acad. Dentistry, Acad. of Periodontology, Sigma Xi, Omicron Kappa Upsilon. Author: with diagnosis staff, Differential Diagnosis of Mouth Diseases, 1943; Handbook of Pulp Symptomatology and Diagnosis, 1943. Home: 450 Riverside Drive. Office: 630 W. 168th St., N.Y.C. 32. Died Oct. 21, 1948.

ZITO, Frank J. (zeeto), lawyer; b. Balt., Aug. 16, 1907; s. Joseph and Anna Marie (Restivo) Z.; student Staunton Mil. Acad., 1922-25, Fordham U., 1926-28, LL.B., 1931; m. Ann Riley, Dec. 20, 1932; children—Peter, Stephen. Admitted to N.Y. bar, 1932, District Columbia, 1947; engaged in admiralty practice Messrs. Hunt, Hill & Betts, N.Y.C., 1932-42; asst. gen. counsel Maritime Adminstrn., 1942-45; now partner Radner, Zito, Kominers & Fort, engaged in practice of admiralty law and problems of steamship industry; prof. admiralty law Georgetown U.; instr. law enforcement Coast Guard. Mem. squadron C, N.G. Cav.; comdr. Coast Guard Auxiliary flotilla 1311. Mem. Maritime Law Assn., Bar Assn. D.C., Soc. Naval Architects and Engrs. Clubs: Whitehall (N.Y.C.); Commercial (San Francisco). Home: 2719 N. Norwood St., Arlington, Va. Office: Tower Bldg., Washington 5. Died Feb. 3, 1955.

ZNANIECKI, Florian Witold (znä-nyĕt'skĭ) sociologist; b. Swiatniki, Poland, Jan. 15, 1882; s. Leon and Amelia (Holtz) Z.; B.A., Univ. of Warsaw; M.A.. U. of Geneva; student Univ. of Zurich, Univ. of Paris; Ph.D., Univ. of Cracow, 1909; m. Emilia Szwejkowska, Sept. 1, 1906; one son, Julius; m. 2d, Eileen Markley, April 26, 1916; one dau., Helena (Mrs. Richard S. Lopata). Dir. Polish Emigrants Protective Assn., 1911-14; lecturer, Univ. of Chicago, 1917-19; prof. sociology, Univ. of Poznan, Poland, 1920-39; vis. prof., Columbia, 1931-38, summer 1939, Julius Beer lecturer, 1939-40; vis. prof., Univ. of Ill., 1939-40, prof. of sociology, 1941—. Decorated Commander Polonia Restituta. Founder, Polish Sociol. Inst and Polish Sociol. Review. Fellow A.A.A.S.; mem. Am. Social. Soc. (pres. 1953-54), Internat. Sociol. Inst., London Sociol. Soc. (vice pres.). Author: The Problem of Values; Humanism and Knowledge; The Fall of Western Civilization; Introduction to Sociology; Sociology of Education, 2 vols.; The City Viewed by Its Inhabitants; The Men of Today and the Civilization of the Future; (all in Polish); (in English) The Polish Peasant, 5 vols. (with W. I. Thomas), 1918-20; Cultural Reality, 1919; Laws of Social Psychology, 1925; The Method of Sociology, 1934; Social Actions, 1936; The Social Role of the Man of Knowledge, 1940 (translation in Spanish, 1944), (in Spanish), Las sociedades de cultura nacional, 1944; Cultural Sciences, Modern Nationalities, 1952; about 30 articles in various languages. Home: 810 W. White St., Champaign, Ill. Died Mar. 23, 1958.

ZOBEL, Alfred Jacob, surgeon; b. San Francisco, Apr. 15, 1873; s. Jacob and Rose (Hart) Z.; M.D., Leland Stanford Jr. U., 1898; m. Maybelle Getz, June 2, 1901 (died Aug. 5, 1923); children—Newton Getz, Dr. Jerome Fremont, Claire Ann; m. 2d, Claire L. Wolfe, May 10, 1925. Asst. police surgeon Emergency Hosp., 1898-99; asso. prof. medicine San Francisco Poly. and Post-Grad. Sch., 1902-05, chief dept. rectal and colonic surgery, 1905—; chief rectal surgeon Mount Zion Hosp., 1932-42; pres. San Francisco Polyclinic, 1920-25. Diplomate Am. Bd. Surgery. Fellow A.C.S., Am. Proctologic Soc. (pres. 1917); mem. A.M.A., San Francisco Med. Soc. (pres. 1927), Alpha Kappa Kappa; hon. mem. Royal Soc. of Medicine, London. Mason (32°, Shriner). Club: San Francisco Commercial. Contbr. chapter on Local Anesthesia, in Cooke's Diseases of the Rectum and Colon, 1914; also papers each year, 1909—; to Trans. Am. Proctologic Soc. Home: 352 Lake St., San Francisco 18. Office: Shreve Bldg., 210 Post St., San Francisco 8. Died Oct. 17, 1949.

ZOFFMAN, George F., business exec.; b. Salinas, Cal., June 4, 1880; s. Alexander N. and Olene (Madsen) Z.; M.E., Stanford, 1907; m. Irene Dowling, Sept. 28 1910; children—George E., Irene M. (Mrs. Nealon). Asst. gen. mgr. Cinco Minas Co., Jalisco, Mexico, 1915-28; pres., gen. mgr. Duval Sulphur & Potash Co., Houston, 1929—. Mem. Am. Inst. Mining and Metall. Engrs., Tex. Acad. Sci., Am. Potash Inst., Am. Mining Congress. Democrat, Episcopalian. Clubs: Petroleum, Houston. Home: 2626 S. Calumet Dr. Office: Niels Esperson Bldg., Houston. Died June 5, 1957; buried Holy Cross Cemetery, San Francisco.

ZON, Raphael, forester; b. Simbirsk, Russia, Dec. 1, 1874; s. Gabriel and Eugenia (Berliner) Z.; B.A., Classical Gymnasium, Simbirsk, 1892; B.S., Imperial U., Kazan, 1896; Cornell U., 1901; m. Anna Puziriskaya, 1903; children—Leo, Henry. Came to U.S., 1897, naturalized, 1903. With Forest Service, U.S. Dept. Agr., 1901—; asst. until 1907, chief of forest investigations, 1907-22, dir. Lake States Forest Expt. Sta., 1922-45; prof. forestry U. Minn. Fellow Soc. Am. Foresters, Originated and developed forest research in U.S. Clubs: Campus (Mpls.); Cosmos (Washington). Author: Forest Resources of the World, 2 vols. (with W. N. Sparhawk), 1923; also numerous govt. bulls. and articles in mags. Home: 2237 Doswell Av., St. Paul 8. Died Oct. 29, 1956.

ZOOK, George Frederick (zōōk), educator; b. Ft. Scott, Kan., Apr. 22, 1885; s. Douglas and Helen (Follenius) Z.; A.B., U. of Kan., 1906, A.M., 1907; Ph.D., Cornell Univ., 1914; Litt.D., Boston, 1934; LL.D., Ohio Wesleyan, 1931, U. of Mich., Duquesne U., Wayne U., Mt. Union Coll., all 1934, U. of Southern California, 1935, Univ. of Pa., 1946, St. Francis College, 1947; University of Akron, University of Pittsburgh, 1948; m. Susie Gant, Aug. 21, 1911. Fellow in European History, U. of Kan., 1906-07; asst. in modern European History, Cornell U., 1907-09; instr. same, Pa. State Coll., 1909-11; traveling fellow in Europe, Cornell U., 1911-12; asst. prof. modern European History, 1912, asso. prof., 1914, prof. 1916-20, Pa. State Coll. With Com. on Pub. Information, Washington, D.C., 1918; asso. dir. sect. on ednl. instrns. of Savings Div., U.S. Treasury Dept., 1919; chief Div. of Higher Edn., U.S. Bur. Edn., 1920-25; pres. University of Akron, 1925-33; U.S. commr. of edn., 1933-34; pres. Am. Council on Edn.

1934-50; senior specialist in edn. Library of Congress since 1951. Member executive com. of National Advisory Com. on Edn., 1929-31; sec. Commn. on Higher Instns., North Central Assn. Colls. and Secondary Schools, 1926-31. Vice chmn. President's Adv. Com. on Edn., 1937; chmn. President's Commn. on Higher Edn., 1946-47; mem. U.S. national commission for UNESCO since 1946; chmn. U.S. ednl. mission to Germany, 1946; U.S. del. 3d Internat. Conf. on UNESCO, Beirut, 1949, 5th Internat. Conf., Florence, 1950; chmn. U.S. delegation to Internat. Conf. of Universities, Utrecht, 1946. Mem. Phi Beta Kappa, Phi Kappa Phi, Omicron Delta Kappa, Kappa Delta Pi, Phi Delta Kappa. Methodist. Club: Cosmos. Author: The Royal Adventurers Trading into Africa, 1919; Principles of Accrediting Higher Institutions (with M. E. Haggerty), 1936; The Role of the Federal Government in Education, 1945; also America at War (illustrated lectures issued by Committee on Public Information), 1918; also various survey reports on higher ednl. institutions in Ark., Okla., Kan., Mass., N.C., etc. Home: 1535 N. Glebe Rd., Arlington, Va. Address: 1785 Massachusetts Av. N.W., Washington. Died Aug. 17, 1951; buried Cedar Hill Cemetery, Washington.

ZORN, Edwin George, clergyman; b. Chicago, Dec. 10, 1892; s. Edward George and Ida (Thompson) Z.; ed. pub. schs. of Chicago; m. Alice Maurer, Oct. 23, 1915; children—Wesley James, Ruth Elizabeth, Paul Benjamin, David Robert. Mem. engring. dept. B. & O. R.R., 1911-13; with Industrial Publications, Inc., 1914-31; exec. sec. Christian Business Men's Com. of Chicago, 1931-38; exec. sec. Independent Fundamental Chs. of Am. Home: 7528 S. Morgan St. Office: 542 Dearborn St., Chgo. 5. Died Aug. 21, 1949.

ZULAUF, Romeo Maxwell, dean; b. New London, Minn., Nov. 17, 1902; s. A. L. and Hattie (Adams) Z.; B.A., Carleton Coll., 1924; M.A., U. Minn., 1930; grad. study Northwestern U., 1936-37, 43-44; Ed.D. Ind. U., 1956; m. Ruth Field, 1926 (dec. 1933); children—Richard F., Nancy A.; m. 2d, Eleanor Parson, 1936. Tchr. social studies, pub. schs. of Deer River and St. Cloud, Minn., also Elmhurst, Ill., 1924-29; instr. Northern Ill. State Tchrs. Coll., 1929-33, asst. prof., 1933-38, asso. prof., 1938-41, dean faculty, 1941-52, dean instrn., 1952—. Mem. N.E.A., Am. Assn. U. Profs., Nat. Soc. for Study Edn., Phi Delta Kappa, Alpha Phi Omega. Home: 597 Normal Rd., DeKalb, Ill. Died July 22, 1957.

ZUPPKE, Robert Carl (zŭp'kĕ), football coach; b. Berlin, Germany, July 2, 1879; s. Franz Simon and Hermine (Bocksbaum) Z.; brought by parents to U.S., 1881; grad. State Normal Sch., Milwaukee, 1901; Ph.B., U. of Wis., 1905; student summer course Art Inst. Chicago, 1904; m. Fanny Tillotson Erwin, June 27, 1908 (died July 1936); m. Leona Ray, Sept. 10, 1956. Director school athletic, Muskegon, Mich., 1906-10, Oak Park, Ill., 1910-13; head football coach Univ. of Ill., 1913-41; teams have won or tied for 7 conference championships in 29 yrs.; nat. football championships, 1914, 19, 23, 27; also prof. phys. edn.; mem. Am. Football Rules Com., 1939-40; mem. sports program coms. Chicago and New York world's fairs. Retired, 1941; professor emeritus, 1941——. Head coach of All Star Football team, 1942. Chairman $2,000,000 stadium drive. University of Illinois, 1922-23; mem. Walter Camp Memorial Com., 1925-26. Mem. Am. Football Coaches Assn. (pres. 1924-25), Kappa Sigma (Alpha Gamma Chapter). Lutheran. Clubs: Rotary, Champaign Country, Muskegon County Country. Author: Football Technique and Tactics, 1922, 24; Coaching Football, 1930. As amateur artist exhibited at Chgo. Artists' Exhbn., 1911, 13, Toledo, O., 1912, 13, Jackson, Miss., 1929, 30, Chicago and New York, 1937, Milwaukee Jour. Hobby Show, 1941, Davenport (Ia.) Art Inst., 1941, 42, one-man shows Palmer House, Chicago, 1937-38, 1940. Elected Nat. Football Hall of Fame, Rutgers, 1951 Wis.; Hall of Fame, Milw., 1951; Helm's Hall of Fame, Los Angeles, 1950.

Home: 305 W. University Av., Champaign, Ill. Died Dec. 22, 1957; buried Roselawn Cemetery.

ZWEMER, Samuel Marinus, missionary, author; b. Vriesland, Mich., Apr. 12, 1867; s. Adrian and Katharina (Boon) Z.; A.B., Hope Coll., Holland, Mich., 1887, A.M., 1890; New Brunswick (N.J.) Theol. Sem., 1890; D.D., Hope, 1904, Rutgers, 1919; LL.D., Muskingum Coll., 1918; ordained clergyman, Reformed Ch. in America, 1890; m. Bagdad, Arabia, Amy E. Wilkes, May 18, 1896; children—Nellie Elizabeth (Mrs. Claude L. Pickens, Jr.), Kathrina (dec.), Ruth (dec.), Raymund L., Amy Ruth (Mrs. Homer N. Violette), Mary Moffatt. Missionary at various stations in Arabia, 1891-1912, and at Cairo, Egypt, 1913-29. Has traveled extensively; crossed Oman Peninsula; visited Sanaa in Yemen twice, during Arab rebellion, 1892, 1904; visited Hofhoof in Hassa, East Arabia, twice, etc.; chmn. and organizer Mohammedan Missionary Conference, Cairo, Egypt, 1906. Now prof. of the history of religion and Christian missions, Princeton Theol. Sem. Editor of the Moslem World (quar. rev.), N.Y.C.; pres. Am. Christian Lit. Soc. for Moslems. Author: Arabia, the Cradle of Islam, 1902; Topsy Turvy Land (with Mrs. Amy E. Zwemer), 1902; Raymund Lull, 1904; Moslem Doctrine of God, 1906; Islam—A challenge to Faith; The Moslem World, 1907; The Moslem Christ, 1911; The Unoccupied Mission Fields, 1910; Zigzag Journeys in the Camel Country, 1912; Childhood in Moslem World, 1915; Mohammed or Christ, 1915; The Disintegration of Islam, 1917; Influence of Animism on Islam, 1920; A Moslem Seeker After God, 1920; Christianity the Final Religion, 1921; Call to Prayer, 1923; The Law of Apostasy in Islam, 1924; Across the World of Islam, 1928; The Glory of the Cross, 1928; Thinking Missions with Christ, 1933; The Origin of Religion, 1935. Fellow Royal Geog. Soc., Victoria Inst.; mem. Royal Asiatic Soc.; hon. Phi Beta Kappa (N.J. chpt., 1923). Home: 48 Mercer St., Princeton, N.J. Office: 156 Fifth Av., N.Y.C. Died Apr. 2, 1952.

ADDENDUM

(Deaths, or dates of death or other revisions, received after the main body of the volume [beginning on page 11] had gone to press.)

ABDUL RAHMAN, Prince Tuanka, king of Malaya (title, Yang di-Pertuan Agong, meaning paramount ruler); s. Yang di-Pertuan Besar (chief of chiefs) of Negri Sembilan, a state composed of nine small states; ed. sch. at Kuala Jampol and coll. at Kuala Kangsor; reader for bar, Inns of Court, London, Eng., 1925; called to bar, 1928. Filled various judicial posts, Malaya, 1930-33; following death of father, elected Yang di-Pertuan Besar of Negri Sembilan, 1933; Free and United Fedn. of Malaya (Johore, Pahang, Negri Sembilan, Selangor, Perak, Kedah, Perlis, Kelantan, Trenggam, Penang, Malacca) became ind. nation within Brit. Commonwealth, 1957; elected constnl. monarch for 5 yr. term, 1957. Decorated Knight Grand Cross Order St. Michael and St. George (Gt. Britain). Address: Royal Palace, Kuala Lumpur, Fedn. of Malaya. Died Apr. 1, 1960.

ADAMS, Annette Abbott, judge; b. Prattville, Cal., Mar. 12, 1877; d. Hiram Brown and Annette Frances (Stubbs) Abbott; grad. Chico (Cal.) State Normal Sch., 1897; B.L., U. of Cal., 1904, J.D., 1912; LL.D., Mills College, Cal., 1950; m. M. H. Adams, August 13, 1906. Principal, Modoc County High Sch., Alturas, Cal., 1907-10; admitted to Cal. bar, 1912; asst. U.S. atty. Northern Dist. of Cal., 1914-18; U.S. atty. same dist. July 25, 1918-June 26, 1920; asst. atty. gen. U.S., June 26, 1920-Aug. 15, 1921; asst. spl. counsel for U.S. in oil litigation, Nov. 1935-Sept. 1941; apptd. spl. asst. to atty. gen. (U.S.) in condemnation proceedings, July 22, 1940, resigned Sept. 30, 1941; appointed presiding justice, Dist. Court of Appeal, 3d Dist. Cal., Mar. 30, 1942, elected for 12-year term, Nov. 3, 1942. Mem. Am. Bar Assn., Am. Law Inst., Am. Assn. U. Women, League Women Voters, Am. Women's Assn. (hon.), Delta Delta Delta. Clubs: California, Woman's Athletic. Home: 1897 11th Av. Chambers. Library and Courts Bldg., Sacramento, Cal. Died Oct. 26, 1956.

ADAMS, Franklin Pierce ("F.P.A."), author; b. Chgo., Ill., Nov. 15, 1881; s. Moses and Clara (Schlossman) A.; grad. Armour Scientific Acad., 1899; student U. Mich., 1899-1900, M.A., 1914; m. Minna Schwartze, Nov. 15, 1904; m. 2d, Esther Sayles Root, May 9, 1925; children—Anthony, Timothy, Persephone, Jonathan. With Chicago Journal, 1903-04, New York Evening Mail, 1904-13, New York Tribune, 1914-21, New York World, 1922-31, New York Herald Tribune, 1931-37; with New York Post, 1938-1941; conducted "Conning Tower" column. Club: Players. Author: Tobogganing on Parnassus, 1911; In Other Words, 1912; By and Large, 1914; Weights and Measures, 1917; Something Else Again, 1920; Overset, 1922; So There!. 1923; So Much Velvet, 1924; Half a Loaf, 1927; Christopher Columbus, 1931; The Diary of Our Own Samuel Pepys, 1935; The Melancholy Lute, 1936; Innocent Merriment (anthology), 1942; Nods and Becks, 1944; F.P.A. Book of Pretorians, 1952. Wrote (in collaboration with O. Henry) musical comedy, Lo, 1909. Mem. cast of Information Please, radio program, 1938—. Address: 16 Gramercy Park, N.Y.C. 3. Died Mar. 23, 1960.

ADAMS, William Edward, clergyman, educator; b. Medina, O., Oct. 15, 1866; s. Samuel Thorne and Sarah Helm (Gardiner) A.; grad. high sch., Medina, 1885; elective studies, Hiram (O.) Coll., 1888-93; grad. Cleveland (O.) Sch. of Expression, 1896; A.B., Richmond (O.) Coll., 1904, A.M., 1906; m. Grace Carlton, July 25, 1893; children—Russel Monroe, Harold Jay, Carlton Fitch, Arlene Marie, Samuel Thorne (dec.), Helen Elizabeth (Mrs. Harry Wright). Successively farm laborer, salesman, teacher pub. schs.; head dept. of speech, Hiram Coll., 1893-97; head of Ft. Wayne (Ind.) Sch. of Expression, 1897-99; lecturer Tri-State Business Coll., Ft. Wayne, Ind., 1898-1900; ordained ministry Disciples of Christ Ch., 1896, and served in various states 20 yrs.; head of speech dept., Spokane U., 1921-30, Whitworth Coll., Spokane, 1930-34. Has lectured in 29 states. Served in ednl. dept. Y.M.C.A., Camp Lewis, Wash., and on Pacific slope, World War. Mem. A.A.A.S. Republican. Mason (32°). Author: A Harmony of Voice Methods for Speech, 1931. Co-editor The Psychogram 2 yrs. Contbr. to periodicals. Also author of verse pub. in "Eminent Poets of America," "American Lyric Poetry," "Poetry of The Machine Age," and "Washington Poets." Home: E. 2724 Pacific Av., Spokane, Wash. Died Mar. 14, 1946.

AHERN, Eugene Leslie (ā'hērn), cartoonist; b. Chicago, Ill., Sept. 16, 1895; s. Eugene William and Mary (Kelly) A.; ed. pub. schs. of Chgo. and Chgo. Art Inst.; m. Jane Susan Lynn, Feb. 17, 1917; children—Eugene (dec.) Nancy Anne. Cartoonist for News Enterprise Assn., Cleveland, O., 1914-36; cartoonist for King Features Syndicate, Inc., N.Y. City, 1936—. Creator of "Room and Board." Mem. Los Angeles Art Assn., Los Angeles Philharmonic Assn., Nat. Cartoonists Soc. Roman Catholic. Club: Bel-Air Country. Home: 10565 Fontenelle, West Los Angeles 24, Cal. Died Mar. 6, 1960.

ALMOND, James Edward, assn. exec.; b. Madison, Ind., Apr. 30, 1889; s. W. S. and Emma J. Almond; B.S., Hanover Coll., 1911, LL.D., 1949; m. Margery E. McLean, Sept. 29, 1915. Newspaper pub., Fargo, N.D., Riverside, Cal., Wabash, Ind.; publicity splist. Am. City Bur. (fund raising counsel), Chgo., N.Y.C., and Portland, Ore., 1923; corp. sec. and v.p., pres. 1936, now chmn. bd.; dir. Business Screen Pub. Co. Mem. Am. Assn. of Fund Raising Counsel (past pres.). Phi Delta Theta. Episcopalian. Clubs: University (Chgo.), Sunset Ridge Country (Winnetka, Ill.). Home: 1519 Hinman Av., Evanston, Ill. Office: 221 N. La Salle St., Chgo.; also 470 Fourth Av., N.Y.C. Died Mar. 13, 1960.*

AMEN, John Harlan (ā'mĕn), lawyer; b. Exeter, N.H., Sept. 15, 1898; s. Harlan Page and Mary (Rawson) A.; grad. Phillips Acad., Exeter, 1915; A.B., Princeton U., 1919; student Harvard Law Sch., 1919-22; m. Marion Cleveland, July 25, 1926; 1 son, Grover Cleveland. Admitted to N.Y. bar, 1923; asso. with Shearman & Sterling, New York, 1923-28; partner Duryee, Zunino & Amen, N.Y., 1928-38; partner Parker & Duryee 1938; mem. Amen, Weisman & Butler, N.Y.C.; special assistant to United States atty. gen. on cases involving violations of federal anti-trust laws, 1928-38, apptd. (Oct. 26, 1938) special prosecutor to supersede dist. atty. of Kings County in connection with investigation of official corruption in Brooklyn; apptd. (Aug. 23, 1940) asst. atty.-gen. of the State of N.Y. to conduct city-wide investigation of contracts for constrn. of pub. highways and sewers in Kings, Queens, New York, Bronx and Richmond Counties. Published: Report on Probation Department of Kings County Court, 1941; Report on Department of Correction in Kings County, 1942; Report of Kings County Investigation (1938-1942), 1942. Conducted investigation of N.Y. City Police Dept. in connection with gambling racket, 1942. Served as 2d lt. U.S. Marine Corps, Reserve Flying Corps, during World War; commd. lt. col., U.S. Army, Aug. 1942; col., 1944—. Asso. trial counsel, chief interrogations div. office U.S. Chief of Counsel in war criminal trials, at Nuernburg, Germany, 1945-46. Awarded Legion of Merit with Oak Leaf Cluster (U.S.); Royal Order of St. Olaf, rank of commander (Norway); Order of the White Lion (Czechoslovakia). Pres. Phillips Exeter Acad. Alumni Assn., 1940-41. Mem. Loyalty Review Bd., Am. Bar Assn., Assn. of Bar of the City of N.Y. Clubs: Ivy, Princeton, River Club of N.Y. Home: 430 E. 57th St. Office: 17 E. 63d St., N.Y. City 21. Died Mar. 10, 1960.

ANDREWS, Roy Chapman, zoölogist, explorer; b. Beloit, Wis., Jan. 26, 1884; s. Charles E. and Cora M. (Chapman) A.; grad. Beloit Coll. Acad., 1902; B.A., Beloit Coll., 1906, hon. Sc.D., 1928; M.A., Columbia, 1913; hon. Sc.D., Brown U., 1926; m. Yvette Borup; children—George Borup, Roy Kevin; m. 2d, Wilhelmina Christmas, Feb. 21, 1935. Dir. Am. Museum of Natural History, retired Jan. 1, 1942, appointed honorary director. Expedition to Alaska, 1908; collected white whales Saquenay River, 1909; special naturalist U.S.S. Albatross, on voyage to Dutch East Indies, Borneo, Celebes, 1909-10; explored N. Korea, 1911-12; with Borden Alaska Expdn., 1913; specialized in study of whales and other water mammals until 1914; leader Asiatic expdns. of Am. Mus. Natural History, 1st expdn., Tibet frontier, S.W. China and Burma, 1916, 17, 2d expdn., N. China and Outer Mongolia, 1919, 3d expdn., Central Asia, 1921-32, Opened the Gobi Desert to use of motor cars for commercial purposes; mapped much new area in the Gobi Desert; made first accurate general map of Mongolia; discovered many geological strata previously unknown; discovered some of the richest fossil fields in the world; also first dinosaur eggs, skulls and parts of the skeleton of the Baluchitherium, and many other fossil mammals and reptiles previously unknown to science. The researches proved Central Asia to be one of the chief centers of the origin and distribution of the world's reptilian and mammalian life. Served in Intelligence Service, U.S., 1918. Awarded Elisha Kent Kane gold medal, Phila. Geog. Soc., 1929; Hubbard gold medal, Nat. Geog. Soc., 1931; Explorers' Club medal, 1932, Charles P. Daly gold medal, Am. Geog. Soc., 1936; Vega gold medal, Royal Swedish Anthropol. and Geog. Soc., 1937; Loczy medal, Hungarian Geog. Soc., 1937; Silver Buffalo Award, Nat. Council, Boy Scouts Am., 1952. Hon. mem. Am. Mus. of Natural History (New York); fellow Nat. Geog. Soc., A.A.A.S., N.Y. Acad. Sciences, Am. Geog. Soc., N.Y. Zoöl. Soc.; mem. Am. Philos. Soc. of Phila., Sigma Chi (awarded Significant Sig medal), Phi Beta Kappa. Mem. numerous other scientific socs. U.S. and fgn. Mem. coll. electors Hall of Fame, N.Y.U. Clubs: Ends of the Earth, Angler's (New York City); Wilderness (Philadelphia); Wayfarer's (Chicago); Explorers' (pres. 1931-35), Doolittle, Boone and Crockett; Peking (Peking). Author many scientific papers, mag. articles, 22 books on exploration, adventure, popular science; among books are: On the Trail of Ancient Man, The New Conquest of Central Asia, Under a Lucky Star, Meet Your Ancestors, Heart of Asia, Beyond Adventure, All About Dinosaurs, All About Whales, Quest of the Snow Leopard. Home: Pondwood Farm, Colebrook, Conn. Office: American Museum of Natural History, N.Y.C. 24. Died Mar. 12, 1960. Cremated.

ATHERTON, Ray, U.S. foreign service; b. Brookline, Mass., Mar. 28, 1883; B.A., Harvard, 1905; studied architecture in Paris, France, 4 yrs.; hon. LL.D., Brown's U., 1944, U. of British Columbia, 1944, U. of Toronto, 1944, McGill U., 1946; married. Engaged in banking, 1907-08; in architect's office, 1914-16; apptd. from Ill. after examination to class 4, sec. of legation, and advanced through classes to class 1, 1929; at Tokyo, 1917-19, Peking, 1919-21; with Philippine Commn., 1921; with Dept. of State, Washington, D.C., 1922-23 and 1924; at Athens, 1923; 1st sec., London, 1924-27; apptd. counselor of Embassy at London, 1927; apptd. U.S. minister to Bulgaria, 1937; adviser London Naval Conf., 1930, 1935; acting chmn. Wheat Advisory Com., London, 1939; apptd. minister to Denmark 1939; acting chief European Div., Department of State, 1940-43; apptd. minister to Canada and minister near Govt. of Luxembourg in Canada, June 1943; also to serve concurrently as minister to Denmark, November 1943; appointed as first American Ambassador to Canada. Apptd. as alternate del. to the U.S.A. delegation to UN Gen. Assembly meeting, Paris, Sept. 1948. Served in Mass. Volunteer Militia 3 yrs. Address: 3017 O St., N.W., Washington, D.C. Died Mar. 16, 1960.

BAILEY, Margaret Emerson, author; b. Providence, R.I.; d. William Whitman and Eliza Randall (Simmons) B.; A.B., Bryn Mawr, 1907; scholarship in English, U. Chgo., 1907-08. Began writing for newspapers, 1919, later wrote essays for Country Life and Atlantic, spl. articles for Bookman and short stories for the Dial. Democrat. Episcopalian. Club: Bryn Mawr (New York). Author: The Value of Good Manners, 1922; Robin Hood's Barn, 1922. Home: 580 St. Nicholas Av., New York, N.Y. Died Oct. 29, 1949.

BARNUM, Gertrude, b. Chester, Ill., Sept. 29, 1866; d. William H. and Clara Letitia (Hyde) B.; ed. high sch., Evanston, Ill., and spl. courses in economics and history, U. Wis. Asst. sec. and treas., Hull House, Chgo., 1889-96; later head resident Henry Booth Settlement, Chgo., and dean of girls, Port Deposit (Md.) Inst.; 1st national sec. of Women's Trade Union League, 1903-04; gen. arbitration and publicity agt. Internat. Ladies Garment Workers' Union, 1911-16; spl. agt. U.S. Industrial Relations Commn., 1914; asst. dir. investigation service, U.S. Dept. Labor, 1918-19; mem. President's Industrial Conf., representing the public, Washington, D.C., Oct. 1919. Member Nat. Women's Suffrage Assn. Clubs: Riverside (Ill.); Woman's (hon.); Woman's City (Los Angeles, Calif.). Home: 2723 Benvenue Av., Berkeley, Calif. Died June 17, 1948.

BOYD, Harry Burton, clergyman; b. Chgo., Ill., Mar. 10, 1882; s. Joseph Warren and Minnie (Brock) B.; B.A., cum laude, Centre Coll., Ky., 1908, D.D., 1928; B.D., McCormick Theol. Sem., 1911; D.D., Hastings (Neb.) Coll., 1922; LL.D., U. of Dubuque, 1928; m. Margaret Elizabeth Denham, Oct. 10, 1911; 1 son, Leslie Randolph. Ordained Presbyn. ministry, 1911; pastor successively Denton, Tex., Olean, N.Y., Iowa City, Ia., until 1918, Park Ch., Erie, Pa., 1919-28, Arch. Street Presbyn. Ch., Phila., 1928-37, First Ch., Indiana, Pa., 1937-55, Garden Crest Ch., St. Petersburg, Fla., 1955—. Served as chaplain 313th Engrs., 88th Div., U.S. Army, 1917-18; sr. chaplain 88th Div., A.E.F., 1918-19; organized first sch. of chaplains held in U.S. Army, Camp Dodge, Ia., Oct. 1917; organized ednl. work of 88th Div., A.E.F., Jan. 1, 1919, enrolling 3,000 students; hon. discharged June 19, 1919. Mem. bd. dirs. U. of Dubuque, Ia., 1926-50, pres. bd., 1927-36; mem. bd. overseers Centre College, 1949—; v.p. Pa. Lord's Day Alliance; trustee and v.p. U.S.S. Niagara Assn.; trustee Western Theol. Sem. 1940-55; del. Pan-Presbyn. Alliance, 1928; commr. Gen. Assembly, 1921, 1932, 1942; moderator Erie Presbytery, 1921, Kitanning Presbytery 1942; del. to Fed. Council of Chs., 1932-34; chmn. Phila. Prohibition Emergency Com., 1933; trustee Pa. Anti-Saloon League, 1935, v.p. 1938-46. Mem. Am. Acad. Polit. and Social Science, Am. Legion. Mem. bd. dirs. Ind. Chapter, Am. Red Cross, 1940, chmn. 1943-45. Mem. Phi Delta Theta. Republican. Mason (33°). Clubs: Ingleside, Kiwanis. Preacher before schools and colls.; contbr. religious press. Home: 305-15th Av. N.E., St. Petersburg, Fla. Died July 11, 1959.

BROWDER, Basil David, textile exec.; b. Henry Co., Va., Mar. 21, 1899; s. Joseph Lee and Patty (Corbin) B.; student Danville Comml. Coll., 1912-14, Alexander Hamilton Inst., 1916-18; m. Louise Barnes, Nov. 9, 1935; 1 stepson, William B. Guerrant. Messenger, typist Dan River Mills, Inc., Danville, Va., 1916-17, sec. to sales mgr., 1917-19; asst. to purchasing agt., 1919-25, mgr. sheeting order dept., 1925-32, mgr. order dept., 1932-38, mgr. bleaching and finishing, 1938-40, asst. to pres., 1940-42, v.p., 1942-49, v.p. charge mfg., 1949-52, exec. v.p., 1952—, dir., 1950—; dir. Anderson Bros. Consol. Cos., Inc. Mem. bd. dirs. So. Industrial Relations Conf.; dir., v.p. Memorial Hosp. Assn.; mem. bd. dirs. Barter Theatre. Dir. Wayles R. Harrison Meml. Fund, United Fund, City Planning Commn. Trustee Averett College. Recipient 1st Citizenship award, Kiwanis, 1943. Mem. Vets. Fgn. Wars, Am. Legion, Am. Assn. Textile Chemists and Colorists, Soc. Am. War Dads, Va. Mfrs. Assn. (dir.), U.S. (policy com.), Danville C.'s of C., National Assn. of Mfrs., Am. Cotton Mfrs. Inst., Newcomen Soc. N.A. Democrat. Methodist (trustee). Clubs: Golf, Rotary (hon.), Lions (pres. 1934), Young Men's, Glen Oak Country, (Danville); Farmington Country (Charlottesville); Commonwealth (Richmond); Golden Horseshoe (Williamsburg); Cape Colony (Virginia Beach). Home: 439 W. Main St. Office: W. Main St., Danville, Va. Died Apr. 1960.

BRUHN, Wilhelm L., paint co. exec.; b. Neumuenster, Germany, Apr. 19, 1900; s. Johannes and Dorothea (Plotz) B.; grad. Kiel (Germany) Bus. Sch., 1919; student univs. Kiel, Berlin, also Sorbonne, Paris; m. Charlotte Rangartz, Aug. 13, 1931; 1 son, Ehrich Walter. Came to U.S., 1926, naturalized, 1935. Exec. sec. Electro-Thermit Corp., Berlin, Germany, 1919-23; fgn. corr., 1923-25; mgr. paint dept. Goldschmidt A.G., Essen, Germany, 1925-26, sales mgr., N.Y.C., 1928-29; various positions, 1926-28; various positions, then Western trade sales mgr. Valspar Corp., N.Y.C. and Chgo., 1929-52, Western mgr., 1958-59, pres., dir., 1959—; owner, operator Hale & Perry, wholesale paint distbrs., Denver, 1952-58; co-founder, sec.-treas. Paint and Wallpaper Distbr. Assn. of Colo., Denver, 1956-58, pres., 1958. Served with F.A., German Army, 1918-19. Home: 500 S. Kensington Av., LaGrange, Ill. Office: 7701 W. 47th St., Lyons, Ill. Died Mar. 16, 1960.

BUGNIAZET, G. M., v.p. and mem. exec. com. Am. Fed. of Labor; sec. Electricians' Union. Address: Am. Fed. of Labor Bldg., Washington, D.C. Died Mar. 25, 1960.

BURNS, Herbert Deschamps, banker; b. Digby, N.S., Can., June 11, 1878; s. Charles Fowler and Sarah Caroline (Brown) B.; student Digby Acad.; D. C.L., U. Kings Coll., 1949; m. Marguerite Williams, Nov. 10, 1903 (dec. 1947); children—Charles F. W., Constance; m. 2d, Alleen Louise Steele, June 15, 1950. Jr. clk. Bank of N.S., Moncton, N.B., 1896-1901, acct., Boston, 1901-03, Montreal, Que., 1903-05, mgr., Kentville, N.S., 1905-06, Woodstock, N.B., 1906, Vancouver, B.C., 1906-15, supt. Western br., Toronto, 1915-16, mgr. Toronto br., 1916-23, asst. gen. mgr., 1923-41, gen. mgr., 1941-44, v.p., dir., 1944-45, pres., 1945-49, chmn. bd., 1949—, honorary president, 1956—; chairman of the board Crown Life Ins. Co.; director National Trust Co., Ltd., Central Can. Investment Co., Toronto Savs. & Loan Co. Mem. Anglican Ch. Mason. Clubs: Vancouver, Toronto, Toronto Golf, York, Halifax; Mt. Royal (Montreal, Que.). Home: 34 Rosedale Rd., Toronto, Ont.; also Pansy Patch, St. Andrews, N.B. Office: 44 King St. W., Toronto, Ont., Can. Died Mar. 28, 1960.

CARRINGTON, Richard Adams, Jr., pub.; b. St. Paul, Minn., July 11, 1889; s. Richard Adams and Emily (Crooks) C.; ed. pub. schs. and St. Paul Acad., Minn.; m. Florence Louise Cooper, Jan. 28, 1938; 1 son, Richard Thomas. Classified advtg. solicitor St. Paul Pioneer Press, 1909, reporter; successively asst. advtg. mgr. Anaconda Standard, Butte, Mont., reporter Kansas City Star, advtg. mgr. Duluth News-Tribune, advtg. dir. and gen. mgr. Omaha Bee, advtg. mgr. Oakland Post-Enquirer, pub. Oakland Post-Enquirer until 1938; pub. Los Angeles Examiner 1938-56; v.p., dir., chmn. exec. com. Hearst Corp., 1956—. Mem. Sigma Delta Chi. Clubs: Athenian-Nile (Oakland, Cal.); Cal.; Los Angeles Stock Exchange, Los Angeles Country. Home: 541 S. Lucerne Blvd., Los Angeles 5; also Koala, Lake Tahoe, Cal. Office: 530 W. Sixth St., Los Angeles 14. Died Mar. 21, 1960.

CARROLL, Howard Joseph, clergyman; b. Pittsburgh, Pa., Aug. 5, 1902; s. William J. and Brigid-mary (Hogan) C.; student Duquesne U., Pittsburgh, Pa., 1919-21; Ph.L., Saint Vincent Coll., Latrobe, Pa., 1923, A.B., 1924; S.T.D., U. of Fribourg (Switzerland), 1928. Ordained priest, Catholic Ch., 1927; asst. pastor, Sacred Heart Ch., Pittsburgh, Pa., 1928-38; instr. in philosophy, Mount Mercy Coll., Pittsburgh, Pa., 1930-38; asst. gen. sec. Nat. Cath. Welfare Conf., Washington, D.C., 1938-44, general secretary, 1944-57; Bishop diocese Altoona-Johnstown, Pa., 1957—. Papal chamberlain, 1943; Domestic Prelate, 1945. Mem. bd. dirs. Community Chests and Councils; sec. bd. trustees Nat. Catholic Community Service; mem. bd. dirs. United Service Organizations. Address: 1211 13th St., Altoona, Pa. Died Mar. 21, 1960.

CLARK, Dwight Edwin, phys. and surg.; b. Mt. Eaton, O., July 28, 1910; s. Clement Nelson and Zena D. (Zaugg) C.; A.B., Western Res. U., 1932; M.S., U. Rochester, 1935, M.D., 1937; m. Eleanor Melander, Dec. 23, 1939; children—Judith Lynn, Elizabeth Ann. Practicing physician, surgeon, 1938—; faculty U. Chgo., 1942—, prof. surgery, 1951—, chmn. surgery, 1958—. Contbr. articles med. publs. Home: 5801 Dorchester Av., Chgo. Died July 24, 1959.

COLCORD, Joanna Carver, social worker; b. at sea, Mar. 18, 1882; d. Capt. Lincoln Alden and Jane French (Sweetser) Colcord; brought to U.S. in 1884; B.S. cum laude, U. of Me., 1906, M.S., 1909, hon. M.A., 1932; certificate, N.Y. Sch. of Social Work, 1911; unmarried. Began as chemist, Agrl. Exptl. Sta., Orono, Me., 1906; asst. dist. sec. New York Charity Organization Soc., 1911, supt. of district work, 1914-25; on leave of absence as field rep. Am. Red Cross, to Virgin Islands, 1920-21; general sec. Minneapolis Family Welfare Assn. and lecturer U. of Minn., 1925-29; dir. charity orgn. dept. Russell Sage Foundation, N.Y., 1929-45. Mem. adv. council Govt. of Virgin Islands, U.S. Dept. of Interior; pres. Minn. Conf. of Social Work, 1929. Mem. Am. Assn. of Social Workers, Phi Kappa Phi, Phi Beta Kappa, Alpha Omicron Pi. Democrat. Conglist. Co-editor: The Long View, 1930. Author: Broken Homes, 1919; Emergency Work Relief (with Kurtz and Koplowitz), 1932; Cash Relief, 1936; Songs of American Sailormen, 1938; Your Community, 1939; Sea Language Comes Ashores, 1945. Home: Searsport, Me. Died Apr. 1960.

DALY, Edwin King, baking; b. Bridgeport, Conn., Nov. 15, 1896; s. Michael J. and Elizabeth (King) D.; student Fordham U.; LL.D., Villanova U., 1955; m. Alice F. Ryan, June 5, 1924; 1 son, Edwin King, Jr. Pres. Horn & Hardart Co., N.Y., 1936, Horn & Hardart Baking Co., 1941. Superior Fire Ins. Co., 1941; dir. Horn & Hardart Co., Horn & Hardart Baking Co., Provident Tradesmens Bank & Trust Company, Philadelphia Electric Company (Phila.); bd. mgrs. Beneficial Mut. Savs. Bank, Phila. Pres. Jos V. Horn Found. Mem. adv. council bd. trustees Chestnut Hill Coll.; trustee of Jefferson Medical Coll., Jefferson Hosp., Drexel Inst. Technology, St. Joseph's College; board mgrs. Chestnut Hill Coll.; dir. Children's Heart Hospital. Knight of Malta, Knight Comdr. Equestrian Order of Holy Sepulchre. Mem. Am.-Irish Hist. Society, Catholic Philopatrian Lit. Inst., Pa. Hist. Soc. Clubs: Racquet. Died Mar. 28, 1960.

DETWEILER, Frederick German, prof. sociology; b. Louisville, Ky., Mar. 4, 1881; s. John Samuel and Sarah Ella (German) D.; grad. Central High Sch., Kansas City, Mo., 1897; B.D., Rochester Theol. Sem., 1909; A.B., Denison U., 1917, A.M., 1919; Ph.D., U. Chgo., 1922; m. Vera Devoir Oswalt, Oct. 25, 1910; children—Frederick Oswalt, Mary Muriel. Ordained Bapt. ministry, 1908; pastor Oberlin, O., 1908-11; gen. sec. Y.P. Dept., Ohio Bapt. Conv., 1911-12; pastor Dayton, O., 1912-15, Galion, 1915-17; instr. sociology, 1917-18, asst. prof., 1918-20, prof., 1920—- dean of men, 1928-37, Denison U., prof. emeritus, 1949. Mem. Am. Social Soc., Ohio Valley Sociol. Soc., Ohio Acad. Science, Phi Beta Kappa, Lambda Chi Alpha. Author: Baptist Young People at Work, 1913; The Negro Press in the United States, 1922. Home: Granville, O. Died Mar. 1960.

DILLON, J. Clifford, advt. exec.; b. N.Y.C., Dec. 14, 1904; s. John J. and Annette E. (Shannon) D.; student Columbia, 1923-24; m. Carol O'Kane, Sept. 8, 1932; children—J. Brian, Stuart J., Donald, Annette E. Feature writer Bklyn. Eagle, 1925-26, N.Y. Herald Tribune, 1926-27; with N.Y. Sun, 1927-39; engaged in advt., 1939—; copy group head Kenyon & Eckhardt, Inc., 1941-43; mem. plans bd. J. Walter Thompson Co., 1943-46; v.p., copy chief Sullivan, Stauffer, Colwell & Bayles, Inc., 1946-51, Dancer-Fitzgerald-Sample, 1951-52; v.p., copy dir. Ward Wheelock Co., Phila., 1953-54; v.p., Compton Advt., Inc., N.Y.C., 1954-55, asst. creative dir., 1955-59, creative dir., chmn. creative bd., 1959—. Mem. N.Y. Hist. Soc., Amateur Trapshooting Assn. Clubs: Phila. Cricket (Chestnut Hill, Pa.); N.Y. Athletic (N.Y.C.); Gipsy Trail (Carmel, N.Y.). Office: 625 Madison Av., N.Y.C. 22. Died Mar. 16, 1960.

DOYLE, Michael Francis, lawyer; b. Philadelphia, Pa.; s. John J. and Mary (Hughes) Doyle; LL.B., U. Penn., 1897; LL.D., Villanova Coll., 1935, St. Johns U., 1944, Nat. U., Ireland, 1959; m. Nancy O'Donoghue, 1918. In gen. practice, including internat. law. Mem. Permanent Court Internat. Arbitration (The Hague), 1938-52; mem. Citizen's Relief Com., Comprehensive Plans Com., Phila.; special agent Dept. of State, 1915; actg. counsellor Am. Legation, Switzerland, Am. Embassy, Vienna, 1915; counsel for Sir Roger Casement, on trial for treason, London, 1916. Spl. asst. chief of ordnance, War Department, 1917-18; counsel various individuals and units Irish revolutionary movement; adviser Irish Free State Com. in drafting Nat. Constn., 1922; counsel 1st Irish delegation to League of Nations, Hayti-San Domingo before State Dept., 1922. Chmn. Am. Com., Geneva, League of Nations, 1920-39; hon. v.p. U.N. Association. Member delegations representing U.S. internat. confs.; 1937; appointed by Pres. mem. Permanent Court Internat. Arbitration, The Hague, 1938; reappointed 1944; v.p. Cath. Assn. Internat. Peace; adviser Interparlimentary Union, London, 1957. Chairman bd. dirs. George Washington Boyhood Home. Dem. Presdl. elector, 1928, 32, 44, 48; chairman Dem. Presdl. electors, inauguration of Pres. Roosevelt, 1933, 41. Pres. Electoral College, U.S., 1945-49, 53, hon. pres., 1957. Trustee Nat. Fund for Med. Edn., James Monroe Found., 1956, Assumption Coll., 1956; mem. adv. com. Xavier U. (La.) Villanova (Pa.) College, 1957; director Christian Muslim Continuing Committee, 1957. Mem. nat., state and local bar assns. and legal socs.; dir. Am. Czeckoslovakia Independence Com.; founder counsel Cath. Near East Welfare Association; v.p. Mexican Commn. against Religious Persecution; hon. master Philadelphia Navy Yard; dir. Catholic Missionary Soc. President Thomas Jefferson Memorial Association; dir. Patrick Henry Memorial Foundation, Recipient numerous civil and secular honors and decorations, 1929—, latest being Cross of Merit (Naval) Spain, 1952; Emmanuel D'Alzon medal Assumption Coll., 1956; apptd. pvt. chamberlain Pope John XXIII; hon. bencher Kings Inns of Court. Ireland. Mem. Am. Peace Soc. (v.p.). Clubs: Penn, Contemporary, Lawyers, Friendly Sons of St. Patrick, others. Home: 1900 S. Rittenhouse Sq. Office: Girard Trust Bldg., Phila. Died Mar. 27, 1960.

DUDLEY, Helena Stuart, settlement worker; b. in Neb., 1958; d. Judson H. and Caroline (Bates) D.; student Mass. Inst. Tech., 1884-5; A.B., Bryn Mawr Coll., 1889. Teacher biology and chemistry, Packer Collegiate Inst., Brooklyn, 1889-92; head worker, Coll. Settlement, Phila., 1892-3; head worker Denison House, Boston Coll. Settlement, 1893-12. Member Consumers' League. Club: Twentieth Century. Address: 11 Florence St., Boston. Died Sept. 30, 1932.

DUNTON, Edith Kellogg ("Margaret Warde"), author; b. Rutland, Vt., Dec. 28, 1875; d. Walter C. and Miriam (Barrett) D.; A.B., Smith Coll., 1897; unmarried. Author: Betty Wales, Freshman, 1904; Betty Wales, Sophomore, 1905; Betty Wales, Junior, 1906; Betty Wales, Senior, 1907; Betty Wales, B.A., 1908; Betty Wales & Co., 1909; Betty Wales on the Campus, 1910; Betty Wales Decides, 1911; Nancy Lee, 1912; Nancy Lee's Spring Term, 1913; Nancy Lee's Lookout, 1915; Nancy Lee's Namesake, 1918; The Holiday Book, 1925; K. Blake's Way, 1929; Biddy and Buddy's Holidays, 1930; Joan Jordan's Job, 1931. Home: Rutland, Vt. Died Dec. 31, 1944.

FAY, Amy, pianist; b. Bayou Goula, La., May 21, 1844; d. Rev. Charles and Charlotte Emily (Hopkins) F.; acad. edn., Cambridge, Mass., and Berlin; studied music in Europe under leading teachers; unmarried. Début at New York, 1876; pianist with Theodore Thomas Orchestra, Cambridge, 1877; played in ann. musical festivals, Worcester; extensive concert tours in U.S.; gave evening piano recitals in New York pub. sch. halls under the Bd. of Edn.; also musical lectures and conversaziones. Introduced in this country the celebrated Deppe Method in the training of piano students. Identified with women's musical clubs, and advancement of women in music generally. Hon. pres. Women's Philharmonic Soc. of New York. Author: Music Study in Germany (20 edits.) and has been transl. into French and German and reprinted in England. Died Feb. 28, 1928.*

FERGUSON, Margaret Clay, botanist; b. Phelps, N.Y., Aug. 20, 1863; d. Robert Bell and Hannah Maria (Warner) F.; B.S., Cornell U., 1899, fellow, 1899-1900, Ph.D., 1901; Sc.D., Mount Holyoke College, 1937. Teacher and prin. pub. schs., 1877-86; in charge Dept. of Science, Harcourt Place Sem., Gambier, O., 1892-93; instr. in botany, 1894-96 and 1902-04, asso. prof. and head dept. of botany, 1904-06, prof. and head of dept., 1906-32, now research prof. botany, Wellesley Coll. Asst. in botany, summer, Cornell, 1901, 02, instr., 1903. Fellow A.A.A.S.; mem. Sigma Xi, Bot. Soc. America, California Acad. of Science, Am. Assn. Univ. Profs., Am. Genetic Assn., Am. Soc. Naturalists, Am. Assn. Univ. Women, Science League of America, Mass. Hort. Soc., Eugenics Soc. of U.S., Am. Micros. Soc. (v.p., 1914), Bot. Soc. America (v.p., 1922; pres. 1929). Author of scientific papers dealing with problems in plant physiology, genetics, cytology and comparative morphology. Home: Wellesley, Mass. Died 1951.

FLEWELLING, Ralph Carlin, architect; b. St. Louis, Mich., May 4, 1894; s. Ralph Tyler and Jennie (Carlin) F.; B.S., Wesleyan U., Middletown, Conn., 1916; grad. stdy Mass. Inst. Tech., 1916-17; m. Carol Hunter, Nov. 19, 1925; 1 son, Ralph Hunter. Practiced architecture in Los Angeles, 1924—; received honor awards from Southern Calif. Chapter A.I.A., and medals and prizes from art associations and national publications for outstanding structures including pub. bldgs., schools and residences. Served in U.S. Army, 1917-19, resigned as capt., 1919. Awarded U.S. Navy Commendation in 1945, for outstanding services rendered in War Construction Program. Fellow Am. Inst. of Architects (past pres. Southern Calif. chap.). Mem. planning and architectural bds., Alpha Delta Phi, Tau Sigma Delta. Author: Town in Transition, 1945. Home: 5147 Oakwood Av., La Canada, Calif. Office: 3112 Los Feliz Blvd., Los Angeles 26, Calif. Died Apr. 1960.

FOX, Norman Arnold, author; b. Sault Ste. Marie, Mich., May 26, 1911; s. Alfred Charles and Florence Pearl (Smith) F.; student pub. schs., Great Falls, Mont.; m. Rosalea Spaulding, July 7, 1949. Bookkeeper, accountant, 1929-38; fiction writer, 1938—. Mem. Western Writers of Am. Author: Gunsight Kid, 1941; gun-Handy, 1941; Six-Gun Syndicate, 1942; The Stampede Kid, 1942; Lord Six-Gun, 1943; Thundering Trail, 1944; Thorson of Thunder Gulch, 1945; Silent in the Saddle, 1945; Valley of Vanishing Riders, 1946; Dead End Trail, 1946; Rider from Yonder, 1947; Cactus Cavalier, 1947; Devil's Saddle, 1948; Feathered Sombrero, 1948; Thirsty Land, 1949; Shadow on the Range, 1949; Stormy in the West, 1950; Phantom Spur, 1950; Tall Man Riding, 1951; Roughshod, 1951; Ghostly Hoofbeats, 1952; Long Lightning, 1953; Rawhide Years, 1953; Broken Wagon, 1954; Night Passage, 1956; Stranger from Arizona, 1956; The Badlands Beyond, 1957; The Valiant Ones, 1957; Rope the Wind, 1958. Contbr. short stories, novelettes, serials, Western action and popular mags. Home: P.O. Box 1762, Great Falls, Mont. Died Mar. 1960.

GADSBY, George M(adill), pub. utility exec.; b. Collinwood, O., May 4, 1886; s. George and Sarah J. (Madill) G.; grad. Marietta (O.) Coll., 1906, M.A., 1907; grad. Mass. Inst. Tech., 1909; Eng. D., Univ. Pitts., 1927; LL.D., Marietta Coll., Marietta, O., 1941, U. Utah, 1952; m. Evelyn C. Crandall, June 19, 1912; children—Craig M., Charles C. Chemist and supt. Warren (Pa.) Water Co., 1909-11; with home office of Am. Water Works & Guaranty Co., Pittsburgh, 1911-13; supt. Ark. Water Co., Little Rock, 1913-15; gen. office work, Am. Water Works & Electric Co., 1915-17; asst. to pres., later v.p., West Penn Power Co., 1917-27, pres., 1927-28; became pres. and gen. mgr. Utah Power & Light Co., 1929, now chairman board; director Western Colorado Power Company. Mem. bd. national Industrial Conf. Bd. Past pres. Edison Elec. Inst.; sec. (Utah Mass. Inst. Tech.; dir. Utah State Inst. Fine Arts. Conglist. Clubs: Rotary, Alta, Country (Salt Lake City), University (N.Y.). Home: 525 B St. Office: 1407 W. North Temple St., Salt Lake City. Died Mar. 29, 1960.

GAUSS, Clarence Edward (gŏs); b. Washington, D.C., Jan. 12, 1887; s. Herman and Emilie J. (Eisenman) G.; ed. high schools, Washington and under pvt. tutors; m. Rebecca Louise Barker, Feb. 3, 1917; 1 son, Charles Barker. Stenographer and Invalid Pensions Com., Nat. Ho. of Rep., Washington, D.C., 1903-06; entered Dept. of State, Aug. 2, 1906; dep. consul gen. at Shanghai, China, 1907-09; returned to Dept. of State at Washington, D.C., v. and dep. consul gen. at Shanghai, 1912-15, in charge, 1915-16; in charge Consulate Gen., Tientsin, July-Sept. 1916; consul at Amoy, 1916-20, at Tsinan, Shantung, China, June 16, 1920-Apr. 1923; consul gen. at Mukden, Manchuria, Aug. 1923-Mar. 1924, at Tientsin, China, 1924-26, Shanghai, 1926-27; Tientsin, 1927-31; assigned to Dept. of State, 1931; counselor of legation at Peiping, China, 1933-35; counselor of embassy and consul gen. at Paris, 1935; consul gen. at Shanghai, 1935-40; minister to Australia, 1940-41; Ambassador to China, Feb. 1941-Dec. 1944; retired from Foreign Service as of June 1, 1945; mem. bd. dirs. Export-Import Bank, Washington, D.C., Dec. 1945—. Home: Wardman Park Hotel. Office: Export-Import Bank, Washington 25, D.C. Died Apr. 1960.

GAY, Maria, operatic mezzo-soprano; b. in Province of Catalonia, Spain; studied sculpture, but later took up violin; spent nearly 6 mos. in jail for singing a revolutionary hymn, at age of 16; sang in concerts, and at Brussels appeared first in opera as Carmen, having learned the part in 5 days; went to Paris and studied under Ada Adiny 1 yr.; m. Giovanni Zentello, tenor singer. Made first appearance in America at Metropolitan Opera House, N.Y., 1906; has gained signal reputation as interpreter of title rôle in "Carmen," as Pilar, in "La Habanera," Dalila, in "Samson et Dalila," Lia in "L'Enfant Prodigue," etc.; a leading member of Boston Opera Co. Died July 29, 1943.*

GRUBBE, Emil Herman, physician, radiologist; b. Chgo., Jan. 1, 1875; s. Albert and Bertha (Reets) G.; tchrs. and pharmacy degrees Valparaiso (Ind.) U.; 1890-92, B.S., 1893, A.M., 1894, Ph. D., 1895, chemist and physicist, 1895-96; M.D., Gen. Med. Coll., Chgo., 1898, Chicago Coll. Medicine and Surgery, 1910; postgrad. Bellevue Hosp., N.Y.C., 1901. Specialist x-ray therapy, 1896—; pioneer application x-ray for treatment of disease, for cure recurrent carcinoma; treatment cancer with x-ray, Jan. 28, 1896, Tb of the skin, Jan. 29, 1896; pioneered use of lead as protection untoward effects x-ray; pioneered design, establishment of hosp. x-ray dept.; dir. Ill. X-Ray and Electro-Therapeutic Lab.; lectr. chemistry and physics Gen. Med. Coll., 1895, adj. prof. chemistry, physics and x-rays, 1896-97, prof. roentgenology, electrotherapeutics dept. Hahnemann Hosp., Chgo., 1896-1919; prof. radiology, x-ray therapeutics and electrophysics Ill. Postgrad. Sch. Electro-Therapeutics, 1899-1921; roentgenologist Chgo. Bapt. Hosp., 1900-16, Pine Sanitarium, 1911-16; cons. staff Peekskill Sanitarium, 1900-06; prof., head dept. roentgenology and electrotherapeutics Chgo. Coll. Medicine and Surgery, 1910-20; cons. physician Frances E. Willard Hosp., 1910-24; prof. roentgenology, phys. therapeutics Jenner Med. Coll., 1914-17; hon. cons. roentgenologist Streeter Meml. Hosp., Chgo., 1938. Del. Internat. Elec. Congress, St. Louis, 1904. Mem. citizens bd. U. Chgo. Recipient award for pioneer work x-ray therapy and electrotherapy Am. Inst. Medicine; citation Chgo. Med. Soc., 1946; award Walter Reed Soc., 1952; citation scroll Chgo. Roentgen Soc., 1956. Diplomate Am. Bd. Radiology, 1937. Fellow A.C.P.; mem. Am. Roentgen Ray Soc., Radiol. Soc. N.A. (founder mem.), A.M.A., Assn. Am Physicians, Nat. Acad. Scis., Am. Assn. Cancer Research, Nat. Soc. Phys. Therapeutics (pres. 1912), Ill., Chgo. med. socs., Chgo. Roentgen Soc., A.A.A.S., Assn. Approved Radiology, Am. Philos. Soc., North Shore (pres. 1939), Am. philatelic socs.; hon. mem. Pioneer Philatelic Soc., Pioneer Philatelic Phalanx. Clubs: Press, Hamilton. Author: A System of Inorganic Chemical Analysis, 1898; X-Ray Treatment —Its Origin, Birth and Early History, 1949. Editor Archives of Electrology and Radiology, 1904-08; asso. editor Am. Electro-Therapeutic and X-Ray Era, 1901-13. Author numerous med. articles, monographs. Home: 1205 Sherwin Av., Chgo. Died. Mar. 26, 1960.

GUÉRARD, Albert Leon (gā-rärd'), author; b. Paris, France, Nov. 3, 1880; s. Marcel Theophile and Marie (Collot) G.; B.A., Paris, 1899; post-grad. studies, London and Sorbonne, Paris; Agrégé, 1906; Litt.D., Geneva College, Beaver Falls, Pa., 1936, Brandeis University, Waltham, Massachusetts, 1957; m. Wilhelmina Macartney, 1907; children—Sidney (dec.), Therina, Albert Joseph. Traveling scholarship in Eng., 1901-03; jr. prof. lit. and examiner in history Paris Normal Sch., 1904-06; instr. Williams Coll., 1906-07; asst. and asso. prof. French, Stanford U., 1907-13, prof. gen. lit., 1925-46, emeritus, 1946—; prof. French, Rice Inst., Houston, 1913-24, U. Cal., So. br., 1924-25; prof. French, U. Chgo., summer 1916, 20, U. Cal., 1921, 22, 26, U. Wis., 1923, U. Hawaii, 1930, U. Ore., 1931; prof. English, Harvard, summer 1949, U. Hawaii, 1950; prof. comparative lit. Brandeis U., 1950-53; lectr. French civilizaton New Sch. for Social Research, 1951, Radcliffe College, 1951-52; associate in Humanities, Stanford, 1957-58. Served with U.S. Army, intelligence and liaison services during World War I; with OWI, 1942-45. Mem. Phi Beta Kappa, Pi Delta Phi, Pi Sigma Alpha. Episcopalian. Decorated Chevalier of Legion of Honor (France); Crown of Rumania. Author: French Prophets of Yesterday, 1913; French Civilization in the XIX Century, 1914; Five Masters of French Romance, 1916; French Civilization from Its Origins to the Close of the Middle Ages, 1920; International Languages, 1921; The Napoleonic Legend, 1923; Honoré de Balzac (pamphlet), 1924; Beyond Hatred, 1925; Life and Death of an Ideal, 1928; L'Avenir de Paris, 1929; Literature and Society, 1935; Art for Art's Sake, 1936; Preface to World Literature, 1940; The France of Tomorrow (de luxe edit.), 1941, (complete), 1942; Napoleon III, 1943; Europe Free and United, 1945; France: A Short History, 1946; What the Teacher Learned (4 vols.), 1948—; Napoleon III, 1955; Napoleon I, 1956; Fossils and Presences, 1957; Joan of Arc, 1957; France: The Biography of a Nation, 1959. Address: 635 Gerona Rd., Stanford, Cal.

HARING, Alexander (hăr'ing), engineer, lawyer; b. Troy, New York, August 19, 1871; s. States S. and Anna M. (Alexander) Haring; C.E., from Rensselaer Polytechnic Institute, Troy, New York, 1895; LL.B., New York U., 1909, LL.M., 1910, J.D., 1911; m. Ethel Chapman, May 29, 1901; 1 son, Forrest Chapman. Began engring. practice, 1895; admitted to N.Y. Bar, 1909; prof. bridge and ry. engring., New York U., 1905-36, with N.Y. World's Fair, 1936-39; sec. Dept. of Public Works, N.Y.C., 1939-40; editor, Engr. Research Office, U.S. Army, 1943-45; private engring. and law practice, 1909—. Mem. Am. Soc. Civil Engrs.; Bronx Soc. Professional Engrs. (pres.), Bull-terrier Club of N.Y. (pres.), Phi Belta Phi. Presbyterian. Club: Rotary of the Bronx (pres.). Author: The Law of Contract, 1910. Home: 2489 Sedgwick Av., Bronx, New York. Died Mar. 14, 1960.

HAWES, Harriet Boyd (Mrs. Charles Henry Hawes), archaeologist; b. at Boston, Oct. 11, 1871; d. Alexander and Harriet Fay (Wheeler) Boyd; A.B., Smith Coll., 1892, M.A., 1901, L.H.D., 1910; student, 1896-97, fellow, 1898-1900, Am. Sch. of Classical Studies, Athens, Greece; m. Charles Henry Hawes, Eng., Mar. 3, 1906; children—Alexander Boyd, Mary Nesbit. Began archaeol. explorations in Greece, 1896, under fellowship of Am. Sch. of Classical Studies, Athens; excavated citadel and tombs of Iron Age (1000 B.C.) at Kavousi, Crete, 1900; as rep. Am. Exploration Soc., Phila., discovered and excavated town and palace of Bronze Age (1600 B.C.) at Gournia, Crete, 1901, 03, 04. Red Cross nurse in Turko-Grecian War, 1897, Spanish-Am. War, 1898; conducted relief work among Serbians, in Corfu, 1915-16; organizer and first dir. of Smith College Relief Unit in dept. of Somme, France, 1917. Life mem. Archaeol. Inst. America. Red Cross decoration from Queen Olga of Greece. Episcopalian. Author: Gournia, Vasiliki and Other Prehistoric Sites on the Isthmus of Hierapetra, Crete (with others), 1908; Crete, the Forerunner of Greece (with C. H. Hawes), 1909. Lecturer in pre-Christian art, Wellesley Coll., 1920-36; acteive in work for New Economics, 1937—. Home: 2 Belfield Rd., Alexandria, Va. Died Mar. 31, 1945.

HICKEY, Jeremiah Griffin, business executive; b. Rochester, N.Y., Nov. 15, 1866; s. Jeremiah and Margaret (Griffin) H.; student parochial schs.; m. Constance J. Duffy, June 21, 1905; children—Walter B. D., Thomas F. G., Margaret (Mrs. John C. Menihan), Jeremiah Griffin (officer U.S.N.), Teresa M. (Mrs. Jerome Doyle), Edward James (officer U.S. Army). Pres. Hickey-Freeman Co., Rochester, N.Y., 1899—. Trustee Montroe County Savings Bank, 1920-32. Pres. Rochester Clothiers Exchange, 1909-11; v.p. Nat. Assn. Clothiers, 1934-36. Dir. Security Trust Co., Rochester, N.Y.; vice chmn. Rochester Bur. Municipal Research; mem. Rochester Park Bd., 1909-15. Fair price commissioner Rochester District under Lever Act, 1920. Member Rochester Chamber of Commerce (past president), Society of Genesee (vice president), Knight of Malta. A founder of The Rochesterians. Clubs: Rochester, Genesee Valley, Country (Rochester, N.Y.). Home: 2100 St. Paul Blvd. Office: 1155 Clinton Av. N., Rochester, N.Y. Died Mar. 29, 1960.

HINES, Frank Thomas, army officer; b. Sale Lake City, Utah, Apr. 11, 1879; s. Frank L. and Martha J. H.; LL.D., Agrl. Coll. of Utah, 1920; LL.D., Lincoln Memorial U., 1927, U. of Ala., 1932; honor grad. Coast Arty. Sch., 1904; grad. C.A. Sch., 1911; LL.D., Bethany College, West Virginia, 1944; m. Nellie M. Vier, Oct. 4, 1900; children—Mrs. Viera H. Kennedy (dec.), Frank T. Jr. Sergt., 1st sergt. Battery B, Utah Light Arty., May 9, 1898-Mar. 22, 1899; commd. 2d lt. Utah Light Arty., 1899; hon. mustered out vols., Aug. 16, 1899; comd. 2d lt. Arty. Corps, U.S. Army, Sept. 20, 1901; promoted through grades to brig. gen. N.A., Apr. 18, 1918. Served in 24 engagements P.I., recommended for Congl. Medal of Honor; was in Europe, 1914, and assisted in returning 3,100 Am. citizens to U.S., after opening of World War; assigned to office of chief of staff as asst. in Embarkation Service, Aug. 5, 1917; apptd. chief of embarkation, Jan. 26, 1918; apptd. chief of Transportation Service, U.S. Army, 1919. With Secretary of War Baker represented U.S. at Interallied Transport Council, London, Sept. 1918; again in England also in France, January 1919, to represent War Department in adjustment of transport matters with allied nations; recommended by Pres. Wilson for permanent appmt. as brig. gen., Dec. 3, 1919; appmt. confirmed, Jan. 7, 1920; resigned from Army, Aug. 31, 1920; apptd. brig. gen. O.R.C., Sept. 7, 1920; dir. U.S. Vets.' Bur., Washington, 1923-30; administrator Vets.' Affairs, 1930-44; retraining and re-employment adminstrn., 1944-45; retired as brig. gen., 1944. Apptd. ambassador to Panama, 1945-48. Former mem. Am. Society Mechanical Engrs. Awarded D.S.M. (both Army and Navy); Companion Order of the Bath (British); Grand Officer Ordre de Léopold (Belgian); Legion of Honor (French); Order of Sacred Treasure, 2d class (Japanese); War Cross (Czechoslovakian). Clubs: Congressional Country, Sulgrave, Army-Navy (Washington, D.C.); Bonneville (Salt Lake City). Home: 3900 Cathedral Av. N.W., Washington 16, D.C. Died Apr. 3, 1960.

HOPEKIRK, Helen, pianist, composer; b. nr. Edinburgh, Scotland; d. Adam and Helen (Croall) H.; studied in Leipzig, later in Vienna under Leschetizky and Nawratil, afterwards in Paris, orchestration under Mandl; m. William Wilson, Aug. 4, 1882 (dec.). Played at Leipzig, Gewandhaus Concerts, Vienna Philharmonic, London Richter Concerts, frequently at Crystal Palace, under August Manns, also with Halle's Manchester orchestra and other European orgns.; appeared with Boston Symphony Orchcestra under Henschel, Nikisch and Gericke, playing her own compositions in Boston and Cambridge under Gericke; played also under Theodor Thomas, Brooklyn Philharmonic, Van der Stucken, NewYork, Brooklyn Philharmonic, Van der Stücken, New York, Cincinnati, Philadelphia festival and with Kneisel Quartette and other Chamber Music organizations in New York, Boston and other cities, in addition to giving many piano recitals. Teacher of piano, Boston. Composer: (piano) Iona Memories; Sundown; Serenata; Shadows; Robin Goodfellow; (violoncello and piano) Romance; (violin and piano) Melody; Romancec; (voice) Six Songs; Five Songs; Reconciliation; Blows the Wind Today; Seventy Scottish Songs (with accompaniments); Dance to Your Shadow and The Sealwoman's Sea Joy (folk songs of the Hebrides, also arranged as solo for piano); Slumber Song (4-part chorus). Address: 31 Allerton St., Brookline (Boston), Mass. Died Nov. 19, 1945.*

HOSKINS, James Dickcason, univ. pres.; b. New Market, Tenn., Jan. 31, 1870; s. William Patton and Mary Olivia Rawls (Mills) H.; B.S., U. of Tenn., 1891, A.M., 1893, LL.B., 1897; U. of Chicago, summer 1900; LL.D., Maryville (Tenn.) College, 1932; LL.D., University of Chattanooga (Tennessee), 1945; Litt.D., Cumberland U., Lebanon, Tenn., 1932; m. Lynn Luella Deming, Nov. 29, 1899; children—Ella Deming (dec.), William Patton. Instr. mathematics, U. of Tenn., 1891-93; 1st asst., Masonic Inst., Ft. Jesup, La., 1893-94; instr. and prin., Knoxville (Tenn.) Classical Sch., 1894-98; prof. history, 1898-99, asso. prin., 1899-1900, Baker-Himel Sch., Knoxville; asst. prof. history, 1900-04, asst. prof. history and economic, 1904-07, prof., 1907—, dean, Dec. 1910—, acting pres. Feb.-July 1919, dean and asst. pres., July 1919-33, acting pres. July 1933-34, pres., 1934-46, president emeritus, 1946—, University of Tennessee. Pres. Tennessee Coll. Assn., 1933-34. Member University Race Commission. Trustee Knoxville Coll. Presbyterian; vice moderator 142d Gen. Assembly Presbyn. Ch. in U.S.A. Mem. Tenn. Textbook Commn., 1936. Pres. Assn. of Land-Grant Colleges and Universities, 1941-42. Member Am. Hist. Assn., Tenn. History Teachers' Assn. (ex-pres.), E. Tenn. Hist. Soc. (pres.), Sons of the Revolution (president Knoxville chapter 1943-44), Phi Kappa Phi, Pi Kappa Alpha. Club: Irving of Knoxville (pres., 1937—). Author of chapters "Tennessee as a State" (1796-1861), and "Tennessee as a Part of the Confederacy" (1861-1865), in The South in the Building of the Nation; editor U. of Tenn. publs., 1900-10. Home: Knoxville, Tenn.

HOWES, Ethel Dench Puffer, educator, author; b. Framingham, Mass., 1872; d. George Dana and Ella (Dench) Puffer; A.B., Smith Coll., 1891; studied univs. of Berlin and Freiburg, 1895-97; Ph.D., Radcliffe Coll., 1902; m. Benjamin A. Howes, Aug. 5, 1908; children—Ellen Dench, Benjamin Thomas. Instr. mathematics, Smith Coll., 1892-95; asst. in psychcology, Radcliffe Coll., 1898-1907; instr. and asso. prof. philosophy, Wellesley Coll., 1901-08; instr. psychcology, Simmons Coll., 1904-07; dir. Smith Coll. Inst. for Coördination of Women's Interests, 1925—. Fellow A.A.A.S.; mem. Am. Philos. Assn., Am. Psychol. Assn., Am. Sociol. Soc., Am. Assn. Univ. Profs., Phi Beta Kappa. Author: Studies in Symmetry, 1902; The Psychology of Beauty, 1905; also mag. articlces on edn. of women, reports White House Conf. on Child Welfare and Protection, 1930, President's Conf. on Home Bldg. and Home Ownership, 1931. Co-author and editor of Publs. Smith Coll. Inst. Home: Scarsdale, N.Y. Died Oct. 28, 1950.

HOYT, Burnham, architect; b. Denver Feb. 3, 1887; s. Wallace and Lydia Jane (Tompkins) H.; ed. pub. schs. Denver, and Beaux-Arts Inst., of Design, N.Y.; A.F.D., Univ. of Denver, 1949; married Mildred Fuller, Mar. 21, 1936. Began as architect, 1923; formerly with George Post, Bertram Goodhue and Pelton, Allen & Collens, all of N.Y.C.; prof. design, N.Y.U., 1929-33; in practice at Denver, 1919—. Designed Riverside Ch., N.Y.C.; Lake Jr. High Sch., Children's Hosp., Albany Hotel, Sch. for Crippled Children, Denver; Penrose Pavilion at Glockner Hosp., Colorado Springs; Broadmoor Swimming Pool, Red Rocks Theatre, Denver Public Library, etc. Recipient Medal of Honor, 7th Congress Pan-Am. Architects, 1950; citation meritorious service, Colo. Gov., 1952; Civis Princeps award Regis College, 1958. Fellow American Institute of Architects; mem. Beaux-Arts Inst. of Design. Clubs: Mile High, Cactus (Denver). Home: 3031 E. Exposition Av., Denver 9. Died Apr. 1960.

HUNT, Duane Garrison, bishop; b. Reynolds, Neb., Sept. 19, 1884; s. Andrew Dixon and Dema Esther (Garrison) H.; A.B., Cornell Coll., Mt. Vernon, Ia., 1907; student U. of Ia. Law Sch., 1911-12, U. Chgo., 1912-13, St. Patricks Sem., Menlo Park, Cal., 1916-20; LL.D., U. Portland, 1935, Columbia Coll., Dubuque, Ia., 1937. Teacher high schs., Ia., 1907-11; teacher pub. speaking, U. Utah, 1913-16, U. of Cal., 1917-18; ordained priest Roman Catholic Ch., 1920; given title monsignor, 1925; consecrated bishop Salt Lake Diocese, 1937. Raised to dignity of Assistant at the Pontifical Throne by Pope Pius XII, May 25, 1946. Mem. Phi Alpha Delta, Pi Kappa Alpha. Rotarian. Author: The People, the Clergy and the Church, 1936. Editor of Intermountain Catholic, 1930-32. Radio speaker on Catholic religion, 1927—. Address: 333 E. South Temple St., Sale Lake City, Utah. Died Apr. 1960.*

HYDE, Ida Henrietta, prof. physiology; b. Davenport, Ia., Sept. 8, 1857; d. Mayer and Babette (Lowenthal) H.; B.S., Cornell U., 1891; fellow Bryn Mawr Coll., 1892; instr., 1893; European fellow, Nat. Assn. Collegiate Alumnae, U. Strassburg, 1894; Ph.D., U. Heidelberg, 1896 (holder Heidelberg table Naples Zoöl. Sta.); research work, U. Berne, 1896, Harvard Med. Sch., 1897; prof. physiology, and research work, Woods Hole Biol. Sta., 1897-99, 1901-07; research work U. Liverpool, 1904; student Rush Med. Coll., Chgo., 1908-12; unmarried. Associate prof. physiology, 1899-05, prof., 1905—, U. Kan. Mem. Am. Physiol. Assn., Am. Biol. Assn., A.A.A.S, Nat. Assn. Collegiate Alumnae, Kan. Assn. Collegiate Alumnae, A.M.A., Women's Ednl. Assn. (Boston); hon. mem. Naples Table Assn. for Promotion of Research. Originator Am. Women's Research Table in Naples Zoöl. Sta., 1907. First Am. woman to receive Ph.D. from a German univ. Author: Outlines of Experimental Physiology, 1905; Laboratory Outlines of Physiology, 1910. Home: Lawrence, Kansas. Died Aug. 22, 1945.

JOHNSON, Albert Rittenhouse, prof. of structural design; b. Lambertville, N.J., Mar. 7, 1880; s. Clark B., and Sallie A. (Green) J.; ed. Delaware Twp. pub. schs.; N.J. State Normal Sch., Trenton, N.J.; B.S., Rutgers U., 1907, C.E., 1925; m R. Ethel Hughes, Aug. 16, 1911; children—Edna Rittenhouse, Elizabeth Ann. Taught in N.J. pub. schs., Jan. 1900 to June 1903; engring. dept. Hudson & Manhattan R.R., 1907-08; U.S. River and Harbor work, 1908; mem. faculty Rutgers U., 1908-50, ret. professor of structural design; worked with McClintic Marshall Constrn. Co., Pottstown, Pa., and N.Y. C., Hughes Foulkrod Constrn. Co., Phila., N.J. State Highway Dept., Trenton, N.J. Mem. Nat. Soc. Engrs., Phi Beta Kappa, Sigma Xi, Tau Beta Pi, Lambda Chi Alpha. Mason. Home: Stockton, Hunterdon Co., N.J. Died Mar. 15, 1960.

JOHNSON, George H., dir. City Stores, Bankers Bond and Mortgage Guaranty Co. of N.Y., Loft Candy Corporation; v.p. Benjamin Franklin Realty & Holding Co. Home: 324 Shadeland Av., Drexel Hills, Pa. Office: 8th and Market Sts., Philadelphia, Pa. Died Oct. 13, 1959.

JOHNSON, Isaac Cureton, naval officer; b. Evergreen, Avoyelles Parish, La., June 20, 1881; s. Isaac Cureton and Alzine (Marshall) J.; ed. La. State U., 1897-1900; B.S., U.S. Naval Acad., 1904; grad. Naval War Coll., 1923, Naval Submarine Sch., 1928; m. Sheila Helena Allen, Sept. 10, 1934. Promoted through grades to rear-adm., 1942 (retired). Decorated Navy Cross, French Legion of Honor, Meixcan Service Medal, World War Victory Medal, Am. Defense Bar. Mem. Sigma Alpha Epsilon. Clubs: New York Yacht; Army and Navy (Washington, D.C.). Home: 2193 W. 25th St., Los Angeles, Cal. died Apr. 3, 1960.*

KATZENTINE, A(rthur) Frank, lawyer; b. Talladega, Ala., Jan. 16, 1902; s. Siegfried Zach and Elizabeth (Rayfield) K.; LL.B., Vanderbilt U., Nashville, Tenn., 1924; m. Ucola Collier, June 11, 1928. Admitted to Florida bar, 1928, practiced in Miami, 1928—; judge Municipal Ct., 1928; mayor, 1932-34; owner Radio Sta. WKAT, WKAT-FM, Muzak, Melody, Inc., Serenade, Mayan Recordings, Inc. Pres., Crime Commission of Greater Miami. Served as lt. col., U.S.A. A.F., World War II. Awarded medal for outstanding community service by U.S. Jr. Chamber of Commerce, 1935. Apptd. lt. col. staff of Gov. of Fla. and col. staff Gov. of Ky., 1934; apptd. col. staff of Gov. of Fla., 1941. Chmn. Organizational com. Inter-Am. Cultural & Trade Center. Mem. S.A.R., Sigma Nu. Democrat. Baptist. Clubs: Com. of 100 (bd. govs.), Surf, Army and Navy (Wash., D.C.); La Gorce Country. Home: 4745 Pine Tree Drive. Office Du Pont Bldg., Miami, Fla. Died Mar. 27, 1960.

KUNKEL, Louis Otto, botanist; b. Mexico, Mo., May 7, 1884; s. Henry and Katie Price (Spencer) K.; B.S. in Edn., U. Mo., 1909, A.B., 1910, A.M., 1911; student Henry Shaw Sch. Botany, St. Louis, 1911-12; Ph.D., Columbia, 1914; grad. study U. Freiburg, Germany, 1915-16; m. Johanna Caroline Wortmann, Sept. 4, 1915; children—Henry George, Otto Wortmann, Walter Relph, Paul Spercer. Asst. in botany U. Mo., 1908-11, Columbia, 1912-13, research asst., 1913-14; pathologist U.S. Dept. Agr., 1914-20; asso. pathologist expt. sta. Hawaiian Sugar Planters Assn., 1920-23; pathologist Boyce Thompson Inst. Plant Research, Yonkers, N.Y., 1923-32; mem. Rockefeller Inst. Med. Research, 1931-49, mem. emeritus, 1949—. Fellow A.A.A.S.; mem. Nat. Acad. Sci., Am. Philos. Soc., Bot. Soc. Am, Am. Phytopathological Soc., Phi Beta Kappa, Sigma Xi, Alpha Zeta, Phi Delta Kappa. Joint author: Filter Viruses, 1928. Home: 122 Voorhees St., Pennington, N.J. Office: Rockefeller Inst. Medical Research, 66th St. and York Av., N.Y.C. 21. Died Mar. 20, 1960.

LEMANN, Monte M., lawyer; b. Donaldsonville, La., Apr. 3, 1884; s. Bernard and Harriet (Friedheim) L.; A.B., Tulane U., 1902, LL.D., 1930; A.B., Harvard U., 1903, LL.B., 1906, LL.D., 1952; married Nettie E. Hyman, December 7, 1921 (died July 1946); children—Thomas Berthelot, Stephen Berthelot; married 2d, Mildred C. Lyons, Oct. 11, 1947. Admitted to Louisiana bar, 1907, since general practice at New Orleans; member firm Monroe & Lemann; professor law (part time) Tulane University, 1910-29, emeritus; asst. chief counsel U.S. Shipping Bd., 1918. Mem. Nat. Commn. on Law Observance and Enforcement (Wickersham Commn.), 1929-31; hon. dir. Tuberculosis Association of New Orleans; trustee Dillard U., Flint-Goodridge Hospital, hon., Touro Infirmary; chmn. bd. advisory editors Tulane Law Review. Member U.S. Supreme Court Advisory Commn. on Rules of Civil Procedure, 1953-57; appointed special master in Arkansas v. Tenn., 1937, and Ill. Waterway case, 1940. Mem. Am. Bar Assn., Am. Law Inst. (council), La. State Bar Assn. (ex-pres.), Nat. Legal Aid Society (ex-dir.), Assn. Bar City N.Y., Harvard Law Sch. Assn., Fgn. Policy Assn., Am. Judicature Society (dir.), La. State Inst., (v.p.), Am. Civil Liberties Union, Harvard Alumni Assn. (ex-v.p.), Am. Jewish Com., Phi Beta Kappa. Clubs: Round Table, New Orleans Country; Harvard (N.Y.C. and La.). Home: 6110 Marquette Pl., New Orleans 18. Office: Whitney Bldg., New Orleans 12. Died Sept. 13, 1959.

LENZ, Sidney S., bridge expert; b. Chgo., Ill., July 12, 1873; s. John J. and Joanna L.; ed. pub. schs.; unmarried. Has held nat. and internat. bridge and whist championships many times; winner of numerous medals, cups and trophies in tournament bridge plays; pres. Lenz, Inc.; v.p. Judge Pub. Co.; bridge editor of Judge. Hon. v.p. U.S. Table Tennis Assn. Author: Lenz on Bridge, Vol. I. 1926, Vol. II, 1927; How's Your Bridge?, 1929; My System of Contract Bidding, 1930; 1-2-3 Official System of Contract Bridge, 1931; Cribbage, 1946. Contbr. to Liberty, Vanity Fair and Famous Features Syndicate. Home: 25 Central Park West, New York, N.Y. Died Apr. 12, 1960.

LEVY, Adele Rosenwald, civic worker; b. Chgo., July 19, 1892; d. Julius and Augusta (Nussbaum) Rosenwald; m. Armand Deutsch, Feb. 11, 1912; children—Armand S., Richard E.; m. 2d, David M. Levy, M.D., June 2, 1927. First chmn. nat. women's div. United Jewish Appeal, 1946-48; Am. del. first WHO conf., Geneva, 1948; pres. N.Y. Assn. for New Americans, 1949-50; mem. exec. com. Mid-Century White House Conf. Children and Youth, 1950; charter mem. N.Y.C. Youth Bd., 1947; mem. N.Y. State Temporary Commn. Youth and Delinquency, 1955; mem. N.Y. State Youth Commn., 1956—. Pres. Citizens' Com. for Children of N.Y. C., Inc., Adele R. Levy Fund, Inc.; v.p. Marion R. Ascoli Fund, Museum Modern Art; trustee Brandeis U., Mt. Sinai Hosp. (N.Y.C.). Cited Outstanding Jewish Woman of 1946; recipient John H. Finley award City Coll., N.Y., 1955. Club: Cosmopolitan (N.Y.C.). Home: 993 Fifth Av., N.Y.C. 28. Office: 100 Park Av., N.Y.C. 17. Died Mar. 12, 1960.

LYDENBERG, Harry Miller, librarian; b. Dayton, O., Nov. 18, 1874; s. Wesley Braxton and Marianna (Miller) L.; A.B., Harvard, 1897; L.H.D., Union Coll., Litt.D., Tufts Coll., 1935, Columbia, 1940, Rochester, 1942; L.H.D., Yale, 1946; m. Madeliene Rogers Day, Jan. 23, 1912; children—John, Mary. Began as cataloguer with Lenox Branch, New York Pub. Library, 1896; in charge manuscripts same library, 1896-99, asst. to dir., 1899-1908; chief reference librarian New York Pub. Library, 1908-27; asst. dir., 1928-34, dir., 1934-41, retired. Director-librarian Biblioteca Benjamin Franklin, Mexico City, 1941-43; dir. Bd. on Internat. Relations, Am. Library Assn., 1943-46. Decorated Knight Order El Sol del Peru, 1947. Hon. mem. Am. Library Assn. (named for Joseph W. Lippincott award, 1949);

mem. Am. Philos. Soc., Am. Antiquarian Soc. Clubs: Century, Grolier, Harvard (N.Y.), Cosmos. Author: History of the N.Y. Pub. Library, 1923; Life of John Shaw Billings, 1924; Paper or Sawdust—A Plea for Good Paper for Good Books, 1924; The Care and Repair of Books (with John Archer), published 1931; Crossing the Line, published 1957. Editor: Archibald Robertson, Lieutenant-General, Royal Engineers, His Diaries and Sketches in America, 1762-1780, 1930. Translator (from the French of André Blum) On the Origin of Paper, 1934; on the Origins of Printing and Engraving, 1940. Address: 145 E. Walnut St., Westerville, O. Died Apr. 1960.

MacFARLAND, Robert Alfred, clergyman; b. Berea, N.C.; s. Simeon DeWitt and Frances Hannah (Sherman) MacF.; grad. Bethel Hill (N.C.) Institute, 1897; B.S., U. of Richmond, 1902, D.D., 1921; B.Th., Southern Bapt. Theol. Sem., 1908; Th.D., Oskaloosa Coll., 1916; m. Lulu Mae Bass, June 3, 1903; children—Burelle, Robert DeWitt, Phoebe Frances. Ordained ministry Bapt. Ch., 1899; pastor Scotland Neck, N.C., 1908-10, 1913-18, Suffolk, Va., 1910-13, Lynchburg, Va., 1918-27, Gaffney, S.C., 1927-33, Rock Hill, 1933-42; pastor-at-large, 1942—. Mem. Virginia Baptist Bd. of Missions and Edn., 1921-27, North Carolina Bapt. Bd. Missions, 1913-18; pres. Va. Bapt. State Conv., 1926-27; mem. S.C. Bapt. Edn. Commn., 1929—; chmn. program and order of business, Southern Bapt. Conv., 1930; mem. S.C. Bapt. Gen. Mission Bd., 1930—; pres. S.C. Baptist State Conv.; pres. S.C. Anti-Saloon League. Preacher annual sermon S.C. Bapt. State Conv., 1931. Trustee Baptist Courier of S.C., Fork Union Military Acad., Wake Forest Coll., Southern Baptist Theol. Sem., Limestone Coll., Furman Univ., Va. Baptist Hosp., N.C. Baptist Orphanage. Democrat. Mason. Mem. Sigma Phi Epsilon (founder 1901). Clubs: Rotary, Crustbreakers. Home: Gaffney, S.C. Died Mar. 15, 1960.

MATTHEWS, Armstrong R., business exec.; b. Nashville, Tenn., May 8, 1902; s. Harley and Edine Rollen (Armstrong) M.; student Montgomery Bell Acad., 1915-20, Vanderbilt U., 1920-21; E.M., Lehigh University, 1925; m. Elizabeth Sampson, June 10, 1937; one daughter, Elizabeth B. Staff engr. Consolidation Coal Co., Fairmont, W.Va., 1926-29, div. supt., 1929-33; staff engr. Phila. and Redding Coal & Iron Co., Pottsville, Pa., 1933-35; supt. Clover Splint Coal Co., Closplint, Ky., 1935-44; exec. v.p. Clinchfield Coal Corp., Dante, Va., 1944-46, pres., 1946-51; pres., dir. Pocahontas Fuel Co., Inc., Pocahontas, Va., 1951-58. Consolidation Pitts. Coal Co., 1956—; dir. Am. Coal Shipping, Incorporated, New York Central Railroad. Mem. Am. Inst. of Mining and Metallurgical Engrs., Sigma Chi. Clubs: Metropolitan, Uptown, Engineers, Pinnacle (N.Y.C.); Duquesne (Pitts.); University, Country (Bluefield, W.Va.). Home: 124 Woodland Rd. Office: Koppers Bldg., Pitts. Died Apr. 2, 1960.

McBRIDE, William Manley, newspaper editor; b. Paterson, N.J., Dec. 1, 1894; s. Andrew and Catherine (Manley) McB.; grad. high sch., Paterson, 1913; m. Mary Cecilia Meade, June 10, 1918; children—Eileen (McLaughlin), Marilyn (McGuire). Reporter Passaic Daily Herald, 1913, mng. editor, 1917-25, editor, 1925-32; mng. editor Herald-News (following merger of city's two newspapers), Passaic, 1932-45, editor, 1946-55, editor emeritus, 1955—. Former pres. of New Jersey Unit, Associated Press; dir. The Passaic Daily News, Passaic Community Chest; mem. Passaic C. of C. Served as private, Psychol. Examining Bd. of Med. Corps, U.S. Army, Camp Dix, N.J., World War I; served as war correspondent Herald-News, Italy, World War II. Mem. N.J. State Press Assn. (life), Am. Legion, Am. Soc. Newspaper Editors. Clubs: Pica, Pennington. Author: "Anybody Here from Jersey?". Home: 155 Albion St., Passaic, N.J. Died Apr. 1960.

McConnell, H(arry) Hugh, ins. exec.; b. Elmira, N.Y., May 5, 1908; s. Harry N. and Carolyn E. (Smith) McC.; student Montclair (N.J.) Acad., 1927, Sheffield Sci. Sch., Yale, 1932; m. Virginia Clutia, June 25, 1937; children—Judith D., Harry Hugh. With Metropolitan Life Ins. Co., N.Y.C., 1945—, asst. v.p., 1948, 3d v.p., 1950, 2d v.p., 1952—; bd. mgrs. Montclair Savings Bank (N.J.); dir. Am. Broadcasting-Paramount Theatres, Inc., St. Regis Paper Co. Home: 58 Melrose Pl., Montclair, N.J. Office: 1 Madison Av., N.Y.C. 10. Died Apr. 11, 1960.

MEIKLE, George Stanley, research dir.; b. Milton Mills, N.H., May 30, 1886; s. George Douglas and Emma Etta (Fox) M.; B.Engring. and Master Civil Engring., Union Coll., Schenectady, N.Y., 1913; m. Louise Juliet Zimmerman (M.D.), Sept. 6, 1910. Chief safety engr., asst. dist. mech. engr. U.S. Steel Corp., 1909-11; scientific research Gen. Electrc Co. Labs., Schenectady, 1912-17; pres. G. S. Meikle Co., cons. scientists and engrs., N.Y. City, 1919-24; research and engring. exec., 1924-28; mem. administrative staff, 1928—, dir. research relations with industry, 1928—, Purdue U.; mem. bd. dirs. and research dir. (officer) Purdue Research Foundation, 1930—; v.p. Better Homes in America, Inc.; v.p. Purdue Aeronautics Corp., Research, education and defense; W.O.C., United States Department of Commerce Coordination and Administration of Univ. and Federal War Research, World War II. Research consultant U.S. Navy, tech. dir. and officer in charge gas mask div. U.S. Army, 1917-19; in charge development submarine dir. for U.S. Navy and model 1919 gas mask for U.S. Army (as civilian), World War I; capt. Chem. Warfare Service O.R.C. Fellow Am. Assn. for Advancement of Science, Internat. Anesthesia Research Soc.; mem. Tippecanoe County Med. Assn. (hon.), Sigma Xi, Tau Beta Pi, Scacbbard and Blade. Republican. Mason (Scottish Rite). Rotarian. Research in physical chemistry, discovering hot cathode gas filled rectifers, "Tungar," and allied devices; research in heat transfer resulting in new formula and discovery of methods and devices for heating houses with liquid and gaseous fuels. Home: 606 Terry Lane, W. Lafayette, Ind. Died Mar. 30, 1960.

MELLETT, Lowell, writer; b. Elwood, Ind., Feb. 22, 1884; s. Jesse and Margaret (Ring) M.; ed. pub. schs.; m. Berthe Knatvold, Mar. 21, 1914. Newspaper work in Indpls., St. Louis, Cin., New York; editor Seattle Sun, 1913-15; mgr. United Press, Washington, D.C., 1916-17; asst. European mgr. same, at London, Eng., 1917; war corr. with Am., French and British armies, 1917-18; mng. editor Collier's Weekly, 1920; editor Washington Daily News, 1921-37; mgr. Scripps-Howard Newspaper Alliance, 1925-37; dir. Nat. Emergency Council, 1937-38; dir. Office of Government Reports, Executive Office of President, 1939-42; administrative asst. to Pres., 1940-44. Clubs: Cosmos, Gridiron, National Press. Contbr. to American and English mags. Home: 1301 Vermont Av., N.W. Office: Evening Star Bldg., Washington, D.C. Died Apr. 6, 1960.

METZMAN, Gustav, railroad exec.; b. Baltimore, Md., June 23, 1886; s. Lewis and Sophia (Schultz) M.; ed. public schools and Polytechnic Inst., Baltimore, Md.; m. Marie S. Hutchinson, Feb. 18, 1933; step children—Mrs. Arthur Pegler, Charles L. Hutchinson. Mem. staff Eastern Presidents' Conf., 1916-17; with New York Central System, 1920—, transportation asst. to vice pres., 1920-22, transportation asst. to pres., 1922-28, mgr. freight transportation, 1929-40, asst. vice pres., Chgo., 1940-42, asst. v.p. and gen. mgr., later v.p. and gen. mgr. in charge Big Four Ry., Cin., 1942-44, v.p. N.Y. Central System, Chgo., 1944, pres., N.Y.C., 1944-52, chmn. bd., 1952—; chmn. bd., dir. Pitts. & Lake Erie R.R., also various subsidiary cos. of N.Y. Central; dir. J. P. Morgan & Co., Railway Equipment & Publ. Co., Century Fed. Savs. & Loan Assn.; trustee Emigrant Indsl. Savs. Bank. Chmn. bd. Am. Ry. Car Inst.; dir. Assn. m. R.R.'s. Served with U.S. R.R., Adminstrn, N.Y., World War I; chief rail div. Transportaton Corps, U.S. Army, Washington, 1942. Lutheran. Clubs: Union League, Cloud (N.Y.); Chicago; Union (Cleve.). Home: 299 Park Av., N.Y.C. 17. Office: 230 Park Av., N.Y.C. 17. Died Apr. 11, 1960.

MEYERS, Carl W., business exec; b. Youngstown, O., June 2, 1891; s. William and Wilhelmina (Consoer) M.; ed. high sch., spl. course in mech. engring.; m. Louise F. Wolf, June 26, 1912; 1 son, Ward C. Began as switchboy Carnegie Steel Co. Youngstown, O., 1907, held various positions, 1907-23, supt. Carnegie Steel Co. McCDonald Mills, 1923-31; with Republic Steel Corp., as supt. rolling mills, Chgo., roll engr., Cleve., asst. dist. mgr., dist. mgr., Central Alloy Dist., Canton and Massillon O., (except for war leaves), 1931-46; pres. Colo. Fuel and Iron Corp., 1946-52, vice chmn. bd. and dir., 1952—; dir. Colo. & Wyo. Ry. Co.; dir. Colo. & Wyo. Telegraph Co., Colo. Fuel and Iron Warehouse Co., Cal. Wire Cloth Corp., Am. Wire Fabrics Corp., Claymont Steel Corp., 1946-52. Mem. bd. dirs. Am. Iron and Steel Inst. (N.Y.) Asst. dir. steel div. WPB, 1943-44. Served as col., U.S. Army, Strategic Bombing Survey Mission, 1945-46. Republican. Lutheran. Clubs: Cloud (N.Y.C.); Madison (Ohio) Golf and Country. Home: Shore Dr., North Madison, O. Office: 575 Madison Av., N.Y.C. 22. Died Apr. 10, 1960.

MOONEY, William M., postmaster; b. at Steubenville, O., Nov. 18, 1870; s. William H. and Amanda (Crawford) M.; grad. high sch., Steubenville; student Duff's Coll., Pittsburgh, Pa., and Boston (Mass.) Conservatory of Music; m. Bessie B. Butterworth, July 3, 1923. With Sherrard and Mooney, bankers, Steubenville, 1890-93; entered govt. service, 1893; paymaster and disbursing officer, Post Office Dept., 1912-20; chief clk. same dept., 1922-23; postmaster Washington, D.C., 1923—. Mem. Washington Bd. of Trade. Presbyn. Mason (K. T., Shriner). Clubs: Nat. Press, Anglers (pres.), Columbia Country, Capital Yaccht. Home: 4407 18th St. N.W., Washington, D.C. Died Apr. 1960.

MOURSUND, Walter Henrik, educator; b. Fredericksburg, Tex., Aug. 13, 1884; s. Albert Waddell and Henrietta Magdalena (Mowinkle) M.; M.D., U. Tex., 1906; LL.D., Baylor U., 1944; m. Freda Adelaide Plate, June 24, 1907; children—Walter H., Thayer (dec.), Waddell, Mildred. Assistant in pathology and bacteriology, Baylor U., 1911-12, prof. physiology, 1912-13, prof. pathology and bacteriology, 1913-14, sec., registrar, 1914-15, prof. pathology, 1914-17, prof. bacteriology, 1920-21, prof. clin. pathology, 1920-27, prof. bacteriology and hygiene, 1924-38, prof. hygiene and preventive medicine, 1938-53, acting dean, 1920-21, 1922-23, dean 1923-53, dean emeritus, Baylor U., 1953—. Served as captain and major, Medical R.C., World War I. Mem. A.M.A., Southern Med. Assn., Tex. State Med. Assn., Harris County Med. Soc. Democrat. Presbyterian. Mason. Author: A History of Baylor University College of Medicine 1900-1953, 1956. Home: 5625 Jackson, Houston 4. Died Nov. 29, 1959.

MUIR, James, banker; b. Peebles, Scotland; student pub. schs., Peebles; D.C.L., Bishop's U., 1953; LL.D., Dalhousie U., 1956, U. Montreal, 1957; m. Phyllis Marguerite Brayley, Sept. 27, 1919; 1 daughter, Heather (Mrs. Yves Levesque). With Commercial Bank of Scotland Limited, Peebles, 1907-10, Chartered Bank of India, London, 1910-12; with Royal Bank of Canada, Moose Jaw, Saskatchewan, 1912-16, supervisor's dept., Winnipeg, Manitoba, 1916, account Grain Exchange br., 1916, head office, 1917-23, insp. supervisor's dept., Winnipeg, 1923-25, asst. supervisor, supervisor's dept., N.Y.C., 1925-28, mgr., Winnipeg, 1928-31, gen. insp. head office 1931-35, asst. gen. mgr., 1935-45, gen. mgr., 1945-48, dir., 1947—, v.p., 1948, pres. 1949-54, chmn. and pres., 1954—; v.p., exec. com. Montreal Trust Co.; dir., mem. exec. com. Standard Brands, Inc., Algoma Steel Corp., Ltd. dir. Met. Life Insurance Co., Westcoast Transmission Co. Limited The Scotsman Publications, Limited (Edinburgh), Canadian Pacific Railway Company, Sogemines, Limited, Trust Corp. of Bahamas, Ltd.; v.p. Royal Bank of Canada Trust Co. Gov., mem. exec. com. Royal Victoria Hospital; gov. Dalhousie U.; life governor, chmn. finance com. Verdun Protestant Hosp.; governor Montreal Gen. Hosp., Royal Edward Laurentian Hospita, Royal Victoria Hosp., Lower Can. College, McGill U.; dir. National Heart Found. Named Freeman of the Royal and Ancient Burgh of Peebles, Scotland, 1952; electted Hon. Chief Eagle Ribs of Blood Indian Tribe of Blackfoot Confederacy. Nat. Trust for Scotland. Clubs: St. James's, Montreal, Mt. Royal, Mt. Bruno Golf and Country, Manitoba (Winnipeg); Matawin Fishing, Royal, Saint Lawrence Yacht, Laval-sur-le-Lac Golf, Toronto, York (Toronto); Rideau (Ottawa); The Brook (N.Y.C.); Seigniory (Montebello); St. Andrews Golf; Lyford Cay (Nassau). Home: 3495 Holton Av. Office: 360 St. James St., W., Montreal, Que., Can. Died Apr. 10, 1960.

NEUBERGER, Richard Lewis (nū'bẽr-gẽr), U.S. senator, author; b. Portland, Ore., Dec. 26, 1912; s. Isaac and Ruth (Lewis) N.; student U. Ore., 1930-35; m. Maurine Brown, Dec. 20, 1945. Newspaperman, writer, 1928—; N.W. corr. N.Y. Times, 1939-54. Mem. Ore. Senate, 13th Dist., 1948-54; U.S. senator from Oregon, 1955—. Served from 2d lt. to capt., AUS, 1942-45. Mem. Am. Polar Soc. (dir.), Soc. Mil. Engrs., Vets. Fgn. Wars, Ore. Grange, Pi Tau Pi. Democrat. Jewish religion. Clubs: City, Tualatin Country (Portland). Author: An Army of the Aged (with Kelley Loe), 1936; Integrity—The Life of George W. Norris (with Stephen B. Kahn), 1937; Our Promised Land, 1938; The Lewis and Clark Expedition, 1951; Royal Canadian Mounted Police, 1953; Adventures in Politics—We go to the Legislature, 1954. Home: 1910 S.W. Clifton St., N.W., Portland, Ore. Died Mar. 9, 1960.

NOMLAND, Ruben, prof.; b. Buxton, N.D., Mar. 8, 1899; s. Knud J. and Sarah (Knutson) N.; B.S., U. of N.D., 1922; M.D., Rush Med. Coll., 1925; fellow in dermatology and syphilology Mayo Found., 1926-28; Hyde Memorial fellow in dermatology Rush Med. Coll., 1928-36; m. Irma Aleshire, 1929; children—Knut Julian, Nancy, David (dec.). Prof. and head dept. of dermatology and syphilology State U. of Ia., 1936—. Fellow Am. Med. Assn.; mem. Chgo. Dermatol. Soc., Soc. for Investigative Dermatology, Am. Dermatologic Assn., Alpha Tau Omega, Alpha Kappa Kappa, Phi Beta Kappa. Contbr. numerous articles to med. jours. Office: University Hospitals, Iowa City, Ia. Died Apr. 13, 1960.

NORD, James Garesché, army officer; b. Fort Lewis, Colo., Oct. 18, 1886; s. Maj. Edward Otho Cresap Ord II, U.S. Army, and Mary Frances (Norton) O.; B.S., U.S. Mil. Acad., West Point, 1909; student Sch. of Musketry, Monterey, Calif., 1910, Inf. Sch., Fort Benning, Ga., 1921-22, Command and Gen. Staff Sch., 1923-24, Army War Coll., 1928-29; m. Irene H. Walsh, Apr. 19, 1927; children—James Garesché, Jr., Marian Eleanor, Edward Otho Cresap. Commd. 2d lt., U.S. Army, 1909, advanced through ranks to maj. gen., 1944; on Mexican border, central Alaska, 1909-17; instr. 1st Plattsburg Camp, 1916; at Culver Mil. Acad., and O.T.C., at Fort Des Moines, Iowa, 1917; with A.E.F., France, 1917-19, participated in Aisne-Marne, St. Mihiel, Argonne campaigns, occupation of Rhineland; operations staff officer, 1st Army Corps and 3d Army; on staff, 9th Corps Area, San Francisco, 1919-21; War Plans Div., War Dept. Gen. Staff, Washington, D.C., 1930-34; instr. Command and Gen. Staff Sch., 1924-28; maj.,

30th Inf., 1929-30; comdg. Ft. Washington, Md., 1934-36; dir., Inf. Bd., Ft. Benning, Ga., 1936-38; comdg. 57th Inf., P.I., 1938-40; sr. instr., Pa. Nat. Guard, June to Oct., 1940; brig. gen., 1st Div., comdg. Army contingents of Spl. Task Force, specializing with Atlantic Fleet in landing operations, 1940-42; comdg. 28th Inf. Div., 1942. Chairman, Joint Brazil-U.S. Defense Commission, June 1942—; U.S. Army delegate on the Inter-American Defense Board, Feb. 1943—. Died Apr. 15, 1960.

PAEPCKE, Walter Paul, corp. ofcl.; b. Chgo., June 29, 1896; s. Hermann and Paula (Wagner) P.; student U. Sch. for Boys, Chgo., Chgo. Latin Sch. for Boys; A.B., Yale, 1917; LL.D. (hon.), U. Denver, Occidental Coll.; L.H.D. (hon.), Trinity Coll., Wesleyan U.; m. Elizabeth H. Nitze, Apr. 16, 1922; children—Walter P. (dec.), Anina H. Woods, Paula A. Zucher, Alice Antonia DeBrul. Began as asst. treas. Chgo. Mill & Lumber Corp., 1929-33; pres. Container Corp. Am., 1926-46, chmn. bd., chief exec. officer, 1946—; pres. The Aspen Co.; dir. U.S. Gypsum Co., Aspen Skiing Corp., Encyclopaedia Britannica, Inc., Encyclopaedia Britannica Films, Inc., Continental Air Lines, Inc., K. W. Battery Co., Inc. Chmn. Aspen Inst. for Humanistic Studies; dir. Council for Financial Aid to Edn., Fund for Advancement Edn.; trustee U. Chgo., Chgo. Orchestral Assn., Art Inst. Chgo. Enlisted USNRF, 1918; later commd. ensign. Mem. Newcomen Soc., Phi Beta Kappa, Alpha Delta Phi. Presbyn. Clubs: Arts, Casino, Mid-Day, Cliff Dwellers, Commonwealth, Commercial, Economic, Chicago, Old Elm, Racquet, Tavern (Chgo.); Links (N.Y.C.); Denver and Cactus (Denver). Home: The Drake, Chgo., 11. Office: 38 S. Dearborn St., Chgo. 3. Died Apr. 4, 1960.

PARKER, Valeria Hopkins, marriage counselor, lecturer and writer; born in Chgo., February 11, 1879; daughter of Anson Smith and Martha (Leath) Hopkins; B.A., Oxford (O.) Coll. (now Miami U.), 1898; M.D., Hering Homeo. Med. Coll., Chgo., 1902; studied in Europe, 1902-05; m. Edward Oliver Parker, M.D., Nov. 25, 1905 (dec.); children —Mason (dec.), Leath (Mrs. Thomas E. Bracken). Apptd. probation officer of home town, Greenwich, Conn., 1913; field sec. Conn. Social Hygiene Assn., 1914-19; joined staff Am. Social Hygiene Assn., 1919-36; exec. sec. U.S. Interdepartmental Social Hygiene Bd., 1921-22; dir. of the Institute on Marriage and the Home, 1936-37; now marriage counselor, N.Y.; lecturer, writer. Supervisor of State Policewomen of Conn., World War; pres. Nat. Council of Women of U.S., 1925-29 (now hon. pres.); etc. Awarded Bishop medal by Miami U. for distinguished service in field of social hygiene, 1938. Mem. Am. Assn. Marriage Counselors; hon. pres. and chmn. social hygiene com. Nat. Council of Women U.S.A. Director American Association Marriage Counsellors. Club: Democratic Womens (3d v.p.) (Greenwich). Mem. Christ Ch. Author: Daughters and Mothers, 1940. Contbr. articles on social hygiene. Address: 211 Park Av., Greenwich, Conn. Died Oct. 24, 1959.

PLOCK, Richard Henry, lawyer; b. Burlington, Ia., Sept. 6, 1908; s. William H. and Helen M. (Atkinson Repass) P.; A.B., Amherst Coll., 1930; LL.B., Harvard, 1933; m. Helen Moulton Swisher, Oct. 6, 1934; children—Richard Henry, Carolyn Ann, Susan Swisher. Admitted to Ia. bar; 1933; now partner Pryor, Hale, Plock, Riley & Jones, Burlington. Chmn. Des Moines County Civil Def. Council, 1950-54. Mem. Ia. Bd. Regents, 1937-59. Mem. Assn. Governing Bds. State Univs. and Allied Instns. (pres. 1945-46, sec. 1949—), C. of C. (pres. 1950-51), Am. Judicature Soc., Am. Law Inst., Am., Ia., Des Moines County (pres. 1946-47) bar assns., Des Moines County Law Library Assn. (pres. 1953), Ia. Hist. Soc., Phi Beta Kappa, Delta Sigma Rho, Delta Kappa Epsilon, Order of Coif. Rep. (county chmn. 1942-46). Conglist. (state moderator 1945-46). Author: Issues in State Control of Higher Education, 1957. Co-author: Partisan Politics on the Campus, 1950. Editor Proc. Assn. Governing Bds., 1949—. Contbr. articles Ia. Law Rev. Home: 515 S. Garfield Av. Office: 321 N. 3d St., Burlington, Ia. Died Apr. 22, 1959.

RAMEY, Homer Alonzo, congressman; b. on farm near Sparta, Morrow County, Ohio, Mar. 2, 1891; student Park Coll., Parkville, Missouri, 1913; LL.B., Ohio Northern U., Ada, O., 1916; honorary LL.D., Lincoln Memorial U., Harrogate, Tennessee; m. Ruby Dearth, Nov. 29, 1915; children—Malcolm Burton, Bernard Curtis. Admitted to Ohio bar, 1916, law practice, Put-in-Bay, O.; mem. Ohio House of Reps., 1920-24; served in Ohio State Senate, 1925-26; judge of Municipal Court of Toledo, O., 1926-43; mem. 78th to 80th Congresses (1943-49), 9th Ohio Dist. Republican. Home: 2102 Parkdale Av., Toledo, O. Office: 1707 House Office Bldg., Washington, D.C. Died Apr. 13, 1960.

RAMSDELL, Edwin George, surgeon; b. New York, N.Y. May 14 1886; s. Edwin Benjamin and Sarah Eloise (Finlayson) R.; A.B., Columbia, 1905, M.D., 1908; m. Bessie Alan Sadler, Dec. 16, 1911; children—Edwin Alan, John Alan. Practicing physician and instr. in surgery, Columbia U. Coll. of Physicians and Surgeons, 1910-17; asst. Surgeon White Plains (N.Y.) Hosp., 1910-19, attending surgeon, 1919-33, surg. dir., 1933—; cons. surgeon Mt. Vernon (N.Y.) Hosp., 1931—, New York Hosp. Westchester Br., 1936—, v.p. and dir. White Plains Med. Center, 1928—, pres. bd., 1942—; gov. White Plains Hosp., chief of staff, 1941—; mem. Westchester County Board of Health, 1931—, pres., 1934—. Mem. bd. Man. Westchester County Dept. of Labs., dir. County Trust Co. Dep. dir. and chief med. officer Civil Defense; dir. Civic and Businessmen's Assn., White Plains. Served in Am. Hosp., Juilly, France, 1915; capt., later maj. A.U.S. Med. Corps, 1917-19; participated in St. Mihiel-Argonne offensive; col. U.S. Med. Res. Corps. Chevalier, Legion of Honor; Croix de Guerre with Palm. Diplomate, Am. Bd. Surgery. Fellow Am. Coll. of Surgeons, N.Y. Acad. of Medicine. Mem. Am. Med. Assn., American Goitre Society. Westchester Surgical Soc., Westchester Cancer Com. (dir.), Med. Editors and Authors Assn., International Surgical Society, Society Older Graduates of Columbia, S.A.R., Alpha Omega Alpha, Phi Gamma Delta. Republican. Methodist. Clubs: University, Columbia (New York); University Rotary (White Plains); Bayhead Yacht (N.J.); Scarsdale Golf; Union Interalliee (Paris). Contbr. of med. articles to profl. jours. Home: 14 Winslow Rd. Office: Medical Centre Bldg., White Plains, N.Y. Died Apr. 12, 1960.

RODENBECK, Adolph Julius, lawyer; b. Rochester, N.Y.; s. Charles T. and Fredericka C. R.; graduate Free Academy, Rochester, 1881, U. Rochester, 1885; law student, Rochester, 1885-87; m. Blanche B. Brown, 1927. Admitted to the bar, Brooklyn, N.Y., 1887; in Europe, 1888; lawyer, Rochester, N.Y., 1888; 2d asst. city atty., 1892, 1st asst., 1892-94; corp. counsel, 1894-98; mem. N.Y. Assembly, 1899-1901; mayor Rochester, 1902-03; judge N.Y. Court of Claims, 1903-12 presiding judge, 1915-16; justice Supreme Court of N.Y., 1916-31. Chmn. Bd. of Statutory Consolidation, State of N.Y., 1904-16. Del.-at-large N.Y. State Constl. Conv., 1915. Mem. Am. Inst. of Law, Alumni Am. Academy of Dramatic Arts of N.Y. City, Delta Kappa Epsilon, Phi Beta Kappa, etc. Mason; Odd Fellow. Club: Oak Hill Country. Author: The Anatomy of the Law, 1925; The Logic of the Christian Faith, 1946. Home: Hotel Sheraton, Rochester, N.Y. Office: 739 Powers Bldg., Rochester, N.Y. Died Apr. 1960.

RUML, Beardsley (rŭml); b. Cedar Rapids, Ia., Nov. 5, 1894; s. Wentzle and Salome (Beardsley) R.; B.S., Dartmouth, 1915; Ph.D., U. Chgo., 1917; m. Lois Treadwell, Aug. 28, 1917; children—Treadwell, Ann, Alvin. Sec. The Scott Co., Phila., 1919-21; asst. to pres. Carnegie Corp. N.Y., 1921-22; dir. Laura Spelman Rockefeller Memorial, 1922-29; trustee, Spelman Fund, N.Y., 1929-48; dean Social Sci. div. and prof. edn. U. Chgo., 1931-33; treas. R. H. Macy & Co., Inc., 1934-45, chmn. bd. 1945-49; formerly chmn. Federal Reserve Bank, N.Y.C.; econ. adv. to government of Puerto Rico. Trustee Museum of Modern Art, Dartmouth College, Fisk U.; trustee and chmn., bus. com., Nat. Planning Assn.; trustee Com. for Econ. Development; dir. Nat. Bur. of Econ. Research; Encyclopedia Britannica, Inc., Gen. Am. Investors Co., Inc., Enterprise Paint Manufacturing Co., Nat. Securities & Research Corp., Peerless Casualty Co. Chmn. Hansen's Lab., Inc., ANTA. Member Psi Upsilon, Phi Beta Kappa, Sigma Xi. Clubs: Century, The Links, The Players (N.Y.C.). Author: Tomorrow's Business, 1945; Memo to A College Trustee, 1959. Address: 342 Madison Av., N.Y.C. 17. Died Apr. 18, 1960.

SCHMITZ, Herbert Eugene, gynecologist, educator; b. Chgo., Oct. 10, 1901; s. Henry and Meta E. (Lenzen) S.; student U. Sch. for Boys and parochial sch.; student U. Wis., 1919-21; B.S., Loyola U., 1923, M.D., 1926; grad. study U. Chgo., 1924, Northwestern, 1928; m. Marion Elizabeth Fry, Apr. 24, 1924; children—Herbert Eugene, Mary Louise, Henry, Nancy Elizabeth, George Francis, Joan Marie, Peter Alfred. Prof., chmn. dept. obstetrics and gynecology Stritch sch. medicine Loyola U.; head dept. obstetrics and gynecology Mercy Hosp.; dir. Mercy Hosp. Inst. Radiation Therapy; prof. gynecology Cook Co. Grad. Sch. Medicine; head dept. obstetrics St. Vincent's Infant and Maternity Hosp.; chief of staff Lewis Meml. Maternity Hosp. Served as pharmacist's mate, U.S. Navy, World War I. Diplomate Am. Bd. Obstetrics and Gynecology. Director Am. Bd. of Obstetrics and Gynecology. Fellow A.C.S. (bd. govs.); mem. A.M.A., Central Assn. Obstetricans, Gynecologists (pres. 1957-58), Illinois, Chgo. med. socs., Am., Central States, Chgo. gynecol. socs., Am. Assn. Obstetricians and Gynecologists (ex-pres.), Soc. of Pelvic Surgeons, Am. Radium Soc., Phi Beta Pi. Roman Catholic. Clubs: Ill. Athletic, Chicago, Edgewater Golf (Chgo.). Home: 2100 W. Pratt Av. Office: 55 E. Washington St., Chgo. Died Apr. 17, 1960.

SHELDON, George Lawson, ex-governor; b. Nehawka, Neb., May 31, 1870; s. Lawson and Julia A. (Pallord) S.; B.L., U. Neb., 1892; A.B., Harvard, 1893; m. Rose Higgins, 1895. Engaged in farming. Capt. Co. B, 3d Neb. Inf., Spanish-Am. War, 1898. Gov. of Neb., 1907-09; received 10 votes for vice-presidential nomination in Rep. Nat. Conv., Chgo., 1908. Mason. Address: Nehawka, Neb. Died Apr. 5, 1960.

STROZIER, Robert Manning, university president; b. McRae, Ga., July 20, 1906; the son of Reuben James and Mattie (Stokes) S.; B.Ph., Emory U., 1929, A.M., 1930; Ph.D., U. Chgo., 1945; m. Margaret Burnett, Dec. 27, 1937; children—Robert Manning, Charles Burnett, Anne Lucille. Prof. Romance languages Georgia State Coll. for Men, Tifton, 1930-33; dean men, prof. French, West Ga. Coll., 1933-40; asso. dean students, asso. prof. Romance langs., U. Ga., 1940-45; asst. dean students, asso. dir. Internat. House, U. Chgo., 1944-45, acting dean div. Humanities, 1947, dean students, asst. prof. Romance langs., 1946-50, dean students, 1950-57, asso. prof., 1950-55, prof., romance langs. and lit., 1955-57; pres. Fla. State U., 1957—. Dir. Army Specialized Tng. Program, U. of Ga., 1944-45. Pres. Internat. House, 1957; Decorated Chevalier de la Legion d'Honneur. Mem. Nat. Assn. Student Personnel Adminstrs. (pres. 1954), Modern Language Assn., Newcomen Soc., Phi Beta Kappa, Sigma Alpha Epsilon, Omicron Delta Kappa. Episcopalian. Rotarian. Home: 1030 W. Tennessee St., Tallahasse, Fla. Died Apr. 20, 1960.

TOMPKINS, H(arold) D., business exec.; b. Kemptville, Ont., Can., Aug. 17, 1893; s. Benjamin A. and Bertha (Richardson) T.; ed. pub. sch., Kemptville, Ont.; m. Elsie V. Judd, Feb. 23, 1929; 1 dau., Susanne Elizabeth. With Firestone Tire & Rubber Co., 1919—, gen. line salesman, 1919, mgr. truck tire sales, Seattle Dist., 1922-25, mgr. truck tire sales West Coast Div., 1925-35, sales mgr. Calif. Div., 1935-40, sales mgr. parent co., Akron, O. 1940-41 v.p. charge sales 1941, now v.p. Mem. Akron C. of C. Rep. Presbyterian. Clubs: portage Country, Akron City (Akron); Mayfield Country (Cleveland); Jonathan (Los Angeles). Home: R.D. Route 2, Hudson, Ohio. Office: 1200 Firestone Parkway, Akron 17. Died Apr. 18, 1960.

VENNEMA, John, lawyer; b. Holland, Mich., Oct. 2, 1871; s. Ame B. W. and Johanna J. (De Swarte) V.; prep. edn., high sch., Holland; Hope Coll.; LL.B., Kent Coll. of Law, 1896; LL.D., Hope Coll., 1930; m. Sybell S. Meyers, Oct. 22, 1902 (dec.); children—Marcelle Dorothy (Mrs. Ashley Anderson Owen), John; m. 2d, Fanny Somerville Maitland, 1941. Admitted to Ill. bar, 1895; mem. firm Harris, Vennema & Bird, 1904-09, Hyde, Vennema & Bird, 1909-14, alon e1914—; attorney for village of Kenilworth, 1909-19. Consul general at Chicago for The Netherlands, 1915-41. Mem. Ill. State and Chgo. bar assns. Decorated Officer Order of Orange-Nassau (Holland); Officer of Oak-Crown (Luxemburg). Ex-pres. Chicago Congl. Club; ex-vice-pres. Chicago Congl. Union. Republican. Episcopalian. Mason (32°). Clubs: Marquette Range Engineers, Ishpeming, Wawonowin Golf. Home: Negaunee, Mich. Died Apr. 16, 1960.

VOGELBACK, William Edward, cons. engr., business exec.; b. N.Y. City, June 9, 1893; s. Louis and Antonia (Hanosey) V.; ed. civil and elec. engring, various tech. schs., N.Y.; M.B.A., U. Chicago; m. Parthenia Carmichael, concert pianiste, Dec. 25, 1920. Mem. engring. staff Sanderson & Porter, 1914-17, asst. Chgo. mgr., 1920-24; ind. cons. engr. 1924—; pres. So. States Power Co., 1926, Standard Tel. Co., 1927-28, Boise (Ida.) Water Co., 1927-28, Am. Engring. & Management Corp., 1927-42, Am. States Pub. Service Co. (also pres. or chmn. of its 34 subsidiaries and affiliates), 1928-33, and several other corps.; pres. and chmn. bd. Union Gas & Electric Co., 1944—. Mem. U. of Ill. Citizens Com.; mem. governing bd., trustee Library of Internat. Relations. Cons. engineer, aircraft, W.P.B., Washington, 1942; central field commissioner, Pacific and China, Dept. of State, 1946. Served with 1st Ill. Cav., Mex. Border, 1916; attended Plattsburg (Arty.), 1917, Sch. Mil. Aeronautics (O.S.U.); commd. in Signal Corps (Aviation), 1918. Mem. bd. assos. Northwestern U.; citizens bd. U. Chgo.; mem. bd. Salvation Army, Chgo. Mem. Am. Inst. E.E., Soc. Am. Mil. Engrs., Ill. and Nat. socs. profl engrs, Beta Gamma Sigma. Profl. engr., N.Y., Ill. Clubs: Racquet, Chicago, Tavern, Chicago Golf; Metropolitan (N.Y.C.). Author: Magnets Light, in Library and Sci. Series, 1933 (editor). Designed and pub. Series Pictorial Maps of various countries; also Panorama Western Theatre of War in Europe, 1940. Home: 232 E. Walton Pl. Office: 230 N. Michigan Av., Chgo. Died Apr. 17, 1960.

WADSWORTH, Augustus Baldwin, physician; b. Bklyn., Oct. 25, 1872; s. Charles David and Clara L. (Blanchard) W.; S.B. in biology, Mass. Inst. Tech., 1893; M.D., Coll. Phys. and Surg., Columbia, 1896; interne St. Luke's Hosp., 1897-99; studied at Berlin and Vienna, June-Oct. 1899; m. Caroline Delano, Apr. 19, 1910; children—Eugene Delano, Augustus Baldwin, Caroline Delano. Asst. in bacteriology and hygiene and alumni fellow in pathology, 1899-1905, instr. bacteriology and hygiene, 1905-08, Alonzo Clark scholar in pathology, 1905-09, asso. in bacteriology, 1908, asst. prof., 1909-13, Coll. Phys. and Surg., New York; asst. physician out-patient dept., 1905-08, cons. bacteriologist, 1909-14, Roosevelt Hosp.; dir. div. of labs. and research, N.Y. State Dept. of Health, Albany, 1914-45; ret. 1945. Am. rep. 2d Internat. Conf. on Serums and Serol. Tests, Health Sect., League of Nations, Paris, 1922. Knight Order of St. Olav. Mem. Assn. Am. Physicians, Am. Assn. Pathologists and Bacteriologists, Soc. Exptl. Medicine and Biology, Am. Assn. of Immunologists, Harvey Soc., N.Y. Acad. Medicine. Clubs: University, Century (New York); Fort Orange (Albany). Contbr. tech. and scientific papers on med., bacteriol. and hygienic subjects. Address: Manchester, Vt. Died June 1954.

WALES, Henry, journalist, war-corr., author; b. Englewood, Bergen Co., N.J., June 14, 1888; s. Henry G. and Frances Jane (Barker) W. Engaged in newspaper work in N.Y.C., San Francisco, Denver and Chgo., went to Europe on outbreak of World War, 1914; with Paris edition of New York Herald, then corr. of New York World, and war corr. Internat. News Service, attached to G.H.Q., A.E.F. After Armistice joined foreign staff of Chicago Tribune, covering Paris Peace Conf.; continued as foreign polit. corr., covering League of Nations, Kapp Putsch, Berlin, Hitler Putsch, Munich, Mussolini's march on Rome, Primo Rivera's dictature in Spain, Zeligowski and Pilsudski coups in Poland, Prince Carol's exile and return Bucharest, Greco-Turk operations, Anatolia and Dardanelles, Hispano-French operations against Riffs and Arabs, restoration outbreaks in Austria and Hungary; toured Russia-Siberia, 1932, investigating 5-year plan, then visited China and Japan; screen writer, Hollywood, 1933. Served as pres. Anglo-Am. Press Assn., Paris. Address: Paris, France. Died Jan. 1960.*

WALLACE, Elizabeth, prof.; b. Bogotá, U.S. of Colombia, S.A., 1865; d. Thomas Freeman and Martha (Torrance) W.; came to U.S., 1874; B.S., Wellesley, 1886; fellow U. Chgo., 1892-93, reader in Spanish, 1893-94; Collége de France, Élève titulaire, at the École des Hautes Études, Paris, 1897. Dean of women, Knox Coll., Ill., 1894-96; instr. and asso. prof. French lit., 1897—, head of Beecher House, 1893-1909, dean in jr. colls., 1905—, U. Chgo. Officier d'Académie conferred by French Govt. Fellow Internat. Inst., Madrid, 1910-11. Mem. Drama League America. Clubs: Fortnightly, Little Room. Author: South American Republics, 1894; La Perfecta Casada, 1902; A Garden of Paris, 1911; Mark Twain and the Happy Island, 1912. Overseas service with Rockefeller Mission and Am. Red Cross in France, 1917-18. Address: University of Chicago, Chicago, Ill. Died Apr. 12, 1960.

WARREN, Althea, librarian; b. Dec. 18, 1886; d. Lansing and Emma Newhall (Blodgett) Warren; Ph.B., U. Chgo., 1908; grad. U. Wis. Library Sch., 1911; Litt.D., Mills College, 1939. Branch librarian Public Library, Chgo., 1911-12; librarian Sears, Roebuck & Co., Chgo., 1912-14; cataloger and reorganizer Pub. Library, San Diego, Cal., 1914-16, city librarian, 1916-26; 1st asst. city librarian Los Angeles Pub. Library, 1926-33, city librarian, 1933-47, ret.; teacher U. So. Cal., Library Sch., 1948—; lectr. U. Mich., 1949-50, U. Wis., 1950-51. Mem. Am. Library Assn. (council 1934-39; pres. 1943-44), Cal. Library Assn. (past pres.), Am. Assn. Adult Edn. (vice-pres.). Dir. nat. campaign to secure books for Army and Navy, 1942. Home: 1849 Campus Road, Los Angeles 41. Died Dec. 20, 1958.

WELLINGTON, C(larence) G(eorge), editor; b. Salina, Kan., Mar. 27, 1890; s. Josiah Dix and Anna (Macy) W.; student Kan. State Coll., 1910-13; m. Gladys Flavia Hazlett, Sept. 18, 1920; children—Joseph Dix, Robert Briggs, Mary Ann (Mrs. Robert Hodgson), John Richard. Reporter Abilene (Kan.) Reflector (now Reflector-Chronicle), 1913-14, Topeka (Kan.) Daily Capital, 1915, Kansas City (Mo.) Star, 1916; night editor Kansas City Star, 1923-42, dir. 1942—; mng. editor, 1947, now exec. editor. Mem. Am. Society of Newspaper Editors (dir.), Sigma Delta Chi (pres. Kansas City profl. chpt. 1948). Rep. Presbyn. Clubs: Kansas City, Saddle and Sirloin (Kansas City). Home: 2901 W. 67th Terrace, Kansas City 13. Office: The Kansas City Star, Kansas City 17, Mo. Died Jan. 20, 1959.

WELLS, Joel Cheney, trustee Am. Optical Co.; b. Southbridge, Mass., Nov. 11, 1874; s. George Washington and Mary Eliza (McGregory) W.; ed. Worcester Acad.; m. Florence Winifred Morse, Nov. 20, 1901; children—John Morse, Gertrude Alice, Florence (dec.); m. 2d, Marion Hengerer Hollister, July 20, 1942. With Am. Optical Co., Southbridge, 1893, clerk, 1902-03; sec., 1903-08, dir. 1908—, v.p., 1913-30, exec. v.p., 1930-37, trustee, 1912—. Pres. and trustee Wells Hist. Museum. Member Mass. S.A.R. Republican. Baptist. Mason (32°). Clubs: Country (Brookline); Union (Boston); Fishers Island; Southbridge; Cohasse Country. Home: Walker Pond, Sturbridge, Mass. Office: care American Optical Co., Southbridge, Mass. Died Jan. 6, 1960.

WHEELER, Harry A., banker; b. Brooklyn, N.Y., May 26, 1866; s. Andrew Martin and Theresa (Van Loon) W.; ed. pub. schs. of Brooklyn; (LL.D., Northwestern U., 1913); m. Emma Lindsay, Sept. 7, 1887; children—Lindsay, Mildred (Mrs. Arthur W. Wakeley). Dist. mgr. 1894-99, v.p., 1899-1901, and pres., 1901-10, Credit Clearing House, Chgo.; v.p. Union Trust Co., 1910-24, pres. 1924-29; chmn. bd. dirs. Mercantile Trust & Savings Bank, 1932-36; v. chmn. bd. First Nat. Bank of Chgo., 1929-31, now dir.; dir. Lumberman's Mutual Casualty Co., Am. Motorist Ins. Co. General secretary Chgo. Assoc. Commerce, 1906-07; chairman, ways and means com., 1908, v.p., 1909, chmn. exec. com., 1910, pres., 1911); chmn. Chgo. Pub. Library Commn., 1909; mem. exec. com. Chgo. Plan Commn., 1910; apptd. by President Taft as mem. Commn. on Second Class Mail Matter, June 1911; declined appmt. on Federal Reserve Bd., 1914. Chmn. Permanent Com. on Relations bet. U.S. and Uruguay. Trustee Garrett Bibl. Inst., 1914— (pres. bd., 1919—). Federal food administrator for Ill., Aug. 1917-18. Pres. C. of C. U.S.A., 1912-13, 1918-19; pres. Ry. Business Assn., 1932—; chmn. bd. govs. Com. on Unemployment, Ill., 1932. Chmn. Nat. Commn. on Unemployment, 1931; mem. White House Industrial Conf., 1919. Clubs: Chicago, Union League, Commercial (pres. 1923). Home: Union League Club. Office: 38 S. Dearborn St., Chicago, Ill. Died Jan. 23, 1960; buried Rosehill Cemetery.

WHITE, Thomas Raeburn, lawyer; b. Dublin, Ind., Aug. 30, 1875; s. William Wilson and Mary Abigail (White) W.; B.L., Earlham Coll., 1896; LL.B., U. Pa., 1899; LL.D., Earlham Coll., Richmond, Ind., 1935; m. Elizabeth Wilson, June 12, 1901 (died Jan. 25, 1921); children—Mary Louise, William Wilson, Thomas Raeburn; m. 2d, Agnes Dorothy Shipley, Jan. 12, 1924; children—David, Dorothy Shipley, Stephen Prevost. Admitted to Pa. bar and U.S. Courts, 1899; lecturer, U. Pa., 1899-1904, asst. prof. law, 1904-05. Trustee Bryn Mawr Coll.; chmn. Com. of 70, 1920-30. Clubs: University, Union League, Rittenhouse, Sunnybrook Golf, Penllyn Country. Author: Commentaries on the Constitution of Pennsylvania, 1907 and many articles in law review mags. Home: Penllyn, Pa. Office: Land Title Bldg., Phila. Died Dec. 1959.

WHITFORD, Robert Naylor, univ. prof.; b. Crawfordsville, Ind., June 28, 1870; s. Matthew Mackie and Julia Dumont (Naylor) W.; A.B., Wabash Coll., 1890, A.M., 1892, Ph.D., 1893, Litt.D., 1935; studied Johns Hopkins, 1892-93, Harvard, Sept.-Dec. 1906, U. Pa., 1908-09; m. Marion Cone, Apr. 26, 1911. Head dept. of English, Lake Forest (Ill.) Acad., 1893-94, Peoria (Ill.) High Sch., 1894-1906; prof. English lit. and dean Am. Internat. Coll., Springfield, Mass., 1906-08; head dept. of English, Blees Mil. Acad., Macon, Mo., Jan.-June 1910; prof. English lit., Toledo U., 1910-38, prof. emeritus, June 1938—, also dir. of graduate study, 1914-29. Mem. Modern Language Assn. Am., Assn. Univ. Profs. (pres. Toledo Chapter, 1935-37), Phi Delta Theta, Phi Beta Kappa (sec.), Shakespeare Am. Assn. Univ. Profs. (pres. Toledo Chapter, 1935-37), Phi Delta Theta, Phi Beta Kappa (sec.). Shakespeare Assn. of Toledo (ex-pres.). Republican. Presbyterian. Author: Motivies in English Fiction, 1918. Editor: Anthology of English Poetry; Beowulf to Kipling, 1903; Goldsmith's Deserted Village and Other Poems, 1905; Goldsmith's She Stoops to Conquer, and The Good-Natured Man, 1930. Home: 2046 Elliott Av., Toledo 6, O. Died Jan. 6, 1959; buried Woodlawn Cemetery, Toledo.

WHITTEMORE, Wyman, surgeon; b. Cambridge, Mass., Apr. 6, 1879; s. John Marshall and Louise Adams (Kelsey) W.; B.S., Harvard, 1901, M.D., 1905; m. Mary Emerson Brooks, Nov. 18, 1911; children—Mary Emerson, Louise Adams. Practiced in Boston, 1905—; cons. surgeon Mass. Gen. Hosp., Mass. Eye and Ear Infirmary, Beth Israel Hosp., Peterboro (N.H.) Hosp., Sturdy Memorial Hosp. (Attleboro, Mass.); now retired. Fellow Am. Surg. Assn.; mem. Am. and Mass. med. assns., Am. Assn. for Thoracic Surgery. Contbr. on surgical subjects. Home: Dublin, N.H.; Boyce, Virginia. Died Jan. 1957.

WILDER, Russell Morse, physician, ret.; b. Cincinnati, O., Nov. 24, 1885; s. William Hamlin and Ella (Taylor) W.; grad. South Side Acad., Chgo., 1903; B.S., U. Chgo., 1907, Ph.D., 1912; M.D, Rush Med. Coll., 1912; grad. study U. of Chgo., 1913, Vienna, 1914; m. Lucy Elizabeth Beeler, Mar. 18, 1911; children—Russell Morse, Thomas Carroll. Instr. in anatomy and pathology, U. of Chgo., 1909-10; began practice at Chgo., 1912; resident Presbyn. Hosp., Chgo., 1915-17; instr. in medicine, Rush Med. Coll., 1915-17; mem. Mayo Clinic, 1919-29; asst. prof. medicine, Mayo Foundation, U. of Minn., 1919-22, asso. prof., 1922-29; prof. of med. and chmn. dept. of medicine, U. of Chgo., 1929-31; prof. med. and head dept. of med., Mayo Foundation, and mem. Mayo Clinic, Rochester, Minn., 1931-50; dir. Nat. Inst. Arthritis and Metabolic Diseases U.S. Pub. Health Service, 1951-53. Served as medical gas officer, A.E.F., 1918-19. Mem. Com. on Med., 1940-46, and chmn., 1940, also mem. Food and Nutrition Bd., 1940-50, and chmn., 1940-41—both of Nat. Research Council. Chief, Civilian Food Requirements Branch, Food Distribution Adminstrn., U.S. War Food Adminstrn., 1943. Recipient Howard Taylor Ricketts award, 1949; Joseph Goldberger award, 1954; Am. Bakers Assn. award, 1956. Member A.M.A. (mem. council on foods; Frank Billings Meml. lectr. 1950), A.C.P. (master 1957), Assn. Am. Physicians, Am. Soc. Clin. Investigation, Am. Physiol. Soc., Minn. Soc. of Internal Medicine, Chgo. Inst. Med., Inst. Nutrition, Am. Diabetes Assn. (pres. 1947), Minn., Washington acads. med. Central Interurban Clin. Club, Sigma Xi, Alpha Omega Alpha, Nu Sigma Nu, Delta Kappa Epsilon. Democrat. Episcopalian. Clubs: University. Author publs. relating to field, also collaborator on several med. books. Asso. editor profl. jours. Home: 705 Eighth Av. S.W. Address: Mayo Clinic, Rochester, Minn. Died Dec. 16, 1959.

WILLIAMS, Othneil Glanville, corp. exec.; b. Geneva, N.Y., Nov. 9, 1900; s. Charles Eliot and Harriet (Glanville) W.; B.S., Mass. Inst. Tech., 1922; m. Janet Sheldon, June 28, 1930; children—Othneil Glanville, Charles Sheldon, Delia Crosby, Eliot Penfield. With Gilbert Clock Corp., Winsted, 1923-57, successively draftsman, asst. supt., works mgr., exec. v.p., treas., pres., 1953-58, chmn., 1957-58; pres. Williams Corp., 1958—. Mem. Clock Mfrs. Assn. Am. (pres. 1951-53). Episcopalian. Home: High Springs, Winsted. Office: Box 686, Winsted, Conn. Died Jan. 1960.

WILLIAMS, Roger, shipbuilding exec.; b. Chatham Centre, N.Y., Nov. 5, 1879; s. A. Ford and Katherine (Van Volkenburgh) W.; grad. U.S. Naval Acad., 1901; m. Frances McIlvaine, Nov. 7, 1906; children—Roger, Frances Randall (Mrs. William C. Chanler), Eveline Wilbor (Mrs. Saxon W. Holt, Jr.). Resigned commission U.S. Navy and joined Internat. Merc. Marine Co., N.Y.C., 1920-30; v.p. and dir. Newport News Shipbuilding & Drydock Company, 1930-46, chmn. exec. com., Aug. 1946—. Served as officer, U.S. Navy, 1901-20. Awarded Sampson medal. Spanish-Am. War and Navy Cross, World War I. Trustee Mariners Mus. Mem. Soc. Naval Architects and Marine Engrs. Episcopalian. Clubs: Army and Navy (Washington); India House, N.Y. Yacht, Century (N.Y.C.). Home: Chatham Centre, N.Y. Office: 90 Broad St., N.Y.C. Died Nov. 1959.

WILSON, William, state ofcl.; b. Chgo., Mar. 3, 1884; s. Charles B. and Hansine (Sorensen) W.; LL.B., Ill. Wesleyan U., 1905, LL.D., 1934; m. Hazel Thriege, Jan. 29, 1913; children—Charles W., James T., Robert J., Barbara Lou (Mrs. T. R. Harris). Admitted to Ill. bar, 1905; practice of law, Chgo., 1905-08, Pontiac, Ill., 1908-09; partner Tuesburg, Wilson & Armstrong, Pontiac, 1912-24; mem. firm Kirkland, Fleming, Green, Martin & Ellis (now Kirkland, Ellis, Hodson, Chaffetz & Masters), Chgo., 1924—; spl. asst. atty. gen., Ill., 1922-23, 1953—; county atty., Livingston County, 1922-24. Trustee, Ill. Wesleyan U. Mem. Am., Ill., Chgo. bar assns., Chgo. Law Inst., Civil War Round Table, Tau Kappa Epsilon. Rep. Methodist. Mason (32°). Clubs: Claxton, Union League, Mid-Day (Chgo.); La Grange Country. Home: 1303 W. 59th St., LaGrange, Ill. Office: Prudential Plaza, Chgo. 1. Died Apr. 3, 1959.

WINTER, Herman, labor union ofcl.; b. Helena, Mont., July 18, 1884; s. Herman and Louise (Huck) W.; student parochial schs.; m. Elizabeth Ashley, Aug. 27, 1907; 1 dau., Mary Louise. Ofcl. Bakery & Confectionery Workers Internat. Union, 1902—, beginning as local sec., successively mem. gen. exec. bd., now pres.; legislative rep. Mo. State Fedn. Labor; pres. Kansas City Central Labor Union; treas. Union Labor Ins. Co.; exec. officer union label trades dept. AFL, now v.p. AFL. Home: 6900 James Reed Rd., Kansas City 29, Mo. Deceased.

WISHART, Charles Frederick (wĭsh'ărt), theologian; b. Ontario, O., Sept. 3, 1870; s. William (D.D.) and Sarah (Irvine) W.; A.B., Monmouth Coll., Ill., 1894; spl. work in oratory, U. Chgo.; grad. Pittsburgh Theol. Sem., 1897; D.D., Monmouth, 1909; LL.D., James Millikin, 1918, Lafayette Coll., 1920, Washington and Jefferson Coll., 1939; Litt.D., Monmouth Coll., 1936, L.H.D., 1937; m. Josephine Long, July 6, 1904; children—James Hunt, Sara Elizabeth, Josephine Bosworth. Winner of the Ill. inter-collegiate oratorical contest, 1893, interstate oratorical contest, Indianapolis, 1894, Purdy scholarship, Pitts. Theol. Sem., 1895; ordained United Presbyn. ministry, 1897; founder 11th U.P. Church, Pitts., and pastor, 1897-1910; prof. systematic theology, Pitts. Theol. Sem., 1910-14; pastor 2d Presbyn. Ch., Chgo., 1914-19; pres. Coll. of Wooster, 1919-44, pres. emeritus 1944—. Pres. Nat. Young People's Christian Union, 1897, General Bd. Edn., Presbyterian Ch. in U.S.A., 1917-19; Presbyn. Bd. Ch. Extension, 1918. Lecturer McCormick Theol. Sem., 1915-17; dir. McCormick Theol. Sem., 1919—, Lane Theol. Sem., 1926—; corporator, Presbyn. Minister Fund, 1923, dir. 1935-44; moderator Gen. Assembly Presbyn. Ch., U.S.A., 1923; moderator Synod of Ohio, Presbyterian Church, U.S.A., 1929; former dir. Bd. Christian Education of Presbyterian Ch. Mem. of Phi Beta Kappa, Delta Sigma Rho, Eta

Sigma Phi, Pi Kappa Lambda. Club: Rotary (Wooster). Author: The Pulpit in Wartime—A Symposium, 1918; The Unwelcome Angel, 1919; The Range Finders, 1921; The God of the Unexpected, 1923; The New Freedom in the Natural Order, 1931; The Book of Day, 1935; Coverdale Speaks, 1935; The Bible in Our Day—A Symposium, 1935; On Going to College —A Symposium, 1938. Home: 827 N. Bever St., Wooster, O. Died Apr. 11, 1960.

WITHEROW, William Porter (wĭth'ẽr-ō), business exec.; b. Pitts., Apr. 15, 1888; s. William and Alice May (Douglass) W.; grad. St. Paul's Sch., Concord, N.H., 1905; Ph.B., Yale, 1908; LL.D., Thiel College; m. Dorothy Dilworth, Dec. 3, 1913; children—William Porter, Mrs. Virginia W. Ahlbrandt. With Jones & Laughlin Steel Co., 1908-10; member Irvin & Witherow, engrs., 1910-14; pres. Witherow Steel Corp., 1914-29; chmn. bd. Donner Steel Co., 1929-30; v.p. Republic Steel Corp., 1930; pres., dir. Steel Products Co., 1932-52, Blaw-Knox Co., 1937-52; pres. Cemenstone Corp.; dir. Pittsburgh and W. Va. Ry. Co., Westinghouse Air Brake Co., Bell Telephone Co. of Pa.; v.p., trustee Dollar Savs. Bank; trustee Northwestern Mutual Life Ins. Co. Tech. adviser Internat. Labor Conf., Geneva, 1936; dir. Nat. Industrial Recovery Board, Washington, 1935; dir. Nat. Indsl. Conf. Bd., 1946-53; mem. Prison Investigation Commn. of Pa., 1953. Dir. Pitts. Bd. Pub. Edn.; mem. Pitts. Sinking Fund Commn. Trustee, sec. Carnegie Inst. of Pitts., Carnegie Inst. of Tech.; trustee Pitts. YMCA. Pres. N.A.M., 1942, chmn. bd. 1943, now dir., hon. v.p.; dir. Internat. C. of C. Mem. Engrs. Soc. of Western Pa., Yale Engrs. Assn. (v.p.), Am. Iron and Steel Inst., Pitts. Regional Planning Assn., Delta Psi. Republican. Presbyn. Clubs: Yale, Duquesne, Fox Chapel Golf, Pittsburgh Golf (Pitts.). Home: 4716 Ellsworth Av., Pitts. 13. Office: Farmers Bank Bldg., Pitts. 22. Died Jan. 1960.

WYATT, Lee B., judge; b. Franklin, Ga., July 13, 1890; s. Smitheul Franklin and Mary Elizabeth (Kent) W.; student Bowdon (Ga.) Coll., 1909-10; LL.B., Mercer U., Macon, Ga., 1914; m. Sara Baker, Dec. 25, 1939. Admitted to bar, 1914, engaged in general practice of law, LaGrange, Ga., 1914-31; city atty., City of LaGrange, 1923-31; mem. Gen. Assembly of Ga., 1917-22; judge of Superior Courts, Coweta Circuit, 1931-42; asso. justice Supreme Court of Ga., 1943-53, presiding justice, 1953—; apptd. mem. of mil. tribunals trying alleged major war criminals at Nürnberg, Germany, appointed for term of six months from Aug. 10th, 1947, on leave of absence from Georgia Supreme Court during this service; pres. LaGrange (Ga.) Theatre Co., Inc.; pres. Home Building Loan Assn.; v.p. LaGrange Banking Co. Mem. Am., Ga., Coweta and Troup Co. bar assns. Mason (Shriner), Elk, Woodmen of World. Home: Greenville Rd., LaGrange, Ga. Office: Judicial Bldg., Atlanta. Died Feb. 1960.

YATMAN, Marion Fay (yăt'mȧn), Rep. nat. committeewoman; b. Framingham, Mass., Mar. 28, 1891; d. Herbert Henry and Nettie (Lowe) Fay; A.B., Radcliffe Coll., 1912, A.M., 1913, Ph.D., 1918; m. Ellis L. Yatman, Oct. 4, 1919; 1 son, Thomas Laurie. Teacher in secondary schools, Detroit and Swampscott, Mass., 1915-17; tchr. history, Carnegie Inst. Tech., Pittsburgh, 1918-19. Mem. R.I. House of Reps., 1936-42; del. to Rep. Nat. Conv., 1940; Rep. nat. committeewoman, 1944—. Mem. adv. com. White House conf. on aging, 1951. Dir. Providence Shelter for Colored Children, 1929—. Pres. Women's Republican Club of R.I., 1943—. Mem. Phi Beta Kappa. Home: 34 Cushing St., Providence, R.I. Died Jan. 1960.